LANGENSCHEIDT'S STANDARD FRENCH DICTIONARY

French-English
English-French

by

KENNETH URWIN

Docteur de l'Université de Paris
Docteur de l'Université de Caen

Enlarged and updated edition 1988

Hodder & Stoughton

© 1968, 1988 Langenscheidt KG, Berlin and Munich
Printed in Germany

First Part

French-English

Contents
Table des matières

Preface

Language has two faces: one looking back, one looking forward. This revised edition of the "Standard French Dictionary" has tried to take both of these aspects into account: In retaining some of yesterday's speech, it will help the user to grapple with the great 19th century authors, whether for school or for pleasure. At the same time, he will find language's path into the future staked out by such words as: *aiguilleur du ciel, alcootest, banlieue-dortoir, écologisme, microprocesseur, organigramme, rétro, télédistribution, etc., etc.*

Needless to say, a great deal of the material old and new is made up of phrases and phraselike expressions covering all registers of speech from everyday language down to slang.

A series of appendices to the dictionary proper gives a list of some common proper names, of common abbreviations, tables of numerals and weights and measures, and a list of model verbs to which the user is referred by the reference number with each verb in the vocabulary. Irregular forms of verbs have been given as separate entries.

The instructions on how to use this dictionary (pages 7–13) should be read carefully: they are intended to increase its practical value.

The phonetic transcription has been given in square brackets after each entry word, using the system of the International Phonetic Association.

It is hoped that this new dictionary will be an instrument for better understanding between peoples.

LANGENSCHEIDT

Préface

La langue a deux visages: l'un est tourné vers le passé, l'autre vers le futur. Cette nouvelle édition du «Standard French Dictionary» s'efforce de tenir compte de ces deux aspects: En gardant une certaine partie du vocabulaire d'hier, il aidera l'utilisateur dans la lecture des auteurs classiques, que ce soit à l'école ou pour son plaisir personnel; mais d'autre part, pour rendre son dû à l'aspect «futuriste» de la langue, de nombreux «mots nouveaux» ont été introduits, comme par ex.: *aiguilleur du ciel, alcootest, banlieue-dortoir, écologisme, microprocesseur, organigramme, rétro, télédistribution, etc., etc.*

Il va sans dire qu'une bonne partie de ce dictionnaire consiste en phrases et expressions idiomatiques appartenant à tous les niveaux de langue.

En complément du dictionnaire proprement dit nous donnons une liste de noms propres, une autre des abréviations les plus courantes, ainsi que des tables d'adjectifs numéraux et de poids et de mesures et une table synoptique des conjugaisons à laquelle renvoie le numéro après chaque verbe. Les formes irrégulières des verbes se trouveront dans le vocabulaire sous forme de mots-souches indépendants.

Nous recommandons aux utilisateurs de lire attentivement les indications pour l'emploi de ce dictionnaire (pages 7–13), ce qui en relevera la valeur pratique.

La prononciation figurée, placée entre crochets à la suite du mot-souche, est indiquée selon la méthode de l'Association Phonétique Internationale.

Puisse ce dictionnaire contribuer à une meilleure compréhension entre les peuples.

LANGENSCHEIDT

Directions for the use of this dictionary
Indications pour l'emploi de ce dictionnaire

1. **Arrangement.** The alphabetic order of the entry word has been observed throughout. Hence you will find, in their proper alphabetic order:

a) the irregular forms of nouns, adjectives, comparatives, adverbs, and those forms of irregular verbs from which the various tenses can be derived. Reflexive or pronominal verbs, however, will be found under the simple infinitive;

b) the various forms of the pronouns;

c) compound words.

2. **Homonyms** of different etymologies have been subdivided by exponents;

e.g. *mousse*[1] ship's boy ...
      mousse[2] moss ...
      mousse[3] blunt ...

3. **Differences in meaning.** The different senses of French words can be distinguished by:

a) explanatory additions given in italics after a translation;

e.g. *tombant* drooping (*moustache, shoulders*); sagging (*branch*); flowing (*hair*);

b) symbols and abbreviations before the particular meaning (see list on pages 10–11). If, however, the symbol or abbreviation applies to all translations alike, it is placed between the entry word and its phonetic transcription.

A semicolon is used to separate one meaning from another which is essentially different.

1. **Classement.** L'ordre alphabétique des mots-souches a été rigoureusement observé. Ainsi on trouvera dans leur ordre alphabétique:

a) les formes irrégulières des noms, des adjectifs, des comparatifs, des adverbes et, des verbes irréguliers, les formes dont on peut dériver les divers temps; toutefois les verbes réfléchis ou pronominaux se trouveront après l'infinitif simple;

b) les formes diverses des pronoms;

c) les mots composés.

2. Les **Homonymes** d'etymologie différente font l'objet d'articles différents distingués par un chiffre placé en haut derrière le mot en question;

p.ex. *mousse*[1] ship's boy ...
       mousse[2] moss ...
       mousse[3] blunt ...

3. **Distinction de sens.** Les différents sens des mots français se reconnaissent grâce à:

a) des additions explicatives, en italique, placées à la suite des versions proposées;

p.ex. *tombant* drooping (*moustache, shoulders*); sagging (*branch*); flowing (*hair*);

b) des symboles ou des définitions en abrégé qui les précèdent (voir liste, pages 10–11). Si, cependant, les symboles ou les abréviations se rapportent à l'ensemble des traductions, ils sont intercalés entre le mot-souche et la transcription phonétique.

Le point-virgule sépare une acception donnée d'une autre essentiellement différente.

8

4. **The gender** of French nouns is always given. In the case of adjectives the gender is not given unless there is a danger of misunderstanding.

5. **Letters in brackets** within an entry word indicate that the word may be spelt with or without the letter bracketed;

e.g. *immu(t)abilité* immutability.

6. **Conjugations of verbs.** The number given in round brackets after each French infinitive refers to the table of conjugations at the end of this volume (pages 570–598).

4. **Le genre grammatical** des noms français est toujours indiqué. Pour les adjectifs le genre est indiqué exceptionnellement pour éviter des malentendus.

5. **Les lettres entre parenthèses** dans les mots-souches indiquent qu'il est permis d'écrire le même mot de deux manières différentes;

p.ex. *immu(t)abilité* immutability.

6. **Conjugaisons des verbes.** Les chiffres donnés entre parenthèses à la suite de chaque verbe français renvoient à la table synoptique des conjugaisons à la fin de ce dictionnaire (pages 570–598).

Key to the symbols and abbreviations
Explication des symboles et des abréviations

1. Symbols

The tilde (~, ~) serves as a mark of repetition. To save space, compound entry words are often given with a tilde replacing one part.

The tilde in bold type (~) replaces the entry word at the beginning of the entry;

e.g. **wagon** ...; **~-poste** = wagon-poste.

The simple tilde (~) replaces:

a) The entry word immediately preceding (which may itself contain a tilde in bold type), or in an illustrative example containing a feminine adjective, that part of the feminine adjective suppressed in the catch-word;

e.g. **abattre** ...; s'~ = s'abattre; **aéro...**; **~statique** ...; *ballon m* ~ = ballon aérostatique; **aphteux, -euse** *adj.*: *fièvre f ~euse* = fièvre aphteuse;

b) within the phonetic transcription, the whole of the pronunciation of the preceding entry word, or of some part of it which remains unchanged;

e.g. **vénérable** [vene'rabl] ...; **vénération** [~ra'sjɔ̃] = [venera'sjɔ̃] ...; **vénérer** [~'re] = [vene're].

The tilde with circle (♀, ♂). When the first letter changes from capital to small or vice-versa, the usual tilde is replaced by a tilde with circle (♀, ♂);

e.g. **saint, sainte** ...; ♀-**Esprit** = Saint-Esprit; **croix** ...; ♀-*Rouge* = Croix-Rouge.

The other symbols used in this dictionary are:

1. Symboles

Le tilde (~, ~) est le signe de la répétition. Afin de gagner de la placé, souvent le mot-souche ou un de ses éléments a été remplacé par le tilde.

Le tilde en caractère gras (~) remplace le mot-souche qui se trouve au début de l'article;

p.ex. **wagon** ...; **~-poste** = wagon-poste.

Le tilde simple (~) remplace:

a) le mot-souche qui précède (qui d'ailleurs peut également être formé à l'aide du tilde en caractère gras), ou dans une expression avec adjectif féminin l'élément de l'adjectif féminin supprimé dans le mot-souche;

p.ex. **abattre** ...; s'~ = s'abattre; **aéro...**; **~statique** ...; *ballon m* ~ = ballon aérostatique; **aphteux, -euse** *adj.*: *fièvre f ~euse* = fièvre aphteuse;

b) dans la transcription phonétique, la prononciation entière du mot-souche qui précède ou la partie qui demeure inchangée;

p.ex. **vénérable** [vene'rabl] ...; **vénération** [~ra'sjɔ̃] = [venera'sjɔ̃] ...; **vénérer** [~'re] = [vene're].

Le tilde avec cercle (♀, ♂). Quand la première lettre se transforme de majuscule en minuscule, ou vice versa, le tilde normal est remplacé par le tilde avec cercle (♀, ♂);

p.ex. **saint, sainte** ...; ♀-**Esprit** = Saint-Esprit; **croix** ...; ♀-*Rouge* = Croix-Rouge.

Les autres symboles employés dans ce dictionnaire sont:

10

F *colloquial,* familier.
V *vulgar,* vulgaire.
† *obsolete,* vieilli.
❦ *botany,* botanique.
⊕ *technology,* technologie; *mechanics,* mécanique.
⚒ *mining,* mines.
⚔ *military,* militaire.
⚓ *nautical,* nautique; *navy,* marine.
✝ *commercial,* commerce; *finance,* finances.

🚂 *railway, Am. railroad,* chemin de fer.
✈ *aviation,* aviation.
♪ *music,* musique.
⌂ *architecture,* architecture.
ϟ *electricity,* électricité.
⚖ *law,* droit.
A' *mathematics,* mathématique.
✓ *agriculture,* agriculture.
🜍 *chemistry,* chimie.
💊 *medicine,* médecine.
▨ *heraldry,* blason.

2. Abbreviations – Abréviations

a. *also,* aussi.
abbr. *abbreviation,* abréviation.
adj. *adjective,* adjectif.
admin. *administration,* administration.
adv. *adverb,* adverbe; *adverbial phrase,* locution adverbiale.
Am. *Americanism,* américanisme.
anat. *anatomy,* anatomie.
approx. *approximately,* approximativement.
archeol. *archeology,* archéologie.
art. *article,* article.
astr. *astronomy,* astronomie.
attr. *attributively,* attribut.
bibl. *biblical,* biblique.
biol. *biology,* biologie.
box. *boxing,* boxe.
Br. *British,* britannique.
ch.sp. *childish speech,* langage enfantin.
cin. *cinema,* cinéma.
cj. *conjunction,* conjonction.
co. *comical,* comique.
coll. *collective,* collectif.
comp. *comparative,* comparatif.
cond. *conditional,* conditionnel.
cost. *costume,* costume.
cuis. *cuisine,* culinary art.
def. *definite,* défini.
dem. *demonstrative,* démonstratif.
dial. *dialectal,* dialectal.
dimin. *diminutive,* diminutif.
eccl. *ecclesiastical,* ecclésiastique.
e.g. *exempli gratia, for example,* par exemple.
esp. *especially,* surtout.
etc. *and so on,* et cætera.
f *feminine,* féminin.
fig. *figuratively,* sens figuré.
foot. *football,* football.
Fr. *French,* français.

fut. *future,* futur.
geog. *geography,* géographie.
geol. *geology,* géologie.
ger. *gerund,* gérondif.
gramm. *grammar,* grammaire.
hist. *history,* histoire.
hunt. *hunting,* chasse.
icht. *ichthyology,* ichtyologie.
imper. *imperative,* impératif.
impers. *impersonal,* impersonnel.
impf. *imparfait,* imperfect.
ind. *indicative,* indicatif.
indef. *indefinite,* indéfini.
inf. *infinitive,* infinitif.
int. *interjection,* interjection.
interr. *interrogative,* interrogatif.
inv. *invariable,* invariable.
Ir. *Irish,* irlandais.
iro. *ironically,* ironiquement.
irr. *irregular,* irrégulier.
journ. *journalism,* journalisme.
ling. *linguistics,* linguistique.
m *masculine,* masculin.
metall. *metallurgy,* métallurgie.
meteor. *meteorology,* météorologie.
min. *mineralogy,* minéralogie.
mot. *motoring,* automobilisme.
mount. *mountaineering,* alpinisme.
myth. *mythology,* mythologie.
n *neuter,* neutre.
neg. *negative,* négatif.
npr. *nom propre,* proper name.
num. *numeral,* numéral.
oft. *often,* souvent.
opt. *optics,* optique.
orn. *ornithology,* ornithologie.
o.s.,o.s. *oneself,* soi-même.
p. *person,* personne.
paint. *painting,* peinture.
parl. *parliament,* parlement.
pej. *pejoratively,* sens péjoratif.
pers. *personal,* personnel.

phls.	*philosophy,* philosophie.	*s.th., s.th.*	*something,* quelque chose.
phot.	*photography,* photographie.		
phys.	*physics,* physique.	*su.*	(= *f* + *m*) *substantif,* noun.
physiol.	*physiology,* physiologie.	*su./f*	*substantif féminin,* feminine noun.
pl.	*plural,* pluriel.		
poet.	*poetic,* poétique.	*su./m*	*substantif masculin,* masculine noun.
pol.	*politics,* politique.		
poss.	*possessive,* possessif.	*sup.*	*superlative,* superlatif.
p.p.	*participe passé,* past participle.	*surv.*	*surveying,* arpentage.
		tel.	*telegraphy,* télégraphie.
p.pr.	*participe présent,* present participle.	*teleph.*	*telephony,* téléphonie.
		telev.	*television,* télévision.
pred.	*predicative,* prédicatif.	*tex.*	*textiles,* industries textiles.
pref.	*prefix,* préfixe.	*thea.*	*theatre,* théâtre.
pres.	*present,* présent.	*(TM)*	*trademark,* marque déposée.
pron.	*pronoun,* pronom.	*typ.*	*typography,* typographie.
prp.	*preposition,* préposition; *prepositional phrase,* locution prépositive.	*univ.*	*university,* université.
		USA	*United States of America,* États-Unis.
p.s.	*passé simple,* past tense.	*usu.*	*usually,* d'ordinaire.
psych.	*psychology,* psychologie.	*v/aux.*	*verbe auxiliaire,* auxiliary verb.
q.	*quelqu'un,* someone.		
qch.	*quelque chose,* something.	*vet.*	*veterinary,* vétérinaire.
qqf.	*quelquefois,* sometimes.	*v/i.*	*verbe intransitif,* intransitive verb.
recip.	*reciprocal,* réciproque.		
rel.	*relative,* relatif.	*v/impers.*	*verbe impersonnel,* impersonal verb.
rfl.	*reflexive,* réfléchi.		
sbj.	*subjunctive,* subjonctif.	*v/t.*	*verbe transitif,* transitive verb.
sc.	*scilicet, namely,* c'est-à-dire.		
Sc.	*Scottish,* écossais.	*vt/i.*	*verbe transitif et intransitif,* transitive and intransitive verb.
sg.	*singular,* singulier.		
sl.	*slang,* argot.	*zo.*	*zoology,* zoologie.
s.o., s.o.	*someone,* quelqu'un.		
sp.	*sports,* sport.		

The phonetic symbols of the International Phonetic Association

Signes phonétiques de l'Association Phonétique Internationale

A. Vowels

Note: In French the vowels are "pure", i.e. there is no slackening off or diphthongization at the end of the sound. Thus, the [e] of *né* [ne] has no tail as in English *nay* [nei].

[ɑ] back vowel, mouth well open, tongue lowered, as in English *father*: long in *pâte* [pɑːt], short in *cas* [kɑ].

[ɑ̃] [ɑ]-sound, but with some of the breath passing through the nose: long in *prendre* [prɑ̃ːdr], short in *banc* [bɑ̃].

[a] clear front vowel, tongue further forward than for [ɑ] and corners of the mouth drawn further back: long in *page* [paːʒ], short in *rat* [ra].

[e] closed vowel, tongue raised and well forward, corners of the mouth drawn back, though not as far as for [i]; purer than the vowel in English *nay, clay*, etc.: *été* [eˈte].

[ɛ] open vowel, tongue less raised and further back than for [e], corners of the mouth drawn back but slightly less than for [e]; purer than the sound in English *bed*: long in *mère* [mɛːr], short in *après* [aˈprɛ].

[ɛ̃] [ɛ]-sound, but with some of the breath passing through the nose: long in *plaindre* [plɛ̃ːdr], short in *fin* [fɛ̃].

[ə] rounded sound, something like the **a** in English *about*: *je* [ʒə], *lever* [ləˈve].

[i] closed vowel, tongue very high, corners of the mouth well back, rather more closed than [i] in English *sea*: long in *dire* [diːr], short in *vie* [vi].

[o] closed vowel, tongue drawn back, lips rounded: no tailing off into [u] or [w] as in English *below*: long in *fosse* [foːs], short in *peau* [po].

[ɔ] open o but closer than in English *cot*, with tongue lower, lips more rounded, mouth more open: long in *fort* [fɔːr], short in *cotte* [kɔt].

[ɔ̃] [ɔ]-sound, but with some of the breath passing through the nose: long in *nombre* [nɔ̃ːbr], short in *mon* [mɔ̃].

[ø] a rounded [e], pronounced rather like the **ir** of English *birth* but closer and with lips well rounded and forward: long in *chanteuse* [ʃɑ̃ˈtøːz], short in *peu* [pø].

[œ] a rounded open e [ɛ], a little like the **ur** of English *turn* but with the tongue higher and the lips well rounded: long in *fleur* [flœːr], short in *œuf* [œf].

[œ̃] the same sound as [œ] but with some of the breath passing through the nose: long in *humble* [œ̃ːbl], short in *parfum* [parˈfœ̃].

[u] closed vowel with back of the tongue raised close to the soft palate and the front drawn back and down, and lips far forward and rounded; rather like the **oo** of English *root* but tighter and without the tailing off into the [w] sound: long in *tour* [tuːr], short in *route* [rut].

[y] an [i] pronounced with the lips well forward and rounded: long in *mur* [myːr], short in *vue* [vy].

B. Consonants

Note: the consonant sounds not listed below are similar to those of English, except that they are much more dry: thus the [p] is not a breathed sound and [t] and [d] are best pronounced with the tip of the tongue against the back of the top teeth, with no breath accompanying the sound.

[j] a rapidly pronounced sound like the **y** in English *yes: diable* [djɑːbl], *dieu* [djø], *fille* [fiːj].

[l] usually more voiced than in English and does not have its 'hollow sound': *aller* [aˈle].

[ɲ] the "n mouillé", an [n] followed by a rapid [j]: *cogner* [kɔˈɲe].

[ŋ] not a true French sound; occurs in a few borrowed foreign words: *meeting* [miˈtiŋ].

[r] in some parts of France the [r] may be sounded like a slightly rolled English [r], but the uvular sound is more generally accepted. It has been described as sounding like a short and light gargle: *ronger* [rɔ̃ˈʒe].

[ʃ] rather like the **sh** of English *shall*, never like the **ch** of English *cheat*: *chanter* [ʃɑˈte].

[ɥ] like a rapid [y], never a separate syllable: *muet* [mɥɛ].

[w] not as fully a consonant as the English [w]. It is half-way between the consonant [w] and the vowel [u]: *oui* [wi].

[ʒ] a voiced [ʃ]; it is like the second part of the sound of **di** in the English *soldier*, i.e. it does not have the [d] element: j'ai [ʒe]; *rouge* [ruːʒ].

C. Use of the sign ˈ to mark stress

The stressed syllable is indicated by the use of ˈ before it. This is to some extent theoretical. Such stress as there is is not very marked and the presence of the ˈ may be considered a reminder that the word should not normally be stressed in any other syllable, especially if the word resembles an English one which *is* stressed elsewhere.

Though a stress-mark is shown for each word, all the words in one breath group will not in fact carry the stress indicated: thus, though *mauvais* may be transcribed [mɔˈvɛ], in *mauvais ami* there is only one main stress, on the *-mi*.

In words of one syllable only, the stress mark is not given.

D. Use of the sign : to mark length

When the sign [ː] appears after a vowel it indicates that the duration of the vowel sound is rather longer than for a vowel which appears without it. Thus the [œ] of *feuille* [fœːj] is longer than the [œ] of *feuillet* [fœˈjɛ]. In unstressed syllables one frequently finds a semi-long vowel but this fine shade of duration has not been marked in the transcription.

A

A, a [a] *m* A, a.

a [a] *3rd p. sg. pres. of* avoir *1.*

à [ᴧ] *prp. place*: at (*table, Hastings*), in (*Edinburgh*), on (*the wall*); *direction*: to, into; *distance*: at a distance of (*10 miles*); *origin*: from, of; *time*: at (*7 o'clock, this moment, his words*); in (*spring*); *sequence*: by (*twos*); for; *agent, instrument, etc.*: on (*horseback*); with; by (means of); *manner*: in; on (*condition, the occasion*); *price*: for (*two dollars*); at, by; *dative, possession*: donner qch. à q. give s.th. to s.o., give s.o. s.th.; grâce à Dieu! thank God!; c'est à moi this is mine; c'est à moi de (*inf.*) it is for me to (*inf.*); un ami à moi a friend of mine; à terre on *or* to the ground; de la tête aux pieds from head to foot; prêt à ready *or* willing to; au secours! help!; à vingt pas d'ici twenty steps *or* paces from here; emprunter (arracher) à borrow (tear) from; c'est bien aimable à vous that's very kind of you; à l'aube at dawn; à la longue at length; au moment de (*inf.*) on (*ger.*); à le voir seeing him; à tout moment constantly; à demain till tomorrow; *int.* see you tomorrow!; à jamais for ever; à partir de ... from ... (on); mot à mot word for word, literal(ly *adv.*); quatre à quatre four at a time; peu à peu little by little; bateau *m* à vapeur steamer, steamboat; maison *f* à deux étages two-storied house; ♪ à quatre mains for four hands; verre *m* à vin wineglass; fait à la main handmade; à voix basse in a low voice; à la nage swimming; peinture *f* à l'huile painting in oil; aux yeux bleus blue-eyed; à dessein on purpose; à regret reluctantly; à merveille excellently; à prix bas at a low price; à mes frais at my expenses; à louer to let; à vendre for sale; à la bonne heure well done!; fine!

abaissement [abɛs'mɑ̃] *m* lowering, sinking; *prices, temperature, etc.*: fall; falling; dropping; *water etc.*: abatement; *ground*: dip; *fig.* humbling, abasement; **abaisser** [abɛ'se] (1b) *v/t.* lower; *fig. a.* reduce; humble, bring low; ⅄ bring down (*a figure*), drop (*a perpendicular*), depress (*an equation*); s'~ fall, drop, go down; *fig.* humble o.s., lower o.s.; *fig.* s' ~ à descend *or* stoop to.

abajoue [aba'ʒu] *f zo.* cheek-pouch; F flabby cheek.

abandon [abɑ̃'dɔ̃] *m* abandonment, forsaking; desertion; neglect; destitution; *rights*: surrender; lack of restraint, absence of reserve; *sp.* withdrawal; à l'~ completely neglected; at random; laisser tout à l'~ leave everything in confusion; **abandonner** [ᴧdɔ'ne] (1a) *v/t.* forsake, abandon; leave; ⅜ surrender; renounce (*a claim, a right*); s'~ lose heart; neglect o.s.; give way *or* vent (to, à); give o.s. up (to, à), indulge (in, à).

abasourdir [abazur'diːr] (2a) *v/t.* stun; *fig.* dumbfound.

abat [a'ba] *m: pluie f d'~* downpour; ~s *pl.* offal *sg.*

abâtardir [abɑtar'diːr] (2a) *v/t.* impair; debase; s'~ deteriorate, degenerate; **abâtardissement** [ᴧdis'mɑ̃] *m* deterioration, degeneration.

abat-jour [aba'ʒuːr] *m/inv.* lampshade; sun-blind; △ skylight.

abattage [aba'taːʒ] *m* knocking down, throwing down; *tree*: felling; clearing; *animals*: slaughter; *fig.* F dressing-down; ~ urgent forced slaughter; **abattant** [ᴧ'tɑ̃] *m counter, table*: flap; trapdoor; ~ de W.-C. lavatory seat; **abattement** [abat'mɑ̃] *m* prostration; dejection; ~ à la base personal allowance; *Am.* exemption; **abattis** [ᴧ'ti] ⚔ abatis; *cuis.* giblets *pl.*; *sl.* ~ *pl.* limbs; *sl.* numéroter ses ~ take stock of o.s.; **abattoir** [ᴧ'twaːr] *m* slaughterhouse; **abattre** [a'batr] (4a) *v/t.* knock down; fell; slaughter, destroy;

🗲 bring *or* shoot down; *fig.* dishearten, depress, demoralize, wear out; ~ *de la besogne* get through a lot of work; *ne te laisse pas* ~ don't let things get you down; s'~ crash; fall; s'~ *sur* beat down on (*rain etc.*); swoop down on, pounce on; *fig.* hail down on; **abattu,e** *fig.* [aba'ty] depressed.

abat-vent [aba'vã] *m*/*inv.* chimney-cowl; 🌿 wind-break, cloche.

abbatial, e, *m*/*pl.* **-aux** [aba'sjal, ~'sjo] abbatial; **abbaye** [abe'ji] *f* abbey; *monks:* monastery; *nuns:* convent; **abbé** [a'be] *m* abbot; *priest; hist.* abbé; **abbesse** [a'bɛs] *f* abbess.

ABC [abe'se] *m* primer; spelling-book; *fig.* rudiments *pl.*

abcès 🞋 [ap'sɛ] *m* abscess.

abdication [abdika'sjo] *f* abdication; renunciation.

abdiquer [abdi'ke] (1m) *v*/*i.* abdicate; *v*/*t.* renounce (*s.th.*).

abdomen [abdɔ'mɛn] *m* abdomen.

abécédaire [abese'dɛːr] *m* spelling-book; primer; *fig.* elements *pl.*

abeille [a'bɛːj] *f* bee; ~ *mâle* drone; ~ *mère, reine f des* ~s queen (bee); ~ *ouvrière* worker (bee).

aberration [abɛra'sjo] *f* aberration.

abêtir [abe'tiːr] (2a) *v*/*t.* make stupid, stupefy; s'~ grow stupid.

abhorrer [abɔ're] (1a) *v*/*t.* loathe, detest.

abîme [a'biːm] *m* abyss, chasm; **abîmer** [abi'me] (1a) *v*/*t.* spoil, damage, ruin; *sl.* beat up, smash; s'~ get spoilt *or* damaged *or* ruined; be plunged (in, *dans*).

abject, e [ab'ʒɛkt] contemptible, mean; abject; **abjection** [~ʒɛk'sjo] *f* baseness, abjection, meanness.

abjurer [abʒy're] (1a) *v*/*t.* abjure; retract, recant.

ablation [abla'sjo] *f* removal, excision.

able *icht.* [abl] *m,* **ablette** *icht.* [a'blɛt] *f* bleak.

ablution [ably'sjo] *f* ablution (*a. eccl.*).

abnégation [abnega'sjo] *f* abnegation, self-denial, self-sacrifice.

abois [a'bwa] *m*/*pl.*: *aux* ~ at bay (*a. fig.*), hard pressed; **aboiement** [abwa'mã] *m* bark(ing), bay(ing).

abolir [abɔ'liːr] (2a) *v*/*t.* abolish, suppress; annul; repeal; **abolition**

[~li'sjo] *f* abolition, suppression; 🕇 *debt:* cancelling; annulment.

abominable [abɔmi'nabl] abominable; heinous (*crime*); **abomination** [~na'sjo] *f* abomination; **abominer** [~'ne] (1a) *v*/*t.* abominate, loathe.

abondamment [abõda'mã] *adv.* of *abondant;* **abondance** [~'dãːs] *f* abundance; *en* ~ plentiful(ly *adv.*); *parler d'*~ extemporize; **abondant, e** [~'dã, ~'dãːt] plentiful, copious; abundant; abounding (in, *en*); **abonder** [~'de] (1a) *v*/*i.* be plentiful; abound (in, *en*).

abonné *m,* **e** *f* [abɔ'ne] *magazine, paper, telephone:* subscriber; *electricity, gas:* consumer; 🚃 *etc.* season-ticket holder, *Am.* commuter; **abonnement** [abɔn'mã] *m* subscription; *carte f d'*~ season-ticket, *Am.* commutation ticket; **abonner** [abɔ'ne] (1a) *v*/*t.:* ~ *q. à qch.* take out a subscription to s.th. for s.o.; s'~ *à* subscribe to; take (out) a season-ticket for.

abord [a'bɔːr] *m* approach, access (to, *de*); manner, address; ~s *pl.* approaches, outskirts; *d'*~ (at) first; *de prime* ~ at first sight; *dès l'*~ from the outset; *d'un* ~ *facile* easy to approach; *tout d'*~ first of all; **abordable** [abɔr'dabl] accessible; 🕇 reasonable (*price*); **abordage** ⚓ [~'daːʒ] *m* boarding, grappling; coming alongside; collision; **aborder** [~'de] (1a) *v*/*i.* ⚓ land, berth; *v*/*t.* ⚓ grapple; run down (*a ship*); *fig.* approach, tackle (*a problem*); *fig.* accost (*s.o.*); s'~ meet.

aborigène [abɔri'ʒɛn] **1.** *adj.* aboriginal; native; **2.** *su.*/*m* aboriginal; ~s *pl.* aborigines.

abortif, -ve [abɔr'tif, ~'tiːv] **1.** *adj.* abortive; 🞋 abortifacient; **2.** *su.*/*m* 🞋 abortifacient.

abouchement [abuʃ'mã] *m* † interview; ⊕ butt-joining; **aboucher** [abu'ʃe] (1a) *v*/*t.* join together; ⊕, *a.* 🞋 connect; ⊕ join end to end; s'~ confer.

aboulie *psych.* [abu'li] *f* aboulia, loss of will-power; **aboulique** *psych.* [~'lik] irresolute.

about ⊕ [a'bu] *m wood:* butt-end; **abouter** ⊕ [abu'te] (1a) *v*/*t.* join end to end; **aboutir** [~'tiːr] (2a) *v*/*i.* lead ([in]to, *à*), end (in, *à*); abut (on, à); ✖ come to a head, burst (*abscess*); *fig.* **aboutissant, e** [˷ti'sɑ̃, ˷'sɑ̃:t] bordering, abutting; **aboutissement** [˷tis'mɑ̃] *m* issue, outcome; *plan*: materialization; ✖ *abscess*: bursting, coming to a head.

aboyer [abwa'je] (1h) *v/i.* bark, bay; **aboyeur** [˷'jœ:r] *m* yelping dog; *fig.* carping critic; tout; dun.

abrasif, -ve ⊕ [abra'zif, ˷'zi:v] *adj.*, *a. su./m* abrasive; **abrasion** ✖ [˷'zjɔ̃] *f* abrasion, scraping.

abrégé [abre'ʒe] *m* summary, précis; **abréger** [˷] (1g) *v/t.* shorten, abbreviate.

abreuver [abrœ've] (1a) *v/t.* water; soak; s'˷ drink (*animal*); quench one's thirst (*person*); **abreuvoir** [˷'vwa:r] *m* horse-pond, trough, watering place (*in a river*).

abréviation [abrevja'sjɔ̃] *f* abbreviation; *a.* ✁ *sentence*: shortening.

abri [a'bri] *m* shelter, cover; ✖ dugout; air-raid shelter; ✖ ˷ atomique atomic shelter; ✖ ˷ bétonné blockhouse, *sl.* pill-box; ⛟ ˷ de mécanicien cab; à l'˷ de sheltered from; screened from; mettre à l'˷ shelter, screen (from, de).

abricot [abri'ko] *m* apricot; **abricotier** [˷kɔ'tje] *m* apricot-tree.

abriter [abri'te] (1a) *v/t.* shelter, screen, protect, shield (from de, contre); s'˷ take shelter *or* refuge.

abrivent [abri'vɑ̃] *m* ✖ sentry-box, shelter; ⚐ screen, matting.

abroger [abrɔ'ʒe] (1e) *v/t.* abrogate, repeal, rescind.

abrupt, e [a'brypt] abrupt; steep, sheer; *fig.* rugged (*style*); blunt (*words*).

abruti *m*, e *f sl.* [abry'ti] fool, idiot; **abrutir** [˷'ti:r] (2a) *v/t.* stupefy, brutalize; s'˷ become sottish; **abrutissement** [˷tis'mɑ̃] *m* brutishness, degradation.

abscisse ⚲ [ap'sis] *f* abscissa.

absence [ap'sɑ̃:s] *f* absence; lack; ˷ d'esprit absent-mindedness; **absent, e** [˷'sɑ̃, ˷'sɑ̃:t] absent; *fig.* absent-minded; **absentéisme** [˷sɑ̃te'ism] *m* absenteeism; **absenter** [˷sɑ̃'te] (1a) *v/t.*: s'˷ absent o.s., stay away; go away from home.

abside △ [ap'sid] *f* apse.

absinthe [ap'sɛ̃:t] *f* absinth; ⚘ wormwood.

absolu, e [apsɔ'ly] absolute; peremptory (*voice*); ⚗ pure (*alcohol*); *phys.* zéro *m* ˷ absolute zero (—459.4° *F.*); **absolument** [apsɔly'mɑ̃] *adv.* absolutely, completely; **absolution** [˷'sjɔ̃] *f* absolution (from, de); **absolutisme** [˷'tism] *m* absolutism; **absolutoire** [˷'twa:r] absolving.

absorber [apsɔr'be] (1a) *v/t.* absorb, soak up; imbibe; consume; *fig.* engross; s'˷ be absorbed (in, dans); **absorption** [˷sɔrp'sjɔ̃] *f* absorption (*a. fig.*).

absoudre [ap'sudr] (4bb) *v/t. eccl., a. fig.* absolve; exonerate; **absous, -te** [˷'su, ˷'sut] *p.p. of* absoudre.

abstenir [apstə'ni:r] (2h) *v/t.*: s'˷ refrain *or* abstain (from, de); *parl.* s'˷ (de voter) abstain (from voting); **abstention** [˷tɑ̃'sjɔ̃] *f* abstention (from, de); renunciation.

abstinence [apsti'nɑ̃:s] *f* abstinence; abstention (from, de); faire ˷ de abstain from (*s.th.*); **abstinent, e** [˷'nɑ̃, ˷'nɑ̃:t] 1. *adj.* abstemious, sober; 2. *su.* total abstainer, teetotaller.

abstraction [apstrak'sjɔ̃] *f* abstraction; ˷s *pl.* vagueness *sg.*; ˷ faite de cela leaving that aside; apart from that; faire ˷ de qch. leave s.th. out of account, disregard s.th.; se perdre dans des ˷s be lost in thought.

abstraire [aps'tre:r] (4ff) *v/t.* abstract, isolate; s'˷ become engrossed (in dans, en); **abstrait, e** [˷'tre, ˷'tret] abstracted; abstract (*idea*); abstruse (*problem, subject*).

abstrus, e [aps'try, ˷'try:z] abstruse; obscure; recondite.

absurde [ap'syrd] 1. *adj.* absurd; 2. *su./m*: tomber dans l'˷ become ridiculous; **absurdité** [˷syrdi'te] *f* absurdity, nonsense.

abus [a'by] *m* abuse, misuse (of, de), error; ˷ de confiance breach of trust; faire ˷ de abuse; overindulge in; **abuser** [aby'ze] (1a) *v/t.* mislead; deceive; s'˷ be mistaken; *v/i.*: ˷ de misuse; take unfair advantage of; impose upon; delude; **abusif, -ve** [˷'zif, ˷'zi:v] excessive; *gramm.* contrary to usage, improper.

abyssal, e [abi'sal, ˷'so] deep-sea...; **abysse** [a'bis] *m* deep sea.

acabit F [aka'bi] *m* quality, nature;

du même ~ tarred with the same brush.

acacia ♀ [aka'sja] *m* acacia.

académicien [akademi'sjɛ̃] *m* academician; **académie** [~'mi] *f* academy; learned society; school (*of art etc.*); *paint.* nude; *in France*: educational district; **académique** [~'mik] academic; pretentious (*style*).

acagnarder [akaɲar'de] (1a) *v/t.*: *s'*~ idle, laze.

acajou [aka'ʒu] *m* mahogany.

acanthe ♀ [a'kɑ̃:t] *f* acanthus (*a.* ⚠), brank-ursine.

acariâtre [aka'rjɑːtr] quarrelsome; peevish; shrewish; nagging.

accablant, e [aka'blɑ̃, ~'blɑ̃:t] overwhelming (*proof, emotions*); crushing, oppressive (*heat*); **accablement** [~blə'mɑ̃] *m* dejection; prostration; ✝ pressure; **accabler** [~'ble] (1a) *v/t.* overwhelm (with, de); overpower, crush.

accalmie [akal'mi] *f* ✕, ⚓, *a. fig.* lull; ✝ slack period.

accaparement [akapar'mɑ̃] *m* hoarding; *fig.* F monopolizing; **accaparer** [~'re] (1a) *v/t.* corner, hoard; *fig.* F monopolize (*the conversation*); *fig.* seize; *fig.* take up (*time, energy, etc.*); *fig.* take up the time (and energy) of (*s.o.*); **accapareur** *m,* **-euse** *f* [~'rœːr, ~'røːz] *supplies*: buyer-up; monopolizer; *fig.* F hoarder; grabber.

accéder [akse'de] (1f) *v/i.*: ~ *à* have access to; accede to (*a request*).

accélérateur, -trice [akselera'tœːr, ~'tris] **1.** *adj.* accelerating; **2.** *su./m* accelerator; ~ *de particules* particle accelerator; **accélération** [~ra'sjɔ̃] *f* acceleration; *work-rhythm*: speeding up; *mot. pédale f d'*~ accelerator; **accélérer** [~'re] (1f) *v/i.* accelerate (*a. mot.*); *mot. sl.* step on the gas; *v/t. fig.* expedite, quicken; *s'*~ become faster.

accent [ak'sɑ̃] *m* accent; stress; emphasis; pronunciation; **accentuation** [aksɑ̃tɥa'sjɔ̃] *f* stress(ing); accentuation; **accentuer** [~'tɥe] (1n) *v/t.* stress; accentuate; emphasize; *fig.* strengthen.

acceptable [aksɛp'tabl] acceptable; satisfactory; **acceptation** [~ta'sjɔ̃] *f* acceptance (*a.* ✝); **accepter** [~'te] (1a) *v/t.* accept; agree to; **accep-**

teur ✝ [~'tœːr] *m* drawee, acceptor; **acception** [~'sjɔ̃] *f* meaning, sense; *sans* ~ *de personne* without respect of persons; *dans toute l'*~ *du mot* in the full meaning or in every sense of the word.

accès [ak'sɛ] *m* access, approach; *anger, fever*: attack; fit; *par* ~ by fits and starts; **accessible** [aksɛ'sibl] accessible; approachable (*person*); **accession** [~'sjɔ̃] *f* accession; adherence; ~ *à la propriété* home ownership; ~ *du travail* rehabilitation; **accessoire** [~'swaːr] **1.** *adj.* accessory; *occupation f* ~ subsidiary occupation, side-line; **2.** *su./m* accessory; subsidiary topic or matter; *thea.* ~*s pl.* properties, *sl.* props.

accident [aksi'dɑ̃] *m* accident (*a. phls.*); ♪ accidental; ~ *de (la) circulation* road accident; ~ *de personne* casualty; ~ *de terrain* unevenness, undulation; *par* ~ accidentally; **accidenté, e** [aksidɑ̃'te] **1.** *adj.* uneven, irregular (*ground*); chequered (*life*); **2.** *su.* injured person, casualty; **accidentel, -elle** [~'tɛl] accidental, unintentional, casual; **accidenter** [~'te] (1a) *v/t.* vary (*one's style*); make picturesque, give variety to (*a landscape*); injure, damage; *s'*~ have an accident; **accidenteur** [~'tœːr] *m* party who causes an or the accident.

acclamation [aklama'sjɔ̃] *f* acclamation, applause; **acclamer** [~'me] (1a) *v/t.* acclaim, applaud, cheer.

acclimatation [aklimata'sjɔ̃] *f* acclimatization; *jardin m d'*~ Zoo; Botanical Gardens *sg.*; **acclimater** [~'te] (1a) *v/t.* acclimatize (to, à); *s'*~ become acclimatized.

accointance [akwɛ̃'tɑ̃:s] *f oft. pej.* intimacy, intercourse; *avoir des* ~*s avec* have dealings with; **accointer** [~'te] (1a) *v/t.*: *s'*~ *de* (*or avec*) *q.* enter into relations with s.o.

accolade [akɔ'lad] *f* embrace; accolade; F hug; *typ. a.* bracket, brace (⏜); **accolage** ⚘ [~'la:ʒ] *m* fastening to an espalier; **accoler** [~'le] (1a) *v/t.* couple, brace, bracket; tie up (*a plant*).

accommodage [akɔmɔ'da:ʒ] *m food*: preparation, dressing; **accommodant, e** [~'dɑ̃, ~'dɑ̃:t] accommodating, easy to deal with, good-natured; **accommodation**

[～da'sjɔ̃] *f* adaptation; **accommodement** [akɔmɔd'mɑ̃] *m* compromise, arrangement; ✝ agreement; **accommoder** [～mɔ'de] (1a) *v/t.* fit, adapt (to, *à*); prepare, dress (*food*); s'～ *à* adapt o.s. to; s'～ *de* put up with, make the best of.

accompagnateur *m*, **-trice** *f* [akɔ̃paɲa'tœːr, ～'tris] ♪ accompanist; escort (of a tour); **accompagnement** [～paɲ'mɑ̃] *m* attendance; accompaniment (*a. ♪*); **accompagner** [～pa'ɲe] (1a) *v/t.* accompany; escort.

accomplir [akɔ̃'pliːr] (2a) *v/t.* accomplish, achieve; complete; **accomplissement** [～plis'mɑ̃] *m* accomplishment, achievement; completion.

accord [a'kɔːr] *m* agreement; harmony; ♪ chord; pitch; *gramm.* concordance, agreement (*a. pol.*); *pol.* treaty; ～ *commercial* trade agreement; d'～ agreed!; d'un commun ～ by common consent, by mutual agreement; tomber d'～ agree, reach an agreement; **accordable** [akɔr'dabl] reconcilable; grantable; ♪ tunable; **accordage** ♪ [～'daːʒ] *m* tuning; **accordailles** [～'dɑːj] *f/pl.* † betrothal *sg.*; **accordéon** ♪ [～de'ɔ̃] *m* accordion; concertina; *fig.* en ～ crumpled (up); **accordéoniste** [～deɔ'nist] *m* accordion player; **accorder** [～'de] (1a) *v/t.* grant; match; ♪, *a. radio:* tune; s'～ agree (*a. gramm.*); harmonize (with, *avec*); **accordeur** *m*, **-euse** *f* ♪ [～'dœːr, ～'døːz] tuner.

accorte [a'kɔrt] *adj./f* pleasing, winsome.

accostable [akɔs'tabl] approachable; **accostage** ⚓ [～'taːʒ] *m* boarding; drawing alongside (of, *de*); **accoster** [～'te] (1a) *v/t.* ⚓ berth; board; ～ q. accost s.o., F go up to s.o.; greet s.o.

accotement [akɔt'mɑ̃] *m* mot., 🚗 shoulder; verge (*of road*); ～ *stabilisé* hard shoulder; ～ *non stabilisé* no hard shoulder, Br. *a.* soft verges; **accoter** [akɔ'te] (1a) *v/t.* lean, rest (against *contre*, *à*; on, *sur*); s'～ lean (against, *contre*); **accotoir** [～'twaːr] *m* armrest.

accouchée [aku'ʃe] *f* woman in childbed; **accouchement** [akuʃ'mɑ̃] *m* confinement; ～ *laborieux* difficult confinement; ～ *sans douleur* painless delivery; **accoucher** [aku'ʃe] (1a) *v/i.* be delivered (of, *de*), give birth (to, *de*); *fig.* ～ *de* qch. bring s.th. forth; *v/t.* deliver (*a woman*); **accoucheur** [～'ʃœːr] *m* obstetrician; **accoucheuse** [～'ʃøːz] *f* midwife.

accouder [aku'de] (1a) *v/t.:* s'～ lean (on one's elbows); **accoudoir** [～'dwaːr] *m* arm-rest, elbow-rest; balustrade, rail.

accouple [a'kupl] *f* leash; **accouplement** [akuplə'mɑ̃] *m* coupling (*a. radio*); pairing; ⚡ connecting; ☀ copulation; ⊕ ～ *articulé* joint coupling; ⚡ ～ *en série* series connection; **accoupler** [～'ple] (1a) *v/t.* couple (up) (*a.* 🐕); ⚡ connect, group; *fig.* join; s'～ mate.

accourcir [akur'siːr] (2a) *v/t.* curtail; shorten; **accourcissement** [～sis'mɑ̃] *m* shortening.

accourir [aku'riːr] (2i) *v/i.* hasten (up), run up.

accoutrement [akutrə'mɑ̃] *m* dress; F get-up; **accoutrer** [～'tre] (1a) *v/t.* equip; rig (*s.o.*) out (in, *de*).

accoutumance [akuty'mɑ̃ːs] *f* habit, use, usage; **accoutumé, e** [～'me] **1.** *adj.* accustomed (to, *à*); *à l'*～*e* usually; **2.** *su.* regular visitor; **accoutumer** [～'me] (1a) *v/t.* accustom (*s.o.*) (to, *à*).

accouvage [aku'vaːʒ] *m* artificial incubation.

accréditer [akredi'te] (1a) *v/t.* accredit (*an ambassador*); confirm (*a story*); credit; authorize; s'～ gain credence; **accréditeur** [～'tœːr] *m* guarantor; surety; **accréditif** [～'tif] *m* ✝ (letter of) credit; credential.

accroc [a'kro] *m* clothes: rent, tear; *fig.* hitch; *fig.* impediment; *sans* ～*s* smooth(ly *adv.*).

accrochage [akrɔ'ʃaːʒ] *m* hooking; *picture:* hanging; accumulation; *box.* clinch; *radio:* picking-up; ⚔ engagement; clash (*with the police*); F squabble; **accroche-cœur** [akrɔʃ'kœːr] *m* kiss-curl; **accrochement** [～'mɑ̃] *m* hooking; *fig.* difficulty; 🚗 coupling; **accrocher** [akrɔ'ʃe] (1a) *v/t.* hang (up) (on, from *à*); collide with (*a vehicle*); hook; catch; ⚓ grapple; ⚔ engage; *radio:* pick up; *sl.* pawn (*a watch*); F buttonhole (*s.o.*); s'～ cling (to, *à*); get

caught (on, *à*); *box.* clinch; ⚓
follow closely; F have a set-to;
accrocheur, -euse [-ˈʃœːr, -ˈʃøːz]
tenacious, persistent; eye-catching,
catchy; *c'est un ~* he's a sticker.
accroire [aˈkrwaːr] (4n) *v/t.*: (en)
faire ~ qch. à q. delude s.o. into
believing s.th.; *s'en faire ~* over-
estimate o.s.
accroissement [akrwasˈmɑ̃] *m*
growth; increase; Ⓐ *function*: increment.
accroître [aˈkrwaːtr] (4o) *v/t.* increase; *v/i. a. s'~* grow.
accroupir [akruˈpiːr] (2a) *v/t.*: *s'~*
crouch (down); squat (down).
accru, e [aˈkry] 1. *p.p. of accroître*;
2. *su./f* accretion, extension.
accu F [aˈky] *m* ⚡ accumulator; battery; *(re)charger (or régénérer) l'~*
charge the accumulator.
accueil [aˈkœːj] *m* reception, greeting; ✝ *faire (bon) ~ à une traite*
hono(u)r a bill; *faire bon ~ à* welcome
(*s.o.*); **accueillant, e** [akœˈjɑ̃,
~ˈjɑ̃ːt] affable; **accueillir** [~ˈjiːr]
(2c) *v/t.* welcome, greet, receive;
✝ hono(u)r *(a bill).*
acculer [akyˈle] (1a) *v/t.* drive into
a corner *or* to the wall; *s'~* set one's
back (against *à, contre*).
accumulateur, -trice [akymyla-
ˈtœːr, ~ˈtris] *su.* hoarder; *fig.* miser;
su./m ⚡ accumulator; **accumuler**
[~ˈle] (1a) *v/t.* accumulate.
accusateur, -trice [akyzaˈtœːr,
~ˈtris] 1. *adj.* incriminating; accus-
ing; 2. *su.* accuser; *su./m* ⚖ *hist. ~*
public Public Prosecutor; **accusation** [~zaˈsjɔ̃] *f* accusation; charge;
accusé, e [~ˈze] 1. *adj.* accused;
prominent (*feature*); 2. *su.* accused;
su./m: ✝ *~ de réception* acknowl-
edgement (of receipt); **accuser**
[~ˈze] (1a) *v/t.* accuse; *fig.* emphasize, bring out; show; ✝ *~ réception* acknowledge receipt (of, *de*); *s'~*
stand out; accuse o.s.
acéphale *zo.* [aseˈfal] acephalous,
headless.
acerbe [aˈsɛrb] tart; *fig.* sharp;
acerbité [asɛrbiˈte] *f* acerbity;
tartness; sharpness.
acéré, e [aseˈre] sharp, keen; *fig.*
mordant (*criticism*); **acérer** [~] (1f)
v/t. steel; *fig.* sharpen, give edge to.
acétate ⚗ [aseˈtat] *m* acetate; *~*
d'alumine acetate of alumina; *~ de*

cuivre verdigris; **acéteux, -euse**
[~ˈtø, ~ˈtøːz] acetous; **acétique**
[~ˈtik] acetic; **acétone** [~ˈtɔn] *f*
acetone; **acétylène** [~tiˈlɛn] *m*
acetylene.
achalandage [aʃalɑ̃ˈdaːʒ] *m* cus-
tom(ers *pl.*); **achalandé, e** [~ˈde]:
bien ~ well-stocked; ✝ with a large
custom (*shop*); **achalander** [~ˈde]
(1a) *v/t.* provide with custom.
acharné, e [aʃarˈne] keen; fierce,
bitter; strenuous; relentless; **acharnement** [~nəˈmɑ̃] *m* tenacity; re-
lentlessness; fury; stubbornness;
acharner [~ˈne] (1a) *v/t.*: *s'~ à* be
intent on; slave at; *s'~ sur (or contre)*
be implacable towards.
achat [aˈʃa] *m* purchase; purchasing; ✝ *pouvoir m d'~* purchasing
power.
acheminement [aʃminˈmɑ̃] *m* progress, course (towards, *vers*); ✝ *etc.*
routing; **acheminer** [~miˈne] (1a)
v/t. put on the way; train (*a horse*); ✝
etc. route, forward (to *sur, vers*); *s'~*
make one's way (towards *vers, sur*).
acheter [aʃˈte] (1d) *v/t.* buy, purchase; *fig.* bribe; *~ qch. à q.* buy s.th.
from s.o.; buy s.th. for s.o., buy s.o.
s.th.; *~ cher (bon marché)* buy at a
high price (cheap); **acheteur** *m*,
-euse *f* [~ˈtœːr, ~ˈtøːz] purchaser,
buyer.
achèvement [aʃɛvˈmɑ̃] *m* completion, conclusion; **achever** [aʃˈve]
(1d) *v/t.* finish, complete; F do for;
s'~ draw to a close; *v/i.*: *~ de (inf.)*
finish (*ger.*).
achillée ♀ [akiˈle] *f* milfoil, yarrow.
achoppement [aʃɔpˈmɑ̃] *m* stumble; knock; *pierre f d'~* stum-
bling-block; **achopper** [aʃɔˈpe] (1a)
v/i. a. s'~ stumble (over *sur*; against,
à); *fig.* come to grief.
achromatique *opt.* [akrɔmaˈtik]
achromatic.
acide ⚗ [aˈsid] 1. *adj.* sharp, tart,
acid; 2. *su./m* acid; *~ chlorhydrique*
hydrochloric acid; *~ sulfurique* sulphuric acid; **acidification** [asidifi-
kaˈsjɔ̃] *f* acidification; **acidimètre**
[~ˈmɛtr] *m* acidimeter; **acidité** [~ˈte]
f acidity, sourness; **acidulé, e**
[asidyˈle] acidulated; *bonbons m/pl.*
~s acid drops; **aciduler** [~] (1a) *v/t.*
turn sour; acidulate.
acier [aˈsje] *m* steel; *~ à précontrainte*
pre-stressed steel; *~ au tungstène*

tungsten steel; ~ *coulé* (*or fondu*) cast steel; ~ *doux* mild steel; ~ *laminé* rolled steel; ~ *spécial* high-grade steel; ~ *trempé* hardened *or* tempered steel; d'~ steel(y), of steel; **aciérage** ⊕ [asje'ra:ʒ] *m* steeling; *bain m* d'~ steel bath; **aciérer** [~'re] (1f) *v/t.* steel, acierate; **aciérie** ⊕ [~'ri] *f* steelworks *usu. sg.*

acné ♂ [ak'ne] *f* acne.

acolyte [akɔ'lit] *m eccl.* acolyte; *fig.* associate, confederate.

acompte [a'kɔ̃:t] *m* down payment, deposit, payment on account; instalment; F *fig.* foretaste; *par* ~s by instalments.

aconit ♀ [akɔ'nit] *m* aconite, monk's-hood.

acoquiner [akɔki'ne] (1a) *v/t. oft. pej.* s'~ *avec q.* take up with s.o.

à-côté [akɔ'te] *m remark:* aside; side-issue; ~s *pl.* purlieus.

à-coup [a'ku] *m* jolt, jerk, sudden stop; *par* ~s by fits and starts; *sans* ~s smooth(ly *adv.*).

acoustique [akus'tik] **1.** *adj.* acoustic; *appareil m* ~ hearing-aid; **2.** *su./f* acoustics *pl.*

acquéreur [ake'rœ:r] *m* purchaser, buyer; acquirer; **acquérir** [~'ri:r] (21) *v/t.* acquire, obtain; win (*esteem, friends*); *fig.* ~ *droit de cité* become naturalized; *v/i.* improve; **acquerrai** [akɛr're] *1st p. sg. fut. of acquérir*.

acquêt 🏛 [a'kɛ] *m* acquisition; ~s *pl.* common property *sg.* (*in marriage*).

acquièrent [a'kjɛ:r] *3rd p. pl. pres. of acquérir;* **acquiers** [~] *1st p. sg. pres. of acquérir.*

acquiescement [akjɛs'mɑ̃] *m* acquiescence (in, *à*); consent; **acquiescer** [akjɛ'se] (1k) *v/i.* acquiesce (in, *à*), agree (to, *à*).

acquis[1] [a'ki] *1st p. sg. p.s. of acquérir.*

acquis[2]**, e** [a'ki, ~'ki:z] **1.** *p.p. of acquérir;* **2.** *adj.* acquired, gained; established (*fact*); **3.** *su./m* attainments *pl.*, experience; **acquisition** [akizi'sjɔ̃] *f* acquisition, acquiring; purchase; *fig.* ~s *pl.* attainments.

acquit [a'ki] *m* discharge, release; 🏛 receipt (for, *de*); ~ *de transit Customs:* transire; *par* ~ *de conscience* for conscience sake; for form's sake; F *par manière d'*~ as

a matter of form; 🏛 *pour* ~ paid, received with thanks; ~s-à-caution *pl.* ~s-à-caution [akiakɔ'sjɔ̃] *m Customs:* permit; **acquittement** [akit'mɑ̃] *m debt:* discharge; 🏛 acquittal; **acquitter** [aki'te] (1a) *v/t.* unburden (*one's conscience*); 🏛 acquit; 🏛 discharge (*a debt*); 🏛 receipt (*a bill, a note*); fulfil (*an obligation*); ~ *q. de qch.* release s.o. from s.th.; s'~ *de* discharge (*a debt*); perform, fulfil (*a duty*).

acre ✒ [akr] *m* acre.

âcre [ɑ:kr] tart, sharp; *fig.* caustic (*remark*); **âcreté** [ɑkrə'te] *f* bitterness, acidity.

acrimonie [akrimɔ'ni] *f* acrimony; bitterness; **acrimonieux, -euse** [~'njø, ~'njø:z] acrimonious, bitter.

acrobate [akrɔ'bat] *su.* acrobat, tumbler; **acrobatie** [~ba'si] *f* acrobatics *pl.;* ~ (*aérienne*) aerobatics *pl.*

acte [akt] *m* act (*a. thea.*); deed (*a.* 🏛); 🏛 title; bill (*of sale*); 🏛 writ; ~s *pl.* learned society: transactions; records; *bibl.* ♀s *pl.* *des Apôtres* Acts of the Apostles; 🏛 ~ *civil* civil marriage; ~ *de décès* death-certificate; ~ *notarié* notarial deed; *faire* ~ *de présence* put in an appearance; *prendre* ~ *de* take note of; **acteur** [ak'tœ:r] *m* actor.

actif, -ve [ak'tif, ~'ti:v] **1.** *adj.* active; busy; alert; **2.** *su./m* 🏛 assets *pl.*, credit (side); *gramm.* active voice. [actinotherapy.\ **actinothérapie** ♂ [aktinɔtera'pi] *f/*

action [ak'sjɔ̃] *f* action, act; exploit; *water:* effect; *machine:* working; *thea.* gesture; 🏛 action, lawsuit; ✕ engagement; 🏛 share-(certificate), *Am.* stock; *eccl.* ~ *de grâces* thanksgiving; 🏛 ~ *de mine* mining-share; *champ m* d'~ sphere of action; **actionnaire** [aksjɔ'nɛ:r] *su.* shareholder, *Am.* stockholder; **actionnariat** [~nar'ja] *m* ~ *ouvrier,* ~ *des salariés* employee) shareholding; **actioner** [~'ne] (1a) *v/t.* 🏛 sue; ⊕ set in motion; operate (*a machine*); urge on; s'~ bestir o.s.

activer [akti've] (1a) *v/t.* stir up, push on; expedite; s'~ busy o.s. (with, *à*); **activité** [~vi'te] *f* activity; briskness.

actrice [ak'tris] *f* actress.

actualité [aktɥali'te] *f* actuality,

reality; topical question; ~s pl. cin. news-reel sg., F news sg.; radio: current events; d'~ topical.

actuel, -elle [ak'tɥɛl] current, present.

acuité [akɥi'te] f acuteness (a. ⚔); sharpness, keenness.

acupuncteur, acuponcteur [akypɔ̃k'tœːr] m acupuncturist; **acupuncture, acuponcture** [~'tyːr] f acupuncture. [angled.\

acutangle Å [aky'tɑ̃ːgl] acute-\

adage [a'daːʒ] m adage, saying, saw.

adamantin, e [adamɑ̃'tɛ̃, ~'tin] adamantine.

adaptabilité [adaptabili'te] f adaptability, adaptableness; **adaptable** [adap'tabl] adaptable; **adaptateur** phot., telev. [~ta'tœːr] m adapter; **adaptation** [~ta'sjɔ̃] f adaptation; adjustment; **adapter** [~'te] (1a) v/t. adapt, adjust (s.th. to s.th., qch. à qch.); s'~ à qch. adapt o.s. to s.th.; fit s.th.

additif [adi'tif] m additive; **addition** [adi'sjɔ̃] f addition; accretion; restaurant: bill, Am. or F check; **additionnel, -elle** [adisjɔ'nɛl] additional; impôt m ~ surtax; **additionner** [~'ne] (1a) v/t. add up, tot up; add (to, à); ~ un liquide de qch. add s.th. to a liquid, mix or dilute a liquid with s.th.; additionné de sucre with sugar added.

adénite ⚔ [ade'nit] f adenitis.

adéno... [adeno] glandular, adeno...

adent ⊕ [a'dɑ̃] m dovetail, tenon.

adepte [a'dɛpt] su. adept; initiate.

adéquat, e [ade'kwa, ~'kwat] adequate.

adhérence [ade'rɑ̃ːs] f adherence; adhesion (a. ⚔, phys.); **adhérent, e** [~'rɑ̃, ~'rɑ̃ːt] 1. adj. adhesive; adherent (to, à); 2. su. adherent, supporter; **adhérer** [~'re] (1f) v/i.: ~ à adhere or cling to; hold (an opinion); join, support (a party); mot. grip (the road).

adhésif, -ve [ade'zif, ~'ziːv] adhesive, sticky; emplâtre m ~ adhesive plaster; **adhésion** [~'zjɔ̃] f adhesion (a. fig.).

adieu [a'djø] 1. int. farewell!; goodbye!; dire ~ à say goodbye or farewell to; fig. give up or renounce (s.th.); 2. su./m: ~x pl. farewell sg., leave-taking sg.; faire ses ~x (à) say good-bye (to); take one's leave (of).

adipeux, -euse [adi'pø, ~'pøːz] adipose, fatty; **adipose** [~'poːz] f adiposis; **adiposité** [~pozi'te] f adiposity, fatness.

adirer ⚖ [adi're] (1a) v/t. lose, mislay (documents).

adjacent, e [adʒa'sɑ̃, ~'sɑ̃ːt] adjacent, contiguous (to, à); être ~ à border on, adjoin; rue f ~e side-street.

adjectif [adʒɛk'tif] m adjective.

adjoindre [ad'ʒwɛ̃ːdr] (4m) v/t. unite, associate; appoint as assistant; enrol(l); s'~ à join with (s.o.); **adjoint, e** [~'ʒwɛ̃, ~'ʒwɛ̃ːt] 1. adj. assistant-...; 2. su./m assistant; ~ au (or du) maire deputy-mayor.

adjonction [adʒɔ̃k'sjɔ̃] f adjunction; ⚠ annexe; gramm. zeugma.

adjudant [adʒy'dɑ̃] m ⚔ company sergeant-major; ⚓ warrant-officer; ⚔ ~-chef regimental sergeant-major; ⚓ ~ de pavillon flag-lieutenant.

adjudicataire [adʒydika'tɛːr] m highest-bidder; auction: purchaser; contractor; **adjudication** [~'sjɔ̃] f adjudication, award; contract: allocation; auction: knocking-down; mettre en ~ invite tenders for; put up for auction.

adjuger [adʒy'ʒe] (1l) v/t. award; auction: knock down.

adjuration [adʒyra'sjɔ̃] f adjuration; imprecation; **adjurer** [~'re] (1a) v/t. adjure, beseech; exorcise (a spirit).

adjuvant [adʒy'vɑ̃] m ⚔ adjuvant, additive; stimulus.

admettre [ad'mɛtr] (4v) v/t. admit; let in; permit.

administrateur [administra'tœːr] m administrator, manager; bank: director; **administratif, -ve** [~'tif, ~'tiːv] administrative; **administration** [~'sjɔ̃] f administration (a. eccl.); management; governing body; civil service; **administratrice** [~'tris] f administratrix; **administré m, e f** [adminis'tre] person under one's administration or jurisdiction; **administrer** [~] (1a) v/t. administer (a. eccl.), conduct, manage, govern; ⚖ ~ des preuves furnish proof.

admirable [admi'rabl] admirable, wonderful; **admirateur, -trice** [admira'tœːr, ~'tris] 1. adj. admiring; 2. su. admirer; **admiratif, -ve**

[ˌ'tif,ˌ'tiːv] admiring; **admiration** [ˌ'sjɔ̃] *f* admiration, wonder; **admirer** [admiˈre] (1a) *v/t.* admire. **admis, e** [adˈmi, ˌ'miːz] **1.** *p.p.* of *admettre*; **2.** *adj.* admitted; accepted; conventional; **admissible** [admiˈsibl] admissible; eligible (to, à); **admission** [ˌ'sjɔ̃] *f* admission; ⊕ inlet; ⊕ *période f d'~* induction stroke.

admonestation [admɔnestaˈsjɔ̃] *f,* **admonition** [ˌni'sjɔ̃] *f* admonition, reprimand; **admonester** [ˌnesˈte] (1a) *v/t.* admonish, reprimand, censure.

ado F [aˈdo] *m* youth, young man.

adolescence [adɔleˈsãːs] adolescence, youth; **adolescent, e** [ˌ'sã, ˌ'sãːt] **1.** *adj.* adolescent; **2.** *su.* adolescent; F teen-ager; *su./m* youth.

adonner [adɔˈne] (1a) *v/t.*: *s'~ à* devote o.s. to; take to (*drink etc.*), become addicted to.

adopter [adɔpˈte] (1a) *v/t.* adopt (*a child, a name, an opinion*); assume (*a name*); *parl.* pass (*a bill*); **adoptif, -ve** [ˌ'tif, ˌ'tiːv] adopted; adoptive (*parent*); **adoption** [ˌ'sjɔ̃] *f* adoption; *bill:* passage; carrying; *fils m par ~* adopted son; *pays m d'~* adopted country.

adorable [adɔˈrabl] adorable; charming; **adorateur, -trice** [ˌraˈtœːr, ˌ'tris] **1.** *su.* adorer, worshipper; F great admirer; **2.** *adj.* adoring; **adoration** [ˌraˈsjɔ̃] *f* adoration, worship; **adorer** [ˌ're] (1a) *v/t.* adore (*a. fig.*); worship (*God*); F dote on.

adossement [adosˈmã] *m* leaning (against à, contre); position back to back; **adosser** [adoˈse] (1a) *v/t.* lean; place back to back; *s'~ à* (*or contre*) lean one's back against.

adouber [aduˈbe] (1a) *v/t.* chess: adjust (*a piece*); *hist.* dub (*s.o.*) ([a] knight).

adoucir [aduˈsiːr] (1a) *v/t.* sweeten; tone down (*a colour*); mitigate; allay (*a pain*); pacify; ⊕ polish (*metal*), rough-polish (*glass*); *s'~* soften; grow softer (*voice*); grow milder (*weather*); grow less (*pain, grief*); **adoucissement** [ˌsisˈmã] *m* softening; alleviation; relief; sweetening.

adresse [aˈdrɛs] *f* address; skill, dexterity; shrewdness; **adresser**

[adrɛˈse] (1a) *v/t.* address; send; direct; refer (to, à); *~ la parole à q.* adress s.o.; *s'~ à* speak to; go and see; inquire at; be intended for; appeal to.

adroit, e [aˈdrwa, ˌ'drwat] dexterous; shrewd.

adulateur, -trice [adylaˈtœːr, ˌ'tris] **1.** *adj.* flattering, fawning; **2.** *su.* sycophant; **adulation** [ˌlaˈsjɔ̃] *f* adulation, sycophancy; **aduler** [ˌ'le] (1a) *v/t.* fawn upon, flatter (*s.o.*).

adulte [aˈdylt] *adj., a. su.* adult, grown-up.

adultération [adylteraˈsjɔ̃] *f* adulteration; **adultère** [adylˈtɛːr] **1.** *adj.* adulterous; **2.** *su./m* adulterer; adultery; *su./f* adulteress; **adultérer** [ˌteˈre] (1f) *v/t.* adulterate; **adultérin, e** [ˌteˈrɛ̃, ˌ'rin] adulterine; ♀ hybrid.

advenir [advəˈniːr] (2h) *v/i., a. impers.* happen, occur, turn out; *advienne que pourra* come what may.

adventice [advãˈtis] adventitious, casual (*a.* ♀); **adventif, -ve** [ˌ'tif, ˌ'tiːv] ♀ growing wild, chance...; accrued (*property*).

adverbe [adˈvɛrb] *m* adverb.

adversaire [advɛrˈsɛːr] *m* adversary, opponent; **adverse** [ˌ'vɛrs] adverse, unfavo(u)rable; ⅔ opposing, other (*party*); *fortune f ~* adversity; **adversité** [ˌvɛrsiˈte] *f* adversity, bad luck.

aérage [aeˈraːʒ] *m* aeration, airing; ventilation (*a.* ⚒); *puits m d'~* air-shaft; **aération** [ˌraˈsjɔ̃] airing, ventilation; **aéré, e** [ˌ're] airy; **aérer** [ˌ're] (1f) *v/t.* air, give (*s.th.*) an airing; aerate; ventilate; *s'~* get some fresh air; **aérien, -enne** [ˌ'rjɛ̃, ˌ'rjɛn] aerial; air-...; *chemin m de fer ~* elevated railway; *défense f ~enne* aerial defence; *voyage m ~* journey by air; **aérifère** [aeriˈfɛːr] air-...

aéro... [aerɔ] flying-..., air-...; *~bus* [ˌ'bys] *m* airbus; **~drome** [ˌdroːm] *m* aerodrome, *Am.* airdrome; **~dynamique** [ˌdinaˈmik] **1.** *adj.* aerodynamic; streamlined; **2.** *su./f* aerodynamics *sg.*; **~gare** [ˌ'gaːr] *f* air terminal; **~gramme** [ˌ'gram] *m* air letter; **~modélisme** [ˌmɔdeˈlism] *m* model aircraft making; **~modéliste** [ˌmɔdeˈlist] *m* model aircraft maker; **~moteur** [ˌmɔˈtœːr] *m* aero-engine;

wind-engine; **~naute** [~'noːt] *m* aeronaut, balloonist; **~nautique** [~no'tik] **1.** *adj.* aeronautical; **2.** *su./f* aeronautics *sg.*; **~plane** [~'plan] *m* aeroplane, aircraft; **~port** [~'pɔːr] *m* airport; **~porté, e** [~pɔr'te]: *troupes f/pl.* **~es** airborne troops; **~postal, e,** *m/pl.* **-aux** [~pɔs'tal, ~'to] airmail...; **~sol** [~'sɔl] aerosol; spray; **~spatial, e** *m/pl.*, **-aux** [~spa'sjal, -'sjo] aerospace ...; **~stat** [~s'ta] *m* airship, balloon; **~station** [~sta'sjo] *f* aeronautics *sg.*; **~statique** [~sta'tik] **1.** *adj.*: *ballon m* **~** balloon; **2.** *su./f* aerostatics *sg.*; **~train** (*TM*) [~'trɛ̃] *m* hovertrain.

affabilité [afabili'te] *f* affability, graciousness (*to avec, envers*); **affable** [a'fabl] affable, gracious.

affadir [afa'diːr] (2a) *v/t.* render tasteless *or* uninteresting; *fig.* disgust; **affadissement** [~dis'mɑ̃] *m* loss of flavo(u)r; growing insipid.

affaiblir [afɛ'bliːr] (2a) *v/t.* weaken; *phot.* reduce (the contrasts of); *s'*~ grow weaker; **affaiblissement** [~blis'mɑ̃] *m* diminution; weakening; reducing; **affaiblisseur** *phot.* [~bli'sœːr] *m* reducing agent *or* bath.

affaire [a'fɛːr] *f* business, affair; question, matter; ⚖ case; transaction; **~s** *pl. a.* belongings; **~s** *pl. étrangères* foreign affairs; *avoir* **~** *à* have to deal with; be faced with (*a problem etc.*); *cela fait l'*~ that will do (nicely); *ce n'est pas petite* **~** it is no trifling matter; *parler* (*d'*)**~s** talk business; *son* **~** *est faite* he is done for; *voilà l'*~ that's it!; **affairé, e** [afɛ're] busy; **affairement** [afɛr'mɑ̃] *m* hurry, bustle; **affairer** [afɛ're] (1a) *v/t.*: *s'*~ busy oneself, be busy; **affairisme** [afɛ'rism] *m* racketeering; **affairiste** [afɛ'rist] *m* racketeer.

affaissement [afɛs'mɑ̃] *m* sinking; *ground:* subsidence; *strength:* breaking up; ⚕ prostration; *fig.* depression; **affaisser** [afɛ'se] (1b) *v/t.* cause to sink; weigh down; *s'*~ sink, subside; give way; cave in; collapse (*a.* ⚕).

affaler [afa'le] (1a) *v/t.* ⚓ haul down; lower; *s'*~ ⚓ be driven ashore; F drop.

affamé, e [afa'me] hungry, ravenous (for, *de*); **affamer** [~] (1a) *v/t.* starve.

affectation [afɛkta'sjo] *f* affectation;

pretence; ✝ appropriation; † predilection; ✗ *etc.* posting, *Am.* assignment; assignment (*to a post*); **affecté** [~'te] affected, F put-on; **affecter** [~'te] (1a) *v/t.* assign; set apart; pretend; assume (*a shape*); move (*s.o.*); affect; have a predilection for; ⚖ burden (*the land*); ⚕ affect, attack; ✗ *etc.* post, *Am.* assign; **affectif, -ve** [~'tif, ~'tiːv] affective; **affection** [~'sjo] *f* affection (*a.* ⚕); fondness, liking; ⚕ disease, complaint; **affectionner** [~sjo'ne] (1a) *v/t.* be fond of, have a liking for; † *s'*~ *à* *q.* become fond of s.o.; *s'*~ *q.* gain s.o.'s affections; **affectueux, -euse** [~'tɥø, ~'tɥøːz] affectionate, fond, loving.

afférent, e [afe'rɑ̃, ~'rɑ̃ːt] relating, relative (to, *à*); accruing.

affermer [afɛr'me] (1a) *v/t.* let; rent (*land*).

affermir [afɛr'miːr] (2a) *v/t.* consolidate, make firm; *fig.* strengthen.

affété, e [afe'te] affected, mincing; **afféterie** [~'tri] *f* affectation, mincing.

affichage [afi'faːʒ] *m* bill-posting; *fig.* F show; *panneau m d'*~ notice-board; **affiche** [a'fif] *f* poster; **afficher** [afi'fe] (1a) *v/t.* post up, placard; *fig.* parade, flaunt; *s'*~ *pour* set up for; **afficheur** [~'fœːr] *m* bill-sticker.

affidé, e [afi'de] **1.** *adj.* † trusty; **2.** *su. pej.* accomplice; secret agent.

affilage ⊕ [afi'laːʒ] *m* whetting, sharpening.

affilée [afi'le]: *d'*~ at a stretch, on end.

affiler [afi'le] (1a) *v/t.* sharpen, whet; ⊕ set (*a saw*); draw (*gold*).

affiliation [afilja'sjo] *f* affiliation; **affilié** *m, e f* [afi'lje] *su.* (affiliated) member, associate; **affilier** [afi'lje] (1o) *v/t.* affiliate (with, *to à*); *s'* ~ *à* join (*a society etc.*).

affiloir [afi'lwaːr] *m* hone; *razor:* strop; *knife:* steel; whetstone.

affinage ⊕ [afi'naːʒ] *m* refining; *fig.* improvement; *cloth:* cropping; *hemp:* hackling; *plank:* fining down; ~ *de surface* surface refinement; **affiner** [~'ne] (1a) *v/t.* refine; improve; point (*needles*); fine (*metals*); fine down (*a plank*); hackle (*hemp*); crop, shear (*cloth*); mature (*wine, cheese*).

affinité [afini'te] *f* affinity (*a.* 🜂), relationship; *fig.* resemblance.

affirmatif, -ve [afirma'tif, ~'ti:v] **1.** *adj.* affirmative; **2.** *su./f* affirmative; *dans l'~ve* in the affirmative; *if so; répondre par l'~ve* answer yes or in the affirmative; **affirmation** [~ma'sjɔ̃] *f* assertion; **affirmer** [~'me] (1a) *v/t.* assert.

affleurer [aflœ're] (1a) *v/t.* level; make flush; be level *or* flush with; *v/i.* be level *or* flush.

afflictif, -ve ⚖ [aflik'tif, ~'ti:v] corporal, bodily; *peine f ~ve* corporal punishment; penal servitude; **affliction** [~'sjɔ̃] *f* affliction, sorrow, distress; **affliger** [afli'ʒe] (11) *v/t.* afflict (with, *de*); distress, grieve; *s'~* grieve, be distressed (at, *de*).

affluence [afly'ɑ̃:s] *f* flow(ing); flood; ✇ afflux; abundance; crowd; *heures f/pl. d'~* peak hours, rush hours; **affluent, e** [~'ɑ̃, ~'ɑ̃:t] **1.** *adj.* † affluent; **2.** *su./m* tributary; **affluer** [~'e] (1n) *v/i.* flow (*a.* ✇); abound; *fig.* crowd, flock; **afflux** [a'fly] *m* afflux, rush.

affolement [afɔl'mɑ̃] *m* panic; *engine:* racing; **affoler** [afɔ'le] (1a) *v/t.* frighten, terrify, throw into a panic; madden; *s'~* (get in a) panic, F get in a flap; go crazy; ✇ *etc.* (begin to) race (*engine etc.*).

affouragement [afuraʒ'mɑ̃] *m* fodder(ing); **affourager** [~ra'ʒe] (1l) *v/t.* fodder (*cattle*).

affranchi, e [afrɑ̃'ʃi] **1.** *adj.* freed; free (from, *of de*); **2.** *su./m* freedman; *su./f* freedwoman; **affranchir** [~'ʃi:r] (2a) *v/t.* free, emancipate; exempt; *post:* frank, prepay, stamp; *s'~ de* get rid of; **affranchissement** [~ʃis'mɑ̃] *m* emancipation; release, exemption; *post:* franking, prepayment; postage.

affres [afr] *f/pl.* pangs, terrors, throes.

affrètement ⚓ [afrɛt'mɑ̃] *m* freighting; charter(ing); **affréter** ⚓ [afre'te] (1f) *v/t.* freight; charter.

affreux, -euse [a'frø, ~'frø:z] frightful, dreadful; ghastly; hideous.

affriander [afriɑ̃'de] (1a) *v/t.* entice, allure; make attractive.

affront [a'frɔ̃] *m* affront, insult; *faire un ~ à* insult; **affronter** [afrɔ̃'te] (1a) *v/t.* confront, face; *fig.* brave; ✇ join face to face.

affublement *pej.* [afyblə'mɑ̃] *m* get-up, rig-out; **affubler** *pej.* [~'ble] (1a) *v/t.* rig out (in, *de*).

affût [a'fy] *m* hiding-place; gun-carriage; *chasser à l'~* stalk; *être à l'~* lie in wait; be on the look-out (for, *de*); **affûter** ✇ [afy'te] (1a) *v/t.* sharpen (*a.* F *fig.*); set (*a saw*); stock with tools; **affûteuse** ✇ [~'tø:z] *f* grinding-machine.

afin [a'fɛ̃] **1.** *prp.: ~ de* (*inf.*) (in order) to (*inf.*); **2.** *cj.: ~ que* (*sbj.*) in order that, so that.

africain, e [afri'kɛ̃, ~'kɛn] *adj., a. su.* ♀ African.

Afrikander [afrikɑ̃'dɛ:r] *m* Afrikander.

agaçant, e [aga'sɑ̃, ~'sɑ̃:t] irritating; provocative; **agacer** [~'se] (1k) *v/t.* irritate, annoy; *s'~* get annoyed; **agacerie** F [agas'ri] *f* provocation, teasing, coquetry.

agapes F [a'gap] *f/pl.* feast.

agate [a'gat] *f* agate.

âge [ɑ:ʒ] *m* age; period; generation; *d'~ à, en ~ de* of an age to; *enfant mf d'~ scolaire* child of school age; *entre deux ~s* middle-aged; *quel ~ avez-vous?, quel est votre ~?* how old are you?; *à ton ~* when I was your age; *retour m d'~* change of life; **âgé, e** [ɑ'ʒe] old, aged; elderly; *~ de deux ans* 2 years old, aged 2.

agence [a'ʒɑ̃:s] *f* agency; *~ de publicité* advertising agency; *~ de voyages* travel agency; *~ générale* general agency; *~ matrimoniale* marriage bureau; **agencement** [aʒɑ̃s'mɑ̃] *m* arrangement, order; *~s pl.* fixtures; **agencer** [aʒɑ̃'se] (1k) *v/t.* arrange; order; fit up.

agenda [aʒɛ̃'da] *m* note-book, memorandum-book; appointment book; diary.

agenouiller [aʒnu'je] (1a) *v/t.: s'~* kneel (down).

agent [a'ʒɑ̃] *m* agent; middleman; medium, agency; (*a. ~ de police*) policeman, (police) constable; *~ de brevet* patent agent; *~ de change* stockbroker, exchange broker; *~ de liaison* liaison officer; *~ de location* house agent; *~ de maîtrise* supervisor; foreman; *~ fiduciaire* trustee; *~ provocateur* agent provocateur.

agglomération [aglɔmera'sjɔ̃] *f* agglomeration; mass; built-up area; *~s pl. urbaines* centres of population, urban districts *or* centres; **aggloméré** [~'re] *m* patent fuel, briquette; *geol.* conglomerate; **agglomérer** [~'re] (1f) *v/t.* agglomerate; bring together; s'~ cohere; cake.

agglutinant, e [aglyti'nɑ̃, ~'nɑ̃:t] **1.** *adj.* adhesive; agglutinative; binding; **2.** *su./m* bond; **agglutinatif, -ve** [~na'tif, ~'ti:v] **1.** *adj. see* *agglutinant 1*; **2.** *su./m* agglutinant; **agglutiner** [~'ne] (1a) *v/t.* agglutinate; bind; s'~ cake, agglutinate.

aggravant, e [agra'vɑ̃, ~'vɑ̃:t] aggravating; **aggravation** [~va'sjɔ̃] *f* worsening; *penalty*: increase; 🏛, ⚖ aggravation; **aggraver** [~'ve] (1a) *v/t.* aggravate; worsen; increase; s'~ worsen.

agile [a'ʒil] agile, nimble; active; **agilité** [aʒili'te] *f* agility, nimbleness.

agio [a'ʒjo] *m* ✝ agio; F jobbery; **agiotage** ✝ [aʒjɔ'ta:ʒ] *m* (stock-)jobbing; **agioter** ✝ [~'te] (1a) *v/i.* gamble, speculate; **agioteur** [~'tœːr] *m* gambler, speculator.

agir [a'ʒiːr] (2a) *v/i.* act; do; operate, work; behave; ~ *bien* (*mal*) *envers* (*or avec*) behave well (badly) towards; 🏛 ~ *contre* prosecute; sue; *il s'agit de savoir si* the question is whether; s'~ *de* be a question of (*s.th.*); **agissant, e** [aʒi'sɑ̃, ~'sɑ̃:t] active; bustling; **agissements** [aʒis'mɑ̃] *m/pl.* doings; machinations; goings-on.

agitateur, -trice [aʒita'tœːr, ~'tris] *su.* agitator; ⊕ mixer; *su./m* 🔧 stirring-rod; **agitation** [~ta'sjɔ̃] *f* agitation (*a. fig.*); stir(ring); shaking, tossing; disturbance; restlessness; excitement; **agité, e** [~'te] restless; excited; perturbed; choppy, rough (*sea*); **agiter** [~'te] (1a) *v/t.* agitate; wave; shake, toss; stir; disturb; debate (*a question*); s'~ move (about); stir; fidget.

agneau [a'ɲo] *m* lamb; **agneler** [aɲə'le] (1d) *v/i.* lamb; **agnelet** † [~'le] *m* lambkin; **agnelin** [~'lɛ̃] *m* *fur*: lambskin.

agonie [agɔ'ni] *f* death agony; *être à l'~* be at the point of death; **agonir** [~'niːr] (2a) *v/t.*: ~ *q. d'injures* heap abuse on s.o.; **agoniser** [~ni'ze] (1a) *v/i.* be at the point of death, be dying.

agrafe [a'graf] *f* hook; clasp; clamp; clip; ⊕ dowel; ⊕ joint; **agrafer** [agra'fe] (1a) *v/t.* hook; clasp; fasten; clip (*papers*); ⊕ dowel; *sl.* nab (= *capture*); **agrafeuse** [~'føːz] *f* stapler.

agraire [a'grɛːr] agrarian; *réforme f* ~ agrarian reform.

agrandir [agrɑ̃'diːr] (2a) *v/t.* increase; enlarge; exalt; exaggerate; s'~ grow larger; **agrandissement** [~dis'mɑ̃] *m* enlargement; increase; rise (in power *etc.*); *phot.* blow-up; **agrandisseur** *phot.* [~di'sœːr] *m* enlarger.

agrarien, -enne [agra'rjɛ̃, ~'rjɛn] *adj., a. su./m* agrarian.

agréable [agre'abl] agreeable, pleasant; pleasing.

agréé [agre'e] *m commercial court*: counsel, attorney.

agréer [~] (1a) *v/t.* accept; approve; allow; *veuillez ~ l'expression de mes sentiments distingués* Yours sincerely; s'~ *à* enjoy; *v/i.* be agreeable (to, *à*).

agrégat ⊕ [agre'ga] *m* aggregate; **agrégation** [~ga'sjɔ̃] *f* ⊕ binding; ⊕ aggregate; admission (*to a society*); *in France*: competitive State examination for appointment as teacher in a *lycée*; **agrégé, e** [~'ʒe] **1.** *adj.* aggregate; *geol.* clastic (*rock*); **2.** *su./m* one who has passed the *agrégation*; **agréger** [~'ʒe] (1g) *v/t.* † admit, incorporate; admit to the title of *agrégé*.

agrément [agre'mɑ̃] *m* consent; approval; pleasure, amusement; charm; ~s *pl.* ornaments; trimmings; *voyage m d'~* pleasure-trip; **agrémenter** [~mɑ̃'te] (1a) *v/t.* adorn.

agrès [a'grɛ] *m/pl.* ⚓ tackle *sg.*, gear *sg.*; *sp.* apparatus *sg.*, fittings.

agresseur [agre'sœːr] *m* aggressor; assailant; **agressif, -ve** [~'sif, ~'siːv] aggressive; **agression** [~'sjɔ̃] *f* aggression; attack; assault; ~s *pl.* stresses *pl.*, strains *pl.*; **agressivité** [agresivi'te] *f* aggressiveness.

agreste [a'grɛst] rural; rustic; uncouth.

agricole [agri'kɔl] agricultural (*labourer, products*); **agriculteur** [~kyl'tœːr] *m* agriculturist; husbandman; farmer; **agriculture** [~kyl'tyːr] *f* agriculture; husbandry.

agriffer [agri'fe] (1a) v/t. F claw; s'~ à claw at; clutch at.

agripper [agri'pe] (1a) v/t. F clutch (at); grab.

agronomie [agrɔnɔ'mi] f husbandry, agronomy.

agrumes [a'grym] m/pl. citrus fruit.

aguerrir [agɛ'riːr] (2a) v/t. harden, season; s'~ grow seasoned; s'~ à (or contre) become hardened to.

aguets [a'gɛ] m/pl.: aux ~ on the watch or look-out.

aguicher sl. [agi'ʃe] (1a) v/t. excite; tantalize; sl. turn (s.o.) on.

ah! [ɑ] int. oh!; ah!

ahaner [aa'ne] (1a) v/i. pant; work hard, toil; hum and haw.

ahurir F [ay'riːr] (2a) v/t. bewilder.

ai [e] 1st p. sg. pres. of avoir 1.

aï zo. [ai] m ai.

aide [ɛːd] su. assistant; help; su./f help, assistance; pol. ~ économique economic aid; à l'~ de to or with the help of; venir en ~ à q., venir à l'~ de q. help s.o.; su./f: ~ ménagère home help; ~-comptable, pl. ~s-comptables [ɛdkɔ'tabl] su. assistant-accountant; ~-maçon, pl. ~s-maçons [~ma'sɔ̃] m hodman; ~-mémoire [~me'mwaːr] m/inv. pocket-book; manual; pol. aide-mémoire; memorandum; aider [ɛ'de] (1b) v/t. help, assist, aid; s'~ de make use of; v/i.: ~ à qch. help (towards) s.th., contribute to s.th.

aie [ɛ] 1st p. sg. pres. sbj. of avoir 1.

aïeul [a'jœl] m grandfather; **aïeule** [~] f grandmother; **aïeuls** [~] m/pl. grandparents; grandfathers; **aïeux** [a'jø] m/pl. ancestors, forefathers.

aigle [ɛgl] su./m eagle; fig. genius; elephant paper; lectern; su./f ⊘ eagle; ✕ standard.

aiglefin icht. [ɛglə'fɛ̃] m haddock.

aiglon [ɛ'glɔ̃] m eaglet.

aigre [ɛːgr] 1. adj. sour, tart; bitter (wind, tone); shrill, sharp (voice, sound); crude (colour); 2. su./m sharpness; **aigre-doux, -douce** [ɛgrə'du, ~'dus] bitter-sweet; fig. subacid; **aigrefin** [~'fɛ̃] m icht. haddock; fig. sharper, swindler; **aigrelet, -ette** [~'lɛ, ~'lɛt] sourish, tart; **aigrette** [ɛ'grɛt] f orn. aigrette (a. cost., ⚜), egret (a. ⚘); tuft; ⚡ a. brush; **aigreur** [ɛ'grœːr] f sourness (a. fig.); fig. ranco(u)r; ⊕ iron: brittleness; ✱ ~s pl. acidity sg. (of

the stomach); heartburn sg.; **aigrir** [ɛ'griːr] (2a) v/t/i. turn sour; v/t. fig. embitter.

aigu, -guë [e'gy] sharp, pointed; ✗, ✗; gramm. acute; fig. intense; bitter; piercing (sound); ♪ high(-pitched).

aigue-marine, pl. **aigues-marines** [ɛgma'rin] su./f, a. adj./inv. aquamarine.

aiguière [e'gjɛːr] f ewer.

aiguillage ✇ [egɥi'jaːʒ] m shunting, Am. switching; points pl., Am. switches pl.; **aiguille** [e'gɥiːj] f needle (a. pine, compass); clock: hand; ⚠ king-post; mountain: point; churchtower: spire; ✇ points pl., Am. switch; **aiguillée** [egɥi'je] f needleful; **aiguiller** [~'je] (1a) v/t. ✇ shunt, Am. switch; fig. direct, steer, orient(ate); **aiguillette** [~'jɛt] f aiguillette, aglet; ✗, ⚓ shoulder-knot; **aiguilleur** ✇ [~'jœːr] m pointsman, Am. switchman; ✗ ~ du ciel air traffic controller; **aiguillier** [~'je] m needle-maker; needle-book; **aiguillon** [~'jɔ̃] m goad; wasp: sting; fig. spur, stimulus; **aiguillonner** [~jɔ'ne] (1a) v/t. goad; fig. spur on; rouse.

aiguiser [eg(ɥ)i'ze] (1a) v/t. whet (a. fig.), sharpen; set (a razor, a saw); fig. excite, quicken.

ail, pl. **⚘ ails**, cuis. **aulx** [aːj, o] m ⚘ allium; cuis. garlic.

aile [ɛl] f wing (a. ✕, sp.); windmill: sail; blade; eccl. aisle; F fin, arm; mot. wing, Am. fender; ✗ ~ en delta delta wing; ✗ ~ en flèche swept-back wing; **ailé, e** [ɛ'le] winged; **aileron** [ɛl'rɔ̃] m pinion; small wing; shark: fin; ✗ aileron; water-wheel: float(-board); ⚠ scroll; **ailette** [ɛ'lɛt] f ⚠ small wing; ⊕ lug; radiator: gill, fin; ventilator: vane; turbine: blade; **ailier** sp. [ɛ'lje] m wing(er).

aillade cuis. [a'jad] f garlic sauce.

aille [aj] 1st p. sg. pres. sbj. of aller 1.

ailleurs [a'jœːr] adv. elsewhere; d'~ from somewhere else; moreover, besides; nulle part ~ nowhere else.

aimable [ɛ'mabl] agreeable, pleasant; amiable, kind; nice.

aimant¹, e [ɛ'mɑ̃, ~'mɑ̃ːt] loving, affectionate.

aimant² [ɛ'mɑ̃] m magnet (a. fig.); ~ long bar magnet; ~ naturel magnetic iron ore; **aimantation** [ɛmɑ̃-

ta'sjɔ̃] *f* magnetization; **aimanter** [ˌ'te] (1a) *v/t.* magnetize; *aiguille f aimantée* magnetic needle.

aimer [ɛ'me] (1b) *v/t.* love; like; be fond of; be in love with; *v/i.* love; ˌ *à (inf.)* like (*ger.*) or to (*inf.*); *j'aimerais* I would like; *j'aimerais mieux* I would prefer *or* rather *or* sooner.

aine *anat.* [ɛn] *f* groin.

aîné, e [ɛ'ne] *adj.*, *a. su.* elder; eldest; first-born; senior; *il est mon ˌ de trois mois* he is 3 months older than I; he is my senior by 3 months; **aînesse** [ɛ'nɛs] *f* primogeniture; seniority; *droit m d'ˌ* law of primogeniture; birthright.

ainsi [ɛ̃'si] **1.** *adv.* thus; so; in this way; ˌ *soit-il!* so be it!; *eccl.*, *a. co.* amen; *pour ˌ dire* so to speak; **2.** *cj.* so; ˌ *que* as well as; like.

air[1] [ɛːr] *m* air; wind; atmosphere (*a. fig.*); *metall.* ˌ *chaud* hot blast; ⊕ ˌ *comprimé* compressed air; ˌ *conditionné* air-conditioned; ˌ *frais* fresh air; *courant m d'ˌ* draught, *Am.* draft; *en l'ˌ* (up) into the air; *en plein ˌ* in the open air; *il y a qch. dans l'ˌ* there is s.th. in the wind; *menaces f/pl. en l'ˌ* empty threats; *mettre à l'ˌ* place in the open; *fig. être en l'ˌ* be in disorder or confusion, be in a mess; *fig.* flanquer (*or* F ficher) *en l'ˌ* throw away; F chuck up *or* out; knock over; *fig.* mettre en l'ˌ throw into confusion; *fig.* paroles *f/pl.* en l'ˌ idle talk; *fig.* projets *m/pl.* en l'ˌ castles in the air; *fig.* vivre de l'ˌ *du temps* live on air.

air[2] [ˌ] *m* air, look, appearance; way, manner; ˌ *de famille* family likeness; *avoir l'ˌ de* look like; *avoir l'ˌ de (inf.)* seem to (*inf.*), look as if (*ind.*); *prendre (or se donner) des ˌs* give o.s. airs.

air[3] ♩ [ˌ] *m* air, tune, melody; aria; ˌ *à boire* drinking song.

aire [ˌ] *f* area; site; (threshing-)floor; △, ♉ area; *eagle:* eyrie; ♐ ˌ *d'atterrissage* landing strip *or* patch; *meteor.* ˌ *de haute (basse) pression* high (low) pressure (area); ˌ *du vent* wind direction; point of the compass.

airelle ♣ [ɛ'rɛl] *f* bilberry, whortleberry, *Am.* huckleberry, blueberry.

airer [ɛ're] (1a) *v/i.* build an eyrie *or* a nest.

aisance [ɛ'zãːs] *f* ease; comfort;

competency; *cabinet m d'ˌs* public convenience, water-closet; **aise** [ɛːz] **1.** *adj.*: *être bien ˌ* be very glad; **2.** *su./f* ease, comfort; † pleasure; *à l'ˌ, à son ˌ* comfortable; well-off; *adv.* comfortably; *en prendre à son ˌ* take it easy; *mal à l'ˌ* ill at ease; **aisé, e** [ɛ'ze] easy; well-to-do, well-off (for money).

aisselle [ɛ'sɛl] *f anat.* armpit; △ haunch; ♀ axilla.

ajointer [aʒwɛ̃'te] (1a) *v/t.* join (together); fit end to end.

ajonc ♣ [a'ʒɔ̃] *m* gorse, furze.

ajour [a'ʒuːr] *m* △ opening; ⊕ perforation; **ajouré, e** [aʒu're] perforated; open-work.

ajournement [aʒurnə'mã] *m* postponement; adjournment; ✕ deferment; **ajourner** [ˌ'ne] (1a) *v/t.* postpone; adjourn; defer; *pol.* table (*a bill*).

ajouter [aʒu'te] (1a) *v/t.* add; ˌ *foi à* believe (*s.th.*).

ajustage ⊕ [aʒys'ta:ʒ] *m* fitting, assembly; fit; ˌ *lâche* (*serré*) loose (tight) fit; **ajustement** [ˌtə'mã] *m* adjusting, adjustment; **ajuster** [ˌ'te] (1a) *v/t.* adjust, fit; adapt; settle, arrange; true up; aim (*a shot, a gun*); ˌ *une montre* put a watch right; *s'ˌ* fit; agree; adapt o.s.; suit o.s.; **ajusteur** [ˌ'tœːr] *m* fitter.

ajutage [aʒy'ta:ʒ] *m* nozzle; jet; *water-works:* a(d)jutage.

alacrité [alakri'te] *f* alacrity; eagerness.

alaire [a'lɛːr] alar, of the wings.

alambic [alã'bik] *m* still; **alambiqué, e** *fig.* [ˌbi'ke] oversubtle, strained.

alanguir [alã'giːr] (2a) *v/t.* make languid; *s'ˌ* languish; flag; grow languid; **alanguissement** [ˌgis-'mã] *m* languor; weakness.

alarme [a'larm] *f* alarm; *donner l'ˌ* sound the alarm; **alarmer** [alar-'me] (1a) *v/t.* alarm, startle; disquiet; worry; *s'ˌ* be(come) alarmed; worry; **alarmiste** [ˌ'mist] *su.*, *a. adj.* alarmist.

albanais, e [alba'nɛ, ˌ'nɛːz] **1.** *adj.* albanian; **2.** *su./m ling.* Albanian; *su.* ♀ Albanian.

albâtre [al'bɑːtr] *m* alabaster.

albatros *orn.*, ♐ [alba'trɔs] *m* albatross. [albino.)

albinos [albi'noːs] *su.*, *a. adj./inv.*)

Albion [al'bjɔ̃] _f_ Britain; _poet._
Albion.
album [al'bɔm] _m_ album; _paint._
sketch-book; picture-book.
albumine _𝔐_ [alby'min] _f_ albumin.
alcali [alka'li] _m_ alkali; ～ _minéral_
soda-ash; ～ _végétal_ potash; ～ _vola-_
til ammonia; **alcalin, e** [～'lɛ̃, ～'lin]
alkaline.
alchimie [alʃi'mi] _f_ alchemy.
alcool [al'kɔl] _m_ alcohol; F spirit(s
_pl._); ～ _dénaturé_ methylated spirits
_pl._; ～ _méthylique_ methyl alcohol;
alcoolique [alkɔ'lik] **1.** _adj._ alcoholic; **2.** _su._ alcoholic; drunkard;
alcooliser [～li'ze] (1a) _v/t._ alco-
holize; fortify (_wine_); **alcoolisme**
[～'lism] _m_ alcoholism; **alcoomètre**
[～'mɛtr] _m_ alcoholometer; **alcoo-**
test [～'test] _m_ breathalyser; breath
test.   [recess.]
alcôve [al'ko:v] _f_ alcove; (bed-)
alcyon _orn._ [al'sjɔ̃] _m_ kingfisher,
halcyon.
aléa [ale'a] _m_ risk, hazard; **aléa-**
toire [～a'twa:r] aleatory; risky;
problematic(al).
alêne ⊕ [a'lɛn] awl.
alentour [alɑ̃'tu:r] **1.** _adv._ around;
2. _su./m:_ ～s _pl._ neighbourhood _sg._,
surroundings.
alerte [a'lɛrt] **1.** _adj._ alert, quick;
watchful; **2.** _int._ look out!; **3.** _su./f_
alarm, alert; warning; ～ _au feu_ fire
alarm; _fausse_ ～ false alarm; **alerter**
[alɛr'te] (1a) _v/t._ alert; warn.
alésage ⊕ [ale'zɑ:ʒ] _m_ boring;
reaming; bore; **aléser** ⊕ [～'ze] (1f)
_v/t._ bore; ream.
alevin [al'vɛ̃] _m_ fry; **alevinier** [～-
vi'nje] _m_ breeding-pond.
alexandrin, e [alɛksɑ̃'drɛ̃, ～'drin]
1. _adj._ Alexandrian; Alexandrine;
2. _su./m prosody:_ alexandrine; _su._ ♀
Alexandrian.
alezan [al'zɑ̃] _su./m, a. adj._ chestnut.
alfa ♀ [al'fa] _m_ alfa(-grass), esparto
(-grass).
algarade [alga'rad] _f_ storm of insults _or_ abuse; dressing-down;
escapade; sally; ✕ † raid.
algèbre [al'ʒɛ:br] _f_ algebra; **algé-**
brique [～ʒe'brik] algebraic.
algérien, -enne [alʒe'rjɛ̃, ～'rjɛn]
adj., a. su. ♀ Algerian.
algue ♀ [alg] _f_ alga; sea-weed.
alibi [ali'bi] _m_ alibi; ～ _de fer_ cast-
iron alibi.

aliénable _𝔤𝔱𝔵_ [alje'nabl] alienable;
aliénation [～na'sjɔ̃] _f_ alienation
(_a._ _𝔤𝔱𝔵_); _𝔐_ mental derangement;
insanity; **aliéné, e** [～'ne] _su., a. adj._
lunatic; **aliéner** [～'ne] (1f) _v/t._ _𝔤𝔱𝔵_
alienate; unhinge (_s.o.'s mind_).
alignement [aliɲ'mɑ̃] _m_ alignment;
building-line; ✕ dressing (_of line_);
aligner [ali'ɲe] (1a) _v/t._ △ align;
lay out in a line; mark out; ✕ dress,
draw up in a line; _s'_～ fall into line;
✕ dress; _non aligné_ nonaligned.
aliment [ali'mɑ̃] _m_ food, nutriment;
𝔤𝔱𝔵 ～s _pl._ alimony _sg._; ～s _pl._ _naturels_
health food (_sg._); **alimentaire**
[alimɑ̃'tɛ:r] alimentary; for food;
nutritional; dietary; **alimentation**
[～ta'sjɔ̃] _f_ feeding, alimentation;
food, diet; nutrition; supplying,
supply; ⊕ feed; ～ _défectueuse_ malnu-
trition; ～ _en essence_ fuelling; _magasin_
_m d'_～ food shop (_Am._ store); _rayon m_
_d'_～ food department; **alimenter**
[～'te] (1a) _v/t._ feed (_a._ ⊕); nourish (_a._
fig.); supply with food; _fig._ keep
alive (_hatred, a quarrel, etc._); ～ _en qch._
supply with s.th.
alinéa [aline'a] _m_ paragraph; _typ._
_en_ ～ indented.
alité, e [ali'te] confined to bed;
alitement [alit'mɑ̃] _m_ confinement
to bed; **aliter** [ali'te] (1a) _v/t._ confine to bed; _s'_～ take to one's bed.
alizé [ali'ze] _m_ trade wind.
allaiter [alɛ'te] (1b) _v/t._ suckle.
allant [a'lɑ̃] _m_ initiative; energy;
F dash; _avoir de l'_～ have plenty of
go.
allécher [ale'ʃe] (1f) _v/t._ entice,
tempt, allure.
allé, e [a'le] **1.** _p.p._ of _aller 1;_ **2.** _su./f_
going; avenue; (tree-lined) walk;
path; passage; drive(way); ～es _pl. et_
venues f/pl. coming _sg._ and going _sg._,
to-and-fro _sg._
allégation [alega'sjɔ̃] _f_ allegation.
allège [al'lɛ:ʒ] _f_ ⚓ lighter; ⚓ barge;
△ breast-wall; △ balustrade.
allégement [alleʒ'mɑ̃] _m_ alleviation
(of, de), relief (from, de); lighten-
ing; ～ _fiscal_ tax relief; **alléger**
[～le'ʒe] (1g) _v/t._ make lighter; light-
en; _fig._ alleviate, relieve.
allégorie [allego'ri] _f_ allegory.
allègre [al'lɛ:gr] lively, brisk; cheerful; **allégrement** [～legrə'mɑ̃] _adv._
of _allègre;_ **allégresse** [～le'grɛs] _f_
joy, cheerfulness; liveliness.

alléguer [alle'ge] (1s) *v/t.* allege;
state; urge; adduce (*evidence etc.*);
quote; cite; ~ l'*ignorance* plead
ignorance.

alléluia [alelɥi'ja] *m* hallelujah,
alleluia(h).

allemand, e [al'mɑ̃, ~'mɑ̃:d] **1.** *adj.*
German; **2.** *su./m ling.* German;
su. ♀ German.

aller [a'le] **1.** (1q) *v/i.* go; depart;
~ (*inf.*) be going to (*inf.*), go and
...; *a.* = *fut.* tense; ~ à *bicyclette*
go by bicycle; ~ à *cheval* ride (a
horse); ~ *bien* (*mal*) be *or* be going
well (badly); ~ *chercher* (go and)
look for; fetch; ~ *diminuant* grow
steadily less; ~ *en chemin de fer* go
by train *or* rail; ~ *en voiture* drive,
ride (in a car), go by car; ~ *se coucher*
go to bed; ~ *sur la cinquantaine* be
going *or* getting on for fifty; ~ *voir*
q. call on s.o.; go and see s.o.;
allons! let's go!; come!; nonsense!; come along!; *ce chapeau*
lui va bien (*mal*) that hat suits
(does not suit) him; *cela me va*
that suits me; *comment allez-vous?*
how are you?; *il va sans dire* it goes
without saying, it is obvious; *il y*
va de ... it is a matter of ...; ... ıs at
stake; *la clef va à la serrure* the key
fits the lock; *n'allez pas croire ...!*
don't believe ...!; don't think ...!;
F *on y va!* coming!; *s'en* ~ go
away, leave, depart; *va!* agreed!;
believe me ...!; **2.** *su./m* ♣ outward journey; 🚋 single ticket; ~ *et*
retour journey there and back;
ticket: return; *à l'~* on the outward
journey; *au pis* ~ if the worst comes
to the worst; *le pis* ~ the last resort.

allergie [alɛr'ʒi] *f* 🩺, *a.* F *fig.*
allergy; **allergique** [~'ʒik] allergic
(to, *à*).

alliable [a'ljabl] miscible; *fig.* compatible; **alliage** [a'lja:ʒ] *m* alloy;
♣ alligation; **alliance** [a'ljɑ̃:s] *f*
alliance; marriage; union; wedding
ring; **allié, e** [a'lje] **1.** *adj.* allied;
2. *su.* ally; relation by marriage;
allier [~] (1o) *v/t.* ally; unite; ⊕
alloy (*metals*); blend (*colours*); *s'*~
marry, be married.

allitération [alitera'sjɔ̃] *f* alliter-
ation.

allô! [a'lo] *int.* hullo!, hello!

allocation [alɔka'sjɔ̃] *f* allocation;
allowance; grant; ~s *pl. familiales*

family allowances; ~ *d'assistance*
subsidy; ~ *de chômage* unemployment benefit; ~ *de maternité* maternity benefit; ~ *vieillesse* old age relief.

allocution [alɔky'sjɔ̃] *f* address,
speech.

allogène [alɔ'ʒɛn] non-native; alien.

allonge [a'lɔ̃:ʒ] *f* extension; eking-
piece; *table:* leaf; meat-hook; *box.*
reach; 🚣 rider; **allongement**
[alɔ̃ʒ'mɑ̃] *m* lengthening; ⊕ elon-
gation; **allonger** [alɔ̃'ʒe] (11) *v/t.*
lengthen; delay; prolong; *sl.* aim
(*a blow*) (at, *à*); *sl.* fork out (*money*);
s'~ stretch (out), grow longer.

allopathie [alɔpa'ti] *f* allopathy.

allouable [a'lwa:bl] grantable; **al-**
louer [a'lwe] (1p) *v/t.* grant;
allocate.

allumage [aly'ma:ʒ] *m* lighting; ⊕
ignition; *mot.* ~ *prématuré* back-
fire; pinking; ~ *raté* misfire; *cou-*
per l'~ switch off the ignition; *re-*
tarder l'~ retard the spark; **allu-**
mé, e *sl.* [~'me] worked-up; **allu-**
me-feu [alym'fø] *m/inv.* fire-lighter;
allume-gaz [~'gɑ:z] *m/inv.* gas-
lighter; **allumer** [aly'me] (1a) *v/t.*
light, kindle, inflame; *v/i.* switch
on (the light); *s'*~ catch fire; light up;
allumette [~'mɛt] *f* match; ~ *de*
sûreté safety match.

allure [a'ly:r] *f* walk, gait; bearing,
manner; demeanour; speed; pace;
appearance; ♣ mode of sailing,
sailing-trim; 🚣 *business:* trend; *à*
toute ~ at full speed; *filer* (*mar-*
cher) *à une* ~ *normale* travel (walk,
go) at a normal speed; *forcer l'*~
increase speed; *fig. prendre une*
bonne ~ take a promising turn;
régler l'~ set the pace.

alluvial, e, *m/pl.* **-aux** *geol.* [ally-
'vjal, ~'vjo] alluvial; **alluvion**
[~'vjɔ̃] *f* alluvium; alluvial (deposit).

almanach [alma'na] *m* almanac;
calendar; ~ *du commerce* commercial directory; *faiseur m d'*~s
weather-prophet.

aloi [a'lwa] *m* standard, quality (*a.*
fig.); *fig. de bon* ~ genuine; sterling;
fig. de mauvais ~ base, worthless;
monnaie f d'~ sterling money.

alors [a'lɔ:r] *adv.* then; at *or* by
that time; in that case; well (then); ~
même que even when *or* though; ~ *que*
at a time when; whereas; *d'*~ of that

time; *jusqu'~* until then; F *et ~?* and what then?; so what?

alouette *orn.* [a'lwɛt] *f* lark.

alourdir [alur'diːr] (2a) *v/t.* make heavy *or* dull; weigh down; s'~ become heavy; **alourdissement** [~dis'mã] *m* heaviness.

aloyau [alwa'jo] *m* sirloin (of beef).

alpaga *zo.* [alpa'ga] *m* alpaca.

alpage [al'paːʒ] *m* pasture on the upper slopes; **alpe** [alp] *f* Alp, height; *geogr. les* ♀s *pl.* the Alps; **alpestre** [al'pɛstr] alpine.

alphabet [alfa'bɛ] *m* alphabet; spelling-book; primer; **alphabétique** [~be'tik] alphabetical.

alpin, e [al'pɛ̃, ~'pin] alpine; ✕ *chasseur m* ~ mountain infantryman; **alpinisme** [alpi'nism] *m* mountaineering; **alpiniste** [~'nist] *su.* mountaineer, F climber.

alsacien, -enne [alza'sjɛ̃, ~'sjɛn] 1. *adj.* Alsatian, of Alsace; 2. *su.* ♀ Alsatian, man (woman) of Alsace.

altérable [alte'rabl] liable to deterioration; ~ *à l'air* which deteriorates on exposure to the air; **altérant, e** [~'rã, ~'rãːt] thirst-making; **altération** [~ra'sjõ] *f* deterioration; weakening; *coinage:* debasing; *colour:* fading; *voice:* faltering; *fig.* misrepresentation.

altercation [altɛrka'sjõ] *f* altercation; dispute.

altéré¹, e [alte're] thirsty (*fig.* for, de).

altéré², e [~] haggard (*face*); faded (*colour*); broken, faltering (*voice*).

altérer¹ [~] (1f) *v/t.* change for the worse; corrupt; debase (*the currency*); taint; spoil; adulterate, tamper with; inflect (*a note*); s'~ change for the worse; deteriorate; break (*voice*); weather (*rock*).

altérer² [~] (1f) *v/t.* make thirsty.

alternance [altɛr'nãːs] *f* alternation (*a. ⚡*); ✓ ~ *des cultures* crop rotation; **alternateur** ⚡ [~na'tœːr] *m* alternator; **alternatif, -ve** [~na'tif, ~'tiːv] alternate; alternative; ⊕ reciprocating; ⚡ *courant m* ~ alternating current; **alternative** [~na'tiːv] *f* alternation; alternative; ~s *pl. saisonnières* seasonal alternation *sg.*; **alterne** [al'tɛrn] alternate (*angle*); **alterner** [~tɛr'ne] (1a) *v/i.* alternate, take turns; *v/t.* rotate (*the crops*); ⊕ break (*a joint*).

Altesse [al'tɛs] *f title:* Highness.

altier, -ère [al'tje, ~'tjɛːr] haughty, proud, lofty; **altimètre** [alti'mɛtr] *m* altimeter; **altitude** [~'tyd] *f* altitude; ✈ ~ *d'utilisation* cruising altitude; ✈ *prendre de l'~* climb.

alto ♪ [al'to] *m voice:* alto; viola; alto saxophone.

altruisme [altry'ism] *m* altruism; **altruiste** [~'ist] 1. *adj.* altruistic; selfless; 2. *su.* altruist.

alumine [aly'min] *f* alumina; **aluminium** [~mi'njɔm] *m* aluminium, *Am.* aluminum.

alun [a'lœ̃] *m* alum; **aluner** [aly'ne] (1a) *v/t.* alum; *phot.* harden (*the negative*).

alunir [aly'niːr] (2a) *v/i.* land on the moon; **alunissage** [~ni'saːʒ] *m* landing on the moon, lunar landing.

alvéole [alve'ɔl] *m* alveolus; *a.* ⊕ cell; *tooth:* socket; cavity.

amabilité [amabili'te] *f* amiability; kindness; ~s *pl.* civilities.

amadou [ama'du] *m* tinder, touchwood, *Am.* punk; **amadouer** [~'dwe] (1p) *v/t.* coax, wheedle; draw, attract (*customers*).

amaigrir [ame'griːr] (2a) *v/t.* make thin; reduce; s'~ lose weight, grow thin; **amaigrissement** [~gris'mã] *m* growing thin; slimming; emaciation; *soil:* impoverishment.

amalgamation [amalgama'sjõ] *f* amalgamation; ✝ merger; **amalgame** [~'gam] *m* amalgam; F mixture; **amalgamer** [~ga'me] (1a) *v/t.* amalgamate.

amande [a'mãːd] *f* almond; kernel; **amandier** [~'dje] *m* almond-tree.

amant, e [a'mã, ~'mãːt] *su.* lover; *su./f* mistress.

amarante ♀ [ama'rãːt] *su./f, a. adj./inv.* amaranth.

amarrage [ama'raːʒ] *m* mooring; docking; **amarre** ⚓ [a'maːr] *f* mooring rope; hawser; ~s *pl.* moorings; **amarrer** [ama're] (1a) *v/t.* moor; make fast; secure; dock; lash (*a hawser*); s'~ moor, make fast; dock.

amas [a'ma] *m* heap; store; crowd; ~ *de neige* snow-drift; **amasser** [ama'se] (1a) *v/t.* heap up; amass; accumulate.

amateur [ama'tœːr] *m* lover (*of music, sports, etc.*); admirer; amateur; **amateurisme** [~tœ'rism] *m sp. etc.* amateurism; *pej.* amateurishness.

amatir [ama'tiːr] (2a) *v/t.* mat; dull; deaden.

amazone [ama'zoːn] *f* amazon; horsewoman; (lady's) riding-habit.

ambages [ăm'baːʒ] *f/pl.* circumlocution; *sans* ~ forthrightly.

ambassade [ămba'sad] *f* embassy; ambassador's staff; *fig.* errand; **ambassadeur** [~sa'dœːr] *m* ambassador; *fig.* messenger; **ambassadrice** [~sa'dris] *f* ambassadress, *a.* ambassador's wife.

ambiance [ă'bjăːs] *f* surroundings *pl.*, environment; atmosphere; **ambiant, e** [ă'bjă, ~'bjăːt] surrounding; *conditions f/pl.* ~es circumstances; environment *sg.*

ambidextre [ăbi'dekstr] 1. *adj.* ambidextrous; 2. *su.* ambidexter.

ambigu, -guë [ămbi'gy] 1. *adj.* ambiguous; equivocal; 2. *su./m* mixture, medley; cold collation; **ambiguïté** [~gui'te] *f* ambiguity.

ambitieux, -euse [ăbi'sjø, ~'sjøːz] 1. *adj.* ambitious; *style m* ~ affected style; 2. *su.* ambitious person; **ambition** [~'sjɔ̃] *f* ambition; **ambitionner** [~sjɔ'ne] (1a) *v/t.* covet; be eager for; *pol.* ~ *le pouvoir* aspire to power; strive for power.

amble [ă:bl] *m* amble, pace; *Am.* single-foot.

ambre [ă:br] *m* amber; ~ *gris* ambergris; **ambrer** [ă'bre] (1a) *v/t.* scent with amber. [♀ wormseed.)

ambroisie [ăbrwa'zi] *f* ambrosia;)

ambulance [ăby'lăs] *f* ambulance (*a. mot.*); ✄ field hospital; **ambulancier** [~lă'sje] *m* ambulance man or driver; **ambulancière** [~lă'sjɛːr] *f* ambulance woman; **ambulant, e** [~'lă, ~'lăːt] 1. *adj.* itinerant, travelling; ambulant; strolling (*player*); 2. *su./m post:* travelling sorter; **ambulatoire** [~la'twaːr] ambulatory.

âme [ɑ:m] *f* soul (*a. fig.*); *fig.* feeling; ⊕ *cable etc.:* core; *girder:* web; ✄ *gun:* bore; *fig.* ~s *pl.* souls, inhabitants; *fig.* ~ *damnée* tool, F stooge; ~ *en peine* soul in Purgatory; *rendre l'*~ breathe one's last.

amélioration [ameljɔra'sjɔ̃] *f* improvement; **améliorer** [~'re] (1a) *v/t.* improve, ameliorate.

amen [a'mɛn] *int., a. su./m/inv.* amen.

aménagement [amenaʒ'mă] *m* arranging; arrangement; adjustment; ✓ parcelling out; development; ~ *du territoire* town and country planning; ~ *intérieur* interior decoration; **aménager** [~na'ʒe] (11) *v/t.* arrange; ✓ parcel out; plan (*a town*); develop (*an area etc.*).

amendable [amă'dabl] improvable; **amende** [a'mă:d] *f* fine; ~ *honorable* amende honorable; *sous peine d'*~ on pain of a fine; *mettre q. à l'*~ fine s.o.; **amendement** [amăd'mă] *m* improvement (*a.* ✓); ✓ manure; *parl.* amendment; **amender** [amă'de] (1a) *v/t.* amend; improve; *s'*~ *a.* mend one's ways.

amenée [am'ne] *f* bringing; ⊕ ~ *d'air* air-intake, air-inlet; **amener** [~] (1d) *v/t.* lead (to, *à*); pull; bring (in, up, down, out); produce; cause; throw (*a number*); ⚓ *pavillon* strike one's flag; ~ *une crise* force an issue; *sl. amène-toi!* come along!; ⚖ *mandat m d'*~ order to appear.

aménité [ameni'te] *f* amenity; charm; *usu. iro.* ~s *pl.* compliments.

amenuisement [amnɥiz'mă] *m* decrease, dwindling, lessening, diminishing; **amenuiser** [amnɥi'ze] (1a) *v/t.* thin down; pare down; *s'*~ decrease, dwindle, lessen, diminish.

amer, -ère [a'mɛːr] bitter (*a. fig.*).

américain, e [ameri'kɛ̃, ~'kɛn] 1. *adj.* American; 2. *su.* ♀ American; **américaniser** [~kani'ze] (1a) *v/t.* Americanize; *s'*~ become Americanized; **américaniste** [~ka'nist] *su.* Americanist.

amerrir ✈ [ame'riːr] (2a) *v/i.* land, alight (*on sea*); splash down; **amerrissage** [~ri'saːʒ] *m* alighting, landing (*on sea*); splashdown.

amertume [amɛr'tym] *f* bitterness (*a. fig.*).

améthyste [ame'tist] *f* amethyst.

ameublement [amœblə'mă] *m* furnishing; (suite of) furniture; *tissu m d'*~ furnishing fabric; **ameublir** [~'bliːr] (2a) *v/t.* ⚖ convert into personalty; bring (*realty*) into the communal estate; ✓ break up (*the soil*); **ameublissement** [~blis'mă] *m* conversion into personalty; *realty:* inclusion in the communal estate; ✓ *soil:* breaking-up.

ameuter [amø'te] (1a) *v/t.* form (*hounds*) into a pack; assemble; stir

up, incite (*the mob*) (against, *contre*); s'~ collect (into a mob); riot.
ami, e [a'mi] **1.** *su.* friend; *société f des* ~s Quakers *pl.*; **2.** *adj.* friendly; *fig.* kindly; **amiable** [a'mjabl] amicable; friendly; *à l'~* amicably; *adj.* private; *vendre à l'~* sell privately.
amiante *min.* [a'mjã:t] *m* asbestos.
amical, e, *m/pl.* -aux [ami'kal, ~'ko] friendly; amicable.
amidon [ami'dõ] *m* starch; **amidonner** [~dɔ'ne] (1a) *v/t.* starch.
amincir [amɛ̃'si:r] (2a) *v/t.* make thinner; make (*s.o.*) look slender; *Am.* slenderize; s'~ grow thinner; **amincissant, e** [~si'sã, ~'sã:t] slimming, *Am.* slenderizing.
amiral [ami'ral] *m* admiral; *vaisseau m ~* flagship; **amirauté** [~ro-'te] *f* admiralship; admiralty; *l'2* the Admiralty.
amitié [ami'tje] *f* friendship; affection; friendliness; ~s *pl.* compliments (= *greetings*); *faites-lui mes* ~s give him my compliments *or* regards; remember me to him; *faites-moi l'~ de* (*inf.*) do me the favo(u)r of (*ger.*).
ammoniac, -que [amɔ'njak] *adj.*: *gaz m ~* ammonia; *sel m ~* sal ammoniac; **ammonisation** *biol.* [~niza'sjõ] *f* ammonification.
amnésie [amne'zi] *f* amnesia, loss of memory.
amnistie [amnis'ti] *f* amnesty; **amnistier** [~'tje] (1o) *v/t.* pardon, grant an amnesty to.
amocher *sl.* [amɔ'ʃe] (1a) *v/t.* make a mess of; bash up.
amoindrir [amwɛ̃'dri:r] (2a) *v/t.* lessen, reduce, decrease; s'~ diminish, grow less; **amoindrissement** [~dris'mã] *m* lessening, reduction, decrease;   [ning amok.}
amok [a'mɔk] *m* amok; person run-}
amollir [amɔ'li:r] (2a) *v/t.* soften; *fig.* weaken; s'~ go soft; weaken; **amollissement** [~lis'mã] *m* softening (*a. fig.*); *fig.* weakening.
amonceler [amõs'le] (1c) *v/t.* pile up; accumulate; **amoncellement** [~sɛl'mã] *m* heap(ing); piling; accumulation; pile.
amont [a'mõ] *m*: *en ~* up-stream; *fig.* beforehand, in advance; *en ~ de* above; *fig.* previous to, before; *voyage m en ~* up journey.

amorçage [amɔr'sa:ʒ] *m* *pump*: priming; *shell*: capping; starting; *fish*: baiting; **amorce** [a'mɔrs] *f* bait; priming; *pump, gun*: primer; *shell*: percussion cap; ✗ fuse; *fig.* beginning; **amorcer** [amɔr'se] (1k) *v/t.* bait; prime (*a pump*); cap (*a shell*); *fig.* begin; ⊕, *a. fig.* s'~ start; ✗ build up (*magnetic field*); **amorçoir** ⊕ [~'swa:r] *m* auger, boring-bit; centre punch.
amorphe [a'mɔrf] amorphous; *fig.* spineless.
amortir [amɔr'ti:r] (2a) *v/t.* deaden (*a noise, a pain*); cushion, absorb (*a shock*); tone down (*a colour*); ✝ pay off, amortize; ✝ write off (*equipment*); △ slake (*lime*); *phys.* damp down; **amortissable** ✝ [~ti'sabl] redeemable; **amortissement** [~tis-'mã] *m* deadening; ✝ depreciation; ✝ redemption; paying-off; *shock*: absorption; **amortisseur** ⊕ [~ti-'sœ:r] *m* damping device; damper; (*a. ~ de choc*) shock absorber.
amour [a'mu:r] *m* love; passion; affection; 2 Cupid, Love; ~s *f/pl.* love *sg.*, delight *sg.*; amours; *l'~ du prochain* love of one's neighbour; *iro. pour l'~ de Dieu* for heaven's sake; **amouracher** [amura'ʃe] (1a) *v/t.* enamour; s'~ *de* fall in love with, become enamoured of; **amourette** [~'rɛt] *f* love affair; ♣ crush; ♀ quaking-grass; ♀ London pride; **amoureux, -euse** [~'rø, ~'rø:z] **1.** *adj.* loving; amorous (*look etc.*); ~ *de* in love with; enamoured of; **2.** *su.* sweetheart; **amour-propre,** *pl.* **amours-propres** [amur'prɔpr] *m* self-respect; *pej.* conceit.
amovible [amɔ'vibl] removable; detachable.
ampérage ✗ [ãpe'ra:ʒ] *m* amperage;
ampère ✗ [ã'pɛ:r] *m* ampere.
amphibie [ãfi'bi] **1.** *adj.* amphibious; ✗ *etc.* combined (*operation*); **2.** *su./m* amphibian; **amphibiens** [ãfi-'bjɛ̃] *m/pl.* amphipia *pl.*, amphibians *pl.*
amphigouri [ãfigu'ri] *m* amphigory; rigmarole.
amphithéâtre [ãfite'ɑ:tr] *m* amphitheatre, *Am.* amphitheater; *univ.* lecture hall.
amphityron [ãfiti'jõ] *npr./m* Amphitryon; *fig.* host, entertainer.

ample [ãpl] ample; spacious, roomy; full, complete; **ampleur** [ã'plœːr] f fullness; *meal*: copiousness; *style*: breadth; *appeal*: generality; ~ *du son* volume of sound; **ampliation** [ãplia'sjõ] f certified copy; **amplificateur** [~fika'tœːr] m *sound*: intensifier; *radio*: amplifier, booster; *phot.* enlarger; **amplification** [~fika'sjõ] f amplification (a. *radio*); development; *phot.* enlargement; *opt.* magnification; *fig.* exaggeration; **amplifier** [~'fje] (1o) v/t. amplify (a. ⚡), develop; *opt.* magnify; *fig.* exaggerate; **amplitude** [~'tyd] f amplitude (a. *phys., astr.*); vastness.

ampoule [ã'pul] f ⚕ flask; ⚡ bulb (a. *thermometer*); *vacuum flask*: container; ⚕ blister; ⚡ ampoule; *phot.* ~ (*de*) *flash* flash; **ampoulé, e** [ãpu'le] blistered; *fig.* bombastic.

amputation [ãpyta'sjõ] f *limb*: amputation, cutting off; *book*: curtailment; **amputé, e** f [~'te] person who has lost a limb; **amputer** [~'te] (1a) v/t. ⚕ amputate; *fig.* cut down.

amulette [amy'lɛt] f amulet, charm.

amusant, e [amy'zã, ~'zãːt] amusing, entertaining; funny; **amusegueule** F [amyz'gœl] m/inv. appetizer (a. *fig.*); cocktail snack; **amusement** [amyz'mã] m entertainment; amusement; pastime; **amuser** [amy'ze] (1a) v/t. amuse, entertain; put off, fool (*creditors*); s'~ a. have fun; *amusez-vous bien!* enjoy yourself; have a good time!; s'~ *de* make fun of, laugh at; **amusette** [~'zɛt] f plaything; diversion.

amygdale *anat.* [amig'dal] f tonsil; **amygdalite** [~da'lit] f tonsillitis.

an [ã] m year; *avoir dix* ~s be ten (years old); *bon* ~, *mal* ~ taking one year with another; *jour m de l'*~ New Year's day; *par* ~ a year, per annum; *tous les trois* ~s every three years.

anabaptiste [anaba'tist] m anabaptist.

anachorète [anakɔ'rɛt] m anchorite, recluse.

anachronisme [anakrɔ'nism] m anachronism.

anal, e, m/pl. **-aux** *anat.* [a'nal, ~'no] anal.

analgésique [analʒe'zik] adj., a. su./m analgesic.

analogie [analɔ'ʒi] f analogy; *par* ~ by analogy (with, *avec*); **analogue** [~'lɔg] **1.** adj. analogous (to, with *à*), similar (to, *à*); **2.** su./m analogue; parallel.

analphabète [analfa'bɛt] adj., a. su. illiterate; **analphabétisme** [~be'tism] m illiteracy.

analyse [ana'liːz] f analysis (a. 🇦, 🇦, etc.); précis, abstract; ✝ ~ *du marché* market analysis; 🩸 ~ *du sang* bloodtest; ~ *du travail* time and motion study; **analyser** [~li'ze] (1a) v/t. analyse (a. 🇦, 🇦, *fig.*); make a précis of; **analytique** [~li-'tik] analytic(al).

ananas [ana'na] m pineapple, ananas.

anarchie [anar'ʃi] f anarchy; *fig.* state of confusion; **anarchique** [~'ʃik] anarchic(al), anarchist(ic); **anarchisme** [~'ʃism] m anarchism; **anarchiste** [~'ʃist] adj., a. su. anarchist.

anathème [ana'tɛm] m anathema; curse.

anatomie [anatɔ'mi] f anatomy; F *fig. une belle* ~ a nice figure (*woman*); **anatomique** [~'mik] anatomical; **anatomiste** [~'mist] m anatomist; **anatomiser** [~mi'ze] (1a) v/t. anatomize.

ancêtre [ã'sɛtr] m ancestor, forefather.

anche ♪ [ãː'ʃ] f reed.

anchois [ã'ʃwa] m anchovy.

ancien, -enne [ã'sjɛ̃, ~'sjɛn] **1.** adj. ancient, old; bygone, past; former, late; senior; ~(ne) *élève* mf old boy (girl); *univ. Am.* alumnus (alumna); ~ *combattant* ex-serviceman, *Am.* veteran; **2.** su./m *eccl.* elder; *les* ♀s *pl.* the Ancients (*Greeks and Romans*); **anciennement** [ãsjɛn'mã] adv. in days of old, formerly; **ancienneté** [~'te] f oldness, antiquity; length of service; *avancer à l'*~ be promoted by seniority.

ancrage [ã'kraːʒ] m anchoring, anchorage; *droit* m *d'*~ anchorage due; **ancre** [ãː'kr] f ⚓ anchor; △ brace; *être à l'*~ ride at anchor; **ancrer** [ã'kre] (1a) v/t. anchor; *fig.* fix firmly.

andalou, -ouse [ãda'lu, ~'luːz] adj., a. su. ♀ Andalusian.

andouille [ã'duːj] f chitterlings *pl.*; *sl.* duffer, mug; **andouiller** *hunt.*

[ădu'je] *m* tine; **andouillette** [˰'jɛt] *f* small chitterling sausage.

androgyne [ădrɔ'ʒin] androgynous; **androphobe** [˰'fɔb] **1.** *adj.* man-hating; **2.** *su.* man-hater.

âne [ɑːn] *m* ass; donkey (*a. fig.*); ⊕ bench-vice; *pont m aux ˰s* child's play.

anéantir [aneă'tiːr] (2a) *v/t.* annihilate; destroy; reduce to nothing; *fig.* overwhelm; **anéantissement** [˰tis'mă] *m* annihilation, destruction; prostration; dejection.

anecdote [anɛk'dɔt] *f* anecdote; **anecdotique** [˰dɔ'tik] anecdotal.

anémie [ane'mi] *f* an(a)emia; **anémier** [˰'mje] (1a) *v/t.* render an(a)emic; F weaken; *s'˰* become an(a)emic; **anémique** [˰'mik] an(a)emic.

anémomètre [anemɔ'mɛtr] *m* anemometer, wind-ga(u)ge.

anémone ⚕ [ane'mɔn] *f* anemone.

ânerie [ɑn'ri] *f* gross blunder; stupidity; F ignorance.

anéroïde [anerɔ'id] aneroid (*barometer*).

ânesse [ɑ'nɛs] *f* she-ass.

anesthésie ⚕ [anɛste'zi] *f* an(a)esthesia; an(a)esthetic; **anesthésier** [˰'zje] (1a) *v/t.* an(a)esthetize; **anethésique** [˰'zik] *adj., a. su./m* an(a)esthetic.

anfractuosité [ăfraktɥozi'te] *f* irregularity; ˰s *pl.* winding(s *pl.*) *sg.*

ange [ɑːʒ] *m* angel; ˰ *gardien* guardian angel; *fig. être aux ˰s* be in the seventh heaven; be overjoyed; *faiseuse f d'˰s* baby-farmer; **angélique** [ăʒe'lik] **1.** *adj.* angelic; **2.** *su./f* ⚕, *cuis.* angelica; ⚕ *˰ sauvage* cow-parsnip; **angélus** [˰'lys] *m* angelus (*a. bell*).

angine ⚕ [ă'ʒin] *f* angina; tonsillitis; ˰ *de poitrine* angina pectoris; **angineux, -euse** [ăʒi'nø, ˰'nøːz] anginal, anginous.

anglais, e [ă'glɛ, ˰'glɛːz] **1.** *adj.* English; **2.** *su./m ling.* English; ♀ Englishman; *les* ♀ *m/pl.* the English; *su./f* ♀ Englishwoman.

angle [ăːgl] *m* angle; ⊕ edge; ♉ ˰ *aigu* (*droit, obtus*) acute (right, obtuse) angle; ˰ *visuel* angle of vision.

anglican, e [ăgli'kă, ˰'kan] **1.** *adj.* Anglican; *l'Église f* ˰*e* the Church of England; **2.** *su.* Anglican.

angliciser [ăglisi'ze] (1a) *v/t.* anglicize; *s'˰* become English; imitate the English; **anglicisme** [˰'sism] *m* Anglicism; English idiom; **angliciste** [˰'sist] *su.*, **anglicisant** *m*, **e** *f* [˰si'ză, ˰'zăːt] student of *or* authority on English language and literature.

anglo... [ăglɔ] Anglo...; ˰**manie** [˰ma'ni] *f* anglomania; ˰**normand, e** [˰nɔr'mă, ˰'măːd] *adj., a. su.* ♀ Anglo-Norman; ˰**phile** [˰'fil] *adj., a. su.* Anglophil(e); ˰**phobe** [˰'fɔb] **1.** *su.* Anglophobe; **2.** *adj.* Anglophobic; ˰**phone** [˰'fɔn] **1.** *adj.* English-speaking; **2.** *su.* English-speaking person; ˰**-saxon, -onne** [˰sak'sɔ̃, ˰'sɔn] *adj., a. su.* ♀ Anglo-Saxon.

angoisse [ă'gwas] *f* anguish, agony; ♉ *a.* spasm; *poire f d'˰* choke-pear; **angoisser** [ăgwa'se] (1a) *v/t.* cause anguish to, distress.

angora [ăgɔ'ra] *adj. a. su.* angora.

anguille *icht.* [ă'giːj] *f* eel; ˰ *de mer* conger-eel; *il y a ˰ sous roche* there's more in it than meets the eye; **anguillère** [ăgi'jɛːr] *f* eel-pond; eel-pot; **anguillule** *zo.* [˰'jyl] *f* eel-worm.

angulaire [ăgy'lɛːr] angular; *angle-...*; *pierre f* ˰ corner-stone; **anguleux, -euse** [˰'lø, ˰'løːz] angular; rugged.

anhélation [anela'sjɔ̃] *f* shortness of breath; **anhéler** [˰'le] (1f) *v/i.* gasp, pant.

anhydre ♋ [a'nidr] anhydrous.

anicroche [ani'krɔʃ] *f* hitch, difficulty; F snag.

ânier *m*, **-ère** *f* [ɑ'nje, ˰'njɛːr] donkey-driver, ass-driver.

aniline ♋ [ani'lin] *f* aniline; *colorant m d'˰* aniline dye.

animadversion [animadvɛr'sjɔ̃] *f* animadversion, reproof.

animal, e, *m/pl.* **-aux** [ani'mal, 'mo] **1.** *su./m* animal; *fig.* dolt; **2.** *adj.* animal, brutish; *règne m* ˰ animal kingdom; **animalcule** [˰mal'kyl] *m* animalcule; **animalier** [˰ma'lje] *m* painter *etc.* of animals; **animaliser** [animali'ze] (1a) *v/t.* animalize; *s'˰* become animalized; **animalité** [˰'te] *f* animality; animal kingdom.

animateur, -trice [anima'tœːr, ˰'tris] **1.** *adj.* animating; **2.** *su.* emcee, *Br. a.* compère; organizer; *fig.* driving force (*person*); **animation** [~'sjɔ̃] *f* animation; coming *or* bringing to life; **animé, e** [ani'me] spirited, lively; ✝ brisk (*market*); *cin.* dessins *m/pl.* ~s animated cartoons; **animer** [~] (1a) *v/t.* animate; liven up; impel, prompt, actuate; light up (*the features*).

animosité [animozi'te] *f* animosity, ranco(u)r, spite.

anis ⚜ [a'ni] anise; aniseed; **aniser** [ani'ze] (1a) *v/t.* flavo(u)r with aniseed.

ankylose ⚕ [ãki'lo:z] *f* anchylosis.

annal, e [an'nal] **1.** *adj.* yearly, lasting for one year; **2.** *su./f:* ~es *pl.* annals, records.

anneau [a'no] *m* ring (*a.* ⊕, *sp.*); *chain:* link; *hair:* ringlet; ~ brisé split ring.

année [a'ne] *f* year; ~ bissextile leap year; ~ civile natural year; ~ scolaire school year, academic year, session; ~-lumière, *pl.* ~s-lumière [~ly-'mjɛ:r] *f* light year.

anneler [an'le] (1c) *v/t.* curl (*the hair*); ring (*a pig*).

annexe [an'nɛks] **1.** *su./f* annex(e), outbuilding; *document:* schedule, supplement; appendix; *letter:* enclosure; *state:* dependency; **2.** *adj.* annexed; école *f* ~ demonstration school; lettre *f* ~ covering letter; **annexer** [annɛk'se] (1a) *v/t.* annex; **annexion** [~'sjɔ̃] *f* annexation.

annihiler [annii'le] (1a) *v/t.* annihilate, destroy; ⅔ annul.

anniversaire [anivɛr'sɛ:r] **1.** *adj.* anniversary; **2.** *su./m* birthday; anniversary; ~ de mariage wedding anniversary; gâteau *m* d'~ birthday cake.

annonce [a'nɔ̃:s] *f* announcement, notice; advertisement; *cards:* call; *fig.* presage, sign; ~s *pl.* encartées inset (advertisements) *sg.*; *journ.* petites ~s *pl.* classified adds; **annoncer** [anɔ̃'se] (1k) *v/t.* announce; foretell; *fig.* indicate; s'~ promise (*well, ill, etc.*); **annonceur** [~'sœ:r] *m* advertizer; **Annonciation** [~sja'sjɔ̃] *f*: l'~ the Annunciation; fête *f* de l'~ Lady Day.

annotateur *m*, **-trice** *f* [anɔta'tœ:r, ~'tris] annotator, commentator; **annotation** [~ta'sjɔ̃] *f* annotating, note, annotation; ✝ inventory of goods attached; **annoter** [~'te] (1a) *v/t.* annotate.

annuaire [a'nɥɛ:r] *m* year-book, annual; almanac; *teleph.* directory; ⚥ militaire Army List; **annuel, -elle** [a'nɥɛl] annual, yearly; ⚥ plante *f* ~elle annual; **annuité** [anɥi'te] *f* annual instalment; (terminable) annuity.

annulable [any'labl] that can be cancelled *or* annulled; ⅔ voidable; defeasible.

annulaire [any'lɛ:r] **1.** *adj.* ringlike, annular; **2.** *su./m* (*a.* doigt *m* ~) ring-finger.

annulation [anyla'sjɔ̃] *f* annulment; ⅔ judgment: setting aside; *sentence:* quashing; **annuler** [~'le] (1a) *v/t.* annul; cancel (*a cheque, a contract*); set aside (*a judgment, a will*); quash (*a sentence*).

anoblir [anɔ'bli:r] (2a) *v/t.* ennoble; raise to the peerage.

anode ⚡ [a'nɔd] *f* anode.

anodin, e [anɔ'dɛ̃, ~'din] **1.** *adj.* anodyne; *fig.* harmless, mild; **2.** *su./m* analgesic, anodyne.

anomalie [anɔma'li] *f* anomaly.

ânon *zo.* [ɑ'nɔ̃] *m* young ass, ass's foal; F ass; **ânonner** [anɔ'ne] (1a) *v/t.* stumble through; mumble through; drone through.

anonymat [anɔni'ma] *m* anonymity; **anonyme** [~'nim] **1.** *adj.* anonymous; unnamed; société *f* ~ limited (-liability) company, *abbr.* Ltd., *Am.* Inc. Ltd.; **2.** *su./m* anonymous writer; anonymity.

anorak [anɔ'rak] *m* anorak.

anorexie ⚕ [anɔrɛk'si] *f* anorexia, loss of appetite; **anorexigène** [anɔrɛksi'ʒɛn] appetite suppressant.

anormal, e, *m/pl.* **-aux** [anɔr'mal, ~'mo] abnormal, irregular.

anse [ã:s] *f* cup *etc.*: handle; ear; *rope:* loop; *geog.* cove, small bay.

antagonisme [ãtagɔ'nism] *m* antagonism; **antagoniste** [~'nist] **1.** *su./m* antagonist, opponent; **2.** *adj.* antagonistic, opposed.

antalgique [ãtal'ʒik] *adj., a. su./m* antalgic; anodyne.

antan [ã'tã] *adv.*: d'~ of yester year.

antarctique [ãtark'tik] **1.** *adj.* antarctic; **2.** *su./m* l'⚥ the Antarctic.

anté... [ãte] pre..., ante...

antébois ⚠ [ãte'bwa] *m* chair-rail.

antécédent, e [ãtese'dã, ~'dã:t] **1.** *adj.* antecedent, preceding; **2.** *su./m* ♫, ♪, *gramm.* antecedent;

~s *pl.* (past) records, antecedents; *sans* ~s *judiciaires* with a clean record, not known to the police.

antéchrist [ãte'krist] *m* Antichrist.

antédiluvien, -enne [ãtedily'vjɛ̃, ~'vjɛn] antediluvian (*a. fig.*).

antenne [ã'tɛn] *f zo.* antenna, F feeler; ⚓ lateen yard; *radio:* aerial; ~ *à cadre* frame aerial; ~ *dirigée* directional aerial; ~ *extérieure* outdoor aerial.

antérieur, e [ãte'rjœːr] anterior, prior, previous (to, *à*).

anthère ♀ [ã'tɛːr] *f* anther.

anthologie [ãtɔlɔ'ʒi] *f* anthology.

anthracite [ãtra'sit] *m* anthracite.

anthrax ♀ [ã'traks] *m* anthrax.

anthropo... [ãtrɔpɔ] anthropo...; ~ide [~'id] *adj., a. su./m* anthropoid; ~logie [~lɔ'ʒi] *f* anthropology; ~logue [~'lɔg] *m* anthropologist; ~morphe [~'mɔrf] 1. *adj.* anthropomorphous; 2. *su./m zo.* anthropoid (ape); ~phage [~'faːʒ] 1. *su./m* cannibal; 2. *adj.* cannibalistic.

anti... [ãti] anti...; *ante*...; ~aérien, -enne [~ae'rjɛ̃, ~'rjɛn] anti-aircraft (*defence etc.*); ~biotique ♀ [~bjɔ-'tik] *m* antibiotic; ~brouillard *mot.* [~bru'jaːr] *adj., a. su./m/inv.* demister; ~chambre [~'ʃãːbr] *f* anteroom, waiting-room; *faire* ~ *chez* wait on, dance attendance on; ~char [~'ʃaːr] *adj.* anti-tank (*missile*); ~choc [~'ʃɔk] *adj./inv.* shockproof; ~chrétien, -enne [~kre'tjɛ̃, ~'tjɛn] anti-christian.

anticipation [ãtisipa'sjɔ̃] *f* anticipation; encroachment (*on rights*); *par* ~ in advance; ~ *de paiement* advance payment; *littérature d'*~ science fiction; *roman d'*~ science fiction novel; **anticiper** [~'pe] (1a) *v/t.* anticipate; foresee; *v/i.:* ~ *sur* anticipate.

anti... ~clérical, e *m/pl.* -aux [ãtikleri'kal, ~'ko] *adj.* anticlerical; ~conceptionnel, -elle [~kɔ̃sɛpsjɔ-'nɛl] contraceptive; ~corps [~'kɔːr] *m* anti-body; ~dater [~da'te] (1a) *v/t.* antedate; ~dépresseur [~deprɛ'sœːr] antidepressant; ~dérapant, e *mot.* [~dera'pã, ~'paːt] 1. *adj.* non-skid; 2. *su./m* non-skid tyre; ~détonant, e *mot.* [~detɔ'nã, ~'nãːt] antiknock; ~dote ♀ [~'dɔt] *m* antidote (to, for, against *à, de*);

~éblouissant, e [~eblui'sã, ~'sãt] anti-dazzle.

antienne [ã'tjɛn] *f* antiphon; anthem; *fig. chanter toujours la même* ~ be always harping on the same string.

anti...: ~fading [ãtifa'diŋ] *m radio:* (*a. dispositif m* ~) automatic volume control; ~gel ⊕ [~'ʒɛl] *m* antifreeze; ~halo *phot.* [~a'lo] 1. *adj./inv.* non-halation..., backing; 2. *su./m* backing.

antilope *zo.* [ãti'lɔp] *f* antelope.

anti...: ~parasite [~para'zit] *m radio:* suppressor; ~pathie [~pa'ti] *f* antipathy (against, to *contre*), aversion (to, *contre*); ~pathique [~pa'tik] disagreeable; ~pode [~'pɔd] *m* antipode; *fig. the* very opposite; ~polluant, e [~pɔlɥ'ã, ~'ãt] non-polluting; ~pollution [~pɔly'sjɔ̃] *f* antipollution; ~pyrine ♀ [~pi'rin] *f* antipyrin.

antiquaille [ãti'kaːj] *f* lumber; fog(e)y; F old stuff, chunk; **antiquaire** [~'kɛːr] *m* antiquary, antique dealer; second-hand bookseller; **antique** [ã'tik] ancient; antique; antiquated; **antiquité** [ãtiki'te] *f* antiquity; ~s *pl.* antiques.

anti...: ~rides [ãti'rid] 1. *adj.* anti-wrinkle; 2. *su./m* anti-wrinkle cream or lotion; ~rouille ⊕ [~'ruːj] *m* anti-rust (composition); ~sémite [~se-'mit] 1. *adj.* anti-Semitic; 2. *su.* anti-Semite; ~septique ♀ [~sɛp'tik] *adj., a. su./m* antiseptic; ~social, e, *m/pl.* -aux [~sɔ'sjal, ~'sjo] antisocial; ~solaire [~sɔ'lɛːr]: *crème f* ~ sun cream; ~spasmodique ♀ [~spasmɔ'dik] antispasmodic; ~tétanique ♀ [~teta'nik] antitetanic; ~thèse [~'tɛːz] *f* antithesis; direct contrary; ~tuberculeux, -euse ♀ [~tybɛrky'lø, ~'løːz] antitubercular; ~vol [~'vɔl] *adj.* (*a. su./m*) anti-theft (device).

antonyme [ãtɔ'nim] 1. *adj.* antonymous; 2. *su./m* antonym.

antre [ã:tr] *m* cave; den, lair.

anurie ♀ [any'ri] *f* anuresis.

anus *anat.* [a'nys] *m* anus.

anxiété [ãksje'te] *f* anxiety, concern; **anxieux, -euse** [~'sjø, ~'sjøːz] anxious, uneasy; eager (to, de).

aorte *anat.* [a'ɔrt] *f* aorta. [ripe.]

août [u] *m* August; **aoûté, e** [u'te] ripe.

apache [a'paʃ] *m* (*usu. in Paris*) hooligan, tough, hoodlum.

apaisement [apɛz'mɑ̃] *m* appeasement; quieting, calming; **apaiser** [apɛ'ze] (1b) *v/t.* appease (*a. one's hunger*), calm, pacify, soothe; quench (*one's thirst*); lull (*a storm*); *s'*~ calm down (*person*); die down.
apanage [apa'na:ʒ] *m* ap(p)anage; prerogative, privilege; exclusive right (to, *de*); **apanager** [~na'ʒe] (1l) *v/t.* endow with an ap(p)anage; **apanagiste** [~na'ʒist] **1.** *adj.* having an ap(p)anage; **2.** *su.* ap(p)anagist.
aparté [apar'te] *m thea.* aside; F private conversation; *en* ~ aside, in a stage-whisper.
apathie [apa'ti] *f* apathy, listlessness; **apathique** [~'tik] apathetic, listless.
apatride [apa'trid] **1.** *su.* stateless person; **2.** *adj.* stateless.
apepsie ⚕ [apɛp'si] *f* dyspepsia, indigestion.
apercevable [apɛrsə'vabl] perceivable, perceptible; **apercevoir** [~sə'vwa:r] (3a) *v/t.* see; *s'*~ *de* notice; realize; become aware of; **aperçu** [~'sy] *m* glimpse; general idea; rough estimate.
apéritif, -ve [aperi'tif, ~'ti:v] **1.** *adj.* appetizing; **2.** *su./m* appetizer; aperitif; *l'heure f de l'*~ cocktail time.
apéro F [ape'ro] *m* aperitif.
apesanteur [apəzɑ̃'tœ:r] *f* weightlessness; *en état d'*~ weightless.
à-peu-près [apø'prɛ] *m* approximation.
apeuré, e [apœ're] frightened.
aphasie ⚕ [afa'zi] *f* aphasia; **aphasique** ⚕ [~'zik] aphasic, speechless.
aphone ⚕ [a'fɔn] voiceless.
aphorisme [afɔ'rism] *m* aphorism.
aphte ⚕ [aft] *m* aphtha; **aphteux, -euse** *vet.*, ⚕ [af'tø, ~'tø:z] *adj.*: *fièvre f* ~*euse* foot-and-mouth disease.
apical, e, *m/pl.* **-aux** ⚒, ⚘, *gramm.* [api'kal, ~'ko] apical.
apicole [api'kɔl] apiarian; **apiculteur** [apikyl'tœ:r] *m* beekeeper, apiarist; **apiculture** [~'ty:r] *f* beekeeping.
apitoiement [apitwa'mɑ̃] *m* pity, compassion; ~ *sur soi-même* self-pity; **apitoyer** [~'je] (1h) *v/t.* move (to pity); *s'*~ *sur* feel pity for (*s.o.*); bewail, lament (*s.th.*).
aplanir [apla'ni:r] (2a) *v/t.* level; smooth; plane; *fig.* remove, smooth (away).
aplatir [apla'ti:r] (2a) *v/t.* make flat, flatten; ⊕ clench (*a rivet*); *fig.* crush; *s'*~ flatten o.s.; *fig.* gravel (before, *devant*).
aplomb [a'plɔ̃] *m* perpendicularity; *fig.* balance, equilibrium; steadiness; coolness; self-possession; *pej.* cheek; *d'*~ vertical(ly *adv.*), upright, plumb; steady (steadily *adv.*); F well, in good shape; △ *prendre l'*~ take the plumb.
apo... [apɔ] apo...; ~**calypse** [~ka'lips] *f* apocalypse; *l'*♀ the Book of Revelation; ~**calyptique** [~kalip'tik] apocalyptic; *fig.* obscure (*style*); ~**cryphe** [~'krif] **1.** *adj.* apocryphal; **2.** *su./m*: ~*s pl. the* Apocrypha.
apode *zo.* [a'pɔd] **1.** *adj.* apodal, footless; **2.** *su./m* apod.
apo...: ~**dictique** [apɔdik'tik] apodictic, indisputable; ~**gée** [~'ʒe] *m astr.* apogee; *fig.* height, zenith, culminating point; ~**logie** [~lɔ'ʒi] *f* apologia; vindication; ~**logiste** [~lɔ'ʒist] *m* apologist; ~**plexie** ⚕ [~plɛk'si] *f* apoplexy; ~**stasie** [~sta'zi] *f* apostasy; *pol.* F ratting; ~**stasier** [~sta'zje] (1o) *v/t.* apostatize from; *v/i.* apostatize; renounce one's faith *or* principles *or* party; ~**stat, e** [~s'ta, ~s'tat] *adj., a. su.* apostate, F turncoat.
apostille [apɔs'tij] *f* marginal recommendation; ⚓ entry (*in log*); † apostil, foot-note, side-note.
apostolat [apɔstɔ'la] *m* apostolate, apostleship; **apostolique** [~'lik] apostolic.
apostrophe [apɔs'trɔf] *f rhetoric, a. gramm.* apostrophe; rude remark; **apostropher** [~trɔ'fe] (1a) *v/t.* address (*s.o.*) sharply.
apothéose [apɔte'o:z] *f* apotheosis; *fig. a.* pinnacle; *thea.* grand finale.
apothicaire [apɔti'kɛ:r] *m*: *compte m d'*~ exorbitant bill.
apôtre [a'po:tr] *m* apostle (*a. fig.*); *faire le bon* ~ play the saint.
apparaître [apa'rɛ:tr] (4k) *v/i.* appear; come into sight; become evident.
apparat [apa'ra] *m* pomp, show.
appareil [apa'rɛ:j] *m* apparatus (*a. fig.*, ⚕, ⌂); ⚕ *wound*: dressing; △ bond; △ *stones*: height; *phot.* camera; ⊕ machinery; ⊕ device; *teleph. etc.* instrument; *radio*: set; pomp, display; *anat.* ~ *digestif*

digestive system; *phot.* ~ *de petit format* miniature camera; ~ *de projection* projector; *teleph. qui est à l'*~*?* who is speaking?; **appareillage** [~rɛ'ja:ʒ] *m* ⚓ getting under way; installation; △ bonding; △ *stones:* drafting; ⚡ *etc.* equipment; ⊕ fixture; ⊕ plant.

appareillement [aparɛj'mɑ] *m* matching (up); pairing.

appareiller[1] [aparɛ'je] (1a) *v/t.* match (up); pair.

appareiller[2] [aparɛ'je] (1a) *v/t.* install; △ bond; △ draft; ⚓ trim (*a sail*); *v/i.* ⚓ get under way; **appareilleur** [~'jœ:r] *m* fitter, trimmer; △ house carpenter; △ foreman mason.

apparemment [apara'mɑ̃] *adv. of apparent;* **apparence** [~'rɑ̃:s] *f* appearance, semblance; *en* ~ outwardly; *sauver les* ~*s* save one's face; **apparent, e** [~'rɑ̃, ~'rɑ̃:t] apparent; conspicuous.

apparenter [aparɑ̃'te] (1a) *v/t.: s'*~ *à* marry into (*the nobility etc.*).

apparier [apa'rje] (1o) *v/t.* pair (off); mate.

appariteur [apari'tœ:r] *m* ⚖ apparitor, usher; *univ.* laboratory assistant.

apparition [apari'sjɔ̃] *f* appearance; apparition; spectre; vision.

apparoir ⚖ [apa'rwa:r] (3b) *v/impers.* appear (from, *de;* that, *que*).

appartement [apart'mɑ̃] *m* flat, *Am.* apartment.

appartenance [apartə'nɑ̃:s] *f:* ~ *à* belonging to; membership of; **appartenant, e** [~'nɑ̃, ~'nɑ̃:t] belonging (to, *à*); **appartenir** [~'ni:r] (2h) *v/i.* belong (to, *à*); *il appartient à q. de faire qch.* it is s.o.'s business *or* it rests with s.o. to do s.th.; *v/t.: s'*~ be one's own master.

appas [a'pɑ] *m/pl.* charms.

appât [a'pɑ] *m* bait; lure; *poultry:* soft food; *mordre à l'*~ take the bait; **appâter** [apɑ'te] (1a) *v/t.* lure, entice; cram (*poultry*).

appauvrir [apo'vri:r] (2a) *v/t.* impoverish; *s'*~ become impoverished; grow poor(er); **appauvrissement** [~vris'mɑ̃] *m* impoverishment; deterioration; ~ *du sang* impoverished blood.

appeau [a'po] *m* decoy(-bird); birdcall.

appel [a'pɛl] *m* call; appeal (*a.* ⚖); ✗ roll-call, call-over, muster; ⊕ ~ *d'air* indraught, intake of air; *teleph.* ~ *local (interurbain)* local call (trunk call); ~ *téléphonique* (tele)phone call; ⚖ *cour f d'*~ Court of Appeal; *faire* ~ *à* have recourse to; ✗ *ordre m d'*~ induction order; **appeler** [ap'le] (1c) *v/t.* call; call to; call up; send for; ~ *l'attention de q. sur qch.* call s.o.'s attention to s.th.; *s'*~ be called; *v/i.:* ~ *d'un jugement* appeal against a sentence; *en* ~ *à* appeal to; **appellation** [apɛla'sjɔ̃] *f* appellation; ✝ ~ *d'origine* indication of origin.

appendice [apɛ̃'dis] *m* appendix (*a.* ⚑, *anat.*); △ annex(e); ⚑ tail; **appendicite** ⚕ [~di'sit] *f* appendicitis.

appentis [apɑ̃'ti] *m* lean-to (roof); penthouse; outhouse.

appert [a'pɛ:r] *3rd p. sg. pres. of apparoir.*

appesantir [apəzɑ̃'ti:r] (2a) *v/t.* make heavy; weigh down; dull; *s'*~ become heavy; *s'*~ *sur* dwell upon; **appesantissement** [~tis'mɑ̃] *m* increase in heaviness *or* dullness.

appétence [ape'tɑ̃:s] *f* appetency, craving (for, of, *after pour*).

appétissant, e [apeti'sɑ̃, ~'sɑ̃:t] appetizing, tempting (*a. fig.*); **appétit** [~'ti] *m* appetite; desire; craving; *ouvrir l'*~ give an edge to the appetite.

applaudir [aplo'di:r] (2a) *v/i.* approve (s.th., *à qch.*); *v/t.* applaud; clap; *s'*~ *de* congratulate o.s. on; **applaudissements** [~dis'mɑ̃] *m/pl.* applause *sg.*; commendation *sg.*

applicable [apli'kabl] applicable (to, *à*); that can be applied; **application** [~ka'sjɔ̃] *f* application; *fig.* diligence; *broderie f* ~ appliqué work; **applique** [a'plik] *f* inlaid work, inlaying; applied ornament; (wall-)bracket; **appliqué, e** [apli'ke] diligent; ⚗ *etc.* applied; **appliquer** [~] (1m) *v/t.* apply; F ~ *une gifle à q.* fetch s.o. one; *fig. s'*~ *à* work hard at; be bent on.

appoint [a'pwɛ̃] *m* contribution; added portion; help, support; (*a. monnaie f d'*~) odd money, (right) change; *d'*~ secondary; extra; *faire l'*~ give the right change; **appointements** [apwɛ̃t'mɑ̃] *m/pl.* emoluments, salary *sg.*

appointer[1] [apwɛ̃'te] (1a) *v/t.* put on a salary (basis).

appointer[2] ⊕ [~] (1a) *v/t.* sharpen.

appontement ⚓ [apɔ̃t'mã] *m* gangplank; wharf; landing-stage; **apponter** [apɔ̃'te] (1a) *v/i.* land on an aircraft carrier.

apport [a'pɔːr] *m* ⚏ contributed property; ✝ contribution; ⚏ initial share; ⚒ bringing up; ✝ *capital m d'~* initial capital; **apporter** [apɔr'te] (1a) *v/t.* bring; exercise (*care*); supply, provide; produce; *~ du retard à* be slow in; *~ du zèle à* show zeal in.

apposer [apo'ze] (1a) *v/t.* affix (to, *à*); put; set (*a seal*); **apposition** [~zi'sjɔ̃] *f* affixing; *gramm.* apposition.

appréciable [apre'sjabl] appreciable; **appréciation** [~sja'sjɔ̃] *f* valuation; estimate; appreciation; **apprécier** [~'sje] (1a) *v/t.* value; estimate; appreciate.

appréhender [apreã'de] (1a) *v/t.* apprehend; dread; seize; **appréhension** [~'sjɔ̃] *f* apprehension; ⚖ arrest.

apprenant *m*, **e** *f* [aprə'nã, ~'nãt] learner, student.

apprendre [a'prãːdr] (4aa) *v/t.* learn; teach (s.o. s.th., *qch. à q.*); *~ à faire qch.* teach s.o. (how) to do s.th.; *~ par cœur* learn by heart.

apprenti *m*, **e** *f* aprã'ti] apprentice; learner; ⚖ *etc.* articled clerk; **apprentissage** [~til'sa:ʒ] *m* apprenticeship; ⚖ *etc.* articles *pl.*

apprêt [a'prɛ] *m* preparation; ⊕ finishing; *cuis.* dressing, seasoning; *paint.* priming, size; *fig.* affectation; **apprêtage** [aprɛ'ta:ʒ] *m* finishing; sizing; **apprêté, e** [~'te] affected; **apprêter** [~'te] (1a) *v/t.* prepare; ⊕ finish; size, prime; starch; *s'~* get ready; be imminent; dress; **apprêteur** *m*, **-euse** *f* [~'tœːr, ~'tøːz] finisher, dresser.

apprivoiser [aprivwa'ze] (1a) *v/t.* tame (*a. fig.*); *fig.* make sociable.

approbateur, -trice [aprɔba'tœːr, ~'tris] **1.** *adj.* approving; **2.** *su.* approver; **approbatif, -tive** [~'tif, ~'tiːv] approving; **approbation** [~'sjɔ̃] *f* approbation, approval; ✝ certifying.

approchant, e † [aprɔ'ʃã, ~'ʃãːt] **1.** *adj.*: *~ de* approximating to; **2.** *appro-*

chant adv., *a. prp.* nearly; **approche** [a'prɔʃ] *f* approach; *les ~s de* the immediate surroundings of (*a town etc.*); **approcher** [aprɔ'ʃe] (1a) *v/t.* bring (*s.th.*) near; *s'~ de* draw *or* come near (to); *v/i.* approach; draw *or* come near.

approfondir [aprɔfɔ̃'diːr] (2a) *v/t.* deepen; *fig.* go deeper into; investigate thoroughly; **approfondissement** [~dis'mã] *m* deepening; *fig.* thorough investigation.

appropriation [aprɔpria'sjɔ̃] *f* appropriation; adaptation (to, *à*); embezzlement; allocation; **approprier** [~pri'e] (1o) *v/t.* appropriate; adapt (to, *à*); *s'~ à* adapt o.s. to; fall in with.

approuver [apru've] (1a) *v/t.* approve (of); consent to; agree to; confirm (*an appointment*); authorize.

approvisionnement [aprɔvizjɔn-'mã] *m* provisioning, supply(ing); stock(ing); **approvisionner** [~zjɔ-'ne] (1a) *v/t.* supply (with, *en*); provision, victual; *s'~* lay in stores.

approximatif, -ve [aprɔksima'tif, ~'tiːv] approximate; **approximation** [~'sjɔ̃] *f* approximation.

appui [a'pɥi] *m* support (*a. fig.*); rest, prop, stay; *à l'~* in support of this; *à l'~ de* in support of; *~(e)-livres*, *pl.* *~s-livres*, *~e-livres* [apɥi'liːvr] *m* book-rest; *~(e)-tête*, *pl.* *~s-tête* [~'tɛːt] *m* headrest; *mot.* head-restraint; **appuyer** [apɥi'je] (1h) *v/t.* support; press; lean, rest (against, *contre*); *v/i.*: *~ sur* rest on; press, push (*a button etc.*), press down; *fig.* emphasize, stress; *~ sur la* (*or ~ à*) *droite* bear to the right; *s'~ sur* lean, rest on *or* against; *fig.* rely on.

âpre [ɑːpr] rough, harsh; biting; keen; *~ à* eager for; ruthless at; *~ au gain* grasping, greedy.

après [a'prɛ] **1.** *prp. space, time*: after; behind; *idea of attack*: at, on to; *~ vous, Madame* after you, Madam; *~ quoi* after which; thereupon; *~ tout* after all; *~ Jésus-Christ* after Christ; *être toujours ~ q.* be always nagging at s.o.; *~ avoir lu ce livre* after reading this book; *d'~* according to; *~ que* after, when; **2.** *adv.* after(wards), later; next; *la semaine d'~* the following week; *une semaine ~* one week later; *~-demain* [aprɛdə'mɛ̃] *adv.*

the day after tomorrow; ~-**guerre** [~'gɛːr] *m* or *f* post-war period; ~-**midi** [~mi'di] *m/inv.* afternoon; ~-**rasage** [~ra'zaːʒ] *adj., a. su./m/inv.* after-shave; ~-**vente** [~'vãːt]: *service m* ~ after-sales service.

âpreté [ɑprə'te] *f* roughness; harshness; sharpness; bitterness; keenness.

à-propos [aprɔ'po] *m* aptness, suitability; opportuneness.

apte [apt] fit(ted) (to, for *à*); apt; **aptitude** [apti'tyd] *f* aptitude; fitness; ⚙ capacity, qualification; ✕ ~s *pl. physiques* physique *sg.*; *mot.* ~ *à conduire* fitness to drive.

apurement ✝ [apyr'mã] *m* audit (-ing); **apurer** [apy're] (1a) *v/t.* audit, pass; discharge (*a liability*).

aquafortiste [akwafɔr'tist] *su.* etcher; **aquaplane** [~'plan] *m* surf-board; **aquaplaning** *mot.* [~pla'niŋ] *m* aquaplaning; **aquarelle** [~'rɛl] *f* aquarelle, water-colo(u)r; **aquarelliste** [~rɛ'list] *su.* aquarellist, water-colo(u)rist; **aquarium** [~'rjɔm] *m* aquarium; **aquatique** [~'tik] aquatic; marshy (*land*).

aqueduc [ak'dyk] *m* aqueduct (*a. anat.*); culvert; **aqueux, -euse** [a'kø, ~'køːz] watery.

aquilin, e [aki'lɛ̃, ~'lin] aquiline; *nez m* ~ Roman nose.

aquilon [aki'lɔ̃] *m* north wind.

arabe [a'rab] **1.** *adj.* Arabian; Arab; Arabic; *chiffre m* ~ Arabic numeral; **2.** *su.* ♀ Arab; *su./m ling.* Arabic; *horse:* Arab; *fig.* Shylock, usurer.

arabesque [ara'bɛsk] *adj., a. su./f* arabesque.

arabique [ara'bik] Arabic; Arabian; *gomme f* ~ gum arabic; *geog. le golfe* ♀ the Arabian gulf.

arable [a'rabl] arable (*land*).

arachide ♀ [ara'ʃid] *f* peanut, ground-nut.

araignée ♀ [arɛ'ɲe] *f zo.* spider; ⊕ grapnel; ⚓ clew; *vehicle:* buggy; *sl. avoir une ~ au plafond* have bats in the belfry; *fig. pattes f/pl. d'~* long thin fingers; scrawl *sg.*; ⊕ grease-channels; *toile f d'~* cobweb; spider's web.

aratoire [ara'twaːr] farming, agricultural.

arbalète [arba'lɛt] *f* cross-bow; **arbalétrier** [~letri'e] *m* cross-bow-man; ⚓ principal rafter.

arbitrage [arbi'traːʒ] *m* arbitration; ✝ arbitrage; *conseil m d'*~ conciliation board; **arbitraire** [~'trɛːr] arbitrary; **arbitre** [ar'bitr] *m* ✝ arbitrator; referee (*a. sp.*); *phls.* libre ~ free will; **arbitrer** [~bi'tre] (1a) *v/t.* arbitrate; *sp.* referee.

arborer [arbɔ're] (1a) *v/t.* hoist (*a flag*); *fig.* wear, display; sport (*a garment*); **arborescence** ♀ [~rɛ'sãːs] *f* arborescence; **arborescent, e** ♀ [~rɛ'sã, ~'sãːt] arborescent; **arboriculteur** ✓ [~rikyl'tœːr] *m* arboriculturist, nurseryman; **arboriculture** ✓ [~rikyl'tyːr] *f* arboriculture.

arbre [arbr] *m* tree; ⊕ spindle, shaft, axle; ⚙ mast; arbor; ⊕ ~ *à cames* cam-shaft; ⊕ ~ *de transmission* propeller shaft; ~ *généalogique* genealogical tree; ~ *manivelle* crank-shaft; ⊕ ~ *primaire* driving shaft; **arbrisseau** [~bri'so] *m* sapling; shrub.

arbuste ♀ [ar'byst] *m* bush, shrub.

arc [ark] *m* bow; △ arch; ⟨, ⊕ arc; ~ *en ogive* ogival arch; ~ *plein cintre* semi-circular arch; ⚙ *avoir de l'*~ sag; ✦ *lampe f à* ~ arc-lamp.

arcade [ar'kad] *f* archway; ⊕ arch; *spectacles:* bridge; ~s *pl.* arcade *sg.*

arcanes [ar'kan] *m/pl.* arcana, mysteries.

arc-boutant, *pl.* **arcs-boutant** [arkbu'tã] *m* △ flying buttress; △, ⊕ stay (*a. fig.*), strut; **arc-bouter** [~'te] (1a) *v/t.* buttress; shore up.

arceau [ar'so] *m* hoop; arch.

arc-en-ciel, *pl.* **arcs-en-ciel** [arkã-'sjɛl] *m* rainbow.

archaïque [arka'ik] archaic; **archaïsme** [~'ism] *m* archaism.

archange [ar'kãːʒ] *m* archangel.

arche[1] [arʃ] *f* arch; hoop.

arche[2] *bibl.* [~] *f* Ark; ~ *d'alliance* Ark of the Covenant.

archéologie [arkeɔlɔ'ʒi] *f* arch(a)eology; **archéologue** [~'lɔg] *m* arch(a)eologist.

archer [ar'ʃe] *m* archer; **archet** ♪, ⊕ [~'ʃɛ] *m* bow.

archétype [arke'tip] **1.** *adj.* archetypal; **2.** *su./m* archetype, prototype.

archevêché [arʃəvɛ'ʃe] *m* archbishopric, archdiocese; archbishop's palace; **archevêque** [~'vɛk] *m* archbishop.

archi... [arʃi] arch...; extremely; to the hilt; ~**bondé, e** [~bɔ̃'de],

~comble [~'kɔ:bl] packed (full); **~duc** [~'dyk] m archduke.

archipel geog. [arʃi'pɛl] m archipelago.

architecte [arʃi'tɛkt] m architect; ~ *paysagiste* landscape gardener; **architecture** [~tɛk'ty:r] f architecture; ~ *de paysage* landscape gardening or design.

archives [ar'ʃi:v] f/pl. archives, records; **archiviste** [~ʃi'vist] su. archivist; ⳨ filing clerk.

arçon [ar'sɔ̃] m saddle-bow; *vider les ~s* be unhorsed; fig. become embarrassed.

arctique [ark'tik] Arctic.

ardemment [arda'mɑ̃] adv. of ardent; **ardent, e** [~'dɑ̃, ~'dɑ̃:t] hot, burning (a. ⚓), scorching; fig. ardent, fervent, eager; fig. être sur des charbons ~s be on tenterhooks; **ardeur** [~'dœ:r] f heat; fig. ardo(u)r; eagerness; horse: mettle; ⚓ ~ d'estomac heartburn.

ardillon [ardi'jɔ̃] m buckle: tongue, catch; typ. pin.

ardoise [ar'dwa:z] f slate; **ardoisé, e** [ardwa'ze] slate-colo(u)red; **ardoisière** [~'zjɛ:r] f slate-quarry.

ardu, e [ar'dy] steep, abrupt; arduous; difficult.

are [a:r] m are.

arène [a'rɛn] f arena; poet. sand.

aréole [are'ɔl] f ♀, ⚓, anat. areola; meteor. nimbus, halo.

arête [a'rɛt] f icht. (fish-)bone; ⊕, mount., etc. edge; mount. crest, ridge; △, ⊕, etc. chamfer; beading; ♀ awn, beard; à ~s vives sharp-edged.

argent [ar'ʒɑ̃] m silver; money; ⊘ argent; ~ comptant cash; ~ de poche pocket-money; ~ en caisse cash in hand; ~ liquide ready money; en avoir pour son ~ have one's money's worth; être à court d'~ be short of money; **argentan** [arʒɑ̃'tɑ̃] m nickel or German silver; **argenté, e** [~'te] silver(ed); silvery; silver-plated; **argenter** [~'te] (1a) v/t. silver; **argenterie** [~'tri] f (silver-)plate.

argentin¹, e [arʒɑ̃'tɛ̃, ~'tin] silvery.

argentin², e [~] adj., a. su. ♀ Argentine.

argenture [arʒɑ̃'ty:r] f mirror: silvering; silver-plating.

argile [ar'ʒil] f clay; ~ réfractaire

fire-clay; **argileux, -euse** [arʒi'lø, ~'lø:z] clayey; argillaceous.

argon ⚛ [ar'gɔ̃] m argon.

argot [ar'go] m. slang; **argotique** [~gɔ'tik] slangy.

arguer [ar'gɥe] (1e) v/t. infer, deduce (from, de); assert; ~ de qch. put s.th. forward (as a reason); ⳨ ~ un acte de faux assert that a document is spurious; v/i. argue; **argument** [argy'mɑ̃] m argument (a. ⚓, a. of a book); plot, summary; ⅋ variable; **argumentation** [~mɑ̃ta'sjɔ̃] f argumentation; **argumenter** [~mɑ̃'te] (1a) v/i. argue (about, à propos de; against, contre; **argutie** [~'si] f quibble.

aride [a'rid] arid, dry; sterile; barren; **aridité** [aridi'te] f aridity, dryness; barrenness.

arien, -enne [a'rjɛ̃, ~'rjɛn] adj., a. su. Arian.

ariette ♪ [a'rjet] f arietta.

aristo sl. [aris'to] m swell; **aristocrate** [~tɔ'krat] su. aristocrat; **aristocratie** [~tɔkra'si] f aristocracy; **aristocratique** [~tɔkra'tik] aristocratic, upper-class.

arithméticien m, **-enne** f [aritmeti'sjɛ̃, ~'sjɛn] arithmetician; **arithmétique** [~'tik] 1. adj. arithmetical; 2. su./f arithmetic.

arlequin [arlə'kɛ̃] m Harlequin; food: scraps pl.; fig. weathercock.

armateur ⚓ [arma'tœ:r] m shipowner; **armature** [~'ty:r] f frame; brace; brassière: boning; ♪ armature; ♪ key-signature; fig. structure.

arme [arm] f arm; weapon; ⚔ branch of the service; ⚔ ~s pl. blanches side-arms; ~ à tir rapide automatic weapon; ~ automatique light machine-gun; ~ de choc striking weapon; ~s pl. spatiales space weapons; sp. faire des ~s fence; **armé, e** [ar'me] adj.: béton m ~ reinforced concrete, ferro-concrete; poutre f ~e trussed beam; verre m ~ wired glass; **armée** [ar'me] f army; forces pl.; ~ de l'air Air Force; ~ de mer Navy; ~ de métier regular army; ~ de terre land forces pl.; ♀ du Salut Salvation Army; **armement** [armə'mɑ̃] m armament, arming; equipment; ⚓ commissioning; ⚓ manning.

arménien, -enne [arme'njɛ̃, ~'njɛn] adj., a. su. ♀ Armenian.

armer [ar'me] (1a) *v/t.* arm (with, *de*); equip; ♻ commission; ♻ man; cock (*a pistol*); ⊕ mount (*a machine*); ⚡ wind (*a dynamo*); ⚡ sheath (*a cable*); set (*an apparatus*); † ~ *q.* *chevalier* dub s.o. knight; s'~ *de* arm o.s. with, *fig.* call upon (*one's courage, patience, etc.*).

armistice [armis'tis] *m* armistice.

armoire [ar'mwa:r] *f* cupboard; wardrobe; locker; ~ *à pharmacie* medicine-chest; ~ *au* (*or à*) *linge* linen-closet.

armoiries ⚔ [armwa'ri] *f/pl.* (coat *sg.* of) arms; armorial bearings.

armorial, e, *m/pl.* -**aux** ⚔ [armɔ-'rjal, ~'rjo] **1.** *adj.* armorial; **2.** *su./m* armorial, book of heraldry; **armorier** ⚔ [~'rje] (1o) *v/t.* emblazon.

armure [ar'my:r] *f* armo(u)r; ⊕ weave; *phys.* magnet: armature; ⚡ *dynamo*: pole-piece; **armurerie** [armyr'ri] *f* manufacture of arms; arms factory; gunsmith's shop; ⚔ armo(u)ry; **armurier** ⚔, ♻ [~'rje] *m* armo(u)rer; gunsmith.

arnica ❀ [arni'ka] *f* arnica.

aromate [arɔ'mat] *m* spice, aromatic; **aromatique** [arɔma'tik] aromatic; **aromatiser** [~ti'ze] (1a) *v/t.* give aroma *or* flavo(u)r to; *cuis.* flavo(u)r; **arome** [a'ro:m] *m* aroma; *cuis.* flavo(u)ring.

aronde ⊕ [a'rɔ̃:d] *f*: *queue f d'~* dovetail.

arpège ♪ [ar'pɛ:ʒ] *m* arpeggio.

arpent [ar'pɑ̃] *m* (*approx.*) acre; **arpentage** [arpɑ̃'ta:ʒ] *m* (land-)surveying; survey; **arpenter** [~'te] (1a) *v/t.* survey, measure (*the land*) *fig.* pace (up and down), stride along; **arpenteur** [~'tœ:r] *m* (land-)surveyor; *orn.* great plover.

arquebuse [arkə'by:z] *f* (h)arquebus.

arqué, e [ar'ke] arched, curved; *jambes* ~*es* bow legs, bandy legs; **arquer** [~] (1m) *v/t.* bend; arch; camber.

arraché [ara'ʃe] *m* *sp.* snatch; *fig. à l'*~ narrow (*victory etc.*); *fig.* obtenir *qch. à l'*~ (just manage to) snatch s.th.; **arrache-clou** ⊕ [araʃ'klu] *m* nail claw, nail wrench; **arrache-pied** [~'pje] *adv.*: *d'*~ relentlessly; fiercely; *travailler d'*~ F work flat out; **arracher** [ara'ʃe] (1a) *v/t.* tear out *or*

away (from, *à*); pull out; extract; draw (*a tooth*); extort (*a confession, money*); **arracheur, -euse** [~'ʃœːr, ~'ʃøːz] *su.* puller; *su./f* ⚡ potato-lifter.

arraisonnement ♻ [arɛzɔn'mɑ̃] *m* boarding; examination (of a bill of health); **arraisonner** ♻ [~zɔ'ne] (1a) *v/t.* hail; board; stop and examine.

arrangement [arɑ̃ʒ'mɑ̃] *m* arrangement (*a.* ♪); settlement, agreement; ✝ composition (*with creditors*); **arranger** [arɑ̃'ʒe] (1l) *v/t.* arrange (*a.* ♪); put in order; tidy, straighten; sort (*cards*); organize; settle (*a dispute, a quarrel*); suit (*s.o.*); *cela m'arrange* that suits me; F *cela s'arrangera* it'll turn out all right; s'~ manage (with, *de*), make do (with, *de*); come to an agreement, ✝ compound (with, *avec*); dress; s'~ *pour faire qch.* see to it that one can do s.th.; **arrangeur** *m*, **-euse** *f* ♪ [~'ʒœːr, ~'ʒøːz] arranger.

arrérager ✝ [arera'ʒe] (1l) *v/i.* get in arrears; **arrérages** ✝ [~'ra:ʒ] *m/pl.* arrears; back-interest *sg.*

arrestation [arɛsta'sjɔ̃] *f* arrest; apprehension; ⚖ ~ *préventive* protective custody.

arrêt [a'rɛ] *m* stop (*a.* ⊕); ⊕ stoppage; stopping; halt; interruption; ⚖ judgment; ⚖ award; *admin.* decree; ⚖ seizure; ⚖ detention; ⚖ arrest; *foot.* tackle; ⊕ *lock*: tumbler; *bus, tram, train*: stop(ping-place); ⚔ ~*s pl.* arrest *sg.*; ⚖ ~ *de mort* death sentence; *chien m d'*~ pointer; *cran m d'*~ safety-catch; *dispositif m d'*~ arresting device; ⚖ *rendre un* ~ deliver judgment; ⊕ *robinet m d'*~ stop-cock; *temps m d'*~ pause, halt; **arrêté** [arɛ'te] *m* order; decree; ordinance; by(e)-law; ✝ ~ *de compte(s)* settlement; **arrêter** [~] (1a) *v/t.* stop; arrest; check; fix, fasten; draw up; decide; ✝ make up, close (*an account*); fasten off (*a stitch*); ~ *les mailles knitting*: cast off; s'~ stop; halt, pause; cease (*noise*); *sans s'*~ *a.* without (a) letup; *v/i.* stop; *hunt.* point (*dog*); ~ *de faire qch.* stop doing s.th.

arrhes [a:r] *f/pl.* deposit *sg.*; earnest (money) *sg.*

arrière [a'rjɛːr] **1.** *adv.*: *en* ~ behind; back, backward(s); in arrears; *être en*

~ be behind; *regarder en* ~ look back; *rester en* ~ lag behind; *faire un pas en* ~ step back(wards); *revenir en* ~ go back; 2. *su./m* back (part), rear; ⚓ stern; *sp.* back; 3. *adj./inv.* back; *mot.* feu *m* (*or lanterne f*) ~ rear-light; *roue f* ~ back-wheel, rear-wheel; *vent m* ~ leading wind; **arriéré, e** [arje're] 1. *adj.* late; in arrears; backward (*child, country*); 2. *su./m* arrears *pl.*; ✝ *faire rentrer des* ~s recover debts.

arrière...: ~-**ban** *hist.* [arjer'bɑ̃] *m* (whole body of) vassals *pl.*; ~-**bouche** [~'buʃ] *f* back of the mouth; ~-**boutique** [~bu'tik] *f* back-shop; ~-**cour** [~'kuːr] *f* backyard; ~-**garde** ⚔ [~'gard] *f* rearguard; ~-**goût** [~'gu] *m* after-taste; ~-**grand'père** [~grɑ̃'pɛːr] *m* great-grandfather; ~-**main** [~'mɛ̃] *f* back of the hand; *horse:* hindquarters *pl.*; back-hand stroke; ~-**neveu** [~nə-'vø] *m* grand-nephew; ~-**pensée** [~pɑ̃'se] *f* ulterior motive; mental reservation; ~-**petit-fils,** *pl.* ~-**petits-fils** [~pəti'fis] *m* great-grandson; ~-**plan** [~'plɑ̃] *m* background; ~-**point** [~'pwɛ̃] *m* backstitch.

arriérer [arje're] (1f) *v/t.* postpone; s'~ fall behind (*person*); get into arrears.

arrière...: ~-**saison** [arjersɛ'zɔ̃] *f* late season *or* autumn, *Am.* late fall; ~-**train** [~'trɛ̃] *m* waggon-body; trailer; *animal:* hindquarter.

arrimer ⚓ [ari'me] (1a) *v/t.* stow; trim (*a ship*); pack (*for transit*).

arrivant *m*, **e** *f* [ari'vɑ̃, ~'vɑ̃:t] arrival, comer; **arrivée** [~'ve] *f* arrival, coming; ⊕ inlet, intake; *sp.* finish; **arriver** [~'ve] (1a) *v/i.* arrive, be (at, à), come; happen; succeed, be successful; ⚓ bear away; ~ *à* (*inf.*) succeed in (*ger.*); manage to (*inf.*); **arriviste** [~'vist] *su.* thruster, (social) climber; careerist.

arrogance [aro'gɑ̃:s] *f* arrogance; haughtiness; **arrogant, e** [~'gɑ̃, ~'gɑ̃:t] arrogant; haughty.

arroger [aro'ʒe] (11) *v/t.*: s'~ arrogate (*s.th.*) to o.s.

arrondir [arɔ̃'diːr] (2a) *v/t.* (make) round; round off (*a. fig. a sum*); round, double; s'~ fill out; become round; **arrondissement** [~dis'mɑ̃] *m* rounding off; roundness; *admin.* district; *admin. town:* ward.

arrosage [aro'za:ʒ] *m* watering, wetting; sprinkling; *cuis.* basting; *wine:* dilution; *rain:* soaking; **arroser** [~'ze] (1a) *v/t.* water; wet (*a. fig.*); sprinkle; moisten; *cuis.* baste; dilute (*wine*); F wash down (*the food*); F *ça s'arrose* that calls for a drink; **arroseur** [~'zœːr] *m* watercart attendant; **arroseuse** [~'zøːz] *f* watercart; ~-*balayeuse* combined street-watering and sweeping lorry *or* truck; **arrosoir** [~'zwaːr] *m* watering-can; sprinkler.

arsenal [arsə'nal] *m* arsenal (*a. fig.*); armo(u)ry; ⚓ dockyard.

arsenic 🜍 [arsə'nik] *m* arsenic.

art [aːr] *m* art; skill; ~s *pl. et métiers m/pl.* arts and crafts; ~s *pl. ménagers* domestic science.

artère [ar'tɛːr] *f* artery (*a. fig.*); thoroughfare; ⚡ feeder; **artériel, -elle** [arte'rjɛl] arterial; **artériosclérose** ⚕ [~rjɔskle'roːz] *f* arteriosclerosis.

artésien, -enne [arte'zjɛ̃, ~'zjɛn] artesian; of Artois; *puits m* ~ artesian well.

arthrite ⚕ [ar'trit] *f* arthritis; gout.

artichaut [arti'ʃo] *m cuis.* artichoke; ⚔ spiked barrier.

article [ar'tikl] *m* article (*a.* ⚘, ✝, *eccl., gramm.*); thing; *treaty:* clause; item; subject, topic; ✝ ~s *pl.* goods; ~s *pl.* de *Paris* fancy goods; *journ.* ~ *de fond* leading article; ~ *de luxe* luxury article; ~ *documentaire* documentary report; à l'~ *de la mort* at the point of death; *faire l'*~ puff one's goods; **articlier** *journ.* [~ti'klje] *m* copy-writer, columnist.

articulaire ⚕ [artiky'lɛːr] articular, of the joints; **articulation** [~la'sjɔ̃] *f anat., speech:* articulation; joint; ⊕ connection; ⚡ node; utterance; **articuler** [~'le] (1a) *v/t.* articulate; link; pronounce distinctly; state clearly.

artifice [arti'fis] *m* artifice; guile; stratagem; expedient; ⚔ ~s *pl.* flares; *feu m d'*~ fireworks *pl.*; flash of wit; **artificiel, -elle** [artifi'sjɛl] artificial; **artificier** [~'sje] *m* pyrotechnist; ⚔ artificer; **artificieux, -euse** [~'sjø, ~'sjøːz] artful, crafty, cunning.

artillerie ⚔ [artij'ri] *f* artillery, ordnance; gunnery; ~ *antiaérienne*

45 assassiner

(*or contre avions*) anti-aircraft artillery; ~ *d'assaut* assault artillery; ~ *lourde* (*or à pied*) heavy artillery; *pièce f d'*~ piece of ordnance; **artilleur** [ˌti'jœːr] *m* artilleryman, gunner.

artimon ⚓ [arti'mɔ̃] *m* mizzen; mizzenmast.

artisan [arti'zɑ̃] *m* artisan; craftsman; working-man; *fig.* creator, agent; **artisanat** [ˌza'na] *m* handicraft; craftsmen *pl.*

artiste [ar'tist] *su.* artist; ♪, *thea.* performer; **artistique** [ˌtis'tik] artistic.

aryen, -enne [a'rjɛ̃, ˌ'rjɛn] *adj., a. su.* ♀ Aryan, Indo-European.

as[1] [a] *2nd p. sg. pres. of avoir 1.*

as[2] [ɑːs] *m* ace (*a. fig.*); *sp.* crack (player *etc.*); *sl. être plein aux* ~ have stacks of money.

asbeste [as'bɛst] *m* asbestos.

ascendance [asɑ̃'dɑ̃ːs] *f* ancestry; *astr.* ascent; **ascendant, e** [ˌ'dɑ̃, ˌ'dɑ̃ːt] **1.** *adj.* upward (*motion etc.*); **2.** *su./m* ascendant; ascendency; *fig.* influence; ~s *pl.* ancestry *sg.*

ascenseur [asɑ̃'sœːr] *m* lift, *Am.* elevator; F *fig. renvoyer l'*~ do a favour in return, return the favour, reciprocate; **ascension** [ˌ'sjɔ̃] *f* ascent; climb; rising; ⊕ *piston:* upstroke; *eccl. l'*♀ Ascension-day; **ascensionniste** [ˌsjɔ'nist] *su.* climber; mountaineer; balloonist.

ascète [a'sɛt] *su.* ascetic; **ascétique** [ase'tik] ascetic; **ascétisme** [ˌ'tism] *m* ascetism.

asepsie ♪ [asɛp'si] *f* asepsis; **aseptique** ♪ [ˌ'tik] aseptic; **aseptiser** ♪ [ˌti'ze] (1a) *v/t.* asepticize.

asexué, e [asɛksɥ'e] *biol.* asexual; sexless. [Asiatic; Asian.]

asiatique [azja'tik] *adj., a. su.* ♀ᶴ

asile [a'zil] *m* asylum; retreat; shelter; † sanctuary; ~ *d'aliénés* mental hospital; ~ *pour animaux* animal home, *Am.* animal shelter.

asocial, e *m/pl.* -**aux** [asɔ'sjal, ˌ'sjo] antisocial.

aspect [as'pɛ] *m* aspect (*a. gramm.*); sight; appearance; look; *fig.* viewpoint.

asperge ♀ [as'pɛrʒ] *f* asparagus.

asperger [aspɛr'ʒe] (1l) *v/t.* sprinkle; spray (with, *de*).

aspérité [asperi'te] *f* asperity, roughness, harshness; unevenness.

asperseur [aspɛr'sœːr] *m* sprinkler; **aspersion** [ˌ'sjɔ̃] *f* aspersion, sprinkling; spraying; **aspersoir** [ˌ'swaːr] *m* ⚭ *watering-can:* rose; *eccl.* aspergillum.

asphaltage [asfal'taːʒ] *m* asphalting; **asphalte** [ˌ'falt] *m* asphalt.

asphyxie [asfik'si] *f* asphyxia(tion), suffocation; **asphyxier** [ˌ'sje] (1o) *v/t.* (*a. s'*~) asphyxiate, suffocate.

aspic [as'pik] *m* zo. asp; *cuis.* aspic; ♀ aspic, French lavender; *fig. langue f d'*~ venomous tongue.

aspirant, e [aspi'rɑ̃, ˌ'rɑ̃ːt] **1.** *adj.* sucking; ⊕ suction-...; **2.** *su.* aspirant, candidate; *su./m* ⚓ officer candidate; ⚓ midshipman; ✂ acting pilot-officer; **aspirateur, -trice** [ˌra'tœːr, ˌ'tris] **1.** *adj.* suction-...; **2.** *su./m* ⊕ suction-conveyor; ⊕ exhaust-fan; aspirator; vacuum cleaner; **aspiration** [ˌra'sjɔ̃] *f* aspiration (*a. gramm.*); *fig.* longing (after, *à*); ⊕ suction; ⊕ inspiration, inhaling; ⊕ intake; **aspirer** [ˌ're] (1a) *v/t.* breathe in; suck in *or* up; *gramm.* aspirate; ✎ inhale; *v/i.:* ~ *à* (*inf.*) aspire to (*inf.*); ~ *à qch.* aspire to s.th.; long for s.th.

aspirine ✎ [aspi'rin] *f* aspirin; *prendre un comprimé d'*~ take an aspirin.

assagir [asa'ʒiːr] (2a) *v/t.* make wiser; steady, sober (down).

assaillant [asa'jɑ̃] *m* assailant; **assaillir** [ˌ'jiːr] (2s) *v/t.* assail, attack; *fig.* beset (with, *de*).

assainir [ase'niːr] (2a) *v/t.* make healthier; cleanse, purify; clean (up); clear (*slums, the atmosphere, etc.*); drain (*marshes*); stabilize (*the economy etc.*); reorganize (*the finances etc.*); **assainissement** [ˌnis'mɑ̃] *m* cleansing, purifying; cleaning (up); clearing; *marshes:* draining; *economy:* stabilization; *finances:* reorganization.

assaisonnement [asezɔn'mɑ̃] *m* seasoning; flavo(u)ring; *salad:* dressing; **assaisonner** [ˌzɔ'ne] (1a) *v/t.* season (with, *de*); flavo(u)r (with, *de*); dress (*salads*).

assassin, e [asa'sɛ̃, ˌ'sin] **1.** *su./m* assassin; murderer; *à l'*~! murder!; *su./f* murderess; **2.** *adj.* murderous; *fig.* provocative; *fig.* deadly; **assassinat** [ˌsi'na] *m* murder; assassination; **assassiner** [ˌsi'ne] (1a) *v/t.*

murder (a. fig.); assassinate; F
pester.

assaut [a'so] m assault, attack; sp.
bout, match; faire ~ de bandy
(words, wit).

assèchement [asɛʃ'mɑ̃] m drying,
draining, drainage; **assécher** [ase-
'ʃe] (1f) v/t. dry; drain.

assemblage [asɑ̃'blaːʒ] m gathering, collection; ⊕ assembly; ⊕
joint; ⚡ connection, coupling; **assemblée** [~'ble] f assembly, meeting; congregation; ~
générale general meeting; ~ plénière plenary assembly; **assembler**
[~'ble] (1a) v/t. assemble (a. ⊕);
gather, call together; convene (a
committee); ✕ muster; ⚡ couple,
connect; join(t); s'~ assemble, meet.

assener [asə'ne] (1d) v/t. strike,
land (a blow).

assentiment [asɑ̃ti'mɑ̃] m agreement, assent, consent; signe m d'~
nod.

asseoir [a'swaːr] (3c) v/t. seat,
place; pitch (a tent); lay (a stone);
establish (a tax); base (an opinion);
on le fit ~ he was asked to take a
seat; s'~ sit down; settle; 🐝 pancake.

assermenté, e [asɛrmɑ̃'te] sworn;
on oath.

assertion [asɛr'sjɔ̃] f assertion.

asservir [asɛr'viːr] (2a) v/t. enslave
(to, à) (a. fig.); subdue; subject;
⊕ synchronize; **asservissement**
[~vis'mɑ̃] m slavery, subjection;
bondage; ⊕ control.

assesseur [asɛ'sœːr] m assessor;
assistant judge.

asseyons [asɛ'jɔ̃] 1st p. pl. pres. of
asseoir.

assez [a'se] adv. enough; rather;
sufficiently; fairly; ~! that's
enough!; that will do!; (en) avoir ~ de
be sick (and tired) of; j'en ai ~! a. I've
had enough of it, F I'm fed up with it.

assidu, e [asi'dy] diligent; assidu-
ous; regular; constant; attentive
(to, auprès de); **assiduité** [~dʇi'te]
f diligence, assiduity; ~s pl. constant attentions or care sg.; **assidû-
ment** [~dy'mɑ̃] adv. of assidu.

assieds [a'sje] 1st p. sg. pres. of asseoir.

assiégeant, e [asje'ʒɑ̃, ~'ʒɑ̃ːt] 1. adj.
besieging; 2. su./m besieger; **assiéger** [~'ʒe] (1g) v/t. besiege (a. fig.);

surround; beset; fig. mob; fig.
dun.

assiérai [asje're] 1st p. sg. fut. of asseoir.

assiette [a'sjɛt] f plate; ⚓ trim;
horse: seat; ⊕ etc. basis; machine:
support; tax: establishment; F il
n'est pas dans son ~ he's out of
sorts, he's not up to the mark; **assiettée** [asje'te] f plate(ful).

assignation [asiɲa'sjɔ̃] f assignation;
⚖ summons, subpoena; **assigner**
[~'ne] (1a) v/t. assign; allot; appoint,
fix (a time); allocate; ✝ earmark (a
sum); ⚖ summon, subpoena.

assimilable [asimi'labl] ⚘ assimilable; comparable (to, à); **assimilation** [~la'sjɔ̃] f assimilation; ✕,
⚓ correlation, equivalence; **assimiler** [~'le] (1a) v/t. assimilate;
compare; give equal status to.

assis¹ [a'si] 1st p. sg. p.s. of asseoir.

assis², e [a'si, ~'siːz] 1. p.p. of asseoir; 2. adj. seated, sitting; être ~
be seated or sitting; 🐝 etc. place f
~e seat; 3. su./f △ foundation; △
bricks: course; cement: layer; rider:
seat; ~es pl. meetings, sessions; ⚖
assizes; ⚖ cour f d'~es Assize
Court.

assistance [asis'tɑ̃ːs] f assistance,
help; audience, spectators pl.; eccl.
congregation; ⚖, eccl. attendance,
presence; ~ judiciaire (free) legal
aid; ~ maritime salvage; ~ publique
public assistance, public relief; ~
sociale (social) welfare work; **assistant, e** [~'tɑ̃, ~'tɑ̃ːt] su. assistant;
usu. ~s pl. spectators, onlookers;
audience sg.; su./f: ~e sociale social
worker; **assister** [~'te] (1a) v/i.:
~ à attend; be present at; v/t.
assist, help, aid (s.o.).

association [asɔsja'sjɔ̃] f association; ✝ partnership; society; union;
⚡ coupling, connection; ~ de bienfaisance charitable organization; ✝
~ en nom collectif (ordinary) partnership; **associé m, e** f [asɔ'sje]
partner; learned society: associate;
✝ ~ commanditaire sleeping partner; **associer** [~] (1o) v/t. associate,
unite; join up; ⚡ connect, couple;
s'~ (à or avec) associate o.s. (with);
join (in s.th.); keep company with;
✝ enter into partnership with.

assoiffé, e [aswa'fe] thirsty; fig. eager
(for, de).

assoirai F [aswa're] *1st p. sg. fut. of* **asseoir;** **assois** F [a'swa] *1st p. sg. pres. of asseoir.*

assolement ⚷ [asɔl'mɑ̃] *m* (crop-)rotation; **assoler** ⚷ [asɔ'le] (1a) *v/t.* rotate the crops on.

assombrir [asɔ̃'briːr] (2a) *v/t.* darken; make gloomy (*a. fig.*); cloud (*a. fig.*); *s'~* darken; become cloudy (*sky*); *fig.* become gloomy.

assommant, e [asɔ'mɑ̃, ~'mɑ̃ːt] F boring; tiresome; **assommer** [~-'me] (1a) *v/t.* fell; stun; knock on the head; knock out; *fig.* bore; *fig.* overcome; **assommoir** [~'mwaːr] *m* † bludgeon; *fig. coup m d'~* staggering blow.

assomption [asɔ̃p'sjɔ̃] *f* assumption; *eccl.* l'Ꝗ the Assumption.

assonance [asɔ'naːs] *f* assonance; **assonant, e** [~'nɑ̃, ~'nɑ̃ːt] assonant.

assorti, e [asɔr'ti] assorted; (*well-, badly-*)matched; † (*well-, badly-*)stocked; ~ *à* matching; **assortiment** [asɔrti'mɑ̃] *m* assortment (*a.* †), range, variety; ⊕ set; *typ.* sorts *pl.*; **assortir** [~'tiːr] (2a) *v/t.* match; *s'~* match (s.th., *à* qch.), go well together.

assoupir [asu'piːr] (2a) *v/t.* make sleepy *or* drowsy; soothe, deaden, lull (*a pain etc.*); *s'~* doze off; wear off (*pain*); **assoupissement** [~pis-'mɑ̃] *m* drowsiness; nap, doze; *fig.* sloth; ⚕ torpor.

assouplir [asu'pliːr] (2a) *v/t.* make supple; break in (*a horse*); *fig. s'~* become more tractable.

assourdir [asur'diːr] (2a) *v/t.* deafen (*a. fig.*); *fig.* deaden, damp, muffle (*a sound*); tone down (*a light etc.*); *gramm.* unvoice (*a consonant*).

assouvir [asu'viːr] (2a) *v/t.* satiate, appease (*one's hunger*); quench (*one's thirst*); † glut (*the market*); *s'~* gorge; become sated (with, *de*).

assoyons F [aswa'jɔ̃] *1st p. pl. pres. of asseoir.*

assujetti, e [asyʒɛ'ti] subject, liable (to, *à*); ~ *à l'assurance* subject to compulsory insurance; ~ *aux droits de douane* liable to duty, dutiable; **assujettir** [~'tiːr] (2a) *v/t.* subjugate, subdue; fix, fasten; secure; make liable (to, *à*); compel (to *inf.*, *à inf.*); **assujettissement** [~tis'mɑ̃] *m* subjugation; securing.

assumer [asy'me] (1a) *v/t.* assume,

take (*a responsibility*) upon o.s.; take up (*duties*).

assurance [asy'rɑ̃ːs] *f* assurance (*a.* †), self-confidence; certainty; security, pledge; safety; † insurance; ~*s pl. sociales* social security *sg.*; ~*-automobile* car insurance; ~*-incendie* fire-insurance; ~ *maladie* health-insurance; ~ *maritime* marine insurance; ~ *au tiers* third-party insurance; ~ *tous risques* comprehensive insurance; ~*-vie,* ~ *sur la vie* life assurance *or* insurance; ~*-vieillesse* old-age insurance; *passer un contrat d'~* take out an insurance policy; **assuré, e** [~'re] 1. *adj.* sure; confident; 2. *su.* † *the* insured; policy-holder; **assurément** [~re'mɑ̃] *adv.* assuredly; **assurer** [~'re] (1a) *v/t.* assure; secure, fasten; make secure; make steady; affirm; ensure (*a result*); † insure; provide, maintain (*a service etc.*); carry out, undertake, handle (*work etc.*); *s'~ a.* make sure (of, *de*; that, *que*); *s'~ de a.* ensure; **assureur** † [~'rœːr] *m* insurers *pl.*, insurance agent; ~ *maritime* underwriter.

aster ⚲, *biol.* [as'tɛːr] *m* aster; **astérisque** *typ.* [~te'risk] *m* asterisk (*).

asthénie ⚕ [aste'ni] *f* debility.

asthmatique ⚕ [asma'tik] *adj., a. su.* asthmatic; **asthme** ⚕ [asm] *m* asthma.

asticot [asti'ko] *m* maggot; F *un drôle d'~* a queer cove *or* chap; **asticoter** F [~kɔ'te] (1a) *v/t.* plague, worry.

astigmate ⚕ [astig'mat] astigmatic.

astiquer [asti'ke] (1m) *v/t.* polish; smarten; [⚲, *anat.* astragalus.]

astragale [astra'gal] *m* ⌂ astragal;∫ **astral, e,** *m/pl.* -aux [as'tral, ~'tro] astral; **astre** [astr] *m* star (*a. fig.*).

astreindre [as'trɛ̃ːdr] (4m) subject; force, compel (to, *à*); bind; *s'~ à* force o.s. to, keep to.

astringent, e ⚕ [astrɛ̃'ʒɑ̃, ~'ʒɑ̃ːt] *adj., a. su./m* astringent.

astro... [astrɔ] astro...; ~*logie* [~lɔ-'ʒi] *f* astrology; ~*logue* [~'lɔg] *m* astrologer; ~*naute* [~'noːt] *m* astronaut, space traveller; ~*nautique* [~no'tik] *f* astronautics *sg.*, space travel; ~*nef* [~'nɛf] *m* space-ship; ~*nome* [~'nɔm] *m* astronomer; ~*nomie* [~nɔ'mi] *f* astronomy; ~*nomique* [~nɔ'mik] astronomical (*year*, *a.* F *price*); ~**physique** [~fi-'zik] **1.** *adj.* astrophysical; **2.** *su./f* astrophysics *sg.*

astuce [as'tys] *f* guile, craftiness; wile, trick; **astucieux, -euse** [~ty-'sjø, ~'sjø:z] crafty, astute, artful.

asymétrique [asime'trik] asymmetrical, unsymmetrical.

asymptote Ⱥ [asɛ̃p'tɔt] **1.** *adj.* asymptotic; **2.** *su./f* asymptote.

atavique [ata'vik] atavistic; *biol.* retour *m* ~ throw-back; **atavisme** [~'vism] *m* atavism.

ataxie ⚕ [atak'si] *f* ataxy, ataxia.

atelier [atə'lje] *m* workshop; studio; (shop *or* workroom) staff; ⚒ working party; *pol.* work-group; ⊕ ~ *de constructions mécaniques* engine works; ~ *de réparations* repair-shop.

atermoiement [atɛrmwa'mɑ̃] *m* † deferment of payment; procrastination; F ~*s* shilly-shallying *sg.*; **atermoyer** [~'je] (1h) *v/t.* † put off, defer (*payment*); *v/i.* temporize, procrastinate; *s'*~ arrange for an extension of time (*with creditors*).

athée [a'te] **1.** *adj.* atheistic; **2.** *su.* atheist; **athéisme** [ate'ism] *m* atheism.

athlète [at'lɛt] *m* (*Am.* track and field) athlete; **athlétique** [atle'tik] athletic; **athlétisme** [~'tism] *m* (*Am.* track and field) athletics *pl.*

atlantique [atlɑ̃'tik] **1.** *adj.* Atlantic; **2.** *su./m* ♀ Atlantic (Ocean).

atlas [at'lɑ:s] *m* atlas; *geog.*, *myth.* ♀ Atlas.

atmosphère [atmɔs'fɛ:r] *f* atmosphere (*a. fig.*); **atmosphérique** [~fe'rik] atmospheric.

atoll *geog.* [a'tɔl] *m* atoll, coral island.

atome [a'to:m] *m* atom (*a. fig.*); *fig.* speck; F *fig.* avoir des ~*s crochus* (*avec q.*) have things in common (with s.o.), be on the same wavelength (with s.o.); **atomique** [atɔ'mik] atomic; *bombe f* ~ atom(ic) bomb; *énergie f* ~ atomic energy; *ère f* ~ atomic age; *pile f* ~ atomic pile; *poids m* ~ atomic weight; **atomiser** [~mi'ze] (1a) *v/t.* atomize; pulverize; **atomiseur** [~mi'zœ:r] *m* spray, atomizer.

atone [a'tɔn] *gramm.* atonic, unstressed; *fig.* dull; vacant; **atonie** ⚕ [atɔ'ni] *f* atony, sluggishness.

atours [a'tu:r] *m/pl.* †, *a. co.* finery *sg.*

atout [a'tu] *m* trump; *fig.* asset, advantage; *jouer* ~ play trumps.

atoxique [atɔ'ksik] non-poisonous.

âtre [ɑ:tr] *m* hearth.

atroce [a'trɔs] atrocious, dreadful; grim; **atrocité** [atrɔsi'te] *f* atrocity; atrociousness.

atrophie ⚕ [atrɔ'fi] *f* atrophy; emaciation; **atrophier** [~'fje] (1o) *v/i.*, *a. s'*~ atrophy.

attabler [ata'ble] (1a) *v/t.*: *s'*~ sit down to table; *fig.* F own up, *usu. Am.* come clean.

attache [a'taʃ] *f* bond, tie, link; cord, strap; ⊕ brace, joint; paper clip; *chien m d'*~ house-dog; ⚓ *pat m d'*~ home pat; **attaché** [ata'ʃe] *m pol.* attaché; **attachement** [ataʃ'mɑ̃] *m* attachment (*a. fig.*); **attacher** [ata'ʃe] (1a) *v/t.* attach; fasten (*a. fig.*); tie; *fig.* attract; *s'*~ *à* attach o.s. to; cling to; apply *or* devote o.s. to; ⚒ *s'*~ *au sol* hold on to the ground; *s'*~ *aux pas de q.* dog s.o.'s footsteps.

attaque [a'tak] *f* attack (*a.* ⚔, ⚒); assault; ⊕, *mot.* drive; *être d'*~ feel fit; **attaquer** [ata'ke] (1m) *v/t.* attack; assail; assault; ⚖ contest (*a will*), sue (*s.o.*); ⊕ operate; F begin; *s'*~ *à* fall upon, attack; *fig.* tackle; *v/i.* attack.

attardé, e [atar'de] **1.** *adj.* belated; backward; old-fashioned; **2.** *su.* late-comer; **attarder** [~] (1a) *v/t.* make late; *s'*~ delay, linger (over, *sur*); *s'*~ *à* (*inf.*) stay (up) late (*ger.*).

atteindre [a'tɛ̃dr] (4m) *v/t.* reach, attain; overtake; hit (*a target*); strike (*a. fig.*); *fig.* affect; *v/i.*: ~ *à* attain (to), achieve; **atteint, e** [a'tɛ̃, ~'tɛ̃:t] **1.** *p.p. of* atteindre; **2.** *su./f* reach; attack (*a.* ⚕), blow, stroke; touch; harm, injury; *hors d'*~*e* out of reach.

attelage [at'la:ʒ] *m* harnessing; yoke, team; ⊕ attachment; 🚃 coupling; **atteler** [~'le] (1c) *v/t.* harness; yoke; connect; 🚃 couple; *s'*~ *à* settle *or* F get down to (*a task*); **attelle** [a'tɛl] *f* ⚕ splint; ~*s pl.* hames.

attenant, e [at'nɑ̃, ~'nɑ̃:t] neighbo(u)ring, adjacent (to, *à*).

attendant [atɑ̃'dɑ̃]: *en* ~ *adv.* meanwhile; *prp.* pending; *en* ~ *que* (*sbj.*) until, till (*ind.*); **attendre** [a'tɑ̃dr] (4a) *v/t.* wait for, await; look for-

49
attroupement

ward to; expect; *attendez voir!*
wait and see!; *faire ~ q.* keep s.o.
waiting; *s'~ à* expect (*s.th.*).
attendrir [atɑ̃'driːr] (2a) *v/t.* soften,
make tender; tenderize (*meat*); *fig.*
touch, move; *s'~ sur* gush over; *se
laisser ~* be moved *or* affected; **at-
tendrissement** [~dris'mɑ̃] *m* emotion; (feeling of) pity.
attendu, e [atɑ̃'dy] **1.** *p.p. of attendre*; **2.** *attendu prp.* considering; on
account of; *~ que* seeing that ...; ⚖
whereas; **3.** *su./m:* *~s pl.* ⚖ reasons
adduced.
attentat [atɑ̃'ta] *m* assassination attempt; attack; outrage; ⚖ *~ à la
pudeur* indecent assault; ⚖ *~ aux
mœurs* indecent behavio(u)r, *Am.*
offense against public morals.
attente [a'tɑ̃ːt] *f* wait(ing); expectation; *contre toute ~* contrary to
expectations; 🕭 *salle f d'~* waiting
room.   [attempt (on, à).]
attenter [atɑ̃'te] (1a) *v/i.* make an⌡
attentif, -ve [atɑ̃'tif, ~'tiːv] (à) attentive (to); heedful (of); careful; mind-
ful; **attention** [~'sjɔ̃] *f* attention,
care; *~!* look out; *faire ~* pay attention (to, à); take care (of, à); **atten-
tisme** [~'tism] *m* wait-and-see attitude *or* policy; waiting game; **atten-
tiste** [~'tist] **1.** *su.* partisan of a wait-
and-see policy; **2.** *adj.* wait-and-see.
atténuant, e [ate'nɥɑ̃, ~'nɥɑ̃ːt] ⚖
mitigating *or* extenuating (*circumstances*); 🎖, ⚒ attenuant; **atténuer**
[~'nɥe] (1n) *v/t.* mitigate, lessen,
soften; *s'~ a.* die down.
atterrer [ate're] (1a) *v/t.* overwhelm, astound, stun.
atterrir [ate'riːr] (2a) *v/i.* ⚓ make
a landfall; ✈ land; **atterrissage**
[~ri'saːʒ] *m* ⚓ landfall; ✈ landing;
✈ *~ forcé* forced landing; ✈ *~ sans
visibilité* instrument landing; ✈
train m d'~ undercarriage.
atterrissement [ateris'mɑ̃] *m* alluvium.
atterrisseur ✈ [ateri'sœːr] *m*
undercarriage; *~ escamotable*
retractable undercarriage.
attestation [atesta'sjɔ̃] *f* attestation;
testimonial; certificate; ⚖ *~ sous
serment* affidavit; **attester** [~'te]
(1a) *v/t.* testify, certify.
attiédir [atje'diːr] (2a) *v/t.* cool (*a.
fig.*); take the chill off; *s'~* (grow)
cool (*a. fig.*).

4 GTW Fr-E

attifer [ati'fe] (1a) *v/t. usu. pej.* dress
(*s.o.*) up; *s'~* get o.s. up, rig o.s. out.
attiger F [ati'ʒe] (1l) *v/i.* exaggerate,
F lay it on.
attique [a'tik] **1.** *adj.* Attic; **2.** *su./m*
△ attic; *su./f:* l'△ Attica.
attirail [ati'raːj] *m* outfit; gear; F
pomp; *pej.* paraphernalia *pl.*
attirance [ati'rɑ̃ːs] *f* attraction; **attirant, e** [~'rɑ̃, ~'rɑ̃ːt] attractive;
engaging; **attirer** [~'re] (1a) *v/t.*
attract; draw; (al)lure; *s'~* win
(*s.th.*).
attiser [ati'ze] (1a) *v/t.* stir up (*a.
fig.*); ⊕ stoke; *fig.* fan, feed; **atti-
soir** [~'zwaːr] *m* poker; ⊕ pricker,
fire-rake.
attitré, e [ati'tre] appointed, regular; customary.
attitude [ati'tyd] *f* attitude (towards,
envers).
attouchement [atuʃ'mɑ̃] *m* contact
(*a.* 🖐), touch(ing).
attractif, -ve [atrak'tif, ~'tiːv] attractive; gravitational (*force*); **attraction** [~'sjɔ̃] *f* attraction (*a. fig.*),
pull; *~s pl.* variety show *sg.*; cabaret
sg., *Am.* floor show *sg.*; *phys. ~ universelle* gravitation.
attrait [a'tre] *m* attractiveness,
charm; inclination (for, *pour*).
attrapade F [atra'pad] *f*, **attrapage**
F [~'paːʒ] *m* tiff, quarrel; blowing-
up, reprimand.
attrape [a'trap] *f* hoax, trick; *object:*
joke (article); **attrape-mouches**
[atrap'muʃ] *m/inv.* flypaper; ⚘
catchfly; *orn.* flycatcher; **attrape-
nigaud** [~ni'go] *m* booby trap; **attraper** [atra'pe] (1a) *v/t.* catch (*a.
🐟*); trap; *fig.* trick; F scold; *se faire ~*
be taken in; get hauled over the coals
(for *ger.*, *pour inf.*).
attrayant, e [atre'jɑ̃, ~'jɑ̃ːt] attractive; engaging.
attribuer [atri'bɥe] (1n) *v/t.* attribute (to, à); assign; allot; *s'~* appropriate; **attribut** [~'by] *m* attribute;
gramm. predicate; emblem; ⚔
badge; **attribution** [~by'sjɔ̃] *f* attribution; allocation; conferment;
~s pl. competence *sg.*, powers, duties.
attrister [atris'te] (1a) *v/t.* sadden;
s'~ become sad; cloud over (*sky*).
attrition [atri'sjɔ̃] *f* abrasion; *eccl.*
attrition (*a.* 🖐).
attroupement [atrup'mɑ̃] *m* ⚖

unlawful assembly; *fig.* mob; **at-trouper** [atru'pe] (1a) *v/t.* gather together; *s'~* flock together; assemble, crowd.

atypique [ati'pik] atypical.

aubade [o'bad] *f* ♪ aubade; F cat-calling.

aubaine [o'bɛn] *f* ⚖ right of escheat; *fig.* godsend, windfall.

aube[1] [o:b] *f* dawn; *eccl.* alb.

aube[2] [~] *f* paddle, float; blade.

aubépine ♀ [obe'pin] *f* hawthorn; whitethorn.

auberge [o'bɛrʒ] *f* inn, tavern; *~ de la jeunesse* youth hostel.

aubergine ♀ [ober'ʒin] *f* egg-plant.

aubergiste [ober'ʒist] *su.* innkeeper; *su./m* landlord; *su./f* landlady.

aucun, e [o'kœ̃, ~'kyn] **1.** *adj.* any; **2.** *pron.* any(one); *with ne or on its own:* none; *d'~s* some (people); **aucunement** [okyn'mɑ̃] *adv.* not at all, by no means.

audace [o'das] *f* audacity (*a. fig.*); daring; boldness; F *payer d'~* face the music; **audacieux, -euse** [oda'sjø, ~'sjø:z] audacious, bold, daring; impertinent.

au-deçà † [odə'sa] *adv.* on this side; **au-dedans** [~'dɑ̃] *adv.* inside, within; *~ de* within; **au-dehors** [~'ɔ:r] *adv.* (on the) outside; *~ de* outside, beyond; **au-delà** [~'la] **1.** *adv.* beyond; *~ de* beyond, on the other side of; **2.** *su./m* beyond; *l'~* the next world; **au-dessous** [~'su] *adv.* below; *~ de* below, under; beneath; **au-dessus** [~'sy] *adv.* above; *~ de* above; *fig.* beyond; **au-devant** [~'vɑ̃] *adv.* forward, ahead; *aller ~ de* go to meet; anticipate; forestall; *aller ~ d'un danger* court danger.

audible [o'di:bl] audible; **audience** [o'djɑ̃:s] *f* attention, interest; ⚖ hearing; audience; *radio etc.*: public; **audiencier** [odjɑ̃'sje] *m* ⚖ usher; F haunter of law-courts; **audiovisuel, -elle** [odjovi'zɥɛl] audiovisual; **auditeur, -trice** [odi'tœːr, ~'tris] *su.* hearer, listener; *univ.* student who attends lectures only; *su./m* ⚖, ⚖ public prosecutor; *admin.* commissioner of audits; *~s m/pl.* audience; **auditif, -ve** [~'tif, ~'ti:v] *anat.* auditory; *appareil m ~* hearing aid; **audition** [~'sjɔ̃] *f* hearing; recital; audition; *~s pl. du*

jour radio: today's program(me) *sg.*; **auditionner** [~sjɔ'ne] (1a) *v/t.* audition (*s.o.*); *v/i.* audition, give an audition; **auditoire** [~'twa:r] *m* audience.

auge [o:ʒ] *f* trough (*a.* ⊕); manger; ⊕ *water-wheel*: bucket; *geol. ~ glaciaire* glacial valley; **auget** [o'ʒɛ] *m* small trough; ⊕ *water-wheel*: bucket.

augmentation [ogmɑ̃ta'sjɔ̃] *f* increase (*a.* ♪, ♀); *prices, wages*: rise; augmentation (*a.* ♪, ♪); *faire une ~ knitting*: make a stitch; **augmenter** [~'te] (1a) *v/t.* increase, augment; raise (*a price, the wages*); *s'~* increase; *v/i.* increase, rise; grow.

augure [o'gyːr] *m* augury, omen; augur; **augurer** [ogy're] (1a) *v/t.* augur; forecast.

auguste [o'gyst] **1.** *adj.* august, majestic; **2.** *su./m circus*: the funny man.

aujourd'hui [oʒur'dɥi] today; (*d'*)*~ en huit* (*quinze*) today week (fortnight).

aumône [o'moːn] *f* alms; charity; **aumônier** [omo'nje] *m* almoner; chaplain (*a.* ✗).

aunaie [o'nɛ] *f* plantation of alders.

aune[1] ♀ [o:n] *m* alder.

aune[2] [~] *f* † ell; F *une figure longue d'une ~* a face as long as a fiddle; **auner** [o'ne] (1a) *v/t.* measure by the ell.

auparavant [opara'vɑ̃] *adv.* before(hand); *d'~* preceding.

auprès [o'prɛ] *adv.* near; close by; *~ de* near, beside; compared with; in the opinion *or* view of, with (*s.o.*).

aurai [ɔ're] *1st p. sg. fut. of avoir* 1.

auréole [ɔre'ɔl] *f* aureole, halo; *phot.* halation.

auriculaire [ɔriky'lɛːr] **1.** *adj.* auricular; ear-...; *doigt m ~* = **2.** *su./m* little finger.

aurifère [ɔri'fɛːr] *adj.* auriferous, gold-bearing; **aurification** [~fika'sjɔ̃] *f tooth*: filling *or Am.* stopping with gold; **aurifier** [~'fje] (1o) *v/t.* fill *or* stop with gold.

aurore [ɔ'rɔːr] **1.** *su./f* dawn (*a. fig.*), daybreak; *myth.* ♀ Aurora; *~ boréale* northern lights *pl.*; **2.** *adj.* golden yellow.

auscultation ✗ [ɔskylta'sjɔ̃] *f* auscultation, sounding (of chest); **aus-**

culter ⚕ [∼'te] (1a) v/t. auscultate, sound.

auspice [ɔs'pis] m auspice, omen; ∼s pl. protection sg.; auspices.

aussi [o'si] **1.** adv. also; too; as well; so; ∼ ... que as ... as; moi ∼ so am (do, can) I, F me too; **2.** cj. therefore; and so; ∼ bien besides, moreover; **aussitôt** [osi'to] **1.** adv. immediately, at once; ∼ que as soon as; **2.** prp. immediately on.

austère [ɔs'tɛ:r] austere, stern; severe; **austérité** [∼teri'te] f austerity, sternness; severity.

austral, e, m/pl. -als or -aux [ɔs-'tral, ∼'tro] southern; **australien, -enne** [∼tra'ljɛ̃, ∼'ljɛn] adj., a. su. ♀ Australian.

austro... [ɔstrɔ] Austro-...

autan [o'tã] m strong south wind.

autant [∼] adv. as much, as many; so much, so many; ∼ dire practically, to all intents and purposes; (pour) ∼ que as far as; d'∼ (plus) que especially as, all the more as; en faire ∼ do the same.

autarcie [otar'si] f autarky; **autarcique** [∼'sik] autarkical.

autel [o'tɛl] m altar.

auteur [o'tœ:r] m author (a. fig.); crime: perpetrator; writer; ♪ composer; ⚖ principal; droit m d'∼ copyright; droits m/pl. d'∼ royalties; femme f ∼ authoress.

authenticité [otãtisi'te] f authenticity, genuineness; **authentique** [∼'tik] authentic, genuine.

auto F [o'to] f (motor-)car.

auto... [oto] auto-..., self-...; motor-...; **∼bus** [∼'bys] m (motor) bus; **∼car** [∼'ka:r] m motor coach; **∼chenille** [∼ʃə'ni:j] f crawler tractor; half-track vehicle.

autochtone [otɔk'tɔn] **1.** adj. autochthonous; aboriginal; **2.** su. autochthon.

auto...: **∼clave** [oto'kla:v] m sterilizer; cuis. pressure-cooker; **∼collant, e** [∼kɔ'lɑ̃, ∼'lɑ̃t] **1.** adj. self-adhesive; **2.** su./m sticker; **∼crate** [∼'krat] m autocrat; **∼cratie** [∼kra'si] f autocracy; **∼cratique** [∼kra'tik] autocratic; **∼détermination** [∼determina'sjɔ̃] f self-determination; **∼didacte** [∼di'dakt] **1.** adj. self-taught; **2.** su. self-taught person; **∼drome** [∼'dro:m] m motor-racing

track; **∼école** [∼e'kɔl] f school of motoring; driving school; **∼gène** [∼'ʒɛn] autogenous; ⊕ soudure f ∼ autogenous or oxy-acetylene welding; **∼gire** ✈ [∼'ʒi:r] m autogiro; **∼graphe** [∼'graf] adj., a. su./m autograph; **∼mate** [∼'mat] m automaton; **∼mation** [∼ma'sjɔ̃] f automation; **∼matique** [∼ma'tik] automatic, self-acting; **∼matisation** ⊕ [∼matisa'sjɔ̃] f automation; **∼matiser** [∼mati'ze] (1a) v/t. automate.

automnal, e, m/pl. -aux [otɔm'nal, ∼'no] autumnal; **automne** [o'tɔn] m autumn, Am. fall.

auto...: **∼mobile** [otɔmɔ'bil] **1.** su./f (motor-)car, Am. automobile; **2.** adj. self-propelling; canot m ∼ motor boat; **∼mobilisme** [∼mɔbi'lism] m motoring; **∼mobiliste** [∼mɔbi'list] su. motorist; **∼motrice** ⚙ [∼mɔ'tris] f rail-motor, Am. rail-car; **∼neige** [∼'nɛ:ʒ] m snowmobile, snowcat; **∼nome** [∼'nɔm] autonomous; independent; self-governing; **∼nomie** [∼nɔ'mi] f autonomy; independence; **∼portrait** [∼pɔr'trɛ] m self-portrait; **∼propulsé, e** [∼prɔpyl'se] self-propelled.

autopsie [otɔp'si] f autopsy.

autorail ⚙ [otɔ'ra:j] m rail-motor, Am. rail-car.

autorisation [otɔriza'sjɔ̃] f authorization; permission; leave; licence; ∼ exceptionnelle special permission or permit; **autorisé, e** [∼'ze] authorized; authoritative (source); **autoriser** [∼'ze] (1a) v/t. authorize; empower; permit; s'∼ de use, rely on; refer to; **autoritaire** [∼tɛ:r] **1.** adj. authoritative; dictatorial; **2.** su./m authoritarian; **autoritarisme** [∼ta'rism] m authoritarianism; **autorité** [∼'te] f authority; (legal) power; control; faire ∼ be an authority (on, en matière de).

auto...: **∼route** [otɔ'rut] f motorway, Am. superhighway; **∼stop** [∼'stɔp] m hitch-hiking; faire de l'∼ hitch-hike, thumb a lift; **∼stoppeur** m, -euse f [∼stɔ'pœ:r, ∼'pø:z] hitch-hiker.

autour[1] orn. [o'tu:r] goshawk.

autour[2] [∼] adv. round, about; ∼ de round, about (s.th.).

autre [o:tr] **1.** adj. other; different; further; ∼ chose something else; d'∼ part on the other hand; l'∼

jour the other day; *nous* ～*s Français* we Frenchmen; *tout* ～ *chose* quite a different matter; *un* ～ *moi-même* my other self; **2.** *pron./indef.* (an-) other; ～*s pl.* others; *à d'*～*s!* nonsense!, tell that to the marines!; *de temps à* ～ now and then; *l'un l'*～ one another, each other; *ni l'un ni l'*～ neither; *tout* ～ anybody else; *un(e)* ～ another (one), one more; **autrefois** [otrə'fwa] *adv.* formerly; **autrement** [～'mɑ̃] *adv.* otherwise; (or) else.

autrichien, -enne [otri'ʃjɛ̃, ～'ʃjɛn] *adj., a. su.* ♀ Austrian.

autruche *orn.* [o'tryʃ] *f* ostrich; *pratiquer la politique de l'*～ stick one's head in the sand.

autrui [o'trɥi] *pron.*, *no pl.*, *usu. after prp.* others, other people.

auvent [o'vɑ̃] *m* penthouse; porchroof; ⚠ weather-board; ⊕, 🚗 hood; *mot.* dash; *mot.* ～*s pl.* louvres.

auxiliaire [oksi'ljɛːr] **1.** *adj.* auxiliary; *bureau m* ～ sub-office; **2.** *su./m* auxiliary (*a. gramm.*).

avachi, e [ava'ʃi] limp, flabby; **avachir** [ava'ʃiːr] (2a) *v/t.* make limp *or* flabby *or* sloppy; *s'*～ go out of shape; become limp *or* flabby *or* sloppy.

aval¹, *pl.* **-s** ✝ [a'val] *m* endorsement.

aval² [～] *m* lower course of stream; *en* ～ downstream; afterwards; *en* ～ *de* below; after; **avalage** [ava'laːʒ] *m* going downstream; *wine:* cellaring.

avalanche [ava'lɑ̃ːʃ] *f* avalanche; *fig.* shower.

avaler [ava'le] (1a) *v/t.* swallow; gulp down; inhale (*the cigarette smoke*); *fig.* swallow, pocket; **avaleur** *m*, **-euse** *f* [～'lœːr, ～'løːz] swallower; F guzzler.

avaliser ✝ [avali'ze] (1a) *v/t.* endorse, back (*a bill*); **avaliste** ✝ [～'list] *m* endorser.

à-valoir [ava'lwaːr] *m/inv.* advance (payment); down payment, deposit.

avance [a'vɑ̃ːs] *f* advance; progress; lead; ⊕ *tool:* feed movement, travel; ✝ loan, advance; *mot.* ～ *à l'allumage* advance of the spark; *à l'*～, *d'*～ in advance, beforehand; *être en* ～ be early; be ahead (of schedule); *faire des* ～ *à* make up to (*s.o.*); **avancée** [avɑ̃'se] *f* projection; **avancement** [avɑ̃s'mɑ̃] *m* advancement; progress; putting forward; promotion;

avancer [avɑ̃'se] (1k) *v/t.* advance (*a.* ✝); hasten (*s.th.*); put on (*a watch*); promote; *fig.* be of help to; *s'*～ advance; move forward; *fig.* commit o.s., F stick one's neck out; *v/i.* advance; be fast (*watch*); be ahead; ⚠ project; ～ *en âge* be getting on (in years).

avanie [ava'ni] *f* affront, snub.

avant [a'vɑ̃] **1.** *prp.* before (*Easter, the end, his arrival*); in front of (*the church*); within, in less than (*three days*); ～ *peu* before long; ～ *Jésus-Christ* before Christ, *abbr.* B.C.; ～ *tout* above all; first of all; ～ *de* (*inf.*) before (*ger.*); ～ *que* (*sbj.*) before; **2.** *adv.* beforehand; previously; forward; far; *d'*～ before, previous; *peu de temps* ～ shortly before; *plus* ～ further, more deeply; *bien* ～ *dans* (*la nuit, la forêt*) far into (the night, the wood); **3.** *cj.:* ～ *que* (*sbj.*) before (*ind.*); ～ *de* (*inf.*) before (*ger.*); **4.** *adj./inv.* front …; *roue f* ～ front wheel; **5.** *int.:* ~ *en* ～*!* forward!; advance!; *mettre en* ～ advance (*an argument etc.*); **6.** *su./m* front; ⚓ bow; *sp.* forward.

avant-… [avɑ̃] fore…

avantage [avɑ̃'taːʒ] *m* advantage; privilege; profit; gain; benefit; *tennis:* vantage; *à l'*～ *de* to the benefit of; **avantager** [～ta'ʒe] (11) *v/t.* favo(u)r; *fig.* flatter (*dress etc.*); **avantageux, -euse** ⚠ [～ta'ʒø, ～'ʒøːz] *adj.* attractive (*price etc.*); profitable; favo(u)rable; conceited.

avant-…: ~**-bec** [avɑ̃'bɛk] *m* ⚠ bridge: pier-head; ⚓ forepeak; ~**-bras** [～'bra] *m/inv.* forearm; ~**-centre** *sp.* [～'sɑ̃ːtr] *m* centre forward; ~**-corps** ⚠ [～'kɔːr] *m* projecting part, projection; ~**-coureur** [～ku'rœːr] **1.** *su./m* forerunner; **2.** *adj.* precursory; *signe m* ～ premonitory sign; ~**-dernier, -ère** [～dɛr'nje, ～'njeːr] *adj. a. su.* last but one; ~**-garde** [～'gard] *f* ⚔ advance(d) guard; vanguard (*a. fig.*); ~**-guerre** [～'gɛːr] *m or f* pre-war period; *d'*～ pre-war; ~**-hier** [～'tjeːr] *m* the day before yesterday; ~**-port** [～'pɔːr] *m* outer harbo(u)r; ~**-poste** ⚔ [～'pɔst] *m* outpost; ~**-projet** [～prɔ'ʒɛ] *m* pilot study; ~**-propos** [～prɔ'po] *m/inv.* preface, foreword; ~**-scène** *thea.* [～'sɛn] *f* proscenium; stage-box; ~**-train** [～'trɛ̃] *m* forecarriage;

⚒ limber; ~-**veille** [~'vɛːj] *f* two days before.

avare [a'vaːr] **1.** *adj.* miserly; stingy; **2.** *su.* miserly person; **avarice** [ava'ris] *f* avarice; stinginess; **avaricieux, -euse** [~ri'sjø, ~'sjøːz] avaricious; stingy.

avarie [ava'ri] *f* ⚓ average; damage; ⊕ breakdown; deterioration; F syphilis; **avarié, e** [~'rje] damaged; injured; spoiled; rotting, bad; **avarier** [~'rje] (1o) *v/t.* spoil; damage; s'~ go bad, rot.

avatar [ava'taːr] *m* avatar; ~s *pl.* ups and downs; vicissitudes.

avec [a'vɛk] **1.** *prp.* with; for, in spite of (*all his riches*); ~ *patience* (*véhémence etc.*) patiently (vehemently *etc.*); ~ *l'âge* with age; ~ *ça* into the bargain; et ~ *ça, Madame,* anything else, Madam ?; ~ *ce temps-là* in this weather; *divorcer d'~ sa femme* divorce one's wife; *distinguer l'ami d'~ le flatteur* distinguish a friend from a flatterer; **2.** *adv.* F with it *or* them, F him, her, them.

avenant[1], **e** [av'nɑ̃, ~'nɑ̃ːt] comely; à l'~ in keeping; ... to match; appropriate.

avenant[2] ⚖ [av'nɑ̃] *m* codicil, rider.

avènement [avɛn'mɑ̃] *m* arrival, coming; *king:* accession; **avenir** [av'niːr] *m* future; à l'~ in (the) future; **avent** *eccl.* [a'vɑ̃] *m* Advent.

aventure [avɑ̃'tyːr] *f* adventure; chance, luck; love affair; à l'~ at random; *dire la bonne* ~ tell fortunes; *parc m d'*~ adventure playground; **aventurer** [avɑ̃ty're] (1a) *v/t.* venture, risk; s'~ venture, take a risk; **aventureux, -euse** [~'rø, ~'røːz] adventurous; hazardous; bold (*theory*); **aventurier, -ère** [~'rje, ~'rjɛːr] **1.** *adj.* adventurous; **2.** *su./m* adventurer; *su./f* adventuress.

avenue [av'ny] *f* avenue; drive.

avéré [ave're] established (*fact etc.*); known, recognized; **avérer** [~] (1f) *v/t.:* s'~ be confirmed; s'~ ... turn out to be ...; prove (to be) ...; show oneself to be ...

avers [a'vɛːr] *m* coin: obverse.

averse [a'vɛrs] *f* shower, downpour.

aversion [avɛr'sjɔ̃] *f* aversion (to, *pour*), dislike (of, for *pour*).

avertir [avɛr'tiːr] (2a) *v/t.* warn (of, *de*); notify; **avertissement**

[~tis'mɑ̃] *m* warning; notification; foreword; ✝ demand note; **avertisseur** [~ti'sœːr] *m* warner; warning signal; *thea.* call-boy; 🚒 signal; *mot.* horn; ~ *d'incendie* fire-alarm.

aveu [a'vø] *m* confession; consent; *homme m sans* ~ disreputable character.

aveugle [a'vœgl] **1.** *adj.* blind; ~ *d'un œil* blind in one eye; **2.** *su.* blind person; *en* ~ blindfold; *les* ~s *pl.* the blind; **aveuglément** [avœgle'mɑ̃] *adv.* blindly; **aveuglement** [~glə'mɑ̃] *m* blindness; **aveugle-né, e** [~glə'ne] **1.** *adj.* blind from birth; **2.** *su.* person blind from birth; **aveugler** [~'gle] (1a) *v/t.* blind; dazzle; ⚓ stop (*a leak*); **aveuglette** [~'glɛt] *adv.:* à l'~ blindly; 🐦 *voler à l'*~ fly blind.

aveulir [avœ'liːr] (2a) *v/t.* enfeeble.

avez [a've] *2nd p. pl. pres. of avoir* **1.**

aviateur *m*, **-trice** *f* [avja'tœːr, ~'tris] aviator; **aviation** [~'sjɔ̃] *f* aviation; flying; air force; aircraft; ~ *civile* civil aviation; ~ *de ligne* air traffic.

aviculteur [avikyl'tœːr] *m* birdfancier; poultry farmer.

avide [a'vid] greedy, eager (for, *de*); **avidité** [avidi'te] *f* greediness; eagerness.

avilir [avi'liːr] (2a) *v/t.* degrade, debase; lower; s'~ lower o.s., demean o.s.; lose value, fall (*in price etc.*); **avilissement** [~lis'mɑ̃] *m* debasement, degradation, depreciation, fall (*in price etc.*).

aviné, e [avi'ne] intoxicated, drunk, F tipsy; **aviner** [~] (1a) *v/t.* season (*a cask*); s'~ get drunk.

avion [a'vjɔ̃] *m* aeroplane, *Am.* airplane; F plane; ~ *à décollage vertical* vertical takeoff aircraft; ~ *à réaction* jet (plane); ~ *bimoteur* (*polymoteur*) two- (multi-)engined aircraft; ~ *de bombardement* bomber; ~ *de chasse* fighter; ~ *de combat* battle plane; ~ *d'entraînement* training plane; ~ *de ligne* airliner; ~ *de reconnaissance* scouting *or* reconnaissance plane; ~ *de transport* transport plane; ~-*fusée* rocket-plane; ~-*taxi* charter plane; ~ *transbordeur* air ferry; *par* ~ by airmail; **avionette** [avjɔ'nɛt] *f* light aeroplane (*Am.* airplane).

aviron [avi'rɔ̃] *m* oar; rowing.

avis [a'vi] *m* opinion; notice, notifi-

cation; advice; warning; ~ *d'expert*
expert opinion; *être d'~ que* feel *or*
think *or* be of the opinion that; *être
de l'~ de q.*, *être du même ~ que q.* be of
or share s.o.'s opinion; *à mon ~* in my
opinion; *jusqu'à nouvel ~* until further notice; *note f d'~* advice note;
sans ~ préalable without notice; *✝
suivant ~* as per advice; *un ~* a piece of
advice; **avisé, e** [avi'se] shrewd;
prudent; *bien ~* well-advised; **aviser**
[~] (1a) *v/t.* catch sight of; notify,
inform; *s'~* realize, notice; *s'~ de*
think about (*s.th.*); take it into one's
head to (*inf.*); *v/i.* decide, take steps;
~ *à* see about (*s.th.*). [sloop.)

aviso ⚓ [avi'zo] *m* dispatch-boat;)
avitaminose 🜍 [avitami'no:z] *f*
avitaminosis, vitamin deficiency.

aviver [avi've] (1a) *v/t.* revive,
brighten; touch up (*a colour*); ⊕
put a keen edge on, sharpen; ⊕
burnish (*metal*); 🜍 ~ *les bords de*
refresh (*a wound*).

avocat¹ ⚖ [avɔ'ka] *m* barrister, counsel; *Am.* counsellor; *Sc.* advocate (*a.
fig.*); ~ *général* (*approx.*) King's *or*
Queen's Counsel.

avocat² ♀ [~] *m* avocado (pear).

avoine [a'vwan] *f* oat(s *pl.*).

avoir [a'vwa:r] (1) **1.** *v/t.* have;
obtain; hold; ~ *en horreur* abhor,
detest; ~ *faim* (*soif*) be hungry
(thirsty); ~ *froid* (*chaud*) be cold
(hot); ~ *honte* be ashamed; ~ *lieu*
happen, take place; *en ~ assez* be
fed up; *en ~ contre* have a grudge
against; *j'ai vingt ans* I am 20
(years old); *qu'avez vous?* what's
the matter with you?; *v/impers.*:
il y a there is, there are; *il y a un an*
a year ago; **2.** *su./m* property; possession; *✝* credit; ~ *à l'étranger* de-
posits *pl.* abroad; ~ *en banque*
credit balance; *doit et ~* debit and
credit.

avoisiner [avwazi'ne] (1a) *v/t.*
border on; be near to.

avons [a'vɔ̃] *1st p. pl. pres. of avoir 1.*

avortement [avɔrtə'mɑ̃] *m* 🜍 miscarriage (*a. fig.*); abortion; ♀ non-
formation; **avorter** [~'te] (1a) *v/i.*
miscarry (*a. fig.*); abort; ♀ develop
imperfectly; *faire ~* procure an
abortion; **avorton** [~'tɔ̃] *m* abortion; F shrimp, *sl.* little squirt.

avouable [a'vwabl] avowable;
avoué [a'vwe] *m* solicitor; attorney;
avouer [~] (1p) *v/t.* admit, acknowledge, confess; *s'~ coupable*
plead guilty.

avril [a'vril] *m* April; *poisson m d'~*
April fool.

axe [aks] *m* axis (*a. pol.*); ⊕ axle;
✠ ~ *balisé* (localizer) beam; ⊕ ~
de pompe pump spindle; *opt.* ~ *optique* axis of vision.

axiome 📐, *phls.*, *fig.* [ak'sjo:m] *m*
axiom.

axonge [ak'sɔ̃:ʒ] *f* lard; grease.

ayant [ɛ'jɑ̃] *p.pr. of avoir 1;* ~
cause, *pl.* **~s cause** ⚖ *su./m* assign;
executor; trustee; ~ **droit**, *pl.* **~s
droit** ⚖ *su./m* rightful claimant;
beneficiary; **ayons** [ɛ'jɔ̃] *1st p.pl.
pres. sbj. of avoir 1.*

azalée ♀ [aza'le] *f* azalea.

azimut [azi'myt] *m* azimuth; *fig. tous
~s* omnidirectional.

azotate 🜍 [azɔ'tat] *m* nitrate; **azote**
🜍 [a'zɔt] *m* nitrogen; **azoté, e**
[azɔ'te] nitrogenous; *engrais m/pl.*
~*s* nitrate fertilizers; **azotite** 🜍
[~'tit] *m* nitrite.

aztèque [az'tɛk] **1.** *adj.* Aztec;
2. *su.* ♀ Aztec; *su./m sl.* little shrimp
of a fellow.

azur [a'zy:r] *m* azure, blue; *pierre f
d'~* lapis lazuli; blue-spar; **azuré, e**
[azy're] azure, (sky-)blue.

azyme [a'zim] **1.** *adj.* unleavened;
2. *su./m* unleavened bread.

B

B, b [be] *m* B, b.

baba[1] [ba'ba] *m* baba (*sponge-cake soaked in rum syrup*).

baba[2] F [⌣] *adj./inv.* flabbergasted.

babeurre [ba'bœːr] *m* buttermilk.

babil [ba'bil] *m child*: prattle; *birds*: twittering; *brook*: babble; **babillage** [babi'jaːʒ] *m child*, *brook*: babbling; *birds*: twittering; **babillard, e** [⌣'jaːr, ⌣'jard] 1. *adj.* talkative, garrulous; 2. *su.* chatterer; *su./f sl.* better; **babiller** [⌣'je] (1a) *v/i.* prattle; babble.

babine [ba'bin] *f zo.* pendulous lip; chop; *f* ⌣s *pl.* lips, chops.

babiole [ba'bjɔl] *f* knick-knack, curio; toy, bauble.

bâbord ⚓ [ba'bɔːr] *m* port (side).

babouche [ba'buʃ] *f* Turkish slipper.

babouin [ba'bwɛ̃] *m zo.* baboon; F imp (= *naughty child*).

bac[1] [bak] *m* ferry(-boat); ⊕ tank, vat; ⚡ *accumulator*: container; *passer q. en* ⌣ ferry s.o. over.

bac[2] F [bak] *m see* baccalauréat; **baccalauréat** [bakalɔre'a] *m* school-leaving certificate.

bacchanale F [baka'nal] *f* orgy; drinking song; **bacchante** [⌣'kɑ̃ːt] *f* bacchante; *fig.* lewd woman.

bâche [bɑ:ʃ] *f* ⊕ tank, cistern; ⊕ casing; ✓ forcing frame; sheet, cover; ⌣ *goudronnée* tarpaulin.

bachelier *m*, **-ère** *f* [baʃə'lje, ⌣'ljɛːr] holder of the school-leaving certificate.

bâcher [bɑ'ʃe] (1a) *v/t.* cover (*with a sheet*); ⊕ case (*a turbine*).

bachique [ba'ʃik] Bacchic; bacchanalian (*scene*); drinking (*song*).

bachot[1] [ba'ʃo] *m* ⚓ wherry, dinghy; ⊕ sieve.

bachot[2] F [ba'ʃo] *m see* baccalauréat; *boîte f à* ⌣ cramming-shop, crammer's; **bachotage** F [⌣ʃɔ'taːʒ] *m* cramming (*for an exam*); *faire du* ⌣ = **bachoter** F [⌣ʃɔ'te] (1a) *v/i.* cram (*for an exam*).

bacille [ba'sil] *m* bacillus; *porteur m de* ⌣s germ-carrier.

bâcle [bɑ:kl] *f* bar; **bâcler** [bɑ'kle] (1a) *v/t.* bar (*a door*); ⚓ block (*a port*); F hurry over (*one's toilet*); F scamp (*a piece of work*).

bactérie [bakte'ri] *f biol.* bacterium; *zo.* bacteria.

badaud *m*, **e** *f* [ba'do, ⌣'doːd] stroller; gaper; *Am.* F rubber-neck.

baderne ⚓ [ba'dɛrn] *f* fender; F *vieille* ⌣ old fog(e)y; ✕ old dug-out.

badigeon [badi'ʒɔ̃] *m* whitewash; distemper; **badigeonnage** [⌣ʒɔ-'naːʒ] *m* whitewashing; distempering; ✖ painting (*with iodine*); **badigeonner** [⌣ʒɔ'ne] (1a) *v/t.* whitewash; distemper; daub; ✖ paint.

badin[1], **e** [ba'dɛ̃, ⌣'din] 1. *adj.* playful; 2. *su.* joker, banterer.

badin[2] ✈ [ba'dɛ̃] *m* air-speed indicator.

badinage [badi'naːʒ] *m* banter.

badine [ba'din] *f* cane, switch.

badiner [badi'ne] (1a) *v/i.* jest; toy (*with*, *avec*).

baffe F [baf] *f* slap (in the face).

bafouer [ba'fwe] (1p) *v/t.* ridicule, scoff at; **bafouillage** [bafu'jaːʒ] *m* stammering; **bafouiller** [⌣'je] (1a) *v/i.* stammer; *sl.* talk nonsense; *mot.* splutter.

bâfrer *sl.* [bɑ'fre] (1a) *vt/i.* guzzle.

bagage [ba'gaːʒ] *m* luggage, *Am.* baggage; ✕ kit; *fig.* stock of knowledge; ⌣s *pl. non accompagnés* luggage *sg.* in advance; *plier* ⌣ pack up and leave; *sl.* decamp; *sl.* die.

bagarre [ba'gaːr] *f* fight(ing); scuffle; brawl; riot; **bagarrer** F [⌣ga're] (1a) *v/t.: se* ⌣ quarrel; fight.

bagatelle [baga'tɛl] *f* trifle, bagatelle; ⌣! nonsense!; F *pour une* ⌣ for a song.

bagne ⚒ [baɲ] *m* convict prison; penal servitude.

bagnole F [ba'ɲɔl] *f* motor car; *vieille* ⌣ jalopy.

bagou(t) F [ba'gu] *m* glibness; *avoir du* ⌣ have the gift of the gab.

bague [bag] *f* ring; *cigar*: band; ⊕ strap; ⊕ ~ *d'arrêt* set collar; **baguenauder** F [~no'de] (1a) *v/i. a. se* ~ go for stroll; stroll about; **baguette** [ba'gɛt] *f* stick, rod; stick of bread; ♪ baton; ⚠ beading; *writing paper*: black border; *stockings*: clock; ~ *magique*, ~ *de fée* magic wand; ♀ ~ *d'or* wall-flower; *passer par les* ~*s* run the gauntlet; **baguier**, **baguier** [ba'gje] *m* ring-case; ring size ga(u)ge.

bahut [ba'y] *m* † trunk, chest; low sideboard; *sl.* school.

bai, e [bɛ] *adj., a. su./m* bay.

baie[1] ♀ [~] *f* berry.

baie[2] *geog.* [~] *f* bay, bight.

baie[3] ⚠ [~] *f* bay, opening.

baignade [bɛ'ɲad] *f* bathe, dip; **baigner** [~'ɲe] (1b) *v/t.* bathe; bath; se ~ bathe; take a bath; *v/i.* steep; *fig. baigné de larmes* suffused with tears (*eyes*); **baigneur, -euse** [~'ɲœːr, ~'ɲøːz] *su.* bather; bathing attendant; *su./f* bathing-wrap, *Am.* bathrobe; **baignoire** [~'ɲwaːr] *f* bath(-tub); *thea.* ground-floor box.

bail, *pl.* **baux** [baːj, bo] *m* lease; ~ *à ferme* farming lease; *prendre à* ~ take a lease of, lease.

bâillement [baj'mɑ̃] *m* yawn(ing); gaping; **bâiller** [ba'je] (1a) *v/i.* yawn; gape; stand ajar (*door*).

bailleur *m*, **-eresse** *f* [ba'jœːr, baj'rɛs] 🏦 lessor; ♈ ~ *de fonds* backer; sleeping or silent partner.

bâillon [bɑ'jɔ̃] *m* gag; *horse*: muzzle; **bâillonner** [~jɔ'ne] (1a) *v/t.* gag (*a. fig.*).

bain [bɛ̃] *m* bath; bathing; F *fig. dans le* ~ in the picture, informed; implicated, involved; *prendre un* ~ *de foule* go on a walkabout; *sortie f de* ~ bath-wrap, *Am.* bath-robe; ~-**douche**, *pl.* ~**s-douches** [~'duʃ] *m* shower(-bath); ~-**marie**, *pl.* ~**s-marie** [~ma'ri] *m* ♒ waterbath; *cuis.* double saucepan, *Am.* double boiler.

baïonnette ✕ [bajɔ'nɛt] *f* bayonet.

baisemain [bɛz'mɛ̃] *m* hand-kissing; **baiser** [bɛ'ze] **1.** *su./m* kiss; **2.** (1b) *v/t.*: ~ *q. à la joue* kiss s.o.'s cheek; *sl. (a. v/i.)* ~ (*q.*) make love (to *s.o.*); **baisoter** F [~zɔ'te] (1c) *v/t.* peck at.

baisse [bɛs] *f* fall (*a. prices*), going down; subsidence; *sight, prices*: decline; *tide*: ebb; *en* ~ falling (*stocks*);

baisser [bɛ'se] (1b) *v/t. usu.* lower; turn down (*the light*); drop (*a curtain*); se ~ bend down; *v/i.* decline; fall; abate (*flood*); ebb (*tide*); burn low (*lamp*).

bajoue [ba'ʒu] *f*: ~*s pl.* cheeks, chaps, chops.

bakélite [bake'lit] *f* bakelite.

bal, *pl.* **bals** [bal] *m* ball; dance; **balade** F [ba'lad] *f* stroll; ramble; **balader** F [bala'de] (1a) *v/t.* take for a walk; carry about; se ~ (take a) stroll; **baladeur, -euse** [~'dœːr, ~'døːz] **1.** *adj.* F wandering; **2.** *su.* wanderer, saunterer; *su./f* trailer (*of car, of tram*); street-barrow; hand-cart; ⚡ inspection lamp.

baladin *m*, **e** *f* [bala'dɛ̃, ~'din] mountebank; F clown.

balafre [ba'lafr] *f* gash, slash; scar; **balafrer** [~la'fre] (1a) *v/t.* gash, slash; scar.

balai [ba'lɛ] *m* broom; brush; *mot. windscreem-wiper*: blade; ~ *mécanique* carpet sweeper; *coup m de* ~ sweep; *fig.* clean sweep.

balance [ba'lɑ̃ːs] *f* balance (*a.* ♈); scales *pl.*, weighing machine; ♈ balance; † hesitation; ♈ ~ *de(s) paiements* balance of payments; ~ *romaine* steelyard; ♈ *faire la* ~ strike the (*fig.* a) balance; *faire pencher la* ~ turn the scales; *astr. la* ♎ Libra, the Balance; *fig. mettre en* ~ weigh up; **balancement** [balɑ̃s'mɑ̃] *m* sway(ing), swing(ing); *fig.* balance; **balancer** [balɑ̃'se] (1k) *v/t.* swing; throw, fling, chuck; F chuck out; balance; *fig.* weigh up; se ~ rock, sway; swing; seesaw; *sl.* se ~ de not to care a damn about; *sl.* je m'en balance *a.* I couldn't care less (about it); **balancier** [~'sje] *m* balancing pole; *mot. crank-shaft*: balancer; *watch*: balance-wheel; *clock*: pendulum; *pump*: handle; ⊕ *beam-engine*: beam; ⊕ fly(-press); **balançoire** [~'swaːr] *f* seesaw; swing.

balayer [balɛ'je] (1i) *v/t.* sweep out or up or away (*a. fig.*); *fig.* clear out; scour (*the sea*); *telev.* scan; **balayette** [~'jɛt] *f* whisk; small brush; **balayeur, -euse** [~'jœːr, ~'jøːz] *su. person*: sweeper; *su./f machine*: sweeper; **balayures** [~'jyːr] *f/pl.* sweepings.

balbutiement [balbysi'mɑ̃] *m* stuttering, stammering; **balbutier**

[ᴧ'sje] (1o) v/i. mumble; stammer; v/t. stutter out, stammer out.

balcon [bal'kɔ̃] m ⚠ balcony; *thea.* dress circle.

baldaquin [balda'kɛ̃] m canopy, baldachin.

baleine [ba'lɛn] f whale(bone); **baleinier** [balɛ'nje] m whaler (*ship, a. man*); whaling; **baleinière** [ᴧ'njɛːr] f whale-boat; ~ de *sauvetage* life-boat.

balise¹ ♀ [ba'liːz] f canna seed.

balise² [ba'liːz] f ⚓ beacon; 🛫 runway light; *mot.* road sign; marker; ~ *flottante* buoy; **baliser** [ᴧli'ze] (1a) v/t. ⚓ beacon; ⚓ buoy; provide with runway lights *or* road signs; mark out.

balistique [balis'tik] **1.** *adj.* ballistic; **2.** *su./f* ballistics *sg.*

baliverne F [bali'vɛrn] f mostly ᴧs pl. nonsense *sg.*

ballade [ba'lad] f ballad.

ballant, e [ba'lɑ̃, ᴧ'lɑ̃ːt] **1.** *adj.* dangling; swinging; slack (*rope*); **2.** *su./m* swing.

ballast [ba'last] m ⊕ ballast; ⚓ ballast-tank; **ballastière** [ᴧlas'tjɛːr] f gravel-pit.

balle¹ [bal] f ball; bullet; shot; ✝ cotton: bale; *pedlar:* pack; *sl.* head; *sl.* franc; ~ de *service tennis:* service-ball.

balle² [ᴧ] f husk, chaff; ♀ glume.

ballerine [bal'rin] f ballet-dancer, ballerina; **ballet** [ba'lɛ] m ballet.

ballon [ba'lɔ̃] m balloon (*a.* 🝔); (foot)ball; 🝔 flask; ⊕ carboy; ⚓ ball-signal; ~ de *plage* beach ball; *fig.* ~ d'essai feeler; ~-sonde test *or* sounding balloon; **ballonnement** [ᴧlɔn'mɑ̃] m swelling; 🩺 distension; 🩺 flatulence; **ballonner** [ᴧlɔ'ne] (1a) vt/i. swell; bulge; distend (*a.* 🩺).

ballot [ba'lo] m pack, bundle; F idiot, chump; **ballottage** *pol.* [balɔ'taːʒ] m second ballot; **ballotter** [ᴧ'te] (1a) v/t. toss (about), shake about; *fig.* être ballotté entre be tossed *or* torn between; v/i. shake; toss; rattle (*door*).

bal(l)uchon F [baly'ʃɔ̃] m bundle.

balnéaire [balne'ɛːr] bath...; watering-...; *station* f ~ watering-place; seaside resort.

balnéothérapie [balneɔtera'pi] f balneotherapy.

balourd, e [ba'luːr, ᴧ'lurd] **1.** *adj.*

---

awkward; **2.** *su.* awkward person; yokel; *su./m* ⊕ unbalance; unbalanced weight; **balourdise** [ᴧlur-'diːz] f awkwardness; F bloomer, stupid mistake.

baltique [bal'tik] **1.** *adj.* Baltic; **2.** *su./f: la* (mer) ♀ *the* Baltic (Sea).

bambin m, **e** f F [bɑ̃'bɛ̃, ᴧ'bin] little child; kid; youngster.

bamboche [bɑ̃'bɔʃ] f puppet; F spree; *faire* ~ go on the spree; *il est* ~ he's a bit merry; **bambocher** F [bɑ̃bɔ'ʃe] (1a) v/i. go on the spree; **bambocheur** m, **-euse** f F [ᴧ'ʃœːr, ᴧ'ʃøːz] reveller.

bambou [bɑ̃'bu] m bamboo(-cane).

ban [bɑ̃] m † proclamation; drum roll; F applause; *mettre au* ~ banish; F send to Coventry; outlaw (from, *de*); *publier les* ᴧs put up *or* publish the bans; *fig. le* ~ *et l'arrière-*~ de ses amis *etc.* all his friends *etc.*

banal, e, *m/pl.* **-als** *fig.* [ba'nal] commonplace, banal; vulgar; **banaliser** [ᴧnali'ze] (1a) v/t. popularize; vulgarize.

banane [ba'nan] f ♀ banana; *sl.* decoration, medal; *sl.* chopper, whirlybird (= *helicopter*); **bananier** [ᴧna'nje] m banana-tree.

banc [bɑ̃] m bench (*a.* ⊕); form, seat; *eccl.* pew; *lathe, oysters, stone:* bed; *sand, mud:* bank; *sand, coral:* shoal; (witness-)box; *fish:* school, shoal; ⊕ ~ d'épreuve testing stand, bench.

bancal, e, *m/pl.* **-als** [bɑ̃'kal] **1.** *adj.* bandy(-legged); unsteady, rickety; **2.** *su.* bandy-legged person.

bandage [bɑ̃'daːʒ] m 🩺 bandaging; bandage; *mot.* tyre, *Am.* tire; ⊕ *spring:* winding up; 🩺 ~ *herniaire* truss.

bande¹ [bɑ̃ːd] f band, strip; stripe; stretch (*of land*); 🩺 bandage; strap; ⊕ *spring:* compression; *cin.* reel; *post:* wrapper; ⚓ list; ~ *dessinée* comic strip; strip cartoon; ~ *magnétique* recording tape; ~ *molletière* puttee; ⊕ ~ *transporteuse* conveyor belt; *enregistrer sur* ~ tape-record; *enregistrer sur* ~ *vidéo* videotape; *sous* ~ *post:* by post.

bande² [ᴧ] f band, gang; party; flock; pack.

bandeau [bã'do] *m* headband; diadem; bandage; **bandelette** [bãd-'let] *f* strip; **bander** [bã'de] (1a) *v/t.* bandage, bind up; wind up, tighten; ⚡ key in; *fig.* ~ *les yeux de* blindfold (*s.o.*); *v/i.* be tight; **banderole** [~'drɔl] *f* streamer; pennant; ✗ *rifle:* sling; *cartoon:* balloon.

bandit [bã'di] *m* bandit; gangster; crook.

bandoulière [bãdu'ljɛ:r] *f* shoulder-strap; *en* ~ slung over the shoulder.

banjo ♪ [bã'ʒo] *m* banjo.

banlieue [bã'ljø] *f* suburbs *pl.*, outskirts *pl.*; *de* ~ suburban; ~-*dortoir* dormitory suburb; **banlieusard** *m*, **e** *f* F [~ljø'za:r, ~'zard] suburbanite.

banne [ban] *f* hamper; coal cart; awning; tarpaulin; ✗ tub, skip; ⚓ *dredger:* bucket; **bannette** [ba-'net] *f* small hamper.

banni, e [ba'ni] **1.** *adj.* banished; **2.** *su.* outcast; outlaw; exile.

bannière [ba'njɛ:r] *f* banner; F *être en* ~ be in shirt-tails.

bannir [ba'ni:r] (2a) *v/t.* outlaw; exile (*from, de*).

banque [bã:k] *f* bank; banking; ~ *du sang* blood bank; ~ *par actions* joint-stock bank; *faire sauter la* ~ break the bank; **banqueroute** ✝ [bã'krut] *f* bankruptcy; failure; *faire* ~ go bankrupt.

banquet [bã'kɛ] *m* banquet, feast.

banquette [bã'kɛt] *f* bench, seat; *earth:* bank; *golf:* bunker.

banquier *m*, **-ère** *f* [bã'kje, ~'kjɛ:r] banker. [ice.\

banquise [bã'ki:z] *f* ice-floe; pack-⌡

baptême [ba'tɛ:m] *m* baptism, christening; *nom m de* ~ Christian name, *Am.* given name; **baptiser** [bati'ze] (1a) *v/t.* baptize, christen; F *fig.* water (down) (*the wine*); **baptismal, e**, *m/pl.* **-aux** [batis'mal, ~'mo], **baptistaire** [~'tɛ:r] baptismal; *extrait m baptistaire* certificate of baptism.

baquet [ba'kɛ] *m* tub, bucket.

bar[1] [ba:r] *m* (public) bar; *au* ~ in the pub.

bar[2] *icht.* [~] *m* bass; perch.

bar[3] *phys.* [~] *m* bar.

baragouin F [bara'gwɛ̃] *m* gibberish; lingo; **baragouiner** F [~gwi'ne] (1a) *vt/i.* jabber, gibber.

baraque [ba'rak] *f* hut, shed; F dump, joint, hole; **baraquement**

[~rak'mã] *m*: ✗ ~*s pl.* hutments; **baraquer** ✗ [~ra'ke] (1m) *vt/i.* hut.

baratin F [bara'tɛ̃] *m* sweet talk; patter, *Am.* malarky; **baratiner** [~ti'ne] (1a) *vt/i.* sweet-talk; *v/t.* chat (*s.o.*) up.

barattage [bara'ta:ʒ] *m* churning; **baratte** [~'rat] *f* churn; **baratter** [~ra'te] (1a) *v/t.* churn.

barbacane [barba'kan] *f* ⊕ draining channel; weep-hole; ⚡ barbican; ⚡ loop-hole.

barbare [bar'ba:r] **1.** *adj.* barbaric; barbarous; uncivilized; **2.** *su./m* barbarian.

barbaresque [barba'rɛsk] *adj.*, *a.* *su./m* Berber.

barbarie [barba'ri] *f* barbarism; barbarity, cruelty; **barbarisme** *gramm.* [~'rism] *m* barbarism.

barbe[1] [barb] *f* beard (*a.* ♀); whiskers *pl.*; mould, mildew; ⊕ burr; F bore, nuisance; ~ *à papa* candyfloss, *Am.* cotton candy; *se faire faire la* ~ get o.s. shaved; (*se*) *faire la* ~ shave.

barbe[2] [~] *m* barb, Barbary horse.

barbeau [bar'bo] *m icht.* barbel; ♀ cornflower; *icht.* ~ *de mer* red mullet; *bleu* ~ cornflower blue; **barbelé, e** [~bə'le] **1.** *adj.* barbed; *fil m de fer* ~ barbed wire; **2.** *su./m:* ~*s pl.* barbed wire entanglement *sg.*

barber *sl.* [bar'be] (1a) *v/t.* bore.

barbet, -ette [bar'bɛ, ~'bɛt] *su.* water-spaniel; *su./m icht.* barbel.

barbiche [bar'biʃ] *f* goatee; short beard.

barbier [bar'bje] *m* barber; **barbifier** F [~bi'fje] (1o) *v/t.* shave; bore; *se* ~ be bored.

barbiturique [barbity'rik] **1.** *adj.* barbituric; **2.** *su./m* barbiturate.

barbotage [barbɔ'ta:ʒ] *m* paddling; splashing; ⊕ splash; *gas:* bubbling; mess, mud; bran mash; *sl.* filching; *sl.* mumbling; **barboter** [~'te] (1a) *v/i.* paddle, splash (about); bubble (*gas*); *v/t.* mumble; *sl.* filch; *sl.* scrounge; **barboteur, -euse** [~-'tœ:r, ~'tø:z] *su.* paddler; *sl.* scrounger; *su./m* ⊕ bubbler; ⊕ stirrer; *su./f* rompers *pl.*; washing machine.

barbouillage [barbu'ja:ʒ] *m* daubing; scrawl(ing), scribble; **barbouiller** [~'je] (1a) *v/t.* daub; smear (with, *de*); sully; scribble, scrawl;

basculer

fig. botch; *se* ~ dirty one's face;
barbouilleur *m*, **-euse** *f* F [~'jœːr,
~'jøːz] dauber; hack.
barbouze F [bar'buːz] *m* secret
(police) agent.
barbu, e [bar'by] bearded (*a.* ♀);
mouldy.
barbue *icht.* [~] *f* brill.
barcasse ♺ [bar'kas] *f* launch; F old
tub.
barda *sl.* [bar'da] *m* ✕ pack, kit;
stuff, things *pl.*
bardane ♥ [bar'dan] *f* burdock.
barde[1] [bard] *m* bard.
barde[2] [~] *f* pack-saddle; *cuis.* slice of
bacon, bard.
bardeau[1] [bar'do] *m* ◬ shingle
(-board), *Am.* clapboard; lath; small
raft.
bardeau[2] [~] *m* hinny.
barder[1] *sl.* [bar'de] (1a): *ça barde*
sparks are flying.
barder[2] [~] (1a) *v/t.* ✕ † arm with
bards; *cuis.* bard (*with bacon*), lard (*a.*
fig.).
bardot [bar'do] *m* hinny; packmule.
barème [ba'rɛm] *m* table, (price) list;
scale; schedule; graph.
barguigner F [bargi'ne] (1a) *v/i.*:
sans ~ without shilly-shallying.
baril [ba'ri] *m* cask(ful); **barillet**
[~ri'jɛ] *m* keg; *revolver*: cylinder;
⊕ barrel; *anat.* middle-ear.
bariolage [barjɔ'laːʒ] *m* motley;
gaudy colo(u)r scheme; **barioler**
[~'le] (1a) *v/t.* variegate; paint in
gaudy colo(u)rs.
barman, *pl.* *a.* **-men** [bar'man,
~'mɛn] *m* barman.
baromètre [barɔ'mɛtr] *m* barometer; F (weather-)glass.
baron [ba'rɔ̃] *m* baron; **baronne**
[~'rɔn] *f* baroness.
baroque [ba'rɔk] **1.** *adj.* quaint; odd;
baroque; **2.** *su./m* ◬ etc. baroque.
baroud F [ba'rud] *m* fight(ing); ~
d'honneur gallant last stand; **barou-
der** F [baru'de] *v/i.* fight.
barouf F [ba'ruf] *m* noise, racket.
barque ♺ [bark] *f* barge, boat.
barrage [ba'raːʒ] *m* barring, closing; dam(ming); *fig.* obstruction;
⊕ barrage (*a.* ✕), weir; ♺ harbour:
boom; ✝ *cheque*: crossing; ✕ *tir m*
de ~ curtain-fire.
barre [baːr] *f* bar (*a.* ♩♩); ⊕ rod;
gold: ingot; ♺ helm; stroke (*of*
the pen); *tex.* stripe; ♪ bar(-line);

(tidal) bore; *sp.* ~*s* *pl.* *parallèles*
parallel bars; *sp.* ~ *fixe* horizontal
bar; *mot.* ~ *de connexion* tie-rod;
♩♩ ~ *des témoins* witness-box; ✟ ~
omnibus (*collectrice*) omnibus-bar;
barreau [ba'ro] *m* bar (*a.* ♩♩);
rail; *ladder*: rung; fire-bar; *être*
reçu au ~ be called to the bar, *Am.*
pass the bar.
barrer [ba're] (1a) *v/t.* bar; secure
with a bar; block (up); dam (*a*
stream); close (*a road*); cross out
(*a word*); ♺ steer; ✟ cross (*a*
cheque); *route f barrée* no thoroughfare; *sl.* *se* ~ skedaddle, make off.
barrette[1] *eccl.* [ba'rɛt] *f* biretta;
cardinal's cap.
barrette[2] [~] *f* hair slide; *medal*: bar.
barreur ♺ [ba'rœːr] *m* helmsman,
cox.
barricader [barika'de] (1a) *v/t.*
barricade; **barrière** [~'rjɛːr] *f* barrier (*a.* 🌫, *a. fig.*); obstacle; *castle*,
🌫 *level-crossing, town*: gate; turnpike; *sp.* starting-post.
barrique [ba'rik] *f* hogshead, cask,
butt.
barrir [ba'riːr] (2a) *v/i.* trumpet
(*elephant*).
bartavelle *orn.* [barta'vɛl] *f* rock
partridge.
bas, basse [ba, baːs] **1.** *adj.* *usu.*
low (*a. fig.*); mean; lower; *basse*
fréquence radio: low frequency; *au*
~ *mot* at the lowest estimate; *à voix*
basse in a low voice; *under one's*
breath; *chapeau* ~ hat in hand;
chapeaux ~*!* hats off!; *en* ~ *âge* of
tender years; *les classes f/pl.* ~*ses*
the lower classes; *prix m* ~ low price(s
pl.); **2.** *su./m* lower part; bottom;
stocking; *fig.* low state; **3.** *bas adv.*
low (down); *ici-*~ here below; *là-*~
down there; over there; *à* ~ ...*!*
down with ...!; *en* ~ (down) below.
basalte *geol.* [ba'zalt] *m* basalt.
basane [ba'zan] *f* sheepskin, basil;
basaner F [~za'ne] (1a) *v/t.* *a. se*
~ tan.
basculant, e [basky'lɑ̃, ~'lɑ̃ːt] rock-
ing, tilting; *pont m* ~ drawbridge;
siège m ~ tip-up seat; **bascule**
[~'kyl] *f* weighing machine; seesaw; *cheval m à* ~ rocking-horse;
weigh-bridge; *wagon m à* ~ tip-
waggon, *Am.* dump-cart; **basculer** [~ky'le] (1a) *vt/i.* rock; seesaw,
Am. teeter; tip (up); topple over; *fig.*

fluctuate; *fig.* ~ *dans* get into; **basculeur** [~ky'lœ:r] *m* rocker; ⊕ rocking-lever.

base [ba:z] *f* base (*a.* ♗, ♙); *surv.* base(-line); bottom; ⊕ bedplate; *fig.* basis, foundation; ~ *aérienne* air-base; ~ *de lancement* rocket launching site; ~ *d'entente* working basis; *sans* ~ unfounded; **baser** [ba'ze] (1a) *v/t.* base, found (on, *sur*); *se* ~ *sur* be grounded on.

bas-fond [ba'fõ] *m* low ground; *fig.* underworld; ♗ shallows *pl.*

basilic [bazi'lik] *m* ♀ basil; *myth., a. zo.* basilisk.

basique ♗ [ba'zik] basic.

basket(-ball) *sp.* [baskɛt('bɔ:l)] *m* basket-ball.

basque[1] [bask] *f* skirt (*of a garment*).

Basque[2] [~] *su.*: *tambour m de* ~ tambourine.

basse [ba:s] *f ♪ part, singer, voice*: bass; ♗ sandbank, shoal; ♗ reef; **~-contre**, *pl.* **~s-contre** ♪ [bas-'kõ:tr] *f* deep bass; **~-cour**, *pl.* **~s-cours** [~'ku:r] *f* farm-yard; **~-courier, -ère** [~ku'rje, ~'rje:r] *su.* farm-hand; *su./m* poultry-boy; *su./f* poultry-maid; **~-fosse**, *pl.* **~s-fosses** [~'fo:s] *f* dungeon; **bassement** [~'mã] *adv.* basely, meanly; **bassesse** [ba'sɛs] *f* baseness; lowness; low deed, mean action.

basset *zo.* [ba'sɛ] *m* basset hound.

basse-taille, *pl.* **basses-tailles** [bas-'ta:j] *f voice*: bass-baritone.

bassin [ba'sɛ̃] *m* basin (*a. geog.*); artificial lake; ⊕ tank; ♗ dock; *anat.* pelvis; *sl.* bore; ♗ ~ *de carénage* careening basin; ~ *de radoub* dry dock; ~ *de retenue* reservoir; ♗ *faire entrer au* ~ dock; **bassinant, e** *sl.* [basi'nã, -'nãt] boring; **bassine** [ba'sin] *f* pan; ~ *à confiture* preserving pan; **bassiner** [basi'ne] (1a) *v/t.* bathe (*a wound*); ✍ spray; warm (*a bed*); *sl.* bore; *sl.* annoy; **bassinoire** [~'nwa:r] *f* warming pan; *sl.* bore; *sl.* large watch.

basson ♪ [ba'sõ] *m* bassoon; *person*:} **baste!** † [bast] *int.* enough of that!

bastille ⚔ [bas'ti:j] *f* small fortress.

bastingage ♗ [bastɛ̃'ga:ʒ] *m* bulwarks *pl.*; rails *pl.*

bastion ⚔, *fig.* [bas'tjõ] *m* bastion; stronghold, bulwark.

bastonnade [bastɔ'nad] *f* bastinado; † flogging.

bastringue *sl.* [bas'trɛ̃:g] *m* low dancing-hall; shindy; paraphernalia.

bas-ventre [ba'vã:tr] *m* lower part of the abdomen.

bât [ba] *m* pack-saddle; *cheval m de* ~ pack-horse.

bataille [ba'ta:j] *f* battle (*a. fig.*); *ordre m de* ~ battle formation *or* order; **batailler** [bata'je] (1a) *v/i.* (*contre*) struggle (with), fight (against); **batailleur, -euse** [~'jœ:r, ~'jø:z] **1.** *adj.* quarrelsome; **2.** *su.* fighter; **bataillon** ⚔, *a. fig.* [bata'jõ] *m* battalion; *chef m de* ~ major.

bâtard, e [ba'ta:r, ~'tard] **1.** *adj.* bastard; *fig.* degenerate; **2.** *su.* bastard; *animal*: mongrel.

bateau ♗ [ba'to] *m* boat, ship; *sl.* ~x *pl.* beetle-crushers; ~ *à vapeur* steamer; ~ *de sauvetage* lifeboat; F *monter un* ~ *à q.* pull s.o.'s leg; **~-citerne**, *pl.* **~x-citernes** ♗ [batosi'tɛrn] *m* tanker; **~-feu**, *pl.* **~x-feux** ♗ [~'fø] *m* lightship; **~-mouche**, *pl.* **~x-mouches** ♗ [~'muʃ] *m* small passenger steamer; **~-phare**, *pl.* **~x-phares** ♗ [~'fa:r] *m* lightship; **~-pilote**, *pl.* **~x-pilotes** ♗ [~pi'lɔt] *m* pilot boat; **~-pompe**, *pl.* **~x-pompes** ♗ [~'põ:p] *m* fireboat.

bateleur, -euse *f* [ba'tlœ:r, ~'tlø:z] knock-about comedian; juggler.

batelier [batə'lje] *m* boatman; ferryman; ~ *de chaland* bargee; **batellerie** [batɛl'ri] *f* lighterage; inland water transport; ~ *fluviale* river fleet.

bâter [ba'te] (1a) *v/t.* saddle (*a pack-horse etc.*); F *c'est un âne bâté* he is a complete fool.

bath *sl.* [bat] *adj./inv.* super, posh, fab.

bâti [ba'ti] *m* frame(work); ⊕ bed, support.

batifoler F [batifɔ'le] (1a) *v/i.* frolic; cuddle (s.o., *avec q.*).

bâtiment [bati'mã] *m* building, edifice; ♗ vessel.

bâtir[1] [ba'ti:r] (2a) *v/t.* build, erect; ~ *un terrain* build on a site; *terrain m à* ~ building site.

bâtir[2] [~] (2a) *v/t.* baste, tack.

bâtisse [ba'tis] *f* masonry; F house, building.

batiste *tex.* [ba'tist] *f* cambric.

bâton [ba'tõ] *m* stick; staff; truncheon; wand of office; ~ *d'encens* joss stick; ~ *de rouge à lèvres* lipstick; ♀ ~

d'or wallflower; ~ *ferré* alpenstock; *à* ~*s rompus* by fits and starts; **bâtonner** [bɑtɔˈne] (1a) *v/t.* beat; **bâtonnet** [~ˈnɛ] *m* short stick; *cuis.* ~*s pl. de poisson* fish fingers, *Am.* fish sticks.

bats [ba] *1st p. sg. pres. of battre*; **battage** [baˈta:ʒ] *m* beating; *butter*: churning; *corn*: threshing; ⚒ field of fire; ⊕ ramming; F plugging, boosting; **battant, e** [~ˈtɑ̃, ~ˈtã:t] **1.** *adj.* banging, pelting (*rain*); *porte f* ~*e* swing-door; folding-door; *fig. tambour* ~ briskly; F *tout* ~ *neuf* brand-new; **2.** *su./m door*: leaf; *bell*: clapper; *fig.* fighter; F *fig.* go-getter; **batte** [bat] *f* beater; beating; beetle, rammer; *cricket*: bat; **battement** [~ˈmɑ̃] *m* beating; clapping; palpitation; pulsation, up and down movement; **batterie** [baˈtri] *f* ✐, ⚒ battery; *drum*: beat, roll; ♪ drums *pl.*, percussion; † scuffle; ⊕ ~ *de chaudières* battery of boilers; ~ *de cuisine* kitchen utensils *pl.*; **batteur** [~ˈtœ:r] *m* beater (*a. cuis.*); *sp.* *cricket*: batsman; ♪ drummer; **batteuse** ✐, ⊕ [~ˈtø:z] *f* thresher; **battoir** [~ˈtwa:r] *m* (linen) beetle; bat (*a. sp.*); F *fig.* (large) hand, paw.

battre [batr] (4a) *v/t.* beat, strike; thrash; thresh; mint (*money*); defeat; scour (*the countryside*); shuffle (*cards*); ~ *q. en brèche* disparage s. o., run s.o. down; *se* ~ fight; *v/i.* throb; clap; bang; **battu, e** [baˈty] **1.** *p.p. of battre*; **2.** *su./f* beat; *admin.* round-up; ⚓ ~ *en mer* scouting cruise.

baudet [boˈdɛ] *m* donkey; ass (*a. fig.*).

bauge [bo:ʒ] *f* wallow; lair (*of wild boar*); *fig.* pigsty.

baume [bo:m] *m* balsam; balm (*a. fig.*).

bauxite ⚒ [bokˈsit] *f* bauxite.

bavard, e [baˈva:r, ~ˈvard] **1.** *adj.* garrulous, talkative; **2.** *su.* chatterbox; gossip; F bore; **bavardage** [bavarˈda:ʒ] *m* gossip; chatter; **bavarder** [~ˈde] (1a) *v/i.* gossip; chatter; tell tales.

bave [ba:v] *f* dribble; slobber; froth; foam; *fig.* venom; **baver** [baˈve] (1a) *v/i.* dribble, slobber; run (*pen*); ✒ ooze; F talk drivel; ~ *sur* cast a slur on; F *fig.* ~ *d'admiration* be agape with admiration; F *fig. en* ~ have a hard time (of it); F *fig. en faire* ~ *à q.*

give s.o. a hard time (of it); *v/t.* F *fig. en* ~ *des ronds de chapeau* gape in astonishment.

bavette [baˈvɛt] *f* bib; F *tailler une* ~ chew the fat; **baveux, -euse** [~ˈvø, ~ˈvø:z] slobbery (*mouth*); runny, wet; *typ.* blurred.

bavure [baˈvy:r] *f* ⊕ burr; ⊕ seam; *writing*: smudge.

bazar [baˈza:r] *m* bazaar; bargain stores; *sl. tout le* ~ the lot, the whole caboodle; **bazarder** *sl.* [~zarˈde] (1a) *v/t.* sell off; get rid of.

béant, e [beˈɑ̃, ~ɑ̃:t] gaping, yawning, wide open.

béat, e [beˈa, ~ˈat] **1.** *adj.* smug, complacent; **2.** *su.* smug *or* complacent person; **béatifier** *eccl.* [beatiˈfje] (1o) *v/t.* beatify; **béatitude** [~ˈtyd] *f* bliss, beatitude; complacency.

beau (*adj. before vowel or h mute* **bel**) *m*, **belle** *f*, *m/pl.* **beaux** [bo, bɛl, bo] **1.** *adj.* beautiful; fine; handsome; *au* ~ *milieu de* right in the middle of; *avoir* ~ (*inf.*) (*inf.*) in vain; *il fait* ~ (*temps*) it is fine; *le* ~ *sexe* the fair sex; **2.** *su./m hist.* beau; *le* ~ the beautiful; *être au* ~ be set fair (*weather*); *faire le* ~ sit up and beg (*dog*); *su./f* beauty; *sp.* deciding game; *la Belle au bois dormant* (the) Sleeping Beauty.

beaucoup [boˈku] *adv.* much, a great deal; many; F *à* ~ *près* by a long chalk; *de* ~ by far.

beau-fils, *pl.* **beaux-fils** [boˈfis] *m* stepson; son-in-law; **beau-frère**, *pl.* **beaux-frères** [~ˈfrɛ:r] *m* brother-in-law; **beau-père**, *pl.* **beaux-pères** [~ˈpɛ:r] *m* father-in-law; stepfather.

beaupré ⚓ [boˈpre] *m* bowsprit.

beauté [boˈte] *f* beauty; *fig.* belle, beauty.

beaux-arts [boˈza:r] *m/pl.* fine arts; **beaux-parents** [~paˈrɑ̃] *m/pl.* parents-in-law.

bébé [beˈbe] *m* baby; doll.

bec [bɛk] *m bird*: beak, bill; ⊕ *tool*: nose; ⊕ nozzle; spout; ♪ mouthpiece; *pen*: nib; F mouth, nose; ⊕ ~ *d'âne* mortise-chisel; ~ *de gaz* gas burner, F lamp-post; F *fig. tomber sur un* ~ (*de gaz*) get *or* be stymied.

bécane F [beˈkan] *f* bike, bicycle.

bécarre ♪ [beˈka:r] *m* natural (sign).

bécasse *orn.* [beˈkas] *f* woodcock.

bec-de-cane, *pl.*   **becs-de-cane**

[bɛkdə'kan] *m* spring lock; slide-bolt; lever handle; ⊕ flat-nosed pliers *pl.*; **bec-de-lièvre**, *pl.* **becs-de-lièvre** [‿'ljɛːvr] *m* harelip.

bêchage [bɛ'ʃaːʒ] *m* digging; F disparagement.

béchamel *cuis.* [beʃa'mɛl] *f* bechamel.

bêche [bɛʃ] *f* spade.

bêche-de-mer, *pl.* **bêches-de-mer** [beʃdə'mɛːr] *m* bêche-de-mer; *gramm.* beach-la-mar.

bêcher [bɛ'ʃe] (1a) *v/t.* dig; F disparage, run (*s.o.*) down, pull (*s.o., s.th.*) to pieces; **bêcheur, -euse** F [bɛ'ʃœːr, -øːz] stuck-up.

bécot [be'ko] *m orn.* small snipe; peck (= *little kiss*); **bécoter** F [bekɔ'te] (1a) *v/t.* give (*s.o.*) a peck.

becqueter [bɛk'te] (1c) *v/t.* peck at; pick up; *sl.* eat; F kiss.

bedaine F [bə'dɛn] *f* belly; paunch.

bedeau *eccl.* [bə'do] *m* verger, beadle.

bedon F [bə'dõ] *m* paunch; **bedonner** F [‿dɔ'ne] (1a) *v/i.* grow paunchy, acquire a corporation.

bée [be] *adj./f:* bouche *f* ‿ gaping, open-mouthed.

beffroi [be'frwa] *m* belfry; ⊕ *dredge:* gantry.

bégayer [begɛ'je] (1i) *v/i.* stammer; *v/t.* stammer out.

bègue [bɛg] **1.** *adj.* stuttering, stammering; être ‿ stammer; **2.** *su.* stutterer, stammerer.

bégueter [beg'te] (1d) *v/i.* bleat (*goat*).

béguin [be'gɛ̃] *m* hood; baby's bonnet; F infatuation; *person:* love; **béguine** [‿'gin] *f eccl.* beguine; F very devout woman.

beige [bɛːʒ] **1.** *adj.* beige; **2.** *su./f* unbleached serge.

beigne *sl.* [bɛɲ] *f* blow; bruise.

beignet *cuis.* [bɛ'ɲɛ] *m* fritter; doughnut.

bel [bɛl] *see beau*; ‿ esprit *m person:* wit; ‿ et bien well and truly, genuinely; le ‿ âge youth; un ‿ âge a ripe old age.

bêlement [bɛl'mɑ̃] *m* bleating; **bêler** [bɛ'le] (1a) *v/i.* bleat (*sheep*).

belette *zo.* [bə'lɛt] *f* weasel.

belge [bɛlʒ] *adj., a. su.* ♀ Belgian; **Belgique** [bɛl'ʒik] *f: sl.* filer en ‿ bolt (*financier*).

bélier [be'lje] *m zo.* ram (*a.* ⊕), *Am.*

buck; ✖ *hist.* battering ram; *astr.* le ♈ Aries, the Ram.

belinogramme [bəlinɔ'gram] *m* telephotograph.

bélître † [be'litr] *m* cad, knave.

bellâtre [bɛ'lɑːtr] **1.** *adj.* foppish; **2.** *su./m* fop.

belle [bɛl] *see beau 1;* à la ‿ étoile in the open; de plus ‿ more than ever; iro. en faire de ‿s be up to s. th. pretty; l'échapper ‿ have a narrow escape; **‿-dame**, *pl.* **‿s-dames** [‿'dam] *f* ♀ deadly nightshade; *zo.* painted lady; **‿-fille**, *pl.* **‿s-filles** [‿'fiːj] *f* stepdaughter; daughter-in-law; **‿-mère**, *pl.* **‿s-mères** [‿'mɛːr] stepmother; mother-in-law; **‿s-lettres** [‿'lɛtr] *f/pl.* belles-lettres, humanities; **‿-sœur**, *pl.* **‿s-sœurs** [‿'sœːr] *f* sister-in-law.

bellicisme [bɛlli'sism] *m* warmongering; **belligérant, e** [‿ʒe'rɑ̃, ‿'rɑ̃ːt] *adj., a. su./m* belligerent; **belliqueux, -euse** [‿'kø, ‿'køːz] bellicose, warlike.

bellot, -otte F [bɛ'lo, ‿'lɔt] dandified; pretty(-pretty). [pinocle.]

belote [bə'lɔt] *f* cards: sort of

belvédère [bɛlve'dɛːr] *m* belvedere; summer-house; vantage-point.

bémol ♩ [be'mɔl] *m* flat.

bénédicité [benedisi'te] *m* grace (before a meal); **bénédiction** [‿dik-'sjõ] *f* blessing.

bénéfice [bene'fis] *m* ✝ profit, gain; benefit; *eccl.* living; **bénéficiaire** [‿fi'sjɛːr] *m* ✝ payee; ⚖, *eccl., etc.* beneficiary; **bénéficier** [‿fi'sje] (1o) *v/i.* profit, benefit (by, de); make a profit (on, sur).

benêt [bə'nɛ] **1.** *adj./m* stupid, silly; **2.** *su./m* simpleton.

bénévole [bene'vɔl] benevolent; gratuitous, unpaid; voluntary.

bénignité [beniɲi'te] *f* kindness; mildness (*a.* ⚕); **bénin, -igne** [be-'nɛ̃, ‿'niɲ] kind, benign; mild (*a.* ⚕).

bénir [be'niːr] (2a) *v/t.* bless; *eccl. a.* consecrate; **bénit, e** [‿'ni, ‿'nit] blessed; consecrated; *eccl.* eau *f* ‿e holy water; **bénitier** *eccl.* [‿ni'tje] *m* holy-water basin.

benne [bɛn] *f* hamper; *dredger:* bucket; ✖ tub, skip; ✖ cage; *telpherway:* bucket seat; ⊕ ‿ preneuse (mechanical) grab; clam-shell bucket; ⊕ (camion *m* à) ‿ basculante tipping waggon.

benoît, e [bən¹wa, ~¹wat] sanctimonious; bland.

benzine [bɛ̃¹zin] *f* benzine; **benzol** 🏠 [~¹zɔl] *m* benzol.

béquille [be¹ki:j] *f* crutch; *bicycle*: stand; ⚓ shore, prop; *marcher avec des ~s* walk on crutches; **béquiller** [~ki¹je] (1a) *v/i.* walk on crutches; *v/t.* ⚓ shore up.

bercail [bɛr¹ka:j] *m/sg.* sheepfold; *eccl.* fold.

berceau [bɛr¹so] *m* cradle (*a. fig., a.* ⚙); ⊕ bed; ⚐ bower, arbo(u)r; **bercer** [~¹se] (1k) *v/t.* rock; lull; soothe; delude (with promises, *de promesses*); **berceuse** [~¹sø:z] *f* cradle; rocking-chair; ♪ lullaby.

béret [be¹rɛ] *m* (*a. ~ de Basque*) beret; *~ écossais* tam-o'-shanter.

berge [bɛrʒ] *f* river, ditch: bank; *mountain*: flank; ✕ rampart.

berger [bɛr¹ʒe] *m* shepherd (*a.fig.*); **bergère** [~¹ʒɛ:r] *f* shepherdess; easy chair; *orn.* wagtail; **bergerie** [~ʒə¹ri] *f* sheep-pen; *paint., prosody:* pastoral; **bergeronnette** *orn.* [~ʒərɔ¹nɛt] *f* wagtail.

berline [bɛr¹lin] *f* saloon (car), *Am.* sedan; † *coach:* Berlin; ✕ truck, tram.

berlue [bɛr¹ly] *f* ✿ false vision; *fig. avoir la ~* get things all wrong.

berne ⚓ [bɛrn] *f: en ~* at half-mast.

berner [bɛr¹ne] (1a) *v/t.* laugh at, chaff; hoax.

bernique[1]! *sl.* [bɛr¹nik] *int.* nothing doing!

bernique[2] *orn.* [~] *f* limpet.

besace [bə¹zas] *f* † double sack; *fig. être réduit à la ~* be reduced to beggary.

bésef *sl.* [be¹zɛf] *see bezef.*

besicles *iro.* [bə¹zikl] *f/pl.* glasses, spectacles.

besogne [bə¹zɔɲ] *f* work; job; **besogneux, -euse** [~zɔ¹nø, ~¹nø:z] needy, hard-up.

besoin [bə¹zwɛ̃] *m* need, want; poverty; *au ~* in case of need; *when required; avoir ~ de* need; *il est ~ (de inf.)* it is necessary (to *inf.*).

bestial, e, *m/pl.* **-aux** [bɛs¹tjal, ~¹tjo] bestial, brutish; **bestialité** [~tjali¹te] *f* brutishness; bestiality; **bestiaux** [~¹tjo] *m/pl.* livestock *sg.*, cattle *sg.*

best-seller [bɛstsɛ¹lœ:r] *m* best seller.

bêta, -asse [bɛ¹ta, ~¹tas] **1.** *adj.* stupid; **2.** *su.* blockhead, ass.

bétail [be¹ta:j] *m/sg.* livestock, cattle.

bête [bɛt] **1.** *su./f* animal; beast; fool; *~s pl. féroces* wild beasts; *~ à cornes* horned beast; *~ de somme* beast of burden; *~ fauve* deer; *~ noire* wild boar; *fig. chercher la petite ~* split hairs; *fig. ma ~ noire* my pet aversion; **2.** *adj.* stupid, silly; **bêtifier** [bɛti¹fje] (1o) *v/i.* play the fool; talk stupidly; **bêtise** [~¹ti:z] *f* stupidity; blunder; nonsense; mere trifle.

béton 🏠 [be¹tɔ̃] *m* concrete; *fig. du ~* absolutely safe *or* reliable; **bétonnière** [~tɔ¹njɛ:r] *f* cement mixer.

bette ⚘ [bɛt] *f* beet; **betterave** ⚘ [bɛ¹tra:v] *f* beet(root); (*a. ~ sucrière*) sugar-beet; *~ fourragère* mangelwurzel.

beuglant *sl.* [bø¹glɑ̃] *m* cheap café-concert; **beuglement** [~glə¹mɑ̃] *m* lowing, mooing; **beugler** [~¹gle] (1a) *v/i.* low; moo.

beurre [bœ:r] *m* butter; *au ~ noir* with browned butter sauce; *sl. c'est du ~* it is child's play; *faire son ~* feather one's nest; F *un œil au ~ noir* a black eye; **beurré** [bœ¹re] *m* butter-pear; **beurrée** [~¹re] *f* slice of bread and butter; **beurrer** [~¹re] (1a) *v/t.* butter; **beurrier, -ère** [~¹rje, ~¹rjɛ:r] **1.** *su./m* butter-dish; **2.** *adj.* butter-producing.

beuverie [bø¹vri] *f* drinking bout.

bévue [be¹vy] *f* blunder, slip; *commettre une ~* drop a brick.

bezef *sl.* [be¹zɛf] *adv.: pas ~* not much.

bi... [bi] bi..., di...

biais, e [bjɛ, bjɛ:z] **1.** *adj.* skew, oblique; **2.** *su./m* ⚙ *etc.* skew; slant; slanting; *fig.* expedient; *de (or en) ~* on the cross, on the slant; *regarder de ~* look askance at; **biaiser** [bjɛ¹ze] (1b) *v/i.* (be on the) slant; skew; *fig.* use evasions.

bibelot [bi¹blo] *m* knick-knack, trinket.

biberon [bi¹brɔ̃] *m* *baby:* feeding (*Am.* nursing) bottle; *invalid:* feeding-cup; F tippler; **biberonner** F [~brɔ¹ne] (1a) *v/i.* tipple.

bibi *sl.* [bi¹bi] *m* I, me, myself; F (woman's) hat.

Bible [bibl] *f* Bible.

biblio... [biblio] biblio...; **~graphie** [~gra'fi] *f* bibliography; **~manie** [~ma'ni] *f* bibliomania; book collecting; **~phile** [~'fil] *m* bibliophile, book-lover; **~thécaire** [~te'kɛːr] *m* librarian; **~thèque** [~'tɛk] *f* library; bookcase; ~ *de prêt* lending library; *fig.* ~ *vivante* walking encyclop(a)edia.

biblique [bi'blik] Biblical.

bicarbonate 🜊 [bikarbɔ'nat] *m* bicarbonate; ~ *de soude* bicarbonate of soda, baking soda.

bicentenaire [bisɑ̃t'nɛːr] *m* bicentenary, *Am.* bicentennial.

biceps *anat.* [bi'sɛps] *m*, *a.* *adj.* biceps.

biche *zo.* [biʃ] *f* hind, doe; *ma* ~ my darling.

bicher *sl.* [bi'ʃe] (1a) *v/i.*: *ça biche!* how goes it?; things alright with you?

bichette *zo.* [bi'ʃɛt] *f* young hind.

bichon *m*, **-onne** *f* [bi'ʃɔ̃, ~'ʃɔn] lapdog; **bichonner** [~ʃɔ'ne] (1a) *v/t.* spruce (*s.o.*) up; titivate.

bichromie [bikrɔ'mi] *f* two-colo(u)r printing.

bicolore [biko'lɔːr] two-colo(u)r; of two colo(u)rs.

bicoque [bi'kɔk] *f* shanty, F dump.

bicorne [bi'kɔrn] **1.** *adj.* two-pointed; **2.** *su./m* cocked hat.

bicyclette [bisi'klɛt] *f* (bi)cycle.

bidasse *sl.* [bi'das] *m* (simple) soldier.

bide *sl.* [bid] *m* belly; flop, washout; lies *pl.*, rubbish, nonsense.

bidet [bi'dɛ] *m* nag; ⊕ trestle; *hygiene:* bidet.

bidoche *sl.* [bi'dɔʃ] *f* meat.

bidon [bi'dɔ̃] **1.** *m* tin, can, drum; ✗ canteen, water-bottle; *sl.* belly; *sl.* rubbish, pack of lies; *c'est pas du* ~ that's the honest truth; **2.** *adj. sl.* fake, mock, sham, phoney.

bidonner *sl.* [bidɔ'ne] (1a) *vt/i.* swig; *v/t.*: *se* ~ split one's sides.

bidonville [bidɔ̃'vil] *m* shanty-town.

bidule F [bi'dyl] *m* thing(umabob).

bief [bjɛf] *m* canal reach; mill-race.

bielle ⊕ [bjɛl] *f* connecting rod.

bien [bjɛ̃] **1.** *adv. usu.* well; right(ly), porper(ly); quite, rather; really, indeed; *adjectivally:* good, nice, fine, all right; ~ *de la peine* much trouble; ~ *des gens* many people; ~ *que* (*sbj.*) (al)though; *aller* ~ be well; *eh* ~! well!; *être* ~ *a.* be on good terms (with s.o., *avec q.*); *se porter* ~ be in good health; *tant* ~ *que mal* so so; *c'est* ~ *de lui!* that's just like him!; **2.** *su./m* good; welfare; possession, property, wealth, estate; goods *pl.*; ~ *public* public *or* common weal; ✝ ~s *pl. de consommation* consumer goods; **~-aimé, e** [~nɛ'me] beloved; **~-dire** [~'diːr] *m* fine words *pl.*, eloquence; **~-être** [~'nɛːtr] *m* wellbeing, comfort; **~faisance** [~fə'zɑ̃ːs] *f* beneficence, charity; *œuvre f ou société f ou association f de* ~ charitable organization, charity; **~faisant, e** [~fə'zɑ̃, ~'zɑ̃ːt] beneficent, charitable; salutary, beneficial; **~fait** [~'fɛ] *m* benefit; service; *fig.* blessing; **~faiteur, -trice** [~fɛ'tœːr, ~'tris] **1.** *su./m* benefactor; *su./f* benefactress; **2.** *adj.* beneficent; **~-fondé** [~fɔ̃'de] *m* merits *pl.* (*of claim etc.*); **~-fonds**, *pl.* **~s-fonds** [~'fɔ̃] *m* real estate; landed property; **~heureux, -euse** [~nœ'rø, ~'røːz] blissful, happy; blessed; **~-jugé** 🏛 [~ʒy'ʒe] *m* proper decision.

biennal, e, *m/pl.* **-aux** [biɛ'nal, ~'no] biennial.

bien-pensant, e [bjɛ̃pɑ̃'sɑ̃, ~'sɑ̃ːt] *adj.*, *a. su.* right-thinking (person).

bienséance [bjɛse'ɑ̃ːs] *f* propriety, decorum; **bienséant, e** [~'ɑ̃, ~'ɑ̃ːt] seemly, decent.

bientôt [bjɛ̃'to] *adv.* soon, before long; *à* ~! so long!

bienveillance [bjɛ̃vɛ'jɑ̃ːs] *f* kindness; goodwill; benevolence; **bienveillant, e** [~'jɑ̃, ~'jɑ̃ːt] kind(ly), benevolent.

bienvenu, e [bjɛ̃və'ny] **1.** *adj.* welcome (to, *à*); **2.** *su.* welcome person; *soyez le* ~! welcome!; *su./f* welcome; *souhaiter la* ~*e à q.* welcome s.o.

bière¹ [bjɛːr] *f* beer; ~ *blonde* pale *or* light ale; ~ *brune* brown ale.

bière² [~] *f* coffin.

biffer [bi'fe] (1a) *v/t.* cross out (*a word*); 🏛 strike out; ~ *les indications inutiles* strike out what does not apply.

bifteck [bif'tɛk] *m* beefsteak; ~ *de porc* pork steak.

bifurcation [bifyrka'sjɔ̃] *f* road etc.: fork; 🚄 junction; **bifurquer** [~'ke] (1m) *v/i. a. se* ~ fork, divide; 🚄 branch off; ⚡ shunt (*current*).

bigame [bi'gam] **1.** *adj.* bigamous; **2.**

su. bigamist; **bigamie** [~ga'mi] *f* bigamy.

bigarré, e [biga're] variegated; **bigarrer** [~'re] (1a) *v/t.* variegate, mottle; **bigarrure** [~'ry:r] *f* motley, variegation.

bigle [bigl] 1. *adj.* squint-eyed; 2. *su.* squint-eyed person.

bigleux, -euse F [bi'glø, ~'glø:z] shortsighted.

bigophone F [bigɔ'fɔn] *m* phone.

bigorne [bi'gɔrn] *f* two-beaked anvil; *anvil:* beak; **bigorner** *sl.* [~gɔr'ne] (1a) *v/t.* smash up; **se** ~ fight.

bigot[1] ✗ [bi'go] *m* mattock.

bigot[2]**, e** [bi'go, ~'gɔt] *adj.* (*a. su.*) sanctimonious (person); **bigoterie** [~gɔ'tri] *f* sanctimoniousness, (religious) bigotry.

bigoudi [bigu'di] *m* (hair) curler.

bigre! *sl.* [bigr] *int.* by Jove!, bosh!; **bigrement** *sl.* [~ə'mɑ̃] *adv.* jolly (well), darn (well).

bijou, *pl.* **-x** [bi'ʒu] *m* jewel, gem; **bijouterie** [biʒu'tri] *f* jewellery, *Am.* jewelry; jeweller's shop; **bijoutier** *m*, **-ère** *f* [~'tje, ~'tjɛ:r] jeweller.

bikini [biki'ni] *m* bikini.

bilan [bi'lɑ̃] *m* ✝ balance sheet; *fig.* outcome; *fig.* consequences *pl.*; *fig.* toll; ✝ *déposer son* ~ file a petition in bankruptcy; *fig. faire le* ~ *(de)* take stock (of).

bilatéral, e, *m/pl.* **-aux** [bilate'ral, ~'ro] bilateral, two-sided.

bilboquet [bilbɔ'kɛ] *m toy:* cup-and-ball; *toy:* tumbler; *typ.* jobwork.

bile [bil] bile, gall; **biler** *sl.* [bi'le] (1a) *v/t.*: *ne te bile pas!* don't worry!; take it easy!; **se** ~ get worked up; **bilieux, -euse** [~'ljø, ~'ljø:z] bilious; *fig.* testy; morose.

bilingue [bi'lɛ̃:g] bilingual.

billard [bi'ja:r] *m* (game of) billards *pl.*; billiard table; billiard room; F operating table; **bille** [bi:j] *f* (*billiard etc.*) ball; marble; billet, block; *sl.* mug (*= face*); *sl.* nut (*= head*); *stylo m à* ~ ball-point pen.

billet [bi'jɛ] *m* note, letter; notice; circular; ticket (*a.* 🎭, *thea.*); ✝ bill; ~ *à ordre* ✝ promissory note; ♱ single bill; ~ *blanc lottery:* blank; ~ *circulaire* tourist ticket; ✝ circular note; ~ *de banque* bank-note, *Am. a.* bill; ~ *de faire part* intimation, notice (*of death, wedding, etc.*);

~ *de faveur* complimentary ticket; ~ *doux* love-letter.

billevesée [bilvə'ze] *f* crazy notion.

billion [bi'ljɔ̃] *m* one million millions, billion; *Am.* one thousand billions, trillion.

billon [bi'jɔ̃] *m* alloy; copper *or* nickel coinage; base coinage; ✗ ridge of earth; **billot** ✗ [bi'jo] *m* block; *tethering:* clog; wheel drag.

bimbeloterie [bɛ̃blɔ'tri] *f* toys *pl.*, knick-knacks *pl.*; (cheap) toy trade.

bimensuel, -elle [bimɑ̃'sɥɛl] fortnightly.

bimoteur [bimɔ'tœ:r] *adj./m* twin-engined.

binaire [bi'nɛ:r] binary.

binard [bi'na:r] *m* (stone-)lorry, dray.

biner [bi'ne] (1a) *v/t.* ✗ hoe; dig *etc.* for a second time; *v/i. eccl.* celebrate two masses in one day; **binette** ✗ [~'nɛt] *f* hoe; *sl.* face, dial, mug.

biniou [bi'nju] *m* Breton pipes *pl.*; *sl.* horn, wind instrument.

binocle [bi'nɔkl] *m* eye-glasses *pl.*; pince-nez; lorgnette.

binôme ⚹ [bi'no:m] *adj., a. su./m* binomial.

biochimie ⚗ [biɔʃi'mi] *f* biochemistry.

biographe [biɔ'graf] *m* biographer; **biographie** [~gra'fi] *f* biography.

biophysique [biɔfi'zik] *f* biophysics *sg.*

biosphère [biɔ'sfɛ:r] *f* biosphere.

biotope [biɔ'tɔp] *m* biotope.

bipartisme *pol.* [bipar'tism] *m* coalition government. [seater.)

biplace [bi'plas] *adj., a. su.* two-)

biplan ✈ [bi'plɑ̃] *m* biplane.

bipolaire ⚡ [bipɔ'lɛ:r] bipolar.

bique [bik] *f* F nanny-goat; *sl.* old hag; *sl.* nag; **biquet** *m*, **-ette** *f* F [bi'kɛ, ~'kɛt] kid.

biréacteur ✈ [bireak'tœ:r] 1. *adj./m* twin-jet; 2. *su./m* twin-jet plane.

bis[1]**, bise** [bi, bi:z] greyish-brown; *à* ~ *ou à blanc* anyhow; *pain m* ~ brown bread.

bis[2] [bis] 1. *adv.* twice; again; encore!; *no. 9* = 9A (*house etc.*); 2. *su./m* encore.

bisaïeul [biza'jœl] *m* great-grandfather; **bisaïeule** [~] *f* great-grandmother.

bisannuel, -elle [biza'nɥɛl] biennial.

bisbille F [bis'bi:j] *f* bickering; *en* ~ at loggerheads (with, *avec*).

biscornu, e F [biskɔr'ny] mis-shapen; distorted; illogical; queer (*idea*).

biscotin [biskɔ'tɛ̃] *m* crisp biscuit; ship's biscuit; **biscotte** [~'kɔt] *f* rusk; **biscuit** [~'kɥi] *m* biscuit, *Am. a.* zwieback; plain cake; ⚜ *ceramics*: biscuit, bisque; ~ *à la cuiller* spongefinger, *Am.* lady-finger; ~ *de mer* ship's biscuit.

bise¹ [bi:z] *f* north wind; *poet.* winter.

bise² F [~] *f* (little) kiss; *faire une* ~ *à q.* give s.o. a (little) kiss.

biseau ⊕ [bi'zo] *m* chamfer, bevel; *en* ~ chamfered, bevelled; **biseauter** [~zo'te] (1a) *v/t.* ⊕ chamfer, bevel; bezel (*gems*); *fig.* mark (*cards*).

biser¹ [bi'ze] (1a) *v/t.* re-dye.

biser² ✶ [~] (1a) *v/i.* darken.

biser³ F [~] (1a) *v/t.* kiss.

bismuth ⚗ [bis'myt] *m* bismuth.

bison *zo.* [bi'zɔ̃] *m* bison.

bisque [bisk] *f cuis.* shellfish soup; **bisquer** F [bis'ke] (1m) *v/i.*: *faire* ~ *q.* rile s.o.

bissac [bi'sak] *m* double wallet.

bissecteur, -trice ⚗ [bisɛk'tœːr, ~'tris] bisecting; **bissection** ⚗ [~'sjɔ̃] *f* bisection.

bisser [bi'se] (1a) *v/t.* encore (*a singer, a song*); repeat; **bissextile** [bisɛks'til] *adj./f*: *année f* ~ leap year; **bissexuel, -elle** ⚥ [~sɛk'sɥɛl] bisexual.

bistourner [bistur'ne] (1a) *v/t.* wrench.

bistre [bistr] **1.** *su./m* bistre; **2.** *adj./inv.* blackish-brown, swarthy.

bistrot [bis'tro] *m* pub, café; pub- *or* café-owner.

bitume [bi'tym] *m* bitumen; **bitumer** [~ty'me] (1a) *v/t.* tar; asphalt.

biture *sl.* [bi'ty:r] *f*: *prendre une* ~ get drunk.

bivouac ✕ [bi'vwak] *m* bivouac.

bizarre [bi'za:r] odd, curious, strange, peculiar; **bizarrerie** [~zar'ri] *f* oddness, peculiarity; whimsicality.

bizut(h) *sl.* [bi'zy] *m* first-year student; beginner.

bla-bla F [bla'bla] *m/inv.* bunkum, *Am.* blah.

blackbouler [blakbu'le] (1a) *v/t.* blackball, turn down.

blafard, e [bla'fa:r, ~'fard] wan, pale.

blague [blag] *f* F joke; trick, practical joke; F stupid mistake, blunder; F stupid thing, nonsense; (~ *à tabac*) tobacco pouch; ~ *à part* joking apart; F *sans* ~? you don't say!; really?; **blaguer** F [bla'ge] (1m) *v/i.* joke; *tu blagues!* impossible!; *v/t.* make fun of, F kid.

blair *sl.* [blɛ:r] *m* nose.

blaireau [blɛ'ro] *m* *zo.* badger; shaving-brush; *paint.* brush.

blairer *sl.* [blɛ're] (1a) *v/t.*: *je ne peux pas le* ~ I can't stand him.

blâmable [bla'mabl] blameworthy; **blâme** [blɑ:m] *m* blame; *admin.* reprimand; **blâmer** [bla'me] (1a) *v/t.* blame; censure; reprimand.

blanc, blanche [blɑ̃, blɑ̃:ʃ] **1.** *adj.* white; clean, pure; blank (*paper, cartridge*); pale (*ale*); *armes f/pl. blanches* side-arms; F *carte f blanche* free hand; *nuit f blanche* sleepless night; *se battre à l'arme blanche* fight with cold steel; **2.** *su.* white; white person; *su./m* blank; white wine; (egg) white; white meat; *chauffer à* ~ make white-hot; *fig.* work (*s.o.*) up, excite (*s.o.*); *saigner à* ~ bleed white; *tirer à* ~ fire blanks; (*signer un*) *chèque en* ~ (sign a) blank cheque; ~-**bec**, *pl.* ~**s-becs** F [blɑ̃'bɛk] *m* callow youth, *Am.* sucker, greenhorn; **blanchâtre** [blɑ̃'ʃɑ:tr] whitish; **blanche** ♪ [blɑ̃:ʃ] *f* minim, *Am.* half note; **blancheur** [blɑ̃'ʃœ:r] *f* whiteness; paleness; purity; **blanchir** [~'ʃi:r] (2a) *v/t.* whiten; bleach; clean; wash, launder; *v/i.* turn white; blanch; fade; **blanchissage** [~ʃi'sa:ʒ] *m* washing; laundering; **blanchisserie** [~ʃis'ri] *f* laundering; laundry; **blanchisseur** [~ʃi'sœ:r] *m* laundryman; ⊕ bleacher; **blanchisseuse** [~ʃi'sø:z] *f* laundress; washerwoman; **blancseing**, *pl.* **blancsseings** [blɑ̃'sɛ̃] *m* blank signature; *fig.* full power(s *pl.*).

blaser [bla'ze] (1a) *v/t.* blunt (*the palate*); surfeit; *se* ~ become indifferent (to *de, sur*).

blason [bla'zɔ̃] *m* coat-of-arms, blazon; heraldry; **blasonner** [~zɔ'ne] (1a) *v/t.* blazon.

blasphémateur, -trice [blasfema-'tœ:r, ~'tris] **1.** *su.* blasphemer; **2.** *adj.* blasphemous; **blasphème** [~'fɛm] *m* blasphemy; **blasphémer** [~fe'me] (1f) *vt/i.* blaspheme.

blatte [blat] *f* cockroach, blackbeetle.

blé [ble] *m* corn; wheat; ~ *de Turquie* maize, *Am.* (Indian) corn; ~ *noir* buckwheat.

blême [blɛːm] wan, pale; ghastly, livid; **blêmir** [blɛˈmiːr] (2a) *v/i.* blanch; grow pale.

blennorragie ✽ blɛnɔraˈʒi] *f* gonorrh(o)ea.

blèse [blɛːz] lisping; *être* ~ = **bléser** [bleˈze] (1f) *v/i.* lisp.

blessant, e [blɛˈsɑ̃, ~ˈsɑ̃ːt] offensive (*remark*); **blesser** [~ˈse] (1a) *v/t.* wound; hurt; offend; *se* ~ *a.* take offence; **blessure** [~ˈsyːr] *f* wound, injury.

blet, blette [blɛ, blɛt] over-ripe.

bleu, bleue, *m/pl.* **bleus** [blø] **1.** *adj.* blue; *cuis.* underdone; *une colère f bleue* a towering rage; *une peur f bleue* a blue funk; *zone f bleue* zone of parking restrictions in the centre of a town; **2.** *su./m* blue; ⊕ blue print; ✽ bruise; F greenhorn; ✕ F recruit; ~s *pl.* overalls; ~ *de Prusse* Prussian blue; ~ *d'outremer* ultramarine; **bleuâtre** [~ˈɑːtr] bluish; **bleuir** [~ˈiːr] (2a) *v/t.* blue; make blue; *v/i.* become blue.

blindage [blɛ̃ˈdaːʒ] *m* ✕, ⚓ armo(u)r plating; ✕ timbering; ⚡ screening; **blindé, e** [~ˈde] **1.** *adj.* armo(u)red; bullet-proof; F *fig.* hardened, immune (to, *contre*); thick-skinned; *sl.* drunk; **2.** *su./m* armo(u)red car; **blinder** [~ˈde] (1a) *v/t.* ✕, ⚓ armo(u)r-plate; ⊕ shore up; timber; F *fig.* harden, make immune *or* indifferent (to, *contre*).

bloc [blɔk] *m* block; (*memo*) pad; mass; *pol.* bloc; ⊕ unit; *sl.* prison, clink; *à* ~ tight, hard, right home; *en* ~ in one piece; in the lump; wholesale; **blocage** [blɔˈkaːʒ] *m* blocking (*a.* ⚡); ▲ rubble; ▲ cement-block foundation; ⊕ jamming, stopping; ~ *des prix* freezing of prices; ~ *des salaires* pay freeze; **bloc-cylindres,** *pl.* **blocs-cylindres** *mot.* [blɔksiˈlɛ̃ːdr] *m* cylinder-block.

blockhaus [blɔˈkoːs] *m/inv.* ✕ block-house; ⚓ conning-tower.

bloc-notes, *pl.* **blocs-notes** [blɔkˈnɔt] *m* (memo) pad, writing pad.

blocus [blɔˈkys] *m* blockade; *hist.* ~ *continental* continental system; *faire le* ~ *de* blockade; *forcer le* ~ run the blockade.

5*

blond, blonde [blɔ̃, blɔ̃ːd] **1.** *adj.* blond, fair; pale (*ale*); **2.** *su./m* blond; *su./f* blonde.

blondin, e [blɔ̃ˈdɛ̃, ~ˈdin] **1.** *adj.* fair-haired; **2.** *su.* fair-haired person.

bloquer [blɔˈke] (1m) *v/t.* block (up); besiege; blockade; ✝ stop (*a cheque*); ⊕ lock; ⊕ jam on (*the brake*); ⛴ close (*a section*); ✝ freeze (*wages, prices*); F lock up; *se* ~ get jammed.

blottir [blɔˈtiːr] (2a) *v/t.*: *se* ~ crouch, squat; nestle.

blouse [bluːz] *f* blouse; smock; overall; *billiards*: pocket; **blouser** [bluˈze] (1a) *v/t.* pocket (*the ball at billiards*); F deceive; **blouson** [~ˈzɔ̃] *m* lumber-jacket; *Am.* windbreaker.

bluet ⚘ [blyˈɛ] *m* cornflower.

bluette [blyˈɛt] *f* trivial story.

bluff F [blœf] *m* bluff; **bluffer** F [blœˈfe] (1a) *v/t.* bluff (*s.o.*); *v/i.* pull a fast one, try it on.

blutage [blyˈtaːʒ] *m* bolting, sifting; **bluter** [~ˈte] (1a) *v/t.* bolt, sift (*flour etc.*); **blutoir** [~ˈtwaːr] *m* bolting-machine; sieve.

boa *zo., cost.* [bɔˈa] *m* boa.

bobard *sl.* [bɔˈbaːr] *m* tall story; lie, fib.

bobèche [bɔˈbɛʃ] *f* candlestick: sconce; *sl.* nut, head.

bobinage ⚡, ⊕ [bɔbiˈnaːʒ] *m* winding; **bobine** [~ˈbin] *f* bobbin, reel, spool; roll; ⚡ coil; ⊕ drum; *sl.* dial, face; **bobiner** [bɔbiˈne] (1a) *v/t.* wind, spool; **bobineuse** [~ˈnøːz] *f* winding-machine.

bobo F [bɔˈbo] *m* hurt; sore; *ch.sp.* bump.

bocage [bɔˈkaːʒ] *m* grove, copse.

bocal [bɔˈkal] *m* jar, bottle (*with wide mouth and short neck*); globe, fish-bowl; *chemist:* show-bottle.

bocard *metall.* [bɔˈkaːr] *m* ore-crusher; **bocarder** [~karˈde] (1a) *v/t.* crush (*ore*).

bock [bɔk] *m* glass of beer.

bœuf [bœf, *pl.* bø] **1.** *su./m* ox; beef; boiled beef; ~ *à la mode* stewed beef; ~ *conservé* corned beef; **2.** *adj. sl.* colossal, fine, *Am.* bully.

boggie ⛢ [bɔˈʒi] *m* bogie, *Am.* truck.

bohème [bɔˈɛm] *adj., a. su.* Bohemian; **bohémien, -enne** *geog.* [~eˈmjɛ̃, ~ˈmjɛn] *adj., a. su.* ♀ Bohemian; gypsy.

boire [bwa:r] (4b) **1.** v/t. drink; soak up, imbibe; fig. pocket (an insult); fig. drink in (s.o.'s words); ~ un coup have a drink; ~ une goutte take a sip; have a nip; v/i. drink; be a drunkard; ~ comme un trou drink like a fish; **2.** su./m drink(ing).

bois [bwɑ] m wood; timber; forest; rifle: stock; ~ pl. stag: horns, antlers; ~ contre-plaqué plywood; ~ de construction (or d'œuvre) timber; ~ de lit bedstead; ♪ les ~ pl. the woodwind sg.; touchez du ~ touch wood!; **boisage** △ etc. [bwa'za:ʒ] m timbering; frame(work); saplings pl.; **boisé, e** [~'ze] (well-)wooded; wainscoted (room); **boisement** [bwaz'mɑ̃] m afforestation; **boiser** [bwa'ze] (1a) v/t. panel; afforest; ⚒ timber, prop; **boiserie** [bwaz'ri] f △ panelling; wainscoting; woodwork.

boisseau [bwa'so] m measure: 13 litres (approx. 1 peck); ⊕ faucet-pipe; △ drain-tile; **boisselier** [~sə-'lje] m bushel-maker; cooper.

boisson [bwa'sɔ̃] m drink; pris de ~ drunk, intoxicated.

boîte [bwat] f box (a. ⊕); tin, Am. can; ⊕ case; F place, room; F joint, dump; F company, firm; F école; sl. prison; mot.~ à gants glove compartment; ~ à ordures litterbin, Am. litterbag; ~ à outils tool-box; ~ aux lettres letter-box, Am. mail-box; ~ de conserves tin, Am. can; F ~ de nuit night-club; mot. ~ de vitesses gearbox, Am. transmission; ~ postale post-office box; en ~ tinned, Am. canned; F fig. mettre q. en ~ pull s.o.'s leg.

boiter [bwa'te] (1a) v/i. limp; **boiteux, -euse** [~'tø, ~'tø:z] lame; rickety (table etc.).

boîtier [bwa'tje] m box-maker; watch-case maker; torch, watch, etc.: case.

boivent [bwa:v] 3rd p. pl. pres. of boire 1.

bol[^1] [bɔl] m ⚒ bole; ✻ bolus.

bol[^2] [~] m bowl; sl. (good) luck; sl. avoir du ~ be lucky; F prendre un ~ d'air get some fresh air; sl. en avoir ras le ~ be fed up with it.

bolchevisme [bɔlʃə'vism] m Bolshevism; **bolcheviste** [~'vist] adj., a. su. Bolshevist.   [car.]

bolide [bɔ'lid] m bolide; mot. racing-J

bombance F [bɔ̃'bɑ̃:s] f feast(ing); junket(ing); carouse.

bombardement [bɔ̃bardə'mɑ̃] m shelling; bombing; bombardment (a. phys.); **bombarder** [~'de] (1a) v/t. shell; bombard; pelt (with, de) (stones, a. fig. questions); F on l'a bombardé ministre he has been pitchforked into a Ministry; **bombardier** [~'dje] m bomber.

bombe [bɔ̃:b] f ✗ bomb; (aerosol) spray; F feast; ~ à hydrogène H-bomb; ~ à retardement time-bomb; ~ nucléaire nuclear bomb; en ~ like a rocket; faire la ~ go on a spree; **bomber** [bɔ̃'be] (1a) v/t. cause to bulge; curve, arch; camber (a road); ~ la poitrine stick out one's chest; ~ le torse throw out one's chest, fig. a. swagger; v/i. a. se~ bulge; swell out.

bon, bonne [bɔ̃, bɔn] **1.** adj. usu. good; nice, kind; proper, right; fit (for, à), apt; benevolent, charitable; dutiful (son); ✝ sound (firm); witty; typ. stet; ~ à manger eatable; ~ marché cheap(ly); ~ mot witticism; à quoi~? what's the use?; à son~ plaisir at his own convenience; at his discretion; de bonne famille of good family; de bonne foi truthful, honest; de bonne heure early; prendre qch. en bonne part take s.th. in good part; pour de ~, tout de ~ in earnest; really; for good; **2.** bon adv. nice; good; il fait~ it's nice and warm (weather); il fait~ (faire qch.) it's nice (to do s.th.); il ne fait pas ~ (faire qch.) it's not advisable (to do s.th.); tenir ~ stand fast or firm, hold out; **3.** su./m voucher, ticket, coupon; ✝ bond, draft; I.O.U., note of hand; ~ de caisse cash voucher; ~ de poste post: postal order; ~ du Trésor Treasury bond.

bonace [bɔ'nas] f lull (before storm).

bon(-)à(-)rien, pl. **bons(-)à(-)rien** [bɔ̃a'rjɛ̃] m good-for-nothing.

bonasse [~] good-hearted; simple-minded.

bonbon [bɔ̃'bɔ̃] m sweet, Am. candy.

bonbonne [bɔ̃'bɔn] f carboy.

bonbonnière [bɔ̃bɔ'njɛ:r] f sweet (-meat)box; fig. snug little dwelling.

bond [bɔ̃] m jump; bound; leap; fig. ~ en avant breakthrough; fig. faire faux ~ à leave in the lurch, let down.

bonde [bɔ̃:d] f ⊕ plug; barrel: bung; bung-hole; sluice-gate; **bondé**

[bɔ̃'de] packed, crammed, chock-full.

bondir [bɔ̃'di:r] (2a) *v/i.* bound, jump; bounce; caper; **bondissement** [~dis'mɑ̃] *m* bounding, leaping; frisking.

bondon ⊕ [bɔ̃'dɔ̃] *m* bung, plug.

bonheur [bɔ'nœ:r] *m* happiness; bliss; good luck; success; *par* ~ luckily; *porter* ~ bring good luck.

bonhomie [bɔnɔ'mi] *f* simple goodheartedness; simplicity; *avec* ~ goodnaturedly; **bonhomme**, *pl.* **bonhommes** [bɔ'nɔm, bɔ̃'zɔm] 1. *su./m* fellow, chap; ~ *de neige* snowman; 2. *adj. inv.* good-humo(u)red.

boni † [bɔ'ni] *m* surplus; profit; **bonification** [bɔnifika'sjɔ̃] *f* improvement, amelioration; † allowance, bonus; *insurance*: ~ *pour non sinistre* no claims bonus; **bonifier** [bɔni'fje] (1o) *v/t.* improve; † make good; † *avoir a discount to*; † *credit* (*s.th.*); **boniment** [~'mɑ̃] *m advertizing*: puff; *pej.* claptrap, humbug.

bonjour [bɔ̃'ʒu:r] *m* good morning; good afternoon.

bonne [bɔn] *f* maid; servant; waitress; ~ *a tout faire* maid of all work, F general; ~ *d'enfants* nursery-maid; **~-maman**, *pl.* **~s-mamans** *ch.sp.* [bɔnma'mɑ̃] *f* grandma, granny.

bonnement [bɔn'mɑ̃] *adv.*: *tout* ~ simply, plainly.

bonnet [bɔ'nɛ] *m* cap; *brassière*: cup; F *avoir la tête près du* ~ be quick-tempered *or* hot-headed; F *gros* ~ bigwig, *Am.* big shot; **bonneterie** [bɔn'tri] *f* hosiery; **bonnetier** *m*, **-ère** *f* [~'tje, ~'tjɛ:r] hosier; **bonnette** [bɔ'nɛt] *f* child's bonnet; *phot.* supplementary lens.

bon-papa, *pl.* **bons-papas** *ch.sp.* [bɔ̃pa'pa] *m* gran(d)dad, grandpa.

bonsoir [bɔ̃'swa:r] *m* good evening; good night.

bonté [bɔ̃'te] *f* goodness, kindness; *ayez la* ~ *de* (*inf.*) be so kind as to (*inf.*).

bonze [bɔ̃:z] *m* bonze (*Buddhist priest*); F bigwig, big shot; *sl. vieux* ~ old dodderer.

borax ⚗ [bɔ'raks] *m* borax.

bord [bɔ:r] *m* edge, border; side; seaside, shore; *river*: bank; tack; *hat*: brim; ✈ ~ *d'attaque* leading edge; ✈ ~ *de fuite* trailing edge; ⚓ *à* ~ on board; **bordage** [bɔr'da:ʒ] *m*

hem(ming), border(ing); ⊕ flanging; ⚓ planking, sheathing; **bordé** [~'de] *m* edging, border; ⚓ planking; ⚓ plating; **bordée** ⚓ [~'de] *f* broadside; tack; watch; *fig. une* ~ *d'injures* a volley of abuse; *courir une* ~ ⚓ make a tack, *fig.* go on the spree.

bordel [bɔr'dɛl] *m* brothel.

bordelais, **e** [bɔrdə'lɛ, ~'lɛ:z] of Bordeaux.

border [bɔr'de] (1a) *v/t.* hem, border (*a dress*); ⊕ flange; ⚓ plank; ⚓ ~ *la côte* keep close to the shore, hug the shore; ~ *un lit* tuck in the bedclothes.

bordereau † [bɔrdə'ro] *m* memorandum; statement; invoice; dispatch note; note, slip; list.

bordure [bɔr'dy:r] *f* border(ing); frame; edge; rim; kerb, *Am.* curb.

bore ⚗ [bɔ:r] *m* boron.

boréal, **e**, *m/pl.* **-als** *or* **-aux** [bɔre'al, ~'o] north(ern).

borgne [bɔrɲ] 1. *adj.* one-eyed, blind in one eye; *fig.* disreputable, shady; 2. *su.* one-eyed person.

borique ⚗ [bɔ'rik] boric.

borne [bɔrn] *f* boundary, limit; boundary-stone; landmark; ⚡ bollard; ∮ terminal; ~ *kilométrique* (*approx.*) milestone; **borné**, **e** [bɔr-'ne] limited; narrow, restricted; **borner** [~'ne] (1a) *v/t.* set limits to; limit; mark the boundary of; *se* ~ *à* content o.s. with, restrict o.s. to; **bornoyer** [~nwa'je] (1h) *v/t.* squint along (*an edge*); *surv.* stake off.

boscot, **-otte** † [bɔs'ko, ~'kɔt] 1. *adj.* hunchbacked; 2. *su.* hunchback.

bosquet [bɔs'kɛ] *m* grove, thicket.

bosse [bɔs] *f* hump; bump; knob; dent; *fig. avoir la* ~ *de* have a gift for; *en* ~ in relief; **bosseler** [~'le] (1c) *v/t.* ⊕ emboss; *fig.* batter; **bosser** *sl.* [bɔ'se] (1a) *v/i.* work hard, *sl.* peg away; **bossoir** ⚓ [~'swa:r] *m* bow; davit; **bossu**, **e** [~'sy] 1. *adj.* hunchbacked; 2. *su.* hunchback; **bossuer** [~'sɥe] (1n) *v/t.* dent, batter.

bot, **bote** [bo, bɔt] *adj.*: *pied m* ~ clubfoot.

botanique [bɔta'nik] 1. *adj.* botanical; 2. *su./f* botany.

botte[1] [bɔt] *f* high boot; *fig.* heel; ~*s pl. à l'écuyère* riding boots; ~*s pl. imperméables* waders; *fig. à propos de* ~*s* without rhyme or reason.

botte[2] [bɔt] *f* bunch; bundle, bale;

wire: coil; **bottelage** [bɔˈtla:ʒ] *m* trussing; **botteler** [~ˈtle] (1c) *v/t.* bundle; bunch; tie up.

botter [bɔˈte] (1a) *v/t.* put boots on, supply (*s.o.*) with boots *or* shoes; *sp.*, *a.* F kick; *le Chat botté* Puss-in-Boots; *sl.* *ça me botte* I like that; o.k.!

bottine [bɔˈtin] *f* (half-)boot; Wellington boot.

botulisme [bɔtyˈlism] *m* botulism.

bouc [buk] *m* he-goat; *beard*: goatee; ~ *émissaire* scapegoat, *Am.* fall guy.

boucan F [buˈkɑ̃] *m* shindy, hullabaloo.

boucaner [bukaˈne] (1a) *v/t.* cure (*by smoke*); F sun-burn; *v/i.* hunt wild animals; be cured *or* smoke-dried; *sl.* kick up a row; **boucanier** F [~ˈnje] *m* buccaneer.

bouche [buʃ] *f* mouth; opening; ⊕ nozzle; ✕ *canon*: muzzle; ✕ ~ *à feu* piece of artillery; ~ *d'eau* hydrant; ⚓ water-crane; ~ *de chaleur* hot-air vent; ~ *d'incendie* fire-hydrant, *Am.* fire-plug; ~ *de métro* underground (*Am.* subway) entrance; *sl.* *ta* ~! shut up!; **bouche-à-bouche** [buʃaˈbuʃ] *m/inv.* mouth-to-mouth artificial respiration, kiss of life.

bouché, e [buˈʃe] blocked; choked; F stupid, dense; F ~ *à l'émeri* absolutely blockheaded.

bouchée [~] *f* mouthful; *cuis.* patty.

boucher[1] [buˈʃe] (1a) *v/t.* stop (up); shut up; cork (*a bottle*).

boucher[2] [buˈʃe] *m* butcher; **bouchère** [~ˈʃɛːr] *f* butcher's wife; **boucherie** [buʃˈri] *f* butcher's shop; butcher's trade; slaughter (*a. fig.*).

bouche-trou [buʃˈtru] *m* stop-gap, substitute; **bouchon** [buˈʃɔ̃] *m* cork, stopper, plug (*a.* ♪); *cask*: bung; *fishing*: float; F † pub; *mot.* (*a.* ~ *de circulation*) traffic jam; ~ *de paille* wisp of straw; **bouchonner** [buʃɔˈne] (1a) *v/t.* rub down (*a horse*); † bundle up; F *fig.* coddle, cosset.

boucle [bukl] *f* buckle; ring; loop; circuit; ear-ring; *hair*: curl, lock; **boucler** [buˈkle] (1a) *v/t.* buckle; loop; curl (*one's hair*); F lock up; *v/i.* curl (*hair*).

bouclier [buˈklje] *m* shield (*a. fig.*).

bouder [buˈde] (1a) *v/i.* sulk; shirk; pass (*at dominoes*); *v/t.* be sulky with; be cool towards; **bouderie** [~ˈdri] *f* sulkiness; **boudeur, -euse** [~ˈdœːr,

~ˈdøːz] **1.** *adj.* sulky; **2.** *su.* sulky person.

boudin [buˈdɛ̃] *m* black pudding, *Am.* blood-sausage; *tobacco*: twist; ⊕ *wheel*: flange; ~ *blanc* white pudding; ⊕ *ressort m à* ~ spiral spring; **boudiner** [budiˈne] (1a) *v/t.* ⊕ coil; F be too tight for (*s.o.*) (*garment*); F se ~ *dans* squeeze o.s. into (*a garment*).

boudoir [buˈdwaːr] *m* boudoir, lady's private room. [ment.)

boue [bu] *f* mud; dirt; slush; sedi-)

bouée ⚓ [buˈe] *f* buoy.

boueur [buˈœːr] *m* scavenger; dustman, *Am.* garbage-collector; street cleaner; **boueux, -euse** [buˈø, ~ˈøːz] muddy; dirty.

bouffant, e [buˈfɑ̃, ~ˈfɑ̃:t] **1.** *adj.* puffed (*sleeve*); full (*skirt*); ample; **2.** *su./m* puff; **bouffarde** F [~ˈfard] *f* pipe.

bouffe[1] [buf] comic.

bouffe[2] *sl.* [~] *f* food, F grub.

bouffée [buˈfe] *f* puff, whiff; 🍃 attack; 🍃 ~ *de chaleur* hot flush; **bouffer** [~] (1a) *v/i.* puff out; *v/t.* F eat (greedily); blue (*money*).

bouffi, e [buˈfi] puffed (with, de), puffy, swollen; turgid (*style*); **bouffir** [~ˈfiːr] (2a) *vt/i.* swell; **bouffissure** [~fiˈsyːr] *f* swelling; *fig.* bombast.

bouffon, -onne [buˈfɔ̃, ~ˈfɔn] **1.** *adj.* farcical; comical; ridiculous; **2.** *su./m* buffoon, clown, fool; **bouffonnerie** [~fɔnˈri] *f* buffoonery.

bouge [buːʒ] *m* hovel, dump; low dive; ⊕ *cask*: bilge; *wall*: bulge; ⚓ camber.

bougeoir [buˈʒwaːr] *m* candlestick.

bouger [buˈʒe] (1l) *v/i.* move, stir; *v/t.* F move.

bougie [buˈʒi] *f* candle; taper; *phys.* candle-power; *mot.* (*a.* ~ *d'allumage*) sparking-plug, *Am.* spark plug.

bougon, -onne F [buˈgɔ̃, ~ˈgɔn] **1.** *adj.* grumpy; **2.** *su.* grumbler.

bougran *tex.* [buˈgrɑ̃] *m* buckram.

bougre *sl.* [bugr] **1.** *su./m* fellow, chap; ~ *d'idiot!* you blooming idiot!; **2.** *int.* gosh!; **bougrement** *sl.* [bugrəˈmɑ̃] *adv.* devilishly; very; **bougresse** *sl.* [~ˈgrɛs] *f* jade.

boui-boui, *pl.* **bouis-bouis** F [bwiˈbwi] *m* low theatre *or* music-hall; low haunt, *Am.* dive.

bouillabaisse [bujaˈbɛs] *f* (*Provençal*) fish-soup.

bouillant, e [buˈjɑ̃, ˌˈjɑ̃ːt] boiling (*a. fig.* with, *de*); hot; *fig.* hotheaded.
bouille *sl.* [buːj] *f* face; head.
bouilli, e [buˈji] 1. *p.p.* of *bouillir*; 2. *su./m* boiled beef; *su./f* gruel; pulp;
bouillir [ˌˈjiːr] (2e) *v/i.* boil; *faire* ~ *l'eau* boil the water; **bouilloire** [bujˈwaːr] *f* kettle, *Am.* teakettle;
bouillon [buˈjɔ̃] *m* bubble; broth (*a. biol.*); soup; restaurant; ✝ unsold copies *pl.*; ~ *d'onze heures* poison(ed drink); *fig. boire un* ~ suffer a loss;
bouillonner [ˌjɔˈne] (1a) *v/i.* bubble; seethe (*a. fig.* with, *de*); *v/t.*: ~ *une robe* gauge a dress; **bouillotte** [ˌˈjɔt] *f* footwarmer; hot-water bottle; *cards*: bouillotte; *sl.* head; kettle, *Am.* teakettle; **bouillotter** [ˌjɔˈte] (1a) *v/i.* simmer.
boulange F buˈlɑ̃ːʒ] bakery trade; **boulanger** [bulɑ̃ˈʒe] 1. *su./m* baker; 2. (11) *v/t.* make (*bread*), bake (*bread*); **boulangerie** [bulɑ̃ʒˈri] *f* bakery; baker's shop; baking.
boule [bul] *f* ball; bowl; *sl.* head; ~ *de neige* snowball; ~*s pl.* Quiès (*TM*) earplugs.
bouleau ♀ [buˈlo] *m* birch; birch-wood.
bouledogue [bulˈdɔg] *m* bulldog.
bouler F [buˈle] (1a) *v/t.* send rolling; *v/i.* roll; *envoyer* ~ send (*s.o.*) packing;
boulet [ˌˈlɛ] *m* bullet; shot; (~ *de canon*) cannon-ball; ✝ *coal*: ovoids *pl.*; *horse*: pastern-joint; **boulette** [ˌˈlɛt] *f* small ball; *cuis.* (~ *de viande*) meat ball; *sl.* blunder.
boulevard [bulˈvaːr] *m* boulevard.
bouleversement [bulvɛrsəˈmɑ̃] *m* overthrow; confusion; **bouleverser** [ˌˈse] (1a) *v/t.* upset (*a. fig.*); throw into confusion; bowl over.
boulier [buˈlje] *m* *billiards:* scoring board; (*a.* ~ *compteur*) abacus.
boulimie ✻ [buliˈmi] *f* abnormal hunger.
boulin [buˈlɛ̃] *m* pigeon-hole; ⚠ putlog(-hole).
bouline ⚓ [buˈlin] *f* bowline; **bouliner** ⚓ [ˌliˈne] (1a) *v/i.* sail close to the wind; *v/t.* haul (*a sail*) to windward.
boulingrin [bulɛ̃ˈgrɛ̃] *m* lawn, grass-plot.
boulon ⊕ [buˈlɔ̃] *m* bolt; pin; **boulonner** [ˌlɔˈne] (1a) *v/t.* bolt (down); *v/i. sl.* swot.
boulot, -otte [buˈlo, ˌˈlɔt] 1. *adj.*

dumpy; 2. *su./m sl.* work; job; **boulotter** F [ˌlɔˈte] (1a) *v/t.* eat; get through (*money*); *v/i.* jog along; *ça boulotte!* things are fine!
boumer *sl.* [buˈme] *v/i.*: *ça boume?* how's things?; *ça boume!* it's going fine!
bouquet [buˈkɛ] *m* bunch of flowers; nosegay; aroma; *wine:* bouquet; *c'est le* ~*!* that takes the cake!; **bouquetière** [bukˈtjɛːr] *f* flower-girl.
bouquetin *zo.* [bukˈtɛ̃] *m* ibex.
bouquin[1] [buˈkɛ̃] *m* old he-goat.
bouquin[2] buˈkɛ̃] *m* old book; F book; **bouquiner** [bukiˈne] (1a) *v/i.* collect old books; pore over old books; F read; **bouquineur** [ˌˈnœːr] *m* lover or collector of old books; **bouquiniste** [ˌˈnist] *m* second-hand bookseller.
bourbe [burb] *f* mud; mire; slime; **bourbeux, -euse** [burˈbø, ˌˈbøːz] muddy; *zo.* mud-...; **bourbier** [ˌˈbje] *m* mire; *fig.* mess.
bourdaine ♀ [burˈdɛn] *f* black alder.
bourde F [burd] *f* fib; blunder.
bourdon[1] [burˈdɔ̃] *m* pilgrim's staff.
bourdon[2] ♪ [burˈdɔ̃] *m* drone (*bass*); tenor *or* great bell; *zo.* bumblebee; *typ.* out; *zo. faux* ~ drone; **bourdonner** [ˌdɔˈne] (1a) *v/i.* hum, buzz; *fig.* murmur; *v/t.* hum (*a tune*); **bourdonneur, -euse** [ˌdɔˈnœːr, ˌˈnøːz] 1. *adj.* humming; 2. *su./m* F humming bird.
bourg [buːr] *m* small market-town; borough; **bourgade** [burˈgad] *f* large village; **bourgeois, e** [ˌˈʒwa, ˌˈʒwaːz] 1. *adj.* middle-class; homely; *pej.* narrow-minded; bourgeois; 2. *su.* citizen; middle-class person; F Philistine; *les petits* ~ the petty bourgeoisie *sg.*; *en* ~ in plain clothes; *su./f* F *la or ma* ~*e* my wife, F the missus; **bourgeosie** [ˌʒwaˈzi] *f* citizens *pl.*; freemen *pl.*; middle-class; *petite* ~ lower middle-class, small shopkeepers *pl.*, tradespeople *pl.*
bourgeon [burˈʒɔ̃] *m* ♀ bud; ✻ pimple; **bourgeonner** [ˌʒɔˈne] (1a) *v/i.* ♀ bud, shoot; ✻ break out into pimples.
bourgeron [burʒəˈrɔ̃] *m* overall; ⚒ fatigue jacket; ⚓ jumper.
bourgmestre [burgˈmɛstr] *m* burgomaster.
bourgogne [burˈgɔɲ] *m* *wine:* bur-

gundy; **bourguignon, -onne** [ˌ-gi'nɔ̃, ˌ'nɔn] *adj., a. su.* ♀ Burgundian.

bourlinguer [burlɛ̃'ge] (1m) *v/i.* ⚓ strain, make heavy weather; *fig.* knock about (*the world*).

bourrache ♀ [bu'raʃ] *f* borage.

bourrade [bu'rad] *f* blow; thrust; unkind word; *gun:* kick; **bourrage** ⊕[ˌ'ra:ʒ] *m* packing; charging; F ˌ *de crâne* bluff, eyewash; *media:* brainwashing.

bourrasque [bu'rask] *f* squall; gust of wind; *fig.* gust, attack.

bourre[1] [bu:r] *f* fluff; waste; padding; stuffing; *fire-arms:* plug; ⊕ ˌ *de soie* floss-silk.

bourre[2] *sl.* [ˌ] *m* cop (= *policeman*).

bourré, e [bu're] packed, crammed, stuffed (with, *de*); chock-full; *sl.* plastered (= *drunk*).

bourreau [bu'ro] *m* executioner; *fig.* tormenter.

bourrée [bu're] *f* bundle of firewood.

bourreler [bur'le] (1c) *v/t.* torture (*a. fig.*); ⊕ fit draught-excluders to (*a door*); **bourrelet** [ˌ'lɛ] *m* pad; wad; draught-excluder; bulge; fold *or* roll (*of flesh*); **bourrelier** [ˌ'lje] *m* saddler; **bourrer** [bu're] (1a) *v/t.* stuff; cram; pad; ram in; *fig.* trounce.

bourriche [bu'riʃ] *f* hamper(ful).

bourricot [buri'ko] *m* (small) donkey; **bourrin** *sl.* [ˌ'rɛ̃] *m* horse, nag; **bourrique** [ˌ'rik] *f* she-ass; *fig.* blockhead; **bourriquet** [ˌri'ke] *m* ass' colt; ⊕ winch.

bourru, e [bu'ry] **1.** *adj.* surly, churlish; **2.** *su./m* curmudgeon; ˌ *bienfaisant* rough diamond.

bourse [burs] *f* purse (*a. fig.*); bag; *zo.* pouch; *univ. etc.* scholarship; ✝ ♀ Stock Exchange; ♀ *du Travail* Labo(u)r Exchange; **boursicot** F [bursi'ko] *m* savings *pl.*, F nest-egg; ✝ purse; **boursier, -ère** [ˌ'sje, ˌ'sjɛ:r] *su. univ. etc.* scholarship-holder; exhibitioner; *su./m* ✝ speculator; paymaster, purse-holder.

boursoufler [bursu'fle] (1a) *v/t.* puff up; bloat; **boursouflure** [ˌ'fly:r] *f* swelling; *paint:* blister; *fig. style:* turgidity.

bous [bu] *1st p. sg. pres. of* bouillir.

bousculade [busky'lad] *f* hustle; scrimmage; **bousculer** [ˌ'le] (1a) *v/t.* knock (*s.th.*) over; jostle (*s.o.*).

bouse [bu:z] *f* cow-dung; **bousiller** F [buzi'je] (1a) *v/t.* botch, bungle (*a piece of work*); ruin, wreck, F bust up, goof up.

boussole [bu'sɔl] *f* compass; ⚡ galvanometer; F *perdre la* ˌ lose one's head; be all at sea.

boustifaille F [busti'fa:j] *f* food, grub.

bout [bu] *m usu.* end (*a. fig.*); extremity; *cigarette:* tip, butt; *pen:* nib; bit, piece; *ground:* patch; *à* ˌ worn out, F all in; *être à* ˌ *de qch.* have run out of s.th.; *à* ˌ *de course* at the end of one's resources; *à* ˌ *de forces* at the end of one's tether; *à* ˌ *portant* point-blank; *au* ˌ *de* after *or* in (*a year*); *au* ˌ *du compte* after all, in the end; *de* ˌ *en* ˌ from beginning to end; ⚓ from stem to stern; *fig. joindre les deux* ˌ*s* make both ends meet; *pousser à* ˌ *try to breaking point*; *venir à* ˌ *de* manage; (be able to) cope with.

boutade [bu'tad] *f* whim; sally; outburst.

boute-en-train [butɑ̃'trɛ̃] *m/inv.* exhilarating fellow, good company; life and soul (*of a party*).

bouteille [bu'tɛ:j] *f* bottle; ⊕ ˌ *à gaz* gas cylinder; ˌ *isolante* (*or thermos*) Thermos flask; *prendre de la* ˌ age (*wine*); *fig.* grow old.

bouter ✝ [bu'te] (1a) *v/t.* push.

bouteroue ⚠ [bu'tru] *f* guard-stone; *bridge:* guard-rail.

boutique [bu'tik] *f* shop; booth; ⊕ set of tools; *parler* ˌ talk shop; **boutiquier** *m*, **-ère** *f* [ˌti'kje, ˌ'kjɛ:r] shopkeeper.

boutoir *zo.* [bu'twa:r] *m* snout (*of boar*); *fig. coup m de* ˌ thrust; cutting remark.

bouton [bu'tɔ̃] *m* button; ♀ bud; 𝕤 pimple; *cost.* stud, link; *door, radio:* knob; ˌ *de puissance radio:* volume control; *appuyer sur le* ˌ press the bell; *tourner le* ˌ switch on *or* off; ˌ-**d'or**, *pl.* ˌ**s-d'or** ♀ [ˌtɔ̃'dɔ:r] *m* butter-cup; **boutonner** [ˌtɔ̃'ne] (1a) *v/t.* button (up); *v/i.* ♀ bud; 𝕤 come out in pimples; **boutonnerie** [ˌtɔn'ri] *f* button trade *or* factory; **boutonnière** [ˌtɔ̃'njɛ:r] *f* buttonhole; 𝕤 incision; **bouton-poussoir**, *pl.* **boutons-poussoirs** [ˌtɔ̃pu'swa:r] *m* push-button; **bou-**

bras

ton-pression, *pl.* boutons-pression [ˌtɔprɛˈsjɔ̃] *m* press-stud.
bouture *♂* [buˈtyːr] *f* cutting.
bouverie [buˈvri] *f* cowshed.
bouvet ⊕ [buˈvɛ] *m* grooving-plane; tonguing-plane.
bouvier, -ère [buˈvje, ˌˈvjɛːr] *su.* cowherd; drover; F boor; *su./f* cowgirl.
bouvreuil *orn.* [buˈvrœːj] *m* bullfinch.
bovin, e [bɔˈvɛ̃, ˌˈvin] bovine; *bêtes f/pl.* ˌes horned cattle.
box, *pl.* boxes [bɔks] *m* horse-box; *mot.* lock-up (garage); *dormitory:* cubicle; F ˌ *des accusés* dock.
boxe *sp.* [ˌ] *f* boxing.
boxer¹ [bɔkˈse] (1a) *vt/i.* box.
boxer² [bɔkˈsœːr] *m* dog: boxer.
boxeur [bɔkˈsœːr] *m* boxer, prizefighter.
boyau [bwaˈjo] *m* hose-pipe; bowel, gut; ✂ communication trench; *fig.* narrow passage.
boycottage [bɔjkɔˈtaːʒ] *m* boycotting; boycotter [ˌˈte] (1a) *vt.* boycott.
bracelet [brasˈlɛ] *m* bracelet; bangle; armlet; ♀ node; ˌ *de montre* watch-strap; ˌ-montre, *pl.* ˌs-montres [ˌlɛˈmɔ̃tr] *m* wristwatch.
brachial, e, *m/pl.* -aux *anat.* [braˈkjal, ˌˈkjo] brachial.
braconnage [brakɔˈnaːʒ] *m* poaching; braconner [ˌˈne] (1a) *v/i.* poach; braconnier [ˌˈnje] *m* poacher.
bractée ♀ [brakˈte] *f* bract.
brader [braˈde] (1a) *v/t.* sell off cheap(ly), undersell.
braguette [braˈgɛt] *f* trousers: fly, flies *pl.*
brai [brɛ] *m* tar, pitch.
braillard, e [braˈjaːr, ˌˈjard] 1. *adj.* brawling; shouting, obstreperous; 2. *su.* bawler; brawler; brailler [ˌˈje] (1a) *vt/i.* bawl; brailleur, -euse [ˌˈjœːr, ˌˈjøːz] 1. *adj.* brawling; shouting; 2. *su.* bawler; brawler.
braire [brɛːr] (4c) *v/i.* bray (*ass*); F cry; *sl.* squeal.
braise [brɛːz] *f* glowing embers *pl.*; live charcoal; cinders *pl.*; *sl.* cash; braiser [brɛˈze] (1b) *v/t. cuis.* braise; *v/i. sl.* pay; braisière *cuis.* [ˌˈzjɛːr] *f* braising-pan.

brait [brɛ] *p.p. of* braire. [(*stag*).ˎ
bramer [braˈme] (1o) *v/i.* bellˏ
brancard [brɑ̃ˈkaːr] *m* stretcher; hand-barrow; ⊕ *carriage:* shaft; brancardier [ˌkarˈdje] *m* stretcher-bearer.
branchage [brɑ̃ˈʃaːʒ] *m coll.* branches *pl.*; branche [brɑ̃ːʃ] *f* branch (*a. fig.*, ♫, ✝); bough; *spectacles:* side; *propeller:* blade; *compass:* leg; *sl.* vieille ˌ old pal; branchement [brɑ̃ʃˈmɑ̃] *m* branching; ⚡ lead, branch-circuit; ⚡ tapping (*of main*); ☎ˌ (*de voie*) junction; brancher [brɑ̃ˈʃe] (1a) *v/t.* ⚡ plug in(to *sur*); ♫, *a. fig.* connect *or* link (up) (with *sur*); *fig.* être branché en direct sur qch. be in immediate touch *or* in close contact with s.th.; F *fig.* être branché be in the know; be well up on things.
branchies *zo.* [brɑ̃ˈʃi] *f/pl.* gills.
branchu, e [brɑ̃ˈʃy] branchy.
brande ♀ [brɑ̃ːd] *f* heather; heath.
brandebourg *cost.* [brɑ̃dˈbuːr] *m* frogs *pl.* and loops *pl.*
brandiller [brɑ̃diˈje] (1a) *vt/i.* dangle. [dish, wave.ˎ
brandir [brɑ̃ˈdiːr] (2a) *v/t.* bran-ˏ
brandon [brɑ̃ˈdɔ̃] *m* (fire-)brand; *fig.* ˌ *de discorde* troublemaker.
branlant, e [brɑ̃ˈlɑ̃, ˌˈlɑ̃ːt] tottering; shaky; loose (*tooth*); branle [brɑ̃ːl] *m* swing; shaking, impulse, start; en ˌ in action, going; branlebas [brɑ̃lˈba] *m/inv.* ⚓ clearing the decks, pipe to quarters; *fig.* commotion; branler [brɑ̃ˈle] (1a) *vt/i.* shake, move; swing; *v/i. a.* rock, be unsteady; be loose (*tooth, tool, etc.*).
braquage [braˈkaːʒ] *m car etc.:* steering; *gun:* aiming, pointing; *car:* rayon de ˌ turning circle.
braque [brak] 1. *su./m* pointer; F mad-cap; 2. *adj.* F silly, *sl.* daft.
braquer [braˈke] (1m) *v/t.* aim, point (*a gun etc.*); *mot. etc.* change the direction of; *v/i. mot.* turn the wheel.
bras [bra] *m* arm; ⊕ handle; ⊕ leg; ⊕ crane: jib; ⊕ˌ *pl.* workmen; hands; ˌ (*de pick-up*) *gramophone:* tone-arm; ˌ dessus, ˌ dessous arm-in-arm; *à* tendus at arm's length; *à* tour de ˌ with might and main; avoir le ˌ long be very influential; couper ˌ et jambes à q. dishearten s.o.; en ˌ de chemise in shirt-sleeves.

braser ⊕ [braˈze] *v/t.* hardsolder.

brasero [brazeˈro] *m* brazier; glowing fire; *fig.* blaze; **brasier** [‿ˈzje] *m* brazier; glowing fire; *fig.* blaze; **brasiller** [‿ziˈje] (1a) *v/i.* sparkle (*sea*); splutter (*meat etc. in pan*); *v/t.* grill.

brassage [braˈsaːʒ] *m* brewing; *fig.* (inter)mixing.

brassard [braˈsaːr] *m* arm-band; armlet.

brasse [bras] *f* ⚓ fathom; *swimming*: stroke; ‿ *sur le dos* (*ventre*) back-(breast-)stroke; **brassée** [braˈse] *f* armful; *swimming*: stroke.

brasser[1] [braˈse] (1a) *v/t.* ⚓ brace; ⚓ swing (*the propeller*).

brasser[2] [braˈse] (1a) *v/t.* brew (*a. fig.*); *metall.* puddle; (inter-)mix; F handle (*an affair*); **brasserie** [brasˈri] *f* brewery; beer-saloon; brewing; restaurant.

brassière [braˈsjɛːr] *f* shoulder-strap; (child's) bodice; ‿ *de sauvetage* life-jacket.

brassin [braˈsɛ̃] *m* brew; mash-tub.

brasure [braˈzyːr] *f* brazed seam; hard solder(ing).

bravache [braˈvaʃ] 1. *su./m* bully; swaggerer; 2. *adj.* blustering, swaggering; **bravade** [‿ˈvad] *f* bravado, bluster; **brave** [braːv] brave; good, honest; F smart; *un ‿ homme* a worthy man; *un homme ‿* a brave man; F *faux ‿ see bravache 1*; **braver** [braˈve] (1a) *v/t.* defy; brave; **bravo** [‿ˈvo] 1. *su./m* cheers *pl.*; 2. *int.* ‿! bravo!; well done!; hear, hear!; **bravoure** [‿ˈvuːr] *f* bravery.

brayer [brɛˈje] 1. *su./m* ⚕ truss; 2. (1i) *v/t.* ⚓ tar; ⚠ sling.

break *mot.* [brɛk] *m* estate (car), *Am.* station wagon.

brebis brəˈbi] *f* ewe; sheep; *fig.* ‿ *galeuse* black sheep.

brèche [brɛʃ] *f* breach; gap; ⚓ hole; *blade*: notch; *fig. battre en ‿* disparage; ‿*dent* [‿ˈdɑ̃] 1. *adj.* gap-toothed; 2. *su.* gap-toothed person.

bredouille [brəˈduːj] unsuccessful; empty-handed; *se coucher ‿* go supperless to bed; **bredouiller** [‿duˈje] (1a) *vt/i.* mumble.

bref, brève [bref, brɛːv] 1. *adj.* brief, short; 2. *su./m eccl.* (papal) brief; 3. *bref adv.* in short, briefly.

bréhaigne † *zo.* [breˈɛɲ] barren (*mare etc.*).

brelan [brəˈlɑ̃] *m cards*: brelan; *cards*: pair royal; gambling den.

breloque [brəˈlɔk] *f* (watch-)charm; ⚔ dismiss; F *battre la ‿* go erratically.

brème [brɛm] *f icht.* bream; *sl.* playing card.

brésilien, -enne [breziˈljɛ̃, ‿ˈljɛn] *adj., a. su.* ♀ Brazilian.

bretailler F [brətɑˈje] (1a) *v/i.* fight on the slightest provocation; fence.

bretelle [brəˈtɛl] *f* (shoulder-)strap; *mot.* link road; *mot.* ‿ *de contournement* bypass; ‿*s pl.* braces, *Am.* suspenders.

breton, -onne [brəˈtɔ̃, ‿ˈtɔn] 1. *adj.* Breton; 2. *su./m ling.* Breton; *su.* ♀ Breton.

bretteur † [brɛˈtœːr] *m* swashbuckler; duellist.

breuvage [brœˈvaːʒ] *m* beverage, drink; ⚕ draught.

brève [brɛːv] *f gramm.* short syllable; ♪ breve; *tel.* dot; *orn.* short tail.

brevet [brəˈve] *m* patent; † warrant; certificate, diploma; ⚔ commission; ‿ *de capacité school:* lower certificate; ⚓ ‿ *de capitaine* master's certificate; ⚔ ‿ *de pilote* pilot's licence; *prendre un ‿* take out a patent; **breveté, e** [brəvˈte] certificated (*teacher etc.*), commissioned (*officer*); **breveter** [‿] (1c) *v/t.* patent; grant a patent to; *fig.* license.

bréviaire *eccl.* [breˈvjɛːr] *m* breviary.

bréviligne [breviˈliɲ] thick-set, squat.

bribes [brib] *f/pl.* scraps; fragments.

bric-à-brac [brikaˈbrak] *m/inv.* odds *pl.* and ends *pl.*; curios *pl.*; curiosity shop.

brick ⚓ [brik] *m* brig.

bricole [briˈkɔl] *f* strap; breast-harness; rebound; F ‿*s pl.* odds and ends, odd jobs; **bricoler** F [‿kɔˈle] (1a) *v/i.* do odd jobs; *v/t.* arrange; **bricoleur** [‿kɔˈlœːr] *m* handy man, *Am.* putterer; potterer.

bride [brid] *f* bridle; rein (*a. fig.*); ⊕ tie, strap; ⊕ flange; ⊕ ‿ *de serrage* clamp(ing) piece; *à ‿ abattue, à toute ‿* at full speed; *lâcher la ‿ à l'émotion* give free rein to one's feelings; *fig. laisser à q. la ‿ sur le cou* give s.o. his head; *fig. tenir la ‿ haute à* keep a tight rein on; be high-handed with; **brider**

[bri'de] (1a) *v/t.* bridle; curb; tie (up); ⊕ flange; *cuis.* truss (*fowl*); *cost.* bind (*a buttonhole*).

bridger [brid'ʒe] (11) *v/i.* play bridge.

bridon [bri'dɔ̃] *m* snaffle.

brie [bri] *m* Brie (cheese).

brièvement [briɛv'mɑ̃] *adv.* briefly, succinctly; **brièveté** [~'te] *f* brevity; concision.

brigade [bri'gad] *f* ✕ brigade; *workers*: gang; *workers*: shift; *police*: squad; **brigadier** [~ga'dje] *m* ✕ corporal; ⊕ foreman; *police*: sergeant.

brigand [bri'gɑ̃] *m* brigand; robber; F ruffian; **brigandage** [~gɑ̃'da:ʒ] *m* highway robbery; plunder.

brigue [brig] *f* intrigue; cabal; **briguer** [bri'ge] (1m) *v/t.* seek, aspire to *or* after; court (*favour*); canvass for (*votes*).

brillant, e [bri'jɑ̃, ~'jɑ̃:t] **1.** *adj.* shining, brilliant, bright; **2.** *su./m* brilliance, brightness; gloss; shine; *diamond*: brilliant; **briller** [~'je] (1a) *v/i.* shine, glisten, sparkle; F ~ *par son absence* be conspicuous for one's absence.

brimade [bri'mad] *f* rag(ging), *Am.* hazing.

brimbaler [brɛ̃ba'le] (1a) *v/i.* dangle; wobble; *v/t.* F carry about.

brimborion [brɛ̃bɔ'rjɔ̃] *m* bauble.

brimer [bri'me] (1a) *v/t.* rag, *Am.* haze; bully.

brin [brɛ̃] *m* grass: blade; *tree*: shoot; ⚓, *rope*: strand; *fig.* bit; touch; **brindille** [~'di:j] *f* twig.

bringue¹ F [brɛ̃:g] *f* spree, F binge, bust; *faire la ~* be *or* go on a spree.

bringue² F [~] *f*: *grande ~* tall (and ugly) woman, F beanpole.

brioche [bri'ɔʃ] *f* brioche; bun; F blunder.

brique [brik] *f* ▲ brick; ✝ *soap*: bar; ~ *de parement* facing brick; ~ *hollandaise* clinker; ~ *tubulaire* hollow brick; *sl.* *bouffer des ~s* not to have a bite; **briquet** [bri'kɛ] *m* cigarette-lighter; tinder-box; *battre le ~* strike a light; **briqueter** [brik'te] (1c) *v/t.* brick; face with bricks *or* with imitation brickwork; **briqueterie** [~'tri] *f* brick-yard; **briquetier** [~'tje] *m* brick-maker; **briquette** [bri'kɛt] *f* briquette.

bris [bri] *m* breaking (*a.* ⚖); ⚓ wreckage; **brisant, e** [bri'zɑ̃, ~'zɑ̃:t] **1.** *adj.* high-explosive; **2.** *su./m* reef; breaker (*wave*).

brise ⚓ [bri:z] *f* breeze.

brise-bise [briz'bi:z] *m/inv.* draught-excluder.

brisées [bri'ze] *f/pl.* tracks; *hunt.* broken boughs; *fig.* *aller sur les ~ de q.* trespass s.o.'s preserves.

brise...: **~-glace** [briz'glas] *m/inv.* ice-breaker; ice-fender; **~-jet** ⊕ [~'ʒɛ] *m/inv.* anti-splash nozzle; **~-lames** ⚓ [~'lam] *m/inv.* breakwater; groyne.

briser [bri'ze] (1a) *v/t.* break; shatter; *fig. a.* crush; *v/i.* break (with, *avec*); *brisons là!* let's leave it at that!; **brise-tout** F [briz'tu] *su./inv. esp.* destructive child; **briseur** *m*, **-euse** *f* [bri'zœːr, ~'zø:z] breaker; ~ *de grève* strikebreaker.

brisure [bri'zy:r] *f* break; *shutter*: folding-joint; ⊘ brisure.

britannique [brita'nik] **1.** *adj.* British; Britannic (*majesty*); **2.** *su.*: *les ~s m/pl.* the British.

broc [bro] *m* jug, pitcher.

brocanter [brɔkɑ̃'te] (1a) *v/i.* deal in second-hand goods; *v/t.* sell (to a second-hand dealer); barter; **brocanteur** *m*, **-euse** *f* [~'tœ:r, ~'tø:z] second-hand dealer; broker.

brocard¹ † [brɔ'ka:r] *m* lampoon.

brocard² *hunt.* [~] *m* yearling roedeer.

brocart † [~] *m* brocade.

broche [brɔʃ] *f* spit; skewer; ⊕ spindle; ⊕ pin; tent-peg; brooch; F knitting-needle; *zo.* boar: tusk; **brocher** [brɔ'ʃe] (1a) *v/t.* stitch; brocade; emboss; *livre broché* paperbound book.

brochet *icht.* [brɔ'ʃɛ] *m* pike.

brochette [brɔ'ʃɛt] *f* skewer; ⊕ pin.

brocheur, -euse [brɔ'ʃœːr, ~'ʃø:z] *su.* stitcher, sewer (*of books*); *su./f* stitching-machine; stapling-machine; **brochure** [~'ʃy:r] *f* booklet, brochure; pamphlet; stitching (*of books*); *tex.* inwoven pattern.

brodequin [brɔd'kɛ̃] *m* half-boot; ✕ ammunition-boot; F *thea.* chausser le ~ take to comedy.

broder [brɔ'de] (1a) *v/t.* embroider (*a. fig.*); **broderie** [~'dri] *f* embroidery (*a. fig.*); *fig.* embellishment; **brodeur** *m*, **-euse** *f* [ˌ‿ˈdœːr, ‿ˈdøːz] embroiderer.

broie [brwa] *f tex.* brake; ✗ brake-harrow; **broiement** [ˌ‿ˈmã] *m* crushing, pulverizing; *tex.* braking.

brome 🜍 [broːm] *m* bromine; **bromique** 🜍 [brɔˈmik] bromic; **bromure** 🜍 [ˌ‿ˈmyːr] *m* bromide.

bronche *anat.* [brɔ̃ːʃ] *f* wind-pipe; bronchus; ‿*s pl.* bronchi(a).

broncher [brɔ̃ˈʃe] (1a) *v/i.* stumble; trip; move; *fig.* falter, flinch; *sans* ‿ without flinching.

bronchite 🞼 [brɔ̃ˈʃit] *f* bronchitis.

bronze [brɔ̃ːz] *m* bronze; *fig.* *cœur m de* ‿ heart of steel; **bronzer** [brɔ̃ˈze] (1a) *v/t.* bronze; tan; *fig.* harden.

brosse [brɔs] *f* brush; paint-brush; ‿*s pl.* brushwood *sg.*; *cheveux m/pl.* *en* ‿ crew-cut *sg.*; *fig. passer la* ‿ *sur* efface; **brosser** [brɔˈse] (1a) *v/t.* brush; scrub; F thrash; F *se* ‿ *(le ventre)* go without; *sl.* have an empty belly; **brosserie** [brɔsˈri] *f* brush-ware; brush-trade; brush-factory; **brossier** [brɔˈsje] *m* brush-maker; dealer in brushes.

brou [bru] *m* husk; ‿ *de noix* walnut stain; walnut liqueur.

brouet [bruˈɛ] *m* (thin) gruel, F skilly; ‿ *noir* black broth.

brouette [bruˈɛt] *f* wheelbarrow; **brouetter** [ˌ‿ɛˈte] (1a) *v/t.* convey in a (wheel)barrow.

brouhaha [bruaˈa] *m* hubbub; hullabaloo; uproar.

brouillage [bruˈjaːʒ] *m radio:* jamming; interference.

brouillamini F [brujamiˈni] *m* muddle.

brouillard [bruˈjaːr] **1.** *su./m* fog; smog; ✝ waste-book; **2.** *adj./m:* *papier m* ‿ blotting-paper; **brouillasser** [ˌ‿jaˈse] (1a) *v/impers.* drizzle.

brouille F [bruːj] *f* disagreement; quarrel; *être en* ‿ *avec* be at loggerheads with; **brouiller** [bruˈje] (1a) *v/t.* mix up; confuse; *radio:* jam; *radio:* interfere with (*a broadcast*); shuffle (*cards*); scramble (*eggs*); *fig.* create dissension between; set at variance; ‿ *du papier* scribble over paper; **brouillerie** [brujˈri] *f* disagreement; **brouilleur** [ˌ‿ˈjœːr] *m radio:* jammer.

brouillon¹, **-onne** [bruˈjɔ̃, ˌ‿ˈjɔn] **1.**

adj. unmethodical; muddle-headed (*person*); *avoir l'esprit* ‿ be muddle-headed; **2.** *su.* muddler; muddle-head.

brouillon² [bruˈjɔ̃] *m* draft, rough copy; scribbling paper; **brouillonner** [ˌ‿jɔˈne] (1a) *v/t.* botch (*an essay etc.*); draft, make a rough copy of.

broussailles [bruˈsaːj] *f/pl.* brush-wood *sg.*, scrub *sg.*, bush *sg.*; *en* ‿ shaggy, unkempt (*hair*); **brousse** [brus] *f the bush (in Australia etc.*).

brout [bru] *m* tender shoots *pl.*; browse(-wood); **brouter** [bruˈte] (1a) *v/t.* browse (on), graze; *v/i.* ⊕ jump (*tool*); **broutille** [ˌ‿ˈtiːj] *f* twig; F trifle.

broyage [brwaˈjaːʒ] *m* pounding, crushing; grinding; *tex.* braking; **broyer** [ˌ‿ˈje] (1h) *v/t.* pound, crush; grind; *tex.* brake; **broyeur** *m*, **-euse** *f* [ˌ‿ˈjœːr, ˌ‿ˈjøːz] pounder; grinder; *tex.* hemp-braker.

brrr! [brrr] *int.* ugh!

bru [bry] *f* daughter-in-law.

bruine [brɥin] *f* drizzle, Scotch mist; **bruinement** [ˌ‿ˈmã] *m* drizzling; **bruiner** [brɥiˈne] (1a) *v/impers.* drizzle; **bruineux**, **-euse** [ˌ‿ˈnø, ˌ‿ˈnøːz] drizzly.

bruire [brɥiːr] (4d) *v/i.* rustle; hum (*machine*); murmur (*brook etc.*); **bruissement** [brɥisˈmã] *m* rumbling; rustling; humming; murmuring; **bruit** [brɥi] *m* noise; clatter, din; rumble; *metal.:* clang; *gun:* report; 🞼 murmur; *fig.* rumo(u)r, report; ‿*s pl.* *parasites radio:* interference *sg.*; ‿ *de fond radio etc.:* background noise; ‿ *sourd* thud; *le* ‿ *court que ...* rumo(u)r has it that ..., it is rumo(u)red that ...; **bruitage** *thea.*, *cin.* [brɥiˈtaːʒ] *m* sound effects *pl.*; **bruiteur** *m*, **-euse** *f* [ˌ‿ˈtœːr, ˌ‿ˈtøːz] sound-effects engineer.

brûlé [bryˈle] *m* smell of burning; **brûle-gueule** F [brylˈgœl] *m/inv.* nosewarmer; **brûle-pourpoint** [ˌ‿purˈpwɛ̃] *adv.:* *à* ‿ point-blank; **brûler** [bryˈle] (1a) *v/t.* burn (*a. fig.*); scorch; 🞼 cauterize; overrun (*a signal*); ✗ nip; 🕮 not to stop at; *sl.* unmask, detect; *fig.* ‿ *ses vaisseaux* burn one's boats; *se* ‿ *la cervelle* blow one's brains out; *v/i.* burn (*a. fig.*), be on fire; catch (*milk*); *fig.* be consumed; F be hot, be roasting; ⁓ de (*inf.*) be eager to (*inf.*); **brûleur, -euse** [⌣'lœːr, ⁓'løːz] *su.* person: burner; *coffee*: roaster; brandy distiller; *su./m gas etc.*: burner; **brûloir** [⌣'lwaːr] *m machine*: coffee roaster; blowlamp; **brûlot** [⌣'lo] *m* ⚓ flare; F *pol.* firebrand; **brûlure** [⌣'lyːr] *f* burn; scald; ⚡ frost-nip; ⚕ ⁓s *pl.* d'estomac heartburn *sg.*

brume [brym] *f* thick fog; (sea-) mist; **brumeux, -euse** [bry'mø, ⁓'møːz] foggy; *fig.* hazy.

brun, brune [brœ̃, bryn] **1.** *adj.* brown; dark (*complexion*); dark-haired; **2.** *su./m* brown; *su./f* brunette; nightfall; **brunâtre** [bry-'naːtr] brownish; **brunir** [⌣'niːr] (2a) *vt/i.* brown; tan; *v/t.* ⊕ burnish, polish; **brunissage** [⌣ni-'saːʒ] *m* burnishing; polishing; (sun)tan.

brusque [brysk] blunt, brusque, abrupt; sudden; rough; sharp; **brusquer** [brys'ke] (1m) *v/t.* be blunt with (*s.o.*); hurry; hustle; precipitate (*s.th.*); **brusquerie** [⌣kə'ri] *f* abruptness, brusqueness.

brut, brute [bryt] raw; crude (*oil*); unrefined (*sugar*); uncut (*diamond*); undressed (*stone*); ✝ *poids m* ⁓ gross weight; **brutal, e** *m/pl.* **-aux** [bry-'tal, ⁓'to] brutal; savage, fierce; harsh (*colour*); brute (*force*); unfeeling; plain, unvarnished (*truth*); **brutaliser** [⌣tali'ze] (1a) *v/t.* ill-treat; bully; **brutalité** [⌣tali'te] *f* brutality; *sp.* rough play; *fig.* suddenness (*of an event etc.*); **brute** [bryt] *f* brute (*a. fig.*); lout.

bruyant, e [brɥi'jɑ̃, ⁓'jɑ̃ːt] noisy, loud; boisterous; *fig.* resounding (*success*).

bruyère [brɥi'jɛːr] *f* heather; heath; briar; *orn.* coq *m* de ⁓ grouse.

bu, e [by] *p.p.* of *boire 1.*

buanderie [bɥɑ̃'dri] *f* wash-house.

bubonique ⚕ [bybɔ'nik] bubonic; *peste f* ⁓ bubonic plague.

buccal, e, *m/pl.* **-aux** [byk'kal, ⁓'ko] buccal, of the mouth.

bûche [byːʃ] *f* log; block; *cuis.* Swiss roll; F blockhead; *ramasser une* ⁓ have a fall, come a cropper.

bûcher[1] [by'ʃe] *m* wood-shed; pile of firewood, wood-stack; pyre.

bûcher[2] [⌣] (1a) *v/t.* ⊕ rough-hew; *sl.* thrash; F swot at, work hard at

or for, *Am.* grind; *v/i.* F work hard; swot, *Am.* grind.

bûcheron [byʃ'rɔ̃] *m* woodcutter, *Am.* lumberjack; **bûcheronne** [⌣'rɔn] *f* woodcutter's wife.

bûcheur *m,* **-euse** *f* F [by'ʃœːr, ⁓'ʃøːz] plodder; swotter, *Am.* grind.

budget [byd'ʒɛ] *m* budget; *admin.* estimates *pl.*; F *boucler son* ⁓ make ends meet; **budgétaire** [⌣ʒe'tɛːr] budgetary; financial (*year etc.*); **budgétisation** [⌣ʒetiza'sjɔ̃] *f* budgeting.

buée [bɥe] *f* steam, vapo(u)r.

buffet [by'fɛ] *m* sideboard; dresser; cupboard; buffet; 🚃 refreshment room; F *danser devant le* ⁓ have a bare cupboard; **buffetier** [byf'tje] *m* refreshment-room manager; **buffetière** [⌣'tjɛːr] *f* refreshment-room manageress.

buffle [byfl] *m zo.* buffalo; buffalo-hide; ⊕ buff-stick; **buffleterie** [⌣ə'tri] *f* leather equipment.

bugle[1] ♩ [bygl] *m* saxhorn.

bugle[2] ♀ [⌣] *f* bugle.

buis ♀ [bɥi] *m* box-tree; box-wood; **buisson** [bɥi'sɔ̃] *m* bush; spinney, thicket; **buissoneux, -euse** [bɥi-sɔ'nø, ⁓'nøːz] bushy; **buissonnier, ère** [⌣'nje, ⁓'njɛːr] *adj.*: *faire l'école* ⁓ère play truant, *Am.* play hooky.

bulbe ♀ [bylb] *m* bulb; **bulbeux, -euse** [byl'bø, ⁓'bøːz] bulbous; ♀ bulbed.

bulldozer [buldɔ'zœːr] *m* bull-dozer.

bulle [byl] *f* bubble; blister; *cartoon*: balloon; *eccl.* papal bull; *faire des* ⁓s blow bubbles.

bulletin [byl'tɛ̃] *m* bulletin; form; voting-paper; report; 🚃 ⁓ de bagages luggage-ticket, *Am.* baggage-check; ✝ ⁓ de commande order-form; ⁓ d'expédition way-bill; ⁓ de santé health report.

bulleux, -euse [by'lø, ⁓'løːz] bubbly; ♀ bullate; ⚡, *geol.* vesicular.

bungalow [bœ̃ga'lo] *m* bungalow.

buraliste [byra'list] *su.* tax collector; tobacconist; clerk.

bure[1] *tex.* [byːr] *f* rough homespun.

bure[2] ⚒ [⌣] *f* shaft (*of a mine*).

bureau [by'ro] *m* writing-table, desk; bureau; office; *admin.* department; board of directors, governing body; *thea.* ⁓x *pl.* *fermés* sold out; ⊕ ∼ *ambulant* travelling post office; ∼ *central* head post office, G.P.O.; *teleph.* exchange; ∼ *de bienfaisance* relief committee; ∼ *de douane* custom-house; *thea.* ∼ *de location* box-office; ∼ *de placement* labo(u)r exchange; (private) employment bureau; ∼ *de poste* post office; ∼ *de renseignements* information bureau; ∼ *de tabac* tobacconist's (shop); ∼ *ministre* knee-hole desk; ✗ *deuxième* ∼ Intelligence (Department); ⚓ Naval Intelligence Division; **bureaucrate** [byro'krat] *m* bureaucrat; F black-coated worker; **bureaucratie** [∼kra'si] *f* bureaucracy, F red tape; **bureaucratiser** [∼krati'ze] (1a) *v/t.* bureaucratize.

burette [by'rɛt] *f* cruet (*a. eccl.*); ⊕ oil-can, oiler; ⚗ burette.

burin ⊕ [by'rɛ̃] *m* burin, etching-needle, graver; cold chisel; engraving; **buriner** [∼ri'ne] (1a) *v/t.* engrave; chisel; *v/i.* F swot.

burlesque [byr'lɛsk] burlesque; comical, ridiculous.

bus [by] *1st p. sg. p.s. of* boire 1.

buse[1] [byːz] *f orn.* buzzard; F blockhead, fool.

buse[2] [∼] *f* ⊕ pipe; nozzle; ✗ air-shaft; *mot.* choke(-tube).

busqué, e [bys'ke] arched, curved; *nez m* ∼ hook nose.

buste [byst] *m* bust; *en* ∼ half-length.

but [by(t)] *m* target; aim; goal (*a. sp.*); purpose; *avoir pour* ∼ aim at, intend; *de* ∼ *en blanc* bluntly; *droit au* ∼ (straight) to the point; *marquer un* ∼ score a goal.

buté, e [by'te] obstinate, mulisk; **buter** [∼] (1a) *v/i.*: ∼ *contre* stumble over (*a. fig.*); bump *or* bang against *or* into, hit; *fig.* ∼ *contre or sur* meet with, come up against (*a difficulty etc.*); *v/t.* prop (up); *fig.* make (*s.o.*) obstinate; *se* ∼ be(come) obstinate; **buteur** [by'tœːr] *m foot.* striker; *sl.* killer.

butin [by'tɛ̃] *m* booty, spoils *pl.*; **butiner** [∼ti'ne] (1a) *vt/i.* † plunder; *v/i.* gather honey (*bee*); *v/t.* gather honey from (*a flower*).

butoir [by'twaːr] *m* ⊕ stop; catch; ⊕ terminal buffer.

butor [by'tɔːr] *m orn.* bittern; F lout, clod.

butte [byt] *f* mound, hillock; bank; ✗ butts *pl.*; *fig. en* ∼ *à* exposed to; **butter** ⚘ [by'te] (1a) *v/t.* earth up; **buttoir** ⚘ [∼'twaːr] *m* ridging-plough, *Am.* ridging-plow.

buvable [by'vabl] drinkable; *sl.* acceptable; **buvard** [∼'vaːr] *m* blotting-paper; **buvette** [∼'vɛt] *f* refreshment bar; *spa:* pump-room; **buveur** *m*, **-euse** *f* [∼'vœːr, ∼'vøːz] drinker; toper; ∼ *d'eau* teetotaller; **buvons** [∼'vɔ̃] *1st p. pl. pres. of* boire 1; **buvoter** F [∼vɔ'te] (1a) *v/t.* sip (*wine*); *v/i.* tipple.

byzantin, e [bizɑ̃'tɛ̃, ∼'tin] Byzantine.

C

C, c [se] *m* C, c.

ça [sa] F *abbr. of cela; c'est* ~*!* that's right!; *et avec* ~*?* anything else?

çà [~] **1.** *adv.* here; hither; ~ *et là* here and there; **2.** *int. (ah)* ~*!* now then!

cabale [ka'bal] *f* cabal; intrigue; clique, faction; **cabaler** [kaba'le] (1a) *v/i.* intrigue; **cabaleur, -euse** [~'lœːr, ~'løːz] **1.** *adj.* intriguing; **2.** *su.* intriguer.

caban [ka'bɑ̃] *m* oilskins *pl.*; dufflecoat.

cabane [ka'ban] *f* hut, shed; cabin; *rabbit:* hutch; *dog:* kennel; **cabanon** [~ba'nɔ̃] *m* small hut; *prison:* cell; *lunatic:* padded cell.

cabaret [kaba'rɛ] *m* night club; † pub(lic house), tavern; **cabaretier** *m*, **-ère** *f* † [~barə'tje, ~'tjeːr] innkeeper; publican.

cabas [ka'bɑ] *m* basket.

cabestan ⊕, ⚓ [kabɛs'tɑ̃] *m* capstan, winch.

cabillau(d) *icht.* [kabi'jo] *m* fresh cod.

cabine [ka'bin] *f* cabin; (~ *téléphonique*) telephone-box, telephonebooth; 👝 (*a.* ~ *d'aiguillage*) signalbox; *cin.* ~ *de projection* projection room; **cabinet** [~bi'nɛ] *m* small room; office; consulting room; practice; 👝 chambers *pl.*; ministry; ~(s *pl.*) (*d'aisances*) water-closet, lavatory; ~ *de groupe* joint practice; ~ *de toilette* dressing-room; ~ (*de travail*) study; *phot.* ~ *noir* dark room.

câble [kɑːbl] *m* cable (*a.* F = *cablegram*); ⚓ ~ *de remorque* hawser; ~ *métallique* wire rope; stranded wire; **câbler** [kɑ'ble] (1a) *v/t.* cable (*a message*); ⚡ wire up; **câblogramme** [~blɔ'gram] *m* cablegram.

caboche [ka'bɔʃ] *f* (hob)nail; ⊕ clout-nail; F head, pate.

cabosse F [ka'bɔs] *f* ⚥ cacao-pod; ⚡ bump, bruise; **cabosser** F [~bɔ'se] (1a) *v/t.* ⚡ bump, bruise; dent.

cabotage ⚓ [kabɔ'taːʒ] *m* coastal navigation; **caboter** [~'te] (1a) *v/i.* coast.

cabotin, e [kabɔ'tɛ̃, ~'tin] **1.** *adj.* theatrical, histrionic, affected; **2.** *su. thea.* ham (actor, *f* actress); *fig.* show-off, play-actor (*f* -actress); **cabotinage** [~ti'naːʒ] *m thea.* hamming; *fig.* showing-off, play-acting; **cabotiner** [~ti'ne] (1a) *v/i. thea.* ham; *fig.* show off, playact.

cabrer [kɑ'bre] (1a) *v/t.* 🐎 elevate; *se* ~ rear (*horse*); 🐎 rear, buck; *fig. se* ~ *contre* jib at, rebel against.

cabri *zo.* [ka'bri] *m* kid; **cabriole** [kabri'ɔl] *f* caper, leap; **cabrioler** [~ɔ'le] (1a) *v/i.* caper; **cabriolet** [~'lɛ] *m mot.* cab(riolet).

cabus [ka'by] *adj./m:* *chou m* ~ headed cabbage.

cacahouète ⚥ [kaka'wɛt] *f*, **cacahuète** ⚥ [~'ɥɛt] *f* peanut.

cacao [kaka'o] *m* ⚥ cacao, ⚡ cocoa; **cacaotier** [~ɔ'tje] *m*, **cacaoyer** [~ɔ'je] *m* cacao-tree.

cacarder [kakar'de] (1a) *v/i.* cackle (*goose*).

cacatoès *orn.* [kakatɔ'ɛs] *m* cockatoo; **cacatois** ⚓ [~'twa] *m* royal (-sail).

cachalot *zo.* [kaʃa'lo] *m* spermwhale, cachalot.

cache [kaʃ] *su./f* hiding-place; *su./m phot.* mask; ⊕ panel, plate; **~cache** [~'kaʃ] *m* hide-and-seek (*a. fig.*); **~col** [~'kɔl] *m/inv.* scarf; **~nez** [~'ne] *m/inv.* muffler; **~poussière** [~pu'sjeːr] *m/inv.* dust-coat.

cacher [ka'ʃe] (1a) *v/t.* hide, conceal; ~ *sa vie* live in retirement; *esprit m caché* reserved person; sly person; *se* ~ hide; **cache-sexe** [kaʃ'seks] *m/inv.* G-string; **cachet** [ka'ʃɛ] *m* seal; stamp; ⚡ trade-mark; mark; F fee; ⚡ cachet; *courir le* ~ give private lessons; **cacheter** [kaʃ'te] (1c) *v/t.* seal; **cachette** [ka'ʃɛt] *f* hiding place, hideout; *en* ~ secretly; by stealth; under the counter (*sale*); **cachot** [~'ʃo] *m* dungeon; ⚡ cell; prison; **cachotterie** [~'tri] *f* mysterious ways *pl.*; *faire des* ~s be secretive; act secretively; **cachottier,**

-ère F [~'tje, ~'tjɛ:r] **1.** *adj.* secretive; **2.** *su.* sly person.

cacique F [ka'sik] *m* candidate who has obtained first place; *fig.* (big) boss, big chief.

caco... [kakɔ] caco...; **~phonique** [~fɔ'nik] cacophonous, discordant.

cactus ♀ [kak'tys] *m*, **cactier** ♀ [~'tje] *m* cactus.

cadastre [ka'dastr] *m* cadastral survey; (public) register of lands; survey.

cadavéreux, -euse [kadave'rø, ~'rø:z] cadaverous, deathlike; deathly pale; **cadavérique** *anat.* [~'rik] cadaveric; *rigidité f* ~ rigor mortis; **cadavre** [ka'dɑ:vr] *m* corpse, *Am. a.* cadaver; *animal:* carcase; *sl.* dead man (= *empty winebottle*).

cadeau [ka'do] *m* present, gift.

cadenas [kad'nɑ] *m* padlock; clasp; ~ *à chiffres* combination-lock.

cadence [ka'dɑ̃:s] *f* cadence (*a.* ♪), rhythm; step; *march:* time; *à la* ~ *de* at the rate of, *fig.* to the tune of.

cadet, -ette [ka'dɛ, ~'dɛt] **1.** *adj.* younger; **2.** *su.* (the) younger, junior; *il est mon* ~ he is my junior (by 3 years, *de 3 ans*), he is younger than I; *su./m* ✕ cadet; *golf:* caddie.

cadran [ka'drɑ] *m* dial; *clock:* face; ~ *solaire* sun-dial; **cadre** [ka:dr] *m usu.* frame; *fig. a.* framework, context; *fig.* setting, surroundings *pl.*; *fig.* scope, limits *pl.*; *personnel:* executive, manager; ✕ officer; *les* ~*s a.* the managerial staff; ~ (*de réception*) *radio:* frame aerial; ~ *orienté radio:* directional aerial; **cadrer** [ka'dre] (1a) *v/i.* tally, agree; fit in.

caduc, -que [ka'dyk] decrepit, decaying; feeble (*voice*); ♈ null, lapsed; ♈ time-barred; ♀ deciduous; **caducité** [~dysi'te] *f* dilapidated state; decrepitude; ♈ nullity; ♈ lapsing; ♀ caducity.

cafard¹ [ka'fa:r] *m zo.* cockroach; F *avoir le* ~ be down in the dumps.

cafard², e [ka'fa:r, ~'fard] **1.** *adj.* sanctimonious; **2.** *su. school:* sneak; *su./m* ✕ *sl.* spy; **cafarder** [~far'de] (1a) *v/i. school:* sneak.

café [ka'fe] **1.** *su./m* coffee; café; ~ *complet* continental breakfast; ~ *crème* white coffee; ~ *nature* (or *noir*) black coffee; **2.** *adj./inv.* coffee-colo(u)red; **~-concert**, *pl.* **~s-con-serts** [~fekɔ'sɛ:r] *m*, F **caf'conc'**

[kaf'kɔ̃:s] *m* café with a cabaret show.

cafetier, -ère [kaf'tje, ~'tjɛ:r] *su.* café-owner; *su./f* coffee-pot; *sl.* head.

cafouillage F [kafu'ja:ʒ] *m* muddle; **cafouiller** F [~'je] (1a) *v/i.* not to work properly, F be on the blink (*machinery etc.*); *fig.* muddle things up, get into a muddle, flounder (*person*); *fig.* get *or* turn into a shambles; **cafouillis** F [~'ji] *m* muddle.

cage [ka:ʒ] *f bird:* cage; hen-coop; ⚠ frame; cover, casing; F prison; ~ *d'ascenseur* lift (*Am.* elevator) shaft; ~ *d'escalier* stair-well; *anat.* ~ *thoracique* chest.

cagne *sl.* [kaɲ] *f school:* class preparing to compete for entrance to the *École normale supérieure.*

cagneux, -euse [ka'nø, ~'nø:z] knock-kneed; **cagnotte** [~'nɔt] *f* pool, kitty.

cagot, e [ka'go, ~'gɔt] **1.** *adj.* sanctimonious; **2.** *su.* bigot; hypocrite; **cagoterie** [kagɔ'tri] *f* cant; **cagotisme** [~'tism] *m* false piety.

cahier [ka'je] *m* paper-book; exercise-book; ♓ defaulters' book; ♰ ~ *des charges* specifications *pl.*

cahin-caha F [kaɛ̃ka'a] *adv.* so-so; middling.

cahot [ka'o] *m vehicle:* jolt, jog; **cahoter** [kaɔ'te] (1a) *vt/i.* jolt along; toss; *vie f cahotée* life of ups and downs; **cahoteux, -euse** [~'tø, ~'tø:z] bumpy (*road*).

cahute [ka'yt] *f* hut; cabin; hovel.

caïd F [ka'id] *m* (big) boss, big chief; gangster boss.

caille *orn* [ka:j] *f* quail.

caillé [kɑ'je] *m* curds *pl.*, curdled milk.

caillebotis [kajbɔ'ti] *m* duck-board(s *pl.*); ♓ grating.

caillebotte [kaj'bɔt] *f* curds *pl.*; **cailler** [kɑ'je] *vt/i.* curdle, clot; congeal (*blood*); *sl.* be cold; *ça caille* it's freezing.

caillette¹ [kɑ'jɛt] *f zo. ruminants:* fourth stomach; *cuis.* rennet.

caillette² F [~] *f* flirt; tart.

caillot [ka'jo] *m* clot.

caillou, *pl.* **-x** [ka'ju] *m* pebble; cobble; **cailloutage** [kaju'ta:ʒ] *m* ⚠ rough-cast, pebble-dash; ⚙ gravel; road-metal; pebble paving; **caillouter** [~'te] (1a) *v/t.* ballast,

metal (a road, a railway-track);
pave with pebbles; **caillouteux,
-euse** [⹁'tø, ⹁'tøːz] stony; pebbly,
shingly (beach); **cailloutis** [⹁'ti] m
gravel; road-metal; pebbled surface; cobbled pavement; rubble.

caisse [kɛs] f case, box; ♱ cash-box;
♱ till; (pay-)desk; thea. pay-box;
♱ fund; ♪, anat. drum; ⊕ body; ✕
sl. prison, cells pl.; ⹁ à eau water-
tank; ♱ ⹁ d'amortissement sinking-
fund; depreciation; ⹁ d'épargne
savings-bank; ⹁ de prêts loan bank;
⹁ enregistreuse cash-register; ∮ ⹁
nationale de l'énergie national grid;
argent m en ⹁ cash in hand; fig.
battre la grosse ⹁ advertize; boost
a product; faire la ⹁ balance the
cash; grosse ⹁ instrument: bass or
big drum; person: bass drummer;
tenir la ⹁ be in charge of the cash;
caissier m, **-ère** f [kɛ'sje, ⹁'sjɛːr]
cashier; treasurer; **caisson** [⹁'sɔ̃] m
box; ⊕ caisson; ✕ ammunition-
waggon; locker; mot. boot; ⚒
bunker.

cajoler [kaʒɔ'le] (1a) v/t. coax,
wheedle; **cajolerie** [⹁ʒɔl'ri] f coaxing, wheedling; **cajoleur, -euse**
[⹁ʒɔ'lœːr, ⹁'løːz] 1. adj. wheedling;
2. su. wheedler.

cal, pl. cals [kal] m callosity; ♀, ⚕
callus.

calamité [kalami'te] f calamity,
disaster; **calamiteux, -euse** [⹁'tø,
⹁'tøːz] calamitous.

calandre [ka'lɑ̃ːdr] f mangle; tex.
calender, roller (a. for paper); mot.
shell; mot. radiator grill; **calandrer**
[⹁lɑ̃'dre] (1a) v/t. mangle; tex. etc.
calender; surface.

calcaire [kal'kɛːr] 1. adj. calcareous;
chalky (soil); hard (water); 2. su./m
limestone; **calcification** ∮ [⹁sifi-
ka'sjɔ̃] f calcification; **calcination**
[⹁sina'sjɔ̃] f calcination; metall.
oxidation; ores: roasting.
calciner [kalsi'ne] (1a) v/t. char;
burn (to cinders or ashes); ⊕ etc.
roast; ⚒ calcine.

calcul [kal'kyl] m reckoning, calcu-
lation; estimate; Ⱥ calculus; Ⱥ
arithmetic; ⚕ calculus, stone; ⹁
biliaire gall-stone; ⹁ mental mental
arithmetic; **calculateur, -trice**
[kalkyla'tœːr, ⹁'tris] 1. adj. scheming; 2. su. person: calculator, reckoner; su./f machine: calculator; **cal-**

culer [⹁'le] (1a) v/t. reckon, calculate; ⹁ de tête work (s.th.) out in one's
head; **calculette** [⹁'lɛt] f pocket or
desk calculator; **calculeux, -euse**
⚕ [⹁'lø, ⹁'løːz] 1. adj. calculous; 2. su.
sufferer from stone.

cale[1] [kal] m hold; quay: slope, slip;
⹁ sèche drydock.

cale[2] [kal] f ⊕ wedge; ⊕, ⚒ chock; ⊕
prop, strut; ⊕ tightening-key; **calé,
e** F [ka'le] clever, bright; difficult,
tough, tricky.

calebasse [kal'bɑːs] f ♀ calabash,
gourd; metall. small ladle; sl. head.

calèche [ka'lɛʃ] f barouche, calash.

caleçon [kal'sɔ̃] m (pair of) under-
pants pl.; ⹁ long long johns pl.; ⹁ de
bain bathing-trunks pl.

calembour [kalɑ̃'buːr] m pun.

calembredaine F [kalɑ̃brə'dɛn] f
nonsense; quibble.

calendrier [kalɑ̃'drje] m calendar;
almanac; ⹁ à éffeuiller tear-off calendar.

cale-pied cycl. [kal'pje] m toe-clip.

calepin [kal'pɛ̃] m notebook.

caler[1] [ka'le] (1a) v/t. ⚓ strike (the
sail); ⚓ house (a mast); v/i. ⚓ draw
water; F climb down.

caler[2] [⹁] (1a) v/t. prop up (a. fig.);
wedge (up), chock (up); ⊕ jam;
mot. stall (an engine); ⊕, ∮ adjust;
F se ⹁ les joues, se les ⹁ have a good
feed; v/i. mot. stall; F idle.

calfat ⚓ [kal'fa] m caulker; **calfater**
[⹁fa'te] (1a) v/t. caulk.

calfeutrer [kalfø'tre] (1a) v/t. stop
up the chinks of (a window etc.);
F se ⹁ shut o.s. up.

calibrage [kali'braːʒ] m tube: cali-
brating; ⊕ ga(u)ging; phot. trimming; **calibre** [⹁'libr] m ✕ calibre
(a. fig.); bore; size; ⊕ tool: ga(u)ge;
template; ⊕ ⹁ pour filetages thread
ga(u)ge; compas m de ⹁ callipers
pl.; **calibrer** [⹁li'bre] (1a) v/t. ⊕
ga(u)ge; calibrate; phot. trim; typ.
cast off. [cup; ♀ calyx; anat. calix.|
calice [ka'lis] m eccl. chalice; fig.⌡

calicot [kali'ko] m tex. calico; sl.
counter-jumper, sales assistant,
Am. sales-clerk.

califourchon [kalifur'ʃɔ̃] adv.: à ⹁
astride.

câlin, e [kɑ'lɛ̃, ⹁'lin] 1. adj. cajoling;
coaxing; caressing, winning (ways);
2. su. wheedler; **câliner** [⹁li'ne] (1a)
v/t. wheedle; caress; pet.

calleux, -euse [ka'lø, ~'lø:z] horny, callous.

calligraphie [kaligra'fi] *f* calligraphy, penmanship.

callosité [kalozi'te] *f* callosity.

calmant, e [kal'mã, ~'mã:t] **1.** *adj.* calming; soothing (*a.* 🎜); **2.** *su./m* 🎜 sedative.

calme¹ [kalm] *m* calm(ness); stillness; *fig.* composure.

calme² [kalm] calm, still, quiet; **calmer** [kal'me] (1a) *v/t.* calm, still, quiet; *fig.* soothe; se ~ calm down.

calomniateur, -trice [kalɔmnja-'tœ:r, ~'tris] **1.** *adj.* slanderous, libellous; **2.** *su.* slanderer, calumniator; **calomnie** [~'ni] *f* calumny, slander, libel; **calomnier** [~'nje] (1o) *v/t.* slander, libel.

calorie *phys.* [kalɔ'ri] *f* calorie; **calorifère** [kalɔri'fɛ:r] **1.** *adj.* heat-conveying; **2.** *su./m* central heating installation; **calorifique** *phys.* [~'fik] calorific, heating; **calorifuge** [~'fy:ʒ] **1.** *adj.* heat-insulating; **2.** *su./m* heat-insulation; ⊕ non-conduction; **calorifugeage** ⊕ [~fy'ʒa:ʒ] *m* heat-insulation; **calorifuger** ⊕ [~fy'ʒe] (1l) *v/t.* insulate.

calot [ka'lo] *m* ⚔ forage-cap; ⊕ small wedge; ⊕ *quarry*: block of stone; *sl.* eye; *ribouler des* ~s be flabbergasted; **calotin** *sl.* [~lɔ'tɛ̃] *m* ardent church-goer; sky-pilot (= *priest*); **calotte** [~'lɔt] *f* skull-cap (*a. eccl.*); ⚔ undress cap; watchcase; F box on the ears; *sl.* clergy; **calotter** [~lɔ'te] (1a) *v/t.* F cuff (*s.o.*); *golf*: top (*the ball*).

calque [kalk] *m* tracing; F copy; **calquer** [kal'ke] (1m) *v/t.* trace (from, *sur*); *needlework*: transfer (*a pattern*); copy; *papier m à* ~ tracing-paper; se ~ *sur q.* copy s.o., model o.s. on s.o.

calumet [kaly'mɛ] *m* 🌿 reed (*of a Red Indian*); *le* ~ *de la paix* the pipe of peace, the calumet.

calvaire [kal'vɛ:r] *m eccl.* stations *pl.* of the Cross; *eccl.* calvary; *fig.* martyrdom; *le* ⚰ (Mount) Calvary.

calvinisme *eccl.* [kalvi'nism] *m* Calvinism.

calvitie [kalvi'si] *f* baldness.

camail *cost.* [ka'ma:j] *m* cape (*a. eccl.*, *a. orn.*), cloak.

camarade [kama'rad] *su.* comrade, fellow, mate, F chum; ~ *de classe*

classmate; **camaraderie** [~ra'dri] *f* comradeship, friendship; clique.

camard, e [ka'ma:r, ~'mard] **1.** *adj.* snub-nosed; **2.** *su./f*: *la* ~e Death.

cambouis [kã'bwi] *m* dirty oil; cart-grease.

cambré, e [kã'bre] bent; cambered, arched; bow-legged; **cambrement** [~brɔ'mã] *m* bending, cambering; **cambrer** [~'bre] (1a) *v/t.* bend; camber; arch; se ~ throw out one's chest; warp (*wood*).

cambriolage [kãbriɔ'la:ʒ] *m* housebreaking; burglary; **cambrioler** [~'le] (1a) *v/t.* break into (*a house*), burgle; **cambrioleur** [~'lœ:r] *m* housebreaker; burglar.

cambrure [kã'bry:r] *f* curve, camber; *foot*: arch.

cambuse [kã'by:z] *f* ⚓ store-room; canteen; *sl.* hovel; low pub(lic house); glory-hole; **cambusier** ⚓ [~by'zje] *m* store-keeper; steward's mate.

came¹ ⊕ [kam] *f* cam; *arbre m à* ~s cam-shaft.

came² *sl.* [~] *f* drug; *sl.* junk; **camé, e** *sl.* [ka'me] *adj.*, *a. su.* drug-addicted (person); *su. sl. a.* junkie.

caméléon *zo.* [kamele'ɔ̃] *m* chameleon.

camélia 🌿 [kame'lja] *m* camelia.

camelot [kam'lo] *m* street hawker; newsvendor; ~ *du roi* young royalist; **camelote** [~'lɔt] *f* cheap goods *pl.*; junk, trash; *de* ~ gimcrack.

caméra [kame'ra] *f* cine-camera.

camérier *eccl.* [kame'rje] *m* chamberlain.

camériste [kame'rist] *f* lady's maid; chamber-maid.

camion [ka'mjɔ̃] *m* waggon; lorry, *Am.* truck; (*a.* ~ *automobile*) motor lorry; ~-**citerne**, *pl.* ~**s-citernes** [~mjɔ̃si'tɛrn] *m lorry*: tanker; ~-**grue**, *pl.* ~**s-grues** [~mjɔ̃'gry] *m* breakdown lorry, *Am.* wrecker; **camionnage** [kamjɔ'na:ʒ] *m* cartage; carting, *Am.* trucking; **camionner** ✝ [~'ne] (1a) *v/t.* cart, carry; truck; **camionette** [~'nɛt] *f* small lorry, *Am.* light truck; **camionneur** [~'nœ:r] *m* lorry-driver, *Am.* truck driver.

camisole [kami'sɔl] *f* sleeved vest; *woman*: dressing jacket; ~ *de force* strait jacket. [mile.⟩

camomille 🌿 [kamɔ'mi:j] *f* camo-⟩

camouflage [kamu'fla:ʒ] *m* disguising; ✕, ⚓ camouflage; **camoufler** [ᴗ'fle] (1a) *v/t.* disguise; ✕, ⚓ camouflage; **camouflet** F [ᴗ'flɛ] *m* insult; snub.

camp [kɑ̃] *m* camp (*a. fig.*); party; *fig.* side; ᴗ *de réfugiés* refugee camp; ᴗ *de vacances* holiday camp; ᴗ *volant* temporary shelter; F *ficher* (*or sl. fouter*) *le* ᴗ clear out; **campagnard, e** [kɑ̃pa'ɲaːr, ᴗ'ɲard] 1. *adj.* country; rustic; 2. *su.* rustic; *su./m* countryman; *su./f* countrywoman; **campagne** [ᴗ'paɲ] *f* open country; countryside; ✕, ⚓, *pol.*, ✝ *etc.* campaign; *à la* ᴗ in the country; *en pleine* ᴗ in the open; **campagnol** *zo.* [ᴗpa'ɲɔl] *m* vole.

campanile △ [kɑ̃pa'nil] *m* belltower; **campanule** ♀ [ᴗ'nyl] *f* campanula.

campé, e [kɑ̃'pe] (*bien* ᴗ) (well) established; well-constructed; wellbuilt; firmly fixed; **campement** ✕ [kɑ̃p'mɑ̃] *m* camping; encampment; camp; camp party; **camper** [kɑ̃'pe] (1a) *vt/i.* encamp; *v/t.* F place; *fig.* arrange; *se* ᴗ *devant etc.* plant o.s. in front of *etc.*; *v/i.* camp; **campeur** *m*, **-euse** *f* [ᴗ'pœːr, -'pøːz] camper; **camping** [ᴗ'piŋ] *m* camping; (*terrain de*) ᴗ camping site; *faire du* ᴗ go camping.

campos F [kɑ̃'po] *m* holiday.

camus, e [ka'my, ᴗ'myːz] snubnosed; pug-nosed.

canadien, -enne [kana'djɛ̃, ᴗ'djɛn] 1. *adj.* Canadian; 2. *su.* ♀ Canadian; *su./f* sheepskin jacket.

canaille F [ka'naːj] 1. *adj.* low, base; cheap; 2. *su./f* bastard; rascal; ✝ rabble.

canal [ka'nal] *m* canal (*a.* ♀, *a. anat.*); channel; ⚓ passage; ⊕ pipe, conduit; ⊕ culvert; △ fluting; *anat.* duct; ⊕ᴗ-*tunnel* underground canal; **canalisation** [ᴗnaliza'sjɔ̃] *f river:* canalization; ⊕ pipeline; ⊕ mains *pl.*

canapé [kana'pe] *m* couch, sofa; *cuis.* canapé, fried slice of bread; ᴗ-**lit**, *pl.* ᴗ**s-lits** [ᴗpe'li] *m* bed-settee.

canard [ka'naːr] *m* duck; drake; F hoax; F false news; sensationalist newspaper, rag; F brandy- *or* coffee-soaked lump of sugar; ♪ wrong note; **canardeau** [kanar'do] *m* duckling; **canarder** [ᴗ'de] (1a) *v/i.* ⚓ pitch; ♪ play *or* sing a wrong note; *v/t.* F snipe

at; **canardière** [ᴗ'djɛːr] *f* duckpond; *duck-shooting:* screen; duckgun; ✕ loop-hole.

canari *orn.* [kana'ri] *m* canary.

canasson *sl. pej.* [kana'sɔ̃] *m* horse; nag.

cancan¹ [kɑ̃'kɑ̃] *m dance:* cancan.

cancan² [kɑ̃'kɑ̃] *m* piece of gossip; ᴗs *pl.* tittle-tattle *sg.*; **cancaner** [kɑ̃ka'ne] (1a) *v/i.* gossip; talk scandal; **cancanier, -ère** [ᴗ'nje, ᴗ'njɛːr] 1. *adj.* tale-bearing; 2. *su. person:* gossip.

cancer [kɑ̃'sɛːr] *m* 🜨 cancer; malignant growth; *astr. le* ♋ Cancer (*a. geog.*), the Crab; **cancéreux, -euse** 🜨 [kɑ̃se'rø, ᴗ'røːz] 1. *adj.* cancerous; 2. *su.* cancer patient; **cancérigène** 🜨 [ᴗri'ʒɛn] carcinogenic, carcinogenous; **cancérologie** 🜨 [ᴗrɔlɔ'ʒi] *f* cancer research; **cancre** [kɑ̃:kr] *m* crab; F dunce, dud.

candeur [kɑ̃'dœːr] *f* artlessness.

candi [kɑ̃'di] 1. *adj./m* candied; 2. *su./m:* ᴗs *pl.* crystallized fruit.

candidat *m*, **e** *f* [kɑ̃di'da, ᴗ'dat] candidate; **candidature** [ᴗda'tyːr] *f* candidature; *poser sa* ᴗ *à* apply for (*a position*).

candide [kɑ̃'did] artless, ingenuous.

cane [kan] *f (female)* duck; **caner** *sl.* [ka'ne] (1a) *v/i.* funk it, chicken out; **caneton** [kan'tɔ̃] *m* duckling.

canette¹ [ka'nɛt] *f orn.* duckling; teal.

canette² [ᴗ] *f* ⊕ faucet; can; bottle; *tex.* spool.

canevas [kan'va] *m* canvas; outline.

caniche *zo.* [ka'niʃ] *m* poodle.

caniculaire [kaniky'lɛːr] sultry; *jours m/pl.* ᴗs dog-days; **canicule** [ᴗ'kyl] *f* dog-days *pl.*; *astr.* dog-star. [knife.]

canif [ka'nif] *m* penknife, pocket-)

canin, e [ka'nɛ̃, ᴗ'nin] 1. *adj.* canine; *exposition f* ᴗe dog-show; *avoir une faim* ᴗe be as hungry as a wolf; *dent f* ᴗe = 2. *su./f* canine (tooth).

caniveau [kani'vo] ⊕ gutter; ⚡ *cables:* conduit; ⚡ main.

canne [kan] *f* ♀ cane, reed; walking-stick; ᴗ *à pêche* fishing rod; ᴗ *à sucre* sugar-cane; *sucre m de* ᴗ cane-sugar; **canneler** [ᴗ'le] (1c) *v/t.* groove; △ flute; corrugate.

cannelle¹ [ka'nɛl] *f* ♀ cinnamon; *fig.* small pieces *pl.*

cannelle² [~] f faucet.
cannelure [kan'ly:r] f groove, channel; ⚘ fluting; corrugation; **canner** [ka'ne] (1a) v/t. cane-bottom; **cannette** [~'nɛt] f see cannelle¹; canette².
cannibale [kani'bal] m cannibal, man-eater.
canon¹ [ka'nɔ̃] m ✕, ⚓ gun, cannon; coll. artillery; key, rifle, watch, etc.: barrel; measuring-glass; sl. glass of wine; ~ à électrons electron gun.
canon² [ka'nɔ̃] m ♀, eccl. canon; **canonial, e**, m/pl. -aux [kanɔ'njal, ~'njo] canonical; of a canon; **canonique** [~'nik] canonical (book, age); F respectable, proper; **canoniser** eccl. [~ni'ze] (1a) v/t. canonize.
canonnade ✕ [kanɔ'nad] f gun-fire; cannonade; **canonner** [~'ne] (1a) v/t. cannonade; batter (a fortress); **canonnier** ✕ [~'nje] m gunner; **canonnière** [~'njɛ:r] f ⚓ gunboat; ⚘ drain-hole; toy: pop-gun.
canot [ka'no] m boat; dinghy; ~ automobile motorboat; ~ de sauvetage lifeboat; ~ glisseur speedboat; ~ pliable folding boat; ~ pneumatique rubber dinghy; **canotage** [kanɔ'ta:ʒ] m rowing, boating, canoeing; faire du ~ row; **canoter** [~'te] (1a) v/i. row; go (in for) boating; **canotier** [~'tje] m boatman; oarsman; cost. straw-hat, boater. [singer, vocalist.)
cantatrice [kɑ̃ta'tris] f (professional)∫
cantharide zo. [kɑ̃ta'rid] f Spanish fly; poudre f de ~s cantharides pl.
cantine [kɑ̃'tin] f ✕ restaurant: canteen; soup-kitchen; equipment-case; **cantinier, -ère** [~ti'nje, ~'njɛ:r] su. canteen-attendant; su./m canteen-manager; su./f canteen-manageress.
cantique eccl. [kɑ̃'tik] m canticle; hymn; sacred song; bibl. le ♌ des ♌s the Song of Songs.
canton [kɑ̃'tɔ̃] m admin. canton, district; 🚂, road: section.
cantonade thea. [kɑ̃tɔ'nad] f wings pl.; thea. parler à la ~ speak to s.o. behind the scenes, speak off; crier à la ~ shout for everybody to hear.
cantonnement [kɑ̃tɔn'mɑ̃] m ✕ quarters pl.; ✕ billeting; **cantonner** [kɑ̃tɔ'ne] (1a) v/t. ✕ billet, quarter; v/i. ✕ be billeted; **cantonnier** [~'nje] m district road-surveyor; roadman; 🚂 permanent-way man.

canule [ka'nyl] f 💉 nozzle; cannula; sl. bore.
caoutchouc [kau'tʃu] m india-rubber; mackintosh, raincoat; mot. etc. tyre; ~s pl. galoshes, Am. rubber overshoes; ~ durci vulcanite; ~ mousse foam rubber; gant m de ~ rubber-glove.
cap [kap] m geog. cape, headland; ⚓, ✕ head; de pied en ~ from head to foot; mettre le ~ sur head for; ⚓, ✕ suivre le ~ fixé be on one's course.
capable [ka'pabl] capable, able; **capacité** [~pasi'te] f capacity (a. ♎); ability; ♎ legal competence.
cape [kap] f cape, cloak; hood; cigar: outer leaf; ⚓ être à la ~ be hove to; rire sous ~ laugh up one's sleeve.
capeline [kap'lin] f sun-bonnet; wide-brimmed hat.
capillaire [kapil'lɛ:r] 1. adj. capillary; artiste m ~ tonsorial artist; 2. su./m ♀ maidenhair fern; **capillarité** phys. [~lari'te] f capillary attraction, capillarity.
capilotade cuis. [kapilɔ'tad] f hash; fig. en ~ bruised; F mettre q. en ~ beat s.o. to a pulp.
capitaine [kapi'tɛn] m captain (a. fig.); ⚓ a. master; ✕, gang, team: leader; sp. ~ d'équipe team captain.
capital, e, m/pl. -aux [kapi'tal, ~'to] 1. adj. capital; fundamental, essential; deadly (sin); peine f ~e capital punishment, death penalty; 2. su./m ✝ capital, assets pl.; ~ d'apport initial capital; ~ d'exploitation working capital; ✝ ~ et intérêt principal and interest; su./f geog. capital; typ. capital (letter); **capitaliser** [~tali'ze] (1a) v/t. ✝ capitalize; v/i. save; **capitalisme** [~ta'lism] m capitalism.
capitation [kapita'sjɔ̃] f poll-tax.
capiteux, -euse [kapi'tø, ~'tø:z] heady (wine); sensuous, F sexy.
capiton ✝ [kapi'tɔ̃] m silk waste; **capitonner** [~tɔ'ne] (1a) v/t. upholster; cost. quilt.
capitulaire [kapity'lɛ:r] capitular(y); **capitulation** [~la'sjɔ̃] f capitulation, surrender; **capituler** [~'le] (1a) v/i. ✕ surrender; capitulate; fig. yield; fig. compromise (with, avec) (one's conscience).
capoc ✝ [ka'pɔk] m kapok.
capon, -onne [ka'pɔ̃, ~'pɔn] 1. adj.

cowardly, afraid; **2.** *su.* coward;
school: sneak.

caporal [kapɔ'ral] *m* ✖ corporal; F
tobacco: shag; ✖ ~ *chef* lance-ser-
geant; **caporalisme** [⌣ra'lism] *m*
narrow militarism.

capot [ka'po] **1.** *su./m mot.* bonnet,
Am. hood; ✝ cowling; *cards*: capot;
⚓ companion(-hatch); **2.** *adj./inv.*
fig. nonplussed; **capotage** [⌣pɔ-
'ta:ʒ] *m mot.* hooding; ✝, *mot.* overturning; ✝ noseover; **capote** [⌣'pɔt]
f greatcoat; bonnet; *mot.* hood, *Am.*
convertible top; *chimney*: cowl; *sl.* ~
anglaise French letter (= *contraceptive*); **capoter** [⌣pɔ'te] (1a) *v/i.*
capsize, overturn; *fig.* fail, founder.

câpre ♀ [kɑ:pr] *f* caper.

capricant, e ♒ [kapri'kɑ̃, ⌣'kɑ̃:t]
bounding; caprisant (*pulse*).

caprice [ka'pris] *m* caprice, whim;
impulse; *geol.* offshoot; ♪ caprice,
capriccio; **capricieux, -euse** [⌣-
pri'sjø, ⌣'sjø:z] capricious; whimsical; wayward (*child*).

capricorne [kapri'kɔrn] *m* capricorn beetle; *astr. le* ♑ Capricorn,
the Goat.

capsule [kap'syl] *f* capsule; *bottle*:
cap, crown-cork; ✖ percussion-
cap; ⚡ *à* ~ dished (*electrode*); **capsuler** [⌣sy'le] (1a) *v/t.* seal, cap (*a
bottle*).

captage [kap'ta:ʒ] *m* water-catch-
ment; collecting (*of waters*); ⚡
picking up; ⊕ recovery (*of by-products*); **captateur** *m*, **-trice** *f* 🔓
[⌣ta'tœr, ⌣'tris] inveigler; **captation** [⌣ta'sjɔ̃] *f* 🔓 inveiglement; ⚡
collecting; collection; *tel.*, *teleph.*
tapping; **capter** [⌣'te] (1a) *v/t.* ⚡
collect; catch (*waters*); ⊕ recover
(*waste*); *radio*: pick up (*a station*);
tel., *teleph.* tap, intercept; captivate
(*s.o.*); win by insidious means; **capteur** [⌣'tœr] *m* ⚓ captor; ⊕ collector; ~ *solaire* solar energy collector; **captieux, -euse** [⌣'sjø, ⌣'sjø:z]
fallacious, specious.

captif, -ve [kap'tif, ⌣'ti:v] **1.** *adj.*
captive; **2.** *su.* prisoner; **captiver**
[⌣ti've] (1a) *v/t.* captivate, charm;
master (*one's feelings*); **captivité**
[⌣tivi'te] *f* captivity.

capture [kap'ty:r] *f* capture;
seizure; ⚓ *a.* prize; **capturer** [⌣ty-
're] (1a) *v/t.* capture; ⚓ seize;
arrest.

capuchon [kapy'ʃɔ̃] *m cost.* hood;
eccl. cowl; *lamp*, *pen*, *etc.*: cap.

capucin [kapy'sɛ̃] *m* Capuchin friar;
capucinade F [⌣si'nad] *f* dull sermon *or* address; **capucine** [⌣'sin] *f*
Capuchin nun; ♀ nasturtium; ⚛
drip-stone; *vehicle*: hood; *rifle*:
band.

caque [kak] *f* keg; herring-barrel;
caquer [ka'ke] (1m) *v/t.* cure and
barrel (*herrings*).

caquet [ka'ke] *m*, **caquetage** [kak-
'ta:ʒ] *m hens*: cackling; F gossip,
chatter; *rabattre le caquet de q.*
show s.o. up; make s.o. sing small;
caqueter [⌣'te] (1c) *v/i.* cackle
(*hen*); F gossip, chatter; gabble;
caqueteur *m*, **-euse** *f* [⌣'tœ:r, ⌣-
'tø:z] *person*: gossip.

car¹ [ka:r] *m* 🚌, *tram*: car; *police*:
van; motor-coach.

car² [⌣] *cj.* for, because.

carabe *zo.* [ka'rab] *m* carabid
(beetle).

carabin *sl.* [kara'bɛ̃] *m* medic.

carabine ✖ [kara'bin] *f* rifle; carbine; **carabiné, e** [⌣bi'ne] sharp,
violent; ⚓ strong; **carabinier**
[⌣bi'nje] *m* † carabineer; *Italy*: soldier of the police militia, constable;
Spain: customs officer.

caracole [kara'kɔl] *f horsemanship*:
caracole, half-turn; *fig.* caper; **caracoler** [⌣kɔ'le] (1a) *v/i. horsemanship*:
caracole; *fig.* caper, gambol.

caractère [karak'tɛ:r] *m* character;
nature; temperament; feature,
characteristic; letter; *typ.* type; *mauvais* ~ bad temper; **caractériel,
-elle** [⌣te'rjɛl] **1.** *adj.* (of) character;
(emotionally) disturbed; **2.** *su.* problem child, (emotionally) disturbed
child; **caractériser** [⌣teri'ze] (1a)
v/t. characterize; *se* ~ *par* be distinguished by; **caractéristique**
[⌣teris'tik] **1.** *adj.* characteristic (of,
de), distinctive; typical (of, de); **2.**
su./f characteristic.

carafe [ka'raf] *f* decanter; water-
bottle; carafe; ✝ *avoir la* ~ make a
forced landing; *rester en* ~ be left in
the lurch; **carafon** [⌣ra'fɔ̃] *m* small
decanter *or* carafe; *wine*: icepail.

carambolage [karãbɔ'la:ʒ] *m* billiards*: cannon, *Am.* carom; *mot.*
crash, pileup; **caramboler** [⌣bɔ'le]
(1a) *v/i.* cannon, *Am.* carom; *v/t.* hit,
crash into; *se* ~ crash (into each

other), collide; **carambouilleur** [~bu'jœ:r] *m* swindler (*who buys things on credit and sells or pawns them at once*).

caramel [kara'mɛl] *m* caramel, burnt sugar; gravy-browning; **caraméliser** [~meli'ze] (1a) *v/t.* caramel(ize) (*sugar*); mix caramel with.

carapater *sl.* [karapa'te] (1a) *v/t.*: se ~ decamp, scram.

carat [ka'ra] *m* carat.

caravane [kara'van] *f* caravan; *mot.* caravan, *Am.* trailer; **caravanier** [~va'nje] *m* caravaneer; **caravansérail** [~vãse'ra:j] *m* caravanserai.

carbonate 🜕 [karbɔ'nat] *m* carbonate; *sl.* washing soda; **carbonater** 🜕 [~bɔna'te] (1a) *v/t.* carbonate; **carbone** [~'bɔn] *m* 🜕 carbon; *papier m* ~ carbon paper; **carbonique** 🜕 [~bɔ'nik] carbonic; **carboniser** [~bɔni'ze] (1a) *v/t.* carbonize, char; *fig.* burn to death.

carburant [karby'rã] *m* motor fuel; **carburateur** *mot.* [~byra'tœ:r] *m* carburettor; **carbure** 🜕 [~'by:r] *m* carbide; **carburé, e** [~by're] carburetted; vaporized (*fuel*).

carcan [kar'kã] *m hist.* iron collar; *fig.* yoke, restraint.

carcasse [kar'kas] *f* carcass; frame(-work); 🜕 shell, skeleton.

carcinome 🟊 [karsi'nɔm] *m* carcinoma.

cardage *tex.* [kar'da:ʒ] *m wool:* carding; *cloth:* teaseling, raising.

cardamine ♀ [karda'min] *f* cardamine; ~ *des prés* mayflower.

cardan ⊕ [kar'dã] *m* universal joint; *arbre m à* ♀ Cardan shaft.

carde [kard] *f* ♀ bur, teasel; ♀ chard; *tex.* carding-brush; ⊕ ~ *métallique* wire-brush; **carder** *tex.* [kar'de] (1a) *v/t.* card, comb (*wool*); teasel (*cloth*); **cardeuse** *tex.* [~'dø:z] *f* carding-machine.

cardiaque 🟊 [kar'djak] **1.** *adj.* cardiac; *crise f* ~ heart attack; *être* ~ have a heart condition; **2.** *su.* sufferer from heart trouble, F heart-case.

cardinal, e *m/pl.* **-aux** [kardi'nal, ~'no] *adj., a. su./m* cardinal.

carême [ka'rɛm] *m* Lent; fast; *comme mars en* ~ without fail; **~prenant**, *pl.* **~s-prenants** [~rɛmprɑ'nɑ̃] *m* Shrovetide; *person:* Shrovetide reveller.

carénage [kare'na:ʒ] *m* ⚓ careening;

careening-place; docking; ✈, *mot.* stream-lining.

carence [ka'rɑ̃:s] *f* 🜕, ✝ insolvency; defaulting; 🟊, *a. fig.* deficiency (of, in *de*); incompetence, inadequacy; *maladie f par* ~ deficiency disease.

carène [ka'rɛn] *f* ⚓ hull; ✈, *mot.* stream-lined body; *pompe f de* ~ bilge-pump; **caréner** [~re'ne] (1f) *v/t.* ⚓ careen; ✈, *mot.* stream-line.

caresse [ka'rɛs] *f* caress; endearment; **caresser** [~rɛ'se] (1a) *v/t.* caress, fondle; *fig.* cherish (*hopes*).

cargaison ⚓ [karge'zɔ̃] *f* cargo; shipping (*of cargo*); **cargo** ⚓ [~'go] *m* cargo-boat, tramp; **carguer** ⚓ [~'ge] (1m) *v/t.* take in (*sail*).

caricature [karika'ty:r] *f* caricature; cartoon; *fig.* travesty.

carie [ka'ri] *f* 🟊 caries; *trees:* blight; ✍ *corn:* stinking smut; **carier** [~'rje] (1o) *v/i. a. se* ~ rot, decay.

carillon [kari'jɔ̃] *m* carillon, chime(s *pl.*); peal; ♪ tubular bells *pl.*; F row; **carillonner** [~jɔ'ne] (1a) *vt/i.* chime; sound; *fête f carillonnée* High Festival; **carillonneur** [~jɔ'nœ:r] *m* carillon player; bell-ringer; change-ringer.

carlin, e [kar'lɛ̃, ~'lin] *adj., a. su.* pug.

carlingue [kar'lɛ̃:g] *f* ⚓ keelson; ✈ fuselage; F cockpit.

carme [karm] *m* Carmelite, White Friar; ~ *déchaussé* discalced Carmelite; **carmélite** [karme'lit] *f nun:* Carmelite.

carmin [kar'mɛ̃] *su./m, a. adj./inv.* carmine.

carminatif, -ve 🟊 [karmina'tif, ~'ti:v] *adj., a. su./m* carminative.

carnage [kar'na:ʒ] *m* slaughter; **carnassier, -ère** [karna'sje, ~'sjɛ:r] **1.** *adj.* carnivorous; **2.** *su./f* game bag; *su./m* carnivore; **carnation** [~'sjɔ̃] *f* flesh tint(s *pl.*).

carnaval, *pl.* **-als** [karna'val] *m* carnival; King Carnival.

carne *sl.* [karn] *f* tough meat; old horse; bad-tempered person; wastrel; slut.

carnet [kar'nɛ] *m* notebook; (*cheque-, ticket-, etc.*) book; ~ *de bal* card; ✝ ~ *de commandes* order book.

carnier [kar'nje] *m* game-bag.

carnivore [karni'vɔ:r] **1.** *adj.* carnivorous; **2.** *su./m*: ~s *pl.* carnivora.

carotte [ka'rɔt] **1.** *su./f* ♀, ✍ carrot;

tobacco: plug; *sl.* trick, swindle; **2.** *adj./inv.* carroty, ginger; **carotter** F [ʌrɔˈte] (1a) *v/t.* steal, F pinch; cheat, F do.

caroube ♀ [kaˈrub] *f* carob; **caroubier** ♀ [ʌruˈbje] *m* carob-tree.

carpe[1] *anat.* [karp] *m* carpus, wrist.

carpe[2] *icht.* [karp] *f* carp; **carpeau** *icht.* [karˈpo] *m* young carp.

carpette[1] [karˈpɛt] *f* rug.

carpette[2] *icht.* [ʌ] *f* young carp.

carquois [karˈkwa] *m* quiver.

carre [kɑːr] *f plank*: thickness; *hat*: crown; *boot*: square toe; **carré, e** [kɑˈre] **1.** *adj.* square; squared (*stone*); *fig.* plain, blunt; **2.** *su./m* square; ✗ patch; *staircase*: landing; *anat.* quadrate muscle; *cuis.* loin; ⚓ ~ des officiers ward-room; mess-room; *su./f sl.* room, digs *pl.*; **carreau** [ʌˈro] *m* small square; *flooring*: tile, flag; floor; (window-)pane; *cards*: diamonds *sg.*; ✗ *mine*: head; (tailor's) goose; † bolt; *à* ~*x* checked (*material*); F *se garder (or tenir) à* ~ take every precaution; **carrefour** [karˈfur] *m* crossroads *pl.*; intersection; square (*in town*).

carrelage [kɑrˈlaːʒ] *m* tiling; **carreler** [ʌˈle] (1c) *v/t.* tile, pave with tiles; square (*paper*); checker; **carrelet** [ʌˈlɛ] *m* square dipping-net; ⊕ large needle; sewing-needle (*of boatmen*); **carreleur** [ʌˈlœːr] *m* tile-layer.

carrément [kɑreˈmɑ̃] *adv.* square (-ly); *fig.* bluntly; straight (out); **carrer** [kɑˈre] (1a) *v/t.* square; *se* ~ swagger; loll (*in a chair*).

carrier [kɑˈrje] *m* quarryman.

carrière[1] [kɑˈrjɛːr] *f* quarry.

carrière[2] [ʌ] *f* course; career; *donner* ~ *à* give free rein to.

carriériste [karjeˈrist] *su.* careerist.

carriole [kɑˈrjɔl] *f* light cart.

carrossable [kɑrɔˈsabl] carriageable, passable (*for vehicles*); **carrosse** [ʌˈrɔs] *m* † coach; *fig.* rouler ~ live in style; **carrosserie** *mot.* [ʌrɔsˈri] *f* body, coachwork.

carrousel [karuˈsɛl] *m* merry-go-round; ✗ tattoo.

carrure [kɑˈryːr] *f* breadth of shoulders.

cartable [karˈtabl] *m* satchel; writing-pad; cardboard portfolio.

carte [kart] *f* card; *restaurant*: menu; map, ⚓ chart; ticket; *fig.* ~ *blanche*

full powers *pl.*; a free hand, a blank cheque; ✗ ~ *d'accès au bord* boarding pass; ~ *d'alimentation* ration book; ~ *de lecteur* reader's ticket; ~ *d'identité* identity card; *mot.* ~ *grise* car licence; ~ *postale* postcard; *mot.* ~ *verte* insurance document, *Br.* green card; *battre les* ~*s* shuffle (the cards); *faire les* ~*s* deal (the cards); *jouer* ~*s sur table* be above-board.

cartel [karˈtɛl] *m* ⏰ ring, cartel, combine; *pol.* coalition.

carte-lettre, *pl.* **cartes-lettres** [kartəˈlɛtr] *f* letter-card.

cartellisation ⊕ [karteliza'sjɔ̃] *f* cartelization.

carter [karˈtɛːr] *m mot.* crank-case; *bicycle*: gear-case.

cartilage [kartiˈlaːʒ] *m anat.* cartilage, F gristle; **cartilagineux, -euse** [ʌlaʒiˈnø, ʌˈnøːz] *anat.* cartilaginous, F gristly; ♀ hard.

cartographe [kartɔˈgraf] *m* map-maker, chart-maker; cartographer; **cartographie** [ʌgraˈfi] *f* cartography; mapping; map collection; **cartomancie** [ʌmɑ̃ˈsi] *f* cartomancy, fortune-telling (by cards).

carton [karˈtɔ̃] *m* cardboard; pasteboard; cardboard box; cardboard portfolio; *art*: cartoon; *phot.* mount; *typ.* cancel; *geog.* inset map; ...*en* ~ *a.* paper...; ~ *bitumé* roofing felt; ~ *ondulé* corrugated cardboard; *fig.* *homme m de* ~ man of straw; **cartonner** [ʌtɔˈne] (1a) *v/t.* bind in boards, case; *cartonné* hardback (*book*); **cartonnerie** [ʌtɔnˈri] *f* cardboard manufactory; cardboard trade; **cartonnier** [ʌtɔˈnje] *m* (cardboard) file; **carton-pâte**, *pl.* **cartons-pâtes** [ʌtɔ̃ˈpaːt] *m* papier mâché.

cartothèque ⏰ [kartɔˈtɛk] *f* card index.

cartouche[1] [karˈtuʃ] *m* ♌, *art*: cartouche.

cartouche[2] [karˈtuʃ] *f* ✗ cartridge; refill (*of ball-pen*); **cartouchière** [ʌtuˈʃjɛːr] *f* ✗ cartridge-pouch; ~ *d'infirmier* first-aid case.

carvi ♀ [karˈvi] *m* caraway.

cas [kɑ] *m* case (*a.* ⚕ = *disease*, *patient*; *a. gramm.*); instance, circumstance; affair; ~ *limite* borderline case; *au* (*or dans le*) ~ *où* (*cond.*) in case *or* in the event of (*ger.*); *au* ~ *où* (*cond.*), *en* ~ *que* (*sbj.*) in case ... should (*inf.*); *dans tous les* ~, *en* *tout* ~ in any case; *en aucun* ~ in no circumstances; *en ce* ~ if so; *faire grand* ~ *de* think highly of (*s.th.*); *faire peu de* ~ *de* set little value on; *le* ~ *échéant* if needed; *selon le* ~ as the case may be.

casanier, -ère [kaza'nje, ~'njɛ:r] *adj., a. su.* stay-at-home.

casaque [ka'zak] *f* coat, jacket; jumper (*of woman*); *F tourner* ~ turn one's coat; **casaquin** [~za'kɛ̃] *m* dressing-jacket; jumper.

cascade [kas'kad] *f* waterfall, falls *pl.*, cascade; *F* gay time; *F* piece of reckless folly; **cascader** [~ka'de] (1a) *v/i.* cascade; **cascadeur** [~ka-'dœ:r] *m* stuntman; acrobat.

case [ka:z] *f* hut, small house; compartment; pigeon-hole; *chessboard*: square; ~ *postale* Post Office box, P.O. box.

caséeux, -euse [kaze'ø, ~'ø:z] cheesy, caseous.

casemate ✠ [kaz'mat] *f* casemate.

caser [ka'ze] (1a) *v/t.* F put; † file (*papers*); marry off; find a job for; put (*s.o.*) up; *se* ~ settle down; find a home (with, *chez*).

caserne ✠ [ka'zɛrn] *f* barracks *pl.*; **caserner** ✠ [~zɛr'ne] (1a) *v/t.* quarter, billet; *v/i.* live in barracks.

casier [ka'zje] *m* compartment; locker; pigeon-hole; filing cabinet; rack, bin; ✠ ~ *judiciaire* police record; *avoir un* ~ *judiciaire vierge* have a clean record.

casino [kazi'no] *m* casino.

casque [kask] *m* helmet; ~*s pl.* d'écoute ear-phones; ~ *blindé* crash helmet; **casqué, e** [kas'ke] helmeted; **casquer** F [~'ke] (1m) *v/i.* foot the bill; *v/t.* fork out (*a sum*); **casquette** [~'kɛt] *f* (peaked) cap.

cassable [ka'sabl] breakable; **cassant, e** [~'sã, ~'sã:t] brittle (*china etc.*); crisp (*biscuit*); curt, short (*manner, voice*); *F* knife-edge (*crease*); *metall.* short; *sl.* ce n'est pas ~, ça n'a rien de ~ it's not exactly tiring work; *F* it's not so hot, it's nothing to write home about; **cassation** [~sa'sjɔ̃] *f* ✠ reversing, quashing, setting aside; ✠ reduction to the ranks; ✠ *cour f de* ~ Supreme Court of Appeal.

casse¹ [ka:s] *f* breakage, damage; *fig.* break; *F* row.

casse² [~] *f typ.* case; ⊕ ladle; *metall.*

crucible; *typ.* *haut* (*bas*) *de* ~ upper (lower) case.

casse³ [~] *f* ♀ cassia; senna.

casse...: ~-*cou* [kas'ku] *m/inv.* dangerous spot; ~-*croûte* [~'krut] *m/inv.* snack; snack-bar; ~-*noisettes* [~nwa'zɛt] *m/inv.*, ~-*noix* [~'nwa] *m/inv.* nutcrackers *pl.*; ~-*pieds* F [~'pje] 1. *su/inv.* bore, F pain in the neck; 2. *adj./inv.* boring; ~-*pipe(s)* F [~'pip] *m/inv.* war; front.

casser [ka'se] (1a) *v/t.* break, smash; crack; F punch (*s.o.'s* nose, *le nez à q.*); ✠ reduce to the ranks; ✠ set aside, quash, reverse; F ~ *sa pipe* kick the bucket (= *die*); *v/i. a. se* ~ break, give way; wear out (*person*).

casserole [kas'rɔl] *f* saucepan, stewpan.

casse-tête [kas'tɛt] *m/inv.* life-preserver (= *loaded stick*); club, truncheon; *fig.* puzzle, head-ache; *fig.* din, uproar.

cassette [ka'sɛt] *f* (jewel-)casket; case; money-box; cassette.

casseur, -euse [ka'sœ:r, ~'sø:z] 1. *adj.* destructive, aggressive (*look etc.*); 2. *su.* breaker; *cars*: scrap dealer; F ~ *d'assiettes* truculent person.

cassis¹ [ka'sis] *m* ♀ black currant; *sl.* head.

cassis² ⊕ [ka'si] *m* cross-drain.

cassonade [kasɔ'nad] *f* brown sugar.

cassure [ka'sy:r] *f* break; fragment.

caste [kast] *f* caste; *esprit m de* ~ class consciousness.

castel † [kas'tɛl] *m* (small) castle.

castillan, e [kasti'jã, ~'jan] *adj., a. su.* ♀ Castilian.

castor *zo.*, ♣ [kas'tɔ:r] *m* beaver.

casuel, -elle [ka'zɥɛl] 1. *adj.* accidental, fortuitous, casual; *gramm.* case-...; ✠ contingent; 2. *su./m* perquisites *pl.*

casuistique [kazɥis'tik] *f* casuistry (*a. fig.*).

cataclysme [kata'klism] *m* cataclysm, disaster; **catalepsie** ✿ [~lep'si] *f* catalepsy; **catalogue** [~-'lɔg] *m* catalogue, list; *faire le* ~ *de* run over the list of; **cataloguer** [~lɔ'ge] (1m) *v/t.* catalogue, list; **catalyser** [~li'ze] (1a) *v/t.* catalyse; **catalyseur** ✿ [~li'zœ:r] *m* catalyst; **cataphote** *mot.* [~'fɔt] *m road:* cat's eye, *Am.* reflector; **cataplasme** ✿ [~'plasm] *m* poultice; **catapulter**

[⁓pyl'te] catapult; **cataracte** [⁓'rakt]
m cataract (*a.* ✵).

catarrhe ✵ [ka'taːr] *m* catarrh; F ⁓
nasal cold in the head; **catarrheux,**
-euse [⁓ta'rø, ⁓'røːz] catarrhous.

catastrophe [katas'trɔf] *f* catastrophe; disaster; **catastrophique**
[⁓trɔ'fik] catastrophic.

catch *sp.* [katʃ] *m* catch-as-catch-can.

catéchiser [kateʃi'ze] (1a) *v/t. eccl.*
catechize; *fig.* coach; lecture; reason
with (*s.o.*).

catégorie [katego'ri] *f* category,
class; **catégoriser** [⁓ri'ze] (1a) *v/t.*
classify.

caténaire ⚡ [kate'nɛːr] 1. *adj.* catenary; 2. *su./f* trolley-wire.

cathédrale [kate'dral] *f* cathedral.

cathode ⚡ [ka'tɔd] *f* cathode; **cathodique** ⚡ [⁓tɔ'dik] cathodic; *tube m à
rayons* ⁓s cathode-ray tube.

catholique [katɔ'lik] 1. *adj.* (Roman)
Catholic; F *pas* (*très or bien*) ⁓ (a bit)
fishy *or* shady, not (quite) straight; 2.
su. (Roman) Catholic.

catimini F [katimi'ni] *adv.*: en ⁓
stealthily; on the sly.

catin F [ka'tɛ̃] *f* prostitute.

catir *tex.* [ka'tiːr] (2a) *v/t.* press,
gloss.

cauchemar [koʃ'maːr] *m* night-
mare; *fig.* pet aversion.

causal, e [ko'zal] causal, causative.

cause [koːz] *f* cause, motive; reason; ⚖ case, trial; *à* ⁓ *de* on account of; *fig.* en ⁓ at stake; involved; *mettre en* ⁓ question (*s.th.*);
pour ⁓ for a good reason; ⚖ *sans* ⁓
briefless (*barrister*).

causer¹ [ko'ze] (1a) *v/t.* cause.

causer² [ko'ze] (1a) *v/i.* talk (*a. fig.* =
blab), chat; **causerie** [koz'ri] *f* talk,
chat; **causette** F [ko'zɛt] *f* little
chat; **causeur, -euse** [⁓'zœːr, ⁓-
'zøːz] 1. *adj.* talkative, chatty; 2. *su.*
talker; *su./f* settee for two.

causticité [kostisi'te] *f* 🜍 causticity; *fig.* caustic humo(u)r; biting
quality (*of a remark etc.*); **caustique**
[⁓'tik] 1. *adj.* 🜍, *a. fig.* caustic; 2.
su./m 🜍 caustic; *su./f opt.* caustic.

cautèle [ko'tɛl] *f* cunning, craftiness;
cauteleux, -euse [kot'lø, ⁓'løːz]
cunning, crafty; wary.

cautère ✵ [ko'tɛːr] *m* cautery; **cautériser** ✵ [⁓teri'ze] (1a) *v/t.* cauterize.

caution [ko'sjɔ̃] *f* security, guaran-

tee; ⚖ bail; ✝ deposit; *être* (*or se
porter*) ⁓ go bail; ✝ stand surety;
fournir ⁓ produce bail; *sujet à* ⁓
unreliable, unconfirmed; **cautionnement** [⁓sjɔn'mã] *m* surety; **cautionner** [⁓sjɔ'ne] (1a) *v/t.* stand
surety for (*s.o.*); ⚖ go bail for; *fig.*
support, back.

cavalcade [kaval'kad] *f* cavalcade;
procession; **cavale** *poet.* [⁓'val] *f*
mare; **cavaler** *sl.* [⁓va'le] (1a) *v/i.*
run; *v/t.* pester (*s.o.*); se ⁓ do a
bunk (= *run away*); **cavalerie**
[⁓val'ri] *f* cavalry; **cavalier, -ère**
[⁓va'lje, ⁓'ljɛːr] 1. *su.* rider; *su./m*
horseman; *dancing*: partner; *chess*:
knight; ⚔ trooper; *su./f* horsewoman; 2. *adj.* haughty; off-hand;
jaunty; ⚡ *perspective f,* ⁓ère iso-
metric projection.

cave [kaːv] 1. *su./f* cellar (*a. fig.*);
vault; ⊕ *coke-oven*: wharf; *cards*:
stake(s *pl.*); 2. *adj.* hollow; *anat.*
veine f ⁓ vena cava; **caveau** [ka'vo]
m cellar, vault; burial vault; **caver**
[⁓'ve] (1a) *v/t.* hollow (out), undermine; put up (*money at cards*); *v/i.*
put up a sum of money; **caverne**
[⁓'vɛrn] *f* cave, cavern; (*thieves'*)
den; ✵ cavity; **caverneux, -euse**
[⁓vɛr'nø, ⁓'nøːz] cavernous; *fig.*
hollow, sepulchral (*voice*); **caviste**
[⁓'vist] *m* cellarman; **cavité** [⁓vi'te]
f cavity, hollow.

ce¹ [s(ə)] *dem./pron./n* it; this; that;
these, those; ce qui (*or que*)
what, which; *c'est pourquoi* therefore; *c'est que* the truth is that;
c'est moi it is I, F it's me.

ce² (*before vowel or h mute* **cet**) *m,*
cette *f*, **ces** *pl.* [sə, sɛt, se] *dem./adj.*
this, that, *pl.* these, those; *ce ...-ci*
this; *ce ...-là* that.

céans [se'ã] *adv.* F here(in); *maître
m de* ⁓ master of the house.

ceci [sə'si] *dem./pron./n* this; ⁓
étant this being the case *or* so.

cécité [sesi'te] *f* blindness.

cédant, e ✝, ⚖ [se'dã, ⁓'dãːt]
1. *su.* assignor, grantor, transferor;
2. *adj.* assigning, granting, trans-
ferring; **céder** [⁓'de] (1f) *vt/i.* give
up, yield; surrender; *v/t.* 🜍 give
off; transfer; sell (*a lease*); ⁓ *le
pas à* give way to; ⁓ *le passage*
give way; *le* ⁓ *à q.* be inferior *or*
second to s.o. (in, *en*).

cédille *gramm.* [se'diːj] *f* cedilla.

cèdre [sɛːdr] *m tree or wood:* cedar.
cédule [se'dyl] *f* script, note; *admin.
taxes:* schedule; summons *sg.*
cégétiste [seʒe'tist] *m* trade-union-
ist (= *member of the C.G.T.*).
ceindre [sɛ̃ːdr] (4m) *v/t.* (*de,* with)
gird; bind; surround; wreathe.
ceinture [sɛ̃'tyːr] *f* belt (*a. fig. of
fortifications, hills, etc.*); girdle;
waist; waistband; enclosure, circle;
~ (*de sécurité*) seat *or* safety belt; ~ *de
sauvetage* lifebelt; ~ *verte* green belt;
🚢 *ligne f de* ~ circle line; **ceinturer**
[sɛ̃ty're] (1a) *v/t.* seize (*s.o.*) round
the waist; *fig.* surround; *foot.* collar
(*s.o.*) low; **ceinturier** [~'rje] *m* belt-
maker; **ceinturon** [~'rɔ̃] *m* waist-
belt, sword-belt.
cela [s(ə)la] **1.** *dem./pron./n* that;
à ~ *près* with that exception; ~ *fait*
thereupon; *c'est* ~ that's right,
that's it; *comment* ~? how?; *et ...
avec tout* ~? and what about ...?;
2. *su./m psych.* id.
céladon [sela'dɔ̃] *su./m, a. adj./inv.*
celadon, parrot-green.
célébration [selebra'sjɔ̃] *f* celebra-
tion; **célèbre** [~'lɛbr] famous, celebrated; **célébrer** [sele'bre] (1f)
v/t. celebrate; extol; **célébrité** [~-
bri'te] *f* celebrity.
celer [sə'le] (1d) *v/t.* conceal.
céleri ❦ [sel'ri] *m* celery; *pied m de*
~ head of celery.
célérité [seleri'te] *f* speed, rapidity,
swiftness.
céleste [se'lɛst] heavenly, celestial;
bleu ~ sky-blue; ♪ *voix f* ~ *organ:*
vox angelica.
célibat [seli'ba] *m* celibacy; **célibataire** [~ba'tɛːr] **1.** *adj.* single; cel-
ibate; **2.** *su./m* bachelor; *su./f* unmarried woman; single girl; spinster.
celle [sɛl] *f see* celui. [cupboard.）
cellier [sɛ'lje] *m* store-room, store-）
cellulaire [sɛly'lɛːr] cellular; *régime
m* ~ solitary confinement; *voiture f*
~ police-van, F Black Maria; **cellule** [~'lyl] *f* cell; F den; *⚡* ~ *au
sélénium* selenium cell; ✈ ~ *d'a-
vion* air-frame; *telev.* ~ *photo-élec-
trique* electric eye; **celluleux,
-euse** [sɛly'lø, ~'løːz] cell(at)ed;
celluloïd(e) ⊕ [~lɔ'id] *m* celluloid;
cellulose ❦, ⳨ [~'loːz] *f* cellulose.
celte [sɛlt] **1.** *adj.* Celtic; **2.** *su.* ♀
Celt; **celtique** [sɛl'tik] **1.** *adj.*
Celtic; **2.** *su./m ling.* Celtic.

celui *m,* **celle** *f,* **ceux** *m/pl.,* **celles**
f/pl. [sə'lɥi, sɛl, sø, sɛl] *dem./pron.*
he (*acc.* him); she (*acc.* her); the
one, that; *pl.* they (*acc.* them);
those; ~*ci etc.* [sɔlɥi'si *etc.*] the
latter; this one; ~*là etc.* [sɔlɥi'la
etc.] the former; that one.
cément *metall.* [se'mɑ̃] *m* cement
(*a. ⚙*), powdered carbon; **cémenter** [~mɑ̃'te] (1a) *v/t. metall.* case-
harden (*steel*); cement (*an armour-
plate*).
cendre [sɑ̃ːdr] *f* cinders *pl.,* ash;
mercredi m des ♀*s* Ash Wednesday;
cendré, e [sɑ̃'dre] **1.** *adj.* ash-grey,
ashy; **2.** *su./f sp.* cinders *pl.*; ⚙
lead ashes *pl.*; **cendreux, -euse**
[~'drø, ~'drøːz] ash-grey, ashy;
gritty; *metall.* brittle (*steel*); **cendrier** [~dri'e] *m* ash-pan; 🚢 ash-
box; ash-tray.
Cendrillon [sɑ̃dri'jɔ̃] *f* Cinderella
(*a. fig.*); *fig.* stay-at-home; F drudge.
Cène [sɛn] *f the* Last Supper; *protestant service: the* Lord's Supper;
the Holy Communion.
censé, e [sɑ̃'se] *:* être ~ *faire qch.* be
supposed to do s.th.; *nul n'est* ~
ignorer la loi ignorance of the law is
no excuse; **censément** [~se'mɑ̃]
adv. supposedly; ostensibly; to all
intents and purposes; **censeur**
[~'sœːr] *m* censor; *lycée:* vice-prin-
cipal; *univ.* proctor; **censurable** †
[~sy'rabl] open to censure; **censure**
[~'syːr] *f* censure; *cin., journ., etc.*
censorship; **censurer** [~sy're] (1a)
v/t. censure; censor.
cent [sɑ̃] **1.** *adj./num.* (a *or* one)
hundred; **2.** *su./m (inv. when followed by another number)* hundred;
cinq pour ~ five per cent; *je vous le
donne en* ~ I give you a hundred
guesses; *trois* ~ *dix* three hundred
and ten; *trois* ~*s ans* three hundred
years; **centaine** [sɑ̃'tɛn] *f* (about)
a hundred.
centaure *myth.* [sɑ̃'tɔːr] *m* centaur.
centenaire [sɑ̃t'nɛːr] **1.** *adj.* a hundred years old; *fig.* ancient, venerable; **2.** *su./m* centenary; *su. person:*
centenarian; **centésimal, e,** *m/pl.*
-aux [sɑ̃tezi'mal, ~'mo] centesimal;
thermomètre m ~ centigrade thermometer.
centi... [sɑ̃ti] centi...; **centiare** [sɑ̃-
'tjaːr] *m measure:* one square metre
(*approx.* 1 1/5 *square yards*); **cen-**

tième [ˌˈtjɛm] **1.** *adj./num., a. su., a. su./m fraction:* hundredth; **2.** *su./f thea.* hundredth performance; **centigrade** [ˌtiˈgrad] centigrade; **centime** [ˌˈtim] *m* ¹/₁₀₀ *of a franc;* **centimètre** [ˌtiˈmɛtr] *m measure:* (*approx.*) ²/₅ inch; tape-measure.

central, e *m/pl.* **-aux** [sɑtral, ˌˈtro] **1.** *adj.* central; **2.** *su./m* telephone-exchange; call-station; *su./f ⚡ (∼ électrique)* powerhouse; power station (*Am.* plant); *⚡ ∼e hydro-électrique* hydro-electric generating station; *∼e nucléaire* (*or atomique*) nuclear power station (*Am.* plant); **centraliser** [ˌtraliˈze] (1a) *v/t. a. se ∼* centralize; **centre** [sɑ̃tr] *m* centre, *Am.* center; middle; *foot. ∼s pl.* insides; *meteor. ∼ de dépression* storm centre; *phys. ∼ de gravitation* (*or d'attraction*) centre of attraction; **centrer** [sɑ̃ˈtre] (1a) *v/t.* centre, *Am.* center; adjust; **centrifuge** [sɑtriˈfy:ʒ] centrifugal; *essoreuse f ∼* rotary dryer; **centripète** [ˌˈpɛt] centripetal; **centriste** *pol.* [sɑ̃ˈtrist] *adj., a. su.* centrist.

centuple [sɑ̃ˈtypl] *su./m, a. adj.* hundredfold; **centupler** [ˌtyˈple] (1a) *vt/i.* increase a hundredfold.

cep *⚘* [sɛp] *m* vine-stock; vine-plant.

cèpe *⚘* [∼] *m* flap mushroom.

cependant [səpɑ̃ˈdɑ̃] **1.** *adv.* meanwhile; **2.** *cj.* however, nevertheless, yet.

céramique [seraˈmik] **1.** *adj.* ceramic; **2.** *su./f* ceramics *pl.*, pottery; **céramiste** [∼ˈmist] *su.* potter.

cérat *⚕* [seˈra] *m* cerate, ointment. **Cerbère** [sɛrˈbɛːr] *m myth., a. fig.* Cerberus.

cerceau [sɛrˈso] *m* hoop; *⚕* cradle (*over bed*); **cercle** [sɛrkl] *m* circle (*a. fig.*), ring (*a. ⊕*); *barrel:* hoop; dial; ring. company, group; *fig.* sphere, range; *geog. ∼ polaire* polar circle; *en ∼s* in the wood (*wine*); *♉ quart m de ∼* quadrant; **cercler** [sɛrˈkle] (1a) *v/t.* encircle, ring; hoop; put a tyre on (*a wheel*).

cercueil [sɛrˈkœːj] *m* coffin; *∼ en plomb* (leaden) shell.

céréale *⚘* [sereˈal] *su./f, a. adj.* cereal.

cérébral, e, *m/pl.* **-aux** [sereˈbral, ∼ˈbro] cerebral, brain…; *fatigue f ∼e* brain-fag.

cérémonial, *pl.* **-als** [seremɔˈnjal] *m* ceremonial; **cérémonie** [ˌˈni] *f* ceremony (*a. fig.*), pomp; formality; *sans ∼* informal(ly *adv.*); **cérémonieux, -euse** [ˌˈnjø, ∼-ˈnjøːz] ceremonious, formal.

cerf [sɛːr] *zo.* stag, hart; *cuis.* venison.

cerfeuil *⚘* [sɛrˈfœːj] *m* chervil. **cerf-volant,** *pl.* **cerfs-volants** [sɛrvɔˈlɑ̃] *m zo.* stag-beetle; (paper) kite.

cerise [səˈriːz] **1.** *su./f ⚘* cherry; *sl.* bad luck; **2.** *adj./inv.* cherry-red; **cerisette** [sɔriˈzɛt] *f* dried cherry; *⚘* winter-cherry; **cerisier** [ˌˈzje] *m* cherry-tree; cherry-wood.

cerne [sɛrn] *m tree:* (age-)ring; ring, circle (*round eyes, wound, etc.*); **cerneau** [sɛrˈno] *m* green walnut; **cerner** [ˌˈne] (1a) *v/t.* encircle, surround; hem in; ring (*a tree etc.*); *fig.* delimit, define (*a problem etc.*); shell (*nuts*); *avoir les yeux cernés* have rings under one's eyes.

certain, e [sɛrˈtɛ̃, ∼ˈtɛn] **1.** *adj.* certain, sure; positive, definite; (*before noun*) one; some; **2.** *pron.* some, certain; **certes** [sɛrt] *adv.* indeed; **certificat** [sɛrtifiˈka] *m* certificate (*a. ⚘*); testimonial; *∼ de bonne vie et mœurs* certificate of good character; *∼ d'origine* dog *etc.*: pedigree; **certification** [ˌfikaˈsjɔ̃] *f* certification; *signature:* witnessing; **certifier** [ˌˈfje] (1o) *v/t.* certify, attest, assure; witness (*a signature*); **certitude** [ˌˈtyd] *f* certainty.

cérumen [seryˈmɛn] *m* ear-wax.

céruse [seˈry:z] *f* white lead; **cérusite** [ˌryˈzit] *f* cerusite.

cerveau [sɛrˈvo] *m* brain; *fig.* mind; *fig.* mastermind; *∼ brûlé* hothead; *rhume m de ∼* cold in the head.

cervelas *cuis.* [sɛrvɔˈla] *m* saveloy.

cervelet *anat.* [sɛrvɔˈlɛ] *m* cerebellum; **cervelle** *anat., cuis.* [∼ˈvɛl] *f* brains *pl.*; *brûler la ∼ à q.* blow s.o.'s brains out; *se creuser la ∼* rack one's brains; *fig. une ∼ de lièvre* a memory like a sieve.

ces [se] *pl. of* ce³.

césarienne *⚕* [sesaˈrjɛn] *adj./f:* (*opération f ∼*) Caesarean (operation).

cessation [sesaˈsjɔ̃] *f* cessation, stoppage, suspension; breach (*of relations*); **cesse** [sɛs] *f: n'avoir pas de ∼ que* not to rest until; *sans ∼* continually; continuously, constantly; **cesser** [sɛ'se] (1a) *vt/i.* cease; leave off; *v/i.: faire ~* put a stop to; **cessez-le-feu** [~selə'fø] *m/inv.* ceasefire; **cessible** 🏛 [~'sibl] transferable; assignable; **cession** [~'sjɔ̃] *f* 🏛 transfer, assignment; ✝ *shares:* delivery; **cessionnaire** ✝ [~sjɔ'nɛːr] *m* transferee, assignee; *bill:* holder.

c'est-à-dire [sɛta'diːr] *cj.* that is to say, i.e.; in other words; F ~ *que* well, actually.

césure [se'zyːr] *f* caesura.

cet *m*, **cette** *f* [sɛt] *see* ce².

cétacé, e zo. [seta'se] **1.** *adj.* cetaceous; cetacean; **2.** *su./m* cetacean.

ceux [sø] *m/pl. see* celui.

chabler [ʃa'ble] (1a) *v/t.* ⊕ hoist (*a load*); ⚓ tow (*a boat*); 🎋 beat (*a walnut-tree*). [Burgundy).⟩

chablis [ʃa'bli] *m* Chablis (= *white*)⟩

chabot *icht.* [ʃa'bo] *m* bullhead, miller's thumb; chub.

chacal, *pl.* **-als** zo. [ʃa'kal] *m* jackal.

chacun, e [ʃa'kœ̃, ~'kyn] *pron./indef.* each (one); everybody.

chafouin, e [ʃa'fwɛ̃, ~'fwin] sly, toxy; sly-looking.

chagrin¹, e [ʃa'grɛ̃, ~'grin] **1.** *su./m* grief, sorrow; trouble; annoyance; **2.** *adj.* sorry; sad; troubled (at, de); distressed (at, de); peevish.

chagrin² [ʃa'grɛ̃] *m* (*a. peau f de ~*) *leather:* shagreen.

chagriner¹ [ʃagri'ne] (1a) *v/t.* grieve, distress; annoy; *se ~* fret.

chagriner² [~] (1a) *v/t.* grain (*leather*).

chahut F [ʃa'y] *m* uproar, row; rag; **chahuter** F [~y'te] (1a) *v/i.* kick up a row; *sl.* boo; *v/t.* rag (*s.o.*); give (*s.o.*) the bird; boo (*s.o.*).

chai [ʃɛ] *m* wine and spirit store.

chaîne [ʃɛn] *f* chain; link(s *pl.*); fetter; necklace; *fig.* sequence, train (*of ideas*); *tex.* warp; ⚓ chain-boom; geog. mountains: range; *mot.* **~s** *pl.* antidérapantes anti-skid chains; ⊕ *travail m à la ~* assembly line work, work on the conveyor belt; **chaîner** [ʃɛ'ne] (1b) *v/t.* △, *surv.* chain; △ tie; **chaînette** [~'nɛt] *f* small chain; ♪ catenary; *point m de ~* chain-stitch; **chaînon** [~'nɔ̃] *m* chain: link; geog. mountains: secondary range.

chair [ʃɛːr] *f* flesh; meat; *fruit:* pulp; *fig. ~ de poule* goose-flesh.

chaire [~] *f* eccl., *a. univ.* chair; eccl. throne; eccl. pulpit; rostrum; tribune.

chaise [ʃɛːz] *f* chair, seat; *hist.* (*a. ~ à porteurs*) sedan-chair; *~ de poste* post-chaise; *~ longue* couch, chaise longue.

chaland¹ [ʃa'lã] *m* lighter, barge.

chaland² *m*, **e** *f* † [ʃa'lã, ~'lã:d] customer (*a. fig.*), purchaser.

chalcographie [kalkɔgra'fi] *f* engraving on metal; engraving studio.

châle [ʃɑːl] *m* shawl.

chalet [ʃa'lɛ] *m* chalet; country cottage; *~ de nécessité* public convenience.

chaleur [ʃa'lœːr] *f* heat (*a. of animals*), warmth; ardo(u)r, zeal; ⊕ *~ blanche* white heat; **chaleureux, -euse** [~lœ'rø, ~'røːz] warm; *fig.* ardent; cordial, hearty (*welcome etc.*); glowing (*colour, terms*).

châlit [ʃa'li] *m* bedstead.

challenge *sp.* [ʃa'lã:ʒ] *m* challenge.

chaloupe ⚓ [ʃa'lup] *f* launch, long-boat.

chalumeau [ʃaly'mo] *m* drinking-straw; ♪, ⊕ pipe; ⊕ blow-lamp.

chalut [ʃa'ly] *m* trawl; drag-net; **chalutier** ⚓ [~ly'tje] *m* person, *boat:* trawler.

chamailler F [ʃamɑ'je] (1a) *v/i.* squabble with; *se ~* squabble (with, avec); be at loggerheads, bicker (with, avec); **chamaillerie** [~maj-'ri] *f* squabble, brawl, scuffle; **chamailleur, -euse** [~mɑ'jœːr, -'jøz] **1.** *adj.* quarrelsome; **2.** *su.* squabbler.

chamarrer [ʃama're] (1a) *v/t.* bedeck; *fig.* embroider; **chamarrure** [~'ryːr] *f* (*tawdry*) decoration.

chambard F [ʃã'bar] *m*, **chambardement** F [~bardə'mã] *m* upheaval, upset; **chambarder** F [~bar'de] (1a) *v/t.* rifle (*a room*); smash up, upset (*a. fig.*).

chambellan [ʃãbɛl'lã] *m* chamberlain.

chambranle △ [ʃã'brãːl] *m* frame; *~ de cheminée* mantelpiece.

chambre [ʃã:br] *f* (*bed*)room; chamber (*a. pol.*, ✝, ⊕); 🏛 division; ⚓ cabin; *mot. ~ à air* inner tube; *~ à un lit* (*deux lits*) single (double) room; *~ d'amis* guest *or* spare room; ✝ *~ de commerce* chamber of commerce; *pol.* ♀ *des députés* House of Commons, *Am.* House of Representatives, *France:* Chamber of Deputies; ♻ ~ *des machines* engineroom; *phot.* ~ *noire* dark room; ~ *sur la cour (rue)* back (front) room; *garder la* ~ be confined to one's room; ♪ *musique f de* ~ chamber music; ⊕ *ouvrier m en* ~ homeworker; garret-craftsman; *fig. stratégiste m en* ~ armchair strategist; **chambrée** [ʃɑ̃'bre] *f* roomful; ✄ barrack-room; *thea.* house; *thea.* takings *pl.*; **chambrer** [~'bre] (1a) *v/t.* lock up in a room; bring (*wine*) to room temperature; **chambrière** [~'brjɛːr] *f* † chambermaid; long whip; *truck etc.:* drag.

chameau [ʃa'mo] *m zo.* camel; 🚂 shunting engine; *sl.* dirty dog *m*, bitch *f*; **chamelier** [~mə'lje] *m* camel-driver; **chamelle** *zo.* [~'mɛl] *f* she-camel.

chamois *zo.* [ʃa'mwa] *m* chamois; chamois *or* shammy leather; *gants m/pl. de* ~ wash-leather gloves; **chamoiser** [~mwa'ze] (1a) *v/t.* chamois, dress (*leather*).

champ [ʃɑ̃] *m* field (*a. fig.*); open country; ground; space; *fig.* range; ⊕ side, edge; ~ *d'activité* scope *or* field of activity; *sp.* ~ *de courses* racecourse, race-track; ~ *de repos* churchyard; ~ *visuel* field of vision; *à tout bout de* ~ the whole time, at every end and turn; *à travers* ~s across country; ⊕ *de* ~ on edge, edgewise.

champagne [ʃɑ̃'paɲ] *su./m* champagne; *su./f: fine* ~ liqueur brandy. **champenois, e** [ʃɑ̃pə'nwa, ~'nwaːz] of Champagne.

champêtre [ʃɑ̃'pɛːtr] rural, rustic.

champignon [ʃɑ̃pi'ɲɔ̃] *m* ♀ mushroom; 🚂 *rail:* head; F *mot.* accelerator pedal; F *mot. appuyer sur le* ~ step on¬ the gas; **champignonnière** [~ɲɔ'njɛːr] *f* mushroom-bed.

champion *m*, -**onne** *f* [ʃɑ̃'pjɔ̃, ~'pjɔn] *sp., fig.* champion; *fig.* supporter; ~ *du monde* world champion; **championnat** [~pjɔ'na] *m* championship.

chançard, e [ʃɑ̃'saːr, ~'sard] **1.** *adj.* lucky; **2.** *su.* lucky person; **chance** [ʃɑ̃ːs] *f* luck, fortune; chance; ~s *pl. égales* equal opportunities *or* chances; *bonne* ~! good luck; *par* ~ by good fortune; *les* ~s *sont contre lui* the odds are against him.

chanceler [ʃɑ̃s'le] (1c) *v/i.* reel, stagger, totter; falter.

chancelier [ʃɑ̃sə'lje] *m* chancellor; *pol. embassy:* secretary; **chancelière** [~sə'ljɛːr] *f* chancellor's wife; foot-muff; **chancellerie** [~sɛl'ri] *f* chancellery.   [risky; lucky.] **chanceux, -euse** [ʃɑ̃'sø, ~'søːz] **chancir** [ʃɑ̃'siːr] (2a) *v/i. a. se* ~ go mo(u)ldy; **chancissure** [~si'syːr] *f* mo(u)ld, mildew.

chancre [ʃɑ̃:kr] *m* 🩺 ulcer; 🌿 F, *a.* ♀ canker; **chancreux, -euse** [ʃɑ̃'krø, ~'krøːz] 🩺 ulcerous; cankerous (*growth*); cankered (*organ*).

chandail [ʃɑ̃'daːj] *m* sweater.

Chandeleur *eccl.* [ʃɑ̃d'lœːr] *f: la* ~ Candlemas; **chandelier** [ʃɑ̃də'lje] *m* candlestick; *person:* chandler; ⊕ boiler: pedestal; **chandelle** [~'dɛl] *f* candle; *cricket, tennis:* skyer, lob; ♠ stay, prop; *à la* ~ by candlelight; *fig. en voir trente-six* ~s see stars; *fig. le jeu n'en vaut pas la* ~ the game is not worth the candle; **chandellerie** [~dɛl'ri] *f* candleworks *usu. sg.*

chanfrein[1] [ʃɑ̃'frɛ̃] *m* blaze (*on a horse's forehead*); horse etc.: forehead.

chanfrein[2] [ʃɑ̃'frɛ̃] *m* bevelled edge; **chanfreiner** ⊕ [~frɛ'ne] (1a) *v/t.* bevel, chamfer.

change [ʃɑ̃:ʒ] *m* ✝ exchange; *hunt.* wrong scent; F false scent; *fig. donner le* ~ *à q.* put s.o. off, sidetrack s.o.; **changeable** [ʃɑ̃'ʒabl] changeable; exchangeable; **changeant, e** [~'ʒɑ̃, ~'ʒɑ̃:t] changing; changeable, variable; unsettled (*weather*); **changement** [ʃɑ̃ʒ'mɑ̃] *m* change, alteration; *mot.* ~ *de vitesse* gear-change, *Am.* gearshift; ~ *de voie* points *pl.*; **changer** [ʃɑ̃'ʒe] (1l) *v/t.* change; exchange (for, *contre*); alter; *se* ~ change (one's clothes); *se* ~ *en* change *or* turn into; *v/i.* change, alter (s.th., *de qch.*); ~ *de train* change (trains); **changeur** [~'ʒœːr] *m* money-changer.

chanoine *eccl.* [ʃa'nwan] *m* canon; **chanoinesse** *eccl.* [~nwa'nɛs] *f* canoness.

chanson [ʃɑ̃'sɔ̃] *f* song; † ~s *pl.* nonsense; **chansonner** [ʃɑ̃sɔ'ne] (1a) *v/t.* write satirical songs about (s.o.); **chansonnette** [~'nɛt] *f* comic song; **chansonnier, -ère** [~'nje, ~'njɛːr] *su.* singer; *su./m* songbook.

chant[1] [ʃɑ̃] *m* ♪ singing; song; *eccl.*
chant; canto; melody; *au* ~ *du coq* at
cock-crow; ~ *de Noël* Christmas
carol.

chant[2] ⊕ [~] *m* edge, side; *de* ~, *sur* ~
on edge, edgewise.

chantage [ʃɑ̃'ta:ʒ] *m* blackmail.

chantepleure [ʃɑ̃tə'plœːr] *f* wine
funnel; colander; watering-can with
a long spout; *cask*: tap; ⚠ *gutter*:
spout; **chanter** [ʃɑ̃'te] (1a) *v/t.* sing;
celebrate; ~ *victoire sur* crow over;
iro. que me chantez-vous là? that's a
fine story!; *v/i.* sing; creak (*door*);
sizzle (*butter*); crow (*cock*); *faire* ~ *q.*
blackmail s.o.; F *si ça vous chante* if it
suits you.

chanterelle[1] [ʃɑ̃'trɛl] *f* ♪ violin: E-
string; decoy-bird; bird-call.

chanterelle[2] ⚘ [~] *f* *mushroom*:
cantharellus.

chanteur *m*, -**euse** *f* [ʃɑ̃'tœːr, ~'tøːz]
singer; *maître m* ~ *hist.* mastersinger;
F blackmailer.

chantier [ʃɑ̃'tje] *m* building site;
(*timber- etc.*) yard; workyard, site; F
mess; *traffic sign*: roadworks; *sur le* ~
in hand.

chantonner [ʃɑ̃tɔ'ne] (1a) *vt/i.* hum.

chantourner ⊕ [ʃɑ̃tur'ne] (1a) *v/t.*
jig-saw; ⊕ *scie f à* ~ bow saw, jig-saw.

chantre [ʃɑ̃:tr] *m* *eccl.* cantor; *poet.*
singer, poet.

chanvre [ʃɑ̃:vr] *m* hemp; cannabis;
chanvrier, -**ère** [ʃɑ̃vri'e, ~'ɛːr] 1. *su.*
hemp-grower; 2. *adj.* hemp-...

chaos [ka'o] *m* chaos, confusion;
chaotique [~o'tik] chaotic.

chaparder F [ʃapar'de] (1a) *v/t.*
scrounge, filch, lift.

chape [ʃap] *f* *eccl.* cope; covering,
layer; *cuis.* dish cover; ⊕ D-joint;
mot. tyre: tread; *mot.* patch (*on tyre*);
⚠ *bridge*: coping; ⊕ *roller*: flange;
pulley-block: strap; **chapeau** [ʃa'po] *m* hat; ⚠ *chimney*:
cowl; ⊕, *a. pen*: cap; ~! well done!,
hats off!; ♪ ~ *chinois* Chinese bells
pl.; ~ *haut de forme* top hat; ~ *melon*
bowler; F *travailler du* ~ talk through
one's hat.

chapelain [ʃa'plɛ̃] *m* chaplain.

chapelet [ʃa'plɛ] *m* rosary; ✝ *beads*,
onions: string; *fig.* string, series; ✗
bombs: stick; **chapelier**, -**ère**
[~pə'lje, ~'ljɛːr] 1. *adj.* hat-...; 2. *su.*
hatter, *Am.* milliner; *su./f* Saratoga
trunk.

chapelle [ʃa'pɛl] *f* chapel; ~ *ardente*
chapel of rest.

chapellerie [ʃapɛl'ri] *f* hat-trade;
hat-shop; **chapelure** *cuis.* [~'plyːr]
f bread crumbs *pl.*

chaperon [ʃa'prɔ̃] *m* hood; ⚠ *wall*:
coping; *roof*: cap-stone; chaperon;
le petit ♀ *rouge* Little Red Riding
Hood; **chaperonner** [~prɔ'ne] (1a)
v/t. hood (*a falcon*); chaperon (*s.o.*);
⚠ put a coping on (*a wall*).

chapiteau [ʃapi'to] *m* ✝ capital;
windmill etc.: cap; *circus*: big top.

chapitre [ʃa'pitr] *m* chapter (*a. eccl.*);
heading, subject; **chapitrer** F [~pi-
'tre] (1a) *v/t.* read (*s.o.*) a lecture,
reprimand.

chapon [ʃa'põ] *m* capon; **chaponner**
[~pɔ'ne] (1a) *v/t.* caponize.

chaque [ʃak] *adj.* each, every.

char [ʃar] *m* waggon; ~ *à bancs* char-
a-banc(s *pl.*); ✗ ~ *blindé* armo(u)red
car; ✗ ~ *d'assaut* tank; ✗ ~ *de
combat* light-armo(u)red car; ♀ *de
l'État* Ship of State; ~ *de triomphe*
triumphal car; ~ *funèbre* hearse.

charabia [ʃara'bja] *m* gibberish.

charade [ʃa'rad] *f* charade.

charançon *zo.* [ʃarɑ̃'sɔ̃] *m* weevil.

charbon [ʃar'bɔ̃] *m* coal; (*a.* ~ *de bois*)
charcoal; ⚘ carbon; 🌿 blight; an-
thrax; ⚘ carbuncle; *fig.* être sur des
~s *ardents* be on tenterhooks; **char-
bonnage** ✗ [~bɔ'na:ʒ] *m* coal
mining; colliery; bunkering; **char-
bonner** [~bɔ'ne] (1a) *v/t.* char, carbonize; *cuis.* burn; sketch *or* blacken
with charcoal; *v/i.* ⚓ coal (*ship*);
charbonnerie [~bɔn'ri] *f* coal
depot; **charbonnier**, -**ère** [~bɔ'nje,
~'njɛːr] 1. *adj.* coal-...; charcoal-...; 2.
su./m coal-man; coal-merchant;
coal-hole; ⚓ collier; ~ *est maître chez
lui* a(n English)man's home is his
castle; *su./f* coal-scuttle; charcoal
kiln; *orn.* great tit; ⚓ coal lighter.

charcuter [ʃarky'te] (1a) *v/t.* cut
(*meat*) into small pieces; F mangle;
🌿 F carve, operate clumsily upon
(*a patient*); **charcuterie** [~'tri] *f*
pork-butcher's shop *or* trade *or*
meat; delicatessen; **charcutier** *m*,
-**ère** *f* [~'tje, ~'tjɛːr] pork-butcher;
F sawbones *sg.* (= *surgeon*).

chardon [ʃar'dɔ̃] *m* thistle; **chardonneret** *orn.* [~dɔn'rɛ] *m* gold-
finch.

charge [ʃarʒ] *f* load, burden; ⚓

loading; ⊕, ⚞⚟, ✂, ✕ *arms*: charge; cost; post, office; responsibility; exaggeration, caricature, *thea.* overacting; ✕ ~ *payante* pay load; ⊕ ~ *utile* useful load; *à* ~ *de* |*revanche* on condition of reciprocity; *être à la* ~ *de* be dependent on *or* depending upon; *femme f de* ~ housekeeper; *pas m de* ~ *marching*: double time; **chargé, e** [ʃar'ʒe] **1.** *adj.* loaded, laden (with, *de*); full (of, *de*); heavy (with, *de*); full, busy (*day*, *schedule*); ✒ coated, furry (*tongue*); troubled, guilty (*conscience*); overloaded, overladen (*a. fig.*); overelaborate (*style etc.*); ~ *de a.* in charge of; **2.** *su./m*: *pol.* ~ *d'affaires* chargé d'affaires, ambassador's deputy; *univ.* ~ *de cours* reader, senior lecturer; **chargement** [~ʒə'mɑ̃] *m* load; ⚓ lading; ⚓ cargo; ✂ charging; **charger** [~'ʒe] (11) *v/t.* (*de*, with) load, burden (*a. fig.*); charge (*a.* ✕, ⚞⚟, ✂); entrust; *post*: register; *thea.* overact; ✈ inflate (*an account*); ~ *q. de coups* drub s.o., belabo(u)r s.o.; se ~ become overcast (*sky*); become coated (*tongue*); *se* ~ *de* take care *or* charge of, see to; se ~ *de* (*inf.*) undertake to (*inf.*), take it upon o.s. to (*inf.*); **chargeur** [~'ʒœːr] *m* loader, ⚓ shipper; stoker; ✂ charger.

chariot [ʃa'rjo] *m* waggon; cart, trolley; ⚓ cradle; ⊕ *crane*: crab; *typewriter*: carriage; *camera*: baseboard; *astr. le grand* ♀ Charles's Wain.

charitable [ʃari'tabl] charitable (to, towards *envers*); **charité** [~'te] *f* charity, love; alms(-giving) *sg.*

charivari [ʃariva'ri] *m* din, noise, hullabaloo.

charlatan *m*, **e** *f* [ʃarla'tɑ̃, ~'tan] charlatan, quack; **charlatanisme** [~ta'nism] charlatanism.

charlotte *cuis.* [ʃar'lɔt] *f* apple charlotte; trifle.

charmant, e [ʃar'mɑ̃, ~'mɑ̃ːt] charming, delightful.

charme[1] ♀ [ʃarm] *m* hornbeam.

charme[2] [ʃarm] *m* charm (*a. fig.*); spell; **charmer** [ʃar'me] (1a) *v/t.* charm (*a. fig.*); delight; **charmeur, -euse** [~'mœːr, ~'møːz] **1.** *adj.* charming; **2.** *su.* charmer.

charmille [ʃar'miːj] *f* hedge; arbo(u)r.

charnel, -elle [ʃar'nɛl] carnal;

sensual; **charnier** [~'nje] *m* charnel-house (*a. fig.*).

charnière [ʃar'njɛːr] *f* hinge; ⊕ ~ *universelle* univeral joint.

charnu, e [ʃar'ny] fleshy.

charogne [ʃa'rɔɲ] *f* carrion; *sl.* *woman*: slut; *man*: scoundrel.

charpente [ʃar'pɑ̃ːt] *f* framework (*a. fig.*); timber-work, steel-work; *house*, *ship*, *etc.*: skeleton; **charpenter** [ʃarpɑ̃'te] (1a) *v/t.* frame (*a. fig.*); **charpenterie** [~'tri] *f* carpentry; carpenter's (shop); timber-yard; **charpentier** [~'tje] *m* carpenter; ~ *de navires* ship-\ **charpie** ✒ [ʃar'pi] *f* lint. [wright.⎰

charretée [ʃar'te] *f* cartload; F *fig. une* ~ *de* loads of, piles of; **charretier** [~'tje] *m* carter; **charrette** [ʃa'rɛt] *f* cart; ~ *à bras* handcart, pushcart, barrow; **charriage** [~'rja:ʒ] *m* carriage; *sl.* swindling; exaggeration, chaffing; **charrier** [~'rje] (1o) *v/t.* cart, carry; *sl.* swindle; make fun of; *v/i.* exaggerate; *sans* ~ joking apart; **charroi** [~'rwa] *m* carriage, cartage; ✕ † ~*s pl.* transport *sg.*; **charron** [~'rɔ̃] *m* wheelwright; cartwright; **charroyeur** [~rwa'jœːr] *m* carter, carrier.

charrue [ʃa'ry] *f* plough, *Am.* plow; *fig. mettre la* ~ *devant les bœufs* put the cart before the horse.

charte [ʃart] *f* charter; deed; *hist. la Grande* ≈ Magna C(h)arta; *École f des* ~*s* School of Pal(a)eography; ~-**partie**, *pl.* ~*s*-**parties** [ʃartəpar'ti] *f* charterparty.

chartreux, -euse [ʃar'trø, ~'trøːz] **1.** *adj.* Carthusian; **2.** *su.* Carthusian; *su./f* Carthusian monastery; *liqueur*: Chartreuse.

chas [ʃa] *m* *needle*: eye.

chasse [ʃas] *f* hunt(ing); (*a.* ~ *au tir*) shooting; game, bag; shooting-season; hunting-ground; ⊕ *wheels*: play; ⊕ flush; ~ *à courre* (stag-) hunting; ~ *d'eau W.C.*: flush, lavatory chain.

châsse [ʃɑːs] *f* eccl. reliquary, shrine; *spectacles*: frame; *sl.* ~*s pl.* eyes.

chasse...: ~-**marée** [ʃasma're] *m/inv.* fish-cart; coasting lugger; ~-**mouches** [~'muʃ] *m/inv.* fly-swatter; *horse*: fly-net; ~-**neige** [~'nɛːʒ] *m/inv.* snow-plough, *Am.* snow-plow; *sp. ski*: stem; *virage m en* ~

stem-turn; **~-pierres** 🚂 [~'pjɛːr] m/inv. cow-catcher.

chasser [ʃa'se] (1a) v/t. hunt, pursue; drive away or out; expel; drive (a nail); v/i. (usu. ~ à courre) hunt, go hunting (s.th., à qch.); drive; mot. skid; ⚓ drag; **chasseresse** poet. [ʃas'rɛs] f huntress; **chasseur** [ʃa'sœːr] m hunter; hotel: page-boy, Am. bell-hop; ✗ rifleman; ⚓ chaser; ✈ fighter; ✈ ~ à réaction jet fighter; **chasseuse** [~'søːz] f huntress.   [bleary-eyed.⟩

chassieux, -euse [ʃa'sjø, ~'sjøːz] **châssis** [ʃa'si] m frame (a. mot., 🚂); mot. chassis; window-sash; paint. stretcher; trunk: tray; ✗ slide; ✈ under-carriage; ✗ forcing frame; typ. chase; thea. scenery: flat; phot. plate-holder; ✈ ~ d'atterrissage landing gear; **~-presse** phot. [~si-'prɛs] m printing-frame.

chaste [ʃast] chaste, pure; **chasteté** [~ə'te] f chastity, purity.

chasuble eccl. [ʃa'zybl] f chasuble.

chat zo. [ʃa] m (tom-)cat; le ♀ botté Puss in Boots.

châtaigne [ʃa'tɛɲ] f ♣ chestnut (a. horse); **châtaigneraie** [ʃatɛ-ɲə'rɛ] f chestnut grove; **châtaignier** [~'ɲje] m chestnut(-tree, -wood); **châtain, e** [ʃa'tɛ̃, ~'tɛn] adj., a. su./m chestnut, brown.

château [ʃa'to] m castle; manor, hall; palace; fig. ~ de cartes house of cards; ~ d'eau water-tower, 🚂 tank; ~x pl. en Espagne castles in the air.

chateaubriand, châteaubriant cuis. [ʃatobri'ɑ̃] m grilled steak, Am. porter-house steak.

châtelain [ʃat'lɛ̃] m castellan; lord (of the manor); **châtelaine** [~'lɛn] f chatelaine (a. cost.); lady (of the manor).

chat-huant, pl. **chats-huants** orn. [ʃa'ɥɑ̃] m tawny or brown owl.

châtier [ʃa'tje] (1o) v/t. punish, chastise; fig. refine (one's style); ~ l'insolence de q. punish s.o. for his impudence.

chatière [ʃa'tjɛːr] f cat-hole (in a door); cat-trap; ventilation hole; fig. secret entrance.

châtiment [ʃati'mɑ̃] m punishment.

chatoiement [ʃatwa'mɑ̃] m sheen; sparkle; glistening.

chaton¹ [ʃa'tɔ̃] m jewel: setting; jewel (in setting).

chaton² [~] m zo. kitten; ♣ catkin.

chatouillement [ʃatuj'mɑ̃] m tickle, tickling; **chatouiller** [ʃatu'je] (1a) v/t. tickle (a. fig.); F thrash; **chatouilleux, -euse** [~'jø, ~'jøːz] ticklish; sensitive, touchy, sore (point); delicate (question).

chatoyer [ʃatwa'je] (1h) v/i. shimmer; glisten; soie f chatoyée shot silk.

châtrer [ʃa'tre] (1a) v/t. castrate, geld; ✗ prune.

chatte [ʃat] f (she-)cat; tabby; **chattemite** F [~'mit] f toady, sycophant; **chatterie** [ʃa'tri] f wheedling; ~s pl. dainties, goodies.

chatterton ✗ [ʃater'tɔn] m insulating or adhesive tape.

chaud, e [ʃo, ʃoːd] **1.** adj. warm; hot; fig. ardent, keen; bitter (tears); avoir ~ be or feel warm; be or feel hot; il fait ~ it is warm or hot; la donner ~e à fill (s.o.) with dismay; servir ~ serve up (a dish) hot; tenir ~ keep warm; **2.** chaud adv. warm etc.; **3.** su./m heat, warmth; **chaudeau** cuis. [ʃo'do] m caudle, eggnog; **chaud-froid,** pl. **chauds-froids** cuis. [ʃo'frwa] m chaud-froid; ~ de ... cold jellied ...;

chaudière ⊕ [ʃo'djɛːr] f boiler; ~ auxiliaire donkey boiler; ~ à vide vacuum pan; **chaudron** [~'drɔ̃] m ca(u)ldron; F old and tinny piano; **chaudronnier** [~drɔ'nje] m brazier; coppersmith; ironmonger.

chauffage [ʃo'faːʒ] m heating; warming; ~ à distance long-distance heating; ~ au pétrole oil heating; ~ central central heating; bois m de ~ firewood; **chauffard** F [~'faːr] m road hog; **chauffe** ⊕ [ʃo:f] f heating; stoking, firing; metall. firechamber; ⊕ activer la ~ fire up.

chauffe...: **~-bain** [ʃof'bɛ̃] m geyser; **~-eau** [ʃo'fo] m/inv. water-heater; **~-pieds** [ʃof'pje] m/inv. foot-warmer; **~-plats** [~'pla] m/inv. dish-warmer, chafing-dish.

chauffer [ʃo'fe] (1a) v/t. warm, heat; ⊕ stoke up (a furnace); fig. boost; fig. cram (s.o. for an examination); sl. pinch, steal; v/i. get warm or hot; ⊕ overheat (bearings etc.); ⊕ get up steam (engine); ~ au pétrole burn oil; sl. se faire ~ get pinched (= arrested); **chaufferette** [~'frɛt] f foot-warmer; dish-warmer; mot. heater; **chaufferie** [~'fri] f metall. reheating furnace;

forge; ⚓ stokehold; **chauffeur,
-euse** [\~'fœːr, \~'føːz] *su. mot.* driver;
su./m mot. chauffeur; ⚓ stoker; *sl.*
crammer, coach (*for examination*);
su./f mot. chauffeuse; fireside chair;
chauffoir [\~'fwaːr] *m* warm-room.

chaufour [ʃoˈfuːr] *m* lime-kiln.

chauler ⚒ [ʃoˈle] (1a) *v/t.* lime (*the
soil*); lime-wash.

chaume [ʃoːm] *m* haulm; *roof:*
thatch; stubble; **chaumière**
[\~ˈmjɛːr] *f* thatched cottage; **chau-
mine** *poet.* [\~ˈmin] *f* cot.

chausse [ʃoːs] *f* wine strainer; † \~s *pl.*
breeches; **chaussée** [ʃoˈse] *f* road-
way; road; causeway; *geog.* reef;
chausse-pied [ʃosˈpje] *m* shoe-
horn; **chausser** [ʃoˈse] (1a) *v/t.* put
on (*shoes etc.*); put shoes on (*s.o.*); fit
(*shoe*); \~ *bien* (*large*) be well-(large-)
fitting; \~ *du 40* take size 40 (in shoes);
se \~ put on (one's) shoes; **chausse-
trape** [ʃosˈtrap] *f hunt.* trap (*a. fig.*);
fig. trick; ♣ starthistle; **chaussette**
[ʃoˈsɛt] *f* sock; **chausson** [\~ˈsɔ̃] *m*
slipper; ballet shoe; boxing shoe;
fencing shoe; gym shoe; **chaussure**
[\~ˈsyːr] *f* shoe, boot.

chauve [ʃoːv] 1. *adj.* bald; 2. *su.* bald
person; **\~-souris**, *pl.* **\~s-souris** *zo.*
[ʃovsuˈri] *f* bat.

chauvin, e [ʃoˈvɛ̃, \~ˈvin] 1. *adj.* jin-
goistic, chauvinist(ic); 2. *su.* chauvinist warmonger; **chauvinisme**
[\~viˈnism] *m* jingoism, chauvinism, F
flag-waving.

chaux [ʃo] *f* lime; \~ *éteinte* slaked
lime; \~ *vive* quicklime; *blanchir à la* \~
whitewash; limewash.

chavirer ⚓ [ʃaviˈre] (1a) *vt/i.* capsize; upset.

chef [ʃɛf] *m* head, principal; chief,
chieftain; master; leader; *cuis.* (*a.* \~
de cuisine) chef (= *male head cook*); ♪
conductor; *fig.* heading; ⚡ count;
fig. authority; ⊕ \~ *d'atelier* shop
foreman; \~ *de bande* ringleader; ⚔ \~
de bataillon major; \~ *de bureau* (comptabilité) chief *or* head clerk (accountant); *sp.* \~ *d'équipe* team leader,
captain; \~ *d'État* chief of State; ⚑
\~ *de gare* station master; ✝ \~ *de rayon*,
\~ *de service* departmental manager *or*
head, floor manager; ⚑ \~ *de train*
guard, *Am.* conductor; *au premier* \~
in the highest degree; in the first
place; *de mon* \~ for myself; on my
own authority; ... *en* \~ ... in chief; \~-

d'œuvre, *pl.* **\~s-d'œuvre** [ʃɛˈdœːvr]
m masterpiece; **\~lieu**, *pl.* **\~s-lieux**
[ʃɛfˈljø] *m* chief town; county town,
Am. county seat.

cheftaine [ʃɛfˈtɛn] *f* scout-mis-
tress.

chemin [ʃəˈmɛ̃] *m* way; road; path;
eccl. \~ *de croix* Way of the Cross;
\~ *de fer* railway, *Am.* railroad; \~ *de
table* (table)runner; \~ *faisant* on the
way; *faire son* \~ make one's way;
fig. get on well; **chemineau** [ʃəmi-
ˈno] *m* tramp, *Am.* hobo; **cheminée** [\~ˈne] *f* chimney; ⚓ funnel;
smoke-stack; ⊕ stack; fireplace;
mantelpiece; **cheminer** [\~ˈne] (1a)
v/i. tramp, plod on; **cheminot** ⚑
[\~ˈno] *m* railwayman; platelayer.

chemise [ʃəˈmiːz] *f* shirt (*of men*);
chemise (*of women*); *book:* wrapper;
folder (*for papers*); ⊕ *boiler etc.*:
jacket; ⊕ \~ *d'eau* water jacket;
chemiserie [\~mizˈri] *f* shirt-mak-
ing; shirt shop; shirt factory;
haberdashery; **chemisette** *cost.*
[ʃəmiˈzɛt] *f* jumper; chemisette (*of
women*); **chemisier, -ère** [\~ˈzje,
\~ˈzjɛːr] *su.* shirt-maker; shirt-seller;
haberdasher; *su./m* shirt-blouse;
jumper.

chênaie [ʃɛˈnɛ] *f* oak-grove.

chenal [ʃəˈnal] *m* channel, fairway;
⊕ mill-race.

chenapan [ʃənaˈpɑ̃] *m* scoundrel.

chêne ♣ [ʃɛːn] *m* oak.

chéneau [ʃeˈno] *m* △ *eaves:* gutter;
mot. drip-mo(u)lding.

chêne-liège, *pl.* **chênes-lièges** [ʃɛn-
ˈljɛːʒ] *m* cork-tree, cork-oak.

chènevière [ʃɛnˈvjɛːr] *f* hemp-field;
chènevis [\~ˈvi] *m* hemp-seed.

chenil [ʃəˈni] *m* dog-kennel (*a. fig.*).

chenille [ʃəˈniːj] *f* caterpillar; *caterpillar tractor:* track; *tex.* chenille.

chenu, e [ʃəˈny] hoary (*hair*); snowy
(*mountain*).

cheptel [ʃɛpˈtɛl] *m* (live-)stock; \~
mort implements *pl.* and buildings
pl.

chèque ✝ [ʃɛk] *m* cheque, *Am.*
check; \~ *barré* crossed cheque; \~
de voyage traveller's cheque; \~ *sans
provision* cheque without cover;
formulaire m de \~ blank cheque;
chéquier [ʃeˈkje] *m* cheque book,
Am. checkbook.

cher, chère [ʃɛːr] 1. *adj.* dear, beloved; expensive; *la vie f chère* high

prices *pl.*; *moins* ~ cheaper; *peu* ~ cheap; **2.** *su./m:* mon ~ my dear friend; *su./f:* ma **chère** my dear; **3.** *cher adv.* dear(ly); *acheter* ~ buy at a high price; *coûter* ~ be expensive; *payer* ~ pay a high price for (*s.th.*); *fig.* smart or pay for; *vendre* ~ sell dear.

chercher [ʃɛr'ʃe] (1a) *v/t.* look for, seek; search; try; *aller* ~ fetch, get; *envoyer* ~ send for; *venir* ~ call for, fetch; F *ça va* ~ *dans les* ... that'll add up to about ...; **chercheur, -euse** [~'ʃœːr, ~'ʃøːz] **1.** *adj.* enquiring; **2.** *su.* seeker; investigator; researcher; *su./m* finder; detector; *radio:* cat's-whisker.

chère [ʃɛːr] *f:* (*la*) bonne ~ good food.

chéri, e [ʃe'ri] **1.** *adj.* dear, cherished; **2.** *su.* darling, dear(est); **chérir** [~'riːr] (2a) *v/t.* cherish, love dearly; **chérot** *sl.* [ʃe'ro] (too) expensive, *Brit.* F pricey; **cherté** [ʃɛr'te] *f* dearness; high price; high prices *pl.*; *la* ~ *de la vie* the high cost of living.

chérubin [ʃery'bɛ̃] *m* cherub.

chétif, -ve [ʃe'tif, ~'tiːv] puny, weak; paltry (*reason*); wretched, pitiful, miserable.

cheval [ʃə'val] *m* horse; *mot.* horse-power; *sp.* ~ de bois vaulting horse; ~ de course race-horse; ✖ ~ de frise cheval de frise; ~ entier stallion; *chevaux pl.* de bois merry-go-round *sg.*; *aller à* ~ ride, go on horseback; *être à* ~ *sur* straddle (*s.th.*); F be well up in; F be a stickler for (*etiquette*); **chevalement** [~val'mã] *m* ⚒ pit-head frame; △ *walls:* shoring; **chevaler** [~va'le] (1a) *v/t.* △ shore up; ⊕ put (*s.th.*) on a trestle; **chevaleresque** [ʃəval'rɛsk] chivalrous; knightly; **chevalerie** [~'ri] *f* chivalry; knighthood; chivalrousness; **chevalet** [ʃəva'lɛ] *m* trestle; ♪ violin etc.: bridge; ⊕, *a. billiards:* rest; *paint.* easel; ⊕ saw-horse; **chevalier** [~'lje] *m* knight; *fig.* ~ d'industrie sharper, swindler; *faire q.* ~ knight s.o.; **chevalière** [~'ljɛːr] *f* signet-ring; **chevalin, e** [~'lɛ̃, ~'lin] equine; **cheval-vapeur**, *pl.* **chevaux-vapeur** ⊕ [ʃəvalva'pœːr, ~vova'pœːr] *m* horse-power; **chevaucher** [~vo'ʃe] (1a) *v/i.* ride on horseback; sit astride; overlap; *v/t.*

ride on; sit astride; *bridge:* span (*a river*).

chevelu, e [ʃə'vly] long-haired; *cuir m* ~ scalp; **chevelure** [~'vlyːr] *f* (head of) hair; *comet:* tail.

chevet [ʃə'vɛ] *m* bed-head; bolster; △ *church:* chevet, apse; *fig.* bedside (*of a sick person*); *lampe f de* ~ bedside lamp; *livre m de* ~ bedside book, *fig.* favo(u)rite reading.

chevêtre [ʃə'vɛːtr] *m* ⚒ (jaw-)bandage; △ trimmer beam.

cheveu [ʃə'vø] *m* (single) hair; ~x *pl.* hair *sg.*; ~x *pl. à la* Jeanne d'Arc bobbed hair (with fringe); ~x *pl.* en brosse crewcut; *sl.* avoir mal aux ~x have a hang-over; *fig.* couper les ~x en quatre split hairs; *de l'épaisseur d'un* ~ by a hair's breadth; F *se prendre aux* ~x have a real set-to; *tiré par les* ~x farfetched; *voilà le* ~! that's the snag!

cheville [ʃə'viːj] *f* peg (*a. violin*), pin (*a.* ⊕); ⊕ bolt; *fig.* padding, *anat.* ankle; ~ ouvrière king-pin, *fig.* mainspring; **cheviller** [~vi'je] (1a) *v/t.* pin, peg, bolt; plug; *fig.* pad.

cheviotte *tex.* [ʃə'vjɔt] *f* wool, *cloth:* cheviot.

chèvre [ʃɛːvr] *f* zo. (she-)goat; ⊕, △ derrick; ⊕ trestle; **chevreau** zo. [ʃə'vro] *m* kid; de (or en) ~ kid-...; **chèvrefeuille** ♀ [ʃɛvrə'fœːj] *m* honeysuckle; **chevrette** [ʃə'vrɛt] *f* zo. kid; roe-doe; ⊕ trivet; F shrimp, prawn; **chevreuil** [~'vrœːj] *m* roebuck; roe-deer; *cuis.* venison; **chevrier** [~'vrje] *m* goatherd; **chevrière** [~'vrjɛːr] *f* goat-girl; **chevron** [~'vrɔ̃] *m* △ rafter; ✖ chevron, stripe; **chevronné, e** [~'ne] experienced, practised, seasoned; veteran...; **chevrotement** [ʃəvrɔt'mã] *m* quavering; **chevroter** [ʃəvrɔ'te] (1a) *v/i.* quaver, quiver, tremble (*voice*); bleat (*goat*); **chevrotine** [~'tin] *f* buckshot.

chez [ʃe] *prp. direction:* to; *place:* at (*s.o.'s house or shop*); with (*my aunt*); in (*a. fig.*); *post:* care of, *abbr. c/o; fig.* among (*the English*); ~ nous in our country; ~ Zola in the works of Zola; être (aller) ~ soi be at (go) home; être (aller) ~ le docteur be at (go to) the doctor's; faire comme ~ soi make o.s. at home; de ~ q. from s.o.'s (house); de ~ soi from home; ~-**moi** (*etc.*) [~'mwa] *m/inv.:* mon ~ my home.

chialer *sl.* [ʃjaˈle] (1a) *v/i.* snivel.

chiasse [ʃjas] *f fly etc.*: dirt; *sl.* drag; *sl. avoir la* ～ have the runs; be in a blue funk.

chic [ʃik] **1.** *su./m* chic, smartness, style; *fig.* knack; **2.** *adj.* smart, stylish; F first-rate, F posh, classy; F decent (*fellow*); *des robes f/pl.* chics smart robes.

chicane [ʃiˈkan] *f* quibbling; chicanery; ⊕ baffle(-plate); ⚔ zigzag trench; **chicaner** [ʃikaˈne] (1a) *v/t.* quibble, cavil; *v/t.* wrangle with (*s.o.*); haggle over (*s.th.*); **chicaneur, -euse** [～ˈnœːr, ～ˈnøːz] **1.** *adj.* argumentative; quibbling; **2.** *su.* quibbler, haggler; litigious person; **chicanier, -ère** [～ˈnje, ～ˈnjɛːr] **1.** *adj.* litigious; quibbling; haggling; **2.** *su.* litigious person; ⚖ barrator.

chiche [ʃiʃ] **1.** *adj.* scanty; niggardly, mean (*person*); **2.** *su./m* ⚘ (*a. pois m*～) chick-pea.

chichis F [ʃiˈʃi] *m/pl.* frills (*a. fig.*); *fig.* affected manners; *faire des* ～ put on airs; make a fuss; create difficulties.

chicorée ⚘ [ʃikɔˈre] *f* chicory; endive (*a. salad etc.*).

chicot [ʃiˈko] *m* tooth, tree: stump.

chicotin [ʃikɔˈtɛ̃] *m* aloes *pl.*; *amer comme* ～ as bitter as gall.

chien [ʃjɛ̃] *m* dog; *gun*: hammer, cock; ～ *d'aveugle* guide dog; ～ *de chasse* hound; *entre* ～ *et loup* in the twilight; ～ *méchant!* beware of the dog!; **chiendent** ⚘ [～ˈdɑ̃] *m* couch-grass; **chienloup,** *pl.* **chiens-loups** *zo.* [～ˈlu] *m* Alsatian, wolf-hound; **chienne** [ʃjɛn] *f* (female) dog; bitch.

chier V [ʃje] (1o) *v/i.* shit.

chiffe [ʃif] *f* rag; *fig.* weakling; **chiffon** [ʃiˈfɔ̃] *m* rag; frippery; scrap; *tex.* chiffon; F *parler* ～*s* talk dress; **chiffonner** [ʃifɔˈne] (1a) *v/t.* ruffle, crumple; *fig.* sully; *fig.* irritate, provoke; *v/i.* pick rags; rake through *or* comb dustbins; do some dressmaking; **chiffonnier, -ère** [～ˈnje, ～ˈnjɛːr] *su.* rag-picker; dustbin-raker; *su./m* bureau, chest of drawers.

chiffre [ʃifr] *m* figure, number, numeral; cipher, code; amount, total; mark; monogram; ～ *d'affaires* turnover; ～ *repère* reference number; **chiffrer** [ʃiˈfre] (1a) *v/i.* calculate;

v/t. number; work out, express in figures; ♪ figure; write in cipher *or* code, encipher, encode; **chiffreur** [～ˈfrœːr] *m* reckoner; cipherer.

chignole [ʃiˈɲɔl] *f* ⊕ hand-drill; F jalopy.

chignon [ʃiˈɲɔ̃] *m* bun, chignon; coil of hair.

chilien, -enne [ʃiˈljɛ̃, ～ˈljɛn] *adj., a. su.* ♀ Chilean.

chimère [ʃiˈmɛːr] *f* chimera; **chimérique** [～meˈrik] visionary.

chimie [ʃiˈmi] *f* chemistry; **chimique** [～ˈmik] chemical; **chimiste** [～ˈmist] *su.* chemist (*not pharmacist*).

chimpanzé *zo.* [ʃɛ̃pɑ̃ˈze] *m* chimpanzee.

chiner[1] *tex.* [ʃiˈne] (1a) *v/t.* shadow (*a fabric*).

chiner[2] F [～] (1a) *v/t.* make fun of, kid, rag.

chinois, e [ʃiˈnwa, ～ˈnwaːz] **1.** *adj.* Chinese; **2.** *su./m ling.* Chinese; ♀ Chinaman; *les* ♀ *m/pl.* the Chinese; *su./f* ♀e Chinese woman; **chinoiserie** [～nwazˈri] *f* Chinese curio; F trick; ～s *pl. administratives* red tape *sg.*

chiper *sl.* [ʃiˈpe] (1a) *v/t.* pinch; swipe; *tennis:* poach (*a ball*).

chipie F [ʃiˈpi] *f* sour woman; shrew.

chipoter F [ʃipɔˈte] (1a) *v/i.* nibble at one's food; haggle, quibble; waste time.

chique [ʃik] *f zo.* chigger, jigger; *tobacco:* quid.

chiqué *sl.* [ʃiˈke] *m* fake, pretence.

chiquenaude [ʃikˈnoːd] *f* flick (of the finger).

chiquer [ʃiˈke] (1m) *v/t.* chew (*tobacco*); *v/i.* chew (tobacco).

chiragre ⚕ [kiˈragr] *f* gout in the hand; **chiromancie** [kirɔmɑ̃ˈsi] *f* palmistry; **chiromancien** *m*, **-enne** *f* [～ˈsjɛ̃, ～ˈsjɛn] palmist.

chirurgical, e, *m/pl.* **-aux** [ʃiryrʒiˈkal, ～ˈko] surgical; **chirurgie** [～ˈʒi] *f* surgery; **chirurgien** [～ˈʒjɛ̃] *m* surgeon.

chlorate ⚗ [klɔˈrat] *m* chlorate; **chlore** [klɔːr] *m* ⚗ chlorine; *sl.* calcium chloride; **chlorhydrique** [klɔriˈdrik] ⚗ *adj.*: *acide m* ～ hydrochloric acid, F spirits *pl.* of salt; **chloroforme** ⚗, ⚕ [～rɔˈfɔrm] *m* chloroform; **chlorose** [～ˈroːz] *f* ⚕, ⚘ chlorosis; ⚘ *a.* etiolation; **chlorotique** ⚕ [～rɔˈtik] chlorotic;

chlorure ⚗ [ᴧ'ry:r] *m* chloride; ᴧ *d'ammonium* sal-ammoniac; ᴧ *de chaux* bleaching powder.

choc [ʃɔk] *m* shock; collision, crash; impact; *de* ᴧ shock-...

chocolat [ʃɔkɔ'la] 1. *su./m* chocolate; ᴧ *à craquer* plain chocolate; 2. *adj./inv.* chocolate; **chocolatier, -ère** [ᴧla'tje, ᴧ'tjɛ:r] 1. *adj.* chocolate; 2. *su.* chocolate-maker, chocolate-seller; *su./f* chocolate-pot.

chœur [kœ:r] *m* △, *eccl.* choir, △ chancel; ♪, *thea.*, *etc.* chorus.

choir [ʃwa:r] (3d) *v/i.* fall.

choisi, e [ʃwa'zi] choice, select(ed); chosen, appointed (*party leader etc.*); **choisir** [ᴧ'zi:r] (2a) *v/t.* choose, pick (from *entre, parmi*); *sp.* toss for (*sides*); **choix** [ʃwa] *m* choice, option; selection; *au* ᴧ as you wish; ✝ all one price; *de* ᴧ choice, *fig.* picked (*man*); ✝ *de premier* ᴧ best quality..., prime (*meat*).

chômage [ʃo'ma:ʒ] *m* unemployment; stoppage; ⊕ shut-down; ⚡ (power) cut; F dole; *en* ᴧ out of work; *en* ᴧ *partiel* on part-time, on short work; **chômer** [ᴧ'me] (1a) *v/i.* take a day off; be idle; be unemployed; *jour m chômé* day off; **chômeur** *m*, **-euse** *f* [ᴧ'mœ:r, ᴧ'mø:z] unemployed worker; *les* ᴧ*s m/pl.* the unemployed.

chope [ʃɔp] *f* tankard.

choper [ʃɔ'pe] (1a) *v/t.* pinch (= steal, *a.* = arrest); *sl.:* nab; *tennis:* chop.

chopine [ʃɔ'pin] *f* half-litre mug; ⊕ *pump:* plunger; **chopiner** F [ᴧpi'ne] (1a) *v/i.* booze.

chopper [ʃɔ'pe] (1a) *v/i.* trip, stumble.

choquant, e [ʃɔ'kɑ̃, ᴧ'kɑ̃:t] shocking, offensive; gross; **choquer** [ᴧ'ke] (1m) *v/t.* shock; offend; bump against; clink (*glasses*); *se* ᴧ come into collision (with, *contre*); be shocked; take offence (at, *de*).

choral, e, *m/pl.* **-als, -aux** [kɔ'ral, ᴧ'ro] 1. *adj.* choral; 2. *su./m* chorale; *su./f* choral society.

chorégraphie [kɔregra'fi] *f* choreography.

choriste [kɔ'rist] *m eccl.* chorister; *opera:* chorus-singer; **chorus** [ᴧ'rys] *m* chorus; *faire* ᴧ chorus one's agreement; echo; repeat in chorus.

chose [ʃo:z] 1. *su./f* thing; matter, affair; property; ᴧ *en question* case in point; ⚖ ᴧ *jugée* res judicata; ᴧ

publique State; *autre* ᴧ something else; *grand-*ᴧ much; *peu de* ᴧ not much, very little; *quelque* ᴧ something; *quelque* ᴧ *de bon* (*nouveau*) something good (new); *su./m* what's-its (his, her)-name, thingumajig; *monsieur* ♀ Mr. What's-his-name; 2. *adj./inv.* F: *tout* ᴧ queer, out-of-sorts.

chou, -x [ʃu] *m* cabbage; *fig.* cabbage-bow; rosette; ᴧ*x pl. de Bruxelles* Brussels sprouts; ᴧ *à la crème* cream puff; ᴧ *frisé* kale; *être bête comme* ᴧ be idiotic; be simplicity itself; *pej.* *feuille f de* ᴧ rag, gutter paper (= *newspaper of no standing*); *mon* ᴧ! (my) dear!; darling!

choucas *orn.* [ʃu'ka] *m* jackdaw.

chouchou *m*, **-oute** *f* [ʃu'ʃu, ᴧ'ʃut] darling, pet; **chouchouter** [ᴧʃu'te] (1a) *v/t.* pamper, pet.

choucroute *cuis.* [ʃu'krut] *f* sauerkraut.

chouette [ʃwɛt] 1. *su./f orn.* owl; 2. F *adj., a. int.* fine, splendid.

chou...: ᴧ-**fleur,** *pl.* ᴧ**x-fleurs** [ʃu-'flœ:r] *m* cauliflower; ᴧ-**navet,** *pl.* ᴧ**x-navets** [ᴧna've] *m* swede; ᴧ-**palmiste,** *pl.* ᴧ**x-palmistes** [ᴧpal-'mist] *m* palm-cabbage; ᴧ-**rave,** *pl.* ᴧ**x-raves** [ᴧ'ra:v] *m* kohlrabi.

choyer [ʃwa'je] (1h) *v/t.* fondle, pet; *fig.* cherish.

chrétien, -enne [kre'tjɛ̃, ᴧ'tjɛn] 1. *adj.* Christian; 2. *su.* Christian; *su./m fig.* good citizen; **chrétienté** [ᴧtjɛ̃'te] *f* Christendom.

Christ [krist] *m* (Jesus) Christ; ♀ crucifix; **christianiser** [kristjani-'ze] (1a) *v/t.* christianize; **christianisme** [ᴧ'nism] *m* Christianity.

chrome [kro:m] *m* ⚗ chromium; ✝ chrome; **chromo** F [krɔ'mo] *m* colo(u)r-print.

chromo... [krɔmo] chromo..., colo(u)r-...

chronique [krɔ'nik] 1. *adj.* ⚕ chronic; 2. *su./f* chronicle; *journ.* report, news *sg.*; **chroniqueur** *m*, **-euse** *f* [ᴧni'kœ:r, ᴧ'kø:z] chronicler; *journ.* reporter; par-writer, paragrapher.

chrono... [krɔnɔ] chrono...; ᴧ-**graphe** [ᴧ'graf] *m* stop-watch; *phys.* chronograph; ᴧ**logie** [ᴧlɔ'ʒi] *f* chronology; ᴧ**logique** [ᴧlɔ'ʒik] chronological; ᴧ**mètre** [ᴧ'mɛtr] *m* chronometer; *sp.* ~ *à déclic* stopwatch; ~**métrer** *sp.* [~me'tre] (1f) *v/t.* time; ~**métreur** [~me'trœːr] *m sp.*, *a.* ⊕ time-keeper; ~**métrie** [~me'tri] *f* chronometry, timemeasurement.

chrysalide *zo.* [kriza'lid] *f* chrysalis, pupa; **chrysanthème** ♀ [~zã'tɛːm] *m* chrysanthemum.

chuchoter [ʃyʃɔ'te] (1a) *vt/i.* whisper; **chuchoterie** [~'tri] *f* whispering.

chut! [ʃyt] *int.* ssh!; hush!

chute [~] *f* fall; spill; *fig.* downfall, overthrow, ruin; ⊕, ✗ shoot; *geog.* falls *pl.*; ~ *d'eau* waterfall; **†** ~ *des prix* drop in prices; *anat.* ~ *des reins* small of the back; ~ *du jour* nightfall; *faire une* ~ (have a) fall.

chuter[1] [ʃy'te] (1a) *v/t.* hush; *thea.* hiss; *v/i.* say hush.

chuter[2] [~] (1a) *v/i.* fall; decrease, diminish; *thea.* (be a) flop; ~ *de deux levées cards:* be two tricks down.

ci [si] **1.** *adv.* here; *cet homme-*~ this man; **2.** *dem./pron. see ceci; comme* ~ *comme ça* so so; ~**après** [~a'prɛ] *adv.* below.

cibiche *sl.* [si'biʃ] *f* cig, *Br.* fag (= *cigarette*).

cible [sibl] *f* target (*a. fig.*); **†** *etc.* target group.

ciboire *eccl.* [si'bwaːr] *m* ciborium.

ciboule ♀ [si'bul] *f* Welsh onion; **ciboulette** ♀ [sibu'lɛt] *f* chive; **ciboulot** *sl.* [~'lo] *m* nut (= *head*).

cicatrice [sika'tris] *f* scar; **cicatriser** [~tri'ze] (1a) *v/t.* heal; *se* ~ heal (up), scar over.

ci...: ~**-contre** [si'kɔ̃ːtr] *adv.* opposite; ~**-dessous** [~'dsu] *adv.* below, hereunder; ~**-dessus** hereinafter; ~**-dessus** [~'dsy] *adv.* above(-mentioned); hereinbefore; ~**-devant** [~'dvã] **1.** *adv.* formerly, previously; **2.** *su./ inv.* aristocrat; F old fogey.

cidre [sidr] *m* cider.

ciel [sjɛl] **1.** *su./m* (*pl.* **cieux**) [sjø]) sky, heaven; (*pl.* **ciels** [sjɛl]) (bed-) tester; ⊕, ✗ roof; (*pl.* **ciels** or **cieux**) climate, sky; **2.** *int.* good heavens! [taper.]

cierge *eccl.* [sjɛrʒ] *m* (wax) candle,

cigale *zo.* [si'gal] *f* cicada.

cigare [si'gaːr] *m* cigar; **cigarette** [~ga'rɛt] *f* cigarette; **cigarière** [~ga'rjɛːr] *f* cigar-maker.

cigogne [si'gɔɲ] *f orn.* stork; ⊕ crank(-lever).

ciguë ♀, ✗ [si'gy] *f* hemlock.

ci-inclus, e [siɛ̃'kly, ~'klyːz], **ci-joint, e** [~'ʒwɛ̃, ~'ʒwɛ̃ːt] **1.** *adj.* enclosed, sub-joined (*letter, copy*); **2.** *ci-inclus, ci-joint adv.* herewith; ~ *la lettre* herewith the letter.

cil [sil] *m* (eye)lash.

cilice [si'lis] *m* hair-shirt.

cilié, e ♀ [si'lje] ciliate; **ciller** [~'je] (1a) *v/t.* blink (one's eyes, *les yeux*).

cime [sim] *f* top, summit; *mountain:* peak.

ciment [si'mã] *m* cement; ~ *armé* reinforced concrete; **cimenter** [simã'te] (1a) *v/t.* cement (*a. fig.*); **cimenterie** [~'tri] *f* cement works *usu. sg.*; **cimentier** [~'tje] *m* cementmaker; cement-worker.

cimeterre [sim'tɛːr] *m* scimitar.

cimetière [sim'tjɛːr] *m* cemetery, graveyard; *mot.* ~ *de voitures* scrapyard.

cimier [si'mje] *m* helmet, *a.* 🏷: crest; *venison:* haunch.

cinabre [si'naːbr] *m* cinnabar; *paint.* vermilion.

ciné F [si'ne] *m* cinema, F films *pl.*, *Am.* movies *pl.*; **cinéaste** [~'ast] *m* cinematographer; film-producer; scenario-writer; **ciné-caméra** [~kame'ra] *f* cine-camera; **ciné-club** [~'klœb] *m* filmclub; **ciné-journal** [~ʒur'nal] *m* news-reel; **cinéma** [~'ma] *m* cinema; F films *pl.*, pictures *pl.*, *Am.* movies *pl.*; F *fig.* playacting, act, show; F *fig.* fuss; ~ *parlant* F talkie; **cinémathèque** [sinema'tɛk] *f* film-library; **cinématique** *phys.* [~'tik] **1.** *adj.* kinematic; **2.** *su./f* kinematics *pl.*; **cinématographe** [~to-'graf] *m* cinematograph, F cinema; **cinématographier** [~tɔgra'fje] (1o) *v/t.* film; **cinématographique** [~tɔgra'fik] cinematographic; film-...; **cinéphile** [~fil] *su.* film enthusiast.

cinéraire [sine'rɛːr] **1.** *adj.* cinerary; **2.** *su./f* ♀ cineraria.

ciné-roman [sinerɔ'mã] *m* film story.

cinétique *phys.* [sine'tik] **1.** *adj.* kinetic; **2.** *su./f* kinetics *pl.*

cingalais, e [sɛ̃ga'lɛ, ~'lɛːz] *adj., a. su.* ♀ Cingalese.

cinglant, e [sɛ̃'glã, ~'glãːt] lashing (*rain*); bitter, biting (*cold, wind, etc.*);

fig. scathing; **cinglé, e** F [~'gle] **1.** *adj.* nutty, nuts (= *mad*); **2.** *su.* crackpot; **cingler** [~'gle] (1a) *v/t.* lash; ⚓ *v/i.* sail; scud along; steer a course.

cinq [sɛ̃:k; *before consonant* sɛ̃] *adj./ num., a. su./m/inv.* five; *date, title:* fifth; **cinquantaine** [sɛ̃kɑ̃'tɛn] *f* (about) fifty; *la* ~ the age of fifty, the fifties *pl.*; **cinquante** [~'kɑ̃:t] *adj./num., a. su./m/inv.* fifty; **cinquantième** [~kɑ̃'tjɛm] *adj./num., a. su.* fiftieth; **cinquième** [~'kjɛm] **1.** *adj./num.* fifth; **2.** *su.* fifth; *su./m* fraction: fifth; fifth, *Am.* sixth floor; *su./f secondary school:* (approx.) second form.

cintre [sɛ̃:tr] *m* △ arch, curve, bend; coat *or* clothes hanger; *thea.* ~s *pl.* flies; **cintré, e** [sɛ̃'tre] arched, curved; *cost.* waisted; F nutty, nuts (= *mad*); **cintrer** ⊕ [~] (1a) *v/t.* bend, curve; arch.

cirage [si'ra:ʒ] *m* waxing, polishing; *boot, shoe, floor, etc.*: polish.

circon... [sirkɔ̃] circum...; ~**cire** [~'si:r] (4e) *v/t.* circumcise; ring (*a tree*); ~**cis, e** [~'si, ~'si:z] *p.p. of circoncire*; ~**cision** [~si'zjɔ̃] *f* circumcision; *tree:* ringing; ~**férence** [~fe'rɑ̃:s] *f* circumference; perimeter; *tree:* girth; ~**flexe** *gramm.* [~'flɛks] circumflex; *accent m* ~ circumflex (accent); ~**locution** [~lɔky'sjɔ̃] *f* circumlocution; ~**scription** [~skrip'sjɔ̃] *f* Ⱥ circumscribing; *admin.* division, district; ~ *électorale* electoral district *or* ward; constituency; ~**scrire** [~s'kri:r] (4e) *v/t.* Ⱥ circumscribe (*a. fig.*); *fig.* limit; ⚡ locate (*a fault*); ~**spect, e** [~s'pɛ, ~s'pɛkt] guarded, circumspect; ~**spection** [~spɛk'sjɔ̃] *f* caution, circumspection; ~**stance** [~s'tɑ̃:s] *f* circumstance; event; ~s *pl.* atténuantes attenuating circumstances; ⚖ ~s *pl. et dépendances f/pl.* appurtenances; *de* ~ occasional; temporary; special; ~**stancié, e** [~stɑ̃'sje] detailed; ~**stanciel, -elle** [~stɑ̃'sjɛl] due to circumstances; *gramm.* adverbial (*complement*); ~**venir** [~v'ni:r] (2h) *v/t.* circumvent; outwit (*s.o.*); † impose on (*s.o.*); ~**vention** † [~vɑ̃'sjɔ̃] *f* imposture, fraud; ~**volution** △, *anat.* [~vɔly'sjɔ̃] *f* convolution.

circuit [sir'kɥi] *m* circuit; circuitous route, roundabout way; circumference; ⚡ *mettre en* ~ connect up; ⚡ *mettre en court* ~ short-circuit; *ouvrir (fermer) le* ~ switch on (off); ~ *imprimé* printed circuit; ⚡ ~ *intégré* integrated circuit.

circulaire [sirky'lɛ:r] *adj., a. su./f* circular; **circulation** [~la'sjɔ̃] *f* air, bank-notes, blood, information, etc.: circulation; ✈, *bank-notes etc.*: currency; traffic; 🚗 running; ~ *interdite* no thoroughfare; **circulatoire** *physiol.* [~la'twa:r] circulatory; *appareil m* ~ circulatory system; **circuler** [~'le] (1a) *v/i.* circulate, flow; ✈ turn over; 🚗 run (*train*); *circulez!* move along!; pass along!

circumnavigation [sirkɔmnaviga'sjɔ̃] *f* circumnavigation.

cire [si:r] *f* wax; *eccl.* taper; ~ *à cacheter*, ~ *d'Espagne* sealing-wax; ~ *à parquet* floor-polish; ~ *d'abeilles* beeswax; **ciré, e** [si're] **1.** *adj.* waxed, polished; *toile f* ~e oilcloth, American cloth; **2.** *su./m* oilskin *pl.*; **cirer** [~'re] (1a) *v/t.* wax; polish; **cireur** [~'rœ:r] *m*, **-euse** [~'rœ:r, ~'rø:z] *su.* polisher; (~ *de chaussures*) shoeblack, *Am.* shoeshine boy; *su./f machine:* waxer, polisher; **cirier, -ère** [~'rje, ~'rjɛ:r] **1.** *adj.* wax...; **2.** *su./m* wax-chandler; ♀ candleberry-tree, *Am.* bayberry.

ciron *zo.* [si'rɔ̃] *m* mite.

cirque [sirk] *m* circus; amphitheatre; cirque (*of mountains*).

cirrhose ⚕ [si'ro:z] cirrhosis.

cirrus *meteor.* [si'rys] *m* cirrus.

cisaille [si'za:j] *f metal:* clippings *pl.*; ⊕ shearing machine; ⊕ guillotine; ~s *pl.* shears; wire-cutter *sg.*; ~s *pl. à haies* hedge-shears, hedge-clippers; **cisailler** [~za'je] (1a) *v/t.* clip; cut; shear (*metal*); *fig.* discredit; cripple (*s.o.'s career*); **ciseau** [~'zo] *m* chisel; ~x *pl.* scissors; ⚡ shears; **ciseler** [siz'le] (1d) *v/t.* chisel; cut; chase (*silver*); tool (*leather*); *fig.* polish (*one's style*); **ciselet** [~'lɛ] *m* small chisel; chasing tool; **ciseleur** [~'lœ:r] *m* chiseler; engraver; chaser; tooler; **ciselure** [~'ly:r] *f* chiseling; chasing; tooling; **cisoires** [si'zwa:r] *f/pl.* bench-shears.

citadelle ⚔ [sita'dɛl] *f* citadel, stronghold; **citadin, e** [~'dɛ̃, ~'din] *su.* citizen; *su./m* townsman; *su./f* townswoman.

citation [sita'sjɔ̃] *f* quotation; ⚔

mention in dispatches; ⚔ summons *sg.*; ⚖ subpoena (*of a witness*).

cité [si'te] *f* city; (large) town; housing estate; *la* ⌕ *London:* the City; *Paris:* the Cité; ~ *lacustre* lakedwelling; ~ *universitaire* students' residential blocks *pl.*; *droit m de* ~ freedom of the city; *fig. avoir droit de* ~ be accepted; be established; **~-dortoir,** *pl.* **~s-dortoirs** [~dɔrt'waːr] *f* dormitory town; **~-jardin,** *pl.* **~s-jardins** [~teʒar'dɛ̃] *f* gardencity.

citer [si'te] (1a) *v/t.* quote, cite; ✕ mention in dispatches; ⚔ summon; ⚖ subpoena (*a witness*).

citerne [si'tɛrn] *f* cistern, tank; 🚃 tank-car.

cithare ♩ [si'taːr] *f* zither; **cithariste** ♩ [~ta'rist] *su.* zither-player.

citoyen *m*, **-enne** *f* [sitwa'jɛ̃, ~'jɛn] citizen.

citrin, e [si'trɛ̃, ~'trin] lemon-yellow; **citrique** 🜍 [~'trik] citric; **citron** [~'trɔ̃] 1. *su./m* 🜍 lemon, citron, lime; F nut (= *head*); ~ *pressé* lemon squash; 2. *adj./inv.* lemon(-colo[u]red); **citronnade** [sitrɔ'nad] *f* lemonade; **citronnier** [~'nje] *m* 🜍 lemon-tree; *wood:* lemon-wood.

citrouille 🜍 [si'truːj] *f* pumpkin.

civet *cuis.* [si'vɛ] *m* stew; ~ *de lièvre* jugged hare.

civette¹ *zo.* [si'vɛt] *f* civet-cat; 🜏 *perfume:* civet.

civette² 🜍 [~] *f* chive.

civière [si'vjɛːr] *f* hand-barrow; stretcher; *coffin:* bier.

civil, e [si'vil] 1. *su./m* ✕ civilian; *eccl.* layman; civil status *or* dress; *dans le* ~ in civil life; *en* ~ in mufti, in plain clothes; 2. *adj.* civil; ✕ civilian; *eccl.* lay; civic; polite (to, towards *à*, *envers*); *année f* ~*e* calendar year; ⚖ *droit m* ~ common law; *état m* ~ civil status; register office; *mariage m* ~ civil marriage; *mort f* ~*e* civil death; **civilisateur, -trice** [siviliza'tœːr, ~'tris] 1. *adj.* civilizing; 2. *su.* civilizer; **civilisation** [~za'sjɔ̃] *f* civilization; **civiliser** [~'ze] (1a) *v/t.* civilize; *se* ~ become civilized; **civilité** [~'te] *f* civility, courtesy; *fig.* ~*s pl.* compliments, kind regards; *faire des* ~*s à* be civil to.

civique [si'vik] civic; civil (*rights*);

patriotic (*song*); *droits m/pl.* ~*s* civic rights, *Am.* citizen rights; *instruction f* ~ civics *sg.*; **civisme** [~'vism] *m* good citizenship.

clabaud [kla'bo] *m* *hunt.* (long-eared) hound; F scandal-monger; **clabaudage** [~bo'daːʒ] *m* *hunt.* babbling; F spiteful gossip; **clabauder** [~bo'de] (1a) *v/i. hunt.* babble; F talk scandal (about, *sur*).

claie [klɛ] *f* ⚸ hurdle; fence; ⊕ screen; ⊕ grid.

clair, e [klɛːr] 1. *adj.* clear; bright; obvious; thin (*silk, soup, wood*); 2. *clair adv.* clearly, plainly; thinly; 3. *su./m* light; *garment:* thin place; *tirer au* ~ decant (*wine*); *fig.* clarify, bring to light; **clairet, -ette** [klɛ'rɛ, ~'rɛt] 1. *adj.* pale, light; thin (*voice*); 2. *su./m* local light red wine; **claire-voie,** *pl.* **claires-voies** [klɛr'vwa] *f* open-work; △ skylight; ⚓ decklight; *eccl.* clerestory; ⚸ *à* ~ thinly; **clairière** [klɛ'rjɛːr] *f* clearing; glade; *linen:* thin place; **clair-obscur,** *pl.* **clairs-obscurs** *paint.* [klɛrɔps'kyːr] *m* chiaroscuro.

clairon ♩ [klɛ'rɔ̃] *m* bugle; *clarinet:* upper register; *person:* bugler; **claironner** [~rɔ'ne] (1a) *v/i.* sound the bugle; trumpet; *v/t. fig.* trumpet abroad.

clairsemé, e [klɛrsə'me] thinly-sown; scattered, sparse; thin (*hair, beard*).

clairvoyance [klɛrvwa'jãːs] *f* perceptiveness; clear-sightedness; **clairvoyant, e** [~'jã, ~'jãːt] perceptive; clear-sighted; clairvoyant.

clamer [kla'me] (1a) *v/t.* protest (*one's innocence etc.*); F cry (*s.th.*) out; **clameur** [~'mœːr] *f* clamo(u)r, outcry; *sea, tempest:* roar(ing).

clan [klã] *m* clan; *fig.* clique.

clandestin, e [klãdɛs'tɛ̃, ~'tin] clandestine, secret; ✕ underground (*forces*); illicit; *fig.* underhand; stealthy; ⚓ *passager m* ~ stowaway; **clandestinité** [~tini'te] *f* secrecy; clandestineness; stealth.

clapet [kla'pɛ] *m* ⊕ valve; 🜍 rectifier.

clapier [kla'pje] *m* rabbit hutch *or* warren; F *fig.* dump, hole.

clapotement [klapɔt'mã] *m*, **clapotis** [klapɔ'ti] *m* *waves:* lapping, plashing; **clapoter** [~'te] (1a) *v/i.* lap, plash; **clapoteux, -euse** [~'tø,

~'tø:z] choppy (*sea*); plashing (*noise*). [one's tongue).⟩
clapper [kla'pe] [1a] *v/i.* click (*with* ⟩
claque [klak] *su./f* smack, slap; *thea.* claque, hired applause; *sl.* death; golosh, *Am.* overshoe; *fig. prendre ses cliques et ses* ~*s* depart quickly, F clear off; *su./m* opera-hat, crush-hat; cocked hat; *sl.* disorderly house; **claquedent** F [~'dã] *m* starveling; **claquement** [~'mã] *m* bullet, whip: smack; door: slam; hands: clapping; teeth: chattering; machine: rattle.
claquemurer [klakmy're] (1a) *v/t.* immure; se ~ shut o.s. up.
claquer [kla'ke] (1m) *v/i.* clap; crack (*whip*); bang, slam (*door*); burn out (*lamp*); F kick the bucket (= *die*); break; snap (*string etc.*); F go bust; F go phut; F come to nothing; ~ *des doigts* snap one's fingers; ~ *des mains* clap; *il claquait des dents* his teeth were chattering; 2. *v/t.* slap, smack; slam, bang; *fig.* burst; wear out, tire out; *thea.* applaud; F blue, blow (*money*); F se ~ tire o.s. out; **claquet** [~'kɛ] *m* (mill-)clapper; **claqueter** [klak'te] (1c) *v/i.* cluck, cackle (*hen*); clapper (*stork*); **claquette** [kla'kɛt] *f* *eccl.* clapper; F chatterbox; (*danse f à*) ~*s* pl. tap-cance sg.; **claqueur** [~'kœ:r] *m* hired clapper.
clarifier [klari'fje] (1o) *v/t.* clarify.
clarine [kla'rin] *f* cattle-bell; **clarinette** ♩ [~ri'nɛt] *f* clarinet; person: clarinettist.
clarté [klar'te] *f* light, clearness; brightness; sun: gleam; glass: transparency; *fig.* lucidity.
classe [klɑ:s] *f* class (*a. sociology*; *a.* 🐟 *etc.*); category; rank; kind; ✗ annual contingent; *primary school*: standard; *secondary school*: form, *Am.* grade; class-room; lessons *pl.*; ~ *moyenne* (*ouvrière*) middle (working) class(es *pl.*); *aller en* ~ go to school; *de première* ~ 🐟 *etc.* first-class (*ticket, compartment*); *fig.* first-rate; *faire la* ~ teach; **classé, e** [kla'se] classified; listed (*building*); **classement** [klɑs'mã] *m* classification; 🌱 *etc.* filing; grading; **classer** [klɑ'se] (1a) *v/t.* classify; 🌱 *etc.* file; catalogue, *Am.* catalog; grade; **classeur** [~'sœ:r] *m* 🌱 file; filing cabinet, *Am.* file case; ⊕ sorter; sizer; ~ *à anneaux* ring binder.

classicisme [klasi'sism] *m* classicism.
classification [klasifika'sjõ] *f* classification; **classifier** [~'fje] (1o) *v/t.* classify.
classique [kla'sik] 1. *adj.* classical (*author, music, period*); classic; standard; *fig.* orthodox; 2. *su./m* classic; classicist (*as opposed to romantic*); *les* ~*s* pl. the (*ancient, French*) classics.
clause 🏛 [klo:z] *f* clause; ~ *additionnelle* rider; additional clause.
claustral, e, *m/pl.* -**aux** [klos'tral, ~'tro] monastic; **claustrophobie** [klostrɔfɔ'bi] *f* claustrophobia.
claveau [kla'vo] *m* 🏛 arch-stone; *vet.* sheep-pox.
clavecin ♩ [klav'sɛ̃] *m* harpsichord.
clavette ⊕ [kla'vet] *f* pin, key, peg, cotter.
clavicule *anat.* [klavi'kyl] *f* clavicle, collar-bone.
clavier ♩ *etc.* [kla'vje] *m* *piano, typewriter*: keyboard; *organ*: manual; *wind-instrument*: range; † key-ring, key-chain.
clayon [klɛ'jõ] *m* wicker-tray (*for cheese*); wattle enclosure; **clayonnage** [~jɔ'na:ʒ] *m* wicker-work; wattle fencing; ⊕ mat; **clayonner** [~jɔ'ne] (1a) *v/t.* protect with wattle fencing; mat.
clé, clef [kle] *f* key (*a. fig.*); 🏛 keystone; 🏛 *beam*: reinforcing piece; ⊕ spanner, wrench; 🔩 switch-key; ♩ clef; ♩ key-signature; ♩ key (*woodwind instrument*); *sp.* wrestling: lock; ~ *à douilles* box-spanner; ~ *à molette* adjustable spanner; ~ *anglaise* monkey-wrench; ~ *crocodile* crocodile spanner; *mot.* ~ *pour roues* wheelbrace; 🔺, *a. fig.* ~ *de voûte* keystone; ~*s en main* ready for immediate occupation (*house etc.*); *fausse* ~ skeleton key; *mettre sous* ~ lock up; *sous* ~ under lock and key.
clématite 🌿 [klema'tit] *f* clematis.
clémence [kle'mã:s] *f* clemency (*a. of weather*); leniency; mercy; **clément, e** [~'mã, ~'mã:t] clement, lenient; merciful; mild (*disease etc.*); *ciel m* ~ mild climate.
clenche [klã:ʃ] *f* (door-)latch.
clerc [klɛ:r] *m* *eccl.* cleric, clergyman; 🏛 clerk; F *être* (*grand*) ~ be an expert on; *faire un pas de* ~ blunder; **clergé** [klɛr'ʒe] *m* clergy *pl.*; **clérical, e**, *m/pl.* -**aux** *eccl., a. pol.*

[kleri'kal, ~'ko] *adj.*, *a. su.*/*m* clerical.
clic! [klik] *int.* click!
clichage [kli'ʃaːʒ] *m typ.* stereotyping; electro-typing; ⚒ caging;
cliché [~'ʃe] *m typ. type:* plate; *illustration:* block; *phot.* negative; *fig.* cliché, stock phrase; **clicher** [~'ʃe] (1a) *v*/*t. typ.* stereotype; take electrotypes of; ⚒ cage; **clicherie** *typ.*, *journ.* [kliʃ'ri] stereotype room; stereotyping shop.
client *m*, **e** *f* [kli'ã, ~'ãːt] client; ✝ customer; *hotel:* guest; **clientèle** [~ã'tɛl] *f* ✝ custom, customers *pl.*; ✝ goodwill; ✝ connection; ✐, ✠ practice; ~ *d'habitués* regular clients *pl. or* customers *pl.*; *donner sa* ~ *à* patronize.
cligner [kli'ɲe] *vt*/*i.* wink; blink; *v*/*t.* screw up (*one's eyes*); **clignotant** *mot.* [kliɲɔ'tã] *m* indicator, trafficator; blinker; *fig.* warning light; **clignoter** [~'te] (1a) *v*/*i.* blink; flicker (*eyelids, light*); twinkle (*star*).
climat [kli'ma] *m* climate; region; *fig.* atmosphere; **climatérique** [klimate'rik] 1. *su.*/*f* climacteric; 2. *adj.* climacteric; *a.* = **climatique** [~'tik] climatic (*conditions*); *station f* ~ health-resort; **climatisation** [~tiza'sjɔ̃] *f* air conditioning; **climatiser** [~ti'ze] (1a) *v*/*t.* air-condition; **climatiseur** [~ti'zœːr] *m* air conditioner; **climatologie** [~tɔlɔ'ʒi] *f* climatology; **climatologique** [~tɔlɔ'ʒik] climatological.
clin [klɛ̃] *m:* ~ *d'œil* wink; *en un* ~ *d'œil* in the twinkling of an eye.
clinicien ✐ [klini'sjɛ̃] *su.*/*m*, *a. adj.*/*m* clinician; **clinique** ✐ [~'nik] 1. *adj.* clinical; 2. *su.*/*f* clinic; nursing home; F surgery (*of a doctor*); teaching hospital.
clinquant, e [klɛ̃'kã, ~'kãːt] 1. *adj.* showy, gaudy, flashy; 2. *su.*/*m* tinsel; ⊕ foil; *fig.* showiness.
clip [klip] *m pen etc.:* clip.
clipper ⚓, ✈ [kli'pœːr] *m* clipper.
clique F [klik] *f* set, clique; gang; ✗ drum and bugle band; **cliquet** ⊕ *etc.* [kli'kɛ] *m* catch; ratchet; **cliqueter** [klik'te] (1c) *v*/*i.* rattle; clink (*glass*); jingle (*keys etc.*); *mot.* pink; **cliquetis** [~'ti] *m metall.* clang, rattle; clatter; *glasses:* clinking; *keys etc.:* jingling; *mot.* pinking.
clisse [klis] *f bottle:* wicker covering; *cheese:* drainer; ✐ splint; **clisser**

[kli'se] (1a) *v*/*t.* wicker (*a bottle*); ✐ put in splints; *bouteille f clissée* demijohn.
clivage [kli'vaːʒ] *m* cleavage; gap, split; **cliver** [kli've] (1a) *v*/*t. a.* se ~ split, cleave.
cloaque [klɔ'ak] *m* cesspool (*a. fig.*); *fig.* sink (*of iniquity*).
clochard F [klɔ'ʃaːr] *m* down-and-out; tramp, *Am.* hobo; **clochardiser** [~ʃardi'ze] (1a) *v*/*t.:* se ~ go to the dogs.
cloche [klɔʃ] *f* bell; ✙ bell-jar; ✐ cloche; ✐ cup (*for blistering*); dish-cover; cloche(-hat); *sl.* idiot; F *la* ~ (the) down-and-outs (in general); ~**pied** [~'pje] *adv.:* *sauter à* ~ hop.
clocher[1] [klɔ'ʃe] *m* church tower; steeple; *fig. de* ~ parochial; *esprit m de* ~ parochialism.
clocher[2] [~] (1a) *v*/*i.* F go *or* be wrong; limp, hobble.
clocheton [klɔʃ'tɔ̃] *m* bell-turret; **clochette** [klɔ'ʃɛt] *f* handbell; ⚘ bell-flower; ~ *d'hiver* snowdrop.
cloison [klwa'zɔ̃] *f* ⚠ partition (wall); ⚓ bulkhead; *mot.* baffle-plate; *fig.* ~ (*étanche impenetrable*) barrier; *fig.* séparé(e)s *par des* ~s étanches in watertight compartments; **cloisonnage** [~zɔ'naːʒ] *m* partition (-ing); **cloisonner** [~zɔ'ne] (1a) *v*/*t.* partition; divide up; compartmentalize.
cloître *eccl.* [klwaːtr] *m* cloister(s *pl.*); monastery; convent; **cloîtrer** [klwa'tre] (1a) *v*/*t.* cloister; *nonne f cloîtrée* enclosed nun.
clope *sl.* [klɔp] *f* cig, *Br.* fag (= *cigarette*).
clopin-clopant F [klɔpɛ̃klɔ'pã] *adv.* hobbling (along); **clopiner** [~pi'ne] (1a) *v*/*i.* hobble, limp.
cloporte *zo.* [klɔ'pɔrt] *m* wood-louse, *Am.* sow-bug.
cloque [klɔk] *f* ✐ lump, swelling; ✐ *corn:* rust; *tree:* blight.
clore [klɔːr] (4f) *vt*/*i.* close; *v*/*t.* enclose (*land*); **clos, close** [klo, kloːz] 1. *p.p.* of *clore*; 2. *adj.* closed; shut in; finished; 3. *su.*/*m* enclosure, close; vineyard; **closerie** [kloz'ri] *f* small estate; small holding; croft; pleasure garden; **clôt** [klo] *3rd p. sg. pres.* of *clore*; **clôture** [~'tyːr] *f* fence, enclosure; closure, closing; end; ✝ *account:* winding up; ✝ *books:*

balancing; **clôturer** [ˌtyˈre] (1a)
v/t. enclose (*land*); ✝ close down (*a
factory*); *pol.* apply the closure to (*a
debate*); ✝ wind up, close.

clou [klu] *m* nail; *fig.* star turn, hit,
highlight; 🌢 boil, carbuncle; *pedestrian crossing*: stud; *sl.* pawn-
shop, *Am.* hock shop; *sl.* clink, jail;
sl. old jalopy; *cuis.* ~ *de girofle* clove;

clouer [kluˈe] (1a) *v/t.* nail; pin
down; rivet; *fig.* tie; *tapis m* **cloué**
fitted carpet; **clouter** [ˌte] (1a) *v/t.*
stud; **clouterie** [ˌtri] *f* nail-
making; nail-works *usu. sg.*; **cloutier** [ˌtje] *m* nail-dealer; nailsmith.

clown [klun] *m* clown; buffoon;
clownerie [ˌri] *f* clownish trick;
clownishness; **clownesque** [klu-
ˈnɛsk] clownish; farcical.

cloyère [klwaˈjɛːr] *f* oyster-basket.

club [klœb] *m* club.

cluse *geol.* [klyːz] *f* transverse valley.

coadjuteur *eccl.* [koadʒyˈtœːr] *m*
coadjutor; **coadjutrice** *eccl.* [ˌˈtris]
f coadjutrix.

coagulation [koagylaˈsjɔ̃] *f* coagulation, congealing; **coaguler** [ˌle]
(1a) *v/t. a.* **se** ~ coagulate, clot;
curdle.

coaliser *pol.* [koaliˈze] (1a) *v/t. a.*
se ~ unite; **coalition** [ˌsjɔ̃] *f*
coalition; *fig.* combine; *ministère
m de* ~ coalition ministry.

coasser [koaˈse] (1a) *v/i.* croak.

coassocié *m*, **e** *f* [koasɔˈsje] co-
partner.

cobaye *zo.*, *fig.* [kɔˈbaːj] *m* guinea-
pig.

cocagne [kɔˈkaɲ] *f:* *mât m de* ~
greasy pole; *pays m de* ~ land of
plenty.

cocaïne [kɔkaˈin] *f* cocaine.

cocasse F [kɔˈkas] comical, droll.

coccinelle *zo.* [kɔksiˈnɛl] *f* lady-
bird.

coccyx *anat.* [kɔkˈsis] *m* coccyx.

coche[1] [kɔʃ] *m* ✝ stage-coach; *faire
la mouche du* ~ buzz around; be a
busy-body; F *manquer le* ~ miss the
boat (= *lose an opportunity*).

coche[2] [ˌ] *f* nick, notch.

coche[3] *zo.* [ˌ] *f* sow.

cocher[1] [kɔˈʃe] (1a) *v/t.* nick, notch;
check off, tick off.

cocher[2] [kɔˈʃe] *m* coachman, F cabby;
cochère [ˌˈʃɛːr] *adj./f:* *porte f* ~
carriage-entrance; main gate.

cochon, -onne [kɔˈʃɔ̃, ˌˈʃɔn] **1.** *su./m*

pig, hog, porker; *fig.* filthy swine; ~
de lait sucking-pig; ~ *d'Inde* guinea-
pig; **2.** *adj. sl.* indecent; filthy; **cochonner** [ˌʃɔˈne] (1a) *v/i.* farrow;
v/t. F botch (*a piece of work*); **co-
chonnerie** [ˌʃɔnˈri] *f* filth; rubbish;
foul trick; hogwash (= *bad food*);
cochonnet [ˌʃɔˈnɛ] *m* young pig;
bowls: jack; *tex.* cylinder.

cockpit ✈ [kɔkˈpit] *m* cockpit.

cocktail [kɔkˈtɛl] *m* cocktail; cocktail
party; ~ *Molotov* Molotov cocktail.

coco [kɔˈko] *su./m* (*a. noix f de* ~)
coco(a)nut; F liquorice water; *sl.*
head; F guy; F darling; F stomach;
✈ *sl.* petrol; *ch.sp.* hen, egg; *su./f*
F snow (= *cocaine*).

cocon [kɔˈkɔ̃] *m* cocoon.

cocorico [kɔkɔriˈko] *m* cock-a-
doodle-doo.

cocotier ♀ [kɔkɔˈtje] *m* coconut
palm.

cocotte[1] [kɔˈkɔt] *f* chuck-chuck
(= *hen*); F darling, ducky, *pej.*
loose woman, tart.

cocotte[2] *cuis.* [ˌ] *f* stew-pan.

coction [kɔkˈsjɔ̃] *f* 🜂 boiling, coction; 🌢 digestion.

cocu F [kɔˈky] *m* cuckold, deceived
husband; **cocufier** F [ˌkyˈfje] (1o)
v/t. cuckold.

codage [kɔˈdaːʒ] *m* (en)coding; **code**
[kɔd] *m* code (*a.* 🜨 *a. tel.*); 🜨 ~ *civil
(pénal, de la route)* civil (penal, highway) code; ~ *postal* postcode, *Am.* zip
code; *mot. se mettre en* ~ dip (*Am.*
dim) the headlights; **coder** [kɔˈde]
(1a) *v/t.* code.

codétenu *m*, **e** *f* 🜨 [kodetˈny] fellow-
prisoner.

codifier [kɔdiˈfje] (1o) *v/t.* 🜨 codify;
tel. etc. code.

coéducation [koedykaˈsjɔ̃] *f* coedu-
cation. [factor.)

coefficient [koefiˈsjɑ̃] *m* coefficient;(

coéquation *admin.* [koekwaˈsjɔ̃] *f*
proportional assessment.

coercitif, -ve 🜨, *phys.* [koɛrsiˈtif,
ˌˈtiːv] coercive.

cœur [kœːr] *m* heart (*a. fig.*);
courage; feelings *pl.*; centre; *cards:*
heart(s *pl.*); 🌢 ~*-poumon m artificiel*
heart-lung machine; 🌢 *arrêt m du* ~
heart failure; *à* ~ *joie* to one's heart's
content; *avoir mal au* ~, *avoir le* ~ *sur
les lèvres* feel sick; *par* ~ by heart; *cela
vous (sou)lève le* ~ that makes you
(feel) sick.

coexistence [koɛgzis'tɑ̃ːs] *f* coexistence (*a. pol.*); **coexister** [~'te] (1a) *v/i.* coexist.

coffrage [kɔ'fraːʒ] *m* 🛠 coffering, lining; shuttering (*for concrete work*); **coffre** [kɔfr] *m* chest, box; coffer; ⚓ moorings *pl.*; ⚓ (mooring-)buoy; case; 🔋 ballast-bed; *mot.* boot; ⚓ form, box (*for concrete work*); ⚓ *navire m à* ~ well-decker; **coffre-fort**, *pl.* **coffres-forts** [~ə'fɔːr] *m* safe; strong-box; **coffrer** [kɔ'fre] (1a) *v/t.* F imprison; 🛠 coffer, line; **coffret** [~'frɛ] *m* casket; (*tool-, work-, etc.*)box.

cogérance [koʒe'rɑ̃ːs] *f* co-administration; joint management; **cogérer** [~'re] (1f) *v/i.* manage jointly; **cogestion** [~'stjɔ̃] *f* joint management; co-management.

cogiter [kɔʒi'te] (1a) *vt/i.* cogitate; think (up).

cognac [kɔ'ɲak] *m* cognac, F brandy. **cognassier** ♀ [kɔɲa'sje] *m* quince-tree.

cognée [kɔ'ɲe] *f* axe, hatchet; **cogner** [~] (1a) *v/t.* hammer in; drive in (*a nail*); knock, hit; bump against; *v/i.* knock (*a. mot.*); bump.

cohabiter [koabi'te] (1a) *v/i.* live together, cohabit.

cohérence [kɔe'rɑ̃ːs] *f* coherence; *avec* ~ coherently; **cohérent, e** [~'rɑ̃, ~'rɑ̃ːt] coherent; **cohésion** [~'zjɔ̃] *f* cohesion; *phys. force f de* ~ cohesive force.

cohue [kɔ'y] *f* crowd, throng, crush; mob.

coi, coite [kwa, kwat] quiet; *se tenir* ~ keep quiet; F lie doggo.

coiffe [kwaf] *f* head-dress; cap; *hat:* lining; ⚓ cap-cover; **coiffé, e** [kwa'fe] *adj.:* être ~ be wearing a hat; have done one's hair; *fig.* be infatuated (with, de); être bien ~ have one's hair well dressed; né ~ born lucky; **coiffer** [~'fe] (1a) *v/t.* cover (*one's head*); *hat:* suit; put on (*a hat*); do (*one's hair*); *fig.* cover (up for) (*s.o.*); *fig.* control (*an organization etc.*); *sp., a. fig.* beat (*an opponent*); *de combien coiffez-vous?* what size in hats do you take?; ~ *sainte Catherine* reach the age of 25 without being married (*woman*); *sp., a. fig.* ~ *q. au poteau* beat s.o. at the post; **coiffeur, -euse** [~'fœːr, ~'føːz] *su.* hairdresser; *su./f* dressing-table;

coiffure [~'fyːr] *f* head-dress; hair-style; hairdressing; ~ *à la Jeanne d'Arc* bobbed hair (with fringe).

coin [kwɛ̃] *m* corner; nook, spot; ground: patch; *coins:* die; ⊕ wedge, chock; *fig.* hallmark, stamp; ~ *du feu* fireside; *dans tous les* ~s *et recoins* in every corner, everywhere; **coincement** ⊕ [kwɛ̃s'mɑ̃] *m* jamming; **coincer** ⊕ [kwɛ̃'se] (1k) *v/t.* wedge; *fig. sl.* corner; arrest; *v/i. a. se* ~ jam, stick.

coïncidence [kɔɛ̃si'dɑ̃ːs] *f* coincidence; ≸ ~ *d'oscillations* surging; **coïncider** [~'de] (1a) *v/i.* coincide. **coing** ♀ [kwɛ̃] *m* quince. **coït** kɔ'it] *m* coitus.

coke [kɔk] *m* coke; *petit* ~ breeze; **cokerie** [kɔ'kri] *f* coking plant.

col [kɔl] *m* neck (*a. fig.*); *cost.* collar; *geog.* pass, col; *fig.* ~ *blanc* (*bleu*) white- (blue-)collar worker; ~ *cassé* (*droit, rabattu*) wing (stand-up, turn-down) collar; ~ *roulé* polo neck, *Am.* turtleneck; *à* ~ *Danton* open-necked (*shirt*); *faux* ~ detachable *or* separate collar.

colchique ♀ [kɔl'ʃik] *m* colchicum. **coléoptère** *zo.* [kɔleɔp'teːr] *m* beetle; ~s *pl.* coleoptera.

colère [kɔ'lɛːr] **1.** *su./f* anger; *en* ~ angry; *se mettre en* ~ become angry; **2.** *adj.* angry; irascible (*person*); **coléreux, -euse** [kɔle'rø, ~'røːz] hot-tempered, irascible; **colérique** [~'rik] choleric.

colifichet [kɔlifi'ʃɛ] *m* trinket; ~s *pl.* rubbish *sg.*; ✝ *rayon m des* ~s fancy goods department.

colimaçon *zo.* [kɔlima'sɔ̃] *m* snail; *en* ~ spiral (*staircase*).

colin *icht.* [kɔ'lɛ̃] *m* hake.

colin-maillard [kɔlɛ̃ma'jaːr] *m* game: blind-man's buff.

colique ⚕ [kɔ'lik] *f* colic; F stomach-ache; *sl. avoir la* ~ have the wind up.

colis [kɔ'li] *m* packet, parcel; luggage; *par* ~ *postal* by parcel post.

collaborateur *m*, **-trice** *f* [kɔllabo-ra'tœːr, ~'tris] collaborator (*a. pol.*); associate; *review:* contributor; **collaboration** [~ra'sjɔ̃] *f* collaboration (*a. pol.*); co-operation; *book:* joint authorship; **collaborer** [~'re] (1a) *v/i.* collaborate, co-operate; contribute (*to a journal etc.*).

collage [kɔ'laːʒ] *m* pasting; gluing;

paper: sizing; F (*unmarried*) cohabitation; *paint.* collage; **collant, e** [~'lɑ̃, ~'lɑ̃:t] **1.** *adj.* sticky, adhesive; *cost.* tight, close-fitting, skintight; *pej.* clinging; **2.** *su./m*: ~s *pl.* tights.

collatéral, e, *m/pl.* **-aux** [kɔllate'ral, ~'ro] **1.** *adj.* collateral; *eccl.* side-(*aisle*); **2.** *su.* relative, collateral; *su./m eccl.* side-aisle.

collateur *eccl.* † [kɔlla'tœ:r] *m* patron (*of a living*); **collation** [~'sjɔ̃] *f* t_{2}^{1} *etc.* granting, conferment; *eccl.* advowson; *typ.* checking, proofreading; *documents*: collation; light meal; **collationner** [~sjɔ'ne] (1a) *v/t.* collate, compare; check; *v/i.* have a light meal.

colle [kɔl] *f* paste, glue; gum; *paper etc.*: size; *fig.* poser, difficult question; *school*: detention; ~ **forte** glue.

collecte [kɔl'lɛkt] *f eccl. etc.* collection; collecting; *eccl. prayer*: collect; *faire une* ~ make a collection; **collecteur** [kɔllɛk'tœ:r] *m* ⚡ collector; ⚡ commutator; ⊕ sewer; *mot.* ~ **d'admission** (*d'échappement*) intake (exhaust) manifold; **collectif, -ve** [~'tif, ~'ti:v] collective; **collection** [~'sjɔ̃] *f* collection; gathering; **collectionner** [~sjɔ'ne] (1a) *v/t.* collect; **collectiviser** [~tivi'ze] (1a) *v/t.* collectivize; communize; **collectivité** [~tivi'te] *f* community; group; common ownership.

collège [kɔ'lɛ:ʒ] *m* college; school; secondary grammar school; ~ **électoral** constituency; electoral body, *Am.* electoral college; *sacré* ~ College of Cardinals.

collégial, e, *m/pl.* **-aux** [kɔle'ʒjal, ~'ʒjo] **1.** *adj.* collegiate; collegial; **2.** *su./f* collegiate church; **collégialité** *pol.*, ✝ *etc.* [~ʒjali'te] *f* collegial administration; **collégien, -enne** [~'ʒjɛ̃, ~'ʒjɛn] *su.* college-student; *su./m* schoolboy; *su./f* schoolgirl.

collègue [kɔl'lɛg] *su.* colleague.

coller [kɔ'le] (1a) *v/t.* stick; paste; glue; size (*paper*); clarify (*wine*); F put, stick (*s.th. in a place*); F plough (*a candidate*); *se* ~ stick; *sl.* cohabit, live (with, *avec*); *v/i.* stick; cling; *sl. ça colle!* all right!; *sl. cela ne colle pas* it is not going properly.

collerette [kɔl'rɛt] *f cost.* collarette; ⊕ *joint, pipe*: flange.

collet [kɔ'le] *m* ⚡, ⊕, *cost.* collar; *cost.* cape; *cuis.* neck, scrag; *tooth*,

violin, ⊕ *screw, chisel*: neck; ⊕ *pipe, etc.*: flange; snare (*for rabbits etc.*); *fig.* ~ **monté** strait-laced person; strait-laced; **colleter** [kɔl'te] (1c) *v/t.* (seize by the) collar; grapple with; *fig.* hug; *se* ~ come to grips; *v/i.* set snares (*for rabbits etc.*).

colleur *m*, **-euse** *f* [kɔ'lœ:r, ~'lø:z] paster; (*bill-*)sticker; *paper*: sizer; *sl. school*: stiff examiner; *sl.* liar.

collier [kɔ'lje] *m* necklace; collar (*a.* ⊕, ⚓, *zo., order*); ~ **de chien** dog collar; *coup m de* ~ *fig.* big effort; ⚡ sudden overload; *fig. reprendre le* ~ be back in harness.

collimateur [kɔlima'tœ:r] *m* collimator; *fig. avoir or prendre dans le* ~ train one's sights on.

colline [kɔ'lin] *f* hill.

collision [kɔlli'zjɔ̃] *f* collision.

collocation [kɔllɔka'sjɔ̃] *f* t_{2}^{1} order of priority of creditors (*in bankruptcy*); *gramm.* collocation.

collodion ♎ [kɔllɔ'djɔ̃] *m* collodion.

colloque [kɔl'lɔk] *m* conference; conversation; parley.

collusion ♎ [kɔlly'zjɔ̃] *f* collusion; **collusoire** ♎ [~'zwa:r] collusive.

collutoire [kɔlly'twa:r] *m* mouthwash.

collyre [kɔl'li:r] *m* eyewash.

colmater [kɔlma'te] (1a) *v/t.* seal (up or off); plug (up); fill in (*holes etc.*); ⚡ warp (*the soil*); ⚒ consolidate.

colocataire [kɔlɔka'tɛ:r] *su.* joint tenant; co-tenant.

colombe *orn.* [kɔ'lɔ̃:b] *f* pigeon; dove (*a. pol.*); **colombier** [kɔlɔ̃'bje] *m* dovecot(e); pigeon-house; **colombin, e** [~'bɛ̃, ~'bin] **1.** *adj.* dove-like; dove-colo(u)red; **2.** *su./m orn.* stock-dove; ⚒ lead ore; *su./f* ⚡ pigeon-dung.

colon [kɔ'lɔ̃] *m* small holder; settler, colonist.

côlon *anat.* [ko'lɔ̃] *m* colon.

colonel ⚔ [kɔlɔ'nɛl] *m* colonel; **colonelle** [~] *f* colonel's wife.

colonial, e, *m/pl.* **-aux** [kɔlɔ'njal, ~'njo] **1.** *adj.* colonial; *denrées f/pl.* ~**es** colonial produce *sg.*; **2.** *su./m* colonial; *su./f* ⚔ colonial troops *pl.*; **colonialisme** *pol.* [~nja'lism] *m* colonialism; **colonie** [~'ni] *f* colony, settlement; ~ **de vacances** holiday camp; **colonisateur, -trice** [kɔlɔniza'tœ:r, ~'tris] **1.** *adj.* colonizing; **2.** *su.* colonizer; **colonisation** [~za'sjɔ̃] *f* colonization, settling; **coloniser** [ˌ'ze] (1a) *v/t.* colonize, settle.

colonne [kɔ'lɔn] *f* △, ✂, column; △ pillar; ⚓ en ˌ line ahead; ˌ *Morris* advertizing column *or* pillar.

colophane [kɔlɔ'fan] *f* rosin.

colorant, e [kɔlɔ'rã, ˌ'rãːt] **1.** *adj.* colo(u)ring; **2.** *su./m* dye; colo(u)ring (matter); **colorer** [ˌ're] (1a) *v/t.* colo(u)r, stain; dye; **colorier** [ˌ'rje] (1o) *v/t.* colo(u)r; coloris [ˌ'ri] *m* colo(u)r(ing); *fig.* hue.

colossal, e, *m/pl.* **-aux** [kɔlɔ'sal, ˌ'so] colossal, gigantic; **colosse** [ˌ'lɔs] *m* colossus; F giant.

colportage [kɔlpɔr'taːʒ] *m* hawking, peddling; **colporter** [ˌ'te] (1a) *v/t.* hawk, peddle; *fig.* spread (*news*); **colporteur** *m*, **-euse** *f* [ˌ'tœːr, ˌ'tøːz] hawker; pedlar, *Am.* peddler; *fig.* newsmonger.

coltiner [kɔlti'ne] (1a) *v/t.* carry (*loads*) (on one's back); F *fig.* se ˌ saddle o.s. with (*s.th., s.o.*); **coltineur** [ˌ'nœːr] *m* heavy porter; ˌ de *charbon* coal-heaver.

colza ♀ [kɔl'za] *m* rape, colza, rapeseed.

coma ✿ [kɔ'ma] *m* coma; **comateux, -euse** ✿ [ˌma'tø, ˌ'tøːz] comatose.

combat [kɔ'ba] *m* ✂ combat, battle, engagement; struggle (*a. fig.*); *fig.* contest; *hors de* ˌ disabled; out of action; **combatif, -ve** [kɔba'tif, ˌ'tiːv] pugnacious; **combattant** [ˌ'tã] *m* combatant, fighting man; fighter; *zo.* game-cock; *ancien* ˌ exservice man, veteran; **combattre** [kɔ'batr] (4a) *vt/i.* fight.

combe [kɔ:b] *f* coomb, dale, dell.

combien [kɔ'bjɛ̃] *adv.* how (many *or* much); ˌ de *temps* how long; ˌ de ... *qui* (*or* que) (*sbj.*) however much ... (*inf.*); F *le* ˌ *sommes-nous?* what day of the month is it?

combinaison [kɔ̃binɛ'zɔ̃] *f* combination, arrangement, plan; *cost.* overalls *pl.*, boiler-suit; *cost.* combinations *pl.*; ✈ flying suit; *woman:* slip; **combinateur** ⚡ [ˌna'tœːr] *m:* ˌ de *couplage* controller; **combine** F [kɔ'bin] *f* plan, scheme; **combiner** [ˌbi'ne] (1a) *v/t.* combine; devise, concoct; se ˌ combine.

comble [kɔ:bl] **1.** *su./m fig.* summit, height; △ roof(ing); *au* ˌ de la joie overjoyed; *de fond en* ˌ from top to

bottom; *mettre le* ˌ *à* crown; *pour* ˌ *to* cap it all; *c'est le or un* ˌ! that beats all!; **2.** *adj.* heaped up; packed (*house, room*); **comblé, e** [kɔ̃'ble] overjoyed; **comblement** [kɔ̃blə'mã] *m* filling in; **combler** [ˌ'ble] (1a) *v/t.* fill (in); ✂, ✝ make good (*a deficit, casualties*); *fig.* fulfill; *fig.* gratify; *fig.* ˌ q. de qch. shower s.th. on s.o.

combustibilité [kɔ̃bystibili'te] *f* inflammability; **combustible** [ˌ'tibl] **1.** *adj.* inflammable; combustible; **2.** *su./m* fuel; **combustion** [ˌ'tjɔ̃] *f* combustion, burning; ˌ *continue* slow combustion.

comédie [kɔme'di] *f* comedy; *fig.* playacting; *fig. jouer la* ˌ playact; **comédien, -enne** [ˌ'djɛ̃, ˌ'djɛn] **1.** *su.* comedian; *su./m* actor; *su./f* actress; **2.** *adj.* theatrical.

comestible [kɔmɛs'tibl] **1.** *adj.* edible, eatable; **2.** *su./m* article of food; ˌs *pl.* provisions, victuals.

comète *astr.* [kɔ'mɛt] *f* comet.

comice [kɔ'mis] *m* show; gathering; *hist.* ˌs *pl.* electoral meeting *sg.*; ˌ *agricole* agricultural show, cattleshow.

comique [kɔ'mik] **1.** *adj.* comic (*actor, author*); comical, funny; **2.** *su./m* comedian, humorist; comic actor; comedy-writer; comedy.

comité [kɔmi'te] *m* committee, board; ˌ *d'arbitrage* arbitration board; ˌ *de surveillance* vigilance committee; *petit* ˌ little *or* informal meeting.

commandant [kɔmã'dã] *m* ✂, ⚓ commanding officer, commander; ✈ squadron-leader; ✂ ˌ de *bataillon*, ˌ *d'escadron* major; ˌ *en chef* commander-in-chief; **commande** [ˌ'mãːd] *f* ✝ order; ⊕, ✈ control; ⊕ lever; *mot.* drive; ✝ *bulletin m de* ˌ order-form; *de* ˌ feigned; *eccl.* of obligation; F essential; *sur* ˌ to order; **commandement** [ˌmãd'mã] *m* ✂, *a. fig.* command; instruction; ⚖ summons *sg.*; *eccl.* commandment; **commander** [ˌmã'de] (1a) *v/t.* command (*a. fig.*), order (s.th. from s.o., qch. *à* q.); control; dominate; ˌ *à* control; se ˌ control o.s.; lead into each other *or* one another (*rooms*); *cela ne se commande pas* it does not depend upon our will; *v/i.* give

orders; **commandeur** [～'dœːr] *m*
order of knighthood: commander.
commanditaire ✝ [kɔmãdi'tɛːr] *m*
sleeping *or Am.* silent partner; **commandite** [～'dit] *f* (*a.* société *f* en ～)
limited partnership; **commandi-
ter** ✝ [～'te] (1a) *v/t.* finance (*an
enterprise*); become a sleeping partner in.
comme [kɔm] **1.** *adv.* as, like; how; in
the way of; ～ ça like that; just (so); F～
ci ～ ça so so; F c'est tout ～ it comes to
the same thing; ～ il faut proper(ly
adv.); **2.** *cj.* as, seeing that; *temporal*:
just as.
commémoratif, -ve [kɔmemɔra'tif,
～'tiːv] commemorative (of, de);
memorial (*service*); fête *f* ～ve festival
of remembrance; **commémora-
tion** [～ra'sjõ] *f* commemoration;
commémorer [～'re] (1a) *v/t.* com-
memorate.
commençant, e [kɔmã'sã, ～'sãːt] **1.**
adj. beginning, early; **2.** *su.* beginner; **commencement** [～mãs'mã]
m beginning, start, outset; **commencer** [～mã'se] (1k) *vt/i.* begin;
start.
commendataire *eccl.* [kɔmãda'tɛːr]
m commendator.
commensal *m*, **e** *f* [kɔmã'sal] companion at table, table-companion;
regular guest.
commensurable ⚖ [kɔmãsy-
'rabl] commensurable (with, to
avec).
comment [kɔ'mã] **1.** *adv.* how;
what: **2.** *int.* what!; why!; F et ～!
and how; **3.** *su./m/inv.* why; les ～
et les pourquoi the whys and the
wherefores.
commentaire [kɔmã'tɛːr] *m* commentary; *fig.* comment; **commentateur** *m*, **-trice** *f* [～ta'tœːr, ～'tris]
commentator; **commenter** [～'te]
(1a) *v/t.* comment upon (*a. fig.* =
criticise).
commérage [kɔme'raːʒ] *m* gossip.
commerçant, e [kɔmɛr'sã, ～'sãːt] **1.**
adj. commercial; business...; mercantile; très ～ very busy (*street*); **2.**
su./m tradesman, merchant; les ～s *pl.*
tradespeople; **commerce** [～'mɛrs]
m trade, commerce; commercial
world; ✝ dealings *pl.*; ～ de détail retail
trade; ～ d'outre-mer overseas trade;
registre *m* du ～ Commercial Register;
commercer [kɔmɛr'se] (1k) *v/i.*

(with, *avec*) trade, deal; *fig.* have
dealings; **commercial, e**, *m/pl.*
-aux [～'sjal, ～'sjo] commercial, trading, business.
commère [kɔ'mɛːr] *f* ✝ *eccl.* godmother; gossip; crony.
commettant [kɔme'tã] *m* ♟✝, ✝
principal; *pol.* ～s *pl.* constituents;
commettre [～'mɛtr] (4v) *v/t.*
commit.
comminatoire [kɔmina'twaːr] com-
minatory; *fig.* threatening.
commis, e [kɔ'mi, ～'miːz] **1.** *p.p.* of
commettre; **2.** *su./m* clerk; agent;
(shop-)assistant; ～ voyageur commercial traveller, *Am.* travelling
salesman.
commisération [kɔmizera'sjõ] *f*
pity; commiseration.
commissaire [kɔmi'sɛːr] *m* commissioner; *police*: superintendent;
⚓ purser; *sp.* steward; ✝ ～ aux
comptes auditor; **～-priseur**, *pl.* **～s-
priseurs** [～serpri'zœːr] *m* auction-
eer; official valuer; **commissariat**
[～sa'rja] *m* commissioner's office;
central police station.
commission [kɔmi'sjõ] *f* commission; *admin. a.* committee, board;
message; errand; faire la ～ à q. give
s.o. the message; **commissionnaire** [～sjɔ'nɛːr] delivery boy or man;
messenger; ✝ commission agent; ～
de transport forwarding agent; ～
en gros factor; **commissionner**
[～sjɔ'ne] (1a) *v/t.* commission.
commissure [kɔmi'syːr] *f* commissure; ～ des lèvres corner of the
mouth.
commode [kɔ'mɔd] **1.** *adj.* convenient; comfortable; handy; easy-
going (*person*); good-natured; **2.** *su./f*
chest of drawers, *Am. a.* highboy;
commodément [kɔmɔde'mã] *adv.*
of commode 1; **commodité** [～di'te] *f*
convenience; comfort; ～s *pl.* public
convenience *sg.*
commotion [kɔmɔ'sjõ] *f* commotion, disturbance; ⚡, ✚ shock; ✚
concussion.
commuer ♟ [kɔ'mɥe] (1p) *v/t.* commute (to, en).
commun, e [kɔ'mœ̃, ～'myn] **1.** *adj.*
common; usual; joint; vulgar; ✝
average, mean (*tare*); chose *f* ～e
common cause; faire bourse ～e pool
resources; sens *m* ～ common sense;
2. *su./m* generality, common run;

common funds *pl.*; † servants *pl.*; ~s *pl.* outbuildings; conveniences; *en* ~ in common; *su./f admin.* commune, (*approx.*) parish; *hist.* 2e Commune (*1789, a. 1871*); *parl. Chambre f des* ~es House of Commons *pl.*; **communal, e,** *m/pl.* **-aux** [kɔmyˈnal, ~ˈno] common; communal; parish ...; **communard** *hist.* [~ˈnaːr] *m* communard (*supporter of the 1871 Paris Commune*); **communauté** [~noˈte] *f eccl., admin., a. fig.* community; ⚖ joint estate; *pol.* 2 French Community; 2 *Économique Européenne* European Economic Community; ~ *de travail school:* group activity; **communément** [~neˈmɑ̃] *adv. of commun 1.*

communiant *m,* **e** *f eccl.* [kɔmyˈnjɑ̃, ~ˈnjɑ̃ːt] communicant; **communicable** [kɔmyniˈkabl] communicable; **communicatif, -ve** [~kaˈtif, ~ˈtiːv] communicative; infectious (*laughter*); **communication** [~kaˈsjɔ̃] *f* communication; message; (telephone) call; *teleph.* ~ *locale* (*interurbaine*) local (long-distance) call; *teleph. donner la* ~ put a call through; *teleph. mauvaise* ~ wrong number; **communier** *eccl.* [kɔmyˈnje] (1o) *v/i.* communicate; *v/t.* administer Holy Communion to (*s.o.*); **communion** [~ˈnjɔ̃] *f* communion (*a. eccl.*); **communiqué** [kɔmyniˈke] *m* official statement, communiqué; *radio:* news *sg.*; bulletin; ~ *de presse* press release; **communiquer** [~] (1m) *vt/i.* communicate; *v/i.* be in communication *or* connection; ~ *avec* lead into; (*faire*) ~ connect; *v/t.:* se ~ spread (to, *à*); be communicative (*person*).

communisant, e [kɔmyniˈzɑ̃, ~ˈzɑ̃ːt] **1.** *adj.* communistic; **2.** *su. pol.* fellow-traveller, communist sympathizer; **communisme** [~ˈnism] *m* communism; **communiste** [~ˈnist] *su., a. adj.* communist.

commutateur ⚡ [kɔmytaˈtœːr] *m* commutator; *light:* switch; **commutation** [~ˈsjɔ̃] *f* commutation (*a.* ⚖); ⚡ changing over; *de* ~ switch-...; **commutatrice** ⚡ [~ˈtris] *f* rotary transformer; **commuter** ⚡ [kɔmyˈte] (1a) *v/t.* change over.

compacité [kɔpasiˈte] *f* compactness; *metal:* density; **compact, e** [~ˈpakt] compact; dense.

compagne [kɔ̃ˈpaɲ] *f* companion; wife; mate; **compagnie** [kɔ̃paˈɲi] *f* company (*a.* ✝, ✂, *a. person*); ⚓ division; society; *de ou en* ~ together; *tenir* ~ *à q.* keep s.o. company; **compagnon** [~ˈɲɔ̃] *m* comrade; mate (*a.* ⊕), partner; ⊕ journeyman; ~ *de route* fellow traveller; **compagnonnage** † [~nɔˈnaːʒ] *m* trade-guild; time of service as journeyman.

comparable [kɔ̃paˈrabl] comparable; **comparaison** [~rɛˈzɔ̃] *f* comparison; simile.

comparaître ⚖ [kɔ̃paˈrɛːtr] (4k) *v/i.* appear; *faire* ~ *devant* bring before.

comparatif, -ve [kɔ̃paraˈtif, ~ˈtiːv] *adj., a. gramm. su./m* comparative; **comparé, e** [~ˈre] comparative (*grammar, history, etc.*); **comparer** [~ˈre] (1a) *v/t.* compare (to, with *à, avec*).

comparse [kɔ̃ˈpars] *m thea.* supernumerary; † super; *fig.* confederate.

compartiment [kɔ̃partiˈmɑ̃] *m* 🚃, ship, ceiling, *etc.:* compartment; partition; division; *draughts, chess, etc.:* square; ~ *de congélation* freezing compartment, freezer.

comparution ⚖ [kɔ̃paryˈsjɔ̃] *f* appearance.

compas [kɔ̃ˈpa] *m* compasses *pl.*; ⚓ *etc.* compass; *mot. hood:* arms *pl.*; standard, scale; ⚓ ~ *à pointes sèches* dividers *pl.*; *surv.* ~ *de relèvement* azimuth compass; ⚓~ *gyroscopique* gyro-compass; **compassé, e** [kɔ̃paˈse] formal, stiff; regular; **compasser** [~] (1a) *v/t.* measure with compasses; *fig.* consider, weigh, study; ⚓ ~ *la carte* prick the chart.

compassion [kɔ̃paˈsjɔ̃] *f* compassion, pity.

compatible [kɔ̃paˈtibl] compatible. **compatir** [kɔ̃paˈtiːr] (2a) *v/i.:* ~ *à* sympathize with; bear with; **compatissant, e** [~tiˈsɑ̃, ~ˈsɑ̃ːt] (*pour, to[wards]*) compassionate, tender; sympathetic; indulgent.

compatriote [kɔ̃patriˈɔt] *su.* compatriot; *su./m* fellow-countryman; *su./f* fellow-countrywoman.

compensateur, -trice [kɔ̃pɑ̃saˈtœːr, ~ˈtris] **1.** *adj.* compensating; ⚡ equalizing (*current*); *phot.* compensating (*filter, screen*); *phys.* pen-

dule m ~ compensation pendulum;
2. *su./m* compensator; ⚒ trimmer;
compensation [₋saˈsjɔ̃] *f* compensation; ⊕, ⚖ balancing; *sp.* handicapping; ✝ *accord m de* ~ barter agreement; ✝ *caisse f de* ~ equalization fund; ✝ *chambre f de* ~ clearing-house; **compenser** [₋ˈse] (1a) *v/t.* compensate, make up for; ⊕ balance; ⚓ adjust (*a compass*); *sp.* handicap.

compère [kɔ̃ˈpɛːr] *m eccl.* godfather; *thea.* compère; *F* accomplice; comrade, pal; *bon* ~ good fellow; ~**-loriot,** *pl.* ~**s-loriots** ⚕ [₋pɛrlɔˈrjo] *m* sty.

compétence [kɔ̃peˈtãːs] *f* competence (*a.* ⚖); skill, ability; **compétent, e** [₋ˈtã, ₋ˈtãːt] competent (*a.* ⚖); **compéter** [₋ˈte] (1f) *v/i.* ⚖ be within the jurisdiction (of, *à*); belong by right (to, *à*).

compétiteur *m,* **-trice** *f* [kɔ̃petiˈtœːr, ₋ˈtris] competitor, candidate, rival (for, *à*); **compétitif, -ve** [₋ˈtif, ₋ˈtiːv] competitive (*prices*); rival; **compétition** [₋ˈsjɔ̃] *f* competition, rivalry.

compiler [kɔ̃piˈle] (1a) *v/t.* compile.

complainte [kɔ̃ˈplɛ̃ːt] *f* lament; ⚖ complaint; plaintive ballad *or* song.

complaire [kɔ̃ˈplɛːr] (4z) *v/i.* be pleasing; ~ *à* please, humo(u)r (*s.o.*); *v/t.:* se ~ take pleasure (in *ger.,* *à inf.;* in s.th., *dans or* en *qch.*); **complaisance** [kɔ̃plɛˈzãːs] *f* obligingness, kindness; self-satisfaction, complacency; ✝ *effet m de* ~ accommodation bill; **complaisant, e** [₋ˈzã, ₋ˈzãːt] obliging; self-satisfied, complacent.

complément [kɔ̃pleˈmã] *m* complement (*a.* ✕, *a. gramm.*); *gramm.* object; **complémentaire** [₋mãˈtɛːr] complementary (*a.* ⚕); supplementary; further (*information*).

complet, -ète [kɔ̃ˈplɛ, ₋ˈplɛt] **1.** *adj.* complete; full (*theatre etc.*); ~! full up; *hotel:* no vacancies; *thea.* full house; *café m* ~ continental breakfast; **2.** *su./m* (*a.* ~*-veston*) suit; *au* (*grand*) ~ whole, entire; **complètement** [₋plɛtˈmã] **1.** *su./m* completion; ✕ bringing up to strength; **2.** *adv.* completely, thoroughly, utterly; **compléter** [₋pleˈte] (1f) *v/t.* complete, fill up; ✕ bring up to strength; replenish (*stores*).

complexe [kɔ̃ˈplɛks] **1.** *adj.* complex; complicated; *gramm., a.* ⚕ compound; **2.** *su./m* complex; **complexé, e** [₋plɛkˈse] **1.** *adj.* suffering from a complex; **2.** *su.* person suffering from a complex.

complexion [kɔ̃plɛkˈsjɔ̃] *f* constitution; temperament.

complexité [kɔ̃plɛksiˈte] *f* complexity.

complication [kɔ̃plikaˈsjɔ̃] *f* complication (*a.* ⚕); complexity.

complice [kɔ̃ˈplis] *adj., a. su.* accessory (to, *de*); accomplice (of, *de*); **complicité** [₋plisiˈte] *f* complicity; ⚖ aiding and abetting, abetment.

compliment [kɔ̃pliˈmã] *m* compliment; congratulation; flattery; ~*s pl.* kind regards; **complimenter** [₋mãˈte] (1a) *v/t.* compliment, congratulate (on *de, sur*).

compliqué, e [kɔ̃pliˈke] complicated, elaborate, intricate; ⚕ compound (*fracture*); **compliquer** [₋] (1m) *v/t.* complicate; ⚕ *la maladie s'est compliquée* complications set in.

complot [kɔ̃ˈplo] *m* plot, conspiracy; *former un* ~ hatch a plot; **comploter** [₋plɔˈte] (1a) *v/t.* plot, scheme (to *inf., de inf.*); *v/i.* conspire.

componction [kɔ̃pɔ̃kˈsjɔ̃] *f* compunction; *F avec* ~ solemnly.

comportement [kɔ̃pɔrtəˈmã] *m* behavio(u)r; *psych. etc. de* ~ behavio(u)ral; **comporter** [kɔ̃pɔrˈte] (1a) *v/t.* consist of, be composed of; comprise, include; *fig.* involve; require; se ~ behave, act.

composant, e [kɔ̃poˈzã, ₋ˈzãːt] *adj., a. su.* component; **composé, e** [₋ˈze] **1.** *adj.* compound (*a.* ⚕ *a. gramm.*); ⚕ composite; *fig.* composed; impassive; *être* ~ *de* be made up of, consist of; **2.** *su./m* compound; **composer** [₋ˈze] (1a) *v/t.* make up; set up; form; compose; arrange; *typ.* set; ⚕ find the resultant of; ~ *son visage* compose one's countenance; se ~ *de* be made up of, consist of; *v/i.* compose music *etc.*; write a composition; come to terms (with, *avec*); **compositeur, -trice** [₋ziˈtœːr, ₋ˈtris] *su.* ♪ composer; *typ.* compositor, type-setter; *su./m typ.* type-setting machine; **composition** [₋ziˈsjɔ̃] *f* making-up; setting-up; formation; composition; composing (*a. typ.*); *typ.* type-setting; *school:* essay; examination (paper); *amener q. à* ⌣ get s.o. to come to terms; *venir à* ⌣ come to terms.

compost ✍ [kɔ̃'pɔst] *m* compost; **composter** [kɔ̃pɔs'te] (1a) *v/t.* ✍ treat with compost; date *or* punch (*a ticket*); **composteur** [⌣'tœːr] *m typ.* composing-stick; dating stamp; dating and numbering machine.

compote [kɔ̃'pɔt] *f* stewed fruit; *en* ⌣ stewed; *fig.* to *or* in a pulp; **compotier** [⌣pɔ'tje] *m* compote-dish; fruit-dish.

compréhensible [kɔ̃preɑ̃'sibl] comprehensible, understandable; **compréhension** [⌣'sjɔ̃] *f* understanding; **comprendre** [kɔ̃'prɑ̃ːdr] (4aa) *v/t.* understand; include; F *je comprends!* I see!

compresse ⚕ [kɔ̃'prɛs] *f* compress; **compresser** F [kɔ̃prɛ'se] (1a) *v/t.* pack; **compresseur** [⌣'sœːr] *m* *mot.* supercharger; road-roller; **compressible** [⌣'sibl] compressible; **compression** [⌣'sjɔ̃] *f* compression; ⊕ crushing; repression; ✝ cutback, restriction.

comprimé ⚕ [kɔ̃pri'me] *m* tablet; **comprimer** [⌣] (1a) *v/t.* compress; *fig.* repress; hold back (*emotions etc.*); ✝ cut back (*expenses etc.*).

compris, e [kɔ̃'pri, ⌣'priːz] **1.** *p.p. of comprendre*; **2.** *adj.* (*inv. before su.*): *non* ⌣ exclusive of; *service m* ⌣ service included; *tout* ⌣ all in; *y* ⌣ including.

compromettre [kɔ̃prɔ'mɛtr] (4v) *v/t.* compromise; endanger, jeopardize; *fig.* implicate; **compromis** [⌣'mi] *m* compromise (*a.* ✝), arrangement (*a.* ✝); **compromission** [⌣mi'sjɔ̃] *f* compromising; compromise.

comptabilité ✝ [kɔ̃tabili'te] *f* bookkeeping, accountancy; counting-house; accountancy department; ⌣ *en partie double* (*simple*) double (single) entry book-keeping; **comptable** [⌣'tabl] **1.** *adj.* accountable, responsible; **2.** *su.* book-keeper, accountant; **comptant** [⌣'tɑ̃] **1.** *adj./m* ready (*cash*); **2.** *su./m* cash, ready money; *au* ⌣ (for) cash; **3.** *adv.* in cash, F on the nail; **compte** [kɔ̃ːt] *m* account; count; reckoning; number; *fig.* profit, advantage; ⌣ *à rebours* rocket; countdown; ⌣ *bloqué* (*courant, ouvert*) blocked (current, open) account; ⌣ *de chèques postaux* postal cheque account; ⌣

d'épargne savings account; ⌣ *de virement* clearing-account; ⌣ *rendu* account, report; *book etc.*: review; *à* ⌣ on account; *fig. à bon* ⌣ cheap; *à ce* ⌣ in that case; *en fin de* ⌣ after all; *mettre qch. sur le* ⌣ de ascribe s.th. to; *régler un* ⌣ settle an account; *se rendre* ⌣ *de* realize; *tenir* ⌣ *de qch.* take s.th. into account; **compte-gouttes** [kɔ̃t'gut] *m/inv.* dropper; ⊕ drip-feed lubricator; **compter** [kɔ̃'te] (1a) *v/t.* reckon, count (up); value; ✝ charge; expect; *v/i.* count, rely (on, *sur*); reckon; **compteur** [⌣'tœːr] *m* meter; register; *person:* counter; ⌣ *à gaz* gas-meter; ⚡ ⌣ *de courant* electricity meter; ⌣ *de Geiger* Geiger counter; *mot.* ⌣ *de stationnement* parking meter; *mot.* ⌣ *de vitesse* speedometer; **comptoir** [⌣'twaːr] *m* ✝ counter; *public house:* bar; ✝ bank; ✝ ⌣ *d'escompte* discount bank.

compulser [kɔ̃pyl'se] (1a) *v/t.* examine, check (*documents*).

compulsif, -ive [kɔ̃pylsif, -iːv] compulsive. [pute.⟩

computer [kɔ̃py'te] (1a) *v/t.* com-⟩

comte [kɔ̃ːt] *m* earl; (non-English) count; **comté** [kɔ̃'te] *m* county; shire; **comtesse** [⌣'tɛs] *f* countess.

con, conne *sl.* [kɔ̃, kɔn] **1.** *adj.* stupid; *il est* ⌣ *comme la lune* he is an absolute idiot; **2.** *su.* idiot; *à la* ⌣ stupid, foolish; lousy.

concasser ⊕ [kɔ̃kɑ'se] (1a) *v/t.* crush, grind, break up; **concasseur** [⌣'sœːr] *m* breaker, crushing-mill.

concave [kɔ̃'kaːv] concave. [grant.⟩

concéder [kɔ̃se'de] (1f) *v/t.* concede,⟩

concentration [kɔ̃sɑ̃tra'sjɔ̃] *f* concentration; condensation; *camp m de* ⌣ concentration camp; **concentré, e** [⌣'tre] **1.** *adj. fig.* reserved; abstracted (*look*); **2.** *su./m* extract; concentrate; **concentrer** [⌣'tre] (1a) *v/t.* concentrate (*a.* ✝); intensify; focus (*light*); *fig.* restrain (*one's feelings*); *se* ⌣ *sur* be centred upon; **concentrique** ⚛ *etc.* [⌣'trik] concentric.

concept [kɔ̃'sɛpt] *m* concept; **conceptible** [kɔ̃sɛp'tibl] conceivable; **conceptif, -ve** [⌣'tif, ⌣'tiːv] conceptive; **conception** [⌣'sjɔ̃] *f* conception (*a. fig.*); idea; ⌣ *du monde* philosophy of life.

concernant [kõsɛrˈnɑ̃] *prp.* concerning, regarding; **concerner** [~ˈne] (1a) *v/t.* concern, regard; *en ce qui concerne* ... with regard to ..., as far as ... is concerned; in matters of ...
concert [kõˈsɛːr] *m* concert; *fig.* agreement; *fig. de ~ (avec)* together (with); in unison (with); *agir de ~* take concerted action; **concertation** [kõsɛrtɑˈsjõ] *f* consultation(s *pl.*), dialog(ue); **concerter** [kõsɛrˈte] (1a) *v/t.* (pre)arrange; plan; *se ~* concert *or* work together; **concerto** ♪ [~ˈto] *m* concerto.
concession [kõsɛˈsjõ] *f* concession, grant; *~ à perpétuité grave*: grant in perpetuity; **concessionnaire** [~sjɔˈnɛːr] **1.** *adj.* concessionary; **2.** *su./m* grantee (*of land*); † licence-holder, concession-holder.
concevable [kõsˈvabl] conceivable; **concevoir** [~ˈvwaːr] (3a) *v/t.* conceive (*a. physiol., a. fig.*); understand; imagine; word (*a message*).
conchoïde ⅍ [kõkɔˈid] *f* conchoid.
concierge [kõˈsjɛrʒ] *su.* door-keeper; caretaker; *su./m* porter; *su./f* portress; **conciergerie** [~sjɛrʒəˈri] *f* caretaker's lodge; post of caretaker; *a. hist.* ♀ *a prison in Paris.*
conciliable [kõsiˈljabl] reconcilable; **conciliabule** [~ljaˈbyl] *m* secret meeting; *eccl.* conventicle; F confabulation; **conciliant, e** [~ˈljɑ̃, ~ˈljɑ̃ːt] conciliatory; **conciliateur** *m*, **-trice** *f* [~ljaˈtœːr, ~ˈtris] peacemaker; **conciliation** [~ljaˈsjõ] *f* conciliation; **concilier** [~ˈlje] (1o) *v/t.* reconcile, conciliate; *se ~* gain, win (*s.o.'s esteem etc.*); *fig.* win (*s.o.*) (over); *se ~ avec* agree with.
concis, e [kõˈsi, ~ˈsiːz] concise, terse; **concision** [~siˈsjõ] *f* concision, terseness, brevity.
concitoyen *m*, **-enne** *f* [kõsitwaˈjɛ̃, ~ˈjɛn] fellow-citizen.
concluant, e [kõklyˈɑ̃, ~ˈɑ̃ːt] conclusive; **conclure** [~ˈklyːr] (4g) *v/t.* conclude (*a. a treaty, a. fig.*), finish; *fig.* infer (from, *de*); *~ à* conclude in favo(u)r of; **conclusion** [~klyˈzjõ] *f* conclusion; end; inference; ⚖ finding; ⚖ *~s pl.* pleas; case *sg.*; ⚖ *déposer des ~s* deliver a statement.
concocter F [kõkɔkˈte] (1a) *v/t.* concoct; work out, devise.
concombre ⚘ [kõˈkõːbr] *m* cucumber.
concomitant, e [kõkɔmiˈtɑ̃, ~ˈtɑːt] concomitant.
concordance [kõkɔrˈdɑ̃ːs] *f* concordance (*a. bibl.*); *gramm.* agreement; **concordant, e** [~ˈdɑ̃, ~ˈdɑ̃ːt] harmonious; **concordat** [~ˈda] *m eccl.* concordat; † bankrupt's certificate.
concorde [kõˈkɔrd] *f* harmony, concord; **concorder** [~kɔrˈde] (1a) *v/i.* concur, agree; † compound with one's creditors.
concourant, e [kõkuˈrɑ̃, ~ˈrɑ̃t] ⅍ *etc.* convergent; concerted (*efforts etc.*); **concourir** [~ˈriːr] (2i) compete; *~ à* contribute to, work towards; **concours** [~ˈkuːr] *m* assistance; help, aid; gathering; competition; competitive examination; show (*of agricultural products, cattle, horses, etc.*); ⅍ convergence; *~ hippique* horse show; *hors ~* not competing (for prize); *fig.* unequalled, outstanding.
concret, -ète [kõˈkrɛ, ~ˈkrɛt] concrete; **concréter** [kõkreˈte] (1f) *v/t. a. se ~* solidify, congeal; **concrétion** [~ˈsjõ] *f* coagulation; concretion (*a.* ⚕).
concubinage [kõkybiˈnaːʒ] *m* concubinage.
concupiscence [kõkypiˈsɑ̃ːs] *f* concupiscence, lust; **concupiscent, e** [~ˈsɑ̃, ~ˈsɑ̃ːt] concupiscent.
concurremment [kõkyraˈmɑ̃] *adv.* jointly; † in competition; ⚖ *venir ~* rank equally; **concurrence** [~ˈrɑ̃ːs] *f* coincidence; competition, rivalry; *~ déloyale* unfair competition; † *faire ~ à* compete with; † *jusqu'à ~ de* to the amount of; *sans ~* unrivalled; **concurrent, e** [~ˈrɑ̃, ~ˈrɑ̃ːt] **1.** *adj.* co(-)operating; rival, competing; **2.** *su.* competitor; candidate (*for a post*).
concussion [kõkyˈsjõ] *f* misappropriation of funds; extortion; **concussionnaire** [~sjɔˈnɛːr] **1.** *adj.* guilty of misappropriation *or* extortion; **2.** *su.* official guilty of misappropriation *or* extortion.
condamnable [kõdɑˈnabl] blameworthy; criminal; guilty; **condamnation** [~naˈsjõ] *f* condemnation; ⚖ sentence; ⚖ conviction; ⚖ *~ à vie* life sentence; **condamner** [~ˈne] (1a) *v/t.* condemn; ⚖ sentence; ⚖ convict; *fig.* blame, censure; ⚓ block up; board up (*a window*).

condensateur ⚡ etc. [kɔ̃dɑ̃saˈtœːr]
m condenser; ~ à *plaques* plate condenser; **condensé** [~ˈse] *m journ.*
digest; précis; sum-up; **condenser**
[~ˈse] (1a) *v/t.* condense; **conden-**
seur ⊕ [~ˈsœːr] *m* condenser.
condescendance [kɔ̃dɛsɑ̃ˈdɑ̃:s] *f*
condescension; *avec* ~ condescend-
ing(ly *adv.*); **condescendre** [~-
ˈsɑ̃:dr] (4a) *v/i.* condescend (to *inf.*, à
inf.); comply (with, à).
condiment [kɔ̃diˈmɑ̃] *m* condiment;
seasoning.
condisciple [kɔ̃diˈsipl] *m* schoolfel-
low; fellow-student.
condition [kɔ̃diˈsjɔ̃] *f* condition (*a.
sp.*); circumstances *pl.*; rank; ~s *pl.*
terms; ~s *pl. de travail* working conditions; ~ *préalable* condition precedent; à ~ on condition, ✝ on approval; à ~ *que* provided *or* providing
(that); *mettre en* ~ *sp. etc.* make fit;
fig. condition; **conditionné, e**
[kɔ̃disjɔˈne] in ... condition; ⚡, *phls.*
conditioned; **conditionnel, -elle**
[~ˈnɛl] *adj., a. gramm. su./m* conditional; **conditionner** [~ˈne] (1a)
v/t. condition (*the air, wool, etc., a.
fig.*); ✝ package.
condoléance [kɔ̃dɔleˈɑ̃:s] *f* condo-
lence; *sincères* ~s *pl.* deepest sympathy *sg.*
conductance ⚡ [kɔ̃dykˈtɑ̃:s] *f* conductivity; **conducteur, -trice** [~-
ˈtœːr, ~ˈtris] **1.** *adj.* ⚡ conducting; ⊕
driving; **2.** *su.* leader; *mot. etc.*
driver; 👮 guard, *Am.* conductor;
su./m ⚡, *phys.* conductor; ⚡ main;
conductibilité ⚡, *phys.* [~tibiliˈte] *f*
conductivity; **conductible** [~ˈtibl]
conductive; **conduction** [~ˈsjɔ̃] *f*
conduction; **conduire** [kɔ̃ˈdɥiːr]
(4h) *v/t.* conduct (*a.* ♪, ⊕); lead (to
à); *mot.* steer (*a.* ⚓), drive; ✝
manage, run; *mot. permis m de* ~
driving licence, *Am.* driver's license;
se ~ behave; **conduisis** [~dɥiˈzi] *1st
p. sg. p.s. of conduire;* **conduisons**
[~dɥiˈzɔ̃] *1st p. pl. pres. of conduire;*
conduit, e [~ˈdɥi, ~ˈdɥit] **1.** *p.p. of
conduire;* **2.** *su./m* conduit, pipe,
passage; *anat.* duct; ~ *principal* main;
~ *souterrain* culvert; drain; *su./f*
guidance; *vehicle:* driving; command, management; ⊕ pipe; *fig.*
behavio(u)r; *mot.* ~ à *gauche* (à *droite*)
left-hand (right-hand) drive; ~ *d'eau*
water-main; channel; ~ *de gaz* gas-

8*

piping; ~ *d'huile* oilduct; *mot.* ~ *en
état d'ivresse* drunken driving.
cône [koːn] *m* cone; ⊕ *a.* bell; ⚓ ~ *de
charge torpedo:* war-head; *en* ~
tapering.
confection [kɔ̃fɛkˈsjɔ̃] *f* making;
manufacture; ✝ ready-made clothes
pl.; ⚗ confection; *cost. de* ~ ready-
made; **confectionner** [~sjɔˈne] (1a)
v/t. make (up) (*a.* ✝ *a balance-sheet*);
manufacture; **confectionneur** *m*,
-euse *f* [~sjɔˈnœːr, ~ˈnøːz] manufacturer; ✝ ready-made clothier.
confédération [kɔ̃federaˈsjɔ̃] *f* (con-)
federation; **confédéré, e** [~ˈre]
1. *adj.* confederate; **2.** *su.* confederate; *su./m: hist. Am. les* ♀s *pl.* the
Confederates; **confédérer** [~ˈre]
(1f) *v/t. a. se* ~ confederate, unite.
conférence [kɔ̃feˈrɑ̃:s] *f* conference;
univ. lecture; ~ *avec projections*
lantern lecture; ~ *de presse* press
conference; *univ.* ~s *pl. pratiques*
seminar *sg.*; *univ. maître m de* ~s
lecturer; **conférencier** *m*, **-ère** *f*
[~rɑ̃ˈsje, ~ˈsjɛːr] member of a conference; lecturer, speaker; **confé-**
rer [~ˈre] (1f) *v/t.* compare (*texts*);
confer (*a degree*); *typ.* check
(*proofs*); *v/i.* confer (with, *avec*);
~ *de* talk about (*s.th.*); talk (*s.th.*)
over.
confesse *eccl.* [kɔ̃ˈfɛs] *f* confession;
confesser [kɔ̃feˈse] (1a) *v/t.* confess (*a. eccl.*); admit; *c'est le diable
à* ~ this is the dickens of a job;
eccl. se ~ confess, go to confession;
confesseur *eccl., a. hist.* [~ˈsœːr] *m*
confessor; **confession** [~ˈsjɔ̃] *f*
confession (*a. eccl.*); admission;
confessionnal *eccl.* [~sjɔˈnal] *m*
confessional(-box); **confessionnel,**
-elle [~sjɔˈnɛl] confessional, denominational.
confiance [kɔ̃ˈfjɑ̃:s] *f* confidence,
trust, reliance; ~ *en soi* self-confidence; *avoir* ~ *en, faire* ~ à have
confidence in, trust; *homme m de* ~
reliable man; confidential agent;
confiant, e [~ˈfjɑ̃, ~ˈfjɑ̃:t] confident,
trusting; **confidence** [~ˈdɑ̃:s] *f* confidence, secret; **confident** [~ˈdɑ̃] *m*
confidant; **confidente** [~ˈdɑ̃:t] *f*
confidante; **confidentiel, -elle**
[~dɑ̃ˈsjɛl] confidential; **confier**
[kɔ̃ˈfje] (1o) *v/t.* entrust; *fig.* confide;
se ~ à put faith in; rely on; *se* ~ *en q.*
put one's trust in s.o.; confide in s.o.

configuration [kɔ̃figyra'sjɔ̃] *f* configuration (*a. astr.*); lie (*of the land*).

confiner [kɔ̃fi'ne] (1a) *v/i.* border (on, *à*); *v/t.* shut (*s.o.*) up (in, *dans*) (*a. fig.*); se ~ seclude o.s.; **confins** [~'fɛ̃] *m/pl.* confines (*a. fig.*), limits.

confire [kɔ̃'fiːr] (4i) *v/t.* preserve (*fruit*); candy (*peels*); pickle (*in salt or vinegar*); steep (*skins*).

confirmatif, -ve [kɔ̃firma'tif, ~'tiːv] corroborative; confirmative; **confirmation** [~ma'sjɔ̃] *f* confirmation (*a. ⚜, eccl., etc.*); **confirmer** [~'me] (1a) *v/t.* confirm (*a. eccl.*); bear out, corroborate.

confis [kɔ̃'fi] *1st p. sg. pres. and p.s. of* confire.

confiscable [kɔ̃fis'kabl] liable to seizure *or* confiscation; **confiscation** [~ka'sjɔ̃] *f* confiscation; seizure, forfeiture.

confiserie [kɔ̃fiz'ri] *f* confectionery; confectioner's (shop); **confiseur** *m*, **-euse** *f* [~fi'zœːr, ~'zøːz] confectioner; **confisons** [~fi'zɔ̃] *1st p. pl. pres. of* confire.

confisquer [kɔ̃fis'ke] (1m) *v/t.* confiscate, seize.

confit, e [kɔ̃'fi, ~'fit] **1.** *p.p. of* confire; **2.** *adj. cuis.* preserved; candied; *fig.* ~ dans (*or en*) steeped in, full of; **confiture** [~fi'tyːr] *f* jam, preserve; F soft soap.

conflagration [kɔ̃flagra'sjɔ̃] *f* conflagration, blaze.

conflit [kɔ̃'fli] *m* conflict; clash; ✝ ~ salarial wages dispute; ✝ ~ social industrial dispute.

confluent, e [kɔ̃fly'ɑ̃, ~'ɑ̃ːt] **1.** *adj.* ⚜, ⚕ confluent; **2.** *su./m* confluence, meeting.

confondre [kɔ̃'fɔ̃ːdr] (4a) *v/t.* confound (*a. fig.*); (inter)mingle; *fig.* confuse; *fig.* disconcert; se ~ blend; be lost; *fig.* be confused.

conformation [kɔ̃fɔrma'sjɔ̃] *f* conformation, structure; **conforme** [~'fɔrm] conformable; true; consonant (with, *à*); identical (with, *à*); ⚜ pour copie ~ certified true copy; **conformément** [kɔ̃fɔrme'mɑ̃] *adv.* in accordance (with, *à*); **conformer** [~'me] (1a) *v/t.* shape, form; *fig.* conform (to, *à*); ✝ ~ les écritures agree the books; se ~ à conform to, comply with; **conformité** [~mi'te] *f* conformity (with, *avec*);

to, *à*); agreement, accordance (with, *avec*).

confort [kɔ̃'fɔːr] *m* comfort; *mot.* pneu *m* ~ balloon tyre; **confortable** [~fɔr'tabl] comfortable; considerable; **conforter** [~fɔr'te] (1a) *v/t.* strengthen, reinforce; confirm.

confraternité [kɔ̃fratɛrni'te] *f* confraternity; (good) fellowship; **confrère** [~'frɛːr] *m* colleague; fellow (-teacher, -doctor, *etc.*); **confrérie** *eccl.* [~fre'ri] *f* confraternity.

confrontation [kɔ̃frɔ̃ta'sjɔ̃] *f* ⚖ confrontation; ⚖ identification; *texts:* comparison; **confronter** [~'te] (1a) *v/t.* confront (with *à*, *avec*); compare (*texts*).

confus, e [kɔ̃'fy, ~'fyːz] confused (*a. fig.*); indistinct (*noise, sight*); obscure (*style*); *fig.* ashamed; **confusément** [kɔ̃fyze'mɑ̃] *adv.* confusedly; indistinctly; F in a jumble; **confusion** [~'zjɔ̃] *f* confusion, disorder; *fig.* embarrassment; *dates, names, etc.:* mistake; ⚕ (*mental*) aberration.

congé [kɔ̃'ʒe] *m* leave (*a. ✕*); holiday; dismissal, notice (to quit, of dismissal, *etc.*); ✕, ⚓ discharge; *admin.* permit; ⚠ congé; ~ de maladie sick leave; ~ de maternité maternity leave; ~s scolaires *pl.* school holidays (*Am.* vacation); ~ payé paid holidays *pl.* (*Am.* vacation); deux jours *m/pl.* de ~ two days off, two days' holiday; donner (son) ~ à q. give s.o. notice; prendre ~ de take leave of; **congédiable** [kɔ̃ʒe'djabl] due for *or* liable to dismissal; **congédier** [~'dje] (1o) *v/t.* dismiss; ✕, ⚓ discharge; ⚓ pay off; ✕ disband (*troops*).

congelable [kɔ̃ʒ'labl] freezable; **congélateur** [kɔ̃ʒela'tœːr] *m* freezer; **congélation** [kɔ̃ʒela'sjɔ̃] *f* freezing; setting; ⚜, ⚕ frost-bite; **congelé, e** [kɔ̃ʒ'le] frozen; chilled (*meat*); **congeler** [~] (1d) *v/t. a.* se ~ freeze (*a. ✝ credits*); congeal; F solidify.

congénère [kɔ̃ʒe'nɛːr] **1.** *adj. biol.* congeneric; *anat.* congenerous; **2.** *su./m biol.* congener; *fig.* lui et ses ~s he and his like.

congénital, e, -aux [kɔ̃ʒeni'tal, ~'to] congenital.

congestion ⚕ [kɔ̃ʒes'tjɔ̃] *f* congestion; ~ pulmonaire pneumonia; **con-**

gestionner [ˌtjɔ'ne] (1a) v/t. ⚙ congest; fig. flush (s.o.'s face).
conglomérat [kɔ̃glɔmeˈra] m geol. pudding-stone; △ cemented gravel; **conglomération** [ˌra'sjɔ̃] f conglomeration; **conglomérer** [ˌ're] (1f) v/t. a. se ~ conglomerate.
conglutiner ⚙ [kɔ̃glyti'ne] (1a) v/t. a. se ~ conglutinate.
congratuler [kɔ̃graty'le] (1a) v/t. congratulate.
congréganiste eccl. hist. [kɔ̃grega-'nist] su. member of the Congregation; **congrégation** eccl. [ˌ'sjɔ̃] f community; protestantism: congregation; brotherhood; College of Cardinals: committee; hist. the Congregation.
congrès [kɔ̃'grɛ] m congress; **congressiste** [ˌgrɛ'sist] su. member of a congress; su./m Am. Congressman.
congru, e [kɔ̃'gry] adequate; suitable; eccl. congruous; fig. portion f ~e short allowance; bare living; **congruent, e** [ˌgry'ɑ̃, ~'ɑ̃ːt] congruent (with, à).
conicité [kɔnisi'te] f conical shape; bullet: taper; **conifère** ♀ [ˌ'fɛːr] 1. adj. coniferous; 2. su./m: ~s pl. conifers; **conique** [kɔ'nik] 1. adj. conical; conic; ⊕ coned, tapering; ⊕ bevel (gearing, pinion); 2. su./f Å (a. section f ~) conic section.
conjecture [kɔ̃ʒɛk'tyːr] f surmise, guess; **conjecturer** [ˌty're] (1a) v/t. surmise, guess.
conjoint, e [kɔ̃'ʒwɛ̃, ~'ʒwɛ̃ːt] 1. adj. united, joint; ⚌ married; Å règle f ~e chain-rule; 2. su./m spouse; ~s pl. husband and wife.
conjonctif, -ve [kɔ̃ʒɔ̃k'tif, ~'tiːv] conjunctive (a. gramm.); anat. connective; **conjonction** [ˌ'sjɔ̃] f conjunction (a. gramm., astr.); union; **conjonctive** anat. [ˌ'tiːv] f conjunctiva; **conjonctivite** ⚙ [ˌti'vit] f conjunctivitis; **conjoncture** [ˌ-'tyːr] f (set or combination of) circumstances pl.; ~ (économique) economic situation; ✝ haute ~ boom; **conjoncturel, -le** [ˌty'rɛl] cyclical; of the economic situation.
conjugaison [kɔ̃ʒygɛ'zɔ̃] f gramm., biol., etc. conjugation; pairing (of guns etc.).
conjugal, e, m/pl. -aux [kɔ̃ʒy'gal, ~'go] conjugal.

conjuguer [kɔ̃ʒy'ge] (1m) v/t. gramm. conjugate; pair (guns etc.).
conjungo F [kɔ̃ʒɔ̃'go] m marriage (formula).
conjurateur [kɔ̃ʒyra'tœːr] m magician; **conjuration** [ˌ'sjɔ̃] f conspiracy, plot; exorcism; F ~s pl. entreaties; **conjuré** m, e f [kɔ̃ʒy're] conspirator; **conjurer** [ˌ] (1a) v/t. conspire, plot; exorcise (spirits); entreat (s.o. to inf., q. de inf.); se ~ conspire (together).
connais [kɔ'nɛ] 1st p. sg. pres. of connaître; **connaissable** [kɔnɛ'sabl] recognizable (by, à); phls. cognizable; **connaissance** [ˌ'sɑ̃ːs] f knowledge, learning; acquaintance (a. person); ⚌ cognizance; ⚙ consciousness; en ~ de cause on good grounds, advisedly; **connaissement** ⚓ [kɔnɛs'mɑ̃] m bill of lading; ~ direct through bill of lading; **connaisseur, -euse** [ˌnɛ-'sœːr, ~'søːz] 1. adj. (of an) expert; 2. su. connoisseur; expert; **connaissons** [ˌnɛ'sɔ̃] 1st p. pl. pres. of connaître; **connaître** [ˌ'nɛːtr] (4k) v/t. know (a. bibl.); be aware of; understand; experience; s'y or se ~ en qch. know all about s.th., be an expert in s.th.; v/i.: ⚌ ~ de take cognizance of; deal with; faire ~ q. à introduce s.o. to.
connard m, e f sl. [kɔ'naːr, ~'nard], **connasse** [ˌ'nas] f idiot, goddamn fool.
connecter [kɔnɛk'te] (1a) v/t. connect (to, with avec); **connectif, -ve** [ˌ'tif, ~'tiːv] 1. adj. anat. connective; 2. su./m ♀ connective.
connexe [kɔ'nɛks] connected; **connexion** [kɔnɛk'sjɔ̃] f connection (a. ⚡); ⚡ lead; Å connex; ⊕ ~ directe positive drive; **connexité** [ˌsi'te] f connexity, relationship.
connivence [kɔni'vɑ̃ːs] f complicity, connivance.
conoïde Å [kɔnɔ'id] adj., a. su./m conoid.
connu, e [kɔ'ny] p.p. of connaître; **connus** [ˌ] 1st p. sg. p.s. of connaître.
conque [kɔ̃ːk] f conch; anat. external ear; △ apse; ⊕ delivery space.
conquérant, e [kɔ̃ke'rɑ̃, ~'rɑ̃ːt] 1. adj. conquering; fig. swaggering; 2. su. conqueror, victor; **conquérir** [ˌ'riːr] (2l) v/t. conquer; fig. win;

conquête [kɔ̃'kɛːt] *f* conquest; **conquis, e** [ˌ'ki, ˌ'kiːz] *p.p. of conquérir.*

consacrer [kɔ̃sa'kre] (1a) *v/t.* consecrate (*a. fig.*); devote (*energies*); hallow (*the memory etc.*); *expression f consacrée* stock phrase, cliché.

consanguin, e [kɔ̃sɑ̃'gɛ̃, ˌ'gin] consanguineous; half-(*brother etc.*); inbred (*horse etc.*); **consanguinité** [ˌgini'te] *f* 🏛 consanguinity; inbreeding.

conscience [kɔ̃'sjɑ̃ːs] *f* consciousness; conscience; ˌ *de soi* self-awareness; *perdre* (*reprendre*) ˌ lose (regain) consciousness; *avoir bonne* (*mauvaise*) ˌ have a clear (bad) conscience; *avoir* ˌ *de* be aware of; **consciencieux, -euse** [ˌsjɑ̃'sjø, ˌ'sjøːz] conscientious; **conscient, e** [ˌ'sjɑ̃, ˌ'sjɑ̃ːt] conscious, aware (of, *de*).

conscription 🏛 [kɔ̃skrip'sjɔ̃] *f* conscription, *Am.* draft; **conscrit** [ˌ'kri] *m* 🏛 conscript, *Am.* draftee; *fig.* novice. [secration.ʃ
consécration [kɔ̃sekra'sjɔ̃] *f* con-ʃ
consécutif, -ve [kɔ̃seky'tif, ˌ'tiːv] consecutive; ˌ *à* following upon.

conseil [kɔ̃'sɛːj] *m* advice; committee, board; 🏛 counsel; ♱ ˌ *d'administration* board of directors; 🏛, ⚓ ˌ *de guerre* council of war; court-martial; ˌ *d'employés* works committee; ˌ *d'entreprise* works council; *pol.* ˌ *de sécurité* Security Council; *pol.* ˌ *des ministres* Cabinet; ♱ ˌ *de surveillance* board of trustees; *admin.* ˌ *général* county council; 🏛 ˌ *judiciaire* guardian; *ingénieur-* *m* consulting engineer; *président m du* ♀ Premier, Prime Minister; **conseiller** [ˌsɛ'je] **1.** (1a) *v/t.* advise; recommend; **2.** *su./m* adviser; *admin.* councillor; ˌ *d'orientation professionnelle* careers adviser, vocational guidance counsellor; ˌ *économique* economic adviser; ˌ *général* county councillor; ˌ *municipal* town *or* city councillor.

consensus [kɔ̃sɛ̃'sys] *m* consensus.

consentement [kɔ̃sɑ̃t'mɑ̃] *m* consent, assent; *du* ˌ *de tous* by universal consent; *par* ˌ *mutuel* by mutual consent; **consentir** [ˌsɑ̃'tiːr] (2b) *v/i.* consent (to, *à*), agree (with, *à*); ⊕ yield (*beam*); *v/t.* authorize; grant; accept (*an opinion*).

conséquence [kɔ̃se'kɑ̃ːs] *f* consequence, result; importance; *de* ˌ *of* importance, important; *en* ˌ consequently; *en* ˌ *de* in consequence of; **conséquent, e** [ˌ'kɑ̃, ˌ'kɑ̃ːt] **1.** *adj.* consistent; following; **2.** *su./m* 🦌, *gramm., phls.* consequent; *par* ˌ consequently.

conservable [kɔ̃sɛr'vabl] that will keep (*food*); **conservateur, -trice** [ˌva'tœːr, ˌ'tris] **1.** *adj.* preservative; *pol.* Conservative; **2.** *su.* keeper, curator, guardian; *pol.* Conservative; **conservation** [ˌva'sjɔ̃] *f* preservation; **conservatisme** [ˌva'tism] *m* conservatism; **conservatoire** [ˌva'twaːr] **1.** *adj.* preservative, of conservation; **2.** *su./m* school, academy (*of music etc.*); conservatoire, *Am.* conservatory.

conserve[1] ⚓ [kɔ̃'sɛrv] *f* convoy; *naviguer de* ˌ sail in company.

conserve[2] [kɔ̃'sɛrv] *f* preserve; tinned food; **conserver** [ˌsɛr've] (1a) *v/t.* preserve, keep; *fig.* maintain; *se* ˌ keep (*food*); *bien conservé* well-preserved.

considérable [kɔ̃side'rabl] considerable; extensive; *fig.* important; **considération** [ˌra'sjɔ̃] *f* consideration; attention; motive; esteem; **considérer** [ˌ're] (1f) *v/t.* consider; contemplate; regard; *hautement considéré* highly respected; *bien considéré* well-thought-of.

consignataire [kɔ̃siɲa'tɛːr] *m* ♱ consignee; 🏛 trustee; depositary; **consignateur** *m*, **-trice** *f* [ˌ'tœːr, ˌ'tris] consignor; shipper; **consignation** [ˌ'sjɔ̃] *f* ♱ consignment; deposit; 🏛 *Caisse f des dépôts et* ˌ*s* Deposit and Consignment Office; *stock m en* ˌ goods *pl.* on consignment; **consigne** [kɔ̃'siɲ] *f* order, instructions *pl.*; 🏛, ⚓ order-board; 🏛 password; 🏛, ⚓ confinement; *school:* detention; 🏛 guardroom; 🚉 left-luggage office, *Am.* baggage room, checkroom; ♱ deposit (on *a bottle etc.* sur); **consigner** [ˌsi'ɲe] (1a) *v/t.* deposit; ♱ consign; ♱ put a deposit on (*a bottle etc.*); 🏛 confine to barracks; *school:* detain (*a pupil*); close, put out of bounds; 🚉 put in the left-luggage office, *Am.* check (*baggage*); ˌ (*par écrit*) set down, record, register; ˌ *sa porte à q.* not to be at home to s.o.

consistance [kɔ̃sis'tɑ̃:s] ƒ consistency; firmness; *fig.* standing, credit;
consister [ˌʌ'te] (1a) *v/i.* consist
(of *en, dans*).
consolant, e [kɔ̃sɔ'lɑ̃, ˌʌ'lɑ̃:t] *see*
consolateur 1; **consolateur, -trice**
[ˌʌla'tœːr, ˌʌ'tris] **1.** *adj.* consoling,
comforting; **2.** *su.* consoler, comforter; **consolation** [ˌʌla'sjɔ̃] ƒ consolation, comfort.
console [kɔ̃'sɔl] ƒ ♪, 🔺, *a. table*:
console.
consoler [kɔ̃sɔ'le] (1a) *v/t.* console,
comfort.
consolider [kɔ̃sɔli'de] (1a) *v/t.* consolidate (*a.* ✝); 🔺 brace (*a wall*);
fund (*a debt*); ✚ unite, heal (*a fracture etc.*); se ˌʌ grow firm; ✚ unite,
heal.
consommateur *m*, **-trice** ƒ [kɔ̃sɔ-
ma'tœːr, ˌʌ'tris] consumer; *café etc.*:
customer; **consommation** [ˌʌma-
'sjɔ̃] ƒ consumption; ✕, ⚓ expenditure; consummation (*a. of marriage*); *café*: drink; ✝ *biens m/pl. de*
ˌʌ consumer goods; *mot. concours m*
de ˌʌ economy run; *impôt m sur la* ˌʌ,
taxe ƒ *de* ˌʌ purchase tax; ✝ *société ƒ*
coopérative de ˌʌ co(-)operative
stores *pl.*; **consommé, e** [ˌʌ'me]
1. *adj.* consummate (*skill*); **2.** *su./m*
cuis. stock; clear soup, broth; **consommer** [ˌʌ'me] (1a) *v/t.* consummate (*a. marriage*); accomplish;
consume, use up.
consomption [kɔ̃sɔ̃p'sjɔ̃] ƒ consumption; destruction (*by fire*); ✚
decline.
consonance ♪, *gramm.* [kɔ̃sɔ'nɑ̃:s] ƒ
consonance; **consonant, e** ♪,
gramm. [ˌʌ'nɑ̃, ˌʌ'nɑ̃:t] consonant;
consonne *gramm.* [kɔ̃'sɔn] ƒ consonant.
consort [kɔ̃'sɔːr] *m* consort; ˌʌs *pl.*
associates, confederates; *prince m* ˌʌ
prince consort; **consortium** [ˌʌsɔr-
'sjɔm] *m* consortium.
conspirateur, -trice [kɔ̃spira'tœːr,
ˌʌ'tris] **1.** *adj.* conspiring; **2.** *su.* conspirator; **conspiration** [ˌʌra'sjɔ̃] ƒ
conspiracy, plot; **conspirer** [ˌʌ're]
(1a) *v/i.* conspire (*a. fig.*), plot; *fig.*
tend.
conspuer [kɔ̃s'pɥe] (1a) *v/t.* decry;
thea. etc. boo; *sp.* barrack.
constamment [kɔ̃sta'mɑ̃] *adv.*
steadfastly; continually, constantly;
constance [ˌʌ'tɑ̃:s] ƒ constancy;

steadiness; perseverance; **constant,
e** [ˌʌ'tɑ̃, ˌʌ'tɑ̃:t] **1.** *adj.* constant; invariable (*a.* Ⅱ); steadfast; patent
(*fact*); **2.** *su./ƒ* ♪, *phys.* constant.
constat [kɔ̃s'ta] *m* certified *or* official
report; established fact; 👫 ˌʌ *d'huissier* affidavit made by process-
server; **constatation** [kɔ̃stata'sjɔ̃] ƒ
establishment, finding (*of facts*);
certified statement; proof (*of identity*); **constater** [ˌʌ'te] (1a) *v/t.*
establish, ascertain; record, state;
certify (*s.o.'s death*); note.
constellation [kɔ̃stɛlla'sjɔ̃] ƒ constellation; **constellé, e** [ˌʌ'le] span-
gled; studded; **consteller** [ˌʌ'le]
(1a) *v/t.* constellate; stud (*with
jewels*).
consternation [kɔ̃stɛrna'sjɔ̃] ƒ consternation, dismay; **consterner**
[ˌʌ'ne] (1a) *v/t.* (fill with) dismay.
constipation ✚ [kɔ̃stipa'sjɔ̃] ƒ constipation; **constiper** ✚ [ˌʌ'pe] (1a)
v/t. constipate.
constituant, e [kɔ̃sti'tɥɑ̃, ˌʌ'tɥɑ̃:t]
1. *adj.* constituent (*a. pol.*); component; **2.** *su.* 👫 constituent; 👫
dowry, annuity: grantor; *pol.* elector; *su./m* constituent part; *pol.*
member of the Constituent Assembly (*1789*); *su./ƒ* ⚭e the Constituent
Assembly (*1789*); **constituer** [ˌʌ-
'tɥe] (1n) *v/t.* constitute; establish;
appoint; settle; 👫 empanel (*the
jury*); set up, institute (*a committee*);
constitutif, -ve [ˌʌty'tif, ˌʌ'tiːv]
constituent; 👫 constitutive; **constitution** [ˌʌty'sjɔ̃] ƒ ✚, *pol.* constitution; establishing; formation;
composition (*a.* 🔬); 👫 briefing (*of
a lawyer*); **constitutionnel, -le**
[ˌʌtysjɔ'nɛl] constitutional.
constricteur *physiol., a. zo.* [kɔ̃s-
trik'tœːr] *adj., a. su./m* constrictor;
constrictif, -ve [ˌʌ'tif, ˌʌ'tiːv] con-
strictive; [constringent.\
constringent, e ✚ [kɔ̃strɛ̃'ʒɑ̃, ˌʌ'ʒɑ̃:t]/
constructeur [kɔ̃stryk'tœːr] *m*
builder, constructor; engineer; ˌʌ *de
maisons* (master-)builder; ˌʌ *mécanicien* manufacturing engineer;
construction [ˌʌ'sjɔ̃] ƒ construction (*a.* 🔺, Ⅱ, *gramm.*); building;
structure; *de* ˌʌ *française* French-
built; *en* ˌʌ on the stocks (*boat*);
société ƒ de ˌʌ building society;
construire [kɔ̃s'trɥiːr] (4h) *v/t.*
construct (*a.* 🔺, Ⅱ, *gramm., a. fig.*);

build; **construisis** [‿trμi'zi] *1st p.
sg. p.s. of construire*; **construisons**
[‿trμi'zɔ̃] *1st p. pl. pres. of construire*; **construit, e** [‿'trμi, ‿'trμit]
p.p. of construire.

consul [kɔ̃'syl] *m* consul; **consulaire** [kɔ̃sy'lɛ:r] consular; **consulat**
[‿'la] *m* consulate.

consultant, e [kɔ̃syl'tɑ̃, ‿'tɑ̃:t]
1. *adj.* consulting, consultant; *avocat m* ‿ chamber counsel; **2.** *su.*
consulter; *ﬡ* consultant; **consultatif, -ve** [‿ta'tif, ‿'ti:v] advisory,
consulting; **consultation** [‿ta'sjɔ̃]
f consultation, conference; *ﬡ*
opinion; **consulter** [‿'te] *v/t.*
consult; se ‿ consider; *v/i.*:
ﬡ ‿ *avec* hold a consultation
with.

consumer [kɔ̃sy'me] (1a) *v/t.* consume; devour; burn; *fig.* se ‿ waste
away; **consumérisme** [‿me'rism]
m consumerism.

contact [kɔ̃'takt] *m* contact (*a. ⚡
etc.*); *⚡ ‿ à fiche* plug; *⚡* F ‿ *de terre*
earth; *mot. clef f de* ‿ ignition key;
entrer en ‿ *avec* get in touch with;
contacter [‿tak'te] (1a) *v/t.* contact;
contacteur *⚡* [‿tak'tœ:r] *m* circuit-
maker; contact-maker.

contage *ﬡ* [kɔ̃'ta:ʒ] *m* contagium;
contagieux, -euse [kɔ̃ta'ʒjø,
‿'ʒjø:z] *ﬡ* contagious; infectious;
catching; **contagion** *ﬡ* [‿'ʒjɔ̃] *f*
contagion; infection.

contaminer [kɔ̃tami'ne] (1a) *v/t.* *ﬡ*
infect; contaminate.

conte [kɔ̃:t] *m* story, tale.

contemplatif, -ve [kɔ̃tɑ̃pla'tif,
‿'ti:v] **1.** *adj.* contemplative; **2.** *su.*
dreamer; **contempler** [‿'ple] (1a)
v/t. contemplate; *fig.* meditate
upon; *v/i.* meditate.

contemporain, e [kɔ̃tɑ̃pɔ'rɛ̃, ‿'rɛn]
adj., a. su. contemporary.

contenance [kɔ̃t'nɑ̃:s] *f* capacity;
content(s *pl.*); *fig.* bearing, countenance; **conteneur** [‿'nœ:r] *m*
container; **contenir** [‿'ni:r] (2h) *v/t.*
contain, hold (*a. ✕*); *fig.* control,
restrain; se ‿ control o.s., keep one's
temper.

content, e [kɔ̃'tɑ̃, ‿'tɑ̃:t] **1.** *adj.* con-
tent(ed); pleased, happy; **2.** *su./m* F
sufficiency; *tout son* ‿ to one's heart's
content; **contentement** [‿tɑ̃t'mɑ̃]
m contentment, satisfaction; **contenter** [‿tɑ̃'te] (1a) *v/t.* content,

satisfy; se ‿ make do, be content
(with, de).

contentieux, -euse [kɔ̃tɑ̃'sjø,
‿'sjø:z] **1.** *adj.* contentious; **2.** *su./m*
ﬡ matters *pl.* in dispute; *✝*, *admin.*
legal department; **contention**
[‿'sjɔ̃] *f* application; *ﬡ* holding; *✝*
dispute.

contenu [kɔ̃t'ny] *m* content(s *pl.*).
conter [kɔ̃'te] (1a) *v/t.* tell, relate;
en ‿ à q. pull s.o.'s leg; *en ‿ de belles* tell tall stories (about, *sur*).

contestable [kɔ̃tɛs'tabl] debatable,
questionable; **contestataire** *pol.*
[‿ta'tɛ:r] **1.** *adj.* anti-establishment;
2. *su.* protester; **contestation**
[‿ta'sjɔ̃] *f* dispute; *pol.* anti-establishment movement; **contester**
[‿'te] (1a) *v/t./i.* dispute; *pol.* protest.

conteur *m*, **-euse** *f* [kɔ̃'tœ:r, ‿'tø:z]
narrator; story-teller; *fig.* romanc-
er, F bit of a liar.

contexte [kɔ̃'tɛkst] *m* context; *ﬡ*
text (*of a deed etc.*); **contextuel, -le**
[‿tɛksty'ɛl] contextual.

contigu, -guë [kɔ̃ti'gy] adjoining;
adjacent (*a. ⅄*); **contiguïté** [‿gμi-
'te] *f* contiguity, adjacency.

continence [kɔ̃ti'nɑ̃:s] *f* continence,
continency; **continent, e** [‿'nɑ̃,
‿'nɑ̃:t] **1.** *adj.* continent, chaste; *ﬡ*
unintermitting (*fever*); **2.** *su./m*
geog. continent; mainland; **continental, e,** *m/pl.* **-aux** [‿nɑ̃'tal, ‿'to]
continental.

contingence [kɔ̃tɛ̃'ʒɑ̃s] *f* *phls.* contingency; *les* ‿s incidents; chance
happenings.

contingent, e [kɔ̃tɛ̃'ʒɑ̃, ‿'ʒɑ̃:t]
1. *adj.* contingent; **2.** *su./m* quota;
ration, allowance; **contingente-
ment** [‿ʒɑ̃t'mɑ̃] *m* quota system;
contingenter [‿ʒɑ̃'te] (1a) *v/t.* fix
quotas for.

continu, e [kɔ̃ti'ny] **1.** *adj.* continuous (*a. ⅄ function*), continual; uninterrupted, unbroken; *⚡* direct
(*current*); *⅄* continued (*fraction*);
2. *su./m* *phys.* continuum; **continuation** [‿nμa'sjɔ̃] *f* continuation;
weather: long spell; *war etc.*: carrying on; **continuel, -elle** [‿'nμɛl]
continual, unceasing; **continuer**
[‿'nμe] (1n) *v/t/i.* continue; carry
on; extend; *v/t.* ‿ *à* (*inf.*) continue
(*ger.*), continue to (*inf.*); *v/t.* prolong;
continuité [‿nμi'te] *f* continuity;
uninterrupted connection; **conti-**

nûment [ˌny'mɑ̃] *adv.* continuously, without a break.
contorsion [kɔ̃tɔr'sjɔ̃] *f* contortion;
ɟ distortion; *faire des* ~*s* pull a
wry face.
contour [kɔ̃'tu:r] *m* contour, outline; *town:* circuit; **contourner**
[ˌtur'ne] (1a) *v/t.* outline; go round;
by-pass (*a town*); distort (*one's
face*); F get round (*the law*).
contraceptif, **-ive** [kɔ̃trasep'tif,
~'ti:v] *adj., a. su./m* contraceptive;
contraception [~'sjɔ̃] *f* contraception.
contractant, e [kɔ̃trak'tɑ̃, ~'tɑ̃:t] **1.**
adj. contracting; **2.** *su.* contracting
party; **contracter** [~'te] (1a) *v/t.*
contract (*debt, habit, illness, marriage, etc.*); incur (*debts*); catch
(*cold*); **contractile** *physiol.* [~'til]
contractile; **contraction** [~'sjɔ̃] *f*
contraction; *road:* narrowing.
contractuel, -elle [kɔ̃trak'tɥɛl] **1.**
adj. contractual; **2.** *su.* employee on
contract; traffic warden, *f a.* F meter
maid.
contradicteur [kɔ̃tradik'tœ:r] *m*
contradictor; opponent; **contradiction** [~'sjɔ̃] *f* contradiction; opposition; **contradictoire** [~'twa:r]
contradictory; inconsistent; conflicting (*with, à*); *jugement m* ~
judgment given after a full hearing.
contraindre [kɔ̃'trɛ̃:dr] (4m) *v/t.*
compel, force; coerce; *fig.* restrain
(*one's feelings etc.*); *se* ~ restrain
o.s.; **contraint, e** [~'trɛ̃, ~'trɛ̃:t]
1. *adj.* cramped (*position, style*);
forced (*smile*); stiff (*manner*);
2. *su./f* compulsion, constraint;
embarrassment; *par* ~*e* under
duress; *sans* ~*e* freely.
contraire [kɔ̃'trɛ:r] **1.** *adj.* contrary,
opposite (*to, à*); averse; *en sens* ~
in the opposite direction; **2.** *su./m*
contrary, opposite; *au* ~ on the
contrary.
contralto ♪ [kɔ̃tral'to] *m* contralto.
contrariant, e [kɔ̃tra'rjɑ̃, ~'rjɑ̃:t]
provoking; tiresome; vexatious;
contrarier [~'rje] (1o) *v/t.* thwart,
oppose; annoy, vex; contrast; **contrariété** [~rie'te] *f* difficulty; annoyance, vexation; clash (*of colours,
interests, etc.*).
contraste [kɔ̃'trast] *m* contrast;
contraster [~tras'te] (1a) *vt/i.*
contrast.

contrat [kɔ̃'tra] *m* contract; *marriage:* settlement; *passer un* ~ enter
into an agreement.
contravention [kɔ̃travɑ̃'sjɔ̃] *f* ✝ infringement; *mot.* parking ticket *or*
fine.
contre [kɔ̃:tr] **1.** *prp.* against; contrary to; (in exchange) for; ✝, *sp.*
versus; ~ *son gré* against his will;
dix ~ *un* ten to one; **2.** *adv.* against;
near; *tout* ~ close by; **3.** *su./m box.*
counter; *cards:* double; *le pour et
le* ~ the pros *pl.* and the cons *pl.*;
règlement m par ~ settlement per
contra.
contre... [kɔ̃tr(ə)] counter...; anti...;
contra...; back...; ~**-accusation** ✝
[kɔ̃trakyza'sjɔ̃] *f* counter-charge;
~**-allée** [~a'le] *f* side-walk, side-lane;
~**-amiral** ⚓ [~ami'ral] *m* rear-
admiral; ~**-assurance** [~asy'rɑ̃:s] *f*
reinsurance; ~**-attaque** ✗ [~a'tak] *f*
counter-attack; ~**balancer** [kɔ̃trə-
balɑ̃'se] (1k) *v/t.* counterbalance;
~**bande** [~'bɑ̃:d] *f* contraband,
smuggling; smuggled goods *pl.*;
faire la ~ smuggle; ~**bandier** [~bɑ̃-
'dje] *m* smuggler; ~**bas** [~'bɑ] *adv.:*
en ~ lower down (than, *de*); down-
wards; ~**basse** ♪ [~'bɑ:s] *f*
doublebass; ~**-bouter** [~bu'te],
~**-buter** [~by'te] (1a) *v/t.* buttress;
~**carrer** [~ka're] (1a) *v/t.* thwart,
counteract; ~**cœur** [~'kœ:r] *adv.:*
à ~ reluctantly; ~**coup** [~'ku] *m*
rebound; recoil; repercussion; *fig.*
side-effects *pl.*; *par* ~ as a result
(*indirect*); ~**dire** [~'di:r] (4p) *v/t.*
contradict; *se* ~ contradict o.s. *or*
each other; ~**dit** [~'di] *adv.: sans*
~ unquestionably.
contrée [kɔ̃'tre] *f* region.
contre...: ~**-écrou** ⊕ [kɔ̃tre'kru] *m*
counter-nut; ~**-épreuve** [~e-
'prœ:v] *f* countercheck, crosscheck;
typ. counterproof; ~**-espionnage**
[~ɛspjɔ'na:ʒ] *m* counter-espionage;
~**-expertise** [~ɛkspɛr'ti:z] *f* counter-
valuation; ~**façon** [kɔ̃trəfa'sɔ̃] *f* forgery, counterfeit; counterfeiting; infringement of copyright; ~**facteur**
[~fak'tœ:r] *m* forger, counterfeiter;
~**faction** [~fak'sjɔ̃] *f* forgery; counterfeiting; ~**faire** [~'fɛ:r] (4r) *v/t.*
imitate, mimic; forge; counterfeit
(*money*); disguise (*one's voice etc.*);
fig. deform; ~**-fiche** ⌂, ⊕ [~'fiʃ] *f*
brace, strut; ~**ficher** *sl.* [~fi'ʃe] *v/t.*:

se ~ de care a damn about; ~-**fil** ⊕ [~'fil] *m*: *à* ~ against the grain; ~**fort** [~'fɔːr] *m* ⚠ buttress; *geog*. spur; *boot*: stiffening; ~*s pl*. foot-hills; ~-**haut** [~'o] *adv*.: en ~ higher up; on a higher level; ~-**jour** [~'ʒuːr] *m* backlightning; *à* ~ against the light; ~-**lettre** 🕮 [~'lɛtr] *f* counter-deed; defeasance; ~**maître** [~'mɛːtr] *m* foreman; ⚓ petty officer; first mate; ~-**mesure** [~mə'zyːr] *f* countermeasure; counterpoise; ~**partie** [~par'ti] *f* opposite view; *fig*. compensation; en ~ in compensation; in return; ~-**pied** *fig*. [~'pje] *m* opposite view; ~-**plaqué** [~pla'ke] *m* plywood; ~-**poids** [~'pwa] *m* counterweight; *clock*: balanceweight; counterpoise; ~-**poil** [~'pwal] *adv*.: *à* ~ the wrong way; ~-**point** ♪ [~'pwɛ̃] *m* counterpoint; ~-**pointe** ⊕ [~'pwɛ̃ːt] *f* tailstock; ~-**poison** [~pwa'zɔ̃] *m* antidote (to, *de*); ~-**porte** [~'pɔrt] *f* ⚠ inner door, *Am*. storm-door; ⊕ *furnace*: shield.

contrer [kɔ̃'tre] (1a) *v/t*. *box*. counter; *cards*: double; *fig*. cross, thwart.

contre...: ~-**rail** 🚂 [kɔ̃trə'raːj] *m* safety-rail; ~-**sceller** [~sɛ'le] (1a) *v/t*. counter-seal; ~**seing** [~'sɛ̃] *m* counter-signature; ~**sens** [~'sãːs] *m* misinterpretation; nonsense; *à* ~ in the wrong way; ~**signataire** [~sijna-'tɛːr] *m* one who countersigns; ~**temps** [~'tɑ̃] *m* mishap; inconvenience; disappointment; ♪ syncopation; *à* ~ at the wrong moment; ♪ out of time; ♪ contra tempo; ~-**terroriste** [~tɛrɔ'rist] *adj*., *a. su*. anti-terrorist; ~-**torpilleur** ⚓ [~torpi'jœːr] *m* destroyer; light cruiser; ~-**valeur** † [~va'lœːr] *f* exchange value; ~-**vapeur** ⊕ [~va'pœːr] *f/inv*. reversed steam; ~**venant** *m*, e *f* 🕮 [~və'nã, ~'nãːt] contravener; offender; ~**venir** [~və'niːr] (2h) *v/i*.: ~ *à* contravene; ~**vent** [~'vã] *m* outside shutter; ⊕ wind-brace; back-draught; ~**ventement** ⊕ [~vãt'mã] *m* wind-bracing; ~**vérité** [~veri'te] *f* ironical statement; untruth; ~-**visite** 🎖 [~vi'zit] *f* check inspection; ~-**voie** 🚂 [~'vwa] *f* wrong side of the train.

contribuable [kɔ̃tri'bɥabl] **1.** *su*. taxpayer; ratepayer; **2.** *adj*. taxpaying; ratepaying; **contribuer** [~'bɥe] (1n) *v/i*. contribute; con-

tribution [~by'sjɔ̃] *f* contribution; *admin*. tax; rate; mettre *à* ~ make use of, have recourse to, use.

contrit, e [kɔ̃'tri, ~'trit] penitent, contrite; **contrition** [~tri'sjɔ̃] *f* penitence, contrition.

contrôle [kɔ̃'troːl] *m* check(ing), inspection; supervision; verification; control; *thea*. box-office; † auditing; *gold*, *silver*: hallmark(ing); *gold*, *silver*: assaying; assay office; ~ *des changes* exchange control; 🖋 ~ *des naissances* birth-control; *coupon m de* ~ *ticket*: stub; **contrôler** [kɔ̃tro'le] (1a) *v/t*. check; verify; examine (*a passport etc*.); stamp (*gold, silver*); control (*s.o*.); **contrôleur** *m*, -**euse** *f* [~'lœːr, ~'løːz] inspector; supervisor; ticket-collector; controller; *métro etc*.: driver; 🚄 ~ (*aérien or de la navigation aérienne*) air traffic controller.

contrordre [kɔ̃'trɔrdr] *m* countermand; *sauf* ~ unless countermanded.

controuvé, e [kɔ̃tru've] forged, spurious.

controverse [kɔ̃trɔ'vɛrs] *f* controversy; **controverser** [~vɛr'se] (1a) *v/t*. debate (*a topic*); controvert (*an opinion*); *v/i*. hold a discussion.

contumace 🕮 [kɔ̃ty'mas] *f*: *par* ~ in absentia.

contus, e 🖋 [kɔ̃'ty, ~'tyːz] contused, bruised; **contusion** [kɔ̃ty'zjɔ̃] *f* contusion, bruise; **contusionner** [~zjɔ'ne] (1a) *v/t*. contuse, bruise.

conurbation [kɔnyrba'sjɔ̃] *f* conurbation; megalopolis.

convaincant, e [kɔ̃vɛ̃'kã, ~'kãːt] convincing; **convaincre** [~'vɛ̃ːkr] (4gg) *v/t*. convince; *fig*. prove (*s.o*.) guilty (of, *de*).

convalescence [kɔ̃valɛ'sãːs] *f* convalescence; être en ~ convalesce; **convalescent, e** [~'sã, ~'sãːt] *adj*., *a. su*. convalescent.

convenable [kɔ̃v'nabl] suitable; decent, seemly; **convenance** [~'nãːs] *f* fitness; propriety; decency; convenience; expediency; *à la* ~ *de q*. to s.o.'s liking; to suit s.o.'s convenience; *mariage m de* ~ marriage of convenience; *par* ~ for the sake of decency; **convenir** [~'niːr] (2h) *v/i*.: ~ *à* suit, fit; ~ *de* agree upon; reach agreement about; admit, acknowledge (*s.th*.); *c'est convenu!*

agreed!; *il convient de* (*inf.*) it is advisable *or* fitting to (*inf.*).

convention [kɔ̃vɑ̃'sjɔ̃] *f* convention; agreement; *pol.* assembly; ∼s *pl.* clauses; ∼ *collective* collective bargaining; **conventionné** [∼sjɔ'ne]: *médecin* ∼ panel doctor; **conventionnel, -elle** [∼sjɔ'nɛl] **1.** *adj.* conventional; **2.** *su./m hist.* member of the National Convention.

conventuel, -elle [kɔ̃vɑ̃'tɥɛl] conventual.

convergence [kɔ̃vɛr'ʒɑ̃:s] *f* convergence; ✗, *a. fig.* concentration; **convergent, e** [∼'ʒɑ̃, ∼'ʒɑ̃:t] converging; ✗ concentrated; **converger** [∼'ʒe] (1l) *v/i.* converge.

convers, e [kɔ̃'vɛːr, ∼'vɛrs] lay...

conversation [kɔ̃vɛrsa'sjɔ̃] *f* conversation, talk; *teleph.* call; **converser** [∼'se] (1a) *v/i.* converse, talk.

conversion [kɔ̃vɛr'sjɔ̃] *f* conversion (*a.* ✞); ✗ wheel(ing), change of front; **converti** *m, e f* [∼'ti] convert; **convertible** [∼'tibl] convertible (into, en); **convertir** [∼'tiːr] (2a) *v/t.* ✞, *eccl.*, *phls.*, *fig.* convert; **convertisseur** [∼ti'sœːr] *m* ⊕ converter; ⚡ transformer.

convexe [kɔ̃'vɛks] convex.

conviction [kɔ̃vik'sjɔ̃] *f* conviction.

convier [kɔ̃'vje] (1o) *v/t.* invite; urge.

convive [kɔ̃'viːv] *su.* guest; table companion.

convocation [kɔ̃vɔka'sjɔ̃] *f* convocation, summons *sg.*; notice of a meeting *or* an appointment; ✗ calling-up papers *pl.*

convoi [kɔ̃'vwa] *m* convoy; 🚂 train; (*a.* ∼ *funèbre*) funeral procession; ∼ *automobile* motor transport column.

convoiter [kɔ̃vwa'te] (1a) *v/t.* covet, desire; **convoitise** [∼'tiːz] *f* covetousness; lust.

convoler *iro.* [kɔ̃vɔ'le] (1a) *v/i.* (re)marry.

convoquer [kɔ̃vɔ'ke] (1m) *v/t.* summon; ✗ call up; *admin.* summon to an interview.

convoyer ✗, ⚓ [kɔ̃vwa'je] (1h) *v/t.* convoy; **convoyeur** [∼'jœːr] *m* ⚓ convoy(-ship); ⚓ convoying officer; ✗ officer in charge of a convoy; ⊕ conveyor, endless belt.

convulser [kɔ̃vyl'se] (1a) *v/t. physiol.* convulse; F frighten into fits; **con-**

vulsif, -ve [∼'sif, ∼'siːv] convulsive; **convulsion** [∼'sjɔ̃] *f* convulsion; spasm.

coopérateur *m*, **-trice** *f* [kɔɔpera-'tœːr, ∼'tris] co(-)operator; **coopératif, -ve** [∼'tif, ∼'tiːv] **1.** *adj.* co(-)-operative; **2.** *su./f* co(-)operative stores *pl.*; ∼*ve immobilière* building society; **coopération** [∼'sjɔ̃] *f* co(-)operation; **coopératisme** [∼-'tism] *m* co(-)operative system; **coopérer** [kɔɔpe're] (1f) *v/i.* co(-)operate.

cooptation [kɔɔpta'sjɔ̃] *f* co-optation; **coopter** [∼'te] (1a) *v/t.* co-opt.

coordinateur *m*, **-trice** *f* [kɔɔrdina'tœːr, -'tris] coordinator; **coordination** [∼'sjɔ̃] *f* coordination.

coordonnées ⚚ [kɔɔrdɔ'ne] *f/pl.* co-ordinates; **coordonner** [∼] (1a) *v/t.* coordinate (with, à); arrange.

copain F [kɔ'pɛ̃] *m* pal, chum, *Am.* buddy.

copeau [kɔ'po] *m* wood shaving; ⊕ ∼*x pl.* turnings.

copiage [kɔ'pjaːʒ] *m school:* copying; **copie** [∼'pi] *f* (carbon) copy, transcript; *fig.* imitation; *phot.* print; *school:* exercise, paper; ∼ *au net* fair copy; **copier** [∼'pje] (1o) *v/t.* copy; *fig.* imitate; *school:* crib (from, sur).

copieux, -euse [kɔ'pjø, ∼'pjøːz] copious, abundant.

copilote ✈ [kopi'lɔt] *m* second pilot, *Am.* co-pilot.

copinage F [kɔpi'naːʒ] *m* cronyism; **copine** F [kɔ'pin] *f girl:* pal, chum; **copiner** F [kɔpi'ne] (1a) *v/i.* be pally; be pals; **copinerie** F [kɔpin-'ri] *f* pallyness; *coll.* the pals *pl.*

copiste [kɔ'pist] *su.* copier, copyist; *fig.* imitator.

copra(h) [kɔ'pra] *m* copra.

copreneur ⚖ [kɔprə'nœːr] *m* cotenant, co-lessee.

coproduction [kɔprɔdyk'sjɔ̃] *n* joint production, coproduction.

copropriétaire [kɔprɔprije'tɛːr] *su.* joint owner, co-owner; **copropriété** [∼'te] *f* joint ownership, co-ownership.

copule *gramm.* [kɔ'pyl] *f* copula.

coq¹ ⚓ [kɔk] *m* ship's cook.

coq² *orn.* [kɔk] *m* cock, *Am.* rooster; *box.* (*a. poids m* ∼) bantam weight; ∼ *de bruyère* (great) grouse; ∼ *d'Inde* see

dindon; être comme un ~ en pâte live
like a fighting cock, be in clover; être
le ~ du village be cock of the walk; ~-
à-l'âne [kɔka'lɑːn] *m*/*inv.* abrupt
jump from one subject to another.

coque [kɔk] *f* egg: shell; ⚓ hull,
bottom; ⊕ *boiler*: body; œuf *m* à la ~
boiled egg.

coquelicot ⚘ [kɔkli'ko] *m* red poppy.

coqueluche [kɔ'klyʃ] *f* 💉 whooping-
cough; *fig.* darling, favo(u)rite.

coqueriquer [kɔkri'ke] (1m) *v*/*i.*
crow.

coquet, -ette [kɔ'kɛ, ~'kɛt] **1.** *adj.*
coquettish; smart, stylish (*hat etc.*);
trim (*garden*); F tidy (*sum*); **2.** *su./f*
flirt; **coqueter** [kɔk'te] (1c) *v*/*i.*
coquette; flirt (with, *avec*); *fig.* toy
(with, *avec*).

coquetier [kɔk'tje] *m* egg-cup; egg-
merchant.

coquetterie [kɔkɛ'tri] *f* coquetry;
affectation; smartness, daintiness.

coquillage [kɔki'jaːʒ] *m* shell-fish;
shell; **coquille** [~'kiːj] *f* egg, *nut*,
oyster, *snail*, *a. fig.*: shell; *typ.* misprint, printer's error; *metall.* chill-
mould; bank paper; *size*: small post;
fig. sortir de sa ~ come out of one's
shell.

coquin, e [kɔ'kɛ̃, ~'kin] **1.** *adj.* roguish; **2.** *su.* rogue; rascal (*a. co.*);
su./f hussy; **coquinerie** [~kin'ri] *f*
roguery; rascality.

cor[1] [kɔːr] *m hunt.* tine; ♪, *a. hunt.*
horn; ♪ horn-player; ♪~ *d'harmonie*
French horn; *fig. à ~ et à cri* insistently; *sonner* (or *donner*) *du ~*
sound the horn.

cor[2] 🦶 [~] *m* corn.

corail, *pl.* **-aux** [kɔ'raːj, ~'ro] *m*
coral; **corailleur** [kɔra'jœːr] *m*
coral fisher; coral worker; coral-
fishing boat; **corallin, e** [~'lɛ̃, ~'lin]
coral-red.

corbeau [kɔr'bo] *m orn.* crow;
raven; △ corbel; F person of ill
omen.

corbeille [kɔr'bɛːj] *f* basket; *thea.*
dress-circle; ⊕ *valve*: cage; 🌱
(round) flower-bed; **corbeillée**
[~bɛ'je] *f* basketful.

corbillard [kɔrbi'jaːr] *m* hearse.

cordage [kɔr'daːʒ] *m* rope; *racket*:
stringing; cord of wood; ⚓ ~s *pl.*
gear *sg.*; **corde** [kɔrd] *f* rope, cord,
line; ♪ string; ♪ chord; 🏋 lift
wire; hangman's rope, *fig.* gallows

sg.; *anat.* ~s *pl.* vocales vocal
c(h)ords.

cordé, e ⚘ *etc.* [kɔr'de] cordate,
heart-shaped.

cordeau [kɔr'do] *m* chalk-line,
string; (measuring) tape; (⚓ tow-)
rope; *tex.* selvedge; ✂, ⚔ fuse;
cordée [~'de] *f mount.* rope (*of
climbers*); ✝ cord (*of wood*); *racket*:
stringing; **cordeler** [kɔrdə'le] (1c)
v/*t.* twist (*hemp etc.*) into rope; **cor-
delette** [~'lɛt] *f* small cord *or*
string; *en* ~s in small plaits;
cordelier [~'lje] *m* Franciscan
friar; **cordelière** [~'ljɛːr] *f* ✝ Franciscan nun; girdle; *typ.* ornamental
border; **corder** [kɔr'de] (1a) *v*/*t.*
twist (*hemp etc.*) into rope; ✝
measure (*wood*) by the cord; string
(*a racket*); twist (*tobacco*); cord (*a
trunk etc.*); **corderie** [~'dri] *f* rope-
making; rope-trade.

cordial, e, *m*/*pl.* **-aux** [kɔr'djal,
~'djo] **1.** *adj.* cordial; 💊 stimulating; **2.** *su./m* cordial; **cordialité**
[~djali'te] *f* cordiality.

cordier [kɔr'dje] *m* rope-maker;
dealer in ropes; ♪ violin: tail-piece;
cordon [~'dɔ̃] *m* cord, string, tape;
(shoe-)lace; door-pull, bell-pull;
line (*of trees etc.*); *admin.* cordon,
edge; *anat.* ~ ombilical navel string,
umbilical cord; **cordon-bleu**, *pl.*
cordons-bleus F *fig.* [~dɔ̃'blø] *m*
first-rate cook; **cordonner** [~dɔ'ne]
(1a) *v*/*t.* twist, cord (*hemp etc.*); edge-
roll (*coins*).

cordonnerie [kɔrdɔn'ri] *f* shoe-
making; shoemaker's shop.

cordonnet [kɔrdɔ'nɛ] *m* braid, cord.

cordonnier [kɔrdɔ'nje] *m* shoemaker; F cobbler.

coréen, -enne [kɔre'ɛ̃, ~'ɛn] *adj.*,
a. su. ♀ Korean.

coriace [kɔ'rjas] tough (*a. fig.*).

coricide 🦶 [kɔri'sid] *m* corn cure.

corindon *min.* [kɔrɛ̃'dɔ̃] *m* corun-
dum.

corinthien, -enne [kɔrɛ̃'tjɛ̃, ~'tjɛn]
1. *adj.* Corinthian; **2.** *su.* ♀ Corinthian; *su./m* △ Corinthian.

cormier ⚘ [kɔr'mje] *m* service
(-tree, -wood).

cormoran *orn.* [kɔrmɔ'rɑ̃] *m* cor-
morant.

cornac [kɔr'nak] *m* mahout, elephant
driver; F *fig.* guide, companion,
chaperon; **cornaquer** F [~na'ke]

(1a) v/t. guide, show (s.o.) around, accompany, chaperon.

corne [kɔrn] f horn (a. fig.); dog's-ear (in a book); ~ à chaussures shoe-horn, shoe-lift; de ~ horn...; **bêtes** f/pl. à ~s horned cattle; **corné, e** [kɔr'ne] **1.** adj. horny; horn...; **2.** su./f anat. cornea; **cornéen, -enne** [~ne'ɛ̃, ~'ɛn] adj.: opt. lentilles f/pl. ~ennes contact lenses.

corneille orn. [kɔr'nɛ:j] f crow, rook.

cornemuse ♪ [kɔrnə'my:z] f bag-pipe(s pl.); **cornemuseur** [~my-'zœ:r] m piper.

corner¹ foot. [kɔr'nɛ:r] m corner.

corner² [kɔr'ne] (1a) v/i. hoot; v/t. fig. trumpet (news etc.); turn down the corner of (a page etc.); **cornet** [~'nɛ] m pastry: horn; icecream: cone; paper bag, screw of paper; ♪ (à pistons) cornet; F se mettre qch. dans le ~ have s.th. to eat; **cornette** [~'nɛt] su./f nun: coif; mob-cap.

corniche [kɔr'niʃ] f rock: ledge; coast road; △ cornice.

cornichon [kɔrni'ʃɔ̃] m gherkin; F nitwit.

cornière [kɔr'njɛ:r] f ⊕ angle(-iron, -bar).

cornouille ♀ [kɔr'nu:j] f cornel-berry; **cornouiller** [~nu'je] m cornel(-tree); ♣ dogwood.

cornu, e [kɔr'ny] horned; spurred (wheat); fig. absurd.

cornue [~] f ♫ etc. retort; metall. steel converter.

corollaire [kɔrɔl'lɛ:r] m ⅄ corollary; ♀ corollary tendril; **corolle** ♀ [~'rɔl] f corolla.

coron [kɔ'rɔ̃] m miners' quarters pl.

coronaire ♫, anat. [kɔrɔ'nɛ:r] coronary; **coronal, e** m/pl. -aux [~'nal, ~'no] coronal.

corporatif, -ve [kɔrpɔra'tif, ~'ti:v] corporat(iv)e; **corporation** [~'sjɔ̃] f corporation; ♣ hist. (trade-)guild.

corporel, -elle [kɔrpɔ'rɛl] corpo-real; corporal (punishment); bodily.

corps [kɔ:r] m body (a. ♫); flesh; matter; ✕ (army) corps; ♣ (battle) fleet; F person, figure; fig. profes-sion; ♖ corpus (of law); ~ à ~ hand to hand; ~ de bâtiment main building; ~ de logis housing unit; ~ de métier g(u)ild; trade associa-tion; ♣ ~ mort (fixed) moorings pl.; à ~ perdu desperately; en ~ in a

body; faire ~ avec be an integral part of; levée f du ~ start of the funeral; ♣ perdu ~ et biens lost with all hands.

corpulence [kɔrpy'lɑ̃:s] f stoutness, corpulence; **corpulent, e** [~'lɑ̃, ~'lɑ̃:t] stout, corpulent; portly.

corpus [kɔr'pys] m corpus; **corpus-cule** [kɔrpys'kyl] m corpuscle; par-ticle.

correct, e [kɔ'rɛkt] correct, proper; accurate; **correcteur** m, **-trice** f [kɔrɛk'tœ:r, ~'tris] corrector, proof-reader; **correctif, -ve** [~'tif, ~'ti:v] adj., a. su./m corrective; **correction** [~'sjɔ̃] f punishment; correction; maison f de ~ reformatory; sauf ~ subject to correction; **correction-nel, -elle** ♖ [~sjɔ'nɛl] **1.** adj. cor-rectional; délit m ~ minor offence; tribunal m ~ = **2.** su./f court of petty sessions, Am. police court.

corrélation [kɔrrela'sjɔ̃] f correla-tion.

correspondance [kɔrɛspɔ̃'dɑ̃:s] f correspondence; ☎ etc. connection; ☎ railway omnibus, transfer coach; cours m par ~ correspondence course; par ~ by letter, by post; vote f par ~ postal vote; voter par ~ vote by post; **correspondancier** m, **-ère** f ✝ [~dɑ̃'sje, ~'sjɛ:r] correspondence clerk; **correspondant, e** [~'dɑ̃, ~'dɑ̃:t] **1.** adj. corresponding; ☎ con-necting; **2.** su. ✝, journ. correspond-ent; pen friend, Am. pen pal; school: parents' representative; **corres-pondre** [kɔrɛs'pɔ̃:dr] (4a) v/i.: ~ à correspond to or with, suit; tally with; communicate with (another room etc.); ~ avec q. be in correspond-ence with s.o.   [passage.]

corridor [kɔri'dɔ:r] m corridor,]

corrigé [kɔri'ʒe] m fair copy; key, crib; **corriger** [~'ʒe] (11) v/t. cor-rect; read (proofs); punish; rectify; cure; **corrigible** [~'ʒibl] corrigible.

corroborer [kɔrrɔbɔ're] (1a) v/t. corroborate, confirm.

corroder [kɔrrɔ'de] (1a) v/t. cor-rode, eat away.

corroi [kɔ'rwa] m leather: currying; **corroierie** [~rwa'ri] f currying; curriery.

corrompre [kɔ'rɔ̃:pr] (4a) v/t. cor-rupt; spoil (the taste); taint (meat); ♖ suborn; se ~ become corrupt(ed) or tainted.

corrosif, -ve [kɔrrɔ'zif, ~'ziːv] *adj.*, *a. su.*/*m* corrosive; **corrosion** [~'zjɔ̃] *f* corrosion; *soil*: erosion; ⊕ pitting.

corroyer [kɔrwa'je] (1h) *v/t.* curry (*leather*); rough-plane (*wood*); weld (*iron*, *steel*); puddle (*clay*); **corroyeur** [~'jœːr] *m* currier; *metall.* blacksmith.

corrupteur, -trice [kɔryp'tœːr, ~-'tris] **1.** *adj.* corrupting; **2.** *su.* corrupter; briber; ⚖ suborner; **corruptible** [~'tibl] corruptible; open to bribery; **corruption** [~'sjɔ̃] *f* corruption; bribery; *Am.* graft; ⚖ subornation; *food*: tainting; *air*, *water*: pollution.

corsage *cost.* [kɔr'saːʒ] *m* bodice; † blouse.

corsaire [kɔr'sɛːr] *m* corsair, privateer.

corse [kɔrs] *adj.*, *a. su.* ♀ Corsican.

corsé, e [kɔr'se] strong; full-bodied (*wine*); spicy (*story*); F substantial.

corselet *zo.*, *a. hist.* [kɔrsə'lɛ] *m* cors(e)let.

corser [kɔr'se] (1a) *v/t.* give body or flavo(u)r to; strengthen; **se ~** take a turn for the worse.

corset [kɔr'sɛ] *m* corset; **corsetière** [~sə'tjɛːr] *f* corsetmaker.

cortège [kɔr'tɛːʒ] *m* procession; retinue, train; **~ funèbre** funeral procession.

cortisone ⚕ [kɔrti'zɔn] *f* cortisone.

corvéable ✕ [kɔrve'abl] liable to fatigue duty; **corvée** [~'ve] *f* ✕ fatigue; ⚓ duty; ✕ fatigue party; *fig.* drudgery, hard work, chore, drag; thankless job.

corvette ⚓ *hist.* [kɔr'vɛt] *f* corvette.

coryphée [kɔri'fe] *m* leader of the ballet, principal dancer; *fig.* party leader, chief.

coryza ⚕ [kɔri'za] *m* cold in the head.

cosmétique [kɔsme'tik] *adj.*, *a. su.*/*m* cosmetic.

cosmique [kɔs'mik] cosmic.

cosmo... [kɔsmɔ] cosmo...; **~drome** [~'droːm] *m* cosmodrome; **~graphie** [~gra'fi] *f* cosmography; **~naute** [~'noːt] *su.* cosmonaut; **~polite** [~pɔ'lit] *adj.*, *a. su.* cosmopolitan.

cosse [kɔs] *f* pod, husk; shell; ⚡ eye or spade terminal; *sl.* laziness; **cossu, e** F [kɔ'sy] rich (*a. fig.*); well-to-do.

costal, e, *m*/*pl.* **-aux** *anat.* [kɔs'tal, ~'to] costal; **costaud, e** *sl.* [~'to, ~'toːd] strong, sturdy; hefty.

costume [kɔs'tym] *m* costume, dress; suit; **~ de bain** bathing-costume; **~ de golf** plus-fours *pl.*; **~ tailleur** tailor-made suit (*for women*); coat and skirt; **costumer** [~ty'me] (1a) *v/t.* dress up; *bal m* costumé fancy-dress ball; **costumier** [~ty-'mje] *m* costumier; ⚖, *univ.* outfitter; *thea.* wardrobe-keeper.

cotation † [kɔta'sjɔ̃] *f* quotation, quoting; **cote** [kɔt] *f* quota; *admin.* assessment; ⚖, †, etc. *document*: identification *or* classification mark; *sp.* odds *pl.*; ⚓ classification; † *prices etc.*: quotation; *school*: mark (*for an essay etc.*); *fig.* rating, standing; popularity; **~ d'alerte** danger mark; F **avoir la ~** be (very) popular.

côte [koːt] *f* ⚕, *anat.*, *cuis.* rib; ⚕ midrib; slope; hill; coast, shore; **~ à ~** side by side.

côté [ko'te] *m* side; direction; **à ~ de** beside; **de ~** sideways; **de mon ~** for my part; **du ~ de** in the direction of; **d'un ~** on one side; **d'un ~ ..., de l'autre ~** on the one hand ..., on the other hand; **la maison d'à ~** next door.

coteau [kɔ'to] *m* slope, hillside; hillock.

côtelé, e *tex.* [kot'le] ribbed; **côtelette** [~'lɛt] *veal*: cutlet; *pork*, *mutton*: chop; F **~s** *pl.* whiskers: mutton-chops.

coter [kɔ'te] (1a) *v/t.* classify, number, letter (*a document*); ⚓ class (*a ship*); quote (*prices*); *admin.* assess.

coterie [kɔ'tri] *f* set, circle, clique.

côtier, -ère [ko'tje, ~'tjɛːr] coast (-ing); coastal; inshore (*fishing*).

cotillon [kɔti'jɔ̃] *m* † petticoat; **courir le ~** flirt with the girls.

cotisation [kɔtiza'sjɔ̃] *f* subscription; contribution; fee; *admin.* assessment; quota; **cotiser** [~'ze] (1a) *v/t.* *admin.* assess; **se ~** subscribe; get up a subscription.

coton [kɔ'tɔ̃] *m* cotton; *a.* **~ hydrophile** cotton wool, *Am.* absorbent cotton; **élever dans du ~** coddle (*a baby*); **cotonnade** [kɔtɔ'nad] *f* cotton fabric; **~s** *pl.* cotton goods; **cotonner** [~'ne] (1a) *v/t.*: **se ~** become covered with down; become woolly (*fruit*); become fluffy (*cloth*); **cotonnerie** [kɔtɔn'ri] *f* cotton growing; cotton-plantation; cotton-mill; **cotonneux, -euse** [~tɔ'nø, ~'nøːz] cottony; woolly (*fruit*, *style*); sleepy

(*pear*); fleecy (*cloud*); **cotonnier,
-ère** [͜tɔ'nje, ͜'njɛːr] *m* 1. *adj*. cotton-...; 2. *su./m* ♀ cotton-plant;
coton-poudre, *pl.* **cotons-
poudre** [͜tɔ'puːdr] *m* guncotton.

côtoyer [kotwa'je] (1h) *v/t*. hug (*the
shore*); keep close to; skirt (*the
forest*); border on (*a. fig.*); *fig.* rub
shoulders with (*s.o.*); se ~ rub
shoulders.

cotte [kɔt] *f* workman's overalls *pl.*;
petticoat; ~ de mailles coat of mail.

cou [ku] *m* neck.

couac ♩ [kwak] *m* squawk.

couard, e [kwaːr, kward] 1. *adj.*
coward(ly); 2. *su.* coward; **couardi-
se** [kwar'diːz] *f* cowardice.

couchage [ku'ʃaːʒ] *m* night's lodging; *clothes*: bedding; sac *m* de ~
sleeping-bag; **couchant, e** [͜'ʃɑ̃,
͜'ʃɑ̃ːt] 1. *su./m* sunset, setting of the
sun; west; 2. *adj.*: chien *m* ~ setter;
fig. crawler, fawner; soleil *m* ~ setting
sun; **couche** [kuʃ] *f* layer; *paint etc.*:
coat; *geol.* (*a. social etc.*) stratum;
napkin, nappy, *Am.* diaper (*for
baby*); ✂ seam; ✦ hotbed; *tree*: ring;
† bed; ~s *pl.* childbirth *sg.*; ~ d'arrêt
barrier layer; ⊕ ~ de roulement running surface; *fausse* ~ miscarriage; F
il en a une ~! what a fathead!; F se
donner une belle ~ drink o.s. blind;
coucher [ku'ʃe] 1. (1a) *v/t*. put to
bed; lay down; beat down; put *or*
write (*s.th.*) down (on, sur); mention
(*s.o.*) (in one's will, sur son testament); ~ qch. en joue aim s.th.; se ~ go
to bed; lie down; set (*sun*); ~ sleep;
2. *su./m* going to bed; *sun*: setting;
coucherie *sl.* [kuʃ'ri] *f oft. pl.* love-
making; **couchette** [͜'ʃɛt] *f* cot; ⚓
bunk; ⬛, ⚓ berth; **coucheur**
[͜'ʃœːr] *m*: mauvais ~ awkward
customer, nasty fellow.

couci-couça [kusiku'sa], **couci-
couci** [͜'si] *adv.* so-so.

coucou [ku'ku] *m* cuckoo(-clock); ♀
F cowslip.

coude [kud] *m* elbow (*a. river, road*);
⊕ *shaft*: crank; coup *m* de ~ nudge;
jouer des ~s elbow one's way; **coudée**
[ku'de] *f* cubit; F avoir ses ~s franches
have elbow-room; *fig.* have a free
hand.

cou-de-pied, *pl.* **cous-de-pied**
[kud'pje] *m* instep.

couder ⊕ [ku'de] (1a) *v/t*. crank (*a
shaft*); bend (*a pipe*) into an elbow;

coudoyer [͜dwa'je] (1h) *v/t*. elbow,
jostle; rub shoulders with.

coudre[1] [kudr] (4l) *v/t*. sew; stitch;
machine *f* à ~ sewing-machine; rester
bouche cousue remain silent.

coudre[2] ♀ [kudr] *m*, **coudrier** ♀
[ku'drje] *m* hazel-tree.

couenne [kwan] *f* bacon-rind; *roast
pork*: crackling; ✦ mole; **couen-
neux, -euse** ✦ [kwa'nø, ͜'nøːz]
buffy (*blood*); angine *f* ~euse diphtheria.

couffe [kuf] *f*, **couffin** [ku'fɛ̃] *m*
basket.

couillon *sl.* [ku'jɔ̃] *m* fool; ~! bloody
fool!

coulage [ku'laːʒ] *m* pouring (*a.
metall.*); *metall.* casting; *liquid*: leak-
ing; ⚓ scuttling; *fig.* leakage; **coulant, e** [͜'lɑ̃, ͜'lɑ̃ːt] 1. *adj.* running;
flowing (*a. style*); *fig.* easy; F easy-
going; F accommodating; 2. *su./m*
sliding ring (*a.* ⊕); ♀ runner; ✂
case-slide.

coule [kul] *adv.*: être à la ~ be wise,
know the ropes, know all the tricks of
the trade, be with it.

coulé [ku'le] *m dancing*: slide; ♩ slur;
billiards: follow-through; ⊕ cast
(-ing); **coulée** [͜] *f writing*: running-
hand; *lava, liquid*: flow; ⊕ casting;
⊕ tapping; *fig.* streak; **couler** [͜]
(1a) *v/t*. pour; ⚓ sink (*a ship*); ♩ slur;
fig. slip; F ruin; se ~ slide, slip; F
fig. se la ~ douce have an easy
time; *v/i.* flow, run; ⚓ founder,
sink; ⊕ run; slip; leak (*pen, vat, etc.*);
fig. slip by (*time*); *fig.* pass over
(*facts*).

couleur [ku'lœːr] *f* colo(u)r (*a. fig.*);
complexion; *cards*: suit; *cin.* en ~(s
pl.) technicolor-...; ✦ pâles ~s *pl.*
chlorosis *sg.*, green-sickness *sg.*; sous
~ de under the pretence of.

couleuvre [ku'lœːvr] *f* grass snake; F
avaler des ~s pocket an insult.

coulis [ku'li] 1. *adj./m*: vent *m* ~
insidious draught; 2. *su./m* ⊕ (liquid)
filling; *cuis.* purée.

coulisse [ku'lis] *f* ⊕ groove, slot; ⊕
slide; ⚔ wooden shoot; *thea.* wing;
backstage; *fig.* background; ✦ outside market; dans les ~s backstage (*a.
fig.*); porte *f* à ~ sliding door; *fig.*
regard *m* en ~ sideglance; **coulisser**
[kuli'se] (1a) *v/t*. fit with slides; *v/i.*
slide; **coulissier** ✦ [͜'sje] *m* outside
broker.

couloir [ku'lwa:r] *m* corridor (*a.* ♟, *geog.*), passage; *parl.* lobby; ⊕ shoot; *cin. film*: track; *water, mountain*: gully; *tennis*: tram-lines *pl.*; ✈ ~ aérien air corridor.

coup [ku] *m* blow, knock; hit; thrust; *knife*: stab; wound; ⊕, *sp.* stroke; sound; beat; *gun etc.*: shot; *wind*: gust; turn; (evil) deed; *sl.* drink, glass (*of wine*); *fig.* influence; ✦ ~ de *chaleur* heat-stroke; F ~ de *fil* (telephone) call, ring; ~ de *filet* haul; ~ de *grâce* finishing stroke, quietus; ✗ ~ de *grisou* firedamp explosion; ~ de *Jarnac* treacherous attack; F low trick; ✗ ~ de *main* surprise attack, raid; ~ de *maître* master stroke; *foot.* ~ d'*envoi* kick-off; place-kick; ~ de *pied* kick; ~ de *poing* blow (with the fist); ✦ ~ de *sang* apoplectic fit, F stroke; ✦ ~ de *soleil* sunburn; ~ d'*essai* trial shot; ~ d'*État* coup d'état; ~ de *téléphone* (telephone) call; ~ de *tête* butt; *fig.* impulsive act; *fig.* ~ de *théâtre* dramatic turn; ~ d'*œil* glance, view; ~ *franc* foot. free kick; *hockey*: free hit; à ~ *sûr* certainly; *après* ~ after the event; as an afterthought; *sp. donner le* ~ *d'envoi* kick off; *donner un* ~ *de brosse* give a brush (down); *donner un* ~ *de main à* help; give a helping hand to; *d'un* (*seul*) ~ at one go; *du premier* ~ at the first attempt; *entrer en* ~ *de vent* burst in, rush in; *être aux cent* ~s be desperate; F *être dans le* ~ be with it; F *monter le* ~ *à* q. deceive s.o.; *pour le* ~ this time; for the moment; *saluer d'un* ~ *de chapeau* raise one's hat to; *tenir le* ~ take it; keep a stiff upper lip; *tout à* ~ suddenly, all of a sudden; *tout d'un* ~ (all) at once; *traduire qch. à* ~s *de dictionnaire* translate s.th., looking up each word in the dictionary.

coupable [ku'pabl] **1.** *adj.* guilty; **2.** *su.* culprit; ⚖ delinquent.

coupage [ku'pa:ʒ] *m* cutting; *wine*: blending; diluting (*of wine with water*); **coupant** [~'pɑ̃] *m* (cutting) edge.

coup-de-poing, *pl.* **coups-de-poing** [kud'pwɛ̃] *m* (~ *américain*) knuckleduster.

coupe¹ [kup] *f* cutting; *trees*: felling; ⊕ *wood etc.*, *a. fig.* cut; section; ~ *des cheveux* haircut; *fig. sous la* ~ *de* q. under s.o.'s control *or* thumb.

coupe² [~] *f* (drinking) cup; *sp.* cup; *sl.* dial, mug.

coupé [ku'pe] *m* brougham; 🚗 coupé (*a. mot.*), half-compartment; **coupée** ⚓ [~] *f* gangway.

coupe...: ~**cigares** [kupsi'ga:r] *m*/*inv.* cigar-cutter; ~**circuit** ⚡ [~sir'kɥi] *m*/*inv.* circuit-breaker; ~**faim** [~'fɛ̃] *m*/*inv.* appetite suppressant; ~**gorge** [~'gɔrʒ] *m*/*inv.* death-trap; ~**jarret** [~ʒa'rɛ] *m* cut-throat; assassin; ~**légumes** [~le'gym] *m*/*inv.* vegetable-cutter; ~**papier** [~pa'pje] *m*/*inv.* paperknife; letter-opener.

couper [ku'pe] (1a) *v*/*t.* cut (*a. tennis*); cut off (*a.* ✗); cut down (*trees*), chop (*wood*); intercept; intersect; interrupt; water down (*wine*); ⚡ switch off; *cards*: trump; *teleph.* ~ *la communication* ring off; *mot.* ~ *l'allumage* switch off the ignition; *se* ~ intersect; F *fig.* give o.s. away; *v*/*i.*: ~ *court* avoid; *sl.* ~ *à* dodge (*s.th.*); F ~ *dans le vif* resort to extreme measures; *teleph. ne coupez pas!* hold the line!

couperet [ku'prɛ] *m* chopper; *guillotine*: blade.

couperose [ku'pro:z] *f* ✦ blotchiness; ♀ ~ *verte* (*bleue*) green (blue) vitriol; **couperosé, e** [~pro'ze] blotchy (*skin*).

coupeur, -euse [ku'pœ:r, ~'pø:z] *su. person*: cutter; *su.*/*f* cutting machine; ✗ header.

couplage [ku'pla:ʒ] *m* ⚡ *etc.* coupling, connection; **couple** [kupl] *m* pair, couple; ⊕ torque, turning moment; **coupler** [ku'ple] (1a) *v*/*t.* couple; ⚡ connect; **couplet** [~'plɛ] *m* verse; ⊕ hinge.

coupoir [ku'pwa:r] *m instrument*: cutter.

coupole [ku'pɔl] *f* cupola, dome; ✗ revolving gun-turret.

coupon [ku'pɔ̃] *m* bread, dividend, *etc.*: coupon; 🚗, *thea.* ticket; *material*: remnant; ⊕ test-bar; ~**réponse** *postal post*: international reply coupon; **coupure** [~'py:r] *f* cut, gash; (newspaper-)cutting, clipping; ⚡, *thea.* cut; paper money; *geol.* fault.

cour [ku:r] *f* court (*a.* ⚖); (court-)yard; ✗ square; *Northern France*: lavatory; *thea.* côté ~ O.P.; ♀ *inter-*

nationale de justice International Court of Justice (at the Hague); faire la ~ à court, woo.

courage [ku'ra:ʒ] m courage, F pluck; valo(u)r; **courageux, -euse** [~ra'ʒø, ~'ʒø:z] brave, courageous, F plucky; zealous.

couramment [kura'mã] adv. fluently; in general use, usually; **courant, e** [~'rã, ~'rã:t] **1.** adj. running; current; ⚓ floating (debt); ⚓ standard (make); chien m ~ hound; **2.** su./m ⚡, water: current; stream; metall. blast; present month, ⚓ instant, abbr. inst.; fig. course; ⚡ ~ alternatif (continu) alternating (direct) current; ~ d'air draught, Am. draft; ⚡ ~ triphasé three-phase current; au ~ (de) conversant (with), acquainted (with), well informed (of or about); être au ~ de a. know all about; mettre q. au ~ (de) inform s.o. (about or of); se tenir au ~ keep up to date; dans le ~ de in the course of; fin ~ at the end of this month; ⚡ ... pour tous ~s A.C./D.C. ...

courbatu, e [kurba'ty] stiff, aching; **courbature** [~'ty:r] f stiffness, muscle soreness; ~s pl. aches and pains.

courbe [kurb] **1.** adj. curved; **2.** su./f curve; sweep; graph; **courber** [kur'be] (1a) vt/i. bend, curve; v/t.: se ~ bend, stoop; **courbette** [~'bɛt] f: fig. faire des ~s à knowtow to; **courbure** [~'by:r] f curve; road: camber; earth, space: curvature; ⊕ beam: sagging; ⊕ double ~ pipe: S-bend.

coureur, -euse [ku'rœ:r, ~'rø:z] su. runner (a. sp.); fig. frequenter (of cafés etc.); fig. hunter (of prizes etc.); su./m: sp. ~ de fond stayer; ~ de jupons skirt-chaser; su./f streetwalker.

courge ♀ [kurʒ] f gourd; pumpkin; Am. squash.

courir [ku'ri:r] (2i) v/i. run; race; flow (blood, river, etc.); fig. be current; ⚓ sail; v/t. run after; pursue; hunt; overrun; sp. run (a race); frequent, haunt; F ~ le cachet give private lessons; ~ le monde travel widely; être fort couru be much sought after.

courlis orn. [kur'li] m curlew.

couronne [ku'rɔn] f crown; coronet; flowers, laurel: wreath; ⊕ wheel: rim; **couronnement** [~rɔn'mã] m

crowning; coronation; **couronner** [~rɔ'ne] (1a) v/t. crown (a. fig.; a. ⚡ a tooth); fig. award a prize to.

courrai [ku're] 1st p. sg. fut. of courir.

courre [ku:r] v/t.: chasse f à ~ hunt(ing); **courrier** [ku'rje] m courier; post, mail; letters pl.; journ. (news, theatrical, etc.) column; faire son ~ deal with one's mail; **courriériste** journ. [~rje'rist] su. columnist.

courroie [ku'rwa] f strap; ⊕ belt; mot. ~ de ventilateur fan belt.

courroucer [kuru'se] (1k) v/t. anger; se ~ get angry; **courroux** poet. [~'ru] m anger.

cours [ku:r] m course; ⚡ △ bricks: course, layer; money: circulation; ⚓ quotation; univ. course (of lectures); school: class(es pl.), lesson; ~ d'eau stream, river; ⚓ ~ des changes rate of exchange; ⚓ ~ du marché mondial price on the world market; au ~ de during, in the course of; en ~ in progress.

course [kurs] f run(ning); race; excursion, trip; ⚓ cruise; ⊕ stroke; errand; ~ à pied (foot-)race; pol. ~ aux armements armaments race; ~ de chevaux horse-race; ~ de côte hill climb; ⊕ ~ d'essay test run; F fig. être dans la ~ be with it; faire des ~s go shopping; rund errands; garçon de ~s errand boy. [charger; steed.〕

coursier [kur'sje] m mill-race; poet.〕

court¹ [ku:r] m (tennis-)court.

court², courte [ku:r, kurt] **1.** adj. short, brief; à ~ (de) short (of); sl. avoir la peau ~e be lazy; **2.** court adv. short; couper ~ cut short; tout ~ simply, only.

courtage ⚓ [kur'ta:ʒ] m brokerage.

courtaud, e [kur'to, ~'to:d] **1.** adj. squat, dumpy; **2.** su. stocky person; **courtauder** [~to'de] (1a) v/t. dock the tail of; crop the ears of.

court...: ~-bouillon, pl. ~s-bouillons cuis. [kurbu'jɔ̃] m wine-sauce in which fish or meat is cooked; ~-circuit, pl. ~s-circuits ⚡ [~sir'kɥi] m short-circuit; ~-circuiter ⚡, a. fig. [~sirkɥi'te] (1a) v/t. short-circuit; fig. a. bypass.

courtepointe [kurtə'pwɛ̃:t] f counterpane.

courtier, -ère ⚓ [kur'tje, ~'tjɛ:r] su. broker; (electoral) agent; su./m: ~ marron ⚓ outside broker; F bucket shop swindler.

courtine [kur'tin] *f* † curtain; ✕ line of trenches; △ façade.

courtisan [kurti'zɑ̃] *m* courtier; **courtisane** [~'zan] *f* courtesan; **courtiser** [~'ze] (1a) *v/t.* pay court to; woo; F suck up to.

courtois, e [kur'twa, ~'twaːz] courteous, polite (to[wards], envers); **courtoisie** [~twa'zi] *f* courtesy.

couru, e [ku'ry] 1. *p.p. of courir;* 2. *adj.* sought after; popular; ♉ accrued (*interest*); **courus** [~] *1st p. sg. p.s. of courir.*

couseuse [ku'zøːz] *f* seamstress; stitcher (*of books*); stitching machine; **cousis** [~'zi] *1st p. sg. p.s. of coudre*[1]; **cousons** [~'zɔ̃] *1st p. pl. pres. of coudre*[1].

cousin[1] [ku'zɛ̃] *m* midge, gnat.

cousin[2] **m, e** *f* [ku'zɛ̃, ~'zin] cousin; **cousinage** F [~zi'naːʒ] *m* cousinship; cousinry; (poor) relations *pl.*

coussin [ku'sɛ̃] *m* cushion; pad; bolster; pillow (*of lacemaker*); **coussinet** [~si'nɛ] *m* small cushion; ⊕ bearing; ♀ F bilberry, huckleberry; ⊕ ~ à *billes* ball-bearings *pl.*; ⬛ ~ de rail (rail-)chair.

cousu, e [ku'zy] 1. *p.p. of coudre*[1]; 2. *adj.* sewn; *fig.* ~ *d'or* rolling in money; ~ (à la) *main* hand-sewn; F ~ *main* solid; excellent, first-rate; *fig. rester bouche* ~*e* keep one's mouth shut.

coût [ku] *m* cost; ~*s pl.* expenses; ~ *de la vie* cost of living; **coûtant, e** [ku'tɑ̃, ~'tɑ̃ːt] *adj.: prix m* ~ cost price.

couteau [ku'to] *m* knife; ♪ blade; *être à* ~*x tirés* be at daggers drawn; **coutelas** [kut'la] *m* ♣ cutlass; *cuis.* broad-bladed knife; *icht.* F swordfish; **coutelier** [kutə'lje] *m* cutler; **coutellerie** [~tɛl'ri] *f* cutlery; cutlery works *usu. sg.*; cutler's shop.

coûter [ku'te] (1a) *vt/i.* cost; *v/i.:* ~ *cher (peu)* be (in)expensive; *coûte que coûte* at all costs; **coûteux, -euse** [~'tø, ~'tøːz] expensive, costly.

coutil *tex.* [ku'ti] *m* twill.

coutre [kutr] *m* ♪ plough-share; (wood-)chopper.

coutume [ku'tym] *f* custom, habit; *avoir* ~ *de* be accustomed to; *comme de* ~ as usual; **coutumier, -ère** [~ty'mje, ~'mjɛːr] customary; ⚖ unwritten (*law*).

couture [ku'tyːr] *f* sewing; dressmaking; seam (*a.* ⊕); F *fig.* angle, aspect; *battre q. à plate* ~ beat s.o. hollow; *haute* ~ high-class dressmaking; *maison f de haute* ~ fashion house; **couturier, -ère** [~tyˈrje, ~'rjɛːr] *su.* dressmaker; *su./f: thea. répétition f des* ~*ères* dress rehearsal.

couvain [ku'vɛ̃] *m* nest of insect eggs; brood-comb (*for bees*); **couvaison** [~vɛ'zɔ̃] *f* brooding time; incubation; **couvée** [~'ve] *f eggs:* clutch; *chicks:* brood.

couvent [ku'vɑ̃] *m nuns:* convent; *monks:* monastery.

couver [ku've] (1a) *v/t.* sit on (*eggs*); hatch (out) (*eggs*); ♉ be sickening for; *fig.* hatch (*a plot*); *fig.* (molly-)coddle (*a child*); *fig.* ~ *des yeux* not to take one's eyes off (*s.o., s.th.*); gloat over (*one's victim*); *v/i.* smoulder (*fire, a. fig.*); *fig.* be brewing; *fig., a.* ♉ develop, be developing.

couvercle [ku'vɛrkl] *m* lid, cover; ⊕ *a.* cap.

couvert, e [ku'vɛːr, ~'vɛrt] 1. *p.p. of couvrir;* 2. *adj.* covered; hidden; obscure; wooded (*country*); overcast (*sky*); *rester* ~ keep one's hat on; 3. *su./m* table things *pl.*; *restaurant:* cover-charge; shelter, cover(ing); *être à* ~ be sheltered, *a. fig.* be safe (from *de*); *le vivre et le* ~ board and lodging; *mettre* (*ôter*) *le* ~ lay (clear) the table; *sous le* ~ *de* under the cover or pretext of; *su./f pottery:* glaze; **couverture** [~vɛr'tyːr] *f* covering; cover; coverage (*a. journ.*); △ roofing; rug, blanket; ♉ security; *fig. sous* ~ *de* under cover or cloak of.

couveuse [ku'vøːz] *f* sitting hen; incubator.

couvi [ku'vi] *adj./m* addled (*egg*).

couvre [ku:vr] *1st p. sg. pres. of couvrir;* ~-**chef** F [kuvrə'ʃɛf] *m* headgear, hat; ~-**feu** [~'fø] *m* curfew; ~-**joint** ⊕ [~'ʒwɛ̃] *m wood:* covering bead; *metall.* flat coverplate; *buttjoint:* welt; ~-**lit** [~'li] *m* bedspread; ~-**pied(s)**, *pl.* ~-**pieds** [~'pje] *m* coverlet; bedspread.

couvreur [ku'vrœːr] *m* △ roofer; *freemason:* tiler; **couvrir** [~'vriːr] (2f) *v/t.* cover (*a. journ.*); △ roof; *post:* refund; *se* ~ cover o.s. (*a. with honour etc.*); put one's hat on; clothe o.s.; become overcast (*sky etc.*).

crabe [krɑ:b] *m* crab.
crac! [krak] *int.* crack!
crachat [kra'ʃa] *m* spit; *ℱ* sputum;
F star (*of an Order*); **craché, e** F
[~'ʃe] *adj.*: ce garçon est son père
tout ~ this boy is the dead spit of
his father; **cracher** [~'ʃe] (1a) *vt/i.*
spit; *v/t.* F cough up, fork out
(*money*); *v/i.* splutter (*pen*); **cra-
cheur** *m*, **-euse** *f* [~'ʃœ:r, ~'ʃø:z]
spitter; **crachoir** [~'ʃwa:r] *m* spit-
toon; F *tenir le* ~ do all the talking,
hold the floor; **crachoter** [~ʃɔ'te]
(1a) *v/i.* sputter.
crack *sp.* [krak] *m* crack (*horse*);
champion; ace.
craie [krɛ] *f* chalk; (*a. bâton m de* ~)
stick of chalk.
craindre [krɛ̃:dr] (4m) *v/t.* fear, be
afraid of; ~ *de* (*inf.*) be afraid of
(*ger.*); † *craint l'humidité inscription*: keep dry *or* in a dry place;
je crains qu'il (*ne*) *vienne* I am
afraid he is coming *or* will come;
je crains qu'il ne vienne pas I am
afraid he will not come; **craignis**
[krɛ'ɲi] *1st p. sg. p.s.* of craindre;
craignons [~'ɲɔ̃] *1st p. pl. pres.* of
craindre; **crains** [krɛ̃] *1st p. sg. pres.*
of craindre; **craint, e** [krɛ̃, krɛ̃:t]
1. *p.p.* of craindre; **2.** *su./f* fear,
dread; *de* ~ *que ...* (*ne*) (*sbj.*) lest;
craintif, -ve [krɛ̃'tif, ~'ti:v] timid,
fearful.
cramoisi, e [kramwa'zi] *adj., a.
su./m* crimson.
crampe *ℱ* [krɑ̃:p] *f* cramp; **crampon** [krɑ̃'pɔ̃] *m* △ cramp(-iron),
staple; *boot sole*: stud; *horseshoe*:
calk; *ℱ* crampon; *ℱ* tendril; F
(clinging) bore; **cramponner** [~
pɔ'ne] (1a) *v/t.* △ clamp; calk (*a
horseshoe*); F pester; buttonhole
(*s.o.*); se ~ *à* cling to.
cran [krɑ̃] *m* notch; *ratchet, rifle,
etc.*: catch; *wheel*: cog; *geol., metall.*
fault; F pluck, guts *pl.*; *hair*: wave; ~
d'arrêt stop; F *être à* ~ be on edge; be
edgy.
crâne[1] [krɑ:n] *m* cranium, skull.
crâne[2] F [krɑ:n] plucky; jaunty; **crânement** F [krɑn'mɑ̃] *adv.* pluckily;
jauntily; F jolly; **crânerie** [~'ri] *f*
pluck; jauntiness, swagger; **crâ-
neur, -euse** F [krɑ'nœ:r, ~-ø:z] **1.** *adj.*
être ~ be a show-off; **2.** *su.* show-off.
crapaud [kra'po] *m* toad (*a. fig. pej.*);
zo. grease; tub easy-chair; *piano*:

baby-grand; F *fig.* brat, urchin; **cra-
paudière** [~po'djɛ:r] *f* toadhole;
swampy place; **crapaudine** [~po-
'din] *f* toadstone; *ℱ* ironwort; ⊕
grating; *bath*: waste hole; *cuis. à la* ~
boned and broiled, spatchcocked.
crapule [kra'pyl] *f* debauchery; dissolute person; blackguard; *coll.* dissolute crowd; **crapuleux, -euse**
[~py'lø, ~'lø:z] dissolute; filthy,
lewd, foul.
craque F [krak] *f* tall story; (whop-
ping) lie.
craquelé, e [kra'kle] crackled (*china,
glass*).
craquelin [kra'klɛ̃] *m biscuit*: crack-
nel; *stocking*: wrinkle; *fig.* shrimp of
a man.
craquelure [kra'kly:r] *f* crack; fine
cracks *pl.*
craquement [krak'mɑ̃] *m* crackling;
creaking; *fingers*: crack; *snow*:
crunching; **craquer** [kra'ke] (1m)
v/i. crack; crackle; crunch (*snow*);
squeak (*shoes etc.*); come apart at the
seams (*clothes, a. fig.*); *fig.* give way;
F *fig.* break down (*person, thing*); *v/t.*
strike (*a match*); **craqueter** [krak-
'te] (1c) *v/i.* crackle; chirp (*cricket*);
clatter (*stork*); **craqueur** *m*, **-euse** *f*
F [kra'kœ:r, ~'kø:z] teller of tall
stories, fibber.
crash *ℱ* [kraʃ] *m* crash-landing.
crasse [kras] **1.** *adj./f* crass (*ignorance*); **2.** *su./f* filth, dirt; *metall.*
dross; meanness; F dirty trick;
crasseux, -euse [kra'sø, ~'sø:z]
dirty, filthy; F mean; **crassier**
[~'sje] *m* slag-heap, tip.
cratère [kra'tɛ:r] *m* crater; ✕ shell-
hole.
cravache [kra'vaʃ] *f* hunting-crop,
riding-whip.
cravate [kra'vat] *f* (neck)tie; ⚓ sling;
⊕ collar; *orn.* ruff; **cravater** [~va'te]
(1a) *v/t.* put a tie on; ⊕ wind round;
se ~ put one's tie on; *sp. etc.* collar
(*s.o.*); *sl.* take *s.o.* for a ride.
crawl *sp.* [kro:l] *m* crawl(-stroke).
crayeux, -euse [krɛ'jø, ~'jø:z]
chalky; *geol.* cretaceous; **crayon**
[~'jɔ̃] *m* pencil; pencil sketch; *ℱ*
carbon-pencil; ~ *à bille* ball-point
pen; ~ *à cils* eyebrow pencil; ~
d'ardoise slate pencil; ~ *de couleur*
colo(u)ring pencil; ~ *feutre* felt(-tip)
pen; ~ (*de rouge*) *à lèvres* lipstick; ~-
lèvres lip-pencil; ~ *noir* lead pencil; ~

pour les yeux eyeliner (pencil); **crayonnage** [∼jɔˈnaːʒ] *m* pencil sketch; **crayonner** [∼jɔˈne] (1a) *v/t.* sketch; make a pencil note of, jot down.

créance [kreˈɑ̃ːs] *f* belief, credence; confidence; ✝ credit; *pol. lettres f/pl.* de∼ credentials; **créancier** *m*, -**ère** *f* [∼ɑ̃ˈsje, ∼ˈsjɛːr] creditor.

créateur, -**trice** [kreaˈtœːr, ∼ˈtris] **1.** *adj.* creative; **2.** *su.* creator; inventor; ✝ issuer; **créatif**, -**ive** [∼ˈtif, ∼ˈtiːv] creative; **création** [∼ˈsjɔ̃] *f* creation (*a. bibl., cost., thea., a. fig.*); establishment; **créativité** [∼tiviˈte] *f* creativeness, creativity; **créature** [∼ˈtyːr] *f* creature; *fig.* tool; ⊦ person.

crécelle [kreˈsɛl] *f* rattle; *fig.* chatterbox.

crèche [krɛʃ] *f* manger; crib (*a. eccl.*); crèche, day-nursery; *sl.* pad (= *home, house room*); **crécher** *sl.* [kreˈʃe] (1f) *v/i.* live, *sl.* hang out; stay.

crédence [kreˈdɑ̃ːs] *f* sideboard; *eccl.* credence-table.

crédibilité [kredibiliˈte] *f* credibility.

crédit [kreˈdi] *m* credit (*a.* ✝, *a. fig.*); *parl.* sum (voted); prestige; *admin.* ∼ *municipal* pawn-office; *à* ∼ on credit; on trust; gratuitously; *faire* ∼ *à* give credit to; **créditer** [∼diˈte] (1a) *v/t.*: ∼ *q. de credit* s.o.'s account with (*a sum*); give s.o. credit for; **créditeur**, -**trice** [∼diˈtœːr, ∼ˈtris] **1.** *su.* creditor; **2.** *adj.* credit-...

credo [kreˈdo] *m/inv.* creed (*a. fig.*).

crédule [kreˈdyl] credulous; **crédulité** [∼dyliˈte] *f* credulity.

créer [kreˈe] (1a) *v/t.* create (*a. fig.*); ✝ make out (*a cheque*), issue (*a bill*); *admin. etc.* appoint, make (*s.o. magistrate etc.*).

crémaillère [kremaˈjɛːr] *f* pot-hook; ⊕ rack; 👟 cog-rail; 👟 (*a. chemin m de fer à* ∼) rack-railway; *pendaison f de* ∼ housewarming (party); *pendre la* ∼ give a house-warming (party).

crémation [kremaˈsjɔ̃] *f* cremation; **crématoire** [∼ˈtwaːr] crematory; *four m* ∼ crematorium.

crème [krɛm] *f* cream (*a. fig.*); *cuis. a.* custard; *fig. the* best; ∼ *fouettée* whipped cream; ∼ *glacée* ice-cream; **crémer** [kreˈme] (1f) *v/i.* cream; **crémerie** [krɛmˈri] *f* creamery, dairy; small restaurant; **crémeux**, -**euse** [kreˈmø, ∼ˈmøːz] creamy; **cré-**

mier, -**ère** [∼ˈmje, ∼ˈmjɛːr] *su.* keeper of a small restaurant; *su./m* dairyman; *su./f* dairymaid; cream-jug.

crémone △ [kreˈmɔn] *f* casement bolt.

créneau [kreˈno] *m* △ crenel; loophole; look-out slit; *fig., a.* ✝ *etc.* gap; slot; *mot.* parking space; *mot. faire un* ∼ get into the *or* a parking space; **créneler** [krɛnˈle] (1c) *v/t.* △ crenel(l)ate (*a wall*); cut loop-holes in (*a wall*); ⊕ tooth, notch; mill (*a coin*); **crénelure** [∼ˈlyːr] *f* indentation; notches *pl.*; ⚲ crenel(l)ing.

crêpage [krɛˈpaːʒ] *m* crimping; ⊦ ∼ *de chignon* fight, set-to (*between women*).

crêpe¹ [krɛp] *m tex.* crape; crêpe (-rubber).

crêpe² *cuis.* [∼] *f* pancake.

crêper [krɛˈpe] (1a) *v/t.* frizz, crimp; ⊦ *se* ∼ *le chignon* tear each other's hair, ∼ fight (*women*).

crépi △ [kreˈpi] *m* rough-cast.

crépine [kreˈpin] *f* fringe; ⊕ *pump*: rose, strainer; **crépins** [∼ˈpɛ̃] *m/pl. shoemaker*: grindery *sg.*; **crépir** [∼ˈpiːr] (2a) *v/t.* crimp; △ roughcast; pebble (*leather*); **crépissure** △ [∼piˈsyːr] *f* rough-cast.

crépitation [krepitaˈsjɔ̃] *f* crackle; 𝒮 crepitation; **crépiter** [∼ˈte] (1a) *v/i.* crackle; sputter (*butter, etc.*); 𝒮 crepitate.

crépon [kreˈpɔ̃] *m tex.* crépon; hairpad; **crépu**, **e** [∼ˈpy] fuzzy (*hair*); crinkled; **crépure** [kreˈpyːr] *f hair*: frizzing, crimping.

crépuscule [krepysˈkyl] *m* twilight, dusk.

cresson [krɛˈsɔ̃] *m* (water)cress; *sl. ne pas avoir de* ∼ *sur la fontaine* have lost one's thatch (= *hair*).

crétacé, **e** *geol.* [kretaˈse] chalky, cretaceous.

crête [krɛt] *f* △, *geog., zo., anat.*, helmet, wave: crest; *mountain*: ridge, summit; *cock*: comb; *fig.* head; **crêté**, **e** *zo.* [krɛˈte] tufted, crested.

crétin *m*, **e** *f* [kreˈtɛ̃, ∼ˈtin] 𝒮 cretin; ⊦ fool; **crétinisme** 𝒮 [∼tiˈnism] *m* cretinism.

cretonne *tex.* [krəˈtɔn] *f* cretonne.

creuser [krøˈze] (1a) *v/t.* hollow out, excavate; dig; sink (*a well*); plough, *Am.* plow (*a furrow*); *fig.* wrinkle;

fig. hollow; se ~ *la tête* (*or la cervelle*) rack one's brains.
creuset ⊕ [krø'zɛ] *m* crucible; *a.fig.* test, trial.
creux, creuse [krø, krø:z] **1.** *adj.* hollow, empty; sunken (*cheeks*); ⊕, 🚂 slack (*period*); *fig.* futile; *assiette f creuse* soup-plate; *heures f/pl. creuses* off-peak hours; **2.** *su./m* hollow; *stomach*: pit; *wave, graph*: trough; F bass voice; ~ *de la main* hollow of the hand.
crevaison [krəvɛ'zɔ̃] *f* bursting (*a.* ⊕, *mot.*); *mot.* puncture; *sl.* death.
crevant, e F [krə'vɑ̃, ~'vɑ̃:t] boring; killing (*work*); very funny (*story*).
crevasse [krə'vas] *f* crack; *wall*: crevice; *glacier*: crevace; *skin*: chap; *metal etc.*: flaw; **crevasser** [~va'se] (1a) *v/t.* crack; chap (*the skin*); se ~ crack; chap (*skin*).
crève F [krɛ:v] *f* death; **~-cœur** [krɛv'kœ:r] *m/inv.* heart-ache, grief.
crever [krə've] (1d) *vt/i.* burst, split; *v/i.* F die (*animal*); F ~ *de faim* starve; F ~ *de rire* split one's sides with laughter; *v/t.* work *or* ride (*a horse*) to death; ~ *le cœur à q.* break s.o.'s heart; F ~ *les yeux à q.* be staring s.o. in the face, be obvious; se ~ *de travail* work o.s. to death.
crevette *zo.* [krə'vɛt] *f* shrimp; prawn.
cri [kri] *m* cry; shriek (*of horror, pain, etc.*); F fashion, style; *hinge, spring*: creak; *bird*: chirp; *mouse*: squeak; ~ *de guerre* war-cry; F *pol. etc.* slogan; *à* ~ *public* by public proclamation; ... *dernier* ~ the latest thing in ...; *pousser un* ~ (*or des* ~*s*) scream; **criailler** [~ɑ'je] (1a) *v/i.* bawl; whine, F grouse; ~ *contre* scold, rail at; **criaillerie** [~ɑj'ri] *f* bawling; whining; scolding; **criant, e** [~'ɑ̃, ~'ɑ̃:t] glaring, crying; **criard, e** [~'a:r, ~'ard] **1.** *adj.* crying; shrill (*voice*); pressing (*debt*); loud (*colour*); **2.** *su.* bawler; *su./f* shrew.
crible [kribl] *m* sieve; ⊕, ⚒ screen; **cribler** [kri'ble] (1a) *v/t.* riddle; *fig.* overwhelm, cover (with, *de*); *être criblé de dettes* be over head and ears in debt; **cribleur** *m*, **-euse** *f* [~'blœ:r, ~'blø:z] riddler; ⊕, ⚒ screener; ⊕ screening machine; **criblure** [~'bly:r] *f* ⚒ screenings *pl.*; siftings *pl.*
cric ⊕ [krik] *m* jack.
cricri F [kri'kri] *m* cricket; chirping.
criée [kri'e] *f* auction; *vente f à la* ~ sale by auction; **crier** [~'e] (1a) *v/i.* cry, call out; scream; squeak (*door, hinge, mouse, shoes*); *v/t.* cry, proclaim; hawk (*wares*); shout (*abuses, orders*); **crieur, -euse** [~'œ:r, ~'ø:z] *su.* shouter; hawker; *su./m thea.* call-boy.
crime [krim] *m* crime; ⚖ felony; ~ *d'État* treason; ~ *d'incendie* arson; **criminaliser** [kriminali'ze] (1a) *v/t.* refer (*a case*) to a criminal court; **criminaliste** [~'list] *su.* criminologist; **criminalité** [~li'te] *f* criminal nature (*of an act*); ⚖ ~ *juvénile* juvenile delinquency; **criminel, -elle** [krimi'nɛl] **1.** *adj.* criminal (*law, action*); guilty (*person*); **2.** *su.* criminal, felon; *su./m* criminal action.
crin [krɛ̃] *m* horsehair; coarse hair; ~ *végétal* vegetable horsehair; *fig.* ... *à tout* ~ (*or tous* ~*s*) out and out ...; F *être comme un* ~ be very touchy.
crincrin F [krɛ̃'krɛ̃] *m* fiddle; fiddler.
crinière [kri'njɛ:r] *f* mane; *helmet*: (horse-)tail; F crop of hair.
crinoline [krinɔ'lin] *f* crinoline.
crique [krik] *f* creek, cove, small bay; ⊕ *metal*: flaw.
criquet [kri'kɛ] *m zo.* locust; *zo.* F cricket; F small pony; *sl. person*: shrimp.
crise ⚕, *pol., fig.* [kri:z] *f* crisis; ⚕ attack; shortage; ⚕ *cardiaque* heart attack; ~ *du logement* housing shortage; ~ *économique* (*mondiale*) (world-wide) slump; *une* ~ *se prépare* things are coming to a head.
crispation [krispa'sjɔ̃] *f* contraction; contortion; tensing (up); twitch(ing); puckering; **crispé, e** [~'pe] tense, strained; uptight; **crisper** [~'pe] (1a) *v/t.* contract; clench (*one's fists*); contort (*one's face*); tense (up); F irritate (s.o.); se ~ *a.* tighten; *a.* pucker up (*face*).
crisser [kri'se] (1a) *v/i.* grate, rasp; squeak (*brakes*); ~ *des dents* grind one's teeth.
cristal [kris'tal] *m* crystal; crystal-glass; **cristallin, e** [~ta'lɛ̃, ~'lin] **1.** *adj.* crystalline; clear as crystal; **2.**

su./m anat. crystalline lens; **cristal-liser** [~tali'ze] (1a) *vt/i.* crystallize.

critère [kri'tɛːr] *m* criterion, test; **critérium** *sp.* [~te'rjɔm] *m* selection match *or* race.

critique [kri'tik] **1.** *adj.* critical; **2.** *su./m* critic; *su./f* criticism; **critiquer** [~ti'ke] (1m) *v/t.* criticize, find fault with; review (*a book*); censure; **critiqueur** *m,* **-euse** *f* [~ti'kœːr, ~'køːz] fault-finder.

croasser [krɔa'se] (1a) *v/i.* croak (*raven, a. fig.*); caw (*crow, rook*).

croc [kro] *m* hook; ⊕ pawl; *zo.* fang.

croc-en-jambe, crocs-en-jambe [krɔkɑ̃'ʒɑ̃:b] *m* trip (up); *donner (or faire) un* ~ *à q.* trip s.o. up.

croche [krɔʃ] *f* ♪ quaver; ⊕ ~s *pl.* crook-bit tongs.

crochet [krɔ'ʃɛ] *m* hook; crochet-hook; skeleton key; *typ.* square bracket; *zo.* fang; *faire un* ~ swerve; make a detour; *fig. vivre aux* ~s *de q.* live off s.o.; **crocheter** [krɔʃ'te] (1d) *v/t.* pick (*a lock*); hook *s.th.* out *or* up; **crocheteur** [~'tœːr] *m* thief: picklock; **crochu, e** [krɔ'ʃy] hooked; crooked (*ideas*); *fig. avoir les doigts* ~es be light-fingered (*thief*); be close-fisted.

crocodile [krɔkɔ'dil] *m zo.* crocodile; 🕪 audible warning system.

croire [krwaːr] (4n) *v/i.* believe (in, *à*; in God, *en Dieu*); *v/t.* believe; think; ~ *q. intelligent* believe s.o. to be intelligent; *à l'en* ~ according to him (her); *faire* ~ *qch. à q.* lead s.o. to believe s.th.; *s'en* ~ be conceited.

crois [krwa] *1st p. sg. pres. of* croire.

croîs [~] *1st p. sg. pres. of* croître.

croisade [krwa'zad] *f* crusade; **croisé, e** [~'ze] **1.** *adj.* crossed; folded (*arms*); double-breasted (*coat*); *tex.* twilled; *mots m/pl.* ~s crossword puzzle; **2.** *su./m* crusader; *tex.* twill; *su./f* crossing; casement window; △ *church:* transept; **croisement** [krwaz'mɑ̃] *m* crossing; intersection; *animals:* interbreeding; cross(-breed); **croiser** [krwa'ze] (1a) *v/t.* cross (*a. ♀, biol.*); fold (*one's arms*); *tex.* twill; *v/i.* ♫ cruise; **croiseur** ♫ [~'zœːr] *m* cruiser; **croisière** [~'zjɛːr] *f* cruise; *vitesse f de* ~ cruising speed; *fig.* pace; **croisillon** [~zi'jɔ̃] *m* cross-piece; ⊕ star-handle.

croissance [krwa'sɑ̃:s] *f* growth; ✝ ~ *zéro* zero growth; **croissant, e** [~'sɑ̃,

~'sɑ̃:t] **1.** *adj.* waxing (*moon*); **2.** *su./m moon:* crescent; *cuis.* croissant; ☽ lune; **croissons** [~'sɔ̃] *1st p. pl. pres. of* croître.

croisure [krwa'zyːr] *f tex.* twill weave; *cost.* cross-over.

croître [krwaːtr] (4o) *v/i.* grow; increase; wax (*moon*); lengthen (*days, shadows*).

croix [krwa] *f* cross (*a. decoration; fig.* = *trial, affliction*); *typ.* dagger, obelisk; ~ *de Lorraine* cross of Lorraine; ✠ ~*-Rouge* Red Cross; *en* ~ crosswise; *fig. avec la* ~ *et la bannière* with great ceremony; F *fig. il faut or c'est la* ~ *et la bannière pour ...* it's the devil's job to ...

croquant¹, e [krɔ'kɑ̃, ~'kɑ̃:t] **1.** *adj.* crisp; **2.** *su./m cuis.* gristle.

croquant² [krɔ'kɑ̃] *m* F clodhopper; unimportant person.

croque au sel [krɔko'sɛl] *adv.:* *manger à la* ~ eat (*s.th.*) with salt only.

croque...: ~*-madame cuis.* [krɔkma'dam] *m/inv.* toasted ham and cheese sandwich with fried egg; ~*-mitaine* F [~mi'tɛn] *m* bog(e)y man; ~*-monsieur cuis.* [~mə'sjø] *m/inv.* toasted ham and cheese sandwich; ~*-mort* F [~'mɔːr] *m* undertaker's mute; ~*-note* F *pej.* [~'nɔt] *m* third-rate musician.

croquer [krɔ'ke] (1m) *vt/i.* crunch; *v/t.* munch; sketch; *fig.* gobble up; ♪ leave out (*notes*); ⚓ hook; F ~ *le marmot* cool one's heels; F *joli à* ~ pretty enough to eat.

croquet¹ [krɔ'kɛ] *m* croquet.

croquet² [krɔ'kɛ] *m* crisp almond-covered biscuit; F snappy person; **croquette** *cuis.* [~'kɛt] *f* croquette; rissole.

croquis [krɔ'ki] *m* sketch.

cross-country *sp.* [krɔskœn'tri] *m* cross-country running.

crosse [krɔs] *f* crook (*a. eccl.*); *eccl.* crozier; *gun:* butt; ⊕ *piston:* cross-head; *sp. golf:* club; *hockey:* stick.

crotale [krɔ'tal] *m antiquity:* crotalum; *zo.* rattlesnake, *Am. a.* rattler.

crotte [krɔt] *f* droppings *pl.*; *cuis. une* ~ *de chocolat* a chocolate; **crotté, e** [krɔ'te] dirty; **crottin** [~'tɛ̃] *m* horse dung.

croulant, e [kru'lɑ̃, ~'lɑ̃:t] **1.** *adj.* tumble-down; ramshackle; **2.** *su./m: vieux* ~ old fossil; ~s *pl.* old people;

crouler [~'le] (1a) *v/i.* totter, crumble; collapse.
croup ♂ [krup] *m* croup.
croupade [kru'pad] *f horsemanship*: croupade; **croupe** [krup] *f animal*: croup, rump; F *person*: rump, bottom, behind; *hill*: crest, brow; △ hip; en~ behind (the rider *or* driver); on the pillion; *monter* en ~ *a.* ride pillion; **croupetons** [~'tɔ̃] *adv.*: à ~ crouching, squatting; **croupi, e** [kru'pi] stagnant (*water*); *fig.* sunk (in, *dans*); **croupier** ✝ [~'pje] *m* broker's backer; *casino*: croupier; **croupière** [~'pjɛːr] *f* crupper; *fig.* ✝ *tailler des* ~*s à* make things difficult for; **croupion** [~'pjɔ̃] *m bird*: rump; F *chicken etc.*: parson's nose; **croupir** [~'piːr] (2a) *v/i.* stagnate; *fig.* ~ *dans* wallow in.
croustade *cuis.* [krus'tad] *f* pie, pasty; **croustillant, e** [krusti'jã, ~'jãːt] crisp; short (*pastry*); crusty (*bread etc.*); *fig.* spicy (*story*); attractive (*woman*); **croustiller** [~'je] (1a) *v/i.* nibble crusts (*with wine*); crunch (*food*); **croûte** [krut] *f* crust (*a.* ♂); *cheese*: rind; ♂ scab; F daub (= *poor picture*); *fig. pej.* old fossil; *pej.* dunce; F *casser la* ~ have a snack; **croûter** F [kru'te] (1a) *v/i.* eat, feed; **croûteux, -euse** ♂ [~'tø, ~'tøːz] covered with scabs; **croûton** [~'tɔ̃] *m* piece of crust; *sl.* dauber (= *poor painter*); *fig. pej.* old fossil.
croyable [krwa'jabl] believable; trustworthy (*person*); **croyance** [~'jãːs] *f* belief; faith; **croyant, e** [~'jã, ~'jãːt] **1.** *adj.* believing; **2.** *su.* believer; *les* ~*s m/pl.* the faithful; **croyons** [~'jɔ̃] *1st p. pl. pres. of* croire.
cru¹, **crue** [kry] raw; uncooked; *fig.* broad; ~ à *l'estomac* indigestible.
cru² [~] *m* wine region; ✔ vineyard; wine, vintage; *fig.* soil; F locality; *de mon* ~ of my own (invention); *du* ~ local (*wine*, F *a. person etc.*); (*vin de*) *grand* ~ great wine.
cru³, **crue** [~] *p.p. of* croire.
crû, **crue**, *m/pl.* **crus** [~] *p.p. of* croître.
cruauté [kryo'te] *f* cruelty (to, *envers*).
cruche [kryʃ] *f* jug, pitcher; *sl.* dolt, duffer; **cruchon** [kry'ʃɔ̃] *m* small jug; *beer*: mug; *sl.* dolt, duffer.

crucial, e, *m/pl.* **-aux** [kry'sjal, ~'sjo] crucial (*a. fig.*), cross-shaped;
crucifiement [krysifi'mã] *m* crucifixion; **crucifier** [~'fje] (1o) *v/t.* crucify; **crucifix** [~'fi] *m* crucifix; **crucifixion** [~fik'sjɔ̃] *f* crucifixion; **cruciforme** [~'fɔrm] cruciform, cross-shaped.
crudité [krydi'te] *f* crudity; coarseness (*of an expression*); indigestibility (*of food*); ~*s pl.* offensive *or* gross passages *or* words; *cuis.* raw vegetables.
crue [kry] *f water*: swelling, rise; flood; en ~ in spate, in flood (*river*).
cruel, -elle [kry'ɛl] cruel (to, *envers*).
crûment [kry'mã] *adv. of* cru¹.
crus [kry] *1st p. sg. p.s. of* croire.
crûs [~] *1st p. sg. p.s. of* croître.
crusse¹ [krys] *1st p. sg. impf. sbj. of* croire.
crusse² [~] *1st p. sg. impf. sbj. of* croître.
crustacé *zo.* [krysta'se] *m* crustacean, F shellfish.
crypte △, ♀, *anat.* [kript] *f* crypt.
crypto... [kriptɔ] crypto...
cubage [ky'baːʒ] *m* cubic content.
cubain, e [ky'bɛ̃, ~'bɛn] *adj., a. su.* ♀ Cuban.
cube [kyb] **1.** *su./m* cube; cubic space; ~*s pl. toy*: building blocks, bricks; **2.** *adj.* cubic; **cuber** [ky'be] (1a) *v/t.* cube; find the cubic contents of; have a cubic content of.
cubilot *metall.* [kybi'lo] *m* smelting cupola.
cubique [ky'bik] **1.** *adj.* cubic; ♣ *racine f* ~ cube root; **2.** *su./f* ♣ cubic (curve); **cubisme** *paint.* [~'bism] *m* cubism; **cubiste** *paint.* [~'bist] *su.*, *a. adj.* cubist.
cubitus *anat.* [kybi'tys] *m* cubitus, ulna.
cueillaison [kœjɛ'zɔ̃] *f* picking, gathering; **cueille** [kœːj] *1st p. sg. pres. of* cueillir; **cueillerai** [kœj're] *1st p. sg. fut. of* cueillir; **cueillette** [kœ'jɛt] *f* picking, gathering; **cueillir** [~'jiːr] (2c) *v/t.* gather, pick; *fig.* win; *fig.* snatch, steal (*a kiss*); F pick (*s.o.*) up; F catch, nab; ~ *q. à froid* catch s.o. off (his *or* her) guard, take s.o. unawares; **cueilloir** [kœj'waːr] *m* fruit-basket; *tool*: fruit-picker.
cuiller, cuillère [kчi'jɛːr] *f* spoon; ⊕ *tool*: spoon-drill; ⊕ scoop; *sl.* fin (=

hand); ~ *à bouche* table-spoon; ~ *à café* coffee-spoon; ~ *à dos d'âne* heaped spoon; ~ *à pot* ladle; **cuillerée** [kɥij're] *f* spoonful.

cuir [kɥiːr] *m* leather; *razor:* strop; *animal:* hide; F faulty liaison (*in speech*); ~ *chevelu* scalp; ~ *de Russie* Russia (leather); F *faire un* ~ drop a brick (= *make an incorrect liaison*); **cuirasse** [kɥi'ras] *f* breast-plate, cuirass; ⚓, *zo.* armo(u)r; **cuirassé, e** [kɥira'se] **1.** *adj.* armo(u)red, armo(u)r-plated; *fig.* hardened (*against, contre*); **2.** *su./m* battleship; **cuirasser** [~'se] (1a) *v/t.* put a cuirass on (*s.o.*); ⚓ armo(u)r; ⊕ protect; *fig.* harden (against, *contre*); **cuirassier** ⚔ [~'sje] *m* cuirassier.

cuire [kɥiːr] (4h) *v/t.* cook; bake (*bread*); fire (*bricks, pottery*); boil (*sugar*); ~ *à l'eau* boil; ~ *au four* bake, roast; *v/i.* cook; be boiling (*a. fig.*); smart (*eyes etc.*); *il lui en cuira* he'll be sorry for it; *faire* ~ cook (*s.th.*); **cuisant, e** [kɥi'zɑ̃, ~'zɑ̃ːt] burning, stinging, smarting; *fig.* bitter (*cold, disappointment*); burning (*desire*); **cuiseur** ⊕ [~'zœːr] *m* burner.

cuisine [kɥi'zin] *f* kitchen; ⚔ cook-house; ⚓ galley; cookery; cooking; ⚔ ~ *roulante* field-kitchen; *faire la* ~ do the cooking; **cuisiner** [~zi'ne] (1a) *vt/i.* cook; *v/t. fig.* F grill (*s.o.*); F cook (*accounts etc.*); **cuisinier, -ère** [~zi'nje, ~'njɛːr] *su.* cook; *su./f* (~ *à gas, électrique* gas, electric) cooker, *Am.* range.

cuisis [kɥi'zi] *1st p. sg. p.s. of cuire;* **cuisons** [~'zɔ̃] *1st p. pl. pres. of cuire.*

cuissard [kɥi'saːr] *m armour:* cuisse; ⊕ (water-)leg; **cuisse** [kɥis] *f* thigh; *cuis. chicken:* leg; **cuisseau** *cuis.* [kɥi'so] *m veal:* fillet of leg.

cuisson [kɥi'sɔ̃] *f* cooking; baking; *sugar:* boiling; *bricks etc., a. fig.:* burning.

cuissot [kɥi'so] *m venison:* haunch.

cuistre [kɥistr] *m* (priggish) pedant; F cad.

cuit, e [kɥi, kɥit] **1.** *p.p. of cuire;* **2.** *su./f* ⊕ *bricks etc.:* baking, firing; *sugar:* boiling; batch (*of baked things*); F *prendre une* ~ get tight (= *drunk*); **cuiter** *sl.* [kɥi'te] (1a) *v/t.:* se ~ get drunk.

cuivre [kɥiːvr] *m* copper; ~ *jaune* brass; ♪ ~s *pl.* brass *sg.*; **cuivré, e** [kɥi'vre] coppery, copper-colo(u)red;

bronzed (*complexion*); *fig.* metallic (*voice*); brassy, blaring; **cuivrer** [~'vre] (1a) *v/t.* copper; **cuivreux, -euse** [~'vrø, ~'vrøːz] coppery; ⊕ cupreous (*ore*); 🜨 cuprous; *fig.* blaring.

cul V [ky] *m* backside, V arse, *Am.* ass; *animal:* haunches *pl.*; F bottom (*of an object*); *cart:* tail; **culasse** [ky'las] *f* ⚔ breech; ⚙ yoke, heel-piece; *mot.* detachable cylinderhead.

culbute [kyl'byt] *f* somersault; tumble, F purler; *sl.* failure; F *faire la* ~ 🜨 fail; *pol.* fall; F make a scoop; **culbuter** [~by'te] (1a) *v/i.* turn a somersault; topple over; tumble; F 🜨 fail; F *pol.* fall; *v/t.* throw over; overthrow (*a. pol.*); upset; knock head over heels; tip; **culbuteur** [~by'tœːr] *m* tipping device; *mot.* rocker-arm, valve-rocker; ⚙ tumbler.

cul...: ~**-de-jatte**, *pl.* ~**s-de-jatte** [kyd'ʒat] *m* legless cripple; ~**-de-lampe**, *pl.* ~**s-de-lampe** [~'lɑ̃ːp] *m* 🜨 pendant; 🜨 bracket, corbel; *typ.* tail-piece; ~**-de-sac**, *pl.* ~**s-de-sac** [~'sak] *m* blind alley (*a fig.*).

culée [ky'le] *f* 🜨 abutment; ⚓ stern-way; **culer** [~'le] (1a) *v/i.* go backwards, back; ⚓ veer astern (*wind*); make stern-way; **culière** [~'ljɛːr] *f* crupper.

culinaire [kyli'nɛːr] culinary.

culminant, e [kylmi'nɑ̃, ~'nɑ̃ːt] *astr.* culminant; *point m* ~ highest point; *glory, power:* height; *power:* zenith; **culmination** *astr.* [~na-'sjɔ̃] *f* culmination; **culminer** [~'ne] (1a) *v/i.* culminate, reach the highest point (*a. fig.*).

culot [ky'lo] *m* ⊕ bottom, base; *fig.* baby of the family; F cheek, nerve, impudence; *tobacco pipe:* dottle; F *avoir du* ~ have a lot of cheek; F *porter la* ~ wear the trousers; F *prendre une* ~ *cards etc.:* lose heavily; **culotte** [ky'lɔt] *f* breeches *pl.*; pants *pl.*; knickers *pl.*, panties *pl.* (*for women*); *beef:* rump; ⚙ breeches *pl.*, Y pipe; F *porter la* ~ wear the trousers; F *prendre une* ~ *cards etc.:* lose heavily; **culotté, e** [kylɔ'te] seasoned (*pipe*); F cheeky; **culotter** [kylɔ'te] (1a) *v/t.* put trousers on; season (*a pipe*).

culpabiliser [kylpabili'ze] (1a) *v/t.* make (*s.o.*) feel guilty; **culpabilité** [~'te] *f* guilt.

culte [kylt] *m* worship; creed, cult; religion; *protestant church:* (church) service; **cultivable** [kylti'vabl] arable; **cultivateur, -trice** [∼va-'tœ:r,∼'tris] **1.** *su.* cultivator; farmer; *su./m* cultivator, light plough; **2.** *adj.* farming; **cultivé, e** [∼'ve] ⚭ cultivated; *fig.* cultured; **cultiver** ⚭ [∼'ve] (1a) *v/t.* cultivate (*a. fig.*); farm, till.

culture [kyl'ty:r] *f* ⚭ cultivation (*a. fig.*), farming, growing; *fish etc.*: breeding; *fig.* culture (*a. of bacteria*); ⚭ ∼s *pl.* crops, cultivated land *sg.*; ∼ *physique* physical culture; **culturel, -elle** [∼ty'rɛl] cultural; **culturisme** [∼ty'rism] *m* bodybuilding; **culturiste** [∼ty'rist] *su.* bodybuilder.

cumin ⚭ [ky'mɛ̃] *m* cum(m)in.

cumul [ky'myl] *m* plurality (*of offices*); 🕮 consecutiveness (*of sentences*); **cumulard** *pej.* [kymy'la:r] *m* pluralist; **cumuler** [∼'le] (1a) *v/t.* hold a plurality of (*offices*); draw (*salaries*) simultaneously.

cupide [ky'pid] greedy, covetous; **cupidité** [∼pidi'te] *f* greed, cupidity. [ing.]

cuprifère [kypri'fɛ:r] copper-bear-]

curable [ky'rabl] curable; **curage** [∼'ra:ʒ] *m teeth:* picking; *drain etc.:* clearing (out); ∼s *pl.* dirt *sg.*; **curatelle** 🕮 [kyra'tɛl] *f* trusteeship, guardianship; **curateur, -trice** [∼'tœ:r, ∼'tris] *su.* 🕮 trustee; guardian (*of a minor*); committee (*of a lunatic*); *su./m* administrator; *su./f* administratrix; **curatif, -ve** [∼'tif, ∼'ti:v] *adj., a. su./m* curative; **cure** [ky:r] *f* care; 🕂, *eccl.* cure; *eccl.* living; ∼ *de rajeunissement* rejuvenation; ∼ *de repos* rest cure.

curé [ky're] *m* parish priest; (Anglican) vicar, rector.

cure-dent [kyr'dɑ̃] *m* toothpick.

curée [ky're] *f hunt.* deer's entrails *pl.* given to the hounds; *fig.* ∼ *des places* scramble for office.

cure...: ∼**ongles** [ky'rɔ̃:gl] *m/inv.* nail-cleaner; ∼**oreille** [kyrɔ're:j] *m* ear-pick; ∼**pipe** [kyr'pip] *m* pipe-cleaner.

curer [ky're] (1a) *v/t.* clean (out); pick (*one's teeth etc.*); dredge (*a river*); **curetage** [kyr'ta:ʒ] *m* scraping; 🕂 curetting; **cureur** [ky'rœ:r] *m* cleaner.

curial, e, *m/pl.* **-aux** *eccl.* [ky'rjal, ∼'rjo] of the parish priest, curé's ...; **curie** *eccl.* [∼'ri] *f* curia.

curieux, -euse [ky'rjø,∼'rjø:z] **1.** *adj.* curious; interested (in, *de*); inquisitive; odd; strange; *curieusement a.* oddly enough; **2.** *su.* curious *or* interested person; *su./m* the odd thing (about, *de*); **curiosité** [∼rjɔzi'te] *f* curiosity; ∼s *pl.* sights (*of a town*).

curiste [ky'rist] *su.* patient taking a cure.

curseur ⊕ [kyr'sœ:r] *m* slide; slider; runner (*a.* ⚭).

cursif, -ve [kyr'sif, ∼'si:v] **1.** *adj.* cursive; cursory; **2.** *su./f writing:* cursive, running hand; *typ.* script.

cuscute ⚭ [kys'kyt] *f* dodder.

cuspide ⚭ [kys'pid] *f* cusp; **cuspidé, e** ⚭ [∼pi'de] cuspidate.

custode [kys'tɔd] *f eccl.* altar-curtain; pyx-cloth; custodial (*for host*); *mot.* ∼ *arrière* rear-window.

cutané, e [kyta'ne] cutaneous; (*disease*) of the skin.

cuvage [ky'va:ʒ] *m*, **cuvaison** [∼vɛ-'zɔ̃] *f* fermenting in vats; vat room; **cuve** [ky:v] *f* vat; ⊕ tank; cistern; *mot.* float-chamber; **cuveau** [ky'vo] *m* small vat; small tank; **cuvée** [∼'ve] *f* vatful; *wine:* growth.

cuveler [ky'vle] (1c) *v/t.* line (*a shaft etc.*).

cuver [ky've] (1a) *vt/i.* ferment, work; **cuvette** [∼'vɛt] *f* wash-basin; bowl; *geol., geog.* basin; *phot.* dish; *W.C.:* pan, bowl; *barometer:* cup; *thermometer:* bulb; *watch:* cap; ⊕ *ball-bearing:* race; ball-socket; **cuvier** [∼'vje] *m* wash-tub.

cyanose [sja'no:z] *f* 🕂 cyanosis; *min.* cyanose; **cyanuration** [∼nyra'sjɔ̃] *f* cyanidization; **cyanure** ⚗ [∼'ny:r] *m* cyanide.

cybernéticien [sibɛrneti'sjɛ̃] *m* cyberneticist; **cybernétique** [∼'tik] **1.** *su./f* cybernetics *sg.*; **2.** *adj.* cybernetic; **cybernétiser** [∼ti'ze] (1a) *v/t.* control cybernetically.

cyclable [si'klabl] for cyclists; *piste f* ∼ cycle path.

cyclamen ⚭ [sikla'mɛn] *m* cyclamen.

cycle [sikl] *m* cycle (*a. fig.*); **cyclique** [si'klik] cyclic(al); **cyclisme** *sp.* [∼'klism] *m* cycling; **cycliste** [∼'klist] **1.** *su.* cyclist; **2.** *adj.* cycling.

cyclo... [siklɔ] cyclo...; **cycloïde** ⚗ [∼'id] *f* cycloid; **cyclomoteur** [∼mɔ'tœ:r] *m* moped, auto-cycle; **cyclomotoriste** [∼mɔtɔ'rist] *su.* moped-rider.

cyclone *meteor.* [si'klɔn] *m* cyclone.
cyclotourisme [siklɔtu'rism] *m* cycle-touring, touring on (bi)cycles.
cyclotron *phys.* [siklɔ'trɔ̃] *m* cyclotron.
cygne *orn.* [siɲ] *m* swan.
cylindrage [silɛ̃'dra:ʒ] *m* rolling (*a.* ⊕); *tex.* calendering; **cylindre** ⊕ [~'lɛ̃:dr] *m* cylinder; roller.
cylindrée *mot.* [silɛ̃'dre] *f* (cubic) capacity; **cylindrer** [~'dre] (1a) *v/t.* ⊕ roll; *tex.* calender; **cylindrique** [~'drik] cylindrical.

cymbale ♪ [sɛ̃'bal] *f* cymbal; **cymbalier** [~ba'lje] *m* cymbalist.
cynique [si'nik] **1.** *adj.* cynical; *phls.* cynic; *fig.* shameless; **2.** *su./m phls.* cynic; *fig.* shameless person; **cynisme** [~'nism] *m phls.* cynicism; *fig.* effrontery.
cynocéphale *zo.* [sinɔse'fal] *m* cynocephalus, dog-faced baboon.
cyprès ♀ [si'prɛ] *m* cypress; **cyprière** [~pri'ɛ:r] *f* cypress-grove.
cyprin *icht.* [si'prɛ̃] *m* carp.
cystite ⚕ [sis'tit] *f* cystitis.

D

D, d [de] *m* D, d.

da [da]: *oui-da!* yes indeed!

d'ac *sl.* [dak] okay, Ok.

dactylo F [dakti'lo] *su. person:* typist; *su./f* typing; F typing pool; **~graphe** [daktilɔ'graf] *su.* typist; **~graphie** [~gra'fi] *f* typing, typewriting; **~graphier** [~gra'fje] (1o) *v/t.* type.

dada F [da'da] *m ch.sp.* gee-gee; *fig.* hobby(-horse), fad.

dadais F [da'dɛ] *m* simpleton.

dague [dag] *f* dagger; ⚓ dirk; ⊕ scraping-knife; *zo. deer:* first antler; *wild boar:* tusk.

daguet *hunt.* [da'gɛ] *m* brocket.

daigner [dɛ'ɲe] (1b) *v/t.* deign (to *inf.*), condescend (to *inf.*).

daim [dɛ̃] *m zo.* deer; buck; ✝ buckskin; *en* ~ suède (*gloves*); **daine** *zo.* [dɛn] *f* doe.

dais [dɛ] *m* canopy.

dallage [da'la:ʒ] *m* paving; flagging; tiled floor; **dalle** [dal] *f* paving-stone; flagstone; floor tile; *sl.* throat; **daller** [da'le] (1a) *v/t.* pave; tile (*the floor*).

daltonien, -enne ♣ [daltɔ'njɛ̃, ~'njɛn] **1.** *adj.* colo(u)r-blind; **2.** *su.* colo(u)r-blind person; **daltonisme** ♣ [~'nism] *m* colo(u)r-blindness.

dam [dɑ̃] *m* ✝ hurt, prejudice; *au (grand)* ~ *de* (much) to the detriment *or* displeasure of.

damas [da'mɑ] *m* Damascus blade; *tex.* damask; ♣ damson; **damasquiner** [~maski'ne] (1a) *v/t.* damascene; **damasser** [~mɑ'se] (1a) *v/t.* damask; *acier m damassé* Damascus steel.

dame [dam] **1.** *su./f* lady (*a. chess*); *cards, chess:* queen; *draughts:* king; ⊕ (paving) beetle; rammer; ~ *de charité* lady visitor; ♀s *pl.* Ladies (= *toilet*); ~ *d'honneur* matron of hono(u)r; ~ *du vestiaire* cloakroom (*Am.* checkroom) attendant, *Am. a.* hatcheck girl; *jeu m de* ~s draughts, *Am.* checkers; **2.** *int.* indeed!; of course!; **~jeanne**, *pl.* **~s-jeannes** [~'ʒan] *f* demijohn; **damer** [da'me]

(1a) *v/t.* crown (*a piece at draughts*); ⊕ ram (*the earth etc.*); *fig.* ~ *le pion à* outdo *or* outwit (*s.o.*).

damier [da'mje] *m* draught-board, *Am.* checker-board; *tex. à* ~ chequered, checked.

damnable [dɑ'nabl] *fig.* detestable, damnable; *eccl.* deserving damnation; **damnation** [~na'sjõ] *f* damnation; **damner** [~'ne] (1a) *v/t.* damn; F *faire* ~ *q.* drive s.o. crazy.

damoiseau [damwa'zo] *m* ✝ squire; F fop; **damoiselle** ✝ [~'zɛl] *f* damsel.

dancing [dɑ̃'siŋ] *m* public dance-hall; supper-club.

dandin F [dɑ̃'dɛ̃] *m* simpleton; **dandiner** [~di'ne] (1a) *v/t.* dandle; *se* ~ waddle; strut.

danger [dɑ̃'ʒe] *m* danger; ~ *de mort!* danger of death!; *en* ~ *de mort* in danger of one's life; **dangereux, -euse** [dɑ̃ʒ'rø, ~'rø:z] dangerous (to, *pour*).

danois, e [da'nwa, ~'nwa:z] **1.** *adj.* Danish; **2.** *su./m ling.* Danish; *zo.* great Dane; *su.* ♀ Dane; *les* ♀ *m/pl.* the Danes.

dans [dɑ̃] *prp. usu.* in (*the street, the house, a moment, a month, the morning, the past*); *place:* within (*the limits*); among (*the crowd*); *direction:* into; *time:* within (*an hour*), during; *condition:* in; with; under (*these circumstances, the necessity*); *source, origin:* out of, from; ~ *la ville* (with)in the town; *entrer* ~ *une pièce* enter a room; ~ *Racine* in Racine; *mettre qch.* ~ *un tiroir* put s.th. in(to) a drawer; ~ *le temps* formerly; *périr* ~ *un accident* be killed in an accident; ~ *le commerce* in trade; ~ *l'embarras* embarrassed; ~ *l'intention de* (*inf.*) with the intention of (*ger.*); *faire qch.* ~ *la perfection* do s.th. to perfection; *avoir foi* ~ have confidence in; *consister* ~ consist of; *puiser* (*boire, manger*) ~ draw (drink, eat) from; *prendre* ~ take from *or* out of.

dansant, e [dɑ̃'sɑ̃, ~'sɑ̃:t] dancing; springy (*step*); lively (*tune*); *thé m* ~ tea-dance, thé dansant; **danse** [dɑ̃:s] *f* dance; dancing; *fig.* F battle; *sl.* thrashing; *♪* ~ *de Saint-Guy* St. Vitus' dance; ~ *macabre* Dance of Death; *salle f de* ~ ballroom; **danser** [dɑ̃'se] (1a) *v/t.* dance; dandle (*a baby*); *v/i.* prance (*horse*); *faire* ~ *q.* dance with s.o.; *fig.* F lead s.o. a dance; **danseur, -euse** [~'sœ:r, ~'sø:z] *su.* dancer; (dance-)partner; ballet-dancer; ~ *de corde* tight-rope dancer; *su./f* ballerina; **dansotter** F [~sɔ'te] (1a) *v/i.* hop, skip.

danubien, -enne *geog.* [dany'bjɛ̃, ~'bjɛn] Danubian.

dard [da:r] *m* † javelin, dart; *zo. bee etc.*: sting (*a. fig.*); *sun*: piercing ray; *flame*: tongue; *♀* pistil; *icht.* dace; **darder** [dar'de] (1a) *v/t.* hurl; shoot forth; *icht.* spear; *fig.* shoot (*a glance*) (at, *sur*).

dare-dare F [dar'da:r] *adv.* posthaste, at top speed.

darne *cuis.* [darn] *f fish*: slice, steak.

dartre [dartr] *f ♂* dartre; scurf; *metall.* scab; **dartreux, -euse** [dar'trø, ~'trø:z] *♂*, *metall.* scabby; *♂* herpetic.

date [dat] *f* date; ~ *limite* deadline; target date; *de longue* ~ of long standing; *en* ~ *de ...* dated ...; *être le premier en* ~ come first; *faire* ~ mark an epoch; *jusqu'à une* ~ *récente* until recently; **dater** [da'te] (1a) *v/i.* date (from, *de*); *à* ~ *de ce jour* from today; from that day; *cela date de loin* it goes a long way back; *v/t.* date (*a letter*); **dateur** [~'tœ:r] *m*, **datographe** [~to'graf] *m watch*: date indicator.

datte *♀*, † [dat] *f* date; *sl. des* ~*s!* not on your life!, *Am.* no dice!; **dattier** *♀* [da'tje] *m* date-palm.

daube *cuis.* [do:b] *f* stew; *en* ~ stewed, braised.

dauber[1] † [do'be] (1a) *v/t.* (*or v/i.* ~ *sur*) *q.* pull s.o. to pieces behind his back; jeer at s.o.

dauber[2] *cuis.* [do'be] (1a) *v/t.* stew, braise; **daubière** *cuis.* [~'bjɛ:r] *f* stew-pan, braising-pan.

dauphin [do'fɛ̃] *m zo.* dolphin; *hist.* Dauphin (= *eldest son of French king*); *fig.* successor; **dauphine** *hist.* [~'fin] *f* Dauphiness, wife of the Dauphin; **dauphinelle** *♀* [~fi'nɛl] *f* delphinium.

davantage [davɑ̃'ta:ʒ] *adv.* more (and more); longer (*space, time*).

davier [da'vje] *m ♂* (extraction) forceps; ⊕ cramp; ♎ davit.

de [də] *prp. usu.* of; *material*: (made) of (*wood*), in (*velvet*); *cause*: of (*hunger*), from (*exhaustion*); with, for (*pain, joy*); *origin*: from (*France, the house*), out of; *distance*: of, from; *direction*: to (*the station*); *place*: at, in; *time*: by (*day, night*); in; for (*ten month*); *agent, instrument*: with (*a stick*); by (*name*); in (*a low voice*); on; *manner*: in (*this way*); *measure, comparison*: by; *price*: for; *partitive article*: *du pain* (some) bread; ~ *la viande* (some) meat; *des légumes* vegetables; *un litre* ~ *vin* a litre of wine; *une douzaine* ~ *bouteilles* a dozen bottles; *la ville* ~ *Paris* the city (of) Paris; *le mois* ~ *janvier* January; *assez* ~ enough; *beaucoup* ~ much (*money*), many (*things*); *moins* ~ less; *pas* ~ no; *peu* ~ few; *plus* ~ more; *tant* ~ so much, so many; *trop* ~ too much, too many; *qch.* ~ *rouge* s.th. red; *genitive, possession*: ~ *mon père* of my father, my father's; ~ *la table* of the table; *le journal d'hier* yesterday's paper; *les œuvres* ~ *Molière* Molière's works; *matériaux* ~ *construction* building materials; *membre du Parlement* Member of Parliament; *habitant des villes* city-dweller; *le meilleur élève* ~ *la classe* the best pupil in the class; *souvenirs d'enfance* childhood memories; *amour* (*crainte*) ~ love (fear) of; *chapeau* ~ *paille* straw hat; *une robe* ~ *soie rouge* a dress in red silk; *mourir* ~ *cancer* (*fatigue*) die of cancer (from fatigue); ~ *haut en bas* from top to bottom; *tirer qch.* ~ *sa poche* take s.th. out of *or* from one's pocket; *saigner du nez* bleed from the nose; *à trois milles* ~ *distance* at a distance of three miles; ~ *... à ...* from ... to ...; *between ... and ...*; *prendre la route* (*le train*) ~ *Bordeaux* take the Bordeaux road (train); *près* ~ near, close to; *d'un côté* on one side; ~ *ce côté* on this side; ~ *nos jours* in our times; ~ *ma vie* in my lifetime; *du temps* ~ *Henri IV* in the days of Henry IV; *à 2 heures* ~ *l'après-*

midi at 2 p.m.; *avancer* (*retarder*) ~ *5 minutes* be 5 minutes fast (slow) (*watch*); *vêtir* (*couvrir*, *orner*) ~ clothe (cover, decorate) with; *se nourrir* (*vivre*) ~ feed (live) on; *frapper* (*toucher*) ~ strike (touch) with; *montrer du doigt* point at; *fig.* scorn; *précédé* ~ preceded by; *trois mètres* ~ *long* (*haut*) three metres long (high); *âgé* ~ *5 ans* 5 years old *or* of age; *plus âgé* ~ *2 ans* older by 2 years; *plus* ~ *6* more than 6; *d'un œil curieux* with an inquiring look *or* eye; *un chèque* (*des marchandises*) ~ *20 F.* a cheque (goods) for 20 F.; ~ *beaucoup* by far; *content* ~ content *or* pleased with; *digne* ~ ...-worthy, worthy of; *fier* ~ proud of; *paralysé d'un bras* paralyzed in one arm; *un jour* ~ *libre* a free day; *un drôle* ~ *bonhomme* an odd chap.

dé[1] [de] *m gaming*: die; *domino*: piece; *golf*: tee; ~*s pl.* dice; *le* ~ *en est jeté* the die is cast.

dé[2] [~] *m* (*a.* ~ *à coudre*) thimble.

déambuler F [deãby'le] (1a) *v/i.* stroll about, saunter.

débâcle [de'ba:kl] *f ice*: breaking up; *fig.* disaster; downfall, collapse; F *pol.* landslide; ✝ crash; **débâcler** [~ba'kle] (1a) *v/t.* ✝ unfasten (*a door etc.*); clear (*a harbour*); *v/i.* break up (*ice*).

déballage [deba'la:ʒ] *m* unpacking; display (*a. fig.*); F *fig.* effusion, outpouring; **déballer** [~'le] (1a) *v/t.* unpack; F *fig.* let out (*emotions, complaints, etc.*), air, display (*knowledge etc.*).

débandade [debã'dad] *f* stampede, flight; rout; *à la* ~ in disorder; **débander** [~'de] (1a) *v/t.* unbend; remove the bandage from (*a wound, the eyes*); ✗ disband; *se* ~ slacken, relax; scatter, disperse (*crowd*); ✗ break into a rout.

débaptiser [debati'ze] (1a) *v/t.* rename.

débarbouiller [debarbu'je] (1a) *v/t.* wash (*s.o.'s*) face; *se* ~ wash one's face; *fig.* get out of difficulties as best one can.

débarcadère [debarka'dɛ:r] *m* ⚓ landing-stage, wharf; ⛟ arrival platform.

débardage ⚓ [debar'da:ʒ] *m* unloading; **débarder** [~'de] (1a) *v/t.* remove (*timber*) from the woods *or*

(*stone*) from the quarry; ⚓ unload, discharge; **débardeur** [~'dœ:r] *m* ⚓ stevedore, docker; *garment*: slipover, *Brit.* tank top.

débarquement [debarkə'mã] *m* ⚓ unloading, discharge; *passengers*: landing; ⛟ F detraining, arrival; **débarquer** [~'ke] (1m) *v/t.* ⚓ unship, unload; land, disembark (*passengers*); *bus etc.*: set down; F dismiss (*s.o.*); *v/i.* ⚓ land, disembark; ⛟ alight, ✗ detrain.

débarras [deba'ra] *m* lumber room, junk room; *bon* ~! good riddance!; **débarrasser** [~ra'se] (1a) *v/t.* clear; relieve (of, *de*); *se* ~ *de* get rid of (*s.o.*, *s.th.*); get clear of (*s.th.*); extricate o.s. from.

débat [de'ba] *m* discussion; debate (*a. pol.*); dispute; ⚖ ~*s pl.* proceedings; court hearing *sg.*

débâter [deba'te] (1a) *v/t.* unsaddle.

débâtir [deba'ti:r] (2a) *v/t.* demolish; take the tacking threads out of (*a dress*).

débattre [de'batr] (4a) *v/t.* debate, discuss; *fig. se* ~ struggle; flounder about (in the water, *dans l'eau*).

débauchage [debo'ʃa:ʒ] *m* laying off, dismissal; **débauche** [de'bo:ʃ] *f* debauch(ery); *fig.* profusion; **débauché, e** [debo'ʃe] **1.** *adj.* debauched; **2.** *su.* debauchee; **débaucher** [~] (1a) *v/t.* ✝ lead (*s.o.*) astray; entice away (*a workman*); F tempt away; lay off (*workmen*).

débile [de'bil] feeble, weak; F foolish, ridiculous; **débilitant, e** [debili'tã, ~'tã:t] debilitating, weakening; **débilité** [~'te] *f* weakness, debility; **débiliter** [~'te] (1a) *v/t.* weaken; debilitate; ⚕ undermine (*the health*).

débinage *sl.* [debi'na:ʒ] *m* disparagement, running down; **débine** *sl.* [~'bin] *f* poverty; **débiner** *sl.* [~bi'ne] (1a) *v/t.* disparage, run (*s.o.*) down; *se* ~ come down in the world; slip quietly away, make o.s. scarce.

débit [de'bi] *m* retailshop; ✝ turnover; sales *pl.*; ⊕ output; ⊕, *a. speaker*: delivery; ✝ debit; *river*: flow; ~ *de boissons* (*de tabac*) pub (tobacconist's [shop]); *avoir un* ~ *facile* be glib, F have the gift of the gab; *portez ... au* ~ *de mon compte* debit me with ...; **débitant** *m*, **e** *f* [debi'tã, ~'tã:t] dealer; **débiter** [~'te] (1a) *v/t.* sell, retail (*a. fig. lies*); cut up (*logs*

etc.); ⊕ yield; reel off (*a poem*); *usu.*
pej. utter (*threats*); *usu. pej.* deliver (*a*
speech); ✝ debit (s.o. with s.th. *qch. à*
q., q. de qch.).

débiteur¹, -trice [debi'tœːr, ~'tris]
1. *su.* debtor; **2.** *adj.* debit...

débiteur² *m*, **-euse** *f* [debi'tœːr,
~'tøːz] retailer; *usu. pej.* utterer,
...monger; ~ de *calomnies* scandal-
monger.

déblai [de'blɛ] *m* cutting, excavation;
excavated material; **déblaiement**
[~blɛ'mã] *m* excavating, excavation, digging out; removal (*of ex-*
cavated material).

déblatérer [deblate're] (1f) *v/t.*
talk, utter; *v/i.* rail (against, *contre*).

déblayer [deblɛ'je] (1h) *v/t.* clear
away, remove; clear (*a. fig.*).

déblocage [deblɔ'kaːʒ] *m* clearing;
✝, ⊕ releasing; **débloquer** [~'ke]
(1m) *v/t.* clear; unblock; ✝, ⊕ release; ✗ relieve (*a place*); unclamp
(*an instrument*).

débobiner [debɔbi'ne] (1a) *v/t.*
unwind, unreel.

déboire [de'bwaːr] *m* nasty after-
taste; disappointment.

déboiser [debwɑ'ze] (1a) *v/t.* clear
of trees; ✗ untimber (*a mine*).

déboîter [debwa'te] (1a) *v/t.* ♣
dislocate; ⊕ disconnect; *v/i. mot.*
filter; haul out of the line.

débonder [debɔ̃'de] (1a) *v/t.* unbung
(*a cask*); open the sluice-gates of
(*a reservoir*); *fig.* ~ son cœur, se ~
pour out one's heart; *v/i. a.* se ~
burst (out).

débonnaire [debɔ'nɛːr] good-natured, easy-going; **débonnaireté**
[~nɛr'te] *f* good nature; good hu-
mo(u)r.

débordé, e [debɔr'de] overflowing;
fig. overwhelmed (with work, *de*
travail); dissipated (*life, man*); **dé-**
bordement [~də'mã] *m* overflowing, flood; *fig.* outburst (*of temper*
etc.); ♣, ✗ outflanking; ~s *pl.* dissipation *sg.*, excess(es *pl.*) *sg.*; **dé-**
border [~'de] (1a) *vt/i.* overflow,
run over; *v/t.* project beyond, stick
out beyond; ✗ outflank; ♣ sheer
off; ⊕ trim.

débotter [debɔ'te] (1a) *v/t.* take off
(*s.o.'s*) boots; *v/i. a.* se ~ take off
one's boots; *fig. au débotté* immediately on arrival.

débouché [debu'ʃe] *m* outlet; open-

ing (*a. fig., a.* ✝); ✝ *a.* market; ✝
créer de nouveaux ~s open up new
markets; **déboucher** [~] (1a) *v/t.*
clear; open, uncork (*a bottle*); *v/i.*
emerge; open (on[to], *sur*); ~ *sur or*
dans a. lead to; end up in.

déboucler [debu'kle] (1a) *v/t.* un-
buckle (*one's belt*); uncurl (*one's*
hair); F release.

débouler [debu'le] (1a) *vt/i.* roll
down; tumble down; *hunt.* bolt.

déboulonner [debulɔ'ne] (1a) *v/t.*
unrivet, unbolt; F debunk.

débourber [debur'be] (1a) *v/t.*
clean (out); haul (*a carriage*) out
of the mire; F get (*s.o.*) out of a
mess.

débourrer [debu're] (1a) *v/t.* remove the stuffing from; break in
(*a horse*); remove the wad from
(*a gun*); clean out (*a pipe*); *fig.*
smarten (*s.o.*) up.

débours [de'buːr] *m* (*usu. pl.*) dis-
bursement; outlay; expenses *pl.*;
rentrer dans ses ~ recover *or* recoup
one's expenses; **débourser** [~bur-
'se] (1a) *v/t.* lay out, spend, dis-
burse; *v/i.* F shell out, fork out.

déboussoler F *fig.* [debusɔ'le] (1a)
v/t. disorient(ate); disconcert.

debout [də'bu] *adv.* upright; standing (up); on its hind legs (*animal*);
~! get up!; *être* ~ be up, be out of
bed; *fig. ne pas tenir* ~ not to hold
water, be fantastic (*theory*); *4 places*
~ *4* standing; *se tenir* ~ stand.

débouter ⚖ [debu'te] (1a) *v/t.* non-
suit; dismiss.

déboutonner [debutɔ'ne] (1a) *v/t.*
unbutton; *manger* (*rire*) à *ventre*
déboutonné eat (laugh) immoder-
ately; *fig. se* ~ unburden o.s.; F
get s.th. off one's chest.

débraillé, e [debrɑ'je] untidy; slovenly (*appearance, voice*); free, rather
indecent (*conversation*); loose (*mor-*
als, life).

débranchement [debrɑ̃ʃ'mã] *m* dis-
connecting; **débrancher** ⚡ [~brã-
'ʃe] (1a) *v/t.* disconnect.

débrayage [debrɛ'jaːʒ] *m mot.* de-
clutching; F strike, *Am.* walkout;
débrayer [~'je] (1i) *v/t.* ⊕ disconnect; *v/i. mot.* declutch; F
knock off work.

débrider [debri'de] (1a) *v/t.* un-
bridle; halt; ♣ incise; F open (*s.o.'s*
eyes); *sans* ~ at a stretch, on end.

débris [de'bri] *m/pl.* debris *sg.*; remains; wreckage *sg.*; fragments; rubble *sg.*; rubbish *sg.*; ⊕ *metal*: scraps.

débrouillard, e F [debru'ja:r, ~'jard] **1.** *adj.* resourceful; **2.** *su.* resourceful *or* smart person; **débrouiller** [~'je] (1a) *v/t.* disentangle; *fig.* clear up; *se* ~ find a way out of difficulties; manage; cope.

débroussailler [debrusɑ'je] (1a) *v/t.* clear of undergrowth; *fig.* clear (up *or* out), unravel.

débucher *hunt.* [deby'ʃe] (1a) *v/t.* drive (*a stag*) from cover; *v/i.* break cover.

débusquer [debys'ke] (1m) drive (*an animal*) out (from cover); drive *or* chase (*s.o.*) out.

début [de'by] *m* beginning, start; first move *etc.*; *thea.* debut, first appearance; *salaire de* ~ starting salary; *faire ses* ~s make a first appearance; **débutant, e** [deby'tɑ̃, ~'tɑ̃:t] *su.* beginner; novice; *su./m thea.* debutant; *su./f* debutante, F deb; **débuter** [~'te] (1a) *v/i.* begin, start; play first (*in a game*).

déc(a)... [dek(a)] dec(a)...

deçà [də'sa] *adv.* on this side; ~ *delà* here and there, on all sides; *en* ~ *de* on this side of.

décacheter [dekaʃ'te] (1c) *v/t.* unseal, open (*a letter*).

décade [de'kad] *f* decade; period of ten days *or* years.

décadence [deka'dɑ̃:s] *f* decadence, decline, decay; **décadent, e** [~'dɑ̃, ~'dɑ̃:t] *adj., a. su.* decadent.

décaèdre ⊕ [deka'ɛ:dr] **1.** *adj.* decahedral; **2.** *su./m* decahedron.

décaféiné, e [dekafei'ne] caffeine-free, decaffeinated.

décagone ⊕ [deka'gɔn] *m* decagon.

décaisser [deke'se] (1b) *v/t.* unpack, unbox; ⊕ pay out; ✓ plant out.

décalage [deka'la:ʒ] *m* shifting; *fig.* gap, discrepancy; lag; **décaler** [~'le] (1a) *v/t.* shift (forward *or* back); move forward; put back.

décalogue [deka'lɔg] *m the* Decalogue, *the* Ten Commandments *pl.*

décalquage [dekal'ka:ʒ] *m*, **décalque** [~'kalk] *m* transfer(ring); tracing (off); **décalquer** [~kal'ke] (1m) *v/t.* transfer; trace off.

décamper [dekɑ̃'pe] (1a) *v/i. fig.* decamp; F clear out, *sl.* vamoose.

décanat [deka'na] *m* deanship.

décanter [dekɑ̃'te] (1a) *v/t.* decant, pour off.

décapage [deka'pa:ʒ] *m*, **décapement** [~kap'mɑ̃] *m* scouring; *metal*: pickling; ~ *au jet de sable* sandblasting; **décapant** [~'pɑ̃] *m* scouring agent *or* solution; paint *or* varnish remover; **décaper** [~ka'pe] (1a) *v/t.* scour; cleanse.

décapiter [dekapi'te] (1a) *v/t.* behead, decapitate; cut the head off (*a.* ✓).

décapotable *mot.* [dekapɔ'tabl] convertible; drop-head (*coupé*).

décapsulateur [dekapsyla'tœ:r] *m* (crown-cork) opener.

décarburer *metall.* [dekarby're] (1a) *v/t.* decarbonize.

décartellisation ✝ [dekartɛliza'sjɔ̃] *f* decartel(l)ization.

décatir [deka'ti:r] (2a) *v/t. tex.* sponge, take the gloss off; F *se* ~ lose one's beauty, age.

décavé, e F [deka've] **1.** *adj.* ruined, F broke (*person*); worn out; haggard (*face*); **2.** *su.* ruined person; **décaver** [~] (1a) *v/t.* win all (*s.o.'s*) money (*at cards etc.*), F clean (*s.o.*) out.

décéder *admin., eccl.* [dese'de] (1f) *v/i.* die, decease.

déceler [desə'le] (1d) *v/t.* reveal, disclose.

décélération [deselerɑ'sjɔ̃] *f* deceleration.

décembre [de'sɑ̃:br] *m* December.

décemment [desa'mɑ̃] *adv. of décent;* **décence** [~'sɑ̃:s] *f* decency, decorum.

décennal, e *m/pl.* -aux [desɛ'nal, ~'no] decennial.

décent, e [de'sɑ̃, ~'sɑ̃:t] decent; modest; seemly; *peu* ~ unseemly.

décentraliser *admin.* [desɑ̃trali'ze] (1a) *v/t.* decentralize.

décentré, e [desɑ̃'tre] off-centre; **décentrer** [~] (1a) *v/t.* throw off centre; *se* ~ move off centre.

déception [desɛp'sjɔ̃] *f* disappointment.

décercler [desɛr'kle] (1a) *v/t.* unhoop.

décerner [desɛr'ne] (1a) *v/t.* award (*a price*) (to, *à*), confer (*an honour*) (on, *à*); ⚖ issue (*a writ etc.*).

décès [de'sɛ] *m admin. etc.* decease, death; ⚖ demise.

décevant, e [desə'vɑ̃, ~'vɑ̃:t] de-

décevoir

décevoir 144

ceptive; disappointing; **décevoir** [√'vwa:r] (3a) *v/t.* deceive; disappoint.

déchaînement [deʃɛn'mã] *m* unbridling; *fig.* outburst; **déchaîner** [√ʃɛ'ne] (1b) *v/t.* let loose (*a. fig.*); se √ break loose; break (*storm*); se √ contre storm at.

déchanter F [deʃã'te] (1a) *v/i.* F change one's tune; F sing small, come down a peg.

décharge [de'ʃarʒ] *f* ⚡, ✗, ⚖, ⊕ discharge; ⚡ output; ✗ volley; ⚖ acquittal; ✝ receipt (*for delivery*); ✝ credit; *fig.* relief, easing; lumberroom, F gloryhole; reservoir; √ (*publique or municipale*) rubbish (*Am.* garbage) dump; ⚖ témoin *m* à √ witness for the defence; ⊕ tuyau *m* de √ outlet; à sa √ in his defence; **déchargeoir** ⊕ [deʃar'ʒwa:r] *m* outlet; waste pipe; **décharger** [√'ʒe] (1l) *v/t.* unload (*a cart, a gun*); ⚓ unlade; discharge (*a.* ⚡, ⚓, ⚖, *a gun*) (at sur, contre); empty (*a boiler, a reservoir*); *admin.* exempt (from, de); ⚖ acquit; *fig.* relieve, ease; *fig.* vent; se √ go off (*gun*); ⚡ run down; *fig.* vent itself (*anger*); se √ de pass off (*a responsibility etc.*) (onto, sur).

décharné, e [deʃar'ne] lean, emaciated, fleshless; gaunt.

déchaumer ✔ [deʃo'me] (1a) *v/t.* plough (*Am.* plow) up the stubble of (*a field*); break (*the ground*).

déchausser [deʃo'se] (1a) *v/t.* take off (*s.o.'s*) shoes and stockings; lay bare (*a tooth, tree roots, etc.*).

dèche *sl.* [dɛʃ] *f* poverty, distress; F dans la √ hard up, broke.

déchéance [deʃe'ã:s] *f* downfall; (moral) decay; *insurance:* expiration; ⚖ forfeiture; lapse (*of a right*).

déchet [de'ʃɛ] *m* loss, decrease; √s *pl.* waste sg. (*a. phys.*), refuse sg., scrap sg.; waste products; √s *pl.* radioactifs radio-active waste sg.; ✝ √ de route loss in transit.

déchiffrer [deʃi'fre] (1a) *v/t.* decipher; decode (*a message*); ♪ read at sight; **déchiffreur, -euse** [√'frœ:r, √'frø:z] su. decipherer; decoder; ♪ sight-reader; su./m: √ de radar radar scanner.

déchiqueter [deʃik'te] (1c) *v/t.* hack, slash, tear to shreds (*a. fig.*), tear up.

déchirant, e [deʃi'rã, √'rã:t] heart-rending; agonizing (*cry, pain, scene*); racking (*cough*); **déchirement** [√ʃir'mã] *m* tearing (*a.* ⚡); laceration; pang, wrench; √ de cœur heartbreak; **déchirer** [deʃi're] (1a) *v/t.* tear (*a. fig.*); tear up; *fig.* rend; **déchirure** [√'ry:r] *f* tear, rent; ⚡ laceration.

déchoir [de'ʃwa:r] (3d) *v/i.* decay, decline, fall off.

déchristianiser [dekristjani'ze] (1a) *v/t.* dechristianize.

déchu, e [de'ʃy] **1.** *p.p.* of déchoir; **2.** *adj.* fallen; expired (*insurance policy*); disqualified.

déci... [desi] deci...

décidé, e [desi'de] decided, determined; resolute, confident (*manner, person*); **décidément** [√de'mã] *adv.* certainly, positively, really; **décider** [√'de] (1a) *v/t.* decide, settle; decide on; √ q. à (*inf.*) persuade s.o. to (*inf.*); *v/i.:* √ de (*inf.*) decide to (*inf.*), make up one's mind to (*inf.*).

décimal, e, *m/pl.* **-aux** [desi'mal, √'mo] *adj., a. su./f* decimal; **décimer** [√'me] (1a) *v/t.* decimate (*a. fig.*); *fig.* deplete; **décimo** [√'mo] *adv.* tenthly.

décisif, -ve [desi'sif, √'si:v] decisive (*battle etc.*); conclusive (*proof*); positive (*tones*); F cock-sure (*person*); **décision** [√'sjõ] *f* decision (*a.* ⚖); *fig.* resolution.

déclamateur, -trice [deklama'tœ:r, √'tris] **1.** *su./m* declaimer; stump orator, F tub-thumper; bombastic writer; **2.** *adj.* see déclamatoire; **déclamation** [√ma'sjõ] *f* declamation; ranting; **déclamatoire** [√ma'twa:r] declamatory; ranting (*speech*); turgid (*style*); **déclamer** [√'me] (1a) *v/t.* declaim; recite (*a poem*); *v/i.* rant; rail (against, contre).

déclaration [deklara'sjõ] *f* declaration; statement; *admin.* registration, notification; √ de revenu income-tax return; **déclarer** [√'re] (1a) *v/t.* declare (*a.* ✝); ⚖ √ coupable find guilty; avez-vous qch. à √? have you anything to declare? se √ declare (for, pour; against, contre); speak one's mind; declare one's love; break out (*fire, war, epidemic, etc.*).

déclasser [deklɑ'se] (1a) *v/t.* bring (*s.o.*) down in the world; ✗ etc. declare obsolete (*a weapon etc.*); ⚓

disrate (*a sailor*); 🚢 transfer from one class to another; *sp.* penalize (*a runner*).

déclencher [deklɑ̃'ʃe] (1a) *v/t.* launch (*an attack*); unlatch (*a door*); ⊕ release (*a. phot.*), disengage, disconnect (*a. ⚡*); F start; **déclencheur** [ˌ∿'ʃœːr] *m* release (*a. phot.*); *phot.* ∿ *automatique* self-timer.

déclic ⊕ [de'klik] *m* catch, pawl, trip-dog, trip pin; nippers *pl.*; *montre f à* ∿ stop-watch.

déclin [de'klɛ̃] *m* decline, decay; *moon, talent:* waning; *year:* fall; *au* ∿ *du jour* at the close of day; *au* ∿ *de sa vie* in his declining years, towards the end of his days; **déclinaison** [dekline'zɔ̃] *f astr.* declination; *⚡* variation; *gramm.* declension; **décliner** [ˌ∿'ne] (1a) *v/i.* deviate; decline; *fig.* fade, fail, wane; *v/t.* decline (*a. gramm.*); refuse; state (*one's name*). [release.]

décliqueter ⊕ [deklik'te] (1c) *v/t.*]
déclive [de'kliːv] **1.** *adj.* sloping; **2.** *su./f* slope; **déclivité** [ˌ∿klivi'te] *f* slope, gradient, incline.

décloisonner [deklwazɔ'ne] (1a) *v/t.* decompartmentalize.

déclouer [deklu'e] (1a) *v/t.* unnail; take down (*a picture*); *sl.* take out of pawn.

décocher [dekɔ'ʃe] (1a) *v/t.* shoot, let fly; let off (*an epigram*); discharge.

décoction [dekɔk'sjɔ̃] *f* decoction.

décoder [dekɔ'de] (1a) *v/t.* decode; decipher.

décoiffer [dekwa'fe] (1a) *v/t.* remove (*s.o.'s*) hat; take (*s.o.'s*) hair down; ruffle (*s.o.'s*) hair.

décollage [dekɔ'laːʒ] *m* unsticking; ✈ takeoff; **décoller** [ˌ∿'le] (1a) *v/t.* unstick; disengage; loosen; se ∿ come loose; *v/i.* ✈ take off; F budge, depart.

décolleté, e [dekɔl'te] **1.** *adj.* low-necked (*dress*); wearing a low-necked dress (*woman*); **2.** *su./m* low neckline; bare neck and shoulders *pl.*; **décolleter** [ˌ∿] (1c) *v/t.* cut out the neck of (*a dress*); ⊕ cut (*a screw*); se ∿ wear a low-necked dress.

décolonisation [dekɔlɔniza'sjɔ̃] *f* decolonization; **décoloniser** [ˌ∿'ze] (1a) *v/t.* decolonize.

décolorer [dekɔlɔ're] (1a) *v/t.* disco(u)r; fade; bleach; se ∿ fade; grow pale (*person*).

décombres [de'kɔ̃br] *m/pl.* rubbish *sg.*; debris *sg.*, *buildings:* rubble *sg.*

décommander [dekɔmɑ̃'de] (1a) *v/t.* cancel (*an invitation etc.*); ✝ countermand; se ∿ excuse o.s. from an invitation; cancel an appointment.

décomposer [dekɔ̃po'ze] (1a) *v/t.* 🜍, ✏, *phys.* decompose; 🜍 analyse; 🜏 split up; distort (*the features*); se ∿ decay; become convulsed (*features*); **décomposition** [ˌ∿zi'sjɔ̃] *f* decomposition; rotting, decay; *features:* distortion; *gramm.* construing.

décompte [de'kɔ̃t] *m* ✝ deduction; balance due; detailed account; *fig.* *éprouver du* ∿ be disappointed (in, *à*); **décompter** [ˌ∿kɔ̃'te] (1a) *v/t.* deduct; calculate (*the interest*); reckon off.

déconcerter [dekɔ̃ser'te] (1a) *v/t.* disconcert; upset (*plans*); ✝ ♪ put out of tune; se ∿ lose one's assurance.

déconfit, e [dekɔ̃'fi, ˌ∿'fit] crestfallen, discomfited; **déconfiture** [ˌ∿fi'tyːr] *f* ruin, failure; insolvency; collapse; defeat.

décongeler [dekɔ̃'ʒle] (1d) *v/t.* defreeze, thaw (out).

décongestionner [dekɔ̃ʒɛstjɔ'ne] (1a) *v/t.* relieve congestion in; clear.

déconnecter [dekɔnɛk'te] (1a) *v/t.* disconnect; *fig.* separate.

déconner *sl.* [dekɔ'ne] (1a) *v/i.* talk a load of bullshit; blunder; *sl.* boob.

déconseiller [dekɔ̃sɛ'je] (1a) *v/t.* advise (*s.o.* against *s.th.*, *qch. à q.*; *s.o.* against *ger.*, *q. de inf.*).

déconsidérer [dekɔ̃side're] (1f) *v/t.* discredit.

décontenancer [dekɔ̃tnɑ̃'se] (1k) *v/t.* put out of countenance, abash; se ∿ lose one's self-assurance.

décontracter [dekɔ̃trak'te] (1a) *v/t.* relax; **décontraction** [ˌ∿'sjɔ̃] *f* relax, cool(ness).

déconvenue [dekɔ̃v'ny] *f* disappointment; discomfiture; *fig.* blow; set-back.

décor [de'kɔːr] *m house:* decoration; *thea.* set(ting), scene; *thea.* ∿*s pl.* scenery *sg.*; *mot. sl. rentrer dans le* ∿ run into a wall *etc.*; **décorateur** *m*, **-trice** *f* [dekɔra'tœːr, ˌ∿'tris] decorator; *thea.* stage-designer; **décoration** [ˌ∿ra'sjɔ̃] *f* decoration

décorer

(a. = medal, insignia, ribbon of an order); **décorer** [ˑˈre] (1a) v/t. decorate; confer a decoration on.

décortiquer [dekɔrtiˈke] (1m) v/t. husk (rice); shell (nuts); peel (fruit).

décorum [dekɔˈrɔm] m decorum, propriety.

découcher [dekuˈʃe] (1a) v/i. sleep out; stay out all night.

découdre [deˈkudr] (41) v/t. unpick (a garment); rip open.

découler [dekuˈle] (1a) v/i.: ˑ de follow or result from.

decoupage [dekuˈpaːʒ] m cutting up or out; carving; cut-out (figure); **découper** [ˑˈpe] (1a) v/t. carve (a chicken); cut up; cut out (a newspaper article, a pattern); ⊕ stamp out, punch; fig. se ˑ stand out (against, sur).

découplé, e [dekuˈple] well-built, strapping; **découpler** [ˑ] (1a) v/t. uncouple (a. ♪), unleash; radio: decouple.

découpoir ⊕ [dekuˈpwaːr] m cutter; **découpure** [ˑˈpyːr] f cutting-out; pinking; newspaper: cutting; geog. indentation.

découragement [dekuraʒˈmã] m discouragement, despondency; **décourager** [ˑraˈʒe] (1l) v/t. discourage; dissuade (from, de); se ˑ lose heart.

décousu, e [dekuˈzy] 1. p.p. of découdre; 2. adj. unstitched, unsewn; fig. disconnected; disjointed; rambling; 2. su./m disconnectedness; **décousure** [ˑˈzyːr] f seam that has come unsewn; gash, rip (from animal's horns etc.).

découvert, e [dekuˈveːr, ˑˈvert] 1. p.p. of découvrir; 2. adj. uncovered; ✗ exposed; ✝ overdrawn (account); 3. su./m ✝ overdraft; ✗ open ground; admin. deficit; à ˑ openly; in the open; ✝ unsecure (credit), short (sale); su./f uncovering; discovery (a. fig.); aller à la ˑe explore, ✗ reconnoitre; **découvreur** [ˑˈvrœːr] m discoverer; **découvrir** [ˑˈvriːr] (2f) v/t. uncover, lay bare, expose; discover; find out, detect; se ˑ take off one's hat; come into sight; come to light (secret, truth); clear up (sky).

décrasser [dekraˈse] (1a) v/t. clean, scrape; ⊕ scale (a boiler); draw (a furnace); decarbonize (an engine);

fig. rub the rough edges off (s.o.), polish (s.o.) up.

décrépir △ [dekreˈpiːr] (2a) v/t. strip the plaster or rough-cast off; **décrépit, e** [ˑˈpi, ˑˈpit] decrepit, senile; **décrépiter** ⚗ [ˑpiˈte] (1a) v/i. decrepitate; **décrépitude** [ˑpiˈtyd] f decrepitude; (senile) decay.

décret [deˈkrɛ] m decree; **décréter** [ˑkreˈte] (1f) v/t. order; declare; decree; **décret-loi**, pl. **décrets-lois** [ˑkrɛˈlwa] m order in council, Am. executive order.

décrire [deˈkriːr] (4q) v/t. describe (a. ✗).

décrocher [dekrɔˈʃe] (1a) v/t. unhook; teleph. lift (the receiver); uncouple; F get, land (o.s.) (s.th.); v/i. teleph. lift the receiver; fig. switch off; fig. hang up one's boots; **décrochez-moi-ça** sl. [ˑʃemwaˈsa] m/inv. reach-me-down; second-hand clothes' shop.

décroissance [dekrwaˈsãːs] f, **décroissement** [ˑkrwasˈmã] m decrease; decline; moon: wane; **décroître** [deˈkrwaːtr] (4o) v/i. decrease, diminish; wane (moon).

décrotter [dekrɔˈte] (1a) v/t. remove the mud from; clean; scrape; F fig. rub the rough edges off (s.o.); **décrotteur** [ˑˈtœːr] m shoe-black; hotel: boots; **décrottoir** [ˑˈtwaːr] m door-scraper; wire-mat.

décru, e [deˈkry] 1. p.p. of décroître; 2. su./f water: fall, subsidence; decrease.

déçu, e [deˈsy] p.p. of décevoir.

déculotter [dekylɔˈte] (1a) v/t. take off (s.o.'s) trousers; se ˑ take off one's trousers; sl. chicken out.

déculpabiliser [dekylpabiliˈze] (1a) v/t. excuse; free from a sense of guilt.

décuple [deˈkypl] 1. adj. tenfold; 2. su./m tenfold; le ˑ de ten times as much as; **décupler** [ˑkyˈple] (1a) vt/i. increase tenfold.

décuver [dekyˈve] (1a) v/t. rack off (wine).

dédaigner [dedɛˈɲe] (1b) v/t. scorn, disdain; **dédaigneux, -euse** [ˑˈɲø, ˑˈnøːz] scornful, disdainful; **dédain** [deˈdɛ̃] m disdain, scorn (of, de); disregard (of, de; for, pour); contempt (for, de).

dédale [deˈdal] m labyrinth (a. fig.).

dedans [dɔˈdã] 1. adv. in, inside, within; en ˑ inside; en ˑ de within;

F *mettre q.* ~ take s.o. in; **2.** *su./m* inside, interior.

dédicace [dedi'kas] *f* dedication (*a. fig.*); *church:* consecration; **dédier** [~'dje] (1o) *v/t.* dedicate (*a. fig.*); *fig.* inscribe (*a book*).

dédire [de'di:r] (4p) *v/t.*: *se* ~ *de* go back upon, retract, take back; break (*an engagement, a promise*); **dédit** [~'di] *m* renunciation; withdrawal; *promise etc.*: breaking; ⚖ forfeit, penalty.

dédommagement [dedɔmaʒ'mã] *m* indemnity; compensation, damages *pl.*; **dédommager** [~ma'ʒe] (11) *v/t.* compensate (for, de).

dédouanement [dedwanmã] *m* customs clearance; **dédouaner** [~'ne] (1a) *v/t.* clear (*goods etc.*) through the customs; *fig.* clear the name of, rehabilitate.

dédoubler [dedu'ble] (1a) *v/t.* divide into two; undouble (*a cloth*); remove the lining of (*a coat etc.*); 🚂 run (*a train*) in two parts.

déductible [dedyk'tibl]: ~ (*de l'impôt* tax-)deductible; **déduction** [~'sjɔ̃] *f* ♱, *phls.* deduction; ♱ allowance.

déduire [de'dɥi:r] (4h) *v/t. phls.* deduce, infer; ♱ deduct, allow.

déesse [de'ɛs] *f* goddess.

défaillance [defa'jã:s] *f* failure, failing; ♨ faint, swoon; ⚖ witness: default; **défaillant, e** [~'jã, ~'jã:t] **1.** *adj.* failing; sinking (*heart*); faltering (*steps*); waning (*light*); ⊕, *fig.* at fault; faint (*person*); defaulting; **2.** *su.* ⚖, ♱ defaulter; **défaillir** [~'ji:r] (2t) *v/i.* fail, lose strength; falter (*courage*); *fig.* sink (*heart*); faint, swoon (*person*); ⚖ fail to appear.

défaire [de'fɛ:r] (4r) *v/t.* undo; ✗ defeat; annul (*a treaty*); unpack; unwrap; *fig.* distort (*the face*); *fig.* upset (*s.o.'s plans*); rid (s.o. of s.th., *q. de qch.*); *se* ~ come undone; undo one's coat; get rid (of, de); **défaite** [~'fɛt] *f* defeat; *fig.* lame excuse, evasion; *fig.* failure; **défaitisme** [defɛ'tism] *m* defeatism, pessimism; **défaitiste** [~'tist] *adj., a. su.* defeatist, pessimist.

défalquer [defal'ke] (1m) *v/t.* deduct; write off (*a debt*).

défausser [defo'se] (1a) *v/t.* straighten; *cards:* *se* ~ discard.

défaut [de'fo] *m* defect; want, lack;

fault, shortcoming; ⊕ flaw; ⚖ default; ♱ ~ *de provision* no funds; *à* ~ *de* for want of, in place of; *hunt.* être en ~ be at fault (*a. fig.*); *faire* ~ be lacking; be missing; be in short supply; *il nous a fait* ~ we have missed him; *sans* ~ faultless, flawless.

défaveur [defa'vœ:r] *m* disfavo(u)r (with,, *auprès de*), discredit; **défavorable** [~vɔ'rabl] unfavo(u)rable.

défécation [defeka'sjɔ̃] *f* ♔, *physiol.* defecation; clarification.

défectif, -ve [defɛk'tif, ~'ti:v] *gramm.* defective; ♱ deficient; **défection** [~'sjɔ̃] *f* defection (from, de); **défectueux, -euse** [~'tɥø, ~'tɥø:z] faulty, defective; **défectuosité** [~tɥozi'te] *f* defect, flaw; faultiness.

défendable [defã'dabl] defensible; tenable; **défendeur** *m*, **-eresse** *f* ⚖ [~'dœ:r, ~'drɛs] defendant; respondent; **défendre** [de'fã:dr] (4a) *v/t.* defend (*a.* ⚖, *a.* ✗); protect; support; forbid; *à son corps défendant* reluctantly; *fig. se* ~ *de* (*inf.*) refrain from (*ger.*), help (*ger.*); F *fig. se* ~ hold one's own; get along *or* by, manage, cope; F *fig. se* ~ *bien en qch.* be good at s.th.

défense [de'fã:s] *f* defence, *Am.* defense; protection; prohibition; *elephant:* tusk; ⚖ defence, plea; ⚓ fender; ~ *de fumer* no smoking; ⚖ *légitime* ~ self-defence; *psych.* ~*s pl.* defence mechanism *sg.*; **défenseur** [defã'sœ:r] *m* defender; *fig.* supporter; ⚖ counsel for the defence; **défensif, -ve** [~'sif, ~'si:v] *adj., a. su./f* defensive.

déférence [defe'rã:s] *f* deference, regard, respect; *par* ~ *pour* in deference to, out of regard for; **déférer** [~'re] (1f) *v/t.* ⚖ submit; remove (*to the Court of Appeal*); inform against (*a criminal*); administer (*an oath*); bestow, confer (*an honour*); *v/i.* defer (to, *à*); comply (with, *à*) (*an order*).

déferler [defɛr'le] (1a) *v/t.* unfurl (*a flag*); set (*sails*); *v/i.* break (*waves*); ✗ F break up (*attack*).

déferrer [defe're] (1a) *v/t.* remove the iron from; unshoe (*a horse*); *fig.* disconcert; ⚓ ~ *un navire* slip anchor.

défeuiller [defœ'je] (1a) *v/t.* strip

(a tree) of its leaves, defoliate; se ~ shed its leaves (tree).

défi [de'fi] m challenge; lancer un ~ à challenge; mettre q. au ~ dare or defy s.o. (to inf., de inf.).

défiance [de'fjɑ̃:s] f suspicion, distrust; ~ de soi-même lack of self-confidence; pol. vote m de ~ vote of no confidence; **défiant, e** [~'fjɑ̃, ~'fjɑ̃:t] distrustful, suspicious; cautious.

déficeler [defis'le] (1c) v/t. untie (a parcel etc.).

déficient, e [defi'sjɑ̃, ~'sjɑ̃:t] adj., a. su. deficient.

déficit [defi'si] m deficit, shortage; deficiency; **déficitaire** [~si'tɛ:r] ✝ showing a deficit; ✓ short (harvest).

défier [de'fje] (1o) v/t. challenge; dare; fig. brave, defy; se ~ de distrust, be on one's guard against; se ~ de soi-même lack self-confidence.

défigurer [defigy're] (1a) v/t. disfigure; fig. distort (the sense, the truth).

défilade F [defi'lad] f procession; **défilé** [~'le] m geog. pass, gorge; march past; parade; **défiler** [~'le] (1a) v/t. unthread; ✕ defilade (a fortress); ✕ conceal (guns, troops); ~ son chapelet speak one's mind; se ~ come unstrung; ✕ take cover; sl. clear off, get out; v/i. ✕ file off; march past.

défini, e [defi'ni] definite (a. gramm.); defined; bien ~ a. clean-cut; **définir** [~'ni:r] (2a) v/t. define; fig. describe; se ~ become clear; **définissable** [defini'sabl] definable; **définitif, -ve** [~'tif, ~'ti:v] 1. adj. definitive, final; à titre ~ permanently; 2. su./f: en ~ve in short; **définition** [~'sjɔ̃] f definition; cross-words: clue; telev. picture: resolution.

déflagration [deflagra'sjɔ̃] f combustion, deflagration.

déflation [defla'sjɔ̃] f deflation.

défleuraison ♀ [deflœrɛ'zɔ̃] f fall(ing) of blossom; **défleurir** [~'ri:r] (2a) v/t. strip (a plant) of its bloom; take the bloom off (a fruit); v/i. a. se ~ lose its blossom.

déflorer [deflɔ're] (1a) v/t. ✓ strip (a plant) of its bloom; deflower (a virgin); fig. F take the freshness off.

défoncer [defɔ̃'se] (1k) v/t. stave

in; break up (the ground, a road); smash in (a door etc.); fig. destroy, F knock the bottom out of (an argument); se ~ break up; collapse (roof); sl. get high (on drugs); sl. défoncé high, stoned.

déformation [defɔrma'sjɔ̃] f deformation (a. ⊕); ⊕ wood: warping; ✗, phot. distortion; **déformer** [~'me] (1a) v/t. deform; ⊕, ✗, phot., phys., a. fig. distort; ⊕ buckle, warp; se ~ warp (wood); get out of shape.

défouler F [defu'le] (1a) v/t.: se ~ release one's pent-up feelings, F let off steam.

défourner [defur'ne] (1a) v/t. draw from the oven or kiln.

défraîchi, e [defrɛ'ʃi] (shop)soiled, Am. shopworn; faded; **défraîchir** [~'ʃi:r] (2a) v/t. take away the freshness of; se ~ lose its freshness; fade.

défrayer [defrɛ'je] (1i) v/t. defray (s.o.'s) expenses; fig. ~ la conversation be the (main) topic or subject of conversation; be the life of the conversation.

défricher [defri'ʃe] (1a) v/t. ✓ clear, reclaim (land); F fig. break new ground in (a subject).

défriser [defri'ze] (1a) v/t. uncurl; fig. disappoint.

défroisser [defrwa'se] (1a) v/t. smooth out.

défroncer [defrɔ̃'se] (1k) v/t. take out the gathers in (a cloth); ~ les sourcils cease to frown.

défroque fig. [de'frɔk] f usu. ~s pl. cast-off clothing sg.; **défroquer** [~frɔ'ke] (1m) v/t. unfrock (a priest).

défunt, e [de'fœ̃, ~'fœ̃:t] 1. adj. deceased; late; 2. su. deceased, Am. decedent.

dégagé, e [dega'ʒe] clear (sky, road); free, unconstrained; off-hand (manner, tone); **dégagement** [~gaʒ'mɑ̃] m clearing; freeing; extrication; relief; emission; passage; escalier m de ~ emergency stairs; ⊕ tuyau m de ~ waste pipe; **dégager** [~ga'ʒe] (1l) v/t. clear; free; extricate; relieve; release (from a promise, d'une promesse); give off, emit (a smell etc.); fig. bring out (an idea etc.); ✗ ~ l'inconnue isolate the unknown quantity; se ~ free o.s.; clear; emanate, be given off; emerge, come out; v/i.: dégagez! clear the way!; bus: gangway!

dégaine F [deˈgɛːn] f (awkward) way of carrying o.s.; gawkiness; **dégainer** [~gɛˈne] (1b) v/t. unsheathe, draw (one's sword); v/i. draw.

déganter [degɑ̃ˈte] (1a) v/t. unglove (one's hand); se ~ take off one's gloves.

dégarnir [degarˈniːr] (2a) v/t. strip; dismantle; unsaddle (a horse); ⚓ unrig; ✄ withdraw the troops from; ✔ thin out (a tree); se ~ be stripped; empty (room); become bald (head); lose its leaves (tree).

dégât [deˈgɑ] m food etc.: waste; ~s pl. damage sg.; havoc sg.

dégauchir ⊕ [degoˈʃiːr] (2a) v/t. rough-plane (wood); dress (a stone); straighten, true up (the machinery); fig. knock the corners off (s.o.).

dégel [deˈʒɛl] m thaw; **dégelée** F [deʒɔˈle] f shower of blows; **dégeler** [~] (1d) vt/i. thaw; unfreeze, defrost; v/t.: F se ~ thaw (person).

dégénérer [deʒeneˈre] (1f) v/i. degenerate (from, de; into, en); **dégénérescence** ✿ [~reˈsɑ̃ːs] f degeneration.

dégingandé, e [deʒɛ̃gɑ̃ˈde] awkward, lanky, ungainly.

dégivrer [deʒiˈvre] (1a) v/t. de-ice, defrost; **dégivreur** [~ˈvrœːr] m de-icer, defroster.

déglacer [deglaˈse] (1k) v/t. thaw; defrost (the refrigerator); unglaze (paper).

déglinguer F [deglɛ̃ˈge] (1m) v/t. knock to pieces, F bust up.

dégluer [deglyˈe] (1a) v/t. remove the sticky substance from; remove the bird-lime from (a bird).

déglutition physiol. [deglytiˈsjɔ̃] f swallowing.

dégobiller sl. [degɔbiˈje] (1a) v/t. bring up (food); v/i. vomit, F spew, puke.

dégoiser F [degwaˈze] (1a) v/t. reel off, spout (a speech etc.).

dégommer [degɔˈme] (1a) v/t. ungum; ⊕ clean off old oil from; F dismiss (s.o.); F beat (s.o.) (at a game); F se faire ~ get the sack.

dégonflé sl. [degɔ̃ˈfle] m funk; **dégonfler** [~] (1a) v/t. deflate; reduce (✿ a swelling, ✝ prices, fig. s.o.'s importance etc.); fig. debunk (s.o.); se ~ go flat (tyre); F back out, F chicken out.

dégorgeoir [degɔrˈʒwaːr] m outlet, outflow; pump: spout; **dégorger** [~ˈʒe] (11) v/t. cleanse; clear, unstop (a pipe etc.); disgorge (a. fig.); v/i. a. se ~ flow out; overflow; ✿ discharge (abscess); become free (pipe etc).

dégot(t)er sl. [degɔˈte] (1a) v/t. find, F unearth; v/i. ~ (bien) look great; ~ mal look awful.

dégouliner F [deguliˈne] (1a) v/i. roll (down); trickle.

dégourdi, e [degurˈdi] 1. adj. lively, sharp, smart; 2. su. brisk person, F live wire; **dégourdir** [~ˈdiːr] (2a) v/t. warm (up), take the stiffness from (one's legs etc.); take the chill off (a liquid); fig. smarten (s.o.) up, F lick (s.o.) into shape; se ~ les jambes stretch one's legs; se ~ a. feel warmer; become more alert; F learn the ropes.

dégoût [deˈgu] m disgust, loathing (for, pour); dislike, repugnance (for, pour); **dégoûtant, e** [deguˈtɑ̃, ~ˈtɑ̃ːt] disgusting, loathsome, repulsive; **dégoûter** [~ˈte] (1a) v/t. disgust, repel; se ~ de take a dislike to, grow sick of.

dégoutter [deguˈte] (1a) v/i. drip, trickle (from, with de).

dégradation [degradaˈsjɔ̃] f degradation (a. phys.); rock: weathering; phys. energy: dissipation; colours etc.: shading off; ⚖ ~ civique loss of civil rights; **dégrader** [~ˈde] (1a) v/t. degrade; ✄ demote, reduce to the ranks; shade off (colours); damage, deface (a building); se ~ deteriorate.

dégrafer [degraˈfe] (1a) v/t. unhook, unfasten.

dégraissage [degrɛˈsaːʒ] m cuis. skimming; (dry-)cleaning; **dégraisser** [~ˈse] (1a) v/t. remove the fat from; cuis. skim; take the grease marks out of (s.o.'s); **dégraisseur** [~ˈsœːr] m person: drycleaner.

degré [dəˈgre] m degree (a. ⚚ etc., a. of parentage); stage; step; rank; ~ centésimal degree centigrade; ~ de congélation freezing point; par ~s by degrees, progressively.

dégréer ⚓ [degreˈe] (1a) v/t. unrig (a mast, a ship); dismantle (a crane).

dégrèvement [degrɛvˈmɑ̃] m abatement of tax; derating; **dégrever** [~grəˈve] (1d) v/t. reduce (a duty, a tax); derate; reduce the assessment on; disencumber (an estate).

dégringolade F [degrɛ̃gɔˈlad] f

tumble, fall; *currency*: collapse;
dégringoler F [~'le] (1a) *vt/i.*
tumble down.

dégriser [degri'ze] (1a) *v/t.* sober
(*s.o.*); *fig.* bring (*s.o.*) to his senses;
se ~ sober up; *fig.* come to one's
senses.   [draw down (*a wire*).)

dégrosser ⊕ [degro'se] (1a) *v/t.*)

dégrossir [degro'si:r] (2a) *v/t.*
rough-hew (*a stone*); rough-plane
(*wood*); rough out (*a plan*); F lick
(*s.o.*) into shape.

dégrouiller *sl.* [degru'je] (1a) *v/t.*:
se ~ hurry up, F get a move on.

déguenillé, e [degəni'je] 1. *adj.*
ragged, tattered; 2. *su.* ragamuffin.

déguerpir [deger'pi:r] (2a) *v/t.* ⟨t⟩
abandon (*one's property etc.*); *v/i.*
move out; clear out, *Am.* beat it;
faire ~ send (*s.o.*) packing.

déguisement [degiz'mã] disguise;
fig. concealment; fancy dress; *sans*
~ openly; **déguiser** [~gi'ze] (1a)
v/t. disguise; conceal; se ~ *a.* put
on fancy dress.

dégustateur *m*, **-trice** *f* [degysta-
'tœ:r, ~'tris] taster; **dégustation**
[~ta'sjõ] *f* tasting; **déguster** [~'te]
(1a) *v/t.* taste; F sip; relish, enjoy.

déhanché, e [deã'ʃe] *horse*: hip-
shot; *fig.* ungainly, slovenly; moving with a loose gait; **déhancher**
[~] (1a) *v/t.*: se ~ dislocate its hip
(*horse*); *fig.* move with a loose gait;
sway one's hips.

déharnacher [dearna'ʃe] (1a) *v/t.*
unharness.

dehors [də'ɔ:r] 1. *adv.* outside, out;
dîner ~ dine out; *en* ~ outside; outwards; *en* ~ *de* outside; in addition
to; *en* ~ *de moi* without my knowledge *or* participation; *mettre q.* ~
turn s.o. out; F sack s.o., *Am.* lay
s.o. off; ⟨t⟩ *toutes voiles* ~ with
every sail set; 2. *su./m* outside, exterior; ~ *pl.* appearances.

déifier [dei'fje] (1o) *v/t.* deify; *fig.*
make a god of; **déité** [~'te] *f* deity.

déjà [de'ʒa] *adv.* already, before.

déjection [deʒɛk'sjõ] *f* ☆ evacuation; ~s *pl. a.* ejecta (*of a volcano*).

déjeter ⊕ [deʒə'te] (1c) *v/t. a.* se ~
warp (*wood*); buckle (*metal*).

déjeuner [deʒœ'ne] 1. (1a) *v/i.* have
breakfast; (have) lunch; 2. *su./m*
lunch; *petit* ~ breakfast; ~**-débat**, *pl.*
~**s-débats** [~nede'ba] *m* working
lunch.

déjouer [de'ʒwe] (1p) *v/t.* thwart;
foil; outwit; elude; baffle.

déjucher [deʒy'ʃe] (1a) *v/t.* unroost
(*hens*); F *fig.* make (*s.o.*) come off
his perch; *v/i.* come off the roost.

déjuger [deʒy'ʒe] (11) *v/t.*: se ~
reverse one's opinion.

delà [də'la] *adv., a. prp.* beyond.

délabré, e [dela'bre] dilapidated;
ramshackle, tumble-down; impaired (*health*); **délabrer** [~] (1a)
v/t. dilapidate, wreck; ruin (*a. one's
health*); se ~ fall into decay (*house*);
become impaired (*health*).

délacer [dela'se] (1k) *v/t.* unlace;
undo (*one's shoes*).

délai [de'lɛ] *m* delay; respite; reprieve; *à bref* ~ at short notice;
dans un ~ *de 2 mois* at a two-months'
notice; ~**-congé**, *pl.* ~**s-congés**
[~lekõ'ʒe] *m* term of notice.

délaisser [delɛ'se] (1b) *v/t.* forsake,
desert; abandon (*a.* ⟨t⟩ *prosecution*); ⟨t⟩ relinquish.   [(*butter*).)

délaiter [delɛ'te] (1b) *v/t.* work)

délarder [delar'de] (1a) *v/t.* remove
the fat from; ⊕ thin down (*wood*);
bevel, chamfer (*an edge*).

délassement [delɑs'mã] *m* rest, relaxation; recreation; **délasser** [~-
lɑ'se] (1a) *v/t.* rest, refresh; se ~
relax.

délateur, -trice [dela'tœ:r, ~'tris]
su. informer, spy; *su./m* ⊕ detector
(*of a lock*); **délation** [~'sjõ] *f* in-
forming, denunciation, squealing.

délavé, e [dela've] washed out;
wishy-washy; weak.

délayer [delɛ'je] (1i) *v/t.* dilute; *fig.*
spin out (*a speech*).

délectable [delɛk'tabl] delectable;
delightful; **délecter** [~'te] (1a) *v/t.*:
se ~ *à* take delight in.

délégataire ⟨t⟩ [delega'te:r] *su.* del-
egatee; **délégateur** *m*, **-trice** *f* ⟨t⟩
[~'tœ:r, ~'tris] delegator; **délégation** [~'sjõ] *f* delegation (*a. coll.*);
⟨t⟩ assignment; **délégué, e** [dele-
'ge] 1. *adj.* deputy..., delegated; 2.
su. delegate; deputy; *su./m*: ⊕ ~
syndical shop steward; ⊕ ~ *du personnel* union steward; **déléguer** [~]
(1s) *v/t.* delegate; ⟨t⟩ *a.* assign.

délester [delɛs'te] (1a) *v/t.* ⚓ *etc.*
unballast; unload; *fig.* relieve (of,
de); ⚡ shed the load.

délétère [dele'te:r] deleterious;
noxious; poison(ous) (*gas, a. fig.*);

fig. pernicious (*doctrine*); offensive (*smell*).

délibératif, -ve [delibera'tif, ‿'tiːv] deliberative; *avoir voix* ‿*ve* be entitled to speak and vote; **délibération** [‿ra'sjõ] *f* deliberation, debate, discussion (on, *sur*); reflection; resolution, vote; **délibéré, e** [‿'re] **1.** *adj.* deliberate; determined; *de propos* ‿ deliberately; **2.** *su./m* ɪ̌ɪ̌ private sitting, consultation; **délibérer** [‿'re] (1f) *v/i.* deliberate; consult together; ponder, reflect (on *de*, *sur*).

délicat, e [deli'ka, ‿'kat] delicate; fragile; dainty; nice, difficult, tricky (*situation*, *question*); fastidious (*eater*); sensitive (*skin*); scrupulous; *peu* ‿ unscrupulous, dishonest; *su./m:* *faire le* ‿ be squeamish; **délicatesse** [‿ka'tɛs] *f* delicacy; fragility; fastidiousness; tact; difficulty; *avec* ‿ tactfully.

délice [de'lis] *su./m* delight; *su./f:* ‿*s pl.* delight *sg.*, pleasure *sg.*; *faire les* ‿*s de* be the delight of; *faire ses* ‿*s de* revel in; **délicieux, -euse** [‿li'sjø, ‿'sjøːz] delicious; delightful.

délictueux, -euse ɪ̌ɪ̌ [delik'tɥø, ‿'tɥøːz] punishable, unlawful; felonious; *acte m* ‿ misdemeano(u)r.

délié, e [de'lje] slim, thin, slender; glib (*tongue*); nimble (*fingers*, *wit*); **délier** [‿] (1o) *v/t.* untie, undo; release; *eccl.* absolve; *sans bourse* ‿ without spending a (half)penny.

délimiter [delimi'te] (1a) *v/t.* delimit; fix the boundaries of; demarcate; define (*powers*).

délinquance ɪ̌ɪ̌ [delɛ̃'kãːs] *f* delinquency; ‿ *juvénile* juvenile delinquency; **délinquant** *m, e f* ɪ̌ɪ̌ [‿'kã, ‿'kãːt] delinquent, offender; trespasser.

délirant, e [deli'rã, ‿'rãːt] frantic, frenzied; rapturous; ✵ delirious; raving; **délire** [‿'liːr] *m* ✵ delirium; *fig.* frenzy; **délirer** [‿li're] (1a) *v/i.* be delirious; rave (*a. fig.*); **délirium tremens** ✵ [‿li'rjɔm tre'mɛ̃ːs] *m* delirium tremens, F d.t.'s.

délit ɪ̌ɪ̌ [de'li] *m* misdemeano(u)r, offence; *en flagrant* ‿ in the act, redhanded.

délivrance [deli'vrãːs] *f* deliverance; release; rescue; ✵ confinement; delivery; certificate, *ticket*, *etc.*: issue; **délivrer** [‿'vre] (1a) *v/t.*

(set) free; deliver (*a.* ✵, *a. a certificate*); release; issue (*a certificate*, *a ticket*); se ‿ *de* free o.s. from.

déloger [delɔ'ʒe] (1l) *v/i.* remove, move house; go away; ✕ march off; *v/t.* oust, drive out; ✕ dislodge.

déloyal, e, *m/pl.* **-aux** [delwa'jal, ‿'jo] disloyal, false; ✝ unfair (*competition*); *sp.* foul; **déloyauté** [‿jo'te] *f* disloyalty, treachery.

déluge [de'lyːʒ] *m* deluge, flood (*a. fig.*); F rain: downpour.

déluré, e [dely're] smart, sharp, knowing; forward, cheeky.

délustrer [delys'tre] (1a) *v/t.* *tex.* take the gloss off (*a cloth*); *fig.* take the shine off; se ‿ lose its gloss; grow shabby; *fig.* fade.

démagogue [dema'gɔg] *m* demagogue.

démailler [dema'je] (1a) *v/t.* unshackle (*a chain*); unpick (*a knitted object*); se ‿ run, ladder (*stocking*); **démailloter** [‿jo'te] (1a) *v/t.* unswaddle (*a baby*).

demain [də'mɛ̃] *adv., a. su./m* tomorrow; *à* ‿*!* good-bye till tomorrow!, F see you to-morrow!; ‿ *en huit* to-morrow week.

démancher [demã'ʃe] (1a) *v/t.* unhaft, remove the handle of (*a tool*); ✵ F dislocate; *fig.* upset; *v/i.* ♪ shift.

demande [də'mãːd] *f* question; enquiry; request (for, *de*); ✝ demand; ɪ̌ɪ̌ claim, action; ‿ *d'emploi* application for a job; ɪ̌ɪ̌ ‿ *en dommages-intérêts* claim for damages; ‿ *en mariage* proposal (of marriage); *à la* ‿ as required; *à la* ‿ *générale* by general request; *sur* ‿ on application *or* request; **demander** [‿mã'de] (1a) *v/t.* ask (for); beg, request; wish, want; order; apply for; ‿ *q.* ask for s.o.; ‿ *qch. à q.* ask s.o. for s.th.; se ‿ wonder.

demandeur[1] *m*, **-euse** [dəmã'dœːr, ‿'døːz] petitioner; applicant (for, *de*); demander; *cards*: declarer; *teleph.* caller.

demandeur[2] *m*, **-eresse** *f* ɪ̌ɪ̌ [dəmã'dœːr, ‿'drɛs] plaintiff.

démangeaison [demãʒɛ'zõ] *f* itching; *fig.* F itch, longing; **démanger** [‿'ʒe] (1l) *v/i.*: ‿ *à q.* itch (*arm*, *leg*, *etc.*); *fig.* *ça me démange de* (*inf.*) I'm dying to (*inf.*).

démantèlement [demãtɛl'mã] *m*

dismantling; **démanteler** [∼mɑ̃t'le] (1d) v/t. dismantle; demolish, raze; break up (a gang).

démantibuler [demɑ̃tiby'le] (1a) v/t. ruin, break up, smash up.

démaquillage [demaki'ja:ʒ] m: crème m de ∼cleansing cream; **démaquillant** [∼'jɑ̃] m make-up remover, cleanser; **démaquiller** [∼'je] (1a) v/t.: se ∼ take off one's make-up.

démarcation [demarka'sjɔ̃] f demarcation, boundary.

démarche [de'marʃ] f step (a. fig.), walk, gait; fig. a. procedure(s pl.); faire des ∼s pour take steps to.

démarquer [demar'ke] (1m) v/t. remove the marks from; ✝ mark down (prices); fig. plagiarize.

démarrage [dema'ra:ʒ] m mot., 🚢 ✗ start; ⚓ unmooring; **démarrer** [∼'re] (1a) vt/i. ⚓ cast off; mot., 🚢, ✗ start; v/i. fig. get moving, get off the ground; faire ∼ mot. start; ⊕ set in motion; **démarreur** ⊕, mot. [∼'rœ:r] m starter.

démasquer [demas'ke] (1m) v/t. unmask (a. ⚔); ⚓ show (a light); fig. ∼ ses batteries show one's hand.

démêlé [deme'le] m dispute; contest; **démêler** [∼'le] (1a) v/t. unravel; comb out (one's hair); fig. make out; clear up; avoir qch. à ∼ avec q. have a bone to pick with s.o.; **démêloir** [∼'lwa:r] m large-toothed comb.

démembrer [demɑ̃'bre] (1a) v/t. dismember; break up.

déménagement [demenaʒ'mɑ̃] m removal, moving (house); voiture f de ∼ furniture van; **déménager** [∼na'ʒe] (11) v/t. (re)move; move the furniture out of (a house); v/i. move house; fig. go out of one's mind; F sa tête déménage he has taken leave of his senses; **déménageur** [∼na'ʒœ:r] m furniture remover.

démence [de'mɑ̃:s] f insanity, madness; 🅰 dementia; ⚖ lunacy.

démener [demə'ne] (1d) v/t.: se ∼ struggle; fling o.s. about; fig. strive hard.

dément, e [de'mɑ̃, ∼'mɑ̃:t] 1. adj. mad; ⚖ lunatic; 2. su. mad person, lunatic.

démenti [demɑ̃'ti] m denial, contradiction; fig. failure; **démentir** [∼'ti:r] (2b) v/t. contradict; deny

(a fact); belie; se ∼ contradict o.s.; fail (to keep one's word).

démérite [deme'rit] m demerit; **démériter** [∼'rite] (1a) v/i. act in a blameworthy manner; ∼ auprès de q. forfeit s.o.'s esteem; ∼ de break faith with (s.o.); become unworthy of (s.th.).

démesuré, e [demezy're] inordinate, beyond measure; excessive; out of all proportion.

démettre [de'mɛtr] (4v) v/t. dislocate; ✝ deprive; ⚖ ∼ q. de son appel dismiss s.o.'s appeal; se ∼ l'épaule dislocate one's shoulder, put one's shoulder out (of joint); se ∼ de qch. give s.th. up, abandon s.th.; se ∼ (de ses fonctions) resign.

démeubler [demœ'ble] (1a) v/t. remove the furniture from.

demeurant [dəmœ'rɑ̃]: au ∼ after all; **demeure** [∼'mœ:r] f dwelling, residence; ✝ delay; à ∼ permanent(ly); dernière ∼ last resting place; ✝ en ∼ in arrears; mettre q. en ∼ de (inf.) call upon s.o. to (inf.); mise f en ∼ summons; **demeuré, e** [∼'mœ:re] mentally retarded; half-witted; **demeurer** [∼mœ're] (1a) v/i. live, reside; stay, stop; en ∼ là stop, leave off.

demi, e [də'mi] 1. adj. (inv. before su.) half, demi-..., semi-...; une demi-heure half an hour, a half-hour; une heure et demie an hour and a half; dix heures et demie half past ten; 2. su./m half; sp. half-back; ∼-**cercle** [dəmi'sɛrkl] m semicircle; surv. demi-circle; ∼-**fond** sp. [∼'fɔ̃] m medium distance; ∼-**frère** [∼'frɛ:r] m half-brother, step-brother; ∼-**gros** ✝ [∼'gro] m wholesale dealing in small quantities; ∼-**jour** [∼'ju:r] m/inv. half-light; ∼-**journée** [∼jur'ne] f part-time work; half-day.

démilitariser [demilitari'ze] (1a) v/t. demilitarize.

demi...: ∼-**monde** [dəmi'mɔ̃:d] m demi-monde; ∼-**mot** [∼'mo] adv.: à ∼ without many words; ∼-**pension** [∼pɑ̃'sjɔ̃] f part board; ∼-**reliure** [rə'ljy:r] f quarter-binding; ∼-**saison** [∼sɛ'zɔ̃] f between-season, mid-season; ∼-**sec** [∼'sɛk] adj./m medium dry (wine); ∼-**sœur** [∼'sœ:r] f half-sister, step-sister; ∼-**solde** ✗ [∼'sɔld] f half pay; ∼-**sommeil** [∼sɔ'mɛ:j] m somnolence; ∼-**soupir** ♪ [∼su'pi:r] m quaver rest.

démission [demi'sjɔ̃] *f* resignation; abdication; *donner sa* ~ hand in one's resignation; **démissionnaire** [~sjɔ'nɛːr] **1.** *adj.* resigning; **2.** *su.* resigner; **démissionner** [~sjɔ'ne] (1a) *v/i.* resign, step down; *fig.* give up.

demi...: ~-**tarif** [dəmita'rif] *m*: (*à* ~ at) half-price *or* half-fare; ~-**teinte** *paint.*, *phot.* [~'tɛ̃ːt] *f* half-tone, half-tint; ~-**ton** ♩ [~'tɔ̃] *m* semitone; ~-**tour** [~'tuːr] *m* half-turn; ✗ about turn; *mot.* U-turn; *faire* ~ turn back; turn about; ✗ about-turn; ⚓ turn a half-circle.

démobiliser ✗ [demɔbili'ze] (1a) *v/t.* demobilize.

démocrate [demɔ'krat] **1.** *adj.* democratic; **2.** *su.* democrat; **démocratie** [~kra'si] *f* democracy; **démocratiser** [~krati'ze] (1a) *v/t.* democratize; *fig.* put in the reach of the average man.

démodé, e [demɔ'de] old-fashioned, out of date, dated, outmoded; **démoder** [~] (1a) *v/t.*: *se* ~ go out of fashion.

démographe [demɔ'graf] *m* demographer; **démographie** [~gra'fi] *f* demography.

demoiselle [dəmwa'zɛl] *f* young lady; spinster; ⊕ paving-beetle; *zo.* dragon-fly; ⚓ rowlock; ~ (*de magasin*) shop-girl; ~ *d'honneur* bridesmaid; maid of hono(u)r.

démolir [demɔ'liːr] (2a) *v/t.* demolish (*a. fig. an argument*), pull down; *fig.* overthrow; *fig.* ruin; F give a good thrashing to (*s.o.*); **démolisseur** [~li'sœːr] *m* demolition worker *or* contractor, wrecker; *fig.* demolisher; **démolition** [~li'sjɔ̃] *f* demolition; ~*s pl.* rubbish *sg.*; rubble *sg.* (*from demolished building*).

démon [de'mɔ̃] *m* demon, devil, fiend; *fig.* imp; *le* ~ *de midi* love in middle age.

démonétiser [demɔneti'ze] (1a) *v/t.* demonetize (*metal*); *fig.* discredit (*s.o.*).

démoniaque [demɔ'njak] *adj.*, *a. su.* demoniac.

démonstrateur *m*, **-trice** *f* [demɔ̃stra'tœːr, ~'tris] ✝ demonstrator; **démonstratif, -ve** [~'tif, ~'tiːv] **1.** *adj.* demonstrative (*a. gramm.*); *peu* ~ undemonstrative, dour; **2.** *su./m gramm.* demonstrative; **démon-**

stration [~'sjɔ̃] *f* demonstration; ✗ show of force.

démontable ⊕ [demɔ̃'tabl] that can be taken to pieces; collapsible (*boat*); **démontage** [~'taːʒ] *m* dismantling; *tyre*: removal; **démonté, e** [~'te] stormy, wild (*sea*); flustered; **démonter** [~'te] (1a) *v/t.* unseat (*a rider*); ⊕ dismantle, take down; *fig.* upset, take aback, fluster; *se* ~ lose countenance; get flustered.

démontrer [demɔ̃'tre] (1a) *v/t.* demonstrate, show.

démoraliser [demɔrali'ze] (1a) *v/t.* demoralize; *fig.* dishearten; ✗ destroy *or* undermine the morale of (*troops etc.*).

démordre [de'mɔrdr] (4a) *v/i.* let go; *fig.* give in; *fig. ne pas* ~ *de* stick to.

démouler [demu'le] (1a) *v/t.* withdraw from the mould; turn out (*a cake*).

démunir [demy'niːr] (2a) *v/t.* deprive (of, *de*); *se* ~ de part with; ✝ run short of.　　　　[muzzle (*a dog*).]
démuseler [demyz'le] (1c) *v/t.* un-}
démystification [demistifika'sjɔ̃] *f* debunking; demystification; **démystifier** [~'fje] (1a) *v/t.* debunk; demystify.

démythifier [demiti'fje] (1a) demythologize; debunk; demystify.

dénatalité [denatali'te] *f* fall in the birth-rate.

dénationaliser [denasjɔnali'ze] (1a) *v/t.* denationalize; *se* ~ lose one's nationality.

dénaturaliser [denatyrali'ze] (1a) *v/t.* denaturalize.

dénaturé, e [denaty're] unnatural; 🜍 *alcool m* ~ methylated spirit; **dénaturer** [~] (1a) *v/t.* adulterate; *fig.* misrepresent, distort; pervert.

dénégation [denega'sjɔ̃] *f* denial; ⚖ traverse.

déni ⚖ [de'ni] denial, refusal.

déniaiser F [denje'ze] (1a) *v/t.* educate (*s.o.*) in the ways of the world; smarten (*s.o.'s*) wits; *fig.* initiate (*s.o.*) sexually.

dénicher [deni'ʃe] (1a) *v/t.* take from the nest; ✗ dislodge; *fig.* unearth, rout out; discover; *v/i.* fly away; F *fig.* clear out, depart.

denier [də'nje] *m* small coin; penny; cent; money; *stockings*: denier; *les* ~*s pl. publics* public funds; *le* ~ *de Saint-Pierre* Peter's pence.

dénier [de'nje] (1o) *v/t.* deny; disclaim; refuse.

dénigrer [deni'gre] (1a) *v/t.* disparage, run (*s.o.*) down.

déniveler [deni'vle] (1c) *v/t.* make uneven (*the surface*); *surv.* determine differences in level.

dénombrement [denɔ̃brə'mã] *m* counting; *population:* census; **dénombrer** [~'bre] (1a) *v/t.* count; take a census of (*the population*).

dénominateur ⅍ [denɔmina'tœːr] *m* denominator; **dénominatif, -ve** [~'tif, ~'tiːv] denominative; **dénomination** [~'sjɔ̃] *f* name, denomination; **dénommer** [denɔ'me] (1a) *v/t.* denominate, call, designate.

dénoncer [denɔ̃'se] (1k) *v/t.* denounce (*a. a treaty*); betray, indicate; expose; ~ q. (*à la police*) inform against s.o.; **dénonciateur, -trice** [~sja'tœːr, ~'tris] 1. *su.* informer; F stoolpigeon; 2. *adj.* telltale, revealing; laying information (*letter*); **dénonciation** [~sja'sjɔ̃] *f* denunciation; information (against, de); notice of termination (*of treaty etc.*).

dénoter [denɔ'te] (1a) *v/t.* denote, show, mark.

dénouement [denu'mã] *m* untying; result, outcome; *difficulty:* solution; *thea. etc.* dénouement; **dénouer** [~'nwe] (1p) *v/t.* untie, unravel, undo; *fig.* clear up; loosen (*limbs, the tongue*); se ~ come undone; end (*story*); loosen (*tongue*).

denrée [dã're] *f usu.* ~s *pl.* commodity *sg.*; produce *sg.*; ~s *pl.* alimentaires food-stuffs; ~s *pl.* coloniales colonial produce *sg.*

dense [dãːs] dense (*a. phys.*); thick; *peu* ~ thin; sparse; **densimètre** *phys.* [dãsi'mɛtr] *m* densimeter, hydrometer; **densité** [~'te] *f* density (*a. phys., a. of population*); *phys.* specific weight.

dent [dã] *f* tooth (*a.* ⊕); *elephant:* tusk; *geog.* jagged peak; ⊕ cog; *fork:* prong; ~ *de lait* (*de sagesse*) milk tooth (wisdom tooth); ~s *pl.* artificielles denture *sg.*; *sl.* avoir la ~ be hungry; *avoir une* ~ *contre* have a grudge against; *être sur les* ~s be worn out; *mal m aux* ~s toothache; *sans* ~s toothless; **dentaire** *anat.* [dã'tɛːr] dental (*art, pulp*); **dental, e**, *m/pl.* **-aux** [~'tal, ~'to] 1. *adj.*

dental (*nerve, consonant*); 2. *su./f gramm.* dental (consonant); **dent-de-lion**, *pl.* dents-de-lion ⚘ [dãd-'ljɔ̃] *f* dandelion; **denté, e** [dã'te] toothed; ⊕ *roue f* ~ *e* cogwheel; **dentelé, e** [dãt'le] jagged, notched; serrated (*a. leaf*); **denteler** [~] (1c) *v/t.* notch; indent (*a. fig.*); **dentelle** [dã'tɛl] *f* lace; wrought ironwork; **dentelure** [dãt'lyːr] *f* indentation; *post:* perforation (*of stamps*); **denter** [dã'te] (1a) *v/t.* ⊕ tooth, cog (*a wheel*); **denticulé, e** [~tiky'le] ⚘ denticulate; ⚠ denticular; **dentier** [~'tje] *m* denture, F plate; set of false teeth; **dentifrice** [~ti'fris] 1. *su./m* dentifrice, tooth-paste; 2. *adj.:* eau *f* ~ mouth-wash; **dentine** *anat.* [~'tin] *f* dentine; **dentiste** [~'tist] *m* dentist; **dentition** [~ti'sjɔ̃] *f* dentition; *baby:* teething; **denture** [~'tyːr] *f* set of (*natural*) teeth; ⊕ teeth *pl.*, cogs *pl.*, gear teeth *pl.*

dénucléarisé, e [denykleari'ze] atom-free (*zone*).

dénuder [deny'de] (1a) *v/t.* lay bare; strip; **dénuement** [~ny'mã] *m* destitution; poverty (*a. fig.*); *room:* bareness; **dénuer** [~'nɥe] (1n) *v/t.* strip (of, de); dénué de devoid of, lacking, ...less.

dépannage [depa'naːʒ] *m* repairing, fixing; repairs *pl.*; *fig.* helping (out); help, relief, F troubleshooting; *mot.* (*a. service m de* ~) breakdown service; **dépanner** [~'ne] (1a) *v/t.* repair, fix; *fig.* help (out), tide over, relief; **dépanneur** *mot.* [~'nœːr] *m* breakdown mechanic; **dépanneuse** *mot.* [~'nøːz] *f* breakdown lorry, *Am.* wrecker. [unpack.]

dépaqueter [depak'te] (1c) *v/t.*

dépareillé, e [deparɛ'je] odd (= *unpaired*); ✝ *articles m/pl.* ~s job lot *sg.*, oddments.

déparer [depa're] (1a) *v/t.* strip (of *ornaments*); divest (*of medals etc.*); *fig.* spoil, mar.

déparier [depa'rje] (1o) *v/t.* remove one of a pair of; separate (*a pair*); *gant m* déparié odd glove.

départ¹ [de'paːr] *m* departure (*a.* ⚔), start; ⚓ sailing; *fig.* start, beginning; *sp.* bloc *m* de ~ starting block; *sp.* lancé flying start; *point m de* ~ starting point (*a. fig.*); *fig. au* ~ in the beginning; at the outset.

départ² [~] *m* division, separation.

départager [departa'ʒe] (1l) *v/t.* decide between; ~ *les voix* give the casting vote.

département [depart'mɑ̃] *m* department (*a. pol. Am.*); *pol.* Ministry; *admin.* department; *fig.* province.

departir [depar'tiːr] (2b) *v/t.* distribute, deal out; *se* ~ *de* abandon, give up.

dépassement [depɑs'mɑ̃] *m* overstepping, going beyond; *credit etc.*: exceeding; **dépasser** [~pɑ'se] (1a) *v/t.* pass, go beyond; exceed (*a. a speed*); overtake (*a car, a person, etc.*); project beyond; *fig.* outshine; *fig.* be beyond (*s.o.'s means etc.*); F *cela me dépasse* it is beyond my comprehension, F it's beyond me; *sp.* ~ *à la course* outrun.

dépassionner [depasjɔ'ne] (1a) *v/t.* take the heat out of (*a discussion etc.*).

dépaver [depa've] (1a) *v/t.* take up the pavement of (*a street*).

dépayser [depei'ze] (1a) *v/t.* take (*s.o.*) out of his element; mislead; *fig.* bewilder.

dépecer [depɔ'se] (1d *a.* 1k) *v/t.* cut up; dismember; break up (*an estate, a ship*).

dépêche [de'pɛːʃ] *f* dispatch; telegram, F wire; **dépêcher** [depɛ'ʃe] (1a) *v/t.* hasten; expedite; dispatch; *se* ~ hurry up, make haste (to *inf.*, *de inf.*).

dépeigner [depɛ'ɲe] (1a) *v/t.* ruffle.

dépeindre [de'pɛ̃ːdr] (4m) *v/t.* depict; describe.

dépenaillé, e [depɔna'je] tattered, ragged.

dépendance [depɑ̃'dɑ̃ːs] *f* dependence; dependency (*of a country*); *fig.* subjection, domination; ~*s pl.* outbuildings, annexes.

dépendre¹ [de'pɑ̃ːdr] (4a) *v/i.* depend (on, *de*); *cela dépend* that depends; *il dépend de vous de (inf.)* it lies with you to (*inf.*).

dépendre² [~] (4a) *v/t.* take down, unhang.

dépens [de'pɑ̃] *m/pl.* cost *sg.*, expense *sg.*, ⚖ costs; *aux* ~ *de q.* at s.o.'s expense.

dépense [de'pɑ̃ːs] *f* expenditure, spending, outlay, expense; *gas, steam, etc.*: consumption; **dépenser** [depɑ̃'se] (1a) *v/t.* spend; consume (*coal etc.*), use (up); *fig. se* ~ exert

o.s.; **dépensier, -ère** [~'sje, ~'sjɛːr] **1.** *su.* storekeeper; *hospital*: dispenser; spendthrift; **2.** *adj.* extravagant, spendthrift.

déperdition [depɛrdi'sjɔ̃] *f* waste; loss; *gas*: escape.

dépérir [depe'riːr] (2a) *v/i.* decline, pine (away), dwindle; **dépérissement** [~ris'mɑ̃] *m* declining, pining, dwindling; decay(ing); deterioration.

dépersonnaliser [depɛrsɔnali'ze] (1o) *v/t.* depersonalize; *se* ~ loose one's personality; become impersonal.

dépêtrer [depɛ'tre] (1a) *v/t.* extricate, free; *se* ~ *de* get o.s. out of (*s.th.*); F *se* ~ *de q.* shake s.o. off.

dépeupler [depœ'ple] (1a) *v/t.* depopulate; thin (*a forest*).

déphasage [defa'zaːʒ] *m phys.* phase difference; *fig.* discrepancy, gap; *fig.* lag; **déphasé, e** [~'ze] *phys.* out of phase; *fig.* disoriented; *fig.* lagging behind; F *fig.* no longer with it.

dépiauter F [depjo'te] (1a) *v/t.* skin; *fig.* dissect (*a book*).

dépilation [depila'sjɔ̃] *f* depilation; removal of hair; **dépilatoire** [~la-'twaːr] **1.** *adj.* depilatory; *pôte f* ~ hair-removing cream; **2.** *su./m* depilatory, hair-remover; **dépiler** [~'le] (1a) *v/t.* remove the hair from.

dépister [depis'te] (1a) *v/t. hunt.* run to earth (*a.* F *fig. s.o.*); *fig.* detect, discover; put off the scent; *fig.* baffle.

dépit [de'pi] vexation, frustration; *en* ~ *de* in spite of; **dépiter** [~pi'te] (1a) *v/t.* annoy; spite; *se* ~ be annoyed *or* vexed (at, *de*).

déplacé, e [depla'se] out of place; displaced; *fig.* misplaced; improper; **déplacement** [~plas'mɑ̃] *m* moving, shifting; movement; displacement, relocation, transfer, removal; travel(ling); ⚓ displacement; ~ *disciplinaire* disciplinary transfer; *frais m/pl. de* ~ travelling expenses; **déplacer** [~pla'se] (1k) *v/t.* displace, shift, move; dislodge; ⚓ have a displacement of; *fig.* transfer (*s.o.*); *se* ~ move; move *or* get around *or* about; travel.

déplaire [de'plɛːr] (4z) *v/i.:* ~ *à* displease; *v/t.:* *se* ~ *à* dislike; **déplaisant, e** [deplɛ'zɑ̃, ~'zɑ̃ːt]

unpleasant, disagreeable; **déplaisir**
[~'ziːr] *m* displeasure; annoyance.

déplanter ✗ [deplɑ̃'te] (1a) *v/t.* dis-
plant; take up (*a plant*); transplant.

dépliant [depli'ɑ̃] *m* folding album;
folder; **déplier** [~'e] (1a) *v/t.* unfold.

déplisser [depli'se] (1a) *v/t.* un-
pleat, take the pleats out of; *se* ~
come out of pleats.

déploiement [deplwa'mɑ̃] *m* un-
folding; *goods, courage, etc.*: display; ✗, ⚓, *troops, etc.*: deploy-
ment.

déplomber [deplɔ̃'be] (1a) *v/t.* unseal; ✗ unstop, *Am.* remove the
filling from (*a tooth*).

déplorable [deplɔ'rabl] deplorable,
lamentable; wretched; **déplorer**
[~'re] (1a) *v/t.* deplore; lament,
mourn.

déployer [deplwa'je] (1h) *v/t.* unfold; display (*a flag, goods, patience,
etc.*); ✗ deploy (*troops*); ⚓ unfurl
(*the sail*).

déplumer [deply'me] (1a) *v/t.* pluck;
se ~ moult; F grow bald.

dépolir ⊕ [depɔ'liːr] (2a) *v/t.* remove
the polish from; grind, frost (*glass*);
se ~ grow dull; *verre m dépoli* ground
or frosted glass.

dépolluer [depɔl'lɥe] (1n) *v/t.* de-
pollute; **dépollution** [depɔly'sjɔ̃] *f*
depolluting.

dépopulation [depɔpyla'sjɔ̃] *f* de-
population; falling population.

déport ✝ [de'pɔːr] *m* backwarda-
tion.

déportation [depɔrta'sjɔ̃] *f* ⚖
transportation; *pol.* deportation;
déportements [depɔrtə'mɑ̃] *m/pl.*
misconduct *sg.*; dissolute life *sg.*;
déporter [~'te] (1a) *v/t.* deport
(*s.o.*); carry away; ⊕ off-set (*a part*);
v/i. ✗ drift.

déposant *m*, **e** *f* [depo'zɑ̃, ~'zɑ̃ːt] ✝
depositor; ⚖ bailor; ⚖ deponent,
witness; **déposer** [~'ze] (1a) *v/t.*
deposit (*s.th., money, required documents*, ⚗ *a sediment, etc.*); lay
down; leave; depose (*a king etc.*);
parl. introduce, table (*a bill*); ⚖
file (*a petition*), prefer (*a charge*),
lodge (*a complaint*); ✝ register (*a
trade-mark*); *v/i.* settle (*wine*); ⚖
give evidence (against, *contre*);
depose (that, *que*); **dépositaire**
[~zi'teːr] *su.* trustee; ⚖ bailee; ✝

agent (for, *de*); **déposition** [~zi-
'sjɔ̃] *f* ⚖, *a. king*: deposition; ⚖
evidence; ⚖ ~ *sous serment* affidavit.

déposséder [depose'de] (1f) *v/t.*
(*de*) dispossess (from), deprive (of);
dépossession [~se'sjɔ̃] *f* dispos-
session.

dépôt [de'po] *m* deposit; ⚖ bail-
ment; *telegram*: handing in; ✝
store; depot (*a.* ✗); ✝ warehouse;
Customs: bond; sediment (*in liquid*); ⚗ depositing; 🚂 *engine*: shed;
police station; ✗ accumulation of
matter; ✝ *trade-mark*: registration;
~ *de marchandises* goods depot;
freight yard; ~ *de mendicité* work-
house; ~ *mortuaire* mortuary; *caisse f
de* ~*s et consignations* Deposit and
Consignment Office; *en* ~ on sale; in
stock; on trust.

dépoter [depo'te] (1a) *v/t.* ✗ plant
out (*seedlings*); unpot (*a plant*);
decant (*wine etc.*).

dépotoir [depo'twaːr] *m* rubbish
(*Am.* garbage) dump; junk room *or*
yard.

dépouille [de'puːj] *f* *animal*: skin;
serpent: slough; ⊕ rake, clearance;
metall. draw; ~*s pl.* spoils, booty *sg.*;
effects; ~ *mortelle* mortal remains *pl.*;
dépouillement [~puj'mɑ̃] *m* de-
spoiling; scrutiny, examination;
votes: count; **dépouiller** [~pu'je]
(1a) *v/t.* skin; strip; plunder; rob;
examine; open (*letters*); count
(votes); *fig.* cast off *or* aside (*one's
pride etc.*); *se* ~ shed its leaves (*tree*);
cast its skin (*serpent*); divest o.s., get
rid (of, *de*).

dépourvoir [depur'vwaːr] (3m) *v/t.*
deprive (of s.th., *de* qch.); **dépourvu, e** [~'vy] 1. *adj.*: ~ *de* lacking, short of, devoid of; 2. *dépourvu*
adv.: *au* ~ unawares.

dépoussiérage [depusje'raːʒ] *m*
dusting; ⊕ dust extraction; *air*: filtering; **dépoussiérer** [~'re] (1a) *v/t.*
remove (the) dust from; dust down;
fig. dust off.

dépravation [deprava'sjɔ̃] *f* *taste
etc.*: depravation; *morals*: depravity;
dépraver [~'ve] (1a) *v/t.* deprave,
corrupt.

dépréciation [depresja'sjɔ̃] *f* depreciation; wear and tear; **déprécier** [~'sje] (1o) *v/t.* depreciate (*a.*
✝), undervalue; belittle, F run

down; devalue (*coinage*); se ~ ✝
depreciate; *fig.* belittle o.s.

déprédateur, -trice [depreda'tœːr,
~'tris] **1.** *su.* depredator; embezzler;
2. *adj.* depredatory; **déprédation**
[~'sjɔ̃] *f* depredation, pillaging;
peculation.

déprendre [de'prɑ̃ːdr] (4q) *v/t.*: se ~
de break away from; free *or* rid o.s.
of; cast off.

dépressif, -ve [depre'sif, ~'siːv]
bearing down; *fig.* depressing; **dépression** [~'sjɔ̃] *f* depression (*a.* ✝,
a. meteor., *a.* fig.); fall (*in value*)
barometer: fall in pressure; ✘ (~
nerveuse nervous) breakdown; **dé-
prime** F [de'prim] *f* depression;
déprimer [depri'me] (1a) *v/t.*
depress; *fig.* lower; se ~ become
depressed.

depuis [də'pɥi] **1.** *prp.* since, for;
from; ~ *quand?* since when?; *je suis
ici* ~ *cinq jours* I have been here for
five days; ~ ... *jusqu'à* from ... (down)
to; **2.** *adv.* since (then); afterwards;
3. *cj.*: ~ *que* since.

dépuratif, -ve [depyra'tif, ~'tiːv]
adj., *a.* *su./m* depurative; **dépurer**
[~'re] (1a) *v/t.* depurate, cleanse (*the
blood*); purify (*water, metal*).

députation [depyta'sjɔ̃] *f* deputa-
tion; membership of Parliament; se
présenter à la ~ stand for Parliament,
Am. run for Congress; **député** [~'te]
m deputy, M.P., *Am.* Congressman;
députer [~'te] (1a) *v/t.* depute;
delegate (*to à, vers*).

déraciner [derasi'ne] (1a) *v/t.*
uproot; *fig.* eradicate.

déraidir [dere'diːr] (2a) *v/t.* take the
stiffness out of; *fig.* relax.

dérailler [derɑ'je] (1a) *v/i.* ⚫ *etc.* go
off the rails; be derailed, leave the
track; F talk wildly; F behave
weirdly; F be on the blink (*machinery*); **dérailleur** [~'jœːr] *m* ⚫
shifting track; *bicycle:* gearshift.

déraison [dere'zɔ̃] *f* unreasonable-
ness; unwisdom; **déraisonnable**
[~zɔ'nabl] unreasonable, irrational;
unwise; foolish; **déraisonner** [~zɔ-
'ne] (1a) *v/i.* talk nonsense; rave
(*sick man*).

dérangement [derɑ̃ʒ'mɑ̃] *m* derangement; disturbance, disorder;
trouble; upset; ✔, ⊕ fault; **déranger** [~rɑ̃'ʒe] (1l) *v/t.* derange; bother; disturb; upset (*a.* fig.); ⊕ put

out of order; se ~ move; take trouble
(to *inf.*, *pour inf.*); lead a wild life;
⊕ get out of order; get upset.

dérapage [dera'paːʒ] *m mot.* skid
(-ding); ⚓ dragging; **déraper** [~'pe]
(1a) *v/t.* ⚓ trip, weigh (*the anchor*);
v/i. ⚓ drag; drag its anchor (*ship*);
mot. skid.

dératé, e F [dera'te] **1.** *adj.* scatter-
brained, harum-scarum; **2.** *su./m*:
courir comme un ~ run like a hare.

derby *sp.* [dɛr'bi] *m* derby, horse-
race; contest.   [more.|

derechef [dərə'ʃɛf] *adv.* again, once|

déréglé [dere'gle] ⊕ out of order;
fig. immoderate; dissolute (*life*);
dérèglement [~ˌrɛglə'mɑ̃] *m* disorder; *pulse:* irregularity; profli-
gacy; dissolute life; **dérégler** [~re-
'gle] (1f) *v/t.* upset, disarrange;
unsettle; ⊕ put out of order; se ~
get out of order; *fig.* get into evil
ways.

dérider [deri'de] (1a) *v/t.* smooth;
unwrinkle; *fig.* cheer (*s.o.*) up.

dérision [deri'zjɔ̃] *f* derision, ridicule; *tourner en* ~ hold up to ridicule; **dérisoire** [~'zwaːr] ridiculous, laughable; *prix m* ~ ridicu-
lously low price.

dérivatif, -ve [deriva'tif, ~'tiːv] *adj.*,
a. *su./m* derivative; **dérivation**
[~'sjɔ̃] *f* ✘, *gramm.* derivation;
watercourse: diversion; ⚫ loop-
(-line); ⚡ shunt(ing); *teleph.* branch-
circuit; ⚛ differentiation; ⚓ drift;
dérive [de'riːv] *f* ⚓ leeway; *aller
à la* ~ drift; **dérivé** ⌃ⱼ, *gramm.*
[deri've] *m* derivative; **dérivée** ⚛
[~] *f* differential coefficient.

dériver¹ [deri've] (1a) *v/i.* drift.

dériver² [~] (1a) *v/t.* divert; ⚡, ⚫
shunt; ✝ free from the board; ✘, ⚛,
gramm. derive; *v/i.* derive *or* be derived (from, *de*); spring (from, *de*).

dériver³ ⊕ [~] (1a) *v/t.* unrivet;
unhead (*a rivet*).

dermatologiste [dɛrmatɔlɔ'ʒist],
dermatologue [~'lɔg] *su.* dermato-
logist.

dernier, -ère [dɛr'nje, ~'njɛːr] **1.**
adj. last, latest; highest, utmost
(*importance etc.*); ✝ closing (*price*);
least (*trouble, worry*); vilest (*of
men*); *le jugement* ~ judgment-day,
the last judgment; *mettre la* ~*ère
main à* give the finishing touch to;
2. *su.* last, latest; **dernièrement**

[ˌnjɛrˈmɑ̃] adv. lately, not long ago, recently.

dérobade [derɔˈbad] f escape; horse: balking; **dérobé, e** [ˌˈbe] hidden, concealed; **dérobée** [ˌˈbe] adv.: à la ~ secretly, on the sly; **dérober** [ˌˈbe] (1a) v/t. steal; hide; cuis. skin (beans), blanch (almonds); se ~ steal away; hide; escape (from, à).

dérogation [derɔgaˈsjɔ̃] f derogation (of, à); faire ~ à deviate from; **déroger** [ˌˈʒe] (1l) v/i. derogate (from, à); deviate (from, à); fig. lower o.s., stoop (to inf., jusqu'à inf.).

dérouiller [deruˈje] (1a) v/t. remove the rust from; fig. polish up.

dérouler [deruˈle] (1a) v/t. unroll; unreel (a cable, a wire); fig. unfold (one's plan); se ~ unroll; come unwound; fig. unfold (scene); fig. occur, develop.

déroute [deˈrut] f rout; fig. ruin; mettre en ~ rout; **dérouter** [ˌruˈte] (1a) v/t. re-route (an aircraft etc.); fig. confuse, disconcert (s.o.), baffle (s.o., s.th.).

derrick [dɛˈrik] m oil-well: derrick.

derrière [dɛˈrjɛːr] **1.** adv. behind, at the back, in the rear; ⚓ astern; ⚓ aft; par ~ from the rear; **2.** prp. behind, at the back of, in the rear of, Am. back of; ⚓ astern of; ⚓ abaft; être ~ q. back s.o. up; **3.** su./m back, rear; F backside, behind, bottom, rump; ✂ ~s pl. rear sg.; de ~ rear..., hind...

derviche [dɛrˈviʃ] m, **dervis** [ˌˈvi] m dervish.

dès [de] prp. from, since; upon (arrival, entry); as early as; ~ demain from tomorrow; ~ lors from then on; ~ que as soon as.

désabonner [dezabɔˈne] (1a) v/t.: se ~ cancel one's subscription (to, à).

désabuser [dezabyˈze] (1a) v/t. disabuse, disillusion; se ~ have one's eyes opened.

désaccord [dezaˈkɔːr] m discord; disharmony; disagreement; discrepancy; fig. en ~ at variance; **désaccorder** [ˌkɔrˈde] (1a) v/t. ♪ put out of tune; radio: detune; fig. set at variance; ♪ se ~ get out of tune.

désaccoupler [dezakuˈple] (1a) v/t. unpair; unleash (hounds).

désaccoutumer [dezakutyˈme] (1a)

v/t.: ~ q. de (inf.) break s.o. of the habit of (ger.).

désaffecté, e [dezafɛkˈte] disused; abandoned.

désaffection [dezafɛkˈsjɔ̃] f loss of affection; disaffection.

désagréable [dezagreˈabl] disagreeable, unpleasant, nasty.

désagréger [dezagreˈʒe] (1a) v/t. disaggregate, disintegrate; geol. weather (rock).

désagrément [dezagreˈmɑ̃] m unpleasantness; nuisance, inconvenience; discomfort.

désajuster [dezaʒysˈte] (1a) v/t. disarrange; ⊕ throw out of adjustment.

désaltérant, e [dezalteˈrɑ̃, ˌˈrɑ̃ːt] thirst-quenching; **désaltérer** [ˌˈre] (1f) v/t. quench (s.o.'s) thirst; refresh, water (a plant).

désamarrer ⚓ [dezamaˈre] (1a) v/t. unmoor.

désamorcer [dezamɔrˈse] (1k) v/t. unprime; defuse (a. fig.); se ~ run dry (pump etc.).

désappointement [dezapwɛtˈmɑ̃] m disappointment; **désappointer** [ˌpwɛˈte] (1a) v/t. disappoint.

désapprendre [dezaˈprɑ̃ːdr] (4aa) v/t. unlearn; forget (a subject, a skill).

désapprobateur, -trice [dezaprɔbaˈtœːr, ˌˈtris] **1.** su. disapprover; **2.** adj. disapproving; **désapprouver** [ˌpruˈve] (1a) v/t. disapprove (of), object to.

désarçonner [dezarsɔˈne] (1a) v/t. unseat (a rider); fig. dumbfound.

désarmement [dezarmaˈmɑ̃] m disarmament; **désarmer** [ˌˈme] (1a) v/t. disarm (a. fig.); ⚓ lay up (a ship); unship (oars); ✂ unload (a gun); uncock (a rifle); v/i. disarm; ⚓ be laid up (ship).

désarrimer ⚓ [dezariˈme] (1a) v/t. unstow (the cargo); put (a ship) out of trim; se ~ shift.

désarroi [dezaˈrwa] m confusion, disorder.

désarticuler [dezartikyˈle] (1a) v/t. dislocate; ✿ disarticulate.

désassembler [dezasɑ̃ˈble] (1a) v/t. take (s.th.) to pieces; disassemble; disconnect (joints, couplings).

désastre [deˈzastr] m disaster; **désastreux, -euse** [ˌzasˈtrø, ˌˈtrøːz] disastrous, calamitous.

désavantage [dezavã'taːʒ] *m* disadvantage; drawback; **désavantager** [ˌ˷ta'ʒe] (11) *v/t.* (put at a) disadvantage; handicap; **désavantageux, -euse** [ˌ˷ta'ʒø, ˷'ʒøːz] unfavo(u)rable.

désaveu [deza'vø] *m* disavowal, denial; repudiation; disclaimer; **désavouer** [ˌ˷'vwe] (1p) *v/t.* disown; disavow; repudiate; disclaim.

désaxé, e [dezak'se] ⊕ out of true (*wheel*); off-centre; offset (*cylinder*); eccentric (*cam, a. fig.*); *fig.* F unbalanced.

desceller [desɛ'le] (1a) *v/t.* unseal, break the seal of; ⊕ loosen; force (*a safe*).

descendance [dɛsã'dãːs] *f* descent; *coll.* descendants *pl.*; **descendant, e** [ˌ˷'dã, ˷'dãːt] **1.** *adj.* descending, downward; ♫ decreasing (*series*); 🚂 up-... (*platform, train*); **2.** *su.* descendant; **descendre** [dɛ'sãːdr] (4a) *v/i.* descend (*a. fig.*), go *or* come down(stairs); fall (*temperature*); alight; get off (*a bus etc.*); dismount (*from a horse*); put up, stay (*at a hotel*); be descended (*from a family etc.*); ~ *chez q.* stay with s.o.; 🚉 ~ *dans* (*or chez*) raid; 💥 ~ en piqué nose-dive; 🚉 ~ *sur les lieux* visit the scene (*of the accident, crime, etc.*); *v/t.* go *or* come down; bring (*s.th.*) down; take (*s.th.*) down (*from a shelf etc.*); lower (*by rope etc., a.* ♪); bring *or* shoot down; set (*s.o.*) down, F drop (*s.o.*) (*at an address*); **descente** [ˌ˷'sãːt] *f* descent; slope; *police:* raid; 🚂 alighting from (*a train*); ⚓ landing; ⚔ prolapse; lowering (*by rope etc.*); taking down (*from the wall etc.*); ⊕ *piston:* downstroke; △ downpipe; *radio:* down-lead; ⚡ run (*on a bank*); ~ *à pic ski:* straight (downhill) run; *paint. etc.* ~ *de croix* descent from the cross; ~ *de lit* (bed-side) rug; 🎿 ~ *piquée* nosedive.

descriptif, -ve [dɛskrip'tif, ˷'tiːv] descriptive; **description** [ˌ˷'sjɔ̃] *f* description.

déséchouer ⚓ [deze'ʃwe] (1p) *v/t.* refloat.

déségrégation *pol.* [desegrega'sjɔ̃] *f* desegregation.

désempar|é, e [dezãpa're] helpless, all at sea; crippled (*vehicle etc.*); ~**er** [˷] (1a) *v/i.:* *sans* ~ without stop-(ping), on end; *v/t.* ⚓ disable; undo.

désemplir [dezã'pliːr] (2a) *v/t.* half-empty; *v/i.:* *ne pas* ~ be always full.

désenchaîner [dezãʃɛ'ne] (1b) *v/t.* unchain, unfetter.

désenchanter [dezãʃã'te] (1a) *v/t.* disenchant; *fig.* disillusion.

désencombrer [dezãkɔ̃'bre] (1a) *v/t.* clear; disencumber.

désenfler [dezã'fle] (1a) *v/t.* reduce the swelling of (*the ankle*); deflate (*a tyre etc.*); *v/i. a. se* ~ go down, become less swollen.

désengager ⊕ [dezãga'ʒe] (11) *v/t.* free from an engagement *or* an obligation.

désengorger ⊕ [dezãgɔr'ʒe] (11) *v/t.* unstop (*a pipe*).

désenivrer [dezãni'vre] (1a) *v/t.* sober (*s.o.*) (up).

désennuyer [dezãnɥi'je] (1h) *v/t.* amuse (*s.o.*); divert (*s.o.*); *se* ~ seek diversion (in *ger., à inf.*; *from, de*).

désenrayer ⊕ [dezãrɛ'je] (1i) *v/t.* release (*a brake etc.*).

désensibiliser [desãsibili'ze] (1a) *v/t.* desensitize.

désenvenimer 💊 [dezãvəni'me] (1a) *v/t.* cleanse (*a wound*).

déséquilibre [dezeki'libr] *m* lack of balance; unbalance; **déséquilibré, e** [dezekili'bre] unbalanced (*a. mind*); out of balance; **déséquilibrer** [ˌ˷] (1a) *v/t.* throw (*s.th.*) off balance; unbalance.

désert, e [de'zɛːr, ˷'zɛrt] **1.** *adj.* deserted; deserted (*island, country*); wild (*country*); lonely (*spot*); **2.** *su./ m* desert, wilderness; **déserter** [dezɛr'te] (1a) *v/t.* desert (*a.* 💥), forsake, abandon; *v/i.* 💥 desert; **déserteur** [ˌ˷'tœːr] *m* deserter; **désertion** [ˌ˷'sjɔ̃] *f* desertion. [lation.]

désescalade [dezɛskalad] *f* de-esca-╮

désespérant, e [dezɛspe'rã, ˷'rãːt] heart-breaking; disheartening; **désespéré, e** [˷'re] desperate; hopeless ; *être dans un état* ~ be past recovery; **désespérément** [ˌ˷re'mã] *adv.* desperately; **désespérer** [ˌ˷'re] (1f) *v/i.* despair (of, *de*); lose hope; lose heart; *v/t.* drive (*s.o.*) to despair; **désespoir** [dezɛs'pwaːr] *m* despair; desperation; *en* ~ *de cause* as a last resource.

désétatiser [dezetati'ze] (1a) *v/t.* denationalize; ⚡ *etc.* decontrol.

déshabillé [dezabi'je] *m* undress; *en* ~ in dishabille; in undress; **déshabiller** [~] (1a) *v/t.* undress, disrobe; strip (*a.* ✦).

déshabituer [dezabi'tɥe] (1n) *v/t.*: ~ q. de (*inf.*) break s.o. of the habit of (*ger.*); se ~ grow unused (to, *de*); break o.s. of the habit (of *ger., de inf.*).

déshériter [dezeri'te] (1a) *v/t.* disinherit; deprive; *les désherités* the underprivileged.

déshonnête [dezɔ'nɛt] improper, immodest; **déshonneur** [~'nœ:r] *m* dishono(u)r, disgrace; **déshonorant, e** [~nɔ'rɑ̃, ~'rɑ̃:t] dishono(u)ring, dishono(u)rable; degrading; disgraceful; **déshonorer** [~nɔ're] (1a) *v/t.* dishono(u)r, disgrace; disfigure (*a picture etc.*).

déshumaniser [dezymani'ze] (1a) *v/t.* dehumanize.

déshydrater ⚗ [dezidra'te] (1a) *v/t.* dehydrate.

désignation [deziɲa'sjɔ̃] *f* designation; appointment (as, *au poste de*); **désigner** [~'ɲe] (1a) *v/t.* designate, indicate; appoint.

désillusionner [dezillyzjɔ'ne] (1a) *v/t.* disillusion, undeceive.

désinence *gramm.* [dezi'nɑ̃:s] *f* ending.

désinfecter [dezɛ̃fɛk'te] (1a) *v/t.* disinfect; decontaminate.

désintégration [dezɛ̃tegra'sjɔ̃] *f* disintegration; *atom:* splitting; *rock:* weathering.

désintéressé, e [dezɛ̃terɛ'se] unselfish; disinterested, unbiased; **désintéressement** [~rɛs'mɑ̃] *m* impartiality; unselfishness; ✝ *partner:* buying out; ✝ *creditor:* paying off; **désintéresser** [~rɛ'se] (1a) *v/t.* ✝ buy out (*a partner*); ✝ pay off (*a creditor*); reimburse (*s.o.*); se ~ de lose interest in; take no part in; take no further interest in; **désintérêt** [~'rɛ] *m* disinterest, indifference.

désintoxiquer [dezɛ̃tɔksi'ke] (1a) *v/t.* ✿ detoxicate; treat for alcoholism *or* drug addiction.

désinvolte [dezɛ̃'vɔlt] free, easy (*bearing, gait*); off-hand, airy (*manner*); rakish; F cheeky (*reply*); **désinvolture** [~vɔl'ty:r] *f* ease, freedom (*of bearing*); off-handedness; F cheek.

désir [de'zi:r] *m* desire, wish; **désirable** [dezi'rabl] desirable; *peu* ~ undesirable; **désirer** [~'re] (1a) *v/t.* desire, wish, want; *laisser à* ~ leave much to be desired; **désireux, -euse** [~'rø, ~'rø:z] (*de*) desirous (of); eager (to).

désister [dezis'te] (1a) *v/t.*: se ~ de withdraw; desist from; renounce.

désobéir [dezɔbe'i:r] (2a) *v/i.*: ~ à disobey; **désobéissance** [~i'sɑ̃:s] *f* disobedience (to, *à*); **désobéissant, e** [~i'sɑ̃, ~'sɑ̃:t] disobedient.

désobligeant, e [dezɔbli'ʒɑ̃, ~'ʒɑ̃:t] disobliging, unfriendly; **désobliger** [~'ʒe] (1l) *v/t.* disoblige (*s.o.*); offend (*s.o.*).

désobstruer [dezɔpstry'e] (1a) *v/t.* free (*s.th.*) of obstructions; ⊕ clear (*a pipe*). [deodorant.]

désodorisant [dezɔdɔri'zɑ̃] *m*⟩

désœuvré, e [dezœ'vre] **1.** *adj.* idle, unoccupied; at a loose end; **2.** *su.* idler; **désœuvrement** [~vrə'mɑ̃] *m* idleness; leisure.

désolant, e [dezɔ'lɑ̃, ~'lɑ̃:t] sad, distressing; troublesome; **désolation** [~la'sjɔ̃] *f* desolation; grief; **désolé, e** [~'le] desolate; very sorry; **désoler** [~'le] (1a) *v/t.* desolate; lay waste; distress, grieve (*s.o.*).

désolidariser [desɔlidari'ze] (1a) *v/t.*: se ~ (*de*) dissociate o.s. (from).

désopilant, e F [dezɔpi'lɑ̃, ~'lɑ̃:t] side-splitting, screaming; **désopiler** *fig.* [~'le] (1a) *v/t.*: se ~ shake with laughter.

désordonné, e [dezɔrdɔ'ne] disorderly; untidy; excessive (*pride, appetite*); immoderate (*appetite*); dissolute (*life, man, etc.*); **désordre** [~'zɔrdr] *m* disorder (*a.* ✿), confusion; *fig.* dissoluteness; ~s *pl.* disturbances, riots; *vivre dans le* ~ lead a wild life.

désorganisation [dezɔrganiza'sjɔ̃] *f* disorganization.

désorienter [dezɔrjɑ̃'te] (1a) *v/t.* mislead; *fig.* bewilder, confuse, disconcert; puzzle; *fig. tout désorienté a.* at a loss, all at sea.

désormais [dezɔr'mɛ] *adv.* from now on, henceforth.

désossé, e [dezɔ'se] boned (*fish etc.*); F boneless, flabby (*person*); **désosser** [~] (1a) *v/t. cuis.* bone (*a fish etc.*); *fig.* take to pieces, dissect (*a book etc.*).

despote [dɛsˈpɔt] *m* despot; **despotique** [ˌpɔˈtik] despotic; **despotisme** [ˌpɔˈtism] *m* despotism.

dessaisir [desɛˈziːr] (2a) *v/t.* ⚖ dispossess; se ~ *de* part with, give up.

dessalé, e *fig.* [desaˈle] knowing, sharp (*person*); **dessaler** [ˌ] (1a) *v/t.* desalinate; *cuis.* soak (*fish*); *fig.* put (*s.o.*) up to a thing or two; *fig.* se ~ learn a thing or two.

dessécher [deseˈʃe] (1f) *v/t.* dry (up); wither (*a plant, a limb*); drain (*a swamp*); parch (*one's mouth*); sear (*the heart*); se ~ dry up; wither.

dessein [dɛˈsɛ̃] *m* design; scheme, plan; intention; à ~ intentionally, on purpose.

desseller [desɛˈle] (1a) *v/t.* unsaddle.

desserrer [desɛˈre] (1a) *v/t.* loosen (*the belt, a screw*); unclamp; unscrew (*a nut*); release (*the brake*); unclench (*one's fist, one's teeth*).

dessert [deˈsɛːr] *m* dessert; **desserte** [ˌˈsɛrt] *f* sideboard; *public transport:* service, servicing.

desservir[1] [desɛrˈviːr] (2b) *v/t.* clear (*the table*); clear (*s.th.*) away; (*a. ~ la table*) clear the table.

desservir[2] [ˌ] (2b) *v/t. public transport:* serve; call at (*a port*, 🚢 *a station*); *eccl.* minister to (*a parish*); lead (in)to (*road etc.*).

desservir[3] [ˌ] (2b) *v/t.* put (*s.o.*) at a disadvantage; harm (*s.o.'s*) interests.

dessiccatif, -ve [desikaˈtif, ˌˈtiːv] drying.

dessiller [desiˈje] *v/t.*: F ~ *les yeux à* (*or de*) *q.* open s.o.'s eyes (*to the truth*).

dessin [deˈsɛ̃] *m* drawing, sketch; △ *etc.* plan; ⊕ draughtsmanship; pattern, design; ~ *à main levée* free-hand drawing; *cin.* ~ *animé* (animated) cartoon; **dessinateur, -trice** [desinaˈtœːr, ˌˈtris] *su.* drawer, sketcher; designer; cartoonist; *su./m* ⊕ draughtsman; *su./f* ⊕ draughtswoman; **dessiner** [ˌˈne] (1a) *v/t.* draw, sketch; design (*material etc.*); lay out (*a garden*); outline; se ~ stand out, be outlined; appear; *fig.* take shape.

dessouder ⊕ [desuˈde] (1a) *v/t.* unsolder; reopen (*a welded seam etc.*).

dessouler [desuˈle] (1a) *v/t.* sober (up); *v/i. a.* se ~ sober up.

dessous [dəˈsu] **1.** *adv.* under(neath), beneath, below; *de* ~ underneath; *en* ~ underneath; *fig.* in an underhand way; **2.** *prp.*: *de* ~ from under; **3.** *su./m* underside, lower part; ~ *pl.* (*women's*) underclothing *sg.*, F undies; *fig.* seamy *or* shady side *sg.*; F *avoir le* ~ be defeated, get the worst of it; **~-de-bras** *cost.* [dəsudɑˈbra] *m/inv.* dress-shield.

dessus [dəˈsy] **1.** *adv.* above, over; on (it, them, *etc.*); *en* ~ at the top, above; *sens* ~ *dessous* in confusion, topsy-turvy; ⚓ *avoir le vent* ~ be aback; *fig.* mettre le doigt ~ hit the nail on the head; **2.** *prp.* † on, upon; *de* ~ from, (from) off; **3.** *su./m* top, upper side; ♩ treble; *thea.* ~ *pl.* flies; *avoir (prendre) le* ~ have (get) the upper hand, have (get) the best of it; ~ *de cheminée* mantelpiece; *fig.* le ~ *du panier* pick of the basket; **~-de-lit** [dəsydˈli] *m/inv.* bedspread, coverlet.

déstabiliser [destabiliˈze] (1a) *v/t.* destabilize, make unstable.

destin [dɛsˈtɛ̃] *m* fate, destiny; **destinataire** [destinaˈtɛːr] *su.* addressee; 🕇 *money order:* payee; *goods:* consignee; **destination** [ˌnaˈsjɔ̃] *f* destination; *à* ~ *de* 🚢 for, to; ⚓ bound for; *post:* addressed to; **destinée** [ˌˈne] *f* destiny; **destiner** [ˌˈne] (1a) *v/t.* destine; intend (for, *à*); se ~ *à* intend to take up, enter (*a profession*).

destituer [destiˈtɥe] (1n) *v/t.* dismiss, discharge; **destitution** [ˌtyˈsjɔ̃] *f* dismissal; removal.

destrier *poet.* [destriˈe] *m* charger, steed.

destroyer ⚓ [dɛstrwaˈjœːr] *m* destroyer.

destructeur, -trice [dɛstrykˈtœːr, ˌˈtris] **1.** *adj.* destructive; destroying; **2.** *su.* destroyer; **destructif, -ve** [ˌˈtif, ˌˈtiːv] destructive (of, *de*); **destruction** [ˌˈsjɔ̃] *f* destruction; demolition.

désuet, -ète [deˈsɥɛ, ˌˈsɥɛt] obsolete (*a. gramm.*), out-of-date; **désuétude** [ˌsɥeˈtyd] *f* disuse; *tomber en* ~ fall into disuse; ⚖ fall into abeyance (*law*), lapse (*right*).

désunion [dezyˈnjɔ̃] *f* disunion; *parts:* separation; *fig.* dissension; **désunir** [ˌˈniːr] (2a) *v/t.* disunite, divide; *fig.* set at variance.

détachant [deta'ʃɑ̃] *m* stain remover.

détachement [detaʃ'mɑ̃] *m* loosening; detachment (*a.* ✕); *fig.* indifference (to, *de*), unconcern.

détacher[1] [deta'ʃe] (1a) *v/t.* detach (*a.* ♪); undo, unfasten; separate; ✕ detail (*a company*); 🕮 uncouple; *fig.* estrange; se ~ come loose; part; stand out (against, *sur*).

détacher[2] [~] (1a) *v/t.* clean, remove stains from.

détail [de'ta:j] *m* detail; particular; *fig.* trifle; 🕇 retail; *marchand m en* ~ retailer; *vendre au* ~ retail; **détaillant** *m*, *e* *f* [deta'jɑ̃, ~'jɑ̃:t] retailer; **détailler** [~'je] (1a) *v/t.* enumerate; itemize (*an account*); relate in detail; cut up; 🕇 (sell) retail.

détaler F [de'ta'le] (1a) *v/i.* decamp, clear out.

détaxation [detaksa'sjɔ̃] *f* tax reduction *or* removal; **détaxe** [de'taks] *f* tax reduction *or* removal *or* refund; **détaxer** [detak'se] (1a) *v/t.* reduce *or* remove the tax on (*s.th.*).

détecteur ⚡ [detɛk'tœ:r] *m* radio: detector; ⚡ ~ *de fuites* fault-finder.

détective [detɛk'ti:v] *m* detective; *phot.* box-camera.

déteindre [de'tɛ̃:dr] (4m) *v/t.* remove the colo(u)r from; *v/i. a.* se ~ fade, lose colo(u)r; run, bleed (*colour*).

dételer [det'le] (1c) *v/t.* unharness; 🕮 uncouple; *v/i.* F stop (working); F knock off; *sans* ~ without a break.

détendre [de'tɑ̃:dr] (4a) *v/t.* loosen, slacken; *fig.* relax (*the mind*); steady (*one's nerves*); calm, reduce (*one's anger*); ⊕ expand (*steam*); se ~ slacken; relax.

détenir [det'ni:r] (2h) *v/t.* hold; detain (*goods, s.o., a.* ⚖).

détente [de'tɑ̃:t] *f* relaxation; slackening; *gun:* trigger; *pol.* détente; *fig.* improvement (*of relations*); ⊕ *steam:* expansion; *mot.* power stroke; *fig. dur à la* ~ close-fisted; *appuyer sur la* ~ press the trigger.

détenteur *m*, **-trice** *f* [detɑ̃'tœ:r, ~'tris] holder (*a. sp.*); detainer (*of goods, property*); **détention** [~'sjɔ̃] *f* detention, imprisonment; 🕇 holding; possession; withholding; ⚖ ~ *préventive* holding *or* remand in custody; ⚖ *maison f de* ~ remand home; house of detention; **détenu**, **e**

[det'ny] **1.** *p.p. of* détenir; **2.** *su.* prisoner.

détergent, **e** [detɛr'ʒɑ̃, ~'ʒɑ̃t] **1.** *adj.* detergent; **2.** *su./m* detergent; cleanser; **déterger** [~'ʒe] (11) *v/t.* cleanse.

détériorer [deterjɔ're] (1a) *v/t.* make worse; spoil; impair, damage; se ~ deteriorate; spoil.

déterminant [detɛrmi'nɑ̃] *m* ⚕ determinant; *gramm.* determiner; **détermination** [~na'sjɔ̃] *f* determination; *fig. a.* resolution; **déterminé**, **e** [~'ne] determined; definite, specific; *fig.* resolute; **déterminer** [~'ne] (1a) *v/t.* determine, settle; ascertain; induce; bring about; ~ q. *à* lead *or* induce s.o. to; ~ *de* (*inf.*) resolve to (*inf.*); se ~ make up one's mind (to *inf., à inf.*); resolve (upon s.th., *à qch.*).

déterrer [detɛ're] (1a) *v/t.* unearth (*a. fig.*); dig up; exhume (*a corpse*).

détersif, **-ve** [detɛr'sif, ~'si:v] *m* detergent; cleansing product.

détestable [detɛs'tabl] detestable, hateful; **détester** [~'te] (1a) *v/t.* hate; detest.

détonateur [detɔna'tœ:r] *m* detonator; *fig.* trigger; **détonation** [~na'sjɔ̃] *f* detonation; *gun:* report; **détoner** [~'ne] (1a) *v/i.* detonate, explode; *faire* ~ detonate; *mélange m détonant* detonating mixture.

détonner [detɔ'ne] (1a) *v/i.* ♪ sing *or* play out of tune; *fig.* clash (*colours*).

détordre [de'tɔrdr] (4a) *v/t.* untwist, unravel; unlay (*a rope*); **détors**, **e** [~'tɔ:r, ~'tɔrs] untwisted; unlaid (*rope*); **détortiller** [~tɔrti'je] (1a) *v/t.* untwist; disentangle.

détour [de'tu:r] *m* detour, roundabout way; ~*s pl.* curves, turns; *sans* ~ straightforward(ly *adv.*); *tours et* ~*s* ins and outs (*a. fig.*), nooks and corners.

détourné, **e** [detur'ne] roundabout (*way*), *fig. a.* indirect; *sentier m* ~ by-path; **détournement** [~nə'mɑ̃] *m* diversion; *money:* embezzlement; *funds:* misappropriation; ⚖ abduction (*of a minor*); ~ *d'avion* highjacking; **détourner** [~'ne] (1a) *v/t.* turn away; divert (*a river, the traffic, etc., fig. s.o.*); avert (*s.o.'s anger, a blow, one's eyes, etc.*); embezzle (*money*); misappropriate (*funds*); entice (*a wife from her husband, s.o. from his* duty); abduct (*a minor*); highjack (*an airplane*); se ~ de turn aside from.

détracteur *m*, **-trice** *f* [detrak'tœːr, ~'tris] detractor, maligner; slanderer.

détraqué, e [detra'ke] out of order; deranged (*mind*); shattered (*health*); F *il est* ~ he is out of his mind; **détraquer** [~] (1m) *v/t.* put out of order; throw (*a machine*) out of gear; *fig.* upset; se ~ break down; F go all to pieces (*person*).

détrempe [de'trãːp] *f* distemper; *metall.* annealing; **détremper** [~trã'pe] (1a) *v/t.* soak; dilute; *metall.* anneal.

détresse [de'trɛs] *f* distress.

détriment [detri'mã] *m* detriment, injury; *au* ~ *de* to the prejudice of.

détritus [detri'tys] *m* detritus, debris; refuse; rubbish.

détroit *geog.* [de'trwa] *m* strait(s *pl.*).

détromper [detrɔ̃'pe] (1a) *v/t.* undeceive, enlighten; F *détrompez-vous!* don't you believe it!; se ~ recognize one's error.

détrôner [detro'ne] (1a) *v/t.* dethrone; *fig.* replace, supersede.

détrousser [detru'se] (1a) *v/t.* rob (*s.o.*); **détrousseur** [~'sœːr] *m* highwayman, footpad.

détruire [de'trɥiːr] (4h) *v/t.* destroy (*a. fig.*); demolish (*buildings, a. arguments*).

dette [dɛt] *f* debt (*a. fig.*); ♀ *publique* National Debt; ~*s pl. actives* assets; ~*s pl. passives* liabilities.

deuil [dœ:j] *m* mourning (*a. clothes, a. time*); bereavement; *fig. faire son* ~ *de qch.* give s.th. up as lost, F say goodbye to s.th.; *porter le* ~ *de q.* mourn for s.o.

deux [dø] *adj./num., a. su./m/inv.* two; *date, title:* second; ~ *fois* twice; ~ *p* double p (*in spelling*); *à nous* ~ between us; *de* ~ *jours l'un, tous les* ~ *jours* every other day, on alternate days; *diviser en* ~ halve; *en* ~ in two (*pieces*); *Georges* ♀ George the Second; *le* ~ *mai* the second of May; *nous* ~ the two of us; *tous (les)* ~ both; **deuxième** [dø'zjɛm] **1.** *adj./num.* second; **2.** *su.* second; *su./m* second, *Am.* third floor; *su./f secondary school:* (*approx.*) fifth form.

deux...: ~**-pièces** [dø'pjɛs] *m* (woman's) two-piece suit; ~**-points**

[~'pwɛ̃] *m/inv.* colon; ~**-roues** [~'ru] *m/inv.* two-wheeled vehicle.

dévaler [deva'le] (1a) *vt/i.* run *or* rush down.

dévaliser [devali'ze] (1a) *v/t.* rob; rifle, burgle (*a house*).

dévalorisation ✝ [devalɔriza'sjɔ̃] *f currency:* devaluation; depreciation, fall in value; **dévaloriser** ✝ [~'ze] (1a) *v/t.* devaluate (*the currency*).

dévaluation ✝ [devalɥa'sjɔ̃] *f* devaluation; **dévaluer** ✝ [~'lɥe] (1n) *v/t.* devaluate.

devancer [dəvã'se] (1k) *v/t.* precede; outstrip, leave (*s.o.*) behind; *fig.* forestall; **devancier** *m*, **-ère** *f* [~'sje, ~'sjɛːr] precursor; predecessor; **devant** [də'vã] **1.** *adv.* in front, ahead, before; **2.** *prp.* in front of, before; ahead of; in the presence of (*s.o.*); *fig.* in the eyes of (*the law*); **3.** *su./m* front, forepart; *gagner les* ~*s* take the lead; *zo. patte f de* ~ foreleg; *prendre les* ~*s* make the first move, forestall the others *etc.*; **devanture** [~vã'tyːr] *f* front; shop window.

dévastateur, -trice [devasta'tœːr, -'tris] devastating; destructive; **dévaster** [~'te] (1a) *v/t.* devastate, lay waste, ravage, wreck.

déveinard F [devɛ'naːr] *m* a man whose luck is out; **déveine** F [~'vɛn] *f* (run of) ill-luck, bad *or* hard luck.

développement [devlɔp'mã] *m* development (*a. phot., a. ⅄*); *Å algebra:* expansion; *pays m en voie de* ~ developing country; **développer** [~lɔ'pe] (1a) *v/t.* develop; expand (*a. ⅄*); spread out; *fig.* amplify, unfold (*a plan*); se ~ develop, expand; spread out.

devenir [dəv'niːr] (2h) *v/i.* become; grow (*tall, sad, etc.*).

dévergondé, e [devɛrgɔ̃'de] **1.** *adj.* profligate; shameless; F extravagant (*style etc.*); **2.** *su.* profligate.

déverrouiller [devɛru'je] (1a) *v/t.* unbolt.

dévers [de'vɛːr] *m* slope, cant; *road:* banking; ⚙ cant, vertical slant.

déversement [devɛrsə'mã] *m water etc.:* discharge; *cart:* tilting; *refuse:* dumping.

déverser [devɛr'se] (1a) *v/t.* pour (out) (*water etc.*); dump (*refuse etc.*); tip (out); unload; *fig.* discharge, empty; se ~ pour, empty; **déversoir**

[~'swa:r] *m* overflow; overfall, waste-weir; *fig.* outlet.

dévêtir [devɛ'ti:r] (2g) *v/t.* undress; take off (*one's coat etc.*); *metall.* open up (*a mould*); se~ *de qch.* divest o.s. of s.th.

déviation [devja'sjɔ̃] *f road:* deviation, diversion; *compass:* variation; ⊕ *tool:* deflection; *fig.* deviation; **deviationniste** [~sjɔ'nist] *adj., a. su.* deviationist.

dévider [devi'de] (1a) *v/t. tex.* unwind; reel; *fig.* reel off; **dévideur** *m*, **-euse** *f tex.* [~'dœ:r, ~'dø:z] reeler; **dévidoir** [~'dwa:r] *m tex.* winder; ⚡ (cable-)drum.

dévier [de'vje] (1o) *v/i.* deviate, swerve; *faire* ~ deflect (*s.th.*); *fig.* divert (*the conversation*); *v/t.* deflect; turn aside (*a blow*); se ~ become crooked; warp (*wood*).

devin [də'vɛ̃] *m* soothsayer; **deviner** [~vi'ne] (1a) *v/t.* guess; foretell, foresee (*the future*); see through (*s.o.*); **devineresse** [~vin'rɛs] *f* fortune teller; **devinette** [dəvi'nɛt] *f* riddle, conundrum; **devineur** *m*, **-euse** *f* [~'nœ:r, ~'nø:z] guesser.

devis [də'vis] *m* estimate; tender.

dévisager [deviza'ʒe] (1l) *v/t.* stare at (*s.o.*).

devise [də'vi:z] *f* motto; ▨ device; ✝ currency; ✝ ~s *pl.* étrangères foreign currency *sg.*; **deviser** [~vi'ze] (1a) *v/i.* chat.

dévisser [devi'se] (1a) *v/t.* unscrew; *sl.* ~ *son billard* die, *sl.* peg out.

dévoiler [devwa'le] (1a) *v/t.* unveil; reveal (*a. fig.*).

devoir [də'vwa:r] **1.** (3a) *v/t.* owe; *v/aux.* have to, must; should, ought to, be to; *j'aurais dû le faire* I should have done it; *je devrais le faire* I ought to do it; **2.** *su./m* duty; *school:* home-work; exercise; ✝ debit; ~s *pl.* respects; *faire ses* ~s do one's homework; *rendre ses* ~s *à* pay one's respects to (*s.o.*).

dévolu, e [devɔ'ly] **1.** *adj.* (*à*) devolved (upon); *eccl.* lapsing (to); **2.** *su./m:* jeter son ~ *sur* have designs on; lay claim to; choose (*s.th.*).

dévorant, e [devɔ'rɑ̃, ~'rɑ̃:t] ravenous (*animal, a. fig.* hunger); consuming (*fire, a. fig. passion*); **dévorer** [~'re] (1a) *v/t.* devour; consume; squander (*a fortune*); F *mot.* ~ *l'espace* eat up the miles.

dévot, e [de'vo, ~'vɔt] **1.** *adj.* devout, pious; *pej.* sanctimonious; **2.** *su.* devout person; *pej.* sanctimonious person; *faux* ~ hypocrite; **dévotion** [~vo'sjɔ̃] *f* devotion; piety; **dévoué, e** [~'vwe] devoted; *votre tout* ~ yours faithfully *or* sincerely; **dévouement** [~vu'mɑ̃] *m* devotion (to, *à*), self-abnegation; **dévouer** [~'vwe] (1p) *v/t.* devote; dedicate.

devoyé, e [devwa'je] *adj., a. su.* delinquent; **dévoyer** [~] (1h) *v/t.* lead (*s.o.*) astray; se ~ go astray.

devrai [də'vre] *1st p. sg. fut. of* devoir 1.

dextérité [dɛksteri'te] *f* dexterity, ability, skill.

dextrose [dɛks'tro:z] *m* dextrose.

diabète ⚕ [dja'bɛt] *m* diabetes; **diabétique** ⚕ [~be'tik] *adj., a. su.* diabetic.

diable [dja:bl] *m* devil; ⊕ (stone-)lorry; trolley; porter's barrow, *Am.* porter's dolly; *comment* (*où, pourquoi*) ~ how (where, why) the devil; *au* ~ *vauvert* at the back of beyond; *bon* ~ not a bad fellow; *tirer le* ~ *par la queue* be hard up; **diablement** F [djablə'mɑ̃] *adv.* devilish; **diablerie** [~blə'ri] *f* devilry; F fun; mischievousness; **diablesse** F [~'blɛs] *f* she-devil; virago, shrew; **diablotin** [~blɔ'tɛ̃] *m imp* (*a.* F = *mischievous child*); cracker; **diabolique** [~bɔ'lik] fiendish, diabolic(al), devilish.

diacre *eccl.* [djakr] *m* deacon.

diadème [dja'dɛm] *m* diadem.

diagnose [djag'no:z] *f* ⚕ diagnosis; ⚕ diagnostics *sg.*; **diagnostic** ⚕ [djagnɔs'tik] *m* diagnosis (*of disease*); *faire le* ~ *de* diagnose; **diagnostique** ⚕ [~'tik] diagnostic; **diagnostiquer** [~ti'ke] (1m) *v/t.* diagnose.

diagonal, e *m/pl.* **-aux** [djagɔ'nal, ~'no] *adj., a.* ⅋ *su./f* diagonal.

diagramme [dja'gram] *m* diagram.

dialecte [dja'lɛkt] *m* dialect.

dialectique [djalɛk'tik] *f* dialectics *pl.*

dialogue [dja'lɔg] *m* dialog(ue); **dialoguer** [~lɔ'ge] (1m) *v/i.* converse, talk; *v/t.* write (*s.th.*) in dialog(ue) form.

diamant [dja'mɑ̃] *m* diamond; **diamanter** [~mɑ̃'te] (1a) *v/t.* set with diamonds; ⊕ diamondize; **dia-**

mantin, e [⁓mɑ̃'tɛ̃,⁓'tin] diamond-like.

diamètre ⚗ [dja'mɛtr] *m* diameter.

diane [djan] *f* ✗ reveille; ⚓ morning watch.

diantre! † [djɑ̃:tr] *int.* deuce!; *sl.* hell!

diapason ♪ [djapa'zɔ̃] *m* diapason, pitch; tuning-fork; *voice:* range; *fig.* au ⁓ (de) in harmony *or* tune (with).

diaphane [dja'fan] diaphanous; transparent.

diaphragme [dja'fragm] *m* ⊕, *anat.* diaphragm; *phot.* diaphragm stop; *gramophone:* sound-box; **diaphragmer** [⁓frag'me] (1a) *v/t.* provide with a diaphragm; *phot.* stop down (*the lens*).

diapositive *phot.* [djapɔzi'ti:v] *f* transparency.

diapré, e [dja'pre] variegated, mottled.

diarrhée 🩺 [dja're] *f* diarrhoea.

diatomique ⚗ [diatɔ'mik] diatomic.

diatribe [dja'trib] *f* diatribe; harangue.

dictaphone [dikta'fɔn] *m* dictaphone.

dictateur [dikta'tœ:r] *m* dictator; *de* ⁓ dictatorial (*tone, attitude, etc.*); **dictature** [⁓'ty:r] *f* dictatorship; **dictée** [⁓'te] *f* dictation; **dicter** [⁓'te] (1a) *v/t.* dictate (*a. fig.*); **diction** [⁓'sjɔ̃] *f* diction; delivery; style; **dictionnaire** [⁓sjɔ'nɛ:r] *m* dictionary; lexicon; ⁓ ambulant walking dictionary; **dicton** [⁓'tɔ̃] *m* saying; proverb.

dièse ♪ [djɛ:z] *m* sharp.

diesel ⊕ [di'zɛl] *m* diesel engine; *équiper de moteurs* ⁓s dieselize.

diéser ♪ [dje'ze] (1f) *v/t.* sharp(en) (*a note*).

diète 🩺 [djɛt] *f* diet (*a. pol.*), regimen; ⁓ absolue starvation diet; **diététique** [djete'tik] dietary.

dieu [djø] *m* god; ♀ God; ♀ *merci* thank God; F thank heaven; *à* ♀ *ne plaise* God forbid; *grâce à* ♀ thanks be to God; *by God's grace; mon* ♀! good heavens!; dear me!; *pour l'amour de* ♀ for Christ's sake.

diffamant, e 🏛 [difa'mɑ̃, ⁓'mɑ̃:t] defamatory; libellous; slanderous; **diffamateur** *m*, **-trice** *f* 🏛 [difama'tœ:r, ⁓'tris] defamer; libeller; slanderer; **diffamation** 🏛 [⁓'sjɔ̃] *f* defamation; ⁓ *écrite* libel; ⁓ *orale*

slander; **diffamatoire** [⁓'twa:r] defamatory; libellous; slanderous; **diffamer** [difa'me] (1a) *v/t.* defame; slander; libel.

différemment [difera'mɑ̃] *adv. of* *différent*; **différence** [⁓'rɑ̃:s] *f* difference; *à la* ⁓ *de* unlike; **différencier** [⁓rɑ̃'sje] (1o) *v/t.* differentiate (*a.* ⚗) (from *de, d'avec*); distinguish (between, *entre*); **différend** [⁓'rɑ̃] *m* dispute; quarrel; difference; **différent, e** [⁓'rɑ̃, ⁓'rɑ̃:t] different; distinct (from, *de*); **différentiel, -elle** [⁓rɑ̃'sjɛl] *adj., a. mot. su./m, a.* ⚗ *su./f* differential; **différer** [⁓'re] (1f) *v/t.* postpone, put off, defer; delay; *v/i.* differ (from, *de*).

difficile [difi'sil] **1.** *adj.* difficult (*a. fig.*); *fig.* hard to please; **2.** *su./m*: *faire le* ⁓ be hard to please; *be* squeamish; **difficulté** [⁓kyl'te] *f* difficulty; *faire des* ⁓s create obstacles, make difficulties, raise objections; **difficultueux, -euse** [⁓kyl'tɥø, ⁓'tɥø:z] over-particular, fussy; squeamish; *fig.* thorny (*business, enterprise*).

difforme [di'fɔrm] deformed; misshapen; **difformité** [⁓fɔrmi'te] *f* deformity, malformation.

diffracter *opt.* [difrak'te] (1a) *v/t.* diffract.

diffus, e [di'fy, ⁓'fy:z] diffused (*light*); *fig.* diffuse (*style etc.*); *éclairs m/pl.* ⁓ sheet lightning *sg.*; **diffuser** [dify'ze] (1a) *v/t.* diffuse (*heat, light*); *radio, rumour:* broadcast; **diffuseur** [⁓'zœ:r] *m* ⊕ spray nozzle; *radio:* broadcaster (*person*); *radio:* cone loud-speaker; **diffusion** [⁓'zjɔ̃] *f* heat, light, news, germs: diffusion; *news:* spreading; *radio:* broadcasting; *disease, germs:* spread; *fig. style:* prolixity, diffuseness.

digérer [diʒe're] (1f) *v/t.* digest (*food, news*); *fig.* swallow (*an insult*); **digestif, -ve** [diʒɛs'tif, ⁓'ti:v] *adj., a. su./m* digestive; **digestion** [⁓'tjɔ̃] *f* digestion.

digital, e, *m/pl.* **-aux** [diʒi'tal, ⁓'to] **1.** *adj.* digital; *empreinte f* ⁓e fingerprint; **2.** *su./f* ♀ digitalis, foxglove.

digne [diɲ] worthy, deserving; dignified (*air*); ⁓ *d'éloges* praiseworthy; **dignitaire** [diɲi'tɛ:r] *m* dignitary; **dignité** [⁓'te] *f* dignity.

digression [digrɛ'sjɔ̃] *f* digression (*a. astr.*).

digue [dig] *f* dike, dam, embankment; jetty; sea-wall; breakwater; *fig.* barrier.

dilapider [dilapi'de] (1a) *v/t.* squander (*a fortune, money*); misappropriate (*trust funds*).

dilatation [dilata'sjɔ̃] *f eye:* dilation; expansion (*a.* △, ⌐ₘ, ⊕ *truck*); *stomach:* distension; **dilater** [∼'te] (1a) *v/t.* dilate, expand; distend (*the stomach*); *fig.* ∼ le cœur gladden the heart; se ∼ dilate, expand; become distended; **dilatoire** ⚖, *a. fig.* [∼'twa:r] dilatory.

dilection [dilɛk'sjɔ̃] *f* dilection; loving-kindness.

dilemme [di'lɛm] *m* dilemma.

dilettante [dilɛt'tɑ̃:t] *su.* dilettante, amateur; **dilettantisme** [dilɛtɑ̃-'tism] *m* dilettantism, amateurism; amateurishness.

diligence † [dili'ʒɑ̃:s] *f* diligence, industry; speed, haste; stage-coach; **diligent, e** [∼'ʒɑ̃, ∼'ʒɑ̃:t] diligent, industrious; speedy; prompt.

diluer [di'lɥe] (1n) *v/t.* dilute (with, *de*); water down; **dilution** [∼ly'sjɔ̃] *f* dilution.

diluvien, -enne [dily'vjɛ̃, ∼'vjɛn] diluvial (*clay, deposit*); diluvian (*fossil*); *fig.* torrential (*rain*).

dimanche [di'mɑ̃:ʃ] *m* Sunday.

dîme [dim] *f* tithe.

dimension [dimɑ̃'sjɔ̃] *f* dimension (*a. fig.*); size; *fig. a.* importance, weight; *prendre les* ∼s *de* measure out; *fig.* understand, seize; *fig.* become, grow *or* develop into.

dîmer [di'me] (1a) *v/i.* levy tithes.

diminuer [dimi'nɥe] (1n) *vt/i.* lessen, diminish; reduce; *v/i.* ↟ go down; abate (*fever, flood*); ⚓ ∼ de *toile* shorten sail; **diminution** [∼ny'sjɔ̃] *f* diminution; reduction (*a. price*); ↟ rebate (*on account*); *dress:* shortening; abatement.

dinanderie [dinɑ̃'dri] *f* brass-ware, copper-ware.

dinde [dɛ̃:d] *f* turkey-hen; *cuis.* turkey; *fig.* stupid woman; **dindon** [dɛ̃'dɔ̃] *m* turkey-cock; *fig.* fool; **dindonneau** [dɛ̃dɔ'no] *m* young turkey; **dindonnier** *m*, **-ère** *f* [∼'nje, ∼'njɛ:r] turkey-keeper.

dîner [di'ne] **1.** (1a) *v/i.* dine, have dinner; **2.** *su./m* dinner(-party);

∼-**débat**, *pl.* ∼s-**débats** [∼nede'ba] *m* working dinner; **dînette** [∼'nɛt] *f* snack (meal); **dîneur, -euse** [∼'nœ:r, ∼'nø:z] *su.* diner; *su./m:* F *un beau* ∼ a good trencherman.

dingo [dɛ̃:go] **1.** *su./m zo.* dingo; **2.** *adj. sl.* crazy, nuts.

dingue *sl.* [dɛ̃:g] **1.** *adj.* crazy, nuts; **2.** *su.* crackpot, loony.

dinguer *sl.* [dɛ̃'ge] (1m) *v/i.: aller* ∼ drop; crash down (*things*), go sprawling (*person*); *envoyer* ∼ send (*s.o.*) packing; send (*s.th.*) flying.

diocèse *eccl.* [djo'sɛ:z] *m* diocese.

dioptrie *phys., opt.* [djɔp'tri] *f* diopter.

diphtérie 𝒮 [difte'ri] *f* diphtheria.

diphtongue *gramm.* [dif'tɔ̃:g] *f* diphthong.

diplomate [diplɔ'mat] *m* diplomat (*a. fig.*); **diplomatie** [∼ma'si] *f* diplomacy (*a. fig.*); diplomatic service; **diplomatique** [∼ma'tik] **1.** *adj.* diplomatic; **2.** *su./f* diplomatics *pl.*; pal(a)eography.

diplôme [di'plo:m] *m* diploma; certificate; **diplômé, e** [∼plo'me] **1.** *adj.* certificated; *ingénieur m* ∼ qualified engineer; **2.** *su.* (*approx.*) graduate.

dire [di:r] **1.** *v/t.* (4p) say; tell; recite (*a poem*); show, reveal; ∼ à q. *de* (*inf.*) tell s.o. to (*inf.*); ∼ du mal *de* speak ill of; ∼ *que oui* (*non*) say yes (no); F *à qui le dites-vous?* don't I know it!; *sl.* you're telling me!; *à vrai* ∼ to tell the truth; *cela ne me dit rien* that conveys nothing to me; it doesn't appeal to me; *cela va sans* ∼ it goes without saying; *c'est-à-*∼ that is to say, i.e.; in other words; *c'est tout* ∼ I need say no more; *dites donc!* I say!; *on dirait que* one (you) would think that; *on le dit riche* he is said to be rich; *on dit* people say; it is said; *pour tout* ∼ in a word; *qu'en dites-vous?* what is your opinion?; *sans mot* ∼ without a word; se ∼ claim to be; be used (*word*); *vouloir* ∼ mean; *vous l'avez dit* exactly; *Am.* F you said it; **2.** *su./m* statement; ⚖ allegation; *au* ∼ *de* according to.

direct, e [di'rɛkt] **1.** *adj.* direct; straight; 🚂 through (*train, ticket*); **2.** *su./m* 🚂 through *or* express train; *radio, telev.:* live broadcast; *en* ∼ live (*broadcast, a. fig.*); *box.* ∼ *du droit*

straight right; **directement** [dirɛk-tǝmɑ̃] directly; straight (away).
directeur, -trice [dirɛk'tœːr, ~'tris] **1.** *su.*/*m* director, manager; *school*: headmaster; principal; *prison*: warden; *journ.* editor; *eccl.* ~ de conscience confessor; ✝ ~ **gérant** managing director; *su.*/*f* directress; manageress; *school*: headmistress; **2.** *adj.* directing, controlling; guiding (*principle*); ⊕ driving; *mot.* steering (*wheel*); **direction** [~'sjɔ̃] *f* direction; *enterprise, war*: conduct; ✝ management; ✝ manager's office; ✝ board of directors; *school*: headship; ⊕ driving; ⊕ steering; course, route; en ~ de bound *or* heading for, ...bound; *train* m en ~ de train for; **directive** [~'tiːv]*f* directive;~s *pl. a.* guidelines; **directoire** [~'twaːr] *m eccl.* directory; *hist.* ♀ Directory; **directrice** [~'tris] *f see directeur.*
dirigeable [diri'ʒabl] **1.** *adj.* dirigible; *antenne f* ~ directional aerial; **2.** *su.*/*m* airship; **dirigeant** [~'ʒɑ̃] *m* ruler, leader; **diriger** [~'ʒe] (1l) *v/t.* direct; ✝ *etc.* manage, F run; *mot.* drive; ⚓, *mot.* steer; ⚓ sail; ♩ conduct; aim (a gun, a. fig. remarks); *journ.* edit; se ~ vers make one's way towards, make for; **dirigisme** *pol.* [~'ʒism] *m* planning, planned economy.
dis [di] *1st p. sg. pres. and p.s. of dire* 1.
discernement [disɛrnǝ'mɑ̃] *m* discernment; discrimination (between...and,de...et de); **discerner** [~'ne] (1a) *v/t.* discern, make out; distinguish, discriminate (between s.th. and s.th., qɛh. de qch.).
disciple [di'sipl] *m* disciple, follower; **discipline** [disi'plin] *f* discipline; *eccl.* scourge; ✗ *compagnie f de* ~ disciplinary company; **discipliner** [~pli'ne] (1a) *v/t.* discipline; *school*: bring under control. [lus.]
discobole *sp.* [disko'bɔl] *m* discobo-/
discontinu, e [diskɔ̃ti'ny] discontinuous; **discontinuer** [~'nɥe] (1n) *vt/i.* discontinue, stop; *sans* ~ without stopping; at a stretch.
disconvenance [diskɔ̃v'nɑ̃ːs] *f* unsuitability; disparity; **disconvenir** [~'niːr] (2h) *v/i.*: ~ de deny; ~ que (*sbj.*) deny that (*ind.*).
discophile [disko'fil] *su.* (gramophone) record fan.

discordance [diskɔr'dɑ̃ːs] *f sounds*: discordance; *opinions etc.*: disagreement, conflict; **discordant, e** [~'dɑ̃, ~'dɑ̃ːt] discordant (*sounds*); conflicting (*opinions etc.*); ♩ out of tune (*instrument*); *geol.* unconformable; **discorde** [dis'kɔrd] *f* discord, dissension; **discorder** [~kɔr'de] (1a) *v/i.* ♩ be discordant; clash (*colours*); disagree (*persons*).
discothèque [diskɔ'tɛk] *f* record library; record collection; disco(thèque).
discoureur *m*, **-euse** *f* [disku'rœːr, ~'røːz] speechifier; talkative person; **discourir** [~'riːr] (2i) *v/i.* discourse; **discours** [dis'kuːr] *m* speech (*a. gramm.*); discourse; talk; language; ~ *improvisé* extempore speech; ~ *inaugural* inaugural address, *Am.* inaugural; *faire un* ~ make a speech; *gramm. partie f du* ~ part of speech.
discourtois, e [diskur'twa, ~'twaːz] discourteous, rude, unmannerly.
discrédit [diskre'di] *m* discredit, disrepute; **discréditer** [~di'te] (1a) *v/t.* bring into discredit; disparage.
discret, -ète [dis'krɛ, ~'krɛt] discreet; ♰, ♫ discrete; cautious; tactful; quiet (*dress, taste, village, etc.*); modest (*request*); *sous pli* ~ under plain cover; **discrétion** [diskre'sjɔ̃] *f* discretion; prudence; tact; à ~ at will; unlimited; ✗ unconditional (*surrender*); *être à la* ~ de be at the disposal of; be at the mercy of; **discrétionnaire** ♰♣ [~sjɔ'nɛːr] discretionary.
discrimination [diskrimina'sjɔ̃] *f* discrimination, differentiation; ~ *raciale* racial discrimination.
disculper [diskyl'pe] (1a) *v/t.* clear (s.o. of s.th., q. de qch.).
discussion [disky'sjɔ̃] *f* discussion, debate; argument; **discuter** [~'te] (1a) *v/t.* discuss, debate; question; ♰♣ sell up (a debtor).
disert, e [di'zɛːr, ~'zɛrt] eloquent.
disette [di'zɛt] *f* scarcity, dearth; shortage (of, de).
diseur, -euse [di'zœːr, ~'zøːz] *su.* speaker, reciter; talker; *su.*/*f thea.* diseuse; ~*euse de bonne aventure* fortune-teller.
disgrâce [dis'grɑːs] *f* disgrace, disfavo(u)r; misfortune; **disgracié, e** [disgra'sje] out of favo(u)r; **disgra-**

cier [~'sje] (1o) *v/t.* dismiss from favo(u)r; disgrace; **disgracieux, -euse** [~'sjø, ~'sjø:z] uncouth, awkward; ungracious (*reply*).

disjoindre [dis'ʒwɛ̃:dr] (4m) *v/t.* sever, separate; *se* ~ come apart; break up; **disjoncteur** ≠ [disʒɔ̃-'tœːr] *m* circuit-breaker; switch (-board); **disjonctif, -ve** *gramm.* [~'tif, ~'tiːv] disjunctive; **disjonction** [~'sjɔ̃] *f* sundering, separation; ⚡ severance.

dislocation [dislɔka'sjɔ̃] *f* ⊕ taking down; ✕ breaking up (*of troops*); ✗ dislocation; *fig.* dismemberment; *geol.* fault; **disloquer** [~'ke] (1m) *v/t.* ✕ break up; ✗ dislocate; *fig.* dismember; disperse; *geol.* fault.

disons [di'zɔ̃] *1st p. pl. pres. of dire 1.*

disparaître [dispa'rɛːtr] (4k) *v/i.* disappear; vanish.

disparate [dispa'rat] **1.** *adj.* ill-assorted, ill-matched; dissimilar; **2.** *su./f* disparity; *colours:* clash; incongruity; **disparité** [~ri'te] *f* disparity.

disparition [dispari'sjɔ̃] *f* disappearance.

dispendieux, -euse [dispã'djø, ~'djø:z] expensive.

dispensaire ✗ [dispã'sɛːr] *m* community clinic; *hospital:* surgery; outpatients' department; **dispensateur** *m*, **-trice** *f* [~pãsa'tœːr, ~'tris] distributor; **dispense** [~'pãːs] *f* exemption; certificate of exemption; *eccl.* dispensation; **dispenser** [~pã'se] (1a) *v/t.* dispense; exempt, excuse (from, *de*); *se* ~ *de* avoid, get out of.

disperser [disper'se] (1a) *v/t.* disperse, scatter; **dispersion** [~'sjɔ̃] *f* dispersion; breaking up; ≠ dissipation; ✕ rout; *phys. light:* scattering.

disponibilité [disponibili'te] *f* availability; disposal; release; ~*s pl.* available funds *or* means *or* time *sg.*; *en* ~ unattached; **disponible** [~'nibl] *f* disposable; available; spare (*time*); ✕ unattached.

dispos, e [dis'po, ~'po:z] fit, in good form; all right; alert (*mind*).

disposer [dispo'ze] (1a) *v/t.* dispose, arrange, lay out; *se* ~ (*à*) prepare (for *s.th.*; to *inf.*); *v/i.:* ~ *de* dispose of; have at one's disposal; ~ *pour* apply to; *vous pouvez* ~ you may go;

dispositif [~zi'tif] *m* ⊕ device, appliance; system; plan; **disposition** [~zi'sjɔ̃] *f* disposition; arrangement; disposal; state (*of mind*), frame of mind; tendency (to, *à*); ~*s pl.* talent *sg.*; *à la* ~ *de q.* at s.o.'s disposal; *à votre entière* ~ *a.* entirely at your service.

disproportion [disprɔpɔr'sjɔ̃] *f* disproportion; **disproportionné, e** [~sjɔ'ne] disproportionate.

dispute [dis'pyt] *f* dispute, quarrel; *chercher* ~ *à* pick a quarrel with; **disputer** [~py'te] (1a) *vt/i.* dispute; contend; *v/i.* argue, quarrel; *v/t. sp.* play (*a match*); fight for (*victory*); F tell (*s.o.*) off; ~ *qch. à q.* contend with s.o. for s.th.; F *se* ~ argue, quarrel, have an argument; **disputeur, -euse** [~py'tœːr, ~'tø:z] **1.** *adj.* contentious, quarrelsome; **2.** *su.* arguer, wrangler.

disquaire [dis'kɛːr] *m* record dealer *or* seller.

disqualifier *sp.* [diskali'fje] (1o) *v/t.* disqualify.

disque [disk] *m* disk; *sp.* discus; 🚦 signal; ⊕ plate; (gramophone) record, album, disc, *Am.* disk; ~*s pl. des auditeurs radio:* listener's requests; *teleph.* ~ *d'appel* dial; ~ *de longue durée*, ~ *microsillon* long-playing record, F long-player; *mot.* ~ *de stationnement* parking disc; *changeur m de* ~*s* record changer.

dissection [disɛk'sjɔ̃] *f* dissection.

dissemblable [disã'blabl] *adj.:* ~ *à* (*or de*) dissimilar to (*s.th.*), unlike (*s.th.*); **dissemblance** [~'blã:s] *f* dissimilarity.

disséminer [disemi'ne] (1a) *v/t.* spread; scatter; disseminate.

dissension [disã'sjɔ̃] *f* discord, dissension; **dissentiment** [~ti'mã] *m* disagreement, dissent.

disséquer [dise'ke] (1s) *v/t.* dissect.

dissertation [disɛrta'sjɔ̃] *f* dissertation; essay; **disserter** [~'te] (1a) *v/i.* discourse (on, *sur*), F hold forth.

dissidence *eccl. etc.* [disi'dã:s] *f* dissidence, dissent; **dissident, e** *eccl.*, *pol.* [~'dã, ~'dã:t] **1.** *adj.* dissident; dissenting; **2.** *su.* dissentient; *eccl.* nonconformist, dissenter.

dissimilitude [disimili'tyd] *f* dissimilarity.

dissimulation [disimyla'sjɔ̃] *f* dis-

sembling, dissimulation; concealment, cover-up; **dissimulé, e** [ᴗ'le] *fig.* hidden; secretive, double-dealing, dissembling; **dissimuler** [ᴗ'le] (1a) *v/t.* conceal, hide; cover up; se ᴗ hide; *vt/i.* dissemble.
dissipateur, -trice [disipa'tœːr, ᴗ'tris] **1.** *su.* spendthrift; **2.** *adj.* wasteful; **dissipation** [ᴗpa'sjɔ̃] *f* dissipation (*a. fig.*); waste; inattention; *school:* fooling; **dissiper** [ᴗ'pe] (1a) *v/t.* dissipate; waste (*money, time*); disperse, dispel (*clouds, fear, a suspicion*); clear up (*a misunderstanding*); divert; se ᴗ disappear; amuse o.s.; *fig.* become dissipated; be inattentive (*pupil*).
dissocier [disɔ'sje] (1o) *v/t.* dissociate.
dissolu, e [disɔ'ly] dissolute; **dissoluble** [ᴗ'lybl] 🔧 soluble; 🔧 dissolvable; **dissolution** [ᴗly'sjɔ̃] *f* 🔧 dissolving; 🔧 solution; ⚖ *a. parl.* dissolution; disintegration; dissoluteness; **dissolvant, e** [disɔl'vɑ̃, ᴗ'vɑ̃ːt] **1.** *adj.* solvent; **2.** *su./m* solvent; ᴗ de vernis à ongles nail-varnish remover.
dissonance [disɔ'nɑ̃ːs] *f* ♪, *a. fig.* dissonance; *fig. a.* clash, discord; **dissonant, e** [ᴗ'nɑ̃, ᴗ'nɑ̃ːt] dissonant; discordant, clashing, jarring.
dissoudre [di'sudr] (4bb) *v/t.* dissolve; ⚖ annul (*a marriage*); **dissous, -te** [ᴗ'su, ᴗ'sut] *p.p.* of dissoudre.
dissuader [disɥa'de] (1a) *v/t.* dissuade (from [doing] s.th., de [*faire*] qch.); **dissuasion** [ᴗ'zjɔ̃] *f* dissuasion; ⚔ arme *f* de ᴗ deterrent weapon.
distance [dis'tɑ̃ːs] *f* distance; *time:* interval; *mot.* ᴗ d'arrêt braking distance; ⚔ ᴗ de tir range; *opt.* ᴗ focale focal length; ⊕ commande *f* à ᴗ remote control; tenir à ᴗ keep (s.o.) at arm's length; **distancer** [ᴗtɑ̃'se] (1k) *v/t.* outrun, outstrip; *fig.* se laisser ᴗ lag behind; **distant, e** [ᴗ'tɑ̃, ᴗ'tɑ̃ːt] distant; *fig. a.* aloof.
distendre ⚕ [dis'tɑ̃ːdr] (4a) *v/t.* distend; pull, strain (*a muscle*); **distension** ⚕ [ᴗtɑ̃'sjɔ̃] *f* distension; *muscle:* straining.
distiller [disti'le] (1a) *v/t.* 🔧, ⊕ distil; ⊕ condense (*water*); *fig.* exude; **distillerie** [ᴗtil'ri] *f* distillery; *trade:* distilling.

distinct, e [dis'tɛ̃(ːkt), ᴗ'tɛ̃ːkt] distinct; separate; clear; **distinctif, -ve** [ᴗtɛ̃k'tif, ᴗ'tiːv] distinctive, characteristic; **distinction** [ᴗtɛ̃k'sjɔ̃] *f* distinction; difference; discrimination; refinement; polished manner.
distingué, e [distɛ̃'ge] distinguished; eminent; refined; smart (*appearance, dress*); sentiments *m/pl.* ᴗs yours truly; **distinguer** [ᴗ] (1m) *v/t.* distinguish; make out; single out; hono(u)r; se ᴗ distinguish o.s.; *fig.* stand out; **distinguo** [ᴗ'go] *m* distinction.
distique [dis'tik] *m Greek or Latin:* dìstich; *French verse:* couplet.
distordre [dis'tɔrdr] (4a) *v/t.* distort; twist (*the ankle etc.*); **distors, e** [ᴗ'tɔːr, ᴗ'tɔrs] distorted (*limb*); **distorsion** [ᴗtɔr'sjɔ̃] *f* distortion.
distraction [distrak'sjɔ̃] *f* absent-mindedness; inattention, distraction; amusement, recreation; ✝ appropriation; ⚖ misappropriation (*of funds*).
distraire [dis'trɛːr] (4ff) *v/t.* separate; ✝ set aside, appropriate; ⚖ misappropriate (*funds etc.*); amuse, entertain; distract (*s.o.'s attention*); **distrait, e** [ᴗ'trɛ, ᴗ'trɛt] inattentive; absent-minded; piéton *m* ᴗ jay-walker.
distribuer [distri'bɥe] (1n) *v/t.* distribute; give out; hand out; deal out; *post:* deliver (*letters*); deal (*cards*); **distributeur, -trice** [ᴗby'tœːr, ᴗ'tris] *su.* distributor; *su./m* ⊕ distributor; booking-clerk, *Am.* ticket agent, ticket clerk; ᴗ (*automatique*) (slot *or* vending) machine; **distribution** [ᴗby'sjɔ̃] *f* distribution; giving out. out; *post:* delivery; *thea.* cast(ing).
district [dis'trik(t)] *m* district, region; *fig.* province.
dit, dite [di, dit] **1.** *p.p.* of dire 1; **2.** *adj.* so-called; autrement ᴗ in other words; **dites** [dit] *2nd p. pl. pres.* of dire 1.
diurétique ⚕ [diyre'tik] *adj., a. su./m* diuretic.
diurne [diyrn] diurnal; day-(*bird*).
divagation [divaga'sjɔ̃] *f* wandering; *fig.* digression; **divaguer** [ᴗ'ge] (1m) *v/i.* wander; *fig.* digress; F ramble, rave. [couch.\
divan [di'vɑ̃] *m* divan; (studio)∫

divergence [diver'ʒɑ̃:s] f divergence (a. ♉, ♀); fig. difference; **diverger** [∼'ʒe] (1l) v/i. diverge, branch off; fig. differ.

divers, e [di'vɛ:r, ∼'vɛrs] diverse, miscellaneous; various; sundry; **diversifier** [diversi'fje] (1o) v/t. diversify, vary; **diversion** [∼'sjɔ̃] f diversion (a. ✗); change; **diversité** [∼si'te] f diversity; variety.

divertir [diver'ti:r] (2a) v/t. divert; amuse; entertain; ✝ misappropriate (funds); **divertissement** [∼tis-'mɑ̃] m entertainment, amusement; pastime; ✝ funds: misappropriation; thea. divertissement.

divette [di'vɛt] f light opera, music hall: singer.

dividende ✝, ♉ [divi'dɑ̃:d] m dividend.

divin, e [di'vɛ̃, ∼'vin] divine (a. fig.); holy; godlike; **divinateur, -trice** [divina'tœ:r, ∼'tris] **1.** su. soothsayer; diviner; **2.** adj. prophetic; **divination** [∼'sjɔ̃] f divination (a. fig.), soothsaying; **divinatoire** [∼'twa:r] diving-...; baguette f ∼ dowsing-rod; **diviniser** [divini'ze] (1a) v/t. deify; fig. glorify; **divinité** [∼'te] f divinity; deity.

diviser [divi'ze] (1a) v/t. divide (a. ♉); separate (from, d'avec); **diviseur** [∼'zœ:r] m ✗ etc. divider; ♉ divisor; ♉ commun ∼ common factor; **divisible** [∼'zibl] divisible; **division** [∼'zjɔ̃] f division (a. ♉, ✗, ⚓, school); section; admin. department; fig. dissension, discord; ♪ double bar; typ. hyphen; biol. ∼ binaire (or cellulaire) binary fission; ∼ du travail division of labo(u)r.

divorce [di'vɔrs] m divorce (a. fig.); fig. disagreement; ⚖ former une demande en ∼ seek a divorce; **divorcer** ⚖ [∼vɔr'se] (1k) v/i. divorce (s.o., [d']avec q.); fig. break (with, [d']avec).

divulgation [divylga'sjɔ̃] f divulgence, disclosure; **divulguer** [∼'ge] (1m) v/t. divulge, disclose, reveal.

dix [dis; before consonant di; before vowel and h mute diz] adj./num., a. su./m/inv. ten; date, title: tenth; **∼-huit** [di'zɥit; before consonant ∼'zɥi] adj./num., a. su./m/inv. eighteen; date, title: eighteenth; **dix-huitième** [∼zɥi'tjɛm] adj./num., a. su. eighteenth; **dixième** [∼'zjɛm]

1. adj./num., a. su., a. su./m fraction: tenth; **dix-neuf** [diz'nœf; before vowel and h mute ∼'nœv] adj./num., a. su./m/inv. nineteen; date, title: nineteenth; **dix-neuvième** [∼nœ'vjɛm] adj./num., a. su. nineteenth; **dix-sept** [dis'sɛt] adj./num., a. su./m/inv. seventeen; date, title: seventeenth; **dix-septième** [∼sɛ-'tjɛm] adj./num., a. su. seventeenth.

dizain [di'zɛ̃] m ten-line stanza; rosary: decade; **dizaine** [∼'zɛn] f (about) ten, half a score; dans la ∼ within ten days.

do ♪ [do] m/inv. do, note: C.

docile [dɔ'sil] docile; amenable; submissive; **docilité** [∼sili'te] f docility; obedience; meekness.

dock [dɔk] m ⚓ dock(yard); ✝ warehouse; **docker** [dɔ'kɛ:r] m docker.

docte [dɔkt] learned (a. iro.).

docteur [dɔk'tœ:r] m doctor; physician; **doctoral, e** [dɔktɔ'ral, ∼'ro] doctoral; fig. pedantic; **doctorat** [∼'ra] m doctorate, Doctor's degree; **doctoresse** [∼'rɛs] f (lady) doctor.

doctrine [dɔk'trin] f doctrine, tenet.

document [dɔky'mɑ̃] m document; **documentaire** [∼mɑ̃'tɛ:r] adj., a. su./m documentary; **documenter** [∼mɑ̃'te] (1a) v/t. document.

dodeliner [dɔdli'ne] (1a) v/i. ∼ de la tête wag one's head.

dodo ch.sp. [do'do] m bye-byes, sleep; bed; faire ∼ (go to) sleep.

dodu, e [dɔ'dy] plump, chubby.

dogme [dɔgm] m dogma, tenet.

dogue zo. [dɔg] m: ∼ anglais mastiff; **doguin** [dɔ'gɛ̃] m zo. pug; ⊕ (lathe-)dog.

doigt [dwa] m finger; zo., anat. digit; ∼ de pied toe; à deux ∼s de on the verge of, within an ace of; fig. mettre le ∼ sur put one's finger on, pinpoint (a problem etc.); montrer du ∼ point at; **doigté** [dwa'te] m ♪ fingering; fig. skill; fig. tact; **doigter** ♪ [∼'te] (1a) v/t. finger (a piece of music); **doigtier** [∼'tje] m finger-stall.

dois [dwa] 1st p. sg. pres. of devoir 1.

doit ✝ [∼] m debit, liability; **doivent** [dwa:v] 3rd p. pl. pres. of devoir 1.

dol ⚖ [dɔl] m fraud.

doléances [dɔle'ɑ̃:s] f/pl. complaints; grievances; **dolent, e** [∼'lɑ̃,

~·'lɑ̃:t] painful (*limb*); plaintive, doleful (*person, voice, etc.*).

doler [dɔ'le] (1a) *v/t.* pare (*wood, skins*); shave (*wood*).

dollar [dɔ'la:r] *m coinage:* dollar.

dolomie [dɔlɔ'mi] *f,* **dolomite** [~'mit] *f* dolomite.

domaine [dɔ'mɛn] *m* domain; realm; estate, property; *fig.* sphere, field; ~ *public* public property.

dôme [do:m] *m* dome; *fig.* canopy; vault (*of heaven*).

domesticité [dɔmɛstisi'te] *f* menial condition; domestic service; *animal:* domesticity; *coll.* staff (of servants); **domestique** [~'tik] **1.** *adj.* domestic; menial; **2.** *su.* servant; domestic; ~s *pl.* staff *sg.* (of servants), household *sg.;* **domestiquer** [~ti'ke] (1m) *v/t.* domesticate; tame; *se* ~ become domesticated.

domicile [dɔmi'sil] *m* residence; ⚖ domicile; *travail m à* ~ home-work; **domiciliaire** [dɔmisi'ljɛ:r] domiciliary; **domicilié, e** [~'lje] domiciled, resident; **domicilier** [~'lje] (1o) *v/t.* domicile; *se* ~ *à* take up residence at.

dominant, e [dɔmi'nɑ̃, ~'nɑ̃:t] **1.** *adj.* dominant, ruling; prevailing, predominating; **2.** *su./f* ♪ dominant; *fig.* dominant feature; **dominateur, -trice** [~na'tœ:r, ~'tris] **1.** *adj.* dominant, ruling; domineering (*attitude, person*); **2.** *su.* ruler; **domination** [~na'sjɔ̃] *f* domination, rule; **dominer** [~'ne] (1a) *v/t.* dominate; master, rule; overlook; *v/i.* rule; predominate; prevail (*opinion*); ~ *sur* rule over; domineer.

dominical, e, *m/pl.* **-aux** [dɔmini-'kal, ~'ko] dominical; Sunday-...; *oraison f* ~ Lord's Prayer.

domino [dɔmi'no] *m cost., game:* domino.

dommage [dɔ'ma:ʒ] *m* damage, injury; ~s *pl.* damage *sg.* (*to property*); ~s *pl. de guerre* war damage (compensation) *sg.;* ⚖ ~s *pl. et intérêts m/pl.* damages; *c'est* ~*!,* *quel* ~*!* what a pity!; *c'est* ~ *que* it's a pity (that); **dommageable** [dɔma'ʒabl] harmful, prejudicial; ⚖ *acte m* ~ tort.

domptable [dɔ̃'tabl] tamable; **dompter** [~'te] (1a) *v/t.* tame; break in (*a horse*); *fig.* subdue (*feelings*); *fig.* reduce (*s.o.*) to obedience;

dompteur *m,* **-euse** *f* [~'tœ:r, ~-'tø:z] tamer (*of animals*); subduer, vanquisher.

don [dɔ̃] *m* gift (*a. fig.*) (for, de), present; ⚖ donation; *fig.* talent (for, de); *faire* ~ *à q. de qch.* make a present of s.th. to s.o.; **donataire** ⚖ [dɔna'tɛ:r] *su.* donee, *Sc.* donatary; **donateur, -trice** [~-'tœ:r, ~'tris] *su.* giver; *su./m* ⚖ donor; *su./f* ⚖ donatrix; **donation** [~'sjɔ̃] *f* donation, gift.

donc [dɔ̃k; dɔ̃] **1.** *adv.* then; just ...; *allons* ~*!* come along!; come, come!, nonsense!; *pourquoi* ~*?* (but) why?; *viens* ~*!* come along!; **2.** *cj.* therefore, so, consequently, then; hence.

donjon [dɔ̃'ʒɔ̃] *m castle:* keep.

donnant, e [dɔ'nɑ̃, ~'nɑ̃:t] generous; ~ ~ tit for tat; **donne** [dɔn] *f cards:* deal; *à qui la* ~*?* whose deal is it?; *fausse* ~ misdeal; **donnée** [dɔ'ne] *f* datum; theme; fundamental idea; ~s *pl.* admitted facts; **donner** [~'ne] (1a) *v/t.* give (*a. advice, orders, an example*), present, bestow; yield (*a. a profit, a harvest, fig. a result*); deal (*cards, a blow*); set (*a problem, a price*); ♂ donate (*blood*); *sl.* give away (*an accomplice*); ~ *à* assign to; confer (*a title*) upon; † ~ *avis* (*quittance*) give notice (a receipt); ~ *de la peine* give trouble; ~ *en mariage* give in marriage; *teleph.* ~ *à q. la communication avec* put s.o. through to; ~ *le bonjour à* wish (*s.o.*) good day; ~ *lieu à* give rise to, cause; ~ *q. pour perdu* give s.o. up for lost; *elle lui donna un enfant* she bore him a child; *se* ~ *à* abandon o.s. to; *se* ~ *de la peine* take pains; *se* ~ *pour* give o.s. out as; *v/i.* give, sag; ⊕, ✂ engage; *cards:* deal; ~ *à entendre* give to understand; ~ *contre* run against; ~ *dans* run into; *sun:* shine into (*a room*); *fig.* have a taste for; ~ *sur* overlook, look out on; lead to; **donneur** *m,* **-euse** *f* [~'nœ:r, ~'nø:z] giver, donor; *cards:* dealer; † seller; ~ *de sang* blood donor; † ~ *d'ordre* principal.

dont [dɔ̃] *pron.* whose, of whom (which); by *or* from *or* among *or* about whom (which).

donzelle F [dɔ̃'zɛl] *f* wench, hussy.

dopage [dɔ'pa:ʒ] *m* doping; **dopant**

[dɔˈpɑ̃] *m* dope; **doper** *sp.* [dɔˈpe] (1a) *v/t.* dope; **doping** *sp.* [dɔˈpiŋ] *m* action: doping; *drug*: dope.

doré, e [dɔˈre] gilt, gilded; golden (*hair etc.*); browned (*meat*); glazed (*cake*).

dorénavant [dɔrenaˈvɑ̃] *adv.* henceforth.

dorer [dɔˈre] (1a) *v/t.* gild; brown (*meat*); glaze (*a cake*); F ~ *la pilule* gild the pill; **doreur** *m*, **-euse** *f* [dɔˈrœːr, ~ˈrøːz] gilder.

dorloter [dɔrlɔˈte] (1a) *v/t.* fondle; pamper; make a fuss of.

dormant, e [dɔrˈmɑ̃, ~ˈmɑ̃ːt] **1.** *adj.* sleeping; ✝, ⚕, *geol.* dormant; stagnant, still (*water*); **2.** *su./m* sleeper; ⊕ casing, frame; **dormeur, -euse** [~ˈmœːr, ~ˈmøːz] *su.* sleeper; *fig.* sluggard; *su./f* stud earring; **dormir** [~ˈmiːr] (2b) *v/i.* sleep, be asleep; ⚕ close (*flower*); ✝ lie idle; *fig.* be still or latent; ~ *comme une souche* (*or une marmotte or un loir*) sleep like a log; ~ *sur les deux oreilles* be absolutely confident; ~ *trop longtemps* oversleep; *histoire f à ~ debout* incredible story; **dormitif, -ve** ✻ [~miˈtif, ~ˈtiːv] **1.** *adj.* soporific; **2.** *su./m* sleeping-draught.

dorsal, e, *m/pl.* **-aux** [dɔrˈsal, ~ˈso] dorsal.

dortoir [dɔrˈtwaːr] *m* dormitory; sleeping-quarters *usu. pl.*

dorure [dɔˈryːr] *f* gilding; gold-braid; *meat*: browning; *cake*: glazing.

doryphore *zo.* [dɔriˈfɔːr] *m* Colorado beetle.

dos [do] *m* back (*a. of chair, page, etc.*); *nose*: bridge; *geog.* ridge; *en ~ d'âne* ridged, high-crowned (*road*); △ ogee; hump-back (*bridge*); *en avoir plein le ~* be fed up with it; *faire le gros ~* arch its back (*cat*); *voir au ~* turn over!; see overleaf.

dosage [doˈzaːʒ] *m* ✻ dosage; 🜍 titration, quantity determination; **dose** [doːz] *f* ✻ dose; 🜍 amount, proportion; *fig.* share; ~ *excessive*, ~ *trop forte* overdosis; **doser** [doˈze] (1a) *v/t.* ✻ determine the dose of; 🜍 titrate; *fig.* measure out.

dossier [doˈsje] *m chair etc.*: back; file, papers *pl.*; documents *pl.*; 🜨 record; ✻ case history.

dot [dɔt] *f* dowry; **dotal, e,** *m/pl.*

-aux [dɔˈtal, ~ˈto] dotal; 🜨 *régime m ~* marriage settlement; **dotation** [~taˈsjɔ̃] *f* endowment; ⊕ etc. equipment; **doter** [~ˈte] (1a) *v/t.* give a dowry to (*a bride*); endow (*a hospital etc.*, *a. fig.*) (with, de).

douaire [dwɛːr] *m* (*widow's*) dower; (*wife's*) jointure; **douairière** [dwɛˈrjɛːr] *su./f*, *a. adj.* dowager.

douane *admin.* [dwan] *f* customs *pl.*; **douanier, -ère** [dwaˈnje, ~ˈnjɛːr] **1.** *adj.* customs-...; **2.** *su./m* customs officer.

doublage [duˈblaːʒ] *m cost.* lining; ⊕ plating; *cin.* dubbing; **double** [dubl] **1.** *adj.* double, twofold; *à ~ face* two-faced (*person*); *à ~ sens* ambiguous; ✝ *en partie ~* by double-entry; *sp. partie f ~ golf*: foursome; **2.** *su./m* double; duplicate; ✝ *en ~* in duplicate; *plier en ~* fold in half *or* in two; ~*s pl.* messieurs tennis: men's doubles; **doublé** [duˈble] *m billiards*: stroke off the cushion; rolled gold; plated ware; **doubler** [~ˈble] (1a) *v/t.* double (*a.* ♘ *a cape*); fold in half *or* in two; *cost.* line; ⊕ *metal*: plate; *cin.* dub; pass, overtake; *thea.* understudy (*a role*); *mot. défense de ~* no overtaking!; *mot. ~ à gauche* overtake *or* pass on the left; ~ *une classe* repeat a class; *v/i.* double; **doublet** [~ˈblɛ] *m* doublet; **doublon** [~ˈblɔ̃] *m* double; doublet; **doublure** [~ˈblyːr] *f cost.* lining; *thea.* understudy; *mot.* overtaking.

douce-amère, *pl.* **douces-amères** ⚕ [dusaˈmɛːr] *f* bitter-sweet, woody nightshade; **douceâtre** [~ˈsɑːtr] sweetish; sickly; **doucement** [dusˈmɑ̃] gently; softly; carefully; smoothly; **doucereux, -euse** [dusˈrø, ~ˈrøːz] sweetish, sickly, cloying; *fig.* smooth-tongued; sugary; **doucet, -ette** [duˈsɛ, ~ˈsɛt] **1.** *adj.* meek; mild; **2.** *su./f* ⚕ lamb's lettuce, corn-salad; **douceur** [~ˈsœːr] *f* sweetness; softness; gentleness; *weather*: mildness; ~*s pl.* sweets, *Am.* candies; *fig. en ~* soft (*landing, transition, etc.*); gently, smoothly; carefully.

douche [duʃ] *f* shower(-bath); ✻ douche; **doucher** [duˈʃe] (1a) *v/t.* give (*s.o.*) a shower-bath; F dowse (*s.o.*); ✻ douche.

doucir [du'si:r] (2a) *v/t.* grind down (*glass or metal*).

douer [dwe] (1p) *v/t.* endow (with, de) (*a. fig.*); être doué *pour* have a natural gift for.

douille [du:j] *f* ⊕, ⚡ socket; ⚡ (bulb-)holder; cartridge case; ⊕ *wheel:* sleeve.

douillet, -ette [du'jɛ, ~'jɛt] soft (*cushion etc., a. person*); *pej.* effeminate, over-delicate.

douleur [du'lœ:r] *f* pain; suffering; grief; **douloureux, -euse** [~lu'rø, ~'rø:z] 1. *adj.* painful; aching; *fig.* sad; *fig.* sorrowful (*look*); *fig.* grievous (*cry, event, loss*); 2. *su./f* F bill, *Am.* check.

doute [dut] *m* doubt, misgiving; suspicion; *mettre (or révoquer)* en ~ (call in) question (*whether, que*); *sans* ~ no doubt; probably; *sans aucun* ~ without (a) doubt, assuredly; **douter** [du'te] (1a) *v/i.* (*a.* ~ de) doubt, question; mistrust; *v/t.:* se ~ de suspect, think; **douteur, -euse** [~'tœ:r, ~'tø:z] 1. *su.* doubter; 2. *adj.* doubting; **douteux, -euse** [~'tø, ~'tø:z] doubtful, dubious; questionable; uncertain.

douve [du:v] *f* ⚒ moat; ⚔ trench; *sp.* water-jump; *tub:* stave.

doux, douce [du, dus] 1. *adj.* soft (*a. fig.; a. iron.; a. drug etc.*); sweet; mild (*a. steel*); gentle; smooth; pleasant (*memories, news*); billet *m* ~ love-letter; eau *f* douce fresh *or* soft water; vin *m* ~ must; 2. *adv.:* F filer doux sing small; submit; *tout doux!* take it easy!; *sl.* en douce on the quiet.

douzaine [du'zɛn] *f* dozen; à la ~ by the dozen; une ~ de fleurs a dozen flowers; **douze** [du:z] *adj./num., a. su./m/inv.* twelve; *date, title:* twelfth; **douzième** [du'zjɛm] *adj./num., a. su.* twelfth.

doyen *m*, **-enne** *f* [dwa'jɛ̃, ~'jɛn] *eccl., univ.* dean; *diplomat:* doyen; *fig.* (*a.* ~ d'âge) senior; **doyenné** [~jɛ'ne] *m* deanery; ⚘ *pear:* doyenne.

draconien, -enne [drakɔ'njɛ̃, ~'njɛn] draconian; harsh.

dragage ⊕ [dra'ga:ʒ] *m* dredging; dragging (*for body*); (*mine-*)sweeping.

dragée [dra'ʒe] *f* sugared almond; sweet; ⚜ dragee; ✗ *sl.* bullet; *fig.* pill; *hunt.* small shot; tenir la ~

haute à make (*s.o.*) pay dearly; **drageoir** [~'ʒwa:r] *m* watch-glass: bezel; comfit-box, comfit-dish.

drageon ⚘ [dra'ʒɔ̃] *m* sucker.

dragon [dra'gɔ̃] *m myth.* dragon (*a. fig.*); *zo.* flying lizard; ✗, *orn.* dragoon; **dragonne** [~'gɔn] *f* sword-knot; *umbrella:* tassel.

drague [drag] *f* ⊕ dredger; grappling-hook; *fishing:* drag-net, dredge; **draguer** [dra'ge] (1m) *v/t.* ⊕ dredge; drag (*a pond*); dredge for (*oysters*); ⚓ sweep for (*mines*); *sl.* (try and) pick up (*a girl etc.*); **dragueur** [~'gœ:r] *m* ⊕ dredger-man; *fishing:* dragman; (*a. bateau m* ~) dredger; ⚓ ~ de mines mine sweeper.

drain [drɛ̃] *m* cloth; drain(ing); drain-pipe; ⚜ drainage tube; ✗ watercourse; **drainage** ⚘, ⚜ [drɛ'na:ʒ] *m* drainage, draining; ✝ drain; **drainer** ⚘, ⚜ [~'ne] (1a) *v/t.* drain.

dramatique [drama'tik] 1. *adj.* dramatic (*a. fig.*); auteur *m* ~ playwright; 2. *su./m* drama (*a. fig.*); **dramatiser** [~ti'ze] (1a) *v/t.* dramatize (*a. fig.*); adapt (*a novel*) for the stage; **dramaturge** [~'tyrʒ] *m* playwright; **drame** [dram] *m* drama (*a. fig.*); play.

drap [dra] *m* cloth; ~ (de lit) sheet; ~ mortuaire pall; F être dans de beaux ~s be in a pretty mess; **drapeau** [dra'po] *m* flag; *telev.* irregular synchronism; ✗ colo(u)rs *pl.*; sous les ~x ✗ in the services; F *fig.* on the side (of, de); **draper** [~'pe] (1a) *v/t.* drape; cover with cloth (*buttons etc.*); se ~ drape o.s. (in, dans) (*a. fig.*); **draperie** [~'pri] *f* drapery; curtains *pl.*; ✗ bunting; **drapier** [~'pje] *m* draper; cloth merchant *or* manufacturer.

drastique ⚜ [dras'tik] *adj., a. su./m* drastic.

drawback ✝ [dro'bak] *m* drawback.

drèche [drɛʃ] *f* draff.

dressage [drɛ'sa:ʒ] *m* preparation; *monument:* erection; ⊕ *stone, wood:* dressing; ⊕ facing; training (*a.* ✗); *horse:* breaking in; **dressement** [drɛs'mã] *m* preparation, drawing up; **dresser** [drɛ'se] (1a) *v/t.* erect (*a monument etc.*); fix up (*a bed*); raise (*one's head*); prick up (*one's ears*); lay, set (*an ambush, the table, a trap*); draw up (*a contract, an* *inventory, a list, a report*); pitch (*a tent*); ✗ lay out (*a camp*); ✗ establish (*a battery*); ⚒ lodge (*a complaint*); ♥ make out (*a cheque*); dish up (*food*); train (*an animal, a person*); break in (*a horse*); ✗ drill (*recruits*); ⊕ line up (*an engine, a machine*); trim (*a hedge*); dress (*wood, a stone*); ⊕ straighten out (*a wire*); ∼ un procès-verbal contre (*or à*) q. take down the particulars of a minor offence, F take s.o.'s name and address; se ∼ rise, get to one's feet; stand on end (*hair*); stand (*monument etc.*); rise on its hind legs (*horse*); **dresseur** *m*, **-euse** *f* [∼'sœːr, ∼'søːz] trainer (*of animals*); adjuster; **dressoir** [∼-'swaːr] *m* dresser, sideboard.

dribbler *sp.* [dri'ble] (1a) *vt/i.* dribble.

drille[1] [driːj] *m*: F bon ∼ grand chap; F *pauvre* ∼ poor devil.

drille[2] ⊕ [∼] *f* hand-drill, drill-brace.

drisse ⚓ [dris] *f* halyard, yard-rope.

drogue [drɔg] *f* drug; *coll.* drugs *pl.*; *pej.* patent medicine; **drogué, e** [drɔ'ge] **1.** *adj.* high (on drugs), *sl.* stoned; **2.** *su.* drug addict; dope fiend; **droguer** [drɔ'ge] (1m) *v/t.* drug (up); dose up; se ∼ take drugs, be on drugs; **droguerie** [∼'gri] *f* chemist's, *Am.* drugstore.

droit, droite [drwa, drwat] **1.** *adj.* straight (*a. line*); right (*angle, hand, side*); upright (*a. fig.*); vertical; stand-up (*collar*); *fig.* honest; au ∼ de at right angles with; ℄ section *f* ∼e cross-section; **2.** *droit adv.* straight; *tout* ∼ straight ahead *or* on; **3.** *su./m* right; privilege; law; fee, charge; ∼s *pl. d'auteur* royalties; ∼s *pl. civiques* civil rights; ♥ ∼s *pl. de magasinage* storage *sg.* (charges); warehouse dues; ∼ *de douane* (customs) duty; ∼ *des gens* law of nations; ∼ *du plus fort* right of the strongest; *à qui de* ∼ to the proper person *or* quarter; *avoir* ∼ à be entitled to; be eligible for; *de* (*bon*) ∼ by right; *être en* ∼ *de* (*inf.*) have a right to (*inf.*), be entitled to (*inf.*); *faire son* ∼ study law; *su./f* right hand; straight line; *à* ∼e on the right; *direction*: to the right; *tenir la* ∼e keep to the right; *pol.* la ℞e the Right, the Conservatives *pl.*; **droitier, -ère** [drwa'tje, ∼'tjɛːr] **1.** *adj.* right-

handed; *pol.* right-wing; **2.** *su.* right-handed person; *pol.* Rightist, Conservative; **droitiste** *pol.* [∼'tist] *adj., a. su.* Rightist; **droiture** [∼'tyːr] *f* uprightness; integrity; honesty.

drolatique [drɔla'tik] comic, humorous; spicy; **drôle** [droːl] **1.** *adj.* funny; odd, queer; F *la* ∼ *de guerre* the phoney war; *un(e)* ∼ *de* a funny, an odd; **2.** *su./m* rascal, knave; **drôlerie** [droːl'ri] *f* jesting, fun; joke, jest, *Am.* gag; **drôlesse** † [droːˈlɛs] *f* hussy.

dromadaire *zo.* [drɔmaˈdɛːr] *m* dromedary.

drosser ⚓, ✈ [drɔ'se] (1a) *v/t.* drive, carry, drift (*wind etc.*).

dru, drue [dry] **1.** *adj.* thick, strong; dense; vigorous; **2.** *dru adv.* thickly; ∼ *et menu* in a steady drizzle (*rain*); (*walk*) with quick, short steps; *tomber* ∼ fall thick and fast.

druide [drɥid] *m* druid.

drupe ♣ [dryp] *f* drupe, stone-fruit.

dû, due, *m/pl.* **dus** [dy] **1.** *p.p.* of *devoir* 1; **2.** *adj.* due; owing; **3.** *su./m* due.

dubitatif, -ve [dybita'tif, ∼'tiːv] dubitative.

duc [dyk] *m* duke; *orn.* horned owl; **ducal, e**, *m/pl.* **-aux** [dy'kal, ∼'ko] ducal; … of a *or* the duke.

ducat † [dy'ka] *m* ducat.

duché [dy'ʃe] *m* duchy, dukedom; **duchesse** [∼'ʃɛs] *f* duchess; *tex.* duchesse lace *or* satin; ♣ duchess pear.

ductile [dyk'til] ductile, malleable (*a. fig.*); *fig.* pliable; **ductilité** [∼-tili'te] *f* malleability; *fig.* docility.

duel[1] *gramm.* [dɥɛl] *m* dual.

duel[2] [dɥɛl] *m* duel; **duelliste** [dɥɛ-'list] *m* duellist.

dum-dum [dum'dum] *f* dum-dum (bullet).

dûment [dy'mã] *adv.* duly, in due form, properly.

dumping ♥ [dœm'piŋ] *m* dumping; *faire du* ∼ dump.

dune [dyn] *f* dune; ∼s *pl.* downs.

dunette ⚓ [dy'nɛt] *f* poop-deck.

duo ♪ [dɥo] *m* duet.

duodénum *anat.* [dɥɔde'nɔm] *m* duodenum.

dupe [dyp] *f* dupe; F gull; *être* ∼ *de* be taken in by; *prendre q. pour* ∼ make a cat's-paw of s.o.; **duper**

[dy'pe] (1a) *v/t.* dupe, fool; take (*s.o.*) in; **duperie** [ˌ'pri] *f* deception, trickery; take-in; **dupeur** [ˌ'pœːr] *m* cheat, swindler, *Am.* sharper; hoaxer.

duplex ⊕ [dy'plɛks] *adj., a. su./m* duplex; **duplicata** [dyplika'ta] *m/inv. copy*: duplicate; **duplicateur** [ˌka'tœːr] *m* duplicator; ⚡ doubler; **duplicatif, -ve** [ˌka'tif, ˌ'tiːv] duplicative; **duplicité** [ˌsi'te] *f* duplicity, double-dealing.

dur, dure [dyːr] **1.** *adj.* hard (*a. fig.*); stiff; tough (*meat, wood*); *fig.* harsh; unfeeling; hardened; *avoir le sommeil* ˌ be a heavy sleeper; *être* ˌ *avec* (*or pour*) *q.* be hard on s.o., be rough with s.o.; *avoir l'oreille* ˌe, *être* ˌ *d'oreille* be hard of hearing; **2.** *dur adv.* hard; **3.** *su./m* F tough guy; hard-liner; F *un* ˌ *à cuire* a tough nut to crack; ⚠ *en* ˌ permanent (*structure etc.*); *su./f*: *coucher sur la dure* sleep on the bare ground *or* on bare boards.

durabilité [dyrabili'te] *f* durability; **durable** [ˌ'rabl] durable, lasting; solid.

durant [dy'rɑ̃] *prp.* during; ˌ *des années* for many years; *sa vie* ˌ his whole life long; *des heures* ˌ for hours (and hours).

durcir [dyr'siːr] (2a) *v/t.* harden; hard-boil (*an egg*); *metall.* chill; *v/i. a. se* ˌ harden; set (*concrete*); **durcissement** [ˌsis'mɑ̃] *m* hardening, toughening; stiffening; *metall.* chilling.

durée [dy're] *f* duration; *machine,* *building, etc.*: wear, life; *de courte* ˌ short-lived; **durer** [ˌ] (1a) *v/i.* last, endure; wear (well) (*goods*); hold out, bear, F stick (it) (*person*); *le temps me dure* time hangs heavily on my hands, I find life dull.

duret, -ette F [dy're, ˌ'rɛt] rather hard; rather tough (*meat*); **dureté** [dyr'te] *f* hardness (*a. fig.*); *meat*: toughness; *fig.* harshness; austerity; ˌ *d'oreille* hardness of hearing; **durillon** [dyri'jɔ̃] *m foot*: corn; *hand*: callosity.

durit *mot.* (*TM*) [dy'rit] *f* radiator hose.

dus [dy] *1st p. sg. p.s. of devoir 1.*

duvet [dy'vɛ] *m* down; *tex.* fluff, nap; F down quilt; **duveté, e** [dyv'te], *a.* **duveteux, -euse** [ˌ'tø, ˌ'tøːz] downy, fluffy.

dynamique [dina'mik] **1.** *adj.* dynamic; **2.** *su./f* dynamics *sg.*; **dynamiser** [ˌmi'ze] (1a) *v/t.* make (more) dynamic; **dynamite** [ˌ'mit] *f* dynamite; **dynamiter** [ˌmi'te] (1a) *v/t.* dynamite; blow up; *fig. a.* F bust (up); **dynamo** ⚡, ⊕ [ˌ'mo] *f* dynamo; ˌ *lumière* (*or d'éclairage*) lighting generator; **dynamomètre** ⊕ [ˌmɔ'mɛtr] *m* dynamometer.

dynastie [dinas'ti] *f* dynasty.

dysenterie ⚕ [disɑ̃'tri] *f* dysentery.

dysfonctionnement ⚕ [disfɔ̃ksjɔn'mɑ̃] *f* dysfunction.

dyspepsie ⚕ [dispɛp'si] *f* dyspepsia, indigestion; **dyspepsique** [ˌpɛp'sik] *adj., a. su.* dyspeptic.

dytique *zo.* [di'tik] *m* water-beetle, dytiscus.

E

E, e [ə] *m* E, e.

eau [o] *f* water; rain; *fruit*: juice; perspiration; *eccl.* ~ bénite holy water; ~ de toilette lotion; ~ du robinet tap water; ♫~ *lourde* heavy water; ♂⃗ ~ oxygénée hydrogen peroxide; ~ potable drinking water; ~ vive spring water, running water; aller aux ~x go to a watering-place; ⚓ faire ~ (spring a) leak; faire de l'~ ⚓, ⛟ (take in) water; ♂⃗ make water; grandes ~x pl., jeux m/pl. d'~x ornamental fountains; river: high water sg.; nager entre deux ~x swim under water; prendre les ~x take the waters (at a spa); ville f d'~ watering-place, spa; ~-de-vie, pl. ~x-de-vie [od'vi] *f* brandy; spirits pl.; ~-forte, pl. ~x-fortes ♫ [o'fɔrt] *f* nitric acid; etching; ~x-vannes [o'van] *f/pl.* liquid manure sg., sewage sg.

ébahir [eba'iːr] (2a) *v/t.* amaze, astound; take (s.o.'s) breath away; s'~ be astounded, wonder (at, de); **ébahissement** [~is'mã] *m* amazement, wonder.

ébarber [ebar'be] (1a) *v/t.* trim (a. ♂⃗); ♂⃗ clip; ⊕ dress.

ébats [e'ba] *m/pl.* frolics, gambols; prendre ses ~ frolic, gambol; **ébattre** [e'batr] (4a): *v/t.*: s'~ frolic, gambol, frisk about.

ébaubi, e [ebo'bi] amazed, astounded.

ébauchage [ebo'ʃaːʒ] *m* roughing out (of s.th.); **ébauche** [e'boːʃ] *f* outline (a. fig.); sketch (a. fig.); rough draft; fig. ghost (of a smile); **ébaucher** [ebo'ʃe] (1a) *v/t.* rough out, sketch (out); roughhew (a stone etc.); fig. give a ghost or a hint of (a smile etc.); s'~ take shape, form, develop.

ébène [e'bɛn] *f* ebony; fig. d'~ jet-black; **ébénier** ♀ [ebe'nje] *m* ebony-tree; **ébéniste** [~'nist] *m* cabinet-maker; **ébénisterie** [~nis-'tri] *f* cabinet-work; cabinet-making.

éberlué, e [ebɛrlɥ'e] flabbergasted.

éblouir [eblu'iːr] (2a) *v/t.* dazzle (a. fig.); **éblouissement** [~is'mã] *m* dazzle; glare; dizziness.

ébonite [ebɔ'nit] *f* ebonite, vulcanite.

éborgner [ebɔr'ɲe] (1a) *v/t.* blind in one eye, put (s.o.'s) eye out; ♪ disbud.

ébouillanter [ebujã'te] (1a) *v/t.* scald.

éboulement [ebul'mã] *m* caving in, collapsing; fall of stone; landslide; **ébouler** [ebu'le] (1a) *v/t.* bring down; s'~ cave in, collapse; slip (cliff, land); **éboulis** [~'li] *m* △ debris; fallen earth; scree.

ébouriffant, e F [eburi'fã, ~'fãːt] amazing, startling; fantastic (story); **ébouriffer** [~'fe] (1a) *v/t.* ruffle (a. fig.), dishevel (s.o.'s hair); fig. amaze.

ébrancher ♪ [ebrã'ʃe] (1a) *v/t.* lop off the branches of (a tree); prune, trim; **ébranchoir** ♪ [~'ʃwaːr] *m* (long-hafted) billhook.

ébranlement [ebrãl'mã] *m* shaking, shock; fig. agitation, commotion; fig. disturbance (a. of the mind); **ébranler** [ebrã'le] (1a) *v/t.* shake (a. fig.); loosen (a tooth); set in motion; disturb; s'~ shake; ring (bells); start, set off; ⚔ move off.

ébrécher [ebre'ʃe] (1f) *v/t.* notch; chip (a plate etc.); jag (a knife); fig. make a hole in (one's fortune); fig. damage (s.o.'s reputation).

ébriété [ebrie'te] *f* drunkenness, intoxication.

ébrouement [ebru'mã] *m* snort (-ing); **ébrouer** [~'e] (1a) *v/t.*: s'~ snort; take a (dust-)bath (bird).

ébruiter [ebrɥi'te] (1a) *v/t.* noise abroad, make known; divulge (a secret); s'~ become known.

ébullition [ebyli'sjõ] *f* boiling; effervescence; fig. turmoil; point m d'~ boiling point.

éburné, e [ebyr'ne] eburnean, like ivory; anat. substance f ~e dentine.

écaille [e'kaːj] *f* ♂⃗, ♀, metall., fig.,

fish: scale; *paint*: flake; *wood*: splinter; *tortoise etc.*: shell; ✝ tortoise-shell.

écailler[1] [ekɑˈje] (1a) *v/t.* scale (*fish, a. metall.*); open (*oysters*); s'~ scale *or* flake off, peel off.

écailler[2], **-ère** [ekɑˈje, ~ˈjɛːr] *su.* oyster-seller; *su./f* oyster-knife.

écailleux, -euse [ekɑˈjø, ~ˈjøːz] scaly; flaky (*paint*).

écale [eˈkal] *f* pea: pod; *nut*: husk; **écaler** [ekaˈle] (1a) *v/t.* shell (*peas*); hull (*walnuts*); shuck (*chestnuts*).

écarlate [ekarˈlat] *adj., a. su./f* scarlet.   [wide (*one's eyes*).]

écarquiller [ekarkiˈje] (1a) *v/t.* open∫

écart [eˈkaːr] *m* gap; divergence; difference; separation; *cards*: discard (-ing); ✂ *range*: error (*a. fig.*); ✝ margin (*of prices*); ⊕ deviation; ⊕ variation; swerve; *fig.* digression; *fig. fancy*: flight; ~ (*de conduite*) misdemeano(u)r; *à l'*~ on one side, apart; aloof; out of the way; *faire un* ~ swerve; shy (*horse*); *gymn.* grand ~ splits *pl.*; *se tenir à l'*~ stand aside *or* aloof; **écarté, e** [ekarˈte] remote; isolated; out-of-the-way; lonely.

écarteler [ekartəˈle] (1d) *v/t.* ✠ *hist.* quarter; *fig.* tear apart; *écartelé entre* torn between.

écartement [ekartəˈmɑ̃] gap, space (between, *de*); ⛟ *track*: gauge; *mot.* wheelbase; ⊕ deflection; **écarter** [~ˈte] (1a) *v/t.* separate; spread; remove; avert; push aside (*a. proposals*); divert (*suspicion etc.*); s'~ move aside; diverge; stray, deviate (from, *de*).

Ecclésiaste [ɛkleˈzjast] *m*: *livre m de l'*~ Ecclesiastes; **ecclésiastique** [~zjasˈtik] **1.** *adj.* ecclesiastical; clerical (*hat etc.*); **2.** *su./m* clergyman, ecclesiastic; *l'*♃ Ecclesiasticus.

écervelé, e [esɛrvəˈle] **1.** *adj.* scatter-brained, wild, flighty; **2.** *su.* scatterbrain, harum-scarum, madcap.

échafaud [eʃaˈfo] *m* scaffolding; *sp. etc.* stand; ✠ scaffold, gallows *pl.*; **échafaudage** [~foˈdaːʒ] *m* ⚠ scaffolding; *fig.* structure; *fig. fortune*: piling up; **échafauder** [~foˈde] (1a) *v/i.* erect a scaffolding; *v/t.* pile up; *fig.* build up; construct.

échalas [eʃaˈla] *m* ✗ vine-prop; hop-pole; *fig.* spindle-shanks (= *lanky person*); **échalasser** [~laˈse] (1a) *v/t.* prop (*the vine etc.*).

échalier [eʃaˈlje] *m* stile; gate.

échalote ⚘ [eʃaˈlɔt] *f* shallot.

échancrer [eʃɑ̃ˈkre] (1a) *v/t.* indent, notch; scallop (*a handkerchief*); cut out (the neck of) (*a dress*); **échancrure** [~ˈkryːr] *f* indentation; cut; *dress*: neckline; notch.

échange [eˈʃɑ̃ːʒ] *m* exchange (*a.* ✝); ✝ barter; *libre* ~ free trade; *en* ~ *de* in exchange *or* return for; **échanger** [eʃɑ̃ˈʒe] (1l) *v/t.* exchange (for *pour*, *contre*) (*a.* ✝); ✝ barter; **échangeur** [~ˈʒœːr] *m* *mot.* interchange; ⊕ exchanger.

échanson [eʃɑ̃ˈsɔ̃] *m* † cup-bearer; butler.

échantillon [eʃɑ̃tiˈjɔ̃] *m* sample (*a. fig.*); specimen; pattern; ⊕ template; ~ *représentatif* adequate sample; **échantillonnage** [~jɔˈnaːʒ] *m* sampling; (collection of) samples *pl.*; **échantillonner** [~jɔˈne] (1a) *v/t.* sample.

échappatoire [eʃapaˈtwaːr] *f* evasion, way out, loop-hole; **échappé, e** [~ˈpe] **1.** *adj.* fugitive, runaway; **2.** *su.* fugitive, runaway; *su./f* escape; (free) space; *sp.* spurt; ~ (*de vue*) vista; ~ *de lumière* burst of light; *par* ~s by fits and starts; **échappement** [eʃapˈmɑ̃] *m* gas etc.: escape; ⊕, *mot.* exhaust; ⊕ outlet; *clock*: escapement; *mot.* *tuyau m* (*pot m*) *d'*~ exhaust-pipe (silencer); **échapper** [eʃaˈpe] (1a) *v/i.* escape; avoid; dodge; defy; *laisser* ~ let slip; set free; *le mot m'a échappé* the word has slipped my memory; *v/t.*: *fig. l'*~ *belle* have a narrow escape *or* F a close shave; s'~ escape (from, *de*); slip out; disappear.

écharde [eˈʃard] *f* splinter.

écharner ⊕ [eʃarˈne] (1a) *v/t.* flesh (*hides*); **écharnoir** [~ˈnwaːr] *m* fleshing knife.

écharpe [eˈʃarp] *f* (shoulder) sash; *cost.* stole, scarf; ⚔ *arm*: sling; *en* ~ diagonally, slantwise; **écharper** [eʃarˈpe] (1a) *v/t.* slash; cut to pieces (*a.* ✂); *tex.* card (*wool*).

échasse [eˈʃɑːs] *f* stilt; *scaffold*: pole; *fig. monté sur des* ~s on one's high horse; **échassier** [eʃaˈsje] *m* *orn.* wader; *fig.* spindle-shanks.

échaudé *cuis.* [eʃoˈde] *m* canary-bread; **échauder** [~ˈde] (1a) *v/t.* scald; *tex.* scour; F fleece (*s.o.*);

fig. se *faire* ~ burn one's fingers; **échaudoir** [~'dwa:r] *m* scalding-room; scalding-tub; *tex.* scouringvat; **échaudure** [~'dy:r] *f* scald.

échauffant, e [eʃo'fã, ~'fã:t] *ℱ* heating; *ℱ* constipating; *fig.* exciting; **échauffement** [eʃof'mã] *m* ⊕ heating; *ℱ* overheating; *ℱ* constipation; *fig.* over-excitement; **échauffer** [eʃo'fe] (1a) *v/t.* overheat (*ℱ*, *a.* a *room*); *ℱ* constipate; ⊕ heat; *fig.* warm; *fig.* inflame; *s'*~ become overheated; warm up; ⊕ get *or* run hot.

échauffourée [eʃofu're] *f* brawl; scuffle; clash; ✕ skirmish, affray.

échéance ✝ [eʃe'ã:s] *f bill:* falling due, term; maturity; date; *tenancy:* expiration; *à longue* ~ long-dated; long-term; **échéant, e** [~'ã, ~'ã:t] ✝ falling due; *le cas* ~ if necessary; should the occasion arise.

échec [e'ʃɛk] *m chess:* check (*a. fig.*); ⊕, *a. fig.* failure; ~*s pl.* chess *sg.*; chessmen; chessboard *sg.*; *voué à l'* ~ doomed to failure.

échelette [eʃ'lɛt] *f cart etc.:* rack; **échelle** [e'ʃɛl] *f ladder (a. fig.):* colours, drawing, map, prices, wages, *etc.:* scale; *stocking:* ladder, run; ~ *double* pair of steps; ~ *mobile (des salaires)* sliding scale (of wages); ~ *sociale* social scale; *faire la courte* ~ *à q.* give s.o. a helping hand; *sur une grande* ~ on a large scale; **échelon** [eʃ'lɔ̃] *m ladder:* rung; *admin.* grade; *fig.* step; ✕ echelon; ♪ degree; *pol. etc. à l'* ~ *le plus élevé* at the highest level; ⊕ *en* ~ stepped (*gearing*); **échelonnement** [eʃlɔn'mã] *m* ✕ echeloning; ⊕ placing at intervals; ✝ spreading (*over a period*); ✗ brushes, *a. fig. holidays:* staggering; **échelonner** [eʃlɔ'ne] (1a) *v/t.* ✕ (draw up in) echelon; space out; place at intervals; ⊕ step (*gears*); ✝ spread (*payments over a period*); stagger (*a. fig. holidays*); grade.

écheniller [eʃni'je] (1a) *v/t.* ✗ clear of caterpillars; *fig.* clean up, free from undesirable elements; **échenilloir** ✗ [~nij'wa:r] *m* tree-pruner; branch-lopper.

écheveau [eʃ'vo] *m* skein, hank; *fig.* maze, jumble; **échevelé, e** [eʃə'vle] dishevelled; tousled; *fig.* wild;

écheveler [~] (1c) *v/t.* dishevel, rumple (*s.o.'s hair*).

échine *anat.* [e'ʃin] *f* backbone, spine; **échiner** [eʃi'ne] (1a) *v/t.* break (*s.o.'s*) back; *fig.* tire (*s.o.*) out; *fig.* thrash (*s.o.*) within an inch of his live; *sl.* ruin; *fig.* s'~ tire o.s. out.

échiquier [eʃi'kje] *m* chess-board; checker pattern; *pol. Br.* ♀ Exchequer; *en* ~ chequerwise.

écho [e'ko] *m* echo; *faire* ~ echo.

échoir [e'ʃwa:r] (3d) *v/i.* ✝ fall due; expire (*tenancy*); fall (*to s.o.'s lot*); *fig.* befall.

échoppe¹ [e'ʃɔp] *f (covered)* stall, booth.

échoppe² ⊕ [~] *f* burin; graver.

échotier *journ.* [eko'tje] *m* gossip-writer, paragraphist; columnist.

échouer [e'ʃwe] (1p) *v/i.* ♣ run aground; *fig.* fail, come to naught; fall through; *fig.* land, end up (in, *dans*); *faire* ~ foil; ruin; thwart; *v/t.* ♣ run (a *ship*) aground; beach.

échu, e [e'ʃy] ✝ due; expired.

écimer ✗ [esi'me] (1a) *v/t.* pollard, top.

éclabousser [eklabu'se] (1a) *v/t.* splash, bespatter (with, *de*); **éclaboussure** [~'sy:r] *f* splash.

éclair [e'klɛ:r] *m* flash of lightning; flash (*a. fig.*); *cuis.* éclair; ~*s pl. de chaleur* heat lightning *sg.*; ✕ *guerre f* ~ blitzkrieg; *visite f* ~ lightning visit; **éclairage** [eklɛ'ra:ʒ] *m* light(ing); ✕, ♣ scouting; ~ *par projecteurs* flood-lighting; ✗ *circuit m d'* ~ light(ing) circuit; **éclairagiste** [~ra-'ʒist] *m* lighting engineer; **éclaircie** [eklɛr'si] *f* fair period; break (*of clouds*); clearing (*in a forest*); *fig.* bright period (*in life*); **éclaircir** [~'si:r] (2a) *v/t.* clear (up); brighten; thin (a *forest*); clarify (a *liquid*); thin out (a *sauce*); *fig.* solve, explain, elucidate; **éclairer** [eklɛ're] (1b) *v/t.* light, illuminate; *fig.* enlighten; ✕ reconnoitre; *s'*~ light up; become clear(er); **éclaireur** [~'rœ:r] *m* ✕, ♣, *etc.* scout.

éclat [e'kla] *m* splinter, chip; burst (*of laughter, of thunder*); explosion; flash (*of gun, light*); brightness, radiance, brilliance (*a. fig.*); *fig.* splendo(u)r; *fig.* glamo(u)r; ~ *de rire* burst of laughter; *faire* ~ create a stir; *faux* ~ tawdriness; *rire aux* ~*s* roar with laughter; **éclatant, e** [ekla'tã, ~'tã:t] brilliant; sparkling, glittering; magnificent; loud (*noise*); *fig.* obvious; **éclater** [ʌ'te] (1a) *v/i.* burst, explode; shatter; break up, split (up); flash (*a. fig.*); shine out *or* forth; clap (*thunder*); break out (*fire, laughter, war*); ⁓ *de rire* burst out laughing; **éclateur** ⚡ [ʌ'tœːr] *m* spark-gap; spark-arrester; ⁓ *à boule* discharger.

éclipse [e'klips] *f* eclipse; *fig.* disappearance; **éclipser** [eklip'se] (1a) *v/t.* eclipse (*a. fig.*); obscure (*a beam*); s'⁓ vanish.

éclisse [e'klis] *f* wedge; 🩹 splint; ⊕ butt-strap; 🚂 fish-plate; **éclisser** [ekli'se] (1a) *v/t.* 🩹 splint; 🚂 fish.

éclopé, e [eklɔ'pe] **1.** *adj.* lame, footsore; **2.** *su.* cripple; lame person.

éclore [e'klɔːr] (4f) *v/i.* hatch (*bird*); ❀ open; ❀ bloom; *fig.* develop, come to light; **éclosion** [eklɔ'zjɔ̃] *f* eggs: hatching; ❀ opening; ❀ blooming; *fig.* birth, dawning.

écluse [e'klyːz] *f* lock; sluice; floodgate; **éclusée** [ekly'ze] *f* lockful; sluicing-water; **écluser** [ʌ'ze] (1a) *v/t.* provide (*a canal*) with locks; pass (*a barge*) through a lock; **éclusier, -ère** [ʌ'zje, ʌ'zjɛːr] **1.** *su.* lock-keeper; **2.** *adj.* lock-...

écœurer [ekœ're] (1a) *v/t.* disgust, sicken, nauseate; *fig.* dishearten.

école [e'kɔl] *f* school (*a. fig.*); ✕, ⚓ drill; ⁓ *confessionnelle* denominational school; ⁓ *de commerce* commercial school; ⁓ *des arts et métiers* industrial school; engineering college; technical school *or* institute; ⁓ *des hautes études commerciales* commercial college (*of university standing*); ⁓ *laïque* undenominational school; ⁓ *libre* private school; ⁓ *maternelle* infant school; kindergarten; ⁓ *mixte* mixed school, *Am.* co-educational school; ⁓ *moyenne* intermediate school; ⁓ *primaire supérieure* central school; ⁓ *professionnelle* training school; ⁓ *secondaire* secondary school; ⁓ *supérieure* college, academy; *faire* ⁓ get a following (*person*); become the accepted thing; attract followers; *faire l'*⁓ (*à*) teach; *faire l'*⁓ *buissonnière* play truant; **écolier, -ère** [ekɔ'lje, ʌ'ljɛːr] *su.* pupil; *su./m* schoolboy; *su./f* schoolgirl.

écologie [ekɔlɔ'ʒi] *f* ecology; **écologique** [ʌ'ʒik] ecological; **écologis-**me [ʌ'ʒism] *m* ecology movement; **écologiste** [ʌ'ʒist] *su.* ecologist.

éconduire [ekɔ̃'dɥiːr] (4h) *v/t.* show out; get rid of; reject (*a suitor*); *être éconduit* meet with a polite refusal.

économat [ekɔnɔ'ma] *m* † stewardship; *school, univ.:* bursarship; *society:* treasurership; steward's (*etc.*) office; **économe** [ʌ'nɔm] **1.** *adj.* economical, thrifty; sparing; **2.** *su.* † steward, housekeeper; treasurer; bursar; **économie** [ekɔnɔ'mi] *f* economy, saving; thrift; management; ⁓*s pl.* savings; ⁓ *dirigée* controlled economy; ⁓ *domestique* domestic economy; housekeeping; ⁓ *politique* political economy; economics *sg.*; *faire des* ⁓*s* save (up); **économique** [ʌ'mik] **1.** *adj.* economic (*doctrine, problem, system*); inexpensive, economical, cheap; **2.** *su./f* economics *sg.*; **économiser** [ʌmi'ze] (1a) *v/t.* economize, save (on, *sur*); **économiste** [ʌ'mist] *m* (political) economist.

écope [e'kɔp] *f* ladle (*a. cuis.*); ⚓ scoop; **écoper** [ekɔ'pe] (1a) *v/t.* bail out; *v/i. sl.* be hit; cop it; get the blame.

écorce [e'kɔrs] *f* tree: bark; *fruit:* rind, peel; *fig.* outside, crust; **écorcer** [ekɔr'se] (1k) *v/t.* bark; peel (*a fruit*).

écorcher [ekɔr'ʃe] (1a) *v/t.* skin, flay; graze, chafe (*the skin*); scrape, scratch; *fig.* murder (*a language*); *fig.* grate on (*the ear*); *fig.* burn (*one's throat*); *fig.* fleece (*a client*); **écorcheur** [ʌ'ʃœːr] *m* flayer; *fig.* fleecer; **écorchure** 🩹 [ʌ'ʃyːr] *f* abrasion, F graze, scratch.

écorner [ekɔr'ne] (1a) *v/t.* break *or* chip the corner(s) off (*s.th.*); dog-ear (*a book*); *fig.* make a hole in (*one's fortune*); **écornifler** F [ʌni'fle] (1a) *v/t.* scrounge; sponge; **écornifleur** *m*, **-euse** *f* F [ʌni'flœːr, ʌ'fløːz] cadger, scrounger; sponger; **écornure** [ʌ'nyːr] *f* chip (*off wood, stone, etc.*).

écossais, e [ekɔ'sɛ, ʌ'sɛːz] **1.** *adj.* Scottish; *étoffe f* ⁓*e* tartan, plaid; **2.** *su./m ling.* Scots; ♀ Scot, Scotsman; *les* ♀ *m/pl.* the Scots; *su./f* ♀ Scot, Scotswoman.

écosser [ekɔ'se] (1a) *v/t.* shell, hull.

écosystème [ekɔsi'stɛm] *m* ecosystem.

écot [e'ko] *m* share (of the bill); *payer chacun son* ~ go Dutch treat, *Am.* go Dutch.

écoulement [ekul'mã] *m* outflow, flow (*a.* 𝄞); (*nasal*) discharge; *bath etc.*: waste-pipe; *crowd*: dispersal; ✝ sale, disposal; ✝ ~ *facile* ready sale; **écouler** [eku'le] (1a) *v/t.* ✝ sell off, dispose of; *s'*~ flow out; pass, elapse (*time*); ✝ sell.

écourter [ekur'te] (1a) *v/t.* shorten, F cut short; dock (*a horse*); crop (*dog's ears*); *fig.* clip (*words*).

écoute[1] [e'kut] *f* listening(-in); *être aux* ~*s* listen (in); *fig.* keep one's ears open (for, *de*); *heures f/pl. de grande* ~ *radio, telev.*: peak listening (viewing) hours; *mettre q. sur* ~(s) tap s.o.'s telephone; *station f d'*~ monitoring station.

écoute[2] ⚓ [~] *f sail*: sheet.

écouter [eku'te] (1a) *v/t.* listen to; pay attention to; *v/i.* listen (in); **écouteur, -euse** [~'tœːr, ~'tøːz] *su. person, a. radio*: listener; *su./m teleph.* receiver; *radio*: head-phone, ear-phone.

écoutille ⚓ [eku'tiːj] *f* hatchway.

écran [e'krã] *m* screen; *phot.* filter; *faire* ~ *à* screen; *fig.* be *or* get in the way of; *le petit* ~ television; *porter à l'*~ film (*a novel, a play*).

écraser [ekra'ze] (1a) *v/t.* crush; *mot.* run over; ✝ F glut (*the market*); *fig.* overwhelm; *fig.* ruin; *mot.* ~ *l'accélérateur* (*or* F *le champignon*) put one's foot hard down (on the accelerator); *mot.* ~ *le frein* slam on the brakes; *s'*~ collapse; break; ✈, *mot.* crash (into, *contre*); *sl.* (*a. v/i.*) keep one's mouth shut, shut up.

écrémer [ekre'me] (1f) *v/t.* cream (*milk, a. fig.*); skim (*milk, molten glass*); *fig.* take the cream of (*s.th.*); *lait m non écrémé* whole milk; **écrémeuse** [~'møːz] *f* separator; creamer; *metall., a. glass-making*: skimmer; **écrémoir** [~'mwaːr] *m* skimmer.

écrêter [ekre'te] (1a) *v/t.* level off *or* down; *fig.* take the edge off.

écrevisse *zo.* [ekrə'vis] *f* crayfish, *Am.* crawfish.

écrier [ekri'e] (1a) *v/t.*: *s'*~ cry (out), shout (out); exclaim.

écrin [e'krɛ̃] *m* (jewel-)case.

écrire [e'kriːr] (4q) *v/t.* write (down); spell (*a word*); **écrivis** [ekri'vi] 1st

p. sg. p.s. of écrire; **écrivons** [~'vɔ̃] 1st *p. pl. pres. of* écrire; **écrit, e** [e'kri, ~'krit] 1. *p.p. of* écrire; 2. *su./m* writing; document; *univ. etc.* written examination; *par* ~ in writing; **écriteau** [ekri'to] *m* bill, poster, placard; notice; notice-board; **écritoire** [~'twaːr] *m* inkstand; *eccl.* scriptorium; **écriture** [~'tyːr] *f* (hand)writing; script; ✝ entry, item; ✝ ~ *en partie double* double entry; ♀ *sainte* Holy Scripture; ⚖, ✝ ~*s pl.* paper *sg.*, documents; books; **écrivailler** F [~vɑ'je] (1a) *v/i.* scribble; be a hack-writer of the poorest kind; **écrivain** [~'vɛ̃] *m* writer, author; *femme f* ~ authoress; woman writer; **écrivassier** F [~va'sje] *m* hack-writer, penny-a-liner.

écrou[1] [e'kru] *m* ⊕ nut, female screw.

écrou[2] ⚖ [~] *m* entry (*on calendar*) of receipt of prisoner into custody; committal to jail; *levée f d'*~ release from prison.

écrouelles ✱ [ekru'ɛl] *f/pl.* scrofula *sg.*

écrouer ⚖ [ekru'e] (1a) *v/t.* imprison; send to prison.

écrouir *metall.* [ekru'iːr] (2a) *v/t.* cold-hammer; cold-draw; cold-harden; cold-roll.

écroulement [ekrul'mã] *m* collapse, falling-in; crumbling; fall (*a. fig.*), *fig.* ruin; **écrouler** [ekru'le] (1a) *v/t.*: *s'*~ collapse (*a. fig.*); fall (down); crumble; break up; give way; come to nothing.

écroûter [ekru'te] (1a) *v/t.* cut the crust off; ⚒ scarify (*land*).

écru, e [e'kry] unbleached, ecru; *soie f* ~ raw silk; *toile f* ~ holland.

écu [e'ky] *m* shield; 🛡 coat of arms; ~*s pl.* plenty *sg.* of money.

écueil [e'kœːj] *m* reef; rock (*a. fig.*); shelf; *fig.* danger.

écuelle [e'kɥɛl] *f* bowl, basin; ⚔ pan; **écuellée** [ekɥe'le] *f* bowlful.

éculer [eky'le] (1a) *v/t.* wear (*one's shoes*) down at the heel.

écume [e'kym] *f* froth; *waves*: foam; jam, metal, *a. fig.*: lather; scum; ~ *de mer* meerschaum; **écumer** [eky'me] (1a) *v/t.* skim; *fig.* scour (the sea[s], *les mers*); *v/i.* foam, froth (*a. metal, a. fig.*); **écumeur** [~'mœːr] *m*: F ~ *de marmites*

sponger, parasite; ~ de mer pirate;
écumeux, -euse [~'mø, ~'møːz]
foamy, frothy; scummy; **écumoire**
[~'mwaːr] f skimmer.

écurage [eky'raːʒ] m cleansing;
cleaning (out); **écurer** [~'re] (1a)
v/t. cleanse, scour; clean (out); pick
(one's teeth).

écureuil zo. [eky'rœːj] m squirrel.
écureur m, **-euse** f [eky'rœːr, ~'røːz]
cleanser, cleaner, scourer.

écurie [eky'ri] f stable; fig. team.
écusson [eky'sɔ̃] m ∅ shield, escutcheon; ⊕ key-plate; ✕ badge; ♀
shield-bud.

écuyer, -ère [ekɥi'je, ~'jɛːr] su.
rider; su./m horseman; riding-
master; △ staircase: hand-rail; ✗
tree: prop; hist. (e)squire; † equer-
ry; su./f horsewoman; bottes f/pl.
à l'~ère riding-boots.

eczéma ✖ [ɛgze'ma] m eczema.
édénien, -enne [ede'njɛ̃, ~'njɛn]
paradisaic.

édenté, e [edã'te] toothless; zo.
edentate; **édenter** [~] (1a) v/t.
break the teeth of; s'~ lose one's
teeth.

édicter ✗ etc. [edik'te] (1a) v/t.
decree; enact (a law).

édifiant, e [edi'fjã, ~'fjãːt] edifying;
édificateur [edifika'tœːr] m builder; **édification** [~'sjɔ̃] f erection,
building; (moral) edification; fig.
F information; **édifice** [edi'fis] m
building, edifice; structure (a. fig.);
édifier [~'fje] (1o) v/t. build, erect;
edify (morally); fig. F enlighten.

édit [e'di] m edict.
éditer [edi'te] (1a) v/t. edit; publish
(a book etc.); **éditeur** [~'tœːr] m
text: editor; book etc.: publisher;
édition [~'sjɔ̃] f edition; publishing (trade); **éditorial, e,** m/pl.
-aux [~tɔ'rjal, ~'rjo] 1. adj. editorial; leading (article); 2. su./m leader;
editorial.

édredon [edrə'dɔ̃] m eiderdown.
éducable [edy'kabl] educable; train-
able (animal); **éducatif, -ve** [~ka'tif,
~'tiːv] educational; educative; **éducation** [~ka'sjɔ̃] f education, schooling; rearing; training (a. animals); ~
physique physical training.
édulcorant [edylkɔ'rã] m sweetener;
édulcorer [~'re] (1a) v/t. sweeten;
🔩 edulcorate.
éduquer [edy'ke] (1m) v/t. educate;

bring up (a child); train (an animal, a
faculty); mal éduqué ill-bred.

éfaufiler [efofi'le] (1a) v/t. unravel.
effacé, e [efa'se] faded; unobtrusive,
inconspicuous; retiring (manners,
person, etc.), retired (life); receding
(chin etc.); **effacer** [~] (1k) v/t.
efface, blot out, erase; fig. outshine,
throw into the shade; s'~ wear away;
fade away; stand aside; keep in the
background, F take a back seat.

effarement [efar'mã] m alarm;
dismay; **effarer** [efa're] (1a) v/t.
frighten, scare; startle; dismay; s'~
be scared (at, by de); take fright (at,
de).

effaroucher [efaru'ʃe] (1a) v/t.
startle; scare away; alarm; fig. shock
(the modesty).

effectif, -ve [efɛk'tif, ~'tiːv] 1. adj.
effective; ✝ active, real; 2. su./m
manpower; ✕ total strength; ⚓
complement; ⊕ stock; **effectuer**
[~'tɥe] (1n) v/t. effect, carry (out),
execute; accomplish; go into (training).

efféminer [efemi'ne] (1a) v/t. render
effeminate; mollycoddle (a child).

effervescence [efɛrvɛ'sãːs] f effervescence; fig. agitation, exite-
ment; restiveness; **effervescent, e**
[~'sã, ~'sãːt] effervescent (liquid);
fig. in a turmoil.

effet [e'fɛ] m effect, result; operation,
action; impression; ✝ bill; ✝ commencement (of policy); ~ secondaire
side effect; ~s pl. things, clothes; ✝
stocks; ✝ bonds; ✝ ~s pl. à payer (à
recevoir) bills payable (receivable); ✝
~s pl. publics government stock sg. or
securities; ✝ ~ à court terme short-
dated bill; à cet ~ with this end in
view, for this purpose; en ~ indeed;
mettre à l'~ put (s.th.) into operation;
prendre ~ become operative; produire
son ~ operate, act; sans ~ ineffective.

effeuiller [efœ'je] (1a) v/t. pluck the
petals off (a flower); thin out the
leaves of (a fruit-tree); fig. destroy bit
by bit; s'~ lose its petals (flower) or
leaves (tree); **effeuilleuse** F [~'jøːz]
stripper.

efficace [efi'kas] effective; efficient
(a. ⊕); **efficacité** [~kasi'te] f ef-
ficacy; efficiency (a. ⊕).
efficience [efi'sjãːs] f efficiency;
efficient, e [~'sjã, ~'sjãːt] efficient.
effigie [efi'ʒi] f effigy.

effilé, e [efi'le] tapering; slender; *tex.* frayed, fringed; *mot.* streamlined; **effiler** [~'le] (1a) *v/t. tex.* fray, unravel; taper; *cuis.* string (beans); **effilocher** *tex.* [~lɔ'ʃe] (1a) *v/t.* ravel out; fray; break (*cotton waste etc.*).

efflanqué, e [eflɑ̃'ke] lean, F skinny, lanky; *fig.* inadequate (*style*).

effleurer [eflœ're] (1a) *v/t.* graze, touch lightly; brush; skim (*the water*); ✍ plough lightly; *fig.* touch lightly upon (*a subject*).

efflorescence [eflɔrɛ'sɑ̃:s] *f* ♀ flowering; 🔥 efflorescence; 🩹 rash, eruption.

effluent, e [efly'ɑ̃, ~'ɑ̃:t] *adj., a. su./m* effluent; **effluve** [e'fly:v] *m* effluvium; exhalation; *fig.* breath; ⚡ ~ *électrique* glow discharge.

effondrement [efɔ̃drə'mɑ̃] *m* collapse (*a.* ♣, *a. fig.*); caving in; ♣ *prices:* slump; ✍ trenching; **effondrer** [~'dre] (1a) *v/t.:* s'~ collapse; cave in; break down.

efforcer [efɔr'se] (1k) *v/t.:* s'~ de or à (*inf.*) do one's best to (*inf.*); strive to (*inf.*).

effort [e'fɔ:r] *m* effort, exertion; pressure; ⊕ stress; ⊕, 🩹 strain; *sp. ball:* spin.

effraction 🔒 [efrak'sjɔ̃] *f* breaking open; *vol m avec* ~ house-breaking (*by day*), burglary (*by night*).

effrayant, e [efrɛ'jɑ̃, ~'jɑ̃:t] terrifying, dreadful, appalling; *fig.* awful; **effrayer** [~'je] (1i) *v/t.* frighten, scare, terrify; s'~ take fright, be frightened (at, *de*).

effréné, e [efre'ne] unbridled, unrestrained.

effriter [efri'te] (1a) *v/t.* crumble; cause to crumble; s'~ crumble.

effroi [e'frwa] *m* terror, fear, fright; dread.

effronté, e [efrɔ̃'te] brazen-faced, impudent, saucy (*child*); **effronterie** [~'tri] *f* effrontery, impudence, impertinence.

effroyable [efrwa'jabl] frightful (*a. fig.*).

effusion [efy'zjɔ̃] *f* effusion (*a. fig.*); outpouring; ~ *de sang* bloodshed; 🩹 haemorrhage; *avec* ~ effusively.

égailler [ega'je] (1a) *v/t. a.* s'~ scatter (*birds*).

égal, e, *m/pl.* **-aux** [e'gal, ~'go] **1.** *adj.* equal; level; smooth; even (*a. fig.*), regular; steady (*pace*); *cela*

m'est ~ it is all the same to me, I don't mind; F *c'est* ~ all the same; **2.** *su.* equal, peer; *su./m: à l'*~ *de* as much as; **égaler** [ega'le] (1a) *v/t.* regard as equal; be equal to, equal; *fig.* compare with, F touch; **égaliser** [egali'ze] (1a) *v/t.* equalize (*a. sp.*); level; make even; ♪ equate; **égalitaire** [~'tɛ:r] *adj., a. su.* egalitarian; **égalité** [~'te] *f* equality; evenness (*a. fig., a.* ♪); *sp. à* ~ equal on points.

égard [e'ga:r] *m* regard, consideration, respect; ~*s pl.* respect *sg.*; attentions (to, *pour*); *à cet* ~ in this respect; *à l'*~ *de* with respect to; *as regards; à mon* ~ concerning me; *à tous* ~*s* in every respect; *eu* ~ *à* considering; *manque m d'*~ lack of consideration; slight; *par* ~ *pour* out of respect for; *sans* ~ *pour* without regard for.

égarement [egar'mɑ̃] *m* mislaying; error; *fig.* (*mental*) aberration; *feelings:* frenzy; *conduct, expression:* wildness; bewilderment; **égarer** [ega're] (1a) *v/t.* mislay; lead astray; mislead; let (*one's eyes*) wander; bewilder; *fig. avoir l'air égaré* look distraught; s'~ lose one's way; go astray; become unhinged (*mind*).

égayer [egɛ'je] (1i) *v/t.* cheer up; enliven; s'~ amuse o.s.; cheer up; make merry (about, *de*).

églantier ♀ [eglɑ̃'tje] *m* wild rose (-bush); ~ *odorant* sweet briar; **églantine** ♀ [~'tin] *f flower:* wild rose; ~ *odorante flower:* sweet briar.

église [e'gli:z] *f* church.

églogue [e'glɔg] *f* eclogue.

égocentrique [egɔsɑ̃'trik] egocentric.

égoïne ⊕ [egɔ'in] *f* compass saw.

égoïsme [egɔ'ism] *m* egoism; selfishness; **égoïste** [~'ist] **1.** *su.* egoist; **2.** *adj.* egoistic; selfish.

égorger [egɔr'ʒe] (1l) *v/t.* cut the throat of; F stick (*a pig*); slaughter, massacre (*people*); *fig.* fleece; **égorgeur** *m,* **-euse** *f* [~'ʒœ:r, ~'ʒø:z] cutthroat; (*pig-*)sticker.

égosiller [egozi'je] (1a) *v/t.:* s'~ bawl; shout; make o.s. hoarse.

égout [e'gu] *m* sewer; **égoutter** [egu'te] (1a) *v/t.* drain (*a.* ✍); strain (*vegetables*); s'~ drain, drip; **égouttoir** [~'twa:r] *m* drainer; *cuis.* platerack.

égrapper [egra'pe] (1a) *v/t.* pick off (*grapes etc.*); ⚒ clean (*ore*).

égratigner [egrati'ɲe] (1a) *v/t.* scratch (*a.* ✒); *fig.* gibe at, F have a dig at; **égratignure** [ˌ'ɲyːr] *f* scratch; *fig.* gibe, F dig.

égrener [egrə'ne] (1d) *v/t.* pick off (*grapes*); shell (*peas, corn*); gin (*cotton*); ripple(*flax*); *tree:* shed(*the leaves*) one by one; *fig.* deal with one by one; s'ˌ drop (away), scatter.

égrillard, e [egri'jaːr, ˌ'jard] ribald, lewd, F dirty.

eh! [e] *int.* hey!; hi!; ˌ *bien!* well!; now then!

éhonté, e [eɔ̃'te] shameless.

éjaculer [eʒaky'le] (1a) *v/t.* ejaculate.

éjection [eʒɛk'sjɔ̃] *f* ejection.

élaborer [elabɔ're] (1a) *v/t.* elaborate, work out (*a. fig.*).

élaguer [ela'ge] (1m) *v/t.* ✒ prune (*a. fig.*); *fig. a.* cut out *or* down.

élan[1] [e'lɑ̃] *m* spring, dash, bound; impetus; *fig.* impulse; *fig.* outburst (*of temper etc.*).

élan[2] *zo.* [ˌ] *m* elk, moose.

élancé, e [elɑ̃'se] (tall and) slim, slender; **élancement** [elɑ̃s'mɑ̃] *m* spring; *fig.* yearning (towards, *vers*); ⚕ twinge, shooting pain; **élancer** [elɑ̃'se] (1k) *v/i.* twinge, throb; *v/t.:* s'ˌ shoot; rush; ⚕ shoot up.

élargir [elar'ʒiːr] (2a) *v/t.* enlarge; widen; broaden (*a. fig.*); *fig., a.* 🔒 release; **élargissement** [ˌʒis'mɑ̃] *m* enlarging; widening, broadening; *fig., a.* 🔒 release.

élasticité [elastisi'te] *f* elasticity; *fig.* springiness; **élastique** [ˌ'tik] **1.** *adj.* elastic; *fig.* flexible; *gomme f* ˌ (india-)rubber; **2.** *su./m* (india-)rubber; *cost.* elastic; rubber band.

électeur [elɛk'tœːr] *m pol.* voter; elector (*a. hist.*); ˌ *par correspondance* absent voter; **électif, -ve** [ˌ'tif, ˌ'tiːv] elective; **élection** [ˌ'sjɔ̃] *f* election (*a. fig.*); *fig.* choice; ˌs *pl. partielles* by-election *sg.*; **électoral, e,** *m/pl.* -aux [ˌtɔ'ral, ˌ'ro] electoral, election …; **électoralisme** *pej.* [ˌtɔra'lism] *m* electioneering; **électorat** [ˌtɔ'ra] *m coll., a. hist.* electorate; franchise; **électrice** [ˌ'tris] *f pol.* electress (*a. hist.*), voter.

électricien [elɛktri'sjɛ̃] *m* electrician; **électricité** [ˌsi'te] *f* electricity; **électrifier** [ˌ'fje] (1o) *v/t.* elec-

trify; **électrique** [elɛk'trik] electric; electrical (*unit*); **électriser** [ˌtri'ze] (1a) *v/t.* electrify (*a. fig.*); *fig.* thrill; *fil m électrisé* live wire.

électro… [elɛktrɔ] electro…; ˌ-aimant [ˌɛ'mɑ̃] *m* electro-magnet; ˌcardiogramme ⚕ [ˌkardjɔ'gram] *m* electrocardiogram; ˌchoc ⚕ [ˌ'ʃɔk] *m treatment:* electric shock.

électrode [elɛk'trɔd] *f* electrode.

électro…: ˌmagnétique [elɛktrɔmaɲe'tik] electromagnetic; ˌménager [ˌmena'ʒe] *adj./m: appareils m/pl.* ˌs domestic electrical equipment *sg.*

électron *phys.* [elɛk'trɔ̃] *m* electron; **électronicien** [ˌtrɔni'sjɛ̃] *m* electronics engineer; **électronique** [ˌtrɔ'nik] **1.** *adj.* electronic; **2.** *su./f* electronics *sg.*

électrophone [elɛktrɔ'fɔn] *m* record player.

électuaire [elɛk'tɥɛːr] *m* electuary.

élégamment [elega'mɑ̃] *adv.* elegantly; **élégance** [ˌ'gɑ̃ːs] *f* elegance; **élégant, e** [ˌ'gɑ̃, ˌ'gɑ̃ːt] **1.** *adj.* elegant, stylish; smart; **2.** *su./m* man of fashion; *su./f* woman of fashion.

élément [ele'mɑ̃] *m* element; ingredient; ⚡ cell; ˌs *pl.* rudiments, first principles, basics; **élémentaire** [ˌmɑ̃'tɛːr] elementary; rudimentary; fundamental, basic.

éléphant *zo.* [ele'fɑ̃] *m* elephant; ˌ *femelle* cow-elephant.

élevage [el'vaːʒ] *m* breeding, rearing; ranch; **élévateur, -trice** [eleva'tœːr, ˌ'tris] **1.** *adj.* lifting; *anat.* elevator (*muscle*); **2.** *su./m* elevator (*a. anat.*); lift; **élévation** [ˌ'sjɔ̃] *f* elevation (*a.* 🔭, 📐); lifting, raising; rise, increase; height; altitude (*a. astr.*); **élévatoire** [ˌ'twaːr] hoisting.

élève [e'lɛːv] *su.* pupil; *univ.* student; apprentice; *su./f* young rearing animal; *cattle etc.:* breeding; ✒ seedling.

élevé, e [el've] high; *fig.* lofty; bred, brought-up; *mal* ˌ ill-bred; **élever** [ˌ've] (1d) *v/t.* raise (*a.* 🔭), lift; 📐 erect, set up; breed (*cattle etc.*); keep (*bees, hens*); bring up (*a child*); 📐 ˌ *au carré (au cube)* square (cube); s'ˌ rise; get up; amount (to, *à*); protest, take a stand (against, *contre*); **éleveur** [ˌ'vœːr] *m* breeder (*of horses, cattle*); ˌ *de* chiens dog-fancier; **élevure** ⚕ [~-'vy:r] *f* pimple, pustule.

élider *gramm.* [eli'de] (1a) *v/t.* elide.

éligible [eli'ʒibl] eligible.

élimer [eli'me] (1a) *v/t. a.* s'~ wear threadbare.

éliminer [elimi'ne] (1a) *v/t.* eliminate (*a.* Ⱥ); get rid of; Ⱥ s'~ cancel out.

élire [e'li:r] (4t) *v/t.* elect, choose; *parl.* return (*a member*).

élision *gramm.* [eli'zjɔ̃] *f* elision.

élitaire [eli'tɛ:r] elitist; **élite** [e'lit] *f* elite, pick, choice, best; *d'~* picked; crack (*team etc.*).

élixir [elik'si:r] *m* elixir.

elle [ɛl] *pron./pers./f subject*: she, it; ~s *pl.* they; *object*: her, it; (to) her, (to) it; ~s *pl.* them; (to) them; à ~ to her, to it; hers, its; à ~s *pl.* to them; theirs; *c'est* ~ it is she, F it's her; *ce sont* ~s *pl.*, F *c'est* ~s *pl.* it is they, F it's them.

ellébore ♣ [elle'bɔ:r] *m* hellebore; ~ *noir* Christmas rose.

elle-même [ɛl'mɛ:m] *pron./rfl.* herself; **elles-mêmes** *pl.* themselves.

ellipse [e'lips] *f gramm.* ellipsis; Ⱥ ellipse; **elliptique** [elip'tik] elliptic(al).

élocution [elɔky'sjɔ̃] *f* elocution.

éloge [e'lɔ:ʒ] *m* praise; eulogy, panegyric.

éloigné, e [elwa'ɲe] remote; distant (*a. relative*); far-off, faraway; far (off *or* away); **éloignement** [elwaɲ-'mɑ̃] *m* distance; remoteness; removal; *fig.* estrangement; **éloigner** [elwa'ɲe] (1a) *v/t.* remove; move (*s.th.*) away; dismiss (*a thought*); avert (*a suspicion, a danger*); postpone; estrange (*s.o.*); s'~ move away, go away; digress; s'~ *du sujet* wander from the subject, divagate.

éloquence [elɔ'kɑ̃:s] *f* eloquence; **éloquent, e** [~'kɑ̃, ~'kɑ̃:t] eloquent.

élucider [elysi'de] (1a) *v/t.* elucidate, clear up.

élucubrations [elykybra'sjɔ̃] *f/pl.* *pej.* wild imaginings.

éluder [ely'de] (1a) *v/t. fig.* evade; shirk (*work*).

Élysée [eli'ze] **1.** *su./m myth.* Elysium; *pol.* Élysée (= *Paris residence of the President of the French Republic*); **2.** *adj. myth.* Elysian (*Fields*).

émacier [ema'sje] (1o) *v/t.* s'~ waste away, become emaciated.

émail, *pl.* **-aux** [e'ma:j, ~'mo] *m* enamel (*a. of teeth*); enamelling material; *phot.* glaze; **émailler** [ema-'je] (1a) *v/t.* enamel; glaze (*porcelain, a. phot.*); *fig.* sprinkle, spangle (with, de).

émanation [emana'sjɔ̃] *f* emanation, efflux.

émancipation [emɑ̃sipa'sjɔ̃] *f* emancipation; **émancipé, e** *fig.* [~'pe] free, forward; **émanciper** [~'pe] (1a) *v/t.* emancipate.

émaner [ema'ne] (1a) *v/i.* emanate, issue, originate.

émarger [emar'ʒe] (1l) *v/t.* make marginal notes in, write in the margin of; *v/i.* † draw one's salary.

émasculation [emaskyla'sjɔ̃] *f* emasculation (*a. fig.*).

embâcle [ɑ̃'ba:kl] *m* obstruction; ice-jam (*in water-way*).

emballage [ɑ̃ba'la:ʒ] *m* packing; package; packaging; *sp.* burst of speed; F blowing-up; ✝ ~ *perdu* (*consigné*) non-returnable (returnable) packing (*or* can, bottle, *etc.*); **emballer** [~'le] (1a) *v/t.* pack (up); wrap up; *mot.* race (*the engine*); thrill, excite; F blow (*s.o.*) up; *sl.* arrest; *sl.* get (*s.o.*) round; s'~ bolt (*horse*); race (*engine*); F get excited; F fly into a temper; *v/i. sp.* spurt; **emballeur** *m*, **-euse** *f* [~'lœ:r, ~'lø:z] packer; *sl.* cajoler.

embarbouiller F [ɑ̃barbu'je] (1a) *v/t.* dirty; *fig.* muddle (*s.o.*); s'~ get muddled.

embarcadère [ɑ̃barka'dɛ:r] *m* ⚓ landing-stage; wharf, quay; 🚄 (departure) platform; **embarcation** [~'sjɔ̃] *f* craft; ship's boat.

embardée [ɑ̃bar'de] *f* swerve.

embargo ⚓, *pol.* [ɑ̃bar'go] *m* embargo.

embarquement [ɑ̃barkə'mɑ̃] *m* ⚓ embarkation; *goods*: shipment; **embarquer** [~'ke] (1m) *v/t.* ⚓ embark; ship (*goods*, F *a. water*); take on board; *v/i. a.* s'~ embark (*a. fig.* upon, *dans*), go aboard.

embarras [ɑ̃ba'ra] *m* obstruction; impediment (*of speech*); difficulty, trouble; embarrassment; ~ *d'argent* money difficulties; ~ *pl.* traffic jam; F *faire des* ~ make a fuss; **embarrasser** [~ra'se] (1a) *v/t.* clutter (up); hinder; bother; put in an awkward position; *fig.* perplex,

puzzle; 🖈 clog (*the digestion*); s'~ de
burden o.s. with.
embasement ⬙ [ãbaz'mã] *m* base;
ground-table.
embauchage [ãbo'ʃaːʒ] *m*, **embauche** [ã'boːʃ] *f* taking on (*of
workmen*); hiring; *labour*: *pas d'embauche* no vacancies; **embaucher**
[ãbo'ʃe] (1a) *v/t.* take on, hire; **embauchoir** [~'ʃwaːr] *m* boot tree.
embaumé, e [ãbo'me] balmy (*air*);
embaumer [~] (1a) *v/t.* embalm
(*a corpse, a. the garden*); scent, perfume; smell of; *v/i.* smell sweet.
embecquer [ãbɛ'ke] (1m) *v/t.* feed
(*a bird*); bait (*the hook*).
embéguiner [ãbegi'ne] (1a) *v/t.*
wrap up (*s.o.'s*) head (in, de); *fig.*
infatuate; s'~ de become infatuated
with (*s.o.*).
embellie [ãbɛ'li] *f* 🕂 lull; fair
period; **embellir** [~'liːr] (2a) *v/t.*
make (look) more attractive; embellish (*a. fig.*); beautify; *fig.* glamorize;
v/i. become better-looking; **embellissement** [~lis'mã] *m* embellishment; improvement in looks.
emberlificoter *sl.* [ãbɛrlifiko'te]
(1a) *v/t.* entangle; get round, cajole;
s'~ get tangled; get in a muddle.
embêtant, e F [ãbɛ'tã, ~'tãːt] annoying, irritating, tiresome; **em-
bêtement** F [ãbɛt'mã] *m* nuisance;
worry; annoyance; F bother; **embêter** F [ãbɛ'te] (1a) *v/t.* annoy;
bore; get on (*s.o.'s*) nerves.
emblave ✔ [ã'blaːv] *f* land sown
with corn; *corn*: sown seed; **em-
blaver** ✔ [ãbla've] (1a) *v/t.* sow
with corn.
emblée [ã'ble] *adv.*: d'~ right away,
then and there, at the first attempt.
emblème [ã'blɛːm] *m* emblem;
symbol; badge.
embob(el)iner F [ãbɔb(l)i'ne] (1a)
v/t. get round, coax.
emboîter [ãbwa'te] (1a) *v/t.* encase;
nest (*boats, boxes, tubes*); pack in
boxes; ⊕ joint; F hiss, hoot; ~ *le
pas à q.* dog s.o.'s footsteps; 🗙 fall
into step with s.o.; *fig.* model o.s.
on s.o.; **emboîture** [~'tyːr] *f* fit;
⊕ socket; ⊕ joint; 🖈 juncture.
embolie 🖈 [ãbɔ'li] *f* embolism.
embonpoint [ãbõ'pwɛ̃] *m* stoutness;
plumpness.
emboucher [ãbu'ʃe] (1a) *v/t.* ♪ put
to one's mouth; *fig. mal embouché*

foul-mouthed;   **embouchure**
[~'ʃyːr] *f* river: mouth; ♪ mouthpiece; opening.
embourber [ãbur'be] (1a) *v/t.* bog;
fig. implicate; s'~ get stuck in the
mud (*etc.*); *fig.* get tied up.
embourgeoiser [ãburʒwa'ze] (1a)
v/t.: s'~ become conventional.
embout [ã'bu] *m* stick, umbrella:
ferrule.
embouteillage [ãbutɛ'jaːʒ] *m* bottling; 🕂 bottling up; *fig.* traffic jam;
⚓ bottleneck; **embouteiller** [~'je]
(1a) *v/t.* bottle; 🕂 bottle up, block
up; *fig.* hold up (*the traffic*); block
(*the road*).
embouter [ãbu'te] (1a) *v/t.* tip, put
a ferrule on.
emboutir [ãbu'tiːr] (2a) *v/t.* ⊕
stamp, press (*metal*); emboss; tip,
put a ferrule on; *mot.* hit, run or
crash into.
embranchement [ãbrãʃ'mã] *m*
junction; branching (off); ⊕, *a. fig.*
branch; 🚋 branch-line; 🚋 siding;
fork (*of a road*); branch-road; *geog.*
spur; **embrancher** [ãbrã'ʃe] (1a)
v/t. join up; s'~ form a junction
(*roads*); branch off (from, sur).
embrasement [ãbraz'mã] *m* conflagration; *fig.* fire; *fig.* burning passion; *pol.*, *fig.* conflagration; **em-
braser** [ãbra'ze] (1a) *v/t.* set on
fire; *fig.* fire; *fig.* set aglow.
embrassade [ãbra'sad] *f* embrace,
hug; kissing; **embrasser** [~'se]
(1a) *v/t.* embrace (*a. fig.*); hug; *fig.*
take up (*a career, a cause*); *fig.* encircle; kiss; include, take in.
embrasure [ãbra'zyːr] *f* embrasure; window-recess; 🕂 gun-port.
embrayage [ãbrɛ'jaːʒ] *m* ⊕ connecting, coupling; *mot. clutch*: engaging; putting (*the engine*) into
gear; *mot.* clutch; *mot.* ~ *à cône* cone
clutch; *mot.* ~ *à disques* multi-disc
clutch; **embrayer** [~'je] (1i) *v/t.* ⊕
connect, couple; throw into gear; F
fig. start, set (*s.th.*) rolling; *v/i. mot.*
let in the clutch; F *fig.* start, begin.
embrigader [ãbriga'de] (1a) *v/t.* 🗙
recruit; *fig.* enrol; F organize.
embrocher [ãbrɔ'ʃe] (1a) *v/t. cuis.*
(put on the) spit; ⚡ wire on to a
circuit; F run (*s.o.*) through.
embrouillage [ãbru'jaːʒ] *m*, **embrouillement** [ãbruj'mã] *m* confusion; tangle; **embrouillamini** F

[ăbrujami'ni] *m* tangle, mess(-up);
embrouiller [ăbru'je] (1a) *v/t.*
tangle (up); muddle (up); *fig.* confuse (*an issue*); *s'~* get into a tangle;
fig. get into a muddle.

embroussaillé, e [ăbrusa'je] covered with bushes; *fig.* tousled; F
complicated.

embruiné, e [ăbrui'ne] ✔ blighted
with cold drizzle; lost in a haze of
rain.

embrumer [ăbry'me] (1a) *v/t.*
shroud with mist *or* haze *or* fog; *fig.*
cloud.

embruns [ă'brœ̃] *m/pl.* sea spray *sg.*,
spindrift *sg.*

embrunir [ăbry'ni:r] (2a) *v/t.*
darken.

embryon [ăbri'jɔ̃] *m* embryo (*a.*
fig.); F insignificant little man.

embûche [ă'by:ʃ] *f* trap, pitfall; †
ambush.

embuer [ă'bɥe] (1n) *v/t.* steam up;
dim (*a. fig.*).

embuscade [ăbys'kad] *f* ambush;
embusqué [~'ke] *m* man in ambush; man under cover; F ✗
shirker, dodger; **embusquer** ✗
etc. [~'ke] (1m) *v/t.* place in ambush
or in wait; *s'~* lie in wait; take
cover; F ✗ shirk.

éméché, e F [eme'ʃe] slightly the
worse for drink *or* F for wear.

émeraude [em'ro:d] *su./f, a.*
adj./inv. emerald.

émerger [emɛr'ʒe] (1l) *v/i.* emerge;
come into view, appear.

émeri [em'ri] *m* emery(-powder).

émérite [eme'rit] emeritus (*professor*); experienced, practised.

émersion [emɛr'sjɔ̃] *f* emergence
(*a. opt.*); *astr.* emersion.

émerveiller [emɛrve'je] (1a) *v/t.*
amaze, fill with wonder; *s'~* marvel,
be amazed (at, de).

émétique ✗ [eme'tik] *adj., a. su./m*
emetic.

émetteur, -trice [eme'tœ:r, ~'tris]
1. *adj.* issuing; *radio:* transmitting,
broadcasting; **2.** *su./m* † issuer;
radio: transmitter; *~ à modulation
de fréquence* V.H.F. transmitter; *~
à ondes courtes* short wave transmitter; *~ de télévision* television
transmitter; *~-récepteur radio:*
transmitter-receiver, F walkie-
talkie; **émettre** [e'mɛtr] (4v) *v/t.*
emit, send out; † issue; utter (*a*

sound, a. counterfeit coins); express
(*an opinion*); *radio:* transmit, broadcast; put forward (*a claim*).

émeute [e'mø:t] *f* riot, disturbance;
émeutier [emø'tje] *m* rioter.

émietter [emjɛ'te] (1a) *v/t.* crumble;
fig. waste.

émigration [emigra'sjɔ̃] *f* emi-
gration; **émigré, e** [~'gre] *su.* expatriate; **émigrer** [~'gre] (1a) *v/i.*
emigrate (*people*); *pol.* fly the
country.

émincé *cuis.* [emɛ̃'se] *m* sliced meat;
émincer [~] (1k) *v/t.* mince, slice
(up) (*meat*).

éminemment [emina'mɑ̃] *adv.* to
a high degree; **éminence** [~'nɑ̃:s] *f*
eminence (*a. fig., a. title*); **éminent, e** [~'nɑ̃, ~'nɑ̃:t] eminent;
high, elevated; *fig.* distinguished.

émissaire [emi'sɛ:r] **1.** *su./m* emissary (*a.* ⊕), messenger; ⊕ outlet;
anat. emissary vein; **2.** *adj.:* *bouc
m ~* scapegoat; **émission** [~'sjɔ̃] *f*
emission; † issue, issuing; uttering
(*of sound, a. of counterfeit coins*);
heat: radiation; *radio:* transmission,
broadcast(ing); *~ de télévision* television transmission.

emmagasiner [ămagazi'ne] (1a)
v/t. † store, warehouse; ⚡, *phys.,
a. fig.* store up.

emmailloter [ămajo'te] (1a) *v/t.*
swaddle (*a baby*); swathe (*one's leg
etc.*).

emmancher [ămɑ̃'ʃe] (1a) *v/t.* fix
a handle to, haft; ⊕ joint (*pipes*);
fig. start (*an affair*).

emmanchure [ămɑ̃'ʃy:r] *f* armhole.

emmêler [ămɛ'le] (1a) *v/t.* tangle;
fig. mix up, get in a tangle *or*
muddle.

emménager [ămena'ʒe] (1l) *v/i.*
move in; *v/t.* move (*s.o., s.th.*) in,
install.

emmener [ăm'ne] (1d) *v/t.* take
(*s.o.*) away, lead (*s.o.*) away *or* out.

emmerdant, e ∨ [ămɛr'dɑ̃, ~'dɑ̃:t]
boring; annoying; **emmerder** ∨
[~'de] (1a) *v/t.* bore (*s.o.*) (stiff); get
on (*s.o.'s*) nerves; bug, give (*s.o.*) a
pain in the neck; *s'~* be bored (stiff).

emmieller [ămjɛ'le] (1a) *v/t.*
sweeten with honey; *fig.* sugar
(*one's words*); ∨ irritate.

emmitoufler [ămitu'fle] (1a) *v/t.*
muffle up (in dans, de).

émoi [e'mwa] *m* emotion, agitation; excitement; commotion; anxiety.

émollient, e 🌿 [emɔ'ljã, ˷'ljã:t] *adj., a. su./m* emollient, counter-irritant.

émoluments [emɔly'mã] *m/pl.* emoluments, pay *sg.*, salary *sg.*

émonder [emɔ̃'de] (1a) *v/t.* 🗡 prune (*a. fig. a book*), trim; *fig.* clean.

émotion [emo'sjɔ̃] *f* emotion; *fig.* agitation, disturbance; 🌿 quickening (*of pulse*); **émotionnable** [˷-sjɔ'nabl] emotional; excitable; **émotionner** F [˷sjɔ'ne] (1a) *v/t.* affect; thrill.

émotivité [emɔtivi'te] *f* emotivity.

émoucher [emu'ʃe] (1a) *v/t.* drive the flies from *or* off; **émouchette** [˷'ʃɛt] *f* fly-net (*for horses*); **émouchoir** [˷'ʃwa:r] *m* fly-whisk; fly-net (*for horses*).

émoudre ⊕ [e'mudr] (4w) *v/t.* grind, sharpen, whet; **émoulu, e** [emu'ly] sharp(ened); *fig. frais* ˷ de fresh from (*school etc.*).

émousser [emu'se] (1a) *v/t.* ⊕ blunt, take the edge off (*a. fig.*); 🗡 remove the moss from; ⊕ *s'*˷ become blunt(ed) (*a. fig.*); lose its edge *or* point.

émoustiller F [emusti'je] (1a) *v/t.* exhilarate, F ginger up; put on one's mettle; *s'*˷ get jolly; cheer up.

émouvant, e [emu'vã, ˷'vã:t] moving, touching; **émouvoir** [˷'vwa:r] (3f) *v/t.* move; affect, touch; stir up, rouse (*the audience, a crowd*).

empailler [ãpa'je] (1a) *v/t.* pack (*s.th.*) in straw; stuff (*a dead animal*); 🗡 cover up with straw.

empaler [ãpa'le] (1a) *v/t.* impale.

empan [ã'pã] *m* span.

empaqueter [ãpak'te] (1c) *v/t.* pack up; wrap up; do up (*a parcel*).

emparer [ãpa're] (1a) *v/t.: s'*˷ de seize, lay hands on; take possession of.

empâté, e [ãpa'te] coated (*tongue*); *fig.* thick (*voice*); bloated (*face*); **empâter** [˷] (1a) *v/t.* make thick; *s'*˷ put on flesh.

empattement [ãpat'mã] *m mot.* wheel base; 🔺 foundation; 🔺 *wall:* footing.

empaumer F [ãpo'me] (1a) *v/t.* trick (*s.o.*), take (*s.o.*) in.

empêchement [ãpɛʃ'mã] *m* obstacle, hindrance; prevention; impediment (*of speech*); *sans* ˷ without let or hindrance; **empêcher** [ãpɛ'ʃe] (1a) *v/t.* prevent (from *ger., de inf.*); stop; hinder; *s'*˷ de refrain from, stop o.s. (from) (*doing s.th.*); *on ne peut s'*˷ de *a.* one cannot help (*doing s.th.*).

empeigne [ã'pɛɲ] *f shoe:* vamp.

empennage 🛩 [ãpɛ'na:ʒ] *m* tail unit; stabilizer(s *pl.*); *bomb:* fin assembly.

empereur [ã'prœ:r] *m* emperor.

empesé, e F [ãpə'ze] stiff, starchy (*manner etc.*); **empeser** [˷] (1d) *v/t.* starch (*linen etc.*); stiffen.

empester [ãpɛs'te] (1a) *v/t.* stink out (*a room*); stink (of).

empêtrer [ãpɛ'tre] (1a) *v/t.* hobble (*an animal*); entangle; *fig.* involve (in, *dans*); *fig.* embarrass (*s.o.*).

emphase [ã'fa:z] *f* bombast, pomposity; *gramm.* emphasis; **emphatique** [ãfa'tik] bombastic, pompous; grandiloquent; *gramm.* emphatic.

empierrer [ãpjɛ're] (1a) *v/t.* metal (*a road*); pave; 🚂 ballast (*a track*).

empiéter [ãpje'te] (1f) *v/i.* trespass, encroach (upon, *sur*) (*a. fig.*); *v/t.* appropriate (from, *sur*).

empiffrer F [ãpi'fre] (1a) *v/t.: s'*˷ de stuff o.s. with.

empiler [ãpi'le] (1a) *v/t.* pile (up); F rob, cheat (out of, *de*); *fig.* F *s'*˷ *dans* pile into.

empire [ã'pi:r] *m* empire; dominion; sway; control; influence; ˷ *sur soi-même* self-control.

empirer [ãpi're] (1a) *v/t.* make (*s.th.*) worse; *v/i.* become *or* grow worse.

empirique [ãpi'rik] **1.** *adj.* empirical, rule-of-thumb; **2.** *su./m* empiricist; **empirisme** [˷'rism] *m* empiricism; *fig.* guess-work.

emplacement [ãplas'mã] *m* buildings etc.: site; place, spot; ⚓ berth (*of a ship*); ⚔ *gun:* emplacement; ⚔(dis)position (*of troops for battle*), station (*of peace-time troops*).

emplâtre [ã'pla:tr] *m* 🌿 plaster; *mot. etc.* patch.

emplette [ã'plɛt] *f* purchase, shopping.

emplir [ã'pli:r] (2a) *v/t. a. s'*˷ fill (up).

emploi [ã'plwa] *m* employment; use; post, job, situation; ˷ *du temps* schedule, timetable; *mode m d'~* directions *pl.* for use; *plein ~* full employment; *sans ~* unemployed, jobless; **employé** *m*, **e** *f* [ãplwa'je] employee; clerk; *shop:* assistant; **employer** [~'je] (1h) *v/t.* employ; use; spend (*time*); *s'~* be used; *s'~ à* apply *or* devote o.s. to ([*doing*] *s.th.*); **employeur** *m*, **-euse** *f* [~'jœːr, ~'jøːz] employer.

empocher [ãpɔ'ʃe] (1a) *v/t.* pocket (*a. fig.*); *fig.* receive, F get.

empoigner [ãpwa'ɲe] (1a) *v/t.* grip (*a. fig.*); grasp, seize; catch, arrest.

empois [ã'pwɑ] *m* starch; *tex.* dressing.

empoisonnant, e F [ãpwazɔ'nã, ~'nãːt] irritating, annoying; *fig.* poisonous; **empoisonner** [~'ne] (1a) *v/t.* poison; *fig.* corrupt; *fig.* bore (*s.o.*) to death; reek of; **empoisonneur, -euse** [~'nœːr, ~'nøːz] **1.** *su.* poisoner; **2.** *adj.* poisonous.

empoissonner [ãpwasɔ'ne] (1a) *v/t.* stock (*a lake etc.*) with fish.

emporté, e [ãpɔr'te] **1.** *adj.* hotheaded, hasty; quick-tempered; **2.** *su.* hot-headed *or* quick-tempered person; **emportement** [~tə'mã] *m* (fit of) anger; *avec ~* angrily; **emporte-pièce** [~tə'pjɛs] *m/inv.* punch; *fig. à l'~* cutting, sarcastic; **emporter** [~'te] (1a) *v/t.* carry away, take away; remove; ✗ *etc.* capture; *plats m/pl. à ~* take-away meals, *Am.* meals to go; *l'~* win, get the upper hand (of, *sur*); prevail (over, *sur*); *l'~ sur a.* get the better of; *fig.* surpass, triumph over; *s'~* lose one's temper, flare up; bolt (*horse*).

empoté, e [ãpɔ'te] **1.** *adj.* awkward, clumsy; **2.** *su.* awkward *or* clumsy person; **empoter** [~] (1a) *v/t.* pot (*jam etc., a.* ✗).

empourprer [ãpur'pre] (1a) *v/t.* tinge with crimson *or* with purple (*grapes*); *s'~* flush (*person*); turn red.

empreindre [ã'prɛ̃ːdr] (4m) *v/t.* imprint, stamp, impress; **empreinte** [ã'prɛ̃t] *f* impress, (im-)print, stamp, impression; *~ digitale* finger-print.

empressé, e [ãprɛ'se] eager; earnest, fervent; willing; fussy; **empressement** [ãprɛs'mã] *m* eagerness, promptness, readiness; hurry; *avec ~* readily; *peu d'~* reluctance; **empresser** [ãprɛ'se] (1a) *v/t.: s'~*

à (*inf.*) be eager to (*inf.*), show zeal in (*ger.*); *s'~ de* (*inf.*) hasten to (*inf.*).

emprise [ã'priːz] *f* hold (on, *sur*); mastery.

emprisonner [ãprizɔ'ne] (1a) *v/t.* imprison; confine (*s.o. to his room*).

emprunt [ã'prœ̃] *m* loan; borrowing; *gramm.* loanword; *nom m d'~* assumed name; ✝ *souscrire à un ~* subscribe to a loan; **emprunté, e** [ãprœ̃'te] assumed; sham; borrowed; derived; stiff, awkward (*manner etc.*); **emprunter** [~'te] (1a) *v/t.* borrow (from, of *à*); assume (*a name*); take (*a road, a track*); **emprunteur** *m*, **-euse** *f* [~'tœːr, ~'tøːz] borrower; ⚖ bailee.

empuantir [ãpɥã'tiːr] (2a) *v/t.* make (*s.th.*) stink; infect (*the air*); *s'~* become foul.

ému, e [e'my] *p.p.* of émouvoir.

émulateur, -trice [emyla'tœːr, ~'tris] emulative, rival; **émulation** [~'sjɔ̃] *f* emulation, rivalry, competition; **émule** [e'myl] *su.* emulator, rival, competitor.

émulsion [emyl'sjɔ̃] *f* emulsion; **émulsionner** [~sjɔ'ne] (1a) *v/t.* emulsify.

en¹ [ã] *prp. place:* in (*France*); at; *direction:* into (*town*); to (*France, town*); *time:* in (*summer*); (with)in (*an hour, two days*); *state:* in (*good health, mourning, prayer, English*); on (*leave, strike, sale*); at (*war, peace*); as, like (*some character*); *change:* into (*decay, oblivion, English*); to (*dust, ashes, pieces*); *material:* of; *ger.:* ~ *dansant* (while) dancing; ~ *attendant* in the meantime; *partir ~ courant* run away; ~ *ne pas* (*ger.*) by not (*ger.*); ~ *ville* in town, *Am.* downtown; ~ *tête* at the head (of, *de*); *aller ~ ville* go to town; ~ *voiture* in a *or* by car; ✍ ~ *voiture!* all aboard!; ~ *avion* by air; ~ *arrière* (*de*) behind; *direction:* ~ *arrière* backward; ~ *avant* in front; *direction:* forward, on; *de ... ~ ...* from ... to ...; ~ (*l'an*) *1789* in 1789; ~ *colère* in anger, angry; ~ *défaut* at fault; ~ *fait* in fact; ~ *hâte* in a hurry; ~ *honnête homme* (*ami*) as *or* like an honest man (a friend); *mettre ~ vente* put up for sale; ~ *vérité* really, actually; ~ *vie* alive, living; *changer*

des livres ~ francs change pounds
into francs; briser ~ morceaux break
to pieces or into bits; ... ~ bois (or)
wooden (gold) ...; escalier m ~ spirale spiral staircase; fertile (riche) ~
fertile (rich) in; ~ l'honneur de in
hono(u)r of; ~ punition de as a punishment for; docteur m ~ droit Doctor of Laws; admirer qch. ~q. admire
s.th. about s.o.; de mal ~ pis from
bad to worse; de plus ~ plus more
and more.

en[2] [~] **1.** adv. from there; on that
account, for it; ~ être plus riche be
the richer for it; j'~ viens I have
just come from here; **2.** pron. genitive: of or about or by or from or
with him (her, it, them); quantity
or inanimate possessor: of it or them;
partitive use: some, any, negative:
not any, none; sometimes untrans-
lated: qu'~ pensez-vous? what do
you think (about it)?, what is your
opinion?; qu'~ dira-t-on? what
will people say (about it)?; il ~
mourut he died of it; il s'~ soucie
he worries about it; j'~ ai cinq I
have five (of them); je vous ~ offre
la moitié I offer you a half or half
of it; j'~ connais qui ... I know
some people who ...; je connais cet
auteur et j'~ ai lu tous les livres I
know this author and have read all
his books; j'~ ai besoin I need it or
some; je n'~ ai pas I have none, I
haven't any; prenez-~ take some;
c'~ est fait the worst has happened;
c'~ est fait de moi I am done for;
je vous ~ félicite! congratulations!;
s'~ aller go away.

enamourer [ănamu're] (1a) v/t.:
s'~ fall in love (with, de).

encablure ⚓ [ăka'bly:r] f cable('s-
length).

encadrement [ăkadrə'mă] m framing; frame(work); setting; **encadrer** [~'dre] (1a) v/t. frame; enclose, surround; ✕ officer (a battalion); ✕ enrol (recruits); ✕ straddle (an objective).

encager [ăka'ʒe] (1l) v/t. put in a
cage; ✕ cage.

encaisse [ă'kɛs] f ✝ cash (in hand);
box. punishment; **encaissé, e**
[ăke'se] encased; deep (valley);
sunken (road); **encaisser** [~] (1b)
v/t. ✝ box, encase; ✍ plant in
tubs; ✝ collect, (en)cash (a bill,

money); ⊕ embank (a river); ballast (a road); fig. swallow (an insult); fig. stand, bear; F ~ une gifle
get one's ears boxed.

encan [ăkă] m (public) auction;
mettre à l'~ put (s.th.) up for auction.

encanailler [ăkanɑ'je] (1a) v/t. degrade; fill (the house) with low
company; s'~ lower o.s.; keep low
company; fig. have one's fling.

encapuchonner [ăkapyʃɔ'ne] (1a)
v/t. put a cowl on; ⊕ cover, hood;
s'~ put a cowl or hood on; fig. become a monk.

encaquer [ăka'ke] (1m) v/t. ✝
barrel; fig. pack (people) like sar-
dines.

encartage [ăkar'ta:ʒ] m insetting;
inset; ✝ card(ing) (of pins); **encar-
ter** [~'te] (1a) v/t. inset; insert (a
loose leaflet); card (pins).

en-cas [ă'kɑ] m/inv. cuis. snack, light
meal; stand-by, thing kept for emer-
gencies; dumpy umbrella.

encastrement ⊕ [ăkastrə'mă] m
fixing; embedding; bed, recess;
casing, frame; rigid fixing; **encastrer** ⊕ [~'tre] (1a) v/t.: ~ dans fit or
sink or embed into; s'~ dans fit into.

encaustique [ăkos'tik] f encaustic;
floor, furniture: wax polish; **en-
caustiquer** [~ti'ke] (1m) v/t. wax,
polish.

encaver [ăka've] (1a) v/t. cellar.

enceindre [ă'sɛ̃:dr] (4m) v/t. surround, gird, enclose.

enceinte[1] [ă'sɛ̃:t] f enclosure; precincts pl.; box. ring; surrounding
wall(s pl.).

enceinte[2] [~] adj./f pregnant.

encens [ă'să] m incense; fig. flattery; **encenser** [ăsă'se] (1a) v/t.
eccl. cense; burn incense to; fig.
flatter; **encenseur** [~'sœ:r] m eccl.
thurifer; fig. flatterer; **encensoir**
[~'swa:r] m thurible, censer; fig.
flattery, fulsome praise.

encéphale ✻ [ăse'fal] m encephalon,
brain; **encéphalite** ✻ [~fa'lit] f
encephalitis.

encerclement [ăsɛrklə'mă] m en-
circling; **encercler** [~'kle] (1a) v/t.
encircle, shut in.

enchaînement [ăʃɛn'mă] chain,
series, linking; dog etc.: chaining
(up); fig. sequence; **enchaîner**
[ăʃɛ'ne] (1b) v/t. chain (a dog, a

prisoner); connect, link up (*a. fig. ideas*); *fig.* captivate; *fig.* curb, en- chain.

enchanté, e [ăʃǎ'te] enchanted; delightful (*place*); *fig.* delighted (at, with *de*; to *inf.*, de *inf.*); ~ de vous voir pleased to meet you; **enchante- ment** [ăʃăt'mǎ] *m* magic; spell; *fig.* charm; *fig.* delight; **enchanter** [ăʃǎ'te] (1a) *v/t.* bewitch; delight; **enchanteur, -eresse** [~'tœːr, ~'trɛs] **1.** *su. fig.* charmer; *su./m* enchanter; *su./f* enchantress; **2.** *adj.* entrancing; enchanting; delight- ful, charming.

enchâsser [ăʃɑ'se] (1a) *v/t.* mount, set (*jewels, a.* ⊕); ⊕, *a. fig.* frame, house; *eccl.* enshrine; **enchâssure** [~'syːr] *f jewel etc.*: setting; ⊕ axle: housing.

enchère [ă'ʃɛːr] *f* bidding, bid; *der- nière (folle)* ~ highest (irrespon- sible) bid; *mettre (or vendre) aux ~s* put up for auction; *vente f aux ~s* auction sale.

enchérir [ăʃe'riːr] (2a) *v/t.* † raise the price of; *v/i.* † grow dearer, go up (*in price*); make a higher bid, go higher; ~ *sur* outbid (*s.o.*); *fig.* out- do (*s.o.*); *fig.* improve on (*s.th.*); **enchérissement** † [~ris'mǎ] *m* rise (in price); **enchérisseur** [~ri- 'sœːr] *m* bidder; *dernier* ~ highest bidder.

enchevêtrer [ăʃve'tre] (1a) *v/t.* halter (*a horse*); *fig.* entangle, con- fuse; △ join (*joists*).

enclave *pol.* [ă'klaːv] *f* enclave; **en- claver** [ăkla've] (1a) *v/t. pol.* enclave (*a territory*); *fig.* hem in, enclose.

enclenche ⊕ [ă'klăːʃ] *f* gab; **enclen- cher** [ăklă'ʃe] (1a) *v/t.* ⊕ engage; throw into gear; ∮ switch on; *fig.* set going.   [prone (to, à).]

enclin, e [ă'klɛ̃, ~'klin] inclined,∫ **enclore** [ă'klɔːr] (4f) *v/t.* enclose; wall in, fence in; **enclos** [ă'klo] *m* enclosure; paddock; sheep-fold; (enclosing) wall.

enclume [ă'klym] *f* anvil (*a. anat.*).

encoche [ă'kɔʃ] *f* notch, nick; slot; ⊕ gab; *avec ~s* thumb-indexed; **enco- cher** [ăkɔ'ʃe] (1a) *v/t.* notch, nick; slot; drive home (*a pin etc.*).

encoffrer [ăkɔ'fre] (1a) *v/t.* lock up (*a. fig.*); *fig.* hoard (*money*).

encoignure [ăkɔ'ɲyːr] *f* corner; corner-cupboard.

encoller [ăkɔ'le] (1a) *v/t.* glue; paste, gum (*paper*); size (*cloth*).

encolure [ăkɔ'lyːr] *f* neck (*a. of horse*); size in collars; neck-line.

encombrant, e [ăkɔ̃'brɑ̃, ~'brɑ̃ːt] cumbersome; bulky (*goods, lug- gage*); **encombre** [ă'kɔ̃ːbr] *m: sans* ~ without difficulty; **encombre- ment** [ăkɔ̃brə'mɑ̃] *m* obstruction; litter; *traffic*: congestion; † glut; *people*: overcrowding; *article*: bulk (-iness); **encombrer** [~'bre] (1a) *v/t.* encumber; obstruct, block up; clutter up; † glut (*the market*); *fig.* saddle with.

encontre [ă'kɔ̃ːtr] *prp.*: à l'~ de against; *aller à l'~ de* run counter to.

encorbellement [ăkɔrbɛl'mǎ] *m* △, ⊕ cantilever; △ corbel-table.

encorder *mount.* [ăkɔr'de] (1a) *v/t.* rope (*climbers*) up; *s'*~ rope up.

encore [ă'kɔːr] **1.** *adv.* still; yet; too, besides; more; once again; ~ *un* another one; ~ *une fois* once again *or* more; *en voulez-vous* ~? do you want some more?; *non seulement ... mais* ~ not only ... but also; *pas* ~ not yet; *quoi* ~? what else?; **2.** *cj.*: ~ *que* (*sbj. or cond.*) although (*ind.*).

encorner [ăkɔr'ne] (1a) *v/t.* gore.

encourager [ăkura'ʒe] (1l) *v/t.* en- courage; cheer up.

encourir [ăku'riːr] (2i) *v/t.* incur; take (*a risk*).

encrasser [ăkra'se] (1a) *v/t.* dirty, soil, grease; ⊕ clog, choke (*a machine*); *mot.* soot up (*a plug*); foul (*a gun*).

encre [ăːkr] *f* ink; ~ *de Chine* Indian ink; ~ *d'imprimerie* printer's ink; ~ *sympathique* invisible ink; **en- crer** *typ.* [ă'kre] (1a) *v/t.* ink; **en- crier** [ăkri'e] *m* ink-pot, ink-well; *typ.* ink-trough.

encroûter [ăkru'te] (1a) *v/t.* crust, encrust; cake with mud *etc.*; △ rough-cast; *fig. s'*~ get into a rut.

encuver [ăky've] (1a) *v/t.* vat.

encyclopédie [ăsiklɔpe'di] *f* ency- clop(a)edia.

endauber *cuis.* [ădo'be] (1a) *v/t.* stew; tin, can.

endémique ✱ [ăde'mik] endemic.

endenter [ădă'te] (1a) *v/t.* tooth, cog (*a wheel*); mesh (*wheels*); indent (*timber*).

endetter [ădɛ'te] (1a) *v/t. a. s'*~ get into debt.

endeuiller [ãdœ'je] (1a) v/t. plunge into mourning; fig. shroud in gloom.
endiablé, e [ãdja'ble] possessed; fig. wild; reckless; fig. mischievous.
endiguer [ãdi'ge] (1m) v/t. dam up (a river); dike (land); fig. stem.
endimanché, e [ãdimã'ʃe] in one's Sunday best.
endive ♀ [ã'di:v] f endive.
endoctriner [ãdɔktri'ne] (1a) v/t. indoctrinate, instruct; F win over (to one's cause).
endolori, e [ãdɔlɔ'ri] sore; tender.
endommager [ãdɔma'ʒe] (1l) v/t. damage; injure.
endormeur m, **-euse** f [ãdɔr'mœ:r, ~'mø:z] fig. humbug, cajoler; swindler; bore; **endormi, e** [~'mi] 1. adj. asleep; sleepy, drowsy; numb (leg etc.); dormant (passion); 2. su. sleeper; fig. sleepyhead; **endormir** [~'mi:r] (2b) v/t. send to sleep; make (s.o.) sleep; numb (the leg etc.); deaden (a pain); fig. bore; fig. lull (a suspicion); fig. hoodwink, beguile (s.o.); s'~ go to sleep (a. fig.); fall asleep; **endormissement** [~mis'mã] m going to sleep; ✠ passing into inconsciousness; sleepiness, somnolence.
endos ✝ [ã'do] m, **endossement** ✝ [ãdos'mã] m endorsement; **endossataire** ✝ [ãdosa'tɛ:r] su. endorsee; **endosser** [~'se] (1a) v/t. ✝ endorse; ✝ back; put on (clothes); fig. assume; ~ qch. à q. saddle s.o. with s.th.; **endosseur** ✝ [~'sœ:r] m endorser.
endroit [ã'drwa] m place, spot; site; side; tex. right side; à l'~ de as regards; par ~s in places.
enduire [ã'dɥi:r] (4h) v/t. 🜂 coat, plaster (with, de) (a. fig.); smear (with, de); **enduit** [ã'dɥi] m paint, tar, etc.: coat, coating; 🜂 coat of plaster, plastering; tex. proofing.
endurance [ãdy'rã:s] f endurance; fig. patience; **endurant, e** [~'rã, ~'rã:t] patient, long-suffering.
endurcir [ãdyr'si:r] (2a) v/t. harden (a. fig. the heart); fig. inure (to, à); s'~ harden (a. fig.); become fit or tough.
endurer [ãdy're] (1a) v/t. endure, bear, tolerate.
énergétique [enɛrʒe'tik] ✹ energizing; ⊕ of energy; **énergie** [~'ʒi] f energy; ⊕ fuel and power; ~ atomi-

que (or nucléaire) atomic or nuclear energy; ⊕ ~ consommée power consumption; **énergique** [~'ʒik] energetic; drastic (measures, steps, remedy); emphatic.
énergumène [enɛrgy'mɛn] su. person in a frenzied state of mind.
énervement [enɛrvə'mã] m exasperation; F state of nerves; **énerver** [~'ve] (1a) v/t. enervate (the body, the will); irritate, annoy; F get on (s.o.'s) nerves.
enfance [ã'fã:s] f childhood; fig. infancy; childishness; dotage; **enfant** [ã'fã] su. child; ~ de chœur eccl. altar boy; F fig. choir boy (= naïve person); ~ gâté spoilt child; fig. pet; fig. ~ terrible enfant terrible; ~ trouvé foundling; d'~ childlike; childish; mes ~s! boys (and girls)!; ⚥ men!; lads!; su./m boy; su./f girl; **enfanter** [ãfã'te] (1a) v/t. give birth to, bear; fig. beget; father (an idea); **enfantillage** [~ti'ja:ʒ] m childishness; fig. ~s pl. baby tricks; **enfantin, e** [~'tɛ̃, ~'tin] childish; infantile.
enfariner [ãfari'ne] (1a) v/t. cuis. flour, cover with flour; fig. être enfariné de have a smattering of.
enfer [ã'fɛ:r] m hell; ~s pl. the underworld sg.; aller un train d'~ go at top speed.
enfermer [ãfɛr'me] (1a) v/t. shut up; lock up; shut in, enclose.
enferrer [ãfɛ're] (1a) v/t. pierce; fig. F s'~ be hoist with one's own petard.
enfiévrer [ãfje'vre] (1f) v/t. make (s.o.) feverish; fig. excite, stir up; s'~ grow feverish; fig. get excited.
enfilade [ãfi'lad] f series; rooms: suite; houses: row; fig. string; **enfiler** [~'le] (1a) v/t. thread (a needle); string (pearls etc.); enter, take (a road etc.); slip on (clothes); F (a. s'~) eat, F get through; drink, F knock back.
enfin [ã'fɛ̃] 1. adv. at last, finally; in short, that is to say; 2. int. at last!; still!
enflammer [ãfla'me] (1a) v/t. inflame; set on fire; strike (a match); fig. stir up; s'~ catch fire; fig. flare up; ✹ inflame.
enfler [ã'fle] (1a) v/t. swell (a. fig.); bloat; puff out (one's cheeks); fig. inflate (one's style); fig. puff (s.o.) up; v/i. a. s'~ swell; **enflure** [ã'fly:r] f ✹ swelling; fig. style: turgidity.

enfoncement [ãfõs'mã] *m door*: breaking open; *nail*: driving in; sinking (*a.* ⊕ *of a pile*); *ground*: hollow; ⚓ recess; ⚓ bay; **enfoncer** [ãfõ'se] (1k) *v/t.* break in *or* open; drive in; thrust; ✕ *etc.* break through; F get the better of; F down (*s.o.*); s'~ plunge; sink, go down; subside; go in; *v/i.* sink; **enfonçure** [~'syːr] *f ground*: hollow; *rock*: cavity; *cask*: bottom. [hide.\

enfouir [ã'fwiːr] (2a) *v/t.* bury;\

enfourchement [ãfurʃə'mã] *m* ⊕ fork link; *wood*: open mortise-joint, slit-and-tongue joint; **enfourcher** [~'ʃe] (1a) *v/t.* get astride, mount (*a bicycle, a horse*); ~ son dada get on to one's pet subject.

enfourner [ãfur'ne] (1a) *v/t.* put in the oven; put in a kiln (*bricks, pottery*); *sl.* gobble (*one's food*).

enfreindre [ã'frɛ̃ːdr] (4m) *v/t.* infringe, break, transgress (*the law*); violate (*a treaty*).

enfuir [ã'fчiːr] (2d) *v/t.*: s'~ flee, run away; escape (from, de); leak (*liquid*).

enfumer [ãfy'me] (1a) *v/t.* fill with smoke; blacken with smoke; smoke out (*bees, animals*).

enfutailler [ãfyta'je] (1a) *v/t.* cask (*wine*).

engagé [ãga'ʒe] **1.** *adj.* ✕ enlisted; *fig.* committed (*literature*); **2.** *su./m* ✕ volunteer; *sp.* entry; **engagement** [ãgaʒ'mã] *m* engagement; promise; bond; pawning; appointment; ✕ enlistment; ✕ skirmish; *sp.* entry; ~s *pl.* liabilities; ✝ sans ~ without obligation; **engager** [ãga-'ʒe] (1l) *v/t.* engage (*a.* ⊕ *machinery*); employ; ✕ enlist; ⊕ take on (*hands*); pawn (*a watch etc.*); pledge (*one's word*); ⚖ institute (*proceedings*); ⊕ put in gear; *fig.* begin, open, ✕ join (*battle*); ⚓ foul (*the anchor etc.*); jam (*a machine*); s'~ undertake, promise (to *inf.*, à *inf.*); commit o.s. (to *inf.*, à *inf.*); take service (with, chez); ⚓ foul; jam (*machine*); ⚓ get out of control; *fig.* enter; *fig.* begin (*battle, discussion*); ✕ enlist; *v/i.* ⊕ (come into) gear.

engainer [ãgɛ'ne] (1b) *v/t.* sheathe; ✿ ensheathe.

engeance *pej.* [ã'ʒãːs] *f* brood, bunch, lot.

engelure ✻ [ãʒ'lyːr] *f* chilblain.

engendrer [ãʒã'dre] (1a) *v/t.* beget; *fig.* engender; produce; generate (*heat*); *fig.* breed (*a disease, contempt*).

engin [ã'ʒɛ̃] *m* machine; tool; device; F gadget, contraption; ✕ ballistic missile; ~s *pl. fishing*: tackle *sg.*

englober [ãglɔ'be] (1a) *v/t.* include, take in; unite, merge.

engloutir [ãglu'tiːr] (2a) *v/t.* swallow; gulp; *fig.* swallow up; *fig.* sink (*money in s.th.*).

engluer [ãgly'e] (1a) *v/t.* lime (*a bird, twigs*); *fig.* trap, ensnare (*s.o.*).

engorger [ãgɔr'ʒe] (1l) *v/t.* block, choke up; ⊕ obstruct; ✻ congest.

engouement [ãgu'mã] *m* ✻ obstruction; *fig.* infatuation (with, pour); **engouer** [~'e] (1a) *v/t.* ✻ obstruct; s'~ ✻ become obstructed; *fig.* become infatuated (with, de).

engouffrer [ãgu'fre] (1a) *v/t.* engulf; F devour (*food*); *fig.* swallow up; s'~ be swallowed up, rush (*wind*); F dive (into, dans).

engoulevent *orn.* [ãgul'vã] *m* nightjar, goatsucker.

engourdir [ãgur'diːr] (2a) *v/t.* (be)numb; *fig.* dull (*the mind*); s'~ grow numb, F go to sleep; *fig.* become sluggish; **engourdissement** [~dis'mã] *m* numbness; *fig.* dullness; ✝ *market*: slackness.

engrais ✔ [ã'grɛ] *m* manure; fattening pasture *or* food; ~ *pl.* azotés nitrate fertilizers, F nitrates; ~ vert manure crop; **engraisser** [ãgrɛ'se] (1a) *v/t.* fatten (*animals*), cram (*poultry*); make(*s.o.*) fat; ✔ manure, fertilize; *v/i.* grow fat; thrive (*cattle*); **engraisseur** [~'sœːr] *m* fattener; *poultry*: crammer.

engranger ✔ [ãgrã'ʒe] (1l) *v/t.* garner, get in (*the corn*).

engraver [ãgra've] (1a) *v/t.* ⚓ strand (*a ship*); cover (*ground*) with sand *or* gravel; ⚓ s'~ ground; run on to the sand; silt up (*harbour*).

engrenage [ãgrə'naːʒ] *m* ⊕ gearing; (toothed) gear; throwing *or* coming into gear; *fig.* network, mesh; **engrener** [~'ne] (1d) *v/t.* feed corn into (*a threshing-machine*); feed (*animals*) on corn; ⊕ (put into) gear, engage (*wheels*); *fig.* start (*s.th.*) off, set (*s.th.*) going; s'~ engage, cog, mesh with one another; *v/i.* be in mesh; **engrenure** ⊕ [∼'ny:r] *f* gear ratio; engaging.

engrosser *sl.* [ãgrɔ'se] (1a) *v/t.* get (*s.o.*) pregnant, *sl.* knock (*s.o.*) up.

engrumeler [ãgrym'le] (1c) *v/t.*: s'∼ clot, curdle.

engueulade *sl.* [ãgœ'lad] *f* telling-off, F dressing-down, blow-up; **engueuler** *sl.* [∼'le] (1a) *v/t.* tell (*s.o.*) off, blow (*s.o.*) up, go for (*s.o.*).

enguirlander [ãgirlã'de] (1a) *v/t.* garland; wreathe (with, *de*); F tell (*s.o.*) off, go for (*s.o.*).

enhardir [ãar'di:r] (2a) *v/t.* embolden; *fig.* encourage (to *inf.*, *à inf.*); s'∼ grow bold, take courage; make bold (to, *à*).

énigmatique [enigma'tik] enigmatic; **énigme** [e'nigm] *f* enigma; *parler par* ∼s speak in riddles.

enivrement [ãnivrə'mã] *m* intoxication; *fig.* elation; **enivrer** [∼'vre] (1a) *v/t.* intoxicate; make (*s.o.*) drunk; *fig.* elate, go to (*s.o.'s*) head; s'∼ get drunk.

enjambée [ãʒã'be] *f* stride; **enjambement** [ãʒãb'mã] *m* prosody: run-on line; enjambment; **enjamber** [ãʒã'be] (1a) *v/t.* bestride (*a horse*, *a. fig.*); stride over (*an object*); *fig.* span, straddle; *v/i.* stride; *prosody:* run on (*line*).

enjeu [ã'ʒø] *m* gambling, *a. fig.*: stake.

enjoindre [ã'ʒwɛ̃:dr] (4m) *v/t.* enjoin, order, direct; call upon.

enjôler [ãʒo'le] (1a) *v/t.* wheedle, coax; cajole; **enjôleur, -euse** [∼'lœ:r, ∼'løːz] **1.** *su.* coaxer, wheedler; cajoler; **2.** *adj.* wheedling, coaxing; cajoling, 🎵 smooth-tongued.

enjoliver [ãʒɔli've] (1a) *v/t.* beautify, embellish; *fig.* embroider (*a story*); **enjoliveur** *mot.* [∼'vœːr] *m* hub cap.

enjoué, e [ã'ʒwe] jaunty, sprightly; playful, lively; **enjouement** [ãʒu-'mã] *m* sprightliness; playfulness.

enlacer [ãla'se] (1k) *v/t.* entwine; interlace; embrace, clasp; ⊕ dowel.

enlaidir [ãlɛ'diːr] (2a) *v/t.* disfigure; make (*s.o.*) ugly; *v/i.* grow ugly.

enlevé, e [ãl've] *paint.* dashed off; ♪ (*played*) con brio; **enlèvement** [ãlɛv'mã] *m* removal; carrying off; kidnapping; abduction; ✕ storming; 🕂 snapping up (*of goods*); **enlever** [ãl've] (1d) *v/t.* remove; take

away *or* off; lift up; carry off (*a. fig. a prize*); kidnap; abduct; deprive (*s.o.* of *s.th.*, *qch. à q.*); *fig.* urge on; ✕ storm; *fig.* do (*s.th.*) brilliantly; ∼ *en arrachant* (*grattant*) snatch (rub) away; s'∼ take off (*balloon etc.*); peel off (*bark*, *paint*, *skin*, *etc.*); boil over (*milk*); *fig.* flare up (*person*); *se faire* ∼ *par* elope with.

enliser [ãli'ze] (1a) *v/t.* get (*a car etc.*) stuck in the sand *etc.*; s'∼ sink (*in a quicksand*); get bogged, get stuck; *fig.* get bogged down.

enluminer [ãlymi'ne] (1a) *v/t.* illuminate; colo(u)r (*a map etc.*); *fig.* flush, redden; **enluminure** [∼'nyːr] *f* illumination; *maps etc.*: colo(u)r-ing; *fig.* redness, high colo(u)r.

enneigé, e [ãnɛ'ʒe] snow-covered, snow-clad; **enneigement** [ãnɛʒ-'mã] *m* condition of the snow; *bulletin m d'*∼ snow report.

ennemi, e [en'mi] **1.** *adj.* enemy ...; holstile (to, *de*); opposing; **2.** *su.* enemy; adversary.

ennoblir [ãnɔ'bliːr] (2a) *v/t.* ennoble (*a. fig.*).

ennui [ã'nɥi] *m* nuisance, annoyance; boredom, tediousness; *fig.* bore; trouble; ∼s *pl.* worries; **ennuyer** [ãnɥi'je] (1h) *v/t.* bore, weary; worry, annoy; s'∼ be bored (with, *de*); long (for, *de*); *fig.* s'∼ *mortellement* be bored to death, *sl.* be bored stiff; **ennuyeux, -euse** [∼'jø, ∼'jøːz] boring, tedious, annoying, vexing.

énoncé [enɔ̃'se] *m* statement; wording; **énoncer** [∼'se] (1k) *v/t.* state, set forth; express; **énonciation** [∼sja'sjɔ̃] *f* stating, declaring; expressing.

enorgueillir [ãnɔrgœ'jiːr] (2a) *v/t.* make (*s.o.*) proud; s'∼ *de* glory in; pride o.s. on.

énorme [e'nɔrm] enormous, tremendous, huge; *pej.* outrageous, shocking; **énormément** [enɔrme-'mã] *adv.* enormously; *fig.* extremely, very; ∼ *de* a great many; **énormité** [∼mi'te] *f* vastness, hugeness; *fig.* enormity; gross blunder; *fig.* shocking thing.

enquérir [ãke'riːr] (2l) *v/t.*: s'∼ *de* inquire *or* ask about; **enquête** [ã'kɛːt] *f* inquiry; investigation; ∼ *par sondage* sample survey; **enquêter** [ãkɛ'te] (1a) *v/i.* make an investigation; hold an inquiry; **enquêteur** *m*, **-euse** *f* [~'tœːr, ~'tøːz] investigator; pollster.

enquiquiner F [ãkiki'ne] (1a) *v/t.* get on (*s.o.'s*) nerves.

enracinement [ãrasin'mã] *m* taking root; *fig.* deep-rootedness; **enraciner** [~si'ne] (1a) *v/t.* ✓ root; ✓, ⚠ dig in; *fig.* implant; s'~ take root; *fig.* become rooted.

enragé, e [ãra'ʒe] **1.** *adj.* mad; rabid (*dog, a. fig. opinions*); *fig.* keen, enthusiastic; wild (*life*); **2.** *su.* enthusiast; **enrager** [~] (1l) *v/i.* be mad (*a. fig.*); fume; *faire* ~ *q.* tease s.o.; drive s.o. wild.

enrayer [ãrɛ'je] (1i) *v/t.* fit (*a wheel*) with spokes; *fig.* check, stem; ⊕ s'~ jam.

enrégimenter [ãreʒimã'te] (1a) *v/t.* enlist; enrol.

enregistrement [ãrəʒistrə'mã] *m* registration; record(ing); entry; registry (*a. admin.*); *cin., radio, gramophone:* recording; *admin.* register office; **enregistrer** [~'tre] (1a) *v/t.* register (*a.* ⚓); record (*a. cin., radio, music*); *sp.* score (*a goal*); **enregistreur, -euse** [~'trœːr, ~'trøːz] **1.** *adj.* recording; registering; **2.** *su./m* (*tape- etc.*)recorder; ✈ ~ *de vol* flight recorder.

enrhumer [ãry'me] (1a) *v/t.* give (*s.o.*) a cold; s'~ catch (a) cold.

enrichi, e [ãri'ʃi] ⊕ *etc.* enriched (*uranium etc.*), improved; *a. su.* newrich, parvenu, upstart; **enrichir** [~'ʃiːr] (2a) *v/t.* enrich (*a. fig.*); make (*s.o.*) wealthy; s'~ grow rich.

enrober [ãrɔ'be] (1a) *v/t.* coat (with, *de*); imbed (in, *de*).

enrôler [ãro'le] (1a) *v/t.* enrol(l), recruit; ✗ enlist; *ls*'~ enrol(l) (in, *dans*); ✗ enlist.

enroué, e [ã'rwe] hoarse, husky; **enrouement** [ãru'mã] *m* hoarseness, huskiness; **enrouer** [ã'rwe] (1p) *v/t.* make hoarse *or* husky; s'~ become hoarse.

enrouiller [ãru'je] (1a) *v/t.* cover with rust.

enroulement [ãrul'mã] *m* rolling up; ⊕, ✓, ✗, *etc.* winding; wrapping up (in, *dans*); **enrouler** [ãru'le] (1a) *v/t.* roll up; ⊕, ✓, ✗, *etc.* wind; wrap up (in, *dans*).

enroutiné, e [ãruti'ne] routineminded; stick-in-the-mud.

enrubanner [ãryba'ne] (1a) *v/t.* decorate with ribbons.

ensabler [ãsa'ble] (1a) *v/t.* ⚓ run (*a ship*) aground; strand; cover (*the soil*) with sand; silt up (*a harbour*); s'~ ⚓ settle in the sand; silt up.

ensacher [ãsa'ʃe] (1a) *v/t.* put into sacks; bag.

ensanglanter [ãsãglã'te] (1a) *v/t.* stain *or* cover with blood.

enseigne [ã'sɛɲ] *su./f* (shop) sign; signboard; *à telle(s)* ~*(s) que* so much so that; *fig. être logé à la même* ~ be in the same boat; *su./m* ✗ † standardbearer; ⚓ sublieutenant, *Am.* ensign.

enseignement [ãsɛɲ'mã] *m* teaching; tuition; education, instruction; *fig.* lesson; ~ *par correspondance* postal tuition; ~ *primaire* (*secondaire, supérieur*) primary (secondary, higher) education; **enseigner** [ãsɛ'ɲe] (1a) *v/t.* teach; *fig.* point out; ~ *qch. à q.* teach s.o. s.th.

ensemble [ã'sãːbl] **1.** *adv.* together; at the same time; **2.** *su./m* whole; unity; *cost.* ensemble, suit, outfit; ⊕ set (*of tools*); ⊕ assembly unit; ⚠ block (*of buildings*); ⚠ *grand* ~ housing scheme *or* development; *dans l'*~ on the whole; *d'*~ comprehensive; combined; ⅍ *théorie f des* ~*s* set theory; *vue f d'*~ general view; **ensemblier** [ãsãbli'e] *m* (interior) decorator.

ensemencer ✓ [ãsmã'se] (1k) *v/t.* sow (with, *en*).

enserrer [ãsɛ're] (1a) *v/t.* squeeze; be too tight for; hem in.

ensevelir [ãsə'vliːr] (2a) *v/t.* bury (*a. fig.*); shroud (*a corpse*).

ensiler ✓ [ãsi'le] (1a) *v/t.* silo, silage.

ensoleillé, e [ãsɔlɛ'je] sunny, sunlit.

ensommeillé, e [ãsɔmɛ'je] sleepy, drowsy.

ensorceler [ãsɔrsə'le] (1c) *v/t.* put a spell on; bewitch (*a. fig.*); **ensorceleur, -euse** [~sə'lœːr, ~'løːz] **1.** *su.* *fig.* charmer; *su./m* sorcerer; *su./f* sorceress; **2.** *adj.* bewitching (*a. fig.*); **ensorcellement** [~sɛl'mã] *m* sorcery, witchcraft; spell.

ensuite [ã'sɥit] *adv.* then, after (-wards), next; *et* ~? what then?

ensuivre [ã'sɥiːvr] (4ee) *v/t.*: s'~ follow, ensue, result (from, *de*).

entablement ⚠ [ãtablə'mã] *m* coping; entablature (*a.* ⊕).

entacher [ɑ̃ta'ʃe] (1a) *v/t.* sully; taint (with, *de*); ⚖ vitiate; *entaché de nullité* void for want of form.

entaille [ɑ̃tɑ:j] *f wood etc.*: notch, nick; groove; *chin etc.*: gash, cut; **entailler** [~tɑ'je] (1a) *v/t.* notch, nick (*wood*); groove; gash, cut (*s.o.'s chin etc.*).

entame [ɑ̃'tam] *f loaf, meat*: outside slice; **entamer** [ɑ̃ta'me] (1a) *v/t.* cut into (*a loaf*); open (*a bottle, a jar of jam, etc., a. fig.*); *fig.* smear (*s.o.'s reputation*); begin, start (*a discussion, a quarrel, etc.*); broach (*a cask, a. fig. a subject*); ⚖ institute (*proceedings*); ⚔ commence (*operations*).

entasser [ɑ̃tɑ'se] (1a) *v/t. a. s'~* pile up; accumulate; crowd together (*people, animals*).

ente [ɑ̃:t] *f* ✓ graft, scion; ⊕ *paintbrush*: handle.

entendement [ɑ̃tɑ̃d'mɑ̃] *m* understanding; **entendre** [ɑ̃'tɑ̃:dr] (4a) *v/t.* hear (*a.* ⚖); understand; intend, mean; attend (*a lecture*); *~ dire que* hear that; *~ parler de* hear of; *~ raison* listen to reason; *laisser ~* hint; *s'~* agree; get on (with, *avec*); get on (together); be heard; *s'~ à* be good at, be an expert at; know all about; **entendu, e** [ɑ̃tɑ̃'dy] **1.** *adj.* agreed; knowing (*smile, etc.*); **2.** *int.* all right; F O.K.; *bien ~!* of course!; **entente** [ɑ̃'tɑ̃:t] *f* understanding; agreement; meaning; ✝ *~ industrielle* combine.

enter [ɑ̃'te] (1a) *v/t.* ✓ graft (*a.* ⊕); ⊕ scarf (*timbers*).

entériner ⚖ [ɑ̃teri'ne] (1a) *v/t.* ratify, confirm.

entérique *anat.* [ɑ̃te'rik] enteric; **entérite** ⚕ [~'rit] *f* enteritis.

enterrement [ɑ̃tɛr'mɑ̃] *m* burial, interment; funeral; **enterrer** [ɑ̃tɛ'ʀe] (1a) *v/t.* bury, inter; *fig.* outlive; *fig.* shelve (*a question*).

en-tête [ɑ̃'tɛ:t] *m* letterhead; heading; *typ.* headline, *Am.* caption; **entêté, e** [ɑ̃tɛ'te] obstinate, stubborn, F pig-headed; **entêtement** [ɑ̃tɛt'mɑ̃] *m fig.* obstinacy, stubbornness, F pig-headedness; **entêter** [ɑ̃tɛ'te] (1a) *v/t. odour*: make (*s.o.*) giddy; go to (*s.o.'s*) head; *s'~* be obstinate; *s'~ à* (*inf.*) persist in (*ger.*).

enthousiasme [ɑ̃tu'zjasm] *m* enthusiasm; *avec* (*sans*) *~* (un)enthusiastically; **enthousiasmer** [~zjas'me] (1a) *v/t.* fill with enthusiasm; *fig.* carry (*s.o.*) away; *s'~* enthuse (over, *pour*); **enthousiaste** [~'zjast] **1.** *adj.* enthusiastic; **2.** *su.* enthusiast (for, *de*).

entichement [ɑ̃tiʃ'mɑ̃] *m* infatuation (for *de, pour*); keenness (on, *pour*); **enticher** [ɑ̃ti'ʃe] (1a) *v/t.*: *s'~ de* become infatuated with.

entier, -ère [ɑ̃'tje, ~'tjɛ:r] **1.** *adj.* whole (*a. number*); entire, complete; total; full (*authority, control, fare, etc.*); *fig.* headstrong; *cheval m ~* stallion; **2.** *su./m* entirety; *en ~* in full; completely.

entité *phls.* [ɑ̃ti'te] *f* entity.

entôler *sl.* [ɑ̃to'le] (1a) *v/t.* rob; fleece, *sl.* con.

entomologie [ɑ̃tɔmɔlɔ'ʒi] *f* entomology.

entonner[1] [ɑ̃tɔ'ne] (1a) *v/t.* barrel (*wine*).

entonner[2] ♪ [~] (1a) *v/t.* begin to sing (*a song*); strike up (*a tune*); *eccl.* intone; *fig.* sing (*s.o.'s praises*).

entonnoir [ɑ̃tɔ'nwa:r] *m* funnel; ⚔ crater; *geog.* hollow; *geol.* sink-hole.

entorse ⚕ [ɑ̃'tɔrs] *f* sprain, wrench; *se donner une ~* sprain one's ankle.

entortiller [ɑ̃tɔrti'je] (1a) *v/t.* twist, wind; wrap up; entangle; *fig.* wheedle, get (*s.o.*) round; F express (*views etc.*) in an obscure fashion; *s'~* twine; *fig.* get entangled.

entourage [ɑ̃tu'ra:ʒ] *m* surroundings *pl.*; setting, frame(work); circle (*of associates, friends, etc.*); attendants *pl.*; ⊕ *machinery*: casing; **entourer** [~'re] (1a) *v/t.* surround (with, *de*); encircle (*a.* ⚔).

entournure *cost.* [ɑ̃tur'ny:r] *f* armhole.

entracte [ɑ̃'trakt] *m thea., cin.* interval, *Am.* intermission; ♪ interlude.

entraide [ɑ̃'trɛ:d] *f* mutual aid; **entraider** [ɑ̃trɛ'de] (1b) *v/t.*: *s'~* help one another.

entrailles [ɑ̃'trɑ:j] *f/pl.* intestines, entrails, bowels; *fig.* pity *sg.*; compassion *sg.*; *~ de la terre* bowels of the earth.

entrain [ɑ̃'trɛ̃] *m* liveliness; spirit, go, mettle.

entraînement [ɑ̃trɛn'mɑ̃] *m* impetus, force, impulse; *fig.* heat (*of*

discussion); ⊕ *machine*: drive; *sp. etc.*
training; **entraîner** [ătrɛˈne] (1a)
v/t. carry away; pull; drag along; *fig.*
lead (*s.o.*), incite (*s.o.*); ⊕ drive; *fig.*
involve; *fig.* give rise to, bring about;
sp. train; *sp.* coach (*a team*); **entra-**
îneur [ˌˈnœːr] *m sp.* trainer; *team*:
coach; pace-maker; ⊕ driving
device; **entraîneuse** [ˌˈnøːz] dance
hostess.

entrave [ăˈtraːv] *f* fetter; shackle;
fig. hindrance, obstacle; **entraver**
[ătraˈve] (1a) *v/t.* fetter, shackle;
fig. impede, hinder.

entre [ăːtr] *prp.* between (*two points
in space or time*); in (*s.o.'s hands
etc.*); among (*others, other things,
my brothers*); out of (*a number*); ~
eux one another, each other; between themselves; *soit dit* ~ *nous*
between ourselves, between you
and me and the lamp-post; ~ *amis*
among friends; ~ *quatre yeux* in
private; ~ *deux ages* middle-aged
(*woman*); ~ *la vie et la mort* between
life and death; *moi* ~ *autres* I for
one; *d'*~ (out) of, (from) among;
l'un (ceux) d'~ *eux* one (these) of
them; *see* nager.

entre...: ~**bâiller** [ătrəbaˈje] (1a)
v/t. half-open; ~**chats** *fig.* [ˌˈʃa]
m/pl. capers; ~**choquer** [ˌʃɔˈke]
(1m) *v/t.* clink (*glasses*); *s'*~ collide;
clash (*a. fig.*); knock against one
another (*bottles etc.*); ~**côte** *cuis.*
[ˌˈkoːt] *f* entrecôte, rib of beef; ~
couper [ˌkuˈpe] (1a) *v/t.* intersect;
fig. interrupt; *s'*~ *la gorge* cut one
another's throats; ~**croiser** [ˌ
krwaˈze] (1a) *v/t. a. s'*~ intersect,
cross; interlock; ~**deux** [ˌˈdø]
m/inv. space between, interspace;
△ partition; *basket-ball*: center
jump; *cost.* insertion; ~**deux-**
guerres [ˌdøˈɡɛːr] *f or m/inv.* the
inter-war years *pl.* (*between World
War I and II*).

entrée [ăˈtre] *f* entry; entrance; admission (*a. ⊕*), access; price of entry;
import (duty); *cuis.* entrée; ⊕ inlet,
intake; *fig.* start, beginning; ✝ receipt; ⚓ arrival (*of ship*); cave, *harbour*: mouth; ~ *en vacances school*:
breaking up; ~ *gratuite* free admission; ~ *latérale* side entrance; *d'*~ (*de
jeu*) from the outset, right from the
beginning, from the very first.

entre...: ~**faites** [ătrəˈfɛt] *f/pl.*: *sur*

ces ~ meanwhile, meantime; ~**fer**
⚡ [ˌˈfɛr] *m* air-gap; ~**filet** [ˌfiˈlɛ] *m
newspaper*: paragraph; ~**gent** [ˌˈʒã]
m tact; worldly wisdom; ~**lacer**
[ˌlaˈse] (1k) *v/t.* interlace; inter-
twine; ~**lacs** [ˌˈla] *m* △ knotwork;
△ tracery; *fig.* tangle; ~**lardé, e**
[ˌlarˈde] streaky; ~**larder** [ˌlarˈde]
(1a) *v/t. cuis.* lard; *fig.* interlard (*a
speech*) (with, *de*); ~**ligne** [ˌˈliɲ] *m*
space between lines; interlineation;
~**mêler** [ˌmɛˈle] (1a) *v/t.* inter-
mingle; intersperse; mix; blend;
fig. intersperse (*a speech*) (with, *de*);
s'~ mingle; *fig. s'*~ *dans* meddle
with; ~**mets** *cuis.* [ˌˈmɛ] sweet;
~**metteur, -euse** [ˌmɛˈtœːr, ˌˈtøːz]
su. go-between; *su./m* ✝ middleman; procurer; *su./f* procuress; ~
mettre [ˌˈmɛtr] (4v) *v/t.*: *s'*~ intervene; act as go-between; ~**mise**
[ˌˈmiːz] *f* intervention; mediation;
~**pont** ⚓ [ˌˈpõ] *m* between-decks;
d'~ steerage (*passenger*); ~**poser** ✝
[ˌpoˈze] (1a) *v/t.* warehouse, store;
put in bond (*at the customs*); ~**po-**
seur ✝ [ˌpoˈzœːr] *m* warehouseman; *customs*: officer in charge of
a bonded store; ~**positaire** ✝ [ˌ
poziˈtɛːr] *m* warehouseman; *customs*: bonder; ~**pôt** [ˌˈpo] *m* ✝
warehouse, store, repository; *customs*: bonded warehouse; ⚔ ammunition: depot; ~ *frigorifique* cold
store; *en* ~ in bond; ~**prenant, e**
[ˌprəˈnã, ˌˈnãːt] enterprising; ~
prendre [ˌˈprãːdr] (4aa) *v/t.* undertake, embark (up)on; contract
for (*work*); *fig.* worry; F *fig.* besiege
(*s.o.*); ~**preneur** [ˌprəˈnœːr] *m* contractor; ~ *de pompes funèbres*
undertaker, *Am.* mortician; ~**prise**
[ˌˈpriːz] *f* undertaking; concern; ✝
contract; attempt; ~ *de transport*
carriers *pl.*

entrer [ăˈtre] (1a) *v/i.* enter, go *or*
come in; take part, be concerned;
be included; ~ *dans* enter; ~ *dans
une famille* marry into a family; ~
en enter upon (*s.th.*) *or* into (*competition*); *fig.* ~ *en jeu* come into
play; ~ *pour beaucoup dans*
play an important role *or* part in;
faire ~ show (*s.o.*) in(to the room);
drive (*s.th. into s.th.*); *v/t.* bring in,
introduce.

entre...: ~**rail** 🚂 [ătrəˈraːj] *m*
ga(u)ge; ~**sol** △ [ˌˈsɔl] *m floor*: mez-

zanine; **~-temps** [ʌ'tɑ̃] **1.** *m*/*inv.* interval; *dans l'~* meanwhile; **2.** *adv.* meanwhile; **~teneur** [ʌtə'nœːr] *m* maintainer; **~tenir** [ʌtə'niːr] (2h) *v*/*t.* maintain; keep up; support; talk to (*s.o.*) (about, de); entertain (*suspicions, doubts*); *s'~* support o.s.; converse, talk (with, *avec*); *sp.* keep o.s. fit; **~tien** [ʌ'tjɛ̃] *m* maintenance; upkeep; conversation; **~toise** ⚠ [ʌ'twaːz] *f* strut, (cross-)brace, cross-piece, tie; **~toisement** ⚠ [ʌtwaz'mɑ̃] *m* (counter)bracing; strutting, staying; **~voir** [ʌ'vwaːr] (3m) *v*/*t.* catch a glimpse of; *fig.* foresee, have an inkling of; *laisser ~* disclose, give to understand; **~vue** [ʌ'vy] *f* interview.

entrouvrir [ɑ̃truˈvriːr] (2f) *v*/*t.* half-open; open (*curtains*) a little; *fig. s'~* yawn (*chasm*).

énumération [enymeraˈsjɔ̃] *f* enumeration; *votes:* counting; *facts:* recital; **énumérer** [ʌ're] (1f) *v*/*t.* enumerate; count (*votes*); recite (*facts*).

envahir [ɑ̃vaˈiːr] (2a) *v*/*t.* overrun; invade; encroach upon; *fig. feeling:* steal or come over (*s.o.*); **envahisseur** [ʌiˈsœːr] *m* invader.

envaser [ɑ̃vaˈze] (1a) *v*/*t.* silt up; choke with mud; ⚓ run on the mud; *s'~* silt up; ⚓ stick in the mud.

enveloppe [ɑ̃ˈvlɔp] *f* post, *a.* ℞: envelope; *parcel:* wrapping; ⊕ casing, jacket, lagging; *mot. tyre:* outer cover, casing; *fig.* exterior; ✐ *cable:* sheathing; *~ à fenêtre* window envelope; **enveloppement** [ɑ̃vlɔpˈmɑ̃] *m* wrapping; ⚕ *~ humide* wet pack; **envelopper** [ɑ̃vlɔˈpe] (1a) *v*/*t.* envelop; wrap (up); cover; ✕ encircle (*the enemy*); ⊕ lag; *fig.* involve; *fig.* wrap, shroud (in, de).

envenimer [ɑ̃vəniˈme] (1a) *v*/*t.* ⚕ poison; aggravate (*a. fig.*); *fig.* embitter (*s.o.*); *s'~* ⚕ fester; *fig.* grow bitter.

enverguer [ɑ̃vɛrˈge] (1m) *v*/*t.* bend (*the sail*); **envergure** [ʌˈgyːr] *f* ⚓ spread of sail; 🦅, *orn., etc.* (wing-)span; spread, breadth; *fig.* calibre; *fig.* scope, scale; *de grande ~ a.* large-scale. [enverrai.]

enverrai [ɑ̃vɛˈre] *1st p. sg. fut. of*⌐

envers[1] [ɑ̃ˈvɛːr] *prp.* to(wards).

envers[2] [ʌ] *m* *tex.* reverse (*a. fig., a. of medal*), wrong side, back; *fig.* seamy side; *à l'~* inside out; *fig.* topsy-turvy.

envi [ɑ̃ˈvi] *adv.*: *à l'~* vying with each other; in emulation.

enviable [ɑ̃ˈvjabl] enviable; **envie** [ɑ̃ˈvi] *f* envy; longing, desire, fancy; 🌿 agnail, F hangnail; 🌿 birthmark; *avoir ~ de* be in the mood for, have a mind to; *faire ~ à q.* make s.o. envious; *porter ~ à q.* envy s.o.; **envier** [ɑ̃ˈvje] (1o) *v*/*t.* envy; long for; covet; begrudge (*s.o. s.th., qch. à q.*); **envieux, -euse** [ɑ̃ˈvjø, ʌˈvjøːz] envious.

environ [ɑ̃viˈrɔ̃] *adv.* about, approximately; **environs** [ʌˈrɔ̃] *m*/*pl.* vicinity *sg.*; surroundings *sg.*, surroundings; *aux ~ de* about (*fifty*), towards (*Christmas*); **environnement** [ʌrɔnˈmɑ̃] *m* surroundings *pl.*; environment; **environner** [ʌrɔˈne] (1a) *v*/*t.* surround; encompass (*a. fig.*).

envisager [ɑ̃vizaˈʒe] (1l) *v*/*t.* envisage; consider, view, contemplate; *~ de* (*inf.*) think of (*ger.*), consider (*ger.*), contemplate (*ger.*).

envoi [ɑ̃ˈvwa] *m* sending, dispatch (*a.* ⚒.); consignment, parcel; *post:* delivery; *~ par bateau* shipment; *coup m d'~ foot.* kickoff; *fig.* (starting) signal; ✝ *lettre f d'~* letter of advice.

envol [ɑ̃ˈvɔl] *m orn.* (taking) flight; 🛩 taking off, takeoff; **envoler** [ɑ̃vɔˈle] (1a) *v*/*t.*: *s'~* fly away; 🛩 take off; *fig.* fly (*time*); ✝ zoom (up) (*prices etc.*).

envoûter [ɑ̃vuˈte] (1a) *v*/*t.* *fig.* put under a spell, bewitch.

envoyé, e [ɑ̃vwaˈje] **1.** *p.p. of envoyer*; **2.** *su.* envoy, messenger; *su.*/*m:journ.* *~ spécial* special correspondent; **envoyer** [ʌ] (1r) *v*/*t.* send; forward; fling, hurl; shoot, fire; *~ chercher* send for; *~ coucher* (*or promener*) send (*s.o.*) packing, send (*s.o.*) about his business; *sl. s'~* get saddled with (*work*); gulp down (*wine*), get outside (*a meal*).

enzyme [ɑ̃ˈzim] *m* enzyme.

éolien, -enne [eɔˈljɛ̃, ʌˈljɛn] **1.** *adj.* Aeolien (*harp etc.*); **2.** *su.*/*f* windmill (*for pumping*); air-motor.

épagneul *m*, **e** *f* [epaˈnœl] spaniel.

épais, e [eˈpɛ, ʌˈpɛːs] thick; dense (*a. fig. mind*); *fig.* dull (*person*); stout (*glass*); **épaisseur** [epɛ'sœːr] *f* thickness; depth; density; *fig.* denseness; **épaissir** [ʌ'siːr] (2a) *v/t.* thicken; *v/i. a.* s'~ thicken, become thick; *cuis.* jell; grow stout (*person*).

épanchement [epɑ̃ʃ'mɑ̃] *blood*: effusion (*a. fig.*); *fig.* outpouring; **épancher** [epɑ̃'ʃe] (1a) *v/t.* pour out; s'~ pour (out); *fig.* open one's heart.

épandage ✓ [epɑ̃'daːʒ] *m* manuring; *champs m/pl.* d'~ sewage farm *sg.*; **épandre** [e'pɑ̃dr] (4a) *v/t.* spread; shed (*light*); pour out (*a liquid*); s'~ spread.

épanoui, e [epa'nwi] ❦ in full bloom; *fig.* beaming; cheerful; **épanouir** [ʌ'nwiːr] (2a) *v/t.* ❦ open (out); s'~ bloom (*flower, a. fig.*); open up; *fig.* light up (*face*).

épargne [e'parɲ] *f* economy, thrift; saving; ✝ *caisse f* d'~ savings bank; *la petite* ~ small investors *pl.*; **épargner** [epar'ɲe] (1a) *v/t.* save (up), economize (on); be sparing with; *fig.* spare (*s.o.*).

éparpiller [eparpi'je] (1a) *v/t. a.* s'~ scatter, disperse.

épars, e [e'paːr, ʌ'pars] scattered; sparse (*population*); dishevelled (*hair*).

épatant, e F [epa'tɑ̃, ʌ'tɑ̃ːt] stunning, wonderful, marvellous, first-rate, *Am.* swell, great; **épater** [ʌ'te] (1a) *v/t.* break off the foot of (*a wineglass*); F amaze, flabbergast; *nez m* épaté flat or squat nose; F ~ *le bourgeois* shock conventional people; **épateur** *m*, **-euse** *f* F [ʌ-'tœːr, ʌ'tøːz] swanker; bluffer.

épaule [e'poːl] *f anat., a. cuis.* shoulder; ⚓ *bows*: luff; *un coup d'*~ a shove; *fig.* a leg-up; *par-dessus l'*~ disdainfully; **épaulement** [epol'mɑ̃] *m geog., a.* ⊕ shoulder; ⚠ revetment wall; **épauler** [epo'le] (1a) *v/t.* support (*a.* ⚠); help (*s.o.*), back (*s.o.*) up; bring (*a gun*) to the shoulder; *v/i.* take aim; **épaulette** [ʌ'lɛt] *f* ✖ epaulette (*a. = commission*); *cost.* shoulder strap.

épave [e'paːv] *f* 🏛 unclaimed object; waif, stray; ⚓ wreck (*a. fig.*), flotsam.

épée [e'pe] *f* sword (*a. tex.*); rapier; swordsman; *coup m* d'~ *dans l'eau* wasted effort.

épeler [ep'le] (1c) *v/t.* spell (*a word*);

spell out (*a message*); **épellation** [epɛlla'sjɔ̃] *f* spelling.

éperdu, e [epɛr'dy] distraught; frantic; beside o.s., wild; desperate; *éperdument amoureux* head over heels in love; *je m'en moque éperdument* I couldn't care less.

éperlan *icht.* [epɛr'lɑ̃] *m* smelt.

éperon [e'prɔ̃] *m* spur (*on rider's heel, a. zo.,* ❦, *geog.*); ⚓ *warship*: ram; *bridge*: cutwater; ⚠ *wall*: buttress; *fig. eyes*: crow's-foot; **éperonné, e** [eprɔ'ne] spurred; ❦ calcarate; crow-footed (*eyes*); **éperonner** [ʌ] (1a) *v/t.* spur (*a. fig.*); ⚓ ram.

épervier [epɛr'vje] *m orn.* sparrow-hawk; *fishing*: cast-net; *pol.* hawk.

éphémère [efe'mɛːr] **1.** *adj.* ephemeral; *fig.* transitory, fleeting; **2.** *su./ m zo.* day-fly.

éphéméride [efeme'rid] *f* tear-off calendar, block-calendar.

épi [e'pi] *m corn, grain*: ear; ❦ spike; *fig.* cluster; ⊕ wharf; 🚂 marshalling tracks *pl.*

épice [e'pis] *f* spice; *pain m* d'~ gingerbread; *quatre* ~s *pl.* allspice *sg.*; **épicé, e** [epi'se] highly spiced; hot; *fig.* spicy (*story*); **épicer** [ʌ] (1k) *v/t.* spice (*a. fig. a story*); **épicerie** ✝ [epis'ri] *f* groceries *pl.*; grocer's (shop), *Am.* grocery; **épicier** *m*, **-ère** *f* [epi'sje, ʌ'sjɛːr] grocer; *fig.* philistine.

épidémie ☣ [epide'mi] *f* epidemic (*a. fig.*).

épiderme [epi'dɛrm] *m* epidermis.

épier [e'pje] (1o) *v/t.* watch (*s.o.*); spy on (*s.o.*); watch or look out for.

épierrer ✓ [epjɛ're] (1a) *v/t.* clear of stones.

épieu [e'pjø] *m* boar-spear; pike.

épigastre *anat.* [epi'gastr] *m* pit of the stomach, epigastrium.

épigone [epi'gɔn] *m* epigone, follower.

épigraphe [epi'graf] *f* epigraph; motto.

épilation [epila'sjɔ̃] *f* depilation; removal of superfluous hairs; *eyebrows*: plucking; **épilatoire** [ʌ-'twaːr] *adj., a. su./m* depilatory.

épilepsie ☣ [epilɛp'si] *f* epilepsy.

épiler [epi'le] (1a) *v/t.* depilate; remove hairs; pluck (*one's eyebrows*).

épilogue [epi'lɔg] *m* epilogue; **épi-**

loguer [ˌlɔ'ge] (1m) (*sur*) carp (at), find fault (with).

épiloir [epi'lwaːr] *m* eyebrow etc.: tweezers *pl.*

épinaie [epi'nɛ] *f* thicket.

épinard ♧ [epi'naːr] *m* (*a. cuis.* ~s *pl.*) spinach.

épine [e'pin] *f* ♧ thorn (*a. fig.*), prickle; ♧ thorn-bush; *anat.* ~ dorsale backbone, spine.

épinette [epi'nɛt] *f* ♪ spinet; ↗ (hen-)coop; ♧ spruce.

épineux, -euse [epi'nø, ~'nøːz] thorny (*a. fig.*); prickly (*a. fig. person*); *fig.* knotty (*problem*).

épingle [e'pɛ̃ːgl] *f* pin; † ~s *pl.* pin-money *sg.*; ~ à chapeau hatpin; ~ à cheveux hairpin; ~ à linge clothes-peg; ~ de cravate tie-pin, *Am.* stick-pin; ~ de nourrice safety-pin; *fig. coup m* d'~ pin-prick; tiré à quatre ~s dapper, spruce, spick and span; *mot. virage m en* ~ à cheveux hairpin bend; **épinglé** [epɛ̃'gle] *m* (*a. velours m* ~) uncut velvet; **épingler** [~'gle] (1a) *v/t.* pin; pin up; *metall.* pierce (*a mould etc.*); F pin (*s.o.*) down; **épinglerie** ⊕ [~glə'ri] *f* pin-factory; **épinglette** [~'glɛt] *f* ⚔ priming-needle; ⚒ boring-tool; **épinglier** [~gli'e] *m* pin-tray.

épinière [epi'njɛːr] *adj./f:* moelle *f* ~ spinal cord.

épinoche *icht.* [epi'nɔʃ] *f* stickle-back.

épique [e'pik] epic.

épiscopal, e, *m/pl.* -**aux** [episkɔ'pal, ~'po] episcopal; cathedral (*city*); **épiscopat** [~'pa] *m* episcopate; *coll.* the bishops *pl.*

épisode [epi'zɔd] *m* episode; *cin. film m* à ~s serial film.

épistolaire [epistɔ'lɛːr] epistolary; être en relations ~s avec q. correspond with s.o.

épitaphe [epi'taf] *f* epitaph.

épithète [epi'tɛt] *f* epithet; *gramm.* attributive adjective.

épître [e'piːtr] *f* epistle; *fig.* (long) letter.

éploré, e [eplɔ're] tearful, in tears.

éployée ▨ [eplwa'je] *adj./f* spread (*eagle*).

éplucher [eply'ʃe] (1a) *v/t.* pick (*a. tex. wool, a. salad*); pare, peel (*a fruit*); prune (*a fruit-tree*); clean (*a. plumage, salad*); preen (*feath-*

ers); ↗ weed (*a field*); *fig.* pick holes in; **éplucheur** *m*, -**euse** *f* [~'ʃœːr, ~'ʃøːz] cleaner; (*wool-*)picker; (*potato-*)peeler; ↗ weeder; F *fig.* faultfinder; **épluchoir** [~-'ʃwaːr] *m* paring-knife; *cuis.* potato-knife; **épluchures** [~'ʃyːr] *f/pl. potatoes etc.:* peelings; *fig.* refuse *sg.*; waste *sg.*

épointé, e [epwɛ̃'te] blunt (*pencil etc.*); hipshot (*horse*); **épointer** [~] (1a) *v/t.* break the point of; blunt (*s.th.*); s'~ lose its point (*pencil etc.*).

éponge [e'pɔ̃ːʒ] *f* sponge; F *fig.* jeter l'~ throw in the towel *or* sponge; *fig.* passer l'~ sur say no more about (*s.th.*); **éponger** [epɔ̃'ʒe] (11) *v/t.* sponge; mop (*the surface, one's brow*); mop up (*a liquid*); sponge down (*a horse*); dab (*one's eyes*); *a. fig.* absorb; *fig.* compensate.

épopée [epɔ'pe] *f* epic (poem).

époque [e'pɔk] *f* epoch, age, era; period; time; à l'~ at the time (of, de); at that time, then; la Belle ♀ that up to 1914; faire ~ mark an epoch; qui fait ~ epoch-making.

épouiller [epu'je] (1a) *v/t.* delouse.

époumoner [epumɔ'ne] (1a) *v/t.* put (*s.o.*) out of breath; s'~ shout o.s. out of breath.

épousailles [epu'zɑːj] *f/pl.* nuptials, wedding *sg.*; **épouse** [e'puːz] *f* wife, spouse; **épousée** [epu'ze] *f* bride; **épouser** [~'ze] (1a) *v/t.* marry, wed; *fig.* take up, espouse (*a cause*); *fig.* embrace (*an idea*); *fig.* fit (*dress etc.*); *fig.* accept, make (*s.th.*) one's own; ~ son temps move with the times; **épouseur** † [~'zœːr] *m* suitor, eligible man.

épousseter [epus'te] (1c) *v/t.* dust; beat (*a carpet etc.*); rub down (*a horse*); **époussette** [epu'sɛt] *f* feather-duster; rag (*for rubbing down a horse*).

époustouflant, e F [epustu'flɑ̃, ~'flɑ̃ːt] extraordinary, amazing.

épouvantable [epuvɑ̃'tabl] horrible, dreadful, terrible; appalling; **épouvantail** [~vɑ̃'taːj] *m* scarecrow; *fig.* bogy, bugbear; *fig. person:* fright; **épouvante** [~'vɑ̃ːt] *f* terror, fright; **épouvanter** [~vɑ̃'te] (1a) *v/t.* scare; appal.

époux [e'pu] *m* husband; ♋ *a.* spouse; les ~ *pl.* ... the ... couple *sg.*

éprendre [e'prɑ̃ːdr] (4aa) *v/t.:* s'~

de become enamo(u)red of; fall in love with (*s.o.*); take a fancy to (*s.th.*).

épreuve [e'prœːv] *f* test (*a.* ⊕, *a. school examination*); proof (*a. typ.*); *phot.* print; *fig.* ordeal, trial; *sp.* event; *à l'~* de proof against (*s.th.*); *à toute* ~ never-failing; ⊕ foolproof; *mettre à l'~* put to the test.

épris, e [e'pri, ~'priːz] **1.** *p.p.* of *éprendre*; **2.** *adj.* in love (with, de).

éprouver [epru've] (1a) *v/t.* try (*a. fig.*); test; put (*s.o.*) to the test; *fig.* feel (*sympathy etc.*), experience (*pain etc., a. fig. a difficulty*); **éprouvette** [~'vɛt] *f* 🜄 test-tube; probe; *metall.* test-piece.

épucer [epy'se] (1k) *v/t.* clean (*a dog etc.*) of fleas.

épuisé, e [epɥi'ze] exhausted; run down; spent (*energy etc.*); ✝ sold out; *typ.* out of print; **épuisement** [epɥiz'mã] *m* exhaustion (⊕, 🜨, *a. fig.*); *cistern, a. fig. finances:* draining; *resources:* depletion; **épuiser** [epɥi'ze] (1a) *v/t.* exhaust; use up; *fig.* wear (*s.o.*) out; *s'~* run out (*provisions etc.*); run dry, dry up (*source*); wear o.s. out; **épuisette** [~'zɛt] *f* 🜨 scoop, bailer; *fisherman:* landing-net.

épuration [epyra'sjõ] *f* purifying; *oil, metal:* refining; *gas:* filtering; *pol.* purge; *morals:* purging; **épuratoire** [~'twaːr] purifying.

épure [e'pyːr] *f* working drawing; diagram (*a.* 🜨).

épurer [epy're] (1a) *v/t.* purify; refine; filter; *pol.* purge; *fig.* expurgate (*a novel*).

équarrir [eka'riːr] (2a) *v/t.* ⊕ square; cut up *or* quarter the carcass of (*a horse*); ⚠ *bois m équarri* squared timber; **équarrisseur** [~ri'sœːr] *m* knacker.

équateur [ekwa'tœːr] *m* equator.

équation 🜨, 🜄, *astr., fig.* [ekwa'sjõ] *f* equation.

équerre [e'kɛːr] *f* square; ⚠ right angle; ⊕ angle-iron; ~ *à coulisses* sliding callipers *pl.*; ~ *à dessin*, ~ *en* T T-square; *d'~* square; *en* ~ square.

équestre [e'kɛstr] equestrian.

équilibrage [ekili'braːʒ] *m* balancing (*a. mot.*); **équilibre** [eki'libr] *m* balance (*a. fig.*); equilibrium; *fig.*

poise; *pol.* ~ *politique* balance of power; **équilibrer** [ekili'bre] (1a) *v/t.* balance; counterbalance; **équilibreur** [~'brœːr] *m see stabilisateur*; **équilibriste** [~'brist] *su.* equilibrist.

équinoxe [eki'nɔks] *m* equinox.

équipage [eki'paːʒ] *m* retinue, suite; 🜨, 🜨 crew; 🜊 train, equipment; *cost.* attire, F get-up; *fig.* state, plight; ⊕ gear, outfit; ⊕ *factory:* plant; *hunt.* pack of hounds; carriage and horses; **équipe** [e'kip] *f* ⊕ *workmen:* gang; ⊕ shift; 🜊 working party; *sp.* team; 🜨 crew; ~ *de nuit* night shift; *esprit m d'~* team spirit; 🜨 *homme m d'~* yardman.

équipée [eki'pe] *f* escapade; sally.

équipement [ekip'mã] *m* 🜊, 🜨, *sp., etc.* equipment; gear; outfit (*a.* ⊕); **équiper** [eki'pe] (1a) *v/t.* equip (*a.* 🜊); fit out; 🜨 man (*a vessel*).

équitable [eki'tabl] equitable, fair, just.

équitation [ekita'sjõ] *f* horsemanship; *école f d'~* riding-school.

équité [eki'te] *f* equity (*a.* ⚖); fairness, fair dealing.

équivalent, e [ekiva'lã, ~'lãːt] *adj., a. su./m* equivalent; **équivaloir** [~'lwaːr] (3l) *v/i.* be equivalent *or* tantamount (to, *à*).

équivoque [eki'vɔk] **1.** *adj.* equivocal; *fig.* dubious; **2.** *su./f* ambiguity; quibble; **équivoquer** [~vɔ'ke] (1m) *v/i.* quibble, equivocate.

érable 🜧 [e'rabl] *m tree, a. wood:* maple.

érafler [era'fle] (1a) *v/t.* graze, scratch; **éraflure** [~'flyːr] *f* graze, abrasion, scratch.

érailler [era'je] (1a) *v/t. tex.* unravel, fray; fret (*a rope*); roughen (*the voice*); graze, chafe (*the skin*); *s'~* become unravelled; fray (*cloth*).

ère [ɛːr] *f* era, epoch.

érection [erek'sjõ] *f statue etc.:* erection (*a. biol.*); *position:* establishment.

éreintement F [erɛ̃t'mã] *m* exhaustion; slating (= *harsh criticism*); **éreinter** [erɛ̃'te] (1a) *v/t.* break the back of (*a horse*); F exhaust; *fig.* slash, cut to pieces; F *être éreinté a.* be all in, be worn out.

erg *phys.* [ɛrg] *m* erg.

ergot [ɛr'go] *m cock:* spur; 🜧 stub; 🜧, 🜧 ergot; ⊕ catch, lug; *electric bulb:* pin; **ergotage** F [ɛrgɔ'taːʒ] *m* quibbling; **ergoté, e** [∿'te] spurred (*cock*, *rye*); ergoted (*corn*); **ergoter** F [∿'te] (1a) *v/i.* quibble (about, *sur*); split hairs; **ergoteur, -euse** [∿'tœːr, ∿'tøːz] **1.** *adj.* quibbling, pettifogging; **2.** *su.* quibbler, pettifogger.

ergothérapie [ɛrgɔteraˈpi] *f* occupational therapy; work therapy.

ériger [eriˈʒe] (1l) *v/t.* erect (*a statue* etc.); establish, found (*an office, a position*); *fig.* exalt, raise (to, *en*); ∿ qch. en *principe* lay s.th. down as a principle; s'∿ en set o.s. up as, pose as.

ermitage [ɛrmiˈtaːʒ] *m* hermitage; **ermite** [∿'mit] *m* hermit; recluse.

éroder [erɔˈde] (1a) *v/t.* erode; wear away; **érosif, -ve** [∿'zif, ∿'ziːv] erosive; **érosion** [∿'zjɔ̃] *f* erosion; eating away (*of metal, rock*).

érogène [erɔˈʒɛn] erogenous.

érotique [erɔˈtik] erotic; **érotisme** [∿'tism] *m* eroticism; ⚥ erotism.

errant, e [ɛˈrɑ̃, ∿'rɑ̃ːt] rambling, roving, wandering; *chevalier* m ∿ knight-errant.

errate *typ.* [ɛraˈta] *m/inv.* errata slip; **erratum,** *pl.* -ta [ɛraˈtɔm, ∿'ta] *m* erratum.

errements [ɛrˈmɑ̃] *m/pl.* ways, methods; *pej.* bad habits; *anciens* ∿ bad old ways; **errer** [ɛˈre] (1b) *v/i.* ramble, roam, wander; stroll ∿(about); *fig.* err, make a mistake; **erreur** [ɛˈrœːr] *f* error; mistake, slip; ∿ *de traduction* mistranslation; *faire*∿ be mistaken, be wrong; *revenir de ses* ∿s turn over a new leaf.

erroné, e [ɛrɔˈne] erroneous, mistaken, wrong.

ersatz [ɛrˈsats] *m* ersatz, substitute.

éructation [eryktaˈsjɔ̃] *f* eructation, F belch(ing).

érudit, e [eryˈdi,∿'dit] **1.** *adj.* erudite, scholarly, learned; **2.** *su.* scholar; **érudition** [∿di'sjɔ̃] *f* erudition, learning, scholarship.

éruptif, -ve ⚕, *geol.* [erypˈtif, ∿'tiːv] eruptive; **éruption** [∿'sjɔ̃] *f* eruption, ⚕ *a.* rash; cutting (*of teeth*).

érysipèle ⚕ [eriziˈpɛl] *m* erysipelas.

es [ɛ] *2nd p. sg. pres. of être 1.*

ès [ɛs] *prp.*: *docteur* m∿ *sciences* doctor of science.

esbroufe [ɛsˈbruf] *f*: F *faire de l'*∿ swank, show off; 🕳 *à l'*∿ snatch-and-grab (*theft*); **esbroufeur** m, **-euse** f

[∿bru'fœːr, ∿'føːz] swanker; hustler; 🕳 snatch-and-grab thief.

escabeau [ɛskaˈbo] *m* stool; pair of steps, step-ladder; **escabelle** [∿'bɛl] *f* stool.

escadre [ɛsˈkadr] *f* ⚓ squadron; ✈ wing; **escadrille** [ɛskaˈdriːj] *f* ⚓ flotilla; ✈ squadron; **escadron** ✕ [∿'drɔ̃] *m* squadron; *chef* m *d'*∿ major.

escalade [ɛskaˈlad] *f* cliff, wall: climbing, scaling; climb; *pol.*, *fig.* escalation; **escalader** [∿la'de] (1a) *v/t.* scale, climb.

escalator [ɛskalaˈtɔːr] *m* escalator.

escale [ɛsˈkal] *f* ⚓ port of call; ✈ stop; call; *faire* ∿ *à* call at; ✈ *sans* ∿ non-stop (*flight*).

escalier [ɛskaˈlje] *m* staircase; stairs *pl.*; ∿ *roulant* escalator; ∿ *tournant* (*or en colimaçon or à vis*) spiral staircase.

escalope *cuis.* [ɛskaˈlɔp] *f* *meat*: scallop; *fish*: steak; escalope.

escamotable [ɛskamɔˈtabl] disappearing, F pull-down (*arm-rest*); ✈ retractable (*undercarriage*); **escamoter** [∿'te] (1a) *v/t.* conjure away; ✈ retract (*the undercarriage*); *fig.* dodge, evade, get round; filch, pinch; **escamoteur** [∿'tœːr] *m* conjuror.

escampette F [ɛskɑ̃ˈpɛt] *f*: *prendre la poudre d'*∿ skedaddle, vamoose, *Am.* *sl.* take a powder.

escapade [ɛskaˈpad] *f* escapade; prank.

escarbille [ɛskarˈbiːj] *f* cinder; ∿s *pl.* clinkers.

escarbot *zo.* [ɛskarˈbo] *m* beetle.

escarboucle [ɛskarˈbukl] *f* carbuncle.

escargot [ɛskarˈgo] *m* snail.

escarmouche ✕ [ɛskarˈmuʃ] *f* skirmish, brush.

escarole ♀ [ɛskaˈrɔl] *f* endive.

escarpe [ɛsˈkarp] *m* cut-throat.

escarpé, e [ɛskarˈpe] sheer (*rock*), steep; **escarpement** [∿pə'mɑ̃] *m* steepness; ✕, *geol.* escarpment; abrupt descent; *mountain*: slope.

escarpin [ɛskarˈpɛ̃] *m* light shoe.

escarpolette [ɛskarpɔˈlɛt] *f* swing.

escarre ⚕ [ɛsˈkaːr] *f* scab; bed-sore.

escient [ɛˈsjɑ̃] *m*: *à bon* ∿ advisedly.

esclaffer [ɛsklaˈfe] (1a) *v/t.*: s'∿ burst out laughing, guffaw.

esclandre [ɛsˈklɑ̃ːdr] *m* scandal; scene.

esclavage [ɛsklaˈvaːʒ] *m* slavery; *fig.*

drudgery; **esclave** [ʌˈklaːv] su. slave; fig. drudge; être ~ de sa parole stick to one's promise.

escoffier sl. [ɛskɔˈfje] (1o) v/t. kill.

escogriffe F [ɛskɔˈgrif] m lanky fellow, F beanpole.

escompte † [ɛsˈkɔ̃ːt] m discount, rebate; à ~ at a discount; **escompter** [ʌkɔ̃ˈte] (1a) v/t. † discount; fig. anticipate; fig. reckon on, bank on.

escorte [ɛsˈkɔrt] f ✗ etc. escort; ⚓ convoy; **escorter** [ʌkɔrˈte] (1a) v/t. escort; ⚓ a. convoy.

escouade ✗ [ɛsˈkwad] f gang, squad.

escrime [ɛsˈkrim] f fencing; faire de l'~ fence; **escrimer** F [ɛskriˈme] v/t.: s'~ fight (with, contre); s'~ à work hard at; try hard to (inf.); **escrimeur** [ʌˈmœːr] m fencer, swordsman.

escroc [ɛsˈkro] m crook; swindler; **escroquer** [ʌkrɔˈke] (1m) v/t. swindle (s.o.); ~ qch. à q. cheat s.o. out of s.th.; **escroquerie** [ʌkrɔˈkri] f fraud; swindling; false pretences pl.

ésotérique [ezɔteˈrik] esoteric.

espace [ɛsˈpaːs] su./m space; space, a. time: interval; room; ⊕ clearance; ~ vert green space or area; ~ vital living space; dans (or en) l'~ de within (a certain time); su./f typ. space; **espacement** [ʌpasˈmɑ̃] m objects, typ.: spacing; **espacer** [ʌpaˈse] (1k) v/t. space; leave a space between; typ., a. fig. space out; s'~ become less frequent (space, a. time).

espadon [ɛspaˈdɔ̃] m † two-handled sword; icht. sword-fish.

espadrille [ɛspaˈdriːj] f rope-soled canvas shoe.

espagnol, e [ɛspaˈɲɔl] 1. adj. Spanish; 2. su./m ling. Spanish; su. ♀ Spaniard; **espagnolette** [ʌɲɔˈlɛt] f espagnolette.

espalier ✔ [ɛspaˈlje] m espalier.

espèce [ɛsˈpɛs] f kind, sort; ⚖ case (in question); ♀, zo., eccl. species; ~s pl. cash sg., specie sg.; ~ de ...! silly ...!; ~ humaine mankind; en ~s in hard cash; en l'~ in the present case (a. ⚖).

espérance [ɛspeˈrɑ̃ːs] f hope; expectation; fig. promise; ⚖ ~s pl. expectations; ~ de vie life expectancy; **espérer** [ʌˈre] (1f) v/t. hope for; ~ que hope that; je l'espère, j'espère I hope so; ~ quand même hope against hope; v/i. hope, trust (in, en).

espiègle [ɛsˈpjɛgl] 1. adj. mischie-

vous, roguish; 2. su. imp; **espièglerie** [ʌpjɛglɔˈri] f mischief; prank; par ~ out of mischief.

espion, -onne [ɛsˈpjɔ̃, ʌˈpjɔn] su. spy; secret agent; su./m concealed microphone; window-mirror; **espionnage** [ɛspjɔˈnaːʒ] m espionage, spying; † ~ industriel industrial espionage; **espionner** [ʌˈne] (1a) v/t. spy (upon).

esplanade [esplaˈnad] f esplanade, promenade.

espoir [ɛsˈpwaːr] m hope; expectation.

esprit [ɛsˈpri] m spirit; mind, intellect; sense; wit; disposition; talent; meaning; soul; ~-de-vin spirit(s pl.) of wine; ~ fort free-thinker; le Saint-♀ the Holy Ghost or Spirit; plein d'~ witty; présence f d'~ presence of mind; rendre l'~ give up the ghost; venir à (sortir de) l'~ de q. cross (slip) s.o.'s mind.

esquif ⚓ poet. [ɛsˈkif] m small boat, skiff.

esquille ⚕ [ɛsˈkiːj] f bone: splinter.

esquimau [eskiˈmo] 1. adj. Esquimo; 2. su. ♀ Esquimo; su./m cuis. choc-ice; cost. child's rompers pl.

esquinter F [ɛskɛ̃ˈte] (1a) v/t. exhaust; tire (s.o.) out; fig. ruin; run (s.o.) down.

esquisse [ɛsˈkis] f sketch; outline, draft; **esquisser** [ʌkiˈse] (1a) v/t. sketch, outline.

esquiver [eskiˈve] (1a) v/t. avoid, evade; dodge; fig. s'~ slip or steal away, F make o.s. scarce.

essai [eˈsɛ] m ⊕, ⚕ trial, essay; test; sp. try; attempt (to, pour); ~ nucléaire atomic test; mot. ~ sur route trial run; à l'~ on trial; coup m d'~ first attempt; faire l'~ de try (s.th.); ✈ pilote m d'~ test pilot.

essaim [eˈsɛ̃] m swarm (a. fig.); **essaimage** [esɛˈmaːʒ] m hiving off (a. fig.); fig. excessive growth; **essaimer** [esɛˈme] (1a) v/i. swarm.

essarter ✔ [esarˈte] (1a) v/t. clear (the ground); grub up (roots etc.).

essayage [esɛˈjaːʒ] m testing; cost. trying on, fitting; **essayer** [ʌˈje] (1i) v/t. try (to inf., de inf.), attempt; ⚕ test; metall. assay; cost. try on; taste; s'~ à try one's hand at; **essayeur** m, -euse f [ʌˈjœːr, ʌˈjøːz] ⊕ tester; analyst; metall. assayer; cost. fitter.

essayiste [ʌˈjist] su. essayist.

esse [ɛs] *f* ⊕ S-hook; S-shaped link *or* hook *etc.*; ♪ *violin*: sound-hole.

essence [e'sãːs] *f* essence; *trees*: species; ♣, ♂, *etc.* oil; petrol, *Am.* gasoline; extract (*of beef etc.*); *fig.* pith; *poste m d'~* filling-station, *Am.* service station; **essentiel, -elle** [esã'sjɛl] **1.** *adj.* essential; **2.** *su./m* main thing.

essieu [e'sjø] *m* axle.

essor [e'sɔːr] *m* flight, soaring; *fig.* scope; *fig.* progress; **essorrer** [esɔ-'re] (1a) *v/t.* dry; wring (*linen*); ~ *à la machine* spin-dry (*linen*); **essoreuse** [~'røːz] *f* ⊕ drainer; *laundry*: wringer, mangle.

essouflé, e [esu'fle] out of breath; breathless; **essoufler** [~] (1a) *v/t.* wind, make (*s.o.*) breathless; *s'~* get out of breath; *fig.* exhaust o.s.

essuie...: **~-glace** *mot.* [esɥi'glas] *m* windscreen wiper, *Am.* windshield wiper; **~-mains** [~'mɛ̃] *m/inv.* (hand-)towel; **~-pieds** [~'pje] *m/inv.* door-mat; **~-verres** [~'vɛr] *m/inv.* glass cloth.

essuyer [esɥi'je] (1h) *v/t.* wipe; dry; mop up; dust; *fig.* suffer (*defeat etc.*); *fig.* meet with (*a refusal*); F ~ *les plâtres* be the first occupant of a new house; *fig.* be first to do the disagreeable job.

est¹ [ɛst] **1.** *su./m* east; *de l'~* east (-ern); *d'~* easterly (*wind*); *l'Ω* the east (*of a country*); *vers l'~* eastward(s), to the east; **2.** *adj./inv.* east(ern); easterly (*wind*).

est² [ɛ] *3rd p. sg. pres. of* être 1.

estacade [ɛsta'kad] *f* ⚓ stockade; ⚓ breakwater; pier; 🎱 coalpit.

estafette [ɛsta'fɛt] *f* courier; ✕ dispatch-rider.

estafilade [ɛstafi'lad] *f* gash; slash.

estagnon [ɛsta'ɲɔ̃] *m* oil-can; (oil-) drum.

estaminet † [ɛstami'nɛ] *m* tavern; pub; bar.

estampe [ɛs'tãːp] *f* print, engraving; ⊕ stamp, punch, die; **estamper** [ɛstã'pe] (1a) *v/t.* stamp, emboss; ⊕ punch; *fig.* fleece (*s.o.*), swindle (*s.o.*); **estampille** [~'piːj] *f* stamp; brand; ✝ trade-mark; **estampiller** [~pi'je] (1a) *v/t.* stamp; brand; ✝ mark (*goods*).

esthète [ɛs'tɛt] *su.* (a)esthete; **esthéticien** *m*, **-enne** *f* [ɛsteti'sjɛ̃, ~'sjɛn] (a)esthetician; beautician; **esthéti-**

que [~'tik] **1.** *adj.* (a)esthetic; **2.** *su./f* (a)esthetics *pl.*

estimable [ɛsti'mabl] estimable; quite good; assessable; **estimateur** [ɛstima'tœːr] *m* estimator; ✝ valuer, appraiser; **estimatif, -ve** [~'tif, ~'tiːv] estimated (*cost etc.*); estimative (*faculty*); *devis m ~* estimate; **estimation** [~'sjɔ̃] *f* estimation; valuation; assessment, appraisal; **estime** [ɛs'tim] *f* esteem, respect; *à l'~* by guesswork; *tenir q. en haute (petite)* ~ hold s.o. in high (low) esteem; **estimer** [~ti'me] (1a) *v/t.* estimate; value, appraise, assess; *fig.* (hold in) esteem; consider, think.

estival, e [ɛsti'val, ~'vo] *m/pl.* **-aux** summer...; ♥ *etc.* estival; **estivant** *m*, **e** *f* [~'vã, ~'vãːt] summer visitor; **estivation** ♥, *zo.* [~va'sjɔ̃] *f* estivation.

estoc [ɛs'tɔk] *m coup m d'~ fencing:* thrust; *frapper d'~ et de taille* cut and thrust; **estocade** [ɛstɔ'kad] *f* † *fencing:* thrust; *fig.* sudden onset; *a. fig.* death-blow, finishing blow.

estomac [ɛstɔ'ma] *m* stomach; ~ *dérangé* upset stomach; *avoir l'~ dans les talons* be faint with hunger; *mal m d'~* stomach-ache; **estomaquer** F [~ma'ke] (1m) *v/t.* take (*s.o.'s*) breath away, stagger (*s.o.*).

estompe [ɛs'tɔ̃ːp] *f* stump; stump drawing; **estomper** [~tɔ̃'pe] (1a) *v/t.* stump, shade off; *fig.* blur; *fig.* tone down (*crudities*); *fig. s'~* grow blurred; loom up.

estrade [ɛs'trad] *f* platform, stage.

estragon ♥, *cuis.* [ɛstra'gɔ̃] *m* tarragon.

estrapade ⚔ † [ɛstra'pad] *f* strappado.

estropié, e [ɛstrɔ'pje] **1.** *adj.* crippled; ✕ disabled; lame; **2.** *su.* cripple; **estropier** [~] (1o) *v/t.* cripple; lame, maim; ✕ disable; *fig.* mangle (*a quotation, a word*), murder (*music, a language*).

estuaire [ɛs'tɥeːr] *m* estuary, *Sc.* firth.

estudiantin, e [ɛstydjã'tɛ̃, ~'tin] student... [geon.]

esturgeon *icht.* [ɛstyr'ʒɔ̃] *m* sturgeon.

et [e] and; *et ... et* both ... and.

étable [e'tabl] *f* cattle-shed, cow-shed; pigsty (*a. fig.*); **établer** [eta-'ble] (1a) *v/t.* stall (*cattle*); stable (*horses*).

établi[1] [eta'bli] *m* work-bench.

établi[2], **e** [eta'bli] established (*fact*); determined (*limit*); **établir** [~'bli:r] (2a) *v/t.* establish (*a.* ⚖); set up (*a business, a statue, sp. a record*); construct, erect; ascertain (*facts*); prove (*a charge*); draw up (*an account, a budget, a plan*); institute (*a rule, a tax, a post*); ⚡ ~ le contact make contact; s'~ become established; establish (o.s.); settle (*in a place*); **établissement** [~blis'mɑ̃] *m* establishment; institution; settlement; ♱ concern, business, firm; ⊕ factory, plant; ♱ *accounts:* drawing up; ♱ *balance:* striking.

étage [e'ta:ʒ] *m* stor(e)y, floor; *fig.* degree, rank; ⊕, *geol.* stage (*a. of rocket*); *geol.* stratum, layer; ⚒ level; *fig.* de bas ~ of the lower classes (*people*); low; *deuxième* ~ second floor, *Am.* third floor; **étager** [eta'ʒe] (1l) *v/t.* range in tiers; terrace (*the ground*); perform (*an operation*) in stages; **étagère** [~'ʒɛ:r] *f* whatnot; shelves *pl.*; shelf.

étai [e'tɛ] *m* ⚓ stay (*a.* ⚓), prop (*a. fig.*), strut; ⚒ pit-prop; **étaiement** ⚓, ⊕ [ete'mɑ̃] *m see* étayage.

étain [e'tɛ̃] *m* tin; pewter; *papier m* d'~ tinfoil; ~ de soudure plumber's solder.

étal, *pl. a.* **étals** [e'tal] *m market:* stall; **étalage** [eta'la:ʒ] *m* ♱ display, show (*a. fig.*); shop window; *fig. a.* parade; **étalagiste** ♱ [~la'ʒist] window dresser; **étalement** [etal'mɑ̃] *m* displaying; spreading(-out); *holidays etc.:* staggering; **étaler** [eta'le] (1a) *v/t.* ♱ display (*a. fig.*), expose for sale; *fig.* show, disclose; stagger (*holidays*); spread (out); s'~ sprawl; spread *or* stretch out.

étalon[1] [eta'lɔ̃] *m* stallion.

étalon[2] [eta'lɔ̃] *m* standard; ~-*or* gold standard; *poids*-~ troy weight; **étalonnage** [~lɔ'na:ʒ] *m* standardization; *tubes etc.:* calibration; ga(u)ging; *radio:* logging; *phot.* grading; **étalonner** [~lɔ'ne] (1a) *v/t.* standardize; calibrate; ga(u)ge; *radio:* log (*stations*); *phot.* grade; stamp (*weights*).

étamer ⊕ [eta'me] (1a) *v/t.* tin; galvanize; silver (*a mirror*); **étameur** [~'mœ:r] *m* tinsmith; *mirrors:* silverer.

étamine[1] [eta'min] *f* butter-muslin;

bolting-cloth; *passer qch. par l'*~ sift s.th. (*a. fig.*).

étamine[2] ⚡ [~] *f* stamen.

étampe ⊕ [e'tɑ̃:p] *f* stamp, die; punch; swage.

étanche [e'tɑ̃:ʃ] (*water-, air*)tight; impervious; ⚡ insulated; ~ à l'eau watertight; **étanchéité** [etɑ̃ʃei'te] *f* watertightness; airtightness; ⚡ d'~ insulating; **étancher** [~'ʃe] (1a) *v/t.* sta(u)nch (*blood*); stem (*a liquid*); quench (*one's thirst*); stop (*a leak*); make watertight *or* airtight.

étang [e'tɑ̃] *m* pond, pool; ~ à poissons fish pond.

étant [e'tɑ̃] *p. pr. of* être 1.

étape [e'tap] *f* ⚔, *a. fig.* stage; halting-place; *fig.* step (towards, *vers*); *par petites* ~s by easy stages; *faire* ~ stop off, stop over.

état [e'ta] *m* state (*a. pol., a. fig.*), condition; *fig.* position; ⚖ status; profession, trade; *hist.* ~s *pl. the* estates; ~ *civil* civil status; *bureau m de l'*~ *civil* register office; ⚖ *en* ~ *de légitime défense* able to plead self-defence; ~ *d'esprit* frame of mind; *en tout* ~ *de cause* in any case; ~ *transitoire* transition stage; *réduit à l'*~ *de* reduced to; *coup m d'*⚶ coup d'état; F *dans tous ses* ~s all of a dither; *en* ~ *de vol* in flying condition (*airplane*); *être en* ~ *de* (*inf.*) be in a position to (*inf.*); *faire* ~ *de* put forward; *homme m d'*⚶ statesman; *hors d'*~ useless; *remettre en* ~ put in order; **étatique** *pol.* [eta'tik] state ...; (of) state control; **étatisation** [etatiza'sjɔ̃] *f* nationalisation (*of industries*); **étatisme** [~'tism] *m* state control; **état-major**, *pl.* **états-majors** [~ma'ʒɔ:r] *m* ⚔ (general) staff; headquarters *pl.*; *fig.* management.

étau ⊕ [e'to] *m* vice, *Am.* vise; ~ *à main* hand-vice; ~-*limeur* shaping-machine.

étayage ⚓, ⊕ [ete'ja:ʒ] *m* shoring, staying, propping (up); buttressing; **étayer** [~'je] (1i) *v/t.* prop (up), shore, stay; support (*a. fig.*).

été[1] [e'te] *p.p. of* être **1**.

été[2] [~] *m* summer; F ~ *de la Saint-Martin* Indian summer.

éteignoir [ete'ɲwa:r] *m candle:* extinguisher; **éteindre** [e'tɛ̃:dr] (4m) *v/t.* extinguish (*the light, a race, etc.*); put out; ⚡ switch off (*the light*); quench (*one's thirst, a.* ⊕ red-hot *iron*); pay off (*a debt*); abolish (*a right*); *fig.* put an end to (*s.o.'s ambition, hope*); *fig.* soften, dim (*the colour, the light*); deaden (*a sound*); allay (*passions*); slake (*lime*); s'∼ die out; go out (*light etc.*); fade, grow dim; die down (*passions*); die, pass away (*person*).

étendage [etɑ̃'da:ʒ] *m* clothes lines *pl.*; drying-yard; **étendard** [∼'da:r] *m* standard, flag; **étendoir** [∼-'dwa:r] *m* clothes line; **étendre** [e'tɑ̃:dr] (4a) *v/t.* extend; stretch; spread (out); lay (*a tablecloth*); expand (*the wings*); dilute (with, **de**); lay (*s.o.*) down; hang (*linen*) out; *cuis.* roll out (*pastry*); *fig.* widen, enlarge; s'∼ spread; stretch (out), extend; stretch out, lie down; **étendu, e** [etɑ̃'dy] **1.** *adj.* extensive; outspread (*wings*); outstretched (*hands*); widespread (*influence*); **2.** *su./f* extent; expanse; voice, knowledge: range; capacity; *speech etc.*: length.

éternel, -elle [eter'nɛl] eternal; everlasting, unending; **éterniser** [eterni'ze] (1a) *v/t.* perpetuate; eternalize; s'∼ last for ever; **éternité** [∼'te] *f* eternity; *fig.* ages *pl.*

éternuer [eter'nɥe] (1n) *v/i.* sneeze.

êtes [ɛt] *2nd p. pl. pres. of* être **1**.

éteule [e'tœl] *f* stubble.

éther [e'te:r] *m* ether; **éthéré, e** [ete're] etherial (*a.* 🜍); **éthériser** 🜍 [∼ri'ze] (1a) *v/t.* etherize.

éthique [e'tik] **1.** *adj.* ethical; **2.** *su./f* ethics *pl.*; moral philosophy.

ethnique [ɛt'nik] ethnic(al).

ethno... [ɛtnɔ] ethno...

éthylène 🜍 [eti'lɛːn] *m* ethylene.

étiage [e'tja:ʒ] *m* low water mark; *fig.* level.

étinceler [etɛ̃s'le] (1c) *v/i.* sparkle (*a. fig. conversation*); gleam (*anger*); twinkle (*star*); **étincelle** [etɛ̃'sɛl] *f* spark; *mot.* ∼ d'allumage ignition spark; **étincellement** [∼sɛl'mɑ̃] *m* sparkling; twinkling (*of the stars*).

étioler [etjɔ'le] (1a) *v/t.*: s'∼ droop, wilt (*plant*); waste away.

étique [e'tik] emaciated.

étiqueter [etik'te] (1c) *v/t.* label; **étiquette** [eti'kɛt] *f* label, ticket, tag; etiquette, ceremony.

étirer [eti're] (1a) *v/t.* stretch; pull out, draw out; ⊕ draw (*metals*).

étoffe [e'tɔf] *f* material, cloth; *fig.* stuff; *avoir l'*∼ *de* have the makings

of; **étoffé, e** [etɔ'fe] plump (*person*); meaty (*style etc.*); rich (*voice*); **étoffer** [∼] (1a) *v/t.* stuff; *fig.* fill out; *cost.* give fulness to; *fig.* s'∼ fill out (*person*).

étoile [e'twal] *f* star (*a. film*); *typ.* asterisk; blaze (*on horse*); ∼ *du berger* evening star; *zo.* ∼ *de mer* starfish; ∼ *filante* shooting *or* falling star; *à la belle* ∼ out of doors, in the open; **étoiler** [etwa'le] (1a) *v/t.* stud with stars; star (*glass etc.*); s'∼ star (*glass etc.*); glow with stars (*sky*).

étole *cost., eccl.* [e'tɔl] *f* stole.

étonnant, e [etɔ'nɑ̃, ∼'nɑ̃:t] astonishing, surprising; **étonnement** [etɔn'mɑ̃] *m* astonishment, surprise, amazement; **étonner** [etɔ'ne] (1a) *v/t.* astonish, amaze; s'∼ be surprised (at *s.th.*, *de qch*; at *ger.*, *de inf.*).

étouffant, e *fig.* [etu'fɑ̃, ∼'fɑ̃:t] stifling; **étouffée** *cuis.* [∼'fe] *f*: *cuire à l'*∼ braise; **étouffement** [etuf'mɑ̃] *m* stifling; suffocation; *scandal*: hushing up; choking sensation; **étouffer** [etu'fe] (1a) *vt/i. a.* s'∼ suffocate, choke, stifle; *v/t. a.* damp (*a sound*); 🜍 quench (*a spark*); hush up (*an affair*); **étouffoir** [∼'fwa:r] *m* charcoal extinguisher; ♪ damper; *fig.* stuffy room.

étoupe [e'tup] *f* tow; oakum; ⊕ packing; **étouper** [etu'pe] (1a) *v/t.* stop; ⊕ pack; ⚓ caulk; **étoupille** [∼'pi:j] *f* ✗ friction-tube; ✗ fuse.

étourderie [eturdə'ri] *f* inadvertence; blunder, careless mistake; oversight; **étourdi, e** [∼'di] **1.** *adj.* thoughtless, scatter-brained; foolish (*reply etc.*); **2.** *su.* scatter-brain; **étourdir** [∼'di:r] (2a) *v/t.* stun, daze; make dizzy; soothe (*a pain etc.*); appease (*one's hunger*); **étourdissement** [∼dis'mɑ̃] *m* dizziness, giddiness; dizzy spell; *mind:* dazing; *pain etc.*: deadening; *fig.* shock, bewilderment.

étourneau [etur'no] *m orn.* starling; F feather-brain.

étrange [e'trɑ̃:ʒ] strange, odd, peculiar; **étranger, -ère** [etrɑ̃'ʒe, ∼'ʒɛ:r] **1.** *adj. pol.* foreign (*a. fig.*); *pej.* alien; strange, unknown; irrelevant (to, *à*); ∼ *à* unacquainted with (*an affair*); a stranger in (*a place*); **2.** *su.* foreigner; stranger; *su./m* foreign parts *pl.*; *à l'*∼ abroad;

étrangeté [etrãʒ'te] *f* strangeness, oddness.

étranglement [etrãglə'mã] *m* strangulation; *pipe, tube:* neck; *fig.* narrow passage; *fig.* goulet *m* (*or* goulot *m*) d'~ bottleneck; **étrangler** [~'gle] (1a) *v/t.* strangle, choke, throttle (*a.* ⊕), stifle; ✗ strangulate; *fig.* constrict; ⊕ throttle down (*the engine*); *v/i.*: ~ de colère choke with rage; ~ de soif be parched.

étrave ⚓ [e'tra:v] *f* stem(-post).

être [ɛ:tr] **1.** (1) *v/i.* be, exist; belong (to, *à*); lie, stand; F go; *passive voice:* be (*seen*); ~ malade be *or* feel sick; *si cela est* if so; *ça y est* it is done; *ç'est ça* that's it; *c'est moi* it is me; *c'en est assez!* enough (of it)!; *lequel sommes-nous?* what is the date today?; *à qui est cela?* whose is it?; *c'est à lui* de (inf.) it is his turn to (inf.); it rests with him to (inf.); ~ de come *or* be from (*a town*); ~ assis sit; ~ debout stand; *j'ai été voir ce film* I have seen this film; *elle-s'est blessée* she has hurt herself; *elle s'est blessé le doigt* she has hurt her finger; *en* ~ *à* (inf.) be reduced to (ger.); *en êtes-vous?* will you join us?; *où en sommes-nous?* how far have we got?; *quoi qu'il en soit* however that may be; *en* ~ *pour* have spent (*s.th.*) to no purpose; *vous y êtes?* do you follow *or* F get it?; *il est* it is (2 o'clock); *il était une fois* once upon a time there was; *est-ce qu'il travaille?* does he work?, is he working?; *elle est venue, n'est-ce pas?* she has come, hasn't she?; *n'était* but for; **2.** *su./m* being, creature; existence.

étreindre [e'trɛ̃:dr] (4m) *v/t.* clasp; grasp; embrace, hug; *fig.* grip; **étreinte** [e'trɛ̃:t] *f* embrace; grasp; grip.

étrenne [e'trɛn] *f*: ~s *pl.* New Year's gift *sg.*; Christmas box *sg.*; *avoir l'~* de = **étrenner** [etrɛ'ne] (1a) *v/t.* wear (*a garment*) *or* use (*s.th.*) for the first time.

êtres [ɛ:tr] *m/pl.*: *les* ~ *d'une maison* the ins and outs of a house.

étrier [etri'e] *m* stirrup (*a.* anat.); *fig.* mettre le pied à l'~ à q. help s.o.

étrille [e'tri:j] *f* curry-comb; **étriller** [etri'je] (1a) *v/t.* curry (*a horse*); F † thrash, trounce.

étriper [etri'pe] (1a) *v/t.* disembowel (*a horse*); draw (*a chicken*); gut (*a fish*).

étriquer [etri'ke] (1m) *v/t.* make too narrow *or* tight; *fig.* curtail (*a speech*); *habit m étriqué* skimped coat.

étroit, e [e'trwa, ~'trwat] narrow (*a. fig.* mind); tight; confined; limited; *fig.* strict (*sense of a word*); *à l'*~ cramped for room; (*live*) economically; **étroitesse** [etrwa'tɛs] *f* narrowness; tightness; ~ d'esprit narrow-mindedness.

étron [e'trɔ̃] *m* turd.

étude [e'tyd] *f* study (*a.* ♪); office; (*barrister's*) chambers *pl.*; prep-room; research; preparation; (*lawyer's*) practice; ✝ ~ du marché (de motivation) marketing (motivation) research; *à l'*~ under consideration; *thea.* under rehearsal; *faire ses* ~s study; **étudiant** *m*, **e** *f* [ety'djã, ~'djã:t] student; undergraduate; **étudier** [~'dje] (1o) *v/t.* study; prepare (*a lesson*); examine, go into, investigate; design; *s'*~ à (inf.) make a point of (ger.); be very careful to (inf.).

étui [e'tɥi] *m* case, cover; *book, hat:* box; ✗ ~ de cartouche cartridge case.

étuve [e'ty:v] *f* 🔥, ⊕, *baths:* sweating-room; sterilizer; drying cupboard; F oven; **étuvée** *cuis.* [ety've] *f*: *cuire à l'*~ steam; **étuver** [~] (1a) *v/t.* steam (*meat*); *cuis.* stew (*vegetables*); ⊕ dry; sterilize.

étymologie [etimɔlɔ'ʒi] *f* etymology.

eu, e [y] *p.p. of avoir* **1.**

eucalyptus 🔥, *a.* ✗ [økalip'tys] *m* eucalyptus.

eucharistie *eccl.* [økaris'ti] *f* Eucharist; Lord's Supper.

eunuque [ø'nyk] *m* eunuch.

euphémique [øfe'mik] euphemistic; **euphémisme** [~'mism] *m* euphemism.

euphonie [øfɔ'ni] *f* euphony.

euphorie [øfɔ'ri] *f* euphoria; **euphorique** [~'rik] euphoric; **euphorisant, e** [~ri'zã, ~'zã:t] *adj.*, *a. su.* euphoriant; **euphoriser** [~ri'ze] (1a) *v/t.* put into a euphoric mood.

européen, -enne [ørɔpe'ɛ̃, ~'ɛn] *adj.*, *a. su.* Ϙ European.

eus [y] *1st p. sg. p.s. of avoir* **1.**

euthanasie [øtana'zi] *f* euthanasia, F mercy-killing.

eux [ø] *pron./pers. m/pl. subject:* they; *object:* them; *à* ~ to them; theirs; *ce sont* ~, F *c'est* ~ it is they, F it's them; *~-mêmes* [~'mɛːm] *pron./rfl.* themselves.

évacuation [evakɥa'sjɔ̃] *f* evacuation (*a.* ⚥, ⚻); *water:* drainage; **évacué** *m*, **e** *f* [eva'kɥe] evacuee; **évacuer** [~] (1n) *v/t.* ⚻, ⚥ evacuate; ⊕ exhaust (*steam*); drain (*water*).

évadé, e [eva'de] *adj., a. su.* fugitive; **évader** [~] (1a) *v/t.: s'*~ escape, run away.

évaluation [evalɥa'sjɔ̃] *f* valuation; estimate; assessment; **évaluer** [~-'lɥe] (1n) *v/t.* value; estimate; assess.

évangélique [evɑ̃ʒe'lik] evangelical; **Évangile** [~'ʒil] *m* Gospel.

évanouir [eva'nwiːr] (2a) *v/t.: s'*~ ⚥ faint, swoon; *fig.* vanish, fade away; *radio:* fade; **évanouissement** [~nwis'mɑ̃] *m* ⚥ faint, swoon; *fig.* disappearance; *radio:* fading; ⚥ *revenir de son* ~ come to.

évaporation [evapɔra'sjɔ̃] *f* evaporation; **évaporé, e** [~'re] **1.** *adj.* scatterbrained; flighty; irresponsible; **2.** *su.* flighty person; **évaporer** [~'re] (1a) *v/t.: s'*~ evaporate.

évasé, e [eva'ze] bell-mouthed; flared (*skirt*); △ splayed; **évaser** [~'ze] (1a) *v/t.* widen the opening of; open out; flare (*a skirt*); △ splay; *s'*~ widen at the mouth; flare (*skirt*); **évasif, -ve** [~'zif, ~'ziːv] evasive; **évasion** [~'zjɔ̃] *f* escape, flight; evasion, quibble; *literature:* escapism; ~ *de prison* jailbreak; *d'*~ escapist (*novel etc.*); ✝ ~ *des capitaux* exodus of capital.

évêché [evɛ'ʃe] *m* bishopric, see; diocese; bishop's palace.

éveil [e'vɛːj] *m* awakening; alertness; *fig.* dawn; *en* ~ on the alert; **éveillé, e** [evɛ'je] awake; wide-awake; alert, bright; **éveiller** [~] (1a) *v/t.* awaken; *fig.* arouse; *s'*~ wake up; *fig.* awaken.

événement [even'mɑ̃] *m* event; occurrence; incident; emergency.

évent [e'vɑ̃] *m* open air; ⊕ vent (-hole); *zo. whale:* blowhole; *beverage:* flatness; *sentir l'*~ smell musty; F *tête f à l'*~ feather-brain.

éventail [evɑ̃'taːj] *m* fan; *fig. salaries:* range; *en* ~ fan-wise.

éventaire [evɑ̃'tɛːr] *m* (hawker's) tray; street stall.

éventé, e [evɑ̃'te] stale, musty; flat (*beer etc.*); *fig.* hare-brained; divulged (*secret*); **éventer** [~] (1a) *v/t.* air; fan; *hunt.* scent, *fig.* get wind of; *fig.* divulge; let (*beer etc.*) grow flat; F *fig.* ~ *la mèche* uncover a plot; *s'*~ go flat or stale; spoil.

éventrer [evɑ̃'tre] (1a) *v/t.* disembowel; *fig.* break or rip open; gut (*a fish*); *mot.* rip (*a tyre*).

éventualité [evɑ̃tɥali'te] *f* possibility, contingency; **éventuel, -elle** [~'tɥɛl] possible, contingent; eventual.

évêque [e'vɛːk] *m* bishop.

évertuer [evɛr'tɥe] (1n) *v/t.: s'*~ strive, do one's utmost (to *inf.*, *à inf.*).

évidemment [evida'mɑ̃] *adv.* of course, certainly; obviously; **évidence** [~'dɑ̃ːs] *f* obviousness, evidence; obvious fact; *à l'*~, *de toute* ~ (quite) obviously; *en* ~ in a prominent or conspicuous position; *se mettre en* ~ push o.s. forward; **évident, e** [~'dɑ̃, ~'dɑ̃ːt] evident, obvious.

évider [evi'de] (1a) *v/t.* hollow out; groove; pink (*cloth, leather*); cut away.

évier [e'vje] *m scullery:* sink.

évincer [evɛ̃'se] (1k) *v/t.* ⚖ evict, eject, dispossess; *fig.* oust (*s.o.*), supplant (*s.o.*).

évitable [evi'tabl] avoidable; **évitement** [evit'mɑ̃] *m* avoidance, shunning; *route f d'*~ bypass (road); *voie f d'*~ siding; **éviter** [evi'te] (1a) *v/t.* avoid; *fig.* spare (*trouble*); *v/i.:* ~ *de* (*inf.*) avoid (*ger.*).

évocateur, -trice [evɔka'tœːr, ~-'tris] evocative (of, de); **évocation** [~'sjɔ̃] *f* evocation (⚖, *a.* spirits, *a.* past); past, spirits: conjuring up.

évoluer [evɔ'lɥe] (1n) *v/i.* develop, evolve; ⚻, ⚓ manœuvre; move; **évolution** [~ly'sjɔ̃] *f* ⚻, ⚓ manœuvre; *biol. etc.* evolution; *fig.* development.

évoquer [evɔ'ke] (1m) *v/t.* evoke (*a.* ⚖), bring to mind; conjure up (*a.* spirits).

ex... [ɛks] former; ex-...; late; ~-*ministre* former minister.

exact, e [ɛg'zakt] exact (*a. science*);

correct, right; true; punctual (*time*).

exacteur [ɛgzak'tœːr] *m* exactor; extortioner; **exaction** [~'sjɔ̃] *f* extortion; *tax*: exaction.

exactitude [ɛgzakti'tyd] *f* exactitude, exactness; accuracy; *time*: punctuality.

exagération [ɛgzaʒera'sjɔ̃] *f* exaggeration; overstatement; **exagérer** [~ʒe're] (1f) *v/t.* exaggerate; overstate; overestimate; *v/i. fig.* go too far.

exaltation [ɛgzalta'sjɔ̃] *f eccl., a. emotion*: exaltation; excitement; over-excitement; **exalté, e** [~'te] **1.** *adj.* heated; excited; overstrung (*person*); **2.** *su.* hot-head; fanatic; **exalter** [~'te] (1a) *v/t.* exalt, praise; excite, rouse (*emotions*); s'~ grow excited; enthuse.

examen [ɛgza'mɛ̃] *m* examination; ⊕ test; ⊕ *machine*: overhaul; survey; investigation; ✝ *accounts*: inspection; *à l'*~ under consideration (*question*); ~ d'entrée entrance examination; ~ de passage end-of-year examination; *mot.* ~ pour le permis de conduire driving test; **examinateur** *m*, **-trice** *f* [~mina'tœːr, ~'tris] examiner; ⊕ inspector; **examiner** [~mi'ne] (1a) *v/t.* examine (*a.* ⚗); scrutinize; look into, investigate; ⊕ overhaul (*a machine*); *fig.* scan; ✝ inspect (*accounts*).

exaspération [ɛgzaspera'sjɔ̃] *f disease, pain, a.* F *fig.*: aggravation; *fig.* exasperation, irritation; **exaspérer** [~'re] (1f) *v/t.* exasperate, irritate, aggravate.

exaucer [ɛgzo'se] (1k) *v/t.* grant, fulfill (*a wish*); hear (*a prayer*).

excavateur *m*, **-trice** *f* ⊕ [ɛkskava'tœːr, ~'tris] excavator, grub; **excavation** [~'sjɔ̃] *f* excavation; hole.

excédant, e [ɛkse'dɑ̃, ~'dɑ̃ːt] surplus; excess (*luggage*); F tiresome (*person*); **excédent** [~'dɑ̃] *m* excess, surplus; ~ de poids excess weight; **excéder** [~'de] (1f) *v/t.* exceed; *fig.* tire, weary (*s.o.*); irritate.

excellence [ɛksɛ'lɑ̃ːs] *f* excellence; ♀ *title*: Excellency; par ~ particularly; pre-eminently; **excellent, e** [~'lɑ̃, ~'lɑ̃ːt] excellent, F first-rate, capital; delicious (*meal etc.*); **exceller** [~'le] (1a) *v/i.* excel (in, en; in *ger.*, *à inf.*).

excentrer ⊕ [ɛksɑ̃'tre] (2a) *v/t.* throw off centre; **excentrique** [~-'trik] **1.** *adj.* ⊕ eccentric (*a. person*); *fig.* odd (*person*); remote (*quarter of a town*); **2.** *su./m* ⊕ eccentric; cam; *lathe*: eccentric chuck; *su.* eccentric, crank.

excepté [ɛksɛp'te] *prp.* except(ing), save; **excepter** [~'te] (1a) *v/t.* except, exclude (from, de); **exception** [~'sjɔ̃] *f* exception (*a.* ⚖); ~ faite de, à l'~ de with the exception of; *pol.* état m d'~ state of emergency; sauf ~ with certain exceptions; **exceptionnel, -elle** [~sjɔ'nɛl] exceptional, uncommon; ✝ prix m ~ bargain.

excès [ɛk'sɛ] *m* excess; powers, mot. speed limit: exceeding; à l'~, avec ~ excessively, to excess; **excessif, -ve** [~sɛ'sif, ~'siːv] excessive, extreme; unreasonable; exorbitant (*price*).

exciser ⚕ [ɛksi'ze] (1a) *v/t.* excise.

excitable [ɛksi'tabl] excitable; **excitant** [~'tɑ̃] **1.** *su./m* stimulant; **2.** *adj.* exciting; **exciter** [~'te] (1a) *v/t.* excite (*a. fig.*); arouse (*emotions*); incite (*s.o., a rebellion, etc.*); cause; s'~ get excited; get worked up.

exclamation [ɛksklama'sjɔ̃] *f* exclamation; point m d'~ exclamation mark; **exclamer** [~'me] (1a) *v/t.*: s'~ exclaim; protest; make an outcry.

exclure [ɛks'klyːr] (4g) *v/t.* exclude (from, de); *fig.* preclude, prevent; s'~ mutuellement be mutually exclusive; **exclusif, -ve** [ɛkskly'zif, ~'ziːv] exclusive; sole (agent, right); **exclusion** [~'zjɔ̃] *f* exclusion; pupil: expulsion; à l'~ de excluding; **exclusivité** [~zivi'te] *f* exclusiveness; sole right (in, de); ... en ~ exclusive ...

excommunier *eccl.* [ɛkskɔmy'nje] (1o) *v/t.* excommunicate.

excorier [ɛkskɔ'rje] (1o) *v/t. a.* s'~ excoriate; peel off.

excrément [ɛkskre'mɑ̃] *m physiol.* excrement; *fig.* scum; **excréter** *physiol.* [~'te] (1f) *v/t.* excrete.

excroissance [ɛkskrwa'sɑ̃ːs] *f* excrescence.

excursion [ɛkskyr'sjɔ̃] *f* excursion, tour, trip; hike; **excursionniste** [~sjɔ'nist] *su.* tourist, tripper; hiker.

excuse [ɛks'kyːz] *f* excuse; ~s *pl.* apology *sg.*, apologies; **excuser** [~ky'ze] (1a) *v/t.* excuse; s'~ apologize (for, *de*); excuse o.s.; † decline an invitation.

exécrable [εgze'krabl] abominable; horrible; disgraceful; **exécration** [‿kra'sjɔ̃] *f* detestation, execration; *fig.* disgrace; **exécrer** [‿'kre] (1f) *v/t.* loathe, detest.

exécutant *m*, e *f* ♪ [εgzeky'tɑ̃, ‿-'tɑ̃:t] performer; executant; **exécuter** [‿'te] (1a) *v/t.* execute (*a.* ✝, *a.* 🕆 *a murderer*, *etc.*), perform (*a.* ♪), carry out (*a. a plan, an order, etc.*); 🕆 distrain on (*a debtor*); ✝ hammer (*a defaulter*); *fig.* slash (*s.o.*); *s'*‿ comply; yield; *fig.* pay up; **exécuteur**-**trice** [‿'tœ:r, ‿'tris] *su. promise etc.*: performer; 🕆 testamentaire executor; *su./m* † executioner; **exécutif, -ve** [‿'tif, ‿'ti:v] *adj., a. su./m* executive; **exécution** [‿'sjɔ̃] *f* execution (*a.* ✝, *a.* 🕆 *of a murderer*), performance (*a.* ♪); *promise*: fulfilment; ‿ forcée 🕆 debtor: distraint; ✝ defaulter: hammering; 🕆 *law:* enforcement; *mettre à* ‿ carry out.

exemplaire [εgzɑ̃'plɛ:r] **1.** *adj.* exemplary; **2.** *su./m* sample, specimen; model, pattern; *book:* copy; *en double* ‿ in duplicate; **exemple** [‿'zɑ̃:pl] *m* example; *par* ‿! for instance; *par* ‿! well I never!; *ah ça par* ‿! well really!; *ah non, par* ‿! no indeed!

exempt, e [εg'zɑ̃, ‿'zɑ̃:t] *adj.* exempt (from, *de*); free; immune; ✝ ‿ *de défauts* perfect; ‿ *d'impôts* tax-free.

exempter [εgzɑ̃'te] (1a) *v/t.* exempt; exonerate; **exemption** [‿'sjɔ̃] *f* exemption; *fig.* freedom.

exercer [εgzɛr'se] (1k) *v/t.* exercise; ✕ *etc.* train, drill; use, exert (*one's influence, one's power*); practise (*a profession, a trade*); *s'*‿ practise (s.th., *à qch.*); drill; be exerted; *fig.* operate; **exercice** [‿'sis] *m* exercise; ✕ drill, training; *influence, power*: use; practice; ✝ ‿ *fiscal* financial year; (*month's, year's*) trading; *sp.* ‿*s pl. aux agrès* apparatus work; *sp.* ‿*s pl. libres* light gymnastics *sg.*

exhalaison [εgzalɛ'zɔ̃] *f* exhalation; ‿*s pl.* fumes; **exhalation** [‿la'sjɔ̃] *f* exhaling, exhalation; **exhaler** [‿'le] (1a) *v/t.* exhale, give out, emit; *fig.*

express, utter; *fig.* give vent to (*one's anger*); *fig.* breathe (*a sigh*).

exhausser [εgzo'se] (1a) *v/t.* raise (by, *de*), heighten.

exhausteur *mot.* [εgzos'tœ:r] *m* suction-pipe; vacuum-feed tank.

exhérédation 🕆 [εgzereda'sjɔ̃] *f* disinheritance; **exhéréder** 🕆 [‿'de] (1f) *v/t.* disinherit.

exhiber [εgzi'be] (1a) *v/t.* 🕆 produce; show (*animals, the ticket, etc.*); *pej.* flaunt, show off; *pej. s'*‿ make an exhibition of o.s.; **exhibition** [‿bi'sjɔ̃] *f* 🕆 production; showing, display, exhibition; (*cattle-etc.*) show.

exhorter [εgzɔr'te] (1a) *v/t.* exhort, urge, encourage.

exhumer [εgzy'me] (1a) *v/t.* exhume, disinter; *fig.* unearth, bring to light.

exigeant, e [εgzi'ʒɑ̃, ‿'ʒɑ̃:t] exacting, hard to please; **exigence** [‿'ʒɑ̃:s] *f* demand; requirement; *fig.* exactingness; ✝ ‿*s pl.* conditions; **exiger** [‿'ʒe] (11) *v/t.* demand; require; **exigible** [‿'ʒibl] due (*payment*).

exigu, -guë [εgzi'gy] exiguous; scanty; slender (*income, means*); **exiguïté** [‿gчi'te] *f* tininess, smallness; slenderness.

exil [εg'zil] *m* exile, banishment; **exilé** *m*, e *f* [εgzi'le] exile; **exiler** [‿] (1a) *v/t.* exile, banish.

existence [εgzis'tɑ̃:s] *f* existence; life; ✝ ‿*s pl.* stock *sg.*; *moyens m/pl. d'*‿ means of subsistence; **existentialisme** *phls.* [‿tɑ̃sja'lism] *m* existentialism; **existentialiste** *phls.* [‿tɑ̃sja'list] *adj., a. su.* existentialist; **exister** [‿'te] (1a) *v/i.* exist, be; be extant.

exode [εg'zɔd] *m* exodus (*a. fig.*); *bibl.* ♀ Exodus; ‿ *rural sociology:* drift to the towns, urban drift.

exonérer [εgzɔne're] (1f) *v/t.* exempt; free; exonerate; remit (*s.o.'s*) fees.

exorbitant, e [εgzɔrbi'tɑ̃, ‿'tɑ̃:t] exorbitant, excessive.

exorciser *eccl.* [εgzɔrsi'ze] (1a) *v/t.* exorcize; lay (*a ghost*).

exotique [εgzɔ'tik] exotic; *fig.* foreign.

expansibilité [εkspɑ̃sibili'te] *f phys.* expansibility; *fig.* expansiveness; **expansible** *phys.* [‿'sibl] expansible; **expansif, -ve** [ʌ'sif, ʌ'si:v] *phys., a. fig.* expansive; *fig.* effusive; **expansion** [ʌ'sjɔ̃] *f phys., a.* ⊕ expansion; *fig.* expansiveness; *culture:* spread; **expansionnisme** [ʌsjɔ'nism] *m* expansionism.

expatrié, e [ɛkspatri'e] exile, expatriate; **expatrier** [ʌ] (1a) *v/t.* expatriate; exile, banish; **s'ʌ** leave one's own country.

expectant, e [ɛkspɛk'tɑ̃, ʌ'tɑ̃:t] expectant; **expectative** [ʌta'ti:v] *f* expectancy; *dans l'ʌ* de waiting for.

expectoration 𝄞 etc. [ɛkspɛktɔra'sjɔ̃] *f* expectoration; sputum; **expectorer** [ʌ're] (1a) *v/t.* expectorate.

expédient, e [ɛkspe'djɑ̃, ʌ'djɑ̃:t] **1.** *adj.* expedient, advisable, proper (to, de); **2.** *su./m* expedient, shift; *vivre d'ʌs* live by one's wits.

expédier [ɛkspe'dje] (1o) *v/t.* dispatch; get rid of; dispose of (*s.th.*) quickly, hurry through; send (off), forward (*mail etc.*), clear (*the customs*); ⚖ draw up (*a contract*); ʌ *qch. par bateau* ship s.th.; **expéditeur** *m*, **-trice** *f* [ɛkspedi'tœ:r, ʌ'tris] sender; ✝ consigner, shipper; forwarding agent; **expéditif, -ve** [ʌ'tif, ʌ'ti:v] expeditious, prompt; **expédition** [ʌ'sjɔ̃] *f* expedition (*a. geog.*), dispatch (*a.* ✝); ✝ sending; ✝ consignment; shipping; copy; **expéditionnaire** [ʌsjɔ'nɛ:r] *m* ✝ sender; ✝ forwarding agent; shipper, consigner.

expérience [ɛkspe'rjɑ̃:s] *f* experience; 𝄞 etc. experiment, test; *par ʌ* from experience.

expérimenté, e [ɛksperimɑ̃'te] experienced; skilled (*workman*); **expérimenter** [ʌ] (1a) *v/t.* test, try; *v/i.* experiment (on, *sur*).

expert, e [ɛks'pɛ:r, ʌ'pɛrt] **1.** *adj.* expert, skilled (in en, *dans*); able; **2.** *su./m* expert (in, at en) (*a.* ⚖); ✝ valuer; *fig.* connoisseur; ✝ ʌ *comptable* chartered accountant; **expertise** [ɛkspɛr'ti:z] *f* ✝ expert appraisal *or* valuation; ⚓ survey; expert evidence; expert opinion; **expertiser** [ʌti'ze] (1a) *v/t.* ✝ value, appraise; ⚓ survey.

expiable [ɛks'pjabl] expiable; **expiation** [ʌpja'sjɔ̃] *f* expiation; *eccl.* atonement (for, de); **expiatoire** [ʌpja'twa:r] expiatory; **expier**

[ʌ'pje] (1o) *v/t.* expiate, atone for, F pay for.

expiration [ɛkspira'sjɔ̃] *f* expiration, breathing out; termination, expiry; ⊕ steam: discharge; **expirer** [ʌ're] (1a) *v/t.* breathe out; *v/i.* expire (*a.* 𝄞), die.

explétif, -ve [ɛksple'tif, ʌ'ti:v] *adj., a. su./m* expletive.

explicable [ɛkspli'kabl] explicable, explainable; **explicatif, -ve** [ʌka'tif, ʌ'ti:v] explanatory; **explication** [ʌka'sjɔ̃] *f* explanation; ʌ *de texte* textual commentary.

explicite [ɛkspli'sit] explicit, plain.

expliquer [ɛkspli'ke] (1m) *v/t.* explain; comment upon (*a text*); account for; **s'ʌ** explain o.s.; be explained; **s'ʌ** *avec* have it out with; *je m'explique* what I mean is this.

exploit [ɛks'plwa] *m* exploit, deed, feat; ⚖ writ, summons *sg.*; ⚖ *signifier un ʌ à* serve a writ on; **exploitable** [ɛksplwa'tabl] workable (*quarry*); ⚒ gettable (*coal*); exploitable (*person*); ⚖ distrainable; **exploitation** [ʌta'sjɔ̃] *f* exploitation (*a. fig.*); ✝ management; ⚒, 🌳, *quarry:* working; farming; *trees:* felling; *fig.* swindling; mine, workings *pl.*; **exploiter** [ʌ'te] (1a) *v/t.* exploit (*a. fig.*); ⚒ work; ✎ cultivate; ✝ manage; *fig.* take advantage of; *fig.* swindle; *v/i.* ⚖ serve a writ.

explorateur, -trice [ɛksplɔra'tœ:r, ʌ'tris] **1.** *adj.* exploratory; **2.** *su.* explorer; **exploration** [ʌra'sjɔ̃] *f* exploration; ⚒ reconnaissance; *telev.* scanning; **explorer** [ʌ're] (1a) *v/t.* explore; 𝄞 probe; ⚒ reconnoitre; *telev., cin.* scan.

exploser [ɛksplo'ze] (1a) *v/i.* ⊕, ⚒, *a. fig.* explode; *faire ʌ* blow up; **explosible** [ʌ'zibl] explosive; detonable; **explosif, -ve** [ʌ'zif, ʌ'zi:v] *adj., a. su./m* explosive; **explosion** [ʌ'zjɔ̃] *f* explosion; ⊕ bursting; ʌ *démographique* population explosion; *moteur m à ʌ* internal combustion engine.

exportation ✝ [ɛkspɔrta'sjɔ̃] *f* exportation; export trade; ʌs *pl.* exports.

exposant, e [ɛkspo'zɑ̃, ʌ'zɑ̃:t] *su.* ⚖ petitioner; *paint. etc.* exhibitor; *su./m* 𝄞 exponent; index; **exposé** [ʌ'ze] *m* report; outline; account;

statement; **exposer** [ʌˈze] (1a) *v/t.* expose; disclose (*plans*); set forth; state; *paint.* exhibit; jeopardize; *s'ʌ* take risks; **exposition** [ʌziˈsjɔ̃] *f* exhibition; *eccl.* exposition; exposure (*to cold, to danger*; *of a baby*; *of a house*); *facts etc.*: statement, exposition.

exprès, expresse [ɛksˈprɛ, ʌˈprɛs] **1.** *adj.* explicit, express, definite; **2.** *exprès adv.* deliberately, on purpose; **3.** *su./m* express messenger; *lettre f exprès* express letter.

express 🚂 [ɛksˈprɛs] *m* express.

expressément [ɛksprɛseˈmã] expressly.

expressif, -ve [ɛksprɛˈsif, ʌˈsiːv] expressive; **expression** [ʌˈsjɔ̃] *f* expression; 🖌, *fig.* *réduire à la plus simple ʌ* reduce to the simplest terms.

exprimer [ɛkspriˈme] (1a) *v/t.* express; put into words, voice; show (*an emotion*); squeeze out (*juice*); *si l'on peut s'ʌ ainsi* if one may put it that way.

expropriation 🏛 [ɛksprɔpriaˈsjɔ̃] *f* expropriation; compulsory purchase; **exproprier** 🏛 [ʌˈe] (1a) *v/t.* expropriate.

expulser [ɛkspylˈse] (1a) *v/t.* expel (*a. an electron, a. a pupil*); eject (*s.o.*); 🏛 evict (*a tenant*); *univ.* send (*a student*) down; ⊕ discharge.

expurger [ɛkspyrˈʒe] (1l) *v/t.* expurgate, bowdlerize (*a book*).

exquis, e [ɛksˈki, ʌˈkiːz] exquisite; **exquisément** [ʌkizeˈmã] *adv.* of exquis.

exsangue [ɛkˈsãːg] an(a)emic, bloodless.

exsuder [ɛksyˈde] (1a) *vt/i.* exude.

extase [ɛksˈtɑːz] *f* ecstasy; *fig.* rapture; 🕊 trance; **extasié, e** [ʌtɑˈzje] enraptured; **extasier** [ʌtɑˈzje] (1o) *v/t.*: *s'ʌ* go into ecstasies (over *devant, sur*).

extenseur [ɛkstãˈsœːr] **1.** *adj./m anat.* extensor; **2.** *su./m anat. muscle*: extensor; *sp.* chest-expander; *trousers*: stretcher; 🔦 shock-absorber; **extensible** [ʌˈsibl] extensible; *metall.* tensile; **extension** [ʌˈsjɔ̃] *f* extent; extension (*a.* 🕊); spreading; stretching; ⊕ *etc.* tension; *gramm. par ʌ* in a wider sense.

exténuer [ɛksteˈnɥe] (1n) *v/t.* exhaust, tire out; † extenuate.

extérieur, e [ɛksteˈrjœːr] **1.** *adj.* exterior, external, outer; *pol.* foreign; *affaires f/pl. ʌes* foreign affairs; **2.** *su./m* exterior (*a. cin.*); outside; *fig.* appearance; *pol.* foreign countries *pl.*

exterminateur, -trice [ɛkstɛrminaˈtœːr, ʌˈtris] **1.** *adj.* exterminating, destroying; **2.** *su.* exterminator, destroyer; **exterminer** [ʌˈne] (1a) *v/t.* exterminate, destroy, wipe out.

externat [ɛkstɛrˈna] *m* day-school; 🏥 non-resident studentship; **externe** [ʌˈtɛrn] **1.** *adj.* external, outer, 🏥 out-(*patient*); 🏥 *usage m ʌ* external application; **2.** *su.* day-pupil; 🏥 non-resident medical student.

extincteur, -trice [ɛkstɛ̃kˈtœːr, ʌˈtris] **1.** *adj.* extinguishing; **2.** *su./m* fire-extinguisher; *ʌ à mousse* foam extinguisher; **extinction** [ʌˈsjɔ̃] *f* extinction; *fire, light*: extinguishing; suppression; termination; *race etc.*: dying out; *voice*: loss; 💥 *ʌ des feux* lights out, *Am.* taps.

extirper [ɛkstirˈpe] (1a) *v/t.* eradicate (*a. fig.*).

extorquer [ɛkstɔrˈke] (1m) *v/t.* extort (from, out of *à*); **extorsion** [ʌtɔrˈsjɔ̃] *f* extortion; blackmail.

extra [ɛksˈtra] **1.** *su./m/inv.* extra; hired waiter; temporary job; **2.** *adj./inv.* extra-special; **3.** *adv.* extra-...

extraction [ɛkstrakˈsjɔ̃] *f* extraction (*a.* 🕊, 🏥, *a. fig.*); *stone*: quarrying; *gold*: winning; *fig.* origin, descent.

extradition 🏛 [ɛkstradiˈsjɔ̃] *f* extradition.

extraire [ɛksˈtrɛːr] (4ff) *v/t.* extract (*a.* 🏛); pull (*a tooth*); quarry (*stone*); win (*gold*); copy out (*a passage*); *fig.* rescue; **extrait** [ʌˈtrɛ] *m* extract; *admin.* (*birth- etc.*) certificate; abstract; † *ʌ de compte* statement of account.

extraordinaire [ɛkstraɔrdiˈnɛːr] **1.** *adj.* extraordinary; uncommon; special; wonderful; queer; **2.** *su./m* extraordinary thing; *the* unusual.

extrapoler [ɛkstrapɔˈle] (1a) *v/t.* extrapolate.

extravagance [ɛkstravaˈgãːs] *f* extravagance; absurdity; *fig. ʌs pl.* nonsense *sg.*; **extravagant, e** [ʌˈgã, ʌˈgãːt] extravagant; absurd; exorbitant, prohibitive (*price*); ex-

14*

travaguer [ˌ‿'ge] (1m) *v/i.* ⚕ rave; *fig.* talk nonsense; act wildly.

extrême [ɛks'trɛːm] **1.** *adj.* extreme; utmost, furthest; drastic (*measures*); intense (*cold, emotions, etc.*); **2.** *su./m* extreme; *à l'*‿ in the extreme; ‿**-onction** *eccl.* [ɛkstremɔ̃k'sjɔ̃] *f* extreme unction; ♀**-Orient** *geog.* [ˌ‿mɔ'rjɑ̃] *m the* Far East; **extrémiste** *pol. etc.* [ɛkstre'mist] *adj., a. su.* extremist; **extrémité** [ˌ‿mi'te] *f* extremity; very end, tip; extreme; plight, straits *pl.*; last moment; point

of death; ‿*s pl.* extremities; extreme measures.

extrinsèque [ɛkstrɛ̃'sɛk] extrinsic.

exubérance [ɛgzybe'rɑ̃ːs] *f* exuberance, luxuriance, superabundance; **exubérant, e** [ˌ‿'rɑ̃, ˌ‿'rɑ̃ːt] exuberant, luxuriant, superabundant; immoderate (*laughter*).

exultation [ɛgzylta'sjɔ̃] *f* exultation, rejoicing; *avec* ‿ exultantly; **exulter** [ˌ‿'te] (1a) *v/i.* exult, rejoice.

ex-voto [ɛksvɔ'to] *m/inv.* votive offering; ex-voto.

F

F, f [ɛf] *m* F, f.

fa ♪ [fa] *m/inv.* fa, *note*: F; ~ *dièse* F sharp; *clef f de* ~ F-clef.

fable [fɑ:bl] *f* fable; story; *fig.* falsehood; *fig.* talk, laughing-stock (*of the town*); **fabliau** [fɑbli'o] *m* Old French literature: fabliau; **fablier** [~'e] *m* book of fables.

fabricant [fabri'kɑ̃] *m* manufacturer; mill-owner; maker; **fabrication** [~ka'sjɔ̃] *f* manufacture; production; *document*: forging; *fig.* fabrication; ~ *en série* mass production; **fabrique** [fa'brik] *f* manufacture; factory, works *usu. sg.*; *paper, cloth*: mill; make; *eccl.* fabric (*of a church*); *eccl.* church council; **fabriquer** [~bri'ke] (1m) *v/t.* ⊕ manufacture; *fig.* make, do; *fig.* fabricate (*a charge, lies, a document*); coin (*a word*); *sl.* cheat, pinch.

fabulation [fabyla'sjɔ̃] *f* fantasizing; fabrication; **fabuler** (1a) *v/i.* fantasize; make up stories (*a. fig.*); **fabuleux, -euse** [faby'lø, ~'lø:z] fabulous (*a. fig.*).

façade [fa'sad] *f* façade; frontage; front; F window-dressing.

face [fas] *f* face; countenance; aspect; front; ⚓, *a.* ♪ *record*: side; surface; *de* ~ full-face (*photo*); *d'en* ~ opposite; *en* ~ *de* in front of; in the presence of; opposite; *faire* ~ *à* face; *fig.* meet; cope with; *pile ou* ~ heads or tails; ~ *à* **face** *telev.* [~a'fas] *m/inv.* encounter; **~-à-main,** *pl.* **~s-à-main** [~a'mɛ̃] *m* lorgnette.

facétie [fase'si] *f* facetious remark; joke; **facétieux, -euse** [~'sjø, ~'sjø:z] facetious, waggish.

facette [fa'sɛt] *f* facet (*a. zo.*).

fâché, e [fɑ'ʃe] sorry; angry, cross (about, *de*; with s.o., *avec* q.); annoyed; offended; **fâcher** [~] (1a) *v/t.* anger, make angry; offend; grieve, pain; *se* ~ get angry; get angry *or* annoyed (with, *contre*); over, *pour*); fall out (with, *avec*); *se* ~ *tout rouge* blow one's top; *Br. a.* go spare; **fâcherie** [fɑʃ'ri] *f* tiff, quarrel; bad

feeling; **fâcheux, -euse** [fɑ'ʃø, ~'ʃø:z] annoying; deplorable, regrettable; awkward (*situation*).

facial, e, *m/pl.* **-aux** [fa'sjal, ~'sjo] facial, face-...

facile [fa'sil] easy; simple; facile; *fig.* pliable; fluent (*tongue*); **facilité** [fasili'te] *f* easiness; ease; readiness; facility (*a.* ✝), aptitude; complaisance; ✝ ~*s pl. de paiement* easy terms; **faciliter** [~] (1a) *v/t.* facilitate, make easy *or* easier (for s.o., *à* q.).

façon [fa'sɔ̃] *f* make; fashioning; way; manner; ~*s pl.* manners, behavio(u)r *sg.*; ceremony *sg.*, fuss *sg.*; affectation *sg.*; *de* ~ *à* so as to; *de* ~ *que* so that; *de la bonne* ~ properly; in fine style; *de ma* ~ of my own composition; *de toute* ~ in any case; *faire des* ~*s* stand on ceremony; *cost. on travaille à* ~ customers' own materials made up; *sans* ~(*s*) simple; off-handed(ly *adv.*); unceremonious(ly *adv.*); without further ado.

faconde [fa'kɔ̃:d] *f* loquaciousness.

façonner [fasɔ'ne] (1a) *v/t.* shape; form, fashion; make (*a dress etc.*); train; ✔ dress (*the soil*); *fig.* mould (*s.o.*); **façonnier, -ère** [~'nje, ~'njɛ:r] **1.** *adj.* fussy; bespoke (*worker*); **2.** *su.* home-worker.

fac-similé [faksimi'le] *m* facsimile, exact copy.

facteur [fak'tœ:r] *m* postman, *Am.* mailman; maker; ♪ instrument maker; ⚓, *a. fig.* factor.

factice [fak'tis] artificial, factitious.

factieux, -euse [fak'sjø, ~'sjø:z] **1.** *adj.* factious, seditious; **2.** *su.* sedition-monger; **faction** [~'sjɔ̃] *f* ✕ faction; sentry-duty, guard, watch; *fig.* faction; *être de* ~ be on sentry-go *or* on guard; **factionnaire** [~sjɔ'nɛ:r] *m* sentry; sentinel.

factotum [faktɔ'tɔm] *m* factotum; man-of-all-work.

factuel, -elle [fakty'ɛl] factual, objective.

facture [fak'ty:r] *f* ✝ workmanship,

make (*of an article*); ✝ bill, invoice;
♩ *instruments*: manufacturing; ♩
organ pipes: scale; **facturer** ✝
[⌣ty're] (1a) *v/t.* invoice; **facturier**
✝ [⌣ty'rje] *m* invoice clerk; sales-
book.

facultatif, -ve [fakylta'tif, ⌣'ti:v]
optional; ⚖ permissive; *arrêt m* ⌣
request stop; **faculté** [⌣'te] *f* faculty (*a. univ*, *a. fig.*); option; power,
ability; ⌣s *pl.* means, resources.

fada F [fa'da] *m* fool; **fadaise**
[fa'dɛ:z] *f* nonsense, *Am. sl.* baloney.

fadasse [fa'das] sickly (*taste*); pale
(*colour*).

fade [fad] insipid, tasteless; washed-
out (*colour*); **fadeur** [fa'dœ:r] *f*
insipidity; *smell*: sickliness; *fig.*
pointlessness; *fig.* ⌣s *pl.* insipid talk
sg. or compliments.

fading [fe'diŋ] *m* radio: fading.

fafiot ✝ *sl.* [fa'fjo] *m* bank-note.

fagot [fa'go] *m* bundle of firewood;
fig. sentir le ⌣ smack of heresy; **fago-
ter** [⌣'te] (1a) *v/t.* ✝ bundle (*firewood*); F dress (*s.o.*) badly.

faible [fɛbl] **1.** *adj.* weak; feeble (*a.
fig.*); faint (*smell, sound, voice*); slight
(*difference, hope, pain*); gentle
(*slope*); slender (*means*); poor (*performance*); lame (*excuse*); **2.** *su./m*
weakness, foible; *person*: weakling;
les économiquement ⌣s *pl.* the lower
income groups; **faiblesse** [fɛ'blɛs] *f*
weakness, feebleness; frailty; ✝
fainting fit; *fig.* weak point; *amount,
number*: smallness; **faiblir** [⌣'bli:r]
(2a) *v/i.* weaken; ⊕ lose power.

faïence [fa'jã:s] *f* earthenware,
crockery; **faïencerie** [⌣jãs'ri] *f*
trade, *a.* works: pottery; crockery
shop; earthenware, crockery; **faïen-
cier** *m*, **-ère** *f* [⌣jã'sje, ⌣'sjɛ:r]
crockery- *or* earthenware-maker *or*
dealer. [*falloir.*]

faille¹ [faj] *3rd p. sg. pres. sbj. of*]
faille² [fa:j] *f* ⚒, *geol.* fault; *fig.* flaw,
weakness.

failli *m*, **e** *f* ⚖ [fa'ji] bankrupt,
faillible [⌣'jibl] fallible; **faillir**
[⌣'ji:r] (2n) *v/i.*: ⌣ *faire qch.* almost *or*
nearly do s.th., all but do s.th.; *j'ai
failli tomber* I nearly fell; ⌣ *à un devoir*
fail in a duty; **faillite** [⌣'jit] *f* bankruptcy; *fig.* failure; *faire* ⌣ go bankrupt; *mettre q. en* ⌣ declare s.o.
bankrupt.

faim [fɛ̃] *f* hunger; *fig.* thirst (for
glory, *de gloire*); *avoir* (*très*) ⌣ be
(very) hungry; *avoir une* ⌣ *canine* (*or
de loup*) be ravenous; *mourir de* ⌣ die
of starvation; F be famished.

faine ⚘ [fɛ:n] *f* beechnut.

fainéant, e [fɛne'ã, ⌣'ã:t] **1.** *adj.*
idle, lazy; slothful; **2.** *su.* idler;
sluggard; **fainéanter** [⌣ã'te] (1a)
v/i. idle, loaf; **fainéantise** [⌣ã'ti:z]
f idleness, laziness.

faire [fɛ:r] (4r) **1.** *v/t.* make (*bread,
a voyage, a declaration, one's bed, a
profit*), do; create; form; beget (*a
child*); make out (*a list,* ✝ *a cheque*);
pay (*attention, a visit*); clean (*one's
shoes*), do (*a room*); pack (*a trunk*);
cover (*a distance*), travel; carry out,
perform (*a.* ⚔ *an operation*); work
(*miracles*); play (*a.* ♩), feign; see to
it (that *ind.*, *que sbj.*); deal (*cards*);
matter; ⚔ run (*a temperature*); ✝
place (*an order*); *thea.* act (*a part*);
F look; *followed by an inf.*: make,
cause, have; ⌣ *attention* take care;
⌣ *de la peine à* hurt (*s.o.'s*) feelings;
⌣ *de la peinture* paint; ⌣ *de q. son
héritier* make s.o. one's heir; ⌣ *du
bien à* do (*s.o.*) good; *mot.* ⌣ *du 150
kilomètres à l'heure* do 150 kilometres per hour; ⌣ *du ski* ski;
⌣ *du sport* go in for sports; *thea.* ⌣
du théâtre be on the stage (*professional*); ⌣ *école* set a fashion; ⌣
entrer show (*s.o.*) in; ⌣ *faire* have
(*s.th.*) done *or* made (by s.o., *à q.*);
⌣ *fortune* make a fortune; ⌣ *la
cuisine* do the cooking; ⌣ *la vaisselle* wash up the dishes; ✝ ⌣ *le
commerce de* deal in; *mot.* ⌣ *le plein*
fill up (with, *de*); ⌣ *mention de*
mention; ⌣ *partie de* form part of;
⌣ *pendre* get (*s.o.*) hanged; ⌣ *sa
philosophie* read philosophy; ⌣
savoir inform (s.o. of s.th., *qch. à
q.*); ⌣ *un sourire à* give (*s.o.*) a
smile; ⌣ *venir* send for; *ça ne fait
rien* it does not matter; *en* ⌣ *trop*
overdo; *faites-lui mes amitiés* give
him my kindest regards; *ne* ⌣ *que
(inf.)* do nothing but (*inf.*); *qu'est-
ce que ça peut nous* ⌣? what is that
to us!; *trois et six font neuf* three
and six are *or* make nine; *se* ⌣ be
done; become; happen; get used
to; *cela ne se fait pas* that is not
done; *comment se fait-il que?* how
does it happen that?, how is it

that?; *il peut se ~ que* it may happen that; *ne vous en faites pas!* don't worry!; don't bother!; *se ~ entendre* make o.s. heard; be heard; **2.** *v/i.* do, act; manage; make (with, de); look; last; *cards:* deal; fit; say, remark; *~ bien de* (*inf.*) do well *or* right to (*inf.*); *~ bien sur dress:* look well on (*s.o.*); *~ de son mieux* do one's best (to *inf.*, *pour inf.*); *elle fait très jeune* she looks quite young; *fit-il* he said, said he; *je ne peux ~ autrement que de* (*inf.*) I cannot but (*inf.*); *laisser ~ q.* let s.o. alone; *qu'y ~?* what can be done about it?; **3.** *v/impers.* be; *il fait chaud (beau, nuit)* it is hot (fine, dark); *il fait bon* (*inf.*) it is nice to (*inf.*); *~-part* [fɛr-'paːr] *m/inv.* notice, announcement; *~-valoir thea., fig.* [~vaˈlwaːr] *m/inv.* foil.

faisable [fəˈzabl] feasible, practicable.

faisan [fəˈzɑ̃] *m* pheasant; **faisan(d)e** [~ˈzan, ~ˈzɑ̃ːd] *f (a. poulef~)* hen-pheasant; **faisandé, e** [fəzɑ̃-ˈde] high; gamy; *fig.* spicy (*story*); **faisandeau** [~ˈdo] *m* young pheasant; **faisander** *cuis.* [~ˈde] (1a) *v/t.* hang (*game etc.*); *se ~* get high; **faisanderie** [~ˈdri] *f* pheasantry; **faisandier** [~ˈdje] *m* pheasant breeder.

faisceau [fɛˈso] *m* bundle; cluster; *rays:* pencil; beam; 📻 *sidings:* group; *~x pl.* fasces; ⚔ *~ d'armes* pile *or* stack of arms; *former (rompre)* les *~x* (un)pile arms.

faiseur *m*, **-euse** *f* [fəˈzœːr, ~ˈzøːz] maker, doer; *fig.* bluffer; *faiseuse d'anges* back-street abortionist; *~ de mariages* matchmaker; *~ d'intrigues* schemer; *~ de vers* versifier; **faisons** [fəˈzɔ̃] *1st p. pl. pres. of faire*; **fait, e** [fɛ, fɛt] **1.** *p.p. of faire*; *c'en est~ de* it's all up with; **2.** *su./m* fact; deed; act; feat, achievement; happening; development; case; matter, point; *au ~* after all; *de (or en) ~* as a matter of fact; actually; *~s pl. divers* news items; news in brief; *du ~ de* on account of; *en ~ de* as regards; *en venir au ~* come to the point, get down to business; *être au ~ de qch.* be informed of s.th., know how s.th. stands; *il est de ~ que* it is a fact that; *mettre q. au ~ de qch.* acquaint s.o.

with s.th.; give s.o. full information about s.th.

faîtage △ [fɛˈtaːʒ] *m* ridge-piece; roof-tree; ridge tiling; roof timbers *pl.*; **faîte** [fɛːt] *m* top, summit; △ ridge; *geog.* crest.

faites [fɛt] *2nd p. pl. pres. of faire*.

faix [fɛ] *m* burden, load.

fakir [faˈkiːr] *m* fakir.

falaise [faˈlɛːz] *f* cliff.

fallacieux, -euse [falaˈsjø, ~ˈsjøːz] fallacious, misleading.

falloir [faˈlwaːr] (3e) *v/impers.* be necessary, be lacking; *il faut que je* (*sbj.*) I must (*inf.*); *il me faut* (*inf.*) I must (*inf.*); *il me faut qch.* I want s.th.; I need s.th.; *comme il faut* proper(ly *adv.*); *il s'en faut de beaucoup* far from it; *peu s'en faut* very nearly; *tant s'en faut* not by a long way; **fallu** [~ˈly] *p.p. of falloir*; **fallut** [~ˈly] *3rd p. sg. p.s. of falloir*. [(stable) lamp.\]

falot¹ [faˈlo] *m* (hand) lantern;∫

falot², e [faˈlo, ~ˈlɔt] wan (*light*); *fig.* dull, dreary (*person*); † odd, quaint.

falsificateur *m*, **-trice** *f* [falsifika-ˈtœːr, ~ˈtris] forger (*of papers*); adulterator (*of food, milk, etc.*); **falsification** [~ˈsjɔ̃] *f* forgery, forging; adulteration; **falsifier** [falsiˈfje] (1o) *v/t.* falsify; forge; adulterate (*food etc.*).

famé, e [faˈme] *adj.:* *bien (mal) ~ of* good (evil) repute.

famélique [fameˈlik] **1.** *adj.* starving, famished; **2.** *su.* starveling.

fameux, -euse [faˈmø, ~ˈmøːz] famous, renowned; celebrated; F first-class, magnificent; capital, *Am.* swell.

familial, e [famiˈljal, ~ˈljo] family...; domestic; **familiariser** [familjariˈze] (1a) *v/t.* familiarize; *se ~ avec* make o.s. familiar with; **familiarité** [~ˈte] *f* familiarity; *fig.* *~s pl.* liberties; **familier, -ère** [famiˈlje, ~ˈljɛːr] **1.** *adj.* family..., domestic; familiar, well-known; intimate; colloquial; *expression f ~ère* colloquialism; **2.** *su.* intimate; regular visitor; **famille** [~ˈmiːj] *f* family; household.

famine [faˈmin] *f* famine, starvation.

fana F [faˈna] **1.** *adj.* enthusiastic, fanatic; **2.** *su.* enthusiast, fan(atic).

fanal [faˈnal] *m* lantern; beacon; ⚓ navigation light; 📻 headlight.

fanatique [fana'tik] **1.** *adj.* fanatical; enthusiastic; **2.** *su.* fanatic; enthusiast; **fanatisme** [ˌ'tism] *m* fanaticism.

fane [fan] *f potatoes*: haulm; *carrots*: top; dead leaves *pl.*; **faner** [fa'ne] (1a) *v/t.* ted, toss (*the hay*); *fig.* cause (*colour etc.*) to fade; **se ~ fade** (*colour*); wither, droop (*flower*); *v/i.* make hay; **faneur, -euse** [ˌ'nœːr, ˌ'nøːz] *su.* haymaker; *su./f* tedder, tedding machine.

fanfare [fɑ̃'faːr] *f trumpets*: flourish; *hunt. etc.* fanfare; brass band; ✕ bugle band; **fanfaron, -onne** [fɑ̃fa'rɔ̃, ˌ'rɔn] **1.** *adj.* boastful, bragging, swaggering; **2.** *su.* swaggerer, braggart, boaster; *su./m: faire le ~* bluster; brag; **fanfaronnade** [ˌrɔ'nad] *f* swagger, boasting; bluster.

fanfreluche [fɑ̃frə'lyʃ] *f* bauble; *cost.* ~s *pl.* fal-lals.

fange [fɑ̃:ʒ] *f* mud; filth, F muck; **fangeux, -euse** [fɑ̃'ʒø, ˌ'ʒøːz] muddy; dirty, filthy.

fanion ✕ [fa'njɔ̃] *m* flag; pennon.

fanon [fa'nɔ̃] *m eccl.* maniple; *ox*: dewlap; *horse*: fetlock; whalebone.

fantaisie [fɑ̃tɛ'zi] *f* imagination; fancy (*a. fig.*); *fig.* whim; ♪ fantasia; *à ma ~* as the fancy takes (took) me; † *articles m/pl. de ~* fancy goods; *de ~* imaginary; † fancy-...; **fantaisiste** [ˌ'zist] **1.** *adj.* fantastic, freakish; **2.** *su.* fanciful person.

fantasmagorie [fɑ̃tasmagɔ'ri] *f* phantasmagoria; *fig.* weird spectacle.

fantasque [fɑ̃'task] odd; whimsical; queer (*person*).

fantassin [fɑ̃ta'sɛ̃] *m* infantryman, foot-soldier.

fantastique [fɑ̃tas'tik] fantastic; weird; *fig.* incredible.

fantoche [fɑ̃'tɔʃ] *m* puppet (*a. fig.*), marionette; *gouvernement ~* puppet government.

fantôme [fɑ̃'toːm] *m* phantom, ghost, spectre; illusion; *le vaisseau ~* the Flying Dutchman.

faon [fɑ̃] *m* fawn; roe calf.

faquin [fa'kɛ̃] *m* cad, scoundrel; low fellow.

faraud, e [fa'ro, ˌ'roːd] **1.** *adj.* full of o.s.; affected; **2.** *su.* swanker.

farce [fars] **1.** *su./f* practical joke, trick; *thea., a. fig.* farce; *cuis.* stuffing, forcemeat; **2.** *adj. sl.* funny, comical; **farceur** *m*, **-euse** *f* [far'sœːr, ˌ'søːz] practical joker; wag, humorist.

farcir *cuis., a. fig.* [far'siːr] (2a) *v/t.* stuff.

fard [faːr] *m* make-up; rouge; *fig.* artifice, camouflage; *parler sans ~* speak plainly *or* candidly; *sl. piquer un ~* blush.

fardeu [far'do] *m* burden (*a. 🏛*), load.

farder [far'de] (1a) *v/t.* make (*s.o.*) up; paint; *fig.* disguise, camouflage; *se ~* make up. [lorry.)

fardier [far'dje] *m* trolley; truck,

farfadet [farfa'dɛ] *m* goblin; elf.

farfelu, e F [farfə'ly] **1.** *adj.* excentric, crazy, F cranky, F far-out; **2.** *su.* eccentric, F nutcase, F srewball.

farfouiller [farfu'je] (1a) *v/i.* rummage (in, among *dans*); *v/t.* explore.

faribole [fari'bɔl] *f* (stuff and) nonsense.

farinacé, e [farina'se] farinaceous; **farine** [fa'rin] *f* flour, meal; *fig.* type, sort; *~ de riz* ground rice; **fariner** *cuis.* [fari'ne] (1a) *v/t.* dust with flour; **farineux, -euse** [ˌ'nø, ˌ'nøːz] **1.** *adj.* farinaceous; floury; flour-covered; **2.** *su./m* farinaceous food.

farouche [fa'ruʃ] wild, fierce; cruel; timid, shy; unsociable, unapproachable.

fart [faːr] *m* ski wax; **farter** [far'te] (1a) *v/t.* wax (*one's skis*).

fascicule [fasi'kyl] *m encyclopaedia etc.*: part, section; ♀, *zo.* bunch; ♀, *zo.* fascic(u)le.

fascinateur, -trice [fasina'tœːr, ˌ'tris] fascinating; **fascination** [ˌ'sjɔ̃] *f* fascination, charm.

fasciner [fasi'ne] (1a) *v/t.* fascinate; *fig.* entrance.

fascisme *pol.* [fa'ʃism] *m* fascism; **fasciste** *pol.* [ˌ'ʃist] *su., a. adj.* fascist.

fasse [fas] *1st p. sg. pres. sbj. of faire*.

faste [fast] *m* pomp, display.

fastes [ˌ] *m/pl. hist.* fasti; F records.

fastidieux, -euse [fasti'djø, ˌ'djøːz] tedious, dull; irksome, tiresome.

fastueux, -euse [fas'tɥø, ˌ'tɥøːz] ostentatious, showy; sumptuous.

fat [fat] **1.** *adj./m* foppish; conceited; **2.** *su./m* fop; conceited idiot.

fatal, e, *m/pl.* **-als** [fa'tal] fatal; *fig.* inevitable; *femme f* ~e vamp; **fatalisme** [fata'lism] *m* fatalism; **fataliste** [~'list] **1.** *adj.* fatalistic; **2.** *su.* fatalist; **fatalité** [~li'te] *f* fatality.

fatidique [fati'dik] prophetic (*utterance*); fateful.

fatigant, e [fati'gɑ̃, ~'gɑ̃:t] tiring; tiresome, tedious; **fatigue** [fa'tig] *f* fatigue (*a.* ⊕, *metall.*); tiredness, weariness; hard work; *fig.* wear (and tear); *brisé* (*or mort*) *de* ~ dog-tired; *de* ~ strong (*shoes*); working (*clothes*); F *tomber de* ~ be worn out; **fatigué, e** [fati'ge] tired, weary; **fatiguer** [~] (1m) *v/t.* tire, make (*s.o.*) tired; overwork; overstrain; *fig.* bore (*s.o.*); *v/i.* ⊕ labo(u)r, strain (*engine etc.*); *se* ~ get tired; tire o.s.

fatras [fa'trɑ] *m* hotchpotch, jumble; lumber.

fatuité [fatɥi'te] *f* conceit, self-satisfaction.

faubourg [fo'bu:r] *m* suburb; outskirts *pl.; fig. ~s pl.* working classes; **faubourien, -enne** [~bu'rjɛ̃, ~-'rjɛn] **1.** *adj.* suburban; *fig.* common (*accent*); **2.** *su.* suburbanite; *fig.* common person.

fauchage [fo'ʃa:ʒ] *m*, **fauchaison** [~ʃɛ'zɔ̃] *f*, **fauche** [fo:ʃ] *f* mowing, cutting; reaping (time); **fauché, e** [fo'ʃe] **1.** *adj.* F broke; **2.** *su./f* (one) day's mowing *or* cutting; swath; **faucher** [~'ʃe] (1a) *v/t.* mow, cut; reap (*corn*); ✄ mow down (*troops*); ✄ sweep by fire; *sl.* pinch, steal; **fauchet** ✗ [~'ʃɛ] *m* hay-rake; bill-hook; **fauchette** ✗ [~'ʃɛt] *f* bill-hook; **faucheur, -euse** [~-'ʃœːr, ~'ʃøːz] *su. person:* reaper; *su./m zo.* harvest-spider; *Am.* daddy-longlegs; *su./f machine:* reaper; **faucheux** *zo.* [~'ʃø] *m* harvest-spider, *Am.* daddy-long-legs.

faucille ✗ [fo'si:j] *f* sickle.

faucon *orn.* [fo'kɔ̃] *m* falcon, hawk (*a. pol.*). [*falloir.*]

faudra [fo'dra] *3rd p. sg. fut. of*]

faufil [fo'fil] *m* tacking *or* basting thread; **faufiler** [fofi'le] (1a) *v/t.* tack, baste; † slip (*s.th., s.o.*) in; *se* ~ creep in, slip in; thread *or* worm one's way (into, *dans*); **faufilure** [~'ly:r] *f* tacked seam; tacking, basting.

faune [fo:n] *su./m myth.* faun; *su./f zo.* fauna.

faussaire [fo'sɛːr] forger; *fig.* falsifier; **fausser** [~'se] (1a) *v/t.* falsify; distort (*facts, ideas, words*); ⊕ force (*a lock etc.*); ⊕ warp, strain; ⊕ put (*s.th.*) out of true; ♪ put (*s.th.*) out of tune; F ~ *compagnie à q.* give s.o. the slip; ~ *parole à q.* break one's promise to s.o.

fausset[1] ♪ [fo'sɛ] *m* falsetto.

fausset[2] ⊕ [~] *m* spigot, vent-plug.

fausseté [fos'te] *f* falseness, falsity; falsehood; *fig.* treachery, duplicity.

faut [fo] *3rd p. sg. pres. of falloir.*

faute [fo:t] *f* fault (*a. tennis*); error, mistake; *foot. etc.* foul; ~ *de* for want of, lacking; ~ *de mieux* for want of anything better; *faire* ~ be lacking; *sans* ~ without fail; **fauter** F † [fo'te] (1a) *v/i.* go wrong.

fauteuil [fo'tœ:j] *m* arm-chair, easy chair; *meeting:* chair; *thea.* stall; *Académie française:* seat; ~ *à bascule* see rocking-chair; ~ *club* club chair; ⚷ ~ *électrique* electric chair; ~ *roulant* wheel chair; Bath chair.

fauteur *m*, **-trice** *f* [fo'tœ:r, ~'tris] instigator; ⚷ abettor.

fautif, -ve [fo'tif, ~'ti:v] faulty, wrong, incorrect; offending.

fauve [fo:v] **1.** *adj.* tawny; musky (*smell*); lurid (*sky*); **2.** *su./m* fawn; *coll.* deer *pl.*; ~*s pl.* wild beasts; deer *pl.*; **fauvette** *orn.* [fo'vɛt] *f* warbler.

faux[1] ✗ [fo] *f* scythe.

faux[2], **fausse** [fo, fo:s] **1.** *adj.* false; untrue, wrong; imitation...; fraudulent; forged (*document*); ♪ out of tune; ~ *col m* detachable *or* loose collar; ~ *frais m/pl.* incidental expenses; *teleph.* ~ *numéro m* wrong number; *fig.* ~ *pas m* blunder; *fausse clef f* skeleton key; ⚕ *fausse couche f* miscarriage; *fausse monnaie f* counterfeit coin(s *pl.*); *faire fausse route* take the wrong road; **2.** *faux adv.* falsely; ♪ out of tune; **3.** *su./m* falsehood; the untrue; ⚷ forgery; ⚷ *s'inscrire en* ~ *contre* deny (*s.th.*); ~**-bourdon** ♪ [fobur-'dɔ̃] *m* faux-bourdon; ~**-fuyant** *fig.* [~fɥi'jɑ̃] *m* subterfuge, evasion; ~**-monnayeur** [~mɔnɛ'jœːr] *m* counterfeiter.

faveur [fa'vœːr] *f* favo(u)r; *à la* ~ *de* by the help of; under cover of (*darkness etc.*); de ~ complimentary (*ticket*); preferential, special (*treatment, price*); en ~ in favo(u)r (of, de); mois *m* de ~ month's grace; **favorable** [favɔ'rabl] favo(u)rable; advantageous (*price etc.*); propitious; **favori, -te** [~'ri, ~'rit] **1.** adj. favo(u)rite; **2.** su. favo(u)rite; su./m: ~s pl. (side-)whiskers; **favoriser** [~ri'ze] (1a) v/t. favo(u)r; promote; **favoritisme** [~ri'tism] *m* favo(u)ritism.

fayot sl. [fa'jo] *m* ♀ kidney-bean; *person:* eager beaver, *pej.* bootlicker.

fébrifuge 🞊 [febri'fy:ʒ] adj., a. su./m febrifuge; **fébrile** [~'bril] feverish (a. fig.).

fécal, e, *m/pl.* **-aux** 🞠 physiol. [fe'kal, ~'ko] f(a)ecal; *matières f/pl.* ~es = **fèces** [fɛs] *f/pl.* physiol., a. 🞠 f(a)eces; 🞠 precipitate sg.; 🞤 stool sg.

fécond, e [fe'kɔ̃, ~'kɔ̃:d] fruitful, fertile; productive (of, en); prolific; **fécondation** [fekɔ̃dɑ'sjɔ̃] f fertilisation; impregnation; ~ artificielle artificial insemination; ~ croisée, a. fig. ~ mutuelle cross-fertilization; **féconder** [fekɔ̃'de] (1a) v/t. fecundate; fertilize; **fécondité** [~di'te] f fertility; fecundity; fruitfulness.

fécule [fe'kyl] f starch, fecula; **féculent, e** [~ky'lɑ̃, ~'lɑ̃:t] **1.** adj. starchy; 🞠 thick; **2.** su./m starchy food.

fédéral, e, *m/pl.* **-aux** [fede'ral, ~'ro] adj., a. su./m federal; **fédéraliser** [~rali'ze] (1a) v/t. federalize; **fédératif, -ve** [~ra'tif, ~'ti:v] federative; **fédération** [~ra'sjɔ̃] f federation; ~ syndicale ouvrière trade union; **fédéré, e** [~'re] adj., a. su./m federate; **fédérer** [~'re] (1f) v/t. a. se ~ federate.

fée [fe] f fairy; conte *m* de ~s fairytale; pays *m* des ~s fairyland; f vieille ~ old hag; **féerie** [~'ri] f fairyland; fairy scene; fig. enchantment; thea. pantomime; fairy-play; **féerique** [~'rik] fairy, magic; fig. enchanting.

feindre [fɛ̃:dr] (4m) v/t. feign, sham, pretend (to inf., de inf.); v/i. limp slightly (*horse*); **feinte** [fɛ̃:t] f pretence, sham; make-believe; bluff; box. etc. feint; horse: slight limp.

fêlé, e [fɛ'le] cracked (a. sl. fig.);

fêler [~] (1a) v/t. crack (a glass etc.); se ~ crack (glass).

félicitation [felisita'sjɔ̃] f congratulation; faire des ~s à q. congratulate s.o.; **félicité** [~'te] f bliss, joy; **féliciter** [~'te] (1a) v/t.: ~ q. de congratulate s.o. on; se ~ de be pleased with; be thankful for.

félin, e [fe'lɛ̃, ~'lin] **1.** adj. zo. feline, cat-...; fig. cat-like; **2.** su./m zo. feline, cat.

félon, -onne hist. [fe'lɔ̃, ~'lɔn] **1.** adj. disloyal, felon; **2.** su./m felon, caitiff; **félonie** hist. [~lɔ'ni] f disloyalty; feudality: felony.

fêlure [fɛ'ly:r] f crack; split; 🞤 skull: fracture; F avoir une ~ be a bit cracked (= crazy).

femelle zo. [fə'mɛl] adj., a. su./f female.

féminin, e [femi'nɛ̃, ~'nin] **1.** adj. feminine; female (sex); woman's ...; womanly; **2.** su./m gramm. feminine (gender); **féminiser** [~ni'ze] (1a) v/t. make feminine (a. gramm.); give a feminine appearance to; **féminisme** [~'nism] *m* feminism; **féministe** [~'nist] su., a. adj. feminist.

femme [fam] **1.** su./f woman; wife; woman ...; ~ de chambre housemaid; ~ de charge housekeeper; ~ de ménage charwoman, cleaner; housekeeper; **2.** adj. female, woman ...; lady ...; **femmelette** F [~'lɛt] f little or weak woman; man: weakling.

fémur anat. [fe'my:r] *m* femur, thigh-bone.

fenaison ✗ [fənɛ'zɔ̃] f haymaking.

fenderie ⊕ [fɑ̃'dri] f metal, wood: splitting into rods; splitting-mill; splitting-machine; cutting shop; **fendeur** [~'dœ:r] *m* splitter; cleaver; F woodcutter; **fendiller** [~di'je] (1a) v/t. a. se ~ crack (wood, a. paint.); crackle (china, glaze); craze (china, concrete, glaze); **fendre** [fɑ̃:dr] (4a) v/t. split, cleave; slit; crack; rend (the air); break through (a crowd); se ~ split, crack; F se ~ la gueule (or la pomme) split one's sides; F se ~ de fork out (a sum); buy, stand (a round etc.); F il ne s'est pas fendu he didn't overspend himself.

fenêtrage [fənɛ'tra:ʒ] *m* windows pl.; **fenêtre** [~'nɛ:tr] f window; ~ à bascule balance or pivoted window; ~ à coulisse (or guillotine) sash-

window; *jeter l'argent par la* ~
throw money down the drain;
fenêtrer ⚹ [⸗nɛ'tre] (1a) *v/t.* put
windows in.

fenil [fə'ni] *m* hayloft.

fenouil ♀ [fə'nu:j] *m* fennel.

fente [fã:t] *f* crack, fissure, split;
slit; chink; gap; crevice; opening;
⊕ slot.

féodal, e, *m/pl.* **-aux** [feɔ'dal, ⸗'do]
feudal; **féodalité** [⸗dali'te] *f*
feudality; feudal system.

fer [fɛ:r] *m* iron; *fig.* sword; (horse-)
shoe; ~s *pl.* fetters, chains; ~ *à
repasser* (flat-)iron; ⊕ ~ *à souder*
soldering-iron; ~ *à* T T-iron; *fig.* ~ *de
lance* spearhead; most important
factor; ~ *électrique* electric iron; ~ *en
barres* bar *or* strip iron; ⚹ *construction f en* ~ ironwork; *de* ~ iron; *donner
un coup de* ~ *à* press, iron; *fil m de* ~
wire.

ferai [fə're] *1st p. sg. fut. of faire.*

fer-blanc, *pl.* **fers-blancs** [fɛr-
'blã] *m* tin(-plate); **ferblanterie**
[fɛrblã'tri] *f* tin-plate; tin goods
pl., tinware; ⊕ tin-shop; **ferblantier** [⸗'tje] *m* tinsmith.

férié [fe'rje] *adj./m*: *jour m* ~ public
holiday; *eccl.* holy day.

férir † [fe'ri:r] (2u) *v/t.* strike; *sans
coup* ~ without striking a blow.

fermage ✿ [fɛr'ma:ʒ] *m* (farm-)
rent; tenant farming.

ferme[1] [fɛrm] **1.** *adj.* firm, steady
(*a.* ✿); rigid; fixed, fast; resolute;
vente f ~ definite sale; **2.** *adv.* firmly; ~! steady!; *frapper* ~ hit hard;
tenir ~ stand firm. [*à* ~ on lease.)

ferme[2] ⚹ [~] *f* farm; farming lease;)

ferme[3] ⚹ [~] *f* truss(ed girder).

fermé [fɛr'me] **1.** *p.p. of fermer;* **2.** *adj.*
shut; locked; closed (*road, shop, etc.*);
closed-in (*area, site, etc.*); ⊕ *etc.* off
(*faucet, tap, radio, switch, etc.*); *fig.*
impenetrable, inscrutable (*face, expression, etc.*); *fig.* exclusive (*circle,
club, society, etc.*); *être* ~ *à qch.* be
impervious to s.th., have no appreciation of s.th.; *être* ~ *à q.* be closed to
s.o. (*career, circle, etc.*).

ferment [fɛr'mã] *m* ferment (*a.
fig.*); *bread:* leaven; **fermentation**
[⸗mãta'sjõ] *f* fermentation; *dough:*
rising; *fig.* unrest, ferment; **fermenter** [⸗'te] (1a) *v/i.* ferment;
rise (*dough*); *fig.* be in a ferment.

fermer [fɛr'me] (1a) *vt/i.* close,

shut; *v/t.* fasten; turn off (*the
electricity, the gas, the light*); clench
(*one's fist*); block (*a game, a.* 🐝);
~ *à clef* lock; ~ *au verrou* bolt; ~ *à
vis* screw (*s.th.*) down; *sl.* **ferme
ça!, la ferme!** shut up!; *v/i.* close
(down) (*firm etc.*); wrap round
(*clothes*).

fermeté [fɛrmə'te] *f* firmness;
steadiness (*a. of purpose*); constancy; *fig.* strength (*of mind*).

fermette [fɛr'met] *f* (*small*) farmhouse; (*small*) rural residence.

fermeture [fɛrmə'ty:r] *f* shutting,
closing; fastening; ~ *éclair* (*or à glissière*) zip fastener, F zip, *Am.* zipper.

fermier, -ère [⸗'mje, ⸗'mjɛ:r] *su.*
farmer; tenant farmer; *su./f a.*
farmer's wife.

fermoir [fɛr'mwa:r] *m* snap; clasp,
fastener, catch; ⊕ firmer (= *sort of
chisel*).

féroce [fe'rɔs] ferocious (*a. fig.*),
fierce, savage, wild; **férocité**
[⸗rɔsi'te] *f* fierceness; ferocity.

ferraille [fɛ'rɑ:j] *f* old iron, scrap
iron; scrap-heap; *mettre à la* ~ scrap;
ferrailleur [⸗rɑ'jœ:r] *m* scrap-iron
dealer; junkdealer; † F swashbuckler; **ferrant** [⸗'rã] *adj./m*:
maréchal-~ *m* farrier; **ferré, e** [⸗'re]
fitted with iron; iron-tipped; studded (*boots, tyres*); F well up (in, *en*);
ferrer [⸗'re] *v/t.* (1a) shoe (*a horse*);
ferret [⸗'rɛ] *m* tag, tab; *min. stone:*
core; **ferronnerie** [⸗rɔn'ri] *f* ironworks; ironmongery; **ferronnier**
[⸗rɔ'nje] *m* ironworker; ironmonger;
ferronnière [⸗rɔ'njɛ:r] *f* frontlet.

ferroutage [fɛru'ta:ʒ] *m* transport:
piggyback (system).

ferroviaire [fɛrɔ'vjɛ:r] railway-...

ferrugineux, -euse 🜍 [fɛryʒi'nø,
⸗'nø:z] ferruginous, iron-...

ferrure [fɛ'ry:r] *f* iron-fitting; ironwork.

ferry-boat [fɛri'bo:t] *m* train ferry.

fertile [fɛr'til] fertile, fruitful, rich
(in, *en*); **fertiliser** [fɛrtili'ze] (1a)
v/t. fertilize; *se* ~ become fertile;
fertilité [⸗'te] *f* fertility; richness;
abundance.

féru, e [fe'ry] **1.** *p.p. of férir;* **2.** *adj.*: ~
de smitten with; set on (*an idea*).

férule [fe'ryl] *f* ♣ giant fennel;
school: cane; *fig. être sous la* ~ *de q.* be
under s.o.'s (iron) rule.

fervent, e [fɛr'vã, ⸗'vã:t] **1.** *adj.*

fervent, earnest, ardent; **2.** *su.*
enthusiast; devotee, ... fan; **ferveur**
[ˌ'vœːr] *f* fervo(u)r, earnestness.

fesse [fɛs] *f* buttock; ~s *pl.* buttocks,
bottom *sg.*; **fessée** [fɛ'se] *f* spank-
ing; **fesse-mathieu** [fɛsmaˈtjø] *m*
skinflint; **fesser** [fɛ'se] (1a) *v/t.*
spank.

festin [fɛsˈtɛ̃] *m* feast, banquet;
festiner [ˌti'ne] (1a) *v/i.* feast.

festival, *pl.* **-als** [fɛstiˈval] *m* festival; **festivité** [ˌviˈte] *f* festivity.

feston [fɛsˈtɔ̃] *m* festoon; *needle-
work*: scallop; *point m de* ~ buttonhole stitch; **festonner** [ˌtɔˈne]
(1a) *v/t.* festoon; scallop (*a hem*);
v/i. sl. stagger about.

festoyer [fɛstwa'je] (1h) *vt/i.* feast.

fêtard *m*, **e** *f* F [fɛˈtaːr, ~ˈtard] reveller, roisterer; **fête** [fɛːt] *f* feast,
festival; holiday; name *or* Saint's
day; festivity; fête; party; ~ *foraine*
fun fair; ~ *des Mères* Mother's Day; ~
du travail Labo(u)r Day; *faire* ~ *à*
welcome; *sl. faire sa* ~ *à q.* beat s.o.
up; make things hot for s.o.; **fête-
Dieu,** *pl.* **fêtes-Dieu** *eccl.* [fɛtˈdjø] *f*
Corpus Christi; **fêter** [fɛˈte] (1a) *v/t.*
keep (*a feast, a holiday*); feast, entertain (*s.o.*); celebrate (*a birthday, an
event*).

fétiche [feˈtiʃ] *m* fetish; *mot.* mascot.

fétide [feˈtid] fetid, stinking, rank;
fétidité [ˌtidiˈte] *f* fetidness, foul-
ness.

fétu [feˈty] *m* straw; F *fig.* rap.

feu¹ [fø] *m* fire (*a. of a gun or rifle*);
flame; fireplace; *fig.* ardo(u)r; heat;
stove: burner; *mot. etc.* light; *mot.* ~
arrière rearlight; ~ *d'artifice* fire-
work(s *pl.*); ~ *de joie* bonfire; *mot.* ~*x*
pl. de signalisation (routière), F ~ *rouge*
traffic lights *pl.*; ~ *follet* will-o'-the-
wisp; *mot.* ~ *vert (rouge)* green (red)
light (*a. fig.*); ⚒ *aller au* ~ go into
action; *à petit* ~ on *or* over a slow fire;
fig. by inches; *arme f à* ~ fire-arm;
coup m de ~ shot; *donner du* ~ *à q.* give
s.o. a light; *fig. donner le* ~ *vert (à q.)*
give (s.o.) the green light; *fig. entrer
dans le* ~ *pour q.* go through fire and
water for s.o.; *faire* ~ fire (at, *sur*); *fig.
faire long* ~ fail; *fig. ne pas faire long* ~
be short-lived; *mettre le* ~ *à qch.* set
fire to s.th., set s.th. on fire; *par le fer
et le* ~ by fire and sword; *prendre* ~
catch fire; *fig.* flare up, fly into a
temper.

feu², **feue** [fø] *adj.* (*inv. before article
and poss. adj.*) late, deceased; *la feue
reine, feu la reine* the late queen.

feuillage [fœ'jaːʒ] *m* leaves *pl.*,
foliage; **feuillaison** ♀ [ˌjɛˈzɔ̃] *f*
foliation; springtime; **feuillard**
[ˌˈjaːr] *m* hoop-wood; hoop-iron;
⊕ metallic ribbon; **feuille** [fœːj] *f*
♀ leaf; *paper*: sheet; *admin.* form;
⚙ chart; ⚏ list; F *journ.* ~ *de chou*
rag; ~ *de paie* wage-sheet; ~ *de
présence* attendance list; ⊕ time-
sheet; ~ *de route* ⚓ way-bill; ⚒
marching orders *pl.*; ⚒ travel warrant; ~ *volante* fly-sheet; **feuillée**
[fœ'je] *f* arbo(u)r; foliage; ⚒ ~s *pl.*
latrines; **feuille-morte** [fœjˈmɔrt]
adj./inv. dead-leaf (*colour*); oak-
leaf brown; russet; **feuillet** [fœˈjɛ]
m book: leaf; *admin.* form; sheet;
⊕ thin sheet, plate; **feuilletage**
cuis. [fœjˈtaːʒ] *m*, **feuilleté** *cuis.*
[ˌˈte] *m* puff paste; **feuilleter** [ˌˈte]
(1c) *v/t.* skim through, thumb
through, turn over the pages of
(*a book*); *cuis.* roll and fold; ⊕
divide into sheets; **feuilleton** [ˌˈtɔ̃]
m journ. feuilleton; serial (story).

feuillette [fœˈjɛt] *f* (*approx.*) half-
hogshead.

feuillu, **e** [fœˈjy] leafy; deciduous
(*forest*).

feutre [føːtr] *m* felt; felt hat; *saddle*:
stuffing; **feutrer** [føˈtre] (1a) *v/t.*
felt; stuff, pad (*a saddle etc.*); *à pas
feutrés* noiselessly; **feutrier** [ˌtriˈe]
m felt-maker.

fève ♀ [fɛːv] *f* bean; **fèverole** ♀
[fɛˈvrɔl] *f* field-bean.

février [fevriˈe] *m* February.

fi! [fi] *int.* fie!; for shame!; ~ *de ...!*
a fig for ...!; *faire* ~ *de* scorn, turn up
one's nose at.

fiabilité [fjabiliˈte] *f* reliability;
fiable [fjabl] reliable.

fiacre [fjakr] *m* cab, hackney carriage.

fiançailles [fjɑ̃ˈsaːj] *f/pl.* engagement *sg.*, betrothal *sg.* (to, *avec*);
fiancé [ˌˈse] *m* fiancé; **fiancée**
[ˌˈse] *f* fiancée; **fiancer** [ˌˈse] (1k)
v/t. betroth; se ~ become engaged
(to, *à*).

fiasco [fjasˈko] *m* fiasco; *faire* ~ turn
out *or* be a fiasco.

fibranne *tex.* [fiˈbran] *f* staple fibre.

fibre [fibr] *f* fibre; *wood*: grain; *fig.*
feeling; ~ *de bois packing*: wood-

wool, *Am.* excelsior; ~ *de verre*
glass-wool; (*la*) ~ *de la poésie* (a)
soul for poetry; *avoir la ~ sensible*
be impressionable; **fibreux, -euse**
[fiˈbrø, ~ˈbrø:z] fibrous, stringy;
fibrille *physiol.* [~ˈbri:j] *f* fibril.

ficeler [fisˈle] (1c) *v/t.* tie up, do up;
sl. dress (*s.o.*) badly; **ficelle** [fiˈsɛl]
1. *su./f* string (*a. fig.*); twine; *sl.*
tricks *pl.*; *sl. connaître toutes les ~s*
know the ropes; **2.** *adj.* wily,
cunning.

fiche [fiʃ] *f iron, wood:* peg, pin;
paper: form, voucher; sheet, slip (*of
paper*); label; index card; *games:*
counter; ⚡ plug; *fig.* scrap; ~ *de paye*
wages slip; ⚡ ~ *femelle* jack; *mettre
qch. sur ~s* card(-index) s.th.; **ficher**
[fiˈʃe] (1a) *v/t.* stick in, drive in; ∆
point (*a wall*); *sl.* do; *sl.* put; *sl.* give;
sl. ~ *q. à la porte* throw s.o. out; *sl.
fichez-moi la paix!* leave me alone!;
sl. fichez(-moi) le camp! clear off!;
clear out!; *sl. se ~ de* make fun of; not
to care (a hang) about; **fichier** ✝
[~ˈʃje] *m* card index; file (*case*); ~ *de
données* data file.

fichoir [fiˈʃwa:r] *m* clothes-peg.

fichtre! *sl.* [fiʃtr] *int.* my word!;
indeed!; hang it!

fichu¹ [fiˈʃy] *m* neck scarf; small
shawl.

fichu², e *sl.* [~] **1.** *p.p.* of *ficher;*
2. *adj.* lost, done for, *sl.* bust; rotten,
sl. lousy; *mal* ~ wretched; out of
sorts.

fictif, -ve [fikˈtif, ~ˈti:v] fictitious;
sham; ✝ *facture f fictive* pro forma
invoice; **fiction** [~ˈsjø] *f* fiction, invention, fabrication.

fidèle [fiˈdɛl] **1.** *adj.* faithful, true,
staunch; exact (*copy*); **2.** *su. eccl. les*
~*s pl.* the congregation *sg.*; the faithful; **fidélité** [~deliˈte] *f* fidelity;
integrity; *de haute* ~ high fidelity, F
hi-fi (*record etc.*).

fiduciaire [fidyˈsjɛ:r] fiduciary;
trust …; *monnaie f* ~ paper money.

fief [fjɛf] *m hist.* fief; *fig.* preserve,
(private) kingdom; **fieffé, e** [fjɛˈfe]
hist. enfeoffed; given in fee (*land*); F
pej. out and out, arrant, thorough-
paced; **fieffer** *hist.* [~] (1a) *v/t.* en-
feoff (*s.o.*); give (*land*) in feoff.

fiel [fjɛl] *m animal:* gall; *person:*
bile; *fig.* spleen; *fig.* bitterness; *sans*
~ without malice.

fiente [fjɑ̃:t] *f* dung; *birds:* drop-

pings *pl.*; **fienter** [fjɑ̃ˈte] (1a) *v/i.*
dung; mute (*birds*).

fier¹ [fje] (1o) *v/t.: se ~ à* trust
(*s.o.*), rely on; *fiez-vous à moi!* leave
it to me!; *ne vous y fiez pas!* don't
count on it!

fier², fière [fjɛ:r] proud; haughty;
fig. magnificent.

fier-à-bras, *pl.* **fier(s)-à-bras**
[fjɛraˈbra] *m* swaggerer, bully.

fierté [fjɛrˈte] *f* pride; haughtiness;
vanity.

fièvre 🐟 [fjɛ:vr] *f* fever; **fiévreux,
-euse** [fjeˈvrø, ~ˈvrø:z] **1.** *adj.* feverish; fever-ridden; *fig.* excited;
2. *su.* fever patient.

fifre ♪ [fifr] *m* fife (*a. player*).

figer [fiˈʒe] (1l) *v/t. a. se* ~ congeal,
coagulate; *se* ~ *a.* set (*face*); *fig.*
freeze (*smile*).

fignoler F [fiɲɔˈle] (1a) *v/i.* finick,
be finicky; *v/t.* fiddle over (*s.th.*)
with extreme care; *se* ~ titivate o.s.

figue 🌿 [fig] *f* fig; F *mi-~,* mi-raisin
wavering; so-so; middling; **figuier**
🌿 [fiˈgje] *m* fig-tree.

figurant, e *f* [figyˈrɑ̃, ~ˈrɑ̃:t]
thea. supernumerary, F super;
extra; walker-on; **figuratif, -ve**
[~raˈtif, ~ˈti:v] figurative; **figuration** [~raˈsjø] *f* figuration, representation; *thea.* extras *pl.*; **figure**
[fiˈgy:r] *f* ⚕, *person:* figure; shape,
form; face; appearance; court-
card; **figuré, e** [figyˈre] **1.** *adj.*
figured (*cloth etc.*); *fig.* figurative;
2. *su./m: au* ~ figuratively; **figurer**
[~ˈre] (1a) *v/t.* represent; *thea.* act,
play the part of; *se* ~ imagine,
fancy; *v/i.* figure, appear; *thea.* ~ *sur
la scène* walk on; **figurine** [~ˈrin] *f*
statuette; ✝ (wax-)model.

fil [fil] *m* thread (*a. fig.*); wire; ⚡
filament; *blade:* edge; *meat, wood:*
grain; *wool:* ply; ∆ ~ *à plomb*
plumb-line; ~ *d'archal* brass wire,
binding wire; ~ *de fer barbelé*
barbed wire; ~ *de la Vierge* gossamer; *au bout du* ~ on the phone;
coup m de ~ ring, call; *donner du* ~
à retordre à give a lot of trouble to;
⚡ *sans* ~ wireless; **filage** [fiˈla:ʒ] *m*
spinning; yarn; *metall.* drawing;
filament [~laˈmɑ̃] *m* ⚕, ⚡ filament;
silk: thread; **filamenteux, -euse** [~-
lamɑ̃ˈtø, ~ˈtø:z] fibrous; *fig.* stringy;
filandière ✝ [~lɑ̃ˈdjɛ:r] *f* spinner;
les sœurs ~s pl. the Fates; **filandre**

[‿'lɑ̃:dr] *f* fibre; ‿*s pl. meat etc.*:
stringy parts; gossamer *sg.*; **filandreux, -euse** [‿lɑ̃'drø, ‿'drø:z]
stringy, tough (*meat*); streaked
(*marble etc.*); *fig.* involved, complicated; **filant, e** [‿'lɑ̃, ‿'lɑ̃:t]
flowing; shooting (*star*); ropy
(*wine*); **filasse** [‿'las] *f* tow; oakum; *sl.* stringy meat; **filateur** *m*,
-trice *f* [‿la'tœ:r, ‿'tris] *tex.* spinner; (spinning-)mill owner; inform-
er, shadower; **filature** [‿la'ty:r] *f*
spinning-mill, cotton-mill; spinning; shadowing.

file [fil] *f* line, file; (‿ *d'attente*) queue,
Am. line; *à la* ‿ in file; *fig.* on end,
without a break; *chef m de* ‿ leader;
en ‿ *indienne* in single file; ⚓ *en ligne
de* ‿ (single) line ahead; **filer** [fi'le]
(1a) *v/t. tex.* spin; draw (*metal*); play
out (*cards*); ⚓ run out (*a cable*); ⚓
slip (*the moorings*); shadow (*s.o.*); *v/i.*
flow smoothly; run (*oil*); rope (*wine*);
smoke (*lamp*); *fig.* slip by, go by; go,
travel; F clear out; ‿ *doux* sing small;
filez! clear out!; go away!; **filerie**
[fil'ri] *f* spinning mill; *metall.* wire
drawing.

filet [fi'lɛ] *m* net; ⊕ *screw*: thread;
cuis. fillet; *water*: trickle; dash (*of
lemon*); 🚂 *etc.* luggage rack; ‿ *à
provisions* string bag; ‿ *de voix* thin
voice; *coup m de* ‿ *fish*: catch, haul;
filetage [fil'ta:ʒ] *m* ⊕ *metal, wire*:
drawing; ⊕ *screw-cutting*; *screw*:
thread(ing); **fileter** [‿'te] (1d) *v/t.* ⊕
draw (*metal, a. wire*); thread, screw
(*a bolt*); poach (*fish with nets*); **fileur**
m, **-euse** *f tex.* [fi'lœ:r, ‿'lø:z]
spinner.

filial, e, *m/pl.* **-aux** [fi'ljal, ‿'ljo]
1. *adj.* filial; **2.** *su./f* ✝ subsidiary
company; ✝, *a.* association: branch;
filiation [‿lja'sjɔ̃] *f* filiation; descendants *pl.*; *fig.* relationship; *en* ‿
directe in direct line.

filière [fi'ljɛ:r] *f* ⊕ die; ⊕ draw-
plate; ⚓ man-rope; *fig.* usual
channels *pl.*; *fig. passer par la* ‿
work one's way up from the bottom; **filiforme** [fili'fɔrm] thread-
like.

filigrane [fili'gran] *m* filigree
(work); *paper, banknotes*: water-
mark.

fille [fi:j] *f* daughter; girl; maid;
spinster; ‿ *publique* prostitute; ‿ *à
papa* rich man's daughter; ‿ *de salle*

hotel etc.: waitress; *jeune* ‿ girl,
young woman; *vieille* ‿ old maid; ‿-
mère, *pl.* ‿**s-mères** [fij'mɛ:r] *f* unmarried mother; **fillette** [fi'jɛt] *f*
little girl; F lass; **filleul, e** [‿'jœl] *su.*
godchild; *su./m* godson; *su./f* god-
daughter.

film [film] *m* film (*a. cin.*); *cin.* F
picture; *Am.* movie; ‿ *documentaire*
documentary (film); ‿ *en couleurs*
colo(u)r film; ‿ *muet* silent film; ‿
parlant talking picture, F talkie; ‿
policier detective film; ‿ *sonore*
sound-film; ‿ *truqué* trick film;
tourner un ‿ make a film; F act in a
film (*person*); **filmer** [fil'me] (1a)
v/t. film; **filmothèque** [‿mɔ'tɛk] *f*
film library *or* collection.

filon [fi'lɔ̃] *m* ⚒ vein, seam, lode;
sl. good fortune; *sl.* cushy job.

filou [fi'lu] *m* pickpocket, thief;
(*card-*)sharper; F swindler; **filouter**
[filu'te] (1a) *v/t.* swindle (s.o. out of
s.th., *q. de qch.*); rob (s.o. of s.th.,
qch. à q.); **filouterie** [‿'tri] *f*
swindle, fraud; picking pockets,
stealing; cheating.

fils [fis] *m* son; F lad, boy; ‿ *à papa*
rich man's son; *fig.* ‿ *de ses œuvres*
self-made man.

filtrage [fil'tra:ʒ] *m liquid*: filtering;
‿ *à interférences radio*: interference
elimination; **filtre** [filtr] *m* filter;
coffee: percolator; *radio*: by-pass,
filter; *bout m* ‿ *cigarette*: filter-tip;
filtrer [fil'tre] (1a) *v/i. a. se* ‿
filter; *v/t.* filter; by-pass (*a radio-
station*).

fin¹ [fɛ̃] *f* end, termination, close,
conclusion; aim, object; ‿ *d'alerte*
all clear; ✝ ‿ *de mois* monthly
statement; *à la* ‿ in the long run;
at last; *à toutes* ‿*s* for all purposes;
en ‿ *de compte*, F *à la* ‿ *des* ‿*s*
when all is said and done; *mettre*
‿ *à* put an end to; *prendre* ‿ come
to an end; *tirer à sa* ‿ be drawing
to a close.

fin², fine [fɛ̃, fin] fine; pure; choice;
slender (*waist etc.*); artful, sly;
small; subtle; keen (*ear*).

final, e, *m/pl.* **-als** [fi'nal] **1.** *adj.*
final (*a. gramm.*); last; eventual;
2. *su./f gramm.* end syllable; ♪ key-
note; ♪ *plainsong*: final; *sp.* finals
pl.

final(e) ♪ [‿] *m* finale.

finance [fi'nɑ̃:s] *f* finance; finan-

cial world; ready money; ~s pl.
resources; *ministère m des* ♀s Exchequer, Treasury (*a. Am.*); **financer** [finɑ̃'se] (1k) v/t. finance;
financier, -ère [~'sje, ~'sjɛːr]
1. *adj.* financial; stock (*market*);
2. *su./m* financier.

finasser F [fina'se] (1a) v/i. finesse;
use subterfuges; **finasserie** [~-
nas'ri] *f* trickery; (piece of) cunning; ~s pl. wiles; **finasseur, -euse**
[~fina'sœːr, ~'søːz], **finassier, -ère**
[~'sje, ~'sjɛːr] **1.** *adj.* cunning,
wily; **2.** *su.* wily person.

finaud, e [fi'no, ~'noːd] **1.** *adj.* cunning, wily; **2.** *su.* wily person.

fine [fin] *f* liqueur brandy.

finesse [fi'nɛs] *f* fineness; *waist*:
slenderness; cunning; shrewdness;
opt., radio, telev.: sharpness; **finette**
tex. [~'nɛt] *f* flannelette.

fini, e [fi'ni] **1.** *adj.* finished (*a. fig.*),
ended, over; ♣, *gramm., etc.* finite;
fig. pej. absolute, complete; **2.** *su./m*
finish; *phls. etc.* finite; **finir** [~'niːr]
(2a) v/i. finish; end; end up; ~ *de
faire qch.* stop doing s.th.; ~ *par faire
qch.* finally or eventually do s.th.; *en
~* avec get over (and done) with; put
an end to; *à n'en plus ~* endless(ly);
finition ⊕ [~ni'sjɔ̃] *f* finishing.

finlandais, e [fɛ̃lɑ̃'dɛ, ~'dɛːz] **1.** *adj.*
Finnish; **2.** *su.* ♀ Finn, Finlander;
finnois, e [fi'nwa, ~'nwaːz] **1.** *adj.*
Finnish; **2.** *su./m ling.* Finnish; *su.*
♀ Finn.

fiole [fjɔl] *f* small bottle; flask; *sl.*
head.

fioritures [fjɔri'tyːr] *f/pl.* hand-
writing, style: flourishes; ♪ grace-
notes.

firmament [firma'mɑ̃] *m* firmament, sky, heavens *pl.*

firme ♀ [firm] *f* firm; *book*: imprint.

fis [fi] *1st p. sg. p.s. of* faire.

fisc [fisk] *m* Exchequer, Treasury;
Inland (*Am.* Internal) Revenue,
taxes *pl.*; **fiscal, e**, *m/pl.* -aux
[fis'kal, ~'ko] fiscal, tax ...

fissile [fi'sil] fissile; **fission** [~'sjɔ̃]
f (*esp. phys.* nuclear) fission; **fissure** [~'syːr] *f* fissure (*a.* ♣), crack,
split, crevice; **fissurer** [~sy're] (1a)
v/t. *a. se* ~ crack, fissure.

fiston *sl.* [fis'tɔ̃] *m* son, youngster.

fistule ♣ [fis'tyl] *f* fistula.

fixage [fik'saːʒ] *m* fixing; **fixateur**

[~sa'tœːr] *m* fixer; **fixation** [~sa-
'sjɔ̃] *f* fixing; *admin.* assessment;
⚡ fixation; attachment; **fixe** [fiks]
1. *adj.* fixed; steady; firm, fast;
stationary; regular (*price*); *arrêt m
~* regular stop; *traffic sign*: all
buses *etc.* stop here; *étoile f ~* fixed
star; **2.** *su./m* fixed salary; **fixe-
chaussettes** [~ʃo'sɛt] *m* suspender, *Am.* sock-suspender, gar-
ter; **fixer** [fik'se] (1a) v/t. fix (*a.
phot.*, ⚡, ♦, *value, time*), fasten;
settle, appoint; hold (*s.o.'s attention*);
decide, determine; keep one's eye
on (*s.th.*), stare at; ⚒ fix, hold; ⚖
assess (*damages*); ~ *les yeux sur*
stare at, look hard at; *se* ~ settle
(down); **fixité** [~si'te] *f* fixity.

flac! [flak] *int.* slap!; crack!; plop!
(*into water*); *faire* ~ plop.

flacon [fla'kɔ̃] *m* bottle; flask; ~ *plat*
hip flask.

flageller [flaʒɛl'le] (1a) v/t. scourge,
lash.

flageoler [flaʒɔ'le] (1o) v/i. tremble,
shake.

flageolet¹ ♪ [flaʒɔ'le] *m* flageolet.

flageolet² *cuis.* [~] *m* (small) kidney
bean, flageolet.

flagorner [flagɔr'ne] (1a) v/t. flatter;
toady to; fawn upon; **flagornerie**
[~nɔ'ri] *f* flattery, F soft soap;
toadying.

flagrant, e [fla'grɑ̃, ~'grɑ̃ːt] flagrant;
striking; *en ~ délit* red-handed, in
the very act.

flair [flɛːr] *m dog*: scent; *fig.* nose;
fig. person: flair; *avoir du ~ pour*
have a flair for; **flairer** [flɛ're] (1b)
v/t. scent (*a. fig.*); smell; *fig.* suspect; *sl.* smell of.

flamand, e [fla'mɑ̃, ~'mɑ̃ːd] **1.** *adj.*
Flemish; **2.** *su./m ling.* Flemish; *su.*
♀ Fleming.

flamant *orn.* [fla'mɑ̃] *m* flamingo.

flambant, e [flɑ̃'bɑ̃, ~'bɑ̃ːt] **1.** *adj.*
blazing; *fig.* brilliant; **2.** *flambant
adv.*: *tout ~ neuf* brandnew; **flambeau** [~'bo] *m* torch; candlestick; candelabra; **flambée** [~'be]
f blaze, blazing fire; *fig.* surge, outburst; ♦ *prices etc.*: zooming *or*
shooting up; **flamber** [~'be] (1a)
v/i. flame, blaze; burn; ⊕ buckle
(*metal rod*); v/t. singe; ✴ sterilize (*a
needle in a flame*); *fig. sl. être flambé*
be done for; **flamboyer** [~bwa'je]
(1h) v/i. blaze (*fire, a. fig.*).

flamme [flɑːm] *f* flame; *fig.* love, passion; ⚔, ⚓ pennon, pennant; *être en ⁓s* be on fire.

flammèche [flaˈmɛʃ] *f* spark.

flan [flɑ̃] *m cuis.* baked-custard tart; ⊕ *etc.* blank; *sl. c'est du ⁓!* that's a load of hooey!

flanc [flɑ̃] *m* flank, side; ⁓ *de coteau* hillside; F *sur le ⁓* laid up; exhausted; *sl. tirer au ⁓* malinger, F swing the lead.

flancher F [flɑ̃ˈʃe] (1a) *v/i.* flinch; give in; F quit, chicken out; ⊕ break down.

flandrin † F [flɑ̃ˈdrɛ̃] *m* lanky fellow.

flanelle *tex.* [flaˈnɛl] *f* flannel.

flâner [flɑne] (1a) *v/i.* stroll; lounge about; loaf; saunter; **flâneur** *m*, **-euse** *f* [⁓ˈnœːr, ⁓ˈnøːz] stroller; lounger, loafer.

flanquer[1] [flɑ̃ˈke] (1m) *v/t.* throw, chuck; deal, land (*a blow*); ⁓ *q. à la porte* chuck s.o. out; give s.o. the sack.

flanquer[2] [flɑ̃ˈke] (1m) *v/t.* ✕, ⚓, *etc.* flank; **flanqueur** ✕ [⁓ˈkœːr] *m* flanker.

flapi, e F [flaˈpi] tired out, fagged out.

flaque [flak] *f* puddle, pool.

flash, *pl.* **flashes** [flaʃ] *m phot.* flash-light; *radio, telev.*: newsflash.

flasque[1] [flask] flabby, limp.

flasque[2] [⁓] *f* ⚓ flask; † powderhorn.

flasque[3] [⁓] *m* ⊕ *lathe etc.*: cheek; support (*of dynamo*); *mot.* wheeldisk.

flatter [flaˈte] (1a) *v/t.* flatter (s.o. on s.th., *q. sur qch.*; s.o. by *or* in *ger.*, *q. de inf.*); humo(u)r (*s.o.*); caress, stroke; **flatterie** [⁓ˈtri] *f* flattery; **flatteur, -euse** [⁓ˈtœːr, ⁓ˈtøːz] **1.** *adj.* flattering; pleasing; **2.** *su.* flatterer; sycophant.

flatulence 🜊 [flatyˈlɑ̃ːs] *f* flatulence, F wind; **flatulent, e** [⁓tyˈlɑ̃, ⁓ˈlɑ̃ːt] flatulent, caused by flatulence; **flatuosité** 🜊 [⁓tɥoziˈte] *f* flatus, F wind.

fléau [fleˈo] *m* flail; *balance*: beam; *fig.* scourge; pest, curse.

flèche[1] [flɛːʃ] *f* arrow; *balance etc.*: pointer; *church*: spire; ⚓ pole; ⊕ *crane*: jib; *en ⁓* swept-back (*wings*); very rapidly, like an arrow; *fig. faire ⁓ de tout bois* use all means; *fig. monter en ⁓* rocket *or* zoom up.

flèche[2] [⁓] *f bacon*: flitch.

flécher [fleˈʃe] (1f) *v/t.* mark with arrows, arrow (*a course etc.*).

fléchir [fleˈʃiːr] (2a) *v/t.* bend; *fig.* move, touch (*s.o.*); *anat.* flex; *v/i.* bend; give way (*a.* ✕); sag (*cable, wire, a.* †); weaken; *fig.* flag, fall off; † go down (*prices*); **fléchissement** [⁓ʃisˈmɑ̃] *m* bending *etc.*; *see* fléchir; **fléchisseur** *anat.* [⁓ʃiˈsœːr] *adj./m*, *a. su./m* flexor.

flegmatique [flɛgmaˈtik] phlegmatic; **flegme** [flɛgm] *m* phlegm; imperturbability, coolness.

flemmard, e *sl.* [flɛˈmaːr, ⁓ˈmard] **1.** *adj.* lazy; **2.** *su.* slacker; **flemme** *sl.* [flɛm] *f* laziness; *avoir la ⁓* not to feel like work, feel lazy; *tirer sa ⁓* idle one's time away.

flet *icht.* [flɛ] *m* flounder.

flétrir[1] [fleˈtriːr] (2a) *v/t.* fade; wilt; wither; *fig.* blight (*s.o.'s hopes*); *se ⁓* fade; wilt, wither (*flowers*).

flétrir[2] [⁓] (2a) *v/t.* condemn; stain, blemish; *hist.* brand.

flétrissure[1] [fletriˈsyːr] *f* fading; withering.

flétrissure[2] [⁓] *f* stain, blemish; *hist.* brand.

fleur [flœːr] *f* flower (*a. fig.*); blossom; bloom (*a. on fruit*); *fig.* prime; ⁓ *de farine* pure wheaten flour; *à ⁓ de* level with; *à ⁓ de peau* skin-deep; *en ⁓* in bloom; F *faire une ⁓ à q.* do s.o. a good turn; **fleuraison** [flœrɛˈzɔ̃] *f* flowering, blooming.

fleurer [flœˈre] (1a) *v/t.* smell of; *v/i.* smell.

fleuret [flœˈrɛ] *m fencing*: foil; *tex.* floss silk; ✕ drill, borer; *tex.* ⁓ *de ...* first-quality ...; **fleurette** [⁓ˈrɛt] *f* small flower; *conter ⁓ à* say sweet nothings to; **fleurir** [⁓ˈriːr] (2o) *v/i.* flower, bloom; *fig.* flourish, thrive; *v/t.* decorate with flowers; *fig.* make florid; **fleuriste** [⁓ˈrist] *adj.*, *a. su.* florist; (*boutique de*) ⁓ flower shop; **fleuron** [⁓ˈrɔ̃] *m* ♀ floret; rosette; ⚓ finial; *typ.* fleuron; *fig. un ⁓ à sa couronne* a feather in one's cap.

fleuve [flœːv] *m* river.

flexible [flɛkˈsibl] **1.** *adj.* flexible; **2.** *su./m* ⚡ flex; **flexion** [⁓ˈsjɔ̃] *f* ⊕, *a. sp.* bending; ⊕ flexion, sagging; *gramm.* inflexion; **flexueux, -euse** [⁓ˈsɥø, ⁓ˈsɥøːz] winding; ♀ flexuose.

flibuster [flibysˈte] (1a) *v/i.* buccaneer; *v/t. sl.* steal, pinch.

flic *sl.* [flik] *m* policeman, copper,

Am. cop; detective; **flicaille** *sl.* [fli'kaj] *f*: *la* ~ the police, *sl.* the fuzz.
flic flac [flik'flak] *int.* crack.
flingot *sl.* [flɛ̃'go] *m* rifle, gun; **flinguer** F [~'ge] (1m) *v/t.* shoot (s.o.), F gun (*s.o.*) down.
flipper[1] [fli'pœ:r] *m* pin-ball machine.
flipper[2] F [fli'pe] (1a) *v/i.* flip.
flirt [flœrt] *m* flirt(ation); **flirter** [flœr'te] (1a) *v/i.* flirt.
floche [flɔʃ] soft, flabby; floss (*silk*).
flocon [flɔ'kɔ̃] *m* snow: flake; *wool:* flock; **floconneux, -euse** [~kɔ'nø, ~'nø:z] fleecy; ⌢ flocculent.
flonflons [flɔ̃'flɔ̃] *m/pl.* blare *sg.*
floraison [flɔrɛ'zɔ̃] *f* flowering, blooming; **floral, e,** *m/pl.* **-aux** [~'ral, ~'ro] floral.
flore [flɔ:r] *f* ♀ flora; *myth.* ♀ Flora.
florès [flɔ'rɛ:s] *m*: *faire* ~ be in vogue; be a success.
floriculture [flɔrikyl'ty:r] *f* flower growing; **florilège** [~'lɛ:ʒ] *m* (verse) anthology.
florissant, e *fig.* [flɔri'sɑ̃, ~'sɑ̃:t] flourishing.
flot [flo] *m* wave; stream; crowd; *fig.* flood; *à* ~ afloat; ⚓ *mettre qch. à* ~ (re)float s.th.; launch s.th.; **flottaison** ⚓ [flɔtɛ'zɔ̃] *f* floating; *ligne f de* ~ *ship:* water-line; **flottant, e** [~'tɑ̃, ~'tɑ̃:t] (*a.* ✝); flowing (*hair*); loose (*garment*); *fig.* irresolute; *fig.* elusive (*personality*); *pol. électeur* ~ floating voter.
flotte[1] [flɔt] *f* ⚓ fleet; F *the* navy; F water, rain.
flotte[2] [~] *f fishing:* float.
flotter [flɔ'te] (1a) *v/i.* float; flow (*hair*), *fig.* waver (*a.* ✕), be irresolute; **flotteur** [~'tœ:r] *m* raftsman; ⊕, *a. fishing:* float; ⚓ anchor buoy.
flottille ⚓ [flɔ'ti:j] *f* flotilla; ~ *de* pêche fishing fleet.
flou, floue [flu] **1.** *adj.* blurred; soft (*hair*); loose-fitting (*garment*); **2.** *su.* / *m* haziness; *phot.* blurring.
flouer *sl.* [flu'e] (1a) *v/t.* swindle; do (*s.o.*).
fluctuation [flyktɥa'sjɔ̃] *f* fluctuation (*a.* ✝); ⊕ ~ *de charge* variation of load; **fluctuer** [~'tɥe] (1n) *v/i.* fluctuate. (*voice*), slender.)
fluet, -ette [fly'ɛ, ~'ɛt] thin (*a.*)
fluide [flɥid] **1.** *adj.* fluid; *fig. a.* (smoothly) flowing; **2.** *su./m* fluid;

fluidifier [flɥidi'fje] (1o) *v/t.* fluidify; **fluidité** [~'te] *f* fluidity.
flûte [fly:t] *f* ♪ flute; tall champagne (*etc.*) glass; long thin roll (*of bread*); *tex.* shuttle; F ~*s pl.* (long, thin) legs; *sl.* ~! dash it!; bother!; *sl. jouer des* ~*s* take to one's heels; **flûter** [fly'te] (1a) *v/i.* ♪ play the flute; *sl.* drink; F *envoyer* ~ *q.* tell s.o. to go to blazes; *voix f flûtée* melodious voice; piping voice; **flûtiste** ♪ [~'tist] *m* fl(a)utist.
fluvial, e, *m/pl.* **-aux** [fly'vjal, ~'vjo] river...; water...
flux [fly] *m* flow; *cards, face:* flush; ⚡, ⚡, ⌢ *metall.* flux; *le* ~ *et le reflux* the ebb and flow; **fluxion** ⚡, *a.* † ⚕ [flyk'sjɔ̃] *f* fluxion, ⚡ *a.* inflammation, swelling; ~ *à la joue* gumboil; ~ *de poitrine* pneumonia.
foc ⚓ [fɔk] *m* jib; *grand (petit)* ~ outer (inner) jib.
focal, e, *m/pl.* **-aux** *phot.*, *opt.*, ⚕ [fɔ'kal, ~'ko] focal; **focalisation** [~kaliza'sjɔ̃] *f* focussing; **focaliser** [~kali'ze] (1a) *v/t.* focus.
foëne [fwɛn] *f* pronged harpoon.
foi [fwa] *f* faith; belief; trust, confidence; *ajouter* ~ *à* believe (in); *de bonne (mauvaise)* ~ *adv.* in good (bad) faith; *adj.* honest (dishonest); *digne de* ~ reliable; *faire* ~ be a proof; be authentic (of, *de*); attest (that, *que*); *ma* ~! upon my word!; *mauvaise* ~ insincerity; unfairness; *sous la* ~ *du serment* on oath.
foie [~] *m* liver; *sl. avoir les* ~*s* be in a funk.
foin[1] [fwɛ̃] **1.** *su./m* hay; *sl.* row; F *avoir du* ~ *dans ses bottes* have feathered one's nest; *faire du* ~ kick)
foin[2]! [~] *int.* bah! [up a row.)
foire[1] [fwa:r] *f* fair; F *fig.* madhouse; F *fig.* ~ *d'empoigne* free-for-all; rat race; *sl. faire la* ~ whoop it up.
foire[2] *sl.* † [~] *f* diarrhoea.
fois [fwa] *f* time, occasion; *une* ~ once; *deux* ~ twice; *trois* ~ three times; *à la* ~ at once; at the same time; *encore une* ~ once more; *une* ~ *que* when.
foison [fwa'zɔ̃] *f* abundance, plenty; *à* ~ in abundance; galore; **foisonner** [~zɔ'ne] (1a) *v/i.* abound (in, with *de*), teem (with, *de*); swell (*earth, lime*); ⊕ buckle (*metal*).
fol [fɔl] *see fou.*
folâtre [fɔ'la:tr] playful, frisky; **folâtrer** [~la'tre] (1a) *v/i.* frolic,

frisk; gambol; F act the fool; **folâ-
trerie** [ˌlɑtrə'ri] *f* playfulness;
sportiveness; frolic; **folichon, -on-
ne** F [ˌli'ʃɔ̃, ˌ'ʃɔn] playful, frolic-
some; wanton; **folie** [ˌ'li] *f* madness; folly; mania; ∼ *des gran-
deurs* megalomania; *aimer q. à la* ∼
love s.o. to distraction. ·

folié, e ⚭ [fɔ'lje] foliate(d); **folio**
typ. etc. [ˌ'ljo] *m* folio; **folioter**
[ˌljɔ'te] (1a) *v/t.* folio, paginate.

folklore [fɔl'klɔːr] *m* folklore.

folle [fɔl] *see fou*; ∼ *farine* flour dust;
follet, -ette [fɔ'lɛ, ˌ'lɛt] (slightly)
mad; scatterbrained; *esprit m* ∼
goblin; *poil m* ∼ down; *see feu*.

folliculaire F [fɔliky'lɛːr] *m* hack
writer; **follicule** ⚭, *anat.* [ˌ'kyl] *m*
follic(u)le.

fomentateur *m*, **-trice** *f* [fɔmɑ̃ta-
'tœːr, ˌ'tris] fomenter; **fomentation** ✿, *a. fig.* [ˌta'sjɔ̃] *f* fomentation; **fomenter** [ˌ'te] (1a) *v/t.* ✿
foment (*a. fig.*); *fig.* stir up.

foncé, e [fɔ̃'se] dark, deep (*colour*);
bleu ∼ dark blue; **foncer** [ˌ'se] (1k)
v/t. make darker, darken, deepen (*a
colour*); bottom (*a cask*); *v/i.* darken,
grow darker; F rush, dash (*at, sur*).

foncier, -ère [fɔ̃'sje, ˌ'sjɛːr] landed,
real (*property*); ground (*landlord,
rent*); *fig.* thorough, fundamental.

fonction [fɔ̃k'sjɔ̃] *f* function (*a. ⚭,
a. ✿*); *fig. en* ∼ *de* in step with, hand
in hand with; *faire* ∼ *de* act as;
fonctionnaire [jɔ̃ksɔ'nɛːr] *m* official; civil servant; office bearer;
fonctionnel, -elle [ˌ'nɛl] function-
al; **fonctionner** [ˌ'ne] (1a) *v/i.*
function (*a. ✿*); ⊕ work (*brake,
machine, etc.*).

fond [fɔ̃] *m* bottom; *sea*: bed; △,
a. fig. foundation, *fig.* basis; *paint.*
background; back, far end; *fig.* gist,
essence; *à* ∼ thoroughly; *à* ∼ *de
train* at top speed; *article m de* ∼
leading article, leader; *au* ∼ after
all; at bottom; *de* ∼ *en comble* from
top to bottom; **fondamental, e,**
m/pl. **-aux** [fɔ̃damɑ̃'tal, ˌ'to] fundamental; radical; essential.

fondant, e [fɔ̃'dɑ̃, ˌ'dɑ̃ːt] **1.** *adj.*
melting; juicy (*fruit*); **2.** *su./m*
fondant; *metall.* flux.

fondateur *m*, **-trice** *f* [fɔ̃da'tœːr,
ˌ'tris] founder; **fondation** [ˌ'sjɔ̃] *f*
founding; foundation (*a. △*); institution; **fondé, e** [fɔ̃'de] **1.** *adj.*

founded, justified; authorized; ✝
funded (*debt*); être ∼ *à* (*inf.*) be entitled to (*inf.*), have reason to (*inf.*);
2. *su./m*: ∼ *de pouvoir* ♟ proxy,
holder of a power of attorney; ✝
managing director; ✝ chief clerk;
fondement [fɔ̃d'mɑ̃] *m* base, foundation; F behind, bottom; *sans* ∼
groundless, unfounded; **fonder**
[fɔ̃'de] (1a) *v/t.* found (*a. ✝, a. fig.*);
✝ start (*a firm, a paper*); ✝ fund
(*a debt*); *fig.* base, justify.

fonderie ⊕, *metall.* [fɔ̃'dri] *f*
foundry; smelting works *usu. sg.*;
founding; **fondeur** [ˌ'dœːr] *m*
founder; smelter; *typ.* ∼ *en caractères* type-founder; **fondre** [fɔ̃:dr]
(4a) *v/t. metall.* smelt; *metall.* cast
(*a bell, a statue*); melt; dissolve;
thaw (*snow*); blend (*colours*); ✝
amalgamate; *v/i.* melt (*a. fig.*); *fig.*
grow thinner; dissolve (*fig.* in, en);
⚡ blow (*fuse*); ∼ *sur* swoop upon,
pounce upon; *fig.* bear down upon
(*s.o.*).

fondrière [fɔ̃dri'ɛːr] *f* bog, quag-
mire; hollow (*in the ground*).

fonds [fɔ̃] *m* land, estate; ✝ stock-
in-trade; fund; ∼ *pl.* cash *sg.*, capital *sg.*; means; ✝ public funds;
✝ ∼ *de commerce* business, goodwill; ✝ ∼ *pl. de roulement* working
capital *sg.*, cash reserve *sg.*; ∼ *perdu*
life annuity; F *à* ∼ *perdu* without
security. [melted cheese.\
fondue *cuis.* [fɔ̃'dy] *f* fondue,/
font [fɔ̃] *3rd p. pl. pres. of faire.*

fontaine [fɔ̃'tɛn] *f* fountain; spring;
eau f de ∼ spring water; F *ouvrir la* ∼
turn on the waterworks (= *start to
cry*); **fontainier** [ˌtɛ'nje] *m* foun-
tain-maker; filter-maker; wellsinker;
admin. turncock.

fonte [fɔ̃:t] *f* melting; *ore*: smelting;
metal: casting; *snow*: thawing; *typ.*
fount; cast iron.

fonts *eccl.* [fɔ̃] *m/pl.* (*a.* ∼ *baptismaux*)
font *sg.*; *tenir* (*or porter*) *sur les* ∼
baptismaux stand sponsor to (*a
child*); *fig.* (help to) launch (*s.th.*).

foot F [fut] *m*, **football** *sp.* [fut'bɔl] *m*
(Association) football, F soccer;
footballeur [ˌbɔ'lœːr] *m* footballer.

for [fɔːr] *m*: ∼ *intérieur* conscience;
dans (*or en*) *mon* ∼ *intérieur* in my
heart of hearts.

forage ⊕, ✕ [fɔ'raːʒ] *m* boring,
drilling; bore-hole.

forain, e [fɔ'rɛ̃, ~'rɛn] **1.** adj. † alien, foreign; itinerant; *fête f* ~*e* fun fair; **2.** su. strolling player; hawker.

forban [fɔr'bɑ̃] m hist. buccaneer, pirate; crook, shark.

forçat [fɔr'sa] m convict; † galley-slave.

force [fɔrs] **1.** su./f strength; might; force (a. ⚔, a. ⊕); power (a. ⊕); authority; ~ *aérienne* (*tactique*) (tactical) air force; ~ *de frappe* ⚔ strike force; fig. force(fulness); ⚡ ~ *majeure* overpowering circumstances pl.; ~ *motrice* ⊕ horsepower; fig. motive power; phys. ~ *vive* kinetic energy; momentum; *à* ~ *de* by dint of, by means of; *à toute* ~ despite opposition, at all costs; *de première* ~ first-class …; *de vive* ~ by sheer force; *un cas de* ~ *majeure* an act of God; **2.** adv. † many, plenty of; **forcément** [fɔrse'mɑ̃] adv. necessarily, inevitably.

forcené, e [fɔrsə'ne] **1.** adj. mad, frantic, frenzied; **2.** su./m madman; su./f madwoman.

forcer [fɔr'se] (1k) v/t. force; compel, oblige; ⚔ take by storm; run (a *blockade*); break open; pick (a *lock*); ⚓, ⊕ strain; ⊕ buckle (a *plate*); increase (*one's pace, speed*); être forcé de (*inf.*) be obliged to (*inf.*); **forcerie** ↗ [~sə'ri] f forcing house; forcing bed.

forer ⊕ [fɔ're] (1a) v/t. bore, drill.

forestier, -ère [fɔrɛs'tje, ~'tjɛːr] **1.** adj. forest-…; forest-clad; forester's …; **2.** su./m forester.

foret ⊕ [fɔ're] m drill; bit; gimlet.

forêt [~] f forest (a. fig.); fig. hair: shock; ~ *vierge* virgin forest.

foreur ⊕ [fɔ'rœːr] m borer, driller; **foreuse** [~'røːz] f ⊕ machine: drill; ⚒ rock-drill.

forfaire [fɔr'fɛːr] (4r) v/i. be false (to, *à*); ~ *à* fail in (*one's duty*).

forfait¹ [fɔr'fɛ] m heinous crime.

forfait² sp. [~] m forfeit, fine; withdrawal; *declarer* ~ sp. scratch (a horse); withdraw from the competition (a. fig.); fig. give up.

forfait³ [fɔr'fɛ] m contract; *à* ~ for a fixed sum; by contract; job-(*work*); (*buy, sell*) as a job lot; *travail m à* ~ contract work; **forfaitaire** [~fɛ'tɛːr] lump (*sum*); **forfaiture** [~fɛ'tyːr] f abuse (*of authority*); breach (*of duty, honour*, etc.).

15*

forfanterie [fɔrfɑ̃'tri] f bragging, boasting.

forge [fɔrʒ] f forge, smithy; ~*s* pl. ironworks *usu. sg.*; **forgeable** [fɔr-'ʒabl] forgeable; **forger** [~'ʒe] (1l) v/t. forge; fig. invent; **forgeron** [~ʒə'rɔ̃] m (black)smith; ironsmith; **forgeur** [~'ʒœːr] m forger.

formaliser [fɔrmali'ze] (1a) v/t.: se ~ take offence (at, *de*); **formaliste** [~'list] **1.** adj. formal, stiff; **2.** su. formalist (a. *phls.*); stickler for formalities; **formalité** [~li'te] f formality); ceremony; *une simple* ~ a pure formality; **format** [fɔr'ma] m size (a. *phot.*); book: format; **formateur, -trice** [~ma'tœːr, ~'tris] **1.** adj. formative; **2.** su. former, maker; **formation** [~ma'sjɔ̃] f formation (a. ⚔, ✈); education; ~ (*professionnelle* vocational) training; **forme** [fɔrm] f form (a. ⚡, sp., fig., typ., a. = hare's *lair*); shape; pattern; mo(u)ld; formality; ⚓ dock; ~*s* pl. manners; *en* ~ fit, up to the mark or to scratch; *par* ~ *d'avertissement* by way of warning; *pour la* ~ for the sake of appearances; *sous (la)* ~ *de* in the form of; *prendre* ~ take shape; *prendre la* ~ *de* take the form or shape of; **formel, -elle** [fɔr'mɛl] formal; strict; categorical; **former** [~'me] (1a) v/t. form; fashion, shape; fig. constitute; mo(u)ld; fig. train (*s.o.*).

formidable [fɔrmi'dabl] formidable, dreadful; F terrific, sl. smashing, *Am.* swell.

formique ↗ [fɔr'mik] formic (*acid* etc.).

formulaire [fɔrmy'lɛːr] m formulary; pharmacopoeia; *admin.* form; **formule** [~'myl] f ⚕, ↗, a. fig. formula; ⚕ recipe; *admin.*, ⚕, *post:* form; **formuler** [~my'le] (1a) v/t. formulate, draw up; lodge (a *complaint*); state precisely; fig. put into words; ⚕ ~ *une ordonnance* write out a prescription.

fornication [fɔrnika'sjɔ̃] f fornication.

fors † [fɔːr] prp. except.

fort, forte [fɔːr, fɔrt] **1.** adj. strong; robust; clever (at, *en*); good (at, *en*); large (*sum*); fig. big; ample (*resources*); thick; stout (*person*); heavy (*beard, rain, sea, soil*); steep (*slope*); high (*fever, wind*); fig. difficult; fig. severe; *à plus* ~*e rai-*

son all the more; *esprit m* ~
free-thinker; *se faire* ~ *de* undertake to; **2.** *fort adv.* very; strongly;
loud(ly); **3.** *su./m* strong part;
strong man; *fig.* strong point; *fig.*
height (*of debate, fever, season*); ✕
fort, stronghold; ~ *de la Halle*
market porter.

forteresse ✕ [fɔrtə'rɛs] *f* fortress;
stronghold (*a. fig.*).

fortifiant, e [fɔrti'fjɑ̃, ~'fjɑ̃:t] **1.** *adj.*
strengthening; invigorating; **2.** *su./m*
tonic; **fortification** [~fika'sjɔ̃] *f*
fortification; **fortifier** [~'fje] (1o)
v/t. ✕, *fig.* fortify; strengthen (*a.
fig.*); invigorate; *se* ~ grow stronger.

fortin ✕ [fɔr'tɛ̃] *m* small fort.

fortuit, e [fɔr'tɥi, ~'tɥit] chance...,
accidental.

fortune [fɔr'tyn] *f* fortune, luck;
chance; wealth; *bonne (mauvaise)* ~
good (bad) luck; *dîner à la* ~ *du pot*
take pot-luck; ⚓ *mât m de* ~ jury-
mast; *sans* ~ poor; *tenter* ~ try
one's luck; **fortuné, e** [fɔrty'ne]
fortunate; well-off, rich.

forure ⊕ [fɔ'ry:r] *f* bore(-hole).

fosse [fo:s] *f* pit, hole; trench;
grave; *lions*: den; *mot.* inspection
pit; **fossé** [fo'se] *m* ditch, trench;
castle: moat; **fossette** [~'sɛt] *f*
dimple.

fossile [fɔ'sil] **1.** *adj.* fossilized (*a.
fig.*); **2.** *su./m* fossil (*a. fig.*).

fossoyer ⚚ [foswa'je] (1h) *v/t.*
trench, drain; **fossoyeur** [~'jœ:r]
m grave-digger.

fou (*adj. before vowel or h mute* **fol**)
m, **folle** *f*, *m/pl.* **fous** [fu, fɔl, fu]
1. *adj.* mad, insane, crazy; *fig.*
enormous, tremendous; silly, foolish; *devenir (rendre q.)* ~ go (drive
s.o.) mad; **2.** *su.* lunatic; *su./m* fool;
madman; *chess*: bishop; ~*s pl. du
volant* reckless drivers; *su./f* madwoman.

fouailler † [fwa'je] (1a) *v/t.* flog;
beat.

foudre¹ [fudr] *m* tun.

foudre² [fudr] *f* thunderbolt; lightning; *coup m de* ~ thunderbolt (*a.
fig.*); *fig.* love at first sight; *fig.* bolt
from the blue; *la* ~ *est tombée* lightning struck (at, *à*); **foudroyer**
[fudrwa'je] (1h) *v/t.* strike (by lightning); *fig.* strike down; *fig.* dumbfound, crush; ~ *du regard* look daggers at.

fouëne [fwɛn] *f see* **foëne**.

fouet [fwɛ] *m* whip; ~ (*à œufs*) (egg)
whisk; **fouetter** [fwɛ'te] (1a) *v/t.*
whip; birch; flog (*a child*); whisk
(*eggs*); *rain*: lash against (*a window*);
v/i. lash (*rain*).

fougère ♀ [fu'ʒɛ:r] *f* fern.

fougue [fug] *f* fire, spirit, dash;
(*youthful*) enthusiasm; **fougueux,
-euse** [fu'gø, ~'gø:z] fiery, mettle-
some, spirited (*horse*); impetuous.

fouille [fu:j] *f* excavation; *fig.* search;
fouillé, e [fu'je] detailed, elaborate;
fouiller [~] (1a) *v/t.* dig, excavate;
search (*s.o.*); *v/i.* rummage; **fouillis**
[~'ji] *m* jumble, mess.

fouinard, e F [fwi'na:r, ~'nard] inquisitive; sneaking; **fouine** *zo.*
[fwin] *f* stone marten; **fouiner** F
[fwi'ne] (1a) *v/i.* nose *or* ferret about.

fouir [fwi:r] (2a) *v/t.* dig; **fouisseur,
-euse** [fwi'sœ:r, ~'sø:z] **1.** *adj.*
burrowing (*animal*); **2.** *su./m* bur-
rower, burrowing animal.

foulage [fu'la:ʒ] *m* pressing; ⊕
cloth, leather: fulling; *metall.* ramming; *typ.* impression.

foulard [fu'la:r] *m* silk neckerchief
or handkerchief; *tex.* foulard.

foule [ful] *f* crowd, multitude,
throng; mob; heaps *pl.*; *tex., cloth,
leather*: fulling; **fouler** [fu'le] (1a)
v/t. tread; trample down; press,
crush; ✂ strain, wrench; *tex.* full;
metall. ram; *fig.* ~ *aux pieds* ride
rough-shod over; **foulerie** [ful'ri] *f*
fulling-mill; **fouleur** *tex.* [fu'lœ:r]
m fuller; **foulior** [~'lwa:r] *m tex.*
fulling-stock; fulling-mill; *metall.*
rammer; **foulon** *tex.* [~'lɔ̃] *m person*: fuller; *terre f à* ~ fuller's earth;
foulure ✂ [~'ly:r] *f* sprain, wrench.

four [fu:r] *m* oven; cooker; ⊕ furnace, kiln; *thea., a.* F failure, F
flop; ~ *à chaux* lime-kiln; *faire* ~
be a failure *or* F a flop; *petits* ~*s*
pl. small fancy cakes.

fourbe [furb] **1.** *adj.* rascally;
double-dealing; **2.** *su.* cheat; **fourberie** [furbə'ri] *f* swindle; deceit,
trickery; *Am.* skulduggery.

fourbi F [fur'bi] *m* equipment, ✕
kit; thingumajig; **fourbir** [~'bi:r]
(2a) *v/t.* furbish, polish up.

fourbu, e [fur'by] tired out, exhausted.

fourche [furʃ] *f* fork; *en* ~ forked;
fourcher [fur'ʃe] (1a) *v/i.* fork,

branch; *fig. la langue m'a fourché* I made a slip of the tongue; **fourchet** [ʌˈʃɛ] *m* fork; *vet.* foot-rot; **fourchette** [ʌˈʃɛt] *f* (table)fork; wishbone; *statistics etc.*: bracket; *prices etc.*: range; *avoir un bon coup de ʌ* be a hearty eater; **fourchon** [ʌˈʃɔ̃] *m* fork: prong; *bough*: fork; **fourchu, e** [ʌˈʃy] forked; cloven (*hoof*).

fourgon¹ [furˈgɔ̃] *m* van, waggon; 🚂 luggage van, *Am.* baggage *or* freight car.

fourgon² [furˈgɔ̃] *m* poker, fire-rake; **fourgonner** [ʌgɔˈne] (1a) *v/t.* poke (*the fire*); *v/i.* poke (the fire); *fig.* poke about (in, *dans*).

fourgonnette *mot.* [furgɔˈnɛt] *f* light van.

fourmi *zo.* [furˈmi] *f* ant; ʌ *blanche* termite; *fig. avoir des ʌs* have pins and needles; **fourmilier** *zo.* [furmiˈlje] *m* ant-eater; **fourmilière** [ʌˈljɛːr] *f* ant-hill, ants' nest; *fig.* swarm, nest; **fourmi(-)lion,** *pl.* **fourmis(-)lions** *zo.* [ʌˈljɔ̃] *m* ant-lion; **fourmiller** [ʌˈje] (1a) *v/i.* swarm, teem (with, *de*); *fig.* tingle.

fournaise *poet., a. fig.* [furˈnɛːz] *f* furnace; **fourneau** [ʌˈno] *m* ⊕ furnace; cooker, stove; 🔨, ⚒ *mine*: chamber; *pipe*: bowl; *sl.* fool, idiot; *metall. haut* ʌ blast-furnace; **fournée** [ʌˈne] *f* ovenful (⊕, *metall.* charge; ⊕ *bricks*: baking; *loaves, a. fig.*: batch.

fourni, e [furˈni] supplied; thick, abundant; bushy (*beard*).

fournier [furˈnje] *m* baker; oven-man; **fournil** [ʌˈni] *m* bakehouse.

fourniment ⚒ [furniˈmɑ̃] *m* kit, equipment; **fournir** [ʌˈniːr] (2a) *v/t.* furnish, supply, equip (with, *de*); provide; ✝ stock (*a shop*); **fournisseur** ✝ [ʌniˈsœːr] *m* supplier, caterer; tradesman; **fourniture** [ʌˈtyːr] *f* supplying; ʌs *pl.* supplies; equipment *sg.*

fourrage [fuˈraːʒ] *m* forage, fodder; ⚒ foraging; **fourrager** [furaˈʒe] (1l) *v/i.* forage; *fig.* rummage, search; *v/t. fig.* ravage; **fourragère** ⚒ [ʌˈʒɛːr] **1.** *su./f* forage waggon; lanyard; shoulder-braid; **2.** *adj./f*: *plante f* ʌ fodder plant.

fourré, e [fuˈre] fur-lined; furry; lined; filled (with, *de*); *fig. coup m* ʌ backhanded blow; *paix f* ʌe sham peace.

fourreau [fuˈro] *m* 🗡 sheath (*a. cost., a. fig.*); case; ⊕ sleeve; ⊕ *cylinder*: liner.

fourrer [fuˈre] (1a) *v/t.* line with fur; stuff, thrust; cram; ⊦ stick, poke; ⊕ pack (*a joint*); se ʌ wrap o.s. up; hide o.s.; thrust o.s.; **fourreur** [ʌˈrœːr] *m* furrier.

fourrier [fuˈrje] *m* 🗡 quartermaster-sergeant; *fig.* forerunner; **fourrière** [ʌˈrjɛːr] *f* pound; *emmener une voiture à la ʌ, mettre une voiture en ʌ* tow a car away.

fourrure [fuˈryːr] *f* fur; skin; lining (*a. mot. brake*); ⊕ *joint*: packing; 🔺 filler-block.

fourvoyer [furvwaˈje] (1h) *v/t.* lead astray, mislead; se ʌ go astray; be mistaken.

foutaise ⊦ [fuˈtɛːz] *f* rubbish, rot.

foutre V [futr] **1.** (4a) *v/t.* throw; give; do; ʌ *la paix à q.* leave s.o. alone; shut up; ʌ *le camp* clear out, go; ʌ *q. dedans* do *or* cheat s.o.; *je m'en fous* I don't care, I don't give a damn; se ʌ *de* not to care a hang *or sl.* a damn about; **2.** *int.* gosh!; damn it!; **foutu, e** ⊦ [fuˈty] damned, *Br. sl.* bloody; done for, finished, *sl.* bust(ed).

fox *zo.* [fɔks] *m* (*a. fox-terrier*) fox terrier; ʌ**-trot** [ʌˈtrɔt] *m/inv.* foxtrot.

foyer [fwaˈje] *m* hearth, fire(-place); *fig.* home; ⊕ fire-box, combustion chamber; *boiler*: furnace; 🔬, 🔬, *phot., phys.* focus; *hotel*: lounge; *fig.* seat, centre; *thea.* ʌ *des artistes* green-room; ʌ *des étudiants* (university) hall of residence; *building*: Students' Union.

frac [frak] *m* dress-coat.

fracas [fraˈka] *m* crash; din, shindy; **fracassant, e** [ʌkaˈsɑ̃, ʌˈsɑ̃ːt] deafening (*noise*); *fig.* sensational, ⊦ shattering, ⊦ thundering; **fracasser** [ʌkaˈse] (1a) *v/t.* shatter; smash to pieces.

fraction [frakˈsjɔ̃] *f* fraction (*a.* 🔺), portion; *pol.* group; 🔺 ʌ *continue* continued fraction; **fractionnaire** [fraksjɔˈnɛːr] fractional; *nombre m* ʌ mixed number; improper fraction; **fractionner** [ʌˈne] (1a) *v/t.* split up; ⊕, 🔬 fractionate; crack (*mineral oils*); fractionize.

fracture [frakˈtyːr] *f* breaking open; *lock*: forcing; 🦴, *geol.* fracture; **fracturer** [ʌtyˈre] (1a) *v/t.* break

open; force (*a lock*); ⚒ fracture, break; ⚒ se ~ un bras fracture or break one's arm.

fragile [fra'ʒil] fragile; brittle; *fig.* weak; ☞ *inscription*: with care; **fragilité** [⁓ʒili'te] *f* fragility; brittleness; *fig.* weakness, frailty.

fragment [frag'mɑ̃] *m* fragment, bit; snatch (*of a song*); **fragmentaire** [⁓mɑ̃'tɛːr] fragmentary; in fragments.

frai [frɛ] *m* spawning (season); spawn; fry.

fraîcheur [frɛ'ʃœːr] *f* freshness (*a. fig.*); coolness; *fig.* bloom (*a. of flowers*); **fraîchir** [⁓'ʃiːr] (2a) *v/i.* grow colder; freshen (*wind*).

frais¹, **fraîche** [frɛ, frɛʃ] **1.** *adj.* fresh; cool; recent; new (*bread*); wet (*paint*); new-laid (*egg*); **2.** *adv.*: frais arrivé just arrived; fleur *f* fraîche cueillie freshly gathered or picked flower; **3.** *su./m* cool; coolness; au ~ in a cool place; de ~ freshly.

frais² [frɛ] *m/pl.* cost *sg.*, expenses; outlay *sg.*; fees; ⚖ costs; charges; ~ de livraison delivery charges; ~ d'entretien maintenance costs, upkeep *sg.*; ☞ ~ de port en plus carriage *sg.* extra; ~ de transport freight charges; carriage *sg.*; aux ~ de at the expense of; faire les ~ de bear the cost of; *fig.* provide the topic(s) of (*a conversation*); peu de ~ small cost *sg.*; ... pour ~ d'envoi postage and packing ...

fraise¹ [frɛːz] *f* ⚘ strawberry; ⚒ strawberry mark, n(a)evus.

fraise² [⁓] *f cuis.* calf, *lamb*: crow; *turkey*: wattle; *collar*: ruff.

fraise³ ⊕ [frɛːz] *f* countersink (bit); mill; ⊕ ~ champignon (or conique) rose bit.

fraiser ⊕ [frɛ'ze] (1a) *v/t.* mill; countersink.

fraiseuse ⊕ [frɛ'zøːz] *f* milling machine. [plant.)

fraisier ⚘ [frɛ'zje] *m* strawberry)

framboise [frɑ̃'bwaːz] *f* raspberry; **framboiser** [frɑ̃bwa'ze] (1a) *v/t.* flavo(u)r with raspberry; **framboisier** ⚘ [⁓'zje] *m* raspberry-bush.

franc¹, **franche** [frɑ̃, frɑ̃ːʃ] **1.** *adj.* frank; free; open, candid; straightforward; fair (*play*); *fig.* real, pure; ~ de port carriage paid; post-free; foot. coup *m* ~ free kick; **2.** franc *adv.* frankly; candidly; pour parler ~ to be frank.

franc² [frɑ̃] *m coin*: franc; pour un ~ de a franc's worth of.

franc³, **franque** [frɑ̃, frɑ̃ːk] **1.** *adj.* Frankish; **2.** *su.* ♀ Frank; *in Levant*: European.

français, **e** [frɑ̃'sɛ, ⁓'sɛːz] **1.** *adj.* French; **2.** *su./m ling.* French; ♀ Frenchman; les ♀ *m/pl.* the French; *su./f* ♀ Frenchwoman.

franchement [frɑ̃ʃ'mɑ̃] *adv.* frankly; openly; straight (out); F really.

franchir [frɑ̃'ʃiːr] (2a) *v/t.* jump over, clear; cross; pass through; ⚓ weather (*a headland*); *fig.* overcome; **franchise** [⁓'ʃiːz] *f* frankness; openness; *city*: freedom; *admin.* exemption; ~ de bagages baggage (*Am.* luggage) allowance; en ~ duty-free; **franchissable** [⁓ʃi'sabl] passable (*river*); negotiable (*hill*).

franciser [frɑ̃si'ze] (1a) *v/t.* gallicize; **franciste** [⁓'sist] *su.* French scholar or specialist.

franc-maçon, *pl.* **francs-maçons** [frɑ̃ma'sɔ̃] *m* freemason; **franc-maçonnerie** [⁓sɔn'ri] *f* freemasonry.

franco ☞ [frɑ̃'ko] *adv.* free (of charge).

francophone [frɑ̃kɔ'fɔn] **1.** *adj.* French-speaking; **2.** *su.* French-speaking person.

franc-tireur, *pl.* **francs-tireurs** [frɑ̃ti'rœːr] *m* ✗ sniper; *fig.* free lance.

frange [frɑ̃ːʒ] *f* fringe; fringe group; **franger** [frɑ̃'ʒe] (11) *v/t.* fringe.

frangin *sl.* [frɑ̃'ʒɛ̃] *m* brother; **frangine** *sl.* [⁓'ʒin] *f* sister.

franquette F [frɑ̃'kɛt] *adv.*: à la bonne ~ without ceremony.

frappage ⊕ [fra'paːʒ] *m* stamping; striking; *coins*: minting; **frappe** [frap] *f* minting; striking; stamp; **frappé**, **e** [fra'pe] iced; **frapper** [⁓'pe] (1a) *v/t.* strike (*a. fig.*), hit; mint (*money*); ice (*a drink*); type (*a letter*); punch (out) (*a design*); F se ~ get alarmed; *v/i.* strike; knock (at the door, à la porte); ~ du pied stamp one's foot; ~ juste strike home; **frappeur** [⁓'pœːr] **1.** *su./m* ⊕ *etc.* striker; *tel.* tapper; ⊕ stamper; puncher; **2.** *adj./m*: esprit *m* ~ rapping spirit.

frasque [frask] *f* escapade.

fraternel, **-elle** [fratɛr'nɛl] fraternal, brotherly; **fraterniser** [⁓ni'ze]

(1a) *v/i.* fraternize (with, *avec*); **fraternité** [‿ni'te] *f* fraternity, brotherhood.
fratricide [fratri'sid] **1.** *su. person*: fratricide; *su./m crime*: fratricide; **2.** *adj.* fratricidal.
fraude [fro:d] *f* fraud, deception; ‿ *fiscale* tax evasion; *faire entrer en* ‿ smuggle in; **frauder** [fro'de] (1a) *v/i.* cheat; *v/t.* defraud, cheat, swindle; **fraudeur, -euse** [‿'dœ:r, ‿'dø:z] **1.** *adj.* fraudulent; **2.** *su.* defrauder; cheat; ‿ *fiscal(e)* tax evader.
frayer [frɛ'je] (1i) *v/t.* rub; clear (*a path, a way*); *se* ‿ *un chemin* make a way for o.s.; *v/i.* spawn (*fish*); ‿ *avec* associate with.
frayeur [frɛ'jœ:r] fright, terror.
fredaine [frə'dɛn] *f* escapade; *faire des* ‿*s* sow one's wild oats.
fredonner [frədɔ'ne] (1a) *v/t.* hum (*a tune*).
frégate [fre'gat] *f* ⚓ frigate; *orn.* frigate-bird.
frein [frɛ̃] *m mot. etc., a. fig.* brake; *fig. a.* curb, restraint; *horse*: bit; ‿ *à air comprimé* air-brake; ‿ *à rétropédalage* back-pedalling brake; 🚗 ‿ *de secours* emergency-brake; ‿*s pl. à disque* disc brakes; ‿ *sur jante* rim-brake; *mettre un* ‿ *à* curb, bridle; *ronger son* ‿ champ the bit; **freinage** [frɛ'na:ʒ] *m* braking; *puissance de* ‿ braking power; *mot. traces f/pl. de* ‿ skid marks; **freiner** [frɛ'ne] (1a) *vt/i. mot.* brake; *v/i. mot.* apply the brakes; *v/t. mot.* apply the brakes to; *fig.* restrain, curb; *fig.* put a brake on, check.
frelater [frəla'te] (1a) *v/t.* adulterate (*food, wine*).
frêle [frɛl] frail, weak.
frelon *zo.* [frə'lɔ̃] *m* hornet.
freluquet F [frəly'kɛ] *m* whipper-snapper.
frémir [fre'mi:r] (2a) *v/i.* tremble, shudder; rustle (*leaves*); quiver (*a. fig. with, de*); **frémissement** [‿mis'mɑ̃] *m* quiver(ing); shudder(ing); *leaves*: rustle; *wind*: sighing.
frêne ♀ [frɛ:n] *m* ash(-tree).
frénésie [frene'zi] *f* frenzy, madness; **frénétique** [‿'tik] *m* frantic; frenzied (*a. fig.*).
fréquemment [freka'mɑ̃] *adv. of fréquent*; **fréquence** [fre'kɑ̃:s] *f* ⚡, ⚡, *etc.* frequency; **fréquent, e** [‿'kɑ̃, ‿'kɑ̃:t] frequent; ⚡ rapid

(*pulse*); **fréquentation** [‿kɑ̃ta'sjɔ̃] *f* frequenting; association (with, *de*); regular attendance (at, *de*); (*a.* ‿*s pl.*) company (*sg.*); **fréquenté, e** [‿kɑ̃'te]: (*très* ‿ very) busy (*place*); *bien* (*mal*) ‿ of good (ill) repute; **fréquenter** [‿kɑ̃'te] (1a) *v/t.* frequent; visit; see (*s.o.*) frequently); attend (*s.th.*) frequently.
frère [frɛ:r] *m* brother; *eccl.* monk; friar; *faux* ‿ traitor, double-crosser.
frérot F [fre'ro] *m* little brother.
fresque [frɛsk] *f* fresco.
fret ⚓ [frɛ] *m* freight; cargo; *prendre à* ‿ charter; **frètement** ⚓ [frɛt'mɑ̃] *m* chartering; **fréter** [fre'te] (1f) *v/t.* freight; charter; fit out (*a ship*); F hire (*a car etc.*); **fréteur** [‿'tœ:r] *m* shipowner; charterer.
frétiller [freti'je] (1a) *v/i.* wriggle; wag (*tail*); *fig.* fidget.
fretin [frə'tɛ̃] *m*: (*le menu* ‿ the small) fry.
freudien, -enne [frø'djɛ̃, ‿'djɛn] Freudian.
friable [fri'abl] crumbly.
friand, e [fri'ɑ̃, ‿'ɑ̃:d] dainty; ‿ *de* partial to; **friandise** [‿ɑ̃'di:z] *f* titbit, delicacy; epicurism.
fric *sl.* [frik] *m* dough (= *money*).
fricandeau *cuis.* [frikɑ̃'do] *m* stewed larded veal; **fricassée** *cuis.* [frika-'se] *f* fricassee, hash; **fricasser** [‿'se] (1a) *v/t. cuis.* fricassee; *fig.* squander; **fricasseur** *m*, **-euse** *f* F [‿'sœ:r, ‿'sø:z] poor cook; *fig.* squanderer; *journ.* ‿ *d'articles* pot-boiler.   [glary.\
fric-frac *sl.* [frik'frak] *m/inv.* bur-\
friche 🌱 [friʃ] *f* fallow land; waste land; *en* ‿ fallow; *fig.* undeveloped.
fricoter F [friko'te] (1a) *vt/i.* stew; cook (up) (*a. fig.*); F *fig. a.* be up to (*s.th.*); **fricoteur** *m*, **-euse** *f* F [‿'tœ:r, ‿'tø:z] schemer; wangler; trafficker.
friction [frik'sjɔ̃] *f* ⊕ friction; *scalp*: massage; ✿ rubbing; *sp.* rub-down; **frictionner** [‿sjɔ'ne] (1a) *v/t.* rub; give (*s.o.*) a rub-down; massage (*s.o.'s scalp*); give (*s.o.*) a dry shampoo.
frigidaire (*TM*) [friʒi'dɛ:r] *m* refrigerator; F *fig. mettre qch. au* ‿ put s.th. on ice *or* into cold storage.
frigidité ✿ [friʒidi'te] *f* frigidity.
frigo F [fri'go] *m* refrigerator, *Br.* F

fridge; **frigorifier** [frigɔriˈfje] (1o) v/t. refrigerate; *viande f frigorifiée* frozen meat; **frigorifique** [ˌʷˈfik] refrigerating, chilling.

frileux, -euse [friˈlø, ˌʷˈløːz] chilly.

frimas [friˈmɑ] m hoar-frost.

frime F [frim] f sham; *pour la ˌʷ for* the sake of appearances.

frimousse F [friˈmus] f little face.

fringale F [frɛ̃ˈgal] f keen appetite.

fringant, e [frɛ̃ˈgɑ̃, ˌʷˈgɑ̃ːt] frisky, lively; *fig.* dashing (*person*).

fringues [frɛ̃ːg] f/pl. togs.

friper [friˈpe] (1a) v/t. crease; crumple; *se ˌʷ get crumpled*; **friperie** [ˌʷˈpri] f old clothes *pl.*; second-hand goods *pl. or* business; old-clothes shop *or* business; *fig.* rubbish; **fripier** m, -**ère** f [ˌʷˈpje, ˌʷˈpjɛːr] dealer in old clothes; second-hand dealer.

fripon, -onne [friˈpɔ̃, ˌʷˈpɔn] 1. *adj.* roguish; 2. *su.* rascal; **friponnerie** [ˌʷpɔnˈri] f (piece of) mischief, prank(s *pl.*).

fripouille F [friˈpuːj] f bad lot, cad.

frire [friːr] (4s) vt/i. (*a. faire ˌʷ*) fry.

frise[1] [friːz] f △ frieze; *thea.* ˌʷs *pl.* borders.

frise[2] *tex.* [ˌʷ] f frieze; *see cheval.*

friselis [frizˈli] m rustle.

friser [friˈze] (1a) v/t. curl; wave; crimp (*cloth*); skim, graze; *fig.* verge on, border on; v/i. curl (*hair*); **frisoir** [ˌʷˈzwaːr] m (hair-)curler; curling-tongs *pl.*

frison[1] [friˈzɔ̃] m curl, ringlet.

frison[2], -**onne** [friˈzɔ̃, ˌʷˈzɔn] *adj., a. su.* ♀ Frisian.

frisquet, -ette F [frisˈkɛ, ˌʷˈkɛt] chilly, *sl.* parky.

frisson [friˈsɔ̃] m shiver, shudder; *pleasure*: thrill; **frissonner** [ˌʷsɔˈne] (1a) v/i. (with, *de*) shiver, shudder; quiver; be thrilled.

frit, e [fri, frit] *p.p. of frire*; **friterie** [friˈtri] f fried-fish shop *or* stall; **frites** F [frit] f/pl. chipped potatoes, F chips, *Am.* French fries, French fried potatoes; **friteuse** [friˈtøːz] f deep-frying pan; **frittage** ⊕ [friˈtaːʒ] m sintering; roasting; **fritter** ⊕ [ˌʷˈte] (1a) v/t. roast; sinter; **friture** [ˌʷˈtyːr] f frying; frying fat; fried fish; *radio, teleph.*: crackling.

frivole [friˈvɔl] frivolous; *fig.* trifling; **frivolité** [ˌʷvɔliˈte] f frivolity; *fig.* trifle; *lace*: tatting.

froc *eccl.* [frɔk] m cowl; frock; **fro-card** *sl.* [frɔˈkaːr] m monk.

froid, froide [frwa, frwad] 1. *adj.* cold (*a. fig. smile, reception*); chilly (*a. fig. manner*); frigid (*style*); *à ˌʷ* in the cold state; when cold (*a. cuis.*); *avoir ˌʷ* be cold (*person*); *battre ˌʷ à* cold-shoulder (*s.o.*); *en ˌʷ avec* on chilly terms with, cool towards; *faire ˌʷ* be cold (*weather*); *prendre ˌʷ* catch a chill; 2. *su./m* cold; *fig.* coldness; ✝ *industrie f du ˌʷ* refrigeration industry; **froideur** [frwaˈdœːr] f coldness; chilliness; indifference; *fig.* chill; ✽ frigidity.

froissement [frwasˈmɑ̃] m crumpling; rustle; bruising; *fig.* conflict; giving *or* taking offence; **froisser** [frwaˈse] (1a) v/t. crumple, crease; *fig.* offend, hurt, ruffle (*s.o.*); *se ˌʷ* take offence (at, *de*); **froissure** [ˌʷˈsyːr] f *cloth, paper*: crumple.

frôlement [frolˈmɑ̃] m light brushing; light touch; **frôler** [froˈle] (1a) v/t. graze; brush against *or* past; *fig.* come near to.

fromage [frɔˈmaːʒ] m cheese; *fig.* F cushy job; *ˌʷ de tête* pork brawn; **fromager, -ère** [ˌʷmaˈʒe, ˌʷˈʒɛːr] 1. *adj.* cheese...; 2. *su.* cheesemonger; cheesemaker; **fromagerie** [ˌʷmaʒˈri] f cheesemonger's (shop); cheese dairy.

froment ✔ [frɔˈmɑ̃] m wheat.

fronce [frɔ̃ːs] f crease; *dress etc.*: gather; **froncement** [frɔ̃sˈmɑ̃] m puckering; *ˌʷ des sourcils* frown; **froncer** [frɔ̃ˈse] (1k) v/t. pucker, wrinkle; gather (*one's skirt etc.*); *ˌʷ les sourcils* frown; scowl; **froncis** [ˌʷˈsi] m skirt, dress: gathering.

frondaison [frɔ̃dɛˈzɔ̃] f foliage, leaves *pl.*; foliation.

fronde [frɔ̃ːd] f sling; (toy) catapult; *hist. la* ♀ the Fronde (*1648 - 1653*); **fronder** [frɔ̃ˈde] (1a) v/t. sling, catapult (*a stone*); hit with a sling; (*a. ˌʷ contre*) scoff at; **frondeur** m, -**euse** f [ˌʷˈdœːr, ˌʷˈdøːz] 1. *su.* slinger; *hist.* member of the Fronde; *fig.* scoffer; F grouser; 2. *adj.* bantering; irreverent.

front [frɔ̃] m front (*a.* ✖); forehead; brow; face; *fig.* impudence, cheek; *pol.* ♀ *populaire* Popular Front; *de ˌʷ* abreast; front-...; head-on (*collision*); at once; *faire ˌʷ à* face (*s.th.*); **frontal, e**, m/pl. -**aux** [frɔ̃ˈtal, ˌʷˈto]

1. *adj.* frontal, front-...; *mot. collision* ⸾e head-on collision; **2.** *su./m horse:* headband; *anat.* frontal (bone);
fronteau [⸾'to] *m horse:* headband; **Δ** frontal; *eccl.* frontlet; **frontière** [⸾'tjɛːr] **1.** *su./f* frontier; border; boundary; **2.** *adj./f: ville f* ⸾ frontier town; **frontispice** [⸾tis'pis] *m* frontispiece (*a.* **Δ**); titlepage.
fronton [frɔ̃'tɔ̃] *m* **Δ** fronton, pediment; *pelota:* front wall.
frottage [frɔ'taːʒ] *m* polishing; rubbing; *flesh:* chafing; *metal:* scouring; **frottée** F [⸾'te] *f* thrashing; **frottement** [frɔt'mã] *m* rubbing; chafing; ⊕ friction; **frotter** [frɔ'te] (1a) *v/t.* rub; chafe (*one's leg*); polish; scour (*metal*); strike (*a match*); F thrash; *paint.* scumble; *fig.* se ⸾ *à q.* associate with s.o.; come up against s.o.; *v/i.* rub; **frottoir** [⸾'twaːr] *m* polishing cloth, polisher; ⊕ friction-plate; ⨍ brush.
frou(-)frou [fru'fru] *m gown:* rustle, swish; **froufrouter** [⸾fru'te] (1a) *v/i.* rustle, swish.
froussard, e *sl.* [fru'saːr, ⸾'sard] **1.** *adj.* cowardly, *sl.* chicken; **2.** *su.* coward; **frousse** *sl.* [frus] *f* fear, F funk; *avoir la* ⸾ be scared.
fructifier [frykti'fje] (1o) *v/i.* bear fruit; **fructueux, -euse** [⸾'tɥø, ⸾'tɥøːz] fruitful, profitable.
frugal, e, *m/pl.* **-aux** [fry'gal, ⸾'go] frugal; **frugalité** [⸾gali'te] *f* frugality.
fruit [frɥi] *m* fruit; *fig.* advantage, profit; *fig.* result; ⚖ profit, revenue; *zo.* ⸾s *pl.* de mer fish and shellfish, *Am.* sea-food *sg.*; ⸾ sec dried fruit; *fig. person:* failure; **fruité, e** [frɥi'te] fruity (*wine, olives*); **fruiterie** [⸾'tri] *f* store-room for fruit; fruiterer's (shop); greengrocery; **fruitier, -ère** [⸾'tje, ⸾'tjɛːr] **1.** *adj.* fruit-bearing; fruit(-*tree*); **2.** *su.* fruiterer, greengrocer; *su./m* store-room for fruit.
frusques *sl.* [frysk] *f/pl.* togs (= *clothes*).
fruste [fryst] rough (*a. fig.*).
frustration [frystra'sjɔ̃] *f* frustration; **frustrer** [frys'tre] (1a) *v/t.* frustrate; ⸾ *q. de qch.* deprive s.o. of s.th.; cheat s.o. out of s.th.
fuel(-oil) [fjul, fju'lɔjl] *m* fuel-oil.
fugace [fy'gas] fleeting, passing, transient.

fugitif, -ve [fyʒi'tif, ⸾'tiːv] **1.** *adj.* fugitive; *fig.* fleeting, passing, transient; **2.** *su.* fugitive.
fugue [fyg] *f* ♪ fugue; running away; *faire une* ⸾ run away.
fuir [fɥiːr] (2d) *v/i.* flee, run away; leak (*barrel*); recede (*forehead, landscape*); *v/t.* avoid, shun; **fuis** [fɥi] *1st p. sg. pres. and p.s. of fuir;* **fuite** [fɥit] *f* flight; escape; *gas, liquid, a. fig.* secrets: leak, leakage; shunning; *mettre en* ⸾ put to flight; *prendre la* ⸾ take to flight, F take to one's heels.
fulgurant, e [fylgy'rã, ⸾'rãːt] flashing; fulgurating (*pain*); **fulguration** [⸾ra'sjɔ̃] *f* flashing; ⚡ fulguration; **fulgurer** [⸾'re] (1a) *v/i.* flash, fulgurate. [smoky, sooty; murky.\
fuligineux, -euse [fyliʒi'nø, ⸾'nøːz]⎰
fulmicoton [fylmikɔ'tɔ̃] *m see cotonpoudre;* **fulmination** *eccl.,* ⚗ [⸾na-'sjɔ̃] *f* fulmination; **fulminer** [⸾'ne] (1a) *vt/i.* fulminate; *v/i.: fig.* ⸾ *contre* fulminate against.
fumage¹ ⚹ [fy'maːʒ] *m* dunging, dressing; manure.
fumage² [⸾] *fish, meat:* smoking.
fume-cigare(tte) [fymsi'gaːr, ⸾ga-'rɛt] *m/inv.* cigar(ette)-holder.
fumée [fy'me] *f* smoke; *soup:* steam; fumes *pl.; fig.* vanity.
fumer¹ [⸾] (1a) *v/t.* smoke (*cigars, fish, meat*); *v/i.* smoke; steam; *fig.* ⸾ *de colère* fume.
fumer² ⚹ [⸾] (1a) *v/t.* manure, dung (*the soil*).
fumerie [fym'ri] *f* † *tobacco etc.:* smoking; *opium:* den; **fumeron** [⸾'rɔ̃] *m* smoky charcoal; **fumet** [fy'mɛ] *m cooking:* aroma; *wine:* bouquet; *cuis.* concentrate; *hunt.* scent; **fumeur** *m,* **-euse** *f* [⸾'mœːr, ⸾'møːz] smoker; *su./m* 🚬 F smoker, smoking compartment; **fumeux, -euse** [⸾'mø, ⸾'møːz] smoky; heady (*wine*); *fig.* hazy.
fumier [fy'mje] *m* manure, dung; dunghill; *fig. mourir sur le* ⸾ die in squalor.
fumiste [fy'mist] *m* stove-setter; F humbug; F practical joker; **fumisterie** [⸾mis'tri] *f* stove-setting; F practical joke; *sl.* monkey business; **fumivore** ⊕ [⸾mi'vɔːr] *m* smoke-consumer; **fumoir** [⸾-'mwaːr] *m* smoking-room; smokehouse (*for curing of fish, meat*).

funèbre [fy'nɛbr] funeral; gloomy, funereal; **funérailles** [fyne'rɑːj] f/pl. funeral sg.; obsequies; **funéraire** [ʌ'rɛːr] funeral; tomb(stone).

funeste [fy'nɛst] fatal, deadly.

funiculaire [fyniky'lɛːr] 1. adj. funicular; 2. su./m funicular railway.

fur [fyːr] m: au ~ et à mesure progressively, gradually; au ~ et à mesure que (as soon) as; (in proportion) as; au ~ et à mesure de according to.

furet [fy're] m zo. ferret; fig. Nosey Parker, Paul Pry; **fureter** [fyr-'te] (1d) v/i. ferret (a. fig.); fig. rummage, nose about; **fureteur, -euse** [ʌ'tœːr, ʌ'tøːz] 1. adj. prying; 2. su. ferreter; fig. rummager; Nosey Parker.

fureur [fy'rœːr] f fury, rage; passion; aimer avec (or à la) ~ be passionately fond of; fig. faire ~ be all the rage; **furibond, e** [ʌri'bɔ̃, ʌ-'bɔ̃ːd] 1. adj. furious; 2. su. furious person; **furie** [ʌ'ri] f fury, rage; fig. avec ~ frantically, wildly; entrer en ~ become furious; **furieux, -euse** [ʌ'rjø, ʌ'rjøːz] furious, mad, raging.

furole [fy'rɔl] f will-o'-the-wisp.

furoncle [fy'rɔ̃ːkl] m furuncle; F boil. [stealthy.]

furtif, -ve [fyr'tif, ʌ'tiːv] furtive,]

fus [fy] 1st p. sg. p.s. of être 1.

fusain [fy'zɛ̃] m ♀ spindle-tree; (drawing-)charcoal; charcoal sketch; **fuseau** [ʌ'zo] m tex. spindle; ⊕ spherical lune; ⊕ roller-chain: link-pin; ⊕ trundle: stave; biol. nucleus spindle; cost. pantalon m ~ tapering or peg-top trousers pl.; ~ horaire time zone; en ~ tapering (at both ends); F fig. jambes f/pl. en ~ spindle-shanks.

fusée¹ [fy'ze] f tex. spindleful; ⊕ spindle.

fusée² [ʌ] f ✗ bomb etc.: fuse; ✗, phys. rocket; ~ éclairante flare; ~ engin booster, carrier vehicle; avion m ~ rocket-propelled aircraft; lancer une ~ send up a flare.

fuselage ✈ [fyz'laːʒ] m fuselage; **fuselé, e** [ʌ'le] spindle-shaped; tapering; mot. stream-lined; **fuseler** [ʌ'le] (1c) v/t. taper; mot. stream-line.

fuser [fy'ze] (1a) v/i. run, spread (colours); fuse, melt; fig. burst out (laughter); ♫ crackle, F fizz; slake (lime); burn slowly (fuse); **fusible** [ʌ'zibl] 1. adj. fusible; 2. su./m ✗ fuse(-wire).

fusil [fy'zi] m rifle, gun; ~ de chasse shotgun; à portée de ~ within gunshot; coup m de ~ shot; **fusilier** ✗ [fyzi'lje] m fusilier; **fusillade** [ʌ'jad] f rifle-fire, fusillade; (execution by) shooting; **fusiller** [ʌ'je] (1a) v/t. shoot; sl. smash (up), mess up.

fusion [fy'zjɔ̃] f fusion (a. fig.), melting; ✝ merger; **fusionner** [ʌzjɔ'ne] (1a) vt/i. a. se ~ amalgamate, merge.

fustiger [fysti'ʒe] (1l) v/t. censure, denounce; fig. flay; † thrash.

fût [fy] m gun: stock; tools etc.: handle; △ chimney, column, etc.: shaft; barrel, cask; box, drum: body; beer: wood; ♀ tree: bole.

futaie [fy'tɛ] f forest; arbre m de haute ~ full-grown tree, timber tree; **futaille** [ʌ'taːj] f cask, tun.

futaine tex. [fy'tɛn] f fustian.

futé, e F [fy'te] sharp, cunning.

futile [fy'til] futile; trifling; **futilité** [ʌtili'te] f futility; ~s pl. trifles.

futur, e [fy'tyːr] 1. adj. future; 2. su./m intended (husband); gramm. future; su./f intended (wife); **futurisme** paint. [ʌty'rism] m futurism; **futuriste** [ʌty'rist] 1. su. futurist; 2. adj. futuristic; **futurologie** [ʌtyrɔlɔ'ʒi] f futurology; **futurologue** [ʌtyrɔ'lɔg] su. futurologist.

fuyant, e [fɥi'jɑ̃, ʌ'jɑ̃ːt] fleeing; fleeting (moment); shifty (eyes); fig. receding (forehead, a. paint. etc. line); **fuyard, e** [ʌ'jaːr, ʌ'jard] 1. su. fugitive; 2. adj. timid; **fuyons** [ʌ'jɔ̃] 1st p. pl. pres. of fuir.

G

G, g [ʒe] *m* G, g.

gabare ⚓ [gaˈbaːr] *f* lighter; trans-port-vessel; drag-net; **gabarier** [ˌba'rje] *m* barge: skipper; bargee, lighterman.

gabarit [gabaˈri] *m* size; *fig.* calibre; *ships*: model; ⊕ template; ⊕ clear-ance; 🚋, ⊕ ga(u)ge; *fig.* sort, kind; *fig. du même* ~ of the same sort.

gabelle† [gaˈbɛl] *f* salt-tax; **gabelou** *pej.* [ˌˈblu] *m* customs officer.

gabier ⚓ [gaˈbje] *m* topman.

gâche¹ ⊕ [gɑːʃ] *f* staple; wall-hook; catch; *pawl*: notch.

gâche² [gɑːʃ] *f* ⊕ trowel; *cuis.* spatula; **gâcher** [gɑˈʃe] (1a) *v/t.* mix (*mortar*); slack, slake (*lime*); *fig.* waste; spoil; bungle (*work*).

gâchette [gɑˈʃɛt] *f lock*: spring-catch; ⊕ pawl; *gun-lock*: tumbler; F *gun*: trigger.

gâcheur, -euse [gɑˈʃœːr, ~ˈʃøːz] *su.* bungler; *su./m* △ builder's labo(u)r-er; **gâchis** [ˌˈʃi] *m* △ wet mortar; mud; F *fig.* mess.

gadget [gaˈdʒɛ(t)] *m* gadget; **gad-getiser** [ˌdʒɛtiˈze] (1a) *v/t.* make a gadget out of; fit up with gadgets; customize (*a car etc.*).   [Gaelic.]
gaélique [gaeˈlik] *adj., a. su./m ling.*

gaffe [gaf] *f* boat-hook; *fishing*: gaff; F *fig.* blunder, bloomer; F *faire une* ~ put one's foot in it, drop a brick; *sl. faire* ~ be careful; **gaffer** [gaˈfe] (1a) *v/t.* hook; gaff (*a fish*); *v/i.* F blunder, drop a brick; **gaffeur** *m*, **-euse** *f* F [ˌˈfœːr, ~ˈføːz] *m* blunderer.

gaga *sl.* [gaˈga] **1.** *su./m* dodderer; **2.** *adj.* doddering, senile.

gage [gaːʒ] *m* ✝ pledge, pawn; *gam-bling*: stake; *fig.* token; forfeit; ~*s pl.* wages, pay *sg.*; *mettre en* ~ pawn; **gager** [gaˈʒe] (11) *v/t.* ✝ guarantee; F bet; **gageur** *m*, **-euse** *f* [ˌˈʒœːr, ~ˈʒøːz] better, wagerer; **gageure** [ˌˈʒyːr] *f* hopeless *or* (almost) im-possible undertaking; ✝ wager, bet.

gagne-pain [gaɲˈpɛ̃] *m/inv.* liveli-hood; bread-winner; **gagne-petit** [ˌpəˈti] *m/inv.* (itinerant) knife-

grinder; cheap-jack; **gagner** [gaˈɲe] (1a) *v/t.* win (*a. fig.*); gain; earn (*a salary etc.*); reach, arrive at; overtake; *v/i.* gain profit (by, *à*); spread (*disease, fire*); **gagneur** *m*, **-euse** *f* [ˌˈɲœːr, ~ˈɲøːz] earner; gainer; winner.

gai, gaie [ge] gay, merry, jolly, cheerful; lively, bright; ⊕ easy (*bolt, tenon*); F *un peu* ~ a bit merry (= *tipsy*); **gaieté** [ˌˈte] *f* cheer-fulness; mirth; ~*s pl.* frolics; es-capades; broad jokes; *de* ~ *de cœur* out of sheer wantonness.

gaillard, e [gaˈjaːr, ~ˈjard] **1.** *adj.* jolly, merry; strong, well (*health etc.*); broad, spicy, risky (*song, story*); **2.** *su./m* fellow, chap; *su./f* wench; bold young woman; **gail-lardise** [ˌjarˈdiːz] *f* jollity; ~*s pl.* broad jokes, risky stories.

gain [gɛ̃] *m* gain, profit; earning; *cards etc.*: winnings *pl.*

gaine [gɛːn] *f* ♀, *anat., a. knife*: sheath; case, casing; corset, girdle; △, ✗ shaft; *geol.* matrix; **gainer** [gɛˈne] (1b) *v/t.* sheathe.

gala [gaˈla] *m* gala, fête; *en grand* ~ in state; *habits m/pl. de* ~ full dress *sg.*; *fig.* one's Sunday best.

galamment [galaˈmɑ̃] *adv. of galant* 1; **galant, e** [ˌˈlɑ̃, ~ˈlɑ̃ːt] **1.** *adj.* courteous, gallant; † gay, elegant; *aventure f* ~*e* (love) affair; *pej. femme* ~*e* woman of easy virtue; *en* ~*e compagnie* with a lady friend (*man*); with a gentleman friend (*woman*); **2.** *su./m* ladies' man; lover; **galanterie** [ˌlɑ̃ˈtri] *f* politeness, attentiveness; love-affair; pretty speech; ~*s pl.* compliments (*to a woman*); **galan-tin** [ˌlɑ̃ˈtɛ̃] *m* dandy.

galaxie *astr.* [galakˈsi] *f* galaxy; *the* Milky Way.

galbe [galb] *m* curve; contour; line(s *pl.*) (*of a car*); shapeliness; **galber** [galˈbe] (1a) *v/t.* shape.

gale [gal] *f* ✿ scabies, *the* itch; *hunt.* mange; *fig.* defect (*in material*); *fig. sl. woman*: shrew.

galène *min.* [ga'lɛn] *f* galena; ~ *de fer* wolfram.

galère [ga'lɛːr] *f* galley; ⊕ barrow; *qu'allait-il faire dans cette* ~? what was he doing there?; F *vogue la* ~! let's risk it!

galerie [gal'ri] *f* 🗡, ⚔, *thea.*, *museum*: gallery; 🗡 drift, level; arcade; *mot.* roof rack; 🗡~ *de roulage* drawing-road.

galérien [gale'rjɛ̃] *m* † galley-slave; † convict; *fig.* drudge.

galet [ga'lɛ] *m* pebble; ⊕ roller; ⊕ pulley; ~*s pl.* shingle *sg.*

galetas [gal'tɑ] *m* garret; hovel.

galette [ga'lɛt] *f* flat cake; *sl.* money.

galeux, -euse [ga'lø, ~'løːz] mangy (*dog*); 🌿 scurfy (*tree*); with the itch (*person*); F *fig.* *brebis f* ~*euse* black sheep.

galimatias [galima'tjɑ] *m* farrago; gibberish.

galle 🌿 [gal] *f* gall(-nut); *noix f de* ~ nut-gall.

gallicanisme *eccl.* [galika'nism] *m* Gallicanism.

gallicisme [gali'sism] *m* gallicism, French turn of phrase.

gallois, e [ga'lwa, ~'lwaːz] **1.** *adj.* Welsh; **2.** *su./m ling.* Welsh; ♀ Welshman; *les* ♀ *m/pl.* the Welsh; *su./f* ♀ Welshwoman.

galoche [ga'lɔʃ] *f* clog; galosh; *Am.* rubber.

galon [ga'lɔ̃] *m* braid; ⚔, ⚓ stripe; **galonner** [~lɔ'ne] (1a) *v/t.* trim with braid *or* lace; braid.

galop [ga'lo] *m* gallop; *fig.* ~ *d'essay* trial run; *fig. au* ~ (very) quickly; *au grand* ~ at full gallop; *au petit* ~ at a canter; **galoper** [galɔ'pe] (1a) *v/i.* gallop; **galopin** [~'pɛ̃] *m* errand-boy; urchin; ⊕ loose pulley.

galure, galurin *sl.* [ga'lyːr, galy'rɛ̃] *m* hat.

galvaniser [galvani'ze] (1a) *v/t.* galvanize; (electro)plate; *fig.* stimulate; **galvanoplastie** ⊕ [~nɔplas-'ti] *f* electroplating.

galvauder [galvo'de] (1a) *v/t.* tarnish, sully; *se* ~ sully one's reputation; lower o.s.

gambade [gɑ̃'bad] *f* gambol, caper; **gambader** [~ba'de] (1a) *v/i.* gambol, caper; frisk.

gamberge *sl.* [gɑ̃'bɛrʒ] *f* thinking, *co.* cerebration; **gamberger** *sl.* [~bɛr'ʒe] (1l) *v/i.* think.

gambiller † F [gɑ̃bi'je] (1a) *v/i.* dance; fidget.

gamelle [ga'mɛl] *f* 🗡 mess tin; billy (can).

gamin, e [ga'mɛ̃, ~'min] *su.* urchin; street-arab; *su./m* little boy; *su./f* little girl; **gaminerie** [~min'ri] *f* child's trick.

gamma *phys.* [ga'ma] *m*: *rayons m/pl.* ~ gamma rays.

gamme [gam] *f* ♪ scale (*a. paint.*); gamut; range; *fig. changer de* ~ change one's tune; † *haut* (*bas*) *de* ~ high-(low-)grade; (un)expensive.

gammé, e [ga'me] *adj.*: *croix f* ~*e* swastika.

gang [gɑ̃ːg] *m* gang.

ganglion *anat.* [gɑ̃gli'ɔ̃] *m* ganglion.

gangrène [gɑ̃'grɛn] *f* 🌿 gangrene; 🌿, *a. fig.* canker; *fig.* corruption; **gangrener** [gɑ̃grə'ne] (1d) *v/t.* 🌿 gangrene, cause mortification in; *fig.* corrupt; **gangreneux, -euse** [~'nø, ~'nøːz] 🌿 gangrenous; 🌿 cankerous. [hooligan.\

gangster [gɑ̃gs'tɛːr] *m* gangster,\

ganse [gɑ̃ːs] *f* braid; piping; loop.

gant [gɑ̃] *m* glove; ~ *de boxe* boxing-glove; ~ *de toilette* washing-glove; *jeter* (*relever*) *le* ~ throw down (take up) the gauntlet; **gantelet** [gɑ̃t'lɛ] *m* gauntlet; **ganter** [gɑ̃'te] (1a) *v/t.* glove; *fig.* suit (*s.o.*); *se* ~ put one's gloves on; buy gloves; **ganterie** [~'tri] *f* glove-making, glove-trade; glove-shop, glove-counter; glove-factory; † *coll.* gloves *pl.*; **gantier** *m*, **-ère** *f* [~'tje, ~'tjɛːr] glover.

garage [ga'raːʒ] *m* *mot.* garage; hangar; shed; 🚂 shunting; ⚓ dock(ing); 🚂 *voie f de* ~ siding; *fig. mettre q. sur une voie de* ~ put s.o. out in the cold; push s.o. aside; **garagiste** *mot.* [~ra'ʒist] *m* garage owner; garage mechanic.

garance [ga'rɑ̃ːs] *f* **1.** *su./f* 🌿 madder(-wort); *dye*: madder; (madder-)red; **2.** *adj./inv.* (madder-)red.

garant, e [ga'rɑ̃, ~'rɑ̃ːt] *su.* surety, bail; security; *se porter* ~ vouch (for, *de*); *su./m* guarantee, authority; **garantie** [garɑ̃'ti] *f* safeguard; guarantee (*a.* †); † warranty, pledge; **garantir** [~'tiːr] (2a) *v/t.* guarantee (*a.* †); † underwrite; vouch for; *fig.* protect.

garce *sl.* [gars] *f* bitch, strumpet.

garçon [gar'sõ] *m* boy, lad; young man; (*a. vieux* ~) bachelor; *café etc.*: waiter; ~ *de bureau* office-messenger; ~ *d'honneur* best man; F *brave* ~ nice fellow; **garçonne** [~'sɔn] *f* bachelor girl; *cheveux m/pl.* (*or coiffure f*) *à la* ~ Eton crop *sg.*; **garçonnet** [~sɔ'nɛ] *m* little boy; **garçonnière** [~sɔ'njɛːr] *f* bachelor apartment *or* rooms *pl.*

garde [gard] *su./f* watch, guard; care, protection; custody, keeping; nurse; *book*: fly-leaf; *book*: end-paper; ~ *à vous!* look out!; ⚔ attention!, 'shun!; ⚔ *de* ~ on guard, on duty; *faire la* ~ keep watch; ⚔ *monter la* ~ mount guard; *prendre* ~ beware, be careful; *être sur ses* ~*s* be on one's guard; *su./m* guardian, watchman; keeper; warden; ~ *champêtre* rural constable; ♀ *des Sceaux* (French) Minister of Justice; **~-barrière,** *pl.* **~s-barrière(s)** 🚂 [gardəba'rjɛːr] gate-keeper; **~-boue** *mot.* [~'bu] *m/inv.* mud-guard, *Am.* fender; **~-chasse,** *pl.* **~s-chasse(s)** [~'ʃas] *m* gamekeeper; **~-corps** [~'kɔːr] *m/inv.* life-line; **~-côte** [~'koːt] *m* coastguard vessel; **~-feu** [~'fø] *m/inv.* fender; **~-fou** [~'fu] *m* parapet; railing, handrail; **~-frein,** *pl.* **~s-frein(s)** 🚂 [~'frɛ̃] brakesman; **~-malade,** *pl.* **~s-malades** [~ma'lad] *su./m* male nurse; *su./f* nurse; **~-manger** [~mã'ʒe] *m/inv.* larder, pantry; meat-safe; **~-nappe,** *pl.* **~s-nappe(s)** [~'nap] *m* table-mat.

garder [gar'de] (1a) *v/t.* keep; preserve; retain; look after; mind; guard; se ~ protect o.s.; refrain (from *ger.*, de *inf.*); take care (not to *inf.*, de *inf.*); baware (of, de); **garderie** [~'dri] *f* day nursery; **garde-robe** [~də'rɔb] *f furniture, clothes*: wardrobe; toilet, watercloset; **gardeur** *m*, **-euse** *f* [~'dœːr, ~'døːz] keeper, minder; preserver; **garde-voie,** *pl.* **~s-voie(s)** 🚂 [~də'vwa] *m* track-watchman; **garde-vue** [~də'vy] *m/inv.* eye-shade; lampshade; **gardien, -enne** [~'djɛ̃, ~'djɛn] **1.** *su.* guardian; keeper; attendant; *prison*: warder, guard; *foot.* ~ *de but* goal-keeper; ~ *de la paix* policeman; **2.** *adj.*: *ange m* ~ guardian angel.

gare[1] [gaːr] siding (⚒, *a. canal, river, a.* 🚢); 🚂 (railway) station; ⚒~

aérienne airport; 🚢 ~ *de triage* marshalling yard; ⚓ ~ *maritime* harbo(u)r-station; ~ *routière* bus station; 🚢 *chef m de* ~ stationmaster.

gare[2]! [~] *int.* look out!; ~ *à* ... beware of ...; ~ *à toi!* just watch it!; *sans crier* ~ without warning.

garenne [ga'rɛn] *su./f* (rabbit-)warren; fishing preserve; *su./m* wild rabbit.

garer [ga're] (1a) *v/t. mot.* park; dock (*a vessel*); se ~ *mot. etc.* pull to one side; move out of the way; F *mot.* park (one's car); take cover (from, de).

gargariser [gargari'ze] (1a) *v/t.*: se ~ gargle; F revel (in, de); **gargarisme** [~'rism] *m* gargle; gargling.

gargote [gar'gɔt] *f* (third-rate) eating house; cook-shop; **gargotier** *m*, **-ère** *f* [~gɔ'tje, ~'tjɛːr] cook-shop owner.

gargouille △ [gar'guːj] *f* gargoyle; water-spout; culvert; **gargouiller** [~gu'je] (1a) *v/i.* gurgle; rumble (*bowels*); F paddle (in the gutter); **gargouillis** [~gu'ji] *m* gurgling.

garnement F [garnə'mã] *m* good-for-nothing, rogue.

garni [gar'ni] *m* furnished room(s *pl.*), F digs *pl.*; **garnir** [~'niːr] (2a) *v/t.* furnish, provide, fit up (with, de); ⚔ occupy, garrison, line (with, de); trim; ⊕ lag (*pipes*); ↑ stock (*a shop*); **garnison** ⚔ [~ni'zõ] *f* garrison; **garniture** [~ni'tyːr] *f* fittings *pl.*; *cost., cuis.* trimming(s *pl.*); ⊕ lagging; ⊕ packing; *mot. brakes, clutch*: lining; *buttons,* ⊕ *pulleys, toilet, etc.*: set.

garrot [ga'ro] *m* ⊕ tongue (*of saw*); ✂ tourniquet; **garrotter** [~rɔ'te] (1a) *v/t.* pinion; bind down; † gar(r)otte.

gars F [gɑ] *m* lad, young fellow, boy.

gascon *m*, **-onne** *f* [gas'kõ, ~'kɔn] **1.** *adj.* Gascon; **2.** *su./m ling.* Gascon; F *faire le* ~ brag, boast; *su.* ♀ Gascon; **gasconnade** [~kɔ'nad] *f* boast(ing), bragging; tall story; **gasconner** [~kɔ'ne] (1a) *v/i.* speak with a Gascon accent; F brag, boast.

gas(-)oil [ga'zɔjl] *m* fuel *or* diesel oil.

gaspiller [gaspi'je] (1a) *v/t.* waste, squander; dissipate; se ~ be wasted.

gastrite ✂ [gas'trit] *f* gastritis.

gastro... [gastrɔ] gastro...; **gas-**

tronome [ˌ'nɔm] *m* gastronome(r).

gâteau [gɑ'to] *m* cake; (open) tart; pudding (*usu. cold*); *fig.* profit; ~ *des Rois* Twelfth-night cake; *fig. partager le* ~ go shares, split the profit.

gâter [gɑ'te] (1a) *v/t.* spoil (*a. fig.*); *fig.* pamper (*a child*); damage; taint (*the meat*); *se* ~ deteriorate; **gâterie** [ˌ'tri] *f* spoiling (*of a child*); over-indulgence; ~*s pl.* goodies; **gâteux, -euse** [ˌ'tø, ˌ'tøːz] **1.** *su.* old dotard; **2.** *adj.* senile, doddering; **gâtisme** ♂ [ˌ'tism] *m* senile decay.

gauche [goːʃ] **1.** *adj.* left; crooked; awkward, clumsy; *à* ~ on *or* to the left; *tourner à* ~ turn to the left; **2.** *su./f* left hand; left-hand side; *tenir sa* ~ keep to the left; **gaucher, -ère** [go'ʃe, ˌ'ʃɛːr] **1.** *adj.* left-handed; **2.** *su.* left-hander; **gaucherie** [goʃ'ri] *f* awkwardness, clumsiness; **gauchir** [go'ʃiːr] (2a) *v/i. a. se* ~ warp (*wood*); buckle (*metal*); *v/t.* warp; buckle; *fig.* distort; **gauchisme** *pol.* [ˌ'ʃism] left-ism; **gauchissement** [ˌʃis'mɑ̃] *m* warping; buckling; *fig.* distortion; **gauchiste** *pol.* [ˌ'ʃist] *adj., a. su.* leftist.

gaudriole F [godri'ɔl] *f* broad joke(s *pl.*).

gaufre *cuis* [goːfr] *f* waffle; ~ *de miel* honeycomb; **gaufrer** [go'fre] (1a) *v/t.* ⊕ emboss (*leather etc.*); crimp (*linen*); corrugate (*iron, paper*); *tex.* diaper; **gaufrette** *cuis.* [ˌ'frɛt] *f* wafer biscuit; **gaufrier** *cuis.* [ˌfri'e] *m* waffle-iron.

gaule [goːl] *f* long pole; (one-piece) fishing rod; **gauler** [go'le] (1a) *v/t.* knock down (*fruit etc. from a tree*); beat (*with a pole*).

gaulois, e [go'lwa, ˌ'lwaːz] **1.** *adj.* of Gaul; Gallic; *fig.* spicy, broad; **2.** *su./m ling.* Gaulish; *su.* ♀ Gaul; **gauloiserie** [ˌlwaz'ri] *f* broad joke *or* story.

gausser [go'se] (1a) *v/t.: se* ~ *de* make fun of.

gave [gaːv] *m* mountain-torrent (*in the Pyrenees*).

gaver [ga've] (1a) *v/t.* cram (*a. fig. a pupil*); ♂ feed forcibly; *se* ~ stuff o.s. (with, *de*); gorge.

gavroche [ga'vrɔʃ] *su. Paris:* street arab, ragamuffin.

gaz [gɑːz] *m* gas; gas works *usu. sg.*; ♂ wind; ~ *d'échappement* exhaust gas; ~ *d'éclairage* (*or de ville*) illuminating gas; ♠ ~ *hilarant* laughing-gas; ♠ ~ *pl. rares* rare gases; *mot. couper les* ~ throttle back; *mot. ouvrir les* ~ open the throttle; F *mot.* mettre les ~ step on the gas; *mot. pédale f de* ~ accelerator.

gaze [ˌ] *f* gauze.

gazéifier [gɑzei'fje] (1o) *v/t.* gasify; aerate (*mineral waters etc.*); **gezéiforme** ♠ [ˌ'fɔrm] gasiform.

gazer¹ [gɑ'ze] (1a) *v/t.* ✗, *tex.* gas; *v/i.* F *mot.* move at top speed, tear *or* speed along; *fig.* go smoothly; F *ça gaze?* things O.K.?

gazer² [ˌ] (1a) *v/t.* cover with gauze; *fig.* draw a veil (of reticence) over.

gazetier † [gazə'tje] *m* journalist; *fig.* newsmonger; **gazette** [ˌ'zɛt] *f* gazette; *person:* gossip(er).

gazeux, -euse [gɑ'zø, ˌ'zøːz] gaseous; ♠ aerated, fizzy; **gazier** [ˌ'zje] *m* gas-worker; gas-fitter; **gazoduc** [ˌzɔ'dyk] *m* gas pipeline; **gazogène** [ˌzɔ'ʒɛn] *m* gas-producer, generator; gasogene; **gazomètre** [ˌzɔ'mɛtr] *m* gasometer, gas-holder.

gazon [ga'zɔ̃] *m* grass; turf; lawn; **gazonner** [ˌzɔ'ne] (1a) *v/t.* turf; *v/i.* sward.

gazouillement [gazuj'mɑ̃] *m* warbling, chirping, *birds:* twittering, *brook etc.:* babbling; *fig.* prattle; **gazouiller** [gazu'je] (1a) *v/i.* warble, chirp, twitter (*birds*); babble (*brook*); *fig.* prattle; *sl.* stink; **gazouillis** [ˌ'ji] *m* see *gazouillement*.

geai *orn.* [ʒɛ] *m* jay.

géant, e [ʒe'ɑ̃, ˌ'ɑ̃ːt] **1.** *su./m* giant; *su./f* giantess; **2.** *adj.* gigantic.

géhenne [ʒe'ɛn] *f* gehenna, hell (*a. fig.*).

geignard, e F [ʒɛ'naːr, ˌ'nard] whining; moaning; **geindre** [ʒɛ̃ːdr] (4m) *v/i.* whine; moan; whimper; complain.

gel [ʒɛl] *m* frost; freezing (*a.* ✝, *a. fig.*); ♠ gel.

gélatine [ʒela'tin] *f* gelatine; **gélatineux, -euse** [ˌti'nø, ˌ'nøːz] gelatinous.

gelée [ʒə'le] *f* frost; *cuis.* jelly; ~ *blanche* hoar-frost; ground frost; ~ *nocturne* night frost; **geler** [ˌ] (1d) *v/t.* freeze (*a.* ✝ *credits*); ✗, ♂ frostbite; *v/i.* freeze, become frozen;

avoir gelé be frozen (*river*); *il gèle blanc* there is a white frost; *on gèle ici* it is freezing (in) here.

gelinotte *orn.* [ʒəli'nɔt] *f* hazel-grouse; fat(tened) pullet.

gélivure [ʒeli'vy:r] *f* frost-crack.

Gémeaux *astr.* [ʒe'mo] *m/pl.*: *les* ～ Gemini; the Twins; **géminé, e** [～mi'ne] 🜨, *biol.* twin; *biol.* geminate; mixed, co-educational (*school*).

gémir [ʒe'mi:r] (2a) *v/i.* groan, moan; lament, bewail; **gémissement** [～mis'mã] *m* groan(ing), moan(ing).

gemme [ʒɛm] *f min.* gem; precious stone; 🜊 (leaf-)bud; resin; *biol.* gemma; *sel m* ～ rock-salt.

gênant, e [ʒɛ'nã, ～'nã:t] inconvenient, in the way; *fig.* awkward (*silence etc.*).

gencive *anat.* [ʒã'si:v] *f* gum.

gendarme [ʒã'darm] *m police militia*: gendarme, constable; F virago; *sl.* red herring; **gendarmer** [ʒãdar'me] (1a) *v/t.*: *se* ～ flare up, be up in arms; **gendarmerie** [～mə'ri] *f* constabulary; barracks *pl.* or headquarters *pl.* of the gendarmes.

gendre [ʒã:dr] *m* son-in-law.

gène *biol.* [ʒɛ:n] *m* gene.

gêne [ʒɛ:n] *f* embarrassment, uneasiness; difficulty; trouble, bother; discomfort; want, financial straits *pl.*; *sans* ～ free and easy; familiar; **gêner** [ʒɛ'ne] (1a) *v/t.* cramp *s.o.'s* style; *fig.* embarrass; inconvenience; hamper, hinder; trouble; *cela vous gêne-t-il?* is that in your way?; is that troubling you?; *la robe me gêne* the dress is too tight for me; *fig. se* ～ put *o.s.* out (to, *pour*); be embarrassed, be shy; squeeze up; *sourire m gêné* embarrassed smile.

général, e, *m/pl.* **-aux** [ʒene'ral, ～'ro] **1.** *adj.* general; *d'une façon* ～*e* broadly speaking; *en* ～ generally; **2.** *su./m* 🗡 general (*a. eccl. of an order*); ～ *de brigade* 🗡 brigadier, *Am.* brigadier general (*a.* 🦌); 🦌 *Br.* Air Commodore; *su./f* 🗡 general's wife; 🗡 alarm; *eccl.* general (*of order of nuns*); *thea.* dress-rehearsal; **généraliser** [～rali'ze] (1a) *v/t.* generalize; **généraliste** 🔱 [～ra'list] *m* (*a. médecin* ～) general practitioner, G.P.); **généralité** [～rali'te] *f* generality.

générateur, -trice [ʒenera'tœ:r, ～'tris] **1.** *adj.* generating; productive; **2.** *su./f* generator; dynamo; *su./m* 🜨 boiler; ～ *à gaz* gas-producer; **génération** [～'sjõ] *f* generation.

généreux, -euse [ʒene'rø, ～'rø:z] generous (*person, fig. heart, help, wine*); liberal; abundant; 🌳 fertile (*soil*); **générosité** [～rozi'te] *f* generosity; liberality; *wine*: body.

genèse [ʒə'nɛ:z] *f* genesis; *bibl. la* ♌ Genesis.

genêt 🜊 [ʒə'nɛ] *m* broom; ～ *épineux* gorse, furze.

génétique [ʒene'tik] **1.** *adj.* genetic; **2.** *su./f* genetics *pl.*

gêneur *m*, **-euse** *f* [ʒɛ'nœ:r, ～'nø:z] intruder; nuisance; spoil-sport.

genevois, e [ʒən'vwa, ～'vwa:z] *adj., a. su.* ♀ Genevese.

genévrier 🜊 [ʒənevri'e] *m* juniper (-tree).

génial, e, *m/pl.* **-aux** [ʒe'njal, ～'njo] inspired, of genius; **génie** [～'ni] *m* spirit, *a. person*: genius; spirit, characteristic; 🗡 engineers *pl.*; ～ *civil* civil engineering; *coll.* civil engineers *pl.*; *mauvais* (*bon*) ～ bad (good) genius.

genièvre [ʒə'njɛ:vr] *m* 🜊 juniper-berry; juniper(-tree); gin.

génisse [ʒe'nis] *f* heifer.

génital, e, *m/pl.* **-aux** [ʒeni'tal, ～'to] genital; *anat. organes m/pl.* ～*aux* genitals.

génocide [ʒenɔ'sid] *m* genocide.

génois, e [ʒe'nwa, ～'nwa:z] *adj., a. su.* ♀ Genoese.

genou, *pl.* **-x** [ʒə'nu] *m* knee; 🜨 *pipe*: elbow-joint; 🜨 (*a. joint m à* ～) ball-and-socket joint; *se mettre à* ～*x* kneel down; **genouillère** [～nu'jɛ:r] *f* knee-pad; *armour, a. horse*: knee-cap; 🜨 *articulation f à* ～ ball-and-socket joint.

genre [ʒã:r] *m* kind, type, sort; *gramm.* gender; *art*: genre; *zo. etc.* genus; *se donner du* ～ put on airs; *le* ～ *humain* mankind.

gens [ʒã] *m/pl.* (*an adj. or participle immediately preceding it is made feminine*; *if, however, both masculine and feminine forms end in a mute e, the adj. is made masculine*) people, folk *sg.*; servants; nations; *les jeunes* ～ the young folks; *tous les* ～ *intéressés* all people interested; *petites* ～ small fry; *vieilles* ～ old folks; ～ *d'église* clergy *pl.*; church people; ～ *de lettres* men of letters; ∼ *de mer* sailors; ∼ *de robe* lawyers; ⚖ *droit m des* ∼ law of nations.

gent †, *a. co.* [∼] *f* race, tribe.

gentiane [ʒɑ̃'sjan] *f* ♀ gentian; gentian-bitters *pl.*

gentil[1] *hist.* [ʒɑ̃'ti] *m* Gentile.

gentil[2], **-ille** [ʒɑ̃'ti, ∼'ti:j] nice; kind; pretty, pleasing; *sois* ∼*!* be good!; **gentilhomme**, *pl.* **gentils-hommes** [ʒɑ̃ti'jɔm, ∼ti'zɔm] *m* nobleman; gentleman (= *man of gentle birth*); **gentillesse** [∼'jɛs] *f* graciousness; politeness; *avoir la* ∼ *de* (*inf.*) be so kind as to (*inf.*); **gentiment** [∼'mɑ̃] *adv.* of gentil[2].

génuflexion *eccl.* [ʒenyflɛk'sjɔ̃] *f* genuflexion; *faire une* ∼ genuflect.

géodésie [ʒeɔde'zi] *f* surveying, geodesy; **géodésique** [∼'zik] geodetic, geodesic; *surv. point m* ∼ triangulation point.

géographe [ʒeɔ'graf] *m* geographer; **géographie** [∼gra'fi] *f* geography; **géographique** [∼gra'fik] geographic(al).

geôle [ʒo:l] *f* gaoler's lodge; † gaol, prison; **geôlier** [ʒo'lje] *m* jailer.

géologie [ʒeɔlɔ'ʒi] geology. [etry.\ **géométrie** ⚗ [ʒeɔme'tri] *f* geom-∫ **géopolitique** [ʒeɔpɔli'tik] **1.** *adj.* geopolitical; **2.** *su./f* geopolitics *sg.*

gérance [ʒe'rɑ̃:s] *f* direction, management; managership; board of directors *or* governors; **gérant, e** [∼'rɑ̃, ∼'rɑ̃:t] *su./m* director; *company:* managing director; manager; *journ. rédacteur-*∼ managing editor; *su./f* manageress.

gerbage [ʒɛr'ba:ʒ] *m sheaves:* binding; *bales etc.:* stacking; **gerbe** [ʒɛrb] *f corn:* sheaf; *flowers, water:* spray; *sparks:* shower, flurry; *fig.* bundle, collection; ✕ cone of fire; **gerber** [ʒɛr'be] (1a) *v/t.* bind (*corn-sheaves*); stack, pile; ✕ bombard; **gerbier** [∼'bje] *m corn:* stack; barn; **gerbière** [∼'bjɛ:r] *f* harvest wain.

gercer [ʒɛr'se] (1k) *vt/i. a. se* ∼ crack (*wood, skin, soil*); chap (*hands*); **gerçure** [∼'sy:r] *f* crack, fissure; *hands:* chap; ⊕ flaw (*in wood*), haircrack (*in metal*).

gérer [ʒe're] (1f) *v/t.* manage, administer; *mal* ∼ mismanage.

gériatrie ⚕ [ʒerja'tri] *f* geriatrics *sg.*

germain[1], **e** [ʒɛr'mɛ̃, ∼'mɛn] full, own (*brother, sister*); first (*cousin*).

germain[2], **e** *hist.* [ʒɛr'mɛ̃, ∼'mɛn] **1.** *adj.* Germanic, Teutonic; **2.** *su.* ♀ German, Teuton; **germanique** [∼ma'nik] *adj., a. su./m ling.* Germanic; **germanisme** [∼ma-'nism] *m* Germanism; German turn of phrase.

germe [ʒɛrm] *m biol.* germ (*a. fig.*); *potato:* eye; *fig.* seed, origin; **germer** [ʒɛr'me] (1a) *v/i.* germinate; sprout, shoot; *fig.* develop; **germination** *biol.* [∼mina'sjɔ̃] *f* germination; **germoir** [∼'mwa:r] *m* 🌱 seed-bed, hot-bed; *brewing:* malt-house.

gérondif *gramm.* [ʒerɔ̃'dif] *m* gerund.

gerzeau ♀ [ʒɛr'zo] *m* corn-cockle.

gésier *zo.* [ʒe'zje] *m* gizzard.

gésir [ʒe'zi:r] (2q) *v/i.* lie; *ci-gît here lies.*

gestation *physiol.* [ʒɛsta'sjɔ̃] *f* (period of) gestation, pregnancy.

geste[1] [ʒɛst] *f* (*a. chanson f de* ∼) medieval verse chronicle; *faits m/pl. et* ∼*s pl.* doings.

geste[2] [ʒɛst] *m* gesture, motion, sign; **gesticulation** [ʒɛstikyla'sjɔ̃] *f* gesticulation.

gestion [ʒɛs'tjɔ̃] *f* administration, management.

gestique [ʒɛs'tik] *f* gestures *pl.*

ghetto [gɛ'to] *m* ghetto (*a. fig.*).

gibbeux, -euse [ʒi'bø, ∼'bø:z] gibbous; humped; **gibbosité** [∼bozi-'te] *f* gibbosity; hump.

gibecière [ʒib'sjɛ:r] *f* game-bag; *school:* satchel.

gibelotte *cuis.* [ʒi'blɔt] *f* fricassee of rabbit *or* hare in white wine.

giberne [ʒi'bɛrn] *f* cartridge-pouch.

gibet [ʒi'bɛ] *m* gibbet, gallows *usu.*)

gibier [ʒi'bje] *m* game. [*sg.*∫

giboulée [ʒibu'le] *f* sudden shower; F *fig.* shower of blows.

giboyer [ʒibwa'je] (1h) *v/i.* go shooting; **giboyeux, -euse** [∼'jø, ∼'jø:z] abounding in game; *pays m* ∼ good game country.

gicler [ʒi'kle] (1a) *v/i.* squirt, spurt; splash; **gicleur** *mot.* [∼'klœ:r] *m* jet; (spray) nozzle.

gifle [ʒifl] *f* slap in the face; box on the ear; **gifler** [ʒi'fle] (1a) *v/t.:* ∼ *q.* slap s.o.'s face; box s.o.'s ears.

gigantesque [ʒigɑ̃'tɛsk] gigantic; **gigantisme** [∼'tism] *m* ⚕ gigantism; *fig.* gigantic proportions *pl.*; *fig.* overexpansion.

gigogne [ʒiˈgɔɲ] **1.** *su./f*: *la mère* ♀ (*approx.*) the Old Woman who lived in a shoe; **2.** *adj.*: *fusée f* ~ multi-stage rocket; *lit m* ~ stowaway bed; *poupée f* ~ nest of dolls; *table f* ~ nest of tables; ⚓ *vaisseau m* ~ mother ship.
gigot [ʒiˈgo] *m cuis.* leg of mutton; *cost. manches f/pl. à* ~ leg-of-mutton sleeves; **gigoter** F [~gɔˈte] (1a) *v/i.* kick; jig.
gigue[1] [ʒig] *f* haunch of venison; gawky girl; F ~*s pl.* legs.
gigue[2] ♪ [~] *f* jig.
gilet [ʒiˈlɛ] *m* waistcoat, vest; *knitwear*: cardigan; ~ *de sauvetage* life-jacket.
gin [dʒin] *m* gin.
gingembre ⚘ [ʒɛ̃ˈʒɑ̃:br] *m* ginger.
gingivite ⚕ [ʒɛ̃ʒiˈvit] *f* gingivitis.
girafe *zo.* [ʒiˈraf] *f* giraffe.
girandole [ʒirɑ̃ˈdɔl] *f chandelier, jewels*: girandole; *flowers*: cluster.
giratoire [ʒiraˈtwa:r] gyratory (*traffic*); *sens m* ~ roundabout.
girofle ⚘ [ʒiˈrɔfl] *m* clove; *cuis. clou m de* ~ clove; **giroflée** [ʒirɔˈfle] *f* stock; wallflower; **giroflier** ⚘ [~fliˈe] *m* clove-tree.
girolle ⚘ [ʒiˈrɔl] *f* mushroom, *usu.* chanterelle.
giron [ʒiˈrɔ̃] *m* lap; ⊕ loose handle; ⚠ tread; *fig.* bosom (*of the Church*).
girouette [ʒiˈrwɛt] *f* weathercock (*a. fig.*), vane.
gisant [ʒiˈzɑ̃] *m arts*: recumbent effigy; **gisement** [ʒizˈmɑ̃] *m geol.* bed, layer, stratum; ⚓ bearing; ⚒ lode, vein; ~*s pl. houillers* coal measures; **gisons** [ʒiˈzɔ̃] *1st p. pl. pres. of* **gésir**; **gît** [ʒi] *3rd p. sg. pres. of* **gésir**.
gitan *m*, **e** *f* [ʒiˈtɑ̃, ~ˈtan] gipsy.
gîte [ʒit] *su./m* resting-place, lodging; *hare*: form; *animal*: lair; *geol.* bed, stratum; ⚒ vein; ⚠ joist; *su./f* ⚓ list; **gîter** [ʒiˈte] (1a) *v/i.* lodge; lie; sleep; ⚓ list; ⚓ run aground.
givrage ✈ [ʒiˈvra:ʒ] *m* icing; **givre** [ʒi:vr] *m* hoar-frost; **givré, e** [ʒiˈvre] rimy; frosted; ✈ iced-up; **givrer** [~] (1a) *v/t.* cover with hoarfrost, frost (*s.th.*) over; frost (*a cake*); ✈ ice up.
glabre [glɑ:br] smooth, hairless; *fig.* clean-shaven (*face*).
glaçage [glaˈsa:ʒ] *m* glazing; *cuis.* icing, frosting; **glace** [glas] *f* ice; ice-cream; *cuis.* icing; *fig.* chill; mirror; (plate-)glass; *mot. etc.* window; ⊕ flaw; ⚓ *pris dans les* ~*s* ice-bound; **glacé, e** [glaˈse] **1.** *adj.* icy (*a. fig. stare, politeness*), freezing; iced (*drink*); chilled (*wine*); frozen; glazed (*paper etc.*); glacé, kid ...; **2.** *su./m* glaze; **glacer** [~] (1k) *v/t.* freeze; glaze; *fig.* chill (*the wine*); surface (*paper etc.*); *cuis.* frost, ice (*a cake*); ✝ polish (*the rice*); *se* ~ freeze; *fig.* run cold;
glacerie [glasˈri] *f* ice-cream trade; glass-works *usu sg.*; **glaceur** ⊕ [glaˈsœ:r] *m paper, material*: glazer; rolling-machine; glazing-pad; **glaciaire** *geol.* [~ˈsjɛ:r] glacial; ice-(age) ...; **glacial, e,** *m/pl.* **-als** [~ˈsjal] icy (*temperature, a. fig.*); frosty (*air*); ice-...; frigid (*style, manner, politeness, zone*); **glacier** [~ˈsje] *m geol.* glacier; ice-cream man; maker of mirrors *or* plate-glass; **glacière** [~ˈsjɛ:r] *f* ice-house; ice-box; refrigerator; 🚃 refrigerator van; **glacis** [~ˈsi] *m* slope; ⚠ ramp; ⚔ *hist.* glacis; *paint.* glaze, scumble; **glaçon** [~ˈsɔ̃] *m* icicle (*a. fig. person*); ice cube; block of ice; **glaçure** [~ˈsy:r] *f pottery etc.*: glaze, glazing.
glaïeul ⚘ [glaˈjœl] *m* gladiolus.
glaire [glɛ:r] *f* white of egg; mucus, phlegm; flaw (*in precious stone*); **glaireux, -euse** [glɛˈrø, ~ˈrø:z] glaireous; full of phlegm (*throat*).
glaise [glɛ:z] *f* clay, loam; **glaiser** [glɛˈze] (1b) *v/t.* line with clay; ⚒ coffer; ⚘ dress (*the soil*) with clay; ⊕ puddle (*a reservoir*); **glaisière** [~ˈzjɛ:r] *f* clay-pit.
glaive [glɛ:v] *m* sword.
glanage ⚘ [glaˈna:ʒ] *m* gleaning.
gland [glɑ̃] *m* ⚘ acorn; *curtain*: tassel; **glandage** [glɑ̃ˈda:ʒ] *m* pannage.
glande ⚘, *anat.* [glɑ̃:d] *f* gland.
glander *sl.* [glɑ̃ˈde], **glandouiller** *sl.* [~duˈje] (1a) *v/i.* hang around; footle around.
glane [glan] *f* gleaning; *pears*: cluster; *onions*: rope; F ~*s pl.* pickings; **glaner** [glaˈne] (1a) *v/t.* glean (*a. fig.*); **glaneur** *m*, **-euse** [~ˈnœ:r, ~ˈnø:z] gleaner; **glanure** [~ˈny:r] *f* gleanings *pl.* (*a. fig.*).
glapir [glaˈpi:r] (2a) *v/i.* yelp; bark (*fox*); **glapissement** [~pisˈmɑ̃] *m* yelping, yapping; *fox*: barking.

glas [glɑ] *m* knell; ✂ *etc.* salvo of guns (*at funeral*).

glauque [glo:k] sea-green; bluish green.

glèbe [glɛb] *f* earth: sod; † land; *hist.* feudal land; *attaché à la* ~ bound to the soil.

glissade [gli'sad] *f* slip; sliding; slide (*on snow etc.*); *dancing*: glide; *geol.* ~ *de terre* landslide; ✈ ~ *sur l'aile* side-slip; ✈ ~ *sur la queue* tail-dive; *mount.* *faire une descente en* ~ glissade; **glissant, e** [~'sã, ~'sã:t] sliding (*a.* ⊕ *joint*); slippery (*a. fig.*); **glissement** [glis'mã] *m* sliding, slipping; gliding; *geol.* landslide; ⊕ *belt*: creeping; **glisser** [gli'se] (1a) *v/i.* slip; slide (*on ice etc.*); glide; *mot.* skid (*wheel*); ⊕ creep (*belt*); ~ *sur* glance off (*s.th.*, *s.o.*); *fig.* not to dwell upon, let pass; *v/t.* slip (*s.th. into s.th., a stitch, etc.*); *se* ~ slip; creep (*a. fig.*); **glissière** [~'sjɛ:r] *f* slide; (*coal-*)shoot; ⊕ slide-bar; *mot.* ~ *de sécurité* crash barrier; **glissoir** [gli'swa:r] *m* ⊕ slide; chute; **glissoire** [~] *f* slide (*on ice etc.*).

global, e, *m/pl.* -**aux** [glɔ'bal, ~'bo] total; overall; global; **globe** [glɔb] *m* globe (*a. ⚡*), sphere; *sun*: orb; *anat.* (eye)ball; ~ *terrestre* terrestrial globe; **globulaire** [glɔby'lɛ:r] **1.** *adj.* globular; **2.** *su./f* ♀ globularia; **globule** [~'byl] *m* globule (*a. ⚫*); *water*: drop; ⊕ *metals*: airhole; ✦ small pill; *blood*: corpuscle; **globuleux, -euse** [~by'lø, ~'lø:z] globular.

gloire [glwa:r] *f* glory; fame; pride; halo; *se faire* ~ *de* glory in; **gloria** [glɔ'rja] *m eccl.* gloria; F coffee with brandy; **gloriette** [~'rjɛt] *f* summer-house, bower; **glorieux, -euse** [~'rjø, ~'rjø:z] **1.** *adj.* glorious; vain, conceited (about, *de*); *eccl.* glorified; **2.** *su./m* braggart; **glorification** [~rifika'sjõ] *f* glorification; **glorifier** [~ri'fje] (1o) *v/t.* glorify; praise; *se* ~ boast (of, *de*); glory (*in gen.*, *de inf.*); **gloriole** [~'rjɔl] *f* vainglory, vanity.

glose [glo:z] *f* gloss, commentary; *fig.* criticism; **gloser** [glo'ze] (1a) *v/t.* gloss; *v/i.*: ~ *sur* find fault with; criticize; gossip about.

glossaire [glɔ'sɛ:r] *m* glossary; vocabulary.

glotte *anat.* [glɔt] *f* glottis.

glouglou [glu'glu] *m* gurgle; *turkey*: gobble; **glouglouter** [~glu'te] (1a)

v/i. cluck (*hen*); gobble (*turkey*); chuckle (*person*).

glouteron ♀ [glu'trõ] *m* burdock.

glouton, -onne [glu'tõ, ~'tɔn] **1.** *adj.* greedy; **2.** *su.* glutton; *su./m zo.* wolverine; **gloutonnerie** [~tɔn-'ri] *f* gluttony.

glu [gly] *f* bird-lime; glue; **gluant, e** [~'ã, ~'ã:t] sticky, gluey; *sl.* *il est* ~ he's a sticker; **gluau** [~'o] *m* lime-twig; snare.

glucose ⚗ [gly'ko:z] *m* glucose.

gluer [gly'e] (1a) *v/t.* lime (*twigs*); *fig.* make sticky.

glume [glym] *f* chaff; ♀ glume.

glutineux, -euse [glyti'nø, ~'nø:z] glutinous.

glycérine [glise'rin] *f* glycerine.

glycine [gli'sin] *f* ♀ wistaria, wisteria; *phot.* glycin(e).

gnangnan [nã'nã] **1.** *adj./inv.* peevish; **2.** *su.* peevish person.

gn(i)ole, gnôle, *a.* **gnaule** *sl.* [nɔl] *f* brandy.

gnome [gno:m] *m* gnome.

go F [go] *adv.*: *tout de* ~ immediately, straight away.

goal *sp.* [gol] *m* goal; goalkeeper.

gobelet [gɔ'blɛ] *m* goblet; cup; mug; **gobeleterie** [gɔblɛ'tri] *f* hollow-glass factory *or* trade *or* ware; **gobeletier** [~'tje] *m* manufacturer of *or* dealer in glass-ware.

gobe-mouches [gɔb'muʃ] *m/inv.* *orn.* fly-catcher; ♀ fly-trap; F simpleton.

gober [gɔ'be] (1a) *v/t.* swallow (*a.* F *fig.* = *believe blindly*); F *fig.* like (*s.o.*) very much; *sl.* catch; F *se* ~ be conceited, think no end of o.s.

goberger [gɔbɛr'ʒe] (1l) *v/t.*: *se* ~ feed well, F have a good tuck-in.

gobeur, -euse *f* [gɔ'bœ:r, ~'bø:z] F simpleton, credulous person.

godaille *sl.* [gɔ'da:j] *f* feast, guzzle; **godailler** F [~dɑ'je] (1a) *v/i.* feast, guzzle; pub-crawl.

godasses *sl.* [gɔ'das] *f/pl.* boots.

godelureau [gɔdly'ro] *m* (*young*) dandy.

goder [gɔ'de] (1a) *v/i.* crease, pucker; bag (*trousers*); **godet** [~'dɛ] *m* mug; cup (*a. ♀*); bowl (*a. of pipe*); ⊕ *dredger*: bucket; *cost.* flare; pucker (*in cloth*).

godiche F [gɔ'diʃ], **godichon, -onne** [~di'ʃõ, ~'ʃɔn] **1.** *adj.* awkward, stupid; **2.** *su.* simpleton; gawk; lout.

godille ⚓ [gɔˈdiːj] *f* stern-oar.
godillot *sl.* [gɔdiˈjo] *m* (military) boot.
goéland *orn.* [gɔeˈlɑ̃] *m* (sea-)gull;
goélette [ˌˈlɛt] *f* ⚓ schooner; ⚓ trysail; *orn.* sea-swallow.
goémon [gɔeˈmɔ̃] *m* seaweed; wrack.
gogo F [gɔˈgo] *m* dupe, *sl.* mug; *fig. à* ~ in abundance; galore; (*money*) to burn.
goguenard, e [gɔgˈnaːr, ˌˈnard] 1. *adj.* bantering; 2. *su.* mocker, chaffer; **goguette** F [gɔˈgɛt] *f*: en ~ on the spree.
goinfre [gwɛ̃ːfr] *m* glutton, guzzler; **goinfrer** [gwɛ̃ˈfre] (1a) *v/t.*: se ~ guzzle (s.th., de qch.); **goinfrerie** [ˌfrɔˈri] *f* gluttony.
goitre 𝕤 [gwaːtr] *m* goitre; **goitreux, -euse** [gwaˈtrø, ˌˈtrøːz] 1. *adj.* goitrous; 2. *su.* goitrous person.
golf *sp.* [gɔlf] *m* golf; F golf-links; *joueur m de* ~ golfer.
golfe *geog.* [ˌˈ] *m* gulf, bay; *anat.* sinus.
gomme [gɔm] *f* gum; india-rubber; **gommer** [gɔˈme] (1a) *v/t.* gum; mix with gum; rub (*s.th.*) out, erase; *fig.* suppress; *fig.* blur; *v/i.* ⊕ jam, stick; **gommeux, -euse** [ˌˈmø, ˌˈmøːz] 1. *adj.* gummy, sticky; 2. *su./m* F toff, swell, *Am.* dude.
gond [gɔ̃] *m* (door-)hinge; F *sortir de ses* ~s fly into a rage *or* off the handle; F *hors de ses* ~s beside oneself.
gondole [gɔ̃ˈdɔl] *f* gondola; 𝕜 *dirigible balloon*: nacelle; 𝕤 eyebath; **gondoler** [ˌdɔˈle] (1a) *v/i. a.* se ~ warp (*wood*); buckle (*metal*); blister (*paint*); *v/t.*: *sl.* se ~ split one's sides with laughter.
gonflage [gɔ̃ˈflaːʒ] *m* inflation; *mot.* blowing-up; **gonflé, e** [ˌˈfle] swollen; puffy; bloated; 𝕤 distended; *pej.* puffed-up; F *il est vraiment* ~ he's got some nerve *or* cheek; F ~ *à bloc* keyed-up; completely sure of oneself, *pej.* cocksure; **gonflement** [ˌflɔˈmɑ̃] *m* inflation, inflating; swelling; bulging; 𝕤 distension; **gonfler** [ˌˈfle] (1a) *v/t.* swell; inflate; blow up; puff out; fill (*the tyres*); 𝕤 distend (*the stomach*); F *mot., a. fig.* soup up; *v/i. a.* se ~ swell (up); become inflated *or* 𝕤 distended; *pej.* se ~ puff o.s. up; **gonfleur** *mot.* [ˌˈflœːr] *m* air-pump.
gonio ⚓, 𝕜 [gɔˈnjo] *m* direction-finder; ~**mètre** [ˌnjɔˈmɛtr] *m* goniometer.
gordien [gɔrˈdjɛ̃] *adj./m*: nœud *m* ~ Gordian knot.
goret [gɔˈrɛ] *m* little pig, piglet; F *fig.* dirty pig.
gorge [gɔrʒ] *f* throat, neck; *woman*: breast, bosom; *geog., a. hunt.* gorge; *geog.* pass, defile; ⊕ *etc.* groove; *axle*: neck; *lock*: tumbler; *à pleine* ~ at the top of one's voice; *mal m à la* ~ sore throat; F *fig. rendre* ~ make restitution; **gorgée** [gɔrˈʒe] *f* draught; gulp; *petite* ~ sip; **gorger** [ˌˈʒe] (1l) *v/t.* gorge; cram (*fowls, a. fig.*); **gorgerette** [ˌʒɔˈrɛt] *f* *orn.* blackcap; *cost.* gorget; **gorget** ⊕ [ˌˈʒe] *m* mo(u)lding plane.
gorille [gɔˈriːj] *m* *zo.* gorilla; F *fig.* bodyguard.
gosier [goˈzje] *m* throat; gullet; *à plein* ~ loudly; *avoir le* ~ *pavé* have a cast-iron throat.
gosse F [gɔs] *su.* kid, youngster.
gothique [gɔˈtik] 1. *adj.* Gothic; 2. *su./m* 𝔸, *ling., art*: Gothic; *su./f typ.* Old English.
gouache *paint.* [gwaʃ] *f* gouache.
gouailler [gwaˈje] (1a) *v/t/i.* chaff; **gouaillerie** [gwajˈri] *f* banter, chaff; **gouailleur, -euse** [gwaˈjœːr, ˌˈjøːz] 1. *adj.* mocking (*tone*); 2. *su.* banterer.
gouape F [gwap] *f* blackguard, hooligan.
goudron [guˈdrɔ̃] *m* tar; ⚓ *a.* pitch; **goudronnage** [ˌdrɔˈnaːʒ] *m* tarring; **goudronner** [ˌdrɔˈne] (1a) *v/t.* tar; **goudronnerie** [ˌdrɔnˈri] *f* tar-works *usu. sg.*; tar-shed; **goudronneux, -euse** [ˌdrɔˈnø, ˌˈnøːz] tarry; gummy (*oil*).
gouffre [gufr] *m* gulf, pit, abyss.
gouge [guːʒ] *f* ⊕ gouge, hollow chisel; ⊕ barrel plane.
gouine *sl.* [gwin] *f* dike, dyke (= *lesbian*).
goujat [guˈʒa] *m* 𝔸 hodman; farmhand; *fig.* boor, cad.
goujon[1] *icht.* [guˈʒɔ̃] *m* gudgeon.
goujon[2] [guˈʒɔ̃] *m* 𝔸 gudgeon (*a.* ⊕ *of a shaft*); ⊕ stud; ⊕ tenon; bolt; ⊕ coak; ⊕ *hinge*: pin(tle); **goujonner** [ˌʒɔˈne] (1a) *v/t.* ⊕ coak, dowel; ⊕ pin, bolt; ⚓ joggle.
goulée [guˈle] *f* *metall.* channel; F mouthful; **goulet** [ˌˈlɛ] *m* neck; ⚓ narrows *pl.*; 𝔸 neck-gutter; **goulot**

[ˌˈlo] *m bottle*: neck; spout; *sl.* mouth; **goulotte** [ˌˈlɔt], **goulette** [ˌˈlɛt] *f* shoot; water-channel; **goulu, e** [ˌˈly] greedy, gluttonous.

goupille ⊕ [guˈpiːj] *f* pin; *(stop-)* bolt; gudgeon; cotter; **goupiller** [ˌpiˈje] (1a) *v/t.* ⊕ pin, key; *sl.* wangle, arrange.

goupillon [gupiˈjɔ̃] *m eccl.* aspergillum; *bottle, gun, lamp*: brush.

gourbi [gurˈbi] *m* (Arab) hut; shack; F funk-hole.

gourd, gourde [guːr, gurd] benumbed; stiff.

gourde [gurd] **1.** *su./f* ♀ gourd, calabash; *(brandy-)*flask; *sl.* blockhead; **2.** *adj. sl.* blockheaded, thick.

gourdin [gurˈdɛ̃] *m* cudgel, club, bludgeon.

gourgandine † F [gurgɑ̃ˈdin] *f* hussy.

gourmand, e [gurˈmɑ̃, ˌˈmɑ̃ːd] **1.** *adj.* greedy, gluttonous; F *fig.* sweet-toothed; **2.** *su.* gourmand, glutton; epicure; **gourmander** [ˌmɑ̃ˈde] (1a) *v/t.* scold, rebuke; *fig.* treat roughly; **gourmandise** [ˌmɑ̃ˈdiːz] *f* greediness, gluttony; ˌs *pl.* sweetmeats.

gourme [gurm] *f hunt.* strangles *pl.*; ♂ impetigo; ♂ teething rash; *jeter sa ˌ* run at the nose *(horse)*; F *fig.* blow off steam; F sow one's wild oats; **gourmé, e** [gurˈme] stiff, formal *(manners)*; aloof *(person)*.

gourmet [gurˈmɛ] *m* gourmet, epicure.

gourmette [gurˈmɛt] *f horse*: curb; curb-bracelet; curb watch-chain; ⊕ polishing-chain.

gousse [gus] *f* pod, shell; *garlic*: clove; **gousset** [guˈsɛ] *m cost.*, *a.* ⊕ gusset; *cost.* fob, waistcoat pocket; ⊕ bracket; ⊕ stayplate.

goût [gu] *m* taste *(a. fig.)*; flavo(u)r; smell; liking, fancy; style, manner; *avoir bon (mauvais) ˌ* taste nice (nasty); *mauvais ˌ* bad taste; **goûter** [guˈte] **1.** (1a) *v/t.* taste; *fig.* enjoy, appreciate; *v/i.* take a snack; picnic; *ˌ à* try, sample *(s.th.)*; *ˌ de* taste *(s.th.)* (for the first time); **2.** *su./m* snack; *Am.* lunch; *meal*: tea.

goutte[1] ♂ [gut] *f* gout.

goutte[2] [gut] *f* drop; speck, *colour*: spot; F sip, drop; *sl.* spot of brandy *etc.*; *ˌ à ˌ* drop by drop; *ne … ˌ* not …

in the least, not … at all; **goutte-à-goutte** ♂ [ˌaˈgut] *m/inv.* drip; *alimenter au ˌ* drip-feed; **gouttelette** [ˌˈlɛt] *f* droplet; **goutter** [guˈte] (1a) *v/i.* drip.

goutteux, -euse ♂ [guˈtø, ˌˈtøːz] **1.** *adj.* gouty; **2.** *su.* sufferer from gout.

gouttière [guˈtjɛːr] *f* ⌂ gutter(ing); drainpipe; spout; shoot; ♂ cradle; ⌂ ˌs *pl.* eaves.

gouvernail [guvɛrˈnaːj] *m* ⚓ rudder *(a.* ✈*),* helm; ✈ ˌ *de direction* vertical rudder; ✈ ˌ *de profondeur* elevator; **gouvernant, e** [ˌˈnɑ̃, ˌˈnɑ̃ːt] **1.** *adj.* governing, ruling; **2.** *su./f* housekeeper; governess; regent; **gouverne** [guˈvɛrn] *f* guidance; ⊕ control; ⚓ steering; ✈ ˌs *pl.* control surfaces; rudders and ailerons; *fig. pour ta ˌ* for your guidance; **gouvernement** [guvɛrnəˈmɑ̃] *m* government; management; governorship; ⚓ steering; **gouvernemental, e,** *m/pl.* **-aux** [ˌnəmɑ̃ˈtal, ˌˈto] governmental; Government-…; **gouverner** [ˌˈne] (1a) *v/t.* govern *(a.* ⊕*, a. gramm.),* rule, control; ⚓ steer; **gouverneur** [ˌˈnœːr] *m* governor.

grabat [graˈba] *m* pallet; wretched bed; *fig. sur un ˌ* in abject poverty.

grabuge F [graˈbyːʒ] *m* row, ructions *pl.*

grâce [grɑːs] *f* grace *(a. eccl., a.* ✝*),* gracefulness; charm; favo(u)r; mercy; ⚖ pardon; *ˌ!* for pity's sake; ˌs *pl.* thanks; *ˌ à* thanks to; *action f de ˌs* thanksgiving; *coup m de ˌ* finishing stroke, quietus; *de mauvaise ˌ* unwillingly, ungraciously; *dire ses ˌs* say grace after a meal; *faire ˌ de qch. à q.* spare s.o. s.th.; *rendre ˌ(s)* give thanks (to s.o. for s.th., *à q. de qch.*); **gracier** [graˈsje] (1o) *v/t.* pardon, reprieve.

gracieuseté [grasjøzˈte] *f* graciousness; kindness; affability; **gracieux, -euse** [ˌˈsjø, ˌˈsjøːz] graceful, pleasing; gracious; courteous; *à titre ˌ* free (of charge), complimentary.

gracile [graˈsil] slender, slim; thin *(voice)*.

gradation [gradaˈsjɔ̃] *f* gradual process; *gramm. ˌ inverse* anti-climax; *par ˌ* gradually; **grade** [grad] *m* rank *(a.* ✗*),* grade *(a.* ♗*);* *univ.*

degree; ⚓ rating; **gradé** [gra'de] *m* ✖ non-commissioned officer, N.C.O.; ⚓ rated man; **gradin** [ˌ'dɛ̃] *m* step; en ˌs in tiers, tier upon tier; **graduation** *phys.* [ˌdɥa-'sjɔ̃] *f* graduating; scale; **graduel, -elle** [ˌ'dɥel] *adj.*, *a. su./m eccl.* gradual; **graduer** [ˌ'dɥe] (1n) *v/t.* graduate; increase gradually; *univ.* confer a degree on.

grailler [grɑ'je] (1a) *v/i.* speak in a husky voice.

graillon [grɑ'jɔ̃] *m* smell of burnt fat; F clot of phlegm; **graillonner** [ˌjɔ'ne] (1a) *v/i. cuis.* catch; taste of burnt fat; F bring up phlegm, hawk.

grain [grɛ̃] *m* grain (*a. of sand, powder, salt*); seed; *coffee:* bean; berry; *rosary etc.:* bead; texture, grain; particle, speck (*a. fig.*); ⚓ squall; ⊕ lining; ⊕ cam-roller; F bee in the bonnet, quirk; ˌ de beauté beauty spot; mole; ˌ de raisin grape; à gros ˌs coarse-grained; F avoir son ˌ be a bit fuddled (= drunk).

graine [grɛn] *f* seed; *silkworm:* eggs *pl.*; monter en ˌ run to seed; *fig.* grow into an old maid; F de la mauvaise ˌ a bad lot; **graineterie** [ˌ'tri] *f* seed-trade; seed-shop; **grainetier** [ˌ'tje] *m* corn-chandler.

graissage [grɛ'saːʒ] *m* greasing, lubrication; oiling; **graisse** [grɛs] *f* grease (*a.* ⊕); fat; *wine:* ropiness; *sl.* money; **graisser** [grɛ'se] (1a) *v/t.* grease, lubricate, oil; get grease on (*clothes*); F ˌ la patte à q. grease s.o.'s palm (= bribe s.o.); *v/i.* become ropy (*wine*); **graisseur** [ˌ'sœːr] *m person:* greaser; ⊕ lubricator, grease-cup; **graisseux, -euse** [ˌ'sø, ˌ'søːz] greasy, oily; fatty; ropy (*wine*).

grammaire [gram'mɛːr] *f* grammar; **grammairien** *m*, **-enne** *f* [ˌmɛ'rjɛ̃, ˌ'rjɛn] grammarian; **grammatical, e,** *m/pl.* **-aux** [ˌmati'kal, ˌ'ko] grammatical.

gramme [gram] *m measure:* gram (-me). [ophone.]

gramophone [gramɔ'fɔn] *m* gram-/

grand, grande [grɑ̃, grɑ̃ːd] **1.** *adj.* great, big; large; tall; high (*building, explosives, wind*); wide, extensive; grown-up; noble; high-class (*wines*); chief; main (*road*); ˌ public *m* general public; au ˌ jour in broad daylight; de ˌ cœur with a will,

heartily, willingly; de ˌ matin early in the morning; en ˌ on a large scale; un ˌ homme a great man; un homme ˌ a tall man; **2.** *su./m* (Spanish) grandee; great man; adult, grown-up; *school:* senior pupil.

grand...: ˌ-chose [grɑ̃'ʃoːz] *su./inv.:* ne ... pas ˌ not much; **grandeur** [ˌ'dœːr] *f* size; height; greatness; magnitude; splendo(u)r; **grandir** [ˌ'diːr] (2a) *v/i.* grow tall; grow up (*child*); increase, grow; *v/t.* make look taller *or* bigger; magnify (*a. fig.*); enlarge.

grand...: ˌ-livre, *pl.* ˌs-livres [grɑ̃'liːvr] *m* ledger; ˌ-mère, *pl.* ˌ(s)-mères [ˌ'mɛːr] *f* grandmother; ˌ-messe *eccl.* [ˌ'mɛs] *f* high mass; ˌ-oncle, *pl.* ˌs-oncles [ˌ'tɔ̃ːkl] *m* great-uncle; ˌ-peine [ˌ'pɛn] *adv.:* à ˌ with great difficulty *or* much trouble; ˌ-père, *pl.* ˌs-pères [ˌ'pɛːr] *m* grandfather; ˌ-route [ˌ'rut] *f* highway, high road; ˌ-rue [ˌ'ry] *f* high *or* main street; ˌs-parents [ˌpa'rɑ̃] *m/pl.* grandparents.

grange [grɑ̃ːʒ] *f* barn; mettre en ˌ garner.

granit [gra'ni] *m* granite; **graniteux, -euse** [ˌni'tø, ˌ'tøːz] granitic.

granivore [grani'vɔːr] granivorous **granulaire** [grany'lɛːr] granular; **granulation** [ˌla'sjɔ̃] *f* granulation (*a.* ✵); *gunpowder:* corning; **granule** [gra'nyl] *m*, **granulé** [grany'le] *m* granule; **granuler** [ˌ'le] (1a) *v/t.* granulate; corn (*gunpowder*); stipple (*an engraving*); **granuleux, -euse** [ˌ'lø, ˌ'løːz] granular.

graphique [gra'fik] **1.** *adj.* graphic; **2.** *su./m* graph; (*a. dessin m* ˌ) diagram.

grappe [grap] *f fruit:* bunch; cluster; ⳨ onions: string; vet. ˌs *pl.* grapes; **grappiller** [grapi'je] (1a) *v/t.* glean (*vineyards*); F pilfer, scrounge; *v/i.* F make petty profits; **grappilleur** *m*, **-euse** *f* [ˌ'jœːr, ˌ'jøːz] gleaner; F pilferer, scrounger; **grappillon** [ˌ'jɔ̃] *m* small bunch *or* cluster.

grappin [gra'pɛ̃] *m* ⚓ grapnel, grappling-iron; ⊕ grab; ⚠ anchor-iron; ˌs *pl.* climbing-irons; F mettre le ˌ sur lay hands on, get hold of.

gras, grasse [grɑ, grɑːs] **1.** *adj.*
fat(ted) (*animal*); fatty (*acid, tissue*);
greasy, oily (*rag, voice*); stout; thick
(*beam, mud, speech, weather*); heavy
(*soil*); rich (*food, coal*); soft (*outline, stone*); 🔥 aliphatic; *typ.* heavy,
bold(-faced); *fig.* broad, smutty;
fromage m ~ cream cheese; *eccl.*
jour m ~ meat day; **2.** *su./m* fat;
⊕ *beam:* thickness; thick (*of thumb*);
~ *de la jambe* calf (of the leg); *faire*
~ eat meat; **gras-double** *cuis.*
[grɑ'dubl] *m* tripe.
grasseyer [grɑsɛ'je] (1a) *v/i.* speak
with a strong guttural r.
grassouillet, -ette F [grɑsu'jɛ, ~'jɛt]
plump, chubby; buxom (*woman*).
gratifiant, e [grati'fjɑ̃, ~'fjɑ̃ːt] gratifying; satisfying; **gratification**
[~fika'sjɔ̃] *f* tip, gratuity; bonus;
gratifier [~'fje] (1o) *v/t.* ~ *q. de qch.*
bestow s.th. upon s.o.; present *or*
favo(u)r *or* hono(u)r s.o. with s.th.;
fig. attribute s.th. to s.o.
gratin [gra'tɛ̃] *m cuis.* cheese topping; cheese-topped dish; F *fig. the*
upper crust; *cuis. au* ~ with cheese
topping; **gratiné, e** *cuis.* with cheese
topping; F hellish, *a* hell of a ...
gratis [gra'tis] *adv.* free (of charge),
gratis.
gratitude [grati'tyd] *f* gratitude;
thankfulness.
gratte [grat] *f* ⊕ scraper; pickings
pl., F perks *pl.*, graft; 🌱 fringe benefits *pl.*; **~-ciel** [~'sjɛl] *m/inv.* sky-
scraper; **~-cul** [~'ky] *m/inv. dog-rose:*
hip; **~-papier** F [~pa'pje] *m/inv.*
penpusher; **~-pieds** [~'pje] *m/inv.*
shoe-scraper; **gratter** [gra'te] (1a)
v/t. scrape; scratch; scrape off; *sp.*
overtake (*a rival*); *sl.* make (*s.th.*) on
the side; *se* ~ scratch (o.s.); *v/i.:* ~ *du*
pied paw the ground (*horse*); **grattoir** [~'twaːr] *m* scraper; **grattures**
[~'tyːr] *f/pl. metal:* scrapings.
gratuit, e [gra'tɥi, ~'tɥit] free; gratuitous; unmotivated; unfounded; un-
provoked (*abuse, insult*); *à titre* ~ free
of charge, gratis; **gratuité** [~tɥi'te] *f*
gratuitousness.
gravatier [grava'tje] *m* rubbish-
carter; **gravats** [~'va] *m/pl.* (plaster)
screenings; *buildings:* rubbish *sg.*
grave [graːv] **1.** *adj.* grave; solemn;
serious, bad; important; ♪ deep,
low; **2.** *su./m* ♪ low register.
graveler [grav'le] (1c) *v/t.* gravel;

graveleux, -euse [~'lø, ~'løːz]
gravelly (*soil*); gritty; 🩺 suffering
from gravel; 🩺 showing traces of
gravel (*urine*); *fig.* smutty (*song etc.*);
gravelle 🩺 [gra'vɛl] *f* gravel; **gra-
velure** [grav'lyːr] *f* smutty story.
graver [gra've] (1a) *v/t.* engrave,
carve; *fig.* ~ *qch. dans sa mémoire*
engrave s.th. on one's memory;
graveur [~'vœːr] *m* engraver;
stone: carver; ~ *sur bois* wood-
engraver.
gravier [gra'vje] *m* gravel, grit; 🩺
~*s pl.* gravel *sg.*
gravir [gra'viːr] (2a) *v/t.* climb,
ascend; mount.
gravitation [gravita'sjɔ̃] *f* gravita-
tion(al pull); **gravité** [~'te] *f phys.*,
a. fig. gravity; *fig.* seriousness; ♪
deepness; **graviter** [~'te] (1a) *v/i.*
revolve (round, *autour de*); move;
gravitate (to, towards *à, vers*).
gravure [gra'vyːr] *f* engraving;
etching; print; ~ *en taille-douce,* ~ *sur*
cuivre copper-plate engraving; ~ *sur*
acier steel engraving.
gré [gre] *m* will, wish, pleasure;
liking, taste; consent; *à mon* ~ as I
please, to suit myself; *au* ~ *de* at the
mercy of (*the winds etc.*); *bon* ~, *mal* ~
willy-nilly; *contre mon* ~ against my
will, unwillingly; *de bon* ~ willingly;
de mon plein ~ of my own accord;
savoir ~ *à q. de qch.* be grateful to s.o.
for s.th.
grec, grecque [grɛk] **1.** *adj.* Greek;
2. *su./m ling.* Greek; *su.* ♀ Greek;
gréco-latin, e [grekɔla'tɛ̃, ~'tin]
Gr(a)eco-Latin.
gredin *m, e* †[grə'dɛ̃, ~'din] scoundrel, rogue.
gréement ⚓, 🚢 [gre'mɑ̃] *m* rig-
ging; gear; **gréer** ⚓, 🚢 [~'e] (1a)
v/t. rig.
greffage 🌱 [grɛ'faːʒ] *m* grafting;
greffe [grɛf] *su./m* ⚖ office of the
clerk of the court; ⚖ registry (*a.* †),
record-office; *su./f* 🌱, 🩺 graft,
grafting; 🩺 ~ *de cœur* heart transplant; **greffer** 🌱, 🩺 [grɛ'fe] (1a)
v/t. graft; **greffier** [~'fje] *m* ⚖
clerk of the court; ⚖, †, *admin.*
registrar; **greffoir** 🌱 [~'fwaːr] *m*
grafting-knife; **greffon** 🌱 [~'fɔ̃] *m*
graft, slip, scion.
grégaire [gre'gɛːr] gregarious; **gré-
garisme** [~ga'rism] *m* gregarious-
ness.

grège [grɛːʒ] *adj./f* raw (*silk*).
grégeois [gre'ʒwa] *adj./m*: feu m ~ Greek fire.
grêle[1] [grɛːl] slender; thin (*a. fig. voice*); *anat.* small (*intestine*).
grêle[2] [grɛːl] *f* hail; *fig.* hail, shower; **grêlé, e** [gre'le] pock-marked; **grêler** [~'le] (1a) *v/impers.* hail; *v/t.* damage by hail; [gre] pock-mark; **grêlon** [~'lɔ̃] *m* hail-stone.
grelot [grə'lo] *m* small bell; sleigh-bell; F *attacher le* ~ bell the cat; **grelotter** [~lɔ'te] (1a) *v/i.* shiver, tremble, shake (with, *de*); tinkle.
grenade [grə'nad] *f* ☿ pomegranate; ✕ grenade; **grenadier** [grəna'dje] *m* ☿ pomegranate(-tree); ✕ grenadier; ✕ bomber; F *woman*: amazon; **grenadille** [~'diːj] *f* ☿ granadilla; ☦ red ebony; **grenadin, e** [~'dɛ̃, ~'din] **1.** *adj.* of Granada; of Granada; **2.** *su./m cuis.* fricassee of chicken; ☿ grenadin; *orn.* African finch; *su./f tex.* grenadine.
grenaille [grə'naːj] *f* small grain; (small) shot; *en* ~ granulated.
grenat [grə'na] **1.** *su./m* garnet; **2.** *adj./inv.* garnet(-red).
greneler [grən'le] (1c) *v/t.* grain (*leather etc.*).
grener [grə'ne] (1d) *v/i.* corn, seed (*cereals etc.*); *v/t.* corn (*gunpowder*); grain (*salt, a. leather, paper*); stipple (*an engraving*).
grènetis [grɛn'ti] *m* milled edge (*of a coin*).
grenier [grə'nje] *m* granary; (*hay-, corn-*) loft; △ attic, garret.
grenouillage [grənu'jaːʒ] *m* (shady) dealings *pl.*, wangling; **grenouille** [grə'nuːj] *f* frog; F kitty, club-money, funds *pl.*, ✕ mess-funds *pl.*; F *manger la* ~ run off with the funds; **grenouillère** [~nu'jɛːr] *f* marsh; froggery; **grenouillette** [~nu'jɛt] *f* ☿ water-crowfoot; ☞ ranula.
grès [grɛ] *m* sandstone; (*a.* ~ *cérame*) stoneware; earthenware; **gréseux, -euse** [gre'zø, ~'zøːz] sandy, gritty; *geol.* sandstone (*rocks*); **grésière** [~'zjɛːr] *f* sandstone quarry; **grésil** [gre'zi(l)] *m* (fine) hail.
grésiller[1] [grezi'je] (1a) *v/impers.* patter (*hail*).
grésiller[2] [~] (1a) *v/i.* crackle (*fire*); sizzle; sputter (*candle*).
grève [grɛːv] *f* seashore; (*sandy*) beach; ⊕ strike, walkout; ~ *bouchon*

disruptive action, selective action; ~ *de la faim* hunger-strike; ~ *perlée* go-slow strike, *Am.* slow-down strike; ~ *sauvage* wildcat strike; ~ *sur le tas* sit-down strike; *faire* ~ be on strike; *faire la* ~ *du zèle* work to rule; *faire une* ~ *de sympathie* come out in sympathy; *se mettre en* ~ walk out.
grever [grə've] (1d) *v/t.* burden (*an estate*) (with, *de*); tɪ̱ entail (*an estate*); tɪ̱ mortgage (*land*); *admin.* rate (*a building*).
gréviste [gre'vist] *su.* striker.
gribouiller [gribu'je] (1a) *vt/i.* daub; scribble; **gribouillis** [~'ji] *m* scrawl, scribble.
grief [gri'ɛf] *m* grievance, ground for complaint; *faire* ~ *à q. de qch.* hold s.th. against s.o.
grièvement [griɛv'mɑ̃]: ~ *blessé(e)* seriously injured.
griffade [gri'fad] *f* scratch (*of claw*); **griffe** [grif] *f* claw (*a.* ⊕); *fig. a.* clutches *pl.*; maker's label; signature (stamp); *a. fig.* stamp; **griffé, e** ☦ [~'fe] with a famous label; **griffer** [~'fe] (1a) *v/t.* scratch, claw; fasten with a clamp; stamp (a signature on).
griffon [gri'fɔ̃] *m* myth. griffin; *orn.* tawny vulture; *dog*: griffon.
griffonnage [grifɔ'naːʒ] *m* scrawl, scribble; **griffonner** [~'ne] (1a) *v/t.* scrawl, scribble; do a rough sketch of; **griffonneur** *m*, **-euse** *f* [~'nœːr, ~'nøːz] scribbler.
grignoter [grinɔ'te] (1a) *v/t.* nibble (at); pick at (*one's food*); gnaw (away) (at); *fig.* eat away (at); *fig.* wear down or out; *fig.* win, get; *v/i.* nibble (at one's food).
grigou F [gri'gu] *m* miser, skinflint.
gril [gril] *m cuis.* grill, gridiron (*a.* ☘, *a.* ♨); ⊕ sluice-gate; grating; *fig. être sur le* ~ be on tenterhooks.
grillade *cuis.* [gri'jad] *f* grill, grilled steak; grilling.
grillage[1] [gri'jaːʒ] *m cuis.* grilling; roasting (*a. metall.*); ⚡ F bulb: burning-out.
grillage[2] [gri'jaːʒ] *m* lattice; (wire) netting *or* fencing; **grillager** [~ja'ʒe] (1l) *v/t.* surround with wire fencing *or* netting; **grille** [griːj] *f* grate (*a.* ⊕); grating; iron gate, railing; ⚡, *radio, fig.* grid; *mot.* grille; *fig.* schedule.
griller[1] [gri'je] (1a) *v/t. cuis.* grill; toast (*bread*); roast (*beans, a.* ⊕ *ore*);

singe (*cloth*); ♒ calcine; scorch, burn; ⚡ burn out, blow (*a bulb, etc.*); *mot.* F race past; F jump (*the traffic lights*), jump, cut out (*a stop etc.*); F smoke (*a cigarette*); F *sp.* outrun (*an opponent*); *v/i.* F *fig.* be roasting (*in the heat*); *fig.* be burning (with s.th., de qch.; to *inf.*, de *inf.*).

griller² [~] (1a) *v/t.* rail in; bar (*a window*).

grillon *zo.* [gri'jɔ̃] *m* cricket.

grill-room [gril'rum] *m* grill-room.

grimace [gri'mas] *f* grimace, wry face; **grimacer** [~ma'se] (1k) *v/i.* make faces, screw one's face up, grimace; simper; *v/t.*: ~ *un sourire* force a smile; **grimacier, -ère** [~ma'sje, ~'sjɛːr] 1. *adj.* grimacing; grinning; affected; 2. *su.* affected person; hypocrite.

grimer *thea.* [gri'me] (1a) *v/t. a.* se ~ make up.

grimoire [gri'mwaːr] *m* book of spells, gibberish; scribble, scrawl.

grimpant, e [grɛ̃'pɑ̃, ~'pɑ̃t] climbing; ⚑ *a.* creeping, trailing; **grimper** [~'pe] (1a) *vt/i.* climb; *v/i.* climb up; ⚑ climb, creep, trail; **grimpereau** *orn.* [~'pro] *m* treecreeper; **grimpette** [~'pɛt] *f* steep slope *or* climb; **grimpeur, -euse** [~'pœːr, ~'pøːz] 1. *adj.* climbing; 2. *su./m orn.* climber; *cyclism*: good hill-climber.

grincement [grɛ̃s'mɑ̃] *m* door, teeth, wheel: grinding, grating; door, gate: creaking; pen: scratch; **grincer** [grɛ̃'se] (1k) *v/i.* grate, grind; gnash (teeth); creak (door); scratch (pen).

grincheux, -euse [grɛ̃'ʃø, ~'ʃøːz] 1. *adj.* grumpy; testy; touchy; crabbed; 2. *su.* grumbler, F grouser.

gringalet F [grɛ̃ga'lɛ] *m* shrimp (= seedy boy); whipper-snapper.

griot [gri'o] *m* ⚑ flour etc.: seconds *pl.*

griotte [gri'ɔt] *f* ⚑ morello cherry; *min.* griotte (= sort of marble flecked with red and brown).

grippage ⊕ [gri'paːʒ] *m* rubbing, friction; jamming; abrasion.

grippe [grip] *f* dislike; ⚕ influenza, F 'flu; *prendre q. en ~* take a dislike to s.o.; **grippé, e** ⚕ [gri'pe] *adj.*: être~have influenza, F have the 'flu; **gripper** [~] (1a) *v/i. a.* se ~ ⊕ seize up, jam; run hot; become abraded; *tex.* pucker; *v/t.* seize,

snatch; **grippe-sou,** *pl.* **grippe-sou(s)** F [grip'su] *m* skinflint, miser.

gris, grise [gri, griːz] grey; dull (*weather, a. fig.*); F tipsy, fuddled; *faire grise mine à* give a cold welcome to; **grisaille** [gri'zaːj] *f paint.* grisaille; greyness; *fig.* dullness; **grisailler** [~zɑ'je] (1a) *v/t.* paint grey; paint (*s.th.*) in grisaille; *v/i.* turn grey (*hair*); **grisâtre** [~'zɑːtr] greyish.

grisbi *sl.* [gris'bi] *m* dough (= money).

griser [gri'ze] (1a) *v/t.* intoxicate, make drunk; se ~ get drunk; **grisette** [~'zɛt] *f* grisette (*a. tex.*).

grisoller [grizɔ'le] (1a) *v/i.* sing (*lark*).

grison¹, -onne [gri'zɔ̃, ~'zɔn] 1. *adj.* of the canton of Grisons; 2. *su.* inhabitant of the canton of Grisons.

grison², -onne † [gri'zɔ̃, ~'zɔn] 1. *adj.* grey(-haired), grizzled; 2. *su./m* grey-beard; donkey; **grisonner** [~zɔ'ne] (1a) *v/i.* turn grey (*hair*).

grisou ⚒ [gri'zu] *m* fire-damp; gas; coup *m* de ~ fire-damp explosion.

grive *orn.* [griːv] *f* thrush; **grivelé, e** [griv'le] speckled; **griveler** [~] (1d) *v/t.* obtain (*a meal etc.*) without being able to pay; **grivèlerie** [grivɛl'ri] *f* sponging; graft; pilfering.

grivois, e [gri'vwa, ~'vwaːz] broad, spicy (*joke, story, etc.*); **grivoiserie** [~vwaz'ri] *f* broad *or* smutty joke or story *etc.*; licentious gesture.

grog [grɔg] *m* grog, toddy.

grognard *hist.* [grɔ'ɲaːr] *m* soldier of Napoleon's Old Guard; **grognement** [grɔɲ'mɑ̃] *m* grunt; growl; snarl; grumbling; **grogner** [grɔ'ɲe] (1a) *v/i.* grunt; growl; grumble; *v/t.* growl out (*s.th.*); **grogneur, -euse** [~'ɲœːr, ~'ɲøːz] 1. *adj.* grumbling; 2. *su./m* grumbler, F grouser; **grognon, -onne** [~'ɲɔ̃, ~'ɲɔn] 1. *adj.* grumbling; peevish; 2. *su./m* grumbler; cross-patch; **grognonner** F [~ɲɔ'ne] (1a) *v/i.* grunt; grumble, grouse; be peevish.

groin [grwɛ̃] *m pig*: snout.

grol(l)e *sl.* [grɔl] *f* shoe.

grommeler [grɔm'le] (1c) *vt/i.* mutter; growl; grumble.

grondement [grɔ̃d'mɑ̃] *m* thunder: rumble, rumbling; *storm*: roar(ing); *sea*: boom; *dog*: growl; **gronder** [grɔ̃'de] (1a) *v/i.* growl (*dog*);

guérite

grumble (at, *contre*); rumble (*thunder*); roar (*sea*, *storm*); *v/t.* scold; **gronderie** [\~'dri] *f* scolding; **grondeur, -euse** [\~'dœːr, \~'døːz] **1.** *adj.* grumbling, scolding; **2.** *su.* grumbler; *su./f* shrew.

groom [grum] *m* page-boy, *Am.* bell-hop.

gros, grosse [gro, groːs] **1.** *adj.* big, large; stout, fat; thick; broad (*humour etc.*); foul (*weather*, *word*); heavy (*rain*, *sea*); swollen (*river*); † *f* pregnant; *fig.* teeming (with, *de*); *fig.* fraught (with, *de*); \~ *bétail* *m* cattle; \~ *doigt* *m* du *pied* big toe; F *grosse légume* *f* big shot; △ \~ *œuvre* *m* foundations *pl.*; main walls *pl.*; *avoir le cœur* \~ be heavy-hearted; **2.** *gros* *adv.* a great deal, a lot; *gagner* \~ earn a lot, make big money; *écrire* \~ write in large letters; **3.** *su./m* bulk, main part; ✗ main body (*of an army*); thickest part; essential (part); *winter etc.*: heart; ✝ *de* \~ wholesale (*price*, *firm*, *business*, *etc.*); *en* \~ rough, broad (*estimate etc.*); (*describe etc.*) roughly, broadly; all told, altogether; (*write*) in large letters; ✝ wholesale (*a. fig.*); ✝ *marchand* *m* en \~ wholesaler; ✝ *faire le* \~ deal in wholesale; *su./f* gross, twelve dozen.

groseille ♀ [gro'zɛːj] *f* currant; \~ *à maquereau* gooseberry; **groseillier** ♀ [\~zɛ'je] *m* currant bush.

gros-grain *tex.* [gro'grɛ̃] *m* grogram.

grossesse ✗ [gro'sɛs] *f* pregnancy; **grosseur** [\~'sœːr] *f* size, bulk; *lips*: thickness; ✗ swelling; **grossier, -ère** [\~'sje, \~'sjɛːr] coarse; gross, crude; rude, unmannerly; rough; boorish; crass (*ignorance*, *stupidity*, *etc.*); **grossièreté** [\~sjɛr'te] *f* coarseness, roughness; rudeness; grossness; coarse language; *dire des* \~s be offensive; **grossir** [\~'siːr] (2a) *v/t.* enlarge, magnify (*a. opt.*, *a. fig.*); swell; *v/i.* grow bigger, increase; put on weight (*person*); **grossissement** [\~sis'mɑ̃] *m* magnification; enlargement; increase, swelling; **grossiste** ✝ [\~'sist] *m* wholesaler; **grossoyer** [\~swa'je] (1h) *v/t.* engross (*a document*).

grotesque [grɔ'tɛsk] **1.** *adj.* grotesque; **2.** *su./m* grotesque person; freak.

grotte [grɔt] *f* grotto; cave.

grouiller [gru'je] (1a) *v/i.* swarm, crawl, teem, be alive (with, *de*); rumble (*belly*); † stir; *v/t.*: *sl.* se \~ hurry up, F get a move on.

groupe [grup] *m persons*, *objects*, *a.* ♪: group; *stars*: cluster; *trees*: clump; *biol.* division; \~ *de* *pression* pressure group; ✗ \~ *sanguin* blood-group; **groupement** [\~'mɑ̃] *m* grouping; group; **grouper** [gru'pe] (1a) *v/t.* group; *se* \~ form a group *or* groups; gather, cluster (round, *autour de*).

gruau [gry'o] *m* flour of wheat; \~ *d'avoine* groats *pl.*; *cuis.* gruel.

grue [gry] *f* *orn.*, *a.* ⊕ crane; F street-walker, prostitute; ⊕ \~ *à* *bras* (*or* *à* *flèche*) jib-crane; 👜 \~ *d'alimentation* water-pillar; F *faire le* *pied* *de* \~ cool one's heels, hang about (*ger.*, *à* *inf.*).

gruger [gry'ʒe] (1l) *v/t.* crunch; F eat; *fig.* sponge on (*s.o.*), fleece (*s.o.*).

grume [grym] *f* log; *bois* *m* de (*or* en) \~ undressed timber.

grumeau [gry'mo] *m* clot; *salt*: speck; **grumeler** [grym'le] (1c) *v/t.*: se \~ clot, curdle; **grumeleux, -euse** [\~'lø, \~'løːz] curdled; gritty (*pear*).

grutier ⊕ [gry'tje] *m* crane-driver.

gruyère [gry'jɛːr] *m* gruyère.

gué [ge] *m* ford; **guéable** [\~'abl] fordable; **guéer** [\~'e] (1a) *v/t.* ford (*a river*, *a stream*); water (*a horse*).

guenille [gə'niːj] *f* rag; F trollop; *en* \~s in rags.

guenon [gə'nɔ̃] *f* *zo.* long-tailed monkey; F ugly woman.

guêpe *zo.* [gɛːp] *f* wasp; **guêpier** [gɛ'pje] *m* wasps' nest; *orn.* bee-eater.

guère [gɛːr] *adv.*: *ne* ... \~ hardly, little, scarcely, not much *or* many.

guéret [ge'rɛ] *m* ploughed land; fallow land.

guéridon [geri'dɔ̃] *m* pedestal table.

guérilla ✗ [geri'ja] *f* guerilla (warfare); **guérillero** ✗ [\~je'ro] *m per-son*: guerilla.

guérir [ge'riːr] (2a) *v/t.* cure; heal (*a wound etc.*); *v/i.* get better, be cured; heal (*wound*); **guérison** [geri'zɔ̃] *f* cure; *wound*: healing; recovery; **guérissable** [\~'sabl] curable; healable; **guérisseur, -euse** [\~'sœːr, \~'søːz] *su.* healer; quack-doctor.

guérite [ge'rit] *f* ✗ sentry box; workman's hut; (*watchman's*) shelter.

guerre [gɛːr] *f* war(fare); *fig.* quarrel; *Grande* ♀ Great War, World War I; *faire la* ~ make war (on, *à*); *faire la* ~ *à qch. a.* fight s.th.; *fig. de bonne* ~ fair; **guerrier, -ère** [gɛ'rje, ~'rjɛːr] **1.** *adj.* warlike; **2.** *su./m* warrior; **guerroyer** [~rwa'je] (1h) *v/i.* wage war.

guet [gɛ] *m* watch; look-out; patrol; *faire le* ~ be on the look-out; ~**apens**, *pl.* ~**s-apens** [gɛta'pɑ̃] *m* ambush, trap.

guêtre [gɛːtr] *f* gaiter; *mot.* patch, sleeve.

guetter [gɛ'te] (1a) *v/t.* lie in wait for, watch for; *fig.* wait (*one's opportunity*); **guetteur** ✕, ♣ [~'tœːr] *m person:* look-out.

gueulard, e F [gœ'laːr, ~'lard] **1.** *adj.* loud-mouthed (*person*); noisy; **2.** *su.* loudmouth, bigmouth; **gueule** [gœl] *f animal, a. sl. person:* mouth; *sl.* face; F look, appearance; *gun:* muzzle; opening; *sl.* casser la ~ à q. break s.o.'s jaw, F sock s.o.; *sl.* ta ~! shut up!; F *avoir une drôle de* ~ look funny; F *avoir de la* ~ look or be great; **gueule-de-loup**, *pl.* **gueules-de-loup** ♀ [~də'lu] snapdragon, antirrhinum; **gueuler** *sl.* [gœ'le] (1a) *vt/i.* bawl; **gueuleton** F [gœl'tɔ̃] *m* blow-out, spread; **gueuletonner** F [~lətɔ'ne] (1a) *v/i.* have a blow-out.

gueusaille F [gø'zaːj] *f* rabble; **gueusard** [~'zaːr] *m* beggar; rascal, rogue.

gueuse *metall.* [gøːz] *f* pig-mo(u)ld; **gueuserie** [gøz'ri] *f* beggary; begging; *fig.* poor show, poor affair.

gueux, gueuse [gø, gøːz] **1.** *adj.* poverty-stricken, poor; **2.** *su.* beggar; tramp, vagabond; *su./f* wench; *courir la* ~ lead a wild life.

gui[1] ♀ [gi] *m* mistletoe.

gui[2] ♣ [~] *m* boom; guy(-rope).

guibolle *sl.* [gi'bɔl] *f* leg.

guichet [gi'ʃɛ] *m post office, bank etc.:* counter, window; wicket, hatch; 🚋 booking office (window); *thea.* box office; *sp. cricket:* wicket; **guichetier** [giʃ'tje] *m prison:* turnkey.

guide[1] [gid] *m* guide (*a.* ✕, *a.* ⊕); guide-book.

guide[2] [~] *f* rein; girl guide.

guide-âne [gi'dɑːn] *m* (handbook of) elementary instructions *pl.*; *writing pad:* black lines *pl.*, ruled guide; **guider** [~'de] (1a) *v/t.* guide; direct, steer; lead; ⊕ control; *se* ~ *sur* use as

a guide; ⊕ *guidé par ordinateur* computer-controlled.

guidon [gi'dɔ̃] *m* ♣ pennant; *cycle:* handle-bar; ✕ *gun:* foresight.

guigne [giɲ] *f* heart-cherry; F *fig.* bad luck; F *avoir la* ~ be out of luck.

guigner F [gi'ɲe] (1a) *v/t.* steal a glance at; have an eye to; ogle (*s.o.*). [(tree).\

guignier ♀ [gi'ɲje] *m* heart-cherry\

guignol [gi'ɲɔl] *m* Punch and Judy show; puppet (show).

guignolet [giɲɔ'lɛ] *m* cherry-brandy.

guignon [gi'ɲɔ̃] *m* bad luck; *avoir du* ~ have a run of bad luck.

guillaume ⊕ [gi'joːm] *m plane:* rabbet.

guillemets [gij'mɛ] *m/pl.* inverted commas, quotation marks.

guilleret, -ette [gij'rɛ, ~'rɛt] gay; broad (*joke*).

guillocher ⊕ [gijɔ'ʃe] (1a) *v/t.* chequer.

guillotine [gijɔ'tin] *f* guillotine (*a. for cutting paper*); *fenêtre f à* ~ sash-window.

guimauve ♀ [gi'moːv] *f* marshmallow.

guimbarde [gɛ̃'bard] *f* ♪ Jew's-harp; ⊕ grooving-plane; *sl.* rattletrap, *Am.* jalopy.

guimpe [gɛ̃p] *f* (*nun's*) wimple; chemisette.

guindage [gɛ̃'daːʒ] *m* ⊕ hoisting; ⊕ *tackle:* hoist; **guindé, e** [~'de] stiff, starchy; strained; stilted (*style*); **guinder** [~'de] (1a) *v/t.* hoist; *fig.* strain; *fig.* make look stiff; *fig. se* ~ become stilted or strained (*story, etc.*); adopt a stiff manner (*person*).

guinguette [gɛ̃'gɛt] *f* suburban tavern; out-of-town inn.

guiper [gi'pe] (1a) *v/t.* wind; wrap; lap (*a.* ⚡); **guipure** [~'pyːr] *f* pillow-lace; ⚡ lapping.

guirlande [gir'lɑ̃d] *f* garland, wreath, festoon; *pearls:* rope.

guise [giːz] *f* manner, way; *à votre* ~! as you like!; please yourself!; *en* ~ *de* by way of, as.

guitare ♪ [gi'taːr] *f* guitar.

gustatif, -ve [gysta'tif, ~'tiːv] gustative; gustatory (*nerve*); **gustation** [~ta'sjɔ̃] *f* tasting.

gutta-percha [gytapɛr'ka] *f* gutta-percha.

guttural, e, *m/pl.* **-aux** [gyty'ral, ~'ro] **1.** *adj.* guttural; throaty

(*voice*); **2.** *su./f gramm.* guttural.
gymnase [ʒim'nɑːz] *m* gymnasium,
F gym; **gymnaste** [ʌ'nast] *su.*
gymnast; **gymnastique** [ʌnas'tik]
1. *adj.* gymnastic; **2.** *su./f* gymnastics *sg.*, F gym; ∼ *rythmique*
eurhythmics *sg.*; *faire de la* ∼ do
gymnastics.
gymnote *icht.* [ʒim'nɔt] *m* electric
eel.
gynécologiste ⚕ [ʒinekɔlɔ'ʒist], **gy-**
nécologue ⚕ [ʌ'lɔg] *su.* gyn(a)ecol-
ogist.
gypaète *orn.* [ʒipa'ɛt] *m* lammer-
geyer.   [plaster of Paris.)
gypse [ʒips] *m min.* gypsum; ✝)
gyrophare [ʒirɔ'faːr] *m* flashing
light; **gyroscope** [ʌ'skɔp] *m* gyroscope; **gyroscopique** [ʌskɔ'pik] gy-
roscopic; ✈ *appareil m* ∼ *de pilotage*
gyro-pilot; ⚓ *compas m* ∼ gyro-compass.

H

(Before the so-called aspirate *h*, marked ***h**, there is neither elision nor liaison.)

H, h [aʃ] *m* H, h.

habile [a'bil] clever; skilful; ⚖ competent (to, *à*); **habileté** [abil'te] *f* skill, ability; cleverness; (clever) trick; **habilité** ⚖ [ɬ 'te] *f* competency; **habiliter** ⚖ [ɬ 'te] (la) *v/t.* entitle (s.o. to *inf.*, *q. à inf.*).

habillage [abi'jaːʒ] *m* dressing; ⊕ assembling; ✟ get-up; **habillement** [abij'mɑ̃] *m* clothing; clothes *pl.*; dress; **habiller** [abi'je] (la) *v/t.* dress; clothe; ✟ get up; cover; *dress:* suit (*s.o.*); s'~ dress (o.s.), get dressed; dress up (as, en); **habilleur** *m*, **-euse** *f* [ɬ 'jœːr, ɬ 'jøːz] *thea. etc.* dresser.

habit [a'bi] *m* (*a.* ~ *de soirée*) dress coat; dress; coat; *eccl.* habit; *eccl.* frock; ~ **vert** green coat (*of the Members of the Académie française*).

habitable [abi'tabl] habitable; **habitacle** [ɬ 'takl] *m* ⚓ binnacle; ✈ cockpit; *poet.* dwelling; **habitant** *m*, **e** *f* [ɬ 'tɑ̃, ɬ 'tɑ̃ːt] inhabitant; occupier (*of a house*); resident; **habitat** ♀, *zo. etc.* [ɬ 'ta] *m* habitat; **habitation** [ɬ ta'sjɔ̃] *f* habitation; dwelling; residence; **habiter** [ɬ 'te] (la) *v/t.* inhabit, live in; *v/i.* dwell, live, reside.

habitude [abi'tyd] *f* habit, custom, practice, use; *avoir l'* ~ *de* be used to (*s.th., doing s.th.*); *avoir l'~ de* (*inf.*) *a.* be in the habit of (*ger.*); *j'ai l'~*, *j'en ai l'~* I am used to it; *d'~* usually; *par* ~ from sheer force of habit; **habitué** *m*, **e** *f* [ɬ 'tɥe] frequenter, regular attendant *or* customer; **habituel, -elle** [ɬ 'tɥɛl] usual; customary; **habituer** [ɬ 'tɥe] (1n) *v/t.*: ~ *q. à* accustom s.o. to *or* get s.o. used to (*s.th., doing s.th.*); s'~ *à* get used to.

***hâblerie** [ɑblə'ri] *f* boasting; ***hâbleur** *m*, **-euse** *f* [ɑ'blœːr, ɬ 'blø:z] boaster.

***hache** [aʃ] *f* axe; ~-**légumes** [ɬ le'gym] *m/inv.* vegetable-cutter; ~-**paille** [ɬ 'paːj] *m/inv.* chaff-cutter.

***hacher** [a'ʃe] (la) *v/t.* chop (up); hash (*meat*); hack up; *fig.* score (*s.o.'s face*); hatch (*a drawing etc.*); ***hachereau** [aʃ'ro] *m* small axe, hatchet; ***hachette** [a'ʃɛt] *f* hatchet; ***hachis** *cuis.* [a'ʃi] *m* hash (*a. fig.*), mince.

***hachisch** [a'ʃiʃ] *m* hashish.

***hachoir** [a'ʃwaːr] *m* chopper; chopping-knife; chopping-board; ***hachure** [a'ʃyːr] *f* hachure, hatching; en ~s hachured.

***hagard, e** [a'gaːr, ~'gard] wild, wild-looking; distraught.

***haï, e** [a'i] *p.p.* of *haïr*.

***haie** [ɛ] *f* hedge(row); *people:* line; *sp.* hurdle; ~ *d'honneur* guard of hono(u)r; *sp. course f de* ~s hurdle-race; *faire la* ~ be lined up.

***haillon** [a'jɔ̃] *m* rag, tatter.

***haine** [ɛːn] *f* hate, hatred; ***haineux, -euse** [ɛ'nø, ~'nøːz] full of hatred.

***haïr** [a'iːr] (2m) *v/t.* hate, detest, loathe.

***haire** [ɛːr] *f* hair-shirt; *tex.* hair-cloth.

***hais** [ɛ] *1st p. sg. pres.* of *haïr*; ***haïs** [a'i] *1st p. sg. p.s.* of *haïr*; ***haïssable** [ai'sabl] hateful, odious; ***haïssent** [a'is] *3rd p. pl. pres.* of *haïr*.

***halage** [a'laːʒ] *m* ⚓ *ship:* hauling; towing; *chemin m de* ~ tow(ing)-path.

***hâle** [ɑːl] *m* tan(ning); sunburn; ***hâlé, e** [ɑ'le] (sun)tanned, sunburnt.

haleine [a'lɛn] *f* breath; *fig.* wind; *à perte d'~* until out of breath; *avoir l'~ courte* be short-winded; *de longue* ~ long and exacting, of long duration; long-term (*plans*); *hors d'~* out of breath; *tenir en* ~ keep (*s.o.*) breathless.

***haler** [a'le] (la) *v/t.* ⚓ haul (in); tow.

***halètement** [alɛt'mɑ̃] *m* panting, gasping; ***haleter** [al'te] (1d) *v/i.* pant; gasp (for breath); puff.

***haleur** ⚓ [a'lœːr] *m* hauler; tower.

***hall** [ɔl] *m* entrance hall; *hotel:*

lounge; *mot.* open garage; ⊕ shop, room; ***hallage** ✝ [aˈlaːʒ] *m* market dues *pl.*; ***halle** [al] *f* (covered) market.
*hallebarde *hist.* [alˈbard] *f* halberd.
*hallier [aˈlje] *m* thicket, copse; ~*s pl.* brushwood *sg.*
hallucinant, e [alysiˈnɑ̃, ~ˈnɑ̃t] hallucinating; *fig.* incredible, staggering; **hallucination** [~naˈsjɔ̃] *f* hallucination; **hallucinogène** [~nɔˈʒɛn] 1. *adj.* hallucinogenic; 2. *su./m* hallucinogen.
*halo [aˈlo] *m meteor.* halo; *phot.* halation; *opt.* blurring.
halogène ⚛ [alɔˈʒɛn] 1. *adj.* halogenous; 2. *su./m* halogen.
*halte [alt] *f* halt (*a.* 🚂), stop; stopping-place; *faire* ~ stop, ✕ halt; ~(-*là*)! stop!, ✕ halt!
haltère [alˈtɛːr] *m* dumbbell.
*hamac ⚓ *etc.* [aˈmak] *m* hammock.
*hameau [aˈmo] *m* hamlet.
hameçon [amˈsɔ̃] *m* (fish) hook; *fig.* bait; *fig. mordre à l'*~ take the bait.
*hampe¹ [ɑ̃ːp] *f flag:* pole; *spear:* shaft; handle; ⚘ stem.
*hampe² *cuis.* [~] *f* (thin) flank of beef.
*hamster [amsˈtɛːr] *m zo.* hamster; F hoarder (*of food*).
*hanap ✝ [aˈnap] *m* hanap, goblet.
*hanche [ɑ̃ːʃ] *f* hip; *horse:* haunch; ⚓ *ship:* quarter.
*handicap [ɑ̃diˈkap] *m sp.* handicap (*a. fig.*); *fig.* disadvantage; ***handicaper** *sp.* [~kaˈpe] (1a) *v/t.* handicap (*a. fig.*); *les handicapés* (*mentaux or physiques*) the (mentally *or* physically) handicapped.
*hangar [ɑ̃ˈgaːr] *m* shed; lean-to; ✈ hangar.
*hanneton [anˈtɔ̃] *m zo.* cockchafer; F *fig.* harum-scarum, scatterbrain.
*hanter [ɑ̃ˈte] (1a) *v/t.* haunt; *maison f hantée* haunted house; ***hantise** [ɑ̃ˈtiːz] *f* obsession; haunting memory.
*happement [apˈmɑ̃] *m* snatching up, seizing; ***happer** [aˈpe] (1a) *v/t.* catch, snatch; *v/i.* cling, stick.
*haquenée [akˈne] *f* hack; ambling mare; *aller à la* ~ amble along.
*haquet [aˈkɛ] *m* dray, waggon (*a.* ✕); ***haquetier** [ak'tje] *m* drayman.
*hara-kiri [arakiˈri] *m* harakiri, happy dispatch.

*harangue [aˈrɑ̃ːg] *f* harangue; ***haranguer** [arɑ̃ˈge] (1m) *v/t.* harangue; F *fig.* lecture (*s.o.*); F hold forth to; ***harangueur** [~ˈgœːr] *m* orator; F tub-thumper.
*haras [aˈrɑ] *m* stud-farm; stud.
*harasser [araˈse] (1a) *v/t.* wear out, exhaust.
*harcèlement [arsɛlˈmɑ̃] *m* harassing, harrying (*a.* ✕); ***harceler** [~səˈle] (1d) *v/t.* harass, harry (*a.* ✕); badger; nag at, be on at.
*harde¹ [ard] *f* herd; *orn.* flock.
*harde² *hunt.* [ard] *f* leash; ***harder** *hunt.* [arˈde] (1a) *v/t.* leash (*the hounds in couples*).
*hardes [ard] *f/pl.* old clothes.
*hardi, e [arˈdi] bold; daring; rash; impudent; ***hardiesse** [~ˈdjɛs] *f* boldness; temerity, daring; rashness; effrontery.
*hareng [aˈrɑ̃] *m* herring; ~ *fumé* kipper; ~ *saur* red herring; ***harengaison** [arɑ̃gɛˈzɔ̃] *f* herring-season; herring-fishing; ˈ**harengère** [~ˈʒɛːr] *f* fishwife.
*hargne [arɲ] *f* ill-temper; aggressiveness; ***hargneux, -euse** [arˈɲø, ~ˈɲøːz] surly; peevish; bad-tempered; aggressive; nagging (*wife*).
*haricot¹ ⚘ [ariˈko] *m* bean; ~ *blanc* haricot bean; ~ *rouge* kidney bean; ~ *vert* French bean; *sl. courir sur le* ~ *à q.* get on s.o.'s nerves.
*haricot² [~] *m* stew, haricot; ~ *de mouton* haricot mutton, *Am.* lamb stew.
*haridelle F [ariˈdɛl] *f* jade, nag.
harmonica ♪ [armɔniˈka] *m* harmonica; mouth-organ.
harmonie [armɔˈni] *f* ♪ harmony (*a. fig.*); *fig.* agreement; ♪ brass and reed band; **harmonieux, -euse** [~ˈnjø, ~ˈnjøːz] harmonious; **harmonique** [~ˈnik] harmonic; **harmoniser** [~niˈze] (1a) *v/t. a. s'*~ harmonize; match (*colours*); **harmonium** ♪ [~ˈnjɔm] *m* harmonium.
*harnacher [arnaˈʃe] (1a) *v/t.* harness; rig (*s.o.*) out; ***harnacheur** [~ˈʃœːr] *m* harness-maker; saddler; groom.
*harnais [arˈnɛ] *m*, ✝ ***harnois** [~ˈnwa] *m horse*, *a. tex.:* harness.
*haro [aˈro] *m* hue and cry; *crier* ~ *sur* denounce.
harpagon [arpaˈgɔ̃] *m* skinflint.
*harpe¹ ♪ [arp] *f* harp.

*harpe² △ [⁓] *f* toothing-stone.
*harpie [ar'pi] *f myth., a. fig.* harpy; *fig.* hell-cat.
*harpin ⚓ [ar'pɛ̃] *m* boat-hook.
*harpiste ♩ [ar'pist] *su.* harpist.
*harpon [ar'pɔ̃] *m* harpoon; △ wall-staple; ***harponner** [⁓pɔ'ne] (1a) *v/t.* harpoon; *fig.* buttonhole (*s.o.*).
*hasard [a'zaːr] *m* chance, luck; risk; hazard (*a. golf*); *à tout* ⁓ at all hazards *or* events; *au* ⁓ at random; ... *de* ⁓ chance ...; *par* ⁓ by chance; ***hasardé, e** [azar'de] risky, foolhardy; bold; hazardous; ***hasarder** [⁓'de] (1a) *v/t.* risk, venture; ***hasardeux, -euse** [⁓'dø, ⁓'døːz] perilous, risky; daring, foolhardy.
*hase *zo.* [ɑːz] *f* doe-hare; doe-rabbit.
*hâte [ɑːt] *f* haste, hurry; *à la* ⁓ in a hurry; hurriedly; *avoir* ⁓ *de* (*inf.*) be in a hurry to (*inf.*); long to (*inf.*); *en* (*toute*) ⁓ with all possible speed; ***hâter** [ɑ'te] (1a) *v/t. a. se* ⁓ hasten, hurry; ***hâtif, -ve** [ɑ'tif, ⁓'tiːv] hasty; premature; early (*fruit etc.*); ***hâtiveau** [ɑti'vo] *m* early fruit (*esp. pear*); early vegetable.
*hauban [o'bɑ̃] *m* ⚓ shroud; △, ⊕ stay; ⚡ (*bracing-*)wire; ***haubaner** [oba'ne] (1a) *v/t.* stay, guy.
*haubert *hist.* [o'bɛːr] *m* hauberk, coat of mail.
*hausse [oːs] *f* rise (*a.* ↑), *Am.* raise; *rifle:* back-sight, rear-sight; ⊕ block, prop; *à la* ⁓ on the rise; ***haussement** [os'mɑ̃] *m* raising; ⁓ *d'épaules* shrug; ***hausser** [o'se] (1a) *v/t.* raise (*a.* ♩; *a. a house, the price, one's voice*); lift; increase; shrug (*one's shoulders*); *v/i.* rise, go up; ⚓ heave in sight; ***haussier** ↑ [o'sje] *m* bull.
*haussière ⚓ [o'sjɛːr] *f* hawser.
*haut, haute [o, oːt] **1.** *adj.* high; elevated; eminent, important; loud (*voice*); erect (*head*); upper (*floor etc.*); *la haute mer* the open sea; *la mer haute* high tide; **2.** *haut adv.* high (up); aloud; haughtily; further back (*in time*); *fig.* ⁓ *la main* easily; ⁓ *les mains!* hands up!; *d'en* ⁓ *adj.* upstairs; upper; *en* ⁓ *adv.* above; upstairs; **3.** *su./m* height; top; summit; *tomber de son* ⁓ fall flat; *fig.* fall; *fig.* be dumbfounded;

vingt pieds de ⁓ 20 feet *or* foot high; *su./f: la haute* the smart set, the upper crust.
*hautain, e [o'tɛ̃, ⁓'tɛn] proud; haughty.
*haut...: ***⁓bois** ♩ [o'bwa] *m* oboe; (*a.* ***⁓boïste** [obɔ'ist] *m*) oboist; ***⁓-de-chausses,** *pl.* ***⁓s-de-chausses** [od'ʃoːs] *m* breeches *pl.*; ***⁓-de-forme,** *pl.* ***⁓s-de-forme** [⁓'fɔrm] *m* top hat.
*haute-contre, *pl.* ***hautes-contre** ♩ [ot'kɔ̃:tr] *f voice:* alto.
*hautement [ot'mɑ̃] *adv.* highly; loudly; loftily; frankly.
*Hautesse [o'tɛs] *f title of sultan:* Highness.
*hauteur [o'tœːr] *f* height; eminence, high place; hill(-top); level; depth; ▵, *astr.* altitude; ♩ pitch; *fig.* arrogance; *fig.* principles *etc.*: loftiness; *être à la* ⁓ *de* be equal to; be a match for; *fig.* be abreast of (*developments, news*); ⚓ be off (*Calais*); ⚡ *prendre de la* ⁓ gain height; *tomber de sa* ⁓ fall flat; F *fig.* be dumbfounded; *sp. saut en* ⁓ high jump.
*haut...: ***⁓-fond,** *pl.* ***⁓s-fonds** [o'fɔ̃] *m sea:* shoal, shallows *pl.*; ***⁓le-cœur** [ol'kœːr] *m/inv.* heave, nausea; *avoir des* ⁓ retch; ***⁓-le-corps** [⁓'kɔːr] *m/inv.* sudden start; ***⁓-lieu,** *pl.* ***⁓s-lieux** [o'ljø] centre, Mecca (*of art etc.*); ***⁓-parleur** [opar'lœːr] *m radio etc.*: loudspeaker; amplifier; ***⁓-relief,** *pl.* ***⁓s-reliefs** [orə'ljɛf] *m arts:* alto-relievo.
*havanais, e [ava'nɛ, ⁓'nɛːz] *adj., a. su.* ♀ Havanese; ***havane** [a'van] **1.** *su./m* Havana (*cigar*); **2.** *adj./inv.* tobacco-colo(u)red; brown.
*hâve [ɑːv] haggard, gaunt; wan.
*havre ⚓ [ɑːvr] *m* harbo(u)r, haven.
*havresac [ɑvrə'sak] *m* ✕ knapsack; tool-bag; *camping:* haversack.
*hayon *mot.* [ɛ'jɔ̃] *m* rear door, tailgate; *a. voiture à* ⁓ *arrière* hatchback.
hé [e] *int.* hi!; I say!; what!
*heaume *hist.* [oːm] *m* helm(et).
hebdomadaire [ɛbdɔma'dɛːr] **1.** *adj.* weekly; **2.** *su./m* weekly (*paper or publication*).
héberger [eber'ʒe] (1l) *v/t.* accommodate, put up, take in, lodge.
hébéter [ebe'te] (1f) *v/t.* stupefy; daze; *fig.* stun; **hébétude** [⁓'tyd] *f fig.* daze, dazed condition; ⚕ hebetude.

hébraïque [ebra'ik] Hebrew, Hebraic; **hébraïsant** *m*, **e** *f* [~i'zã, ~'zã:t] Hebraist; **hébreu** [e'brø] *adj./m*, *a. su./m ling.* Hebrew.
hécatombe [eka'tɔ̃:b] *f* hecatomb; F *fig. persons:* (great) slaughter.
hectare [ɛk'ta:r] *m* hectare (2.47 *acres*).
hectique ⚕ [ɛk'tik] hectic.
hecto... [ɛktɔ] hecto...; **~gramme** [~'gram] *m* hectogram(me); **~litre** [~'litr] *m* hectolitre (2.75 *bushels*); **~mètre** [~'mɛtr] *m* hectometre.
***hein!** F [ɛ̃] *int.* what?; isn't it?; did I not?, *etc.*
hélas! [e'lɑ:s] *int.* alas!
***héler** [e'le] (1f) *v/t.* hail (*a ship, a taxi*).
hélianthe ⚘ [e'ljã:t] *m* sunflower, helianthus.
hélice [e'lis] *f* ⚹, *anat.* helix (*a.* = *snail*); ⚓ screw; ⚓, ✈ propeller; Archimedean screw; *escalier m en* ~ spiral staircase; *en* ~ helical (ly *adv.*); ⚓ *vaisseau m à* ~ screw-steamer.
hélicoptère ✈ [elikɔp'tɛ:r] *m* helicopter.
hélio... [eljɔ] helio...; **~graphe** *astr.* [~'graf] *m* heliograph; **~gravure** [~gra'vy:r] *f* photogravure; heliogravure; **~scope** *astr.* [~s'kɔp] *m* solar prism; **~thérapie** ⚕ [~tera'pi] *f* sunlight *or* sun ray treatment; **~trope** ⚘ [~'trɔp] *m* heliotrope.
héliport ✈ [eli'pɔ:r] *m* heliport.
hélium ⚗ [e'ljɔm] *m* helium.
helvétien, -enne [ɛlve'sjɛ̃, ~'sjɛn] *adj., a. su.* ⚲ Swiss; **helvétique** [~'tik] Helvetic (*confederation*), Swiss.
***hem!** [ɛm] *int.* ahem!; hm!
héma... [ema], **hémat(o)...** [emat(o)] h(a)ema..., h(a)emat(o)...; blood...; **hématite** *min.* [ema'tit] *f* h(a)ematite; ~ *rouge* red iron.
hémi... [emi] hemi...; **~cycle** ⚠ [~'sikl] *m* hemicycle; **~sphère** [emis'fɛ:r] *m* hemisphere.
hémo... [emɔ] h(a)em(o)... **~globine** *physiol.* [~glɔ'bin] *f* h(a)emoglobin; **~philie** ⚕ [~fi'li] *f* h(a)emophilia; **~rragie** ⚕ [~ra'ʒi] *f* h(a)emorrhage; **~rroïdes** ⚕ [~rɔ'id] *f/pl.* h(a)emorrhoids, piles.
***henné** ⚘ [ɛn'ne] *m* henna (*a. for hair*); *teindre au* ~ henna.
***hennir** [ɛ'ni:r] (2a) *v/i.* whinny, neigh; ***hennissement** [ɛnis'mã] *m* whinny(ing), neigh(ing).
hépatique [epa'tik] **1.** *adj.* hepatic; **2.** *su.* ⚕ hepatic; *su./f* ⚘ hepatica, liverwort; **hépatite** [~'tit] *f* ⚕ hepatitis; *min.* hepatite.
hepta... [ɛpta] hepta...
héraldique [eral'dik] heraldic, armorial.
***héraut** [e'ro] *m* herald (*a. fig.*).
herbacé, e ⚘ [ɛrba'se] herbaceous; **herbage** [~'ba:ʒ] *m* grass-land; pasture; grass; *cuis.* green stuff; **herbager** [~ba'ʒe] *m* grazier; **herbe** [ɛrb] *f* grass; herb; weed; ~*s pl. potagères* pot herbs; *en* ~ unripe; *fig.* budding; *fines* ~*s pl.* herbs for seasoning; *mauvaise* ~ weed; *fig.* bad lot; *couper l'*~ *sous le pied de q.* cut the ground from under s.o.'s feet; *déjeuner sur l'*~ (have a) picknick; *manger son blé en* ~ spend one's money before getting it; **herbeux, -euse** [~'bø, ~'bø:z] grassy; **herbicide** [~bi'sid] *m* weed-killer; **herbivore** *zo.* [~bi'vɔ:r] **1.** *adj.* herbivorous; **2.** *su./m* herbivore; **herboriser** [~bɔri'ze] (1a) *v/i.* go botanizing; gather plants *or* herbs; **herboriste** [~bɔ'rist] *su.* herbalist; **herbu, e** [~'by] **1.** *adj.* grassy; **2.** *su./f* light grazing-land.
***hère** [ɛ:r] *m*: *pauvre* ~ poor devil.
héréditaire [eredi'tɛ:r] hereditary; **hérédité** [~'te] *f* heredity; ⚖ (right of) inheritance.
hérésie [ere'zi] *f* heresy; **hérétique** [~'tik] **1.** *adj.* heretical; **2.** *su.* heretic.
***hérissé, e** [eri'se] bristling (with, *de*); spiked (with, *de*); prickly; bristly (*moustache*); ***hérisser** [~'se] (1a) *v/t.* bristle up; cover with spikes; ruffle (*its feathers*); *se* ~ stand on end (*hair*); bristle (up) (*a. fig.*); ***hérisson** [~'sɔ̃] *m zo.* hedgehog; ⊕ brush.
héritage [eri'ta:ʒ] *m* inheritance, heritage; **hériter** [~'te] (1a) *vt/i.* inherit; ~ (*de*) *qch.* inherit s.th. (from s.o., *de q.*); **héritier, -ère** [~'tje, ~'tjɛ:r] *su.* heir; *su./f* heiress.
hermétique [ɛrme'tik] hermetic; (air-, water)tight; light-proof; impenetrable.
hermine *zo.* [ɛr'min] *f* ermine (*a.* ✝ *fur*), stoat.
***herniaire** ⚕ [ɛr'njɛ:r] hernial; *bandage m* ~ truss; ***hernie** ⚕ [~'ni] *f* hernia, rupture.
héroïne [erɔ'in] *f* heroine; ⚗ hero-

in; **héroïque** [ʌ'ik] heroic (*a.* ⚔); **héroïsme** [ʌ'ism] *m* heroism.
***héron** *orn.* [e'rɔ̃] *m* heron.
***héros** [e'ro] *m* hero.
herpès ✠ [ɛr'pɛs] *m* herpes.
***herse** [ɛrs] *f* ⚔ harrow; △ portcullis; *thea.* ⸗s *pl.* battens; ***herser** ⚔ [ɛr'se] (1a) *v/t.* harrow.
hésitation [ezita'sjɔ̃] *f* hesitation; hesitancy; faltering; misgiving; **hésiter** [ʌ'te] (1a) *v/i.* hesitate, waver; falter (*in speaking*).
hétéro... [etero] hetero...; ⸗**clite** [ʌ'klit] hcteroclite, irregular; *fig.* odd, strange; ⸗**doxe** [ʌ'dɔks] heterodox, unorthodox; ⸗**gène** [ʌ'ʒɛn] heterogeneous; *fig.* incongruous; mixed (*society*).
***hêtre** ⚘ [ɛ:tr] *m* beech.
heure [œ:r] *f* hour; time; moment; period; ... o'clock; *six* ⸗s *pl.* 6 o'clock; ⸗ *d'été* summer time; ⚒ ⸗ *H* zero hour; ⸗ *légale* standard time; ⸗s *pl.* *supplémentaires* overtime *sg.*; *à l'*⸗ on time, punctual(ly *adv.*); *à l'*⸗ (*de*) ... in the ... age; in the ... fashion; *à la bonne* ⸗! well done!; fine!; *tout à l'*⸗ a few minutes ago; in a few minutes; presently; *à tout à l'*⸗! so long!; see you later!; F *c'est l'*⸗ time's up!; *de bonne* ⸗ early; *quelle* ⸗ *est-il?* what time is it?; *livre m d'*⸗s book of hours; prayer-book.
heureux, -euse [œ'rø, ⸗'rø:z] happy, glad, pleased, delighted; lucky; successful; fortunate (*accident, position, etc.*); apt (*expression, phrase, word*).
***heurt** [œ:r] *m* blow, knock, shock; *fig. sans* ⸗ smoothly; ***heurté, e** [œr'te] clashing (*colours*); ***heurter** [ʌ'te] (1a) *vt/i.* knock, hit, strike; jostle; *v/t.* run into; collide with; *fig.* offend (*s.o.'s feelings*); ⚔ ram, strike; *v/i. a. se* ⸗ collide; clash (*colours*); ***heurtoir** [ʌ'twa:r] *m* knocker; ⊕ stop; ⊕ tappet; ⚒ buffer.
hexagonal, e, *m/pl.* **-aux** ⚗ [ɛgzagɔ'nal, ⸗'no] hexagonal; **hexagone** [ʌ'gɔn] *m* ⚗ hexagon; *fig. l'*⸗ France.
hiatus [ja'tys] *m ling.* hiatus; *fig.* gap; *fig.* break.
hibernal, e, *m/pl.* **-aux** [iber'nal, ⸗'no] winter-...; hibernal; wintry; **hibernant, e** [ʌ'nɑ̃, ʌ'nɑ̃:t] hibernating; **hiberner** [ʌ'ne] (1a) *v/i.* hibernate.

***hibou** *orn.* [i'bu] *m* owl; *jeune*⸗ owlet.
***hic** [ik] *m*: *voilà le* ⸗! there's the snag!
***hideux, -euse** [i'dø, i'dø:z] hideous.
hiémal, e, *m/pl.* **-aux** [je'mal, ⸗'mo] winter-...
hier [je:r] *adv.* yesterday; ⸗ *soir* yesterday evening, last night; *d'*⸗ very recent; F *fig. né d'*⸗ green.
***hiérarchie** [jerar'ʃi] *f* hierarchy; ***hiérarchique** [ʌ'ʃik] hierarchical; *voie f* ⸗ official channels *pl.*
hiéroglyphe [jerɔ'glif] *m* hieroglyph; *fig.* scrawl.
hilarant, e [ila'rɑ̃, ʌ'rɑ̃:t] mirthprovoking; **hilarité** [ʌri'te] *f* hilarity, laughter, mirth.
hippique [ip'pik] equine, horse-...; *concours m* ⸗ horse-show; racemeeting, *Am.* race-meet; **hippisme** [ʌ'pism] *m* horse-racing.
hippo... [ipɔ] hippo...; horse...; ⸗**campe** *zo.* [ʌ'kɑ̃:p] *m* sea-horse; hippocampus; ⸗**drome** [ʌ'dro:m] *m* hippodrome; circus; race-course, race-track; ⸗**mobile** [ʌmɔ'bil] horsedrawn; ⸗**potame** *zo.* [ʌpɔ'tam] *m* hippopotamus.
hirondelle [irɔ̃'dɛl] *f orn.* swallow.
hirsute [ir'syt] hirsute, hairy; *fig.* boorish, rough.
hispanique [ispa'nik] Hispanic, Spanish.
hispide ⚘ [is'pid] hispid; hairy.
***hisser** [i'se] (1a) *v/t.* hoist (*a.* ⚓); *se* ⸗ *a.* pull o.s. up.
histoire [is'twa:r] *f* history; story; F fib, invention; *faire des* ⸗s make a todo; F⸗ *de* (*faire qch.*) just to (*do s.th.*); **historien** [ʌtɔ'rjɛ̃] *m* historian; chronicler; narrator; **historier** [ʌ'rje] (1o) *v/t.* illustrate; embellish (*a. fig.*); **historiette** [ʌ'rjɛt] *f* anecdote; short story; **historique** [ʌ'rik] **1.** *adj.* historic(al); **2.** *su./m* historical record *or* account.
histrion [istri'ɔ̃] ham (actor).
hiver [i'vɛ:r] *m* winter; **hivernage** [ivɛr'na:ʒ] *m* ⚓ laying up for the winter; winter season; winter quarters *pl.*, ⚓ winter harbo(u)r; *tropics:* rainy season, wintering (*of cattle*); **hivernal, e**, *m/pl.* **-aux** [ʌ'nal, ʌ'no] winter-...; wintry (*weather*); **hivernant m, e f** [ʌ'nɑ̃, ʌ'nɑ̃:t] winter visitor; **hiverner** [ʌ'ne] (1a) *v/i.*

winter; hibernate (*animal*); v/t.
↗ plough before winter.
*hobereau [ɔ'bro] m orn. hobby; F
small country squire, squireen.
*hochement [ɔʃ'mɑ̃] m shake or nod
(*of the head*); ***hochequeue** orn.
[~'kø] m wagtail; ***hocher** [ɔ'ʃe] (1a)
v/t.:~ la tête shake or nod one's head;
*hochet [ɔ'ʃɛ] m rattle (*for babies*);
toy, bauble.
*hockey sp. [ɔ'kɛ] m hockey; ~ sur
glace ice-hockey; ***hockeyeur** sp.
[ɔkɛ'jœːr] m hockey-player.
hoir 𝄢 [wa:r] m heir; **hoirie** 𝄢
[wa'ri] f inheritance, succession.
*holà [ɔ'la] 1. int. hallo!; stop!; 2.
m/inv.: mettre le~ à qch. put a stop to
s.th.
*holding † [ɔl'diŋ] m holding
company.
*hold-up [ɔl'dœp] m/inv. hold-up.
*hollandais, e [ɔlɑ̃'dɛ, ~'dɛːz] 1. adj.
Dutch; 2. su./m ling. Dutch; ♀
Dutchman; les ♀ m/pl. the Dutch;
su./f ♀ Dutchwoman.
*Hollande [ɔ'lɑ̃:d] su./m Dutch
cheese; su./f tex. Holland.
holocauste [ɔlɔ'ko:st] m holocaust;
fig. sacrifice.
*homard zo. [ɔ'ma:r] m lobster.
homélie [ɔme'li] f eccl. homily; F
fig.sermon, lecture.
homicide [ɔmi'sid] 1. su. person:
homicide; su./m crime: homicide;
~ par imprudence (or involontaire)
manslaughter; ~ volontaire (or prémédité) murder; 2. adj. homicidal.
hommage [ɔ'ma:ʒ] m homage; token
of esteem; ~s pl. compliments; ~
de l'auteur with the author's compliments; rendre ~ do homage,
pay tribute (to, à); **hommasse**
F [ɔ'mas] mannish, masculine
(*woman*); **homme** [ɔm] m man;
mankind; ~ d'affaires businessman;
~ d'État statesman; ⊕ ~ de métier
craftsman; ~-grenouille, pl. ~s-
grenouilles [~grə'nu:j] m frogman;
~-sandwich, pl. ~s-sandwichs
[~sɑ̃'dwitʃ] m sandwich-man.
homo... [ɔmɔ] homo...; ~gène
[~'ʒɛn] homogeneous; ~généiser
[~ʒenei'ze] (1a) v/t. homogenize;
~logue [~'lɔg] 1. adj. homologous; 2.
su./m homologue; person: counterpart, opposite number; ~loguer 𝄢
[~lɔ'ge] (1m) v/t. confirm, endorse;
ratify (*a decision*); prove (*a will*);

~**nyme** gramm. [~'nim] 1. adj.
homonymous; 2. su./m homonym;
~**sexuel, -elle** [~sɛk'sɥɛl] adj. a. su.
homosexual.
*hongre [ɔ̃:gr] 1. adj./m gelded; 2.
su./m gelding; ***hongrois, e** [ɔ̃'grwa,
~'grwa:z] 1. adj. Hungarian; 2. su./m
ling. Hungarian; su. ♀ Hungarian.
honnête [ɔ'nɛːt] honest; upright,
decent; respectable; courteous,
well-bred; seemly (*behaviour*); reasonable (*price*); virtuous (*woman*); ~s
gens m/pl. decent people; **honnêteté** [ɔnɛt'te] f honesty; integrity; politeness; respectability (*of
behaviour*); † fairness; price etc.:
reasonableness; (*feminine*) modesty.
honneur [ɔ'nœ:r] m hono(u)r; ~s pl.
hono(u)rs, preferments; regalia;
avoir l'~ have the hono(u)r (of ger.,
de inf.); † beg (to inf., de inf.); †
faire ~ à hono(u)r, meet (*a bill, an
obligation*); ✕ rendre les ~s present
arms (to, à).
*honnir † [ɔ'ni:r] (2a) v/t. disgrace;
spurn; revile; honni soit qui mal
y pense evil be to him who evil
thinks.
honorabilité [ɔnɔrabili'te] f respectability; **honorable** [~'rabl]
hono(u)rable; respectable, credit-
able, † reputable; **honoraire**
[~'rɛ:r] 1. adj. honorary; 2. su./m: ~s
pl. fee(s pl.) sg., honorarium sg.; 𝄢
retainer sg.; **honorer** [~'re] (1a) v/t.
hono(u)r (a. †); respect; do hono(u)r
to; † meet; s'~ de pride o.s. on;
honorifique [~ri'fik] honorary
(*title*).
*honte [ɔ̃:t] f (sense of) shame; dis-
hono(u)r, disgrace; fig. reproach;
avoir ~ be ashamed (of, de); faire ~
à put to shame; **honteux, -euse**
[ɔ̃'tø, ~'tø:z] ashamed; disgraceful,
shameful, scandalous; bashful.
hôpital [ɔpi'tal] m 🏥 hospital; poor-
house, (*orphan's*) home; ✕ ~ militaire (de campagne) station (field)
hospital.
*hoquet [ɔ'kɛ] m hiccough, hiccup;
emotion: gasp (*of surprise etc.*); ***hoqueter** [ɔk'te] (1c) v/i. hiccup;
have the hiccups.
horaire [ɔ'rɛ:r] 1. adj. time...;
hour-...; ⊕ per hour, hourly;
2. su./m time-table; ~ souple flexible
working hours pl.
*horde [ɔrd] f horde.

horizon [ɔri'zɔ̃] *m* horizon (*a. fig.*); panorama, view; *fig. à l'~ 2000 etc.* in *or* for the year 2000 *etc.*; **horizontal, e,** *m/pl.* **-aux** [∽zɔ̃'tal, ∽'to] horizontal.

horloge [ɔr'lɔ:ʒ] *f* clock; ⊕ ∽ *centrale* master clock; ∽ *normande* grandfather('s) clock; *teleph.* ∽ *parlante* speaking clock, Tim; **horloger** [∽lɔ'ʒe] *m* watch-maker, clockmaker; **horlogerie** [∽lɔʒ'ri] *f* watchmaking, clock-making; watchmaker's (shop).

hormis [ɔr'mi] *prp.* except.

hormone *physiol.* [ɔr'mɔn] *f* hormone.

horoscope [ɔrɔs'kɔp] *m* horoscope; *faire (or tirer) un* ∽ cast a horoscope.

horreur [ɔ'rœ:r] *f* horror; *avoir* ∽ *de* loathe; abhor; hate; *avoir en* ∽ detest, hold in abhorrence; *faire* ∽ *à* disgust; horrify; **horrible** [ɔ'ribl] horrible, dreadful; appalling; **horripiler** [ɔripi'le] (1a) *v/t.* give (*s.o.*) gooseflesh; F make (*s.o.'s*) flesh creep; F *fig.* exasperate.

*****hors** [ɔ:r] *prp.* out of; outside (*the town*); beyond, but, save (*two, this*); *⚔ ∽ circuit* cut off; ∽ *concours* hors concours; *sp.* ∽ *jeu* offside; ∽ *ligne* (*or classe*) outstanding; ✝ ∽ *vente* no longer on sale; *mettre* ∽ *la loi* outlaw (*s.o.*); ∽ (*de*) *pair* peerless; ∽ *de* outside; out of (*breath, danger, fashion, hearing, reach, sight, use*); beyond (*dispute, doubt*); ∽ *d'affaire* out of the wood; ∽ *de combat* disabled; out of action; ∽ *de propos* illtimed; irrelevant (*remark*); ∽ *de saison* unseasonable; ∽ *de sens* out of one's senses; ∽ *de soi* beside o.s. (*with rage*); ∽ *d'ici!* get out!; *qch. est* ∽ *de prix* the price of s.th. is prohibitive.

*****hors...:** ***~-bord** [ɔr'bɔ:r] *m/inv.* outboard motor boat, F speed-boat; ***~-d'œuvre** [∽'dœ:vr] *m/inv. art etc.:* irrelevant matter; *cuis.* horsd'œuvre, side dish; ***~-jeu** *sp.* [∽'ʒø] *m/inv.* off side; ***~-la-loi** [∽la'lwa] *m/inv.* outlaw; ***~-saison** [∽sɛ'zɔ̃] *adj./inv.* off-season (*tariff etc.*); ***~-texte** [∽'tɛkst] *m/inv.* (full page) plate (*in a book*).

hortensia ♀ [ɔrtɑ̃'sja] *m* hydrangea.

horticole [ɔrti'kɔl] horticultural; **horticulture** [∽kyl'ty:r] *f* horticulture, gardening.

hosanna [ɔzan'na] *int., a. su./m* hosanna.

hospice [ɔs'pis] *m* hospice; almshouse; (*orphan's*) home; **hospitalier, -ère** [ɔspita'lje, ∽'ljɛ:r] **1.** *adj.* hospitable; hospital-...; **2.** *su./m eccl.* hospitaller; *su./f eccl.* Sister of Mercy; **hospitaliser** [∽li'ze] (1a) *v/t.* send *or* admit to a hospital *or* home, hospitalize; **hospitalité** [∽li'te] *f* hospitality; *donner l'*∽ *à q.* give s.o. hospitality, F put s.o. up.

hostie [ɔs'ti] *f bibl.* (sacrificial) victim; *eccl.* host.

hostile [ɔs'til] hostile; **hostilité** [∽tili'te] *f* hostility (*against, contre*); enmity; ✗ ∽s *pl.* hostilities.

hôte, hôtesse [o:t, o'tɛs] *su.* guest, visitor, lodger; *su./m* host; landlord; *su./f* hostess; landlady; ✈ *hôtesse de l'air* air hostess.

hôtel [o'tɛl] *m* hotel; ∽ (*particulier*) (private) mansion; ∽ *de ville* town hall, city hall; ∽ *garni* residential hotel; *pej.* lodgings *pl.*, lodging-house; *maître m d'*∽ head waiter; *private house:* butler; ***~-Dieu,** *pl.* ***~s-Dieu** [otɛl'djø] *m* principal hospital; **hôtelier, -ère** [otə'lje, ∽'ljɛ:r] *su.* innkeeper; hotel-keeper; *su./m* landlord; *su./f* landlady; **hôtellerie** [otɛl'ri] *f* hostelry, inn; hotel trade.

*****hotte** [ɔt] *f* basket; pannier; (*bricklayer's*) hod; ⊕ hopper; ⌂ hood.

*****houblon** ♀ *etc.* [u'blɔ̃] *m* hop(s *pl.*); *****houblonner** [ublɔ'ne] (1a) *v/t.* hop (*beer*); *****houblonnier, -ère** [∽'nje, ∽'njɛ:r] **1.** *adj.* hop-(growing); **2.** *su./f* hop-field.

*****houe** ⚹ [u] *f* hoe; *****houer** [u'e] (1a) *v/t.* hoe.

*****houille** [u:j] *f* coal; *fig.* ∽ *blanche* water-power; *****houiller, -ère** ✗ [u'je, ∽'jɛ:r] **1.** *adj.* coal-...; carboniferous; *production f* ∽*ère* output of coal; **2.** *su./f* coal-mine, pit, colliery; *****houilleux, -euse** [u'jø, ∽'jø:z] carboniferous, coal-bearing.

*****houle** [ul] *f* swell, surge, billows *pl.* *****houlette** [u'lɛt] *f* (shepherd's *etc.*) crook; ⚹ trowel; *metall.* hand-ladle.

*****houleux, -euse** [u'lø, ∽'lø:z] swelling, surging (*a. fig.*), billowing; ⚓ rather rough (*sea*); *fig.* stormy (*meeting*).

*****houp!** [up] *int.* up!; off you go!

*****houppe** [up] *f orn., a. feathers,**

hair, wool: tuft; tassel, bob; pompom; *orn.*, *a. hair, tree*: crest; (powder-)puff; *hair:* topknot; ***houpper** [u'pe] (1a) *v/t.* tuft; trim with tufts *or* pompoms; *tex.* comb (*wool*); ***houppette** [u'pɛt] *f* small tuft; powder-puff.

*hourra [u'ra] 1. *int.* hurrah!; 2. *su./m: pousser des* ∼s cheer.

*houspiller [uspi'je] (1a) *v/t.* scold, tell (*s.o.*) off; rag (*s.o.*) (*audience etc.*); handle (*s.o.*) roughly.

*houssaie [u'sɛ] *f* holly-grove.

*housse [us] *f* furniture cover, *Am.* slip-cover; dust-sheet; horse-cloth; *cost.* (protective) bag; ***housser** [u'se] (1a) *v/t.* dust (*furniture*).

*houssine [u'sin] *f furniture, riding:* switch; ***houssiner** [usi'ne] (1a) *v/t.* switch.

*houssoir [u'swa:r] *m* featherduster; whisk.

*houx ♀ [u] *m* holly.

*hoyau ⚓ [wa'jo] *m* grubbing-hoe, mattock.

*hublot ⚓ [y'blo] *m* port-hole, scuttle; air-port; *faux* ∼ dead-light.

*huche [yʃ] *f* kneading-trough; bin; ⊕ hopper.

*hue! [y] *int.* gee up!; *a. to a horse:* to the right!; *fig. tirer à* ∼ *et à dia* pull in opposite directions.

*huée [y'e] *f hunt. etc.* hallooing; *fig.* boo, hoot; ∼s *pl.* booing *sg.*, jeers; ***huer** [y'e] (1a) *v/t.* boo *or* jeer (*s.o.*); *v/i.* hoot (*owl*).

*huguenot, e [yg'no, ∼'nɔt] 1. *adj. eccl.* Huguenot; 2. *su. eccl.* Huguenot; *su./f cuis.* pipkin.

huilage [ɥi'la:ʒ] *m* oiling, lubrication; *metall.* oil-tempering; **huile** [ɥil] *f* oil; ⌐m, ⚶ ∼ *de foie de morue* cod-liver oil; ∼ *de graissage* (*de machine*) lubricating (engine) oil; ∼ *minérale* mineral oil, petroleum; ∼ *végétale* vegetable oil; F *les* ∼s *pl.* the big pots (= *important people*); *eccl. les saintes* ∼s *pl. extreme unction:* the holy oil *sg.*; **huiler** [ɥi'le] (1a) *v/t.* oil, lubricate; *fig. huilé* working *or* running smoothly; **huilerie** [ɥil'ri] *f* oil-works *usu. sg.*; oil-store; **huileux, -euse** [ɥi'lø, ∼'lø:z] oily, greasy; **huilier** [∼'lje] *m* ⊕ oil-can; oil-merchant; *cuis.* oil-cruet; cruet-stand.

huis [ɥi] *m* † door; 🎗 *à* ***∼** *clos* in camera; F *à* ∼ *clos* in private; 🎗

ordonner le ***∼** *clos* clear the court; **huisserie** △ [ɥis'ri] *f* door-frame; **huissier** [ɥi'sje] *m* usher; 🎗 bailiff, process-server.

*huit [ɥit; *before consonant* ɥi] *adj./ num.*, *a. su./m/inv.* eight; *date, title:* eighth; *d'aujourd'hui en* ∼ today week; *tous les* ∼ *jours* once a week; every week; ***huitain** [ɥi'tɛ̃] *m* octet; ***huitaine** [∼'ten] *f* (about) eight; week; ***huitième** [∼'tjɛm] 1. *adj./ num.* eighth; 2. *su.* eighth; *su./m fraction:* eighth; *su./f secondary school:* (*approx.*) second form.

huître [ɥi:tr] *f* oyster; F *fig.* ninny; **huîtrier, -ère** [ɥitri'e, ∼'ɛ:r] 1. *adj.* oyster-...; 2. *su./f* oyster-bed.

*hulotte *orn.* [y'lɔt] *f* brown owl, common wood-owl.

humain, e [y'mɛ̃, ∼'men] 1. *adj.* human; humane; 2. *su./m: les* ∼s *pl.* mankind *sg.*; human beings; **humaniser** [ymani'ze] (1a) *v/t.* humanize; *s'*∼ become (more) human; *fig.* become more sociable; **humanitaire** [∼'te:r] *adj.*, *a. su.* humanitarian; **humanité** [∼'te] *f* humanity; kindness; mankind; ∼s *pl.* classical studies, *the* humanities.

humble [œ̃:bl] humble; lowly; meek; ∼ *serviteur* humble servant.

humecter [ymɛk'te] (1a) *v/t.* moisten, damp, wet; *s'*∼ become moist.

*humer [y'me] (1a) *v/t.* breathe in (*the air, a perfume*); sip (*tea, coffee*); swallow (*a raw egg*).

humeur [y'mœ:r] *f* mood; disposition, temperament; temper; bad temper; ill humo(ur); 🎗 † ∼s *pl.* body fluids; *avec* ∼ crossly; peevishly; *de bonne* (*mauvaise*) ∼ in a good (bad) mood; *être or se sentir d'*∼ *à faire qch.* be in the mood to do *or* for doing s.th.; feel like doing s.th.

humide [y'mid] damp; humid; **humidité** [ymidi'te] *f* dampness; moisture; humidity.

humilier [ymi'lje] (1o) *v/t.* humiliate, humble; **humilité** [∼li'te] *f* humility.

humoriste [ymɔ'rist] 1. *adj.* humorous (*writer*); 2. *su.* humorist; **humoristique** [∼ris'tik] humorous.

humour [y'mu:r] *m* (sense of) humo(u)r;   [mo(u)ld.]

humus ⚓ [y'mys] *m* humus, leaf)

*hune ⚓ [yn] *f* top; ***hunier** ⚓ [y'nje] *m* topsail.

*huppe [yp] *f orn.* hoopoe: *bird*: crest, tuft; ***huppé, e** [y'pe] *orn.* tufted, crested; F *fig.* smart; F *les gens m/pl.* ~s the swells.

*hure [yːr] *f* head (*usu. of boar*); *salmon*: jowl; *cuis.* brawn, *Am.* headcheese; *sl.* (ugly) head.

*hurlement [yrlə'mɑ̃] *m animal*: howl(ing); roar; bellow; ***hurler** [~'le] (1a) *v/i.* howl; roar; *v/t.* bawl out; ***hurleur, -euse** [~'lœːr, ~-'løːz] **1.** *adj.* howling; **2.** *su.* howler; *su./m zo. monkey*: howler.

hurluberlu [yrlybɛr'ly] *m* scatterbrain; harum-scarum.

*hussard ⚔ [y'saːr] *m* hussar; ***hussarde** [y'sard] *f dance*: hussarde; *à la* ~ cavalierly.

*hutte [yt] *f* hut, cabin, shanty.

hybride [i'brid] *adj.*, *a. su./m* hybrid; **hybridité** [ibridi'te] *f* hybrid character, hybridity.

hydratation ♔ [idrata'sjɔ̃] *f* hydration; **hydrater** [~'te] (1a) *v/t.* hydrate, moisturize.

hydraulique [idro'lik] **1.** *adj.* hydraulic; water-...; **2.** *su./f* hydraulics *sg.*

hydravion [idra'vjɔ̃] *m* seaplane; ~ *à* coque flying boat.

hydro... [idrɔ] hydro...; water-...; **~carbure** ♔ [~kar'byːr] *m* hydrocarbon; **~céphalie** ✶ [~sefa'li] *f* hydrocephaly, F water on the brain; **~fuge** [~'fyːʒ] waterproof; **~gène** ♔ [~'ʒɛn] *m* hydrogen; **~glisseur** [~gli'sœːr] *m* hovercraft; **~mel** [~'mɛl] *m* hydromel; **~phile** [~'fil] absorbent (*cotton*); **~phobie** ✶ [~fɔ'bi] *f* rabies; **~pisie** ✶ [~pi'zi] *f* dropsy; **~thérapie** ✶ [~tera'pi] *f* hydrotherapy; water-cure.

hyène *zo.* [jɛn] *f* hyena.

hygiène [i'ʒjɛn] *f* hygiene; *admin.* health; **hygiénique** [iʒje'nik] hygienic, sanitary; healthy; *papier m* ~ toilet paper; **hygiéniste** [~'nist] *su.* hygienist, authority on public health.

hygromètre *phys.* [igrɔ'mɛtr] *m* hygrometer; **hygrométricité** *phys.* [~metrisi'te] *f* humidity; humidity-absorption index.

hymen [i'mɛn] *m anat.* hymen; *poet.* = **hyménée** *poet.* [ime'ne] *m* marriage.

hymne [imn] *su./m* patriotic song; national anthem; *su./f eccl.* hymn.

hyper... [ipɛr] hyper...; **~bole** [~-'bɔl] *f* ♔ hyperbola; *gramm.* hyperbole; **~critique** [~kri'tik] hypercritical; **~métrope** ✶ [~me'trɔp] hypermetropic; long-sighted; **~tension** ✶ [~tɑ̃'sjɔ̃] *f* hypertension; *a.* ~ *artérielle* high blood pressure; **~trophie** ✶ [~trɔ'fi] *f* hypertrophy.

hypnose [ip'noːz] *f* hypnosis; trance; **hypnotiser** [ipnɔti'ze] (1a) *v/t.* hypnotize; **hypnotiseur** [~ti'zœːr] *m* hypnotist; **hypnotisme** [~'tism] *m* hypnotism.

hypo... [ipɔ] hypo...; **~crisie** [~kri'zi] *f* hypocrisy; cant; **~crite** [~'krit] **1.** *adj.* hypocritical; **2.** *su.* hypocrite; **~thécaire** [~te'kɛːr] ... on mortgage; mortgage-...; *créancier m* ~ mortgagee; **~thèque** [~'tɛk] *f* mortgage; *prendre* (*purger*) *une* ~ raise (pay off *or* redeem) a mortgage; **~théquer** [~te'ke] (1f) *v/t.* mortgage; secure (*a debt*) by mortgage; **~thèse** [~'tɛːz] *f* hypothesis; F theory.

hystérie ✶ [iste'ri] *f* hysteria; **hystérique** ✶ [~'rik] hysteric(al).

I

I, i [i] *m* I, i; *i grec* y.

iambe [jã:b] *m* iambus; iambic; ~s *pl.* satirical poem *sg.*; **iambique** [jã-'bik] iambic.

ibérique *geog.* [ibe'rik] Iberian, Spanish.

iceberg [is'bɛrg] *m* iceberg.

ichtyo... [iktjɔ] ichthyo..., fish-...; ~**colle** [~'kɔl] *f* fish-glue, isinglass; ~**phage** [~'fa:ʒ] **1.** *adj.* fish-eating; **2.** *su.* ichthyophagist; ~**saure** [~'sɔ:r] *m* ichthyosaurus.

ici [i'si] *adv.* here; now, at this point; *teleph.* ~ *Jean* John speaking; ~ *Londres radio*: London calling; this is London; *d'*~ *(à) lundi* by Monday; *d'*~ *(à) trois jours* within the next three days; *d'*~ *demain* by tomorrow; *d'*~ *là* by that time, by then; in the meantime; *d'*~ *peu* before long; *jusqu'* ~ *place*: as far as here; *time*: up to now; *par* ~ here(abouts); this way; *près d'*~ nearby; ~-**bas** [isi'bɑ] *adv.* on earth, here below.

iconoclaste [ikɔnɔ'klast] **1.** *adj.* iconoclastic; **2.** *su.* iconoclast; **iconolâtrie** [~la'tri] *f* image-worship.

icosaèdre Å [ikɔza'ɛ:dr] *m* icosahedron.

ictère ⚕ [ik'tɛ:r] *m* jaundice; **ictérique** [~te'rik] **1.** *adj.* jaundiced (*eyes, person*); icteric (*disorder*); **2.** *su.* sufferer from jaundice.

idéal, e, *m/pl.* -**als,** -**aux** [ide'al, ~'o] **1.** *adj.* ideal; **2.** *su./m* ideal.

idée [i'de] *f* idea; notion; intention, purpose; mind, head; suggestion, hint; ~ *fixe* fixed idea, obsession.

idem [i'dɛm] *adv.* idem; ditto.

identifier [idãti'fje] (1o) *v/t.* identify; *s'*~ *à* identify o.s. with; **identique** [~'tik] identical (with, *à*); **identité** [~ti'te] *f* identity; *carte f d'*~ identity card.

idéologie [ideɔlɔ'ʒi] *f* ideology (*a. pol.*).

idiomatique [idjɔma'tik] idiomatic; **idiome** [i'djo:m] *m* idiom; language.

idiot, e [i'djo, ~'djɔt] **1.** *adj.* ⚕ idiot; *fig.* idiotic, absurd; **2.** *su.* ⚕ idiot (*a. fig.*), imbecile; *fig.* fool; **idiotie** [idjɔ'si] *f* ⚕ idiocy; *fig.* piece of nonsense; **idiotisme** [~'tism] *m* idiom(atic expression).

idoine [i'dwan] appropriate.

idolâtre [idɔ'lɑ:tr] **1.** *adj.* idolatrous; *fig.* être ~ de be passionately fond of, worship; **2.** *su./m* idolater; *su./f* idolatress; **idolâtrer** [~la'tre] (1a) *v/i.* worship idols; *v/t. fig.* be passionately fond of, worship; **idolâtrie** [~la'tri] *f* idolatry; **idole** [i'dɔl] *f* idol, image.

if ♀ [if] *m* yew (tree).

ignare [i'ɲa:r] **1.** *adj.* illiterate, ignorant; **2.** *su.* ignoramus.

igné, e [ig'ne] igneous; **ignicole** [igni'kɔl] **1.** *adj.* fire-worshipping; **2.** *su.* fire-worshipper; **ignifuge** [~fy:ʒ] **1.** *adj.* fireproof; non-inflammable; **2.** *su./m* fireproof(ing) material; **ignifuger** [~fy'ʒe] (1l) *v/t.* fireproof; **ignition** [~'sjõ] *f* ignition. [wretched.\

ignoble [i'ɲɔbl] ignoble, base; vile;\

ignominie [iɲɔmi'ni] *f* ignominy, shame, disgrace; **ignominieux, -euse** [~'njø, ~'njø:z] ignominious, shameful, disgraceful.

ignorance [iɲɔ'rã:s] *f* ignorance; **ignorant, e** [~'rã, ~'rã:t] **1.** *adj.* ignorant (of, *de*), uneducated; **2.** *su.* ignoramus; **ignorer** [~'re] (1a) *v/t.* be unaware of, not to know (about); *ne pas* ~ *que* not to be unaware that (*ind.*), know quite well that (*ind.*).

il [il] **1.** *pron./pers./m* he, it, she (*ship etc.*); ~s *pl.* they; **2.** *pron./impers.* it; there; *il est dix heures* it is 10 o'clock; *il vint deux hommes* two men came.

île [i:l] *f* island; isle.

illégal, e, *m/pl.* -**aux** [ille'gal, ~'go] illegal, unlawful.

illégitime [illeʒi'tim] illegitimate (*child*); unlawful (*marriage*); *fig.* spurious; *fig.* unwarranted; **illégitimité** [~timi'te] *f* illegitimacy.

illettré, e [illɛ'tre] illiterate, uneducated.

illicite [illi'sit] illicit; *sp.* foul.

illico F [ili'ko] *adv.* at once, straightaway.

illimité, e [illimi'te] unlimited.

illisible [illi'zibl] illegible; unreadable (*book*).

illogique [illɔ'ʒik] illogical.

illuminant, e [illymi'nã, ~'nã:t] illuminating; **illuminer** [~'ne] (1a) *v/t.* illuminate, flood-light (*buildings*); light up (*a. fig.*); *fig.* enlighten (*s.o.*).

illusion [illy'zjõ] *f* illusion; delusion; **illusionner** [~zjo'ne] (1a) *v/t.* delude; deceive; s'~ delude o.s.; labo(u)r under a delusion; **illusoire** [~'zwa:r] illusory.

illustration [illystra'sjõ] *f* illustration; illustrating; † renown, illustriousness; **illustre** [~'lystr] illustrious, renowned, famous; **illustré** [illys'tre] *m* pictorial (paper), F magazine; **illustrer** [~] (1a) *v/t.* illustrate; † elucidate; s'~ win fame.

îlot [i'lo] *m* islet, small island; *houses:* block.

ilote *hist.* [i'lɔt] *m* helot.

image [i'ma:ʒ] *f* image; picture; **imagé, e** [ima'ʒe] colo(u)rful (*style*); **imagerie** [imaʒ'ri] *f* imagery; **imaginable** [imaʒi'nabl] imaginable; **imaginaire** [~'nɛ:r] imaginary (*a. A*); fictitious; **imaginatif, -ve** [~na'tif, ~'ti:v] imaginative; **imagination** [~na'sjõ] *f* imagination; fancy; **imaginer** [~'ne] (1a) *v/t.* imagine, picture; think up; s'~ imagine; imagine *or* picture o.s.

imbécile [ɛ̃be'sil] 1. *adj.* imbecile, half-witted; *fig.* idiotic; 2. *su.* imbecile; *fig.* idiot, F fat-head, *Am. sl.* nut; **imbécilité** [~sili'te] *f* imbecility; *fig.* stupidity; ~s *pl.* nonsense *sg.*

imberbe [ɛ̃'bɛrb] beardless; F callow.

imbiber [ɛ̃bi'be] (1a) *v/t.* impregnate (with, *de*); s'~ *de* soak up; become saturated with; F drink.

imbu, e [ɛ̃'by]: ~ *de* full of; steeped in.

imbuvable [ɛ̃by'vabl] undrinkable.

imitable [imi'tabl] imitable; worthy of imitation; **imitateur, -trice** [imita'tœ:r, ~'tris] 1. *adj.* imitative; 2. *su.* imitator; **imitatif, -ve** [~'tif,

~'ti:v] imitative; **imitation** [~'sjõ] *f* imitation; *money:* counterfeiting; *signature:* forgery; à l'~ *de* in imitation of; **imiter** [imi'te] (1a) *v/t.* imitate; copy.

immaculé, e [immaky'le] immaculate; unstained.

immanent, e *phls.* [imma'nã, ~'nã:t] immanent. [able.]

immangeable [ɛ̃mã'ʒabl] uneat-]

immanquable [ɛ̃mã'kabl] infallible, inevitable; which cannot be missed (*target etc.*).

immatériel, -elle [immate'rjɛl] immaterial; † intangible.

immatriculation [immatrikyla'sjõ] *f* registration; *univ. etc.* enrolment, matriculation; *mot.* numéro *m* d'~ registration (*Am.* license) number.

immaturité [immatyri'te] *f* immaturity.

immédiat, e [imme'dja, ~'djat] immediate; dans l'~ for the moment.

immémorial, e, *m/pl.* **-aux** [immemɔ'rjal, ~'rjo] immemorial.

immense [im'mã:s] immense, huge, vast; *sl.* terrific (= *wonderful*); **immensité** [~mãsi'te] *f* immensity; vastness.

immerger [immɛr'ʒe] (11) *v/t.* immerse.

immérité, e [immeri'te] unmerited, undeserved.

immersion [immɛr'sjõ] *f* immersion; *submarine:* submergence; *astr.* occultation.

immeuble [im'mœbl] 1. *adj.* 🏛 real; 2. *su./m* 🏛 real estate, realty; † building, house; ~ *tour* tower block.

immigrant, e [immi'grã, ~'grã:t] *adj., a. su.* immigrant; **immigration** [~gra'sjõ] *f* immigration; **immigré** *m*, **e** *f* [~'gre] immigrant; **immigrer** [~'gre] (1a) *v/i.* immigrate.

imminence [immi'nã:s] *f* imminence; **imminent, e** [~'nã, ~'nã:t] imminent, impending.

immiscer [immi'se] (1k) *v/t.*: s'~ dans interfere with; **immixtion** [immik'sjõ] *f* interference.

immobile [immɔ'bil] motionless, unmoving; *fig.* steadfast, unshaken; **immobilier, -ère** 🏛 [immɔbi'lje, ~'ljɛ:r] (real) estate (*agency, agent*); **immobiliser** [~li'ze] (1a) *v/t.* immobilize; fix in position; † tie up *(capital)*; s'~ stop; come to a standstill; **immobilisme** [~'lism] *m* ultra-conservatism; **immobilité** [~li'te] *f* immobility.

immodéré, e [immɔde're] immoderate, excessive.

immodeste [immɔ'dɛst] immodest; shameless.

immoler [immɔ'le] (1a) *v/t.* sacrifice, immolate.

immonde [im'mɔ̃:d] filthy, foul; unclean *(animal, eccl. spirit)*; **immondices** [~mɔ̃'dis] *f/pl.* rubbish *sg.*, refuse *sg.*, dirt *sg.*

immoral, e, m/pl. -aux [immɔ'ral, ~'ro] immoral; **immoralité** [~rali-'te] *f* immorality; immoral act.

immortaliser [immɔrtali'ze] (1a) *v/t.* immortalize; **immortalité** [~tali'te] *f* immortality; **immortel, -elle** [~'tɛl] **1.** *adj.* immortal; everlasting, imperishable; **2.** su. ♀ everlasting flower; *su./m:* ♀s *pl.* immortals, F members of the Académie française.   [vated.|

immotivé, e [immɔti've] unmoti-/ **immuable** [im'mɥabl] unalterable, unchanging.

immuniser ✻ [immyni'ze] (1a) *v/t.* immunize; **immunité** [~'te] *f* immunity (from, *contre*); *admin.* exemption from tax.

immuno-dépresseur ✻ [immynɔdeprɛ'sœ:r] *m* immuno-suppressive drug.

immu(t)abilité [immɥabili'te, ~mytabili'te] *f* immutability, fixity.

impact [ɛ̃'pakt] *m* impact; effect.

impair, e [ɛ̃'pɛ:r] **1.** *adj.* ♀ odd; *anat.* unpaired *(organ)*, single *(bone)*; ✖ down *(line)*; **2.** *su./m* F bloomer, blunder.

impalpable [ɛ̃pal'pabl] impalpable, intangible.

impardonnable [ɛ̃pardɔ'nabl] unpardonable; unforgivable.

imparfait, e [ɛ̃par'fɛ, ~'fɛt] **1.** *adj.* imperfect; unfinished; **2.** *su./m gramm.* imperfect (tense).

imparité [ɛ̃pari'te] *f* inequality; ♀ oddness.

impartial, e, m/pl. -aux [ɛ̃par'sjal, ~'sjo] impartial, unprejudiced, unbiassed.

impasse [ɛ̃'pɑ:s] *f* dead end, blind alley; 'no through road'; *fig.* impasse, deadlock; ✝ *(a. ~ budgétaire)* budget deficit; *faire une ~ cards:*

finesse; *fig. faire l'~ sur qch.* neglect *s.th.* consciously.

impassibilité [ɛ̃pasibili'te] *f* impassiveness, impassibility; **impassible** [~'sibl] impassive, unmoved; unimpressionable.

impatience [ɛ̃pa'sjɑ̃:s] *f* impatience; **impatient, e** [~'sjɑ̃, ~'sjɑ̃:t] impatient; *eager* (to *inf.*, *de inf.*); **impatienter** [~sjɑ̃'te] (1a) *v/t.* irritate, annoy; s'~ lose patience; grow impatient.

impayable [ɛ̃pɛ'jabl] † invaluable; F *fig.* screamingly funny; **impayé, e** ✝ [~'je] unpaid *(debt)*; dishono(u)red *(bill)*.   [infallible.|

impeccable [ɛ̃pɛ'kabl] impeccable;∫ **impénétrable** [ɛ̃pene'trabl] impenetrable (by, *à*); impervious (to, *à*); *fig.* inscrutable; close *(secret)*.

impénitence [ɛ̃peni'tɑ̃:s] *f* impenitence; **impénitent, e** [~'tɑ̃, ~'tɑ̃:t] impenitent, unrepentant.

imper F [ɛ̃'pɛr] *m* *(abbr. of imperméable)* raincoat.

impératif, -ve [ɛ̃pera'tif, ~'ti:v] *adj., a. su./m* imperative.

impératrice [ɛ̃pera'tris] *f* empress.

imperceptible [ɛ̃pɛrsɛp'tibl] imperceptible, undiscernible.

imperfection [ɛ̃pɛrfɛk'sjɔ̃] *f* imperfection; incompleteness; defect, flaw, fault; faultiness.

impérial, e, m/pl. -aux [ɛ̃pe'rjal, ~'rjo] **1.** *adj.* imperial; **2.** *su./f* top; *bus, tram:* top-deck, outside; *beard:* imperial; **impérialisme** [~rja-'lism] *m* imperialism; **impérieux, -euse** [~'rjø, ~'rjø:z] imperious; domineering; peremptory; urgent, pressing.   [able, undying.|

impérissable [ɛ̃peri'sabl] imperish-/ **imperméable** [ɛ̃pɛrme'abl] **1.** *adj.* impermeable; watertight, waterproof; impervious (to, *à*); **2.** *su./m* rain-coat; waterproof.

impersonnel, -elle [ɛ̃pɛrsɔ'nɛl] impersonal.

impertinence [ɛ̃pɛrti'nɑ̃:s] *f* impertinence; rudeness, cheek; ⚖ irrelevance; **impertinent, e** [~'nɑ̃, ~'nɑ̃:t] **1.** *adj.* impertinent; cheeky, pert; ⚖ irrelevant; **2.** *su./m* impertinent fellow; *su./f* saucy girl.

imperturbable [ɛ̃pɛrtyr'babl] unruffled; imperturbable, phlegmatic.

impétrant, e ⚖ [ɛ̃pe'trɑ̃, ~'trɑ̃:t] *su.* grantee.

impétueux, -euse [ɛ̃pe'tɥø, ~'tɥø:z] impetuous; hot-headed, precipitate, impulsive; **impétuosité** [~tɥozi'te] *f* impetuosity; impulsiveness.

impitoyable [ɛ̃pitwa'jabl] pitiless (to[wards] *à*, *envers*); merciless; relentless.

implacable [ɛ̃pla'kabl] implacable, unrelenting (towards *à*, *à l'égard de*, *pour*).

implanter [ɛ̃plɑ̃'te] (1a) *v/t.* plant; *fig.* implant; ⚓ graft; *s'~* take root.

implication [ɛ̃plika'sjɔ̃] *f* implication; *phls.* contradiction; *~s pl.* consequences; **implicite** [~'sit] implicit; implied, tacit; **impliquer** [~'ke] (1m) *v/t.* involve; imply; implicate.

implorer [ɛ̃plɔ're] (1a) *v/t.* implore, beseech.

imploser [ɛ̃plɔ'ze] (1a) *v/i.* implode; **implosion** [~'zjɔ̃] *f* implosion.

impoli, e [ɛ̃pɔ'li] impolite, discourteous; rude (to *envers*, *avec*); **impolitesse** [~li'tɛs] *f* impoliteness, discourtesy; rudeness.

impolitique [ɛ̃pɔli'tik] impolitic; ill-advised.

impondérable [ɛ̃pɔ̃de'rabl] *adj.*, *a. su./m* imponderable.

impopulaire [ɛ̃pɔpy'lɛ:r] unpopular; **impopularité** [~lari'te] *f* unpopularity.

importance [ɛ̃pɔr'tɑ̃:s] *f* importance; size, extent; **important, e** [~'tɑ̃, ~'tɑ̃:t] 1. *adj.* important; considerable; weighty; *fig. pej.* self-important, F bumptious; 2. *su.*: F *faire l'~* give o.s. airs; *su./m* main thing, essential point.

importateur, -trice † [ɛ̃pɔrta'tœ:r, ~'tris] 1. *su.* importer; 2. *adj.* importing; **importation** † [~'sjɔ̃] *f* importation; *~s pl. goods:* imports.

importer[1] [ɛ̃pɔr'te] (1a) *v/t.* † import; *fig.* introduce.

importer[2] [~] (1a) *v/i.* matter; be important; *n'importe!* it doesn't matter!; never mind!; *n'importe quoi* no matter what, anything; *qu'importe?* what does it matter?

importun, e [ɛ̃pɔr'tœ̃, ~'tyn] 1. *adj.* importunate; tiresome; unwelcome; untimely (*request*); 2. *su. person:* nuisance; bore; **importunément** [ɛ̃pɔrtyne'mɑ̃] *adv.* of *importun 1*; **importuner** [~'ne] (1a) *v/t.* importune; bother, pester (with,

de); inconvenience; **importunité** [~ni'te] *f* importunity.

imposable [ɛ̃po'zabl] taxable; **imposant, e** [~'zɑ̃, ~'zɑ̃:t] imposing; commanding; **imposer** [~'ze] (1a) *v/t.* prescribe, impose; force (*an opinion, one's viewpoint*) (upon, *à*); *admin.* tax, rate; *eccl.* lay on (*hands*); *~ du respect à* q. fill s.o. with respect; *~ silence à* q. enjoin silence on s.o.; *s'~* assert o.s.; be essential; *v/i.: en ~ à* q. impress s.o.; *en ~* be imposing; **imposition** [~zi'sjɔ̃] *f* taxation; rating.

impossibilité [ɛ̃posibili'te] *f* impossibility (*a. = impossible thing*); **impossible** [~'sibl] impossible; F fantastic.

imposteur [ɛ̃pɔs'tœ:r] *m* impostor; F sham; **imposture** [~'ty:r] *f* imposture; deception.

impôt [ɛ̃'po] *m* tax, duty; taxation.

impotence [ɛ̃pɔ'tɑ̃:s] *f* impotence; helplessness; **impotent, e** [~'tɑ̃, ~'tɑ̃:t] 1. *adj.* impotent; crippled, helpless; 2. *su.* cripple, invalid.

impraticable [ɛ̃prati'kabl] impracticable; impassable (*road*); *sp.* unplayable (*tennis court etc.*).

imprécation [ɛ̃preka'sjɔ̃] *f* curse.

imprécis, e [ɛ̃pre'si, ~'si:z] vague; unprecise.

imprégner [ɛ̃pre'ɲe] (1f) *v/t.* impregnate (*a. fig.*) (with, *de*).

imprenable ✕ [ɛ̃prə'nabl] impregnable.

imprésario [ɛ̃presar'jo] *su.* impresario.

imprescriptible ⚖ [ɛ̃prɛskrip'tibl] indefeasible.

impression [ɛ̃prɛ'sjɔ̃] *f fig.*, *a. book*, *seal:* impression; *tex.*, *typ. book:* printing; *wind:* pressure; *footsteps:* imprint; *coins:* stamping; (*colour-*) print; *paint.* priming; *envoyer à l'~* send to press; **impressionnable** [ɛ̃presjɔ'nabl] impressionable; **impressionnant, e** [~'nɑ̃, ~'nɑ̃:t] impressive; moving (*sight, voice*); stirring (*news*); **impressionner** [~'ne] (1a) *v/t.* impress, affect, move; make an impression on; **impressionnisme** [~'nism] *m* impressionism; **impressionniste** [~'nist] *su.* impressionist.

imprévisible [ɛ̃previ'zibl] unforeseeable, unpredictable; **imprévision** [~'zjɔ̃] *f* lack of foresight.

imprévoyance [ɛ̃prevwa'jɑ̃:s] *f*

lack of foresight; improvidence;
imprévu, e [ɛ̃pri'vy] unforeseen,
unexpected.

imprimé [ɛ̃pri'me] *m* printed paper
or book; ~s *pl. post*: printed matter
sg.; **imprimer** [~'me] (1a) *v/t. typ.,
tex.* print; impress (*a seal*); communicate, impart (*a movement*);
paint. prime; **imprimerie** [ɛ̃prim-
'ri] *f* printing; printing-house;
printing-press; **imprimeur** [ɛ̃pri-
'mœːr] *m* printer; **imprimeuse**
[~'møːz] *f* (small) printing-machine.

improbable [ɛ̃prɔ'babl] improbable, unlikely; **improbateur, -tri-
ce** [~ba'tœːr, ~'tris] disapproving;
improbation [~ba'sjɔ̃] *f* strong
disapproval.

improbité [ɛ̃prɔbi'te] *f* dishonesty.
improductif, -ve [ɛ̃prɔdyk'tif,
~'tiːv] unproductive; ✝ idle (*assets,
money*).

impromptu [ɛ̃prɔ̃p'ty] 1. *adj./inv.*
extempore (*speech*); impromptu,
scratch (*meal*); 2. *adv.* without preparation, off the cuff; out of the blue;
3. *su./m* ♪ impromptu.

impropre [ɛ̃'prɔpr] wrong; unfit,
unsuitable (for, *à*); **impropriéte**
[ɛ̃prɔprie'te] *f* impropriety; incorrectness.

improuvable [ɛ̃pru'vabl] unprov-
able.

improviser [ɛ̃prɔvi'ze] (1a) *vt/i.* im-
provise; *v/i.* speak extempore; F ad-
lib; **improviste** [~'vist] *adv.*: *à l'~*
unexpectedly, by surprise; with-
out warning.

imprudence [ɛ̃pry'dɑ̃ːs] *f* imprudence; rashness; imprudent act;
imprudent, e [~'dɑ̃, ~'dɑ̃ːt] imprudent, rash; unwise.

impudence [ɛ̃py'dɑ̃ːs] *f* impudence;
effrontery; impudent act; **impudent, e** [~'dɑ̃, ~'dɑ̃ːt] 1. *adj.* impudent; 2. *su.* impudent person;
impudeur [~'dœːr] *f* shamelessness;
lewdness; effrontery; **impudicité**
[~disi'te] *f* indecency; **impudique**
[~'dik] indecent; shameless.

impuissance [ɛ̃pɥi'sɑ̃ːs] *f* power-
lessness, helplessness; impotence
(*a.* ♂); *dans l'~ de* (*inf.*) powerless
to (*inf.*); **impuissant, e** [~'sɑ̃,
~'sɑ̃ːt] powerless, helpless; vain
(*effort*); ♂ impotent.

impulsif, -ve [ɛ̃pyl'sif, ~'siːv] impulsive; **impulsion** [~'sjɔ̃] *f* ⚡, ⊕,

a. fig. impulse; F stimulus; *fig.*
prompting; *force f d'~* impulsive
force.

impunément [ɛ̃pyne'mɑ̃] *adv.* with
impunity; *fig.* harmlessly; **impuni,
e** [~'ni] unpunished; **impunité**
[~ni'te] *f* impunity.

impur, e [ɛ̃'pyːr] impure, tainted;
unclean; **impureté** [ɛ̃pyr'te] *f* impurity, unchastity.

imputable [ɛ̃py'tabl] imputable,
ascribable (to, *à*); ✝ chargeable (to,
sur); **imputer** [~'te] (1a) *v/t.*
impute, ascribe (to, *à*); ✝ ~ *une
somme à* (*or sur*) *un compte* charge a
sum to an account.

imputrescible [ɛ̃pytre'sibl] incorruptible; rot-proof.

inabordable [inabɔr'dabl] unapproachable, inaccessible; prohibitive (*price*).

inacceptable [inaksɛp'tabl] unac-
ceptable.

inaccessible [inaksɛ'sibl] inaccessible; impervious (to, *à*) (*flattery,
light, rain*).

inaccompli, e [inakɔ̃'pli] unaccom-
plished, unfulfilled.

inaccordable [inakɔr'dabl] ungrant-
able (*favour*).

inaccoutumé, e [inakuty'me] unac-
customed (to, *à*); unusual.

inachevé, e [inaʃ've] incomplete,
unfinished.

inactif, -ve [inak'tif, ~'tiːv] inactive;
idle (*a.* ✝ *capital*); ✝ dull (*market*);
🜔 inert; **inaction** [~'sjɔ̃] *f* inaction,
idleness; ✝ dullness; **inactivité**
[~tivi'te] *f* inactivity; ✝ dullness; 🜔
inertness.

inadapté, e [inadap'te] 1. *adj.* not
adapted (to, *à*); maladjusted; 2. *su.*
maladjusted person; misfit.

inadmissible [inadmi'sibl] inadmissible.

inadvertance [inadvɛr'tɑ̃ːs] *f* inadvertence, oversight; *par ~* inadvertently.   [able.]

inaliénable [inalje'nabl] inalien-
inaltérable [inalte'rabl] unchanging, unvarying; which does not
deteriorate.

inamovible [inamɔ'vibl] irremov-
able; for life (*post*); built in (*furniture etc.*); *agencements m/pl.* ~s
fixtures.

inanimé, e [inani'me] inanimate,
lifeless; unconscious.

inanité [inani'te] *f* futility; inane remark.

inanition [inani'sjɔ̃] *f* starvation.

inaperçu, e [inapɛr'sy] unnoticed.

inappréciable [inapre'sjabl] inappreciable (*quantity*); *fig.* invaluable.

inapte [i'napt] unfit (for, *à*); unsuited (to, *à*); incapable (of *ger.*, *à inf.*); **inaptitude** [inapti'tyd] *f* inaptitude; unfitness (for, *à*).

inassouvi, e [inasu'vi] unappeased (*hunger*); unslaked, unquenched (*thirst*); *fig.* unsatisfied.

inattaquable [inata'kabl] unattackable; unassailable; irrefutable; irreproachable.

inattendu, e [inatɑ̃'dy] unexpected.

inattentif, -ve [inatɑ̃'tif, ~'tiːv] inattentive (to, *à*); heedless (of, *à*).

inaugurer [inogy're] (1a) *v/t.* inaugurate, open; unveil (*a monument*); *fig.* usher in (*an epoch*).

inavoué, e [ina'vwe] unacknowledged.

incalculable [ɛ̃kalky'labl] countless, incalculable.

incandescence [ɛ̃kɑ̃de'sɑ̃ːs] *f* incandescence, glow; ≠ *lampe f à* ~ glow-lamp.

incapable [ɛ̃ka'pabl] incapable (of *ger.*, *de inf.*); unfit (to *inf.*, *de inf.*); **incapacité** [~pasi'te] *f* incapacity (*a.* ⚖); unfitness; incompetency.

incarcération [ɛ̃karsera'sjɔ̃] *f* incarceration, imprisonment; **incarcérer** [~'re] (1f) *v/t.* incarcerate, imprison.

incarnadin, e [ɛ̃karna'dɛ̃, ~'din] incarnadine, flesh-pink; **incarnat, e** [~'na, ~'nat] fleshcolo(u)red, rosy; **incarnation** [~na'sjɔ̃] *f* incarnation; *fig.* personification; ✱ *nail:* ingrowing; **incarné, e** [~'ne] incarnate; *fig.* personified; ✱ ingrowing (*nail*); **incarner** [~'ne] (1a) *v/t.* incarnate; *fig.* personify; ✱ *s'*~ grow in (*nail*).

incartade [ɛ̃kar'tad] *f* prank; freak; (*verbal*) outburst.

incassable [ɛ̃ka'sabl] unbreakable.

incendiaire [ɛ̃sɑ̃'djɛːr] **1.** *adj.* incendiary (*bomb*); *fig.* inflammatory; **2.** *su.* incendiary; fire-brand; **incendie** [~'di] *m* fire; ⚖ ~ *volontaire* arson; **incendié** *m*, **e** *f* [~'dje] person rendered homeless by fire; **incendier** [~'dje] (1o) *v/t.* set (*s.th.*) on fire, burn (*s.th.*) down.

incertain, e [ɛ̃sɛr'tɛ̃, ~'tɛn] un-

certain, doubtful; unreliable; undecided (about, *de*) (*person*); unsettled (*weather*); **incertitude** [~ti'tyd] *f* uncertainty, doubt; *result:* inaccuracy; *fig.* indecision; unsettled state (*of the weather*).

incessamment [ɛ̃sesa'mɑ̃] *adv.* incessantly; at any moment; without delay, at once; **incessant, e** [~'sɑ̃, ~'sɑ̃ːt] ceaseless, unceasing, incessant.

inceste [ɛ̃'sɛst] **1.** *adj.* incestuous; **2.** *su./m* incest; *su.* see *incestueux* 2; **incestueux, -euse** [ɛ̃sɛs'tɥø, ~'tɥøːz] **1.** *adj.* incestuous; **2.** *su.* incestuous person.

inchiffrable [ɛ̃ʃi'frabl] immeasurable (*wealth etc.*); *fig.* invaluable.

incidemment [ɛ̃sida'mɑ̃] *adv. of incident* 1; **incidence** [~'dɑ̃ːs] *f* incidence; consequence, effect; **incident, e** [~'dɑ̃, ~'dɑ̃ːt] **1.** *adj.* incidental; *opt.* incident; **2.** *su./m* incident; occurrence; ⚖ point of law; *fig.* difficulty, hitch; ~ *de parcours* mishap, (minor) setback; ~ *technique* technical hitch.

incinération [ɛ̃sinera'sjɔ̃] *f* incineration; cremation; **incinérer** [~'re] (1f) *v/t.* incinerate; cremate.

inciser [ɛ̃si'ze] (1a) *v/t.* make an incision in; ✱ lance (*an abscess*); **incisif, -ve** [~'zif, ~'ziːv] **1.** *adj.* incisive, cutting; *dent f* ~*ve* = **2.** *su./f tooth:* incisor; **incision** [~'zjɔ̃] *f* incision; ✱ *abscess:* lancing. [instigate, urge (on).]

inciter [ɛ̃si'te] (1a) *v/t.* incite;

incivil, e [ɛ̃si'vil] uncivil, rude; **incivilité** [~vili'te] *f* incivility, rudeness; rude remark.

inclinaison [ɛ̃klinɛ'zɔ̃] *f* incline, slope; ⚓ *ship:* list; ~ *magnétique* magnetic dip; **inclination** [~na'sjɔ̃] *f* inclination (*a. fig.*); *body:* bending; *head:* nod; *fig.* bent; **incliner** [~'ne] (1a) *v/t.* incline (*a. fig.*), slope; bend; nod (*one's head*); *s'*~ slant; bow; *fig.* yield (to, *devant*); ⚓ heel; 🏦 bank; *v/i.* incline (*a. fig.*); lean; ⚓ list.

inclure [ɛ̃'klyːr] (4g) *v/t.* include; *letter:* enclose; **inclus, e** [ɛ̃'kly, ~'klyːz] **1.** *adj.* enclosed; *la lettre ci-*~*e* enclosed letter; **inclusif, -ve** [ɛ̃kly'zif, ~'ziːv] inclusive.

incognito [ɛ̃kɔɲi'to] *adv., a. su./m* incognito.

incohérent, e [ɛkɔe'rɑ̃, ~'rɑ̃:t] incoherent (*a. phys.*), rambling.
incolore [ɛkɔ'lɔ:r] colo(u)rless (*a. fig.*); *fig.* insipid.
incomber [ɛkɔ̃'be] (1a) *v/i.*: ~ *à* be incumbent upon; devolve upon.
incombustible [ɛkɔ̃bys'tibl] incombustible, fireproof.
incommensurable [ɛkɔmɑ̃sy'rabl] Å incommensurable; irrational (*root*); incommensurate; *fig.* enormous, huge.
incommode [ɛkɔ'mɔd] inconvenient; uncomfortable; troublesome; unwieldy (*object*); **incommodément** [ɛkɔmɔde'mɑ̃] *adv.* inconveniently, uncomfortably; **incommoder** [~'de] (1a) *v/t.* inconvenience, hinder; disturb, trouble; *food etc.*: disagree with (*s.o.*); **incommodité** [~di'te] *f* inconvenience; discomfort; awkwardness.
incomparable [ɛkɔ̃pa'rabl] incomparable, unrivalled.
incompatible [ɛkɔ̃pa'tibl] incompatible.
incomplet, -ète [ɛkɔ̃'plɛ, ~'plɛt] incomplete, unfinished.
incompréhensible [ɛkɔ̃preɑ̃'sibl] incomprehensible; **incompréhensif, -ve** [~'sif, ~'si:v] uncomprehending; unwilling *or* unable to understand; **incompréhension** [~'sjɔ̃] *f* incomprehension; unwillingness *or* inability to understand.
incompris, e [ɛkɔ̃'pri, ~'pri:z] misunderstood; unappreciated.
inconcevable [ɛkɔ̃sə'vabl] unimaginable, unthinkable.
inconciliable [ɛkɔ̃si'ljabl] irreconcilable.
inconditionnel, -le [ɛkɔ̃disjɔ'nɛl] unconditional, unreserved; unquestioning.
inconduite [ɛkɔ̃'dɥit] *f* misbehavio(u)r; loose living; ♂ misconduct.
incongelable [ɛkɔ̃ʒ'labl] unfreezable; non-freezing.
incongru, e [ɛkɔ̃'gry] incongruous; improper, unseemly; **incongruité** [~grɥi'te] *f* incongruity; unseemliness; **incongrûment** [~gry'mɑ̃] *adv. of incongru.*
inconnu, e [ɛkɔ'ny] **1.** *adj.* unknown (to *à*, *de*); **2.** *su.* unknown, stranger; *su./f* Å unknown (quantity).
inconscience [ɛkɔ̃'sjɑ̃:s] *f* unconsciousness; ignorance (of, *de*); **inconscient, e** [~'sjɑ̃, ~'sjɑ̃:t] **1.** *adj.* unconscious; **2.** *su.* unconscious person; *su./m psych. the* unconscious.
inconséquence [ɛkɔ̃se'kɑ̃:s] *f* inconsequence, inconsistency; thoughtlessness.
inconsidéré, e [ɛkɔ̃side're] inconsiderate (*person*); rash, ill-considered.
inconsistant, e [ɛkɔ̃sis'tɑ̃, ~'tɑ̃:t] unsubstantial; loose (*ground*); soft (*mud*); *fig.* inconsistent.
inconsolable [ɛkɔ̃sɔ'labl] unconsolable; disconsolate (*person*).
inconstance [ɛkɔ̃s'tɑ̃:s] *f* inconstancy, fickleness; changeableness (*of weather*); *biol.* variability; **inconstant, e** [~'tɑ̃, ~'tɑ̃:t] inconstant, fickle; changeable (*weather*); *biol.* variable.
inconstitutionnel, -elle [ɛkɔ̃stitysjɔ'nɛl] unconstitutional.
incontestable [ɛkɔ̃tɛs'tabl] indisputable, unquestionable, beyond (all) question; **incontesté, e** [~'te] undisputed.
incontinence [ɛkɔ̃ti'nɑ̃:s] *f* incontinence (*a.* ♂); **incontinent, e** [~'nɑ̃, ~'nɑ̃:t] **1.** *adj.* incontinent; unchaste; **2.** *incontinent adv.* † forthwith.
inconvenance [ɛkɔ̃v'nɑ̃:s] *f* unsuitableness; impropriety; indecency.
inconvénient [ɛkɔ̃ve'njɑ̃] *m* disadvantage, drawback; inconvenience; *fig.* objection; *si vous n'y voyez pas d'~* if you dont mind, if you have no objections.
inconvertible [ɛkɔ̃vɛr'tibl] inconvertible (*a.* ♥); **inconvertissable** [~ti'sabl] *fig.* incorrigible; past praying for; ♥ inconvertible.
incorporation [ɛkɔrpɔra'sjɔ̃] *f* incorporation; ✗ enrolment; **incorporel, -elle** [~'rɛl] incorporeal; ♂ intangible (*property*); **incorporer** [~'re] (1a) *v/t.* incorporate; mix (with *à*, *avec*, *dans*); ✗ draft (*men*).
incorrect, e [ɛkɔ'rɛkt] incorrect; wrong; inaccurate; indecorous; **incorrection** [~rɛk'sjɔ̃] *f* incorrectness; error; wrong act; indecorousness.
incorrigible [ɛkɔri'ʒibl] incorrigible; *fig.* ⊢ hopeless.   [ruptible.⎰
incorruptible [ɛkɔryp'tibl] incor⎰

incrédibilité [ɛ̃kredibili'te] *f* in-
credibility; **incrédule** [ʌʹdyl] **1.** *adj.*
incredulous; sceptical (about, of *à*
l'égard de); *eccl.* unbelieving; **2.** *su.*
eccl. unbeliever; **incrédulité** [ʌdy-
li'te] *f* incredulity; *eccl.* unbelief.

incrimination [ɛ̃krimina'sjɔ̃] *f* (in-)
crimination; indictment; charge;
incriminer [ʌʹne] (1a) *v/t.* accuse,
charge; *fig.* impeach (*s.o.'s conduct*).

incrochetable [ɛ̃krɔʃ'tabl] burglar-
proof.

incroyable [ɛ̃krwa'jabl] **1.** *adj.* incredible; **2.** *su./m hist.* beau; **incroyance** [ʌʹjãːs] *f* unbelief; **in-
croyant, e** [ʌʹjã, ʌʹjãːt] **1.** *adj.* unbelieving; **2.** *su.* unbeliever.

incrustation [ɛ̃krysta'sjɔ̃] *f* incrustation; ⊕ inlaid work; ⊕
boiler: fur(ring); **incruster** [ʌʹte]
(1a) *v/t.* incrust; ⊕ inlay (with,
de); △ line; form a crust on; *fig.*
s'ʌ become ingrained (*in the mind*);
outstay one's welcome.

incubateur [ɛ̃kyba'tœːr] *m* incubator; **incubation** [ʌʹsjɔ̃] *f eggs, a.* ♂:
incubation; *hens*: sitting.

incube [ɛ̃'kyb] *m* incubus, night-
mare.

inculper [ɛ̃kyl'pe] (1a) *v/t.* charge,
indict.

inculquer [ɛ̃kyl'ke] (1m) *v/t.* in-
culcate, instil (into, *à*).

inculte [ɛ̃'kylt] uncultivated, wild;
waste (*land*); *fig.* rough; *fig.* unkempt (*hair*).

incunable [ɛ̃ky'nabl] *m* early printed
book; ʌs *pl.* incunabula.

incurable [ɛ̃ky'rabl] *adj., a. su.* incurable; **incurie** [ʌʹri] *f* carelessness, negligence.

incursion [ɛ̃kyr'sjɔ̃] *f* inroad, foray,
raid; *fig.* excursion (into, *dans*).

indébrouillable [ɛ̃debru'jabl] impossible to disentangle; *fig.* inextricable.

indécence [ɛ̃de'sãːs] *f* indecency;
indécent, e [ʌʹsã, ʌʹsãːt] indecent;
improper.

indéchiffrable [ɛ̃deʃi'frabl] undeci-
pherable; *fig.* illegible; *fig.* unin-
telligible.

indécis, e [ɛ̃de'si, ʌʹsiːz] undecided;
irresolute; blurred, vague (*outline*
etc.); indecisive (*battle, victory*);
indécision [ʌsi'zjɔ̃] *f* indecision;
uncertainty.

indéfini, e [ɛ̃defi'ni] indefinite; un-

defined; **indéfinissable** [ʌni'sabl]
indefinable; nondescript.

indéfrisable [ɛ̃defri'zabl] *f* permanent wave.

indélébile [ɛ̃dele'bil] indelible; kiss-
proof (*lipstick*).

indélibéré, e [ɛ̃delibe're] uncon-
sidered.

indélicat, e [ɛ̃deli'ka, ʌʹkat] indelicate, coarse; tactless (*act*); dishonest.

indémaillable [ɛ̃demɑ'jabl] ladder-
proof, non-run (*stocking*).

indemne [ɛ̃'dɛmn] undamaged; un-
injured; without loss; free (from,
de); **indemnisation** [ɛ̃demniza'sjɔ̃]
f indemnification; **indemniser**
[ʌʹze] (1a) *v/t.* indemnify, compensate (for, *de*); **indemnité** [ʌʹte]
f indemnity; compensation; allowance; ʌ *de déplacement* travel allowance; ʌ *de maladie* sick pay; ʌ *journa-
lière* daily allowance.

indéniable [ɛ̃de'njabl] undeniable.

indépendamment [ɛ̃depãda'mã]
adv. of indépendant; **indépendance** [ʌʹdãːs] *f* independence (of
de, à l'égard de); **indépendant, e**
[ʌʹdã, ʌʹdãːt] independent (of, *de*);
free (from, *de*); self-contained (*flat*
etc.). [ineradicable.]

indéracinable *fig.* [ɛ̃derasi'nabl]

indéréglable [ɛ̃dere'glabl] fool-
proof (*machine etc.*).

indescriptible [ɛ̃deskrip'tibl] indescribable (F *a. fig.*).

indestructible [ɛ̃destryk'tibl] indestructible.

indéterminé, e [ɛ̃determi'ne] un-
determined; indeterminate (♉, *a.*
fig.).

index [ɛ̃'dɛks] *m* forefinger, index
(finger); *book*: index; pointer; *eccl.*
the Index; *fig.* black list; *mettre à l'ʌ*
blacklist.

indicateur, -trice [ɛ̃dika'tœːr, ʌʹtris]
1. *adj.* indicatory; ʌ *de* indicating
(*s.th.*); **2.** *su./m* ⊕ indicator, ga(u)ge,
pointer; 🚂 guide, time-table; directory (*of streets etc.*); informer,
police spy; ʌ *de pression* pressure-
ga(u)ge; *mot.* ʌ *de vitesse* speedometer; **indicatif, -ve** [ʌʹtif, ʌʹtiːv]
1. *adj.* indicative; **2.** *su./m radio etc.*:
station-signal; signature-tune; 📻
call sign; *gramm.* indicative; **indication** [ʌʹsjɔ̃] *f* indication; information; sign, token; mark; ♉

declaration; ⌇s *pl.* ⚡ *etc.* instructions; ⊕ particulars; *thea.* ⌇s *pl.*
scéniques stage-directions.
indice [ɛ̃'dis] *m* indication, sign; *opt.*,
⚕ index; *fig.* clue; rating, grading; ⌇
de popularité popularity rating.
indicible [ɛ̃di'sibl] unspeakable; unutterable; *fig.* indescribable.
indien, -enne [ɛ̃'djɛ̃, ⌇'djɛn] **1.** *adj.*
Indian; **2.** *su.* ♀ Indian; *su./f tex.*
printed calico; *tex.* chintz.
indifférence [ɛ̃dife'rɑ̃:s] *f* indifference, apathy (towards, *pour*); **indifférent, e** [⌇'rɑ̃, ⌇'rɑ̃:t] indifferent (*a.* ⚕) (to, *à*); unaffected
(by, *à*); unconcerned; ⚕ neutral
(*salt etc.*); unimportant. [*fig.*)]
indigence [ɛ̃di'ʒɑ̃:s] *f* poverty (*a.*)
indigène [ɛ̃di'ʒɛn] **1.** *adj.* indigenous (to, *à*); native; ⚘ homegrown; **2.** *su.* native.
indigent, e [ɛ̃di'ʒɑ̃, ⌇'ʒɑ̃:t] **1.** *adj.*
poor, needy; **2.** *su.* pauper; *su./m:*
les ⌇s *pl.* the poor.
indigeste [ɛ̃di'ʒɛst] indigestible;
stodgy (*a. fig.*); **indigestion** ⚡
[⌇ʒɛs'tjɔ̃] *f* indigestion; F *fig. avoir*
une ⌇ *de* be fed up with.
indignation [ɛ̃diɲa'sjɔ̃] *f* indignation.
indigne [ɛ̃'diɲ] unworthy (of, *de*;
to *inf.*, *de inf.*).
indigner [ɛ̃di'ɲe] (1a) *v/t.* make
(*s.o.*) indignant; *s'*⌇ be indignant
(with, at *contre*, *de*).
indignité [ɛ̃diɲi'te] *f* unworthiness;
vileness; indignity.
indigo [ɛ̃di'go] *m* indigo.
indiquer [ɛ̃di'ke] (1m) *v/t.* indicate;
point out; recommend; *fig.* show;
fix.
indirect, e [ɛ̃di'rɛkt] indirect; *pej.*
underhand; ⚖ circumstantial; ⚡
éclairage m ⌇ concealed lighting.
indiscipliné, e [ɛ̃disipli'ne] undisciplined; unmanageable; unruly;
out of hand.
indiscret, -ète [ɛ̃dis'krɛ, ⌇'krɛt] indiscreet; tactless; *fig.* prying (*look*).
indiscutable [ɛ̃disky'tabl] indisputable, unquestionable.
indispensable [ɛ̃dispɑ̃'sabl] **1.** *adj.*
indispensable (to, for *à*); essential;
unavoidable; **2.** *su./m the* necessary.
indisponible [ɛ̃dispɔ'nibl] unavailable; ⚖ inalienable.
indisposé, e [ɛ̃dispo'ze] unwell, indisposed; **indisposer** [⌇'ze] (1a) *v/t.*

make (*s.o.*) unwell; *fig.* antagonize,
irritate, annoy; *fig.* ⌇ *q. contre* make
s.o. hostile to; **indisposition** [⌇zi-
'sjɔ̃] *f* indisposition; upset.
indisputable [ɛ̃dispy'tabl] unquestionable.
indissociable [ɛ̃disɔ'sjabl] inseparable.
indissoluble [ɛ̃disɔ'lybl] ⚕ insoluble; *fig.* indissoluble.
indistinct, e [ɛ̃dis'tɛ̃(:kt), ⌇'tɛ̃:kt]
indistinct; faint; dim, hazy.
individu [ɛ̃divi'dy] *m* individual
(*a. pej.*); **individualiser** [⌇dɥali'ze]
(1a) *v/t.* particularize; individualize; **individualiste** [⌇dɥa'list]
1. *adj.* individualistic; **2.** *su.* individualist; **invididualité** [⌇dɥali-
'te] *f* individuality; **individuel,
-elle** [⌇'dɥɛl] individual, personal;
private; separate.
indivis, e [ɛ̃di'vi, ⌇'vi:z] joint;
par ⌇ jointly; **indivisible** [⌇vi'zibl]
indivisible; ⚖ joint.
indocile [ɛ̃dɔ'sil] unmanageable, intractable; **indocilité** [⌇sili'te] *f* intractability.
indolence [ɛ̃dɔ'lɑ̃:s] *f* ⚡, *a. fig.* indolence; sloth; **indolent, e** [⌇'lɑ̃,
⌇'lɑ̃:t] **1.** ⚡, *a. fig.* indolent; *fig.*
apathetic; *fig.* sluggish; **2.** *su.* idler.
indolore ⚡ [ɛ̃dɔ'lɔ:r] painless.
indomptable [ɛ̃dɔ̃'tabl] unconquerable; *fig.* indomitable; uncontrollable.
indu, e [ɛ̃'dy] undue (*haste*); unseasonable (*remark*); *à une heure* ⌇e at
some ungodly hour.
indubitable [ɛ̃dybi'tabl] unquestionable, undeniable.
inductance [ɛ̃dyk'tɑ̃:s] *f* inductance; **inducteur, -trice** ⚡ [⌇'tœ:r,
⌇'tris] **1.** *adj.* inducing (*current*); inductive (*capacity*); **2.** *su./m* inductor;
field-magnet; **induction** ⚡, *phls.*
[⌇'sjɔ̃] *f* induction.
induire [ɛ̃'dɥi:r] (4h) *v/t.* infer, induce; *fig.* lead (into, *à*); ⌇ *q. en erreur*
mislead s.o.; **induit** [ɛ̃'dɥi] **1.** *adj./m*
induced; **2.** *su./m* ⚡ induced circuit;
armature.
indulgence [ɛ̃dyl'ʒɑ̃:s] *f* indulgence
(*a. eccl.*); forbearance; **indulgent, e**
[⌇'ʒɑ̃, ⌇'ʒɑ̃:t] *adj.*: ⌇ *pour* indulgent
to, lenient with.
indûment [ɛ̃dy'mɑ̃] *adv.* unduly;
improperly.
industrialiser [ɛ̃dystriali'ze] (1a)

v/t. industrialize; **industrie** [ᴗ'tri] *f* industry; trade, manufacture; *fig.* activity; † *fig.* skill, ingenuity; ᴗ-*clef* key-industry; ᴗ *minière* mining industry; *co. exercer sa coupable* ᴗ practise one's disreputable trade; **industriel, -elle** [ᴗtri'ɛl] **1.** *adj.* industrial; **2.** *su./m* manufacturer; industrialist; **industrieux, -euse** [ᴗtri'ø, ᴗ'ø:z] industrious, busy; skil(l)ful.

inébranlable [inebrɑ̃'labl] unshakable.

inédit, e [ine'di, ᴗ'dit] unpublished; novel, new; original.

ineffable [ine'fabl] ineffable, beyond expression.

inefficace [inefi'kas] ineffective; unavailing; **inefficacité** [ᴗkasi'te] *f* inefficacy; ineffectiveness.

inégal, e, *m/pl.* **-aux** [ine'gal, ᴗ'go] unequal; irregular (*pulse etc.*); uneven (*ground, temper*); changeable (*moods, wind*); **inégalité** [ᴗgali'te] *f* inequality (*a.* 𝔸); irregularity; unevenness.

inéligible [ineli'ʒibl] ineligible.

inéluctable [inelyk'tabl] inescapable.

inemployé, e [inɑ̃plwa'je] unemployed; not made use of.

inepte [i'nɛpt] inept, fatuous, stupid; **ineptie** [inɛp'si] *f* ineptitude; stupidity, ineptness.

inépuisable [inepɥi'zabl] inexhaustible.

inerte [i'nɛrt] inert (*mass, a.* 🔬); inactive (🔬, *a.* mind); *fig.* sluggish; *fig.* passive (*resistance*); **inertie** [inɛr'si] *f phys. etc., a. fig.* inertia; *fig.* listlessness; *fig.* passive resistance; *force f d'*ᴗ inertia, vis inertiae.

inespéré, e [inɛspe're] unhoped-for, unexpected.

inestimable [inɛsti'mabl] invaluable; without price.

inévitable [inevi'tabl] inevitable; unavoidable.

inexact, e [inɛg'zakt] inexact; inaccurate; unpunctual; **inexactitude** [ᴗzakti'tyd] *f* inexactitude; inaccuracy; unpunctuality.

inexcusable [inɛksky'zabl] inexcusable.

inexistant, e [inɛgzis'tɑ̃, ᴗ'tɑ̃:t] nonexistent.

inexorable [inɛgzɔ'rabl] inexorable, unrelenting.

inexpérience [inɛkspe'rjɑ̃:s] *f* lack of experience; **inexpérimenté, e** [ᴗrimɑ̃'te] unskilled (*worker*); untested, untried; inexperienced (*person*).

inexplicable [inɛkspli'kabl] inexplicable.

inexploré, e [inɛksplɔ're] unexplored.

inexprimable [inɛkspri'mabl] inexpressible; unspeakable (*pleasure etc.*).

inexpugnable [inɛkspyg'nabl] impregnable.

inextinguible [inɛkstɛ̃'gɥibl] inextinguishable (*fire*); unquenchable; *fig.* uncontrollable.

inextirpable [inɛkstir'pabl] ineradicable.

inextricable [inɛkstri'kabl] inextricable.

infaillible [ɛ̃fa'jibl] infallible.

infaisable [ɛ̃fɔ'zabl] unfeasible; impracticable.

infamant, e [ɛ̃fa'mɑ̃, ᴗ'mɑ̃:t] defamatory; ignominious; **infâme** [ɛ̃'fɑ:m] infamous; vile (*deed, quarter, slum*); foul (*behaviour, deed*); **infamie** [ɛ̃fa'mi] *f* infamy, dishono(u)r; vile deed *or* thing; ᴗ*s pl.* abuse *sg.*, infamous accusations.

infant [ɛ̃'fɑ̃] *m* infante; **infante** [ɛ̃'fɑ̃:t] *f* infanta; **infanterie** ✗ [ɛ̃fɑ̃'tri] *f* infantry; **infanticide** [ᴗti'sid] **1.** *adj.* infanticidal; **2.** *su. person:* infanticide; *su./m crime:* infanticide; **infantile** [ᴗ'til] infantile (*disease, mortality*); *fig.* childish; **infantiliser** *psych.* [ᴗtili'ze] (1a) *v/t.* make infantile.

infarctus 💊 [ɛ̃fark'tys] *m* infarct(ion); ᴗ *du myocarde* coronary (thrombosis).

infatigable [ɛ̃fati'gabl] indefatigable, untiring.

infatuer [ɛ̃fa'tɥe] (1n) *v/t.* infatuate; *s'*ᴗ *de* become infatuated with.

infécond, e [ɛ̃fe'kɔ̃, ᴗ'kɔ̃:d] barren; *fig.* unfruitful.

infect, e [ɛ̃'fɛkt] stinking; noisome (*smell*); filthy (*book, a. fig. lie, weather*); **infecter** [ɛ̃fɛk'te] (1a) *v/t.* infect; pollute; stink of; **infection** [ᴗ'sjɔ̃] *f* infection; stench.

inférer [ɛ̃fe're] (1f) *v/t.* infer (from, *de*).

inférieur, e [ɛ̃fe'rjœ:r] **1.** *adj.* inferior; lower; ᴗ *à* below; **2.** *su.* in-

ferior; subordinate; **inférioriser** [~rɔri'ze] (1a) v/t. regard as inferior; **infériorité** [~rɔri'te] f inferiority; *complexe m d'*~ inferiority complex.
infernal, e, m/pl. **-aux** [ɛ̃fɛr'nal, ~'no] infernal (a. fig.); fig. devilish; ✷ *pierre f* ~e lunar caustic.
infertile [ɛ̃fɛr'til] infertile, barren.
infestation [ɛ̃fɛsta'sjɔ̃] f infestation; **infester** [~'te] (1a) v/t. infest (with, de) (a. fig.).
infidèle [ɛ̃fi'dɛl] **1.** adj. unfaithful; inaccurate; infidel; unbelieving; **2.** su. unbeliever; infidel; **infidélité** [~deli'te] f infidelity (to, envers); unfaithfulness; inaccuracy; unbelief.
infiltration [ɛ̃filtra'sjɔ̃] f infiltration (a. ✷); **infiltrer** [~'tre] (1a) v/t.: s'~ infiltrate (a. ✕, a. ✷); filter in, seep in (a. fig.).
infime [ɛ̃'fim] lowly; lowest, least; minute, tiny.
infini [ɛ̃fi'ni] **1.** adj. infinite; endless; **2.** su./m infinity; *the* infinite; à l'~ endless(ly); **infiniment** [~ni-'mɑ̃] adv. infinitely; F extremely; **infinité** [~ni'te] f ⅄ etc. infinity; fig. host.
infirme [ɛ̃'firm] **1.** adj. infirm; disabled, crippled; fig. weak; **2.** su. invalid; cripple; **infirmer** [ɛ̃fir'me] (1a) v/t. fig. weaken; disprove; ⅄ quash; **infirmerie** [~mə'ri] f infirmary; sick-room; ⚓ sick-bay; **infirmier** [~'mje] m (hospital-)attendant; male nurse; ✕ medical orderly; ambulance man; **infirmière** [~'mjɛːr] f nurse; **infirmité** [~mi'te] f infirmity; disability; fig. weakness.
inflammable [ɛ̃fla'mabl] inflammable, Am. a. flammable; easily set on fire (a. fig.); **inflammation** [~ma-'sjɔ̃] f inflammation (a. ✷); ignition; **inflammatoire** [~ma'twaːr] inflammatory.
inflation ✝ etc. [ɛ̃fla'sjɔ̃] inflation.
infléchir [ɛ̃fle'ʃiːr] (2a) v/t. bend, inflect; **infléchissement** [~ʃis'mɑ̃] m modification.
inflexible [ɛ̃flɛk'sibl] inflexible; **inflexion** [~'sjɔ̃] f inflection, inflexion (a. ⅄, opt., gramm.); *voice:* modulation; *body:* bow.
infliger [ɛ̃fli'ʒe] (1l) v/t. inflict.
inflorescence ⚘ [ɛ̃flɔrɛ'sɑ̃ːs] f inflorescence.

influence [ɛ̃fly'ɑ̃ːs] f influence; **influencer** [~ɑ̃'se] (1k) v/t. influence; **influent, e** [~'ɑ̃, ~'ɑ̃ːt] influential; **influer** [~'e] (1a) v/i.: ~ sur influence.
in-folio typ. [ɛ̃fɔ'ljo] m/inv., a. adj.}
[inv. folio.]
informaticien [ɛ̃fɔrmati'sjɛ̃] m computer scientist.
information [ɛ̃fɔrma'sjɔ̃] f information; inquiry; ~s pl. radio: news (-bulletin) sg.; newscast sg.
informatique [ɛ̃fɔrma'tik] f computer science; data processing; **informatisation** [~tiza'sjɔ̃] f computerization; **informatiser** [~ti'ze] (1a) v/t. computerize.
informe [ɛ̃'fɔrm] unformed; shapeless, unshapely; 𝄐 irregular, informal.
informel, -le [ɛ̃fɔr'mɛl] informal; casual.
informer [ɛ̃fɔr'me] (1a) v/t. inform, notify; s'~ inquire (about, de; of, from auprès de); v/i.: 𝄐 ~ contre inform against; ~ de, ~ sur investigate, inquire into.
infortune [ɛ̃fɔr'tyn] f misfortune; adversity; **infortuné, e** [~ty'ne] unfortunate, unlucky.
infraction [ɛ̃frak'sjɔ̃] f infraction; *right, treaty, etc.:* infringement; 𝄐 offence; *duty, peace:* breach (of, à).
infranchissable [ɛ̃frɑ̃ʃi'sabl] impassable; fig. insuperable (difficulty).
infrarouge [ɛ̃fra'ruːʒ] infra-red.
infrastructure [ɛ̃frastryk'tyːr] f infrastructure; 🌱 ground organization; ⊕ etc. substructure.
infroissabilité tex. [ɛ̃frwasabili'te] f crease-resistance; **infroissable** tex. [~'sabl] uncreasable.
infructueux, -euse [ɛ̃fryk'tɥø, ~'tɥøːz] unfruitful, barren; fig. unavailing, fruitless.
infus, e [ɛ̃'fy, ~'fyːz] fig. innate, intuitive; *avoir la science* ~e know things by intuition; **infuser** [ɛ̃fy'ze] (1a) v/t. infuse (a. fig. life); brew (tea); v/i. infuse; draw (tea); **infusible** [~'zibl] non-fusible; **infusion** [~'zjɔ̃] f infusion; herb tea; **infusoires** [~'zwaːr] m/pl. infusoria.
ingambe [ɛ̃'gɑ̃ːb] active, nimble.
ingénier [ɛ̃ʒe'nje] (1o) v/t.: s'~ à tax one's ingenuity to, F go all out to; **ingénieur** [~'njœːr] m engineer; ~ de l'État Government civil engi-

neer; ~ *du son radio*: sound engineer, *Am.* sound man; ~ *mécanicien* mechanical engineer; **ingénieux, -euse** [~'njø, ~'njøːz] in-
genious; clever; **ingéniosité**
[~njozi'te] *f* ingenuity; cleverness.
ingénu, e [ɛ̃ʒe'ny] 1. *adj.* ingenuous,
artless, unsophisticated; 2. *su.* artless person; *su./f thea.* ingénue;
ingénuité [~nɥi'te] *f* artlessness,
ingenuousness.
ingérence [ɛ̃ʒe'rãːs] *f* interference;
ingérer [~'re] (1f) *v/t.* ingest; F
consume (*a meal*); *s'~ dans* interfere
in, meddle in.
ingrat, e [ɛ̃'gra, ~'grat] ungrateful
(to[wards], *envers*; for, *à*); thankless (*task*); unpleasant (*work*); un-
promising; ✒, *fig.* unproductive;
âge m ~ awkward age; **ingratitude**
[ɛ̃grati'tyd] *f* ingratitude; thankless-
ness; ✒, *fig.* unproductiveness.
ingrédient [ɛ̃gre'djã] *m* ingredient.
inguérissable [ɛ̃geri'sabl] incurable.
ingurgiter [ɛ̃gyrʒi'te] (1a) *v/t.* ✒
ingurgitate; F swallow.
inhabile [ina'bil] unskilful, inexpert; ⚖ incompetent; **inhabileté**
[~bil'te] *f* lack of skill (in, *à*); clumsiness; **inhabilité** ⚖ [~bili'te] *f*
incapacity, disability; incompetency.
inhabitable [inabi'tabl] uninhabit-
able; **inhabité, e** [~'te] uninhab-
ited; untenanted (*house*).
inhalateur ✒ [inala'tœːr] *m* inhaler;
(*oxygen-*)breathing apparatus; **inhaler** ✒ [~'le] (1a) *v/t.* inhale.
inhérence [ine'rãːs] *f* inherence (in,
à); **inhérent, e** [~'rã, ~'rãːt] inherent (in, *à*); intrinsic.
inhiber [ini'be] (1a) *v/t.* physiol.,
psych. inhibit; ⚖ prohibit; **inhibition** [~bi'sjõ] *f* ⚖ prohibition;
physiol., psych. inhibition.
inhospitalier, -ère [inɔspita'lje, ~-
'ljeːr] inhospitable.
inhumain, e [iny'mɛ̃, ~'men] in-
human; cruel.   [inter.]
inhumer [iny'me] (1a) *v/t.* bury,)
inimaginable [inimaʒi'nabl] unimaginable.
inimitable [inimi'tabl] inimitable.
inimitié [inimi'tje] *f* hostility (*a.
fig.*); enmity.
ininflammable [inɛ̃fla'mabl] non-
inflammable, uninflammable.

inintelligence [inɛ̃teli'ʒãːs] *f* lack
of intelligence; **inintelligent, e**
[~'ʒã, ~'ʒãːt] unintelligent; obtuse;
inintelligible [~'ʒibl] unintelligi-
ble.
inique [i'nik] iniquitous; **iniquité**
[iniki'te] *f* iniquity (*a. eccl., a. fig.*).
initial, e, m/pl. -aux [ini'sjal, ~'sjo]
adj., a. su./f initial; *adj. a.* starting,
first; **initiateur, -trice** [~sja'tœːr,
~'tris] 1. *adj.* initiatory; initiation...;
2. *su.* initiator; originator; **initia-
tique** [~sja'tik] initiatory (*rite etc.*);
initiative [~sja'tiːv] *f* initiative; **initier** [~'sje] (1o) *v/t.* initiate (*a. fig.*).
injecter [ɛ̃ʒɛk'te] (1a) *v/t.* inject
(with *de, avec*); impregnate (*wood*);
injecté de sang bloodshot (*eye*); *s'~*
become bloodshot (*eye*); **injection**
[~'sjõ] *f* ✒, ⊕ injection; *wood:* impregnation.
injonction ⚖ [ɛ̃ʒõk'sjõ] *f* injunction;
order.
injure [ɛ̃'ʒyːr] *f* insult; ravages *pl.* (*of
time*); † wrong, injury, ⚖ tort; *~s pl.*
abuse *sg.*; **injurier** [ɛ̃ʒy'rje] (1o) *v/t.*
insult, abuse; call (*s.o.*) names; **injurieux, -euse** [~'rjø, ~'rjøːz] insulting, abusive (towards, *pour*); † ⚖
tortious.
injuste [ɛ̃'ʒyst] 1. *adj.* unjust, unfair
(to, *envers*); unrighteous (*person*);
2. *su./m* wrong; **injustice** [ɛ̃ʒys'tis]
f injustice, unfairness; **injustifiable** [~ti'fjabl] unwarrantable, un-
justifiable.
inlassable [ɛ̃la'sabl] tireless; *fig.*
untiring.
inné, e [in'ne] innate.
innocemment [inɔsa'mã] *adv.* of
innocent 1; **innocence** [~'sãːs] *f* innocence; **innocent, e** [~'sã, ~'sãːt]
1. *adj.* innocent; simple, artless;
2. *su.* simple *or* artless person; **innocenter** [~sã'te] (1a) *v/t.* clear
(*s.o.*) (of, *de*), prove (*s.o.*) innocent;
justify.   [ness.]
innocuité [innɔkɥi'te] *f* harmless-)
innombrable [innõ'brabl] innu-
merable, countless.
innovation [innɔva'sjõ] *f* innovation; **innover** [~'ve] (1a) *vt/i.* in-
novate; *v/i.* introduce innovations
(in, *en*); break new ground.
inoccupé, e [inɔky'pe] unoccupied;
vacant; unemployed; idle (*person*).
in-octavo *typ.* [inɔkta'vo] *m/inv., a.
adj./inv.* octavo.

inoculer [inɔky'le] (1a) v/t. 𝒮, a. fig. inoculate, infect (s.o. with s.th., qch. à q.).

inodore [inɔ'dɔːr] odo(u)rless; 𝒬 scentless.

inoffensif, -ve [inɔfã'sif, ~'siːv] inoffensive; harmless.

inondation [inɔ̃da'sjɔ̃] f inundation; flood; fig. deluge; **inonder** [~'de] (1a) v/t. inundate; flood (a. 🜉); fig. deluge (with, de); F soak.

inopérant, e 🜪 [inɔpe'rã, ~'rãːt] inoperative.

inopiné, e [inɔpi'ne] unforeseen, sudden.

inopportun, e [inɔpɔr'tœ̃, ~'tyn] inopportune; untimely; **inopportunément** [~tyne'mã] adv. of inopportun.

inorganisation [inɔrganiza'sjɔ̃] f disorganization, lack of organization.

inoubliable [inubli'abl] unforgettable.

inouï, e [i'nwi] unheard of; extraordinary.

inoxydable [inɔksi'dabl] rust-proof; rustless; stainless (steel).

inqualifiable [ɛ̃kali'fjabl] beyond words; fig. indescribable; fig. scandalous.

in-quarto typ. [ɛ̃kwar'to] m/inv., a. adj./inv. quarto.

inquiet, -ète [ɛ̃'kjɛ, ~'kjɛt] restless; uneasy; anxious; **inquiétant, e** [ɛ̃kje'tã, ~'tãːt] alarming, disturbing; fig. disquieting; **inquiéter** [~'te] (1f) v/t. alarm, disturb; make (s.o.) uneasy; s'~ worry (about, de); **inquiétude** [~'tyd] f disquiet; uneasiness, anxiety; restlessness.

insaisissable [ɛ̃sɛzi'sabl] unseizable; elusive; imperceptible (difference, sound, etc.); 🜪 not attachable.

insalissable [ɛ̃sali'sabl] dirt-proof.

insalubre [ɛ̃sa'lybr] unhealthy; insanitary; **insalubrité** [~lybri'te] f unhealthiness; insanitary condition.

insanité [ɛ̃sani'te] f insanity; fig. nonsense.

insatiable [ɛ̃sa'sjabl] insatiable.

insciemment [ɛ̃sja'mã] adv. unconsciously.

inscription [ɛ̃skrip'sjɔ̃] f inscription; registration, enrolment; univ. matriculation; 🜉 script; 🜨 maritime seaboard conscription; **inscrire** [~'kriːr] (4q) v/t. inscribe,

write down; register; enroll; s'~ register.

inscrutable [ɛ̃skry'tabl] inscrutable.

insecte [ɛ̃'sɛkt] m insect, Am. F bug; **insecticide** [ɛ̃sɛkti'sid] **1.** adj. insecticidal; poudre f ~ insect-powder; **2.** su./m insecticide; pesticide; **insectivore** zo. [~'vɔːr] **1.** su./m insectivore; **2.** adj. insectivorous.

insécuriser [ɛ̃sekyri'ze] (1a) v/t. make (s.o.) feel unsure or uncertain, give (s.o.) a feeling of insecurity.

insensé, e [ɛ̃sã'se] **1.** adj. mad (a. fig.); fig. senseless; fig. crazy (idea, plan); **2.** su./m madman; su./f madwoman.

insensibilisation 𝒮 [ɛ̃sãsibiliza'sjɔ̃] f an(a)esthetization; **insensibiliser** 𝒮 [~'ze] (1a) v/t. an(a)esthetize; **insensibilité** [~'te] f insensibility (a. fig.); insensitiveness; callousness, indifference; **insensible** [ɛ̃sã'sibl] insensible; insensitive; indifferent; imperceptible (difference).

inséparable [ɛ̃sepa'rabl] **1.** adj. inseparable; **2.** su. inseparable companion; su./m: orn. ~s pl. love-birds.

insérer [ɛ̃se're] (1f) v/t. insert; **insertion** [ɛ̃sɛr'sjɔ̃] f insertion.

insidieux, -euse [ɛ̃si'djø, ~'djøːz] insidious (a. 𝒮 disease); crafty (person).

insigne¹ [ɛ̃'siɲ] distinguished (by, for par); signal (favour); pej. notorious; glaring.

insigne² [~] m ✕, sp., etc. badge; ~s pl. insignia; ~s pl. de la royauté royal insignia.

insignifiant, e [ɛ̃siɲi'fjã, ~'fjãːt] insignificant; trifling; trivial.

insinuer [ɛ̃si'nɥe] (1n) v/t. insinuate (a. fig.); 🜪 insert (a probe etc.); s'~ insinuate o.s.; worm one's way (into, dans).

insipide [ɛ̃si'pid] insipid; tasteless (food); fig. dull, uninteresting; **insipidité** [~pidi'te] f food: tastelessness, lack of taste; fig. insipidity, dullness; tameness.

insistance [ɛ̃sis'tãːs] f insistence (on ger., à inf.); avec ~ insistently; **insister** [~'te] (1a) v/i. insist (on ger. à, pour inf.); ~ sur stress; persist in.

insociable [ɛ̃sɔ'sjabl] unsociable.

insolation [ɛ̃sɔla'sjɔ̃] f 𝒮 sunstroke; sun-bathing; phot. daylight printing.

insolence [ɛ̃sɔ'lãːs] f insolence; im-

pertinence; impudence; **insolent, e**
[ˌ'lɑ̃, ˌ'lɑ̃:t] insolent, impertinent;
overbearing.

insoler [ɛ̃sɔ'le] (1a) v/t. expose (s.th.)
to the sun; *phot.* print by daylight.

insolite [ɛ̃sɔ'lit] unusual; strange.

insoluble [ɛ̃sɔ'lybl] insoluble (a.
fig.).

insolvable † [ɛ̃sɔl'vabl] insolvent.

insomnie [ɛ̃sɔm'ni] f insomnia,
sleeplessness.

insondable [ɛ̃sɔ̃'dabl] unsoundable
(*sea*); *fig.* unfathomable.

insonorisé, e [ɛ̃sɔnɔri'ze] sound-
proof(ed); **insonoriser** [ˌ] (1a) v/t.
soundproof.

insouciance [ɛ̃su'sjɑ̃:s] f unconcern;
jauntiness; carelessness; **insouciant, e** [ˌ'sjɑ̃, ˌ'sjɑ̃:t] unconcerned,
carefree, jaunty; thoughtless; **insoucieux, -euse** [ˌ'sjø, ˌ'sjø:z]
carefree; unconcerned (about, de).

insoumis, e [ɛ̃su'mi, ˌ'mi:z] 1. *adj.*
unsubdued; unruly, refractory; insubordinate; ✗ absent; 2. *su./m* ✗
absentee.

insoutenable [ɛ̃sut'nabl] untenable,
indefensible; unbearable (*pain*).

inspecter [ɛ̃spɛk'te] (1a) v/t. ✗ etc.
inspect; † examine (*accounts*); **inspecteur** [ˌ'tœ:r] m factory, mines,
police, school, sanitary, taxes: inspector; *works:* overseer; † examiner; shop-walker, *Am.* floorwalker; **inspection** [ˌ'sjɔ̃] f inspection; examination; inspectorate; ✗
muster parade.

inspiration [ɛ̃spira'sjɔ̃] f inspiration
(*a. fig.*); **inspirer** [ˌ're] (1a) v/t.
inspire (s.o. with s.th., qch. à q.)
(*a. fig.*); *fig.* prompt (to *inf.*, de
inf.).

instabilité [ɛ̃stabili'te] f instability
(*a. fig.*); **instable** [ˌ'tabl] unstable;
fig. unreliable.

installation [ɛ̃stala'sjɔ̃] f installation; setting (in); moving in, setting
up house *or* shop; putting in; ⊕
equipment; ⊕ plant; ⊕ ~ d'aérage
ventilation plant; **installer** [ˌ'le]
(1a) v/t. install; put in *or* up; ⊕ etc. fit
up; fit out; furnish (*a house*); *fig.*
establish, settle; s'~ settle down;
settle in; set up house *or* shop.

instamment [ɛ̃sta'mɑ̃] *adv.* ear-
nestly; urgently.

instance [ɛ̃s'tɑ̃:s] f *admin.*, ⚖ authority; ⚖ (legal) proceedings *pl.*; ~s

pl. entreaties; *en* ~ *de* on the point of;
instant, e [ˌ'tɑ̃, ˌ'tɑ̃:t] 1. *adj.* pressing; imminent; 2. *su./m* moment,
instant; *à l'*~ just now; immediately;
instantané, e [ˌtɑ̃ta'ne] 1. *adj.*
instantaneous; instant (*coffee etc.*); 2.
su./m phot. snapshot; **instantanéi-
té** [ˌtɑ̃tanei'te] f instantaneousness.

instar [ɛ̃s'ta:r] m: *à l'*~ *de* after the
manner of, like.

instauration [ɛ̃stɔra'sjɔ̃] f founding; establishment; **instaurer** [ˌ-
're] (1a) v/t. found; establish.

instigateur m, **-trice** f [ɛ̃stiga'tœ:r,
ˌ'tris] instigator (of, de); inciter (to,
de); **instigation** [ˌ'sjɔ̃] f instigation.

instiller ⚗ [ɛ̃sti'le] (1a) v/t. instil (a.
fig.), drop (*liquid in the eye*).

instinct [ɛ̃s'tɛ̃] m instinct; d'~, *par* ~
instinctively; **instinctif, -ve** [ˌtɛ̃k-
'tif, ˌ'ti:v] instinctive.

instituer [ɛ̃sti'tɥe] (1n) v/t. institute;
establish; *admin.*, a. ⚖ appoint (*an
heir etc.*); **institut** [ˌ'ty] m institute;
eccl. order; *eccl.* rule; **instituteur,
-trice** [ˌty'tœ:r, ˌ'tris] su. school-
teacher; **institution** [ˌty'sjɔ̃] f institution; **institutionnaliser** [ˌtysjɔ-
nali'ze] (1a) v/t. institutionalize.

instructeur [ɛ̃stryk'tœ:r] 1. *su./m*
instructor (a. ✗), teacher; 2. *adj./m*:
⚖ *juge* m ~ examining magistrate;
instructif, -ve [ˌ'tif, ˌ'ti:v] in-
structive; **instruction** [ˌ'sjɔ̃] f instruction; education; ✗ training (*of
troops*); ⚖ preliminary investigation,
judicial inquiry; ~s *pl.* instructions,
directions; ~ *civique* civics *sg.*; ~
publique state education; *avoir de l'*~
be well educated; **instruire** [ɛ̃s-
'trɥi:r] (4h) v/t. inform; educate,
teach; ✗ train (*troops etc.*); ✗ drill
(*troops*); ⚖ investigate; **instruit, e**
[ɛ̃s'trɥi, ˌ'trɥit] educated, learned.

instrument [ɛ̃stry'mɑ̃] m instrument (a. ♪, a. ⚖), tool (a. *fig.*); ⚖
deed; **instrumenter** [ˌmɑ̃'te] (1a)
v/t. ♪ score; v/i. ⚖ draw up a document; ~ *contre* order proceedings
to be taken against.

insu [ɛ̃'sy] m: *à l'*~ *de* without the
knowledge of, unknown to.

insubmersible [ɛ̃sybmɛr'sibl] un-
sinkable.

insubordination [ɛ̃sybɔrdina'sjɔ̃] f
insubordination; **insubordonné, e**
[ˌdɔ'ne] insubordinate.

insuccès [ɛ̃syk'sɛ] *m* failure.

insuffisance [ɛ̃syfi'zɑ̃:s] *f* insufficiency; *fig.* unsatisfactoriness; **insuffisant, e** [˷'zɑ̃, ˷'zɑ̃:t] insufficient; inadequate; *fig.* incompetent.

insuffler [ɛ̃sy'fle] (1a) *v/t.* inflate (*a balloon etc.*); ♣ spray (*one's throat*); *fig.* inspire (s.o. with s.th., *qch. à q.*).

insulaire [ɛ̃sy'lɛ:r] **1.** *adj.* insular; **2.** *su.* islander.

insuline ♣ [ɛ̃sy'lin] *f* insulin.

insulte [ɛ̃'sylt] *f* insult; **insulter** [ɛ̃syl'te] (1a) *v/t.* insult; *v/i.*: † ˷ *à* abuse, revile; be an insult to.

insupportable [ɛ̃sypɔr'tabl] unbearable; insufferable (*person*); intolerable; F aggravating.

insurgé, e [ɛ̃syr'ʒe] *adj., a. su.* insurgent, rebel; **insurger** [˷] (1l) *v/t.*: s'˷ revolt, rebel (against, *contre*).

insurmontable [ɛ̃syrmɔ̃'tabl] insurmountable, insuperable.

insurrection [ɛ̃syrɛk'sjɔ̃] *f* insurrection, rebellion, rising.

intact, e [ɛ̃'takt] intact; undamaged; untouched; *fig.* unblemished (*reputation*).

intarissable [ɛ̃tari'sabl] inexhaustible; never-failing; long-winded (*talker*).

intégral, e, *m/pl.* **-aux** [ɛ̃te'gral, ˷'gro] **1.** *adj.* integral (*a.* Å√), full, complete; **2.** *su./f* Å√ integral; *music etc.*: complete works *pl.* or series; **3.** *su./m* crash helmet; **intégralement** [˷gral'mɑ̃] fully, in full; **intégrant, e** [˷'grɑ̃, ˷'grɑ̃:t] integral (*part etc.*); **intégration** [˷gra'sjɔ̃] *f* integration; **intègre** [ɛ̃'tɛgr] upright, honest; incorruptible; **intégrer** [ɛ̃te'gre] (1f) *v/t.* integrate; **intégrité** [ɛ̃tegri'te] *f* integrity.

intellect [ɛ̃tɛl'lɛkt] *m* intellect; **intellectuel, -elle** [˷lɛk'tɥɛl] *adj., a. su.* intellectual.

intelligence [ɛ̃tɛli'ʒɑ̃:s] *f* intelligence; understanding; *d'˷ avec* in agreement *or* collusion with; *en bonne (mauvaise)* ˷ on good (bad) terms; **intelligent, e** [˷'ʒɑ̃, ˷'ʒɑ̃:t] intelligent; clever; **intelligible** [˷'ʒibl] intelligible; *fig.* distinct.

intempérance [ɛ̃tɑ̃pe'rɑ̃:s] *f* intemperance; **intempérant, e** [˷'rɑ̃, ˷'rɑ̃:t] intemperate; **intempérie** [˷'ri] *f weather*: inclemency; ˷s *pl.* bad weather *sg.*

intempestif, -ve [ɛ̃tɑ̃pɛs'tif, ˷'ti:v] untimely, unseasonable.

intendance [ɛ̃tɑ̃'dɑ̃:s] *f* intendance; stewardship; ✕ Commissariat; *pol.* (*approx.*) domestic affairs *pl.*; **intendant** [˷'dɑ̃] *m* intendant; steward; ✕ Commissariat officer; ♣ paymaster; *school*: bursar.

intense [ɛ̃'tɑ̃:s] intense; severe (*cold, pain*); powerful; deep (*colour*); ⚡ strong (*current*); heavy (*flow*); high (*fever*); bitter (*cold*); **intensif, -ive** [ɛ̃tɑ̃'sif, ˷'i:v] intensive; **intensifier** [ɛ̃tɑ̃si'fje] (1a) *v/t.* (*a.* s'˷) intensify; **intensité** [ɛ̃tɑ̃si'te] *f* intensity; severity; strength; *light*: brilliance; *colour*: depth, richness; *cold*: bitterness; *wind*: force.

intenter ⚖ [ɛ̃tɑ̃'te] (1a) *v/t.* bring (*an action*); institute (*proceedings*).

intention [ɛ̃tɑ̃'sjɔ̃] *f* intention; aim, purpose; *à ton* ˷ for you; **intentionné, e** [˷sjɔ'ne] ...-disposed, ...-intentioned; *bien* ˷ well-intentioned, well-meaning; **intentionnel, -elle** [˷sjɔ'nɛl] intentional, wilful.

inter... [ɛ̃tɛr] inter...; **˷agir** [˷a'ʒi:r] (2a) *v/i.* interact; **˷allié, e** *pol.* [˷a'lje] interallied; **˷calaire** [˷ka-'lɛ:r] intercalated; intercalary (*day etc.*); **˷caler** [˷ka'le] (1a) *v/t.* intercalate; insert; ⚡ cut in; **˷céder** [˷se-'de] (1f) *v/t.* intercede (on s.o.'s behalf, *pour q.*; with s.o., *auprès de q.*); **˷cepter** [˷sɛp'te] (1a) *v/t.* intercept; ⊕ shut off (*steam*); **˷ception** [˷sɛp'sjɔ̃] *f* interception; ⊕ *steam*: shutting off; **˷cesseur** [˷sɛ'sœ:r] *m* intercessor; **˷cession** [˷sɛ'sjɔ̃] *f* intercession; **˷changeable** [˷ʃɑ̃'ʒabl] interchangeable; **˷continental, e** *m/pl.* **-aux** [˷kɔ̃tinɑ̃'tal, ˷'to] intercontinental (*a.* ✕ *missile*); **˷dépendance** [˷depɑ̃'dɑ̃:s] *f* interdependence; **˷diction** [˷dik'sjɔ̃] *f* interdiction; **˷dire** [˷'di:r] (4p) *v/t.* prohibit, forbid; *fig.* bewilder, dumbfound; *eccl.* (lay under an) interdict; *admin.* suspend; **˷disciplinaire** [˷disipli'nɛ:r] interdisciplinary; **˷dit, e** [˷'di, ˷'dit] **1.** *adj.* forbidden; bewildered, perplexed, taken aback; **2.** *su./m eccl.* interdict.

intéressé, e [ɛ̃terɛ'se] **1.** *adj.* interested; selfish; **2.** *su.* interested party; **interessement** † [˷rɛs'mɑ̃] *m* (*workers'*) profit-sharing (scheme); **intéresser** [˷rɛ'se] (1b) *v/t.* interest; concern; s'~ take an interest (in, à); **intérêt** [~'rɛ] *m* interest (*a.* ✝); advantage; *par* ~ out of selfishness; ✝ *à* ~ *fixe* fixed-interest; *sans* ~ uninteresting; ✝ interest-free.

interférence *phys., fig.* [ɛ̃tɛrfe'rɑ̃ːs] *f* interference (*a. radio*).

interfolier [ɛ̃tɛrfɔ'lje] (1o) *v/t.* interleave (*a book*).

intérieur, e [ɛ̃te'rjœːr] **1.** *adj.* interior, inner; inward; *geog., a.* ⚓ inland...; *admin., pol.* domestic, home...; **2.** *su./m* interior, inside; home; *sp.* inside; *d'~* domestic, domesticated (*person*).

intérim [ɛ̃te'rim] *m/inv.* interim; *par* ~ *adj.* interim; *adv.* temporarily; **intérimaire** [~ri'mɛːr] **1.** *adj.* temporary, acting; **2.** *su.* locum tenens; deputy; F temp.

inter...: **~jection** [ɛ̃tɛrʒɛk'sjɔ̃] *f* interjection; ⚖ *d'appel* lodging of an appeal; **~jeter** [~ʒə'te] (1c) *v/t.* interject; ⚖ ~ *appel* appeal; **~ligne** [~'liɲ] *su./m* space (between two lines); *su./f typ.* lead; **~ligner** [~li'ɲe] (1a) *v/t.* interline; *typ.* lead out; **~linéaire** [~line'ɛːr] interlinear; **~locuteur** *m*, **-trice** *f* [~ɔky'tœːr, ~'tris] interlocutor; *conversation*: speaker; questioner; ~ *valable pol. etc.* valid representative; *fig.* worthy opponent; **~lope** [~'lɔp] **1.** *adj.* ✝ illegal, dishonest; *fig.* shady, dubious; **2.** *su./m* smuggler; blockade-runner; **~loquer** *fig.* [~lɔ'ke] (1m) *v/t.* disconcert, nonplus; **~mède** [~'mɛd] *m* medium; *thea.* interlude; **~médiaire** [~me'djeːr] **1.** *adj.* intermediate; ✝ middleman's ...; ⊕ *arbre m* ~ countershaft; **2.** *su./m* intermediary, go-between; medium; ✝ middleman; agent; *par l'~ de* through (the medium of).

interminable [ɛ̃tɛrmi'nabl] never-ending, interminable.

intermittence [ɛ̃tɛrmi'tɑ̃ːs] *f* intermittence; *par* ~ intermittently; **intermittent, e** [~'tɑ̃, ~'tɑ̃ːt] intermittent (*a.* ✽ *fever*); ✽ irregular (*pulse*); ⚡ make-and-break (*current*).

internat [ɛ̃tɛr'na] *m* living-in; boarding-school; ✽ post of assistant house-physician *or* house-surgeon, *Am.* internship; *coll.* boarders *pl.*

international, e, *m/pl.* **-aux** [ɛ̃tɛrnasjɔ'nal, ~'no] **1.** *adj.* international; **2.** *su. sp.* international; *su./f* International (Working Men's Association); *song*: Internationale.

interne [ɛ̃'tɛrn] **1.** *adj.* internal; inner; municipal (*law*); ⚓ interior (*angle*); resident; **2.** *su. school*: boarder; ✽ resident medical student in a hospital; **internement** [ɛ̃tɛrnə'mɑ̃] *m admin.* internment; *lunatic*: confinement; **interner** [~'ne] (1a) *v/t. admin.* intern; shut up, confine (*a lunatic*).

inter...: **~pellateur** *m*, **-trice** *f* [ɛ̃tɛrpɛla'tœːr, ~'tris] interpellator; **~pellation** [~pɛla'sjɔ̃] *f* peremptory question(ing); interruption; ⚖ challenge; *parl.* interpellation; **~peller** [~pɛ'le] (1a) *v/t.* interpellate; ⚖ *etc.* challenge; ⚖ *etc.* call upon (*s.o.*) to answer; **~phone** [~'fɔn] *m* intercom; **~planétaire** [~plane'tɛːr] interplanetary; **~polateur** *m*, **-trice** *f* [~pɔla'tœːr, ~'tris] interpolator; **~polation** [~pɔla'sjɔ̃] *f* interpolation; **~poler** [~pɔ'le] (1a) *v/t.* interpolate; **~poser** [~pɔ'ze] (1a) *v/t.* interpose; ⚖ *personne f interposée* intermediary; third party fraudulently hold out as a principal; *par ... interposé* through ..., by ..., with the help of ...; *s'~* interpose *or* place o.s. (between, *entre*); **~position** [~pozi'sjɔ̃] *f* interposition; *fig.* intervention; ⚖ *de personnes* fraudulent holding out of a third party as principal; **~prétation** [~preta'sjɔ̃] *f* interpreting; interpretation (*a. thea.,* ♪*, etc.*); explanation; **~prète** [~'prɛt] *su.* interpreter; *fig.* exponent; **~préter** [~pre'te] (1f) *v/t.* interpret; expound; read (*a signal*); *mal* ~ misconstrue; **~professionnel, -elle** [~prɔfɛsjɔ'nɛl] (*salaries*) in comparable professions; **~rogateur, -trice** [ɛ̃tɛrɔga'tœːr, ~'tris] **1.** *adj.* interrogative; questioning; **2.** *su.* questioner; interrogator; *school*: examiner; **~rogatif, -ive** *gramm.* [~rɔga'tif, ~'tiːv] *adj., a. su./m* interrogative; **~rogation** [~rɔga'sjɔ̃] *f* interrogation; question; questioning; *point m d'~* question-mark; **~rogatoire** [~rɔga'twaːr] *m* ⚖ interrogatory, examination (*of an accused*); ⚖ questioning; **~roger** [~rɔ'ʒe] (1l) *v/t.* interrogate, question; examine; *fig.* consult; **~rompre** [~'rɔ̃ːpr] (4a) *v/t.* interrupt; break (*a. journey, a.* ⚡); suspend, stop, cut short; ⊕ shut off (*steam*); **~rupteur, -trice** [~ryp-

ˈtœːr, ~ˈtris] **1.** *adj.* interrupting; **2.**
su. interruptor; *su./m* ⚡ switch,
circuit breaker; **~ruption** [~rypˈsjõ]
f interruption; stopping; *communications:* severing; *work:* stopping; ⚡
current: breaking; ⊕ *steam:* shutting
off; *sans* ~ without a break; **~section**
[~sɛkˈsjõ] *f* ⚶ *etc.* intersection; *track,
road:* crossing; **~stellaire** [~steˈlɛːr]
interstellar; **~stice** [ɛtɛrsˈtis] *m* interstice; chink; **~urbain, e** [ɛtɛryr-
ˈbɛ̃, ~ˈbɛn] interurban; *teleph.*
trunk(-*call, -line, etc.*); **~valle** [~ˈval]
m interval (*a.* ♩); space, gap; *time:*
period; ⚡ clearance; *dans l'*~ in the
meantime; *par* ~s off and on, at
intervals; **~venir** [~vəˈniːr] (2h) *v/i.*
intervene, interfere; *fig.* occur, happen; **~vention** [~vãˈsjõ] *f* intervention (*a.* ♂♀); interference; ⚡ operation; ⚡ ~ *chirurgicale* surgical intervention; **~vertir** [~vɛrˈtiːr] (2a) *v/t.*
invert (*an order, a.* ♪); **~view** [~ˈvju]
f interview(ing); **~viewer 1.** (1a) *v/t.*
[~vjuˈve] interview; *interviewé*(e) in-
terviewee; **2.** *su./m* [~vjuˈvœːr] interviewer.

intestin, e [ɛtɛsˈtɛ̃, ~ˈtin] **1.** *adj.* internal; civil (*war*); **2.** *su./m anat.*
intestine, bowel, gut; ~ *grêle* small
intestine; *gros* ~ large intestine;
intestinal, e, *m/pl.* -aux [~tiˈnal,
~ˈno] intestinal.

intimation [ɛtimaˈsjõ] *f* intimation;
admin. notice; ⚖ notice of appeal;
intime [ɛˈtim] intimate, close;
inner; private; **intimer** [ɛtiˈme]
(1a) *v/t.* intimate; notify; ⚖ summons (*s.o.*) to appear before the
Court of Appeal.

intimider [ɛtimiˈde] (1a) *v/t.* in-
timidate; frighten; threaten; F
bully.

intimité [ɛtimiˈte] *f* intimacy; privacy; *fig.* depths *pl.*; *dans l'*~ privately, in private life; in privacy.

intitulé [ɛtityˈle] *m book etc.*: title;
chapter: heading; *deed:* premises *pl.*;
intituler [~] (1a) *v/t.* entitle, call.

intolérable [ɛtɔleˈrabl] intolerable,
unbearable; **intolérance** [~ˈrãːs] *f*
intolerance; **intolérant, e** [~ˈrã,
~ˈrãːt] intolerant.

intonation [ɛtɔnaˈsjõ] *f speech:*
intonation; *voice:* modulation,
pitch.

intoxication ⚕ [ɛtɔksikaˈsjõ] *f*
poisoning; ~ *alimentaire* food poi-

soning; **intoxiquer** ⚕ [~ˈke] (1m)
v/t. poison.

intraitable [ɛtrɛˈtabl] unmanageable; obstinate, inflexible; ⚕ beyond treatment.

intramusculaire [ɛtramyskyˈlɛːr]
1. *adj.* intramuscular; **2.** *su./f* intramuscular injection.

intransigeant, e [ɛtrãziˈʒã, ~ˈʒãːt]
1. *adj.* uncompromising; peremptory (*tone*); *pol.* intransigent; **2.** *su.
pol.* die-hard.

intransitif, -ve *gramm.* [ɛtrãziˈtif,
~ˈtiːv] intransitive.

intraveineux, -euse ⚕ [ɛtravɛˈnø,
~ˈnøːz] **1.** *adj.* intravenous; **2.** *su./f*
intravenous injection.

intrépide [ɛtreˈpid] intrepid, fear-
less; *pej.* brazen; **intrépidité** [~pi-
diˈte] *f* intrepidity, fearlessness.

intrigant, e [ɛtriˈgã, ~ˈgãːt] **1.** *adj.*
scheming; **2.** *su.* intriguer, schemer;
intrigue [ɛˈtrig] *f* intrigue; machination; plot (*a.* thea., *novel, etc.*);
love-affair; **intriguer** [ɛtriˈge] (1m)
v/i. plot, intrigue; *v/t.* puzzle, intrigue (*s.o.*).

intrinsèque [ɛtrɛ̃ˈsɛk] intrinsic;
specific (*value*).

introducteur *m*, **-trice** *f* [ɛtrɔdyk-
ˈtœːr, ~ˈtris] introducer; **introduction** [~dykˈsjõ] *f* introduction;
ushering in; ⊕ *steam:* admission;
book: preface; **introduire** [~ˈdɥiːr]
(4h) *v/t.* introduce; usher in, show
in; ⊕ admit (*steam*); s'~ get in,
enter.

introniser [ɛtrɔniˈze] (1a) *v/t.* en-
throne; *fig.* establish (*a fashion*); s'~
establish o.s.; become established
(*fashion*).

introuvable [ɛtruˈvabl] undiscover-
able.

intrus, e [ɛˈtry, ~ˈtryːz] **1.** *adj.* in-
truding; **2.** *su.* intruder; ⚖ trespasser; F *reception etc.*: gate-crasher;
intrusion [ɛtryˈzjõ] *f* intrusion.

intuitif, -ve [ɛtɥiˈtif, ~ˈtiːv] intuitive; **intuition** [~ˈsjõ] *f* intuition, insight.

inusable [inyˈzabl] everlasting;
proof against wear.

inusité, e [inyziˈte] unusual; not in
use (*word*).

inutile [inyˈtil] useless; pointless;
needless; unnecessary; superfluous;
inutilisable [inytiliˈzabl] unser-
viceable, unemployable (*person*);

worthless; **inutilisé, e** [~ˈze] un-used; **inutilité** [~ˈte] f uselessness; futility; useless thing.

invaincu, e [ɛ̃vɛ̃ˈky] unbeaten; un-vanquished; unconquered.

invalide [ɛ̃vaˈlid] **1.** adj. invalid (a. ✠), infirm; ✗ disabled; rickety (chair etc.); **2.** su. invalid; su./m disabled soldier, pensioner; **inva-lider** [ɛ̃valiˈde] (1a) v/t. ✠ invali-date; quash (elections); pol. unseat (a member of Parliament etc.); **in-validité** [~diˈte] f infirmity; dis-ablement; ✗ invalidism; ✠ in-validity.

invariable [ɛ̃vaˈrjabl] invariable, unchanging. [ance.↓

invariance A̸ [ɛ̃vaˈrjɑ̃ːs] f invari-↲

invasion [ɛ̃vaˈzjɔ̃] f invasion.

invective [ɛ̃vɛkˈtiːv] f invective; ~s pl. abuse sg.; **invectiver** [~tiˈve] (1a) v/t. rail at, abuse (s.o.); v/i.: ~ contre rail at, revile, inveigh against.

invendable ✝ [ɛ̃vɑ̃ˈdabl] unsale-able, unmerchantable.

inventaire [ɛ̃vɑ̃ˈtɛːr] m inventory; ✝ stock-list; faire son ~ take stock; **inventer** [~ˈte] (1a) v/t. invent; **inventeur, -trice** [~ˈtœːr, ~ˈtris] **1.** adj. inventive; **2.** su. inventor; discoverer; ✠ finder; **inventif, -ve** [~ˈtif, ~ˈtiːv] inventive; **invention** [~ˈsjɔ̃] f invention; imaginative ca-pacity; **inventorier** ✝ [~tɔˈrje] (1o) v/t. inventory, list; value (bills etc.); take stock of.

inverse [ɛ̃ˈvɛrs] adj., su./m opposite; inverse; reverse; **inverser** [ɛ̃vɛrˈse] (1a) vt/i. reverse (a. ⚡); **inverseur** [~ˈsœːr] m ⚡ reverser; ⊕ reversing device or handle; **inversible** [~ˈsibl] reversible; **inversion** [~ˈsjɔ̃] f A̸, gramm. inversion; ⚡ current: rever-sal; **invertir** [~ˈtiːr] (2a) v/t. reverse (a. ⚡ the current); invert.

investigateur, -trice [ɛ̃vɛstigaˈtœːr, ~ˈtris] **1.** adj. investigating; searching (a. glance); **2.** su. investigator, in-quirer; **investigation** [~ˈsjɔ̃] f in-vestigation, inquiry.

investir [ɛ̃vɛsˈtiːr] (2a) v/t. invest; ✗ a. blockade; **investissement** [~tis-ˈmɑ̃] m investment; **investisseur** [~tiˈsœːr] investor.

invétérer [ɛ̃veteˈre] (1f) v/t.: s'~ become inveterate, become deep-rooted.

invincible [ɛ̃vɛ̃ˈsibl] invincible; fig. insuperable (difficulty).

inviolable [ɛ̃vjɔˈlabl] inviolable; burglar-proof (lock); immune (dip-lomat, etc.).

invisible [ɛ̃viˈzibl] invisible.

invitation [ɛ̃vitaˈsjɔ̃] f invitation; sans ~ uninvited(ly adv.); sur l'~ de at the invitation of; **invite** [ɛ̃ˈvit] f invitation, inducement; cards: lead; **invité** m, e f [ɛ̃viˈte] guest; **inviter** [~] (1a) v/t. invite (to inf., à inf.); ask, request; fig. tempt; cards: call for.

invivable F [ɛ̃viˈvabl] unlivable-with, unbearable (person); impossible to live in (building etc.).

invocation [ɛ̃vɔkaˈsjɔ̃] f invocation.

involontaire [ɛ̃vɔlɔ̃ˈtɛːr] involun-tary.

invoquer [ɛ̃vɔˈke] (1m) v/t. invoke; call upon; put forward (an excuse, a reason, etc.).

invraisemblable [ɛ̃vrɛsɑ̃ˈblabl] un-likely, improbable; **invraisem-blance** [~ˈblɑ̃ːs] f unlikelihood, improbability. [nerable.↓

invulnérable [ɛ̃vylneˈrabl] invul-↲

iode ♑, ✗ [jɔd] m iodine; **ioder** [jɔˈde] iodize; **iodique** [~ˈdik] iodic.

ion ♑, ⚗, phys. [jɔ̃] m ion.

ionique¹ △ [jɔˈnik] Ionic.

ionique² [jɔˈnik] phys. ionic; radio: thermionic (tube, valve); **ionisation** ♑, phys. [~nizaˈsjɔ̃] f ionization.

iouler ♪ [juˈle] (1a) v/i. yodel.

irai [iˈre] 1st p. sg. fut. of aller 1.

irascible [iraˈsibl] irritable, testy; quick-tempered.

iris [iˈris] m ⚘, anat., phot. iris; poet. rainbow; ⚘ a. flag; **irisation** [iriza-ˈsjɔ̃] f iridescence; **irisé, e** [~ˈze] iridescent; **iriser** [~ˈze] (1a) v/t. make iridescent.

irlandais, e [irlɑ̃ˈdɛ, ~ˈdɛːz] **1.** adj. Irish; **2.** su./m ling. Irish; ♀ Irish-man; les ♀ pl. the Irish; su./f ♀ Irishwoman.

ironie [irɔˈni] f irony; **ironique** [~ˈnik] ironic(al); **ironiser** [~niˈze] (1a) v/i. speak ironically.

irradiation [irradjaˈsjɔ̃] f ✗, phys. irradiation; phot. halation; **irradier** [~ˈdje] (1o) v/i. radiate, spread (pain, etc.); v/t. irradiate.

irraisonnable [irrɛzɔˈnabl] irra-tional.

irréalisable [irrealiˈzabl] unrealiz-

able (a. ✝); impracticable; **irréalité**
[~'te] f unreality.
irrécusable [irreky'zabl] unimpeachable; unchallengeable.
irréductible [irredyk'tibl] ⚕, ⚜
irreducible; *fig.* unshakable.
irréel, -elle [irre'ɛl] unreal.
irréfléchi, e [irrefle'ʃi] thoughtless;
unthinking, rash (*person*).
irrégularité [irregylari'te] f irregularity; unevenness; **irrégulier,
-ère** [~'lje, ~'ljɛːr] irregular; uneven;
erratic.
irrémédiable [irreme'djabl] incurable; *fig.* irreparable; irremediable,
past remedy.
irréparable [irrepa'rabl] irreparable; *fig.* irretrievable.
irrépréhensible [irrepreɑ̃'sibl]
blameless.
irrépressible [irrepre'sibl] uncontrollable; irrepressible.
irréprochable [irrepro'ʃabl] irreproachable; ⚖ unimpeachable.
irrésistible [irrezis'tibl] irresistible.
irrésolu, e [irrezo'ly] irresolute;
unsolved (*problem*); **irrésolution**
[~ly'sjɔ̃] f indecision, irresolution.
irrespectueux, -euse [irrɛspɛk-
'tɥø, ~'tɥøːz] disrespectful (to
[-wards] *pour, envers*).
irresponsabilité [irrɛspɔ̃sabili'te] f
irresponsibility; **irresponsable**
[~'sabl] irresponsible.
irrétrécissable *tex.* [irretresi'sabl]
unshrinkable; *rendre* ~ sanforize.
irréversible [irevɛr'sibl] irreversi-
ble.
irrévocable [irrevo'kabl] irrevoca-
ble; absolute (*decree*).
irrigateur [irriga'tœːr] m 🪠 hose
(-pipe); water-cart; ⚕ *wounds:* irri-
gator; ⚕ douche, enema; **irrigation** [~ga'sjɔ̃] f 🪠, ⚕ irrigation; 🪠
flooding; ⚕ douching; **irriguer**
[~'ge] (1m) v/t. 🪠, ⚕ irrigate; 🪠
water; ⚕ douche.
irritable [irri'tabl] irritable; touchy
(*person*); sensitive (*skin*); **irritant,
e** [~'tɑ̃, ~'tɑ̃ːt] irritating; ⚕ irritant;
irriter [~'te] (1a) v/t. irritate; ⚕
inflame; s'~ become angry (at,
with s.o. *contre q.*; at s.th., *de qch.*);
⚕ become inflamed.
irruption [irryp'sjɔ̃] f irruption; invasion; inrush; *river:* overflow,
flood; *faire* ~ burst *or* barge in (on
s.o., *chez q.*).

isard *zo.* [i'zaːr] m izard, (Pyrenean)
wild goat.
islamique [isla'mik] Islamic; **isla-
misme** [~'mism] m Islam(ism).
islandais, e [islɑ̃dɛ, ~'dɛːz] **1.** *adj.*
Icelandic; **2.** *su./m ling.* Icelandic; *su.*
♀ Icelander.
isobare *meteor.* [izo'baːr] f isobar;
isocèle ⚕ [~'sɛl] isosceles; **isochro-
ne** ⊕ [~'krɔn], **isochronique** ⊕
[~krɔ'nik] isochronous.
.isolant, e [izo'lɑ̃, ~'lɑ̃ːt] **1.** *adj.* isolat-
ing; ⚡ insulating; *bouteille* f ~e
vacuum *or* thermos flask; **2.** *su./m*
insulator; insulating material; **iso-
lateur** ⚡ [~la'tœːr] m insulator; **isolé, e** [~'le] isolated; lonely; lone;
remote, out-of-the-way; **isolement**
[izɔl'mɑ̃] m ⚜, ⊕, *a. fig.* isolation; ⚡
insulation; **isolément** [izɔle'mɑ̃]
adv. separately; **isoler** [~'le] (1a) v/t.
isolate (*a.* ⚗) (from *d'avec, de*); ⚡
insulate; **isoloir** [~'lwaːr] m polling
booth.
isomère [izo'mɛːr] **1.** *adj.* ⚗, ♀
isomerous, isomeric; **2.** *su./m* ⚗
isomer.
isotope ⚗, *phys.* [izo'tɔp] m isotope.
israélien, -enne [israe'ljɛ̃, ~'ljɛn]
adj., a. su. ♀ Israeli; **israélite** [~'lit]
1. *adj.* Jewish, of the Israelites; **2.**
su. ♀ Israelite, Jew.
issu, e [i'sy] **1.** *adj.:* ~ *de* descended
from; born of; **2.** *su./f* issue, end;
upshot; result; outlet; ⊕ ~es *pl.*
by-products; *à l'*~e *de* at the end
of; after; *sans* ~e blind (*alley*).
isthme *géog., anat.* [ism] m isthmus.
italien, -enne [ita'ljɛ̃, ~'ljɛn] **1.** *adj.*
Italian; **2.** *su./m ling.* Italian; *su.* ♀
Italian; **italique** *typ.* [~'lik] *adj., a.
su./m* italic.
item [i'tɛm] *adv.* item, also.
itératif, ve [itera'tif, ~'tiːv] *gramm.*
iterative; ⚖ repeated.
itinéraire [itine'rɛːr] **1.** *adj.* road-...,
direction-...; **2.** *su./m* itinerary;
route; guide-book; **itinérant,
e** [~'rɑ̃, ~'rɑ̃ːt] itinerant; ✕
mobile.
ivoire [i'vwaːr] m ivory; **ivoirerie**
[ivwarə'ri] f ivory work *or* trade.
ivraie ♀ [i'vrɛ] f cockle, darnel;
bibl. tares *pl.*
ivre [iːvr] drunk (with, *de*); intoxicated; *fig.* mad (with, *de*); **i-
vresse** [i'vrɛs] f drunkenness, in-

toxication; *fig.* ecstasy; **ivrogne, -esse** [i'vrɔɲ, ivrɔ'ɲɛs] **1.** *adj.* addicted to drink; drunken; **2.** *su.* drunkard, toper, *sl.* boozer; **ivrognerie** [ivrɔɲ'ri] *f* (habitual) drunkenness.

J

J, j [ʒi] *m* J, j.

jabot [ʒa'bo] *m bird*: crop; *cost. blouse, shirt*: frill; ruffle, jabot; **jaboter** F † [~bɔ'te] (1a) *v/i.* jabber, chatter.

jacasse [ʒa'kas] *f zo.* magpie; F † chatterbox; **jacasser** [~ka'se] (1a) *v/i.* chatter, gossip; **jacasserie** [~kas'ri] *f* gossip.

jachère ✔ [ʒa'ʃɛːr] *f* fallow; **jachérer** ✔ [~ʃe're] (1f) *v/t.* plough up (*fallow land*); fallow (*land*).

jacinthe [ʒa'sɛ̃ːt] *f* ✿ hyacinth; *min.* jacinth; ✿ ~ des bois bluebell.

jack ⚡ [ʒak] *m* jack.

jacobin, e [ʒakɔ'bɛ̃, ~'bin] *su. hist.* Jacobin; *fig.* sympathizer with radical democracy.

Jacques [ʒɑːk] *npr./m* James; *sl.* faire le ⚥ play the fool.

ja(c)quot *orn.* [ʒa'ko] *m parrot*: Poll(y).

jactance [ʒak'tɑ̃ːs] *f* boast(ing); **jacter** *sl.* [~'te] (1a) *v/i.* boast; brag.

jade *min.* [ʒad] *m* jade.

jadis [ʒa'dis] *adv.* formerly, long ago; *de ~ a.* of old.

jaillir [ʒa'jiːr] (2a) *v/i.* gush, spurt out; shoot *or* burst forth; fly (*sparks*); flash (*light*); **jaillissement** [~jis-'mɑ̃] *m* gushing *etc.* [jet-black.

jais *min.* [ʒɛ] *m* jet; noir comme du ~╛

jalon [ʒa'lɔ̃] *m* surveying staff; (range-)pole; ✗ aiming-post; *fig.* planter (*or* poser) des ~s (*or* les premiers ~s) pave the way *or* prepare the ground (for de, pour); **jalonner** [~lɔ'ne] (1a) *v/t.* stake out; *fig.* mark; *fig.* be a landmark in (*a period*).

jalouser [ʒalu'ze] (1a) *v/t.* be jealous of (*s.o.*); **jalousie** [~'zi] *f* jealousy; Venetian blind; screen; ✿ sweet-william; ~ du métier professional jealousy; **jaloux, -ouse** [ʒa'lu, ~'luːz] jealous; envious; *fig.* eager (for, de).

jamais [ʒa'mɛ] *adv.* ever; never; ~ de la vie! out of the question!; ~ plus never again; à (*or* pour) ~ for ever; ne ... ~ never.

jambage [ʒɑ̃'baːʒ] *m* ⚠ *door*: jamb; *door, window*: post; *fireplace*: cheek, jamb; foundation-wall; *writing*: down-stroke; **jambe** [ʒɑ̃:b] *f* leg; *glass*: stem; ⚠ *brickwork*: stone pier; ⚠ ~ de force strut, prop; *mot.* stay-rod; à toutes ~s at top speed; cela me fait une belle ~! a fat lot of good that does me; *sp.* jeu *m* de ~s foot-work; prendre ses ~s à son cou take to one's heels; **jambé, e** [ʒɑ̃'be] *adj.*: bien ~ with shapely legs; **jambette** [~'bɛt] *f* small leg; ⚠ stanchion; **jambier, -ère** [~'bje, ~'bjɛːr] 1. *adj. anat.* tibial; 2. *su./f* elastic stocking; legging; *sp.* shinguard; **jambon** [~'bɔ̃] *m* ham; œufs *m/pl.* au ~ ham and eggs; **jambonneau** [~bɔ'no] *m* knuckle of ham; small ham.

jamboree [ʒɑ̃bɔ're] *m* jamboree.

jansénisme *eccl.* [ʒɑ̃se'nism] *m* Jansenism.

jante [ʒɑ̃:t] *f wheel*: felloe; rim.

janvier [ʒɑ̃'vje] *m* January.

japon [ʒa'pɔ̃] *m* Japan porcelain; **japonais, e** [~pɔ'nɛ, ~'nɛːz] 1. *adj.* Japanese; 2. *su./m ling.* Japanese; *su.* 2 Japanese; les 2 *m/pl.* the Japanese.

japper [ʒa'pe] (1a) *v/i.* yelp.

jaquette [ʒa'kɛt] *f* morning coat; (*lady's*) jacket; *book etc.*: (dust) cover.

jardin [ʒar'dɛ̃] *m* garden; ~ alpin rock-garden; ~ anglais landscape garden; ~ d'enfants kindergarten; *thea.* côté *m* ~ prompt-side; **jardinage** [ʒardi'naːʒ] *m* gardening; *diamond*: flaw; ~ paysagiste landscape gardening; **jardiner** [~'ne] (1a) *v/i.* garden; **jardinet** [~'nɛ] *m* small garden; **jardinier, -ère** [~'nje, ~'njɛːr] 1. *adj.* garden...; 2. *su.* gardener; ~ paysagiste landscape gardener; *su./f* flower stand; window-box; spring cart; *orn.* ortolan; ~ère d'enfants kindergarten teacher; *cuis.* à la ~ère garnished with vegetables.

jargon [ʒarˈgɔ̃] *m* jargon; slang; *fig.* gibberish; **jargonner** [~gɔˈne] (1a) *v/i.* talk jargon.

jarre [ʒaːr] *f* (earthenware) jar; ⚡ ~ *électrique* Leyden jar.

jarret [ʒaˈrɛ] *m anat. man:* back of the knee; *horse:* hock; *cuis. beef:* shin; *veal:* knuckle; ⊕ *pipe:* elbow; 🔺 bulge; **jarretelle** [ʒarˈtɛl] *f* suspender; *Am. a.* garter; **jarretière** [~ˈtjɛːr] *f* garter.

jars *orn.* [ʒaːr] *m* gander.

jaser [ʒaˈze] (1a) *v/i.* chatter, talk; gossip; **jaseur, -euse** [~ˈzœːr, ~ˈzøːz] **1.** *adj.* talkative; **2.** *su.* chatterbox; gossip; tale-bearer.

jasmin ♀ [ʒasˈmɛ̃] *m* jasmine.

jaspe *min.* [ʒasp] *m* jasper; ~ *sanguin* bloodstone; **jaspé, e** [ʒasˈpe] marbled, veined.

jatte [ʒat] *f* bowl; *milk:* pan, basin; **jattée** [ʒaˈte] *f* bowlful; *milk:* panful.

jauge [ʒoːʒ] *f* ga(u)ge (*a.* ⊕); ga(u)ging-rod; *mot.* (~ *d'huile*) dipstick; (~ *d'essence*) petrol ga(u)ge, *Am.* gasoline ga(u)ge; ⚓ tonnage; **jauger** [ʒoˈʒe] (11) *v/t.* ga(u)ge (*a.* ⊕); measure; *fig.* size up.

jaunâtre [ʒoˈnɑːtr] yellowish; sallow (*face*); **jaune** [ʒoːn] **1.** *adj.* yellow; **2.** *adv.: rire* ~ give a sickly smile; **3.** *su./m* yellow; *egg.:* yolk; F blackleg, scab, *Am.* strike-braker; **jaunet, -ette** [ʒoˈnɛ, ~ˈnɛt] yellowish; **jaunir** [~ˈniːr] (2a) *vt/i.* yellow; **jaunisse** 🩺 [~ˈnis] *f* jaundice.

Javel [ʒaˈvɛl] *m: eau f de* ~ liquid bleach (and disinfectant).

javeler [ʒavˈle] (1c) *v/t.* 🌾 lay (*corn*) in swaths; *v/i.* turn yellow; **javelle** 🌾 [ʒaˈvɛl] *f corn:* swath; bundle.

javelot [ʒavˈlo] *m* javelin.

jazz [dʒaːz] *m* jazz. I

je [ʒə] *pron./pers.* I

jeannette F [ʒaˈnɛt] *f* sleeve-board.

je-m'en-fichisme F [ʒəmɑ̃fiˈʃism], **je-m'en-foutisme** F [~fuˈtism] *m/inv.* couldn't-care-less attitude.

je(-)ne(-)sais(-)quoi [ʒənseˈkwa] *m/inv.* indefinable something.

jerrycan *mot.* [dʒɛriˈkan] *m* petrolcan.

jet [ʒɛ] *m* throw, cast(ing); jet (*a. gas, nozzle, etc.*); *liquid:* gush, spurt; *light:* flash; ⚓, 🔩 jetsam; ♀ shoot, sprout; *metall.* casting; ✈ jet (aeroplane); ~ *de sable* sandblast; ⚔ *armes*

f/pl. de ~ projectile *or* missile weapons; *du premier* ~ at the first try; **jetable** [ʒəˈtabl] disposable, throwaway; **jetée** [ʒəˈte] *f* jetty; breakwater; **jeter** [~ˈte] (1c) *v/t.* throw, fling, hurl; throw away; ⚓ drop (*anchor*), jettison (*goods*); 🔺 lay (*the foundations*); 🎣 discharge; utter (*a cry, a threat*); give off (*sparks*); se ~ *river:* flow (into, *dans*); se ~ *sur* pounce on; se ~ *vers* rush towards; **jeton** [~ˈtɔ̃] *m* counter; token; *teleph.* ~ *de téléphone* telephone token.

jeu [ʒø] *m* game; play (*a.* ⊕); gambling; fun; *thea.* acting; *tools etc.:* set; *machine etc., a. fig.* working; ⊕ clearance; *fig.* action; *fig.* interaction; ♪ *organ:* stop; *cards:* pack, *Am.* deck; *thea.* ~*x pl. de scène* stage business *sg.*; ~ *de mots* pun, play on words; ~ *d'esprit* witticism; *cacher son* ~ hide one's cards; *être en* ~ be at stake; *entrer en* ~ come into play; *mettre en* ~ stake; *il a beau* ~ *de (or pour) (inf.)* it's easy for him to (*inf.*).

jeudi [ʒøˈdi] *m* Thursday; ~ *saint* Maundy Thursday.

jeun [ʒœ̃] *adv.: à* ~ on an empty stomach, fasting.

jeune [ʒœn] **1.** *adj.* young; youthful; younger, junior; *fig.* new; recent; unripe, early (*fruit*); ~ *fille* girl; ~ *homme* youth, lad; **2.** *su.* young person *or* animal; *su./m: les* ~*s pl.* the young *pl.*; youth (*coll.*) *sg.*

jeûne [ʒøːn] *m* fast(ing), abstinence; **jeûner** [ʒøˈne] (1a) *v/i.* fast (from, *de*).

jeunesse [ʒœˈnɛs] *f* youth; boyhood, girlhood; *fig.* youthfulness, freshness; F girl; ~ *scolaire* schoolchildren *pl.*; **jeunet, -ette** F [~ˈnɛ, ~ˈnɛt] very young.

jiu-jitsu [dʒydʒitˈsy] *m* ju-jutsu.

joaillerie [ʒɔajˈri] *f* jewellery; jeweller's business; **joaillier** *m*, **-ère** *f* [ʒɔaˈje, ~ˈjɛr] jeweller.

job F [ʒɔb] *m* job, employment.

jobard F [ʒɔˈbaːr] *m* dupe, F mug; **jobarder** [ʒɔbarˈde] (1a) *v/t.* fool, dupe; **jobarderie** [~ˈdri] *f* gullibility.

jociste [ʒɔˈsist] *su. member of the Jeunesse ouvrière chrétienne.*

jocrisse [ʒɔˈkris] *m* fool; clown; F mug.

joie [ʒwa] *f* joy; delight; pleasure; ~

journée

de vivre joy in life; *fille de* ~ prostitute.

joignis [ʒwaˈɲi] *1st p. sg. p.s. of joindre*; **joignons** [~ˈɲɔ̃] *1st p. pl. pres. of joindre*; **joindre** [ʒwɛ̃ːdr] (4m) *v/t.* join (*a.* ⊕); unite, combine; bring together; clasp (*one's hands*); ✝ attach (*to a letter*); adjoin (*a house etc.*); ✝ *etc.* **pièces** *f/pl. jointes* enclosures; *se* ~ *à* join (in); *v/i.* meet; **joins** [ʒwɛ̃] *1st p. sg. pres. of joindre*; **joint, e** [ʒwɛ̃, ʒwɛ̃ːt] **1.** *p.p. of joindre*; **2.** *su./m* ⚠, ⊕, ⚡, *anat., geol.* joint; join; *metall.* seam; ⊕ *piston:* packing; ⊕ ~ *à rotule* ball-and-socket joint; *mot.* ~ *de culasse* gasket; *sans* ~ seamless; F *trouver le* ~ find a way (to, *inf.*, *pour inf.*; *of ger.*, *de inf.*); **jointé, e** [ʒwɛ̃ˈte] jointed; pasterned (*horse*); **jointif, -ve** ⚠ [~ˈtif, ~ˈtiːv] placed edge to edge; joined; **jointoyer** ⚠ [~twaˈje] (1h) *v/t.* point; grout; **jointure** [~ˈtyːr] *f* ⊕, *anat.* joint; *fingers:* knuckle.

joli, e [ʒɔˈli] pretty; nice; **joliet, -ette** [~ˈljɛ, ~ˈljɛt] rather pretty; **joliment** [~liˈmɑ̃] *adv.* prettily; *fig.* well; F awfully; F pretty.

jonc 🌿 [ʒɔ̃] *m* rush; Malacca cane; *droit comme un* ~ straight as a die; **jonchaie** 🌿 [ʒɔ̃ˈʃɛ] *f* rush bed; caneplantation; **joncher** [~ˈʃe] (1a) *v/t.* strew (with, *de*); *fig.* litter; **jonchère** [~ˈʃɛːr] *f see jonchaie*.

jonction [ʒɔ̃kˈsjɔ̃] *f* junction (*a.*⊕, *a.* 🚂); ⚡ connector; joining, meeting; 🚃 joinder.

jongler [ʒɔ̃ˈgle] (1a) *v/i.* juggle (*a. fig.*); **jonglerie** [~gləˈri] *f* juggling; *fig.* trick(ery); **jongleur** [~ˈglœːr] *m* juggler; cheat, charlatan; ✝ jongleur.

jonque ⚓ [ʒɔ̃ːk] *f* junk.

jouable ♪, *thea., etc.* [ʒwabl] playable; **jouailler** F [ʒwaˈje] (1a) *v/i. cards:* play for love; ♪ *piano:* strum, *violin:* scrape.

joue [ʒu] *f* cheek; ~ *contre* ~ cheek by jowl; *mettre en* ~ take aim at.

jouer [ʒwe] (1p) *v/t.* play (*a.* ♪, *thea., a game, cards*); back (*a horse*); stake, bet (*money*); pretend to be; imitate (*s.o.*); look like (*wool*); F fool (*s.o.*); *se* ~ *de* take (*s.th.*) in one's stride; make light of; *v/i.* play; gamble (on the Stock Exchange), speculate; ⊕ work, run well (*ma-*

chine); ⊕ have too much play; ~ *à* play (*a play, cards, football, at soldiers, etc.*); ~ *de* ♪ play (*an instrument*); *fig.* use, make use of; *à qui de* ~? *cards:* whose turn is it?; *faire* ~ set in motion; release; **jouet** [ʒwɛ] *m* toy; plaything (*a. fig.*); **joueur, -euse** [ʒwœːr, ʒwøːz] **1.** *su.* player; gambler; ✝ speculator, operator; ✝ ~ *à la hausse* (*à la baisse*) bull (bear); **2.** *adj.* fond of playing *or* gambling.

joufflu, e [ʒuˈfly] chubby. [beam.\
joug [ʒu] *m* yoke (*a.* ⊕); *balance:*\
jouir [ʒwiːr] (2a) *v/i.* enjoy o.s.; ~ *de* enjoy (*s.th.*); **jouissance** [ʒwiˈsɑ̃ːs] *f* enjoyment; ✝ fruition, right to interest *etc.*

joujou, pl. -x F [ʒuˈʒu] *m* toy, plaything; *faire* ~ *avec* play with.

jour [ʒuːr] *m* day(light); daytime; light (*a. fig.*); dawn, daybreak; opening, gap; *sewing:* open-work; *fig.* aspect; ~ *de fête* holiday; ~ *de l'an* New Year's Day; ~ *ouvrable* working-day; *à* ~ *sewing:* openwork ...; ✝ posted, up to date; *au grand* ~ in broad daylight; *fig.* publicly; *au* ~ *le* ~ from day to day; *au point* (*or lever*) *du* ~ at daybreak; *de* ~ by day; *de nos* ~*s* nowadays; *donner le* ~ *à* give birth to; *du* ~ *au lendemain* overnight; *at a moment's* notice; ⚔ *être de* ~ be on duty for the day; *l'autre* ~ the other day; *fig. mettre au* ~ reveal, disclose; *par* ~ per *or a or* each day; *cuis. plat m du* ~ today's special dish; *petit* ~ morning twilight; *sous un nouveau* ~ in a new light; *tous les* (*deux*) ~*s* every (other) day; *un* ~ one day (*in the past*), some day (*in the future*); *un* ~ *ou l'autre* sooner or later; *vivre au* ~ *le* ~ live from hand to mouth; *see voir.*

journal [ʒurˈnal] *m* record, diary; journal (*a.* ✝); ✝ day-book; ⚓, ⊕ log-book; newspaper; ~ *financier* (*officiel*) financial (official) gazette; ~ *parlé radio:* news(-bulletin), *Am.* newscast; *le* ~ *du jour* today's paper; **journalier, -ère** [ʒurnaˈlje, ~ˈljɛːr] **1.** *adj.* daily; variable (*character*); **2.** *su./m* day-labo(u)rer, journeyman; **journalisme** [~ˈlism] *m* journalism; **journaliste** [~ˈlist] *su.* journalist; reporter; ✝ journalizer.

journée [ʒurˈne] *f* day; daytime; day's work *or* journey; *à la* ~ by the day; *femme f de* ~ charwoman, F daily; **journellement** [~nɛl'mã] *adv.* daily, every day.

joute [ʒut] *f* contest; † joust, tilt; **jouter** [ʒu'te] (1a) *v/i.* fight; † joust, tilt.

jovial, e, *m/pl.* -als, -aux [ʒɔ'vjal, ~'vjo] jolly, jovial; good-natured; **jovialité** [~vjali'te] *f* joviality, jollity.

joyau [ʒwa'jo] *m* jewel (*a. fig.*).

joyeux, -euse [ʒwa'jø, ~'jøːz] merry, joyful, cheerful.

jubé △, *eccl.* [ʒy'be] *m* rood-screen, rood-loft.

jubilaire [ʒybi'lɛːr] jubilee-...; **jubilation** F [~la'sjɔ̃] *f* jubilation; **jubilé** [~'le] *m* jubilee; fiftieth anniversary; golden wedding; **jubiler** [~'le] (1a) *v/i.* be delighted, rejoice; F gloat.

jucher [ʒy'ʃe] (1a) *vt/i.* perch (*bird, a. fig. person*); roost; **juchoir** [~-'ʃwaːr] *m* perch, hen-roost.

judaïque [ʒyda'ik] Judaic (*law*); Jewish (*history*); **judaïser** [~i'ze] (1a) *v/i.* Judaize; **judaïsme** [~'ism] *m* Judaism.

Judas [ʒy'dɑ] *m* Judas (*a. fig.*); F traitor; ♀ spy-hole, Judas(-hole) (*in a door*).

judicature [ʒydika'tyːr] *f* judicature; judgeship; **judiciaire** [~'sjɛːr] judicial, legal; *poursuites f/pl.* ~s legal proceedings; **judicieux, -euse** [~'sjø, ~'sjøːz] judicious, sensible; discerning; *peu* ~ injudicious; ill-advised.

judo *sp.* [ʒy'do] *m* judo.

juge [ʒy:ʒ] *m* judge (*a. fig.*); *sp.* umpire; ~ *d'instruction* examining magistrate; **jugement** [ʒyʒ'mã] *m* judgment; ⚖ *case*: trial; sentence (*on criminal*), *civil case*: award; *fig.* opinion; *fig.* discrimination, good sense; *eccl.* ~ *dernier* Last Judgment, doomsday (*a. fig.*); ⚖ ~ *par défaut* judgment by default; ⚖ *passer en* ~ stand trial; **jugeote** F [ʒy'ʒɔt] *f* common sense; **juger** [~'ʒe] (1l) *v/t.* judge; ⚖ *a.* pass sentence on; ⚖ *try* (*for, pour*); *fig.* think; ~ *à propos de* think it proper to; *mal* ~ misjudge (*s.o.*).

jugulaire [ʒygy'lɛːr] **1.** *adj.* jugular; **2.** *su./f* *anat.* jugular (vein); *helmet etc.*: chin strap; **juguler** [~'le] (1a) *v/t.* † strangle; *fig.* nip (*s.th.*) in the

bud; *fig.* check, stop; *fig.* stifle, put down; ✴ jugulate.

juif, juive [ʒɥif, ʒɥiːv] **1.** *adj.* Jewish; **2.** *su./m eccl.* (*practising*) Jew; ♀ Jew; *petit* ~ funny bone; *su./f* ♀ Jewess.

juillet [ʒɥi'jɛ] *m* July.

juin [ʒɥɛ̃] *m* June.

juiverie [ʒɥi'vri] *f* Jewry; *coll. the* Jews *pl.*

Jules [ʒyl] *m sl.* man, guy; F boyfriend.

julienne [ʒy'ljɛn] *f cuis.* vegetable soup; ♥ rocket.

jumeau, -elle, *m/pl.* -aux [ʒy'mo, ~'mɛl, ~'mo] **1.** *adj.* twin; **2.** *su.* twin; *su./f:* ~*elles pl. opt.* binoculars; opera-glasses; ⊕ cheeks; *lathe-bed*: slide-bars; **jumelage** [ʒym'laːʒ] *m* twinning (*of towns*); **jumelé, e** [~'le] twin; coupled.

jument [ʒy'mã] *f* mare.

jumping *sp.* [dʒœm'piŋ] *m* jumping.

jungle [ʒɔ̃:gl] *f* jungle.

jupe [ʒyp] *f* skirt; **jupe-culotte,** *pl.* **jupes-culottes** [~ky'lɔt] *f* culotte, divided skirt; **jupon** [ʒy'pɔ̃] *m* petticoat; slip, *Am.* half-slip; *Sc.* kilt; *fig.* women *pl.*; *courir le* ~ be a skirt-chaser, run after women.

juré, e [ʒy're] **1.** *adj.* sworn; **2.** *su./m* juror, juryman; ~*s pl.* jury; **jurement** [ʒyr'mã] *m* swearing, oath; **jurer** [ʒy're] (1a) *v/t.* swear; vow; *v/i.* curse; *fig.* clash (*colours*); **jureur** [~'rœːr] *m* swearer.

juridiction [ʒyridik'sjɔ̃] *f* ⚖ jurisdiction; venue; *fig.* province; **juridique** ⚖ [~'dik] judicial; legal.

jurisconsulte ⚖ [ʒyriskɔ̃'sylt] *m* jurist; legal expert; **jurisprudence** ⚖ [~pry'dãːs] *f* jurisprudence; statute law; case-law; (*legal*) precedents *pl.*

juriste ⚖ [ʒy'rist] *m* jurist; legal writer.

juron [ʒy'rɔ̃] *m* oath, swear-word.

jury [ʒy'ri] *m* ⚖ jury; *univ. etc.* board of examiners; selection committee.

jus [ʒy] *m* juice; *cuis.* gravy; *sl.* coffee; ⚡ *sl.* juice (= *current*); *sl.* petrol, *Am.* gas; *sl.* elegance; *cuis.* *arroser de* ~ baste (*meat*); *mot. sl.* *donner du* ~ step on the gas.

jusant ⚓ [ʒy'zã] *m* ebb(-tide).

jusqu'au-boutisme *pol. etc.* [ʒysko-bu'tism] *m* extremism; **jusqu'au-boutiste** *pol. etc.* [~'tist] *su.* whole-hogger; die-hard; **jusque** [ʒysk(ə)] *prp.* (*usu. jusqu'à*) until, till; as far as (to), up *or* down to; *jusqu'à ce que* (*sbj.*) until; *jusqu'au bout* to the (bitter) end; *jusqu'ici* thus *or* so far. **juste** [ʒyst] **1.** *adj.* just, legitimate, fair; proper, fit; accurate; exact (*word*); tight (*fit*); right (*time, watch, word*); ∼-*milieu m* happy *or* golden mean; *au* ∼ exactly; **2.** *adv.* rightly; just; precisely; ♪ true; scarcely; *à 10 heures* ∼ at ten (o'clock) sharp; **justement** [ʒystə'mã] rightly; just, precisely; **justesse** [∼'tɛs] *f* exactness; accuracy; *de* ∼ just, barely, by a hair's breadth; **justice** [∼'tis] *f* justice; equity; legal proceedings *pl.*; *aller en* ∼ go to law; *poursuivre en* ∼ take legal action against; *se faire* ∼ revenge o.s.; commit suicide; **justiciable** [∼ti-'sjabl] *adj.*: ∼ *de* amenable to (*a. fig.*); open to (*criticism*); **justicier,** -**ère** [∼ti'sje, ∼'sjɛːr] *adj., a. su.* justiciary.

justificatif, -**ve** [ʒystifika'tif, ∼'tiːv] **1.** *adj.* justificatory; *pièce f* ∼*ve* = **2.** *su./m* supporting document; ✝ voucher; **justification** [∼fika'sjɔ̃] *f* justification; **justifier** [∼'fje] (1o) *v/t.* justify, vindicate; *se* ∼ clear o.s.; *v/i.*: ∼ *de* give proof of.

jute *tex.* [ʒyt] *m* jute.

juteux, -**euse** [ʒy'tø, ∼'tøːz] **1.** *adj.* juicy; F *fig.* lucrative; **2.** *su./m* ✗ *sl.* company sergeant-major.

juvénile [ʒyve'nil] juvenile; youthful; **juvénilité** [∼nili'te] *f* youthfulness.

juxtaposer [ʒykstapo'ze] (1a) *v/t.* juxtapose, place side by side.

K

K, k [ka] *m* K, k.
kakatoès *orn.* [kakatɔˈɛs] *m* cockatoo.
kaki *tex.* [kaˈki] *su./m, a. adj./inv.* khaki.
kangourou *zo.* [kãguˈru] *m* kangaroo.
kaolin [kaɔˈlɛ̃] *m* china clay, kaolin.
karaté [karaˈte] *m* karate.
képi [keˈpi] *m* peaked cap, kepi.
kermesse [∼] *f* village fair; church bazaar.
kérosène [kerɔˈzɛn] *m* paraffin(-oil), *Am.* kerosene.
khâgne [kaɲ] *f see* cagne.
kibboutz [kiˈbuts] *m* kibbutz.
kidnapper [kidnaˈpe] (1a) *v/t.* kidnap; **kidnappeur** *m*, **-euse** *f* [∼ˈpœːr, ∼ˈpøːz] kidnapper.
kif kif *sl.* [kifˈkif] *adj./inv.* same; the same thing, much of a muchness.
kiki *sl.* [kiˈki] *m* throat, neck.
kilo... [kilɔ] kilo...; **∼cycle** ⚡ [∼ˈsikl] *m* kilocycle; **∼(gramme)** [∼(ˈgram)] *m measure:* kilogram(me); **∼métrage** [∼meˈtraːʒ] *m* measuring *or* length in kilometres, mileage; **∼mètre** [∼ˈmɛtr] *m measure:* kilometre, *Am.* kilometer; **∼métrer** [∼meˈtre] (1f)

v/t. measure in kilometres; mark (*a road*) with kilometre stones; **∼watt** ⚡ [∼ˈwat] *m* kilowatt; **∼-heure** kilowatt-hour.
kimono *cost.* [kimɔˈno] *m* kimono; *manche f* ∼ Magyar sleeve.
kinésithérapeute [kineziteraˈpøːt] *su.* physiotherapist; **kinésithérapie** [∼ˈpi] *f* physiotherapy.
kiosque [kjɔsk] *m* kiosk; *band:* stand; *flower, newspaper:* stall; ⚓ house; ⚓ *submarine:* conning tower.
kirsch [kirʃ] *m* kirsch(wasser).
kitchenette [kitʃəˈnɛt] *f* kitchenette.
klaxon *mot. etc.* [klakˈsɔ̃] *m* horn, hooter, klaxon; **klaxonner** [∼sɔˈne] (1a) *v/i.* hoot, sound the horn; *v/t.* hoot at.
kleptomane [klɛptɔˈman] *adj., a. su.* kleptomaniac; **kleptomanie** [∼maˈni] *f* kleptomania.
knock-out *box.* [nɔˈkaut] **1.** *su./m/inv.* knock-out; **2.** *adj./inv.:* mettre q. ∼ knock s.o. out.
krach ✝ [krak] *m* crash.
kyrielle ⊢ [kiˈrjɛl] *f* rigmarole; long list (of, *de*).
kyste ⚕ [kist] *m* cyst.

L

L, 1 [ɛl] *m* L, l.

la¹ [la] *see* le.

la² ♪ [~] *m/inv.* la, *note:* A; donner le ~ give the pitch.

là [la] *adv. place:* there; *time:* then; ~ où where; ce livre-~ that book; c'est ~ que that is where; de ~ hence; ~-**bas** [~'ba] *adv.* over there.

labeur [la'bœ:r] *m* labo(u)r, toil; *typ.* bookwork.

labial, e, *m/pl.* **-aux** [la'bjal, ~'bjo] *adj., a. su./f* labial (*a. gramm.*).

labile [la'bil] ♀, ♈ labile; *fig.* unstable; *fig.* untrustworthy (*memory*).

laborantine [laborɑ̃'tin] *f* female laboratory assistant; **laboratoire** [~ra'twa:r] *m* ♈ laboratory; *metall. furnace:* hearth; ~ de langues language laboratory; ~ spatial space lab; **laborieux, -euse** [~'rjø, ~'rjø:z] laborious, hardworking; working (*classes*).

labour [la'bu:r] *m* ploughing, tillage; ~s *pl.* ploughed land *sg.*; cheval *m* de ~ plough-horse; **labourable** [labu-'rabl] arable; plough-...; **labourage** [~'ra:ʒ] *m* ploughing, tilling; **labourer** [~'re] (1a) *v/t.* plough, till; *fig.* furrow, gash, slash (into), dig into; *fig.* lacerate; **laboureur** [~'rœ:r] *m* ploughman; farm-hand.

labyrinthe [labi'rɛ̃:t] *m* labyrinth (*a. anat.*); maze.

lac [lak] *m* lake; F dans le ~ in a fix, in the soup.

laçage [la'sa:ʒ] *m* lacing (up); **lacer** [~'se] (1k) *v/t.* lace (up); ♣ belay (*a rope*).

lacérer [lase're] (1f) lacerate; tear; slash.

lacet [la'sɛ] *m* (*shoe- etc.*) lace; *hunt.* noose, snare (*a. fig.*); *road:* hairpin bend; en ~s winding (*road*).

lâchage [lɑ'ʃa:ʒ] *m* release; F friends: dropping; **lâche** [lɑ:ʃ] **1.** *adj.* loose, slack; lax (*discipline, style*); cowardly; **2.** *su./m* coward; **lâcher** [lɑ'ʃe] (1a) *v/t.* release (*a. mot.*), loosen, slacken; let go of; *fig.* give up, *a. friend:* drop; let out (*a curse, an*

oath, *a secret*); ⊕ blow off (*steam*); *fig.* ~ pied give way; *v/i.* become loose; give way; snap (*rope etc.*); *sp.* F give up; **lâcheté** [lɑʃ'te] *f* cowardice; **lâcheur** *m*, **-euse** *f* F [lɑ'ʃœ:r, ~'ʃø:z] fickle person; quitter.

lacis ⚔, *anat., etc.* [la'si] *m* network.

laconique [lakɔ'nik] laconic.

lacrymal, e, *m/pl.* **-aux** [lakri'mal, ~'mo] tear-...; **lacrymogène** [~mɔ-'ʒɛn] tear-exciting; gaz *m* ~ tear-gas.

lacs [lɑ] *m* noose, snare; *fig.* trap.

lacté, e [lak'te] milky; milk-(*diet, fever*); *anat.* lacteal; voie *f* ~e Milky Way, Galaxy; **lactose** ♈ [~'to:z] *f* lactose, milk-sugar.

lacune [la'kyn] *f* gap, blank.

lacustre [la'kystr] lacustrine (*a. zo.*); cité *f* ~ lake-dwelling.

lad *sp.* [lad] *m* stable-boy.

là-dessous [lat'su] *adv.* underneath, under there; **là-dessus** [~'sy] *adv.* thereupon (*place, a. time*); on that.

ladite [la'dit] *see* ledit.

ladre [lɑ:dr] **1.** *adj.* stingy, mean; **2.** *su./m* skinflint, miser; **ladrerie** [lɑdrə'ri] *f* stinginess, meanness.

lai, e [lɛ] **1.** *adj. eccl.* lay-...; **2.** *su./m eccl.* layman; lay; **laïc, -ique** [la'ik] *adj., a. su. see* laïque; **laïcisation** [laisiza'sjɔ̃] *f* secularisation; **laïciser** [~'ze] (1a) *v/t.* secularize; **laïcité** [~'te] *f* secularity, undenominationalism.

laid, e [lɛ, lɛ:d] ugly; plain (*face*); *Am.* homely; mean (*deed*); **laideron** F [lɛ'drɔ̃] *mf* plain woman *or* girl; **laideur** [~'dœ:r] *f* ugliness; *face:* plainness, *Am.* homeliness.

laie¹ [lɛ] *f* wild sow.

laie² [~] *f* ride; forest-path.

lainage [lɛ'na:ʒ] *m* fleece; woollen article; *tex.* teaseling; ♈ ~s *pl.* woollens, woollen goods; **laine** [lɛn] *f* wool; *carpet:* pile; ~ artificielle àrtificial wool; ~ peignée worsted; **lainer** *tex.* [lɛ'ne] (1b) *v/t.* teasle, nap; **laineux, -euse** [~'nø, ~'nø:z] fleecy; woolly (*hair, sheep, a.* ♀); **lainier, -ère** [~'nje, ~'njɛ:r]

1. *adj.* wool(len); **2.** *su.* manufacturer of woollens.

laïque [la'ik] **1.** *adj.* secular; undenominational (*school*); **2.** *su./m* layman; ~s *pl.* laity; *su./f* laywoman.

laisse [lɛs] *f* leash, lead; *fig.* tenir q. en ~ keep s.o. in leading-strings.

laissé(e)-pour-compte, *pl.* laissé(e)s-pour-compte **1.** *adj.* ✝ returned; unsold; *a. fig.* rejected; **2.** *su.* ✝ returned *or* unsold article; *a. fig.* reject.

laisser [lɛ'se] (1b) *v/t.* leave; let, allow, permit; abandon, quit; ~ là q. leave s.o. in the lurch; ~ là qch. give s.th. up; *v/i.*: ~ à désirer leave much to be desired; ~ à penser give food for thought; **~-aller** [lɛsea'le] *m/inv.* unconstraint; carelessness; **~-faire** *pol. etc.* [~'fɛːr] *m* inaction, non-interference; **laissez-passer** [~pa'se] *m/inv.* pass, permit.

lait [lɛ] *m* milk; ~ de chaux whitewash; ~ en poudre powdered milk; cochon *m* de ~ sucking-pig; **laitage** [lɛ'taːʒ] *m* dairy products *pl.*; **laitance** [~'tãːs] *f*, **laite** [lɛt] *f* milt; soft roe; **laité, e** [lɛ'te] soft-roed; **laiterie** [~'tri] *f* dairy; dairy-farming; **laiteux, -euse** [~'tø, ~'tøːz] milky; 🜨 lacteal, milk-...; **laitier, -ère** [~'tje, ~'tjɛːr] **1.** *adj.* milk-...; dairy-...; **2.** *su./m* milk-man; ⊕ slag; *su./f* milk-woman; milkmaid; dairymaid; milk-cart.

laiton [lɛ'tɔ̃] *m* (yellow) brass.

laitue 🜨 [lɛ'ty] *f* lettuce; ~ pommée cabbage-lettuce.

laïus F [la'jys] *m* speech.

lama[1] [la'ma] *m* Buddhism: lama.

lama[2] *zo.* [~] *m* llama.

lambeau [lã'bo] *m* shred, bit, scrap; rag.

lambin, e F [lã'bɛ̃, ~'bin] **1.** *adj.* dawdling, slow; **2.** *su.* dawdler; **lambiner** F [~bi'ne] (1a) *v/i.* dawdle.

lambrequin [lãbrə'kɛ̃] *m* valance, pelmet.

lambris △ [lã'bri] *m* wood: wainscoting, panelling; marble, stone: wall-lining; **lambrissage** △ [lãbri'saːʒ] *m* wainscoting, panelling; *room*: lining; **lambrisser** △ [~'se] (1a) *v/t.* wainscot, panel; line (*a room*); plaster (*attic walls*).

lame [lam] *f metal*: thin plate, strip; *sword, razor,* 🜨 *leaf, etc.*: blade; ⚡ *accumulator etc.*: plate; ⚓ wave;

feather: vane; blind: slat; (metallic) foil; **lamelle** [la'mɛl] *f* lamella; scale, flake; metal: thin sheet; blind: slat; ~s *pl.* à parquet steel shavings; **lamelleux, -euse** [~mɛ'lø, ~'løːz] fissile, F flaky; lamellate(d) (*fungus etc.*).

lamentable [lamã'tabl] deplorable, lamentable; grievous (*error*); pitiful; full of woe (*voice*); **lamentation** [~ta'sjɔ̃] *f* lamentation; **lamenter** [~'te] (1a) *v/t.*: se ~ lament, deplore (s.th., de qch.).

lamette [la'mɛt] *f metal*: small plate; small blade.

laminer [lami'ne] (1a) *v/t.* ⊕ laminate, roll (*metal*); calender (*paper*); throttle (*steam*); *fig.* reduce, cut down, curtail; **laminoir** ⊕ [~'nwaːr] *m* rolling mill; *fig.* passer au ~ put (*s.o.*) *or* go through the mill.

lampadaire [lãpa'dɛːr] *m street*: street lamp *or* light; room: standard lamp, *Am.* floor lamp; lamp post.

lampe [lãːp] *f* lamp; radio: valve; telev. tube; ~ à arc arc-light; ~ amplificatrice radio: amplifying valve; ⊕ ~ à souder blowlamp, blowtorch; ~ de chevet bedside lamp; ⚒ ~ de mineur safety-lamp; ~ de poche flashlamp, electric torch; ~ témoin pilot-lamp; ~ triode three-electrode lamp.

lampée [lã'pe] *f water etc.*: draught, *Am.* draft; d'une seule ~ at one gulp; **lamper** [~] (1a) *v/t.* gulp down, F swig (*a drink*).

lampion [lã'pjɔ̃] *m decorations*: fairy-light; Chinese lantern; **lampiste** [~'pist] *m* lamp-maker; lamplighter; F underling.

lamproie *icht.* [lã'prwa] *f* lamprey.

lampyre *zo.* [lã'piːr] *m* fire-fly, glow-worm.

lance [lãːs] *f* spear; lance; waterhose: nozzle; railing: spike; ~ d'incendie fire hose; ⊕ ~ hydraulique monitor; *fig.* rompre une ~ (*or* des ~s) avec cross swords with (*s.o.*); **lancée** [lã'se] *f* momentum; continuer sur sa ~ keep up the momentum (*a. fig.*); keep up, be (still) going strong.

lance...: **~-eau** [lã'so] *m/inv.* water cannon; **~-flammes** ⚔ [lãs'flaːm] *m/inv.* flame-thrower; **~-grenades** ⚔ [~grə'nad] *m/inv.* grenadethrower; **lancement** [~'mã] *m* throwing; *Am.* baseball: pitch; ⚓ launching (*a. rocket, a. fig.*); bomb:

releasing; *propeller*: swinging; ✈ floating; **lancer** [lã'se] **1.** (1k) *v/t.* throw, fling, hurl; *Am. baseball*: pitch (*a ball*); launch (⚓, ✈ *an article, a rocket, fig. an attack, a. fig. a person*); ⚓ fire (*a torpedo*); utter (*an oath*); emit (*smoke, steam*); set (*a dog on s.o.*); ⚡ switch on; *mot.* start; 🎯 swing (*the propeller*); ✈ float (*a company*); *fig.* crack (*a joke*); se ~ rush, dash, dart; *fig.* se ~ *dans* go or launch (out) into; **2.** *su./m sp.* throw; **lance-torpilles** ⚓ [lãstɔr'piːj] *m/inv.* torpedo tube.

lancette ♰, ⚕ [lã'sɛt] *f* lancet.

lanceur *m*, **-euse** *f* [lã'sœːr, ~'søːz] thrower; *cricket*: bowler; *Am. sp. baseball*: pitcher; ✈ promoter, floater; *fig.* initiator; **lancier** ⚔ [~'sje] *m* lancer.

lancinant, e [lãsi'nã, ~'nãːt] shooting, throbbing (*pain*).

landau, *pl.* **-s** [lã'do] *m* pram, *Am.* baby carriage; landau.

lande [lãːd] *f* heath, moor.

langage [lã'gaːʒ] *m* language; speech; ~ *chiffré* coded text.

lange [lãːʒ] *m* baby's napkin; ~s *pl.* swaddling-clothes (*a. fig.*).

langoureux, -euse [lãgu'rø, ~'røːz] languid, languishing.

langouste *zo.* [lã'gust] *f* lobster; F crayfish.

langue [lãːg] *f* tongue; language; ~ *d'arrivée* target language; ~ *de départ* source language; ~ *maternelle* native language, mother tongue; ~ *verte* slang; *avoir la ~ bien pendue* have a glib tongue; *de ~ anglaise* English-speaking (*country*); *donner sa ~ aux chats* give up (*a riddle etc.*); *ne pas avoir sa ~ dans sa poche* have a quick *or* ready tongue; **languette** [lã'gɛt] *f metal, wood*: small tongue; strip; *shoe,* ⊕ *joint, a.* ♪: tongue; ⊕ feather; *balance*: pointer.

langueur [lã'gœːr] *f* languor; listlessness.

languir [lã'giːr] (2a) *v/i.* languish, pine; *thea.* drag; *fig.,* ✈ be dull; **languissant, e** [~gi'sã, ~'sãːt] languid, listless; languishing (*look etc.*); ✈ dull.

lanière [la'njɛːr] *f* thong, lash.

lansquenet [lãskə'nɛ] *m* lansquenet (*a. card game*).

lanterne [lã'tɛrn] *f* lantern; *opt.* ~ *à projections* slide projector; ~ *rouge*

rear light; *fig.* tail-ender; ~ *vénitienne* Chinese lantern; **lanterneau** [lãtɛr'no] *m* ⚠ staircase: skylight; 🚢 *Am.* monitor roof; **lanterner** F [~'ne] (1a) *v/i.* dawdle; *v/t.* put (*s.o.*) off; pester (*s.o.*); **lanternier** [~'nje] *m* lantern-maker; lamp-lighter.

lanugineux, -euse ♀ [lany3i'nø, ~'nøːz] downy.

lapalissade [lapali'sad] *f* truism, glimpse of the obvious.

laper [la'pe] (1a) *v/t.* lap.

lapereau [la'pro] *m* young rabbit.

lapidaire [lapi'dɛːr] *adj., a. su./m* lapidary; **lapidation** [~da'sjɔ̃] *f* stoning; **lapider** [~'de] (1a) *v/t.* stone to death; F throw stones at; *fig.* hurl (*abuse etc.*); **lapidifier** [~di'fje] (1o) *v/t.* petrify.

lapin, e [la'pɛ̃, ~'pin] *su./m* rabbit; F chap; ~ *de choux* (*or domestique*) tame rabbit; ~ *de garenne* wild rabbit; ~ *mâle* buck rabbit; ✈ *peau f de* ~ cony; F *poser un* ~ *à q.* fail to turn up; *su./f* doe; **lapinière** [~pi'njɛːr] *f* rabbit-hutch; rabbit-warren.

lapis(-lazuli) [la'pis, ~pislazy'li] *m min.* lapis lazuli; *colour*: bright blue.

lapon, -onne [la'põ, ~'pɔn] **1.** *adj.* Lapp(ish); **2.** *su./m ling.* Lapp(ish); *su.* ♀ Laplander, Lapp.

laps [laps] *m*: ~ *de temps* lapse *or* space of time; **lapsus** [la'psys] *m pen, tongue*: slip; *memory*: lapse.

laque [lak] *su./f* lac; *paint.* lake; hair spray; *su./m* lacquer; **laquer** [la'ke] (1m) *v/t.* lacquer, japan.

laquelle [la'kɛl] *see lequel.*

larbin F [lar'bɛ̃] *m* flunkey.

larcin ♰ [lar'sɛ̃] *m* larceny; pilfering.

lard [laːr] *m* bacon; back-fat; F *faire du* ~ grow stout; **larder** [lar'de] (1a) *v/t. cuis.* (inter)lard (*a. fig.*); *fig.* assail (with, *de*); **lardoire** [~'dwaːr] *f cuis.* larding-pin; ⚔ *pile*: shoe; **lardon** [~'dõ] *m cuis.* piece of larding bacon; *fig.* cutting remark, jibe; F kid, baby; **lardonner** [~dɔ'ne] (1a) *v/t. cuis.* cut (*bacon*) into strips; *fig.* taunt.

large [larʒ] **1.** *adj.* broad; wide; big; ample; loose-fitting (*suit etc.*); **2.** *adv.* broadly; **3.** *su./m* breadth, width; room, space; ⚓ open sea; offing; *au* ~! keep away!; **largesse** [lar'ʒɛs] *f* liberality; bounty, largesse; **largeur** [⁓'ʒœ:r] f breadth, width; ⚓ arch: span; ⁓ d'esprit broadness of mind.

largue ⚓ [larg] slack (rope); free, large (wind); **larguer** [lar'ge] (1m) v/t. ⚓ let go or cast off (a rope); unfurl (a sail); ✈ release (bombs); drop (a. fig.); F fig. chuck up (one's job etc.), chuck (out) (principles etc.).

larme [larm] f tear; teardrop; fig. drop; fig. ⁓s pl. de crocodile crocodile tears; **larmier** [lar'mje] m ⚙ dripstone; anat. eye: corner; **larmoyant, e** [larmwa'jã, ⁓'jã:t] weeping; tearful, pej. maudlin; **larmoyer** [⁓'je] (1h) v/i. fig. pej. weep.

larron [la'rõ] m † thief; s'entendre comme ⁓s en foire be as thick as thieves.

larve biol. [larv] f larva, grub.

laryngite [larɛ̃'ʒit] f laryngitis; **laryngoscope** ⚕ [⁓gɔs'kɔp] m laryngoscope; **laryngotomie** ⚕ [⁓gɔtɔ'mi] f laryngotomy; **larynx** anat. [la'rɛ̃:ks] m larynx.

las, lasse [lɑ, lɑ:s] tired, weary.

lascar [las'ka:r] m lascar; F (smart) fellow.

lascif, -ve [la'sif, ⁓'si:v] lascivious, lewd; **lasciveté** [⁓siv'te] f lasciviousness, lewdness.

lasser [lɑ'se] (1a) v/t. tire; fig. exhaust; se ⁓ grow weary (of, de); **lassitude** [⁓si'tyd] f weariness, lassitude.

latent, e [la'tã, ⁓'tã:t] ⚕, phys., phot., etc. latent; fig. concealed.

latéral, e, m/pl. -aux [late'ral, ⁓'ro] lateral; side-...

latin, e [la'tɛ̃, ⁓'tin] 1. adj. Latin; ⚓ lateen (sail); les nations f/pl. ⁓es the Latin peoples; 2. su./m ling. Latin.

latitude [lati'tyd] f geog., fig. latitude; fig. freedom; geog. par 10° de ⁓ Sud in latitude 10° South.

latrines [la'trin] f/pl. latrines.

latte [lat] f lath; floor: board; **latter** [la'te] (1a) v/t. lath; ⊕ lag; **lattis** [⁓'ti] m lathwork.

laudanum [loda'nɔm] m laudanum.

laudatif, -ve [loda'tif, ⁓'ti:v] laudatory.

lauréat, e [lɔre'a, ⁓'at] 1. adj. laureate; 2. su. laureate, prize-winner.

laurier ♀, a. fig. [lɔ'rje] m laurel; ⁓-rose pl. ⁓s-roses ♀ [⁓rje'ro:z] m common oleander.

lavable [la'vabl] washable; ⁓ en ma-

chine machine-washable; **lavabo** [⁓va'bo] m wash-stand; lavatory; ✗ baths pl.; **lavage** [⁓'va:ʒ] m washing; pol. ⁓ de cerveau brain-washing; terre f de ⁓ alluvium; faire (subir) un ⁓ de cerveau à q. brainwash s.o.

lavande ♀ [la'vã:d] f lavender.

lavandière [lavã'dje:r] f washerwoman; laundress; **lavasse** F [⁓'vas] f watery soup; slops pl., dishwater, hog-wash.

lave geol. [la:v] f lava.

lave-glace, pl. lave-glaces [lav'glas] m windscreen (Am. windshield) washer; **lave-mains** [⁓'mɛ̃] m/inv. hand-basin; **lavement** [⁓'mã] m eccl. washing; ⚕ enema; **laver** [la've] (1a) v/t. wash; scrub (a. 🐾 ⊕); bathe (a wound); fig. clear; F ⁓ la tête à tell (s.o.) off, Am. call (s.o.) down; **laverie** [lav'ri] f launderette; **lavette** [⁓'vɛt] f dish-mop; dishcloth; **laveur, -euse** [⁓'vœ:r, ⁓'vø:z] su. person: washer, ⊕, 🐾 gas: scrubber; su./m ⊕ scrubber; su./f washing-machine; **lave-vaisselle** [lavvɛ'sɛl] m/inv. dish washer; **lavis** paint. [la'vi] m washing; wash-tint; wash-drawing; **lavoir** [⁓'vwa:r] m wash-house, ✗ washing-plant; ⁓ de cuisine scullery; **lavure** [⁓'vy:r] f (a. ⁓ de vaisselle) dishwater.

laxatif, -ve ⚕ [laksa'tif, ⁓'ti:v] adj., a. su./m laxative, aperient; **laxisme** [la'ksism] m laxity, laxness; **laxité** [laksi'te] f laxity.

layette [lɛ'jɛt] f packing-case; (baby's) layette, baby-linen.

lazaret ⚓ [laza'rɛ] m lazaret(to) (a. = quarantine station).

lazulite min. [lazy'lit] f see lapis (-lazuli).

le m, la f, les pl. [lə, la, le] 1. art./def. the; 2. pron./pers. him, her, it; pl. them.

lé [le] m tex. width, breadth; ⚓ tow-path.

leader pol., journ., sp. [li'dœ:r] m leader.

lèche [lɛʃ] f F bread etc.: thin slice; sl. faire de la ⁓ à suck up to; ⁓-cul V [⁓'ky] m/inv. arse-crawler; ⁓frite [⁓'frit] f dripping-pan.

lécher [le'ʃe] (1f) v/t. lick; fig. overpolish, elaborate (one's style); **lécheur m, -euse f** [⁓'ʃœ:r, ⁓'ʃø:z] † gourmand; pej. toady; **lèche-vitrines** F [lɛʃvi'trin] m/inv. window-

shopping; *faire du* ~ go window-shopping, window-shop.
leçon [lə'sɔ̃] *f* reading; *school, a. fig.*: lesson; *univ.* lecture; ~ *particulière* private lesson.
lecteur *m*, **-trice** [lɛk'tœːr, ~'tris] reader; *univ.* foreign assistant; *typ.* proof-reader; **lecture** [~'tyːr] *f* reading (*a. parl., a.* ⊕); reading matter; *avoir de la* ~ be well read; *faire la* ~ *à q.* read to s.o.
ledit *m*, **ladite** *f*, **lesdits** *m/pl.*, **lesdites** *f/pl.* [lə'di, la'dit, le'di, le'dit] *adj.* the aforesaid, the above-mentioned, the said ...
légal, e *m/pl.* **-aux** [le'gal, ~'go] legal; forensic (*medicine*); *monnaie f* ~*e* legal tender; **légaliser** [legali'ze] (1a) *v/t.* legalize; attest, certify (*a declaration, a signature*); **légalité** [~'te] *f* legality, lawfulness.
légat *hist., a. eccl.* [le'ga] *m* legate; **légataire** 🏛 [lega'tɛːr] *su.* legatee; heir; ~ *universel* residuary legatee; **légation** *eccl., pol.* [~'sjɔ̃] *f* legation.
légendaire [leʒɑ̃'dɛːr] **1.** *adj.* legendary; F epic (*struggle, fight*); **2.** *su./m* legendary; **légende** [~'ʒɑ̃:d] *f* legend (*a. coins, illustrations, etc.*); *typ.* caption; *diagram, map, etc.*: key.
léger, -ère [le'ʒe, ~'ʒɛːr] light (*a. wine*); slight (*error, pain*); weak (*tea, coffee*); mild (*beer, tobacco*); *fig.* flighty (*conduct, woman*); *fig.* frivolous; free (*talk*); *à la légère* lightly; unthinkingly, too hastily; *prendre à la légère* a. make light of; **légèreté** [leʒɛr'te] *f* lightness *etc., see léger.*
légion [le'ʒjɔ̃] *f* ✗ *etc.* legion; *fig.* host; ~ *d'Honneur* Legion of Hono(u)r; ✗ ~ *étrangère* Foreign Legion; **légionnaire** [~ʒjɔ'nɛːr] *m hist.* legionary; ✗ soldier of the Foreign Legion; member of the Legion of Hono(u)r.
législateur *m*, **-trice** *f* [leʒisla'tœːr, ~'tris] legislator; **législatif, -ve** [~'tif, ~'tiːv] legislative; **législation** [~'sjɔ̃] *f* legislation; law; **législature** [~'tyːr] *f* legislature; period of office of a legislative body; **légiste** [le'ʒist] **1.** *su./m* legist, jurist; **2.** *adj.*: *médecin m* ~ medical expert.
légitimation [leʒitima'sjɔ̃] *f child*: legitimation; official recognition;

légitime [~'tim] **1.** *adj.* legitimate, lawful; *fig.* justifiable; sound (*inference*); ~ *défense f* self-defence; **2.** *su./f* 🏛 child's portion; *sl.* wife; **légitimer** [~ti'me] (1a) *v/t.* legitimate; *fig.* justify; *admin. etc.* recognize; **légitimité** [~timi'te] *f* legitimacy; lawfulness.
legs [lɛ] *m* legacy; bequest; **léguer** [le'ge] (1s) *v/t.* bequeath (*a. fig.*), leave.
légume [le'gym] *m* vegetable; ♀ pod; **légumier, -ère** [legy'mje, ~'mjɛːr] **1.** *adj.* vegetable...; **2.** *su./m* vegetable dish; **légumineux, -euse** ♀ [~mi'nø, ~'noːz] **1.** *adj.* leguminous; **2.** *su./f* leguminous plant.
lendemain [lɑ̃d'mɛ̃] *m* next day, day after; *fig.* morrow; *fig.* future; *fig.* consequences; *le* ~ *matin* the next morning; *fig. sans* ~ short-lived.
lénifier 💊 [leni'fje] (1o) *v/t.* soothe, assuage, alleviate; **lénitif, -ve** 💊 [~'tif, ~'tiːv] **1.** *adj.* lenitive; soothing; **2.** *su./m* lenitive.
lent, lente [lɑ̃, lɑ̃:t] slow; slow-burning (*powder*).
lente [lɑ̃:t] *f louse*: nit.
lenteur [lɑ̃'tœːr] *f* slowness; ~*s pl.* slowness *sg.*; dilatoriness *sg.*
lentille [lɑ̃'tiːj] *f* ♀ lentil; *opt.* lens; ⊕, *clock pendulum*: bob, ball; ~*s pl. face*: freckles, spots; *opt.* ~*s pl.* cornéennes contact lenses.
léonin, e [leɔ'nɛ̃, ~'nin] leonine; *fig. part f* ~*e* lion's share; **léopard** *zo.* [~'paːr] *m* leopard.
lépidoptères [lepidɔp'tɛːr] *m/pl.* lepidoptera.
lèpre 💊 [lɛpr] *f* leprosy (*a. fig.*); **lépreux, -euse** [le'prø, ~'prøːz] **1.** *adj.* leprous; **2.** *su.* leper; **léproserie** 💊 [~prɔz'ri] *f* leper-hospital.
lequel *m*, **laquelle** *f*, **lesquels** *m/pl.*, **lesquelles** *f/pl.* [lə'kɛl, la'kɛl, le'kɛl] **1.** *pron./rel.* who, whom, which; **2.** *pron./interr.* which (one)?; **3.** *adj.* which.
lérot *zo.* [le'ro] *m* garden dormouse, leriot.
les [le] *see le.*
lès [le] *prp.* near ... (*only in place names*).
lesbienne [lɛs'bjɛn] *f* lesbian.
lèse-majesté 🏛 [lɛzmaʒɛs'te] *f* high treason, lese-majesty; **léser** [le'ze] (1f) *v/t.* wrong (*s.o.*); injure (*a. fig. s.o.'s pride*); *fig.* damage.

lésine [le'zin] f stinginess; **lésiner** [~zi'ne] (1a) v/i. be stingy; ~ sur haggle over; **lésinerie** [~zin'ri] f stinginess.

lésion [le'zjɔ̃] f injury (a. ⚖️); 🩹 lesion.

lessivage [lɛsi'va:ʒ] m washing; ⊕ boiler: cleaning; ⊕, ⚒ leaching; **lessive** [~'si:v] f wash(ing); ✝ washing powder; faire la ~ do the laundry; jour m de ~ washing-day; **lessivé, e** F [lɛsi've] washed out, all in; **lessiver** [~] (1a) v/t. wash, scrub (the floor); clean (a boiler); ⊕, ⚒ leach; sl. clean (s.o.) out.

lest ⚓ [lɛst] m ballast.

leste [~] light, nimble, agile; fig. unscrupulous; fig. broad (humour).

lester [lɛs'te] (1a) v/t. ballast; weight (a net).

léthargie [letar'ʒi] f lethargy; **léthargique** [~'ʒik] lethargic.

letton, -onne [le'tɔ̃, ~'tɔn] 1. adj. Lettonian; geog. Latvian; 2. su./m ling. Lettish; su. ♀ Lett.

lettre [lɛtr] f letter; ~s pl. literature sg., letters; ⚖️ ~s pl. de procuration letters of procuratory; ~s pl. patentes letters patent; ~ chargée (or recommandée) post: registered letter; hist. ~ de cachet order under the king's private seal; ✝ ~ de change bill of exchange; pol. ~ de commerce business letter; pol. ~ de créance credentials pl.; ~ de crédit letter of credit; ~ de faire-part notice (of wedding etc.); ~ de voiture way-bill, consignment note; à la ~, au pied de la ~ literally; en toutes ~s in full; homme m (femme m) de ~s man (woman) of letters; lever les ~s post: collect the post; F passer comme une ~ à la poste go off smoothly; go through easily; **lettré, e** [lɛ'tre] well-read, literate.

leu [lø] m: à la queue ~ in single file.

leur [lœ:r] 1. adj./poss. their; 2. pron./pers. them; (to) them; 3. pron./poss.: le (la) ~, les ~s pl. theirs, their own; 4. su./m theirs, their own; les ~s pl. their (own) people.

leurre [lœ:r] m fish, a. fig.: bait; fig. illusion, deception; **leurrer** [lœ're] (1a) v/t. bait (a fish); decoy; allure; fig. deceive, delude, take in; se ~ delude o.s.

levage [lə'va:ʒ] m hoisting, raising; dough: rising; appareil m de ~ hoist.

levain [lə'vɛ̃] m yeast; leaven (a.fig.).

levant [lə'vɑ̃] m east; **levantin, e** [~vɑ̃'tɛ̃, ~'tin] adj., a. su. ♀ Levantine.

levé [lə've] m ♪ up beat; surv. survey; **levée** [~'ve] f thing, ⚒ siege: raising; thing, ban, embargo: lifting; meeting: closing; ⚖️ court: rising; ⚒ levy(ing); embankment, causeway; post: collection; ⚒ camp: striking; ⚓ anchor: weighing, sea: swell; removal; ⊕ piston: travel, cam, valve: lift, cam, cog; cards: trick; **lever** [~'ve] 1. (1d) v/t. lift; raise (a. ⚒); adjourn, close (a meeting); levy (⚒, a. taxes); shrug (one's shoulders); post: collect; post: clear (a letter-box); ⚒ etc. strike (a. camp); ⚓ weigh (anchor); remove (a bandage, a difficulty, a doubt); cards: pick up (a trick); se ~ rise, stand up; clear (weather); v/i. 🌱 shoot; rise (dough); 2. su./m person, thing, sum: rising; thea. curtain: rise; (royal) levee; surv. surveying; **lève-tard** [lɛv'ta:r] su./inv. late riser; **lève-tôt** [lɛv'to] su./inv. early riser.

levier [lə'vje] m lever; mot. ~ du changement de vitesse gear lever.

levraut [lə'vro] m leveret, young hare.

lèvre [lɛ:vr] f lip (a. 🌱); crater: rim; geol. fault: wall; ~s pl. wound: lips; se mordre les ~s d'avoir parlé regret having spoken.

levrette [lə'vrɛt] f greyhound bitch; **lévrier** [le'vrje] m greyhound.

levure [lə'vy:r] f yeast; ~ artificielle baking-powder.

lexicographe [lɛksikɔ'graf] m lexicographer; **lexicographie** [~gra'fi] f lexicography.

lez [le] see lès.

lézard [le'za:r] m zo. lizard; fig. idler, lounger; faire le ~ bask in the sun; **lézarde** [~'zard] f chink, crevice, crack; **lézarder** [~zar'de] (1a) v/t. crack, split; v/i. F bask in the sun; F lounge.

liage [lja:ʒ] m binding, tying, fastening; **liaison** [ljɛ'zɔ̃] f † joining; connection (a. ✝); relationship; contact; dealings pl.; fig. link; 🔺 mortar, cement; ⚒, gramm. liaison (a. = intimacy); ♪ slur; **liant, liante** [ljɑ̃, ljɑ̃:t] 1. adj. elastic; good-natured, sociable; 2. su./m sociability; flexibility, springiness; 🔺 binding agent.

liarder † [ljar'de] (1a) v/i. pinch and scrape; count every halfpenny.

liasse [ljas] f bundle, packet; wad.

libation [liba'sjɔ̃] f libation; F faire d'amples ⁓s drink deeply.

libelle [li'bɛl] m lampoon; ⚖ libel; **libeller** [libɛl'le] (1a) v/t. draw up (a cheque, a document); make out (a cheque); **libelliste** [⁓'list] m lampoonist.

libellule zo. [libɛl'lyl] f dragon-fly, (devil's) darning-needle.

liber ♀ [li'bɛːr] m bast, inner bark.

libéral, e, m/pl. **-aux** [libe'ral, ⁓'ro] 1. adj. liberal; broad; generous; 2. su./m liberal; **libéralisme** pol. [libera'lism] m liberalism; **libéralité** [⁓li'te] f liberality; fig. generosity; **libérateur, -trice** [⁓'tœːr, ⁓'tris] 1. adj. liberating; 2. su. liberator, deliverer; rescuer; **libération** [⁓'sjɔ̃] f liberation; ⚖ discharge (a. ✕), release; ✝ payment in full; **libérer** [libe're] (1f) v/t. liberate; set free; ⚖, ✕ discharge; ✕ exempt from military service; ✝ free (s.o. of a debt); se ⁓ de free o.s. from; ✝ liquidate (a debt); **libertaire** [libɛr'tɛːr] su. a. adj. libertarian; **liberté** [⁓'te] f liberty, freedom; ⊕ piston: clearance; ⁓ de la presse freedom of the press; ⁓ religieuse freedom of worship; prendre des ⁓s avec take liberties with; prendre la ⁓ de (inf.) take the liberty of (ger.); **libertin, e** [⁓'tɛ̃, ⁓'tin] 1. adj. dissolute; licentious; 2. su. libertine; **libertinage** [⁓ti'naːʒ] m dissolute behavio(u)r or ways pl.; licentiousness.

libidineux, -euse [libidi'nø, ⁓'nøːz] lewd, lustful; **libido** psych. [⁓'do] f libido.

libraire [li'brɛːr] su. bookseller; **⁓-éditeur,** pl. **⁓s-éditeurs** [⁓brɛredi-'tœːr] m publisher; **librairie** [⁓brɛ-'ri] f bookshop; book-trade; publishing house.

libre [libr] free; clear (passage etc.); independent (school); temps m ⁓ spare time; ⁓ à vous de (inf.) you are welcome or at liberty to (inf.); teleph. pas ⁓ line engaged, Am. line busy; **⁓-échange** [libre'ʃãːʒ] m free(-)trade; **⁓-échangiste** [⁓ʃã'ʒist] m free-trader; **⁓-service,** pl. **⁓s-services** [librəsɛr'vis] m self-service; self-service store or restaurant, etc.

librettiste thea. [librɛ'tist] m librettist; **libretto** thea. [⁓'to] m libretto.

lice [lis] f † lists pl.; fig. entrer en ⁓ contre enter the lists against, have a tilt at.

licence [li'sãːs] f fig., a. admin. licence; univ. degree of licentiate; fig. licentiousness; ⁓ poétique poetic licence; prendre des ⁓s avec take liberties with; **licencié** m, e f [lisã'sje] licentiate; univ. bachelor (of arts etc.); ✝ licensee; **licenciement** ✕ etc. [⁓si'mã] m disbanding; **licencier** [⁓'sje] (1o) v/t. disband; ⊕ lay off (workmen); **licencieux, -euse** [⁓'sjø, ⁓'sjøːz] licentious.

lichen ♀ [li'kɛn] m lichen. [(up).⎱
licher sl. [li'ʃe] (1a) v/t. lick; drink⎰

licite [li'sit] licit, lawful.

licol [li'kɔl] m halter.

licorne [li'kɔrn] f ⚡, myth. unicorn; icht. ⁓ de mer narwhal.

licou [li'ku] m see licol.

lie [li] f lees pl.; dregs pl. (a. fig.).

liège [ljɛːʒ] m ♀ cork oak; cork; float; **liégeux, -euse** [lje'ʒø, ⁓'ʒøːz] cork-like.

lien [ljɛ̃] m tie (a. ⊕), bond, link; ⊕ metal: strap, band; ⁓s pl. chains; **lier** [lje] (1o) v/t. bind (a. ⚖), fasten, tie; connect, link (ideas, questions, topics); cuis. thicken (a sauce); ⁓ connaisance avec strike up an acquaintance with; se ⁓ avec make friends with.

lierre ♀ [ljɛːr] m ivy.

liesse [ljɛs] f rejoicing, jollity.

lieu [ljø] m place; locality; spot; fig. grounds pl., reason, cause; ♋ locus; site; ⁓x pl. premises; ⁓x pl. (d'aisance) privy sg., toilet sg.; gramm. ⁓x pl. communs commonplaces; au ⁓ de instead of; au ⁓ que whereas; avoir ⁓ take place, occur; donner ⁓ à give rise to; en haut ⁓ in high places; en premier ⁓ in the first place, first of all; il y a (tout) ⁓ de (inf.) there is (every) reason for (ger.); sur les ⁓x on the premises; F on the spot.

lieue [ljø] f measure: league.

lieur, -euse [ljœːr, ljøːz] su. person: binder; su./f (mechanical) binder.

lieutenance [ljøt'nãːs] f lieutenancy; **lieutenant** [⁓'nã] m ✕ lieutenant; ⚓ ⁓ de vaisseau lieutenant; **⁓-colonel** ✕ lieutenant-colonel; ✈ wing-commander.

lièvre zo. [ljɛːvr] m hare.

liftier [lifˈtje] m lift boy, Am. elevator operator.

ligament anat. [ligaˈmã] m ligament; **ligamenteux, -euse** [‿mã-ˈtø, ‿ˈtøːz] ligamentous; **ligature** [‿ˈtyːr] f binding, tying; ✂, typ. ligature; ⚓, ✄ splice; ♪ tie; **ligaturer** [‿tyˈre] (1a) v/t. bind; ✄ ligature; ♪ tie.

lignage [liˈɲaːʒ] m lineage; **lignard** ✕ F [‿ˈɲaːr] m soldier of the line, infantryman; **ligne** [liɲ] f line, row; ✈ flight; geog. the equator; (‿ de pêche) fishing (Am. fish) line; ‿ aérienne ✈ overhead line; airline; à la ‿! new paragraph!, indent!; F elle a de la ‿ she has a good figure; sp. dernière ‿ droite home straight or stretch; ⚙ grande ‿ main line; hors ‿ incomparable; lire entre les ‿s read between the lines; pêcher à la ‿ angle; **lignée** [liˈɲe] f line(age); stock; descendants pl.

ligneux, -euse [liˈɲø, ‿ˈɲøːz] ligneous, woody; **lignifier** [‿ɲiˈfje] (1o) v/t. a. se ‿ turn into wood; **lignite** min. [‿ˈɲit] m lignite, brown coal.

ligoter [ligɔˈte] (1a) v/t. tie up.

ligue [lig] f league; **liguer** [liˈge] (1m) v/t. league; **ligueur** hist. [‿ˈgœːr] m leaguer.

lilas ♀ [liˈla] su./m, a. adj./inv. lilac.

limace [liˈmas] f zo. slug; ⊕ Archimedean screw; **limaçon** [‿maˈsõ] m zo. snail; anat. cochlea; ‿ de mer periwinkle; escalier m en ‿ spiral staircase.

limaille ⊕ [liˈmaːj] f filings pl.

limande [liˈmãːd] f icht. dab; ⊕ graving piece.

limbe [lɛ̃ːb] m astr. rim; ♈, ♀ limb; ♀ leaf: lamina; eccl. ‿s pl. limbo sg.; fig. dans les ‿s rather vague, in the air.

lime ⊕ [lim] f file; ‿ à ongles nailfile; ‿ d'émeri emery board; enlever à la ‿ file (s.th.) off; **limer** [liˈme] (1a) v/t. file; fig. polish; **limeuse** ⊕ [‿ˈmøːz] f filing-machine.

limier [liˈmje] m zo. bloodhound; F sleuth.

limitatif, -ve [limitaˈtif, ‿ˈtiːv] limiting, restrictive; **limitation** [‿siˈsjõ] f limitation, restriction; ‿ des naissances birth-control; **limite** [liˈmit] 1. su./f limit; boundary (a. sp.); ‿ d'élasticité elastic limit, tensile strength; sans ‿ de durée a. open-end(ed); 2. adj.: cas m ‿ border-line case; vitesse f ‿ maximum speed, speed limit; **limiter** [limiˈte] (1a) v/t. limit; restrict; **limitrophe** [‿ˈtrɔf] (de) adjacent (to); bordering (on); pays m ‿ borderland.

limoger [limɔˈʒe] (1l) v/t. supersede (a general etc.); dismiss.

limon[1] [liˈmõ] m mud, slime, alluvium.

limon[2] [‿] m cart etc.: shaft; ⚓ string-board.

limon[3] ♀ [liˈmõ] m sour lime; **limonade** [limɔˈnad] f lemonade; **limonadier** m, -ère [‿naˈdje, ‿ˈdjɛːr] bar-keeper; dealer in soft drinks, Am. soda-fountain keeper.

limoneux, -euse [limɔˈnø, ‿ˈnøːz] muddy (water); geol. alluvial; ♀ growing in mud; bog-...

limousine [limuˈzin] f rough woollen coat or cloak; mot. † limousine; **limousiner** ⚓ [‿ziˈne] (1a) v/t. build in rubble work.

limpide [lɛ̃ˈpid] clear, transparent, limpid; **limpidité** [‿pidiˈte] f limpidity; clarity.

lin [lɛ̃] m ♀ flax; tex. linen; **linaire** ♀ [liˈnɛːr] f linaria, F toad-flax; **linceul** [lɛ̃ˈsœl] m shroud.

linéaire [lineˈɛːr] linear; ⊕ dessin m ‿ geometrical drawing; mesure f ‿ measure of length; **linéament** [‿aˈmã] m feature (a. fig.).

linette ♀ [liˈnet] f linseed.

linge [lɛ̃ːʒ] m linen, calico; ‿ de corps underwear; ‿ de table table linen; ‿ sale dirty linen (a. fig.); **linger** m, -ère [lɛ̃ˈʒe, ‿ˈʒɛːr] su. linen-draper; su./f wardrobe keeper; seamstress; **lingerie** [lɛ̃ʒˈri] f underwear; ✝ linen-drapery; ✝ linen-trade; linen-room.

lingot metall. [lɛ̃ˈgo] m ingot; **lingotière** metall. [‿gɔˈtjɛːr] f ingot-mo(u)ld.

lingual, e, m/pl. **-aux** [lɛ̃ˈgwal, ‿ˈgwo] lingual; **linguiste** [‿ˈgɥist] su. linguist; **linguistique** [‿gɥisˈtik] 1. adj. linguistic; 2. su./f linguistics sg.

linier, -ère [liˈnje, ‿ˈnjɛːr] 1. adj. linen...; flax...; 2. su./f flax-field.

liniment ✚ [liniˈmã] m liniment.

linoléum [linɔleˈɔm] m linoleum; oilcloth.

linon tex. [liˈnõ] m lawn; buckram.

linotte *orn.* [li'nɔt] *f* linnet; red poll; F *tête f de* ~ feather-brain.
linteau △ [lɛ̃'to] *m* lintel.
lion [ljɔ̃] *m* lion (*a.* F); F celebrity; *astr. le* ♌ Leo, the Lion; *fig. part f du* ~ lion's share; **lionceau** [ljɔ̃-'so] *m* lion cub; **lionne** [ljɔn] *f* lioness.
lippe [lip] *f* thick lower lip; F *faire la* ~ pout; **lippée** † [li'pe] *f* feast; **lippu, e** [~'py] thick-lipped.
liquéfaction ♒ *etc.* [likefak'sjɔ̃] *f* liquefaction; **liquéfier** ♒ *etc.* [~'fje] (1o) *v/t.* liquefy; reduce to the liquid state; *se* ~ liquefy.
liquette F [li'kɛt] *f* shirt.
liqueur [li'kœːr] *f* liquor, drink; liqueur; ♒ solution, liquid.
liquidateur ⚖ [likida'tœːr] *m* liquidator; **liquidation** [~'sjɔ̃] *f* liquidation; ✝ Stock Exchange: settlement; ✝ clearance sale; ⚖ † ~ *judiciaire* winding up.
liquide [li'kid] **1.** *adj.* liquid (*a. gramm., a.* ✝ *debt*); ready (*money*); *actif m* ~ liquid assets *pl.*; **2.** *su./m* liquid; drink; *su./f gramm.* liquid consonant; **liquider** [~ki'de] (1a) *v/t.* liquidate (*a. fig.*); ✝ settle (*an account, a. fig. a question*); ✝ sell off (*goods*); *fig.* get rid of; *se* ~ *avec* clear off one's debt to.
liquoreux, -euse [liko'rø, ~'røːz] liqueur-like; sweet (*wine*); **liquoriste** [~'rist] *m* wine and spirit merchant.
lire¹ [liːr] (4t) *v/i.* read (about, *sur*); *v/t.* read; *cela se lit sur votre visage* it shows in your face; *je vous lis difficilement* I have difficulty with your handwriting.
lire² [~] *f Italian currency*: lira.
lis ♀ [lis] *m* lily; ▨ *fleur f de* ~ fleur-de-lis.
liséré [lize're] *m* border, edging; piping, binding; **lisérer** [~] (1d) *v/t.* border, edge; pipe.
liseron ♀ [liz'rɔ̃] *m* bindweed, convolvulus.
liseur, -euse [li'zœːr, ~'zøːz] *su.* great reader; *su./f* reading stand; *book*: dust jacket; reading-lamp; *cost.* bed jacket; **lisibilité** [~zibili'te] *f* legibility; **lisible** [~'zibl] legible; *fig.* readable (*book*).
lisière [li'zjɛːr] *f tex.* selvedge, list; *field, forest*: edge; *country, field*: border; *fig.* leading-strings *pl.*

lisons [li'zɔ̃] *1st p. pl. pres. of* lire¹.
lissage [li'saːʒ] *m* ⊕ polishing; *metal*: burnishing.
lisse¹ [lis] smooth, polished; glossy.
lisse² ⚓ [~] *f* rail; *hull*: ribband.
lisser [li'se] (1a) *v/t.* smooth, polish; burnish (*metal*); glaze (*paper*); *bird*: preen (*its feathers*); *se* ~ become smooth; **lissoir** ⊕ [~'swaːr] *m* smoother; polishing-iron.
liste [list] *f* list; roll; register; ⚔ roster; ⚖ *jury*: panel; ~ *civile* civil list; ~ *électorale* register of voters; ~ *noire* blacklist; *mettre sur la* ~ *noire a.* blacklist.
listeau [lis'to] *m*, **listel** [~'tɛl] *m* △ listel, fillet; *coin*: rim; ⚓ sheer rail.
lit [li] bed (*a.* △, ⊕, *river, etc.*); *river*: bottom; *geol.* layer, stratum; ~ *de camp* camp-bed; *hist.* ~ *de justice king's throne in old French parliament*; ~ *de mort* death-bed; ~ *d'enfant* cot; ~ *de plume* feather bed; *fig.* comfortable job; ⚓ ~ *du vent* wind's eye; ~ *escamotable* folding-bed; *chambre f à deux* ~*s* twin-bedded room; *enfant mf du second* ~ child of the second marriage; *faire* ~ *à part* sleep apart; *garder le* ~ be confined to one's bed.
litanie [lita'ni] *f* litany; *eccl.* ~*s pl.* litany *sg.*; F *la même* ~ the old, old story; the same refrain.
liteau [li'to] *m* △ batten, rail; *tex.* stripe.
literie [li'tri] *f* bedding.
litho... [lito] litho...; ~**graphe** [~'graf] *m* lithographer; ~**graphie** [~gra'fi] *f* lithography; lithograph.
litière [li'tjɛːr] *f* litter; *fig.* faire ~ de trample underfoot.
litigant, e ⚖ [liti'gɑ̃, ~'gɑ̃ːt] litigant; **litige** [~'tiːʒ] *m* dispute; ⚖ (law-) suit; *en* ~ under dispute, at issue; **litigieux, -euse** [~ti'ʒjø, ~'ʒjøːz] litigious.
litre [litr] *m measure*: litre, *Am.* liter.
littéraire [lite'rɛːr] literary; **littéral, e**, *m/pl.* **-aux** [~'ral, ~'ro] literal (*a.* ⚖); ⚖ documentary (*evidence*); **littérateur** [~ra'tœːr] *m* man of letters; **littérature** [~ra-'tyːr] *f* literature; ~ *professionnelle* technical literature.
littoral, e, *m/pl.* **-aux** [lito'ral, ~'ro] **1.** *adj.* coastal, littoral; **2.** *su./m* coast-line; shore.

liturgie *eccl.* [lityr'ʒi] *f* liturgy;
liturgique *eccl.* [ʌ'ʒik] liturgical.

liure [ljy:r] *f cart-load etc.*: lashing.

livide [li'vid] livid; ghastly; **lividité** [ʌvidi'te] *f* lividness; ghastliness.

livrable ✝ [li'vrabl] deliverable; ready for delivery; **livraison** [ʌvrɛ-'zɔ̃] *f* ✝ delivery; *book*: instalment; ✝ ~ à *domicile* home delivery.

livre[1] [li:vr] *m* book; ⚓ ~ *de bord* logbook; ~ *de cuisine* cookery book, *Am.* cookbook; ~ *de raison* register; record; *pol.* ~ *jaune* (*approx.*) blue book; à ~ *ouvert* at sight; *tenir les* ~*s* keep the accounts; ✝ *tenue f des* ~*s* book-keeping; *see grand-livre.*

livre[2] [~] *f money, weight*: pound.

livrée [li'vre] *f* livery; *coll.* servants *pl.*

livrer [~] (1a) *v/t.* deliver; give away (*a secret etc.*); ~ à give *or* hand over to, deliver up to; *se* ~ à give o.s. up to; confide in; indulge in; engage in; carry out; ⚔ ~ *bataille* give battle.

livret [li'vrɛ] *m* booklet; ♪ libretto; (*bank-*)book; *school*: record-book; (*student's*) handbook.

livreur ✝ [li'vrœ:r] *m* delivery-man, delivery-boy; **livreuse** [li'vrø:z] *f* delivery-girl; delivery-van.

lobe [lɔb] *m* ♀, *anat.* lobe; ~ *de l'oreille* earlobe; **lobé, e** ♀ [lɔ'be] lobed, lobate; **lobule** ♀, *anat.* [~'byl] *m* lobule.

local, e, *m/pl.* **-aux** [lɔ'kal, ~'ko] **1.** *adj.* local; **2.** *su./m* premises *pl.*; site; room; **localiser** [lɔkali'ze] (1a) *v/t.* locate; localize; **localité** [ʌli'te] *f* locality, place; **locataire** [~'tɛ:r] *su.* tenant, occupier; ⚖ lessee; lodger; hirer; **locatif, -ve** [~'tif, ~'ti:v] rental; tenant's ...; *réparations f/pl.* ~*ves* repairs for which the tenant is liable; **location** [~'sjɔ̃] *f* hiring; letting, renting; tenancy; *thea. etc.* booking; ~ *de livres* lending-library; *bureau m de* ~ box-office; booking-office (*a.* 🎭); **location-vente,** *pl.* **locations-ventes** [~sjɔ̃'vã:t] *f* hire-purchase system.

loch ⚓ [lɔk] *m* log.

lock-out ⊕ [lɔ'kaut] *m/inv.* lock-out.

locomobile [lɔkɔmɔ'bil] **1.** *adj.* travelling; locomotive; **2.** *su./f* transportable steam-engine, locomobile; **locomotif, -ve** [~'tif, ~-'ti:v] **1.** *adj.* ⊕, *a. physiol.* locomotive; transportable; **2.** *su./f* locomotive, engine; *fig.* pacemaker; *fig.* dynamic element; **locomotion** [~'sjɔ̃] *f* locomotion.

locuste *zo.* [lɔ'kyst] *f* locust.

locution [lɔky'sjɔ̃] *f* expression, phrase.

lof ⚓ [lɔf] *m* windward side; *sail*: luff; **lofer** ⚓ [lɔ'fe] (1a) *v/i.* luff.

loge [lɔ:ʒ] *f* hut; cabin; *freemason, gardener, porter*: lodge; *dog*: kennel; *thea.* box; *thea.* (*artist's*) dressing-room; ♀ cell, loculus; **logeable** [lɔ'ʒabl] fit for occupation (*house*); *mot.* comfortable; **logement** [lɔʒ-'mã] *m* lodging, housing; accommodation; ⚔ billeting; ⚔ quarters *pl.*; ⊕ bed, seating; ✝ container; **loger** [lɔ'ʒe] (1l) *v/t.* lodge, house; ⚔ billet, quarter; put; ⊕ fix, fit, set; *v/i.* lodge, live; ⚔ *be* quartered; ~ *en garni* live in lodgings; **logette** [~'ʒɛt] *f* small lodge; *thea.* small box; **logeur** [~'ʒœ:r] *m* landlord, lodging-house keeper; ⚔ householder (*on whom a soldier is billeted*); **logeuse** [~'ʒø:z] *f* landlady.

logiciel [lɔʒi'sjɛl] *m computer*: software.

logicien *m*, **-enne** *f* [lɔʒi'sjɛ̃, ~'sjɛn] logician; **logique** [~'ʒik] **1.** *adj.* logical; **2.** *su./f* logic.

logis [lɔ'ʒi] *m* abode, home, dwelling; hostelry; *fig. la folle du* ~ imagination. [tics *sg.*)

logistique(s) [lɔʒis'tik] *f*/(*pl.*) logis-)

loi [lwa] *f* law; rule; *mettre hors la* ~ outlaw; *parl. projet m de* ~ bill; *se faire une* ~ *de* (*inf.*) make a point of (*ger.*); ~**-cadre,** *pl.* ~**s-cadres** [~'ka:dr] *f* skeleton law.

loin [lwɛ̃] *adv.* far, distant (from, de); ~ *de* (*inf.*) far from (*ger.*); *aller trop* ~ overdo it, go too far; *au* ~ far away; *bien* ~ very far; far back (*in the past*); further on (*in the book etc.*); *de* ~ at a distance; from afar; *de* ~ *en* ~ at long intervals, now and then; **lointain, e** [~'tɛ̃, ~'tɛn] **1.** *adj.* far (off), distant, remote; **2.** *su./m* distance; *dans le* ~ in the distance.

loir *zo.* [lwa:r] *m* dormouse.

loisible [lwa'zibl] permissible; *il lui est* ~ *de* (*inf.*) he is at liberty to (*inf.*); **loisir** [~'zi:r] *m* leisure; spare time; ~*s pl.* leisure activities; à ~ at leisure, leisurely.

lombaire *anat.* [lɔ̃'bɛːr] lumbar; **lombes** *anat.* [lɔ̃:b] *m/pl.* lumbar region *sg.*; loins.

londonien, -enne [lɔ̃dɔ'njɛ̃, ~'njɛn] 1. *adj.* London ...; 2. *su.* ♀ Londoner.

long, longue [lɔ̃, lɔ̃:g] 1. *adj.* long; thin (*sauce*); ~ *à croître* slow-growing; ✝ *à* ~ *terme* long-dated (*bill*); *de longue main* well in advance; *être* ~ *à* (*inf.*) be long in (*ger.*); 2. *long adv.*: *fig. en dire* ~ speak volumes; *en savoir* ~ know a lot (about, *sur*); 3. *su./m* length; *de* ~ *en large* to and fro; *deux pieds de* ~ two feet long; *le* (*or au*) ~ *de* (all) along; *tomber de tout son* ~ fall full length; *su./f gramm.* long syllable; *cards:* long suit; *à la longue* in the long run; at length.

longanimité [lɔ̃ganimi'te] *f* forbearance; long-suffering.

long-courrier ✈ [lɔ̃ku'rje] *m* long-distance plane.

longe [lɔ̃:ʒ] *f* tether; *whip*: thong; longe; *cuis. veal, venison*: loin.

longer [lɔ̃'ʒe] (11) *v/t.* pass *or* go along; skirt (*the coast, a wall*); **longeron** [lɔ̃ʒ'rɔ̃] *m* 🔺 stringer; longitudinal girder; ✈ *fuselage*: longeron, *wing*: spar.

longévité [lɔ̃ʒevi'te] *f* longevity, long life.

longitude *geog.* [lɔ̃ʒi'tyd] *f* longitude; **longitudinal, e,** *m/pl.* **-aux** [~tydi'nal, ~'no] longitudinal, lengthwise; ⚓ fore-and-aft.

longtemps [lɔ̃'tɑ̃] *adv.* long, a long time; *il y a* ~ long ago.

longueur [lɔ̃'gœːr] *f* length (*a. sp.*); *fig. film, novel, etc.*: tedious passage; *à* ~ *de* all (*day, year, etc.*) long; throughout the (*day, year, etc.*); for (*days, years, etc.*); *phys.* ~ *d'onde radio*: wavelength; *a. fig. être sur la même* ~ *d'onde(s)* be on the same wavelength.

longue-vue, *pl.* **longues-vues** [lɔ̃g-'vy] *f* telescope, field-glass.

looping ✈ [lu'piŋ] *m* loop(ing); *faire un* ~ loop (the loop).

lopin [lɔ'pɛ̃] *m ground*: patch, plot.

loquace [lɔ'kwas] talkative; garrulous; **loquacité** [~kwasi'te] *f* loquacity, talkativeness.

loque [lɔk] *f* rag.

loquet [lɔ'kɛ] *m* latch; *knife*: clasp; **loqueteau** [lɔk'to] *m* catch, small latch.

loqueteux, -euse [lɔk'tø, ~'tøːz]

1. *adj.* ragged, in tatters; 2. *su.* tatterdemalion.

lorgner [lɔr'ɲe] (1a) *v/t.* ogle, leer at; *fig.* have one's eye on; stare at; **lorgnette** [~'ɲet] *f* opera-glasses *pl.*; **lorgnon** [~'ɲɔ̃] *m* eye-glasses *pl.*; pince-nez.

loriot *orn.* [lɔ'rjo] *m* oriole.

lorrain, e [lɔ'rɛ̃, ~'rɛn] 1. *adj.* of *or* from Lorraine; 2. *su.* ♀ Lorrainer.

lors [lɔːr] *adv.*: ~ *de* at the time of; ~ *même que* even when; *dès* ~ since that time; consequently; *pour* ~ so ...; **lorsque** [lɔrsk(ə)] *cj.* when.

losange ⩗ [lɔ'zɑ̃:ʒ] *m* rhomb(us); *en* ~ diamond-shaped.

lot [lɔ] *m* portion, share, lot (*a. fig.*); prize; *gros* ~ first prize, jackpot; **loterie** [lɔ'tri] *f* lottery (*a. fig.*); draw, raffle.

lotier 🌿 [lɔ'tje] *m* lotus.

lotion [lɔ'sjɔ̃] *f* 🎇, ⊕ washing; 🎇 lotion; ~ *capillaire* hairwash; **lotionner** [~sjɔ'ne] (1a) *v/t.* wash, bathe; sponge.

lotir [lɔ'tiːr] (2a) *v/t.* parcel out (✝, *a. an estate*); divide up (into lots *or* plots); ~ *q. de qch.* allot s.th. to s.o.; **lotissement** [~tis'mɑ̃] *m* lot, plot; (housing) development; ✝ parcelling out; dividing into lots; *estate*: apportionment.

loto [lɔ'to] *m* lotto; lotto set.

louable [lwabl] laudable, praiseworthy (for, *de*).

louage [lwa:ʒ] *m* hiring out; hire; ✂ chartering; *de* ~ hired; ✂ charter...

louange [lwɑ̃:ʒ] *f* praise; **louanger** [lwɑ̃'ʒe] (11) *v/t.* praise, extol; **louangeur, -euse** [~'ʒœːr, ~'ʒøːz] 1. *adj.* adulatory; 2. *su.* adulator, lauder. [ligan.)

loubar(d) [lu'baːr] *m* young hoo-)

louche[1] [luʃ] ✝ squinting; crosseyed; *fig.* dubious, shady, F fishy, funny.

louche[2] [~] *f* (soup-)ladle; ⊕ reamer.

loucher [lu'ʃe] (1a) *v/i.* squint; **loucherie** [luʃ'ri] *f* squint.

louchet [lu'ʃe] *m* draining-spade.

louer[1] [lwe] (1p) *v/t.* rent, hire; book, reserve (*a place, seats*).

louer[2] [~] (1p) *v/t.* praise; commend (s.o. for s.th., *q. de qch.*); *se* ~ *de* be very pleased with (*s.o., s.th.*); congratulate o.s. on (*ger., de inf.*).

loueur[1] *m*, **-euse** *f* [lwœːr, lwøːz] hirer out.

loueur², **-euse** [~] 1. *adj.* flattering; 2. *su.* flatterer.

loufoque F [lu'fɔk] loony, daft, F dippy.

loulou *zo.* [lu'lu] *m* Pomeranian.

loup [lu] *m zo.* wolf; *fig.* (black velvet) mask; ⚔ gas-mask: face-piece; ~ *de mer icht.* sea-perch; F old salt; *à pas de ~* stealthily; *entre chien et ~* in the twilight; *hurler avec les ~s* do in Rome as the Romans do; *jeune ~* ambitious young manager; **~-cervier**, *pl.* **~s-cerviers** [~sɛr'vje] *m zo.* lynx; *fig.* profiteer.

loupe [lup] *f* ⚕ wen; ♀ excrescence; *opt.* lens, magnifying-glass.

loupé ⊕ [lu'pe] defective (*piece*); **louper** F [~'pe] (1a) *v/t.* mess up; bungle, botch; miss (*one's train, an occasion, etc.*).

loup-garou, *pl.* **loups-garous** [luga'ru] *m myth.* werewolf; F *fig.* bear; F bogy.

lourd, lourde [lu:r, lurd] heavy; clumsy; *fig.* dull (*mind etc.*); sultry, close (*weather*); **lourdaud, e** [lur-'do, ~'do:d] 1. *adj.* clumsy, awkward; dull-witted; 2. *su.* lout; clod; blockhead; **lourdeur** [~'dœ:r] *f* heaviness; clumsiness.

loustic F [lus'tik] *m* wag.

loutre [lutr] *f zo.* otter; ✝ sealskin.

louve *zo.* [lu:v] *f* she-wolf; **louveteau** [luv'to] *m* wolf-cub (*a. Boy Scouts*).

louvoyer [luvwa'je] (1h) *v/i.* ⚓ tack; *fig.* manœuvre; *fig.* hedge.

loyal, e, *m/pl.* **-aux** [lwa'jal, ~'jo] fair, straightforward, sincere; faithful; ⚖ true; **loyauté** [~jo'te] *f* fairness; honesty; loyalty (to, *envers*).

loyer [lwa'je] *m* rent; ✝ money: price.

lu, e [ly] *p.p. of* lire¹.

lubie [ly'bi] *f* whim, fad.

lubricité [lybrisi'te] *f* lubricity, lust; **lubrifiant, e** ⊕ [~'fjɑ̃, ~'fjɑ̃:t] 1. *adj.* lubricating; 2. *su./m* lubricant; **lubrification** [~fika'sjɔ̃] *f* lubrication; greasing; **lubrifier** [~'fje] (1o) *v/t.* lubricate; grease, oil; **lubrique** [ly'brik] lustful, lewd; wanton.

lucane [ly'kan] *m* lucanus, stag beetle.

lucarne [ly'karn] *f* dormer *or* attic window; gable-window.

lucide [ly'sid] lucid (*a.* ⚕), clear; **lucidité** [~sidi'te] *f* lucidity (*a.* ⚕); ⚕ sanity; clearness.

luciole *zo.* [ly'sjɔl] *f* firefly, glowworm.

lucratif, -ve [lykra'tif, ~'ti:v] lucrative; **lucre** [lykr] *m* lucre, profit.

ludique [ly'dik] play ...

luette *anat.* [lɥɛt] *f* uvula.

lueur [lɥœ:r] *f* gleam, glimmer (*a. fig.*); flash.

luge [ly:ʒ] *f* toboggan, sledge, *Am.* sled; **luger** [ly'ʒe] (1l) *v/i.* toboggan, sledge, *Am.* sled; **lugeur** *m*, **-euse** *f* [~'ʒœ:r, ~'ʒø:z] tobogganer.

lugubre [ly'gybr] dismal, gloomy; ominous.

lui¹ [lɥi] *p.p. of* luire.

lui² [~] *pron./pers. subject:* he; *object:* him, her, it; (to) him, (to) her, (to) it; *à ~* to him, to her, to it; his, hers, its; *c'est ~* it is he, F it's him; **~-même** [~'mɛ:m] *pron./rfl./m* himself, itself.

luire [lɥi:r] (4u) *v/i.* shine, gleam; *fig.* dawn (*hope*); **luisant, e** [lɥi'zɑ̃, ~'zɑ̃:t] 1. *adj.* shining; gleaming; glossy (*surface*); 2. *su./m* gloss, shine; **luisis** [~'zi] *1st p. sg. p.s. of* luire; **luisons** [~'zɔ̃] *1st p. pl. pres. of* luire.

lumière [ly'mjɛ:r] *f* light; ⊕ port; *fig.* (*a. ~s*) knowledge; *à la ~ de* by (*fig.* in) the light of; **lumignon** [lymi'ɲɔ̃] *m* candle-end; poor light; **luminaire** [~'nɛ:r] *m coll.* lighting; **luminescence** [~nɛ'sɑ̃:s] *f* luminescence; *éclairage m par ~* fluorescent lighting; **luminescent, e** [~nɛ'sɑ̃, ~'sɑ̃:t] luminescent; **lumineux, -euse** [~'nø, ~'nø:z] luminous; *phys.* light (*-wave*); bright, brilliant (*a. fig. idea*); illuminated (*advertisement*); **luminosité** [~nozi'te] *f* luminosity; brightness; radiance.

lunaire [ly'nɛ:r] 1. *adj.* lunar; 2. *su./f* ♀ lunaria; **lunaison** *astr.* [~nɛ'zɔ̃] *f* lunation; **lunatique** [~na'tik] ✝ moonstruck; *fig.* capricious, whimsical.

lunch [lœ̃:ʃ] *m* lunch(eon); snack; **luncher** [lœ̃'ʃe] (1a) *v/i.* lunch; have a snack.

lundi [lœ̃'di] *m* Monday; F *faire le ~* take Monday off.

lune [lyn] *f* moon; *poet.* month; *~ de miel* honeymoon; *clair m de ~* moonlight; *être dans la ~* be in the clouds; *promettre la ~* promise the moon and stars; **luné, e** [ly'ne]: *bien (mal) ~*

well- (ill-)disposed; in a good (bad) mood.

lunetier [lynˈtje] *m* spectacle-maker; optician; **lunette** [lyˈnɛt] *f* telescope; *sp.* wrestling; glasses; *mot. etc.* goggles; 🚋 cab-window; ⊕ die; ⊕ *lathe*: back-rest; ⁓s *pl. de soleil* sunglasses; **lunetterie** [lynɛˈtri] *f* spectacle-making; making of optical instruments.

lunule [lyˈnyl] *f anat.*, *a.* ⚕ lunule, lunula; *finger-nail*: half-moon.

lupanar [lypaˈnaːr] *m* brothel.

lupin ♀ [lyˈpɛ̃] *m* lupin.

lurette F [lyˈrɛt] *f*: *il y a belle* ⁓ *a long time ago.*

luron [lyˈrɔ̃] *m* (jolly) fellow; **luronne** [⁓ˈrɔn] *f* (lively) lass.

lus [ly] *1st p. sg. p.s. of* lire[1].

lustre[1] *poet.* [lystr] *m* lustre, period of five years.

lustre[2] [lystr] *m* lustre (*a.fig.*), gloss; chandelier; **lustrer** [lysˈtre] (1a) *v/t.* glaze, gloss; F make shiny (*with wear*); **lustrine** *tex.* [⁓ˈtrin] *f* (silk) lustrine; cotton lustre; *manches f/pl. de* ⁓ oversleeves.

lut ⊕ [lyt] *m* luting; **luter** ⊕ [lyˈte] (1a) *v/t.* lute, seal with luting.

luth ♪ [lyt] *m* lute; **lutherie** [lyˈtri] *f* stringed-instrument trade *or* industry.

luthérien, -enne *eccl.* [lyteˈrjɛ̃, ⁓ˈrjɛn] *adj.*, *a. su.* Lutheran.

luthier [lyˈtje] *m* lute-maker; stringed-instrument maker *or* seller.

lutin, e [lyˈtɛ̃, ⁓ˈtin] **1.** *adj.* mischievous, impish; **2.** *su./m* imp (*a. fig. child*), elf, goblin; **lutiner** [⁓tiˈne] (1a) *v/t.* tease; pester.

lutrin *eccl.* [lyˈtrɛ̃] *m* lectern; *coll.* succentors *pl.*

lutte [lyt] *f* fight; struggle; conflict; *sp.* wrestling; *sp.* ⁓ *à la corde* tug-of-war; *pol.* ⁓ *des classes* class war *or* struggle; **lutter** [lyˈte] (1a) *v/i.* fight, struggle; *sp.*, *a. fig.* wrestle; **lutteur** *m*, **-euse** *f* [⁓ˈtœːr, ⁓ˈtøːz] wrestler; *fig.* fighter.

luxation 🩺 [lyksaˈsjɔ̃] *f* luxation, dislocation.

luxe [lyks] *m* luxury; wealth; *fig.* profusion; *de* ⁓ luxury, de luxe.

luxer 🩺 [lykˈse] (1a) *v/t.* luxate, dislocate.

luxueux, -euse [lykˈsɥø, ⁓ˈsɥøːz] luxurious; sumptuous (*feast*).

luxure [lykˈsyːr] *f* lewdness, lechery; **luxuriant, e** [⁓syˈrjɑ̃, ⁓ˈrjɑ̃ːt] luxuriant; **luxurieux, -euse** [⁓syˈrjø, ⁓ˈrjøːz] lecherous, lewd.

luzerne ♀ [lyˈzɛrn] *f* lucern(e), *Am.* alfalfa; **luzernière** 🌱 [⁓zɛrˈnjɛːr] *f* lucern(e)-field.

lycée [liˈse] *m* (state) grammar-school; **lycéen, -enne** [⁓seˈɛ̃, ⁓seˈɛn] *su.* pupil at a *lycée*; *su./m* grammar-schoolboy; *su./f* grammar-schoolgirl.

lymphe 🩺 [lɛ̃ːf] *f* lymph.

lynchage [lɛ̃ˈʃaː3] *m* lynching; **lyncher** [⁓ˈʃe] (1a) *v/t.* lynch.

lynx *zo.* [lɛ̃ks] *m* lynx; *aux yeux de* ⁓ lynx-eyed.

lyre [liːr] *f* ♪ lyre; ⊕ quadrant; ⚓ *rowlock*: stirrup; *orn. oiseau-*⁓ lyre-bird; **lyrique** [liˈrik] **1.** *adj.* lyric (-al); **2.** *su./m* lyric poet; **lyrisme** [⁓ˈrism] *m* lyricism.

lys ♀ [lis] *m* lily.

M

M, m [ɛm] *m* M, m.
ma [ma] *see* mon.
maboul, e F [ma'bul] **1.** *adj.* cracked, dippy; **2.** *su.* loony.
macabre [ma'ka:br] gruesome; ghastly; *danse f ~* dance of Death.
macadamiser [makadami'ze] (1a) *v/t.* macadamize (*a road*).
macaque *zo.* [ma'kak] *m* macaque.
macaron *cuis.* [maka'rɔ̃] *m* macaroon; **macaroni** [~rɔ'ni] *m/inv.* *cuis.* macaroni; F dago (= *Italian*).
macédoine [mase'dwan] *f ~ de fruits*) fruit salad; *fig.* miscellany, *pej.* hotchpotch; *~ de légumes* mixed (diced) vegetables *pl.*
macérer [mase're] (1f) *v/t.* soak, steep; *fig.* mortify (*the flesh*).
Mach *phys.* [mak] *npr.*: *nombre m de ~* mach (number).
mâche [mɑ:ʃ] *f horses*: mash; ♀ corn-salad.
mâchefer ⊕ [maʃ'fɛ:r] *m* clinker, slag; *lead*: dross.
mâcher [ma'ʃe] (1a) *v/t.* chew; munch; *~ à q. la besogne* half-do s.o.'s work for him; *ne pas ~ ses mots* not to mince matters.
machin F [ma'ʃɛ̃] *m* thing, gadget; what's-his-name.
machinal, e, *m/pl.* **-aux** [maʃi'nal, ~'no] mechanical, unconscious; **machinateur** [~na'tœ:r] *m* plotter, schemer; **machination** [~na'sjɔ̃] *f* machination, plot; **machine** [ma-'ʃin] *f* machine; engine (*a.* 🚢); dynamo; F thing, gadget; *~s pl.* machinery *sg.*; *~ à calculer* calculating machine, calculator; *~ à écrire* typewriter; *~ à photocopier* photocopier; *~ à sous* slot-machine; **machine-outil,** *pl.* **machines-outils** [~ʃinu-'ti] *f* machine-tool; **machiner** [~ʃi-'ne] (1a) *v/t.* scheme, plot; hatch; *machiné à l'avance* put-up (*affair*); **machinery** [~ʃin'ri] *f* machinery, ⚓ engine-room; **machiniste** [~ʃi-'nist] *m* bus driver; *thea.* scene shifter.
mâchoire [ma'ʃwa:r] *f* jaw (*a.* ⊕); ⊕

vice; ⊕ flange; *mot. ~s pl.* (brake-)shoes; **mâchonner** [~ʃɔ'ne] (1a) *v/t.* mumble; mutter; chew; *animal*; champ (*fodder*); **mâchure** [~'ʃy:r] *f tex.* flaw; *fruit, flesh*: bruise; **mâchurer** [~ʃy're] (1a) *v/t.* soil, stain; *typ.* smudge; chew, munch.
macis ♀, *cuis.* [ma'si] *m* mace.
maçon [ma'sɔ̃] *m* 🔺 mason; F free-mason.
mâcon [ma'kɔ̃] *m* Mâcon (= *wine of Burgundy*).
maçonner [masɔ'ne] (1a) *v/t.* 🔺 build; face (*with stone*); wall up (*a door, a window*); **maçonnerie** [~sɔn'ri] *f* 🔺 masonry; 🔺 stonework; F freemasonry; **maçonnique** [~sɔ-'nik] masonic.
macro... [makrɔ] macro...; **~biotique** [~bjɔ'tik] macrobiotic; **~biotisme** [~bjɔ'tism] *m* macrobiotics *sg.*; **~céphale** *zo.*, ♀ [~se'fal] macro-cephalic, large-headed; **~cosme** [~'kɔsm] *m* macrocosm.
macule [ma'kyl] *f* spot, blemish, stain; *astr.* sun-spot; **maculer** [~ky'le] (1a) *v/t.* maculate; stain; *typ.* mackle; *v/i. a. se ~* mackle, blur.
madame, *pl.* **mesdames** [ma'dam, me'dam] *f* Mrs.; madam; F lady.
madeleine [mad'lɛn] *f* ♀ (*sort of*) pear; *cuis.* sponge-cake.
mademoiselle, *pl.* **mesdemoiselles** [madmwa'zɛl, medmwa'zɛl] *f* Miss; young lady.
madère [ma'dɛ:r] *m* Madeira (wine).
Madone [ma'dɔn] *f* Madonna.
madras 🌿, *tex.* [ma'dra:s] *m* Madras (handkerchief).
madré, e [ma'dre] **1.** *adj.* mottled; spotted; *fig.* sly, wily; **2.** *su. fig.* sly fox.
madrier 🔺 [madri'e] *m* timber; plank.
madrilène [madri'lɛn] **1.** Madrilenian; of Madrid; **2.** *su.* ♀ inhabitant of Madrid.
maestria [maestri'ja] *f* skill.
mafflu, e F [ma'fly] heavy-jowled.
magasin [maga'zɛ̃] *m* shop, *Am.*

store; warehouse, store; *camera, rifle*: magazine; ⚒ armo(u)ry; ~ *à succursales multiples* chain stores *pl.*; ✝ *grand* ~ department store; ✝ *en* ~ in stock; **magasinage** [~zi'na:ʒ] *m* warehousing, storing; storage (charges *pl.*); **magasinier** [~zi'nje] *m* warehouseman, store-keeper.

magazine [maga'zin] *m* (illustrated) magazine.

mage [ma:ʒ] **1.** *su./m* magus; seer; **2.** *adj.*: *bibl. les Rois* m/*pl.* ♗s the Three Wise Men, the (Three) Magi; **magicien** *m*, **-enne** *f* [maʒi-'sjɛ̃, ~'sjɛn] magician; wizard; **magie** [~'ʒi] *f* magic (*a. fig.*); **magique** [~'ʒik] magic(al) (*a. fig.*).

magistral, e, *m/pl.* **-aux** [maʒis'tral, ~'tro] magisterial; *fig.* pompous; *fig.* masterly (*work*); F first-rate; ⚔ magistral; **magistrat** [~'tra] *m* magistrate, judge; **magistrature** [~tra'ty:r] *f* magistrature; magistracy; ~ *assise* Bench, judges *pl.*; ~ *debout* public prosecutors *pl.*

magma [mag'ma] *m geol.* magma; *fig.* muddle.

magnanime [mana'nim] magnanimous; **magnanimité** [~nimi'te] *f* magnanimity.

magnat [mag'na] *m* magnate.

magnésie ⚗ [mane'zi] *f* magnesia, magnesium oxide; *sulfate* m *de* ~ Epson salts *pl.*

magnésite [mane'zit] *f* magnesite, meerschaum.

magnésium [mane'zjɔm] *m* ⚗ magnesium; *phot.* flash-light.

magnétique [mane'tik] magnetic; **magnétisme** [~'tism] *m* magnetism; **magnétite** *min.* [~'tit] *f* lodestone, magnetite; **magnéto** [~'to] *f* magneto; **magnétophone** [~tɔ'fɔn] *m* tape recorder; ~ *à cassettes* cassette recorder; **magnétoscope** [~tɔ-'skɔp] *m* video(-tape) recorder; **magnétoscoper** (1a) *v/t.* video-tape.

magnificence [manifi'sã:s] *f* magnificence, splendo(u)r; ~s *pl.* lavishness *sg.*; **magnifier** [~'fje] (1a) *v/t.* magnify, glorify, glamorize; **magnifique** [~'fik] magnificent, splendid; *fig.* marvellous.

magnolia ♣ [manɔ'lja] *m*, **magnolier** ♣ [~'lje] *m* magnolia(-tree).

magot¹ [ma'go] *m zo.* barbary ape; macaque; *fig.* ugly man.

magot² F [~] *m* savings *pl.*, hoard.

magouille *sl.* [ma'guj] *f* dealings *pl.*, tricks *pl.*; wangle; graft.

mahométan, e [maɔme'tã, ~'tan] *adj.*, *a. su.* Mohammedan, Moslem; **mahométisme** [~'tism] *m* Mohammedanism.

mai [mɛ] *m* May; may-pole.

maie [~] *f* kneading-trough.

maigre [mɛ:gr] **1.** *adj.* thin, lean; meagre, scanty (*meal, a. fig.*); **2.** *su./m meat*: lean; *icht.* meagre; *faire* ~ fast, abstain from meat; **maigrelet, -ette** [mɛgrə'lɛ, ~'lɛt] rather thin, slight; **maigreur** [~-'grœ:r] *f* thinness; emaciation; *fig.* meagreness, poorness; **maigrir** [~'gri:r] (2a) *v/i.* grow thin; lose weight; *v/t.* make thinner; ⊕ thin (*wood*).

mail [ma:j] *m* ⊕ sledge-hammer; avenue; ✝ *club, game*: mall.

maille¹ [ma:j] *f* stitch; *chain*: link; (chain-)mail; *net*: mesh; *feather*: speckle; *vine etc.*: bud; ⊕ two-handed mallet; *à larges* (*petites*) ~s wide-(close-)meshed.

maille² [~] *f*: *avoir* ~ *à partir avec q.* have a bone to pick with s.o.

maillechort [maj'ʃɔ:r] *m* nickel *or* German silver.

mailler [ma'je] (1a) *v/t.* net; ⚓ lace; ⊕ shackle (*chains*); ⊕ make (*s.th.*) in lattice-work; *v/i.* ♀ bud; *a. se* ~ become speckled (*partridge etc.*).

maillet [ma'jɛ] *m* mallet, maul; *sp.* polo-stick; croquet mallet.

maillon [ma'jɔ̃] *m chain*: link; *tex.* mail; ⚓ shackle; **maillot** [ma'jo] *m* swaddling-clothes *pl.*; *sp. football*: jersey; *rowing, running*: vest; ~ *de bain woman*: swimsuit; *man*: bathing trunks *pl.*

main [mɛ̃] *f* hand (*a cards; a. = handwriting*); ✝ *paper*: quire; *cards*: deal; ~ *courante* handrail; *à la* ~ in the *or* one's hand; (*do s.th.*) by hand; *à* ~ *levée* freehanded; *à pleines* ~s lavishly; *avoir la* ~ *cards*: have the lead *or* deal; *bas* (*haut*) *les* ~s! hands off (up)!; *battre des* ~s clap (one's hands); *fig. de bonnes* ~s on good authority; *en* ~ under control; *in* hand; *en un tour de* ~ straight off, F in a jiffy; *en venir aux* ~s come to blows *or* grips; *fait à la* ~ handmade; *la* ~ *dans la* ~ hand in hand; *payer de la* ~ *à* *la* ~ pay direct without formalities; *mettre la* ~ *sur* lay hands on; *prêter la* ~ lend a hand; *savoir de longue* ~ have known for a long time; *serrer la* ~ *à q.* shake hands with s.o.; *sous la* ~ to hand, at hand, handy; *sous* ~ underhanded(ly *adv.*); ~**-d'œuvre**, *pl.* ~**s-d'œuvres** ⊕ [~'dœːvr] *f* labo(u)r; manpower; ~**forte** [~'fɔrt] *f*: *prêter* ~ give assistance (*to the police etc.*); ~**levée** ⚖ [~lə've] *f* withdrawal; ~**mise** [~'miːz] *f* seizure (*of, sur*); ⚖ distraint; ~**morte** ⚖ [~'mɔrt] *f* mortmain.

maint, mainte *poet.* [mɛ̃, mɛ̃ːt] many a; *maintes fois* many a time.

maintenance [mɛ̃t'nɑ̃s] *f* maintenance.

maintenant [mɛ̃t'nɑ̃] *adv.* now; *dès* ~ from now on, henceforth.

maintenir [mɛ̃t'niːr] (2h) *v/t.* maintain (*a. fig.*); keep; support; uphold; *se* ~ continue; remain; hold one's own; **maintien** [mɛ̃'tjɛ̃] *m* maintenance; bearing, carriage; *perdre son* ~ lose countenance.

maire [mɛːr] *m* mayor; **mairie** [mɛ'ri] *f* town hall; mayoralty.

mais [mɛ] 1. *cj.* but; ~ *non!* no indeed!; not at all!; ~ *oui!* sure!, of course!; 2. *adv.*: *je n'en puis* ~ I am completely exhausted; I don't know what to say.

maïs ♠ [ma'is] *m* maize, Indian corn, *Am.* corn.

maison [mɛ'zɔ̃] *f* house; home; household; family; ♥ (*a.* ~ *de commerce*) firm; ~ *close* brothel; ~ *d'arrêt* gaol, lock-up; ~ *de commission* commission agency; ~ *de rapport* apartment house; ~ *de santé* nursing home; mental hospital; ~ *du Roi* Royal Household; ~ *jumelle* semidetached house; ♥ ~ *mère* head office; *de bonne* ~ of a good family; *la* ~ *des Bonaparte* the House of Bonaparte; *tenir* ~ *ouverte* keep open house; **maisonnée** [mɛzɔ'ne] *f* household, family; **maisonnette** [~'nɛt] *f* cottage, small house.

maître, -esse [mɛːtr, mɛ'trɛs] 1. *su./m* master (*a. fig.*); *fig.* ruler; owner; *school:* teacher; ⚓ petty officer; ⚖ *title given to lawyers:* maître; ~ *d'armes* fencing-master; *univ.* ~ *de conférences* lecturer; ~ *d'hôtel* headwaiter; ⚓ chief steward; ~ *d'œuvre* foreman; *être* ~ *de* be in control of;

have at one's disposal; *être passé* ~ *en* be a past master of *or* in; *su./f* mistress; 2. *adj.* ♠, ⊕, *etc.*, *a. fig.* principal, main; ~**autel**, *pl.* ~**s-autels** *eccl.* [mɛtro'tɛl] *m* high altar; **maîtrisable** [~tri'zabl] controllable; **maîtrise** [~'triːz] *f* mastership; *fig.* feeling, profession, *etc.*: mastery; command, control; **maîtriser** [~tri'ze] (1a) *v/t.* master, overcome; *se* ~ control o.s.

majesté [maʒɛs'te] *f* majesty; **majestueux, -euse** [~'tɥø, ~'tɥøːz] majestic, stately.

majeur, e [ma'ʒœːr] 1. *adj.* major (*a.* ⚖, ♪, *phls.*), greater; *fig.* main, chief; *devenir* ~ reach one's majority; 2. *su./m* ♪ major; middle finger; **major** ✗ [ma'ʒɔːr] *m* regimental adjutant; ~ *de place* town major; ~ *général* chief of staff; **majoration** [~ʒɔra'sjɔ̃] *f* over-estimation; increase; *admin.* advancement; **majordome** [~ʒɔr'dɔm] *m* major-domo, steward; **majorer** [maʒɔ're] (1a) *v/t.* over-estimate; ♥ add to (*a bill*); increase; **majorité** [~ri'te] *f* majority (*a.* ⚖); ⚖ coming of age; ✗ adjutancy.

majuscule [maʒys'kyl] 1. *adj.* capital (*letter*); 2. *su./f* capital letter.

mal [mal] 1. *su./m* evil; hurt, harm; pain; ♥ disease; wrong; ~ *à l'estomach* stomachache; ~ *aux reins* backache; ~ *de cœur* nausea, sickness; ~ *de l'air* air sickness; ~ *de mer* seasickness; ~ *de tête* headache; ~ *du pays* homesickness; *avoir* ~ *au ventre* have a stomachache; *avoir du* ~ *à faire qch.* have difficulty (in) doing s.th.; *donner du* ~ *à q.* give s.o. some trouble; *faire* ~ (*à q.*) hurt (s.o.); *faire du* ~ *à q.* harm s.o.; ♥ *haut* ~ epilepsy; *prendre* ~ be taken ill; *se donner du* ~ take pains *or* trouble; 2. *adv.* badly; ill; uncomfortable; ~ *à l'aise* ill at ease; ~ *à propos* inopportunely, at the wrong time; ~ *fait* badly made; botched (*work*); *être* ~ be uncomfortable; be wrong; *pas* ~ good-looking, presentable (*person*); quite good; F *pas* ~ *de* a good many, a lot of; *prendre* ~ *qch.* take offence at s.th.; *se sentir* ~ feel ill; *se trouver* ~ faint.

malade [ma'lad] 1. *adj.* ill, sick; diseased; 2. *su.* patient; sick person; **maladie** [mala'di] *f* disease; illness, sickness; ailment; ~ *de carence* deficiency disease, vitamin deficiency; ~ *infantile* childhood disease; *fig.* teething troubles *pl.*; **maladif, -ve** [ˌ~'dif, ˌ~'diːv] sickly, ailing.

maladresse [malaˈdrɛs] *f* clumsiness; blunder; **maladroit, e** [ˌ~'drwa, ˌ~'drwat] **1.** *adj.* clumsy, awkward; **2.** *su.* duffer; blunderer; awkward person.

malais, e [maˈlɛ, ˌ~'lɛːz] **1.** *adj.* Malay(an); **2.** *su./m ling.* Malay(an); *su.* ♀ Malay(an).

malaise [maˈlɛːz] *f* uneasiness; discomfort; *fig.* unrest; **malaisé, e** [ˌ~lɛˈze] difficult.

malappris, e [malaˈpri, ˌ~'priːz] **1.** *adj.* ill-mannered; **2.** *su.* ill-mannered person.

malavisé, e [malaviˈze] **1.** *adj.* ill-advised; injudicious (*person*); **2.** *su.* blunderer.

malaxage [malakˈsaːʒ] *m* mixing; *dough:* kneading; **malaxer** [ˌ~'se] (1a) *v/t.* mix; knead (*dough*); **malaxeur** ⊕ [ˌ~'sœːr] *m* (cement) mixer; mixing machine.   [uncouth.]

malbâti, e [malbɑˈti] misshapen;

malchance [malˈʃɑːs] *f* bad luck; mishap; **malchanceux, -euse** [ˌ~ʃɑ̃sø, ˌ~'søːz] **1.** *adj.* unlucky, luckless; **2.** *su.* unlucky person.

maldonne [malˈdɔn] *f cards:* misdeal; error, mistake; misunderstanding.

mâle [mɑːl] **1.** *adj.* male (♀, ⊕ *screw*, *person*); *zo.* buck (*rabbit*), dog (*fox, wolf*), bull (*elephant*); *orn.* cock; *fig.* virile; manly; **2.** *su./m* male.

malédiction [maledikˈsjɔ̃] *f* curse.

maléfice [maleˈfis] *m* evil spell; **maléfique** [ˌ~'fik] evil; maleficent.

malencontre † [malɑ̃ˈkɔ̃ːtr] *f* mishap; **malencontreux, -euse** [malɑ̃kɔ̃ˈtrø, ˌ~'trøːz] unfortunate, awkward.

malentendu [malɑ̃tɑ̃ˈdy] *m* misunderstanding.

mal-être [malˈɛːtr] *m* (feeling of) discomfort; uneasiness.

malfaçon [malfaˈsɔ̃] *f* bad workmanship; defect; **malfaire** [malˈfɛːr] (4r) *v/i.* do evil; **malfaisant, e** [ˌ~fəˈzɑ̃, ˌ~'zɑ̃ːt] harmful; mischievous; evil-minded (*person*); **malfaiteur** *m*, **-trice** *f* [ˌ~fɛˈtœːr, ˌ~'tris] malefactor; offender.

malfamé, e [malfaˈme] ill-famed; notorious.

malformation [malfɔrmaˈsjɔ̃] *f* malformation (*a.* 𝔰°).

malgré [malˈgre] *prp.* despite, in spite of; ~ *moi* against my will; ~ *tout* still.

malhabile [malaˈbil] clumsy; inexperienced (in *ger.*, *à inf.*).

malheur [maˈlœːr] *m* bad luck; misfortune; unhappiness; ~ *à lui!* woe betide him!; *quel* ~! what a pity!; **malheureux, -euse** [ˌ~lœˈrø, ˌ~'røːz] **1.** *adj.* unlucky, unhappy; unfortunate; *fig.* poor; *fig.* paltry; **2.** *su.* unfortunate person; *pauvre* ~! poor soul!

malhonnête [malɔˈnɛt] dishonest; *fig.* impolite; indecent (*gesture*); **malhonnêteté** [ˌ~nɛtˈte] *f* dishonesty; *fig.* rudeness; *gesture:* indecency.

malice [maˈlis] *f* malice; *fig.* trick; *ne pas voir* ~ *à* not to see any harm in; **malicieux, -euse** [ˌ~liˈsjø, ˌ~'sjøːz] mischievous; waggish, sly (*remark etc.*).

malignité [maliɲiˈte] *f* malignity (*a.* 𝔰°); piece of spite; **malin, -igne** [ˌ~'lɛ̃, ˌ~'liɲ] **1.** *adj.* malignant (*a.* 𝔰°); wicked; *fig.* cunning, sharp, sly; *fig.* clever, smart; *fig.* difficult; **2.** *su. fig.* shrewd person; *su./m: le* ♀ the Devil.

malingre [maˈlɛ̃ːgr] sickly, weakly.

malintentionné, e [malɛ̃tɑ̃sjɔˈne] **1.** *adj.* evil-minded, ill-intentioned; **2.** *su.* evil-minded person.

malique 🜍 [maˈlik] malic (*acid*).

mal-jugé ⚖ [malʒyˈʒe] *m* miscarriage of justice.

malle [mal] *f* trunk; ⚓ mail-boat; (*dé)faire sa* ~ (un)pack.

malléable [malleˈabl] malleable (*a. fig.*); *fig.* pliant.

malle-poste, *pl.* **malles-poste** [malˈpɔst] *f* mail-coach; **malletier** [malˈtje] *m* trunk-maker; **mallette** [maˈlɛt] *f* suitcase; attaché case; small case.

malmener [malməˈne] (1d) *v/t.* illtreat, maltreat, handle roughly.

malotru, e [malɔˈtry] **1.** *adj.* uncouth; vulgar; **2.** *su.* boor, churl.

malpeigné, e [malpɛˈɲe] unkempt, untidy (*person*).

malpropre [malˈprɔpr] dirty (*a. fig.*); slovenly (*appearance*); **malpropreté** [ˌ~prɔprəˈte] *f* dirtiness (*a. fig.*); dirt; slovenliness; ~*s pl.* dirty stories, F smut *sg.*

malsain, e [mal'sɛ̃, ~'sɛn] unhealthy; unwholesome (*a. fig.*); dangerous (*coast*); *fig.* unsound.

malséant, e [malse'ɑ̃, ~'ɑ̃:t] unbecoming, unseemly.

malsonnant, e [malsɔ'nɑ̃, ~'nɑ̃:t] offensive.

malt [malt] *m* malt; **malter** [mal'te] (1a) *v/t.* malt; **malterie** [~'tri] *f* malting; malt-house; **malteur** [~'tœːr] *m* maltster; **maltose** ⚗, ⊕ [~'toːz] *m* maltose.

maltraiter [maltrɛ'te] (1a) *v/t.* ill-treat, maltreat; handle roughly; batter.

malveillance [malvɛ'jɑ̃:s] *f* malevolence, ill will, spite (to[wards] *pour, envers*); **malveillant, e** [~'jɑ̃, ~'jɑ̃:t] ill-willed; malicious; spiteful.

malversation ⚖ [malvɛrsa'sjɔ̃] *f* embezzlement; breach of trust.

malvoisie [malvwa'zi] *mf wine*: malmsey.

maman [ma'mɑ̃] *f* mam(m)a, mummy, *Am. a.* mom.

mamelle [ma'mɛl] *f* breast; *cow etc.*: udder; teat; **mamelon** [mam-'lɔ̃] *m* nipple (*a.* ⊕ *for oiling*); *person, a. animal*: teat; ⊕ boss; *geog.* rounded hillock; **mamelonné, e** [~lɔ'ne] mamillate; hilly.

mamel(o)uk [mam'luk] *m* mameluke.

m'amie †, **ma mie** [ma'mi] *f* my dear.

mamillaire [mamil'lɛ:r] mamillary; **mammaire** *anat.* [~'mɛ:r] mammary; **mammifère** *zo.* [~mi'fɛ:r] **1.** *adj.* mammalian; **2.** *su./m* mammal.

mamours [ma'mu:r] *m/pl.* billing *sg.* and cooing *sg.*, caresses.

mammouth *zo.* [ma'mut] *m* mammoth.

manant [ma'nɑ̃] *m* boor; yokel; † villager.

manche[1] [mɑ̃:ʃ] *m* handle; haft; (*broom-*)stick; *whip*: stock; ♪ *violin*: neck; 𝄞 ~ *à balai* joy-stick; *jeter le* ~ *après la cognée* give up.

manche[2] [~] *f* sleeve; *water*: hose; (*air-*)shaft; *geog.* strait; *sp.* heat; *tennis*: set; *cards*: hand; 𝄞 ~ *à air* wind sock; *la* ⚥ the (English) Channel; F *faire la* ~ beg (for alms).

mancheron [mɑ̃ʃ'rɔ̃] *m plough*: handle; *cost.* cuff; short sleeve; **manchette** [mɑ̃'ʃɛt] *f* cuff; wrist-band; *journ.* headline; *sl.* ~*s pl.* handcuffs; **manchon** [~'ʃɔ̃] *m* muff; ⊕ casing, sleeve; gas-mantle.

manchot, e [mɑ̃'ʃo, ~'ʃɔt] **1.** *adj.* one-armed; *fig.* awkward with one's hands, F ham-fisted; **2.** *su.* one-armed person; *su./m orn.* penguin.

mandant [mɑ̃'dɑ̃] *m* ⚖ principal; employer; *pol.* constituent.

mandarin [mɑ̃da'rɛ̃] mandarin (*a. fig., pej.*); **mandarinat** [mɑ̃dari'na] *m* mandarinate.

mandarine ⚘ [mɑ̃da'rin] *f* mandarin(e), tangerine.

mandat [mɑ̃'da] *m* mandate; commission; ⚖ power of attorney; ⚖ warrant; ✝ draft, order; *sous* ~ mandated (*territory*); **mandataire** [mɑ̃da'tɛ:r] *su.* agent; ⚖ attorney; trustee; *pol.* mandatory; **mandat-carte,** *pl.* **mandats-cartes** [~'kart] *m post*: money order (*in post-card form*); **mandater** [~'te] (1a) *v/t.* give a mandate to; write a money order for (*a sum*); **mandat-poste,** *pl.* **mandats-poste** [~'pɔst] *m* postal money order.

mandement [mɑ̃d'mɑ̃] *m eccl.* pastoral letter; instructions *pl.*; **mander** [mɑ̃'de] (1a) *v/t.* instruct (*s.o.*); summon (*s.o.*); *journ.* *on mande* ... it is reported ...

mandibule *anat.* [mɑ̃di'byl] *f* mandible.

mandoline ♪ [mɑ̃dɔ'lin] *f* mandolin(e).

mandragore ⚘ [mɑ̃dra'gɔːr] *f* mandragora, F mandrake.

mandrin ⊕ [mɑ̃'drɛ̃] *m* mandrel; chuck; punch.

manducation [mɑ̃dyka'sjɔ̃] *f* mastication; *eccl.* manducation.

manège [ma'nɛ:ʒ] *m* riding school; *fig.* trick, stratagem; (*a.* ~ *de chevaux de bois*) roundabout, merry-go-round.

mânes [ma:n] *m/pl.* manes, spirits (*of the departed*).

manette ⊕ [ma'nɛt] *f* lever (*a. mot.*); *Morse*: key.

manganèse ⚗, *min., metall.* [mɑ̃ga-'nɛːz] *m* manganese.

mangeable [mɑ̃'ʒabl] edible, eatable; **mangeaille** [~'ʒa:j] *f* † feed (*for animals*); F food, F grub; **mangeoire** [~'ʒwa:r] *f* manger; feeding-trough; **manger** [mɑ̃'ʒe] **1.** (11) *vt/i.* eat; *v/t.* corrode (*metal*); squander (*money*); mumble (*words*); *fig.* use up, consume (*coal, gas, petrol, etc.*); **2.** *su./m* food; **mangetout** [mãʒ'tu] *m/inv.* † spendthrift; ♀ French bean; **mangeur** *m*, **-euse** *f* [mã'ʒœ:r, ~'ʒø:z] eater; *fig.* devourer; **mangeure** † [~'ʒy:r] *f* place eaten (*by mice, moths, etc.*).

maniabilité [manjabili'te] *f* handiness; manageableness; ⚞, *mot.* manœuvrability; **maniable** [~'njabl] manageable, manœuvrable; handy (*tool*); *fig.* tractable.

maniaque [ma'njak] **1.** *adj.* finnicky, fussy; fanatic; suffering from a mania; **2.** *su.* ⚥ maniac; **manie** [~'ni] *f* mania; funny habit.

maniement [mani'mã] *m* management; handling; **manier** [~'nje] (1o) *v/t.* manage; handle.

manière [ma'njɛ:r] *f* manner (*a. paint. etc.*), way; *fig.* mannerisms *pl.*; ~*s pl.* manners; *à la* ~ *de* after the manner of; *de* ~ *à* so as to; *de* ~ *que* so that; *d'une* ~ *ou d'une autre* somehow or other; *en aucune* ~ in no way; *en* ~ *de* by way of; *faire des* ~*s* be affected; affect reluctance; **maniéré, e** [manje're] affected; *paint. etc.* mannered; *fig.* genteel (*voice etc.*); **maniérisme** [~'rism] *m* mannerism.

manieur [ma'njœ:r] *m* controller; *pej.* ~ *d'argent* financier; financial adventurer.

manif F [ma'nif] *f* (*abbr. of manifestation*) demo; **manifestant, e** *pol.* [manifɛs'tã, ~'tãt] **1.** *adj.* demonstrating; **2.** *su.* demonstrator; **manifestation** [~ta'sjɔ̃] *f* manifestation; *pol.* demonstration; *eccl.* revelation; **manifeste** [~'fɛst] **1.** *adj.* manifest, obvious; ⚖ overt; **2.** *su./m* manifesto; ♻ manifest; **manifester** [~fɛs'te] (1a) *v/t.* show, manifest; reveal; *se* ~ appear; show o.s.; *v/i. pol.* demonstrate.

manigance F [mani'gã:s] trick, scheme; F monkey business; dealings *pl.*; **manigancer** F [~gã'se] (1k) *v/t.* plot, scheme.

manipulateur [manipyla'tœ:r] *m* handler; *tel.* sending key; *radio:* sender; **manipulation** [~la'sjɔ̃] *f* manipulation; handling; **manipuler** [~'le] (1a) *v/t.* manipulate (*a. fig.*), handle; ♻, *tel.* operate (*a key etc.*).

manitou F [mani'tu] *m* boss, tycoon.

manivelle ⊕ [mani'vɛl] *f* crank (-handle).

manne¹ [man] *f* basket; (*baby's*) bassinet.

manne² [~] *f* *bibl.* manna; *fig.* godsend.

mannequin¹ [man'kɛ̃] *m* small hamper.

mannequin² [man'kɛ̃] *m* ⚥, *paint.* manikin; *paint.* lay figure; *cost.* dummy; mannequin; *fig.* puppet; **mannequiner** *paint.* [~ki'ne] (1a) *v/t.* pose (*s.o.*) unnaturally.

manœuvrabilité [manœvrabili'te] *f* manœuvrability; ♻ shunting, ⚞ switching; **manœuvrable** [~'vrabl] manageable; workable; **manœuvre** [ma'nœ:vr] *su./f* working; operation; ♻ shunting, Am. switching; ✕, ♻ manœuvre (*a. fig.*); exercise; ✕, ♻ movement; *fig.* intrigue; *su./m* (manual) labo(u)rer; unskilled worker; *fig.* hack; **manœuvrer** [manœ'vre] (1a) *v/t.* work (*a machine etc.*); ♻ shunt, marshal; *vt/i.* manœuvre (*a.* ✕, ♻, *fig.*); **manœuvrier, -ère** [~vri'e, ~'ɛ:r] skilful; capable.

manoir [ma'nwa:r] *m* country-house; *hist.* manor.

manomètre ⊕ [manɔ'mɛtr] *m* manometer.

manouvrier [manuvri'e] *m* day-labo(u)rer.

manque [mã:k] *m* lack, want; deficiency, shortage; *fig.* emptiness; *drugs etc., a. fig.* (symptôme *m* de) ~ withdrawal (symptom); ~ *de* for lack of; ~ *de foi* breach of faith; ~ *de parole* breaking of one's promise; F *à la* ~ poor, fifth-rate; **manqué, e** [mã'ke] unsuccessful; **manquement** [mãk'mã] *m* failure₂ lapse; ~ *à* breach of; **manquer** [mã'ke] (1m) *v/t.* miss (*a. fig.*); spoil (*one's life, a picture*); *se* ~ miss one another; *v/i.* lack; be absent; be missing; fail; ~ *à q.* be missed by s.o.; ~ *à qch.* fail in s.th.; commit a breach of s.th.; ~ *de qch.* lack s.th., not to have s.th.; *ne pas* ~ *de rien* lack for nothing; ~ (*de*) *faire qch.* nearly do s.th.; *j'ai manqué* (*de*) *tomber* I nearly fell; *ne pas* ~ *de* (*inf.*) not to fail to (*inf.*).

mansarde △ [mã'sard] *f* attic, garret(-window); *roof:* mansard.

mansuétude [mãsɥe'tyd] *f* gentleness, meekness.

mante [mã:t] *f* (*woman's*) sleeveless

cloak; *zo.* ~ *religieuse* (*or prie-Dieu*) praying mantis.

manteau [mã'to] *m* coat; cloak (*a. fig.*); mantle (*a. zo.*); ⊕ casing; ⚙ mantelpiece; *sous le* ~ on the quiet, secretly; **mantelet** [mãt'lɛ] *m cost.* tippet, mantlet; ⚓ port-lid; **mantille** *cost.* [mã'tiːj] *f* mantilla.

manucure [many'kyːr] *su.* manicurist; **manucurer** [⹀ky're] (1a) *v/t.* manicure.

manuel, -elle [ma'nɥɛl] **1.** *adj.* manual; **2.** *su./m* handbook, manual; text-book; ~ *d'entretien* instruction handbook.

manufacture [manyfak'tyːr] *f* (manu)factory; ⊕ plant; **manufacturer** [⹀ty're] (1a) *v/t.* manufacture; **manufacturier, -ère** [⹀ty-'rje, ⹀'rjeːr] **1.** *adj.* manufacturing; **2.** *su./m* manufacturer; mill-owner.

manuscrit, e [manys'kri, ⹀'krit] **1.** *adj.* manuscript; hand-written; **2.** *su./m* manuscript.

manutention [manytã'sjõ] *f* control; handling; ⚖, ⚓ store-keeping; stores *pl.*; bakery; **manutentionner** [⹀sjɔ'ne] (1a) *v/t.* handle; ⚖, ⚓ store; bake.

mappemonde [map'mõːd] *f* map of the world.

maquereau [ma'kro] *m icht.* mackerel; V pimp.

maquette [ma'kɛt] *f* model (*a. thea.*); ⊕ mock-up; *book:* dummy; *metall.* bloom.

maquignon [maki'ɲõ] *m* horse-dealer; *pej.* shady dealer *or* go-between; **maquignonnage** [⹀ɲɔ'naːʒ] *m* horse-dealing; *pej.* sharp practice; **maquignonner** [⹀ɲɔ'ne] (1a) *v/t.* fake up (*a horse*); arrange (*s.th.*) by sharp practices, F work, *sl.* cook.

maquillage [maki'jaːʒ] *m* make-up; **maquiller** [⹀'je] (1a) *v/t.* make up; *phot.* work up; *fig.* disguise; *se* ~ make up; **maquilleur** *m*, **-euse** *f* [⹀'jœːr, ⹀'jøːz] *thea.* make-up artist; *fig.* faker.

maquis [ma'ki] *m* scrub; *fig.* maze; jungle; ⚔ underground forces *pl.*, maquis; *prendre le* ~ go underground.

maraîcher, -ère [marɛ'ʃe, ⹀'ʃɛːr] **1.** *adj.* market-(gardening)...; *culture f mâraichère* market gardening, *Am.* truck farming; **2.** *su./m* market-gardener, *Am.* truck farmer.

marais [ma'rɛ] *m* marsh; bog; swamp.

marasme [ma'rasm] *m* ⚕ marasmus, wasting; *fig.* depression (*a.* ✝).

marathon *sp.* [mara'tõ] *m* marathon (*a. fig.*).

marâtre [ma'rɑːtr] *f* step-mother; cruel *or* unnatural mother.

maraude [ma'roːd] *f* plundering, looting; filching; F *en* ~ cruising, crawling (*taxi*); **marauder** [⹀ro-'de] (1a) *v/i.* plunder; filch; F cruise (*taxi*).

marbre [marbr] *m* marble; *typ.* press-stone; ⊕ (sur)face-plate; *typ. sur le* ~ in type; **marbrer** [mar-'bre] (1a) *v/t.* marble; *fig.* mottle; **marbrerie** [⹀brə'ri] *f* marble-cutting, marble-work; marble-mason's yard; **marbrier, -ère** [⹀bri'e, ⹀'eːr] **1.** *adj.* marble...; **2.** *su./m* marble-cutter; monumental mason; *su./f* marble-quarry; **marbrure** [⹀'bryːr] *f* marbling; *fig.* mottling.

marc [maːr] *m* grapes *etc.:* marc; (*tea-*)leaves *pl.*, (*coffee-*)grounds *pl.*

marcassin *zo.* [marka'sɛ̃] *m* young wild boar.

marchand, e [mar'ʃã, ⹀'ʃã:d] **1.** *adj.* saleable, marketable; trade (*name, price*); shopping (*centre*); commercial (*town*); ⚓ merchant (*navy, ship*); **2.** *su.* dealer, shopkeeper; (*coster-, fish-, iron-*)monger; ~ *d'anti-quités* antique dealer; ~ *des quatre-saisons* costermonger; ~ *de tabac* tobacconist; ~ *en* (*or au*) *détail* retailer; ~ *en gros* wholesaler; **marchandage** [marʃã'daːʒ] *m* bargaining; **marchander** [⹀'de] (1a) *v/t.* haggle with (s.o., q.); bargain for (s.th., *qch.*); beat (*s.o.*) down; ⊕ subcontract (*a job*); *ne pas* ~ not to spare; **marchandeur** *m*, **-euse** *f* [⹀'dœːr, ⹀'døːz] bargainer; ⊕ subcontractor of labo(u)r; **marchandise** [⹀'diːz] *f* merchandise, wares *pl.*, goods *pl.*; 🚃 *train m de* ~*s* goods train, *Am.* freight train.

marche¹ [marʃ] *f* walk; ⚖, ♪ march; tread; step, stair; 🚃, 🚃 *machine, train:* running; *fig. events, stars, time, etc.:* course; *fig.* (rate of) progress; ~ *arrière mot.* reversing; 🚃 backing; *en* ~ *etc.* moving...; ⊕ running; *en état de* ~ in working order; ⊕, *a. fig. mettre en* ~ start, set going, set in motion.

marche[2] *geog.* [∼] *f* border(land); march(-land).

marché [mar'ʃe] *m* market (*a. financial*); deal, bargain; ✝ *à terme* time-bargain; ∼ *au comptant* cash transaction; ✝, *pol.* ♀ *commun* Common Market; ∼ *des changes* exchange market; ∼ *du travail* labo(u)r market; ∼ *intérieur (étranger)* home (foreign) market; ∼ *noir* black market; (*à*) *bon* ∼ cheap(ly); (*à*) *meilleur* ∼ more cheaply; cheaper; *le bon* ∼ the cheapness (of, *de*); (*aller*) *faire son* ∼ go shopping; *fig. par-dessus le* ∼ into the bargain.

marchepied [marʃə'pje] *m vehicle:* footboard; *mot.* running-board; *wagon:* tail-board; step-ladder; *fig.* stepping-stone.

marcher [mar'ʃe] (1a) *v/i.* walk, go (*a.* 🚂 *engine*); ✗ *etc.* march; ⊕ ∼ run (*a.* 🚂 *train*), work; *fig.* F swallow; ⚓ sail, head (for, *vers*); ⊕ ∼ *à vide* run idle; ∼ *sur les pas de q.* follow in s.o.'s footsteps; ∼ *sur les pas de q.* tread on s.o.'s feet; *faire* ∼ run (*a house,* ∼ *a business*); F *faire* ∼ *q.* pull s.o.'s leg; F (*je ne*) *marche pas!* nothing doing!; F *ne pas se laisser* ∼ *sur les pieds* not to let o.s. be put upon; *ma montre ne marche plus* my watch is broken; **marcheur, -euse** [∼'ʃœːr, ∼'ʃøːz] **1.** *adj.* walking; ⚓ *bon* ∼ fast-sailing; **2.** *su.* walker; *su./m:* F *vieux* ∼ old rake.

marcotte 🌿 [mar'kɔt] *f* layer; runner; **marcotter** 🌿 [∼kɔ'te] (1a) *v/t.* layer.

mardi [mar'di] *m* Tuesday; ∼ *gras* Shrove Tuesday.

mare [maːr] *f* pond; pool (*a. fig.*).

marécage [mare'kaːʒ] *m* bog, swamp; fen, marshland; **marécageux, -euse** [∼ka'ʒø, ∼'ʒøːz] boggy, swampy, marshy.

maréchal ✗ [mare'ʃal] *m* marshal; (*a.* ∼-*ferrant*) farrier; ∼ *des logis cavalry:* sergeant; ∼ *des logis-chef* battery *or* squadron sergeant-major; **maréchalat** [∼ʃa'la] *m* marshalship; **maréchalerie** [∼ʃal-'ri] *f* horse-shoeing; smithy.

marée [ma're] *f* tide; ✝ fresh fish; *fig.* flood, wave, surge; ∼ *basse (haute)* low (high) tide, low (high) water; *grande* ∼ springtide; *la* ∼ *descend (monte)* the tide is going out (coming in).

marelle [ma'rɛl] *f game:* hopscotch.

marémoteur, -trice [maremɔ'tœːr, ∼'tris] tidal (*energy*); *usine* ∼*trice* tidal power station.

mareyeur *m,* **-euse** *f* [marɛ'jœːr, ∼'jøːz] fishmonger.

margarine ✝ [marga'rin] *f* margarine.

marge [marʒ] *f* border, edge; margin (*a. fig., a.* ✝); *fig.* scope; ∼ *bénéficiaire* profit margin; ∼ *de sécurité* safety margin; *fig. en* ∼ (*de*) on the fringe (of); **margelle** [mar'ʒɛl] *f well:* curb(-stone); **margeur** [∼-'ʒœːr] *m typ.* layer-on; *typewriter:* margin stop; **marginal, e** *m/pl.* -*aux* [∼ʒi'nal, ∼'no] marginal.

margotin [margɔ'tɛ̃] *m* bundle of firewood.

margouillis F [margu'ji] *m* mud, slush; mess.

margoulin F [margu'lɛ̃] *m* petty tradesman; swindler; (small-time) crook.

marguerite 🌿 [margə'rit] *f* daisy; *grande* ∼ marguerite, ox-eye daisy; *petite* ∼ daisy.

mari [ma'ri] *m* husband; **mariable** [∼'rjabl] marriageable, F in the marriage market; **mariage** [∼'rjaːʒ] *m* marriage; wedding; matrimony; ∼ *d'amour* love match; **marié, e** [∼'rje] **1.** *adj.* married; **2.** *su./m* bridegroom; *su./f* bride; **marier** [∼'rje] (1o) *v/t.* marry (*a. fig.*), give *or* join in marriage; *fig.* join; *fig.* blend (*colours*); se ∼ marry, get married; *fig.* harmonize (with, *à*); **marieur** *m,* **-euse** *f* [∼'rjœːr, ∼'rjøːz] matchmaker.

marihuana [mariɥa'na], **marijuana** [mariʒɥa'na] *f* marijuana.

marin, e [ma'rɛ̃, ∼'rin] **1.** *adj.* marine (*plant*); sea...; nautical; **2.** *su./m* sailor; moist wind (*in South-Eastern France*); F ∼ *d'eau douce* land-lubber.

marinade [mari'nad] *f* pickle; brine; *cuis.* marinade.

marine [ma'rin] **1.** *adj./inv.* navy (-blue); **2.** *su./f* ⚓ navy; ⚓ seaman-ship; *paint.* seascape; ∼ *de guerre* Navy; ∼ *marchande* merchant service *or* navy, *Am.* merchant marine.

mariner *cuis.* [mari'ne] (1a) *v/t.* marinade; pickle.

marinier, -ère [mari'nje, ∼'njɛːr] **1.** *adj.* naval; **2.** *su./m* waterman, bargee; *su./f swimming:* side-stroke.

marionnette [marjɔ'nɛt] *f* puppet

(*a. fig.*); *théâtre m de* ~s puppet-show.

marital, e, *m/pl.* **-aux** [mari'tal, ~'to] marital; **maritalement** [~tal-'mã] *adv.* maritally; *vivre* ~ live together as husband and wife.

maritime [mari'tim] maritime (♀, *law, power, province*); shipping (*agent, intelligence*); naval (*dock-yard*); marine (*insurance*); seaborne (*trade*); seaside (*town*). [tern.]

maritorne [mari'tɔrn] *f* slut, slat-

marivaudage [marivo'da:ʒ] *m* preciosity in writing; mild flirting.

marjolaine ♀ [marʒɔ'lɛn] *f* marjoram.

marmaille F *coll.* [mar'mɑ:j] *f* children *pl.*, F kids *pl.*

marmelade [marmə'lad] *f* compote (*of fruit*); (*orange*) marmalade; F mess; *fig. en* ~ pounded to a jelly.

marmite [mar'mit] *f* pan; (cook-ing-)pot; ✗ F heavy shell; ~ *à pression* (*or de Papin*) pressure-cooker; ~ *norvégienne* hay-box; F *faire bouillir la* ~ keep the pot boiling; **marmiton** [~mi'tõ] *m* cook's boy; (*pastry-cook's*) errand-boy.

marmonner [marmɔ'ne] (1a) *v/t.* mumble, mutter.

marmoréen, -enne [marmɔre'ɛ̃, ~'ɛn] marmoreal, marble...; **marmoriser** ⚗ [~ri'ze] (1a) *v/t.* marmarize.

marmot [mar'mo] *m* F brat; F *cro-quer le* ~ cool one's heels; wait.

marmotte [mar'mɔt] *f zo.* marmot, *Am.* woodchuck; ✝ case of samples; head-scarf.

marmotter [marmɔ'te] (1a) *v/t.* mumble, mutter.

marmouset [marmu'ze] *m fig.* F whipper-snapper, little chap; ⊕ fire-dog.

marne ✗, *geol.* [marn] *f* marl; **marner** [mar'ne] (1a) *v/t.* ✗ marl; *v/i.* ⚓ rise (*tide*).

marocain, e [marɔ'kɛ̃, ~'kɛn] *adj., a. su.* ♀ Moroccan.

maronner [marɔ'ne] (1a) *vt/i.* growl, mutter.

maroquin [marɔ'kɛ̃] *m* morocco (-leather); *pol.* F ministerial port-folio; **maroquiner** [~ki'ne] (1a) *v/t.* give a morocco finish to; make (*skin*) into morocco-leather; **maroquinerie** [~kin'ri] *f* fancy leather goods *pl.*

marotte [ma'rɔt] *f* (*fool's*) cap and bells *pl.*; *hairdresser etc.*: dummy head; F fad, F bee in the bonnet.

maroufle[1] ✝ [ma'rufl] *m* lout, hoo-ligan.

maroufle[2] [ma'rufl] *f* strong paste; **maroufler** [~ru'fle] (1a) *v/t.* re-mount (*a picture*); prime, size (*can-vas*); ✂ tape (*a seam*).

marquant, e [mar'kã, ~'kã:t] out-standing, prominent; **marque** [mark] *f* mark (*a.* ✝, *a. fig.*); ✝ brand, make (*a. mot.*); ✝ tally; *sp.* score; *fig.* token; *fig.* highest quality; ~ *au crayon* pencil mark; ~ *de fa-brique*, ~ *de fabrication* trade mark; brand (name); ~ *déposée* registered trademark; *de* ~ distinguished (*per-son*); ✝ F choice, best quality; **mar-quer** [mar'ke] (1m) *v/t.* mark; stamp; brand; *sp.* score (*goals, points*); *fig.* denote, indicate; *fig.* show (*one's age, one's feelings*); *fig.* emphasize; ascertain (*facts*); *fig.* watch, keep a watch on (*one's oppo-nent etc.*); ♪ ~ *la mesure* beat time; *v/i.* be outstanding; F ~ *mal* make a bad impression; **marqueter** [~kə'te] (1c) *v/t.* speckle; inlay (*wood*); **mar-queterie** [~kə'tri] *f* inlaid work, marquetry; *fig.* patchwork.

marqueur, -euse [mar'kœːr, ~'køːz] *su.* marker; *sp.* scorer.

marquis [mar'ki] *m* marquis, mar-quess; **marquise** [~'kiːz] *f* title: marchioness; marquee; awning, canopy.

marraine [ma'rɛn] *f* godmother; *eccl., a. fig.* sponsor.

marrant, e *sl.* [ma'rã, ~'rã:t] screamingly funny; odd.

marre *sl.* [ma:r] *f*: *en avoir* ~ be fed up (with, *de*); **marrer** *sl.* [ma're] (1a) *v/t.*: *se* ~ (have a good) laugh, F split one's sides.

marri, e ✝ [ma'ri] grieved.

marron[1] [ma'rõ] **1.** *su./m* ♀ (*edible*) chestnut; F blow; ♀ ~ *d'Inde* horse-chestnut; **2.** *adj./inv.* brown; chest-nut(-coloured).

marron[2], **-onne** [ma'rõ, ~'rɔn] un-qualified; unlicensed (*taxi-driver, trader, etc.*).

maronnier ♀ [marɔ'nje] *m* chestnut (-tree).

mars [mars] *m* March; *astr.* Mars; ✗ ~ *pl.* spring wheat *sg.*

marsouin [mar'swɛ̃] *m zo.* porpoise;

⚓ forecastle awning; ⚔ F colonial infantry soldier.

marsupial *m*, **-e** *f*, *m/pl.* **-aux** *zo.* [marsy'pjal, ~'pjo] *adj.*, *a. su./m* marsupial.

marteau [mar'to] *m* hammer (*a. ♪, a. anat.*); (*door-*)knocker; *clock:* striker; *icht.* hammerhead; ~ *pneumatique* pneumatic drill; ~**pilon**, *pl.* ~**x-pilons** *metall.* [~topi'lɔ̃] *m* power-hammer; forging-press.

martel [mar'tɛl] *m* † hammer; *fig.* se mettre ~ *en tête* worry; **marteler** [~tə'le] (1d) *v/t.* hammer; pound; *fig.* ~ *ses mots* speak each word with emphasis.

martial, e, *m/pl.* **-aux** [mar'sjal, ~'sjo] martial (*a. law*); soldierly; **martien, -enne** [~'sjɛ̃, ~'sjɛn] *adj.*, *a. su.* ♀ Martian.

martinet¹ [marti'nɛ] *m* ⊕ tilt-hammer; (*small*) whip.

martinet² *orn.* [~] *m* swift, martlet.

martin-pêcheur, *pl.* **martins-pê-cheurs** *orn.* [martɛ̃pɛ'fœːr] *m* king-fisher.

martre *zo.* [martr] *f* marten.

martyr *m*, **e** *f* [mar'tiːr] martyr; *enfant m* ~ battered child; **martyre** [~'tiːr] *m* martyrdom; *fig.* agonies *pl.*; **martyriser** [~tiri'ze] (1a) *v/t. eccl.* martyr; *fig.* torment; *fig.* make a martyr of.

marxiser [marksi'ze] (1a) *v/t.* make Marxist; se ~ become Marxist; **marxisme** *pol.* [mark'sism] *m* Marxism; **marxiste** *pol.* [~'sist] *adj.*, *a. su.* Marxist.

mas [mɑs] *m* small farmhouse.

mascarade [maska'rad] *f* masquer-ade (*a. fig.*).

mascaret [maska'rɛ] *m* bore, tidal wave.

mascotte [mas'kɔt] *f* mascot, charm.

masculin, e [masky'lɛ̃, ~'lin] **1.** *adj.* masculine; male; **2.** *su./m gramm.* masculine.

masochiste [mazɔ'fist] *su.* mas-ochist.

masque [mask] *m* mask (*a. fig.*); *fig.* cloak, cover; *thea.* masque; mas-querader; ~ *à gaz* gas-mask, respi-rator; **masquer** [mas'ke] (1m) *v/t.* mask; *fig.* conceal; ⚓ back (*a sail*).

massacrant, e [masa'krɑ̃, ~'krɑ̃ːt] *adj.*: *humeur f* ~*e* bad *or* F foul temper; **massacre** [~'sakr] *m* mas-

sacre; slaughter (*a. fig.*); **massa-crer** [masa'kre] (1a) *v/t.* massacre, slaughter; *fig.* make a hash of, ruin; murder (*music*); *tennis:* kill (*a ball*); **massacreur** *m*, **-euse** *f* [~'krœːr, ~'krøːz] slaughterer; *fig.* bungler; *fig. music:* murderer.

massage ⚕ [ma'saːʒ] *m* massage.

masse¹ [mas] *f* ⊕ sledge-hammer; (*ceremonial*) mace.

masse² [~] *f* ⚔, *phys.*, *fig.* mass; † bulk; ⚡ fund; ⚖ earth; *persons*, *water:* body; *fig.* crowd, heap; *en* ~ in a body; as a whole; *fig.* mass..., a great number of.

massé [ma'se] *m billiards:* massé (shot).

massepain [mas'pɛ̃] *m* marzipan.

masser¹ [ma'se] (1a) *v/t.* mass (*people*); se ~ form a crowd.

masser² [ma'se] (1a) *v/t.* ⚕ mas-sage; rub down (*a horse*); **masseur** [~'sœːr] *m* (*a.* ~ *kinésithérapeute*) masseur; **masseuse** [~'søːz] *f* mas-seuse.

massicot¹ ⚗, ⊕ [masi'ko] *m* yellow lead.

massicot² [~] *m books:* guillotine, trimmer.

massier [ma'sje] *m* mace-bearer.

massif, -ve [ma'sif, ~'siːv] **1.** *adj.* massive, bulky; heavy; solid (*gold*); **2.** *su./m* clump, cluster; △ block, solid mass; *geog.* mountain mass.

massue [ma'sy] *f* club (*a. zo.*, ⚕); *fig. en coup de* ~ sledge-hammer (*arguments*).

mastic [mas'tik] *m iron etc.:* mastic; *glazier:* cement; putty; *tooth:* fill-ing, stopping.

masticateur [mastika'tœːr] **1.** *adj./m* masticatory; **2.** *su./m* masticator; **masticatoire** [~'twaːr] **1.** *adj.* mas-ticatory; **2.** *su./m* ⚕ masticatory; chewing-gum.

mastiquer¹ [masti'ke] (1m) *v/t.* masticate; chew.

mastiquer² [~] (1m) *v/t.* ⊕ cement; stop (*a hole, a. a tooth*); putty (*a window*).

mastroquet F [mastrɔ'kɛ] *m* public-house keeper, F pub-keeper.

masure [ma'zyːr] *f* hovel, shack.

mat¹, mate [mat] *adj.* dull, flat, lustre-less (*colour*); heavy (*bread, dough*).

mat² [~] *adj./inv.* checkmated; *être* ~ be checkmate; *faire* ~ checkmate (*s.o.*).

mât [mɑ] *m* ⚓ mast; (*tent-*)pole; ⚓ strut; ~ *de pavillon* flagstaff, flagpole; 🚩 ~ *de signaux* signalpost; ⚓ *navire m à trois* ~*s* threemaster.

matador [mata'dɔːr] *m* matador; *fig.* magnate; *fig.* bigwig.

matamore [mata'mɔːr] *m* swashbuckler.

match, *pl. a.* **matches** *sp.* [matʃ] *m* match; ~ *de championnat* league match; ~ *de retard* match in hand; ~ *retour* return match.

matelas [mat'la] *m* mattress; ⊕ ~ *d'air* air-cushion; ~ *pneumatique* air-bed, air-mattress; **matelasser** [matla'se] (1a) *v/t.* pad; stuff; *porte f matelassée* baize door; **matelassier** *m*, **-ère** *f* [~'sje, ~'sjɛːr] mattress-maker; mattress-cleaner; **matelassure** [~'syːr] *f* padding, stuffing.

matelot [mat'lo] *m* sailor; **matelote** [~'lɔt] *f cuis.* matelote; † (*approx.*) hornpipe; *à la* ~ sailor-fashion.

mater[1] [ma'te] (1a) *v/t.* mat, dull; ⊕ hammer; work (*the dough*).

mater[2] [~] (1a) *v/t.* (check)mate (*at chess*); *fig.* subdue, humble.

mâter ⚓ [mɑ'te] (1a) *v/t.* mast; rig (*booms*); up-end (*a boat*).

matérialiser [materjali'ze] (1a) *v/t. a. se* ~ materialize; **matérialisme** [~'lism] *m* (~ *dialectique* dialectic) materialism; **matérialiste** 1. *adj.* materialistic; 2. *su.* materialist; **matériau** △ [~'rjo] *m* material; **matériaux** ⊕, △, *fig.* [~'rjo] *m/pl.* materials; **matériel, -elle** [~'rjɛl] 1. *adj.* material; physical; *fig.* sensual; ⚡ *dommages m/pl.* ~*s* damage *sg.* to property; *vie f* ~*elle* necessities *pl.* of life; 2. *su./m* ⊕ plant; apparatus; *school, a.* ⚓: furniture; *war:* material; *computer:* hardware; ~ *humain* manpower; men *pl.*; 🚩 ~ *roulant* rolling stock.

maternel, -elle [matɛr'nɛl] maternal; mother (*tongue*); *école f* ~*elle* infant school; **maternité** [~ni'te] *f* maternity, motherhood; maternity hospital.

mathématicien *m*, **-enne** *f* [matemati'sjɛ̃, ~'sjɛn] mathematician; **mathématique** [~'tik] 1. *adj.* mathematical; 2. *su./f:* ~*s pl.* mathematics; ~*s pl. spéciales* higher mathematics.

matière [ma'tjɛːr] *f* material; matter,

substance; *fig.* subject; *fig.* grounds *pl.* (*oft.* ⚡); *anat.*, *fig.* ~ *grise* grey matter; ~*s pl. premières* raw material *sg.*; ⊕~*s plastiques* plastics; *en* ~ *de* as regards; in matters of; *en la* ~ on the subject; *entrer en* ~ broach the subject; *table f des* ~*s* table of contents.

matin [ma'tɛ̃] 1. *su./m* morning; *au* ~ in the morning; *de bon* (*or grand*) ~, *au petit* ~ early in the morning; 2. *adv.* early.

mâtin [mɑ'tɛ̃] *su./m* mastiff hound.

matinal, e, *m/pl.* **-aux** [mati'nal, ~'no] morning...; early; *être* ~ be an early riser (*person*); **matinée** [~'ne] *f* morning, forenoon; morning's work; *cost.* wrapper; *thea.* matinee, afternoon performance; *faire la grasse* ~ sleep late, F have a lie in; **matines** *eccl.* [ma'tin] *f/pl.* mat(t)ins; **matineux, -euse** [mati'nø, ~'nøːz] 1. *adj.* early rising; 2. *su.* early riser; **matinier, -ère** [~'nje, ~'njɛːr] *adj.:* *l'étoile f* ~*ère* the morning star. {⊕ hammer.}

matir [ma'tiːr] (2a) *v/t.* mat, dull;

matois, e [ma'twa, ~'twaːz] 1. *adj.* sly, foxy, cunning; 2. *su.* crafty person.

matou *zo.* [ma'tu] *m* tom-cat.

matraquage [matra'kaːʒ] *m* bludgeoning, *etc.*; *see matraquer*; **matraque** [ma'trak] *f* bludgeon; rubber truncheon; **matraquer** [matra'ke] (1a) *v/t.* bludgeon, beat (*s.o.*) up; *fig.* overcharge (*customer, etc.*), overburden (*tax-payer etc.*); *fig.* bombard (*the public*); *fig.* plug (*a song, etc.*).

matriarcat [matriar'ka] *m* matriarchy; **matrice** [~'tris] 1. *su./f* matrix; ⊕ die; ⊕ master record; *typ.* type mo(u)ld; *anat.* womb, uterus; 2. *adj.* primary (*colour*); mother (*church, tongue*); **matricer** ⊕ [matri'se] (1k) *v/t.* stamp (out); swage; **matricide** [~'sid] 1. *su.* person: matricide; *su./m* crime: matricide; 2. *adj.* matricidal.

matricule [matri'kyl] *su./f* roll, register; registration; *su./m* registration or reference number; ✕ regimental number; *sl.* *ça devient mauvais pour son* ~ his number is up, things are going to be hot for him.

matrimonial, e, *m/pl.* **-aux** [matrimɔ'njal, ~'njo] matrimonial.

matrone [ma'trɔn] *f* matron.

maturation [matyra'sjɔ̃] *f* ripening; *tobacco:* maturing.

mâture ⚓ [mɑ'tyːr] f masting; coll. masts pl.; sheer-legs pl.

maturité [matyri'te] f maturity; ripeness; avec ～ after mature consideration.

matutinal, e, m/pl. **-aux** [matyti-'nal, ～'no] matutinal.

maudire [mo'diːr] (4p) v/t. curse; fig. grumble about; **maudit, e** [～'di, ～'dit] **1.** p.p. of maudire; **2.** adj. (ac)cursed; fig. execrable, damnable.

maugréer [mogre'e] (1a) v/i. curse; fig. grumble (about, at contre).

maure [mɔːr] **1.** adj./m Moorish; **2.** su./m ♀ Moor; **mauresque** [mɔ-'rɛsk] **1.** adj. Moorish; △ Moresque; **2.** su./f ♀ Moorish woman.

mausolée [mozɔ'le] m mausoleum.

maussade [mo'sad] surly, sullen; fig. depressing, dull (weather); irritable (person, tone); **maussaderie** [～sa'dri] f sullenness; irritability, peevishness.

mauvais, e [mɔ've, ～'veːz] **1.** adj. bad (a. influence, news, ⌘ season); evil, wicked; wrong; ill; nasty, unpleasant; offensive (smell); ✶ severe (illness); ～e excuse lame excuse; ～e foi dishonesty; unfairness; ～e tête unruly or obstinate 'person; de ～e humeur in a bad temper; **2.** mauvais adv.: il fait ～ the weather is bad; sentir ～ smell bad, stink.

mauve [moːv] su./f ♀ mallow; su./m, a. adj. mauve, purple.

mauviette [mo'vjɛt] f orn. skylark; fig. frail person; **mauvis** orn. [～'vi] m redwing.

maxillaire anat. [maksil'lɛːr] m jaw-bone; ～ supérieur maxilla.

maximal, e, m/pl. **-aux** [maksi'mal, ～'mo] maximal; **maxime** [mak'sim] f maxim; **maximiser** [～simi'ze] (1a) v/t. maximize; **maximum**, pl. a. **maxima** [～si'mɔm, ～'ma] su./m, a. adj. maximum; porter au ～ maximize.

mayonnaise cuis. [majɔ'nɛːz] f mayonnaise.

mazout [ma'zut] m fuel oil; crude oil.

me [mə] **1.** pron./pers. me; to me; ～ voici! here I am!; **2.** pron./rfl. myself, to myself.

méandre [me'ɑ̃ːdr] m wind(ing), bend; faire des ～s meander, wind (river).

mec F [mɛk] m gay, fellow.

mécanicien [mekani'sjɛ̃] m mechanic; engineer; ⚙ engine driver, Am. engineer; **mécanique** [～'nik] **1.** adj. mechanical; **2.** su./f mechanics sg.; mechanism, (piece of) machinery; engineering; phys. ～ ondulatoire wave-mechanics sg.; **mécaniser** [～ni'ze] (1a) v/t. mechanize; turn (s.o.) into a machine; **mécanisme** [～'nism] m mechanism; machinery.

mécano ⊕ F [meka'no] m mechanic.

méchamment [meʃa'mɑ̃] adv. of méchant; **méchanceté** [～ʃɑ̃s'te] f nastiness; meanness; malice, spite; spiteful remark or action; **méchant, e** [～'ʃɑ̃, ～'ʃɑ̃ːt] **1.** adj. nasty; mean; bad; spiteful; fig. † poor, sorry, paltry; il n'est pas ～ he's all right; he's harmless; **2.** su./m naughty boy; su./f naughty girl.

mèche¹ [mɛʃ] f candle, lamp: wick; ✂ match fuse; whip: cracker, Am. snapper; hair: lock; ⊕ bit, drill; éventer la ～ discover a secret; vendre la ～ let the cat out of the bag, sl. blow the gaff.

mèche² F [～] f: de ～ avec in collusion with; hand in glove with; il n'y a pas ～! it can't be done!

mécompte [me'kɔ̃ːt] m miscalculation, mistake in reckoning, error; fig. disappointment.

méconnaissable [mekɔnɛ'sabl] unrecognizable; hardly recognizable; **méconnaissance** [～nɛ'sɑ̃ːs] f failure to recognize; **méconnaître** [～'nɛːtr] (4k) v/t. refuse to recognize, cut; fig. not to appreciate; fig. underrate; fig. disown.

mécontent, e [mekɔ̃'tɑ̃, ～'tɑ̃ːt] dissatisfied, discontented (with, de); annoyed (at, de; that, que); **mécontentement** [～tɑ̃t'mɑ̃] m dissatisfaction (with, de); displeasure, annoyance (at, de); pol. disaffection; **mécontenter** [～tɑ̃'te] (1a) v/t. dissatisfy; displease, annoy.

mécréant, e [mekre'ɑ̃, ～'ɑ̃ːt] **1.** adj. unbelieving; heterodox; **2.** su. unbeliever; misbeliever; miscreant.

médaille [me'daːj] f medal; badge; △ medallion; **médaillé, e** [meda-'je] **1.** adj. decorated; holding a medal; **2.** su. medallist; medal-winner, prize-winner; **médaillier** [～'je] m medal cabinet; collection of medals; **médailliste** [～'jist] m collector of medals; medal-maker; **médaillon** [∼'jõ] *m* medallion; locket; *journ.* inset; *cuis.* butter: pat; *cuis.* medaillon.

médecin [met'sɛ̃] *m* doctor, physician; ⚓ ∼ *du bord* ship's doctor; ∼ *légiste* medical expert; ∼ *traitant* doctor in charge of the case; *femme f* ∼ lady doctor; **médecine** [∼'sin] *f* medicine; ∼ *légale* forensic medicine.

media, média [me'dja] *m/pl.* (mass) media.

médian, e [me'djɑ̃, ∼'djan] median; middle...; *foot.* half-way (*line*); **médiat, e** [∼'dja, ∼'djat] mediate; **médiateur, -trice** [medja'tœːr, ∼'tris] 1. *adj.* mediatory; 2. *su.* mediator; intermediary; *pol.* ombudsman; **médiation** [∼'sjõ] *f* mediation.

médical, e, *m/pl.* **-aux** [medi'kal, ∼'ko] medical; **médicalisation** [∼kaliza'sjõ] *f* medical care; **medicaliser** [∼kali'ze] (1a) *v/t.* provide medical care for; **médicament** [medika'mɑ̃] *m* medicament, F medicine; **médicamenter** [∼mɑ̃'te] (1a) *v/t.* doctor, dose (*s.o.*); **médicamenteux, -euse** [∼mɑ̃'tø, ∼'tøːz] medicinal; **médicastre** [medi'kastr] *m* quack (doctor); **médication** [∼ka'sjõ] *f* medical treatment, medication; **médicinal, e,** *m/pl.* **-aux** [∼si'nal, ∼'no] medicinal; **médico-legal, e,** *m/pl.* **-aux** [∼kole'gal, ∼'go] medico-legal.

médiéval, e, *m/pl.* **-aux** [medje'val, ∼'vo] medi(a)eval; **médiéviste** [∼'vist] *su.* medi(a)evalist.

médiocre [me'djɔkr] mediocre; poor, second-rate; indifferent; **médiocrité** [∼djɔkri'te] *f* mediocrity; F *person*: second-rater.

médire [me'diːr] (4p) *v/i.*: ∼ *de q.* slander s.o., speak ill of s.o., F run s.o. down; **médisance** [medi'zɑ̃s] *f* slander; scandal-mongering; **médisant, e** [∼'zɑ̃, ∼'zɑ̃:t] 1. *adj.* slanderous; backbiting; 2. *su.* slanderer; scandal-monger.

méditatif, -ve [medita'tif, ∼'tiːv] meditative; contemplative, pensive; **méditation** [∼ta'sjõ] *f* meditation (*a. eccl.*); cogitation, thought; **méditer** [∼'te] (1a) *v/i.* meditate; *v/t.* contemplate (*s.th.*).

méditerrané, e *geog.* [mediterra'ne] mediterranean.

médium [me'djɔm] *m psychics:* medium; ♪ middle register.

médius *anat.* [me'djys] *m* middle finger.

médullaire ♀, *anat.* [medyl'lɛːr] medullary.

méduse [me'dyːz] *f* jelly-fish; **méduser** [∼dy'ze] (1a) *v/t.* dumbfound; petrify.

meeting *sp., pol.* [mi'tiŋ] *m* meeting.

méfaire † [me'fɛːr] *v/i.* occurs only in *inf.* do wrong; **méfait** [∼'fɛ] *m* misdeed; *fig.* ill or damaging effect, ravages *pl.*

méfiance [me'fjɑ̃:s] *f* distrust; **méfiant, e** [∼'fjɑ̃, ∼'fjɑ̃:t] suspicious, distrustful; **méfier** [∼'fje] (1o) *v/t.*: *se* ∼ be on one's guard; *se* ∼ *de* be suspicious of, distrust; look out for, watch.

mégalo... [megalo] megalo...; **∼mane** [∼'man] *su.* megalomaniac; **∼manie** [∼ma'ni] *f* megalomania; **∼pole** [∼'pɔl] *f* megalopolis.

mégaphone [mega'fɔn] *m* megaphone.

mégarde [me'gard] *f*: *par* ∼ inadvertently; accidentally.

mégatonne [mega'tɔn] *f* megaton.

mégère [me'ʒɛːr] *f* shrew, termagant.

mégot F [me'go] *m cigarette:* fag end, *Am.* butt; *cigar:* stump; (poor) cigar; **mégoter** F [∼gɔ'te] (1a) *v/i.* skimp (on, *sur*).

meilleur, e [mɛ'jœːr] 1. *adj.* better; *le* ∼ the better (*of two*), the best (*of several*); 2. *su./m* best (thing).

mélancolie [melɑ̃kɔ'li] *f* melancholy, gloom; ✲ melancholia; **mélancolique** [∼'lik] mournful, gloomy, melancholy; ✲ melancholic.

mélange [me'lɑ̃:ʒ] *m* mixture, blend; *cards:* shuffling; ∼*s pl.* miscellany *sg.*; ∼ *réfrigérant* freezing-mixture; **mélanger** [melɑ̃'ʒe] (1l) *v/t. a. se* ∼ mix; blend; **mélangeur** [∼'ʒœːr] *m* mixing-machine, mixer.

mélasse [me'las] *f* molasses *pl.*, treacle; *sl. dans la* ∼ in the soup.

mêlée [mɛ'le] *f* ✖ mêlée, fray; scuffle; scramble; *sp. rugby:* scrum; **mêler** [∼] (1a) *v/t.* mix; mingle, blend; ∼ *q. à* (*or dans*) involve s.o. in; *se* ∼ *à* join; mix with; *se* ∼ *de* meddle in, interfere in or with; dabble in (*politics*).

méninge

mélèze ♣ [me'lɛ:z] *m* larch.

mélilot ♣ [meli'lo] *m* sweet clover, melilot.

méli-mélo, *pl.* **mélis-mélos** F [melime'lo] *m* jumble; clutter; hotchpotch.

mellifère [mɛlli'fɛ:r] honey-bearing; **mellifique** [‿'fik] mellific, honey-making; **melliflue** *fig.* [‿'fly] mellifluous, honeyed.

mélodie [melɔ'di] *f* ♩ melody, tune; melodiousness; **mélodieux, -euse** [‿'djø, ‿'djø:z] melodious, tuneful; **mélodique** ♩ [‿'dik] melodic; **mélodrame** [‿'dram] *m* melodrama; **mélomane** [‿'man] **1.** *adj.* mad on music; **2.** *su.* melomaniac.

melon [mə'lɔ̃] *m* ♣ melon; bowler (hat).

membrane [mã'bran] *f* ♣, *anat.*, ⊕ membrane; *zo.* duck, goose, etc.: web; **membraneux, -euse** [‿bra-'nø, ‿'nø:z] membranous.

membre [mã:br] *m* member; *body:* limb; ♣ rib; **membré, e** [mã'bre] *adj.:* bien ‿ well-limbed; **membru, e** [‿'bry] strong-limbed; biglimbed; **membrure** [‿'bry:r] *f coll.* limbs *pl.*, ⚓ ribs *pl.*; 𝄞 frame.

même [mɛ:m] **1.** *adj.* same; *after noun:* self, very; ce ‿ soir the same evening; ce soir ‿ this very evening; en ‿ temps at the same time; la bonté ‿ kindness itself; les ‿s personnes the same persons; *see* vousmême; **2.** *adv.* even; à ‿ de (*inf.*) able to (*inf.*), in a position to (*inf.*); boire à ‿ la bouteille drink out of the bottle; de ‿ in the same way, likewise; de ‿ que like, (just) as; pas ‿ not even; quand ‿ even if; all the same; tout de ‿ all the same; voire ‿ ... indeed ...

mémère F [me'mɛ:r] *f* mother; mum(my); grandmother, F granny.

mémoire[1] [me'mwa:r] *f* memory; de ‿ by heart, from memory; de ‿ d'homme within living memory; en ‿ de in memory of.

mémoire[2] [‿] *m* memorandum; memorial; memoir, dissertation; 🕮 abstract; ‿s *pl.* transactions; ♀s *pl.* (historical) memoirs.

mémorable [memɔ'rabl] memorable, noteworthy; **mémorial** [‿'rjal] *m* Gazette; ♀ memoirs *pl.*; **mémorialiste** [‿rja'list] *m* memorialist.

menace [mə'nas] *f* threat, menace; **menacer** [‿na'se] (1k) *v/t.* threaten (with, de).

ménage [me'na:ʒ] *m* housekeeping; housework; † set of furniture; *fig.* household, family; *fig.* married couple; faire bon ‿ (avec) get on well (with); faire le ‿ do the housework; faux ‿ unmarried couple living together; femme *f* de ‿ charwoman, cleaner; être heureux en ‿ be happily married; jeune ‿ newly married couple; monter son ‿ set up house; tenir le ‿ de keep house for; **ménagement** [‿naʒ'mã] *m* care; consideration, caution.

ménager[1] [mena'ʒe] (1l) *v/t.* save; use economically, make the most of; arrange; provide.

ménager[2], **-ère** [mena'ʒe, ‿'ʒɛ:r] **1.** *adj.* domestic; *fig.* thrifty, sparing (of, de); enseignement *m* ‿ domestic science; **2.** *su./f* housewife; housekeeper; canteen of cutlery; cruet-stand; **ménagerie** [‿naʒ'ri] *f* menagerie.

mendiant, e [mã'djã, ‿'djã:t] **1.** *adj.* mendicant; *su.* beggar; *su./m:* F les quatre ‿s *pl.* figs, raisins, almonds and hazel-nuts as dessert; **mendicité** [‿disi'te] *f* begging; beggary; beggardom; **mendier** [‿'dje] (1o) *v/i.* beg; *v/t.* beg for; ‿ des compliments fish for compliments; **mendigot** F [‿di'go] *m* beggar.

meneau ⌂ [mə'no] *m* mullion; à ‿x mullioned.

menée [mə'ne] *f* hunt. track; *fig.* manœuvre, intrigue.

mener [‿] (1d) *v/t.* lead; take, get (s.o. to, q. à); 🐎 draw (a line); *fig.* run, control, manage; steer (a boat); ‿ qch. à bien (or à bonne fin) see s.th. through; ‿ par le bout du nez lead by the nose; cela peut le ‿ loin that may take him a long way; *v/i.* lead (to, à).

ménestrel *hist.* [menɛs'trɛl] *m* minstrel; **ménétrier** [‿ne'trje] *m* village musician, fiddler.

meneur [mə'nœ:r] *m* leader; ringleader; driver; *pej.* agitator, fomenter; ‿ de jeu emcee, *Br. a.* compère; quizmaster.

menhir *geol.* [me'ni:r] *m* menhir.

méninge [menɛ̃ʒ] *m anat.* meninx; F ‿s *pl.* brains; F se creuser les ‿s rack one's brains; F se fatiguer les ‿s

overtax one's brains; **méningite** ⚕
[menɛ̃'ʒit] *f* meningitis.

ménisque *anat.* [me'nisk] *m* meniscus.

ménopause ⚕ [menɔ'poːz] *f* menopause.

menotte [mə'nɔt] *f* ⊕ handle; *mot.
etc.* link; F little hand; ~s *pl.* handcuffs.

mensonge [mã'sɔ̃ːʒ] *m* lie, falsehood; *fig.* delusion; ~ *officieux* (*or
pieux*) white lie; **mensonger, -ère**
[~sɔ̃'ʒe, ~'ʒɛːr] untrue; false; *fig.*
illusory.

mensualité [mãsu̯ali'te] *f* monthly
payment *or* instalment; monthly
salary; **mensuel, -elle** [~'su̯ɛl] 1.
adj. monthly; 2. *su.* employee paid
by the month.

mensurations [mãsyra'sjɔ̃] *f/pl.*
measurements.

mental, e, *m/pl.* **-aux** [mã'tal, ~'to]
mental; *restriction f* ~e mental reservation; **mentalité** [~tali'te] *f* mentality.

menterie F [mã'tri] *f* lie, F fib;
menteur, -euse [~'tœːr, ~'tøːz] 1.
adj. lying; deceptive, false; 2. *su.* liar,
F fibber.

menthe ♀ [mãːt] *f* mint.

mention [mã'sjɔ̃] *f* mention; *faire ~
de* = **mentionner** [~sjɔ'ne] (1a) *v/t.*
mention; name.

mentir [mã'tiːr] (2b) *v/i.* lie (to, *à*).

menton [mã'tɔ̃] *m* chin; **mentonnet** [mãtɔ'nɛ] *m* ⊕ catch; ⊕ lug;
🚂 flange; **mentonnière** [~'njɛːr] *f*
(*bonnet-*)string; ⚕ chin-bandage; ✕
check-strap; ♪ *violin*: chin-rest.

mentor [mɛ̃'tɔːr] *m* mentor.

menu, e [mə'ny] 1. *adj.* small; fine;
minute (*details, fragments*); slim,
slender (*figure*); petty, trifling;
2. *menu adv.* small, fine; *hacher ~
mince*; *chop* (*s.th.*) up small; 3. *su./m*
detail; *meal*: menu; ~ *à prix fixe*
table d'hôte; *par le ~* in detail.

menuiser [mənɥi'ze] (1a) *v/t.* cut
(*wood*) down; *v/i.* do woodwork;
menuiserie [~nɥiz'ri] *f* woodwork,
carpentry; joiner's shop; **menuisier** [~nɥi'zje] *m* joiner; carpenter.

méphitique [mefi'tik] noxious,
foul; *gaz m* ~ choke-damp.

méplat, e [me'pla, ~'plat] 1. *adj.*
flat; ⚔ flat-laid; in planks (*wood*);
2. *su./m* flat part; *geol. rock*: ledge.

méprendre [me'prãːdr] (4aa) *v/t.*:

se ~ sur be mistaken about, misjudge; *fig. à s'y ~* to the life; *il n'y
a pas à s'y ~* there can be no mistake.

mépris [me'pri] *m* contempt, scorn;
au ~ de in defiance of, contrary to;
méprisable [mepri'zabl] contemptible; **méprisant, e** [~'zã,
~'zãːt] scornful, contemptuous.

méprise [me'priːz] *f* mistake.

mépriser [mepri'ze] (1a) *v/t.* despise; scorn.

mer [mɛːr] *f* sea; tide; ~ *haute* high
tide; *haute ~* open sea; *porter de
l'eau à la ~* carry coals to Newcastle.

mercanti F [mɛrkã'ti] *m* profiteer;
mercantile [~'til] profit-minded,
mercenary; *esprit m ~* (absolute)
profit-mindedness.

mercenaire [mɛrsə'nɛːr] 1. *adj.*
mercenary (*a.* ✕); 2. *su./m* hireling;
✕ mercenary.

mercerie [mɛrsə'ri] *f* haberdashery;
haberdasher's (shop), *Am.* notions
shop.

merci [mɛr'si] 1. *adv.* thank you,
thanks (for, *de*); ~ *bien,* ~ *beaucoup*
many thanks, thank you very much;
2. *su./m* thanks *pl.*; *su./f* mercy; *à la ~
de* at the mercy of; *crier ~* cry mercy,
beg for mercy; *sans ~* pitiless(ly
adv.), merciless(ly *adv.*).

mercier *m,* **-ère** *f* [mɛr'sje, ~'sjɛːr]
haberdasher; small-ware dealer.

mercredi [mɛrkrə'di] *m* Wednesday.

mercure ⚕ [mɛr'kyːr] *m* mercury,
quicksilver; **mercureux** ⚕ [~ky'rø]
adj./m mercurous.

mercuriale [mɛrky'rjal] *f* ♀ market-
prices *pl.*; F *fig.* reprimand.

mercuriel, -elle [mɛrky'rjɛl] mercurial.

merde V [mɛrd] 1. *su./f* shit; 2. *int.*
hell!; **merdier** *sl.* [mɛr'dje] *m* (hell
of a) mess.

mère [mɛːr] *f* mother (*a. fig.*); ⊕ die;
mo(u)ld; *fig.* source, root; ~(-)*célibataire* unmarried mother; ~ *patrie*
mother country; ♀ *maison f ~* head
office.

méridien, -enne [meri'djɛ̃, ~'djɛn]
1. *adj. geog.* meridian; midday;
astr. transit; 2. *su./m* meridian; *su./f*
meridian line; midday nap; sofa;
méridional, e, *m/pl.* **-aux** [~djo-
'nal, ~'no] 1. *adj.* south(ern); me-

ridional; **2.** *su.* southerner; merid-
ional.

meringue *cuis.* [mə'rɛ̃:g] *f* meringue.

mérinos ✝, *zo.* [meri'nos] *m* me-
rino.

merise ♀ [mə'ri:z] *f* wild cherry;
merisier [⁓ri'zje] *m* wild cherry
(-tree).

mérite [me'rit] *m* merit; quality;
ability; *sans* ⁓ undeserving; **mériter** [meri'te] (1a) *vt/i.* deserve,
merit; **méritoire** [⁓'twa:r] merito-
rious, praiseworthy, commendable.

merlan [mɛr'lɑ̃] *m icht.* whiting; *sl.*
hairdresser; **merle** [mɛrl] *m orn.*
blackbird; F *fig.* ⁓ *blanc* rara avis;
F *fig. fin* ⁓ sly fellow.

merluche [mɛr'lyʃ] *f icht.* hake;
✝ dried cod.

merrain [mɛ'rɛ̃] *m* ⊕ stave-wood;
wood for cooperage; *deer's antlers*:
beam.

merveille [mɛr'vɛːj] *f* marvel, wonder; *à* ⁓ magnificently, F fine; **merveilleux, -euse** [⁓vɛ'jø, ⁓'jø:z]
marvellous, wonderful; supernatural.

mes [me] *see* mon.

més... [mez] mis...; **⁓alliance** [me-
za'ljɑ̃:s] *f* misalliance.

mésange *orn.* [me'zɑ̃:ʒ] *f* tit(mouse);
mésangette [⁓zɑ̃'ʒɛt] *f* bird-trap.

mésaventure [mezavɑ̃'ty:r] *f* mis-
adventure, mishap, mischance.

mesdames [me'dam] *pl. of madame;* **mesdemoiselles** [medmwa-
'zɛl] *pl. of mademoiselle.*

mésentente [mezɑ̃'tɑ̃:t] *f* misunderstanding, disagreement.

mésentère *anat.* [mezɑ̃'tɛ:r] *m*
mesentery.

mésestimer [mezɛsti'me] (1a) *v/t.*
underestimate; hold (*s.o.*) in low
esteem.

mésintelligence [mezɛ̃teli'ʒɑ̃:s] *f*
disagreement; *en* ⁓ *avec* at loggerheads with.

mesquin, e [mɛs'kɛ̃, ⁓'kin] mean,
stingy; **mesquinerie** [⁓kin'ri] *f*
meanness; pettiness.

mess ✗ [mɛs] *m* mess.

message [mɛ'sa:ʒ] *m* message (*a.
fig.*); **messager** *m*, **-ère** *f* [⁓sa'ʒe,
⁓'ʒɛ:r] messenger, *fig.* harbinger;
messageries [⁓saʒ'ri] *f/pl.* delivery
or distribution service *sg.*; shipping
(company) *sg.*

messe *eccl., a.* ♪ [mɛs] *f* mass.

messeoir [mɛ'swa:r] (3k) *v/i.* be
unbecoming (to, *à*).

Messie *bibl.* [mɛ'si] *m* Messiah.

messieurs [mɛ'sjø] *pl. of monsieur.*

mesurable [məzy'rabl] measurable;
mesurage [⁓'ra:ʒ] *m* measurement;
mesure [mə'zy:r] *f* measure; measurement; extent, degree; step; *fig.*
moderation; *verse:* metre; ♪ time;
♪ bar; *à* ⁓ one by one; in proportion; *à* ⁓ *que* (in proportion) as;
donner sa ⁓ show what one is capable of; *en* ⁓ *de* in a position to;
outre ⁓ excessively, beyond measure; *poids m/pl. et* ⁓*s pl.* weights
and measures; *prendre des* ⁓*s contre*
take steps *or* measures against; *fig.*
prendre la ⁓ *de q.* size s.o. up;
prendre les ⁓*s de q.* take s.o.'s measurements; *fig. sans* ⁓ boundless; *sur* ⁓
to measure; to order; **mesurer**
[məzy're] (1a) *v/t.* measure; calculate; *fig.* estimate; se ⁓ *avec* pit o.s.
against; **mesureur** [⁓'rœ:r] *m person, machine:* measurer; ga(u)ge; ♀
metre.

méta... [meta] meta...

métairie [mete'ri] *f* small farm.

métal [me'tal] *m* metal; ⁓ *brut* (*commun*) raw (base) metal; **métallifère** [metalli'fɛ:r] metalliferous;
métallique [⁓'lik] metallic; wire
(*rope*); ✝ *encaisse f* ⁓ gold reserve;
métalliser ⊕ [⁓li'ze] (1a) *v/t.*
cover with metal, plate; metallize;
métallo F [⁓'lo] *m* metal-worker;
métallurgie ⊕ [⁓lyr'ʒi] *f* metallurgy; smelting; **métallurgiste** ⊕
[⁓lyr'ʒist] *m* metallurgist; metal-
worker.

méta...: ⁓morphose [metamɔr'fo:z]
f metamorphosis, transformation;
⁓morphoser [⁓mɔrfo'ze] (1a) *v/t.*
metamorphose; se ⁓ change; **⁓-
phore** [⁓'fɔ:r] *f* metaphor; image;
⁓phorique [⁓fɔ'rik] metaphorical;
⁓physique [⁓fi'zik] *f* metaphysics
sg.; **⁓psychique** [⁓psi'ʃik] *f* para-
psychology; **⁓stase** ✚ [⁓'sta:z] *f*
metastasis.

métayer [mete'je] *m* metayer, tenant
farmer; *Am.* share-cropper.

métempsycose [metɑ̃psi'ko:z] *f*
metempsychosis.

météo [mete'o] *su./f* weather report;
meteorological office; *su./m* meteor-
ologist; weather man; **météore**
[⁓'ɔ:r] *m* meteor; **météorisme** [⁓ɔ-

'rism] *m* 🐟 meteorism; flatulence; *vet.* hoove; **météorologie** [~ɔrɔlɔ-'ʒi] *f* meteorology.

métèque *pej.* [meˈtɛk] *m sl.* wop, *Br. sl.* wog.

méthode [meˈtɔd] *f* method, system; way; **méthodique** [~tɔˈdik] methodical, systematic.

méticuleux, -euse [metikyˈlø, ~ˈløːz] meticulous, punctilious, F fussy.

métier [meˈtje] *m* job; trade; craft; profession; (~ *à tisser* weaving) loom.

métis, -isse [meˈtis] **1.** *su.* half-breed; *dog:* mongrel; **2.** *adj.* half-bred; cross-bred; mongrel (*dog*).

métrage [meˈtraːʒ] *m* measurement; metric length; *cin.* court (*long*)~ short (full-length) film; **mètre** [mɛtr] *m* metre, *Am.* meter; rule, yardstick; ~ *à ruban* tape measure; ~ *carré* square metre; ~ *cube* cubic metre; ~ *pliant* folding rule; **métrique** [~ˈtrik] **1.** *adj.* metric; **2.** *su./f* metrics *sg.*

métro F [meˈtro] *m* underground railway, tube, *Am.* subway.

métro...: ~**logie** [metrɔlɔˈʒi] *f* metrology; ~**manie** [~maˈni] *f* metromania; ~**nome** ♪ [~ˈnɔm] *m* metronome.

métropole [metrɔˈpɔl] *f* metropolis; capital; mother country; **métropolitain, e** [~pɔliˈtɛ̃, ~ˈtɛn] **1.** *adj.* metropolitan; **2.** *su./m* metropolitan; *eccl.* archbishop; underground railway.

mets¹ [mɛ] *m* food; dish; ~ *tout préparé* ready-to-serve meal.

mets² [~] *1st p. sg. pres. of* mettre.

mettable [mɛˈtabl] wearable (*clothes*); **metteur** [~ˈtœːr] *m* ⊕ setter; 🎬 (*plate-*)layer; ~ *en scène thea.* producer; *cin.* director.

mettre [mɛtr] (4v) *v/t.* put; place, set; lay (*a. the table*); put on (*clothes*); translate (into, *en*); bet (on, *sur*); *fig.* suppose, assume; ~ *à l'aise* put (*s.o.*) at his ease; ⚡ ~ *à la terre* earth; ~ *au point* adjust; *opt.* focus (*a lens*); *fig.* clarify (*an affair*); ~ *bas* lamb (*sheep*), litter, whelp (*bitch*), foal (*mare*), farrow (*pig*), calve (*cow*); ~ *de côté* save; ~ *deux heures à* (*inf.*) take two hours to (*inf.*); ~ *en colère* make angry; ~ *en jeu* bring into play *or* discussion; ⊕ ~ *en marche* start (*a. fig.*); *typ.* ~ *en pages* make up; *thea.* ~ *en*

scène stage; *mettons que ce soit vrai* let us suppose this to be true *or* that this is true; *se* ~ place o.s., stand; *se* ~ *à* (*inf.*) begin (*ger.*, to *inf.*); start (*ger.*), take to; *se* ~ *à l'œuvre* set to work; *se* ~ *en colère* get angry; *se* ~ *en gala* put on formal dress; *se* ~ *en route* start out; *se* ~ *ensemble* live together (*unmarried couple*); *se* ~ *en tête de* (*inf.*) take it into one's head to (*inf.*); *s'y* ~ set about it.

meublant, e [mœˈblɑ̃, ~ˈblɑ̃ːt] decorative, effective, nice; **meuble** [mœbl] **1.** *adj.* movable; loose (*ground*); 🏛 *biens m/pl.* ~s movables; **2.** *su./m* piece of furniture; ~s *pl.* furniture *sg.*; **meublé, e** [mœˈble] **1.** *adj.*: (*non*) ~ (un)furnished; **2.** *su./m* furnished room; **meubler** [~] (1a) *v/t.* furnish; fig. fill (with, *de*).

meule¹ [mœːl] *f* hay: stack, rick; *charcoal:* pile; *bricks:* clamp; 🌱 *mushrooms:* bed.

meule² [mœːl] *f* ⊕ millstone; grindstone; ~ *de fromage* large round cheese; **meuler** ⊕ [mœˈle] (1a) *v/t.* grind; **meulerie** [møl-'ri] *f* millstone-factory, grindstone-factory; **meulier** ⊕ [møˈlje] *m* millstone-maker, grindstone-maker; **meulière** ⊕ [~ˈljɛːr] *f* millstone grit; millstone quarry.

meulon [møˈlɔ̃] *m* small haystack; *corn:* stook; (*hay*)cock.

meunerie [mønˈri] *f flour:* milling; **meunier** [møˈnje] miller; **meunière** [~ˈnjɛːr] *f* woman mill-owner, *a.* miller's wife.

meurent [mœːr] *3rd p. pl. pres. of* mourir; **meurs** [~] *1st p. sg. pres. of* mourir; **meurt-de-faim** F [mœrdəˈfɛ̃] *m/inv.* starveling; *de* ~ starvation (*wage*).

meurtre [mœrtr] *m* murder; 🏛 non-capital murder, *Am.* murder in the second degree; *au* ~! murder!; *fig. c'est un* ~ it is a downright shame; **meurtrier, -ère** [mœrtriˈe, ~ˈɛːr] **1.** *adj.* murderous; guilty of murder (*person*); **2.** *su./m* murderer; *su./f* murderess; △ loophole.

meurtrir [mœrˈtriːr] (2a) *v/t.* bruise; **meurtrissure** [~triˈsyːr] *f* bruise. [*voir.*]

meus [mø] *1st p. sg. pres. of* mou-

meute [møːt] *f* pack; *fig.* mob.

meuvent [mœːv] *3rd p. pl. pres. of* mouvoir.

mévendre ✝ † [meˈvãːdr] (4a) *v/t.* sell at a loss; **mévente** ✝ [ˌˈvãːt] *f* goods: sale at a loss; slump.

mezzanine [mɛdzaˈnin] *f* mezzanine (floor).

mi ♪ [mi] *m/inv.* mi, *note*: E.

mi... [mi] *adv.* half, mid, semi-; ˌ-clos half open; *à* ˌ-chemin half-way; *la* ˌ-janvier mid-January; *sp. poids m* ˌ-lourd light-heavy weight.

miaou [mjau] *m* miaow, mew.

miasme [mjasm] *m* miasma.

miauler [mjoˈle] (1a) *v/i.* mew, miaow.

mica *min.* [miˈka] *m* mica; **micelle** *biol.* [miˈsɛl] *m* micella.

miche [miʃ] *f* round loaf.

micheline 🚃 [miʃˈlin] *f* rail-car.

micmac F [mikˈmak] *m* intrigue; underhand work.

micro F [miˈkro] *m radio*: microphone, F mike; *au* ˌ on the air.

micro... [mikrɔ] micro...

microbe [miˈkrɔb] *m* microbe, F germ.

microcéphale [mikrɔseˈfal] *adj., a. su.* microcephalic.

micron [miˈkrõ] *m measure*: micron (1/1000 *mm*).

micro...: ˌ**cosme** [ˌkrɔˈkɔsm] *m* microcosm; ˌ**phone** [mikrɔˈfɔn] *m* microphone; ˌ**processeur** [ˌkrɔprɔsɛˈsœːr] *m* microprocessor; ˌ**scope** [ˌkrɔsˈkɔp] *m* microscope; ˌ**sillon** [ˌkrɔsiˈjõ] *m* microgroove; long-playing record.

midi [miˈdi] *m* midday, noon, twelve o'clock; *fig.* heyday (*of life*); ˌ *et demi* half past twelve; *plein* ˌ high noon; *geog. le* ♀ the South of France; **midinette** F [ˌdiˈnɛt] *f* dressmaker's assistant, midinette.

mie [mi] *f bread*: soft part, cumb.

miel [mjɛl] *m* honey; **miellé, e** [mjɛˈle]honeyed; honey-colo(u)red; **mielleux, -euse** [ˌˈlø, ˌˈløːz] like honey; *fig.* honeyed (*words*); bland (*smile*); smooth-tongued (*person*).

mien, mienne [mjɛ̃, mjɛn] **1.** *pron./ poss.*: *le* ˌ, *la* ˌne, *les* ˌs *m/pl.*, *les* ˌnes *f/pl.* mine; **2.** *adj./poss.* † of mine; *un* ˌ *ami* a friend of mine; **3.** *su./m* mine, my own; *les* ˌs *pl.* my (own) people.

miette [mjɛt] *f* crumb; *fig.* piece, bit.

mieux [mjø] **1.** *adv.* better; rather; *aimer* ˌ prefer; ✈ *aller* ˌ feel *or* be better; *à qui* ˌ ˌ one trying to outdo the other; *de* ˌ *en* ˌ better and better; *je ne demande pas* ˌ *que de* (*inf.*) I shall be delighted to (*inf.*); *le* ˌ (the) best; *tant* ˌ all the better; *valoir* ˌ be better; *vous feriez* ˌ *de* (*inf.*) you had better (*inf.*); **2.** *su./m* best; ✈ *change for the better; au* ˌ as well as possible, ✝ at best; *faire de son* ˌ do one's best.

mièvre [mjɛːvr] delicate; *fig.* affected (*style*); **mièvrerie** [mjɛvrəˈri] *f* delicateness; *fig. style etc.*: affectation.

mignard, e [miˈɲaːr, ˌˈɲard] affected, mincing; dainty; **mignardise** [ˌɲarˈdiːz] *f* affectation; *style*: finicalness; ✿ (garden) pink; **mignon, -onne** [ˌˈɲõ, ˌˈɲɔn] **1.** *adj.* dainty, sweet, nice, cute; *péché m* ˌ besetting sin; **2.** *su.* darling, pet; **mignoter** † [ˌɲɔˈte] (1a) *v/t.* caress; pet.

migraine [miˈgrɛn] *f* migraine, sick headache.

migrant, e [miˈgrã, ˌˈgrãːt] **1.** *adj.* migrant; **2.** *su.* migrant (worker); **migrateur, -trice** [migraˈtœːr, ˌˈtris] *orn.* migratory; migrant (*person*); **migration** [ˌˈsjõ] *f* migration; **migratoire** [ˌˈtwaːr] migratory.

mijaurée [miʒɔˈre] *f* affected woman.

mijoter [miʒɔˈte] (1a) *v/t.* let (*s.th.*) simmer (*a. fig. an idea*); hatch (*a plot*); *fig. se* ˌ be brewing; *v/i.* simmer.

mil [mil] *adj./inv.* thousand (*only in dates*).

milan *orn.* [miˈlã] *m* kite.

mildiou ✿, ✔ [milˈdju] *m* mildew.

miliaire ✖ [miˈljɛːr] miliary (*fever*).

milice ✖ [miˈlis] *f* militia; **milicien** ✖ [ˌliˈsjɛ̃] *m* militiaman.

milieu [miˈljø] *m* middle; *phys.* medium; *fig.* circle, sphere; *fig.* environment; *fig.* (social) background; *fig.* middle course; *the* underworld; *au* ˌ *de* in the middle of.

militaire [miliˈtɛːr] **1.** *adj.* military; ♪ martial; **2.** *su./m* military man; soldier; **militant, e** [miliˈtã, ˌˈtãːt] **1.** *adj.* militant; **2.** *su.* fighter (for, de); militant; **militariser** [ˌtariˈze] (1a) *v/t.* militarize; **militarisme** [ˌtaˈrism] *m* militarism; **militer** [ˌˈte]

(1a) *v/i.* militate (against, *contre*; in favo[u]r of *pour, en faveur de*); be a militant.

mille [mil] **1.** *adj./num./inv.* (a or one) thousand; **2.** *su./m/inv.* thousand; *sp.* bull's eye; *mettre dans le ~* hit the bull's eye; F *fig.* be bang on target; *su./m* mile.

mille-feuille [mil'fœːj] *f* ♀ yarrow; *cuis.* mille-feuille (*sort of puff pastry*); **millénaire** [mille'nɛːr] **1.** *adj.* millennial; **2.** *su./m* one thousand; thousand years, millennium.

mille...: ~-pattes *zo.* [mil'pat] *m/inv.* centipede, millepede; **~(-)pertuis** ♀ [~pɛr'tɥi] *m* St. John's wort.

millésime [mille'zim] *m* date (*on coin*); ⊕ year of manufacture.

millet ♀ [mi'jɛ] *m* (wood) millet-grass; *grains m/pl. de ~* bird-seed, canary-seed.

milliaire [mi'ljɛːr] milliary; *borne f ~* milestone; **milliard** [~'ljaːr] *m* milliard, one thousand million(s *pl.*), *Am.* billion; **millième** [~'ljɛm] *adj., a. su., a. su./m* fraction: thousandth; **millier** [~'lje] *m* (about) a thousand; **million** [~'ljɔ̃] *m* million.

mime [mim] *m* mimic; *thea. hist.* mime; **mimer** [mi'me] (1a) *v/t.* mime (*a scene*); mimic (*s.o.*).

mimétisme *zo.* [mime'tism] *m* mimicry. [ling.}

mimi [mi'mi] *m* pussy; F pet, dar-}

mimique ♀ [mi'mik] mimic.

mimosa ♀ [mimo'za] *m* mimosa.

minable *fig.* [mi'nabl] seedy, shabby.

minauder [mino'de] (1a) *v/i.* simper, smirk; **minauderie** [~'dri] *f* simpering, smirking.

mince [mɛ̃ːs] thin; slender, slight, slim; F *~ alors!* hell!

mine[1] [min] *f* appearance, look; *~s pl.* simperings; *avoir bonne (mauvaise) ~* look well (ill); look good (bad); *faire ~ de (inf.)* make as if to (*inf.*); make a show of (*s.th.; doing s.th.*).

mine[2] [min] *f* ✕, ⚒, ⚓, *fig.* mine; *pencil:* lead; *fig.* store; *~ de houille* colliery, coal-mine; *~ de plomb* graphite; *faire sauter une ~* spring a mine; **miner** [mi'ne] (1a) *v/t.* ✕ mine; *fig.* undermine, consume; **minerai** ✕ [min'rɛ] *m* ore.

minéral, e, *m/pl.* **-aux** [mine'ral, ~'ro] **1.** *adj.* mineral; inorganic (*chemistry*); *eau f ~e* mineral water; spa water; **2.** *su./m* mineral; **minéraliser** [~rali'ze] (1a) *v/t.* mineralize; **minéralogie** [~ralɔ'ʒi] *m* mineralogy; **minéralogique** [~ralɔ'ʒik] mineralogical; *mot. numéro m ~* registration (*Am.* license) number; *mot. plaque f ~* number plate.

minet *m,* **-ette** *f* [mi'nɛ, ~'nɛt] puss(ycat); F pet, darling; young trendy.

mineur[1] *m* [mi'nœːr] **1.** *adj.* minor, (*a.* ♪♭, ♪); **2.** *su.* ♪♭, ♪ minor; *su./f* minor premise; assumption.

mineur[2] [~] *m* ✕ miner; ✕ sapper.

miniature [minja'tyːr] *f* miniature; **miniaturiser** [~tyri'ze] (1a) *v/t.* miniaturize; **miniaturiste** [~ty-'rist] *adj., a. su.* miniaturist.

minier, -ère [mi'nje, ~'njɛːr] **1.** *adj.* mining; **2.** *su./f* open-cast mine.

mini-jupe [mini'jyp] *f* miniskirt.

minimal, e, *m/pl.* **-aux** [mini'mal, ~'mo] minimal; **minime** [~'nim] tiny; *fig.* trivial; **minimiser** [~ni-mi'ze] (1a) *v/t.* minimize, play down; **minimum,** *pl. a.* **minima** [~ni-'mɔm, ~'ma] **1.** *su./m* minimum; *~ vital* minimum living wage; **2.** *adj.* minimum.

ministère [minis'tɛːr] *m* agency; *pol., a. eccl.* ministry; *pol.* office, government department; service; *pol.* ♀ Office; Ministry; ♀ *de la Défense nationale* Ministry of Defence, *Am.* Department of Defense; ♀ *des Affaires étrangères* Foreign Office, *Am.* State Department; ⚖ ♀ *public* Public Prosecutor; **ministre** [~'nistr] *m pol., a.* protestantism: minister; ♀ *de la Défense nationale* Minister of Defence, *Am.* Secretary of Defense; ♀ *des Affaires étrangères* Foreign Secretary, *Am.* Secretary of State; ♀ *des Finances France:* Minister of Finance, *Britain:* Chancellor of the Exchequer, *Am.* Secretary of the Treasury.

minium ♎ [mi'njɔm] *m* minium; red lead.

minois F [mi'nwa] *m* pretty face.

minorité [minɔri'te] *f* minority; ⚖ infancy; *pol. mettre en ~* defeat (*the government*).

minoterie [minɔ'tri] *f* flour-mill;

mitonner

flour-milling; **minotier** [ˌ‑'tje] *m* (flour-)miller.

minuit [mi'nɥi] *m* midnight; ~ et *demi* half past twelve (at night).

minuscule [minys'kyl] **1.** *adj.* tiny; small (*letter*); **2.** *su./f* small letter, *typ.* lower-case letter.

minute [mi'nyt] **1.** *su./f* minute; *deed, judgment*: draft; record; *à la* ~ this instant; to the minute; while you wait; **2.** *int.* wait a bit!; **minuter** *admin.* [miny'te] (1a) *v/t.* time; **minuterie** [ˌ‑'tri] *f* clocks *etc.*: motion work; ♪ time switch.

minutie [miny'si] *f* (attention to) minute detail; **minutieux, -euse** [ˌ‑'sjø, ˌ‑'sjøːz] detailed, painstaking, thorough.

mioche F [mjɔʃ] *su.* urchin; kid(die), tot.

mi-parti, e [mipar'ti] equally divided; halved.

miracle [mi'raːkl] *m* miracle (*a.fig.*); **miraculeux, -euse** [ˌ‑raky'lø, ˌ‑'løːz] miraculous; F marvellous.

mirage [mi'raːʒ] *m* mirage; *fig.* illusion; **mire** [miːr] *f* ✕ aiming; *gun*: bead; *surv.* pole, levelling-rod; *telev.* test-card, test-pattern; *point m de* ~ ✕ aim; *fig.* cynosure; **mirer** [mi're] (1a) *v/t.* aim at; *surv.* take a sight on; ☩ candle (*an egg*); hold (*cloth*) against the light; *se* ~ look at o.s.; be reflected.

mirifique F [miri'fik] wonderful.

mirliton [mirli'tɔ̃] *m* ♪ toy flute; *cuis.* cream puff; *vers m/pl. de* ~ doggerel.

mirobolant, e F [mirɔbɔ'lɑ̃, ˌ‑'lɑ̃ːt] marvellous; staggering.

miroir [mi'rwaːr] *m* mirror, looking-glass; *mot.* ~ *rétroviseur* driving mirror; **miroitement** [ˌ‑rwat'mɑ̃] *m* flash; gleam; *water*: shimmer; **miroiter** [mirwa'te] (1a) *v/i.* flash; glitter; sparkle; *fig. faire* ~ *qch. à q.* paint s.th. in glowing colo(u)rs for s.o.

miroton *cuis.* [mirɔ'tɔ̃] *m* re-heated beef in onion sauce.

mis¹ [mi] *1st p. sg. p.s. of* mettre.

mis², e [mi, miːz] *p.p. of* mettre.

misaine ⚓ [mi'zɛn] *f* foresail; *mât m de* ~ foremast.

misanthrope [mizɑ̃'trɔp] **1.** *su./m* misanthropist; **2.** *adj.* misanthropic.

miscible [mi'sibl] miscible.

mise [miːz] *f* placing, putting; *auc-*

tion: bid; *gamble*: stake; dress, attire; ☩ outlay; ~ *à la retraite* retirement; ✄ ~ *à la terre* earthing; ⚒ ~ *à l'eau* launching; ~ *à mort bullfight*: kill (of the bull); ~ *à pied* sacking; ~ *au point* adjustment; *phot.* focussing; ~*-bas* dropping (*of young animals*); ☩ ~ *de fonds* putting up of money; ⊕ ~ *en fabrication* putting into production; ~ *en liberté* release; ⊕ ~ *en marche* starting; ~ *en ondes* radio adaptation; *typ.* ~ *en pages* making up; ~ *en plis hair*: setting; *mot.* ~ *en route* starting up; *thea.* ~ *en scène* staging, production; ~ *en service* commencement of service; ~ *en train* start(ing); ☩ ~ *en vente* putting up for sale; *ne pas être de* ~ be out of place *or* season; **miser** [mi'ze] (1a) *v/t.* bid; stake; *v/i.* count (on, *sur*).

misérable [mize'rabl] **1.** *adj.* miserable; *fig.* wretched; *fig.* mean (*action*); **2.** *su.* (poor) wretch; **misère** [ˌ‑'zɛːr] *f* misery; poverty; *fig.* trifle.

miséricorde [mizeri'kɔrd] **1.** *su./f* mercy, forgiveness; **2.** *int.* mercy!; **miséricordieux, -euse** [ˌ‑kɔr'djø, ˌ‑'djøːz] merciful (to, *envers*).

missel *eccl.* [mi'sɛl] *m* missal.

missile ✕ [mi'sil] *m* (guided) missile; ~ *de croisière* cruise missile.

mission [mi'sjɔ̃] *f* mission; **missionnaire** [ˌ‑sjɔ'nɛːr] *m* missionary; **missive** [ˌ‑'siːv] *f* missive, letter.

mistigri F [misti'gri] *m* puss.

mistral [mis'tral] *m* mistral (*cold north-east wind in Provence*).

mitage [mi'taːʒ] *m* spoiling (of the countryside) through architectural development.

mitaine [mi'tɛn] *f* mitten.

mite [mit] *f* moth; *cheese*: mite; **mité, e** [mi'te] moth-eaten; **miter** [ˌ‑] (1a) *v/t.* spoil (*the countryside*) through architectural development.

mi-temps [mi'tɑ̃] *f sp.* half-time; interval; ☩ *à* ~ half-time (*work*).

miteux, -euse F [mi'tø, ˌ‑'tøːz] shabby; seedy (*person*).

mitiger [miti'ʒe] (1l) *v/t.* mitigate; relax (*a law etc.*).

miton ✿ F [mi'tɔ̃] *m*: *onguent m* ~ *mitaine* harmless but useless ointment.

mitonner [mitɔ'ne] (1a) *v/i.* simmer; *v/t.* let (*s.th.*) simmer; *fig.* hatch.

mitoyen, -enne [mitwa'jɛ̃, ~'jɛn] common (*to two things*), ⚔ party (*wall*).

mitraille ✕ [mi'trɑːj] *f* grape-shot; F coppers *pl.* (= *small change*); **mitrailler** ✕ [mitrɑ'je] (1a) *v/t.* machine-gun, strafe, rake with fire; **mitraillette** ✕ [~'jɛt] *f* submachine-gun; **mitrailleur** ✕ [~'jœːr] **1.** *su./m* machine-gunner; **2.** *adj./m*: fusil *m* ~ Bren gun; **mitrailleuse** ✕ [~'jøːz] *f* machine-gun.

mitre [mitr] *f* (*bishop's*) mitre; ⚔ chimney-cowl; **mitron** [mi'trɔ̃] *m* journeyman baker; ⚔ chimney-pot.

mixage [mik'saːʒ] *m* (sound) mixing; **mixer**[1] [~'se] (1a) *v/t.* mix (*sounds*); **mixer**[2] [~'sœːr] *m* (food) mixer; **mixte** [mikst] mixed; 🕮 combined; ~ double *m tennis:* mixed doubles *pl.*; enseignement *m* ~ co-education; **mixtion** 🜍 [miks'tjɔ̃] *f* mixture; *drugs:* compounding; **mixtionner** 🜍 [~tjɔ'ne] (1a) *v/t.* compound (*drugs*); **mixture** 🜍, 💊 [~'tyːr] *f* mixture.

mobile [mɔ'bil] **1.** *adj.* mobile; movable (*a. feast*); moving (*object, target, etc.*); detachable; *fig.* inconstant; ✕ colonne *f* ~ flying column; **2.** *su./m* moving body; ⊕ moving part; *fig.* motive; *fig.* mainspring; premier ~ *person:* prime mover; **mobilier, -ère** [~bi'lje, ~'ljɛːr] **1.** *adj.* 🏦 movable; 🏦 personal (*action, estate*); 🕆 transferable; **2.** *su./m* furniture; suite.

mobilisation [mɔbiliza'sjɔ̃] *f* ✕, 🏦 mobilization; 🕆 realization; 🕆 liquidation; **mobiliser** [~'ze] (1a) *v/t.* ✕, 🏦 mobilize; ✕ call up; 🕆 realize (*an indemnity*); 🕆 liquidate (*capital*).

mobilité [mɔbili'te] *f* mobility; *fig. temperament etc.:* fickleness.

mobylette (*TM*) [mɔbi'lɛt] *f* moped.

moche F [mɔʃ] ugly; F lousy; rotten; poor, shoddy; F awful.

modal, e, *m/pl.* **-aux** [mɔ'dal, ~'do] modal; **modalité** [~dali'te] *f* phls. modality; 🎵 form of scale; ~s *pl.* 🕆 terms and conditions; 🏦 restrictive clauses.

mode [mɔd] *su./m* 🎵, phls. mood (*a. gramm.*); mode, method; ✍ d'emploi directions *pl.* for use; 🕆 ~ de paiement method of payment; *su./f* fashion; à la ~ fashionable, stylish, F in; à la ~ de in the style of; *cuis.* ... fashion; à la dernière ~ in the latest fashion.

modèle [mɔ'dɛl] **1.** *su./m* model (*a. fig.*), pattern; prendre q. pour ~ model o.s. on s.o.; **2.** *adj.* model ...

modelé [mɔd'le] *m* relief; contours *pl.*; **modeler** [~'le] (1d) *v/t.* model (on, sur); mo(u)ld; shape; **modeleur** ⊕ [~'lœːr] *m* pattern-maker.

modérateur, -trice [mɔdera'tœːr, ~'tris] **1.** *su.* moderator, restrainer; *su./m* ⊕ regulator; 🎇, phys. moderator; (*volume-*)control; **2.** *adj.* moderating, restraining; **modération** [~ra'sjɔ̃] *f* moderation, restraint; price, tax, 🏦 sentence: reduction; **modéré, e** [~'re] *adj.* moderate; sober; conservative (*estimate*); **modérer** [~'re] (1f) *v/t.* moderate, restrain; check; reduce (*the price etc.*); se ~ abate (*weather*).

moderne [mɔ'dɛrn] modern; **moderniser** [mɔdɛrni'ze] (1a) *v/t.* modernize; **moderniste** [~'nist] modernist; **modernité** [~ni'te] *f* modernity; modern times *pl.*

modeste [mɔ'dɛst] modest; unpretentious; quiet; moderate (*price*); **modestie** [~dɛs'ti] *f* modesty; unpretentiousness.

modicité [mɔdisi'te] *f means:* modesty; *prices:* reasonableness.

modifiable [mɔdi'fjabl] modifiable; **modificateur, -trice** [~fika'tœːr, ~'tris] modifying; **modification** [~fika'sjɔ̃] *f* modification, alteration; **modifier** [~'fje] (1o) *v/t.* modify (*a. gramm.*); alter; 🕆 rectify (*an entry*).

modique [mɔ'dik] reasonable, moderate (*price*); slender, modest (*means*).

modiste [mɔ'dist] *f* milliner, modiste.

modulateur 🎇 [mɔdyla'tœːr] *m* modulator; **modulation** [~'sjɔ̃] *f* modulation (🎵, *a. voice*); *voice:* inflexion; **module** [mɔ'dyl] *m* 𝔸 modulus; ⚔ module; unit; size; **moduler** [~dy'le] (1a) *vt/i.* modulate.

moelle [mwal] *f* marrow; 🌿 pith (*a. fig.*); *anat.* medulla; ~ épinière spinal cord; **moelleux, -euse** [mwa'lø, ~'løːz] marrowy (*bone*); 🌿 pithy; *fig.* soft; *fig.* mellow (*light, voice*).

moellon [mwa'lɔ̃] *m* quarry-stone; ~ de roche rock rubble.

mœurs [mœrs] *f/pl.* morals; manners, ways, customs; *animals*: habits.

mohair [mɔ'ɛːr] *m* mohair.

moi [mwa] **1.** *pron./pers. subject*: I; *object*: me; (to) me; à ~ to me; mine; *c'est ~* it is I, F it's me; *de vous à ~* between you and me; *il a vu mon frère et ~* he has seen my brother and me; **2.** *su./m* ego, self.

moignon [mwa'ɲɔ̃] *m* stump (*of amputated limb*).

moi-même [mwa'mɛːm] *pron./rfl.* myself.

moindre [mwɛ̃:dr] less(er); *le* (*la*) ~ the least; the slightest; **moindrement** [mwɛ̃drə'mɑ̃] *adv.*: *pas le* ~ not in the least.

moine [mwan] *m* monk; *fig.* F bedwarmer, hot-water bottle; *metall.* blister; **moineau** *orn.* [mwa'no] *m* sparrow; *sl.* fellow; **moinerie** *usu. pej.* [mwan'ri] *f* friary; monkery; **moinillon** F [mwani'jɔ̃] *m* young monk.

moins [mwɛ̃] **1.** *adv.* less (than, que); fewer; ~ de deux less than two; à ~ de (*inf.*), à ~ que ... (ne) (*sbj.*) unless; *au* ~ at least; de ~ en ~ less and less; *du* ~ at least (= *at all events*); *le* ~ (the) least; **2.** *prp.* minus, less; *cinq heures* ~ *dix* ten minutes to five; **3.** *su./m* ⅄ minus (sign); ~-**value** ✝ [ˌva'ly] *f* depreciation.

moire *tex.* [mwaːr] *f* moire; watered silk; **moirer** *tex.*, *a.* ⊕ [mwa're] (1a) *v/t.* moiré.

mois [mwa] *m* month; month's pay; ✝ *à un* ~ *de date* one month after date; *par* ~, *tous les* ~ monthly; *tous les* ~ every month.

moisi, e [mwa'zi] **1.** *adj.* mo(u)ldy; musty (*smell, taste*); **2.** *su./m* mo(u)ld, mildew; *sentir le* ~ smell musty; **moisir** [ˌˈziːr] (2a) *vt/i.* mildew; *v/i.* *a. se* ~ go mo(u)ldy; F vegetate; **moisissure** [ˌzi'syːr] *f* ✗ mildew, mo(u)ld; mustiness.

moisson [mwa'sɔ̃] *f* harvest, crop (*a. fig.*); harvest-time; **moissonner** [mwasɔ'ne] (1a) *v/t.* harvest, reap (*a. fig.*), gather; **moissonneur** [ˌˈnœːr] *m* harvester, reaper; **moissonneuse** [ˌˈnøːz] *f* harvester, reaper (*a. machine*); ~-**batteuse** combine-harvester; ~-**lieuse** *machine*: self-binder.

moite [mwat] moist, damp; clammy; ✝ limp; **moiteur** [mwa'tœːr] *f* moistness; ✗ perspiration.

moitié [mwa'tje] **1.** *su./f* half; F better half (= *wife*); à ~ *chemin* half-way; à ~ *prix* (at) half-price; *se mettre de* ~ *avec q.* go halves with s.o.; **2.** *adv.* half.

mol [mɔl] *see* mou 1.

molaire [mɔ'lɛːr] *adj., a. su./f* molar.

môle [moːl] *m* mole, breakwater; pier.

moléculaire [mɔleky'lɛːr] molecular; **molécule** [ˌˈkyl] *f* molecule; ⚗ ~-**gramme** gram(me-)molecule.

molester [mɔlɛs'te] (1a) *v/t.* molest.

molette [mɔ'lɛt] *f* spur: rowel; ⊕ cutting-wheel; *paint.* small pestle; ✗ winding-pulley; *lighter*: wheel; *clef f à* ~ adjustable spanner.

mollasse F [mɔ'las] soft, flabby; slow (*person*); *su./m* molle [mɔl] *see* mou 1; **mollesse** [mɔ'lɛs] *f* softness, flabbiness; slackness; indolence; **mollet, -ette** [ˌˈlɛ, ˌˈlɛt] **1.** *adj.* softish; soft-boiled (*egg*); tender (*feet*); *pain m* ~ roll; **2.** *su./m leg*: calf; **molletière** [mɔl'tjɛːr] *f* puttee; **mollir** [mɔ'liːr] (2a) *v/i.* soften; slacken; *fig.* get weak; ✗ give ground; ✝ get easier (*price of commodity*).   [F slowcoach.]

mollusque *zo.* [mɔ'lysk] *m* mollusc;)

mollo! [mɔ'lo] *int.* easy!; gently!; *vas-y* ~! easy does it!

molosse [mɔ'lɔs] *m* watch-dog; mastiff.

môme *sl.* [moːm] *su. child*: kid, brat.

moment [mɔ'mɑ̃] *m* moment (*a. phys.*); *au* ~ *où* (*or que*) since; *par* ~s now and again; *pour le* ~ for the time being; **momentané, e** [ˌˈmɑ̃ta'ne] momentary; temporary (*absence*).

momerie [mɔm'ri] *f* mummery; *fig.* affectations *pl.*

momie [mɔ'mi] *f* mummy; F old fogy; F bag of bones; **momifier** [ˌmi'fje] (1o) *v/t.* mummify.

mon *m*, **ma** *f*, *pl.* **mes** [mɔ̃, ma, me] *adj./poss.* my.

monacal, e, *m/pl.* **-aux** *eccl.* [mɔna'kal, ˌˈko] monac(h)al; **monachisme** *eccl.* [ˌˈkism] *m* monasticism.

monarchie [mɔnar'ʃi] *f* monarchy; **monarchiste** [ˌˈʃist] *adj., a. su.* monarchist; **monarque** [mɔ'nark] *m* monarch.

monastère [mɔnas'tɛːr] *m* monastery; *nuns:* convent; **monastique** [ˌˈtik] monastic.

monceau [mɔ̃'so] *m* heap, pile.

mondain, e [mɔ̃'dɛ̃, ˌˈdɛn] **1.** *adj.* mundane, worldly; fashionable; **2.** *su.* wordly-minded person; *su./m* man-about-town; *su./f* society woman; *police: la* ♀ the vice squad; **mondanité** [ˌdani'te] *f* worldliness; love of social functions; **monde** [mɔ:d] *m* world (*a. fig.*); people; *fig.* society; *au bout du* ～ at the back of beyond; *dans le* ～ *entier* all over the world; *homme m du* ～ man of good breeding; *il y a du* ～ there is a crowd; *recevoir du* ～ entertain (guests); *tout le* ～ everyone; *fig. un* ～ *de lots pl.* of; *vieux comme le* ～ as old as the hills; **mondial, e,** *m/pl.* -**aux** [mɔ̃'djal, ˌˈdjo] worldwide; world (*war*); **mondialisation** [mɔ̃djaliza'sjɔ̃] *f* establishing *or* application on a worldwide basis; spread(ing) throughout the world; **mondialiser** [ˌˈze] (1a) *v/t.* establish *or* apply on a worldwide basis; (*a. se* ～) spread throughout the world.

monégasque [mɔne'gask] of Monaco.

monétaire [mɔne'tɛːr] monetary; **monétisation** [ˌtiza'sjɔ̃] *f* minting.

moniteur [mɔni'tœːr] *m school, telev.* monitor; *sp.* coach; ✈ *plane:* instructor; **monition** *eccl.* [ˌˈsjɔ̃] *f* monition; **monitoire** *eccl.* [ˌˈtwaːr] *m* (*a. lettre f* ～) monitory (letter).

monnaie [mɔ'nɛ] *f* money; (small) change; currency; ✝ ～ *forte* hard currency; *donner la* ～ *de* give change for, change (*a note etc.*); **monnayer** [ˌnɛ'je] (1i) *v/t.* mint, coin; **monnayeur** [ˌnɛ'jœːr] *m* minter, coiner.

mono [mɔ'no] *f, a. adj. short for monophonie, monophonique:* mono; *en* ～ (in) mono.

mon(o)... [mɔn(ɔ)] mon(o)...; **monobloc** [mɔnɔ'blɔk] cast *or* made in one piece.

monocle [mɔ'nɔkl] *m* monocle.

mono...: ～**game** [mɔnɔ'gam] monogamous; ～**gamie** [ˌga'mi] *f* monogamy; ～**gramme** [ˌ'gram] *m* monogram; *initials pl.*; ～**logue** [ˌ'lɔg] *m* monologue; ～**loguer** [ˌlɔ'ge] (1m) *v/i.* soliloquize.

monôme ⚹ [mɔ'noːm] *m* monomial.

mono...: ～**phasé, e** ⚡ [mɔnɔfa'ze] single-phase; ～**phonie** [ˌfɔ'ni] *f* monaural reproduction; *en* ～ (in) mono; ～**phonique** [ˌfɔ'nik] monaural, mono(phonic); ～**place** ✈, *mot.* [ˌ'plas] *m* single-seater; ～**plan** ✈ [ˌ'plɑ̃] *m* monoplane; ～**pole** [ˌ'pɔl] *m* monopoly; ～**poliser** [ˌpɔli'ze] (1a) *v/t.* monopolize; ～**rail** 🚄 [ˌ'rɑːj] *adj., a. su./m* monorail; ～**syllabe** [ˌsi'lab] *m* monosyllable; ～**théisme** [ˌte'ism] *m* monotheism; ～**tone** [ˌ'tɔn] monotonous; ～**tonie** [ˌtɔ'ni] *f* monotony.

monseigneur, *pl.* **messeigneurs** [mɔ̃sɛ'ɲœːr, mɛsɛ'ɲœːr] *m* My Lord; *archbishop, duke:* Your Grace; *prince:* Your Royal Highness; His Lordship; His Grace; His Royal Highness; **monsieur,** *pl.* **messieurs** [mə'sjø, mɛ'sjø] *m* Mr.; sir; gentleman; man; *in letters:* Dear Sir; ～ *le Président* Mr. President.

monstre [mɔ̃:str] **1.** *su./m* monster (*a. fig.*); freak of nature; ～ *sacré* (super)star; **2.** *adj.* colossal, huge; **monstrueux, -euse** [mɔ̃stry'ø, ˌˈøːz] monstrous; huge; frightful; **monstruosité** [ˌozi'te] *f* monstrosity; *fig.* enormity; [the Alps.]

mont [mɔ̃] *m* mount(ain); *les* ～*s pl.*) **montage** [mɔ̃'taːʒ] *m* putting up; *loads, materials:* hoisting; ⊕ *machine:* assembling; *gun, phot., etc.:* mounting; ⚡ wiring, connecting up; *gems, scene, etc.:* setting; *mot. tyre:* fitting (on); *cin. film:* editing; ⊕ *chaîne f de* ～ assembly line.

montagnard, e [mɔ̃ta'ɲaːr, ˌˈɲard] **1.** *adj.* mountain..., highland...; **2.** *su.* mountaineer, highlander; **montagne** [ˌ'taɲ] *f* mountain; *la* ～ the mountains *pl.*; ～*s pl. russes* switchback *sg.*; **montagneux, -euse** [ˌta'nø, ˌˈnøːz] mountainous, hilly.

montaison [mɔ̃tɛ'zɔ̃] *f salmon:* run-up; **montant, e** [ˌˈtɑ̃, ˌˈtɑ̃:t] **1.** *adj.* rising; uphill; 🚂 up (*train, platform*); *cost.* high-necked; **2.** *su./m* reckoning, account: total; *tide:* flow, rising; *ladder:* upright; (*tent-*)pole; *stair:* riser; (*gate-*)post; leg; (*lamp-*)post.

mont-de-piété, *pl.* **monts-de-piété** [mɔ̃dəpje'te] *m* pawn-shop.

monte...: ~-charge [mɔ̃t'ʃarʒ] *m/
inv.* hoist; goods-lift; **~-pente** [~-
'pãːt] *m* ski-lift; **~-plats** [~'pla] *m/
inv.* service-lift, *Am.* dumb-waiter.
monté, e [mɔ̃'te] **1.** *adj.* mounted (*a.
police*); equipped; F *fig. coup m ~*
plot, put-up job; *fig. être ~* have a
grudge (against, *contre*); **2.** *su./f*
rising; rise; ascent; climb, gradient;
⚡, *mot.* climbing; **monter** [~'te]
(1a) *v/i.* climb (up), ascend, mount;
go upstairs; rise (*anger, price, sun,
barometer, tide*); amount (to, *à*)
(*cost, total*); boil up (*milk*); ~ *à* (*or
sur*) *un arbre* climb a tree; ~ *dans
un train* get on a train, *Am.* board
a train; ~ *en avion* get into a plane;
~ *sur un navire* go aboard a ship;
faire ~ raise (*prices*); *v/t.* mount (*a.
phot., a.* ⚔ *guard*), climb, go up
(*the stairs, a hill*); ride (*a horse*); ⚓
set up (*a factory*); take up, carry
up; turn up (*a lamp, etc.*); equip;
wind up (*a watch*); assemble (*a
machine*); *thea.* stage (*a play*); *fig.*
plan, plot; F ~ *la tête à q.* work s.o.
up (against, *contre*); ~ *son ménage*
set up house; *se ~* amount (to, *à*);
monteur *m*, **-euse** *f* [~'tœːr, ~'tøːz]
⊕ setter; *cin.* cutter; *thea.* producer;
⊕, ⚙ fitter; **monticule** [~ti'kyl] *m*
hillock; *ice:* hummock.

montre [mɔ̃ːtr] *f* show, display;
shop-window; show-case; watch,
mot. clock; *mot. etc. course f contre
la ~* race against the clock; *faire ~
de* display; **~-bracelet,** *pl.* **~s-bra-
celets** [mɔ̃trəbras'le] *f* wrist-watch;
montrer [mɔ̃'tre] (1a) *v/t.* show;
display; indicate, point out; *se ~*
show o.s., *fig.* prove (o.s.); turn out;
appear.

montueux, -euse [mɔ̃'tɥø, ~'tɥøːz]
hilly, mountainous; **monture** [~-
'tyːr] *f horse, picture:* mount; ⊕
mounting, assembling; *gem:* setting; *spectacles:* frame; *gun etc.:*
handle, stock; *sans ~* rimless (*spectacles*).

monument [mɔny'mã] *m* monument (*a. fig.*), memorial; public
building; ~s *pl. town:* sights; ~ *funéraire* monument (*over tomb*);
monumental, e, *m/pl.* **-aux** [~mã-
'tal, ~'to] monumental; F huge,
enormous.

moquer [mɔ'ke] (1m) *v/t.: se ~ de*
make fun of; F *s'en ~* not to care (a

21*

damn); **moquerie** [mɔk'ri] *f* mockery; ridicule; jeer.
moquette¹ [mɔ'kɛt] *f* decoy(-bird).
moquette² [~] *f* fitted carpet, wall-
to-wall carpet(ing); *tex.* moquette.
moqueur, -euse [mɔ'kœːr, ~'køːz]
1. *adj.* mocking; derisive; **2.** *su.*
mocker; *su./m orn.* mocking-bird.
moraine *geol.* [mɔ'rɛn] *f* moraine.
moral, e, *m/pl.* **-aux** [mɔ'ral, ~'ro]
1. *adj.* moral; *fig.* mental; **2.** *su./m*
morale; (moral) nature; *su./f* mor-
als *pl.*; ethics; *fables etc.:* moral;
moralisateur, -trice [mɔraliza-
'tœːr, ~'tris] moralizing (*person*);
edifying; **moraliser** [~li'ze] *vt/i.*
moralize; *v/t.* F lecture, preach at
(*s.o.*); **moraliste** [~'list] *su.* moralist; **moralité** [~li'te] *f* good (moral) conduct, morality; morals *pl.*;
story: moral; *thea.* morality(-play).
moratoire [mɔra'twaːr] ⚖ mora-
tory; ⚓ *intérêts m/pl.* ~s interest *sg.*
on over-due payments.
morbide [mɔr'bid] morbid, sickly;
paint. delicate (*flesh-tints*); **morbi-
desse** *paint.* [~bi'dɛs] *f* delicacy of
flesh-tints, morbidezza; **morbidité**
[~bidi'te] *f* morbidity.
morceau [mɔr'so] *m* piece, morsel;
bit, scrap; *avoir qch. pour un ~ de pain*
get s.th. for a song; **morceler**
[~sə'le] (1c) *v/t.* cut up (into pieces);
divide (*land, an estate*); **morcellement** [~sɛl'mã] *m* cutting up; *land,
estate:* parcelling out.
mordache ⊕ [mɔr'daʃ] *f* clamp;
chuck: jaw, grip.
mordacité [mɔrdasi'te] *f* 🜍 corro-
siveness; *fig.* causticity, mordancy;
mordant, e [mɔr'dã, ~'dãt] biting;
scathing, caustic; **mordicus** F
[mɔrdi'kys] *adv.* stoutly, doggedly.
mordiller [mɔrdi'je] (1a) *v/t.* nibble;
puppy etc.: bite playfully.
mordoré, e [mɔrdɔ're] *adj., a. su./m*
bronze, reddish brown.
mordre [mɔrdr] (4a) *v/t.* bite; ⊕
catch; *acid:* corrode (*metal*); *se ~ les
lèvres* bite one's lips; *v/i.* bite (*a. fig.*);
⊕ catch, engage (*wheel*); *fig. ~ à* get
one's teeth into; take to (*a subject*);
mordu, e F [mɔr'dy] **1.** *adj.* madly in
love (with, *de*); mad *or* crazy *or* wild
(about, *de*); **2.** *su.* fan, freak, buff; *un
~ du film* a film freak.
more [mɔːr] *adj./m, a. su./m* ♀ *see
maure;* **moreau, -elle,** *m/pl.* **-eaux**

[mɔ'ro, ⁓'rɛl, ⁓'ro] **1.** *adj.* black (*horse*); **2.** *su./f* ♀ morel, black nightshade; **moresque** [⁓'rɛsk] *adj.*, *a. su./f see* **mauresque.**

morfondre [mɔr'fɔ̃:dr] (4a) *v/t.* freeze; *se* ⁓ wait, F cool one's heels; *fig.* be bored.

morgue[1] [mɔrg] *f* haughtiness, arrogance.

morgue[2] [⁓] *f* mortuary, morgue.

moribond, e [mɔri'bɔ̃, ⁓'bɔ̃:d] **1.** *adj.* moribund, dying; **2.** *su.* dying person; *su./m: les* ⁓s *pl.* the dying.

moricaud, e [mɔri'ko, ⁓'ko:d] **1.** *adj.* dark-skinned, dusky; **2.** *su.* blackamoor; F darky.

morigéner [mɔriʒe'ne] (1f) *v/t.* lecture (*s.o.*); tell (*s.o.*) off.

morille ♀ [mɔ'ri:j] *f fungus:* morel.

morillon [mɔri'jɔ̃] *m* ♀ black grape; *orn.* tufted duck; ⚒ rough emerald.

mormon, -onne [mɔr'mɔ̃, ⁓'mɔn] *adj., a. su.* Mormon.

morne [mɔrn] gloomy; dismal (*scene, existence*); bleak (*scenery*).

morose [mɔ'ro:z] morose; surly; forbidding (*aspect*); **morosité** [⁓rozi-'te] *f* moroseness, surliness; gloominess.

morphine ⚕ [mɔr'fin] *f* morphia, morphine; **morphinisme** ⚕ [⁓fi-'nism] *m* morphinism; **morphinomane** [⁓fino'man] *adj., a. su.* morphia addict, F drug-fiend, *Am.* dope-fiend.

morphologie [mɔrfɔlɔ'ʒi] *f* morphology; **morphologique** [⁓'ʒik] morphological.

mors [mɔ:r] *m harness:* bit; ⊕ *vice:* jaw; *fig. prendre le* ⁓ *aux dents* lose one's temper, get mad.

morse *zo.* [mɔrs] *f* walrus.

morsure [mɔr'sy:r] *f* bite; *fig.* sting.

mort[1] [mɔ:r] *f* death; *à* ⁓ deadly; *attraper la* ⁓ catch one's death; *avoir la* ⁓ *dans l'âme* be sick at heart; *mourir de sa belle* ⁓ die in bed.

mort[2]**, e** [mɔ:r, mɔrt] **1.** *p.p. of* **mourir; 2.** *adj.* dead; stagnant (*water*); *paint.* nature *f* ⁓e still life; *poids m* ⁓ dead weight; *point m* ⁓ *mot.* neutral (*gear*); *fig.* dead-lock; **3.** *su.* dead person; *su./m* dummy (*at cards*); *faire le* ⁓ be dummy; *fig.* sham dead; *jour m des* ♀s All Souls' Day; ⁓s *pl. et blessés m/pl.* casualties.

mortadelle [mɔrta'dɛl] *f* Bologna sausage.

mortaise ⊕ [mɔr'tɛ:z] *f* mortise.

mortalité [mɔrtali'te] *f* mortality; **mort-aux-rats** [mɔro'ra] *f* ratsbane; **mortel, -elle** [mɔr'tɛl] **1.** *adj.* mortal; fatal (*accident, wound*); *fig.* deadly, boring; **2.** *su.* mortal; **morte-saison,** *pl.* **mortes-saisons** ⚬ [mɔrtse'zɔ̃] *f* slack season, off-season.

mortier △, ⚔ [mɔr'tje] *m* mortar.

mortification [mɔrtifika'sjɔ̃] *f* ⚕, *eccl., fig.* mortification; ⚕ gangrene; *cuis.* game: hanging; *fig.* humiliation; **mortifier** [⁓'fje] (1o) *v/t.* mortify (*the body, one's passions, fig. s.o.*); ⚕ gangrene; *cuis.* hang (*game*); ⚕ *se* ⁓ mortify, gangrene; **mort-né, e** [mɔr'ne] **1.** *adj.* still-born (*child, a. fig. project*); **2.** *su.* still-born baby; **mortuaire** [mɔr'tɥɛ:r] mortuary; death...; *drap m* ⁓ pall; *extrait m* ⁓ death certificate; *maison f* ⁓ house of the deceased.

morue *icht.* [mɔ'ry] *f* cod; ⁓ *sèche* salt cod; *huile f de foie de* ⁓ cod-liver oil.

morve [mɔrv] *f vet.* glanders *pl.*; (nasal) mucus, V snot; **morveux, -euse** [mɔr'vø, ⁓'vø:z] **1.** *adj. vet.* glandered; F snotty; **2.** *su.* F greenhorn.

mosaïque[1] *bibl.* [mɔza'ik] Mosaic.

mosaïque[2] [mɔza'ik] *f flooring, a. telev.:* mosaic; mosaic; **mosaïste** [⁓'ist] *su.* worker in mosaic.

moscoutaire *pej.* [mɔsku'tɛ:r] **1.** *adj.* Communist; **2.** *su.* F Bolshie.

mosquée [mɔs'ke] *f* mosque.

mot [mo] *m* word; note, line (= *short letter*); saying; ⚔ password; ⁓s *pl. croisés* crossword (puzzle) *sg.*; ⁓ *à* ⁓ word for word; ⚔, *fig.* ⁓ *d'ordre* keyword, watchword; *à* ⁓s *couverts* by hints; *au bas* ⁓ at the lowest estimate; *avoir des* ⁓s *avec q.* fall out with s.o.; *bon* ⁓ witticism; *en un* ⁓ in a word, in a nutshell; *jouer sur les* ⁓s play upon words; *ne pas souffler* ⁓ keep one's mouth shut; *prendre q. au* ⁓ take s.o. at his word; *sans* ⁓ *dire* without a word.

motard F [mɔ'ta:r] *m* motor cyclist; courtesy cop.

motel [mɔ'tɛl] *m* motel.

moteur, -trice [mɔ'tœ:r, ⁓'tris] **1.** *adj.* motive, driving; *anat.* motory; **2.** *su./m* ⊕ motor; engine; *fig.*

moulineur

(prime) mover, driving force; ~ *à* *combustion interne*, ~ *à explosion* internal combustion engine; ~ *à deux temps* two-stroke engine; ~ *à injection* injection engine; ~ *à réaction* jet engine; ~ *fixe* stationary engine.

motif, -ve [mɔ'tif, ~'tiːv] **1.** *adj.* motive; **2.** *su./m* motive; *fig.* grounds *pl.*; ♩ theme; *needlework:* pattern.

motion [mɔ'sjɔ̃] *f* motion; *parl.* ~ *de* *confiance* (*censure*) motion of confidence (no-confidence).

motivation [mɔtiva'sjɔ̃] *f* motivation; **motiver** [~'ve] (1a) *v/t.* motivate; cause; ꝏ give the reasons for.

moto F [mɔ'to] *f* motor cycle, F motor bike.

moto... motor...; power-driven...; ~**culteur** [mɔtɔkyl'tœːr] *m* power-driven cultivator; ~**culture** [~kyl'tyːr] *f* mechanized farming; ~**cyclette** [~si'klɛt] *f* motor cycle; ~ *à sidecar* motor cycle combination; *faire de la* ~ motor-cycle; ~**cycliste** [~si'klist] *su.* motor cyclist; ~**glisseur** ⚓ [~gli'sœːr] *m* speed-boat; ~**godille** ⚓ [~gɔ'diːj] *f* out-board slung motor; **motoriser** [mɔtɔri'ze] (1a) *v/t.* motorize.

mot-souche, *pl.* **mots-souches** *typ.* [mo'suʃ] *m* catchword.

motte [mɔt] *f* mound; *earth:* clod; *lawn, peat:* sod; *butter:* pad.

motus! [mɔ'tys] *int.* keep it quiet!

mou (*adj. before vowel or h mute* **mol**) *m,* **molle** *f, m/pl.* **mous** [mu, mɔl, mu] **1.** *adj.* soft; *fig.* weak; flabby (*flesh*); slack (*rope*); close (*weather*); calm, smooth (*sea*); lights *pl.* **2.** *su./m* belt, rope, *etc.:* slack; *cuis.* lights *pl.*

mouchard *pej.* [mu'ʃaːr] *m* (police) informer, F stool-pigeon; F *school:* sneak; **moucharder** [~ʃar'de] (1a) *v/t.* spy on (*s.o.*); *school:* sneak on; *v/i.* spy; sneak (*at school*); **mouche** [muʃ] *f* fly; *foil:* button; *target:* bull's-eye; spot, speck; patch (*on face*); beauty-spot; *faire* ~ hit the bull's-eye; *faire d'une* ~ *un éléphant* make a mountain out of a molehill; *fig. pattes f/pl. de* ~ handwriting: scrawl; *prendre la* ~ get angry; F *quelle* ~ *le pique?* what is biting him?

moucher [mu'ʃe] (1a) *v/t.* wipe (*s.o.'s*) nose; snuff (*a candle*); ⊕

trim; *fig.* snub (*s.o.*); *se* ~ blow *or* wipe one's nose.

moucherolle *orn.* [muʃ'rɔl] *f* fly-catcher.

moucheron[1] [muʃ'rɔ̃] *m* gnat, midge; F kid.

moucheron[2] [~] *m candle:* snuff.

moucheter [muʃ'te] (1c) *v/t.* spot, fleck; button (*a foil*); **mouchette** [mu'ʃɛt] *f* ⊕ mo(u)lding-plane; ~*s* *pl.* snuffers; **moucheture**[muʃ'tyːr] *f* spot, speckle, fleck; *zo.* ermine: tail.

mouchoir [mu'ʃwaːr] *m* handkerchief; ⊕ triangular wooden bracket; ~ *de tête* head square; **mouchure** [~'ʃyːr] *f* (nasal) mucus; *candle:* snuff; *rope:* frayed end.

moudre [mudr] (4w) *v/t.* grind.

moue [mu] *f* pout; *faire la* ~ pout, look sulky.

mouette *orn.* [mwɛt] *f* gull.

moufle [mufl] *f* ⊕ set of pulleys; (block and) tackle; △ tie, clamp; ~*s* *pl.* mitts; ≠ wiring gloves.

mouflon *zo.* [mu'flɔ̃] *m* moufflon, wild sheep.

mouillage [mu'jaːʒ] *m* moistening, dampening; *wine:* watering; ⚓ anchoring; **mouiller** [~'je] (1a) *v/t.* wet, damp, moisten; water (*wine etc.*); ⚓ moor (*a ship*); ⚓ drop (*the anchor*); *gramm.* palatalize (*a consonant*); *se* ~ get wet; grow moist (*with tears*); **mouillure** [~'jyːr] *f* wetting; damp-mark; *gramm.* palatalization.

moulage [~] *m* ⊕ cast(ing); *metall.* founding; △ plaster mo(u)lding.

moulant, e [mu'lɑ̃, ~'lɑ̃ːt] skintight (*dress*).

moule[1] [mul] *m* ⊕ mo(u)ld; matrix; *jeter en* ~ cast.

moule[2] [mul] *f* mussel; F fat-head; F lazy-bones *sg.*

moulé, e [mu'le] mo(u)lded, cast; *écriture moulée* block letters *pl.*

mouler [mu'le] (1a) *v/t.* cast; mo(u)ld; *metall.* found; *fig.* fit tightly; ~ *sur* model (*s.th.*) on; **mouleur** [~'lœːr] mo(u)lder, caster.

moulière [mu'ljɛːr] *f* mussel-bed.

moulin [mu'lɛ̃] *m* mill (*a.* ⊕); ~ *à café* coffee-mill; **mouliner** [muli'ne] (1a) *v/t. tex.* throw (*silk*); *insects:* eat into (*wood*); **moulinet** [~'nɛ] *m* winch; *fishing-rod:* reel; turnstile; *fencing, a. stick:* twirl; ~ *à musique* toy musical box; **mou-**

lineur *tex.* [ˌˈnœːr] *m*, **moulinier** *tex.* [ˌˈnje] *m* silk-thrower.

moulons [muˈlɔ̃] *1st p. pl. pres. of moudre*; **moulu, e** [ˌˈly] **1.** *adj. fig.* F tired out; aching all over; **2.** *p.p. of moudre*.

moulure △, ⊕ [muˈlyːr] *f* mo(u)lding; profiling.

moulus [muˈly] *1st p. sg. p.s. of moudre*.

mourant, e [muˈrɑ̃, ˌˈrɑ̃ːt] **1.** *adj.* dying; faint (*voice*); languishing (*voice*); F screamingly funny; **2.** *su.* dying person; **mourir** [ˌˈriːr] (2k) *v/i.* die; die out (*fire*); die away (*sound*); fall (*hope*); ~ avant l'âge come to an untimely end; être à ~ de rire be screamingly funny; ennuyer q. à ~ bore s.o. to death; *v/t.*: se ~ be dying; die away.

mouron [muˈrɔ̃] *m* ♀ (~ rouge) scarlet pimpernel; ♀ ~ blanc (or des oiseaux) chickweed; *sl.* hair; *sl.* se faire du ~ worry (o.s. sick).

mourrai [murˈre] *1st p. sg. fut. of mourir*; **mourus** [muˈry] *1st p. sg. p.s. of mourir*.

mousquet ✗ [musˈkɛ] *m* musket; **mousquetade** [muskəˈtad] *f* musket-shot; *musket-shots*: volley; **mousquetaire** ✗ [ˌˈtɛːr] *m* musketeer; **mousqueton** [ˌˈtɔ̃] *m* snaphook; ✗ † artillery carbine.

mousse[1] [mus] *m* ship's boy; cabin-boy.

mousse[2] [ˌ] *f* ♀ moss; *beer*: froth; *sea*: foam; *soap*: lather; *cuis.* mousse.

mousse[3] [ˌ] blunt.

mousseline [musˈlin] **1.** *su./f tex.* muslin; **2.** *adj./inv.*: *cuis.* pommes *f/pl.* ~ mashed potatoes; verre *m* ~ muslin-glass.

mousser [muˈse] (1a) *v/i.* froth; lather (*soap*); effervesce, fizz (*champagne*); F faire ~ q. crack s.o. up; **mousseux, -euse** [ˌˈsø, ˌˈsøːz] **1.** *adj.* mossy; foaming; sparkling (*wine*); **2.** *su./m* sparkling wine.

mousson [muˈsɔ̃] *f* monsoon.

moussu, e [muˈsy] mossy; ♀ rose *f* ~e moss-rose.

moustache [musˈtaʃ] *f* moustache; *cat*: whiskers *pl.*; **moustachu, e** [ˌtaˈʃy] moustached.

moustiquaire [mustiˈkɛːr] *f* mosquito-net; **moustique** *zo.* [ˌˈtik] *m* mosquito; gnat.

moût [mu] *m grapes*: must; unfermented wine.

moutarde ♀, *a. cuis.* [muˈtard] *f* mustard; **moutardier** [ˌtarˈdje] *m* mustard-pot; mustard-maker; F se croire le premier ~ du pape think no end of o.s.

mouton [muˈtɔ̃] *m* sheep; *cuis.* mutton; ~s *pl.* fleecy clouds; *sea*: white horses; revenons à nos ~s let us get back to the subject; **moutonner** [ˌtɔˈne] (1a) *v/i.* foam, break into white horses (*sea*); ciel *m* moutonné mackerel sky; **moutonnerie** [ˌtɔnˈri] *f* stupidity; **moutonneux, -euse** [mutɔˈnø, ˌˈnøːz] fleecy (*sky*); frothy, covered with white horses (*sea*); **moutonnier, -ère** [ˌˈnje, ˌˈnjɛːr] ovine; *fig.* sheep-like, easily led.

mouture [muˈtyːr] *f* grinding, milling; milling dues *pl.*

mouvance [muˈvɑ̃ːs] *f* domain, sphere (of influence); mobility; instability; **mouvant, e** [muˈvɑ̃, ˌˈvɑ̃ːt] moving; shifting (*sands*); loose (*ground*); *fig.* changeable; sables *m/pl.* ~s quicksand *sg.*; **mouvement** [muvˈmɑ̃] *m* movement (*a.* ♪); motion (*a. phys.*); ♥, *a. fig.* change; ♥ *market*: fluctuation; *roads etc.*: traffic; ⊕ *machine*: action, works *pl.*; *fig.* impulse; *fig.* outburst; ~ clandestin underground movement; ⊕ ~ perdu idle motion; ~ perpétuel perpetual motion; ~ populaire popular uprising; ~ syndical trade-unionism; ⚓ faire un faux ~ strain o.s. or a muscle; **mouvementé, e** [ˌmɑ̃ˈte] lively; busy; eventful (*life*); undulating (*ground*).

mouvoir [muˈvwaːr] (3f) *v/t.* ⊕ drive; ⚓ propel (a *ship*); *fig.* move; *fig.* urge, drive, prompt; se ~ move; **mouvrai** [ˌˈvre] *1st p. sg. fut. of mouvoir*.

moyen, -enne [mwaˈjɛ̃, ˌˈjɛn] **1.** *adj.* middle; mean, average; medium (*size, quality*); ♀ Age Middle Ages *pl.*; classe *f* ~enne middle class; du ♀ Age medi(a)eval; **2.** *su./m* means *sg.*, way, manner; medium; ♠ mean; ⚖ grounds *pl.* of a claim; ~s *pl.* resources; au ~ de by means of; il (n')y a (pas) ~ de (*inf.*) it is (im)possible to (*inf.*); pas ~! nothing doing!; le ~ de (*inf.*) how could one (*inf.*); *su./f* average, mean; *examination*: passmark; *en ~enne* on an average; **moyenâgeux, -euse** F [~jɛna'ʒø, ~'ʒøːz] (*pej.* sham-)medi(a)eval, historic; *fig.* antiquated; **moyennant** [~jɛ'nɑ̃] *prp.* for (*money etc.*); *~ quoi* in return for which.

moyeu[1] [mwa'jø] *m wheel*: hub, nave.

moyeu[2] [~] *m* preserved plum.

mû, mue, *m/pl.* **mus** [my] *p.p. of* mouvoir.

muance [mɥɑ̃ːs] *f voice*: breaking.

mucilage ꬳ [mysi'laːʒ] *m* gum, mucilage; **mucilagineux, -euse** [~laʒi'nø, ~'nøːz] mucilaginous, viscous.

mucosité [mykozi'te] *f* mucus.

mue [my] *f birds*: mo(u)lt(ing); *snakes*: sloughing; *animals*: shedding of coat *etc.*; mo(u)lting-season; *hens*: coop; *voice*: breaking; **muer** [mɥe] (1n) *v/i.* mo(u)lt (*birds*); slough (*snake*); shed its coat *etc.* (*animal*); break (*voice*); cast its antlers (*stag*).

muet, -ette [mɥɛ, mɥɛt] 1. *adj.* dumb; mute; 2. *su.* dumb *or* mute person.

mufle [myfl] *m animal*: muzzle, nose; *fig.* F boor, lout; F mug (= *face*); **muflerie** F [myflə'ri] *f* boorishness; **muflier** ꬳ [~fli'e] *m* snapdragon.

mugir [my'ʒiːr] (2a) *v/i.* bellow (*bull, a.* F *person with rage*); low (*cow*); howl (*wind*); roar (*sea, a. fig.*); **mugissement** [~ʒis'mɑ̃] *m* bellowing *etc.*

muguet [my'gɛ] *m* ꬳ lily of the valley; ꬳ thrush.

mulâtre *m*, **-tresse** *f* [my'lɑːtr, ~la'trɛs] mulatto.

mule[1] [myl] *f* mule, slipper; ꬳ kibe.

mule[2] *zo.* [~] *f* (she-)mule.

mulet[1] *zo.* [my'lɛ] *m* mule.

mulet[2] *icht.* [~] *m* grey mullet.

muletier [myl'tje] *m* muleteer.

mulot *zo.* [my'lo] *m* field-mouse.

mulsion [myl'sjɔ̃] *f* milking.

multi... [mylti] multi(-)...; many- ...; **~colore** [~kɔ'lɔːr] many-col-o(u)red, multi-colo(u)red; **~latéral, e,** *m/pl.* **-aux** [~late'ral, ~'ro] multilateral.

multiple [myl'tipl] 1. *adj.* multiple; multifarious; 2. *su./m* multiple; **multiplication** [~tiplika'sjɔ̃] *f* multiplication; ⊕, *mot.* gear(-ratio); *fig.* increase; **multiplier** [~tipli'e]

(1a) *vt/i.* multiply; *v/t.*: ⊕ *~ la* vitesse gear up.

multitude [mylti'tyd] *f* multitude; crowd.

municipal, e, *m/pl.* **-aux** [mynisi-'pal, ~'po] municipal; bye-(*law*); local, town...; *conseil m ~* town council; **municipalité** [~pali'te] *f* municipality, township.

munificence [mynifi'sɑ̃ːs] *f* munificence; bounty; **munificent, e** [~'sɑ̃, ~'sɑ̃ːt] munificent; bounteous.

munir [my'niːr] (2a) *v/t.* equip, provide (with, *de*); **munitions** [myni-'sjɔ̃] *f/pl.* ✗ ammunition *sg.*; *~ de bouche* provisions.

muqueux, -euse [my'kø, ~'køːz] mucous.

mûr, mûre [myːr] ripe; mature (*age, mind, wine*).

mur [myːr] *m* wall; ✗ *~ du son* sound barrier; **murage** [my'raːʒ] *m* walling (in); bricking up; **muraille** [~'rɑːj] *f* high *or* thick wall; ⚓ *ship*: side; **mural, e,** *m/pl.* **-aux** [~'ral, ~'ro] mural; *carte f ~e* wall-map.

mûre ꬳ [myːr] *f* mulberry; blackberry.

murer [my're] (1a) *v/t.* wall in; wall *or* block up.

mûrier ꬳ [my'rje] *m* mulberry (-bush *or* -tree); *~ sauvage* bramble.

mûrir [my'riːr] (2a) *vt/i.* ripen, mature (*a. fig.*); *v/t. fig.* meditate, think out thoroughly.

murmure [myr'myːr] *m* murmur (-ing); whisper; **murmurer** [~my-'re] (1a) *vt/i.* murmur; whisper; babble (*child, stream*); *fig.* complain.

mûron ꬳ [my'rɔ̃] *m* blackberry; wild raspberry.

mus [my] *1st p. sg. p.s. of* mouvoir.

musaraigne *zo.* [myza'rɛɲ] *f* shrewmouse.

musard, e [my'zaːr, ~'zard] 1. *adj.* idling; 2. *su.* idler; **musarder** F [~zar'de] (1a) *v/i.* idle; fritter away one's time.

musc [mysk] *m* musk; *zo.* musk-deer.

muscade ꬳ [mys'kad] *f* nutmeg.

muscadet [myska'dɛ] *m* (*sort of*) muscatel (wine).

muscardin *zo.* [myskar'dɛ̃] *m* dormouse.

muscat [mys'ka] *m* muscat (grape *or* wine); musk-pear.

muscle [myskl] *m* muscle; *fig.*
brawn; **musclé, e** [mys'kle] muscular; brawny; athletic; sinewy (*a.
fig.*); *fig.* powerful, strong; *fig.*
strong-arm (*politics etc.*); **muscler**
[~] (1a) *v/t.* develop the muscles of;
fig. strengthen; **musculaire** [~ky-
'lɛ:r] muscular; **musculeux, -euse**
[~ky'lø, ~'lø:z] muscular; *cuis.* sinewy (*meat*). [mug (= *face*).\
museau [my'zo] *m* muzzle; snout; F\
musée [my'ze] *m* museum.
museler [myz'le] (1c) *v/t.* muzzle (*a.
fig.*); **muselière** [~zə'ljɛ:r] *f* muzzle.
muser [my'ze] (1a) *v/i.* dawdle; fritter away one's time.
musette [my'zɛt] *f horse*: nose-bag;
✗ haversack; ♪ country bagpipe;
bal m ~ popular dance-hall.
musical, e, *m/pl.* **-aux** [myzi'kal,
~'ko] musical; **music-hall** [myzi-
'ko:l] *m* music-hall; variety; **musicien, -enne** [myzi'sjɛ̃, ~'sjɛn]
1. *adj.* musical; **2.** *su.* musician;
performer, player; **musique** [my-
'zik] *f* music; ✗ *etc.* band; ~ *enregistrée* recorded music.
musqué, e [mys'ke] musky; musk;
fig. paroles f/pl. ~*es* honeyed words;
poire f ~*e* musk-pear; *rose f* ~*e*
musk-rose.
musulman, e [myzyl'mã, ~'man]
adj., a. su. ♀ Moslem, Mohammedan.
mutabilité [mytabili'te] *f* instability; ♙ alienability; **mutation**
[~ta'sjɔ̃] *f* change, alteration; ♪, *biol.*
mutation; ♪ *violin-playing:* shift;
personnel, property: transfer; **muter**
[~'te] (1a) *v/t.* transfer (*an official
etc.*).
mutilation [mytila'sjɔ̃] *f person,
book, statue, etc.*: mutilation; *person*: maiming; *book, statue, etc.*:
defacement; **mutilé** [~'le] *m*: ~ *de
guerre* disabled ex-serviceman; ~
du travail disabled workman; **muti-**

ler [~'le] (1a) *v/t.* mutilate; maim;
deface.
mutin, e [my'tɛ̃, ~'tin] **1.** *adj.* mischievous; † insubordinate; **2.** *su./m*
mutineer; **mutiner** [~ti'ne] (1a)
v/t.: *se* ~ rise in revolt, rebel; be
unruly; ✗ mutiny; **mutinerie**
[~tin'ri] *f* rebellion; ✗ mutiny; unruliness; pertness.
mutisme [my'tism] *m* silence.
mutualité [mytɥali'te] *f* mutuality,
reciprocity; **mutuel, -elle** [my-
'tɥɛl] **1.** *adj.* mutual; *pari m* ~
totalizator, F tote; *secours m/pl.* ~*s*
mutual benefit; *société f de
secours* ~ friendly society; **2.** *su./f*
mutual insurance company.
myocarde *anat.* [mjɔ'kard] *m* my-
ocardium; **myocardite** ⚕ [~kar-
'dit] *f* myocarditis.
myope ⚕ [mjɔp] **1.** *adj.* myopic,
near-sighted, short-sighted; **2.** *su.*
near-sighted *or* short-sighted person; **myopie** ⚕ [mjɔ'pi] *f* myopia,
near-sightedness, short-sighted-
ness. [forget-me-not.\
myosotis ⚘ [mjɔzɔ'tis] *m* myosotis,\
myrte ⚘ [mirt] *m* myrtle; **myrtille**
⚘ [mir'til] *f* whortleberry, bilberry,
Am. blueberry, huckleberry.
mystère [mis'tɛ:r] *m* mystery (*a.
thea.*), secret; secrecy; **mystérieux,
-euse** [~te'rjø, ~'rjø:z] mysterious;
enigmatic; **mysticisme** [~ti'sism]
m mysticism; **mystification** [~tifi-
ka'sjɔ̃] *f* hoax; mystification; **mystifier** [~ti'fje] (1o) *v/t.* hoax, fool;
mystify; **mystique** [~'tik] **1.** *adj.*
mystic; **2.** *su.* mystic; *su./f* mystical
theology *or* doctrine.
mythe [mit] *m* myth (*a. fig.*); legend;
mythique [mi'tik] mythical; **mythologie** [mitɔlɔ'ʒi] *f* mythology;
mythologique [~lɔ'ʒik] mytholog-
ical; **mythologue** [~'lɔg] *m* mythol-
ogist; **mythomane** *psych.* [~'man]
adj., a. su. mythomaniac.

N

N, n [ɛn] *m* N, n.
nabab [na'bab] *m* nabob.
nabot, e [na'bo, ~'bɔt] 1. *su.* dwarf, midget; 2. *adj.* dwarfish.
nacelle [na'sɛl] *f* ⚓ skiff, wherry; ✈ cockpit; *airship:* gondola; *balloon:* basket.
nacre [nakr] *f* mother of pearl; **nacré, e** [na'kre] pearly; **nacrer** [~] (1a) *v/t.* give a pearly sheen to.
nage [na:ʒ] *f* swimming; rowing; stroke; ~ *à la brasse* breast-stroke; ~ *libre* free style; ~ *sur le dos* backstroke; *à la* ~ by swimming; *donner la* ~ *rowing:* set the stroke; F (*tout*) *en* ~ bathed in perspiration; **nageoire** [na'ʒwa:r] *f icht.* fin; *whale:* paddle; float; *sl.* arm; **nager** [~'ʒe] (11) *v/i.* swim; row; float; ~ *dans l'opulence* be rolling in money; *v/t.:* ~ *le crawl* swim the crawl; **nageur** *m*, **-euse** *f* [~'ʒœ:r, ~'ʒø:z] swimmer; rower.
naguère [na'gɛ:r] *adv.* lately, a short time ago.
naïf, -ve [na'if, ~'i:v] naïve, artless, unaffected; unsophisticated, simple.
nain, naine [nɛ̃, nɛn] 1. *su.* dwarf, midget; 2. *adj.* dwarf(ish); stunted.
nais [nɛ] *1st p. sg. pres. of naître;* **naissance** [nɛ'sɑ̃:s] *f* birth; *fig.* origin; *fig.* beginning; *acte m de* ~ birth-certificate; *Français de* ~ French-born; ~ *des cheveux* hair line; *fig. prendre* ~ originate; **naissant, e** [~'sɑ̃, ~'sɑ̃:t] dawning; *fig. a.* incipient; **naissent** [nɛs] *3rd p. pl. pres. of naître;* **naître** [nɛ:tr] (4x) *v/i.* be born; dawn; *fig.* originate, begin; *faire* ~ give rise to, cause.
naïveté [naiv'te] *f* naïvety, ingenuousness; simpleness; ingenuous remark.
naja *zo.* [na'ʒa] *m* cobra. [*woman*).\
nana *sl.* [na'na] *f* chick (= *girl,*∫
nantir [nɑ̃'ti:r] (2a) *v/t.* ⚖ *creditor:* secure; *fig.* provide (with, *de*); *bien nanti* well-off (for money); *les nantis* the well-to-do; **nantissement** [~tis'mɑ̃] *m* security; lien, hypothecation.

napalm ⚗, ⚔ [na'palm] *m* napalm.
naphte ⚗ [naft] *m* naphtha.
nappe [nap] *f* (table)cloth; cover; *ice, water, etc.:* sheet; ~ *de pétrole* oil slick; **napperon** [na'prɔ̃] *m* (table)mat; ~ *individuel* place mat.
naquis [na'ki] *1st p. s.g. p.s. of naître.*
narcisse ⚘ [nar'sis] *m* narcissus; ~ *des bois* daffodil; **narcissique** [~si'sik] narcissistic; **narcissisme** [~si'sism] *m* narcissism.
narcose ⚕ [nar'ko:z] *f* narcosis; **narcotique** [~kɔ'tik] *adj., a. su./m* narcotic.
nard ⚘ [na:r] *m* (spike)nard.
narguer [nar'ge] (1m) *v/t.* flout; jeer at (*s.o.*).
narine [na'rin] *f anat.* nostril.
narquois, e [nar'kwa, ~'kwa:z] mocking.
narrateur *m*, **-trice** *f* [nara'tœ:r, ~'tris] narrator, teller, relater; **narratif, -ve** [~'tif, ~'ti:v] narrative; **narration** [~'sjɔ̃] *f* narration, narrative; **narrer** [na're] (1a) *v/t.* narrate, relate.
narval, *pl.* **-als** *zo.* [nar'val] *m* narwhal.
nasal, e, *m/pl.* **-aux** [na'zal, ~'zo] *adj., a. su./f gramm.* nasal; **nasaliser** *gramm.* [~zali'ze] (1a) *v/t.* nasalize.
naseau [~'zo] *m* nostril; **nasillard, e** [nazi'ja:r, ~'jard] nasal, twanging; **nasiller** [~'je] (1a) *v/i.* speak through one's nose *or* with a twang; *v/t.* twang (*s.th.*) (out).
nasse [nas] *f* eel-pot; trap (*a. fig.*).
natal, e, *m/pl.* **-als** [na'tal] native; birth...; **natalité** [~tali'te] *f* birth-rate, natality.
natation [nata'sjɔ̃] *f* swimming; **natatoire** [~'twa:r] *zo.* natatory; *icht. vessie f* ~ air-bladder, swimming-bladder.
natif, -ve [na'tif, ~'ti:v] 1. *adj.* native (*a.* ⚒); natural, innate; 2. *su.* native.
nation [na'sjɔ̃] *f* nation; *bibl. les* ~*s pl.* the Gentiles; **national, e**, *m/pl.* **-aux** [~sjɔ'nal, ~'no] 1. *adj.*

national; 2. *su./m:* ∼*s pl.* nationals; *su./f* (*a.* route *f* ∼*e*) highway; main road; **nationalisation** [nasjɔnaliza-'sjɔ̃] *f* nationalization; **nationalisme** *pol.* [∼'lism] *m* nationalism; **nationaliste** *pol.* [∼'list] **1.** *su.* nationalist; **2.** *adj.* nationalistic; **nationalité** [∼li'te] *f* nationality; nation.

nativité *eccl.*, *astr.* [nativi'te] *f* nativity.

natte [nat] *f* (*straw- etc.*) mat(ting); *hair:* plait, braid; F pigtail; **natter** [na'te] (1a) *v/t.* cover (*s.th.*) with mats; plait (*one's hair, straw*).

naturalisation [natyraliza'sjɔ̃] *f pol.* naturalization; ♥, *zo.* acclimatizing; **naturaliser** [∼li'ze] (1a) *v/t.* naturalize; ♥, *zo.* acclimatize; stuff, mount (*an animal*); se ∼ become naturalized; **naturalisme** *paint. etc.* [∼'lism] *m* naturalism; **naturaliste** [∼'list] **1.** *su.* naturalist; taxidermist; **2.** *adj.* naturalistic; **naturalité** [∼li'te] *f* naturalness.

nature [na'ty:r] **1.** *su./f* nature; kind; type; disposition, temperament; *paint.* d'après ∼ from nature; de ∼ à (*inf.*) likely to (*inf.*), such as to (*inf.*); lois *f/pl.* de la ∼ laws of nature; de ∼, par ∼ by nature, naturally; payer en ∼ pay in kind; **2.** *adj./inv.* plain; café *m* ∼ black coffee; **naturel, -elle** [naty'rɛl] **1.** *adj.* natural; **2.** *su./m* disposition, nature; naturalness; native; au ∼ realistically, true to life; *cuis.* plain; **naturiste** [∼'rist] **1.** *su.* naturist; **2.** *adj.* naturistic.

naufrage [no'fra:ʒ] *m* shipwreck (*a. fig.*); faire ∼ be shipwrecked; **naufragé, e** [nofra'ʒe] **1.** *adj.* shipwrecked; castaway; **2.** *su.* shipwrecked person; castaway; **naufrageur** [∼'ʒœ:r] *m* wrecker.

nauséabond, e [nozea'bɔ̃, ∼'bɔ̃:d] nauseous, foul; evil-smelling; **nausée** [∼'ze] *f* nausea; seasickness; *fig.* loathing; **nauséeux, -euse** [∼ze'ø, ∼'ø:z] nauseous; loathsome.

nautique [no'tik] ♣ nautical; sea-...; aquatic (*sports*); **nautonier** [∼tɔ-'nje] *m* ferryman, pilot.

naval, e, *m/pl.* **-als** [na'val] naval, nautical; constructions *f/pl.* ∼es ship-building *sg.*

navarin *cuis.* [nava'rɛ̃] *m* mutton stew with turnips.

navet [na'vɛ] *m* turnip; F *paint.* daub; F rubbish, tripe.

navette[1] [na'vɛt] *f eccl.* incense boat; ⊕ shuttle; 🚗 *etc.* shuttle service; ∼ spatiale space shuttle; *fig.* faire la ∼ shuttle; come and go; ply.

navette[2] ♥ [∼] *f* rape.

navigabilité [navigabili'te] *f* navigability; *ship:* seaworthiness; ✈ airworthiness; **navigable** [∼'gabl] navigable; seaworthy (*ship*); ✈ airworthy; **navigateur** [∼ga'tœ:r] **1.** *adj./m* seafaring; **2.** *su./m* navigator; sailor; **navigation** [∼ga'sjɔ̃] *f* navigation, sailing; ∼ intérieure inland navigation; **naviguer** [∼'ge] (1m) *vt/i.* ♣, ✈ navigate; ♣ steer.

naviplane ♣ [navi'plan] *m* hovercraft.

navire ♣ [na'vi:r] *m* ship, vessel; ♣ ∼ de commerce merchantman; ∼-**citerne**, *pl.* ∼**s-citernes** ♣ [∼vir-si'tern] *m* tanker; ∼-**école**, *pl.* ∼**s-écoles** ♣ [∼vire'kɔl] *m* training ship; ∼-**hôpital**, *pl.* ∼**s-hôpitaux** ♣ [∼virɔpi'tal, ∼'to] *m* hospital-ship.

navrant, e [na'vrɑ̃, ∼'vrɑ̃:t] heart-rending, heart-breaking; **navré, e** [∼'vre] deeply grieved; heart-broken; **navrer** [∼'vre] (1a) *v/t.* grieve (*s.o.*) deeply; j'en suis navré! I am awfully *or* F terribly sorry!

ne [nə] *adv.*: ne ... guère not ... much, scarcely; ne ... jamais never; ne ... pas not; ne ... plus no more, no longer; ne ... plus jamais never again; ne ... point not (at all); ne ... que only.

né, née [ne] **1.** *p.p. of* naître; **2.** *adj.* born; *fig.* cut out (for, pour); bien ∼ of a good family; *fig.* être ∼ coiffé be born with a silver spoon in one's mouth.

néanmoins [neɑ̃'mwɛ̃] *adv.* nevertheless, however; yet.

néant [ne'ɑ̃] *m* nothing(ness), naught; *admin.* nil; 🏛 mettre à ∼ dismiss; réduire à ∼ reduce to naught; **néantiser** [∼ɑ̃ti'ze] (1a) *v/t.* destroy; reduce to nothing.

nébuleux, -euse [neby'lø, ∼'lø:z] **1.** *adj.* nebulous; cloudy (*a. liquid*), misty (*sky, view*); *fig.* gloomy (*face*); F *fig.* obscure; **2.** *su./f astr.* nebula; **nébulosité** [∼lozi'te] *f* haziness (*a. fig.*); patch of haze *or* mist.

nécessaire [nesɛ'sɛ:r] **1.** *adj.* neces-

sary (to, for *à*); requisite; **2.** *su./m*
necessaries *pl.*; outfit, kit, set; ~ *de*
toilette toilet bag; **nécessité** [‿si'te] *f*
necessity, need; indigence; **nécessiter** [‿si'te] (1a) *v/t.* necessitate,
entail, require; **nécessiteux, -euse**
[‿si'tø, ‿'tø:z] **1.** *adj.* needy; **2.** *su./m*:
les ~ *pl.* the needy.

nécro... [nekrɔ] necro...; ~**loge**
[‿'lɔ:ʒ] *m* obituary list; death-roll;
~**logie** [‿lɔ'ʒi] *f* obituary; ~**logue**
[‿'lɔg] *m* necrologist; ~**mancie**
[‿mã'si] *f* necromancy; ~**pole**
[‿'pɔl] *f* necropolis, city of the dead.

nécrose [ne'kro:z] *f* 🎖 necrosis; ♀
canker.

nectar ♀, *a. myth.* [nɛk'ta:r] *m*
nectar.

néerlandais, e [neɛrlã'dɛ, ‿'dɛ:z]
1. *adj.* Dutch, Netherlandish;
2. *su.* ♀ Netherlander; *su./m* ♀ Dutchman; *su./f* ♀ Dutchwoman.

nef [nɛf] *f church*: nave; *poet.* ship.

néfaste [ne'fast] ill-omened; ill-
starred; ill-fated; disastrous.

nèfle ♀ [nɛfl] *f* medlar; *sl. des* ~*s!* not
likely!

négatif, -ve [nega'tif, ‿'ti:v] **1.** *adj.*
negative (*a.* ⚡); *phot.* épreuve *f* ~*ve* =
2. *su./m phot.* negative; *su./f* negative; *dans la* ~*ve* in the negative; if
not; *répondre par la* ~*ve* say no; *se
tenir sur la* ~*ve* maintain a negative
attitude; **négation** [‿'sjɔ̃] *f* nega-
tion, denial; *gramm.* negative.

négligé, e [negli'ʒe] **1.** *adj.* neglected;
slovenly (*dress, style*); careless (*appearance, dress*); **2.** *su./m* undress;
informal dress; dishabille; négligé;
négligeable [‿'ʒabl] negligible (*a.*
⚡); trifling; **négligence** [‿'ʒã:s] *f*
negligence, neglect; oversight; **négligent, e** [‿'ʒã, ‿'ʒã:t] negligent,
careless; **négliger** [‿'ʒe] (1l) *v/t.*
neglect; overlook; disregard; slight
(*s.o.*); *se* ~ become careless *or*
slovenly.

négoce [ne'gɔs] *m* trade, business;
négociable [‿negɔ'sjabl] negotiable; market (*value*); **négociant**
[‿'sjã] *m* (wholesale) merchant;
trader; **négociateur, *m* -trice** *f*
[‿sja'tœ:r, ‿'tris] negotiator; **négociation** [‿sja'sjɔ̃] *f* negotiation (*a.*
⚡); ♱ transaction; ⚔ parley; **négocier** [‿'sje] (1o) *vt/i.* negotiate; *mot.* ~
un virage negotiate a bend.

nègre [nɛgr] *m* negro; F ghost

(writer); (*barrister's*) devil; *fig.* tra-
vailler comme un ~ work like a slave;
négresse [ne'grɛs] *f* negress; **négrier** [negri'e] *m* slave trader; ⚓ (*a.
bateau m* ~) slave ship; *fig.* slave
driver; **négrillon** F [‿'jɔ̃] *m* negro
boy; F piccaninny; **négrillonne** F
[‿'jɔn] *f* negro girl.

neige [nɛ:ʒ] *f* snow (*a. sl.* = *cocaine*);
~*s pl.* éternelles perpetual snow *sg.*;
🏔 ~ *carbonique* dry ice; ~ *croûteuse*
(*poudreuse*) crusted (powdery)
snow; *boule f de* ~ snowball;
🚂 *train m de* ~ winter sports train;
neiger [ne'ʒe] (11) *v/impers.* snow;
neigeux, -euse [‿'ʒø, ‿'ʒø:z]
snowy; snow-covered; snow-white.

nénuphar ♀ [neny'fa:r] *m* water-
lily.

néo... [neɔ] neo-...; ~**logisme** [‿lɔ-
'ʒism] *m* neologism.

néon 🏔 [ne'ɔ̃] *m* neon; *éclairage m
au* ~ neon lighting.

néphrétique 🎖 [nefre'tik] **1.** *adj.*
nephritic; **2.** *su.* sufferer from ne-
phritis; **néphrite** [‿'frit] *f* 🎖 ne-
phritis; *min.* jade; 🎖 ~ *chronique*
Bright's disease.

népotisme [nepɔ'tism] *m* nepotism.

nerf [nɛ:r] *m anat.* nerve; *fig.*
vigo(u)r, F guts *pl.*; *fig.* ~ *de bœuf*
cosh; life-preserver; *fig. avoir du* ~ be
vigorous; *avoir ses* ~*s*, F *avoir les* ~*s en
pelote or en boule* be on edge; *le* ~ *de la
guerre* the sinews *pl.* of war; *porter* (*or
donner or* F *taper*) *sur les* ~*s à q.* get on
s.o.'s nerves.

nerprun ♀ [nɛr'prœ̃] *m* buckthorn.

nerveux, -euse [nɛr'vø, ‿'vø:z] nervous; sinewy; *anat.* nerve...; excitable, highly-strung (*person*); *fig.*
virile (*style etc.*); **nervin** 🎖 [‿'vɛ̃]
adj./m, a. su./m nervine; **nervosis-
me** 🎖 [‿vɔ'zism] *m* nervous predisposition; **nervosité** [‿vozi'te]
f nervousness; irritability; irritation;
nervure [‿'vy:r] *f leaf etc.*: vein; △,
⊕ rib.

net, nette [nɛt] **1.** *adj.* clean; neat;
clear; clear-cut, distinct; ♱ net; **2.**
net adv. plainly, flatly; clearly; *refuser* ~ refuse point-blank; **3.** *su./m*:
copie f au ~ fair copy; *mettre qch. au* ~
make a fair copy of s.th.; **netteté**
[nɛtə'te] *f* cleanness; (*bodily*) cleanliness; *fig.* image, sound: clarity; dis-
tinctness; *fig.* decidedness; **nettoie-
ment** [nɛtwa'mã] *m* cleaning; clear-

ing; **nettoyage** [~'ja:ʒ] m ⊕ scaling; ⚒ mopping-up; ~ à sec dry-cleaning; **nettoyer** [~'je] (1h) v/t. clean; clear; ⊕ scale; ⚒ mop up; F rifle (*a house*, *s.o.*); F clean out; ~ à sec dry-clean; **nettoyeur** m, **-euse** f [~'jœːr, ~'jøːz] cleaner.

neuf[1] [nœf; *before vowel or h mute* nœv] adj./num., a. su./m/inv. nine; date, title: ninth.

neuf[2], **neuve** [nœf, nœːv] **1.** adj. new; fig. inexperienced; **2.** su./m new; quoi de ~? what's new?; remettre à ~ do up (like new); repeindre à ~ redecorate.

neurasthénie [nøraste'ni] f neurasthenia; **neurasthénique** 𝒮 [~'nik] adj., a. su. neurasthenic; **neurologue** 𝒮 [nørɔ'lɔg] m neurologist, nerve specialist; **neurone** [nø'rɔn] m neuron.

neutraliser [nøtrali'ze] (1a) v/t. neutralize; **neutraliste** pol. [~'list] adj., a. su. neutralist; **neutralité** [~li'te] f neutrality; 𝒮 neutral state; **neutre** [nøːtr] **1.** adj. neuter (a. gramm.); 𝒮, pol., a. colour: neutral; **2.** su. pol. neutral; su./m gramm. neuter.

neutron phys. [nø'trɔ̃] m neutron.

neuvaine eccl. [nœ'vɛn] f novena; **neuvième** [~'vjɛm] adj./num., a. su., a. su./m fraction: ninth.

névé geol. [ne've] m névé, firn.

neveu [nɔ'vø] m nephew; ~x pl. descendants.

névralgie 𝒮 [nevral'ʒi] f neuralgia; **névralgique** [~'ʒik] 𝒮 neuralgic; fig. point m ~ sore spot.

névr(o)... [nevr(ɔ)] neur(o)...

névrose [ne'vroːz] f neurosis; **névrosé, e** [nevrɔ'ze] adj., a. su. neurotic; **névrotique** [~'tik] neurotic.

nez [ne] m nose; animal: snout; ⚓, ✈ bow, nose; scent; F ~ à ~ face to face; au ~ de q. under s.o.'s nose; fig. avoir le ~ fin be shrewd; F avoir q. dans le ~ bear s.o. a grudge; mener par le bout du ~ twist (s.o.) round one's little finger; mettre le ~ dans poke one's nose into.

ni [ni] cj. nor, or; ni ... ni neither ... nor; ni moi non plus nor I (either).

niable [njabl] deniable; ⚖ traversable.

niais, e [njɛ, njɛːz] **1.** adj. simple, silly; Am. dumb; **2.** su. fool; simpleton; Am. dumbbell; **niaiserie** [njɛz'ri] f foolishness, silliness.

niche[1] [niʃ] f trick, practical joke.

niche[2] [niʃ] f niche, recess; ~ à chien kennel; **nichée** [ni'ʃe] f nestful; brood; **nicher** [~] (la) v/i. nest; F fig. live, hang out; v/t.: se ~ (build it's) nest; fig. nestle; fig. lodge o.s. (thing), put o.s. (person).

nichrome metall. [ni'krɔm] m chrome-nickel steel.

nickel 𝒮 [ni'kɛl] m nickel; **nickelage** ⊕ [ni'kla:ʒ] m nickel-plating; **nickeler** ⊕ [~'kle] (1c) v/t. nickel (-plate).

nicotine 𝒮 [nikɔ'tin] f nicotine.

nid [ni] m nest; fig. thieves: den; tex. ~ d'abeilles honeycomb, Am. waffle weave; mot. ~-de-poule pothole (on a road); **nidification** [nidifika'sjɔ̃] f nest-building.

nièce [njɛs] f niece.

nielle [njɛl] su./f ✿ wheat: earcockle; ✿ nigella; su./m ⊕ niello, inlaid enamel-work; **nieller** [njɛ'le] (la) v/t. ✿ blight, smut; ⊕ (inlay with) niello; ✿ se ~ smut; **niellure** [~'lyːr] f ✿ blighting; ⊕ niellowork.

nier [nje] (1o) v/t. deny; repudiate (a debt); on ne saurait ~ que there can be no denying that.

nigaud, e [ni'go, ~'goːd] **1.** adj. simple, silly; **2.** su. simpleton, booby, ass; **nigauderie** F [~go'dri] f stupidity; simplicity.

nimbe [nɛ̃ːb] m nimbus, halo; **nimbé, e** [nɛ̃'be] haloed.

nipper F [ni'pe] (la) v/t. rig (s.o.) out; **nippes** F [nip] f/pl. old clothes; togs.

nippon, e [ni'pɔ̃, ~'pɔn] adj., a. su. ♀ Japanese, Nipponese.

nique F [nik] f: faire la ~ à cook a snook at (s.o.); treat (s.th.) with contempt.

nitouche [ni'tuʃ] f: sainte ~ (little) hypocrite; F goody-goody.

nitrate 𝒮 [ni'trat] m nitrate; ~ de ... ... nitrate; **nitre** 𝒮 [nitr] m nitre, saltpetre; **nitré, e** [ni'tre] nitrated; **nitro-...**; **nitreux, -euse** [~'trø, ~'trøːz] nitrous; **nitrière** [nitri'ɛːr] f saltpetre-bed; nitreworks usu. sg.; **nitrification** [~fika'sjɔ̃] f nitrification; **nitrifier** [~'fje] (1o) v/t. a. se ~ nitrify; **nitrique** [ni'trik] nitric (acid).

nitro... [nitrɔ] nitro(-)...; **~gène** 𝒮 [~'ʒɛn] m nitrogen.

nitruration ⚛ [nitryra'sjɔ̃] f nitrid-
ing.   [nival.)
nivéal, e, m/pl. -aux ⚥ [nive'al,‿'o])
niveau [ni'vo] m level (a. ⊕); fig.
standard; ⊕ ga(u)ge; ~ d'eau wa-
ter-level; ~ de maçon plumb-level;
mot. ~ d'essence petrol gauge, Am.
gasoline level gage; ~ de vie standard of living; pol. ~ le plus élevé
highest level; fig. au ~ de on a par
with; de ~ level (with, avec); 🚂
passage m à ~ level crossing, Am.
grade crossing; **niveler** [niv'le] (1c)
v/t. level, even up; ⊕ true up; survey (the ground); **niveleur** [‿'lœ:r]
m leveller (a. fig.); **nivellement**
[nivɛl'mɑ̃] m land: surveying;
ground, a. fig.: levelling.
nobiliaire [nɔbi'ljɛ:r] **1.** adj. nobil-
iary; **2.** su./m peerage-list; **noble**
[nɔbl] **1.** adj. noble; lofty (style);
2. su./m nobleman; su./f noble-
woman; **noblesse** [nɔ'blɛs] f nobility (a. fig.).
noce [nɔs] f wedding; wedding-
party; ~s pl. d'argent (d'or) silver
(golden) wedding sg.; F faire la ~ go
on the spree or sl. the binge; voyage m
de ~s honeymoon (trip); **noceur** m,
-euse f F [nɔ'sœ:r, ‿'sø:z] reveller;
fast liver.
nocif, -ve [nɔ'sif, ‿'si:v] harmful,
noxious; **nocivité** [‿sivi'te] f harmfulness.
noctambule [nɔktɑ̃'byl] su. late-
nighter, night bird; † sleepwalker;
nocturne [‿'tyrn] **1.** adj. nocturnal;
by night; **2.** su./m orn. nocturnal
(bird of prey); ♩ nocturne.
Noël [nɔ'ɛl] m (oft. la [fête de]~)
Christmas; yule-tide; Christmas
present; ♩♀ (Christmas) carol; arbre
m de~ Christmas tree; le Père~, le Bon
homme ~ Father Christmas, Santa
Claus; joyeux ~! merry Christmas!
nœud [nø] m knot (a. ⚓); band: bow;
fig. tie, bond; fig. matter, play, question, etc.: crux; ⚥, ♣, ⚢, astr., phys.
node; 🚂 junction; ~ de tisserand
weaver's knot; ~ papillon bow tie.
noir, noire [nwa:r] **1.** adj. black;
dark; fig. gloomy (thoughts); fig. illegal, illicit; sl. dead drunk; avoir des
idées noires have the blues; cuis. beurre m ~ browned butter sauce; blé m ~
buckwheat; **2.** su./m black (man);
negro; colour: black; dark(ness); ~ de
fumée lampblack; fig. ~ sur blanc in

black and white; au ~ illegally, illicitly; broyer du ~ be in the dumps;
mettre dans le ~ hit the mark; prendre
le ~ go into mourning; travailler au ~
moonlight; voir tout en ~ look on the
black side of things; su./f black
woman; negress; ♩ crotchet; **noirâtre** [nwa'rɑ:tr] blackish, darkish;
noiraud, e [‿'ro, ‿'ro:d] **1.** adj.
swarthy; **2.** su. swarthy person;
noirceur [nwar'sœ:r] f blackness;
darkness; fig. gloominess; fig. foul-
ness; crime: heinousness; **noircir**
[‿'si:r] (2a) v/t. blacken (a. fig.);
make gloomy (a picture, the sky,
thoughts); se ~ darken; v/i. turn black
or dark; **noircissure** [‿si'sy:r] f
smudge.
noise [nwa:z] f: chercher ~ à (try to)
pick a quarrel with.
noisetier ⚥ [nwaz'tje] m hazel(-tree,
-bush); **noisette** [nwa'zɛt] **1.** su./f
⚥ hazel-nut; **2.** adj./inv. (a. couleur
f ~) (nut-)brown; hazel (eyes);
noix [nwa] f ⚥ walnut; ⚥, a. ⚡
nut; ⊕ half-round groove; sl. head;
sl. fellow; ~ de terre peanut;
cuis. ~ de veau round shoulder of
veal.
nom [nɔ̃] m name; gramm. noun;
fig. reputation; ~ de baptême Christian or baptismal name, Am. given
name; ~ de famille family name;
surname; ~ de guerre assumed
name; ~ de jeune fille maiden name; ~
de plume pen-name; ✝ ~ déposé
registered trade name; ✝ ~ social
name of (the) firm or company; de ~
by name; décliner ses ~ et prénoms
give one's full name; du ~ de called,
by the name of; petit ~ Christian
name, Am. given name.
nomade [nɔ'mad] **1.** adj. wandering;
nomadic; **2.** su. nomad.
nombrable [nɔ̃'brabl] countable;
nombre [nɔ̃:br] m number (a.
gramm.); ~ cardinal cardinal number; ~ entier integer; whole number; ~ impair (pair, premier) odd
(even, prime) number; bon ~ de a
good many ...; du ~ de one of; bibl.
les ⚥s pl. Numbers; sans ~ countless; **nombrer** [nɔ̃'bre] (1a) v/t.
count, number; **nombreux, -euse**
[‿'brø, ‿'brø:z] numerous; manifold; rhythmic, harmonious.
nombril [nɔ̃'bri] m anat. navel; ⚥
fruit: eye.

nomenclature [nɔmãklaˈtyːr] *f* nomenclature; list.

nominal, e, *m/pl.* **-aux** [nɔmiˈnal, ˌˈno] nominal; of names; *appel m* ~ roll-call; ✝ *valeur f* ~e face-value; **nominatif, -ve** [ˌna'tif, ˌ'tiːv] 1. *adj.* nominal; of names; ✝ registered (*securities*); 2. *su./m gramm.* nominative; **nomination** [ˌna'sjɔ̃] *f* nomination; appointment.

nommé, e [nɔ'me] 1. *adj.* appointed (*day*); *à point* ~ in the nick of time; 2. *su.: le* ~ X, *la* ~*e* X the person named X; *su./m: un* ~ *Jean* one John; **nommément** [ˌme'mã] *adv.* by name; especially; **nommer** [ˌ'me] (1a) *v/t.* name; mention; appoint (*to a post*); *se* ~ be called; give one's name.

non [nɔ̃] *adv.* no; not; ~ *pas!* not at all!; ~ (*pas*) *que* (*sbj.*) not that (*ind.*); *dire que* ~ say no; *ne* ... *pas* ~ *plus* not ... either.

non... [nɔ̃; *before vowel* nɔn] non-...; **~-activité** [nɔnaktivi'te] *f* non-activity; *mettre en* ~ suspend.

nonagénaire [nɔnaʒe'nɛːr] *adj., a. su.* nonagenarian.

non-agression *pol.* [nɔnagrɛ'sjɔ̃] *f* non-aggression; *pacte m de* ~ non-aggression pact. [*papal nuncio.*]

nonce [nɔ̃ːs] *m* nuncio; ~ *apostolique*]

nonchalance [nɔ̃ʃa'lãːs] *f* nonchalance; languidness; **nonchalant, e** [ˌ'lã, ˌ'lãːt] nonchalant, unconcerned, languid.

non...: **~-combattant** ⚔ [nɔ̃kɔ̃ba-'tã] *m* non-combattant; **~-conducteur, -trice** [ˌkɔ̃dyk'tœːr, ˌ'tris] 1. *adj.* non-conducting; 2. *su./m* non-conductor; **~-conformisme** *eccl.* [ˌkɔ̃fɔr'mism] *m* nonconformity, dissent; **~-conformiste** [ˌkɔ̃fɔr'mist] *m* non-conformist (*a. fig.*); **~-engagé, e** *pol.* [ˌãga'ʒe] 1. non-aligned; 2. *su./m* non-aligned country; **~-ingérence** [nɔnɛ̃ʒe'rãːs] *f*, **~-intervention** [nɔnɛ̃tɛrvã'sjɔ̃] *f* non-intervention; non-interference; **~-lieu** ⚖ [nɔ̃'ljø] *m* no true bill; *rendre une ordonnance de* ~ dismiss the charge.

nonne †, *co.* [nɔn] *f* nun.

nonobstant [nɔnɔp'stã] 1. *prp.* notwithstanding; 2. *adv.* † for all that.

nonpareil, -eille [nɔ̃pa'rɛːj] 1. *adj.* matchless, unparalleled; 2. *su./f* apple, *a. typ.:* nonpareil.

non...: **~-retour** [nɔ̃rə'tuːr] *m: point*

m de ~ point of no return; **~-réussite** [ˌrey'sit] *f* failure; *plan:* miscarriage; **~-sens** [ˌ'sãːs] *m* meaningless act *or* expression; **~-valeur** [ˌva'lœːr] *f* worthless object; unproductive land; F passenger (= *incompetent employee etc.*); *admin.* possible deficit; **~-violence** [ˌvjɔ'lãs] *f* nonviolence.

nord [nɔːr] 1. *su./m* north; ⚓ north wind; *du* ~ north(ern); northerly (*wind*); *le* ⚓ the north (*of a country*); *fig. perdre le* ~ lose one's bearings; *vers le* ~ northward(s), to the north; 2. *adj./inv.* northern (*latitudes etc.*); northerly (*wind*); **~-est** [nɔ'rɛst] 1. *su./m* north-east; 2. *adj./inv.* north-east; north-eastern (*region*); north-easterly (*wind*); **~-ouest** [nɔ'rwɛst] 1. *su./m* north-west; 2. *adj./inv.* north-west; north-western (*region*); north-westerly (*wind*).

noria [nɔ'rja] *f* ⊕ chain-pump; bucket-conveyor; *fig.* line, chain, string.

normal, e, *m/pl.* **-aux** [nɔr'mal, ˌ'mo] 1. *adj.* normal; usual; standard (*measures etc.*); natural; *École f* ~*e* (teachers') training college; 2. *su./f* norm; normal (*a. Ⓐ*); *au-dessous de la* ~ above average; *revenir à la* ~ get back to normal; **normalien** *m*, **-enne** *f* [nɔrma'ljɛ̃, ˌ'ljɛn] student at an *École normale*; **normalisation** [ˌliza'sjɔ̃] *f* standardization; **normaliser** [ˌli'ze] (1a) *v/t.* standardize; normalize.

normand, e [nɔr'mã, ˌ'mãːd] 1. *adj.* Norman; F *réponse f* ~*e* non-committal answer; 2. *su.* ♀ Norman.

norme [nɔrm] *f* norm, standard.

norvégien, -enne [nɔrve'ʒjɛ̃, ˌ'ʒjɛn] *adj., a. su.* ♀ Norwegian.

nos [no] *pl. de notre.*

nostalgie [nɔstal'ʒi] *f* ✻ nostalgia; *fig.* homesickness; *fig.* yearning; **nostalgique** [ˌ'ʒik] nostalgic; *fig.* homesick.

notabilité [nɔtabili'te] *f* notability (*a. person*); *fig.* prominent person; **notable** [nɔ'tabl] 1. *adj.* notable; considerable; distinguished; 2. *su./m* person of distinction *or* note; *hist.* Notable.

notaire [nɔ'tɛːr] *m* notary (public).

notamment [nɔta'mã] *adv.* particularly, especially.

notarial, e, _m/pl._ **-aux** [nɔtaˈrjal,
~ˈrjo] notarial; **notarié, e** [~ˈrje]
adj.: acte _m_ ~ deed executed and
authenticated by a notary.
notation ♪, ♫ [nɔtaˈsjɔ̃] _f_ notation.
note [nɔt] _f_ note (a. ♪, _pol._, _fig._),
memo(randum); minute; anno-
tation; _school_: mark; _journ._ notice; ✝
account, bill; _prendre_ ~ _de_ note, make
a note of; _prendre des_ ~s jot down
notes; **noter** [nɔˈte] (1a) _v/t._ note,
make a note of; jot down; take notice
of; ♪ write down.
notice [nɔˈtis] _f_ note, notice.
notification [nɔtifikaˈsjɔ̃] _f_ notification, notice; **notifier** [~ˈfje] (1o)
_v/t._ intimate (s.th. to s.o., _qch. à q._);
notify (s.o. of s.th., _qch. à q._).
notion [nɔˈsjɔ̃] _f_ notion, idea; ~s _pl._
smattering _sg._; **notoire** [~ˈtwaːr]
well-known; manifest; _pej._ notorious; **notoriété** [~tɔrjeˈte] _f_ noto-
riety; _person_: repute.
notre, _pl._ **nos** [nɔtr, no] _adj./poss._
our.
nôtre [noːtr] **1.** _pron./poss._: _le_ (_la_)
~, _les_ ~s _pl._ ours; **2.** _su./m_ ours,
our own; _les_ ~s _pl._ our (own) people.
nouage [nwaːʒ] _m_ tying; _bone_: knitting.
nouba _sl._ [nuˈba] _f_: _faire la_ ~ go on a
binge, live it up.
noué, e [nwe] knotty (_joint_); _fig._
stunted (_mind etc._); **nouer** [nwe]
(1p) _v/t._ tie (up); knot; _fig._ enter into
(_conversation, relations_); _se_ ~ become
knotted; _fig._ be formed; build up;
_v/i._ set (_fruit_); **nouet** _cuis._ [nwɛ] _m_
bag of herbs; **noueux, -euse** [nwø,
nwøːz] knotty; ⚜ arthritic (_rheuma-
tism_); gnarled (_hands, stem_).
nougat _cuis._ [nuˈga] _m_ nougat.
nouille [nuːj] _f cuis._ noodle; F gutless
individual, drip, idiot.
nourrain [nuˈrɛ̃] _m_ fry, young fish;
nourrice [~ˈris] _f_ (wet-)nurse; ⊕,
⚒ service-tank; _mot._ feed-tank;
mettre un enfant en ~ put a child
out to nurse; **nourricerie** [~risˈri]
_f_ stock-farm; silkworm nursery;
baby-farm; **nourricier, -ère** [~-
riˈsje, ~ˈsjɛːr] nutritious, nutritive;
foster-(_father, mother_); **nourrir**
[~ˈriːr] (2a) _v/t._ feed, nourish;
suckle, nurse (_a baby_); _fig._ harbo(u)r
(_hope, thoughts_); foster (_hatred_);
cherish (_hope, a grudge_); strengthen;
maintain (_a fire_); _se_ ~ _de_ live on;

_v/i._ be nourishing; **nourrissage**
[nuriˈsaːʒ] _m cattle_: rearing; **nourrissant, e** [~ˈsɑ̃, ~ˈsɑ̃ːt] nourishing;
nutritious; rich (_food_); **nourrisseur** [~ˈsœːr] _m_ dairyman; ⊕ feed-
roll; **nourrisson** [~ˈsɔ̃] _m_ suckling,
nursling; foster-child; **nourriture**
[~ˈtyːr] _f_ feeding; food; board, keep;
_la_ ~ _et le logement_ board and lodging.
nous [nu] **1.** _pron./pers. subject_: we;
object: us; (to) us; _à_ ~ to us; ours;
ce sont ~, F _c'est_ ~ it is we, F it's
us; **2.** _pron./rfl._ ourselves; **3.** _pron./
recip._ each other; one another;
~-**mêmes** [~ˈmɛːm] _pron./rfl._ ourselves.
nouveau (_adj. before vowel or h mute_
-**el**) _m,_ -**elle,** _m/pl._ -**aux** [nuˈvo,
~ˈvɛl, ~ˈvo] **1.** _adj._ new; recent, fresh;
new-style; another, further; novel;
~_eaux riches m/pl._ nouveaux riches,
newly rich; _le plus_ ~ latest; _qch._ (_rien_)
_de_ ~ s.th. (nothing) new; _quoi de_ ~?
what's the news?; **2.** _nouveau adv._:
_à_ ~ anew, afresh; _de_ ~ again;
nouveau-né, e [nuvoˈne] **1.** _adj._
new-born; **2.** _su./m_ new-born child;
nouveauté [~ˈte] _f_ newness, novel-
ty; latest model; innovation; ✝ ~s
_pl._ fancy goods; linen-drapery _sg._;
nouvel [nuˈvɛl] **1.** _adj. see nouveau 1;_
~ _an m_ New Year; **nouvelle** [nu-
ˈvɛl] **1.** _adj. see nouveau 1;_ **2.** _su./f_
news _sg._, tidings _pl._; short story;
avoir des ~s _de q._ hear from _or_ of
s.o.; **nouvelliste** [~vɛˈlist] _su._
short-story writer; _journ._ F par
writer.
novateur, -trice [nɔvaˈtœːr, ~ˈtris]
1. _adj._ innovating; **2.** _su._ innovator.
novembre [nɔˈvɑ̃ːbr] _m_ November.
novice [nɔˈvis] **1.** _adj._ inexperienced
(in _à, dans_), new (to _à, dans_); **2.** _su._
novice (_a. eccl., a. fig._); _fig._ tyro, beginner; _profession_: probationer; **noviciat** [~viˈsja] _m_ noviciate; F apprenticeship.
noyade [nwaˈjad] _f_ drowning.
noyau [nwaˈjo] _m fruit_: stone, kernel; _phys., biol., fig._ nucleus (_a. atom
etc._); ⊕ _wheel_: hub; _metall._, _a._ ⚒
core; △ newel; _fig._ group; _pol._ cell;
fig. ~ _dur_ hard core; ✓ _fruit m à_ ~
stone-fruit; **noyautage** [~joˈtaːʒ] _m_
pol. infiltration (into, _de_); _metall._
coring.
noyer¹ [nwaˈje] (1h) _v/t._ drown

(*a*. F *fig*.); flood (*a. mot*.), inundate, immerse; ⊕ countersink (*a screw*); ⊕ bed (*s.th*.) in cement; se ~ *suicide*: drown o.s.; *accident*: be drowned; *fig*. be steeped (in, *dans*); ⊕ *vis f* noyée countersunk screw.

noyer² ⚲ [~] *m* walnut(-tree).

nu, nue [ny] **1.** *adj*. naked, nude, bare; *fig*. unadorned; ~-*pieds*, *pieds* ~*s* barefoot(ed); **2.** *su./m* nude; nudity; △ bare part; **3.** *adv*.: *à nu* bare; *mettre à nu* expose, lay bare; de-nude; *monter à nu* ride (*a horse*) bareback.

nuage [nɥaːʒ] *m* cloud; *sans* ~*s* cloudless (*sky*), *fig*. perfect (*bliss*); **nuageux, -euse** [nɥa'ʒø, ~'ʒøːz] cloudy, overcast; *fig*. hazy (*idea*).

nuance [nɥãːs] *f* shade (*a. fig*.), hue; *fig*. tinge; *fig*. nuance, shade of meaning; **nuancer** [nɥã'se] (1k) *v/t*. shade (with, *de*); vary (*the tone*); express slight differences in.

nubile [ny'bil] nubile, marriageable.

nucléaire *phys*. [nykle'ɛːr] nuclear (*a. armament*); **nucléon** *phys*. [~'lɔ̃] *m* nucleon.

nudisme [ny'dism] *m* nudism; **nudiste** [~'dist] *su*. nudist; **nudité** [~di'te] *f* nudity, nakedness; *paint*. nude; △ bareness.

nue [ny] *f* high cloud; ~*s pl*. skies (*a. fig*.); *porter aux* ~*s* praise to the skies; *fig. tomber des* ~*s* be thunderstruck; **nuée** [nɥe] *f* storm-cloud; *fig*. cloud; swarm, host.

nuire [nɥiːr] (4u *a*. h) *v/i*.: ~ *à* harm, hurt; be injurious to; **nuisance** [nɥi'zãːs] *f environment etc*.: nuisance; **nuisant, e** [nɥi'zã, ~'zãːt] harmful, polluting; **nuisibilité** [nɥizibili'te] *f* harmfulness; **nuisible** [~'zibl] harmful, injurious.

nuit [nɥi] *f* night; *de* ~ by night; *passer la* ~ stay overnight (with, *chez*); **nuitée** [nɥi'te] *f* night's work; *hotel etc*.: overnight stay; **nuiteux**

m, **-euse** *f* [nɥi'tø, ~'tøːz] person working by night.

nul, nulle [nyl] **1.** *adj*. no, not one; void, null; *sp*. drawn (*game*); non-existent; ⚖ invalid (*marriage*); **2.** *pron./indef*. no(t) one, nobody; **nullement** [nyl'mã] *adv*. not at all; **nullité** [nyli'te] *f* ⚖ nullity, invalidity; *fig*. nothingness; non-existence; *person*: nonentity; *fig*. incapacity.

numéraire [nyme'rɛːr] **1.** *adj*. legal (*tender*); numerary (*value*); **2.** *su./m* specie; cash; currency; **numéral, e**, *m/pl*. **-aux** [~'ral, ~'ro] numeral; **numérateur** ⚲ [~ra'tœːr] *m* numerator; **numération** ⚲ [~ra'sjɔ̃] *f* numeration; number system; **numérique** [~'rik] numerical; digital; **numéro** [~'ro] *m* number; *periodical*: issue, copy; ✝ size; F person, fellow; (~ *de téléphone*) telephone number; F ~ *deux* second-best; ~ *de vestiaire* cloak-room ticket; F ~ *un* first-class; **numérotage** [~rɔ'taːʒ] *m* numbering; *book*: paging; **numéroter** [~rɔ'te] (1a) *v/t*. number; paginate (*a book*); **numéroteur** [~rɔ'tœːr] *m* numbering machine *or* stamp.

numismate [nymis'mat] *m* numismatist; **numismatique** [~ma'tik] *f* numismatics *sg*.

nuptial, e, *m/pl*. **-aux** [nyp'sjal, ~'sjo] bridal; wedding...

nuque [nyk] *f* nape *or* F scruff of the neck. [nanny.⟨

nurse [nœrs] *f* children's nurse, F⟨

nutritif, -ve [nytri'tif, ~'tiːv] nourishing, nutritive; nutritional; food...; **nutrition** [~'sjɔ̃] *f* nutrition; **nutritionel, -le** [~sjɔ'nɛl] nutritional.

nylon *tex*. [ni'lɔ̃] *m* nylon.

nymphe [nɛ̃ːf] *f myth*. nymph (*a. fig*.); *zo*. pupa, chrysalis; **nymphéa** ⚲ [nɛ̃fe'a] *m* water-lily; nymphea; **nymphette** [nɛ̃'fɛt] *f* nymph.

O

O, o [o] *m* O, o.
ô! [o] *int.* oh!
oasis [oa'zis] *f* oasis (*a. fig.*).
obédience [ɔbe'djɑ̃:s] *f eccl.* dutiful submission, obedience; F submission; de même ~ of the same (*religious etc.*) persuasion; d'~ *communiste* of Communist allegiance.
obéir [ɔbe'i:r] (2a) *v/i.:* ~ *à* obey; comply with (*s.th.*); yield to; ⚓, *mot.* respond to; ⚓ answer; *se faire* ~ compel obedience (from, *par*); **obéissance** [~i'sɑ̃:s] *f* obedience; submission (*to authority*); *fig.* pliancy; **obéissant, e** [~i'sɑ̃, ~i'sɑ̃:t] obedient; submissive; *fig.* pliant. [lisk.\
obélisque *archeol.* [ɔbe'lisk] *m* obe-\
obérer [ɔbe're] (1f) *v/t.* burden with debt; s'~ run deep into debt.
obèse [ɔ'bɛ:z] **1.** *adj.* obese, stout; **2.** *su.* obese *or* stout person; **obésité** [ɔbezi'te] *f* obesity, corpulence.
obit *eccl.* [ɔ'bit] *m* obit; **obituaire** [ɔbi'tɥɛ:r] *m* obituary list.
objecter [ɔbʒɛk'te] (1a) *v/t.* raise as an objection (to, *à*); ~ *qch. à q.* allege *or* hold s.th. against s.o.; **objecteur** [~'tœ:r] *m:* ✗ ~ *de conscience* conscientious objector; **objectif, -ve** [~'tif, ~'ti:v] **1.** *adj.* objective; **2.** *su./ m opt.* objective; *phot.* lens; ✗, ⚓ target; *fig.* aim, object; **objection** [~'sjɔ̃] *f* objection; **objectiver** *phls.* [~ti've] (1a) *v/t.* objectify; **objectivité** [~tivi'te] *f* objectivity.
objet [ɔb'ʒɛ] *m* object (*a. gramm., phls., a. fig.*); thing; subject(-matter); *fig.* purpose, aim; *gramm.* complement; ✝ article; ~s *pl.* *trouvés* lost property *sg.*; *remplir son* ~ reach one's goal.
obligataire ✝ [ɔbliga'tɛ:r] *m* bondholder, debenture-holder; **obligation** [~'sjɔ̃] *f* obligation, duty; ✝ bond, debenture; favo(u)r; gratefulness; **obligatoire** [~'twa:r] obligatory; compulsory; binding (*agreement, decision*); *enseignement m* ~ compulsory education; ✗ *service m*

militaire ~ compulsory military service.
obligé, e [ɔbli'ʒe] **1.** *adj.* obliged, compelled (to *inf.*, *de inf.*); necessary, indispensable; inevitable; *fig.* grateful; **2.** *su.* person under an obligation; ✝ obligor; **obligeamment** [~ʒa'mɑ̃] *adv.* of *obligeant*; **obligeance** [~'ʒɑ̃:s] *f* kindness; *avoir l'~ de* (*inf.*) be so kind as to (*inf.*); **obligeant, e** [~'ʒɑ̃, ~'ʒɑ̃:t] obliging; kind; **obliger** [~'ʒe] (1l) *v/t.* oblige, bind (to, *à*); compel (to, *de*); do (*s.o.*) a favo(u)r; s'~ *à* bind o.s. to.
oblique [ɔ'blik] **1.** *adj.* oblique; slanting; *fig. regard m* ~ sidelong glance; **2.** *su./f* oblique line; **obliquer** [ɔbli'ke] (1m) *v/i.* turn off (to[wards] *à*, *vers*); **obliquité** [~ki'te] *f* obliqueness.
oblitération [ɔblitera'sjɔ̃] *f* obliteration; *stamp:* cancellation; ⚙ obstruction; **oblitérer** [~'re] (1f) *v/t.* obliterate; cancel (*a stamp*); ⚙ obstruct (*a vein*).
oblong, -gue [ɔ'blɔ̃, ~'blɔ̃:g] oblong.
obnubiler [ɔbnybi'le] (1a) *v/t.* cloud, obnubilate (*the mind*); obsess (*idea etc.*).
obole [ɔ'bɔl] *f* ✝ obol(us); F farthing; (*widow's*) mite; *apporter son* ~ *à* contribute one's mite to.
obombrer [ɔbɔ̃'bre] (1a) *v/t.* cloud over.
obscène [ɔp'sɛn] obscene; smutty; **obscénité** [~seni'te] *f* obscenity; smuttiness.
obscur, e [ɔps'ky:r] dark; gloomy (*weather*); obscure (*a. fig.*); abstruse (*argument etc.*); dim (*horizon, light*); humble (*person*); **obscurantisme** [~kyrɑ̃'tism] *m* obscurantism; **obscuration** *astr.* [~kyra'sjɔ̃] *f* occultation; **obscurcir** [~kyr'si:r] (2a) *v/t.* obscure; darken; dim (*the view*); **obscurcissement** [~kyrsis-'mɑ̃] *m* darkening; dimming; obscuring; **obscurément** [~kyre'mɑ̃] *adv.* of *obscur*; **obscurité** [~kyri'te]

f obscurity (*a. fig.*); darkness; *fig.* vagueness. [importune, pester.]

obséder [ɔpse'de] (1f) *v/t.* obsess;

obsèques [ɔp'sek] *f/pl.* funeral *sg.*, obsequies; **obséquieux, -euse** [ɔpse'kjø, ~'kjøːz] obsequious, fawning; **obséquiosité** [~kjozi'te] *f* obsequiousness.

observable [ɔpsɛr'vabl] observable; **observance** [~'vãːs] *f* observance (*a. eccl.*); **observateur, -trice** [~va'tœːr, ~'tris] 1. *adj./m* observant; 2. *su.* observer; ✕, ✊ spotter; **observation** [~va'sjɔ̃] *f* observation; *eccl., law, rule:* observance; reprimand; **observatoire** [~va'twaːr] *m astr.* observatory; ✕ observation post; **observer** [~'ve] (1a) *v/t.* serve, keep (*feast, law, rule, sabbath*); watch; notice; *faire ~ qch. à q.* draw s.o.'s attention to s.th.; *s'~* be careful *or* cautious.

obsessif, -ve [ɔpse'sif, ~'siːv] obsessive; **obsession** [~'sjɔ̃] *f* obsession.

obstacle [ɔps'takl] *m* obstacle; *sp.* hurdle; *sp. course f d'~s* obstacle *or* hurdle race; *faire~ à* stand in the way of; hinder; obstruct.

obstétrique ✊ [ɔpste'trik] 1. *adj.* obstetric(al); 2. *su./f* obstetrics *sg.*

obstination [ɔpstina'sjɔ̃] *f* obstinacy; perversity; pig-headedness; **obstiné, e** [~'ne] obstinate, stubborn; persistent; pig-headed; **obstiner** [~'ne] (1a) *v/t.: s'~* show obstinacy; *s'~ à* (*inf.*) persist in (*ger.*).

obstructif, -ve [ɔpstryk'tif, ~'tiːv] *pol.* obstructive; ✊ obstruent; **obstruction** [~'sjɔ̃] *f* ✊, *pol.* obstruction; *pol.* filibustering; ✊ stoppage; **obstructionnisme** *pol.* [~sjɔ̃'nism] *m* obstructionism, filibustering; **obstruer** [ɔpstry'e] (1a) *v/t.* obstruct, block; ⊕ choke.

obtempérer [ɔptãpe're] (1f) *v/i.: ~ à* comply with, obey.

obtenir [ɔptə'niːr] (2h) *v/t.* obtain, get; **obtention** [~tã'sjɔ̃] *f* obtaining.

obturateur, -trice [ɔptyra'tœːr, ~'tris] 1. *adj.* obturating, closing; 2. *su./m* ✕, *anat.* obturator; *phot.* shutter; ⊕ stop-valve; *mot.* throttle; **obturation** [~ra'sjɔ̃] *f* ✊ obturation; closing; sealing; *tooth:* filling; **obturer** [~'re] (1a) *v/t.* stop, seal, obturate; fill (*a tooth*).

obtus, e [ɔp'ty, ~'tyːz] Ⱥ, *a. fig.* obtuse; blunt; *fig.* dull; **obtusangle** Ⱥ [~ty'zã:gl] obtuse-angled.

obus [ɔ'by] *m* ✕ shell; *mot.* valve-plug; *~ à balles* shrapnel; *~ non éclaté* unexploded shell, dud; *~ perforant* armo(u)r-piercing shell; **obusier** ✕ [ɔby'zje] *m* howitzer.

obvier [ɔb'vje] (1o) *v/i.: ~ à* prevent.

oc [ɔk] *adv.: langue f d'~* Langue d'oc, Old Provençal.

occasion [ɔka'zjɔ̃] *f* opportunity, chance; occasion; *fig.* reason (for, de); † bargain; *à l'~* when the chance occurs; *à l'~ de* on the occasion of; *d'~* second-hand; cheap; *par ~* occasionally; **occasionner** [~zjɔ̃'ne] (1a) *v/t.* cause, give rise to.

occident [ɔksi'dã] *m* west, occident; **occidental, e,** *m/pl.* **-aux** [~dã'tal, ~'to] 1. *adj.* west(ern); occidental; 2. *su.* occidental; westerner.

occiput *anat.* [ɔksi'pyt] *m* occiput, back of the head.

occire † [ɔk'siːr] (4y) *v/t.* kill, slay; **occis, e** [~'si, ~'siːz] *p.p. of* occire.

occlusion [ɔkly'zjɔ̃] *f* stoppage, obstruction; ⊕ *valve:* closure; ✍ ✊ occlusion.

occultation *astr.* [ɔkylta'sjɔ̃] *f* occultation; **occulte** [ɔ'kylt] occult; secret; hidden; **occultisme** [ɔkyl-'tism] *m* occultism.

occupant, e [ɔky'pã, ~'pãːt] 1. *adj.* occupying, in occupation; *fig.* engrossing (*work*); 2. *su./m* occupant; ⚖, ✕ occupier; **occupation** [~pa'sjɔ̃] *f* occupation; profession; employment, work; ✕ *forces f/pl. d'~* occupying forces; *sans ~* unemployed; **occuper** [~'pe] (1a) *v/t.* occupy (*a.* ✕); employ (*workers etc.*); *s'~* keep (o.s.) busy; *s'~ à* be engaged in; *s'~ de* see to (*s.th.*); take care of; deal with; be in charge of; look after; attend to (*customer*); be interested in.

occurrence [ɔky'rãːs] *f* occurrence; happening; emergency, juncture; *en l'~* at this juncture; *in or F under the circumstances; in the present case.

océan [ɔse'ã] *m* ocean, sea (*a. fig.*); F *l'~* ♀ the Atlantic; **océanien, -enne** [~a'njɛ̃, ~'njɛn] 1. *adj.* Oceanian, Oceanic; 2. *su.* ♀ South Sea Islander; **océanique** [~a'nik] oceanic, ocean...

ocelot *zo.* [ɔs'lo] *m* ocelot.

ocre [ɔkr] *f* ochre; **ocrer** [ɔ'kre] (1a) *v/t.* ochre; **ocreux, -euse** [ɔ'krø, ~'krø:z] ochrous.

oct... [ɔkt], **octa...** [ɔkta], **octo...** [ɔktɔ] oct..., octa..., octo...; **octaèdre** [ɔkta'ɛ:dr] 1. *adj.* octahedral; 2. *su./m* ⚛ octahedron.

octane ⚗ [ɔk'tan] *m* octane.

octant ⚓, *astr.*, *surv.* [ɔk'tɑ̃] *m* octant.

octobre [ɔk'tɔbr] *m* October.

octogénaire [ɔktɔʒe'nɛ:r] *adj.*, *a. su.* octogenarian.

octogone ⚛ [ɔktɔ'gɔn] *m* octagon.

octroi [ɔk'trwa] *m* concession, grant; city toll; toll-house; **octroyer** [~trwa'je] (1h) *v/t.* grant; bestow (on, *à*).

octuple [ɔk'typl] eightfold; octuple.

oculaire [ɔky'lɛ:r] 1. *adj.* ocular; eye(-*witness*); 2. *su./m* opt. eyepiece; **oculiste** ✱ [~'list] *m* oculist.

odeur [ɔ'dœ:r] *f* odo(u)r (*a. fig.*), smell, scent.

odieux, -euse [ɔ'djø, ~'djø:z] 1. *adj.* odious; hateful; heinous (*crime*); 2. *su./m* odiousness; odium.

odontalgie ✱ [ɔdɔ̃tal'ʒi] *f* toothache, odontalgia.

odorant, e [ɔdɔ'rɑ̃, ~'rɑ̃:t] fragrant, sweet-smelling; scented; **odorat** [~'ra] *m* (sense of) smell; **odoriférant, e** [~rife'rɑ̃, ~'rɑ̃:t] fragrant, odoriferous.

œcuménique [ekyme'nik] (o)ecumenical.

œil, *pl.* **yeux** [œ:j, jø] *m* eye; *bread, cheese:* hole; notice, attention; *à l'~* by the eye; *sl.* on credit *or* tick; *à l'~ nu* with the naked eye; *à mes yeux* in my opinion; *avoir l'~ à qch.* see to s.th.; *avoir l'~ sur* keep an eye on; *coup m d'~* glance; *entre quatre yeux* in confidence; *être tout yeux* be all eyes; *F faire de l'~* ogle; tip s.o. the wink; *fermer les yeux sur* shut one's eyes to; *perdre des yeux* lose sight of; *F pour vos beaux yeux* for love, for your pretty face; *sauter aux yeux* be obvious; *sous mes yeux* before my face; **~-de-bœuf,** *pl.* **~s-de-bœuf** [œjdə'bœf] *m* bull's-eye window; **~-de-perdrix,** *pl.* **~s-de-perdrix** ✱ [~pɛr'dri] *m* soft corn; **œillade** [œ'jad] *f* wink, glance.

œillère [œ'jɛ:r] *f* blinker (*a. fig.*), *Am.*

blind; ✱ eye-bath; **œillet** [œ'jɛ] *m* eyelet(-hole); 🌸 pink, carnation; **œilleton** [œj'tɔ̃] *m* ✔ eyebud; *phot.* eye; ✖ *rifle sight:* peephole; **œillette** 🌸 [œ'jɛt] *f* oil-poppy.

œsophage *anat.* [ezɔ'fa:ʒ] *m* (o)esophagus, gullet.

œstre *zo.* [ɛstr] *m* oestrus; bot-fly.

œstrogène [østrɔ'ʒɛn] *m* (o)estrogen.

œuf [œf, *pl.* ø] *m* egg; *biol.* ovum; *icht.* spawn, roe; ~s *pl.* *brouillés* scrambled eggs; ~s *pl.* *sur le plat* fried eggs; ~ *à la coque* (soft-)boiled egg; ~ *dur* hard-boiled egg; *blanc m d'~* white of egg; *fig. dans l'~* in the bud; *jaune m d'~* egg-yolk.

œuvre [œ:vr] *su./f* work; effect; product(ion); (*welfare*) society; occupation; ~s *pl.* works (*a. eccl.*); *bois m d'~* timber; *se mettre à l'~* start working; *su./m* ⚛ main work; *writer:* complete works *pl.*; ♪ opus; *grand ~* philosopher's stone; ⚛ *gros ~* foundations *pl.* and walls *pl.*; **œuvrer** [œ'vre] (1a) *v/i.* work.

offense [ɔ'fɑ̃:s] *f* insult; ⚖ contempt (of Court, *à la Cour*); *eccl.* sin; **offenser** [ɔfɑ̃'se] (1a) *v/t.* offend; injure; *s'~* take offence (at, *de*); **offenseur** [~'sœ:r] *m* offender; **offensif, -ve** [~'sif, ~'si:v] *adj.*, *a.* ✖ *su./f* offensive.

offert, e [ɔ'fɛ:r, ~'fɛrt] *p.p.* of offrir; **offertoire** *eccl.* [ɔfɛr'twa:r] *m* offertory.

office [ɔ'fis] *su./m* office (*a. fig.*); agency, bureau; service (*a. eccl.*, *a. fig. = turn*); *d'~* officially; automatically; *faire ~ de* act as; *su./f* butler's pantry; servants' hall; **officiant** *eccl.* [ɔfi'sjɑ̃] *m* officiating priest; officiant; **officiel, -elle** [~'sjɛl] official; formal (*call*).

officier [ɔfi'sje] 1. (1o) *v/i.* officiate; 2. *su./m* officer; **officière** [~'sjɛ:r] *f* woman officer (*in the Salvation Army*); **officieux, -euse** [~'sjø, ~'sjø:z] unofficial; *à titre ~* unofficially.

officinal, e, *m/pl.* **-aux** ✱ [ɔfisi'nal, ~'no] medicinal; **officine** [~'sin] *f* ✱ dispensary; chemist's shop, *Am.* drugstore; F *fig.* den.

offrande *usu. eccl.* [ɔ'frɑ̃:d] *f* offering; **offrant** [ɔ'frɑ̃] *m:* *au plus ~* to the highest bidder; **offre** [ɔfr] 1. *1st p. sg. pres. of offrir;* 2. *su./f* offer; ⚖ tender; *auction:* bid; *journ.* ~s *pl.* *d'emploi* situations vacant; *l'~ et la*

demande supply and demand; **offrir**
[ɔ'friːr] (2f) v/t. offer; give (to, à);
expose (to, à); hold out (one's hand
etc.); bid (at an auction); ~ le mariage
à propose to; s'~ a. present itself
(occasion etc.); s'~ treat o.s. to
s.th.; buy o.s. s.th.; s'~ à faire qch.
offer or volunteer to do s.th.

offset typ. [ɔf'sɛt] m/inv. offset.

offusquer [ɔfys'ke] (1m) v/t. obscure (the view, a. fig.); offend; s'~
take offence (at, de).

ogival, e, m/pl. **-aux** △ [ɔʒi'val,
~'vo] ogival, pointed, Gothic;
ogive [ɔ'ʒiːv] f △ ogee, ogive;
Gothic or pointed arch; △ vault:
rib; ✗ war-head.

ogre [ɔgr] m ogre; manger comme
un ~ eat like a horse; **ogresse**
[ɔ'grɛs] f ogress.

oh! [o] int. oh!

ohé! [o'e] int. hi!; hullo!; ⚓ ahoy!

oie zo. [wa] f goose.

oignon [ɔ'ɲɔ̃] m onion; ♀ bulb; ♫
bunion; F turnip (= watch); en
rang d'~s in a row; **oignonade** cuis.
[ɔɲɔ'nad] f onion-stew; **oigno-
nière** [~'njɛːr] f onion-bed.

oindre [wɛ̃:dr] (4m) v/t. oil; eccl.
anoint; **oint, ointe** bibl., a. eccl.
[wɛ̃, wɛ̃:t] adj., a. su./m anointed.

oiseau [wa'zo] m bird; △ (bricklayer's) hod; F fellow, Am. guy; ~ de
passage bird of passage; ~ de proie
bird of prey; à vol d'~ as the crow
flies; vue f à vol d'~ bird's-eye view;
~-mouche, pl. **~x-mouches** orn.
[~zo'muʃ] m humming-bird; **oiseler** [waz'le] (1c) v/i. go bird-
catching; **oiselet** [~'lɛ] m small bird;
oiseleur [~'lœːr] m fowler, bird-
catcher; **oiselier** [wazə'lje] m birdfancier; bird-seller; **oisellerie**
[~zɛl'ri] f bird-catching; bird-
breeding; bird-shop.

oiseux, -euse [wa'zø, ~'zøːz] idle (a.
fig.); fig. useless; **oisif, -ve** [~'zif,
~'ziːv] idle (a. ✞); unemployed; unoccupied; **oisiveté** [~ziv'te] f idleness; sloth.

oison [wa'zɔ̃] m gosling.

oléagineux, -euse [ɔleaʒi'nø,
~'nøːz] oily, oleaginous; ♀ oil-
yielding; **oléoduc** [ɔleo'dyk] m
pipeline.

olfactif, -ve [ɔlfak'tif, ~'tiːv] olfac-
tory; **olfaction** physiol. [~'sjɔ̃] f
olfaction.

oligarchie [ɔligar'ʃi] f oligarchy.

olivacé, e [ɔliva'se] olive-green;
olivaie [~'vɛ] f olive-grove; **oli-
vaire** [~'vɛːr] olive-shaped; **olivai-
son** [~vɛ'zɔ̃] f olive-harvest; **olivâtre** [~'vɑːtr] olive (colour); sallow (complexion); **olive** [ɔ'liːv]
1. su./f ♀ olive; 2. adj./inv. olive-
green; **oliverie** [ɔli'vri] f olive-oil
factory; **olivier** ♀ [~'vje] m olive-
tree; olive-wood; bibl. Mont m des
♀s Mount of Olives.

olympien, -enne [ɔlɛ̃'pjɛ̃, ~'pjɛn]
Olympian; fig. godlike; **olympique**
[~'pik] Olympic; Jeux m/pl. ♀s
Olympic games.

ombelle ♀ [ɔ̃'bɛl] f umbel; en ~ =
ombellé, e ♀ [ɔ̃bɛl'le] umbellate.

ombilical, e, m/pl. **-aux** [ɔ̃bili'kal,
~'ko] umbilical.

ombrage [ɔ̃'braːʒ] m shade; fig. offence, umbrage; porter ~ à q. offend
s.o.; prendre ~ de qch. take umbrage
or offence at s.th.; **ombrager**
[ɔ̃bra'ʒe] (1l) v/t. (give) shade; **ombrageux, -euse** [~'ʒø, ~'ʒøːz] shy
(horse); touchy, sensitive (person);
ombre [ɔ̃:br] f shadow (a. fig.);
shade (a. myth., a. paint.); fig. dark;
fig. obscurity; fig. a. hint, suspicion;
~s pl. chinoises shadow-show sg.; fig.
~ d'une chance the ghost of a chance;
à l'~ in the shade; à l'~ de in the shade
of; fig. under cover of; rester dans l'~
stay in the background; sl. à l'~ in
jail; **ombrelle** [ɔ̃'brɛl] f sunshade,
parasol; **ombrer** [ɔ̃'bre] (1a) v/t.
shade; darken (the eyelids); **om-
breux, -euse** [ɔ̃'brø, ~'brøːz] shady.

omelette cuis. [ɔm'lɛt] f omelet(te).

omettre [ɔ'mɛtr] (4v) v/t. omit, leave
out; ~ de (inf.) fail to (inf.); **omission** [ɔmi'sjɔ̃] f omission; oversight.

omni... [ɔmni] omni...; **~bus** [~'bys]
m (omni)bus; ➄ train m ~ stopping or
local train, Am. accommodation
train; **~potence** [~pɔ'tɑ̃:s] f omnipotence; **~potent, e** [~pɔ'tɑ̃, ~'tɑ̃:t]
omnipotent; **~présent, e** [~pre'zɑ̃,
~'zɑ̃t] omnipresent; [der-blade.)
omoplate anat. [ɔmɔ'plat] f shoul-)

on [ɔ̃] pron. one, people pl.; you;
somebody; ~ dit que it is said that.

once¹ [ɔ̃:s] f measure: ounce; F fig.
scrap, bit.

once² zo. [~] f snow-leopard, ounce.

oncial, e, m/pl. **-aux** [ɔ̃'sjal, ~'sjo]
adj., a. su./f uncial.

oncle [ɔ̃:kl] *m* uncle.
onction [ɔ̃k'sjɔ̃] *eccl.*, *a. fig. pej.* unction; **onctueux, -euse** [ˌ~'tɥø, ˌ~'tɥø:z] creamy, rich; smooth; oily (*surface*, *a. pej. manner*); *fig.* unctuous (*speech*).
onde [ɔ̃:d] *f* wave (*a. hair*, *a. radio*); undulation; ˌ~s *pl.* moyennes radio: medium waves; *phys.* ~ sonore sound wave; ~ *ultra-courte* ultrashort wave; *grandes* ˌ~s *pl.* radio: long waves; *longueur f d'*~ wavelength; *mettre en* ˌ~s radio: put on the air; **ondé, e** [ɔ̃'de] **1.** *adj.* wavy (*hair, surface*); undulating; watered (*silk*); **2.** *su./f* heavy shower; **ondin** *m*, **e** *f* [ɔ̃'dɛ̃, ˌ~'din] water-sprite.
on-dit [ɔ̃'di] *m/inv.* rumo(u)r, hearsay.
ondoiement [ɔ̃dwa'mɑ̃] *m* undulation; *eccl.* emergency *or* private baptism; **ondoyant, e** [ˌ~'jɑ̃, ˌ~'jɑ̃:t] undulating, wavy; swaying (*crowd*); *fig.* changeable; **ondoyer** [ˌ~'je] (1h) *v/i.* undulate, wave; sway (*crowd*); fall in waves (*hair*); *v/t. eccl.* baptize privately (*a child*); **ondulation** [ɔ̃dyla'sjɔ̃] *f* ground, *water*: undulation; *hair:* wave; ⊕ *metal etc.*: corrugation; **ondulatoire** *phys.* [ˌ~la'twa:r] undulatory; wave-(*motion*); **ondulé, e** [ˌ~'le] undulating (*ground*); corrugated (*metal etc.*); wavy, waved (*hair*); *tôle f* ˌ~e corrugated iron; **onduler** [ˌ~'le] (1a) *v/i.* undulate, ripple; *v/t.* wave (*one's hair*); ⊕ corrugate; **onduleux, -euse** [ˌ~'lø, ˌ~'lø:z] wavy, sinuous.
onéreux, -euse [ɔne'rø, ˌ~'rø:z] onerous; troublesome; *fig.* heavy; *à titre* ~ subject to liabilities; ⚖ for valuable consideration.
ongle [ɔ̃:gl] *m* (finger)nail; *zo.* claw; *eagle, falcon, etc.:* talon; ~ *des pieds* toenail; *jusqu'au bout des* ˌ~s to the fingertips; **onglée** [ɔ̃'gle] *f* numbness of the fingertips; **onglet** [ɔ̃'glɛ] *m* thimble; *book:* tab, thumb-index; ⚖ ungula; ⊕ mitre; **onglier** [ɔ̃gli'e] *m* manicure-set; ˌ~s *pl.* nail-scissors.
onguent [ɔ̃'gɑ̃] *m* ointment, salve.
ongulé, e *zo.* [ɔ̃gy'le] **1.** *adj.* ungulate, hoofed; **2.** *su./m:* ˌ~s *pl.* ungulates, ungulata.
ont [ɔ̃] *3rd. p. pl. pres. of avoir 1.*
onze [ɔ̃:z] **1.** *adj./num.*, *a. su./m/inv.*

eleven; *date*, *title:* eleventh; **2.** *su./ m/inv. foot.* team; **onzième** [ɔ̃- 'zjɛm] *adj./num.*, *a. su.* eleventh.
opacité [ɔpasi'te] *f* opacity; *fig.* denseness.
opale [ɔ'pal] **1.** *su./f* opal; **2.** *adj./inv.* opalescent; opal (*glass*); **opalin, e** [ɔpa'lɛ̃, ˌ~'lin] *adj.*, *a. su./f* opaline.
opaque [ɔ'pak] opaque.
opéra [ɔpe'ra] *m* opera; *building:* opera-house.
opérable ⚕ [ɔpe'rabl] operable.
opéra-comique, pl. opéras-co-miques ♪, *thea.* [ɔperakɔ'mik] *m* light opera.
opérateur, -trice [ɔpera'tœ:r, ˌ~'tris] *su.* operator; *su./m cin.* cameraman; ⚕ operating surgeon; **opération** [ˌ~'sjɔ̃] *f* ⚕, ♣, ✕, *a. fig.* operation; ✝ transaction; ⚕ *salle f d'*~ operating theatre; **opérationnel, -le** [ˌ~sjɔ'nɛl] operational; **opératoire** ⚕ [ˌ~'twa:r] operating; postoperative; *médicine f* ~ *subject:* surgery.
opercule [ɔpɛr'kyl] *m* cover; lid (*a.* ⚓); *icht.* gill-cover.
opérer [ɔpe're] (1f) *v/t.* operate, effect; ♣, ✞ₙ✕ carry out; ⚕ operate on (*s.o.*) (for, de); s'~ take place; *v/i.* act; work.
opérette ♪ [ɔpe'rɛt] *f* operetta; musical comedy.
ophtalmie ⚕ [ɔftal'mi] *f* ophthalmia.
ophtalmo... ⚕ [ɔftalmɔ] ophthalmo...; ˌ~**scope** [ˌ~mɔs'kɔp] *m* ophthalmoscope.
opiacé, e [ɔpja'se] opiated.
opiner [ɔpi'ne] (1a) *v/i.* be of (the) opinion (that, *que*); decide, vote; ~ *du bonnet* nod assent; **opiniâtre** [ˌ~'njɑ:tr] obstinate, stubborn; **opiniâtrer** [ˌ~nja'tre] (1a) *v/t.:* s'~ remain stubborn; persist (in, *dans*; in *ger.*, *à inf.*); **opiniâtreté** [ˌ~njatra'te] *f* obstinacy, stubbornness; **opinion** [ˌ~'njɔ̃] *f* opinion; *à mon* ~ in my opinion; *avoir bonne* (*mauvaise*) ~ *de* think highly (poorly) of.
opiomane [ɔpjɔ'man] *su.* opiumeater; opium addict; **opium** [ɔ- 'pjɔm] *m* opium.
opportun, e [ɔpɔr'tœ̃, ˌ~'tyn] opportune, timely; advisable; **opportunément** [ɔpɔrtyne'mɑ̃] *adv. of opportun*; **opportunisme** [ˌ~'nism] *m* opportunism; **opportuniste** *pol.*

[ˌ'nist] **1.** *adj.* time-serving; **2.** *su.*
opportunist; time-server; **opportunité** [ˌni'te] *f* timeliness; opportuneness; advisability.

opposant, e [ɔpoˈzɑ̃, ˌ'zɑ̃:t] **1.** *adj.*
opposing, adverse; **2.** *su.* opponent;
opposé, e [ˌ'ze] **1.** *adj.* opposed;
opposite (*a.* Ⓐ); *fig.* contrary;
2. *su./m* opposite (of, de); *à l'*ˌ *de*
contrary to, unlike; **opposer** [ˌ'ze]
(1a) *v/t.* oppose; contrast (with, *à*);
*s'*ˌ *à* be opposed to; resist (*s.th.*);
opposition [ˌzi'sjɔ̃] *f* opposition
(*a. parl., astr.*); contrast; *être en* ˌ
avec clash with; **oppositionnel, -le**
[ˌzisjɔˈnɛl] **1.** *adj.* oppositional; **2.** *su.*
oppositionist.

oppresser [ɔprɛˈse] (1a) *v/t.* oppress
(*a.* 🏥); *fig.* depress; **oppresseur**
[ˌ'sœ:r] *m* oppressor; **oppressif,
-ve** [ˌ'sif, ˌ'si:v] oppressive; **oppression** 🏥 [ˌ'sjɔ̃] *f* oppression (*a.
fig.*); difficulty in breathing.

opprimer [ɔpriˈme] (1a) *v/t.* oppress, crush.

opprobre [ɔˈprɔbr] *m* opprobrium,
shame, disgrace.

optatif, -ve [ɔptaˈtif, ˌ'ti:v] *adj., a.
su./m gramm.* optative.

opter [ɔpˈte] (1a) *v/i.* opt; choose; ˌ
pour decide in favo(u)r of.

opticien [ɔptiˈsjɛ̃] *m* optician.

optimal, e *m/pl.* **-aux** [ɔptiˈmal,
ˌ'mo] optimal; **optimiser** [ɔptimiˈze] (1a) *v/t.* optimize; **optimisme** [ɔptiˈmism] *m* optimism;
optimiste [ˌ'mist] **1.** *adj.* optimistic; sanguine (*disposition*); **2.** *su.*
optimist.

option [ɔpˈsjɔ̃] *f* option (on, sur) (*a.*
♱); choice (between *de*, entre); **optionnel, -le** [ɔpsjɔˈnɛl] optional.

optique [ɔpˈtik] **1.** *adj.* optic; optical;
2. *su./f* optics *sg.*; optical device;
*illusion f d'*ˌ optical illusion.

opulence [ɔpyˈlɑ̃s] *f* affluence;
wealth (*a. fig.*); **opulent, e** [ˌ'lɑ̃,
ˌ'lɑ̃:t] opulent, wealthy; abundant; F
buxom (*figure*).

opuscule [ɔpysˈkyl] *m* pamphlet;
short treatise.

or¹ [ɔ:r] **1.** *su./m* gold; *de l'*ˌ *en barres*
as good as ready money; *d'*ˌ
gold(en); *rouler sur l'*ˌ be rolling in
money.

or² [ˌ] *cj.* now, well (now).

oracle [ɔˈra:kl] *m* oracle.

orage [ɔˈra:ʒ] *m* storm (*a. fig.*);

orageux, -euse [ɔraˈʒø, ˌ'ʒø:z]
stormy (*a. fig. debate*); thundery
(*weather*); threatening (*sky etc.*).

oraison [ɔrɛˈzɔ̃] *f* prayer; oration;
ˌ *dominicale* Lord's Prayer; ˌ *funèbre* funeral oration.

oral, e *m/pl.* **-aux** [ɔˈral, ˌ'ro]
1. *adj.* oral; **2.** *su./m* oral examination.

orange [ɔˈrɑ̃:ʒ] **1.** *su./f* 🍊 orange;
su./m colour: orange; **2.** *adj./inv.*
orange (*colour*); **orangé, e** [ɔrɑ̃ˈʒe]
adj., a. su./m orange; **orangeade**
[ˌ'ʒad] *f* orangeade, orange squash;
orangeat [ˌ'ʒa] *m* candied orange-peel; **oranger** [ˌ'ʒe] *m* 🍊 orange-tree; orange-seller; **orangerie**
[ɔrɑ̃ʒˈri] *f* orangery; orange-grove.

orang-outan(g) *zo.* [ɔrɑ̃uˈtɑ̃] *m*
orang-(o)utang.

orateur [ɔraˈtœ:r] *m* orator, speaker;
spokesman; **oratoire** [ˌ'twa:r]
1. *adj.* oratorical; **2.** *su./m eccl.*
oratory; (private) chapel; **oratorio**
♪ [ˌtɔˈrjo] *m* oratorio.

orbe¹ △ [ɔrb] *adj.:* *mur m* ˌ blind
wall.

orbe² [ɔrb] **1.** *su./m* orb; globe,
sphere; **orbite** [ɔrˈbit] *f* orbit;
anat. eye: socket; *mettre (or placer) en*
(*or sur*) ˌ put into orbit; **orbiter**
[ɔrbiˈte] (1a) *v/i.* orbit.

orchestre ♪ [ɔrˈkɛstr] *m* orchestra; ˌ
à cordes string orchestra; *chef m d'*ˌ
conductor; bandmaster; **orchestrer** [ˌkɛsˈtre] (1a) *v/t.* ♪ orchestrate,
score; *fig.* organize; *fig.* mastermind.

orchidée 🌺 [ɔrkiˈde] *f* orchid.

ordalie † [ɔrdaˈli] *f* ordeal.

ordinaire [ɔrdiˈnɛ:r] **1.** *adj.* ordinary, usual, customary; Ⓐ vulgar
(*fractions*); average; *peu* ˌ uncommon, unusual; *mot. essence f* ˌ regular petrol (*Am.* gas); ♱ *tribunal m* ˌ
civil court; *vin m* ˌ table wine; **2.**
su./m daily fare; ✗ mess; *eccl.*
Ordinary; *à l'*ˌ, *d'*ˌ as a rule, usually;
*sortir de l'*ˌ be out of the ordinary.

ordinateur [ɔrdinaˈtœ:r] *m* computer.

ordination *eccl.* [ɔrdinaˈsjɔ̃] *f* ordination.

ordonnance [ɔrdɔˈnɑ̃:s] *f* order (*a.*
♱); arrangement; 🏥 prescription;
pol., admin. statute; ✗ † orderly; ♱
ˌ (*de paiement*) order to pay; **ordonnateur, -trice** [ˌnaˈtœ:r, ˌ'tris]
1. *su.* director; organizer; **2.** *adj.*

managing; **ordonnée** ♣ [⁓'ne] f ordinate; **ordonner** [⁓'ne] (1a) v/t. order, command; arrange; direct; ⚕ prescribe; tidy; eccl., a. admin. ordain; v/i. dispose (of, de).

ordre [ɔrdr] m order; sequence; orderliness; (social) estate; class, sort; command; eccl. ⁓s pl. Holy Orders; ✝ ⁓ d'achat purchase permit; ⁓ du jour agenda; admin. ⁓ public law and order; fig. de l'⁓ de in the region of (2000); fig. de premier ⁓ first-class, outstanding; jusqu'à nouvel ⁓ until further notice; ✗ mot m d'⁓ password; numéro m d'⁓ serial number; ✗ porté (or cité) à l'⁓ du jour mentioned in dispatches.

ordure [ɔr'dy:r] f dirt, filth; ⁓s pl. refuse sg., rubbish, Am. garbage; **ordurier, -ère** [⁓dy'rje, ⁓'rjɛ:r] filthy; scurrilous; obscene (book); lewd.

oreillard, e zo. [ɔrɛ'ja:r, ⁓'jard] 1. adj. lop-eared; 2. su./m longeared bat; **oreille** [ɔ'rɛːj] f ear; metall. lug, flange; vase: handle; book: dog's ear; fig. hearing; fig. heed; avoir de l'⁓ have a good ear (for music); ♪ avoir l'⁓ absolue have perfect pitch; avoir l'⁓ dure be hard of hearing; être tout ⁓s be all ears; faire la sourde ⁓ turn a deaf ear; F se faire tirer l'⁓ need a lot of persuading; tirer les ⁓s à (or de) pull (s.o.'s) ears; **oreille-d'ours**, pl. **oreilles-d'ours** ♣ [ɔrɛj'durs] f bear's ear; **oreiller** [ɔrɛ'je] m pillow; **oreillette** [⁓'jɛt] f anat. auricle; cap: ear-flap; **oreillons** ⚕ [⁓'jɔ̃] m/pl. mumps sg.

ores [ɔ:r] adv.: d'⁓ et déjà from now on.

orfèvre [ɔr'fɛ:vr] m goldsmith; **orfèvrerie** [⁓fɛvrə'ri] f goldsmith's trade or shop; gold plate.

orfraie orn. [ɔr'frɛ] f osprey.

organe [ɔr'gan] m anat., a. fig. organ; fig. voice; ⊕ ⁓s pl. de commande controls; **organigramme** [ɔrgani-'gram] m organization chart; flow chart or diagram(me); **organique** [ɔrga'nik] organic; **organisateur, -trice** [⁓niza'tœ:r, ⁓'tris] 1. su. organizer; 2. adj. organizing; **organisation** [⁓niza'sjɔ̃] f organization; setting up; setup; **organisationnel, -le** [⁓nizasjɔ'nɛl] organizational; **organiser** [⁓ni'ze] (1a) v/t.

organize; arrange; set up; s'⁓ settle down, get into working order; **organisme** [⁓'nism] m organism; **organiste** ♪ [⁓'nist] su. organist.

orgasme physiol. [ɔr'gasm] m orgasm.

orge ♣ [ɔrʒ] su./f barley; su./m: ⁓ mondé hulled barley; ⁓ perlé pearlbarley; **orgeat** [ɔr'ʒa] m orgeat (sort of syrup); **orgelet** ⚕ [⁓ʒə'lɛ] m eyelid: stye.

orgie [ɔr'ʒi] f orgy; colours etc., fig.: riot; fig. profusion.

orgue ♪ [ɔrg] su./m organ; ⁓ de Barbarie barrel-organ; su./f: eccl. ⁓s pl. organ sg.; les grandes ⁓s pl. the grand organ sg.

orgueil [ɔr'gœːj] m pride; dignity; pej. arrogance; **orgueilleux, -euse** [⁓gœ'jø, ⁓'jøːz] proud; pej. arrogant.

orient [ɔ'rjɑ̃] m Orient, East; pearl: water; **oriental, e,** m/pl. **-aux** [ɔrjɑ̃-'tal, ⁓'to] 1. adj. oriental, east(ern); orient (jewel); 2. su. oriental; **orientation** [⁓tɑ'sjɔ̃] f orientation; bearings pl.; ground· lie, lay; aspect; pol. trend; ⁓ professionnelle vocational guidance; **orienter** [⁓'te] (1a) v/t. orient (a house etc.); train, point (a gun, an instrument); direct (a. radio), guide; antenne f orientée radio: directional aerial; s'⁓ find one's bearings; fig. s'⁓ vers turn towards.

orifice [ɔri'fis] m hole, opening; ⊕ port.

origan ♣ [ɔri'gɑ̃] m origanum.

originaire [ɔriʒi'nɛːr] originating (in, from de); native; innate; **original, e,** m/pl. **-aux** [⁓'nal, ⁓'no] 1. adj. original; novel (idea); inventive (mind); fig. queer; 2. su. eccentric; su./m text etc.: original; **originalité** [⁓nali'te] f originality; fig. eccentricity; **origine** [ɔri'ʒin] f origin; birth; fig. source; dès l'⁓ from the outset; **originel, -elle** [⁓ʒi'nɛl] eccl. etc. original (sin, grace); primordial; fundamental.

oripeaux [ɔri'po] m/pl. rags.

ormaie [ɔr'mɛ] f elm-grove; **orme** ♣ [ɔrm] m tree, a. wood: elm; fig. attendez-moi sous l'⁓! you can wait for me till the cows come home!

ornement [ɔrnə'mɑ̃] m ornament, adornment; trimming; ♪ grace (-note); ✗ badge; eccl. ⁓s pl. vestments; *sans* ~s plain (*style*); **ornemental, e** *m/pl.* **-aux** [~mã'tal, ~'to] ornamental, decorative; **ornementer** [~mã'te] (1a) *v/t.* ornament; **orner** [ɔr'ne] (1a) *v/t.* decorate, ornament; adorn (*a. fig.*).

ornière [ɔr'njɛːr] *f* rut (*a. fig.*); ⊕ groove.

ornitho... [ɔrnitɔ] ornitho...; **~logie** [~lɔ'ʒi] *f* ornithology.

orphelin, e [ɔrfə'lɛ̃, ~'lin] **1.** *adj.* orphan(ed); ~ *de père* (*mère*) fatherless (motherless); **2.** *su.* orphan; **orphelinat** [~li'na] *m* orphanage.

orteil *anat.* [ɔr'tɛːj] *m* (big) toe.

ortho... [ɔrtɔ] orth(o)...; **~doxe** [~'dɔks] **1.** *adj.* orthodox; conventional; correct; **2.** *su.* orthodox; **~graphe** [~'graf] *f* spelling, orthography; **~graphier** [~gra'fje] (1o) *v/t.* spell (*a word*) correctly; *mal* ~ mis-spell; **~pédie** ✋ [~pe'di] *f* orthop(a)edy; **~phonie** [~fɔ'ni] *f* correct pronunciation; ✋ speech therapy.

ortie ⚘ [ɔr'ti] *f* nettle; **ortier** ✋ [~'tje] (1o) *v/t.* urticate.

ortolan *orn.* [ɔrtɔ'lɑ̃] *m* ortolan.

orvet *zo.* [ɔr'vɛ] *m* slow-worm.

os [ɔs, *pl.* o] *m* bone; *fig. trempé jusqu'aux* ~ soaked to the skin.

oscillation [ɔsilla'sjɔ̃] *f* oscillation; *machine*: vibration; *pendulum*: swing; *fig.* fluctuation, change; **osciller** [~'le] (1a) *v/i.* oscillate, sway; swing (*pendulum*); ✞ fluctuate; *fig.* waver.

osé, e [o'ze] bold, daring.

oseille ⚘ [ɔ'zɛːj] *f* sorrel.

oser [o'ze] (1a) *v/t.* dare.

oseraie ✎ [oz'rɛ] *f* osier-bed; **osier** ⚘ [o'zje] *m* osier, willow; wicker.

osmose [ɔs'moːz] *f* osmosis.

ossature *anat.*, ⊕, *fig.* [ɔsa'tyːr] *f* skeleton, frame; **osselet** [ɔs'lɛ] *m* knucklebone; *anat.* ossicle; **ossements** [~'mã] *m/pl.* bones, remains; **osseux, -euse** [ɔ'sø, ~'søːz] bony; **ossification** ✋ [ɔsifika'sjɔ̃] *f* ossification; **ossifier** [ɔ'fje] (1o) *v/t. a.* s'~ ossify; **ossuaire** [ɔ'sɥɛːr] *m* ossuary, charnel-house.

ostensible [ɔstã'sibl] open, patent; **ostensoir** *eccl.* [~'swaːr] *m* monstrance; **ostentation** [~ta'sjɔ̃] *f* ostentation, show.

ostéo... [ɔsteɔ] osteo...

ostracisme [ɔstra'sism] *m* ostra-

cism; *frapper q. d'~* ostracize s.o.

ostréicole [ɔstrei'kɔl] oyster-...; **ostréiculteur** [~kyl'tœːr] *m* oyster-breeder; **ostréiculture** [~kyl'tyːr] *f* oyster-breeding.

ostrogot(h), e [ɔstrɔ'go, ~'gɔt] **1.** *adj.* Ostrogothic; *fig.* barbarous; **2.** *su.* ♂ Ostrogoth; *fig.* barbarian, vandal.

otage [ɔ'taːʒ] *m* hostage (for, *de*); *fig.* guarantee.

otalgie ✋ [ɔtal'ʒi] *f* ear-ache.

otarie *zo.* [ɔta'ri] *f* sea-lion.

ôter [o'te] (1a) *v/t.* remove, take away; take off (*one's gloves etc.*); Å deduct, subtract (*a number*).

otite ✋ [ɔ'tit] *f* otitis; ~ *moyenne* tympanitis.

oto-rhino ✋ [ɔtɔri'no], **oto-rhinolaryngologiste** [ɔtɔrinɔlarɛ̃gɔlɔ-'ʒist] *su.* ear, nose and throat specialist.

ottoman, e [ɔtɔ'mã, ~'man] **1.** *adj.* Ottoman; **2.** *su.* ♀ Ottoman; *su./m tex.* grogram; *su./f* divan, ottoman.

ou [u] *cj.* or; *ou ... ou* either ... or; *ou bien* or else; *si ... ou* whether ... or.

où [u] **1.** *adv. place, direction*: where; *time*: when; **2.** *pron./rel. place, direction*: where; *time*: when, on which; *fig.* at or in which; *d'où* whence, where ... from; hence, therefore; *par où?* which way?

ouaille [wa'j] *f* ✝, *a. dial.* sheep; *fig., eccl.* ~s *pl.* flock *sg.*

ouate [wat] *f* wadding; cotton-wool; ~ *hydrophile* absorbent cotton-wool; **ouater** [wa'te] (1a) *v/t.* wad, pad; *fig.* soften (*a sound*); *cost.* quilt.

oubli [u'bli] *m* forgetfulness; forgetting; oblivion; oversight, omission.

oublie [~] *f* wafer; cornet.

oublier [ubli'e] (1a) *v/t.* forget; overlook; miss (*an occasion*); neglect; *faire* ~ live down; *n'oubliez pas* remember; s'~ forget o.s.; indulge (in, *à*); **oubliettes** [~'ɛt] *f/pl.* secret dungeon *sg.*, oubliette *sg.*; **oublieux, -euse** [~'ø, ~'øːz] forgetful, unmindful (of, *de*).

oued [wɛd] *m* wadi, watercourse.

ouest [wɛst] **1.** *su./m* west; *de l'*~ west(ern); *d'*~ westerly (*wind*); *vers l'*~ westward(s), to the west; **2.** *adj./inv.* west(ern); westerly (*wind*); **ouf!** [uf] *int.* phew! [(*wind*).√

oui [wi] **1.** *adv.* yes; *dire que* ~ say

yes; *mais* ~! certainly!; yes indeed!;
2. *su./m/inv.* yes.
ouiche! *sl.* [wiʃ] *int.* not on your
life!
ouï-dire [wi'diːr] *m/inv.* hearsay;
par ~ by hearsay; **ouïe** [wi] *f* (sense
of) hearing; ⊕ ear; ~s *pl.* ♪ sound-
holes; *icht.* gills (*of a fish*); **ouïr**
[wiːr] (2r) *v/t.* hear.
ouragan [ura'gɑ̃] *m* hurricane.
ourdir [ur'diːr] (2a) *v/t.* *tex.* warp;
fig. weave (*an intrigue*), hatch (*a
plot*).
ourler [ur'le] (1a) *v/t.* hem; ⊕ lap-
joint; **ourlet** [~'lɛ] *m* hem; *fig.*
edge; ⊕ lap-joint.
ours [urs] *m* *zo.* bear (*a. fig.*); ~ *blanc*
polar bear; ~ *en peluche* Teddy
bear; **ourse** [~] *f* *zo.* she-bear;
astr. la Grande ♀ the Great Bear,
Charles's Wain; *astr. la Petite* ♀
the Little Bear; **oursin** *zo.* [ur'sɛ̃]
m sea-urchin; **ourson** *zo.* [~'sɔ̃] *m*
bear cub.
oust(e)! F [ust] *int.* get a move on!;
out you go!
outarde *orn.* [u'tard] *f* bustard;
Canada goose.
outil [u'ti] *m* tool; **outillage** [uti-
'jaːʒ] *m* tool set *or* kit; ⊕ equipment, plant, machinery; **outiller**
[~'je] (1a) *v/t.* equip with tools;
⊕ fit out (*a factory*); **outilleur**
[~'jœːr] *m* tool-maker.
outrage [u'traːʒ] *m* outrage; ⚖ ~ *à
magistrat* contempt of court; **outrager** [utra'ʒe] (1l) *v/t.* outrage; insult; violate (*a woman*); **outrageux, -euse** [~'ʒø, ~'ʒøːz] insulting,
scurrilous.
outrance [u'trɑ̃ːs] *f* excess; *à* ~ to
the bitter end; to the death (*war*);
outrancier, -ère [utrɑ̃'sje, ~'sjɛːr]
1. *adj.* extreme; 2. *su.* extremist.
outre[1] [uːtr] *f* water-skin.
outre[2] [uːtr] 1. *prp.* beyond; in addition to; 2. *adv.*: *en* ~ moreover,
furthermore; *passer* ~ not to take
notice (of, *à*); *passer* ~ *à a.* disregard,
ignore; *percer q. d'*~ *en* ~ run s.o.
through; ~**cuidance** [utrəkɥi'dɑ̃ːs] *f*
bumptiousness, overweening conceit; ~**cuidant, e** [~'dɑ̃, ~'dɑ̃ːt]
bumptious, overweening; ~**mer**
[~'mɛːr] *m* lapis lazuli; *colour:* ultramarine; ~**mer** [~'mɛːr] *adv.* overseas...; ~**passer** [~pɑ'se] (1a) *v/t.*
exceed; go beyond.

outrer [u'tre] (1a) *v/t.* exaggerate;
tire out; *outré de colère* provoked
to anger, infuriated.
ouvert, e [u'vɛːr, ~'vɛrt] 1. *p.p. of
ouvrir*; 2. *adj.* open (*a. fig.*, *a.* ✗
war, *city*); quick (*mind*); *fig. à bras
~s with open arms; ✝ *compte m* ~
open account, open credit; **ouverture** [uvɛr'tyːr] *f* opening; aper-
ture; ♪ overture; ⊕ ~s *pl.* ports.
ouvrable [u'vrabl] workable; *jour
m* ~ working day; **ouvrage** [u'vraːʒ]
m work; *fig.* workmanship; product; **ouvrager** [uvra'ʒe] (1l) *v/t.*
⊕ work; *tex.* embroider.
ouvre [uːvr] *1st p. sg. pres. of ouvrir*.
ouvré, e [u'vre] wrought (*iron*);
worked (*timber*); *tex.* figured.
ouvre-boîtes [uvrə'bwat] *m/inv.*
tin-opener, *Am.* can-opener;
ouvre-bouteilles [~bu'tɛːj] *m/inv.*
bottle-opener; **ouvre-lettres** [~-
'lɛtr] *m/inv.* letter-opener.
ouvrer [u'vre] (1a) *v/t.* work; *tex.*
diaper, figure.
ouvreur, -euse [u'vrœːr, ~'vrøːz] *su.*
opener; *su./f thea.* usherette (*a. cin.*);
box-attendant; *tex. machine:* cotton-
opener.
ouvrier, -ère [uvri'e, ~'ɛːr] 1. *su.*
worker; operator; factory-worker; ~
agricole farm-hand; ✗ ~ *au jour* surface hand; ~ *aux pièces* piece-worker;
su./m: ~ *qualifié* skilled workman; ~
simple unskilled worker; *su./f*
factory-girl; *zo.* worker (bee *or* ant);
2. *adj.* working (*class*); workmen's
...; *labo(u)r...*; worker (*ant, bee*);
ouvriérisme [~e'rism] *m* worker
control.
ouvrir [u'vriːr] (2f) *v/t.* open (*a. fig.*);
unfasten; turn on (*the gas, a tap*); *fig.*
begin; open (*s.th.*) up; ♪ break (*the
circuit*); ✗ lance (*a boil*); *fig.* s'~ *à q.*
confide in s.o.; talk freely to s.o.; *v/i.*
a. s'~ open. [charity workshop.\
ouvroir [u'vrwaːr] *m* workroom;}
ovaire ♀, *anat.* [ɔ've:r] *m* ovary.
ovale [ɔ'val] *adj.*, *a.* *su./m* oval.
ovation [ɔva'sjɔ̃] *f* ovation; *faire
une* ~ *à q.* give s.o. an ovation.
ove [ɔːv] *m* △ ovolo; egg-shaped
section; **ové, e** [ɔ've] egg-shaped.
ovi... [ɔvi] ovi..., ovo...
ovin, e [ɔ'vɛ̃, ~'vin] ovine.
ovipare *zo.* [ɔvi'paːr] oviparous.
ovni [ɔv'ni] *m* (= *objet volant non identifié*) Ufo.

ovule *biol.* [ɔ'vyl] *m* ovum; ♀ ovule.
ox(y)... [ɔks(i)] ox(y)...
oxycoupeur [ɔksiku'pœːr] *m* oxyacet-
ylene burner.
oxydable 🜍 [ɔksi'dabl] oxidizable;
  oxydation 🜍 [~da'sjɔ̃] *f* oxidization;
  oxyde 🜍 [ɔk'sid] *m* oxide; ~ de

carbone carbon monoxide; **oxyder**
🜍 [~si'de] (1a) *v/t. a. s'~* oxidize.
oxygène 🜍 [ɔksi'ʒɛn] *m* oxygen;
  oxygéné, e [~ʒe'ne] 🜍 oxygenated;
  F *cheveux m/pl.* ~s peroxided hair;
  eau f ~e hydrogen peroxide.
ozone 🜍 [ɔ'zɔn] *m* ozone.

P

P, p [pe] *m* P, p.

pacage [pa'ka:ʒ] *m* pasturage; grazing; **pacager** [ˎka'ʒe] (11) *v/t.* pasture, graze.

pachyderme zo. [paʃi'dɛrm] **1.** *adj.* thick-skinned; **2.** *su./m* pachyderm.

pacificateur, -trice [pasifika'tœːr, ˎ'tris] **1.** *adj.* pacifying; **2.** *su.* peacemaker; **pacification** [ˎ'sjɔ̃] *f* pacification, pacifying; **pacifier** [pasi'fje] (1o) *v/t.* pacify (*a country*); calm (*the crowd, s.o.'s mind*); **pacifique** [ˎ'fik] **1.** *adj.* pacific; peaceful, quiet; *l'océan m* ♀ = **2.** *su./m*: *le* ♀ the Pacific (Ocean).

pacotille [pakɔ'tiːj] *f* ⚓ shoddy goods *pl.*; *fig.* cheap stuff, rubbish, junk; *de* ˎ cheap; jerry-built (*house*).

pacte [pakt] *m* pact, agreement; **pactiser** [pakti'ze] (1a) *v/i.* come to terms; compromise (with, *avec*).

paf F [paf] **1.** *int.* slap!; **2.** *adj.* F tight (= *drunk*).

pagaie [pa'gɛ] *f* paddle.

pagaïe F, **pagaille** F [pa'ga:j] *f* disorder, mess; *fig.* chaos.

paganiser [pagani'ze] (1a) *vt/i.* paganize; **paganisme** [ˎ'nism] *m* paganism; heathendom.

pagayer [pagɛ'je] (1i) *vt/i.* paddle.

page¹ [pa:ʒ] *m* page(-boy).

page² [pa:ʒ] *f book*: page, leaf; *à la* ˎ in the know, up to date; **paginer** [paʒi'ne] (1a) *v/t.* paginate.

pagne [paɲ] *m* loin-cloth.

paie [pɛ] *f* pay(ment), wages *pl.*; *enveloppe f de* ˎ pay envelope; *jour m de* ˎ pay-day; **paiement** [ˎ'mɑ̃] *m* payment; ˎ *anticipé* advance payment *or* instalment; ˎ *au comptant* cash payment; ˎ *contre livraison* cash on delivery; ˎ *partiel* part-payment; *suspendre ses* ˎ*s* suspend payment.

païen, -enne [pa'jɛ̃, ˎ'jɛn] *adj., a. su.* pagan, heathen.

paillage ✗ [pɑ'ja:ʒ] *m* mulching.

paillard, e *sl.* [pɑ'ja:r, ˎ'jard] **1.** *adj.* ribald, lewd; **2.** *su./m* rake; *su./f*

wanton; **paillardise** [ˎjar'di:z] *f* lechery; lewd talk.

paillasse¹ [pɑ'jas] *m* buffoon, clown.

paillasse² [pɑ'jas] *f* straw mattress, palliasse; ⚛ bench; **paillasson** [ˎja'sɔ̃] *m* mat; matting; **paille** [pɑ:j] **1.** *su./f* straw; ⊕ *iron:* shavings *pl.*; ⊕, *gem, glass, metal, a. fig.*: flaw; *fig.* poverty; ˎ *de fer* steel wool; *fig. homme m de* ˎ man of straw, tool, Am. front; *tirer à la courte* ˎ draw lots; **2.** *adj./inv.* straw-colo(u)red; **paillé, e** [pɑ'je] flawed, flawy; scaly (*metal*); straw-colo(u)red; **pailler** [ˎ'je] (1a) *v/t.* mulch; (cover with) straw; **2.** *su./m* farm-yard; straw-yard; straw-stack; **paillet** [ˎ'jɛ] *m* pale red wine; **pailleter** [paj'te] (1c) *v/t.* spangle (with, *de*); **paillette** [pa'jɛt] *f* sequin, spangle; *mica, soap:* flake; *metall.* scale; *jewel:* flaw; grain of golddust; **pailleux, -euse** [pɑ'jø, ˎ'jø:z] strawy; ⊕ flawy; **paillis** [ˎ'ji] *m* mulch; **paillotte** [ˎ'jɔt] *f* straw hut.

pain [pɛ̃] *m* bread; loaf; *soap:* cake, tablet; *butter:* pat; *sugar:* lump; *fig.* livelihood; *sl.* punch, blow; ˎ *à cacheter* wafer, seal; ˎ *bis* brown bread; ˎ *complet* whole-meal bread; ˎ *d'épice* gingerbread; *petit* ˎ roll.

pair, paire [pɛ:r] **1.** *adj.* equal; Å even (*number*); **2.** *su./m* equality; ✝ par; *parl.* peer; *person:* equal; *au* ˎ *in* return for board and lodging, au pair; *de* ˎ together, hand in hand (with, *avec*); *hors* (*de*) ˎ peerless, unrivalled; *fig. être au* ˎ *de* be up to date *or* schedule with; *parl. la Chambre des* ♀*s* the (House of) Lords *pl.*

paire [pɛ:r] *f* pair; *birds etc.*: brace; *fig. faire la* ˎ be two of a kind.

pairesse [pɛ'rɛs] *f* peeress; **pairie** [ˎ'ri] *f* peerage.

paisible [pɛ'zibl] peaceful, quiet.

paître [pɛ:tr] (4k) *v/t.* graze (*cattle*); drive to pasture; feed on (*grass*); *v/i.* feed, graze; pasture, browse; F *envoyer q.* ˎ send s.o. packing.

paix [pɛ] *f* peace; quiet; *fig.* reconciliation; ~ *donc!* keep quiet!; ~ *séparée* separate peace; *faire la* ~ make peace; F *ficher la* ~ *à q.* leave s.o. alone, let s.o. be.

pal, *pl.* **pals** [pal] *m* pale (*a.* ⬜), stake.

palabre [pa'labr] *f or m* palaver; F speech.

paladin [pala'dɛ̃] *m* paladin, knight; knight-errant.

palais[1] [pa'lɛ] *m* (*royal or bishop's*) palace; *coll.* lawyers *pl.*; ~ *de justice* law-courts *pl.*

palais[2] ♀, *anat.*, *fig.* [~] *m* palate; *anat.* voile *m* du ~ soft palate.

palan ♣, ⊕ [pa'lɑ̃] *m* pulley-block, tackle; set of pulleys.

palanche [pa'lɑ̃:ʃ] *f* yoke (*for carrying buckets etc.*).

palangre [pa'lɑ̃:gr] *f* trawl-line, *Am.* trawl.

palanque [pa'lɑ̃:k] *f* stockade.

palanquin [palɑ̃kɛ̃] *m* palanquin.

palatal, e, *m/pl.* **-aux** [pala'tal, ~'to] *adj.*, *a. su./f* palatal; **palatin, e** *anat.* [pala'tɛ̃, ~'tin] palatine.

pale[1] *eccl.* [pal] *f* chalice-cover, pall.

pale[2] [~] *f* ♣, ⚓, *cin.* blade (*a. fan*); *fan:* vane; ⊕ arm.

pâle [pɑ:l] pale, pallid; wan; ashen (*complexion*); *fig.* colo(u)rless (*style*); ✗ *sl.* sick; *fig.* sickly (*smile*).

palefrenier [palfrə'nje] *m* groom; stable-boy; ostler; **palefroi** † [~'frwa] *m* palfrey.

paléo... [paleɔ] pal(a)eo...; **paléontologie** [~ɔ̃tɔlɔ'ʒi] *f* pal(a)eontology.

paleron [pal'rɔ̃] *m* ox *etc.*: shoulder-blade; *cuis.* chuck.

palet [pa'lɛ] *m game:* quoit.

paletot [pal'to] *m* overcoat; *sl.* tomber sur le ~ *à q.* jump on s.o., pitch into s.o.

palette [pa'lɛt] *f paint., a. fig.* palette; *cuis.* shoulder; ⊕ *wheel etc.:* paddle; † pallet.

pâleur [pɑ'lœ:r] *f* pallor, paleness; *moon:* wanness.

palier [pa'lje] *m* ⌂ stairs: landing; ⊕ bearing; ⊕ pillow-block; ⚓, 🚂, *mot.* level; *sur le même* ~ on the same floor; **palière** ⌂ [~'ljɛ:r] *adj./f* top (*step*).

palinodie [palinɔ'di] *f* recantation.

pâlir [pɑ'li:r] (2a) *v/i.* (grow) pale; *fig.* fade; *v/t.* make pale; bleach (*colours*).

palissade [pali'sad] *f* palisade,

fence; ✗ stockade; **palissader** [~sa'de] (1a) *v/t.* fence in, enclose; ✗ stockade; ⚘ hedge in (*a field*).

palissandre [pali'sɑ̃:dr] *m* rosewood.

palisser ⚘ [pali'se] (1a) *v/t.* train (*vine etc.*).

palliatif, -ve [pallja'tif, ~'ti:v] *adj.*, *a. su./m* palliative.

pallier [pal'lje] (1o) *v/t.* palliate.

palmarès [palma'rɛs] *m* prize-list, hono(u)rs list.

palme[1] [palm] *f* ♀ palm(-branch); *fig.* palm; *skin diving etc.:* flipper.

palme[2] † [~] *m measure:* hand('s-breadth).

palmé, e [pal'me] ♀ palmate; *orn.* web-footed.

palmer ⊕ [pal'mɛ:r] *m* micrometer ga(u)ge.

palmeraie [palmə'rɛ] *f* palm-grove; **palmette** [~'mɛt] *f* ⌂ palm-leaf, palmette; ⚘ fan-shaped espalier; **palmier** ♀ [~'mje] *m* palm-tree; **palmipède** *zo.* [~mi'pɛd] *adj.*, *a. su./m* palmipede; **palmite** [~'mit] *m* palm-marrow; **palmure** *orn.* [~'my:r] *f* web.

palombe *orn.* [pa'lɔ̃:b] *f* ring-dove, wood-pigeon.

palonnier [palɔ'nje] *m* ⊕ *carriage etc.:* swingle-bar; *mot.* compensation bar; ⚓ rudder-bar.

pâlot, -otte [pɑ'lo, ~'lɔt] palish; peaky.

palpable [pal'pabl] palpable (*a. fig.*); tangible; *fig.* obvious; **palpe** [palp] *m zo.* feeler; *icht.* barbel; **palper** [pal'pe] (1a) *v/t.* feel; ✠ palpate; F pocket (*money*).

palpitant, e [palpi'tɑ̃, ~'tɑ̃:t] **1.** *adj.* fluttering (*heart*); throbbing; *fig.* thrilling; **2.** *su./m sl.* ticker (= heart); **palpitation** [~ta'sjɔ̃] *f* throb(bing); ✠ palpitation; fluttering; **palpiter** [~'te] (1a) *v/i.* palpitate; throb, beat (*heart*); flutter; *fig.* thrill (with, *de*).

paltoquet F † [paltɔ'ke] *m* lout; whipper-snapper.

paludéen, -enne [palyde'ɛ̃, ~'ɛn] marsh...; ✠ malarial (*fever*); **paludisme** ✠ [~'dism] *m* malaria, marsh fever; **palustre** [pa'lystr] paludous; swampy (*ground*).

pâmer [pɑ'me] (1a) *v/t.*: † se ~ faint; se~ *de qch.* be overcome with s.th.; se ~ *de joie a.* be in raptures; se ~ *de rire* split one's sides with laughter; **pâmoison** †, *co.* [~mwa'zɔ̃] *f* swoon.

papelard

pampa [pɑ̃'pa] *f* pampas *pl.*

pamphlet [pɑ̃'flɛ] *m* lampoon; **pamphlétaire** [ˌflɛ'tɛːr] *m* pamphleteer, lampoonist.

pamplemousse ♀ [pɑ̃plə'mus] *m* grapefruit; shaddock.

pampre ♀ [pɑ̃ːpr] *m* vine-branch, vine-shoot.

pan[1] [pɑ̃] *m* cost. flap; coat-tail; △ wall: piece, section; (wooden) partition, framing; building, prism, nut: side; sky: patch.

pan[2]! [ˌ] *int.* bang!; slap!

pan... [pɑ̃; before vowel pan] pan...

panacée [pana'se] *f* panacea, cure-all.

panachage [pana'ʃaːʒ] *m* election: splitting one's vote; **panache** [ˌ'naʃ] *m* plume, tuft (on a helmet etc.); smoke: wreath; fig. gallantry; mot. etc. faire ~ turn over; **panaché, e** [pana'ʃe] **1.** adj. mixed (salad, ice); **2.** su./m shandy(gaff); **panacher** [ˌ] (1a) v/t. variegate; election: split (one's votes).

panade [pa'nad] *f* cuis. panada; F dans la ~ in need; in the soup.

panais ♀ [pa'nɛ] *m* parsnip.

panama [pana'ma] *m* panama hat, F (fine-)straw hat.

panaris ♀ [pana'ri] *m* whitlow.

pancarte [pɑ̃'kart] *f* placard, bill; sign; notice.

pancréas anat. [pɑ̃kre'ɑːs] *m* pancreas.

panda zo. [pɑ̃'da] *m* panda.

panégyrique [paneʒi'rik] *m* panegyric; faire le ~ de panegyrize (s.o.).

paner cuis. [pa'ne] (1a) v/t. cover with bread-crumbs; **paneterie** [pan'tri] *f* bread-pantry; ✗, school, etc.: bread-store; **panetier** [ˌ'tje] *m* bread-store keeper; **panetière** [ˌ'tjɛːr] *f* bread-cupboard; sideboard.

panier [pa'nje] *m* basket (a. sp.); ~ à salade salad washer; sl. Black Maria, prison van; fig. ~ percé spendthrift; F le dessus du ~ the pick of the bunch; **panier-repas,** pl. **paniers-repas** [ˌrə'pa] *m* packed lunch, lunchpack.

panifiable [pani'fjabl] bread-...; farine *f* ~ bread-flour; **panification** [ˌfika'sjɔ̃] *f* panification; **panifier** [ˌ'fje] (1o) v/t. turn (flour) into bread.

panique [pa'nik] adj., a. su./f panic; **paniquer** [ˌni'ke] (1a) v/t. (throw into a) panic; se ~ = v/i. (get into a) panic.

panne[1] tex. [pan] *f* plush.

panne[2] [ˌ] *f* lard, hog's fat.

panne[3] [ˌ] *f* mot. etc. breakdown; ⚡ etc. current, engine: failure; être en ~ be stuck; être en ~ de ... have run out of ...; laisser en ~ leave (s.o.) in the lurch; tomber en ~ break down.

panne[4] △ [ˌ] *f* pantile; roof: purlin.

panneau [pa'no] *m* wood, a. paint.: panel; board; ⚑ ground-signal; ⚓ hatch; ✗ glass frame; F snare, trap.

panneton ⊕ [pan'tɔ̃] *m* key: web; (window-)catch.

panoplie [panɔ'pli] *f* set (of tools, toys, etc.); outfit; ✗ armoury; fig. package, (whole) set, variety.

panorama [panɔra'ma] *m* panorama.

panse [pɑ̃ːs] *f* F belly (a. ⚗ retort etc.); zo. first stomach, paunch.

pansement ⚕ [pɑ̃s'mɑ̃] *m* wound: dressing; **panser** [pɑ̃'se] (1a) v/t. groom, rub down (a horse); ⚕ dress (a wound), tend (a wounded man).

pansu, e [pɑ̃'sy] pot-bellied.

pantalon [pɑ̃ta'lɔ̃] *m* trousers pl., Am. pants pl.; (woman's) knickers pl.; slacks pl.

panteler [pɑ̃'tle] (1c) v/i. pant.

panthère zo. [pɑ̃'tɛːr] *f* panther.

pantin [pɑ̃'tɛ̃] *m* toy: jumping-jack; fig. puppet.

panto... [pɑ̃tɔ] panto...; **~graphe** [ˌ'graf] *m* drawing, a. ✗: pantograph; lazy-tongs pl.

pantois [pɑ̃'twa] adj./m flabbergasted.

pantomime [pɑ̃tɔ'mim] *f* dumb show; pantomime.

pantouflard [pɑ̃tu'flaːr] *m* stay-at-home type; **pantoufle** [ˌ'tufl] *f* slipper; fig. en ~s in a slipshod way; **pantouflerie** ⊕ [ˌtuflə'ri] *f* slipper-making.

paon orn. [pɑ̃] *m* peacock (a. fig.); **paonne** orn. [pan] *f* peahen; **paonneau** [pa'no] *m* pea-chick.

papa F [pa'pa] *m* papa, dad(dy); fig. à la ~ in leisurely fashion; fig. de ~ old, antiquated, old-fashioned; (good) old; grandfather's ...

papal, e, m/pl. **-aux** [pa'pal, ~'po] papal; **papauté** [~po'te] *f* papacy; **pape** eccl., a. fig. [pap] *m* pope.

papelard, e F [pa'plaːr, ~'plard] **1.** adj. sanctimonious; **2.** su./m

sanctimonious person; **papelardise**
F [⹂plarˈdiːz] *f* cant, sanctimoniousness.

paperasse [paˈpras] *f* red tape; useless paper(s *pl.*); **paperasserie** [⹂-
prasˈri] *f* accumulation of old papers; F red tape, red-tapism; **paperassier** [⹂praˈsje] *m* bureaucrat.

papeterie [papˈtri] *f* paper-mill;
paper trade; stationery; stationer's
(shop); **papetier, -ère** [⹂ˈtje, ⹂-
ˈtjɛːr] **1.** *su.* stationer; paper-manu-
facturer; **2.** *adj.* paper(-making);
papier [paˈpje] *m* paper; document; ✝ bill(s *pl.*); ∼ *à calquer* tracing-paper; ∼ *à la cuve* hand-made
paper; ∼ *à lettres* letter-paper; ∼ *à musique* music-paper; ∼ *bible* (*or indien*)
India paper; ∼ *buvard* blotting paper; ∼ *carbone* carbon paper; ∼ *couché* art paper; ∼ *d'emballage* brown
paper; ∼ *de verre* sand-paper, glass-
paper; ∼ *-émeri* emery-paper; ∼ *-
filtre* filter-paper; ∼ *hygiénique* toi-
let-paper; ∼ *peint,* ∼ *-tenture* wallpaper; ∼ *pelure* tissue-paper; ∼ *-
monnaie* [⹂pjemɔˈnɛ] *m* paper
money.

papille ♀, *anat.* [paˈpiːj] *f* papilla.

papillon [papiˈjɔ̃] *m zo.* butterfly;
cost. butterfly bow, bow-tie; leaflet;
(parking) ticket; *poster:* fly-bill;
inset map; *document:* rider; ✝ label,
tag; ⊕ butterfly-valve; ⊕ wing-nut;
mot. throttle; F *fig.* ∼*s pl.* noirs gloomy
thoughts; **papillonner** [⹂jɔˈne] (1a)
v/i. flutter; F flit from subject to
subject; **papillotte** [⹂ˈjɔt] *f* curl-
paper; frill (*round ham etc.*); twist of
paper; **papilloter** [⹂jɔˈte] (1a) *v/i.*
blink (*eyes, light*); *cin.* flicker; *fig.*
glitter.

paprika ♀, *cuis.* [papriˈka] *m* red
pepper.

papule ✿, ♀ [paˈpyl] *f* papula, papule; **papuleux, -euse** [⹂pyˈlø, ⹂-
ˈløːz] papulose, F pimply.

papyrus [papiˈrys] *m* papyrus.

pâque [pɑːk] *f* (*Jewish*) Passover.

paquebot ⚓ [pakˈbo] *m* (passen-
ger-)liner; packet-boat.

pâquerette ♀ [pɑˈkrɛt] *f* daisy.

Pâques [pɑːk] *su./m* Easter; *su./f:*
∼ *pl. closes* Low Sunday *sg.*; ∼ *pl.
fleuries* Palm Sunday *sg.*; *faire ses*
♀ make one's Easter communion.

paquet [paˈkɛ] *m* parcel, package;
pack; bundle; ⚓ ∼ *de mer* heavy sea;

faire son ∼ *or ses* ∼*s* pack one's bags;
lâcher son ∼ *à q.* give s.o. a piece of
one's mind; (y) *mettre le* ∼ give all one
has got; *risquer le* ∼ chance the lot;
paqueter [pakˈte] (1c) *v/t.* make up
into a parcel; **paqueteur** *m,* **-euse** *f*
✝, ⊕ [⹂ˈtœːr, ⹂ˈtøːz] packer.

par [par] *prp. place:* by (*sea*),
through (*the door, the street*); via
(*Calais*); over; to; *time:* on (*a fine
evening, a summer's day*); in (*the
rain*); *motive:* from; through; out
of (*friendship, curiosity*); *agent:* by;
instrument: by (*mail, telephone,
train, boat, etc.*); *distribution:* per
(*annum, capita*), each; a (*day, week,
etc.*); in (*hundreds, numerical order*);
∼ *eau et* ∼ *terre* by land and sea;
∼ *monts et* ∼ *vaux* over hill and
dale; ∼ *où?* which way?; ∼ *toute la
terre* (*ville*) all over the world
(town); *regarder* (*jeter*) ∼ *la fenêtre*
look (throw) out of the window;
tomber ∼ *terre* fall to the ground;
∼ *un beau temps* in fine weather; ∼
bonheur (*malheur*) by good (ill) fortune, (un)fortunately; ∼ *hasard* by
chance; ∼ *pitié!* for pity's sake!;
vaincu ∼ *César* conquered by Caesar; *Phèdre* ∼ *Racine* Phèdre by
Racine; ∼ *soi-même* (by *or* for) oneself; *célèbre* ∼ famous for; ∼ *conséquent* consequently; ∼ *droit et raison* by rights; ∼ *avion post:* via air-
mail; *venir* ∼ *air à* fly to; *prendre* ∼
la main take by the hand; *jour* ∼
jour day by day; *deux* ∼ *deux* two
by two; *commencer* (*finir etc.*) ∼
(*inf.*) begin (end) by (*ger.*); F ∼
trop court (much *or* far) too short;
de ∼ by, in conformity with (*the
conditions, nature, etc.*); *de* ∼ *le roi*
by order of the King; in the King's
name; ∼*-ci* here; ∼*-là* there; ∼*-ci*
∼*-là* hither and thither; now and
then; ∼ *derrière* from behind; ∼*-
dessous* under, beneath; ∼*-dessus*
over (*s.th.*); ⚖ ∼*-devant* before, in
presence of.

para ✗ F [paˈra] *m* paratrooper.

para...: ∼**bole** [paraˈbɔl] *f* parable;
♉ parabola.

parachever [paraʃˈve] (1d) *v/t.* perfect.

para...: ∼**chute** [paraˈʃyt] *m* ✈ parachute; ✗ *cage:* safety device; ∼**-
chuter** [⹂ʃyˈte] (1a) *v/t.* (drop by)
parachute; *fig.* pitchfork (s.o. into, *q.*

dans); ~**chutiste** [~ʃyˈtist] *m* para-
chutist; paratrooper.
parade [paˈrad] *f box., a. fencing*:
parry; *horse*: checking; reply, repartee; ⚔ parade (*a. fig.*); *fig.* show;
faire ~ *de* show off, display; *lit m de*
~ lying-in-state bed; **parader**
[~raˈde] (1a) *v/i.* strut (about).
paradigme *gramm.* [paraˈdigm] *m*
paradigm.
paradis [paraˈdi] *m* paradise; *thea.*
gallery, F the gods *pl.*; ✝ ~ *fiscal* tax
haven; **paradisiaque** [~diˈzjak]
paradisiac; of paradise; **paradisier**
orn. [~diˈzje] *m* bird of paradise.
paradoxal, e, *m/pl.* **-aux** [paradɔk-
ˈsal, ~ˈso] paradoxical; **paradoxe**
[~ˈdɔks] *m* paradox.
parafe [paˈraf] *m see paraphe*; **parafer** [~raˈfe] *see* parapher.
paraffine 🜋 [paraˈfin] *f* paraffin.
parafoudre ⚡ [paraˈfudr] *m* light-
ning-arrester; *magneto*: safety-gap.
parage[1] † [paˈraːʒ] *m* birth, descent;
de haut ~ of high lineage.
parage[2] [~] *m*: ~*s pl.* ⚓ latitudes;
regions; vicinity *sg.*, quarters; *dans
les* ~*s de* ... *a.* in the ... area, near ...;
dans les ~ (around) here.
paragraphe [paraˈgraf] *m* paragraph.
parais [paˈrɛ] *1st p. sg. pres. of paraître*; **paraissons** [~rɛˈsɔ̃] *1st p. pl.
pres. of paraître*; **paraître** [~ˈrɛːtr]
(4k) *v/i.* appear; seem; look; be visible; come out (*book etc.*); *vient de* ~
just out (*book*); *v/impers.*: *à ce qu'il
paraît* apparently; *il paraît que* (*ind.*)
it seems that; *il paraît que oui* (*non*) it
appears so (not).
parallèle [paralˈlɛl] **1.** *adj.* parallel;
fig. unofficial (*institution etc.*);
second, side (*job etc.*); alternative
(*medicine etc.*); **2.** *su./f* Å, ⚔ parallel;
su./m geog., ⚡, *a. fig.* parallel; **paral-
lélépipède** Å [~lelepiˈpɛd] *m* paral-
lelepiped; **parallélisme** [~leˈlism]
m parallelism (between ... and *de* ...
à, entre ... *et*); **parallélogramme**
Å [~leloˈgram] *m* parallelogram.
para...: ~**lyser** [paraliˈze] (1a) *v/t.* 🜃
paralyse (*a. fig.*); *fig.* cripple; ~**lysie**
🜃 [~ˈzi] *f* paralysis; † palsy; ~ *agitante*
Parkinson's disease; ~**lytique** 🜃
[~ˈtik] *adj., a. su.* paralytic; ~**mètre**
Å, *a. fig.* [paraˈmɛtr] *m* parameter;
~**militaire** [paramiliˈtɛːr] *m* semi-
military.

parangon [parɑ̃ˈgɔ̃] *m* paragon,
model; flawless gem; *typ.* gros ~
double pica.
parapet [paraˈpɛ] *m* ⚠, ⚔ parapet; ⚔
breastwork.
paraphe [paˈraf] *m signature*: flourish; initials *pl.*; **parapher** [~raˈfe]
(1a) *v/t.* initial.
para...: ~**phrase** [paraˈfrɑːz] *f* paraphrase; *fig.* circumlocution; ~**phraser** [~fraˈze] (1a) *v/t.* paraphrase;
fig. add to (*a story etc.*); ~**plégie** 🜃
[~pleˈʒi] *f* paraplegia; ~**pluie** [~ˈplɥi]
m umbrella (*a.* ⚔, ⚔); ~**site** [~ˈzit] **1.**
adj. ♀, *⚡* parasitic; **2.** *su./m* ♀, *biol.,
zo., fig.* parasite; *fig.* sponger; ~*s pl.
radio*: atmospherics; ~**sol** [~ˈsɔl] *m*
parasol, sunshade; *mot.* visor; ~**tonnerre** [~tɔˈnɛːr] *m* lightning-con-
ductor; lightning-rod; ~**typhoïde**
🜃 [~tifɔˈid] *f* paratyphoid fever;
~**vent** [~ˈvɑ̃] *m* folding screen.
parbleu! [parˈblø] *int.* rather!; of
course!
parc [park] *m* park; enclose; *horses*:
paddock; *cattle*: pen; *sheep*: fold;
oysters: bed; ⊕ *coal*: yard; 🛢, ⚔
depot; *child*: playpen; ✝, *a. fig.*
stock; *mot.* ~ *de stationnement* car
park, *Am.* parking lot; **parcage**
[parˈkaːʒ] *m mot.* parking; *cattle*:
penning; *sheep*: folding; *oysters*:
laying down; *mot.* ~ *interdit* no
parking.
parcellaire [parsɛlˈlɛːr] divided into
small portions; **parcelle** [~ˈsɛl] *f
land*: lot, plot; small fragment; *fig.*
grain; **parceller** [~sɛˈle] (1a) *v/t.*
divide into lots; portion out; **par-
celliser** [~sɛliˈze] (1a) *v/t.* divide *or*
split up.
parce [pars] *cj.*: ~ *que* because.
parchemin [parʃəˈmɛ̃] *m* parchment; *bookbinding*: vellum; F ~*s pl.
univ.* diplomas; 🜍 title-deeds; **parcheminé, e** [parʃəmiˈne] *fig.* parchment-like, dried; wizened (*skin*);
parcheminer [~ˈne] (1a) *v/t.* give a
parchment finish to; *se* ~ shrivel up;
become parchment-like; **parche-
mineux, -euse** [~ˈnø, ~ˈnøːz]
parchment-like.
parcimonie [parsimɔˈni] *f* parsi-
mony, stinginess; **parcimonieux,
-euse** [~ˈnjø, ~ˈnjøːz] parsimonious,
stingy.
parc(o)mètre [park(ɔ)ˈmɛtr] *m*
parking meter.

parcourir [parku'ri:r] (2l) *v/t.* travel through; traverse (*a.* ⚡); cover (*a distance*); skim, look through (*a book, papers, etc.*); *eye*: survey; **parcours** [~'ku:r] *m* distance covered; *sp., golf, river*: course; ⊕ path; trip, journey.

pardessus [pardə'sy] *m* overcoat, top-coat.

par-devers [pardə'vɛ:r] in the presence of, before; in one's possession; *garder qch.* ~ *soi* keep s.th. to o.s.

pardi! † [par'di] *int.* of course!; rather!

pardon [par'dɔ̃] **1.** *su./m* pardon (*a. eccl.*); forgiveness; *eccl.* pilgrimage (*in Brittany*); **2.** *int.*: ~! excuse me!; ~? I beg your pardon?; **pardonnable** [~dɔ'nabl] forgivable, excusable; **pardonner** [~dɔ'ne] (1a) *v/t.* pardon, forgive; excuse; *je ne pardonne pas que vous l'ayez visité* I cannot forgive your having visited him.

pare...: ~**-balles** [par'bal] *adj./inv.* bullet-proof; ~**-boue** *mot.* [~'bu] *m/inv.* see garde-boue; ~**-brise** *mot.* [~'bri:z] *m/inv.* windscreen, *Am.* windshield; ~**-chocs** *mot.* [~'ʃɔk] *m/inv.* bumper; ~**-étincelles** [~etɛ̃'sɛl] *m/inv.* fire-guard; 🔥 spark-catcher; ~**-feu** [~'fø] *m/inv.* forest: fire-break.

pareil, -eille [pa'rɛ:j] **1.** *adj.* like, similar; such (a); *sans* ~ unrivalled, unequalled; **2.** *su.* equal, like; peer; match; *su./f rendre la ~eille à* pay (*s.o.*) back in his own coin.

parement [par'mɑ̃] *m* adorning; ornament; *cost., a.* 🔺 facing; 🔺 stone: face; ⊕, *cuis.* dressing; kerb-stone, curb-stone.

parent, e [pa'rɑ̃, ~'rɑ̃:t] *su.* relative; relation; *su./m*: ~*s pl.* parents, father and mother; **parental, e,** *m/pl.* **-aux** [parɑ̃'tal, ~'to] parental; **parenté** [~rɑ̃'te] *f* relationship, kinship.

parenthèse [parɑ̃'tɛ:z] *f* parenthesis, digression; *typ.* bracket; *entre* ~s in brackets; *fig.* incidentally.

parer [pa're] (1a) *v/t.* ornament, adorn; dress (*meat, vegetables*); ⚓ clear (*the anchor*); ⚓ steer clear of, clear; ward off, parry; avoid; pull up (*a horse*); *se* ~ deck o.s. out (in, de); *fig.* show off; *v/i.*: ~ *à* provide against *or* for; obviate (*a difficulty*); avert (*an accident*).

pare-soleil [parsɔ'lɛ:j] *m/inv.* sun-visor (*a. mot.*).

paresse [pa'rɛs] *f* laziness, idleness; *mind, a.* 💩 bowels, *etc.*: sluggishness; **paresseux, -euse** [~rɛ'sø, ~'sø:z] **1.** *adj.* sluggish; lazy, idle; **2.** *su.* lazy *or* idle person; *su./m zo.* sloth.

pareur *m,* **-euse** *f* ⊕ [pa'rœ:r, ~-'rø:z] finisher, trimmer.

parfaire [par'fɛ:r] (4r) *v/t.* complete, finish; make up (*a total of money*); **parfait, e** [~'fɛ, ~'fɛt] **1.** *adj.* perfect; *fig.* thorough, utter; 🕇 full (*payment*); F capital; (c'est) ~! splendid!; **2.** *su./m gramm.* perfect; *cuis.* ice-cream; **parfaitement** [~fɛt'mɑ̃] *adv.* perfectly; thoroughly; ~! precisely!; exactly!

parfois [par'fwa] *adv.* sometimes, now and then.

parfum [par'fœ̃] *m* perfume, scent; fragrance; *sl. être au* ~ be in the know; *sl. mettre q. au* ~ put s.o. in the picture, wise s.o. up; **parfumer** [~fy'me] (1a) *v/t.* perfume, scent; *se* ~ use scent; **parfumerie** [~fym'ri] *f* parfumery; **parfumeur** *m,* **-euse** *f* 🕇 [~fy'mœ:r, ~'mø:z] perfumer.

pari [pa'ri] *m* bet, wager; *sp.* betting; ~ *mutuel* totalizator system, F tote; **pariade** *orn.* [~'rjad] *f* pairing; pairing season; pair; **parier** [~'rje] (1o) *vt/i.* bet (on, *sur*); wager.

pariétaire 🌿 [parje'tɛ:r] *f* wall-pellitory; **pariétal, e,** *m/pl.* **~aux** [~-'tal, ~'to] **1.** 🌿, *anat.* parietal; *paint.* mural; **2.** *su./m anat.* parietal bone.

parieur *m,* **-euse** *f* [pa'rjœ:r, ~'rjœ:z] better, punter.

Parigot *m,* **e** *f* F [pari'go, ~'gɔt] Parisian; **parisien, -enne** [~'zjɛ̃, ~'zjɛn] *adj., a. su.* ♀ Parisian.

paritaire [pari'tɛ:r] *adj.*: *réunion f* ~ round-table conference; **parité** [~'te] *f* parity; equality; ⚖ evenness.

parjure [par'ʒy:r] **1.** *adj.* perjured; **2.** *su. person*: perjurer; *su./m* perjury; **parjurer** [~ʒy're] (1a) *v/t.*: *se* ~ perjure o.s.

parking *mot.* [par'kiŋ] *m* parking; car park, *Am.* parking lot.

parlant, e [par'lɑ̃, ~'lɑ̃:t] speaking (*a. fig.*); *fig.* talkative; *cin.* sound (*film*); *fig.* expressive; *fig.* eloquent, that speaks for itself; **parlé, e** [~'le] spoken (*language*).

parlement [parlə'mɑ̃] *m* parliament; **parlementaire** [parləmã-'tɛːr] **1.** *adj.* parliamentary, *Am.* Congressional; *drapeau m* ~ flag of truce; **2.** *su./m* member of parliament, *Am.* Congressman; negotiator; **parlementarisme** *pol.* [~ta'rism] *m* parliamentary government; **parlementer** [~'te] (1a) *v/i.* parley.

parler [par'le] **1.** (1a) *v/i.* speak, talk (to, *à*; of, about *de*); be on speaking terms (with, *à*); *les faits parlent* the facts speak for themselves; *on m'a parlé de* I was told about; *sans* ~ *de* let alone ...; *v/t.* speak (*a language*); ~ *affaires* (F *boutique, politique, raison*) talk business (F shop, about politics, sense); *se* ~ be spoken (*language*); **2.** *su./m* speech; dialect; way of speaking; **parleur, -euse** [~'lœːr, ~'løːz] *su.* talker; **parloir** [~'lwaːr] *m* parlo(u)r; **parlote** F [~'lɔt] *f* chitchat.

parmesan [parmə'zã] *m* Parmesan (cheese).

parmi [par'mi] *prp.* among; amid.

parodie [parɔ'di] *f* parody; skit ([up]on, *de*); **parodier** [~'dje] (1o) *v/t.* parody, burlesque.

paroi [pa'rwa] *f biol.*, ⊕ boiler, cylinder, *a.* rock, tent: wall; 🜨 partition-wall; *case, stomach, tunnel:* lining; *thea.* flat.

paroisse [pa'rwas] *f* parish; parish church; **paroissial, e,** *m/pl.* -**aux** [parwa'sjal, ~'sjo] parochial; parish-...; **paroissien, -enne** [~'sjɛ̃, ~'sjɛn] *su.* parishioner; *su./m* prayerbook; F *drôle de* ~ queer stick.

parole [pa'rɔl] *f* word; remark; promise, 🜨 parole; *fig.* speech; eloquence; saying; *bourse:* have the floor; *donner la* ~ *à q.* call upon s.o. to speak.

parpaing 🜨 [par'pɛ̃] *m* parpen; breeze-block.

Parque *myth.* [park] *f* one of the Fates; *les* ~ the Fates, the Parcae.

parquer [par'ke] (1m) *v/t.* enclose; pen (*cattle*); fold (*sheep*); put (*a horse*) in paddock; *mot.*, 🜨 park; *v/i. a. se* ~ park; **parquet** [~'kɛ] *m* 🜨 floor(ing); *mirror:* backing; 🜨 public prosecutor's department; 🜨 well; † official market; *bourse:* Ring; **parqueter** ⊕ [parkə'te] (1c) *v/t.* lay a floor in (*a room*); parquet; **parqueterie** ⊕ [~'tri] *f* laying of

floors; ~ *en mosaïque* inlaid floor; inlaying; **parqueteur** ⊕ [~'tœːr] *m* parquet-layer.

parrain [pa'rɛ̃] *m* godfather; sponsor (*a. fig.*).

parricide [pari'sid] **1.** *adj.* parricidal; **2.** *su. person:* parricide; *su./m crime:* parricide.

parsemer [parsə'me] (1d) *v/t.* strew, sprinkle (with, *de*); *fig.* stud, spangle.

part [paːr] *f* share (*a.* ✝); part; portion (*a.* 🜨); place; *food:* helping, *cake:* piece; *à* ~ apart, separately; *à* ~ *cela* apart from that; except for that; *à* ~ *entière* full (*member etc.*); entirely, fully; *à* ~ *soi* in one's own heart, to o.s.; *autre* ~ elsewhere; *d'autre* ~ besides; *de la* ~ *de* on behalf of; from; *de ma* ~ from me; on my part; *de* ~ *en* ~ through and through; *de* ~ *et d'autre* on both sides (of, *de*), on either side; *d'une ... d'autre* ~ on the one hand ... on the other hand; *faire* ~ *de qch. à q.* inform s.o. of s.th.; *faire la* ~ *de* take into account; *nulle* ~ nowhere; *pour ma* ~ as to me, for one; *prendre* ~ *à* take part in, join in; *quelque* ~ somewhere; **partage** [par'taːʒ] *m* division, sharing; 🜨, *a. pol.* partition; share, portion, lot (*a. fig.*); *geog. ligne f de* ~ *des eaux* watershed, *Am.* divide; *échoir en* ~ *à q.* fall to s.o.'s lot; **partager** [~ta'ʒe] (11) *v/t.* divide (up); share (*a. fig. an opinion*); *se* ~ be divided; differ; *être bien (mal) partagé* be well (ill) provided for *or* endowed.

partance ⛴, 🚂 [par'tãːs] *f* departure; *en* ~ *pour* (bound) for.

partant[1] [par'tã] *cj.* therefore, hence.

partant[2] [par'tã] *m* departing traveller; party leaving; *sp.* starter, runner.

partenaire [partə'nɛːr] *m* partner (*a. sp., cin., etc.*).

parterre [par'tɛːr] *m* ✿ flower-bed; *thea.* pit.

parti[1], **e** [par'ti] away; gone; F tipsy; *... est bien (mal)* ~ *...* had a good (bad) start.

parti[2] [par'ti] *m pol., fig.* party; *fig.* side; *marriage:* match; *fig.* choice, decision, option; *fig.* course of action, solution; ~ *pris* bias, set purpose; *prendre* ~ (*pour*) take sides (with); *prendre un* ~ come to a decision; *prendre le* ~ *de* (*inf.*) decide to (*inf.*); *prendre son* ∼ *de* resign o.s. to; *tirer* ∼ *de* turn (*s.th.*) to account; utilize; use; **partial, e,** *m*/*pl.* **-aux** [∼'sjal, ∼'sjo] biased; partial (to, *envers*); **partialité** [∼sjali'te] *f* partiality (for, to *envers*); bias.

participation [partisipa'sjɔ̃] *f* participation; ♥, *a. fig.* share (in, *à*); ♥ ∼ *majoritaire* controlling interest; **participe** *gramm.* [∼'sip] *m* participle; **participer** [∼si'pe] (1a) *v*/*i.* participate, (have a) share (in, *à*); take part (in, *à*); ∼ *de* partake of; resemble.

particulariser [partikylari'ze] (1a) *v*/*t.* particularize; specify; *se* ∼ (*par*) be distinguished (by); **particularité** [∼'te] *f* particularity; (distinctive) feature; characteristic.

particule [parti'kyl] *f* particle (*a. phys., a. gramm.*).

particulier, -ère [partiky'lje, ∼'ljɛ:r] **1.** *adj.* particular, special; unusual; private (*collection, room, etc.*); **2.** *su.* private individual; *su.*/*m* private life; *en* ∼ privately; particularly.

partie [par'ti] *f* part (*a.* ♪); *pleasure, hunt., a.* ♣♣: party; *cricket, foot., tennis:* match; ♥ line of business; ♣♣ ∼ *civile* plaintiff; ♥ ∼ *simple* (*double*) single (double) entry; *en grande* ∼ largely; *en* ∼ in part, partly; *faire* ∼ *de* be one of, belong to; **partiel, -elle** [∼'sjɛl] partial, incomplete.

partir [par'ti:r] (2b) *v*/*i.* go (away); start; leave (for, *pour*); set out; go off (*a. gun etc.*); *hunt.* rise; come off (*button etc.*); ∼ *en voyage* go on a journey; *à* ∼ *de* (starting) from.

partisan, e [parti'zã, ∼'zan] **1.** *su.* partisan, follower; supporter, advocate; *j'en suis* ∼ I am (all) for it; *su.*/*m* ✗ *soldier:* guerilla; *guerre f de* ∼*s* guerilla warfare; **2.** *adj.* party ...

partitif, -ve *gramm.* [parti'tif, ∼'ti:v] partitive (*article*). [quarter.⎰

partition [parti'sjɔ̃] *f* ♪ score; ⊘⎰

partout [par'tu] *adv.* everywhere; ∼ *où* wherever; *rien* ∼ *tennis:* love all.

partouze *sl.* [par'tu:z] *f* orgy.

paru, e [pa'ry] *p.p. of paraître.*

parure [pa'ry:r] *f* adornment; ornament; *jewels etc.:* set; ⊕ parings *pl.*

parus [pa'ry] *1st p. sg. p.s. of paraître.*

parution [pary'sjɔ̃] *f* book: publication.

parvenir [parvə'ni:r] (2h) *v*/*i.:* ∼ *à* arrive; reach; succeed in (doing s.th., *faire qch.*); **parvenu** *m,* **e** *f* [∼'ny] upstart.

parvis [par'vi] *m* △ square (*in front of church*); *bibl., a. fig.* court.

pas [pɑ] **1.** *su.*/*m* step (*a. dancing, a. of staircase*), pace, gait, walk; footprint; *door:* threshold; *geog.* pass(age); ♣, *fig.* straits *pl.*; ⊕ *screw:* thread; *fig.* move; distance (*between seats, rows, etc.*); *fig.* precedence; *fig.* difficulty, obstacle; ∼ *à* ∼ step by step; ∼ *cadencé* measured step; ✗, *sp.* ∼ *gymnastique* double; *à grands* ∼ apace, quickly; *mot. aller au* ∼ go dead slow; *à* ∼ *de loup* stealthily; *au* ∼ at a walking pace; *faux* ∼ slip (*a. fig.*); *fig.* (social) blunder; *geog. le* ∼ *de Calais* the Straits *pl.* of Dover; ∼ *de porte* key money; *ceder le* ∼ *à* give way to; *être dans un mauvais* ∼ be in a bad patch; *prendre le* ∼ *sur* take the lead from, outstrip; ✗, *sp. marquer le* ∼ mark time; **2.** *adv.* not; *ne ... pas* not; *ne ... pas de* no; *ne ... pas un* not (a single) one; *ne ... pas non plus* nor or not ... either.

pascal, e, *m*/*pl.* **-als, -aux** [pas'kal, ∼'ko] paschal; Easter (*vacation*).

pas-d'âne ♀ [pɑ'dɑ:n] *m*/*inv.* coltsfoot.

pasquinade † [paski'nad] *f* lampoon.

passable [pɑ'sabl] passable, acceptable; middling; *mention f* ∼ *examination:* pass; **passade** ⸖ [∼'sad] *f* passing fancy; F brief love affair; **passage** [∼'sa:ʒ] *m* passage (*a. in a book*); ☜, *mountains, river, etc.:* crossing; way; *mountain:* pass; △ arcade; ⚡ flow; *fig.* transition; ☜ ∼ *à niveau* level crossing, *Am.* grade crossing; *psych.* ∼ *à vide* blank; ∼ *clouté* pedestrian crossing, *Am.* crosswalk; ∼ *souterrain* subway; ∼ *supérieur* railway bridge; *de* ∼ migratory (*bird*); *fig.* passing, casual; *être de* ∼ *à* be passing through (*a town etc.*), be in (*a town etc.*) at the moment; **passager, -ère** [∼sa'ʒe, ∼'ʒɛ:r] **1.** *adj.* of passage (*bird*); passing (*a. fig.*); **2.** *su.* ♣, ✈ passenger; **passant, e** [∼'sã, ∼'sã:t] **1.** *su.* passer-by; **2.** *adj.* busy, frequented (*road*); **passavant** [∼sa'vã] *m* ♣ gangway; *admin.* permit; *customs:* transire.

passe [pɑ:s] *f* ♣, ☜, *fencing, foot:*

pass; *bonne (mauvaise)* ～ good (bad) position; *en* ～ *de (inf.)* in a fair way to *(inf.)*, on the point of *(ger.)*; *mot m de* ～ password.

passé, e [pɑ'se] **1.** *su./m* past; 🏦 record; *gramm.* past (tense); **2.** *adj.* past; over; faded *(colour)*; last *(week etc.)*; **3.** *prp.* after, beyond.

passe...: ～**-bouillon** *cuis.* [pɑsbu-'jɔ̃] *m/inv.* soup-strainer; ～**car-reau** [～ka'ro] *m* sleeve-board; ～**-debout** *hist.* [～də'bu] *m/inv.* transire; ～**-droit** [～'drwa] undeserved privilege; unfair promotion.

passéisme [pase'ism] *m* clinging to the past; **passéiste** [～'ist] *adj.* (a. *su.* person) clinging to the past.

passe...: ～**-lacet** [～la'se] *m* bodkin; ～**-lait** *cuis.* [～'lɛ] *m/inv.* milk strainer.

passement [pas'mɑ̃] *m cost.* lace; *chair etc.*: braid; **passementer** [～mɑ̃'te] (1a) *v/t.* trim with lace; braid *(furniture)*; **passementier** *m*, **-ère** *f* [～mɑ̃'tje, ～'tjɛːr] dealer in trimmings.

passe...: ～**-montagne** [pɑsmɔ̃'taɲ] *m* Balaclava helmet; ～**-partout** [～par'tu] **1.** *su./m/inv.* passkey, master key; *phot.* slip-in mount; ⊕ crosscut saw; compass-saw; **2.** *adj./inv.* all-purpose; general-purpose; *pej.* nondescript; ～**-passe** [～'pɑs] *m/inv.* legerdemain, sleight-of-hand; *tour m de* ～ conjuring trick; ～**-plats** [～'pla] *m/inv.* service-hatch; ～**poil** *cost.* [～'pwal] *m* piping, braid; ～**port** [～'pɔːr] *m admin.* passport; ⚓ sea-letter; ～**-purée** *cuis.* [～py're] *m/inv.* potato masher.

passer [pɑ'se] (1a) **1.** *v/i.* pass (a. *time*); go (to, *à*); be moved *(pupil)*; become, ✗ be promoted; fade *(colour)*, vanish; pass away, die; *fig.* wear off *(success etc.)*; go by, elapse *(time)*; be transmitted *or* handed down *(heritage, tradition)*; ✈ fly (over, *sur*); 🏦 ～ *à la douane* go through the customs; ～ *chez q.* call at s.o.'s *or* on s.o.; ～ *en proverbe* become proverbial; *mot.* ～ *en seconde* change into second gear; ～ *par* go through; *road:* go over *(a mountain)*; ～ *pour* be thought to be, be considered *(s.th.)*, seem; ～ *sur* overlook *(a fault)*; *faire* ～ pass *(s.th.)* on (to, *à*); while away *(the time)*; get rid of; *j'en passe I*

am skipping over many items; *laisser* ～ let *(s.o.)* pass; miss *(an opportunity)*; *passons!* no more about it!; *se faire* ～ *pour* pose as; **2.** *v/t.* pass; cross; go past; hand (over) (to, *à*); slip *(s.th. into a pocket)*; slip on, put on *(a garment)*; omit, leave out; overlook, excuse *(a mistake)*; spend *(time)*; sit for *(an examination)*; vent *(one's anger)* (on, *sur*); *cuis.* strain *(a liquid)*, sift *(flour)*; 🏦 place *(an order)*; *parl.* pass *(a bill)*; ～ *en fraude* smuggle in; *elle ne passera pas le jour* she will not live out the day; *se* ～ pass, go by *(time)*; happen, take place; pass away, cease; abate *(anger)*; fade *(colour)*; *se* ～ *de* do without *(s.th., qch.; ger., inf.)*.

passereau *orn.* [pas'ro] *m* sparrow.

passerelle [pas'rɛl] *f* footbridge; 🚢 gangway; catwalk; ⊕ crane: platform; ⚓ bridge; *fig.* (inter)link.

passe...: ～**-temps** [pɑs'tɑ̃] *m/inv.* pastime; hobby; ～**-thé** [～'te] *m/inv.* tea-strainer.

passeur [pɑ'sœːr] *m* ferryman; smuggler.

passible 🏦 [pɑ'sibl] liable (to, de).

passif, -ve [pɑ'sif, ～'siːv] **1.** *adj.* passive (a. *gramm.*); *fig.* blind *(obedience)*; *défense f* ～ve Civil Defence; Air Raid Precautions *pl.*; 🏦 *dettes f/pl.* ～ves liabilities; **2.** *su./m gramm.* passive (voice); 🏦 liabilities *pl.*

passion [pɑ'sjɔ̃] *f* passion (for, de) (a. 🎵, *eccl.*, a. *fig.*); **passionnant, e** [pasjɔ'nɑ̃, ～'nɑ̃ːt] thrilling; fascinating; **passionné, e** [～'ne] **1.** *adj.* passionate, impassioned (for, *pour*); enthusiastic (about, de); **2.** *su.* enthusiast, F fan; **passionnel, -elle** [～'nɛl] *adj.:* 🏦 *crime m* ～ crime due to sexual passion; **passionner** [～'ne] (1a) *v/t.* rouse, excite; *fig.* fascinate; *se* ～ become passionately fond (of, *pour*); get excited.

passivité [pasivi'te] *f* passivity.

passoire *cuis.* [pɑ'swaːr] *f* strainer.

pastel [pas'tɛl] *m* crayon; pastel drawing; *bleu m* ～ pastel blue.

pasteur [pas'tœːr] *m* shepherd; *eccl.* pastor.

pasteuriser [pastœri'ze] (1a) *v/t.* pasteurize *(milk)*.

pastiche [pas'tiʃ] *m* pastiche; parody; **pasticher** [ˌti'ʃe] (1a) *v/t.* copy the style of; parody.

pastille [pas'tiːj] *f* pastille, lozenge.

pastis [pas'tis] *m* aniseed aperitif; F muddle.

pastoral, e, *m/pl.* **-aux** [pastɔ'ral, ˌ'ro] **1.** *adj.* pastoral; episcopal (*ring*); **2.** *su./f* pastoral; **pastorat** [ˌ'ra] *m* pastorate.

pastourelle [pastu'rɛl] *f poem:* pastoral.

pat [pat] *su./m, a. adj./m* stalemate.

pataquès [pata'kɛːs] *m* faulty liaison (*in speech*).

patate [pa'tat] *f* 🌱 sweet potato; F spud (= *potato*); *sl.* idiot, fathead.

patati* [pata'ti] *int.:* et ~ et patata and so forth and so on.

patatras* [pata'tra] *int.* crash!

pataud, e [pa'to, ˌ'toːd] **1.** *su.* clumsy puppy; F lout; **2.** *adj.* clumsy, loutish.

patauger [pato'ʒe] (1l) *v/i.* flounder (*a. fig.*); paddle, wade (*in sea*); **pataugeoire** [ˌ'ʒwaːr] *f* paddling pool.

pâte [paːt] *f* paste; dough; *paper:* pulp; *fig.* stuff; *fig.* type; ~s *pl.* alimentaires Italian pastes; ~ dentifrice tooth-paste; F une bonne ~ a good sort; F une ~ molle a softy, a spineless individual; vivre comme un coq en ~ live like a fighting cock; **pâté** [pa'te] *m cuis.* pie; *liver:* paste; *fig. trees etc.:* clump, cluster; *ink:* blot; ~ de maisons block (of houses); ~ (de sable) sandcastle; **pâtée** [ˌ] *f hens:* mash; dog food; *fig.* coarse food; F hiding, threshing.

patelin F [pat'lɛ̃] *m* native village; small place.

patelinage [patli'naːʒ] *m* smooth words *pl.*, F blarney; **pateliner** F [ˌli'ne] (1a) *v/t.* cajole (*s.o.*); wheedle; *v/i.* blarney; **patelinerie** [ˌlin'ri] *f see* patelinage.

patelle [pa'tɛl] *f zo., anat., archeol.* patella; *zo.* limpet, barnacle.

patène *eccl.* [pa'tɛn] *f* paten.

patenôtre [pat'noːtr] *f* Lord's prayer; ⚒ bucket elevator; ~s *pl.* rosary *sg.*, F beads.

patent, e [pa'tɑ̃, ˌ'tɑ̃ːt] **1.** *adj.* patent; obvious; *hist.* Lettres *f/pl.* ~es Letters patent; **2.** *su./f* licence; ✝ *etc.* tax; ⚓ (*a.* ~e de santé) bill of health; **patenté, e** [ˌtɑ̃'te] **1.** *adj.* licensed; **2.** *su.* licensee.

pater *eccl.* [pa'tɛːr] *m/inv.* Lord's prayer; paternoster.

patère [ˌ] *f* hat-peg, coat-peg; curtain-hook.

paterne [pa'tɛrn] benevolent; **paternel, -elle** [patɛr'nɛl] paternal; fatherly; **paternité** [ˌni'te] *f* paternity, fatherhood.

pâteux, -euse [pa'tø, ˌ'tøːz] pasty; cloudy (*jewel*); thick (*voice etc.*); coated (*tongue*).

pathétique [pate'tik] **1.** *adj.* pathetic (*a. anat.*), moving, touching; **2.** *su./m* pathos, *the* pathetic.

pathogène 🔬 [patɔ'ʒɛn] pathogenic; **pathologie** 🔬 [ˌlɔ'ʒi] *f* pathology; **pathologique** 🔬 [ˌlɔ'ʒik] pathological.

pathos [pa'tɔs] *m* pathos; emotionalism.

patibulaire [patiby'lɛːr] gallows...; *fig.* hang-dog (*look*).

patience [pa'sjɑːs] *f* patience; forbearance; (jig-saw) puzzle; prendre ~ be patient; **patient, e** [ˌsjɑ̃, ˌ'sjɑ̃ːt] *adj., a. su.* patient; **patienter** [ˌsjɑ̃'te] (1a) *v/i.* be patient; wait patiently.

patin [pa'tɛ̃] *m* skate; *sledge:* runner; ⊕ *brake, wheel:* shoe; brake-block; ⊕ *rail:* flange; *staircase:* sleeper; ~ à roulettes roller-skate; **patinage** [ˌti'naːʒ] *m* skating; *wheel, belt:* slipping.

patine [pa'tin] *f* bronze: patina.

patiner[1] [pati'ne] (1a) *v/t.* give a patina to.

patiner[2] [pati'ne] (1a) *v/i.* skate; slip (*wheel, belt*); skid (*wheel*); *fig.* get nowhere (fast), make no progress; **patinette** [ˌ'nɛt] *f* scooter; **patineur** *m*, **-euse** *f* [ˌ'nœːr, ˌ'nøːz] skater; **patinoire** [ˌ'nwaːr] *f* skating-rink.

pâtir [pɑ'tiːr] (2a) *v/i.* suffer (from, de); vous en pâtirez you will rue it.

pâtisser [pɑti'se] (1a) *v/i.* make pastry; **pâtisserie** [ˌtis'ri] *f* pastry; pastry shop; pastry-making; cakes *pl.*; **pâtissier** *m*, **-ère** *f* [ˌti'sje, ˌ'sjeːr] pastry-cook.

patois [pa'twa] *m* dialect, patois; F jargon.

patouiller F [patu'je] (1a) *v/i.* flounder, splash (*in the mud*).

patraque F [pa'trak] **1.** *su./f* worn-out machine; *person:* old crock;

2. adj. seedy (person); worn-out (machine).

pâtre [pɑːtr] m shepherd; herdsman.

patriarcal, e, m/pl. -aux [patriar-'kal, ~'ko] patriarchal; **patriarche** [~'arʃ] m patriarch (a. eccl.).

patricien, -enne [patri'sjɛ̃, ~'sjɛn] adj., a. su. patrician.

patrie [pa'tri] f fatherland; native or mother country; fig. home.

patrimoine [patri'mwan] m patrimony, inheritance; **patrimonial, e,** m/pl. -aux [~mɔ'njal, ~'njo] patrimonial.

patriote [patri'ɔt] **1.** adj. patriotic (person); **2.** su. patriot; **patriotique** [~ɔ'tik] patriotic (sentiments, song, etc.); **patriotisme** [~ɔ'tism] m patriotism.

patron [pa'trɔ̃] m master, F boss; head (of a firm); hotel: proprietor; protector; eccl. patron (saint); cost. pattern; ⊕ template; ✝ model; **patronage** [patrɔ'naːʒ] m patronage (a. ✝); support; eccl. young people's club; **patronal, e,** m/pl. -aux [~'nal, ~'no] eccl. patronal (festival); patron (saint); ✝ employers' ...; **patronat** [~'na] m protection; ✝ coll. employers pl.; **patronne** [pa'trɔn] f mistress; protectress; eccl. patroness; **patronner** [patrɔ'ne] (1a) v/t. patronize, sponsor, support; **patronnesse** [~'nɛs] adj./f patroness.

patrouille ⚔ [pa'truːj] f patrol; **patrouiller** ⚔ [patru'je] (1a) v/i. (go on) patrol; **patrouilleur** [~'jœːr] m ⚓ patrol-boat; ⚜ scout; ⚔ member of a patrol.

patte [pat] f zo. paw (a. F = hand); orn. foot; insect: leg; ⊕ cramp, hook; ⊕ flange; clamp; ⚓ anchor: fluke; cost. strap; envelope, a. pocket: flap; F authority, power; F ~s pl. de mouche writing: scrawl; faire ~ de velours draw in its claws (cat); fig. speak s.o. fair; F tomber sous la ~ de q. fall into s.o.'s clutches; **~d'oie,** pl. **~s-d'oie** [~'dwa] f crossroads pl.; wrinkle: crow's-foot.

pâturage [pɑty'raːʒ] m grazing; pasture(-land); pasturage; **pâture** [~'tyːr] f fodder; food (a. fig.); pasture; **pâturer** [~ty're] (1a) vt/i. graze.

pâturin ♦ [pɑty'rɛ̃] m meadowgrass, Am. spear-grass.

paturon [paty'rɔ̃] m horse: pastern.

paume [poːm] f palm of hand.

paumé, e F [po'me] miserable, wretched; fig. lost, at a loss; a. su. down(-)and(-)out; derelict.

paupérisme [pope'rism] m pauperism.

paupière [po'pjɛːr] f eyelid.

paupiette cuis. [po'pjɛt] f (beef- or veal-)olive.

pause [poːz] f pause, break; foot. half time; ♪ rest; (lunch- etc.)interval; **~café** coffee break; **pauser** [po'ze] (1a) v/i. pause; ♪ dwell (on a note).

pauvre [poːvr] **1.** adj. poor; needy; scanty (vegetation); fig. slight (chance); unfortunate; **2.** su./m poor man; admin. pauper; **pauvresse** [po'vrɛs] f poor woman; admin. pauper; **pauvret** m, **-ette** f fig. [~'vrɛ, ~'vrɛt] person: poor little thing; **pauvreté** [~vrə'te] f poverty (a. fig.), destitution.

pavage [pa'vaːʒ] m paving; pavement.

pavaner [pava'ne] (1a) v/t.: se ~ strut; F show off.

pavé [pa've] m paving-stone, paving-block; pavement; highway; fig. the streets pl.; F thick (boring) book; heavy tome; **pavement** [pav'mɑ̃] m see pavage; **paver** [pa've] (1a) v/t. pave; **paveur** [~'vœːr] m paver.

pavillon [pavi'jɔ̃] m pavilion; lodge, house; ✝ bed: canopy; gramophone, loud-speaker: horn; funnel: mouth; teleph. mouthpiece; ⚓ flag, colo(u)rs pl.; ♪ trumpet: bell; anat. auricle, external ear.

pavois [pa'vwa] m hist. (body-)shield; ⚓ bulwark; coll. flags pl.; élever sur le ~ hist. raise to the throne; fig. extol; **pavoiser** [~vwa'ze] (1a) v/t. deck with flags; v/i. put out (the) flags; a. fig. wave the banners.

pavot ♦ [pa'vo] m poppy.

payable [pɛ'jabl] payable; **payant, e** [~'jɑ̃, ~'jɑ̃t] **1.** adj paying; charged for; with a charge for admission; fig. profitable; **2.** su. payer; ✝ drawee; **paye** [pɛːj] f see paie; **payement** [pɛj'mɑ̃] m see paiement; **payer** [pɛ'je] (1i) v/t. pay; pay for (an article, a. fig.); ✝ defray (expenses); settle (a debt); fig. reward (for, de); ~ cher pay dear, fig. be sorry for; ~ de retour reciprocate (an affection etc.); trop payé overpaid; trop peu payé underpaid; se ~ be paid or recompensed; se ~ de paroles be satisfied by mere words; **payeur, -euse** [~'jœːr, ~'jøːz] su. payer; su./m ⚹, ⚓ paymaster; bank: teller.

pays [pe'i] m country; land; region; home, native land; F fellow-countryman; mal m du ~ homesickness; vin m du ~ local wine; **paysage** [pei'zaːʒ] m landscape, scenery; fig. scene; **paysagiste** [~za'ʒist] m landscape painter; landscape gardener; **paysan, -anne** [~'zɑ̃, ~'zan] adj., a. su. peasant, rustic; **paysannat** [~za'na] m, **paysannerie** [~zan'ri] f peasantry; farmers pl.; **payse** F [pe'iz] f fellow-countrywoman.

péage [pe'aːʒ] m toll; tollgate; autoroute f à ~ toll motorway, Am. turnpike (road); **péagiste** [pea'ʒist] su. toll collector.

peau [po] f ⚹, anat., a. fruit, sausage, milk: skin; ✝ pelt, hide; ✝ leather; fruit: peel; faire ~ neuve change clothes; fig. turn over a new leaf; ♀-**Rouge**, pl. ♀x-**Rouges** [~'ruːʒ] m Red Indian, redskin.

peccable [pɛk'kabl] liable to sin.

peccadille [pɛka'diːj] f peccadillo.

pechblende ⚛, phys. [pɛʃ'blɛ̃ːd] f pitchblende.

pêche[1] ⚹ [pɛːʃ] f peach.

pêche[2] [~] f fishing; fishery; catch; ~ à la ligne angling; aller à la ~ go fishing.

péché [pe'ʃe] m sin; fig. indiscretion, error; ~ mignon little weakness; **pécher** [~] (1f) v/i. sin; fig. offend (against, contre); fig. err.

pêcher[1] [pɛ'ʃe] m peach-tree.

pêcher[2] [pɛ'ʃe] (1a) v/t. fish for; drag up (a corpse); fig. find, pick up; v/i.: ~ à la ligne angle; **pêcherie** [pɛʃ'ri] f fishing-ground.

pêcheur, -eresse [pe'ʃœːr, peʃ'rɛs] 1. adj. sinning; sinful; 2. su. sinner.

pêcheur, -euse [pɛ'ʃœːr, ~'ʃøːz] 1. adj. fishing; 2. su./m fisherman; su./f fisherwoman.

pectoral, e, m/pl. -aux [pɛktɔ'ral, ~'ro] pectoral; cough-(lozenge, syrup).

péculat [peky'la] m embezzlement, peculation; **péculateur** [~la'tœːr] m embezzler, peculator.

pécule [pe'kyl] m savings pl., F nest-egg; ⚹, ⚓ gratuity.

pécuniaire [peky'njɛːr] pecuniary, financial.

pédagogie [pedagɔ'ʒi] f pedagogy; **pédagogique** [~gɔ'ʒik] pedagogic; **pédagogue** [~'gɔg] su. pedagogue.

pédale [pedal] f cycle, a. ♪: pedal; ⊕ treadle; sl. queer, gay; mot. ~ d'embrayage clutch (pedal); sl. perdre les ~s get all mixed up; **pédaler** [peda'le] (1a) v/i. pedal; F cycle; **pédaleur** m, -**euse** f F [~'lœːr, ~'løːz] pedalist; cyclist; **pédalier** [~'lje] m cycle: crank gear; ♪ pedal-board; **pédalo** F [~'lo] m pedal-craft.

pédant, e [pe'dɑ̃, ~'dɑ̃ːt] 1. adj. pedantic, priggish; 2. su. pedant, prig; **pédanterie** [pedɑ̃'tri] f pedantry; priggishness; **pédantesque** [~'tɛsk] pedantic; **pédantisme** [~'tism] m see pédanterie.

pédé sl. [pe'de] m gay, queer.

pédestre [pe'dɛstr] pedestrian; **pédestrement** [~dɛstrə'mɑ̃] adv. on foot.

pédiatre ⚕ [pe'dja:tr] m p(a)ediatrist; **pédiatrie** ⚕ [~dja'tri] f p(a)ediatrics pl.

pédiculaire [pediky'lɛːr] pediculous, lousy; ✿ maladie f ~ phthiriasis; **pédicule** biol. [~'kyl] m pedicle; **pédiculé, e** [~ky'le] pediculate.

pédicure [pedi'kyːr] su. chiropodist; **pédologie** [pedɔlɔ'ʒi] f subject: child psychology.

pègre [pɛːgr] f coll. thieves pl., underworld, gangsterdom.

peignage tex. [pɛ'naːʒ] m combing, carding; **peigne** [pɛɲ] m comb (a. ⊕); shell-fish: scallop, clam; tex. wool: card; hemp: hackle; ~ de chignon back-comb; se donner un coup de ~ run a comb through one's hair; fig. passer qch. au ~ fin go through or over s.th. with a fine-tooth comb; **peigné, e** [pɛ'ɲe] 1. adj. combed; fig. affected (style); bien ~ trim; mal ~ unkempt; 2. su./m tex. worsted; su./f tex. cardful (of wool etc.); F fig. thrashing; **peigner** [~'ɲe] (1a) v/t. comb (a. tex.); tex. card (wool), hackle (hemp); polish (one's style); **peigneur, -euse** tex. [~'ɲœːr, ~'ɲøːz] su. wool-comber; su./f wool-combing machine; hackling-machine; **peignier** [~'ɲje] m comb-maker; ✝ comb-seller; **peignoir** [~'ɲwaːr] m (lady's) dressing gown; morning wrapper; ~ de bain bath-

penchant

wrap; **peignures** [ₓˈɲyːr] *f*/*pl.* combings.

peinard, e F [pɛˈnaːr, ₓˈnard] *adj.* quiet; cushy (*job etc.*); **se tenir** (*or rester*) ₓ keep quiet *or* out of trouble.

peindre [pɛ̃ːdr] (4m) *v*/*t.* paint; ₓ *au pistolet* spray (*with paint*); *fig.* ₓ *en beau* paint (*things*) in rosy colo(u)rs; F *se* ₓ make up.

peine [pɛn] *f* sorrow; trouble, difficulty; effort; punishment; pain; *à* ₓ hardly, scarcely; *à grand-*ₓ with difficulty; *en valoir la* ₓ be worth while; *être en* ₓ *de* be at a loss to; *faire de la* ₓ *à* hurt (*s.o.*); *sous* ₓ *de* under pain of; **peiner** [pɛˈne] (1a) *v*/*t.* pain, hurt, grieve; *fig.* tire; *v*/*i.* toil; labo(u)r (*a. mot. engine*).

peintre [pɛ̃ːtr] *m* painter; artist; ₓ *en bâtiments house*: painter and decorator, house-painter; *femme f* ₓ woman artist; **peinture** [pɛ̃ˈtyːr] *f* painting; paint(work); ₓ *au pistolet* spray-painting; *prenez garde à la* ₓ! wet paint!; **peinturer** [ₓtyˈre] (1a) *v*/*t.* paint; daub; **peinturlurer** F [ₓtyrlyˈre] (1a) *v*/*t.* daub (with colo[u]r); paint in all the colo(u)rs of the rainbow.

péjoratif, -ve [peʒɔraˈtif, ₓˈtiːv] pejorative; disparaging; *au sens* ₓ in a disparaging sense.

pékin [peˈkɛ̃] *m* F ✕ civilian; F ✕ *en* ₓ in civvies.

pékiné, e *tex.* [pekiˈne] candy-striped.

pelade ⚕ [pɔˈlad] *f* alopecia.

pelage, e [pɔˈlaːʒ] *m* pelt, coat, fur; **pelé, e** [pɔˈle] 1. *adj.* peeled (*fruit, tree-bark*); bald (*person*); 2. *su.* F bald-pate, bald person.

pêle-mêle [pɛlˈmɛl] 1. *adv.* higgledy-piggledy, in confusion; 2. *su.*/*m*/*inv.* disorder, jumble.

peler [pɔˈle] (1d) *vt*/*i.* peel.

pèlerin, e [pɛlˈrɛ̃, ₓˈrin] *su.* pilgrim; *su.*/*m orn.* peregrine falcon; *icht.* basking shark; *su.*/*f cost.* cape; **pèlerinage** [ₓriˈnaːʒ] *m* (place of) pilgrimage; *aller en* ₓ go on a pilgrimage.

pélican [peliˈkɑ̃] *m orn.* pelican; ⊕ *bench*: holdfast. [coat.]

pelisse [pɔˈlis] *f* pelisse, fur-lined⌋

pellagre ⚕ [pɛlˈlaːgr] *f* pellagra.

pelle [pɛl] *f* ⊕ shovel, scoop; *oar*: blade; (*child's*) spade; ₓ *à poussière* dust-pan; ⊕ ₓ *mécanique* grab;

shovel-dredger; F *fig. ramasser une* ₓ come a cropper (*off a horse, a. fig.*); have a spill (*off a cycle*); **pelletée** [ₓˈte] *f* shovelful, spadeful; **pelleter** [ₓˈte] (1c) *v*/*t.* shovel; turn with a shovel.

pelleterie [pɛlˈtri] *f* ⊕ fur-making; ✝ fur-trade; *coll.* peltry.

pelleteur *m*, **-euse** *f* [pɛlˈtœːr, ₓˈtøːz] shovel excavator.

pelletier *m*, **-ère** *f* [pɛlˈtje, ₓˈtjɛːr] furrier.

pelliculaire [pɛlliˈkyˈlɛːr] pellicular (*metal*); **pellicule** [ₓˈkyl] *f* (thin) skin; *phot.*, *a.* ice, oil: film; *scalp*: dandruff, scurf.

pelotage [pɔlɔˈtaːʒ] *m string, wool, etc.*: winding into balls; *billiards*: knocking the balls about; F petting; **pelote** [ₓˈlɔt] *f string, wool*: ball; *cotton-wool*: wad; (pin) cushion; *game*: pelota; *fig. faire sa* ₓ feather one's nest; make one's pile; **peloter** [pɔlɔˈte] (1a) *v*/*t.* ✝ wind (*s.th.*) into a ball; F handle (*s.o.*) roughly; F pet (*a girl*); F paw (*a woman*); F flatter (*s.o.*); F *se* ₓ pet, neck; **peloton** [ₓˈtɔ̃] *m string, wool*: ball; ✕ squad, platoon; *fig.* group; *sp. runners*: bunch, field, main body; ₓ *de tête sp.* leaders *pl.* (*a. fig.*), *fig.* front-runners *pl.*; ₓ *d'exécution* firing squad *or* party; **pelotonner** [ₓtɔˈne] (1a) *v*/*t.* wind (*s.th.*) into a ball; *se* ₓ curl up, roll o.s. up; huddle together.

pelouse [pɔˈluːz] *f* lawn; grass-plot; turf, *a. golf*: green.

peluche *tex.* [pɔˈlyʃ] *f* plush; *ours m en* ₓ teddy bear; **pelucher** [pɔlyˈʃe] (1a) *v*/*i.* become fluffy; shed fluff; **pelucheux, -euse** [ₓˈʃø, ₓˈʃøːz] shaggy; fluffy.

pelure [pɔˈlyːr] *f fruit*: peel; *vegetable*: paring, peeling; *cheese*: rind; F overcoat, outer garment(s *pl.*).

pénal, e [peˈnal, ₓˈno] **-aux** penal; penalty (*clause*); **pénalisation** *sp.* [penalizaˈsjɔ̃] *f* penalizing; *area*: penalty; **pénalité** *sp.*, *a.* ⚖ [ₓˈte] *f* penalty; **penalty** *foot.* [peˈnalˈti] *m* penalty (kick).

pénates [peˈnat] *m*/*pl.* penates, household gods; *fig.* home *sg.*

penaud, e [pɔˈno, ₓˈnoːd] shamefaced, abashed, crestfallen.

penchant, e [pɑ̃ˈʃɑ̃, ₓˈʃɑ̃ːt] 1. *adj.* sloping, leaning; *fig.* declining; 2. *su.*/*m* slope; (*hill*)side; *fig.* inclination, propensity (to, for *à*), tendency; *fig.* fondness (for s.o., *pour* q.); **pencher** [~'ʃe] (1a) *v/t.* tip, tilt (*s.th.*); bend (*one's head*); se ~ lean (over); bend (down); *v/i.* tilt, lean (over); be slanting; *fig.* se ~ sur study, look into; *fig.* incline, be inclined (to, vers).

pendable [pɑ̃'dabl] † meriting the gallows; *fig.* outrageous; **pendaison** [dɛ'zɔ̃] *f* *death*: hanging; **pendant, e** [~'dɑ̃, ~'dɑ̃:t] 1. *adj.* hanging; lop-(*ears*); flabby (*cheeks*); ₤₺ pending; 2. *su./m* pendant; *fig.* fellow, counterpart; 3. *pendant prp.* during; for (2 *days*, 3 *miles*); ~ que while, whilst; **pendard, e** F [~'da:r, ~'dard] *su.* gallows-bird; rogue; *su./f* hussy.

pendeloque [pɑ̃d'lɔk] *f* ear-drop; F *cloth*: shred; ~s *pl.* pendants; *chandelier*: drops; **pendentif** [pɑ̃dɑ̃'tif] *m necklace*, *a.* ⚯: pendant; △ pendentive; en ~ hanging; **penderie** [~'dri] *f* hanging-wardrobe; hanging cupboard.

pendiller [pɑ̃di'je] (1a) *v/i.* dangle.

pendre [pɑ̃:dr] (4a) *vt/i.* hang (on, from *à*); *dire pire* (*or pis*) *que* ~ *de q.* sling mud at s.o.; run s.o. down; **pendu, e** [pɑ̃'dy] 1. *p.p.* of *pendre*; 2. *adj.* hanged; hanging (on, from *à*); 3. *su.* person who has been hanged *or* who has hanged himself.

pendulaire [pɑ̃dy'lɛ:r] swinging; pendular (*motion*); **pendule** [~'dyl] *su./m phys. etc.* pendulum; *su./f* clock; **pendulette** [~dy'lɛt] *f* small clock.

pêne [pɛ:n] *m lock*: bolt; latch.

pénétrable [pene'trabl] penetrable; **pénétrant, e** [~'trɑ̃, ~'trɑ̃:t] penetrating; keen (*glance, intelligence, wind*); pervasive (*smell*); acute (*person*); **pénétration** [~tra'sjɔ̃] *f* penetration (*a. fig.*); *fig.* insight, shrewdness; **pénétrer** [~'tre] (1f) *v/t.* penetrate; *fig.* fathom (*a secret*); permeate (with, de); *v/i.* penetrate; enter; force one's way.

pénible [pe'nibl] painful; hard, laborious.

péniche ⚓ [pe'niʃ] *f* barge; lighter; ⚔ ~ *de débarquement* landing-craft.

pénicillé, e [penisil'le] penicillate; **pénicilline** ⚕ [~'lin] *f* penicillin.

péninsulaire [penɛ̃sy'lɛ:r] peninsu-

lar; **péninsule** *geog.* [~'syl] *f* peninsula.

pénis *anat.* [pe'nis] *m* penis.

pénitence [peni'tɑ̃:s] *f* penitence, repentance; *eccl.* penance; *mettre q. en* ~ *school*: make s.o. stand in the corner; **pénitencerie** *eccl.* [~tɑ̃s'ri] *f* penitentiary(ship); **pénitencier** [~tɑ̃'sje] *m eccl.*, ₤₺ penitentiary; ₤₺ reformatory; **pénitent, e** [~'tɑ̃, ~'tɑ̃:t] *adj., a. su.* penitent; **pénitentiaux** [~tɑ̃'sjo] *adj./m/pl.* penitential (*psalms*); **pénitentiel, -elle** [~tɑ̃'sjɛl] penitential, (*works*) of penance.

pennage [pɛn'na:ʒ] *m* plumage.

penne[1] ⚓ [pɛn] *f* peak.

penne[2] [pɛn] *f* quill-feather; wing-feather, tail-feather; *arrow*: feather; *tex.* warp end; **penné, e** ♀ [pe'ne] pennate, pinnate; **pennon** [~'nɔ̃] *m* pennon; *arrow*: feather.

pénombre [pe'nɔ̃:br] *f* half-light; penumbra; obscurity (*a. fig.*).

pensant, e [pɑ̃'sɑ̃, ~'sɑ̃:t] thinking; *mal* ~ heretical; *see bien-pensant*.

pensée[1] ♀ [pɑ̃'se] *f* pansy.

pensée[2] [pɑ̃'se] *f* thought; idea; *fig.* mind; intention; **penser** [~'se] (1a) *v/i.* think (of, *à*); remember; intend; *fig.* expect; *faire* ~ remind (s.o. of s.th., *q. à qch.*); *pensez à faire cela* don't forget to do this; *sans y* ~ thoughtlessly; *v/t.* think, believe; consider; think out; *elle pense venir* she means to come; *qu'en pensez-vous?* what do you think of it?; **penseur** [~'sœ:r] *m* thinker; *libre* ~ free-thinker; **pensif, -ve** [~'sif, ~'si:v] pensive, thoughtful.

pension [pɑ̃'sjɔ̃] *f* pension, allowance; boarding house; boarding school; (charge for) board and lodging; ~ *alimentaire* maintenance allowance; **pensionnaire** [pɑ̃sjɔ-'nɛ:r] *su.* boarding house, *school*: boarder; *hotel*: resident; ⚕ inmate; **pensionnat** [~'na] *m* boarding school; *school*: hostel; *coll.* boarders *pl.*; **pensionner** [~'ne] (1a) *v/t.* pension off. [tion.\
pensum [pɛ̃'sɔm] *m school*: imposi-⌡
pent(a)... [pɛt(a)] pent(a)...; five...;
pentathlon *sp.* [pɛta'tlɔ̃] *m* pentathlon.

pente [pɑ̃:t] *f* slope, incline; gradient; *river*: fall; △ *roof*: pitch; *fig.* bent, propensity.

Pentecôte [pãt'ko:t] _f_ Whitsun (-tide); Pentecost; _dimanche m de la ~_ Whit Sunday.

pénultième [penyl'tjɛm] **1.** _adj._ penultimate; **2.** _su./f gramm._ penult, last syllable but one.

pénurie [peny'ri] _f_ shortage, scarcity; _fig._ poverty, need.

pépère F [pe'pɛ:r] **1.** _su./m_ granddad; _gros ~_ big, quiet fellow; chubby child; **2.** _adj._ F quiet; cosy; cushy.

pépie [pe'pi] _f disease of birds_: pip; F _fig. avoir la ~_ have a terrible thirst.

pépiement [pepi'mã] _m_ chirp(ing), cheep(ing); **pépier** [~'pje] (1o) _v/i._ chirp, cheep.

pépin [pe'pɛ̃] _m fruit_: pip; F snag; F umbrella, F brolly; _sl. avoir un ~ pour_ be in love with, F be smitten by; **pépinière** [pepi'njɛ:r] _f ✓_ seed-bed; _✓_, _a. fig._ nursery; **pépiniériste** [~nje'rist] _m_ nurseryman.

pépite [pe'pit] _f gold_: nugget.

pepsine [pɛp'sin] _f_ pepsin.

péquin F [pe'kɛ̃] _m see_ **pékin.**

perçage [pɛr'sa:ʒ] _m_ piercing, boring; _cask_: tapping.

percale _tex._ [pɛr'kal] _f_ cambric; percale; **percaline** [~ka'lin] _f tex._ percaline; _calico; bookbinding_: cloth.

perçant, e [pɛr'sã, ~'sã:t] piercing; penetrating, keen (_cold, mind, etc._); **perce** [pɛrs] _f ⊕_ borer, drill; _♪ flute_: hole; _en ~ broached_ (_cask_); _mettre en ~_ broach; **perce-bois** _zo._ [~'bwa] _m/inv._ wood-borer; **percée** [pɛr'se] _f_ opening; _✗, a. fig._ break-through; _metall._ tap-hole; _furnace_: tapping; **percement** [~sə'mã] _m_ piercing; boring; perforation; opening; **perce-neige** ❀ [pɛrs'nɛ:ʒ] _f/inv._ snowdrop; **perce-oreille** _zo._ [pɛrsɔ'rɛ:j] _m_ earwig.

percepteur, -trice [pɛrsɛp'tœ:r, ~'tris] **1.** _adj._ perceiving; **2.** _su./m_ collector of taxes; **perceptibilité** [~tibili'te] _f_ perceptibility; _sound_: audibility; _tax_: liability to collection; **perceptible** [~'tibl] perceptible; audible (_sound_); collectable, collectible (_tax_); **perceptif, -ve** [~'tif, ~'ti:v] perceptive; **perception** [~'sjɔ̃] _f_ perception; _admin. taxes, etc._: collection; collectorship (of taxes).

percer [pɛr'se] (1k) _v/t._ pierce; _fig._ penetrate; break through; perforate; make a hole in (_a wall etc._);

broach (_a cask_); sink (_a well_); ⊕ drill, punch; _♪_ lance (_an abscess_); _v/i._ pierce; come through; **perceur, -euse** [~'sœ:r, ~'sø:z] _su._ borer; driller; puncher; _su./f_ drill (-ing-machine).

percevable [pɛrsə'vabl] perceivable; leviable (_tax_); **percevoir** [~'vwa:r] (3a) _v/t._ perceive; hear (_a sound_); collect (_taxes, fares, etc._).

perche¹ _icht._ [pɛrʃ] _f_ perch.

perche² [pɛrʃ] _f_ pole; F lanky individual; _fig. tendre la ~ à q._ give s.o. a helping hand; _sp. saut m à la ~_ pole vault; **percher** [pɛr'ʃe] (1a) _v/i. a. se ~_ perch, roost; F _fig._ live, F hang out; _v/t._ F put, stick (_somewhere_); **percheur, -euse** [~'ʃœ:r, ~'ʃø:z] perching; roosting; _oiseau m ~_ percher; **perchoir** [~'ʃwa:r] _m_ perch, roost.

perclus, e [pɛr'kly, ~'kly:z] anchylosed; stiff; lame; paralyzed (_a. fig._).

perçoir ⊕ [pɛr'swa:r] _m_ punch, drill; gimlet.

percolateur [pɛrkɔla'tœ:r] _m coffee_: percolator.

percussion [pɛrky'sjɔ̃] _f ✗_, _♪_, _a. gun_: percussion; **percutant, e** [~'tã, ~'tã:t] percussive; _fig._ that strikes home; _fig._ trenchant; **percuter** [~'te] (1a) _v/t._ strike; hit; _✗_ percuss; _v/i.: ~ contre_ crash into, hit; **percuteur** [~'tœ:r] _m_ fuse, _gun_: hammer; _fuse_: plunger.

perdable [pɛr'dabl] losable; **perdant, e** [~'dã, ~'dã:t] **1.** _adj._ losing; _billet m ~ ticket_: blank; **2.** _su._ loser; **perdition** [~di'sjɔ̃] _f eccl._ perdition; _⚓ en ~_ sinking; in distress; **perdre** [pɛrdr] (4a) _v/t._ lose; waste (_time, pains_); get rid of; be the ruin of; _~ la pratique_ get out of practice; _~ q. de vue_ lose sight of s.o.; _je m'y perds_ I can't make head or tail of it; _se ~_ be lost; disappear; lose one's way; be wasted; go bad; be wrecked; _v/i._ lose; ⊕ _etc._ leak.

perdreau [pɛr'dro] _m orn._ young partridge; _cuis._ partridge; **perdrix** _orn._ [~'dri] _f_ partridge.

perdu, e [pɛr'dy] **1.** _p.p. of_ **perdre;** **2.** _adj._ lost; waisted; _fig._ ruined; ⊕, _△_ sunk; _phys._ idle (_motion_); _✗_ stray (_bullet_); loose (_woman_); spare (_time_); out-of-the-way, god-forsaken (_place_); _à corps ~_ desperately; recklessly; *crier comme un ~* shout like a madman; *reprise f ~e* invisible darn.

père [pɛːr] *m* father (*a. fig.*); *eccl.* ♀ Father; *~s pl.* forefathers; *~ de famille* paterfamilias; *~ spirituel* father confessor; F *le ~ ... old ...; Dumas ~* Dumas Senior; *ses ~ et mère* his parents.

pérégrination [peregrina'sjɔ̃] *f* peregrination.

péremption ⚖ [perãp'sjɔ̃] *f* striking out of an action by reason of failure to comply with a time-limitation; **péremptoire** [~'twaːr] peremptory (*tone, a.* ⚖ *exception*); decisive (*argument*); ⚖ strict (*time-limit*).

perenniser [perɛni'ze] (1a) *v/t.* perpetuate; **pérennité** [~'te] *f* everlastingness.

péréquation *admin.* [perekwa'sjɔ̃] *f* equalization; standardizing; adjustment; balancing (out).

perfectibilité [pɛrfɛktibili'te] *f* perfectibility; **perfectible** [~'tibl] perfectible; **perfection** [~'sjɔ̃] *f* perfection; *à (or dans) la ~* to perfection; **perfectionnement** [~sjɔn-'mɑ̃] *m* improvement; perfecting; **perfectionner** [~sjɔ'ne] (1a) *v/t.* improve; perfect.

perfide [pɛr'fid] false; treacherous (*to, envers*); perfidious; **perfidie** [~fi'di] *f* perfidy, (act of) treachery.

perforage ⊕ [pɛrfɔ'raːʒ] *m see perforation*; **perforateur, -trice** [~ra-'tœːr, ~'tris] 1. *adj.* perforating; 2. *su./m* perforator; *su./f* ⊕ boring *or* drilling machine; card punch; **perforation** [~ra'sjɔ̃] *f* perforation (*a.* ⚕); drilling; *mot. etc.* puncture, puncturing; **perforer** [~'re] (1a) *v/t.* perforate; ⊕ drill, bore through; punch (*leather, paper*); *mot.* puncture; **perforeuse** [~'røːz] *f see perforatrice*.

performance [pɛrfɔr'mɑ̃ːs] *f* performance.

pergola [pɛrgɔ'la] *f* pergola.

péri... [peri] peri...; **~carde** *anat.* [~'kard] *m* pericardium; **~cardique** ⚕ [~kar'dik] pericardial; **~cardite** ⚕ [~kar'dit] *f* pericarditis; **~carpe** ♀ [~'karp] *m* pericarp, seed-vessel.

péricliter [perikli'te] (1a) *v/i.* be in jeopardy *or* F in a bad way.

péril [pe'ril] *m* peril, danger; risk; *au ~ de* at the risk of; **périlleux,**

-euse [~ri'jø, ~'jøːz] perilous, dangerous.

périmé, e [peri'me] out-of-date; expired (*ticket etc.*); ⚖ barred by limitation.

périmètre [peri'mɛtr] *m* ♀ perimeter; *fig.* sphere.

périnée *anat.* [peri'ne] *m* perineum.

période [pe'rjɔd] *su./f* time, a. astr., geol., gramm., ♂, a. phys. wave: period; ♪ phase; ♪ phrase; age, era, epoch; *su./m poet.* point; zenith; **périodicité** [perjɔdisi'te] *f* periodicity; **périodique** [~'dik] 1. *adj.* periodic(al); intermittent; ♂ recurrent (*fever*); 2. *su./m* periodical.

péri...: **~oste** *anat.* [pe'rjɔst] *m* periosteum; **~ostite** ⚕ [~rjɔs'tit] *f* periostitis; **~pétie** [peripe'si] *f* sudden change; **~s** *pl.* vicissitudes; **~phérie** [~fe'ri] *f* ♀ periphery, circumference; *town:* outskirts *pl.*; **~phérique** [~fe'rik] 1. *adj.* peripheral; outlying (*district etc.*); *mot. boulevard m ~* = 2. *su./m* ring road, circular route; **~phrase** *gramm.* [~'fraːz] *f* periphrasis; circumlocution; *par ~* periphrastically; **~phrastique** *gramm.* [~fras'tik] periphrastic.

périr [pe'riːr] (2a) *v/i.* perish, die; ⚓ be wrecked, be lost.

périscope [peris'kɔp] *m* periscope; **périscopique** [~kɔ'pik] periscopic.

périssable [peri'sabl] perishable; **périssoire** [~'swaːr] *f* canoe.

péri...: **~style** 🏛 [peris'til] *m* peristyle; *eccl.* cloisters *pl.*; **~toine** *anat.* [peri'twan] *m* periton(a)eum; **~tonite** ♂ [~tɔ'nit] *f* peritonitis; **~urbain, e** [~yr'bɛ̃, ~'bɛn] suburban, suburb ...

perle [pɛrl] *f* pearl (*a. typ.*); bead (*a. fig. of dew*); *fig.* maid, wife, *etc.*: jewel; F *school:* howler; **perlé, e** [pɛr'le] set with pearls; *fig.* pearly; ♪ *etc.* exquisitely executed; **perler** [~'le] (1a) *v/t.* pearl (*an article, a. barley*); set with pearls; *v/i.* execute perfectly; *v/i.* stand in beads (*sweat*); bead (*sugar*); **perlier, -ère** [~'lje, ~'ljɛːr] pearl-bearing; pearl-...

perlimpinpin [pɛrlɛ̃pɛ̃'pɛ̃] *m*: *poudre f de ~* quack powder; *fig.* magic cure-all.

permanence [pɛrma'nɑ̃ːs] *f* permanence; office *etc.* always open to the public; *en ~* permanently; **perma-**

nent, e [~'nɑ̃, ~'nɑ̃:t] **1.** *adj.* permanent; *fig.* lasting; *admin.* standing (*committee, order*); *cin.* non-stop (*performance*); **2.** *su./f* permanent wave, perm; **permanenter** [~manɑ̃'te] (1a) *v/t.* perm.

perméable [pɛrme'abl] permeable, pervious.

permettre [pɛr'mɛtr] (4v) *v/t.* permit, allow; authorize; *se* ~ *de* (*inf.*) venture to (*inf.*), take the liberty of (*ger.*); **permis, e** [~'mi, ~'mi:z] **1.** *p.p. of permettre*; **2.** *adj.* permitted, allowed; lawful; **3.** *su./m* permit; licence; *mot.* ~ *de conduire* driving licence, *Am.* driver's license; ~ *de séjour* residence permit; **permissif, -ve** [~mi'sif, ~'si:v] permissive; **permission** [~mi'sjɔ̃] *f* permission; ✕, ⚓ leave (of absence); ✕ ~ *de détente* furlough after strenuous service; **permissionnaire** [~misjɔ'nɛ:r] *m* permit holder; ✕ soldier on leave; ⚓ liberty man.

permutable [pɛrmy'tabl] interchangeable; **permutation** [~ta'sjɔ̃] *f* exchange of posts; ♙ *etc.* permutation; **permuter** [~'te] (1a) *v/t.* exchange (*posts etc.*); ♭ change over; ♙ *etc.* permute; *v/i.* exchange posts (with, *avec*).

pernicieux, -euse [pɛrni'sjø, ~'sjø:z] pernicious, injurious.

péronnelle F *pej.* [perɔ'nɛl] *f* silly goose.

péroraison [perɔrɛ'zɔ̃] *f* peroration; **pérorer** [~'re] (1a) *v/i.* hold forth; F speechify.

peroxyde ⚗ [pɛrɔk'sid] *m* peroxide.

perpendiculaire [pɛrpɑ̃diky'lɛ:r] upright; ♙ perpendicular (to, *à*) (*a.* △ *style*).

perpétration [pɛrpetra'sjɔ̃] *f* perpetration; **perpétrer** [~'tre] (1f) *v/t.* perpetrate, commit.

perpétuel, -elle [pɛrpe'tɥɛl] perpetual, everlasting; for life; **perpétuer** [~'tɥe] (1n) *v/t.* perpetuate; **perpétuité** [~tɥi'te] *f* perpetuity; *à* ~ in perpetuity; for life (⚖ *sentence*).

perplexe [pɛr'plɛks] perplexed (*person*); perplexing (*situation*); **perplexité** [~.plɛksi'te] *f* perplexity.

perquisition ⚖ [pɛrkizi'sjɔ̃] *f* search; ~ *domiciliaire* search of a house; **perquisitionner** ⚖ [~sjɔ-'ne] (1a) *v/i.* (carry out a) search.

perron ⚓ [pɛ'rɔ̃] *m* front steps *pl.*

perroquet [pɛrɔ'kɛ] *m orn.* parrot; ⚓ *sail:* topgallant; **perruche** [~'ryʃ] *f orn.* parakeet; hen-parrot; (~ *ondulée*) budgerigar; ⚓ mizzen topgallant sail.

perruque [pɛ'ryk] *f* wig; F *fig. vieille* ~ fogey; **perruquier** † [~ry-'kje] *m* wig-maker; barber.

persan, e [pɛr'sɑ̃, ~'san] **1.** *adj.* Persian; **2.** *su./m ling.* Persian; *su.* ♀ Persian; **perse** *tex.* [pɛrs] *f* chintz.

persécuter [pɛrseky'te] (1a) *v/t.* persecute; F *fig.* harass; **persécuteur, -trice** [~'tœ:r, ~'tris] **1.** *adj.* persecuting; *fig.* troublesome; **2.** *su.* persecutor; **persécution** [~'sjɔ̃] *f* persecution; *fig.* importunity.

persévérance [pɛrseve'rɑ̃:s] *f* perseverance (in *ger., à inf.*); **persévérant, e** [~'rɑ̃, ~'rɑ̃:t] persevering (in *ger., à inf.*); dogged (*work*); **persévérer** [~'re] (1f) *v/i.* persevere.

persienne [pɛr'sjɛn] *f* Venetian blind; slatted shutter.

persiflage [pɛrsi'fla:ʒ] *m* mockery; **persifler** [~'fle] (1a) *v/t.* make fun of, mock; **persifleur, -euse** [~'flœ:r, ~'flø:z] **1.** *adj.* mocking; **2.** *su.* mocker.

persil ♀ [pɛr'si] *m* parsley; **persillade** *cuis.* [~si'jad] *f* beef salad with parsley-sauce; **persillé, e** [~si'je] blue(-moulded) (*cheese*); spotted with green; marbled (*meat*).

persistance [pɛrsis'tɑ̃:s] *f* persistence (in *ger., à inf.*); ♗, *a. fig.* continuance; **persistant, e** [~'tɑ̃, ~-'tɑ̃:t] persistent (*a.* ♀ *leaves*); dogged (*effort*); *fig.* lasting; steady (*rain*); **persister** [~'te] (1a) *v/i.* persist (in s.th., *dans qch.*; in *ger., à inf.*); *la pluie persiste* it keeps on raining.

personnage [pɛrsɔ'na:ʒ] *m* personage; person of distinction; *thea. etc.* character; *pej.* individual, person; **personnaliser** [~nali'ze] (1a) *v/t.* personalize; give a personal touch to; **personnalité** [~nali'te] *f* personality; person of distinction; *fig.* ~s *pl.* personal remarks, personalities; **personne** [pɛr'sɔn] **1.** *su./f* person (*a. gramm.*); one's self; body, appearance; ⚖ *morale* corporate body, artificial person; *jeune* ~ young lady; **2.** *pron./indef./m/inv.* anybody, anyone; (*with negative*) not anyone, nobody; *qui l'a vu?* ~! who saw him? no one!; **personnel, -elle** [pɛrsɔ-'nɛl] **1.** *adj.* personal (*a.* ♗, *gramm.*); selfish, self-(*interest etc.*); not transferable (*ticket*); **2.** *su./m* staff, personnel; ⚓ complement; ✂ ~ *à terre* (*or rampant*) ground staff *or* crew; ~ *enseignant school:* staff, *univ.* academic staff, *Am.* faculty; **personnification** [~nifika'sjɔ̃] *f* personification; impersonation; **personnifier** [~ni'fje] (1o) *v/t.* personify; impersonate.

perspectif, -ve [pɛrspɛk'tif, ~'tiːv] **1.** *adj.* perspective; **2.** *su./f* perspective; *fig.* outlook; prospect; vista; *en* ~ in view.

perspicace [pɛrspi'kas] shrewd, perspicacious; **perspicacité** [~kasi'te] *f* perspicacity, shrewdness, insight.

persuader [pɛrsɥa'de] (1a) *v/t.* persuade; (*of, de;* to *inf.*, *de inf.*); convince; **persuasif, -ve** [~'zif, ~'ziːv] persuasive; **persuasion** [~'zjɔ̃] *f* persuasion; conviction.

perte [pɛrt] *f* loss, ruin; waste; leakage; ✗ ~s *pl.* casualties; ~ *sèche* dead loss; ✝ *à* ~ at a loss; *à* ~ *de vue* as far as the eye can see; F *fig.* endlessly; *en pure* ~ to no purpose; *être en* ~ *de 10 F* be 10 francs down *or* out of pocket; *être en* ~ *de vitesse* ✂ lose lift, *fig.* lose momentum.

pertinence [pɛrti'nãːs] *f* pertinence; **pertinent, e** [~'nã, ~'nãːt] pertinent, relevant; judicious.

pertuis [pɛr'tɥi] *m* sluice; *metall.* tap-hole; *geog.* channel; *river:* narrows *pl.*; *geog.* pass.

perturbateur, -trice [pɛrtyrba-'tœːr, ~'tris] **1.** *adj.* disturbing; **2.** *su.* disturber; interferer; **perturbation** [~'sjɔ̃] *f* perturbation, agitation; ~s *pl. atmosphériques radio:* atmospherics.

péruvien, -enne [pery'vjɛ̃, ~'vjɛn] *adj., a. su.* ♀ Peruvian.

pervenche ♀ [pɛr'vãːʃ] *f* periwinkle.

pervers, e [pɛr'vɛːr, ~'vɛrs] **1.** *adj.* perverse; perverted; **2.** *su.* ♂ pervert; **perversion** [~vɛr'sjɔ̃] *f* perversion; **perversité** [~vɛrsi'te] *f* perversity; **pervertir** [~vɛr'tiːr] (2a) *v/t.* corrupt; pervert.

pesage [pə'zaːʒ] *m* weighing; *turf:* weighing-in; weighing-in room; paddock; **pesamment** [~za'mã] *adv.* of *pesant 1;* **pesant, e** [~'zã,

~'zãːt] **1.** *adj.* heavy; *fig.* ponderous (*style*); *fig.* dull (*mind*); **2.** *su./m* weight; **pesanteur** [~zã'tœːr] *f* weight; *phys.* gravity; heaviness; *fig.* clumsiness; *fig.* dullness.

pèse... [pɛz] ...ometer; ...-scales *pl.*; ~-*bébé* [~be'be] *m* baby-scales *pl.*

pesée [pə'ze] *f* weighing; *faire la* ~ *de* weigh (*s.th.*); **pèse-lettre** [~'lɛtr] *m* letter scales *pl.*; **pèse-personnes** [~pɛr'sɔn] *m* (bathroom) scales *pl.*; **peser** [pə'ze] (1d) *v/t.* weigh; consider; *v/i. fig.* lie *or* weigh heavy (on *sur, à*); ~ *à q. a.* weigh s.o. down; ~ *sur a.* press hard on (*a lever*); **pesette** [~'zɛt] *f* assay scales *pl.*; **peseur** *m*, **-euse** *f* [~'zœːr, ~'zøːz] weigher; **peson** [~'zɔ̃] *m* balance.

pessimisme [pɛsi'mism] *m* pessimism; **pessimiste** [~'mist] **1.** *adj.* pessimistic; **2.** *su.* pessimist.

peste [pɛst] *f* plague (*a. fig.*), pestilence; F *fig.* pest, nuisance; F ~! confound it!; *vet.* ~ *bovine* cattle-plague; ♟ ~ *bubonique* bubonic plague, *hist.* Black Death; ~ *soit de lui* a plague on him!; **pester** [pɛs-'te] (1a) *v/i.* rave, storm (at, *contre*); **pestiféré, e** [pɛstife're] **1.** *adj.* plague-stricken; **2.** *su.* plague-stricken person; **pestilence** ♟ † [~'lãːs] *f* pestilence; **pestilentiel, -elle** [~lã'sjɛl] pestilential.

pet [pɛ] *m* ∨ fart; *cuis.* ~-*de-nonne* doughnut, fritter.

pétale ♀ [pe'tal] *m* petal.

pétarade [peta'rad] *f* fireworks: crackle; *mot.* back-fire; ✗ random firing; **pétard** [pe'taːr] *m* ✗ shot; ⚙ detonator; *firework:* cracker; F sensational news; *sl.* backside, bum; F *faire du* ~ kick up a row; **péter** [~'te] (1f) *v/i.* crack (*fire, gun*); pop (*cork*); ∨ fart; **pétillant, e** [~ti'jã, ~'jãt] sparkling; fizzy, bubbly (*liquid*); **pétiller** [~ti'je] (1a) *v/i.* crackle (*fire etc.*); sparkle (*champagne, eyes*); *fig.* scintillate (with wit, *d'esprit*).

petiot, e F [pə'tjo, ~'tjɔt] **1.** *adj.* tiny, little; **2.** *su./m* little boy; *su./f* little girl.

petit, e [pə'ti, ~'tit] **1.** *adj.* small, little; slight (*sound*); minor (*nobility, subject*); *school:* lower (*forms*); tight (*shoes*); short; young (*a. zo.*); petty, trifling; *pej.* mean; ~ *à* ~ little by little; ~*e industrie* smaller industries

pl.; ~*es gens pl.* humble people; **2.** *su.*
child, kid; *zo.* cub, young; **petit-
déjeuner** F [⸝tideʒø'ne] (1a) *v/i.*
(have) breakfast; **petite-fille,** *pl.*
petites-filles [⸝tit'fi:j] *f* grand-
daughter; **petitement** [⸝tit'mɑ̃]
poorly; pettily; meanly; **petitesse**
[⸝ti'tɛs] *f* smallness, littleness; *pej.*
meanness, pettiness; mean trick;
petit-fils, *pl.* **petits-fils** [⸝ti'fis] *m*
grandson; **petit-gris,** *pl.* **petits-
gris** [⸝ti'gri] *m zo.* miniver; † *fur:*
squirrel.
pétition [peti'sjɔ̃] *f* petition; **pétitionnaire** [⸝sjɔ'nɛ:r] *su.* petitioner;
pétitionner [⸝sjɔ'ne] (1a) *v/i.*
petition.
petit...: ~-**lait,** *pl.* ~**s-laits** [pɔti'lɛ]
m whey; ~-**maître,** *pl.* ~**s-maîtres**
[⸝'mɛ:tr] *m* fop; ~-**nègre** F [⸝'nɛ:gr]
m: parler ~ talk pidgin; ~-**neveu,**
pl. ~**s-neveux** [⸝nɔ'vø] *m* grand-
nephew; ~**s-enfants** [⸝zɑ̃'fɑ̃] *m/pl.*
grandchildren; ~-**suisse,** *pl.* ~**s-
suisses** *cuis.* [⸝'sɥis] *m* small cream
cheese.
peton F [pɔ'tɔ̃] *m* tiny foot, F tootsy.
pétrel *orn.* [pe'trɛl] *m* petrel.
pétrification [petrifika'sjɔ̃] *f* petri-
faction; **pétrifier** [⸝'fje] (1o) *v/t.*
petrify; F dumbfound; *se* ~ petrify.
pétrin [pe'trɛ̃] *m* kneading-trough; F
fig. mess; F *dans le* ~ in a mess *or* fix;
pétrir [⸝'tri:r] (2a) *v/t.* knead;
mo(u)ld (*clay, a. s.o.'s mind*); **pé-
trissage** [petri'sa:ʒ] *m* kneading;
clay, a. fig. mind: mo(u)lding; **pé-
trisseur, -euse** [⸝'sœ:r, ⸝'sø:z] *su.*
kneader; *su./f* kneading-machine.
pétrochimie [petrɔʃi'mi] *f* petro-
chemistry; **pétrochimique** [⸝'mik]
petrochemical; **pétrochimiste**
[⸝'mist] *su.* petrochemist.
pétrole [pe'trɔl] *m* petroleum; mineral oil; paraffin, *Am.* kerosene; ~
brut crude oil; *puits m de* ~ oil-well;
pétrolier, -ère [petrɔ'lje, ⸝'ljɛ:r]
1. *adj.* oil-...; **2.** *su./m* (*a. navire m*
~) tanker; **pétrolifère** [⸝li'fɛ:r]
oil-bearing; oil-(*belt, field, well*).
pétulance [pety'lɑ̃:s] *f* liveliness;
horse: friskiness; **pétulant, e** [⸝'lɑ̃,
⸝'lɑ̃:t] lively; frisky (*horse*).
peu [pø] **1.** *adv.* little; few; *before
adj.:* un-..., not very; ~ *à* ~ bit by
bit, little by little; ~ *de* little (*bread
etc.*), few (*people, things, etc.*); ~ *de
chose* nothing much; ~ *d'entre eux*

few of them; *à* ~ *près* approximately, nearly; *depuis* ~ of late;
pour ~ *que* (*sbj.*) however little (*ind.*),
if ever (*ind.*); *quelque* ~ rather,
slightly; *sous* (*or dans*) ~ before long;
tant soit ~ ever so little, a little bit;
viens un ~! come here!; **2.** *su./m*
little, bit; want, lack; *le* ~ *de* ... the
little ..., the lack of ...; *un* ~ *de*
a bit of.
peuplade [pœ'plad] *f* small tribe,
people; **peuple** [pœpl] *m* people;
nation; **peupler** [pœ'ple] (1a) *v/t.*
populate (with, *de*); stock (*with animals etc.*); *fig.* fill; *se* ~ become
populated; fill up with people; ⸝ *v/i.*
multiply, breed.
peuplier ♀ [pœpli'e] *m* poplar.
peur [pœ:r] *f* fear, dread; *avoir* ~ be
afraid (of, *de*), be scared (of, *de*); *de* ~
de (*faire*) *qch.* for fear of (doing) s.th.;
de ~ *que* ... (*ne*) (*sbj.*) for fear of (*ger.*);
faire ~ *à* frighten (*s.o.*); **peureux,
-euse** [pœ'rø, ⸝'rø:z] fearful; timid.
peut-être [pø'tɛ:tr] *adv.* perhaps,
maybe; **peuvent** [pœ:v] *3rd p. pl.
pres. of pouvoir 1*; **peux** [pø] *1st p. sg.
pres. of pouvoir 1*.
phagocyter [fagɔsi'te] (1a) *v/t. biol.*
phagocytose; *fig.* absorb.
phalange [fa'lɑ̃:ʒ] *f anat., a.* ♀
phalanx; *fig.* host.
phalène *zo.* [fa'lɛn] *f* moth.
phallocrate [falɔ'krat] *m* male
chauvinist; **phallocratie** [⸝kra'si] *f*
male chauvinism.
phare [fa:r] *m* lighthouse; ⚓,
beacon; ♣, *mot.* headlight, head-
lamp; *mot.* ~*s pl.* code dipped *or*
dimmed headlights, *Am. a.* dim-
mers; *mot. baisser les* ~*s* dim *or* dip
the headlights.
pharisaïque [fariza'ik] pharisaic(al);
pharisaïsme [⸝za'ism] *m* phari-
saism (*a. fig.*); **pharisien** [⸝'zjɛ̃] *m*
pharisee (*a. fig.*); *fig.* self-righteous
person; *fig.* hypocrite.
pharmaceutique [farmasø'tik]
1. *adj.* pharmaceutic(al); **2.** *su./f*
pharmaceutics *sg.*; **pharmacie** [⸝-
'si] *f* pharmacy; chemist's (shop),
Am. drugstore; medicine-chest;
pharmacien *m*, **-enne** *f* [⸝'sjɛ̃,
⸝'sjɛn] chemist, *Am.* druggist;
pharmacologie [⸝kɔlɔ'ʒi] *f* phar-
macology; **pharmacopée** [⸝kɔ'pe]
f pharmacopoeia.
phase [fa:z] *f* phase (*a.* ✵, ✦, *fig.*).

phénicien, -enne [feni'sjɛ̃, ~'sjɛn]
1. *adj.* Phoenician; **2.** *su./m ling.*
Phoenician; *su.* ♀ Phoenician.
phénique ⚕ [fe'nik] *adj.*: *acide m* ~
= **phénol** ⚕ [~'nɔl] *m* phenol,
carbolic acid.
phénomène [fenɔ'mɛn] *m* phenom-
enon; *fig.* wonder; freak.
philanthrope [filɑ̃'trɔp] *su.* philan-
thropist.
philatélie [filate'li] *f* stamp-collect-
ing, philately; **philatéliste** [~'list]
su. stamp-collector, philatelist.
philippique [fili'pik] *f* philippic.
Philistin [filis'tɛ̃] *m* Philistine (*a.
fig.*).
phil(o)... [fil(ɔ)] phil(o)...
philo...: ~**logie** [filɔlɔ'ʒi] *f* philology;
~**logue** [~'lɔg] *su.* philologist; ~
sophe [~'zɔf] **1.** *su.* philosopher;
2. *adj.* philosophical; ~**sophie** [~
zɔ'fi] *f* philosophy; *faire sa* ~ be in
the philosophy class (= [*approx.*]
lower 6th form); ~**sophique** [~zɔ-
'fik] philosophic(al).
philtre [filtr] *m* philtre.
phlébite ✣ [fle'bit] *f* phlebitis.
phobie *psych.* [fɔ'bi] *f* phobia.
phonétique [fɔne'tik] **1.** *adj.* phonetic; **2.** *su./f* phonetics *pl.*; **phonique**
[~'nik] phonic; sound (*signal*).
phonographe [fɔnɔ'graf] *m*, F **pho-
no** [~'no] *m* gramophone, record-
player, *Am. a.* phonograph.
phoque [fɔk] *m zo.* seal; ✝ sealskin.
phosphate ⚕, ✗ [fɔs'fat] *m* phosphate; **phosphore** ⚕ [~'fɔ:r] *m*
phosphorus; **phosphoré, e** [fɔsfɔ-
're] containing phosphorus, phos-
phorated, phosphuretted (*hydrogen*); **phosphorescence** [~rɛ'sɑ̃:s] *f*
phosphorescence; **phosphores-
cent, e** [~rɛ'sɑ̃, ~'sɑ̃:t] phosphorescent; **phosphoreux, -euse** ⚕ [~
'rø, ~'rø:z] phosphorous; **phosphorique** ⚕ [~'rik] *adj./m* phos-
phoric; **phosphorite** *min.* [~'rit] *f*
phosphorite; **phosphure** ⚕ [fɔs-
'fy:r] *m* phosphide; **phosphuré, e**
⚕ [~fy're] phosphuretted.
photo F [fɔ'to] *f* photograph, F
photo; *faire de la* ~ go in for photography.
photo... [fɔtɔ] photo...; ~**calque** ⊕
[~'kalk] *m* blue print; ~**chimie**
[~ʃi'mi] *f* photochemistry; ~**chro-
mie** [~krɔ'mi] *f* colo(u)r photography; photochromy; ~**copie** [~kɔ'pi]

f photocopy; ~**copier** [~kɔ'pje] (1o)
v/t. photocopy; ~**copieur** [~kɔ'pjœ:r]
m photocopier; ~**électrique** *phys.*
[~elɛk'trik] photoelectric; ~**gène**
phys. [~'ʒɛn] photogenic; ~**génique**
[~ʒe'nik] actinic; *cin.*, *phot.* photogenic; ~**graphe** [~'graf] *m* photographer; ~**graphie** [~gra'fi] *f* photograph, F photo; photography; ~
aérienne aerial photography; ~
graphier [~gra'fje] (1o) *v/t.* photograph, take a photo(graph) of; *se
faire* ~ have one's photo(graph)
taken; ~**graphique** [~gra'fik] photographic; *appareil m* ~ camera; ✗
reconnaissance f ~ photoreconnais-
sance; ~**gravure** [~gra'vy:r] *f* pro-
cess, *a.* *print*: photogravure; ~**lithographie** [~litɔgra'fi] *f* photolithog-
raphy; photolithograph; ~**mètre**
[~'mɛtr] *m* photometer, light meter;
~**pile** [~'pil] *f* solar battery; ~
sensible [~sɑ̃'sibl] photosensitive;
~**stoppeur** [~stɔ'pœ:r] *m* street
photographer; ~**thérapie** ✣ [~tera-
'pi] *f* phototherapy; light-cure;
~**tropisme** ♀ [~trɔ'pism] *m* photo-
tropism; ~**type** ⊕ [~'tip] *m* photo-
type; collotype; ~**typie** ⊕ [~ti'pi] *f*
process: collotype.
phrase [frɑ:z] *f* sentence; ♪ phrase;
phraséologie [frazeɔlɔ'ʒi] *f* phra-
seology; **phraséologique** [~'ʒik]
phraseological; **phraser** [frɑ'ze]
(1a) *vt/i.* phrase (*a.* ♪); **phraseur** *m*,
-**euse** *f* F [~'zœ:r, ~'zø:z] phrasemon-
ger, speechifier.
phrénologie [frenɔlɔ'ʒi] *f* phrenol-
ogy; **phrénologique** [~'ʒik] phren-
ological; **phrénologiste** [~'ʒist]
m phrenologist.
phtisie ✣ [fti'zi] *f* phthisis; consumption.
phyllo... *zo.* [filɔ] phyllo...; ~**xéra**
[~lɔkse'ra] *m* phylloxera.
physicien *m*, -**enne** *f* [fizi'sjɛ̃, ~'sjɛn]
physicist.
physico... [fiziko] physico...; physical (*chemistry*).
physio... [fizjɔ] physio...; ~**logie**
[~lɔ'ʒi] *f* physiology; ~**logique** [~
lɔ'ʒik] physiological; ~**logiste** [~lɔ-
'ʒist] *su.* physiologist; ~**nomie** [~nɔ-
'mi] *f* physiognomy; appearance;
countenance; *fig.* aspect, character.
physique [fi'zik] **1.** *adj.* physical;
bodily; **2.** *su./f* physics *sg.*; ~
nucléaire nuclear physics *sg.*; *su./m*

physique; constitution; appearance.
phyto... [fitɔ] phyto...; **phytopte**
zo. [ˌ~ˈtɔpt] m rust-mite.

piaffement [pjafˈmɑ̃] m horse: paw-
ing, piaffer; **piaffer** [pjaˈfe] (1a)
v/i. paw the ground (horse); prance
(horse); fig. ~ d'impatience fidget;
piaffeur, -euse [ˌ~ˈfœːr, ˌ~ˈføːz]
prancing, high-stepping (horse); fig.
fidgety; swaggering.

piaillard, e F [pjɑˈjaːr, ˌ~ˈjard] **1.** adj.
cheeping (bird); squalling (child);
2. su. squalling child; **piailler** [ˌ~-
ˈje] (1a) v/i. cheep (bird); squeal,
screech (child, animal); **piaillerie**
[pjɑjˈri] f birds: (continuous) cheeping; children etc.: squealing, screech-
ing; **piailleur** m, **-euse** f [pjɑˈjœːr,
ˌ~ˈjøːz] bird: cheeper; child etc.:
squealer, squaller.

pianino ♪ [pjaniˈno] m pianino; **pianiste** ♪ [ˌ~ˈnist] su. pianist; **piano**
[ˌ~ˈno] **1.** adv. ♪ piano; F fig. gently,
easy; **2.** su./m piano(forte); ~ à queue
grand piano; ~ droit upright piano;
jouer du ~ play the piano well; **pianoter** F
[ˌ~nɔˈte] (1a) v/i. ♪ tinkle (on the
piano); fig. drum one's fingers (on,
sur).

piaule sl. [pjol] f digs pl. (= lodgings); **piauler** [pjoˈle] (1a) v/i.
cheep (chicks); whine, pule (children).

pic¹ [pik] m ✗ etc. pick(axe); geog., a.
⚓ peak; cards: pique (at piquet); ~
pneumatique pneumatic drill; à ~
perpendicular(ly adv.), sheer; just at
the right moment or time.

pic² orn. [~] m woodpecker.

picaillons sl. [pikaˈjɔ̃] m/pl. dough
sg. (= money). [(novel).]

picaresque [pikaˈrɛsk] picaresque⟩

pichet [piˈʃɛ] m pitcher, jug.

pickpocket [pikpɔˈkɛt] m pickpocket.

pick-up [piˈkœp] m/inv. radio:
pickup, record-player.

picorer [pikɔˈre] (1a) vt/i. peck (at).

picoté, e [pikɔˈte] pitted (face etc.);
picotement [ˌ~ˈmɑ̃] m smarting
(sensation); prickling; **picoter** [ˌ~te]
(1a) v/t. make smart; prickle; peck
(at) (bird).

picotin [pikɔˈtɛ̃] m measure: peck.

pie¹ [pi] **1.** su./f orn. magpie; **2.** adj./
inv. piebald (horse).

pie² [~] adj./f: œuvre f ~ charitable
deed, good work.

pièce [pjɛs] f piece; bit, fragment;
cost. patch; wine: cask, barrel; tex.
roll; money: coin, piece; ⊕ machine: part; thea. play; room (in a
house);fig. mo(u)ld; ⚖ document (in
a case); ⊕, mot., etc. ~s pl. de rechange spare parts; ⊕ ~s pl. dé-
tachées attendant parts; ~ d'eau
ornamental lake; ~ de résistance
cuis. principal dish; fig. principal
feature; à la ~ in ones, separately;
5 F (la) ~ 5 F each; mettre en ~s
break or tear (s.th.) to pieces; tout
d'une ~ all of a piece.

pied [pje] m ⚕, anat., column, glass,
measure, mountain, stocking, tree,
verse, wall: foot; foothold; footing
(a. ✗); furniture: leg; ♀ stalk;
wine-glass: stem; camera etc.: stand,
rest; asparagus, lettuce, etc.: head;
hunt. track; ~ à coulisse slide ga(u)ge,
sliding cal(l)ipers pl.; ~ plat flat-
foot; à ~ on foot; walking; au ~
de la lettre literal(ly adv.); au ~ levé
off the cuff; at a moment's notice;
avoir ~ have a footing; sl. c'est le ~!
that's great!; coup m de ~ kick; en ~
full-length (portrait); F faire du ~
play footsie (with à, avec); F lever le ~
make o.s. scarce; get out; F mettre q.
à ~ dismiss or F sack s.o.; mettre sur ~
establish, set up; prendre (perdre) ~
gain a (lose one's) foothold; **~-à-
terre** [ˌ~taˈtɛːr] m/inv. temporary
lodging; town apartment; **~-bot,**
pl. **~s-bots** [ˌ~ˈbo] m club-footed
person; **~-d'alouette,** pl. **~s-
d'alouette** [ˌ~daˈlwɛt] m larkspur,
delphinium; **~de-biche,** pl. **~s-de-
biche** [ˌ~dəˈbiʃ] m bell-pull; ⊕ nail-
claw; sewing-machine: presser-foot;
⚕ molar forceps; **~-de-chèvre,** pl.
~s-de-chèvre ⊕ [ˌ~dəˈʃɛːvr] m footing; **~-de-poule** tex. [ˌ~dəˈpul] m
broken-check; **~-droit,** pl. **~s-
droits** [ˌ~ˈdrwa] △ arch, bridge: pier;
side-wall; window: jamb.

piédestal [pjedɛsˈtal] m pedestal.

pied-noir, pl. **pieds-noirs** F [pje-
ˈnwaːr] m European settler in
Algeria.

piège [pjɛːʒ] m trap (a. fig.); prendre
au ~ trap; tendre un ~ à set a trap for;
piéger [pjeˈʒe] (1g) v/t. trap (a. fig.
s.o.); booby-trap (s.th.).

pie-grièche, pl. **pies-grièches** [pi-
griˈɛʃ] f orn. shrike; F fig. woman:
shrew.

pierraille [pjɛ'rɑ:j] f rubble; road metal; **pierre** [pjɛ:r] f stone (a. ♟); ~ à briquet flint; △ ~ de taille freestone; ashlar; ~ fine semi-precious stone; ~ précieuse precious stone, gem; **pierreries** [pjɛrə'ri] f/pl. precious stones, gems, jewels; **pierrette** [ɔ'rɛt] f small stone; thea. pierrette; **pierreux, -euse** [ɔ'rø, ɔ'røːz] stony; gravelly (river-bed); gritty (pear); ♟ calculous; ♟ suffering from calculus.

pierrot [pjɛ'ro] m thea. pierrot, clown; F orn. cock-sparrow; F fellow.

piété [pje'te] f piety; devotion.

piétiner [pjeti'ne] (1a) v/t. trample (s.th.) underfoot; ✗, ⊕ tread; v/i. stamp; (a. ~ sur place) mark time.

piétisme [pje'tism] m pietism; **piétiste** [ɔ'tist] 1. su. pietist; 2. adj. pietistic.

piéton, -onne [pje'tɔ̃, ɔ'tɔn] 1. su. pedestrian; 2. adj. = **piétonnier, -ère** [ɔtɔ'nje, ɔ'njɛːr] pedestrian, for pedestrians; rue f (or aire f or zone f) piétonne (or piétonnière) pedestrian precinct.

piètre F [pjɛtr] wretched, poor (a. fig.); fig. lame (excuse).

pieu [pjø] m stake, pile, post; sl. bed; **pieuter** sl. [ɔ'te] (1a) v/rfl.: se ~ hit the sack.

pieuvre zo. [pjœːvr] f octopus, squid, devil-fish.

pieux, -euse [pjø, pjøːz] pious, devout; dutiful (child); ⚖ charitable (bequest).

pif¹ F [pif] m nose.

pif²! [ɔ] int.: ~ ~!, ~ paf! bang, bang!

pif(f)er sl. [pi'fe]: je ne peux pas le ~ I can't stand him; **pifomètre** [pifɔ'mɛːtr] m instinct, intuition; au ~ by guesswork; by chance.

pige [piːʒ] f measuring rod; journ. etc. à la ~ (paid) by the line; sl. faire la ~ à do better than, outdo.

pigeon [pi'ʒɔ̃] m orn. pigeon (a. F fig.); △ builder's plaster; ~ voyageur carrier-pigeon; **pigeonne** orn. [ɔ'ʒɔn] f hen-pigeon; **pigeonneau** [piʒɔ'no] m young pigeon; F fig. dupe; **pigeonnier** [ɔ'nje] m pigeon-house, dovecot(e).

piger sl. [pi'ʒe] (1l) vt/i. cotton on (to, à), get (it), get the message (= understand); look (at).

pigment [pig'mɑ̃] m skin etc.: pigment.

pigne ♀ [piɲ] f fir-cone, pine-cone.

pignocher F [piɲɔ'ʃe] (1a) v/i. pick (at one's food).

pignon [pi'ɲɔ̃] m △ gable; ⊕ pinion; ⊕ cogwheel; ♀ pine seed; fig. avoir ~ sur rue be well set up.

pignouf F [pi'nuf] m rotten cad; miser.

pilage [pi'laːʒ] m pounding, crushing.

pilastre △ [pi'lastr] m pilaster; newel.

pile¹ [pil] f pile, heap; △ bridge: pier; phys. (atomic, nuclear) pile; ⚡ battery; ⊕ beating-trough; sl. thrashing; ⚡ ~ sèche dry cell.

pile² [ɔ] f reverse (of a coin); ~ ou face heads pl. or tails pl.; jouer à ~ ou face toss up; F exactly, just, right; F s'arrêter ~ stop short or dead.

piler [pi'le] (1a) v/t. pound, crush, grind (almonds, pepper); F beat.

pileux, -euse zo., a. ♀ [pi'lø, ɔ'løːz] pilose, hairy.

pilier [pi'lje] m △ pillar (a. fig.), column; bridge: pier; fig. frequenter (of a place).

pillage [pi'jaːʒ] m looting, pillaging; mettre au ~ plunder; **pillard, e** [ɔ'jaːr, ɔ'jard] 1. adj. pillaging; pilfering; 2. su. looter, plunderer; **piller** [ɔ'je] (1a) v/t. pillage, loot, plunder; fig. steal from (an author); fig. ransack (a book, a work); **pilleur, -euse** [ɔ'jœːr, ɔ'jøːz] 1. adj. looting; pilfering; 2. su. looter; plunderer; ⚓ ~ d'épaves wrecker.

pilon [pi'lɔ̃] m ⊕ rammer; metall. stamper; pestle; F wooden leg; cuis. fowl: drumstick; mettre au ~ pulp (a book); **pilonner** [ɔlɔ'ne] (1a) v/t. pound; ⊕ ram; metall. stamp (ore); ✗ shell, ✈ bomb, a. fig. bombard.

pilori [pilɔ'ri] m pillory.

pilot [pi'lo] m △ pile; salt-pans: heap of salt.

pilotage [pilɔ'taːʒ] m ⚓ pilotage (a. ✈); ✈ flying; ✈ ~ sans visibilité blind flying, flying on instruments; **pilote** [ɔ'lɔt] 1. su./m ⚓, ✈, etc., a. fig. pilot; fig. leader, guide; ✈ ~ automatique automatic pilot, gyro-pilot; ~ d'essai test-pilot; 2. adj. pilot (project etc.), experimental; ♣ low-priced (drink etc.).

piloter [pilɔ'te] (1a) v/t. ⚓, ✈ pilot;

🗲 fly (a plane); fig. guide, show (round Paris, dans Paris).

pilotis [pilɔ'ti] m pile-work; piling.

pilule ⚕, a. fig. [pi'lyl] f pill.

pimbêche F [pɛ̃'bɛʃ] f stuck-up woman or girl.

piment [pi'mɑ̃] m ⚕, a. cuis. pimento, Jamaica pepper; cuis. red pepper; fig. spice; **pimenter** [ˌmɑ̃'te] (1a) v/t. cuis. season with pimento; fig. give spice to (a story).

pimpant, e [pɛ̃'pɑ̃, ˌ'pɑ̃:t] smart; fresh and trim; spruce.

pin ⚕ [pɛ̃] m pine(-tree), fir(-tree); ~ sylvestre Scotch fir; pomme f de ~ fir-cone, pine-cone.

pinacle [pi'nakl] m pinnacle; fig. height of power or fame; F porter au ~ praise (s.o.) to the skies.

pinailler sl. [pina'je] (1a) v/i. quibble.

pinard F [pi'na:r] m wine.

pinasse ⚓ [pi'nas] f pinnace.

pince [pɛ̃:s] f ⊕ pincers pl., pliers pl.; riveting, sugar, etc.: tongs pl.; ✂ clip (a. bicycle, paper, etc.); ⊕ crowbar; zo. crab, lobster: claw; sl. fig. paw, hand; cost. dart, pleat; zo. ~s pl. herbivora: incisors; ~ à épiler tweezers pl.; ~ à linge clothes peg (Am. pin); ~ à ongles nail clippers pl.

pincé, e [pɛ̃'se] 1. adj. prim, affected; stiff (voice); tight-lipped (smile); 2. su./f pinch (of salt etc.).

pinceau [pɛ̃'so] m (paint-)brush; opt. light: pencil; fig. touch.

pincement [pɛ̃s'mɑ̃] m pinch(ing); plucking; twinge; j'ai eu un ~ au cœur my heart missed a beat; **pince-monseigneur**, pl. **pinces-monseigneur** [pɛ̃smɔ̃sɛ'nœːr] m crowbar, jemmy; **pince-nez** [ˌ'ne] m/inv. pince-nez, eye-glasses pl.; **pincer** [pɛ̃'se] (1k) v/t. pinch; nip; grip; purse (one's lips); F arrest; ♪ pluck (the strings); en ~ pour have a crush on (s.o.); **pince-sans-rire** F [pɛ̃ssɑ̃'ri:r] m/inv. man of dry and sly humo(u)r; **pincettes** [pɛ̃'sɛt] f/pl. tweezers; (fire) tongs; **pinçon** [ˌ'sɔ̃] m pinch mark.

pineraie ⚕ [pin'rɛ] f, **pinède** ⚕ [pi'nɛd] f see pinière.

pingouin orn. [pɛ̃'gwɛ̃] m auk, razorbill.

pingre F [pɛ̃:gr] 1. adj. miserly, stingy, near; 2. su. skinflint; **pingrerie** F [pɛ̃grə'ri] f stinginess.

pinière ⚕ [pi'njɛ:r] f pine-wood, fir-grove.

pinson orn. [pɛ̃'sɔ̃] m finch.

pintade [pɛ̃'tad] f orn. guinea-fowl; F stuck-up woman.

pinte [pɛ̃:t] f measure: (French) pint, (approx.) English quart; **pinter** sl. [pɛ̃'te] (1a) v/i. tipple, booze; v/t. swill (beer etc.).

piochage [pjɔ'ʃa:ʒ] m swotting; **pioche** ⊕ [pjɔʃ] f pick(axe); **piocher** [pjɔ'ʃe] (1a) vt/i. dig (with a pick); F fig. grind; v/t. F fig. swot at; v/i. F fig. swot; **piocheur, -euse** [ˌʃœ:r, ˌʃø:z] su. F person: swot, Am. grind; su./m ⊕ navvy, digger; su./f ⊕ steam-digger.

piolet mount. [pjɔ'lɛ] m ice-axe.

pion [pjɔ̃] m chess: pawn; draughts: man; F school: usher, supervisor (of preparation).

pioncer sl. [pjɔ̃'se] (1k) v/i. sleep.

pionnier ⚒ [pjɔ̃'nje] m pioneer (a. fig.).

pipe [pip] f pipe (a. measure for wine); ⚡, gas, liquid: tube; **pipeau** [pi'po] m ♪ (reed-)pipe; bird-call; birds: limed-twig, snare; **pipée** [ˌ'pe] f bird-snaring (with bird-calls).

pipe-line [pajp'lajn] m oil: pipe-line.

piper [pi'pe] (1a) v/t. lure (with bird-calls); fig. † trick, dupe (s.o.); load (a dice); mark (a card).

pipette ⚗ [pi'pɛt] f pipette.

pipeur [pi'pœ:r] m bird-lurer; F sharper, cheat.

pipi ch.sp. [pi'pi] m: faire ~ wee.

piquant, e [pi'kɑ̃, ˌ'kɑ̃:t] 1. adj. pricking; stinging (nettle, a. remark); biting (remark, wind); tart (wine); pungent (smell, taste); fig. piquant (a. sauce), stimulating; cuis. hot (spice); mot m ~ witty remark, quip; 2. su./m plant: sting; porcupine: quill; sauce etc.: bite; fig. piquancy; fig. point; **pique** [pik] su./f † ✗ pike; pointed tip; pique, ill feeling; su./m cards: spade(s pl.); **piqué, e** [pi'ke] 1. adj. quilted (garment); sour (wine); ♪ staccato (note); 🗲 nose-(dive); cuis. larded (meat); F cracked, dotty; moth-eaten; 2. su./m quilting; piqué; 🗲 nose-dive, vertical dive; **pique-assiette** F [pika'sjɛt] m sponger; **pique-**

feu [pik'fø] m/inv. fire-rake, poker;
pique-nique [ˌ'nik] m picnic;
pique-notes [ˌ'nɔt] m/inv. spike-
file; **piquer** [pi'ke] (1m) vt/i.
prick; sting; v/t. nettle, wasp, fig.
remark: sting (s.o.); make (eyes,
tongue) smart; moths, worms: eat
into; tex. quilt; pink (silk); stick
(into, dans); fig. offend; arouse
(s.o.'s curiosity); cuis. lard; fig.
interlard (an account, a story);
ℱ ~ q. à qch. give an injection of
s.th. to s.o.; ℱ ~ un animal put an
animal to sleep; ~ une tête dive, take a
header; F ~ un soleil blush; se ~ get
mildewy; turn sour; fig. get offended; se ~ de pride o.s. on; have
pretensions to; v/i.: ~ des deux spur
one's horse; ~ sur head for; 🛩 etc.
dive down on.
piquet[1] [pi'kɛ] m peg, stake, post; ✗
picket; ~ de grève strike picket.
piquet[2] [ˌ] m cards: piquet; pack of
piquet cards.
piqueter [pik'te] (1c) v/t. stake out (a
camp, a. surv., a. 🔺); peg out; spot,
dot; 🛠 picket (a factory etc.).
piquette [pi'kɛt] f second wine; poor
wine; **piqueur, -euse** [ˌ'kœːr,
ˌ'køːz] su. stitcher, sewer; su./m hunt.
whip(per-in); groom; outrider; ⚒
hewer; 🚂 plate-layer; **piqûre**
[ˌ'kyːr] f sting, prick; (flea-)bite; ℱ
injection; puncture; spot; books,
leather, etc.: stitching, sewing.
pirate [pi'rat] m pirate; ~ de l'air
highjacker; **pirater** [pi'ra'te] (1a)
v/i. practise piracy; pirate; **piraterie** [ˌ'tri] f piracy (a. fig.); ~ aérienne
highjacking.
pire [piːr] worse; au ~ if the worst
comes to the worst; le ~ (the) worst.
piriforme [piri'fɔrm] pear-shaped.
pirogue [pi'rɔg] f (dug-out) canoe.
pirouette [pi'rwɛt] f toy: whirligig;
horsemanship, a. dancing: pirouette;
pirouetter [ˌrwɛ'te] (1a) v/i. pirouette; twirl.
pis[1] zo. [pi] m udder.
pis[2] [pi] adv. worse; le ~ (the) worst;
~-aller [piza'le] m/inv. stopgap, last
resource.
piscicole [pisi'kɔl] piscicultural;
pisciculteur [ˌkyl'tœːr] m pisci-
culturist; **pisciculture** [ˌkyl'tyːr] f
pisciculture, fish-breeding; **pisci-
forme** [ˌ'fɔrm] pisciform, fish-
shaped.

piscine [pi'sin] f swimming-pool;
public baths pl.; † fish-pond.
piscivore [pisi'vɔːr] piscivorous.
pisé 🔺 [pi'ze] m puddled clay.
pissat [pi'sa] m (animal) urine; **pis-
senlit** ⚘ [ˌsɑ̃'li] m dandelion; F fig.
manger les ~s par la racine be pushing
up the daisies (= be dead); **pisser** ∨
[ˌ'se] (1a) v/i. piss, pee; **pissoir** ∨
[ˌ'swaːr] m urinal; **pissotière** ∨
[ˌsɔ'tjɛːr] f urinal.
pistache ⚘ [pis'taʃ] f pistachio-nut;
pistachier ⚘ [ˌta'ʃje] m pistachio
tree.
piste [pist] f track; race-track; race-
course; circus: ring; hunt., a. fig.
trail, scent; clue, lead; 🛩 tarmac; 🛩
~ d'atterrissage landing-strip; 🛩
d'envol runway; cin. ~ sonore sound-
track; **pister** [pis'te] v/t. hunt. track;
tail (s.o.).
pistil ⚘ [pis'til] m pistil.
pistolet [pistɔ'le] m pistol; gun; a. ~
pulvérisateur spray gun.
piston [pis'tɔ̃] m ⊕ piston; ♪ valve; ♪
cornet; fig. influence, F pull; ⊕
course f du ~ piston-stroke; **piston-
ner** F [ˌtɔ'ne] (1a) v/t. pull strings for
(s.o.).
pitance [pi'tɑ̃ːs] f (allowance of)
food; **piteux, -euse** [ˌ'tø, ˌ'tøːz]
piteous, sorry, woeful.
pithécanthrope [pitekɑ̃'trɔp] ~m
pithecanthrope, ape-man.
pitié [pi'tje] f pity (on, de).
piton [pi'tɔ̃] m ⊕ eye-bolt, ring-
bolt; F large nose; geog. peak; mount.
piton, peg; ~ à vis screweye.
pitoyable [pitwa'jabl] pitiful; pitia-
ble; poor.
pitre [pitr] m clown (a. pej. fig.);
pitrerie [pitrə'ri] f buffoonery.
pittoresque [pitɔ'rɛsk] 1. adj. picturesque; graphic (description, style);
2. su./m picturesqueness; vividness.
pivert orn. [pi'vɛːr] m green woodpecker.
pivoine ⚘ [pi'vwan] f peony.
pivot [pi'vo] m ⊕ pivot (a. ✗ sl.),
pin, axis; lever: fulcrum; fig. central figure etc.; ⚘ tap-root; F ~s pl.
legs; **pivoter** [ˌvɔ'te] (1a) v/i.
pivot; turn, swivel; ✗ wheel; ⚘
form tap-roots; F faire ~ drill, put
(s.o.) through it.
placage [pla'kaːʒ] m ⊕ veneer(ing);
metal: plating; ♪ patchwork; **placard** [ˌ'kaːr] m cupboard; 🔺 door:

panel; poster, bill; *typ. proof*: galley; **placarder** [ˌkar'de] (1a) *v/t.* post (*a bill*); stick (*a poster*) on a wall.

place [plas] *f* place, position; space, room; seat (*a. 🚢, thea., etc.*); square; (*taxi-*)stand; job, employment; rank; ✕ ~ *d'armes* parade-ground; ✕ ~ *forte* fortified town; fortress; *à la* ~ *de* instead of; *à votre* ~ if I were you; † *faire la* ~ canvass for orders; *par* ~*s* here and there; *sur* ~ on the spot; **place-ment** [plas'mɑ̃] *m* placing; † sale, disposal; † *money*: investing, investment.

placer [pla'se] (1k) *v/t.* place; put; find employment for; † sell, dispose of; † invest (*money*); seat (*s.o.*); show (*s.o.*) to a seat; F *il n'a pu* ~ *un mot* he couldn't get a word in; *se* ~ find a job; sell (*article*).

placet 🛐🛐 [pla'sɛ] *m* claim; petition.

placeur, -euse [pla'sœːr, ~'søːz] *su.* manager of an employment agency; steward (*at meetings*); † placer, seller; *su./f thea.* usherette, attendant.

placide [pla'sid] placid, calm; **placidité** [ˌsidi'te] *f* calmness, serenity, placidity.

placier *m*, **-ère** *f* [pla'sje, ~'sjɛːr] † agent, canvasser; *admin.* clerk in charge of letting market pitches.

plafond [pla'fɔ̃] 1. *su./m* ceiling (*a. fig., a. 🛫*); *mot.* maximum speed; ✕ roof; ⚓ *hold*: floor; ⊕ *canal*: bottom; 2. *adj.* maximum, ceiling; **plafonner** [ˌfɔ'ne] (1a) *v/t.* 🛦 ceil; *v/i.* reach a maximum; *mot.* reach one's top speed; 🛫 fly at the ceiling; † reach the ceiling (*of, à*) (*prices*); **plafonnier** [ˌfɔ'nje] *m* ceiling-light; *mot.* roof-light.

plage [plaːʒ] *f* beach, shore; seaside resort; surface; place; area, zone; period (*of time*); section, portion; range; ~ *arrière* ⚓ quarter-deck; *mot.* back shelf.

plagiaire [pla'ʒjɛːr] *m* plagiarist (*from, de*); **plagiat** [ˌ'ʒja] *m* plagiarism, plagiary; **plagier** [ˌ'ʒje] (1o) *v/t.* plagiarize, F crib from.

plaid [plɛd] *m tex., cost.* plaid; travelling-rug.

plaider [plɛ'de] (1a) *v/i.* plead; litigate, go to court; *v/t.* plead; **plaideur** *m*, **-euse** *f* 🛐🛐 [ˌ'dœːr, ~'døːz]

litigious person; **plaidoirie** 🛐🛐 [ˌdwa'ri] *f* counsel's speech; **plaidoyer** [ˌdwa'je] *m* 🛐🛐 defence speech; *fig.* plea, argument (*for, en faveur de*).

plaie [plɛ] *f* wound; sore (*a. fig.*); scourge; *bibl., fig.* plague.

plaignant, e 🛐🛐 [plɛ'ɲɑ̃, ~'ɲɑ̃ːt] *adj., a. su.* plaintiff; complainant.

plain, plaine [plɛ̃, plɛn] *adj.*: *de* ~-*pied* on a level (*with, avec*), on the same floor; *fig.* straight; ~-**chant**, *pl.* ~**s-chants** ♪ [plɛ̃'ʃɑ̃] *m* plainsong.

plaindre [plɛ̃ːdr] (4m) *v/t.* pity, be sorry for; † grudge; *se* ~ complain;] **plaine** [plɛn] *f* plain. [grumble.│

plainte [plɛ̃ːt] *f* complaint (*a.* 🛐🛐); reproach; lamentation; **plaintif, -ve** [plɛ̃'tif, ~'tiːv] plaintive; querulous (*person, voice*).

plaire [plɛːr] (4z) *v/i.*: ~ *à* please; *à Dieu ne plaise* God forbid (*that, que*); *v/impers.*: *cela lui plaît* he likes that; *plaît-il?* I beg your pardon?; *qu'il vous plaise ou non* if you like it or not; *s'il vous plaît, s'il te plaît* please; *v/t.*: *se* ~ delight (*in, à*); enjoy o.s.; be happy; please one another.

plaisamment [plɛza'mɑ̃] *adv. of plaisant 1*; **plaisance** [ˌ'zɑ̃ːs] *f*: *de* ~ pleasure-(*boat, ground*); country (*seat*), in the country (*house*); **plaisant, e** [ˌ'zɑ̃, ~'zɑ̃ːt] 1. *adj.* pleasant; amusing; † ridiculous; 2. *su./m the* amusing part (*of s.th.*); *mauvais* ~ practical joker; **plaisanter** [plɛzɑ̃'te] (1a) *v/i.* joke; *pour* ~ for fun, for a joke; *v/t.* chaff (*s.o.*); **plaisanterie** [ˌ'tri] *f* joke; *mauvaise* ~ silly joke; *par* ~ for fun; **plaisantin** [ˌ'tɛ̃] *m* joker.

plaisir [plɛ'ziːr] *m* pleasure (*a. fig.*); delight; amusement; favo(u)r; *à* ~ at will; without cause; *avec* ~ willingly; *de* ~ pleasure-...; *faire* ~ *à* please; *les* ~*s pl. de la table* the pleasures of the palate; *menus* ~*s pl.* little luxuries; *par* ~ for pleasure.

plaisons [plɛ'zɔ̃] *1st p. pl. pres. of plaire*; **plaît** [plɛ] *3rd p. sg. pres. of plaire*.

plan, plane [plɑ̃, plan] 1. *adj.* plane (*a.* 🛦), level, flat; 2. *su./m* 🛦, 🛦, 🛫, ✒, *opt.* plane; ⊕ *plane*: sole; ✕ *fire*: line; 🛫 *wing*; *fig.* level, sphere; plan; rank, importance; 🛦 *etc., fig.* plan; draft, drawing; *cin. gros* ~ close-up; F *laisser q. en* ~ leave s.o. in the lurch; *premier* ~ *thea.* down-stage; *paint.* foreground; *fig.* first importance; *second* ~ *paint.* middle ground; *fig.* background, *fig.* second rank.

planche [plã:ʃ] *f* board; plank; (*book-*)shelf; ⊕ plate, block; ✔ *(flower- etc.)*bed; *thea.* ~*s pl.* boards, stage *sg.*; ⚓ ~ *de débarquement* gang-plank; *faire la* ~ *swimming:* float (on one's back); ⚓, ✝ *jours m/pl. de* ~*s* lay days; **planchéier** [plãʃeˈje] (1a) *v/t.* board (over); floor (*a room*); **plancher** [ˌ'ʃe] 1. *su./m* (*boarded*) floor; ⚓ planking; ✂, *mot.* floor-board; F ~ *des vaches* terra firma; F *débarrasser le* ~ clear out (= *go away*); F *mot. mettre le pied au* ~ step on it; 2. *adj.* bottom, minimum (*price etc.*); **planchette** [ˌ'ʃɛt] *f* small board *or* plank.

plan-concave *opt.* [plãkõˈka:v] planoconcave; **plan-convexe** *opt.* [ˌ'vɛks] planoconvex.

plane ⊕ [plan] *f* drawing-knife; turning-chisel.

plané, e ✈ [plaˈne] gliding; *vol m* ~ glide, volplane; *birds:* soaring.

planer[1] [plaˈne] (1a) *v/t.* ⊕ make even; plane (*wood*).

planer[2] [ˌ] (1a) *v/i.* ✈ glide; soar (*bird*); hover (*bird, mist, a. fig.*).

planétaire [planeˈtɛ:r] 1. *adj.* planetary; 2. *su./m* planetarium; **planète** *astr.* [ˌ'nɛt] *f* planet.

planeur [plaˈnœ:r] *m* ✈ glider; ⊕ *metals:* planisher; **planeuse** ⊕ [ˌ'nø:z] *f* planing-machine; planishing-machine.

planification *pol.* [planifikaˈsjõ] *f* planning; **planifier** [ˌ'fje] (1a) *v/t.* plan; *économie f planifiée* planned economy.

planimétrie ⚗ [planimeˈtri] *f* planimetry; **planimétrique** [ˌ'trik] planimetric(al).

planning [plaˈniŋ] *m* planning (*a. pol.*); ~ *familial* family planning.

planque *sl.* [plãk] *f* hideaway; cushy job; **planquer** *sl.* [plãˈke] (1m) *v/t.* hide; *se* ~ take cover; hide; lie flat.

plant ✔ [plã] *m* sapling; slip; (*nursery*) plantation; **plantage** ✔ [plãˈta:ʒ] *m* planting; plantation.

plantain ♀ [plãˈtɛ̃] *m* plantain.

plantation [plãtaˈsjõ] *f* planting; plantation; *fig.* setting up, erection; **plante** [plã:t] *f* ♀ plant; *anat. foot:*

sole; ~ *d'appartement* indoor plant; ~ *marine* seaweed; *jardin m des* ~*s* botanical gardens *pl.*, F zoo; **planter** [plãˈte] (1a) *v/t.* plant; fix, set up; F *fig.* ~ *là* run out on (*s.o.*); jilt (*s.o.*); chuck (up); *se* ~ take (up) a stand; **planteur** [ˌ'tœ:r] *m* planter; **planteuse** [ˌ'tø:z] *f* planting-machine.

plantigrade *zo.* [plãtiˈgrad] *adj., a. su./m* plantigrade.

plantoir ✔ [plãˈtwa:r] *m* dibble.

planton ⚔ [plãˈtõ] *m* orderly.

plantule ♀ [plãˈtyl] *f* plantlet, plantling.

plantureux, -euse [plãtyˈrø, ˌ'rø:z] plentiful, copious; fertile, rich (*country*); *fig.* buxom (*woman*).

plaque [plak] *f* sheet; *metal, a. phot.:* plate; *marble:* slab; *engine, a.* ⚙: bed-plate; (*ornamental*) plaque; badge; ~ *commémorative* (votive) tablet; *mot.* ~ *de police*, ~ *minéralogique* number plate; ~ *de porte* (*rue*) name plate (street plate); ~ *d'identité* identification plate, ⚔ identity disc; ~ *tournante* 🚂 turntable; *fig.* centre; **plaqué** ⊕ [plaˈke] *m* plated metal; electroplate; veneered wood; **plaquer** [ˌ'ke] (1m) *v/t.* ⊕ plate (*metal*); ⊕ veneer (*wood*); ✔ lay down (*turf*); *foot.* tackle; ♪ strike (*a chord*); F run out on (*s.o.*); jilt (*s.o.*); chuck (up); **plaquette** [ˌ'kɛt] *f* *metal, wood:* small plate; *stone, marble:* thin slab; brochure; **plaqueur** [ˌ'kœ:r] *m* ⊕ *metal:* plater; *wood:* veneerer; *foot.* tackler.

plastic ⚗ [plasˈtik] *m* explosive gelatine; **plasticité** [ˌtisiˈte] *f* plasticity; **plastique** [ˌ'tik] 1. *adj.* plastic; 2. *su./f* plastic art; *fig.* figure; *su./m* ⊕ plastic goods *pl.*

plastron [plasˈtrõ] *m* ⚔ breast-plate; ⊕ drill-plate; fencing-jacket; *fig.* butt; *cost.* woman's modesty-front; *cost.* man's shirt-front; **plastronner** [ˌtrɔˈne] (1a) *v/i.* F strut, put on side.

plat, plate [pla, plat] 1. *adj.* flat (*a. fig.*); level; smooth (*sea*); straight (*hair*); low-heeled (*shoes*); empty (*purse*); plain (*water*); *fig.* dull; *fig.* poor, paltry; *calme m* ~ dead calm; 2. *su./m* flat part (*of s.th.*); oar; tongue: blade; *book:* board; *cuis.* dish; *cuis.* course; *à* ~ flat; F *fig.* washed out, all in; F *mettre les pieds dans le* ~ put

one's foot in it; *tomber à ~* fall flat on
one's face, *thea.* fall flat *(play)*.

platane ♀ [pla'tan] *m* plane-tree;
faux ~ sycamore, great maple.

plateau [pla'to] *m* tray; platform;
thea. stage; *geog.* plateau; *balance*:
scale; ⊕ (bed-)plate; ⊕ table.

plate-bande, *pl.* **plates-bandes**
[plat'bã:d] *f* ✗ flower-bed; (grass)
border; △ plat band; F *plates-
bandes pl.* preserves, private ground
sg.

platée [pla'te] *f* △ concrete: foundation; F dishful.

plate-forme, *pl.* **plates-formes**
[plat'fɔrm] *f bus, a. fig.*: platform;
⚙ *engine*: foot-plate.

platine [pla'tin] *su./f lock, watch*:
plate; *typewriter, printing press*:
platen; *record player*: turntable;
deck; *su./m* ⚛ *min.* platinum; **pla-
tiné, e** [~ti'ne] platinized; *une blonde
~e* a platinum blonde.

platitude [plati'tyd] *f* platitude,
commonplace remark; *fig.* servility;
style: flatness.

plâtrage [pla'tra:ʒ] *m* ⊕ plastering;
△ plaster-work; F rubbish; **plâ-
tras** [~'tra] *m* debris (of building
materials); **plâtre** [pla:tr] *m* plaster; plaster cast; plaster-work;
battre comme ~ beat *(s.o.)* to a jelly;
💊 *mettre en ~* (put into) plaster;
plâtrer [pla'tre] (1a) *v/t.* plaster;
fig. patch up; 💊 (put into) plaster;
plâtreux, -euse [~'trø, ~'trø:z]
plastery; chalky *(soil, water)*; gypse-
ous; **plâtrier** [~tri'e] *m* plasterer;
calciner of gypsum; **plâtrière** [~tri-
'ɛ:r] *f* gypsum-quarry, gypsum-
kiln; chalk-pit.

plausible [plo'zibl] plausible; specious.

plèbe [plɛb] *f the* plebs; *the* common people *pl.*; **plébéien, -enne**
[plebe'jɛ̃, ~'jɛn] *adj., a. su.* plebeian;
plébiscite [plebi'sit] *m* plebiscite;
plébisciter [~si'te] (1a) *v/t.* vote for
by plebiscite; vote for *or* elect *or*
approve (of) by an overwhelming
majority; F measure *(s.o.'s)* popularity.

plein, pleine [plɛ̃, plɛn] **1.** *adj.* full
(of, *de*); filled (with, *de*); high *(sea,
tide)*; open *(country, street)*; big
with young *(animal)*; solid *(brick,
wood, tyre, wire)*; *~ emploi see
plein-emploi*; *fig. pleine saison the*

height of the season; *de son ~ gré*
of one's own free will; *en ~ air* in the
open; *en ~ jour* in broad daylight;
fig. publicly, openly; ⚓ *en pleine
mer* on the open sea; *en pleine rue* in
the open street; openly; **2.** *su./m*
full part; *building*: solid part; ✗
etc. bull's-eye; fill(ing); *battre son ~*
be at the full *(tide)*; *fig.* be in full
swing *(party, season, etc.)*; *mot.
faire le ~* fill up with petrol *or Am.*
gas, fill up the tank; **plein-emploi**
[plɛnã'plwa] *m* full employment;
plein-temps [plɛ̃'tã] **1.** *adj./inv.*
full-time; **2.** *m/inv.* full-time job.

plénier, -ère [ple'nje, ~'njɛ:r] complete, absolute; ⚛ *eccl.* plenary;
plénipotentiaire [plenipotã'sjɛ:r]
adj., a. su./m plenipotentiary; **plénitude** [~'tyd] *f* fullness; com-
pleteness.

plénum, plenum [ple'nɔm] *m*
plenum.

pléonasme [pleo'nasm] *m* pleonasm.

pléthore [ple'tɔ:r] *f* ⚕, *a. fig.*
plethora; *fig.* (super)abundance;
pléthorique [~to'rik] ⚕ plethoric,
full-blooded; *fig.* (super)abundant.

pleur [plœ:r] *f* tear; **pleurard, e**
[plœ'ra:r, ~'rard] **1.** *adj.* whimpering; whining *(voice)*; tearful; **2.** *su.*
whiner; F cry-baby; **pleure-mi-
sère** [plœrmi'zɛ:r] *su./inv.* person
who is always pleading poverty;
pleurer [plœ're] (1a) *v/t.* weep for,
mourn for; *v/i.* weep; cry (for,
de; over, *sur*) *(a. fig.)*; water, run
(eyes); ⊕ *etc.* drip; ⚡ bleed.

pleurésie ⚕ [plœre'zi] *f* pleurisy.

pleureur, -euse [plœ'rœ:r, ~'rø:z]
1. *adj.* tearful, lachrymose; weeping
(person, rock, ♀ willow); **2.** *su.*
weeper; whimperer; *su./f* hired
mourner; **pleurnicher** F [plœrni-
'ʃe] (1a) *v/i.* whimper, whine, snivel;
pleurnicherie [~niʃ'ri] *f* whining;
pleurnicheur, -euse [~ni'ʃœ:r,
~'ʃø:z] **1.** *adj.* whining, whimpering,
peevish; **2.** *su.* whiner, whimperer;
F cry-baby.

pleut [plø] *3rd p. sg. pres. of pleuvoir.*

pleutre [plø:tr] *m* cad; coward.

pleuvoir [plø'vwa:r] (3g) *v/impers.*
rain; *il pleut à verse* it is pouring (with
rain), it is raining hard; *v/i. fig.* pour
in; **pleuvra** [~'vra] *3rd p. sg. fut. of
pleuvoir.*

plèvre *anat.* [plɛ:vr] *f* pleura.

plexus *anat.* [plɛkˈsys] *m*: ~ solaire solar plexus.

pli [pli] *m* fold, pleat; wrinkle; (*a. faux* ~) crease; ✝ cover, envelope; *bridge, whist*: trick; *arm, leg*: bend; *fig.* habit; *ground*: undulation; ~*s pl.* non repassés unpressed pleats; *faire des ~s* crease (up); *faire des ~s à* pleat (*s.th.*); F *cela ne fait pas un ~* that's for sure; *fig.* prendre un ~ acquire a habit; ✝ *sous ce* ~ enclosed, herewith; ✝ *sous* ~ *séparé* under separate cover; **pliable** [~ˈabl] foldable, folding; pliable, flexible (*a. fig.*); **pliant, e** [~ˈɑ̃, ~ˈɑ̃:t] **1.** *adj.* pliant, flexible; folding; *fig.* docile; *mot. capote f* ~*e* collapsible hood; **2.** *su./m* folding-stool, camp-stool.

plie *icht.* [pli] *f* plaice.

plier [pliˈe] (1a) *v/t.* fold (up); bend; bow (*one's head*); *se* ~ *à* submit to; *fig.* give o.s. up to; *v/i.* bend; yield (*a.* ⚔); **plieur, -euse** [~ˈœ:r, ~ˈø:z] *su.* folder; *su./f* folding-machine.

plinthe △ *etc.* [plɛ̃:t] *f* plinth.

plioir [pliˈwa:r] *m* bookbinding: folder; paper-knife; *fishing-line*: winder.

plisser [pliˈse] (1a) *v/t.* pleat; crumple; crease; corrugate (*metal, paper*); pucker up (*one's face etc.*); *v/i.* crease, pucker; hang in or have folds; **plissure** [~ˈsy:r] *f* pleating; pleats *pl.*

pliure [pliˈy:r] *f* fold; bend; *bookbinding*: folding.

plomb [plɔ̃] *m* lead; △ lead sink; ⚡ fuse; ✝ lead seal; ⚓ plummet; *hunt. etc.* shot; *typ.* metal, type; *fig.* weight; *à* ~ vertically; upright; straight down; *mine f de* ~ black-lead, graphite; *sommeil m de* ~ heavy sleep; *tomber à* ~ fall plumb *or* vertically; **plombage** [plɔ̃ˈba:ʒ] *m* leading, plumbing; ✝ sealing; *teeth*: stopping, filling; **plomba-gine** [~baˈʒin] *f* graphite, plum-bago; **plombé, e** [~ˈbe] leaded (*a. cane*); leaden (*sky*); livid (*complex-ion*); **plomber** [~ˈbe] (1a) *v/t.* cover *or* weight with lead; glaze (*pottery*); stop, fill (*a tooth*); △ plumb; ✝ seal; *fig.* give a livid hue to; **plomberie** [~ˈbri] *f* plumb-ing; lead industry; lead-works *usu. sg.*; plumber's (shop); **plombier** [~ˈbje] *m* lead-worker; plumber;

plombifère [~biˈfɛ:r] lead-bearing; lead (*glaze*).

plongeant, e [plɔ̃ˈʒɑ̃, ~ˈʒɑ̃:t] plung-ing; from above (*view*); **plongée** [~ˈʒe] *f* plunge, dive; diving; slope; *ground*: dip; ~ *sous-marine* (skin) diving; **plongeoir** [~ˈʒwa:r] *m* diving-board; **plongeon** [~ˈʒɔ̃] *m* dive; *orn.* diver; *faire le* ~ dive; *fig.* make up one's mind, F take the plunge; **plonger** [~ˈʒe] (1l) *vt/i.* plunge; *v/t.* dip (into, *dans*); *se* ~ immerse o.s.; *fig.* être plongé dans be absorbed in; *v/i.* dive; ⚓ submerge (*submarine*); dip (*ground, a.* ⚔ *seam*); ⚓ ~ *du nez* pitch; **plongeur, -euse** [~ˈʒœ:r, ~ˈʒø:z] **1.** *adj.* diving; **2.** *su. person*: diver; dish-washer, washer-up (*in a restaurant*); *su./m orn.* diver; ⊕ plunger.

plot ⚡ [plo] *m* stud, terminal; plug.

plouc, plouk, plouque F *pej.* [pluk] **1.** *su./m* rustic, country bumpkin; provinciality, provincialism; **2.** *adj./inv.* rustic, provincial.

ploutocratie [plutɔkraˈsi] *f* plutoc-racy.

ployable [plwaˈjabl] pliable; **ployer** [~ˈje] † (1h) *vt/i.* bend; *v/i.* give way.

plu¹ [ply] *p.p. of* plaire.

plu² [~] *p.p. of* pleuvoir.

pluie [plɥi] *f* rain (*a. fig.*); *fig.* shower; ~(*s pl.*) acide(s) acid rain; *craint la* ~! keep dry!; F *fig.* faire la ~ *et le beau temps* rule the roost.

plumage [plyˈma:ʒ] *m* plumage; **plumard** *sl.* [~ˈma:r] *m* bed; **plu-me** [plym] *f* feather; pen; pen-nib; *homme m de* ~ man of letters; **plu-meau** [plyˈmo] *m* feather duster; **plumée** [~ˈme] *f poultry*: plucking; **plumer** [~ˈme] (1a) *v/t.* pluck (*poultry*); F fleece (*s.o.*); **plumet** [~ˈme] *m* ⚔ *helmet*: plume; **plumier** [~ˈmje] *m* pen(cil) box; pen tray; **plumitif** *pej.* [~miˈtif] *m* penpush-er; scribbler.

plupart [plyˈpa:r] *f*: *la* ~ most, the majority, the greater part; *la* ~ *des gens, la* ~ *du monde* most people; *la* ~ *du temps* most of the time; generally; *pour la* ~ mostly.

pluralité [plyraliˈte] *f* plurality; *votes*: majority.

pluri... [plyri] pluri..., multi...

pluriel, -elle *gramm.* [plyˈrjɛl] **1.** *adj.* plural; **2.** *su./m* plural; *au* ~ in the plural.

plus¹ [ply; *oft.* plys *at end of word-group; before vowel* plyz] **1.** *adv.* more; ⅍ plus; ~ ... ~ ... the more ... the more ...; ~ *confortable* more comfortable; ~ de more than (*2 days*); ~ de soucis! no more worries!; ~ *grand* bigger; ~ *haut!* speak up!; ~ *que* more than (*he*); ~ *rien* nothing more; de ~ further(more); de ~ en ~ more and more; en ~ in addition (to, de); extra; *le* ~ *confortable* most comfortable; *le* ~ *grand* biggest; *moi non* ~ nor I, F me neither; ne ... ~ no more, no longer; not again; *non* ~ (not) either; *rien de* ~ nothing else *or* more; *sans* ~ simply, only, nothing more; *tant et* ~ any amount, plenty; **2.** *su./m:* le ~ the most, the best; *au* ~ at the best, at most; *tout au* ~ at the best, at the very most.

plus² [ply] *1st p. sg. p.s. of* plaire.

plusieurs [ply'zjœːr] *adj./pl./pl., a. pron./indef./pl.* several; some.

plus-que-parfait *gramm.* [plyskə-par'fɛ] *m* pluperfect.

plus-value ⅍, *pol.* [plyva'ly] *f* appreciation, increment value; betterment; extra-payment; *impôt m sur la* ~ (*approx.*) capital gains tax.

plut [ply] *3rd p. sg. p.s. of* pleuvoir.

plutonium ⚛ [plyto'njɔm] *m* plutonium.

plutôt [ply'to] *adv.* rather, sooner (than, *que*); on the whole.

pluvial, e, *m/pl.* -**aux** [ply'vjal, ~'vjo] rain-...; rainy (*season*); **pluvier** *orn.* [~'vje] *m* plover; **pluvieux, -euse** [~'vjø, ~'vjøːz] rainy; wet; of rain; **pluviomètre** *meteor.* [~vjɔ'mɛtr] *m* rain-ga(u)ge, udometer.

pneu, *pl.* **pneus** [pnø] *m mot.* tyre, *Am.* tire; express letter; ~ *antidérapant* non-skid tyre; **pneumatique** [~ma'tik] **1.** *adj.* air-..., pneumatic; **2.** *su./m* (pneumatic) tyre; (*a. carte f* ~) express letter.

pneumonie ⚕ [pnømɔ'ni] *f* pneumonia; **pneumonique** ⚕ [~'nik] pneumonic.

pochade [pɔ'ʃad] *f* rapid *or* rough sketch. [drunk.)

pochard, e [pɔ'ʃaːr, ~'ʃard] *adj., su.)*

poche [pɔʃ] *f* pocket; sack; case; pouch; *geol.* pot-hole; *geol.* washout; *cost.* pucker, F bag; *fig.* isolated case(s *pl.*); ~ *d'air* ✈ air-pocket; ⊕

airlock; *argent m de* ~ pocket-money; **pochée** [pɔ'ʃe] *f* pocketful; **pocher** [~'ʃe] (1a) *v/t. cuis.* poach; *fig.* black (*s.o.'s eye*); dash off (*an essay*, *a sketch, etc.*); *cost.* make baggy at the knees; **pochetée** [pɔʃ'te] *f* pocketful; *sl.* stupid (person); **pochette** [pɔ'ʃɛt] *f* small pocket; handbag, sachet; *matches:* book; fancy handkerchief; ⅍ pocket-set (*of mathematical instruments*).

podagre ⚕ [pɔ'dagr] **1.** *su.* gouty person; *su./f* podagra; **2.** *adj.* gouty.

podomètre [pɔdɔ'mɛtr] *m* pedometer.

poêle¹ [pwɑːl] *m* (funeral-)pall.

poêle² [pwɑːl] *m* stove, cooker.

poêle³ [pwɑːl] *f* frying-pan; F *fig. tenir la queue de la* ~ be in charge *or* control; **poêlée** [pwɑ'le] *f* panful.

poêlier [pwɑ'lje] *m* dealer in stoves and cookers; stove-setter.

poêlon [pwɑ'lɔ̃] *m* small saucepan; casserole.

poème [pɔ'ɛːm] *m* poem; **poésie** [~e'zi] *f* (piece of) poetry; **poète** [~'ɛt] *m* poet; *femme f* ~ woman poet, poetess; **poétereau** [pɔe'tro] *m* poetaster; **poétesse** [~'tɛs] *f* poetess; **poétique** [~'tik] **1.** *adj.* poetic(al); **2.** *su./f* poetics *sg.*; **poétiser** [~ti'ze] (1a) *v/i.* write poetry; *v/t.* poet(ic)ize.

poids [pwɑ] *m* weight; heaviness; *fig.* importance; load; *fig.* burden; ✝ ~ *brut* gross weight; *box.* ~ *coq* bantam weight; *box.* ~ *léger* lightweight; ~ *lourd box.* heavy-weight; *mot.* heavy lorry *or* truck; *box.* ~ *mi-lourd* light heavy-weight; ~ *mort* dead weight; *box.* ~ *mouche* fly-weight; *box.* ~ *moyen* middle-weight; ✝ ~ *net* net weight; *box.* ~ *plume* feather-weight; ⚛ ~ *spécifique* specific gravity; ✈ ~ *utile* payload; ~ *vif* live weight; *sp. lancer m* (*or lancement m*) *du* ~ shot put; *fig. ne pas faire le* ~ not to measure up.

poignant, e [pwa'nɑ̃, ~'nɑ̃ːt] poignant; keen; *fig.* heart-breaking.

poignard [pwa'naːr] *m* dagger; **poignarder** [~nar'de] (1a) *v/t.* stab; *fig.* wound (*s.o.*) deeply; **poigne** F [pwaɲ] *f* grip, grasp; **poignée** [pwa'ɲe] *f* handful (*a. fig.*); *door etc.:* handle; *sword:* hilt; ⊕ *tool:* haft; ~ *de main* handshake; **poignet** [~'ɲɛ] *m* wrist; *cost.* cuff; *shirt:* wristband.

poil [pwal] *m* hair; fur, coat (*of animal*); *tex. cloth*: nap; *velvet*: pile; ♀ down; *brush*: bristle; F *à* ~ naked; F *au* ~ great, fantastic; perfectly, fine; F *de bon* (*mauvais*) ~ in a good (bad) mood; **poilu, e** [pwa'ly] 1. *adj.* hairy, shaggy; 2. *su./m* ✗ F French soldier.

poinçon ⊕ [pwɛ̃'sɔ̃] *m* (brad)awl; punch; stamp; *silver etc.*: (hall-) mark; embroidery: pricker; **poinçonner** [pwɛ̃sɔ'ne] (1a) *v/t.* prick; punch (*a. tickets*); stamp; hall-mark (*silver etc.*); **poinçonneur** [~'nœːr] *m* puncher; **poinçonneuse** [~'nøːz] *f* ⊕ stamping-machine; ⑯ ticket-punch.

poindre [pwɛ̃ːdr] (4m) *v/t.* † sting; *v/i.* dawn (*day*[*light*]); *fig.* come up, appear; ♀ sprout.

poing [pwɛ̃] *m* fist.

point[1] [pwɛ̃] *m* ✏, ♉, *phys.*, *typ.*, *sp.*, *fig.*, *time*, *place*: point; *gramm.* full stop, *Am.* period; ✂, needle-work: stitch; *opt.* focus; ♩ score; *school*: mark; speck; dot (*a. on letter i*); *cards*, *dice*: pip; *fig.* extent, degree; *fig.* state, condition; *cost.* lace; *fig.* ~ *chaud* hot spot, trouble spot; ~ *d'arrêt* stopping place; ✂ ~ *de côté* stitch in one's side; ✂ ~ *de suture* stitch (*in a wound*); ~ *de vue* point of view, viewpoint; ~ *d'exclamation* exclamation mark; ~ *d'interrogation* question mark; ~ *du jour* daybreak; *fig.* ~ *faible* weak point; *fig.* ~ *noir* problem; difficulty; weak spot *or* link; ~-*virgule* semicolon; *à ce* ~ *que* so much so that; *à* ~ in the right condition; in the nick of time; medium-cooked (*meat*); *au* ~ *mot.* in neutral; *fig.* at a standstill; *sp.* *battre aux* ~*s* beat (*s.o.*) on points; *de* ~ *en* ~ in every particular; *deux* ~*s* colon; *en tout* ~ in every way, on all points; *être sur le* ~ *de* (*inf.*) be about to (*inf.*); ⚓ *faire le* ~ take the ship's position; *mauvais* ~ *school*: bad *or* poor mark; *mettre au* ~ *opt.* focus; *mot. etc.* tune (*the engine*); restate (*a question*); clarify (*an affair*); *sur ce* ~ on that score *or* head.

point[2] [~] *adv.*: *ne* ... ~ not ... at all; ~ *du tout!* not at all.

pointe [pwɛ̃ːt] *f* point; *arrow etc.*: tip; *bullet*: nose; *spire*, *tree*: top; touch (*of bronchitis etc.*, *a. fig.*); *geog.* head-land, *land*: tongue; *day*: break; witticism; *fig.* peak, maximum; ~ *des pieds* tiptoe; ⊕ ~ *sèche* etching-needle; dry-point engraving; F *avoir une* ~ *de vin* be slightly excited with drink; *fig.* *de* ~ top, leading; top, maximum; latest (*developments etc.*); décolleté *m en* ~ V-neck; *en* ~ pointed (*beard*); tapering; *fig.* top, leading; *heures f/pl. de* ~ peak hours.

pointer[1] [pwɛ̃'te] (1a) *v/t.* prick up (*one's ears*); sharpen (*a pencil*); ♩ dot (*a note*); *v/i.* ♀ sprout, come up; rear (*horse*); rise, soar (*bird*, *spire*).

pointer[2] [pwɛ̃'te] (1a) *v/t.* aim (*a gun etc.*); check (off) (*items*, *names*); prick; F *se* ~ turn up, show up; *v/i.* clock in *or* out (*worker*); **pointillé, e** [pwɛ̃ti'je] *su./m* dotted line; stippling; **pointiller** [~'je] (1a) *v/t.* dot; stipple; **pointilleux, -euse** [~'jø, ~'jøːz] particular (about, *sur*); finicky; touchy.

pointu, e [pwɛ̃'ty] pointed, sharp; *fig.* shrill (*voice*); *fig.* touchy (*disposition*); **pointure** [~'tyːr] *f collars*, *shoes*, *etc.*: size.

poire [pwaːr] *f* ♀ pear; ⚡ bulb; ⚡ pear-switch; *sl.* mug, sucker, F head; ~ *à poudre* powder-flask; F *garder une* ~ *pour la soif* put s.th. by for a rainy day; **poiré** [pwa're] *m* perry.

poireau [pwa'ro] *m* ♀ leek; F waiting person; F *faire le* ~ = **poireauter** F [~rɔ'te] (1a) *v/i.* be kept waiting, F cool *or* kick one's heels; **poirée** ♀ [~'re] *f* white beet.

poirier ♀ [pwa'rje] *m* pear-tree.

pois [pwa] *m* ♀ pea; *tex.* polka dot; ~ *pl. cassés* split peas; ~ *chiche* chick-pea; *tex.* ~ spotted, dotted; *cuis.* *petits* ~ *pl.* green peas.

poison [pwa'zɔ̃] *m* poison.

poissant, e F [pwa'sã, ~'sãːt] importunate, a pest.

poissard, e [pwa'saːr, ~'sard] 1. *adj.* vulgar; 2. *su./f* fishwife; foul-mouthed woman; *langue f de* ~*e* F Billingsgate.

poisse F [pwas] *f* bad luck; **poisser** [pwa'se] (1a) *v/t.* make sticky; ⊕ pitch; F nab (*s.o.*); **poisseux, -euse** [~'sø, ~'søːz] sticky.

poisson [pwa'sɔ̃] *m* fish; ~ *d'avril* April Fool trick *or* joke; ~ *rouge* goldfish; *faire un* ~ *d'avril à* make an April Fool of (*s.o.*); *astr. les* ⚋*s pl.* Pisces, the Fishes; **poisson-~-chats** *icht.* [~sɔ̃'ʃa] *m* cat-fish; **poissonnerie** [~sɔn'ri] *f* fish-market;

poltron

fish-shop; **poissonneux, -euse** [⌂sɔ'nø, ⌂'nøːz] teeming with fish; **poissonnier, -ère** [⌂sɔ'nje, ⌂'njɛːr] su. fishmonger; su./f fishkettle.

poitrail [pwa'traːj] m zo. breast; co. (human) chest; **poitrinaire** ⚕ [⌂tri'nɛːr] adj., a. su. consumptive; **poitrine** [⌂'trin] f breast, chest; woman: bust.

poivrade cuis. [pwa'vrad] f dressing of oil, vinegar and pepper; **poivre** [pwaːvr] m pepper; F ⌂ et sel grey-haired (person); grain m de ⌂ peppercorn; **poivré, e** [pwa'vre] peppery, hot (food); pungent (smell); stiff (price); fig. spicy (story); **poivrer** [⌂'vre] (1a) v/t. pepper; F spice (a story etc.); **poivrier** [⌂vri'e] m pepper-box; ♀ pepper-plant; **poivrière** [⌂vri'ɛːr] f pepper-pot; pepper-box (a. ⚔.); pepper-plantation; **poivron** [⌂'vrɔ̃] m pimento, allspice; **poivrot** F [⌂'vro] m drunkard.

poix [pwa] f pitch; cobbler's wax.

polaire ⚡, ⚑, geog. [pɔ'lɛːr] polar; **polarisation** phys. [pɔlariza'sjɔ̃] f polarization; **polariser** [⌂'ze] (1a) v/t. phys. polarize; fig. focus, centre; **polarité** phys. [⌂'te] f polarity.

pôle [poːl] m pole; geog. ⌂ Nord (Sud) North (South) Pole.

polémique [pɔle'mik] 1. adj. polemic; 2. su./f polemic; eccl. polemics pl.; **polémiquer** [⌂mi'ke] (1m) v/i. polemize.

poli, e [pɔ'li] 1. adj. polished (a. fig.); burnished (metal); glossy; fig. polite; fig. urbane, elegant; 2. su./m polish, gloss.

police[1] [pɔ'lis] f police, constabulary; policing; regulations pl.; ⌂ de la circulation traffic police; ⌂ fluviale river police; ⌂ judiciaire (approx.) Criminal Investigation Department, C.I.D.; agent m de ⌂ policeman; appeler ⌂(-)secours dial 999; ✕ bonnet m de ⌂ forage cap; fiche f de ⌂ registration form (at a hotel); ✕ salle f de ⌂ guard-room.

police[2] [⌂] f insurance policy; ✝ ⌂ de chargement bill of lading; ⌂ flottante floating policy.

policer ✝ [pɔli'se] (1k) v/t. bring law and order to; organize; civilize.

polichinelle [pɔliʃi'nɛl] m Punch; F buffoon; secret m de ⌂ open secret.

policier, -ère [pɔli'sje, ⌂'sjɛːr] 1. adj.

police...; detective (film, novel); 2. su./m policeman; detective; detective novel.

poliment [pɔli'mɑ̃] adv. of poli 1.

poliomyélite ⚕ [pɔljɔmje'lit] f poliomyelitis, F polio; infantile paralysis.

polir [pɔ'liːr] (2a) v/t. polish (a. fig.); make glossy; burnish (metal); fig. refine; **polisseur, -euse** [pɔli'sœːr, ⌂'søːz] su. polisher; su./f polishing machine; **polissoir** [⌂'swaːr] m ⊕ tool: polisher; polishing machine; buff-stick; nail-polisher.

polisson, -onne [pɔli'sɔ̃, ⌂'sɔn] 1. adj. naughty; pej. indecent; saucy; 2. su. naughty child, scamp; dissolute person; **polissonner** [⌂sɔ'ne] (1a) v/i. run the streets (child); behave or talk lewdly; **polissonnerie** [⌂sɔn'ri] f child: mischievousness; indecent act; smutty story; depravity.

polissure [pɔli'syːr] f polish(ing).

politesse [pɔli'tɛs] f politeness, courtesy; ⌂s pl. civilities.

politicien m, -enne f usu. pej [pɔliti'sjɛ̃, ⌂'sjɛn] politician; **politique** [⌂'tik] 1. adj. political; fig. prudent; wary; fig. diplomatic; homme m ⌂ politician; 2. su./m politician; su./f politics; policy; ⌂ de clocher parish-pump politics; ⌂ de la porte ouverte open-door policy; ⌂ extérieure (intérieure) foreign (home) policy; **politiquer** F [⌂ti'ke] (1m) v/i. dabble in politics; talk politics; **politologie** [pɔlitɔlɔ'ʒi] f political science; **politologue** [⌂'lɔg] su. political scientist.

polka [pɔl'ka] f ♪ dance: polka; ⊕ quarryman's hammer.

pollen ♀ [pɔl'lɛn] m pollen; **pollinique** ♀ [⌂li'nik] pollinic; pollen-(sac, tube); **pollinisation** ♀ [⌂liniza'sjɔ̃] f fertilisation, pollinization.

polluant, e [pɔl'lɥɑ̃, ⌂'lɥɑ̃t] 1. adj. polluting; 2. su./m pollutant, polluting agent; **polluer** [⌂'lɥe] (1n) v/t. pollute; defile; eccl. profane; **pollution** [⌂ly'sjɔ̃] f pollution (a. ⚕); eccl. profanation.

polochon sl. [pɔlɔ'ʃɔ̃] m bolster.

polonais, e [pɔlɔ'nɛ, ⌂'nɛːz] 1. adj. Polish; 2. su./m ling. Polish; su. ♀ Pole; su./f ♪ dance: polonaise.

poltron, -onne [pɔltrɔ̃, ⌂'trɔn] 1. adj. timid; cowardly; craven; 2. su.

coward, craven, *sl.* funk; **poltronnerie** [ˌtrɔn'ri] *f* timidity; cowardice.

poly... [pɔli] poly...; **~clinique** [ˌ-
kli'nik] *f* polyclinic; **~copier** [ˌkɔ-
'pje] (1o) *v/t.* duplicate, *Am.* mimeo-
graph; **~èdre** Ⓐ [ˌ'ɛ:dr] 1. *adj.* poly-
hedral; 2. *su./m* polyhedron; **~game**
[ˌ'gam] 1. *adj.* polygamous; ♀ poly-
gamic; 2. *su.* polygamist; **~gamie**
[ˌga'mi] *f* polygamy; **~glotte** [ˌ'glɔt]
adj., a. su. polyglot; **~gone** [ˌ'gɔn] 1.
adj. polygonal; 2. *su./m* polygon; ✕
artillery: shooting-range; **~mère** Ⓐ
[ˌ'mɛːr] polymeric; **~nôme** Ⓐ
[ˌ'noːm] *m* polynomial.

polype [pɔ'lip] *m zo.* polyp; ♂ pol-
ypus; **polypeux, -euse** [ˌli'pø, ˌ-
'pøːz] polypous.

poly...: **~phonie** ♪ [pɔlifɔ'ni] *f* po-
lyphony; **~phonique** ♪ [ˌfɔ'nik]
polyphonic; **~technicien** [ˌtɛkni-
'sjɛ̃] *m* student at the *Ecole polytechnique;* **~technique** [ˌtɛk'nik]: ⚷ *f or
Ecole f ~* Academy of Engineering;
~valance [ˌva'lɑ̃ːs] *f* ⚷ poly-
valency; ⊕ *etc., a. fig.* versatility,
flexibility; **~valant, e** [ˌva'lɑ̃, ˌ'lɑ̃ːt]
⚷ polyvalent; ⊕ *etc., a. fig.* versatile,
flexible, multi-purpose.

pomiculteur [pɔmikyl'tœːr] *m* fruit
grower.

pommade [pɔ'mad] *f* pomade, po-
matum, *(hair-)*cream; F *passer de la ~
à* soft-soap *(s.o.);* **pommader**
[ˌma'de] (1a) *v/t.* pomade, put cream
on *(one's hair).*

pommard [pɔ'maːr] *m* Pommard *(a
red burgundy).*

pomme [pɔm] *f* apple; ♀ pome;
lettuce etc.: head; *bedstead, stick:*
knob; *sprinkler etc.:* rose; F head; ~ *de
discorde* bone of contention; ~ *de
terre* potato; ~*s pl. chips* potato
crisps, *Am.* chips; ~*s pl. frites* Br.
chips, *Am.* French fries, French
fried potatoes; ~*s pl. mousseline*
mashed potatoes; F *tomber dans les ~s*
pass out (= *faint*); **pommé, e**
[pɔ'me] 1. *adj.* rounded; F *downright
(fool);* first-rate; *chou m ~* white-
heart cabbage; *laitue f ~e* cabbage
lettuce; 2. *su./m* cider.

pommeau [pɔ'mo] *m* pommel;
fishing-rod: butt.

pommelé, e [pɔm'le] dappled; *ciel
m ~* mackerel sky; *gris ~* dapple-
grey; **pommelle** ⊕ [pɔ'mɛl] *f*

grating *(over pipe);* **pommer** [ˌ-
'me] (1a) *v/i. a. se ~* form a head
(cabbage, lettuce, etc.); **pomme-
raie** ⚹ [pɔm'rɛ] *f* apple-orchard;
pommette [pɔ'mɛt] *f* knob; *anat.*
cheek-bone; **pommier** [ˌ'mje] *m*
apple-tree; **pomologie** [ˌmɔlɔ'ʒi] *f*
pomology.

pompe[1] [pɔ̃ːp] *f* pomp, ceremony;
entrepreneur m de ~s funèbres funeral director, undertaker, *Am.*
mortician.

pompe[2] [pɔ̃ːp] *f* ⊕ pump; *mot. ~ à
essence* petrol-pump, *Am.* gas-
pump; *sl.* shoe, boot; ~ *à graisse*
grease-gun; ~ *à incendie* fire-engine;
~ *à pneumatique* tyre-pump; tyre-
inflator; ~ *aspirante* suction-pump;
~ *aspirante-foulante* lift-and-force
pump; F *à toute ~* at top speed, at full
tilt; F *sp.* *faire des ~s* do push-ups;
pomper [pɔ̃'pe] (1a) *v/t.* pump *(a.
fig.);* suck up *or* in; F tire out;
pompette F [ˌ'pɛt] tipsy.

pompeux, -euse [pɔ̃'pø, ˌ'pøːz]
pompous; stately; high-flown *(style).*

pompier [pɔ̃'pje] 1. *su./m* fireman;
les ~s pl. the fire brigade *sg.;* 2. *adj.* F
corny; high-falutin' *(style);* **pom-
piste** *mot.* [ˌ'pist] *m* pump attendant.

pompon [pɔ̃'pɔ̃] *m* pompon, tuft;
powder-puff; F *iro. avoir (or tenir) le ~*
surpass everyone; **pomponner**
[ˌpɔ'ne] (1a) *v/t.* dress up, F doll up.

ponant *hist.* [pɔ'nɑ̃] *m* West; Occident.

ponce [pɔ̃ːs] *f (a. pierre f ~)* pumice-
stone; *drawing:* pounce.

ponceau[1] ⚠ [pɔ̃'so] *m* culvert.

ponceau[2] [ˌ] 1. *su./m* corn-poppy;
poppy-red; 2. *adj./inv.* poppy-red.

poncer ⊕ [pɔ̃'se] (1k) *v/t.* pumice;
floor etc.: sand-paper; rub down
(paint); pounce *(a drawing);* **pon-
ceux, -euse** [ˌ'sø, ˌ'søːz] 1. *adj.*
pumiceous; 2. *su./f* ⊕ sand-paper-
ing machine; **poncif, -ve** [ˌ'sif,
ˌ'siːv] 1. *adj.* conventional; trite;
stereotyped *(effect, plot);* 2. *su./m*
conventionalism; *fig.* conventional
piece of writing.

ponction ♂ [pɔ̃k'sjɔ̃] *f* puncture;
blister: pricking; **ponctionner** [ˌ-
sjɔ'ne] (1a) *v/t.* puncture; tap; prick
(a blister).

ponctualité [pɔ̃ktɥali'te] *f* punctuality; **ponctuation** *gramm.* [ˌ'sjɔ̃]

f punctuation; **ponctuel, -elle** [pɔ̃k'tɥɛl] punctual; *phys.* pinpoint (*a. fig.*); *fig.* isolated, selective, individual; **ponctuer** [~'tɥe] (1n) *v/t.* punctuate; emphasize (*a spoken word*).

pondaison [pɔ̃dɛ'zɔ̃] *f* eggs: laying.

pondérable [pɔ̃de'rabl] ponderable; **pondérateur, -trice** [~ra'tœːr, ~'tris] stabilizing; balancing; **pondération** [~ra'sjɔ̃] *f* balance (*a. fig.*); *fig.* level-headedness; **pondéré, e** [~'re] level-headed.

pondeur, -euse [pɔ̃'dœːr, ~'døːz] 1. *adj.* (egg-)laying; 2. *su. fig.* prolific producer (*of novels etc.*); *su./f hen:* layer; **pondoir** [~'dwaːr] *m* nest-box; *hens:* laying-place; **pondre** [pɔ̃ːdr] (4a) *v/t.* lay (*an egg*); F *fig.* produce, bring forth.

poney *zo.* [pɔ'nɛ] *m* pony.

pongiste [pɔ̃'ʒist] *su.* table tennis player.

pont [pɔ̃] *m* △, ⊕, *fig.* bridge; ⊕, *mot.* axle; ⚓ deck; ~s *pl. et chaussées f/pl.* Highways Department *sg.* (*in France*); ⊕ ~ *à bascule* weigh-bridge; ~ *aérien* air-lift; *mot.* ~ *arrière* rear-axle; *mot.* ~ *élévateur garage:* repair *or* car ramp; ~ *roulant* ⊕ travelling crane; 🚋 traverser; △ ~ *suspendu* suspension-bridge; △ ~ *tournant* swing-bridge; *fig. couper les* ~s burn one's boats; **pontage** [pɔ̃'taːʒ] *m* bridge-building; bridging; ⚓ by-pass.

ponte[1] [pɔ̃ːt] *f* eggs: laying; eggs *pl.*

ponte[2] [~] *m* cards: punter; F top brass, V.I.P.

ponter [pɔ̃'te] (1a) *v/i.* cards: punt.

pontife [pɔ̃'tif] *m* pontiff; *fig.* pundit; *souverain m* ~ pope, sovereign pontiff; **pontifical, e,** *m/pl.* **-aux** [pɔ̃tifi'kal, ~'ko] *adj., a. su./m* pontifical; **pontificat** [~fi'ka] *m* pontificate; **pontifier** [~'fje] (1o) *v/i.* pontificate (*a. fig.*).

pont-levis, *pl.* **ponts-levis** [pɔ̃lə'vi] *m* drawbridge.

ponton [pɔ̃'tɔ̃] *m* ✗ pontoon; ⚓ lighter; *in river etc.:* floating landing stage; † hulk; **pontonnier** ✗ [~tɔ'nje] *m* pontoneer.

popeline *tex.* [pɔ'plin] *f* poplin.

popote F [pɔ'pɔt] 1. *su./f* cooking; ✗ cook-shop; ✗ (*field-*)mess; *faire la* ~ do the cooking; 2. *adj.* stay-at-home, quiet.

populace *pej.* [pɔpy'las] *f* populace, rabble; **populacier, -ère** F [~la-'sje, ~'sjɛːr] vulgar, common.

populage ♀ [pɔpy'laːʒ] *m* marsh marigold.

populaire [pɔpy'lɛːr] 1. *adj.* popular (with, *auprès de*); 2. *su./m* common people; herd; **populariser** [pɔpy-lari'ze] (1a) *v/t.* popularize; make (*s.o.*) popular; **popularité** [~'te] *f* popularity; **population** [pɔpyla-'sjɔ̃] *f* population; ~ *active* working population; **populeux, -euse** [~'lø, ~'løːz] populous; crowded (*city etc.*); **populo** F [~'lo] *m* common people, riff-raff.

porc [pɔːr] *m* pig, hog; *cuis.* pork; *fig.* (dirty) swine.

porcelaine [pɔrsə'lɛn] *f* china (-ware); porcelain; ~ *de Limoges* Limoges ware; **porcelainier, -ère** [~lɛ'nje, ~'njɛːr] 1. *adj.* china...; porcelain...; 2. *su./m* porcelain manufacturer.

porcelet [pɔrsə'lɛ] *m* piglet, *ch.sp.* piggy.

porc-épic, *pl.* **porcs-épics** *zo.* [pɔr-ke'pik] *m* porcupine, *Am.* hedgehog.

porche △ [pɔrʃ] *m* porch, portal.

porcher [pɔr'ʃe] *m* swine-herd; **porchère** [~'ʃɛːr] *f* swine-maiden; **porcherie** [~ʃə'ri] *f* pig-farm; pigsty (*a. fig.*).

pore [pɔːr] *m* pore; **poreux, -euse** [pɔ'rø, ~'røːz] porous; unglazed (*pottery etc.*).

porion ✗ [pɔ'rjɔ̃] *m* overman.

pornographie [pɔrnɔgra'fi] *f* pornography.

porosité [pɔrozi'te] *f* porosity.

porphyre [pɔr'fiːr] *m min.* porphyry; ⚒ slab; **porphyrique** *min.* [~fi'rik] porphyritic.

porreau [pɔ'ro] *m see poireau.*

port[1] [pɔːr] *m* ⚓, 🚢 port; harbo(u)r; haven (*a. fig.*); ~ *d'attache* port of registry; ~ *de* (*or à*) *marée* tidal harbo(u)r; ~ *de mer* seaport; ~ *franc* free port; *arriver à bon* ~ ⚓ come safe into port; *fig.* arrive safely; *capitaine m de* ~ harbo(u)r-master; *entrer au* ~ come into port.

port[2] [pɔːr] *m* carrying; *goods etc.:* carriage; *letter, parcel:* postage; ⚓ *ship:* tonnage; *transport, telegram, etc.:* charge; *decorations, uniform:* wearing; *person:* bearing, carriage; ~ *dû* carriage forward; ~

payé carriage *or* postage paid; **portable** [pɔr'tabl] portable; *cost.* wearable; **portage** [ˌ'taːʒ] *m* ✝ conveyance, transport; ⚓ portage; ⊕ bearing. [door.⟩

portail ⚠ [pɔr'taːj] *m* portal; main⟩

portant, e [pɔr'tɑ̃, ˌ'tɑ̃ːt] **1.** *adj.* ⊕ bearing, carrying; *fig. bien (mal)* ~ in good (bad) health; **2.** *su./m* ⊕ stay, strut; *box, trunk:* handle; *thea.* framework (*of a flat*); **portatif, -ve** [ˌta'tif, ˌ'tiːv] portable.

porte [pɔrt] **1.** *su./f* ⚠, *a.* ⊕ door (*a. fig.*); gate (*a.* ⚓); doorway, entrance; *geog.* pass, gorge; ~ *à deux battants* folding-door; ~ *cochère* carriage entrance, gateway; ⚒ ~ *d'aérage* trap, air-gate; ~ *vitrée* glass door; *écouter aux* ~s eavesdrop; *mettre* (*or* F *flanquer*) *q. à la* ~ turn s.o. out; give s.o. the sack; *nous habitons* ~ *à* ~ we are next-door neighbo(u)rs; **2.** *adj.:* *anat. veine f* ~ portal vein.

porte...: ~(-)**à**(-)**faux** [pɔrta'fo] *m:* *en* ~ in an unstable position; ~**aiguilles** [ˌe'gɥiːj] *m/inv.* needle case; ~**avions** ⚓ [ˌa'vjɔ̃] *m/inv.* aircraft carrier; ~**bagages** [ˌba'gaːʒ] *m/inv.* luggage (*Am.* baggage) rack; ~**billets** [ˌbi'jɛ] *m/inv.* note case, *Am.* billfold; ~**bonheur** [ˌbɔ'nœːr] *m/inv.* talisman, lucky charm; mascot; ~**bouteilles** [ˌbu'tɛːj] *m/inv.* bottle rack; ~**cigarettes** [ˌsiga'rɛt] *m/inv.* cigarette case; ~**clefs** [ˌ'kle] *m/inv.* key ring; *hotel:* key rack; ~**drapeau** ⚒ [ˌdra'po] *m/inv.* colo(u)r bearer.

portée [pɔr'te] *f* bearing; ⚠ span; *gun:* range; *voice:* compass; *arm:* reach; ♪ stave; *animals:* litter; *fig.* comprehension; *fig.* meaning, consequences *pl.*, implications *pl.*; *à* (*la*) ~ (*de*) within reach (of); *hors de* (*la*) ~ (*de*) without reach (of); *à* (*hors de*) ~ *de voix* within (out of) earshot; *être à la* ~ *de a.* be within the understanding of (*s.o.*); *vues f/pl. à longue* ~ farsighted policy *pl.*

porte...: ~**enseigne** [pɔrtɑ̃'sɛɲ] *m/inv.* colo(u)r-bearer; ~**faix** [ˌ'fɛ] *m* (street-)porter; *docks:* stevedore.

porte-fenêtre, *pl.* **portes-fenêtres** ⚠ [pɔrtə'fnɛːtr] *f* French window.

porte...: ~**feuille** [pɔrtə'fœːj] *m documents, a. pol.:* portfolio; wallet, note-case, *Am.* bill-fold; ✝ ~ *titres*

investments *pl.*, securities *pl.*; ~**habits** [pɔrta'bi] *m/inv.* hall-stand; ~**malheur** [ˌma'lœːr] *m/inv.* bringer of bad luck, F Jonah; ~**manteau** [ˌmɑ̃'to] *m* coat-rack, hatstand; ~**mine** [ˌ'min] *m/inv.* pencil-case; propelling pencil; ~**monnaie** [ˌmɔ'nɛ] *m/inv.* purse; ~**parapluies** [ˌpara'plɥi] *m/inv.* umbrella-stand; ~**parole** [ˌpa'rɔl] *m/inv.* spokesman, F mouthpiece; ~**plume** [pɔrtə'plym] *m/inv.* penholder.

porter [pɔr'te] (1a) *v/t.* carry; bear; wear (*clothing*); take; strike, deal (*a blow*); ⚖ bring (*a charge, a complaint*); ✝ charge; ✝ place (*to s.o.'s credit*); ✝ post (*in ledger*); produce (*fruit etc.*); ⚒ shoulder (*arms*); *fig.* lead (*s.o.*) (*to, à*); *fig.* increase (*the number, the price, the temperature*); *fig.* have (*an affection, an interest*), bear (*the responsibility, witness*); *se* ~ proceed (to, *à*); feel, be (*well, unwell etc.*); *se* ~ *bien* (*mal*) *a.* be in good (bad) health; *se* ~ *comme un charme* be as fit as a fiddle; *se* ~ *candidat* stand as candidate; *pol.* run (for, *à*); *se* ~ *garant de* vouch for; *v/i.* bear (*a. fig.*), rest (on, *sur*); deal (with, *sur*); carry (*sound etc.*); hit the mark, strike home (*shot, a. fig. insult, etc.*); ⚕ be pregnant; be with young (*animal*); *fig.* ~ *à la tête* go to the head (*wine*); ~ *sur les nerfs* get on one's nerves.

porte...: ~**respect** [pɔrtrɛs'pɛ] *m/inv.* defensive weapon; ~**savon** [ˌsa'vɔ̃] *m or m/inv.* soap-dish, soapholder; ~**serviettes** [ˌsɛr'vjɛt] *m/inv.* towel-rack.

porteur, -euse [pɔr'tœːr, ˌ'tøːz] **1.** *su.* porter; *letter, message, news, etc.:* bearer; ⚕ (*germ-*)carrier; *su./m* ✝ bearer, payee (*of cheque*) (*stock-, share*)holder; *au* ~ (*payable*) to bearer (*cheque*); **2.** *adj.* pack-(*animal*); ⊕ bearing; suspension-...; carrier (*wave, rocket*).

porte-voix [pɔrtə'vwa] *m/inv.* speaking-tube; megaphone.

portier, -ère [pɔr'tje, ˌ'tjɛːr] *su.* doorman; gatekeeper; porter; *su./f mot., a.* 🚗 door; door-curtain; **portillon** [ˌti'jɔ̃] *m* wicket(-gate); small gate.

portion [pɔr'sjɔ̃] *f* portion, share, part; *meal:* helping; F ~ *congrue* bare living.

portique [pɔr'tik] *m* portico, porch; ⊕ gantry; *sp.* crossbar.

porto [pɔr'to] *m wine*: port.

portrait [pɔr'trɛ] *m paint.* portrait; face; *fig.* likeness; *fig.* description; character-sketch, profile; ~ *robot* identikit (picture); **portraitiste** [pɔrtrɛ'tist] *su.* portrait-painter; **portraiturer** [~ty'rre] (1a) *v/t.* portray.

portugais, e [pɔrty'gɛ, ~'gɛːz] 1. *adj.* Portuguese; 2. *su./m ling.* Portuguese; *su.* ♀ Portuguese; *les* ♀ *m/pl.* the Portuguese.

posage ⊕ [po'zaːʒ] *m* placing; fixing; *bricks, pipes*: laying; **pose** [poːz] *f* ⊕ placing; fixing; *bricks, pipes*: laying; ✕ posting; *phot.* time-exposure; *fig.* posture; pose; *fig.* affectation; *prendre une* ~ adopt *or* strike an attitude; **posé, e** [po'ze] *fig.* sedate, staid, grave; steady (*bearing, person, voice*); sitting (*bird*); **posemètre** *phot.* [poz'mɛtr] *m* exposure meter; **poser** [po'ze] (1a) *v/t.* place, put (*a. a question, a motion*), lay (*a.* △ *bricks, pipes, carpet,* 🚃 *rails, etc.*); lay down (*a book, a. fig. a principle*); hang (*curtains*); set (*a problem*); ⊕ fix, fit; ✕ ~ *les armes* lay down one's arms; ~ *q.* establish s.o.'s reputation; *posons le cas que* let us suppose that; *se* ~ *fig.* achieve a certain standing; ✈︎ land (*plane*); *se* ~ *comme* pass o.s. off as, claim to be; *v/i.* rest, lie; *paint.* pose (*a. fig.*), sit; F *fig.* put it on, *Am.* put on dog; *fig.* ~ *pour* claim to be; **poseur, -euse** [~'zœːr, ~'zøːz] *su.* affected person; attitudinizer; *su./m pipes, a. mines*: layer; (*bill-*)sticker.

positif, -ve [pozi'tif, ~'tiːv] 1. *adj.* ⚭, ⚡, *gramm., phys., phot.* positive; real, actual; matter-of-fact, practical (*person*); 2. *su./m phot., gramm., phot.* positive; ♪ choir-organ.

position [pozi'sjɔ̃] *f* position; situation (*a. fig.*); job; (*physical*) posture, attitude; (*social*) standing; ~ *clé* key position; *feux m/pl. de* ~ ✈︎ navigation lights; ⚓︎ riding lights; *mot.* parking lights; *prendre* ~ *sur* take up a definite stand about.

posologie ⚕ [pozɔlɔ'ʒi] *f* dosage, directions *pl.* for use.

possédé, e [pɔse'de] 1. *adj.* possessed

(by, *de*; *fig. a.* with, *pour*); 2. *su./m* madman, maniac; *su./f* madwoman;

posséder [~] (1f) *v/t.* possess (*a. fig.*); own; have; *fig. passion, influence*: dominate; have a thorough knowledge of; *fig. se* ~ contain o.s., control o.s.

possesseur [pɔse'sœːr] *m* owner, possessor; **possessif, -ve** *gramm.* [~'sif, ~'siːv] *adj., a. su./m* possessive; **possession** [~'sjɔ̃] *f* possession (*a. by a demon*); *fig.* thorough knowledge (*of a subject*); ~ *de soi* self-control.

possibilité [pɔsibili'te] *f* possibility; **possible** [~'sibl] 1. *adj.* possible; *le plus* ~ as far as possible; as many *or* much as possible; *le plus vite* ~ as quickly as possible; 2. *su./m* what is possible; *faire tout son* ~ do all one can (*to inf., pour inf.*).

post... [pɔst] post...

postal, e, *m/pl.* **-aux** [pɔs'tal, ~'to] postal; *sac m* ~ mail-bag.

postdater [pɔstda'te] (1a) *v/t.* post-date.

poste[1] [pɔst] *f* post; mail; postal service; post office; ~ *aérienne* air-mail; ~ *restante* to be called for, *Am.* general delivery; *mettre à la* ~ post, *Am.* mail (*a letter*); *par la* ~ by post.

poste[2] [~] *m* post (*a.* ✕); job; position; *pilot*: cockpit; ✕, ⊕, ⚓︎, *police, fire, radio, tel., etc.*: station; *radio, teleph.*: set; *teleph.* extension; ✝ entry; ✝ item; *mot.* (*filling*) station, (*petrol*) pump; ✕ ~ *avancé* advanced post, outpost; 🚃 ~ *d'aiguillage* signal-box; ✈︎ ~ *de contrôle* control tower; ~ *de secours* first-aid post; ✕ regimental aid post; ~ *de télévision* television set; ~ *de T.S.F.* radio; ~ *téléphonique* telephone-station; *conduire q. au* ~ take s.o. to the police station.

poster [pɔs'te] (1a) *v/t.* post, *Am.* mail (*a letter*); post, station (*a sentry*).

postérieur, e [pɔste'rjœːr] 1. *adj.* posterior; subsequent (*time*); hind (-er) (*place*); back (*vowel*); 2. F *su./m* posterior, F backside.

postérité [pɔsteri'te] *f* posterity; descendants *pl.*; *la* ~ generations *pl.* to come.

postface [pɔst'fas] *f book*: postscript.

posthume [pɔs'tym] posthumous.

postiche [pɔs'tiʃ] 1. *adj.* false (*hair*

etc.); imitation (*pearl*); 2. *su./m* hair-piece; postiche.

postier *m*, **-ère** *f* [pɔs'tje, ~'tjɛ:r] post-office employee; **postillon** [~ti'jõ] *m* postilion; F *speech*: splutter(ing).

post...: ~position [pɔstpozi'sjõ] *f* postposition; **~scolaire** [~skɔ'lɛ:r] after-school; *class, school*: continuation ...; **~scriptum** [~skrip-'tɔm] *m/inv*. postscript, P.S.

postulant *m*, **e** *f* [pɔsty'lɑ̃, ~'lɑ̃:t] *post*: applicant, candidate; *eccl.* postulant; **postulat** [~'la] *m* postulate, assumption; **postulation** [~la'sjõ] *f* postulation; **postuler** [~'le] (1a) *v/t.* apply for (*a post*); postulate; *v/i.* ⚖ conduct a (law)suit.

posture [pɔs'ty:r] *f* posture, attitude; *fig.* position.

pot [po] *m* pot; jar, jug, can; ⚗ crucible; ~ *à eau* water jug, ewer; ~ *à fleurs* flower-pot; ~ *à lait* milk-can, milk-jug; ~ *de chambre* chamber(-pot); ~ *de fleurs* pot of flowers; *fig.* découvrir le ~ aux roses smell out the secret; *manger à la fortune du* ~ take pot luck; F *fig.* tourner autour du ~ beat about the bush.

potable [pɔ'tabl] drinkable, fit to drink; F fair, acceptable; *eau f* ~ drinking water.

potache F [pɔ'taʃ] *m* secondary-school boy, grammar-school boy.

potage [pɔ'ta:ʒ] *m* soup; *fig. pej. pour tout* ~ in all; **potager, -ère** [~ta'ʒe, ~'ʒɛ:r] 1. *adj.* pot-(*herbs*); kitchen (*garden*); 2. *su./m* (*a. jardin* ~) kitchen *or* vegetable garden.

potasse [pɔ'tas] *f* ⚗ potash; ⚗ (impure) potassium carbonate; **potasser** F [pɔta'se] (1a) *v/t.* swot at *or* for; **potassique** ⚗ [~'sik] potassium...; potassic (*salt*); **potassium** ⚗ [~'sjɔm] *m* potassium.

pot-au-feu [pɔto'fø] 1. *su./m/inv.* stock-pot; beef-broth; boiled beef and vegetables; 2. *adj.* stay-at-home; **pot-bouille** † *sl.* [po'bu:j] *f*: *faire* ~ *ensemble* live together; **pot-de-vin,** *pl.* **pots-de-vin** F [pod'vɛ̃] *m* tip, gratuity; *pej.* bribe; *pej.* hush-money, *Am. sl.* take-off.

pote *sl.* [pɔt] *m* pal, *Am.* buddy.

poteau [pɔ'to] *m* post (*a. sp.*), stake; pole; ⚒ pit-prop; *sl.* pal, *Am.*

buddy; ~ *indicateur* sign-post; ~ *télégraphique* telegraph pole.

potée [pɔ'te] *f* potful, jugful; *beer*: mugful; ⊕ emery, putty, *etc.*: powder.

potelé, e [pɔt'le] plump, chubby; dimpled.

potence [pɔ'tɑ̃:s] *f* gallows *usu. sg.*, gibbet; ⚒, ⊕ arm, cross-piece; ⊕ *crane*: jib; *mériter la* ~ deserve hanging.

potentat [pɔtɑ̃'ta] *m* potentate; † F magnate.

potentialiser ⚕ *etc.* [pɔtɑ̃sjali'ze] (1a) *v/t.* potentiate, increase the effect of; **potentiel, -elle** [~'sjɛl] *adj., a. su./m* potential (*a. gramm.*).

poterie [pɔ'tri] *f* pottery (*a. works*); earthenware; ~ *d'étain* pewter; **potiche** [~'tiʃ] *f* vase of Chinese *or* Japanese porcelain; F *fig.* figurehead; **potier** [~'tje] *m* potter; ~ *d'étain* pewterer.

potin [pɔ'tɛ̃] *m* pewter; pinchbeck; F gossip; F din, rumpus; ~ *jaune* brass; **potiner** F [pɔti'ne] (1a) *v/i.* gossip; **potinier, -ère** [~'nje, ~'njɛ:r] 1. *adj.* gossipy; 2. *su.* scandalmonger, gossip; *su./f* gossip-shop.

potion ⚕ [po'sjõ] *f* potion, draught.

potiron ♣ [pɔti'rõ] *m* pumpkin.

pot-pourri, *pl.* **pots-pourris** [popu-'ri] *m cuis.* meat-stew; ♪ pot-pourri (*a. perfume*), medley.

pou, *pl.* **poux** [pu] *m* louse; (*bird-*)mite; (*sheep-*)tick.

pouah! [pwa] *int.* ugh!

poubelle [pu'bɛl] *f* refuse-bin, *Am.* garbage-can; dustbin.

pouce [pu:s] *m* thumb; † *measure*: inch (*a. fig.*); big toe; *manger sur le* ~ have a snack; *mettre les* ~s knuckle under, give in; *s'en mordre les* ~s regret it bitterly; *se tourner les* ~s twiddle one's thumbs; **poucettes** [pu'sɛt] *f/pl.* thumb-cuffs; † *torture*: thumb-screw *sg.*; **poucier** [~'sje] *m* ⚙ thumb-stall; ⊕ *latch*: thumb-piece.

pouding *cuis.* [pu'diŋ] *m* pudding.

poudre [pu:dr] *f* powder; dust (*a. fig.*); ⚔ (gun)powder; ⚔ ~ *de mine* blasting powder; *café m en* ~ instant coffee; *il n'a pas inventé la* ~ he won't set the Thames on fire; *fig. jeter de la* ~ *aux yeux de q.* throw dust in s.o.'s eyes; bluff s.o.;

réduire en ~ pulverize; *sucre m en* ~ castor sugar; **poudrer** [pu'dre] (1a) *v/t.* (sprinkle [*s.th.*] with) powder; **poudrerie** [ˌdrə'ri] *f* (gun)powder-factory; **poudreux, -euse** [ˌ'drø, ˌ'drøːz] 1. *adj.* dusty; powdery; *neige f* ~*euse* = 2. *su/f* powder snow; **poudrier** [ˌdri'e] *m* powder-case, powder-box; *compact*; **poudrière** [ˌdri'jɛːr] *f esp. fig.* powder keg; **poudrin** [ˌ'drɛ̃] *m see embrun*; **poudroyer** [ˌdrwa'je] (1h) *v/i.* form *or* send up clouds of dust.

pouf [puf] 1. *int. sound of falling*: plop!; plump!; *feelings*: phew!; 2. *su./m cushion*: pouf; puff (= *exaggerated advertisement*); **pouffant, e** F [pu'fɑ̃, ˌ'fɑ̃ːt] screamingly funny; **pouffer** [ˌ'fe] (1a) *v/i.* (*a.* ~ *de rire*) burst out laughing.

pouffiasse *sl.* [puf'jas] *f* whore, tart; slattern, slut; fat woman.

pouillerie *sl.* [puj'ri] *f* abject poverty; filthy hole.

pouilles [puːj] *f/pl.*: *chanter* ~ *à* jeer at.

pouilleux, -euse [pu'jø, ˌ'jøːz] lousy, lice-infested; F wretched.

poulailler [pula'je] *m* hen-house, hen-roost; F *thea.* gallery, gods *pl.*; **poulaillerie** [ˌlaj'ri] *f* poultry-market.

poulain [pu'lɛ̃] *m zo.* foal, colt; ⊕ skid; slide-way.

poulaine [pu'lɛn] *f* ⚓ head; *hist. souliers m/pl. à la* ~ shoes with long pointed toes.

poularde *cuis.* [pu'lard] *f* fowl; fat (-tened) pullet; **poule** [pul] *f* hen; *cuis.* fowl; *games*, *a. fencing*: pool; *races*: sweepstake; F girl; F tart, prostitute; ~ *d'Inde* turkey-hen; F ~ *mouillée* milksop; *fig. chair f de* ~ goose-flesh; **poulet** [pu'lɛ] *m* chicken; F love-letter; *sl.* copper (− *policeman*); **poulette** [pu'lɛt] 1. *su./f zo.* pullet; F girl; 2. *adj.*: *cuis. sauce f* ~ sauce of butter, yolk of egg and vinegar.

pouliche *zo.* [pu'liʃ] *f* filly.

poulie ⊕ [pu'li] *f* pulley; block; driving wheel.

pouliner [puli'ne] (1a) *v/i.* foal.

poulot *m*, **-otte** *f* F [pu'lo, ˌ'lɔt] darling, pet (*addressing children*).

poulpe *zo.* [pulp] *m see pieuvre*.

pouls ⚕ [pu] *m* pulse; *prendre le* ~ *à q.* feel *s.o.*'s pulse; F *fig. tâter le* ~ *à q.*

sound *s.o.*; F *se tâter le* ~ reflect, hesitate.

poumon [pu'mɔ̃] *m anat.* lung; ⚕ ~ *d'acier* iron lung.

poupard [pu'paːr] *m* baby in long clothes; baby-doll.

poupe ⚓ [pup] *f* stern, poop; *avoir le vent en* ~ ⚓ have the wind astern; *fig.* have the wind in one's sails, be on the road to success.

poupée [pu'pe] *f* doll; puppet; F chick (= *girl*); bandaged finger.

poupin, e [pu'pɛ̃, ˌ'pin] chubby; *visage* ~ baby face.

poupon *m*, **-onne** *f* F [pu'pɔ̃, ˌ'pɔn] baby; **pouponner** F [pupɔ'ne] (1a) *v/t.* coddle (*a child etc.*); **pouponnière** [ˌ'njɛːr] *f* babies' room (*in day-nursery*); day-nursery; infants' nursery.

pour [puːr] 1. *prp.* for (*s.o.*, *this reason*, *negligence*, *ten dollars*, *the moment*, *Christmas*, *ever*); on account of, because of, for the sake of; instead of; in favo(u)r of; considering; as; (al)though, in spite of, for; calculated *or* of a nature to (*inf.*); about to (*inf.*); ✝ per (*cent*); *du respect* ~ consideration for; *prendre* ~ take for; *passer* ~ be looked upon as; *see partir*; ~ *le plaisir (la vie)* for fun (life); ~ *ma part* as for me; ~ *moi* in my opinion; ~ *(ce qui est de) cela* as far as that goes; *see amour*; *il fut puni* ~ *avoir menti* he was punished for lying *or* because he had lied; ~ *être riche il ... though* he is rich he ...; in spite of being rich he ...; *être* ~ (*inf.*) be on the point of (*ger.*); ~ *affaires* on business; ~ *de bon* seriously, in earnest; ~ *le moins* at least; ~ *ainsi dire* so to speak, as it were; ~ *important qu'il soit* however important it may be; ~ *peu que* (*sbj.*) if ever (*ind.*); however little (*ind.*); ~ *que* (*sbj.*) so *or* in order that; *être* ~ *beaucoup (peu) dans qch.* play a big (small) part in s.th.; *être* ~ be in favo(u)r of; *sévère* ~ hard on, strict with; 2. *su./m*: *le* ~ *et le contre* the pros *pl.* and cons *pl.*

pourboire [pur'bwaːr] *m* tip, gratuity.

pourceau [pur'so] *m* pig, hog, swine.

pour-cent ✝ [pur'sɑ̃] *m/inv.* percentage, rate per cent; **pourcen-**

tage † [~sɑ̃'taːʒ] *m* percentage; rate.
pourchasser [purʃa'se] (1a) *v/t.*
pursue; *fig.* chase; hound (*a debtor etc.*).

pourfendeur *iro.* [purfɑ̃'dœːr] *m* destroyer; **pourfendre** *iro.* [~'fɑ̃ːdr] (4a) *v/t.* attack, fight (against).

pourlécher F [purle'ʃe] (1f) *v/t.*: se ~ lick; se ~ *les babines* lick one's chops.

pourparlers [purpar'le] *m/pl.* (*diplomatic*) talks, negotiations; ✕ parley *sg.*

pourpoint *cost.* † [pur'pwɛ̃] *m* doublet.

pourpre [purpr] **1.** *su./f* dye, robe, *a. fig.*: purple; *su./m* dark red, crimson; ♂ purpura; **2.** *adj.* dark red, crimson, purple; **pourpré, e** [pur'pre] crimson; purple.

pourquoi [pur'kwa] **1.** *adv.*, *cj.* why; *c'est* ~ therefore; that's why; **2.** *su./m/inv.*: *le* ~ the reason (for, de).

pourrai [pu're] *1st p. sg. fut. of* pouvoir 1.

pourri, e [pu'ri] **1.** *adj.* rotten (with, de) (*fruit, wood, a. fig.*); bad (*egg, meat*); addled (*egg*); dank (*air*); damp (*weather*); putrid (*flesh*); **2.** *su./m* rotten part, bad patch (*of fruit etc.*); **pourrir** [~'riːr] (2a) *vt/i.* rot; *v/i.* go bad *or* rotten; rot (away) (*wood etc.*); addle (*egg*); *fig.* ~ *en prison* rot in goal; **pourriture** [~ri'tyːr] *f* decay, rot(ting); putrefaction; *fig.* rottenness, corruption.

poursuite [pur'sɥit] *f* pursuit (*a. fig.*); chase; ~*s pl.* legal action *sg.*; prosecution *sg.*; **poursuivant, e** [~sɥi'vɑ̃, ~'vɑ̃ːt] **1.** *su.* pursuer; ⚖ plaintiff; prosecutor; **2.** *adj.* prosecuting; **poursuivre** [~'sɥiːvr] (4ee) *v/t.* pursue (*a.* ✕, *a. fig.*); *fig.* continue, go on with; ⚖ sue (*s.o.*); prosecute (*s.o.*).

pourtant [pur'tɑ̃] *cj.* nevertheless, (and) yet.

pourtour [pur'tuːr] *m* periphery; precincts *pl.*; *thea.* gangway round the stalls; *avoir cent mètres de* ~ be 100 metres round.

pourvoi ⚖ [pur'vwa] *m* appeal; petition (for mercy, *en grâce*); **pourvoir** [~'vwaːr] (3m) *v/t.* provide, supply, furnish (with, de); ⚖ *se* ~ appeal (to the Supreme Court, *en cassation*); *se* ~ *en grâce* petition

for mercy; *v/i.*: ~ *à* provide for; ~ *à un emploi* fill a post; **pourvoyeur** *m*, **-euse** *f* [~vwa'jœːr, ~'jøːz] provider; caterer; contractor. [(that).﹚
pourvu [pur'vy] *cj.*: ~ *que* provided﹚
poussah [pu'sa] *m* toy: tumbler; *fig.* pot-bellied man.

pousse [pus] *f* leaves, hair, etc.: growth; *teeth*: cutting; ✿ (*young*) shoot; *wine*: ropiness; **~-café** F [~ka'fe] *m/inv.* liqueur (*after coffee*), F chaser; **~-cailloux** ✕ *sl.* [~ka'ju] *m/inv.* foot-slogger (= *infantrymen*); **poussé, e** [pu'se] advanced; extensive, thorough (*studies etc.*); highly developped; elaborate; exaggerated; **poussée** [~] *f* ⊕, ✕ thrust; *phys.* pressure (*a. business*); *fig.* push, shove; *fig.* upsurge; ✿ growth; ♂ outbreak; ✿ growth; **pousse-pousse** [pus'pus] *m/inv.* rickshaw (*in the East*); push-chair; **pousser** [pu'se] (1a) *v/t.* push, shove; push (*the door*) to, push (*a bolt*) across; drive (*a tunnel*); jostle (*s.o.*); *fig.* carry (to, *jusqu'à*); *fig.* urge on (*a crowd, a horse*); incite (*a crowd, s.o.*); *fig.* utter (*a cry*), heave (*a sigh*); extend (*one's studies*); push (*s.o.*) on; ✿ put forth (*roots, leaves*); *se* ~ push o.s. forward; push one's way to the front; *v/i.* push, apply pressure; ✿ grow (*a. hair etc.*); *fig.* make one's way, push on; **poussette** [~'sɛt] *f* game: push-pin; baby-carriage; push-chair.

poussier [pu'sje] *m* coal-dust; **poussière** [~'sjɛːr] *f* dust; speck of dust; *water*: spray, spindrift; ✿ ~ *fécondante* pollen; *mordre la* ~ bite the dust; F *fig.* 300 F et des ~s threehundred odd francs; **poussiéreux, -euse** [~'sje'rø, ~'røːz] dusty; dust-colo(u)red.

poussif, -ve [pu'sif, ~'siːv] broken-winded (*horse etc.*); F shortwinded (*person*).

poussin [pu'sɛ̃] *m* chick; *cuis.* spring chicken; **poussinière** [~si'njɛːr] *f* chicken-coop; incubator.

poussoir [pu'swaːr] *m* electric bell, clock, etc.: push; ⊕, *mot.* push-rod; ✕ *machine-gun*: button.

poutrage △ [pu'traːʒ] *m* framework, beams *pl.*; **poutre** △ [puːtr] *f* beam; joist; *metal*: girder; **poutrelle** △ [pu'trɛl] *f* small beam; girder.

pouvoir [pu'vwaːr] **1.** (3h) v/t. be able; can; be possible; cela se peut bien it is quite possible; il se peut que (sbj.) it is possible that (ind.); puis-je? may I?; n'en ~ plus be worn out; be at the end of one's resources; **2.** su./m power; en mon (son etc.)~ (with)in my (his etc.) power.

pragmatique [pragma'tik] **1.** adj. pragmatic; **2.** su./f hist. Pragmatic Sanction; **pragmatisme** [~'tism] m pragmatism.

prairie [prɛ'ri] f meadow; grassland, Am. prairie.

praline cuis. [pra'lin] f burnt almond; praline; **praliner** cuis. [~li'ne] (1a) v/t. brown, crisp (almonds).

praticable [prati'kabl] practicable; feasible (idea, plan); negotiable, passable (road etc.); **praticien** m, -enne f [~sjɛ̃, ~'sjɛn] ✍, ꭗꭜ practitioner; practician; **pratiquant, e** eccl. [~'kɑ̃, ~'kɑ̃ːt] practising (Catholic etc.), churchgoing; **pratique** [pra'tik] **1.** adj. practical; convenient; useful; **2.** su./f practice (a. eccl.); habit, use; experience; mettre en ~ put into practice; **pratiquer** [~ti'ke] (1m) v/t. practise (✍, ꭗꭜ, a. a religion, etc.); exercise (a profession); put into practice (a rule, virtues, etc.); carry out; ⚠ make, cut (a hole, a path, etc.); se ~ be the practice.

pré [pre] m (small) meadow.

pré... [~] pre...; prae..., ante..., fore...

préalable [prea'labl] **1.** adj. previous; preliminary; **2.** su./m prerequisite, (pre)condition; † preliminary; au ~ = **préalablement** [~labla'mɑ̃] first, beforehand.

préambule [preɑ̃'byl] m preamble (to, de).

préau [pre'o] m yard; school: covered playground.

préavis [prea'vi] m previous (or advance) notice; warning; donner son ~ give (one's) notice.

prébende eccl. [pre'bɑ̃ːd] f prebend.

précaire [pre'kɛːr] precarious; delicate (health); **précarité** [~kari'te] f precariousness.

précaution [preko'sjɔ̃] f precaution; caution; care; avec ~ cautiously; warily; **précautionner** [~-'sjɔ'ne] (1a) v/t. warn, caution; se ~ contre take precautions against.

précédemment [preseda'mɑ̃] adv.

previously, before; **précédent, e** [~'dɑ̃, ~'dɑ̃ːt] **1.** adj. preceding, previous, prior; former; **2.** su./m precedent; ꭗꭜ ~s pl. case-law sg.; sans ~ unprecedented; **précéder** [~'de] (1f) v/t. precede; go before; fig. take precedence over, have precedence of.

précepte [pre'sɛpt] m precept; **précepteur** m, -trice f [presɛp-'tœːr, ~'tris] tutor; teacher; **préceptoral, e,** m/pl. -aux [~tɔ'ral, ~'ro] tutorial; **préceptorat** [~tɔ-'ra] m tutorship.

prêche [prɛːʃ] m protestantism: sermon; fig. protestantism; **prêcher** [prɛ'ʃe] (1a) v/t. preach (a. fig.); preach to (s.o.); v/i. preach; fig. ~ à q. de (inf.) exhort s.o. to (inf.); ~ d'exemple (or par l'exemple) set an example; **prêcheur** m, -euse f fig. [~'ʃœːr, ~'ʃøːz] sermonizer; **prêchi-prêcha** F [~ʃipre'ʃa] m preachifying.

précieux, -euse [pre'sjø, ~'sjøːz] **1.** adj. precious; valuable; fig. affected (style etc.); **2.** su. affected person; **préciosité** [~sjozi'te] f preciosity, affectation.

précipice [presi'pis] m precipice.

précipitamment [presipita'mɑ̃] adv. in a hurry, headlong; **précipitation** [~ta'sjɔ̃] f (violent) haste, hurry, precipitancy; 🜍 phys., meteor. precipitation; **précipité, e** [~'te] **1.** adj. precipitate; hasty; ✍ racing (pulse); headlong (flight); **2.** su./m 🜍 etc. precipitate; **précipiter** [~'te] (1a) v/t. throw (down); hurl (down); fig. plunge (into war, despair, etc.); quicken, hasten; precipitate (events, a. 🜍); se ~ rush (at, upon sur).

précis, e [pre'si, ~'siːz] **1.** adj. precise, accurate, exact; definite (explanation, reason, time); à dix heures ~es at ten o'clock precisely or F sharp; **2.** su./m summary, précis, abstract; **précisément** [presize'mɑ̃] adv. of précis 1; **préciser** [~'ze] (1a) v/t. state precisely; define; specify; make clear; se ~ become clear(er); **précision** [~'zjɔ̃] f precision, accuracy, exactness; ~s pl. detailed information sg., particulars.

précité, e [presi'te] above(-mentioned), aforesaid.

précoce [pre'kɔs] precocious (child, talent, a. ♀); early (♀, a. season); fig.

premature; **précocité** [‿kɔsi'te] f precocity; earliness.

précompte ✝ [pre'kɔ̃:t] m previous deduction; **précompter** [‿kɔ̃'te] (1a) v/t. deduct beforehand.

préconçu, e [prekɔ̃'sy] preconceived; idée f ‿e preconception.

préconiser [prekɔni'ze] (1a) v/t. recommend; advocate.

préconstruction △ [prekɔ̃stryk-'sjɔ̃] f prefabrication.

précontraint, e ⊕ [prekɔ̃'trɛ̃, ‿'trɛ̃:t] prestressed (concrete).

précurseur [prekyr'sœ:r] **1.** su./m forerunner, precursor; harbinger (of spring); **2.** adj./m premonitory.

prédécesseur [predesɛ'sœ:r] m predecessor.

prédestination [predɛstina'sjɔ̃] f predestination; **prédestiné, e** [‿'ne] foredoomed; fig. fated (to, à); **prédestiner** [‿'ne] (1a) v/t. predestine (to, à) (a. fig.).

prédicateur m, **-trice** f [predika-'tœ:r, ‿'tris] preacher; **prédication** [‿'sjɔ̃] f preaching; sermon.

prédiction [predik'sjɔ̃] f prediction; forecast; **prédire** [‿'di:r] (4p) v/t. predict, prophesy, foretell; forecast.

prédisposer 💰, a. fig. [predispo'ze] (1a) v/t. predispose; ‿ contre prejudice (s.o.) against (s.o.); **prédisposition** 💰, a. fig. [‿zi'sjɔ̃] f predisposition.

prédominance [predɔmi'nɑ̃:s] f predominance, prevalence; **prédominant, e** [‿'nɑ̃, ‿'nɑ̃:t] predominant, prevalent, prevailing; **prédominer** [‿'ne] (1a) v/i. predominate, prevail (over, sur); v/t. take pride of place over.

prééminence [preemi'nɑ̃:s] f preeminence (over, sur); **prééminent, e** [‿'nɑ̃, ‿'nɑ̃:t] pre-eminent.

préemption [preɑ̃p'sjɔ̃] f preemption; droit m de ‿ preemptive right.

préexistant, e [preɛksis'tɑ̃, ‿'tɑ̃:t] pre-existent, pre-existing.

préfabriqué, e [prefabri'ke] prefabricated; maison f ‿e prefab (-ricated house); **préfabriquer** [‿] (1m) v/t. prefabricate.

préface [pre'fas] f preface (a. eccl.); foreword, introduction (to à, de); **préfacer** [‿fa'se] (1k) v/t. write a preface to.

préfectoral, e, m/pl. **-aux** [prefɛk-tɔ'ral, ‿'ro] prefectorial; of the or a prefect; **préfecture** [‿'ty:r] f hist. prefectship; hist, a. admin. prefecture; admin. Paris police headquarters pl.

préférable [prefe'rabl] preferable (to, à), better (than, à); **préférence** [‿'rɑ̃s] f preference (a. ✝); 💰💰 priority; de ‿ in preference (to, à), preferential (tariff), ✝ preference (shares); **préférer** [‿'re] (1f) v/t. prefer.

préfet [pre'fɛ] m hist., a. admin. prefect; civil administrator; ‿ de police chief commissioner of the Paris police; ‿ des études school: master in charge of discipline; ⚓ ‿ maritime port-admiral; **préfète** F [‿'fɛt] f prefect's wife.

préfixe gramm. [pre'fiks] m prefix; **préfixer** [‿fik'se] (1a) v/t. fix (a date etc.) in advance; gramm. prefix.

préhistoire [preis'twa:r] f prehistory; **préhistorique** [‿tɔ'rik] prehistoric.

préjudice [preʒy'dis] m prejudice, harm; wrong, damage; 💰💰 tort; au ‿ de to the detriment of; sans ‿ de without prejudice to; **préjudiciable** [preʒydi'sjabl] prejudicial, detrimental (to, à); 💰💰 tortious; **préjudiciaux** 💰💰 [‿'sjo] adj./m/pl.: frais m/pl. ‿ security sg. for costs; **préjudiciel, -elle** 💰💰 [‿'sjɛl] interlocutory; **préjudicier** [‿'sje] (1o) v/i. be prejudicial or detrimental (to, à); ‿ à injure.

préjugé [preʒy'ʒe] m prejudice; bias; presumption; 💰💰 (legal) precedent; sans ‿s unprejudiced; **préjuger** [‿] (1l) v/t. (or v/i.: ‿ de) prejudge, judge in advance.

prélasser F [prela'se] (1a) v/t.: se ‿ lounge, loll (in a chair etc.); strut.

prélat eccl. [pre'la] m prelate.

prélèvement [prelɛv'mɑ̃] m previous deduction; deduction, amount deducted; blood, gas, ore, etc.: sample; **prélever** [prel've] (1d) v/t. deduct in advance; levy; take (a sample [a. 💰 of blood]) (from, à).

préliminaire [prelimi'nɛ:r] **1.** adj. preliminary (to, de); **2.** su./m preliminary; ‿s pl. document: preamble sg.

prélude ♩, a. fig. [pre'lyd] m prel-

ude; **préluder** [ˌly'de] (1a) v/i. ♪
(play a) prelude; fig. ~ à lead up to,
serve as prelude to.

prématuré, e [prematy're] premature, untimely; **prématurément**
[ˌre'mɑ̃] adv. of prématuré.

préméditation [premedita'sjɔ̃] f
premeditation; avec ~ wilfully; 🏛
with malice aforethought; **prémédité, e** [ˌ'te] deliberate; **préméditer** [ˌ'te] (1a) v/t. premeditate.

prémices [pre'mis] f/pl. first fruits;
cattle: firstlings; † fig. beginnings.

premier, -ère [prə'mje, ˌ'mjɛːr]
1. adj. first (time, place, position,
rank); fig. leading, best; title: the
first; ⅍ prime (number); admin.
etc. principal, head (clerk); former
(of two); mot. ˌère vitesse f first or
low gear; ~ livre m school: primer;
pol. ~ ministre m Prime Minister;
au ~ coup at the first attempt; ce
n'est pas le ~ venu he isn't just anybody; le ~ venu the first comer; les
cinq ˌs pl. the first five; Napoléon
Iᵉʳ Napoleon I, Napoleon the
First; partir le ~ be the first to
leave; **2.** su./m first; first, Am. second floor; en ~ in the first place;
thea. jeune ~ leading man; le ~ du
mois the first of the month; su./f
secondary school: (approx.) sixth
form; thea. first night or performance; cin., a. fig. première; mot. first
(gear); 🚃 first class (carriage); thea.
jeune ˌère leading woman; 🚢 voyager
en ˌère travel first (class); **premièrement** [ˌmjɛr'mɑ̃] adv. first; in the
first place; **premier-né, premier-
née** or **première-née**, m/pl.
premiers-nés [ˌmje'ne, ˌmjɛr'ne]
adj., a. su./m first-born.

prémilitaire [premilitɛːr] premil-
itary (training).

prémisse [pre'mis] f logic: premise,
premiss.

prémonition [premɔni'sjɔ̃] f pre-
monition; **prémonitoire** 🩺
[ˌ'twaːr] premonitory.

prémunir [premy'niːr] (2a) v/t. put
(s.o.) on his guard, forewarn (s.o.)
(against, contre); se ~ take precautions (against, contre).

prenable [prə'nabl] pregnable; **prenant, e** [ˌ'nɑ̃, ˌ'nɑ̃ːt] captivating;
absorbing; † partie f ˌe payee;
recipient.

prénatal, e, m/pl. **-als** or **-aux**
25*

[prena'tal, ˌ'to] prenatal, antenatal.

prendre [prɑ̃ːdr] (4aa) **1.** v/t. take
(a. lessons, a degree, a road, ✂ a
town), grasp; catch (fire, a cold,
the train), trap (a rat); steal; seize;
accept; eat (a meal), have (tea, a
meal); pick up; engage (a servant);
take (up) (time); handle, treat; 🌾
choose; buy (a ticket); ✂ conquer;
✂ etc. capture; ~ à mentir catch
(s.o.) in a lie; ~ corps put on weight;
~ en amitié take to (s.o.); ⚓ ~ le
large put to sea; ~ mal misunder-
stand; take (s.th.) badly; ~ plaisir à
take pleasure in; ~ pour take (s.o.)
for; ~ q. dans sa voiture give s.o. a
lift; ~ rendez-vous avec make an
appointment with; ~ sur soi take
(s.th.) upon o.s.; pour qui me pre-
nez-vous? what do you take me
for?; se laisser ~ let o.s. be taken
in; se ~ be caught; cling (to, à);
set (liquid); curdle (milk); se ~ à
undertake (a task), begin; fig. s'en
~ à find fault with (s.o.); fig. s'y ~
manage, go about things; **2.** v/i.
set (plaster etc.); congeal, freeze;
curdle (milk); cuis. thicken; cuis.
catch (milk in pan); take root (tree);
take (fire); fig. be successful; ça ne
prend pas that cock won't fight;
preneur m, **-euse** f [prə'nœːr,
ˌ'nøːz] taker; 🏛 lessee; 🌾 buyer,
purchaser; chèque: payee; **prennent** [prɛn] 3rd p. pl. pres. of prendre.

prénom [pre'nɔ̃] m first or Christian
name, Am. given name; **prénom-
mé, e** [prenɔ'me] above-named;
prénommer [ˌ] (1a) v/t.: se ~ be
called.

prenons [prə'nɔ̃] 1st p. pl. pres. of
prendre.

préoccupation [preɔkypa'sjɔ̃] f pre-
occupation; anxiety, concern; **préoccuper** [ˌ'pe] (1a) v/t. preoccupy;
worry, trouble; se ~ de concern o.s.
with; be concerned about, worry or
care about.

préparateur m, **-trice** f [prepara-
'tœːr, ˌ'tris] preparer; experiments:
demonstrator; assistant; **préparatifs** [ˌ'tif] m/pl. preparations; **préparation** [ˌ'sjɔ̃] f preparation (a.
🩺 etc.) (for, à); preparing; ⊕ dressing; typ. ouvrage m en ~ work to
appear shortly; **préparatoire** [ˌ-
'twaːr] preparatory (a. school); preliminary; **préparer** [prepa're] (1a)

v/t. prepare (for, *à*); train (*for a career*); coach (*a pupil*); prepare for (*an examination*); draw up (*a speech*); ⊕ dress; make (*tea etc.*); se ~ prepare (o.s.) (for, *à*); get ready; *fig.* be in the wind, be brewing (*event*).

prépondérance [prepɔ̃deˈrɑ̃:s] *f* preponderance (over, *sur*); *avoir la* ~ preponderate; **prépondérant, e** [~ˈrɑ̃, ~ˈrɑ̃:t] preponderant; leading (*part, role*); casting (*vote*).

préposé *m,* **e** *f* [prepoˈze] official in charge; employee, attendant; postman, *Am.* mailman; **préposer** [~] (1a) *v/t.* appoint (as *comme, pour*; to, *à*).

préposition *gramm.* [prepoziˈsjɔ̃] *f* preposition; **prépositionnel, -elle** *gramm.* [~sjɔˈnɛl] prepositional.

pré(-)retraite [prerəˈtrɛt] *f* early retirement.

prérogative [prerɔgaˈtiːv] *f* prerogative; *parl.* privilege.

près [prɛ] **1.** *adv.* near, close (at hand); *à beaucoup* ~ by far; *à cela* ~ except for that; *à cela* ~ *que* except that; *à peu de chose* ~ little short of; *à peu* ~ nearly; about; *fig. au plus* ~ to the nearest point; *de* ~ closely; from close to; (*fire*) at close range; *ici* ~ near by, quite near, close at hand; *regarder de plus* ~ take a closer look, examine more closely; *tout* ~ very near, quite close; **2.** *prp.* near; to; *ambassadeur m* ~ *le Saint-Siège* ambassador to the Holy See; ~ *de* near, close to (*Paris, the station*), by; nearly (*two hours, two o'clock, ten pounds, three miles*), almost; ⚓ *courir* ~ *du vent* sail close to the wind; *il était* ~ *de tomber* he was on the point of falling.

présage [preˈzaːʒ] *m* portent, foreboding; omen; **présager** [~zaˈʒe] (1l) *v/t.* portend, bode; foresee.

pré-salé, *pl.* **prés-salés** [presaˈle] *m* salt-marsh sheep; *cuis.* salt-marsh mutton.

presbyte 🩺 [prezˈbit] *adj.*, *a. su.* long-sighted; **presbytéral, e**, *m/pl.* **-aux** [prezbiteˈral, ~ˈro] priestly; **presbytère** *eccl.* [~ˈtɛːr] *m* presbytery; *protestantism:* vicarage, rectory, *Sc.* manse; **presbytie** 🩺 [~ˈsi] *f* long-sightedness.

prescience [preˈsjɑ̃:s] *f* foreknowledge.

préscolaire [preskɔˈlɛːr] preschool.
prescriptible 🏛 [preskripˈtibl] prescriptible; **prescription** [~ˈsjɔ̃] *f* ⊕, *admin.* regulation(s *pl.*); 🏛 prescription; ⊕~s *pl.* specifications; **prescrire** [presˈkriːr] (4q) *v/t.* prescribe (*s.o.'s conduct, a rule, a.* 🩺), lay down (*the law, a time, s.o.'s conduct, etc.*); 🏛 bar (*by statute of limitations etc.*); 🏛 *se* ~ *par* be barred at the end of (*5 years*).

préséance [preseˈɑ̃:s] *f* precedence (of, over *sur*).

présélection [preselɛkˈsjɔ̃] *f* preselection.

présence [preˈzɑ̃:s] *f* presence (at, *à*); ~ *d'esprit* presence of mind; *en* ~ face to face (with, *de*); *faire acte de* ~ put in *or* enter an appearance.

présent¹, e [preˈzɑ̃, ~ˈzɑ̃:t] **1.** *adj.* present (at, *à*); current; ~! present!; *esprit m* ~ ready wit; *gramm.* *temps m* ~ present (tense); **2.** *su./m* present (time *or gramm.* tense); *à* ~ just now, at present; *les* ~*s pl.* exceptés present company *sg.* excepted; *pour le* ~ for the time being, for the present; *quant à* ~ as for now; *su./f: la* ~*e* this letter.

présent² [preˈzɑ̃] *m* present, gift; *faire* ~ *de* make a present of; **présentable** F [prezɑ̃ˈtabl] presentable; **présentateur** *m,* **-trice** *f* [~taˈtœːr, ~ˈtris] presenter; *show, etc.:* host, emcee; **présentation** [~taˈsjɔ̃] *f* 🩺, ✝, 🩺, *eccl., thea., court:* presentation; introduction (to s.o., *à q.*); ⚔ trooping (the colo[u]r, *du drapeau*); ✝ *à* ~ on demand, at sight.

présentement ✝ [prezɑ̃tˈmɑ̃] *adv.* now, this minute; at present.

présenter [prezɑ̃ˈte] (1a) *v/t.* present (*a.* ⚔, ✝, *a.* difficulties, ⚔ *arms*), offer; show; introduce (*formally*); nominate (*a candidate*) (for, *pour*); produce (*one's passport*); *parl.* table (*a bill*); submit (*a conclusion*); *cin. etc.* ~ *q.* (*en vedette*) star s.o.; *je vous présente ma femme* may I introduce my wife?; *se* ~ appear; arise (*problem, question*); occur; present o.s.; ⚔ report (o.s.); introduce o.s.; *se* ~ *chez q.* call on s.o.; *se* ~ *bien* (*mal*) look good (not too good); *v/i.:* ~ *bien* (*mal*) have a pleasant (an unattractive) appearance; **présentoir** [~ˈtwaːr] *m* display stand *or* shelf.

préservateur, -trice [prezɛrva-'tœːr, ~'tris] preserving (from, *de*); **préservatif, -ve** [~'va'tif, ~'tiːv] **1.** *adj.* preservative; **2.** *su./m* preservative; ♂ condom; **préservation** [~va'sjɔ̃] *f* preservation, protection; **préserver** [~'ve] (1a) *v/t.* preserve, protect (from, *de*).

présidence [prezi'dãːs] *f* presidency; President's house; † board; ✝, *a.* admin. chairmanship; **président** *m, e f* [~'dã, ~'dãːt] president; *admin.* chairman; ⚖ presiding judge; **présidentiel, -elle** [~dã-'sjɛl] **1.** *adj.* presidential; **2.** *su./f pol.* ~*les pl.* presidential elections; **présider** [~'de] (1a) *v/t.* preside over *or* at (*s.th.*); *fig.* direct; *v/i.*: ~ *à* preside at *or* over.

présomptif, -ve [prezɔ̃p'tif, ~'tiːv] presumptive; ⚖ *héritier m* ~ heir apparent; **présomption** [~'sjɔ̃] *f* presumption (*a.* ⚖, *a. fig. pej.*); **présomptueux, -euse** [~'tɥø, ~'tɥøːz] presumptuous; self-conceited, self-important.

presque [presk(ə)] *adv.* almost, nearly; **presqu'île** *geog.* [pres'kil] *f* peninsula.

pressage ⊕ [pre'saːʒ] *m* pressing; **pressant, e** [~'sã, ~'sãːt] pressing, urgent; earnest (*request*); **presse** [pres] *f* ⊕, *journ., typ.* press; pressing-machine; crowd, throng; haste; *business*: pressure; *exemplaire m du service de* ~ review copy; *heures f/pl. de* ~ rush hours; *sous* ~ in the press (*book*); **pressé, e** [pre'se] hurried (*style, words*); in a hurry (*person*); crowded, close; ⊕ pressed; urgent (*letter, task*); *citron m* ~ (fresh) lemon squash; **presse-bouton** [presbu'tɔ̃] *adj./inv.* push-button; automatic; **presse-citron** [pressi-'trɔ̃] *m/inv.* lemon-squeezer; **presse-étoffe** [~e'tɔf] *m/inv.* sewing-machine: presser-foot; **presse-étoupe** ⊕ [~e'tup] *m/inv.* stuffing box.

pressentiment [presãti'mã] *m* presentiment; foreboding; F feeling, *Am.* hunch; **pressentir** [~'tiːr] (2b) *v/t.* have a presentiment of; sound (*s.o.*) (out) (on, *sur*); *faire* ~ foreshadow (*s.th.*).

presse...: ~**pantalon** [prespãta'lɔ̃] *m/inv.* trouser-press; ~**papiers** [~pa'pje] *m/inv.* paper-weight;

~**-purée** [~py're] *m/inv.* potato-masher.

presser [pre'se] (1a) *v/t.* press (*a.* ⊕, *a. fig.*), squeeze; hasten (one's steps, *le pas*); hurry (*s.o.*); push on, urge on (*a horse etc.*); *cuis.* squeeze; *se* ~ crowd, press; throng; hurry, hasten; *v/i.* press; be urgent; *rien ne presse* there is no hurry.

pressing [prɛ'siŋ] *m* (steam) pressing.

pression [prɛ'sjɔ̃] *f* pressure (*a.* ⊕, *meteor., mot., a. fig.*); *cost.* snap fastener; ♂ ~ *artérielle* blood pressure; *bière f à la* ~ draught (*Am.* draft) beer; *faire* ~ *sur* press (*s.th.*) down, press (down) on (*s.th.*); *fig. a.* exercer *une* ~ *sur* put pressure on (*s.o.*), pressurize (*s.o.*); **pressoir** [~'swaːr] *m* (wine- *etc.*)press; **pressurage** [presy'raːʒ] *m* pressing; F *fig.* extortion; **pressurer** [~'re] (1a) *v/t.* press (*grapes*); press out (*juice*); F *fig.* extort money from; **pressureur** [~'rœːr] *m* pressman; **pressuriser** [~ri'ze] (1a) *v/t.* pressurize.

prestance [prɛs'tãːs] *f* fine presence, commanding appearance; **prestataire** [~ta'tɛːr] *su.* person receiving benefits *or* allowances; ~ *de services* service(s) (*trade etc.*); **prestation** [~ta'sjɔ̃] *f* dues: prestation; *money*: lending; (*insurance-*)benefit; service; *sp., thea. etc., a. fig.* performance; ⚖ ~ *de serment* taking (of) the oath; ~*s pl. en nature* allowances in kind.

preste [prɛst] nimble, quick; F ~! quick!; **prestesse** [prɛs'tɛs] *f* quickness, nimbleness; alertness.

prestidigitateur [prɛstidiʒita'tœːr] *m* conjurer; juggler; **prestidigitation** [~'sjɔ̃] *f* conjuring, sleight of hand; juggling.

prestige [prɛs'tiːʒ] *m* prestige; *fig.* influence; **prestigieux, -euse** [~ti-'ʒjø, ~'ʒjøːz] prestigious.

présumable [prezy'mabl] presumable; **présumer** [~'me] (1a) *v/t.* presume; assume; *il est à* ~ *que* the presumption is that; *trop* ~ *de* overestimate (*s.th.*); *trop* ~ *de soi* be too presuming.

présure [pre'zyːr] *f* rennet.

prêt[1] [prɛ] *m* loan; *wages*: advance; ⚔ pay; ~ *à intérêt* loan at interest; ~ *sur gage* loan against security.

prêt[2], **prête** [prɛ, prɛt] ready (for

s.th., *à qch.*; to *inf.*, *à inf.*); prepared; ~ *à* on the verge of.

pretantaine F [pretɑ̃'tɛn] *f: courir la* ~ gad about.

prêt-à-porter [prɛtapɔr'te] *m coll.* ready-to-wear *or* ready-made clothes *pl. or* clothing.

prêt-bail, *pl.* **prêts-baux** *pol.* [prɛ-'ba:j], ~'bo] *m* lease-lend, lend-lease.

prétendant, e [pretɑ̃'dɑ̃, ~'dɑ̃:t] *su.* candidate (for, *à*); *su./m* pretender (*to throne*); suitor; **prétendre** [~'tɑ̃:dr] (4a) *v/t.* claim; assert, affirm, maintain; intend; *v/i.* lay claim (to, *à*); aspire (to, *à*); **prétendu, e** [~tɑ̃'dy] **1.** *adj.* alleged; *pej.* so-called; **2.** *su.* F (*my*) intended.

prête-nom *usu. pej.* [prɛt'nɔ̃] *m* man of straw, figure-head, F front.

pretentaine [pretɑ̃'tɛn] *f see pretantaine.*

prétentieux, -euse [pretɑ̃'sjø, ~'sjø:z] pretentious; conceited; **prétention** [~'sjɔ̃] *f* pretension (*a. fig.*), claim; *fig.* conceit.

prêter [prɛ'te] (1a) *v/t.* lend, *Am.* loan; take (*an oath*); attribute; *fig.* credit (s.o. with s.th., *qch. à q.*); ~ *à* impart to; *se* ~ *à* lend o.s. to; be a party to; *v/i.* give (*gloves etc.*); ~ *à* give rise to.

prétérit *gramm.* [prete'rit] *m* (*English*) preterite.

prêteur *m*, **-euse** *f* [prɛ'tœ:r, ~'tø:z] lender; ~ *sur gages* pawnbroker; ₤ pledgee.

prétexte [pre'tɛkst] *m* pretext, excuse; *prendre* ~ *que* put forward as a pretext that; *sous* ~ *que* on the plea *or* under the pretext that; **prétexter** [~tɛks'te] (1a) *v/t.* plead; allege; give (*s.th.*) as a pretext.

prétoire [pre'twa:r] *m hist.* praetorium; ₤ court.

prêtraille † *pej.* [prɛ'trɑ:j] *f* priests *pl.*; shavelings *pl.*; **prêtre** [prɛtr] *m* priest; ~*-ouvrier* worker priest; **prêtresse** [prɛ'trɛs] *f* priestess; **prêtrise** [~'tri:z] *f* priesthood.

preuve [prœ:v] *f* proof (*a.* A, ₤, *fig.*); ₤, *a. fig.* evidence; signs *pl.*; *faire* ~ *de* show, display; *faire la* ~ *de* prove; *faire ses* ~*s* prove o.s. *or* itself.

preux † [prø] **1.** *adj.* valiant, gallant; **2.** *su./m/inv.* valiant knight.

prévaloir [preva'lwa:r] (3l) *v/i.* prevail (against, *sur*); *faire* ~ make good (*a claim, one's right*), win people over

to (*an idea, an opinion*); *v/t.*: *se* ~ *de* take advantage of; exercise (*a right*); pride o.s. on.

prévaricateur, -trice [prevarika-'tœ:r, ~'tris] **1.** *adj.* unjust; **2.** *su.* unjust judge; person guilty of a breach of trust; **prévarication** [~ka'sjɔ̃] *f* maladministration of justice; breach *or* abuse of trust; **prévariquer** [~'ke] (1m) *v/i.* be unjust (*judge*); betray one's trust.

prévenance [prev'nɑ̃:s] *f* kindness, (kind) attention; **prévenant, e** [~'nɑ̃, ~'nɑ̃:t] kind, attentive, considerate (to, *envers*); prepossessing (*manners etc.*); **prévenir** [~'ni:r] (2h) *v/t.* forestall; prevent (*an accident, danger, illness*); anticipate (*a wish*); warn; *admin.* inform, give notice; prepossess; *pej.* prejudice; **préventif, -ve** [prevã'tif, ~'ti:v] ❀, *a.* ₤ preventive; deterrent (*effect*); ₤ *détention f* ~ve remand in custody, detention awaiting trial; **prévention** [~'sjɔ̃] *f* prevention; prepossession, *pej.* prejudice; ₤ custody; ~ *routière* road safety; **préventionnaire** ₤ [~sjɔ-'nɛ:r] *su.* prisoner on remand; **préventorium** ❀ [~to'rjɔm] *m* observation sanatorium; **prévenu, e** [prev-'ny] **1.** *p.p. of prévenir*; **2.** *adj.* prepossessed; prejudiced; **3.** *su.* accused; prisoner.

prévisible [previ'zibl] foreseeable; **prévision** [~'zjɔ̃] *f* forecast (*a. meteor.*); anticipation; expectation; **previsionnel, -elle** [~zjɔ'nɛl] forward-looking; **previsionniste** † [~zjɔ'nist] *su.* forecaster.

prévoir [pre'vwa:r] (3m) *v/t.* forecast (*a. the weather*), foresee, anticipate; plan, provide for; lay down (*s.th.*) (in advance).

prévôt [pre'vo] *m* ₤, *a. hist.* provost; ✗ assistant provost marshal; ~ *de salle fencing:* assistant fencing-master; **prévôté** [~vo'te] *f hist.* provostship; *hist.* provostry; ✗ military police (establishment *or* service).

prévoyance [prevwa'jɑ̃:s] *f* foresight; precaution; ~ *sociale* national insurance; *mesures f/pl. de* ~ precautionary measures; *société f de* ~ provident society; **prévoyant, e** [~'jɑ̃, ~'jɑ̃:t] provident; careful, cautious; far-sighted.

prie-Dieu [pri'djø] *m/inv.* prayer stool, prie-Dieu, praying-desk; **prier** [✓'e] (1a) *v/t.* pray; ask, entreat, beg, beseech; invite (*to dinner etc.*); *je vous* (en) *prie!* please (do)!; don't mention it!; *les priés m/pl.* the guests; *sans se faire* ✓ willingly, readily; *se faire* ✓ require pressing, need persuading; **prière** [✓'ɛːr] *f* prayer; request, entreaty; ✓ *de* (ne pas) (*inf.*) please (do not) (*inf.*).

prieur *eccl.* [pri'œːr] *m* prior; **prieure** *eccl.* [✓'œːr] *f* prioress; **prieuré** [✓œ're] *m* priory; priorship.

primaire [pri'mɛːr] primary; simplistic; simple-minded (*person*).

primat [pri'ma] *m eccl.* primate; *fig.* pre-eminence; **primates** *zo.* [✓'mat] *m/pl.* primates; **primatie** *eccl.* [✓ma'si] *f* primacy; **primauté** [✓mo'te] *f* primacy (*a. eccl.*); priority.

prime¹ [prim] *f* ✝ premium; ✝ subsidy; ✝, ⊕ bonus; ✝ free gift; *fig. faire* ✓ be highly appreciated.

prime² [prim] **1.** *adj.* ♣ prime; *fig.* first; ✓ *jeunesse* earliest youth; *de* ✓ *abord* at first; *de* ✓ *saut* at the first attempt; **2.** *su./f eccl., a. fencing:* prime.

primer¹ [pri'me] (1a) *v/i.* prevail; have priority; ⊕, *a. astr.* prime; *v/t.* surpass; take precedence of; have *or* take priority over; *la force prime le droit* might is right.

primer² [✓] (1a) *v/t.* award a prize to; ✝ give a bonus to.

primerose ♀ [prim'roːz] *f* hollyhock.

primesautier, -ère [primso'tje, ✓-'tjɛːr] impulsive; ready.

primeur [pri'mœːr] *f* ✝ freshness, newness; ✓*s pl.* ✓ early vegetables *or* fruit; *avoir la* ✓ *d'une nouvelle* be the first to hear a piece of news; **primeuriste** ✓ [✓mœ'rist] *m* grower of early vegetables *or* fruit.

primevère ♀ [prim'vɛːr] *f* primula; primrose.

primitif, -ve [primi'tif, ✓'tiːv] primitive; first, early; original, pristine; *gramm.* primary (*tense*).

primo [pri'mo] *adv.* first, in the first place; **primogéniture** [✓mɔ-ʒeni'tyːr] *f* primogeniture.

primordial, e, *m/pl.* **-aux** [primɔr'djal, ✓'djo] primordial; *fig.* of primary importance.

prince [prɛ̃ːs] *m* prince.

princeps [prɛ̃'sɛps] *adj.:* *édition f* ✓ first edition.

princesse [prɛ̃'sɛs] *f* princess; **princier, -ère** [✓'sje, ✓'sjɛːr] princely.

principal, e, *m/pl.* **-aux** [prɛ̃si'pal, ✓'po] **1.** *adj.* principal (*fig., a.* ♣, ♪, *gramm.*), chief, main; **2.** *su./m school:* head(master); *admin.* chief clerk; ✝ principal; *fig.* main thing; **principalat** [✓pa'la] *m school:* headship; **principat** *hist.* [✓'pa] *m* principate; **principauté** [✓po'te] *f* principality.

principe [prɛ̃'sip] *m* principle; *en* ✓ in principle; *par* ✓ on principle; *sans* ✓*s* unprincipled (*person*).

printanier, -ère [prɛ̃ta'nje, ✓'njɛːr] spring...; **printemps** [✓'tɑ̃] *m* spring; springtime (*a. fig.*); *fig.* heyday.

priorat [prio'ra] *m* priorate, priorship.

prioritaire [priɔri'tɛːr] **1.** *adj.* having priority, priority...; **2.** *su.* priority-holder; **priorité** [✓'te] *f* priority; *mot. a.* right of way; *de* ✓ *mot.* major (*road*); ✝ preference (*shares*).

pris¹ [pri] *1st p. sg. p.s. of prendre*.

pris², e [pri, priːz] **1.** *p.p. of prendre;* **2.** *adj.:* *bien* ✓ well-proportioned (*figure*), well-built (*man*); ✓ *de sommeil* drowsy.

prise [priːz] *f* hold, grip (*a. fig.*), grasp; ⚒ taking (*a. phot.*); ⚒ *town:* capture; ⚓ prize; ⊕ *machine:* mesh, engagement; ✝ *parcels:* collection; *cement etc.:* setting; *snuff:* pinch; *fish:* catch; ⊕ *ore:* sample; *analysis:* specimen, sample; ⊕ *air, steam, etc.:* intake; ✓ *d'air* ⊕ air-inlet; ✈ *air scoop;* ✓ *d'eau* intake of water; tap, cock; *hydrant;* ⚒ water-crane; F ✓ *de bec* squabble; ⚖ ✓ *de corps* arrest; ⚡ ✓ *de courant* wall-plug, socket, power point; *trolley:* current collector; ✓ *de sang* blood specimen; ⚡ ✓ *de terre* earth-connection; ✓ *de vues* taking of photographs, photography; *cin.* shooting; *avoir* ✓ *sur* have a hold over *or* on; *fig. donner* ✓ *à* lay ✓. to; *en* ✓ ⊕ engaged, in gear; ⚓ holding (*anchor*); *fig. en* ✓ *directe avec* in close contact with, in touch with; *être aux* ~*s avec* be at grips with; *faire* ~ set (*cement*); *faire une* ~ *à* (*or sur*) tap (*river*, ⚓ *coil, cable*); *lâcher* ~ let go; F *fig.* give in.

prisée 🖤 [pri'ze] *f* valuation; appraisal.

priser[1] [pri'ze] (1a) *v/t.* inhale, snuff, take; *v/i.* take snuff.

priser[2] [~] (1a) *v/t.* value, appreciate, prize.

priseur[1] *m*, **-euse** *f* [pri'zœːr, ~'zøːz] snuff-taker.

priseur[2] 🖤 [pri'zœːr] *m goods*: appraiser; valuer.

prismatique [prisma'tik] prismatic; **prisme** [prism] *m* prism.

prison [pri'zɔ̃] *f* prison; gaol, *Am.* jail; ✗, ⚓ cell(s *pl.*); imprisonment, ✗ F cells *pl.*; **prisonnier, -ère** [~zɔ'nje, ~'njɛːr] 1. *su.* prisoner; *se constituer* ~ give o.s. up (to the police); 2. *adj.* ✗ captive; 🖤 imprisoned.

privatif, -ve *gramm.* [priva'tif, ~'tiːv] *adj.*, *a. su./m* privative; **privation** [~'sjɔ̃] *f* 🖤, ✗, *fig.* deprivation, loss; *fig.* privation; 🖤 forfeiture.

privautés *pej.* [privo'te] *f/pl.* familiarity *sg.*, liberties.

privé, e [pri've] 1. *adj.* private; 2. *su./m* private life; private sector; *en* ~ privately; in private life.

priver [pri've] (1a) *v/t.* deprive; *se* ~ *de* do without; stint o.s. of.

privilège [privi'lɛːʒ] *m* privilege; **privilégier** [~le'ʒje] (1o) *v/t.* privilege; favo(u)r, prefer, give preference to.

prix [pri] *m* price, cost; value (*a. fig.*); prize; reward; *sp.* challenge-cup race, prize race, stakes *pl.*; ✝ *exchange*: rate; ~ *courant* market or current price; price-list; ~ *de revient* cost price; ~ *de vente* selling price; ~ *fait* (*or fixe*) fixed price; ~ *fort* list price; ~ *homologué* established price; ~ *régulateur* standard of value; ~ *unique* one-price store; ~ *unitaire* unit-price; *à* ~ *d'ami* cheap; *à aucun* ~ not at any price, on no account; *à tout* ~ at all costs; *à vil* ~ at a low price, F dirt cheap; *dernier* ~ lowest price, F rock-bottom price; *faire un* ~ quote a price (to, *à*); *hors de* ~ at ransom prices; ~ *fixe* F [~'fiks] *m* restaurant with a fixed-price meal.

pro F [pro] *m* pro(fessional).

probabilité [prɔbabili'te] *f* probability (*a.* 🅰); *selon toute* ~ in all probability; **probable** [~'babl] probable, likely.

probant, e 🖤 *etc.* [prɔ'bɑ̃, ~'bɑ̃ːt] probative; conclusive; **probation** [~ba'sjɔ̃] *f* probation; **probatoire** [~ba'twaːr] probative; **probe** [prɔb] honest; of integrity (*man*); **probité** [prɔbi'te] *f* probity, integrity.

problématique [prɔblema'tik] 1. *adj.* problematical; questionable; 2. *su./f* problem(s *pl.*); **problème** [~'blɛm] *m* problem (*a.* 🅰, *a. fig.*); puzzle.

procédé [prɔse'de] *m fig.* proceeding; conduct; *billiard cue*: tip; ⊕ process; ~*s pl.* behaviour *sg.*; *bons* ~*s pl.* civilities; *manquer aux* ~*s* be ill-mannered; **procéder** [~'de] (1f) *v/i.* proceed (from, *de*); 🖤 against, *contre*; to, *à*); arise (from, *de*); act; **procédure** [~'dyːr] *f* procedure (*a.* 🖤); 🖤 proceedings *pl.*

procès [prɔ'sɛ] *m* 🖤 (legal) proceedings *pl.*; legal action; trial; ~ *civil* (law)suit; ~ *criminel* (criminal) trial; **processif, -ve** [~sɛ'sif, ~'siːv] litigious; procedural (*form*).

procession [prɔse'sjɔ̃] *f eccl. etc.* procession; parade; *fig.* cars, visitors: string; **processionnaire** *zo.* [prɔsɛsjɔ'nɛːr] 1. *adj.* processionary; 2. *su./f zo.* processionary caterpillar; **processional** *eccl.* [~'nal] *m* processional; **processionnel, -elle** [~'nɛl] processional (*hymn etc.*); **processionnellement** [~nɛl'mɑ̃] *adv.* in procession.

processus [prɔse'sys] *m anat., a. fig.* process; progress; method.

procès-verbal 🖤 [prɔsɛvɛr'bal] *m* official report, statement; *mot.* parking ticket; *meeting*: proceedings *pl.*; *dresser* (*un*) ~ *contre q.* make a report on s.o., take s.o.'s name and address; *mot.* book (*a motorist*).

prochain, e [prɔ'ʃɛ̃, ~'ʃɛn] 1. *adj.* next (*in a series*); nearest; near; impending (*departure, storm, etc.*); 2. *su./m* neighbo(u)r, fellow-creature; **prochainement** [~ʃɛn'mɑ̃] *adv.* soon, shortly; **proche** [prɔʃ] 1. *adj.* near, close; 2. *adv.*: *de* ~ *en* ~ by degrees; 3. *su./m*: ~*s pl.* relatives.

proclamation [prɔklama'sjɔ̃] *f* proclamation; *faire une* ～ issue a proc-lamation; **proclamer** [～'me] (1a) *v/t.* proclaim (*a. fig.*); declare, announce.   [create.]

procréer [prɔkre'e] (1a) *v/t.* pro-

procuration [prɔkyra'sjɔ̃] *f* ♱, *a.* ⚖ procuration, power of attorney; *par* ～ by proxy *or* procuration; **procurer** [～'re] (1a) *v/t. a. se* ～ obtain, get, procure; **procureur** [～'rœːr] *m* ⚖ procurator, proxy; *eccl.* bursar; ⚖ attorney; ⚲ *de la République* (*approx.*) Public Prosecutor, *Am.* district attorney; ～ *général* (*approx.*) Attorney General.

prodigalité [prɔdigali'te] *f* prodigality; extravagance, lavishness.

prodige [prɔ'diːʒ] **1.** *su./m* prodigy; marvel (*a. fig.*); **2.** *adj.*: *enfant mf* ～ infant prodigy; **prodigieux, -euse** [～di'3jø, ～'3jøːz] prodigious, stupendous.

prodigue [prɔ'dig] **1.** *adj.* prodigal (*a. pej.*); lavish (of, with *de*), profuse (in, *de*); spendthrift; *bibl.* *l'enfant m* ～ the Prodigal Son; **2.** *su.* spendthrift, prodigal; **prodiguer** [～di'ge] (1m) *v/t.* lavish; be unsparing of; squander; *se* ～ set out to please.

prodrome [prɔ'droːm] *m* prodrome (to, *de*); ⚕ premonitory symptom; *fig.* preamble (to, *de*).

producteur, -trice [prɔdyk'tœːr, ～'tris] **1.** *adj.* productive (of, *de*); producing; ⊕ generating (*apparatus*); **2.** *su.* producer; ✓ *a.* grower; **productible** [～'tibl] producible; **productif, -ve** [～'tif, ～'tiːv] productive, fruitful; **production** [～'sjɔ̃] *f* production (*a.* ⚖, ♩, ⊕, *cin.*); ♩, gas, steam: generation; ⊕ output; product; ⚖ growth; **productivité** [～tivi'te] *f* productivity; **produire** [prɔ'dɥiːr] (4h) *v/t.* produce (*a.* ⚖ *evidence, a. cin.*); ♱, ✓ yield; ⊕ turn out (*products*); generate (♩, gas, steam); *fig.* give rise to; *fig.* bring about; *se* ～ take place, happen, occur; **produit** [～'dɥi] *m* 兑, ⊕, ♒ product; ✓ produce; proceeds *pl.* (*of sale*), receipts *pl.*; ♱ yield; ～ *accessoire* (*or secondaire*) by-product; ～ *d'un capital* yield of a capital sum; ♱ ～ *manufacturé* manufacture(d product); ♱ ～ *national brut* gross national product; ♱ ～ *ouvré* finished article.

proéminence [prɔemi'nɑ̃ːs] *f* prominence; protuberance; **proéminent, e** [～'nɑ̃, ～'nɑ̃ːt] prominent; projecting.

profanateur *m*, **-trice** *f* [prɔfana-'tœːr, ～'tris] desecrator; **profanation** [～'sjɔ̃] *f* desecration; **profane** [prɔ'fan] **1.** *adj.* profane; secular (*history, art, theatre, etc.*); sacrilegious; impious; **2.** *su.* layman (*a. fig.*); F *fig.* outsider; **profaner** [～fa'ne] (1a) *v/t.* profane; desecrate (*a church, a tomb*); *fig.* degrade (*one's talent etc.*).

proférer [prɔfe're] (1f) *v/t.* utter; pour forth (*insults*).

professer [prɔfɛ'se] (1a) *v/t.* profess; be a professor of (*a subject*); practise (*law, medicine, etc.*); **professeur** [～'sœːr] *m* teacher, master; (*a. femme f* ～) secondary school: mistress; *univ.* professor, lecturer; ～ *d'athéisme* avowed *or* open atheist; **profession** [～'sjɔ̃] *f eccl.*, *a. fig.* profession; occupation; trade; *de* ～ by profession; *fig.* habitual (*drunkard*); *sans* ～ of private means (*person*); **professionnaliser** [～sjɔna-lize] (1a) *v/t.*: *se* ～ become *or* go professional; acquire (a) professional character; **professionnel, -elle** [～sjɔ'nɛl] **1.** *adj.* professional; vocational; ⚕ occupational (*disease*); *enseignement m* ～ vocational training; **2.** *su. usu. sp.* professional; **professorat** [～sɔ'ra] *m* secondary school: post of teacher; *univ.* professorship; *coll.* teaching profession, teachers *pl.*; *univ.* professoriate.

profil [prɔ'fil] *m* profile; outline; △ *etc.* section; *geog.* contour; **profilé, e** [prɔfi'le] **1.** *adj.* ✈, ⚓, *mot.* streamlined; **2.** *su./m* ⊕, *mot., etc.* section; **profiler** [～] (1a) *v/t.* ⊕ shape; draw (*s.th.*) in section; profile; *mot.* streamline; *se* ～ be silhouetted (against *contre, sur, à*).

profit [prɔ'fi] *m* ♱ profit (*a. fig.*); *fig.* advantage, benefit; ♱ ～*s pl. et pertes f/pl.* profit *sg.* and loss *sg.*; *mettre qch. à* ～ turn s.th. to account, take advantage of s.th.; **profitable** [prɔfi'tabl] profitable, advantageous; **profiter** [～'te] (1a) *v/i.* profit (by, *de*); *fig.* grow, thrive; *fig.* wear well (*material etc.*), be economical; ～ *à q.* benefit s.o.; be profitable to s.o.; ～ *de* take advantage of, make the most of; **profiteur** *pej.* [ˌ‿'tœːr] *m* profit-taker; F profiteer; F ‿ *de guerre* war profiteer.

profond, e [prɔ'fɔ̃, ‿'fɔ̃ːd] **1.** *adj.* deep (*a. fig. sigh, sleep*); *fig.* profound; **2.** *profond adv.* deep; **3.** *su./m* depth(s *pl.*); *au* ‿ *de la nuit* in the dead of night; **profondément** [ˌ‿fɔ̃de'mɑ̃] *adv. of profond 1*; **profondeur** [ˌ‿fɔ̃-'dœːr] *f* depth (*a. fig.*); *en* ‿ in depth; thorough(going); in-depth.

profus, e [prɔ'fy, ‿'fyːz] profuse; **profusément** [prɔfyze'mɑ̃] *adv. of profus*; **profusion** [‿'zjɔ̃] *f* profusion; abundance; *fig.* lavishness; *fig. à* ‿ lavishly.

progéniture [prɔʒeni'tyːr] *f* progeny, offspring.

prognose ⚕ [prɔg'noːz] *f* prognosis.

programme [prɔ'gram] *m* programme, *Am.* program (*a. pol., radio, data processing*); *pol.* platform; *univ. etc.* examination: syllabus; ‿ *des auditeurs radio*: request program(me); ‿ *d'études* curriculum; **programmateur, -trice** [prɔgrama'tœːr, ‿'tris] *su. radio (person), su./m data processing (machine)*: programmer; **programmation** [ˌ‿ma'sjɔ̃] *f radio, data processing*: programming; **programmer** [‿'me] *vt/i.* (1a) *data processing, etc.*: program; *fig. a.* plan; **programmeur** *m*, **-euse** *f* [‿'mœːr, ‿'møːz] *data processing (person)*: programmer.

progrès [prɔ'grɛ] *m* progress; advancement; *faire des* ‿ progress, make headway; **progresser** [prɔ-grɛ'se] (1a) *v/i.* progress, make headway, advance; *fig.* improve; **progressif, -ve** [‿'sif, ‿'siːv] progressive; forward; gradual; graduated (*tax*); **progression** [‿'sjɔ̃] *f* progress; progression (*a.* ♬); advance(ment); increase; **progressiste** *pol.* [‿'sist] *adj., a. su.* progressive.

prohiber [prɔi'be] (1a) *v/t.* forbid, prohibit; *hunt. temps m prohibé* close season; **prohibitif, -ve** [prɔi-bi'tif, ‿'tiːv] prohibitive (*price etc.*); prohibitory (*law etc.*); **prohibition** [‿'sjɔ̃] *f* prohibition; ‿*s pl. de sortie* ban *sg.* on exports; **prohibition-niste** [ˌ‿sjɔ'nist] *adj., a. su./m* prohibitionist.

proie [prwa] *f* prey (*a. fig.*); *être en* ‿ *à* be a prey to, be consumed by (*hatred etc.*), be tortured by (*pains, remorse, etc.*).

projecteur [prɔʒɛk'tœːr] *m* projector; floodlight; spot(light); searchlight; **projectif, -ve** [‿'tif, ‿'tiːv] projective; **projectile** [‿'til] *adj., a. su./m* projectile; missile; **projection** [‿'sjɔ̃] *f* projection (*a.* △, ♬); △ plan; (lantern) slide; **projecture** △ [‿'tyːr] *f* projection.

projet [prɔ'ʒɛ] *m* project, plan; draft; scheme; *parl.* ‿ *de loi* government bill; *état m de* ‿ planning stage; **projeter** [prɔʒ'te] (1c) *v/t.* project; throw; cast (*a shadow*); *fig.* plan, contemplate, intend; *se* ‿ stand out; be cast (*shadow*); jut out (*cliff etc.*).

prolétaire *pol.* [prɔle'tɛːr] *m* proletarian; **prolétariat** [ˌ‿ta'rja] *m coll.* proletariate; **prolétarien, -enne** [ˌ‿ta'rjɛ̃, ‿'rjɛn] proletarian.

prolifération [prɔlifera'sjɔ̃] *f* proliferation; **proliférer** [‿fe're] (1f) *v/i.* proliferate; **prolifique** [‿'fik] prolific.

prolixe [prɔ'liks] prolix, diffuse; F *fig.* long-winded; **prolixité** [ˌ‿liksi-'te] *f* prolixity; F *fig.* verbosity.

prologue [prɔ'lɔg] *m* prolog(ue) (*to, de*).

prolongation [prɔlɔ̃ga'sjɔ̃] *f time*: prolongation; *leave, stay, ticket*: extension; *sp.* extra time; **prolonge** ⚔ [prɔ'lɔ̃ːʒ] *f* ammunition waggon; lashing-rope; **prolongement** [ˌ‿lɔ̃ʒ'mɑ̃] *m space*: prolongation; extension; **prolonger** [ˌ‿lɔ̃'ʒe] (1l) *v/t.* prolong, extend (*in time or space*); ⚕ protract (*a disease*); ♬ produce (*a line*); ⚓ coast (along); *se* ‿ continue; extend; be protracted.

promenade [prɔm'nad] *f* walk(ing); stroll (*on foot*), drive (*in a car*), sail (*in a boat*), ride (*on a bicycle*); trip, excursion; *place*: promenade, avenue; ⚔ ‿ (*militaire*) route march; *faire une* ‿ go for *or* take a walk; **promener** [‿'ne] (1d) *v/t.* take (*s.o.*) for a walk *or* a drive etc.; exercise (*an animal*); take, conduct; *fig.* run (*one's hand, one's eyes*) (*over, sur*); cast (*one's mind, one's thoughts*) (*over, sur*); *envoyer* ‿ *q.* send s.o. about his business; *se* ‿ walk, go for a walk *or* ride etc.; *fig.* rove, wander (*eyes, gaze*); *va te* ‿! get away with you!; **promeneur** *m*,

-euse *f* [\\'nœːr, \\'nøːz] walker, stroller; tripper; *thea.* promenader; **promenoir** [\\'nwaːr] *m* promenade, covered walk; ♪ promenade deck; ♣ lobby.

promesse [prɔ'mɛs] *f* promise; assurance; ✝ promissory note; *manquer à sa* ~ break one's promise; **prometteur, -euse** [\\~me'tœːr, \\~'tøːz] **1.** *adj.* free with his (her, *etc.*) promises; *fig.* promising, full of promise, attractive; **2.** *su.* person free with his (her) promises, ready promiser; **promettre** [\\'mɛtr] (4v) *v/t.* promise (*a. fig.*); *fig.* bid fair to (*inf.*); *se* ~ *qch.* promise o.s. s.th.; look forward to s.th.; *v/i.* look *or* be promising; **promis, e** [\\'mi, \\~'miːz] **1.** *p.p. of* promettre; **2.** *adj.* promised; engaged (*to be married*); *la terre* ~e the Promised Land (*a. fig.*); **3.** *su.* betrothed, F intended.

promiscuité [prɔmiskɥi'te] *f* promiscuity; *en* ~ promiscuously.

promission *bibl., a. fig.* [prɔmi'sjɔ̃] *f*: *la terre de* ~ the Promised Land.

promontoire *geog.* [prɔmɔ̃'twaːr] *m* promontory; headland.

promoteur, -trice [prɔmɔ'tœːr, \\~'tris] **1.** *adj.* promoting; **2.** *su.* promoter; (*a.* ~*-constructeur*, ~ *de construction*) property developer; ✝ ~ *de ventes* sales promoter; **promotion** [\\~mɔ'sjɔ̃] *f* promotion; *school:* class (= *year*); *coll.* persons *pl.* promoted; ✝ special offer; ✝ ~ *des ventes* sales promotion; ✝ *en* ~ on special offer; ~ *ouvrière or sociale* rise in the social scale, social advancement; **promotionnel, -elle** ✝ [\\~mɔsjɔ'nɛl] promotion(al); **promouvoir** [\\~mu-'vwaːr] (3f) *v/t.* promote.

prompt, prompte [prɔ̃, prɔ̃ːt] prompt, quick, speedy, ready; ~ *à se décider* quick to make up one's mind; **promptitude** [prɔ̃ti'tyd] *f* promptness, promptitude, quickness; readiness.

promu, e [prɔ'my] *p.p. of* promouvoir.

promulgation [prɔmylga'sjɔ̃] *f law:* promulgation; *decree:* publication; **promulguer** [\\~'ge] (1m) *v/t.* promulgate (*a law*); publish, issue (*a decree*).

prône *eccl.* [proːn] *m* sermon; **prôner** [pro'ne] (1a) *v/t. eccl.* preach to; *fig.* extol, crack (*s.th., s.o.*) up; read (*s.o.*) a lecture, scold; **prôneur** *m*, **-euse** *f* [\\'nœːr, \\~'nøːz] extoller, *sl.* booster.

pronom *gramm.* [prɔ'nɔ̃] *m* pronoun; **pronominal, e,** *m/pl.* **-aux** *gramm.* [\\~nɔmi'nal, \\~'no] pronominal.

prononçable [prɔnɔ̃'sabl] pronounceable; **prononcé, e** [\\~'se] **1.** *adj.* pronounced (*a. fig.*); *fig.* marked; **2.** *su./m* ♣ decision; **prononcer** [\\~'se] (1k) *v/t.* pronounce; ♣ pass (*sentence*); make (*a. a speech*); *fig.* mention (*a name*); *mal* ~ mispronounce (*a word etc.*); *se* ~ give one's opinion *or* decision; come to a decision (on, about *sur*); be pronounced (*word*); *v/i.* pronounce; ~ *sur* rule upon, adjudicate upon (*a question*); ♣ give one's verdict on; **prononciation** [\\~sja-'sjɔ̃] *f gramm.* pronunciation; ♣ *sentence:* passing; *verdict:* bringing in; *speech:* delivery.

pronostic [prɔnɔs'tik] *m* prognostic(ation); forecast; *turf:* (*tipster's*) selection; ⚕ prognosis; **pronostiquer** [\\~ti'ke] (1m) *v/t.* foretell; ⚕ prognose, give a prognosis; forecast (*the weather*); **pronostiqueur** *m*, **-euse** *f* [\\~ti'kœːr, \\~'køːz] prognosticator.

propagande [prɔpa'gãːd] *f* propaganda; publicity; advertising; *de* ~ propaganda ...; **propagandisme** [\\~gã'dism] *m* propagandism; **propagandiste** [\\~gã'dist] *su.* propagandist.

propagateur, -trice [prɔpaga'tœːr, \\~'tris] **1.** *adj.* propagating; **2.** *su.* propagator; *news, germs, etc.*: spreader; **propagation** [\\~ga'sjɔ̃] *f* propagation, spread(ing); *phys.* ~ *des ondes* wave propagation; **propager** [\\~'ʒe] (11) *v/t.* propagate (*biol., phys., a. fig.*); spread (*news, germs*); *fig.* popularize; *se* ~ propagate; spread; *phys.* be propagated.

propane ♫ [prɔ'pan] *m* propane.

propension [prɔpã'sjɔ̃] *f* propensity, tendency.

prophète [prɔ'fɛt] *m* prophet, seer; *fig.* prophesier; **prophétesse** [prɔ-fe'tɛs] *f* prophetess; **prophétie** [\\~'si] *f* prophecy; **prophétique** [\\~'tik] prophetic; **prophétiser** [\\~ti'ze] (1a) *v/t.* prophesy, foretell.

prophylactique ✇ [prɔfilak'tik] prophylactic; **prophylaxie** ✇ [ˌˈsi] f prophylaxis; prevention of disease.

propice [prɔ'pis] propitious (to, *à*; for s.th., *à qch.*); favo(u)rable (to, *à*).

propitiation [prɔpisja'sjõ] f propitiation; **propitiatoire** [ˌˈtwaːr] propitiatory; F *don m ~ sop* (to Cerberus).

proportion [prɔpɔr'sjõ] f proportion (with, *avec*); ratio; *fig. ~s pl.* size *sg.*, dimensions; *à ~ que* in proportion as; *en ~ de* in proportion or relation to; **proportionnel, -elle** [ˌsjɔ'nɛl] 1. *adj.* proportional; A̸ *moyenne f ~elle* mean proportional; 2. *su./f* A̸ proportional; **proportionner** [ˌsjɔ'ne] (1a) *v/t.* proportion or adjust or adapt (to, *à*); *bien proportionné* well-proportioned.

propos [prɔ'po] m purpose; topic; remark; convenience; *~ pl.* talk *sg.*; *à ~* relevant, pertinent, timely; *à ~!* by the way!; *à ~ de* about; regarding, concerning, in connection with; *à ~ de rien* for no reason at all; *à ce ~* in this connection; *à tout~* at every (end and) turn; *changer de ~* change the subject; *hors de ~* irrelevant (*comment*); ill-timed; *juger à ~* think fit; *mal à ~* inopportunely, at the wrong moment; **proposable** [prɔpo'zabl] worthy of consideration; **proposer** [ˌˈze] (1a) *v/t.* propose; suggest; offer (*a solution, money*); put forward (*a candidate, s.o. as a model*); *se ~* propose or offer o.s. (as, *comme*); *se ~ de* (*inf.*) propose or intend to (*inf.*); *se ~ pour* (*inf.*) offer to (*inf.*); **proposition** [ˌzi'sjõ] f offer, proposal; A̸, *phls.*, ♪ proposition; *gramm.* clause; motion (*to be voted upon*).

propre [prɔpr] 1. *adj.* proper, correct; peculiar (to, *à*); characteristic (of, *à*); own; fit, able (to, *à*) calculated (to, *à*); clean; neat; housetrained, *Am.* housebroken (*animal*); toilet-trained, clean (*child*); *~ à rien* good for nothing; *~ maison f* own house; *maison f ~* clean house; *en ~s termes* in so many words; 2. *su./m* nature, characteristic, peculiarity; *gramm.* literal sense; *~ à rien* good-for-nothing; *iro. c'est du ~!* that's a fine thing!; **propret, -ette** † [prɔ'prɛ, ~'prɛt] neat, tidy; **propreté** [ˌprə'te] f cleanness; neatness; cleanliness.

propriétaire [prɔprie'tɛːr] *su./m* proprietor, owner; landlord; *su./f* landlady; proprietress; **propriété** [ˌˈte] f property (*a. phys.*); estate; ownership; *fig.* characteristic, property; *language, words, etc.*: correctness; *~ immobilière* real estate; *~ littéraire* copyright.

proprio F [prɔpri'o] m proprietor; owner; landlord.

propulser [prɔpyl'se] (1a) *v/t.* propel; ✇ *propulsé par réaction* rocket-powered; **propulseur** [ˌˈsœːr] 1. *adj./m* propulsive, propelling, propellent; 2. *su./m* propeller; **propulsif, -ve** [ˌˈsif, ˌˈsiːv] propulsive, propelling; **propulsion** [ˌˈsjõ] f propulsion; *~ par réaction* rocket-propulsion.

prorata [prɔra'ta] m/inv. proportion; *au ~* pro rata (*payment*); *au ~ de* in proportion to, proportionately to.

prorogation [prɔrɔga'sjõ] f *parl.* prorogation; ⚖ etc. extension of time; *fig.* prolongation; **proroger** [ˌˈʒe] (1l) *v/t. parl.* adjourn, prorogue; ⚖, ✝ extend (*a time-limit*), prolong.

prosaïque [prɔza'ik] prosaic; *fig.* unimaginative, dull; **prosaïsme** [ˌˈism] m prosaic style; *fig.* dullness; **prosateur** [ˌˈtœːr] m prose-writer.

proscription [prɔskrip'sjõ] f proscription; banishment; *fig.* abolition; **proscrire** [ˌˈkriːr] (4q) *v/t.* proscribe; *fig.* abolish; *fig.* forbid; **proscrit** m, e f [ˌˈkri, ˌˈkrit] proscript, outlaw, exile.

prose [proːz] f prose; *eccl.* sequence.

prosélyte [prɔze'lit] m proselyte.

prospecter [prɔspɛk'te] (1a) *v/t.* ⚒ prospect; ✝ canvass; **prospecteur** ⚒ etc. [ˌˈtœːr] m prospector; **prospectif, -ve** [ˌˈtif, ˌˈtiːv] 1. *adj.* prospective; forward-looking; 2. *su./f* forecasting (the future); research into the future development; **prospection** [ˌˈsjõ] f ⚒ etc. prospecting; prospection; ✝ canvassing; **prospectus** [ˌˈtys] m prospectus; leaflet; brochure; handbill.

prospère [prɔs'pɛːr] prosperous, thriving; favo(u)rable (*circumstances etc.*); well-to-do (*person*); **prospé-**

rer [ˌpe're] (1f) *v/i.* prosper, thrive; succeed; **prospérité** [ˌperi'te] *f* prosperity; ✝ *vague f de* ～ boom.

prostate *anat.* [prɔ'stat] *f* prostate (gland).

prosterner [prɔstɛr'ne] (1a) *v/t.*: se ～ prostrate o.s.; bow down (before, to *devant*); F kowtow (to, *devant*).

prostituée [prɔsti'tɥe] *f* prostitute, whore; **prostituer** [ˌ'tɥe] (1a) *v/t.* prostitute (*a. fig.*); **prostitution** [ˌty'sjɔ̃] *f* prostitution (*a. fig.*).

prostration [prɔstra'sjɔ̃] *f* prostration (*a. 𝔰*); 𝔰 exhaustion; **prostré, e** [ˌ'tre] prostrate; 𝔰 exhausted.

protagoniste *thea., a. fig.* [prɔtagɔ-'nist] *m* protagonist.

protecteur, -trice [prɔtɛk'tœːr, ～'tris] **1.** *adj.* ⊕, *a. pol.* protective; protecting; *fig. pej.* patronizing; **2.** *su.* protector; patron; ～ *de l'environnement* environmentalist; **protection** [ˌ'sjɔ̃] protection (against, from *contre*); patronage, influence; wire-pulling; ～ *civile* civil defence; F *air m de* ～ patronizing air; **protectionnisme** *pol.* [ˌsjɔ'nism] *m* protectionism; **protectionniste** *pol.* [ˌsjɔ'nist] *adj., a. su.* protectionist; **protectorat** [ˌtɔ'ra] *m* protectorate.

protégé [prɔte'ʒe] *m* favo(u)rite; protégé; **protégée** [ˌte'ʒe] *f* protégée; **protège-oreilles** [ˌtɛʒɔ'rɛːj] *m/inv.* ear-protector; **protéger** [ˌte'ʒe] (1g) *v/t.* protect (from, *contre*); *fig.* be a patron of; patronize.

protéine [prɔte'iːn] *f* protein; **protéique** [ˌ'ik] protein..., proteinic.

protestant, e [prɔtɛs'tɑ̃, ～'tɑ̃ːt] *adj., a. su.* Protestant; **protestantisme** *pol.* [ˌtɑ̃'tism] *m* Protestantism; **protestataire** *pol.* [ˌta'tɛːr] *su.* objector; **protestation** [ˌta'sjɔ̃] *f* protest (against, *contre*); protestation (*of friendship, innocence, etc.*); **protester** [ˌ'te] (1a) *v/t.* protest (*a.* ✝ *a bill*); *v/i.*: ～ *contre* challenge; protest against; ～ *de qch.* protest s.th.; **protêt** [prɔ'tɛ] *m* protest.

prothèse 𝔰 [prɔ'tɛːz] *f* prosthesis; artificial limb; (*a.* ～ *dentaire*) false teeth *pl.*, denture.

prot(o)... [prɔt(ɔ)] prot(o)...

protocolaire [prɔtɔkɔ'lɛːr] formal; of etiquette; **protocole** [ˌ'kɔl] *m* protocol; ceremonial; F etiquette; *pol.* chef *m du* ～ Chief of Protocol.

prototype [prɔtɔ'tip] *m* prototype.

protubérance [prɔtybe'rɑ̃ːs] *f* protuberance; (*solar*) prominence; knob.

protuteur *m*, **-trice** *f* 𝔱 [prɔty-'tœːr, ～'tris] acting guardian.

prou [pru] *adv.*: *ni peu ni* ～ none or not at all; *peu ou* ～ more or less.

proue ⚓ [ˌ] *f* prow, bows *pl.*

prouesse [pru'ɛs] *f* prowess; ～*s pl.* exploits.

prouvable [pru'vabl] provable; **prouver** [ˌ've] (1a) *v/t.* prove.

provenance [prɔv'nɑ̃ːs] *f* source, origin; ✝ product; produce; 🚂 *en* ～ *de* from; **provenir** [ˌ'niːr] (2h) *v/i.*: ～ *de* arise from, come from; originate in.

proverbe [prɔ'vɛrb] *m* proverb; **proverbial, e** *m/pl.* **-aux** [ˌvɛr-'bjal, ～'bjo] proverbial.

providence [prɔvi'dɑ̃ːs] *f* providence; F *fig.* guardian angel; **providentiel, -elle** [ˌdɑ̃'sjɛl] providential; *fig.* opportune, heavensent.

province [prɔ'vɛ̃ːs] *f* provinces *pl.*; *fig. de* ～ provincial, *pej.* countrified; **provincial, e,** *m/pl.* **-aux** [ˌvɛ̃'sjal, ～'sjo] **1.** *adj.* provincial; *fig. pej.* countrified; **2.** *su., a. su./m eccl.* provincial.

proviseur [prɔvi'zœːr] *m* lycee: headmaster; **provision** [ˌ'zjɔ̃] *f* provision, stock, supply; *finance:* funds *pl.*, cover; 🚂 sum paid into court; *faire ses* ～*s* go shopping; *par* ～ provisional; *sac m à* ～*s* shopping-bag; **provisoire** [ˌ'zwaːr] provisional; temporary; acting (*official etc.*); **provisorat** [ˌzɔ'ra] *m* lycee: headmastership.

provocant, e [prɔvɔ'kɑ̃, ～'kɑ̃ːt] provocative (*a. fig.*); *fig.* enticing; **provocateur, -trice** [ˌka'tœːr, ～'tris] **1.** *adj.* provocative; **2.** *su.* aggressor; instigator; provoker; **provocation** [ˌka'sjɔ̃] *f* provocation; instigation; *crime:* incitement; challenge; 𝔰 *sleep etc.:* inducement; **provoquer** [ˌ'ke] (1m) *v/t.* provoke; incite (to, *à*); 𝔰 induce (*sleep etc.*); *fig.* cause, bring about; *fig.* arouse (*suspicion etc.*).

proxénète [prɔkse'nɛt] *su./m* procurer; *su./f* procuress.

proximité [prɔksimi'te] *f* proximity; nearness; ～ *de parenté* near relationship; *à* ~ near at hand; *à* ~ *de* close to.

prude [pryd] **1.** *adj.* prudish; **2.** *su./f* prude.

prudemment [pryda'mã] *adv.* of *prudent*; **prudence** [~'dã:s] *f* care-(fulness), cautiousness; prudence; discretion; wisdom; **prudent, e** [~'dã, ~'dã:t] careful, cautious; prudent; discreet; *fig.* wise, advisable (to *inf.*, *de inf.*).

pruderie [pryd'ri] *f* prudery, prudishness; **prud'homme** [~'dɔm] *m* man of integrity, *fig.* wise man; *conseil m des* ~*s* conciliation board.

prudhommerie [prydɔm'ri] *f* pomposity.

pruine [prɥin] *f* bloom (*on fruit*).

prune [pryn] **1.** *su./f* plum; F *fig. pour des* ~*s* for nothing; **2.** *adj./inv.* plum-colo(u)red; **pruneau** [pry'no] *m* prune; F ✕ (*rifle-*)bullet; *sl.* black eye; **prunelaie** [✗] [pryn'lɛ] *f* plum orchard; **prunelée** [~'le] *f* plum jam; **prunelle** [pry'nɛl] *f* ♀ sloe; ♀, *a. tex.* prunella; *anat.* eye: pupil; *fig.* apple (*of the eye*); **prunellier** ♀ [~nɛ'lje] *m* blackthorn, sloetree; **prunier** ♀ [~'nje] *m* plum-tree.

prurigineux, -euse ✗ [pryriʒi'nø, ~'nø:z] pruriginous; **prurit** ✗ [~'ri(t)] *m* pruritus, itching.

Prusse [prys] *f:* *bleu m de* ~ Prussian blue; **prussien, -enne** [pry'sjɛ̃, ~'sjɛn] *adj., a. su.* ♀ Prussian; **prussique** ✗ [~'sik] *adj.:* *acide m* ~ prussic acid.

psalmiste ✗ [psal'mist] *m* psalmist; *bibl. le* ♀ *the* Psalmist (= *king David*); **psalmodie** [~mɔ'di] *f eccl.* psalmody; intoned psalm; F *voice:* singsong; **psalmodier** [~mɔ'dje] (1o) *vt/i.* intone, chant; *v/t.* F *fig.* drone (*s.th.*) out; **psaume** [pso:m] *m* psalm; **psautier** [pso'tje] *m* psalter.

pseud(o)... [psød(ɔ)] pseud(o)...

pseudonyme [psødɔ'nim] *m* assumed name; pseudonym; nom de plume; stage name.

ps(it)t! [ps(i)t] *int.* psst!; I say!

psittacisme ✗ [psita'sism] *m* psittacism, parrotry; **psittacose** ✗ [~'ko:z] *f* psittacosis; parrot disease.

psych... [psik] psych(o)...; **~analyse** ✗ [psikana'li:z] *f* psychoanalysis;

psychanalyser [~li'ze] (1a) *v/t.* psychoanalyze; **~analyste** ✗ [~'list] *m* psychoanalyst; **~analytique** ✗ [~li'tik] psychoanalytic(al).

psyché [psi'ʃe] *f* cheval-glass.

psych...: **~iatre** [psi'kja:tr] *m* psychiatrist; **~iatrie** [psikja'tri] *f* psychiatry; **~iatrique** [~'trik] psychiatric; *hôpital m* ~ *a.* mental hospital.

psychique [psi'ʃik] psychic; **psychisme** [~'ʃism] *m* psychism.

psycho... [psikɔ] psycho...; **~logie** [~lɔ'ʒi] *f* psychology; ~ *des enfants* (*foules*) child (mass) psychology; **~logique** [~lɔ'ʒik] psychological (*a.* F *fig. moment*); **~logue** [~'lɔg] *su.* psychologist; **~pathe** ✗ [~'pat] *su.* psychopath.

psychose [psi'ko:z] *f* ✗ psychosis; obsessive fear; ~ *de guerre* war scare.

psycho...: **~somatique** [psikɔsɔma'tik] **1.** *adj.* psychosomatic; **2.** *su./f* psychosomatics *sg.*; **~thérapeute** [~tera'pø:t] *su.* psychotherapist; **~thérapie** [~tera'pi] *f* psychotherapy; **~trope** [~'trɔp] **1.** *adj.* psychotropic; **2.** *su./m* psychotropic (substance).

ptomaïne ✗, ♀ [ptɔma'in] *f* ptomaine.

pu [py] *p.p. of pouvoir* 1.

puant, e [pɥã, pɥã:t] stinking; foul (*a. fig.*); F conceited; **puanteur** [pɥã'tœ:r] *f* stench, stink.

pubère [py'bɛ:r] pubescent; **pubertaire** [~bɛr'tɛ:r] (of) puberty; adolescent; *l'âge m* ~ puberty; **puberté** [~bɛr'te] *f* puberty.

pubescent, e ♀ [pybɛ'sã, ~'sã:t] pubescent, downy.

pubien, -enne *anat.* [py'bjɛ̃, ~'bjɛn] pubic; **pubis** *anat.* [~'bis] *m* pubis.

publiable [pybli'able] publishable; **public, -que** [~'blik] **1.** *adj.* public; *la chose* ~*que* the state, the government; *la vie* ~*que* public life, politics *pl.*; *maison f* ~*que* brothel; **2.** *su./m* public; *thea. etc.* audience; *en* ~ in public; *le grand* ~ the general public; F the man in the street; **publication** [pyblika'sjɔ̃] *f* publication; publishing; *en cours de* ~ printing (*book*); **publiciste** [~'sist] *su.* publicist; public relations officer; **publicitaire** [~si'tɛ:r] **1.** *adj.* publicity-...; advertising...; promotion...; **2.** *su./m* publicity man;

publicité [~si'te] f publicity; public relations pl.; advertising; ~ aérienne sky-writing; ~ lumineuse illuminated advertising; bureau m de ~ advertising agency; exemplaires m/pl. de ~ press copies; **publier** [~'e] (1a) v/t. publish; make public; release (news); proclaim.

puce [pys] 1. su./f flea; F marché m aux ~s flea market; F secouer les ~s à give (s.o.) a good hiding; 2. adj./inv. puce.

pucelle [py'sɛl] f maiden, virgin; la ♀ (d'Orléans) the Maid of Orleans, Joan of Arc.

puceron ✔ [pys'rɔ̃] m plant-louse; aphis.

pucier sl. [py'sje] m bed.

pudeur [py'dœ:r] f modesty; decency; reserve; sans ~ shameless(ly adv.); **pudibond, e** [~di'bɔ̃, ~'bɔ̃:d] prudish; **pudicité** [~disi'te] f modesty; bashfulness; chastity; **pudique** [~'dik] modest, bashful; chaste.

puer [pɥe] (1n) v/i. stink, reek, smell; v/t. smell of; stink of.

puériculture [pɥerikyl'ty:r] f rearing of children; infant care; **puéril, e** [~'ril] puerile, childish (a. argument etc.); âge m ~ childhood; **puérilité** [~rili'te] f childishness; puerility (a. fig.).

pugilat [pyʒi'la] m pugilism; F setto, fistfight; **pugiliste** [~'list] m pugilist, boxer, F pug.

puîné, e [pɥi'ne] 1. adj. younger; 2. su./m younger brother; su./f younger sister.

puis¹ [pɥi] adv. then, afterwards, next; et ~ and then; moreover; et ~ après? what then?; what about it?, so what?

puis² [~] 1st p. sg. pres. of pouvoir 1.

puisage ⊕ [pɥi'za:ʒ] m pumping up; **puisard** [~'za:r] m ⊕ sump; **puisatier** [~za'tje] m well digger; **puiser** [~'ze] (1a) v/t. draw (from à, dans) (a. fig.); dip (into, dans).

puisque [pɥisk(ə)] cj. since, as; seeing that.

puissamment [pɥisa'mã] adv. powerfully; fig. extremely; **puissance** [~'sã:s] f fig., a. ⊕, ⚡, ⚛, eccl., pol., radio: power; force; fig. influence; ⚖, fig. authority; phys. ~ en bougies candle-power; ~ lumineuse searchlight: candle-power; pol. ~ mondiale world(-)power; **puissant, e** [~'sã, ~'sã:t] powerful; strong; weighty (argument); thick (coalseams).

puisse [pɥis] 1st p. sg. pres. sbj. of pouvoir 1.

puits [pɥi] m well; ⚒ shaft; ⊕, ⚒ pit; ~ d'aérage air-shaft; cuis. ~ d'amour cream-puff; jam-puff; fig. ~ de science person: mine of information. [sweater.]

pull-over [pyloˈvœ:r] m pullover;

pulluler [pyly'le] (1a) v/i. swarm, teem; multiply rapidly.

pulmonaire [pylmɔ'nɛ:r] 1. adj. pulmonary; 2. su./f ♣ lungwort.

pulpe [pylp] f pulp; finger etc.: pad; **pulpeux, -euse** [pyl'pø, ~'pø:z] pulpy, pulpous.

pulsatif, -ve [pylsa'tif, ~'ti:v] pulsatory; throbbing (pain); **pulsation** [~'sjɔ̃] f pulsation (a. ⚡, a. phys.); heart: throb(bing), beat (-ing); **pulsatoire** ⚔ [~'twa:r] pulsatory.

pulsion psych. [pyl'sjɔ̃] f urge, drive; ~ sexuelle sexual urge.

pulsoréacteur ✈ [pylsɔreak'tœ:r] m intermittent jet; pulsojet.

pulvérisateur [pylveriza'tœ:r] m pulverizer; spray, atomizer; liquids: vaporizer; **pulvériser** [~'ze] (1a) v/t. pulverize (a. fig. s.o.); F sp. smash (a record); mot. etc., a. fig. atomize (petrol, liquids); **pulvérulence** [pylvery'lã:s] f powderiness; dustiness; **pulvérulent, e** [~'lã, ~'lã:t] powdery; dusty.

puma zo. [py'ma] m puma, cougar.

punais, e [py'nɛ, ~'nɛ:z] 1. adj. foulsmelling; 2. su./f zo. bug; drawing-pin, Am. thumbtack.

punch [pɔ̃:ʃ] m punch.

punique hist. [py'nik] Punic; fig. foi f ~ treachery.

punir [py'ni:r] (2a) v/t. punish (with, de); **punissable** [pyni'sabl] punishable; **punition** [~'sjɔ̃] f punishment; games: forfeit.

pupillaire anat., ⚖ [pypil'lɛ:r] pupil(l)ary; **pupillarité** ⚖ [~lari'te] f wardship.

pupille¹ [py'pil] su. ⚖ ward; orphanage-child; ~ de la nation war orphan (in France).

pupille² anat. [~] f eye: pupil.

pupitre [py'pitr] m desk; ♪ (music-) stand; eccl. lectern; ⊕ ~ de commande control desk; ⚡, thea. ~ de distribution (or commutation) switch-desk.

pur, pure [pyːr] pure (*a. fig.*), spotless; *fig.* clear (*conscience etc.*); *fig.* innocent, chaste (*girl*); *fig.* sheer, downright; *zo.* ~ *sang* thoroughbred; *folie f pure* utter folly.

purée [py're] *f cuis. vegetables:* mash; mashed potatoes *pl.*; thick soup; *sl. être dans la* ~ be in the soup, be hard up.

pureté [pyr'te] *f* purity (*a. fig.*); chastity; *fig.* clearness.

purgatif, -ve [pyrga'tif, ~'tiːv] *adj., a. su./m* purgative; **purgation** [~'sjɔ̃] *f* ⚕, *eccl.* purgation; ⚕ purging; ⚕ purge; **purgatoire** *eccl.* [~'twaːr] *m* purgatory (*a. fig.*); **purge** [pyrʒ] *f* ⚕ purge (*a. pol.*), purgative; ⚖ *mortgage:* redemption; ⊕ blow-off; *tex.* cleaning; **purgeoir** ⊕ [pyr'ʒwaːr] *m* filtering-tank; **purger** [~'ʒe] (1l) *v/t.* purge (*fig., a.* ⚕), cleanse; ⚖ serve (*a sentence*); ⊕, *a. fig.* clear; se ~ take a purgative; *fig.* clear o.s.

purification [pyrifika'sjɔ̃] *f* purification (*a. eccl.*); cleansing; **purifier** [~'fje] (1o) *v/t.* purify, cleanse; refine (*metal*); ⊕ disinfect (*the air etc.*).

purin ✓ [py'rɛ̃] *m* liquid manure.

purisme [py'rism] *m* purism; **puriste** [~'rist] 1. *su.* purist; 2. *adj.* puristic.

puritain, e [pyri'tɛ̃, ~'tɛn] 1. *su.* Puritan; 2. *adj.* puritan(ical) (*a. fig.*); **puritanisme** [~ta'nism] *m* puritanism (*a. fig.*).

purpurin, e [pyrpy'rɛ̃, ~'rin] purplish; crimson. [thoroughbred.)

pur-sang [pyr'sɑ̃] *m/inv. horse:*)

purulence ⚕ [pyry'lɑ̃ːs] *f* purulence; **purulent, e** ⚕ [~'lɑ̃, ~'lɑ̃ːt] purulent; *foyer m* ~ abscess.

pus¹ ⚕ [py] *m* pus, matter.

pus² [~] *1st p. sg. p.s. of pouvoir 1.*

pusillanime [pyzilla'nim] pusillanimous; faint-hearted; **pusillanimité** [~nimi'te] *f* faint-heartedness.

pustule ⚕ [pys'tyl] *f* pustule; **pustulé, e** ⚕ [~ty'le], **pustuleux, -euse** ⚕ [~ty'lø, ~'løːz] pustulous.

putain V [py'tɛ̃] *f* whore; ~! goddamn it!

putatif, -ve [pyta'tif, ~'tiːv] putative; reputed.

putois *zo.* [py'twa] *m* polecat.

putréfaction [pytrefak'sjɔ̃] *f* putrefaction, decay; **putréfier** [~'fje] (1o) *v/t.* putrefy, rot, decompose; se ~ putrefy; **putrescence** [pytrɛ-'sɑ̃ːs] *f* putrescence; ⚕ sepsis; **putrescent, e** [~'sɑ̃, ~'sɑ̃ːt] putrescent; **putrescible** [~'sibl] liable to putrefaction; **putride** [py'trid] putrid; tainted. [*Auvergne*).)

puy *geog.* [pɥi] *m* peak (*in the*)

puzzle [pœzl] *m* jig-saw puzzle.

pygmée [pig'me] *m* pygmy.

pyjama [piʒa'ma] *m* (pair of) pyjamas *pl.*, *Am.* pajamas *pl.*

pylône [pi'loːn] *m* ⚡ pylon (*a.* ⚠), mast; ⛴, ⚒ post.

pyramidal, e, *m/pl.* **-aux** [pirami-'dal, ~'do] pyramidal; **pyramide** ⚠, ⚒ [~'mid] *f* pyramid; ~ *des âges statistics:* age pyramid.

pyrite *min.* [pi'rit] *f* pyrites.

pyro... [pirɔ] pyro...; ~**gravure** [~gra'vyːr] *f* poker-work; ~**ligneux** ⚒ [~li'nø] *adj.: acide m* ~ pyroligneous acid; ~**mane** [~'man] *su.* pyromaniac; ~**phore** ⚒, *zo.* [~'fɔːr] *m* pyrophorus.

pyrosis ⚕ [pirɔ'zis] *m* pyrosis, heartburn.

pyro...: ~**technicien** [pirɔtɛkni'sjɛ̃] *m* pyrotechnist; ~**technie** [~tɛk'ni] *f* pyrotechnics *pl.*

pyroxyle ⚒ [pirɔk'sil] *m* pyroxyline; gun-cotton.

Pyrrhus [pi'rys] *npr./m: victoire f à la* ~ Pyrrhic victory.

python *zo. etc.* [pi'tɔ̃] *m* python; **pythonisse** [~tɔ'nis] *f* prophetess; clairvoyante.

Q

Q, q [ky] *m* Q, q.

quadragénaire [kwadraʒe'nɛ:r] *adj., a. su.* quadragenarian.

quadrangulaire [kwadrᾰgy'lɛ:r] *A̸* *etc.* quadrangular; **△** four-cornered.

quadrant *A̸* [ka'drᾰ] *m* quadrant; **quadrature** [kwadra'ty:r] *f* *A̸*, *astr.* quadrature; *A̸ circle*: squaring (*a. fig.*).

quadri... [kwadri] quadri...; **⁓folié, e** ♃ [⁓fɔ'lje] quadrifoliate.

quadrilatère *A̸ etc.* [kwadrila'tɛ:r] *su./m, a. adj.* quadrilateral.

quadrillage [kadri'ja:ʒ] *m* cross-ruling; cross-gridding; chequerwork; squares *pl.*; *fig.* cover(ing), control(ling); **quadrille** [⁓'dri:j] *m* ♪ *dance, a. cards*: quadrille; **quadriller** [⁓dri'je] (1a) *v/t.* square (*paper etc.*); grid (*map*); chequer; *fig.* cover (*an area etc.*); (bring under) control.

quadri...: **⁓moteur** *✦* [kwadrimɔ-'tœ:r] **1.** *adj./m* four-engined; **2.** *su./m* four-engined plane; **⁓phonie** [⁓fɔ'ni] *f* quadrophony; *en ⁓* in quadrophonic sound; **⁓réacteur** *✦* [⁓reak'tœ:r] *m* four-engined jet plane.

quadrupède [kwadry'pɛd] **1.** *adj.* four-footed, quadruped; **2.** *su./m* quadruped.

quadruple [kwa'drypl] *adj., a. su./m* quadruple, fourfold; **quadruplé(e)s** [⁓dry'ple] *su./pl.* quadruplets; **quadrupler** [⁓] (1a) *vt/i.* quadruple; increase fourfold.

quai [ke] *m* quay, wharf; **🚋** platform; embankment (*along a river*); *droits m/pl. de ⁓* quayage (dues) *sg.*

qualifiable [kali'fjabl] subject to qualification; describable (as, *de*); **qualificatif, -ve** *gramm.* [⁓fika'tif, ⁓'ti:v] **1.** *adj.* qualifying; **2.** *su./m* qualifier; **qualification** [⁓fika'sjɔ] *f* qualification (*a. sp.*); calling; *gramm.*, **†** qualifying; description, designation; **qualifié, e** [⁓'fje] qualified (to, *pour*); **⊕** skilled (*workman*); **🕱**

aggravated (*larceny*); **qualifier** [⁓'fje] (1o) *v/t.* call, style (by, *de*; s.o. s.th., *q. de qch.*); qualify (*a. gramm.*); *se ⁓* call o.s.; qualify (for, *pour*); **qualitatif, -ve** [⁓ta'tif, ⁓'ti:v] qualitative; **qualité** [⁓'te] *f* quality, property; nature; qualification; *fig.* capacity (as, *de*); title; *avoir ⁓ pour* be qualified to; *de première ⁓* first-rate; *en (sa) ⁓ de* in his capacity as; **†** *gens m/pl. de ⁓* gentlefolk.

quand [kᾱ] **1.** *adv.* when; *depuis ⁓?* how long?, since when?; *pour ⁓ est ...?* when is ...?; **2.** *cj.* when; *⁓ même* none the less, nevertheless; even though.

quant à [kᾱ'ta] *prp.* as for; as regards; in relation to.

quantième [kᾱ'tjɛm] *m* day of the month, date.

quantifier [kᾱti'fje] (1o) *v/t.* quantify.

quantique *phys.* [kwᾰ'tik] *adj.*: *mécanique f ⁓* quantum mechanics.

quantitatif, -ve [kᾰtita'tif, ⁓'ti:v] *🐑 etc.* quantitative; *gramm.* (*adjective*) of quantity, (*adverb*) of degree; **quantité** [⁓'te] *f* quantity.

quantum, *pl.* **-ta** [kwᾰ'tɔm, ⁓'ta] *m* *A̸*, *🐑*, *🜨*, *phys.* quantum; *phys.* *théorie f des quanta* quantum theory.

quarantaine [karᾱ'tɛn] *f* (about) forty; **⚓** quarantine; *la ⁓* the age of forty, the forties *pl.*; *mettre q. en ⁓ 🌶, ⚓* quarantine s.o.; *fig.* send s.o. to Coventry; **quarante** [⁓'rᾱ:t] **1.** *adj./num.*, forty; **2.** *su./m/inv.* forty; *les ♀ the Forty (members of the Académie française)*; *⁓-cinq tours m record*: single; **quarantième** [⁓'tjɛm] *adj./num., a. su.* fortieth.

quart [ka:r] *m A̸ etc.* quarter; **⚓** point (of the compass); **⚓** watch; *♪ ⁓ de soupir* semiquaver rest; *⁓ d'heure* quarter of an hour; *fig. passer un mauvais ⁓ d'heure* have a hard time (of it); *faire passer un mauvais ⁓ d'heure à q.* give s.o. a hard time; *deux heures moins le ⁓* a quarter to two; *le ⁓ a sonné* it has struck quarter past; *un*

~ (de livre) a quarter (of a pound); fig. aux trois ~s almost (completely); fig. les trois ~s de most (of); fig. au ~ de tour immediately, straight off; fig. un petit ~ d'heure a few minutes; **quarte** [kart] 1. adj./f ♂ quartan (fever); 2. su./f ♩ fourth; fencing: carte, quart(e).

quartier [kar'tje] m quarter; (fourth) part; piece, portion; venison: haunch; bacon: gammon; stone: block; district, neighbo(u)rhood; fig. mercy, clemency; ✗ quarters pl.; ~ chic residential quarter; ✗ ~ général headquarters pl.; ~ ouvrier working-class district; ✗ demander ~ ask for or cry quarter; ✗ faire ~ give quarter; ~**-maître**, pl. ~s-**maîtres** [~tje'mɛːtr] m ⚓ leading seaman; ✗ † quartermaster.

quarto [kwar'to] adv. fourthly.

quartz min. [kwarts] m quartz; **quartzeux, -euse** min. [kwart'sø, ~'søːz] quartzose; quartz (sand).

quasi [ka'zi] adv. almost, practically; quasi; ~**-délit** ᵗᵗ [~zide'li] m technical offence; **quasiment** F [~zi-'mã] adv. almost, practically.

Quasimodo eccl. [kazimɔ'do] f Low Sunday.

quaternaire ⚛, ♁ₘ, geol., etc. [kwater'nɛːr] quaternary.

quatorze [ka'tɔrz] adj./num., a. su./m/inv. fourteen; date, title: fourteenth; **quatorzième** [~tɔr-'zjɛm] adj./num., a. su. fourteenth.

quatrain [ka'trɛ̃] m quatrain.

quatre [katr] adj./num., a. su./m/inv. four; date, title: fourth; à ~ pas d'ici close by; à ~ pattes on all fours; entre ~ yeux between you and me; pol. les ♀ Grands the Big Four; ~**-mâts** ⚓ [katra'mɑ] m/inv. four-master; ~**-saisons** [~sɛ'zɔ̃] f/inv. (sort of) strawberry; see marchand 2; ~**-temps** eccl. [~'tã] m/pl. ember days; ~**-vingt-dix** [~vɛ̃'dis; before consonant ~'di; before vowel or h mute ~'diz] adj./num., a. su./m/inv. ninety; ~**-vingt-dixième** [~vɛ̃di-'zjɛm] adj./num., a. su. ninetieth; ~**-vingtième** [~vɛ̃'tjɛm] adj./num., a. su. eightieth; ~**-vingts** [~'vɛ̃] adj./num., a. su./m (loses its -s when followed by another number) eighty; quatre-vingt-un eighty-one; **quatrième** [katri'ɛm] 1. adj./num. fourth; 2. su. fourth; su./m fraction:

fourth, quarter; fourth, Am. fifth floor; su./f secondary school: (approx.) third form.

quatuor ♩ [kwa'tɥɔːr] m quartet; ~ à cordes string quartet.

que [kə] 1. pron./interr. what?; how (many)!; ~ cherchez-vous?, qu'est-ce que vous cherchez? what are you looking for?; ~ c'est beau! how beautiful it is!; ~ de monde! what a lot of people!; ~ faire? what can (could) be done?; qu'est-ce ~ c'est ~ cela? what's that?; qu'est-ce ~ la littérature? what is literature?; 2. pron./rel. whom, that; which; what; (autant) ~ je sache so far as I know; je ne sais ~ dire I don't know what to say; je sais ce qu'il veut I know what he wants; le jour qu'il vint the day (when) he came; l'homme ~ j'aime the man (whom or that) I love; misérable ~ tu es! wretch that you are!; you wretch!; 3. cj. that; so that; when; whether; replacing another cj. to avoid its repetition: puisque vous le dites et ~ nous le croyons since you say so and we believe it; ~ (sbj.) ... ~ (sbj.) whether (ind.) ... or (ind.); ~ la lumière soit! let there be light!; ~ le diable l'emporte! to hell with him!; approchez ~ je vous regarde come closer and let me look at you; aussi ... ~ as ... as; d'autant plus ... ~ all the more ... as or because; il ne partira pas sans ~ cela ne soit fait he will not leave before it is done; il y a ... ~ since ...; je crois ~ oui I think so; ne ... ~ only, but; non (pas) ~ (sbj.) not that (ind.); plus ~ more than; tel ~ such as; tel ~ je suis as I am; un tel vacarme ~ such a row that.

quel, quelle f, **quels** m/pl., **quelles** f/pl. [kɛl] 1. adj./interr. what; who; which; what (a)!; quelle bonté! how kind!; quelle heure est-il? what time is it?; ~ que (sbj.) whatever (ind.); quelle que soit son influence whatever his influence (may be); ~s que soient ces messieurs whoever these gentlemen may be; 2. adj./indef. whatever; whoever; whichever.

quelconque [kɛl'kɔːk] adj./indef. any whatever; some ... or other; ordinary, commonplace; indifferent, poor.

quelque [kɛlk(ə)] 1. adj. some, any;

~s *pl.* some, (a) few; ~ **chose** something, anything; ~ **peu** something; ~ ... **qui** (*or* **que**) (*sbj.*) whatever (*ind.*); **ne** ... ~ **chose** not ... anything; **2.** *adv.* some, about; ~ **peu** somewhat, a little; ~ ... **que** (*sbj.*) however (*adj.*); ~**fois** [kɛlkə'fwa] *adv.* sometimes, now and then.

quelqu'un *m, e f, m/pl.* **quelques-uns** [kɛl'kœ̃, ~'kyn, ˌkɔ'zœ̃] *pron./indef.* someone, anyone; somebody, anybody; *pl.* some, any; ~! ✝ shop!; F *W.C.*: engaged!; ~ **des** ... one (*or* other) of the ...; **être** ~ be s.o. (important).

quémander [kemɑ̃'de] (1a) *v/i.* beg (from, à); *v/t.* beg for; **quémandeur**, *m* -**euse** *f* [~'dœːr, ~'døːz] importunate beggar; (*place*-)hunter.

qu'en-dira-t-on [kɑ̃dira'tɔ̃] *m/inv.* what people will say; public opinion.

quenelle *cuis.* [kə'nɛl] *f* (*fish-, meat-*)ball.

quenotte F [kə'nɔt] *f* tooth.

quenouille [kə'nuːj] *f* distaff; ⚲ cat's-tail; *fig.* **tomber en** ~ fall to the distaff side.

querelle [kə'rɛl] *f* quarrel; dispute; ~ **d'Allemand** groundless quarrel; **quereller** [kərɛ'le] (1a) *v/t.* quarrel with (*s.o.*), nag (*s.o.*); **se** ~ quarrel; fall out (with, *avec*); **querelleur**, -**euse** [~'lœːr, ~'løːz] **1.** *adj.* quarrelsome; nagging (*wife*); **2.** *su.* quarrelsome person.

quérir [ke'riːr] (2v) *v/t.: aller* ~ go and fetch, go for; *envoyer* ~ send for; *venir* ~ come and fetch, come for.

question [kɛs'tjɔ̃] *f* question; matter; ⚖ issue; ⚖ *hist.* torture; ~ **d'actualité** topic of the moment *or* day; ~ **en suspens** outstanding question, question still unresolved; ~-**piège** trick question, loaded question; *ce n'est pas la* ~ that is not the point; *il est* ~ *de* it is a question of; there is talk of; *mettre qch. en* ~ challenge s.th.; question s.th.; ... *ne fait pas* ~ there is no doubt about ...; **questionnaire** [kɛstjɔ'nɛːr] *m* list of questions; quiz; questionnaire; **questionner** [~'ne] (1a) *v/t.* question (*s.o.*); **questionneur**, -**euse** [~'nœːr, ~'nøːz] **1.** *adj.* inquisitive; **2.** *su.* inquisitive person; *su./m: c'est un éternel* ~ he never stops asking questions.

quête [kɛt] *f* quest, search; *hunt.*

tracking (*by dogs*); *eccl. etc.* collection; *en* ~ *de* in search of; *fig.* looking for (*information*); **quêter** [kɛ'te] (1a) *v/t.* collect; F *fig.* seek (for); *hunt.* seek (*game*); *v/i.* take up a collection; **quêteur** *m*, -**euse** *f* [~'tœːr, ~'tøːz] collector (*of alms*); *eccl.* taker-up of the collection.

quetsche [kwɛtʃ] *f* damson.

queue [kø] *f* ⚲, *zo., astr., etc.* tail; *pan*: handle; *cost. dress*: train; (*billiard*-)cue; *fig.* bottom, (tail) end; *people*: queue, *Am.* line; rear; ⚲ stalk; *tool, button*: shank; *en* ~ in the rear; *fig.* at the bottom *or* tail-end; *faire (la)* ~ queue up, form a queue, *Am.* line up, stand in line; *mot. faire une* ~ *de poisson* cut in (on, à); *fig. finir en* ~ *de poisson* fizzle out; *n'avoir ni* ~ *ni tête* be disconnected (*story*); ♪ *piano m à* ~ grand piano; ~-**d'aronde**, *pl.* ~**s-d'aronde** ⊕ [~da'rɔ̃ːd] *f* dovetail; ~-**de-cochon**, *pl.* ~**s-de-cochon** ⊕ [~dkɔ'ʃɔ̃] *f* auger-bit, gimlet; ~-**de-morue**, *pl.* ~**s-de-morue** [~dmɔ'ry] *f* (*painter's*) flat brush; F evening dress, tails *pl.*; ~-**de-pie**, *pl.* ~**s-de-pie** [~d'pi] *f* swallow-tail coat; ~-**de-rat**, *pl.* ~**s-de-rat** [~d'ra] *f* ⊕ rattail(ed file); reamer; (*sort of*) snuffbox.

qui [ki] **1.** *pron./interr. subject: persons*: who, *two persons*: which; *things*: which *or* what; *object: persons*: whom; *things*: which; ~ **des deux?** which of the two?; ~ **est-ce** ~ **chante?** who sings?, who is singing?; ~ **est-ce que tu as vu?** who(m) did you see?; à ~ to whom? à ~ **est ce livre?** whose book is this?; whom does this book belong to?; **de** ~ whose?; of *or* from whom?; **2.** *pron./rel. subject: persons*: who, that; (he *or* anyone) who; *things*: which, that; what; *after prp.*: *persons*: whom; *things*: which; ~ **pis est** what is worse; ~ **que ce soit** whoever it is; anyone; à ~ **mieux mieux** vying with one another; **ce** ~ what; which; *n'avoir* ~ **tromper** have no one to deceive; **3.** *pron./indef.* some; ~ ..., ~ ... some ..., some *or* others ...

quia ✝ [kɥi'a] *adv.: être à* ~ be nonplussed; *mettre* (*or* **réduire**) à ~ nonplus.

quiconque [ki'kɔ̃k] *pron./indef.* whoever, anyone who; anybody.

quidam [ki'dam] *m*: un ～ an individual, someone.

quiétude [kᵐ ie'tyd] *f* quietude.

quignon [ki'ɲɔ̃] *m* *bread*: chunk, hunk.

quille[1] ⚓ [ki:j] *f* keel.

quille[2] [ki:j] *f* *sp.* skittle, ninepin; *sl.* leg; *fig.* recevoir *q.* comme un chien dans un jeu de ～s give s.o. a cold welcome; **quillier** *sp.* [ki'je] *m* skittle-alley.

quinaire [kᵐ i'nɛ:r] ⚕ quinary; ⚕, *zo.* pentamerous.

quincaille [kɛ̃'ka:j] *f* ✝ (piece of) hardware, ironmongery; F *coins*: coppers *pl.*; **quincaillerie** ✝ [～kɑj'ri] *f* hardware, ironmongery; hardware shop; **quincaillier** ✝ [～kɑ'je] *m* hardware merchant, ironmonger.

quinconce [kɛ̃'kɔ̃s] *m*: en ～ staggered; zigzag.

quinine ⚕, ⚗ [ki'nin] *f* quinine.

quinquagénaire [kᵤ ɛ̃kwaʒe'nɛ:r] *adj.*, *a. su.* quinquagenarian.

quinquennal, e, *m/pl.* **-aux** [kᵤ ɛ̃kᵤ ɛn'nal, ～'no] five-year (*plan*).

quinquina ⚗ [kɛ̃ki'na] *m* cinchona, quinquina.

quint ✝ [kɛ̃] *adj./m* fifth; Charles ♀ Charles V.

quinte [kɛ̃:t] *f* *cards*: quint; *fencing*: quinte; ♪ fifth; F *fig.* whim; *coughing*: fit.

quintessence [kɛ̃tɛ'sɑ̃:s] *f* quintessence; **quintessencier** [～sɑ̃'sje] (1o) *v/t.* refine.

quintette ♪ [kɛ̃'tɛt] *f* quintet(te).

quinteux, -euse [kɛ̃'tø, ～'tø:z] crotchety, cantankerous (*person*); restive (*horse*); ⚕ fitful.

quintuple [kɛ̃'typl] *adj.*, *a. su./m* quintuple, fivefold; **quintupler** [～ty'ple] (1a) *vt/i.* increase fivefold, quintuple.

quinzaine [kɛ̃'zɛn] *f* (about) fifteen; fortnight; fortnight's pay; **quinze** [kɛ̃:z] *adj./num.*, *a. su./m/inv.* fifteen; *date, title*: fifteenth; ～ jours

a fortnight; **quinzième** [kɛ̃'zjɛm] *adj./num.*, *a. su.* fifteenth.

quiproquo [kipro'ko] *m* misunderstanding; mistake.

quittance ✝ [ki'tɑ̃:s] *f* receipt; donner ～ à give (*s.o.*) a receipt in full; *fig.* forgive (*s.o.*); **quittancer** ✝ [～tɑ̃'se] (1k) *v/t.* receipt.

quitte [kit] *adj.* free, clear (of, de); discharged (from, de); être ～ be quits, be even; en être ～ pour qch. get or come off with s.th.; *adj./inv.*: ～ à (*inf.*) even if (*ind.*); il le fera ～ à perdre son argent he will do it even if he loses his money.

quitter [ki'te] (1a) *v/t.* leave (*a person, a place*); resign (*a post*); give up (*a post, business, a. fig.*); take off (*one's coat, hat, etc.*); *teleph.* ne quittez pas! hold the line, please!

quitus ✝, ⚖ [ki'tys] *m* full discharge; receipt in full.

qui-vive [ki'vi:v] *m/inv.* ✕ (*sentry's*) challenge; *fig.* être sur le ～ be on the qui vive *or* on the alert.

quoi [kwa] **1.** *pron./interr. things*: what; de neuf? what's the news?; ～ donc! what!; **2.** *pron./rel.* what; ～ que (*sbj.*) whatever (*ind.*); ～ qu'il en soit be that as it may; avoir de ～ have the wherewithal; avoir de ～ vivre have enough to live on; (il n'y a) pas de ～! don't mention it!; you're welcome!; sans ～ ... otherwise, or else; un je-ne-sais-～ (or je ne sais ～) a(n indescribable) something, just something.

quoique [kwak(ə)] *cj.* (al)though.

quolibet [kɔli'bɛ] *m* gibe.

quote-part [kɔt'pa:r] *f* quota, share.

quotidien, -enne [kɔti'djɛ̃, ～'djɛn] **1.** *adj.* daily, everyday; ⚕ quotidian; **2.** *su./m* daily (*paper*); **quotidienneté** [～djɛn'te] *f* everyday life.

quotient [kɔ'sjɑ̃] *m* ⚕ quotient; *pol.*, *admin.* quota; *psych.* ～ intellectuel intelligence quotient, *abbr.* I. Q.

quotité [kɔti'te] *f* share, portion, amount.

R

R, r [ɛːr] *m* R, r.

rabâchage [rabɑˈʃaːʒ] *m* tiresome repetition; rigmarole; **rabâcher** [ɹˈʃe] (1a) *v/i.* repeat the same thing over and over again; *v/t.* repeat (*s.th.*) over and over again; **rabâcheur, -euse** [ɹˈʃœːr, ɹˈʃøːz] *su.* person who repeats the same thing over and over again.

rabais [raˈbɛ] *m* ✝ *price:* reduction, discount; *au* ∼ at a discount *or* reduced price; **rabaisser** [ɹbɛˈse] (1a) *v/t.* lower; ✝ depreciate (*the coinage*); *fig.* belittle; humble (*s.o., s.o.'s pride*).

rabat [raˈba] *m cost.* bands *pl.*; *handbag etc.:* flap; ⊕ rabbet; ∼**-joie** [ɹbaˈʒwa] *m/inv.* spoil-sport, wet blanket; **rabattage** [ɹbaˈtaːʒ] *m* ✝ *prices:* lowering; *hunt.* beating (*for game*); heading back (*of game*); *fig.* heading off (*of people*); ✗ cutting back; **rabatteur** [ɹbaˈtœːr] *m* ✝ tout; *hunt.* beater; **rabattre** [ɹˈbatr] (4a) *v/t.* fold back *or* down; lower (*a. fig.*); *fig.* reduce; ✗ cut back; *hunt.* beat up (*game*); head (*game*) back; *fig.* head off (*people*); tone down (*a colour*); lower (*the price, s.o.'s pride, one's claims*); ∼ *qch. de* take *s.th.* off (*the price etc.*); *fig.* en ∼ climb down; *mot. etc.* se ∼ get back into the inside lane; *se ∼ sur* fall down upon; *fig.* fall back on.

rabbin [raˈbɛ̃] *m* rabbi.

rabibocher ⊢ [rabiboˈʃe] (1a) *v/t.* patch up; *fig.* reconcile (*two adversaries*); se ∼ make it up.

rabiot *sl.* [raˈbjo] *m food:* extra; overtime; extra time.

rabique ✗ [raˈbik] rabic.

râble [rɑːbl] *m zo.* hare *etc.:* back; *cuis. hare:* saddle; **râblé, e** [rɑˈble] thick-backed (*hare*); broad-backed, strapping, strong (*person*).

rabonnir [rabɔˈniːr] (2a) *vt/i.* improve.

rabot ⊕ [raˈbo] *m* plane; ∼ *en caoutchouc* squeegee; **raboter** [rabɔˈte] (1a) *v/t.* ⊕ plane (*wood*); *fig.* polish;

sl. filch, *Am.* lift (*s.o.'s money*); **raboteur** ⊕ [ɹˈtœːr] *m* planer; **raboteuse** ⊕ [ɹˈtøːz] *f* planing-machine; **raboteux, -euse** [ɹˈtø, ɹˈtøːz] rough; knotty (*wood*); uneven (*road*); rugged (*country, a. fig. style*).

rabougri, e [rabuˈgri] stunted, dwarfed (*person, a. plant*); scraggy (*vegetation*); **rabougrir** [ɹˈgriːr] (2a) *v/t.* stunt the growth of; *v/i. a.* se ∼ become stunted.

rabouter [rabuˈte] (1a), **raboutir** [ɹˈtiːr] (2a) *v/t.* join end to end.

rabrouer ⊢ [rabruˈe] (1a) *v/t.* scold, F dress down; snub.

racaille [raˈkɑːj] *f people:* riff-raff, scum; *things:* trash.

raccommodage [rakɔmɔˈdaːʒ] *m* mending, repairing; *socks etc.:* darning; repair; darn; **raccommodement** [ɹmɔdˈmɑ̃] *m* reconciliation; *quarrel:* mending; **raccommoder** [ɹmɔˈde] (1a) *v/t.* mend, repair; darn (*socks etc.*); *fig.* reconcile; se ∼ *avec* make it up with (*s.o.*); **raccommodeur,** *m* **-euse** *f* [ɹmɔˈdœːr, ɹˈdøːz] repairer, mender.

raccord [raˈkɔːr] *m* ⊕ joint, connection; link; ⚠ join (*a. picture etc.*); linking up; touch-up; **raccordement** [rakɔrdəˈmɑ̃] *m* ⊕, ⚠ joining, linking, connection; 🚂 *voie f de* ∼ slip line; **raccorder** [ɹˈde] (1a) *v/t.* join, connect, link (up).

raccourci, e [rakurˈsi] **1.** *adj.* shortened; abridged (*account*); ⚲ oblate; bobbed (*hair*); short (*stature*); *fig. à bras* ∼(*s*) with might and main; **2.** *su./m* abridgement; short cut (*to somewhere*); *en* ∼ in a few words, briefly; **raccourcir** [ɹˈsiːr] (2a) *v/t.* shorten; cut short (*a speech*); curtail; abridge (*an account, a story*); *v/i.* grow shorter; *tex.* shrink; **raccourcissement** [ɹsisˈmɑ̃] *m* shortening; abridgement; *tex.* shrinking.

raccroc [raˈkro] *m billiards:* fluke;

fig. par ~ by chance; **raccrocher** [rakrɔ'ʃe] (1a) *v/t.* hang up again; F get hold of (*s.o.*, *s.th.*); F solicit, accost (*s.o.*); *se* ~ clutch (at, *à*); *fig.* link (with); F recoup one's losses; *v/i.* *teleph.* hang up, ring off.

race [ras] *f* race; *zo.* species, breed; *fig.* breeding; **racé, e** [ra'se] thoroughbred (*a. fig.*); pure(bred).

racer [re'sœːr] *m* racing-horse; *mot.* racing-car.

rachat [ra'ʃa] *m* repurchase; *goods:* buying in; *annuity, covenant, loan, option, a. eccl.:* redemption; *policy, value:* surrender; **rachetable** [raʃ-'tabl] ♰ redeemable; *eccl.* atonable (*sin*); **racheter** [~'te] (1d) *v/t.* buy back; ♰ buy (*s.th.*) in; redeem (♰ *annuity, debt, loan, a. fig.*); ransom (*a prisoner*); atone for (*one's sins, a. fig.*); ♰ surrender (*a policy*); buy more of (*s.th.*).

rachitique 𝒮 [raʃi'tik] rachitic, rickety; **rachitisme** 𝒮 [~'tism] *m* rachitis, rickets.

racinage [rasi'naːʒ] *m coll.* (edible) roots *pl.*; *tex.* walnut dye; *bookbinding:* tree-marbling; **racine** [~'sin] *f* ✎, ♀, ♐, *ling.*, *a. fig.* root; *mountain:* foot; **raciner** [~si'ne] (1a) *v/i.* ♀ (take) root; *v/t. tex.* dye with walnut; *bookbinding:* marble.

racisme [ra'sism] *m* racialism, racism; **raciste** [~'sist] *adj., a. su.* racialist, racist.

racle ⊕ [rɑːkl] *f* scraper.

raclée F [rɑ'kle] *f* hiding, thrashing, dressing-down; **racler** [~'kle] (1a) *v/t.* scrape; make a clean sweep of; ✎ thin out; *se la gorge* clear one's throat; *v/i.*: ♪ ~ *du violon* scrape on the fiddle; **raclette** [~'klɛt] *f* ⊕ scraper; ✎ hoe; *phot.* squeegee; **racloir** ⊕ [~'klwaːr] *m* scraper; **racloire** [~'klwaːr] *f* ⊕ spokeshave; tongue scraper; **raclure** [~'klyːr] *f* scrapings *pl.*

racolage [rakɔ'laːʒ] *m* ✕, ♰ recruiting; *fig.* enlisting; *prostitute:* soliciting; **racoler** [~'le] (1a) *v/t.* ✕, ♰ recruit; *fig.* enlist; *fig.* tout for; *prostitute:* solicit; **racoleur** [~'lœːr] *m* tout; **racoleuse** [~'løːz] *f* prostitute, streetwalker.

raconter [rakɔ̃'te] (1a) *v/t.* tell, relate; **raconteur** *m*, **-euse** *f* [~'tœːr, ~'tøːz] (story-)teller.

racornir [rakɔr'niːr] (2a) *v/t.* harden, toughen; *se* ~ harden; grow hard or horny; *fig.* grow callous; *fig.* shrivel up.

radar [ra'daːr] *m* radar (set); **radariste** [~da'rist] *m* radar operator.

rade ⚓ [rad] *f* roads *pl.*, roadstead; *fig. laisser en* ~ abandon.

radeau [ra'do] *m* raft; ~ *de sauvetage* life raft.

radiaire [ra'djɛːr] radiate(d); **radial, e**, *m/pl.* **-aux** ♐, *anat.* [~'djal, ~'djo] radial; **radiance** [~'djɑ̃ːs] *f* radiance; radiant heat; **radiant, e** [~'djɑ̃, ~'djɑ̃ːt] *adj., a. su./m* radiant; **radiateur** [~dja-'tœːr] *m* radiator.

radiation[1] *phys.* [radja'sjɔ̃] *f* radiation.

radiation[2] [~] *f* striking out; *debt etc.:* cancellation; ♰ *solicitor:* striking off; *barrister:* disbarment.

radical, e, *m/pl.* **-aux** [radi'kal, ~'ko] **1.** *adj.* radical (*a.* ♐, ♀, ♏, *pol., gramm.*); **2.** *su./m* radical; ♐ root(-sign); *gramm.* root; **radicaliser** [~kali'ze] (1a) *v/t.* radicalize; intensify; **radicelle** ♀ [~'sɛl] *f* radicle.

radié, e [ra'dje] radiate(d), rayed.

radier[1] *etc.* [ra'dje] *m* floor, base, bed; level; *basin, dock:* apron; (*foundation-*)raft; *tunnel:* invert.

radier[2] [~] (1o) *v/t.* strike out, erase; delete; cancel.

radieusement [radjøz'mɑ̃] radiantly; brilliantly; gloriously; **radieux, -euse** [~'djø, ~'djøːz] radiant (*a. fig.*).

radin *sl.* [ra'dɛ̃] stingy.

radio [ra'djo] *su./f* radio; radio set; 𝒮 X-ray photograph; *à la* ~ on the radio; *su./m* radio(tele)gram; radio operator.

radio... [radjo] radio...; ~**actif, -ve** *phys.* [~ak'tif, ~'tiːv] radioactive; ~**conducteur** ⚡ [~kɔ̃dyk'tœːr] *m* radio conductor; ~**détection** [~detɛk'sjɔ̃] *f* radiodetection; ~**diffuser** [~dify'ze] (1a) *v/t.* broadcast; ~**diffusion** [~dify'zjɔ̃] *f* broadcasting; ~**électricité** radio, *a. phys.* [~elɛk-trisi'te] *f* radioelectricity; ~**élément** *phys.* [~ele'mɑ̃] *m* radioactive element, radio-element; ~**goniométrie** [~gɔnjome'tri] *f* direction-finding; ~**gramme** [~'gram] *m* ⚡ radiogram; 𝒮 X-ray photograph; skiagraph; ~**graphe** [~'graf] *su.* radiographer; **~graphie** 📷 [~gra'fi] *f* radiography; X-ray photograph(y); **~graphier** [~gra'fje] (1o) *v/t.* X-ray; **~guidage** [~gi'da:ʒ] *m* 🎯 radio control; *mot.* traffic news *pl.*; **~guidé, e** [~gi'de] radiocontrolled; **~journal** [~ʒur'nal] *m radio*: news bulletin; **~logie** 📷, *a. phys.* [~lɔ'ʒi] *f* radiology; **~logue** 📷 [~'lɔg] *m*, **~logiste** 📷 [~lɔ'ʒist] *m* radiologist; **~mètre** *phys.* [~'mɛtr] *m* radiometer; **~phare** 🎯 [~'fa:r] *m* radio beacon; **~phonie** [~fɔ'ni] *f* radiotelephony; **~phonique** [~fɔ'nik] wireless ...; radio...; **~phono** [~fɔ'no] *m instrument, furniture*: radiogram; **~repérage** [~rəpe'ra:ʒ] *m* radiolocation; **~reporter** [~rəpɔr'tɛ:r] *m* (radio) commentator; **~réveil,** *pl.* **~s-réveils** [~re'vɛj] *m* clock radio; **~scopie** 📷 [~skɔ'pi] *f* radioscopy; **~télégramme** 📷 [~tele'gram] *m* radiotelegram; **~télégraphie** 📷 [~telegra'fi] *f* radiotelegraphy; **~téléphonie** [~telefɔ'ni] *f* radiotelephony; **~(-)télévisé, e** [~televi'ze] broadcast on both radio and television; **~thérapie** 📷 [~tera'pi] *f* radiotherapy.

radis 🌱 [ra'di] *m* radish; F *ne pas avoir un ~* be penniless, F be broke.

radium ⚛ [ra'djɔm] *m* radium; **~térapie** 📷 [~djɔmtera'pi] *f* radium treatment, radium-therapy.

radius *anat., a. zo.* [ra'djys] *m* radius.

radotage [radɔ'ta:ʒ] *m* drivel, twaddle; dotage; **radoter** [~'te] (1a) *v/i.* talk nonsense; drivel; be in one's dotage; **radoteur** *m*, **-euse** *f* [~'tœ:r, ~'tø:z] dotard; driveller.

radoub ⚓ [ra'du] *m* repair; *bassin m de ~* graving-dock, dry dock; **radouber** ⚓ [~du'be] (1a) *v/t.* repair the hull of; dock.

radoucir [radu'si:r] (2a) *v/t.* calm (*a. fig.*); make (*s.th.*) milder or softer; se ~ become milder or softer.

rafale [ra'fal] *f* squall; *wind*: (strong) gust; ✖ *gun-fire*: burst; ~ *de pluie* cloud-burst.

raffermir [rafer'mi:r] (2a) *v/t.* harden, make firm(er); *fig.* strengthen; *fig.* fortify; se ~ harden (*a.* ✝ *prices*); ✝ level off (*prices*); 📷 improve; **raffermissement** [~mis'mã] *m* hardening (*a.* ✝ *of prices*); *fig.* strengthening; *fig.* improvement.

raffinage ⊕ [rafi'na:ʒ] *m sugar, petrol, etc.*: refining; *oil*: distilling; **raffiné, e** [~fi'ne] refined (*sugar, petrol, a. fig.*); *fig.* subtle; **raffinement** [~fin'mã] *m fig.* refinement; *fig.* subtlety; ⊕ *sugar, petrol, etc.*: refining; *oil*: distilling; **raffiner** [~fi'ne] (1a) *v/t.* refine (*a.* ⊕, *a. fig.*); *v/i.* be punctilious *or* overnice (on, *upon* sur); **raffinerie** ⊕ [~fin'ri] *f* refinery; (sugar-)refining; oil distillery; **raffineur** *m*, **-euse** *f* ⊕ [~fi'nœ:r, ~'nø:z] refiner.

raffoler F [rafɔ'le] (1a) *v/i.*: ~ *de* be passionately fond of, F be mad about; dote on.

raffut F [ra'fy] *m* row, din.

raffûter ⊕ [rafy'te] (1a) *v/t.* reset, sharpen (*a tool*).

rafiot ⚓ [ra'fjo] *m* skiff.

rafistoler F [rafistɔ'le] (1a) *v/t.* patch (*s.th.*) up.

rafle[1] 🌱 [rɑ:fl] *f grapes etc.*: stalk; *maize*: cob.

rafle[2] [rɑ:fl] *f police etc.*: raid, round-up; swipe.

rafraîchir [rafrɛ'ʃi:r] (2a) *v/t.* cool; renovate; freshen up; refresh (*a. one's memory*); revive; brush up (*a subject*); restore (*a painting*); *v/i.* cool; grow cooler (*weather*); **rafraîchissement** [~ʃis'mã] *m* ⊕ *etc.* cooling; *memory*: refreshing; *subject*: brushing up; *painting etc.*: restoring; ~*s pl.* refreshments; **rafraîchisseur** [~ʃi'sœ:r] *m*, **rafraîchissoir** [~ʃi'swa:r] *m* cooler.

ragaillardir F [ragajar'di:r] (2a) *v/t.* cheer (*s.o.*) up.

rage [ra:ʒ] *f* rage, fury; *fig.* mania; violent pain; 📷 rabies; *faire ~* rage, be raging; **rager** [ra'ʒe] (11) *v/i.* rage; be infuriated; **rageur, -euse** [~'ʒœ:r, ~'ʒø:z] violent-tempered; choleric; angry.

raglan *cost.* [ra'glɑ̃] *m* raglan.

ragot[1], **e** [ra'go, ~'gɔt] **1.** *adj.* squat, stocky (*person, a. horse*); **2.** *su./m hunt.* boar in its third year.

ragot[2] F [ra'go] *m* tittle-tattle, gossip.

ragoût [ra'gu] *m cuis.* stew; † *fig.* relish, spice; **ragoûtant, e** [ragu'tã, ~'tã:t]: *peu ~* unsavo(u)ry; unpleasant; unpalatable.

ragréer [ragre'e] (1a) *v/t.* finish, polish; 🔺 clean down (*brickwork*); ⚓ re-rig; *fig.* restore.

rai [rɛ] *m light*: ray; *wheel*: spoke.

raid [rɛd] *m mot.* long-distance run *or* ✈ flight; *mot.* (long-distance) endurance test; ✗, ✈ raid.

raide [rɛd] **1.** *adj.* stiff (*a. manner*); rigid; tight (*rope*); straight (*flight, hair*); steep (*path, slope, stair, a. fig. remark*); F *fig.* unyielding (*character*); **2.** *adv.* steep(ly); hard; *tomber* ~ *mort* drop stone dead; **raideur** [rɛˈdœːr] *f* stiffness (*a. of manner*); rigidity; *rope:* tautness; *path, slope, stair:* steepness; *character, temperament:* inflexibility; *avec* ~ violently; stubbornly; **raidir** [~ˈdiːr] (2a) *v/t.* stiffen (*a. fig.*); tighten (*a rope*); *se* ~ brace o.s.; *v/i. a. se* ~ grow stiff; harden; **raidissement** [~disˈmã] *m* stiffening; tautening.

raie[1] [rɛ] *f* line; streak; stripe; scratch; *hair:* parting; ✔ furrow; *anat., a.* ✔ ridge.

raie[2] *icht.* [~] *f* skate, ray.

raifort ♀ [rɛˈfɔːr] *m* horse-radish.

rail [rɑːj] *m* rail; railway, *Am.* railroad; ~ *conducteur* live rail.

railler [rɑˈje] (1a) *v/t.* laugh at (*s.o.*); make fun of (*s.o.*); twit (*s.o.*); *se* ~ *de* make fun of; *v/i.* joke; **raillerie** [rɑjˈri] *f* banter; jest; scoffing; ~ *à part* joking aside; *entendre la* ~ be able to take a joke; *ne pas entendre* ~ be very touchy, be unable to take a joke; **railleur, -euse** [rɑˈjœːr, ~ˈjøːz] **1.** *adj.* bantering, mocking; *su.* scoffer; banterer.

rainette [rɛˈnɛt] *f zo.* tree-frog; ♀ *apple:* pippin.

rainure ⊕ [rɛˈnyːr] *f* groove; slot.

raire [rɛːr] (4ff) *v/i.* bell (*stag*).

rais [rɛ] *m see* rai.

raisin [rɛˈzɛ̃] *m* grape(s *pl.*); ~s *pl. de Corinthe* currants; ~s *pl. de Smyrne* sultanas; ~s *pl. secs* raisins; **raisiné** [~ziˈne] *m* grape jam.

raison [rɛˈzõ] *f* reason; sense; satisfaction; justice, right; proof, ground; justification; motive; ⚖ claim; *A* ratio; ✝ ~ *sociale* name, style (*of a firm*); *à* ~ *de* at the rate of; *à plus forte* ~ so much *or* all the more; *avec* (*juste*) ~ rightly, with good reason; *avoir* ~ be right; *avoir* ~ *de* get the better of; get the upper hand of; *comme de* ~ as one might expect; of course; *en* ~ *de* in proportion to; because of; *parler* ~ talk sense; **raisonnable** [~zɔˈnabl] sensible, reasonable (*a.* ✝); rational; adequate; fair; **raisonné, e** [~zɔˈne]

reasoned; descriptive (*catalogue*); **raisonnement** [~zɔnˈmã] *m* reasoning; argument; *pas de* ~s! don't argue!; **raisonner** [rɛzɔˈne] (1a) *v/i.* reason, argue (about, *sur*); *v/t.* reason with (*s.o.*); weigh (*actions*); **raisonneur, -euse** [~ˈnœːr, ~ˈnøːz] **1.** *adj.* reasoning; *fig.* argumentative; **2.** *su.* reasoner; *fig.* argumentative person; *su./m: faire le* ~ argue.

rait [rɛ] *p.p./inv. of* raire.

rajeunir [raʒœˈniːr] (2a) *v/t.* make younger, rejuvenate; renovate; *se* ~ make o.s. look younger; *v/i.* get *or* look younger; **rajeunissement** [~nisˈmã] *m person:* rejuvenation; renovation.

rajouter [raʒuˈte] (1a) *v/t.* add.

rajustement [raʒystəˈmã] *m* readjustment, setting right; ✝ ~ *des salaires* wage adjustment; **rajuster** [~ˈte] (1a) *v/t.* readjust, set to rights; *fig.* settle (*a quarrel*).

râle [rɑːl] *m orn.* rail; (*a.* **râlement** [rɑlˈmã] *m*) ✗ râle; *throat:* rattle; death-rattle.

ralenti [ralãˈti] *m* slow motion *or* speed; *au* ~ slow(ly *adv.*); *tourner au* ~ idle, tick over; **ralentir** [~ˈtiːr] (2a) *vt/i. a. se* ~ slow down; relax; **ralentissement** [~tisˈmã] *m* slowing down, slackening; decrease.

râler [rɑˈle] (1a) *v/i.* groan; be in one's death agony; F grouse, fume (with anger, *de colère*); **râleur** *m*, **-euse** *f* F [~ˈlœːr, ~ˈløːz] grouser.

ralliement [raliˈmã] *m* ✗ rally(ing); ✗, ⚓ assembly; *mot m de* ~ password; *point m de* ~ rallying-point; **rallier** [~ˈlje] (1o) *v/t.* ✗, ⚓ assemble (*troops, ships*); ✗, ⚓ rejoin (*a unit, a ship*); *fig.* win, attract (*support, votes, etc.*); *se* ~ *à* rally to; ⚓ hug (*the shore*).

rallonge [raˈlõːʒ] *f* ⊕ extension-piece; *table:* extension-leaf; ✝ additional sum *or* payment; *une* ~ *de ...* an additional ...; *table f à* ~s extension table; **rallongement** [~lõʒˈmã] *m* extension; **rallonger** [~lõˈʒe] (1l) *v/t.* lengthen; eke out; *cuis.* thin (*a sauce*).

rallumer [ralyˈme] (1a) *v/t.* relight; *fig.* revive (*an emotion*); *se* ~ rekindle; break out again (*war*); *fig.* revive (*emotion*).

rallye *mot. etc.* [raˈli] *m* race-meeting, rally.

randonneur

ramage [ra'ma:ʒ] *m tex.* floral design; *orn.* song, warbling; **ramager** *orn.* [∿ma'ʒe] (11) *v/t.* sing, warble.

ramassage [rama'sa:ʒ] *m* gathering; collection; picking up; ∿ *scolaire* school bus service; *point de* ∿ pick-up point; **ramassé, e** [∿'se] stocky (*person, horse*); ⊕, *a. fig.* compact; **ramasse-miettes** [∿mas'mjet] *m/inv.* crumb-tray, crumb-scoop; **ramasser** [rama'se] (1a) *v/t.* gather (together); collect; pick up (*an object*); *fig.* ∿ *une bûche* come a cropper; *se* ∿ collect; pick o.s. up; *fig.* crouch (*animal*); *fig.* gather o.s. (*for an effort*); **ramassis** [∿'si] *m* pile; F *people:* pack.

rame[1] ⚓ [ram] *f* oar.

rame[2] [∿] *f* † *paper:* ream; 🚋 *coaches*, ⚓ *barges etc.*: string; 🚋 train.

rame[3] ✗ [∿] *f* stick, prop.

rameau [ra'mo] *m* ♉ bough; ♉ twig; *geog., a. family, science, etc.*: branch; ✗ vein; *zo.* ∿x *pl.* antlers; ∿ *d'olivier* olive-branch (*a. fig.*); *eccl.* (*dimanche m des*) ♉x Palm Sunday; **ramée** [∿'me] *f* leafy branches *pl.*, arbo(u)r; small wood (*for burning etc.*).

ramender [ramã'de] (1a) *v/t.* mend (*nets*); ✗ manure again; renew the gilt of (*a picture-frame*).

ramener [ram'ne] (1d) *v/t.* bring back; ⚓, *a. fig.* reduce (to, *à*); draw (down, back, *etc.*); *fig.* restore (*peace*); *fig.* win (*s.o.*) over; *sl.* ∿ *sa fraise* (*or gueule*), *la* ∿ protest; talk big; *se* ∿ amount, come down (to, *à*); F turn up, come (back).

ramequin *cuis.* [ram'kɛ̃] *m* ramekin, ramequin (= *mixture of cheese, eggs, etc.*).

ramer[1] ✗ [ra'me] (1a) *v/t.* stick; prop (up).

ramer[2] [ra'me] (1a) *v/i.* row; **rameur, -euse** [∿'mœ:r, ∿'mø:z] *su.* rower; *su./m* oarsman; *su./f* oarswoman.

rameux, -euse ♉ [ra'mø, ∿'mø:z] ramose; branching; **ramier** *orn.* [∿'mje] *m* ring-dove, wood-pigeon; **ramification** [∿mifika'sjõ] *f* ramification (*a. fig.*); branch(ing); **ramifier** [∿mi'fje] (1o) *v/t.:* *se* ∿ ramify; branch out; **ramille** [∿'mi:j] *f* twig; ∿s *pl. fire-lighting:* small wood *sg.*

ramolli, e [ramɔ'li] softened; F *fig.* soft-headed; **ramollir** [∿'li:r] (2a) *v/t.* soften; *se* ∿ soften, grow soft;

ramollissement [∿lis'mã] *m* softening; 🕮 ∿ *cérébral* softening of the brain.

ramoner [ramɔ'ne] (1a) *v/t.* sweep (*the chimney*); ⊕ scour, clear; *mount.* climb (*a chimney*); **ramoneur** [∿'nœ:r] *m* (chimney-)sweep.

rampant, e [rã'pã, ∿'pã:t] **1.** *adj.* △ sloping; ♉, *zo.* creeping; *zo.* crawling; *fig.* cringing; *fig.* pedestrian (*style*); **2.** *su./m* △ sloping part; **rampe** [rã:p] *f* slope, incline; inclined plane; gradient; *Am. road:* grade; △, 🚋, ✗ ramp; *stairs:* handrail; *thea.* limelight (*a. fig.*); footlights *pl.*; ✗ runway lights *pl.*; ∿ *de lancement* launching ramp; **ramper** [rã'pe] (1a) *v/i.* creep (*a.* ♉, *zo., a. person*); crawl (*zo., person, a.* F *fig.*); *fig.* fawn (*person*); ♉ trail; *fig.* lurk.

ramponneau F [rãpɔ'no] *m* blow.

ramure [ra'my:r] *f* branches *pl.*; *stag:* antlers *pl.*

rancard *sl.* [rã'ka:r] *m* info, tip-off; meeting, date; **rancarder** [∿kar'de] (1a) *v/t.* inform, tip (*s.o.*) off; make a date with, date (*s.o.*); *se* ∿ get the info (about, *sur*).

rancart F [rã'ka:r] *m:* *mettre au* ∿ discard; throw on the scrap-heap; F chuck out; shelve (*a project*); *admin.* retire (*s.o.*).

rance [rã:s] **1.** *adj.* rancid; **2.** *su./m: sentir le* ∿ smell rancid.

ranch, *pl.* ranches [rã:ʃ] *m* ranch.

ranche [rã:ʃ] *f ladder:* peg; **rancher** [rã'ʃe] *m* peg-ladder, pole-ladder.

rancir [rã'si:r] (2a) *v/i.* become rancid; **rancissure** [∿si'sy:r] *f* rancidness.

rancœur [rã'kœ:r] *f* ranco(u)r; resentment.

rançon [rã'sõ] *f* ransom; *fig.* price; **rançonner** [rãsɔ'ne] (1a) *v/t.* hold to ransom; ransom (*s.o.*); † F fleece; **rançonneur, -euse** F [∿'nœ:r, ∿'nø:z] extortionate.

rancune [rã'kyn] *f* grudge; *garder* (*de la*) ∿ *à q.* bear s.o. a grudge (for, *de*); *sans* ∿! no offence!; no hard feelings!; **rancunier, -ère** [∿ky'nje, ∿'njɛ:r] **1.** *adj.* spiteful; **2.** *su.* spiteful person; person bearing a grudge.

randonnée [rãdɔ'ne] *f* tour, excursion, (*long*) trip; outing; hike; **randonneur** *m*, **-euse** *f* [∿'nœ:r, ∿'nø:z] hiker; excursionist.

rang [rã] *m* row, line; order; class; tier; ✗, *a. fig.* rank; F *fig. de premier* ～ first-rate, first-class; **rangé, e** [rɑ'ʒe] **1.** *adj.* tidy; steady (*person*); orderly; (*a. bien* ～) well-ordered; ✗ pitched (*battle*); **2.** *su./f* row, line; *thea. figures*: set; **ranger** [～] (11) *v/t.* (ar)range; ✗ draw up, marshal; put (*s.th.*) away; tidy (*objects, a room*); *fig.* rank (among, *parmi*); ⚓ hug (*the coast*); *fig.* steady (*s.o.*); restrain; keep back (*a crowd*); *mot.* park (*one's car*); se ～ line up, get into rows or line; *fig.* settle down (*in life, behaviour, etc.*); *mot.* pull over; *fig.* make way (*person*); *fig.* se ～ à fall in with, come round to.

ranimer [rani'me] (1a) *v/t. a.* se ～ revive; *fig.* cheer up.

rapace [ra'pas] rapacious (*a. fig.*); predatory; **rapacité** [～pasi'te] *f* rapacity; *avec* ～ rapaciously.

rapatriement [rapatri'mã] *m* repatriation; **rapatrier** [～'e] (1a) *v/t.* repatriate.

râpe [rɑːp] *f* ⊕ rasp, rough file; *cuis.* grater; ♀ *grapes etc.*: stalk; **râper** [rɑ'pe] (1a) *v/t.* ⊕ rasp; grind (*snuff*); *cuis.* grate; wear threadbare (*clothes*); **râpé** threadbare (*clothes*).

rapetasser F [rapta'se] (1a) *v/t.* patch up; cobble (*shoes*); *fig.* botch up.

rapetisser [rapti'se] (1a) *v/t.* make (*s.th.*) smaller; shorten (*clothes*); *v/i. a.* se ～ become smaller; shorten; *tex.* shrink.

râpeux, -euse [rɑ'pø, ～'pøːz] rough; raspy (*tongue*); harsh (*voice, wine*).

rapiat, e F [ra'pja, ～'pjat] **1.** *adj.* stingy; **2.** *su.* skinflint.

rapide [ra'pid] **1.** *adj.* rapid, fast, swift; steep (*slope*); **2.** *su./m geog.* rapid; ⚟ express (train); **rapidité** [～pidi'te] *f* swiftness, speed; *slope*: steepness.

rapiéçage [rapje'saːʒ] *m* patching (-up); patchwork; **rapiécer** [～'se] (1f *a.* 1k) *v/t.* patch.

rapière † [ra'pjɛːr] *f* rapier.

rapin † F [ra'pɛ̃] *m* art student; *pej.* dauber (= *painter*).

rapine [ra'pin] *f* rapine; *pej.* graft; **rapiner** [～pi'ne] (1a) *vt/i.* pillage.

rappareiller [raparɛ'je] (1a) *v/t.* match, complete (*a set*).

rapparier [rapa'rje] (1o) *v/t.* match, complete (*a pair*).

rappel [ra'pɛl] *m pol. etc.* recall; reminder; ✝ *money*: calling in; ✗ back pay; ✚ (*injection de* ～) booster (shot); *thea.* curtain call; call (*to order*); ⊕ backmotion; *fig.* touch, suspicion; *mount.* faire une descente en ～ rope down; *touche f de* ～ *type-writer*: backspacer; **rappeler** [～'ple] (1c) *pol., a. fig.* recall; *thea.* call for (*an actor*); remind (s.o. of s.th., *qch. à q.*); ⊕ draw back; *teleph.* ring back; *fig.* restore (s.o. *to health*); *parl.* ～ à l'ordre call to order; se ～ recall, remember (*s.th.*).

rappliquer [rapli'ke] (1m) *v/t.* reapply; *v/i.* F come or go back.

rapport [ra'pɔːr] *m* ✝, ⊕ return, yield; ✝ *etc.* report; statement, account; ⅄, *a. mot.* ratio; connection (with, *avec*); relation; *fig.* resemblance; ～s *pl.* intercourse *sg.*; *fig.* en ～ avec in keeping or touch with; F faire des ～s tell tales; *maison f de* ～ apartment house; *mettre q. en* ～ avec put s.o. in touch with; *par* ～ à in relation to; compared with; *sous tous les* ～s in every respect or way; **rapporter** [rapɔr'te] (1a) *v/t.* bring back; *hunt.* retrieve; ⚖ restore; ⚖, *admin.* revoke; ⊕ join, add; ✝ yield, produce; *fig.* get; report (*a fact, an observation, etc.*); *fig.* ～ à relate to; ascribe to; se ～ à relate to; s'en ～ à rely on; *v/i.* pay, be profitable; F tell tales; present a report (on, about *sur*); **rapporteur, -euse** [～'tœːr, ～'tøːz] **1.** *adj.* sneaking; **2.** *su.* sneak, telltale; *su./m committee, conference*: rapporteur; ✗, ⚖ judge advocate; ⅄ protractor.

rapprendre [ra'prɑ̃ːdr] (4aa) *v/t.* learn or teach (*s.th.*) again.

rapprochement [raprɔʃ'mã] *m* bringing together; comparison; connection; closeness; *fig.* reconciliation; *pol.* rapprochement, re-establishment of harmonious relations; **rapprocher** [～prɔ'ʃe] (1a) *v/t.* bring together; bring (*s.th.*) near again; bring (*things*) closer together; put (*s.th.*) nearer (to, *de*); compare, put together; *fig.* reconcile; se ～ get closer or draw near(er) (to, *de*); *fig.* become reconciled (with, *de*); *fig.* se ～ de be close to.

rapt F⚤ [rapt] *m* abduction of a minor; kidnapping.

râpure [rɑ'py:r] *f* filings *pl.*; raspings *pl.*

raquette [ra'kɛt] *f sp.* racket, ping-pong: snowshoe; ♣ prickly pear.

rare [ra:r] rare (*a.* ☜, *phys.*, *fig.*); *fig.* singular, uncommon; ☞ slow (*pulse*); thin, scanty (*hair etc.*); **raréfaction** [rarefak'sjɔ̃] *f phys.* rarefaction; ⊹ growing scarcity; **raréfier** [~'fje] (1o) *v/t. phys.* rarefy; ⊹ *etc.* make scarce; se ~ rarefy; grow scarce(r); **rareté** [rar'te] *f phys.*, *a. fig.* rarity; ⊹, *a. fig.* scarcity; singularity; rare occurrence.

ras¹, rase [rɑ, rɑ:z] **1.** *adj.* close-cropped (*hair, head*); close-shaven (*cheek, chin, beard*); *fig.* blank, bare; open (*country*); full (*measure*); à ~ bord to the brim; brim-full; *faire table rase* make a clean sweep; *cuis.* *une cuillerée* ~e a level spoonful; **2.** *adv.*: *coupé* (*or taillé*) ~ cut short; **3.** *prp.*: à (*or au*) ~ de level *or* flush with.

ras² [rɑ] *m see raz.*

rasade [rɑ'zad] *f* brim-full glass; *verser une* ~ à fill (*s.o.'s*) glass to the brim; **rasage** [~'za:ʒ] *m beard*: shaving; *tex. cloth*: shearing; **rasemottes** ⚔ [raz'mɔt] *m/inv.*: *voler en* ~ hedge-hop; **raser** [rɑ'ze] (1a) *v/t.* shave; *tex.* shear (*cloth*); ⊹ *fig.* bore (*s.o.*); ✂ raze (*to the ground*); *fig.* graze, skim; *crème f à* ~ shaving cream; *se* ~ shave; F *fig.* be bored; *rasé de près* clean-shaven, close-shaven; **raseur** *m*, **-euse** *f* [~'zœ:r, ~'zø:z] shaver; *tex.* shearer; F *fig.* bore, *Am. sl.* bromide; **rasibus** F [~zi'bys] *adv.* very close (to, *de*); **rasoir** [~'zwa:r] **1.** *su./m* razor; *tex.* knife; ~ *de sûreté* safety razor; *fig. au* ~ perfectly; **2.** *adj.* F boring.

rassasier [rasa'zje] (1o) *v/t.* satisfy; satiate (with, *de*); cloy (with, *de*); se ~ take one's fill.

rassemblement [rasɑ̃blə'mɑ̃] *m* collecting; gathering; crowd; ✗ parade; **rassembler** [~'ble] (1a) *v/t.* (re)assemble; gather together (again); *fig.* muster (*strength*); ✗ parade. [down again.)

rasseoir [ra'swa:r] (3c) *v/t.*: *se* ~ sit ∫

rasséréner [rasere'ne] (1f) *v/t.*: *se* ~ become serene again.

rassis, e [ra'si, ~'si:z] settled, calm; sedate; stale (*bread*).

rassurer [rasy're] (1a) *v/t.* reassure; △ strengthen.

rastaquouère F [rasta'kwɛ:r] *m* flashy adventurer.

rat [ra] *m zo.* rat; F *fig.* miser; F *fig.* ~ *de bibliothèque* book-worm; ~ *de cave* exciseman; ~ *d'eglise* frequent church-goer; ~ *d'hôtel* hotel thief.

rata *sl.* [ra'ta] *m* stew.

ratage [ra'ta:ʒ] *m* failure, F washout, flop; messing-up.

ratatiner [ratati'ne] (1a) *v/t. a. se* ~ shrivel, shrink; crinkle up (*parchment*).

ratatouille *sl.* [rata'tu:j] *f* stew; skilly.

rate¹ [rat] *f anat.* spleen; *zo.*, *anat.* milt; F *dilater la* ~ *de q.* make s.o. shake with laughter; F *ne pas se fouler la* ~ take things easy.

rate² *zo.* [~] *f* (*female*) rat.

raté, e [ra'te] **1.** *adj.* botched (*work*); miscarried; *coup m* ~ failure; **2.** *su. person*: failure, F washout; *su./m* ⊕, *mot.* misfire.

râteau [rɑ'to] *m* ⚒ *etc.* rake; F large comb; ⊕ *lock*: wards *pl.*; **râteler** [rɑt'le] (1c) *v/t.* ⚒ rake (up); **râtelier** [rɑtə'lje] *m* rack; F (set of) false teeth *pl.*, denture.

rater [ra'te] (1a) *v/i. mot.* misfire (*a. fig.*); fail to go off (*gun*); *fig.* fail; *v/t.* miss; mess up, spoil; fail in (*an examination, attempt, etc.*).

ratiboiser *sl.* [ratibwa'ze] (1a) *v/t.* pinch (= *steal*) (from s.o., *à q.*); clean (*s.o.*) out; ruin, wreck (*s.o.*).

ratière [ra'tjɛ:r] *f* rat-trap.

ratification [ratifika'sjɔ̃] *f* ratification; **ratifier** [~'fje] (1o) *v/t.* ratify; approve.

ratiner *tex.* [rati'ne] (1a) *v/t.* freeze (*cloth*).

ratiociner *pej.* [rasjɔsi'ne] (1a) *v/i.* reason, quibble.

ration [ra'sjɔ̃] *f* ration(s *pl.*), allowance; *physiol.* intake.

rationaliser [rasjɔnali'ze] (1a) *v/t.* rationalize; **rationalisme** [~'lism] *m* rationalism; **rationaliste** *phls.* [~'list] *adj.*, *a. su.* rationalist; **rationalité** [~li'te] *f* rationality.

rationnel, -elle [rasjɔ'nɛl] rational (*a.* ♠); F *fig.* sensible.

rationnement [rasjɔn'mɑ̃] *m* rationing; **rationner** [~sjɔ'ne] (1a) *v/t.* ration (*a. fig.*).

ratisser [rati'se] (1a) *v/t.* ✿ rake; ✿

hoe; scrape (*skins, potatoes*); *fig.* comb (*police etc.*); F rake in, grab; F clean (*s.o.*) out; **ratissoire** [~'swa:r] *f ⚹* hoe; *⚹* rake; scraper.

raton [ra'tɔ̃] *m zo.* little rat; F darling; *zo.* ~ *laveur* rac(c)oon.

rattachement [rataʃ'mɑ̃] *m* linking up; *pol.* union; **rattacher** [~ta'ʃe] (1a) *v/t.* (re)fasten; tie up (again); *fig.* connect; *fig.* bind; se ~ be fastened; *fig.* be connected (with, à).

rattraper [ratra'pe] (1a) *v/t.* catch again; recover (*one's health, one's money*); catch up on (*time*); overtake; *fig.* make good, make up for (*an error etc.*), compensate; ⊕ take up (*play*); se ~ à catch hold of (*a branch etc.*); *fig.* se ~ make up for it; catch up.

raturage [raty'ra:ʒ] *m* erasing; crossing out; **rature** [~'ty:r] *f* erasure; crossing out; **raturer** [~ty're] (1a) *v/t.* erase; cross out; scrape (*parchment*).

rauque [ro:k] hoarse; harsh.

ravage [ra'va:ʒ] *m* ravages *pl.*, havoc; **ravager** [~va'ʒe] (1l) *v/t.* ravage, lay waste; devastate; play havoc with.

ravalement [raval'mɑ̃] *m building*: re-surfacing, refurbishing; **ravaler** [~va'le] (1a) *v/t.* swallow (again *or* down); F *fig.* take back (*a statement*); ⊕, *fig.* reduce (to, à); *fig.* lower, disparage; ⚹ re-surface, refurbish (*a wall, a building*); *⚹* cut back, trim; *fig.* se ~ lower o.s.

ravauder [ravo'de] (1a) *v/t.* mend, patch; darn (*socks etc.*); botch; **ravaudeur** *m*, **-euse** *f* [~'dœːr, ~'døːz] mender; patcher; botcher.

rave ⚹ [ra:v] *f* rape.

ravi, e [ra'vi] enraptured; F delighted (with s.th., *de qch.*; to *inf.*, *de inf.*).

ravier [ra'vje] *m* radish-dish, hors-d'œuvres dish; **ravière** *⚹* [~'vjɛːr] *f* radish-bed; turnip-field.

ravigote *cuis.* [ravi'gɔt] *f* ravigote sauce; **ravigoter** F [~gɔ'te] (1a) *v/t.* revive, refresh, F buck (*s.o.*) up.

ravilir [ravi'liːr] (2a) *v/t.* degrade, debase.

ravin [ra'vɛ̃] *m*, **ravine** [~'vin] *f*, **ravinée** [ravi'ne] *f* ravine, gully; **raviner** [~] (1a) *v/t.* cut channels in (*the ground*).

ravir [ra'viːr] (2a) *v/t.* carry off, abduct; steal; *fig.* charm, delight; à ~ delightfully.

raviser [ravi'ze] (1a) *v/t.*: se ~ change one's mind; think again.

ravissant, e [ravi'sɑ̃, ~'sɑ̃:t] ravishing; enchanting; delightful, lovely; **ravissement** [~vis'mɑ̃] *m* carrying off; *fig.* rapture; **ravisseur** [~vi-'sœːr] *m* plunderer; abductor (*of a woman*); kidnapper (*of a child*).

ravitaillement [ravitaj'mɑ̃] *m* supplying (with, en); ⊕ refuel(l)ing; **ravitailler** [~tɑ'je] (1a) *v/t.* supply (with, en); *mot. etc.* refuel; se ~ get fresh supplies; ⊕ refuel; **ravitailleur** [~tɑ'jœːr] *m ⚓* supply ship; ⚓ parent ship; ✈ refuelling aircraft.

raviver [ravi've] (1a) *v/t.* revive; brighten up; se ~ revive; break out again (*struggle*).

ravoir [ra'vwaːr] *v/t.* occurs only in *inf.* get (*s.th.*) back again; have (*s.th.*) again.

rayer [rɛ'je] (1i) *v/t.* scratch (*a surface*); stripe (*cloth etc.*); ⊕ groove (*a cylinder*); rifle (*a gun*); rule (*paper*); strike out, cross out.

rayon[1] [rɛ'jɔ̃] *m book-case*: shelf; *store*: department; *fig.* speciality, F line, field; ~ *de miel* honeycomb.

rayon[2] [rɛ'jɔ̃] *m phys., a. fig.* ray; *sun, light*: beam; A radius (*a. fig.*); *wheel*: spoke; *⚹* drill; *⚹* lettuce *etc.*: row; *⚕* ~*s pl.* X X-rays; (*grand*) ~ *d'action* (long) range; **rayonnage** [rɛjɔ'na:ʒ] *m* set of shelves; **rayonnant, e** [~jɔ'nɑ̃, ~'nɑ̃:t] radiant (*heat, a. fig.*); *fig.* beaming (*face*); *phys.* radio-active (*matter*).

rayonne *tex.* [rɛ'jɔn] *f* rayon.

rayonnement [rɛjɔn'mɑ̃] *m phys.* radiation; *astr., fig.* radiance; **rayonner** [~jɔ'ne] (1a) *v/i. phys. u. fig.* radiate; *fig.* shine (forth); *fig.* beam (with, de); tour, go touring.

rayure [rɛ'jyːr] *f tex.* stripe; streak; *glass etc.*: scratch; ⊕ groove; *gun*: rifling; erasure, striking out.

raz [rɑ] *m* strong current, race; ~ *de marée* tidal wave (*a. fig.*); *fig.* landslide; *fig.* flood.

razzia [ra(d)'zja] *f* raid, razzia.

re... [rə], **ré...** [re] re-...; ... again; ... back.

ré ♪ [re] *m/inv.* re, *note*: D.

réacteur [reak'tœːr] *m ⚡, phys.* reactor; *mot.* engine; F jet.

réactif, -ve [~'tif, ~'tiːv] **1.** *adj.* reactive; test-(*paper*); **2.** *su./m* reagent; **réaction** [∿'sjɔ̃] *f pol.*, ⊕ reaction; *rifle:* kick; 🛠 jet; 🚟 *physiol.*, *etc.* test; *phys.* ∼ *en chaîne* chain reaction; *avion m à* ∼ *jet* (plane); **réactionnaire** *pol.* [∿sjɔ-'nɛːr] *adj.*, *a. su.* reactionary.

réadmettre [read'mɛtr] (4p) *v/t.* re-admit; **réadmission** [∿mi'sjɔ̃] *f* readmittance.

réagir [rea'ʒiːr] (2a) *v/i.* react (to, *à*; on, *sur*).

réalisable [reali'zabl] realizable; available (*assets*); feasible (*plan*); **réalisateur, -trice** [∿za'tœːr, ∿'tris] *su.* realizer; *shares:* seller; *plan:* worker out; *su./m. cin.* director; **réalisation** [∿za'sjɔ̃] *f* realization; *shares:* selling out; carrying out, performing; production; **réaliser** [∿'ze] (1a) *v/t.* realize; achieve; produce; sell out (*shares*); carry out (*a plan*); se ∼ be realized; come true; **réalisme** [rea'lism] *m* realism; **réaliste** [∿'list] **1.** *adj.* realist(ic); **2.** *su.* realist; **réalité** [∿li'te] *f* reality; ∼s *pl.* facts; *en* ∼ really, actually.

réanimation [reanima'sjɔ̃] *f* resuscitation; **réanimer** [∿'me] (1a) *v/t.* resuscitate, revive.

réapparaître [reapa'rɛːtr] (4k) *v/i.* reappear; **réapparition** [∿ri'sjɔ̃] *f* reappearance.

réapprovisionner [reaprɔvizjɔ'ne] (1a) *v/t.* restock (with, *en*).

réarmement [rearmə'mã] *m* ✂ rearming; rearmement; ⚓ refitting; **réarmer** [∿'me] (1a) *v/t.* ✂ rearm; reload (*a gun*); ⚓ refit.

réassigner ⚖ [reasi'ɲe] (1a) *v/t.* re-summon.

réassortir ✝ [reasɔr'tiːr] (2a) *v/t.* restock; match up.

réassurer ✝ [reasy're] (1a) *v/t.* re-insure, reassure.

rebaptiser [rəbati'ze] (1a) *v/t.* re-baptize (*child*); rename (*s.th.*).

rébarbatif, -ve [rebarba'tif, ∿'tiːv] forbidding, grim; *fig.* crabbed (*style*); surly (*disposition*).

rebâtir [rəba'tiːr] (2a) *v/t.* △ re-build; *fig.* reconstruct.

rebattre [rə'batr] (4a) *v/t.* beat again; reshuffle (*cards*); F *fig.* repeat over and over again; *avoir les oreilles rebattues de* be sick of hearing (*s.th.*); *sentier m rebattu* beaten track.

rebelle [rə'bɛl] **1.** *adj.* rebellious; ✂ obstinate; ⊕ refractory (*ore*); un-ruly (*spirit*); **2.** *su.* rebel; **rebeller** [∿bɛ'le] (1a) *v/t.*: *se* ∼ rebel, rise (against, *contre*); **rébellion** [rebɛ-'ljɔ̃] *f* rebellion, revolt, rising.

rebiffer F [rəbi'fe] (1a) *v/t.*: *se* ∼ bristle (up); get one's back up.

reboisement [rəbwaz'mã] *m* reaf-forestation; **reboiser** [∿bwa'ze] (1a) *v/t.* reafforest (*land*).

rebond [rə'bɔ̃] *m* bounce; rebound; **rebondi, e** [rəbɔ̃'di] chubby, plump; **rebondir** [∿'diːr] (2a) *v/i.* rebound; bounce; *fig.* get going again.

rebord [rə'bɔːr] *m* edge, rim, border; (*window-*)sill; ⊕ flange; *cost.* hem.

reboucher [rəbu'ʃe] (1a) *v/t.* stop (*s.th.*) up again; recork (*a bottle*); fill up.

rebours [rə'buːr] *m*: *à* (*or au*) ∼ against the grain; *fig.* the wrong way; backwards; contrary (to, *de*).

rebouter ✂ [rəbu'te] (1a) *v/t.* set (*a broken leg*); **rebouteur** ✂ [∿'tœːr] *m*, **rebouteux** ✂ [∿'tø] *m* bone-setter.

rebras [rə'bra] *m glove:* gauntlet; *book jacket:* flap.

rebrousse-poil [rəbrus'pwal] *adv.*: *à* ∼ against the nap; the wrong way (*a.* F *fig.*); **rebrousser** [∿bru'se] (1a) *v/t.* brush up (*one's hair, tex.*); ruffle up; F *fig.* rub (*s.o.*) the wrong way; ∼ *chemin* retrace one's steps; turn back.

rebuffade [rəby'fad] *f* rebuff, snub.

rébus [re'bys] *m* picture-puzzle.

rebut [rə'by] *m* rejection; ✝ *etc.* reject; ⊕ waste, rubbish; *fig.* scum; *post:* dead letter; ✝ *marchandises f/pl. de* ∼ trash *sg.*; *mettre au* ∼ dis-card; put on the scrap-heap; throw out; ⊕ scrap; **rebutant, e** [rəby'tã, ∿'tãːt] tiresome; forbidding; **rebu-ter** [∿'te] (1a) *v/t.* repel; discourage, take the heart out of; se ∼ be(come) discouraged.

récalcitrant, e [rekalsi'trã, ∿'trãːt] *adj.*, *a. su.* recalcitrant.

recaler [rəka'le] (1a) *v/t.* wedge again (*furniture*); ⊕ reset; F fail, F plough (*a candidate*).

récapituler [rekapity'le] (1a) *v/t.* recapitulate, sum up, summarize.

recel ⚖ [rə'sɛl] *m*, **recèlement** ⚖ [∿sɛl'mã] *m stolen goods:* receiving;

criminal: harbo(u)ring; concealment; **receler** [rəsə'le] (1d) *v/t.* ⚖ receive; harbo(u)r; conceal (*a. fig.*); **receleur** *m*, **-euse** *f* ⚖ [~'lœ:r, ~'lø:z] receiver (of stolen goods), F fence. [lately, of late.]

récemment [resa'mã] *adv.* recently.

recensement [rəsã:s'mã] *m admin.* census; *admin.* record; *admin. votes*: count(ing); ✝ (new) inventory; *fig.* review; ✗ registration; **recenser** [rəsã'se] (1a) *v/t. admin.* take a census of; count (*votes*); record; ✗ register; ✝ inventory; **recension** [~'sjõ] *f text*: recension.

récent, e [re'sã, ~'sã:t] recent, fresh, new.

recéper [rəse'pe] (1f) *v/t.* ⚡ cut down *or* back; ⊕ cut down to level.

récépissé [resepi'se] *m* receipt; acknowledgment.

réceptacle [resεp'takl] *m* receptacle (*a.* ♣); ⊕ steam, waters: collector; **récepteur, -trice** [~'tœ:r, ~'tris] **1.** *adj.* receiving; *appareil m* ~ *tel.*, *teleph.* receiver; *radio*: set; **2.** *su./m* ⊕, *tel.*, *teleph.* receiver; *radio*: set; ⊕ *machine*: driven part; *teleph.* décrocher (*raccrocher*) *le* ~ lift (hang up) the receiver; **réceptif, -ve** [~'tif, ~'ti:v] receptive; **réception** [~'sjõ] *f* receipt; *tel.*, *teleph.*, *telev.*, *a. hotel, a. at court*: reception; welcome; *thea.* acceptance (*of a new play*); **réceptionner** [~sjo'ne] (1a) *v/t.* check and sign for; **réceptionniste** [~sjo'nist] *su.* receptionist; **réceptivité** [~tivi'te] *f* receptivity; ✝ *en état de* ~ liable to infection.

récession [resε'sjõ] *f* recession (*a.* ✝).

recette [rə'sεt] *f* ✝ receipts *pl.*, returns *pl.*; *thea. etc.* takings *pl.*; ✝ acceptance; receipt; *admin.* collectorship; *cuis.* recipe; ✝ bills, debts: collection; ✗ landing; *garçon m de* ~ bank-messenger; *thea. etc.* faire ~ be a (box-office) hit; be a success.

recevable [rəsə'vabl] admissible (*a.* ⚖); ✝ fit for acceptance; **receveur, -euse** [~'vœ:r, ~'vø:z] *su.* receiver; *admin.* collector; *tel.* addressee; *su./m bus, tram*: conductor; (post)master; *su./f* (post)mistress; *thea.* usherette; *bus, tram*: conductress; **recevoir** [~'vwa:r] (3a) *v/t.* receive; *fig.* welcome; admit (*pu-

pils, a. fig. customs), promote (*to a higher class*); accept (*an excuse*); être reçu à (*inf.*) be permitted *or* authorized to (*inf.*); être reçu à un examen pass an examination; être reçu avocat (*médecin*) qualify as a barrister (doctor); *v/i.* hold a reception, be at home; **recevrai** [~'vre] *1st p. sg. fut. of* recevoir.

rechange [rə'ʃã:ʒ] *m*: de~ spare (*part etc.*); alternative (*plan etc.*); des vêtements de ~ a change of clothes; **rechanger** [~ʃã'ʒe] (1l) *v/t.* (ex)change (*s.th.*) again.

rechaper *mot.* [rəʃa'pe] (1a) *v/t.* retread (*a tyre*).

réchapper [reʃa'pe] (1a) *v/i.*: ~ de escape from; get over (*s.th.*); ✝ recover from (*an illness*).

recharger [rəʃar'ʒe] (1l) *v/t.* reload; ⚡ recharge; refill (*a pen, a lighter, etc.*).

réchaud [re'ʃo] *m* hot-plate; chafing-dish; ~ à alcool spirit-stove; ~ à gaz gas-oven, gas-cooker; ~ à pétrole oil-stove.

réchauffé [reʃo'fe] *m cuis.* warmed-up dish; *fig.* rehash; *fig.* old *or* stale news; **réchauffer** [~'fe] (1a) *v/t.* (re)heat; warm up *or Am.* over (*food*); *fig.* warm (*s.o.'s heart*); *fig.* reawaken (*s.o.'s enthusiasm etc.*); se ~ warm o.s. up; **réchauffeur** ⊕ [~'fœ:r] *m* (pre-)heater; **réchauffoir** [~'fwa:r] *m* hot-plate.

rechausser [rəʃo'se] (1a) *v/t.* fit (*s.o.*) with new shoes; *mot.* fit (*a car*) with new tyres; ⚡ bank up the foot of (*a tree etc.*); ⚠ line the foot of (*a wall*).

rêche [rεʃ] rough; difficult (*person*).

recherche [rə'ʃεrʃ] *f* search; research, investigation; ⚖ enquiry; *fig. style*: studied elegance; ⚖ ~ de (la) paternité affiliation; à la ~ de in search of; *fig. sans* ~ unaffected, easy; **recherché, e** [rəʃεr'ʃe] sought after; ✝ in demand; studied (*elegance, style*); *fig.* choice, exquisite (*dress etc.*); *fig.* strained (*interpretation, style*); **rechercher** [~] (1a) *v/t.* search for, seek; look for; *fig.* court (*praise, a woman*); try to obtain; ✝ find (*the value of s.th.*).

rechigné, e [rəʃi'ɲe] sour (*look etc.*); sour-tempered, surly (*person*); **rechigner** [~] (1a) *v/i.* jib, balk (at, *devant*; at *ger.*, à *inf.*); look sour; *sans* ~ with a good grace.

rechute 🩺, *eccl.* [rə'ʃyt] *f* relapse.

récidive [resi'diːv] *f* 🩺 recurrence; ⚖ repetition of an offence; **récidiver** [∼di've] (1a) *v/i.* 🩺 recur; ⚖ commit an offence for the second time, relapse into crime; **récidiviste** ⚖ [∼di'vist] *su.* second *or* habitual offender, recidivist.

récif ⚓, *geog.* [re'sif] *m* reef.

récipiendaire [resipjɑ̃'dɛːr] *su.* newly elected member; **récipient** [∼'pjɑ̃] *m* container, receptable; ⊕ air-pump *etc.*: receiver; ⊕ cistern.

réciprocité [resiprɔsi'te] *f* reciprocity; interchange; **réciproque** [∼'prɔk] **1.** *adj.* reciprocal (*a.* ⚖, *phls.*, *gramm.*), mutual; ⚖ inverse (*ratio*), converse (*proposition*); et ∼ment and vice versa; **2.** *su./f* ⚖, *phls.* converse; *fig.* la ∼ the same; the opposite, the reverse.

récit [re'si] *m* account; narrative; ♪ recitative; ♪ *organ:* swell-box; **récital**, *pl.* -als ♪ [∼'tal] *m* recital; **récitant** *m*, e *f* [∼'tɑ̃, ∼'tɑ̃t] *radio*, *telev.*, *etc.*: narrator; **récitateur** *m*, -trice *f* [∼ta'tœːr, ∼'tris] reciter; **récitatif** ♪ [∼ta'tif] *m* recitative; **récitation** [∼ta'sjɔ̃] *f* recitation; **réciter** [∼'te] (1a) *vt/i.* recite.

réclamant *m*, e *f* [rekla'mɑ̃, ∼'mɑ̃ːt] complainer; ⚖ claimant; **réclamation** [∼ma'sjɔ̃] *f* complaint (*a. admin.*); objection; ⚖ claim; *bureau m des* ∼s claims department; **réclame** [re'klaːm] *f* advertising; advertisement; *pej.* blurb; *typ.* catchword; ∼ *lumineuse* illuminated sign; *faire de la* ∼ advertise, boost one's goods; **réclamer** [∼kla'me] (1a) *v/t.* claim (from, *à*); demand (*s.th.*) back; call for; require; *se* ∼ *de* appeal to; *fig.* use (*s.o.*) as one's authority; *v/i.*: ∼ *contre* complain of; protest against; ⚖ appeal against.

reclassement [rəklas'mɑ̃] *m* reclassifying, re-classification; regrouping; *admin.* regrading; **reclasser** [∼klɑ'se] (1a) *v/t.* re-classify; regroup; regrade.

reclus, e [rə'kly, ∼'klyːz] **1.** *adj.* cloistered; 2. recluse; **réclusion** [rekly'sjɔ̃] *f* seclusion, retirement; ⚖ solitary confinement with hard labo(u)r.

récognition *phls.* [rekɔgni'sjɔ̃] *f* recognition.

recoiffer [rəkwa'fe] (1a) *v/t.* do (*s.o.'s*) hair (again); se ∼ do one's hair (again); put one's hat on again.

recoin [rə'kwɛ̃] *m* nook, cranny.

reçois [rə'swa] *1st p. sg. pres. of* recevoir; **reçoivent** [∼'swaːv] *3rd p. pl. pres. of* recevoir.

récolement ⚖ [rekɔl'mɑ̃] *m* verification; *depositions:* reading; **récoler** ⚖ [∼kɔ'le] (1a) *v/t.* check; read over a deposition to (*a witness*).

récollection *eccl.* [rekɔlɛk'sjɔ̃] *f* recollection.

recoller [rəkɔ'le] (1a) *v/t.* re-glue; re-paste; F plough (again) (*in an examination*).

récolte [re'kɔlt] *f* harvest, crop; harvesting, F *fig.* collection; *fig.* profits *pl.*; **récolter** [∼kɔl'te] (1a) *v/t.* harvest; gather in; *fig.* collect.

recommandable [rəkɔmɑ̃'dabl] to be recommended; estimable (*person*); *fig.* advisable; **recommandation** [∼da'sjɔ̃] *f* recommendation; *fig.* instruction, advice; *post:* registration; **recommander** [∼'de] (1a) *v/t.* recommend; *fig.* advise; *fig.* bring (*to s.o.'s attention*); *post:* register; se ∼ remind o.s. to; se ∼ de give (*s.o.*) as a reference; *post:* en recommandé by registered post (*Am.* mail).

recommencer [rəkɔmɑ̃'se] (1k) *vt/i.* begin again, start afresh.

récompense [rekɔ̃'pɑ̃ːs] *f* reward (for, de); *iro.* punishment; *show etc.:* prize, award; en ∼ in return (for, de); **récompenser** [∼pɑ̃'se] (1a) *v/t.* reward, recompense (for, de).

recomposer [rəkɔ̃po'ze] (1a) *v/t.* ⚗ recompose; *typ.* reset.

recompter [rəkɔ̃'te] (1a) *v/t.* recount, count again.

réconciliable [rekɔ̃si'ljabl] reconcilable; **réconciliateur** *m*, -trice *f* [∼lja'tœːr, ∼'tris] reconciler; **réconciliation** [∼lja'sjɔ̃] *f* reconciliation; **réconcilier** [∼'lje] (1o) *v/t.* reconcile; se ∼ *à* make one's peace with (*a. eccl.*); make it up with (*s.o.*).

reconduction ⚖ [rəkɔ̃dyk'sjɔ̃] *f* *lease:* renewal; *tacite* ∼ renewal of lease by tacit agreement; **reconduire** [∼'dɥiːr] (4h) *v/t.* escort (*s.o.*) (back); lead back; show (*s.o.*) to the door; ⚖ renew (*a lease*); **reconduite** [∼'dɥit] *f* escorting (s.o.) (back); showing (s.o.) to the door.

réconfort [rekɔ̃'fɔːr] *m* comfort, consolation; **réconfortant** [ˌfɔr-'tɑ̃] *m* tonic, stimulant; **réconforter** [ˌfɔr'te] (1a) *v/t.* cheer (s.o.) up, comfort; strengthen.

reconnaissable [rəkɔnɛ'sabl] recognizable (by, from *à*); **reconnaissance** [ˌ'sɑ̃ːs] *f* recognition; ⚔ *etc.* reconnaissance, reconnoitring; ✝ note of hand, F I.O.U.; ⚖, *fig.* acknowledgment; *fig.* gratitude; ⚖ bastard: affiliation; **reconnaissant, e** [ˌ'sɑ̃, ˌ'sɑ̃ːt] grateful (for, de; to, envers); **reconnaître** [rəkɔ-'nɛːtr] (4k) *v/t.* recognize (a. ⚖, *a. pol. a government*); know again; ✝ credit; *fig.* acknowledge; ⚔, ✗, *etc.* reconnoitre; ⚓ identify (a ship); *fig.* be grateful for; *fig.* se ~ collect one's thoughts; get one's bearings.

reconquérir [rəkɔ̃ke'riːr] (21) *v/t.* reconquer; win back (*a. fig.*); **reconquête** [ˌ'kɛːt] *f* reconquest.

reconstituant, e [rəkɔ̃sti'tɥɑ̃, ˌ'tɥɑːt] *adj., a. su./m* tonic, restorative; **reconstituer** [ˌ'tɥe] (1n) *v/t.* reconstitute; reconstruct (*a crime*); restore (⚠ *an edifice, fig. s.o.'s health*).

reconstruction [rəkɔ̃stryk'sjɔ̃] *f* reconstruction, rebuilding; **reconstruire** [ˌ'trɥiːr] (4h) *v/t.* reconstruct, rebuild.

recoquiller [rəkɔki'je] (1a) *v/t. a.* se ~ curl up; shrivel up; *page f* recoquillée dog-eared page.

record [rə'kɔːr] **1.** *su./m sp. etc.* record; ⊕ maximum output; *sp.* détenir le ~ hold the record; **2.** *adj./inv.* record…; bumper (*crop*); **recordman**, *pl.* -men [ˌkɔrd-'man, ˌ'mɛn] *m* record-holder.

recoucher [rəku'ʃe] (1a) *v/t.* put (s.o.) to bed again; lay down again; se ~ go back to bed.

recoudre [rə'kudr] (4l) *v/t.* sew up or on again; *fig.* link up.

recoupe [rə'kup] *f stone, metal, etc.*: chips *pl.*, chippings *pl.*; *food:* scraps *pl.*; ⚸ second crop; ✝ *flour:* sharps *pl.*; **recouper** [ˌku'pe] (1a) *v/t.* cut (again); intersect; ⚠ step; blend (*wines*); cross-check; confirm, support (*a declaration etc.*); se ~ intersect, overlap; match up, tally

(*declarations etc*); *v/i.* cards: cut again.

recourbement [rəkurbə'mɑ̃] *m* bending; **recourber** [ˌ'be] (1a) *v/t.* bend (again or down).

recourir [rəku'riːr] (2i) *v/i.* run back; ~ *à* turn to (s.o.); resort to, have recourse to; **recours** [ˌ'kuːr] *m* recourse; resort; ⚖ appeal (for mercy, en grâce).

recouvrement[1] [rəkuvrə'mɑ̃] *m* covering, coating.

recouvrement[2] [rəkuvrə'mɑ̃] *m* debt, health, strength, etc.: recovery; ~s *pl.* outstanding debts; **recouvrer** [ˌ'vre] (1a) *v/t.* recover, regain; collect (*a tax, a debt, etc.*).

recouvrir [rəku'vriːr] (2f) *v/t.* recover, cover (s.th.) again (with, de); cover (*a. fig.*); coat; ⊕ overlap.

récréatif, -ve [rekrea'tif, ˌ'tiːv] recreational; entertaining; light (*reading*); **récréation** [ˌ'sjɔ̃] *f* recreation; *school:* play.

recréer [rəkre'e] (1a) *v/t.* recreate; re-establish.

récréer [rekre'e] (1a) *v/t.* entertain, amuse; refresh; se ~ take some recreation.

récrépir [rekre'piːr] (2a) *v/t.* ⚠ replaster; rough-cast again; F *fig.* patch up, touch up.

récrier [rekri'e] (1a) *v/t.*: se ~ (*sur*) cry out, exclaim (against); object (to).

récrimination [rekrimina'sjɔ̃] *f* recrimination; **récriminer** [ˌ'ne] (1a) *v/i.* remonstrate (against, *contre*).

récrire [re'kriːr] (4q) *v/t.* rewrite; *v/i.* reply by letter.

recroître ⚘ [rə'krwaːtr] (4o) *v/i.* grow again.

recroqueviller [rəkrɔkvi'je] (1a) *v/t.*: se ~ curl up, shrivel up (*leaf etc.*) curl or huddle o.s. up (*person*).

recrû, -crue [rə'kry] **1.** *su./m copsewood:* new growth; **2.** *p.p.* of recroître.

recrudescence [rəkrydɛ'sɑ̃ːs] *f* recrudescence; fresh outbreak; **recrudescent, e** [ˌ'sɑ̃, ˌ'sɑ̃ːt] recrudescent.

recrue ⚔, *pol., fig.* [rə'kry] *f* recruit; **recruter** ⚔, *pol., fig.* [rəkry'te] (1a) *v/t.* recruit; se ~ be recruited; **recruteur** [ˌ'tœːr] *m* recruiter; recruiting officer.

rectangle ⅄ [rɛk'tɑ̃:gl] 1. *adj.* right-angled; 2. *su./m* rectangle; **rectangulaire** ⅄ [⹁tɑ̃gy'lɛ:r] rectangular, right-angled.

recteur, -trice [rɛk'tœ:r, ⹁'tris] 1. *adj.* guiding; *orn.* tail(-*feather*); 2. *su./m univ.* rector, vice-chancellor.

rectificateur ⌁, ⨍ [rɛktifika'tœ:r] *m* rectifier; **rectificatif, -ve** [⹁'tif, ⹁'ti:v] 1. *adj.* rectifying; 2. *su./m* corrigendum (*to a circular*); **rectification** [⹁'sjɔ̃] *f* rectification; *alcohol:* rectifying; *fig.* correction; **rectifier** [rɛkti'fje] (1o) *v/t.* straighten; correct (*an error, a price,* ⚒ *the range*); ⌁, ⅄, *a. fig.* rectify; *fig.* put (*s.th.*) right; ⊕ adjust (*a machine etc.*); ⊕ true up (*on the lathe*).

rectiligne [rɛkti'liɲ] rectilinear; linear (*movement*); *fig.* unswerving.

rectitude [rɛkti'tyd] *f* straightness; *fig.* rectitude; *fig.* correctness.

recto [rɛk'to] *m page:* recto; *book:* right-hand page.

reçu, e [rə'sy] 1. *su./m* receipt; *au* ⹁ *de* (up)on receipt of; 2. *adj.* received, accepted, recognized; 3. *p.p. of* recevoir.

recueil [rə'kœ:j] *m* collection; anthology; ⚖ compendium, digest; **recueillement** [⹁kœj'mɑ̃] *m* collectedness; meditation; **recueillir** [⹁kœ'ji:r] (2c) *v/t.* collect, gather; ✓, *a. fig.* reap; *fig.* give shelter to (*s.o.*), take (*s.o.*) in; obtain (*information*); se ⹁ collect one's thoughts; meditate.

recuire [rə'kɥi:r] (4h) *v/t.* recook, cook (*s.th.*) again; ⊕ reheat; ⊕ anneal (*glass*), temper (*steel*).

recul [rə'kyl] *m* retirement; backward movement; *rifle:* kick; *cannon:* recoil; **reculade** [rəky'lad] *f* retreat (*a.* ⚒, *fig.*), falling back; **reculé, e** [⹁'le] remote, distant; **reculer** [⹁'le] (1a) *v/i.* move *or* draw back; back (*car, horse*); *fig.* shrink (from, *devant*); *v/t.* move back; set back; *fig.* postpone; **reculons** [⹁'lɔ̃] *adv.:* à ⹁ backwards.

récupérateur ⊕ [rekypera'tœ:r] *m* regenerator; *oil:* extractor; **récupération** [⹁ra'sjɔ̃] *f loss:* recoupment; ⊕, *a.* ⚒ recovery; ⊕ retrieval, salvage, reprocessing; rehabilitation; **récupérer** [⹁'re] (1f) *v/t.*

recover; recoup (*a loss*); ⊕ retrieve, salvage, reprocess (*materials*); rehabilitate (*persons*); bring (*a satellite*) back to earth; *v/i. a.* se ⹁ recuperate; recover.

récurer [reky're] (1a) *v/t.* scour; clean; **récureur** [⹁'rœ:r] *m* scourer.

reçus [rə'sy] *1st p. sg. p.s. of* recevoir.

récusable ⚖ [reky'zabl] challengeable; impeachable (*evidence, witness*); **récuser** ⚖ [⹁'ze] (1a) *v/t.* challenge, object to (*a witness*); impeach (*s.o.'s evidence*); se ⹁ declare o.s. incompetent, decline to give an opinion.

recyclage [rəsi'kla:ʒ] *m* reorientation; retraining; ⊕ recycling, reprocessing; **recycler** [⹁'kle] (1a) *v/t.* reorient; retrain; ⊕ recycle, reprocess.

rédacteur, -trice [redak'tœ:r, ⹁-'tris] *su.* writer, author; drafter; *journ.* sub-editor; *journ.* ⹁ en chef editor; **rédaction** [⹁'sjɔ̃] *f* drafting; *journ.* editorial staff; *journ.* editing; *journ.* (newspaper) office; *school:* composition, essay.

reddition [redi'sjɔ̃] *f* surrender; ✝ rendering (*of an account*).

redécouvrir [rədeku'vri:r] (2f) *v/t.* rediscover.

redemander [rədmɑ̃'de] (1a) *v/t.* ask for (*s.th.*) again *or* back; ask for more of (*s.th.*).

rédempteur, -trice [redɑ̃p'tœ:r, ⹁'tris] 1. *adj.* redeeming; 2. *su.* redeemer; **rédemption** [⹁'sjɔ̃] *f* redemption (*a. eccl.*).

redescendre [rədɛ'sɑ̃:dr] (4a) *v/i.* go *or* come down again; ⚓ back (*wind*); fall (*barometer*); *v/t.* bring down again; take (*s.th.*) down again; ⹁ l'escalier go downstairs again.

redevable [rəd'vabl] 1. *adj.* indebted (for, *de*); être ⹁ *de qch. à q.* owe s.o. s.th.; 2. *su.* debtor; **redevance** [⹁'vɑ̃:s] *f* charge, fee; (*author's*) royalty; *admin.* tax, dues *pl.*; **redevoir** [⹁'vwa:r] (3a) *v/t.* owe a balance of.

rédhibition ⚖ [redibi'sjɔ̃] *f* annulment of sale (*owing to latent defect*); **rédhibitoire** [⹁'twa:r] *adj.* ⚖ redhibitory (*defect*); *fig.* crippling, dooming (*defect etc.*); *vice m* ⹁ *a.* latent defect that makes a sale void.

rédiger [redi'ʒe] (1l) *v/t.* draw up, draft, write; *journ.* edit.

rédimer [redi'me] (1a) *v/t.* redeem; se ~ de redeem o.s. from; compound for (*a tax*).

redingote *cost.* [rədɛ̃'gɔt] *f* frock-coat.

redire [rə'diːr] (4p) *v/t.* repeat; say *or* tell again; *v/i.*: avoir (*or* trouver *or* voir) à ~ à find fault with; take exception to, criticize; **rediseur** *m*, **-euse** *f* [ˌdi'zœːr, ˌ'zøːz] repeater; **redite** [ˌ'dit] *f* repetition, tautology; **redites** [ˌ'dit] 2nd *p. pl. pres.* of redire.

redondance [rədɔ̃'dãːs] *f* redundancy; **redondant, e** [ˌ'dã, ˌ'dãːt] redundant.

redonner [rədɔ'ne] (1a) *v/t.* give (*s.th.*) again; restore (*s.th., a. strength*); *v/i.* return, come on again; ~ dans fall back into; la pluie redonne de plus belle the rain is coming on again worse than ever.

redoubler [rədu'ble] (1a) *v/t.* redouble; *cost.* reline; ~ une classe *school*: stay down; *v/i.* increase (*fever*); ~ d'efforts strive harder than ever.

redoutable [rədu'tabl] formidable; to be feared (by, à).

redoute [rə'dut] *f* ✗ redoubt; *dancing-hall*: gala evening.   [dread.\

redouter [rədu'te] (1a) *v/t.* fear,

redressement [rədrɛs'mã] *m fig.* rectification; ⊕, *fig.* straightening; ⚡ rectifying; ♥, *opt., phot.* correction; **redresser** [rədrɛ'se] (1a) *v/t.* re-erect (*a statue*); raise (*a pole*); ⚓ right (*a boat*); set right (*a wrong etc.*); ✗ lift the nose of; *a. fig.* rectify; ⊕ straighten out, true; se ~ stand up again; draw o.s. up; right itself (*boat*); ✗ flatten out; *fig.* mend one's ways; **redresseur** [ˌ'sœːr] *m* ⚡ rectifier; ⚡ commutator; ⊕ straightener; *fig.* righter (*of wrongs*).

redû, -due [rə'dy] 1. *p.p.* of redevoir; 2. *su./m* ♥ balance due.

réducteur, -trice [redyk'tœːr, ˌ'tris] 1. *adj.* reducing; 2. *su./m* 🔬, *phot.* reducer; reducing camera *or* apparatus; ⊕, *mot.* reducing gear; **réductibilité** [ˌtibili'te] *f* reducibility; **réductible** ♪, 🔬, ♥ [ˌ'tibl] reducible; **réductif, -ve** 🔬 [ˌ'tif, ˌ'tiːv] reducing; **réduction** [ˌ'sjɔ̃] *f* decrease; ♥, ♪, 🔬, ⚡, metall., admin., phot., paint., a. fig. reduc-

tion, *taxes, wages, production, etc.*: *a.* cut; ⚡ *voltage*: stepping down; ⊕ gearing down; ⚡ *sentence*: mitigation; **réduire** [re'dɥiːr] (4h) *v/t.* reduce; lessen; cut down (*expenses*); subjugate; ⚡ step down; ⊕ gear down; se ~ à keep (o.s.) to; *fig.* come *or* F boil down to; **réduit** [ˌ'dɥi] 1. *su./m* retreat, nook; *pej.* hovel; ✗ keep; 2. *adj./m*: à prix ~ at a reduced price.

réédifier [reedi'fje] (1o) *v/t.* rebuild; re-erect.

rééditer [reedi'te] (1a) *v/t.* republish; *cin.* remake (*a film*); **réédition** [ˌ'sjɔ̃] *f* re-issue; *cin. a.* re-make.

rééducatif, -ve 🔬 [reedyka'tif, ˌ'tiːv] occupational (*therapy*); **rééducation** 🔬 [ˌka'sjɔ̃] *f* re-education; rehabilitation; **rééduquer** 🔬 [ˌ'ke] (1m) *v/t.* re-educate; rehabilitate.

réel, -elle [re'ɛl] 1. *adj.* real (*a.* ⚡ *action, estate*); actual; ♥ (in) cash; 2. *su./m* reality, *the* real.

réélection [reelɛk'sjɔ̃] *f* re-election; **rééligible** [ˌli'ʒibl] re-eligible; **réélire** [ˌ'liːr] (4t) *v/t.* re-elect.

réescompte ♥ [reɛs'kɔ̃ːt] *m* rediscount; **réescompter** ♥ [ˌkɔ̃'te] (1a) *v/t.* rediscount.

réévaluation [reevalɥa'sjɔ̃] *f* revaluation; **réévaluer** [ˌ'lɥe] (1n) *v/t.* revalue.

réexpédier [reɛkspe'dje] (1o) *v/t.* send back; forward, send on.

refaire [rə'fɛːr] (4r) *v/t.* remake; do *or* make (*s.th.*) again; mend, repair; 🔬 restore to health; F swindle, do (*s.o.*), dupe; F steal (from, à); se ~ 🔬 recuperate; ♥ retrieve one's losses; **refait, e** F [ˌ'fɛ, ˌ'fɛt] duped.

réfection [refɛk'sjɔ̃] *f* remaking; ⚠ rebuilding; repair(ing); 🔬 recuperation; **réfectoire** [ˌ'twaːr] *m* refectory, dining-hall.

refend [rə'fã] *m* splitting; ⊕ *bois m de* ~ wood in planks; ⚠ *mur m de* ~ partition-wall; **refendre** [ˌ'fãːdr] (4a) *v/t.* split; rip (*timber*); slit (*leather*).

référé ⚡ [refe're] *m* summary procedure; provisional order; **référence** [ˌ'rãːs] *f* reference (*a. of a servant*); ♥ pattern-book; ♥ sample-book; *fig.* allusion; *ouvrage m de* ~ reference book; **référendaire** [ˌ-

rǎ'dɛːr] *m* ⚖ *commercial court*: chief clerk; *hist. grand ~* Great Referendary; **référendum** [ʌr̃ɛ-'dɔm] *m* referendum; strike ballot; **référer** [ʌ're] (1f) *v/t. se ~ à* refer to (*s.th.*); ask (*s.o.'s*) opinion; consult; *en ~ à q.* submit the matter to s.o.

refermer [rɔfɛr'me] (1a) *v/t.* shut (again), close (again); *se ~* close up (*wound*); shut (again).

réfléchi, e [refle'ʃi] thoughtful (*person*); considered (*action, opinion*); ⚖ premeditated (*crime*); *gramm.* reflexive; *tout ~* everything considered; **réfléchir** [ʌ'ʃiːr] (2a) *v/t.* reflect; *se ~* curl back; *phys.* be reflected; reverberate (*sound*); *v/i.* consider; reflect (on *à, sur*); **réfléchissement** *phys.* [ʌʃis'mã] *m* reflection; *sound:* reverberation; **réflecteur** [reflɛk'tœːr] *m* ⚡, *mot., phys.* reflector; *fig.* searchlight; **reflet** [rɔ'flɛ] *m* reflection; glint, gleam, glimmer; *picture, etc.:* highlight; **refléter** [ʌfle'te] (1f) *v/t.* reflect, throw back (*colour, light*); *fig. se ~ sur* be reflected on (*s.o.*).

réflexe *phys., physiol.* [re'flɛks] *adj., a. su./m* reflex; **réflexion** [ʌflɛk'sjɔ̃] *f phys., a. fig.* reflection; *fig.* thought; *toute ~ faite* everything considered.

refluer [rɔfly'e] (1a) *v/i.* flow back; ebb (*tide*); *fig.* fall back; *fig.* pour (into, *dans*); **reflux** [ʌ'fly] *m tide:* ebb; ebbtide; flowing back; *fig. crowd etc.:* falling back.

refondre [rɔ'fɔ̃ːdr] (4a) *v/t.* ⊕ remelt; *metall., a. fig.* recast; *fig.* remodel; ⚓ refit (*a ship*); **refonte** [ʌ'fɔ̃ːt] *f* remelting; recasting (*a. fig.*); reorganization; ⚓ refit(ting).

réformable [refɔr'mabl] reformable; ⚔ liable to discharge; ⚖ reversible; **réformateur, -trice** [ʌma'tœːr, ʌ'tris] **1.** *adj.* reforming; **2.** *su.* reformer; **réformation** [ʌma'sjɔ̃] *f* reformation (*a. eccl.*); **réforme** [re'fɔrm] *f* reform(ation); ⚔, ⚓ discharge; *horse:* casting; *eccl. la ♀ the Reformation; ⚔ mettre à la ~ discharge (s.o.); cast (a horse); dismiss, cashier (an officer); **réformé, e** [refɔr'me] **1.** *su. eccl.* protestant; ⚔ person invalided out of the service; **2.** *adj. eccl.* reformed; ⚔ discharged (*soldier*).

reformer [rɔfɔr'me] (1a) *v/t.* reform, form anew.

réformer [refɔr'me] (1a) *v/t.* reform, amend; ⚔, ⚓ invalid (*s.o.*) out of the service; dismiss; cashier (*an officer*); retire (*an officer*); cast (*a horse*); ⚖ reverse (*a judgment*).

refoulement [reful'mã] *m* driving back; *fig.* repression (*a. psych.*); **refouler** [rɔfu'le] (1a) *v/t.* drive back, repel; *fig.* repress (*a. psych.*), hold back, force back.

réfractaire [refrak'tɛːr] **1.** *adj.* refractory (*a.* ⊕ *ore*), rebellious, recalcitrant; ⊕ fire-proof; proof (against, *à*); **2.** *su.* refractory person; ⚔ defaulter, *Am.* draft-dodger; **réfraction** *phys., opt.* [ʌ'sjɔ̃] *f* refraction; *indice m de ~* refractive index.

refrain [rɔ'frɛ̃] *m* refrain (*a. fig.*); F *fig. le même ~* the same old story.

refrènement [rɔfrɛn'mã] *m instincts:* curbing; **refréner** [ʌfre'ne] (1f) *v/t.* curb, restrain.

réfrigérant, e [refriʒe'rã, ʌ'rãːt] **1.** *adj.* refrigerating, cooling; freezing; ⚗ refrigerant; ⊕ cooler-...; **2.** *su./m* ♨ condenser; refrigerator; ⚗ refrigerant; **réfrigérateur** [ʌra'tœːr] *m* refrigerator; *fig. mettre qch. au ~* put s.th. on ice *or* in cold storage; **réfrigératif, -ve** ⚗ [ʌra'tif, ʌ'tiːv] *adj., a. su./m* refrigerant; **réfrigération** [ʌra'sjɔ̃] *f* refrigeration; *meat.:* chilling; **réfrigérer** [ʌ're] (1f) *v/t.* refrigerate; cool; chill (*meat*).

refroidir [rɔfrwa'diːr] (2a) *v/t.* cool, chill; ⊕, *a. fig.* quench (*metal, a.* one's enthusiasm, one's sympathy); *sl.* kill; ⊕ *refroidi par l'air* air-cooled (*engine*); ⚗ *se ~* catch a chill; *v/i. a. se ~* grow cold; cool off (*a. fig.*); **refroidissement** [ʌdis'mã] *m* cooling (down); ⚗ chill; *temperature:* drop.

refuge [rɔ'fyːʒ] *m* refuge; shelter (*a. admin.*); *birds:* sanctuary; traffic island; *mot.* lay-by; *fig.* pretext, F way out; **réfugié m, e** *f* [refy'ʒje] refugee; **réfugier** [ʌ] (1o) *v/t.: se ~* take refuge; seek shelter; *fig.* have recourse (to, *dans*).

refus [rɔ'fy] *m* refusal; denial; rejection; ✝ *~ m d'acceptation* nonacceptance; *essuyer un ~* meet with a refusal; **refuser** [ʌfy'ze] (1a) *vt/i.* refuse, decline; *v/t.* ⚔ reject (*a* *man*); fail (*a candidate*); ~ de (*inf.*), se ~ à (*inf.*) refuse to (*inf.*); se ~ à qch. resist s.th., object to s.th.

réfutation [refyta'sjɔ̃] *f* refutation; proof to the contrary; **réfuter** [~'te] (1a) *v/t.* refute; disprove.

regagner [rəga'ɲe] (1a) *v/t.* regain; win back; recover; return to (*a place*).

regain [rə'gɛ̃] *m* ✶ aftergrowth, second growth; *fig.* renewal, revival; ~ de vie new lease of (*Am.* on) life.

régal, *pl.* -als [re'gal] *m* treat; delight; **régalade** [~ga'lad] *f*: boire à la ~ drink without the lips coming into contact with the glass *or* bottle.

régalage ⊕ [rega'la:ʒ] *m* levelling.

régale [re'gal] 1. *adj./f*: ✶ eau *f* ~ aqua regia; 2. *su./f hist.* royal prerogative. [*ground*).\

régaler[1] [rega'le] (1a) *v/t.* level (*the*

régaler[2] [~] (1a) *v/t.* treat (*s.o.*) to a (fine) meal; ~ q. de qch. treat s.o. to s.th.; se ~ have a fine meal *etc.*; *fig.* enjoy o.s.; se ~ de feast on; treat o.s. to.

regard [rə'ga:r] *m* look, glance; *sewer etc.*: man-hole; inspection hole; peep-hole; *geol.* inlier; *fig.* attention, eyes *pl.*; au ~ de compared to; en ~ de opposite, facing; **regardant, e** F [rəgar'dã, ~'dã:t] stingy, niggardly; **regarder** [~'de] (1a) *v/t.* look at, watch; glance at; face, look on to; *telev.* look in; *fig.* consider (as, *comme*); *fig.* concern; ~ fixement stare at; cela me regarde that is my business; *v/i.* (have a) look; ~ à pay attention to (*s.th.*); look through (*s.th.*); ~ par (à) la fenêtre look through (in at) the window; ~ fixement stare.

régate [re'gat] *f* regatta; *cost.* sailor-knot tie.

regel [rə'ʒɛl] *m* renewed frost.

régence [re'ʒã:s] *f* regency; fob-chain.

régénération [reʒenera'sjɔ̃] *f* regeneration; ⊕ reclamation; ... à ~ regenerative ...; **régénérer** [~'re] (1f) *v/t.* regenerate; ⊕ reclaim.

régent, e [re'ʒã, ~'ʒã:t] *su.* regent; *su./m* † *collège*: form-master; **régenter** [~ʒã'te] (1a) *v/t.* † teach; F *fig.* lord it over.

régicide [reʒi'sid] 1. *adj.* regicidal; 2. *su. person*: regicide; *su./m crime*: regicide.

régie [re'ʒi] *f* administration; management; state control; excise-office.

regimber [rəʒɛ̃'be] (1a) *v/i.* balk (at, *contre*); kick (against, at *contre*).

régime [re'ʒim] *m* organization; regulations *pl.*; system; ⊕ *engine*: normal running; *mot.* speed; ✶ diet; *gramm.* object; ✿ *bananas etc.*: bunch; *hist. Ancien* ♀ Ancien Regime (*before 1789*); *gramm.* cas *m* ~ objective case; ✶ mettre au ~ put (*s.o.*) on a diet; suivre un ~ (follow a special) diet.

régiment [reʒi'mã] *m* ✕ regiment; F *fig.* host; **régimentaire** ✕ [~mã-'tɛ:r] regimental; army-...; troop (*train*).

région [re'ʒjɔ̃] *f* region (*a. anat.*); area; *phys.* field; ~ désertique desert region; ~ vinicole wine-producing district; **régional, e**, *m/pl.* -aux [~ʒjɔ'nal, ~'no] regional, local.

régir [re'ʒi:r] (2a) *v/t.* pol., gramm., fig. govern; ⊕ direct, manage; **régisseur** [~ʒi'sœ:r] *m* manager; *thea.* stage-manager; *cin.* assistant director; ✶ *farm*: bailiff; *estate*: agent.

registre [rə'ʒistr] *m* register (*a.* ♪), record; † account-book; ⊕ log-book; ⊕ *chimney etc.*: damper; ⊕ *steam engine*: throttle; ~ de l'état civil register of births, deaths and marriages; tenir ~ de keep a record of, note (down).

réglable [re'glabl] adjustable; **réglage** [~'gla:ʒ] *m* ⊕ regulating, adjustment; *speed*: control; *paper*: ruling; *radio*: tuning; **règle** [regl] *f* rule; ⊕ ruler, rule; *surv.* measuring rod; ✶ ~s *pl.* menses; ♀ ~ à calcul slide rule; ♀ ~ de trois rule of three; de ~ usual, customary; en ~ in order, straight; **réglé, e** [re'gle] regular; steady (*pace*, *person*); △ uniform (*courses*); ruled (*paper*); fixed (*hour etc.*); **règlement** [reglə'mã] *m* admin., ✕ *etc.* regulation(s *pl.*); rule; † settlement; **réglementaire** [regləmã'tɛ:r] regular, prescribed; regulation-...; *pas* ~ against the rules; **réglementation** [~ta'sjɔ̃] *f* regulation; regulating, control; ~ de la circulation traffic regulations *pl.*; **réglementer** [~'te] (1a) *v/t.* regulate, control; make rules for; **régler** [re'gle] (1f) *v/t.* ⊕, *a. fig.* regulate; ⊕, ✝ adjust; *fig.* settle (*a quarrel, a question,* ✝ *an account*); ✝ settle (up), pay (up); rule (*paper*); *mot.* tune (*an engine*); ~ *sur* model on; adjust to.

réglet [re'glɛ] *m* carpenter's rule; ⚠ reglet; **réglette** [~'glɛt] *f typ.* reglet; small rule; (*metal*) strip; *slide-rule*: slide; *mot.* ~-*jauge* dipstick.

réglisse ♀, ✿ [re'glis] *f* liquorice.

réglure [re'gly:r] *f paper:* ruling.

règne [rɛɲ] *m* ♀, *zo.* kingdom; *pol.*, *a. fig.* reign; **régner** [re'ɲe] (1f) *v/i.* reign (*a. fig.*), rule; *fig.* prevail.

regorger [rəɡɔr'ʒe] (1l) *v/i.* overflow; abound (in, *de*); be crowded (with, *de*); *v/t.* bring up (*food*); *fig.* disgorge.

regratter [rəɡra'te] (1a) *v/t.* ⚠ scrape, rub down (*a wall*); *v/i.* ✝ F huckster.

régresser [reɡrɛ'se] (1a) *v/i.* decrease, decline, fall off; **régressif**, -ve [~'sif, ~'si:v] regressive; **régression** [~'sjɔ̃] *f* regression; *biol.* retrogression; *biol.* throw-back; *sales etc.*: drop.

regret [rə'ɡrɛ] *m* regret (for, of *de*); *à* ~ regretfully, with regret; *avoir* ~ *de* (*inf.*) regret to (*inf.*); **regrettable** [rəɡrɛ'tabl] regrettable; unfortunate; **regretter** [~'te] (1a) *v/t.* regret; be sorry (that *ind.*, *que sbj.*; for *ger.*, *de inf.*); miss, mourn (for).

regroupement [rəɡrup'mɑ̃] *m* regrouping; **regrouper** [~ɡru'pe] (1a) *v/t.* regroup.

régulariser [reɡylari'ze] (1a) *v/t.* regularize; put (*s.th.*) in order; ⚖ put into legal form; **régularité** [~'te] *f* regularity; *temper:* evenness; punctuality; **régulateur**, **-trice** [reɡyla'tœ:r, ~'tris] **1.** *adj.* regulating; ✝ buffer-(*stocks*); **2.** *su./ m* regulator; *watch:* balance-wheel; **régulier**, **-ère** [~'lje, ~'ljɛ:r] **1.** *adj.* regular (*a.* ⚓, *gramm.*); steady; even, equable (*temper*); **2.** *su./m* ⚔, *eccl.* regular.

régurgiter [reɡyrʒi'te] (1a) *v/t.* regurgitate.

réhabilitation [reabilita'sjɔ̃] *f* rehabilitation (*a. fig.*); *bankrupt:* discharge; ⚠ modernization (*of buildings etc.*); **réhabiliter** [~'te] (1a) *v/t.* reinstate; discharge (*a bankrupt*); *fig.* rehabilitate; *fig.* bring back into

favo(u)r; ⚠ modernize (*buildings etc.*); *se* ~ clear one's name.

réhabituer [reabi'tɥe] (1n) *v/t.* reaccustom (to, *à*).

rehaussement [rəos'mɑ̃] *m* raising (*a. prices*); *fig.* enhancing; **rehausser** [~o'se] (1a) *v/t.* raise; increase (*one's courage*); *fig.* enhance, set off (*one's beauty, a colour, one's merit*).

réimporter [reɛ̃pɔr'te] (1a) *v/t.* reimport.

réimposer [reɛ̃po'ze] (1a) *v/t.* reimpose (*a tax*); tax (*s.o.*) again.

réimpression [reɛ̃prɛ'sjɔ̃] *f* reprint (-ing); **réimprimer** [~pri'me] (1a) *v/t.* reprint.

rein [rɛ̃] *m anat.* kidney; ~*s pl.* back *sg.*, loins; ⚠ *arch:* sides; ♂ ~ *artificiel* kidney machine; ♂ ~ *flottant* floating kidney; *avoir les* ~*s solides* be sturdy; F *fig.* be wealthy; *avoir mal aux* ~*s* have backache; *casser les* ~*s à q.* ruin s.o.

réincorporer [reɛ̃kɔrpɔ're] (1a) *v/t.* reincorporate.

reine [rɛn] *f* queen; ~-**claude**, *pl.* ~s-**claudes** ♀ [~'klo:d] *f* greengage; ~-**des-prés**, *pl.* ~s-**des-prés** ♀ [~de-'pre] *f* meadow-sweet; ~-**marguerite**, *pl.* ~s-**marguerites** ♀ [~mar-ɡə'rit] *f* china aster; **reinette** ♀ [rɛ'nɛt] *f apple:* pippin; ~ *grise* russet.

réinsérer [reɛ̃se're] (1f) *v/t.* reinsert; *fig.* reintegrate (*persons*); **réinsertion** [~sɛr'sjɔ̃] *f* reinsertion; *fig.* reintegration.

réintégration [reɛ̃teɡra'sjɔ̃] *f admin. person:* reinstatement; ⚖ reintegration; ⚖ *conjugal rights:* restitution; *residence:* resumption; **réintégrer** [~'ɡre] (1f) *v/t. admin.* reinstate (*a person*); ⚖ reintegrate; return to, resume (*one's domicile*).

réitératif, -ve [reitera'tif, ~'ti:v] reiterative; second (*summons*); **réitérer** [~'re] (1f) *v/t.* repeat, reiterate.

reître [rɛ:tr] *m* ruffianly soldier.

rejaillir [rəʒa'ji:r] (2a) *v/i.* gush out; spurt; be reflected (*light*); spring; *fig.* fall (upon, *sur*), reflect (on, *sur*).

rejet [rə'ʒɛ] *m* throwing out; *food:* throwing up; ⚖ dismissal; *fig.*, *parl.*, ♂ *etc.* rejection; ✝ transfer; ♀ shoot; **rejetable** [rəʒ'tabl] rejectable; **rejeter** [~'te] (1c) *v/t.* throw back *or* again; fling back (*a.* ⚔ *the enemy*);

throw up (*a. food*); reject (*s.o.'s advice, parl. a. bill, an offer, a. ⚓ etc.*); 🛠 dismiss; ⚓ transfer; cast off (*stitches*); shift (*a. fig. the blame etc.*); ⚘ throw out (*shoots*); ~ la responsabilité sur throw *or* cast the responsibility on; **rejeton** [rəˈtɔ̃] *m* ⚘ (off)shoot; *fig.* offspring, scion.

rejoindre [rəˈʒwɛ̃ːdr] (4m) *v/t.* rejoin (*a.* ⚔); catch (*s.o.*) up; se ~ meet (again).

réjoui, e [reˈʒwi] **1.** *adj.* jolly, jovial, merry; **2.** *su./m:* gros ~ merry *or* jovial fellow; **réjouir** [~ˈʒwiːr] (2a) *v/t.* cheer, delight; entertain, amuse (*the company*); se ~ rejoice (at, in de), be delighted (at, de); enjoy o.s., make merry; **réjouissance** [~ʒwiˈsãːs] *f* rejoicing; ⚓ makeweight.

relâche[1] [rəˈlaːʃ] *m* rest, respite; *thea.* ~! closed!; *thea.* faire ~ be closed; *sans* ~ without respite.

relâche[2] ⚓ [~] *f* (port of) call; faire ~ put into port.

relâché, e [rəlaˈʃe] relaxed; slack (*rope*); *fig.* loose; **relâchement** [~laʃˈmɑ̃] *m* relaxing, slackening; *fig.* relaxation (*a.* ⚓, *a. from work*); *bowels, conduct:* looseness; **relâcher** [~laˈʃe] (1a) *v/t.* loosen (*a.* ⚓ *the bowels*), slacken; *fig.* relax; release (*a* ⚓ *prisoner*); ~ le temps make the weather milder; se ~ grow milder; *v/i.* ⚓ put into port.

relais [rəˈlɛ] *m* ⚡ *radio:* relay; ⊕ shift; *mot.* ~ des routiers truck stop; *sp.* course *f* de (*or par*) ~ relay race; prendre le ~ (*de*) take over (from); sans ~ without relay.

relance [rəˈlãs] *f* boost(ing), stimulation; revival, relaunching; **relancer** [rəlãˈse] (1k) *v/t.* throw back *or* again; return (*a ball*); *hunt.* start (*the quarry*) again; *fig.* pester (*s.o.*); *mot.* restart (*the engine*); *fig.* boost, stimulate; *fig.* revive, relaunch.

relaps, e *eccl.* [rəˈlaps] **1.** *adj.* relapsed; **2.** *su.* apostate, relapsed heretic.

relater [rəlaˈte] (1a) *v/t.* relate, recount; report.

relatif, -ve [rəlaˈtif, ~ˈtiːv] relative (*a. gramm.*); ~ à referring to, connected with, related to; **relation** [~ˈsjɔ̃] *f* relation; connection; account, report; ~s *pl.* acquaintances; ⚓ ~s *pl. publiques* public relations; **relativiser** [~tiviˈze] (1a) *v/t.* relativize; see

(*s.th.*) in (its true) perspective; **relativité** [~tiviˈte] *f* relativity; *phys.* théorie *f* de la ~ relativity theory.

relaxer [rəlakˈse] (1a) *v/t.* relax; 🛠 release; se ~ relax.

relayer [rəlɛˈje] (1i) *v/t.* relieve, take over from; take turns with; ⚡, *tel., radio:* relay; se ~ take turns; work in shifts; *v/i.* change horses.

relégation 🛠 [rəlegaˈsjɔ̃] *f* relegation; **reléguer** [~ˈge] (1s) *v/t.* relegate; *fig.* banish; *fig.* remove.

relent [rəˈlɑ̃] *m* musty smell *or* taste; unpleasant smell.

relevant, e [rəlˈvɑ̃, ~ˈvɑ̃ːt] *adj.:* ~ de dependent on; within the jurisdiction of.

relève [rəˈlɛːv] *f* ⚔, ⚓ relief; F relieving troops *pl.*; ⚔ guard: changing; **relevé, e** [rəlˈve] **1.** *adj.* raised (*head etc.*); turned up (*sleeve, trousers, etc.*); *fig.* high; lofty; noble (*sentiment*); *cuis.* highly seasoned; *fig.* spicy (*story*); **2.** *su./m* abstract, summary; ⚓ statement; *admin.* return; survey; *cost.* tuck; *cuis.* remove (= *course after soup*); ~ du gaz gas-meter reading; *su./f* ⚓ afternoon; **relèvement** [rəlɛvˈmɑ̃] *m* raising again; picking up; bankrate, temperature, wages: rise; raising (*a.* ⚓ bank-rate etc.); ⚓, *surv.* bearing; ⚓, *fig.* recovery, improvement; ⚓ account: making out; ⚔ sentry: relieving; wounded: collecting; **relever** [rəlˈve] (1d) *v/t.* raise (*a.* ⚓ prices, wages, etc.); lift; pick up (*from the ground*); ⚔ rebuild; ⚓ take the bearings of; *surv.* survey; *fig.* bring into relief, set off, enhance; ⚓ make out (*an account*), put up (*a price*); read (*the meter*); *fig.* call attention to, notice; *fig.* accept (*a challenge*); relieve, take over from (*s.o.*); *fig.* release (from, de); *cuis.* season; se ~ get up; rise (*a. fig.*); ⚓, *a. fig.* revive, recover; take turns; *v/i.:* ~ de be dependent on; *admin.* be a matter for; pertain to; arise from; ⚓ have just recovered from.

reliage [rəˈljaːʒ] *m* binding; joining; *casks:* hooping.

relief [rəˈljɛf] *m* relief (*a. fig.*); *fig.* prominence; relief (*a.* ⚓ *map*); *fig.* mettre en ~ set off, throw into relief.

relier [rəˈlje] (1o) *v/t.* bind (*a. books*); join; connect (*a.* ⚡, teleph., ☎); tie (*s.th.*) up again; hoop (*a cask*); **re-lieur, -euse** [rə'ljœːr, ~'ljøːz] *su.* (book)binder; *su.*/*f* bookbinding machine.

religieux, -euse [rəli'ʒjø, ~'ʒjøːz] 1. *adj.* religious; sacred (*music*), church ...; 2. *su.*/*m* monk; *su.*/*f* nun; **religion** [~'ʒjɔ̃] *f* religion; *fig.* sacred duty; *entrer en* ~ enter into religion, take the vows; **religiosité** [~ʒjozi-'te] *f* religiosity; *fig.* scrupulousness (in *ger.*, *à inf.*).

reliquaire [rəli'kɛːr] *m* reliquary, shrine.

reliquat [rəli'ka] *m* ⚕ residue; ✝ *account*: balance; ⚕ after-effects *pl.* **relique** [rə'lik] *f* relic; F *fig.* garder *comme une* ~ treasure.

relire [rə'liːr] (4t) *v*/*t.* re-read.

reliure [rə'ljyːr] *f* (book)binding; ~ *en toile* cloth binding.

relouer [rəlu'e] (1a) *v*/*t.* re-let; renew the lease of.

reluire [rə'lɥiːr] (4u) *v*/*i.* gleam; glisten, glitter; *faire* ~ polish (*s.th.*); **reluisant, e** [~lɥi'zɑ̃, ~'zɑ̃ːt] gleaming, shining; glittering; well-groomed (*horse*).

reluquer [rəly'ke] (1m) *v*/*t.* eye, ogle; have one's eye on; covet.

remâcher [rəmɑ'ʃe] (1a) *v*/*t.* chew again; *fig.* turn (*s.th.*) over in one's mind; brood over.

remailler [rəmɑ'je] (1a) *v*/*t.* mend a ladder in (*a stocking*).

remanent, e ⚡, *phys.* [rəma'nɑ̃, ~'nɑ̃ːt] remanent, residual.

remaniement *pol.* [rəmani'mɑ̃] *m* reshuffle; **remanier** [~'nje] (1o) *v*/*t.* rehandle; ⚠ retile (*a roof*), re-lay (*a pavement, pipes, etc.*); *fig.* recast; *fig.* adapt (*a play etc.*).

remarier [rəma'rje] (1o) *v*/*t.* a. se ~ remarry, marry again.

remarquable [rəmar'kabl] remarkable (for, *par*); distinguished (by, *par*); outstanding (for, *par*), astonishing; **remarque** [~'mark] *f* remark; note; ⚓ landmark; **remarquer** [~mar'ke] (1m) *v*/*t.* notice, note; re-mark; remark, observe; *faire* ~ *qch. à q.* point s.th. out to s.o.; *se faire* ~ attract attention; make o.s. conspicuous.

remballer [rɑ̃ba'le] (1a) *v*/*t.* re-pack; pack up again.

rembarquer [rɑ̃bar'ke] (1m) *vt*/*i.* ⚓ re-embark; *v*/*i.* a. se ~ go to sea

again; *v*/*t.*: F *fig.* se ~ *dans* embark again upon (*s.th.*).

remblai [rɑ̃'blɛ] *m* embankment; filling up *or* in; banking (up); *material*: filling; ⊕ slag dump; **rem-blayer** [~blɛ'je] (1i) *v*/*t.* fill (up); bank (up).

remboîter ⚕ [rɑ̃bwa'te] (1a) *v*/*t.* set (*a bone*).

rembourrage [rɑ̃bu'raːʒ] *m* stuffing, padding; upholstering; **rem-bourrer** [~'re] (1a) *v*/*t.* stuff, pad, upholster.

remboursable ✝ [rɑ̃bur'sabl] re-payable; redeemable (*annuity, stock, etc.*); **remboursement** ✝ [~sə'mɑ̃] *m* reimbursement, repayment; *annuity, stock*: redemption; *livraison f contre* ~ *post*: cash on delivery; **rembourser** [~'se] (1a) *v*/*t.* reimburse, repay; redeem (*stocks etc.*).

rembrunir [rɑ̃bry'niːr] (2a) *v*/*t.*: se ~ darken; cloud over; become gloomy.

remède [rə'mɛd] *m* remedy, cure (for, *à*) (*a. fig.*); *porter* ~ *à* remedy; *sans* ~ beyond remedy; **remédiable** [rəme'djabl] remediable; **remédier** [~'dje] (1o) *v*/*i.*: ~ *à* remedy, cure; ⚙ stop (*a leak*).

remembrement *admin.* [rəmɑ̃brə-'mɑ̃] *m* regrouping of lands.

remémorer [rəmemo're] (1a) *v*/*t.* remind (s.o. of s.th., *qch. à q.*); se ~ call (*s.th.*) to mind.

remerciements [rəmɛrsi'mɑ̃] *m*/*pl.* thanks; **remercier** [~'sje] (1o) *v*/*t.* thank (for, *de*); dismiss (*an employee*); *je vous remercie* thank you.

remettre [rə'mɛtr] (4v) *v*/*t.* put (*s.th.*) back again, replace; *cost.* put (*s.th.*) on again; return; restore; *fig.* calm (*s.o.'s mind*), reassure (*s.o.*); ⚕ set (*a bone*); deliver; hand over (*a. a command, an office*); tender (*one's resignation*); pardon (*an offence*); remit (*a penalty, a. sins*); ✝ give a discount of, allow; *fig.* postpone; ~ *au hasard* leave to chance; F ~ *ça* begin again; ~ *en état* overhaul; se ~ return; *fig.* recover (from, *de*); *s'en* ~ *à q.* rely on s.o. (for, *de*); leave it to s.o.

réminiscence [remini'sɑ̃ːs] *f* reminiscence.

remise [rə'miːz] *su.*/*f* putting back; postponement; *thea.* revival; *pointer*, ⚕ *bone*: setting; ✝ remittance; ✝ discount (of, *de*; on, *sur*); restoration; *post*: delivery; *debt, penalty*: remission; *duties, office, ticket*: handing over; coach-house; 🚗 (*engine*-)shed; ~ *à neuf* renovation; ~ *de bagages* luggage (*Am.* baggage) reclaim; F *sous la* ~ on the shelf; *su./m* livery carriage; **remiser** [~mi'ze] (1a) *v/t.* put (*a vehicle*) away; lay (*s.th.*) aside; F *fig.* superannuate (*s.o.*); F snub (*s.o.*); *hunt.* se ~ take cover.

rémissible [remi'sibl] remissible; **rémission** [~'sjɔ̃] *f debt, sin*: remission; 💊 abatement, remission; *sans* ~ unremitting(ly *adv.*).

rémittence 💊 [remi'tɑ̃:s] *f* abatement, remission; **rémittent, e** 💊 [~'tɑ̃, ~'tɑ̃:t] remittent.

remmailler [rɑ̃ma'je] (1a) *v/t.* see *remailler.*

remodelage [rəmɔd'la:ʒ] *m* remodelling; reorganization; **remodeler** [~'le] (1d) remodel, reshape; reorganize.

remontage [rəmɔ̃'ta:ʒ] *m* going up; *furniture*: assembling; ⚓ ascending; ⊕ *machine etc.*: (re)assembling, refitting; ✈ *shop*: restocking; *wine*: fortifying; *clock*: winding up; *shoes*: vamping; *à* ~ *automatique* self-winding (*watch*); **remontant, e** [~'tɑ̃, ~'tɑ̃:t] **1.** *adj.* ascending; ♀ remontant; 💊 *etc.* stimulating, tonic; **2.** *su./m* 💊 stimulant, tonic, F pick-me-up; **remonte** [rə'mɔ̃:t] *f salmon*: ascent, running; *coll. fish*: run; ⚔ *cavalry*: remount(ing); **remontée** [~mɔ̃'te] *f road*: climb; ⛷ climbing; **remonte-pente** *mount.* [~mɔ̃t'pɑ̃:t] *m see* monte-pente; **remonter** [rə-mɔ̃'te] (1a) *v/i.* go up (again) (*a.* ✈); get (*into a car, on a horse, etc.*) again; rise (*into a car, on a horse, etc.*) again; rise (*barometer*); re-ascend (the throne, *sur le trône*); get higher (*sun*); *fig.* date *or* go back (to, *à*); ⚓ flow (*tide*), come round (*wind*); *v/t.* go up (again), climb up (again); raise (up); take (*s.th.*) up; pull up (*socks, trousers*); ⚔ remount (*s.o.*); wind up (*a watch*); ⊕ reassemble; refit, reset; ✈ restock; *thea.* put (*a play*) on again; refurnish (*a house*); F *fig.* cheer (*s.o.*) up; se ~ recover one's strength *or* spirits; get in a new supply (of, de); **remontoir** ⊕ [~'twa:r] *m watch*: winder; *clock, watch*: key.

remontrance [rəmɔ̃'trɑ̃:s] *f* reprimand, reproof.

remontrer [rəmɔ̃'tre] (1a) *v/t.* show (again); point out; *v/i.: en* ~ *à q.* show *or* prove one knows better than s.o., prove one's superiority to s.o.

remordre [rə'mɔrdr] (4a) *v/t.* bite again; *v/i.: en* ~ *à* take up *or* tackle again; **remords** [~'mɔ:r] *m* remorse; twinge of conscience.

remorque [rə'mɔrk] *f* ⚓, *mot.* tow(ing); tow-rope; ⚓ vessel in tow; *mot.* trailer; *prendre en* ~ tow; *être en* ~ be on tow; **remorquer** [rəmɔr'ke] (1m) *v/t.* ⚓, *mot.* tow; pull; **remorqueur, -euse** [~'kœ:r, ~'kø:z] **1.** *adj.* towing; 🚗 relief (*engine*); **2.** *su./m* tug(boat); towboat.

rémoulade *cuis.* [remu'lad] *f* remoulade-sauce.

rémouleur ⊕ [remu'lœ:r] *m* (*scissors-, etc.*)grinder.

remous [rə'mu] *m water, wind*: eddy; *tide*: swirl; *crowd*: movement; ⚓ *ship*: wash; *river*: rise in level; ✈ slip-stream.

rempailler [rɑ̃pa'je] (1a) *v/t.* reseat (*a rush-bottomed chair*); restuff (*with straw*).

rempart [rɑ̃'pa:r] *m* 🛡 rampart; *fig.* bulwark.

rempiler [rɑ̃pi'le] (1a) *v/t.* pile up again; *v/i.* ⚔ *sl.* re-engage, re-enlist.

remplaçant, e *m, e f* [rɑ̃pla'sɑ̃, ~'sɑ̃:t] *person*: substitute, deputy; 💊, *eccl.* locum tenens, F locum; **remplacement** [~plas'mɑ̃] *m* replacement; substitution; ... *de* ~ refill ...; spare ...; *en* ~ *de* in place of; **remplacer** [~pla'se] (1k) *v/t.* replace (by, *par*); take the place of; supersede (*an official, a rule*); appoint a successor to (*an official, a diplomat*); deputize for.

rempli *cost.* [rɑ̃'pli] *m dress*: tuck; *hem or seam*: turning; **remplier** *cost.* [~pli'e] (1a) *v/t.* put a tuck in (*a dress etc.*); lay (*a hem, a seam*).

remplir [rɑ̃'pli:r] (2a) *v/t.* fill (up), refill (with, de); *admin.* complete, fill in *or* up (*a form*); *fig.* fulfil (*a hope, a promise*), perform (*a duty*), comply with (*formalities*); *thea.* play (*a part*); se ~ fill; **remplissage** [~pli'sa:ʒ] *m* filling (up); ⚔ infilling; 🛡 *etc.* filling (in); *fig.* padding, F radio: fill-up.

remploi [rɑ̃'plwa] *m* re-use, using again; re-employment; ⚖ reinvestment; **remployer** [~plwa'je] (1h) *v/t.* re-use; use again; employ (*s.o.*) again; reinvest (*money*).

remplumer [răply'me] (1a) *v/t.*: se ~ F put on flesh again, get better, recover; F get back on one's feet (*financially*); *orn.* grow new feathers.

rempocher [răpɔ'ʃe] (1a) *v/t.* put (*s.th.*) back in one's pocket.

remporter [răpɔr'te] (1a) *v/t.* take *or* carry back; carry off *or* away; *fig.* win, gain (*a prize, a victory*).

rempoter ✍ [răpɔ'te] (1a) repot.

remuage [rə'mɥa:ʒ] *m* moving, removal; shaking (up), stirring (up); *wine:* settling of the deposit; **remuant, e** [~'mɥɑ̃, ~'mɥɑ̃:t] restless; bustling; **remue-ménage** [~myme-'na:ʒ] *m/inv.* bustle, commotion, stir; **remue-méninges** [~myme-'nɛ̃:ʒ] *m/inv.* brainstorming; **remuement** [~my'mɑ̃] *m* moving; *furniture, earth:* removal; *fig.* stir, commotion; **remuer** [~'mɥe] (1n) *v/t.* move (*furniture, one's head, a. fig. s.o.'s heart, etc.*); stir (*coffee, tea*); *fig.* stir up (*a crowd*); *dog:* wag (*its tail*); se ~ move, stir; bestir o.s., F get a move on; *v/i.* move; budge; be loose (*tooth*).

remugle [rə'my:gl] *m* musty smell.

rémunérateur, -trice [remynera-'tœ:r, ~'tris] **1.** *adj.* remunerative; profitable; **2.** *su.* rewarder; **rémunération** [~ra'sjɔ̃] *f* remuneration, payment (for, *de*); **rémunératoire** ⚖ [~ra'twa:r] for services rendered (*money*) by way of recompense; **rémunérer** [~re] (1f) *v/t.* remunerate, reward; pay for (*services*).

renâcler [rəna'kle] (1a) *v/i.* snort (*horse*); sniff (*person*); *fig.* turn up one's nose (at, *à*); F *fig.* be reluctant; jib (at, *à*).

renaissance [rənɛ'sɑ̃:s] *f* rebirth; revival; *art etc.:* ♀ Renaissance, Renascence; **renaître** [~'nɛ:tr] (4x) *v/i.* be born again; *fig.* reappear; *fig.* revive (*arts, hope, etc.*).

rénal, e, *m/pl.* **-aux** ⚕, *anat.* [re'nal, ~'no] renal; *calcul m* ~ renal calculus.

renard [rə'na:r] *m zo.* fox; ⊕ *sl.* strike-breaker, F blackleg; ⊕, ⚓ dog(-hook); F *fig.* fin ~ sly dog; **renarde** *zo.* [~'nard] *f* vixen, she-fox; **renardeau** *zo.* [rənar'do] *m* fox-cub; **renardière** [~'djɛ:r] *f* fox-hole, fox's earth, burrow.

---

renchéri, e [răʃe'ri] **1.** *adj.* dearer; F particular, fastidious; **2.** *su.* fastidious person; *su./m:* faire le ~ be squeamish; put on airs; **renchérir** [~'ri:r] (2a) *v/t.* raise the price of; *v/i.* get dearer, go up in price; ~ *sur* go one better than (*s.o.*); improve upon (*s.th.*); **renchérissement** [~ris'mɑ̃] *m* increase *or* rise in price; **renchérisseur** [~ri'sœ:r] *m* outdoer; outbidder; ⚘ runner up of prices.

rencogner F [răkɔ'ɲe] (1a) *v/t.* drive *or* push (*s.o.*) into a corner; se ~ huddle (o.s.) up.

rencontre [răˈkɔ̃:tr] *f* ♠, person, streams: meeting; ⚔, persons: encounter; ⚘, *mot.* collision; ⚔ skirmish; *fig.* occasion; *aller à la ~ de* go to meet; *de* ~ casual; chance ...; **rencontrer** [~kɔ̃'tre] (1a) *v/t.* meet; ⚔, *mot.* collide with; *fig.* come across; find; ⚔ encounter; *fig.* meet with, come up against; se ~ meet; ⚘, *mot.* collide; *fig.* happen; *fig.* appear (*person*); *fig.* agree (*persons, ideas*).

rendement [răd'mɑ̃] *m* ✍, ⚘, ⚔ yield; ⊕ *works, men:* output; ⊕ efficiency (*a. of machines*); ⊕, ⚓, *mot.* performance; *sp. time:* handicap; ~ *maximum* maximum output *or* speed.

rendez-vous [răde'vu] *m* rendez-vous (*a.* ⚔); appointment; F date; meeting-place; haunt; ~ *social* collective bargaining.

rendormir [rădɔr'mi:r] (2b) *v/t.* put to sleep again; se ~ fall asleep again.

rendre [ră:dr] (4a) *v/t.* return, give back; restore (*s.o.'s liberty, s.o.'s health*); give (*an account, change,* ⚖ *a verdict*); pay (*homage*); *fig.* convey (*the meaning*), translate; render (⚘ *an account, services*); ⚖ pronounce (*judgment*); ♩ perform, play; ⚘ deliver; ⚘, ✍, ⊕ yield, produce; ⚔ surrender (*a fortress*); ⚘ throw up, vomit; ~ (*adj.*) make (*adj.*); ~ *compte de* account for; *fig.* ~ *justice à* do (*s.o.*) justice; ⚖ ~ *la justice* dispense justice; ~ *les derniers devoirs à* pay (*s.o.*) the last hono(u)rs; ~ *nul* nullify; vitiate (*a contract*); se ~ go (to, *à*); *fig.* yield, give way; ⚔ surrender; *v/i.* be productive *or fig.* profitable; ⚘ vomit; work, run (*engine*); ~ *à* lead to (*way*); **rendu, e** [ră'dy] **1.** *adj.* arrived;

exhausted; **2.** *su./m paint. etc.* rendering; **†** returned article; F *un prêté pour un ~* tit for tat.
rendurcir [rɑ̃dyr'siːr] **(2a)** *v/t. a. se ~* harden.
rêne [rɛn] *f* rein (*a. fig.*); *lâcher les ~s* slacken the reins; *give a horse its head.* [gade, turncoat.)
renégat *m, e f* [rəne'ga, ~'gat] rene-)
rénette ⊕ [re'nɛt] *f* tracing-iron; *leather*: race-knife; *horse's hoof*: paring-knife.
renfermé, e [rɑ̃fɛr'me] **1.** *adj. fig.* uncommunicative; **2.** *su./m* fustiness; *odeur f de ~* fusty *or* stale smell; *sentir le ~* smell fusty *or* stuffy; **renfermer** [~] **(1a)** *v/t.* shut *or* lock up (again); enclose; *fig.* contain, include; *fig.* confine (*to dans, en*); *fig.* hide; *se ~* (*dans, en*) confine o.s. (to); withdraw (into *o.s., silence*).
renflé, e [rɑ̃'fle] bulging, swelling; **renflement** [rɑ̃flə'mɑ̃] *m* bulging, bulge, swelling; **renfler** [~'fle] **(1a)** *v/t.* swell (out); *se ~* bulge (out), swell (out).
renflouer [rɑ̃flu'e] **(1a)** *v/t.* ⚓ refloat; *fig.* put in funds.
renfoncement [rɑ̃fɔ̃s'mɑ̃] *m* knocking in (*of s.th.*) again; △ recess, hollow; denting; *paint.* effect of depth; **renfoncer** [~fɔ̃'se] **(1k)** *v/t.* knock *or* push (further) in; △ recess, set back; dent; pull down (*one's hat*).
renforçateur *phot.* [rɑ̃fɔrsa'tœːr] *m* intensifier; **renforcement** [~sa-'mɑ̃] *m* △, ✗ strengthening (*a. fig. opinion*); reinforcing; *phys. sound*: magnification; *phot.* intensification; **renforcer** [~'se] **(1k)** *v/t.* reinforce; ⊕ *a.* strengthen; increase (*the sound, the expenditure*); *phot.* intensify; *phys.* magnify; **renfort** [rɑ̃'fɔːr] *m* ✗, ⊕, *etc.* reinforcement(s *pl.*); *de ~* stiffening...; *à grand ~ de* with a great deal of.
renfrogné, e [rɑ̃frɔ'ɲe] sullen, sulky; **renfrogner** [~] **(1a)** *v/t.: se ~* scowl; frown.
rengager [rɑ̃ga'ʒe] **(1l)** *v/t.* re-engage; *v/i., a. se ~* ✗ re-enlist.
rengaine F [rɑ̃'gɛːn] *f* old refrain, (*the same*) old story; **rengainer** [~gɛ'ne] **(1a)** *v/t.* † put up (*the sword*); F withhold, hold back, save.
rengorger [rɑ̃gɔr'ʒe] **(1l)** *v/t.: se ~* puff o.s. up, give o.s. airs.

rengraisser [rɑ̃grɛ'se] **(1a)** *v/t.* fatten up again; *v/i.* grow fat again.
renier [rə'nje] **(1o)** *v/t. eccl.* deny; abjure (*one's faith*); disown (*a friend, an opinion*); repudiate (*an action, an opinion*).
reniflement [rəniflə'mɑ̃] *m* sniff(ing); **renifler** [~'fle] **(1a)** *v/t.* sniff (*s.th.*) (up); *fig.* scent; *v/i.* sniff; snivel (*child*); **renifleur** *m*, **-euse** *f* F [~'flœːr, ~'fløːz] sniffer.
rénitence ✗ [reni'tɑ̃ːs] *f* resistance to pressure; **rénitent, e** [~'tɑ̃, ~'tɑ̃ːt] renitent.
renne *zo.* [rɛn] *m* reindeer.
renom [rə'nɔ̃] *m* fame, renown; **renommé, e** [rənɔ'me] **1.** *adj.* famed, renowned, famous (for, *pour*); **2.** *su./f* fame, renown; reputation; *esp.* ⚜ report; rumo(u)r; **renommer** [~] **(1a)** *v/t.* re-elect, re-appoint; † praise.
renoncement [rənɔ̃s'mɑ̃] *m* renouncing; renunciation (*a.* ⚜); *~ à soi-même* self-denial; **renoncer** [rənɔ̃'se] **(1k)** *v/i.: ~ à* give up, renounce, abandon; waive (*a claim, a right*); **renonciation** [~sja'sjɔ̃] *f* renunciation.
renoncule ⚘ [rənɔ̃'kyl] *f* ranunculus; *~ âcre* crowfoot; buttercup.
renouement [rənu'mɑ̃] *m* renewal; **renouer** [~'e] **(1a)** *v/t.* re-knot; tie up again; *fig.* renew; resume (*a conversation*).
renouveau [rənu'vo] *m* spring (-time); renewal; *~ catholique* Catholic (literary) revival; **renouveler** [~nuv'le] **(1c)** *v/t.* renew; revive (*a custom, a lawsuit, a quarrel*); *fig.* transform; † repeat (*an order*); *mot.* fit a new set of (*tyres*); *se ~* be renewed; happen again; **renouvellement** [~nuvel'mɑ̃] *m* renovation; replacement; renewal; *fig.* increase.
rénovateur, -trice [renɔva'tœːr, ~'tris] **1.** *adj.* renovating; **2.** *su.* renovator, restorer; **rénovation** [~'sjɔ̃] *f* renovation, restoration; renewal; reform; (*religious*) revival; **rénover** [~'ve] **(1a)** *v/t.* renovate, restore; renew; reform.
renseigné, e [rɑ̃sɛ'ɲe] (well-)informed (about, *sur*); **renseignement** [~sɛɲ'mɑ̃] *m* (piece of) information; *teleph. ~s* inquiries; *bureau m de ~s* information bureau *or Am.* booth, inquiry office;

prendre des ~*s sur* make inquiries about; ✕ *service m de* ~*s* Intelligence Corps; **renseigner** [~sɛ'ɲe] (1a) *v/t.* inform (*s.o.*), give (*s.o.*) information (about, *sur*); give (*s.o.*) directions; *se* ~ inquire, find out (about, *sur*).

rentabiliser [rɑ̃tabili'ze] (1a) *v/t.* make profitable, make pay; **rentabilité** [rɑ̃tabili'te] *f* profitableness; **rentable** [rɑ̃'tabl] profitable.

rente [rɑ̃ːt] *f* revenue; annuity, pension; stock(s *pl.*), bonds *pl.*; ~*s pl.* (private) income *sg.*; ~ *foncière* ground rent; ~ *perpétuelle* perpetuity; ~ *viagère* life annuity; **rentier** *m*, **-ère** *f* [~'tje, ~'tjɛːr] stockholder; annuitant; person living on private means; *petit* ~ small investor.

rentrant, e [rɑ̃'trɑ̃, ~'trɑ̃ːt] **1.** *adj.* ⚔ re-entrant; 🚗 retractable; ⊕ inset; **2.** *su. sp.* new player; **rentré, e** [rɑ̃'tre] suppressed (*anger*); sunken (*eyes, cheecks*); **rentrée** [~] *f* return, home-coming; re-entry (*a.* ♪); ✍ *crops:* gathering; *school etc.:* re-opening; *parl.* re-assembly; 🌱 *taxes etc.:* collection; 🌱 *money:* receipt; *air etc.:* entry; *actor etc.:* comeback; **rentrer** [~] (1a) *v/i.* re-enter (*a. thea., a.* ♪); come *or* go in (again); return; come *or* go home; re-open (*school etc.*); *parl.* re-assemble; go back to school (*child*); 🌱 come in (*money*); ~ *dans* be included in, be part of; get back, recover (*rights etc.*); crash into (*a wall, car, etc.*); ~ *en fonctions* resume one's duties; *v/t.* take *or* bring *or* get *or* pull in; put away; ✍ gather in (*crops*); 🌱 re-enter (*in an account*); *fig.* suppress (*a desire, one's tears*); 🚗 retract (*the undercarriage*).

renversable [rɑ̃vɛr'sabl] reversible; capsizable (*boat etc.*); **renversant, e** F [~'sɑ̃, ~'sɑ̃ːt] staggering, stunning; **renverse** [rɑ̃'vɛrs] *f* ⚓ *tide:* turn; *à la* ~ backwards; **renversement** [rɑ̃vɛrsə'mɑ̃] *m* reversal (*a. phys.*); ♪, *opt., phls., geol.* inversion; ⊕ reversing; ⚓ *tide:* turn(ing); *wind:* shift(ing); overturning; *fig.* disorder; *fig., a. pol.* overthrow; **renverser** [~'se] (1a) *v/t.* reverse (*a.* ✕, ♪, ⊕ *an engine, the steam, mot.*); ♪, *opt., phls.* invert; turn upside down; knock down; knock over; overturn, upset; spill; *fig., a.*

pol. overthrow; F *fig.* amaze; F ~ *les rôles* turn the tables; *se* ~ fall over; overturn; lie back (*in a chair*); *v/i.* F spill over.

renvoi [rɑ̃'vwa] *m* return(ing), sending back; *ball, sound:* throwing back; *tennis:* return; *heat, light:* reflecting; ⚽ belch; ♪ repeat (sign); *servant:* dismissal; adjournment; 🌱, *pol., typ.* reference; 🌱 transfer; 🌱 remand; **renvoyer** [~vwa'je] (1r) *v/t.* return (*a. tennis*), send back; throw back (*a ball, a sound*); reflect (*heat, light*); dismiss (*s.o.*); postpone; adjourn; *pol.* refer; 🌱 defer; 🌱 remand.

réoccuper [reɔky'pe] (1a) *v/t.* re-occupy.

réorganiser [reɔrgani'ze] (1a) *v/t.* reorganize.

réouverture [reuvɛr'tyːr] *f* reopening; resumption.

repaire [rə'pɛːr] *m animals, a. fig.:* den; *fig. criminal:* haunt; hideout.

repaître [rə'pɛːtr] (4k) *v/t.* feed (*a. fig.*); *se* ~ eat one's fill; *se* ~ *de* feed on; *fig.* indulge in (*vain hopes*); wallow in (*blood*).

répandre [re'pɑ̃ːdr] (4a) *v/t.* spill, shed; spread (*light, news*); scatter (*flowers, money, sand, etc.*); give off (*heat, a smell*); *il s'est répandu que* the rumo(u)r has spread that; *fig. se* ~ go out, be seen in society; **répandu, e** [~pɑ̃'dy] widespread, widely held (*opinion*); well known.

réparable [repa'rabl] reparable; *cost.* repairable; remediable.

reparaître [rəpa'rɛːtr] (4k) *v/i.* reappear; 🌱 recur.

réparateur, -trice [repara'tœːr, ~'tris] **1.** *adj.* repairing; restoring; **2.** *su.* repairer; repairman; **réparation** [~ra'sjɔ̃] *f* repair(ing); *fig.* amends *pl.*; (*legal*) redress; ✕ ~*s pl.* reparations; 🌱 ~ *civile* compensation; *foot. coup m de pied de* ~ penalty kick; **réparer** [~'re] (1a) *v/t.* mend, repair, *Am.* fix; *fig.* make good (*losses, wear*); *fig.* make amends for, put (*s.th.*) right.

repartie [rəpar'ti] *f* repartee; retort; ~ *spirituelle* witty rejoinder; *avoir de la* ~, *avoir la* ~ *facile* be quick at repartee; **repartir** [~'tiːr] (2b) *v/i.* set out *or* leave again; retort, reply.

répartir [repar'tiːr] (2a) *v/t.* share out, distribute (amongst, *entre*);

admin. assess; ✝ allot (*shares*);
répartition [‿ti'sjɔ̃] *f* distribution
(*a.* 🗲); apportionment, division,
sharing out; *errors:* frequency;
admin. assessment; allocation; ✝
allotment.

repas [rə'pɑ] *m* meal; *petit* ~ snack.

repassage [rəpα'sa:ʒ] *m* repassing;
water, mountains: recrossing;
clothes: ironing; *lessons:* revision;
⊕ sharpening; **repasser** [‿'se] (1a)
v/i. pass again; call again (on s.o.,
chez q.); cross over again (to, *en*); *v/t.*
repass; cross (*the sea etc.*) again;
iron (*clothes*); go over (*in the mind,
a lesson, an outline, accounts, etc.*);
take (*s.o.*) back; ⊕ sharpen, whet;
fer m à ~ iron; **repasseur** [‿'sœ:r]
m (*knife- etc.*)grinder; ⊕ examiner;
repasseuse [‿'sø:z] *f* woman, *a.*
machine: ironer.

repayer [rəpɛ'je] (1i) *v/t.* repay;
pay back.

repêchage [rəpɛ'ʃa:ʒ] *m* fishing up
or out; *fig.* giving a helping hand (to,
de); *univ., school:* supplementary examination, F resit; **repêcher** [‿'ʃe]
(1a) *v/t.* fish up *or* out; *fig.* come to
the rescue of, help (*s.o.*) out; give
(*s.o.*) a second chance; *school:* let
(*s.o.*) through, give (*s.o.*) a chance to
scrape through.

repeindre [rə'pɛ̃:dr] (4m) *v/t.*
repaint.

repenser [rəpɑ̃'se] (1a) *v/i.* think
again (about, of *à*); y ~ think it over.

repentant, e [rəpɑ̃'tɑ̃, ~'tɑ̃:t] repentant; **repenti, e** [~'ti] *adj., a. su.*
repentant, penitent; **repentir**
[~'ti:r] **1.** (2b) *v/t.:* se ~ (de *qch.*)
repent ([of] s.th.), be sorry (for s.th.);
2. *su./m* repentance.

repérage [rəpe'ra:ʒ] *m* marking with
guide *or* reference marks; locating.

répercussion [repɛrky'sjɔ̃] *f* repercussion; consequences *pl.*; *phys.
sound:* reverberation; **répercuter**
[~'te] (1a) *v/t.* reverberate; send *or*
throw back, reflect (*heat, light, etc.,
a. fig.*); *fig.* pass on (*costs etc.*) (to,
sur); se ~ *phys.* reverberate; *fig.* have
repercussions.

repère [rə'pɛ:r] *m* (reference *or*
guide) mark; *surv.* benchmark; *cin.*
synchronizing mark; *point m de* ~
landmark (*a. fig.*); **repérer** [~pe're]
(1f) *v/t.* mark with guide *or* reference
marks; fix *or* adjust by guide marks;

✕., ⚓ *etc.* locate; spot; se ~ get *or* take
one's bearings.

répertoire [repɛr'twa:r] *m* index,
list; *thea., a. fig.* repertory; *thea.*
repertoire; *fig.* ~ *vivant* mine of information.

repeser [rəpə'ze] (1d) *v/t.* re-weigh.

répéter [repe'te] (1f) *v/t.* repeat; do
or say again; con (*a lesson, thea.
a part*); *thea.* rehearse (*a play*);
mirror: reflect; **répéteur** [~'tœ:r]
m teleph. repeater; *phys.* reflector;
reproducer; **répétiteur, -trice**
[~ti'tœ:r, ~'tris] *su.* private tutor;
su./m school: assistant-master; ⚓
repeating ship; *teleph.* repeater;
su./f school: assistant-mistress; **répétition** [~ti'sjɔ̃] *f* repetition; recurrence; private lesson; *thea.* rehearsal; *picture etc.:* reproduction,
replica; *thea.* ~ *générale* dress rehearsal; ✕ *fusil m à* ~ repeating
rifle; *montre f à* ~ repeater (watch).

repeupler [rəpœ'ple] (1a) *v/t.* re-
people; 🌿 replant; restock (*a pond,
a river, etc.*).

repiquer [rəpi'ke] (1m) *v/t.* prick
(*s.th.*) again; repair (*a road*); *cost.*
restitch; 🌿 prick *or* plant out; *sl.*
catch *or* F nab again; *v/i.:* F ~ *au plat*
have a second helping; F ~ *au truc*
begin again.

répit [re'pi] *m* respite; F *fig.* breath-
er; *sans* ~ incessant(ly *adv.*).

replacer [rəpla'se] (1k) *v/t.* replace;
✝ reinvest; find a new position for (*a
servant*).

replanter [rəplɑ̃'te] (1a) *v/t.* replant.

replâtrer [rəplɑ'tre] (1a) *v/t.* 🔺 replaster; *fig.* patch up.

replet, -ète [rə'plɛ, ~'plɛt] stoutish;
réplétion [reple'sjɔ̃] *f* repletion.

repli [rə'pli] *m cost.* fold (*a. of
ground*), crease; *rope, snake:* coil;
river: bend, winding; ✕ falling back;
repliable [rəpli'abl] folding; collapsible (*boat, chair*); **repliement**
[~'mɑ̃] *m* re-folding, turning up;
bending back; ✕ falling back; *fig.*
withdrawal (into o.s.); **replier** [~'e]
(1a) *v/t. a.* se ~ fold up; coil up; bend
back; ✕ withdraw (*outposts*); se ~ ✕
fall back; *fig.* retire (within o.s., *sur
soi-même*).

réplique [re'plik] *f* rejoinder, retort;
thea. cue; *work of art etc.:* replica;
cin. retake; ♪ counterpoint: answer;
fig. sans ~ unanswerable (*argument*);

répliquer [⌃pli'ke] (1m) *v/i.* retort; answer back.

reploiement [rəplwa'mɑ̃] *m see* repliement.

répondant [repɔ̃'dɑ̃] *m* ⚖ surety, guarantor; *eccl.* server; *servir de* ⌃ *à q.* stand surety for s.o.; F *avoir du* ⌃ have money behind one, *a. fig.* have something to fall back on; **répondeur** *teleph.* [⌃'dœːr] *m (a.* ⌃ *téléphonique)* answering machine; **répondre** [⌃'pɔ̃:dr] (4a) *v/t.* answer, reply; *eccl.* make the responses at *(mass)*; *v/i.* ⊕ *etc., a. fig.* respond; ⌃ *à* answer; comply with, satisfy; correspond to, match; ⌃ *de* answer for; be responsible for; guarantee; **réponse** [⌃'pɔ̃:s] *f* answer, reply; *phys., physiol., a. fig.* response; *options:* declaration; ⚖⌃*s pl. de droit* judicial decisions; ⌃ *payée* reply paid.

report [rə'pɔːr] *m* ✝ carrying forward; ✝ amount carried forward; transfer; postponement; **reportage** *journ.* [rəpɔr'taːʒ] *m* report(ing); article, story; coverage; (live) commentary.

reporter¹ [rəpɔr'te] (1a) *v/t.* carry or take back; transfer *(a. phot.)*, transmit; ✝ carry forward; ✝ *Stock Exchange:* continue; *fig.* postpone (to, until *à*).

reporter² *journ.* [rəpɔr'tɛːr] *m* reporter; ⌃ *sportif* sports reporter *or* commentator.

repos [rə'po] *m* rest, repose; peace *(of mind etc.);* ♪ pause; resting-place; *stair:* landing; ⚔ ⌃*!* stand easy!; *au* ⌃ at rest *(a. machine);* still; **reposé, e** [⌃po'ze] **1.** *adj.* rested, refreshed; restful, quiet; fresh *(complexion); à tête* ⌃*e* at leisure; deliberately; **2.** *su./f animal:* lair; **repose-pied** [⌃poz'pje] *m/inv.* foot-rest; **reposer** [rəpo'ze] (1a) *v/t.* place, put, lay; 🔫 re-lay *(a track);fig.* rest; ⚔ *reposez armes!* order arms!; *se* ⌃ (take a) rest; rely ([up]on, *sur);* settle *(bird, wine, etc.); fig. se* ⌃ *sur ses lauriers* rest on one's laurels; *v/i.* lie, rest; be at rest; *fig.* ⌃ *sur* rest on, be based on; *ici re-pose* here lies; **reposoir** *eccl.* [⌃-'zwaːr] *m* temporary altar, station.

repoussant, e [rəpu'sɑ̃, ⌃'sɑ̃:t] repulsive; offensive, obnoxious *(odour);* **repousser** [⌃'se] (1a) *v/t.* push back *or* away, repel; ⚔, *a. fig.*

repulse *(an attack, an offer); pol., a. fig.* reject *(a bill, overtures);* ⊕ chase *(metal),* emboss *(leather); v/i.* 🌱 shoot (up) again; grow again *(hair);* recoil *(gun);* resist *(spring);* **repoussoir** [⌃'swaːr] *m* cuticle remover; *paint.* strong piece of foreground; *fig.* foil.

répréhensible [repres̃'sibl] reprehensible; **répréhension** [⌃'sjɔ̃] *f* reprehension.

reprendre [rə'prɑ̃:dr] (4aa) *v/t.* take again; recapture; get *(s.th.)* back; pick *(s.o.)* up (again); *fig.* recover *(senses, strength, taste, tongue);* take back *(an object, a gift, a promise, a servant, etc.);* resume *(a talk, one's work);* repeat *(an operation); thea.* revive *(a play); fig.* catch *(cold,* F *s.o.)* again; *fig.* reprove *(s.o.);* put on again *(one's summer clothes); v/i.* begin again; 🪡, ✝ improve; 🪡 heal again *(wound);* 🌱 take root (again); set again *(liquid);* reply; come in again *(fashion).*

représailles [rəpre'zɑːj] *f/pl.* reprisal(s *pl.) sg.; user de* ⌃ make reprisals.

représentable [rəprezɑ̃'tabl] representable; *thea.* performable; **représentant, e** [⌃'tɑ̃, ⌃'tɑ̃:t] **1.** *adj.* representative; **2.** *su.* representative; *su./m* ✝ agent, traveller; ⌃ *exclusif de* sole agent for; **représentatif, -ve** [⌃ta'tif, ⌃'tiːv] representative (of, de); **représentation** [⌃ta'sjɔ̃] *f* ⚖, *paint., pol., fig.* representation; *thea.* performance, show; ✝ agency; *admin.* official entertainment; *fig.* protest; **représenter** [⌃'te] (1a) *v/t.* re-present; ⚖, ✝, *pol., fig.* represent; stand for; symbolize; *thea.* perform, give *(a play),* take the rôle of *(a character); paint.* depict, portray; *fig.* describe (as, *comme);* introduce *(s.o.)* again; recall *(s.o.);* point *(s.th.)* out (to, *à); fig. se* ⌃ *qch.* imagine *or* picture s.th.; *v/i.* have a good presence; keep up appearances.

répressif, -ve [reprɛ'sif, ⌃'siːv] repressive; **répression** [⌃'sjɔ̃] *f* repression.

réprimable [repri'mabl] repressible.

réprimandable [reprimɑ̃'dabl] deserving (of) censure; **réprimande**

[~'mã:d] *f* reprimand, rebuke; **ré-primander** [~mã'de] (1a) *v/t.* reprimand, rebuke, reprove (for, de).

réprimer [repri'me] (1a) *v/t.* repress.

repris, e [rə'pri, ~'pri:z] **1.** *p.p. of reprendre*; **2.** *adj.* recaptured; **3.** *su./m*: ~ de *justice* old offender; habitual criminal; F old lag, *Am.* repeater; *su./f* recapture, recovery; *talks, work*: resumption; *thea. play,* ⊕ *business*: revival; *box.* round; *foot.* second half; ♪ repetition; *fig.* renewal; 𝕏 fresh attack; *mot. engine*: pick-up; *cost.* darn(ing), mend(ing); repairing, mending; ~e *perdue* invisible mending; *à plusieurs* ~es again and again; on several occasions; ⊕ *valeur f de* ~ trade-in value; ⊕ *prendre qch. en* ~ take s.th. as a trade-in; **repriser** [~pri'ze] (1a) *v/t.* mend, darn; **repriseuse** [~'zø:z] *f* mender, darner.

réprobateur, -trice [reprɔba'tœ:r, ~'tris] reproachful; reproving; **réprobation** [~'sjɔ̃] *f* reprobation, censure; *fig.* (howl of) protest.

reprochable [rəprɔ'ʃabl] reproachable, blameworthy; **reproche** [~'prɔʃ] *m* reproach; reproof; *sans* ~ blameless, unimpeachable; **reprocher** [~prɔ'ʃe] (1a) *v/t.*: ~ *qch. à q.* reproach *or* blame s.o. for s.th.; grudge s.o. s.th.

reproducteur, -trice [rəprɔdyk'tœ:r, ~'tris] **1.** *adj.* reproductive; **2.** *su./m* stud animal; **reproductible** [~'tibl] reproducible; **reproduction** [~'sjɔ̃] *f* 𝕏, *zo., etc.* reproduction; ⊕ reproducing; copy; replica; 𝕣𝕥 *droits m/pl. de* ~ copyright *sg.*; **reproduire** [rəprɔ'dɥi:r] (4h) *v/t.* reproduce; produce *(s.th.)* again; copy; *se* ~ *fig.* recur; *zo. etc.* reproduce, breed.

reprographie [rəpɔgra'fi] *f* reprography; **reprographier** [~'fje] (1o) *v/t.* reproduce, copy.

réprouvable [repru'vabl] blamable; blameworthy; **réprouvé, e** [~'ve] *su.* outcast; *su./m*: *eccl. les* ~*s pl.* the damned; **réprouver** [~'ve] (1a) *v/t.* reprobate *(a. eccl.)*; *fig.* disapprove of; *eccl.* damn.

reps *tex.* [rɛps] *m* rep.

reptile *zo.* [rɛp'til] *adj., a. su./m* reptile.

repu, e [rə'py] **1.** *p.p. of repaître*; **2.** *adj.* satiated, full.

républicain, e [repybli'kɛ̃, ~'kɛn] *adj., a. su.* republican; **république** [~'blik] *f* republic *(a. fig.)*.

répudier [repy'dje] (1o) *v/t.* repudiate *(an opinion, one's wife)*; 𝕣𝕥 relinquish *(a succession)*.

répugnance [repy'ɲɑ̃:s] *f* repugnance; dislike (of, to *pour*); loathing (of, for *pour*); *fig.* reluctance (to *inf.*, *à inf.*); *avec* ~ reluctantly; **répugnant, e** [~'ɲɑ̃, ~'ɲɑ̃:t] repugnant, loathsome, disgusting; **répugner** [~'ɲe] (1a) *v/i.*: ~ *à q.* be repugnant to s.o., disgust s.o.; ~ *à faire qch.* be loath to do s.th.; *il me répugne de (inf.)* I am loath *or* reluctant to *(inf.)*.

répulsif, -ve [repyl'sif, ~'si:v] repulsive; **répulsion** *phys., a. fig.* [~'sjɔ̃] *f* repulsion (for, *pour*).

réputation [repyta'sjɔ̃] *f* reputation, F character; *(good or bad)* name; *connaître q. de* ~ know s.o. by reputation; **réputer** [~'te] (1a) *v/t.* think, consider, hold.

requérant, e 𝕣𝕥 [rəke'rɑ̃, ~'rɑ̃:t] **1.** *su.* plaintiff; petitioner; applicant; **2.** *adj.*: *partie f* ~*e* applicant; petitioner; claimant; **requérir** [~ke'ri:r] (2l) *v/t.* ask (for); claim, demand; *fig.* require; 𝕏 requisition; call upon *(s.o.)* for help; **requête** [~'kɛt] *f* request, petition; demand; 𝕣𝕥 ~ *civile* appeal against a judgment.

requin *icht.* [rə'kɛ̃] *m* shark *(a.* F = *swindler)*.

requis, e [rə'ki, ~'ki:z] **1.** *adj.* required, necessary, requisite; **2.** *p.p. of requérir*; **3.** *su./m* labo(u)r conscript.

réquisition [rekizi'sjɔ̃] *f* requisition(ing) *(a.* 𝕏*)*; levy; demand; **réquisitionner** [~sjɔ'ne] (1a) *v/t.* requisition; seize, commandeer; **réquisitoire** 𝕣𝕥 [~'twa:r] *m* charge, indictment.

rescapé, e [rɛska'pe] **1.** *adj.* rescued; **2.** *su.* survivor; rescued person.

rescinder 𝕣𝕥 [rɛsɛ̃'de] (1a) *v/t.* rescind, annul; avoid *(a contract)*; **rescision** 𝕣𝕥 [~si'zjɔ̃] *f* rescission, annulment; *contract*: avoiding.

rescousse [rɛs'kus] *f*: *aller (venir) à la* ~ *de* go (come) to the rescue of.

réseau [re'zo] *m* 📷, *teleph., roads,*

lace, a. fig.: network; *teleph., fig.*
area (served); ⚡ mains *pl.*; 📻,
rivers, roads: system; ✂ barbed wire
etc.: entanglement; *opt.* diffraction
grating; *anat. nerves*: plexus.
résection ✂ [resɛk'sjɔ̃] *f* resection.
réséda ⚘ [reze'da] *m* reseda.
réséquer ✂ [rese'ke] (1s) *v/t.* resect.
réservation [rezɛrva'sjɔ̃] *f* reservation; 📻 ～ *faite de* without prejudice to; **réserve** [～'zɛrv] *f* 📻, 📻,
eccl., a. fig. reservation; ✖, ⚓, ✝,
📻, *pol.*, ⊕ *power*: re-
serve; *fig.* caution; 📻 *(legal)* portion; ✖ *officier m de* ～ reserve officer; *fig. sans* ～ unreserved(ly *adv.*),
unstinted *(praise)*; 📻 *sous* ～ without prejudice; *sous* ～ *de* subject to;
réservé, e [rezɛr've] *resp.*
cautious; stand-offish; shy; 📻 *tous
droits* ～*s* all rights reserved; **réserver** [～'ve] (1a) *v/t.* reserve; set
(s.th.) aside; save *(s.th.)* up; set
apart *(money for a specific purpose)*;
réserviste ✖ [～'vist] *m* reservist;
réservoir [～'vwa:r] *m* reservoir;
container; *(fish-)*pond; ⊕, *mot.*
tank; ⊕ *(grease-)*box; ✖, *mot.* ～ *de
secours* reserve tank.
résidant, e [rezi'dɑ̃, ～'dɑ̃:t] resident;
eccl. residentiary; **résidence** [～-
'dɑ̃:s] *f* residence; residential flats
pl.; ～ *principale (secondaire)* main
(second) home; **résident** *admin.*
[～'dɑ̃] *m* resident; **résidentiel, -elle**
[～dɑ̃'sjɛl] residential *(quarter)*; **résider** [～'de] (1a) *v/i.* live, dwell,
reside (at, *à*; in, *dans*); *fig.* lie (in
dans, en); **résidu** [～'dy] *m* 🪚 ⊕, ⚗
residue; ⚗ remainder.
résignation 📻, *eccl. etc.*, *a. fig.*
[reziɲa'sjɔ̃] *f* resignation; **résigné, e**
[～'ɲe] resigned (to, *à*); meek; **résigner** [～'ɲe] (1a) *v/t.* resign *(s.th.)*;
give *(s.th.)* up; ～ *le pouvoir* abdicate
(king); lay down office; *se* ～ resign
o.s. (to, *à*).
résilier 📻 [rezi'lje] (1o) *v/t.* cancel,
annul; terminate *(a contract)*.
résille [re'zi:j] *f* hair-net.
résine [re'zin] *f* resin; **résineux,
-euse** [～zi'nø, ～'nø:z] resinous;
coniferous *(forest)*.
résistance [rezis'tɑ̃:s] *f* ⚡, ⊕, ✖,
pol., fig. resistance; ⊕ *materials*:
strength; *fig.* opposition; *fig.* stam-
ina, endurance; *pol.* ♀ underground
movement; ⚡ ～ *de fuite de grille*

radio: grid-leak; *faire* ～ offer *or*
put up resistance; **résistant, e**
[～'tɑ̃, ～'tɑ̃:t] **1.** *adj.* resistant; strong;
tough; fast *(colour)*; hard-wearing;
⊕ *très* ～ *a.* heavy-duty ...; ～ *à la
chaleur* heat-proof; **2.** *su. pol.*
member of the *Résistance (1939—45
war)*; **résister** [～'te] (1a) *v/i.*: ～ *à*
resist; ⚓ weather *(a storm)*; ⊕ take *(a
stress)*; *fig.* bear; hold out against.
résolu, e [rezɔ'ly] **1.** *adj.* resolute;
determined (to, *à*); **2.** *p.p. of* résoudre; **résolus** [～] *1st p. sg. p.s. of* résoudre; **résolutif, -ve** ✂ [rezɔly'tif,
～'ti:v] *adj. a. su./m* resolvent; **résolution** [～'sjɔ̃] *f* 🪚, 𝄃, ♪, *admin.*,
a. fig. resolution; *fig.* resolve, determination; 📻 *contract*: avoidance,
termination; *prendre la* ～ *de* determine to; *admin. prendre une* ～ pass
a resolution; **résolutoire** 📻 [～-
'twa:r] *(condition)* of avoidance; **ré-
solvons** [rezɔl'vɔ̃] *1st p. pl. pres. of*
résoudre.
résonance [rezɔ'nɑ̃:s] *f* resonance;
radio a. tuning; **résonnement**
[～zɔn'mɑ̃] *m* resounding, reverberation, re-echoing; **résonner** [～zɔ'ne]
(1a) *v/i.* resound, reverberate, ring;
be resonant *(room)*; echo *(sound)*.
résorber ✂ [rezɔr'be] (1a) *v/t.* re-
(ab)sorb; **résorption** ✂ [～zɔrp'sjɔ̃]
f re(ab)sorption.
résoudre [re'zudr] (4bb) *v/t.* resolve
(a. ♪ a dissonance, fig. a difficulty); 𝄃
solve *(a. fig. a problem)*; *fig.* decide
on; settle *(a question)*; 📻 rescind,
avoid; *se* ～ *à (inf.)* decide to *(inf.)*,
make up one's mind to *(inf.)*; **résous**
🪚 [～'zu] *p.p./m of* résoudre.
respect [rɛs'pɛ] *m* respect; ～ *de soi*
self-respect; *sauf votre* ～ with all
(due) respect; *saving your presence*;
tenir q. en ～ keep s.o. at arm's length
or in check; **respectable** [rɛspɛk-
'tabl] respectable *(a. fig.)*; *fig. a.* fair-
sized, sizeable; **respecter** [～'te] (1a)
v/t. respect; *se* ～ have self-respect;
respectif, -ve [～'tif, ～'ti:v] respective; **respectueux, -euse** [～'tɥø,
～'tɥø:z] respectful (towards, *envers*;
of, *de*); dutiful *(child)*.
respirable [rɛspi'rabl] respirable;
respiration [～ra'sjɔ̃] *f* respiration,
breathing; **respiratoire** [～ra'twa:r]
breathing; respiratory; *exercice m* ～
breathing exercise; **respirer** [～'re]
(1a) *v/i.* breathe; *fig.* breathe again;

fig. take breath, get one's breath; *v/t.* breathe (in), inhale; *fig.* radiate, exude.

resplendir [rɛsplā'di:r] (2a) *v/i.* be resplendent, glitter (with, *de*); *fig.* glow (with, *de*); **resplendissant, e** [‿di'sã, ‿'sã:t] resplendent; **resplendissement** [‿dis'mã] *m* splendo(u)r, resplendence, brightness.

responsabilité [rɛspõsabili'te] *f* responsibility, liability (*a.* 𝔱𝔱) (for, *de*); accountability; 𝔱𝔱 ~ *civile* civil liability; **responsable** [‿'sabl] responsible, accountable (for s.th., *de qch.*; for s.o., *pour q.*; to *devant, envers*); *rendre q.* ~ *de* hold s.o. responsible for, blame s.o. for.

resquiller F [rɛski'je] (1a) *v/i.* get in on the sly; fiddle a free ride; *v/t.* avoid paying for.

ressac ⚓ [rə'sak] *m* backwash, undertow; surf.

ressaisir [rəsɛ'zi:r] (2a) *v/t.* recapture, seize again; recover possession of; *se* ~ recover o.s.; recover one's balance.

ressasser [rəsɑ'se] (1a) *v/t.* repeat (*a story etc.*) over and over; keep going back over (*a story etc.*); keep turning over (*memories etc.*).

ressaut [rə'so] *m* ⚒ projection; shelf (*along a track*); *geol.* rockstep; *geog.* sharp rise.

ressemblance [rəsã'blã:s] *f* likeness; resemblance (to, *avec*); **ressemblant, e** [‿'blã, ‿'blã:t] lifelike, true to life; **ressembler** [‿'ble] (1a) *v/i.*: ~ *à* resemble, look like; *ils se ressemblent* they are alike.

ressemeler [rəsəm'le] (1c) *v/t.* resole (*a shoe*).

ressentiment [rəsãti'mã] *m* resentment (against, *contre*; at, *de*); *avec* ~ resentfully; **ressentir** [‿'ti:r] (2b) *v/t.* feel, experience (*an emotion, pain, etc.*); resent (*an insult etc.*); *fig. se* ~ *de* feel the (after)effects of.

resserre [rə'sɛr] *f* shed; **resserré, e** [rəsɛ're] narrow, confined; **resserrement** [‿sɛr'mã] *m* contraction; tightening; closing up; narrowness; **resserrer** [‿sɛ're] (1b) *v/t.* (*a. se* ~) tighten (up); contract; close (up); *se* ~ *a.* narrow, grow narrow(er); *se* ~ *autour de* close in on.

ressort¹ [rə'sɔ:r] *m* elasticity; ⊕ spring; *fig.* incentive, motive; ~ *à boudin* (*à lames*) spiral (laminated)

spring; *faire* ~ act as a spring; be elastic; *fig. faire jouer tous les* ~*s* leave no stone unturned.

ressort² [‿] *m* 𝔱𝔱 competence, jurisdiction; *fig.* scope; *en dernier* ~ 𝔱𝔱 without appeal; *fig.* in the last resort.

ressortir¹ [rəsɔr'ti:r] (2b) *v/i.* go *or* come out again; *fig.* stand out, be thrown into relief; *fig.* result, follow (from, *de*); *v/t.* bring *or* take out again.

ressortir² [rəsɔr'ti:r] (2a) *v/i.* 𝔱𝔱 be within the jurisdiction (of, *à*); *fig.* pertain (to, *à*); **ressortissant** *m*, -e *f* [‿ti'sã, ‿'sã:t] national (*of a country*), subject.

ressource [rə'surs] *f* resource(fulness); expedient; ⚒ pull-out; ~*s pl.* resources, means; funds; *en dernière* ~ in the last resort.

ressouvenir [rəsuv'ni:r] (2h) *v/t.*: *se* ~ *de* remember, recall.

ressuer [rə'sɥe] (1n) *v/i.* △, *metall.* sweat; ⊕ *faire* ~ roast (*ore*).

ressusciter [rəsysi'te] (1a) *vt/i.* resuscitate, revive; *v/t.* raise from the dead; *v/i.* rise from the dead.

restant, e [rɛs'tã, ‿'tã:t] **1.** *adj.* remaining, left; 𝔱𝔱 surviving; **2.** *su.* survivor; *su./m* remainder, rest; ✝ *account:* balance.

restaurant [rɛstɔ'rã] *m* restaurant; *manger au* ~ eat out; **restaurateur, -trice** [‿ra'tœ:r, ‿'tris] *su.* restorer; *su./m* restaurateur, keeper of a restaurant; **restauration** [‿ra'sjõ] *f* restoration; **restaurer** [‿'re] (1a) *v/t.* restore; ✳ *etc.* set (*s.o.*) up again; *se* ~ take refreshment; ✳ feed up.

reste [rɛst] *m* rest, remainder, remnant (*a pl.*); ~*s pl.*, *cuis.* remnants, leavings; left-overs; mortal remains; *au* ~, *du* ~ moreover; *de* ~ (*time, money, etc.*) to spare; *en* ~ ✝ in arrears; *fig.* indebted (to, *avec*); **rester** [rɛs'te] (1a) *v/i.* remain; be left (behind); stay; *en* ~ *là* leave it at that; *(il) reste à savoir si* it remains to be seen whether.

restituable [rɛsti'tɥabl] repayable; restorable; **restituer** [‿'tɥe] (1n) *v/t.* restore (*a text, s.th. to s.o.*); return; restitute; 𝔱𝔱 reinstate (*s.o.*); **restitution** [‿ty'sjõ] *f* restoration (*of a text, a. of s.th. to s.o.*); 𝔱𝔱 restitution; return.　　[side restaurant.]

restoroute (*TM*) [rɛstɔ'rut] *m* road-⌇

restreindre [rɛsˈtrɛ̃:dr] (4m) v/t. restrict, limit, cut down; fig. se ~ à limit o.s. to; **restrictif, -ve** [ˌtrik-ˈtif, ˌ̃ti:v] restrictive; **restriction** [ˌtrikˈsjɔ̃] f restriction (a. fig.); limitation; fig. ~ mentale mental reservation; **restringent, e** [ˌtrɛ̃ˈʒɑ̃, ̃ˈʒɑ̃:t] adj., a. su./m astringent.

restructurer [rəstryktyˈre] (1a) v/t. restructure.

résultante Å, phys. [rezylˈtɑ̃:t] f resultant; **résultat** [ˌ̃ˈta] m result (a. Å), issue; effect; avoir pour ~ result in; **résulter** [ˌ̃ˈte] (1a) v/i. (3rd persons only) result, follow (from, de); il en résulte que it follows that.

résumé [rezyˈme] m summary, précis; en ~ to sum up, in short; **résumer** [ˌ̃] (1a) v/t. summarize; sum up (⚛, arguments, etc.); se ~ sum up; fig. amount, F boil down (to, à).

résurrection [rezyrɛkˈsjɔ̃] f resurrection; fig. revival.

retable △, eccl. [rəˈtabl] m reredos, altar-piece.

rétablir [retaˈbli:r] (2a) v/t. re-establish; restore (a. ✕); reinstate (an official); ✚ recover (one's health); fig. retrieve (one's fortune, a position, one's reputation); se ~ recover (a. ✚); ✝ revive; **rétablissement** [ˌblisˈmɑ̃] m re-establishment; restoration; reinstatement; ✚ recovery (a. fig.); ✝ revival.

retailler [rətɑˈje] (1a) v/t. recut (a. ⊕); resharpen (a pencil); prune (a tree) again.

rétamé, e F [retaˈme] worn out; stoned (= drunk); broke; bust(ed); **rétamer** ⊕ [ˌ̃ˈme] (1a) v/t. re-tin; re-coat; F fig. clean (s.o.) out; **rétameur** [ˌ̃ˈmœ:r] m tinker.

retaper F [rətɑˈpe] (1a) v/t. touch up, recast; straighten (a bed); retrim (a hat etc.); fig. restore (s.o.); F buck (s.o.) up; plough (a candidate); se ~ recover; F buck up.

retard [rəˈta:r] m delay; lateness; child, harvest: backwardness; ⚡, ⊕, ✚ lag; ♪ suspension; être en ~ be late; be slow (clock etc.); be behind (with, dans or pour); be backward; être en ~ sur be behind (the fashion, the times); ma montre est en ~ de cinq minutes my watch is 5 minutes slow; **retardataire** [rətardaˈtɛ:r] 1. adj. late; ✝ in arrears; behindhand; backward

(child, country, etc.); 2. su. latecomer; laggard; ✝ etc. person in arrears; ✕, ✚ defaulter; **retardadeur, -trice** [ˌtœ:r, ̃ˈtris] retarding; **retardation** phys. [ˌ̃ˈsjɔ̃] f retardation, negative acceleration; **retardement** [rətardəˈmɑ̃] m delay; retarding; F à ~ after the event, afterwards; bombe f à ~ delayed-action bomb; **retarder** [ˌ̃ˈde] (1a) v/t. delay, retard; make late; defer (an event, payment); put back (a clock); v/i. be late; be slow, lose (clock); ⚡, ✚ lag; ~ sur son temps be behind the times.

reteindre [rəˈtɛ̃:dr] (4m) v/t. redye.

retéléphoner [rətelefɔˈne] (1a) v/i.: ~ (à q.) phone (s.o.) again, call (s.o.) back.

retenir [rətˈni:r] (2h) v/t. hold back; detain (s.o.); keep; hold (s.o., s.o.'s attention); withhold (wages); fig. remember; book (a seat, a room); engage (a servant etc.); fig. repress, hold back (a sob, tears, one's anger, etc.); restrain (from ger., de inf.); se ~ control o.s.; refrain (from, de); se ~ à clutch at (s.th.); **rétention** [retɑ̃ˈsjɔ̃] f ✗, a. ⚛ case: retention; ⚛ pledge: retaining.

retentir [rətɑ̃ˈti:r] (2a) v/i. (re-) sound, ring, echo; fig. ~ sur affect; **retentissement** [ˌtisˈmɑ̃] m re-sounding, echoing; fig. repercussion (of an event); fig. stir.

retenu, e [rətˈny] restrained, reserved; discreet; low-key(ed); **retenue** [ˌ̃] f money: deduction; stoppage; Å carry over; school: detention; holding back; reservoir; dam; ✚ guy(-rope); fig. discretion; modesty; fig. actions, speech: restraint.

réticence [retiˈsɑ̃:s] f reticence; hesitation, reluctance.

réticule [retiˈkyl] m opt. graticule; hand-bag, reticule; **réticulé, e** [ˌ̃ky'le] reticulated.

rétif, -ve [reˈtif, ̃ˈti:v] restive, stubborn (a. fig.).

rétine anat. [reˈtin] f eye: retina; **rétinite** [ˌ̃tiˈnit] f ✗ retinitis; min. pitchstone.

retiré, e [rətiˈre] retired, secluded, solitary; remote; in retirement; **retirer** [ˌ̃] (1a) v/t. withdraw; take out; extract (a bullet, a cork); derive, get (profit); obtain; ✝ take up (a bill); fig. take back (an insult, a

promise, etc.); *fig.* give shelter to
(*s.o.*); *typ.* reprint (*a book*); fire (*a
gun*) again; take out, *Am.* check
out (*luggage*); ~ de la circulation
call in (*currency*); se ~ retire, withdraw; ebb (*tide*), recede (*sea*), subside (*waters*).

retombée [rǝtɔ̃'be] *f* fallout; ⚓ *arch*
etc.: springing; *fig.* ~s *pl.* repercussions, consequences, effect(s) (*sg.*);
fig. spin-off (*sg.*); *phys.* ~s *pl.* radio-
actives fallout *sg.*; **retomber** [~] (1a)
v/i. fall (down) again; fall (back);
dans lapse into; *fig.* ~ sur *blame, glory*:
fall upon.

retoquer F [rǝtɔ'ke] (1m) *v/t.* fail,
F plough (*a candidate*).

retordoir ⊕ [rǝtɔr'dwaːr] *m instrument*: twister; **retordre** [~'tɔrdr]
(4a) *v/t.* wring out again; *tex.*
twist; *fig.* donner du fil à ~ à q. give
s.o. trouble.

retorquer [rǝtɔr'ke] (1m) retort;
turn (*an argument*); cast back (*an
accusation*).

retors, e [rǝ'tɔːr, ~'tɔrs] *tex.*
twisted; curved (*beak*); *fig.* crafty;
rascally.

retouche [rǝ'tuʃ] *f paint. etc.* retouch; *phot.* retouching; ⊕ finishing, dressing; **retoucher** [~tu'ʃe]
(1a) *v/t. paint., phot., etc.* retouch;
⊕ finish, dress; *v/i.*: ~ à meddle
with (*s.th.*) (again).

retour [rǝ'tuːr] *m* return (*a.* ⚓
wall, ✝, ♪, *sp., post, a. fig.*); going
back; ♪, *life, feeling, fortune, opinion, rope*: turn; *fig. feeling, fortune,
opinion, etc.*: change; ♪, ♪ recurrence; ✝ dishono(u)red bill; ♪, *biol.*
reversion; ♪ ~ d'âge critical age,
change of life; *mot.* ~ de flamme
back-fire; ♪ ~ par la terre earth
return; à son ~ on his return; ⚮
billet *m* de ~ return ticket; en ~ de
in return *or* exchange for; être de
~ be back; être sur le ~ be past one's
prime, F be getting on; *sp. match
m* ~ return match; **retourne** [~-
'turn] *f cards*: turn-up; trumps *pl.*;
retourner [~tur'ne] (1a) *v/i.* return; go back; *fig.* recoil (upon,
sur); ♪, *biol.* revert; *de quoi re-
tourne-t-il?* what is it all about?;
il retourne cœur cards: hearts are
trumps; *v/t.* turn (*s.th.*) inside out;
turn (*hay, one's head, omelette, ship,
a. fig. argument, etc.*); turn over (*an*

idea, *the soil*); turn up (*a card*);
twist (*s.o.'s arm*); *cuis.* mix (*salad*);
fig. upset, disturb (*s.o.*); return
(*s.th. to s.o., qch. à q.*); se ~ turn
(round *or* over); round (on, *contre*);
change (*opinion*); F s'en ~ go back.

retracer [rǝtra'se] (1k) *v/t.* retrace;
mark (*s.th.*) out again; *fig.* bring to
mind, recall; se ~ recur.

rétracter [retrak'te] (1a) *v/t.* retract; draw in; withdraw (*an opinion etc.*); ♪♪ rescind (*a decree*); se ~
tex. shrink; ♪, *a. fig.* retract; **rétractile** [~'til] retractile; **rétraction** [~'sjɔ̃] *f* contraction; ♪ retrac-
tion.

retrait [rǝ'trɛ] *m* ⊕ *metal, wood,
etc.*: shrinkage, contraction; withdrawal (*a.* ✝, *parl.*); *licence, ticket,
order, etc.*: cancelling; ⚓ recess;
♪♪ redemption; en ~ sunk (*panel*),
recessed (*shelves*), set·back (*house*).

retraite [rǝ'trɛt] *f* ⚮, ♣ retreat (*a.
fig.*); withdrawal; ⚒ tattoo; retirement, superannuation; pension, ⚒,
♣ retired pay; *animals*: lair; ✝ re-
draft; ⚓ offset; *caisse f de* ~ superannuation fund; en ~ retired; *mettre q. à la* ~ retire s.o., pension s.o.
off; *prendre sa* ~ retire; **retraité, e**
[rǝtrɛ'te] **1.** *adj.* pensioned off;
superannuated; ⚒, ♣ on the retired list; **2.** *su.* pensioner.

retraitement ⊕ [rǝtrɛt'mɑ̃] *m*
reprocessing; **retraiter**[1] [rǝtrɛ'te]
(1a) *v/t.* treat *or* handle again; ⊕
reprocess.

retraiter[2] [~] (1a) *v/t.* pension (*s.o.*)
off, retire (*s.o.*); superannuate (*s.o.*);
⚒, ♣ place on the retired list.

retranchement [rǝtrɑ̃ʃ'mɑ̃] *m* cutting off; *pension*: docking; suppression; ⚒ entrenchment; **retrancher**
[~trɑ̃'ʃe] (1a) *v/t.* cut off (from, de);
remove (from, de); cut out (*a. fig.*); ⚒
entrench; ♪ deduct; se ~ retrench; ⚒
entrench o.s.; dig o.s. in; *fig.* take
refuge (behind, *derrière*).

retransmettre [rǝtrɑ̃s'mɛtrǝ] (4v)
v/t. radio: broadcast; *telev.* show;
retransmission [~mi'sjɔ̃] *f* broadcast; showing.

rétrécir [retre'siːr] (2a) *vt/i. a.* se ~
narrow; contract; *tex.* shrink; **rétrécissement** [~sis'mɑ̃] *m* narrowing; contraction (*a. opt.*); *tex.*
shrinking; ♪ stricture.

retremper [rǝtrɑ̃'pe] (1a) *v/t.* soak

(s.th.) again; ⊕ retemper (steel, a. fig. one's mind, etc.); fig. strengthen (s.o.); se ~ be toned up; get new strength.

rétribuer [retri'bɥe] (1n) v/t. pay, remunerate; **rétribution** [~by'sjɔ̃] f remuneration, payment; salary; sans ~ honorary.

rétro [re'tro] **1.** adj. reminiscent of times past; la vogue ~ nostalgia; **2.** su./m nostalgia; mot. (= rétroviseur) back-view mirror.

rétro... [retro] retro...; **~actif, -ve** [~aktif, ~'ti:v] retroactive, retrospective; admin. avec effet ~ (à) backdated (to) (measure etc.); **~action** [~ak'sjɔ̃] f retroaction; ✟, radio: feedback; **~céder** [~se'de] (1f) v/t. ⚖ retrocede; redemise; ✟ return (a commission); **~fusée** ⚔ [~fy'ze] f retrorocket; braking-rocket; **~grade** [~'grad] retrograde, backward; **~grader** [~gra'de] (1a) v/i. move backwards; regress; retrograde; fall back; mot. change (Am. shift) down (from ... to ..., de ... en ...); v/t. admin. ✗ etc. demote; **~pédalage** [~peda'la:ʒ] m bicycle: back-pedalling; **~spectif, -ve** [~spɛk'tif, ~'ti:v] retrospective.

retrousser [rətru'se] (1a) v/t. turn up (a sleeve, one's trousers, one's moustache); tuck up (one's skirt); curl up (one's lips); nez m retroussé turned-up or snub nose.

retrouvailles [rətru'vɑ:j] f/pl. reunion, reconciliation; **retrouver** [~'ve] (1a) v/t. find (again); rediscover (s.th.); meet (s.o.) again; return to (a place); recover (one's health, one's strength); aller ~ go and see (s.o.) again; se ~ find o.s. back; a. s'y ~ find one's way.

rétro...: **~version** ✗ [retrɔvɛr'sjɔ̃] f retroversion; **~viseur** mot. [~vi-'zœ:r] m driving mirror, rear-view mirror.

rets hunt. [rɛ] m net.

réunifier [reyni'fje] (1o) v/t. reunify. **réunion** [rey'njɔ̃] f reunion; meeting; ✗, a. pol. union; gathering; party, function; **réunir** [~'ni:r] (2a) v/t. (re)unite; join (to, with à); join together, link; collect (money, water); ✗ raise (troops).

réussir [rey'si:r] (2a) v/i. succeed (in ger., à inf.; at or in s.th., dans qch.); be a success (thea. etc.); ⚘ thrive; ~ à pass (an examination); v/t. be suc-

cessful in; carry (s.th.) out well; **réussite** [~'sit] f ✟ result, outcome; success; cards: patience.

revacciner ✗ [rəvaksi'ne] (1a) v/t. revaccinate.

revaloir [rəva'lwa:r] (3l) v/t. pay back in kind; repay; **revalorisation** [rəvaloriza'sjɔ̃] f ✟ revalorization, revaluation; fig. reassertion of the value of; **revaloriser** [~'ze] (1a) v/t. ✟ revalorize, revalue; fig. reassert the value of.

revanche [rə'vɑ̃:ʃ] f revenge; return; en ~ in return; on the other hand; **revancher** [~vɑ̃'ʃe] (1a) v/t.: se ~ have one's revenge; revenge o.s. (for, de).

rêvasser [rɛva'se] (1a) v/i. muse (on, à), day-dream (about, à); **rêvasserie** [~vas'ri] f musing, daydream(ing); **rêvasseur** m, -euse f [~va'sœ:r, ~'sø:z] day-dreamer; **rêve** [rɛ:v] m dream (a. fig.); faire un ~ have a dream.

revêche [rə'vɛʃ] harsh, rough; ⊕ difficult to work (stone, wood); brittle (iron); fig. cantankerous, crabby; sour (face).

réveil [re'vɛ:j] m waking, awakening; religion: revival; ✗ reveille; alarm(-clock); fig. fâcheux ~ rude awakening; **réveille-matin** [~vɛjma'tɛ̃] m/inv. alarm(-clock); **réveiller** [revɛ'je] (1a) v/t. (a)wake; waken (a. fig.); rouse (a. fig.); ✗ turn out; se ~ wake up, awake (person); fig. be awakened or aroused; **réveillon** [~'jɔ̃] m midnight supper (usu. on Christmas Eve and New Year's Eve).

révélateur, -trice [revela'tœ:r, ~-'tris] **1.** adj. revealing; tell-tale (sign); phot. developing (bath); **2.** su. revealer; su./m phot. developer; ⊕ detector; **révélation** [~la-'sjɔ̃] f revelation; ✟ eye-opener; ✗ information; bibl. ♀s pl. the Revelation sg.; **révéler** [~'le] (1f) v/t. reveal (a. eccl.), disclose, ✟ let out (a secret); fig. show; phot. develop.

revenant [rəvə'nɑ̃] m ghost; F fig. stranger; il y a des ~s ici this place is haunted.

revendeur m, -euse f ✟ [rəvɑ̃'dœ:r, ~'dø:z] retailer; second-hand dealer. **revendication** [rəvɑ̃dika'sjɔ̃] f claim, demand; **revendiquer** [~'ke] (1m) v/t. claim, demand; assume (a *responsibility*); claim (*an attempt, an attack, etc.*).

revendre [rə'vãːdr] (4a) *v/t.* resell; † sell out; F *fig.* spare; *en ~ à* outwit (*s.o.*), be too much for (*s.o.*).

revenez-y [rəvne'zi] *m/inv.* renewal, revival, return; F *avoir un goût de ~* be very more-ish.

revenir [rəv'niːr] (2h) *v/i.* return, come back *or* again (*a. fig.*); recover (from, *de*); cost (*s.o. s.th., à q. à qch.*); *fig.* amount (to, *à*); *fig.* fall by right (to, *à*); *∦ ~ à soi* come round; *~ à qch.* amount *or* come down to s.th.; *cela revient au même* it amounts *or* comes to the same thing; *~ de* get over (*s.th.*); *~ sur* retrace (*one's steps*); go back on (*a decision, a promise*); go back over (*the past, an affair, etc.*); *cuis.* faire *~* brown (*meat*); ... *ne me revient pas* I don't like the look of ...; I cannot recall ...; *ne pas en ~* be unable to get over it.

revente [rə'vãːt] *f* re-sale; † *stock:* selling-out.

revenu [rəv'ny] *m person:* income; *State:* revenue; † yield; *metall.* tempering; *admin.* *impôt m sur le ~* income tax; **revenue** *⚹* [*~*] *f* new growth; young wood.

rêver [re've] (1a) *v/i.* dream (about, of *de*); *~ à* think about, ponder over; *~ de* long for; *v/t.* dream of; *fig.* imagine; *fig.* desire ardently.

réverbère [rever'bɛːr] *m* heat, lamp, *etc.*: reflector; street-lamp; **réverbérer** [*~*be're] (1f) *v/t.* reflect (*light*); re-echo (*a sound*).

reverdir [rəver'diːr] (2a) *v/t.* make *or* paint green again; *v/i.* turn green again; F *fig.* grow young again (*person*).

révérence [reve'rãːs] *f* reverence (*a.* ♀ *title*); bow; curtsey; F *parler with all due respect; tirer sa ~* take one's leave; **révérenciel, -elle** [*~*rã'sjɛl] reverential; **révérencieux, -euse** [*~*rã'sjø, *~*'sjøːz] ceremonious; over-polite (*person*); **révérend, e** *eccl.* [*~*'rã, *~*'rãːd] Reverend; **révérendissime** *eccl.* [*~*rãdi-'sim] Most *or* Right Reverend; **révérer** [*~*'re] (1f) *v/t.* revere, (hold in) reverence.

rêverie [rev'ri] *f* reverie; dreaming.

revers [rə'vɛːr] *m* coin, fencing, *a. fig.* fortune: reverse; *hand, page:* back; *tex.* wrong side; *cost. coat:*

lapel; *trousers:* turn-up, *Am.* cuff; *stocking:* turn-down, top; ⚔ uniform: facing; *fig.* set-back; backhanded blow; *sp.* back-hand stroke; **reverser** [rəver'se] (1a) *v/t.* pour (*s.th.*) out again; pour (*s.th.*) back; *fig.* shift (on, to *sur*); † transfer; **réversible** [rever'sibl] reversible; *⚖* revertible; **réversion** *⚖*, *biol.* [*~*'sjõ] *f* reversion (to, *à*).

revêtement [rəvet'mã] *m* △ facing, coating, sheathing; *road:* surface; △, *a.* ⚒ revetment; ⚡ *flex:* cover; ⊕ *wood:* veneer(ing); △ *mur m de ~* retaining wall, revetment wall; **revêtir** [*~*ve'tiːr] (2g) *v/t.* (re-)clothe; dress (in, *de*); *fig.* invest (with, *de*); *cost.* put on; *fig.* assume (*a form, a shape, etc.*); △ face, coat, cover; ⊕ lag (*a boiler*); ⚒ revet; † *~ qch. de sa signature* sign s.th.; affix one's signature to s.th.

rêveur, -euse [re'vœːr, *~*'vøːz] **1.** *adj.* dreamy; dreaming. **2.** *su.* (day-)dreamer.

revient [rə'vjɛ̃] *m: prix m de ~* cost (price).

revirement [rəvir'mã] *m* †, *a. fig.* sudden change *or* turn; † *debt etc.*: transfer; *⚓* going about; **revirer** [*~*vi're] (1a) *v/i.* *⚓* go about; *fig.* change sides.

réviser [revi'ze] (1a) *v/t.* revise; † audit (*accounts*); *⚖* review; ⊕, *mot.* recondition, overhaul; inspect; **réviseur** [*~*'zœːr] *m* reviser; examiner; *typ.* proof-reader; † auditor; **révision** [*~*'zjõ] *f* revision; audit(ing); *⚖* review; ⊕, *mot.* overhaul(ing); ⊕ inspection; *typ.* proof-reading; ⚔ *conseil m de ~* recruiting board, *Am.* draft board; military appeal court; **révisionnisme** *pol.* [*~*zjõ-'nism] *m* revisionism.

revitaliser [rəvitali'ze] (1a) *v/t.* revitalize; *crème f revitalisante* nourishing cream.

revivifier [rəvivi'fje] (1o) *v/t.* revitalize, revive.

revivre [rə'viːvr] (4hh) *v/i.* live again, come alive again; *fig.* revive; *v/t.* live (*s.th.*) over again.

révocable [revo'kabl] revocable; removable (*official*); **révocation** [*~*ka'sjõ] *f* *⚖* *will:* revocation, *law:* repeal; *admin. order:* cancellation, *official:* removal, dismissal; **révocatoire** [*~*ka'twaːr] revocatory.

revoici F [rəvwa'si] *prp.*: *me* ~! here I am again!; **revoilà** F [~'la] *prp.*: *le* ~ *malade!* there he is, ill again!

revoir [rə'vwa:r] **1.** (3m) *v/t.* see again; meet (*s.o.*) again; revise; inspect; ⚙ review; *typ.* read (*proofs*); go over (*accounts etc.*) again; **2.** *su./ m*: *au* ~ good-bye.

révoltant, e [revɔl'tɑ̃, ~'tɑ̃:t] shocking, revolting; **révolte** [~'vɔlt] *f* revolt, rebellion; ✕, ⚓ mutiny; **révolté, e** [revɔl'te] **1.** *adj.* in revolt; **2.** *su.* rebel, insurgent; ✕, ⚓ mutineer; **révolter** [~] (1a) *v/t.* rouse to rebellion, cause to revolt; F *fig.* revolt, shock, disgust; *se* ~ revolt, rebel (*a. fig.*); ✕, ⚓ mutiny.

révolu, e [revɔ'ly] past, bygone (*time*); full (*year*), completed (*period of time*); **révolution** [revɔly'sjɔ̃] *f* ⚛, *pol.*, *fig.* revolution; *astr.* rotation; **révolutionnaire** [~sjɔ'nɛːr] *adj.*, *a. su.* revolutionary; **révolutionner** [~sjɔ'ne] (1a) *v/t.* revolutionize (*a. fig.*); F *fig.* stir up.

revolver [revɔl'vɛːr] *m* revolver, gun; ⊕ *lathe*: turret.

révoquer [revɔ'ke] (1m) *v/t.* revoke, cancel (*an order*); dismiss, remove (*an official*); recall (*an ambassador*); ~ *en doute* question (*s.th.*), call (*s.th.*) in question.

revue [rə'vy] *f* review (= *survey*, *a.* ✕, *journ.*); inspection (*a.* ✕); *journ.* magazine, periodical; *thea.* revue; F *nous sommes de* ~ we'll meet again; we often meet; *passer en* ~ review, run over (*s.th.*); ✕ be reviewed *or* inspected; **revuiste** *thea.* [~'vɥist] *su.* composer of revues.

révulsé, e [revyl'se] *adj.*: *l'œil* ~ with turned-up eyes; **révulsif, -ve** ⚕ [~'sif, ~'si:v] *adj.*, *a. su./m* revulsive; counter-irritant; **révulsion** ⚕ [~'sjɔ̃] *f* revulsion; counter-irritation.

rez-de-chaussée [retʃo'se] *m/inv.* street level; ground floor, *Am.* first floor; *au* ~ on the ground *or Am.* first floor.

rhabiller [rabi'je] (1a) *v/t.* dress (*s.o.*) again; provide (*s.o.*) with new clothing; *fig.* refurbish; ⊕ repair; ⚘ renovate; *se* ~ get dressed again; F *il peut aller se* ~ he'd better give up; **rhabilleur** [~'jœːr] *m* repairer; watch repairer.

rhénan, e [re'nɑ̃, ~'nan] Rhine ..., Rhenish.

rhéostat ⚡ [reɔs'ta] *m* rheostat.

rhétoricien † [retɔri'sjɛ̃] *m* rhetorician; **rhétorique** [~'rik] *f* rhetoric; † (*a. classe f de* ~) *school*: top classical form (*preparing for first part of the baccalauréat*).

Rhin *geog.* [rɛ̃] *m*: *vin m du* ~ hock.

rhino... [rinɔ] rhino...; **~céros** *zo.* [~se'rɔs] *m* rhinoceros; **~logie** ⚕ [~lɔ'ʒi] *f* rhinology; **~plastie** ⚕ [~plas'tie] *f* rhinoplasty; **~scopie** ⚕ [~skɔ'pi] *f* rhinoscopy.

rhodanien, -enne *geog.* [rɔda'njɛ̃, ~'njɛn] of the Rhone.

rhombe ⚛ [rɔ̃:b] *m* rhomb(us); **rhombique** [rɔ̃'bik] rhombic; **rhomboïdal, e,** *m/pl.* **-aux** [~bɔi-'dal, ~'do] rhomboidal.

rhubarbe ♧ [ry'barb] *f* rhubarb.

rhum [rɔm] *m* rum.

rhumatisant, e ⚕ [rymati'zɑ̃, ~-'zɑ̃:t] *adj.*, *a. su.* rheumatic; **rhumatismal, e,** *m/pl.* **-aux** ⚕ [~tis-'mal, ~'mo] rheumatic; **rhumatisme** ⚕ [~'tism] *m* rheumatism, F rheumatics *pl.*; ~ *articulaire* rheumatoid arthritis.

rhume ⚕ [rym] *m* cold; ~ *de cerveau* (*poitrine*) cold in the head (on the chest); ~ *des foins* hayfever; *prendre un* ~ catch (a) cold.

ri [ri] *p.p. of rire* †; **riant, e** [rjɑ̃, rjɑ̃:t] smiling (*person, face, a. countryside*); pleasant (*thought*). [*su.* ribald.] **ribaud, e** † [ri'bo, ~'bo:d] *adj.*, *a.*

riblons ⊕ [ri'blɔ̃] *m/pl.* swarf *sp.*

ribote F [ri'bɔt] *f* drunken bout; *sl.* binge; *être en* ~ be tipsy; be on the spree.

ribouldingue F [ribul'dɛ̃:g] *f* spree.

ricaner [rika'ne] (1a) *v/i.* snigger; sneer; laugh derisively; **ricaneur, -euse** [~ka'nœːr, ~'nø:z] **1.** *su.* sneerer; **2.** *adj.* derisive, sneering.

ric-(à-)rac F [rik(a)'rak] *adv.* strictly, exactly; punctually.

richard *m*, **e** *f* F [ri'ʃaːr, ~'ʃard] wealthy person; **riche** [riʃ] **1.** *adj.* rich (in en, de) (*a. fig.*); wealthy; *fig.* valuable, handsome (*present*); F *fig.* fine, first-class; **2.** *su.* rich person; *su./m*: *bibl. le mauvais* ~ Dives; *les* ~*s pl.* the rich; **richesse** [ri'ʃes] *f* wealth; riches *pl.*; *fig.* opulence; ⚘ *soil*: richness; *vegetation*: exuberance; **richissime** F

[∿ʃi'sim] extremely rich, F rolling in money.

ricin ♀ [ri'sɛ̃] m castor-oil plant; *huile f de* ∿ castor oil.

ricocher [riko'ʃe] (1a) v/i. glance off; ricochet (*bullet etc.*); **ricochet** [∿'ʃɛ] m rebound; ✗ ricochet; *fig.* par ∿ indirectly; *faire* ∿ rebound (*a. fig.*); *faire des* ∿s play drakes and ducks.

rictus [rik'tys] m ♣ rictus; F grin.

ride [rid] f *face, forehead:* wrinkle; *geol. ground:* fold; *sand, water:* ripple; *sand:* ridge; ♣ (shroud) lanyard; **rideau** [ri'do] m curtain; *Am. a.* drape; ✗, ♣, ♠, *a. fig.* screen; *thea.* (drop-)curtain; ⊕ roll-top, roll-shutter; ∿! that's enough!; ∿ de fer *thea.* safety curtain; *pol.* Iron Curtain; *fig.* tirer le ∿ sur draw a veil over.

ridelle [ri'dɛl] f *cart, truck:* rail.

rider [ri'de] (1a) v/t. wrinkle; ripple (*water, sand*); ⊕ corrugate (*metal*); ♣ tighten (*the shrouds*).

ridicule [ridi'kyl] **1.** *adj.* ridiculous; **2.** *su./m* absurdity; ridiculous aspect; ridicule; *tourner en* ∿ (hold up to) ridicule; **ridiculiser** [∿kyli'ze] (1a) v/t. make ridicule, deride.

rien [rjɛ̃] **1.** *su./m* mere nothing, trifle; F tiny bit; **2.** *pron./indef.* anything; nothing; not ... anything; ∿ de nouveau nothing new; ∿ du tout nothing at all; ∿ moins que nothing less than; *cela ne fait* ∿ that does not matter; *de* ∿! don't mention it!; *en moins de* ∿ in less than no time; *il ne dit jamais* ∿ he never says a thing; *il n'y a* ∿ à faire it can't be helped; *obtenir pour* ∿ get for a song; *plus* ∿ nothing more; *sans* ∿ dire without (saying) a word.

rieur, -euse [rjœːr, rjøːz] **1.** *adj.* laughing; merry; mocking; **2.** *su.* laugher.

rififi *sl.* [rifi'fi] m fight, brawl; trouble.

riflard[1] F [ri'flaːr] m umbrella, F brolly.

riflard[2] [∿] m ⊕ *metal:* coarse file; *wood:* jack-plane; paring chisel; plastering trowel.

rigide [ri'ʒid] rigid, stiff (*a. fig.*); fixed (*axle*); tense (*muscle, cord*); **rigidifier** [∿ʒidi'fje] (1o) v/t. make rigid; harden; **rigidité** [∿ʒidi'te] f rigidity, stiffness (*a. fig.*); tenseness.

rigolade F [rigo'lad] f fun, lark.

rigolage ✗ [rigo'laːʒ] m *field:* trenching.

rigolard, e *sl.* [rigo'laːr, ∿'lard] fond of a lark; full of fun, jolly.

rigole [ri'gol] f ✗ trench, ditch; ✗, ⊕ channel; ✗ trough.

rigoler F [rigo'le] (1a) v/i. laugh; enjoy o.s.; **rigoleur, -euse** [∿'lœːr, ∿'løːz] **1.** *adj.* jolly; fond of fun; **2.** *su.* jolly person; person fond of fun; laugher; **rigolo, -ote** F [∿'lo, ∿'lɔt] **1.** *adj.* funny, comical; queer, odd; **2.** *su./m* funny fellow; F card; F revolver; *Am.* gun.

rigorisme [rigo'rism] m rigorism, strictness; **rigoriste** [∿'rist] **1.** *adj.* rigorous; strict; **2.** *su.* rigorist; rigid moralist; **rigoureux, -euse** [rigu'rø, ∿'røːz] rigorous; strict; severe (*climate, punishment*); close (*reasoning*); **rigueur** [∿'gœːr] f rigo(u)r, severity; *fig.* strictness; *fig. reasoning:* closeness, accuracy; à la ∿ strictly; if really necessary, *sl.* at a push; de ∿ obligatory, compulsory.

rillettes *cuis.* [ri'jɛt] f/pl. potted pork mince *sg.*

rimailler † [rima'je] (1a) v/i. write doggerel, dabble in poetry; **rimailleur** † [∿'jœːr] m poetaster, rhymester; **rime** [rim] f rhyme; *fig.* sans ∿ ni raison without rhyme or reason; **rimer** [ri'me] (1a) v/t. put into rhyme; v/i. rhyme (with, *avec*); **rimeur** [∿'mœːr] m rhymer, versifier.

rinçage [rɛ̃'saːʒ] m rinsing.

rinceau [rɛ̃'so] m ♠ foliage; ⊘ branch.

rince-bouteilles [rɛ̃sbu'tɛːj] m/inv. bottle washer; **rince-doigts** [∿'dwa] m/inv. finger bowl; **rincée** [rɛ̃'se] f *sl.* thrashing; F downpour; **rincer** [∿'se] (1k) v/t. rinse; *sl.* clean (*s.o.*) out; *rain:* soak (*s.o.*); *sl.* se ∿ la dalle wet one's whistle; *sl.* se ∿ l'œil get an eyeful; **rinceur** m, **-euse** f [∿'sœːr, ∿'søːz] washer, rinser; **rinçure** [∿'syːr] f slops *pl.* (*a.* F = very thin wine).

ring *box.* [riŋ] m ring.

ringard ⊕ [rɛ̃'gaːr] m poker.

ripaille F † [ri'pɑːj] f revelry; *faire* ∿ carouse; **ripailleur** m, **-euse** f F † [∿pɑ'jœːr, ∿'jøːz] reveller, carouser.

ripoliner [ripoli'ne] (1a) v/t. (paint with) enamel.

riposte [ri'pɔst] *f* retort, smart reply; *sp.* counter; **riposter** [ˌpɔs-'te] (1a) *v/i.* retort; *sp.* counter, riposte; *fig.* ~ *à* counteract.

riquiqui F [riki'ki] *m* shrimp (= *undersized man*).

rire [riːr] **1.** (4cc) *v/i.* laugh (at, de); jest, joke; smile (on, at *à*); make light (of, de); ~ *au nez de q.* laugh in s.o.'s face; ~ *dans sa barbe* chuckle to o.s.; ~ *jaune* give a sickly smile; *à crever de* ~ killingly funny; *éclater de* ~ burst out laughing; *je ne ris pas* I am in earnest; *pour* ~ for fun, as a joke; comic (*paper*); mock (*action, king*); *se* ~ *de* take (*s.th.*) in one's stride; † make fun of, laugh at; **2.** *su./m* laugh(ter); *fou* ~ uncontrollable laughter.

ris[1] ⚓ [ri] *m* reef (*in a sail*).

ris[2] *cuis.* [~] *m*: ~ *de veau* sweetbread.

ris[3] [ri] *1st p. sg. p.s. of rire* 1; **risée** [ri'ze] *f* derision; *person:* laughing stock; ⚓ light sqall; **risette** [~'zɛt] *f* (*child's*) smile; *faire (la)* ~ smile (at, *à*), give a smile; **risible** [~'zibl] ludicrous (*a. person*); ridiculous.

risotto *cuis.* [rizɔ'to] *m* risotto (*Italian rice dish*).

risque [risk] *m* risk; ~ *du métier* occupational hazard; ~ *pour la santé* health hazard; **risqué, e** [ris'ke] risky; daring, risqué (*joke, etc.*); † *à ses* ~*s et périls* at one's own risk; *à tout* ~ at all hazards; *au* ~ *de* (*inf.*) at the risk of (*ger.*); **risquer** [ris'ke] (1m) *v/t.* risk; venture (*a question etc.*); ~ *le coup* take a chance, chance it; *v/i.:* ~ *de* (*inf.*) run the risk of (*ger.*); be likely to (*inf.*); **risque-tout** [~kə'tu] *m/inv.* daredevil.

rissole *cuis.* [ri'sɔl] *f* rissole; (*fish-*) ball; **rissoler** *cuis.* [~sɔ'le] *vt/i.* brown (*meat*).

ristourne † [ris'turn] *f* repayment; refund; rebate; **ristourner** † [~tur'ne] (1a) *v/t.* repay; refund.

rite *eccl. etc.* [rit] *m* rite.

ritournelle [ritur'nɛl] *f* ♪ ritornello; F *fig. la même* ~ the same old story.

ritualiser [rityali'ze] (1a) *v/t.* ritualize; **rituel, -elle** [ri'tɥɛl] *adj., a. su./m* ritual, ceremonial.

rivage [ri'vaːʒ] *m river:* bank; *lake, sea:* shore, beach.

rival, e *m/pl.* **-aux** [ri'val, ~'vo] *adj., a. su.* rival; **rivaliser** [rivali'ze] (1a) *v/i.:* ~ *avec* rival; compete with,

vie with; **rivalité** [~'te] *f* rivalry, competition.

rive [riːv] *f river:* bank; *lake, river:* side; *lake,* † *sea:* shore; *forest:* edge.

river ⊕ [ri've] (1a) *v/t.* rivet; clinch (*a nail*); F ~ *son clou à q.* settle s.o.'s hash.

riverain, e [ri'vrɛ̃, ~'vrɛn] **1.** *adj.* riverside...; riparian; bordering on a road *etc.*; **2.** *su.* riverside resident; riparian owner; dweller along a road *etc.*

rivet ⊕ [ri'vɛ] *m* rivet; *nail:* clinch; **rivetage** ⊕ [riv'taːʒ] *m* riveting; clinching.

rivière [ri'vjɛːr] *f* river; stream (*a. fig.*); *sp.* water-jump; rivière (*of diamonds*).

rixe [riks] *f* brawl, fight; affray.

riz [ri] *m* rice; *cuis.* ~ *au lait* rice pudding; ~ *glacé* polished rice; **rizerie** [riz'ri] *f* rice-mill; **rizière** [ri'zjɛːr] *f* rice-field, rice-swamp.

roadster *mot.* [rɔds'tœːr] *m* two-seater, *Am.* roadster.

rob [rɔb] *m cards:* rubber; *faire un* ~ play a rubber.

robe [rɔb] *f* dress, frock; gown (*a. 🎓, a. univ.*); *animal:* coat; *bird:* plumage; *onion, potato, sausage:* skin; *cigar:* outer leaf; 🎓 legal profession; ~ *de chambre* dressing-gown; **robin** F *pej.* [rɔ'bɛ̃] *m* lawyer.

robinet [rɔbi'nɛ] *m* tap, *Am.* faucet; ~ *d'arrêt* stop cock; ~ *mélangueur* mixer tap; **robinetterie** [~nɛ'tri] *f* plumbing.

robot [rɔ'bo] *m* robot; ✈ pilotless plane; **robotiser** [rɔbɔti'ze] (1a) *v/t.* robotize; ⊕ *a.* automate; *fig. a.* turn (*s.o.*) into a robot.

robre [rɔbr] *m see* rob.

robuste [rɔ'byst] robust, sturdy; ♀ hardy; *fig.* firm (*faith etc.*); **robustesse** [~bys'tɛs] *f* sturdiness; strength; hardiness.

roc [rɔk] *m* rock (*a. fig.*).

rocade [rɔ'kad] *f road:* bypass.

rocaille [rɔ'kaːj] *f* rock-work; rubble; † rococo; *jardin m de* ~ rock-garden; **rocailleux, -euse** [~kɑ'jø, ~'jøːz] rocky, stony, pebbly; *fig.* rugged, rough.

rocambolesque [rɔkɑ̃bɔ'lɛsk] fantastic.

roche [rɔʃ] *f* rock; boulder; ⚒ ~ *mère*

matrix, parent-rock; *fig.* cœur *m* de ~ heart of stone; **rocher** [rɔ'ʃe] *m* (mass of) rock; *anat.* otic bone.

rochet[1] *eccl.* [rɔ'ʃɛ] *m* rochet.

rochet[2] [~] *m* ⊕ ratchet; *tex.* bobbin; ⊕ roue *f* à ~ ratchet-wheel.

rocheux, -euse [rɔ'ʃø, ~'ʃøːz] rocky; stony.

rococo [rɔkɔ'ko] **1.** *su./m* rococo; **2.** *adj./inv.* rococo; *fig.* antiquated.

rodage [rɔ'da:ʒ] *m* ⊕ grinding; *mot.*, *a. fig.* running in; **rodé, e** [~'de] ⊕ run in; *fig.* broken in; *fig.* running well *or* smoothly; **roder** [~'de] (1a) *v/t. mot.* run in (*an engine, a. fig.*); grind in (*valves*).

rôder [ro'de] (1a) *v/i.* loiter; prowl (about); ⚓ veer (at anchor, *sur son ancre*); **rôdeur** *m.* **-euse** *f* [~'dœːr, ~'døːz] prowler.   [ging; bluster.)

rodomontade [rɔdɔmɔ̃'tad] *f* brag-∫

rogations *eccl.* [rɔga'sjɔ̃] *f/pl.* Rogation days; **rogatoire** ⚖ [~'twaːr] rogatory; *commission f* ~ commission (*issued by foreign court*) to take evidence for that court, Commission Rogatoire.

rogatons F [rɔga'tɔ̃] *m/pl.* food: scraps, left-overs.

rogne F [rɔɲ] *f* (bad) temper; se mettre en ~ blow one's top (*Am. a.* one's stack).

rogner [rɔ'ɲe] (1a) *v/t.* trim, pare; clip (*claws, a. fig. the wings*); cut down (*s.o.'s salary*); *v/i. sl.* be in a temper, be cross; grumble; **rogneuse** ⊕ [~'ɲøːz] *f* trimming-machine.

rognon *usu. cuis.* [rɔ'ɲɔ̃] *m* kidney.

rognures [rɔ'ɲyːr] *f/pl.* clippings, cuttings; trimmings; scraps.

rogomme F [rɔ'gɔm] *m* spirits *pl.*; voix *f* de ~ drunkard: husky voice.

rogue [rɔg] haughty, arrogant.

roi [rwa] *m* king (*a. cards, chess*); jour *m* des ♔s Twelfth-night.

roide [rwad] *see* raide.   [wren.)

roitelet [rwat'lɛ] *m* petty king; *orn.*∫

rôle [ro:l] *m* *thea.*, *a. fig.* part, rôle; *thea.* ~ principal title rôle; *thea.* ~ secondaire supporting part; à tour de ~ in turn.

romain, e [rɔ'mɛ̃, ~'mɛn] **1.** *adj.* Roman; **2.** *su./m ling.* Roman; *typ.* roman, primer; *su.* ♀ Roman.

romaine[1] [rɔ'mɛn] *f* balance: steel-yard.

romaine[2] ♀ [~] *f* Cos lettuce.

romaïque [rɔma'ik] *adj.*, *a. su./m ling.* Romaic; modern Greek.

roman, e [rɔ'mɑ̃, ~'mɑ:d] **1.** *adj.* Romance; ▲ Norman (*in England*), Romanesque; **2.** *su./m ling.* Romance; novel; (*medieval*) romance; *usu.* ~s *pl.* fiction *sg.*; ~ à thèse tendenz novel.

romance ♪ [rɔ'mɑ̃:s] *f* song, ballad; ~ sans paroles song without words.

romanche *ling.* [rɔ'mɑ̃:ʃ] *m* Ro(u)-mansh.

romancier *m,* **-ère** *f* [rɔmɑ̃'sje, ~'sjɛːr] novelist; fiction-writer; **roman-cycle,** *pl.* **romans-cycles** [~'sikl] *m* saga (novel).

romand, e *geog.* [rɔ'mɑ̃, ~'mɑ̃:d] *adj.*: la Suisse ~e French(-speaking) Switzerland.

romanesque [rɔma'nɛsk] **1.** *adj.* romantic; **2.** *su./m fig.* romance; **roman-feuilleton,** *pl.* **romans-feuilletons** *journ.* [rɔmɑ̃fœj'tɔ̃] *m* serial (story); **roman-fleuve,** *pl.* **romans-fleuves** [~'flœ:v] *m* saga (novel), river novel.

romanichel *m,* **-elle** *f* [rɔmani'ʃɛl] gipsy; Romany.

romaniser [rɔmani'ze] (1a) *vt/i.* Romanize (*a. eccl.*); **romaniste** [~'nist] *su. eccl., a. ling.* Romanist; *ling.* student of the Romance languages; **romantique** [rɔmɑ̃-'tik] **1.** *adj.* Romantic; *fig.* imaginative; **2.** *su.* Romantic; **roman-tisme** [~'tism] *m* Romanticism.

romarin ♀ [rɔma'rɛ̃] *m* rosemary.

rompre [rɔ̃:pr] (4a) *v/t.* break (*s.th.*) in two; break (⚡ circuit, one's neck, *object, peace, promise, silence,* ✗ *step*); ⚖ *hist.* break on the wheel; break up (*an alliance,* ✗ *an attack, the road, etc.*); ✗ scatter (*a regiment*); break off (*a conversation, an engagement*); disrupt (✗ *an army, fig. unity*); burst (*an artery, the river banks*); break in (*an animal*); ✝ cancel; *fig.* disturb, upset; *fig.* interrupt; *fig.* deaden (*a shock*); *fig.* accustom (*s.o.*) (to, à); se ~ break; snap; accustom *or* harden o.s. (to, à); *v/i.* break; ✗, *a. sp.* give ground; ✗ rompez! dismiss!; **rompu, e** [rɔ̃'py] **1.** *p.p. of* rompre; **2.** *adj.* broken; broken in; ~ à used to, hardened to; experienced in (*business*); ~ de fatigue worn out; à bâtons ~s by fits and starts.

romsteck *cuis.* [rɔms'tɛk] *m* rump-steak.

ronce [rɔ̃:s] *f* ♀ bramble branch; ⊕ wood grain: curl; F ⤳*s pl.* thorns; *fig.* difficulties; ⤳ *artificielle* barbed wire; **ronceraie** [⤳'rɛ] *f* ground covered with brambles.

ronchonner F [rɔ̃ʃɔ'ne] (1a) *v/i.* grumble, grouse; hum (*radio-set*); **ronchonneur** *m*, **-euse** *f* F [⤳'nœːr, ⤳'nøːz] grumbler.

rond, ronde [rɔ̃, rɔ̃:d] **1.** *adj.* round; plump (*face, person*); *fig.* brisk (*wind*); *fig.* straight, honest (*person*); F tipsy, tight, *Am.* high; **2.** *rond adv.*: ⊕ *etc., a. fig.* tourner ⤳ run smoothly; *fig. qu'est-ce qui ne tourne pas* ⤳ what's wrong?; **3.** *su./m* circle, round, ring; *bread etc.*: slice; *butter*: pat; ⊕ washer; F *des* ⤳*s pl.*, *le* ⤳ money, F cash; *en* ⤳ in a circle; *su./f* ✕ *etc.*, *dance*, *a. song*: round; ♪ semibreve; *script*: round hand; *à la* ⤳*e around*; (*do s.th.*) in turn; **rond-de-cuir**, *pl.* **ronds-de-cuir** [⤳d-'kɥiːr] *m* round leather cushion; pen-pusher, clerk; bureaucrat; **rondeau** [rɔ̃'do] *m poem*: rondeau; ♪ rondo; ✓ roller; **rondelet, -ette** [rɔ̃d'lɛ, ⤳'lɛt] plumpish; nice round (*sum*); **rondelle** [rɔ̃'dɛl] *f* disc; slice; ⊕ washer; ⊕ (*ball-*)race; **rondeur** [⤳'dœːr] *f* roundness (*a. fig. style*); fullness; *figure*: curve; *fig.* straightforwardness, frankness; **rondin** [⤳'dɛ̃] *m* log; billet; *iron*: round bar; **rond-point**, *pl.* **ronds-points** [rɔ̃'pwɛ̃] *m* road: *mot.* roundabout, *Am.* traffic circus.

ronflant, e [rɔ̃'flɑ̃, ⤳'flɑ̃:t] snoring (*person*); throbbing, roaring, rumbling (*noise*); resounding (*titles, voice*); *fig.* pretentious, bombastic; **ronflement** [⤳flə'mɑ̃] *m* snore; snoring; *noise*: roar(ing), boom (-ing); *machine, top, a. radio*: hum; **ronfler** [⤳'fle] (1a) *v/i.* snore (*sleeper*); roar, boom; hum; *sl.* prosper; **ronfleur, -euse** [⤳'flœːr, ⤳'fløːz] *su.* snorer; *su./m* ⚡ buzzer.

rongeant, e [rɔ̃'ʒɑ̃, ⤳'ʒɑ̃:t] ⚗ corroding; ✗ rodent; ⚗ gnawing (*worries*); **ronger** [⤳'ʒe] (1l) *v/t.* gnaw; *worms etc.*: eat into; ⚗ corrode; pit (*metal*); *fig.* erode; *fig.* fret (*s.o.'s heart*); se ⤳ *les ongles* bite one's nails; *fig.* rongé de tormented by (*grief*); worn by (*care*); **rongeur,**

-euse [⤳'ʒœːr, ⤳'ʒøːz] **1.** *adj. zo., a.* ✗ rodent; *fig.* gnawing (*care, worry*); **2.** *su./m zo.* rodent.

ronron [rɔ̃'rɔ̃] *m cat*: purr(ing); F *machine*: hum; **ronronner** [⤳rɔ'ne] (1a) *v/i.* purr (*cat, engine*); ⊕, *radio, etc.*: hum.

roquer [rɔ'ke] (1m) *v/i. chess*: castle.

roquet [rɔ'kɛ] *m* pug(-dog); mongrel, *Am.* yellow dog.

roquette¹ ✕ [rɔ'kɛt] *f* rocket.

roquette² ♀ [⤳] *f* rocket.

rosace ⚠ [rɔ'zas] *f* rose-window; (*ceiling-*)rose; **rosacé, e** [⤳za'se] **1.** *adj.* rosaceous; **2.** *su./f*: ⤳*s pl.* rosaceae; **rosage** ♀ [⤳'zaːʒ] *m* rhododendron; **rosaire** *eccl.* [⤳'zɛːr] *m* rosary; **rosâtre** [⤳'zɑːtr] pinkish.

rosbif *cuis.* [rɔs'bif] *m* roast beef.

rose [roːz] **1.** *su./f* ♀ rose; ⚠ rose-window; ⚓ ⤳ *des vents* compass-card; ♀ ⤳ *sauvage* dog-rose; *su./m* rose (*colo(u)r*), pink; *voir tout* (*or la vie*) *en* ⤳ see things (*or the world*) through rose-colo(u)red glasses; **2.** *adj.* pink; rosy; **rosé, e** [⤳'ze] **1.** *adj.* rose-pink, rosy; rose, rosé (*wine*); **2.** *su./m wine*: rosé.

roseau [rɔ'zo] *m* ♀ reed; *fig.* (broken) reed.

rose-croix [roz'krwa] *m/inv.* Rosicrucian.

rosée [rɔ'ze] *f* dew.

roseraie [roz'rɛ] *f* rose garden; **rosette** [rɔ'zɛt] *f ribbon*: bow; rosette (*a. = decoration*); red ink or chalk; ⊕ burr; **rosier** ♀ [⤳'zje] *m* rose tree, rose bush.

rossard *sl.* [rɔ'saːr] *m* skunk, beast (= *objectionable individual*).

rosse [rɔs] **1.** *su./f* † F *horse*: nag; *see* rossard; **2.** *adj.* nasty; beastly; cynical (*comedy*).

rossée F [rɔ'se] *f* thrashing; **rosser** F [⤳] (1a) *v/t.* give (*s.o.*) a thrashing.

rossignol [rɔsi'ɲɔl] *m orn.* nightin-gale; ✝ F piece of junk, old stock; F white elephant; ⊕ skeleton-key; ⚓ whistle.

rossinante F [rosi'nɑ̃:t] *f* worn-out old hack, Rosinante.

rossolis [rɔsɔ'li] *m* ♀ sundew; *cordial*: rosolio.

rot *sl.* [ro] *m* belch.

rôt [⤳] *m* roast (meat).

rotateur, -trice [rɔta'tœːr, ⤳'tris] **1.** *adj.* rotatory; **2.** *su./m anat.* rotator; *biol.* rotifer; **rotatif, -ve**

[ˌˈtif, ˌˈtiːv] **1.** *adj.* rotary; **2.** *su./f* *typ.* rotary (printing-)press; **rotation** [ˌˈsjɔ̃] *f* rotation (*a.* Ⓐ, ✎); ⚕ ˌ du stock merchandise turnover; **rotativiste** *typ.* [ˌtiˈvist] *m* rotary printer; **rotatoire** [ˌˈtwaːr] ⊕ rotatory (*a. phys. power*); rotational (*force*); *phys.* rotary (*polarization*).

roter *sl.* [rɔˈte] (1a) *v/i.* belch, bring up wind; *j'en rotais* it took my breath away.

rôti *cuis.* [roˈti] *m* roast (meat); ˌ de bœuf (porc) roast beef (pork); **rôtie** [ˌ] *f* (round of) toast; ˌ à l'anglaise Welch rarebit.

rotin [rɔˈtɛ̃] *m* ⚘ rattan; rattan cane.

rôtir [roˈtiːr] (2a) *vt/i.* roast (*a. fig.*); *fig.* scorch; *cuis.* prêt(e) à ˌ oven-ready; *v/t.* toast (*bread*); **rôtissage** [ˌtiˈsaːʒ] *m* roasting; **rôtisserie** [ˌtisˈri] *f* cook-shop; **rôtisseur** *m*, **-euse** *f* [rotiˈsœːr, ˌˈsøːz] seller of roast meats; cook-shop keeper; **rôtissoire** *cuis.* [ˌˈswaːr] *f* Dutch oven; roaster.

rotonde [rɔˈtɔ̃ːd] *f* △ rotunda; 🚂 engine shed; en ˌ circular; **rotondité** [ˌtɔ̃diˈte] *f* rotundity; F stoutness.

rotor ✎, ✈ [rɔˈtɔːr] *m* rotor.

rotule [rɔˈtyl] *f* *anat.* knee-cap; ⊕ ball-and-socket joint; *mot.* (*steering*-)knuckle.

roture [rɔˈtyːr] *f* commoner's condition; *coll.* commons *pl.*; **roturier, -ère** [ˌtyˈrje, ˌˈrjɛːr] **1.** *adj.* common, plebeian; **2.** *su.* commoner; self-made man.

rouage ⊕ [rwaːʒ] *m* wheels *pl.* (*a. fig.*); work(s *pl.*); cog-wheel, gear-wheel; *fig.* cog.

rouan, -anne *zo.* [rwɑ̃, rwan] roan.

rouanne ⊕ [rwan] *f* rasing-knife; scribing-compass; carpenter's auger.

roublard, e F [ruˈblaːr, ˌˈblard] **1.** *adj.* wily, crafty; **2.** *su.* wily *or* crafty person; **roublardise** F [ˌblarˈdiːz] *f* cunning; piece of trickery.

rouble [rubl] *m* Russian coinage: r(o)uble.

roucouler [rukuˈle] (1a) *vt/i.* coo; *v/t. fig.* warble (*a song*).

roue [ru] *f* wheel; ˌ arrière (avant) back (front) wheel; *mot.* ˌ de secours spare wheel; ˌ directrice *mot.* steering-wheel; *cycl.* front wheel; ˌ motrice driving wheel; faire la ˌ *orn.* spread its tail (*peacock etc.*); *sp.* turn cart-wheels; ✗ wheel about; *fig.* swagger; *mot. freins m/pl. sur quatre* ˌs four-wheel brakes; mettre (or jeter) des bâtons dans les ˌs de q. put a spoke in s.o.'s wheel; sur ˌs wheeled, on wheels; **roué, e** [rwe] **1.** *su.* cunning *or* artful person; *su./m* rake, roué; **2.** *adj.* cunning, artful; exhausted; **rouelle** [rwɛl] *f* round slice; *veal*: fillet, *beef*: round.

rouennerie *tex.* [rwanˈri] *f* printed cotton goods *pl.*

rouer [rwe] (1p) *v/t.* coil (*a rope*); ⚖ *hist.* break (*s.o.*) on the wheel; *fig.* ˌ de coups thrash (*s.o.*) soundly, beat (*s.o.*) black and blue; **rouerie** [ruˈri] *f* trick; piece of trickery; **rouet** [rwɛ] *m* small wheel; spinning-wheel; ⊕ pulley-wheel; ⊕ *pully:* sheave; *lock:* scutcheon; ⚓ gin.

rouge [ruːʒ] **1.** *adj.* red (with, de); ruddy (*cheek*); red-hot (*metal etc.*); ˌ brique brick-red; ˌ sang blood-red; **2.** *adv.:* *fig.* voir ˌ see red; **3.** *su./m* *colour:* red; F red wine; ˌ à lèvres, bâton m de ˌ lipstick; ⊕ au ˌ at red heat, red-hot; porter au ˌ make (*s.th.*) red-hot; se mettre du ˌ put on rouge; *traffic:* passer au ˌ jump the lights; *su. pol. person:* red; **rougeâtre** [ruˈʒaːtr] reddish; **rougeaud, e** F [ˌˈʒo, ˌˈʒoːd] **1.** *adj.* red-faced; **2.** *su.* red-faced person; **rouge-gorge,** *pl.* **rouges-gorges** *orn.* [ruʒˈgɔrʒ] *m* robin (redbreast).

rougeole [ruˈʒɔl] *f* 💊 measles *sg.*; ⚘ filed-cowwheat.

rouge-queue, *pl.* **rouges-queues** *orn.* [ruʒˈkø] *m* redstart; **rouget** [ruˈʒɛ] *m* *icht.* red mullet; gurnard; *vet.* swine-fever; *zo.* harvest-bug; **rougeur** [ˌˈʒœːr] *f* redness; *face:* blush, flush; blotch, red spot (*on the skin*); **rougir** [ˌˈʒiːr] (2a) *vt/i.* redden; turn red; *fig.* flush; *v/t.* make (*s.th.*) red-hot, bring (*s.th.*) to a red heat; *v/i.* blush.

rouille [ruːj] *f* rust (*a.* ✎); ⚘ mildew; **rouillé, e** [ruˈje] rusty (*a. fig.*), rusted; ⚘ mildewed; **rouiller** [ˌˈje] (1a) *v/t.* rust (*a.* ✎); ⚘ mildew, blight; see ˌ rust; ⚘ go mildewed; *fig.* get out of practice; **rouillure** [ˌˈjyːr] *f* rustiness; ⚘ rust, blight.

rouir [rwiːr] (2a) *v/t.* ret, steep (*flax etc.*); **rouissage** [rwiˈsaːʒ] *m* retting, steeping.

roulade [ruˈlad] *f* roll; ♪ (vocal) flourish, roulade; **roulage** [⁓ˈlaːʒ] *m* ✔, *a. mot.* rolling; *goods:* carriage; haulage; cartage; (road) traffic; ✝ haulage firm; **roulant, e** [⁓ˈlɑ̃, ⁓ˈlɑ̃ːt] **1.** *adj.* rolling; sliding (*door*); good, smooth (*road*); smooth-running (*car*); ✝ floating, working (*capital*), going (*concern*); F screamingly funny; ✕, *fig.* feu *m* ⁓ running fire; **2.** *su./m* les ⁓s train *or* truck crews; **3.** *su./f* (*a.* cuisine *f* ⁓e) field kitchen; **rouleau** [⁓ˈlo] *m* roll; ⊕ *etc.* roller; *rope etc.*: coil; *phot.* spool; *tobacco:* twist; *hair:* curler, roller; (⁓ à pâtisserie) rolling pin; ⁓ hygiénique toilet roll; *fig.* être au bout de son ⁓ be at one's wit's end; **roulement** [rulˈmɑ̃] *m* rolling; ⊕ *machine:* running; rumble, rattle; ⊕ (⁓ à billes) ball bearings *pl.*; ⊕ rolling (mechanism), race; ♪ *drum:* roll; ✝ *capital:* circulation; *fig.* alternation; ✕ run, taxying; *mot.* bande *f* de ⁓ tread; ✈ chemin *m* de ⁓ runway; par ⁓ in rotation; **rouler** [ruˈle] (1a) *v/t.* roll (along *or* about *or* up); ling. roll (*one's r's*), trill; *fig.* turn over (*in one's mind*); F cheat, fleece (*s.o.*); F ⁓ sa bosse knock about the world; se ⁓ roll; F se ⁓ par terre (de rire) fall about laughing; *v/i.* roll (*a.* ♏); roll about *or* along *or* over; travel; wander; *mot.* ride, drive (along); ✈ taxi; ⊕, *mot.* run; ✝ circulate (*money*); take turns, rotate; vary (between, entre); ⁓ sur turn upon, depend on; be rolling in (*money*).

roulette [ruˈlɛt] *f* small wheel; *chair etc.*: caster, truckle; *tram:* trolley-wheel; ⚙ dentist's drill; Å cycloid; *game:* roulette; bathchair; F aller comme sur des ⁓s go like clockwork; *sp.* patin *m* à ⁓s roller-skate.

rouleur, -euse [ruˈlœːr, ⁓ˈløːz] *su.* travelling journeyman; worker who keeps changing jobs; *barrow:* wheeler; *su./m* ✕ trammer, haulier; *zo.* vine-weevil; *su./f* *zo.* leaf-roller; F low prostitute; **roulier, -ère** [⁓ˈlje, ⁓ˈljɛːr] **1.** *adj.* carrying; **2.** *su./m* carrier, carter; **roulis** ♏ [⁓ˈli] *m* roll(ing); **roulotte** [⁓ˈlɔt] *f* (gipsy-)van; *mot.* caravan, trailer;

roulure [⁓ˈlyːr] *f* ⊕ *metal:* rolled edge; *timber:* cup-shake; *sl.* low prostitute.

roumain, e [ruˈmɛ̃, ⁓ˈmɛn] **1.** *adj.* Rumanian; **2.** *su./m ling.* Rumanian; *su.* ♀ Rumanian.

roupie¹ [ruˈpi] *f Indian coinage:* rupee.

roupie² [⁓] *f* † drop of mucus; *fig.* bit of trash; F ce n'est pas de la ⁓ de sansonnet that's not half bad.

roupiller F [rupiˈje] (1a) *v/i.* snooze, doze; *sl.* sleep; **roupilleur** F [⁓ˈjœːr] *m* snoozer; **roupillon** F [⁓ˈjɔ̃] *m* snooze; nap; piquer un ⁓ have a snooze.

rouquin, e F [ruˈkɛ̃, ⁓ˈkin] **1.** *adj.* red-haired, sandy-haired; **2.** *su.* red-haired *or* sandy-haired person, redhead.

rouspéter F [ruspeˈte] (1f) *v/i.* resist, show fight; protest; complain; **rouspéteur** F [⁓ˈtœːr] *m* complainer; quarrelsome fellow; *Am. sl.* griper, sorehead.

roussâtre [ruˈsɑːtr] reddish; **rousseur** [⁓ˈsœːr] *f hair etc.:* redness; tache *f* de ⁓ freckle.

roussi [ruˈsi] *m:* sentir le ⁓ smell of burning; *fig.* smack of heresy (*opinion, statement*); be something of a heretic (*person*).

roussin † [ruˈsɛ̃] *m* cart-horse; cob; *sl.* cop(per) (= *policeman*); *sl.* police-spy, *Am. sl.* stool pigeon.

roussir [ruˈsiːr] (2a) *vt/i.* turn brown; scorch, singe (*linen*); *cuis.* brown.

routage [ruˈtaːʒ] *m post:* sorting; routing.

route [rut] *f* road(way); path; route (*a.* ✕, ♏, ✈); course (*a.* ♏); ✕ chanson *f* de ⁓ marching song; en ⁓ on the way; ♏ on her course; ✝ on the road; en ⁓! off you go!; let's go!; 🚌 right away!; ♏ full speed ahead!; faire ⁓ sur make for; faire fausse ⁓ go astray, take the wrong road; *fig.* be on the wrong track; mettre en ⁓ start (up); se mettre en ⁓ set out; ♏ get under way.

router [ruˈte] (1a) *v/t. post:* sort; route.

routier, -ère [ruˈtje, ⁓ˈtjɛːr] **1.** *adj.* road-...; carte *f* ⁓ère road-map; réseau *m* ⁓ highway network; voie *f* ⁓ère traffic lane; carriage-way; **2.** *su./m* track-chart; *mot.* long-distance driver; *cyclist*: (road) racer; *boy scout*: rover; F *vieux* ~ old stager; *su./f* roadster; road-map; traction-engine; **routine** [~'tin] *f* routine; red tape; *par* ~ as a matter of routine; *de* ~ routine ...; **routinier, -ère** [~ti'nje, ~'njɛːr] **1.** *adj.* routine (*activities*); who works to a routine (*person*); F in a rut; **2.** *su.* routinist; lover of routine; F *fig.* stick-in-the-mud.

rouvre ⚙ [ruːvr] **1.** *adj.*: *chêne m* ~ = **2.** *su./m* Austrian *or* Russian oak, robur.

rouvrir [ru'vriːr] (2f) *vt/i.* reopen.

roux, rousse [ru, rus] **1.** *adj.* russet; reddish(-brown); red (*hair*); *cuis.* brown(ed) (*butter, sauce*); *lune f rousse* April moon; *vents m/pl.* ~ cold winds of April; **2.** *su.* red-haired *or* sandy person; *su./m colour*: russet; reddish-brown; *cuis.* brown sauce; browning; brown(ed) butter.

royal, e, *m/pl.* **-aux** [rwa'jal, ~'jo] royal, regal; kingly; crown (*prince*); *fig.* (*suivre*) *la voie* ~ (take) the royal road; **royaliste** [~ja'list] *adj., a. su.* royalist; **royaume** [~'joːm] *m* kingdom; realm (*a. fig.*); **royauté** [~jo'te] *f* royalty; kingship.

ru [ry] *m* water-course; gully; brook.

ruade [rɥad] *f horse*: kick, lashing out.

ruban [ry'bɑ̃] *m* ribbon (*a.* ✂, *a. typewriter, decorations*), band; tape; measuring-tape; ~ *adhésif* adhesive tape; ~ *bleu* ♣ Blue Ribbon; *fig.* first place *or* prize; *fig.* (sign of) superiority; ~ *d'acier* steel band; *mot.* ~ *de frein* brake band; ⚡ ~ *isolant* insulating (*Am. a.* friction) tape; ~ *magnétique* (*or de magnétophone*) recording tape; ⊕ ~ *roulant* conveyor belt; ⊕ *scie f à* ~ band saw; **rubaner** [ryba'ne] (1a) *vt.* trim (*s.th.*) with ribbons; cut (*s.th.*) (in)to ribbons; ⚡ tape (*a wire*); **rubanier, -ère** [~'nje, ~'njɛːr] ribbon-...

rubéfier ⚡ [rybe'fje] (1o) *vt.* rubefy; **rubicond, e** [~bi'kɔ̃, ~'kɔ̃ːd] florid, rubicund, redfaced.

rubigineux, -euse [rybiʒi'nø, ~'nøːz] rusty, rust-colo(u)red.

rubis [ry'bi] *m min.* ruby; *watch*: jewel; *faire* ~ *sur l'ongle* drain to the dregs; *montre f montée sur* ~ jewelled watch; *payer* ~ *sur l'ongle* pay to the last farthing *or Am.* last cent.

rubrique [ry'brik] *f journ.* column; heading, rubric.

ruche [ryʃ] *f* (bee-)hive; *cost.* ruching, ruche, frill; **rucher** [ry'ʃe] **1.** (1a) *vt/t. cost.* ruche, frill; **2.** *su./m* apiary.

rude [ryd] rough (*cloth, path, sea, skin, wine*); hard (*blow, brush, climb, task, times, weather*); severe (*blow, cold, shock, trial, weather, a. fig.*); harsh (*voice, a. fig.*); primitive (*people etc.*); *fig.* brusque; F enormous; **rudement** [~'mɑ̃] *adv.* roughly etc. *see rude*; F extremely, awfully, real (= *very*).

rudesse [ry'dɛs] *f* roughness; hardness; severity; harshness; primitiveness; brusqueness, abruptness.

rudiment [rydi'mɑ̃] *m anat., biol., zo., etc.* rudiment; *fig.* ~s *pl. a.* grounding *sg.*; **rudimentaire** [~mɑ̃'tɛːr] rudimentary.

rudoyer [rydwa'je] (1h) *v/t.* treat roughly; bully.

rue¹ [ry] *f* street, thoroughfare; ~ *à sens unique* one-way street; ~ *barrée!* no thoroughfare; ~ *commerçante* shopping street.

rue² ⚙ [~] *f* rue.

ruée [rɥe] *f* rush, stampede.

ruelle [rɥɛl] *f* lane, alley; space between bed and wall.

ruer [rɥe] (1n) *v/i.* lash out, kick; *se* ~ (*sur*) fling o.s. (at); rush (at, to); **rueur, -euse** [rɥœːr, rɥœːz] **1.** *adj.* kicking (*horse*); **2.** *su. horse*: kicker.

rugby *sp.* [ryg'bi] *m* rugby (football).

rugir [ry'ʒiːr] (2a) *v/i.* roar (*a. fig.*); howl (*storm, wind*); **rugissement** [~ʒis'mɑ̃] *m* roar(ing); *storm, wind*: howl(ing).

rugosité [rygozi'te] *f* roughness, ruggedness; corrugation; *ground*: unevenness; **rugueux, -euse** [~'gø, ~'gøːz] rough, rugged; corrugated; gnarled (*tree, trunk*).

ruine [rɥin] *f* ruin (*a. fig.*); downfall (*a. fig.*); *fig.* fall; *tomber en* ~s fall in ruins; **ruiner** [rɥi'ne] (1a) *v/t.* ruin (*a. fig.*), destroy; ✝ bankrupt (*s.o.*); disprove (*a theory*); *se* ~ ruin o.s. (*person*); *fig.* go to ruin (*thing*); **ruineux, -euse** [~'nø, ~'nøːz] ruinous; *fig.* disastrous.

ruisseau [rɥi'so] *m* brook; stream (*a. fig. of blood*); street, *a. fig. pej.*: gutter; **ruisseler** [rɥis'le] (1c) *v/i.* stream (with, *de*), run (down);

trickle; drip; **ruisselet** [↙'lɛ] *m*
rivulet, brooklet; **ruissellement**
[rɥisɛl'mɑ̃] *m* streaming, running;
trickling; dripping; *fig. jewels:*
glitter, shimmer.

rumeur [ry'mœːr] *f* distant sound;
confused noise; *traffic:* hum; uproar; *fig.* rumo(u)r, report.

ruminant, e *zo.* [rymi'nɑ̃, ↙'nɑ̃:t]
adj., a. su./m ruminant; **ruminer**
[↙'ne] (1a) *v/t.* ruminate (*fig.* on an
idea, *une idée*); *fig.* ponder; *v/i. zo.,*
fig. chew the cud, ruminate.

rune [ryn] *f* rune; **runique** [ry'nik]
runic.

ruolz [ry'ɔls] *m* electroplate(d
ware).

rupestre [ry'pɛstr] ♀ rupestral,
rock-dwelling; rock-(*drawings*).

rupin, e F [ry'pɛ̃, ↙'pin] **1.** *adj.* first-
rate, *Am.* swell; wealthy (*person*);
2. *su./m* swell, toff, nob.

rupteur ⚡ [ryp'tœːr] *m* circuit-
breaker; **rupture** [↙'tyːr] *f dam:*
breaking (*a. ⚡ circuit*), bursting; ⚕
blood-vessel: rupture; *bone:* fracture; *battle, engagement, negotiations:* breaking off; ⚖ *contract,
promise:* breach; *road surface:*
breaking up; *fig.* falling out, quarrel
(*between persons*); 🚛 ~ de charge
dividing of load; ⚖ ~ de promesse
de mariage breach of promise;
charge f de ~ breaking load.

rural, e, *m/pl.* **-aux** [ry'ral, ↙'ro]
1. *adj.* rural, country...; **2.** *su.* peasant.

ruse [ryːz] *f* ruse, trick, wile; ⚔ ~
de guerre stratagem; *en amour la* ~
est de bonne guerre all's fair in love
and war; *user de* ~ practise deceit;
rusé, e [ry'ze] artful, wily, crafty,
cunning; **ruser** [↙] (1a) *v/i.* use
guile; resort to trickery.

rush [rœʃ] *m sp.* (final) spurt, sprint;
fig. rush.

russe [rys] **1.** *adj.* Russian; **2.** *su./m
ling.* Russian; *su.* ♀ Russian;
russifier [rysi'fje] (1o) *v/t.* Russian-
ize.

russo... [rysɔ] Russo...; **~phile** [↙'fil]
adj., a. su. Russophile.

rustaud, e [rys'to, ↙'to:d] **1.** *adj.*
boorish, loutish, uncouth; **2.** *su.*
boor, lout; F bumpkin; **rusticité**
[↙tisi'te] *f* rusticity; boorishness;
primitiveness; ♀ hardiness; **rustique** [↙'tik] **1.** *adj.* rustic (*a. fig.*);
country...; *fig.* countrified, unrefined; ♀ hardy; **2.** *su./m* ⚒ bush-
hammer; **rustiquer** ⚒ [↙ti'ke]
(1m) *v/t.* give a rustic appearance
to; **rustre** [rystr] **1.** *adj.* boorish,
loutish, churlish; **2.** *su./m* boor,
lout, churl; F bumpkin.

rut [ryt] *m animals:* rut(ting), heat;
être en ~ be in *or* on heat (*female*);
rut (*male*).

rutilant, e [ryti'lɑ̃, ↙'lɑ̃:t] glowing
red; gleaming (*a. fig.*); ⚒ rutilant;
fig. glittering; **rutiler** [↙'le] (1a) *v/i.*
glow, gleam (red).

rythme [ritm] *m* rhythm; **rythmique** [rit'mik] rhythmic.

S

S, s [ɛs] *m* S, s; *s... sl.* = *sacré*.
sa [sa] *see* son[1].
sabbat [sa'ba] *m eccl.* Sabbath; *fig.*
 witches' sabbath; F *fig.* din, racket;
 sabbatique [⹁ba'tik] sabbatical.
sabine ♀ [sa'bin] *f* savin(e).
sabir *ling.* [sa'biːr] *m* Levant: lingua
 franca. [ing.]
sablage ⊕ [sɑ'blaːʒ] *m* sand-blast-⹁
sable[1] [sɑːbl] *m* sand; ✱ gravel;
 sand-glass; ∼ mouvant quicksand; bâtir sur le∼ build on sand; F être sur le∼
 be broke; be down and out.
sable[2] *zo.* [∼] *m* sable.
sablé *cuis.* [sɑ'ble] *m* shortbread;
 sabler [∼'ble] (1a) *v/t.* sand, gravel
 (*a path*); ⊕ cast (*s.th.*) in a
 sandmo(u)ld; ⊕ sand-blast; F *fig.*
 swig (*a drink*); **sableur** [∼'blœːr] *m*
 ⊕ sand-mo(u)lder; F *fig.* hard drinker; **sableux, -euse** [∼'blø, ∼'bløːz]
 1. *adj.* sandy; 2. *su./f* ⊕ sand-jet;
 sablier [⹁bli'e] *m* sand-man; sand-
 box, sand-sifter; sand-glass; *cuis.*
 egg-timer.
sablière[1] ⚠ [sɑbli'ɛːr] *f* plate;
 stringer.
sablière[2] [sɑbli'ɛːr] *f* sand-pit;
 gravel-pit; 🚂 sand-box; **sablon**
 [∼'blɔ̃] *m* fine sand; **sablonner** [sɑ-
 blɔ'ne] (1a) *v/t.* sand; *metall.* sprinkle with welding sand; **sablonneux, -euse** [∼'nø, ∼'nøːz] sandy;
 gritty (*fruit*); **sablonnière** [∼'njɛːr]
 f sand-pit, gravel-pit; *metall.* sand-
 box.
sabord ⚓ [sa'bɔːr] *m* port(hole);
 scuttle; **saborder** [⹁bɔr'de] (1a) *v/t.*
 ⚓ scuttle; *fig.* shut down, wind up (*a
 company etc.*); se ∼ ⚓ scuttle one's
 ship; *fig.* shut down.
sabot [sa'bo] *m* sabot (*a.* ⚔, ⊕);
 wooden shoe *or* clog; *zo.* hoof; ⊕, ⚡
 mot. (*brake-, contact-, etc.*)shoe; F
 dud; *toy:* top; *mot.* ∼ (de Denver)
 (*TM*) Denver shoe; *mot.* ∼ de pare-
 choc overrider; F *fig.* dormir comme
 un ∼ sleep like a log; **sabotage**
 [sabɔ'taːʒ] *m work:* scamping, bun-
 gling; scamped *or* bungled work;

(act of) sabotage (*during strikes etc.*);
 saboter [∼'te] (1a) *v/i.* bungle one's
 work; commit acts of sabotage; *v/t.*
 ⊕ shoe (*a pile*); 🚂 chair (*a sleeper*);
 fig. bungle (*one's work etc.*); ⊕ sabotage (*a job, machinery*); **saboteur**
 m, **-euse** *f* [∼'tœːr, ∼'tøːz] ⊕ saboteur; *work:* bungler, botcher; **sa-
 botier** [∼'tje] *m* sabot-maker.
sabre [sɑːbr] *m* sabre, broadsword;
 icht. sword-fish; ∼ au clair (with)
 drawn sword; coup *m* de ∼ sabre cut;
 slash; F *fig.* traîneur *m* de ∼ sabre-
 rattler; **sabrer** [∼'bre] (1a) *v/t.*
 sabre; slash; F botch, scamp (*one's
 work*); F *fig.* make drastic cuts in (*a
 play etc.*); **sabretache** ✗ [⹁brə'taʃ] *f*
 sabretache; **sabreur** [∼'brœːr] *m* †
 dashing cavalry officer; F *work:*
 scamper.
sac[1] [sak] *m coal, flour, etc.:* sack; bag;
 ✗ kit-bag, knapsack; rucksack; *zo.*
 pouch; *anat.* sac; *geol.* pocket;
 (*wind-*)cone; sackcloth; ∼ à main
 handbag, *Am. a.* purse;∼ de couchage
 sleeping-bag; ∼ de voyage travelling-
 case; ∼ en bandoulière shoulder-bag;
 ∼ en papier paper-bag; F homme *m* de
 ∼ et de corde thorough scoundrel; F
 c'est dans le ∼ it's in the bag; F vider
 son ∼ get it off one's chest.
sac[2] [∼] *m* pillage, sacking.
saccade [sa'kad] *f* jerk; par ∼s in
 jerks; *fig.* by fits and starts; **saccadé, e** [saka'de] jerky; irregular.
saccage [sa'kaːʒ] *m* sacking; havoc;
 saccager [saka'ʒe] (1l) *v/t.* sack;
 create havock in; upset; **saccageur**
 m, **-euse** *f* [∼'ʒœːr, ∼'ʒøːz] plunderer.
saccharate 🜍 [sakka'rat] *m* saccharate; **saccharide** 🜍 [∼'rid] *m*
 saccharide; **saccharifier** 🜍 [∼ri-
 'fje] (1o) *v/t.* saccharify; **saccha-
 rin, e** [∼'rɛ̃, ∼'rin] *adj., a. su./f* sac-
 charine; **saccharose** 🜍 [∼'roːz] *m*
 saccharose.
sacerdoce [saser'dɔs] *m* priesthood
 (*a. coll.*); **sacerdotal, e,** *m/pl.* **-aux**
 [⹁dɔ'tal, ∼'to] priestly; sacerdotal;
 fig. priestlike.

sachant [sa'ʃɑ̃] *p.pr. of* savoir 1; **sache** [saʃ] *1st p. sg. pres. sbj. of* savoir 1.

sachée [sa'ʃe] *f* sackful, bagful; **sachet** [ʌ'ʃɛ] *m* small bag; *scent:* sachet; ~ de thé teabag.

sacoche [sa'kɔʃ] *f* satchel, wallet; *mot., bicycle, etc.:* tool-bag; ⚒ saddle-bag.

sacramental *eccl.* [sakramɑ̃'tal] *m* sacramental; **sacramentel, -elle** [ʌ'tɛl] *eccl.* sacramental; *fig.* ritual.

sacre [sakr] *m king:* anointing, coronation; *bishop:* consecration.

sacraliser [sakrali'ze] (1a) *v/t.* make or consider (*s.th., s.o.*) sacred; **sacralité** [ʌ'te] *f* sacredness; **sacré, e** [sa'kre] holy (*orders, scripture*); sacred (*spot, vessel, a. fig.*); *anat.* sacral; *sl.* (*before su.*) confounded, damned; **sacre-bleu!** [ʌkrə'blø] *int.* damn (it)!; **sacrement** *eccl.* [ʌkrə'mɑ̃] *m* sacrament; *derniers* ~s *pl.* last rites; *fréquenter les* ~s be a regular communicant; **sacrer** [ʌ'kre] (1a) *v/t.* anoint, crown (*a king*); consecrate (*a bishop*); *v/i.* F curse.

sacrificateur *m,* **-trice** *f* † [sakrifi-ka'tœːr, ʌ'tris] sacrificer; **sacrifice** [ʌ'fis] *m* sacrifice (*a. fig.*); *eccl.* saint ~ Blessed Sacrament; **sacrifier** [ʌ'fje] (1o) *v/t.* sacrifice (*a.* ✝, *a. fig.*); *fig.* give (*s.th.*) up (to, for à); *se* ~ devote o.s. (to, à); *v/i.* sacrifice; conform (to, à); **sacrilège** [ʌ'lɛːʒ] **1.** *adj.* sacrilegious, impious; **2.** *su.* sacrilegious person; *su./m* sacrilege.

sacripant [sakri'pɑ̃] *m* F scoundrel, knave; † braggart.

sacristain *eccl.* [sakris'tɛ̃] *m* sacristan; sexton; **sacristi!** [ʌ'ti] *int.* Good Lord!; hang it!; **sacristie** *eccl.* [ʌ'ti] *f* sacristy, vestry.

sacro... [sakrɔ] sacro-... (*a. anat.*); ~-**saint, e** [ʌ'sɛ̃, ʌ'sɛ̃ːt] sacrosanct.

sacrum *anat.* [sa'krɔm] *m* sacrum.

sadique [sa'dik] **1.** *adj.* sadistic; **2.** *su.* sadist; **sadisme** [ʌ'dism] *m* sadism.

safari [safa'ri] *m* safari; ~-*photo* photographic safari.

safran [sa'frɑ̃] **1.** *su./m* ♀, *cuis.* saffron; ♣ crocus; **2.** *adj./inv.* saffron (-colo[u]red); **safraner** *cuis.* [ʌfra-'ne] (1a) *v/t.* (colo[u]r *or* flavo[u]r with) saffron.

sagace [sa'gas] sagacious; shrewd; **sagacité** [ʌgasi'te] *f* sagacity; shrewdness; *avec* ~ sagaciously.

sage [saːʒ] **1.** *adj.* wise; prudent; discreet (*person, conduct*); well-behaved; good (*child*); modest (*woman*); **2.** *su./m* wise man, sage; ~-**femme,** *pl.* ~**s-femmes** [saʒ-'fam] *f* midwife; **sagesse** [sa'ʒɛs] *f* wisdom; discretion; good behavio(u)r; *woman:* modesty; *la* ~ (*d'*)*après coup* hindsight.

sagittaire [saʒi'tɛːr] *su./m hist.* archer; *astr. le* ♑ Sagittarius, the Archer; *su./f* ♀ sagittaria, arrowhead.

sagou *cuis.* [sa'gu] *m* sago.

sagouin, e [sa'gwɛ̃, ʌ'gwin] *su. zo.* squirrel-monkey; *su./m* F slovenly fellow; *su./f* F slattern, slut.

sagoutier ♀ [sagu'tje] *m* sago-palm.

saignant, e [sɛ'ɲɑ̃, ʌ'ɲɑ̃ːt] bleeding; *cuis.* underdone, rare (*meat*); F *fig.* sensational, F hot; **saignée** [ʌ'ɲe] *f* ✠ bleeding; *anat.* (~ *du bras*) bend of the arm; *drainage:* ditch; *fig. resources:* drain, loss(es *pl.*); ⊕ (*oil-*)groove; **saigner** [ʌ'ɲe] (1b) *vt/i.* bleed (*a. fig.*); ⊕*, fig.* drain; tap.

saillant, e [sa'jɑ̃, ʌ'jɑ̃ːt] **1.** *adj.* △ projecting; prominent; *fig.* outstanding, striking; **2.** *su./m* ⚒ salient; **saillie** [ʌ'ji] *f* spurt, bound; ⚒ sally (*a. fig. wit*); *zo.* covering; *fig.* outburst; *paint.* prominence; △ projection; ⊕ lug; *en* ~ projecting; bay(-*window*); *faire* ~ project; protrude; *par* ~s by leaps and bounds.

saillir¹ [sa'jiːr] (2a) *v/i.* spurt out, gush out; ⚒ (make a) sally; *v/t. zo.* cover (*a mare*).

saillir² [ʌ] (2p) *v/i.* project; *paint. etc.* stand out.

sain, saine [sɛ̃, sɛn] healthy (*person, climate, a. sp.*); sound (*doctrine, horse, fruit, timber, views,* ♥, ♣, *etc.*); wholesome (*food*); ⚓ clear; ~ *et sauf* safe and sound; **sain(-)bois** ♀ [sɛ̃'bwa] *m* spurge-flax.

saindoux *cuis.* [sɛ̃'du] *m* lard.

sainfoin ♀, ⚹ [sɛ̃'fwɛ̃] *m* sainfoin.

saint, sainte [sɛ̃, sɛ̃ːt] **1.** *adj.* holy; *eccl.* saintly; consecrated (*building, ground, etc.*); ♀ *Jean* St. John; F *toute la sainte semaine* all the blessed week; **2.** *su.* saint; *su./m:* les ~s *pl. de glace* the Ice *or* Frost Saints; *le* ~ *des* ~s the Holy of

Holies; ~-bernard zo. [sɛ̃bɛr-'naːr] m/inv. St. Bernard; ~-crépin [~kre'pɛ̃] m shoemaker's tools pl.; fig. possessions pl.; 2-Esprit [~tes-'pri] m Holy Ghost; sainteté [sɛ̃-tə'te] f holiness, saintliness; fig. sanctity.

saint...: ~-frusquin F [sɛ̃frys'kɛ̃] m/inv. possessions pl.; tout le ~ the whole caboodle; ~-glinglin F [~glɛ̃'glɛ̃]: à la ~ never; ~-office eccl. [~tɔ'fis] m Holy Office; 2-Père eccl. [~'pɛːr] m the Holy Father, the Pope; 2-Siège eccl. [~'sjɛːʒ] m the Holy See; 2-Sylvestre [~sil'vɛstrə]: la ~ New Year's Eve.

sais [sɛ] 1st p. sg. pres. of savoir 1.

saisi ⚖ [sɛ'zi] m distrainee; saisie [~] f seizure (a. ⚖); ⚖ distraint; saisine [~'zin] f ⚖ livery of seisin; ⚓ etc. lashing; boat: sling; saisir [~'ziːr] (2a) v/t. seize; catch hold of; ⚖ attach; distrain upon (goods); foreclose (a mortgage); ⚓ stow (anchors, boats); cuis. cook (meat) at high temperature; fig. catch, grasp; understand; ~ q. de refer (s.th.) to s.o.; vest s.o. with; se ~ de seize upon (a. fig.); saisissable [~zi'sabl] seizable; attachable; fig. distinguishable; saisissant, e [~zi'sã,~'sãːt] striking; gripping (scene, spectacle, speech); piercing (cold); saisissement [~zis'mã] m † seizure; sudden chill; shock, emotion.

saison [sɛ'zɔ̃] f season; tourist season; time: period; ~ hivernale winter season; (hors) de ~ (un)seasonable, (in)opportune; la ~ bat son plein it is the height of the season; saisonnier, -ère [~zɔ'nje, ~'njɛːr] 1. adj. seasonal; 2. su. seasonal worker.

salade [sa'lad] f salad; lettuce; fig. confusion, jumble; sl. panier m à ~ Black Maria (= prison van); saladier [~la'dje] m salad-bowl.

salage [sa'laːʒ] m salting; † salt-tax.

salaire [sa'lɛːr] m wage(s pl.) (a. fig.); pay; fig. reward; ~ de base basic wage; les gros ~s pl. the top earners.

salaison [salɛ'zɔ̃] f salting; bacon: curing; salt provisions pl.; marchand m de ~s dry-salter.

salamandre [sala'mãːdr] f zo. salamander; ⊕ slow-combustion stove.

salami [sala'mi] m salami; fig. métho-

de f (ou tactique f) du ~ salami tactics sg.

salangane orn. [salã'gan] f salangane; cuis. nid m de ~ bird's nest.

salant [sa'lã] adj./m salt-...

salariat [sala'rja] m salaried or wage-earning classes pl.; salarié, e [~'rje] 1. adj. wage-earning (person); paid (work); 2. su. wage-earner; pej. hireling; salarier [~'rje] (1o) v/t. pay wages to (s.o.).

salaud sl. [sa'lo] m dirty person; fig. bastard, Br. a. bugger; sale [sal] dirty (a. fig.); fig. foul.

salé, e [sa'le] 1. adj. salt(ed); fig. spicy, coarse (story); biting (comment etc.); F stiff (price, ⚖ sentence); 2. su./m salt pork; petit ~ pickled pork.

salement [sal'mã] adv. dirtily; meanly, nastily; sl. very, extremely.

saler [sa'le] (1a) v/t. salt (a. fig.); cure (bacon); fig. fleece, overcharge (s.o.).

saleté [sal'te] f dirt(iness), filth(iness); fig. indecency; dirty story; fig. dirty trick; fig. dire des ~s talk smut.

salicylate ⚗ [salisi'lat] m salicyclate; salicylique [~'lik] salicylic.

salière [sa'ljɛːr] f table: salt-cellar; Am. saltshaker; kitchen: salt-box.

saligaud m, e f sl. [sali'go, ~'goːd] dirty dog, skunk, rotter; sloven.

salin, e [sa'lɛ̃, ~'lin] 1. adj. saline, salty; salt (air); 2. su./m salt-marsh; ⊕, ⚗ (crude) potash; 2. su./f salt-pan, salt works usu. sg; rock-salt mine; salinier [~li'nje] m salter; salt-mine owner; † salt merchant.

salir [sa'liːr] (2a) v/t. dirty, soil; fig. sully; se ~ get dirty or soiled; fig. tarnish one's reputation; salissant, e [~li'sã, ~'sãːt] dirty(ing); tex. etc. easily soiled.

salivaire anat. [sali'vɛːr] salivary; salivation ⚕ [~va'sjɔ̃] f salivation; salive [sa'liːv] f saliva; F perdre sa ~ waste one's breath; saliver [~li-'ve] (1a) v/i. salivate.

salle [sal] f hall; (large) room; hospital: ward; thea. (a. ~ de spectacle) auditorium, F house; ~ à manger dining-room; ~ d'attente waiting-room; ~ de bain(s) bathroom; ~ de classe class-room, schoolroom; ⚔ ~ de police guard-room; ~ des pas perdus lobby, waiting-hall.

salmigondis [salmigɔ̃'di] m cuis.

salmagundi, ragout; *fig.* hotch-potch.

salmis *cuis.* [sal'mi] *m* salmi; ragout *(of roasted game).*

saloir [sa'lwaːr] *m* salting-tub.

salon [sa'lɔ̃] *m* drawing-room; ♣ *etc.* saloon, cabin; *(tea-)*room; ♀ exhibition; *fig.* ⁓s *pl.* society *sg.*, fashionable circles; ♀ *de l'automobile* motor-show; *fréquenter les* ⁓*s* move in high society; **salonnier** [⁓lɔ'nje] *m* art critic; critic of the *Salon (the annual art exhibition in Paris).*

salopard *sl.* [salɔ'paːr] *m* unprepossessing person; **salope** *sl.* [⁓'lɔp] *f* tart; bitch; **saloper** F [salɔ'pe] (1a) *v/t.* mess up, *sl.* goof up; **saloperie** F [salɔ'pri] *f* filth; rubbish, trash; mess; bungled piece of work; ⁓s *pl.* smut *sg.*, dirt *sg.*; *faire une* ⁓ *à* play a dirty trick on; **salopette** [⁓'pɛt] *f* overall(s *pl.*); dungarees *pl.*

salpêtre [sal'pɛːtr] *m* saltpetre, potassium nitrate, nitre.

salsifis ♀, *cuis.* [salsi'fi] *m* salsify.

saltimbanque [saltɛ̃'bãːk] *m* (travelling) showman; *pol., fig.* charlatan, mountebank; † tumbler.

salubre [sa'lyːbr] salubrious, healthy; wholesome *(food etc.)*; **salubrité** [⁓lybri'te] *f* salubrity, healthiness; *food etc.*: wholesomeness; ⁓ *publique* public health.

saluer [sa'lɥe] (1n) *v/t.* bow to; salute *(a.* ✕, ♣*)*, greet *(s.o.)*; *fig.* welcome; ♣ ⁓ *du pavillon* dip the flag to.   [*(of the sea air)*.\

salure [sa'lyːr] *f* saltness; salt tang\

salut [sa'ly] *m* safety; *eccl., a. fig.* salvation; greeting; bow; ✕ salute; ♣ *flag:* dipping; ✕ *colour:* lowering; *eccl.* Benediction (of the Blessed Sacrament); ⁓*!* hullo!; how do you do?; *Armée f du* ♀ Salvation Army; **salutaire** [saly'tɛːr] salutary, wholesome, beneficent; **salutation** [⁓ta'sjɔ̃] *f* greeting; bow; *agréez mes meilleures* ⁓*s end of letter:* yours faithfully; **salutiste** [⁓'tist] *su.* Salvationist, member of the Salvation Army.

salve [salv] *f* ✕ salvo; *guns:* salute; *fig.* round *(of applause).*

samedi [sam'di] *m* Saturday; ⁓ *saint* Holy Saturday, Saturday before Easter.

sanctificateur, -trice [sãktifika-'tœːr, ⁓'tris] **1.** *adj.* sanctifying;

2. *su.* sanctifier; *su./m:* le ♀ the Holy Ghost; **sanctification** [⁓fika'sjɔ̃] *f* sanctification; *Sabbath:* observance; **sanctifier** [⁓'fje] (1o) *v/t.* sanctify, make holy; observe *(the Sabbath)*; *que votre nom soit sanctifié* hallowed be Thy name.

sanction [sãk'sjɔ̃] *f* sanction *(a. pol.)*; approval; penalty, punishment; **sanctionner** [⁓sjɔ'ne] (1a) *v/t.* sanction; approve; punish.

sanctuaire [sãk'tɥɛːr] *m* sanctuary *(a. fig.)*; **sanctus** *eccl.*, ♪ [⁓'tys] *m Mass:* sanctus.

sandal, *pl.* **-als** [sã'dal] *m see santal.*

sandale [sã'dal] *f* sandal; gym-shoe.

sandow *(TM)* [sã'dɔf] *m* elastic; *sp.* chest-expander.

sandre *icht.* [sãːdr] *f* pike-perch.

sandwich, *pl. a.* **-es** [sã'dwitʃ] *m* sandwich; *sl. faire* ⁓ play gooseberry.

sang [sã] *m* blood; race, lineage; kinship, relationship; *biol. à* ⁓ *chaud (froid)* warm-blooded (cold-blooded) *(animal)*; F *avoir le* ⁓ *chaud* be quick-tempered; ✳ *coup m de* ⁓ (apoplectic) fit; *droit m du* ⁓ birthright; ✳ *écoulement m de* ⁓ h(a)emorrhage; *être tout en* ⁓ be covered with blood; *se faire du mauvais* ⁓ worry; ⁓**-froid** [⁓'frwa] *m* composure, self-control; *de* ⁓ in cold blood, cold-bloodedly; *accompli de* ⁓ cold-blooded *(murder etc.).*

sanglant, e [sã'glã, ⁓'glãːt] bloody; blood-covered; blood-red; *fig.* bitter *(attack, criticism, tears, etc.)*; deadly *(insult).*

sangle [sãːgl] *f* strap; *(saddle-)* girth; *fit m de* ⁓ camp-bed; **sangler** [sã'gle] (1a) *v/t.* strap; girth *(a horse)*; strike *(s.o.)*; fasten the webbing on *(a bed, a chair).*

sanglier *zo.* [sãgli'e] *m* wild boar.

sanglot [sã'glo] *m* sob; **sangloter** [⁓glɔ'te] (1a) *v/i.* sob.

sangsue *zo., fig.* [sã'sy] *f* leech.

sanguin, e [sã'gɛ̃, ⁓'gin] blood...; of blood; full-blooded *(person)*; red-faced *(person)*; **sanguinaire** [⁓gi'nɛːr] **1.** *adj.* bloodthirsty *(person)*; bloody *(fight)*; **2.** *su./f* ♀ blood-root; **sanguine** [⁓'gin] *f* blood-orange; red h(a)ematite, red chalk; *min.* bloodstone; *paint.* red chalk (drawing); **sanguinolent, e** [⁓ginɔ'lã, ⁓'lãːt] blood-red; ✳ sanguinolent.

sanie 450

sanie ⚕ [sa'ni] *f* pus, F matter;
sanieux, -euse ⚕ [∼'njø, ∼'njø:z]
sanious.

sanitaire [sani'tɛːr] 1. *adj.* sanitary;
✗ hospital (train), ambulance (aeroplane); 2. *su./m* (*a.* ∼s *pl.*) sanitation;
(bathroom) plumbing; bathroom.

sans [sɑ̃] *prp.* without; free from
or of; ...less; un...; ∼ *hésiter* without hesitating *or* hesitation; *non* ∼
peine not without difficulty; ∼ *plus*
tarder without further delay; ∼
bretelles strapless; ∼ *cesse* ceaseless; ∼ *doute* doubtless, no doubt;
∼ *exemple* unparalleled; ∼ *faute*
without fail; faultless; ∼ *le sou*
penniless; ∼ *que* (*sbj.*) without (*ger.*);
∼ *cela*, ∼ *quoi* but for that; *see mot*;
∼-abri [∼za'bri] *m/inv.* homeless
person; **∼-atout** [∼za'tu] *m* cards:
no trumps; **∼-cœur** F [∼'kœːr] *su./
inv.* heartless person; **∼-culotte**
hist. [∼ky'lɔt] *m* sansculotte (= *extreme republican*); **∼-façon** [∼fa'sɔ̃]
m/inv. straightforwardness, blunt-
ness; **∼-fil** [∼'fil] *f/inv.* wireless
message; **∼-filiste** [∼fi'list] *su.* wireless enthusiast; wireless operator;
∼-gêne [∼'ʒɛn] *su./inv.* off-handed
or unceremonious person; *su./m/*
inv. pej. off-handedness; F cheek;
∼-le-sou F [∼lə'su] *su./inv.* penniless
person.

sansonnet *orn.* [sɑ̃sɔ'nɛ] *m* starling.
sans...: **∼-parti** *pol.* [∼par'ti] *su./inv.*
independent; **∼-souci** [sɑ̃su'si]
adj./inv. carefree; unconcerned; **∼-
travail** [∼tra'vaj] *su./inv.* jobless
person.

santal, *pl.* -als ♀ [sɑ̃'tal] *m* sandal-
wood.

santé [sɑ̃'te] *f* health; *à votre* ∼!
cheers!; your health!; *être en bonne* ∼
be well; *maison f de* ∼ private hospital, nursing home; mental hospital; *médecin m de (la)* ∼ medical
officer of health, F M.O.H.; *service m*
de (la) ∼ Health Service, ✗ medical
service, ⚓ quarantine service.

saoul [su] *see* soûl.
sape [sap] *f* ✗ *etc.* sap(ping); under-
mining (*a. fig.*); **saper** [sa'pe] (1a)
v/t. sap, undermine (*a. fig.*).

sapeur ✗ [sa'pœːr] *m* sapper;
pioneer; **∼-pompier**, *pl.* **∼s-pom-
piers** [∼pœrpɔ̃'pje] *m* fireman;
sapeurs-pompiers pl. fire-brigade.

saphir *min.*, *a. orn.* [sa'fiːr] *m* sap-

phire; **saphirine** *min.* [∼fi'rin] *f*
sapphirine.

sapientiaux *bibl.* [sapjɑ̃'sjo] *adj./m/*
pl.: *Livres m/pl.* ♀ wisdom-literature
sg.

sapin [sa'pɛ̃] *m* ♀ fir(-tree), spruce;
† deal; F coffin; *faux* ∼ pitch-pine;
F *toux f qui sent le* ∼ churchyard
cough; **sapinière** ♀ [∼pi'njɛːr] *f*
fir-plantation.

saponacé, e [sapɔna'se] sapona-
ceous, soapy; **saponaire** ♀ [∼'nɛːr] *f*
saponaria, *usu.* soapwort; **saponi-
fier** [∼ni'fje] (1o) *v/t. a. se* ∼ saponify.

sapristi! † F [sapris'ti] *int.* Good
Lord!; hang it!

sarbacane [sarba'kan] *f* blow-pipe.
sarcasme [sar'kasm] *m* sarcasm;
sarcastic remark; **sarcastique** [∼-
kas'tik] sarcastic.

sarcelle *orn.* [sar'sɛl] *f* teal.
sarclage ✔ [sar'klaːʒ] *m* weeding;
sarcler [∼'kle] *v/t.* ✔ weed; hoe
(up); *fig.* weed out; **sarcloir** ✔
[∼'klwaːr] *m* hoe; **sarclure** ✔ [∼-
'klyːr] *f* (uprooted) weeds *pl.*

sarcome ⚕ [sar'koːm] *m* sarcoma.
sarcophage [sarkɔ'faːʒ] *m* sarcoph-
agus.

sarde [sard] 1. *adj.* Sardinian; 2.
su./m ling. Sardinian; *su.* ♀ Sardinian; **sardine** [sar'din] *f* ✗ pil-
chard; † sardine; ✗ F N.C.O.'s
stripe; **sardinerie** [∼din'ri] *f* sar-
dine-packing factory *etc.*; **sar-
dinier, -ère** [∼di'nje, ∼'njɛːr] *su.*
sardine fisher; sardine packer *or*
curer; *su./m* sardine-net; sardine-
boat. [*bibl.* sardine stone.]

sardoine *min.* [sar'dwan] *f* sard;
sardonique [sardɔ'nik] sardonic.
sargasse ♀ [sar'gas] *f* sargasso.
sarigue *zo.* [sa'rig] *m* sarigue;
South America: opossum.

sarment ♀ [sar'mɑ̃] *m* vine-shoot;
bine; **sarmenteux, -euse** ♀ [∼mɑ̃-
'tø, ∼'tøːz] sarmentous; *vine*: climbing.

sarrasin, e [sara'zɛ̃, ∼'zin] 1. *adj. hist.*
Saracen; 2. *su. hist.* ♀ Saracen; *su./m*
✔ buckwheat; *su./f* ✗, ⚓ portcullis.
sarrau, *pl. a.* -s *cost.* [sa'ro] *m*
overall, smock.
sarriette ♀ [sa'rjɛt] *f* savory.
sas ⊕ [sɑ] *m* sieve, riddle, screen;
(*air-*)lock; lock-chamber; ⚓ *submarine*: flooding-chamber; *passer*
au ∼ sift, bolt (*s.th.*).

sasse [sɑːs] *f* ⚓ bailing-scoop, bailer; ⊕ *flour*: bolter.

sassement [sɑsˈmɑ̃] *m* ⚓ passing through a lock; ⊕ sifting, screening, *flour etc.*: bolting; **sasser** [sɑˈse] (1a) *v/t.* ⚓ pass (*a boat*) through a lock; ⊕ sift (*a. fig.*), screen, bolt (*flour etc.*); jig (*ore*); *fig.* examine in detail.

satané, e F [sataˈne] confounded; **satanique** [ˌˈnik] satanic; *fig.* diabolical.

satellisation [satɛlizaˈsjɔ̃] *f satellite*: putting into orbit; *fig.* making into or becoming a satellite; **satelliser** [ˌliˈze] (1a) *v/t.* put (*a satellite*) into orbit; *fig.* make a satellite of (*a country etc.*); **satellite** [ˌˈlit] *m astr.*, *phys.*, *a. fig.* satellite.

satiété [sasjeˈte] *f* satiety; à ~ to repletion, to satiety.

satin 🟊, *tex.* [saˈtɛ̃] *m* satin; *bois m de* ~ satinwood; **satinade** 🟊, *tex.* [satiˈnad] *f silk*: satinette; **satinage** [ˌˈnaːʒ] *m* ⊕ glazing; *tex.* satining; *paper*: surfacing; *phot. print*: burnishing; **satiné, e** [ˌˈne] **1.** *adj.* satiny; glazed (*leather, paper*); *geol.* satin-(*spar, stone*); **2.** *su./m* gloss; **satiner** [ˌˈne] (1a) *v/t.* satin, glaze; surface (*paper*); press (*linen, paper*); *phot.* burnish; **satinette** 🟊, *tex.* [ˌˈnɛt] *f* (*cotton*) satinette, sateen; **satineur, -euse** *tex.* [ˌˈnœːr, ˌˈnøːz] *su.* satiner, glazer; *su./f* satining-machine, glazing-machine.

satire [saˈtiːr] *f* satire (on, *contre*); lampoon; satirizing; **satirique** [satiˈrik] **1.** *adj.* satiric(al); **2.** *su./m* satirist; **satiriser** [ˌriˈze] (1a) *v/t.* satirize.

satisfaction [satisfakˈsjɔ̃] *f* satisfaction (*a. fig.*); *fig.* amends *pl.* (for *pour, de*); *eccl.* atonement (for, *de*); **satisfaire** [ˌˈfɛːr] (4r) *v/t.* satisfy (*a. fig.*); make amends to (*s.o.*); *v/i. eccl.* make atonement; ~ à satisfy; *fig.* meet (*an objection etc.*); *fig.* fulfil (*a duty*); **satisfaisant, e** [ˌfə-ˈzɑ̃, ˌˈzɑ̃ːt] satisfactory, satisfying; **satisfait, e** [ˌˈfɛ, ˌˈfɛt] satisfied, pleased (with, *de*).

saturable ⚛, *phys.* [satyˈrabl] saturable; **saturer** [ˌˈre] (1a) *v/t.* ⚛, *phys.* saturate (with, *de*); *fig.* satiate.

saturnin, e ⚗ [satyrˈnɛ̃, ˌˈnin]

29*

lead-...; **saturnisme** ⚗ [ˌˈnism] *m* lead-poisoning.

satyre [saˈtiːr] *m myth.* satyr; *zo.* satyr butterfly.

sauce [soːs] *f cuis.*, *a. tobacco*: sauce; *cuis.* gravy; *drawing*: lamp-black; ~ *tomate* tomato sauce; F *dans la* ~ in the soup; **saucée** F [soˈse] *f rain*: downpour; *fig.* dressing-down, F telling-off; **saucer** [ˌˈse] (1k) *v/t.* dip (*s.th.*) in the sauce; soak (*a. F fig.*); F scold, tell (*s.o.*) off; **saucière** [ˌˈsjɛːr] *f* sauce-boat; gravy-boat.

saucisse [soˈsis] *f* (*fresh*) sausage; *sl.* fat-head; idiot; F *ne pas attacher son chien avec des* ~s be careful with one's money.

saucisson [sosiˈsɔ̃] *m* (*dry, smoked, etc.*) sausage; **saucissonnage** F *fig.* [ˌsoˈnaːʒ] *m* splitting (up); **saucissonner** F [ˌsoˈne] (1a) *v/i.* have a snack; picknick.

sauf, sauve [sof, soːv] **1.** *adj.* safe, unhurt; unscathed; **2.** *sauf prp.* except, but; save; in the absence of; ~ à (*inf.*) subject to (*ger.*); ~ *erreur ou omission* errors and omissions excepted; ~ *imprévu* except for unforeseen circumstances; ~ *que* (*sbj.*) except that (*ind.*); ~-**conduit** [sofkɔ̃ˈdɥi] *m* safe-conduct, pass.

sauge ♘, *cuis.* [soːʒ] *f* sage.

saugrenu, e [sogrəˈny] preposterous, ridiculous.

saulaie ♘ [soˈlɛ] *f* willow-plantation; **saule** ♘ [soːl] *m* willow; ~ *pleureur* weeping willow; **saulée** [soˈle] *f* row of willows.

saumâtre [soˈmɑːtr] brackish; F nasty; sour (*person*).

saumon [soˈmɔ̃] **1.** *su./m icht.* salmon; ⊕ *lead*: pig; ⊕ *metal*: ingot, block; **2.** *adj./inv.* salmon-pink; **saumoné, e** [somɔˈne] salmon; *icht. truite f* ~*e* salmon-trout; **saumoneau** *icht.* [ˌˈno] *m* young salmon; parr.

saumure [soˈmyːr] *f* pickling brine; pickle; **saumurer** [ˌmyˈre] (1a) *v/t.* pickle in brine; brine (*anchovies, meat*).

sauna [soˈna] *m* sauna.

saupoudrage [sopuˈdraːʒ] *m* sprinkling; *fig.* scattering; **saupoudrer** [ˌˈdre] (1a) *v/t.* sprinkle, powder (with, *de*); dust (with, *de*); *fig.* scatter; *fig.* stud (*the sky, a speech*) (with, *de*); **saupoudreuse** [ˌˈdrøːz] *f*,

saupoudroir [ʌˈdrwaːr] *m* sprinkler. [herring.]

saur [soːr] *adj./m:* hareng *m* ~ red⌡

saurai [soˈre] *1st p. sg. fut. of savoir* 1.

saurer [soˈre] (1a) *v/t.* kipper, cure (*herrings*); **sauret** [ʌˈrɛ] *adj./m* lightly cured (*herring*); **saurin** [ʌˈrɛ̃] *m* bloater.

saut [so] *m* leap, jump; (*water*)fall; *sp.* ~ à la perche pole-jump; *sp.* ~ d'ange swallow-dive; *sp.* ~ de haie hurdling; *sp.* ~ en hauteur (longueur) high (long) jump; ~ en parachute parachute jump; *sp.* ~ périlleux somersault; F *au* ~ *du lit* on getting out of bed; *faire le* ~ give way; take the plunge; F *faire un* ~ *chez* pop round to (*a shop etc.*); *par* ~s *et par bonds* by leaps and bounds; *fig.* jerkily; ~**-de-lit**, *pl.* ~**s-de-lit** *cost.* [ʌd'li] *m* dressing-gown; **saute** [soːt] *f* price, temperature: jump; sudden change; *wind, a. fig.*: shift; **saute-mouton** *sp. etc.* [sotmu'tɔ̃] *m* leap-frog; *jouer à* ~ play leapfrog; **sauter** [soˈte] (1a) 1. *v/i.* jump, leap (*a. fig.* for joy, de joie); ⚓ shift, veer (*wind*); blow up (*explosive, mine, etc.*); ⚡ blow (*fuse*); ✝ go bankrupt, fail; ~ *aux yeux* be obvious; *faire* ~ blow (*s.th.*) up; ⚡ blow (*a fuse*); burst (*a boiler*); blast (*a rock*); spring (*a trap*); burst (*a button, a lock*); *fig.* dismiss, F fire (*an official*); *fig. pol.* bring down (*the government*); *v/t.* jump (over), leap (over); *fig.* skip, omit; ⚡ blow (*a fuse*); toss (*a child, a. cuis. a pancake*); *cuis.* fry quickly; **sauterelle** [ʌˈtrɛl] *f zo.* grasshopper; F *fig.* (*a. grande* ~) beanpole; **sauterie** [ʌˈtri] *f* jumping, hopping; F (*informal*) dance, F hop; **sauteur, -euse** [ʌˈtœːr, ʌˈtøːz] 1. *adj.* jumping, leaping; *fig.* unreliable (*person*); 2. *su.* jumper (*a. sp.*), leaper; *circus:* tumbler; *fig.* unreliable individual; *su./f cuis.* shallow pan; **sautiller** [ʌtiˈje] (1a) *v/i.* hop, jump (about); throb (*heart*); *fig.* be jerky (*style*).

sautoir [soˈtwaːr] *m sp.* hurdle; St. Andrew's cross, ▨ saltire; *cost.* neckerchief (*worn crossed in front*); long chain worn round the neck; *en* ~ diagonal; *porter en* ~ wear (*s.th.*) crosswise; carry (*a haversack etc.*) with the straps crossed over the chest; *porter un ordre en* ~ wear an order round one's neck.

sauvage [soˈvaːʒ] 1. *adj.* wild (*a. zo., a.* ♀, *a. fig.*); savage; *fig.* shy; *fig.* unsociable; *fig.* unauthorized, illegal; wildcat (*strike*); 2. *su.* (*f a.* **sauvagesse** [ʌvaˈʒɛs]) savage; unsociable person; **sauvageon** ♂ [ʌvaˈʒɔ̃] *m* wilding; grafting: wild stock; **sauvagerie** [ʌvaʒˈri] *f* savagery; *fig.* unsociability; shyness; **sauvagine** [ʌvaˈʒin] *su./f coll. orn.* waterfowl *pl.*; ✝ common pelts *pl.*

sauvegarde [sovˈgard] *f* safeguard (*a. fig.*), protection; safety; safeconduct; ⚓ life-line; **sauvegarder** [ʌgarˈde] (1a) *v/t.* safeguard, protect; keep up (*appearances*).

sauve-qui-peut [sovkiˈpø] *m* stampede; headlong flight; **sauver** [soˈve] (1a) *v/t.* save, rescue (from, de); keep up (*appearances*); ⚓ salvage, salve; *sauve qui peut!* every man for himself!; *se* ~ escape (from, de); ✝ recoup o.s.; *fig.* run away, F clear out, *Am.* F beat it; **sauvetage** [sovˈtaːʒ] *m* life-saving; rescue; ⚓ salvage; *bateau m* (*or canot m*) *de* ~ lifeboat; *ceinture f de* ~ lifebelt; **sauveteur** [ʌˈtœːr] 1. *su./m* rescuer; lifeboatman; ⚓ salvager; 2. *adj./m:* *bateau m* ~ lifeboat; ⚓ salvage vessel; **sauvette** [soˈvɛt]: *à la* ~ hurriedly, hastily, with undue haste; unauthorized, illicit (*hawking etc.*); *hawk etc.* illicitly, without authorization; **sauveur** [soˈvœːr] *m* saver, preserver; *eccl.* ♀ Savio(u)r, Redeemer.

savamment [savaˈmɑ̃] *adv.* learnedly; knowingly, wittingly; with full knowledge.

savane ♂ [saˈvan] *f* savanna(h).

savant, e [saˈvɑ̃, ʌˈvɑ̃ːt] 1. *adj.* learned (in, en); scholarly, erudite; performing (*dog*); *fig.* clever, skilful; 2. *su.* scholar; scientist.

savate [saˈvat] *f* old shoe; *sp.* French *or* foot boxing; F bungler, clumsy workman; F *traîner la* ~ be down at heel; **savetier** ✝ [savˈtje] *m* cobbler.

saveur [saˈvœːr] *f* flavo(u)r, taste; *fig.* zest, pungency; *sans* ~ insipid, tasteless.

savoir [saˈvwaːr] 1. (3i) *v/t.* know (of), be aware of, know how; be able to; learn, get to know; ~ *l'anglais* know English; ~ *vivre* know how to behave; *autant (pas) que je sache* as far as I know (not that I know of); *faire* ~ *qch. à q.* inform s.o. of s.th.; *je ne saurais* (*inf.*) I cannot (*inf.*), I could not (*inf.*); *ne ~ que* (*inf.*) not to know what to (*inf.*); *sans le ~* unintentionally; *v/i.* know; know how; (*à*) *~ to wit, namely*; *c'est à ~ that remains to be seen*; **2.** *su./m* knowledge, learning, erudition, scholarship; **~-faire** [savwar'fɛːr] *m/inv.* ability; know-how; skill(s *pl.*); **~-vivre** [~'viːvr] *m/inv.* good manners *pl.*; (good) breeding.

savon [sa'vɔ̃] *m* soap; F *fig.* rebuke, F telling-off; *~ à barbe* shaving-soap; *~ de Marseille* yellow soap, scrubbing-soap; *bulle f de ~* soap bubble; *donner un coup de ~ à* give (*s.th.*) a wash; F *passer un ~ à q.* dress s.o. down, F tell s.o. off; *pain m de ~* cake of soap; **savonnage** [savɔ'naːʒ] *m* washing, soaping; **savonner** [~'ne] (1a) *v/t.* soap; wash (*clothes*); lather (*one's face before shaving*); F dress (*s.o.*) down; *tex.* se ~ wash; **savonnette** [savɔ'nɛt] *f* cake of soap; **savonneux, -euse** [~'nø, ~'nøːz] soapy; **savonnier, -ère** [~'nje, ~'njɛːr] **1.** *adj.* soap...; **2.** *su./m* soap-maker; soap-berry(-tree).

savourer [savu're] (1a) *v/t.* enjoy; *fig.* savo(u)r; **savoureux, -euse** [~'rø, ~'røːz] tasty, savo(u)ry; *fig.* enjoyable; *fig.* racy (*story*).

savoyard, e [savwa'jaːr, ~'jard] *adj., a. su.* ♀ Savoyard.

saxe [saks] *m* Dresden china.

saxifrage ♀ [saksi'fraːʒ] *f* saxifrage.

saxon, -onne [sak'sɔ̃, ~'sɔn] *adj., a. su.* ♀ Saxon.

saynète *thea.* [sɛ'nɛt] *f* sketch; short comedy.

sbire [sbiːr] *m* henchman; F cop (= *policeman*).

scabieux, -euse [ska'bjø, ~'bjøːz] *adj., a. su./f* scabious.

scabreux, -euse ♀ [ska'brø, ~'brøːz] *fig.* scabrous (*behaviour, tale*); risky; difficult, F ticklish (*work*); delicate (*question*); indelicate (*allusion*); rough (*path*).

scaferlati [skaferla'ti] *m* ordinary cut tobacco.

scalène ♀, *anat.* [ska'lɛn] *adj., a. su./m* scalene.

scalpe [skalp] *m* trophy: scalp.

scalpel ♀ [skal'pɛl] *m* scalpel.

scandale [skã'dal] *m* scandal; *fig.* disgrace, shame; *faire ~ create a*

scandal; **scandaleux, -euse** [skãda'lø, ~'løːz] scandalous, disgraceful; notorious; **scandaliser** [~li'ze] (1a) *v/t.* shock, scandalize; se ~ de be shocked at.

scander [skã'de] (1a) *v/t.* scan (*a verse*); ♪ stress; *fig.* punctuate (*with, de*).

scandinave [skãdi'naːv] *adj., a. su.* ♀ Scandinavian.

scaphandre [ska'fãːdr] *m* diving suit; space suit; *~ autonome* aqualung; *casque m de ~* diver's helmet; **scaphandrier** [~fãdri'e] *m* deep-sea diver.

scapulaire [skapy'lɛr] *adj.* anat., a. su./m *eccl.* scapular.

scarabée zo. [skara'be] *m* beetle; *hist. Egypt:* scarab.

scarificateur [skarifika'tœːr] *m* ✔ scarifier; ⚙ scarificator; **scarifier** [~'fje] (1o) *v/t.* scarify.

scarlatine ⚙ [skarla'tin] *f* (*a. fièvre f ~*) scarlet fever.

sceau [so] *m* seal (*a. fig.*); *fig.* mark; admin. *le ~ de l'État* the Great Seal.

scélérat, e [sele'ra, ~'rat] **1.** *adj.* villainous (*person*); outrageous (*act*); **2.** *su.* villain, scoundrel; **scélératesse** [~ra'tɛs] *f* villainy.

scellé ⚖ [se'le] *m* seal; **sceller** [~] (1a) *v/t.* seal; F ratify; ⚙ bed (*a post etc., in concrete etc.*); plug (*a nail in the wall etc.*).

scénario [sena'rjo] *m* thea., cin. scenario; cin. script; cin. screenplay; *fig. le ~ habituel* the usual pattern; **scénariste** [~'rist] *su.* scenario writer; cin. script-writer; **scène** [sɛn] *f* thea. stage; *fig.* drama; play, a. F *fig.*: scene; *fig. faire une ~ create a scene*; *mettre en ~ stage (a play); mise f en ~ production*; (stage) setting; **scénique** [se'nik] *adj.* scenic; stage...; indications *f/pl.* *~s* stage directions.

sceptique [sɛp'tik] **1.** *adj.* sceptical, Am. skeptical; **2.** *su.* sceptic, Am. skeptic.

sceptre [sɛptr] *m* sceptre; *fig.* power.

schéma [ʃe'ma] *m* diagram; (sketch-) plan; design; **schématique** [~ma'tik] *adj.* schematic.

schisme [ʃism] *m* schism.

schiste geol. [ʃist] *m* shale, schist; **schisteux, -euse** geol. [ʃis'tø, ~'tøːz] schistose; *coal:* slaty.

schlague [ʃlag] *f* ✗ † flogging; beating.

schlitte [ʃlit] *f* wood-sledge (*for transport of lumber down mountain*); *Am.* dray; **schlitteur** [ʃli'tœːr] *m* lumberman (*in charge of a* ~).

schnaps F [ʃnaps] *m* brandy.

schnock *sl.* [ʃnɔk] *m* (old) fathead.

schooner ⚓ [sku'nœːr] *m* schooner.

sciable ⊕ [sjabl] fit for sawing; **sciage** ⊕ [sja:ʒ] *m* sawing; (*a. bois m de* ~) sawn timber; **sciant, e** F [sjã, sjã:t] boring; *fig.* irritating.

sciatique ♠ [sja'tik] **1.** *adj.* sciatic; **2.** *su./m* sciatic nerve; *su./f* sciatica.

scie ⊕ [si] *f* saw; *sl.* bore, nuisance; *fig.* catchword, cliché; *fig.* catch tune, hit tune; ~ *à chantourner* compass-saw; ~ *à main* hand-saw; ~ *à manche* pad-saw; ~ *à ruban* band-saw; ~ *circulaire* circular saw, *Am.* buzz-saw; *trait m de* ~ sawcut.

sciemment [sja'mã] *adv.* knowingly, intentionally; **science** [sjã:s] *f* knowledge, learning; science; ~*s pl. naturelles* natural science *sg.*; *homme m de* ~ scientist, man of science; **science-fiction** [sjãsfik-'sjɔ̃] *f* science fiction; **scientifique** [sjãti'fik] **1.** *adj.* scientific; **2.** *su.* scientist.

scier [sje] (1o) *v/t.* ⊕ saw; ✓ saw off (*a branch*); F ~ *le dos à* bore (*s.o.*) stiff; **scierie** ⊕ [si'ri] *f* sawmill; **scieur** [sjœːr] *m* ⊕ sawyer; ~ *de long* pit sawyer.

scille [sil] *f* ♀ scilla; ♠ squills *pl.*

scindement [sɛ̃d'mã] *m* splitting up; **scinder** [sɛ̃'de] (1a) *v/t.* split up, divide; *se* ~ split (*pol. party*).

scintillation [sɛ̃tilla'sjɔ̃] *f*, **scintillement** [sɛ̃tij'mã] *m* sparkling, scintillation (*a. fig.*); *star:* twinkling; *cin.* flicker(ing); **scintiller** [sɛ̃ti'je] (1a) *v/i.* sparkle, scintillate (*a. fig.*); twinkle (*star*); *cin.* flicker.

scion [sjɔ̃] *m* ✓ shoot, scion; *fishing-rod:* tip.

scirpe ♀ [sirp] *m* bulrush, clubrush.

scissile *min.* [si'sil] scissile; **scission** [si'sjɔ̃] *f* scission, split, division; *faire* ~ secede; **scissipare** *biol.* [sisi'paːr] fissiparous, scissiparous; **scissiparité** *biol.* [~pari'te] *f* fissiparity, scissiparity; **scissure** *anat. etc.* [si'syːr] *f* fissure, cleft.

sciure ⊕ [sjy:r] *f* (*saw*)dust.

scléreux, -euse ♠ [skle'røˌ ~'røːz] sclerous; **sclérose** [~'roːz] *f* ♠ sclerosis; *fig.* ossification; **sclérosé, e** [~rɔ'ze] ♠ sclerotic; *fig.* ossified; **sclérotique** *anat.* [rɔ'tik] *adj., a. su./f* sclerotic.

scolaire [skɔ'lɛːr] school...; **scolariser** [~lari'ze] (1a) *v/t.* provide with schools *or* schooling; **scolarité** [~lari'te] *f* schooling; *années f/pl. de* ~ school years; **scolastique** *phls.* [~las'tik] **1.** *adj.* scholastic; **2.** *su./m* scholastic, schoolman; *su./f* scholasticism.

scolopendre [skɔlɔ'pãːdr] *f zo.* centipede; ♀ hart's-tongue.

sconse ✝ [skɔ̃:s] *m* skunk (fur).

scooter [sku'tœːr] *m* scooter.

scorbut [skɔr'by] *m* scurvy; **scorbutique** ♠ [~by'tik] *adj., a. su.* scorbutic.

score *sp.* [skɔr] *m* score.

scorie [skɔ'ri] *f* slag, scoria; *iron:* dross.

scorpion [skɔr'pjɔ̃] *m zo.* scorpion; *astr. le* ♋ Scorpio, the Scorpion.

scorsonère ♀ [skɔrsɔ'nɛːr] *f* scorzonera, black salsify.

scout, e [skut] **1.** *su./m* boy-scout **2.** *adj.* scout...; **scoutisme** [sku-'tism] *m* boy-scout movement, scouting.

scribe [skrib] *m hist.* (*Jewish*) scribe; copyist; F pen-pusher.

script *cin.* [skript] *m* film-script; ~**-girl** *cin.* [~'gœːrl] *f* continuity-girl.

scriptural, e, m/pl. -aux [skripty-'ral, ~'ro] scriptural; ✝ *monnaie f* ~*e* deposit currency.

scrofulaire ♀ [skrɔfy'lɛːr] *f* figwort; **scrofule** ♠ [~'fyl] *f* scrofula; **scrofuleux, -euse** ♠ [~fy'lø, ~'løːz] scrofulous (*person*); strumous (*tumour*).

scrupule [skry'pyl] *m weight, a. fig.:* scruple; *avoir des* ~*s à* (*inf.*) have scruples about (*ger.*); *sans* ~ unscrupulous(ly *adv.*); **scrupuleux, -euse** [~py'lø, ~'løːz] scrupulous (about, over *sur*); punctilious; *peu* ~ unscrupulous.

scrutateur, -trice [skryta'tœːrˌ ~'tris] **1.** *adj.* searching; **2.** *su./m* scrutinizer, investigator; *pol. etc., ballot etc.:* teller; **scruter** [~'te] (1a) *v/t.* scrutinize; investigate; search (*one's memory*); **scrutin** [~'tɛ̃] *m* poll; *admin.* vote; voting; ~ *public* (*secret*) open (secret) vote;

dépouiller le ~ count the votes;
tour m *de* ~ ballot.
sculpter [skyl'te] (1a) *v/t.* sculpture, carve (out of, *dans*); **sculp-**
teur [~'tœ:r] m sculptor; ~ *sur bois*
wood-carver; **sculpture** [~'ty:r] f
sculpture; ~ *sur bois* wood-carving.
se [sə] **1.** *pron./rfl.* oneself; himself,
herself, itself; themselves; *to ex-*
press passive: ~ *vendre* be sold; ~
roser be(come) pink; **2.** *pron./recip.*
each other, one another.
séance [se'ã:s] f seat; sitting (*a.*
paint.), session, meeting; *cin.* performance; ~ *plénière* (*de clôture*)
plenary (closing) session; *fig.* ~
tenante immediately; **séant, e** [~'ã,
~'ã:t] **1.** *adj.* in session, sitting; *fig.*
seemly, fitting; becoming (to, *à*); **2.**
su./m F posterior; *se mettre sur son* ~
sit up (*in bed*).
seau [so] m pail, bucket; *biscuit:*
barrel; ~ *à charbon* coal-scuttle; F
il pleut à ~*x* it is raining in bucket-
fuls.
sébacé, e [seba'se] sebaceous.
sébile [se'bil] f wooden bowl.
sec, sèche [sek, sɛʃ] **1.** *adj.* dry (*a.*
wine, fig. remark); dried (*cod, rai-*
sins); lean (*person, horse*); sharp
(*blow, answer, remark, tone*); *fig.*
harsh, unsympathetic; barren; ✝
dead (*loss*); split (*peas*); hard (*cash*);
cards: bare (*ace, king, etc.*); **2. sec**
adv.: boire ~ drink neat; drink hard;
brûler ~ burn like tinder; *parler* ~
not to mince one's words; *rire* ~
laugh harshly; *à* ~ dry; dried up;
F hard-up, broke; **3.** *su./m être à* ~ be
dried (up), be dry; F be broke; *mettre*
à ~ dry (up *or* out); drain; F clean
(*s.o.*) out; **4.** *su./f* ⚓ flat; *sl.* fag (=
cigarette); *sl.* piquer une sèche be
stumped (*in oral examination*), get no
marks (*in examination*).
sécante ⚕ [se'kã:t] f secant; **séca-**
teur ✔ [~ka'tœ:r] m pruning shears
pl., secateurs *pl.*
sécession [sesɛ'sjõ] f secession; *faire*
~ secede (from, *de*); **sécessionniste**
[~sjɔ'nist] *adj., a. su.* secessionist.
séchage [se'ʃa:ʒ] m drying; ⊕
wood: seasoning; F *univ. lecture:*
cutting; **sèche-cheveux** [sɛʃə'ʃvø]
m/inv. hair-drier; **sécher** [se'ʃe]
(1f) *v/i.* (become) dry; F waste away
(with, *de*); F be stumped (*in an ex-*

amination); *sl.* smoke; *faire* ~ dry;
⊕ season (*wood*); *v/t.* dry; ⊕
season (*wood*); F *univ.* cut (*a lec-*
ture); F fail (*a candidate*); **séche-**
resse [seʃ'rɛs] f dryness; drought;
person, horse: leanness; *answer,*
remark, tone: curtness; *fig. heart:*
coldness; *fig. style etc.*: bareness;
sécherie [~'ri] f drying-floor; *ma-*
chine: drier; ♨ seed-kiln; **sécheur**
⊕ [se'ʃœ:r] m drier; **sécheuse**
[~'ʃø:z] f steam-drier; **séchoir**
[~'ʃwa:r] m ⊕ drying-room; dry-
ing-ground; ⊕ drier; clothes-
horse, airer.
second, e [sə'gõ, ~'gõ:d] **1.** *adj.*
second (*a. fig.*); **2.** *su.* (the) second;
su./m second in command, princi-
pal assistant; ⚓ first mate, first
officer, *sl.* number one; *box., a.*
duel: second; ⚕ second floor, *Am.*
third floor; ⚓ ~ *maître* petty officer; *su./f* ⚕, ♫, *time:* second; ⊟
second (class); *secondary school:*
(*approx.*) fifth form; *typ.* revise;
secondaire [səgõ'dɛ:r] **1.** *adj.*
secondary; *fig. a.* subordinate, minor; **2.** *su./m* ⚡ secondary winding;
seconder [~'de] (1a) *v/t.* second,
support; further (*s.o.'s interests*).
secouer [sə'kwe] (1p) *v/t.* shake (*a.*
fig.); shake down *or* off; knock out
(*a pipe*); F *fig.* rouse (*s.o.*); F *se* ~
get a move on; rouse o.s.
secourable [səku'rabl] helpful;
ready to help; **secourir** [~'ri:r] (2i)
v/t. aid, succo(u)r, help; **secouriste**
[~'rist] *su.* first-aid worker; voluntary ambulance worker; **secours**
[sə'ku:r] m help, assistance; aid; ⚕
~ *pl.* relieving force *sg.*, relief troops;
au ~! help!; *de* ~ relief-...; spare
(*wheel*); emergency (*exit, landing-*
ground); ⚕, ⚚ premier ~ first aid.
secousse [sə'kus] f bump, jolt, jerk;
⚡, *a. fig.* shock.
secret, -ète [sə'krɛ, ~'krɛt] **1.** *adj.*
secret, concealed; *fig.* reticent;
2. *su./m* secret; secrecy; ⚔ solitary
confinement; ⊕ desk *etc.*: secret
spring; ~ *postal* secrecy of correspondence; *en* ~ in secret, in secrecy; privately; *su./f* prayer: secret;
secrétaire [səkre'tɛ:r] *su. person:*
secretary; *su./m furniture:* secre-
taire, writing-desk; *orn.* secretary-
bird; ~ *d'État* Secretary of State;
~ *particulier* private secretary;

secrétairerie [ˌterəˈri] *f* secretary's staff; secretariat; *pol.* chancery, registry; **secrétariat** [ˌtaˈrja] *m* secretariat, secretary's office; secretaryship.

secréter *physiol.* [sekreˈte] (1f) *v/t.* secrete; **sécréteur, -trice** *or* **-euse** *physiol.* [ˌˈtœːr, ˌˈtris, ˌˈtøːz] secretory; **sécrétion** *physiol.* [ˌˈsjɔ̃] *f* secretion; **sécrétoire** *physiol.* [ˌˈtwaːr] secretory.

sectaire [sɛkˈtɛːr] *adj.*, *a. su.* sectarian; **secte** [sɛkt] *f* sect.

secteur [sɛkˈtœːr] *m* ⚡, ⊕, ✕, *astr.* sector; *admin.* district, area; ⚡ mains *pl.*; ⚓ (*steering-*)quadrant.

section [sɛkˈsjɔ̃] *f* section (*a.* ⚡, △); cutting, docking; ✕ *infantry:* platoon, *artillery:* section; ✕ *ammunition:* column; ⚓ subdivision; *admin.* branch; *bus, tram:* stage; *admin.* ~ de vote polling-district; **sectionnel, -elle** [sɛksjoˈnɛl] sectional; **sectionner** [ˌˈne] (1a) *v/t.* divide into sections; cut, sever.

séculaire [sekyˈlɛːr] secular (= *once in 100 years*); century-old; *fig.* time-hono(u)red, ancient; **séculariser** [ˌlariˈze] (1a) *v/t.* secularize; convert (*a church etc.*) to secular use; **sécularité** [ˌlariˈte] *f* secularity; *eccl.* secular jurisdiction; **séculier, -ère** [ˌˈlje, ˌˈljɛːr] *adj.*, *su./m* secular.

sécuriser [sekyriˈze] (1a) *v/t.* give (*s.o.*) a feeling of security, make (*s.o.*) feel (more) secure; **sécurité** [ˌˈte] *f* security; *admin.*, *mot.*, *a.* ⊕ safety; *pol.* ~ *collective* collective security; ~ *routière* road safety; ⊕ *etc.* de ~ safety ...   [*a. su./m* sedative.]

sédatif, -ve ⚕ [sedaˈtif, ˌˈtiːv] *adj.*⟩

sédentaire [sedɑ̃ˈtɛːr] sedentary (*life, profession*); settled, sedentary (*people etc.*); settled, fixed; *orn.* non-migrant; **sédentariser** [ˌtariˈze] (1a) *v/t.* make sedentary, settle (*a tribe etc.*).

sédiment [sediˈmɑ̃] *m* sediment, deposit; **sédimentaire** *geol. etc.* [ˌmɑ̃ˈtɛːr] sedimentary; aqueous (*rock*); **sédimentation** [ˌmɑ̃taˈsjɔ̃] *f* sedimentation.

séditieux, -euse [sediˈsjø, ˌˈsjøːz] **1.** *adj.* seditious; mutinous; **2.** *su.* seditionist, fomenter of sedition; **sédition** [ˌˈsjɔ̃] *f* sedition; *en* ~ in revolt.

séducteur, -trice [sedykˈtœːr, ˌˈtris] **1.** *adj.* seductive, alluring; tempting (*look, word*); **2.** *su.* seducer; **séductible** [ˌˈtibl] seducible; **séduction** [ˌˈsjɔ̃] *f* seduction (*a.* ⚖); *fig.* attraction; **séduire** [seˈdɥiːr] (4h) *v/t.* seduce (*a.* ⚖); suborn, bribe (*a witness*); *fig.* attract (*s.o.*), fascinate (*s.o.*); **séduisant, e** [ˌdɥiˈzɑ̃, ˌˈzɑ̃ːt] seductive, tempting; *fig.* attractive, fascinating.

segment [sɛɡˈmɑ̃] *m* ⚡, *zo.* segment; ⊕ (*piston-*)ring; caterpillar tyre: joint; **segmentaire** [ˌmɑ̃ˈtɛːr] ⚡ segmentary; △, *anat.* segmental; **segmenter** [ˌmɑ̃ˈte] (1a) *v/t. a.* se ~ segment, divide into segments.

ségrégation [seɡreɡaˈsjɔ̃] *f* segregation (*a. pol.*); isolation; **ségrég(u)é, e** [ˌˈɡe] segregated.

seiche *zo.* [sɛʃ] *f* cuttle-fish; *os m de* ~ cuttle-bone.

séide [seˈid] *m* henchman; blind supporter.

seigle ♀ [sɛɡl] *m* rye; ~ *ergoté* spurred rye.

seigneur [sɛˈɲœːr] *m* lord; noble; lord of the manor; *faire le (or vivre en) grand* ~ live like a lord; *eccl.* le ♀ the Lord; **seigneurial, e** *m/pl.* -aux † [sɛɲœˈrjal, ˌˈrjo] seigniorial, manorial; *maison f* ~e manor-house; **seigneurie** [ˌˈri] *f* lordship; manor.

seille [sɛːj] *f* pail, bucket.

sein [sɛ̃] *m* breast; bosom; *au* ~ *de* within; in the midst of.

seine [sɛn] *f* *fishing:* seine, drag-net.

seing ⚖ [sɛ̃] *m* signature, † sign manual; *acte m sous* ~ *privé* simple contract; private agreement.

séisme [seˈism] *m* earthquake, seism.

seize [sɛːz] *adj./num.*, *a. su./m/inv.* sixteen; *date, title:* sixteenth; **seizième** [sɛˈzjɛm] **1.** *adj./num.*, *a. su.* sixteenth.

séjour [seˈʒuːr] *m* stay; *place:* abode, residence, dwelling; ⚖ *interdiction f de* ~ prohibition from entering certain localities; *permis m de* ~ residence permit; **séjournant, e** [ˌʒurˈnɑ̃, ˌˈnɑ̃ːt] *su.* visitor, guest; **séjourner** [ˌʒurˈne] (1a) *v/i.* stay, reside; stop; remain.

sel [sɛl] *m* salt (*a.* 🜔); *fig.* wit; ~*s pl.* smelling-salts; *prendre qch. avec un* *grain de* ∼ take s.th. with a grain of salt.

select F [se'lɛkt] select; *réunions f/pl.* selects exclusive parties.

sélecter F ✝ [selɛk'te] (1a) *v/t.* choose; **sélecteur** [∼'tœːr] *m* ✗, *a. radio:* selector; **sélectif, -ve** [∼'tif, ∼'tiːv] selective; **sélection** [∼'sjɔ̃] *f* selection (*a.* ♪, ✗, *radio, biol., a. sp.*); choice; **sélectionner** [∼sjɔ'ne] (1a) *v/t.* select, choose; **sélectivité** [∼tivi'te] *f radio:* selectivity.

sélénique ⚗, *astr.* [sele'nik] selenic; **sélénium** ⚗ [∼'njɔm] *m* selenium; **sélénographie** [∼nɔgra'fi] *f* selenography.

self [sɛlf] *f* F self-service restaurant; ✗ (*a. bobine f de* ∼) inductance-coil; **∼-induction** ✗ [∼ɛdyk'sjɔ̃] *f* self-induction; inductance.

selle [sɛl] *f* ⊕, *mot., cuis., horse, bicycle:* saddle; ♠ plate; *physiol.* motion, stool; ∼ *anglaise* hunting saddle; *physiol. aller à la* ∼ go to stool; F *mettre q. en* ∼ give s.o. a helping hand; **seller** [se'le] (1a) *v/t.* saddle (*a horse*); **sellette** [se'lɛt] *f* stool, seat; ⊕ slung cradle; *fig. mettre* (*or tenir*) *q. sur la* ∼ cross-examine s.o., F carpet s.o.; **sellier** [se'lje] *m* saddler.

selon [sə'lɔ̃] **1.** *prp.* according to; ∼ *moi* in my opinion; *c'est* ∼ *!* it all *or* that depends!; **2.** *cj.:* ∼ *que* according as, depending upon whether.

Seltz [sɛlts] *m: eau f de* ∼ soda-water.

semailles [sə'maːj] *f/pl.* sowing *sg.*; seeds.

semaine [sə'mɛn] *f* week; ⊕, ✝ working week; ✗ *etc.* duty for the week; week's pay; ∼ *anglaise* five and a half day (working) week; ∼ *sainte* Holy Week; *à la* ∼ by the week; *en* ∼ during the week; *être de* ∼ be on duty for the week.

sémantique [semɑ̃'tik] **1.** *adj.* semantic; **2.** *su./f* semantics *pl.*

sémaphore [sema'fɔːr] *m* semaphore; ⚓ signal-station (*on land*).

semblable [sɑ̃'blabl] **1.** *adj.* similar (to, *à*) (*a.* ♣ *triangles*); alike; like (*a.* ♣ *terms*); such; **2.** *su.* like, equal; fellow; *su./m: nos* ∼*s pl.* our fellow-men; **semblablement** [∼blablə-'mɑ̃] *adv.* in like manner; **semblant** [∼'blɑ̃] *m* appearance, look; *fig.* show (of, *de*); *faire* ∼ pretend (to *inf.*, *de inf.*); make a show (of

s.th., *de qch.*); *faux* ∼ pretence; *sans faire* ∼ *de rien* as if nothing had happened; surreptitiously; **sembler** [∼'ble] (1a) *v/i.* seem, appear; *il me semble* I think; *que vous en semble?* what do you think (about it)?

semelle [sə'mɛl] *f shoe:* sole; *stocking:* foot; *mot. tyre:* tread; ⊕ bed; ♠ foundation; ∼ *de liège* cork insole; *battre la* ∼ stamp one's feet (to warm them); kick one's heels; *remettre des* ∼*s à* re-sole.

semence [sə'mɑ̃ːs] *f* seed (*a. fig.*); *physiol.* semen; ⊕ (tin)tack; ∼ *de perles* seed-pearls *pl.*; **semer** [∼'me] (1d) *v/t.* ✓ sow (*a. fig. discord etc.*); scatter; *fig.* disseminate, spread (*a rumour*); squander (*one's money*); F lose; F shake off, drop (*s.o.*).

semestre [sə'mɛstr] *m* half-year; six months' duty *or* pay *or* ✗ leave of absence; *univ. etc.* semester; **semestriel, -elle** [∼mɛstri'el] half-yearly; lasting six months.

semeur, -euse [sə'mœːr, ∼'møːz] *su.* sower (*a. fig. of discord*); *fig.* spreader (*of rumours*).

semi... [səmi] semi...; **∼-brève** ♪ [∼'brɛːv] *f* semibreve, *Am.* whole note; **∼-conducteur** ✗ [∼kɔ̃dyk-'tœːr] *m* semi-conductor; **∼-coke** [∼'kɔk] *m* coalite.

sémillant, e [semi'jɑ̃, ∼'jɑ̃ːt] vivacious.

séminaire [semi'nɛːr] *m* seminary; *fig.* training centre; *fig.* colloque, symposium; *univ.* seminar; *petit* ∼ secondary school run by priests.

séminal, e [semi'nal] *m/pl.* -aux [semi'nal, ∼'no] seminal.

semi-remorque [səmirə'mɔrk] *f* articulated truck, *Am.* trailer truck.

semis ✓ [sə'mi] *m* sowing; seedling; seed-bed.

semi-ton ♪ [səmi'tɔ̃] *m* semitone; **semi-voyelle** *gramm.* [∼vwa'jɛl] *f* semivowel.

semoir ✓ [sə'mwaːr] *m* sowing-machine; seed-drill; seeder.

semonce [sə'mɔ̃ːs] *f fig.* reprimand; ⚓ *coup m de* ∼ warning shot; **semoncer** (1k) *v/t.* † reprimand, F read (*s.o.*) a lecture; ⚓ call upon (*a ship*) to heave to *or* to show her flag.

semoule *cuis.* [sə'mul] *f* semolina.

sempiternel, -elle [sɑ̃piter'nɛl] sempiternal, everlasting.

sénat [se'na] *m* senate(-house); **sé-nateur** [sena'tœːr] *m* senator.

séneçon ♧ [sen'sɔ̃] *m* groundsel.

sénevé ♧ [sen've] *m* black mustard.

sénile ⚕ [se'nil] senile; **sénilité** ⚕ [⁓nili'te] *f* senility, senile decay.

sens [sãːs] *m fig. smell etc.*: sense; *fig.* opinion; understanding; judg(e)-ment; meaning; direction (*a.* ♀); way; ⁓ *de la musique* musicianship; ⁓ *de l'orientation* sense of direction; ⁓ *dessus dessous* upside down; ⁓ *devant derrière* back to front; ⁓ *interdit* no entry; ⁓ *moral* moral sense; ⁓ *unique* one-way street; *à mon* ⁓ in my view *or* opinion; *le bon* ⁓, *le* ⁓ *commun* common sense; *plaisirs m/pl. des* ⁓ sensual pleasures; **sensation** [sãsa-'sjɔ̃] *f* sensation; (*physical*) feeling; *à* ⁓ sensational (*news*); **sensationnel, -elle** [⁓sjɔ'nɛl] sensational; *fig.* thrilling; *roman m* ⁓ thriller; **sensé, e** [sã'se] sensible, intelligent; practical.

sensibiliser [sãsibili'ze] (1a) *v/t.* sensitize; *fig.* make sensitive (to, *à*); *sensibilisé à* alive to; ...-minded; **sensibilité** [⁓'te] *f* sensitiveness (*a. phot.*); *fig.* feeling, compassion; **sensible** [sã'sibl] sensitive (*ear, instrument, phot. paper, skin, spot, a. fig.* to *pain etc.*); tender (*flesh, spot*); responsive; susceptible; *fig.* appreciative (of, *à*); *fig.* sympathetic; perceptible, real (*difference, progress*); *phot.* sensitized (*paper*); ♪ *note f* ⁓ leading note *or Am.* tone; **sensiblerie** [⁓siblə'ri] *f* sentiment(ality); F sob-stuff.

sensitif, -ve [sãsi'tif, ⁓'tiːv] **1.** *adj.* sensitive; *anat.* sensory; **2.** *su./f* ♧ sensitive plant; F very sensitive woman *or* girl; **sensitivité** [⁓tivi'te] *f* sensitivity.

sensoriel, -elle [sãsɔ'rjɛl] sensorial, sensory.

sensualisme *phls.* [sãsɥa'lism] *m* sensualism; **sensualiste** *phls.* [⁓'list] **1.** *adj.* sensual; **2.** *su.* sensualist; **sensualité** [⁓li'te] *f* sensuality; sensuousness; **sensuel, -elle** [sã'sɥɛl] sensual; sensuous.

sentence [sã'tãːs] *f* maxim; ⚖ sentence; (*a.* ⁓ *arbitrale*) award; **sentencieux, -euse** [⁓tã'sjø, ⁓'sjøːz] sententious.

senteur *hunt.* [sã'tœːr] *f* scent (*a. poet. = perfume*).

sentier [sã'tje] *m* footpath; path (*a. fig.*); ⁓ *battu* beaten track.

sentiment [sãti'mã] *m* feeling (*a. fig.*); emotion; consciousness, sense; *fig.* opinion, sentiment; ⁓ *d'infériorité* sense of inferiority; *avoir le* ⁓ *de a.* be aware of; *voilà mon* ⁓ that is my opinion; **sentimental, e,** *m/pl.* **-aux** [⁓mã'tal, ⁓'to] sentimental; **sentimentalité** [⁓mãtali'te] *f* sentimentality.

sentine ⚓ [sã'tin] *f ship*: well; cesspit (*a. fig.*); *fig.* sink of iniquity.

sentinelle ✗ [sãti'nɛl] *f* sentry; guard, watch; *faire* ⁓ mount guard; F *fig. faire la* ⁓ be on the watch.

sentir [sã'tiːr] (2b) *v/t.* feel; be conscious of, be alive to; smell (*a. fig.*); taste of, smack of (*s.th.*); F *je ne peux pas le* ⁓ I can't stand him; *vin m qui sent le bouchon* corked wine; *se* ⁓ feel; *ne pas se* ⁓ *de joie* be beside oneself with joy; *v/i.* smell (bad, *mauvais*; *bon*, good).

seoir [swaːr] (3k) *v/i.*: ⁓ *à q.* become s.o.

sépale ♧ [se'pal] *m* sepal.

séparable [sepa'rabl] separable (from, *de*); **séparateur, -trice** [separa'tœːr, ⁓'tris] **1.** *adj.* separating, separative; **2.** *su./m* ⊕ separator; **séparation** [⁓'sjɔ̃] *f* ⊕, ⚒ ⚒, *a. fig.* separation (from, *d'avec*); parting; *fig. family, meeting:* breaking up; division; ⚒ ⚒ *de biens* separate maintenance; ⚒ ⚒ *de corps* judicial separation; *pol.* ⁓ *des pouvoirs* separation of powers; ⚠ *mur m de* ⁓ partition wall; **séparatiste** [⁓'tist] **1.** *adj.* separatist; **2.** *su.* separatist, separationist; secessionist; **séparément** [separe'mã] *adv.* separately; **séparer** [⁓'re] (1a) *v/t.* separate (from, *de*); part; drive apart; divide; *fig.* distinguish (from, *de*); *se* ⁓ part (company); break up (*assembly*); divide; *se* ⁓ *de* part with.

sépia [se'pja] *f zo., colour:* sepia; *zo.* cuttle-fish; *paint.* sepia drawing.

sept [sɛt] *adj./num., a. su./m/inv.* seven; *date, title:* seventh; **septain** [sɛ'tɛ̃] *m* seven-line stanza; ⊕ seven-strand rope (*holding clock weights*); **septante** † [sɛp'tãːt] *adj./num., a. su./m/inv.* seventy; *bibl. version des* ♀ Septuagint; **septembre** [⁓'tãːbr] *m* September; **septembrisades** *hist.* [⁓tãbri'zad] *f/pl.* September massacres (*1792 in Paris*); **septénaire** [ˌteˈnɛːr] *adj.*, *a. su./m* septenary; **septennal, e,** *m/pl.* -aux [ˌtɛnˈnal, ˌˈno] septennial; **septennat** [ˌtɛnˈna] *m* septennate.

septentrion *poet.* [sɛptɑ̃triˈɔ̃] *m* north; **septentrional, e,** *m/pl.* -aux [ˌˈnal, ˌˈno] 1.*adj.* north(ern); 2. *su.* northerner.

septicémie ⚕ [sɛptiseˈmi] *f* septic(a)emia; blood-poisoning; **septicémique** ⚕ [ˌseˈmik] septic(a)emic; **septicité** ⚕ [ˌsiˈte] *f* septicity.

septième [sɛˈtjɛm] 1. *adj./num.* seventh; 2. *su.* seventh; *su./m fraction:* seventh; *su./f* ♪ seventh; *school:* top form of lower school.

septique ⚕ [sɛpˈtik] septic; *fosse f* ~ septic tank.

septuagénaire [sɛptɥaʒeˈnɛːr] *adj.*, *a. su.* septuagenarian.

septuple [sɛpˈtypl] *adj.*, *a. su./m* sevenfold; septuple; **septupler** [ˌtyˈple] (1a) *vt/i.* increase sevenfold, septuple.

sépulcral, e, *m/pl.* -aux [sepylˈkral, ˌˈkro] sepulchral; **sépulcre** [ˌˈpylkr] *m* sepulchre; *le saint* ~ the Holy Sepulchre.

sépulture [sepylˈtyːr] *f* burial; tomb; burial-place.

séquelles [seˈkɛl] *f/pl.* after-effects; aftermath *sg.*

séquence [seˈkɑ̃ːs] *f* sequence.

séquestration [sekɛstraˈsjɔ̃] illegal confinement; **séquestre** 🏛 [ˌˈkɛstr] *m* impoundment; *mettre sous* ~ impound; **séquestrer** [ˌkɛsˈtre] (1a) *v/t.* confine (*s.o.*) illegally; hold (*s.o.*) captive; 🏛 impound (*property*); *fig. se* ~ sequester o.s.

serai [səˈre] *1st p. sg. fut. of* être 1.

sérail [seˈraːj] *m* seraglio.

sérancer *tex.* [serɑ̃ˈse] (1k) *v/t.* heckle, comb (*flax*).

séraphin [seraˈfɛ̃] *m* seraph; ~s *pl.* seraphim; **séraphique** [ˌˈfik] seraphic.

serbe [sɛrb] 1. *adj.* Serb(ian); 2. *su./m ling.* Serb(ian); *su.* ♀ Serb(ian).

serein, e [səˈrɛ̃, ~ˈrɛn] 1. *adj.* serene, calm (*a. fig.*); *fig.* tranquil; ⚕ *goutte f* ~e amaurosis; 2. *su./m* evening dew.

sérénade ♪ [sereˈnad] *f* serenade.

sérénissime [sereniˈsim] *title:* (Most) Serene; **sérénité** [ˌˈte] *f*

serenity (*a. title*); calmness; tranquillity.

séreux, -euse ⚕ [seˈrø, ~ˈrøːz] serous.

serf, serve [sɛrf, sɛrv] 1. *adj.* in bondage; *condition f serve* serfdom; 2. *su.* serf; *su./m* bond(s)man; *su./f* bond(s)woman.

serfouette ✗ [sɛrˈfwɛt] *f* combined hoe and fork; **serfouir** ✗ [~ˈfwiːr] (2a) *v/t.* hoe; loosen (*the soil*).

serge *tex.* [sɛrʒ] *f* serge.

sergent [sɛrˈʒɑ̃] *m* ✗ *etc.* sergeant; ⊕ cramp, clamp; ⚓ ~ *d'armes* (*approx.*) ship's corporal; † ~ *de ville* policeman; ✗ ~-*major*, ~-*chef infantry:* quartermaster-sergeant.

sériciculteur [serisikylˈtœːr] *m* silk-worm breeder; **sériciculture** [~ˈtyːr] *f* silkworm breeding.

série [seˈri] *f* series; sequence; *tools etc.:* set; *sp. race:* heat; *billiards:* break; *en* ~, *par* ~ in series; ✝ *fait en* ~ mass-produced; ✝ *fin f de* ~ remnants *pl.*; *fig. hors* ~ extraordinary; *fig. la* ~ *noire* one disaster after another, a run of hard luck; *fig.* ~ *noire* crime-thriller (*atmosphere, style, etc.*); eerie, sinister; **sérier** [~ˈrje] (1o) *v/t.* arrange, classify.

sérieux, -euse [seˈrjø, ~ˈrjøːz] 1. *adj.* serious; grave; earnest; genuine (*offer, purchaser*); *fig. peu* ~ irresponsible (*person*); 2. *su./m* gravity, seriousness; *thea.* serious rôle; *garder son* ~ preserve one's gravity; *prendre au* ~ take (*s.th.*) seriously.

serin [səˈrɛ̃] *m orn.* serin; canary; F fool; *Am.* sap; greenhorn; **seriner** [səriˈne] (1a) *v/t.* teach (*a canary*) to sing; F *fig.* drum (*a rule etc.*) (into s.o., *à* q.); F ♪ thump out, grind out (*a tune*).

seringue [səˈrɛ̃ːg] *f* ✗, ⚕ syringe; *mot.* ~ *à graisse* grease-gun; **seringuer** [ˌrɛ̃ˈge] (1m) *v/t.* syringe (*the ear etc.*), inject (*a drug*); squirt (*a liquid*).

serment [sɛrˈmɑ̃] *m* oath; *faux* ~ perjury; *prêter* ~ take an oath; *sous* ~ sworn (*evidence*).

sermon [sɛrˈmɔ̃] *m* sermon; *fig.* lecture; **sermonner** F [ˌmɔˈne] (1a) *vt/i.* sermonize; *v/t.* reprimand; **sermonneur, -euse** F [ˌmɔˈnœːr, ~ˈnøːz] 1. *adj.* fault-finding; 2. *su.* fault-finder.

sérosité *physiol.* [seroziˈte] *f* serosity; **sérothérapie** ⚛ [⌣rɔtera'pi] *f* serotherapy.

serpe ⚘ [sɛrp] *f* bill-hook.

serpent [sɛr'pã] *m* ♪, zo., astr., fig. serpent; zo., fig. snake; ~ à lunettes cobra; ~ à sonnettes rattlesnake; **serpentaire** [sɛrpã'tɛːr] su./m orn. secretary-bird; su./f ♀, ⚛ serpentaria, snake-root; **serpenteau** [⌣'to] *m* zo. young snake; firework: serpent, squib; **serpenter** [⌣'te] (1a) v/i. (a. aller en serpentant) wind, meander; **serpentin, e** [⌣'tɛ̃, ⌣'tin] **1.** adj. serpentine; **2.** su./m ⊕ coil; ticker tape, paper streamer; su./f ♀ snake-wood; min. serpentine.

serpette ⚘ [sɛr'pɛt] *f* bill-hook; pruning-knife.

serpillière [sɛrpi'jɛːr] *f* tex. packing-cloth; tex. dish-cloth; F apron made from sacking.

serpolet ♀ [sɛrpo'lɛ] *m* wild thyme.

serrage ⊕ [sɛ'raːʒ] *m* tightening; gripping; mot. ~ des freins braking.

serre [sɛːr] *f* ⚘ greenhouse, glasshouse, conservatory; ⚘ (a. ~ chaude) hot-house; grip; orn. claw, talon; ⊕, ⚛ clip; ⊕ mo(u)ld press.

serré, e [sɛ're] **1.** adj. tight; close-grained (wood); compact; narrow (defile etc.); close (buildings, ⚔ order, reasoning, texture, translation, sp. finish); tightly packed (people etc.); **2.** serré adv.: jouer ~ play cautiously; vivre ~ live on a tight budget.

serre...: ~**-file** [sɛr'fil] m/inv. ⚔ file closer; ⚓ rear ship; marcher en ~ bring up the rear; ~**fils** [⌣'fil] m/inv. ⚡ binding-srew; ⚡ clamp; ~**freins** [⌣'frɛ̃] m/inv. ⚄ brakesman; ⊕ brake-adjuster; ~**joint** ⊕ [⌣'ʒwɛ̃] *m* cramp; screw-clamp.

serrement [sɛr'mã] *m* squeezing; ⚒ dam; ~ de main handshake; hand pressure; fig. ~ de cœur pang; **serre-papiers** [sɛrpa'pje] m/inv. file (for papers); **serrer** [sɛ're] (1b) v/t. press, squeeze; grasp (s.o.'s hand), grip; put (away); tighten (a knot, ⊕ a screw); fig. compress, condense; ⚔ close (the ranks); skirt (the coast, a wall); sp. jostle (other runners etc.); crowd (s.o.'s car); mot. ~ à droite keep (to the) right; ~ q. de près follow close behind s.o.; ~ la main à shake hands with; ~ les dents clench one's teeth; serrez-vous! sit closer!; F move up!; se ~ crowd, stand (sit etc.) close

together; tighten (lips); fig. feel a pang, contract (heart); **serre-tête** [sɛr'tɛːt] m/inv. headband; skullcap.

serrure [sɛ'ryːr] *f* lock; **serrurerie** [sɛryrə'ri] *f* locksmith's trade; lock-smith's (shop); lock-mechanism; metal-work; **serrurier** [⌣'rje] *m* locksmith; metal-worker.

serte [sɛrt] *f* gem: mounting or setting (in a bezel); **sertir** [sɛr'tiːr] (2a) v/t. set (a gem) (in a bezel); set (window-panes) (in, de); **sertissage** [sɛrti'saːʒ] *m* gem: setting; panes: setting in lead; **sertisseur** [⌣'sœːr] *m* setter; **sertissure** [⌣'syːr] *f* bezel; setting.

sérum ⚛ [se'rɔm] *m* serum.

servage [sɛr'vaːʒ] *m* serfdom; bondage.

serval, pl. **-als** zo. [sɛr'val] *m* serval, tiger-cat.

servant, e [sɛr'vã, ⌣'vãːt] **1.** adj. serving; eccl. lay (brother); **2.** su./m ⚔ gunner; tennis: server; su./f servant; dumb waiter, dinner-waggon; ⊕ prop; ⊕ (bench-)vice.

serveur [sɛr'vœːr] m waiter; **serveuse** [⌣'vøːz] *f* waitress.

serviabilité [sɛrvjabili'te] *f* obligingness; **serviable** [⌣'vjabl] obliging, helpful (person); **service** [⌣'vis] *m* service (a. ⚔, ✝, eccl., tennis); ⚔, ⚓ guard etc.: duty; hotel: service charge; ✝, admin. department; cuis. meal: course; tools: set; ~ compris service included; ~ de table dinner-service; ~ diplomatique diplomatic service, Am. corps; ~ divin divine service; ⚔ ~ obligatoire compulsory (military) service; ~s pl. publics public services; ⚔ être de ~ be on duty; ✝ libre ~ self-service; rendre (un) ~ à q. do s.o. a good turn.

serviette [sɛr'vjɛt] *f* (table) napkin, serviette; towel; briefcase, portfolio; ~-éponge Turkish towel; ⚛ ~ hygiénique sanitary towel or Am. napkin.

servile [sɛr'vil] servile; abject (to, envers); menial (duties); slavish (imitation); **servilité** [⌣vili'te] *f* servility.

servir [sɛr'viːr] (2b) v/t. serve (a dish, s.o. at table, ✝ a customer, one's country, a. tennis a ball); help, assist; be in the service of; wait on; cards: deal; ✝ supply; pay (a rent); eccl. ~ la messe serve at mass; hunt.

~ *un sanglier au couteau* dispatch a boar with a knife; *se* ~ help o.s. to food; *se* ~ *de* use; *v/i.* serve (*a.* ⚔); be used (as, *de*); be in service; be useful; *à quoi cela sert-il?* what's the good of that?; *à quoi cela sert-il de* (*inf.*)?, *à quoi sert de* (*inf.*)? what is the good of (*ger.*)?; **serviteur** [~vi'tœːr] *m* servant; ~! no thank you; **servitude** [~vi'tyd] *f* servitude; slavery; *fig.* tyranny; 𝔱𝔱 easement; *fig.* obligation.

servo... ⊕ [sɛrvo] servo(-assisted) ..., power(-assisted) ...; **~commande** [~kɔ'mɑ̃d] *f* servo-control; **~direction** [~dirɛk'sjɔ̃] *f* servo- *or* power steering; **~moteur** [~mɔ'tœːr] *m* servo-motor.

ses [se] *see* son[1].

sessile ♀ *etc.* [sɛ'sil] sessile.

session 𝔱𝔱, *parl.* [sɛ'sjɔ̃] *f* session.

set [sɛt] *m tennis*: set; *table*: place mat.

sétacé, e [seta'se] bristly, setaceous.

séton 𝕤, *zo.* [se'tɔ̃] *m* seton; *plaie f en* ~ flesh wound.

seuil [sœːj] *m phys., psych., fig.* fame, *door*: threshold; doorstep.

seul, seule [sœl] *adj. before su.* one, only, single; very, mere; *after su.* or *verb* alone, lonely; *before art.* only; ... alone; *comme un* ~ *homme* like one man; *un homme* ~ a single *or* lonely man; **seulement** [~'mɑ̃] *adv.* only; solely; but; *ne ... pas* ~ not even; *si* ~ ... if only ...; **seulet, -ette** F [sœ'lɛ, ~'lɛt] alone; lonely.

sève [sɛːv] *f* ♀ sap; *fig.* vigo(u)r, pith.

sévère [se'vɛːr] severe (*a. fig.*); stern; strict (*discipline, morals*); hard (*person, climate*); **sévérité** [~veri'te] *f* severity (*a. fig.*); *person, look*: sternness; *fig. taste*: austerity; *discipline, morals*: strictness; 𝔱𝔱 ~*s pl.* harsh sentences.

sévices [se'vis] *m/pl.* cruelty *sg.*, ill treatment; **sévir** [~'viːr] (2a) *v/i.* rage (*plague, war*); ~ *contre* deal severely with.

sevrage [sə'vraːʒ] *m child, lamb*: weaning; **sevrer** [~'vre] (1d) *v/t.* wean (*a child, a lamb*); 🗲 separate; *fig.* deprive (of, *de*).

sexagénaire [sɛksaʒe'nɛːr] *adj., a. su.* sexagenarian.

sex-appeal [sɛksa'piːl] *m* sex-appeal.

sexe [sɛks] *m* sex; F *le beau* ~, *le* ~ *faible* the fair *or* weaker sex, women *pl.*; *le* ~ *fort* the strong sex, men *pl.*; *des deux* ~*s* of both sexes.

sextuor ♪ [sɛks'tɥɔːr] *m* sextet.

sextuple [sɛks'typl] *adj., a. su./m* sixfold, sextuple; **sextupler** [~ty-'ple] (1a) *vt/i.* increase sixfold, sextuple.

sexuel, -elle [sɛk'sɥɛl] sexual.

seyant, e [sɛ'jɑ̃, ~'jɑ̃ːt] becoming.

shake-hand [ʃɛk'hɑ̃d] *m/inv.* handshake.

shaker [ʃɛ'kœːr] *m* cocktail-shaker.

shampooing [ʃɑ̃'pwɛ̃] *m* shampoo; *faire un* ~ *à* shampoo.

shooter [ʃu'te] (1a) *v/i. foot.* shoot; *sl. se* ~ shoot (up), fix (*drug addict*).

short *cost.* [ʃɔrt] *m* shorts *pl.*

shot *foot.* [ʃɔt] *m* shot.

shunt 🗲 [ʃœ̃ːt] *m* shunt; ~ *de grille* grid leak; **shunter** 🗲 [ʃœ̃'te] (1a) *v/t.* shunt.

si[1] [si] *cj.* if; whether; suppose; ~ *ce n'est que* were it not that; if it were not that; ~ *je ne me trompe* if I am not mistaken; ~ *tant est que* (*sbj.*) if it happens that (*ind.*).

si[2] [~] *adv.* so, so much; *answer to negative question*: yes; ~ *bien que* so that; with the result that; ~ *fait!* yes indeed!; ~ *riche qu'il soit* however rich he may be.

si[3] ♪ [~] *m/inv.* si; *note*: B; ~ *bémol* B flat.

siamois, e [sja'mwa, ~'mwaːz] Siamese; 𝕤 *frères m/pl.* ~, *sœurs f/pl.* ~*es* Siamese twins.

sibérien, -enne [sibe'rjɛ̃, ~'rjɛn] Siberian.

sibilant, e 𝕤 [sibi'lɑ̃, ~'lɑ̃ːt] sibilant.

siccatif, -ve [sika'tif, ~'tiːv] **1.** *adj.* (quick-)drying, siccative; **2.** *su./m* siccative; quick-drying substance.

side-car [sajd'kaːr] *m* motor-cycle combination; side-car.

sidéral, e, *m/pl.* **-aux** [side'ral, ~'ro] *astr.* sidereal; **sidérer** F [~'re] (1a) *v/t.* stagger, shatter.

sidérose [side'roːz] *f min.* siderite; 𝕤 siderosis; **sidérostat** *astr.* [~rɔs'ta] *m* siderostat; **sidérotechnie** [~rɔtɛk'ni] *f* metallurgy of iron; **sidérurgie** [~ryr'ʒi] *f* metallurgy of iron; **sidérurgique** [~ryr'ʒik] ironworking; *usine f* ~ ironworks *usu. sg.*

siècle [sjɛkl] *m* century; *eccl.* world(ly life); *fig.* period, time, age;

F *il y a un* ~ *que* it's ages since; ♀ *des lumières* age of enlightenment; *Grand* ♀ *the* age of Louis XIV.
sied [sje] *3rd p. sg. pres. of seoir.*
siège [sjɛːʒ] *m* chair etc., ⊕, *disease, government, parl.*: seat; centre (*of activity, learning, etc.*); ✝ office; ⚔ siege; ⚖ *judge*: bench; *eccl.* (*episcopal*) see; *chair*: bottom; *mot. etc.* ~ *arrière* back-seat; ~ *du cocher* coachman's box; ✝ ~ *social* head office, registered office; **siéger** [sje'ʒe] (1g) *v/i.* sit (⚖, *a.* in Parliament, *au parlement*); ✝ have its head office; ✝ be seated; *eccl.* hold one's see (*bishop*).
sien, sienne [sjɛ̃, sjɛn] **1.** *pron./poss.*: *le* ~, *la* ~*ne, les* ~*s pl., les* ~*nes pl.* his, hers, its, one's; **2.** *su./m* his *or* her *or* its *or* one's own; *les* ~*s pl.* his *or* her *or* one's (own) people; *su./f: faire des* ~*nes* lark (about).
sieste [sjɛst] *f* siesta; F nap; *faire la* ~ take a nap.
sieur ⚖ [sjœːr] *m: le* ~ ... Mr. ...
sifflant, e [si'flɑ̃, ~'flɑ̃ːt] **1.** *adj.* hissing; wheezing (*breath*); whistling (*note*); *gramm.* sibilant; **2.** *su./f gramm.* sibilant; **sifflement** [~flə-'mɑ̃] *m person, a.* arrow, *bullet, wind*: whistle, whistling; *gas, goose, steam*: hiss(ing); *cuis., a.* ♪ sizzling; *breathing*: wheezing; **siffler** [~'fle] (1a) *v/i.* whistle; hiss; *cuis., a.* ♪ sizzle; ♪ wheeze; blow a whistle; ♪ pipe; *v/t.* whistle (*a tune*); whistle to (*a dog*); whistle for (*a taxi*); ♪ pipe; *thea.* hiss, boo; F swig (*a drink*); **sifflet** [~'flɛ] *m* whistle, ♪ pipe; *thea.* hiss, catcall; ~ *d'alarme* alarm-whistle; *coup m de* ~ (blast of the) whistle; *sl.: couper le* ~ *à q.* cut s.o.'s throat; *fig.* nonplus s.o.; *donner un coup de* ~ blow a whistle; ⊕ *en* ~ slantwise; bevelled; **siffleur, -euse** [~'flœːr, ~'fløːz] **1.** *adj.* whistling; wheezy (*horse*); hissing (*serpent*); **2.** *su.* whistler; *thea.* hisser, booer; *su./m orn.* widgeon; **sifflotement** [~flɔt'mɑ̃] *m* soft whistling; **siffloter** [~flɔ'te] (1a) *vt/i.* whistle softly *or* under one's breath.
sigillaire [siʒil'lɛːr] sigillary; signet (-*ring*); **sigillé, e** [~'le] sigillate(d).
sigisbée †, *co.* [siʒis'be] *m* gallant.
sigle [sigl] *m* shorthand: outline; abbreviation; ~*s pl.* sigla (*in old manuscripts*).

signal [si'ɲal] *m* signal; *teleph.* (*dialling*) tone; ~ *à bras* hand signal, ⚔ *etc.* semaphore signal; ⚑ ~ *avancé* distant signal; ~ *d'alarme* alarm-signal, ⚑ communication cord; *teleph.* ~ *d'appel* calling signal; ~ *de danger* (*détresse*) danger (distress) signal; ~ *horaire radio*: time signal, F pips *pl.*; ~ *lumineux* traffic-light; **signalé, e** [siɲa'le] outstanding; *pej.* notorious; **signalement** [~ɲal-'mɑ̃] *m* description; particulars *pl.*; **signaler** [siɲa'le] (1a) *v/t.* signal (*a train etc.*); *fig.* indicate; point out (*s.th. to s.o., qch. à q.*), draw attention to; describe, give a description of (*s.o.*); report (to, *à*); **signalétique** *admin.* [~le'tik] descriptive; **signalisation** [~liza'sjɔ̃] *f* signalling; signals *pl.*, signal system; *mot.* ~ *routière* road signs *pl.*; *panneau m de* ~ road sign.
signataire [siɲa'tɛːr] *su.* signatory; **signature** [siɲa'tyːr] *f* signature; *apposer sa* ~ *à* set one's hand to; **signe** [siɲ] *m* sign; (*bodily, punctuation*) mark; ⚔ insignia (*of rank*); ~ *de tête* (*des yeux*) nod (wink); *faire* ~ *à* beckon to; *signer* [si'ɲe] (1a) *v/t.* sign; *se* ~ cross o.s.; **signet** [~'ɲɛ] *m* bookmark.
significatif, -ve [siɲifika'tif, ~'tiːv] significant (*a.* ♪ *figure*); **signification** [~'sjɔ̃] *f* meaning; sense; ⚖ notice, petition, writ, *etc.*: service; **signifier** [siɲi'fje] (1o) *v/t.* mean, signify; ⚖ serve (*a writ etc.*); ~ *qch. à q.* make s.th. known to s.o., inform s.o. of s.th.; *qu'est-ce que cela signifie?* what is the meaning of this? (*indicating disapproval*).
silence [si'lɑ̃ːs] *m* silence; stillness; *fig.* secrecy; ♪ rest; *garder le* ~ keep silent (about, *sur*); *passer qch. sous* ~ pass s.th. over in silence; *say nothing about s.th.*; **silencieux, -euse** [~lɑ̃'sjø, ~'sjøːz] **1.** *adj.* silent; still (*evening etc.*); **2.** *su./m mot.* silencer.
silex *min.* [si'lɛks] *m* flint, silex.
silhouette [si'lwɛt] *f* silhouette; outline; profile; **silhouetter** [~lwɛ-'te] (1a) *v/t.* silhouette, outline; *phot.* block out; *se* ~ stand out (against, *contre*).
silicate ♪ [sili'kat] *m* silicate; ~ *de potasse* water-glass; **silice** ♪ [~'lis] *f* silica; **siliceux, -euse** [sili'sø,

~'sø:z] siliceous; **silicium** ⚛ [~-'sjɔm] *m* silicon; **siliciure** ⚛ [~-'sjy:r] *m* silicide.

sillage [si'ja:ʒ] *m* ⚓ wake; ✈, *fig.* trail; *fig. marcher dans le ~ de* follow in (*s.o.'s*) footsteps.

sillet ♩ [si'jɛ] *m* violin etc.: nut.

sillon [si'jɔ̃] *m* furrow; *anat., a. gramophone:* groove; *poet.* ~s *pl.* fields; **sillonner** [~jɔ'ne] (1a) *v/t.* furrow (*a. one's forehead*); *fig.* criss-cross.

silo [si'lo] *m* silo; *potatoes:* clamp; **silotage** ✓ [~lɔ'ta:ʒ] *m* ensilage.

silphe zo. [silf] *m* carrion-beetle.

silure icht. [si'ly:r] *m* silurus, catfish.

simagrée F [sima'gre] *f* pretence; ~s *pl.* affectation *sg.*; affected airs; *faire des* ~s put on airs.

simien, -enne zo. [si'mjɛ̃, ~'mjɛn] *adj., a. su./m* simian; **simiesque** [~'mjɛsk] simian; ape-like.

similaire [simi'lɛ:r] similar (*a.* ⚕); like; **similairement** [~lɛr'mɑ̃] *adv.* in like manner; **similarité** [~lari-'te] *f* similarity, likeness; **simili** [~'li] *m* imitation; **similitude** [~li-'tyd] *f* similitude; similarity (*a.* ⚕); *gramm.* simile.

simonie eccl. [simɔ'ni] *f* simony.

simoun [si'mun] *m* wind: simoom.

simple [sɛ̃:pl] **1.** *adj.* simple; single (*a.* 🎫 ticket); ⚓, ⚓ ordinary; *fig.* elementary; plain (*food, dress*); *fig.* simple(-minded); half-witted; **2.** *su./m* the simple; simple-minded person, simpleton; *tennis:* single; ♣ ~s *pl.* medicinal herbs, simples; ~ *messieurs tennis:* men's single (s *pl.*); **simplicité** [sɛ̃plisi'te] *f* simplicity; *fig.* simple-mindedness; ~s *pl.* naïve remarks; **simplification** [~fika'sjɔ̃] *f* simplification; **simplifier** [~'fje] (1o) *v/t.* simplify; ⚕ reduce to its lowest terms; *se* ~ become simple(r); **simpliste** [sɛ̃'plist] **1.** *adj.* simplistic; over-simple; **2.** *su.* person who over-simplifies.

simulacre [simy'lakr] *m* image; *fig.* pretence, semblance; ✈ flight simulator; ~ *de combat* sham fight.

simulateur *m*, **-trice** *f* [simyla'tœ:r, ~'tris] shammer; ✗ malingerer; ⊕ simulator; **simulation** [~'sjɔ̃] *f* simulation; ✗ malingering; **simulé, e** [simy'le] feigned (*illness*); fictitious; sham (*fight*); **simuler** [~] (1a) *v/t.* simulate; feign (*illness*).

simultané, e [simulta'ne] simul-

taneous; **simultanéité** [~nei'te] *f* simultaneity; **simultanément** [~ne'mɑ̃] *adv. of* simultané.

sinapisme ✿ [sina'pism] *m* mustard-plaster, sinapism.

sincère [sɛ̃'sɛ:r] sincere; **sincérité** [~seri'te] *f* sincerity, frankness; genuineness.

singe [sɛ̃:ʒ] *m* zo. monkey; zo. ape (*a.* F *fig.* = *imitator*); ⊕ hoist; F bully (beef); *sl.* boss; F *faire le* ~ monkey about; *laid comme un* ~ as ugly as sin; **singer** [sɛ̃'ʒe] (1l) *v/t.* mimic, ape; **singerie** [sɛ̃ʒ'ri] *f* monkey trick; grimace; ~s *pl. a.* airs and graces.

singulariser [sɛ̃gylari'ze] (1a) *v/t.* make (*s.o.*) conspicuous; render (*s.o.*) singular; *se* ~ make o.s. conspicuous; **singularité** [~'te] *f* singularity; peculiarity; eccentricity, oddness; **singulier, -ère** [sɛ̃gy'lje, ~'ljɛ:r] **1.** *adj.* singular (*a.* ⚕); peculiar; unusual; strange; conspicuous; single (*combat*); **2.** *su./m* gramm. singular; *au* ~ in the singular.

sinistre [si'nistr] **1.** *adj.* sinister; ominous, threatening; **2.** *su./m* disaster, catastrophe; fire; loss (*from fire etc.*); **sinistré, e** [~nis'tre] **1.** *adj.* (disaster-)stricken; shipwrecked; homeless (*through fire, bombs, etc.*); bomb-damaged (*house etc.*); **2.** *su.* victim (*of a disaster*).

sinon [si'nɔ̃] *cj.* otherwise, if not; except (that, *que*).

sinueux, -euse [si'nɥø, ~'nɥø:z] sinuous; winding (*path, river*); **sinuosité** [~nɥozi'te] *f* winding; meandering; bend (*in river*); **sinus** [~'nys] *m* anat. sinus; ⚕ sine; **sinusite** ✿ [~ny'zit] *f* sinusitis.

sionisme [sjɔ'nism] *m* Zionism; **siphon** [si'fɔ̃] *m* phys. etc. siphon; ⚠ drain etc.: trap.

sire [si:r] *m* king: Sire, Sir; † lord; † *pauvre* ~ *person:* sorry specimen.

sirène [si'rɛn] *f* ⚓, ⊕, *myth.*, zo., *fig.* siren; ⚓, ⊕ hooter; ⚓ foghorn.

sirocco [sirɔ'ko] *m* wind: sirocco.

sirop [si'ro] *m* syrup; (fruit) cordial; ⚕ *a.* mixture.

siroter [sirɔ'te] (1a) *v/t.* F sip; *v/i. sl.* tipple.

sirupeux, -euse [siry'pø, ~'pø:z] syrupy; F *fig.* sloppy, sentimental.

sis, e [si, si:z] *p.p. of* seoir.

sismique [sis'mik] seismic.

sismo... [sismɔ] seismo...; **~graphe** [~'graf] m seismograph.

site [sit] m setting; site, spot; △, ✕ lie of the ground; ~ *propre* bus lane; ✕ angle m de ~ angle of sight.

sitôt [si'to] adv. as or so soon; ~ *après* immediately after; ~ *dit*, ~ *fait* no sooner said than done; ~ *que* as soon as; *ne ... pas de* ~ not ... for a long time.

situation [sitɥa'sjɔ̃] f situation; position; fig. job, post; location; bearing; ♱, ✕, *admin.* return, report; ~ *économique* economic position; ~ *sociale* station in life; **situé, e** [si'tɥe] situated (at, *à*); **situer** [~] (1n) v/t. situate, place; locate (a. fig.).

six [sis; *before consonant* si; *before vowel and h mute* siz] *adj./num.*, *a. su./m/inv.* six; *date, title:* sixth; *à la* ~*-quatre-deux* in a slapdash way; **sixain** [si'zɛ̃] m *prosody:* six-line stanza; *cards:* packet of six packs; **sixième** [~'zjɛm] **1.** *adj./num.* sixth; **2.** *su.* sixth; *su./m fraction:* sixth; sixth, *Am.* seventh floor; *su./f secondary school:* (approx.) first form; **sixte** ♪ [sikst] f sixth.

sizain [si'zɛ̃] m see **sixain**.

skating [skɛ'tiŋ] m roller-skating; skating-rink.

ski [ski] m ski; skiing; ~ *nautique* water skiing; *faire du* ~ = **skier** [~'e] (1a) v/i. ski; **skieur** m, **-euse** f [~'œːr, ~'øːz] skier.

slalom [sla'lɔm] m sp. slalom; fig. zigzag (movement); sp. *descente en* ~ slalom descent; *faire du* ~ = **slalomer** [~lɔ'me] (1a) v/i. sp. slalom; fig. zigzag (one's) way, dodge in and out.

slave [slaːv] **1.** adj. Slavonic; **2.** su./m ling. Slavonic; su. ⌀ Slav; **slavisme** [sla'vism] m Slavism.

slip [slip] m women: panties pl.; men: (short) pants pl.

sloop ⚓ [slup] m sloop.

slovaque [slɔ'vak] adj., a. su. ⌀ Slovak; **slovène** [~'vɛn] adj., a. su. ⌀ Slovene.

smash [smaʃ] m tennis: smash.

smoking [smɔ'kiŋ] m dinner-jacket, *Am.* tuxedo.

snob [snɔb] **1.** adj. snobbish, swanky; swell; **2.** su./m snob; vulgar follower of fashion; **snober** [snɔ'be] (1a) v/t. look down on (*s.o.*); cold-shoulder, cut (*s.o.*); **snobisme**

[~'bism] m vulgar following of fashion; snobbery.

sobre [sɔbr] abstemious (*person*); sober; frugal (*eater, meal*); fig. ~ *de* sparing of; **sobriété** [sɔbrie'te] f abstemiousness; moderation (*in drinking, eating, speech*).

sobriquet [sɔbri'kɛ] m nickname.

soc ✒ [sɔk] m ploughshare.

sociabilité [sɔsjabili'te] f sociability; **sociable** [~'sjabl] sociable, companionable; *il est* ~ he is a good mixer.

social, e, m/pl. **-aux** [sɔ'sjal, ~'sjo] social; ♱ registered (*capital, name of company*); ♱ trading, financial (*year*); *assistante* f ~*e* social worker; ♱ *raison* f ~*e* (registered) name of company or firm; **socialisation** pol. [sɔsjaliza'sjɔ̃] f socialization; **socialiser** pol. [~li'ze] (1a) v/t. socialize; **socialisme** pol. [~'lism] m socialism; **socialiste** [~'list] **1.** adj. socialist; socialistic (*doctrine*); **2.** su. socialist.

sociétaire [sɔsje'tɛːr] su. (full) member; ♱ shareholder; **société** [~'te] f society; company (a. ♱); association, club; ~ *anonyme* company limited by shares; ~ *à responsabilité limitée* (sort of) limited company; ~ *d'abondance* affluent society; ~ *de consommation* consumer society; ~ *de masse* mass society; ⌀ *des Nations* League of Nations; ~ *en commandite* (*par actions*) limited partnership; ~ *en nom collectif* firm; private company; ~ *filiale* daughter (company); ~ *par actions* company limited by shares; *acte* m de ~ deed of partnership.

sociologie [sɔsjɔlɔ'ʒi] f sociology; **sociologique** [~'ʒik] sociological; **sociologue** [~'lɔg] su. sociologist.

socle [sɔkl] m △ base (a. fig.); column: plinth; *wall:* footing; ⊕ bed-plate (*of engine etc.*); bracket; stand.

socque [sɔk] m clog.

socquettes [sɔ'kɛt] f/pl. (*ladies'*) ankle socks.

soda [sɔ'da] m fizzy drink.

sodium ⚗ [sɔ'djɔm] m sodium.

sœur [sœːr] f sister (a. eccl.); eccl. nun; ~ *de lait* foster-sister.

sofa [sɔ'fa] m sofa, settee.

soi [swa] pron. oneself; himself, herself, itself; *amour* m de ~ self-love; *cela va de* ~ that goes without saying;

être chez ~ be at home; en (or de) ~ in itself; ~-**disant** [ˌdiˈzɑ̃] **1.** adj./inv. so-called; **2.** adv. supposedly, apparently; ostensibly.

soie [swa] f silk; (hog-)bristle; ⊕ crank: pin; ⊕ tool etc.: tongue; ✝ ~ artificielle artificial silk; rayon; ~ grège raw silk; **soierie** ✝ [ˌˈri] f silk (fabric); silk trade; silk factory.

soif [swaf] f thirst (a. fig. for, de); avoir ~ be thirsty.

soigné, e [swaˈɲe] neat, trim; well-groomed (appearance); cuis. first-rate (meal); **soigner** [ˌˈɲe] (1a) v/t. look after; ⚕ nurse (a sick person); ⚕ doctor: attend (a patient); fig. elle soigne sa mise she dresses with care; ⚕ se faire ~ have treatment; **soigneux, -euse** [ˌˈɲø, ˌˈɲøːz] careful (of, de; to inf., de inf.); neat; painstaking.

soi-même [swaˈmɛːm] oneself.

soin [swɛ̃] m care, pains pl.; neatness, tidiness; ~s pl. ⚕ etc. attention sg.; aux bons ~s de post: care of, c/o.; par les ~s de thanks to, by courtesy of; premiers ~s pl. first aid sg.; avoir (or prendre) ~ de take care of (s.th.); take care to (do s.th.), be or make sure to (do s.th.).

soir [swaːr] m evening; afternoon; du matin au ~ from morning to night; le ~ in the evening; sur le ~ towards evening; tous les ~s every evening; **soirée** [swaˈre] f duration; period: evening; (evening) party; thea. evening performance; ~ d'adieu farewell party; ~ dansante dance; thea. ~ unique one-night stand.

sois [swa] 1st p. sg. pres. sbj. of être 1; **soit 1.** adv. [swat] (let us) suppose...; say...; ~! all right!, agreed!; ainsi ~-il so be it!, amen!; tant ~ peu ever so little; **2.** cj. [swa]: ~ ... ~ ..., ~ ... ou ... either ... or ...; whether ... or ...; ~ que (sbj.) whether (ind.).

soixantaine [swasɑ̃ˈtɛn] f (about) sixty; la ~ the age of sixty, the sixties pl.; **soixante** [ˌˈsɑ̃ːt] adj./ num., a. su./m/inv. sixty; **soixante-dix** [ˌsɑ̃tˈdis; before consonant ˌˈdi; before vowel and h mute ˌˈdiz] adj./ num., a. su./m/inv. seventy; **soi-xante-dixième** [ˌsɑ̃tdiˈzjɛm] adj./ num., a. su. seventieth; **soixan-tième** [ˌsɑ̃ˈtjɛm] adj./num., a. su. sixtieth.

30 GTW Fr-E

soja ♀ [sɔˈja] m soya-bean, Am. soy-bean.   [f de ~ G-clef.\
sol¹ ♪ [sɔl] m/inv. sol; note: G; clef\
sol² [sɔl] m earth, ground; ✗ soil; field; ~-**air** ✗ [ˌˈɛːr] adj./inv. ground-to-air (missile).

solaire [sɔˈlɛːr] solar; sun(-dial, glasses); ⚜ sun-ray (treatment).

soldat usu. ✗ [sɔlˈda] m soldier; ~ de plomb toy or tin soldier; ♀ inconnu the Unknown Warrior; les simples ~s pl. the rank sg. and file sg.; se faire ~ join the army; simple ~ private; **soldatesque** pej. [ˌdaˈtɛsk] **1.** adj. barrack-room ...; **2.** su./f soldiery.

solde¹ ✗, ⚓ [sɔld] f pay.

solde² ✝ [ˌ] m account: balance; job lot, remnant; ~s pl. (clearance) sale sg.; ~ créditeur (débiteur) credit (debit) balance.

solder¹ ✗, ⚓ [sɔlˈde] (1a) v/t. pay.

solder² [ˌ] (1a) v/t. balance (accounts); settle (a bill, an account); sell off, clear (goods); remainder (a book); se ~ par (or en) show (a profit, deficit, etc.); end (up) in (failure etc.).

sole¹ ↙ [sɔl] f break.

sole² [ˌ] f vet. sole; ⊕ bed-plate; ⊕ furnace: hearth; ⚠ sleeper; ⚓ boat: flat bottom.

sole³ icht. [ˌ] f sole.

solécisme gramm., a. fig. [sɔleˈsism] m solecism.

soleil [sɔˈlɛːj] m sun; sunshine; eccl. monstrance; ♀ sunflower; firework: Catherine-wheel; ⚜ coup m de ~ sunstroke; sunburn; il fait (du) ~ the sun is shining; **soleilleux, -euse** [ˌlɛˈjø, ˌˈjøːz] sunny.

solennel, -elle [sɔlaˈnɛl] solemn; fig. grave (tone); **solenniser** [ˌniˈze] (1a) v/t. solemnize; **solennité** [ˌniˈte] f solemnity; eccl. ceremony; ~s pl. celebrations.

solfège ♪ [sɔlˈfɛːʒ] m sol-fa; **solfier** ♪ [ˌˈfje] (1o) v/t. sol-fa.

solidage ♀ [sɔliˈdaːʒ] m golden-rod.

solidaire [sɔliˈdɛːr] ⊕ etc. interde-pendent; ⚖ joint and several; être ~ (de) show solidarity (with); ⊕ etc. be bound up (with); **solidariser** [sɔlidariˈze] (1a) v/t.: se ~ show solidarity (with, avec); make common cause; **solidarité** [ˌˈte] f solidarity; ⚖ joint responsibility; grève f de ~ sympathetic strike.

solide [sɔ'lid] **1.** *adj.* solid (*body, earth, food, foundation, wall*, a. ✚ *angle*); fast (*colour*); strong (*flow, cloth, building, person*); ✝ sound (*a. reason*); *fig.* reliable; **2.** *su./m* solid (*a.* ✚); △ solid ground *or* foundations *pl.*; **solidification** [sɔlidifika'sjɔ̃] *f* solidifying; **solidifier** [~'fje] (1o) *v/t.* se ~ solidify; **solidité** [~'te] *f* solidity; *building, friendship*, a. *tex.*: strength; *fig.* soundness (*of judgment*, a. ✝).

soliloque [sɔli'lɔk] *m* soliloquy.

solipède *zo.* [sɔli'pɛd] solid-ungulate; whole-hoofed.

soliste [sɔ'list] **1.** *su.* soloist; **2.** *adj.* solo (*violin etc.*).

solitaire [sɔli'tɛːr] **1.** *adj.* solitary, lonely; lonesome; ✻ *ver m* ~ tapeworm; **2.** *su.* solitary, recluse; loner, lone wolf; *su./m* diamond, a. *game:* solitaire; *zo.* old boar.

solitude [sɔli'tyd] *f* solitude, loneliness; lonely spot.

solive △ [sɔ'liːv] *f* beam, joist; **soliveau** △ [~li'vo] *m* small joist.

sollicitation [sɔllisita'sjɔ̃] *f* entreaty, earnest request; ⚡ attraction, *magnet:* pull; ⚡ application (*to the judge*); **solliciter** [~'te] (1a) *v/t.* seek, request, ask *or* beg for; appeal to; solicit; urge; attract; **solliciteur** *m*, **-euse** *f* [~'tœːr, ~'tøːz] applicant (for, de); petitioner; **sollicitude** [~'tyd] *f* concern, solicitude; anxiety (for, pour).

solo [sɔ'lo] **1.** *su./m* ♪ (*pl. a.* **-li** [~'li]) solo; **2.** *adj./inv.* solo (*cycle, violin, etc.*).

solstice [sɔls'tis] *m* solstice; **solsticial, e**, *m/pl.* **-aux** [~ti'sjal, ~'sjo] solstitial.

solubilité [sɔlybili'te] *f* solubility; *fig.* solvability; **soluble** [~'lybl] soluble (*a. fig.*); **solution** [~ly'sjɔ̃] *f* ↥, ✚, ⚗, a. *fig.* solution; resolution; ⚡ discharge (*of obligation*); ~ de continuité gap; break; ✁ fault.

solvabilité ✝ [sɔlvabili'te] *f* solvency; **solvable** ✝ [~'vabl] solvent; **solvant** ↥ [~'vɑ̃] *m* solvent.

sombre [sɔ̃ːbr] dark, gloomy; dull, murky (*sky, weather*); dim (*light*); melancholy (*face, temperament, thoughts*).

sombrer [sɔ̃'bre] (1a) *v/i.* ⚓, a. *fig.* founder; sink; *fig.* fail.

sommaire [sɔ'mɛːr] **1.** *adj.* summary (*a.* ⚡), brief, concise; *fig.* improvised; **2.** *su./m* summary, synopsis; **sommation** [~ma'sjɔ̃] *f* ⚡ demand; notice; summons *sg.*; warning; ✚ summation.

somme¹ [sɔm] *f* sum, amount; ~ globale lump *or* global sum; ~ toute ... on the whole ...; en ~ in short.

somme² [~] *f* burden; bête *f* de ~ beast of burden; mulet *m* de ~ pack-mule.

somme³ [sɔm] *m* nap; faire un ~ take a nap, F have a snooze; **sommeil** [sɔ'mɛːj] *m* sleep, slumber; sleepiness; avoir ~ feel *or* be sleepy; **sommeiller** [~mɛ'je] (1a) *v/i.* be asleep; doze; *fig.* lie dormant.

sommelier [sɔmə'lje] *m* butler; cellarman; *restaurant:* wine-waiter.

sommer¹ [sɔ'me] (1a) *v/t.* summon; call on (*s.o.*) (to *inf.*, de *inf.*); ✗ call upon (*a place*) to surrender.

sommer² ✚ [~] (1a) *v/t.* find the sum of.

sommes [sɔm] *1st p. pl. pres. of* être 1.

sommet [sɔ'mɛ] *m* summit (*a. pol.*), top (*a. fig.*); ✚, △ apex; ✚, ✗ vertex; *head, arch:* crown; *wave:* crest; *fig.* zenith, height; ✚ ~ du poumon apex of the lung; *pol.* conférence *f* au ~ summit conference.

sommier¹ [sɔ'mje] *m* ✝ cash-book; *admin.* register; les ~s criminal records office.

sommier² [~] *m* pack-horse; △ *arch:* springer; *floor:* cross-beam; *door:* lintel; ⊕ *machine:* bed; ⬛ bolster; ♪ *organ:* wind-chest; *piano:* string-plate; (*a.* ~ élastique *or* à ressorts) spring-mattress, box-mattress.

sommité [sɔmi'te] *f* summit; tip; ⚘ top; *fig. person:* leading figure.

somnambule [sɔmnɑ̃'byl] **1.** *adj.* somnambulant; **2.** *su.* somnambulist, sleep-walker; **somnambulisme** [~nɑ̃by'lism] *m* somnambulism, sleep-walking; **somnifère** [~ni'fɛːr] **1.** *adj.* sleep-inducing; ✻ soporific; F boring; **2.** *su./m* ✻ sleeping drug; sleeping pill.

somnolence [sɔmnɔ'lɑ̃ːs] *f* sleepiness, somnolence; **somnolent, e** [~nɔ'lɑ̃, ~'lɑ̃ːt] sleepy, drowsy.

somptuaire [sɔ̃p'tɥɛːr] sumptuary; **somptueux, -euse** [~'tɥø, ~'tɥøːz] sumptuous; *fig.* magnificent; **somptuosité** [~tɥozi'te] *f* sumptuousness, magnificence.

son[1] *m*, **sa** *f*, *pl.* **ses** [sɔ̃, sa, se] *adj./poss.* his, her, its, one's.

son[2] [sɔ̃] *m* sound, noise; *phys. mur m de* ~ sound-barrier.

son[3] ✿ [~] *m* bran; F *tache f de* ~ freckle.

sonate ♪ [sɔ'nat] *f* sonata; **sonatine** ♪ [~na'tin] *f* sonatina.

sondage [sɔ̃'daːʒ] *m* ⚓ boring; ⚒ sounding; ⚒ probing; ⊕ drill-hole; *fig.* survey; (*a.* ~ *d'opinion* opinion) poll; *enquête f par* ~ sampling survey; *fig.* faire des ~s make a spot check; **sonde** [sɔ̃ːd] *f* sounding-rod; ⚓ lead; ⚓ sounding(s *pl.*); ⚒ probe; ⚒ drill(er), borer; **sonder** [sɔ̃'de] (1a) *v/t.* sound (⚓, ⚒ *a patient, a. fig.*); ⚒ probe (*a wound, a. fig.*); *fig.* investigate; *fig.* explore.

songe [sɔ̃ːʒ] *m* dream (*a. fig.*); ~**creux** [sɔ̃ʒ'krø] *m/inv.* dreamer; **songer** [sɔ̃'ʒe] (11) *v/i.* dream (of, de); think (of, à); *songez donc!* just fancy!; **songerie** [sɔ̃ʒ'ri] *f* reverie; (day)dream(ing); **songeur, -euse** [sɔ̃'ʒœːr, ~'ʒøːz] 1. *adj.* pensive; dreamy; thoughtful; 2. *su.* dreamer.

sonique [sɔ'nik] sonic; sound ...; *barrière f* ~ sound barrier.

sonnaille [sɔ'naːj] *f* cattle-bell; **sonnailler** [~na'je] 1. *su./m* bell-wether; 2. (1a) *v/i.* ring the bell all the time; **sonnant, e** [~'nɑ̃, ~'nɑ̃ːt] striking; *fig.* resounding; hard (*cash*); *à trois heures* ~es on the stroke of three; **sonner** [~'ne] (1a) *v/t.* sound (*a.* ⚒); ring (*a bell*); strike (*the hour*); ring for (*s.o., a. church service*); *fig.* ne pas ~ mot not to utter a word; *v/i.* sound; ring (*bell, coin*); strike (*clock*); *gramm.* be sounded *or* pronounced; *fig.* ~ bien (*creux*) sound well (hollow); *dix heures sonnent* it is striking 10; *dix heures sont sonnées* it has struck 10; *les vêpres sonnent* the bell is ringing for vespers; **sonnerie** [sɔn-'ri] *f* bells: ringing; *church etc.*: bells *pl.*; alarm (mechanism); ⊕ striking mechanism; ♪, *teleph., etc.* bell; ✕ (bugle-)call.

sonnet [sɔ'nɛ] *m* sonnet.

sonnette [sɔ'nɛt] *f* (house-)bell; hand-bell; ⊕ pile-driver; *cordon m de* ~ bell-pull; *coup m de* ~ ring; **sonneur** [sɔ'nœːr] *m* bell-ringer; *tel.* sounder; ✕ bugler.

sono F [sɔ'no] *f* P.A. (system); **sono-**
re [~'nɔːr] resonant; *phys.* acoustic; resounding, loud; ringing (*voice*); *gramm.* voiced (*consonant*); *bande f* ~ sound track; *phys.* onde *f* ~ sound-wave; **sonorisation** [~nɔriza'sjɔ̃] *f* (fitting with a) P.A. (system); **sonorité** [~nɔri'te] *f* sonority; *instrument etc.*: tone, sound; *room*: acoustics *pl.*

sont [sɔ̃] *3rd p. pl. pres. of* être 1.

sophisme [sɔ'fism] *m* sophism; *logic*: fallacy.

sophistication [sɔfistika'sjɔ̃] *f* use of sophistry; sophistication; † *wine etc.*: adulteration; **sophistique** [sɔfis'tik] 1. *adj.* sophistic(al); 2. *su./f* sophistry; **sophistiqué, e** [~ti'ke] sophisticated; highly developed; **sophistiquer** [~ti'ke] (1m) *v/t.* sophisticate; *se* ~ become (more) sophisticated; **sophistiqueur** [~ti'kœːr] *m* quibbler.   [*su./m* soporific.]

soporifique [sɔpɔri'fik] *adj., a.]

soprano, *pl. a.* **-ni** ♪ [sɔpra'no, ~'ni] *m* soprano (*voice, a. singer*).

sorbe ✿ [sɔrb] *f* rowanberry.

sorbet *cuis.* [sɔr'bɛ] *m* sorbet, water-ice; † sherbet.

sorbier ✿ [sɔr'bje] *m* sorb; ~ *sauvage* rowan(-tree), mountain-ash.

sorcellerie [sɔrsɛl'ri] *f* witchcraft, sorcery; **sorcier** [~'sje] *m* sorcerer; wizard; *fig.* brilliant mind; **sorcière** [~'sjɛːr] *f* sorceress; witch; *fig. vieille* ~ old hag.

sordide [sɔr'did] sordid, squalid; filthy; *fig.* base; **sordidité** [~didi'te] *f* sordidness.

sornettes [sɔr'nɛt] *f/pl.* nonsense *sg.*; idle talk *sg.*; *conter des* ~ talk nonsense.

sort [sɔːr] *m* fate, destiny; lot; chance, fortune; spell; *fig. jeter un* ~ *sur* cast a spell on *or* over; *tirer au* ~ draw lots; **sortable** [sɔr'tabl] presentable; **sorte** [sɔrt] *f* sort (*a. typ.*), kind; way, manner; *de la* ~ of that sort; in that way; *de* ~ *que* so that; *en quelque* ~ in a way, to some extent; *en* ~ *que* so that; *toutes* ~*s de* all sorts of.

sortie [sɔr'ti] *f* going out; exit; outlet (*a.* ⊕); ⊕ *a.* outflow; leaving; *admin. goods*: issue; ✝ export(ation); ✕ sortie, sally; outing, trip, excursion; *fig.* outburst; ~ *de secours* emergency exit; ~ *s pl. de fonds* outgoings; *à la* ~ *de* on leaving; *cost.* ~ *de bain* bathrobe.

30★

sortilège [sɔrti'lɛːʒ] *m* witchcraft; spell.

sortir[1] [sɔr'tiːr] **1.** (2b) *v/i.* go or come out, leave; ♀, ✓, etc. come up; come through (*tooth*); stand out, protrude (from, de); ~ de come from; come of (*a good family*); have been at (*a school*); get out of (*one's bed, a difficulty*); *fig.* deviate from (*a subject*); F ~ de (*inf.*) have just done or finished (*ger.*); ✗ ~ de *l'hôpital* be discharged from or *Am.* the hospital; ⚑ ~ *des rails* jump the metals; *être sorti* be out; *thea.* sort exit; *v/t.* bring or take or put or send out; ✗ bring out (*a product*), release (*a film etc.*), publish (*a book*); F throw (*s.o.*) out; F come out with (*a remark, joke, etc.*); **2.** *su./m:* au ~ de on leaving; *fig.* at the end of.

sortir[2] ⚖ [~] (2a, *3rd pers. only*) *v/t.* take, have (*effect*).

sosie F [sɔ'zi] *m* (*person's*) double.

sot, sotte [so, sɔt] **1.** *adj.* stupid, foolish; disconcerted; **2.** *su.* fool; **sottise** [sɔ'tiːz] *f* folly, stupidity; stupid act or saying; insult.

sou [su] *m* sou (= 5 *centimes*); *sans le* ~ penniless.

soubassement [subas'mã] *m* ⚠ sub-foundation; base (a. ⊕); ⊕ base-plate; *geol.* bed-rock; *bed:* valance; *fig.* substructure.

soubresaut [subrə'so] *m* jerk; sudden start; *vehicle:* jolt; ✗ ~s *pl.* trembling *sg.*

soubrette [su'brɛt] *f thea.* soubrette, maid-servant; F † maid.

souche [suʃ] *f ✓ tree etc.:* stump; ✓, *a. fig.* stock; ✗ *virus:* strain; ⚠ (*chimney-*)stack; *eccl.* candle-stock; *fig.* blockhead; *fig.* head (*of a family*); ✗ *cheque, ticket:* counterfoil, stub; *carnet m à* ~s counterfoil book, *Am.* stub-book; *fig. faire* ~ found a family or a line.

souci[1] ♀ [su'si] *m* marigold.

souci[2] [su'si] *m* care; worry; concern; **soucier** [~'sje] (1o) *v/t.* trouble (*s.o.*); se ~ be anxious; *ne se* ~ *de rien* care for nothing; se ~ de *trouble o.s. about;* care for or about; mind about; **soucieux, -euse** [~'sjø, ~'sjøːz] anxious, concerned (about, de; to *inf.*, de *inf.*); *fig.* worried.

soucoupe [su'kup] *f* saucer; F ~ *volante* flying saucer.

soudable ⊕ [su'dabl] that can be

soldered or welded; **soudage** ⊕ [~'daːʒ] *m* soldering; welding.

soudain, e [su'dɛ̃, ~'dɛn] **1.** *adj.* sudden; **2.** *soudain adv.* suddenly, all of a sudden; **soudaineté** [~den-'te] *f* suddenness.

soudard *usu. pej.* [su'daːr] *m* † old soldier, F old sweat; *fig.* ruffian.

soude [sud] *f* ♠, ✗, ⊕ soda; ♀ saltwort; ⚗ ~ *caustique* caustic soda.

souder [su'de] (1a) *v/t.* ⊕ solder, weld; *fig.* join; *lampe f à* ~ blowlamp.

soudoyer [sudwa'je] (1h) *v/t.* hire (the services of); *fig.* bribe, buy (*s.o.*) (over).

soudure ⊕ [su'dyːr] *f* solder; soldering; welding; soldered joint; weld, (*welded*) seam; ✗, ⊕, *inner tube, etc.:* F join; *fig. faire la* ~ bridge the gap.

soue [su] *f* pigsty.

souffert, e [su'fɛːr, ~'fɛrt] *p.p. of souffrir.*

soufflage [su'flaːʒ] *m* ⊕ glass-blowing; ⊕ *furnace:* blast; **soufflante** ⊕ [~'flãːt] *f* blower; **souffle** [sufl] *m* breath (a. ✗); breathing; blast; *fig.* inspiration; ✗ murmur; *sp., fig.* wind; *à bout de* ~ out of breath; *trouver son second (ou deuxième)* ~ *sp., a. fig.* get one's second wind; **soufflé** *cuis.* [su'fle] *m* soufflé; **soufflement** [~flə'mã] *m* blowing; **souffler** [~'fle] (1a) *v/i.* blow (*person, a. wind*); pant; get one's breath; *v/t.* blow (♩ *the organ,* ⊕ *glass*); inflate; blow up (*a balloon, a. the fire*); *thea.* prompt; *fig.* whisper; *fig.* breathe (*a word, a sound*); blow out (*a candle*); F trick (s.o. out of s.th., qch. *à* q.); F foment (*a strife*); *fig.* ~ *le chaud et le froid* blow hot and cold; **soufflerie** [~flə'ri] *f* forge, a. ♩ *organ:* bellows *pl.*; ⊕ blower; ⊕ wind-tunnel; **soufflet** [~'flɛ] *m* bellows *pl.* (a. *phot.*); ⊕ fan; 🚃 concertina vestibule; *carriage:* (*folding*) hood; ♩ swell; *cost.* gusset, gore; *fig.* slap, box on the ear; *fig.* affront; **souffleter** [~flə'te] (1c) *v/t.* slap (s.o.) in the face; *fig.* insult; **souffleur, -euse** [~'flœːr, ~'fløːz] *su.* blower; *thea. etc.* prompter; *vet. horse:* roarer; *su./m* ⊕ blower; ✗ blow-out; **soufflure** [~'flyːr] *f glass:* bubble; *metall.* flaw, blowhole; *paint:* blister.

souffrance [su'frãːs] *f* suffering; ⚖ sufferance; ✗ *en* ~ suspended (*busi-*

ness); held up (*post etc.*); outstanding (*bill etc.*); **souffrant, e** [₌'frɑ̃, ₌'frɑ̃:t] suffering, in pain; ✻ unwell, ill; **souffre** [sufr] *1st p. sg. pres. of souffrir*; **souffre-douleur** [₌frə-du'lœ:r] *su./inv.* drudge; scapegoat; laughing-stock.

souffreteux, -euse [sufrə'tø, ₌'tø:z] destitute; sickly (*child etc.*).

souffrir [su'fri:r] (2f) *vt/i.* suffer; *v/t.* bear (*a. fig.*); permit, allow; *v/i. fig.* be grieved (to *inf., de inf.*); be injured.

soufre [sufr] *m* ⚗ *etc.* sulphur; ～ *en poudre, fleur f de* ～ flowers *pl.* of sulphur; *fig. sentir le* ～ smack of heresy; **soufrer** [su'fre] (1a) *v/t.* treat with sulphur; ⊕, *tex.* sulphur (*a. matches*).

souhait [swɛ] *m* wish; *à* ～ to one's liking; **souhaitable** [swɛ'tabl] desirable; **souhaiter** [₌'te] (1a) *v/t.* wish.

souillard [su'ja:r] *m* ⊕ sink-hole; ⊕ sink-stone; ⚠ strut; **souillarde** [₌'jard] *f* scullery; **souille** [su:j] *f* (*wild boar's*) wallow; ⚓ bed; **souiller** [su'je] (1a) *v/t.* soil (with, *de*); pollute; stain (*a. fig.*); *fig.* tarnish (*one's reputation etc.*); **souillon** [₌'jɔ̃] *su.* sloven; *woman:* slut; **souillure** [₌'jy:r] *f* stain (*a. fig.*); spot; *fig.* blemish; ⚗ impurity.

soûl, soûle F [su, sul] **1.** *adj.* drunk; surfeited (with, *de*); satiated; **2.** *su./m* fill (*a. fig.*); *dormir tout son* ～ have one's sleep out.

soulagement [sulaʒ'mɑ̃] *m* relief (*a.* ⊕); **soulager** [₌la'ʒe] (1l) *v/t.* relieve; *se* ～ relieve o.s. (*of a burden, a.* F *fig.*); relieve one's mind.

soûlard *m*, **e** *f* [su'la:r, ₌'lard], **soûlaud** *m*, **e** *f* [₌'lo, ₌'lo:d] drunkard, soaker; **soûler** [₌'le] (1a) *v/t.* satiate, glut (*s.o.*) (with, *de*); F make (*s.o.*) drunk; F get on (*s.o.'s*) nerves, bore (*s.o.*); F *se* ～ get drunk.

soulèvement [sulɛv'mɑ̃] *m* ground, stomach, *a. fig. people:* rising; ⚓ sea: swell(ing); *fig.* general protest; *geol.* upheaval; ✻ ～ *de cœur* nausea; **soulever** [sul've] (1d) *v/t.* raise (*a. fig. an objection, a question, etc.*); lift (up); *fig.* provoke (*an emotion*); *fig.* rouse (*people*) to revolt; F steal, *sl.* lift; *fig.* ～ *le cœur à q.* make s.o. sick; *se* ～ rise (*a.* in revolt); raise o.s.; turn (*stomach*).

soulier [su'lje] *m* shoe; ～*s pl. de ski* ski-boots; ～ *ferré* (*plat*) spiked (low-heeled) shoe; ～ *Richelieu* lace-up shoe; *être dans ses petits* ～*s* be on pins and needles; be ill at ease.

soulignement [suliɲ'mɑ̃] *m* underlining; *fig.* stressing; **souligner** [₌li'ɲe] (1a) *v/t.* underline; *fig.* stress, emphasize.

soumettre [su'mɛtr] (4v) *v/t.* subdue (*s.o., one's feelings, a. a country*); *fig.* subject (s.o. to s.th., *q. à qch.*); *fig.* submit (*an idea, a plan, a request*) (to s.o., *à q.*); *se* ～ *à* submit to, comply with; **soumis, e** [₌'mi, ₌'mi:z] submissive, obedient; dutiful; **soumission** [₌mi'sjɔ̃] *f* ✗, *pol.* submission, surrender; obedience (to, *à*); ✝ tender (for, *pour*); **soumissionnaire** ✝ [sumisjɔ'nɛ:r] *m* tenderer; *finance:* underwriter; **soumissionner** ✝ [₌'ne] (1a) *v/t.* tender for; *finance:* underwrite.

soupape ⊕ [su'pap] *f* valve; *bath etc.:* plug; *fig.* safety-valve; ～ *à papillon* throttle-valve; ～ *d'admission* intake valve; ～ *d'échappement* outlet valve; *mot.* exhaust-valve; *✦* ～ *électrique* rectifier.

soupçon [sup'sɔ̃] *m* suspicion; *fig.* inkling, idea, hint; *fig., a. cuis.* touch, dash; *liquid:* drop; *fig. pas un* ～ *de* not a shadow of, not the ghost of; **soupçonner** [₌sɔ'ne] (1a) *v/t.* suspect; surmise; **soupçonneux, -euse** [₌sɔ'nø, ₌'nø:z] suspicious.

soupe [sup] *f* soup; F, *a.* ✗ meal; F food, *sl.* grub; sop (*for soaking in soup, wine, etc.*); ～ *à l'oignon* onion-soup; F ～ *populaire* soup kitchen; F *monter* (*or s'emporter*) *comme une* ～ *au lait* flare up; F *être* ～ *au lait* be irritable; F *être trempé comme une* ～ be wet through.

soupente [su'pɑ̃:t] *f* ⊕ support; ⚠ loft, garret; closet.

souper [su'pe] **1.** *v/i.* (1a) have supper; *sl. fig. j'en ai soupé* I'm fed up with it; **2.** *su./m* supper.

soupeser [supə'ze] (1d) *v/t.* feel the weight of; weigh (*s.th.*) in the hand.

soupière [su'pjɛ:r] *f* soup-tureen.

soupir [su'pi:r] *m* sigh; ♪ crotchet rest; ♪ (*demi-*)*quart m de* ～ (demi-)semiquaver rest; ♪ *demi-*～ quaver rest; **soupirail,** *pl.* **-aux** [supi-'ra:j, ₌'ro] *m* air-hole; vent (*in air-*

shaft etc.); ventilator; **soupirant** F [~'rɑ̃] suitor, admirer; **soupirer** [~'re] (1a) *v/i.* sigh; ~ *après* (*or pour*) long *or* sigh for.

souple [supl] supple; flexible; *fig.* compliant, docile; **souplesse** [su'plɛs] *f* suppleness; flexibility; *fig.* adaptability; *fig. character*: pliability.

souquenille † [suk'ni:j] *f* smock.

source [surs] *f* source (*a. fig.*); spring; *fig.* origin; ~ *jaillissante* gusher; *de bonne* ~ on good authority; *prendre sa* ~ *dans river*: rise in; **sourcier** [sur'sje] *m* water-diviner.

sourcil [sur'si] *m* eyebrow; *froncer les* ~s frown; **sourciller** [~si'je] (1a) *v/i.* knit one's brows, frown; *fig.* flinch; *ne pas* ~ F not to turn a hair, *Am.* never to bat an eyelid; **sourcilleux, -euse** [~si'jø, ~'jø:z] finicky, pernickety; supercilious.

sourd, sourde [su:r, surd] **1.** *adj.* deaf; dull (*blow, colour, noise, pain, thud*); low (*cry*); hollow (*voice*); *fig.* hidden, veiled (*hostility*); *fig.* underhand; *gramm.* voiceless; F ~ *comme un pot* deaf as a (door-)post; *faire la sourde oreille* turn a deaf ear; *lanterne f sourde* dark-lantern; **2.** *su.* deaf person.

sourdine [sur'din] *f* ♪ mute; ♪ damper; *en* ~ ♪ muted; *fig.* softly; *fig.* on the quiet; *fig. mettre une* ~ *à qch.* tone s.th. down.

sourd-muet, sourde-muette [sur-'mɥɛ, surd'mɥɛt] **1.** *adj.* deaf-and-dumb; **2.** *su.* deaf-mute.

sourdre [surdr] (4dd) *v/i.* spring; *a. fig.* arise.

souriant, e [su'rjɑ̃, ~'rjɑ̃:t] smiling.

souriceau [suri'so] *m* young mouse; **souricière** [~'sjɛ:r] *f* mouse-trap; *fig.* (police-)trap.

sourire [su'ri:r] **1.** (4cc) *v/i.* smile; *pej.* smirk; ~ *à q.* smile at s.o.; *fig.* appeal *or* be attractive to s.o.; **2.** *su./m* smile.

souris [su'ri] *f* mouse.

sournois, e [sur'nwa, ~'nwa:z] underhand; deceitful; **sournoiserie** [~nwaz'ri] *f* underhand manner *or* trick; deceitfulness.

sous [su] *prp. usu.* under (*the table, s.o.'s command, etc.*); underneath; below; at (*the equator*); in (*the tropics, the rain, a favourable light*); within (*three months*); ~ *clé* under

lock and key; ~ *les drapeaux* with the colo(u)rs; ~ *enveloppe* under cover, in an envelope; ~ *le nom de* by the name of; ~ *peine de* on pain of; ~ *peu* before long, shortly; ~ *ce pli* enclosed; ~ *prétexte de* on the pretext of; ~ *le rapport de* in respect of; ~ (*le règne de*) *Louis XIV* under *or* in the reign of Louis XIV; *passer* ~ *silence* pass (*s.th.*) over in silence; ~ *mes yeux* before my eyes; *see* **cape**; **main**.

sous... [su; suz] sub..., under...; ~**-aide** [su'zed] *su.* sub-assistant; ~**-alimenté, e** [~zalimɑ̃'te] undernourished, underfed; ~**-arrondissement** [~zarɔ̃dis'mɑ̃] *m* sub-district; ~**-bail** [su'ba:j] *m* sub-lease; ~**-bois** [~'bwa] *m* undergrowth.

souscripteur ✝ [suskrip'tœ:r] *m* shares, periodical, etc.: subscriber; cheque: drawer; **souscription** [~'sjɔ̃] *f* subscription (for shares, *à des actions*); signature; (*public*) fund; **souscrire** [sus'kri:r] (4q) *v/i.*: ✝, *a.* subscribe ~ *à* subscribe to; ~ *pour* subscribe (*a sum of money*); **souscrit, e** ✝ [~'kri, ~'krit] subscribed (*capital*).

sous...: ~**-cutané, e** ⚕ [sukyta'ne] subcutaneous; ~**-développé, e** [~devlɔ'pe] underdeveloped; ~**-emploi** [suzɑ̃'plwa] *m* underemployment; ~**-entendre** [~ɑ̃'tɑ̃:dr] (4a) *v/t.* understand (*a. gramm.*); imply; ~**-entendu** [~zɑ̃tɑ̃'dy] *m* implication; innuendo; allusion; overtone; ~**-entente** [~zɑ̃'tɑ̃:t] *f* mental reservation; ~**-equipé, e** [~zeki'pe] underequipped; ~**-estimer** [~zesti-'me] (1a) *v/t.* underestimate; ~**-exposer** *phot.* [~zɛkspo'ze] (1a) *v/t.* under-expose; ~**-fifre** F [su'fifr] *m* underling; sidekick; ~**-locataire** [~lɔka'tɛ:r] *su.* subtenant, sublessee; ~**-location** [~lɔka'sjɔ̃] *f* sub-letting; sub-lease; ~**-louer** [~'lwe] (1p) *v/t.* sub-let; sub-lease; rent (*a house*) from a tenant; ~**-main** [~'mɛ̃] *m/inv.* blotting-pad, writing-pad; *en* ~ secretly, behind the scenes; ~**-maître** [~'mɛ:tr] *m* assistant master; ~**-maîtresse** [~mɛ'trɛs] *f* assistant mistress; ~**-marin, e** ⚓ [~ma'rɛ̃, ~'rin] *adj., a. su./m* submarine; ~**-officier** [suzɔfi'sje] *m*, F ~**-off** [~'zɔf] *m* ✗ non-commissioned officer, N.C.O.; ⚓ petty officer; ~**-ordre**

speaker

[~'zɔrdr] *m* ♀ sub-order; *admin.* subordinate; *en* ~ subordinate(ly *adv.*);
~-payer [~pɛ'je] (1i) *v/t.* underpay;
~-pied [su'pje] *m* trouser-strap;
gaiters: under-strap; **~-préfet** [~pre'fɛ] *m* sub-prefect; **~-produit** ⊕ [~prɔ'dɥi] *m* by-product; spin-off; **~-prolétariat** [~prɔletar'ja] *m* under-privileged class; **~-secrétaire** [~sɔkre'tɛːr] *m* under-secretary of State, *d'État*; **~signé, e** [~si'ɲe] **1.** *adj.* undersigned; **2.** *su.* undersigned; *je* ~ ... I the undersigned ...;
~-sol [~'sɔl] *m* ✔ subsoil; ⚠ basement; basement-flat; ⚒ underground; *richesses f/pl.* de ~ mineral resources; **~-tendre** [~'tãdr] (4a) *v/t.* ⚡ subtend; *fig.* underlie.
soustraction [sustrak'sjɔ̃] *f* removal, abstraction (*a.* ⚬); ⚡ subtraction; **soustraire** [~'trɛːr] (4ff) *v/t.* remove; withdraw; ⚡ subtract (from, *de*); *fig.* shield (s.o. from s.th., *q. à qch.*); *se* ~ *à* escape from; avoid (*a duty*).
sous...: **~-traitance** [sutrɛ'tãːs] *f* subcontracting; **~-traitant** [~trɛ'tã] *m* subcontractor; **~-traiter** [~trɛ'te] (1a) *v/t.* subcontract; **~-ventrière** [~vãtri'ɛːr] *f* saddle-girth; belly-band; **~-verge** [~'vɛrʒ] *m/inv.* offhorse; ✝ *fig.* underling; **~-vêtement** [~vɛtmã] *m* undergarment.
soutache ✂, *a. cost.* [su'taʃ] *f* braid.
soutane *eccl.* [su'tan] *f* cassock, soutane; *fig. la* ~ holy orders *pl.*, F the cloth.
soute [sut] *f* ⚓ store-room; ✈ ~ *à bombes* bomb-bay; ~ *à charbon* coal-bunker; ~ *aux poudres* (powder-)magazine.
soutenable [sut'nabl] bearable; tenable (*opinion, theory, a.* ⚔ ✝); **soutenance** [~'nãːs] *f thesis*: maintaining; **soutènement** [suten'mã] *m* support(ing); ⚠ de ~ retaining (*wall*), relieving (*arch*); **souteneur** [sut'nœːr] *m* procurer; **soutenir** [sut'niːr] (2h) *v/t.* support; hold (*s.th.*) up; back (*s.o.*) (*financially*); keep up (*a conversation, a credit, a part*); maintain, assert (*a fact*); uphold (*an opinion, a theory, a thesis*); *fig.* endure, bear (*a comparison*), stand; **soutenu, e** [~'ny] sustained; unflagging (*attention,*

effort, interest); ✝ steady (*market*); *fig.* lofty (*style*).
souterrain, e [sutɛ'rɛ̃, ~'rɛn] **1.** *adj.* underground; *a.fig.* subterranian; **2.** *su./m* underground passage.
soutien [su'tjɛ̃] *m* support(ing); *person*: supporter; *fig.* mainstay; **~-gorge,** *pl.* **~s-gorge** *cost.* [~tjɛ̃'gɔrʒ] *m* brassière, F bra.
soutirer [suti're] (1a) *v/t.* draw off (*wine etc.*); *fig.* get (s.th. out of s.o., *qch. à q.*).
souvenir [suv'niːr] **1.** (2h) *v/t.*: *se* ~ de remember, recall; *v/impers.*: *il me souvient de* (*inf.*) I remember (*ger.*); **2.** *su./m* memory, remembrance; souvenir, keepsake.
souvent [su'vã] *adv.* often; *assez* ~ fairly often; *peu* ~ seldom, not often.
souverain, e [su'vrɛ̃, ~'vrɛn] **1.** *adj.* sovereign; supreme; **2.** *su.* sovereign; **souveraineté** [~vrɛn'te] *f* sovereignty; territory (*of a sovereign*).
soviet *pol.* [sɔ'vjɛt] *m* Soviet; **soviétique** [~vje'tik] **1.** *adj.* Soviet; **2.** *su.* ♀ Soviet citizen.
soya ♀ [sɔ'ja] *m see soja.*
soyeux, -euse [swa'jø, ~'jøːz] **1.** *adj.* silky, silken; **2.** *su./m* silk manufacturer.
soyons [swa'jɔ̃] *1st p. pl. pres. sbj. of* être **1.**
spacieux, -euse [spa'sjø, ~'sjøːz] spacious, roomy.
spadassin [spada'sɛ̃] *m* hired killer; ✝ swordsman.
spalter [spal'tɛːr] *m painting*: graining-brush.
sparadrap ⚕ [spara'dra] *m* sticking or adhesive plaster, *Am. a.* Band-Aid (*TM*).
spasme ⚕ [spasm] *m* spasm; **spasmodique** ⚕ [spasmɔ'dik] spasmodic, spastic.
spath *min.* [spat] *m* spar; ~ *fluor* fluorite.
spatial, e, *m/pl.* **-aux** [spa'sjal, ~'sjo] spatial; space ...; *navire m* ~ space craft.
spatule [spa'tyl] *f* ⚕ spatula; ⊕ spoon tool; *sp.* ski-tip; *orn.* spoonbill; **spatulé, e** [~ty'le] spatulate.
speaker, speakerine [spi'kœːr, ~kə'rin] *su. radio*: announcer; newscaster, newsreader; *su./m parl.* speaker.

spécial, e, *m/pl.* **-aux** [spe'sjal, ~-'sjo] **1.** *adj.* special, particular; ⚔ *armes f/pl.* ~es technical arms; **2.** *su./f school:* higher mathematics class; **spécialiser** [spesjali'ze] (1a) *v/t.* particularize; ear-mark (*funds*); se ~ *dans* specialize in, make a special study of, *Am.* major in; **spécialiste** [~'list] *su.* specialist (*a.* 🎨); expert; ⚒ tradesman; **spécialité** [~li'te] *f* speciality; special study; ⚓ special duty; ⚓ specialized branch; ~ *pharmaceutique* patent medicine.

spécieux, -euse [spe'sjø, ~'sjø:z] specious; plausible.

spécification [spesifika'sjɔ̃] *f* specification; *raw material:* working up; **spécificité** [~fisi'te] *f* specificity (*a.* 🎨); **spécifier** [~'fje] (1o) *v/t.* specify; lay down; stipulate; determine (*s.th.*) specifically; **spécifique** [~-'fik] **1.** *su./m* specific (for, de); **2.** *adj.* specific; *phys. poids m* ~ specific gravity.

spécimen [spesi'mɛn] **1.** *su./m* specimen, sample; **2.** *adj.* specimen (*copy*).

spéciosité [spesjozi'te] *f* speciousness.

spectacle [spɛk'takl] *m* spectacle, sight; *pej.* exhibition; *thea.* play, show; "~s" *pl.* «entertainment»; *le (monde du)* ~ show business; *fig. se donner en* ~ make an ass of o.s.; *taxe f sur les* ~s entertainment tax.

spectateur, -trice [spɛkta'tœ:r, ~'tris] *su.* spectator; witness (*of an accident, an event, etc.*); *su./m:* thea. ~s *pl.* audience *sg.*

spectral, e, *m/pl.* **-aux** [spɛk'tral, ~'tro] spectral (*a.* 🎨); spectrum (*analysis*); *opt.* of the spectrum; *fig.* ghostly; **spectre** [spɛktr] *m* spectre; ghost (*a. fig.*); *opt., a. phys.* spectrum; **spectroscopie** *phys.* [spɛktrɔskɔ'pi] *f* spectroscopy.

spéculaire [speky'lɛ:r] **1.** *adj.* specular; *psych.* mirror (*writing*); *pierre f* ~ mica; **2.** *su./f* ♀ specularia.

spéculateur, -trice [spekyla-'tœ:r, ~'tris] ♈, *a. fig.* speculator; *fig.* theorizer; **spéculatif, -ve** [~'tif, ~'ti:v] ♈, *a. fig.* speculative; *fig.* contemplative; **spéculation** [~'sjɔ̃] *f* ♈, *a. fig.* speculation; *fig.* theory, conjecture; *fig.* cogitation; **spéculer** [speky'le] (1a) *v/i.* ♈, *a. fig.*

speculate (*fig.* on, ♈ in *sur*; ♈ for, *à*).

spéléologie [speleɔlɔ'ʒi] *f* spel(a)eology; cave hunting; F pot-holing; **spéléologue** [~'lɔg] *m* spel(a)eologist; cave hunter; F pot-holer.

spencer *cost.* [spɛ̃'sɛ:r] *m* spencer.

sperme *physiol.* [spɛrm] *m* sperm, semen.

sphère [sfɛ:r] *f* sphere (*a.* 🝞, *fig.*); *geog.* globe; **sphéricité** [sferisi'te] *f* sphericity, curvature; **sphérique** [~'rik] **1.** *adj.* spherical (*a.* 🝞); **2.** *su./m* 🎈 spherical balloon.

sphinx [sfɛ̃:ks] *m* sphynx (*a. fig.*); *zo.* hawk-moth.

spic ♀ [spik] *m* spike-lavender.

spider *mot.* [spi'dɛ:r] *m* dick(e)y (seat).

spinal, e, *m/pl.* **-aux** *anat.* [spi'nal, ~'no] spinal.

spinelle *min.* [spi'nɛl] *m* spinel.

spiral, e, *m/pl.* **-aux** [spi'ral, ~'ro] **1.** *adj.* spiral; **2.** *su./f* spiral; *en* ~e spiral(ly *adv.*), winding; *su./m* ⊕ *watch:* hairspring; **spire** [spi:r] *f* single turn, whorl (*a.* 🐚); 🐚 *bobbin:* one winding.

spirée ♀ [spi're] *f* spiraea.

spirite [spi'rit] **1.** *adj.* spiritualistic; **2.** *su.* spiritualist; **spiritisme** [spiri'tism] *m* spirit(ual)ism; **spiritualiser** [~tɥali'ze] (1a) *v/t.* spiritualize; 🝞 † distil; **spiritualité** [~tɥali'te] *f* spirituality; **spirituel, -elle** [~'tɥɛl] spiritual (*a. eccl., phls., etc.*); *fig.* witty, humorous; **spiritueux, -euse** [~'tɥø, ~'tɥø:z] **1.** *adj.* spirituous; **2.** *su./m* spirit(uous liquor); *les* ~ *pl.* spirits.

spleen † [splin] *m* spleen, melancholy.

splendeur [splã'dœ:r] *f* splendo(u)r; brilliance, brightness; *fig.* grandeur, glory; **splendide** [~'did] splendid; brilliant; *fig.* magnificent.

spoliateur, -trice [spɔlja'tœ:r, ~-'tris] **1.** *adj.* spoliatory (*law, measure*); **2.** *su.* despoiler; **spoliation** [~lja'sjɔ̃] *f* despoilment; **spolier** [~'lje] (1o) *v/t.* despoil, rob (of, de). [dee.]

spondée [spɔ̃'de] *m* prosody: spon-]

spongiaires [spɔ̃'ʒjɛ:r] *m/pl.* spongiae; **spongieux, -euse** [~-'ʒjø, ~-'ʒjø:z] spongy; *anat.* ethmoid (*bone*); **spongiosité** [~ʒjozi'te] *f* sponginess.

spontané, e [spɔ̃ta'ne] spontaneous; ⚮ voluntary (*confession*); ⚮ self-sown; **spontanéite** [˷nei'te] *f* spontaneity; **spontanément** [˷ne-'mɑ̃] *adv. of* spontané.

sporadique ⚮, ⚮ [spɔra'dik] sporadic; **spore** ⚮, *biol.* [spɔ:r] *f* spore.

sport [spɔ:r] *m* sport; ˷*s pl. nautiques* aquatic sports; *le* ˷ sports *pl.*; **sportif, -ve** [spɔr'tif, ˷'ti:v] **1.** *adj.* sporting; sports...; **2.** *su.* follower of sports, F sports fan; *su./m* sportsman; *su./f* sportswoman; **sportsman**, *pl.* **sportsmen** [spɔrts'man, ˷'men] *m* sportsman; **sportswoman**, *pl.* **sportswomen** [˷wu'man, ˷'men] *f* sportswoman.

spot [spɔt] *m* radio, TV, *etc.*: spot; spot(light).

spoutnik [sput'nik] *m* sputnik.

sprat *icht.* [sprat] *m* sprat.

sprint *sp.* [sprint] *m* sprint; **sprinter** *sp.* **1.** [sprin'tœ:r] *su./m* sprinter; **2.** [˷'te] (1a) *v/i.* sprint.

spumeux, -euse [spy'mø, ˷'mø:z] frothy, foamy.

squale *icht.* [skwal] *m* dog-fish.

squame [skwam] *f skin*: scale; *bone*: exfoliation; squama; **squameux, -euse** [skwa'mø, ˷'mø:z] ⚮, *anat.*, *etc.* scaly; squamous (*a.* ⚮).

square [skwa:r] *m* (public) square (with garden).

squelette [skə'let] *m* skeleton (*a. fig.*); ⚓ carcass; *fig. book, plot*: outline; **squelettique** [˷le'tik] skeletal; *fig.* skeleton-like.

stabilisateur, -trice [stabiliza'tœ:r, ˷'tris] **1.** *adj.* stabilizing; **2.** *su./m* ⚒ *etc.* stabilizer; **stabilisation** [˷za'sjɔ̃] *f* stabilization; ⚒ standstill; ⊕ annealing; **stabiliser** [˷'ze] (1a) *v/t.* stabilize (*a.* ✝ *the currency*); ⊕ anneal; *se* ˷ become steady; **stabilité** [˷'te] *f* stability; **stable** [stabl] stable; steady; *fig.* lasting.

stade [stad] *m sp.* stadium; *sp.* athletic club; ⚮, *a. fig.* stage, period.

stage [sta:ʒ] *m* (period of) probation; training period *or* course; ⚖ articles *pl.*; **stagiaire** [sta'ʒjɛ:r] *adj.*, *su.* trainee.

stagnant, e [stag'nã, ˷'nã:t] stagnant (*a.* ✝); **stagnation** [˷na'sjɔ̃] *f* stagnation (*a.* ✝); ⚓ *compass*: slowness; ✝ dullness.

stalle [stal] *f eccl.*, *thea.*, *stable*, *etc.*: stall; *stable*: box.

staminé, e ⚮ [stami'ne] stamened, staminate.

stance [stã:s] *f* stanza.

stand [stã:d] *m* races, show, exhibition: stand; ˷ *de tir* shooting-gallery, rifle range.

standard [stã'da:r] **1.** *su./m teleph.* switchboard; *fig.* standard (of living, de vie); **2.** *adj.* standard; **standardisation** ⊕ [stãdardiza'sjɔ̃] *f* standardization; **standardiser** ⊕ [˷di'ze] (1a) *v/t.* standardize; **standardiste** *teleph.* [˷'dist] *su.* switchboard operator.

standing [stã'diŋ] *m* (social) status, standing, reputation; (de) grand ˷ luxury (flat, apartment, etc.).

starter [star'tɛ:r] *m sp.* starter; *mot.* choke.

station [sta'sjɔ̃] *f* ⚒, ⚓, ⚮, radio, 🕮 underground: station; stop, halt; (taxi-)rank; bus, tram: (fare) stage; (holiday) resort; ⚮ ˷ centrale power station; ˷ climatique health resort; ˷ de correspondance underground railway: interchange station; en ˷ standing; faire une ˷ break one's journey; **stationnaire** [˷sjɔ'nɛ:r] **1.** *adj.* stationary; **2.** *su./m* ⚓ guard ship; **stationnement** *mot.* [˷sjɔn'mã] *m* parking; ˷ bilatéral parking on both sides; ˷ interdit road sign: no parking; no waiting; ˷ unilatéral parking on one side only; **stationner** [˷sjɔ'ne] (1a) *v/i.* stop; halt; stand; park (car); ⚒ be stationed; défense f de ˷ no parking; **station-service**, *pl.* **stations-service** *mot.* [˷sjɔsɛr'vis] *f* service station; repair station.

statique [sta'tik] **1.** *adj.* static; **2.** *su./f* ⊕ statics *sg.*

statisticien [statisti'sjɛ̃] *m* statistician; **statistique** [˷'tik] **1.** *adj.* statistical; **2.** *su./f* statistics *sg.*

statuaire [sta'tɥɛ:r] **1.** *adj.* statuary; **2.** *su./m person*: sculptor; *su./f art*: statuary; sculptress; **statue** [˷'tɥ] *f* statue; image.

statuer [sta'tɥe] (1n) *v/t.* decree, enact; rule; *v/i.*: ˷ sur qch. decide s.th., give judgment on s.th.

stature [sta'ty:r] *f* stature; height.

statut [sta'ty] *m* ⚖ statute; regulation; charter; *pol.* status; constitution; **statutaire** [˷ty'tɛ:r] statutory; ✝ qualifying (*share*).

stéarine ⚗ [stea'rin] *f* stearin(e); **stéarique** ⚗ [˷'rik] stearic.

steeple-chase *sp.* [stiplə'tʃɛz] *m* *track*: hurdle-race.

stellaire [stɛl'lɛːr] **1.** *adj. astr.* stellar; **2.** *su./f* ♀ starwort.

sténo... [stenɔ] steno...; **~dactylographe** [~daktilɔ'graf], F **~dactylo** [~dakti'lo] *su.* shorthand-typist; **~gramme** [~'gram] *m* shorthand report; **~graphe** [~'graf] *su.* shorthand writer; stenographer; **~graphie** [~gra'fi] *f* shorthand; **~type** [~'tip] *su./m* stenotype; *su./f* shorthand typewriter; **~typiste** [~ti'pist] *su.* stenotypist.

stentor [stã'tɔːr] *npr./m*: *fig. voix f de* ~ stentorian voice.

steppe *geog.* [stɛp] *f* steppe.

stercoraire [stɛrkɔ'rɛːr] *m zo.* dung-beetle; *orn.* skua.

stère [stɛːr] *m measure of wood*: stere, cubic metre; *bois m de* ~ cordwood.

stéréo [stere'o] *f*, *a. adj. short for stéréophonie, stéréophonique*: stereo; *en* ~ (in) stereo.

stéréo... [stereɔ] stereo...; **~métrie** Ⓐ [~me'tri] *f* stereometry; **~métrique** Ⓐ [~me'trik] stereometric; **~phonie** [~fɔ'ni] *f* stereophony, stereo (sound); **~phonique** [~fɔ'nik] stereophonic; **~scope** *opt.* [stereɔ-s'kɔp] *m* stereoscope; **~scopique** [~skɔ'pik] stereoscopic; **~type** *typ.* [stereɔ'tip] **1.** *adj.* stereotype; stereotyped (*book*); **2.** *su./m* stereotype (plate); **~typer** [~ti'pe] (1a) *v/t.* stereotype; *expression f* stéréotypée hackneyed phrase; *sourire m* stéréotype fixed smile; **~typie** [~ti'pi] *f* stereotypy; stereotype foundry.

stérile [ste'ril] ♂, ♀, *zo.*, *a. fig.* sterile, barren (*a. woman*); childless (*marriage*); *fig.* fruitless, vain (*effort*); **stériliser** [sterili'ze] (1a) *v/t.* sterilize (*a.* ♂); **stérilité** [~'te] *f* sterility; barrenness (*a. fig.*).

sternum *anat.* [stɛr'nɔm] *m* sternum, breast-bone.

sternutation ♂ [stɛrnyta'sjɔ̃] *f* sternutation, sneezing; **sternutatoire** ♂ [~'twaːr] *adj.* sternutatory; sneezing(-*powder*).

stéthoscope ♂ [stetɔs'kɔp] *m* stethoscope.

stick [stik] *m* ✗ swagger-stick; (*riding-*)switch.

stigmate [stig'mat] *m* ♂, ♀, *a. fig.* stigma; ♂ *wound*: scar, mark; *small-pox*: pock-mark; *fig.* stain (on

character); *eccl.* ~*s pl.* stigmata; **stigmatique** [~ma'tik] stigmatic; *opt.* anastigmatic; **stigmatiser** [~mati'ze] (1a) *v/t. eccl.*, *a. fig.* stigmatize (with, *de*); ♂ pock-mark (*s.o.*); *fig.* brand (*s.o.*).

stimulant, e [stimy'lã, ~'lãːt] **1.** *adj.* stimulating; **2.** *su./m* ♂ stimulant; *fig.* stimulus, incentive; **stimulateur, -trice** [~la'tœːr, ~'tris] **1.** *adj.* stimulative; **2.** *su./m*: ♂ ~ *cardiaque* pacemaker; **stimuler** [~'le] (1a) *v/t.* stimulate; *fig.* incite, give a stimulus to; **stimulus** ♂, *biol.* [~'lys] *m* stimulus.

stipendier *pej.* [stipã'dje] (1o) *v/t.* hire, buy (*s.o.*).

stipulation ⚖ [stipyla'sjɔ̃] *f* condition; stipulation; **stipuler** [~'le] (1a) *v/t.* stipulate.

stock ✝ [stɔk] *m* stock; **stockage** [stɔ'kaːʒ] *m* ✝ stocking; storing; **stocker** [~'ke] (1a) *v/t.* ✝ stock, store; ✗ stockpile (*bombs*).

stoïcien, -enne *phls.* [stɔi'sjɛ̃, ~'sjɛn] **1.** *adj.* stoic(al); **2.** *su.* stoic; **stoïcisme** *phls.*, *a. fig.* [~i'sism] *m* stoicism; **stoïque** [~'ik] **1.** *adj. fig.* stoic(al); **2.** *su.* stoic.

stolon ♀ [stɔ'lɔ̃] *f* stolon, runner, sucker.

stomacal, e *m/pl.* -aux [stɔma'kal, ~'ko] gastric; stomach-(*pump, tube*); **stomachique** ♂, *anat.* [~'ʃik] *adj.*, *a. su./m* stomachic.

stop [stɔp] **1.** *int.* stop!; **2.** *su./m* mot. stop sign; brake light, *Am.* stoplight; F hitchhiking, hitching.

stoppage [stɔ'paːʒ] *m cost.* invisible mending; *stockings*: invisible darning; **stopper** [~'pe] (1a) *v/t.* stop; check; *cost.* repair by invisible mending; *v/i.* (come to a) stop; **stoppeur, -euse** [~'pœːr, ~'pøːz] *su. cost.* fine-darner, invisible mender; F hitchhiker.

store [stɔːr] *m* blind; awning.

strabique ♂ [stra'bik] **1.** *adj.* squint-eyed, F cross-eyed; **2.** *su.* squinter; **strabisme** [~'bism] *m* squinting, strabism(us).

strangulation [strãgyla'sjɔ̃] *f* strangulation.

strapontin [strapɔ̃'tɛ̃] *m bus, taxi, thea.*: folding seat, jump seat; *fig.* back seat, minor role.

strass [stras] *m* paste jewellery, strass.

stratagème ✗, *a. fig.* [strata'ʒɛm] *m* stratagem.

stratégie ✗, *a. fig.* [strate'ʒi] *f* strategy; **stratégiste** [∼'ʒist] *m* strategist.

stratifié, e [strati'fje] (1o) stratified; ⊕ laminated; **stratigraphie** *geol.* [∼tigra'fi] *f* stratigraphy; **stratosphère** *meteor.* [∼tɔs'fɛ:r] *f* stratosphere.

stress *psych.* [strɛs] *m* stress; **stressant, e** [strɛ'sɑ̃, ∼'sɑ̃:t] stress (*situation, etc.*), full of stress.

strict, stricte [strikt] strict (*a. fig.*); *fig.* severe; exact; **striction** [strik'sjɔ̃] *f* ♣ constriction; ♈ striction.

strident, e [stri'dɑ̃, ∼'dɑ̃:t] strident, harsh, shrill.

stridulant, e [stridy'lɑ̃, ∼'lɑ̃:t] stridulant, chirring; **stridulation** [∼la'sjɔ̃] *f* stridulation, chirring; **striduleux, -euse** ♣ [∼'lø, ∼'lø:z] stridulous.

strie [stri] *f* groove; ♌, ♈, *anat., geol.* stria; colour: streak; **strier** [stri'e] (1a) *v/t.* score, scratch; ♈, *geol.* striate; ♌ flute, groove; ⊕ corrugate (*iron*); streak; **striure** [∼'y:r] *f see* strie.   [strophe.‌]

strophe [strɔf] *f* stanza, verse;‌

structure [stryk'ty:r] *f* structure; ∼(s) *d'accueil* reception facilities *pl.*; *psych.* ∼ *de comportement* behavio(u)r pattern; ∼ *gonflable* air hall; **structurel, -elle** [∼ty'rɛl] structural.

strychnine ♣ [strik'nin] *f* strychnine.

stuc ♌ [styk] *m* stucco; **stucateur** [styka'tœ:r] *m* stucco-worker.

studieux, -euse [sty'djø, ∼'djø:z] studious; devoted to study.

studio [sty'djo] *m* radio, *a. cin.*: studio; one-roomed flat, flatlet, *Am.* studio apartment.

stupéfaction [stypefak'sjɔ̃] *f* stupefaction; amazement; **stupéfait, e** [∼'fɛ, ∼'fɛt] stupefied; amazed (at, de); **stupéfiant, e** [∼'fjɑ̃, ∼'fjɑ̃:t] 1. *adj.* stupefying (♣, *a. fig.*); *fig.* astounding; 2. *su./m* ♣ drug, narcotic; **stupéfier** [∼'fje] (1o) *v/t.* ♣, *a. fig.* stupefy; *fig.* astound; **stupeur** [sty'pœ:r] *f* stupor; *fig.* amazement.

stupide [sty'pid] 1. *adj.* stupid, *Am.* F dumb; dumbfounded; silly, foolish; 2. *su.* stupid person; dolt; **stupidité** [∼pidi'te] *f* stupidity; folly.

stuquer ♌ [sty'ke] (1m) *v/t.* stucco.

style [stil] *m* ♀, ♌, *fig.*, *a.* sun-dial: style; etching-needle; *sun-dial:* gnomon; **styler** [sti'le] (1a) *v/t.* train, form; F school (*s.o.*) (in, *à*).

stylet [sti'lɛ] *m* stiletto; ♣ stylet, probe.

styliser [stili'ze] (1a) *v/t.* stylize; **styliste** [sti'list] *su.* stylist; **stylistique** [∼lis'tik] *f* stylistics *sg.*

stylo [sti'lo] *m* pen; F fountain pen; ∼ (*à*) *bille*, ∼-*bille* ball-point pen; ∼(-)*feutre* felt-tip pen; **stylographe** [∼lɔ'graf] *m* fountain pen.

styptique ♣ [stip'tik] *adj.*, *a. su./m* styptic, astringent.

su, e [sy] 1. *p.p. of savoir*; 2. *su./m*: *au vu et au* ∼ *de* to the knowledge of.

suaire [sɥɛ:r] *m* shroud; *eccl. saint* ∼ vernicle, veronica.

suant, e [sɥɑ̃, sɥɑ̃:t] sweaty; *sl.* boring, deadly dull.

suave [sɥa:v] sweet; bland (*manner, tone*); soft (*shade*); mild (*cigar*); **suavité** [sɥavi'te] *f* sweetness, softness; *manner, tone:* blandness, suavity.

sub... [syb] sub...

subalterne [sybal'tɛrn] 1. *adj.* subordinate; inferior; 2. *su./m* underling; ✗ subaltern.

subconscience [sybkɔ̃'sjɑ̃:s] *f* subconsciousness; **subconscient, e** [∼'sjɑ̃, ∼'sjɑ̃:t] 1. *adj.* subconscious; 2. *su./m*: *le* ∼ the subconscious.

subdiviser [sybdivi'ze] (1a) *v/t.* subdivide; **subdivision** [∼'zjɔ̃] *f* subdivision.

subéreux, -euse ♀ [sybe'rø, ∼'rø:z] suberose; corky; *enveloppe f* ∼*euse* cortex.

subir [sy'bi:r] (2a) *v/t.* undergo; suffer (*death, defeat, a penalty*); submit to (*a law, a rule*); come under (*an influence*); put up with, endure.

subit, e [sy'bi, ∼'bit] sudden, unexpected.

subjectif, -ve [sybʒɛk'tif, ∼'ti:v] subjective.

subjonctif, -ve *gramm.* [sybʒɔ̃k'tif, ∼'ti:v] 1. *adj.* subjunctive; 2. *su./m* subjunctive; *au* ∼ in the subjunctive.

subjuguer [sybʒy'ge] (1m) *v/t.* captivate, thrill; † subdue (*a. fig.*); *fig.* master (*one's feelings*).

sublimation ♣, *psych.* [syblima'sjɔ̃] *f* sublimation; **sublime** [∼'blim] 1. *adj.* sublime (*a. anat., fig.*); lofty; 2. *su./m the* sublime; **sublimé** ♣

[sybli'me] *m* sublimate; **sublimer**
[~] (1a) *v/t.* ⚗ sublimate (*a. psych.*),
sublime; **sublimité** [syblimi'te] *f*
sublimity.
submerger [sybmɛr'ʒe] (11) *v/t.*
submerge; flood (*a field, a village, a
valley*); immerse (*an object in water*);
swamp (*a boat, a field*); *fig.* inundate,
overwhelm (with, *de*); *submergé de
besogne* snowed under *or* inundated
with work; **submersible** [~'sibl]
adj., su./m ⚓ † submarine; **submersion** [~'sjɔ̃] *f* submersion, submergence; ⚓ sinking; ✈ flooding;
mort f par ~ death by drowning.
subordination [sybɔrdina'sjɔ̃] *f*
subordination; **subordonné, e** [~-
dɔ'ne] **1.** *adj.* subordinate, dependent (*a. gramm.*); **2.** *su.* subordinate,
underling; **subordonner** [~dɔ'ne]
(1a) *v/t.* subordinate; *fig.* regulate
(according to, in the light of *à*).
suborner [sybɔr'ne] (1a) *v/t.* suborn
(*a.* 🏛 *a witness etc.*); bribe; **su-
borneur, -euse** [~'nœːr, ~'nøːz]
1. *adj.* persuasive; **2.** *su.* 🏛 suborner.
subreptice [sybrɛp'tis] surrepti-
tious; clandestine; **subreption** 🏛
[~'sjɔ̃] *f* subreption.
subroger 🏛 [sybrɔ'ʒe] (11) *v/t.* sub-
rogate; appoint (*s.o.*) as deputy;
subrogé tuteur m surrogate guardian.
subséquemment [sypseka'mɑ̃] *adv.*
subsequently; in due course; **subséquent, e** [~'kɑ̃, ~'kɑ̃ːt] subsequent.
subside [syp'sid] *m* grant, allowance;
subsidiaire [si'djɛːr] subsidiary,
accessory, additional (to, *à*).
subsistance [sybzis'tɑ̃ːs] *f* subsistence; keep; ~s *pl.* provisions, supplies; *mis en* ~ attached to another
unit for rations; **subsistant, e** [~'tɑ̃,
~'tɑ̃ːt] **1.** *adj.* subsisting, extant; **2.**
su./m soldier attached (*to a unit*) for
rations; **subsister** [~'te] (1a) *v/i.*
subsist; exist, continue, be extant;
live (on, *de*); *moyens m/pl. de* ~ means
of subsistence.
substance [syps'tɑ̃ːs] *f* substance (*a.
fig.*); ⊕ *etc.* material; *fig.* gist; *anat.* ~
grise grey matter; *en* ~ substantially;
substantiel, -elle [~tɑ̃'sjɛl] substantial; nourishing (*food*).
substantif, -ve [sypstɑ̃'tif, ~'tiːv] **1.**
adj. substantive (*a. gramm.*); **2.** *su./m*
gramm. substantive, noun.

substitué, e [sypsti'tɥe] supposti-
tious (*child*); **substituer** [~'tɥe] (1n)
v/t. substitute (for, *à*); *se* ~ *à* substitute for, act as substitute for (*s.o.*);
take the place of; **substitut** [~'ty] *m*
deputy; 🏛 locum tenens, F locum; 🏛
deputy public prosecutor; **substitution** [~ty'sjɔ̃] *f* substitution (for,
à); mix-up.
substrat [syps'tra] *m* substratum.
substruction 🏛 [sypstryk'sjɔ̃] *f*
foundation, substructure; under-
pinning; **substructure** 🏛 [~'tyːr] *f*
substructure.
subterfuge [syptɛr'fyːʒ] *m* subterfuge; evasion, shift.
subtil, e [syp'til] subtle; fine, nice
(*distinction, point*); **subtiliser** [syp-
tili'ze] (1a) *v/t.* subtilize; F steal,
filch, pinch; *v/i.:* ~ *sur* subtilize on
(*a question*); **subtilité** [~'te] *f*
subtlety; *distinction:* fineness; ~s *pl.*
a. niceties.
suburbain, e [sybyr'bɛ̃, ~'bɛn] suburban.
subvenir [sybvə'niːr] (2h) *v/i.:* ~ *à*
provide for; **subvention** [sybvɑ̃'sjɔ̃]
f subsidy, subvention; **subvention-
nel, -elle** [~sjɔ'nɛl] subventionary;
subventionner [~sjɔ'ne] (1a) *v/t.*
subsidize.
subversif, -ve [sybvɛr'sif, ~'siːv]
subversive, destructive (of, *de*);
subversion [~'sjɔ̃] *f* subversion;
overthrow.
suc [syk] *m* juice; 💧 sap; *fig.* essence,
pith.
succédané, e [sykseda'ne] *adj., a.
su./m* substitute (for, *de*); **succéder**
[~'de] (1f) *v/i.:* ~ *à* succeed, follow;
replace; 🏛 come into (*a fortune*); ~ *au
trône* succeed to the throne.
succès [syk'sɛ] *m* success; hit; *à* ~
successful; *avec (sans)* ~ *a.* (un)suc-
cessfully.
successeur [syksɛ'sœːr] *m* successor
(to, of *de*); **successible** 🏛 [~'sibl]
entitled to inherit *or* succeed; **successif, -ve** [~'sif, ~'siːv] successive;
in succession; 🏛 ... of succession;
succession [~'sjɔ̃] *f* succession;
series; 🏛 inheritance; **successivement** [~siv'mɑ̃] *adv.* in succession; one after another, consec-
utively; **successoral, e,** *m/pl.* -**aux**
[~sɔ'ral, ~'ro] relating to a succession; death (*duties*).
succin [syk'sɛ̃] *m* yellow amber.

succinct, e [syk'sɛ̃, ~'sɛ̃:(k)t] succinct, concise, brief.

succion [syk'sjɔ̃] *f* suction; sucking (*of a wound*).

succomber [sykɔ̃'be] (1a) *v/i.* succumb (*fig.* to, *à*); *fig.* yield (to, *à*) (*grief, temptation, etc.*); be overcome; die.

succube [sy'kyb] *m* succubus.

succulence [syky'lɑ̃:s] *f* succulence; tasty morsel; **succulent, e** [~'lɑ̃, ~'lɑ̃:t] succulent (*food, morsel, a.* ♀, *a. fig. style*); tasty (*morsel*).

sucer [sy'se] (1k) *v/t.* suck; *fig. avec le lait* imbibe (*s.th.*) from infancy; **sucette** [~'sɛt] *f* ⊕ sucker; ♱ lollipop, F lolly; **suceur, -euse** [~'sœ:r, ~'sø:z] **1.** *adj.* sucking; *zo.* suctorial; **2.** *su.* sucker; *su./m* ⊕ vacuum cleaner: nozzle, sucker; *zo.* ~s *pl.* suctoria; **suçoir** *zo.* [~'swa:r] *m* organ: sucker; **suçon** F [~'sɔ̃] *m* barley-sugar stick; kiss-mark, mark left by sucking (*on the skin*); **suçoter** F [~sɔ'te] (1a) *v/t.* suck (at).

sucrage ⊕ [sy'kra:ʒ] *m* sugaring, sweetening; **sucrase** ♱, ♀ [~'kra:z] *f* invert sugar; **sucrate** ♱ [~'krat] *m* sucrate; **sucre** [sykr] *m* sugar; ~ *de betterave* beet sugar; ~ *de lait* lactose; ~ *de raisin* grape sugar; ~ *en morceaux* (*poudre*) lump (castor) sugar; **sucré, e** [sy'kre] **1.**adj. sweet; **2.** *su./f: faire la ~e* be all honey or sweetness; **sucrer** [~'kre] (1a) *v/t.* sugar, sweeten; *fig. a.* sugar-coat; *sl.* stop, cut; *se ~* help o.s. to sugar; *sl.* line one's pockets; **sucrerie** [~krə'ri] *f* sugar-refinery; ~s *pl.* confectionery *sg.*, sweets, *Am.* candies; **sucrier, -ère** [~kri'e, ~'ɛ:r] **1.** *adj.* sugar-...; **2.** *su.* sugar-refiner, sugar-boiler; *su./m* sugar-bowl, sugar-basin; **sucrin** [~'krɛ̃] *m* sugary melon.

sud [syd] **1.** *su./m* south; ⚓ south wind; *du ~* south(ern); *le* ♀ the south (*of a country*); *vers le ~* southward(s), to the south; **2.** *adj./inv.* southern (*latitudes*); southerly (*wind*).

sudation ♣ [syda'sjɔ̃] *f* sudation, sweating; **sudatoire** [~'twa:r] **1.** *adj.* sudatory; **2.** *su./m* hot-air bath; sweating-room.

sud-est [sy'dɛst] **1.** *su./m* south-east; **2.** *adj./inv.* south-east; south-eastern (*region*); south-easterly (*wind*).

sudiste *Am. hist.* [sy'dist] **1.** *su./m* southerner (*in Civil War*); **2.** *adj.* southern. [*su./m* sudorific.\
sudorifique ♣ [sydɔri'fik] *adj., a.)*

sud-ouest [sy'dwɛst] **1.** *su./m* south-west; **2.** *adj./inv.* south-west; south-western (*region*); south-westerly (*wind*).

suède ♱ [suɛd] *m*: *de* (or *en*) ~ suède (*gloves*); **suédois, e** [sue'dwa, ~'dwa:z] **1.** *adj.* Swedish; **2.** *su./m ling.* Swedish; *su.* ♀ Swede.

suée [sue] *f* F sweat(ing); *sl.* drag, pain; **suer** [~] (1n) *v/i.* sweat (*a. wall, a. fig.* = *toil*); perspire; F *faire ~ q.* get on s.o.'s nerves; bore s.o.; make s.o. sick; F *se faire ~* be bored, get cheesed off; *v/t.* sweat (*iron, a horse, etc.*); *fig.* reek of; *fig. ~ sang et eau* toil hard, F sweat blood; **suette** ♣ [suɛt] *f* fever; **sueur** [suœ:r] *f* sweat, perspiration.

suffi [sy'fi] *p.p.* of *suffire*; **suffire** [~'fi:r] (4i) *v/i.* suffice, be sufficient; *fig. ~ à* meet (*expenses*); *v/impers.*: *il suffit que* it is enough that; **suffisamment** [syfiza'mɑ̃] *adv.* sufficiently, enough; **suffisance** [~'zɑ̃:s] *f* sufficiency; *pej.* (self-)conceit, self-importance; *à* (or *en*) ~ in plenty; **suffisant, e** [~'zɑ̃, ~'zɑ̃:t] **1.** *adj.* sufficient, adequate; *pej.* conceited, self-important; **2.** *su.* conceited person; **suffisons** [~'zɔ̃] *1st p. pl. pres.* of *suffire*.

suffixe *gramm.* [sy'fiks] **1.** *su./m* suffix; **2.** *adj.* suffixed.

suffocant, e [syfɔ'kɑ̃, ~'kɑ̃:t] suffocating, stifling; **suffocation** [~ka'sjɔ̃] *f* suffocation, choking; **suffoquer** [~'ke] (1m) *v/t.* suffocate; choke; *v/i.* choke (with, de).

suffragant, e [syfra'gɑ̃, ~'gɑ̃:t] *adj., a. su./m* suffragan; **suffrage** [~'fra:ʒ] *m pol., a. eccl.* suffrage; *pol.* vote; franchise; *fig.* approbation, approval.

suffusion ♣ [syffy'zjɔ̃] *f* suffusion (*usu. of blood*); flush.

suggérer [sygʒe're] (1f) *v/t.* suggest; inspire; **suggestif, -ve** [~ʒes'tif, ~'ti:v] suggestive; **suggestion** [~ʒes'tjɔ̃] *f* suggestion.

suicidaire [suisi'dɛ:r] **1.** *adj.* suicidal; **suicide-prone,** with suicidal tendencies (*person*); **2.** *su.* person with suicidal tendencies; **suicide** [sɥi'sid] suicide; **suicidé** *m,* **e** *f* [sɥisi'de] *person:* suicide; **suicider** [~] (1a) *v/t.:* se ~ commit suicide.

suie [sɥi] *f* soot.

suif [sɥif] *m* tallow; *cuis.* (*mutton*) fat; *sl.* **suiffer** [sɥi'fe] (1a) *v/t.* tallow; grease; **suiffeux, -euse** [~'fø,~'fø:z] tallowy; greasy.

suint [sɥɛ̃] *m* ⊕ yolk, wool grease; glass gall; *laines f/pl.* en ~ greasy wool *sg.*; **suintant, e** [sɥɛ̃'tɑ̃, ~'tɑ̃:t] oozing; sweating; **suinter** [~'te] (1a) *v/i.* ooze, sweat; ⚓ leak; exude; *v/t. fig.* ooze (*hatred*).

suis¹ [sɥi] *1st p. sg. pres. of* être **1.**

suis² [~] *1st p. sg. pres. of suivre.*

suisse [sɥis] **1.** *adj.* Swiss; **2.** *su./m eccl.* beadle, (*approx.*) verger; *hotel:* porter; ♀ Swiss; *les* ♀s *pl.* the Swiss; *petit* ~ small cream cheese; **Suissesse** [sɥi'sɛs] *f* Swiss (woman).

suite [sɥit] *f* continuation; retinue, train, followers *pl.*; sequence, series; *fig.* result, consequence; sequel; *fig.* coherence; ✝ ~ *à* with reference to; ✗ *à la* ~ on pension; *à la* ~ *de* following (*s.th.*); in (*s.o.'s*) train; *de* ~ in succession, on end; ✝ at once; *donner* ~ *à* give effect to, carry out (*a decision*); ✝ carry out (*an order*); *et ainsi de* ~ and so on; *manquer* (*d'esprit*) *de* ~ lack method or coherence; *par la* ~ later on, eventually; *par* ~ therefore, consequently; *par* ~ *de* as a result of, because of; *tout de* ~ at once, immediately.

suitée [sɥi'te] *adj./f: jument f* ~ mare and foal; wild sow with her young.

suivant, e [sɥi'vɑ̃, ~'vɑ̃:t] **1.** *adj.* following, next; **2.** *su.* follower; *su./m* attendant, follower; *su./f* lady's-maid; *thea.* soubrette; **3.** *suivant prp.* following, along; *fig.* according to; ~ *que* according as; **suivi, e** [~'vi] **1.** *p.p. of suivre*; consistent; steady, regular; coherent (*speech, reasoning, story, etc.*); *très* (*peu*) ~ very popular (unpopular); (not) widely followed; well- (poorly) attended; **suivre** [sɥi:vr] (4ee) *v/t.* follow; take (*a course*); practise (*a profession*); succeed, come after; attend (*lectures etc.*); ~ *des yeux* look after (*s.o.*); ~ *la*

mode keep up with fashion; *v/i.* follow, come after; *à* ~ to be continued; *faire* ~ *post:* forward (*a letter*); (*prière de*) *faire* ~ please forward.

sujet, -ette [sy'ʒe, ~'ʒɛt] **1.** *adj.* subject (to, *à*); **2.** *su. pol.* subject; *su./m* subject (*a. gramm.*, *♪*, *a. fig.*); theme; (subject-)matter; reason (for, de); *fig.* individual, person; *à ce* ~ on this matter, about this; *au* ~ *de* about, concerning, with reference to (*a.* ✝); *mauvais* ~ *person:* bad lot; *school:* bad boy; **sujétion** [syʒe'sjɔ̃] *f* subjection; constraint.

sulfamide ⚕ [sylfa'mid] *f* sulpha drug, sulphonamide; **sulfate** 🜍 [~'fat] *m* sulphate; **sulfure** 🜍 [~'fy:r] *m* sulphide; **sulfurer** [sylfy're] (1a) *v/t.* sulphurate; treat (*vines*) with sulphide; **sulfureux, -euse** [~'rø, ~'rø:z] sulphureous; sulphurous; sulphur...; **sulfurique** 🜍 [~'rik] sulphuric (*acid*).

sultan [syl'tɑ̃] *m* sultan; scent sachet; **sultanat** [~ta'na] *m* sultanate; **sultane** [~'tan] *f* sultana.

super [sy'pɛ:r] **1.** *su./m* high-octane petrol *or* Am. gasoline, F super; **2.** *adj./inv.* F super, fantastic, great.

super... [sypɛr] super-...

superbe [sy'pɛrb] **1.** *adj.* superb; fine, magnificent; **2.** † *su./f* pride, vainglory.

super...: ~**carburant** *mot.* [sypɛr-karby'rɑ̃] *m* high-octane petrol *or* Am. gasoline, F super; ~**cherie** [~ʃə'ri] *f* swindle, fraud, deceit; ~**fétation** [~feta'sjɔ̃] *f physiol.* superfetation; *words etc.:* superfluity; ~**ficie** [~fi'si] *f* area; surface (*a. fig.*); ~**ficiel, -elle** [~fi'sjɛl] superficial (*a. fig.*); ~**fin, e** [~'fɛ̃, ~'fin] superfine; ~**flu, e** [~'fly] **1.** *adj.* superfluous; useless; **2.** *su./m* superfluity; ~**fluité** [~flɥi'te] *f* superfluity; *fig.* ~s *pl.* extras, F luxuries; ~**forteresse** ✈ [~fɔrtə'rɛs] *f* superfortress.

supérieur, e [sype'rjœ:r] **1.** *adj.* superior (*a. fig.*); upper, higher (*a. ♪, zo.*); ✝ of superior quality; ~ *à* superior to; above; **2.** *su.* superior; **supériorité** [~rjɔri'te] *f* superiority (*a. fig.*); *eccl.* superiorship; seniority (in age, *d'âge*).

super...: ~**latif, -ve** [sypɛrla'tif, ~'ti:v] **1.** *adj.* superlative; **2.** *su./m gramm.* superlative; *au* ~ *gramm.* in the superlative; *fig.* superlatively; ~**marché** ✝ [~marˈʃe] *m* supermarket; ~**posable** [~poˈzabl] super-(im)posable; ~**poser** [~poˈze] (1a) *v/t.* super(im)pose (on, *à*); ~**position** [~poziˈsjɔ̃] *f* superimposition; ₳ superposition; *cin.* double exposure; ~(-)**puissance** *pol.* [~pɥiˈsãːs] *f* superpower; ~**sonique** ☁️ [~sɔˈnik] supersonic; *bang m* ~ sonic boom *or* bang; ~**stitieux, -euse** [~stiˈsjø, ~ˈsjøːz] superstitious; ~**stition** [~stiˈsjɔ̃] *f* superstition; *fig.* mania, obsession; ~**structure** [~strykˈtyːr] *f* 🔺, ⚓ superstructure; 🚂 permanent way; ~**viser** [~viˈze] (1a) *v/t.* supervise, control; ~**vision** [~viˈzjɔ̃] *f* control, supervision.

supplanter [syplɑ̃ˈte] (1a) *v/t.* supplant, supersede.

suppléant, e [sypleˈɑ̃, ~ˈɑ̃ːt] **1.** *adj.* deputy ...; acting ...; **2.** *su.* deputy; supply teacher; 🚂 locum; ~*s pl. a.* temporary staff *sg.*; **suppléer** [~ˈe] (1a) *v/t.* supply; make up; complete; deputize for; replace, take the place of; *v/i.*: ~ *à* make up for; remedy; **supplément** [~ˈmɑ̃] *m* supplement (*a.* ₳, *a. book*); addition; extra charge, 🚂 excess (fare); *restaurant:* extra course; **supplémentaire** [~mɑ̃ˈtɛːr] extra, additional; supplementary; ₳ supplemental; ♪ leger (*line*); ⊕ *heures f/pl.* ~*s* overtime *sg.*; 🚂 *train m* ~ relief train; **supplétif, -ve** [~ˈtif, ~ˈtiːv] suppletive, suppletory; ⚔️ auxiliary.

suppliant, e [sypliˈɑ̃, ~ˈɑ̃ːt] **1.** *adj.* suppliant, pleading, imploring; **2.** *su.* suppli(c)ant; **supplication** [~kaˈsjɔ̃] *f* supplication, entreaty.

supplice [syˈplis] *m* torture; *fig. a.* agony, torment; ₰ *dernier* ~ capital punishment; *fig.* être au ~ be on tenterhooks; be agonized; **supplicier** [~pliˈsje] (1o) *v/t. a. fig.* torture; torment.

supplier [sypliˈe] (1a) *v/t.* beseech, implore, beg; **supplique** [syˈplik] *f* petition.

support [syˈpɔːr] *m* support (*a. fig.*); stand, pedestal; **supportable** [sypɔrˈtabl] tolerable, bearable; *fig.* fairly good, moderate; **supporter** [~ˈte] (1a) *v/t.* support; tolerate; withstand; bear, endure; put up with.

supposé, e [sypoˈze] supposed; es-

timated (*number etc.*); **supposer** [~ˈze] (1a) *v/t.* suppose; imply, presuppose; *à* ~ *que, en supposant que* supposing (that); **supposition** [~ziˈsjɔ̃] *f* supposition, surmise; ₰ *will:* forging, setting up (*of a supposititious child*); production of forged document(s), assumption (*of a false name*).

suppositoire ⚕️ [sypoziˈtwaːr] *m* suppository.

suppôt *fig.* [syˈpo] *m* tool, instrument; henchman; ~ *du Satan* (*or du diable*) hellhound.

suppression [sypreˈsjɔ̃] *f* suppression; ⚽ stoppage; *difficulty:* removal; ₰ ~ *d'enfant* concealment of birth; **supprimer** [sypriˈme] (1a) *v/t.* suppress; end; abolish; stop; cut out; do away with; *fig.* omit; *typ.* delete; ₰ conceal; F kill (*s.o.*); cancel (*a train etc.*).

suppurant, e ⚕️ [sypyˈrɑ̃, ~ˈrɑ̃ːt] suppurating; **suppuratif, -ve** ⚕️ [~raˈtif, ~ˈtiːv] *adj., a. su./m* suppurative; **suppuration** ⚕️ [~raˈsjɔ̃] *f* suppuration, running; **suppurer** [~ˈre] (1a) *v/i.* suppurate, run.

supputer [sypyˈte] (1a) *v/t.* calculate, reckon; work out (*expenses, interest*).

supra... [sypra] supra..., super...

suprématie [sypremaˈsi] *f* supremacy; **suprême** [~ˈprɛm] **1.** *adj.* supreme; highest; *fig.* last (*honours, hour, request*); **2.** *su./m cuis.* supreme.

sur[1] [syr] *prp. usu.* on (*a chair, the Thames, my word, my honour*); upon; *destination:* towards (*evening, old age*); *measurement:* by; *number:* out of; *succession:* after; *tomber* ~ hit upon; *donner* ~ *la rue* look on to the street; ~ *la droite* on *or* to the right; ~ *place* on the spot; *avoir de l'argent* ~ *soi* have money on *or* about one; ~ *ce* thereupon, and then; ~ *quoi* whereupon, and then; *un impôt* ~ a tax on; *travailler* ~ work on (*wood etc.*); *être* ~ *un travail* be at a task; *8* ~ *10* 8 out of 10; *measurement:* 8 by 10; *une fois* ~ *deux* every other time; *juger* ~ *les apparences* judge by appearances; *coup* ~ *coup* blow after blow; *revenir* ~ *ses pas* turn back; *fermer la porte* ~ *soi* close the door behind one; ~ *toute(s) chose(s)* above all; *lire qch.* ~ *le journal* read s.th. in the paper; ~ *un ton sévère* in a grave voice; *retenir* ~ keep (*s.th.*)

back out of; stop (*s.th.*) out of (*s.o.'s wages*); *autorité f* ~ authority over.

sur², **sure** [syːr] sour; tart.

sur... [syr] over-...; super...; supra...; sur...

sûr, **sûre** [syːr] sure (of, *de*); safe; reliable (*person*, ⊕, *information*, *a. weather*); *fig.* unerring; *fig.* certain, unfailing; ~ *de soi* self-confident; *à coup* ~ for certain, definitely; *bien* ~! certainly!; surely!, *Am.* sure!; F *pour* ~ of course.

surabondance [syrabɔ̃'dɑ̃ːs] *f* superabundance; ✝ glut; **surabondant**, **e** [~'dɑ̃, ~'dɑ̃ːt] superabundant; superfluous; **surabonder** [~'de] (1a) *v/i.* overflow (with *de*, *en*); ✝ be glutted (with *de*, *en*).

suraigu, **-guë** [syre'gy] highpitched, (very) shrill.

suranné, **e** [syra'ne] old-fashioned; superannuated; out of date.

surbaisser [syrbɛ'se] (1b) *v/t.* △ depress; *mot.* undersling.

surcharge [syr'ʃarʒ] *f* overload; extra *or* excess load; *fig.* extra work; ~ *de bagages* excess luggage (*Am.* baggage); *manuscript etc.*: alteration, correction; **surcharger** [~ʃar'ʒe] (1l) *v/t.* overload (*a.* ⚡), overburden; ⚡ overcharge (*an accumulator*); *post:* overprint (*a stamp*); *typ.* interline; write over (*other words in a line*); *fig.* overtax (*s.o.*).

surchauffe [syr'ʃof] *f* overheating; ⊕ superheat(ing); **surchauffer** [syrʃo'fe] (1a) *v/t.* overheat; superheat (*steam*); burn (*iron*).

surchoix [syr'ʃwa] *m* finest quality.

surclasser *sp.* [syrklɑ'se] (1a) *v/t.* outclass.

surcontrer [syrkɔ̃'tre] *v/t. cards:* redouble.

surcoupe [syr'kup] *f cards:* overtrumping; **surcouper** [~ku'pe] (1a) *v/t. cards:* overtrump.

surcroît [syr'krwa] *m* increase; *un* ~ *de qch.* an added s.th.; *par* ~ in addition.

surdi-mutité 𝕘 [syrdimyti'te] *f* deaf-and-dumbness; **surdité** 𝕘 [~'te] *f* deafness.

surdos [syr'do] *m horse:* back-band; *porter:* carrying-pad.

surdoué, **e** [syr'dwe] exceptionally gifted.

sureau 𝕘 [sy'ro] *m* elder.

surélever [syrel've] (1d) *v/t.* △, ✝

heighten, raise; ✝ put up, boost (*prices*); *road-building:* bank (*a road bend*).

surenchère [syrɑ̃'ʃɛːr] *f auction:* higher bid, outbidding; overbid; *fig.* exaggerated promises *pl.*; *fig. une* ~ *de violences* ever-increasing violence; **surenchérir** [~ʃe'riːr] (2a) *v/i.* rise higher in price; *auction:* bid higher; ~ *sur q.* outbid s.o.; *fig. a.* go one better than s.o.; **surenchérisseur** *m*, **-euse** *f* [~ʃeri'sœːr, ~'søːz] outbidder.

surentraînement *sp.* [syrɑ̃trɛn'mɑ̃] *m* over-training.

surestimer [syrɛsti'me] (1a) *v/t.* over-estimate; overrate (*s.o.*).

suret, **-ette** [sy'rɛ, ~'rɛt] sourish.

sûreté [syr'te] *f* safety; security (*a.* ✝); *fig. blow*, *foot*, *hand*, *stroke:* sureness; *judgment etc.:* soundness; *memory:* reliability; ~ *de soi* self-assurance; *de* ~ safety-...; *la* ♀ the Criminal Investigation Department, the C.I.D., *Am.* the Federal Bureau of Investigation, the F.B.I.

surexcitation [syrɛksita'sjɔ̃] *f* over-excitement; 𝕘 over-stimulation; **surexciter** [~'te] (1a) *v/t.* over-excite (*s.o.*); over-stimulate (*a.* 𝕘).

surexposer *phot.* [syrɛkspo'ze] (1a) *v/t.* over-expose.

surface [syr'fas] *f* surface; ⚓ surface area; area; ⚓ *faire* ~ surface (*submarine*).

surfaire [syr'fɛːr] (4r) *v/t.* overrate (*a book*, *a writer*); ✝ charge too much for.

surfer [sœr'fe] (1a) *v/i.* surf(ride); go surfing; **surfeur** *m*, **-euse** *f* [~'fœːr, ~'føːz] surfer, surfrider.

surgelé, **e** [syrʒə'le] deep-frozen; quick-frozen.

surgeon 𝕘 [syr'ʒɔ̃] *m* sucker; *pousser des* ~*s* sucker; **surgir** [~'ʒiːr] (2a) *v/i.* appear (suddenly); loom up; spring up; *fig.* arise.

surhausser [syro'se] (1a) *v/t.* △ raise; 🐎 cant; ✝ force up the price of.

surhomme [sy'rɔm] *m* superman; **surhumain**, **e** [~ry'mɛ̃, ~'mɛn] superhuman.

surimposer [syrɛ̃po'ze] (1a) *v/t.* superimpose; ✝ overtax, increase the tax on.

surimpression *phot.* [syrɛ̃prɛ'sjɔ̃] *f* double exposure.

surin sl. [syˈrɛ̃] m dagger, knife; **suriner** † sl. [ˌri'ne] (1a) v/t. knife (s.o.), murder (s.o.).

surintendant, e [syrɛ̃tãˈdã, ˌdãːt] su. superintendent, overseer; su./f superintendent's wife; lady-in-waiting in chief.

surir [syˈriːr] (2a) v/i. turn sour.

surjet [syrˈʒɛ] m seam: whipping; **surjeter** [ˌʒəˈte] (1c) v/t. whip (a seam).   [once, on the spot.)

sur-le-champ [syrləˈʃã] adv. at once, on the spot.

surlendemain [syrlãdˈmɛ̃] m day after the morrow, second day (after s.th., de qch.).

surmenage [syrməˈnaːʒ] m over-work(ing); **surmener** [ˌne] (1d) v/t. overwork; work (s.o.) too hard; override (a horse); ⊕, ∮ overrun.

surmontable [syrmɔ̃ˈtabl] sur-mountable; **surmonter** [ˌte] (1a) v/t. rise above (a. fig.); surmount (a building, a. fig. feelings, an obstacle); fig. overcome (an enemy, feelings); se ˌ control o.s.; surmonté de crowned by, surmounted by.

surnager [syrnaˈʒe] (1l) v/i. float on the surface; fig. linger (on).

surnaturel, -elle [syrnatyˈrɛl] **1.** adj. supernatural; fig. uncanny, extraordinary; **2.** su./m: le ˌ the supernatural.

surnom [syrˈnɔ̃] m nickname; appellation, name; hist. agnomen.

surnombre [syrˈnɔ̃ːbr] m excess number; ˌ des habitants overpopulation; en ˌ extra; supernumerary.

surnommer [syrnɔˈme] (1a) v/t. call (s.o. s.th., q. qch.); nickname.

surnuméraire [syrnymeˈrɛːr] adj., a. su./m supernumerary.

suroffre † [syˈrɔfr] f better offer.

suroît ⚓ [syˈrwa] m south-west; hat, a. wind: sou'wester.

surpasser [syrpɑˈse] (1a) v/t. surpass (a. fig.); be higher than; be taller than (a person); fig. exceed, outdo.

surpaye [syrˈpɛːj] f overpayment; bonus, extra pay; **surpayer** [ˌpɛ-ˈje] (1i) v/t. overpay (s.o.); pay too much for (s.th.).

surpeuplé, e [syrpœˈple] overpopulated (area); **surpeuplement** [ˌpləˈmã] m overpopulation.

sur(-)place [syrˈplas] m: faire du ˌ mark time.

surplis eccl. [syrˈpli] m surplice.

surplomb [syrˈplɔ̃] m overhang; en ˌ overhanging; **surplombement** [ˌplɔ̃bˈmã] m overhang(ing); **surplomber** [ˌplɔ̃ˈbe] (1a) vt/i. overhang; v/t. jut out over (s.th.).

surplus [syrˈply] m surplus, excess; remainder; au ˌ besides; moreover; en ˌ excess ..., surplus ...

surprenant, e [syrprəˈnã, ˌnãːt] surprising, astonishing, amazing; **surprendre** [ˌˈprãːdr] (4aa) v/t. surprise; astonish, amaze; come upon (s.o.); catch (s.o.) (unawares); pay (s.o.) a surprise visit; overhear (a conversation, a remark); intercept (a glance, a letter); ˌ la bonne foi de q. abuse s.o.'s good faith.

surprime † [syrˈprim] f insurance: extra premium.

surprise [syrˈpriːz] f surprise; ✗ surprise attack; fig. surprise-packet, lucky dip; par ˌ by surprise.

sur(-)prix [syrˈpri] m excessive price; overcharge.

surproduction [syrprɔdykˈsjɔ̃] f overproduction.

surrégénérateur phys. [syreʒenera'tœːr] m: (a. ˌ rapide) fast breeder.

sursalaire [syrsaˈlɛːr] m bonus; extra pay.

sursaturer ⚗ [syrsatyˈre] (1a) v/t. supersaturate.

sursaut [syrˈso] m start, jump; s'éveiller en ˌ wake with a start.

surseoir [syrˈswaːr] (3c) v/i.: 🕱 ˌ à stay (a judgment, proceedings), suspend (a judgment); defer, postpone; il a été sursis à qch. s.th. has been postponed; **sursis, e** [ˌˈsi, ˌˈsiːz] **1.** p.p. of surseoir; **2.** su./m 🕱 delay; suspension of sentence; ✗ call-up: deferment; **sursitaire** ✗ [ˌsiˈtɛːr] m deferred conscript.

surtaux [syrˈto] m over-assessment; **surtaxe** [syrˈtaks] f surtax; post: postage due, surcharge; admin. over-assessment; **surtaxer** [ˌtak-'se] (1a) v/t. surtax; post: surcharge (a letter); admin. over-assess, over-tax.

surtout¹ [syrˈtu] adv. above all; particularly, especially.

surtout² [ˌ] m dinner table: centre-piece; metall. mantle; light hand-cart; † overcoat.

surveillance [syrvɛˈjãːs] f super-

vision; ⊕ inspection; ✠ surveillance; *sous la ~ de la police* under
police supervision; **surveillant, e**
[~'jɑ̃, ~'jɑ̃:t] *su.* supervisor, overseer; 🕮 inspector; ✝ shop-walker,
Am. floorwalker; *examination*: in-
vigilator; *su./f* ✠ (*ward-)sister*;
surveille [syr've:j] *f*: *la ~ de* two
days before ...; **surveiller** [~ve'je]
(1a) *v/t.* supervise; superintend;
tend (*a machine*); ⊕ inspect, test;
examination: invigilate; *fig.* keep an
eye on, watch; ✠ *liberté f surveillée*
probation.
survenir [syrvə'ni:r] (2h) *v/i.* occur,
happen; take place; set in (*complications etc.*); arrive unexpectedly
(*person*).
survente ✝ [syr'vɑ̃:t] *f* overcharge.
survie [syr'vi] *f* survival; ✠ (presumption of) survivorship; ✝ expectation of life; **survivance** [~vi'vɑ̃:s]
f survival (*a. biol., a. fig.*); *estate*:
reversion; **survivant, e** [~vi'vɑ̃,
~'vɑ̃:t] 1. *adj.* surviving; 2. *su.* survivor; **survivre** [~'vi:vr] (4hh) *v/i.*:
~ à outlive, survive.
survol [syr'vɔl] *m* ✠ flight over; *cin.*
panning; **survoler** ✠ [~vɔ'le] (1a)
v/t. fly over.
survolté, e [syrvɔl'te] ⚡ boosted; *fig.*
(over)excited, worked up.
sus¹ [sy] *1st p. sg. p.s. of savoir 1.*
sus² [sy(s)] 1. *adv.*: *courir ~ à* rush at
(*s.o.*); *en ~ (de)* in addition (to); 2. *int.*
come on!; *~ à ...! at (s.o.)!*, away with
(*s.th.*)!
susceptibilité [syseptibili'te] *f* sus-
ceptibility, sensitiveness, touchi-
ness; **susceptible** [~'tibl] susceptible; sensitive, touchy; *~ de* capable
of; liable to.
susciter [sysi'te] (1a) *v/t.* cause,
give rise to; provoke, stir up (*a
rebellion*); en ~ (*envy*); raise up.
suscription [syskrip'sjɔ̃] *f letter*:
address.
susdit, e ✠ [sys'di, ~'dit] *adj., a.
su.* aforesaid, above-mentioned;
susmentionné, e ✠ [~mɑ̃sjɔ'ne]
see susdit.
susnommé, e ✠ [sysnɔ'me] *adj.,
a. su.* above-named, afore-named.
suspect, e [sys'pɛ, ~'pɛkt] 1. *adj.*
suspicious; suspect (*person*); *~ de*
suspected of; 2. *su.* suspect; **sus-
pecter** [~pɛk'te] (1a) *v/t.* suspect
(*s.o.*); doubt (*s.th.*).

suspendre [sys'pɑ̃:dr] (4a) *v/t.* suspend (*a. a judgment, payment*); hang
up; *fig.* defer; *fig.* interrupt; **suspendu, e** [~pɑ̃'dy] hanging (on,
from *à*); *mot. bien* (*mal*) *~* with a good
(poor) suspension (*car*); **suspens**
[~'pɑ̃] *m*: *en ~* in suspense (*a.* ✝);
outstanding (*question, a.* ✝ *bills*);
suspense [sys'pɛns] *m* suspense;
suspensif, -ve [syspɑ̃'sif, ~'si:v]
suspensive; *gramm.* points *m/pl.* *~s*
points of suspension; **suspension**
[~'sjɔ̃] *f* suspension; hanging (*a.* ✠);
(hanging) lamp; *mot.* springs *pl.*; *~
d'armes* truce; armistice; suspension
of hostilities; ⚓ *en ~* in suspension;
gramm. points *m/pl. de ~* points of
suspension; **suspensoir** [~'swa:r] *m*
suspensory bandage; jockstrap.
suspicion ✠ *etc.* [syspi'sjɔ̃] *f* suspicion; *en ~* suspected.
sustentateur, -trice ✠ [systɑ̃ta-
'tœ:r, ~'tris] lifting; main (*wing*);
sustentation [~ta'sjɔ̃] *f* † suste-
nance; ✠ lift(ing force); **sustenter**
[~'te] (1a) *v/t.*: F *se ~* take suste-
nance.
susurrer [sysy're] (1a) *vt/i.* whisper,
murmur.
suture [sy'ty:r] *f* ✠, *anat.* suture; ✠
wound: stitching; *fig. etc.* join.
suzerain, e [syz're, ~'rɛn] 1. *adj.*
paramount; 2. *su.* suzerain; **suzeraineté** [~rɛn'te] *f* lordship; suzerainty; ✠ suzerain (state).
svelte [svɛlt] slender, slim; **sveltesse** [svɛl'tɛs] *f* slenderness, slimness.
sweater *cost.* [swi'tœ:r] *m* sweater.
swing ♪, *a. box.* [swiŋ] *m* swing;
swinguer ♪ [swiŋ'ge] (1a) swing (*a.
fig.*).
sybaritique [sibari'tik] sybaritic;
voluptuary; **sybaritisme** [~'tism]
m sybaritism.
sycomore ♀ [sikɔ'mɔ:r] *m* sycamore.
sycophante [sikɔ'fɑ̃:t] *m* sycophant,
F toady.
syllabaire [silla'bɛ:r] *m* spelling
book; **syllabe** [~'lab] *f* syllable;
syllabique [~la'bik] syllabic.
sylphe [silf] *m*, **sylphide** [sil'fid] *f*
sylph; *taille f de sylphide* sylph-like
waist.
sylvain [sil'vɛ̃] *m* sylvan, silvan;
~s pl. genii of the woods; **sylvestre**
♀ [~'vɛstr] woodland (*tree*);
wood (*plant*), growing in the woods;
sylviculteur [silvikyl'tœ:r] *m* syl-

viculturist; **sylviculture** [ₓ'ty:r] *f* forestry, sylviculture.

symbiose [sē'bjo:z] *f* symbiosis.

symbole [sē'bɔl] *m* symbol; emblem; *eccl.* ♀ creed; **symbolique** [sēbɔ'lik] symbolic(al); **symboliser** [ₓli'ze] (1a) *v/t.* symbolize; **symbolisme** [ₓ'lism] *m* symbolism; **symboliste** [ₓ'list] **1.** *adj.* symbolistic; **2.** *su.* symbolist.

symétrie [sime'tri] *f* symmetry; *sans* ~ unsymmetrical; **symétrique** [ₓ'trik] symmetrical.

sympa F [sē'pa] *adj./inv.* nice, likable; **sympathie** [sēpa'ti] *f* sympathy (*a.* ♣, *physiol.*); *fig.* liking, congeniality; **sympathique** [ₓ'tik] sympathetic (*a.* ♣, *physiol.*); nice, likable (*person*); attractive; *fig.* congenial (*task*, *work*); invisible (*ink*); *il m'est* ~ I like him, I take to him; **sympathisant, e** [ₓti'zɑ̃, ₓ'zɑ̃:t] **1.** *adj.* sympathizing; **2.** *su./m pol.* fellow-traveller; sympathizer; **sympathiser** [ₓti'ze] (1a) *v/i. fig.* blend, harmonize, go together; sympathize (with, *avec*).

symphonie ♪ [sēfɔ'ni] *f* symphony; **symphoniste** ♪ [ₓ'nist] *m* composer of symphonies; orchestral player.

symposium [sēpɔ'zjɔm] *m* symposium.

symptôme [sēp'to:m] *m* ♣, *a. fig.* symptom; *fig.* sign.

syn... [*before vowel* sin...; *before consonant* sē...] syn...; **ₓchronique** [sēkrɔ'nik] synchronological; synchronistic; **ₓchronisateur** *mot.* [ₓniza'tœ:r] *m* synchromesh (device); **ₓchronisation** [ₓniza'sjɔ̃] *f* synchronization; **ₓchroniser** [ₓni'ze] (1a) *v/t.* synchronize (*a. cin.*); *ᵬ* parallel; **ₓchronisme** [ₓ'nism] *m* synchronism; *ᵬ*, *phys.* step; synchrony (*a. cin.*); **ₓcope** [sē'kɔp] *f* ♣, *gramm.* syncope; ♣ fainting fit, blackout; ♪ syncopation; ♪ syncopated note; **ₓcoper** [ₓkɔ'pe] (1a) *v/t.* ♪, *gramm.* syncopate.

syndic [sē'dik] *m* managing agent; ♣♣ receiver; **syndical, e** *m/pl.* **-aux** [sēdi'kal, ₓ'ko] trade-union (*movement*); **†** *chambre f* ₓₑ (*approx.*) Stock Exchange Committee; **syndicali-**

sation [ₓkaliza'sjɔ̃] *f* unionization; **syndicaliser** [ₓkali'ze] (1a) *v/t.* unionize; **syndicalisme** [ₓka'lism] *m* trade unionism; **syndicaliste** [ₓka'list] *su.* trade unionist; **syndicat** [ₓ'ka] *m* trade union; syndicate, association; receivership, trusteeship (*in bankruptcy*); ~ *d'initiative* tourist information bureau; **syndiqué, e** [ₓ'ke] **1.** *adj.* associated; belonging to a (trade) union; union-...; **2.** *su.* trade unionist; union member; **syndiquer** [ₓ'ke] (1m) *v/t.* unionize; form (*men*) into a trade union; *se* ~ combine; form a syndicate *or* trade-union.

syndrome [sē'drɔm] *m* syndrome.

synodal, e, *m/pl.* **-aux** [sinɔ'dal, ₓ'do] synodical; synodal (*examiner*); **synode** *eccl.* [ₓ'nɔd] *m* synod; **synodique** [ₓnɔ'dik] synodic(al).

synonyme [sinɔ'nim] **1.** *adj.* synonymous (with, *de*); **2.** *su./m* synonym; **synonymie** [ₓni'mi] *f* synonymity; **synonymique** [ₓni'mik] **1.** *adj.* synonymic; **2.** *su./f* synonymy, synonymics *sg.*

synoptique [sinɔp'tik] synoptic.

syntaxe *gramm.* [sē'taks] *f* syntax; **syntaxique** *gramm.* [ₓtak'sik] syntactic(al).

synthèse [sē'tɛ:z] *f* synthesis; **synthétique** [sēte'tik] synthetic; **synthétiser** [ₓti'ze] (1a) *v/t.* synthesize.

syntonisation [sētɔniza'sjɔ̃] *f radio:* tuning; *bobine f de* ~ tuning-coil; **syntoniser** [ₓ'ze] (1a) *v/t. radio:* tune in.

syphilis ♣ [sifi'lis] *f* syphilis.

syrien, -enne [si'rjɛ̃, ₓ'rjɛn] *adj., a. su.* ♀ Syrian.

systématique [sistema'tik] systematic; methodical; *fig.* hide-bound; **systématiser** [ₓti'ze] (1a) *v/t.* systematize; **système** [sis'tɛm] *m* system; *phot.* (*back*, *front*) lens; *fig.* device; ⊕ *etc.* set; F ~ *D* resourcefulness; wangling; ♀ *décimal* (*métrique*) decimal (metric) system; *anat.* ~ *nerveux* nervous system; *fig. esprit m de* ~ pigheadedness; **systémique** [ₓte'mik] systemic.

systole ♣ [sis'tɔl] *f* systole.

T

T, t [te] *m* T, t; ⊕ *fer m en T* T-iron; tee; ⊕ *poutre f en double T* I-section, H-beam.

ta [ta] *see* ton¹.

tabac [ta'ba] **1.** *su./m* ♀, *a.* ✝ tobacco; ∼ *à chiquer* chewing tobacco; ∼ *à fumer* (smoking) tobacco; ∼ *à priser* snuff; ⌀s *pl.* (State) Tobacco Department *sg.*; *bureau m* (*or débit m*) *de* ∼ tobacconist's (shop); *sl. faire un* ∼ be a hit; F *passer* (*q.*) *à* ∼ *see* tabasser; *prendre du* ∼ take snuff; **2.** *adj./inv.* snuff-colo(u)red; **tabagie** [taba'ʒi] *f* ✝ smoking-room; place smelling of stale tobacco-smoke; **tabagisme** [∼'ʒism] *m* nicotine-poisoning; **tabasser** F [∼'se] (1a) *v/t.* handle (*s.o.*) roughly, beat (*s.o.*) up; **tabatière** [∼'tjɛːr] *f* snuff-box.

tabernacle [tabɛr'nakl] *m* tabernacle.

table [tabl] *f* table; *stone:* slab, tablet; *teleph.* switchboard; index; ∼ *à rallonges* extending table; ⅍ ∼ *de multiplication* multiplication table; ∼ *des matières* table of contents; ♪ ∼ *d'harmonie violin:* belly; ∼ *d'hôte* set dinner, table d'hôte; *pol. etc.* ∼ *ronde* round table conference; *à* ∼! dinner is served!; *mettre la* ∼ lay the table; *sainte* ∼ Lord's table, altar; *se mettre à* ∼ sit down at table; *sl.* talk, come clean; **tableau** [ta'blo] *m paint. etc.* picture, painting; *thea.* tableau; *thea. a. fig.* scene; view; *notices, a. ♂, sp.:* board; *hotel:* key-board; (∼ *noir*) blackboard; list, table; ♂, *a.* ⚖ jurors: panel; ⚖ solicitors: roll, *barristers:* list; *typ.* table; 🚂 train indicator; *fig.* description; ∼ *d'annonces* notice-board, *Am.* bulletin-board; ∼ *de bord mot.* dashboard; ✈ instrument panel; ⚡ ∼ *de distribution* switchboard; *mot.* ∼ *de graissage* lubrication chart; F *au* ∼ in the bag; **tableautin** [∼blo'tɛ̃] *m* small picture; **tablée** [∼'ble] *f* (tableful of) guests *pl.*; **tabler** [∼'ble] (1a) *v/i.:* ∼ *sur* count on.

tabletier ✝ [tablə'tje] *m* dealer in *or* maker of fancy articles and inlaid work; **tablette** [∼'blɛt] *f* shelf; *stone:* slab; (window-)sill; *sideboard etc.:* (flat) top; *joist:* bearing surface; ♀ plate; ♂ lozenge; *chocolate:* bar; ∼ *de cheminée* mantelpiece; *rayez ça de vos* ∼s! you can forget that!; don't count on that!; **tabletterie** [∼blɛt'tri] *f* fancy-goods *pl.* (industry); inlaid work.

tablier [tabli'e] *m* apron, *child:* pinafore; *bridge:* road(way); ⊕ *etc.* shutter; *fig. rendre son* ∼ resign; give notice.

tabou, e [ta'bu] **1.** *adj.* taboo; forbidden; **2.** *su./m* taboo.

tabouret [tabu'rɛ] *m* (foot)stool.

tabulaire [taby'lɛːr] *tabular;* **tabulateur** [∼la'tœːr] *m* tabulator; **tabulatrice** [∼la'tris] *f machine:* tabulator.

tac [tak] *m mill:* clack; *sword-blades:* click; *riposter du* ∼ *au* ∼ *fencing:* parry with the riposte; *fig.* give tit for tat.

tache [taʃ] *f* stain (*a. fig.*), spot; mark; ink, *a. fig.:* blot; *colour:* blob, patch; *fig.* blemish; *fruit:* bruise; ∼ *de naissance* birthmark; ∼ *de rousseur face etc.:* freckle; ∼ *de suie* smut; *fig. faire* ∼ jar, be out of place.

tâche [taːʃ] *f* task, job; *ouvrier m à la* ∼ jobbing workman; piece-worker; *prendre à* ∼ *de* (*inf.*) undertake to (*inf.*), make a point of (*ger.*); *travailler à la* ∼ do piece-work.

tacher [ta'ʃe] (1a) *v/t.* stain (*a. fig.*), spot; *fig.* tarnish (*s.o.'s reputation*); *se* ∼ get one's clothes stained; stain, spot (*cloth*).

tâcher [ta'ʃe] (1a) *v/i.* try (to *inf.*, *de inf.*); labo(u)r, toil (at, *à*); ∼ (*à ce*) *que* (*sbj.*) try to (*inf.*); **tâcheron** [taʃ'rɔ̃] *m* jobbing workman; △ sub-contractor, jobber.

tacheter [taʃ'te] (1c) *v/t.* fleck, mottle speckle.

tachy... [taki] tachy...; tacho...; ∼**mètre** ⊕ [∼'mɛtr] *m* speedometer, tachometer.

tacite [ta'sit] tacit; implied; **taciturne** [⌣si'tyrn] taciturn; reserved; close-mouthed.

tacot F [ta'ko] *m mot.* old rattletrap, banger, crate.

tact [takt] *m* (sense of) touch; *fig.* tact; *manque m de* ⌣ tactlessness.

tacticien ✕ *etc.* [takti'sjɛ̃] *m* tactician.

tactile [tak'til] tactile.

tactique [tak'tik] **1.** *adj.* tactical; **2.** *su./f* ✕, *a. fig.* tactics *pl.*

taffetas *tex.* [taf'ta] *m* taffeta.

taie [tɛ] *f* (pillow-)case, slip; ✍ albugo, white speck (*on the eye*).

taillade [ta'jad] *f* slash, gash, cut; **taillader** [⌣ja'de] (1a) *v/t.* slash (*a. cost., a. fig.*); **taillage** [⌣'ja:ʒ] *m file, gear*: cutting; **taillant** [⌣'jɑ̃] *m blade, tool*: (cutting) edge; **taille** [tɑ:j] *f* cutting; ✍ *plant*: pruning; *hedge*: clipping; *stone*: hewing; *hair, tool, clothes*: cut; *blade*: edge; *fig.* size, dimensions *pl.*; *person*: height, stature; waist, figure; waist(line); *cost. à* ⌣ *haute* (*basse*) high-waisted (low-waisted); F *de* ⌣ big; *grandes* ⌣*s pl.* outsizes; *par rang de* ⌣ in order of size *or* height; *être de* ⌣ *à* (*inf.*) be capable of (*ger.*); **taille-crayon** [tajkrɛ'jɔ̃] *m/inv.* pencil sharpener; **taille-douce**, *pl.* **tailles-douces** [⌣'dus] *f* copperplate (engraving); **tailler** [tɑ'je] (1a) *v/t.* cut (*gem, hair, lawn, stone*); hew (*a stone*); trim (*one's beard*); ✍ prune (*a plant*), clip (*a hedge*); ⊕ mill (*gears*); sharpen (*a pencil*); carve (*in a rock etc., a. fig. a way*); hew (*the enemy to pieces*); *bien taillé* well set-up (*person*); *cost.* well-cut; *v/i. cards*: deal; **taillerie** [taj'ri] *f* gem-cutting; gem-cutter's workshop; **tailleur** [tɑ'jœ:r] *m* ⊕ cutter; *cost.* tailor; *gaming*: banker; *cost.* (*a. costume m* ⌣) tailor-made costume; ⌣-*pantalon m* trouser suit, pant(s) suit; **taillis** [⌣'ji] *m* copse; brushwood; **tailloir** [taj'wa:r] *m* trencher; ◬ abacus.

tain ⊕ [tɛ̃] *m mirrors*: silvering; *iron*: tin-bath; foil.

taire [tɛ:r] (4z) *v/t.* suppress, hush (*s.th.*) up, say nothing about, not to mention (*s.th.*); *faire* ⌣ silence, hush; *se* ⌣ be silent, say nothing; stop talking; *taisez-vous!* be quiet!; **taisons** [tɛ'zɔ̃] *1st p. pl. pres. of taire*; **tait** [tɛ] *3rd p. sg. pres. of taire.*

talc *min.* [talk] *m* talc; French chalk; talcum powder; **talcique** [tal'sik] talcose.

talent [ta'lɑ̃] *m* talent (*fig., a. ancient weight*); aptitude; *de* ⌣ talented, gifted; **talentueux, -euse** F [⌣lɑ̃-'tɥø, ⌣'tɥø:z] talented.

talion [ta'ljɔ̃] *m* retaliation.

talisman [talis'mɑ̃] *m* talisman.

talle ✍ [tal] *f* sucker; *wheat etc.*: tiller; **taller** ✍ [ta'le] (1a) *v/i.* throw out suckers; tiller (*wheat*).

taloche [ta'lɔʃ] *f* ⊕ (*plasterer's*) hawk; F cuff, clout; **talocher** F [⌣lɔ'ʃe] (1a) *v/t.* cuff, clout.

talon [ta'lɔ̃] *m foot, shoe,* ⚓ rudder, ⊕ *tool, rifle, mast, a.* ♪ *violin bow*: heel; spur; ⊕ catch; clip; *mot. tyre*: bead(ing); ⊕ *axle, bayonet*: shoulder; *axle*: flange; *loaf*: end; *bread, cheese*: remnant; *cards etc.*: stock, pile; ⚜ counterfoil, stub; ⌣ ⌣*s pl. aiguille* stiletto heels; *tourner les* ⌣*s* take to one's heels; **talonner** [talɔ'ne] (1a) *v/t.* follow (on the heels of); dog (*s.o.*); spur on, urge on (*a horse, a. fig. a person*); dun (*s.o.*); *v/i.* ⚓ touch; strike; **talonnette** [⌣'nɛt] *f* heel.

talqueux, -euse *min.* [tal'kø, ⌣'kø:z] talcose.

talus [ta'ly] *m* slope; bank, embankment; *en* ⌣ sloping.

talweg *geol.* [tal'vɛg] *m* thalweg.

tamanoir *zo.* [tama'nwa:r] *m* great ant-eater.

tamarin ♀ [tama'rɛ̃] *m* tamarind; tamarind-tree; **tamarinier** ♀ [⌣ri-'nje] *m* tamarind-tree.

tambouille *sl.* [tɑ̃'bu:j] *f* kitchen (staff); cooking.

tambour [tɑ̃'bu:r] *m* ♪, ✕, ✕, ⊕ *oil,* ⚡ *cable, mot. brake,* ◬ *column*: drum; *person*: drummer; ⚡ *coil*: cylinder; ◬ *hotel etc.*: revolving door; *embroidery*: frame; ♪ ⌣ *de basque* tambourine (*with jingles*); ⌣ *de ville* town-crier; *fig. mener q.* ⌣ *battant* treat s.o. with a high hand; *sans* ⌣ *ni trompette* quietly, on the quiet; **tambourin** [tɑ̃bu'rɛ̃] *m* ♪ tambourine (*without jingles*); (*Provençal*) long, narrow drum; *ball-games*: tambourine-like racquet; **tambouriner** [⌣ri'ne] (1a) *vt/i.* drum (*a. fig.*).

tamis [ta'mi] *m* sieve; *liquids*: strainer; ⊕ screen; *cinders etc.*:

riddle; *flour:* bolter; *passer au* ~
sift (*a. fig.*); **tamiser** [tami'ze] (1a)
v/t. sift, sieve; strain; filter (*air,
light, a. liquid*); bolt (*flour*); *fig.*
soften (*the light*); *lumière tamisée*
subdued *or* soft(ened) light; **tamiseur** *m,* **-euse** *f* [~'zœːr, ~'zøːz]
person: sifter, screener; strainer.

tampon [tɑ̃'pɔ̃] *m* △ *wall,* ♠, *bath,
wash-basin, cask, metall:* plug;
inking, polishing, a. ♠ *cotton-wool:*
pad; *paper, cotton-wool, etc.:* wad;
rubber stamp; 🚂 (*a.* ~ *de choc*)
buffer; ~ *buvard* hand-blotter; ~ *encreur* inking pad, stamp pad; *coup m*
de ~ collision; F *fig.* thump; *pol. Etat
m* ~ buffer State; **tamponnement**
[~pɔn'mɑ̃] *m* 🚂, *mot.* collision; dab-
bing (*with a pad*); F thumping; **tamponner** [~pɔ'ne] (1a) *v/t.* mop, dab
(*with a handkerchief, a pad, etc.*); 🚂
etc. collide with; *mot.* bump into;
stamp (*a letter etc.*); ⊕ plug.

tam-tam [tam'tam] *m* ♪ tom-tom; ♪
(*Chinese*) gong; *fig.* fuss, to-do.

tan [tɑ̃] *m* tanner's bark.

tancer [tɑ̃'se] (1k) *v/t.* scold, F tell
(*s.o.*) off.

tanche *icht.* [tɑ̃ːʃ] *f* tench.

tandem [tɑ̃'dɛm] *m* tandem (bicycle); *fig.* twosome, pair, couple; *fig.*
partnership; *fig.* combination; *en* ~
tandem; *fig.* together.

tandis [tɑ̃'di] *cj.:* ~ *que* whereas
(*emphasizing difference*); while.

tangage ⚓, ✈ [tɑ̃'gaːʒ] *m* pitch
(-ing).

tangent, e [tɑ̃'ʒɑ̃, ~'ʒɑ̃ːt] 1. *adj.* ⋀
tangent(ial) (*to,* à); 2. *su./f* ⋀ tangent; F *prendre la* ~*e, s'échapper par la*
~*e* make off; dodge the issue; wriggle
out; **tangenter** [~ʒɑ̃'te] (1a) *v/t.* run
along(side), border, skirt; **tangible**
[~'ʒibl] tangible.

tanguer ⚓, ✈ [tɑ̃'ge] (1m) *v/i.*
pitch, rock; be down by the head.

tanière [ta'njɛːr] *f* den, lair (*a. fig.*);
(*fox-*)hole, earth.

tank ✕ [tɑ̃ːk] *m* tank; **tankiste** ✕
[tɑ̃'kist] *m* member of a tank crew.

tannant, e [ta'nɑ̃, ~'nɑ̃ːt] tanning;
F tiresome; boring.

tanne [tan] *f* ♠ *face:* blackhead; ⊕
leather: spot.

tanné, e [ta'ne] 1. *adj.* tan(ned); 2.
su./m colour: tan; **tanner** [~] (1a) *v/t.*
⊕ tan; F irritate; pester; F thrash
(*s.o.*); F ~ *le cuir à q.* tan s.o.'s hide;

tannerie ⊕ [tan'ri] *f* tannery; *trade:*
tanning; **tanneur** ⊕ [ta'nœːr] *m*
tanner; **tan(n)in** [~'nɛ̃] *m* tannin;
tan(n)iser ⊕ [~ni'ze] (1a) *v/t.* treat
(*s.th.*) with tannin.

tan-sad [tɑ̃'sad] *m* pillion.

tant [tɑ̃] *adv.* so much; so *or* as
many; so; as much, as hard (as,
que); so *or* as long (as, *que*); ~ *bien
que mal* somehow (or other); ~ *de
fois* so often; ~ *heureuse qu'elle pa-
raisse* however happy she may
seem; ~ *il y a que* the fact remains,
however, that; ~ *mieux!* so much
the better!; F *good!*; ~ *pis!* so much
the worse!; what a pity!; F too bad!;
~ *s'en faut* far from it; ~ *s'en faut
que* (*sbj.*) far from (*ger.*); ~ *soit peu*
ever so little; even a little; somewhat; *en* ~ *que* in so far as (+ *verb*);
considered as (+ *su.*); *si* ~ *est que*
if indeed.

tante [tɑ̃ːt] *f* aunt; *sl.* queer, nancy-
boy; F *chez ma* ~ pawned, in pawn.

tantième ♦ [tɑ̃'tjɛm] *m* percentage,
share.

tantinet F [tɑ̃ti'ne] *m:* *un* ~ a little,
a bit.

tantôt [tɑ̃'to] 1. *adv.* presently,
soon, by and by; a little while ago,
just now; ~ ... ~ ... now ... now ...,
sometimes ... sometimes ...; *à* ~*!*
good-bye for the present!; F so
long!; 2. *su./m* F afternoon.

taon *zo.* [tɑ̃] *m* gad-fly, horse-fly.

tapage [ta'paːʒ] *m* noise; din; *fig.*
row; fuss; F touching (*s.o. for
money*); *faire du* ~ make a stir
(*news*); **tapageur, -euse** [~pa'ʒœːr,
~'ʒøːz] 1. *adj.* noisy, rowdy; *cost.*
flashy; *fig.* blustering (*manner,
speech*); 2. *su.* rowdy, roisterer;
brawler; noisy person; ⚖ disturber
of the peace; **tape** [tap] *f* slap; F †
ramasser une ~ fail, F flop; **tapé, e**
[ta'pe] 1. *adj.* dried (*fruit*); *fig.* first-
class; *sl.* crazy, nutty; *réponse f* ~*e*
smart answer; 2. *su./f*F lots *pl.,* heaps
pl.; tons *pl.;* children: horde; **tape-
à-l'œil** F [tapa'lœj] 1. *adj.* showy,
flashy; 2. *su./m* show, window-
dressing; **tapecul** [tap'ky] *m* seesaw, *Am.* teeter-totter; gig; *pej. carriage:* rattletrap; **taper** [ta'pe] (1a)
v/t. plug, stop (up); F smack, slap;
slam (*the door*); ♪ thump out (*a tune*),
beat (*a drum*); type (*a letter etc.*); dab
on (*paint*); F touch (*s.o.*) (for, *de*); *sl.*

se ~ qch. put s.th. away (= *eat, drink*); do s.th.; saddle o.s. with s.th.; *sl. tu peux te ~!* nothing doing!; *sl.* you've had it!; *v/i.* knock; hit; bang; ~ *dans l'œil à* take (*s.o.'s*) fancy; ~ *du pied* stamp (one's foot); ~ *sur q.* slate s.o., pitch into s.o.; F ~ *sur le ventre à q.* give s.o. a dig in the waistcoat; **tapette** [~'pɛt] f gentle tap; ⊕ bat (*for corking bottles*); fly-swatter; carpet-beater; F chatter-box; *sl.* queer, fairy, nancy-boy; F *avoir une de ces ~s* (*or une fière ~*) be a real chatterbox; **tapeur** [~'pœːr] m cadger; piano strummer.

tapinois [tapi'nwa] *adv.*: *en ~* quietly, on the sly.

tapioca [tapjɔ'ka] m tapioca; *cuis.* tapioca soup.

tapir[1] [ta'piːr] (2a) *v/t.*: *se ~* crouch; hide (o.s. away); *être tapi* crouch; hide, be hidden; *fig.* lurk.

tapir[2] *zo.* [~] m tapir.

tapis [ta'pi] m carpet; cloth; ⚡ ~ *chauffant* electrically heated mat; ⊕ ~ *roulant* endless belt, assembly line; ~ *vert* (gaming) table; *fig. mettre sur le ~* bring (*s.th.*) up (for discussion); **tapisser** [~pi'se] (1a) *v/t.* paper (*a room*); hang (*a wall*) with tapestry; *fig.* cover, line; **tapisserie** [~pis'ri] f tapestry, hangings *pl.*; tapestry-weaving; tapestry-work; wall-paper; *fig. faire ~* be a wall-flower (*at a dance*); *pantoufles f/pl. en ~* carpet-slippers; **tapissier, -ère** [~pi'sje, ~'sjɛːr] *su.* tapestry-maker; *furniture*: upholsterer; crewel-worker; *su./f* delivery-van; covered waggon.

tapon † [ta'pɔ̃] m plug, stopper; *en ~* screwed up.

tapoter F [tapɔ'te] (1a) *v/t.* tap; pat; strum (*a tune*); drum (*on the table*).

taquer *typ.* [ta'ke] (1m) *v/t.* plane (down); **taquet** [~'kɛ] m ⊕ wedge, angle-block; *metall.* lug; ⚓ cleat.

taquin, e [ta'kɛ̃, ~'kin] **1.** *adj.* (fond of) teasing; **2.** *su.* tease; **taquiner** [~ki'ne] (1a) *v/t.* tease; *fig.* worry; **taquinerie** [~kin'ri] f teasing (disposition).

tarabiscoté, e [tarabiskɔ'te] ⊕ grooved; *fig.* over-elaborate (*style*).

tarabuster F [tarabys'te] (1a) *v/t.* pester (*person*); worry, bother (*thing, idea, etc.*).   [tare.]

tarage ✝ [ta'raːʒ] m allowance for⟩

tarare ✓ [ta'raːr] m winnower.

taratata! F [tarata'ta] *int.* fiddle-sticks!

taraud ⊕ [ta'ro] m (screw-)tap; **taraudage** ⊕ [taro'daːʒ] m nut etc.: tapping; screw-cutting; screw-pitch; **tarauder** [~'de] (1a) *v/t.* ⊕ tap, cut; *a. fig.* pierce; **taraudeuse** ⊕ [~'døːz] f machine: screw-cutter, thread-cutter.

tard [taːr] **1.** *adv.* late; *au plus ~* at the latest; *il se fait ~* it is getting late; *pas plus ~ que ... only ..., not later than ...*; *tôt ou ~* sooner or later; **2.** *su./m*: *sur le ~* late in the day; *fig.* late in life; **tarder** [tar'de] (1a) *v/i.* delay; *il me tarde de* (*inf.*) I am anxious to (*inf.*); *ne pas ~ à* (*inf.*) not to have to wait long before (*ger.*); *sans* (*plus*) *~* without (further) delay; **tardif, -ve** [~'dif, ~'diːv] late; belated (*apology, regret*); *fig.* slow (to, *à*); backward (*fruit, a. fig. intelligence*); **tardigrade** *zo.* [~di'grad] *adj., a. su./m* tardigrade; **tardillon** [~di'jɔ̃] m animal: latest born; *fig.* Benjamin (*of a family*); **tardiveté** [~div'te] f lateness; slowness; backwardness.

tare [taːr] f ✝ tare; *fig.* defect, flaw, taint; ✝ *faire la ~* allow for the tare; **taré, e** [ta're] spoiled, damaged; *with a defect; a. fig.* tainted; *fig.* corrupt.

tarantelle ♪ *etc.* [tarɑ̃'tɛl] f tarantella.

tarentule *zo.* [tarɑ̃'tyl] f tarantula; *fig. être piqué* (*or mordu*) *de la ~* be very excited.

tarer ✝ [ta're] (1a) *v/t.* tare.

targette ⊕ [tar'ʒɛt] f sash-bolt; flat door-bolt.

targuer [tar'ge] (1m) *v/t.*: *se ~ de* pride o.s. on (s.th., *qch.*; doing, *faire*); claim (*a privilege*).

tarière ⊕ [ta'rjɛːr] f auger; drill; 🪚 borer.

tarif [ta'rif] m price-list, tariff; rate(s *pl.*); schedule of charges; ~ *différentiel* (*préférentiel*) differential (preferential) tariff; ~ *postal* postage (rates *pl.*); ~ *réduit* reduced tariff; *plein ~ goods*: full tariff; *person*: full fare; **tarifaire** [tari'fɛːr] tariff-...; **tarifer** [~'fe] (1a) *v/t.* fix the rate of (*a duty, a tariff*); fix the price of (*goods*); **tarification** [~fika'sjɔ̃] f tariffing.

tarin sl. [ta'rɛ̃] m conk (= nose).

tarir [ta'riːr] (2a) v/t. dry up; fig. exhaust; v/i. a. se ~ dry up, run dry; fig. cease; **tarissement** [~ris-'mɑ̃] m drying up; fig. exhausting.

tarot [ta'ro] m cards: tarot pack; ~s pl. cards, game: tarots.

tarse anat. [tars] m tarsus; F human foot: instep; **tarsien, -enne** anat. [tar'sjɛ̃, ~'sjɛn] tarsal.

tartan tex. [tar'tɑ̃] m tartan.

tartarinade F [tartari'nad] f boast.

tarte cuis. [tart] f (open) tart; flan; **tartelette** cuis. [~'lɛt] f tartlet; **tartine** [tar'tin] f slice of bread and butter or jam etc.; F fig. rigmarole; long-winded speech or article or sermon; **tartiner** [~ti'ne] (1a) v/t. spread (bread) (with, de); butter (bread); spread (butter etc.) (on, sur); fromage m à ~ cheese spread.

tartrate 🜍 [tar'trat] m tartrate; **tartre** [tartr] m tartar (a. 🜍, a. dental); ⊕ boiler: scale, fur; **tartreux, -euse** [tar'trø, ~'trøːz] tartarous; ⊕ furry, scaly; **tartrique** 🜍 [~'trik] tartaric (acid).

tartufe [tar'tyf] m hypocrite; **tartuferie** [~ty'fri] f (piece of) hypocrisy, cant.

tas [tɑ] m heap, pile (a. fig. of things); fig. crowd, lot; lies, a. people: pack; ⊕ hand or small anvil; mettre en ~ pile up; sur le ~ on the job, at work.

tasse [tɑːs] f cup; ~ à café coffee-cup; ~ de café cup of coffee.

tasseau [tɑ'so] m ⟁ bracket; (supporting) batten; brick foundation.

tassée [tɑ'se] f cupful.

tassement [tɑs'mɑ̃] m sinking; settling; subsidence; ✝, fig. fall(-off), drop; **tasser** [tɑ'se] (1a) v/t. cram together; pack (tightly); shake down; se ~ crowd together; squeeze up; ⟁ settle; ⟁ sink, subside; ✝ weaken; shrink, grow smaller (with age) (person); F fig. settle down, come out in the wash.

tâter [tɑ'te] (1a) v/t. touch, feel; grope for (s.th.); fig. feel out, explore, try; 🜩 feel (the pulse); v/i.: ~ à (or de) taste, try; fig. ~ de try (one's hand at) (work); **tâte-vin** [tɑt'vɛ̃] m/inv. instrument: wine-taster; sampling-tube.

tatillon, -onne F [tati'jɔ̃, ~'jɔn] 1. adj. niggling, finicky; over-particular; 2. su. fusspot; busybody; **tatillonner** F [~jɔ'ne] (1a) v/i. niggle, fuss over details; be meddlesome.

tâtonner [tɑtɔ'ne] (1a) v/i. feel one's way (a. fig.); grope; fumble; **tâtonneur m, -euse** f [~tɔ'nœːr, ~'nøːz] groper, fumbler; **tâtons** [~'tɔ̃] adv.: à ~ gropingly; marcher etc. à ~ grope one's way.

tatou zo. [ta'tu] m armadillo.

tatouage [ta'twaːʒ] m tattooing; design: tattoo; **tatouer** [~'twe] (1p) v/t. tattoo; **tatoueur** [~'twœːr] m tattooist.

taudis [to'di] m hovel; wretched room; squalid hole; ~ pl. slums.

taule [toːl] f see tôle.

taupe [toːp] f zo. mole; 🜊 moleskin; F myope comme une ~ (as) blind as a bat; sl. pej. vieille ~ old hag; **taupinière** [~pi'njeːr] f molehill.

taureau [tɔ'ro] m bull; astr. le ♉ Taurus, the Bull; avoir un cou de ~ be bull-necked; course f de ~x bull-fight; **taurillon** [~ri'jɔ̃] m bull-calf; **tauromachie** [~rɔma'fi] f bull-fighting. [redundancy.⟩

tautologie [totɔlɔ'ʒi] f tautology,⟩

taux [to] m rate (a. ✝); ✝ fixed price; ⊕ ratio; 🜍 proportion, amount; ✝ ~ de change (rate of) exchange; ~ de charge load per unit area; ~ de la mortalité death-rate; ✝ ~ d'escompte bank rate; ✝ ~ d'intérêt rate of interest; au ~ de at the rate of.

tavelé, e [tav'le] marked; spotted, speckled; **tavelure** [~ly:r] f mark; spot, speckle.

taverne [ta'vɛrn] f tavern; public house, F pub; café-restaurant.

taxateur [taksa'tœːr] m assessor; 🜨 taxing master; **taxation** [~'sjɔ̃] f fixing of prices etc.; admin., a. 🜨 taxation; admin. assessment; **taxe** [taks] f admin. tax, duty; rate; fixed price; ✝ controlled price; **taxer** [tak'se] (1a) v/t. tax; put a tax on (goods); fix (the price); fix the price or rate of; fig. accuse (of, de).

taxi [tak'si] m taxi(-cab), cab; ~-mètre** [~si'mɛtr] m taximeter; ~-phone** teleph. [~si'fɔn] m (public) call-box.

tayloriser ⊕ [tɛlɔri'ze] (1a) v/t. Taylorize; **taylorisme** ⊕ [~'rism] m Taylorism.

tchécoslovaque [tʃekɔslɔ'vak] *adj.*, *a. su.* ♀ Czechoslovak; **tchèque** [tʃɛk] **1.** *adj.* Czech; **2.** *su./m ling.* Czech; *su.* ♀ Czech.

te [tə] **1.** *pron./pers.* you; to you; **2.** *pron./rfl.* yourself, to yourself.

té [te] *m letter:* T; T-square; **⚠** tee-iron.

technicien *m*, **-enne** *f* [tɛkni'sjɛ̃, ~'sjɛn] technician; **techni(ci)ser** [~(si)'ze] (1a) *v/t.* ⊕ mechanize; *fig.* technicalize; **technicité** [~si'te] *f* technicality; **technique** [tɛk'nik] **1.** *adj.* technical; **2.** *su./f* technique; ~ *électrique* electrical engineering; **technocrate** [~'krat] *m* technocrat; **technocratie** [~nɔkra'si] *f* technocracy; **technocratique** [~nɔkra'tik] technocratic; **technologie** [~nɔ-b'ʒi] *f* technology; **technologique** [~nɔb'ʒik] technological.

te(c)k ♀, ✝ [tɛk] *m* teak.

tectrice *orn.* [tɛk'tris] *adj./f:* plumes *f/pl.* ~s tectrices.

tégument ♀, *anat.*, *zo.* [tegy'mɑ̃] *m* tegument.

teigne [tɛɲ] *f zo.* moth; ✿ tinea, scalp-disease; ♀ scurf; *vet.* thrush; F *fig.* pest; **teigneux, -euse** [tɛ'ɲø, ~'ɲøːz] **1.** *adj.* suffering from scalp-disease; **2.** *su.* person suffering from scalp-disease.

teignis [tɛ'ɲi] *1st p. sg. p.s.* of *teindre;* **teignons** [~'ɲɔ̃] *1st p. pl. pres.* of *teindre;* **teindre** [tɛ̃:dr] (4m) *v/t.* dye (blue *etc.*, en bleu *etc.*); stain (*a. fig.*); se ~ dye one's hair; **teins** [tɛ̃] *1st p. sg. pres.* of *teindre;* **teint, teinte** [tɛ̃, tɛ̃:t] **1.** *p.p.* of *teindre;* **2.** *su./m* dye, colo(u)r; complexion; *tex.* bon (*or grand*) ~ fast colo(u)r; *fig.* partisan *m* bon ~ staunch supporter; *petit* ~ fading dye; *su./f* tint, hue, shade; *fig.* touch, tinge; **teinter** [tɛ̃'te] (1a) *v/t.* tint; *fig.* tinge (with, de); **teinture** [~'ty:r] *f tex.*, *a. hair:* dye(ing); *phot. etc.* tinting; colo(u)r, hue; *fig.* touch; ⚕, ✿ tincture; **teinturerie** ⊕ [~tyr'ri] *f* (dry) cleaner's, cleaners *pl.*; dye-works *usu. sg.*; dyeing; **teinturier** [~ty'rje] *m* (dry) cleaner, dyer.

tel *m*, **telle** *f*, **tels** *m/pl.*, **telles** *f/pl.* [tɛl] **1.** *adj./indef.* such; so great; like; as; ~ *maître*, ~ *valet* like master, like man; ~ *que* (such) as; like; such that; ~ *quel* ordinary; just as he *or* it is *or* was; ✝ with all faults;

à telle ville in such and such a town; *de telle sorte que* in such a way that; *il n'y a rien de* ~ *que* there's nothing like; *un* ~ *repas* such a meal; **2.** *pron./indef.* (such a) one; some; *Monsieur un* ~ (*or Un* ♀) Mr. So-and-so; *Madame une telle* (*or Une Telle*) Mrs. So-and-so; ~ *qui* he who.

télautographe [telotɔ'graf] *m* telewriter.

télé F [te'le] television, *Br.* F telly.

télé... [tele] tele...; **~commande** [~kɔ'mɑ̃:d] *f* remote control; **~commander** [~kɔmɑ̃'de] (1a) *v/t.* operate by remote control; **~communication** [~kɔmynika'sjɔ̃] *f* telecommunication; **~distribution** [~distriby'sjɔ̃] *f* cable television; **~enseignement** [~ɑ̃sɛɲ'mɑ̃] *m* educational broadcast *or* television program(me)s *pl.*; **~férique** [~fe'rik] *m see téléphérique;* **~génique** *telev.* [~ʒe'nik] telegenous; **~gramme** [~'gram] *m* telegram, F wire; **~graphe** [~'graf] *m* telegraph; **~graphie** [~gra'fi] *f* telegraphy; ~ *sans fil*, *abbr.* T.S.F. wireless; radio; **~graphier** [~gra'fje] (1o) *vt/i.* telegraph, wire; **~graphique** [~gra'fik] telegraphic; *mandat m* ~ telegraph(ic) money order; *poteau m* ~ telegraph-pole; *réponse f* ~ reply by wire *or* cable; **~graphiste** [~gra'fist] *su.* telegraph operator; telegraph boy *or* messenger; **~guidé, e** [~gi'de] radio-controlled; guided (*missile*); **~imprimeur** [~ɛ̃pri'mœːr] *m* teleprinter; **~mètre** *phot.* [~'mɛtr] *m* rangefinder; **~objectif** *phot.* [~ɔbʒɛk'tif] *m* telephoto lens; **~phérique** [~fe'rik] *m* telpher railway; cableway; cable car; **~phone** [~'fɔn] *m* telephone, F phone; ~ *intérieur* house telephone, internal telephone, F intercom; *annuaire m du* ~ telephone directory *or* F book; *appeler q. au* ~ ring s.o. up; *avez-vous le* ~? are you on the phone?; **~phoner** [~fɔ'ne] (1a) *vt/i.* (tele)phone (s.o., *à* q.); **~phonie** [~fɔ'ni] *f* telephony; ~ *sans fil* radiotelephony; **~phonique** [~fɔ-'nik] telephone...; telephonic; *cabine f* (*or cabinet m*) ~ telephone booth, call-box; **~phoniste** [~fɔ'nist] *su.* telephone operator.

télescopage [telɛskɔ'paʒ] *m* smashing up; concertinaing; telescoping;

traffic: ~ *en serie* pile-up; **télescope** [~'kɔp] *m* telescope; **télescoper** 🚋 *etc.* [~kɔ'pe] (1a) *v/t.* smash up, crash into; *se* ~ concertina, telescope.

télé...: ~**scripteur** ✒ [teleskrip'tœːr] *m* teleprinter; ~**spectateur** *m,* **-trice** *f telev.* [~spɛkta'tœːr, ~'tris] (tele-)viewer; ~**viser** [~vi'ze] (1a) *v/t.* televise; ~**viseur** [~vi'zœːr] *m* television set; televisor; ~**vision** [~vi'zjɔ̃] *f* television; ~ *en couleurs* colo(u)r television; ~ *par câble* cable television.

télex [te'lɛks] *m* telex; **télexer** [~lɛk'se] (1a) *v/t.* telex.

tellement [tɛl'mɑ̃] *adv.* so, in such a way; to such an extent.

tellure 🜊 [tɛl'lyːr] *m* tellurium; **tellureux, -euse** 🜊 [tɛlly'rø, ~'røːz] tellurous; **tellurien, -enne** [~'rjɛ̃, ~'rjɛn] tellurian; earth...

téméraire [teme'rɛːr] **1.** *adj.* rash (*a. fig. judgment etc.*), reckless; daring; **2.** *su.* rash person; dare-devil; **témérité** [~ri'te] *f* temerity, rashness, recklessness; piece of daring; bold speech.

témoignage [temwa'ɲaːʒ] *m* ⚖ *etc.* evidence (*a. fig.*); ⚖ hearing (of witness); *eccl.* witness; *fig.* proof; *fig. en* ~ *de* as a token of; *porter* ~ certify; *rendre* ~ bear witness (to, *à*); **témoigner** [~'ɲe] (1a) *vt/i.* testify; *v/i.* bear witness; *v/t.* show; bear witness to; **témoin** [tem'wɛ̃] **1.** *su./m* witness; *duel:* second; boundary mark; 🜊 reference solution; sample; *sp.* stick (*etc. in relay race*); ⚖ ~ *à charge* (*décharge*) prosecution (defence) witness; ~ *oculaire* eye witness; **2.** *adj./inv.* pilot..., test...; control...; *appartement m* ~ show flat; *lampe f* ~ warning light.

tempe *anat.* [tɑ̃ːp] *f* temple.

tempérament [tɑ̃pera'mɑ̃] *m* temperament; constitution; disposition; ✝ *à* ~ by instal(l)ments, on the instal(l)ment plan; *vente f à* ~ hire-purchase; sale on the instalment plan.

tempérance [tɑ̃pe'rɑ̃ːs] *f* temperance, moderation; **tempérant, e** [~'rɑ̃, ~'rɑ̃ːt] temperate, moderate; 🜊 sedative; **température** [~ra'tyːr] *f* temperature; 🜊 (*boiling-, freezing-*)point; *fig.* feeling; 🜊 *avoir de la* ~ have a temperature; **tempéré, e**

[~'re] temperate, moderate (*climate, a. fig. speech*); *fig.* sober, restrained; ♪ equally tempered; *geog.* **zone** *f* ~*e* temperate zone; **tempérer** [~'re] (1f) *v/t.* moderate, temper (*a. fig.*); *se* ~ moderate.

tempête [tɑ̃'pɛːt] *f wind, a. fig.*: storm; ⚓ hurricane; **tempêter** F [~pɛ'te] (1a) *v/i.* rant and rave, storm, rage; **tempétueux, -euse** [~pe'tɥø, ~'tɥøːz] stormy, tempestuous (*a. fig.*).

temple [tɑ̃ːpl] *m* temple (*a. hist.* ⚘); *protestantism:* church, chapel; *freemasonry:* lodge; **templier** [tɑ̃pli'e] *m* Knight Templar; F *jurer comme un* ~ swear like a trooper.

temporaire [tɑ̃pɔ'rɛːr] temporary; provisional; **temporal, e,** *m/pl.* **-aux** *anat.* [tɑ̃pɔ'ral, ~'ro] **1.** *adj.* temporal; **2.** *su./m* temporal (bone).

temporalité *eccl.* † [tɑ̃pɔrali'te] *f* temporality; **temporel, -elle** [~'rɛl] **1.** *adj.* secular; temporal (= *not eternal, not spiritual*); **2.** *su./m* temporal power; revenue, temporalities *pl.* (*of a benefice*).

temporisateur, -trice [tɑ̃pɔriza'tœːr, ~'tris] **1.** *adj.* temporizing; **2.** *su.* temporizer; ⊕ *welding:* timer; **temporisation** [~za'sjɔ̃] *f* temporization, temporizing; **temporiser** [~'ze] (1a) *v/i.* temporize, delay action deliberately, play for time, stall.

temps¹ [tɑ̃] *m* time (*a.* ♪); while; times *pl.*; ♪, ⊕ phase; *mot. etc.* stroke; ♪ *a.* beat; *gramm.* tense; *à deux* ~ two-stroke (*engine*); *à* ~ in (the nick of) time; *avec le* ~ in (the course of) time; *de mon* ~ in my time; *de* ~ *à autre* (or *en* ~) now and then, from time to time; *en même* ~ at the same time; *en* ~ *de guerre* in wartime; *entre*~ meanwhile; *être de son* ~ keep up with the times; *gagner du* ~ play for time; *il est grand* ~ it is high time (to *inf.*, *de inf.*; that *ind.*, *que sbj.*); *le bon vieux* ~ the good old days *pl.*; *les* ~ *pl. sont durs* times are hard; *le* ~, *c'est de l'argent* time is money; *à deux* ~ duple time; (*ne pas*) *avoir le* ~ *de* (*inf.*) have (no) time to (*inf.*).

temps² [tɑ̃] *m* weather; *quel* ~ *fait-il?* what is the weather like?; *il fait beau* (*mauvais*) ~ the weather is fine (bad).

tenable [tə'nabl] ✕, *a. fig.* tenable;

habitable (*house*); *fig.* pas ~ unbearable.

tenace [tə'nas] tenacious; clinging
(*perfume*, *a.* ⚓); adhesive; stiff
(*soil*); tough (*metal*); *fig.* stubborn,
persistent; retentive (*memory*); **ténacité** [tenasi'te] *f* tenacity (*a.fig.*);
stickiness; *soil*: stiffness; *metal*:
toughness; *fig.* stubbornness; dog-
gedness; *memory*: retentiveness;
avec ~ tenaciously; stubbornly.

tenaille ⊕ [tə'naːj] *f* tongs *pl.*;
clamp; pliers *pl.*; pincers *pl.* (*a.* ⚔);
tenailler *fig.* [ˌ~na'je] (1a) *v/t.*
torture.

tenancier [tənɑ̃'sje] *m* manager;
tenant-farmer; keeper; † freeholder;
tenant, e [ˌ~nɑ̃, ˌ~'nɑ̃ːt] **1.** *adj.*: séance *f* ~e during the sitting; *fig.* then
and there; **2.** *su./m* supporter; *sp.* title
etc.: holder; *bet*: taker; 🏛 d'un seul ~
all in one block; continuous; ~s *pl.*
lands bordering on an estate; ~s *pl.* et
aboutissants *m/pl.* estate: adjacent
parts; *fig.* the full details, the ins and
outs.

tendance [tɑ̃'dɑ̃ːs] *f* tendency; lean-
ings *pl.*; drift, trend; à ~ tendentious
(*book*); avoir ~ à tend to, be inclined
to; **tendancieux, -euse** [ˌ~dɑ̃'sjø,
ˌ~'sjøːz] tendentious; 🏛 leading
(*question*).

tender 🚂 [tɑ̃'dɛːr] *m* tender.

tenderie *hunt.* [tɑ̃'dri] *f* (*bird-*)
snare; setting of snares (*for birds*).

tendeur, -euse [tɑ̃'dœːr, ˌ~'døːz] *su.*
carpet: layer; wallpaper: hanger;
hunt. snares: setter; *su./m* ⊕ tight-
ener; (*trouser- etc.*)stretcher; (*shoe-*)
tree; *mot.* tension-rod; ~ de chaine
chain-adjuster.

tendineux, -euse [tɑ̃di'nø, ˌ~'nøːz]
anat. tendinous; *cuis.* stringy (*meat*).

tendoir [tɑ̃'dwaːr] *m* clothes-line;
tex. tenter.

tendon *anat.* [tɑ̃'dɔ̃] *m* tendon,
sinew.

tendre[1] [tɑ̃ːdr] (4a) *v/t.* stretch;
hang (*wallpaper*), paper (*a room*);
lay (*a carpet, a snare*); pitch (*a
tent*); spread (*a net, a sail*); hold
out (*one's hand*); offer (*one's hand
etc.*); *fig.* strain; ~ l'oreille prick up
one's ears; *v/i.*: ~ à tend towards *s.th.*
or to *do s.th.*; aim at *s.th.* or to *do s.th.*

tendre[2] [tɑ̃ːdr] tender (*heart, meat,
skin, years, youth*); soft (*colour,
grass, metal, pencil, stone, wood,*

etc.); early (*childhood, years*); *fig.*
affectionate, fond; **tendresse** [tɑ̃-
'drɛs] *f* tenderness; love; ~s *pl.*
caresses, endearments; **tendron**
[ˌ~'drɔ̃] *m* ⚓ tender shoot; *cuis.*
gristle; F *fig.* little *or* young girl.

tendu, e [tɑ̃'dy] **1.** *p.p.* of tendre[1];
2. *adj.* stretched; tight; taut; tense,
strained (*a. fig.*).

ténèbres [te'nɛːbr] *f/pl.* darkness
sg. (*a.fig.*), gloom *sg.*; *eccl.* tenebrae;
ténébreux, -euse [ˌ~ne'brø, ˌ~'brøːz]
dark, gloomy; lowering (*sky*); *fig.*
deep, sinister; obscure (*style*).

teneur[1], **-euse** [tə'nœːr, ˌ~'nøːz] *su.*
holder; *su./m*: ⚓ ~ de livres book-
keeper.

teneur[2] [tə'nœːr] *f* tenor (*of book,
conduct, etc.*); ⊕, 🜚 percentage,
amount; *solution*: strength; *min.*
grade; (*gold- etc.*)content; 🜚 ~ en
alcool alcoholic content.

ténia 🐛, *zo.* [te'nja] *m* taenia, tapeworm; **ténifuge** 🐛 [ˌ~ni'fy:ʒ] *adj.*,
a. su./m t(a)enifuge.

tenir [tə'niːr] (2h) **1.** *v/t.* hold (*a. a
meeting*); have, possess; grasp (*a. =
understand*); retain; *fig.* have in
hand, control; manage, run (*a
firm*); keep; contain (*a pint*); *fig.*
accommodate, seat (*200 persons*);
⚓ support; occupy, take up; consider, think; regard (as, *pour*); ⚓
hug (*the coast*); *thea.* take, play
(*a rôle*); † stock (*goods*); take (on)
(*a bet*); ~ compte de take (*s.th.*) into
account; ~ en respect hold in awe;
~ l'eau be watertight; ~ le lit stay
in bed; † ~ les livres do the book-
keeping; ~ sa langue hold one's
tongue; ~ sa promesse keep one's
word; *mot.* ~ (bien) la route hold the
road well; ~ son tempérament de son
père have got one's temper from
one's father; ~ tête à resist; tenez
votre droite keep to the right; se ~
keep (*quiet*); remain (*standing*); be;
s'en ~ à keep to; be satisfied with; **2.**
v/i. hold; hold firm; ⚔ hold out;
remain; *fig.* last; † be held (*market*);
🏛 sit; border (on, à) (*land*); *fig.* be
joined (to, à); be akin to (*s.o. on ger.*, à
inf.); ~ à value (*s.th.*); be due to,
depend on; ~ à ce que (*sbj.*) be
anxious that (*ind.*); ~ bon (*or ferme*)
stand firm; hold out; ⚓ hold tight; ~
de take after (*s.o.*), be akin to (*s.th.*); ~
pour be in favo(u)r of; en ~ pour be

fond of (*s.o.*), stick to (*s.th.*); *je n'y tiens pas* I don't care for it, F I am not keen (on it); *ne pouvoir plus y* ~ be unable to stand it; *tiens!, tenez!* look (here)!; here!; *tiens! well!; really?*

tennis [tɛ'nis] *m* (lawn) tennis; tennis court; *pl.* (*a. chaussures f de* ~) plimsolls, *Am.* sneakers; ~ *de table* table tennis.

tenon [tə'nɔ̃] *m* ⊕ tenon; ⊕ lug; ⚓ nut.

ténor ♪ [te'nɔːr] *m* tenor; *fort* ~ heroic tenor.

tenseur [tɑ̃'sœːr] *adj., a. su./m* Ⱥ, *anat.* tensor; **tension** [~'sjɔ̃] *f phys.*, ⚡, *etc., a. fig.* tension; ⊕, *⚡ blood, steam:* pressure; *⚡ voltage;* ♱ *prices:* hardness, firmness; *⚕ (a. ~ artérielle)* blood-pressure; *⚡ ~ de service* operating potential; *⚕ avoir de la* ~ have high blood pressure; *⚡ sous* ~ live (*wire*); **tensiomètre** [~sjɔ'mɛːtr] *m* blood pressure meter.

tentacule *zo.* [tɑ̃ta'kyl] *m* tentacle.

tentant, e [tɑ̃'tɑ̃, ~'tɑ̃ːt] tempting, alluring; **tentateur, -trice** [tɑ̃ta-'tœːr, ~'tris] 1. *adj.* tempting; 2. *su./m* tempter; *su./f* temptress; **tentation** [~'sjɔ̃] *f* temptation (*to inf., de inf.*); **tentative** [~'tiːv] *f* attempt (at, de); ⚖ ~ *d'assassinat* attempted murder.

tente [tɑ̃ːt] *f* tent; *fair etc.:* booth; ⚓ awning; *dresser une* ~ pitch a tent.

tenter [tɑ̃'te] (1a) *v/t.* tempt (*s.o.*); put to the test; ⚔ ~ *l'assaut de* attempt (*a place*); *être tenté de* (*inf.*) be tempted to (*inf.*); *v/i.:* ~ *de* (*inf.*) try to (*inf.*), attempt to (*inf.*).

tenture [tɑ̃'tyːr] *f* (paper-)hanging; tapestry; hangings *pl.;* wallpaper.

tenu, e [tə'ny] 1. *p.p. of tenir;* 2. *su./f* holding (*a.* ⚖); ♱ *books, shop, etc.:* keeping; *fig.* shape; *person:* bearing; behavio(u)r; ⊕ maintenance; ⚖ *etc.* sitting; *cost., a.* ⚔ dress; ♱ *market, prices:* firmness; ♪ sustained note; ⚔ ~*e de campagne* battle-dress; ~ *de détente* leisure wear; *mot.* ~*e de route* road-holding qualities *pl.;* ~*e de soirée* evening dress; ~*e de ville* morning *or* street dress; ⚔ walking-out dress; *de la* ~*e!* *school etc.:* behave yourself!; ⚔ *en grande* (*petite*) ~*e* in full dress (undress); *en petite,* ~ *en* ~ *légère* in light clothing; F scantily dressed.

ténu, e [te'ny] thin, slender; *fig.* fine; **ténuité** [~nɥi'te] *f* tenuous-ness; slenderness; thinness (*a. of a liquid*); sand, *a. fig.:* fineness.

ter [tɛːr] *adv.* three times, ♪ ter; for the third time; *in house numbers:* 3ter 3b.

tercet ♪ [tɛr'sɛ] *m* triplet (*a. prosody*).

térébenthène ♠ [terebɑ̃'tɛn] *m* terebenthene; **térébenthine** ♠ [~'tin] *f* turpentine.

térébrant, e [tere'brɑ̃, ~'brɑ̃ːt] *zo.* boring; ⚕ terebrating (*pain*).

tergiversation [tɛrʒivɛrsa'sjɔ̃] *f* equivocation; beating about the bush; **tergiverser** [~'se] (1a) *v/i.* shilly-shally; beat about the bush.

terme [tɛrm] *m* end, conclusion; *statue:* terminus; ⚖ quarter; quarter's rent; quarter day; ⚔, ♱, *⚡* time; ♱ *stocks etc.:* settlement; delay (*for payment*); ♱ *price:* instalment; *expression*, Ⱥ, *phls.*, ⚖ *contract:* term; ⚖ ~*s pl.* wording *sg.;* conditions; ~ *de métier* technical term; *à* ~ in due time; *à court* (*long*) ~ ♱ short- (long-)dated; *fig.* short- (long-)term (*policy etc.*); ♱ *demander un* ~ *de grâce* ask for time to pay; *en* ~*s de commerce* in commercial language; *en propres* ~*s* in so many words; *fig. être en bons* ~*s avec* be on good terms with; ♱ *opérations f/pl. à* ~ forward deals; *vente f* (*achat m*) *à* ~ credit sale (purchase).

terminaison [tɛrminɛ'zɔ̃] *f* ending, termination (*a. gramm.*); **terminal, e**, *m/pl.* -**aux** *adj., a. su./m* [~'nal, ~'no] terminal; **terminer** [~'ne] (1a) *v/t.* terminate; end, finish, complete; *se* ~ come to an end; *gramm. se* ~ *en* end in.

terminologie [tɛrminɔlɔ'ʒi] *f* terminology; **terminologique** [~'ʒik] terminological.

terminus ⚙ *etc.* [tɛrmi'nys] 1. *su./m* terminus; 2. *adj.:* gare *f* ~ (railway) terminus.

termite *zo.* [tɛr'mit] *m* termite, white ant; **termitière** [~mi'tjɛːr] *f* termitary.

ternaire [tɛr'nɛːr] ♠, Ⱥ ternary; ♪ triple (*measure*). [two treys *pl.*]

terne¹ [tɛrn] *m lottery:* tern; *dice:*)

terne² [tɛrn] dull; colo(u)rless; tarnished (*metal etc.*); **ternir** [tɛr'niːr] (2a) *v/t.* tarnish (*metal etc., a. fig. s.o.'s honour, s.o.'s reputation*); *fig.* dull; *se* ~ become tarnished *or* dull;

ternissure [‿ni'sy:r] *f* tarnish; dullness; *metal:* dull spot.

terrain [tɛ'rɛ̃] *m* ground; soil, land; terrain; ✗ *(parade- etc.)*ground; *foot.* field; *cricket:* ground; *golf:* course; ⚠ site; *geol.* rock formation; *(ne plus) être sur son* ‿ be in one's element (out of one's depth).

terrasse [tɛ'ras] *f* terrace; bank; ⚠ flat roof; *café:* pavement (area); *assis à la* ‿ sitting outside the café; *en* ‿ terraced; **terrassement** [‿ras'mɑ̃] *m* banking; earthwork; **terrasser** [‿ra'se] (1a) *v/t.* embank, bank up; throw *(s.o.)* down, floor, down *(s.o.)*; lay *(s.o.)* low; *fig.* overwhelm; **terrassier** [‿ra'sje] *m* excavation *or* road worker.

terre [tɛ:r] *f* earth (*a.* ⚡), ground; ✔ soil; ⊕ loam; clay; ⚓ land, shore; property, estate; *fig.* world; ‿ *à* ‿ prosaic, down-to-earth; ‿ *cuite* terracotta; ‿ *ferme* mainland; firm land, terra firma; ✗ *armées f/pl. de* ‿ land forces; F *avoir les pieds sur* ‿ *have* both feet firmly on the ground; *de* ‿ earth(en)...; ⚡ *mettre à la* ‿ earth; *mettre pied à* ‿ alight; *toucher* ‿ land; *se coucher par* ‿ lie on the ground; *tomber par* ‿ fall (flat).

terreau ✔ [tɛ'ro] *m* vegetable-mo(u)ld; compost; leaf-mo(u)ld.

terre-neuvas [tɛrnœ'va] *m* Newfoundland fishing-boat *or* fisherman; **terre-neuve** *zo.* [‿'nœ:v] *m/inv.* Newfoundland dog; **terre-neuvien** [‿nœ'vjɛ̃] *m see terre-neuvas.*

terre-plein [tɛr'plɛ̃] *m* earth platform, terrace; 🚗 road-bed; ✗ terreplein.

terrer [tɛ're] (1a) *v/t.* ✔ earth up; warp (*a field*); spread mo(u)ld over; ⊕ clay (*sugar*); *tex.* full; *se* ‿ ✗ entrench o.s., ✗ lie flat on the ground; go to earth (*fox*); burrow (*rabbit*); **terrestre** [‿'rɛstr] ♀, *zo.* terrestrial; ♀ ground-...; ✗ land-... (*a. insurance*); *fig.* earthly, worldly.

terreur [tɛ'rœ:r] *f* terror (*a. fig.*), dread; *hist. la* ♀ the (Reign of) Terror.

terreux, -euse [tɛ'rø, ‿'rø:z] earthy; *fig.* grubby, dirty; *fig.* muddy (*colour, complexion*).

terrible [tɛ'ribl] terrible (*a. fig.*), dreadful, frightful.

terrien, -enne [tɛ'rjɛ̃, ‿'rjɛn] **1.** *adj.* landed (*proprietor*); country..., of the soil; **2.** *su.* earthling; ⚓ landsman, *pej.* land-lubber.

terrier [tɛ'rje] *m* (*rabbit-*)hole, (*fox-*) earth; *zo.* terrier.

terrifier [teri'fje] (1o) *v/t.* terrify.

terri(l) ✗ [tɛ'ri] *m* heap, tip.

terrine *cuis.* [tɛ'rin] *f* earthenware vessel *or* pot; potted meat; **terrinée** [‿ri'ne] *f* potful; panful.

territoire [teri'twa:r] *m* territory; area of jurisdiction; *anat.* area; **territorial, e,** *m/pl.* -aux [‿tɔ'rjal, ‿'rjo] **1.** *adj.* territorial; **2.** *su./m* ✗ territorial (soldier); *su./f* ✗ territorial army; **territorialité** [‿tɔrjali-'te] *f* territoriality.

terroir ✔ [tɛ'rwa:r] *m* soil; *sentir le* ‿ smack of the soil.

terroriser [tɛrɔri'ze] (1a) *v/t.* terrorize; **terrorisme** [‿'rism] *m* terrorism; **terroriste** *pol.* [‿'rist] *adj., a. su.* terrorist.

tertiaire *geol. etc.* [tɛr'sjɛ:r] tertiary.

tertre [tɛrtr] *m* mound, hillock.

tes [te] *see* ton[1].

tessiture ♪ [tesi'ty:r] *f* tessitura.

tesson [tɛ'sɔ̃] *m* potsherd; *glass etc.:* fragment.

test[1] ⚘ *etc.* [tɛst] *m* test; ‿ *mental* intelligence test.

test[2] [tɛst] *m zo.* shell, test; ♀ *seed:* testa, skin; **testacé, e** *zo.* [tɛsta'se] testaceous.

testament [tɛsta'mɑ̃] *m* ⚖ will, testament; *bibl.* Ancien (Nouveau) ♀ Old (New) Testament; **testamentaire** ⚖ [‿mɑ̃'tɛ:r] testamentary; **testateur** ⚖ [‿'tœ:r] *m* testator *m*; **testatrice** ⚖ [‿'tris] *f* testatrix.

tester[1] ⚖ [tɛs'te] (1a) *v/i.* make a will.

tester[2] ⚘ *etc.* [‿] (1a) *v/t.* test.

testicule *anat.* [tɛsti'kyl] *m* testicle.

testimonial, e, *m/pl.* -aux [tɛsti-mɔ'njal, ‿'njo] oral (*evidence*); deponed to by a witness; *lettre f* ‿e testimonial.

têt 🜊 [tɛ] *m* small fire-clay cup, crucible.

tétanos [teta'nɔs] *m* ⚘ tetanus, lockjaw; *vet.* stag-evil.

têtard [tɛ'ta:r] *m zo.* tadpole; *sl.* child, kid; **tête** [tɛ:t] *f* head (*a.* = leader; *a.* = person); *fig.* face; *fig.* intelligence; *fig.* memory; *fig.* self-possession; *fig.* mind, reason; *page, class, tree, etc.:* top; *column, vehicle:*

front; *chapter*: heading; *foot.* header; ∼ *carrée* stubborn person, *sl.* squarehead; ∼ *chercheuse* rocket etc.: homing device; *fig.* trail blazer; ∼ *de bielle* ⊕ crank-head; *mot.* big end; ⚓ ∼ *de ligne* rail-head; ✕ ∼ *de pont* bridge-head; *iro.* ∼ *d'œuf* egghead; ∼ *nue* bareheaded; *agir* ∼ *baissée* act blindly; *avoir la* ∼ *chaude (froide)* be hot- (cool-)headed; *calculer de* ∼ work (*s.th.*) out in one's head; *coup* m *de* ∼ rash action; *de* ∼ from memory; *faire à sa* ∼ go one's own way; *en* ∼ *à* ∼ privately; *faire la* ∼ *à* frown at; be sulky with; *faire une* ∼ look glum; *forte* ∼ strong-minded *or* unmanageable person; *sp. gagner d'une* ∼ win by a head; *la* ∼ *la première* head first, headlong; *piquer une* ∼ dive; *se mettre en* ∼ *de* (*inf.*) take it into one's head to (*inf.*); *se monter la* ∼ get worked up; F *se payer la* ∼ *de q.* make fun of s.o.; take s.o. for a ride; *tenir* ∼ *à* stand up to, hold one's own against; *un homme de* ∼ a capable man; ∼-**à-tête** [tɛta'tɛːt] *m/inv.* tête-à-tête; private interview; sofa; ∼-**bêche** [tɛt'bɛʃ] *adv.* head to tail; ∼-**de-loup,** *pl.* ∼**s-de-loup** [∼d'lu] *f* wall-broom; longhandled brush.

tétée [te'te] *f* (*baby's*) feed; suck; **téter** [∼] (1f) *v/t. baby*: suck; *v/i.* suck (*baby*).

têtière [tɛ'tjɛːr] *f* infant's cap; antimacassar; ⚓ *sail*: head; *horse*: headstall.

tétin [te'tɛ̃] *m* nipple; **tétine** [∼'tin] *f animal*: teat, dug; **téton** F [∼'tɔ̃] *m* (*woman's*) breast.

tétra... [tetra] tetra...; four-...; ∼**èdre** Ⓐ [∼'ɛdr] 1. *adj.* tetrahedral; 2. *su./m* tetrahedron; ∼**phonie** [∼fɔ'ni] *f* quadrophony.

tétras *orn.* [te'tra] *m* grouse.

tette [tɛt] *f animal*: teat, dug.

têtu, e [tɛ'ty] 1. *adj.* stubborn, obstinate; 2. *su.* stubborn *or* obstinate person; *su./m* ⊕ granitehammer.

teuf-teuf [tœf'tœf] *m/inv.* puffpuff (= *train*); motor-car, *Am.* automobile.

teuton, -onne [tø'tɔ̃, ∼'tɔn] 1. *adj.* Teutonic; 2. *su.* ♀ Teuton; **teutonique** [∼tɔ'nik] Teutonic (*a. Order*).

texte [tɛkst] *m* text.

textile [tɛks'til] 1. *adj.* textile; 2. *su./m* textile (industries *pl.*).

textuaire [tɛks'tɥɛːr] textual; **textuel, -elle** [∼'tɥɛl] textual; word-for-word (*quotation*); **texture** [∼'tyːr] *f* texture; *fig.* construction, make-up.

thalweg *geol.* [tal'vɛg] *m* thalweg.

thaumaturge [toma'tyrʒ] *m* miracle-worker; thaumaturge; **thaumaturgie** [∼tyr'ʒi] *f* thaumaturgy.

thé [te] *m* tea; tea-party; *boîte* f *à* ∼ tea-caddy, tea-canister; *heure* f *du* ∼ tea-time.

théâtral, e, *m/pl.* -**aux** [tea'tral, ∼'tro] theatrical; *fig.* spectacular; *pej.* stagy; **théâtraliser** [∼trali'ze] (1a) *v/t.* put on the stage, dramatize; **théâtralisme** [∼tra'lism] *m* theatricalism, theatricalness; **théâtre** [∼'ɑːtr] *m* theatre, *Am.* theater (*a.* ✕ *of war*); stage, F boards *pl.*; scene (*a. fig.*); *fig.* setting; dramatic art; plays *pl.* (*of s.o.*); ∼ *en plein air,* ∼ *de verdure* open-air theatre; *coup* m *de* ∼ sensational development; *faire du* ∼ go *or* be on the stage; *fig.* playact.

thébaïde [teba'id] *f* solitary retreat; wilderness; **thébaïque** 🜚 [∼'ik] thebaic; opium...; **thébaïsme** 🜚 [∼'ism] *m* opium poisoning, thebaism.

théière [te'jɛːr] *f* teapot.

théine 🜚 [te'in] *f* theine.

théisme *phls.* [te'ism] *m* theism.

thématique [tema'tik] 1. *adj.* thematic; 2. *su./f* subject; **thème** [tɛm] *m* theme (*a.* ♪); topic; ♪ subject; *gramm.* stem; ✕, ⚓ scheme; *school*: prose (composition).

théo... [teo] theo...; ∼**cratie** [∼kra'si] *f* theocracy; ∼**dolite** *surv.* [∼dɔ'lit] *m* theodolite; ∼**logie** [∼lɔ'ʒi] *f* theology; *univ. a.* divinity; *docteur* m *en* ∼ doctor of divinity, D.D.; ∼**logien** m, -**enne** *f* [∼lɔ'ʒjɛ̃, ∼'ʒjɛn] theologian; ∼**logique** [∼lɔ'ʒik] theological.

théorème Ⓐ [teɔ'rɛm] *m* theorem.

théoricien, -enne *f* [teɔri'sjɛ̃, ∼'sjɛn] theoretician, theorist; **théorie** [∼'ri] *f* theory; **théorique** [∼'rik] theoretical; **théoriser** [∼ri'ze] (1a) *vt/i.* theorize.

théosophe [teɔ'zɔf] *su.* theosophist.

thérapeute 🜚 [tera'pøːt] *m* therapeutist; **thérapeutique** [∼pø'tik] 1. *adj.* therapeutic; 2. *su./f* therapy; therapeutics *pl.*; ∼ *de choc* shock-treatment; **thérapie** 🜚 [∼'pi] *f* therapy; ~ *occupationnelle* occupational therapy; ~ *de groupe* group therapy.

thermal, e, *m/pl.* -**aux** [tɛr'mal, ~'mo] thermal; *eaux f/pl.* ~*es* hot springs; *station f* ~*e* spa; **thermalisme** [~ma'lism] *m* balneology; hydrotherapeutics *sg.*; running and organization of spas; **thermes** [tɛrm] *m/pl.* thermal baths; *hist. Greece and Rome*: thermae, public baths; **thermique** *phys.* [tɛr'mik] thermal, thermic; heat (*engine*).

thermo... [tɛrmɔ] thermo-...; ~**électrique** *phys.* [~elɛk'trik] thermo-electric(al); ~**gène** *physiol.* [~'ʒɛn] thermogenic; heat-producing; ~ *ouate f* ♀ thermogene (wool); ~**mètre** [~'mɛtr] *m* thermometer; ~**nucléaire** *phys.* [~nykle'ɛːr] thermonuclear; ~**siphon** *phys.* [~si'fɔ̃] *m* thermo-siphon; ~**stat** [~s'ta] *m* thermostat; ~**thérapie** ♣ [~tera'pi] *f* heat treatment.

thésauriser [tezɔri'ze] (1a) *v/i.* hoard; amass money; *v/t.* hoard, pile up, amass.

thèse [tɛːz] *f* thesis (*a. univ.*); argument.

thon *icht.* [tɔ̃] *m* tunny(-fish), tuna.

thoracique *anat.* [tɔra'sik] thoracic; **thorax** [~'raks] *m anat.* chest; thorax (*a. of insect*).

thrombose ♣ [trɔ̃'boːz] *f* thrombosis.

thuriféraire [tyrife'rɛːr] *m eccl.* thurifer, censer-bearer; *fig.* fawner; sycophant.

thym ♀ [tɛ̃] *m* thyme.

tiare [tja:r] *f* (papal) tiara; papacy.

tibia *anat.* [ti'bja] *m* shin(-bone), tibia.

tic [tik] *m* ♣ tic, twitch; *fig.* mannerism.

ticket [ti'kɛ] *m* ticket; *cloak-room etc.*: check; (*ration-*)coupon; 🚃 ~ *de quai* platform ticket; ♣ ~ *modérateur* patient's contribution, portion paid by the insured.

tic-tac [tik'tak] *m/inv.* tick-tack; click-clack; *clock*: tick(-tock); *heart*: pit-a-pat; **tictaquer** [~ta'ke] (1m) *v/i.* tick (away) (*clock*); go pit-a-pat (*heart*).

tiède [tjɛd] tepid; lukewarm (*a. fig.*); warm (*wind*); **tiédeur** [tje'dœːr] *f* tepidity; lukewarmness (*a. fig.*); *fig.* indifference; **tiédir** [~'diːr] (2a) *v/i.*

become tepid *or* lukewarm; *v/t.* take the chill off; make tepid *or* lukewarm.

tien *m*, **tienne** *f* [tjɛ̃, tjɛn] **1.** *pron./ poss.*: *le* ~, *la* ~*ne*, *les* ~*s pl.*, *les* ~*nes pl.* yours; † thine; **2.** *su./m* your own; *les* ~*s pl.* your (own) people.

tiendrai [tjɛ̃'dre] *1st p. sg. fut. of* **tenir**; **tiennent** [tjɛn] *3rd p. pl. pres. of* **tenir**; **tiens** [tjɛ̃] *1st p. sg. pres. of* **tenir**.

tierce [tjɛrs] *f* ♪, ♮, *astr.* third; *eccl.* terce; *cards, fencing*: tierce; *typ.* final revise; **tiercé** [tjɛr'se] *m* bet to forecast the first three horses in a race; **tiers, tierce** [tjɛːr, tjɛrs] **1.** *adj.* third; *hist.* ~ *état m* third estate, commonalty; ♣ *fièvre f tierce* tertian (ague); **2.** *su./m* third (part); third person; ♣⋅♪ third party; **Tiers-Monde** [tjɛːr'mɔ̃d] *m*: *le* ~ the Third World; **tiers-point** [tjɛr'pwɛ̃] *m* ⊕ triangular file; △ *vaulting*: intersection of two ribs.

tige [ti:ʒ] *f* ♀ stem, stalk; *tree*: trunk; *column*: shaft; ⊕ rod; *boot*: upper; ⚓ anchor, *a. key*: shank; *fig. family*: stock; ⊕ ~ *du piston* piston-rod.

tignasse F [ti'ɲas] *f hair*: mop.

tigre *zo.* [tigr] *m* tiger; **tigré, e** [ti'gre] striped (*fur*); spotted (*skin*); tabby (*cat*); **tigresse** *zo.* [~'grɛs] *f* tigress.

tilde *typ.* [tild] *m* tilde (~).

tillac ⚓ [ti'jak] *m* deck.

tilleul [ti'jœl] *m* ♀ linden, lime (-tree); *infusion*: lime-blossom tea.

timbale [tɛ̃'bal] *f* ♪ kettledrum; *cuis.* pie-dish; *metal* drinking-cup; F *décrocher la* ~ carry off the prize; ♪ *les* ~*s pl. orchestra*: the timpani; **timbalier** ♪ [~ba'lje] *m* kettledrummer; *orchestra*: timpanist.

timbre [tɛ̃:br] *m date, postage, etc.*: stamp; *bicycle, clock, etc.*: bell; *fig. voice etc.*: timbre; ~ *fiscal* revenue stamp; ~ *humide* rubber stamp; F *avoir le* ~ *fêlé* be cracked *or* crazy; **timbré, e** [tɛ̃'bre] sonorous (*voice*); *admin.* stamped (*paper*); ⊕ tested (*boiler*); F *fig.* cracked, crazy, daft; **timbre-poste,** *pl.* **timbres-poste** [~brə'pɔst] *m* postage stamp; **timbre-quittance,** *pl.* **timbres-quittance** [~brəki'tɑ̃:s] *m* receipt stamp; **timbrer** [~'bre] (1a) *v/t.* stamp (*a passport, paper*); post-mark (*a let-*

ter); ⊕ test (*a boiler*); **timbreur** [ˌ'brœːr] *m* stamper.

timide [ti'mid] timid; shy; apprehensive; **timidité** [ˌmidi'te] *f* timidity; shyness; diffidence (in *ger.*, *à inf.*).

timon [ti'mɔ̃] *m* *plough*: beam; *vehicle*: pole; *fig.* helm; ⚓ † tiller; **timonerie** [ˌmɔn'ri] *f* ⚓ steering; ⚓ wheel-house; 🚗, *mot.* steering-gear, brake-gear; ⚓ *maître m de* ˌ quartermaster; *Royal Navy*: yeoman of signals; **timonier** [ˌmɔ'nje] *m vehicle*: wheel-horse; ⚓ helmsman; ⚓ quartermaster; ⚓ signalman.

timoré, e [timɔ're] timorous.

tinctorial, e, *m/pl.* **-aux** [tɛ̃ktɔ'rjal, ˌ'rjo] ⊕ tinctorial; dye(-*stuffs, -woods*).

tins [tɛ̃] *1st pr. sg. p.s. of* tenir.

tintamarre F [tɛ̃ta'maːr] *m* din, noise; *fig.* publicity, fuss; **tintement** [tɛ̃t'mɑ̃] *m bell*: ringing; *glasses, small bells*: tinkle; *coins*: jingle; 🎵 tinnitus, buzzing (*in the ears*); **tinter** [tɛ̃'te] (1a) *v/t.* ring, toll (*the bell*); ring the bell for (*mass etc.*); *v/i.* ring, toll (*bell*); tinkle (*glasses, small bells, etc.*); jingle (*coins*); 🎵 buzz (*ears*); *fig.* tingle, burn (*ears*); **tintouin** F [ˌ'twɛ̃] *m* trouble, worry.

tique *zo.* [tik] *f* tick.

tiquer [ti'ke] (1m) *v/i.* *vet.* be a crib-biter, crib; F twitch (*face etc.*); wince; F *sans* ˌ without turning a hair.

tiqueté, e 🌸, *orn., etc.* [tik'te] variegated, speckled.

tiqueur *m,* **-euse** *f* *psych.* [ti'kœːr, ˌ'køːz] person with a tic.

tir [tiːr] *m* shooting; musketry; *artillery*: gunnery; fire, firing; shooting-match; rifle-range; (*a. jeu m de* ˌ) shooting gallery; ˌ *à la cible* target-practice; ˌ *à volonté* individual fire; ˌ *sur zone* barrage; *à* ˌ *rapide* quick-firing (*gun*); *ligne f de* ˌ line of fire.

tirade [ti'rad] *f* tirade; *thea.* long declamatory speech; 🎵 run.

tirage [ti'raːʒ] *m* drawing, pulling, hauling; *chimney etc.*: draught, Am. draft; wire-drawing; *stone*: quarrying; *lottery*: draw; *typ., phot.* action, *a.* number printed: printing; *journ.* circulation; *book*: (print) run; *fig.* disagreement, friction; ˌ *à part* off-

print; ˌ *au sort* drawing lots; *cheval m de* ˌ draught horse; **tiraillement** [ˌrɑj'mɑ̃] *m* tugging, pulling; *fig.* disagreement, friction; 🌸 ˌ*s pl.* d'estomac pangs of hunger, F aching void *sg.*; **tirailler** [ˌrɑ'je] (1a) *v/t.* pull about; tug at; *fig.* pester (*s.o.*); *v/i.* blaze away, shoot at random; 🏹 ˌ *contre snipe* at; **tirailleur** [ˌrɑ'jœːr] *m* 🏹, *a. fig.* skirmisher; **tirant** [ˌ'rɑ̃] *m* drawstring; bootstrap; *strap etc.*: pull; ⊕ rod; △ tie-beam; tie-rod; ⚓ ˌ *d'eau* draught.

tire [tiːr] *f*: *voleur m à la* ˌ pickpocket.

tiré, e [ti're] **1.** *adj.* haggard, drawn; *fig.* ˌ *par les cheveux* far-fetched; **2.** *su./m* 🎵 drawee; *su./f*: F *une* ˌ a long haul, quite a distance; quite a lot.

tire...: ˌ**-au-flanc** *sl.* [tirɔ'flɑ̃] *m/inv.* skirker; ˌ**-balle** 🎵 [ˌ'bal] *m* bullet-forceps; ˌ**-botte** [ˌ'bɔt] *m* bootjack; boot-hook; ˌ**-bouchon** [ˌbu'ʃɔ̃] *m* corkscrew; *hair*: ringlet; *en* ˌ corkscrew (*curls*); ˌ**-bouton** [ˌbu'tɔ̃] *m* button-hook; ˌ**-clou** ⊕ [ˌ'klu] *m* nail-puller; ˌ**-d'aile** [ˌ'dɛl] *adv.*: *à* ˌ at full speed, swiftly; ˌ**-fesses** F [ˌ'fɛs] *m/inv.* ski tow; ˌ**-larigot** F [ˌlari'go] *adv.*: *à* ˌ to one's heart's content; *boire à* ˌ drink heavily or like a fish; ˌ**-ligne** [ˌ'liɲ] *m* drawing pen; ⊕ scriber.

tirelire [tir'liːr] *f* moneybox; piggy bank; *sl.* tummy (= *stomach*); *sl.* nut (= *head*); *sl.* mug (= *face*).

tire-pied [tir'pje] *m* shoe-horn, shoe-lift; (*shoemaker's*) stirrup; **tirer** [ti're] (1a) *v/t.* pull, drag; draw (*a. a wire, a line, wine*; *a.* 🎵 a cheque, money; *a.* ⚓ 10 feet; *fig.* lots); tug; stretch; pull off (*boots*); raise (*one's hat*) (to, *devant*); 🎵 pull out (*a tooth*); take out (*s.th. from somewhere*); *fig.* derive, get; fire (*a gun etc.*), let off (*a firearm*); *hunt.* shoot at (*an animal*); *typ.* pull (*a proof*), run off (*copies*); *gramm.* borrow (*a word*) (from Greek, du grec); ˌ *du sang à* take a blood specimen from (*s.o.*); ˌ *en longueur* stretch (*s.th.*) out; ˌ *la langue* put one's tongue out; *phot.* F ˌ *le portrait de* snap (*s.o.*); ˌ *les cartes* tell fortunes (by the cards); ˌ *les conséquences* draw the consequences; ˌ *plaisir* (*vanité*) *de* derive pleasure from (take pride in); ˌ *son origine* de spring from; ✝ ~ *une lettre de change sur* draw a bill on (*s.o.*); *film m tiré d'un roman* film adapted from a novel; *se* ~ extricate o.s. (from, *de*); F beat it; F *l'année se tire* the year is drawing to its close; *s'en* ~ get off; pull through; make ends meet; scrape through; *se* ~ *d'affaire* pull through, get out of trouble; 2. *v/i.* pull (at, on *sur*); draw (*chimney, oven, etc.*); tend (to *à, sur*), verge (on *à, sur*); go, make (for, *vers*); shoot, fire (at, *sur*); ✝ ~ *à découvert* overdraw one's account; ~ *à sa fin* draw to a close; run low (*stock*); ⚓ F ~ *au flanc* swing the lead, malinger; ~ *au large* ⚓ stand out to sea; F *fig.* beat it, clear off; ~ *au sort* draw lots; ~ *en longueur* drag on; ~ *sur le rouge* shade into *or* border on red; ~ *sur une cigarette* (*sa pipe*) draw on a cigarette (suck one's pipe); **tiret** *typ.* [~'rɛ] *m* hyphen; dash; **tirette** [~'rɛt] *f* draw-cords *pl.*, curtain cords *pl.*; *mot.* (bonnet) fastener; *desk:* writing-slide; **tireur, -euse** [~'rœːr, ~'røːz] *su.* ⊕, ✝, *a. beer, etc.:* drawer; *typ.* (*proof-*) puller; *gun:* firer; shooter; marksman, shot; *phot.* printer; pickpocket; *su./f phot.* printing-box; ~*euse de cartes* fortune-teller.

tiroir [ti'rwaːr] *m* desk, table, *etc.:* drawer; ⊕, *a.* slide-rule: slide; slide-valve; *à* ~*s* episodic (*play, novel*); F *nom m à* ~*s* double-barrel(l)ed name; ~-**caisse**, *pl.* ~**s-caisses** [~rwar'kɛs] *m* till.

tisane [ti'zan] *f* infusion; (*herb-*)tea; **tisanerie** [~zan'ri] *f hospital:* patients' kitchen.

tison [ti'zɔ̃] *m* fire-brand; half-burned log; fusee; **tisonné, e** [tizɔ'ne] with black spots (*horse's coat*); **tisonner** [~'ne] (1a) *vt/i.* poke, stir; *v/t. fig.* fan (*a quarrel*); **tisonnier** [~'nje] *m* poker; ⊕ ~*s pl.* firing tools.

tissage *tex.* [ti'saːʒ] *m* weaving; weave, mesh; cloth-mill; **tisser** *tex., a. fig.* [~'se] (1a) *v/t.* weave; **tisserand** *tex.* [tis'rɑ̃] *m* weaver; **tisserin** *orn.* [~'rɛ̃] *m* weaver-bird; **tisseur** *m*, **-euse** *f* [ti'sœːr, ~'søːz] weaver; **tissu, e** [~'sy] 1. *adj. fig.* woven, made up; 2. *su./m tex.* fabric, textile, cloth; *fig.* texture; *biol., a. fig.* lies *etc.*: tissue; **tissu-éponge**, *pl.* **tissus-éponges** [~sye-

'pɔ̃ːʒ] *m* terry (cloth), towelling; **tissure** *tex., a. fig.* [~'syːr] *f* texture.

titane ⚗ [ti'tan] *m* titanium; **titanesque** [~ta'nesk], **titanique** [~ta-'nik] titanic.

titiller [titil'le] (1a) *v/t.* tickle, titillate.

titrage [ti'traːʒ] *m* ⚗, ⊕ titration; *metall.* assaying; ⊕ thread, wire: sizing; *cin.* insertion of the titles; **titre** [ti:tr] *m book, claim, eccl., gold, honour, nobility, office, song:* title; *book:* title-page; *chapter, page:* heading; *journ.* headline; *school:* certificate (*a.* ✝); *univ.* diploma; ✝ bond; *admin.* pass (*a.* ⚔), voucher; ⚖ deed; *fig.* claim; ⚗ strength, *alcohol:* degree; *metall. ore:* content; *coinage:* standard; ⊕ *thread, wire:* size; ~*s pl.* qualifications (for, *à*); ✝ stocks and shares, securities; *typ.: courant* running headline; ~ *de créance* proof of debt; *à* ~ *de* by right *or* virtue of; as a (*friend*); *à* ~ *d'office* ex officio; *à* ~ *gratuit* free; as a favo(u)r; *à juste* ~ rightly, deservedly; *en* ~ titular; on the permanent staff; *fig.* acknowledged; *typ. faux* ~ half-title; *or m au* ~ standard gold; **titrer** [ti'tre] (1a) *v/t.* confer a title on (*s.o.*); give a title to; *cin.* title (*a film*); ⚗, ⊕ titrate; *metall.* assay; *journ.* run as a headline; *wine etc.:* ~ *10°* be 10° proof.

tituber [tity'be] (1a) *v/i.* stagger, lurch, reel.

titulaire [tity'lɛːr] 1. *adj.* titular (*a. eccl.*); full, regular (*member*); 2. *su.* holder; *passport:* bearer; *su./m eccl.* incumbent; *univ.* regular professor.

toast [tɔst] *m* toast; *porter un* ~ propose a toast ((to, *à*); **toaster** [tɔs'te] (1a) *v/t.* toast (*s.o.*), drink to (*s.o.'s*) health.

toboggan [tɔbɔ'gɑ̃] *m* toboggan; *mot.* overpass; *piste f de* ~ toboggan-run.

toc [tɔk] 1. *int.* tap, tap!; rat-rat! (*at door*); 2. *su./m sound:* tap, rap; ⊕ (*lathe-*)carrier; ⊕ catch; F sham jewellery; ✝ *en* ~ pinchbeck; 3. *adj./inv. sl.* touched, crazy.

tocante F [tɔ'kɑ̃ːt] *f* watch, F ticker.

tocsin [tɔk'sɛ̃] *m* alarm(-bell, -signal).

toge [tɔːʒ] *f hist. Rome:* toga; ⚖, *univ.* gown; ⚖ robe.   [hubbub.}

tohu-bohu [tɔybɔ'y] *m* confusion;}

toi [twa] *pron./pers. subject*: you; *object*: you; (to) you; *à ~* to you; yours.

toile [twal] *f* linen; cloth; *paint.* canvas; (oil) painting; (*spider's*) web; *thea.* curtain; ⚓ sail; ✕ tent; *~s pl. hunt.* toils; ♰ *~ à matelas* tick(ing); *~ à sac* sackcloth; *~ à voiles* sail-cloth; *~ cirée* ♰ oilcloth, American cloth; ⚓ oilskin; ♰ *~ de coton* cotton(-cloth); *thea., a. fig. ~ de fond* backdrop; *~ métallique* wire gauze; *reliure f en ~* cloth binding; **toilerie** ♰ [~'ri] *f* linen *or* textile trade; linen goods *pl.*; **toilettage** [twale'ta:ʒ] *m* grooming (*of pets*); *fig.* touch-up; **toilette** [~'lɛt] *f* toilet, washing; dressing; dressing table; (*woman's*) dress, costume; wash-stand; *~s pl.* toilet, lavatory; *faire sa ~* have a wash, get washed; *objets pl. de ~* toilet accessories; **toilier, -ère** [~'lje, ~'ljɛ:r] **1.** *adj.* linen...; **2.** *su./m* ♰ linen dealer *or* manufacturer. [yourself.)

toi-même [twa'mɛ:m] *pron./rfl.*

toise [twa:z] *f* measuring apparatus; *fig.* standard (of comparison); † *measure*: fathom; **toiser** [twa'ze] (1a) *v/t.* measure; △, *surv.* survey for quantities; *fig.* eye (*s.o.*) from head to foot, weigh (*s.o.*) up.

toison [twa'zɔ̃] *f* fleece; F *fig.* shock of hair.

toit [twa] *m* roof (*a.* ✕); house-top; *mot. ~* ouvrant sunshine roof; *fig. crier sur les ~s* shout (*s.th.*) from the housetops; **toiture** [twa'ty:r] *f* roof (-ing).

tokai, tokay [tɔ'kɛ] *m wine*: Tokay.

tôle [to:l] *f* ⊕ sheet-metal, sheet-iron; (*galvanized, enamelled, etc.*) iron; plate; boiler-plate; *sl.* clink (= *prison*); *~ ondulée* corrugated iron.

tolérable [tɔle'rabl] tolerable, bearable; **tolérance** [~'rɑ̃:s] *f* ⊕, ✹, *coinage, a. fig.*: tolerance; ⊕ limits *pl.*, margin; *admin.* allowance; (*religious*) toleration; **tolérant, e** [~'rɑ̃, ~'rɑ̃:t] tolerant; **tolérer** [~'re] (1f) *v/t.* tolerate (*a.* ✹ *a drug*); *fig.* overlook; F bear, endure.

tôlerie [tol'ri] *f* sheet-iron and steelplate goods *pl. or* trade *or* works *usu. sg.*

tolet ⚓ [tɔ'lɛ] *m* thole-pin.

tôlier [to'lje] *m* ♰ sheet-iron merchant; sheet-iron worker; *sl.* innkeeper; *sl. hotel*: boss.

tomate ♀ [tɔ'mat] *f* tomato.

tombale [tɔ̃'bal] *adj./f: pierre f ~* tombstone.

tombant, e [tɔ̃'bɑ̃, ~'bɑ̃:t] falling; drooping (*moustache, shoulders*); sagging (*branch*); flowing (*hair*); *à la nuit ~e* at nightfall.

tombe [tɔ̃:b] *f* tomb, grave; tombstone; **tombeau** [tɔ̃'bo] *m* tomb; *fig.* death.

tombée [tɔ̃'be] *f* rain: fall; *à la ~ de la nuit* (*or du jour*) at nightfall; **tomber** [~'be] (1a) **1.** *v/i.* fall (*a.* ✕, *a. fig.* hair, night, government, *etc.*); tumble (down), fall (down); decline; drop (*a.* ✹ *fever*); decrease; subside (*rage, wind, a. fever*); die down (*feelings, fire, storm*); flag (*conversation*); *fig.* fail; *thea.* fall flat (*play*); ✕ crash; *fig.* become; *fig.* go out of fashion; *fig.* drop in (on, *chez*); *~ à rien* come to nothing; *~ bien* (*or juste*) happen *or* come at the right moment; *~ d'accord* reach agreement, agree; *~ dans le ridicule* make a fool of o.s.; *~ de fatigue* be ready to drop; *~ en disgrâce* fall into disgrace; *~ le mardi* fall on a Tuesday (*festival*); *~ mal* be inopportune; *~ malade* (*mort, amoureux*) fall ill (dead, in love); *~ sur* meet (with), run *or* come across; ✕ fall on (*the enemy*); *faire ~* bring down; *cards:* drop; *il tombe de la neige* it is snowing; *laisser ~* drop (*s.th., one's voice*, F *s.o.*); give up, discard; F *les bras m'en tombent* I am flabbergasted; **2.** *v/t. wrestling:* throw (*s.o.*); ⊕ turn up *or* down (*the edge of a plate etc.*); *thea.* bring about the failure of, F kill; F *~ la veste* slip off one's jacket; *sl. ~ une femme* lay a woman; **tombereau** [tɔ̃'bro] *m* (tip-)cart; ✪ open truck; truckload; *hist.* tumbrel; *~ à ordures* dust-cart; **tombeur** [~'bœ:r] *m sp.* wrestler; F *~ de femmes* ladykiller.

tombola [tɔ̃bɔ'la] *f* lottery, raffle.

tome [to:m] *m* tome, (large) volume.

ton¹ *m*, **ta** *f*, *pl.* **tes** [tɔ̃, ta, te] *adj./poss.* your.

ton² [tɔ̃] *m* voice, *paint., phot.*, ✹, *a.* ♪ instrument, *a. fig.* tone; *paint., phot.* tint; *~* shade, colo(u)r; *fig.* form; ♪ pitch; ♪ key; ♪ mode; *fig. le bon ~* good form; *être de bon ~* be good form, be in good taste;

donner le ~ ♪ give the pitch; *fig.* set the tone *or* the fashion; *être dans le ton*, *avoir le* ~ ♪ be in tune; *fig.* tone in, match; *fig.* fit in; *ne pas être dans le* ~ ♪ be out of tune; *fig.* clash; *fig.* be out of place; ♣ *donner du* ~ (*à q.*) brace (*s.o.*) up, act as a tonic (on *s.o.*); **tonal, e,** *m/pl.* **-als** ♪ [tɔˈnal] tonal; **tonalité** [ˌnaliˈte] *f* ♪, *paint.*, *phot.* tonality; *radio*: tone.

tondage [tɔ̃ˈdaːʒ] *m vet.* dipping; shearing (*a. tex.*); **tondaille** [ˌˈdɑːj] *f* (sheep-)shearing; **tondaison** [ˌdɛˈzɔ̃] *f see* tonte; **tondeur, -euse** [ˌˈdœːr, ˌˈdøːz] *su.* shearer; *vet.*, *a.* ✂ clipper; *su./f* shears *pl.*; ✂ lawn-mower; *hair, dog's coat*: clippers *pl.*; **tondre** [tɔ̃ːdr] (4a) *v/t. vet.*, *a.* ⊕ shear; *sheep*: crop (*the grass*); clip (*dog, hair, hedge, horse*); *fig.* fleece (*s.o.*).

tonicité ♣ [tɔnisiˈte] *f* tonicity; **tonifier** ♣ [ˌniˈfje] (1o) *v/t.* tone up, brace; **tonique** [ˌˈnik] **1.** *adj.* tonic (♣, *a.* gramm.); *accent m* ~ stress, tonic; **2.** *su./m* ♣ tonic; *su./f* ♪ tonic, key-note.

tonitruant, e *fig.* [tɔnitryˈɑ̃, ˌˈɑ̃ːt] thundering; violent (*wind*); **tonitruer** *fig.* [ˌˈe] (1a) *v/i.* thunder.

tonnage ⚓ [tɔˈnaːʒ] *m* tonnage; displacement.

tonnant, e [tɔˈnɑ̃, ˌˈnɑ̃ːt] thundering (*a. fig. voice*).

tonne [tɔn] *f measure*: metric ton; tun, cask; **tonneau** [tɔˈno] *m* cask, barrel; governess-cart; *mot.* tonneau; ✗ toll, horizontal spin; *au* ~ draught (*beer*); **tonnelage** [tɔnˈlaːʒ] *m* cooperage; ✝ *marchandises f/pl. de* ~ goods in barrels; **tonnelet** [ˌˈlɛ] *m* keg (*a.* ⚓); small cask; *oil*: drum; **tonnelier** ⊕ [tɔnəˈlje] *m* cooper; **tonnelle** [ˌˈnɛl] *f* △ barrel-vault, semicircular arch; *fig.* bower; *hunt.* tunnel-net; **tonnellerie** ⊕ [ˌnɛlˈri] *f* cooperage; cooper's shop.

tonner [tɔˈne] (1a) *v/i.* thunder (*a. fig.*); *fig.* boom (out); **tonnerre** [ˌˈnɛːr] *m* thunder (*a. fig.*); † thunderbolt, lightning; *coup m de* ~ thunderclap, peal of thunder; *fig.* thunderbolt; F *du* ~ (*de Dieu*) terrific, a hell of a ...

tonsure [tɔ̃ˈsyːr] *f* tonsure; *fig.* priesthood; **tonsurer** [ˌsyˈre] (1a) *v/t.* tonsure.

tonte [tɔ̃ːt] *f* (sheep-)shearing; shearing-time; *tex.* shearing; ✂ clipping; *lawn*: mowing.

tonton F [tɔ̃ˈtɔ̃] *m* uncle.

tonus [tɔˈnys] *m* ♣ tonus, tone; *fig.* energy.

topaze *min.* [tɔˈpaːz] *f* topaz; ~ *brûlée* (*occidentale*) pink (false) topaz.

tope! [tɔp] *int.* agreed!; done!; **toper** *fig.* [tɔˈpe] (1a) *v/i.* agree; shake hands on it.

topinambour ♀, *cuis.* [tɔpinɑ̃ˈbuːr] *m* Jerusalem artichoke.

topique [tɔˈpik] **1.** *adj.* local (*a.* ♣); *fig.* to the point, relevant; **2.** *su./m* ♣ local *or* topical remedy; *phls.* commonplace.

topographe [tɔpɔˈgraf] *m* topographer; **topographie** [ˌgraˈfi] *f* topography; surveying; topographical map *or* plan; **topographique** [ˌgraˈfik] topographic(al); ordnance (*map, survey*).

toquade F [tɔˈkad] *f* passing craze, infatuation.

toquante F [tɔˈkɑ̃ːt] *f* watch, F ticker.

toque *cost.* [tɔk] *f* chef, jockey, univ., ✝: cap; (*woman's*) toque.

toqué, e F [tɔˈke] crazy, cracked, nuts; ~ *de* infatuated with, *sl.* mad about (*a hobby, a woman, etc.*); **toquer** [ˌˈ] (1m) *v/t.* drive (*s.o.*) crazy; *fig.* infatuate; *se* ~ lose one's head (over, for).

torche [tɔrʃ] *f* torch; straw pad; **torcher** [tɔrˈʃe] (1a) *v/t.* wipe (*s.th.*) (clean); daub (*the wall*), cover (*the floor, the wall*) with cobmortar; F *fig.* polish off, do (*s.th.*) quickly; *pej.* botch, scamp (*one's work*); **torchère** [ˌˈʃɛːr] *f* candelabra; **torchette** [ˌˈʃɛt] *f* wisp of straw (*for cleaning*); house flannel; *tex.* hank; **torchis** △ [ˌˈʃi] *m* cob; **torchon** [ˌˈʃɔ̃] *m* (kitchen) cloth; (~ *à vaisselle*) dish towel; duster; floor cloth; F *fig.* rag (= *bad newspaper*); *coup de* ~ wipe; *a. fig.* clean-up; F *fig.* fight, quarrel; **torchonner** F [ˌʃɔˈne] (1a) *v/t.* wipe; *sl.* botch, scamp (*one's work*).

tordage [tɔrˈdaːʒ] *m* twisting; *tex. etc.* twist; **tordant, e** F [ˌˈdɑ̃, ˌˈdɑ̃ːt] screamingly funny; **tord-boyaux** F [tɔrbwaˈjo] *m/inv.* strong (but poor) brandy, *sl.* rot-gut; rat poison; **tordeur, -euse** [tɔrˈdœːr, ˌˈdøːz] *su. tex. person*: twister; *su./f* ⊕ cable-twisting machine; *zo.* leafroller moth; **tordoir** ⊕ [∼'dwaːr] *m* rope-twister, rack-stick; cable-twisting machine; *laundry*: wringer; oil-mill; **tordre** [tɔrdr] (4a) *v/t.* ⊕ twist; wring (*hands, s.o.'s neck, clothes, a. fig. s.o.'s heart*); distort, twist (*one's features, the mouth, the meaning*); ⊕ buckle (*metal*); se ∼ twist, writhe; (*a. se ∼ de rire*) roar with laughter; **tordu, e** [tɔr'dy] twisted; bent; crooked; warped (*a. fig. mind*); F nuts, crazy, loony.

toréador [tɔrea'dɔːr] *m* bull-fighter.

torgn(i)ole F [tɔr'ɲɔl] *f* slap, blow.

tornade [tɔr'nad] *f* tornado; *fig.* torrent of abuse.

toron [tɔ'rɔ̃] *m* rope: strand; *straw*: wisp.

torpeur [tɔr'pœːr] *f* torpor; **torpide** [∼'pid] torpid.

torpille ⚓, ⚡, *a. icht.* [tɔr'piːj] *f* torpedo; **torpiller** ⚓ [∼pi'je] (1a) *v/t.* torpedo (*a ship, a. fig. a scheme*); **torpilleur** ⚓ [∼pi'jœːr] *m* destroyer; *person*: torpedo man.

torréfacteur [tɔrrefak'tœːr] *m* (coffee-)roaster; **torréfaction** [∼fak'sjɔ̃] *f* (coffee-)roasting; torrefaction; **torréfier** [∼'fje] (1o) *v/t.* roast (*coffee etc.*); torrefy; *sun*: scorch (*s.o.*).

torrent [tɔ'rɑ̃] *m* torrent (*a. figs.*); *fig. abuse, light, tears*: flood; **torrentiel, -elle** [tɔrɑ̃'sjɛl] torrential; **torrentueux, -euse** [∼'tɥø, ∼'tɥøːz] torrent-like, torrential.

torride [tɔ'rid] *geog.* torrid; *fig.* scorching (*heat*).

tors, torse [tɔːr, tɔrs] **1.** *adj.* twisted, 🏛 wreathed (*column*); crooked, bandy; cou ∼ wry neck; **2.** *su./m rope etc.*: twist; (twisted) cord; **torsade** [tɔr'sad] *f hair*: twist, coil; twisted cord; en ∼ coiled (*hair*); **torsader** [∼sa'de] (1a) *v/t.* twist (together); coil (*hair*).

torse [tɔrs] *m* trunk, torso; chest.

torsion [tɔr'sjɔ̃] *f rope, wire, etc.*: twisting; *phys.*, ⚙, *mot.* torsion; moment *m* de ∼ torque.

tort [tɔːr] *m* wrong; mistake, error, fault; damage, harm; à ∼ wrongly; à ∼ ou à raison rightly or wrongly; avoir ∼ be wrong; dans (or en) son ∼ in the wrong, at fault; donner ∼ à blame, lay the blame on; prove (to be) wrong; faire (du) ∼ à q. harm s.o., do s.o. harm; be detrimental to s.o.

torticolis ⚡ [tɔrtikɔ'li] *m* crick (in the neck); stiff neck.

tortillard, e [tɔrti'jaːr, ∼'jard] *m* small local railway; **tortille** [∼'tiːj] † *f* winding path (*in a wood etc.*); **tortillement** [∼tij'mɑ̃] *m* twist(ing); *worm, a. fig.*: wriggling; *fig.* quibbling, subterfuge; **tortiller** [∼ti'je] (1a) *v/t.* twist (up); twiddle; twirl (*one's moustache*); se ∼ wriggle; writhe, squirm; *v/i. fig.* wriggle (a)round; ∼ des hanches swing *or* F wiggle one's hips; **tortillon** [∼ti'jɔ̃] *m hair, paper*: twist; *market porter*: headpad.

tortionnaire [tɔrsjɔ'nɛːr] **1.** *adj.* torture-…, of torture; *fig.* wicked; **2.** *su./m* torturer.

tortis [tɔr'ti] *m* twisted threads *pl.*; torsel.

tortu, e † [tɔr'ty] crooked.

tortue [tɔr'ty] *f zo.* tortoise; F à pas de ∼ at a snail's pace; *cuis.* soupe *f* à la ∼ turtle-soup.

tortueux, -euse [tɔr'tɥø, ∼'tɥøːz] tortuous (*a. fig. conduct*), winding; twisted (*tree*); *fig.* crooked (*conduct, person*); *fig.* wily (*person*).

torture [tɔr'tyːr] *f* torture; **torturer** [∼ty're] (1a) *v/t.* torture; *fig.* twist, strain (*the sense, a text*); se ∼ l'esprit rack one's brains.

torve [tɔrv] menacing; forbidding; regard *m* ∼ grim look; scowl.

tôt [to] *adv.* soon; early; ∼ ou tard sooner or later; au plus ∼ at the earliest; le plus ∼ possible as soon as possible; pas de si ∼ not so soon.

total, e, *m/pl.* -aux [tɔ'tal, ∼'to] **1.** *adj.* total, complete; **2.** *su./m* (sum) total; au ∼ on the whole; **totalisateur** [tɔtaliza'tœːr] *m* adding-machine; *turf*: totalizator; **totalisation** [∼za'sjɔ̃] *f* totalization; totting up, adding up; **totalisatrice** [∼za'tris] *f* cash register; **totaliser** [∼'ze] (1a) *v/t.* totalize, tot up, add up; **totalitaire** [∼'tɛːr] totalitarian; **totalitarisme** [∼ta'rism] *m* totalitarianism; **totalité** [∼'te] *f* whole, total; en ∼ wholly.

toton [tɔ'tɔ̃] *m* teetotum; F faire tourner q. comme un ∼ twist s.o. round one's little finger.

touage ⚓ [twa'ʒ] *m* chain-towage (dues *pl.*); kedging.

touaille [twa'j] *f* roller-towel.

toubib F [tu'bib] *m* doctor, F doc.

touchant, e [tu'ʃã, ~'ʃãːt] **1.** *adj.*
touching, moving; **2.** *su./m* touching
thing (about s.th., *de qch.*); **3.** †
touchant prp. concerning, about,
with regard to; **touchau** [tu'ʃo] *m*
(*goldsmith's*) touch-needle, test-
needle; **touche** [tuʃ] *f* touch (*a.
paint., sp.*); *typewriter, ♪ piano*: key;
♪ violin etc.: fingerboard; *paint. etc.,
a. fig.* style, manner; *foot.* throw-in;
foot. (*a. ligne f de ~*) touch-line;
fencing, billiards: hit; *♪ ~s pl. guitar*:
frets; *tel. ~ d'interruption* break-key;
arbitre m de ~ foot. linesman; *rugby*:
touch-judge; *pierre f de ~* touchstone
(*a. fig.*); *sl. avoir une drôle de ~* look
funny; *sur la ~ sp.* on the sidelines;
fig. out in the cold; *fig.* aloof;
touche-à-tout [tuʃa'tu] *su./inv.*
dabbler; meddler; Jack of all trades;
toucheau [~'ʃo] *m see touchau*; **toucher** [~'ʃe] **1.** (1a) *v/t.* touch, hit (*a
ball, ✕ the mark, an opponent*); feel;
contact, reach (*s.o.*); receive, draw
(*money*); † collect (*a bill*); *fig.* move
(*s.o.*) (*to tears etc.*); deal with, touch
on, allude to (*a matter, a question*);
strike (*a. ♣ rock*); *v/i.: ~ à* border on
(*a place, a. fig.*); be in contact with
(*s.th.*); be near to (*an age, a place, a.
fig.*); reach to; *fig.* affect (*interests,
question, welfare*); ♣ call at; *~ à sa fin*
be drawing to a close; *défense f de ~!*
hands off!; F *touchez là!* shake hands
on it!; F *put it there!*; shake!; **2.** *su./m*
touch (*a. ♪ of a pianist*); feel; **tou-
chette** *♪* [~'ʃɛt] *f guitar etc.*: fret,
stop; **toucheur** [~'ʃœːr] *m* (cattle-)
drover.

toue ♣ [tu] *f river barge*; **touée** [twe]
f ♣ warping-cable; *cable, rope, ship
at anchor*: scope; *fig.* stretch, length;
touer ♣ [~] (1p) *v/t.* chain-tow; take
in tow.

touffe [tuf] *f grass, hair*: tuft; *hay,
straw*: wisp; *flowers*: bunch; *trees*:
clump; **touffeur** [tu'fœːr] *f room*:
stifling heat; F fug; **touffu, e** [~'fy]
bushy (*beard etc.*); thickly wooded
(*scenery*); close, tangled (*thicket*);
fig. abstruse; that is heavy reading
(*book*).

toujours [tu'ʒuːr] *adv.* always, ever;
still; nevertheless, anyhow; *~ est-il
que* the fact remains that; *pour* (*or
à*) *~* for ever.

toundra *geog.* [tun'dra] *f tundra*.
toupet [tu'pɛ] *m tuft of hair*; *person,*

a. horse: forelock; F *fig.* impudence,
cheek; *faux ~* toupet.
toupie [tu'pi] *f* (spinning-)top; peg-
top; ⊕ mo(u)lding lathe; *~ d'Allemagne* humming-top; F *vieille ~* old
frump; **toupiller** [tupi'je] (1a) *v/t.*
⊕ shape (*wood*); *v/i.* spin round;
bustle about.
toupillon [tupi'jõ] *m* (*small*) bunch.
tour[1] [tuːr] *f tower*; *chess*: castle,
rook; high-rise *or* tower block; *fig. ~
d'ivoire* ivory tower.

tour[2] [~] *m* ⊕ machine, key, phrase,
order, *fig.*: turn; ⊕ revolution;
(*potter's*) wheel; ⊕ lathe; circuit,
circumference; *cost.* size, measurement; turning, winding; *face*: outline; *affairs*: course; trip, walk,
stroll; *♂, a. road*: twist; *♂* sprain;
sp. tennis: round; *fig.* feat; trick;
fig. manner, style; *~ à ~* by turns;
sp. ~ cycliste cycle race; *~ de force*
feat (*of strength or skill*); *~ de main*
knack, skill; *fig.* tricks *pl.* of the
trade; *sp. ~ de piste* lap; *cost. ~ de
poitrine man*: chest measurement;
woman: bust measurement; *♂ ~ de
reins* crick in the back; *cost. ~ de
taille* waist measurement; *à mon ~* in
my turn; *à ~ de bras* with all one's
might; *à ~ de rôle* in rotation; *c'est
(à) son ~* it is his turn; *en un ~ de
main* in a twinkling, straight away;
♣ *faire le ~* swing the ship; capsize; *faire le ~ de* go round (*the
world etc.*); *faire un mauvais ~ à q.*
play a dirty trick on s.o.; *faire un
~* take a stroll; *fermer à double ~*
double-lock (*a door*); *par ~ de faveur* out of one's (proper) turn.

touraille ⊕ [tu'raːj] *f malt-kiln*.
tourbe[1] † *pej.* [turb] *f mob, rabble*.
tourbe[2] [turb] *f peat, turf*; **tourbeux, -euse** [tur'bø, ~'bøːz] *♂*
peaty, boggy; *marais m ~* peat-bog;
tourbier [~'bje] *m peat-worker*;
tourbière [~'bjɛːr] *f peat-bog*.
tourbillon [turbi'jõ] *m whirlwind*;
dust: swirl; whirlpool; eddy; *astr.,
fig.* vortex; *fig.* whirl; *fig.* round; *~ de
neige* snowstorm; **tourbillonner**
[~jɔ'ne] (1a) *v/i.* swirl; whirl round.
tourelle [tu'rɛl] *f* ⊿, ✕, ♣, ⊕, ✇
turret; ⊕ *lathe*: capstan.
tourie [tu'ri] *f carboy*.
tourisme [tu'rism] *m tourism*; touring; holiday travel; tourist industry;
bureau m de ~ travel agency; *voiture f*

de ~ touring car; **touriste** [~'rist] *su.* tourist; **touristique** [~ris'tik] travel ...; touristic, tourist ...

tourment [tur'mɑ̃] *m* torment, torture (*a. fig.*); *fig.* agony, anguish; ~s *pl. hunger*: pangs; **tourmente** [~'mɑ̃:t] *f* storm (*a. fig.*); *fig.* turmoil; ~ de neige blizzard; **tourmenter** [turmɑ̃'te] (1a) *v/t.* torture, torment; *fig.* worry, trouble; *fig.* pester, harry; ♣ *wind*: toss (*a ship*) about; *fig.* overelaborate (*a picture, a theme, etc.*); se ~ worry, fret; **tourmenteur, -euse** [~'tœ:r, ~'tø:z] tormenting; **tourmentin** ♣ [~'tɛ̃] *m* storm-jib.

tournage [tur'na:ʒ] *m* ⊕ turning (*on a lathe*); ♣ belaying; *cin.* shooting; **tournailler** F [~na'je] (1a) *v/i.* wander up and down *or* about; **tournant, e** [~'nɑ̃, ~'nɑ̃:t] **1.** *adj.* turning; revolving; winding (*path, road*); spiral (*staircase*); **2.** *su./m road, river*: turning, bend; (*street*) corner; winding; *mill*: water-wheel; *fig.* turning point; F *fig.* avoir (*or* rattraper*) q. au ~ pay s.o. back; **tournebroche** [turnə'brɔʃ] *m* roasting jack; † turnspit; **tourne-disque** [~'disk] *m grammophone*: turntable; **tournedos** *cuis.* [~'do] *m* tournedos; fillet steak; **tournée** [tur'ne] *f admin., a.* ♣ round; ⚡ circuit; *thea.* tour; *fig.* round (of drinks); F *fig.* thrashing; faire la ~ de visit, do the round of, F do; **tournemain** † [~nə'mɛ̃] *m:* en un ~ in a twinkling, straight away; **tourner** [~'ne] (1a) **1.** *v/t.* turn; rotate (*a wheel*); turn round (*a corner*); wind (*s.th. round s.th.*); ⚡ shape, fashion; *cuis.* stir (*a liquid*); ♣ make fast (*a hawser*); *cin.* shoot, make (*a film*), actor: star in (*a film*); ⚡ outflank; *fig.* evade (*a difficulty, a law*), get round (*a. ⚡*); *fig.* turn over (*a. a page*), revolve (*a problem*); convert (into, *en*); ~ la tête (l'estomac) à q. turn s.o.'s head (stomach); se ~ turn (round); change (into, *en*); **2.** *v/i.* turn; go round, revolve; ⊕ run, go; spin (*top*); wind (*path, road*); *fig.* whirl (*head*); change (*weather, wind*); shift (*wind*); *cin.* film; turn (sour) (*milk etc.*); *fig.* turn out (*badly, well*); *fig.* ~ à become, tend to(wards); ~ à droite turn to the right; ~ au beau turn fine; *mot.* ~ au ralenti idle, tick over; bien tourné handsome, well set-up; il tourne cœur *cards*: the turn-up is

hearts; la tête me tourne I feel giddy, my head is spinning; mal ~ go to the bad; **tournerie** ⊕ [~nə'ri] *f* turner's shop.

tournesol [turnə'sɔl] *m* 🌻 sunflower; 🜛 litmus.

tournette [tur'nɛt] *f tex.* reel; squirrel's cage; turn-table; ⊕ circular glass-cutter; **tourneur, -euse** [~'nœ:r, ~'nø:z] **1.** *adj.* dancing (*dervish*); **2.** *su./m* ⊕ turner; ⊕ lathe operator; **tournevent** [~nə'vɑ̃] *m* chimney-jack; chimney-cowl; **tournevis** ⊕ [~nə'vis] *m* screwdriver.

tourniole 🜛 F [tur'njɔl] *f* whitlow (*round a nail*).

tourniquet [turni'kɛ] *m* turnstile; † revolving stand; 🗡 sprinkler; ⊕ catch; *shutter*: button; 🗡 vane; 🗡 tourniquet; ⚡ F passer au ~ be court-martialled.

tournis *vet.* [tur'ni] *m sheep*: staggers *pl.*

tournoi [tur'nwa] *m sp. etc.* tournament; *whist*: drive; **tournoiement** [turnwa'mɑ̃] *m* spinning, whirling; *water*: swirling; *bird*: wheeling; 🗡 dizziness; **tournoyer** [~'je] (1h) *v/i.* spin; turn round and round, whirl; swirl (*water*); wheel (*bird*); *fig.* quibble.

tournure [tur'ny:r] *f fig.* turn (*of events etc.*); shape; cast; *phrase*: turn; ⊕ *lathe*: turning(s *pl.*); ~ d'esprit cast of mind; way of thinking; prendre une meilleure ~ take a turn for the better.

tourte [turt] *f cuis.* (covered) pie *or* tart; F dolt, duffer; **tourteau** [tur'to] *m* round loaf; cattle-cake, oil-cake; edible crab; ⊕ centre-boss.

tourtereau *orn.* [turtə'ro] *m* young turtle-dove (*a. fig.*); **tourterelle** *orn.* [~'rɛl] *f* turtle-dove.

tourtière *cuis.* [tur'tjɛ:r] *f* pie-dish; baking-tin.

tous [tu; tus] *see* tout.

Toussaint *eccl.* [tu'sɛ̃] *f: la ~* All Saints' Day; la veille de la ~ Hallowe'en.

tousser [tu'se] (1a) *v/i.* cough; **tousseur** *m*, **-euse** *f* [~'sœ:r, ~'sø:z] cougher; **toussoter** [~sɔ'te] (1a) *v/i.* give little coughs; have a slight cough.

tous-temps [tu'tɑ̃] *adj./inv.* all-weather.

tout *m*, **toute** *f*, **tous** *m/pl.*, **toutes**
f/pl. [tu, tut, tu, tut] **1.** *adj. before
unparticularized noun*: all, any,
every; *sole*, only; *intensive*: very,
most, utmost, extreme; *before
particularized su./sg.*: all, the whole
(of); *before particularized su./pl.*:
all, every, every one of; *with numerals*: all; *with numeral + su./pl.*
every + *su./sg.*; ~ *homme* every *or*
any man; *pour toute nourriture* as
sole food; *de toute fausseté* completely false; *toute la (une) ville* the
(a) whole town; ~ *le monde* everyone; ~ *Paris* all *or* the whole of
Paris; *toutes les semaines* every
week; *tous les cinq* all five; *tous les
deux* both; *toutes les cinq (deux)
semaines* every fifth (other) week;
2. *pron./indef.* [*m/pl.* tus] all; everything; ~ *est là* everything is there;
après ~ after all; *bonne f à* ~ *faire*
maid of all work; *c'est (or voilà)* ~
that is all; *c'est* ~ *dire* that's the
long and the short of it; *et* ~ *et* ~
and all the rest of it; *nous tous* all
of us; *six fois en* ~ six times in all;
3. *su./m* the whole, all; the main
thing; ⅄ (*pl.* **touts** [tu]) total; *du*
~ *au* ~ completely, entirely; *pas
du* ~ not at all; **4.** *adv.* (*before adj./f
beginning with consonant or aspirate
h, agrees as if adj.*) quite, completely;
all; very; ready(*-cooked, -made,
etc.*); right; stark (*naked, mad*);
straight (*ahead, forward*); ~ *à coup*
suddenly; ~ *à fait* completely; ~ *à
l'heure* a few minutes ago; in a few
minutes; ~ *au plus* at the very most;
~ *autant* quite as much *or* many;
~ *d'abord* at first; ~ *de même* all *or*
just the same; ~ *de suite* at once,
immediately; *restaurant*: in a
moment; ~ *d'un coup* at one fell
swoop; ~ *en* (*ger.*) while (*ger.*); ~
petits enfants very young children;
~ *sobre qu'il paraît* however sober
he seems *or* may seem, sober though
he seems *or* may seem; *à* ~ *à l'heure!*
see you later!; *c'est* ~ *un* it's all the
same; *elle est tout contente* (*hon-
teuse*) she is quite content (a-
shamed); *elle est tout étonnée* she
is quite astonished.

tout-à-l'égout [tutale¹gu] *m/inv.*
main-drainage,   direct-to-sewer
drainage.

toute [tut] *see* **tout;** **~fois** [~¹fwa]

cj. however, still, nevertheless;
~-puissance *eccl.* [~pчi¹sã:s] *f*
omnipotence.   [wow.)

toutou *ch.sp.* [tu¹tu] *m* doggie, bow-)

tout(-)va F [tu¹va]: *à* ~ enormous,
unbounded, super; (*adv.*) enormously, F like crazy.

tout-venant [tuvə¹nã] *m* ⁰ un-
screened coal; ✝ ungraded products;
fig. hoi polloi.

toux [tu] *f* cough; *accès m (or quinte f)*
de ~ fit of coughing.

toxicité [tɔksisi¹te] *f* toxicity; **toxi-
cologie** 🐍 [~kɔlɔ¹ʒi] *f* toxicology;
toxicomane 🐍 [~kɔ¹man] **1.** *su.*
dope fiend; drug-addict; **2.** *adj.*
drug-addicted;   **toxicomanie** 🐍
[~kɔma¹ni] *f* dope-habit; drug-habit;
toxine 🐍 [tɔk¹sin] *f* toxin; **toxique**
[~¹sik] **1.** *adj.* toxic; poisonous; **2.**
su./m poison.

trac F [trak] *m* fright; *thea.* stage-
fright; *avoir le* ~ get the wind up; *tout
à* ~ without reflection.

tracas [tra¹kɑ] *m* bother, worry,
trouble; **tracasser** [~ka¹se] (1a) *v/t.*
bother, worry; *se* ~ worry, fret
(about, *pour*); **tracasserie** [~kas¹ri] *f*
worry; harassment; **tracassier,
-ère** [~ka¹sje, ~¹sjɛ:r] **1.** *adj.* vexatious; irksome; **2.** *su.* fussy person;
troublesome person.

trace [tras] *f* trace; *vehicle*: track;
animal, person: trail; footprints *pl.*;
fig. footsteps *pl.*; *burn, suffering*:
mark; *fig.* sign; **tracé** [tra¹se] *m*
tracing, sketching; *town etc.*: layout;
road: lie; ⅄ graph; △ *etc.* outline,
drawing, plan; **tracer** [~] (1k) *v/t.*
trace; mark out; ⅄ plot (*a curve, a
graph*); draw (*a line, a plan*); sketch
(*an outline, a plan*); *fig.* open up (*a
route etc.*); *fig.* show (*the way*); *v/i. sl.*
get a move on; **traceret** ⊕ [tras¹rɛ]
m scriber, tracing-awl; **traceur,
-euse** [tra¹sœ:r, ~¹sø:z] *su., a. adj.* ⊕,
✗, *etc.* tracer.

trachée [tra¹ʃe] *f* ❧, *zo.* trachea; ❧
duct; F *anat.* = ~-**artère**, *pl.* ~**s-
artères** *anat.* [~ʃear¹tɛ:r] *f* trachea,
windpipe; **trachéite** 🐍 [~ke¹it] *f*
tracheitis; **trachéotomie** 🐍
[~keɔtɔ¹mi] *f* tracheotomy; **tracho-
me** 🐍 [~¹kɔ:m] *m* trachoma.

traçoir ⊕ [tra¹swa:r] *m see* **traceret.**

tract [trakt] *m* tract; leaflet.

tractations *pej.* [trakta¹sjõ] *m f/pl.*
dealings.

tracté, e [trak'te] tractor-drawn; **tracteur** [~'tœ:r] *m* tractor; **traction** [~'sjɔ̃] *f* traction; pulling; draught, *Am.* draft; *sp.* pull-up; *sp.* press-up, push-up; 🚋 rolling-stock department; *mot.* (*a.* ~ *avant*) car with front-wheel drive; ⊕ *etc. essai m de* ~ tension test; **tractoriste** [~tɔ-'rist] *su.* tractor driver.

tradition [tradi'sjɔ̃] *f* tradition; 🕱 delivery; folklore; *de* ~ traditional; **traditionaliste** [~sjɔna'list] *su.* traditionalist; **traditionnel, -elle** [~sjɔ'nɛl] traditional; standing (*joke etc.*); habitual.

traducteur *m*, **-trice** *f* [tradyk'tœ:r, ~'tris] translator; **traduction** [~'sjɔ̃] *f* translation; interpretation; **traduire** [tradɥi:r] (4h) *v/t.* translate (into, *en*); *fig.* render, convey, express; 🕱 ~ *en justice* summon, sue, prosecute; *se* ~ *par* be translated by; *fig.* find it's expression in, be expressed by; **traduisible** [~dɥi'zibl] translatable; 🕱 ~ *en justice* liable to prosecution *or* to be sued.

trafic [tra'fik] *m* traffic (*a. fig. pej.*); trading; *teleph.* ~ *interurbain* trunk traffic; *faire le* ~ *de* traffic in; **traficotage** [~fikɔ'ta:ʒ] *m* trafficking, underhand(ed) dealings *pl.*; **trafiquant** [trafi'kɑ̃] *m* trader; trafficker (in *de, en*) (*a. pej.*); **trafiquer** [~'ke] (1m) *v/i.* trade, deal (in, *en*); *usu. pej.* traffic; *pej. fig.* ~ *de* make profit out of, sell; *v/t.* F doctor (*s.th.*) (up); **trafiqueur** *pej.* [~'kœ:r] *m* trafficker (in *de, en*).

tragédie [traʒe'di] *f* tragedy (*a. figs.*); **tragédien** [~'djɛ̃] *m* tragedian, tragic actor; **tragédienne** [~'djɛn] *f* tragic actress, tragedienne; **tragicomique** [traʒikɔ'mik] tragi-comic; **tragique** [tra'ʒik] 1. *adj.* tragic; F *ce n'est pas* (*si*) ~ (*que ça*) that's not so bad; 2. *su./m* tragic aspect (*of an event*); tragedy (*a.* = *tragic art*); tragic poet; *prendre au* ~ make a tragedy of (*s.th.*).

trahir [tra'i:r] (2a) *v/t.* betray; disclose; deceive (*s.o.*); *fig. strength*: fail (*s.o.*); be false to (*one's oath*); not to come up to (*expectations, hopes*); **trahison** [~i'zɔ̃] *f* treachery, perfidy; betrayal (of, *de*); 🕱 treason; *haute* ~ high treason.

traille [trɑ:j] *f* trail-ferry; ferry-cable.

train [trɛ̃] *m* 🚋 train; *vehicles etc.*: string; *tyres, wheels*: set; *admin. laws, decrees etc.*: set, batch, series; *metall.* rolls *pl.*; ⊕ gear; (*timber-*, *Am. lumber-*)raft, float; *zo. horse*: quarters *pl.*; pace (*a. sp.*), speed; *fig.* mood; 🚋 ~-*auto* car sleeper train; 🚋 ~ *correspondant* connection; 🚋 ~ *de banlieue* (*ceinture*) suburban (circle) train; ~ *de derrière* (*devant*) *horse*: hind- (fore-) quarters *pl.*; ⊕ ~ *de laminoir* rolling-mill; 🚋 ~ *de marchandises* (*plaisir, voyageurs*) goods, *Am.* freight (excursion, passenger) train; ⊕ ~ *d'engrenages* gear train; ⊕ ~ *de roues* wheel train; 🚋 ~ *direct* (*or express*) through *or* express train; 🚋 ~ *omnibus* slow *or Am.* accommodation train; 🚋 ~ *rapide* fast express (train); *fig. à fond de* ~ at top speed; *aller son petit* ~ jog along; *fig. dans le* ~ up to date, F in the swim; *en bon* ~ in a good state, doing *or* going well; *être en* ~ *de* (*inf.*) be (engaged in) (*ger.*); be in a mood for (*ger. or su.*); ⚥ F *le* ♀ (*approx.*) (Royal) Army Service Corps; *mal en* ~ out of sorts; *fig. manquer le* ~ miss the bus; *mener grand* ~ live in great style; *sp. mener le* ~ set the pace; *mettre en* ~ set (*s.th.*) going; *typ.* make ready; *fig. monter dans* (*or prendre*) *le* ~ (*en marche*) jump on the bandwagon.

traînage [trɛ'na:ʒ] *m* hauling; sleighing; sleigh transport; ⁰ haulage; *telev.* streaking; **traînant, e** [~'nɑ̃, ~'nɑ̃:t] dragging; trailing (*robe*); *fig.* sluggish; **traînard, e** [~'na:r, ~'nard] *su.* dawdler, *Am.* F slowpoke; *su./m* ⚔ straggler; ⊕ *lathe*: carriage; **traînasser** [~na'se] (1a) *v/t.* † drag out; spin out; *v/i.* hang about; dawdle; **traîne** [trɛ:n] *f dress*: train; *fishing*: dragnet; *à la* ~ in tow (*a. fig.*); lagging behind; **traîneau** [trɛ'no] *m* sleigh, sledge; **traînée** [~'ne] *f blood, light, smoke, snail*: trail; *gunpowder*: train; *fishing*: ground-line; *sl.* prostitute; **traîner** [~'ne] (1b) *v/t.* draw, drag, pull; tow (*a barge*); drawl out (*words*); drag out (*an affair, an existence, a speech*); ~ *la jambe* limp; *se* ~ crawl; drag o.s. along; *fig.* linger; drag (*time*); *v/i.* trail; *fig.* linger on (*a. ☞ illness*); hang about; dawdle; lag behind; languish; flag; remain unpaid (*account*); lie around, lie about (*things*); ~ *en longueur* drag on;

traîneur, -euse [ˌ-'nœːr, ˌ-'nøːz] *su.*
dawdler; ~ *de cafés* person who is
hanging about the cafés; *su./m*
hauler, dragger; ~ *de sabre* swashbuckler; sabre-rattler.

train-poste, *pl.* **trains-poste(s)**
[trɛ̃'pɔst] *m* mail-train.

train-train F [trɛ̃'trɛ̃] *m* (daily)
round; (humdrum) routine.

traire [trɛːr] (4ff) *v/t.* milk (*a cow*);
draw (*milk*); **trait, traite** [trɛ, trɛt]
1. *p.p. of* traire; 2. *su./m* pull(ing);
arrow: shooting; *dart:* throwing;
arrow, dart; *pen:* stroke; mark, line;
liquid: draught, *Am.* draft; gulp;
light: shaft, beam; *fig.* act; stroke (*of
genius*); characteristic touch; trait (*of
character*); *appearance:* feature; *fig.*
reference, relation; *paint.* outline,
contour; ~ *d'esprit* witticism; ~
d'union hyphen; *avoir* ~ *à* have reference to, refer to; *boire d'un seul* ~
drink (*s.th.*) at one gulp *or* F go;
cheval m de ~ draught-horse, *Am.*
draft-horse, cart-horse; *su./f road:*
stretch; *journey:* stage; ✝ *bank:* bill,
draft; *bill:* drawing; trade; milking;
~*e des blanches* white-slave traffic; ~*e
des Noirs* slave-trade; *d'une (seule)* ~
at a stretch; in one go.

traitable [trɛ'tabl] treatable; manageable; *fig.* tractable.

traité [trɛ'te] *m* treatise (on *de, sur*);
pol. etc. treaty, agreement.

traitement [trɛt'mɑ̃] *m* treatment
(*a.* ♪); salary; ⚒ *etc.* pay; ⊕ *material:*
processing; ~ *initial* starting *or* initial
salary; *mauvais* ~*s pl.* illtreatment *sg.*;
maltreatment *sg.*; ~ *des données* data
processing; **traiter** [trɛ'te] (1a) *v/t.*
treat (♪, ⊕, *s.o., a. fig.*); call (*s.o.
s.th., q. de qch.*); entertain (*s.o.*); deal
with; discuss (*a subject*); negotiate
(*business, a deal, a marriage, etc.*); ~ *q.
de prince* address s.o. as prince; *v/i.*
negotiate, treat (for *de, pour*); with,
avec); ~ *de* deal with (*a subject*);
traiteur [ˌ-'tœːr] *m banquet:* caterer;
restaurant keeper.

traître, -esse [trɛːtr, trɛ'trɛs] 1. *adj.*
treacherous (*a. fig.*); *fig.* dangerous;
vicious (*animal*); *ne pas dire un* ~ *mot*
not to say a (single) word; 2. *su./m*
traitor; *thea.* villain; *prendre q. en* ~
attack s.o. when he is off his guard;
su./f traitress; **traîtreusement**
[trɛtrøz'mɑ̃] *adv. of* traître 1; **traîtrise** [ˌ-'triːz] *f* treachery.

trajectoire *phys.*, Å, *etc.* [traʒɛk-
'twaːr] *su./f, a. adj.* trajectory.

trajet [tra'jɛ] *m* 🚌, *mot. etc.* journey;
⚓, *anat., tex.* passage; *channel etc.:*
crossing; *mot. etc.* ride; ✈ flight; ⚡,
a. phys. artery, nerve, projectile, *etc.:*
course.

tralala [trala'la] *m* ♪ tra la la; F *fig.*
fuss, ceremony; *en grand* ~ all dressed
up, F dressed up to the nines.

tram F [tram] *m* tram(car), *Am.*
streetcar, trolley(-car).

trame [tram] *f tex.* woof, weft; *fig.*
frame(work); *fig.* texture; *phot.*
ruled screen; *telev.* frame; *fig.* plot;
tramer [tra'me] (1a) *v/t. tex.* weave
(*a. fig. a plot*); *fig.* plot; *fig.* hatch (*a
plot*); *fig. il se trame qch.* s.th. is
brewing.

traminot [trami'no] *m* tramway employee, *Am.* streetcar employee.

tramontane [tramɔ̃'tan] *f* ⚓ north
wind; north; *astr.* North Star; *fig.*
perdre la ~ lose one's bearings.

tramway [tram'wɛ] *m* tramway;
tram(car), *Am.* streetcar, trolley
(-car); *remorque f de* ~ trailer (of a
tramcar).

tranchant, e [trɑ̃'ʃɑ̃, ˌ-'ʃɑ̃ːt] 1. *adj.*
cutting; sharp (*tool, edge, a. fig. tone,
voice*); *fig.* trenchant (*argument etc*);
glaring (*colour, a. fig. contradiction*);
⊕ *outil m* ~ edgetool; 2. *su./m* edge;
knife: cutting edge; *fig.* argument *m à
deux* ~*s* argument that cuts both
ways; **tranche** [trɑ̃ːʃ] *f bread, meat,
etc., a. fig.:* slice; *book, coin, plank:*
edge; *wheel:* face; ⊕ *tools:* set; ✦
ridge; ✝ *shares:* block; *fig.* portion;
Å *section; bacon:* rasher; *couper en* ~*s*
slice; *en* ~*s* sliced, in slices; ⊕ *par la* ~
edgeways; *sl. s'en payer une* ~ have a
lot of fun; **tranché, e** [trɑ̃'ʃe] 1. *adj.*
distinct, sharp; 🔲 tranché; 2. *su./f*
trench (*a.* ✕); ⚓, *forest etc.:* cutting;
⚡ ~*es pl.* gripes; colic *sg.*; **tranche-
fil** [trɑ̃ʃ'fil] *m horse:* curbchain;
tranchefile [ˌ-'fil] *f book:* headband; **tranchelard** *cuis.* [ˌ-'laːr] *m*
cook's knife; **tranchemontagne**
[ˌ-mɔ̃'taɲ] *m* blusterer, fire-eater;
tranche-pain [ˌ-'pɛ̃] *m/inv.* bread-
cutter; **trancher** [trɑ̃'ʃe] (1a) *v/t.*
slice, cut; cut off; *fig.* cut short;
settle (*a question*) once and for all;
settle (*a difficulty, a problem, a quarrel*); ~ *le mot* speak out, speak plainly;
v/i. cut; contrast sharply (with, *sur*);

fig. take drastic action; † *fig.* ~ *de* set up for *or* as; **tranchoir** [~'ʃwaːr] *m* cutting board.

tranquille [trã'kil] tranquil; calm, still, quiet; *fig.* easy (*a.* ♥ *market*); untroubled (*mind*); *laissez-moi* ~ leave me alone; **tranquillisant** ♣ [trãkili'zã] *m* tranquil(l)izer; **tranquilliser** [~'ze] (1a) *v/t.* calm (*s.o.*, *one's mind*, *etc.*); reassure (*s.o.*) (about, *sur*); *se* ~ calm down; *fig.* set one's mind at rest; **tranquillité** [~'te] *f* tranquil(l)ity, calm, stillness, quiet; peace (*of mind*).

trans... [trãs, trãz] trans...; **~action** [trãzak'sjɔ̃] *f* ♥ transaction; ♥ deal; ⚖️ settlement, arrangement; ♥, ⚖️ composition; compromise (*a. pej.*); **~s** *pl.* dealings; transactions (*of a learned society*); **~atlantique** [~zatlã'tik] 1. *adj.* transatlantic; 2. *su./m* Atlantic liner; deck-chair; **~bahuter** F [~bay'te] (1a) *v/t.* lug (along); shift (around); **~bordement** [trãsbɔrdə'mã] *m* ⚓ transshipment; *river:* ferrying across; *goods, passengers:* transfer; *trucks etc.:* traversing; **~border** [~'de] (1a) *v/t.* tranship; ferry across (*a river*); 🚂 transfer (*goods, passengers*); traverse; **~bordeur** [~'dœːr] *m* travelling platform; (*a. pont m* ~) transporter-bridge; 🚂 train-ferry; **~cendance** *phls.* [trãssã'dãːs] *f* transcendency, transcendence; **~cendant, e** [~'dã, ~'dãːt] *phls.*, *a. fig.* transcendent; Ⱥ transcendental.

transcription [trãskrip'sjɔ̃] *f* transcription (*a.* ♪); copy, transcript; **transcrire** [~'kriːr] (4q) *v/t.* transcribe (*notes*, *a. a text*, *a.* ♪); copy (out).

transe [trãːs] *f* (hypnotic) trance; **~s** *pl.* fear *sg.*, fright *sg.*

transept Ⱥ *eccl.* [trã'sɛpt] *m* transept.

trans...: **~férer** [trãsfe're] (1f) *v/t.* transfer; (re)move from one place to another; relocate; move (*an appointment, a date*); *eccl.* translate (*a bishop*); ⚖️ convey (*an estate*); **~fert** [~'fɛːr] *m* transference; transfer (*a. phot.*, ♥); relocation; ⚖️ *estate:* conveyance; **~figuration** [~figyra-'sjɔ̃] *f* transfiguration; **~figurer** [~figy're] (1a) *v/t.* transfigure; *se* ~ be(come) transfigured; **~formable** [trãsfɔr'mabl] transformable; *mot.*

convertible; **~formateur, -trice** [~ma'tœːr, ~'tris] 1. *adj.* transforming; 2. *su./m* ⚡ transformer; **~formation** [~ma'sjɔ̃] *f* transformation (into, *en*); *phls.* conversion; *de* ~ ⚡ transformer ...; ⊕ processing ...; **~former** [~'me] (1a) *v/t.* transform, convert (*a. foot.*, *a. phls.*), change (into, *en*); *se* ~ change, turn (into, *en*); **~formisme** *biol. etc.* [~'mism] *m* transformism; **~formiste** [~'mist] *su. phls. etc.* transformist; *thea.* quick-change artist; **~fuge** [trãs-'fyːʒ] *m* renegade; defector; **~fuser** *usu.* ♣ [~fy'ze] (1a) *v/t.* transfuse; **~fusion** [~fy'zjɔ̃] *f:* (~ *sanguine or de sang* blood-)transfusion; **~gresser** [~grɛ'se] (1a) *v/t.* transgress, infringe, break (*a law etc.*); **~humer** [trãzy'me] (1a) *v/t.* move (*flocks*) to *or* from the Alpine pastures; *v/i.* move to *or* from the hills.

transi, e [trã'zi] (~ *de froid*) chilled to the bone; ~ *de peur* paralyzed with fear.

transiger [trãzi'ʒe] (1l) *v/i.* compromise (*a. fig.*); come to terms (with, *avec*).

transir [trã'siːr] (2a) *v/t.* chill; benumb; *fig.* paralyse (with, *de*); *v/i.* be chilled to the bone; be paralysed with fear.

transistor [trãzis'tɔr] *m radio:* transistor; **transistoriser** [~tɔri'ze] (1a) *v/t.* transistorize.

transit [trã'zit] *m* ♥ transit; 🚂 through traffic; **transitaire** ♥ [trãzi'tɛːr] 1. *adj.* relating to transit of goods; (*country*) across which goods are conveyed in transit; 2. *su./m* forwarding *or* transport agent; **transiter** ♥ [~'te] (1a) *v/t.* convey (*goods*) in transit; *v/i.* be in transit; **transitif, -ve** [~'tif, ~'tiːv] *gramm.* transitive; *geol.* transitional; **transition** [~'sjɔ̃] *f* transition; ♪ modulation; *geol. de* ~ transitional; **transitoire** [~'twaːr] transitory, transient; temporary; *gramm.* glide (*consonant, vowel*).

trans...: **~lation** [trãsla'sjɔ̃] *f* transfer; ⊕, *eccl.* translation; ⊕ shifting; *tel.* retransmission; ⚖️ conveyance; **~lucide** [~ly'sid] semitransparent, translucent; **~lucidité** [~lysidi'te] *f* semi-transparency, translucence; **~metteur** [~mɛ'tœːr] *m* transmitter; ⚓ signals (officer)

sg.; ⚓ ship's telegraph; ~**mettre**
[~'mɛtr] (4v) v/t. transmit (tel.,
radio, a. heat, light, a message); pass
on (a disease, a message); hand down
(to other generations); ♊ convey,
transfer; ♊ assign (a patent, shares);
~**migration** [~migra'sjɔ̃] f people,
soul: transmigration; ~**migrer** [~-
mi'gre] (1a) v/i. transmigrate; ~-
missibilité [~misibili'te] f trans-
missibility; ♊ transferability; ~-
missible [~mi'sibl] transmissible; ~
♊ etc. transferable; ~**mission** [~-
mi'sjɔ̃] f message, order, a. ⊕, ♂,
phys., radio, tel.: transmission; disease, message, order: passing on; ⊕
drive, (transmission) gear, shafting;
♊ transfer, conveyance; ♊ patent,
shares: assignment; foot. passing;
✖, ⚓ ~s pl. signals; mot. ~ par
chaîne chain-drive; ~**muable** [~-
'mɥabl] transmutable (into, en);
~**muer** [~'mɥe] (1n) v/t. transmute
(into, en); ~**mutabilité** [~mytabi-
li'te] f transmutability (into, en);
~**mutable** [~my'tabl] transmutable
(into, en); ~**mutation** [~myta'sjɔ̃] f
transmutation (into, en); ~**océanique** [trãzɔsea'nik] transoceanic; ~
paraître [trãspa'rɛtr] (4k) v/i.
show through; ~**parence** [~pa'rãːs]
f transparency; ~**parent, e** [~pa'rã,
~'rãːt] **1.** adj. transparent (a. fig.); **2.**
su./m transparent screen; writing-
pad: guide-lines pl.; ~**percer** [~pɛr-
'se] (1k) v/t. pierce (through); run
(s.o.) through; transfix; fig. pierce
(s.o. to the heart, le cœur à q.); fig.
rain: soak.
transpiration [trãspira'sjɔ̃] f ♂
perspiring; perspiration, sweat; ♀,
phys., physiol., a. fig. transpiration;
en ~ in a sweat; **transpirer** [~'re]
(1a) v/i. ♂ perspire, sweat; ♀,
physiol., a. fig. transpire; fig. leak
(out) (news, secret).
trans...: ~**plantable** ♀, ♂ [trãsplã-
'tabl] transplantable; ~**plantation**
[~plãta'sjɔ̃] f transplanting, transplantation; ~**planter** ♀, ✔, ♂, fig.
[~plã'te] (1a) v/t. transplant; ~**port**
[~'pɔːr] m ⚓ transport, carriage; ✔,
♊ conveyance; ♊ assignment; ✝
account: transfer, balance brought
forward; ⚓ troop-ship, transport;
fig. anger: (out)burst; delight, joy:
transport, ecstasy; ♂ ~ au cerveau
brain-storm;   light-headedness;

stroke; ~ d'aviation aircraft transport; ♊ ~ sur les lieux visit to the
scene (of the occurrence); ✝ compagnie f de ~ forwarding company;
⊕ courroie f de ~ conveyor-belt;
de ~ ⊕ conveyor-...; geol. alluvial
(deposit); ~**portable** [~pɔr'tabl]
transportable; ♂ fit to be moved
(patient); ~**portation** [~pɔrta'sjɔ̃] f
✝ goods: conveyance; ✝, ♊ transportation; ~**porter** [~pɔr'te] (1a)
v/t. transport; carry, convey; bring;
fig. carry (s.o.) away; transporté de
joie beside o.s. with joy, enraptured;
se ~ betake o.s.; ♊ se ~ sur les lieux
visit the scene (of the occurrence);
~**porteur** [~pɔr'tœːr] m ✝ carrier; ⊕
conveyor; ~ aérien overhead runway,
cableway; ~**posable** [~po'zabl]
transposable; ~**poser** [~po'ze] (1a)
v/t. typ., ♪, ♫, ♯, etc. transpose; ~**posi-
teur** ♪ [~pozi'tœːr] m (a. instrument
m ~) transposing instrument; ~**position** [~pozi'sjɔ̃] f transposition; cin.
dubbing; ~**sibérien, -enne** geog.
[~sibe'rjɛ̃, ~'rjɛn] trans-Siberian; ~
substantiation eccl. [~sypstãsja-
'sjɔ̃] f transubstantiation; ~**suder**
[~sy'de] (1a) vt/i. transude; v/i. ooze
through; fig. emanate (from, de);
~**vasement** [~vaz'mã] m liquid:
decanting; ~**vaser** [~va'ze] (1a) v/t.
decant; se ~ siphon; ~**versal, e,** m/pl.
-**aux** [~vɛr'sal, ~'so] **1.** adj. cross
(-section), transverse (a. anat.
muscle), transversal; ⚓ athwartship;
♯ coupe f ~e cross-section; **2.** su./f ♯
transversal; ~**versalement** [~vɛr-
sal'mã] adv. transversely, crosswise;
⚓ athwartship.
trapèze [tra'pɛːz] m ♯ trapezium; sp.
trapeze; anat. (a. muscle m ~) trape-
zius; **trapéziste** sp. [~pe'zist] su.
trapeze-artist; trapezist; **trapézoï-
de** ♯ [~pezɔ'id] m trapezoid.
trappe [trap] f trap-door; thea., a.
hunt. trap; ⊕ etc. hatch; **trappeur**
[tra'pœːr] m trapper.
trapu, e [tra'py] thick-set, stocky,
squat.
traque hunt. [trak] f game: beating;
traquenard [~'naːr] m trap (a. fig.);
pitfall; fig. être pris dans son propre ~
fall into one's own trap; **traquer**
[tra'ke] (1m) v/t. beat (the wood) for
game; beat up (game); track down (a
criminal); surround, hem (s.o.) in;
traqueur hunt. [~'kœːr] m beater.

trauma *psych.*, ✒ [tro'ma] *m* trauma; **traumatique** [troma'tik] traumatic; **traumatiser** [⁓ti'ze] (1a) *v/t.* traumatize; **traumatisme** [⁓'tism] *m* traumatism; *psych.* traumatic experience.

travail[1] *vet.* [tra'va:j] *m* frame, sling.

travail[2], *pl.* -aux [tra'va:j, ⁓'vo] *m* work; ⚒, ⚓, *pol.* labo(u)r; ⊕, *physiol.*, *a.* *wine*: working; ✒ childbirth; employment; piece of work, F job; workmanship; business; ⊕ power; ⁓ à la tâche piece-work; ⁓ en série mass production; ⁓ intellectuel (manuel) brain-work (manual work); accident *m* du ⁓ accident at work; être sans ⁓ be out of work; ⚒ ⁓aux *pl.* forcés hard labo(u)r *sg.*; **travailler** [trava'je] (1a) *v/i.* work (on, *sur*); be at work; strive, endeavo(u)r; practise (*musician etc.*); train; work, ferment (*wine*); warp, shrink (*wood*); fade (*colour*); be active (*mind, volcano*); ⊕ be stressed (*beam*); strain (*cable, ship, etc.*); ♱ produce interest (*capital*); *v/t.* work (*a.* ⚒, ⊕); torment (*s.o., s.o.'s mind*); ⊕ shape, fashion; knead (*dough*); overwork (*a horse*); work (hard) at, study (*a subject*); *phot.* work up; *fig.* tamper with; **travailleur, -euse** [⁓'jœ:r, ⁓'jø:z] 1. *adj.* hard-working, industrious; 2. *su.* worker; *su./m* workman, labo(u)rer; ⁓ de force heavy worker; ⁓ intellectuel (manuel) brain-worker (manual worker); *su./f* (*lady's*) worktable; *zo.* worker (bee); **travaillisme** *pol.* [⁓'jism] *m* Labour; **travailliste** *pol.* [⁓'jist] 1. *adj.* Labour ...; 2. *su./m* member of the Labour party; *parl.* Labour member.

travée △ [tra've] *f* bay (*a. of a bridge*); span; row (of seats).

travers [tra'vɛ:r] 1. *su./m* † breadth; *fig.* fault, failing; † ⁓ de doigt finger's breadth; 2. *adv.*: de ⁓ askew, awry; (*look*) askance; *fig.* wrong; en ⁓ (de) across (*s.th.*); 3. *prp.*: à ⁓, au ⁓ de through (*s.th.*); à ⁓ champs across country; **traversable** [⁓vɛr'sabl] traversable; fordable (*river*); **traverse** [⁓'vɛrs] *f* △ traverse beam or girder; *ladder*: rung; transom; 🛏 sleeper, *Am.* tie; *mot. etc.* cross-member; ⊕ crosshead; ✗ groundsill; ⚓ harbour: bar; *fig.* set-back; (*a. chemin m de ⁓*) crossroad, short cut; cross-street; **traversée** [travɛr'se] *f*

⚓, 🚢 crossing; ⚓ voyage, passage; *mount.* traverse; *fig.* ⁓ du désert time in the wilderness; bad patch; low ebb; **traverser** [⁓'se] (1a) *v/t.* cross (*a. fig.*); pass or go through; △ *bridge*: span (*a river*); **traversier, -ère** [⁓'sje, ⁓'sjɛ:r] cross-..., crossing; ferry(-*boat*); ⚓ leading (*wind*); ♪ transverse (*flute*); **traversin** [⁓'sɛ̃] *m carpentry*: cross-bar, cross-piece; *balance*: beam; *bed*: bolster; **traversine** [⁓'sin] *f* cross-bar, cross-beam; ⚓ gangplank.

travesti, e [travɛs'ti] 1. *adj.* disguised; fancy-dress (*ball*); burlesqued; 2. *su./m* fancy dress; *thea.* man's part (played by a woman) (*or vice versa*); transvestite; **travestir** [⁓'ti:r] (2a) *v/t.* misrepresent, distort; se ⁓ put on fancy dress; dress up (as, *en*); **travestisme** [⁓'tism] *m* transvestism; **travestissement** [⁓tis'mã] *m* disguise; disguising; *fig.* travesty, misrepresentation (*of a fact*).

trayeur [trɛ'jœ:r] *m* milker; **trayeuse** [⁓'jø:z] *f* milkmaid; milking-machine; **trayon** [⁓'jõ] *m cow*: teat, dug.

trébuchant, e [treby'ʃã, ⁓'ʃã:t] stumbling; staggering; of full weight (*coin*); **trébucher** [⁓'ʃe] (1a) *v/i.* stumble (*a. fig.*), stagger; turn the scale (*coin*); *fig.* trip; *v/t.* test (*a coin*) for weight; **trébuchet** [⁓'ʃe] *m* assay or precision balance; trap (*for small birds*).

tréfiler ⊕ [trefi'le] (1a) *v/t.* wiredraw; **tréfilerie** ⊕ [⁓fil'ri] *f* wiredrawing (mill); **tréfileur** ⊕ [⁓fi-'lœ:r] *m* wire-drawer.

trèfle [trɛfl] *m* ♣ clover; △, ♣ trefoil; *cards*: club(s *pl.*); ♣ ⁓ blanc shamrock; *mot.* croisement *m* en ⁓ cloverleaf (crossing); *jouer* ⁓ play a club, play clubs; **tréflière** ⚒ [trefli'ɛ:r] *f* clover-field.

tréfonds [tre'fõ] *m fig.* (inmost) depths *pl.*

treillage [trɛ'ja:ʒ] *m* trellis; latticework; wire netting; wire fencing; **treillager** [⁓ja'ʒe] (1l) *v/t.* trellis; lattice (*a wall, a window*); enclose with wire netting.

treille [trɛ:j] *f* vine-arbo(u)r; ♣ climbing vine, grape-vine; F jus *m* de la ⁓ juice of the grape, wine.

treillis [trɛ'ji] *m* trellis(-work), lattice; grid (*for maps etc.*); *tex.* glazed calico; *tex.* coarse canvas, sackcloth; ✕ fatigue-dress, fatigues *pl.*; **treillisser** [⹁ji'se] (1a) *v/t.* see *treillager.*

treize [trɛːz] **1.** *adj./num.* thirteen; *date, title*: thirteenth; ∼ *à la dou-zaine* baker's dozen; **2.** *su./m/inv.* thirteen; **treizième** [trɛ'zjɛm] *adj./num., a. su.* thirteenth.

tremblaie ♀ [trɑ̃'blɛ] *f* aspen grove; **tremblant, e** [trɑ̃'blɑ̃, ∼'blɑ̃ːt] **1.** *adj.* trembling (with, de); quak-ing, shaking (*ground, voice*); qua-vering (*voice*); flickering (*light*); shaky (*bridge, a. fig. person*); quiv-ering (*face*); **2.** *su./m* ♪ *organ*: tremolo (stop); **tremble** ♀ [trɑ̃'bl] *m* aspen; **tremblement** [trɑ̃blə-'mɑ̃] *m* trembling, shaking, quiver-ing; *voice*: quaver(ing); *fig. horror*: shudder(ing); ♪ tremolo; ♫, *a. fig. emotion*: tremor; ∼ *de terre* earth-quake, earth tremor; F *tout le* ∼ the whole shoot *or* caboodle; **trem-bler** [⹁'ble] (1a) *v/i.* tremble, shake, quiver (with, de); quaver (♪, *a. voice*); flicker (*light*); flutter (*bird's wings*); *fig.* tremble, be afraid; ∼ *que* (*sbj.*) be terrified lest (*cond.*); **trembleur, -euse** [⹁'blœːr, ⹁'bløːz] *su.* trembler; *fig.* timid *or* anxious person; *su./m* ⚡ make-and-break; *tel., teleph.* buzzer; **trembloter** [⹁blɔ'te] (1a) *v/i.* quiver, quaver (*voice*); flicker (*light*); flutter (*wings*); shiver (with, de).

trémière ♀ [tre'mjɛːr] *adj./f*: *rose f* ∼ hollyhock.

tremolo [tremɔ'lo] *m* ♪ tremolo; *fig.* quaver.

trémousser [tremu'se] (1a) *v/t.*: *se* ∼ wiggle; fidget (*child etc.*); jig about.

trempage [trɑ̃'paːʒ] *m* ⊕ soaking, steeping; *typ. paper*: damping; **trempe** [trɑ̃ːp] *f* ⊕ soaking, steep-ing; quenching; *metall.* tempering, hardening; *steel*: temper; *fig.* cal-ibre, stamp; F thrashing; hiding; ∼ *de surface* casehardening; **trempée** [trɑ̃'pe] soaked, drenched, wet (through); *metall.* tempered; *fig.* sturdy, energetic; **tremper** [⹁'pe] (1a) *v/t.* soak; drench; dip (*the pen in ink*); dip, *Am.* dunk (*bread, biscuit in a liquid*); ⊕ *etc.* quench; *typ.* damp (*paper*); dilute (*wine*) with water; *v/i.* soak; *fig.* be a party (to, *dans*); **trem-**

pette [⹁'pɛt] *f*: *faire* ∼ dunk a biscuit *etc.* in one's wine *or* coffee *etc.*; F have a dip.

tremplin [trɑ̃'plɛ̃] *m sp. etc.* spring-board; diving-board; *ski*: platform; *fig.* stepping-stone (to, *pour*).

trémulation [tremyla'sjɔ̃] *f* vi-bration, trepidation; ♫ tremor.

trentaine [trɑ̃'tɛn] *f* (about) thirty; *la* ∼ the age of thirty, the thirties *pl.*; **trente** [trɑ̃ːt] *adj./num., a. su./m/inv.* thirty; *date, title*: thirtieth; ∼*-trois tours m* long-playing record, album; **trentième** [trɑ̃'tjɛm] *adj./num., a. su.* thirtieth.

trépan [tre'pɑ̃] *m* ♫, ⊕ trepan; ⊕ rock-drill; *a.* = **trépanation** ♫ [⹁pana'sjɔ̃] *f* trepanning; **trépaner** [⹁pa'ne] (1a) *v/t.* ♫ trepan; ⊕ drill *or* bore into (*rock*).

trépas *poet.* [tre'pɑ] *m* death, de-cease; **trépassé, e** [trepa'se] *adj., a. su.* dead, departed; deceased; **tré-passer** [⹁] (1a) *v/i.* die, pass away.

trépidation [trepida'sjɔ̃] *f* ♫, *a. fig.* trembling; *fig.* flurry, agitation; trepidation, vibration.

trépied [tre'pje] *m* tripod; *cuis.* trivet.

trépigner [trepi'ɲe] (1a) stamp one's feet; jump (for joy, *de joie*); dance (with, *de*); *v/t.* trample (*the earth*).

trépointe [tre'pwɛ̃t] *f shoe*: welt.

très [trɛ] *adv.* very, most; very much.

trésaille [tre'zaːj] *f* ⊕ crosspiece.

Très-Haut [trɛ'o] *m/inv.*: *le* ∼ the Almighty, God.

trésor [tre'zɔːr] *m* treasure (*a. fig.*); treasure-house; *eccl.* relics *pl.* and ornaments *pl.*; ⚖ treasure-trove; *pol.* ♀ Treasury; ∼*s pl.* wealth *sg.*; F *dépenser des* ∼*s pour* spend a for-tune on; **trésorerie** [⹁zɔr'ri] *f* treasury; treasurer's office; treas-urership; *pol.* ♀ Treasury; *Britain*: Exchequer; **trésorier, -ère** [⹁zɔ-'rje, ∼'rjɛːr] *su.* treasurer; *su./m ad-min., a.* ✕ paymaster; *su./f admin.* paymistress.

tressage [trɛ'saːʒ] *m* plaiting, braid-ing.

tressaillement [trɛsaj'mɑ̃] *m* sur-prise: start; *fear*: shudder; *pleasure, joy*: thrill; *pain*: wince; **tressaillir** [⹁sa'jiːr] (2s) *v/i.* quiver, flutter (*heart*); ∼ *de start* (*etc.*) with; shud-der with (*fear*); thrill with (*joy*); wince with (*pain*).

tressauter [treso'te] (1a) *v/i.* jump (with fear, surprise, *etc.*); jolt, jump about (*things*).

tresse [trɛs] *f* hair, straw: tress, plait; *yarn*, *a.* ⚡: braid; **tresser** [trɛ'se] (1a) *v/t.* plait (*hair*, *straw*); braid (*yarn*, *a.* ⚡); weave (*a basket*, *flowers*, *a garland*); **tresseur** *m*, **-euse** *f* [⌐'sœ:r, ⌐'sø:z] braider, plaiter.

tréteau [tre'to] *m* trestle, support; *thea.* ⌐*x pl.* stage *sg.*

treuil ⊕ [trœ:j] *m* winch, windlass.

trêve [trɛ:v] *f* truce; *fig.* respite; *sans* ⌐ unremittingly, relentlessly; ⌐ *de ...* enough of ..., no more ...; ⌐ *de plaisanteries!* no more joking!

tri [tri] *m* sorting.

triade [tri'ad] *f* triad.

triage [tri'a:ʒ] *m* sorting; selecting; ⚒ grading; 🚂 *gare f de* ⌐ marshalling yard.

triangle [tri'ɑ̃:gl] *m* ♇, ♪, *astr.* triangle; ⚓ triangular flag; ≠ three-phase mesh; set square, *Am.* triangle; **triangulaire** [triɑ̃gy'lɛ:r] triangular; *pol.* three-cornered (*contest*); **triangulation** *surv.* [⌐la'sjɔ̃] *f* triangulation.

trias *geol.* [tri'ɑ:s] *m* trias; **triasique** *geol.* [⌐a'zik] triassic.

tribal, e [tri'bal] tribal.

tribord ⚓ [tri'bɔ:r] *m* starboard; *à* (*or par*) ⌐ to starboard. [ily.)

tribu [tri'by] *f* tribe; *zo.* sub-fam-)

tribulation [tribyla'sjɔ̃] *f* tribulation; *fig.* trial; F worry, trouble.

tribun [tri'bœ̃] *m* *hist.* tribune; *fig.* popular orator; demagogue.

tribunal [triby'nal] *m* ⚖, ✕, *a.* *admin.* tribunal; ⚖ (law-)court; *judges*: bench; ⌐ *arbitral* (*de commerce*) arbitration (commercial) court; ⌐ *de première instance* court of first instance; (*approx.*) County Court; ⌐ *de simple police* magistrate's court, F police-court; ⌐ *pour enfants* juvenile court; **tribune** [⌐'byn] *f* rostrum, (*speaker's*) platform; ♱ (*organ*) loft; ♪, *eccl.*, *etc.* gallery; *turf*: grand stand; *fig.* forum; ⌐ *de la presse* press galery; *parl. monter à la* ⌐ address the House.

tribut [tri'by] *m* tribute (*a. fig.*); *fig.* reward; **tributaire** [⌐by'tɛ:r] tributary (*a. geog.*).

tricar *mot.* [tri'ka:r] *m* motor-tricycle; three-wheeler.

tricher [tri'ʃe] (1a) *vt/i.* cheat; **tricherie** [triʃ'ri] *f* cards *etc.*: cheating; trickery; **tricheur** *m*, **-euse** *f* [tri'ʃœ:r, ⌐'ʃø:z] cheat, trickster; *cards*: sharper.

trichine 🦠 [tri'ʃin, ⌐'kin] *f* trichina; thread-worm; **trichinose** 🦠 [⌐ki-'no:z] *f* trichinosis.

trichromie *phot.*, *typ.* [trikrɔ'mi] *f* three-colo(u)r process.

tricolore [triko'lɔ:r] tricolo(u)r(ed); *drapeau m* ⌐ tricolo(u)r, French (national) flag.

tricorne [tri'kɔrn] **1.** *adj. zo.* three-horned; *cost.* tricorn (*hat*); **2.** *su./m* tricorn, three-cornered hat.

tricot [tri'ko] *m* knitting; *tex.* stockinet; 🧥 knitwear; jersey, sweater, pullover; (*a.* ⌐ *de corps*) vest, *Am.* undershirt; **tricotage** [trikɔ'ta:ʒ] *m* knitting; **tricoter** [⌐'te] (1a) *v/t.* knit; F *se* ⌐ make off; *v/i.* F *fig.* move or walk fast; F dance; **tricoteur**, **-euse** [⌐'tœ:r, ⌐'tø:z] *su.* knitter; *su./f* knitting-machine; ⊕ knitting-loom.

trictrac [trik'trak] *m* backgammon (-board); *dice*: rattle.

tricycle [tri'sikl] *m* tricycle; three-wheeled vehicle.

trident [tri'dɑ̃] *m* *myth. etc.* trident; ✔ three-pronged pitch-fork; ♇ trident curve; fish-spear.

tridimensionnel, -elle [tridimɑ̃sjɔ-'nɛl] threedimensional.

trièdre ♇ [tri'edr] **1.** *adj.* trihedral; **2.** *su./m* trihedral, trihedron.

triennal, e *m/pl.* **-aux** [triɛn'nal, ⌐'no] triennial; **triennat** [⌐'na] *m* triennium; three-year term of office.

trier [tri'e] (1a) *v/t.* sort (out); *tex.* pick; 🚂 marshal (*trucks*); *fig.* choose, select; **trieur**, **-euse** [⌐-'œ:r, ⌐'ø:z] *su. person*: sorter; *tex.* (*wool-*)picker; *su./m* ⊕ screening-machine; separator, sorter; *su./f* wool-picking machine; *computer*: sorter.

trifolié, e 🌿 [trifɔ'lje] three-leaved, trifoliate.

trigone ♇ [tri'gɔn] trigonal, three-cornered; **trigonométrie** ♇ [⌐gɔ-nɔme'tri] *f* trigonometry.

trilatéral, e *m/pl.* **-aux** [trilate'ral, ⌐'ro] trilateral, three-sided.

trilingue [tri'lɛ̃:g] trilingual.

trille ♪ [tri:j] *m* trill; **triller** ♪ [tri'je] (1a) *vt/i.* trill.

trillion [tri'ljõ] *m* a million of billions, trillion, *Am.* a billion of billions, quintillion.

trilogie [trilɔ'ʒi] *f* trilogy.

trimard † *sl.* [tri'maːr] *m* high road; **trimarder** *sl.* [trimar'de] (1a) *v/i.* be on the tramp; *v/t.* carry, F lug; **trimardeur** *sl.* [ˌ'dœːr] *m* tramp, *Am.* hobo.

trimbaler F [trɛ̃ba'le] (1a) *v/t.* carry about, F tote about; trail (*s.o.*) along; have (*s.o.*) in tow; F lug (*s.th.*) about.

trimer F [tri'me] (1a) *v/i.* drudge, toil.

trimestre [tri'mɛstr] *m* quarter, three month; quarter's rent *or* salary; *univ.*, *school*: term, *Am.* session; term's fees *pl.*, *Am.* sessional fees *pl.*; **trimestriel, -elle** [ˌmɛstri'ɛl] quarterly; trimestrial.

trimoteur ✈ [trimɔ'tœːr] **1.** *adj./m* three-engined; **2.** *su./m* three-engined aeroplane.

tringle [trɛ̃ːgl] *f* rod; 🛏 bar; ⚓ *etc.* (*wooden*) batten; 📐 square mo(u)lding, tringle.

trinité [trini'te] *f* trinity (*a.* ♀ *eccl.*).

trinôme ♀ [tri'noːm] *adj.*, *a. su./m* trinomial.

trinquart ⚓ [trɛ̃'kaːr] *m* herring-boat.

trinquer [trɛ̃'ke] (1m) *v/i.* clink *or* touch glasses (with, *avec*); (have a) drink (with, *avec*); F *fig.* hobnob (with, *avec*); *sl.* get the worst of it, suffer.

trio [tri'o] *m* ♪ *etc.* trio.

triode [tri'ɔd] *f* (*a.* lampe *f* ˌ) *radio*: three-electrode lamp, triode.

triolet [triɔ'lɛ] *m* ♪ triplet; *prosody*: triolet.

triomphal, e, *m/pl.* **-aux** [triɔ̃'fal, ˌ'fo] triumphal; **triomphalement** [ˌfal'mɑ̃] *adv.* triumphantly; **triomphant, e** [ˌ'fɑ̃, ˌ'fɑ̃ːt] triumphant; **triomphateur, -trice** [ˌfa'tœːr, ˌ'tris] **1.** *adj.* triumphing; **2.** *su./m* (triumphant) victor; winner; **triomphe** [tri'ɔ̃ːf] *m* triumph; *arc m* de ˌ triumphal arch; **triompher** [ˌɔ̃'fe] (1a) *v/i.* triumph (over, de); *fig.* rejoice, exult (over, de); ˌ dans excel in *or* at; ˌ de a. overcome, get over (*s.th.*).

tripaille F [tri'paːj] *f* garbage; (*butcher's*) offal.

triparti, e [tripar'ti], **tripartite** [ˌ'tit] tripartite; *pol.* three-party

(*government*), three-power; **tripartition** [ˌti'sjɔ̃] *f* tripartition.

tripe [trip] *f cuis.* (*usu.* ˌs *pl.*) tripe; *cigar*: core; F ˌs *pl.* guts; *tex.* ˌ de *velours* velveteen; **triperie** [tri'pri] *f* tripe-shop, tripe trade; **tripette** F [ˌ'pɛt] *f:* ça ne *vaut pas* ˌ it's not worth a cent.

triphasé, e ⚡ [trifɑ'ze] three-phase, triphase.

tripier [tri'pje] *m* tripe-dealer, tripe-seller.

triple [tripl] **1.** *adj.* threefold, treble; triple (*a.* ♀, ♏, *astr.*); F *fig.* out-and-out (*fool*); **2.** *su./m* treble; **triplé** *m*, **e** *f* [tri'ple] *children*: triplet; **tripler** [ˌ] (1a) *vt/i.* treble; increase threefold.

triporteur [tripɔr'tœːr] *m* carrier-tricycle; (*commercial*) tri-car.

tripot [tri'po] *m* gambling house, dive; **tripotage** [tripɔ'taːʒ] *m* messing about *or* round; *fig.* intrigue; tampering (*with accounts, the cash, etc.*); **tripotée** *sl.* [ˌ'te] *f* hiding, beating; lots *pl.* (*of people, things*); **tripoter** [ˌ'te] (1a) *v/i.* mess about *or* around; rummage about; *v/t.* finger, fiddle with, play with; meddle with (*s.th.*); paw (*s.o.*); *fig.* be up to; **tripoteur** [ˌ'tœːr] *m* intriguer; mischief-maker; shady speculator.

triptyque [trip'tik] *m art*: triptych; *admin.* triptyque; *fig.* three-part plan *etc.*

trique F [trik] *f* cudgel, big stick; *maigre* (*or* sec) *comme un coup de* ˌ as thin as a rake.

triqueballe † [trik'bal] *m* timber-cart; logging-wheels *pl.*

triquer [tri'ke] (1m) *v/t.* sort (*timber*); beat, thrash (*s.o.*).

trisaïeul [triza'jœl] *m* great-great grandfather; **trisaïeule** [ˌ] *f* great-great grandmother.

trisannuel, -elle [triza'nɥɛl] triennial.

trisection [trisɛk'sjɔ̃] *f* trisection.

trisser[1] *sl.* [tri'se] (1a) *v/t.:* se ˌ clear off.

trisser[2] [ˌ] (1a) *v/i.* call for a second encore; *v/t.* encore twice.

triste [trist] sad; sorrowful, melancholy (*face, news, person*); downcast (*expression, face, person*); dull (*life, weather*); gloomy, dreary (*life, room, scene, weather*); painful (*duty,* *news*); *fig.* sorry, poor; **tristesse** [tris'tɛs] *f* sadness; gloom; *life, room, scene, weather*: gloominess, dreariness; *scenery*: bleakness.

triton[1] *zo.* [tri'tɔ̃] *m* water-salamander, newt; *mollusc*: trumpet-shell.

triton[2] *♩* [~] *m* tritone.

trituration ⊕ [trityra'sjɔ̃] *f* trituration, grinding; **triturer** ⊕ [~'re] (1a) *v/t.* grind (up); knead, pommel; manipulate; F se ~ *la cervelle* rack one's brains.

trivalence ⚛ [triva'lɑ̃:s] *f* trivalence; **trivalent, e** ⚛ [~'lɑ̃, ~'lɑ̃:t] trivalent.

trivial, e, *m/pl.* **-aux** [tri'vjal, ~'vjo] trite, hackneyed; vulgar, coarse; **trivialité** [~vjali'te] *f* triteness, vulgarity, coarseness, vulgarism.

troc [trɔk] *m* barter, exchange; F swop(ping), *Am.* swap(ping).

trochée [trɔ'ʃe] *m prosody*: trochee.

troène ♀ [trɔ'ɛn] *m* privet.

troglodyte [trɔglɔ'dit] *m zo.*, *orn.* troglodyte; *person*: caveman, cave-dweller.

trogne [trɔɲ] *f* bloated face.

trognon [trɔ'ɲɔ̃] *m fruit*: core; *cabbage*: stump, stalk; *sl.* darling; F *fig. jusqu'au* ~ completely, utterly.

trois [trwa] **1.** *adj./num.* three; *date, title*: third; **2.** *su./m/inv.* three; ♣ *règle f de* ~ rule of three; **~-étoiles** [trwaze'twal] *adj.* (*a. su./inv.*) three-star (*restaurant or hotel, etc.*); **troisième** [~'zjɛm] **1.** *adj./num.*, *a. su.* third; **2.** *su./m fraction*: third; third (*Am.* fourth) floor; *su./f secondary school*: (*approx.*) fourth form; **trois-mâts** ⚓ [trwa'mɑ] *m/inv.* three-master; **trois-pieces** *cost.* [~'pjɛs] *m/inv.* three-piece suit; **trois-quarts** [~'ka:r] *m/inv.* ♩ three-quarter violin; three-quarter length coat; *rugby*: three-quarter; **trois-six** ♱ [~'sis] *m* proof spirit.

trolley [trɔ'lɛ] *m* ⊕ trolley, runner; ♂ trolley(-pole and wheel); **~bus** [~lɛ'bys] *m* trolley-bus.

trombe [trɔ:b] *f meteor.* waterspout; *fig.* stream, torrent; ~ *d'eau* cloud-burst; *fig. en* ~ like a whirlwind; *entrer (passer) en* ~ burst in (dash by).

trombine *sl.* [trɔ̃'bin] *f* face; head.

trombone [trɔ̃'bɔn] *m* ♩ trombone; (wire) paper-clip; **tromboniste** ♩ [~bɔ'nist] *m* trombonist.

trommel ⊕, ⚒ [trɔ'mɛl] *m* revolving screen; drum.

trompe [trɔ̃:p] *f* ♩ horn (*a. mot.*); *zo.* proboscis, *elephant*: trunk; *anat.* tube; ~*s pl. utérines* Fallopian tubes.

trompe-la-mort F [trɔ̃pla'mɔ:r] *su./inv.* death-dodger; **trompe-l'œil** [~'plœ:j] *m/inv. art*: trompe-l'œil; *fig.* eyewash, window dressing; **tromper** [~'pe] (1a) *v/t.* deceive; cheat; mislead; delude (about, *sur*); be unfaithful to (*one's husband or wife*); outwit, elude (*the law, a watch*); *fig.* beguile (*one's grief, one's hunger, the time*); *fig.* run counter to (*hopes, intentions*); *se* ~ be wrong; make a mistake; *se* ~ *de chemin* take the wrong road; **tromperie** [~'pri] *f* deceit, deception; illusion; piece of deceit.

trompeter [trɔ̃p'te] (1c) *v/t.* trumpet abroad (*a. fig.*); *fig.* divulge; *v/i.* sound the trumpet; scream (*eagle*).

trompette [trɔ̃'pɛt] *su./f* trumpet; *en* ~ turned-up (*nose*); *su./m* = **trompettiste** [~pɛ'tist] *m* trumpeter.

trompeur, -euse [trɔ̃'pœ:r, ~'pø:z] **1.** *adj.* deceitful (*person*); lying (*tongue, words*); *fig.* deceptive (*appearance etc.*); **2.** *su.* deceiver; cheat; betrayer.

tronc [trɔ̃] *m* ♣, ⚛, *anat.* trunk; ♀ *tree*: bole; ⚛ *column*: drum; *eccl.* collection-box; alms-box; ♣ frustum; ♣ ~ *de cône* truncated cone; **tronche** *sl.* [trɔ̃ʃ] *f* head; **tronçon** [~'sɔ̃] *m* stump; piece; length; offcut; ⚙, *tel., etc.* section; **tronconique** ♣ [~kɔ'nik] in the shape of a truncated cone; **tronçonner** [~sɔ'ne] (1a) *v/t.* cut up; cut into lengths *or* sections.

trône [tro:n] *m* throne; *monter sur le* ~ ascend the throne; **trôner** [tro'ne] (1a) *v/i.* sit enthroned; F *fig.* sit in state, lord it.

tronquer [trɔ̃'ke] (1m) *v/t.* ⚛, ♣ truncate; *fig.* shorten; *fig.* cut down.

trop [tro] *adv.* too much *or* many; too, over-...; unduly; too long *or* far; too often; too well; *de* ~ too many; *être de* ~ be unwelcome, be in the way; *ne ... que* ~ far too ...; *only* too ...; *par* ~ altogether *or* really too ...

trophée [trɔ'fe] *m* trophy.

trophique *physiol.* [trɔ'fik] trophic; digestive (*trouble*).

tropical, e, *m/pl.* **-aux** [trɔpi'kal,

~'ko] tropical (*climate, heat, plant*); **tropique** *astr., geog.* [~'pik] *m* tropic.

trop-plein [trɔ'plɛ̃] *m* overflow; waste-pipe; overflow-pipe; *fig.* superabundance.

troquer [trɔ'ke] (1m) *v/t.* exchange, barter, F swop, *Am.* swap (for, *contre*).

troquet F [trɔ'kɛ] *m* (*small*) café.

trot [tro] *m* trot; *aller au* ~ trot; F *au* ~ quickly; *prendre le* ~ break into a trot; **trotte** F [trɔt] *f* (*a good*) distance; **trotte-menu** † [~mə'ny] *adj./inv.* scampering; *poet. la gent* ~ mice *pl.*; **trotter** [trɔ'te] (1a) *v/i.* trot; scamper (about); F *fig.* be on the move *or* go; ~ *par* (*or dans*) *la tête de q.* haunt s.o. (*tune*); *v/t.*: F se ~ be off; **trotteur, -euse** [~'tœːr, ~'tøːz] 1. *adj.* walking(-*costume etc.*); 2. *su.* *horse:* trotter; *fig.* quick walker; *su./f* *clock, watch:* second hand; **trotti-ner** [~ti'ne] (1a) *v/i.* trot short (*horse*); jog along (*on a horse*); *fig.* toddle (*child*); *fig.* trot about; **trotti-nette** [~ti'nɛt] *f* scooter; **trottoir** [~'twaːr] *m* pavement, footpath, *Am.* sidewalk; ~ *cyclable* cycle path; F *pej.* *faire le* ~ walk the streets.

trou [tru] *m* hole; *needle:* eye; gap (*a. fig.*); *anat.* foramen; *thea.* (*prompt-er's*) box; ✈ ~ *d'air* air pocket; ⊕~ *de* *graissage* oil-hole; *fig. boucher un* ~ pay off a debt; *faire* (*or créer*) *le* ~ *sp.* break clear; *fig.* outdistance one's rivals; F *faire un* ~ *à la lune* do a moonlight flit; abscond.

troublant, e [tru'blɑ̃, ~'blɑ̃ːt] disturbing; disquieting; unsettling; **trouble** [trubl] 1. *adj.* blurred, hazy; cloudy (*liquid etc.*); confused; murky (*light, sky, etc.*); dim (*eyes, light*); 2. *su./m* confusion, disorder; agitation, distress; discord, dissension; *fig.* uneasiness, turmoil; ~*s* *pl.* *pol.* unrest *sg.*, disturbances; 🏛 trouble *sg.*, disorders; **trouble-fête** [trublə'fɛːt] *su./inv.* spoilsport; wet blanket; **troubler** [~'ble] (1a) *v/t.* disturb; cloud (*a liquid*); *fig.* inter-rupt; *fig.* perplex, disconcert; make (*s.o.*) uneasy; ruffle (*s.o.*); *se* ~ become cloudy *or* overcast (*sky*); falter (*voice*); become flustered (*person*); show concern.

trouée [tru'e] *f* gap, break; ✕ breach, break-through; **trouer** [~] (1a) *v/t.*

make a hole *or* holes in; *fig.* pit (with, *de*); *fig.* make gaps in; *se* ~ wear into holes, develop holes; *être troué* have a hole *or* holes (in it).

trouille *sl.* [truːj] *f* fear, jitters *pl.*; *avoir la* ~ have the wind up, be in a blue funk.

troupe [trup] *f* people: troop (*a.* ✕), band; *pej.* gang; *thea.* company, troupe; ✕ regiment; ✕ men *pl.*; cattle, deer, etc.: herd; geese, sheep: flock; *flies:* swarm; *birds:* flight; ✕ ~*s* *pl.* forces, troops; **troupeau** [tru-'po] *m cattle etc.:* herd; *geese, sheep, a. fig., eccl.:* flock; *fig.* set, pack; **trou-pier** † F [~'pje] *m* soldier; *jurer comme un* ~ swear like a trooper.

trousse [trus] *f* † bundle; *hay:* truss; ⊕, 🔧 *instruments, tools:* case, kit; ~ *à* *pharmacie* first-aid box *or* kit; ~ *de* *maquillage* vanity case *or* bag; ~ *à* *outils* toolkit; ~ *de toilette* toilet bag, sponge bag; ~ *de voyage* travelling case; *aux* ~*s de* on (*s.o.'s*) heels, after (*s.o.*); **trousseau** [tru'so] *m* keys etc.: bunch; outfit; *bride:* trousseau; *metall.* sweep; **trousse-queue** [trus'kø] *m/inv. horse:* tail-case; **trousser** [tru'se] (1a) *v/t.* tuck up; turn up (*one's trousers*); *cuis.* truss (*fowl*); *metall.* sweep (*a mould*); F *fig.* dash (*s.th.*) off.

trouvable [tru'vabl] that can be found, findable; **trouvaille** [~'vaːj] *f* (*lucky*) find, godsend; **trouver** [~'ve] (1a) *v/t.* find; discover; hit *or* come upon; meet (with); *fig.* consider, think; ~ *bon* (*mauvais*) (dis)approve; ~ *bon de* (*inf.*) think fit to (*inf.*); ~ *la mort* meet one's death; *aller* (*venir*) ~ *q.* go (come) and see s.o.; *comment trouvez-vous* ...? what do you think of ...?; *enfant m trouvé* foundling; *objets m/pl. trouvés* lost property *sg.*; *vous trouvez?* do you think so?; *se* ~ be (present, situated); feel (*better etc.*); happen; *il se trouve que* ... it happens that; **trouvère** [~'vɛːr] *m* minstrel; **trouveur** *m*, **-euse** *f* [~'vœːr, ~'vøːz] discoverer; finder.

truand [try'ɑ̃] *m* crook, villain; † begger; **truander** F [~ɑ̃'de] *v/t.* (1a) swindle, do.   [shove-net.↑

truble [trybl] *f* fishing: hoop-net,↓

truc F [tryk] *m* knack, hang; dodge; trick; thingummy, thing, gadget.

trucage [try'kaːʒ] *m* faking; cheating; fake; F *accounts:* cooking; *cin.* trick picture; ⚔ dummy work; *pol. elections:* gerrymandering.

truchement [tryʃ'mɑ̃] *m* † interpreter; *fig.* go-between; *fig.* means of expression; *par le* ~ *de* through.

trucider F [trysi'de] (1a) *v/t.* massacre, kill.

truc(k) 📞 [tryk] *m* truck.

truculent, e [tryky'lɑ̃, ~'lɑ̃ːt] col-o(u)rful.

truelle [try'ɛl] *f* ⚒, ⊕, *etc.* trowel; *cuis.* (*fish-)slice;* **truellée** [~ɛ'le] *f* trowelful.

truffe [tryf] *f* ⚘, *cuis.* truffle; *dog:* nose; F idiot; **truffer** [try'fe] (1a) *v/t. cuis.* stuff with truffles; *fig.* truffé de full of, bristling with; **trufficulteur** [~fikyl'tœːr] *m* truffle-grower; **truffier, -ère** [~'fje, ~'fjɛːr] 1. *adj.* truffle-...; 2. *su./m* truffle-grower; *su./f* truffle-bed.

truie [trɥi] *f* sow.

truisme [try'ism] *m* truism.

truite *icht.* [trɥit] *f* trout; ~ *saumonée* salmon trout; **truité, e** [trɥi'te] spotted; speckled; crackled (*china*).

trumeau [try'mo] *m* ▲ pier; pierglass; *cuis.* leg of beef.

truquage [try'kaːʒ] *m see trucage;* **truquer** [~'ke] (1m) *v/t.* fake; F fiddle with, fix; cook (*accounts*); *pol.* gerrymander (*elections*); *v/i.* cheat; sham; **truqueur** *m*, **-euse** *f* [~'kœːr, ~'køːz] *person:* fraud, humbug; faker (*of antiques etc.*).

trust ✝ [trœst] *m* trust; **truster** ✝ [trœs'te] (1a) *v/i.* trust; *v/t.* monopolize (*a. fig.*).

tsar [tsaːr] *m* tsar, czar; **tsarine** [tsa'rin] *f* tsarina, czarina; **tsariste** [~'rist] *adj., a. su.* tsarist, czarist.

tsé-tsé *zo.* [tse'tse] *f* tsetse-fly.

tu¹ [ty] *pron./pers.* you.

tu², e [~] *p.p. of* taire.

tuable [tɥabl] fit for slaughter (*animal*); **tuant, tuante** F [tɥɑ̃, tɥɑ̃ːt] killing (*work*); splitting (*headache*); *fig.* exasperating; boring (*person*).

tub [tœb] *m* tub, bath.

tuba [ty'ba] *m* ♪ tuba; *sp.* snorkel.

tubage [ty'baːʒ] *m* ⊕, ▲, *₰*, *vet.* tubing; *shaft, well:* casing; **tube** [tyb] *m* ⚘, 📞, ⊕ boiler, ⚓ torpedo, *anat., paint., phys., telev.,* † toothpaste, *etc.:* tube; ⊕, ▲ pipe; *radio:*

valve; *anat.* duct; *sl.* hit (song); *sl.* (tele)phone; 📞 ~ *à essai* test-tube; *telev.* ~ *de prise de vue* camera tube; *sl. coup de* ~ phone call; F buzz.

tuber [ty'be] (1a) *v/t.* ⊕, *₰*, *vet.* tube (*boiler, bore-hole, larynx, well*); ⊕ case (*a shaft*).

tubercule [tybɛr'kyl] *m* ⚘ tuber; *₰* tubercle; **tuberculé, e** *biol.* [~ky'le] tubercled, tuberculate(d); **tuberculeux, -euse** [~ky'lø, ~'løːz] 1. *adj.* ⚘ tubercular; *₰* tuberculous; 2. *su.* *₰* tubercular patient; consumptive; **tuberculose** *₰* [~ky'loːz] *f* tuberculosis.

tubéreux, -euse ⚘ [tybe'rø, ~'røːz] tuberose; **tubérosité** [~rozi'te] *f* tuberosity. [tubular.]

tubulaire ⚘, ▲, ⊕, 📞 [tyby'lɛːr]
tubulure [tyby'lyːr] *f* ⊕ pump *etc.:* pipe; nozzle; *bottle:* neck; *mot.* manifold.

tue-chien ⚘ [ty'ʃjɛ̃] *m/inv.* meadow-saffron; **tue-mouches** [~'muʃ] *m/inv.* ⚘ fly agaric; fly-swatter; (*a. papier m* ~) fly-paper; **tuer** [tɥe] (1n) *v/t.* kill (*a. fig. time*); *butcher:* slaughter; *fig.* bore (*s.o.*) to death; *fig.* while away (*one's time*); ⚔ *tué à l'ennemi* killed in action; *se* ~ kill o.s.; commit suicide; be killed; *fig.* wear o.s. out (in, with *à*); **tuerie** [ty'ri] *f fig.* slaughter, massacre; slaughter-house; **tue-tête** [~'tɛt] *adv.: à* ~ at the top of one's voice; **tueur** *m*, **tueuse** *f* [tɥœːr, tɥøːz] killer, slayer, slaughterer (*a. fig.*).

tuf [tyf] *m geol.* tufa; *fig.* foundation, bed-rock; *geol.* ~ *volcanique* tuff.

tuile [tɥil] *f* tile; F *fig.* (piece of) bad luck, blow; **tuileau** [tɥi'lo] *m* broken tile; piece of tile; **tuilerie** ⊕ [tɥil'ri] *f* tileworks *usu. sg.*, tilery; **tuilier** ⊕ [tɥi'lje] *m* tiler, tile maker.

tulipe [ty'lip] *f* ⚘ tulip; ⚡ (tulip-shaped) lamp-shade; **tuilipier** ⚘ [~li'pje] *m* tulip-tree.

tulle *tex.* [tyl] *m* tulle; net.

tuméfaction *₰* [tymefak'sjɔ̃] *f* swelling, tumefaction; **tuméfié, e** *₰* [~'fje] (1o) swollen.

tumeur *₰* [ty'mœːr] *f* tumo(u)r, F growth; swelling.

tumulaire [tymy'lɛːr] tomb..., grave...; tumular(y).

tumulte [ty'mylt] *m* tumult, uproar; *passions, politics:* turmoil; *business:* rush, bustle; riot; **tumultueux,**

-euse [～myl'tɥø, ～'tɥøːz] tumultuous, riotous; *fig.* noisy, rowdy.

tumulus [tymy'lys] *m* tumulus, barrow.

tungstène 🝆ₒ *metall.* [tœks'tɛn] *m* tungsten, wolfram; *acier m au* ～ tungsten steel.

tunique [ty'nik] *f* 🜊, ✕, *cost.* tunic; *eccl.* tunicle.

tunnel [ty'nɛl] *m* tunnel (*a. fig.*); ～ *aérodynamique* wind tunnel.

turban *cost.* [tyr'bɑ̃] *m* turban.

turbin F [tyr'bɛ̃] *m* work, job, F grind.

turbine ⊕ [tyr'bin] *f* turbine; *vacuum cleaner:* rotary fan.

turbiner F [tyrbi'ne] (1a) *v/i.* work, toil; *school:* swot, grind; **turbineur** F [～'nœːr] *m* hard worker.

turbocompresseur ⊕, 🜄 [tyrbɔkɔ̃prɛ'sœːr] *m* turbo-compressor, turbo-supercharger; **turbopropulseur** 🜄 [～prɔpyl'sœːr] *m* propeller turbine; *avion m à* ～ turboprop aircraft; **turboréacteur** 🜄 [～reak'tœːr] *m* turbo-jet engine.

turbot *icht.* [tyr'bo] *m* turbot.

turbulence [tyrby'lɑ̃ːs] *f* turbulence (*a. phys.*); *child:* boisterousness; *fig.* unruliness; **turbulent, e** [～lɑ̃, ～'lɑ̃ːt] turbulent; boisterous (*child, wind*); wild (*sea*); stormy (*life*); *fig.* unruly (*people*).

turc, turque [tyrk] **1.** *adj.* Turkish; † *fig.* hard-hearted, harsh; **2.** *su./m ling.* Turkish; *su.* ♀ Turk; *tête f de* ♀ scapegoat; *try-your-strength machine* (*at a fair*).

turf [tyrf] *m* racecourse; turf, racing; **turfiste** [tyr'fist] *su.* racegoer.

turgide [tyr'ʒid] turgid, swollen.

turion 🜊 [ty'rjɔ̃] *m* turion.

turlupin † [tyrly'pɛ̃] *m* buffoon, clown; **turlupinade** † [～pi'nad] *f* piece of low buffoonery; low pun; **turlupiner** [～pi'ne] (1a) *v/t.* F worry; bother; *v/i.* † play the clown, act the buffoon.

turlututu F [tyrlyty'ty] **1.** *su./m* ♪ (*sort of*) toy flute; **2.** *int.* fiddlesticks!; hoity-toity!

turne F [tyrn] *f* digs *pl.*; den, room; dilapidated house; *quelle* ～! what a hole!; what a dump!

turnep(s) 🜊 [tyr'nɛp(s)] *m* kohlrabi.

turpitude [tyrpi'tyd] *f* turpitude; depravity; smut(ty talk *or* story); foul deed.

turquin [tyr'kɛ̃] *adj./m:* *bleu* ～ bluish-grey, slate-blue.

turquoise [tyr'kwaːz] **1.** *su./f stone:* turquoise; **2.** *adj./inv.* turquoise (*colour*).

tus [ty] *1st p. sg. p.s. of taire.*

tussilage 🜊 [tysi'laːʒ] *m* coltsfoot.

tutélaire [tyte'lɛːr] tutelary; guardian ...; **tutelle** [～'tɛl] *f* ✰ guardianship, tutelage; *pol.* trusteeship; *fig.* protection.

tuteur, -trice [ty'tœːr, ～'tris] *su.* ✰ guradian; *fig.* protector; *su./m* 🜊 prop, stake; **tuteurage** ✔ [～tœ'raːʒ] *m* staking.

tutoiement [tytwa'mɑ̃] *m* use of *tu* and *toi* (*as a sign of familiarity*); **tutoyer** [～'je] (1h) *v/t.* address (*s.o.*) as *tu*; be on familiar terms with (*s.o.*).

tutu [ty'ty] *m* ballet-skirt.

tuyau [tɥi'jo] *m* pipe, tube; *cost.* fluting, goffer; 🜊 stalk; *pipe:* stem; *chimney:* flue; F *fig.* tip, wrinkle, hint; ✔ ～ *d'arrosage* garden-hose; *mot.* ～ *d'échappement* exhaust (pipe); tailpipe; ～ *d'écoulement* drain pipe; ～ *de jonction* (*or communication*) connecting pipe; ～ *de poêle* stovepipe; *sl.* top-hat; ～ *d'incendie* firehose; *fig. dire qch. à q. dans le* ～ *de l'oreille* whisper s.th. in s.o.'s ear; **tuyautage** [tɥijo'taːʒ] *m* ⊕ piping, tubing; pipes *pl.*; pipe-line; *cost.* fluting, goffering; F *fig.* tipping (*off*); **tuyauter** [～'te] (1a) *v/t.* flute (*linen*); F give (*s.o.*) a tip; *fer m à* ～ goffering iron *or* tongs *pl.*; **tuyauterie** [～'tri] *f* pipe and tube works *usu. sg. or* factory *or* trade; *cost.* fluting, goffering.

tuyère [tɥi'jɛːr] *f* ⊕ nozzle; 🜄 ～ *d'éjection* outlet jet, *Am.* jet outlet.

tympan [tɛ̃'pɑ̃] *m* 🜂, *anat.* tympanum; *anat.* (ear-)drum; ⊕ pinion; *hydraulics:* scoop-wheel; treadmill; *typ.* tympan; *fig. crever le* ～ *à q.* split s.o.'s ears; **tympanisme** 🝄 [tɛ̃pa'nism] *m* tympanites; **tympanon** ♪ [～'nɔ̃] *m* dulcimer.

type [tip] **1.** *su./m* type (*a. typ., fig.*); standard model *or* pattern; ✝ sample; F fellow, chap, guy; **2.** *adj.* typical; standard ...; **typesse** *sl.* [ti'pɛs] *f* female.

typhique 🝄 [ti'fik] typhous; **typhoïde** 🝄 [～fo'id] **1.** *adj.* typhoid; **2.** *su./f* typhoid (fever).

typhon *meteor.* [ti'fɔ̃] *m* typhoon.

typhus ⚕ [ti'fys] *m* typhus.

typique [ti'pik] typical (of, *de*); symbolical.

typographe [tipɔ'graf] *m* typographer, printer; **typographie** [ˌɡra'fi] *f* typography; letterpress printing; printing-works *usu. sg.*; **typographique** [ˌɡra'fik] typographical; *erreur f* ~ misprint.

tyran [ti'rɑ̃] *m* tyrant (*a. fig.*); *orn.* king-bird; **tyrannicide** [tirani'sid] *su. person:* tyrannicide; *su./m act:*

tyrannicide; **tyrannie** [ˌ'ni] *f* tyranny (*a. fig.*); **tyrannique** [ˌ'nik] tyrannical (*a. fig.*); **tyranniser** [ˌni'ze] (1a) *v/t.* tyrannize (*s.o.*); oppress (*s.o.*); rule (*s.o.*) with a rod of iron; *fig.* bully (*s.o.*).

tyrolien, -enne [tirɔ'ljɛ̃, ˌ'ljɛn] **1.** *adj.* Tyrolese; **2.** *su.* ♀ Tyrolese; *les* ♀s *m/pl.* the Tyrolese; *su./f* ♪ yodelled melody; ♪ Tyrolienne.

tzar [tsa:r] *etc. see tsar etc.*

tzigane [tsi'gan] *su.* Hungarian gipsy, Tzigane.

U

U, u [y] *m* U, u; ⊕ *fer m en* U U-girder.

ubiquité [ybikɥi'te] *f* ubiquity; *avoir le don d'~* be everywhere at the same time.

ubuesque [yby'ɛsk] grotesque.

ukase *pol., a. fig.* [y'kɑːz] *m* ukase, edict.

ulcération ♀ [ylsera'sjɔ̃] *f* ulceration; **ulcère** ♀ [~'sɛːr] *m* ulcer; sore; *~ à l'estomac* stomach ulcer; **ulcérer** [ylse're] (1f) *v/t.* ♀ ulcerate; *fig.* embitter; **ulcéreux, -euse** [~'rø, ~'røːz] ulcerated; ulcerous.

ultérieur, e [ylte'rjœːr] ulterior; further; subsequent (to, *à*), later (*time*).

ultimatum [yltima'tɔm] *m* ultimatum; **ultime** [~'tim] ultimate, final; **ultimo** [~ti'mo] *adv.* lastly, finally.

ultra *pol.* [yl'tra] *m* extremist, ultra.

ultra... [yltra] ultra...; **~court, e** *phys.* [~'kuːr, ~'kurt] ultra-short (*wave*); **~montain, e** [~mɔ̃'tɛ̃, ~'tɛn] **1.** *adj. geog., pol., eccl.* ultramontane; **2.** *su. eccl., pol.* ultramontanist, Vaticanist; **~sensible** [~sã'sibl] high-speed (*film*); **~(-)son** *phys.* [~'sɔ̃] *m* ultra-sound; **~sonore** *phys.* [~sɔ'nɔːr] ultrasonic; supersonic; **~violet, -ette** *opt.* [~vjɔ'lɛ, ~'lɛt] ultraviolet.

ululer [yly'le] (1a) *v/i.* hoot (*owl*).

un, une [œ̃, yn] **1.** *art./indef.* a, *before vowel:* an; *fig.* someone like; such a (*in int. as intensive*); *not translated before abstract nouns qualified by an adj.: avec une grande joie* with great joy; *~ de ces jours* one of these days; *~ jour ou l'autre* some day or other; **2.** *adj./num./inv.* one; *une fois* once; *une heure* one o'clock; *~ jour sur deux* every other day; *c'est tout ~* it makes no difference; *de deux choses l'une* (it's) one thing or the other; **3.** *su.* one; *~ à ~* one by one; *ne faire qu'~* be as one; be hand in glove; *su./f:journ. la une* page one; *su./m: le un* (number) one; *thea.* first act; **4.** *pron./indef.* one; *les ~s les autres* one

another, each other; *les ~s ..., les autres ... some ..., others ...; l'~ l'autre* one another, each other.

unanime [yna'nim] unanimous (in s.th., *dans qch.*; in *ger. à, pour inf.*); **unanimité** [~nimi'te] *f* unanimity; *à l'~* unanimously, with one voice.

uni, e [y'ni] **1.** *p.p. of unir*; **2.** *adj.* smooth; level, even (*ground*); regular; plain (*colour, a. tex.*); *fig., a. pol.* united; close(-knit) (*family etc.*); **3.** *su./m* plain or simple material.

unicellulaire ♀, *a. zo.* [ynisɛly'lɛːr] unicellular.

unicité [ynisi'te] *f* uniqueness; *phls.* oneness.

unicolore [yniko'lɔːr] unicolo(u)red; one-colo(u)red.

unicorne [yni'kɔrn] **1.** *adj.* single-horned; **2.** *su./m* 🦄, *zo., myth.* unicorn.

unidirectionnel, -elle [ynidirɛksjɔ'nɛl] unidirectional.

unième [y'njɛm] *adj./num., a. su. in compounds:* first; *vingt et ~* twenty-first.

unification [ynifika'sjɔ̃] *f* unification; ⊕, ↑ *companies:* amalgamation, merger; ↑ standardization; **unifier** [~'fje] (1o) *v/t.* unify; ⊕, ↑ amalgamate, merge (*companies*); ↑ standardize.

uniforme [yni'fɔrm] **1.** *adj.* uniform, unvarying; flat (*rate*); *fig.* monotonous; **2.** *su./m* ⚔, ⚓, school, *etc.:* uniform; **uniformément** [yniforme'mã] *adv. of uniforme* 1; **uniformiser** [~mi'ze] (1a) *v/t.* standardize; make (*s.th.*) uniform; **uniformité** [~mi'te] *f* uniformity; *fig.* consistency; evenness.

unijambiste [yniʒã'bist] *su.* one-legged person.

unilatéral, e, *m/pl.* **-aux** ♀, ⚕, *pol., etc.* [ynilate'ral, ~'ro] unilateral.

union [y'njɔ̃] *f* union; combination; *admin.* association; marriage; ⊕ coupling, union-joint; *fig.* agreement.

unipare *biol.* [yni'paːr] uniparous.
uniphasé, e *ℰ* [ynifa'ze] monophase; single-phase.
unipolaire *ℰ* [ynipɔ'lɛːr] unipolar, single-pole ...
unique [y'nik] unique; single, alone; only; ✕, *pol.* united; *fig.* unrivalled; *fig. pej.* impossible; *seul et ∼* one and only; **uniquement** [ynik'mã] *adv.* solely; simply; merely.
unir [y'niːr] (2a) *v/t.* unite (with, *à*); combine (with, *à*); join in marriage; *s'∼* (*à, avec*) unite (with); combine (with); be joined in marriage.
unisson [yni'sõ] *m* ♪ unison; *à l'∼* in unison (with, *de*); *fig.* in harmony *or* keeping (with, *de*).
unitaire [yni'tɛːr] unitary; unitarian (*a. eccl.*); ⚛, ✝ unit-...; **unitarisme** *eccl.* [∼ta'rism] *m* Unitarianism; **unité** [∼'te] *f* ✕, ⚛ unit; ⚛ one; ⚛, *phls.*, *fig.*, *thea.* unity; *fig.* consistency, uniformity; ✝ *prix m de l'∼* price of one.
univalent, e *ℰ* [yniva'lã, ∼'lãːt] univalent, monovalent.
univers [yni'vɛːr] *m* universe; **universaliser** [ynivɛrsali'ze] (1a) *v/t.* universalize; **universalité** [∼sali'te] *f* universality; whole (*a.* ⚖), entirety; **universel, -elle** [∼'sɛl] universal (*a. phls.*, ⊕); ⊕ *etc. a.* all-purpose, general-purpose; world (-wide); ⚖ residuary (*legatee*); *fig. homme m ∼* all-rounder; *ℰ remède m ∼* panacea.
universitaire [ynivɛrsi'tɛːr] 1. *adj.* university ...; academic; 2. *su.* academic; **université** [∼'te] *f* university.
univoque [yni'vɔk] univocal; *fig.* unequivocal (*language, proof, words*); *fig.* uniform.
Untel [ɛ̃'tɛl] *m*: *Monsieur (Madame)* ∼ Mr (Mrs) so-and-so.
uppercut *box.* [ypɛr'kyt] *m* uppercut.
uranate *🜍* [yra'nat] *m* uranate; **urane** *🜍* [y'ran] *m* uranium oxide; **uranite** *min.* [yra'nit] *f* uranite; **uranium** *🜍* [∼'njɔm] *m* uranium.
urbain, e [yr'bɛ̃, ∼'bɛn] urban; town ...; city ...; urbane; **urbaniser** [∼ni'ze] (1a) *v/t.* urbanize; **urbanisme** [∼'nism] *m* urbanism; town planning, *Am.* city planning; **urbaniste** [∼'nist] *m* urbanist; town planner, *Am.* city planner; **urbanis-**

tique [∼ni'stik] urbanistic, town-planning ...; **urbanité** [∼ni'te] *f* urbanity.
urée *🜍* [y're] *f* urea; **urémie** *🜏* [yre'mi] *f* ur(a)emia; **urétérite** *🜏* [∼te'rit] *f* ureteritis; **urètre** *anat.* [y'rɛːtr] *m* urethra.
urgence [yr'ʒãːs] *f* urgency; *🜏 etc.* emergency; *affairs:* pressure; *d'∼* immediately; emergency...; *en cas d'∼* in case of *or* in an emergency; *il y a (grande) ∼* it is (very) urgent; **urgent, e** [∼'ʒã, ∼'ʒãːt] urgent, pressing; *🜏 cas m ∼* emergency; **urger** F [∼'ʒe] (11) *v/i.* be urgent; *rien n'urge* there's no hurry.
urinaire *anat.* [yri'nɛːr] urinary; **urinal** *🜏* [∼'nal] *m (day-, bed-)* urinal; **urine** *physiol.* [y'rin] *f* urine; **uriner** [yri'ne] (1a) *v/i.* urinate, make water; **urinoir** [∼'nwaːr] *m* (public) urinal.
urique *🜍* [y'rik] uric.
urne [yrn] *f* urn; (*∼ électorale*) ballot box; *∼ funéraire* cinerary urn; *aller (or se rendre) aux ∼s* go to the polls.
urologie *🜏* [yrɔlɔ'ʒi] *f* urology; **urologiste** *🜏* [∼'ʒist] *m* urologist.
urticacées ♀ [yrtika'se] *f/pl.* urticaceae; **urticaire** *🜏* [∼'kɛːr] *f* urticaria, nettle-rash.
us [ys] *m/pl.*: *∼ et coutumes f/pl.* ways and customs.
usage [y'zaːʒ] *m* use (*a.* ⚖), employment; *cost.*, *carpet, etc.*: service, wear; *fig.* custom; usage; *fig.* practice; *∼ du monde* good breeding; *🜏 ∼ externe* for external use; *à ∼s multiples* multi-purpose; *à l'∼ de* intended for; *faire ∼ de* use; *faire bon ∼ de* put to good use; *hors d'∼* disused; *il est d'∼ de (inf.)* it is usual to (*inf.*); **usagé, e** [yza'ʒe] second-hand; worn (*clothes*); used; **usager, -ère** [∼'ʒe, ∼'ʒɛːr] 1. *su.* user; ⚖ *pasturage:* common; 2. *adj.* in everyday use; ⚖ *customs:* for personal use; **usant, e** [y'zã, y'zãːt] wearing; exhausting; tiresome (*person*); **usé, e** [y'ze] worn (out); *cost.* threadbare, shabby; frayed (*rope*); *fig.* hackneyed, commonplace; worn-out (*horse*); exhausted (*soil*); **user** [∼] 1. (1a) *v/t.* use up; consume (*fuel*); wear out; spoil (*one's eyes etc.*); waste (*one's youth*); *s'∼* wear away *or* out; *fig.* be spent; *v/i.*: *∼ de* use; make use of; resort to (*tricks, violence*).

usinage ⊕ [yzi'na:ʒ] *m* machining, tooling; **usine** [y'zin] *f* works *usu. sg.*, factory, plant; *tex.*, *metall.*, *paper*: mill; ∼ *atomique* atomic plant; ∼ *électrique* power station, powerhouse; ∼ *hydraulique* waterworks *usu. sg.*; **usiner** [yzi'ne] (1a) *v/t.* ⊕ machine, tool; process.

usité, e [yzi'te] in use, current.

ustensile [ystɑ̃'sil] *m* utensil, implement; tool.

usuel, -elle [y'zɥɛl] usual, customary; common; *langue f* ∼*elle* everyday language.

usufruit ꝺ [yzy'frɥi] *m* usufruct; life interest; **usufruitier, -ère** ꝺ [∼frɥi'tje, ∼'tjɛ:r] **1.** *adj.* usufructuary; **2.** *su.* tenant for life; usufructuary. [orbitant.\

usuraire [yzy'rɛ:r] usurious; ex-∫

usure[1] [y'zy:r] *f* ⊕, *cost.*, *furnishings*, *etc.*: wear (and tear); *geol.*, *gramm.* erosion; ⚔ *guerre f d'*∼ war of attrition; F *avoir q. à l'*∼ wear s.o. down (in the end).

usure[2] [y'zy:r] *f* usury; *fig. rendre avec* ∼ repay (*s.th.*) with interest; **usurier** *m*, **-ère** *f* [yzy'rje, ∼'rjɛ:r] usurer.

usurpateur, -trice [yzyrpa'tœ:r, ∼'tris] **1.** *adj.* usurping; *fig.* encroaching; **2.** *su.* usurper; **usurpation** [∼'sjɔ̃] *f* usurpation (of, *de*); *fig.* encroachment (upon, *de*); **usurpatoire** [∼'twa:r] usurpatory; **usurper** [yzyr'pe] (1a) *v/t.* usurp (*the throne, a title*) (from, *sur*); *v/i. fig.* encroach (upon, *sur*).

ut ♪ [yt] *m/inv.* ut; *note*: C; *clef f d'*∼ C-clef.

utérin, e [yte'rɛ̃, ∼'rin] 🖈🅑, 🜨 uterine; 🖈🅑 half(-*brother*, -*sister*) on the mother's side.

utile [y'til] **1.** *adj.* useful; of service; *fig.* convenient; *en temps* ∼ in (good) time; in due course; **2.** *su./m the* useful; *joindre l'*∼ *à l'agréable* combine business with pleasure; **utilisable** [ytili'zabl] usable; utilizable; available (*ticket*); **utilisateur** [∼za-'tœ:r] *m* user; **utilisation** [∼za'sjɔ̃] *f* utilization; turning (*of s.th.*) to account; use; **utiliser** [∼'ze] (1a) *v/t.* make use of; use; utilize; **utilitaire** [∼'tɛ:r] *adj.*, *a. su.* utilitarian; **utilitarisme** [∼ta'rism] *m* utilitarianism; **utilité** [∼'te] *f* utility, usefulness; use; service, useful purpose; *thea.* small *or* minor part; *actor*: utility man.

utopie [ytɔ'pi] *f* utopia; *d'*∼ utopian; **utopique** [∼'pik] *adj.*, *a. su.* utopian; **utopiste** [∼'pist] *su.* utopian, utopist.

utricule *anat.* [ytri'kyl] *m* utricle.

uval, e, *m/pl.* **-aux** [y'val, ∼'vo] grape-...

uvulaire *anat.* [yvy'lɛ:r] uvular.

V

V, v [ve] *m* V, v; *double v* W, w.
va! [va] *int.* to be sure!; believe me!;
well!; good!; ~ *pour cette somme!*
done (at that price)!; agreed (at that
figure)!
vacance [va'kɑ̃:s] *f* vacancy; vacant
post; ~s *pl.* holidays; vacation *sg.*
(*Am. a. univ.*), *parl.* recess *sg.*; *gran-*
des ~s long holidays *etc.*; **vacancier**
m, -ière *f* [~kɑ̃'sje, ~'sjɛːr] holiday-
maker, *Am.* vacationist; **vacant, e**
[~'kɑ̃, ~'kɑ̃:t] vacant, unoccupied
(*house, post, seat, etc.*); ⚖ in abeyance
(*estate*).
vacarme [va'karm] *m* uproar, din,
racket, row.
vacation ⚖ [vaka'sjɔ̃] *f* attendance,
sitting; *rights etc.*: abeyance; ~s *pl.*
fees; *law-courts*: vacation *sg.*
vaccin ⚕ [vak'sɛ̃] *m* vaccine; **vacci-**
nal, e, *m/pl.* -**aux** ⚕ [vaksi'nal, ~'no]
vaccinal; **vaccination** ⚕ [~na'sjɔ̃] *f*
vaccination; inoculation; **vaccine**
⚕ [vak'sin] *f* cowpox; **vacciner** ⚕
[~si'ne] (1a) *v/t.* vaccinate; inoculate.
vache [vaʃ] **1.** *su./f* cow; ✝ cowhide;
sl. fat woman, V cow; *woman*: bitch;
sl. man etc.: swine; F *le plancher m des*
~s terra firma, dry land; F *fig. manger*
de la ~ enragée have a hard time of it;
F *parler français comme une ~ espagno-*
le murder the French language; **2.**
adj. sl. harsh; bad; mean, foul; **va-**
chement *sl.* [vaʃ'mɑ̃] terribly, real,
damned; (*rain etc.*) damned hard;
vacher *m*, -ère *f* [va'ʃe, ~'ʃɛːr] cowherd; **vacherie** [vaʃ'ri] *f* cowshed,
cowhouse; *sl.* dirty trick; nasty
remark; **vachette** ✝ [va'ʃɛt] *f* leather: calfskin.
vacillant, e [vasi'jɑ̃, ~'jɑ̃:t] unsteady;
swaying; staggering; flickering
(*flame*); shaky (*hand, ladder*); *fig.*
undecided; uncertain (*health*); **va-**
cillation [~ja'sjɔ̃] *f* unsteadiness;
flame: flickering; shakiness; *fig.*
wavering, vacillation; **vacillatoire**
[~ja'twaːr] vacillatory; **vaciller**
[~'je] (1a) *v/i.* be unsteady; sway (to
and fro); stagger; be shaky; flicker

(*light*); twinkle (*star*); *fig.* vacillate,
waver.
vacuité [vakɥi'te] *f* emptiness, vacu-
ity; **vacuum** [~'kɥɔm] *m* vacuum.
vade-mecum [vademe'kɔm] *m/inv.*
vade-mecum; companion (= *book*).
vadrouille [va'druːj] *f* ⚓ swab; F
stroll; **vadrouiller** F [vadru'je] (1a)
v/i. stroll *or* roam (about *or* around);
vadrouilleur, -euse [~'jœːr, ~'jøːz]
1. *adj.* strolling; roaming (the
streets); **2.** *su.* stroller; roamer.
va-et-vient [vae'vjɛ̃] *m/inv.* comings
and goings *pl.*; movement to and fro;
backward and forward motion, *Am.*
back and forth motion; ⚓ shuttle-
service; ⊕ reciprocating gear; ⚡
two-way switch; *faire le ~ entre* 🚢,
bus, etc.: ply between.
vagabond, e [vaga'bɔ̃, ~'bɔ̃:d] **1.** *adj.*
vagabond; wandering; roving (*a.*
fig.); **2.** *su.* vagabond; vagrant,
tramp; **vagabondage** [~bɔ̃'da:ʒ] *m*
wandering; vagrancy; **vagabonder**
[~bɔ̃'de] (1a) *v/i.* be a vagabond;
wander, roam (*a. fig.*).
vagin *anat.* [va'ʒɛ̃] *m* vagina.
vagir [va'ʒiːr] (2a) *v/i.* wail (*newborn*
infant); squeak (*hare*); **vagisse-**
ment [~ʒis'mɑ̃] *m* new-born infant:
vagitus, wail; *hare*: squeak(ing).
vague[1] [vag] *f* ⚓ wave (*a. fig., a.* ⚔);
billow; ⚡ current, *fig.* anger: surge;
fig. la nouvelle ~ the new wave; F *fig.*
faire des ~s cause a stir; F *fig. pas de*
~s! no fuss!
vague[2] [~] **1.** *adj.* vague; hazy; indeterminate; dim (*memory*); loose
(-fitting) (*garment*); **2.** *su./m* vagueness.
vague[3] [~] **1.** *adj.* vacant, empty (*look,*
stare); **2.** *su./m* empty space; *fig.*
vacancy.
vaguemestre [vag'mɛstr] *m* ⚔ post-
orderly; ⚓ postman.
vaguer [va'ge] (1m) *v/i.* roam,
wander.
vaillamment [vaja'mɑ̃] *adv. of*
vaillant; **vaillance** [~'jɑ̃:s] *f* val-
o(u)r, courage, gallantry; **vaillant,**

e [ᴧˈjᾰ, ᴧˈjᾱːt] valiant, brave, courageous; ✕ gallant; stout (*heart*); F
fig. in good health.
vaille [vaj] *1st p. sg. pres. sbj. of*
valoir.
vain, vaine [vɛ̃, vɛn] **1.** *adj.* vain;
empty (*promise, title, words, etc.*);
useless (*effort*); conceited (*person*);
2. *vain adv.:* en ᴧ vainly, in vain.
vainc [vɛ̃] *3rd p. sg. pres. of vaincre;*
vaincre [vɛ̃ːkr] (4gg) *v/t.* conquer
(*a. fig. an emotion, hardship, etc.*);
defeat, beat (*s.o.*) (*a. sp.*); *fig.* outdo;
vaincu, e [vɛ̃ˈky] **1.** *p.p. of vaincre;* **2.**
su. defeated person *or* party; *sp. etc.*
loser; **vainqueur** [ᴧˈkœːr] **1.** *su./m*
victor, conqueror; *sp. etc.* winner; **2.**
adj. victorious; **vainquis** [ᴧˈki] *1st p.*
sg. p.s. of vaincre; **vainquons** [ᴧˈkɔ̃]
1st p. pl. pres. of vaincre.
vairon [vɛˈrɔ̃] **1.** *adj./m:* 🐟, *vet.* wall-
eyed; *yeux m/pl.* ᴧs eyes of different
colo(u)rs; **2.** *su./m icht.* minnow.
vais [vɛ] *1st p. sg. pres. of aller 1.*
vaisseau [vɛˈso] *m* 🚢 ⚓, 🌿, *anat.,*
cuis. vessel; ⚓ ship; 🌿, *anat.* duct,
canal; 🔱 *building:* body; *church:*
nave; *anat.* ᴧ sanguin blood-vessel; ᴧ
spatial spacecraft; *fig.* brûler ses ᴧx
burn one's boats; ᴧ-**école,** *pl.* ᴧx-
écoles [ᴧsoeˈkɔl] *m* training ship.
vaisselier [vɛsəˈlje] *m furniture:*
dresser; **vaisselle** [ᴧˈsɛl] *f dishes pl.;*
tableware; crockery, china; *eau f de* ᴧ
dishwater; *faire la* ᴧ do the washing-
up, wash up, *Am.* wash the dishes.
val, *pl.* **vals,** *a.* **vaux** [val, vo] *m* vale,
dale; *par monts et par vaux* up hill and
down dale.
valable [vaˈlabl] valid (*a. fig.*).
valdinguer *sl.* [valdɛ̃ˈge] *v/i. see din-*
guer.
valence 🜨 [vaˈlɑ̃ːs] *f* valency.
valenciennes [valɑ̃ˈsjɛn] *f* Valenciennes (lace).
valériane 🌿, 🌸 [valeˈrjan] *f* vale-
rian; **valérianelle** 🌸 [ᴧrjaˈnɛl] *f*
lamb's-lettuce.
valet [vaˈlɛ] *m* (m̃an-)servant; *cards:*
knave, jack; ⊕ door-counter-
weight; ⊕ clamp, dog; *mirror, etc.,*
a. 🪞: stand; *fig.* toady; ᴧ de chambre valet, man-servant; ✒ ᴧ de
ferme farm-hand.
valétudinaire [valetydiˈnɛːr] *adj.,*
a. su. valetudinarian.
valeur [vaˈlœːr] *f* value (*a.* 🜨, 🗡,
phls., fig.), worth; asset (*a. fig.*); 🎵

note: length; ✕ valo(u)r, gallantry;
🗡 ᴧs *pl.* shares, securities; 🗡 ᴧs
pl. actives assets; ✕ ᴧ *militaire*
fighting qualities *pl.*; ⚓ ᴧ *nautique*
seaworthiness; 🗡 ᴧ *nominale* face
value; *de* ᴧ valuable; *fig.* of value;
able (*person*); *mettre en* ᴧ enhance
the value of; develop (*the soil*);
reclaim (*a marsh*); *fig.* emphasize,
bring out; *objets m/pl. de* ᴧ valu-
ables; **valeureux, -euse** ✕ [ᴧlœˈrø,
ᴧˈrøːz] brave, gallant, valiant.
validation [validaˈsjɔ̃] *f* validation;
law: ratifying; **valide** [ᴧˈlid]
valid; healthy; *fig.* sound; ✕ fit (*for*
service); F *fig.* peu ᴧ off colo(u)r;
valider [valiˈde] (1a) *v/t.* validate;
authenticate (*a document*); ratify
(*a contract*); **validité** [ᴧdiˈte] *f* valid-
ity.
valise [vaˈliːz] *f* suitcase; (*diplomatic*)
bag; *faire sa* ᴧ (*or ses* ᴧs) pack one's
suitcase(s) *or* one's bags (*a. fig.*).
vallée [vaˈle] *f* valley; **valleuse**
[ᴧˈløːz] *f* small dry valley; **vallon**
[ᴧˈlɔ̃] *m* small valley; dale, vale; **val-**
lonné, e [ᴧbˈne] undulating; **val-**
lonnement [ᴧbnˈmɑ̃] *m* undulation.
valoir [vaˈlwaːr] (3l) *v/i.* be worth; be
profitable; be as good as; be equal to;
apply, hold, be valid; 🗡 à ᴧ on
account (of, *sur*); *ça vaut la peine* (*de*
inf.) it's worth while (*ger.*); *ça vaut le*
coup it's worth trying; *faire* ᴧ make
the most of (*s.th.*); 🗡 invest prof-
itably; 🗡 exploit, make productive;
fig. emphasize, bring out; *v/t.:* ᴧ *qch.*
à q. earn *or* win s.o. s.th.; *se faire* ᴧ
make the most of o.s.; *v/impers.:* il
vaut mieux (*inf.*) it's better to (*inf.*);
mieux vaut tard que jamais better late
than never.
valorisation [valɔrizaˈsjɔ̃] *f* 🗡, *fig.*
increase in value *or* importance; **va-**
loriser [ᴧˈze] (1a) *v/t.* increase the
value *or* importance of; upgrade.
valse 🎵 [vals] *f* waltz; F *aller* ᴧ go
flying *or* crash (against, *contre*); F
envoyer ᴧ send (*s.th.*) flying; send
(*s.o.*) packing; F *faire* ᴧ juggle
around; *faire* ᴧ *l'argent* spend money
like water; **valseur, -euse** [ᴧˈsœːr,
ᴧˈsøːz] **1.** *adj.* waltzing; **2.** *su.* waltzer.
valu, e [vaˈly] **1.** *p.p. of valoir;* **2.** *su./f*
see moins-value; plus-value; **valus** [ᴧ]
1st p. sg. p.s. of valoir.
valvaire 🌸 *etc.* [valˈvɛːr] valvar, val-

vate; **valve** [valv] *f anat., mot., metall., radio,* ⚓, ⚡: valve; **valvé, e** ⚓ [val've] valvate; **valvule** [ₙ'vyl] *f valvule; anat.* valve.

vamp [vã:mp] *f* vamp; **vamper** [ₙ'pe] (1a) *v/t.* vamp, seduce (by coquetry).

vampire [vã'pi:r] *m zo., a. fig.* vampire; *fig.* blood-sucker; **vampirique** [ₙpi'rik] vampiric; blood-sucking.

van [vã] *m* 🜊 winnowing-basket; fan; winnowing-machine; ⚒ van (-ning-shovel); 🜊 *passer au* ~ winnow. [ism.]

vandalisme [vãda'lism] *m* vandal-]

vanesse *zo.* [va'nɛs] *f* vanessa.

vanille ⚓, *cuis.* [va'ni:j] *f* vanilla; *à la* ~ vanilla ...; **vanillé, e** *cuis.* [ₙni'je] vanilla(-flavo[u]red); **vanillerie** 🜊 [ₙnij'ri] *f* vanilla-plantation; **vanillier** [vani'je] *m* vanilla plant; **vanilline** 🝛, ⊕ [ₙ'jin] *f* vanillin.

vanité [vani'te] *f* vanity; *fig.* futility; *pej. tirer* ~ *de* pride o.s. on; **vaniteux, -euse** [ₙ'tø, ₙ'tø:z] **1.** *adj.* vain, conceited; **2.** *su.* conceited person.

vannage[1] [va'na:ʒ] *m* 🜊 winnowing, sifting; ⚒ *ore:* vanning; F *fig.* exhaustion.

vannage[2] ⊕ [ₙ] *m water-gate:* sluice-gates *pl.; turbine:* gating; **vanne** [van] *f* sluice(-gate), water-gate; *turbine:* gate; (overflow) weir; *mot. etc.* valve; *fan, ventilator:* shutter.

vanneau *orn.* [va'no] *m* lapwing, (green) plover.

vanner[1] [va'ne] (1a) *v/t.* 🜊 winnow, sift; ⚒ van; *fig.* exhaust, wear out, tire out.

vanner[2] ⊕ [ₙ] (1a) *v/t.* fit sluices in; gate (*a turbine*).

vannerie [van'ri] *f* basket-making; 🌱 wicker-work, basket-work.

vanneur [va'nœ:r] *m* 🜊 winnower; ⚒ vanner (*a. machine*); **vanneuse** 🜊 [ₙ'nø:z] *f* winnowing-machine.

vannier [va nje] *m* basket-maker.

vannure 🜊 [va'ny:r] *f* chaff, husks *pl.*

vantail, *pl.* **-aux** [vã'ta:j, ₙ'to] *m* door, shutter, *etc.:* leaf.

vantard, e [vã'ta:r, ₙ'tard] **1.** *adj.* boastful, bragging; **2.** *su.* bragger, braggart; *Am. sl.* blow-hard, *Am.*

sl. wind-jammer; **vantardise** [ₙtar'di:z] *f* bragging; boasting; piece of bluff; **vanter** [ₙ'te] (1a) *v/t.* vaunt, extol; F boost, crack up; *se* ~ (*de*) boast (of); **vanterie** [vã'tri] *f* bragging; boast(ing).

va-nu-pieds [vany'pje] *m/inv.* tramp, hobo; beggar.

vap(e)(s) *sl.* [vap] *f/(pl.):* etre dans la *vap*(e) (*or les vap*[e]s) be in a daze.

vapeur [va'pœ:r] *su./f* steam; vapo(u)r; fumes *pl.;* ⊕ *machine f à* ~ steam engine; *su./m* ⚓ steamer, steamship; **vaporeux, -euse** [vapɔ'rø, ₙ'rø:z] vaporous, misty; steamy; *fig.* hazy; *fig.* nebulous; **vaporisateur** [ₙriza'tœ:r] *m* vaporizer; atomizer; scent-spray; ⊕ evaporator; **vaporiser** [ₙri'ze] (1a) *v/t.* vaporize; atomize, spray (*a liquid*); F spray (*s.th.*) with scent; *tex.* steam (*cloth*); *se* ~ vaporize; spray o.s.

vaquer [va'ke] (1m) *v/i.* † be vacant; ⚖, *parl.* not to be sitting; ~ *à* attend to; be occupied with; see to; ~ *à ses affaires a.* go about one's business.

varan *zo.* [va'rã] *m* varan, monitor.

varappe *mount.* [va'rap] *f* rock climbing; rock climb.

varech ⚓ [va'rɛk] *m* seaweed, wrack.

vareuse [va'rø:z] *f* (pea *or* sports) jacket; ⚔ tunic.

variabilité [varjabili'te] *f* variability; *weather, a. fig.* mood: changeableness; **variable** [ₙ'rjabl] **1.** *adj.* ⚓, *astr., gramm., biol.* variable; changeable (*weather, a. mood*); *fig.* fickle; ⚕ unequal (*pulse*); **2.** *su./f* ⚓ variable; **variant, e** [ₙ'rjã, ₙ'rjã:t] **1.** *adj.* variable, inconstant; **2.** *su./f text:* variant, different reading; **variation** [ₙrja'sjɔ̃] *f* variation (*a.* ♪).

varice ⚕ [va'ris] *f* varix; varicose vein. [varicella.]

varicelle ⚕ [vari'sɛl] *f* chicken-pox,]

varié, e [va'rje] varied; various; variegated (*colours etc.*); miscellaneous (*news, items, objects*); ⊕ variable (*motion*); **varier** [ₙ'rje] (1o) *v/t.* vary; variegate (*colours*); ♪ make variations on (*an air*); *v/i.* vary; 🌱 fluctuate (*market*); *fig.* ~ *sur* be at variance on, disagree over; **variété** [ₙrje'te] *f* variety; *scenery:* varied nature; *opinions:* diversity; 🌱 range; *thea.* ~s *pl.* variety theatre *sg.*

variole [va'rjɔl] *f* ⚕ smallpox, variola; *vet.* (cow-, sheep-)pox; **variolé, e** [varjɔ'le] pock-marked; **varioleux, -euse** ⚕ [~'lø, ~'løːz] 1. *adj.* variolous; 2. *su.* smallpox patient; sufferer from smallpox; **variolique** ⚕ [~'lik] variolous.

variomètre ⚡ [varjɔ'mɛtr] *m* variometer.

variqueux, -euse ⚕ [vari'kø, ~'køːz] varicose.

varlope ⊕ [var'lɔp] *f* trying-plane; **varloper** ⊕ [~lɔ'pe] (1a) *v/t.* try up (*a plank*).

vasculaire ⚕, *anat.* [vasky'lɛːr], **vasculeux, -euse** ⚕, *anat.* [~'lø, ~'løːz] vascular; ⚕ **pression** *f* **vasculaire** blood-pressure.

vase[1] [vɑːz] *m* vase; vessel, receptacle; ~ **de nuit** chamber; *fig.* **en** ~ **clos** in seclusion.

vase[2] [~] *f* mud, silt.

vaseline 🜪 [vaz'lin] *f* vaseline, petroleum jelly, *Am.* petrolatum; **enduire de** ~ vaseline.

vaseux, -euse [va'zø, ~'zøːz] muddy, silty; F *fig.* woolly (*ideas*); *sl. fig.* seedy, ill.

vasistas [vazis'tas] *m* fanlight (*over door*), *Am.* transom.

vaso-moteur, -trice *anat.* [vazɔmɔ'tœːr, ~'tris] vaso-motor.

vasque [vask] *f* fountain: basin.

vassal, e, *m/pl.* **-aux** [va'sal, ~'so] 1. *adj.* vassal; ~ **de** (*region*) under the suzerainty of; 2. *su.* vassal; **vassalité** [~sali'te] *f*, **vasselage** [vas'laːʒ] *m* vassalage; *fig.* bondage.

vaste [vast] 1. *adj.* vast, immense; comprehensive; *anat.* vastus; 2. *su./m anat.* vastus; **vastitude** [~i'tyd] *f* vastness; vastity.

va-t-en-guerre [vatɑ̃'gɛr] 1. *su./inv.* sabre-rattler; 2. *adj.* sabre-rattling.

vaticinateur, -trice [vatisina'tœːr, ~'tris] 1. *adj.* prophetic; 2. *su./m* prophet; *su./f* prophetess; **vaticination** [~na'sjɔ̃] *f* prophecy; pompous predictions *pl.*; **vaticiner** [~'ne] (1a) *v/i.* prophesy; make pompous predictions.

va-tout [va'tu] *m/inv.* the whole of one's stakes; **jouer son** ~ stake one's all.

vaudeville [vod'vil] *m* light comedy.

vaudois, e [vo'dwa, ~'dwaːz] *adj.*, *a. su.* 2 Vaudois; *eccl. hist.* Waldensian.

vaudrai [vo'dre] *1st p. sg. fut. of valoir.*

vau-l'eau [vo'lo] *adv.*: † **à** ~ downstream; *fig.* **aller à** ~ go to rack and ruin.

vaurien, -enne [vo'rjɛ̃, ~'rjɛn] *su.* bad lot; F *child:* rascal; *su./m* waster, ne'er-do-well; *su./f* worthless woman.

vautour *orn.* [vo'tuːr] *m* vulture (*a. fig.*).

vautrer [vo'tre] (1a) *v/t.*: **se** ~ wallow (in, *dans*) (*pig, a. fig. person*); F *fig.* sprawl (*on a sofa, etc.*); revel (in, *dans*).

vau-vent *hunt.* [vo'vɑ̃] *adv.*: **à** ~ down (the) wind; (*fly*) before the wind.

vaux [vo] *1st p. sg. pres. of valoir.*

va-vite [va'vit]: **à la** ~ in a hurry, hurriedly; carelessly.

veau [vo] *m* calf; *meat:* veal; 🠋 calf(-leather); F *person:* clod, lout; F *fig.* gutless person *or* car; ~ **marin** seacalf, seal; *fig.* **adorer le** ~ **d'or** worship the golden calf; F **pleurer comme un** ~ blubber; *cuis.* **tête** *f* **de** ~ calf's-head.

vecteur ⚑ [vɛk'tœːr] *adj.*, *a. su./m* vector.

vécu, e [ve'ky] *p.p. of vivre 1.*

vécus [~] *1st p. sg. p. s. of vivre 1.*

vedettariat *thea. etc.* [vɔdɛta'rja] *m* stardom; *the* stars (*pl.*); **vedette** [vɔ'dɛt] *f thea., cin. etc.* star; ⚓ patrol boat, scout; motor boat; **en** ~ F *fig.* in the forefront, in the limelight; *typ.*, *journ.* in bold type; **attraction** *f* ~ highlight.

végétal, e, *m/pl.* **-aux** [veʒe'tal, ~'to] 1. *adj.* plant(-life); vegetable (*butter, kingdom*); 2. *su./m* plant; **végétarien, -enne** [~ta'rjɛ̃, ~'rjɛn] *adj.*, *a. su.* vegetarian; **végétarisme** [~ta-'rism] *m* vegetarianism.

végétatif, -ve [veʒeta'tif, ~'tiːv] vegetative; **végétation** [~ta'sjɔ̃] *f* vegetation; growth; ⚕ ~**s** *pl.* adénoïdes adenoids; **végéter** [~'te] (1d) *v/i.* † ⚘ grow; ⚘, *a. fig.* vegetate.

véhémence [vee'mɑ̃ːs] *f* vehemence; **avec** ~ vehemently; **véhément, e** [~'mɑ̃, ~'mɑ̃ːt] vehement; *fig.* violent.

véhiculaire [veiky'lɛːr] vehicular (*language*); **véhicule** [~'kyl] *m* vehicle (*a. fig.*); *fig. a.* medium; **véhiculer** [~ky'le] (1a) *v/t.* convey, carry; cart.

veille [vɛːj] *f* staying up (*at night*); wakefulness, waking; *eccl.* vigil; eve (of, *de*), day before; *fig.* verge, brink; (night) watch; *fig.* **à la** ~ **de** on the brink *or* eve *or* point of; *la* ~ *de Noël* Christmas Eve; **veillée** [vɛˈje] *f* evening (spent in company); watch; *fig.* ~ *d'armes* night before combat; **veiller** [~ˈje] (1a) *v/i.* stay *or* sit up (late); remain *or* lie awake; *eccl.* keep vigil; ✕ watch, be on the lookout; stand by; ~ *à* see to; attend to; ~ *à ce que* (*sbj.*) see to it *or* make sure that (*ind.*); ~ *sur* look after, watch over; *v/t.* watch over, attend to (*a patient etc.*); *Am.* wake (*a corpse*); **veilleur** [~ˈjœːr] *m*: (~ *de nuit* night) watchman; **veilleuse** [~ˈjøːz] *f* watcher; night light; *mot.* sidelight; *gas:* pilot light; *mettre en* ~ turn down (*the gas etc.*); dim (*a light*); *fig.* put (*a project etc.*) on ice.

veinard, e [vɛˈnaːr, ~ˈnard] **1.** *adj.* lucky; **2.** *su.* lucky person; **veine** [vɛn] *f* ♥, *anat., geol., a. fig.* vein (*a.* = *marking in marble, wood, etc.*); ✕ *ore:* lode; *coal:* seam; *fig.* inspiration; *fig.* mood; F (good) luck; *avoir de la* ~ be lucky; *être en* ~ *de* ... be in a ... mood, be in the mood for ...; **veiné, e** [vɛˈne] veined; grained (*door*); **veiner** ⊕ [~ˈne] (1a) *v/t.* grain, vein (*paintwork*); **veineux, -euse** [~ˈnø, ~ˈnøːz] ⊕ veiny (*wood etc.*); *anat., physiol.* venous; ♥ venose, veiny; **veinule** [~ˈnyl] *f anat. etc.* veinlet; venule; ✕ thread (*of ore*).

vélaire *gramm.* [veˈlɛːr] **1.** *adj.* velar; uvular (*R*); **2.** *su./f* velar (consonant). **vêler** [vɛˈle] (1b) *v/i.* calve (*cow*). **vélin** [veˈlɛ̃] *m* vellum (paper). **velléité** [velei'te] *f* stray impulse; slight inclination; vague desire; *fig.* hint (*of a smile etc.*).

vélo F [veˈlo] *m* (push-)bike, wheel; *aller à* ~ cycle, F bike, wheel. **vélocité** [velosi'te] *f* speed, velocity; **vélodrome** [~ˈdroːm] *m* cycle-racing track, velodrome; **vélomoteur** [~moˈtœːr] *m* light motor-cycle; motor-assisted bicycle.

velours [vəˈluːr] *m* velvet; *gramm.* faulty liaison; *tex.* ~ *à côtes* corduroy; ~ *de coton* velveteen; ~ *de soie* silk velvet; **velouté, e** [vəluˈte] **1.** *adj.* velvety; mellow (*wine*); downy (*cheek, peach*); *phot.* velvet-surface (*paper*); **2.** *su./m* softness, velvetiness; *fruit:* bloom; *tex.* velvet braid; *cuis.* rich thick gravy soup; *tex.* (*a.* ~

de laine) velours; **velouter** [~ˈte] (1a) *v/t.* give a soft *or* velvety appearance to (*s.th.*); *fig.* soften (*an outline*); *se* ~ soften, mellow; **velouteux, -euse** [~ˈtø, ~ˈtøːz] soft, velvety; **veloutier** [~ˈtje] *m* velvet-maker.

velu, e [vəˈly] hairy; ⚠ uncut, rough; ♥ pubescent, villous.

vélum [veˈlɔm] *m* awning. **venaison** *cuis.* [vənɛˈzɔ̃] *f* venison. **vénal, e** *m/pl.* **-aux** [veˈnal, ~ˈno] venal (*a.* *pej.*); *pej.* mercenary, corrupt(ible); ✝ *valeur f* ~*e* market value; **vénalité** [~naliˈte] *f* venality; *pej.* corruptibility.

venant, e [vəˈnã, ~ˈnãːt] **1.** *adj.* thriving; **2.** *su./m*: *à tout* ~ to all and sundry, to anyone.

vendable [vãˈdabl] saleable, marketable.

vendange [vãˈdãːʒ] *f* grape-gathering; wine-harvest; (*a.* ~*s pl.*) *season:* vintage; **vendangeoir** [vãdãˈʒwaːr] *m* grape-basket; **vendanger** [~ˈʒe] (1t) *vt/i.* vintage; *v/t.* gather the grapes of; *v/i.* harvest grapes; gather the grapes; **vendangeur** *m*, **-euse** *f* [~ˈʒœːr, ~ˈʒøːz] vintager; wine-harvester.

venderesse ⚖ [vãˈdrɛs] *f* vendor. **vendetta** [vɛ̃dɛtˈta] *f* vendetta. **vendeur** [vãˈdœːr] *m* ✝ vendor (*a.* ⚖), seller; shop assistant, *Am.* sales clerk; salesman; **vendeuse** ✝ [~ˈdøːz] *f* seller, shop assistant, *Am.* sales clerk; saleswoman; **vendre** [vãːdr] (4a) *v/t.* sell (for, *à*); *à* ~ for sale; *se* ~ sell, be sold (at, for *à*). **vendredi** [vãdrəˈdi] *m* Friday; *le* ~ *saint* Good Friday.

vendu, e [vãˈdy] **1.** *su./m* traitor; **2.** *p.p. of* **vendre**.

venelle [vəˈnɛl] *f* alley. **vénéneux, -euse** [veneˈnø, ~ˈnøːz] poisonous (*a.* ☙ ♥).

vénérable [veneˈrabl] **1.** *adj.* venerable; **2.** *su./m* *freemasonry:* Worshipful Master; **vénération** [~raˈsjɔ̃] *f* veneration; **vénérer** [~ˈre] (1f) *v/t.* venerate; revere.

vénerie [venˈri] *f* hunting; venery. **vénérien, -enne** ⚥ [veneˈrjɛ̃, ~ˈrjɛn] venereal.

venette ✝ *sl.* [vəˈnɛt] *f* funk. **veneur** [vəˈnœːr] *m* huntsman. **vengeance** [vãˈʒãːs] *f* revenge; vengeance; *tirer* ~ *de* be revenged for (*s.th.*); take vengeance on (*s.o.*);

venu

venger [ʌ̃'ʒe] (1l) *v/t.* avenge (for, *de*); se ~ take (one's) revenge (for, *de*); be revenged (on s.o., *de* q.); **vengeur, -eresse** [vɑ̃'ʒœːr, vɑ̃ʒ'rɛs] **1.** *su.* avenger; **2.** *adj.* avenging.

véniel, -elle *eccl.* [ve'njɛl] venial (*sin*).

venimeux, -euse [vəni'mø, ʌ̃'møːz] *zo., a. fig.* venomous; *zo.* poisonous (*serpent, bite*); *fig.* malicious; **venimosité** [ʌ̃mozi'te] *f* sting, a. *fig.*: venomousness; **venin** *zo., fig.* [və-'nɛ̃] *m* venom.

venir [və'niːr] (2h) *v/i.* come, be coming; arrive; grow (*a.* ⚥, *child, tooth*); *fig.* issue, be descended (from, *de*); occur, happen (to *inf.*, *à inf.*); ~ *à* reach (*maturity*); ~ *à bien* be successful; ~ *au monde* be born; ~ *de ce que* (*ind.*) result from (*ger.*); ~ *de dire* have just said; ~ *prendre* come and fetch (*s.o.*); *à* ~ future (*event, state*), (*years*) to come; *bien* ~ thrive; *d'où cela vient-il?* what's the reason for that?; *en* ~ *aux coups* come to blows; *en* ~ *aux faits* get down to business; *être bien* (*mal*) *venu* be (un)welcome; *typ.* be well (badly) produced (*book*); *be* (un)successful; *être mal venu à* (*inf.*) be inappropriate *or* unseemly to (*inf.*); *faire* ~ send for; grow (*wheat*); *où voulez-vous en* ~? what are you getting *or* driving at?; *se faire bien* ~ *de q.* ingratiate o.s. with s.o.; *s'en* ~ come *or* go along; *v/impers.* come; happen; occur; *d'où vient-il que* (*ind.*)? how is it that (*ind.*)?; *est-il venu q.?* has anyone called?; *il est venu quatre hommes* four men have come.

vénitien, -enne [veni'sjɛ̃, ʌ̃'sjɛn] **1.** *adj.* Venetian; *blond m* ~ Titian red; **2.** *su.* ♀ Venetian.

vent [vɑ̃] *m* wind; ~ *arrière* tailwind; ~ *debout* headwind; ~ *de travers* crosswind; *aller comme le* ~ go like the wind; ⚓ *au* ~ *de* to windward of; *fig.* *avoir* ~ *de* get wind of; *coup m de* ~ gust of wind, squall; *fig.* *en coup de* ~ very fast; F *fig.* *dans le* ~ trendy, hip, hep, with(-)it; ♪ *instrument m à* ~ wind instrument; *prendre le* ~ see how the land lies.

vente [vɑ̃ːt] *f* ✝ sale; ✝ *fig.* business; timber; *timber*: felling; ~ *forcée* compulsory sale; ~ *publique* public sale; auction; *de* ~ *difficile* hard to sell; *en* ~ on sale; *typ.* out (*book*); *en* ~ *chez* sold by; *en* ~ *libre* off the ration; unrationed; *être de bonne* ~ sell well; *mettre en* ~ offer (*s.th.*) for sale; publish, issue (*a book*).

venter [vɑ̃'te] (1a) *v/impers.*: *il vente* it is windy, it is blowing; *qu'il pleuve ou qu'il vente* (come) rain or shine, in all weathers; **venteux, -euse** [ʌ̃'tø, ʌ̃'tøːz] windy; windswept (*region*).

ventilateur [vɑ̃tila'tœːr] *m* ventilator; ⚡ *etc.* fan; ~ *soufflant* blower; **ventilation** [ʌ̃la'sjɔ̃] *f* ventilation; ✝ apportionment; ⚖ separate valuation; **ventiler** [ʌ̃'le] (1a) *v/t.* ventilate, air (*a. fig.*); ✝ apportion; ⚖ value separately; *mal ventilé* stuffy (*room*).

ventis [vɑ̃'ti] *m/pl.* wind-fallen trees.

ventosité ⚕, *vet.* [vɑ̃tozi'te] *f* flatulence.

ventouse [vɑ̃'tuːz] *f* ⚕ cupping glass; ⊕ *etc.* suction pad; *zo.* leech, octopus: sucker; **ventouser** ⚕ [ʌ̃tu'ze] (1a) *v/t.* cup (*a patient*).

ventral, e, *m/pl.* **-aux** [vɑ̃'tral, ʌ̃'tro] ventral; **ventre** [vɑ̃:tr] *m* abdomen, belly; stomach, paunch; *pregnant woman*: womb; ⊕, *furnace,* ⚓ *sail, ship*: belly; ⚠, *fig.* bulge; ⚡, *phys.* antinode; ~ *à terre* at full speed; *à plat* ~ flat on one's face *or* one's stomach; *avoir* (*prendre*) *du* ~ be (grow) stout; *faire* ~ bulge (out) (⊕ *vessel,* ⚠ *wall*); F *fig.* *taper sur le* ~ *à q.* be overfamiliar *or* chummy with s.o.; **ventrebleu!** [vɑ̃trə'blø] *int.* zounds!; **ventrée** [vɑ̃'tre] *f lambs*: fall; *animals*: litter; F bellyful.

ventricule *anat.* [vɑ̃tri'kyl] *m* ventricle.

ventrière [vɑ̃tri'ɛːr] *f* ⚕ binder, abdominal belt; ⚠ cross-tie, purlin; ⚓ bilge-block.

ventriloque [vɑ̃tri'lɔk] **1.** *adj.* ventriloquial, ventriloquous; **2.** *su.* ventriloquist; **ventriloquie** [ʌ̃lɔ'ki] *f* ventriloquism, ventriloquy.

ventripotent, e F [vɑ̃tripɔ'tɑ̃, ʌ̃'tɑ̃t] big-bellied; corpulent.

ventru, e [vɑ̃'try] corpulent; big-bellied (*a. bottle*); ⊕ dished (*outwards*).

venu, e [və'ny] **1.** *p.p. of venir;* **2.** *adj.*: *bien* (*mal*) ~ well- (poorly) developed; (un)timely (*remark etc.*); *être* *mal* ~ *de* (*or à*) (*inf.*) be in no position to (*inf.*); *su.* (*first, last, new-*)comer; *le premier* ~ *a.* anybody; *su./f* arrival; coming; *water*: inflow; *tree etc.*: growth; ~ *au monde* birth; ✶ *d'une belle* ~ well-grown; *fig. tout d'une* ~ straight.

vêpres *eccl.* [vɛːpr] *f/pl.* vespers; evensong *sg.*

ver [vɛːr] *m* worm (*a. fig. person*); maggot, grub; ~ *à soie* silk-worm; ~ *blanc* grub; ~ *de terre* earthworm; ~ *luisant* glow-worm; ✿ ~ *solitaire* tapeworm; *tirer les* ~*s du nez à q.* worm secrets out of s.o.

vérace [veˈras] veracious; **véracité** [~rasiˈte] *f* veracity, truth(fulness).

véranda △ [verɑ̃ˈda] *f* veranda(h), *Am.* porch.

verbal, e, *m/pl.* **-aux** [vɛrˈbal, ~ˈbo] verbal; ⚖ oral (*contract*); *see procès-verbal*; **verbalisation** ⚖ [vɛrbalizaˈsjɔ̃] *f* official entry of an offence; F taking of (*s.o.'s*) name and address (*by police*); **verbaliser** [~ˈze] (1a) *v/i. admin.* draw up an official report (*of an offence etc.*); ~ *contre police*: take (*s.o.'s*) name and address; *v/t.i.* verbalize; **verbe** [vɛrb] *m gramm.* verb; *eccl.* ♀ *the* Word; F *avoir le* ~ *haut* be loud of speech; *fig.* be overbearing; **verbeux, -euse** [vɛrˈbø, ~ˈbøːz] verbose, long-winded; **verbiage** [~ˈbjaːʒ] *m* verbosity; verbiage, wordiness; **verbosité** [~boziˈte] *f* verbosity, wordiness.

verdâtre [vɛrˈdɑːtr] greenish; **verdelet, -ette** [~dəˈlɛ, ~ˈlɛt] greenish; slightly acid (*wine*); **verdet** ♠ [~ˈdɛ] *m* verdigris; **verdeur** [~ˈdœːr] *f* greenness (*a. of wood*); *wine etc.*, *a. fig.* remarks: acidity; *old person*: vigo(u)r.

verdict ⚖ [vɛrˈdikt] *m* verdict (*against, contre*; for, *en faveur de*).

verdier *orn.* [vɛrˈdje] *m* greenfinch; **verdir** [~ˈdiːr] (2a) *v/t.* make *or* paint (*s.th.*) green; *v/i.* ♀ become green; ♠ become covered with verdigris; **verdoyant, e** [vɛrdwaˈjɑ̃, ~ˈjɑ̃ːt] verdant, green; greenish (*colour*); **verdoyer** [~ˈje] (1h) *v/i.* become green; take on a green colo(u)r.

verdunisation [vɛrdynizaˈsjɔ̃] *f* *water*: chlorination; **verduniser** [~ˈze] (1a) *v/t.* chlorinate (*water*).

verdure [vɛrˈdyːr] *f* greenness; ♀

greenery, verdure; *cuis.* greenstuff, pot-herbs *pl.*; **verdurier** [~dyˈrje] *m* greengrocer.

véreux, -euse [veˈrø, ~ˈrøːz] wormy (*fruit*); *fig.* bad (*debts*), shady (*company, firm, person*); shaky (*case*).

verge [vɛrʒ] *f* † rod; *anat.* penis.

vergé, e [vɛrˈʒe] **1.** *adj. tex.* streaky, unevenly dyed; *tex.* corded; laid (*paper*); **2.** *su./m* ~ *blanc* cream-laid paper.

verger [vɛrˈʒe] *m* orchard.

vergeté, e [vɛrʒəˈte] streaky; ⊘ paly; **vergette** [~ˈʒɛt] *f* switch, cane; *drum*: hoop; *feathers, twigs*: whisk; ⊘ pallet.

verglacé, e [vɛrglaˈse] iced-over, icy (*road*); **verglas** [~ˈgla] *m* black ice; thin coating of ice.

vergogne [vɛrˈgɔɲ] *f* shame; *sans* ~ shameless(ly *adv.*).

vergue ⚓ [vɛrg] *f* yard; ~ *de misaine* foreyard; *bout m de* ~ yard-arm; *grande* ~ main yard.

véridique [veriˈdik] veracious, truthful (*account, person*); **vérifiable** [~ˈfjabl] verifiable; **vérificateur, -trice** [verifikaˈtœːr, ~ˈtris] **1.** *su./m* *weights etc.*: inspector, examiner; ⊕ ga(u)ge, calipers *pl.*; *mot.* ~ *de pression tyres*: pressure-ga(u)ge; ♱ ~ *comptable* auditor; **2.** *adj.*⊕ testing; verifying; **vérificatif, -ve** [~ˈtif, ~ˈtiːv] verificatory; verifying-...; **vérification** [~ˈsjɔ̃] *f* checking, verification; check; confirming; confirmation; **vérifier** [veriˈfje] (1o) *v/t.* check, verify; confirm, bear out; ♱ audit (*accounts*).

vérin ⊕, *mot.* [veˈrɛ̃] *m* jack.

véritable [veriˈtabl] true; real, genuine (*a. fig.*); *fig. usu. pej.* downright.

vérité [veriˈte] *f* truth; fact; *fig.* truthfulness, sincerity; *à la* ~ as a matter of fact; F *c'est la* ~ *vraie* it's the honest truth; *dire la* ~ tell the truth; *en* ~ really, truly.

verjus [vɛrˈʒy] *m* verjuice (*grape*); **verjuté, e** [~ʒyˈte] acid, sour (*a. fig.*).

vermeil, -eille [vɛrˈmɛːj] **1.** *adj.* ruby (*lips*), bright red; rosy (*cheek*); **2.** *su./m* silver-gilt, vermeil; vermeil varnish.

vermicelle *cuis.* [vɛrmiˈsɛl] *m* vermicelli *pl.*

vermiculaire [vɛrmikyˈlɛːr] ver-

micular (*a. physiol.*); *anat.* vermi-
form (*appendix*); **vermiculé, e**
[～ky'le] ⚠ vermiculate(d); *zo. etc.*
vermiculate; **vermiculure** ⚠ *etc.*
[～ky'ly:r] *f* vermiculation; **vermifuge** ✻ [～'fy:3] *adj., a. su./m* vermifuge.
vermillon [vɛrmi'jõ] **1.** *su./m* vermilion (*a. colour*); bright red;
2. *adj./inv.* bright red; **ver-
millonner** [～jɔ'ne] (1a) *v/t.* paint
(*s.th.*) bright red; rouge (*one's
cheeks*).
vermine [vɛr'min] *f* vermin (*usu.
= lice, fleas*); F *fig.* rabble; **vermineux, -euse** ✻ [vɛrmi'nø, ～'nø:z]
caused by worms, verminous (*disease*); **vermisseau** *zo.* [～'so] *m*
small earthworm; **vermivore** *zo.*
[～'vɔ:r] vermivorous; **vermouler**
[vɛrmu'le] (1a) *v/t.*: se ～ become
worm-eaten (*wood*); **vermoulu, e**
[～'ly] worm-eaten (*wood*); *fig.* decrepit; out-of-date; **vermoulure**
[～'ly:r] *f* worm-holes *pl.*; *wood*:
worm-eaten state; wood dust (*from
wormhole*); *fig.* decrepitude.
vermouth [vɛr'mut] *m* vermouth.
vernaculaire [vɛrnaky'lɛ:r] *adj., a.
su./m* vernacular.
vernal, e, *m/pl.* **-aux** ♀, *astr., etc.*
[vɛr'nal, ～'no] vernal.
verni, e [vɛr'ni] varnished; patent
(*leather*); F lucky.
vernier ♀, *astr., surv.* [vɛr'nje] *m*
vernier; sliding-ga(u)ge.
vernir [vɛr'ni:r] (2a) *v/t.* varnish;
japan (*iron, leather*); polish (*furniture*); glaze (*pottery*); *fig.* gloss over;
vernis [～'ni] *m* varnish; polish;
gloss (*a. fig.*); glaze; ～ à ongles nail
varnish; ～ au tampon French polish;
vernis-émail, *pl.* **vernis-émaux**
[vɛrnie'ma:j, ～'mo] *m* Japan enamel;
vernissage [～'sa:3] *m* ⊕ varnish
(-ing) glaze; glazing; *exhibition*:
varnishing-day; ～ au tampon
French-polishing; **vernisser** ⊕ [～-
'se] (1a) *v/t.* glaze (*pottery*).
vérole ✻ [ve'rɔl] *f* V pox (= *syphilis*); *petite* ～ *see* variole; **vérolé, e**
✻ V [～rɔ'le] poxed (= *syphilitic*).
véronal ⚕ [verɔ'nal] *m* veronal; bar-
bitone.
véronique [verɔ'nik] *f* ♀ speedwell;
eccl. veronica, vernicle.
verrai [vɛ're] *1st p. sg. fut.* of voir.
verrat *zo.* [vɛ'ra] *m* boar.

verre [vɛ:r] *m* glass; glassful; *opt.
lens*; ～ armé wired *or* reinforced
glass; ～ à vin wine glass; ✻ ～ de
contact contact lens; *mot.* ～ de sûreté
safety glass; ～ de vin glass of wine; ～
soluble water-glass; boire (*or prendre*)
un ～ have a drink; se noyer dans un ～
d'eau make a mountain out of a
molehill; **verré, e** [vɛ're] *adj.*: papier
m ～ glass-paper; sand-paper; **verrerie** [vɛr'ri] *f* ⊕ glass-works *usu. sg.*;
⊕ glass-making; ✝ glassware; ～
allant au four flame-proof glassware;
verrier [vɛ'rje] **1.** *su./m* glassmaker;
glass-blower; glass-rack; **2.** *adj./m*:
peintre *m* ～ artist in stained glass;
verrière [～'rjɛ:r] *f* glass (casing);
eccl. etc. stained glass window; 🚂
station: glass-roof; **verrine** [～'rin] *f*
glass (casing); *barometer*: glass; ⚓
lantern; **verroterie** [～rɔ'tri] *f* glass
trinkets *pl.*; small glassware; glass
beads *pl.*
verrou [vɛ'ru] *m* bolt; *shot-gun*:
breech-bolt; ～ de blocage switch-
lock; 🔒 sous les ～s under lock and
key; **verrouiller** [～ru'je] (1a) *v/t.*
bolt (*a door etc.*); ⊕ lock; lock (*s.o.*)
in *or* up; se ～ bolt o.s. in.
verrue ✻ [vɛ'ry] *f* wart; **verruqueux, -euse** [～ry'kø, ～'kø:z]
✻ warty; ♀ warted; ✻, ♀ verru-
cose.
vers[1] [vɛ:r] *m poetry*: line, verse;
～ *pl.* blancs blank verse *sg.*
vers[2] [～] *prp. direction*: to, towards
(*a place*); *time*: towards; about
(*3 o'clock*), around (*noon, Easter*);
～ l'époque about the time; ～ l'est
eastwards, towards the east.
versant [vɛr'sã] *m* slope; *hill etc.*:
side; *canal etc.*: sloping bank.
versatile *fig.* [vɛrsa'til] changeable,
fickle; **versatilité** [～tili'te] *f* changeableness, fickleness, inconstancy.
verse [vɛrs] *adv.*: à ～ in torrents; il
pleut à ～ it is pouring; **versé, e**
[vɛr'se] versed, practised (in, dans);
Verseau *astr.* [vɛr'so] *m*: le ～
Aquarius, the Water-bearer.
versement [vɛrsə'mã] *m liquid*:
pouring (out); ✝ paying in, deposit,
payment; instalment; carnet *m* de ～s
paying-in book; en (*or par*) ～s (*échelonnés*) in *or* by instalments; **verser**
[～'se] (1a) *v/t.* pour (out); overturn (*a
vehicle etc.*); tip (*a truck*); shed
(*blood, light, tears*); ✝ pay (in), de-

posit (*money*); ✗ assign (*men*); *v/i.* turn over; upset; *fig.* ~ *dans* lapse into.

verset [vɛr'sɛ] *m bibl. etc.* verse; *typ.* versicle.

verseur, -euse [vɛr'sœːr, ~'søːz] 1. *adj.* ⊕ *etc.* pouring, pour-through; 2. *su.* pourer; *su./f* coffee-pot.

versicolore [vɛrsiko'lɔːr] variegated, versicolo(u)r(ed); chameleon-like.

versificateur *m,* **-trice** *f* [vɛrsifika-'tœːr, ~'tris] versifier; **versification** [~fika'sjɔ̃] *f* versification; **versifier** [~'fje] (1o) *v/t.* write in verse; put (*prose*) into verse; *v/i.* versify; write poetry.

version [vɛr'sjɔ̃] *f* version; *school:* translation into one's own language.

verso [vɛr'so] *m* verso, back (*of a sheet of paper*); *au* ~ overleaf, on the back.

vert, verte [vɛːr, vɛrt] 1. *adj.* green; unripe (*fruit*); sharp, young (*wine*); raw (*hide*); callow (*youth*); hale and hearty (*old man*); *fig.* severe (*reprimand, punishment*); sharp (*reply*); smutty, spicy (*story*); *haricots m/pl.* ~s French beans; *langue f* ~*e* slang; *en dire* (*or raconter*) *des* ~*es* (*et de pas mûres*) tell some spicy things; 2. *su./m colour,* ⚕ *a. min.:* green; (green) grass; *golf:* putting-green; *wine:* sharpness; *inv.* when used *adjectivally in compounds:* une robe ~ *foncé* a dark green dress; *des rideaux* ~ *olive* olive-green curtains; ~-**de-gris** [vɛrdə'gri] *m* verdigris; ~-**de-grisé,** **e** [~gri'ze] coated *or* covered with verdigris.

vertébral, e, *m/pl.* **-aux** anat. [vɛr-te'bral, ~'bro] vertebral; *colonne f* ~*e* spine, backbone, spinal column; **vertèbre** anat. [~'tɛːbr] *f* vertebra; **vertébré, e** zo. [~te'bre] *adj., a. su./m* vertebrate.

vertement [vɛrtə'mɑ̃] *adv.* sharply; sternly.

vertical, e, *m/pl.* **-aux** [vɛrti'kal, ~'ko] 1. *adj.* vertical; perpendicular; upright; 2. *su./f* ⚕ vertical; **verticalité** [~kali'te] *f* perpendicularity, uprightness.

verticille ⚕ [vɛrti'sil] *m* verticil, whorl; **verticillé, e** ⚕ [~si'le] verticillate, whorled.

vertige [vɛr'tiːʒ] *m* giddiness, dizziness, vertigo; fear of heights; *avoir le* ~ feel dizzy; *cela me donne le* ~ it makes me (feel) dizzy; **vertigi-**

neux, -euse [~tiʒi'nø, ~'nøːz] dizzy, giddy (*hight, speed*); breathtaking; **vertigo** *vet.* [~ti'go] *m* (blind) staggers *pl.*

vertu [vɛr'ty] *f* virtue; chastity; virtuous woman; *substance:* property; *en* ~ *de* by virtue of; because of; in accordance with; thanks to; *faire de nécessité* ~ make a virtue of necessity; **vertueux, -euse** [~'tɥø, ~'tɥøːz] virtuous; chaste (*woman*).

verve [vɛrv] *f* (witty) eloquence; † zest, verve, spirits *pl.,* F go; *être en* ~ have got going, be in brilliant form.

verveine ⚕ [vɛr'vɛn] *f* verbena, vervain.

vésanie † [veza'ni] *f* insanity; madness.

vesce ⚕ [vɛs] *f* vetch, tare.

vésicant, e ✗ [vezi'kɑ̃, ~'kɑ̃ːt] *see* **vésicatoire** 1; **vésicatoire** ✗ [~ka-'twaːr] 1. *adj.* vesicatory, blistering; 2. *su./m* blister, vesicatory; **vésiculaire** ⚕, zo. [~ky'lɛːr] vesicular (*a.* ✗); bladder-like; **vésicule** [~'kyl] *f* anat. etc. vesicle, bladder (*a. icht.*); metall. blister; anat. ~ *biliaire* gall bladder.

vespasienne [vɛspa'zjɛn] *f* street urinal.

vespéral, e, *m/pl.* **-aux** [vɛspe'ral, ~'ro] 1. *adj.* evening-...; 2. *su./m eccl.* vesperal.

vesse *sl.* [vɛs] *f* silent fart; ~-**de-loup,** *pl.* ~**s-de-loup** ⚕ [~də'lu] *f* puffball.

vessie [vɛ'si] *f* anat., a. foot. bladder; F blister (*filled with serum*); ✗ ~ *à glace* ice-bag; icht. ~ *natatoire* air-bladder, swim(ming)-bladder; *fig. prendre des* ~*s pour des lanternes* believe that the moon is made of green cheese, not to know chalk from cheese.

vestale [vɛs'tal] *f* vestal (virgin).

veste cost. [vɛst] *f* short jacket; *fig. remporter une* ~ fail; *fig., pol. etc. retourner sa* ~ turn one's coat, change sides *or* one's party; **vestiaire** [vɛs'tjɛːr] *m thea. etc.* cloakroom, *Am.* check-room; hat-and-coat rack; 🚇 robing-room; ✗, sp. etc. changing-room.

vestibule [vɛsti'byl] *m* (entrance-) hall; vestibule (*a. anat.*).

vestige [vɛs'tiːʒ] *m* relic, remnant, vestige.

veston [vɛs'tɔ̃] *m cost.* (*man's*) jacket; ⚓ monkey-jacket; *complet m* ~

lounge suit; *être en* ~ wear a lounge suit.

vêtement [vɛt'mã] *m* garment; ~*s pl.* clothes; dress *sg.*; *eccl.* vestments; ~*s pl. de dehors* outdoor things; ~*s pl. de dessous* underwear; ~*s pl. de deuil* mourning *sg.*; window's weeds.

vétéran [vete'rã] *m* ✕ *etc.* veteran; *school etc.*: pupil repeating a course.

vétérinaire [veteri'nɛːr] 1. *adj.* veterinary; 2. *su./m* veterinary surgeon, F vet, *Am.* veterinarian.

vétillard *m*, **e** *f* † [veti'jaːr, ~'jard] *see* **vétilleur, -euse**; **vétille** [~'tiːj] *f* trifle; **vétilleur** *m*, **-euse** *f* [~'jœːr, ~'jøːz] quibbler; niggler; **vétilleux, -euse** [~'jø, ~'jøːz] punctilious, particular (*person*).

vêtir [vɛ'tiːr] (2g) *v/t.* clothe, dress (in, *de*); se ~ dress o.s. (in, *de*); put on one's clothes.

veto [ve'to] *m/inv.* veto; *droit m de* ~ power of veto; *mettre son* ~ *à* veto (*s.th.*).

vêts [vɛ] *1st p. sg. pres. of* **vêtir**; **vêtu, e** [vɛ'ty] *p.p. of* **vêtir**; **vêture** [~'tyːr] *f* clothing; † clothes *pl.*; *eccl.* taking of the habit (*monk*) or of the veil (*nun*).

vétuste [ve'tyst] timeworn; decrepit; **vétusté** [~tys'te] *f* decrepitude.

veuf, veuve [vœf, vœːv] 1. *adj.* widowed; *être* (*or rester*) ~ *de q.* be left s.o.'s widow(er); bereft of; 2. *su./m* widower; *su./f* widow; *orn.* widowbird, whidah-bird.

veuille [vœj] *1st p. sg. pres. sbj. of* **vouloir** 1.

veule [vøːl] feeble, flabby (*person etc.*); drab (*life*); toneless, flat (*voice*); ♥ sickly (*plant*).

veulent [vœl] *3rd p. pl. pres. of* **vouloir** 1.

veulerie [vøl'ri] *f person etc.*: listlessness, flabbiness; *life*: drabness; dullness; *voice*: flatness.

veuvage [vœ'vaːʒ] *m woman*: widowhood; *man*: widowerhood.

veux [vø] *1st p. sg. pres. of* **vouloir** 1.

vexant, e [vɛk'sã, ~'sãːt] annoying, upsetting; **vexateur, -trice** [vɛksa-'tœːr, ~'tris] 1. *adj.* vexatious; 2. *su.* vexer; **vexation** [~'sjõ] *f* humiliation; harassing, harassment; **vexatoire** [~'twaːr] humiliating; harassing; **vexer** [vɛk'se] (1a) *v/t.* upset, annoy; se ~ get upset or annoyed; se ~ become vexed or annoyed or chagrined (at, *de*).

via [vi'a] *prp. before place-name*: via, by way of.

viabilité [vjabili'te] *f* viability; *road*: practicability; **viable** [vjabl] viable.

viaduc [vja'dyk] *m* viaduct.

viager, -ère [vja'ʒe, ~'ʒɛːr] 1. *adj.* for life; life ...; *rente f* ~*ère* life annuity; *rentier m* ~ annuitant; 2. *su./m* life income; *en* ~ at life income.

viande [vjãːd] *f* meat; F substance; ~ *fraîche* (*frigorifiée*) fresh (frozen or chilled) meat; ~*s pl. froides restaurant*: cold buffet; *conserve f de* ~ preserved meat.   [(*deer*).\

viander *hunt.* [vjã'de] (1a) *v/i.* graze

viatique [vja'tik] *m eccl.* viaticum, last sacrament; *fig.* money or provisions *pl.* for a journey; *fig.* resource.

vibrant, e [vi'brã, ~'brãːt] vibrating; *fig.* ringing, resonant (*voice, tone*); *fig.* rousing (*speech*); **vibrateur** ⚡ [vibra'tœːr] *m* buzzer, vibrator; **vibration** [~'sjõ] *f* vibration; ⚡ flutter(ing); *voice*: resonance; **vibrer** [vi'bre] (1a) *v/i.* vibrate; ⚡ *appel m vibré* buzzer call; *faire* ~ make (*s.th.*) vibrate; *fig.* thrill; **vibreur** ⚡ [~'brœːr] *m* vibrator, make-and-break; buzzer.

vibromasseur ⚡ [vibrɔma'sœːr] *m massage*: vibrator.

vicaire [vi'kɛːr] *m parish*: curate, assistant priest; † deputy; ~ *de Jésus-Christ* the Vicar of Christ, *le Pope*; ~ *général, grand* ~ vicar-general; **vicariat** *eccl.* [~ka'rja] *m* curacy; vicariate.

vice [vis] *m* vice; defect, fault; ~ *de conformation* defect in build; malformation; ⚖ ~ *de forme* legal flaw; ~ *propre* inherent defect.

vice-... [vis] vice-...; ~**consul** [~kõ-'syl] *m* vice-consul; ~**président** [~prezi'dã] *m* vice-president; ~**roi** [~'rwa] *m* viceroy.

vichy [vi'ʃi] *m* vichy water.

viciateur, -trice [visja'tœːr, ~'tris] vitiating; *fig.* contaminating; **viciation** [~'sjõ] *f* vitiation (*a.* ⚖); *air*: contamination; *fig.* morals *etc.*: corruption; **vicier** [vi'sje] (1o) *v/t.* vitiate (*a.* ⚖); corrupt, taint, spoil; *air m vicié* stale or foul air; se ~ become tainted; **vicieux, -euse** [~'sjø, ~'sjøːz] vicious (*a. fig. circle*); depraved (*person*); defective; faulty (*expression, reasoning*); restive, bad-tempered (*horse*).

34 GTW Fr-E

vicinal, e, *m/pl.* **-aux** [visi'nal, ~'no] local, by(-road).

vicissitude [visisi'tyd] *f* vicissitude; ~s *pl.* ups and downs.

vicomte [vi'kɔ̃:t] *m* viscount; **vicomté** [vikɔ̃'te] *f* viscountcy; viscounty; **vicomtesse** [~'tɛs] *f* viscountess.

victime [vik'tim] *f* victim (a. *fig.*); disaster: casualty; être ~ de be a or the victim of; be down with (*bronchitis*); *fig.* labo(u)r under (*a delusion etc.*).

victoire [vik'twa:r] *f* victory; remporter la ~ gain a or the victory (over, sur); win the day; **victoria** [~tɔ'rja] *su./f* carriage: Victoria; *su./m:* ♀ ~ regia victoria regia, watermaize; **victorieux, -euse** [~tɔ'rjø, ~'rjø:z] victorious (over, de); triumphant (over, de); *fig.* decisive (*proof*).

victuailles F [vik'tɥɑ:j] *f/pl.* eatables, victuals.

vidage [vi'da:ʒ] *m* emptying; F *fig.* dismissal; **vidange** [~'dɑ̃:ʒ] *f* emptying; draining; *mot.* oil change; ~s *pl.* sewage *sg.*; en ~ broached (*cask*), opened (*bottle*); *mot.* faire la ~ change the oil; **vidanger** [vidɑ̃'ʒe] (11) *v/t.* empty; drain; clean out; **vidangeur** [~'ʒœ:r] *m* nightman; **vide** [vid] **1.** *adj.* empty; blank (*space*); *fig.* vain; ~ de sens (de)void of meaning; avoir le cerveau ~ feel light-headed (*from lack of food*); **2.** *su./m* (empty) space; blank (*in document*); gap (*between objects, a. fig.*); *phys.* vacuum, space; *fig.* vacancy, emtptiness; *fig.* nothingness; à ~ empty; ⚡ no-load; ✛ emballé sous ~ vacuum-packed; frapper à ~ miss (the mark, the nail, *etc.*); ⊕ marcher à ~ run light; *mot.* tourner à ~ tick over, idle; **vide-bouteille** [~bu'tɛ:j] *m* siphon; † countrylodge; **vide-citron** [~si'trɔ̃] *m* lemon-squeezer.

vidéo [vide'o] **1.** *adj.* video(-)...; **2.** *su./f* video; videofrequency; **vidéophone** [~ɔ'fɔn] *m* videophone.

vide-ordures [vidɔr'dy:r] *m/inv.* rubbish shoot; **vide-poches** [~'pɔʃ] *m/inv.* tidy; *mot.* glove compartment; **vide-pomme** [~'pɔm] *m/inv.* apple corer; **vider** [vi'de] (1a) *v/t.* empty; drain; clear out; clear (*a forest*); *fig.* exhaust; F *fig.* dismiss, sack (*s.o.*); F chuck (*s.o.*) out; gut, clean (*fish*); draw (*poultry*); stone (*fruit*), core (*an apple*); bail out (*a boat*); *fig.* settle (*an argument, a question*); ✛ make up (*accounts*); ~ les arçons be thrown (*from a horse*); **videur** [~'dœ:r] *m* F bouncer.

vidimer [vidi'me] (1a) *v/t.* attest (*a copy*); **vidimus** [~'mys] *m* vidimus, attested copy.

viduité [vidɥi'te] *f* widowhood.

vidure [vi'dy:r] *f* poultry: entrails *pl.*, fish: guts *pl.*; ~s *pl.* rubbish *sg.*

vie [vi] *f* life; lifetime; way of life; livelihood, living; biography; *fig.* animation, spirit; ~ moyenne expectation of life; ⊕ ~ utile *machine*: life; à ~ for life; de ma ~ in all my life; donner la ~ à give birth to (*a child, fig. a project*); être en ~ be alive; F jamais de la ~! never!; F not on your life!; sans ~ lifeless.

vieil [vjɛ:j] see vieux 1; **vieillard** [vjɛ'ja:r] *m* old man; ~s *pl.* old people; **vieille** [vjɛ:j] see vieux; ~ fille *f* old maid, spinster; **vieillerie** [vjɛj'ri] *f* old clothes *pl.*; old stuff (= furniture etc.; a. fig.); *fig.* outdated ideas; **vieillesse** [vjɛ'jɛs] *f* old age; coll. old people *pl.*; *fig.* custom, wine, etc.: age; **vieillir** [~'ji:r] (2a) *v/t.* age; *v/i.* grow old; age; *fig.* go out of fashion; **vieillissement** [~jis'mɑ̃] *m* ageing; *fig.* obsolescence; **vieillot, -otte** F [~'jo, ~'jɔt] oldish; wizened (*face*); *fig.* old-fashioned.

vielle ♪ † [vjɛl] *f* hurdy-gurdy.

viendrai [vjɛ̃'dre] *1st p. sg. fut. of* venir; **viennent** [vjɛn] *3rd p. pl. pres. of* venir; **viens** [vjɛ̃] *1st p. sg. pres. of* venir.

vierge [vjɛrʒ] **1.** *su./f* virgin, maiden; *astr.* la ♍ Virgo, the Virgin; **2.** *adj.* virgin (*forest, gold, soil*); *fig.* clean, spotless, pure; blank (*page*); *phot.* unexposed (*film*); ~ de clear of.

vieux (*adj. before vowel or h mute* **vieil** *m,* **vieille** *f, m/pl.* **vieux** [vjø, vjɛ:j, vjø] **1.** *adj.* old; aged; ~ jeu old-fashioned; **2.** *su./m* old man; old things *pl.*; mon ~! old boy!; prendre un coup de ~ grow old overnight; *su./f* old woman.

vif, vive [vif, vi:v] **1.** *adj.* alive, living; *fig.* lively (*imagination*); brisk (*action, discussion, fire, game, pace*); sharp (*wind*); bright (*colour*); quick (*temper, wit*); de vive force by main force; eau *f* vive running water; vive arête sharp edge; vives *eaux pl.* spring tide *sg.;* **2.** *su./m* ⚥ living person; living flesh; *paint.* life; *fig. fight:* thick, heart; *blesser au ~* wound to the quick; *entrer dans le ~ du sujet* get to the heart of the matter; *pris sur le ~* taken from (real) life; lifelike; **vifargent** [vifar'ʒɑ̃] *m* quicksilver, mercury.

vigie [vi'ʒi] *f* look-out (post).

vigilamment [viʒila'mɑ̃] *adv. of vigilant;* **vigilance** [~'lɑ̃:s] *f* vigilance; caution; **vigilant, e** [~'lɑ̃, ~'lɑ̃:t] vigilant, watchful, alert; **vigile** [vi-'ʒil] *su./f eccl.* vigil; *su./m* watchman.

vigne [viɲ] *f* ⚥ vine; ✔ vineyard; ✔~ *blanche* clematis; ✔~ *de Judée* woody nightshade; ✔ ~ *vierge* Virginia creeper; *cep m de ~* vinestock; *fig. dans les ~s du Seigneur* in one's cups (= *drunk*); **vigneron** [viɲə'rɔ̃] *m* wine-grower; vine-dresser; **vignette** [~'ɲɛt] *f* vignette; ✝ manufacturer's label; *typ.* engraving; *admin. packet of cigarettes etc.:* revenue band or seal; *mot. (a. ~ de l'impôt) approx.* road tax disc; **vignettiste** [viɲɛ'tist] *m* vignettist; **vigneture** [viɲə'ty:r] *f* ornamental border of vine-leaves (*round miniatures*); **vignoble** [vi-'ɲɔbl] **1.** *su./m* ✔ vineyard; vineyards *pl.* (*of a region*); **2.** *adj.* wine ...

vigogne *zo., a. tex.* [vi'gɔɲ] *f* vicuña.

vigoureux, -euse [vigu'rø, ~'rø:z] vigorous, strong; powerful (*blow*); *fig.* energetic; **vigueur** [~'gœ:r] *f* vigo(u)r, strength; *fig.* force; *en ~* in force; *entrer (mettre) en ~* come (put) into force.

vil, vile [vil] base (*a. metal*), vile; *à ~ prix* at a low price, F dirt cheap.

vilain, e [vi'lɛ̃, ~'lɛn] **1.** *adj.* ugly; nasty, unpleasant; dirty (*trick*); *fig.* mean (*person, deed*); **2.** *su.* blackguard, villain; ✝ villein; F naughty child; *su./m* F *fig.* trouble.

vilebrequin [vilbrə'kɛ̃] *m* ⊕ brace (and bit); wimble; ⊕, *mot.* crankshaft.

vilenie [vil'ni] *f* meanness; *fig.* abuse; vile story; dirty trick, mean action. [ify: run (*s.o.*) down.)

vilipender [vilipɑ̃'de] (1a) *v/t.* vili-)

villa [vi'la] *f* villa; country-house; cottage; **village** [~'la:ʒ] *m* village; **villageois, e** [~la'ʒwa, ~'ʒwa:z] **1.** *adj.* rustic, country-...; **2.** *su.* villager; *su./m* countryman; *su./f* countrywoman.

34*

ville [vil] *f* town, city; *~ maritime* town on the sea, seaside town; *~ natale* hometown; *à la ~* in town (= *not in the country*); *aller en ~* go (in)to town; *diner en ~* dine out; *en ~ post:* Local.

villégiature [vileʒja'ty:r] *f* stay in the country; holiday (*away from town*); *en ~* on holiday.

vin [vɛ̃] *m* wine; *~ chaud* mulled wine; *~ de marque* vintage wine; *~ de pays* local wine; *~ ordinaire* table *or* dinner wine; *grand ~* wine from a famous vineyard; vintage wine; *gros (petit) ~* full-bodied *or* heavy (light) wine; *offrir un ~ d'honneur à* give an official reception in hono(u)r of; *entre deux ~s* slightly tipsy; **vinage** [vi'na:ʒ] *m* wine *etc.:* fortifying; **vinaigre** [~'nɛ:gr] *m* vinegar; *tourner au ~* turn sour (*a. fig.*); **vinaigrer** [vinɛ'gre] (1a) *v/t.* season with vinegar; *fig.* give an acid edge to; **vinaigrerie** [~grə-'ri] *f* vinegar factory *or* trade; vinegar-making; **vinaigrette** *cuis.* [~'grɛt] *f* vinegar sauce; French dressing, oil and vinegar dressing; **vinaigrier** [~gri'e] *m* vinegar-maker; vinegar-merchant; vinegar-cruet; **vinasse** [~'nas] *f* poor, thin wine, F plonk; 🚂 residuary liquor.

vindicatif, -ve [vɛ̃dika'tif, ~'ti:v] vindictive; spiteful; ⚥ punitive; **vindicte** [~'dikt] *f* ⚥ prosecution; F *fig.* obloquy.

vinée [vi'ne] *f* wine-crop, vintage; ✔ fruit-branch of a vine; **viner** ⊕ [~'ne] (1a) *v/t.* fortify (*wine etc.*); **vineux, -euse** [~'nø, ~'nø:z] vinous; wine-flavo(u)red; wine-colo(u)red; full-bodied (*wine*); vintage (*year*).

vingt [vɛ̃; *before vowel and h mute, and when followed by another numeral* vɛ̃:t] *adj./num., a. su./m/inv.* twenty; *date, title:* twentieth; *~ et un* twenty-one; *~-deux* twenty-two; **vingtaine** [vɛ̃'tɛn] *f* (about) twenty; score; **vingtième** [~'tjɛm] *adj./num., a. su./m fraction:* twentieth.

vinicole [vini'kɔl] wine-growing; **viniculture** [~kyl'ty:r] *f* viniculture, wine-growing; **vinification** ⊕ [~fika'sjɔ̃] *f* vinification; **vinique** [vi'nik] vinic (*alcohol etc.*); **vinosité** [~nozi'te] *f* wine: flavo(u)r and strength, vinosity.

vins [vɛ̃] *1st p. sg. p.s. of venir.*

viol ⚥ [vjɔl] *m* rape; violation.
violacé, e [vjɔlaˈse] **1.** *adj.* purplish-blue; blue (*person*); **2.** *su./f*: ♀ ~s *pl.* violaceae; **violacer** [~] (1k) *v/i.* become covered with purplish spots; become purplish.
violateur, -trice [vjɔlaˈtœːr, ~ˈtris] *su.* violator (*a. fig.*); *fig.* breaker (*of law, Sabbath, etc.*); *su./m* † ⚥ ravisher; **violation** [~ˈsjɔ̃] *f* violation (*a. fig.*); *fig.* breach; *Sabbath:* breaking; ~ **de domicile** violation of privacy (*of one's home*).
violâtre [vjɔˈlɑːtr] purplish.
viole ♪ [vjɔl] *f* ~ viol; ~ **d'amour** viola d'amore.
violemment [vjɔlaˈmɑ̃] *adv. of violent*; **violence** [~ˈlɑːs] *f* violence, force; ⚥ duress; *faire* ~ *à* do violence to (*a. fig.*); violate (*a woman*); **violent, e** [~ˈlɑ̃, ~ˈlɑ̃t] violent (*a. death*); fierce; *fig.* intense; F *fig. c'est un peu* ~! that's a bit thick!; **violenter** [~lɑ̃ˈte] (1a) *v/t.* do violence to; ⚥ rape, ravish (*a woman*); **violer** [~ˈle] (1a) *v/t.* violate; *fig.* break; ⚥ rape, ravish (*a woman*).
violet, -ette [vjɔˈlɛ, ~ˈlɛt] **1.** *adj.* violet, purple; *inv. in compounds:* ~ *évêque* bishop's-purple; **2.** *su./m* colour: violet; *su./f* ♀ violet; *sl. faire sa* ~ play the shrinking violet.
violon [vjɔˈlɔ̃] *m* ♪ instrument, *a. player:* violin; F fiddle; ⊕ fiddle-block; F jail, *sl.* quod, clink; *fig.* ~ *d'Ingres* (*artistic*) hobby; *fig. aller plus vite que les* ~s jump the gun; **violoncelle** ♪ [~lɔ̃ˈsɛl] *m* (violon)-cello; cellist; **violoncelliste** ♪ [~lɔ̃-sɛˈlist] *su.* (violon)cellist; **violoniste** ♪ [~lɔˈnist] *su.* violinist.
viorne ♀ [vjɔrn] *f* viburnum.
vipère [viˈpɛːr] *f* zo. viper, adder; *fig. langue f de* ~ venomous tongue; **vipéridés** zo. [viperiˈde] *m/pl.* viperidae, viper family *sg.*; **vipérin, e** [~ˈrɛ̃, ~ˈrin] **1.** *adj.* viperine; *fig.* venomous (*tongue*); **2.** *su./f* zo. viperine snake; ♀ viper's bugloss.
virage [viˈraːʒ] *m* turning; *road etc.:* turn, bend, corner; ⚡, *mot., etc.* sweeping round; 🏦 bank(ing); *sl. racing-track:* bank(ed corner); *mot.* turning space; ♣ going about; *phot.* toning; *tex.* changing of colo(u)r; ⟲ reversal; *fig.* change (*of direction or policy*); ~ *à droite* right turn; right-hand bend; ~ *à*

visibilité réduite blind corner; *prendre un* ~ take a corner; ~**-fixage**, *pl.* ~s**-fixages** *phot.* [~raʒfikˈsaːʒ] *m* combined toning and fixing.
viral, e *m/pl.* **-aux** [viˈral, ~ˈro] viral; virus (*disease*); infectious.
vire [viːr] *f* winding mountain track.
virée [viˈre] *f* trip, tour; joyride; **virement** [virˈmɑ̃] *m* ♣ tide, *a. fig.:* turn; ✝ transfer; *banque f de* ~ clearing bank; **virer** [viˈre] (1a) *v/i.* turn; *mot.* (take a) corner; ⚡ bank; ♣ heave; *phot.* tone; change colo(u)r; ~ *au bleu* turn blue; *v/t.* ✝ transfer (*money*); *phot.* tone; F chuck (*s.o.*) (out).
vireux, -euse [viˈrø, ~ˈrøːz] noxious, poisonous; malodorous, F stinking.
virevolte [virˈvɔlt] *f* half turn; spinning round; *fig.* sudden change, about-turn; **virevolter** [~vɔlˈte] (1a) *v/i.* spin round.
virginal, e, *m/p.* **-aux** [virʒiˈnal, ~ˈno] **1.** *adj.* virginal, maidenly; **2.** *su./m* ♪ virginal; **virginité** [~niˈte] *f* virginity; maidenhood.
virgule [virˈgyl] *f* gramm. comma; 𝐴 (decimal) point.
viril, e [viˈril] male (*clothing, sex*); *fig.* manly; virile; *âge m* ~ manhood; *anat. membre m* ~ penis; **viriliser** [viriliˈze] (1a) *v/t.* make (*s.o.*) look like a man; make a man of (*s.o.*); **virilité** [~ˈte] *f* virility; manliness, manhood.
viro-fixateur *phot.* [virɔfiksaˈtœːr] **1.** *adj./m* toning and fixing; **2.** *su./m* toning and fixing bath.
virole [viˈrɔl] *f* ⊕ handle, stick, tube; ferrule; ⊕ *machine:* collar; *pipes:* thimble-joint; **viroler** [~rɔˈle] (1a) *v/t.* ferrule.
virtualité [virtɥaliˈte] *f* potentiality; virtuality; **virtuel, -elle** [~tɥˈɛl] potential; virtual; **virtuellement** [~tɥɛlˈmɑ̃] *adv.* potentially; virtually, practically.
virtuose [virˈtɥoːz] *su.* virtuoso; **virtuosité** [~tɥoziˈte] *f* virtuosity.
virulence 𝟈, *a. fig.* [viryˈlɑːs] *f* virulence; **virulent, e** 𝟈, *a. fig.* [~ˈlɑ̃, ~ˈlɑ̃t] virulent; **virus** 𝟈 [viˈrys] *m* virus (*a. fig.*); *fig.* plague; *fig.* mania; ~ *filtrant* filterable virus; *maladie f à* ~ virus disease.
vis¹ [vis] *f* screw; ~ *de rappel* adjusting screw; ~ *sans fin* endless screw; *pas m*

de ~ thread of screw; F *fig. serrer la* ~ *à q.* put the screw on s.o.

vis² [vi] *1st p. sg. pres. of vivre 1.*

vis³ [~] *1st p. sg. p.s. of voir.*

visa [vi'za] *m passport*: visa; *document*: signature; *supervisor etc.*: initials *pl.*; *cheque*: certification; *bill*: sighting; ~ *d'entrée* entry visa; ~ *de sortie* exit visa; ~ *de transit* transit visa.

visage [vi'za:ʒ] *m* face; countenance; *à* ~ *découvert* openly; *fig. à* ~ *humain* humane, fit for human beings; *faire bon (mauvais)* ~ *à* be friendly (unfriendly) towards, smile (frown) on (*s.o.*); F *trouver* ~ *de bois* find nobody at home; meet with a closed door; **visagiste** [viza'ʒist] *su.* beautician.

vis-à-vis [viza'vi] **1.** *adv.* opposite; **2.** *prp.*: ~ *de* opposite, facing; *fig.* in relation to, with respect to; **3.** *su./m* person opposite; partner (*at cards etc.*); S-shaped couch.

viscéral, e, *m/pl.* **-aux** *anat.* [vise-'ral, ~'ro] visceral; **viscère** *anat.* [~'sɛːr] *m* internal organ; ~s *pl.* viscera.

viscose ⚗, ⊕, ✝ [vis'ko:z] *f* viscose; **viscosité** [~kozi'te] *f* viscosity; stickiness.

visée [vi'ze] *f* aim (*a. fig.*); ✂, *surv.* aim(ing); sight(ing); ~s *pl.* aims, designs.

viser¹ [vi'ze] (1a) *v/i.* aim (at, *à*) (*a. fig.*); *v/t.* aim at (*a. fig.*); *surv.* sight; *fig.* relate to, have (*s.th.*) in view; *fig.* refer to (*s.o.*), allude to (*s.o.*); *sl.* (take a) look at; ~ *q. à la tête* aim at s.o.'s head.

viser² [~] (1a) *v/t.* visa (*a passport*); initial, sign (*a document*); certify (*a cheque*); 🏷 stamp (*the ticket when a journey is broken*).

viseur [vi'zœːr] *m gun*: sights *pl.*; *phot.* view-finder.

visibilité [vizibili'te] *f* visibility; conspicuousness (*of s.th.*); **visible** [~'zibl] visible; *fig.* evident, obvious; *fig.* able to receive (company), at home (to visitors) (*person*).

visière [vi'zjɛːr] *f helmet*: visor; *cap*: peak; eyeshade; ⊕ inspection-hole; *fig. rompre en* ~ *avec q.* contradict s.o. flatly; quarrel openly with s.o.

vision [vi'zjɔ̃] *f* vision (*a. eccl.*); sight; *fig.* fantasy; phantom; imagination; *trouble m de la* ~ eyesight

trouble; **visionnaire** [~zjɔ'nɛːr] *adj., a. su.* visionary.

visitation *eccl.* [vizita'sjɔ̃] *f: la* ♎ (the Feast of) the Visitation; **visite** [~'zit] *f* visit (*a. ⚕*); (*social or ceremonial*) call; *admin.* inspection; *customs*: examination; ✛ medical examination; 🔍 search; 🔍 ~ *domiciliaire* domiciliary visit; *heures f/pl. de* ~ calling hours; *hospital*: visiting hours; *rendre* ~ *à* pay (*s.o.*) a visit; **visiter** [vizi'te] (1a) *v/t.* visit; *admin.* inspect, examine; 🔍 search; **visiteur, -euse** [~'tœːr, ~'tøːz] **1.** *adj.* visiting; *infirmière f* ~*euse* visiting nurse; **2.** *su.* visitor, caller; ⊕, *admin., etc.* inspector; *customs*: searcher; ✛ representative; *su./f:* ~*euse de santé* health visitor.

vison [vi'zɔ̃] *m zo.* (American) mink; ✛ mink.

visqueux, -euse [vis'kø, ~'køːz] viscous; sticky; gooey, slimy (*a. fig.*).

vissage ⊕ [vi'sa:ʒ] *m* screwing (on *or* down); **visser** [~'se] (1a) *v/t.* ⊕ screw (on, down, in, *etc.*); F clamp down on.

visualiser [vizɥali'ze] (1a) *v/t.* visualize; make visible; **visuel, -elle** [vi'zɥɛl] visual; *champ m* ~ field of vision.

vital, e, *m/pl.* **-aux** [vi'tal, ~'to] vital (*a. fig. question*); **vitaliser** [vitali'ze] (1a) *v/t.* vitalize; **vitalité** [~'te] *f* vitality.

vitamine [vita'min] *f* vitamin.

vite [vit] **1.** *adv.* quickly, rapidly, fast; soon; **2.** *adj.* fast, swift.

vitellus [vitɛl'lys] *m* ♀, *biol.* vitellus; *biol.* yolk.

vitesse [vi'tɛs] *f* speed; quickness; rapidity, swiftness; *phys.* bullet, light, sound: velocity, speed; *mot.* gear; ~ *imposée* prescribed speed; *mot.* ~ *limitée* traffic sign: speed limit, no speeding; *mot. boîte f de* ~s gear-box, *Am.* transmission; *grande (petite)* ~ high (low) speed; *mot. indicateur m de* ~ speedometer; *mot. première (quatrième)* ~ first (fourth) gear; bottom (top) gear; *à toute* ~ at top speed; *en* ~ quickly; in a hurry; *prendre q. de* ~ outrun s.o.

viticole [viti'kɔl] vine-...; viticultural; **viticulteur** [~kyl'tœːr] *m* vine-grower, viticulturist; **viticulture** [~kyl'ty:r] *f* vine-growing, viticulture.

vitrage [vi'tra:ʒ] *m* windows *pl.*; glass work; glass door; glass partition; glass roof; ⊕ glazing; net curtain; **vitrail**, *pl.* **-aux** [ₓ'tra:j, ₓ'tro] *m* leaded glass window; *eccl.* stained glass window; **vitre** [vitr] *f* pane (of glass); window-pane; F *fig. casser les* ₓ*s* kick up a fuss; **vitré, e** [vi'tre] ⊕ glazed; ⚷, *anat.*, *etc.* vitreous; **vitrer** [ₓ'tre] (1a) *v/t.* ⊕ glaze (*a door, a window, etc.*); **vitrerie** [ₓtrə'ri] *f* glazing, glaziery; **vitreux, -euse** [ₓ'trø, ₓ'trø:z] vitreous (*a.* ⚹); glassy; **vitrier** [vitri'e] *m* glass maker; ⊕ glazier; **vitrière** [ₓ'ɛ:r] *f* metal window framing; **vitrifiable** [ₓ'fjabl] vitrifiable; **vitrification** [ₓfika'sjõ] *f* vitrification; **vitrifier** [ₓ'fje] (1o) *v/t.* vitrify; ~ *par fusion* fuse; *se* ~ vitrify; **vitrine** [vi'trin] *f* shop-window; glass case, showcase, display case.

vitriol ⚗ [vitri'ɔl] *m* vitriol (*a. fig.*); *fig. au* ~ biting, caustic (*remark*); **vitriolé, e** ⚗ [ₓ'le] vitriolized; **vitrioler** [ₓ'le] (1a) *v/t.* vitriolize; throw vitriol at (*s.o.*); *tex.* sour (*fabric*); **vitrioleur** *m*, **-euse** *f* [ₓ'lœ:r, ₓ'lø:z] vitriol-thrower.

vitupération [vitypera'sjõ] *f* vituperation, abuse; **vitupérer** [ₓ're] (1f) *v/t.* abuse; ~ *contre* rail against.

vivace [vi'vas] long-lived; ⚘ perennial; ⚘ hardy; *fig.* enduring; *fig.* inveterate; **vivacité** [ₓvasi'te] *f* promptness; alertness; *fig. combat, discussion:* heat; *fig.* hastiness; *colour, feelings, etc.:* vividness; *fig.* liveliness; *horse:* mettle; *avec* ~ vivaciously.

vivandier, -ère † [vivã'dje, ₓ'djɛ:r] *su.* canteen-keeper; *su./f* vivandière.

vivant, e [vi'vã, ₓ'vã:t] **1.** *adj.* living (*a. fig.*), alive; modern (*language*); *fig.* lively (*scene etc.*); vivid (*account, picture, etc.*); **2.** *su./m:* *les* ~*s* the living; *bon* ~ man who enjoys life; easy-going fellow; *de son* ~ in his lifetime.

vivat [va'vat] **1.** *int.* hurrah!; **2.** *su./m* hurrah; ~*s* *pl.* cheers.

vive *icht.* [vi:v] *f* weever, sting-fish.

viveur [vi'vœ:r] *m* pleasure-seeker; fast liver.

vivier [vi'vje] *m* fishpond, fish tank.

vivificateur, -trice [vivifika'tœ:r, ₓ'tris] vivifying; invigorating; **vivi-**

fication [ₓ'sjõ] *f* reviving; **vivifier** [vivi'fje] (1o) *v/t.* vitalize; enliven; give life to; invigorate; **vivipare** [ₓ'pa:r] **1.** *adj.* ⚘, *zo.* viviparous; **2.** *su. zo.* viviparous animal; **vivisection** [ₓsɛk'sjõ] *f* vivisection.

vivoter [vivɔ'te] (1a) *v/i.* live from hand to mouth; rub *or* struggle along; **vivre** [vi:vr] (4hh) *v/i.* live (on, *de*; at, in *à*); be alive; subsist, exist; *fig.* survive, last (*memory etc.*); F *apprendre à* ~ *à* teach (*s.o.*) manners; *avoir beaucoup vécu* have seen life; *difficile à* ~ difficult to get along with; ⚔ *qui vive?* who goes there?; *qui vivra verra* time will show; *se laisser* ~ take life as it comes, take life *or* things easy; *vive ...!* long live ...!; hurrah for (*s.th.*)!; *v/t.* live (*one's life*); live through (*experiences*); **2.** *su./m* † living; food; ~*s* *pl.* provisions; ⚔ rations; *le* ~ *et le couvert* board and bed; *le* ~ *et le logement* board and lodging.

vizir [vi'zi:r] *m* vizi(e)r.

vlan!, v'lan! [vlã] *int.* slap-bang!

vocable [vɔ'kabl] *m* word, term; *eccl. sous le* ~ *de* dedicated to; **vocabulaire** [ₓkaby'lɛ:r] *m* vocabulary; word-list.

vocal, e, *m/pl.* **-aux** [vɔ'kal, ₓ'ko] vocal (*a. anat., a.* ♪); **vocalique** *gramm.* [vɔka'lik] vocalic, vowel-...; **vocalisation** *gramm., a.* ♪ [ₓliza-'sjõ] *f* vocalization; **vocalise** ♪ [ₓ-'li:z] *f* exercise in vocalization; *faire des* ~*s* vocalize; **vocaliser** *gramm., a.* ♪ [ₓli'ze] (1a) *vt/i.* vocalize; **vocalisme** *gramm., a.* ♪ [ₓ'lism] *m* vocalism; **vocation** [ₓ'sjõ] *f* vocation.

vociférations [vɔsifera'sjõ] *f/pl.* shouts, yells; outcries; **vociférer** [ₓ're] (1f) *v/i.* shout, yell, scream (at, *contre*); vociferate (against, *contre*).

vodka [vɔd'ka] *f* vodka.

vœu [vø] *m* vow; *fig.* wish, desire.

vogue [vɔg] *f* fashion, F rage, craze; *dial. eccl.* patronal festival; *être en* ~ be popular, be in fashion, F be in; *entrer (mettre) en* ~ come (bring) into fashion.

voguer [vɔ'ge] (1m) *v/i.* sail (*boat, cloud*); float, drift; *fig. vogue la galère!* let's risk *or* chance it!

voici [vwa'si] *prp.* here is, here are; F ~! look!; ~ *un an que je suis ici* I

have been here for a year; *me* ~*!*
here I am!

voie [vwa] *f* way (*a. fig.*), road;
path; *anat.* duct, tract; *fig.* means
pl., course; 🚉 railway, *Am.* railroad;
⚡ circuit; 🛠 (*dry, wet, etc.*) process; ~ *aérienne* air-route, airway;
~ *de communication* road, thoroughfare; line of communication;
✈ ~ *de départ* runway; ~*s pl. de
droit* legal channels; ⚖ ~*s pl. de
fait* assault *sg.* and battery *sg.*; *fig.*
~*s et moyens* ways and means;
🎺 ~*s pl. respiratoires* respiratory
tract *sg.*; ⚒ ~ *d'eau* leak; 🚉 *à deux*
~*s* double-track (*line*); 🚉 *à ~ normale* (*étroite*) standard-ga(u)ge
(narrow-ga[u]ge) (*line*); 🚉 *à ~
unique* single-track (*line*); *en* ~ *de*
in process of; *under* (*repair*); *par*
~ *de fig.* by (means of); 🚉 *via*;
par ~ *ferrée* by rail(way).

voilà [vwa'la] *prp.* there is, there are;
that is, those are; ~*!* here you are!; ~
ce que je dis that's what I say; ~ *qui est
drôle* that's funny; ~ *tout* that's all; ~
un an que je suis ici I have been here
for a year; *en* ~ *assez!* that's enough!;
me ~*!* here I am!

voilage [vwa'la:ʒ] *m* net curtain(s
pl.); *tex.* veiling, net; **voile** [vwal]
su./m veil (*a. fig., a. eccl.*); *fig.* cloak;
fig. blur; *tex.* voile; *phot.* fog; ⊕
buckle, warping; *anat.* ~ *du palais*
soft palate; *sous le* ~ *de* under the
cloak of; *su./f* ⚓ sail; *fig.* ship; *bateau
m à* ~*s* sailing boat; *faire* ~ set sail (for,
pour); *grand-*~ mainsail; F *mettre les*
~*s* clear out; **voiler** [vwa'le] (1a) *v/t.*
veil (*a.* ♪ *one's voice*); shade, dim (*the
light*); *fig.* cloak, hide; *phot.* fog; ⊕
buckle, warp; ⚓ rig (*a ship*) with
sails; *fig. voix f voilée* husky voice; *fig.
se* ~ become overcast (*sky*); *v/i. a. se* ~
⊕ go out of true; warp (*wood*); **voi-
lerie** ⚓ [vwal'ri] *f* sail-making; sail-
loft; **voilette** *cost.* [vwa'lɛt] *f* (hat-)
veil; **voilier** [~'lje] *m* ⚓ sailing ship,
sailing boat; sail-maker; *bâtiment m
bon* ~ good sailer; **voilure** [~'ly:r] *f* ⚓
sails *pl.*; ✈ wings *pl.*, wing surface;
⊕ rod, wheel: buckling; *wood*:
warping.

voir [vwa:r] (3m) *v/t.* see; perceive;
watch; observe; remark; witness (*an
incident*); visit; inspect; examine; 🩺
attend (*a patient*); 🩺 consult (*a physician*); *fig.* consider, take a view of

(*s.th.*); *fig.* understand; *fig.* experience, go through (*misfortunes*); F
tolerate, stand; ~ *à* (*inf.*) see to it that
(*ind.*); ~ *le jour* be born; ~ *venir q.* see
s.o. coming; *fig.* see what s.o. is up
to; *à ce que je vois* from what I see;
aller ~ (go and) see (*s.o.*), look (*s.o.*)
up; visit; *cela se voit* that's obvious;
c'est à ~ that remains to be seen; F
écoutez ~ just listen; *être bien* (*mal*) *vu
de* be in s.o.'s good (bad) books; *faire*
~ show; *laisser* ~ betray, reveal;
n'avoir rien à ~ *avec* (*or à*) have
nothing to do with; 🩺 *se faire* ~ *par le
médecin* get examined; *venir* ~ call on
(*s.o.*).

voire [vwa:r] *adv.* † truly; (*a.* ~
même) (and) even, indeed.

voirie [vwa'ri] *f* highway system;
system of roads; *admin.* Roads
Department, *Am.* Highway Divi-
sion; highway maintenance; refuse
(*Am.* garbage) collection; refuse
(*Am.* garbage) dump.

voisin, e [vwa'zɛ̃, ~'zin] **1.** *adj.* neigh-
bo(u)ring; adjacent; next (*building,
house, room, etc.*); ~ *de* in the vicinity
of; *fig.* similar to, akin to, approximating to; **2.** *su.* neighbo(u)r; **voisinage** [~zi'na:ʒ] *m* neighbo(u)rhood;
vicinity; surroundings *pl.*; *bon* ~
neighbo(u)rliness; **voisiner** [~zi'ne]
(1a) *v/i.* be adjacent, be side by side;
be neighbo(u)rly, be on friendly
terms (with, *avec*).

voiturage † [vwaty'ra:ʒ] *m* carriage,
conveyance; cost of conveyance;
voiture [~'ty:r] *f* carriage, conveyance, vehicle; *mot.* car, *Am. a.* automobile; † van; † cart; 🚉 coach,
Am. car; † goods *pl.*, *Am.* freight; 🚉
~ *à marchandises* goods truck, *Am.*
freight car; ~ *carénée* streamlined car
or *Am.* automobile; ~ *de livraison*
delivery van; ~ *d'enfant* perambulator, F pram, *Am.* baby carriage; ~ *de
place* taxi; ~ *de remise* hired carriage;
~ *des quatre saisons* costermonger's
barrow; 🚉 ~ *directe* through carriage; F ~*-pie* radio patrol car; ~
publique public conveyance; 🚉
~*-restaurant* dining car, diner; *en* ~*!*
all aboard!; take your seats!; **voitu-
rée** [~ty're] *f people*: carriageful;
goods: cart-load, van-load; **voiturer**
[~ty're] (1a) *v/t.* convey, carry
(*goods*); *fig.* drive; **voiturette** [~ty-
'rɛt] *f mot.* baby car; light car; trap;

voiturier, -ère [ₙty'rje, ₙ'rjɛːr] **1.** *adj.* carriageable; carrying; carriage (*-drive*); **2.** *su./m* ✝ carrier.

voix [vwa] *f* voice (*a. gramm., a. ♪*); ♪ part; speech; tone; *fig.* opinion; *parl., pol.* vote; *à haute* ∼ aloud; ∼ *basse* softly, in a low voice; *pol. aller aux* ∼ vote; *de vive* ∼ by word of mouth; *fig. demeurer sans* ∼ remain speechless; *donner de la* ∼ give tongue, bark (*hounds*); *mettre qch. aux* ∼ put s.th. to the vote.

vol¹ [vɔl] *m* theft, larceny, robbery; ∼ *à l'américaine* confidence trick; ∼ *à l'étalage* shop-lifting; ∼ *avec effraction* housebreaking and larceny.

vol² [vɔl] *m orn.,* ✇ flying; flight (*a. distance, a. fig., a. birds*); locusts: swarm; ∼ *à voile* gliding; ∼ *d'acrobatie* stunt flying; ∼ *de nuit* nightflight; ∼ *habité* manned spaceflight; ∼ *plané* ✇ glide; *orn.* soaring flight; *à* ∼ *d'oiseau* as the crow flies; bird's-eye (*view*); *au* ∼ on the wing; *prendre son* ∼ ✇ take off; *orn.* take wing, fly off; **volage** [vɔ'laːʒ] fickle, inconstant.

volaille [vɔ'laːj] *f* poultry; *cuis.* fowl; **volailler** [ₙla'je] *m* poulterer; poultry-yard.

volant, e [vɔ'lɑ̃, ₙ'lɑ̃ːt] **1.** *adj.* flying; *fig.* loose, floating (*dress*); portable; ✔ wander(*-plug*); **2.** *su./m* game: shuttlecock; ⊕ fly-wheel; ⊕ *lathe etc.:* hand-wheel; *mot.* steering-wheel, F wheel; *cost.* flounce; ✝ ∼ *de sécurité* reserve fund; *mot. prendre le* ∼ drive, take the wheel.

volatil, e [vɔla'til] volatile.

volatile [∼] *m, a. f* fowl; ✝, *co.* bird, winged creature.

volatiliser [vɔlatili'ze] (1a) *v/t. a. se* ∼ volatilize.

vol-au-vent *cuis.* [vɔlo'vɑ̃] *m/inv.* vol-au-vent (*small filled puff-pie*).

volcan [vɔl'kɑ̃] *m* volcano; **volcanique** [ₙka'nik] volcanic; *fig.* fiery; **volcanisme** *geol.* [ₙka'nism] *m* volcanism; (*a slam or vole.*)

vole [vɔl] *f: faire la* ∼ cards: make

volée [vɔ'le] *f* bird, bullet, stairs: flight; *birds:* flight, flock; ✗ volley, ⚓ broadside; *bells:* peal; *blows etc.:* shower; thrashing, hiding; ∼ *basse tennis:* low volley; ∼ *haute tennis:* smash; *à la* ∼ in the air; *catch etc.* in mid air; *fig.* at random; *a. à toute* ∼ with full force; *entre bond et* ∼ *tennis:*

on the half-volley; *fig.* at a lucky moment; ✝ *fig. la haute* ∼ the upper ten *pl.*; *fig. de haute* ∼ top-flight, top-notch (*people*).

voler¹ [vɔ'le] (1a) *vt/i.* steal; *v/t.* rob (*s.o.*); swindle, cheat (*s.o.*).

voler² [∼] (1a) *v/i.* ✇*, orn.* fly (*a. fig.*); *fig.* rush; ∼ *à voile* glide; *v/t. hunt.* fly (*a hawk*); fly at (*the quarry*).

volerie¹ ✝ [vɔl'ri] *f* robbery; larceny.

volerie² *hunt.* [∼] *f* hawking.

volet [vɔ'lɛ] *m window, a. phot., mot., etc.:* shutter; *mot.* flap; *mot.* butterfly-valve; ✔ *etc.* indicator: disk; sorting-board; *fig. trier sur le* ∼ select (*persons*) carefully; screen (*candidates*).

voleter [vɔl'te] (1c) *v/i. orn.* flit (*a. fig. person*); flutter.

voleur, -euse [vɔ'lœːr, ₙ'løːz] **1.** *adj.* thieving; pilfering; *fig.* rapacious; **2.** *su.* thief; (*sheep- etc.*)stealer; *fig.* robber; *su./m: au* ∼*!* stop thief!

volière [vɔ'ljɛːr] *f* aviary; large bird-cage; pigeon-run.

volige ⌂ [vɔ'liːʒ] *f* batten; lath; roofing-strip; **voliger** ⌂ [ₙli'ʒe] (1l) *v/t.* batten; lath.

volitif, -ve [vɔli'tif, ₙ'tiːv] volitional; **volition** [∼'sjɔ̃] *f* volition.

volontaire [vɔlɔ̃'tɛːr] **1.** *adj.* voluntary; spontaneous; *fig.* self-willed, obstinate; **2.** *su./m* ✗ volunteer; **volonté** [∼'te] *f* will; will-power; *fig.* pleasure, desire; ∼*s pl.* ✝ (*last*) will *sg.* and testament *sg.*; *fig.* whims; *à* ∼ at pleasure, at will; *en faire à sa* ∼ have one's own way; *montrer de la bonne* (*mauvaise*) ∼ show (un)willingness; **volontiers** [∼'tje] *adv.* willingly, with pleasure; *fig.* readily, easily.

volt ✔ [vɔlt] *m* volt; **voltage** ✔ [vɔl'taːʒ] *m* voltage; **voltaïque** ✔ [∼ta'ik] voltaic.

voltaire [vɔl'tɛːr] *m* Voltaire chair (*= high-backed armchair*).

volte [vɔlt] *f* horsemanship, *a.* fencing: volt; *sp.* vaulting; ∼**-face** [∼'fas] *f/inv.* volte-face; about-face; right-about turn.

voltige [vɔl'tiːʒ] *f* horsemanship: trick-riding; *sp.* exercises *pl.* on the flying trapeze; leaping-rope; **voltiger** [ₙti'ʒe] (1l) *v/i. orn.* flit (*a. fig.*); fly about; flutter; *sp.* perform on the flying trapeze; *horsemanship:* do trick-riding; **voltigeur** [ₙti-

'ʒœːr] *m sp.* performer on the flying trapeze (*etc.*); ✕ light infantryman.
volubile [vɔly'bil] ♀ voluble (*a. person*), turning; *fig.* glib; fluent; **volubilis** ♀ [ˌbi'lis] *m* morning glory; **volubilité** [ˌbili'te] *f* volubility; *fig.* glibness.
volume [vɔ'lym] *m* volume; tome; Å, *phys., etc.* volume, mass; ✝, ⚓ bulk; **volumineux, -euse** [ˌlymi-'nø, ˌnøːz] voluminous (*a. fig.*); bulky, large.
volupté [vɔlyp'te] *f* (sensual) pleasure; **voluptueux, -euse** [ˌtɥø, ˌtɥøːz] **1.** *adj.* voluptuous; **2.** *su.* sensualist.
volute [vɔ'lyt] *f shell, a.* Δ: volute; Δ, *a.* ♪ *violin:* scroll; *fig. smoke etc.*: curl.
vomique ♀, ✸ [vɔ'mik] *adj.*: noix *f* ∼ nux vomica; **vomir** [ˌ'miːr] (2a) *v/t.* ✸ vomit; *fig.* belch forth; *v/i.* be sick, ✸ vomit; **vomissement** ✸ [ˌmis'mɑ̃] *m action*: vomiting; vomit; **vomitif, -ve** ✸ [ˌmi'tif, ˌ'tiːv] *adj., a. su./m* emetic.
vont [vɔ̃] *3rd. p. pl. pres. of aller* 1.
vorace [vɔ'ras] voracious; **voracité** [ˌrasi'te] *f* voracity; *avec* ∼ voraciously. [(-ring).]
vortex [vɔr'tɛks] *m* whorl; vortex∫
vos [vo] *pl. of votre.*
vosgien, -enne [vo'ʒjɛ̃, ˌ'ʒjɛn] of the Vosges.
votant, e [vɔ'tɑ̃, ˌ'tɑ̃:t] **1.** *adj.* voting; **2.** *su.* voter; *su./m:* liste *f des* ∼s electoral roll; **votation** [ˌta'sjɔ̃] *f* voting; **vote** [vɔt] *m* vote; voting; poll, ballot; *parl. bill:* division; passing (of a bill, *d'une loi*); result (of the voting *or* ballot); **voter** [vɔ-'te] (1a) *v/i.* vote; *v/t.* vote (*money*); pass (*a bill*); ∼ *des remerciements à* pass a vote of thanks to.
votif, -ve *eccl. etc.* [vɔ'tif, ˌ'tiːv] votive.
votre, *pl.* **vos** [vɔtr, vo] *adj./poss.* your.
vôtre [voːtr] **1.** *pron./poss.*: le (*la*) ∼, les ∼s *pl.* yours; F *à la* ∼ cheerio!; your health!; *je suis des* ∼s I am on your side; **2.** *su./m* yours, your own; *les* ∼s *pl.* your (own) people.
voudrai [vu'dre] *1st p. sg. fut. of vouloir* 1.
vouer [vwe] (1p) *v/t.* dedicate; vow; pledge; *fig.* devote (*one's life, one's time*).

vouloir [vu'lwaːr] **1.** (3n) *v/t.* want; need; require; claim; ∼ *bien* be willing; ∼ *dire* mean (to say); *se* ∼ ... want *or* claim to be ...; be meant to be ...; *je voudrais* ... I would like ...; *Dieu veuille que* God grant that; *je le veux bien* I am quite willing; *je veux que cela soit* I insist that it shall be so; *je veux que ce soit fait* I want this to be done; *le moteur ne voulut pas marcher* the engine refused to work; *sans le* ∼ unintentionally; *veuillez me dire* please tell me; *v/i.*: *en* ∼ *à* bear (*s.o.*) a grudge; have designs on (*s.th.*); **2.** *su./m* will; *bon (mauvais)* ∼ good (ill) will; *de son bon* ∼ of one's own accord; **voulu, e** [ˌ'ly] *p.p. of vouloir* 1; **voulus** [ˌ'ly] *1st p. sg. p.s. of vouloir* 1.
vous [vu] **1.** *pron./pers. subject*: you; *object*: you; (to) you; *à* ∼ to you; yours; **2.** *pron./rfl.* yourself, yourselves; **3.** *pron./recip.* each other, one another; ∼**-même** [ˌ'mɛːm] *pron./rfl.* yourself; ∼s *pl.* yourselves.
vousseau Δ [vu'so] *m,* **voussoir** Δ [ˌ'swaːr] *m* arch-stone, voussoir; **voussure** Δ [ˌ'syːr] *f arch*: curve; *ceiling etc.*: arching; **voûte** [vut] *f* Δ arch, vault (*a. fig.*); archway; *anat.* mouth: roof, *skull*: dome; *fig.* ∼ *céleste* canopy of heaven; *en berceau* barrel vault(ing); ∼ *en ogive* ogive vault; **voûté, e** [vu'te] Δ vaulted, arched; *anat.* round (*shoulders*); round-shouldered, bent (*person*); **voûter** [ˌ] (1a) *v/t. fig.* bend; *v/t. a. se* ∼ vault; arch.
vouvoyer [vuvwa'je] (1h) *v/t.* address (*s.o.*) as *vous*.
voyage [vwa'jaːʒ] *m* journey; tour, trip; run (*in a car*); ⚓ voyage; ✈ flight; ∼ *à pied* walk; ∼ *circulaire* circular trip; ∼ *d'affaires* business trip; ∼ *d'agrément* pleasure trip; ∼ *de retour* return journey; ∼ *surprise* mystery tour; ∼ *touristique* conducted tour; ... *de* ∼ travelling-...; *il est en* ∼ he is travelling; *partir en* ∼ go on a journey, F go away; **voyager** [ˌja'ʒe] (1l) *v/i.* travel (*a.* ✝); (make a) journey; *fig.* get about; *orn.* migrate; *il a beaucoup voyagé* he has travelled widely; **voyageur, -euse** [ˌja'ʒœːr, ˌ'ʒøːz] **1.** *su.* traveller; ⚓, 🚌, *etc.* passenger; fare (*in a taxi*); ✝ (*a. commis*

m ~) commercial traveller; **2.** *adj.*
travelling; migratory (*bird*); *pigeon
m* ~ homing pigeon, carrier-pigeon.
voyant, e [vwaˈjɑ̃, ~ˈjɑ̃:t] **1.** *adj.*
who can see (*person*); *fig.* loud,
gaudy (*colour etc.*); conspicuous
(*building, landmark, etc.*); **2.** *su.*
sighted person, person who can see;
clairvoyant; † seer; *su./m* mark; ⊕
sighting-slit; *surv.* sighting-board.
voyelle *gramm.* [vwaˈjɛl] *f* vowel.
voyons [vwaˈjɔ̃] *1st p. pl. pres. of* voir.
voyou [vwaˈju] *m* street-arab; hoo-
ligan, loafer, *Am.* hoodlum.
vrac [vrak] *m:* † en ~ in bulk; loose;
fig. higgledy-piggledy, in a jumble.
vrai, vraie [vrɛ] **1.** *adj.* true; truthful; sta(u)nch, loyal (*friend*); *fig.* real,
genuine; *fig. usu. pej.* downright,
regular; F (*pour*) de ~ really; in
earnest; **2.** *vrai adv.* truly; really;
à ~ dire as a matter of fact; strictly
speaking; dire ~ tell the truth; ~
de ~! F honestly!; *sl.* cross my
heart!; **3.** *su./m* truth; *au* ~ really;
être dans le ~ be right; **vraiment**
[~ˈmɑ̃] *adv.* really, truly; indeed;
vraisemblable [~sɑ̃ˈblabl] **1.** *adj.*
likely, probable; **2.** *su./m* probability; what is probable; **vraisemblance** [~sɑ̃ˈblɑ̃:s] *f* probability,
likelihood; *story etc.*: verisimilitude;
selon toute ~ in all probability.
vrille [vriːj] *f* ⊕ gimlet, borer; ⚘
tendril; ✵ spin; ✵ tomber en ~
go into a spin; **vrillé, e** [vriˈje]
1. *adj.* ⊕ bored; ⚘ tendrilled, with
tendrils; *tex.* twisted, kinked;
curled; **2.** *su./f* ⚘ bindweed; **vriller** [~ˈje] (1a) *v/t.* ⊕ bore; *v/i. tex.*
twist, kink; snarl; ascend in a
spiral (*rocket etc.*); **vrillette** *zo.*
[~ˈjɛt] *f* death-watch beetle.
vrombir [vrɔ̃ˈbiːr] (2a) *v/i.* buzz
(*insect, engine*); ⊕, ✵ hum (*a. top*);
throb; **vrombissement** [~bisˈmɑ̃]
m insect, engine: buzz(ing); ⊕, ✵,
top: hum(ming); ⊕ throb(bing);
mot. purr(ing).
vu, vue [vy] **1.** *p.p. of* voir; **2.** *vu*

prp. considering, seeing (that, *que*);
~ que *a.* since; ⅔ whereas; **3.** *su./m*
sight; *au* ~ de tous openly; *au* ~ et
au su de tous to everybody's knowledge.
vue [~] *f* sight; eyesight; appearance, look; view; purpose, intention;
idea, notion; *cin.* (lantern)slide; *à* ~
♩, ✝ at sight; free-hand (*drawing*); *à*
~ de within sight of; *à* ~ d'œil visibly;
fig. roughly, at a rough estimate; *à la*
~ de in the *or* at the sight of; *à*
première ~ at first sight; ✝ *à* trois jours
de ~ three days after sight; *fig.* avoir
des ~s sur have one's eye(s) on; *avoir*
en ~ have in mind; have it in mind (*to
do*); avoir la ~ courte be shortsighted;
avoir ~ sur look out on, face; *connaître*
q. de ~ know s.o. by sight; en ~ in
sight; *fig.* conspicuous; *fig.* prominent (*person*); en ~ de with a view to;
for the purpose of; in order to; *garder*
q. *à* ~ keep a close watch on s.o.;
perdre de ~ lose sight of; *point m* de ~
point of view; *prise f* de ~s photography; *cin.* film-shooting.
Vulcain [vylˈkɛ̃] *m astr., myth.* Vul-
can; *zo.* ♀ red admiral; **vulcaniser**
⊕ [~kaniˈze] (1a) *v/t.* vulcanize,
cure.
vulgaire [vylˈgɛːr] **1.** *adj.* vulgar (*a.
pej.*); common; general; *pej.* low,
coarse; *langue f* ~ vernacular;
2. *su./m* common people *pl.*; *fig.
pej.* vulgarity; **vulgariser** [vylga-
riˈze] (1a) *v/t.* popularize; *pej.*
coarsen; se ~ become common;
grow vulgar; **vulgarité** [~ˈte] *f*
vulgarity.
vulnérabilité [vylnerabiliˈte] *f* vul-
nerability; **vulnérable** [~ˈrabl]
vulnerable; **vulnéraire** [~ˈrɛːr]
1. *adj.* ✿ vulnery, healing; **2.** *su./f*
⚘ kidney-vetch; **vulnérant, e**
[~ˈrɑ̃, ~ˈrɑ̃:t] wounding.
vultueux, -euse ✿ [vylˈtɥø, ~ˈtɥøːz]
bloated, red and puffy (*face*); **vul-
tuosité** ✿ [~tɥoziˈte] *f* face: puffi-
ness.
vulve *anat.* [vylv] *f* vulva.

W

W, w [dublə'və] *m* W, w.

wagon 🚃 [va'gɔ̃] *m* carriage, coach, *surt. Am.* car; *goods*: waggon, truck; ~ de *marchandises* goods-van, *Am.* freight-car; ~ *frigorifique* refrigerator van *or* car; *monter en* ~ get into *or* board the train; ~-**bar**, *pl.* ~**s-bars** [vagɔ̃'ba:r] *m* refreshment-car; ~-**citerne**, *pl.* ~**s-citernes** [~si'tɛrn] *m* tank-car, tank-waggon; ~-**lit**, *pl.* ~**s-lits** [~'li] *m* sleeping-car, F sleeper, *Am.* pullman.

wagonnet [vagɔ'ne] *m* tip-truck, tip-waggon, *Am.* dump-truck.

wagon...: ~-**poste**, *pl.* ~**s-poste** [vagɔ̃'pɔst] *m* mail-van, *Am.* mail-car; ~-**restaurant**, *pl.* ~**s-restaurants** [~rɛstɔ'rɑ̃] *m* dining-car; restaurant-car; ~-**salon**, *pl.* ~**s-salons** [~sa'lɔ̃] *m* saloon(-car), *Am.* obser-vation-car, parlor-car; ~-**tombereau**, *pl.* ~**s-tombereaux** [~tɔ̃'bro] *m* tipping-car.

wallon, -onne [va'lɔ̃, ~'lɔn] **1.** *adj.* Walloon; **2.** *su./m ling.* Walloon; *su.* ♀ Walloon.

waters F [wa'tɛ:r] *m/pl.* water-closet *sg.*, W.C. *sg.*, toilet *sg.*

watt ⚡ [wat] *m* watt; ~-**heure**, *pl.* ~**s-heures** ⚡ [wa'tœ:r] *m* watt-hour; ~**man**, *pl.* ~**men** [wat'man, ~'mɛn] *m* electric tram *or* train: driver, *Am.* motorman.

week-end [wi'kɛnd] *m* week-end; **weekendard** *m*, **e** *f* F [~kɛn'da:r, ~'dard] week-ender.

western *cin.* [wɛs'tœrn] *m* western (film).

wigwam [wig'wam] *m* wigwam.

wisigoth, e [vizi'go, ~'gɔt] **1.** *adj.* Visigothic; **2.** *su.* ♀ Visigoth.

X

X, x [iks] *m* X, x; *l'X sl.* the *École polytechnique; phys. rayons m/pl.* X X-rays; ☞ *passer aux rayons X* X-ray.

xénophobe [ksenɔ'fɔb] *adj., a. su.* xenophobe; **xénophobie** [ˌfɔ'bi] *f* xenophobia.

xérès [ke'rɛs] *m* sherry.

xylo... [ksilɔ] xylo...; **ˌgraphe** [ˌ'graf] *m* xylographer, wood-engraver; **ˌgraphie** [ˌgra'fi] *f* wood-engraving; wood-cut; **ˌphage** *zo.* [ˌ'faːʒ] **1.** *su./m* xylophagan, xylophage; **2.** *adj.* xylophagous; **ˌphone** ♩ [ˌ'fɔn] *m* xylophone.

Y

Y, y [i'grɛk] *m* Y, y.

y [i] **1.** *adv.* there, here; *fig.* in, at home; *il y a* there is, there are; *il y a deux ans* two years ago; *je l'y ai rencontré* I met him there; *on y va!* come on!; **2.** *pron.* to or by *or* at *or* in it (him, her, them); *ça y est* that's it; *il n'y gagna rien* he gained nothing by it; *il n'y peut rien* there's nothing he can do about it; *il y va de* it is a matter of; *je n'y suis pour rien* I had nothing to do with it; *pendant que j'y pense* by the way; *vous y êtes? do you follow?*; F do you get it?

yacht ⚓ [jak] *m* yacht.

ya(c)k *zo.* [jak] *m* yak.

yaourt *cuis.* [ja'ur(t)] *m* yog(h)urt, yaourt.   [ilex.⎱

yeuse ♣ [jø:z] *f* holm-oak, holly-oak,⎰

yeux [jø] *pl.* of *œil.*   [Yiddish.⎱

yiddish [(j)i'diʃ] *adj.*, *a. su./m*⎰

yodler ♪ [jɔd'le] (1a) *v/i.* yodel.

yoga [jɔ'ga] *m* yoga.

yogourt *cuis.* [jɔ'gurt] *m see* yaourt.

yole ⚓ [jɔl] *f* yawl, gig.

yougoslave [jugɔ'sla:v] *adj.*, *a. su.* ♀ Jugoslav, Yugoslav.

youpin, e F *pej.* [ju'pɛ̃, ~'pin] **1.** *su.* Yid (= *Jew*); **2.** *adj.* Jewish.

youyou ⚓ [ju'ju] *m* dinghy.

ypérite ♠ [ipe'rit] *f* yperite, mustard-gas; **ypréau** ♣ [ipre'o] *m* wych-elm; white poplar.

Z

Z, z [zɛd] *m* Z, z.

zanzibar [zɑ̃zi'baːr] *m* dice-throwing (*for drinks*).

zazou F [za'zu] *m* hepcat.

zèbre [zɛbr] *m* zo. zebra; F chap, *Am.* guy; **zébrer** [ze'bre] (1f) *v/t.* streak; mark (*s.th.*) with stripes; **zébrure** [⌣'bryːr] *f* stripe; zebra markings *pl.*, stripes *pl.*

zébu zo. [ze'by] *m* zebu.

zélateur, -trice [zela'tœːr, ⌣'tris] **1.** *su.* zealot, zealous worker (for, de); **2.** *adj.* zealous; **zèle** [zɛːl] *m* zeal, enthusiasm (for, *pour*); F *faire du* ⌣ make a show of zeal; go beyond one's orders; **zélé, e** [ze'le] **1.** *adj.* zealous; **2.** *su.* zealot; **zélote** *bibl.* [⌣'lɔt] *m* zealot; **zélotisme** [⌣lɔ-'tism] *m* zealotry.

zénith [ze'nit] *m* zenith (*a. fig.*).

zéphire *tex.* [ze'fiːr] *adj.*: *laine f* ⌣ zephyr; **zéphyr** [⌣'fiːr] *m* zephyr; soft breeze; **zéphyrien, -enne** [⌣- fi'rjɛ̃, ⌣'rjɛn] zephyr-like.

zéro [ze'ro] **1.** *su./m* nought, cipher; *scale:* zero; *sp. tennis:* love, *cricket:* duck; F nobody, nonentity; ⚡ off (*on cooker etc.*); *fig. partir de* ⌣ start from scratch; **2.** *adj./inv.: à* ⌣ *heure* at midnight; **zérotage** *phys.* [⌣ro-'taːʒ] *m* determination of the zero point; *thermometer etc.:* calibration.

zeste [zɛst] *m* *lemon etc.:* peel, twist; F *fig. cela ne vaut pas un* ⌣ it's not worth a straw; **zester** [zɛs-'te] (1a) *v/t.* peel (*a lemon etc.*).

zézaiement [zeze'mɑ̃] *m* lisp(ing); **zézayer** [⌣ze'je] (1i) *vt/i.* lisp.

zibeline zo., ⚡ [zi'blin] *f* sable.

zigouiller *sl.* [zigu'je] (1a) *v/t.* knife, kill; ⚔ bayonet; cut to pieces.

zig(ue) *sl.* [zig] *m* chap, *Am.* guy.

zigzag [zig'zag] *m* zigzag (*a.* ⚔, ⚓); ⊕ lazy-tongs *pl.*; ⊕ *disposé en* ⌣ staggered; *en* ⌣ zigzag...; forked (*lightning*); **zigzaguer** [⌣za'ge] (1m) *v/i.* zigzag; flit about (*bat*); *mot.* drive erratically.

zinc [zɛ̃ːg] *m* zinc; ⚓ spelter; F counter, bar; ⚔ *sl.* (heavy) aeroplane.

zinguer [zɛ̃'ge] (1m) *v/t.* metall. coat with zinc; galvanize (*iron*); ⚠ etc. cover (*s.th.*) with zinc; **zingueur** [⌣'gœːr] *m* ⊕ zinc-worker; ⚠ zinc-roofer.

zinzin *sl.* [zɛ̃'zɛ̃] **1.** *su./m* thingummy, thingamajig, contraption; dance hall; **2.** *adj.* cracked, nuts.

zippé, e [zi'pe] with a zip(per).

zizanie [ziza'ni] *f* ⚡ zizania, Indian rice; *fig.* discord; *fig. semer* (*or mettre*) *la* ⌣ stir up ill-feeling.

zodiacal, e, *m/pl.* *aux astr.* [zɔdja-'kal, ⌣'ko] zodiacal; **zodiaque** *astr.* [⌣'djak] *m* zodiac.

zona ⚕ [zɔ'na] *m* shingles *pl.*; **zone** [zoːn] *f* ⚡, ⚔, *geog.* zone; ⚔, *geog.* belt; *admin.* area; F outskirts *pl.* of Paris; *fig.* ⌣ *sombre* grey zone; ⌣ *de silence radio:* skip zone, silent zone.

zoo F [zɔ'ɔ] *m* zoo.

zoo... [zɔɔ] zoo...; **⌣logie** [⌣lɔ'ʒi] *f* zoology; **⌣logique** [⌣lɔ'ʒik] zoological; **⌣phytes** *biol.* [⌣'fit] *m/pl.* zoophytes; phytozoa; **⌣tomie** [⌣tɔ'mi] *f* zootomy, comparative anatomy.

zostère ⚡ [zɔs'tɛːr] *f* sea-wrack, grass-wrack, *Am.* eel-grass.

zouave ⚔ *hist.* [zwaːv] *m* zouave (= French colonial infantryman).

zozoter F [zɔzɔ'te] (1a) *v/i.* lisp.

zut! *sl.* [zyt] *int.* anger, disappointment: hang it!; dash it!; darn it!

Proper names with pronunciation and explanation

Noms propres avec leur prononciation et notes explicatives

A

Abyssinie [abisi'ni] f: l'~ Abyssinia (former name of Ethiopia).

Académie [akade'mi] f: ~ française the French Academy.

Achille [a'ʃil] m Achilles.

Adam [a'dɑ̃] m Adam.

Adélaïde [adela'id] f Adelaide.

Adolphe [a'dɔlf] m Adolf, Adolphus.

Adour [a'duːr] French river.

Adriatique [adria'tik] f: l'~ (or la mer ~) the Adriatic (Sea).

Afghanistan [afganis'tɑ̃] m: l'~ Afghanistan.

Afrique [a'frik] f: l'~ Africa; l'~ du Sud South Africa.

Agathe [a'gat] f Agatha.

Agen [a'ʒɛ̃] capital of the department of Lot-et-Garonne.

Agnès [a'nɛs] f Agnes.

Aimée [ɛ'me] f Amy.

Ain [ɛ̃] French river; department of eastern France.

Aisne [ɛn] French river; department of northern France.

Aix-en-Provence [ɛksɑ̃prɔ'vɑːs] former capital of the province of Provence.

Ajaccio [aʒak'sjo] capital of the department of Corse.

Alain [a'lɛ̃] m Allen.

Alain-Fournier [alɛ̃fur'nje] French writer.

Albanie [alba'ni] f: l'~ Albania.

Albert [al'bɛːr] m Albert.

Albi [al'bi] capital of the department of Tarn.

Albion poet. [al'bjɔ̃] f Albion, Britain.

Alembert, d' [dalɑ̃'bɛːr] French philosopher and mathematician.

Alençon [alɑ̃'sɔ̃] capital of the department of Orne.

Alexandre [alɛk'sɑ̃:dr] m Alexander.

Alger [al'ʒe] Algiers (capital and port of Algeria); Algier (department of Algeria).

Algérie [alʒe'ri] f: l'~ Algeria.

Allemagne [al'maɲ] f: l'~ Germany; l'~ de l'Est East Germany; l'~ de l'Ouest West Germany; l'~ fédérale the Federal Republic of Germany.

Allier [a'lje] French river; department of central France.

Alpes [alp] f/pl. Alps; ~-de-Haute-Provence [alpdəotprɔ'vɑ̃:s] f/pl. department of southeastern France; Hautes-~ [ot'salp] f/pl. department of southeastern France; ~-Maritimes [~mari'tim] f/pl. department of southeastern France.

Alphonse [al'fɔ̃:s] m Alphonso; Alfonso.

Alsace [al'zas] f: l'~ Alsace, Alsatia (old province of France).

Amboise [ɑ̃'bwaːz] French town in the Loire valley with a famous castle.

Amélie [ame'li] f Amelia.

Amérique [ame'rik] f: l'~ America; l'~ centrale Central America; l'~ du Nord North America; l'~ du Sud South America.

Amiens [a'mjɛ̃] capital of the department of Somme; former capital of the province of Picardie.

Ampère [ɑ̃'pɛːr] French physicist.

Anatole [ana'tɔl] m Christian name.

Andorre [ɑ̃'dɔːr] *f* Andorra.

André [ɑ̃'dre] *m* Andrew.

Andrée [ɑ̃'dre] *f Christian name.*

Aneto [ane'to]: *pic m d'∼ highest peak of the Pyrénées.*

Angers [ɑ̃'ʒe] *capital of the department of Maine-et-Loire; former capital of the province of Anjou.*

Angleterre [ɑ̃glə'tɛːr] *f*: *l'∼* England.

Anglo-Normandes [ɑ̃glɔnɔr'mɑ̃:d]: *les îles f/pl. ∼* the Channel Islands.

Angoulême [ɑ̃gu'lɛm] *capital of the department of Charente; former capital of the province of Angoumois.*

Anjou [ɑ̃'ʒu] *m old province of France.*

Anne [ɑːn] *f* Ann(e).

Annecy [an'si] *capital of the department of Haute-Savoie; lac m d'∼ French lake.*

Annette [a'nɛt] *f* Annie, Nancy, Nanny, Nan.

Anouilh [a'nuːj] *French writer.*

Antarctique [ɑ̃tar(k)'tik] *m*: *l'∼* the Antarctic.

Antibes [ɑ̃'tib] *French health resort on the Mediterranean.*

Antoine [ɑ̃'twan] *m* Ant(h)ony.

Anvers [ɑ̃'vɛːr; *Belgian:* ∼'vɛrs] Antwerp.

Apennins [apɛn'nɛ̃] *m/pl.* Apennines.

Aquitaine [aki'tɛn] *f old province of France.*

Arabe [a'rab]: *République f* ♀ *unie* United Arab Republic.

Arabie [ara'bi] *f*: *l'∼* Arabia; *l'∼ Saoudite* Saudi Arabia.

Aragon [ara'gɔ̃] *French poet.*

Archimède [arʃi'mɛd] *m* Archimedes (*Greek scientist*).

Arctique [ark'tik] *m*: *l'∼* the Arctic.

Ardèche [ar'dɛʃ] *French river; department of southern France.*

Ardennes [ar'dɛn] *f/pl. department of northeastern France.*

Argentine [arʒɑ̃'tin] *f*: *l'∼* Argentina, the Argentine.

Ariège [a'rjɛ:ʒ] *French river; department of southern France.*

Aristide [aris'tid] *m* Aristides.

Aristote [aris'tɔt] *m* Aristotle (*Greek philosopher*).

Arnaud [ar'no] *m Christian name.*

Arras [a'rɑːs] *capital of the department of Pas-de-Calais; former capital of the county of Artois.*

Artus [ar'tys] *m*: *le roi ∼* King Arthur.

Artois [ar'twa] *m former French county.*

Asie [a'zi] *f*: *l'∼* Asia; *l'∼ Mineure* Asia Minor.

Athènes [a'tɛn] *f* Athens.

Atlantique [atlɑ̃'tik] *m*: *l'∼* (*or l'océan m ∼*) the Atlantic (Ocean).

Aube [o:b] *French river; department of east-central France.*

Auch [o:ʃ] *capital of the department of Gers; former capital of the duchy of Gascogne.*

Aude [o:d] *French river; department of southern France.*

Auguste [ɔ'gyst] *m* Augustus.

Aurigny [ɔri'ɲi] Alderney (*one of the Channel Islands*).

Aurillac [ɔri'jak] *capital of the department of Cantal.*

Australie [ɔstra'li] *f*: *l'∼* Australia.

Autriche [o'triʃ] *f*: *l'∼* Austria.

Auvergne [ɔ'vɛrɲ] *f old province of France.*

Auxerre [ɔ'sɛːr] *capital of the department of Yonne.*

Aveyron [avɛ'rɔ̃] *French river; department of southern France.*

Avignon [avi'ɲɔ̃] *capital of the department of Vaucluse.*

Azay-le-Rideau [azɛlri'do] *famous French castle.*

B

Bahamas [baa'mas] *f/pl.*: *les (îles f/pl.) ∼* the Bahamas, the Bahama Islands.

Bâle [bal] Basle, Basel.

Balkans [bal'kɑ̃] *m/pl.*: *les ∼* the Balkan Peninsula *sg.*

Baltique [bal'tik]: *la mer ∼* the Baltic Sea.

Balzac [bal'zak] *French writer.*

Barbe [barb] *f* Barbara.

Bar-le-Duc [barlə'dyk] *capital of the department of Meuse.*

Barrès [ba'rɛs] *French writer.*

Barthélemy [bartelə'mi] *m* Bartholomew.

Basque [bask]: *le pays ∼* the Basque Provinces *pl.* (*in Spain*); the Basque Region (*in France*).

Basse-Terre [bas'tɛːr] *capital of the overseas department of Guadeloupe.*

Bastille [bas'tiːj] *f state prison destroyed in 1789.*

Baudelaire [bod'lɛːr] *French poet.*

Baudouin [bo'dwɛ̃] *m* Baldwin.

Bavière [ba'vjɛːr] *f*: *la ∼* Bavaria.

Bayeux [ba'jø] *French town.*

Béarn [be'arn] *m old province of France.*

Beaumarchais [bomar'ʃɛ] *French writer.*

Beauvais [bo'vɛ] *capital of the department of Oise.*

Belfort [bɛl'fɔːr] *capital of the Territoire de* ~; **Territoire** *m* **de** ~ [tɛritwardəbɛl'fɔːr] *department of eastern France.*

Belgique [bɛl'ʒik] *f: la* ~ *Belgium.*

Belgrade [bɛl'grad] *capital of Yugoslavia.*

Benjamin [bɛ̃ʒa'mɛ̃] *m Benjamin.*

Benoît [bə'nwa] *m Benedict.*

Bergson [bɛrk'sɔn] *French philosopher.*

Berlin [bɛr'lɛ̃] *Berlin.*

Berlioz [bɛr'ljoːz] *French composer.*

Bernadotte [bɛrna'dɔt] *French Marshal.*

Bernanos [bɛrna'noːs] *French Catholic writer.*

Bernard [bɛr'naːr] *m Bernard.*

Berne [bɛrn] *Bern(e).*

Berry [bɛ'ri] *m old province of France.*

Berthe [bɛrt] *f Bertha.*

Bertrand [bɛr'trɑ̃] *m Bertram, Bertrand.*

Besançon [bəzɑ̃sɔ̃] *capital of the department of Doubs; former capital of the province of Franche-Comté.*

Beyrouth [be'rut] *Beirut.*

Birmanie [birma'ni] *f: la* ~ *Burma.*

Bizet [bi'zɛ] *French composer.*

Blanc [blɑ̃]: *mont m* ~ *highest peak of the Alpes.*

Blanche [blɑ̃:ʃ] *f Blanche.*

Blois [blwa] *capital of the department of Loir-et-Cher with a famous castle.*

Blum [blum] *French socialist.*

Bohême [bɔ'ɛm] *f: la* ~ *Bohemia.*

Bolivie [bɔli'vi] *f: la* ~ *Bolivia.*

Bonaparte [bɔna'part] *French (Corsican) family; see Napoléon.*

Bonn [bɔn] *capital of the Federal Republic of Germany.*

Bordeaux [bɔr'do] *capital of the department of Gironde.*

Bossuet [bɔ'sɥɛ] *French prelate, orator and writer.*

Bouches-du-Rhône [buʃdy'roːn] *f/pl. department of southeastern France.*

Bouddha [bu'da] *m Buddha.*

Boulogne-sur-Mer [bulɔɲsyr'mɛːr] *French port and town.*

Bourbons *hist.* [bur'bɔ̃] *m/pl. Bourbons (French royal house).*

Bourbonnais [burbɔ'nɛ] *m old province of France.*

Bourg [burk] *capital of the department of Ain.*

Bourges [burʒ] *capital of the department of Cher; former capital of the province of Berry.*

Bourget [bur'ʒɛ]: *lac m du* ~ *French lake;* **Le** ~ [ləbur'ʒɛ] *airport of Paris.*

Bourgogne [bur'gɔɲ] *f: la* ~ *Burgundy (old province of France).*

Braille [bra:j] *Frenchman who invented the alphabet named after him.*

Braque [brak] *French painter.*

Brésil [bre'zil] *m: le* ~ *Brazil.*

Brest [brɛst] *French port and town.*

Bretagne [brə'taɲ] *f: la* ~ *Brittany (old province of France).*

Briand [bri'ɑ̃] *French state man.*

Brigitte [bri'ʒit] *f Bridget.*

Broglie, de [də'brɔːi] *name of two French physicists.*

Bruges [bry:ʒ] *Belgian port and town.*

Bruxelles [bry'sɛl] *Brussels.*

Bucarest [byka'rɛst] *Bucharest.*

Budapest [byda'pɛst] *capital of Hungary.*

Bulgarie [bylga'ri] *f: la* ~ *Bulgaria.*

C

Caen [kɑ̃] *capital of the department of Calvados.*

Cahors [ka'ɔːr] *capital of the department of Lot.*

Caire, Le [lə'kɛːr] *Cairo.*

Calais [ka'lɛ] *French port and town; le Pas de* ~ *the Straits pl. of Dover.*

Californie [kalifɔr'ni] *f: la* ~ *California.*

Calvados [kalva'doːs] *m department of northern France.*

Calvin [kal'vɛ̃] *famous French Protestant reformer.*

Camargue [ka'marg] *f region in the delta of the Rhône.*

Cambodge [kɑ̃'bɔdʒ] *m: le* ~ *Cambodia.*

Cambrai [kɑ̃'brɛ] *French town.*

Cameroun [kam'run] *m: le* ~ *Cameroon.*

Camus [ka'my] *French writer.*

Canada [kana'da] *m: le* ~ *Canada.*

Canaries [kana'ri] *f/pl.: les (îles f/pl.)* ~ *the Canary Islands.*

Cannes [kan] *French health resort on the Mediterranean.*

Cantal [kɑ̃'tal] *m department of central France.*

Cap [kap] *m: le ~ Cape Town.*

Capétiens *hist.* [kape'sjɛ̃] *m/pl.* Capetians (*French royal house*).

Caroline [karɔ'lin] *f Caroline.*

Carolingiens *hist.* [karɔlɛ̃'ʒjɛ̃] *m/pl.* Carolingians (*French royal house*).

Carpates [kar'pat] *f/pl.* Carpathians.

Catherine [ka'trin] *f Catherine, Katharine, Katherine, Kathleen.*

Caucase [ko'kɑːz] *m Caucasus.*

Cayenne [ka'jɛn] *capital of the overseas department of Guyane française.*

Cécile [se'sil] *f Cecilia, Cecily.*

Centre ['sɑtr(ə)] *m: le ~ Central France.*

Cervin [sɛr'vɛ̃] *le mont m ~ the Matterhorn.*

César [se'zaːr] *m: (Jules) ~ Julius Caesar.*

Cévennes [se'vɛn] *f/pl. mountain range of France.*

Cézanne [se'zan] *French painter.*

Chagall [ʃa'gal] *French painter.*

Châlons-sur-Marne [ʃalɔ̃syr'marn] *capital of the department of Marne.*

Chambéry [ʃɑ̃be'ri] *capital of the department of Savoie; former capital of the province of Savoie.*

Chambord [ʃɑ̃'bɔːr] *famous French castle.*

Champagne [ʃɑ̃'paɲ] *f old province of France.*

Champ-de-Mars [ʃɑ̃d'mars] *m area of Paris between the École militaire and the Seine.*

Champs-Elysées [ʃɑ̃zeli'ze] *m/pl. famous Paris avenue.*

Chantilly [ʃɑ̃ti'ji] *French town with famous castle; a. famous race course.*

Charente [ʃa'rɑ̃t] *f French river; department of western France;* **~-Maritime** [ʃarɑ̃tmari'tim] *f department of western France.*

Charles [ʃarl] *m Charles.*

Charlot [ʃar'lo] *m Charlie, Charley;* F *cin.* Charlie Chaplin.

Charlotte [ʃar'lɔt] *f Charlotte.*

Chartres [ʃartr] *capital of the department of Eure-et-Loir.*

Chartreuse [ʃar'trøːz] *f: la Grande-~ famous monastery near Grenoble.*

Chateaubriand [ʃatobri'ɑ̃] *French writer.*

Châteauroux [ʃato'ru] *capital of the department of Indre.*

Chaumont [ʃo'mɔ̃] *capital of the department of Haute-Marne.*

Chenonceaux [ʃənɔ̃'so] *famous French castle.*

Cher [ʃɛːr] *m French river; department of central France.*

Cherbourg [ʃɛr'buːr] *French port and town.*

Chili [ʃi'li] *m: le ~ Chile, Chili.*

Chine [ʃin] *f: la ~ China.*

Chirac [ʃi'rak] *French politician.*

Christine [kris'tin] *f Christina, Christine.*

Christophe [kris'tɔf] *m Christopher.*

Citroën [sitrɔ'ɛn] *French industrialist.*

Claire [klɛːr] *f Clara, Clare.*

Claudel [klo'dɛl] *French Catholic writer.*

Clemenceau [klemɑ̃'so] *French statesman.*

Clermont-Ferrand [klɛrmɔ̃fɛ'rɑ̃] *capital of the department of Puy-de-Dôme; former capital of the province of Auvergne.*

Cocteau [kɔk'to] *French writer.*

Cognac [kɔ'nak] *French town.*

Colbert [kɔl'bɛːr] *French statesman.*

Colette [kɔ'lɛt] *French authoress.*

Collège de France [kɔlɛʒdə'frɑːs] *famous institution of higher education in Paris.*

Colmar [kɔl'maːr] *capital of the department of Haut-Rhin.*

Colombie [kɔlɔ̃'bi] *f: la ~ Colombia.*

Comédie-Française [kɔmedifrɑ̃-'sɛːz] *f National Theatre of France.*

Concorde [kɔ̃'kɔrd] *place f de la ~ one of the most famous squares in Paris.*

Congo [kɔ̃'go] *m African river.*

Constance [kɔ̃s'tɑːs] *m/f Constance;* le lac *m* de ~ the lake of Constance.

Copenhague [kɔpɛ'nag] Copenhagen.

Corée [kɔ're] *f: la ~ Korea.*

Corneille [kɔr'nɛːj] *French classical dramatist.*

Cornouailles [kɔr'nwaːj] *f/pl.: les ~ Cornwall sg.*

Corot [kɔ'ro] *French painter.*

Corrèze [kɔ'rɛːz] *f French river; department of central France.*

Corse [kɔrs] *f: la ~ Corsica (French island; department of France).*

Costa Rica [kɔstari'ka] *m Costa Rica.*

Côte d'Argent [kotdar'ʒɑ̃] *f part of French Atlantic coast.*

Côte d'Azur [kotda'zy:r] *f part of French Mediterranean coast.*

Côte d'Émeraude [kotdem'ro:d] *f part of French Channel coast.*

Côte-d'Ivoire [kotdi'vwa:r] *f: la ~ the Ivory Coast.*

Côte-d'Or [kot'dɔ:r] *f department of east-central France.*

Côtes-du-Nord [kotdy'nɔ:r] *f/pl. department of northwestern France.*

Coulomb, de [dəku'lɔ̃] *French physicist.*

Couperin [ku'prɛ̃] *family of French musicians.*

Courbet [kur'bɛ] *French painter.*

Couve de Murville [kuvdəmyr'vil] *French politician.*

Crète [krɛt] *f: la ~ Crete.*

Creuse [krø:z] *f French river; department of central France.*

Crimée [kri'me] *f: la ~ the Crimea.*

Cuba [ky'ba] *f: Cuba.*

Cupidon [kypi'dɔ̃] *m Cupid (Roman god of Love).*

Curie [ky'ri] *name of two eminent French physicists, discoverers of radium.*

D

Daguerre [da'gɛ:r] *French inventor of the earliest photographic process.*

Dalmatie [dalma'si] *f Dalmatia.*

Danemark [dan'mark] *m: le ~ Denmark.*

Daniel [da'njɛl] *m Daniel.*

Danton [dɑ̃'tɔ̃] *French revolutionary.*

Danube [da'nyb] *m Danube.*

Dardanelles [darda'nɛl] *f/pl.: les ~ the Dardanelles.*

Daudet [do'dɛ] *French writer.*

Daumier [do'mje] *French lithographer.*

Dauphiné [dofi'ne] *m old province of France.*

David [da'vid] *m David (a. French painter).*

Deauville [do'vil] *French health resort on the Channel.*

Debré [də'bre] *French politician.*

Debussy [dəby'si] *French composer.*

Degas [də'ga] *French painter.*

Delacroix [dəla'krwa] *French painter.*

Denis [də'ni] *m Den(n)is.*

Descartes [de'kart] *French philosopher.*

Deux-Sèvres [dø'sɛ:vr] *department of western France.*

Diane [djan] *f Diana.*

Diderot [didə'ro] *French philosopher.*

Dieppe [djɛp] *French port and town.*

Digne [diɲ] *capital of the department of Alpes-de-Haute-Provence.*

Dijon [di'ʒɔ̃] *capital of the department of the Côte-d'Or; former capital of the province of Bourgogne.*

Dinard [di'na:r] *French health resort on the Channel.*

Dominicaine [dɔmini'kɛn]: *la République f ~ the Dominican Republic.*

Dominique [dɔmi'nik] *m Dominic.*

Don Quichotte [dɔ̃ki'ʃɔt] *m Don Quixote.*

Dordogne [dɔr'dɔɲ] *f French river; department of southwestern France.*

Dorothée [dɔrɔ'te] *f Dorothea, Dorothy.*

Doubs [du] *m French river; department of eastern France.*

Douvres [du:vr] *Dover.*

Draguignan [dragi'nɑ̃] *capital of the department of Var.*

Dresde [drɛsd] *Dresden.*

Dreyfus [drɛ'fys] *French army officer convicted of treason and imprisoned, but cleared in 1906.*

Drôme [dro:m] *f French river; department of southeastern France.*

Dublin [du'blɛ̃] *capital of the Republic of Ireland.*

Duhamel [dya'mɛl] *French writer.*

Dumas [dy'ma] *name of two French writers.*

Dunant [dy'nɑ̃] *Swiss merchant, founder of the Red Cross.*

Dunkerque [dœ̃'kɛrk] *Dunkirk (French port and town).*

Durance [dy'rɑ̃:s] *f French river.*

E

Écosse [e'kɔs] *f Scotland.*

Edimbourg [edɛ̃'bu:r] *Edinburgh.*

Edmond [ɛd'mɔ̃] *m Edmund.*

Édouard [e'dwa:r] *m Edward.*

Égée [e'ʒe] *f: la mer ~ the Aegaean Sea.*

Égypte [e'ʒipt] *f: l'~ Egypt.*

Eiffel [ɛ'fɛl] *French engineer.*

Elbe [ɛlb] *f: l'île d'~ Elba (scene of Napoleon's exile).*

Éléonore [eleɔ'nɔ:r] *f Eleanor, Elinor.*

Élisabeth [eliza'bɛt] f Elizabeth.

Élysée [eli'ze] m palace in Paris, official residence of the President of the Republic.

Émile [e'mil] m Christian name.

Émilie [emi'li] f Emily.

Épinal [epi'nal] capital of the department of Vosges.

Équateur [ekwa'tœːr] m: l'~ Ecuador.

Escaut [ɛs'ko] m the Scheldt.

Ésope [e'zɔp] m Aesop (Greek fabulist).

Espagne [ɛs'paɲ] f Spain.

État français [etafrɑ̃'sɛ] m name of the Pétain regime.

États-Unis d'Amérique [etazynidame'rik] m/pl. the United States (of America), the U.S.A.

Éthiopie [etjɔ'pi] f: l'~ Ethiopia.

Étienne [e'tjɛn] m Stephen.

Euclide [ø'klid] Euclid (Greek mathematician).

Eugène [ø'ʒɛn] m Eugene.

Eugénie [øʒe'ni] f Eugenia.

Euphrate [ø'frat] m the Euphrates.

Eure [œːr] French river; department of northern France; ~-et-Loir [œre-'lwaːr] department of northern France.

Europe [ø'rɔp] f: l'~ Europe.

Eustache [øs'taʃ] m Eustace.

Ève [ɛːv] f Eve, Eva.

Évreux [e'vrø] capital of the department of Eure.

Extrême-Orient [ɛkstrɛmɔr'jɑ̃] m: l'~ the Far East.

F

Fauré [fo're] French composer.

Félix [fe'liks] m Felix.

Fénelon [fenə'lɔ̃] French prelate and writer.

Ferdinand [fɛrdi'nɑ̃] m Ferdinand.

Finistère [finis'tɛːr] m department of northwestern France.

Finlande [fɛ̃'lɑ̃ːd] f: la ~ Finland.

Flandre [flɑ̃'dr] f: la ~ (or les ~s) Flanders sg. (old province of France).

Flaubert [flo'bɛːr] French writer.

Flessingue [fle'sɛ̃ːg] Flushing.

Florence [flɔ'rɑ̃s] f Florence.

Foch [fɔʃ] French Marshal.

Foix [fwa] capital of the department of Ariège; former county and its capital; old province of France.

Fontainebleau [fɔ̃tɛn'blo] famous French castle.

Fort-de-France [fɔrdə'frɑ̃s] capital of the overseas department of Martinique.

Fragonard [fragɔ'naːr] French painter.

France¹ [frɑ̃ːs] f: la ~ France.

France² [frɑ̃ːs] French writer.

Franche-Comté [frɑ̃ʃkɔ̃'te] f old province of France.

Franck [frɑ̃ːk] French composer.

François [frɑ̃'swa] m Francis.

Françoise [frɑ̃'swaːz] f Frances.

Frédéric [frede'rik] m Frederick.

G

Gabon [ga'bɔ̃] m: le ~ Gabon.

Gabriel [gabri'ɛl] m Gabriel.

Galles [gal] f: le pays m de ~ Wales.

Gambetta [gɑ̃be'ta] French politician.

Gand [gɑ̃] Ghent.

Gange [gɑ̃ːʒ] m the Ganges.

Gap [gap] capital of the department of Hautes-Alpes.

Gard [gaːr] m French river; department of southern France.

Garonne [ga'rɔn] f French river; Haute-~ [otga'rɔn] f department of southwestern France.

Gascogne [gas'kɔɲ] f: la ~ Gascony; le golfe de ~ the Bay of Biscay.

Gauguin [go'gɛ̃] French painter.

Gaule [go:l] f: la ~ Gaul.

Gaulle, de [də'go:l] French general and president.

Gautier [go'tje] French poet.

Gay-Lussac [gɛly'sak] French scientist.

Gênes [ʒɛn] f Genoa.

Genève [ʒə'nɛːv] f Geneva.

Geneviève [ʒən'vjɛːv] f Genevieve, Winifred.

Geoffroi [ʒɔ'frwa] m Geoffrey, Jeffery, Godfrey.

Georges [ʒɔrʒ] m George.

Gérard [ʒe'raːr] m Gerald.

Germaine [ʒɛr'mɛn] f Christian name.

Gers [ʒɛːr] m French river; department of southwestern France.

Gertrude [ʒɛr'tryd] f Gertrude.

Gévaudan [ʒevo'dɑ̃] m former French county.

Ghana [ga'na] m: le ~ Ghana.

Gide [ʒid] French writer.

Gilbert [ʒil'bɛːr] m Gilbert.

Gilles [ʒil] *m* Giles.

Giraudoux [ʒiro'du] *French writer.*

Gironde [ʒi'rɔ̃:d] *f French river; department of southwestern France.*

Giscard d'Estaing [ʒiskardɛs'tɛ̃] *French president.*

Gobelins, les [legɔ'blɛ̃] *m/pl. famous tapestry factory in Paris.*

Goncourt [gɔ̃'ku:r] *name of two French writers.*

Gounod [gu'no] *French composer.*

Grande-Bretagne [grãdbrə'taɲ] *f: la ~* Great Britain.

Grandlieu [grã'ljø]: *lac m de ~ French lake.*

Grèce [grɛs] *f: la ~* Greece.

Grégoire [gre'gwa:r] *m* Gregory.

Grenoble [grə'nɔbl] *capital of the department of Isère; former capital of the province of Dauphiné.*

Greuze [grø:z] *French painter.*

Grisons [gri'zɔ̃] *m/pl.: les ~* (the Canton of) Grisons.

Groenland [grɔɛn'lã:d] *m: le ~* Greenland.

Groningue [grɔ'nɛ̃:g] Groningen.

Guadeloupe [gwad'lup] *f French overseas department.*

Guatemala [gwatema'la] *m: le ~* Guatemala.

Guebwiller [gɛbvi'lɛ:r]: *ballon m de ~ highest peak of the Vosges.*

Guéret [ge'rɛ] *capital of the department of Creuse; former capital of the province of Marche.*

Guernesey [gɛrnə'zɛ] Guernsey (*one of the Channel Islands*).

Gui [gi] *m* Guy.

Guillaume [gi'jo:m] *m* William, Will.

Guillotin [gijɔ'tɛ̃] *French physician who first proposed the use of the guillotine.*

Guinée [gi'ne] *f: la ~* Guinea.

Guise, de [də'gi:z] *French noble family.*

Guitry [gi'tri] *French actor and playwright.*

Guizot [gi'zo] *French statesman and historian.*

Guy [gi] *m* Guy.

Guyane [gɥi'jan] *f: la ~* Guiana; *~ française* [gɥijanfrã'sɛ:z] *f French overseas department.*

Guyenne [gɥi'jɛn] *f: la ~* Guienne; *~ et Gascogne* [gɥijɛnegas'kɔɲ] *old province of France.*

H

Hainaut [*ɛ'no] *m province of southern Belgium.*

Haïti [ai'ti] *f* Haiti.

Halles [*al] *f/pl: les ~ quarter of Paris, formerly with the principal market.*

Hambourg [ã'bu:r] *f* Hamburg.

Haussmann [os'man] *French administrator.*

Havane [*a'van] *f: la ~* Havana.

Havre, Le [lə'*a:vr] *m French port and town.*

Haye, La [la'*ɛ] the Hague.

Hélène [e'lɛn] *f* Helen.

Helsinki [ɛlsiŋ'ki] *capital of Finland.*

Henri [ã'ri] *m* Henry.

Henriette [ã'rjɛt] *f* Harriet.

Hérault [e'ro] *m French river; department of southern France.*

Hercule [ɛr'kyl] *m* Hercules.

Hilaire [i'lɛ:r] *m* Hilary.

Hildegarde [ildə'gard] *f* Hildegard.

Hippolyte [ipɔ'lit] *m Christian name.*

Hoche [*ɔʃ] *French revolutionary general.*

Hollande [*ɔ'lã:d] *f: la ~* Holland.

Homère [ɔ'mɛ:r] *m* Homer (*Greek poet*).

Honduras [*ɔndy'ra:s] *m: le ~* Honduras.

Hongrie [*ɔ̃'gri] *f: la ~* Hungary.

Hortense [ɔr'tã:s] *f* Hortense.

Hôtel-Dieu [otɛl'djø] *m name of the oldest hospital in Paris.*

Hugo [*y'go] *French writer.*

Hugues [yg] *m* Hugh.

I

Ibert [i'bɛ:r] *French composer.*

If [if] *m small island near Marseilles, former state prison.*

Île-de-France [ildə'frã:s] *f old province of France.*

Ille-et-Vilaine [ilevi'lɛn] *department of northwestern France.*

Inde [ɛ̃:d] *f: l'~* India.

Indien [ɛ̃'djɛ̃]: *océan m ~* Indian Ocean.

Indochine [ɛ̃dɔ'ʃin] *f: l'~* Indo-China.

Indonésie [ɛ̃dɔne'zi] *f: l'~* Indonesia.

Indre [ɛ̃:dr] *French river; department*

* Before the so-called aspirate h, marked *, there is neither elision nor liaison.

of central France; ~-**et-Loire** [ɛ̃dre-
ˈlwaːr] *department of central France*.
Indus [ɛ̃ˈdys] *m the Indus*.
Ingres [ɛ̃ːgr] *French painter*.
Invalides, Les [lezɛ̃vaˈlid] *m/pl.
army pensioners' hospital in Paris; its
church contains the tomb of Napoleon*.
Iphigénie [ifiʒeˈni] *f Iphigenia*.
Irak, Iraq [iˈrak] *m: l'~ Irak, Iraq*.
Iran [iˈrɑ̃] *m: l'~ Iran*.
Irène [iˈrɛn] *f Irene*.
Irlande [irˈlɑ̃ːd] *f: l'~ Ireland; l'~ du
Nord Northern Ireland*.
Isabelle [izaˈbɛl] *f Isabel*.
Isère [iˈzɛːr] *French river; department
of southeastern France*.
Islande [isˈlɑ̃ːd] *f: l'~ Iceland*.
Israël [israˈɛl] *m Israel*.
Italie [itaˈli] *f: l'~ Italy*.

J

Jacquard [ʒaˈkaːr] *inventor of the
loom named after him*.
Jacqueline [ʒɑˈklin] *f Jacqueline*.
Jacques [ʒɑːk] *m James*.
Jamaïque [ʒamaˈik] *f: la ~ Jamaica*.
Japon [ʒaˈpɔ̃] *m: le ~ Japan*.
Jaurès [ʒɔˈrɛs] *French politician and
orator*.
Jean [ʒɑ̃] *m John;* ~-**Jacques** [~ˈʒɑːk]
m Christian name; ~-**Paul** [~ˈpɔl] *m
Christian name;* ~ **sans Terre** [~sɑ̃-
ˈtɛːr] *m John Lackland (English king)*.
Jeanne [ʒɑːn] *f Jean, Joan;* ~ **d'Arc**
[ʒanˈdark] *f Joan of Arc*.
Jeanneton [ʒanˈtɔ̃] *f Jenny*.
Jeannette [ʒaˈnɛt] *f Jenny, Janet*.
Jeannot [ʒaˈno] *m Jack, Johnny*.
Jérôme [ʒeˈroːm] *m Jerome*.
Jersey [ʒɛrˈzɛ] *one of the Channel
Islands*.
Jérusalem [ʒeryzaˈlɛm] *Jerusalem*.
Jésus [ʒeˈzy], **Jésus-Christ** [ʒezy-
ˈkri] *m Jesus (Christ)*.
Joliot-Curie [ʒɔljokyˈri] *name of two
French physicists*.
Jordanie [ʒɔrdaˈni] *f: la ~ Jordan*.
Joseph [ʒɔˈzɛf] *m Joseph*.
Joséphine [ʒozeˈfin] *f Josephine (first
wife of Napoleon I)*.
Jourdain [ʒurˈdɛ̃] *m: le ~ the Jordan*.
Juin [ʒɥɛ̃] *French Marshal*.
Jules [ʒyl] *m Julius*.
Julie [ʒyˈli] *f Julia, Juliet, Gill, Jill*.
Julien [ʒyˈljɛ̃] *m Julian*.
Julienne [ʒyˈljɛn] *f Juliana; Gillian*.

Juliette [ʒyˈljɛt] *f Juliet*.
Jura [ʒyˈra] *m mountain department of
eastern France*.

K

Karpates [karˈpat] *f/pl. Carpathians*.
Kenya [keˈnja] *m: le ~ Kenya*.
Kléber [kleˈbeːr] *French general*.
Koweït [kɔˈwɛjt] *Kuweit*.
Kremlin [krɛmˈlɛ̃] *m the Kremlin*.

L

La Boétie [labɔeˈsi] *French writer*.
La Bruyère [labryˈjɛːr] *French mor-
alist*.
La Chaise [laˈʃɛːz] *French Jesuit*.
Laclos [laˈklo] *French writer*.
La Fayette, de [dəlafaˈjɛt] *French
general and statesman; French woman
writer*.
Laffitte [laˈfit] *French financier*.
La Fontaine [lafɔ̃ˈtɛn] *French fabu-
list*.
Lamarck [laˈmark] *French naturalist*.
Lamartine [lamarˈtin] *French poet*.
Lamennais [lamˈnɛ] *French philoso-
pher*.
La Motte-Picquet [lamɔtpiˈkɛ]
French naval commander.
Landes [lɑ̃ːd] *f/pl. department of
southwestern France*.
Languedoc [lɑ̃gˈdɔk] *m old province
of France*.
Laon [lɑ̃] *capital of the department of
Aisne*.
Laos [laˈoːs] *m: le ~ Laos*.
Laplace [laˈplas] *French physicist*.
Laponie [lapɔˈni] *f: la ~ Lapland*.
La Rochefoucauld [larɔʃfuˈko]
French moralist.
Larousse [laˈrus] *French lexicogra-
pher*.
Laure [lɔːr] *f Laura*.
Laurent [lɔˈrɑ̃] *m Laurence*.
Lausanne [loˈzan] *Swiss town*.
Laval [laˈval] *capital of the department
of Mayenne; French politician*.
Lavoisier [lavwaˈzje] *French chemist*.
Law [lo; *Fr.* laːs] *Scottish financier,
controller-general of the French fi-
nances*.
Lazare [laˈzaːr] *m Lazarus*.
Leconte de Lisle [ləkɔ̃tdəˈlil] *French
poet*.
Le Corbusier [ləkɔrbyˈzje] *French
architect*.

Léman [le'mɑ̃] *m*: *le lac m* ⌣ the lake of Geneva, Lake Leman.
Leningrad [lenin'grad] *town of the U.S.S.R.*
Léon [le'ɔ̃] *m* Leo.
Léonard [leɔ'na:r] *m* Leonard.
Léopold [leɔ'pɔl] *m* Leopold.
Lesage [lə'sa:ʒ] *French writer.*
Lesseps [le'sɛps] *French diplomat who conceived the idea of the Suez Canal.*
Leyde [lɛd] Leyden.
Liban [li'bɑ̃] *m*: *le* ⌣ Lebanon.
Libéria [liber'ja] *m*: *le* ⌣ Liberia.
Libye [li'bi] *f*: *la* ⌣ Libya.
Liège [ljɛ:ʒ] *Belgian town.*
Lille [lil] *capital of the department of Nord.*
Limoges [li'mɔ:ʒ] *capital of the department of Haute-Vienne; former capital of the province of Limousin; renowned for its porcelain.*
Limousin [limu'zɛ̃] *m old province of France.*
Lisbonne [liz'bɔn] *f* Lisbon.
Lise [li:z], **Lisette** [li'zɛt] *f* Betty; Lizzie.
Lisieux [li'zjø] *French town, place of pilgrimage.*
Littré [li'tre] *French lexicographer.*
Livourne [li'vurn] Leghorn.
Loire [lwa:r] *f French river; department of central France;* **Haute-**⌣ [ot'lwa:r] *f department of central France;* ⌣**-Atlantique** [lwaratlɑ̃'tik] *f department of northwestern France.*
Loiret [lwa'rɛ] *m French river; department of central France.*
Loir-et-Cher [lware'ʃɛ:r] *department of central France.*
Londres [lɔ̃:dr] London.
Lons-le-Saunier [lɔ̃lso'nje] *capital of the department of Jura.*
Lorrain [lɔ'rɛ̃] *French painter.*
Lorraine [lɔ'rɛn] *f old province of France.*
Lot [lɔt] *m French river; department of southern France;* ⌣**-et-Garonne** [⌣ega-'rɔn] *department of southwestern France.*
Loti [lɔ'ti] *French writer.*
Louis [lwi] *m* Lewis.
Louise [lwi:z] *f* Louisa, Louise.
Lourdes [lurd] *French town, place of pilgrimage.*
Louvre [lu:vr] *m former royal palace in Paris, now famous museum.*
Lozère [lɔ'zɛ:r] *f department of southeastern France.*

Luc [lyk] *m* Luke.
Lucette [ly'sɛt] *f diminutive of Lucie.*
Lucie [ly'si] *f* Lucy; Lucia.
Lucien [ly'sjɛ̃] *m* Lucian.
Lucienne [ly'sjɛn] *f Christian name.*
Lully [lyl'li] *French composer.*
Lumière [ly'mjɛ:r] *name of two French chemists, inventors of the cinematograph.*
Luxembourg [lyksɑ̃'bu:r] *m* Luxemb(o)urg; *palace and gardens in Paris.*
Lydie [li'di] *f* Lydia.
Lyon [ljɔ̃] Lyons (*capital of the department of Rhône; former capital of the province of Lyonnais*).
Lyonnais [ljɔ'nɛ] *m old province of France.*

M

Mac-Mahon [makma'ɔ̃] *French Marshal.*
Mâcon [mɑ'kɔ̃] *capital of the department of Saône-et-Loire.*
Madagascar [madagas'ka:r] *f* Madagascar.
Madeleine [mad'lɛn] *f* Madeleine; *bibl.* Magdalen.
Madelon [mad'lɔ̃] *f diminutive of Madeleine.*
Madère [ma'dɛ:r] *f* Madeira.
Madrid [ma'drid] *capital of Spain.*
Maeterlinck [metɛr'lɛ̃:k] *Belgian writer.*
Maginot [maʒi'no] *French politician.*
Mahomet [mao'mɛ] *m* Mahomet.
Maillol [ma'jɔl] *French sculptor.*
Maine [mɛn] *f French river; m old province of France;* ⌣**-et-Loire** [⌣e-'lwa:r] *department of western France.*
Mainfroi [mɛ̃'frwa] *m* Manfred.
Maintenon, de [dəmɛt'nɔ̃] *French marquise, secret wife of Louis XIV.*
Majorque [ma'ʒɔrk] *f* Majorca.
Malaisie [male'zi] *f*: *la* ⌣ Malaysia.
Malaysia [male'zja] *f*: *la* ⌣ Malaysia.
Malebranche [mal'brɑ̃:ʃ] *French metaphysician.*
Malherbe [ma'lɛrb] *French poet.*
Mallarmé [malar'me] *French poet.*
Malmaison [malmɛ'zɔ̃] *residence of Joséphine after her divorce from Napoleon I.*
Malraux [mal'ro] *French writer.*
Malte [malt] *f* Malta.
Manche [mɑ̃:ʃ] *f*: *la* ⌣ the English

Channel; *department of northwestern France.*

Manet [ma'nɛ] *French painter.*

Manon [ma'nɔ̃] *f* Moll.

Mans, Le [lə'mɑ̃] *capital of the department of Sarthe; former capital of the province of Maine.*

Marat [ma'ra] *French revolutionary.*

Marc [mark] *m* Mark.

Marcel [mar'sɛl] *m Christian name.*

Marche [marʃ] *f old province of France.*

Margot [mar'go] *f* Maggie, Margot, Peg(gy).

Marguerite [margə'rit] *f* Margaret.

Marie [ma'ri] *f* Mary.

Maritain [mari'tɛ̃] *French philosopher.*

Marivaux [mari'vo] *French playwright.*

Marne [marn] *f French river; department of northeastern France;* **Haute-~** [ot'marn] *f department of northeastern France.*

Maroc [ma'rɔk] *m: le ~* Morocco.

Marseille [mar'sɛ:j] Marseilles *(capital of the department of Bouches-du-Rhône).*

Marthe [mart] *f* Martha.

Martin du Gard [martɛ̃dy'ga:r] *French writer.*

Martinique [marti'nik] *f French overseas department.*

Massif central [masifsɑ̃'tral] *m upland area of France.*

Mathilde [ma'tild] *f* Mathilda, Maud.

Matignon [mati'nɔ̃]: *l'hôtel m ~ residence of the French Prime Minister.*

Matisse [ma'tis] *French painter.*

Mat(t)hieu [ma'tjø] *m* Mat(t)hew.

Maupassant [mopa'sɑ̃] *French writer.*

Mauriac [mɔ'rjak] *French writer.*

Maurice [mɔ'ris]: *l'île f ~* Mauritius.

Mauritanie [mɔrita'ni] *f: la ~* Mauritania.

Maurois [mɔ'rwa] *French writer.*

Maurras [mɔ'ras] *French writer.*

Maxime [mak'sim] *m Christian name.*

Maximilien [maksimi'ljɛ̃] *m* Maximilian.

Mayenne [ma'jɛn] *f French river; department of northwestern France.*

Mecque [mɛk] *f: la ~* Mecca.

Médicis [medi'sis] Medici *(Florentine noble family).*

Méditerranée [mediɛra'ne] *f: la ~* the Mediterranean.

Melun [mə'lœ̃] *capital of the department of Seine-et-Marne.*

Mende [mɑ̃:d] *capital of the department of Lozère.*

Menton [mɑ̃'tɔ̃] *French tourist centre on the Mediterranean.*

Mérimée [meri'me] *French writer.*

Mérovingiens *hist.* [merɔvɛ̃'ʒjɛ̃] *m/pl.* Merovingians *(French royal family).*

Metz [mɛs] *capital of the department of Moselle.*

Meurthe [mœrt] *f French river; former department of northeastern France;* **~-et-Moselle** [~emɔ'zɛl] *department of northeastern France.*

Meuse [mø:z] *f French river; department of northeastern France.*

Mexico [mɛksi'ko] Mexico City.

Mexique [mɛk'sik] *m: le ~* Mexico.

Mézières [me'zjɛ:r] *capital of the department of Ardennes.*

Michel [mi'ʃɛl] *m* Michael.

Michelet [miʃ'lɛ] *French historian.*

Milan [mi'lɑ̃] *m* Milan.

Millet [mi'lɛ; mi'jɛ] *French painter.*

Minorque [mi'nɔrk] *f* Minorca.

Mirabeau [mira'bo] *revolutionary orator.*

Mistral [mis'tral] *Provençal poet.*

Mitterand [mitɛ'rɑ̃] *French president.*

Mohammed [mɔa'mɛd] *see Mahomet.*

Molière [mɔ'ljɛ:r] *French writer of comedies.*

Mollet [mɔ'lɛ] *French politician.*

Monaco [mɔna'ko] *m* Monaco.

Monet [mɔ'nɛ] *French painter.*

Mongolie [mɔ̃gɔ'li] *f: la ~* Mongolia.

Monique [mɔ'nik] *f* Monica.

Montaigne [mɔ̃'tɛɲ] *French moralist.*

Montalembert [mɔ̃talɑ̃'bɛ:r] *French politician and writer.*

Montauban [mɔ̃to'bɑ̃] *capital of the department of Tarn-et-Garonne.*

Montcalm, de [dəmɔ̃'kalm] *French general in Canada.*

Mont-de-Marsan [mɔ̃dmar'sɑ̃] *capital of the department of Landes.*

Montespan [mɔ̃tɛs'pɑ̃] *mistress of Louis XIV.*

Montesquieu [mɔ̃tɛs'kjø] *French writer and constitutionalist.*

Montherlant [mɔ̃tɛr'lɑ̃] *French writer.*

Montmartre [mɔ̃'martr] *part of Paris famous for its night life.*

Montparnasse [mɔ̃par'naːs] *famous artistic quarter of Paris.*

Montpellier [mɔ̃pə'lje] *capital of the department of Hérault.*

Montréal [mɔ̃re'al] *Montreal.*

Moravie [mɔra'vi] *f: la ~ Moravia.*

Morbihan [mɔrbi'ɑ̃] *m department of western France.*

Morvan [mɔr'vɑ̃] *m mountain range of France.*

Moscou [mɔs'ku] *Moscow.*

Moselle [mɔ'zɛl] *f French river; department of northeastern France.*

Moulins [mu'lɛ̃] *capital of the department of Allier; former capital of the province of Bourbonnais.*

Moyen-Orient [mwaɛnɔr'jɑ̃] *m: le ~ the Middle East.*

Mozambique [mɔza'bik] *m: le ~ Mozambique.*

Munich [my'nik] *m Munich.*

Musset [my'sɛ] *French writer.*

N

Nancy [nɑ̃'si] *capital of the department of Meurthe-et-Moselle.*

Nanette [na'nɛt] *f Nancy.*

Nantes [nɑ̃:t] *French port; capital of the department of Loire-Atlantique.*

Naples ['naplə] *m, f Naples.*

Napoléon [napole'ɔ̃]: *~ Iᵉʳ Napoleon I (emperor of the French).*

Navarre [na'vaːr] *f former kingdom.*

Necker [ne'kɛːr] *French financier.*

Neige [nɛ:ʒ]: *crêt m de la ~ highest peak of the Jura.*

Népal [ne'pal] *m: le ~ Nepal.*

Nerval [nɛr'val] *French writer.*

Nevers [nɔ'vɛːr] *capital of the department of Nièvre; former capital of the province of Nivernais.*

Nicaragua [nikara'gwa] *m: le ~ Nicaragua.*

Nice [nis] *capital of the department of Alpes-Maritimes.*

Nicolas [nikɔ'la] *m Nicholas.*

Nicolette [nikɔ'lɛt] *f Christian name.*

Nièvre [njɛ:vr] *f French river; department of central France.*

Niger [ni'ʒɛːr] *m Niger.*

Nigeria [niʒɛr'ja] *m, f: le (or la) ~ Nigeria.*

Nil [nil] *m Nile.*

Nîmes [nim] *capital of the department of Gard.*

Ninon [ni'nɔ̃] *f Nina.*

Niort [njɔːr] *capital of the department of Deux-Sèvres.*

Nivernais [nivɛr'nɛ] *m old province of France.*

Nord [nɔːr] *m department of northern France; la mer du ~ the North Sea.*

Normandie [nɔrmɑ̃'di] *f: la ~ Normandy (old province of France).*

Norvège [nɔr'vɛːʒ] *f: la ~ Norway.*

Notre-Dame [nɔtrə'dam] *metropolitan church of Paris.*

Nouvelle-Calédonie [nuvɛlkaledɔ'ni] *f: la ~ New Caledonia.*

Nouvelle-Zélande [nuvɛlze'lɑ̃d] *f: la ~ New Zealand.*

O

Océanie [ɔsea'ni] *f: l'~ Oceania.*

Oise [waːz] *French river; department of northern France.*

Olivier [ɔli'vje] *m Oliver.*

Oran [ɔ'rɑ̃] *town and department of Algeria.*

Orléanais [ɔrlea'nɛ] *m old province of France.*

Orléans [ɔrle'ɑ̃] *capital of the department of Loiret; former capital of the province of Orléanais; hist. branch of the French royal house of Bourbon.*

Orly [ɔr'li] *airport of Paris.*

Orne [ɔrn] *French river; department of northern France.*

Orphée [ɔr'fe] *m Orpheus.*

Oslo [ɔs'lo] *capital of Norway.*

Ottawa [ɔta'wa] *capital of Canada.*

Ouganda [ugɑ̃'da] *m: l'~ Uganda.*

Oural [u'ral] *Ural.*

P

Pacifique [pasi'fik] *m: le (or l'océan) ~ the Pacific (Ocean).*

Pagnol [pa'ɲɔl] *French writer.*

Pakistan [pakis'tɑ̃] *m: le ~ Pakistan.*

Palestine [palɛs'tin] *f: la ~ Palestine.*

Panamá [pana'ma] *m: le ~ Panama.*

Panthéon [pɑ̃te'ɔ̃] *m Pantheon (building in Paris in the crypt of which are buried some of France's greatest men).*

Paraguay [para'gɛ] *m: le ~ Paraguay.*

Paris [pa'ri] *m capital of France; capital of the department of Seine; former capital of the province of Ile-de-France.*

Parmentier [parmɑ̃'tje] *French economist and agronomist.*

Pascal [pas'kal] *French mathematician, physicist, and philosopher.*

Pas-de-Calais [pɑdka'lɛ] *m department of northern France.*

Pasteur [pas'tœːr] *French chemist and biologist.*

Patrice [pa'tris], **Patrick** [pa'trik] *m* Patrick.

Pau [po] *capital of the department of Basses-Pyrénées; former capital of the province of Béarn.*

Paul [pɔl] *m* Paul.

Pays-Bays [pei'ba] *m/pl.*: *les ~ the* Netherlands.

Pékin [pe'kɛ̃] Pekin(g).

Père-Lachaise [pɛrla'ʃɛːz] *m main cemetery of Paris, named after La Chaise.*

Périgord [peri'gɔr] *m former county of France.*

Périgueux [peri'gø] *capital of the department of Dordogne; former capital of the county of Périgord.*

Pérou [pe'ru] *m*: *le ~* Peru.

Perpignan [pɛrpi'nɑ̃] *capital of the department of Pyrénées-Orientales; former capital of the province of Roussillon.*

Perrault [pɛ'ro] *French writer of fairy tales.*

Perrier [pɛ'rje] *French naturalist.*

Perse *hist.* [pɛrs] *f*: *la ~* Persia.

Persique [pɛr'sik]: *le golfe ~* Persian Gulf.

Pétain [pe'tɛ̃] *French Marshal and politician.*

Peugeot [pø'ʒo] *French industrialist.*

Phèdre [fɛdr] *f* Phaedra.

Philippe [fi'lip] *m* Philip.

Philippines [fili'pin] *f/pl.*: *les ~ the* Philippines.

Picardie [pikar'di] *f old province of France.*

Picasso [pika'so] *Spanish painter.*

Piccard [pi'kaːr] *Swiss physicist.*

Pierre [pjɛːr] *m* Peter.

Pissarro [pisa'ro] *French painter.*

Platon [pla'tɔ̃] *m* Plato (*Greek philosopher*).

Pleyel [plɛ'jɛl] *family of musicians.*

Poincaré [pwɛ̃ka're] *French statesman.*

Poitiers [pwa'tje] *capital of the department of Vienne; former capital of the province of Poitou.*

Poitou [pwa'tu] *m old province of France.*

Pologne [pɔ'lɔɲ] *f*: *la ~* Poland.

Polynésie [poline'zi] *f*: *la ~* Polynesia.

Pompadour [pɔ̃pa'duːr] *mistress of Louis XV.*

Pompidou [pɔ̃pi'du] *French president.*

Port-Royal [pɔrrwa'jal] *French abbey, centre of jansenism.*

Portugal [pɔrty'gal] *m*: *le ~* Portugal.

Poussin [pu'sɛ̃] *French painter.*

Prague [prag] *capital of Czechoslovakia.*

Prévost [pre'vo] *French writer.*

Privas [pri'va] *capital of the department of Ardèche.*

Proche-Orient [prɔʃɔr'jɑ̃] *m*: *le ~ the* Near East.

Proudhon [pru'dɔ̃] *French philosopher.*

Proust [prust] *French writer.*

Provence [prɔ'vɑ̃ːs] *f old province of France.*

Prud'hon [pry'dɔ̃] *French painter.*

Prusse [prys] *f*: *la ~* Prussia.

Puy [pɥi]: *Le ~ capital of the department of Haute-Loire; ~-de-Dôme* [~d'doːm] *m department of central France.*

Pyrénées [pire'ne] *f/pl.* Pyrenees; **Basses-~** [baspire'ne] *f/pl. department of southwestern France;* **Hautes-~** [otpire'ne] *f/pl. department of southwestern France; ~* **Orientales** [pirenezɔrjɑ̃'tal] *f/pl. department of southwestern France.*

Q

Quai d'Orsay [kedɔr'sɛ] *m French Ministry of Defence.*

Quartier latin [kartjela'tɛ̃] *m the student quarter of Paris.*

Quatre-Cantons [katrəkɑ̃'tɔ̃]: *le lac m des ~ the* Lake of Lucerne.

Québec [ke'bɛk] Quebec.

Queneau [kə'no] *French writer.*

Quesnay [ke'nɛ] *French physiocrat.*

Quimper [kɛ̃'pɛːr] *capital of the department of Finistère; former capital of the county of Cornouaille.*

R

Rabelais [ra'blɛ] *French writer.*

Rachel [ra'ʃɛl] *f* Rachel.

Racine [ra'sin] *French classical dramatist.*

Rambouillet [rɑ̃bu'jɛ] *French town with a famous castle.*

Rameau [ra'mo] *French composer.*

Raoul [ra'ul] *m* Ralph; Rudolph.

Ravel [ra'vɛl] *French composer.*

Raymond [rɛ'mɔ̃] *m* Raymond.

Réaumur [reo'my:r] *French naturalist and physicist.*

Récamier [reka'mje] *French woman whose salon under the Restoration was famous.*

Reims [rɛ̃s] Rheims (*French town*).

Renan [rə'nɑ̃] *French writer.*

Renaud [rə'no] *m* Reginald.

Renault [rə'no] *French industrialist.*

René [rə'ne] *m Christian name.*

Renée [rə'ne] *f Christian name.*

Rennes [rɛn] *capital of the department of Ille-et-Vilaine; former capital of the province of Bretagne.*

Renoir [rə'nwa:r] *French painter.*

Réunion [rey'njɔ̃] *f French overseas department.*

Reykjavik [rɛkja'vik] *capital of Iceland.*

Rhénanie [rena'ni] *f: la ~ the Rhineland.*

Rhin [rɛ̃] *m* Rhine; **Bas-~** [bɑ'rɛ̃] *m department of eastern France;* **Haut-~** [o'rɛ̃] *m department of eastern France.*

Rhodésie [rɔde'zi] *f: la ~ Rhodesia.*

Rhône [ro:n] *m French river; department of southeastern France.*

Richard [ri'ʃa:r] *m* Richard; **~ Cœur de Lion** [riʃarkœrdə'ljɔ̃] *m* Richard the Lionhearted.

Richelieu [riʃə'ljø] *French cardinal and statesman.*

Rimbaud [rɛ̃'bo] *French poet.*

Rivarol [riva'rɔl] *French writer.*

Robert [rɔ'bɛ:r] *m* Robert.

Robespierre [rɔbɛs'pjɛ:r] *French revolutionary.*

Rochelle, La [larɔ'ʃɛl] *capital of the department of Charente-Maritime; former capital of the province of Aunis.*

Roche-sur-Yon, La [larɔ'sy'rjɔ̃] *capital of the department of Vendée.*

Rodez [rɔ'dɛ:z] *capital of the department of Aveyron; former capital of the province of Rouergue.*

Rodin [rɔ'dɛ̃] *French sculptor.*

Rodolphe [rɔ'dɔlf] *m* Ralph, Rudolph.

Roger [rɔ'ʒe] *m* Roger.

Rohan [rɔ'ɑ̃] *French general and Calvinist leader; French cardinal.*

Roland [rɔ'lɑ̃] *French woman and republican whose salon had considerable influence in the 18th century.*

Rolland [rɔ'lɑ̃] *French writer.*

Romains [rɔ'mɛ̃] *French writer.*

Rome [rɔm] *f* Rome.

Ronsard [rɔ̃'sa:r] *French poet.*

Rostand [rɔs'tɑ̃] *French dramatist.*

Rouault [rwo] *French painter.*

Roubaix [ru'bɛ] *French town.*

Rouen [rwɑ̃] *French port; capital of the department of Seine-Maritime; former capital of the province of Normandie.*

Rouergue [rwɛrg] *m old province of France.*

Rouget de Lisle [ruʒɛd'lil] *author of the Marseillaise.*

Roumanie [ruma'ni] *f: la ~ Rumania.*

Rousseau [ru'so] *Swiss-born French philosopher.*

Roussillon [rusi'jɔ̃] *old province of France.*

Ruanda [rwɑ̃'da, rwan'da] *m: le ~ Rwanda.*

Rude [ryd] *French sculptor.*

Russie [ry'si] *f: la ~ Russia.*

S

Sade [sad] *French writer.*

Sahara [saa'ra] *m: le ~ the Sahara.*

Saint-Barthélemy, la [lasɛ̃bartelə-mi] *f Massacre of St. Bartholomew.*

Saint-Brieuc [sɛ̃bri'ø] *capital of the department of Côtes-du-Nord.*

Saint-Cloud [sɛ̃'klu] *French town with famous race-course.*

Saint-Denis-de-la-Réunion [sɛ̃-dnidəlarey'njɔ̃] *capital of the overseas department of Réunion.*

Sainte-Beuve [sɛ̃t'bœ:v] *French writer.*

Sainte-Hélène [sɛ̃te'lɛn] *f* Saint Helena.

Saintes [sɛ̃:t] *former capital of the province of Saintonge.*

Saint-Etienne [sɛ̃te'tjɛn] *capital of the department of Loire.*

Saint-Exupéry [sɛ̃tɛksype'ri] *French writer.*

Saint-Germain-des-Prés [sɛ̃-ʒɛrmɛ̃de'pre] *very old church and* *popular quarter of Paris*; **Saint-Germain-en-Laye** [～ã'lɛ] *French town with a famous castle.*

Saint-Just [sɛ̃'ʒyst] *French revolutionary.*

Saint-Laurent [sɛ̃lɔ'rã] *m the St. Lawrence.*

Saint-Lô [sɛ̃'lo] *capital of the department of Manche.*

Saint-Malo [sɛma'lo] *French port and town.*

Saint-Marin [sɛma'rɛ̃] *m San Marino.*

Saintonge [sɛ̃'tõːʒ] *old province of France.*

Saint-Pétersbourg [sɛpetɛr'sbuːr] *St. Petersburg (former name of Leningrad).*

Saint-Saëns [sɛ̃'sãːs] *French composer.*

Saint-Simon [sɛ̃si'mõ] *French economist and philosopher.*

Salvador, El [ɛlsalva'dɔːr] *m El Salvador.*

Salzbourg [salz'buːr] *f Salzburg.*

Sancy [sã'si]: *puy m de ～ highest peak of the Massif central.*

Sand [sã, sãːd] *French woman writer.*

Saône [soːn] *f French river*; **Haute-～** [ot'soːn] *f department of eastern France*; **～-et-Loire** [sone'lwaːr] *department of east-central France.*

Sardaigne [sar'dɛɲ] *f: la ～ Sardinia.*

Sarre [sar] *f: la ～ the Saar.*

Sarthe [sart] *f French river; department of northwestern France.*

Sartre [sartr] *French philosopher.*

Savoie [sa'vwa] *f: la ～ Savoy (department of southeastern France; old province of France)*; **Haute-～** [otsa'vwa] *f department of eastern France.*

Saxe [saks] *f: la ～ Saxony.*

Scandinavie [skãdina'vi] *f: la ～ Scandinavia.*

Scudéry [skyde'ri] *French woman writer.*

Ségur [se'gyːr] *French woman writer.*

Seine [sɛn] *f French river; department of northern France*; **～-et-Marne** [～e'marn] *department of northern France*; **～-et-Oise** [～e'waːz] *department of northern France*; **～-Maritime** [～mari'tim] *department of northern France.*

Serbie [sɛr'bi] *f: la ～ Serbia.*

Seurat [sø'ra] *French painter.*

Sévigné [sevi'ɲe] *French woman writer.*

Sèvres [sɛːvr] *French town renowned for its porcelain.*

Sibérie [sibe'ri] *f: la ～ Siberia.*

Sicile [si'sil] *f: la ～ Sicily.*

Sieyès [sje'jɛs] *French politician.*

Silésie [sile'zi] *f: la ～ Silesia.*

Sisley [sis'lɛ] *French painter.*

Slovaquie [slɔva'ki] *f: la ～ Slovakia.*

Sluter [sly'tɛːr] *Burgundian sculptor.*

Sofia [sɔ'fja] *capital of Bulgaria.*

Somme [sɔm] *f French river; department of northern France.*

Sophie [sɔ'fi] *f Sophia, Sophy.*

Sorbonne [sɔr'bɔn] *f seat of the faculties of letters and science of the University of Paris.*

Soubise [su'biːz]: *hôtel m de ～ the National Archives in Paris.*

Soudan [su'dã] *m: le ～ the Sudan.*

Staël [stɑl] *French woman writer.*

Stendhal [stɛ̃'dal] *French writer.*

Stockholm [stɔ'kɔlm] *capital of Sweden.*

Strasbourg [straz'buːr] *Strasb(o)urg (capital of the department of Bas-Rhin; former capital of the province of Alsace).*

Suède [sɥɛd] *f: la ～ Sweden.*

Suez [sɥeːz] *m Suez.*

Suisse [sɥis] *f: la ～ Switzerland.*

Sully [syl'li] *French politician.*

Sully Prudhomme [syllipry'dɔm] *French poet.*

Suzanne [sy'zan] *f Susan, F Sue.*

Sylvestre [sil'vɛstr] *m Sylvester.*

Syrie [si'ri] *f: la ～ Syria.*

T

Taine [tɛn] *French philosopher and historian.*

Talleyrand-Périgord [talɛrãperi'gɔːr] *French statesman.*

Tamise [ta'miːz] *f: la ～ the Thames.*

Tanger [tã'ʒe] *Tangier.*

Tarbes [tarb] *capital of the department of Hautes-Pyrénées.*

Tarn [tarn] *m French river; department of southern France*; **～-et-Garonne** [～ega'rɔn] *department of southwestern France.*

Tchad [tʃad] *m: le ～ the Republic of Chad.*

Tchécoslovaquie [tʃekɔslɔva'ki] *f: la ～ Czechoslovakia.*

Téhéran [tee'rã] *m* Teheran.
Teilhard de Chardin [tɛjardǝʃar-'dɛ̃] *French Jesuit and philosopher.*
Tel-Aviv [tɛla'vif] *city in West Israel.*
Terre de Feu [tɛrdeʹfø] *f: la ~* Tierra del Fuego.
Terre-Neuve [tɛrʹnœːv] Newfoundland.
Texas [tɛk'sas] *m: le ~* Texas.
Thaïlande [tajʹlãːd] *f: la ~* Thailand.
Théophile [teɔʹfil] *m* Theophilus.
Thérèse [teʹrɛːz] *f* Theresa.
Thibau(l)t [tiʹbo] *m* Theobald.
Thierry [tjɛʹri] *m* Theodoric *(Christian name);* French historian.
Thomas [tɔʹma] *m* Thomas.
Tibet [tiʹbɛ] *m: le ~* Tibet.
Tigre [tigr] *m the* Tigris.
Tirana [tiraʹna] *capital of Albania.*
Tocqueville [tɔkʹvil] *French politician and writer.*
Tokyo [tɔʹkjo] *m* Tokyo.
Toulon [tuʹlɔ̃] *French port and town.*
Toulouse [tuʹluːz] *capital of the department of Haute-Garonne; former capital of the province of Languedoc;*
~-Lautrec [tuluzloʹtrɛk] *French painter.*
Touraine [tuʹrɛn] *f old province of France.*
Tours [tuːr] *capital of the department of Indre-et-Loire; former capital of the province of Touraine.*
Trocadéro [trɔkadeʹro] *m formerly building on the heights of Passy, Paris, replaced by the Palais de Chaillot.*
Trouville [truʹvil] *French health resort on the Channel.*
Troyes [trwa] *capital of the department of Aube; former capital of the province of Champagne.*
Tuileries [tɥilʹri] *f/pl.: les ~ gardens and former royal palace in Paris.*
Tulle [tyl] *capital of the department of Corrèze.*
Tunisie [tyniʹzi] *f: la ~* Tunisia.
Turquie [tyrʹki] *f: la ~* Turkey.

U

Union soviétique [ynjɔ̃sɔvjeʹtik] *f: l'~* the Soviet Union.
Uruguay [yryʹgɛ] *m: l'~* Uruguay.
Utrillo [ytriʹjo] *French painter.*

V

Valadon [valaʹdɔ̃] *French woman painter.*

Valence [vaʹlãːs] *m capital of the department of Drôme; f* Valencia *(Spain).*
Valéry [valeʹri] *French writer.*
Valois *hist.* [vaʹlwa] *m/pl.* French royal house.
Van Gogh [vanʹgɔg] *Dutch painter.*
Vanne [van] *f French river.*
Vannes [van] *f capital of the department of Morbihan.*
Var [vaːr] *m French river; department of southeastern France.*
Varsovie [varsɔʹvi] Warsaw.
Vatican [vatiʹkã] *m: le ~* the Vatican.
Vaucluse [voʹklyːz] *department of southeastern France.*
Vaud [vo] *m: le canton de ~* Vaud.
Vaugelas [voʒʹla] *French grammarian.*
Vauvenargues [vovʹnarg] *French moralist.*
Vendée [vãʹde] *f French river; department of western France.*
Venezuela [venezɥeʹla] *m: le ~* Venezuela.
Venise [vǝʹniz] *f* Venice.
Verdun [vɛrʹdœ̃] *French town.*
Verhaeren [vɛʹrarǝn] *Belgian poet.*
Verlaine [vɛrʹlɛn] *French poet.*
Véronique [verɔʹnik] *f* Veronica.
Versailles [vɛrʹsaːj] *capital of the department of Seine-et-Oise with famous royal palace.*
Vesoul [vǝʹzul] *capital of the department of Haute-Saône.*
Vichy [viʹʃi] *French health resort; seat of Pétain government.*
Victor [vikʹtɔːr] *m* Victor.
Vienne [vjɛn] *f* Vienna *(capital of Austria);* French river; department of west-central France; m town of Isère, near Grenoble; **Haute-~** [otʹvjɛn] *f department of central France.*
Viêt-nam [vjɛtʹnam] *m: le ~* Vietnam.
Vigny [viʹɲi] *French writer.*
Vilaine [viʹlɛn] *f French river.*
Villon [viʹlɔ̃, viʹjɔ̃] *French poet.*
Vincennes [vɛ̃ʹsɛn] *suburb of Paris; famous castle and wood.*
Vlaminck [vlaʹmɛ̃ːk] *French painter.*
Voltaire [vɔlʹtɛːr] *French philosopher.*
Vosges [voːʒ] *f/pl. mountain range; department of eastern France.*

W

Wallonie [walɔʹni] *f French speaking part of Belgium.*

Waterloo [vatɛr'lo] *Belgian village, scene of famous defeat of Napoleon.*

Watteau [va'to] *French painter.*

Weygand [ve'gɑ̃] *Belgian-born French general.*

Y

Yémen [je'mɛn] *m: le* ~ Yemen.

Yonne [jɔn] *f French river; department of central France.*

Yougoslavie [jugɔsla'vi] *f: la* ~ Yugoslavia, Jugoslavia.

Ypres [ipr] *Belgian town.*

Yves [iːv] *m Christian name.*

Z

Zaïre [za'iːr] *m: le* ~ Zaïre.

Zambèze [zɑ̃'bɛːz] *m the* Zambezi.

Zambie [zɑ̃'bi] *f: la* ~ Zambia.

Zola [zɔ'la] *French writer.*

Zurich [zy'rik] *m* Zurich.

Common French Abbreviations
Abréviations françaises usuelles

A

A *ampère* ampere.

A 2 *Antenne deux* channel two (*on French television*).

A.A. *antiaérien* A.A., anti-aircraft.

ac., à cte. *acompte* payment on account.

a.c. *argent comptant* ready money.

A.C.F. *Automobile Club de France* Automobile Association of France.

act. *action* share.

A.D.A.V. *avion à décollage et atterrissage vertical* V.T.O.(L.), vertical take-off (and landing) (aircraft).

à dr. *à droite* on *or* to the right.

A.d.S. *Académie des Sciences* Academy of Science.

AELE *Association européenne de libre échange* EFTA, European Free Trade Association.

AF *Air France* (*French airline*); *anciens francs* old francs.

A.F. *Allocations familiales* family allowance.

A.F.P. *Agence France-Presse* French press agency.

A.G. *Assemblée générale* general meeting; G.A., General Assembly.

à g. *à gauche* on *or* to the left.

AIH *Association internationale de l'hôtellerie* IHA, International Hotel Association.

A.J. *auberge de la jeunesse* youth hostel.

AME *Accord monétaire européen* EMA, European Monetary Agreement.

A.N.P.E. *Agence nationale pour l'emploi* national employment bureau.

A.O.C. *appellation d'origine contrôlée* guaranteed vintage.

A.P. *à protester* to be protested; *Assistance publique* Public Assistance.

ap. J.-C. *après Jesus-Christ* A.D., anno Domini.

arr. *arrondissement* district.

A.S. *Assurances sociales* social insurance; *association sportive* sports club.

a/s. *aux soins de* c/o., care of.

av. *avenue* avenue; *avoir* credit.

av. J.-C. *avant Jésus-Christ* B.C., before Jesus Christ.

B

B *bougie* candle-power.

B. *balle* bale; *billet* bill.

B.C.G. *vaccin bilié Calmette-Guérin* (*antitubercular vaccine*).

B.D. *bande dessinée* cartoon; comic.

Bd. *boulevard* boulevard.

BENELUX *Belgique-Nederland-Luxembourg* BENELUX, Belgium, Netherlands, Luxemb(o)urg.

B. ès L. (*or* **Sc.**) *Bachelier ès Lettres* (*or Sciences*) (*approx.*) Advanced Level of the General Certificate of Education in Arts (*or* Science).

B.F. *Banque de France* Bank of France.

B.O. *Bulletin officiel* Official Bulletin.

B.P. *boîte postale* POB, Post Office Box.

B.P.F. *bon pour francs* value in francs.

B.R.I. *Banque de règlements internationaux* B.I.S., Bank for International Settlements.

B.S.G.D.G. *breveté sans garantie du gouvernement* patent.

C

C *cent* hundred; °**C** *degré Celsius* degree centigrade.

c. *centime* (*hundredth part of a franc*).

C.A. *courant alternatif* A.C., alternating current; *chiffre d'affaires* turnover.

c.-à-d. *c'est-à-dire* i.e., that is to say.

C.A.F. *coût, assurance, fret* c.i.f., cost, insurance, freight.

cal *calorie* calory.

C.A.P. *Certificat d'aptitude professionnelle (certificate granted to a qualified apprentice).*

C.C. *corps consulaire* consular corps; *compte courant* a/c, current account.

CCI *Chambre de Commerce Internationale* ICC, International Chamber of Commerce.

C.C.P. *compte chèques postaux* postal cheque account.

C.D. *corps diplomatique* diplomatic corps.

CE *Conseil de l'Europe* Council of Europe.

CECA *Communauté européenne du charbon et de l'acier* E.C.S.C., European Coal and Steel Community.

CED *Communauté européenne de défense* E.D.C., European Defence Community.

CEE *Communauté économique européenne* E.E.C., European Economic Community.

CEEA *Commission européenne de l'énergie atomique* EURATOM, European Atomic Energy Commission.

C.E.G. *collège d'enseignement général (Secondary Modern School).*

CERN *Organisation européenne pour la recherche nucléaire* European Organisation for Nuclear Research.

C.E.S. *collège d'enseignement secondaire (Secondary School).*

C.E.T. *collège d'enseignement technique (a technical college).*

Cf. *conférez* cf., compare.

C.F.D.T. *Confédération française (et) démocratique du travail (a major association of French trade unions).*

C.F.T.C. *Confédération française des travailleurs chrétiens* French Confederation of Christian Workers.

C.G.A. *Confédération générale de l'agriculture* General Confederation of Agriculture.

C.G.C. *Confédération générale des cadres* General confederation of higher administrative staffs.

C.G.T. *Confédération générale du travail* General confederation of Labour, *(approx.)* T.U.C., Trade Union(s) Congress.

ch *cheval(-vapeur)* H.P., h.p., horsepower.

ch.d.f. *chemin de fer* Ry., railway.

ch.-l. *chef-lieu* capital.

CICR *Comité international de la Croix-Rouge* ICRC., International Committee of the Red Cross.

Cⁱᵉ., Cie. *Compagnie* Co., Company.

CIO *Comité international olympique* IOC., International Olympic Committee.

CISL *Confédération internationale des syndicats libres* ICFTU, International Confederation of Free Trade Unions.

cl *centilitre* centilitre, *Am.* centiliter.

cm *centimètre* centimetre, *Am.* centimeter.

C.N.P.F. *Conseil national du patronat français (employers' association).*

C.N.R. *Conseil national de la Resistance* National Resistance Council.

C.N.R.S. *Centre national de la recherche scientifique (approx.)* S.R.C., Scientific Research Centre.

COE *Conseil œcuménique des églises* WCC, World Council of Churches.

cour. *courant* inst., instant.

C.Q.F.D. *ce qu'il fallait démontrer* Q.E.D., quod erat demonstrandum which was to be proved.

C.-R.F. *Croix-Rouge française* French Red Cross.

CRI *Croix-Rouge internationale* IRC, International Red Cross.

C.R.S. *Compagnies républicaines de sécurité (state security police; member of the C.R.S.).*

cᵗ. *courant* inst., instant.

C.V. *cheval-vapeur* H.P., h.p., horsepower; *cette ville* this town.

D

D.A.T. *Défense aérienne du territoire* Air Space Defence.

D.C.A. *défense contre avions* A.A., anti-aircraft (defence).

D.D.T. *Dichlorodiphényltrichloroéthane* DDT, dichlorodiphenyltrichloroethane.

dép. *départ* departure; *député(e)* member of Parliament, *Am.* representative.

dépt. *département* administrative department.

der. *dernier* ult., ultimo.

dest. *destinataire* addressee, consignee.

D.E.U.G. [døg] *diplôme d'études universitaires générales* certificate of general studies at university level.

D.G.S.E. *Direction générale de la sécurité extérieure* (*counterintelligence agency*).

D.I.T. *défense intérieure du territoire* (*internal defence*).

div. *dividende* dividend.

D.M. *Docteur Médecin* Doctor of Medicine.

do *dito* ditto.

D.O.M. *départements d'outre-mer* overseas administrative departments.

D.O.M.-T.O.M., Dom-Tom [dɔm-ˈtɔm] *départements, territoires d'outre--mer* overseas administrative departments and territories.

D.P.L.G. *Diplômé par le gouvernement* state certificated.

Dr *Docteur* Dr., Doctor (*university degree*).

dr. *droit* right.

D.S.T. *Direction de la surveillance du territoire* (*counterintelligence service*).

dt *doit* debit.

dz *douzaine* doz., dozen.

E

E. *est* E., east.

E.-M. *État-major* H.Q., Headquarters.

E.N.A. *École nationale d'administration* national administrative school.

E.N.S. *École normale supérieure* Training College for secondary school teachers.

E.N.S.I. *Écoles nationales supérieures d'ingénieurs* state colleges of advanced engineering.

env. *environ* about.

e.o.o.e. *erreur ou omission exceptée* E. & O.E., errors and omissions excepted.

etc. *et cætera* etc., etcetera.

Ęts *établissements* establishments.

É.-U. *États-Unis* U.S.A., United States.

E.V. *en ville* Local (*on envelopes*).

ex. *exemple* example; *exercice* year's trading.

ex. att. *exercice attaché* cum dividend.

Exc. *Excellence* Excellency (*title*).

exD. *ex-dividende* ex div., ex dividend.

exp. *expéditeur* consigner.

ext. *externe* external; *extérieur* exterior.

F

F *franc* franc; **°F** *degré Fahrenheit* degree Fahrenheit.

F.A.B. *franco à bord* f.o.b., free on board.

FB *franc(s) belge(s)* Belgian franc(s).

f.c(t). *fin courant* at the end of this month.

Fco *franco* free, carriage paid.

F.E.N. *Fédération de l'éducation nationale* National Education Federation (*autonomous professional union*).

FF *franc(s) français* French franc(s).

F.F.I. *Forces françaises de l'intérieur* French Forces of the Interior.

F.F.L. *Forces françaises libres* Free French Forces.

F.I.A.A. *Fédération internationale d'athlétisme amateur* I.A.A.F., International Amateur Athletic Federation.

FIFA *Fédération internationale de football association* (*federation controlling international football competitions*).

fig. *figure* figure.

FISE *Fonds des Nations Unies pour l'enfance* UNICEF, United Nations Children's Fund.

FIT *Fédération internationale des traducteurs* IFT, International Federation of Translators.

F.M. *fréquence modulée, modulation de fréquence* F.M., frequency modulation.

FMI *Fond monétaire international* IMF, International Monetary Fund.

FMPA *Fédération mondiale pour la protection des animaux* WFPA, World Federation for the Protection of Animals.

F.N.A.C. *Fédération nationale d'achats des cadres* (*department store [chain] for high-quality goods*).

F.O. *Force Ouvrière* (*a Socialist trade union*).

fo *franco* free, carriage paid.

F.O.Q. *franco à quai* f.a.s., free alongside ship.

F.O.R. *franco sur rail* f.o.r., free on rail.

F.O.T. *franco en wagon* f.o.t., free on truck.

f.p. *fin prochain* at the end of next month.

fque *fabrique* make.

FR 3 *France trois* channel three (*on French television*).

fro *franco* free, carriage paid.

Frs *Frères* Bros., Brothers.

FS *franc(s) suisse(s)* Swiss franc(s).

F.S. *faire suivre* please forward (*on letters*).

F.S.M. *Fédération syndicale mondiale* WFTU, World Federation of Trade Unions.

G

g *gramme* gramme, *Am.* gram; *gravité* gravity.

g. *gauche* left.

G.C. (*route de*) *grande communication* (*approx.*) B-road.

G(r.)C. *Grand'Croix* Grand Cross (*of the Legion of Honour*).

G.D.F. *Gaz de France* (*French Gas Board*).

G.O. *grandes ondes* L.W., long wave(s).

G.V. *grande vitesse* per passenger train.

H

h *heure* hour, o'clock.

ha *hectare* hectare.

H.B.M. *habitations à bon marché* property to let at low rents.

H.C. *hors concours* not competing.

H.E.C. (*École des*) *Hautes Études commerciales* School of Advanced Commercial and Management Studies, Paris; *heure de l'Europe Centrale* CET, Central European Time.

H.F. *haute fréquence* high frequency.

H.L.M. *habitations à loyer modéré* property to let at moderate rents.

H.T. *haute tension* high tension.

I

Ibid. *ibidem* ibid., in the same place, ibidem.

Id. *idem* id., same, idem.

I.D.S. *Initiative de défense stratégique* S.D.I., Strategic Defense Initiative.

I.F.O.P. [i'fɔp] *Institut français d'opinion publique* (*state institute monitoring public opinion*).

ing(én.). *ingénieur* engineer.

I.N.P.I. [in'pi] *Institut national de la propriété industrielle* French Patent office.

I.N.S.E. [in'se] *Institut national des statistiques et des études économiques* national institute for statistics and economic research.

int. *interne* internal; *intérieur* interior.

I.U.T. *Institut universitaire de technologie* (*a technical college*).

I.V.G. *interruption volontaire de grossesse* voluntary termination of pregnancy.

J

j *jour* day.

J.A.C. *Jeunesse agricole chrétienne* Christian Agricultural Youth.

J.-B. *Jean-Baptiste* John the Baptist.

J.-C. *Jésus-Christ* J.C., Jesus (Christ).

Je *Jeune* Jun., Junior.

J.E.C. *Jeunesse étudiante chrétienne* Y.C.S., Young Christian Students.

J.-J. *Jean-Jacques* John James.

J.O. *Journal officiel* Official Gazette.

J.O.C. *Jeunesse ouvrière chrétienne* YCW, Young Christian Workers.

K

kg *kilogramme* kilogramme, *Am.* kilogram.

km *kilomètre* kilometre, *Am.* kilometer.

km:h *kilomètres par heure* kilometres (*Am.* -meters) per hour.

kV *kilovolt* k.v., kilovolt.

kW *kilowatt* k.w., kilowatt.

kWh *kilowatt-heure* kilowatt-hour.

L

l *litre* litre, *Am.* liter.

lat. *latitude* latitude.

L. ès L. *licencié ès lettres* (*approx.*) B.A., Bachelor of Arts.

L. ès Sc. *licencié ès sciences* (*approx.*) B.Sc., Bachelor of Science.

Lieut. *lieutenant* Lieut., Lieutenant.

ll. *lignes* ll., lines.

loc. cit. *loco citato* at the place cited.

long. *longitude* longitude.

Lt *lieutenant* Lt., Lieutenant.

Lt-Col. *lieutenant-colonel* Lt.-Col., Lieutenant-Colonel.

M

M. *Monsieur* Mr., Mister.
m *mètre* metre, *Am.* meter.
m. *mort* died.
mb *millibar* millibar.
md(e) *marchand*(e) merchant.
Me *Maître* (*barrister's title of address*).
mg *milligramme* milligramme, *Am.* milligram.
Mgr *Monseigneur* Monsignor.
M.L.F. *Mouvement de libération des femmes* Women's Liberation Movement.
Mlle *Mademoiselle* Miss.
Mlles *Mesdemoiselles* the Misses.
MM. *Messieurs* Messrs.
mm *millimètre* millimetre, *Am.* millimeter.
Mme *Madame* Mrs., Mistress.
Mmes *Mesdames* Mesdames.
mn *minute* minute.
Mon *maison* firm.
M.R.P. *Mouvement Républicain Populaire* Popular Republican Movement.
M/S *navire à moteur Diesel* M.S., motorship.
ms *manuscrit* MS., manuscript.
mss *manuscrits* MSS, manuscripts.
M.T.S. *mètre-tonne-seconde* metre (*Am.* meter)-ton-second.
MV *maladie vénérienne* V.D., venereal disease.
mV *millivolt* millivolt.

N

N. *nord* N., North; *nom* name.
n/... *notre, nos* our.
n. *notre* our.
N.B. *notez bien* N.B., note well.
N.-D. *Notre-Dame* Our Lady.
N.D.L.R. *note de la rédaction* editor's note.
N.E. *nord-est* N.E., north-east.
NF *nouveaux francs* new francs.
N.F. *norme française* French Standard.
No., no *numéro* number.
N.O., N.W. *nord-ouest* N.W., Northwest.
n/sr. *notre sieur* ... our Mr. ...
N.U. *Nations Unies* U.N., United Nations.
n/v. *notre ville* our town.

O

O. *ouest* W., west; *officier* Officer (*of an Order*).

OAA *Organisation pour l'alimentation et l'agriculture* F.A.O., Food and Agriculture Organization.
OACI *Organisation de l'aviation civile internationale* ICAO, International Civil Aviation Organization.
OAS *Organisation de l'Armée Secrète* Secret Army Organization.
O.C. *ondes courtes* s.w., short wave(s).
OCDE *Organisation de coopération et de développement économiques* O.E.C.D., Organization for Economic Co-operation and Development.
OECE *Organisation européenne de coopération économique* O.E.E.C., Organization for European Economic Co-operation.
OIC *Organisation internationale du commerce* ITO, International Trade Organization.
OIN *Organisation internationale de normalisation* ISO, International Organization for Standardization.
OIPC *Organisation internationale de police criminelle* ICPO, INTERPOL, International Criminal Police Organization.
OIR *Organisation internationale pour les réfugiés* IRO, International Refugee Organization.
OIT *Organisation internationale du travail* ILO, International Labour Organization.
O.L.P. *Organisation de libération de la Palestine* PLO, Palestine Liberation Organization.
OMS *Organisation mondiale de la santé* WHO, World Health Organization.
O.N.M. *Office national météorologique* Meteorological Office.
ONU *Organisation des Nations Unies* UNO, United Nations Organization.
op. cit. *opere citato* in the work quoted.
O.P.E.P. [ɔˈpep] *Organisation des pays exportateurs de pétrole* OPEC, Organization of Petroleum Exporting Countries.
O.S *ouvrier spécialisé* semi-skilled worker.
OTAN *Organisation du Traité de l'Atlantique Nord* NATO, North Atlantic Treaty Organization.
OTASE *Organisation du Traité de défense collective pour l'Asie du Sud-Est*

SEATO, Southeast Asia Treaty Organization.

OTC *onde très courte* VHF, very high frequency.

P

P. *Père* Fr., Father.

p. *pour* per; *par* per; *page* page.

P.C. *Parti Communiste* Communist Party; *poste de commandement* Headquarters.

p.c. *pour cent* %, per cent.

p/c. *pour compte* on account.

P.C.B. *physique, chimie, biologie* physics, chemistry, biology.

P.C.C., p.c.c. *pour copie conforme* true copy.

P.C.V. [pese've] *paiement contre vérification* (*a. communication f en* ∿) reverse charge call.

p.d. *port dû* carriage forward.

P.(-)D.G. *président-directeur général* chairman (of the board).

P. et T. *postes et télécommunications* (*approx.*) The Post Office.

p.ex. *par exemple* e.g., for example.

P.G. *Prisonnier de guerre* P.O.W., Prisoner of War.

P.J. *Police judiciaire* (*approx.*) C.I.D., Criminal Investigation Department.

pl. *planche* plate, full-page illustration.

P.M. *police militaire* MP, M.P., Military Police.

p.m. *poids mort* dead weight.

P.M.E. *petites et moyennes entreprises* small businesses.

PMI *Protection maternelle et infantile* MCH, Maternal and Child Health; *petites et moyennes industries* small industries.

P.M.U. *Pari mutuel urbain* local tote.

P.N.B. *produit national brut* gross national product.

P.O. *par ordre* by order.

pp. *pages* pages.

p.p. *port payé* carriage paid.

P.p.c. *pour prendre congé* to take leave.

prov. *province* province.

P.-S. *post-scriptum* P.S., postscript.

P.S.V. *pilotage sans visibilité* instrument flying, blind flying.

P.T.T. *Postes, Télégraphes, Téléphones* (French) G.P.O., General Post Office.

P.V. *petite vitesse* per goods train.

P.-V. *procès-verbal* (*see main dictionary*).

Q

q. *carré* square; *quintal* quintal.

Q.G. *Quartier général* H.Q., Headquarters.

Q.I. *quotient intellectuel* I.Q., intelligence quotient.

qq. *quelque* some; *quelqu'un* someone.

qqf. *quelquefois* sometimes.

Q.S. *quantité suffisante* sufficient quantity.

R

R, r. *rue* Rd., road, street.

R.A.T.P. *régie autonome des transports parisiens* (*Paris Public Transport Board*).

R.A.U. *République arabe unie* United Arab Republic.

RB (*envoi*) *contre remboursement* C.O.D., cash on delivery.

R.C. *registre du commerce* register of trade.

r.d. *rive droite* right bank.

R.D.A. *République démocratique allemande* G.D.R., German Democratic Republic.

Rem. *remarque* annotation.

R.E.R. *Réseau express régional* (*commuter-train network*).

R.F. *République française* French Republic.

R.F.A. *République fédérale d'Allemagne* G.F.R., German Federal Republic.

r.g. *rive gauche* left bank.

R.N. *route nationale* (*approx.*) National Highway.

R.P. *réponse payée* R.P., reply paid; *Révérend Père* Rev. Fr., Reverend Father; *Représentation proportionnelle* P.R., proportional representation.

R.P.F. *Rassemblement du Peuple Français* Rally of the French People (*de Gaull's party*).

R.P.R. *Rassemblement pour la République* Rally for the Republic (*Gaullist party*).

R.S.V.P. *répondez, s'il vous plaît* the favour of an answer is requested.

Rte *route* road.

R.T.F. *Radiodiffusion-télévision française* French Radio and Television.

S

S. *sud* S., south; *Saint* St., Saint.

s. *seconde* s., second.

S.A. *Société anonyme* Co Ltd., limited company; *Am.* Inc., Incorporated.

S.A.R.L. *société à responsabilité limitée* limited liability company.

s.b.f. *sauf bonne fin* under usual reserve.

S.C.E. *service contre-espionnage* C.I.C., Counter Intelligence Corps.

s.d. *sans date* n.d., no date.

SDN *Société des Nations* L of N, League of Nations.

S.-E. *sud-est* S.E., southeast.

s.e. ou o. *sauf erreur ou omission* E. & O.E., errors and omissions excepted.

S.E. *Son Excellence* His Excellency (*Minister's title of address*).

S.F. *sans frais* no expenses; *sience-fiction* science fiction.

S.F.I.O. *Section française de l'internationale ouvrière* French section of the Workers' International (*unified Socialist Party*).

SG *Secrétaire général* SG, Secretary General.

S.G.D.G. *sans garantie du gouvernement* (*patent*) without government guarantee.

S.I. *Syndicat d'initiative* Travel and Tourist Bureau *or* Association.

S.I.D.A. [si¹da] *syndrome immunodéficitaire acquis* AIDS, Acquired Immunity Deficiency Syndrome.

S.J. *Société de Jésus* SJ, Society of Jesus.

s.l.n.d. *sans lieu ni date* n. p. or d., no place or date.

S.M. *Sa Majesté* H.M., His (Her) Majesty.

S.M.E. *Système monétaire européen* European Monetary System.

S.M.I.G. *salaire minimum interprofessionnel garanti* guaranteed minimum wage.

S.N.C.F. *Société nationale des chemins de fer français* French National Railways.

S.-O. *sud-ouest* S.W., southwest.

S.O.F.R.S. [sɔ¹frɛs] *Société française d'enquêtes par sondage* (*a French institute for opinion-polling and market research*).

S.P.A. *Société protectrice des animaux* (*French*) Society for the Prevention of Cruelty to Animals.

S.R. *service de renseignement* Intelligence (Service *or* Department).

SS. *Saints* Saints.

S.S. *Sa Sainteté* His Holiness; *sécurité sociale* Social Security.

S/S *navire à vapeur* S.S., steamship.

st *stère* cubic metre, *Am.* meter.

St(e) *Saint(e)* St., Saint.

Sté *société* company.

S.V.P., s.v.p. *s'il vous plaît* please.

T

t *tonne* ton.

t. *tour* revolution; *tome* volume.

TB *tuberculose* TB, tuberculosis.

T.C.F. *Touring Club de France* Touring Club of France.

tél. *téléphone* telephone.

TF 1 *Télévision française* un channel one (*on French television*).

T.G.V. *train à grande vitesse* high-speed train.

T.N.P. *Théâtre National Populaire* (*one of the Paris theatres subsidized by the State*).

T.N.T. *trinitrotoluène* TNT, trinitrotoluene.

t.p.m. *tours par minute* r.p.m., revolutions per minute.

tr/s *tours par seconde* revolutions per second.

T.S.F. *Télégraphie sans fil* wireless telegraphy; wireless (set).

T.S.V.P. *tournez, s'il vous plaît* P.T.O., please turn over.

T.T.C. *toutes taxes comprises* all taxes included.

T.U. *temps universel* G.M.T., Greenwich mean time.

T.V. *télévision* TV, television.

T.V.A. *taxe à la valeur ajoutée* V.A.T., value-added tax.

U

UEO *Union européenne occidentale* WEU, Western European Union.

UEP *Union européenne de paiements* EPU, European Payments Union.

U.E.R. *unité d'enseignement et de recherche* area of study.

U.H.T. *ultra-haute température* ultra-high temperature.

UIE *Union internationale des étudiants* IUS, International Union of Students.

UIJS *Union internationale de la jeunesse socialiste* IUSY, International Union of Socialist Youth.

UIP *Union interparlementaire* IPU, Inter-parliamentary Union.

UIT *Union internationale des télécommunications* ITU, International Telecommunication Union.

U.N.E.D.I.C. *Union nationale pour l'emploi dans l'industrie et le commerce (unemployment insurance scheme).*

U.N.E.F. *Union nationale des étudiants de France* French National Union of Students.

UNESCO *Organisation des Nations Unies pour l'éducation, la science et la culture* UNESCO, United Nations Educational, Scientific, and Cultural Organization.

U.R.S.S. [yrs] *Union des républiques socialistes soviétiques* U.S.S.R., Union of Soviet Socialist Republics.

V

V *volt* V, volt.

v. *votre, vos* your; *voir, voyez* see; *vers* verse; *verset* versicle.

v/ *votre, vos* your.

Var. *variante* variant.

V.D.Q.S. *vin délimité de qualité supérieure (medium-quality wine).*

Ve *veuve* widow.

vo *verso* verso, back of the page.

vol. *volume* volume.

V/Réf. *votre référence* your reference.

vv. *vers* ll., lines.

Vve *veuve* widow.

W

W *watt* watt.

W. *ouest* W., west.

Wh *watt-heure* watt-hour.

W.L. *Wagons-lits* sleeping cars.

W.R. *Wagons-restaurants* dining cars.

X

X. *anonym* anonymous.

X.P. *exprès payé* express paid.

Z

Z.I. *zone industrielle* industrial area.

Z.U.P. *zone à urbaniser en priorité* priority development area *or* zone.

Numerals
Nombres

Cardinal Numbers — Nombres cardinaux

0 zéro *nought, zero, cipher*	60 soixante *sixty*
1 un, une *one*	70 soixante-dix *seventy*
2 deux *two*	71 soixante et onze *seventy-one*
3 trois *three*	72 soixante-douze *seventy-two*
4 quatre *four*	80 quatre-vingts *eighty*
5 cinq *five*	81 quatre-vingt-un *eighty-one*
6 six *six*	90 quatre-vingt-dix *ninety*
7 sept *seven*	91 quatre-vingt-onze *ninety-one*
8 huit *eight*	100 cent *a or one hundred*
9 neuf *nine*	101 cent un *one hundred and one*
10 dix *ten*	200 deux cents *two hundred*
11 onze *eleven*	211 deux cent onze *two hundred and eleven*
12 douze *twelve*	
13 treize *thirteen*	1000 mille *a or one thousand*
14 quatorze *fourteen*	1001 mille un *one thousand and one*
15 quinze *fifteen*	1100 onze cents *eleven hundred*
16 seize *sixteen*	1967 dix-neuf cent soixante-sept *nineteen hundred and sixty-seven*
17 dix-sept *seventeen*	
18 dix-huit *eighteen*	
19 dix-neuf *nineteen*	2000 deux mille *two thousand*
20 vingt *twenty*	1 000 000 un million *a or one million* [*million*⟩
21 vingt et un *twenty-one*	2 000 000 deux millions *two*⟩
22 vingt-deux *twenty-two*	1 000 000 000 un milliard *one thousand millions, Am. one billion*
30 trente *thirty*	
40 quarante *forty*	
50 cinquante *fifty*	

Ordinal Numbers — Nombres ordinaux

1er le premier, 1re la première *the first*	15e quinzième *fifteenth*
	16e seizième *sixteenth*
2e le deuxième, la deuxième *the second*	17e dix-septième *seventeenth*
	18e dix-huitième *eighteenth*
3e le *or* la troisième *the third*	19e dix-neuvième *ninteenth*
4e quatrième *fourth*	20e vingtième *twentieth*
5e cinquième *fifth*	21e vingt et unième *twenty-first*
6e sixième *sixth*	22e vingt-deuxième *twenty-second*
7e septième *seventh*	30e trentième *thirtieth*
8e huitième *eighth*	31e trente et unième *thirty-first*
9e neuvième *ninth*	40e quarantième *fortieth*
10e dixième *tenth*	41e quarante et unième *forty-first*
11e onzième *eleventh*	50e cinquantième *fiftieth*
12e douzième *twelfth*	51e cinquante et untième *fifty-first*
13e treizième *thirteenth*	
14e quatorzième *fourteenth*	60e soixantième *sixtieth*

61e soixante et unième *sixty-first*
70e soixante-dixième *seventieth*
71e soixante et onzième *seventy-first*
72e soixante-douzième *seventy-second*
80e quatre-vingtième *eightieth*
81e quatre-vingt-unième *eighty-first*

90e quatre-vingt-dixième *nine-tieth*
91e quatre-vingt-onzième *ninety-first*
100e centième *hundredth*
101e cent unième *hundred and first*
200e deux centième *two hundredth*
1000e millième *thousandth*

Fractions — Fractions

½ (un) demi *one half;* la moitié (*the*) half
1½ un et demi *one and a half*
⅓ un tiers *one third*
⅔ (les) deux tiers *two thirds*
¼ un quart *one quarter*
¾ (les) trois quarts *three quarters*

⅕ un cinquième *one fifth*
⅝ (les) cinq huitièmes *five eighths*
⁹⁄₁₀ (les) neuf dixièmes *nine tenths*
0,45 zéro, virgule, quarante-cinq *point four five*
17,38 dix-sept, virgule, trente-huit *seventeen point three eight*

French weights and measures
Mesures françaises

Linear Measures — Mesures de longueur

km	kilomètre	=	1000 m =	0.6214 mi.
hm	hectomètre	=	100 m =	109 yd. 1 ft. 1 in.
dam	décamètre	=	10 m =	32.808 ft.
m	mètre	=	1 m =	3.281 ft.
dm	décimètre	=	$\frac{1}{10}$ m =	3.937 in.
cm	centimètre	=	$\frac{1}{100}$ m =	0.394 in.
mm	millimètre	=	$\frac{1}{1000}$ m =	0.039 in.
µm or **µ**	micron	=	$\frac{1}{1\,000\,000}$ m =	0.000039 in.
	mille marin	=	1852 m =	6080 ft.

Square Measures — Mesures de surface

km²	kilomètre carré	=	1 000 000 m² =	0.3861 sq. mi.
hm²	hectomètre carré	=	10000 m² =	2.471 acres
dam²	décamètre carré	=	100 m² =	119.599 sq. yd.
m²	mètre carré	=	1 m² =	1.196 sq. yd.
dm²	décimètre carré	=	$\frac{1}{100}$ m² =	15.5 sq. in.
cm²	centimètre carré	=	$\frac{1}{10\,000}$ m² =	0.155 sq. in.
mm²	millimètre carré	=	$\frac{1}{1\,000\,000}$ m² =	0.002 sq. in.

Land Measures — Mesures de surfaces agraires

ha	hectare	=	100 a or	10000 m² =	2.471 acres
a	are	=	dam² or	100 m² =	119.599 sq. yd.
ca	centiare	=	$\frac{1}{100}$ a or	1 m² =	1.196 sq. yd.

Cubic Measures — Mesures de volume

m³	mètre cube	=	1 m³ =	35.32 cu. ft.
dm³	décimètre cube	=	$\frac{1}{1000}$ m² =	61.023 cu. in.
cm³	centimètre cube	=	$\frac{1}{1\,000\,000}$ m² =	0.061 cu. in.
mm³	millimètre cube	=	$\frac{1}{1\,000\,000\,000}$ m³ =	0.00006 cu. in.

Measures of Capacity — Mesures de capacité

hl	hectolitre	=	100 l =	22.01 gals.
dal	décalitre	=	10 l =	2.2 gals.
l	litre	=	1 l =	1.76 pt.
dl	décilitre	=	$\frac{1}{10}$ l =	0.176 pt.
cl	centilitre	=	$\frac{1}{100}$ l =	0.018 pt.
ml	millilitre	=	$\frac{1}{1000}$ l =	0.002 pt.
st	stère	=	1 m³ =	35.32 cu. ft. (of wood)

Weights — Poids

t	tonne	=	1 t *or* 1000 kg =	19.68	cwt.
q	quintal	=	¹/₁₀ t *or* 100 kg =	1.968	cwt.
kg	kilogramme	=	1000 g =	2.205	lb.
hg	hectogramme	=	100 g =	3.527	oz.
dag	décagramme	=	10 g =	5.644	dr.
g	gramme	=	1 g =	15.432	gr.
dg	décigramme	=	¹/₁₀ g =	1.543	gr.
cg	centigramme	=	¹/₁₀₀ g =	0.154	gr.
mg	milligramme	=	¹/₁₀₀₀ g =	0.015	gr.

Former Measures — Anciennes mesures

aune f	=	1,188 m	ell★
pied m	=	0,3248 m	foot
pouce m	=	¹/₁₂ pied *or* 27,07 mm	inch
ligne f	=	¹/₁₂ pouce *or* 2,258 mm	line
livre f	=	489,50 g; F 500 g	pound
lieue f	=	4 km	league
arpent m	=	42,21 a	acre

Conjugation of French verbs
Conjugaison des verbes français

In this section specimen verb-tables are set out. Within the body of the Dictionary every infinitive is followed by a number in brackets, *e.g.* (1a), (2b), (3c), *etc.* This number refers to the appropriate model or type in the following pages. (1a), (2a), (3a), (4a) are the **regular** verbs of their conjugation. Others have some irregularity or other special feature.

How to Form the Tenses

Impératif. Take the 2nd person singular and the 1st and 2nd persons plural of the *Indicatif présent*. In verbs of the 1st Conjugation the singular imperative has no final **s** unless followed by *en* or *y*.

Imparfait. From the 1st person plural of the *Indicatif présent*: replace **-ons** by **-ais** etc.

Participe présent. From the 1st person plural of the *Indicatif présent*: replace **-ons** by **-ant**.

Subjonctif présent. From the 3rd person plural of the *Indicatif présent*: replace **-ent** by **-e** etc.

Subjonctif imparfait. To the 2nd person singular of the *Passé simple* add **-se** etc.

Future simple. To the *Infinitif présent* add **-ai** etc.

Conditionnel présent. To the *Infinitif présent* add **-ais** etc.

★The English 'translation' given does not mean that the English measure of that name is exactly the same length, etc., as the French, e.g. the French *pouce* is 27,07 mm and the English *inch* is 25,4 mm.

Auxiliary Verbs

(1) être

A. Indicatif

I. Simple Tenses

Présent

	sg.	pl.
	je suis	nous sommes
	tu es	vous êtes
	il est	ils sont

Imparfait

	sg.	pl.
	j'étais	nous étions
	tu étais	vous étiez
	il était	ils étaient

Passé simple

	sg.	pl.
	je fus	nous fûmes
	tu fus	vous fûtes
	il fut	ils furent

Futur simple

	sg.	pl.
	je serai	nous serons
	tu seras	vous serez
	il sera	ils seront

Conditionnel présent

	sg.	pl.
	je serais	nous serions
	tu serais	vous seriez
	il serait	ils seraient

Participe présent

étant

Participe passé

été

II. Compound Tenses

Passé composé

j'ai été

Plus-que-parfait

j'avais été

Passé antérieur

j'eus été

Futur antérieur

j'aurai été

Conditionnel passé

j'aurais été

Participe composé

ayant été

Infinitif passé

avoir été

B. Subjonctif

I. Simple Tenses

Présent

	sg.	pl.
	que je sois	que nous soyons
	que tu sois	que vous soyez
	qu'il soit	qu'ils soient

Imparfait

	sg.	pl.
	que je fusse	que nous fussions
	que tu fusses	que vous fussiez
	qu'il fût	qu'ils fussent

Impératif

sois — soyons — soyez

II. Compound Tenses

Passé

que j'aie été

Plus-que-parfait

que j'eusse été

Auxiliary Verbs

(1) avoir

A. Indicatif

I. Simple Tenses

Présent

sg. j'ai
tu as
il a[1]

pl. nous avons
vous avez
ils ont

Imparfait

sg. j'avais
tu avais
il avait

pl. nous avions
vous aviez
ils avaient

Passé simple

sg. j'eus
tu eus
il eut

pl. nous eûmes
vous eûtes
ils eurent

Futur simple

sg. j'aurai
tu auras
il aura

pl. nous aurons
vous aurez
ils auront

Conditionnel présent

sg. j'aurais
tu aurais
il aurait

pl. nous aurions
vous auriez
ils auraient

Participe présent

ayant

Participe passé

eu (*f* eue)

II. Compound Tenses

Passé composé

j'ai eu

Plus-que-parfait

j'avais eu

Passé antérieur

j'eus eu

Futur antérieur

j'aurai eu

Conditionnel passé

j'aurais eu

Participe composé

ayant eu

Infinitif passé

avoir eu

B. Subjonctif

I. Simple Tenses

Présent

sg. que j'aie
que tu aies
qu'il ait

pl. que nous ayons
que vous ayez
qu'ils aient

Imparfait

sg. que j'eusse
que tu eusses
qu'il eût

pl. que nous eussions
que vous eussiez
qu'ils eussent

Impératif

aie — ayons — ayez

II. Compound Tenses

Passé

que j'aie eu

Plus-que-parfait

que j'eusse eu

---

[1] a-t-il?

(1 a) blâmer

First Conjugation

I. Simple Tenses

Présent

sg. je blâme
tu blâmes
il blâme[1]

pl. nous blâmons
vous blâmez
ils blâment

Passé simple

sg. je blâmai
tu blâmas
il blâma

pl. nous blâmâmes
vous blâmâtes
ils blâmèrent

Participe passé

blâmé, e

Infinitif présent

blâmer

[1] blâme-t-il?

Impératif

blâme[2]
blâmons
blâmez

Imparfait

sg. je blâmais
tu blâmais
il blâmait

pl. nous blâmions
vous blâmiez
ils blâmaient

Participe présent

blâmant

Futur simple

sg. je blâmerai
tu blâmeras
il blâmera

pl. nous blâmerons
vous blâmerez
ils blâmeront

[2] blâmes-en
blâmes-y

Conditionnel présent

sg. je blâmerais
tu blâmerais
il blâmerait

pl. nous blâmerions
vous blâmeriez
ils blâmeraient

Subjonctif présent

sg. que je blâme
que tu blâmes
qu'il blâme

pl. que nous blâmions
que vous blâmiez
qu'ils blâment

Subjonctif imparfait

sg. que je blâmasse
que tu blâmasses
qu'il blâmât

pl. que nous blâmassions
que vous blâmassiez
qu'ils blâmassent

II. Compound Tenses

(*Participe passé* with the help of **avoir** and **être**)

1. Actif

Passé composé: j'ai blâmé
Plus-que-parfait: j'avais blâmé
Passé antérieur: j'eus blâmé
Futur antérieur: j'aurai blâmé
Conditionnel passé: j'aurais blâmé

2. Passif

Présent: je suis blâmé
Imparfait: j'étais blâmé
Passé simple: je fus blâmé
Passé composé: j'ai été blâmé
Plus-que-parf.: j'avais été blâmé
Passé antérieur: j'eus été blâmé
Futur simple: je serai blâmé
Futur antérieur: j'aurai été blâmé
Conditionnel présent: je serais blâmé
Conditionnel passé: j'aurais été blâmé
Impératif: sois blâmé
Participe présent: étant blâmé
Participe composé: ayant été blâmé
Infinitif présent: être blâmé
Infinitif passe: avoir été blâmé

	Infinitif	Remarks	Présent de l'indicatif	Présent du subjonctif	Passé simple	Futur simple	Impératif	Participe passé
(1b)	aimer	Unstressed *ai-* may be pronounced [ɛ] or [e]	aime aimes aime aimons aimez aiment	aime aimes aime aimions aimiez aiment	aimai aimas aima aimâmes aimâtes aimèrent	aimerai aimeras aimera aimerons aimerez aimeront	aime aimons aimez	aimé, e
(1c)	appeler	The final consonant of the stem is doubled and [ə] becomes [ɛ] before a mute syllable (including the *fut.* and *cond.*)	appelle appelles appelle appelons appelez appellent	appelle appelles appelle appelions appeliez appellent	appelai appelas appela appelâmes appelâtes appelèrent	appellerai appelleras appellera appellerons appellerez appelleront	appelle appelons appelez	appelé, e
(1d)	amener	The **e** [ə] of the stem becomes **è** when stressed and also in the *fut.* and *cond.*	amène amènes amène amenons amenez amènent	amène amènes amène amenions ameniez amènent	amenai amenas amena amenâmes amenâtes amenèrent	amènerai amèneras amènera amènerons amènerez amèneront	amène amenons amenez	amené, e
(1e)	arguer	In this particular verb a mute **e** after the **u** is written **ë** and an **i** after the **u** is written **ï**	arguë arguës arguë arguons arguez arguënt	arguë arguës arguë arguions arguiez arguënt	arguai arguas argua arguâmes arguâtes arguèrent	arguërai arguëras arguëra arguërons arguërez arguëront	arguë arguons arguez	argué, e

	Infinitif	Remarks	Présent de l'indicatif	Présent du subjonctif	Passé simple	Futur simple	Impératif	Participe passé
(1f)	céder	The **é** of the stem becomes **è** when stressed, i.e. **not** in the *fut.* or *cond.*	cède cèdes cède cédons cédez cèdent	cède cèdes cède cédions cédiez cèdent	cédas cédas céda cédâmes cédâtes cédèrent	céderai céderas cédera céderons céderez céderont	cède cédons cédez	cédé, e
(1g)	abreger	The **é** of the stem becomes **è** when stressed, i.e. **not** in the *fut.* or *cond.* In addition, between the **g** and **a** or **o**, an **e** is inserted in the spelling but is not pronounced	abrège abrèges abrège abrégeons abrégez abrègent	abrège abrèges abrège abrégions abrégiez abrègent	abrégeas abrégeas abrégea abrégeâmes abrégeâtes abrégèrent	abrégerai abrégeras abrégera abrégerons abrégerez abrégeront	abrège abrégeons abrégez	abrégé, e
(1h)	employer	The **y** of the stem becomes **i** when followed by **a** mute **e** (including the *fut.* and *cond.*)	emploie emploies emploie employons employez emploient	emploie emploies emploie employions employiez emploient	employai employas employa employâmes employâtes employèrent	emploierai emploieras emploiera emploierons emploierez emploieront	emploie employons employez	employé, e

	Infinitif	Remarks	Présent de l'indicatif	Présent du subjonctif	Passé simple	Futur simple	Impératif	Participe passé
(1i)	payer	The **y** of the stem may be written **y** or **i** when followed by a mute **e** (including the *fut.* and *cond.*)	paie, paye paies, payes paie, paye payons payez paient, -yent	paie, paye paies, payes paie, paye payons payez paient, -yent	payai payas paya payâmes payâtes payèrent	paierai, paye.. paieras paiera paierons paierez paieront	paie, paye.. payons payez	payé, e
(1k)	menacer	**c** takes a cedilla (ç) before **a** and **o** to preserve the [s] sound	menace menaces menace menaçons menacez menacent	menace menaces menace menacions menaciez menacent	menaçai menaças menaça menaçâmes menaçâtes menacèrent	menacerai menaceras menacera menacerons menacerez menaceront	menace menaçons menacez	menacé, e
(1l)	manger	Between the **g** of the stem and an ending beginning **a** or **o**, a mute **e** is inserted to preserve the [ʒ] sound	mange manges mange mangeons mangez mangent	mange manges mange mangions mangiez mangent	mangeai mangeas mangea mangeâmes mangeâtes mangèrent	mangerai mangeras mangera mangerons mangerez mangeront	mange mangeons mangez	mangé, e
(1m)	conjuguer	The mute **u** at the end of the stem remains throughout, even before **a** and **o**.	conjugue conjugues conjugue conjuguons conjuguez conjuguent	conjugue conjugues conjugue conjuguions conjuguiez conjuguent	conjuguai conjuguas conjugua conjuguâmes conjuguâtes conjuguèrent	conjuguerai conjugueras conjuguera conjuguerons conjuguerez conjugueront	conjugue conjuguons conjuguez	conjugué, e

	Infinitif	Remarks	Présent de l'indicatif	Présent du subjonctif	Passé simple	Futur simple	Impératif	Participe passé
(1 n)	saluer	The **u** of the stem, pronounced [u], becomes [y] when stressed and in the *fut.* and *cond.*	salue salues salue saluons saluez saluent	salue salues salue saluions saluiez saluent	saluai saluas salua saluâmes saluâtes saluèrent	saluerai salueras saluera saluerons saluerez salueront	salue saluons saluez	salué, *e*
(1 o)	châtier	The **i** of the stem, pronounced [j], becomes [i] when stressed and in the *fut.* and *cond.* The 1st and 2nd persons pl. of the *pres. sbj.* and of the *impf. ind.* are **-iions, -iiez.**	châtie châties châtie châtions châtiez châtient	châtie châties châtie châtiions châtiiez châtient	châtiai châtias châtia châtiâmes châtiâtes châtièrent	châtierai châtieras châtiera châtierons châtierez châtieront	châtie châtions châtiez	châtié, *e*
(1 p)	allouer	The **ou** of the stem, pronounced [w], becomes [u] when stressed and in the *fut.* and *cond.*	alloue alloues alloue allouons allouez allouent	alloue alloues alloue allouions allouiez allouent	allouai allouas alloua allouâmes allouâtes allouèrent	allouerai alloueras allouera allouerons allouerez alloueront	alloue allouons allouez	alloué, *e*
(1 q)	aller		vais vas va allons allez vont	aille ailles aille allions alliez aillent	allai allas alla allâmes allâtes allèrent	irai iras ira irons irez iront	va (vas-y) allons allez	allé, *e*

	Infinitif	Remarks	Présent de l'indicatif	Présent du subjonctif	Passé simple	Futur simple	Impératif	Participe passé
(1r)	envoyer	Like (1h) but with an irregular *fut.* and *cond.*	envoie envoies envoie envoyons envoyez envoient	envoie envoies envoie envoyions envoyiez envoient	envoyai envoyas envoya envoyâmes envoyâtes envoyèrent	enverrai enverras enverra enverrons enverrez enverront	envoie envoyons envoyez	envoyé, *e*
(1s)	léguer	The **é** of the stem becomes **è** when stressed, i.e. **not** in the *fut.* or *cond.* In addition, the mute **u** at the end of the stem remains throughout, even before **a** and **o**.	lègue lègues lègue léguons léguez lèguent	lègue lègues lègue léguions léguiez lèguent	léguai léguas légua léguâmes léguâtes léguèrent	léguerai légueras léguera léguerons léguerez légueront	lègue léguons léguez	légué, *e*

Second Conjugation

Note the cases in which the verb stem is lengthened by ...**iss**...

I. Simple Tenses

Présent

sg. je punis
tu punis
il punit

pl. nous punissons
vous punissez
ils punissent

Passé simple

sg. je punis
tu punis
il punit

pl. nous punîmes
vous punîtes
ils punirent

Participe passé

puni, e

Infinitif présent

punir

Impératif

punis
punissons
punissez

Imparfait

sg. je punissais
tu punissais
il punissait

pl. nous punissions
vous punissiez
ils punissaient

Participe présent

punissant

Futur simple

sg. je punirai
tu puniras
il punira

pl. nous punirons
vous punirez
ils puniront

Conditionnel présent

sg. je punirais
tu punirais
il punirait

pl. nous punirions
vous puniriez
ils puniraient

Subjonctif présent

sg. que je punisse
que tu punisses
qu'il punisse

pl. que nous punissions
que vous punissiez
qu'ils punissent

Subjonctif imparfait

sg. que je punisse
que tu punisses
qu'il punît

pl. que nous punissions
que vous punissiez
qu'ils punissent

(2a) **punir**²,

II. Compound Tenses

Participe passé with the help of **avoir** and **être**; *see* (1a)

saillir is used only in the 3rd persons of the simple tenses. *P.pr.* **saillant**

¹) **saillir** is used only in the 3rd persons of the simple tenses. *P.pr.* **saillant**

	Infinitif	Remarks	Présent de l'indicatif	Présent du subjonctif	Passé simple	Futur simple	Impératif	Participe passé
(2b)	sentir	No stem lengthening by ...iss... The last consonant of the stem is lost in the 1st and 2nd persons sg. of the *pres. ind.* and the sg. *imper.*	sens sens sent sentons sentez sentent	sente sentes sente sentions sentiez sentent	sentis sentis sentit sentîmes sentîtes sentirent	sentirai sentiras sentira sentirons sentirez sentiront	sens sentons sentez	senti, *e*
(2c)	cueillir	*Pres., fut.* and derivatives like (1a)	cueille cueilles cueille cueillons cueillez cueillent	cueille cueilles cueille cueillions cueilliez cueillent	cueillis cueillis cueillit cueillîmes cueillîtes cueillirent	cueillerai cueilleras cueillera cueillerons cueillerez cueilleront	cueille cueillons cueillez	cueilli, *e*
(2d)	fuir	No stem lengthening by ...iss... Note the alternation between the **y** and **i**: y appears in 1st and 2nd persons pl. of *pres. ind.*, *pres. sbj.*, and *imper.*, in the *p.pr.* and throughout the *impf. ind.*	fuis fuis fuit fuyons fuyez fuient	fuie fuies fuie fuyions fuyiez fuient	fuis fuis fuit fuîmes fuîtes fuirent	fuirai fuiras fuira fuirons fuirez fuiront	fuis fuyons fuyez	fui, *e*

	Infinitif	Remarks	Présent de l'indicatif	Présent du subjonctif	Passé simple	Futur simple	Impératif	Participe passé
(2 e)	bouillir	*Pres. ind.* and derivatives like (4 a)	bous bous bout bouillons bouillez bouillent	bouille bouilles bouille bouillions bouilliez bouillent	bouillis bouillis bouillit bouillîmes bouillîtes bouillirent	bouillirai bouilliras bouillira bouillirons bouillirez bouilliront	bous bouillons bouillez	bouilli, *e*
(2 f)	couvrir	*Pres.* and derivatives like (1 a); *p.p.* in **-ert**	couvre couvres couvre couvrons couvrez couvrent	couvre couvres couvre couvrions couvriez couvrent	couvris couvris couvrit couvrîmes couvrîtes couvrirent	couvrirai couvriras couvrira couvrirons couvrirez couvriront	couvre couvrons couvrez	couvert, *e*
(2 g)	vêtir	As (2 b) but keeps the final consonant of the stem throughout the *pres. ind.* and the *imper.* and has *p.p.* in **-u**	vêts vêts vêt vêtons vêtez vêtent	vête vêtes vête vêtions vêtiez vêtent	vêtis vêtis vêtit vêtîmes vêtîtes vêtirent	vêtirai vêtiras vêtira vêtirons vêtirez vêtiront	vêts vêtons vêtez	vêtu, *e*
(2 h)	venir	Note that the ...**en**... of the *inf.* becomes ...**ien**... in the *fut.* and *cond.*, and when stressed except in the *p.s.* where it becomes ...**in**... [ɛ̃]. Note too the ...**d**... inserted in the *fut.* and *cond.*	viens viens vient venons venez viennent	vienne viennes vienne venions veniez viennent	vins vins vint vînmes vîntes vinrent	viendrai viendras viendra viendrons viendrez viendront	viens venons venez	venu, *e*

	Infinitif	Remarks	Présent de l'indicatif	Présent du subjonctif	Passé simple	Futur simple	Impératif	Participe passé
(2i)	courir	*Pres., p.p., fut.* and derivatives as in (4a) *p.s.* like (3a); ...**rr**... in *fut.* and *cond.*	cours cours court courons courez courent	coure coures coure courions couriez courent	courus courus courut courûmes courûtes coururent	courrai courras courra courrons courrez courront	cours courons courez	couru, *e*
(2k)	mourir	*Pres., fut.* and derivatives as in (4a) with change of ...**ou**... to ...**eu**... in the sg. and the 3rd person pl. of the *pres.*; *p.s.* like (3a); ...**rr**... in *fut.* and *cond.*	meurs meurs meurt mourons mourez meurent	meure meures meure mourions mouriez meurent	mourus mourus mourut mourûmes mourûtes moururent	mourrai mourras mourra mourrons mourrez mourront	meurs mourons mourez	mort, *e*
(2l)	acquérir	*Pres.* and derivatives as in (4a) with change of ...**ér**... to ...**ier**... (*ind.*) and ...**ièr**... (*sbj.*) [jɛri] when stressed; *p.p* in ...**is**; *fut.* and *cond.* in ...**err**..., not ...**érir**...	acquiers acquiers acquiert acquérons acquérez acquièrent	acquière acquières acquière acquérions acquériez acquièrent	acquis acquis acquit acquîmes acquîtes acquirent	acquerrai acquerras acquerra acquerrons acquerrez acquerront	acquiers acquiérons acquérez	acquis, *e*

	Infinitif	Remarks	Présent de l'indicatif	Présent du subjonctif	Passé simple	Futur simple	Impératif	Participe passé
(2 m)	haïr	Regular except that it loses trema from the i in the sg. of the *pres. ind.* and of the *imper.* with a corresponding change of pronunciation	hais [ɛ] hais haït haïssons haïssez haïssent	haïsse haïsses haïsse haïssions haïssiez haïssent	haïs [aˑ] haïs haït haïmes haïtes haïrent	haïrai haïras haïra haïrons haïrez haïront	hais [ɛ] haïssons haïssez	haï, e
(2 n)	faillir	Defective verb			faillis faillis faillit faillîmes faillîtes faillirent	faillirai failliras faillira faillirons faillirez failliront		failli, e
(2 o)	fleurir	Regular (like 2a) but in the sense of *prosper* has *p.pr.* **florissant** and *impf. ind.* **florissais,** etc.	fleuris fleuris fleurit fleurissons fleurissez fleurissent	fleurisse fleurisses fleurisse fleurissions fleurissiez fleurissent	fleuris fleuris fleurit fleurîmes fleurîtes fleurirent	fleurirai fleuriras fleurira fleurirons fleurirez fleuriront	fleuris fleurissons fleurissez	fleuri, e
(2 p)	saillir	Defective verb. *P.pr.* **saillant**	saille saillent	saille saillent		saillera sailleront		sailli, e

Infinitif	Remarks	Présent de l'indicatif	Présent du subjonctif	Passé simple	Futur simple	Impératif	Participe passé
(2q) gésir	Defective verb. Used only in *pres.* and *impf. ind. P.pr.* **gisant**	— — gît gisons gisez gisent					
(2r) ouïr	Defective verb						ouï, *e*
(2s) assaillir	*Pres.* and occasionally *fut.* and their derivatives like (1a)	assaille assailles assaille assaillons assaillez assaillent	assaille assailles assaille assaillions assailliez assaillent	assaillis assaillis assaillit assaillîmes assaillîtes assaillirent	assaillirai assailliras assaillira assaillirons assaillirez assailliront	assaille assaillons assaillez	assailli, *e*
(2t) défaillir	Like (2s). But there is an old 3rd person sg. *pres. ind.* **défaut** in addition	défaille défailles défaille défaillons défaillez défaillent	défaille défailles défaille défaillions défailliez défaillent	défaillis défaillis défaillit défaillîmes défaillîtes défaillirent	défaillirai défailliras défaillira défaillirons défaillirez défailliront	défaille défaillons défaillez	défailli, *e*
(2u) férir	Defective verb						féru, *e*
(2v) quérir	Defective verb						

(3a) recevoir

Third Conjugation

I. Simple Tenses

	Présent		Impératif		Futur simple		Subjonctif présent
sg.	je reçois tu reçois il reçoit		reçois recevons recevez	*sg.*	je recevrai tu recevras il recevra	*sg.*	que je reçoive que tu reçoives qu'il reçoive
pl.	nous recevons vous recevez ils reçoivent			*pl.*	nous recevrons vous recevrez ils recevront	*pl.*	que nous recevions que vous receviez qu'ils reçoivent

	Imparfait				Conditionnel présent		Subjonctif imparfait
sg.	je recevais tu recevais il recevait			*sg.*	je recevrais tu recevrais il recevrait	*sg.*	que je reçusse que tu reçusses qu'il reçût
pl.	nous recevions vous receviez ils recevaient			*pl.*	nous recevrions vous recevriez ils recevraient	*pl.*	que nous reçussions que vous reçussiez qu'ils reçussent

Passé simple

sg. je reçus
tu reçus
il reçut

pl. nous reçûmes
vous reçûtes
ils reçurent

Participe présent

recevant

Participe passé[1]

reçu, e

Infinitif présent

recevoir

II. Compound Tenses

Participe passé with the help of **avoir** and **être;** *see* (1 a)

---

[1] **devoir** and its derivative **redevoir** have **dû, due,** *m/pl.* **dus** and **redû, redue,** *m/pl.* **redus**

	Infinitif	Remarks	Présent de l'indicatif	Présent du subjonctif	Passé simple	Futur simple	Impératif	Participe passé
(3b)	apparoir	Defective verb	il appert					
(3c)	asseoir	There are alternative forms; *pres. ind.* **assois, assoie** etc.; *pres. sbj.* **assoie** etc.; *fut.* **assoirai** etc.; *imper.* **assois, assoyez; assoyons, assoyez;** *p.pr.* **assoyant;** *impf. ind.* **assoyais**	assieds assieds assied asseyons asseyez asseyent	asseye asseyes asseye asseyions asseyiez asseyent	assis assis assit assîmes assîtes assirent	assiérai assiéras assiéra assiérons assiérez assiéront	assieds asseyons asseyez	assis, e
	surseoir		sursois sursois sursoit sursoyons sursoyez sursoient	sursoie sursoies sursoie sursoyions sursoyiez sursoient	sursis sursis sursit sursîmes sursîtes sursirent	surseoirai surseoiras surseoira surseoirons surseoirez surseoiront	sursois sursoyons sursoyez	sursis, e
(3d)	choir	Defective verb. No *p.pr.* There are alternative forms: *fut.* **cherrai** etc.	chois chois choit		chus chus chut chûmes chûtes churent	choirai choiras choira choirons choirez choiront		chu, e

	Infinitif	Remarks	Présent de l'indicatif	Présent du subjonctif	Passé simple	Futur simple	Impératif	Participe passé
	déchoir	Defective verb. No impf. ind. and no p.pr.	déchois déchois déchoit déchoyons déchoyez déchoient	déchoie déchoies déchoie déchoyions déchoyiez déchoient	déchus déchus déchut déchûmes déchûtes déchurent	déchoirai déchoiras déchoira déchoirons déchoirez déchoiront		déchu, e
	échoir	Defective verb. P.pr. échéant. Impf. ind. il échoyait or échéait. There are alternative forms: fut. il écherra, ils écherront	il échoit ils échoient	qu'il échoie	il échut ils échurent	il échoira ils échoiront		échu, e
(3e)	falloir	Impersonal verb	il faut	qu'il faille	il fallut	il faudra		fallu inv.
(3f)	mouvoir	The ...ou... of the stem becomes ...eu... when stressed. **Promouvoir** is used chiefly in the inf., p.p. (**promu, e**) and compound tenses; **émouvoir** has p.p. **ému, e**	meus meus meut mouvons mouvez meuvent	meuve meuves meuve mouvions mouviez meuvent	mus mus mut mûmes mûtes murent	mouvrai mouvras mouvra mouvrons mouvrez mouvront	meus mouvons mouvez	mû, mue

	Infinitif	Remarks	Présent de l'indicatif	Présent du subjonctif	Passé simple	Futur simple	Impératif	Participe passé
(3g)	pleuvoir	Impersonal verb	il pleut	qu'il pleuve	il plut	il pleuvra		*plu inv.*
(3h)	pouvoir	In the *pres. ind.* the 1st person can also be **je puis** and the interrogative is **puis-je** not **peux-je**. No *imper.* In the sg. and 3rd person pl. the **...ou...** of the stem becomes **...eu...** when stressed	peux peux peut pouvons pouvez peuvent	puisse puisses puisse puissions puissiez puissent	pus pus put pûmes pûtes purent	pourrai pourras pourra pourrons pourrez pourront		*pu inv.*
(3i)	savoir	*P.pr.* **sachant**	sais sais sait savons savez savent	sache saches sache sachions sachiez sachent	sus sus sut sûmes sûtes surent	saurai sauras saura saurons saurez sauront	sache sachons sachez	*su, e*
(3k)	seoir	Defective verb. *P.pr.* **seyant** or **séant**. *Impf. ind.* is **il seyait, ils seyaient**	il sied ils siéent	il siée ils siéent		il siéra ils siéront		*sis, e*

	Infinitif	Remarks	Présent de l'indicatif	Présent du subjonctif	Passé simple	Futur simple	Impératif	Participe passé
(31)	valoir	**Prévaloir** forms its pres. sbj. regularly: **que je prévale**, etc. Note the fut. and cond. with **...d...**	vaux vaux vaut valons valez valent	vaille vailles vaille valions valiez vaillent	valus valus valut valûmes valûtes valurent	vaudrai vaudras vaudra vaudrons vaudrez vaudront		valu, e
(3m)	voir	Alternation between **i** and **y** as in (2d). **Pourvoir** and **prévoir** have fut. and cond. in **...oir...**; **pourvoir** has p.s. **pourvus**	vois vois voit voyons voyez voient	voie voies voie voyions voyiez voient	vis vis vit vîmes vîtes virent	verrai verras verra verrons verrez verront	vois voyons voyez	vu, e
(3n)	vouloir	The **...ou...** of the stem becomes **...eu...** when stressed. Note the fut. and cond. with **...d...**	veux veux veut voulons voulez veulent	veuille veuilles veuille voulions vouliez veuillent	voulus voulus voulut voulûmes voulûtes voulurent	voudrai voudras voudra voudrons voudrez voudront	veuille veuillons veuillez	voulu, e

Fourth Conjugation

In the regular 4th Conjugation verbs, the stem does not change

I. Simple Tenses

(4a) vendre

Présent[1]

sg. je vends
tu vends
il vend[2]

pl. nous vendons
vous vendez
ils vendent

Passé simple

sg. je vendis
tu vendis
il vendit

pl. nous vendîmes
vous vendîtes
ils vendirent

Participe passé

vendu, e

Infinitif présent

vendre

Impératif

vends
vendons
vendez

Imparfait

sg. je vendais
tu vendais
il vendait

pl. nous vendions
vous vendiez
ils vendaient

Participe présent

vendent

Futur simple

sg. je vendrai
tu vendras
il vendra

pl. nous vendrons
vous vendrez
ils vendront

Conditionnel présent

sg. je vendrais
tu vendrais
il vendrait

pl. nous vendrions
vous vendriez
ils vendraient

Subjonctif présent

sg. que je vende
que tu vendes
qu'il vende

pl. que nous vendions
que vous vendiez
qu'ils vendent

Subjonctif imparfait

sg. que je vendisse
que tu vendisses
qu'il vendît

pl. que nous vendissions
que vous vendissiez
qu'ils vendissent

II. Compound Tenses

Participe passé with the help of **avoir** and **être;** *see* (1a)

---

[1] **battre** and its derivatives have **bats, bats, bat** in the sg.; the pl. is regular: **battons,** etc.
[2] **rompre** and its derivatives have **il rompt.**

	Infinitif	Remarks	Présent de l'indicatif	Présent du subjonctif	Passé simple	Futur simple	Impératif	Participe passé
(4b)	boire	Note the ...v... in some forms and the ...u... [y] which appears instead of ...oi... The *p.s.* endings are as in (3a). *P.pr.* **buvant**	bois bois boit buvons buvez boivent	boive boives boive buvions buviez boivent	bus bus but bûmes bûtes burent	boirai boiras boira boirons boirez boiront	bois buvons buvez	bu, e
(4c)	braire	Defective verb. *Impf. ind.* is **il brayait**	il brait ils braient			il braira ils brairont		brait
(4d)	bruire	Defective verb. *Impf. ind.* is **bruissait** or **bruyait**	il bruit ils bruissent			il bruira		
(4e)	circoncire	Goes like (4i) except for *p.p.* **circoncis, e**	circoncis circoncis circoncit circoncisons circoncisez circoncisent	circoncise circoncises circoncise circoncisions circoncisiez circoncisent	circoncis circoncis circoncit circoncîmes circoncîtes circoncirent	circoncirai circonciras circoncira circoncirons circoncirez circonciront	circoncis circoncisons circoncisez	circoncis, e
(4f)	clore	Defective verb. Note the circumflex in the 3rd person sg. *pres. ind.* **clôt. Enclore** is conjugated like **clore,** but has all forms of the *pres. ind.*	je clos tu clos il clôt	close closes close closions closiez closent		clorai cloras clora clorons clorez cloront	clos	clos, e

	Infinitif	Remarks	Présent de l'indicatif	Présent du subjonctif	Passé simple	Futur simple	Impératif	Participe passé
	éclore	Defective verb	il éclôt ils éclosent	qu'il éclose qu'ils éclosent		il éclora ils écloront		éclos, e
(4g)	conclure	P.s. as in (3a). **Reclure** is used only in the *inf.*, the *p.p.* (**reclus, e**) and the *compound tenses*	conclus conclus conclut concluons concluez concluent	conclue conclues conclue concluions concluiez concluent	conclus conclus conclut conclûmes conclûtes conclurent	conclurai concluras conclura conclurons conclurez concluront	conclus concluons concluez	conclu, e
(4h)	conduire	**Luire, reluire, nuire** have not **t** in the *p.p.*	conduis conduis conduit conduisons conduisez conduisent	conduise conduises conduise conduisions conduisiez conduisent	conduisis conduisis conduisit conduisîmes conduisîtes conduisirent	conduirai conduiras conduira conduirons conduirez conduiront	conduis conduisons conduisez	conduit, e
(4i)	suffire	**Confire** has *p.p.* **confit, e**	suffis suffis suffit suffisons suffisez suffisent	suffise suffises suffise suffisions suffisiez suffisent	suffis suffis suffit suffîmes suffîtes suffirent	suffirai suffiras suffira suffirons suffirez suffiront	suffis suffisons suffisez	suffi *inv.*

	Infinitif	Remarks	Présent de l'indicatif	Présent du subjonctif	Passé simple	Futur simple	Impératif	Participe passé
(4k)	connaître	The î keeps its circumflex only in the 3rd person sg. pres. ind. and in the fut. and cond.; p.s. ends as in (3a). **Repaître** goes like **connaître**, **paître** has no p.s. and no p.p.	connais connais connaît connaissons connaissez connaissent	connaisse connaisses connaisse connaissions connaissiez connaissent	connus connus connut connûmes connûtes connurent	connaîtrai connaîtras connaîtra connaîtrons connaîtrez connaîtront	connais connaissons connaissez	connu, e
(4l)	coudre	Note that **...s...** replaces **...d...** before a vowel	couds couds coud cousons cousez cousent	couse couses couse cousions cousiez cousent	cousis cousis cousit cousîmes cousîtes cousirent	coudrai coudras coudra coudrons coudrez coudront	couds cousons cousez	cousu, e
(4m)	craindre	Note alternation of nasal **n** and **n mouillé** (**gn**); also **...d...** before the **...r...** only in the inf., fut. and cond. **Oindre** has only inf. and p.p.; **poindre** has only inf., 3rd person sg. pres. ind., fut. and cond., and the compound tenses	crains crains craint craignons craignez craignent	craigne craignes craigne craignions craigniez craignent	craignis craignis craignit craignîmes craignîtes craignirent	craindrai craindras craindra craindrons craindrez craindront	crains craignons craignez	craint, e

| Infinitif | Remarks | Présent | | Passé simple | Futur simple | Impératif | Participe passé |
		de l'indicatif	du subjonctif				
(4n) croire	P.s. ends as in (3a). Accroire occurs only in the *inf.*	crois crois croit croyons croyez croient	croie croies croie croyions croyiez croient	crus crus crut crûmes crûtes crurent	croirai croiras croira croirons croirez croiront	crois croyons croyez	cru, e
(4o) croître	The **i** keeps its circumflex only in the pres. ind. sg., imper. sg., and the fut. and cond. **Décroître** and **accroître** have no circumflex in p.s. or p.p.	croîs croîs croît croissons croissez croissent	croisse croisses croisse croissions croissiez croissent	crûs crûs crût crûmes crûtes crûrent	croîtrai croîtras croîtra croîtrons croîtrez croîtront	croîs croissons croissez	crû, crue *m/pl.* crus
(4p) dire	**Redire** is conjugated like **dire**. The other derivatives of **dire** have **...disez** in the 2nd person pl. pres. *ind.* and *imper.*, except **maudire** which is conjugated like (2a) but has *p.p.* **maudit, e**	dis dis dit disons dites disent	dise dises dise disions disiez disent	dis dis dit dîmes dîtes dirent	dirai diras dira dirons direz diront	dis disons dites	dit, e

	Infinitif	Remarks	Présent de l'indicatif	Présent du subjonctif	Passé simple	Futur simple	Impératif	Participe passé
(4 q)	écrire	Note the ...v... which appears when the verb-ending begins with a vowel	écris écris écrit écrivons écrivez écrivent	écrive écrives écrive écrivions écriviez écrivent	écrivis écrivis écrivit écrivîmes écrivîtes écrivirent	écrirai écriras écrira écrirons écrirez écriront	écris écrivons écrivez	écrit, e
(4 r)	faire	**Malfaire** is used only in the *inf.* and **forfaire** and **parfaire** only in the *inf.*, *p.p.* and compound tenses	fais fais fait faisons faites font	fasse fasses fasse fassions fassiez fassent	fis fis fit fîmes fîtes firent	ferai feras fera ferons ferez feront	fais faisons faites	fait, e
(4 s)	frire	Defective verb	fris fris frit			frirai friras frira frirons frirez friront	fris	frit, e
(4 t)	lire	*P.s.* ends as in (3a)	lis lis lit lisons lisez lisent	lise lises lise lisions lisiez lisent	lus lus lut lûmes lûtes lurent	lirai liras lira lirons lirez liront	lis lisons lisez	lu, e

	Infinitif	Remarks	Présent de l'indicatif	Présent du subjonctif	Passé simple	Futur simple	Impératif	Participe passé
(4 u)	luire	See (4 h). *P.s.* and *impf. sbj.* are rarely used						
(4 v)	mettre	Note that one **t** drops in the *pres. ind.* sg. and *imper.* sg.	mets mets met mettons mettez mettent	mette mettes mette mettions mettiez mettent	mis mis mit mîmes mîtes mirent	mettrai mettras mettra mettrons mettrez mettront	mets mettons mettez	mis, e
(4 w)	moudre	Note that **...l...** replaces **...d...** before a vowel	mouds mouds moud moulons moulez moulent	moule moules moule moulions mouliez moulent	moulus moulus moulut moulûmes moulûtes moulurent	moudrai moudras moudra moudrons moudrez moudront	mouds moulons moulez	moulu, e
(4 x)	naître	Note that **...ss...t...** replaces **...t...** in the *pres. ind.* pl. and its derivatives; note the circumflex in *il* **naît** in the *fut.* and *cond.*, and the *p.p.* **né.** In **renaître** the *p.p.* and the compound tenses are not used	nais nais naît naissons naissez naissent	naisse naisses naisse naissions naissiez naissent	naquis naquis naquit naquîmes naquîtes naquirent	naîtrai naîtras naîtra naîtrons naîtrez naîtront	nais naissons naissez	né, e

	Infinitif	Remarks	Présent de l'indicatif	Présent du subjonctif	Passé simple	Futur simple	Impératif	Participe passé
(4y)	occire	Defective verb						occis, *e*
(4z)	plaire	P.s. ends as in (3a). **Taire** has no circumflex in **il tait**; *p.p.* **tu, e**	plais plais plaît plaisons plaisez plaisent	plaise plaises plaise plaisions plaisiez plaisent	plus plus plut plûmes plûtes plurent	plairai plairas plaira plairons plairez plairont	plais plaisons plaisez	plu *inv.*
(4aa)	prendre		prends prends prend prenons prenez prennent	prenne prennes prenne prenions preniez prennent	pris pris prit prîmes prîtes prirent	prendrai prendras prendra prendrons prendrez prendront	prends prenons prenez	pris, *e*
(4bb)	résoudre	**Absoudre** has *p.p.* **absous, absoute**, but no *p.s.* or *impf. sbj.* **Dissoudre** goes like **absoudre**	résous résous résout résolvons résolvez résolvent	résolve résolves résolve résolvions résolviez résolvent	résolus résolus résolut résolûmes résolûtes résolurent	résoudrai résoudras résoudra résoudrons résoudrez résoudront	résous résolvons résolvez	résolu, *e* In 🜊 résous
(4cc)	rire	P.p. as in (2a)	ris ris rit rions riez rient	rie ries rie riions riiez rient	ris ris rit rîmes rîtes rirent	rirai riras rira rirons rirez riront	ris rions riez	ri *inv.*

Infinitif	Remarks	Présent de l'indicatif	Présent du subjonctif	Passé simple	Futur simple	Impératif	Participe passé
(4dd) sourdre	Defective verb. The past tenses are rare	il sourd ils sourdent	qu'il sourde qu'ils sourdent	il sourdit ils sour- dirent	il sourdra ils sourdront		
(4ee) suivre	Note the p.p. **suivi, e**. **S'ensuivre** occurs only in the 3rd person of each tense	suis suis suit suivons suivez suivent	suive suives suive suivions suiviez suivent	suivis suivis suivit suivîmes suivîtes suivirent	suivrai suivras suivra suivrons suivrez suivront	suis suivons suivez	suivi, e
(4ff) traire	Defective verb. No *impf. sbj.*; **raire** goes like **traire**; p.p. **rait** is *inv.*	trais trais trait trayons trayez traient	traie traies traie trayions trayiez traient		trairai trairas traira trairons trairez trairont	trais trayons traiyez	trait, e
(4gg) vaincre	No **t** in the 3rd person sg. *pres. ind.* Note **c** is replaced by **qu** before a vowel except in the p.p. **vaincu, e**	vaincs vaincs vainc vainquons vainquez vainquent	vainque vainques vainque vainquions vainquiez vainquent	vainquis vainquis vainquit vainquîmes vainquîtes vainquirent	vaincrai vaincras vaincra vaincrons vaincrez vaincront	vaincs vainquons vainquez	vaincu, e
(4hh) vivre	Note omission of the final **v** of the stem in the *pres. ind.* sg., the *p.s.* and the *p.p.*	vis vis vit vivons vivez vivent	vive vives vive vivions viviez vivent	vécus vécus vécut vécûmes vécûtes vécurent	vivrai vivras vivra vivrons vivrez vivront	vis vivons vivez	vécu, e

Second Part

English-French

Contents

Table des matières

Preface

Language has two faces: one looking back, one looking forward. This revised edition of the "Standard French Dictionary" has tried to take both of these aspects into account: In retaining some of yesterday's speech, it will help the user to grapple with the great 19th century authors, whether for school or for pleasure. At the same time, he will find language's path into the future staked out by such words as: *acceleration lane, acid rain, antipollution device, cassette recorder, chat show, deejay, ecocide, typing pool, etc., etc.*

Needless to say, a great deal of the material old and new is made up of phrases and phraselike expressions covering all registers of speech from everyday language down to slang. Irregular forms of verbs and nouns have been put in their proper alphabetic position to help the beginner.

After each entry word the phonetic transcription has been given, using the system of the International Phonetic Association. For English entry words syllabification has been indicated by centred dots. American English, both spelling and usage, has been the object of particular attention.

We recommend the user to read carefully pages 603–604 – instructions on how to use the dictionary, which should increase its practical value. On page 605 ff. there is the explanation of the devices used to save space without sacrificing clarity.

A series of appendices to the dictionary proper gives lists – of proper names, of common abbreviations, of numerals, weights and measures – as well as a list of irregular verbs and an introduction to the conjugations of English verbs.

LANGENSCHEIDT

Préface

La langue a deux visages: l'un est tourné vers le passé, l'autre vers le futur. Cette nouvelle édition du «Standard French Dictionary» s'efforce de tenir compte de ces deux aspects: En gardant une certaine partie du vocabulaire d'hier, il aidera l'utilisateur dans la lecture des auteurs classiques, que ce soit à l'école ou pour son plaisir personnel; mais d'autre part, pour rendre son dû à l'aspect «futuriste» de la langue, de nombreux «mots nouveaux» ont été introduits, comme par ex.: *acceleration lane, acid rain, antipollution device, cassette recorder, chat show, deejay, ecocide, typing pool, etc., etc.*

Il va sans dire qu'une bonne partie de ce dictionnaire consiste en phrases et expressions idiomatiques appartenant à tous les niveaux de langue. Les formes irrégulières des verbes et des substantifs sont mises à leur place alphabétique pour aider les débutants.

À la suite de chaque mot-souche la prononciation est indiquée entre crochets selon le système de l'Association Phonétique Internationale. En outre, pour les mots-souches anglais la division en syllabes est marquée par des points à l'intérieur des mots. L'américain, tant dans son orthographe que dans ses idiotismes, a été l'objet d'une attention spéciale et détaillée.

Nous recommandons la lecture attentive des pages 603/604 – indications pour l'emploi du dictionnaire qui en releveront la valeur pratique. A la page 605 ss. on trouvera l'explication des expédients auxquels on a eu recours pour gagner de la place sans nuire à la clarté.

En complément du dictionnaire proprement dit on trouvera des listes – de noms propres, d'abréviations usuelles, de nombres, de poids, de mesures, – ainsi qu'une liste des verbes irréguliers et une introduction aux conjugaisons des verbes anglais.

LANGENSCHEIDT

Directions for the use of this dictionary
Indications pour l'emploi de ce dictionnaire

1. **Arrangement.** The alphabetic order of the entry words has been observed throughout. Hence you will find, in their proper alphabetic order:

a) the irregular forms of verbs, nouns, comparatives and superlatives;

b) the various forms of the pronouns;

c) compounds.

2. **Homonyms** of different etymologies have been subdivided by exponents;

e.g. *March*[1] mars ...
march[2] marche ...
march[3] marche ...

3. **Vocabulary.** Some of the numerous nouns ending in ...*er*, ...*ing*, ...*ism*, ...*ist* or ...*ness* and adjectives formed with *in*... or *un*... have not been listed in this dictionary. In order to find out their meanings, look up the radical.

4. **Differences in meaning.** The different senses of English words have been distinguished by:

a) explanatory additions given in italics after a translation;

e.g. **a·bate** ...(ra)baisser (*le prix*); ... tomber (*vent*); ...
an·cient 2. *the* ∼*s pl.* les anciens *m|pl.* (*grecs et romains*);

b) symbols and abbreviations before the particular meaning (see list on pages 605–607). If, however, the symbol or abbreviation applies to all translations alike, it is placed

1. **Classement.** L'ordre alphabétique des mots-souches a été rigoureusement observé. Ainsi on trouvera dans leur ordre alphabétique:

a) les formes irrégulières des verbes, des noms, des comparatifs et des superlatifs;

b) les formes diverses des pronoms;

c) les mots composés.

2. Les **homonymes** d'étymologie différente font l'objet d'articles différents distingués par un chiffre placé en haut derrière le mot en question;

p.ex. *March*[1] mars ...
march[2] marche ...
march[3] marche ...

3. **Vocabulaire.** De nombreux noms à terminaison en ...*er*, ...*ing*, ...*ism*, ...*ist* ou ...*ness*, ainsi que beaucoup d'adjectifs formés à l'aide des préfixes *in*... ou *un*... n'ont pas été inclus dans ce dictionnaire. Pour trouver leurs sens il faut chercher les radicaux appropriés.

4. **Distinction de sens.** Les différents sens des mots anglais se reconnaissent grâce à:

a) des additions explicatives, en italique, placées à la suite des versions proposées;

p.ex. **a·bate** ...(ra)baisser (*le prix*); ... tomber (*vent*); ...
an·cient 2. *the* ∼*s pl.* les anciens *m|pl.* (*grecs et romains*);

b) des symboles ou des définitions en abrégé qui les précèdent (voir liste pages 605–607). Si, cependant, les symboles ou abréviations se rapportent à l'ensemble des tra-

between the entry word and its phonetic transcription.

A semicolon separates a given meaning from another one which is essentially different.

5. **Letters in brackets** within an entry word indicate that in most cases in British English the word is spelt with the letter bracketed, in American English without.

6. The **indication of the parts of speech** has been omitted when it is obvious.

7. **Syllabification** has been indicated by centred dots in all entry words of more than one syllable. If, however, a syllabification dot coincides with a stress mark the former is left out.

8. In order to save space we have omitted:

a) *to* before English infinitives;

b) the phonetic transcriptions of compounds whose component parts are separate entry words with transcriptions;

c) the phonetic transcriptions of entry words having one of the endings listed on page 611. In this case the entry word itself takes the stress mark.

9. **Preterite and past participle** of irregular verbs have been given as separate entries. [*irr.*] given after the infinitive of each irregular verb refers to the list of the strong and irregular weak verbs at the end of this volume (pages 1257–1260). Irregular forms of compound verbs, however, have not been listed; instead, their infinitive has been supplemented by [*irr.*] and the respective radical in round brackets;

e.g. **un·der·stand** [*irr.* (*stand*)].

ductions, ils sont intercalés entre le mot-souche et la transcription phonétique.

Le point-virgule sépare une acception d'une autre essentiellement différente.

5. Les **lettres entre parenthèses** dans les mots-souches indiquent que dans la plupart des cas en anglais britannique le mot s'écrit avec cette lettre, pendant qu'en anglais américain sans cette lettre.

6. **L'indication des différentes fonctions des mots** est omise lorsqu'elle est évidente.

7. Les **points de séparation de syllabes** à l'intérieur des mots-souches de plus d'une syllabe indiquent après quelles syllabes le mot peut se diviser. Si, cependant, le point de séparation coïncide avec l'apostrophe d'accentuation, on laisse de côté le point.

8. Afin de gagner de la place, nous avons omis:

a) *to* devant les infinitifs anglais;

b) la transcription phonétique de mots composés dont les parties composantes sont données en tant que mots-souches individuels avec leurs transcriptions;

c) les transcriptions phonétiques de mots-souches possédant l'une des terminaisons mentionnées page 611. L'apostrophe d'accentuation de ces mots se trouve à l'intérieur même du mot-souche.

9. Le **prétérite et le participe passé** des verbes irréguliers se trouvent dans le vocabulaire sous forme de mots-souches individuels. [*irr.*] après l'infinitif de chaque verbe irrégulier renvoie à la liste des verbes forts et verbes faibles irréguliers à la fin de ce dictionnaire (pages 1257–1260). Les formes irrégulières des verbes composés sont supprimées; au lieu de quoi leurs infinitifs sont supplementés par [*irr.*] et leurs radicaux;

p.ex. **un·der·stand** [*irr.* (*stand*)].

Key to the symbols and abbreviations
Explication des symboles et des abréviations

1. Symbols

The tilde (∼, ∼) serves as a mark of repetition. To save space, compound entry words are often given with a tilde replacing one part.

The tilde in bold type (∼) replaces the entry word at the beginning of the entry;

e.g. **day** ...; '**∼·book** = daybook.

The simple tilde (∼) replaces:

a) the entry word immediately preceding (which itself may contain a tilde in bold type);

   e.g. **half** ...; ∼ *a crown* = half a crown;
   day ...; '**∼·light** ...; ∼*-saving time* = daylight-saving time;

b) within the phonetic transcription, the whole of the pronunciation of the preceding entry word, or of some part of it which remains unchanged;

   e.g. **bill**[1] [bil] ...; **bill**[2] [∼] ...; **pil·lar** ['pilə] ...; **pil·lared** ['∼ləd] = ['piləd].

The tilde with a circle (≗, ≗).

When the first letter changes from small to capital or vice-versa, the usual tilde is replaced by a tilde with circle (≗, ≗);

e.g. **grand** ...; ≗ *Duchess* = Grand Duchess; **can·dle** ...; '≗·**mas** = Candlemas.

□ after an adjective indicates that the adjective takes the regular adverbial form;

e.g. **bit·ter** □ = bitterly; **a·ble** □ = ably; **hap·py** □ = happily.

1. Symboles

Le tilde (∼, ∼) est le signe de la répétition. Afin de gagner de la place, souvent le mot-souche ou un de ses éléments a été remplacé par le tilde.

Le tilde en caractère gras (∼) remplace le mot-souche qui se trouve au début de l'article;

p.ex. **day** ...; '**∼·book** = daybook.

Le tilde simple (∼) remplace:

a) le mot-souche qui précède (qui d'ailleurs peut également être formé à l'aide du tilde en caractère gras);

   p.ex. **half** ...; ∼ *a crown* = half a crown;
   day ...; '**∼·light** ...; ∼*-saving time* = daylight-saving time;

b) dans la transcription phonétique, la prononciation entière ou la partie qui demeure inchangée;

   p.ex. **bill**[1] [bil] ...; **bill**[2] [∼] ...; **pil·lar** ['pilə] ...; **pil·lared** ['∼ləd] = ['piləd].

Le tilde avec cercle (≗, ≗).

Quand la première lettre se transforme de minuscule en majuscule ou vice versa, le tilde normal est remplacé par le tilde avec cercle (≗, ≗);

p.ex. **grand** ...; ≗ *Duchess* = Grand Duchess; **can·dle** ...; '≗·**mas** = Candlemas.

□ placé après un adjectif signifie qu'à partir de lui un adverbe régulier peut se former;

p.ex. **bit·ter** □ = bitterly; **a·ble** □ = ably; **hap·py** □ = happily.

($\sim$ally) after an adjective indicates that an adverb is formed by affixing -ally to the entry word;

e.g. **ar·o·mat·ic** ($\sim$ally) = aromatically.

When there is but one adverbial form for adjectives ending in both -ic and -ical, this is indicated in the following way:

his·tor·ic, his·tor·i·cal □,

i.e. historically is the adverb of both adjectives.

The other symbols used in this dictionary are:

F *familier*, colloquial.
V *vulgaire*, vulgar.
† *vieilli*, obsolete.
⚘ *botanique*, botany.
⊕ *technologie*, technology; *mécanique*, mechanics.
⚒ *mines*, mining.
✕ *militaire*, military.
⚓ *nautique*, nautical; *marine*, navy.
✝ *commerce*, commercial; *finances*, finance.

($\sim$ally) placé après un adjectif signifie qu'à partir de lui un adverbe peut se former en ajoutant -ally au mot-souche;

p.ex. **ar·o·mat·ic** ($\sim$ally) = aromatically.

Quand il n'y a qu'un seul adverbe pour des adjectifs à terminaison en -ic et -ical, c'est indiqué de manière suivante:

his·tor·ic, his·tor·i·cal □,

c.-à-d. historically est l'adverbe des deux adjectifs.

Les autres symboles employés dans ce dictionnaire sont:

🚂 *chemin de fer*, railway, *Am.* railroad.
✈ *aviation*, aviation.
♪ *musique*, music.
⌂ *architecture*, architecture.
⚡ *électricité*, electricity.
⚖ *droit*, law.
Å *mathématique*, mathematics.
⚲ *agriculture*, agriculture.
⚗ *chimie*, chemistry.
⚕ *médecine*, medicine.
⊘ *blason*, heraldry.

2. Abbreviations – Abréviations

a.	*aussi*, also.	*co.*	*comique*, comical.
abr.,	*abréviation*, abbreviation.	*coll.*	*collectif*, collective.
abbr.		*comp.*	*comparatif*, comparative.
adj.	*adjectif*, adjective.	*cond.*	*conditionnel*, conditional.
admin.	*administration*, administration.	*cons.*	*consonne*, consonant.
		cost.	*costume*, costume.
adv.	*adverbe*, adverb.	*cuis.*	*cuisine*, culinary art.
alp.	*alpinisme*, mountaineering.	*cycl.*	*cyclisme*, cycling.
Am.	Americanism, *américanisme*.	*dém.*	*démonstratif*, demonstrative.
anat.	*anatomie*, anatomy.		
Angl.	*Angleterre*, England.	*dial.*	*dialectal*, dialectal.
approx.	*approximativement*, approximately.	*eccl.*	*ecclésiastique*, ecclesiastical.
		écoss.	*écossais*, Scottish.
art.	*article*, article.	*enf.*	*enfantin*, childish speech.
astr.	*astronomie*, astronomy.	*èquit.*	*èquitation*, horsemanship.
attr.	*attribut*, attributively.	*etc.*	*et caetera*, and so on.
bibl.	*biblique*, biblical.	*É.-U.*	*États-Unis*, U.S.A.
biol.	*biologie*, biology.	*f*	*féminin*, feminine.
box.	*boxe*, boxing.	*fig.*	figuratively, *sens figuré*.
Brit.	British, *britannique*.	*foot.*	*football*, football.
cin.	*cinéma*, cinema.	*Fr.*	French, *français*.
cj.	*conjonction*, conjunction.	*fut.*	*futur*, future.

géog.	*géographie,* geography.		*p.pr.*	*participe présent,* present participle.
géol.	*géologie,* geology.			
gér.	*gérondif,* gerund.		*préf.*	*préfixe,* prefix.
gramm.	*grammaire,* grammar.		*prét.*	*prétérit,* preterite.
gymn.	*gymnastique,* gymnastics.		*pron.*	*pronom,* pronoun.
hist.	*histoire,* history.		*prov.*	*provincialisme,* provincialism.
icht.	*ichtyologie,* ichthyology.			
impér.	*impératif,* imperative.		*prp.*	*préposition,* preposition.
impf.	*imparfait,* imperfect.		*p.s.*	*passé simple,* past tense.
ind.	*indicatif,* indicative.		*psych.*	*psychologie,* psychology.
indéf.	*indéfini,* indefinite.		*q., q.*	*quelqu'un,* someone.
inf.	*infinitif,* infinitive.		*qch., qch.*	*quelque chose,* something.
int.	*interjection,* interjection.			
interr.	*interrogatif,* interrogative.		*qqfois*	*quelquefois,* sometimes.
inv.	*invariable,* invariable.		*rel.*	*relatif,* relative.
Ir.	*Irish, irlandais.*		*sbj.*	*subjonctif,* subjunctive.
iro.	*ironiquement,* ironically.		*sc.*	*scilicet,* namely, *c'est-à-dire.*
irr.	*irrégulier,* irregular; *see page 604.*		*sg.*	*singulier,* singular.
			sl.	slang, *argot.*
journ.	*journalisme,* journalism.		*s.o.*	someone, *quelqu'un.*
ling.	*linguistique,* linguistics.		*souv.*	*souvent,* often.
m	*masculin,* masculine.		*sp.*	*sport,* sports.
mes.	*mesure,* measure.		*s.th.*	something, *quelque chose.*
métall.	*métallurgie,* metallurgy.		*str.*	strictly taken, *au sens étroit.*
météor.	*météorologie,* meteorology.			
min.	*minéralogie,* mineralogy.		*su.*	*substantif,* substantive; *nom,* noun.
mot.	motoring, *automobilisme.*			
myth.	*mythologie,* mythology.		*sup.*	*superlatif,* superlative.
n	*neutre,* neuter.		*surt.*	*surtout,* especially.
nég.	*négatif,* negative.		*surv.*	surveying, *arpentage.*
npr.	*nom propre,* proper name.		*tél.*	*télégraphie,* telegraphy.
opt.	*optique,* optics.		*téléph.*	*téléphonie,* telephony.
orn.	*ornithologie,* ornithology.		*télév.*	*télévision,* television.
o.s.	oneself, *soi-même.*		*tex.*	*industries textiles,* textiles.
parl.	*parlement,* parliament.		*théâ.*	*théâtre,* theatre.
peint.	*peinture,* painting.		*(TM)*	trademark, *marque déposée.*
péj.	*sens péjoratif,* pejoratively.		*typ.*	*typographie,* typography.
pers.	*personnel,* personal.		*univ.*	*université,* university.
p.ex.	*par exemple,* for example.		*usu.*	usually, *d'ordinaire.*
p.ext.	*par extension,* more widely taken.		*v/aux.*	*verbe auxiliaire,* auxiliary verb.
pharm.	*pharmacie,* pharmacy.			
phls.	*philosophie,* philosophy.		*vét.*	*vétérinaire,* veterinary.
phot.	*photographie,* photography.		*v/i.*	*verbe intransitif,* intransitive verb.
phys.	*physique,* physics.			
physiol.	*physiologie,* physiology.		*v/impers.*	*verbe impersonnel,* impersonal verb.
pl.	*pluriel,* plural.			
poét.	*poétique,* poetic.		*v/rfl.*	*verbe réfléchi,* reflexive verb.
pol.	*politique,* politics.		*v/t.*	*verbe transitif,* transitive verb.
poss.	*possessif,* possessive.			
p.p.	*participe passé,* past participle.		*vt/i.*	*verbe transitif et intransitif,* transitive and intransitive verb.
			zo.	*zoologie,* zoology.

The phonetic symbols
of the International Phonetic Association

Signes phonétiques
de l'Association Phonétique Internationale

A. Voyelles et Diphtongues

[ɑ:] a long, clair, postérieur, comme dans pâte, âme, pâle: *far* [fɑ:], *father* ['fɑ:ðə].

[ʌ] n'existe pas en français. A bref, obscur, sans que les lèvres ne s'arrondissent. Se forme à l'avant de la bouche, ouvertement: *butter* ['bʌtə], *come* [kʌm], *colour* ['kʌlə], *blood* [blʌd], *flourish* ['flʌriʃ], *twopence* ['tʌpəns].

[æ] clair, plutôt ouvert, pas trop bref. On relève la langue vers la partie antérieure du palais dur, en appliquant les lèvres contre les dents: *fat* [fæt], *man* [mæn].

[ɛə] e ouvert, semi-long, pas trop ouvert; ne se trouve en anglais que devant le r qui apparaît en tant que [ə] après l'e ouvert: *bare* [bɛə], *pair* [pɛə], *there* [ðɛə].

[ai] a clair entre le [ɑ:] et le [æ], et un i plus faible, ouvert. La langue s'élève à demi comme pour prononcer l'i: *I* [ai], *lie* [lai], *dry* [drai].

[au] a clair entre le [ɑ:] et le [æ], et un [u] plus faible, ouvert: *house* [haus], *now* [nau].

[e] e court à demi ouvert, un peu moins pur que l'e dans paix: *bed* [bed], *less* [les].

[ei] e à demi ouvert, tendant à finir en i; la langue se soulève à demi comme pour prononcer l'i: *date* [deit], *play* [plei], *obey* [o'bei].

[ə] son glissant, semblable à l'e muet du français debout, mais plus rapide: *about* [ə'baut], *butter* ['bʌtə], *connect* [kə'nekt].

[i:] i long, comme ça vie, bible, mais un peu plus ouvert qu'en français; se prononce avec redoublement dans le sud de l'Angleterre, la langue se soulevant lentement pour prononcer l'i: *scene* [si:n], *sea* [si:], *feet* [fi:t], *ceiling* ['si:liŋ].

[i] i court, ouvert, qui n'existe pas en français; s'articule avec les lèvres lâches: *big* [big], *city* ['si-ti].

[iə] i à demi ouvert, semi-long, finissant en [ə]: *here* [hiə], *hear* [hiə], *inferior* [in'fiəriə].

[ɔ:] son ouvert, long, entre l'a et l'o: *fall* [fɔ:l], *nought* [nɔ:t], *or* [ɔ:], *before* [bi'fɔ:].

[ɔ] son ouvert, court, entre l'a et l'o, un peu comme [ɑ:] très bref, les muscles peu tendus: *god* [gɔd], *not* [nɔt], *wash* [wɔʃ], *hobby* ['hɔ-bi].

[ɔi] o ouvert et i ouvert plus faible. La langue se soulève à demi comme pour prononcer l'i: *voice* [vɔis], *boy* [bɔi], *annoy* [ə'nɔi].

[o] o fermé rapide: *obey* [o'bei], *molest* [mo'lest].

[ou] o long, à demi ouvert, finissant en [u] faible; lèvres non arrondies, langue non soulevée: *note*

[nout], *boat* [bout], *below* [bi'lou].

[ə:] n'existe pas en français; un peu comme l'[œ:] dans peur, mais les lèvres ne s'avancent ni s'arrondissent: *word* [wə:d], *girl* [gə:l], *learn* [lə:n], *murmur* ['mə:mə].

[u:] [u] long comme dans poule, mais sans que les lèvres s'arrondissent; se prononce souvent comme [u] long, à demi ouvert, se terminant en [u] fermé: *fool* [fu:l], *shoe* [ʃu:], *you*

[ju:], *rule* [ru:l], *canoe* [kə'nu:].

[u] [u] rapide: *put* [put], *look* [luk], *careful* ['kɛəful].

[uə] [u] à demi ouvert et à demi long, se terminant en [ə]: *poor* [puə], *sure* [ʃuə], *allure* [ə'ljuə].

Parfois on emploie les nasales françaises suivantes: [ɑ̃] comme dans *détente*, [ɔ̃] comme dans *bonbon*, et [ɛ̃] comme dans *vin*.

La **longueur d'une voyelle** se traduit par [:], p.ex. *ask* [ɑ:sk], *astir* [əs'tə:].

B. Consonnes

[r] ne se prononce que devant les voyelles. Tout à fait différent du r vélaire français. Le bout de la langue forme avec la partie antérieure du palais un passage étroit, par lequel le souffle, voisé, passe, sans pourtant que le son soit roulé. A la fin d'un mot, r ne se prononce qu'en liaison avec la voyelle initiale du mot suivant: *rose* [rouz], *pride* [praid], *there is* [ðɛər'iz].

[ʒ] ch sonore, comme g dans génie, j dans journal: *gentle* ['dʒentl], *jazz* [dʒæz], *large* [lɑ:dʒ], *azure* ['æʒə].

[ʃ] ch sourd, comme dans champ, cher: *shake* [ʃeik], *fetch* [fetʃ], *chivalrous* ['ʃivlrəs].

[θ] n'existe pas en français; résulte de l'application de la langue contre les incisives supérieures: *thin* [θin], *path* [pɑ:θ], *method* ['meθəd].

[ð] le même son sonorisé: *there* [ðɛə], *breathe* [bri:ð], *father* ['fɑ:ðə].

[s] sifflante sourde, comme dans sourd, sot: *see* [si:], *hats* [hæts], *decide* [di'said].

[z] sifflante sonore, comme dans chose, zèle: *zeal* [zi:l], *rise* [raiz], *horizon* [hə'raizn].

[ŋ] n'existe pas en français (sauf dans quelques mots empruntés à l'anglais comme *meeting*); se prononce comme pour une voyelle nasale mais en abaissant le voile du palais vers la fin, de sorte à produire une espèce de n guttural: *ring* [riŋ], *singer* ['siŋə], *finger* ['fiŋgə], *ink* [iŋk].

[w] [u] rapide, prononcé lèvre contre lèvre; se forme avec la bouche dans la même position que u elle allait prononcer [u:]: *will* [wil], *swear* [swɛə], *queen* [kwi:n].

[f] labiale sourde: *fat* [fæt], *tough* [tʌf], *effort* ['efət].

[v] labiale sonore: *vein* [vein], *velvet* ['velvit].

[j] son rapide comme l'i dans diable ou l'y dans yeux: *onion* ['ʌnjən], *yes* [jes], *filial* ['filjəl].

La prononciation des autres consonnes correspond à peu près à celle du français, mais en anglais les occlusives sont plus plosives.

C. Apostrophes d'accentuation

L'accentuation des mots anglais est indiquée par le signe ['] devant la syllabe à accentuer; p.ex. **on·ion** ['ʌnjən]. Si deux des syllabes d'un mot donné se trouvent pourvues d'une apostrophe d'accentuation, à faut les accentuer également tous les deux; p.ex. **up·stairs** ['ʌp'stɛəz], cependant, souvent on n'accentue que l'une des deux syllabes, selon la position du mot dans l'ensemble de la phrase, ou en langue emphatique; p.ex. *upstairs* dans *"the upstairs rooms"* [ðɪ ˈʌpstɛəz ˈrumz] et *"on going upstairs"* [ɔn ˈgouiŋ ʌpˈstɛəz].

Dans les mots-souches composés, dont les éléments sont donnés dans le dictionnaire en tant que mots-souches indépendants avec leurs transcriptions phonétiques, et dans les mots-souches qui possèdent l'une des terminaisons mentionnées sous D, l'apostrophe d'accentuation est donnée dans le mot-souche lui-même. L'accentuation est indiquée également dans le mot-souche, si on ne donne qu'une partie de la transcription phonétique et que l'accent ne porte pas sur la première syllabe de la partie phonétique remplacée par un tilde; p.ex. **ad'min·is·tra·tor** [ʌtə]. Si, cependant, l'accent porte sur la première syllabe ou sur une partie phonétique transcrite, l'apostrophe d'accentuation n'est pas donnée dans le mot-souche, mais se trouve dans la partie entre crochets; p.ex. **ac·cu·rate** [ˈ~rit], **ad·a·man·tine** [~ˈmæntain].

D. Syllabes finales sans symboles phonétiques

Afin de gagner de la place, nous donnerons ici les terminaisons les plus fréquentes des mots-souches avec leur transcription phonétique; par conséquent, ils figurent, sauf exception, dans le dictionnaire sans transcription phonétique. Ces terminaisons ne se trouvent pas transcrites non plus, quand elles sont précédées d'une consonne qui n'a pas été donnée dans les symboles phonétiques du mot précédent, mais qui en français, comme en anglais, demande le même signe phonétique; p.ex. -tation, -ring.

-ability [-əbiliti]	-ent [-e(ə)nt]	-ize [-aiz]
-able [-əbl]	-er [-ə]	-izing [-aiziŋ]
-age [-idʒ]	-ery [-əri]	-less [-lis]
-al [-(ə)l]	-ess [-is]	-ly [-li]
-ally [-(ə)li]	-fication [-fikeiʃ(ə)n]	-ment(s) [-mənt(s)]
-an [-(ə)n]	-ial [-(ə)l]	-ness [-nis]
-ance [-(ə)ns]	-ible [-əbl]	-oid [-ɔid]
-ancy [-ənsi]	-ian [-(jə)n]	-oidic [-ɔidik]
-ant [-ənt]	-ic(s) [-ik(s)]	-or [-ə]
-ar [-ə]	-ical [-ik(ə)l]	-ous [-əs]
-ary [-(ə)ri]	-ily [-ili]	-ry [-ri]
-ation [-eiʃ(ə)n]	-iness [-inis]	-ship [-ʃip]
-cious [-ʃəs]	-ing [-iŋ]	-(s)sion [-ʃ(ə)n]
-cy [-si]	-ish [-iʃ]	-sive [-siv]
-dom [-dəm]	-ism [-iz(ə)m]	-ties [-tiz]
-ed [-d; -t; -id]*	-ist [-ist]	-tion [-ʃ(ə)n]
-edness [-dnis;	-istic [-istik]	-tious [-ʃəs]
-tnis; -idnis]	-ite [-ait]	-trous [-trəs]
-ee [-iː]	-ity [-iti]	-try [-tri]
-en [-n]	-ive [-iv]	-y [-i]
-ence [-(ə)ns]	-ization [-aizeiʃ(ə)n]	

Pour la prononciation de l'américain, voir à la page 613.

---

* [-d] après voyelles et consonnes sonores; [-t] après consonnes sourdes; [-id] après d et t finals.

The spelling of American English
L'orthographe de l'américain

L'orthographe de l'anglais de l'Amérique (AA) se distingue de l'anglais britannique (AB) par les particularités suivantes:

1. L'**u** tombe dans la terminaison **-our**; p.ex. col*o*r, hum*o*r, hon*o*rable, fav*o*r.

2. **-er** au lieu de l'AB **-re** dans les syllabes finales; p.ex. cent*er*, fib*er*, theat*er*, mais pas dans massacre.

3. Le redoublement de la consonne finale **l** ne se produit que quand l'accent principal porte sur la syllabe finale; d'où p.ex. AA counci*l*or, jewe*l*ry, quarre*l*ed, trave*l*ed, woo*l*en au lieu de l'AB councillor, jewellery, quarrelled, travelled, woollen; d'autre part on trouve en AA enroll(s), fulfill(s), skillful, installment au lieu de l'AB enrol(s), fulfil(s), skilful, instalment.

4. En AA **s** au lieu du **c** en AB, surtout dans la syllabe finale **-ence**; p.ex. defe*n*se, offe*n*se, lice*n*se, mais aussi en AA practice et practise en tant que verbe.

5. On simplifie et on abandonne couramment les terminaisons d'origine étrangère; p.ex. dialog(*ue*), prolog(*ue*), catalog(*ue*), program(*me*), envelop(*e*).

6. La simplification d'**ae** et d'**œ** ou **oe** en **e** est également courante; p.ex. an(*a*)emia, an(*a*)esthesia, man*e*uvers = AB manœuvers, subp(*o*)ena.

7. On préfère la terminaison **-ction** à **-xion**; p.ex. conne*ction*, infle*ction*.

8. On trouve fréquemment une simplification des consonnes; p.ex. wag*o*n, kidna*p*er, worshi*p*er, benefi*t*ed pour l'AB waggon, kidnapper, worshipper, benefitted.

9. L'AA préfère **o** à **ou**; p.ex. m*o*(u)ld, sm*o*(u)lder, pl*o*w au lieu de l'AB plough.

10. L'**e** muet disparaît dans des mots comme abridg(*e*)ment, judg(*e*)ment, acknowledg(*e*)ment.

11. L'AA utilise le préfixe **in-** au lieu de **en-** plus souvent que l'AB; p.ex. *in*close, *in*case.

12. L'AA préfère l'orthographe suivante dans des cas particuliers: *check* = AB cheque, *hello* = AB hallo, *cozy* = AB cosy, *mustache* = AB moustache, *skeptic* = AB sceptic, *peddler* = AB pedlar, *gray* = AB grey, *tire* = AB tyre.

13. A côté de although, through, on trouve les formules familières *altho*, *thru*.

The pronunciation of American English
La prononciation de l'américain

L'anglais de l'Amérique (AA), en ce qui concerne l'intonation, le rythme et le son, se distingue de l'anglais britannique (AB) par les particularités suivantes:

1. **Intonation:** L'AA est plus monotone que l'AB.

2. **Rythme:** Des mots à une ou plusieurs syllabes après la syllabe principale accentuée ['] ont en AA un accent secondaire très marqué [ˌ], que les mots en AB n'ont pas ou n'ont que dans une faible mesure; p.ex. dictionary [AA ˈdikʃəˌnɛri = AB ˈdikʃənri], secretary [AA ˈsekrəˌtɛri = AB ˈsekrətri]; en AA, les voyelles courtes accentuées s'allongent (*American drawl*); p.ex. food [AA fuːd = AB fud], capital [AA ˈkæːpətəl = AB ˈkæpitl]; en AA, la syllabe inaccentuée (après une syllabe accentuée) subit un affaiblissement qui adoucit p, t, k en b, d, g; p.ex. property [AA ˈprabərti = AB ˈprɔpəti], united [AA juˈnaidid = AB juːˈnaitid].

3. Une autre particularité courante dans la façon de parler américaine, par opposition à l'AB, c'est la **nasalisation** avant et après une consonne nasale [m, n, ŋ] (*nasal twang*), ainsi que la prononciation plus fermée de [e] et de [o] en tant que premier élément d'une diphtongue; p.ex. home [AA hoːm], take [AA teːk].

4. Le **r** écrit à la finale après une voyelle, ou entre une voyelle et une consonne, se prononce clairement (r rétrofléchi); p.ex. car [AA kɑːr = AB kɑː], care [AA kɛr = AB kɛə], border [AA ˈbɔːrdər = AB ˈbɔːdə].

5. L'**o** [AB ɔ] se prononce en AA un peu comme l'**a** voilé [AA ɑ]; p.ex. dollar [AA ˈdɑlər = AB ˈdɔlə], college [AA ˈkɑlidʒ = AB ˈkɔlidʒ], lot [AA lɑt = AB lɔt], problem [AA ˈprɑbləm = AB ˈprɔbləm]; dans de nombreux cas [ɑ] et [ɔ] peuvent exister simultanément.

6. L'**a** [AB ɑː] donne [æ] ou [æː] en AA dans des mots du genre pass [AA pæ(ː)s = AB pɑːs], answer [AA ˈæ(ː)nsər = AB ˈɑːnsə], dance [AA dæ(ː)ns = AB dɑːns], half [AA hæ(ː)f = AB hɑːf], laugh [AA læ(ː)f = AB lɑːf].

7. L'**u** [AB juː] après consonne dans les syllabes qui portent l'accent principal donne en AA [uː]; p.ex. Tuesday [AA ˈtuːzdi = AB ˈtjuːzdi], student [AA ˈstuːdənt = AB ˈstjuːdənt], mais pas dans music [AA, AB = ˈmjuːzik], fuel [AA, AB = ˈfjuːəl].

8. Le suffixe **-ile** (en AB de préférence [-ail]) s'abrège en AA très souvent en [-əl] ou [-il]; p.ex. futile [AA ˈfjuːtəl = AB ˈfjuːtail], textile [AA ˈtekstil] = AB ˈtekstail]; quant à [-əl] ou [-il] il n'y a pas de prononciation obligatoire.

9. La terminaison **-ization** (AB le plus souvent [-aiˈzeiʃən]) se prononce en AA de préférence [-əˈzeiʃən]. Cette différence de sons correspond au rapport des prononciations AA (préférée) [ə] et AB (standard) [i]; p.ex. editor [AA ˈedətər = AB ˈeditə], basket [AA ˈbæ(ː)skət = AB ˈbɑːskit].

A

A, a [ei] A *m*, a *m*.

a *gramm.* [ei; ə] *article*: un(e *f*); **20 miles a day** 20 milles par jour; **2 shillings a pound** 2 shillings la livre.

A 1 ['ei'wʌn] F de première qualité.

a·back [ə'bæk] masqué (*voile*); F **taken ~** déconcerté, interdit, étonné.

ab·a·cus ['æbəkəs], *pl.* **-ci** ['‿sai] boulier *m* compteur; △ abaque *m*.

a·baft ⚓ [ə'bɑːft] **1.** *adv.* sur l'arrière; **2.** *prp.* en arrière de.

a·ban·don [ə'bændən] abandonner (*a. sp.*), délaisser (*q.*), renoncer à (*un projet*); **~ o.s. to** se livrer à; **a'ban·doned** *adj.* dévergondé; abandonné; **a'ban·don·ment** abandon (-nement) *m*.

a·base [ə'beis] abaisser; F ravaler (*q.*); **a'base·ment** abaissement *m*; humilité *f*.

a·bash [ə'bæʃ] confondre, déconcerter, interdire; **~ed** *at* confus de; **a'bash·ment** confusion *f*, embarras *m*.

a·bate [ə'beit] *v/t.* diminuer; faire cesser (*la douleur*); (r)abattre (*l'orgueil*); (ra)baisser (*le prix*); ⚖ annuler; mettre fin à (*un abus*); *v/i.* diminuer, s'affaiblir, s'apaiser, se modérer; tomber (*vent*); baisser (*prix*); **a'bate·ment** diminution *f*, affaiblissement *m*; *prix, eaux*: baisse *f*; *tempête*: apaisement *m*.

ab·a(t)·tis ✕ [ə'bætis] abattis *m*.

ab·at·toir [æbətwɑː] abattoir *m*.

ab·ba·cy ['æbəsi] dignité *f* d'abbé; **'ab·bess** abbesse *f*; **ab·bey** ['æbi] abbaye *f*; **ab·bot** ['æbət] abbé *m*, supérieur *m*.

ab·bre·vi·ate [ə'briːvieit] abréger (*a. Å*); **ab·bre·vi'a·tion** abréviation *f*.

ABC ['ei'biː'siː] ABC *m*; 🚂 indicateur *m* alphabétique; abécédaire *m*; **~ warfare** guerre *f* atomique, bactériologique (*ou* microbienne) et chimique.

ab·di·cate ['æbdikeit] *v/t.* abdiquer (*le trône*); renoncer à (*un droit*); ré-

signer (*une fonction*); *v/i.* abdiquer; **ab·di·ca·tion** abdication *f*, démission *f*.

ab·do·men *anat.* ['æbdəmen; 🩺 æb-'doumen] abdomen *m*; ventre *m*; **ab·dom·i·nal** [æb'dɔminl] abdominal (-aux *m/pl.*).

ab·duct [æb'dʌkt] enlever; **ab'duc·tion** enlèvement *m*; **ab'duc·tor** ravisseur *m*.

a·be·ce·dar·i·an [eibiːsiː'dɛəriən] **1.** abécédaire; ignorant; **2.** élève *mf* d'une classe élémentaire.

a·bed [ə'bed] au lit, couché.

ab·er·ra·tion [æbə'reiʃn] aberration *f*.

a·bet [ə'bet] encourager; prêter assistance à; (*usu.* **aid and ~**) être le complice de; **a'bet·ment** encouragement *m*; complicité *f* (dans, *in*); **a'bet·tor** complice *mf*; fauteur (-trice *f*) *m* (de, *in*).

a·bey·ance [ə'beiəns] suspension *f*; ⚖ **in ~** en suspens, pendant; vacant (*estate*).

ab·hor [əb'hɔː] abhorrer; **ab·hor·rence** [əb'hɔrns] horreur *f*, aversion *f* (pour, *of*); **hold in ~** avoir en horreur; **ab'hor·rent** □ répugnant (à, *to*); incompatible (avec, *to*); contraire (à, *to*).

a·bide [ə'baid] [*irr.*] *v/i.* demeurer; **~ by** rester fidèle à (*une promesse*), maintenir; *v/t.* attendre; **I cannot ~ him** je ne peux pas le sentir *ou* supporter; **a'bid·ing** □ permanent.

a·bil·i·ty [ə'biliti] capacité *f*; **to the best of one's ~** de son mieux; **a'bil·i·ties** *pl.* intelligence *f*; aptitude *f*.

ab·ject □ ['æbdʒekt] misérable; servile; **ab'jec·tion**, **ab'ject·ness** abjection *f*, misère *f*.

ab·jure [əb'dʒuə] abjurer; renoncer à.

a·blaze [ə'bleiz] en flammes; *a. fig.* enflammé (de, *with*).

a·ble □ ['eibl] capable; habile; compétent; ⚖ apte; **be ~ to** (*inf.*) être à même de (*inf.*); pouvoir (*inf.*); **~ to**

pay en mesure de payer; ⁓**bod·ied** ['⁓'bɔdid] robuste; ✕ bon pour le service; ♏ ⁓ *seaman* matelot *m* de deuxième classe.

ab·lu·tion [ə'bluːʃn] ablution *f.*

ab·ne·gate ['æbnigeit] renoncer à; faire abnégation de (*droits etc.*); **ab·ne'ga·tion** renoncement *m*; désaveu *m*; (*a. self-*⁓) abnégation *f* de soi.

ab·nor·mal □ [æb'nɔːml] anormal (-aux *m/pl.*); **ab'nor·ma·li·ty** caractère *m* anormal; difformité *f.*

a·board ♏ [ə'bɔːd] à bord (de); *Am.* 🚋, 🚂, *bus, tram: all*⁓! en voiture!; ♏ embarquez!

a·bode [ə'boud] 1. *prét. et p.p. de abide*; 2. demeure *f*; résidence *f*; séjour *m.*

a·bol·ish [ə'bɔliʃ] abolir, supprimer; **a'bol·ish·ment**, **ab·o·li·tion** [æbə'liʃn] suppression *m*, suppression *f*; **ab·o'li·tion·ist** abolitionniste *mf.*

A-bomb ['eibɔm] *see atomic bomb.*

a·bom·i·na·ble □ [ə'bɔminəbl] abominable; **a·bom·i'na·tion** abomination *f*, horreur *f.*

ab·o·rig·i·nal [æbə'ridʒənl] □ aborigène, indigène, primitif (-ive *f*); **ab·o'rig·i·nes** [⁓niːz] *pl.* aborigènes *m/pl.*

a·bort *biol.* [ə'bɔːt] avorter; ✕, *espace:* ⁓ *a mission* interrompre *ou* abandonner une mission; **a'bor·tion** avortement *m*; *fig.* œuvre *f* manquée; monstre *m*; *procure* ⁓ faire avorter; **a'bor·tive** □ abortif (-ive *f*); avorté (*projet*); mort-né (*projet*).

a·bound [ə'baund] abonder (en *with, in*); foisonner (de *with, in*).

a·bout [ə'baut] 1. *prp.* autour de; environ, presque; au sujet de; ⁓ *the house* quelque part dans la maison; ⁓ *the streets* dans les rues; *I had no money* ⁓ *me* je n'avais pas d'argent sur moi; ⁓ *ten o'clock* vers 10 heures; *he is* ⁓ *my height* il a à peu près la même taille que moi; *talk* ⁓ *business* parler affaires; *what are you* ⁓? qu'est-ce que vous faites là?; *send s.o.* ⁓ *his business* envoyer promener q.; 2. *adv.* tout autour; à l'entour; çà et là; de ci, de là; *be* ⁓ *to do* être sur le point de faire; *a long way* ⁓ un long détour; *bring* ⁓ accomplir; faire naître; *come* ⁓ arriver; *right* ⁓! demi-tour!; ⁓ *turn!* demi-tour à droite!

a·bove [ə'bʌv] 1. *prp.* au-dessus de, par-dessus; au delà de; *fig.* supérieur à; ⁓ *300* plus de 300; ⁓ *all (things)* surtout; *be* ⁓ *s.o. in* surpasser q. par (*l'intelligence etc.*); *fig. it is* ⁓ *me* cela me dépasse; 2. *adv.* en haut; là-haut; au-dessus; *over and* ⁓ en outre; 3. *adj.* précédent; *the* ⁓ *points* ce qui a été mentionné plus haut, les remarques précédentes; 4. *su.:* *the* ⁓ le susdit; **a'bove-'board** loyal (-aux *m/pl.*), franc(he *f*); **a'bove-'ground** au-dessus de terre; vivant; **a'bove-'men·tioned** susmentionné, (cité) ci-dessus.

ab·ra·ca·dab·ra [æbrəkə'dæbrə] baragouin *m.*

ab·rade [ə'breid] user par le frottement; écorcher (*la peau*).

ab·ra·sion [ə'breiʒn] frottement *m*; attrition *f*; 🩹 écorchure *f*, excoriation *f*; *monnaies:* frai *m*; **ab'ra·sive** ⊕ abrasif *m.*

a·breast [ə'brest] de front; côte à côte; ⁓ *of* (*ou with*) à la hauteur de; *keep* ⁓ *of* marcher de pair avec.

a·bridge [ə'bridʒ] abréger; *fig.* restreindre; **a'bridg(e)·ment** raccourcissement *m*; abrégé *m*, résumé *m*; restriction *f.*

a·broad [ə'brɔːd] à l'étranger, en voyage; sorti (*de la maison*); *there is a report* ⁓ le bruit court que; *the thing has got* ⁓ la nouvelle s'est répandue; F *he is all* ⁓ il est tout désorienté.

ab·ro·gate ['æbrogeit] abroger; **ab·ro'ga·tion** abrogation *f.*

ab·rupt □ [ə'brʌpt] brusque, précipité; saccadé, abrupt (*style*); à pic (*montagne*); **ab'rupt·ness** brusquerie *f*; *chemin:* raideur *f.*

ab·scess ['æbsis] abcès *m.*

ab·scond [æb'skɔnd] s'évader (de, *from*), s'enfuir; se soustraire à la justice; F décamper, filer.

ab·sence ['æbsns] absence *f*; éloignement *m* (de, *from*); ⁓ *of mind* distraction *f*; *leave of* ⁓ permission *f*, congé *m.*

ab·sent 1. □ ['æbsnt] absent, manquant; *fig.* = '⁓-'mind·ed □ distrait; 2. [æb'sent]: ⁓ *o.s.* s'absenter (de, *from*); **ab·sen·tee** [æbsn'tiː] absent(e *f*) *m*; ⁓ *ballot* vote *m* par correspondance; ⁓ *voter* électeur (-trice *f*) *m* par correspondance; **ab·sen'tee·ism** absence *f* de l'ate-

lier; absentéisme *m*; F carottage *m*.
ab·sinth ['æbsinθ] absinthe *f*.
ab·so·lute ☐ ['æbsəluːt] absolu; autoritaire; ♪♫ irrévocable; F achevé (*coquin etc.*); **'ab·so·lute·ness** caractère *m* absolu; **ab·so·lu·tion** absolution *f*; **'ab·so·lut·ism** *hist.* absolutisme *m*.
ab·solve [əb'zɔlv] absoudre (de, *from*), remettre (*un péché*); dispenser, affranchir (de, *from*).
ab·sorb [əb'sɔːb] absorber; amortir (*un choc*); résorber (*un excédent*); *fig.* engloutir; ~ed *in* absorbé dans; tout entier à; **ab'sorb·ent** absorbant (*a. su./m*).
ab·sorp·tion [əb'sɔːpʃn] absorption *f*; *choc*: amortissement *m*; *fig.* engloutissement *m*; *esprit*: absorbement *m*. .
ab·stain [əb'stein] s'abstenir (de, *from*); ~ *from meat* faire maigre; *parl.* ~ (*from voting*) s'abstenir (de voter); **ab'stain·er** (*souv. total* ~) abstème *mf*.
ab·ste·mi·ous ☐ [əb'stiːmiəs] sobre, tempérant.
ab·sten·tion [æb'stenʃn] abstinence *f* (de, *from*); *parl.* abstention *f*.
ab·ster·gent [əb'stəːdʒnt] **1.** abstergent (*a. su./m*); **2.** ♂ détersif *m*.
ab·sti·nence ['æbstinəns] abstinence *f* (de, *from*); *total* ~ abstinence *f* complète; **'ab·sti·nent** ☐ abstinent, sobre.
ab·stract 1. ['æbstrækt] ☐ abstrait; F abstrus (*a*.); **2.** [~] abstrait *m*; résumé *m*, abrégé *m*; *gramm.* ~ (*noun*) nom *m* abstrait; *in the* ~ du point de vue abstrait, en théorie; **3.** [æb'strækt] *v/t.* soustraire (à, *from*); détourner (*l'attention*); dérober (à, *from*); résumer (*un livre*); ⌐ₘ extraire; **ab'stract·ed** ☐ *fig.* distrait, rêveur (-euse *f*); **ab'strac·tion** *papiers etc.*: soustraction *f*; vol *m*; *phls.* abstraction *f*; distraction *f* (*d'esprit*); ⌐ₘ extraction *f*.
ab·struse ☐ [æb'struːs] *fig.* abstrus, obscur; caché; **ab'struse·ness** obscurité *f*, caractère *m* abstrus *etc.*
ab·surd ☐ [əb'sɔːd] absurde, déraisonnable; F idiot; **ab'surd·i·ty** absurdité *f*; absurde *m*.
a·bun·dance [ə'bʌndəns] abondance *f*, affluence *f*; épanchement *m* (*du cœur*); **a'bun·dant** ☐ abondant, copieux (-euse *f*); ~ *in* abondant

en; **a'bun·dant·ly** abondamment.
a·buse 1. [ə'bjuːs] abus *m*; insultes *f/pl*; **2.** [~z] abuser de, mésuser de, faire abus de; maltraiter (*q.*); dénigrer (*q.*); injurier; **a'bu·sive** ☐ abusif (-ive *f*); injurieux (-euse *f*) (*propos*); *be* ~ dire des injures (à, *to*).
a·but [ə'bʌt] aboutir (à, *upon*), confiner (à, *upon*); △ s'appuyer (contre *on*, *against*); **a'but·ment** △ arc-boutant (*pl.* arcs-boutants) *m*; *pont*: butée *f*; *voûte*: pied-droit (*pl.* pieds-droits) *m*; **a'but·ter** propriétaire *m* limitrophe.
a·bysm [ə'bizm] *see* abyss; **a'bys·mal** ☐ insondable; **a·byss** [ə'bis] abîme *m*, gouffre *m*.
a·ca·cia ♀ [ə'keiʃə] acacia *m*.
ac·a·dem·ic, ac·a·dem·i·cal ☐ [ækə'demik(l)] académique; *academic freedom* liberté *f* de l'enseignement; *academic year* année *f* universitaire; **a·cad·e'mi·cian** [əkædə'miʃn] académicien *m*; **ac·a'dem·ics** *pl.* discussion *f* abstraite.
a·cad·e·my [ə'kædəmi] académie *f*.
a·can·thus [ə'kænθəs] ♀ acanthe *f*; △ (feuille *f* d')acanthe *f*.
ac·cede [æk'siːd] ~ *to* accueillir (*une demande*); entrer en possession de (*une charge*); monter sur (*le trône*).
ac·cel·er·ate [æk'seləreit] (s')accélérer; *v/t. fig.* activer; **ac·cel·er·a·tion** accélération *f*; *mot.* ~ *lane* rampe *f* d'accès; **ac'cel·er·a·tor** *mot.* accélérateur *m*.
ac·cent 1. ['æksnt] accent *m*; ♪ temps *m* fort; temps *m* marqué; ton *m*; voix *f*; **2.** [æk'sent] accentuer (*a. fig.*) appuyer sur, souligner.
ac·cen·tu·ate [æk'sentjueit] accentuer; faire ressortir; **ac·cen·tu·a·tion** accentuation *f*.
ac·cept [ək'sept] accepter; agréer (*des vœux*); (*ou* ~ *of*) ♀ accepter, prendre en recette; admettre; **ac·cept·a·ble** ☐ [ək'septəbl] acceptable, agréable (à, *to*); **ac'cepta·ble·ness** acceptabilité *f*; **ac'cept·ance** acceptation *f*; accueil *m* favorable; réception *f*; ♀ *article*: réception *f*; *traite*: acceptation *f*; **ac·cep·ta·tion** [æksep'teiʃn] acception *f*, signification *f* (*d'un mot*); **ac'cept·ed** ☐ reconnu, admis; **ac'cept·er, ac'cept·or** acceptant(e *f*) *m*; ♀ tiré *m*; accepteur *m*.

ac·cess ['ækses] **1.** accès *m* (*a.* ♀, *a. ordinaire*), abord *m* (à, to); entrée *f*; *easy of* ~ abordable; ~ *to power* accession *f* au pouvoir; **2.** *ordinateur:* accéder à; **ac'ces·sa·ry** complice *m*, fauteur *m* (de, to); *see accessory 2;* **ac·ces·si·bil·i·ty** [~i'biliti] accessibilité *f*; **ac'ces·si·ble** □ [~əbl] accessible (à, to); **ac'ces·sion** admission *f* (*d'air*); entrée *f* en fonctions; arrivée *f* (*à un âge*); accroissement *m*; ~ *to the throne* avènement *m* au trône.

ac·ces·so·ry [æk'sesəri] **1.** □ accessoire, subsidiaire (à, to); **2.** accessoire *m*; *accessories* pl. objets *m/pl.* de toilette; accessoires *m/pl.* (*a. théâ.*); *see accessary.*

ac·ci·dence *gramm.* ['æksidəns] morphologie *f*.

ac·ci·dent ['æksidənt] accident *m*; *terrain:* inégalité *f*; *machine:* avarie *f*; ~ *insurance* assurance *f* contre les accidents; *by* ~ accidentellement; par hasard; *be killed in an* ~ perdre la vie dans un accident; **ac·ci·den·tal** [æksi'dentl] **1.** □ accidentel(le *f*), fortuit; accessoire; ~ *death* mort *f* accidentelle; **2.** accessoire *m*; ♪ signe *m* accidentel, accident *m*.

ac·claim [ə'kleim] acclamer.

ac·cla·ma·tion [æklə'meiʃn] acclamation *f*; *by* ~ par acclamation.

ac·cli·mate *surt. Am.* [ə'klaimit] *see acclimatize.*

ac·cli·ma·ti·za·tion [əklaimətai-'zeiʃn] acclimatation *f*; **ac'cli·ma·tize** acclimater; habituer.

ac·cliv·i·ty [ə'kliviti] montée *f*; côte *f*; rampe *f*; pente *f*.

ac·com·mo·date [ə'kɔmədeit] accommoder, conformer; adapter; arranger (*une querelle*); prêter (qch. à q., s.o. with s.th.); recevoir, loger; ~ *o.s. to* s'accommoder à; **ac'com·mo·dat·ing** □ complaisant; peu difficile (sur, about); **ac·com·mo·da·tion** adaptation *f*; arrangement *m*; *dispute:* ajustement *m*; compromis *m*; logement *m*; prêt *m* (*d'argent*); *Am.* ~*s* pl. hébergement *m*, hôtels *m/pl.*; ♥ ~ *bill* billet *m* de complaisance; *seating* ~ nombre *m* de places assises; *Am.* ~ *train* train *m* omnibus.

ac·com·pa·ni·ment [ə'kʌmpəni-mənt] accompagnement *m*; accessoires *m/pl.*; **ac'com·pa·nist** ♪ accompagnateur (-trice *f*) *m*; **ac'com·pa·ny** accompagner; *ac-*

companied with accompagné de, par.

ac·com·plice [ə'kɔmplis] complice *mf* (de, in), fauteur (-trice *f*) *m* (de, in).

ac·com·plish [ə'kɔmpliʃ] accomplir; venir à bout de; mener à bonne fin (*une tâche etc.*); réaliser (*un projet*); **ac'com·plished** achevé; doué; **ac'com·plish·ment** accomplissement *m*; réalisation *f*; *usu.* ~*s* pl. talents *m/pl.*, arts *m/pl.* d'agrément.

ac·cord [ə'kɔːd] **1.** accord *m*, consentement *m*; ✝ consentement *m* mutuel; *with one* ~ d'un commun accord; *of one's own* ~ de sa propre volonté; **2.** *v/i.* concorder (avec, with); *v/t.* concéder; **ac'cord·ance** conformité *f*, accord *m*; *in* ~ *with* conformément à, suivant; **ac'cord·ant** □ (with, to) conforme (à), d'accord (avec); **ac'cord·ing:** ~ *to* selon, suivant, d'après; ~ *as* selon que; **ac'cord·ing·ly** en conséquence; donc.

ac·cor·di·on ♪ [ə'kɔːdjən] accordéon *m*.

ac·cost [ə'kɔst] aborder, accoster.

ac·cou·cheur [æku:'ʃɔː], *f* **ac·cou·'cheuse** [~z] accoucheur (-euse *f*) *m*.

ac·count [ə'kaunt] **1.** calcul *m*, compte *m*, note *f*; récit *m*, relation *f*; valeur *f*; *blocked* ~ compte *m* bloqué; *current* ~ compte *m* courant; ~ *agreed upon* compte *m* arrêté; *payment on* ~ acompte *m*, versement *m* à compte; *sale for the* ~ vente *f* à terme; *statement of* ~ relevé *m* de compte; *of no* ~ de peu d'importance; *on no* ~ dans aucun cas; *on his* ~ à cause de lui, pour lui; *on* ~ *of* à cause de; *sl. be no* ~ ne pas compter; *find one's* ~ *in* trouver son compte à; *have* (*ou hold*) *an* ~ *with* avoir un compte chez; *have a bank* ~ avoir un compte en banque; *lay one's* ~ *with* compter sur; *place to s.o.'s* ~ verser au compte de q.; *take into* ~, *take* ~ *of* tenir compte de; *leave out of* ~ négliger; *turn to* ~ tirer parti de; *keep* ~*s* tenir les livres; *call to* ~ demander compte (à q. de qch.); *give* (*ou render*) *an* ~ *of* rendre raison de; faire un rapport sur; expliquer (*qch.*); F *give a good* ~ *of o.s.* s'acquitter bien; *make* (*little*) ~ *of* faire (peu de) cas de; **2.** *v/i.*

~ *for* expliquer (*qch.*); rendre raison de; justifier (de); *sp.* avoir à son actif; *v/t.* estimer, tenir pour; *be much* (*little*) ~ *ed of* être beaucoup (peu) estimé; **ac·count·a'bil·i·ty** responsabilité *f*; **ac'count·a·ble** □ responsable; redevable (de, *for*); **ac'count·ant** comptable *m*; *chartered* ~, *Am. certified public* ~ expert *m* comptable diplômé; **ac'count-book** livre *m* de comptes.

ac·cou·tred [əˈkuːtəd] accoutré; équipé; **ac·cou·tre·ments** [əˈkuːtəmənts] *pl.* équipement *m*.

ac·cred·it [əˈkredit] accréditer (*q.*, *qch.*, *a.* un ambassadeur auprès d'un gouvernement); ~ *s.th. to s.o.*, ~ *s.o. with s.th.* mettre qch. sur le compte de q.   [ment *m*.\

ac·cre·tion [æˈkriːʃn] accroisse-\

ac·crue [əˈkruː] provenir, dériver (de, *from*); ✝ s'accumuler (*intérêts*).

ac·cu·mu·late [əˈkjuːmjuleit] (s')accumuler; (s')amonceler; *v/t.* amasser (*de l'argent*); **ac·cu·mu·la·tion** accumulation *f*, amoncellement *m*; amas *m*; **ac·cu·mu·la·tive** □ [əˈkjuːmjulətiv] qui s'accumule; **ac'cu·mu·la·tor** accumulateur (-trice *f*) *m*; *phys.* accumulateur *m*.

ac·cu·ra·cy [ˈækjurəsi] exactitude *f*; fidélité *f*; **ac·cu·rate** □ [ˈ~rit] exact, juste; fidèle.

ac·curs·ed [əˈkɔːsid], **ac·curst** [əˈkɔːst] *usu.* F *fig.* maudit; exécrable.

ac·cu·sa·tion [ækjuːˈzeiʃn] accusation *f*; ✝ incrimination *f*; **ac·cu·sa·tive** *gramm.* [əˈkjuːzətiv] (*a.* ~ *case*) accusatif *m*; **ac·cu·sa·to·ry** [əˈkjuːzətəri] accusateur (-trice *f*); **ac·cuse** [əˈkjuːz] accuser (*q.* de qch., *s.o. of s.th.*), ✝ incriminer (*q.*) (auprès de *before*, *to*); *the* ~*d* le (la) prévenu(e *f*) *m*; **ac'cus·er** accusateur (-trice *f*) *m*.

ac·cus·tom [əˈkʌstəm] accoutumer (à, *to*); **ac'cus·tomed** habitué, accoutumé (à, *to*); *be* ~ *to do*(*ing*) *a.* avoir coutume *ou* avoir l'habitude de faire; *get ou become* ~ *to* (*doing*) *s.th.* s'habituer *ou* s'accoutumer à (faire) qch.

ace [eis] as *m* (*a. sl. fig.*, *usu.* un aviateur); *Am.* F ~ *in the hole fig.* encore une ressource; *within an* ~ *of* à deux doigts de.

a·cer·bi·ty [əˈsɔːbiti] aigreur *f*; *ton*: âpreté *f*.

ac·e·tate [ˈæsiteit] acétate *m*; **a·cetic** [əˈsiːtik] acétique; ~ *acid* acide *m* acétique; **a·cet·i·fy** [əˈseti-fai] (s')acétifier; **ac·e·tone** [ˈæsi-toun] acétone *f*; **ac·e·tous** [ˈ~təs] acéteux (-euse *f*); *fig.* aigre; **a·cet·y·lene** [əˈsetiliːn] acétylène *m*.

ache [eik] 1. faire mal à; 2. douleur *f*.

a·chieve [əˈtʃiːv] atteindre à, parvenir à; réaliser (*un but*); accomplir (*un exploit*); acquérir (*de l'estime*); **a'chieve·ment** accomplissement *m*; *projet:* exécution *f*; exploit *m*.

ach·ing [ˈeikiŋ] 1. □ douloureux (-euse *f*); 2. douleur *f*, mal *m*.

ach·ro·mat·ic [ækroˈmætik] (~*ally*) achromatique.

ac·id [ˈæsid] 1. aigre; ~ *rain* pluies *f/pl.* acides; 2. acide *m* (*a.* = LSD); **'ac·id·head** *sl.* acidomane *mf*; **a·cid·i·fy** [əˈsidifai] (s')acidifier; **a'cid·i·ty** acidité *f*; *fig.* aigreur *f*; **ac·i·do·sis** [æsiˈdousis] acidose *f*; **a·cid·u·late** [əˈsidjuleit] aciduler; ~*d drops* bonbons *m/pl.* acidulés *ou* anglais; **a·cid·u·lous** [əˈsidjuləs] acidulé.

ac·knowl·edge [əkˈnɔlidʒ] reconnaître (pour, *as*); répondre à (*un salut*); accuser réception de (*une lettre*); s'avouer; **ac'knowl·edg(e)-ment** reconnaissance *f*; aveu *m*; ~*s pl.* remerciements *m/pl.*; *usu.* ✝ accusé *m* de réception; reçu *m*, quittance *f*.

ac·me [ˈækmi] comble *m*; apogée *m*.

ac·ne ✻ [ˈækni] acné *f*.

a·cock [əˈkɔk] d'un air de défi.

ac·o·nite ♀ [ˈækonait] aconit *m*.

a·corn ♀ [ˈeikɔːn] gland *m*.

a·cous·tic, **a·cous·ti·cal** [əˈkuːs-tik(l)] acoustique; sonore; **a'cous·tics** *usu. sg.* acoustique *f*.

ac·quaint [əˈkweint] informer; ~ *s.o. with s.th.* apprendre qch. à q.; *be* ~*ed with* connaître; *become* ~*ed with* faire *ou* lier connaissance avec; **ac'quaint·ance** connaissance *f*; ~ *with* connaissance de.

ac·qui·esce [ækwiˈes] (*in*) acquiescer (à); accepter (*qch.*); **ac·qui·es·cence** (*in*) acquiescement *m* (à); assentiment *m* (à); soumission *f* (à); **ac·qui·es·cent** □ consentant; résigné.

ac·quire [əˈkwaiə] acquérir (*a. fig.*); ~*d taste* goût *m* acquis; **ac'quire·ment** acquisition *f* (de, *of*); talent *m; usu.* ~*s pl.* connaissances *f/pl.*

ac·qui·si·tion [ækwi'ziʃn] acquisition *f;* **ac·quis·i·tive** □ [æ'kwizitiv] apte *ou* âpre au gain.

ac·quit [ə'kwit] acquitter, absoudre (de, of); ~ *o.s.* of s'acquitter de; ~ *o.s. well (ill)* se bien (mal) acquitter; **ac'quit·tal** ᵼᵗᶻ décharge *f; devoir:* exécution *f;* **ac'quit·tance** ✝, ᵼᵗᶻ acquit *m,* acquittement *m.*

a·cre ['eikə] acre *f; (approx.)* arpent *m;* † champ *m.*

ac·rid □ ['ækrid] âcre; mordant *(style).*

ac·ri·mo·ni·ous □ [ækri'mounjəs] acrimonieux (-euse *f),* atrabilaire; **ac·ri·mo·ny** ['ækriməni] acrimonie *f,* aigreur *f.*

ac·ro·bat ['ækrobæt] acrobate *mf;* **ac·ro'bat·ic** (~*ally*) acrobatique; **ac·ro'bat·ics** *pl.* acrobatie *f;* ✠ acrobaties *f/pl.* aériennes.

a·cross [ə'krɔs] **1.** *adv.* à travers, en travers; de l'autre côté, en croix; **2.** *prp.* à travers, sur; en travers de; *come* ~, *run* ~ rencontrer; tomber sur.

act [ækt] **1.** *v/i.* agir (en, *as;* sur, on); prendre des mesures; se comporter; fonctionner; opérer; *théâ.* jouer; ~ *(up)on* exercer une action sur, agir sur; *Am.* F ~ *up* devenir insoumis; *v/t.* représenter, jouer *(un rôle, une pièce);* **2.** acte *m;* action *f; théâ.* acte *m;* loi *f,* décret *m;* ~*s pl.* actes *m/pl.;* ♀ *of God* force *f* majeure; ♀*s pl. of the Apostles* les Actes *m/pl.* des Apôtres; **'act·a·ble** jouable; **'act·ing 1.** action *f; théâ.* acteur: jeu *m; pièce:* exécution *f;* **2.** suppléant; intérimaire; provisoire; gérant.

ac·tion ['ækʃn] action *f (a. théâ.);* acte *m; cheval:* allure *f;* procès *m;* combat *m,* bataille *f;* mécanisme *m; couleurs:* jeu *m;* gestes *m/pl.;* ~ *radius* rayon *m* d'action; *bring an* ~ *against* intenter une action *ou* un procès à *ou* contre; *take* ~ prendre des mesures; **'ac·tion·a·ble** actionnable, sujet(te *f)* à procès.

ac·ti·vate ['æktiveit] activer; *phys.* rendre radioactif (-ive *f).*

ac·tive □ ['æktiv] actif (-ive *f);* alerte; agile; vif (vive *f);* ✝ ~ *partner* commanditer *m;* **ac'tiv·i·ty** *(souv. pl.)* activité *f;* occupation *f; surt.* ✝ mouvement *m; in full* ~ en pleine activité; *intense* ~ activité *f* intense.

ac·tor ['æktə] acteur *m;* **ac·tress** ['æktris] actrice *f.*

ac·tu·al □ ['æktjuəl] réel(le *f),* véritable; actuel(le *f),* présent; **ac·tual·i·ty** [æktju'æliti] réalité *f;* actualité *f;* **ac·tu·al·ize** ['æktjuəlaiz] réaliser; **ac·tu·al·ly** ['æktʃuəli] en fait; réellement; en réalité; à vrai dire.

ac·tu·ar·y ['æktjuəri] actuaire *m.*

ac·tu·ate ['æktjueit] mettre en action; animer (q. à, *s.o.* to).

a·cu·men [ə'kju:men] finesse *f* (d'esprit).

ac·u·punc·ture ['ækjupʌŋtʃə] acu-} [puncture *f.]*

a·cute □ [ə'kju:t] aigu (-uë *f) (a. ✗, a. angle, pointe, accent, son);* vif (vive *f) (douleur);* fin *(ouïe, esprit);* qui sévit *(crise);* **a'cute·ness** angle: aiguïté *f; son:* acuité *f; douleur etc.:* intensité *f; ouïe:* finesse *f; esprit:* pénétration *f.*

ad F [æd] *see advertisement.*

ad·age ['ædidʒ] maxime *f.*

ad·a·mant ['ædəmənt] *fig.* inflexible; insensible (à, to); **ad·aman·tine** [ˌ~'mæntain] adamantin; *fig. see adamant.*

a·dapt [ə'dæpt] adapter (à to, for); accommoder; adapter *(un texte)* (de, from); **a·dapt·a'bil·i·ty** souplesse *f;* **a'dapt·a·ble** adaptable; commode; **ad·ap'ta·tion** adaptation *f* (à, to); appropriation *f;* **a'dap·ter** *radio:* (bouchon *m* de) raccord *m; télév.* adaptateur *m.*

add [æd] *v/t.* ajouter; joindre; ~ *in* inclure; ~ *up* additionner; *v/i.* ~ *to* augmenter; accentuer; ~ *up* to se totaliser par.

ad·den·dum [ə'dendəm], *pl.* **-da** [ˌ~də] addenda *m;* supplément *m.*

ad·der ['ædə] vipère *f.*

ad·dict 1. [ə'dikt]: ~ *o.s.* s'adonner (à, to), se livrer (à, to); **2.** ['ædikt] *(opium etc.* ~) -mane *mf;* **ad'dict·ed** adonné (à, to); *become* ~ to s'adonner à *(la boisson etc.),* s'abandonner à *(un vice).*

add·ing ['ædiŋ] (d')arithmétique.

ad·di·tion [ə'diʃn] addition *f;* adjonction *f; bâtiment:* rajout *m; ville:* extension *f; Am. terrain:* agrandissement *m;* ~ to addition à; *he had an* ~ *to his family* sa famille vient d'augmenter; *in* ~ en outre; *in* ~ to en plus de; **ad'di·tion·al** additionnel(le *f),* supplémentaire; nouveau

(-el *devant une voyelle ou un h muet*; -elle *f*; -aux *m/pl.*); de plus.

ad·di·tive ['æditiv] additif *m*.

ad·dle ['ædl] **1.** (se) pourrir (*œufs*); *v/t.* fig. troubler (*le cerveau, la tête etc.*); **2.** pourri (*œuf*); trouble, brouillé (*cerveau*).

ad·dress [ə'dres] **1.** adresser; haranguer (*une foule*); (*a.* ~ *o.s. to*) adresser la parole à (*q.*); ~ *o.s. to s.th.* entreprendre qch.; se mettre à qch.; **2.** adresse *f*; habileté *f*; *parl.* profession *f* de foi; supplique *f*; abord *m*; discours *m*; *give an* ~ faire une allocution; *pay one's* ~*es to* faire la cour à (*une femme*); **ad·dress·ee** [ædre'si:] destinataire *mf*; **ad·dress tag** étiquette *f* d'adresse.

ad·e·noids ≈ ['ædinɔidz] *pl.* végétations *f/pl.* adénoïdes.

ad·ept ['ædept] **1.** expert (à *at, in*); versé (dans *at, in*); **2.** adepte *mf*; initié(e *f*) *m*; expert *m* (en, *in*); *F be an* ~ *at* être expert à.

ad·e·qua·cy ['ædikwəsi] suffisance *f*; **ad·e·quate** □ ['~kwit] suffisant; juste; raisonnable.

ad·here [əd'hiə] (*to*) adhérer (à), se coller (à); *fig.* persister (dans), s'en tenir (à); observer (*une règle etc.*); donner son adhésion (à) (*un parti etc.*); **ad'her·ence** (*to*) adhérence *f*, adhésion *f* (à); fidélité *f* (à) (*un parti*); observance *f* (de) (*une règle*); **ad'her·ent 1.** adhérent; **2.** adhérent(e *f*) *m*; partisan *m*.

ad·he·sion [əd'hi:ʒn] *see adherence*; *fig.* adhésion *f*; *phys.* adhérence *f*; *give one's* ~ donner son adhésion (à, *to*).

ad·he·sive [əd'hi:siv] adhésif (-ive *f*) collant; tenace; ~ *plaster*, ~ *tape* sparadrap *m*, emplâtre *m* adhésif.

a·dieu [ə'dju:] **1.** adieu!; **2.** adieu *m*.

ad·i·pose ['ædipous] adipeux (-euse *f*); gras(se *f*).

ad·it ['ædit] accès *m*; ⚒ galerie *f*.

ad·ja·cen·cy [ə'dʒeisənsi] contiguïté *f*; *adjacencies pl.* voisinage *m* immédiat; **ad'ja·cent** □ (*to*) contigu (-uë *f*) (à), attenant (à); limitrophe (de).

ad·jec·ti·val □ [ædʒek'taivl] adjectif (-ive *f*); **ad·jec·tive** ['ædʒiktiv] adjectif *m*.

ad·join [ə'dʒɔin] avoisiner (*qch.*), toucher (à); **ad'join·ing** contigu (-uë *f*); avoisinant.

ad·journ [ə'dʒə:n] (s') ajourner; *v/t.* remettre, différer; lever (*une séance*) (jusque, *to*); **ad'journ·ment** ajournement *m*; remise *f*.

ad·judge [ə'dʒʌdʒ] juger; ⚖ décider, déclarer (*coupable etc.*); condamner (à, *to*); **ad'judge·ment** décision *f*.

ad·ju·di·cate [ə'dʒu:dikeit] *see adjudge*; **ad·ju·di·ca·tion** jugement *m*; décision *f*; arrêt *m*.

ad·junct ['ædʒʌŋkt] accessoire *m*; adjoint(e *f*) *m*; *gramm.* complément *m*.

ad·ju·ra·tion [ædʒuə'reiʃn] adjuration *f*; **ad·jure** [ə'dʒuə] conjurer (de, *to*).

ad·just [ə'dʒʌst] ajuster; arranger; arrêter (*un compte*); régler (*un différend*); agencer (*une machine*); ajuster (*une balance*); *fig.* ~ *to* adapter à; ~*ing screw* vis *f* de serrage; **ad'just·a·ble** □ réglable, ajustable; **ad'just·ment** ajustement *m*; arrangement *m*; règlement *m*; réglage *m*; correction *f*; accommodement *m*.

ad·ju·tan·cy ⋈ ['ædʒutənsi] fonctions *f/pl.* de capitaine adjudant major; **ad·ju·tant** capitaine *m* adjudant major.

ad-lib *Am.* ⨍ [æd'lib] improviser.

ad·meas·ure·ment [æd'meʒəmənt] mensuration *f*; mesurage *m*.

ad·min·is·ter [əd'ministə] *v/t.* administrer (*pays, affaires, sacrement, médicament*); assermenter; appliquer (*la loi*); ~ *justice*, ~ *the law* dispenser *ou* rendre la justice; *v/i.* pourvoir aux besoins (de *q.*, *to s.o.*); **ad·min·is·tra·tion** administration *f*; gestion *f*; prestation *f* (*d'un serment*); *surt. Am.* Administration *f*, Gouvernement *m*; ~ *of justice* administration *f* de la justice; **ad'min·is·tra·tive** [~trətiv] administratif (-ive *f*); d'administration; **ad'min·is·tra·tor** [~treitə] administrateur *m*; gérant *m*; ⚖ curateur *m*.

ad·mi·ra·ble □ ['ædmərəbl] admirable, excellent.

ad·mi·ral ['ædmərəl] amiral *m*; ♀ *of the Fleet* amiral *m* commandant en chef; **'ad·mi·ral·ty** amirauté *f*; *First Lord of the* ♀ ministre *m* britannique de la marine.

ad·mi·ra·tion [ædmi'reiʃn] admiration *f*.

ad·mire [əd'maiə] admirer; s'extasier devant; **ad'mir·er** admirateur (-trice *f*) *m*; adorateur (-trice*f*) *m*.

ad·mis·si·bil·i·ty [ədmisə'biliti] admissibilité *f*; **ad'mis·si·ble** □ admissible; recevable; **ad'mis·sion** admission *f*, accès *m* (à, to); entrée *f*; confession *f*, aveu *m*; F prix *m* d'entrée.

ad·mit [əd'mit] *v/t.* admettre (à, dans to, into); laisser entrer; avoir de la place pour; reconnaître (*une faute etc.*); ⚖ *surt. Am.* ~ to the bar inscrire au tableau des avocats; *v/i.*: ~ of permettre, comporter; *it* ~*s of no excuse* il est sans excuse; **ad'mit·tance** entrée *f*; accès *m*; *no* ~! entrée interdite!; **ad'mit·ted·ly** de l'aveu de tous; de son propre aveu.

ad·mix·ture [əd'mikstʃə] mélange *m*, dosage *m*; *pharm.* mixtion *f*.

ad·mon·ish [əd'mɔniʃ] admonester; exhorter (à, to); prévenir (de, of); **ad·mo·ni·tion** [ædmə'niʃn] remontrance *f*; avertissement *m*; **ad·mon·i·to·ry** □ [əd'mɔnitəri] de remontrances; d'avertissement.

a·do [ə'du:] agitation *f*, activité *f*, embarras *m*, bruit *m*; difficulté *f*; *without much* ~ sans difficulté; sans embarras.

a·do·be [ə'doubi] adobe *m*.

ad·o·les·cence [ædo'lesns] adolescence *f*; **ad·o'les·cent** *adj.*, *a. su./mf* adolescent(e *f*) *m*.

a·dopt [ə'dɔpt] adopter; *fig.* choisir, adopter, embrasser; *fig.* F chiper; ~*ed country* pays *m* ou patrie *f* d'adoption; **a'dop·tion** adoption *f*; choix *m*; **a'dop·tive** adoptif (-ive *f*); ~ *country* pays *m* ou patrie *f* d'adoption.

a·dor·a·ble [ə'dɔːrəbl] adorable; **ad·o·ra·tion** [ædɔː'reiʃn] adoration *f*; F amour *m*; **a·dore** [ə'dɔː] adorer; **a'dor·er** adorateur (-trice *f*) *m*.

a·dorn [ə'dɔːn] orner, parer; **a'dorn·ment** ornement *m*, parure *f*; ornementation *f*.

a·drift [ə'drift] ⚓ à la dérive; *fig.* loin du compte; *turn s.o.* ~ abandonner q., mettre q. sur le pavé.

a·droit [ə'drɔit] adroit; **a'droit·ness** adresse *f*.

ad·u·late ['ædjuleit] aduler, flatter (*q.*); **ad·u'la·tion** adulation *f*; **'ad·u·la·tor** adulateur (-trice *f*) *m*;

'ad·u·la·to·ry adulateur (-trice *f*).

a·dult ['ædʌlt] *adj.*, *a. su./mf* adulte *mf*.

a·dul·ter·ant [ə'dʌltərənt] adultérant *m*; **a'dul·ter·ate** 1. [~reit] adultérer; *fig.* altérer; 2. [~it] adultéré; falsifié; altéré; **a·dul·ter·a·tion** [ədʌltə'reiʃn] adultération *f*; altération *f*; **a'dul·ter·a·tor** falsificateur (-trice *f*) *m*; **a'dul·ter·er** adultère *m*; **a'dul·ter·ess** adultère *f*; **a'dul·ter·ous** □ adultère; **a'dul·ter·y** adultère *m*.

ad·um·brate ['ædʌmbreit] ébaucher, esquisser; laisser entrevoir; † voiler; **ad·um'bra·tion** ébauche *f*, esquisse *f*; pressentiment *m*.

ad·vance [əd'vɑːns] 1. *v/i.* s'avancer; avancer (*en âge*); monter (*en grade*); hausser (*prix*); *biol.* évoluer; *v/t.* avancer; mettre en avant (*des opinions*); augmenter, hausser (*le prix*); élever (*en grade*); faire avancer; 2. marche *f* en avant; ⚔ avance *f*; progrès *m*; avancement *m* (*en grade*); *prix*: hausse *f*; *in* ~ d'avance, en avance; en avant; *be in* ~ *of s.o.* devancer q.; 3. avant-; **ad'vanced** *adj.* avancé; supérieur (*cours, école, etc.*); ~ *English* anglais *m* supérieur; **ad'vance·ment** avancement *m*; progrès *m*.

ad·van·tage [əd'vɑːntidʒ] avantage *m* (*a. au tennis*); dessus *m*; profit *m*; *gain an* ~ *over* se procurer un avantage sur; *gain the* ~ *over* l'emporter sur; *take* ~ *of* profiter de (*qch.*); abuser de (*la crédulité de*) (*q.*); *to* ~ avantageusement; **ad·van·ta·geous** □ [ædvən'teidʒəs] avantageux (-euse *f*) (*pour*, to); utile.

ad·vent ['ædvənt] arrivée *f*; ♀ *eccl.* Avent *m*; **ad·ven·ti·tious** □ [ædven'tiʃəs] adventice; accidentel(le *f*); accessoire.

ad·ven·ture [əd'ventʃə] 1. aventure *f*, entreprise *f*; † spéculation *f* hasardée; 2. (se) hasarder; **ad'ven·tur·er** aventurier *m*; spéculateur*m*; **ad'ven·tur·ess** [~əris] intrigante *f*; **ad'ven·tur·ous** □ aventureux (-euse *f*); audacieux (-euse *f*); entreprenant (*personne*).

ad·verb ['ædvəːb] adverbe *m*; **ad·ver·bi·al** □ [əd'vəːbjəl] adverbial (-aux *m/pl.*).

ad·ver·sar·y ['ædvəsəri] adversaire *m*; ennemi(e *f*) *m*; **ad·verse** □

['və:s] adverse; contraire; ennemi (de, to), hostile (à, to); opposé; défavorable; ~ *balance* déficit *m*; **ad·ver·si·ty** [əd'və:siti] adversité *f*, infortune *f*.

ad·vert [əd'və:t]: ~ *to* faire allusion à; parler de.

ad·ver·tise ['ædvətaiz] faire de la réclame (pour); *v/t.* annoncer, faire savoir, faire connaître; *v/i.* insérer une annonce; ~ *for* chercher par voie d'annonce; **ad·ver·tise·ment** [əd-'və:tismənt] publicité *f*; *journal*: annonce *f*; affiche *f* (*sur un mur*); réclame *f*; **ad·ver·tis·er** ['ædvətaizə] auteur *m* d'une annonce; faiseur *m* de réclame; **'ad·ver·tis·ing**: ~ *agency* agence *f* de publicité; ~ *campaign* campagne *f* publicitaire; ~ *designer* dessinateur *m* publicitaire; ~ *film* film *m* publicitaire; ~ *manager* chef *m* de la publicité; ~ *media* supports *m/pl.* publicitaires; ~ *medium* organe *m* de publicité.

ad·vice [əd'vais] conseil *m*, -s *m/pl.*; avis *m*; ✝ lettre *f ou* note *f* d'avis; *usu.* ~s *pl.* nouvelles *f/pl.*; *on the* ~ *of* sur le conseil de, suivant les conseils de; *take medical* ~ consulter un médecin; **ad'vice-boat** ⚓ aviso *m*.

ad·vis·a·ble □ [əd'vaizəbl] recommandable; **ad'vise** *v/t.* recommander (*qch.*); conseiller (*q.*); conseiller (à q. de *inf.*, *s.o. to inf.*); prévenir (de, of; que, that); ✝ aviser de; *v/i.* se consulter; ~ *with* consulter (*q.*), se consulter avec (*q.*); ~ *on* renseigner (*q.*) sur; **ad'vised** □ réfléchi (*acte*); **ad'vis·ed·ly** [~idli] à dessein; **ad'vis·er** conseiller (-ère *f*) *m*; **ad'vi·so·ry** [~əri] consultatif (-ive *f*); ♀ *Board* conseil *m* consultatif.

ad·vo·ca·cy ['ædvəkəsi] fonction *f* d'avocat; appui *m* (donné à une cause); **ad·vo·cate 1.** ['~kit] avocat *m*; *fig.* défenseur *m*, partisan *m*; **2.** ['~keit] plaider en faveur de (*qch.*); appuyer (*une cause*); préconiser.

adze ⊕ [ædz] (h)erminette *f*.

ae·gis ['i:dʒis] *fig.* égide *f*.

ae·on ['i:ən] éon *m*; *fig.* éternité *f*.

a·er·at·ed ['eiəreitid] aéré (*pain*); gazeux (-euse *f*) (*eau*).

a·e·ri·al ['ɛəriəl] **1.** □ aérien(ne *f*); ~ *camera* aérophoto *m*; ~ *survey* prise *f*

de vue aérienne; ~ *view* vue *f* aérienne; **2.** *radio*, *télév.*: ~ antenne *f*; *high* ~ antenne *f* haute; *mains* ~ antenne *f* secteur; *outdoor* ~ antenne *f* d'extérieur; ~ *mast* mât *m* d'antenne.

a·er·ie ['ɛəri] aire *f*.

aero... [ɛərə] aéro-; **a·er·o·bat·ics** [~'bætiks] *pl.* acrobaties *f/pl.* (aériennes); **a·er·o·drome** ['ɛərədroum] aérodrome *m*; **a·er·o·gram** ['~græm] radiogramme *m*; **a·er·o·lite** ['~lait] aérolithe *m*; **a·er·o·naut** ['~nɔ:t] aéronaute *m*; **a·er·o'nau·tic, a·er·o'nau·ti·cal** □ aéronautique; **a·er·o'nau·tics** *sg.* aéronautique *f*; **a·er·o·plane** ['~plein] aéroplane *m*, avion *m*; **a·er·o·sol (can)** ['~sɔl] aérosol *m*, atomiseur *m*; **a·er·o·space in·du·stry** industrie *f* aérospatiale; **a·er·o·stat** ['~oustæt] aérostat *m*; **a·er·o'sta·tic** aérostatique.

aes·thete ['i:sθi:t] esthète *mf*; **aes·thet·ic, aes·thet·i·cal** □ [i:s-'θetik(l)] esthétique; **aes'thet·ics** *sg.* esthétique *f*.

a·far [ə'fɑ:] (*surt.* ~ *off*) au loin, éloigné; *from* ~ de loin.

af·fa·bil·i·ty [æfə'biliti] affabilité *f*; **af·fa·ble** □ ['æfəbl] affable, courtois.

af·fair [ə'fɛə] affaire *f*; *love* ~ affaire *f* de cœur; F affaire *f*, chose *f*; ~ *of honour* affaire *f* d'honneur; duel *m*.

af·fect [ə'fekt] atteindre, attaquer, toucher; influer sur (*qch.*); affliger; concerner; altérer (*la santé*); ⚕ intéresser (*un organe*); affecter (*une manière*); *he* ~*s the freethinker* il pose au libre penseur; *he* ~*s to sleep* il affecte de dormir; **af·fec·ta·tion** [æfek'teifn] affectation *f*, simulation *f* (de, of); *langage*: afféterie *f*; *style*: mièvrerie *f*; **af·fect·ed** □ [ə'fektid] atteint (*santé*); disposé (pour q., *towards* s.o.); ému; touché; affecté, maniéré (*style*, *maintien*, *etc.*); minaudier (-ère *f*) (*personne*); simulé; **af'fec·tion** affection *f* (a. ⚕) (pour for, *towards*); tendresse *f* (pour, for); impression *f*; **af'fec·tion·ate** □ [~ʃənit] affectueux (-euse *f*), aimant; **af'fec·tive** affectif (-ive *f*).

af·fi·ance [ə'faiəns] **1.** confiance *f* (en, in); **2.** fiancer (avec, to).

af·fi·da·vit [æfi'deivit] attestation *f*

par écrit; *make an* ~ faire une déclaration sous serment.

af·fil·i·ate [ə'filieit] affilier (*un membre*) (*à une société* to, *with a society*); 🕇🕇, *a. fig.* attribuer la paternité de (*q., a. qch.*) (à, on); ~ *o.s. with* s'affilier à; *Am.* fraterniser avec; ~d company filiale *f*; **af·fil·i'a·tion** affiliation *f* (*à une société etc.*); 🕇🕇 légitimation *f*; *Am. usu.* ~s *pl.* attaches *f/pl.* (*politiques*).

af·fin·i·ty [ə'finiti] parenté *f*; affinité *f* (*a.* 🕇, *a. fig.*).

af·firm [ə'fə:m] affirmer, soutenir; 🕇🕇 confirmer; **af·fir·ma·tion** [æfə:-'meiʃn] affirmation *f*; assertion *f*; 🕇🕇 confirmation *f*; **af·firm·a·tive** ☐ [ə'fə:mətiv] **1.** affirmatif (-ive *f*); 2. affirmative *f*; *answer in the* ~ répondre affirmativement *ou* que oui.

af·fix 1. ['æfiks] addition *f*; 2. [ə'fiks] attacher (à, to); apposer (*un sceau, un timbre*) (sur, à).

af·flict [ə'flikt] affliger, tourmenter; ~ed with affligé de; **af'flic·tion** affliction *f*; calamité *f*; infirmité *f*.

af·flu·ence ['æfluəns] affluence *f*; abondance *f*; **'af·flu·ent** ☐ **1.** abondant, riche (en, in); opulent, riche; 2. affluent *m*.

af·flux ['æflʌks] afflux *m*; concours *m* (*de gens*).

af·ford [ə'fɔːd] avoir les moyens de; être en mesure de; disposer de (*le temps*); offrir; *I can* ~ *it* mes moyens me le permettent.

af·for·est [æ'fɔrist] (re)boiser; **af·for·est'a·tion** (re)boisement *m*.

af·fran·chise [ə'fræntʃaiz] affranchir.

af·fray [ə'frei] bagarre *f*; rixe *f*.

af·front [ə'frʌnt] **1.** offenser; faire rougir (*q.*); **2.** affront *m*, offense *f*; *put an* ~ *upon, offer an* ~ *to* faire (un) affront *ou* une avanie à (*q.*).

a·fi·cio·na·do [əfisjə'nɑːdou] aficionado *m*, amateur *m*, fana *m*.

a·field [ə'fiːld] aux champs; à la campagne; *far* ~ très loin.

a·fire [ə'faiə] en feu, embrasé; *set* ~ mettre le feu à.

a·flame [ə'fleim] en flammes, embrasé; *set* ~ mettre en flammes, faire brûler.

a·float 🕇 *a. fig.* [ə'flout] à flot (*a. fig.* = *quitte de dettes*); sur l'eau, à la mer; à bord; en circulation (*idée, bruit*); 🕇 en cours; *keep* ~ se maintenir à flot; *set* ~ lancer (*un navire, un journal, etc.*).

a·foot [ə'fut] à pied; en mouvement, sur pied; *be* ~ être en route *ou* marche *ou* train.

a·fore 🕇 [ə'fɔː] *see* before; **a'fore·men·tioned** [~menʃnd], **a'fore·named** [~neimd], **a'fore·said** susdit, précité; **a'fore·thought** prémédité; *with malice* ~ avec préméditation.

a·fraid [ə'freid] pris de peur, effrayé; *be* ~ *of* avoir peur de, craindre (*q., qch.*); F *I am* ~ *I have to go* je crains bien que je doive partir.

a·fresh [ə'freʃ] de *ou* à nouveau.

Af·ri·caans [æfri'kɑːns] africaans *m* (= *patois hollandais parlé au Cap*); **Af·ri·can** ['~kən] **1.** africain; **2.** Africain(e *f*) *m*; *surt. Am.* nègre; **Af·ri·can·der** [~'kændə] Afrikander *m*.

Af·ro ['æfrou] **1.** afro; **2.** coiffure *f* afro.

aft 🕇 [ɑːft] à *ou* sur l'arrière.

aft·er ['ɑːftə] **1.** *adv.* après; plus tard; ensuite; **2.** *prp. temps:* après; *lieu:* après; à la suite de; *manière:* suivant, selon, d'après; ~ *all* après tout, enfin; *I'll go* ~ *him* j'irai le chercher; *time* ~ *time* à maintes reprises; ~ *having seen him* après l'avoir vu; **3.** *cj.* après que; **4.** *adj.* subséquent; futur; 🕇 arrière; '~**birth** arrière-faix *m/inv.*; '~**crop** regain *m*; seconde récolte *f*; '~**din·ner** d'après dîner; '~**ef·fect** répercussion *f*; '~**glow** dernières lueurs *f/pl.* du couchant; '~**grass**, '~**math** 🗡 regain *m*; *fig.* suites *f/pl.*; '~**hours** le temps *m* après la fermeture (des magasins, cafés, *etc.*); '~**noon** après-midi *m/inv.*; *fig.* ~ (*of life*) déclin *m* de la vie; *this* ~ cet après-midi.

aft·ers F ['ɑːftəz] *pl.* dessert *m*.

after...: '~**sales serv·ice** service *m* après-vente; '~**sea·son** arrière-saison *f*; '~**shave (lo·tion)** lotion *f* après-rasage, after-shave *m*; '~**taste** arrière-goût *m*; '~**thought** réflexion *f* après coup; '~**wards** ['~wədz] après, plus tard; ensuite; par la suite.

a·gain [ə'gen] encore; encore une fois, de nouveau; en outre, d'autre part; ~ *and* ~, *time and* ~ maintes et maintes fois; *as much* (*ou many*) ~ deux fois autant; *twice as much* ~

trois fois autant; *now and* ~ de temps en temps; de temps à autre. **a·gainst** [ə'genst] *prp.* contre; à l'encontre de; *fig.* en prévision de; *as* ~ comparé à; ~ *the wall* contre le mur; ~ *a background* sur un fond; *over* ~ vis-à-vis de; F *run* ~ rencontrer (*q.*) par hasard.

a·gape [ə'geip] bouche *f* bée.

ag·ate *min.* ['ægət] agate *f*; *Am.* marbre *m*; *Am. typ. see ruby.*

a·ga·ve ♀ [ə'geivi] agave *m*.

age [eidʒ] **1.** âge *m*; époque *f*, siècle *m*; génération *f*; F éternité *f*; (*old*) ~ vieillesse *f*; *at the* ~ *of* à l'âge de; *in the* ~ *of Queen Anne* à l'époque de ou du temps de la reine Anne; *of* ~ majeur; *over* ~ trop âgé; *under* ~ mineur; *what is your* ~? quel âge avez-vous?; *when I was your* ~ quand j'avais ton âge, à ton âge; *act ou be your* ~! tu n'es plus un(e) enfant!; F *wait for* ~s attendre des éternités; *come of* ~ atteindre sa majorité; **2.** vieillir; **age brack·et** groupe *m ou* catégorie *f ou* tranche *f* d'âge; **a·ged** ['~id] âgé, vieux (vieil *devant une voyelle ou un h muet*; vieille *f*; vieux *m/pl.*); [eidʒd]: ~ *twenty* âgé de vingt ans; **age group** → *age bracket;* **'age·less** toujours jeune; **'age-old** séculaire.

a·gen·cy ['eidʒənsi] action *f*, opération *f*; entremise *f*, intermédiaire *m*; agent *m* (*naturel*); agence *f*, bureau *m.* [du jour.]

a·gen·da [ə'dʒendə] *sg.* ordre *m*ƒ

a·gent ['eidʒənt] agent *m*, représentant(e *f*) *m*; régisseur *m* (*d'une propriété*); mandataire *mf*; commis *m* voyageur; 🚃 *Am.* chef *m* de gare; 🚉 agent *m*.

ag·glom·er·ate [ə'glɔməreit] (s')agglomérer; **ag·glom·er·a·tion** agglomération *f*.

ag·glu·ti·nate 1. [ə'gluːtineit] (s'ag-) glutiner (*a.* ⚕, *gramm.*); **2.** [~nit] agglutiné; **ag·glu·ti·na·tion** [~-'neiʃn] agglutination *f* (*a.* ⚕, *gramm.*).

ag·gran·dize [ə'grændaiz] agrandir; exagérer; **ag·gran·dize·ment** [~dizmənt] agrandissement *m*.

ag·gra·vate ['ægrəveit] aggraver; empirer; envenimer (*une querelle*); F agacer (*q.*); **ag·gra·va·tion** aggravation *f*; envenimement *m*; F agacement *m*.

40 GTW E-Fr

ag·gre·gate 1. ['ægrigeit] (s')agréger (à, to); *v/i.* F s'élever à *ou* au total de; **2.** □ ['~git] collectif (-ive *f*); global (-aux *m/pl.*), total (-aux *m/pl.*); ⚕, *géol., etc.* agrégé; **3.** [~] ensemble *m*, total *m*; masse *f*; *in the* ~ dans l'ensemble; **ag·gre·ga·tion** [~'geiʃn] agrégation *f*; assemblage *m*.

ag·gres·sion [ə'greʃn] agression *f*; **ag'gres·sive** □ [ə'gresiv] agressif (-ive *f*); militant; casseur (*air*); ~ *war* guerre *f* offensive; *take* (*ou assume*) *the* ~ prendre l'offensive; **ag'gres·sive·ness** agressivité *f*; **ag'gres·sor** agresseur *m*.

ag·grieve [ə'griːv] chagriner, blesser.

ag·gro *Brit. sl.* ['ægrou] agressivité *f*; violences *f/pl*.

a·ghast [ə'gɑːst] consterné; stupéfait (de, *at*).

ag·ile □ ['ædʒail] agile, leste.

a·gil·i·ty [ə'dʒiliti] agilité *f*

ag·i·o † ['ædʒiou] agio *m*; **ag·i·o·tage** ['ædʒiʊtidʒ] agiotage *m*.

ag·i·tate ['ædʒiteit] *v/t.* agiter, remuer; agiter (*une question*); *fig.* émouvoir, troubler; *v/i.* faire de l'agitation (en faveur de, *for*); **ag·i·ta·tion** agitation *f*; mouvement *m*; émotion *f*, trouble *m*; discussion *f*; *insidious* ~ menées *f/pl.* insidieuses; **'ag·i·ta·tor** agitateur *m*; meneur *m*; fauteur *m* de troubles.

ag·let ['æglit] ferret *m*.

a·glow [ə'glou] enflammé; *fig.* resplendissant.

ag·nail ⚘ ['ægneil] envie *f*.

ag·nate ['ægneit] **1.** agnat(e *f*) *m*; **2.** agnat.

a·go [ə'gou]: *a year* ~ il y a un an; *it is a year* ~ il y a un an (que, *since*); *long* ~ il y a longtemps.

a·gog [ə'gɔg] en émoi; dans l'expectative (de, *for*).

ag·o·nize ['ægənaiz] *v/t.* torturer, mettre au supplice; *v/i.* être au supplice *ou* au martyre; **'ag·o·niz·ing** □ atroce; navrant.

ag·o·ny ['ægəni] angoisse *f*; paroxysme *m* (*de joie*); (~ *of death, mortal* ~) agonie *f*; *journ.* F ~ *column* annonces *f/pl.* personnelles.

a·grar·i·an [ə'grɛəriən] **1.** agrarien(ne *f*) *m*; **2.** agraire.

a·gree [ə'griː] *v/i.* consentir; tomber d'accord; s'accorder; (*upon, on*) convenir (de), accepter (*qch.*);

tomber d'accord (sur); admettre (que, *that*); être du même avis (que q., *with s.o.*); ~ to consentir à, accepter (*qch.*); ~ to differ différer à l'amiable; *v/t.* ♣ faire accorder (*les livres*), faire cadrer (*un compte*); be ~d être d'accord (sur, *on*; que, *that*); ~d! d'accord!, soit!; a'**gree·a·ble** ☐ agréable (à, *to*); aimable (envers, *to*); F consentant (à, *to*); a'**gree·a·ble·ness** amabilité *f*; *endroit*: agrément *m*; a'**gree·ment** accord *m*; conformité *f*, concordance *f*; convention *f*, contrat *m*; traité *m*; come to an ~ arriver à une entente; make an ~ passer un contrat (avec q., *with s.o.*).

ag·ri·cul·tur·al [ægri'kʌltʃərəl] agricole (*produit, nation*); agriculteur (*peuple*); **ag·ri·cul·ture** ['~tʃə] agriculture *f*; **ag·ri·cul·tur·ist** [~tʃərist] agriculteur *m*, agronome *m*.

a·ground ⚓ [ə'graund] échoué; run ~ échouer; mettre (*un navire*) à la côte.

a·gue ['eigju:] fièvre *f* (intermittente); '**a·gu·ish** fiévreux (-euse *f*); impaludé (*personne*); *fig.* frissonnant.

ah [ɑ:] ah!, ha!, heu!

a·head [ə'hed] en avant, sur l'avant; straight ~ droit devant; ~ of s.o. en avant de q.; go ~ aller de l'avant; avancer; go ~! marchez!; allez-y!; continuez!

a·hoy ⚓ [ə'hɔi] ho *ou* ohé, du canot!

aid [eid] 1. aider, secourir; venir en aide à; 2. aide *f*, secours *m*; by (*ou* with) the ~ of avec l'aide de (*q.*); à l'aide de (*qch.*); ~s and appliances moyens *m/pl.*

aide-de-camp ✗ ['eiddə'kã:ŋ], *pl.* **aides-de-camp** ['eidzdə'kã:ŋ] officier *m* d'ordonnance.

ai·grette ['eigret] aigrette *f*.

ai·guil·lette ✗ [eigwi'let] aiguillette *f*.

ail [eil] *v/i.* être souffrant; *v/t.* faire souffrir (*q.*); what ~s him? qu'est-ce qu'il a?; '**ail·ing** souffrant, indisposé; '**ail·ment** mal *m*, maladie *f*.

aim [eim] 1. *v/i.* viser (*qch.*); *fig.* ~ at viser (à *inf.*; *qch., s.th.*); *surt. Am.* ~ to (*inf.*) aspirer à (*inf.*); *v/t.*: ~ a gun (*ou* blow) at viser (*q.*); ~ remarks at parler à l'adresse de; 2. action *f* de viser; but *m*; *fig.*

dessein *m*, visées *f/pl.*; but *m*; take ~ viser; '**aim·less** ☐ sans but.

ain't F [eint] = are not, am not, is not, have not, has not.

air¹ [ɛə] 1. air *m*; souffle *m*; brise *f*; by ~ en avion, par la voie des airs; in the open ~ au grand air; castles in the ~ châteaux *m/pl.* en Espagne; be in the ~ être en l'air; *fig.* se préparer; war in the ~ guerre *f* aérienne; on the ~ radiodiffusé; à la radio; be on (off) the ~ (ne pas) radiodiffuser; go on (off) the ~ commencer (terminer) une émission; put on the ~ mettre en ondes, émettre; ~ supply entrée *f* d'air; take the ~ prendre l'air; ✈ décoller; 2. aérer (*une chambre, le linge*); mettre à l'air; bassiner (*un lit*); ventiler (*une question*); faire parade de (*son savoir, ses opinions*); ~ o.s. prendre l'air.

air² [~] air *m*, mine *f*, apparence *f*; give o.s. ~s se donner des airs; with an ~ d'un grand geste; ~s and graces minauderies *f/pl.*

air³ ♪ [~] air *m*, mélodie *f*.

air...: '**~-base** base *f* d'aviation; '**~-bath** bain *m* d'air; '**~-bed** matelas *m* pneumatique; '**~-blad·der** vésicule *f* (aérienne); vessie *f* natatoire; '**~-borne** ✗ en vol; ✗ aéroporté; '**~-brake** frein *m* à air comprimé; ~ **bus** aérobus *m*, airbus *m*; ~ **car·go** fret *m* aérien; '**~-cham·ber** *biol.* chambre *f* à air; ⊕ cloche *f* d'air; '**~-con·di·tioned** climatisé; '**~-con·di·tion·er** climatiseur *m*; '**~-cooled** (*moteur*) à refroidissement par l'air; '**~-craft** avion *m*, -s *m/pl.*; ~ carrier porte-avions *m/inv.*; '**~-cush·ion** coussin *m* à air; '**~-drop** 1. parachuter; 2. parachutage *m*; '**~-field** champ *m* d'aviation; '**~-force** aviation *f*; ♀ **Force** armée *f* de l'air; ~ **freight** fret *m* aérien; transport *m* par air; by ~ par voie aérienne, par avion; '**~-gun** fusil *m* à vent; ~ **host·ess** see stewardess.

air·i·ness ['ɛərinis] situation *f* aérée; bonne ventilation *f*; *fig.* légèreté *f* d'esprit, gaieté *f*.

air·ing ['ɛəriŋ] ventilation *f*; aérage *m*; *vêtements*: éventage *m*; give s.th. an ~ aérer qch.; that room needs an ~ il faut aérer cette pièce; take an ~ faire un (petit) tour, prendre l'air.

air...: '**~-jack·et** gilet *m* de sauvetage; ⊕ chemise f d'air; ~ **let·ter** lettre f par avion, aérogramme m; '~**lift** pont m aérien; '~**line** ligne f aérienne; service m de transports aériens; trajet m à vol d'oiseau; ~ **lin·er** avion m de ligne; ~ **mail** poste f aérienne; '~**man** aviateur m; '~**me¹chan·ic** mécanicien m d'avion; '~**mind·ed** ayant le sens de l'air; '~**pas·sen·ger** passager (-ère f) m; '~**pipe** ⊕ tuyau m d'air; '~**plane** surt. Am. avion m; ~ **pilot** pilote m (d'avion); '~**pock·et** 🛪 trou m d'air; '~**port** aéroport m; '~**pump** pompe f à air; '~**raid** ⚔ raid m aérien; ~ **precautions** défense f anti-aérienne; ~ **shelter** abri m; '~**ship** dirigeable m; '~**sick**: be ~ avoir la nausée; '~**strip** piste f d'atterrissage; ~ **ter·mi·nal** 🛪 aérogare f; '~**tight** (à clôture) hermétique; sl. ~ **case** thèse f inébranlable; '~**traf·fic** **con·'trol·ler** contrôleur m de la navigation aérienne, aiguilleur m du ciel; '~**tube** tuyau m à air; '~**way** voie f aérienne; '~**wom·an** aviatrice f; '~**wor·thy** navigable.

air·y □ ['ɛəri] bien aéré; léger (-ère f); désinvolte; fig. en l'air.

aisle △ [ail] nef f latérale; bas-côté m; passage m (entre bancs).

aitch [eitʃ] h m.

aitch·bone ['eitʃboun] culotte f (de bœuf).

a·jar [ə'dʒɑ:] entrouvert, entre-bâillé; fig. en désaccord (avec, with).

a·kim·bo [ə'kimbou] (les poings) sur les hanches.

a·kin [ə'kin] apparenté (à, avec to).

al·a·bas·ter ['æləbɑ:stə] 1. albâtre m; 2. d'albâtre.

a·lack † [ə'læk] hélas!; ~-a-day! ô jour malheureux!

a·lac·ri·ty [ə'lækriti] empressement m, alacrité f; promptitude f.

a·larm [ə'lɑ:m] 1. alarme f, alerte f; avertisseur m, signal m; fig. agitation f; réveille-matin m/inv.; ~-gun canon m d'alarme; give the ~, raise an ~ donner l'alarme, alerter; 2. alarmer (a. fig.); alerter; a'**larm-bell** tocsin m; timbre m avertisseur; a'**larm-clock** réveille-matin m/inv., réveil m; a'**larm-cord** cordon m de la sonnette d'alarme; a'**larm·ist** alarmiste mf (a. adj.).

a·lar·um [ə'lɛərəm] alerte f; réveille-matin m/inv.; timbre m.

40*

a·las [ə'lɑ:s] hélas!, las!

alb eccl. [ælb] aube f.

Al·ba·ni·an [æl'beinjən] 1. albanais; 2. Albanais(e f) m.

al·be·it [ɔ:l'bi:it] quoique, bien que.

al·bi·no biol. [æl'bi:nou] 1. albinos mf; 2. blanc(he f) (animal).

al·bum ['ælbəm] album m (a. = disque).

al·bu·men, al·bu·min ⚗ ['ælbjumin] albumen m; blanc m d'œuf; al'**bu·mi·nous** albumineux (-euse f).

al·chem·ic, al·chem·i·cal □ [æl'kemik(l)] alchimique; al·che·mist ['ælkimist] alchimiste m; 'al·che·my alchimie f.

al·co·hol ['ælkəhɔl] alcool m; al·co·'hol·ic alcoolique (adj., mf); 'al·co·hol·ism alcoolisme m; al·co·hol·ize ['~laiz] alcooliser.

al·cove ['ælkouv] alcôve f; niche f; tonnelle f (de jardin).

al·der ♀ ['ɔ:ldə] aune m.

al·der·man ['ɔ:ldəmən] alderman m, magistrat m municipal; **al·der·man·ship**['~mənʃip] fonctions f/pl. d'alderman; magistrature f.

ale [eil] ale f; bière f anglaise.

a·lee ⚓ [ə'li:] sous le vent.

a·lem·bic ⚗ [ə'lembik] alambic m.

a·lert [ə'lə:t] 1. □ alerte, éveillé; actif (-ive f); 2. alerte f; on the ~ sur le qui-vive; éveillé; a'**lert·ness** vigilance f; promptitude f.

al·fal·fa ♀ [æl'fælfə] luzerne f.

al·ga ♀ ['ælgə], pl. -gae [~dʒi:] algue f.

al·ge·bra ⅍ ['ældʒibrə] algèbre f; **al·ge·bra·ic** [~'breiik] algébrique.

a·li·as ['eiliæs] 1. autrement nommé; 2. nom m d'emprunt. [excuse f.\

al·i·bi ['ælibai] alibi m; Am. F]

al·ien ['eiljən] 1. étranger (-ère f); fig. ~ to contraire à; qui répugne à; 2. étranger (-ère f) m; 'al·ien·a·ble aliénable, mutable; al·ien·ate ['~eit] aliéner (des biens); fig. détacher, éloigner (de, from), (s')aliéner (q.); al·ien·a·tion biens, cœur: aliénation f; désaffection f; ~ of mind égarement m d'esprit; 'al·ien·ist 🕮 aliéniste m.

a·light¹ [ə'lait] allumé; en feu.

a·light² [~] descendre; mettre pied à terre; se poser (oiseau); 🛪 atterrir; amerrir.

a·lign [ə'lain] v/t. aligner (a. surv.);

mettre en ligne; ~ o.s. with se ranger du côté de; v/i. s'aligner; a'lign-ment alignement m (a. surv.).

a·like [ə'laik] 1. adj. semblable, pareil(le f); 2. adv. semblablement; de la même manière; de même.

al·i·ment ['ælimənt] aliment m; al·i·men·ta·ry [~'mentəri] alimentaire; ~ canal tube m ou canal m alimentaire; al·i·men'ta·tion alimentation f.

al·i·mo·ny ['æliməni] pension f alimentaire; aliments m/pl.

a·line(·ment) [ə'lain(mənt)] see align(ment).

al·i·quot ⚗ ['ælikwɔt] (partie f) aliquote f.

a·live [ə'laiv] vivant, en vie; sensible (à, to), conscient (de, to); fig. éveillé; ⚡ sous tension; no man ~ personne au monde; F look ~! dépêchez-vous!; F man ~! par exemple!; grand Dieu!; be ~ to avoir conscience de; be ~ with grouiller de.

al·ka·li ⚗ ['ælkəlai] alcali m; al·ka·line ['~lain] alcalin; make ~ alcaliser.

all [ɔ:l] 1. adj. tout; sans exception; entier (-ère f); ~ day (long) (pendant) toute la journée; ~ kind(s) of books toutes sortes de livres; for ~ that toutefois, cependant; see above; after; 2. su. tout m; totalité f; my ~ mon tout; ~ of them eux tous; at ~ quoi que ce soit; aucunement; not at ~ (pas) du tout; for ~ (that) I care pour ce que cela me fait; for ~ I know autant que je sache; 3. adv. tout; entièrement; ~ at once tout à coup; tout d'un coup; ~ the better tant mieux; ~ but à peu près, presque; ~ right en règle; en bon état; entendu!; bon!; c'est ça!

all-A·mer·i·can [ɔ:lə'merikən] 1. relevant entièrement des É.-U.; 2. sp. champion m américain.

al·lay [ə'lei] apaiser, calmer; modérer; dissiper (des soupçons); apaiser (la faim, la soif).

al·le·ga·tion [æle'geiʃn] allégation f; al·lege [ə'ledʒ] alléguer; prétendre; al'leged allégué; prétendu; présumé.

al·le·giance [ə'li:dʒns] fidélité f (à, to), obéissance f (à, to); oath of ~ serment m d'allégeance.

al·le·gor·ic, al·le·gor·i·cal □ [æle-'gɔrik(l)] allégorique; al·le·go·rize ['æligəraiz] allégoriser; 'al·le·go·ry allégorie f.

al·le·lu·ia [æli'lu:jə] alléluia m.

al·ler·gic [ə'lɔ:dʒik] a. fig. allergique (à to); al·ler·gy ['ælədʒi] allergie f.

al·le·vi·ate [ə'li:vieit] alléger, soulager; apaiser (la soif); al·le·vi'a·tion allégement m, soulagement m; adoucissement m.

al·ley ['æli] jardin: allée f; ruelle f, ville: passage m; Am. ruelle f latérale; see back ~; see blind; a. skittle-~; F that is right down his ~ c'est son rayon; '~·way Am. ruelle f.

All Fools' Day ['ɔ:l'fu:lzdei] le premier avril.

al·li·ance [ə'laiəns] alliance f; apparentage m; form an ~ s'allier (avec, with).

al·li·ga·tor zo. ['æligeitə] alligator m.

all-in ['ɔ:l'in] mixte; ... tous risques; tout compris; Am. F fini, sl. fichu.

al·lit·er·ate [ə'litəreit] allitérer; al·lit·er'a·tion allitération f.

all-met·al ⊕ ['ɔ:l'metl] tout métal.

al·lo·cate ['æləkeit] allouer, assigner; distribuer; al·lo'ca·tion allocation f; répartition f (des dépenses); part f assignée; [tion f.]

al·lo·cu·tion [ælo'kju:ʃn] allocu-]

al·lo·di·al □ [ə'loudjəl] allodial (-aux m/pl.).

al·lop·a·thist ✝ [ə'lɔpəθist] allopathe mf; al'lop·a·thy allopathie f.

al·lot [ə'lɔt] assigner, attribuer; affecter (qch.) (à, for); répartir; al'lot-ment attribution f; somme: affectation f; ✕ délégation f de solde; partage m; distribution f; portion f; terre: lopin m.

all-out ['ɔ:l'aut] avec toute son énergie, de toutes ses forces.

al·low [ə'lau] permettre; admettre; tolérer; laisser; Am. F opiner; he is ~ed to be on lui reconnaît (su.); ~ for tenir compte de; avoir égard à; F it ~s of no excuse c'est impardonnable; al'low·a·ble □ admissible, admis, légitime; al'low·ance 1. tolérance f; pension f alimentaire; rente f; argent m de poche; ✕ nourriture: indemnité f; frais m/pl.; rabais m, remise f; marge f; ⊕ tolérance f; make ~ for s.o. se montrer indulgent envers q.; make ~ for s.th. faire la part de qch.; 2. faire une rente à; rationner (le pain etc.).

al·loy [ə'lɔi] **1.** alliage *m*; *fig.* mélange *m*; **2.** (s')allier; *v/t. fig.* altérer, diminuer, porter atteinte à.

all...: '~-'**pur·pose** universel(le *f*), à tout faire; '~-'**red** entièrement britannique; '~-'**round** universel(le *f*), complet (-ète *f*); à tout usage; ✝ global (-aux *m/pl.*).

All Saints' Day ['ɔːl'seintsdei] la Toussaint *f*.

All Souls' Day ['ɔːl'soulzdei] la fête *f* des morts.

all-star *sp. Am.* ['ɔːl'staː] composé de joueurs de premier ordre.

al·lude [ə'luːd] faire allusion (à, *to*).

al·lure [ə'ljuə] attirer; séduire; **al-'lure·ment** attrait *m*; appât *m*; séduction *f*; **al'lur·ing** □ attrayant, séduisant.

al·lu·sion [ə'luːʒn] allusion *f* (à, *to*); **al'lu·sive** □ allusif (-ive *f*); faisant allusion (à, *to*).

al·lu·vi·al □ [ə'luːvjəl] alluvial (-aux *m/pl.*) (*terrain*); alluvien(ne *f*) (*gîte*); **al'lu·vi·on** [~ən] alluvion *f*; **al'lu·vi·um** [~əm], *pl.* **-ums, -vi·a** [~vjə] alluvion *f*; lais *m*.

all-weath·er ['ɔːl'weðə] tous-temps; *sp.* ~ *court* (terrain *m* en) quick *m* (*TM*).

al·ly[1] [ə'lai] (s')allier (à, avec *to*, *with*); *v/t.* apparenter (*des familles*); *allied to fig.* allié à *ou* avec; de la même nature que; **2.** ['ælai] allié *m*, coallié *m*.

al·ly[2] ['æli] grosse bille *f*; calot *m*.

al·ma·nac ['ɔːlmənæk] almanach *m*.

al·might·i·ness [ɔːl'maitinis] toute-puissance *f*; **al'might·y 1.** □ tout-puissant (toute-puissante *f*); **2.** F rudement; **3.** ♩ *le* Tout-Puissant.

al·mond ['ɑːmənd] amande *f*.

al·mon·er ['ɑːmənə] aumônier (-ère *f*) *m*.

al·most ['ɔːlmoust] presque, à peu près.

alms [ɑːmz] *usu. sg.* aumône *f*; '~-**bag** aumônière *f*; '~-**house** asile *m* de vieillards *ou* d'indigents.

al·oe ♀, *a. pharm.* ['ælou] aloès *m*.

a·loft [ə'lɔft] ♩ en haut (*dans la mâture*); *fig.* en l'air; ✈ en vol.

a·lone [ə'loun] seul; *let* (*ou leave*) ~ laisser (*q.*) tranquille; *let it* ~! n'y touchez pas!; *let* ~ sans compter; sans parler de.

a·long [ə'lɔŋ] **1.** *adv.*: *move* ~ avancer; *come* ~! venez donc; *stride* ~ avan-

cer à grandes enjambées; *all* ~ depuis longtemps; tout le temps; ~ *with* avec; F *get* ~ *with you!* filez!; allons donc!; **2.** *prp.* le long de; **a'long'shore** le long de la côte; **a'long'side 1.** ♩ *adv.* bord à bord, contre à contre; **2.** *prp.* ♩ accosté de long de; *fig.* tout près de.

a·loof [ə'luːf] à l'écart; distant; ♩ au large; *keep* ~ se tenir éloigné (de, *from*); *stand* ~ s'abstenir; **a'loof·ness** réserve *f* (à l'égard de, *from*).

a·loud [ə'laud] à haute voix; tout haut.

alp [ælp] **1.** alpe *f*; **2.** *the* ~s *pl.* les Alpes *f/pl.*; **al·pen·stock** ['ælpinstɔk] alpenstock *m*; bâton *m* ferré.

al·pha·bet ['ælfəbit] alphabet *m*; **al·pha·bet·ic, al·pha·bet·i·cal** □ [~-'betik(l)] alphabétique.

Al·pine ['ælpain] alpin; alpestre (*climat etc.*); ☀ ~ *sun* rayons *m/pl.* ultraviolets; **al·pin·ist** ['~pinist] alpiniste *mf*.

al·read·y [ɔːl'redi] déjà; dès à présent.

Al·sa·tian [æl'seiʃən] **1.** alsacien (-ne *f*); **2.** Alsacien(ne *f*) *m*; (a. ~ *wolf-hound*) chien-loup (*pl.* chiens-loups) *m*.

al·so ['ɔːlsou] aussi; encore; également; *équit.* ~ *ran* non classé.

al·tar ['ɔːltə] autel *m*; '~-**piece** retable *m*; tableau *m* d'autel.

al·ter ['ɔːltə] changer; *v/t.* modifier; remanier (*un texte*); *Am.* F châtrer (*un animal*); **'al·ter·a·ble** variable; modifiable; **al·ter·a·tion** [~'reiʃn] changement *m*, modification *f* (à, *to*); remaniement *m*.

al·ter·cate ['ɔːltəkeit] se quereller; **al·ter·ca·tion** dispute *f*, querelle *f*.

al·ter·nate 1. ['ɔːltəneit] (faire) alterner; ⚡ *alternating current* courant *m* alternatif; **2.** □ [ɔːl'təːnit] alternatif (-ive *f*), alterné; *on* ~ *days* tous les deux jours; **3.** [~] *Am.* suppléant(e *f*) *m*; remplaçant(e *f*) *m*; **al·ter·na·tion** [~'neiʃn] alternation *f*; alternance *f*; **al'ter·na·tive** [~nətiv] **1.** □ alternatif (-ive *f*); second, autre; ⊕ d'emprunt (*route*); **2.** alternative *f*; autre parti *m* (*entre deux*); *I have no* ~ je n'ai pas le choix; **al·ter·na·tor** ⚡ ['~neitə] alternateur *m*.

al·though [ɔːl'ðou] quoique, bien que.

al·tim·e·ter [æl'timitə] altimètre
m.

al·ti·tude ['æltitju:d] altitude *f*; élévation *f*; hauteur *f*; ~ recorder alti-
traceur *m*. [contralto *m*.}

al·to ♪ ['æltou] alto *m*; *femme*;}

al·to·geth·er [ɔ:ltə'geðə] **1.** tout à
fait, entièrement; en tout; somme
toute; F tous ensemble; **2.** F *in the* ~
tout nu, F à poil.

al·tru·ism ['æltruizm] altruisme *m*;
'**al·tru·ist** altruiste *mf*; **al·tru'is-
tic** (~ally) altruiste.

al·um 🜍 ['æləm] alun *m*; **a·lu·mi-
na** [ə'lju:minə] alumine *f*; **al·u-
min·i·um** [ælju'minjəm], *Am.* **al-
u·mi·num** [ə'lu:minəm] aluminium *m*; ~ *acetate* acétate *m* d'aluminium; **a'lu·mi·nous** [ə'lju:mi-
nəs] alumineux (-euse *f*).

a·lum·nus [ə'lʌmnəs], *pl.* **-ni** [~nai]
m; **a'lum·na** [~nə], *pl.* **-nae** [~ni:]
f élève *mf* (*d'un collège*); étudiant(e
f) *m* (*à une université*); gradué(e *f*)
m; *Am. sp.* ancien équipier *m*.

al·ve·o·lar [æl'viələ] alvéolaire.

al·ways ['ɔ:lwəz] toujours; tout le
temps; *as* ~ comme toujours, F
comme d'habitude.

a·mal·gam [ə'mælgəm] amalgame
m; **a'mal·gam·ate** [~meit] (s')a-
malgamer; fusionner; **a·mal·gam-
'a·tion** amalgamation *f*; mélange *m*;
🜨 fusion *f*.

a·man·u·en·sis [əmænju'ensis], *pl.*
-ses [~si:z] secrétaire *mf*.

am·a·ranth ♣ ['æmərænθ] amarante *f*.

a·mass [ə'mæs] amasser, accumuler.

am·a·teur ['æmətə:] amateur *m*; dilettante *m*; **am·a'teur·ish** d'amateur.

am·a·tive ['æmətiv], **am·a·to·ry**
['~təri] amoureux (-euse *f*); érotique; d'amour.

a·maze [ə'meiz] stupéfier, confondre; **a'maze·ment** stupéfaction *f*,
stupeur *f*; **a'maz·ing** ☐ stupéfiant, étonnant.

Am·a·zon ['æməzn] Amazone *f*; *fig.*
♀ femme *f* hommasse; **Am·a·zo·ni-
an** [~'zounjən] d'Amazone; *géog.*
de l'Amazone.

am·bas·sa·dor [æm'bæsədə] ambassadeur *m*; **am·bas·sa·do·ri·al**
[~'dɔ:riəl] ambassadorial (-aux
m/pl.), d'ambassadeur; **am'bas·sa-
dress** [~dris] ambassadrice *f*.

am·ber ['æmbə] **1.** ambre *m*; **2.** am-
bré; jaune; d'ambre; **am·ber·gris**
['~gri:s] ambre *m* gris.

am·bi·dex·trous ☐ ['æmbi'deks-
trəs] ambidextre; *fig.* fourbe.

am·bi·ent ['æmbiənt] ambiant.

am·bi·gu·i·ty [æmbi'gjuiti] ambiguïté *f*; équivoque *f*; **am'big·u·ous**
☐ ambigu(ë *f*), équivoque; incertain; obscur.

am·bi·tion [æm'biʃn] ambition *f*
(*de, to*); ~s *pl.* ambitions *f/pl.*;
visées *f/pl.*; **am'bi·tious** ☐ ambitieux (-euse *f*) (*de of, to*); prétentieux (-euse *f*) (*style*).

am·ble ['æmbl] **1.** amble *m*, entre-
pas *m*; **2.** aller (à) l'amble; traque-
narder; *fig.* marcher d'un pas tranquille; ~ *up* s'approcher d'un pas
tranquille; '**am·bler** flâneur (-euse
f) *m*; cheval *m* ambleur.

am·bro·si·a [æm'brouziə] ambroisie *f*; **am'bro·si·al** ☐ ambrosiaque;
fig. délicieux (-euse *f*).

am·bu·lance ['æmbjuləns] ambulance *f*; hôpital *m* ambulant; *attr.*
sanitaire; ~ *box* infirmerie *f* porta-
tive; *Am.* F ~ *chaser* avoué *qui
guette les accidents pour faire poursuivre le responsable en dommages-
intérêts*; ~ *man* ambulancier *m*; ~
station poste *m* d'ambulance; poste
m de secours; '**am·bu·lant** ambulant.

am·bu·la·to·ry ['æmbjulətəri] **1.**
ambulant, mobile; ⚕ ambulatoire;
2. promenoir *m*, préau *m*; *eccl.*
déambulatoire *m*.

am·bus·cade [æmbəs'keid], **ambush** ['æmbuʃ] **1.** guet-apens (*pl.*
guets-apens) *m*; embuscade *f*; *lay
(ou make) an* ~ dresser une embuscade (à q., *for* s.o.); **2.** *v/t.*
attirer (*q.*) dans un piège; *v/i.* s'embusquer.

a·mel·io·rate [ə'mi:liəreit] (s')amé-
liorer; **a·mel·io·ra·tion** amélioration *f*.

a·men ['ɑ:'men] amen; ainsi soit-il.

a·me·na·ble ☐ [ə'mi:nəbl] soumis,
docile (à, *to*); ⚖ justiciable.

a·mend [ə'mend] *v/t.* amender; réformer; ⚖ corriger; *parl.* modifier,
amender; *v/i.* s'amender; **a'mend-
ment** modification *f*; ⚖ rectification *f*; *parl.* amendement *m* (*Am. a.
article ajouté à la Constitution des
É.-U.*); **a'mends** [~dz] *sg.* répara-

tion *f*; make ~ for réparer (*un tort*); compenser (*un défaut*).

a·men·i·ty [ə'mi:niti] *lieu*: aménité *f*; charme *m*; amabilité *f*; **amenities** *pl.* commodités *f/pl.* (*de l'existence*); civilités *f/pl.*

a·merce † [ə'mə:s] confisquer (*des terres*); mettre à l'amende.

A·mer·i·can [ə'merikən] **1.** américain; ~ *cloth* toile *f* cirée; ~ *leather* molesquine *f*; *Am.* ~ *Legion* association *f* des anciens combattants des deux guerres mondiales; *tourisme*: ~ *plan* pension *f* complète; **2.** Américain(e *f*) *m*; **a'mer·i·can·ism** américanisme *m*; **a'mer·i·can·ize** (s')américaniser.

Am·er·in·di·an [æmər'indjən], **Am·er·ind** ['æmərind] Indien *m* indigène de l'Amérique.

am·e·thyst *min.* ['æmiθist] améthyste *f*.

a·mi·a·bil·i·ty [eimjə'biliti] amabilité *f* (envers, to); **'a·mi·a·ble** ☐ aimable (envers, to).

am·i·ca·ble ☐ ['æmikəbl] amical (-aux *m/pl.*); bien disposé; **'am·i·ca·ble·ness** disposition *f* amicale.

a·mid(st) [ə'mid(st)] *prp.* au milieu de; parmi; entre.

a·mid·ships ⚓ [ə'midʃips] par le travers, au milieu du navire.

a·miss [ə'mis] mal; de travers; mal à propos; *take* ~ prendre (*qch.*) en mauvaise part; *it would not be* ~ (*for him*) *to* il ne (lui) ferait pas mal de; *what is* ~ *with him?* qu'est-ce qu'il a?

am·i·ty ['æmiti] amitié *f*; concorde *f*.

am·me·ter ⚡ ['æmitə] ampèremètre *m*.

am·mo·ni·a [ə'mounjə] ammoniaque *f*; *liquid* ~ (solution *f* aqueuse d')ammoniaque *f*; F alcali *m* volatil; **am'mo·ni·ac** [~æk], **am·mo·ni·a·cal** [æmo'naiəkl] ammoniac (-aque *f*); *see sal.*

am·mu·ni·tion ⚔ [æmju'niʃn] **1.** munitions *f/pl.* de guerre; **2.** d'ordonnance; ~ *boots* chaussures *f/pl.* de munition; ~ *bread* pain *m* de guerre.

am·nes·ty ['æmnesti] **1.** amnistie *f*; **2.** amnistier.

a·moe·ba *zo.* [ə'mi:bə] amibe *f*.

a·mong(st) [ə'mʌŋ(st)] *prp.* parmi, entre; *from* ~ d'entre; *be* ~ être du nombre de; *they have it* ~ *them* ils l'ont en commun.

a·mor·al [æ'mɔrəl] amoral (-aux *m/pl.*).

am·o·rous ☐ ['æmərəs] amoureux (-euse *f*) (de, of); érotique (*poésie*).

a·mor·phous [ə'mɔ:fəs] *min.* amorphe; *fig.* sans forme; vague.

am·or·ti·za·tion [əmɔ:ti'zeiʃn] amortissement *m*; **am'or·tize** [~taiz] amortir.

a·mount [ə'maunt] **1.** ~ *to* s'élever à, monter à; revenir à; se réduire à; **2.** somme *f*, montant *m*, total *m*; quantité *f*; valeur *f*; *to the* ~ *of* à la valeur de; jusqu'à concurrence de.

a·mour [ə'muə] intrigue *f* galante.

am·pere ⚡ ['æmpɛə] ampère *m*.

am·phet·a·mine [æm'fetəmi:n] amphétamine *f*.

am·phib·i·an ✕, *zo.* [æm'fibiən] **1.** amphibie *m*; **2.** = **am'phib·i·ous** ☐ amphibie.

am·phi·the·a·tre ['æmfiθiətə] amphithéâtre *m*.

am·ple ☐ ['æmpl] ample, large; vaste; gros(se *f*); grand; abondant; **'am·ple·ness** ampleur *f*; abondance *f*.

am·pli·fi·ca·tion [æmplifi'keiʃn] amplification *f* (*a. poét.*, *a. phys.*); *gramm. attribut*: extension *f*; **am·pli·fi·er** ['~faiə] *radio*: amplificateur *m*; haut-parleur *m*; **am·pli·fy** ['~fai] *v/t.* amplifier (*a. radio*); développer; exagérer; *v/i.* discourir; *radio*: ~*ing valve* lampe *f* amplificatrice; **am·pli·tude** ['~tju:d] amplitude *f* (*a. phys.*); ampleur *f*.

am·poule ['æmpu:l] ampoule *f*.

am·pu·tate ⚕ ['æmpjuteit] amputer, faire l'amputation de; **am·pu·'ta·tion** amputation *f*.

a·muck [ə'mʌk] *run* ~ tomber dans la folie meurtrière de l'amok; *fig.* faire les cent coups; *run* ~ *at* (*ou on ou against*) *fig.* s'emballer contre.

am·u·let ['æmjulit] amulette *f*.

a·muse [ə'mju:z] amuser, divertir, faire rire, égayer; distraire; **a'muse·ment** amusement *m*; divertissement *m*; distraction *f*; ~ *arcade* lunapark *m*; ~ *park* parc *m* d'attraction; *fête* *f* foraine; *for* ~ pour se distraire; pour (faire) rire; **a'mus·ing** ☐ amusant, divertissant (pour, to).

am·y·la·ceous [æmi'leiʃəs] amylacé.

an *gramm.* [æn; ən] *article*: un(e *f*).

an·a·bap·tist [ænə'bæptist] anabaptiste *mf*.

a·nach·ro·nism [əˈnækrənizm] anachronisme *m*.

a·n(a)e·mi·a [əˈniːmjə] anémie *f*; **a·n(a)e·mic** anémique.

an·(a)es·the·si·a [ænisˈθiːzjə] anesthésie *f*; **an·(a)es·thet·ic** [~ˈθetik] (~*ally*) anesthésique (*a. su./m*).

a·n(a)es·the·tist [æˈniːsθitist] anesthésiste *mf*; **a·n(a)es·the·tize** [æˈniːsθitaiz] anesthésier, insensibiliser.

an·a·log·ic, an·a·log·i·cal □ [ænəˈlɔdʒik(l)] analogique; **a·nal·o·gous** [əˈnæləgəs] analogue (*with*, *to*); **a·nal·o·gy** [əˈnæləgi] analogie *f* (*avec with*, *to*; *entre*, *between*).

an·a·lyse [ˈænəlaiz] analyser; faire l'analyse de (*a. gramm*.); **a·nal·y·sis** [əˈnæləsis], *pl.* -**ses** [~siːz] analyse *f*; *compte*: dépouillement *m*; *gramm*. analyse *f* logique; **an·a·lyst** [ˈænəlist] analyste *mf*; *public* ~ analyste *m* officiel.

an·a·lyt·ic, an·a·lyt·i·cal □ [ænəˈlitik(l)] analytique.

an·ar·chic, an·ar·chi·cal □ [æˈnɑːkik(l)] anarchique; **an·ar·chism** [ˈænəkizm] anarchisme *m*; **an·arch·ist** [ˈænəkist] anarchiste *mf*; **an·arch·y** anarchie *f*; désordre *m*.

a·nath·e·ma [əˈnæθimə] anathème *m*; malédiction *f*; **a·nath·e·ma·tize** anathématiser, frapper d'anathème; F maudire.

an·a·tom·i·cal □ [ænəˈtɔmikl] anatomique; **a·nat·o·mist** [əˈnætəmist] anatomiste *mf*; **a·nat·o·mize** anatomiser; disséquer; **a·nat·o·my** anatomie *f*; dissection *f*; F *fig*. squelette *m*.

an·ces·tor [ˈænsistə] ancêtre *m*; aïeul (*pl.* -eux) *m*; **an·ces·tral** [~ˈsestrəl] *biol*. ancestral (-aux *m/pl*.); héréditaire, de famille; **an·ces·tress** [ˈænsistris] ancêtre *f*; aïeule *f*; **an·ces·try** race *f*; lignage *m*; aïeux *m/pl*.

an·chor [ˈæŋkə] ⚓, *a. fig*. **1.** ancre *f*; *at* ~ à l'ancre; mouillé; **2.** *v/t*. ancrer, mettre à l'ancre; *v/i*. jeter l'ancre, mouiller; **an·chor·age** ancrage *m*, mouillage *m*.

an·cho·ret [ˈæŋkəret], **an·cho·rite** [~rait] anachorète *m*.

an·chor·man [ˈæŋkəˈmæn] *radio*, *télév*.: présentateur-réalisateur *m* (*pl.* présentateurs-réalisateurs).

an·cho·vy [ænˈtʃouvi] anchois *m*.

an·cient [ˈeinʃənt] **1.** ancien(ne *f*); antique; **2.** *the* ~*s pl.* les anciens *m/pl*. (*grecs et romains*); **an·cient·ly** anciennement; jadis.

an·cil·lar·y [ænˈsiləri] *fig*. subordonné, ancillaire (à, *to*); accessoire (à, *to*).

and [ænd; ənd] et; *thousands* ~ *thousands* des milliers et des milliers; *there are flowers* ~ *flowers* il y a des fleurs et encore des fleurs; *try* ~ *take it* tâchez de le prendre.

and·i·ron [ˈændaiən] landier *m*; chenet *m*.

an·ec·do·tal [ænekˈdoutl], **an·ec·dot·i·cal** □ [~ˈdotikl] anecdotique; **an·ec·dote** [ˈænikdout] anecdote *f*.

an·e·lec·tric *phys*. [æniˈlektrik] anélectrique.

an·e·mom·e·ter [æniˈmɔmitə] anémomètre *m*.

a·nem·o·ne [əˈneməni] anémone *f*.

an·er·oid [ˈænərɔid] (baromètre *m*) anéroïde *m*.

a·new [əˈnjuː] de nouveau; à nouveau.

an·gel [ˈeindʒl] ange *m*; **an·gel·ic, an·gel·i·cal** □ [ænˈdʒelik(l)] angélique.

An·gles [ˈæŋglz] *pl.* Angles *m/pl*.

An·gli·can [ˈæŋglikən] **1.** anglican; *Am. a.* anglais; **2.** anglican(e *f*) *m*.

An·gli·cism [ˈæŋglisizm] anglicisme *m*; idiotisme *m* anglais.

an·gling [ˈæŋgliŋ] pêche *f* à la ligne.

An·glo-Sax·on [ˈæŋglouˈsæksn] **1.** Anglo-Saxon(ne *f*) *m*; **2.** anglo-saxon(ne *f*).

an·go·ra [æŋˈgɔːrə] (laine *f*) angora *m*; (*a.* ~ *cat*) (chat *m*) angora *m*.

an·gry [ˈæŋgri] fâché, irrité, courroucé (*contre q.*, *with s.o.*; de qch. *about s.th.*); ⚓ irrité, enflammé.

an·guish [ˈæŋgwiʃ] angoisse *f*; douleur *f*; *fig*. supplice *m*.

an·gu·lar [ˈæŋgjulə] angulaire; anguleux (-euse *f*) (*visage*); *fig*. maigre, décharné; ~ *point* ⚓ sommet *m*; **an·gu·lar·i·ty** [~ˈlæriti] angu-

larité f; fig. caractère m anguleux.
an·hy·drous ⚗ [æn'haidrəs] anhydre; sec (sèche f), tapé (*fruits*).
an·ile ['einail] de vieille femme.
an·i·line ⚗ ['ænilin] aniline f; ～ *dyes pl.* colorants m/pl. d'aniline.
an·i·mad·ver·sion [ænimæd'və:ʃn] censure f, blâme m; **an·i·mad·vert** [～'və:t] critiquer, censurer, blâmer (qch., *on s.th.*).
an·i·mal ['æniməl] 1. animal m; bête f; 2. animal (-aux m/pl.); *Brit.* ～ *home* asyle m pour animaux; *zo.* ～ *kingdom* règne m animal; ～ *lover* ami(e f) m des animaux; *Am.* ～ *shelter* asyle m pour animaux; ～ *spirits pl.* verve f, entrain m; **an·i·mal·cule** [～'mælkju:l] animalcule m; **an·i·mal·ism** ['～məlizm] animalité f; *biol.* animalisme m; **an·i·mal·i·ty** animalité f.
an·i·mate 1. ['ænimeit] animer; stimuler; mouvementer; 2. ['～mit], *usu.* **an·i·mat·ed** ['～meitid] animé (*a. fig.*); doué de vie; ～ *cartoon* dessins m/pl. animés.
an·i·ma·tion [æni'meiʃn] animation f; vivacité f; chaleur f; entrain m; stimulation f.
an·i·mos·i·ty [æni'mɔsiti], *a.* **an·i·mus** ['æniməs] animosité f.
an·ise ♀ ['ænis] anis m; **an·i·seed** ['～si:d] (graine f d')anis m; *attr.* à l'anis. [astragale m.)
an·kle ['æŋkl] cheville f; ～ *bone*)
an·klet ['æŋklit] bracelet m de jambe; manille f (de forçat); *Am.* socquette f.
an·nals ['ænlz] *pl.* annales f/pl.; *fig.* archives f/pl.
an·neal ⊕ [ə'ni:l] recuire, adoucir (*un métal etc.*); *fig.* tempérer.
an·nex 1. [ə'neks] annexer (à, *to*); ajouter; joindre; ～ *to* poser (*des conditions*) à; 2. ['æneks] annexe f; dépendance f; adjonction f; **an·nex·a·tion** annexion f (de, *of*); mainmise f (sur, *of*).
an·ni·hi·late [ə'naiəleit] anéantir; annihiler; *see annul*; **an·ni·hi·la·tion** anéantissement m; annihilation f; *see annulment*.
an·ni·ver·sa·ry [æni'və:səri] anniversaire m.
an·no·tate ['ænouteit] annoter; commenter; accompagner de remarques; **an·no·ta·tion** annotation f; commentaire m; note f.

an·nounce [ə'nauns] annoncer; faire connaître; **an·nounce·ment** annonce f; avis m; faire-part m/inv.; **an·nounc·er** *radio*: speaker m.
an·noy [ə'nɔi] contrarier; gêner; molester; vexer; **an·noy·ance** contrariété f; chagrin m; ennui m; **an·noyed** contrarié, ennuyé, vexé; **an·noy·ing** □ contrariant, ennuyeux (-euse f), ennuyant.
an·nu·al ['ænjuəl] 1. □ annuel(le f) (*a.* ♀); ～ *ring* ♀ couche f annuelle; 2. ♀ plante f annuelle; *livre:* annuaire m.
an·nu·i·tant [ə'njuitənt] rentier (-ère f) m; **an·nu·i·ty** rente f (annuelle); ♱ (*a.* ～ *bond*) obligation f; *see life*.
an·nul [ə'nʌl] annuler, résilier; dissoudre (*un mariage*); abroger (*une loi*).
an·nu·lar □ ['ænjulə] annulaire.
an·nul·ment [ə'nʌlmənt] annulation f, résiliation f; dissolution f; abrogation f.
an·nun·ci·a·tion [ənʌnsi'eiʃn] proclamation f, annonce f; *eccl.* Annonciation f; **an·nun·ci·a·tor** [～ʃieitə] annonciateur m; *Am.* bouton m (*de sonnerie*).
an·ode ⚡ ['ænoud] 1. anode f; 2. de plaque; ～ *potential* tension f de plaque.
an·o·dyne ⚕ ['ænodain] anodin (*a. su./m*); calmant (*a. su./m*).
a·noint [ə'nɔint] *surt. eccl.* oindre; sacrer; *fig.* graisser.
a·nom·a·lous □ [ə'nɔmələs] anomal (-aux m/pl.); F exceptionnel(le f), anormal (-aux m/pl.), irrégulier (-ère f); **a·nom·a·ly** anomalie f.
a·non [ə'nɔn] bientôt, tout à l'heure; *ever and* ～ de temps en temps.
an·o·nym·i·ty [ænə'nimiti] anonymat m, anonyme m; **a·non·y·mous** □ [ə'nɔniməs] anonyme; inconnu.
an·oth·er [ə'nʌðə] encore un(e); un(e) autre; un(e) second(e); *just such* ～ un autre du même genre; F *tell me ou us* ～! à d'autres!, tu ne le crois pas toi-même!
an·swer ['ɑ:nsə] 1. v/t. répondre (*qch.*) (à q., *s.o.*); faire réponse à; remplir (*un but*); obéir (*à la barre*); répondre à (*une accusation*); ～ *the bell* (*ou door*) aller *ou* venir ouvrir; v/i. répondre (à q., *to s.o.*; à qch., *to s.th.*;

à une question, *to a question*); ne pas réussir; F~ back répliquer, répondre avec impertinence; *don't ~ back!* ne réponds pas!; ~ *for* être responsable de; répondre de (*q.*), se porter garant de (*q.*, *qch.*); ~ *to the name of* s'appeler; **2.** réponse *f* (à; *to*); Å solution *f*; ½ réplique *f*, réfutation *f*; '**an·swer·a·ble** □ responsable; comptable.

ant [ænt] fourmi *f*.

an't [ɑ:nt] F = *are not, am not; sl. ou prov.* = *is not.*

an·tag·o·nism [æn'tægənizm] antagonisme *m* (entre, *between*); opposition *f* (à, *to*; avec, *with*); **an'tag·o·nist** adversaire *m*; antagoniste *m*; **an·tag·o'nis·tic** (~ally) opposé, contraire (à, *to*); adverse; **an'tag·o·nize** éveiller l'hostilité de (*q.*); s'opposer à; contrarier (*une force*).

ant·arc·tic [ænt'ɑ:ktik] antarctique; ♀ *Circle* cercle *m* polaire antarctique.

an·te *Am.* [ænti] *poker:* **1.** première mise *f*; **2.** F (*usu. ~ up*) *v/t., a. v/i.* ouvrir (le jeu); *v/i. fig.* donner son obole.

an·te·ced·ence [ænti si:dəns] priorité *f*; antériorité *f*; *astr.* antécédence *f*; **an·te'ced·ent 1.** □ antécédent; antérieur (à, *to*); **2.** antécédent *m* (*a. gramm.*); thème *m*; *his ~s pl.* ses ancêtres *m/pl.*; son passé *m.*

an·te·cham·ber ['æntitʃeimbə] antichambre *f.*

an·te·date ['ænti'deit] antidater (*un document*); précéder, venir avant.

an·te·di·lu·vi·an ['æntidi'lu:vjən] antédiluvien(ne *f*) (*a. su./mf*).

an·te·lope *zo.* ['æntiloup] antilope *f.*

an·te·na·tal [ænti'neitl] prénatal.

an·ten·na [æn'tenə], *pl.* **-nae** [~ni:] *zo., radio, télév.:* antenne *f*; limaçon: corne *f.*

an·te·ri·or [æn'tiəriə] antérieur (à, *to*).

an·te·room ['æntirum] antichambre *f*, vestibule *m.*

an·them ['ænθəm] *eccl.* antienne *f*, motet *m*; hymne *m.*

ant-hill ['ænthil] fourmilière *f.*

an·thol·o·gy [æn'θɔlədʒi] *fig.* anthologie *f*, florilège *m.*

an·thra·cite *min.* ['ænθrəsait] anthracite *m*; F houille *f* sèche; **an·thrax** ['ænθræks] *vét.* charbon *m.*

an·thro·poid ['ænθrəpoid] anthropoïde (*a. su./m*); **an·thro·po·log·i-**

cal □ [ænθrəpə'lɔdʒikəl] anthropologique; **an·thro·pol·o·gist** [~'pɔlədʒist] anthropologiste *mf*, -logue *mf*; **an·thro'pol·o·gy** [~dʒi] anthropologie *f*; **an·thro·poph·a·gy** [ænθrə'pɔfədʒi] anthropophagie *f.*

anti... [ænti] *préf.* anti-; anté-; contre-.

an·ti-air·craft ['ænti'eəkra:ft]: ~ *alarm* alerte *f* (aux avions); ~ *defence* défense *f* contre avions; D.C.A.; ~ *gun* canon *m* antiaérien.

an·ti·bi·ot·ic 𝒮 ['æntibai'ɔtik] antibiotique (*a. su./m*).

an·tic ['æntik] **1.** □ † grotesque; **2.** bouffonnerie *f*, singerie *f*; ~*s pl.* gambades *f/pl.*

An·ti·christ ['æntikraist] Antéchrist *m.*

an·tic·i·pate [æn'tisipeit] anticiper (*un paiement*; sur *les événements*); devancer; prévoir; s'attendre à; se promettre; escompter (*un résultat*); **an·tic·i'pa·tion** anticipation *f*; prévision *f*; attente *f*; expectative *f*; *payment by ~* paiement *m* par anticipation; *in ~* d'avance; *Thanking you in ~* Avec mes *ou* nos remerciements anticipés; **an'tic·i·pa·to·ry** [~peitəri] anticipé, anticipatif (-ive *f*); par anticipation.

an·ti·cler·i·cal ['ænti'klerikəl] anticlérical.

an·ti·cli·max ['ænti'klaimæks] anticlimax *m.*

an·ti·cor·ro·sive a·gent ['æntikə-'rousiv'eidʒənt] antirouille *m.*

an·ti·cy·clone *météor.* ['ænti'saikloun] anticyclone *m.*

an·ti·daz·zle mot. ['ænti'dæzl] antiaveuglant; ~ *headlights pl.* phares-code *m/pl.*

an·ti·dote ['æntidout] antidote *m*, contrepoison *m* (de, contre *against*; for, *to*).

an·ti·freeze mot. ['ænti'fri:z] antigel *m.*

an·ti·fric·tion ['ænti'frikʃn] antifriction *f*; *attr.* ⊕ antifriction.

an·ti·ha·lo *phot.* ['ænti'heilou] antihalo *m* (*a. su./m*).

an·ti·ic·er ⊕, ✈ ['ænti'aisə] antigivreur *m.*

an·ti·knock mot. ['ænti'nɔk] (produit *m*) antidétonant.

an·ti·mo·ny *min.* ['æntiməni] antimoine *m.*

an·tip·a·thy [æn'tipəθi] antipathie *f*

(pour, contre *against*, *to*); aversion *f* (pour q., *against* s.th.).

an·tip·o·dal [æn'tipədl] situé aux antipodes; **an·ti·pode** ['ᴗpoud], *pl.* **an·tip·o·des** [ᴗ'tipədiːz] chose *f* diamétralement opposée; rebours *m*; ᴗs *pl.* géog. antipodes *m/pl.*

an·ti·pol·lu·tion de·vice ['æntipə-'luʃəndi'vais] équipement *m* antipollution.

An·ti·py·rin [ænti'paiərin] antipyrine *f*, analgésine *f*.

an·ti·quar·i·an [ænti'kwɛəriən] archéologique, de l'antique; **an·ti·quar·y** ['ᴗkwəri] archéologue *m*; amateur *m* d'antiquités; antiquaire *m*; **an·ti·quat·ed** ['ᴗkweitid] vieilli, désuet (-ète *f*); suranné, démodé. **an·tique** [æn'tiːk] **1.** □ antique; ancien(ne *f*); suranné; **2.** antiquité *f*; objet *m* antique; **an·tiq·ui·ty** [ᴗ'tikwiti] antiquité *f* (*romaine etc.*); ancienneté *f*; antiquities *pl.* antiquités *f/pl.*

an·ti·rust ['ænti'rʌst] antirouille *m*. **an·ti·sem·ite** [ænti'siːmait] antisémite (*a. su./mf*); **an·ti-Se·mit·ic** ['ᴗsi'mitik] antisémite; **an·ti-sem·i·tism** [ᴗ'semitizm] antisémitisme *m*.

an·ti·sep·tic [ænti'septik] antiseptique (*a. su./m*).

an·ti-skid *mot.* ['ænti'skid] antidérapant.

an·tith·e·sis [æn'tiθisis], *pl.* **-ses** [ᴗsiːz] antithèse *f*; contraire *m*; **an·ti·thet·ic, an·ti·thet·i·cal** □ [ᴗ-'θetik(l)] antithétique.

ant·ler ['æntlə] *cerf etc.*: andouiller *m*; ᴗs *pl.* bois *m* (*pl.*).

an·to·nym *gramm.* ['æntənim] antonyme *m*.

A num·ber 1 *Am.* F *see* A 1.

a·nus *anat.* ['einəs] anus *m*.

an·vil ['ænvil] enclume *f*; *fig.* chantier *m*, métier *m*.

anx·i·e·ty [æŋ'zaiəti] inquiétude *f*; soucis *m/pl.*; *fig.* désir *m* (de *inf.*; *to inf.*); *fig.* sollicitude *f* (pour, *for*); ✿ anxiété *f*; ᴗ *dream* rêve *m* anxieux. **anx·ious** □ ['æŋkʃəs] inquiet (-ète *f*), soucieux (-euse *f*) (sur, de, au sujet de *about*); désireux (-euse *f*) (de *inf.*, *to inf.*); impatient (de *inf.*, *to inf.*).

an·y ['eni] **1.** *adj.*, *a. pron.* un(e *f*); tout(e *f*); n'importe quel(le *f*);

n'importe lequel (laquelle *f*); *are there* ᴗ *nails?* y a-t-il des clous?; *not* ᴗ aucun, nul; **2.** *adv.* ne se traduit pas d'ordinaire; 'ᴗ·bod·y, 'ᴗ·one quelqu'un(e *f*); n'importe qui; tout le monde; quiconque; (*avec négation*) personne; *not* ᴗ personne; 'ᴗ·how **1.** *cj.* en tout cas; **2.** *adv.* n'importe comment; 'ᴗ·thing quelque chose; (*avec négation*) rien; ᴗ *but* rien moins que; 'ᴗ·way *see* anyhow; 'ᴗ·where n'importe où.

a·pace [ə'peis] vite; à grands pas.

a·part [ə'pɑːt] à part; de côté; écarté; ᴗ *from* en dehors de; hormis que; *joking* ᴗ plaisanterie à part; *set* ᴗ *for* mettre de côté pour; réserver à; **a'part·ment** salle *f*, chambre *f*; pièce *f*; *Am.* appartement *m*; ᴗs *pl.* logement *m*; *Am.* ᴗ *hotel* hôtel *m* meublé avec *ou* sans service; *Am.* ᴗ *house* maison *f* de rapport.

ap·a·thet·ic [æpə'θetik] (ᴗally) indifférent; 'ap·a·thy apathie *f*, indifférence *f*; nonchalance *f*.

ape [eip] **1.** (grand) singe *m*; *Am.* F *go* ᴗ devenir fou (folle *f*); **2.** imiter, singer.

a·peak ⚓ [ə'piːk] à pic, dérapé (*ancre*).

a·pe·ri·ent [ə'piəriənt] **1.** laxatif (-ive *f*); relâchant; **2.** laxatif *m*; relâchant *m*.

ap·er·ture ['æpətjuə] ouverture *f*.

a·pex ['eipeks], *pl.* 'a·pex·es, a·pi·ces ['eipisiːz] sommet *m*; *fig.* apogée *m*.

aph·o·rism ['æfərizm] aphorisme *m*; **aph·o·ris·tic** (ᴗally) aphoristique.

a·pi·ar·y ['eipiəri] rucher *m*; **a·pi·cul·ture** ['ᴗkʌltʃə] apiculture *f*.

a·piece [ə'piːs] chacun(e *f*); la pièce.

ap·ish □ ['eipiʃ] simiesque; imitateur (-trice *f*).

A·poc·ry·pha *bibl.* [ə'pɔkrifə] *pl.* les Apocryphes *m/pl.*; **a'poc·ry·phal** apocryphe.

ap·o·gee *astr.* ['æpodʒiː] apogée *m*.

a·pol·o·get·ic [əpɔlə'dʒetik] **1.** (ᴗally) d'excuse; *eccl.* apologétique (*livre*); **2.** *eccl. usu.* ᴗs *pl.* apologétique *f*; **a·pol·o·gist** apologiste *m*, défenseur *m*; **a'pol·o·gize** s'excuser (de, *for*; auprès de, *to*); **a'pol·o·gy** excuses *f/pl.*; apologie *f*, justification *f* (de, for); *fig.* semblant *m* (de, for); F (mauvais) substitut *m* (de, for); **make an ~** présenter des excuses.

ap·o·plec·tic, ap·o·plec·ti·cal □ [æpə'plektik(l)] apoplectique (*personne*); d'apoplexie; **'ap·o·plex·y** apoplexie *f*; congestion *f* cérébrale.

a·pos·ta·sy [ə'pɒstəsi] apostasie *f*; **a'pos·tate** [~stit] apostat (*a. su./m*); relaps(e *f*) *m*; **a'pos·ta·tize** [~stətaiz] apostasier (qch., *from s.th.*).

a·pos·tle [ə'pɒsl] apôtre *m*; **ap·os·tol·ic, ap·os·tol·i·cal** □ [æpə-'stɔlik(l)] apostolique.

a·pos·tro·phe *gramm.*, *a. rhétorique*: [ə'pɒstrəfi] apostrophe *f*; **a'pos·tro·phize** apostropher; *gramm.* mettre une apostrophe à.

a·poth·e·car·y † [ə'pɒθikəri] apothicaire *m*, pharmacien *m*.

a·poth·e·o·sis [əpɒθi'ousis] apothéose *f*.

ap·pal [ə'pɔːl] épouvanter; consterner; **ap'pall·ing** épouvantable, effroyable.

ap·pa·ra·tus [æpə'reitəs], *pl.* **-tus·es** [~təsiz] appareil *m*, dispositif *m*; attirail *m*; **~ exercises** *pl.* gymnastique *f* aux agrès.

ap·par·el [ə'pærəl]: **wearing ~** vêtements *m/pl.*, habits *m/pl.*

ap·par·ent □ [ə'pærənt] apparent, évident, manifeste; *see heir*; **ap·pa·ri·tion** [æpə'riʃn] apparition *f*; fantôme *m*, revenant *m*.

ap·peal [ə'piːl] **1.** faire appel (à, to); demander (qch., *for s.th.*; à, to); interjeter appel; se pourvoir en cassation; **~ to** attirer, séduire; ⚖ invoquer l'aide de (*la loi*); appeler de (*un jugement*); *see country*; **2.** appel *m*; recours *m*; *fig.* prière *f*, supplication *f*; attrait *m*; ⚖ **court of ~** cour *f* d'appel; **lodge ou file an ~** interjeter appel, se pourvoir en appel; **notice of ~** intimation *f*; **right of ~** droit *m* d'appel; **~ for mercy** demande *f* de grâce; **ap'peal·ing** □ suppliant; émouvant; sympathique.

ap·pear [ə'piə] paraître (*a. livres*); se montrer; se présenter; apparaître; sembler; ⚖ comparaître; **~ for** plaider pour (*q.*); **ap'pear·ance** apparition *f*; entrée *f*; *livre*: parution *f*; apparence *f*; ⚖ comparution *f*; **~s** *pl.* dehors *m/pl.*; **keep up** (*ou save*) **~s** sauver *ou* garder les apparences; **make one's ~** débuter;

paraître; **put in an ~** faire acte de présence; **to all ~s** selon toute apparence.

ap·pease [ə'piːz] apaiser, calmer (*l'agitation, une douleur*); assouvir (*la faim*); **ap'pease·ment** apaisement *m*; assouvissement *m*; **~ policy** politique *f* d'apaisement.

ap·pel·lant [ə'pelənt] appelant(e *f*) (*a. su./m/f*); **ap'pel·late** [~lit] d'appel; **ap·pel·la·tion** [æpe'leiʃn] appellation *f*, nom *m*, désignation *f*, titre *m*; **ap'pel·la·tive** *gramm.* [ə'pelətiv] (*a. ~ name*) nom *m* commun *ou* générique.

ap·pend [ə'pend] attacher, joindre; apposer (*une signature, un sceau*); annexer (*un document*); **ap'pend·age** accessoire *m*, apanage *m* (de, to); annexe *f*; *anat.* appendice *m*; **ap·pen·dec·to·my** *Am.* [~-'dektəmi] appendicectomie *f*; **ap·pen·di·ci·tis** [~disaitis] appendicite *f*; **ap'pen·dix** [~diks], *pl.* **-dix·es, -di·ces** [~disiːz] appendice *m*; ⚕ appendice *m* (vermiculaire).

ap·per·tain [æpə'tein]: **~ to** appartenir à; incomber à; convenir à.

ap·pe·tence, ap·pe·ten·cy ['æpitəns(i)] (for, after, of) appétence *f*; désir *m* (de); convoitise *f* (pour).

ap·pe·tite ['æpitait] (for) appétit *m* (de); *fig.* désir *m* (de), soif *f* (de); **~ suppressant** coupe-faim *m/inv.*, anorexigène *m*.

ap·pe·tiz·er ['æpitaizə] apéritif *m*; **'ap·pe·tiz·ing** alléchant, appétissant.

ap·plaud [ə'plɔːd] *v/i.* applaudir, battre des mains; *v/t.* applaudir (*q.*; *aux efforts de q.*).

ap·plause [ə'plɔːz] applaudissements *m/pl.*; approbation *f*.

ap·ple ['æpl] pomme *f*; **'~-cart** voiture *f* à bras; F **upset s.o.'s ~** bouleverser les plans de q.; **~ pie** tourte *f* aux pommes; **'~-pie:** F **~ order** rangé en ordre parfait; **'~-pol·ish** *sl.* flatter, flagorner (*q.*); **'~-sauce** compote *f* de pommes; *Am. sl.* flagornerie *f*; *int.* chansons!; **'~-tree** pommier *m*.

ap·pli·ance [ə'plaiəns] appareil *m*; instrument *m*; dispositif *m*; **~s** *pl.* attirail *m*.

ap·pli·ca·bil·i·ty [æplikə'biliti] applicabilité *f*; **'ap·pli·ca·ble** (à, to) applicable; approprié; **'ap·pli·cant**

candidat(e *f*) *m* (à, *for*); postu-
lant(e *f*) *m* (de, *for*); **ap·pli·ca·tion**
(to) application *f* (à, sur); apposition *f* (à); *frein:* serrage *m*; assiduité
f; demande *f* (de, *for*); sollicitation
f (de, *for*); ~ *form* bulletin *m* de
demande; ✍ *for external* ~ pour
l'usage externe; (*letter of*) ~ (lettre *f*
de) demande *f* d'emploi; *make an* ~
formuler *ou* faire une demande.
ap·ply [ə'plai] *v/t.* (to) appliquer
(*qch.* sur *qch.*); faire l'application de
(*qch.* à *qch.*); coller (sur); serrer
(*le frein*); mettre en pratique; affecter (*un paiement*) (à); ~ *o.s. to*
s'attacher à; *v/i.* (to) s'appliquer
(à); s'adresser (à); avoir recours (à);
~ *for* poser sa candidature à, solliciter (*qch.*); *applied science* science
f appliquée *ou* expérimentale.
ap·point [ə'pɔint] nommer (q.
gouverneur, *s.o. governor*); dési-
gner(pour *inf.*, to *inf.*); fixer, assigner
(*l'heure, un endroit*); arrêter (*un
jour*); prescrire (que, *that*); *well* ~ed
bien installé, bien équipé; **ap'point-
ment** rendez-vous *m*; entrevue *f*;
nomination *f*; désignation *f*; charge
f, emploi *m*; ~s *pl.* aménagement *m*,
installation *f*; équipement *m*; †
émoluments *m/pl.*; ~ *book* agenda *m*,
calepin *m*; *by special* ~ *to* (*fournisseur*)
breveté *ou* attitré de.
ap·por·tion [ə'pɔːʃn] répartir; assigner (à, *to*); **ap'por·tion·ment**
partage *m*, répartition *f*; allocation *f*.
ap·po·site □ ['æpəzit] approprié
(à, *to*); juste; *be* ~ *to* convenir à;
'**ap·po·site·ness** justesse *f*; à-
propos *m*.   [tion *f*.\
ap·po·si·tion [æpə'ziʃn] apposi-⌐
ap·prais·al [ə'preizl] évaluation *f*;
ap'praise [~'preiz] priser, estimer;
ap'praise·ment évaluation *f*, estimation *f*; **ap'prais·er** estimateur
m, priseur *m*.
ap·pre·ci·a·ble □ [ə'priːʃəbl] appréciable; sensible; **ap'pre·ci·ate**
[~ʃieit] *v/t.* apprécier, faire cas de;
estimer; évaluer; hausser la valeur
de; *v/i.* augmenter de valeur; **ap-
pre·ci·a·tion** appréciation *f* (de,
of); estimation *f* (de, *of*); évaluation
f; amélioration *f*; hausse *f*; plus-
value *f*; **ap'pre·ci·a·tive** □ [~ʃtiv],
ap'pre·ci·a·to·ry [~ʃətəri] appréciateur (-trice *f*); sensible (à, *of*); *be* ~
of apprécier; être sensible à.

ap·pre·hend [æpri'hend] arrêter;
saisir; *poét.* comprendre; *poét.* redouter; **ap·pre·hen·si·ble** □ [~-
'hensəbl] appréhensible; perceptible; **ap·pre'hen·sion** arrestation
f; prise *f* de corps; perception *f*;
compréhension *f*; appréhension *f*,
crainte *f*; **ap·pre'hen·sive** □ perceptif (-ive *f*); timide, craintif
(-ive *f*); *be* ~ redouter (*qch., of
s.th.*); craindre (*qch., of s.th.*; *pour*
q., *for s.o.*; *que, that*).
ap·pren·tice [ə'prentis] **1.** appren-
ti(e *f*) *m*; **2.** placer en apprentissage
(*chez, to*); ~*d to* en apprentissage
chez; **ap'pren·tice·ship** [~tiʃip]
apprentissage *m*.
ap·prise [ə'praiz]: ~ *s.o. of s.th.* apprendre qch. à q.; prévenir q. de
qch.   [condition.\
ap·pro ☩ ['æprou]: *on* ~ à l'essai, à⌐
ap·proach [ə'proutʃ] **1.** *v/i.* (s')ap-
procher; *fig.* approcher (de, *to*); ⚓
atterrir; *v/t.* (s')approcher de; aborder (*q.*); entrer en communication
avec (*q.*); *fig.* faire une démarche
auprès de (*q.*) (au sujet de, *about*);
fig. s'attaquer à, aborder (*un problème*); **2.** approche *f*; approches
f/pl.; venue *f*; voie *f* d'accès; accès
m; abord *m*; *fig.* rapprochement *m*;
ap'proach·a·ble accessible; abordable.
ap·pro·ba·tion [æpro'beiʃn] approbation *f*; consentement *m*.
ap·pro·pri·ate **1.** [ə'prouprieit]
(s')approprier; s'emparer de; *parl.*
affecter, consacrer (à *to*, *for*); **2.** □
[~iit] (to) approprié (à); convenable,
propre (à); à propos; **ap·pro·pri·a·-
tion** appropriation *f*; crédit *m*,
budget *m*; affectation *f* de fonds;
parl. ♀ *Committee* commission *f* du
budget.
ap·prov·a·ble [ə'pruːvəbl] louable;
ap'prov·al approbation *f*; ratification *f*; *on* ~ à l'essai, à l'examen;
ap'prove approuver; ratifier;
(*a.* ~ *of*) agréer; ~ *o.s.* † faire ses
preuves; **ap'proved** □ autorisé,
approuvé; **ap'prov·er** ⚖ complice
m qui dénonce ses camarades.
ap·prox·i·mate **1.** [ə'prɔksimeit]
(se) rapprocher (de, *to*); **2.** □ [~mit]
rapproché, proche, voisin (de, *to*);
approximatif (-ive *f*); **ap'prox·i·-
mate·ly** [~mitli] environ, à peu
près; **ap·prox·i·ma·tion** [~'meiʃn]

rapprochement *m*; approximation *f*;
ap·prox·i·ma·tive □ [~mətiv] approximatif (-ive *f*).

ap·pur·te·nance [ə'pəːtinəns] *usu.*
~s *pl.* accessoires *m/pl.*, attirail *m.*

a·pri·cot ♀ ['eiprikɔt] abricot *m*;
arbre: abricotier *m.*

A·pril ['eiprəl] avril *m*; *make an*
~*-fool of s.o.* faire un poisson
d'avril à q.

a·pron ['eiprən] tablier *m* (*a. mot.*);
théâ. avant-scène *f*; '~*-string* cordon *m* de tablier; *fig.* *be tied to her*
~*s* être pendu à ses jupes; être tenu
en laisse.

ap·ro·pos ['æprəpou] **1.** à propos
(de, *of*), opportun; **2.** à-propos *m.*

apt [æpt] juste, fin; heureux
(-euse *f*) (*expression etc.*); enclin (à,
to); susceptible (de, *to*); habile (à,
at); intelligent; apte, propre (à, *to*);
~ *to take fire* sujet à prendre feu;
qui prend feu facilement; **ap·ti·tude** ['~titjuːd], **'apt·ness** justesse
f, à-propos *m*; penchant *m*, tendance *f* (à, *to*); talent *m* (pour, *for*);
aptitude test test *m* d'aptitude.

aq·ua for·tis ⚗ ['ækwə'fɔːtis] eau-
forte (*pl.* eaux-fortes) *f.*

aq·ua·lung ['ækwəlʌŋ] scaphandre
m autonome.

aq·ua·ma·rine *min.* [ækwəmə'riːn]
aigue-marine (*pl.* aigues-marines) *f.*

aq·ua·plane ['ækwəplein] **1.** aquaplane *m*; **2.** faire de l'aquaplane; *mot.*
faire de l'aquaplaning; **aq·ua·plan·
ing** *mot.* [~'pleiniŋ] aquaplaning
m.

aq·ua·relle [ækwə'rel] aquarelle *f.*

a·quar·i·um [ə'kwɛəriəm], *pl.*
-ums, -i·a [~iə] aquarium *m.*

A·quar·i·us *astr.* [ə'kwɛəriəs] le
Verseau.

a·quat·ic [ə'kwætik] **1.** aquatique;
~ *sports see aquatics*; **2.** plante *f*
ou animal *m* aquatique; **a'quat·ics**
pl. sports *m/pl.* nautiques.

aq·ua·tint ['ækwətint] aquatinte *f.*

aq·ue·duct ['ækwidʌkt] aqueduc *m.*

a·que·ous ['eikwiəs] □ aqueux
(-euse *f*); *géol.* sédimentaire.

aq·ui·line nose ['ækwilain'nouz]
nez *m* aquilin *ou* busqué.

Ar·ab ['ærəb] Arabe *mf*; (*cheval m*)
arabe *m*; *sl.* *street* ♀ gamin *m* des
rues; gavroche *m*; **ar·a·besque**
[~'besk] **1.** *usu. pl.* arabesque *f*, -s
f/pl.; **2.** arabesque, dans le style arabe; **A·ra·bi·an** [ə'reibjən] **1.** arabe;
The ~ *Nights* les Mille et Une Nuits;
2. Arabe *mf*; **Ar·a·bic** ['ærəbik]
1. arabe; *gum* ♀ gomme *f* arabique;
2. *ling.* arabe *m.*

ar·a·ble ['ærəbl] **1.** labourable;
2. (*ou* ~ *land*) terre *f* arable *ou* labourable.

a·rach·nid [ə'ræknid] arachnide *m.*

ar·bi·ter ['ɑːbitə] arbitre *m* (*a. fig.*);
ar·bi·trage ✝ [ɑːbi'trɑːʒ] arbitrage *m*; **'ar·bi·tral** **tri'bu·nal**
tribunal *m* arbitral; **ar'bit·ra·ment**
[~trəmənt] arbitrage *m*; **'ar·bi·
trar·i·ness** arbitraire *m*; **'ar·bi·
trar·y** □ arbitraire; **ar·bi·trate**
['~treit] arbitrer (*a. v/i.*); juger;
trancher (*un différend*); **ar·bi'tra·
tion** arbitrage *m*; procédure *f*
arbitrale; ~ *court* tribunal *m* arbitral; ✝ ~ *of exchange* arbitrage *m* du
change; **'ar·bi·tra·tor** ['~ treitə] ⅌
arbitre *m*; arbitre-juge *m*; **ar·bi·
tress** ['~tris] *femme*: arbitre *m.*

ar·bor ['ɑːbə] ⊕, *roue, meule*: arbre
m; *tour*: mandrin *m*; ♀ *Day Am.*
jour *m* où on est tenu de planter un
arbre; **ar·bo·re·al** [ɑː'bɔːriəl], **ar·
'bo·re·ous** d'arbre(s); arboricole
(*animal*); **ar·bo·res·cent** □ [ɑːbo-
'resnt] arborescent; **ar·bo·ri·cul·
ture** ['ɑːborikʌltʃə] arboriculture *f.*

ar·bour ['ɑːbə] tonnelle *f*, charmille *f*; *vine* ~ treille *f.*

arc ⚡, *astr., etc.* [ɑːk] arc *m* (⚡ électrique); **ar·cade** [ɑː'keid] arcade *f*,
-s *f/pl.*; galerie *f*, -s *f/pl.*; passage *m.*

ar·ca·num [ɑː'keinəm], *pl.* **-na** [~nə]
arcane *m*, secret *m.*

arch[1] [ɑːtʃ] **1.** *surt.* △ voûte *f*, arc
m; cintre *m*; *pont*: arche *f*; ~*-sup·
port* cambrure *f*; **2.** (se) voûter;
v/t. bomber (*a. v/i.*); arquer, cintrer; cambrer.

arch[2] [~] □ espiègle; malin (-igne
f); malicieux (-euse *f*).

arch[3] [~] insigne, grand; archi-.

ar·ch(a)e·o·log·i·cal □ [ɑːkiə'lɔdʒi-
kəl] archéologique; **ar·ch(a)e·ol·o·
gist** [ɑːki'ɔlədʒist] archéologue
su./mf; **ar·ch(a)e·ol·o·gy** archéologie *f.*

ar·cha·ic [ɑː'keiik] (~*ally*) archaïque;
'ar·cha·ism archaïsme *m.*

arch·an·gel ['ɑːkeindʒl] archange *m.*

arch·bish·op ['ɑːtʃ'biʃəp] archevêque *m*; **arch·bish·op·ric** [~rik] archevêché *m*; archiépiscopat *m.*

arch·dea·con [ˈɑːtʃˈdiːkən] archidiacre *m*.

arch·duch·ess [ˈɑːtʃˈdʌtʃis] archiduchesse *f*; **ˈarchˈduch·y** archiduché *m*.

arch·duke [ˈɑːtʃˈdjuːk] archiduc *m*.

arch·er [ˈɑːtʃə] archer *m*; **ˈarch·er·y** tir *m* à l'arc.

ar·chi·di·ac·o·nal [ɑːkidaiˈækənl] d'archidiacre.

ar·chi·e·pis·co·pal [ɑːkiˈpiskəpl] archiépiscopal (-aux *m/pl*.); métropolitain.

ar·chi·pel·a·go [ɑːkiˈpeligou] *géog*. archipel *m*.

ar·chi·tect [ˈɑːkitekt] architecte *m*; *fig*. auteur *m*, artisan *m*; **ar·chi·tec·ton·ic** [ˌ-ˈtɔnik] (ˌ-ally) architectonique; architectural (-aux *m/pl*.); *fig*. directeur (-trice *f*); **ar·chi·tec·ture** [ˈ-tʃə] architecture *f*.

ar·chives [ˈɑːkaivz] *pl*. archives *f/pl*.

arch·ness [ˈɑːtʃnis] espièglerie *f*; malice *f*.

arch·way [ˈɑːtʃwei] passage *m* voûté; porte *f* cintrée; portail *m*.

arc·lamp ⚡ [ˈɑːklæmp] lampe *f* à arc.

arc·tic [ˈɑːktik] **1.** arctique; *fig*. glacial (-als *m/pl*.); ♀ *Circle* cercle *m* polaire; ♀ *Ocean* (océan *m*) Arctique *m*; **2.** ~s *pl*. snowboots *m/pl*.

ar·den·cy [ˈɑːdənsi] ardeur *f*; **ˈar·dent** □ *usu*. *fig*. ardent; *fig*. fort; ~ *spirits pl*. alcool *m*, spiritueux *m/pl*.

ar·do(u)r [ˈɑːdə] *fig*. ardeur *f*; chaleur *f*.

ar·du·ous [ˈɑːdjuəs] ardu (*sentier*, *travail*); rude (*travail*); escarpé (*chemin*); pénible; laborieux (-euse *f*).

a·re·a [ˈɛəriə] aire *f*, superficie *f*; surface *f*; région *f*, territoire *m*; terrain *m* vide; *cinéma etc*.: parterre *m*; cour *f* d'entrée en sous-sol; zone *f*; *Am*. *téléph*. ~ *code* numéro *m* de présélection; *danger* ~ zone *f* dangereuse; *foot*. *goal* ~ surface *f* de but; ⚽ *judicial* ~ ressort *m* judiciaire; *foot*. *penalty* ~ surface *f* de réparation; *prohibited* ~ zone *f* interdite; ~ *bell* sonnette *f* de la porte de service.

a·re·na [əˈriːnə] arène *f*; champ *m* (*a*. *fig*.); *fig*. théâtre *m*.

aren't F [ɑːnt] = *are not*.

a·rête *alp*. [æˈreit] arête *f*.

ar·gent [ˈɑːdʒənt] argenté; ▨ (d')argent.

Ar·gen·tine [ˈɑːdʒəntain] argentin; Argentin(e *f*) *m*.

ar·gil [ˈɑːdʒil] argile *f*; **ar·gil·la·ceous** [ˌ-ˈleiʃəs] argileux (-euse *f*), argillacé.

Ar·go·naut [ˈɑːgənɔːt] argonaute *m*; *Am*. chercheur *m* d'or en Californie.

ar·gu·a·ble [ˈɑːgjuəbl] discutable; soutenable; **ar·gue** [ˈ-gjuː] *v/t*. discuter, débattre; raisonner sur; prouver, démontrer; ~ *s.o. into doing s.th.* persuader à q. de faire qch.; ~ *s.o. out of doing s.th.* dissuader q. de faire qch.; *v/i*. argumenter (sur, *about*); discuter; raisonner; (se) disputer; plaider; ~ *from* tirer argument de.

ar·gu·ment [ˈɑːgjumənt] argument *m*; raisonnement *m*; débat *m*, discussion *f*, dispute *f*; **ar·gu·men·ta·tion** [ˌ-menˈteiʃn] argumentation *f*; **ar·gu·men·ta·tive** □ [ˌ-tətiv] disposé à argumenter; critique.

a·ri·a ♪ [ˈɑːriə] aria *f*.

ar·id [ˈærid] aride (*a*. *fig*.); **aˈrid·i·ty** aridité *f*.

Ar·ies *astr*. [ˈɛəriəs] le Bélier.

a·right [əˈrait] bien, correctement.

a·rise [əˈraiz] [*irr*.] *fig*. s'élever, surgir (de, *from*); se produire; *bibl*. ressusciter; **aˈris·en** *p.p*. *de arise*.

ar·is·toc·ra·cy [ærisˈtɔkrəsi] aristocratie *f*; *fig*. élite *f*; **a·ris·to·crat** [ˈ-təkræt] aristocrate *mf*; **a·ris·to·crat·ic**, **a·ris·to·crat·i·cal** □ aristocratique.

a·rith·me·tic [əˈriθmətik] arithmétique *f*, calcul *m*; **ar·ith·met·i·cal** □ [ˌ-ˈmetikl] arithmétique; **a·rith·me·ti·cian** [ˌ-məˈtiʃən] arithméticien(ne *f*) *m*.

ark [ɑːk] arche *f*; *bibl*. ♀ *of the Covenant* Arche *f* d'alliance.

arm¹ [ɑːm] bras *m*; *fauteuil*: accoudoir *m*; *within* ~'s *reach* à portée de la main; *keep s.o. at* ~'s *length* tenir q. à distance; *infant in* ~s bébé *m*; F *poupon m*; *take s.o. to* (*ou in*) *one's* ~s prendre q. dans ses bras.

arm² [~] **1.** arme *f*; ~s *pl*. armes *f/pl*.; ▨ armes *f/pl*., armoiries *f/pl*.; *see coat* 1; ~s *race* course *f* aux armements; ~s *reduction* désarmement *m*; ~s (*reduction*) *talks* pourparlers *m/pl*. *ou* négociations *f/pl*. sur le désarmement; *be* (*all*) *up in* ~s être en révolte; se gendarmer *ou* s'élever (contre, *against*); *take up* ~s prendre les armes; **2.** (s')armer; *fig.* (se) nantir de; *v/t.* ⊕ armer; renforcer; ⚦ ~ed spinifère.

ar·ma·da [ɑːˈmɑːdə] flotte *f* de guerre; *hist.* the (Invincible) ♀ l'(Invincible) Armada *f.*

ar·ma·ment [ˈɑːməmənt] armement *m*; munitions *f/pl.* de guerre; ⚓ artillerie *f; (a. naval ~)* armements *m/pl.* navals; flotte *f* navale; ~s industry industrie *f* d'armements.

ar·ma·ture [ˈ~tjuə] armure *f (a.* ⚦, zo.); ⚓, *phys.* armature *f; phys.* induit *m.*

arm·chair [ˈɑːmˈtʃɛə] fauteuil *m*; ~ strategist, ~ politician stratège *m* du café du commerce.

armed [ɑːmd] *à ou* aux bras ...

Ar·me·ni·an [ɑːˈmiːnjən] **1.** arménien(ne *f*); **2.** Arménien(ne *f*) *m.*

arm·ful [ˈɑːmful] brassée *f.*

ar·mi·stice [ˈɑːmistis] armistice *m (a. fig.).*

arm·let [ˈɑːmlit] bracelet *m*; brassard *m (de parti politique etc.).*

ar·mo·ri·al [ɑːˈmɔːriəl] armorial (-aux *m/pl.*), héraldique.

ar·mo(u)r [ˈɑːmə] **1.** ✗ armure *f*, blindés *m/pl.*; cuirasse *f (a. fig., zo.);* scaphandre *m*; **2.** cuirasser; blinder; ~ed car automitrailleuse *f*, char *m* blindé; ~ed train train *m* blindé; ~ed turret tourelle *f* blindée; '~-clad, '~-plat·ed blindé, cuirassé; 'ar·mo(u)r·er armurier *m (a.* ✗, ⚓); 'ar·mo(u)r·y magasin *m* d'armes; *caserne:* armurerie *f; fig.* arsenal *m; Am.* fabrique *f* d'armes; *Am.* salle *f* d'exercice.

arm·pit [ˈɑːmpit] aisselle *f*; 'arm·rest accoudoir *m*, accotoir *m.*

ar·my [ˈɑːmi] armée *f; fig.* foule *f*; ~ chaplain aumônier *m* militaire; ~ command staff état-major *m (pl.* états-majors) *m); Salvation* ♀ Armée *f* du Salut; *see service;* '~-a·gent, '~-bro·ker, '~-con·trac·tor fournisseur *m* de l'armée; '~-corps corps *m* d'armée; '~-list ✗ Annuaire *m* militaire.

a·ro·ma [əˈroumə] arôme *m*; bouquet *m*; **ar·o·mat·ic** [ærəˈmætik] (~ally) aromatique; balsamique.

a·rose [əˈrouz] *prét. de* arise.

a·round [əˈraund] **1.** *adv.* autour, à l'entour; d'alentour; *Am.* F par ici, dans ces parages; *Am.* sur pied;

2. *prp.* autour de; *surt. Am.* F environ, presque.

a·rouse [əˈrauz] *usu. fig.* éveiller; stimuler (*q.*); soulever (*une passion*).

ar·rack [ˈærək] arac(k) *m.*

ar·raign [əˈrein] accuser, inculper; traduire en justice; *fig.* s'en prendre à; **ar'raign·ment** mise *f* en accusation; interpellation *f* de l'accusé.

ar·range [əˈreindʒ] *v/t.* arranger; ranger; régler (*des affaires*); ♪ adapter, arranger; fixer (*un jour*); ménager (*des effets*); ♫ ordonner; *v/i.* prendre ses dispositions (pour for, to); convenir (de, to); s'arranger (pour for, to); ~ for s.th. to be there prendre des mesures pour que qch. soit là; **ar'range·ment** arrangement *m*, disposition *f*, aménagement *m*; ♪ arrangement *m*, adaptation *f*; accord *m*; ~ compromis *m*; make one's ~s prendre ses dispositions.

ar·rant □ [ˈærənt] insigne, achevé; ~ knave franc coquin *m.*

ar·ray [əˈrei] **1.** rangs *m/pl.*; *fig.* étalage *m*, rangée *f; poét.* atours *m/pl.*, parure *f;* **2.** ranger, mettre en ordre; déployer (*des troupes etc.*); *poét.* revêtir, parer (de, in).

ar·rear [əˈriə] arrérages *m/pl.*; arriéré *m*; ~s of rent arriéré *m* de loyer; be in ~s s'arriérer; **ar'rear·age** retard *m; Am.* ~s *pl.* arrérages *m/pl.*, dettes *f/pl.*

ar·rest [əˈrest] **1.** arrestation *f*; prise *f* de corps; ✗, ⚓ arrêts *m/pl.*; suspension *f*, mouvement: arrêt *m*; under ~ aux arrêts; **2.** arrêter (*criminel, mouvement, regard, attention, etc.*); appréhender (*q.*) au corps; fixer (*l'attention, le regard*); surseoir à (*un jugement*).

ar·riv·al [əˈraivl] arrivée *f*; ⚓ arrivage *m*; ⚓ entrée *f (du vaisseau);* ~s *pl.* nouveaux venus *m/pl. ou* arrivés *m/pl.*; ~ platform quai *m* de débarquement; on ~ à l'arrivée; To await ~ ne pas faire suivre; **ar'rive** arriver; parvenir; ~ at arriver à; atteindre (*a. un âge*); parvenir à.

ar·ro·gance [ˈærəgəns] arrogance *f*; morgue *f*; **ar·ro·gant** □ arrogant; **ar·ro·gate** [ˈærogeit] (s')attribuer (*qch.*) (à tort); (*usu.* ~ to o.s.) s'arroger, usurper (*qch.*).

ar·row [ˈærou] flèche *f; surv.* flèche *f* d'arpenteur; '~-head pointe *f* de

flèche; broad ~ marque f de l'État
(britannique); ~·**root** ['ærərʊːt] ♣
marante f; cuis. arrow-root (en
ar·row·y ['æroui] en forme de
flèche.

arse sl. [ɑːs] derrière m; sl. cul m.

ar·se·nal ['ɑːsinl] arsenal m.

ar·se·nic ['ɑːsnik] arsenic m; **ar·sen·ic** ⚗ [ɑː'senik] arsénique; **ar'sen·i·cal** arsenical (-aux m/pl.).

ar·son ['ɑːsn] crime m d'incendie.

art¹ [ɑːt] art m; adresse f, habileté f; fig. artifice m; finesse f; péj. astuce f; ~ critic critique mf d'art; ~ dealer marchand m d'objets d'art; Master of ♌s (abbr. M.A.) maître m ès arts, agrégé m de lettres; applied ~s arts m/pl. industriels; fine ~s les beaux-arts m/pl.; liberal ~s arts m/pl. libéraux; ~s and crafts arts m/pl. et métiers m/pl.; Faculty of ♌s Faculté f des Lettres; journal: ~s page page f littéraire.

art² † [~] tu es.

ar·te·ri·al [ɑː'tiəriəl] artériel(le f); ~ road artère f, grande voie f de communication; **ar·te·ri·o·scle·ro·sis** [ɑː'tiəriouskliə'rousis] artériosclérose f (a. fig.); **ar·ter·y** ['ɑːtəri] artère f (a. fig.); traffic ~ artère f de circulation.

ar·te·sian well [ɑː'tiːzjən'wel] puits m artésien.

art·ful ['ɑːtful] adroit, habile, ingénieux (-euse f); rusé.

ar·thrit·ic ✨ [ɑː'θritik] arthritique; **ar·thri·tis** [ɑː'θraitis] arthrite f.

ar·ti·choke ['ɑːtiʃouk] artichaut m; Jerusalem ~ topinambour m.

ar·ti·cle ['ɑːtikl] 1. ♣, ⚡, ⚕, eccl., gramm., etc. article m; ⚔, ⚓ code m; objet m; ~ of clothing vêtement m, article m ou pièce f d'habillement; ~s pl. of apprenticeship contrat m d'apprentissage; ~s pl. of association acte m de société; contrat m de société; 2. placer comme apprenti (chez, to); accuser (de, for); be ~ed faire son apprentissage (chez to, with).

ar·tic·u·late 1. [ɑː'tikjuleit] v/t. articuler (anat., a. mots); énoncer (des mots); v/i. s'articuler (os); 2. □ [~lit], a. **ar'tic·u·lat·ed** [~leitid] net(te f), distinct; surt. zo. articulé (a. langage); Brit. mot. ~ lorry semi-remorque m; **ar·tic·u'la·tion** articulation f; netteté f d'énonciation.

ar·ti·fice ['ɑːtifis] artifice m, ruse f;

adresse f, habileté f; **ar'tif·i·cer** artisan m, ouvrier m; artificier m; ⚒ mécanicien m; ✂ **ar·ti·fi·cial** □ [~'fiʃəl] artificiel(le f); simili-; factice (larmes); ~ manure engrais m/pl. chimiques; ⚗ ~ person personne f juridique ou morale; ~ respiration respiration f artificielle; ~ silk soie f artificielle; ~ stone simili m.

ar·til·ler·y [ɑː'tiləri] artillerie f; **ar'til·ler·y·man** artilleur m.

ar·ti·san [ɑːti'zæn] artisan m, ouvrier m.

art·ist ['ɑːtist] artiste mf, surt. (artiste-)peintre [pl. (artiste-)peintres] m; **ar·tiste** [ɑː'tiːst]artiste mf; **ar·tis·tic, ar·tis·ti·cal** □ [~'tistik(l)] artistique; artiste (tempérament).

art·less □ ['ɑːtlis] sans art; naturel (-le f), sans artifice; naïf (-ïve f), candide; **'art·less·ness** naturel m, simplicité f; naïveté f, candeur f.

art·y ['ɑːti] prétentieux (-euse f); péj. pseudo-artistique.

Ar·y·an ['ɛəriən] 1. aryen(ne f), japhétique; 2. Aryen(ne f) m.

as [æz, əz] 1. adv., a. cj. aussi, si; comme; puisque, étant donné que; tout ... que; au moment où; (au-)tant que; ~ good ~ aussi bon que; ~ far ~ aussi loin que; autant que; ~ if, ~ though comme si; as if (gér.) comme pour (inf.); ~ it were pour ainsi dire; ~ well aussi, également; opportun; ~ well ~ de même que; comme; ~ yet jusqu'ici, jusqu'à présent; (~) cold ~ ice glacé, glacial (-als m/pl.); fair ~ she is si belle qu'elle soit; so kind ~ to do assez aimable pour faire; such ~ to (inf.) de sorte à (inf.), de façon que; such ~ tel que, tel; par exemple; 2. prp. ~ for, ~ to quant à; ~ from à partir de (telle date), depuis; ⚓ ~ per conformément à, suivant.   [amiante m.)

as·bes·tos [æz'bestɔs] asbeste m,)

as·cend [ə'send] v/i. monter, s'élever (à, jusqu'à to); remonter (généalogie); v/t. monter (un escalier); gravir (une colline etc.); monter sur (le trône); remonter (un fleuve); **as'cend·an·cy, as'cend·en·cy** ascendant m, pouvoir m, influence f (sur, over); suprématie f; **as'cend·ant, as'cend·ent** 1. ascendant; 2. see ascendancy; astr. ascendant m; F position f prééminente; be in the ~ être à l'ascendant; prédominer.

as·cen·sion [ə'senʃn] *surt. astr., Am.*
a. montagne, ballon, etc.: ascension *f*;
♀ (*Day*) jour *m* de l'Ascension.

as·cent [ə'sent] *montagne, ballon*:
ascension *f*; montée *f*; pente *f*,
rampe *f*.

as·cer·tain [æsə'tein] constater;
s'informer de; **as·cer'tain·a·ble** □
vérifiable; dont on peut s'assurer;
as·cer'tain·ment constatation *f*;
vérification *f*.

as·cet·ic [ə'setik] **1.** (*~ally*) ascétique; **2.** ascète *mf*; **as'cet·i·cism**
[*~*tisizəm] ascétisme *m*.

as·crib·a·ble [əs'kraibəbl] imputable, attribuable; **as'cribe** imputer,
attribuer.

a·sep·tic 🗲 [æ'septik] aseptique (*a.
su./m*).

ash¹ [æʃ] ♀ frêne *m*; *mountain ~* sorbier *m* sauvage.

ash² [*~*] *usu. ~es pl.* cendre *f*, *-s f/pl.*;
Ash Wednesday mercredi *m* des
Cendres.

a·shamed [ə'ʃeimd] honteux (*-euse
f*), confus; *be* (*ou feel*) *~ of* avoir
honte de; être honteux (*-euse f*) de;
be ~ of o.s. avoir honte.

ash·can *Am.* ['æʃkæn] boîte *f* à ordures, poubelle *f*.

ash·en¹ ['æʃn] de frêne, en frêne.

ash·en² [*~*] de cendres; cendré;
gris; terreux (*-euse f*) (*visage*);
blême.

ash·lar ['æʃlə] pierre *f* de taille;
moellon *m* d'appareil.

a·shore [ə'ʃɔː] à terre; échoué; *run ~,
be driven ~* s'échouer; faire côte.

ash·tray ['æʃtrei] cendrier *m*.

ash·y ['æʃi] cendreux (*-euse f*);
couvert de cendres; gris; blême.

A·si·at·ic [eiʃi'ætik] **1.** asiatique,
d'Asie; **2.** Asiatique *mf*.

a·side [ə'said] **1.** de côté; à part; à
l'écart; *théâ.* en aparté; *~ from Am.*
à part, en plus de; **2.** à-côté *m*;
théâ. aparté *m*.

as·i·nine ['æsinain] asine; F stupide.

ask [ɑːsk] *v/t.* demander (*qch., s.th.*;
qch. à q., *s.o. s.th.*; que *that*); *a.*
inviter (à, *to*); solliciter (qch. de q.,
s.o. for s.th.); prier (q. de *inf., s.o.
to inf.*); *~ (s.o.) a question* poser une
question (à q.); *v/i.: ~ about* se renseigner sur; *~ after* s'informer de,
demander des nouvelles de; *~ for*
demander (*qch.*); demander à voir
(*q.*); *sl. he ~s for it* il ne l'a pas volé;

it is ~ to be had for the ~ing il n'y a
qu'à le demander.

a·skance [əs'kæns], **a'skant, askew** [əs'kjuː] de côté, de travers,
obliquement; *fig.* de guingois.

a·slant [ə'slɑːnt] de biais, de travers.

a·sleep [ə'sliːp] endormi, plongé
dans le sommeil; engourdi (*pied
etc.*); *be ~* être endormi, dormir;
see fall.

a·slope [ə'sloup] en pente, en talus.

asp¹ *zo.* [æsp] aspic *m*.

asp² [*~*] *see* aspen.

as·par·a·gus ♀ [əs'pærəgəs] asperge *f, cuis.* *-s f/pl.*

as·pect ['æspekt] exposition *f*, vue *f*;
aspect *m*, air *m*; point *m* de vue;
the house has a southern ~ la maison
est exposée au sud *ou* a une exposition sud.

as·pen ['æspən] tremble *m*; *attr.* de
tremble.

as·per·gill ['æspədʒil], **as·per·gil-
lum** *eccl.* [*~*'dʒiləm] goupillon *m*.

as·per·i·ty [æs'periti] âpreté *f*; sévérité *f*; rudesse *f*; aspérité *f* (*du style,
a. fig.*).

as·perse [əs'pəːs] asperger; *fig.*
calomnier, dénigrer; salir (*la réputation*); **as·per·sion** [əs'pəːʃn]
aspersion *f; fig.* calomnie *f*.

as·phalt ['æsfælt] **1.** asphalte *m*; F
bitume *m*; **2.** d'asphalte; bitumé.

as·phyx·i·a 🗲 [æs'fiksiə] asphyxie *f*;
as'phyx·i·ate [*~*ieit] asphyxier;
as·phyx·i'a·tion asphyxie *f*.

as·pic ['æspik] aspic *m*; ♀ grande
lavande *f*.

as·pir·ant [əs'paiərənt] aspirant(e *f*)
m (à *to, after, for*); candidat(e *f*) *m*; *~
officer* candidat *m* au rang d'officier;

as·pi·rate ['æspərit] **1.** *gramm.*
aspiré; **2.** *gramm.* aspirée *f*; **3.** ['*~*-
reit] aspirer (*a. ⊕, 🗲*); **as·pi'ration** aspiration *f* (*a. ⊕, 🗲*); ambition *f*; visée *f*; **as'pire** [əs'paiə]
aspirer, viser (à *to, after, at*); ambitionner (*qch.*).

as·pi·rin *pharm.* ['æspərin] aspirine
f; F comprimé *m* d'aspirine.

as'pir·ing □ [əs'paiəriŋ] ambitieux
(*-euse f*).

ass¹ [æs] âne(sse *f*) *m*; *make an ~ of o.s.*
faire des âneries; se donner en spectacle.

ass² *Am. sl.* [æs] derrière *m, sl.* cul *m*.

as·sail [ə'seil] assaillir, attaquer; *fig.*
s'attaquer à; accabler de; *crainte,*

doute, etc.: saisir, envahir (*q.*); frapper (*l'œil etc.*); ~ *s.o. with questions* assaillir *ou* harceler *ou* bombarder q. de questions; **as'sail·a·ble** attaquable; mal défendable; **as'sail·ant, as'sail·er** assaillant(e *f*) *m*; agresseur *m*.

as·sas·sin [ə'sæsin] assassin *m*; **as-'sas·si·nate** [⁓neit] assassiner; **as·sas·si'na·tion** assassinat *m*.

as·sault [ə'sɔːlt] **1.** assaut *m* (*a.* ⚔.); ⚔ attaque *f*; ⚖ tentative *f* de voie de fait; agression *f*; *see* battery; *indecent*; **2.** attaquer, assaillir; ⚖ se livrer à des voies de fait sur (*q.*); ⚔ livrer l'assaut à.

as·say [ə'sei] **1.** *métal etc.*: essai *m*; **2.** *v/t.* essayer, titrer;*v/i.* *Am.* titrer; **as'say·er** essayeur *m*.

as·sem·blage [ə'semblidʒ] réunion *f*; rassemblement *m*; ⊕ montage *m*, assemblage *m*; **as'sem·ble** (s')assembler; (se) rassembler (*troupes*); (se) réunir; *v/t.* ⊕ assembler, monter; **as'sem·bler** ⊕ monteur (-euse *f*) *m*; ajusteur (-euse *f*) *m*; **as'sem·bly** assemblée *f*; assemblement *m*, réunion *f*; ⚔ (sonnerie *f* du) rassemblement *m*; ⊕ montage *m*, assemblage *m*; (*a.* ~ *shop*) salle *f* *ou* atelier *m* de montage; *moving* ~ *belt* chaîne *f* de montage; *Am.* ~ *line* banc *m* de montage; *Am. pol.* ~ *man* député *m*.

as·sent [ə'sent] **1.** assentiment *m*, consentement *m*;**2.**: ~ *to* acquiescer, accéder à; admettre (*qch.*).

as·sert [ə'səːt] affirmer (*que, that*); (*surt.* ~ *o.s.*) soutenir ses droits; (~ *o.s. s'*) imposer; **as'ser·tion** assertion *f*, affirmation *f*; revendication *f* (*de droits*); **as'ser·tive** □ péremptoire; *gramm.* assertif (-ive *f*); impérieux (-euse *f*); **as'ser·tor** celui (celle *f*) qui affirme; défenseur *m*.

as·sess [ə'ses] estimer, évaluer; répartir (*un impôt*); fixer (*une somme*); coter, taxer (à *in, at*); **as'sess·a·ble** □ évaluable (*dommage*); imposable (*propriété*); **as'sess·ment** répartition *f*; évaluation *f*; cotisation *f*; côte *f*; **as'ses·sor** assesseur *m*; contrôleur *m* (*des contributions*).

as·set ['æset] ✝ avoir *m*, actif *m*; *fig.* atout *m*, avantage *m*, valeur *f*; ~*s* *pl.* biens *m/pl.*; ✝ actifs *m/pl.*; ~*s pl. and liabilities pl.* actif et passif *m*.

*41***

as·sev·er·ate [ə'sevəreit] affirmer; **as·sev·er'a·tion** affirmation *f*.

as·si·du·i·ty [æsi'djuiti] assiduité *f*, diligence *f* (à, *in*); *assiduities pl.* petits soins *m/pl.*; **as·sid·u·ous** assidu; diligent.

as·sign [ə'sain] **1.** assigner; consacrer; attribuer; donner (*la raison de qch.*); ⚖ transférer, céder; **2.** ⚖ ayant droit (*pl.* ayants droit) *m*; **as-'sign·a·ble** □ assignable, attribuable; cessible; **as·sig·na·tion** [æsig'neiʃn] attribution *f*; rendez-vous *m*; *see* assignment; **as·sign·ee** [æsi'niː] *see* assign 2; délégué(e *f*) *m*; ⚖ syndic *m*; ⚖ séquestre *m*; **as·sign·ment** [ə'sainmənt] allocation *f*; citation *f*; *surt. Am.* désignation *f*, nomination *f*; *univ.* tâche *f* assignée, devoir *m*; ⚖ transfert *m*, cession *f*; **as·sign·or** [æsi'nɔː] ⚖ cédant(e *f*) *m*.

as·sim·i·late [ə'simileit] (*to, with*) (s')assimiler (à) (*a. physiol.*); *v/t.* comparer (à); **as·sim·i'la·tion** assimilation *f* (*a. physiol.*); comparaison *f*.

as·sist [ə'sist] *v/t.* aider; prêter assistance à; secourir; *v/i.* ~ *at* prendre part à; assister à; **as'sist·ance** aide *f*, secours *m*, assistance *f*; **as'sist·ant 1.** qui aide; adjoint (*a, to*); sous-; **2.** adjoint(e *f*) *m*, auxiliaire *mf*; ✝ commis *m*, employé(e *f*) *m*.

as·size ⚖ [ə'saiz] assises *f/pl.*; ~*s pl.* (cour *f* d')assises *f/pl.*

as·so·ci·a·ble [ə'souʃjəbl] associable (à, *with*); **as·so·ci·ate 1.** [⁓ʃieit] (s')associer (avec, *with*);*v/i.* s'affilier (à, *with*); ~ *in* s'associer pour (*qch.*); fréquenter (*q.*); **2.** [⁓ʃiit] associé; adjoint; **3.** [⁓] associé *m* (*a.* ✝); adjoint *m*; compagnon *m*, camarade *mf*; membre *m* correspondant (*d'une académie*); professeur *m* adjoint; **as·so·ci·a·tion** [⁓si'eiʃən] association *f* (*a. d'idées*); fréquentation *f*; société *f*, amicale *f* (*d'étudiants etc.*); ~ *football* football *m* association.

as·so·nance ['æsənəns] assonance *f*.

as·sort [ə'sɔːt] *v/t.* assortir; classer, ranger; ✝ assortir; *v/i.* (*with*) (s')assortir (avec); aller ensemble; **as'sort·ment** assortiment *m*; classement *m*; ✝ assortiment *m*, choix *m*.

as·suage [ə'sweidʒ] apaiser (*la faim, un désir, etc.*); calmer; soulager; assoupir (*la souffrance*); **as-'suage·ment** apaisement *m*, soulagement *m*, adoucissement *m*.

as·sume [ə'sjuːm] prendre; affecter; revêtir; assumer (*une charge etc.*); simuler; présumer, supposer; **as'sum·ing** □ présomptueux (-euse *f*); **as·sump·tion** [ə'sʌmpʃn] action *f* de prendre; entrée *f* en fonctions; affectation *f*; arrogance *f*; hypothèse *f*; *eccl.* ♀ Assumption *f*; on the ~ that en supposant que; **as'sump·tive** □ hypothétique; admis; arrogant.

as·sur·ance [ə'ʃuərəns] affirmation *f*; promesse *f*; assurance *f* (*a.* = *sûreté; aplomb*); *péj.* hardiesse *f*; *Brit.* life ~ assurance-vie *f* (*pl.* assurances-vie); **as'sure** assurer; assurer la vie de; s'assurer sur la vie; ~ *s.o.* of *s.th.* assurer q. de qch., assurer qch. à q.; **as'sured 1.** assuré (*a.* = *certain; a.* = *sûr de soi*); *péj.* affronté; **2.** assuré(e *f*) *m*; **as'sur·ed·ly** [~ridli] assurément, sans aucun doute; avec assurance, d'un ton assuré; **as'sur·er** [~rə] assuré(e *f*) *m*.

As·syr·i·an [ə'siriən] **1.** assyrien(ne *f*); **2.** Assyrien(ne *f*) *m*.

as·ter ♀ ['æstə] aster *m*; **as·ter·isk** ['~risk] *typ.* astérisque *m*.

a·stern ⚓ [ə'stəːn] à *ou* sur l'arrière.

asth·ma ['æsmə] asthme *m*; **asth·mat·ic** [~'mætik] **1.** *a.* asth·mat·i·cal □ asthmatique; **2.** asthmatique *mf*.

as·tig·mat·ic [æstig'mætik] (~ally) *opt.* astigmate; **a'stig·ma·tism** [~mətizm] astigmatisme *f*.

a·stir [ə'stəː] animé; debout; agité.

as·ton·ish [əs'tɔniʃ] étonner, surprendre; be ~ed être étonné, s'étonner (de *at, to*); **as'ton·ish·ing** □ étonnant, surprenant; **as'ton·ish·ment** étonnement *m*, surprise *f*. [stupéfier.\

as·tound [əs'taund] confondre;∫

as·tra·gal △ ['æstrəgəl] astragale *m*, chapelet *m*.

as·tra·khan [æstrə'kæn] *fourrure:* astrakan *m*.

as·tral ['æstrəl] astral (-aux *m/pl.*).

a·stray [ə'strei] égaré; *péj.* dévoyé; go ~ s'égarer; *péj.* se dévoyer.

a·stride [ə'straid] à califourchon (sur, *of*); ride ~ aller jambe deçà, jambe delà (*sur un cheval etc.*).

as·trin·gent □, ♂ [əs'trindʒənt] astringent (*a. su./m*); styptique (*a. su./m*).

as·trol·o·ger [əs'trɔlədʒə] astrologue *m*; **as·trol·o·gy** [əs'trɔlədʒi] astrologie *f*; **as·tro·naut** ['æstro-nɔːt] astronaute *mf*; **as·tro·nau·tics** [æstrə'nɔːtiks] *sg.* astronautique *f*; **as·tron·o·mer** [əs'trɔnəmə] astronome *m*; **as·tro·nom·i·cal** □ [æstrə'nɔmikl] astronomique; **as·tron·o·my** [əs'trɔnəmi] astronomie *f*.

as·tute □ [əs'tjuːt] avisé, fin; *péj.* rusé, astucieux (-euse *f*); **as'tute·ness** finesse *f*, pénétration *f*; *péj.* astuce *f*.

a·sun·der [ə'sʌndə] éloignés l'un de l'autre; en deux.

a·sy·lum [ə'sailəm] asile *m*, refuge *m*; hospice *m*; F maison *f* d'aliénés.

a·sym·me·try [æ'simitri] asymétrie *f*, dissymétrie *f*.

at [æt; ət] *prp.* à; en (*guerre, mer*); (au)près de; sur (*demande*); *après certains verbes comme rire, se réjouir, s'étonner:* de; ~ the door à la porte; sur le seuil; ~ *my* expense à mes frais; ~ *my* aunt's chez ma tante; run ~ *s.o.* se jeter sur q.; ~ *day-break* au jour levant; ~ *night* la nuit; ~ *table* à table; ~ *a low price* à un bas prix; ~ *all events* en tout cas; ~ *school* à l'école; 2 ~ *a time* 2 par 2; ~ *peace* en paix; ~ *the age of* à l'âge de; ~ *one blow* d'un seul coup; ~ *five o'clock* à cinq heures; ~ *Christmas* à Noël. [visme *m*.\

at·a·vism *biol.* ['ætəvizm] ata-∫

a·tax·y ♂ [ə'tæksi] ataxie *f*, incoordination *f*.

ate [et] *prét. de* eat 1.

a·the·ism ['eiθiizm] athéisme *m*; **'a·the·ist** athée *mf*; **a'the·is·tic, a·the·is·ti·cal** □ athéistique; athée.

ath·lete ['æθliːt] athlète *m*; ♂ ~'s foot pied *m* de l'athlète; ~'s heart cardiectasie *f*; **ath·let·ic** [~'letik] athlétique; F sportif (-ive *f*); ~ heave effort *m* vigoureux; ~ sports *pl.* sports *m/pl.* athlétiques; **ath'let·ics** *pl.*, **ath'let·i·cism** [~tisizm] athlétisme *m*.

at-home [ət'houm] réception *f*; soirée *f*.

a·thwart [ə'θwɔːt] **1.** *prp.* en travers de; **2.** *adv.* en travers (*a.* ⚓); ⚓ par le travers.

a-tilt [ə'tilt] incliné, penché; sur l'oreille (*chapeau*).

At·lan·tic [ət'læntik] **1.** atlantique; **2.** (*a.* ~ *Ocean*) (océan *m*) Atlantique *m*.

at·las ['ætləs] atlas *m*; △ atlante *m*.

at·mos·phere ['ætməsfiə] atmosphère *f* (*a. fig.*); **at·mos·pher·ic,** **at·mos·pher·i·cal** □ [~'ferik(l)] atmosphérique; **at·mos'pher·ics** *pl.* radio: parasites *m/pl.*, perturbations *f/pl.* atmosphériques.

at·oll géog. [ə'tɔl] atoll *m*; île *f* de corail.

at·om ⚛, phys. ['ætəm] atome *m* (*a. fig.*); **a·tom·ic** [ə'tɔmik] atomique; ~ *age* (*bomb, energy, number, warfare, weight*) âge *m* (bombe *f*, énergie *f*, nombre *m*, guerre *f*, poids *m*) atomique; ~ *fission* fission *f* de l'atome; ~-*powered* actionné par l'énergie atomique; ~ *pile* (*ou reactor*) pile *f* atomique, réacteur *m* nucléaire; ~ *research* recherche *f* atomique, recherches *f/pl.* nucléaires; ~ *waste* déchets *m/pl.* nucléaires; **at·om·ism** ['ætəmizm] atomisme *m*; **at·om'is·tic** (~ally) atomistique; **'at·om·ize** pulvériser (*un liquide*); vaporiser; **'at·om·iz·er** pulvérisateur *m*, atomiseur *m*; **'at·o·my** surt. fig. squelette *m*.

a·tone [ə'toun]: ~ *for* expier (*qch.*), racheter (*qch.*); **a·tone·ment** expiation *f*, réparation *f*.

a·ton·ic [æ'tɔnik] ♪ atonique; gramm. atone; **at·o·ny** ['ætəni] atonie *f*; ♪ aveulissement *m*.

a·top F [ə'tɔp] en haut, au sommet; ~ *of* en haut de.

a·tro·cious □ [ə'trouʃəs] atroce; F affreux (-euse *f*); **a·troc·i·ty** [ə'trɔsiti] atrocité *f* (*a. fig.*).

at·ro·phy ♪ ['ætrəfi] **1.** atrophie *f*; contabescence *f*; **2.** (s')atrophier.

at·tach [ə'tætʃ] *v/t.* (*to*) attacher (*chose, valeur, sens, etc.*) (à); lier, fixer (à); annexer (*un document*) (à); imputer (*une responsabilité*) (à); ajouter (*de la foi*) (à); prêter (*de l'importance*) (à); ⚖ arrêter (*q.*); saisir (*qch.*); ~ *o.s. to* s'attacher à; ~ *value to* attacher du prix à; *v/i.* s'attacher (à, *to*); **at'tach·a·ble** qui peut être attaché (à, *to*); ⚖ saisissable; **at·ta·ché** [ə'tæʃei] attaché *m*; ~ *case* mallette *f* (*pour documents*); **at·tached** [ə'tætʃt]: *be* ~ *to* être atta-

ché à, tenir à; faire parti de, être adjoint à; ~ *house* maison *f* individuelle standard; **at'tach·ment** action *f* d'attacher; attachement *m* (*pour, for*); attache *f*, lien *m*; affection *f* (*pour, for*); ⊕, *machine:* accessoire *m*; attelage *m*; ⚖ saisie-arrêt (*pl.* saisies-arrêts) *f*; contrainte *f* par corps.

at·tack [ə'tæk] **1.** attaquer (*a. fig.*); s'attaquer à (*un travail, un repas, etc.*); *maladie:* s'attaquer à (*q.*); **2.** assaut *m*; attaque *f* (*a.* ♪); attentat *m* (*à la vie*); ♪ crise *f*; accès *m*; *heart* ~ crise *f* cardiaque; **at'tack·er** agresseur *m*; attaquant(e *f*) *m*.

at·tain [ə'tein] *v/t.* atteindre, arriver à (*a. fig.*); acquérir (*des connaissances*); *v/i.:* ~ *to* atteindre à; atteindre (*un âge*); **at'tain·a·ble** accessible; **at'tain·der** ⚖ confiscation *f* de biens et mort *f* civile; **at'tain·ment** arrivée *f*; fig. réalisation *f*; ~s *pl.* connaissance *f*, -s *f/pl.*, savoir *m*.

at·taint ⚖ [ə'teint] frapper (*q.*) de mort civile; fig. attaquer; souiller.

at·tar ['ætə] essence *f* de roses.

at·tem·per [ə'tempə] tremper; adoucir; modérer; accorder (avec, *to*).

at·tempt [ə'tempt] **1.** essayer (de, *to*), tâcher (de, *to*); ~ *the life of* attenter à la vie de; **2.** tentative *f*, essai *m*, effort *m* (de, *to*); attentat *m* (contre la vie de q., *[up]on s.o.'s life*).

at·tend [ə'tend] *v/t.* assister à; aller à; servir; visiter; soigner (*un malade*); accompagner; suivre (*un cours*); *v/i.* faire attention; assister; se charger (de, *to*); s'appliquer (à, *to*); ~ *on* visiter, soigner (*un malade*); ~ *to* s'occuper de (*affaires etc.*); **at'tend·ance** hôtel, magasin, etc.: service *m*; présence *f*; assistance *f* (à, *at*); ♪ soins *m/pl.* (pour, *on*), visites *f/pl.* (à, *on*); assiduité *f* (*aux cours, à l'école*); *hours pl. of* ~ heures *f/pl.* de présence; *be in* ~ être de service (auprès de, *on*); F *dance* ~ faire les trente-six volontés (de, *on*); **at'tend·ant 1.** qui accompagne, qui sert, qui suit (q., *[up]on s.o.*); qui assiste; concomitant; **2.** serviteur *m*, domestique *mf*; surveillant(e *f*) *m*; théâ. ouvreuse *f*; gardien(ne *f*) *m*; appariteur *m*; ⊕ surveillant *m*, soigneur *m*; ~s *pl.* personnel *m*.

at·ten·tion [ə'tenʃn] attention *f (a. fig.* = *civilité*); ✘ ~! garde à vous!; *see call; give; pay;* **at'ten·tive** □ attentif (-ive *f*) (à, to); soucieux (-euse *f*) (de, to); *fig.* empressé (auprès de, to).

at·ten·u·ate [ə'tenjueit] atténuer (*a. fig.*); amincir; raréfier (*un gaz etc.*); ténu; **at'ten·u·at·ed** atténué; amaigri; **at·ten'u·a·tion** atténuation *f*; amaigrissement *m*.

at·test [ə'test] attester, certifier (*a. fig.*); (*a. v/i.* ~ to) témoigner de; affirmer sous serment; ⚖ assermenter (*q.*); *surt.* ✘ faire prêter serment à (*q.*); **at·tes·ta·tion** [ætes-'teiʃn] attestation *f*; témoignage *m*; prestation *f* de serment; *surt.* ✘ assermentation *f*; **at·test·er**, **at·test·or** [ə'testə] témoin *m* (⚖ instrumentaire); ⚖ certificateur *m*.

At·tic ['ætik] 1. attique (*a.*); 2. ♀ mansarde *f*, F grenier *m*; ♀s *pl.* combles *m/pl.*; étage *m* mansardé.

at·tire *poét.* [ə'taiə] 1. vêtir; parer; 2. costume *m*, vêtements *m/pl.*

at·ti·tude ['ætitju:d] attitude *f* (envers, to[wards]); pose *f*; position *f* (*d'un avion en vol*); strike an ~ poser, prendre une attitude dramatique; ~ *of mind* disposition *f* d'esprit; manière *f* de penser; **at·ti·tu·di·nize** poser; faire des grâces.

at·tor·ney [ə'tɔ:ni] mandataire *mf*; *Am.* avoué *m*; ⚖ *Am. circuit* ~, *district* ~ procureur *m* de la République; *letter (ou warrant) of* ~ procuration *f*; *power of* ~ pouvoirs *m/pl.*; ♀ *General* avocat *m* du Gouvernement; procureur *m* général; *Am.* chef *m* du Ministère de Justice.

at·tract [ə'trækt] attirer (*a. l'attention*); *fig.* séduire; avoir de l'attrait pour; **at'trac·tion** [~kʃn] attraction *f*; *fig.* attrait *m*; *théâ.* attraction *f*; clou *m* (*du spectacle*); **at'trac·tive** [~tiv] □ *usu. fig.* attrayant, attirant; *théâ.* alléchant; **at'trac·tive·ness** attrait *m*, charme *m*.

at·trib·ut·a·ble [ə'tribjutəbl] imputable; **at·tri·bute 1.** [ə'tribju:t] imputer, attribuer (*une qualité, des vertus*); 2. ['ætribju:t] attribut *m*, qualité *f*; apanage *m*; symbole *m*; *gramm.* épithète *f*; **at·tri·bu·tion** [ætri'bju:ʃn] attribution

f, imputation *f* (à, to); affectation *f* (*à un but*); compétence *f*; **at·trib·u·tive** *gramm.* [ə'tribjutiv] 1. □ qualificatif (-ive *f*); 2. épithète *f*.

at·tri·tion [ə'triʃn] attrition *f*; usure *f* par le frottement; ⊕ usure *f*, *machine*: fatigue *f*; *war of* ~ guerre *f* d'usure.

at·tune [ə'tju:n] ♪ accorder, *fig.* harmoniser (avec, to).

au·burn ['ɔ:bən] châtain roux, blond ardent; acajou.

auc·tion ['ɔ:kʃn] 1. (*a. sale by* ~) vente *f* aux enchères; vente *f* à l'encan; *sell by* (*Am. at*) ~, *put up for* ~ vendre aux enchères; vendre à la criée (*du poisson etc.*); 2. (*usu.* ~ *off*) vendre aux enchères; **auc·tion·eer** [~ʃə'niə] commissaire-priseur (*pl.* commissaires-priseurs) *m*.

au·da·cious □ [ɔ:'deiʃəs] audacieux (-euse *f*), hardi; *péj.* effronté, cynique; **au·dac·i·ty** [ɔ:'dæsiti] audace *f*; hardiesse *f* (*a. péj.*); *péj.* effronterie *f*, cynisme *m*.

au·di·bil·i·ty [ɔ:di'biliti] perceptibilité *f*; **au·di·ble** ['ɔ:dəbl] perceptible; intelligible (*voix etc.*).

au·di·ence ['ɔ:djəns] audience *f* (avec of, with); assistance *f*, assistants *m/pl.* (*à une réunion*); public *m*, spectateurs *m/pl.* (*au théâtre*); auditeurs *m/pl.* (*au concert*).

audio... ['ɔ:diou] audio...; **au·di·o·fre·quen·cy** [~'fri:kwənsi] *radio:* audiofréquence *f*; **au·di·o·phile** ['~fail] amateur *m* de hi-fi; **au·di·o·vis·u·al aids** [~'vizjuəl eidz] support *m* audio-visuel.

au·dit ['ɔ:dit] 1. *comptes:* vérification *f*; 2. vérifier, apurer (*des comptes*); *univ.* † assister à (*un cours*); **au·di·tion** audition *f*; **'au·di·tor** commissaire *m* aux comptes; expert *m* comptable; auditeur *m* (*surt. univ.*); **au·di·to·ri·um** [~'tɔ:riəm] salle *f*; *eccl.* parloir *m*; *Am.* salle *f* (*de concert, de conférence, etc.*); **au·di·to·ry** ['~təri] 1. auditif (-ive *f*); de l'ouïe; 2. auditoire *m*; auditeurs *m/pl.*; *see* auditorium.

au·ger ⊕ ['ɔ:gə] perçoir *m*; tarière *f*.

aught [ɔ:t] quelque chose *m*; *for* ~ *I care* pour ce qui m'importe; *for* ~ *I know* autant que je sache.

aug·ment [ɔ:g'ment] *v/t.* augmenter, accroître; *v/i.* augmenter, s'accroître; **aug·men'ta·tion** augmentation *f*, accroissement *m*; **aug-'ment·a·tive** □ [ˌˈtətiv] augmentatif (-ive *f*).

au·gur [ˈɔːgə] 1. augure *m*; 2. augurer; prédire; *v/i.* être de bon *ou* de mauvais augure; **au·gu·ry** [ˈɔːgjuri] augure *m*; F présage *m*; science *f* des augures.

Au·gust 1. [ˈɔːgəst] août *m*; 2. ♀ □ [ɔːˈgʌst] auguste, imposant; **Au·gus·tan** [ɔːˈgʌstən] d'Auguste; *littérature anglaise*: de la reine Anne.

auk *orn.* [ɔːk] pingouin *m*.

aunt [ɑːnt] tante *f*; ♀ *Sally* jeu *m* de massacre; **aunt·ie, aunt·y** F [ˈˌti] tata *f*; ma tante.

au pair [əuˈpɛə] (*a.* ~ *girl*) jeune fille *f* au pair.

au·ral [ˈɔːrəl] de l'oreille.

au·re·ole [ˈɔːrioul] *eccl., astr.* auréole *f*; *saint*: gloire *f*.

au·ri·cle *anat.* [ˈɔːrikl] auricule *f*; **au·ric·u·la** ♀ [əˈrikjulə] auricule *f*; **au·ric·u·lar** □ [ɔːˈrikjulə] auriculaire; de l'oreille, des oreillettes du cœur; ~*witness* témoin *m* auriculaire.

au·rif·er·ous [ɔːˈrifərəs] aurifère.

au·rist ♀ [ˈɔːrist] auriste *m*.

au·rochs *zo.* [ˈɔːrɔks] bœuf *m* urus.

au·ro·ra [ɔːˈrɔːrə] Aurore *f* (*fig.* ♀); ~ *borealis* aurore *f* boréale; **au·ro·ral** auroral (-aux *m/pl.*); de l'aurore.

aus·cul·ta·tion ♀ [ɔːskəlˈteiʃn] auscultation *f*.

aus·pice [ˈɔːspis] augure *m*, ~*s pl.* auspices *m/pl.*; **aus·pi·cious** □ [ˈpiʃəs] propice; prospère, heureux (-euse *f*).

Aus·sie F [ˈɔsi] 1. Australien(ne *f*) *m*; 2. australien(ne *f*).

aus·tere □ [ɔsˈtiə] austère, frugal (-aux *m/pl.*) (*repas*); sans luxe (*chambre etc.*); cénobitique (*vie*); **aus·ter·i·ty** [ˈteriti] austérité *f*; sévérité *f* de goût; absence *f* de luxe; ~ *budget* budget *m* d'austérité.

aus·tral [ˈɔːstrəl] austral (-als *ou* -aux *m/pl.*).

Aus·tra·lian [ɔsˈtreiljən] 1. australien(ne *f*); 2. Australien(ne *f*) *m*.

Aus·tri·an [ˈɔstriən] 1. autrichien (-ne *f*); 2. Autrichien(ne *f*) *m*.

au·tarch·y [ˈɔːtɑːki] autarchie *f* (= *souveraineté*); *Am. see autarky.*

au·tark·y [ˈɔːtɑːki] autarcie *f*.

au·then·tic [ɔːˈθentik] (~*ally*) authentique; digne de foi; **au'then·ti·cate** [ˌkeit] certifier, légaliser,

valider, viser (*un acte etc.*); établir l'authenticité de; **au·then·ti·ca·tion** certification *f*; validation *f*; **au·then·tic·i·ty** [ˌˈtisiti] authenticité *f*; crédibilité *f*.

au·thor [ˈɔːθə] auteur *m* (*a. fig.*); écrivain *m*; **au·thor·ess** [ˈɔːθəris] femme *f* auteur; femme *f* écrivain; **au·thor·i·tar·i·an** [ɔːθriˈtɛəriən] autoritaire (*a. su./m*); **au'thor·i·ta·tive** □ [ˌtətiv] autoritaire; péremptoire; qui fait autorité (*document*); de bonne source; **au'thor·i·ta·tive·ness** autorité *f*; ton *m* autoritaire; **au'thor·i·ty** autorité *f* (*sur, over*); ascendant *m* (*sur, over*); domination *f*; autorisation *f*, mandat *m* (de *inf.*, to *inf.*); qualité *f* (pour *inf.*, to *inf.*); expert *m* (dans qch., on s.th.); source *f* (*de renseignements*); *surt.* ~*s pl.* l'administration *f*; on good ~ de bonne source; on the ~ of sur la foi de (*q.*); I have it on the ~ of Mr. X je le tiens de Monsieur X; **au·thor·i·za·tion** [ɔːθəraiˈzeiʃn] autorisation *f*; pouvoir *m*; mandat *m*; **'au·thor·ize** autoriser, sanctionner; donner mandat à; **'au·thor·ship** profession *f ou* qualité *f* d'auteur; *livre*: paternité *f*.

au·tism [ˈɔːtizm] autisme *m*; **au·tis·tic** [ɔːˈtistik] autistique.

au·to [ˈɔːtou] auto(mobile) *f*.

auto... [ˈɔːto] auto-.

au·to·bi·og·ra·pher [ɔːtɔbaiˈɔgrəfə] autobiographe *m*; **'au·to·bi·o·'graph·ic, 'au·to·bi·o'graph·i·cal** □ [ˌˈgræfik(l)] autobiographique; **au·to·bi·og·ra·phy** [ˌˈɔgrəfi] autobiographie *f*;   [*torcade.*]

au·to·cade *Am.* [ɔːtoukeid] *see* mo-]

au·to·car [ˈɔːtoukɑː] autocar *m*.

au·toch·thon [ɔːˈtɔkθən] autochthone *m* (= *aborigène*); **au'toch·tho·nous** autochthone.

au·toc·ra·cy [ɔːˈtɔkrəsi] autocratie *f*; **au·to·crat** [ˈɔːtəkræt] autocrate *m*; **au·to·crat·ic, au·to·'crat·i·cal** □ autocratique; autocrate (*personne*); absolu (*caractère*).

au·tog·e·nous weld·ing ⊕ [ɔːˈtɔdʒənəsˈweldiŋ] soudure *f* (à l'autogène.

au·to·gi·ro ✈ [ˈɔːtouˈdʒaiərou] autogyre *m*.

au·to·graph [ˈɔːtəgraːf] 1. autographe *m*; ~ *album* keepsake *m*; 2. signer, dédicacer; ⊕ autographier; **au·to·graph·ic** [ˌ‿ˈgræfik] (*ally*) autographe; ⊕ autographique; **au·tog·ra·phy** [ɔːˈtɔgrəfi] autographe *m*; ⊕ autographie *f*.

au·to·mat *Am*. [ˈɔtəmæt] restaurant *m* à distributeurs automatiques; **aut·o·mate** [ˈ‿meit] automatiser; **au·to·mat·ic** [ˌ‿ˈmætik] (*ally*) **1.** automatique; inconscient; ~ *machine* distributeur *m*; ~ *telephone* (téléphone *m*) automatique *m*; *mot.* ~ *transmission* transmission *f* automatique; **2.** *Am.* automatique *m*; **au·tom·a·tion** ⊕ automatisation *f*; **au·tom·a·ton** [ɔːˈtɔmətən], *pl.* **-tons, -ta** [ˌ‿tə] automate *m* (*a. fig.*).

au·to·mo·bile *surt. Am.* [ˈɔːtəməbiːl] automobile *f*; F voiture *f*.

au·ton·o·mous [ɔːˈtɔnəməs] autonome; **au·ton·o·my** autonomie *f*.

au·top·sy [ˈɔːtəpsi] autopsie *f*.

au·to·type ⊕ [ˈɔːtətaip] fac-similé *m*.

au·tumn [ˈɔːtəm] automne *m*; **au·tum·nal** [ɔːˈtʌmnəl] automnal (-aux *m/pl.*); d'automne.

aux·il·ia·ry [ɔːgˈziljəri] **1.** auxiliaire, subsidiaire (à, *to*); **2.** (*a.* ~ *verb*) *gramm.* verbe *m* auxiliaire; *auxiliaries pl.* (troupes *f/pl.*) auxiliaires *m/pl.*

a·vail [əˈveil] **1.** servir (à), être utile (à) (*q.*); ~ *o.s. of* profiter de (*qch.*); user de (*qch.*); saisir (*une opportunité*); **2.** avantage *m*, utilité *f*; *of no* ~ inutile; *of what* ~ *is it?* à quoi bon?; à quoi sert (*de inf., to inf.*)?; **a·vail·a·bil·i·ty** disponibilité *f*; *billet*: durée *f*, validité *f*; **a·vail·a·ble** □ disponible; libre; accessible; valable, bon(ne *f*), valide; **a·vail·ments** *pl.* disponibilités *f/pl.*

av·a·lanche [ˈævəlɑːnʃ] avalanche *f*.

av·a·rice [ˈævəris] avarice *f*; mesquinerie *f*; **av·a·ri·cious** □ avare, avaricieux (-euse *f*).

a·venge [əˈvendʒ] venger; prendre la vengeance de (*q.*); ~ *o.s.* (*ou be* ~ *d*) (*up*)on se venger de *ou* sur; *avenging angel* divinité *f* vengeresse; **a·veng·er** vengeur (-eresse *f*) *m*.

av·e·nue [ˈævinjuː] avenue *f*; chemin *m* d'accès; promenade *f* plantée d'arbres; *Am.* boulevard *m*.

a·ver [əˈvəː] avérer, affirmer, déclarer; *a*: alléguer.

av·er·age [ˈævəridʒ] **1.** moyenne *f*; ⚓ avarie *f*; ⚓ *general* ~ avaries *f/pl.* communes; ⚓ *particular* ~ avarie *f*

particulière; *on an* ~ en moyenne; **2.** □ moyen(ne *f*); *fig.* ordinaire, normal (-aux *m/pl.*); **3.** prendre *ou* faire *ou* établir la moyenne (de, *of*); donner une moyenne (de, *at*).

a·ver·ment [əˈvəːmənt] affirmation *f*; *a* allégation *f*; preuve *f*.

a·verse □ [əˈvəːs] opposé (à *to*, *from*); ennemi (de); **a'verse·ness**, **a'ver·sion** aversion *f* (pour *to*, *from*); répugnance *f* (à); *he is my aversion* il est mon cauchemar.

a·vert [əˈvəːt] détourner (*a. fig.*); écarter.

a·vi·a·ry [ˈeivjəri] volière *f*.

a·vi·ate ✈ [ˈeivieit] voler; **a·vi·a·tion** aviation *f*; vol *m*; ~ *ground* aérodrome *m*; **a·vi·a·tor** aviateur (-trice *f*) *m*.

av·id □ [ˈævid] avide (de *of*, *for*); **a·vid·i·ty** [əˈviditi] avidité *f* (de, pour *for*).

av·o·ca·do ♀ [ævouˈkɑːdou] (*a.* ~ *pear*) avocat *m*.

av·o·ca·tion [ævoˈkeiʃn] occupation *f*; vocation *f*; profession *f*; métier *m*.

a·void [əˈvoid] éviter; se soustraire à; se dérober à; *a* résoudre, annuler, résilier (*un contrat etc.*); **a'void·a·ble** évitable; **a'void·ance** action *f* d'éviter; *usu. eccl.* vacance *f*; *a* *contrat etc.*: résolution *f*, annulation *f*, résiliation *f*.

av·oir·du·pois ✝ [ævədəˈpoiz] poids *m* du commerce; *Am. sl.* poids *m*, pesanteur *f*.

a·vouch [əˈvautʃ] garantir; reconnaître; *see* **avow**.

a·vow [əˈvau] reconnaître; s'avérer; déclarer; **a'vow·al** aveu *m*; **a'vow·ed·ly** [ˌ‿idli] franchement, ouvertement.

a·wait [əˈweit] attendre (*a. fig.*).

a·wake [əˈweik] **1.** éveillé; attentif (-ive *f*); *be* ~ *to* avoir conscience de; *wide* ~ bien *ou* tout éveillé; *fig.* averti, avisé; **2.** [*irr.*] *v/t.* (*usu.* **a'wak·en**) éveiller; réveiller; ~ *s.o. to* ouvrir les yeux à q. sur; *v/i.* se réveiller, s'éveiller; prendre conscience (de qch., *to* s.*th.*).

a·ward [əˈwɔːd] **1.** adjudication *f*, sentence *f* arbitrale; récompense *f*; *Am.* bourse *f*; *a* dommages-intérêts *m/pl.*; **2.** adjuger, décerner; accorder; conférer (*un titre etc.*).

a·ware [əˈwɛə]: *be* ~ avoir connaissance (de, *of*); avoir conscience (de, of); ne pas ignorer (qch., *of s.th.*; que, *that*); become ~ *of* prendre connaissance *ou* conscience de; se rendre compte de; **a'ware·ness** conscience *f*.

a·wash ⚓ [ə'wɔʃ] à fleur d'eau; ras (*écueil*); *fig.* inondé.

a·way [ə'wei] (au) loin; dans le lointain; absent; à une distance de; *do* ~ *with* supprimer; ~ *with it!* emportezle!; ~ *with you!* allez-vouz-en!; *Am.* F ~ *back* il y a (déjà) longtemps; dès (*une date*); *I cannot* ~ *with it* je ne peux pas sentir cela.

awe [ɔ:] crainte *f*, terreur *f* (de, of); *qqfois* respect *m* (pour, of); terreur *f* religieuse; effroi *m* religieux; **awe·some** ['~səm] *see awful*; **'awe-struck** frappé d'une terreur profonde religieuse *ou* mystérieuse; intimidé.

aw·ful □ ['ɔ:ful] redoutable, effroyable; F fameux (-euse *f*); fier (-ère *f*), affreux (-euse *f*); **'aw·ful·ness** caractère *m* terrible; solennité *f*.

a·while [ə'wail] un moment; pendant quelque temps.

awk·ward □ ['ɔ:kwəd] gauche, maladroit; gêné; fâcheux (-euse *f*), gênant; incommode, peu commode; **'awk·ward·ness** gaucherie *f*; maladresse *f*; manque *m* de grâce; embarras *m*; inconvénient *m*.

awl [ɔ:l] alêne *f*, poinçon *m*.

awn ⚘ [ɔ:n] barbe *f*, barbelure *f*.

awn·ing ['ɔ:niŋ] ⚓, *a. voiture*: tente *f*; *boutique*: banne *f*; *théâtre, hôtel*: marquise *f*; ⚓ tendelet *m*.

a·woke [ə'wouk] *prét. et p.p. de awake* 2.

a·wry [ə'rai] de travers; de guingois; *go* ~, *turn* ~ aller de travers.

axe [æks] **1.** hache *f*; F *the* ~ coupe *f*; traitement, personnel, *etc.*: réductions *f/pl.*; *have an* ~ *to grind* avoir un intérêt personnel à servir; **2.** *v/t.* F faire des coupes dans; mettre à pied (*des fonctionnaires*).

ax·i·om ['æksiəm] *principe:* axiome *m*; **ax·i·o'mat·ic** (~ally) axiomatique; F évident.

ax·is ['æksis], *pl.* **ax·es** ['~si:z] axe *m*.

ax·le ⊕ ['æksl] tourillon *m*; arbre *m*; (*a.* ~-*tree*) essieu *m*.

ay(e) [ai] **1.** *parl.* oui; ⚓ ~, ~! bien (monsieur)!; **2.** oui *m*; *parl.* voix *f* pour; *the* ~*s have it* le vote est pour.

a·za·lea ⚘ [ə'zeiljə] azalée *f*.

az·i·muth *astr.* ['æziməθ] azimut *m*; ~ *instrument* compas *m* de relèvement; **az·i·muth·al** [~'mju:θl] azimutal (-aux *m/pl.*).

a·zo·ic *géol.* [ə'zouik] azoïque.

az·ure ['æʒə] **1.** d'azur, azuré; **2.** azur *m*.

B

B, b [biː] B *m*, b *m*.

baa [baː] **1.** bêler; **2.** bêlement *m*.

Bab·bitt *Am.* ['bæbit] philistin *m*; affreux bourgeois *m*; ⊕ ♀ *metal* métal *m* blanc antifriction.

bab·ble ['bæbl] **1.** babiller; jaser; murmurer; gazouiller; raconter (*qch.*) en babillant; **2.** babil(lage) *m*, babillement *m*; bavardage *m*, jaserie *f*; murmure *m*; **'bab·bler** bavard(e *f*) *m*; jaseur (-euse *f*) *m*.

babe [beib] *poét.* petit(e) enfant *m(f)*.

Ba·bel ['beibl] *bibl.* Tour *f* de Babel; *fig.* brouhaha *m*, vacarme *m*.

ba·boon *zo.* [bə'buːn] babouin *m*.

ba·by ['beibi] **1.** bébé *m*; poupon(ne *f*) *m*; poupard *m*; F *it's your* ~ c'est votre affaire; F *be left holding the* ~ rester avec l'affaire sur les bras; **2.** d'enfant, de bébé, petit; ~ **act** *usu. plead* (*ou play*) *the* ~ *Am.* plaider son inexpérience; appuyer sa défense sur sa minorité; ~ **boom** montée *f* en flèche des naissances; **'~-car·riage** *Am.* voiture *f* d'enfant; **'~-farm·er** personne *f* qui prend des enfants en nourrice; *péj.* faiseuse *f* d'anges; ~ **grand** ♪ piano *m* (à) demi-queue; **'ba·by·hood** ['~hud] première enfance *f*; bas âge *m*; **'ba·by·ish** □ puéril; de bébé.

Bab·y·lo·ni·an [bæbi'lounjən] **1.** babylonien(ne *f*); **2.** Babylonien(ne *f*) *m*.

ba·by...: **'~-mind·er** nourrice *f*; **'~-sit** [*irr.* (*sit*)] veiller sur un enfant; faire du baby-sitting; **'ba·by'sit·ter** baby-sitter *m*, garde-bébé *mf* (*pl.* gardes-bébés).

bac·ca·lau·re·ate [bækə'lɔːriit] baccalauréat *m*; *univ. usu.* licence *f* (*ès lettres, ès sciences, etc.*).

Bac·cha·nal ['bækənl] *see* Bacchant; **'Bac·cha·nals** *pl.*, **Bac·cha·na·li·a** [~'neiljə] *pl.* bacchanales *f/pl.*; **Bac·cha·na·li·an** **1.** bachique; **2.** *fig.* noceur *m*.

Bac·chant ['bækənt] adorateur *m* de Bacchus; (*a.* **Bac·chante** [bə'kænti]) bacchante *f*.

bach·e·lor ['bætʃələ] célibataire *m*, garçon *m*; *hist.* bachelier *m*; *univ.* licencié(e *f*) *m*; ~ *girl* garçonne *f*; **bach·e·lor·hood** ['~hud] célibat *m*; vie *f* de garçon.

bac·il·la·ry [bə'siləri] bacillaire; **ba·cil·lus** [~əs], *pl.* **-li** [~lai] bacille *m*.

back [bæk] **1.** *su. personne, animal*: dos *m*; reins *m/pl.*; revers *m*; *chaise*: dossier *m*; *salle, armoire, scène*: fond *m*; *tête, maison*: derrière *m*; *foot., maison*: arrière *m*; (*at the*) ~ *of* au fond de; *put one's* ~ *into it* y aller de tout son cœur; F *put s.o.'s* ~ *up* mettre q. en colère; faire rebiffer q.; **2.** *adj.* arrière, de derrière; sur le derrière (*pièce*); sur la cour (*chambre d'hôtel*); *gramm.* vélaire; ~ *formation* dérivation *f* régressive; ~ *issue* ancien numéro *m*, ancien volume *m*; ~ *pay* (*ou salary*) rappel *m* de traitement; **3.** *adv.* en arrière; de retour; **4.** *v/t.* renforcer (*un mur, une carte*); endosser (*un livre*); parier sur, miser sur (*un cheval*); appuyer, (*a.* ~ *up*) soutenir; servir de fond à; reculer (*une charrette*); faire (re)culer (*un cheval*); refouler (*un train*); mettre en arrière (*une machine*); ✝ endosser (*un effet*); financer (*q.*); ⚓ ~ *the sails* masquer les voiles; ~ *water*, ~ *the oars* ramer à rebours; scier; ~ *up* prêter son appui à (*qch., q.*); *v/i.* aller en arrière; marcher à reculons; reculer (*cheval*); faire marche arrière (*voiture*); ravaler (*vent*); F se dégager (*de, out of*); F ~ *down* en rabattre; rabattre (*de, from*); **'~-ache** mal *m* aux reins; ~ **al·ley** *Am.* rue *f* misérable (*dans le bas quartier*); **'~-bas·ket** hotte *f*; **'~-bench·er** membre *m* du Parlement sans portefeuille; **'~-bend** *sp.* pont *m*; **'~-bite** [*irr.* (*bite*)] médire de (*q.*); **'~-board** dossier *m*; ⚓ planche *f* à dos; **'~-bone** échine *f*; colonne *f* vertébrale; *fig.* caractère *m*, fermeté *f*; *to the* ~ *fig.* à la moelle des os; **'~-chat** impertinence *f*, répliques *f/pl.* impertinentes; **'~-cloth** *théâ.*

toile *f* de fond; '**∼∙date** antidater; ∼*d to* avec effet rétroactif à, avec rappel à compter de; '∼-'**door** porte *f* de derrière; *fig.* petite porte *f*; '**∼∙drop** *théâ.* toile *f* de fond; **backed** ∼ à dos, à dossier; *phot.* ocré (*plaque*); ∼ **en∙trance** entrée *f* de derrière; '**back∙er** parieur (-euse *f*) *m*; partisan *m*; ✝ donneur *m* d'aval; commanditaire *m*. **back...**: '∼-**fire** *mot.* 1. pétarde *f*; 2. pétarder; ∼'**gam∙mon** trictrac *m*; jacquet *m*; '∼'**ground** fond *m*, arrière-plan *m*; '∼-'**hand 1.** coup *m* fourré; *tennis:* revers *m*; 2. déloyal (-aux *m/pl.*); de revers; '∼-'**hand∙ed** renversé; *fig.* équivoque; '∼-'**hand∙er** *see* back-hand 1; riposte *f* inattendue; '∼∙**lash** contre-coup *m*, répercussion(s *pl.*) *f*, *fig. a.* réaction *f* brutale; '∼-**log** réserve *f*; arriéré *m*; '∼-**pack** sac *m* à dos; '∼-**pay** rappel *m* de salaire; '∼-'**ped∙al** contre-pédaler; ∼*ling* brake frein *m* par contre-pédalage; '∼'**side** derrière *m*; '∼-**sight** hausse *f*; *surv.* coup *m* arrière; '∼-**slap∙per** *Am.* luron *m*; '∼'**slide** [*irr.* (slide)] retomber dans l'erreur *m*; rechuter; '∼'**slid∙er** relaps(e *f*) *m*; '∼'**slid∙ing** récidive *f*; '∼-**stage** derrière la scène, dans les coulisses; '∼'**stairs** escalier *m* de service; '∼-**stitch 1.** point *m* arrière; 2. coudre à points de piqûre; ∼ **street** rue *f* latérale, petite rue *f*; ∼ *abortionist* faiseuse *f* d'anges; '∼-**stroke** (*ou* ∼ *swimming*) nage *f* sur le dos; ∼ **talk** *Am.* impertinence *f*; ∼ **to back** *sp. Am.* F l'un après l'autre; ∼ **to front** sens devant derrière; '∼-**track** *Am.* F *fig.* s'en retourner (*chez soi etc.*).

back∙ward ['bækwəd] **1.** *adj.* attardé, arrière (*personne*); en arrière, rétrograde; en retard; peu empressé (à *inf.*, *in gér.*); **2.** *adv.* (*a.* '**back∙wards**) en arrière; *walk backwards and forwards* aller et venir; **back∙ward'a∙tion** ✝ *Br.* déport *m*; '**back∙ward∙ness** retard *m*; hésitation *f*, lenteur *f* (*a. d'intelligence*); tardiveté *f*.

back...: '∼-**wa∙ter** eau *f* arrêtée; bras *m* de décharge; remous *m*; '∼-**wheel** roue *f* arrière; roue *f* motrice; ∼ *drive* pont *m* arrière; '∼-**woods** *pl.* forêts *f/pl.* de l'intérieur (de l'Amérique du Nord); '∼-**woods∙man** colon *m* des forêts (de l'Amérique du Nord).

ba∙con ['beikən] lard *m*; F *save one's* ∼ sauver sa peau; se tirer d'affaire; *sl.* *bring home the* ∼ revenir triomphant; décrocher la timbale.

bac∙te∙ri∙al □ [bæk'tiəriəl] bactérien(ne *f*); **bac∙te∙ri∙o∙log∙i∙cal** □ [bæktiəriə'lɔdʒikl] bactériologique; **bac∙te∙ri∙ol∙o∙gist** [∼'ɔlədʒist] bactériologiste *m/f*; **bac'te∙ri∙um** [∼iəm], *pl.* -**ri∙a** [∼riə] bactérie *f*.

bad □ [bæd] mauvais; triste (*affaire*); avarié (*viande*); piteux (-euse *f*) (*état*); méchant (*enfant*); grave (*accident*); malade; faux (fausse *f*) (*monnaie*); vilain (*mot. a. Am.*); F *not* ∼ pas mal du tout; *not too* ∼ comme ci comme ça; *things are not so* ∼ ça ne marche pas si mal; *he is* ∼*ly off* il est mal loti; ∼*ly wounded* gravement blessé; F *want* ∼*ly* avoir grand besoin de.

bade [beid] *prét.* de bid 1.

badge [bædʒ] insigne *m*; *fig.* symbole *m*.

badg∙er ['bædʒə] **1.** *zo.* blaireau *m*; **2.** tracasser, harceler, importuner.

bad∙lands *Am.* ['bæd'lændz] *pl.* terres *f/pl.* incultivables.

bad∙min∙ton *sp.* ['bædmintən] badminton *m*.

bad∙ness ['bædnis] mauvaise qualité *f*; mauvais état *m*; méchanceté *f* (*d'une personne*).

bad-tem∙pered ['bæd'tempəd] grincheux (-euse *f*); acariâtre.

baf∙fle ['bæfl] dérouter (*q., des soupçons*); faire échouer (*un projet etc.*); confondre; dépister; *it* ∼*s description* il défie toute description; **baf∙fling** déconcertant.

bag [bæg] **1.** sac *m*; sacoche *f*; bourse *f*; F poche *f* (*sous l'œil*); *chasse:* tableau *m*; *sl.* ∼*s pl.* pantalon *m*; *Am.* F *it's in the* ∼ c'est dans le sac; *depart* ∼ *and baggage* emporter ses cliques et ses claques; **2.** (se) gonfler, bouffer; *v/t.* mettre en sac; F chiper, voler; *chasse:* abattre, tuer.

bag∙a∙telle [bægə'tel] bagatelle *f*; billard *m* anglais.

bag∙gage ['bægidʒ] *Am.* bagages *m/pl.*; ∼ **al∙low∙ance** franchise *f* de bagages; ∼ **car** 🚃 fourgon *m* aux bagages; '∼-**check** bulletin *m* de bagages; '∼-**rack** *auto:* galerie *f*, 🚃 porte-bagages *m/inv.*; ∼ **re∙claim** (guichet *m* de) remise *f* des bagages; ∼ **room** consigne *f*.

bag·ging ['bægiŋ] mise *f* en sac; toile *f* à sac.

bag·gy ['bægi] bouffant; pendant (*joues*); formant poches (*pantalon*).

bag...: '**~·man** F commis *m* voyageur; '**~·pipe** cornemuse *f*; '**~·snatch·er** voleur *m* à la tire.

bail¹ [beil] **1.** garant *m*; caution *f*; ⚖ *admit to* ~ accorder la liberté provisoire sous caution à (*q.*); *be* (*ou go ou stand*) ~ *for* fournir caution pour; **2.** cautionner; ~ *out* se porter caution pour (*q.*).

bail² ⚓ [~] écoper.

bail³ [~] *cricket:* ~*s pl.* bâtonnets *m/pl.*, barrettes *f/pl.*

bail⁴ [~] *baquet etc.*: poignée *f*.

bail·a·ble ⚖ ['beiləbl] admettant l'élargissement *m* sous caution.

bail·ee ⚖ [bei'li:] dépositaire *m*; emprunteur (-euse *f*) *m*.

bail·er ⚓ ['beilə] **1.** écope *f*; **2.** écoper.

bail·iff ['beilif] 🖉 régisseur *m*, intendant *m*; ⚖ agent *m* de poursuites, huissier *m*.

bail·ment ⚖ ['beilmənt] dépôt *m* (*de biens*); mise *f* en liberté sous caution.

bail·or ['beilə] déposant *m*; prêteur (-euse *f*) *m*; ⚖ caution *f*.

bairn *écoss.* [bɛən] enfant *mf*.

bait [beit] **1.** amorce *f*; appât *m* (*a. fig.*); *a. fig.* take the ~ mordre à l'hameçon; **2.** *v/t.* amorcer (*un piège, une ligne, etc.*); faire manger (*un cheval pendant une halte*); *fig.* harceler; importuner; *v/i.* se restaurer; s'arrêter pour se refraîchir.

bait·ing ['beitiŋ] harcelage *m*; amorcement *m*.

baize † [beiz] serge *f*; tapis *m* vert.

bake [beik] **1.** (faire) cuire; *v/i.* boulanger; F brûler; ~*d potatoes pl.* pommes *f/pl.* (de terre) au four; **2.** soirée *f*; '**~·house** fournil *m*, boulangerie *f*.

ba·ke·lite ⊕ ['beikəlait] bakélite *f*.

bak·er ['beikə] boulanger *m*; '**bak·er·y** boulangerie *f*; '**bak·ing** rôtissant, desséchant (*soleil*); F brûlant; ~ *hot* torride; '**bak·ing-pow·der** poudre *f* à lever; '**bak·ing-soda** bicarbonate *m* de soude.

bak·sheesh ['bækʃi:ʃ] bakchich *m*.

bal·a·lai·ka ♪ [bælə'laikə] balalaïka *f*.

bal·ance ['bæləns] **1.** balance *f*; *fig.* équilibre *m*, aplomb *m*; *montre:* balancier *m*, *a. horloge:* régulateur *m*;

† solde *m*; bilan *m*; *surt. Am.* F reste *m*; ~ *in hand* solde *m* créditeur; ~ *of payments* balance *f* des paiements; ~ *of trade* balance *f* commerciale; *see strike* 2; **2.** *v/t.* balancer; équilibrer, stabiliser; compenser; faire contrepoids à; † balancer, solder; dresser le bilan de; *v/i.* se faire équilibre; se balancer; '**~-sheet** † bilan *m*.

bal·co·ny ['bælkəni] balcon *m*; *théâ.* deuxième balcon *m*.

bald [bɔ:ld] chauve; *fig.* nu; dénudé.

bal·da·chin ['bɔ:ldəkin] baldaquin *m*.

bal·der·dash ['bɔ:ldədæʃ] bêtises *f/pl.*, balivernes *f/pl.*

bald...: '**~·head**, '**~·pate** tête *f* chauve; '**~·head·ed** à la tête chauve; *go* ~ *into* faire (*qch.*) tête baissée; '**bald·ness** calvitie *f*; *fig.* nudité *f*; *surt. style:* sécheresse *f*.

bale¹ † [beil] balle *f*, ballot *m*.

bale² ⚓ [~] *v/t.* écoper; *v/i.* ✈ ~ *out* sauter en parachute.

bale·fire ['beilfaiə] † feu *m* d'alarme; *see bonfire*; bûcher *m* funéraire.

bale·ful □ ['beilful] sinistre; funeste.

balk [bɔ:k] **1.** bande *f* de délimitation; billon *m*; *fig.* obstacle *m*; **2.** *v/t.* contrarier; entraver; éviter (*un sujet*); se soustraire à; frustrer; *v/i.* refuser; reculer (*devant, at*); regimber (*contre, at*).

Bal·kan ['bɔ:lkən] balkanique, des Balkans.

ball¹ [bɔ:l] **1.** *cricket, tennis, hockey, fusil, etc.*: balle *f*; *croquet, neige:* boule *f*; *foot., enfant:* ballon *m*; *billard:* bille *f*; *laine, ficelle:* pelote *f*, peloton *m*; *canon:* boulet *m*; *Am. baseball:* coup *m* manqué; F *be on the* ~ être à la hauteur (de la situation); connaître son affaire; *keep the* ~ *rolling* soutenir la conversation; *Am.* F *play* ~ coopérer (*avec, with*); **2.** (s')agglomérer.

ball² [~] (*pl.* -s) *m*; F *fig. have a* ~ s'amuser bien; *open the* ~ ouvrir le bal (*a. fig.*).

bal·lad ['bæləd] ballade *f*; ♪ romance *f*; '**~·mon·ger** chansonnier *m*.

ball-and-sock·et ⊕ ['bɔ:lən'sɔkit]: ~ *joint* joint *m* à rotule.

bal·last ['bæləst] **1.** ⚓ lest *m*; *fig.* esprit *m* rassis; 🚊 ballast *m*, empierrement *m*; *mental* ~ sens *m* rassis; **2.** lester; ⚓ ballaster.

ball...: '~-**bear·ing(s** *pl.*) ⊕ roulement *m* à billes; '~-**boy** *tennis*: ramasseur *m* de balles.

bal·let ['bælei] ballet *m*.

bal·lis·tics [bə'listiks] *usu. sg.* balistique *f*.

bal·loon [bə'luːn] **1.** 🎈, *a.* ⚗ ballon *m*; △ pomme *f*; *mot.* ~ *tyre* pneu *m* ballon *ou* confort; **2.** monter en ballon; bouffer; se ballonner; **bal'loon fab·ric** entoilage *m*; **bal-'loon·ist** aéronaute *m*, aérostier *m*.

bal·lot ['bælət] **1.** (tour *m* de) scrutin *m*; vote *m*; *parl.* tirage *m* au sort; **2.** voter au scrutin; tirer au sort; ~ *for* tirer (*qch.*) au sort; tirer au sort pour; '~-**box** urne *f*.

ball-point-pen ['bɔːlpɔint'pen] stylo *m* à bille.

ball-room ['bɔːlrum] salle *f* de bal; *hôtel*: salle *f* de danse.

bal·ly·hoo *Am.* [bæli'huː] grosse réclame *f*; battage *m*. [déver (*q.*).]

bal·ly·rag F ['bæliræg] faire enrager; reliure (douce *f*).

balm [bɑːm] baume *m* (*a. fig.*).

bal·mor·al [bæl'mɔrl] (béret *m*) balmoral *m*; (brodequin *m*) balmoral *m*.

balm·y □ ['bɑːmi] balsamique; *fig.* embaumé, doux (douce *f*); F toqué.

ba·lo·ney *Am. sl.* [bə'louni] sottises *f/pl.*; foutaise *f*.

bal·sam ['bɔːlsəm] baume *m*; **bal·sam·ic** [~'sæmik] (~*ally*) balsamique.

bal·us·ter ['bæləstə] balustre *m*.

bal·us·trade [bæləs'treid] balustrade *f*; *fenêtre etc.*: accoudoir *m*; garde-corps *m/inv.*

bam·boo [bæm'buː] bambou *m*.

bam·boo·zle F [bæm'buːzl] frauder (de, *out of*); amener par ruse (à, *into*).

ban [bæn] **1.** ban *m*, proscription *f*; *eccl.* interdit *m*; **2.** interdire (*qch.* à q., *s.o. from s.th.*); mettre (*un livre*) à l'index.

ba·nan·a 🍌 [bə'nɑːnə] banane *f*; *Am.* ~ *split* banane *f* à la glace.

band [bænd] **1.** bande *f*; lien *m*; *chapeau etc.*, *frein*: ruban *m*; raie *f*; *deuil*: brassard *m*; ⊕ *roue*: bandage *m*; *reliure*: nerf *m*, nervure *f*; *radio*: bande *f*; ♪ orchestre *m*, musique *f* (*militaire*); **2.** bander; fretter (*un four etc.*); ~ *o.s.*, *be* ~*ed* se bander; *péj.* s'ameuter.

band·age ['bændidʒ] **1.** bandage *m*; bande *f*; bandeau *m*; pansement *m*; *first aid* ~ bandage *m*; pansement *m*; **2.** bander; mettre un pansement à (*une plaie*). [sparadrap *m*.]

Band-Aid (*TM*) *Am.* ['bændeid]/

ban·dan·(n)a [bæn'dɑːnə] foulard *m*; F mouchoir *m*.

band-box ['bændbɔks] carton *m* à chapeaux; carton *m* de modiste; *look as if one came out of a* ~ être tiré à quatre épingles.

ban·dit ['bændit] bandit *m*, brigand *m*; '**ban·dit·ry** brigandage *m*.

band-mas·ter ['bændmɑːstə] chef *m* d'orchestre *ou* de musique *etc.*

ban·dog † ['bændɔg] mâtin *m*.

ban·do·leer [bændə'liə] bandoulière *f*; cartouchière *f*.

bands·man ['bændzmən] musicien *m*; fanfariste *m*; '**band·stand** kiosque *m* à musique; '**band·wag·on** *Am.* F *pol.* char *m* des musiciens; *fig.* cause *f* victorieuse; *get into* (*ou on*) *the* ~ se ranger du bon côté.

ban·dy ['bændi] **1.** *sp.* jeu *m* de crosse; ~-*ball* hockey *m*; **2.** (se) renvoyer (*balle*, *paroles*, *reproches*, *etc.*); échanger (*des coups*, *des plaisanteries*); (*a.* ~ *about*) faire courir (*des bruits*); '~-**leg·ged** bancal (-als *m/pl.*).

bane [bein] *fig.* tourment *m*, malheur *m*; † poison *m*; **bane·ful** □ ['beinful] *fig.* funeste; pernicieux (-euse *f*).

bang [bæŋ] **1.** boum! pan!; *go* ~ éclater; **2.** exactement, pile; directement, en plein; **3.** coup *m*; détonation *f*; *porte*: claquement *m*; **4.** frapper; (faire) claquer *ou* heurter à (*la porte*); battre (*le prix*); *sl.* baiser; '**bang·er** pétard *m*; F vieux tacot *m*; F saucisse *f*; ~*s and mash* saucisses *f/pl.* à la purée.

ban·gle ['bæŋgl] bracelet *m* de poignet *ou* de cheville.

bang-on ['bæŋ'ɔn] exactement, tout juste; *it's* ~ *a.* c'est au poil; il tombe pile; ~ *time* à l'heure pile.

bangs *Am.* [bæŋz] *pl.* coiffure: franges *f/pl.*

bang-up F ['bæŋ'ʌp] première classe; chic *adj./inv. en genre*.

ban·ish ['bæniʃ] bannir; proscrire; '**ban·ish·ment** exil *m*, proscription *f*.

ban·is·ters ['bænistəz] *pl.* balustres *m/pl.*; rampe *f*.

ban·jo ♩ ['bændʒou] banjo *m*.

bank [bæŋk] **1.** talus *m*; terrasse *f*; *sable, brouillard, huîtres*: banc *m*; *rivière*: berge *f*; *nuages*: couche *f*; ✝, *a. jeu*: banque *f*; ~ *of deposit* banque *f* de dépôt; ~ *of issue* banque *f* d'émission; *joint-stock* ~ banque *f* sous forme de société par actions; **2.** *v/t*. endiguer; terrasser; ⊕ surhausser (*un virage*); ✝ déposer en banque; ✈ pencher; incliner sur l'aile; *v/i*. s'entasser, s'amonceler; avoir un compte de banque (*chez, with*); ✈ virer, pencher l'avion; ~ *on* compter sur, miser sur; ~ *up* (s')amonceler; **'bank·a·ble** bancable, négociable en banque; **'bank-ac·count** compte *m* en banque; **'bank-bill** effet *m*; *Am. see* banknote; **'bank·er** banquier *m* (*a. jeu*); *jeu*: tailleur *m*; **bank hol·i·day** jour *m* férié; **'bank·ing 1.** (affaires *f*/*pl.* de) banque *f*; ✈ virage *m* incliné; **2.** de banque, en banque; ~ *charges pl.* frais *m*/*pl.* de banque; ~ *hours pl.* heures *f*/*pl.* d'ouverture des banques; ~ *house* maison *f* de banque; **'bank·note** billet *m* de banque; **'bank·rate** taux *m* officiel *ou* de la Banque *ou* de l'escompte; **bank·rupt** ['~rəpt] **1.** (commerçant *m*) failli *m*; *frauduleux* ~ banqueroutier (-ère *f*) *m*; ~'s *estate* masse *f* des biens (de la faillite); *go* ~ faire faillite; **2.** failli; banqueroutier (-ère *f*); *fig.* ~ *in* (*ou of*) dépourvu de (*une qualité*); **3.** mettre (*q.*) en faillite; **bank·rupt·cy** ['~rəptsi] faillite *f*; *frauduleux* ~ banqueroute *f*; *declaration of* ~ déclaration *f* de faillite.

ban·ner ['bænə] **1.** bannière *f* (*a. eccl.*); étendard *m*; **2.** *Am.* excellent, de première classe; principal (-aux *m*/*pl.*).

banns [bænz] *pl.* bans *m*/*pl.* (*de mariage*); *put up the* ~ (faire) publier les bans; *call the* ~ *of* annoncer le mariage de (*q.*).

ban·quet ['bæŋkwit] **1.** banquet *m*; dîner *m* de gala; **2.** *v/t*. offrir un banquet *etc.* à (*q.*); *v/i*. F faire festin; ~*ing hall* salle *f* de banquet; **'ban·quet·er** banqueteur (-euse *f*) *m*.

ban·shee *écoss., Ir.* [bæn'ʃiː] fée *f* de mauvais augure.

ban·tam ['bæntəm] coq *m* (poule *f*) Bantam; *fig.* nain *m*; *sp.* ~ *weight* poids *m* coq.

ban·ter ['bæntə] **1.** badinage *m*; raillerie *f*; **2.** badiner; railler; **'ban·ter·er** railleur (-euse *f*) *m*.

bap·tism ['bæptizm] baptême *m*; ~ *of fire* baptême *f* du feu; **bap·tis·mal** [bæp'tizməl] de baptême; baptistaire (*registre*).

bap·tist ['bæptist] (ana)baptiste *mf*; **bap·tis·ter·y** ['~tistri] baptistère *m*; **bap·tize** [~'taiz] baptiser (*a. fig.*).

bar [baː] **1.** barre *f* (*a. métal, a. sable, port*); traverse *f*; bar *m*, estaminet *m*; *savon*: brique *f*; *or*: lingot *m*; ♩ barre *f*; mesure *f*; ✝ lame *f*; ⚖ barre *f* (*des accusés*), barreau *m* (*des avocats*); *théâ. etc.*: buvette *f*; *fig.* empêchement *m*; *sp. horizontal* ~ barre *f* fixe; ⚖ *be called to the* ~ être reçu avocat; *prisoner at the* ~ accusé(e *f*) *m*; *stand at the* ~ paraître à la barre; **2.** barrer; griller (*une fenêtre*); bâcler (*une porte*); interdire, exclure (de, *from*); rayer (*de lignes*); empêcher (q. de *inf.*, *s.o. from gér.*); ~ *out* barrer la porte à; **3.** excepté, sauf, à l'exception de; ~ *none* sans exception; ~ *one* sauf un(e).

barb [baːb] *hameçon*: barbillon *m*; *flèche*: barbelure *f*; *plume*: barbe *f*; *fig.* trait *m* acéré; ⚜ ~*s pl.* arêtes *f*/*pl.*

bar·bar·i·an [baː'bɛəriən] barbare (*a. su.*/*mf*); **bar·bar·ic** [~'bærik] (~*ally*) barbare; rude; **bar·ba·rism** ['~bərizm] barbarie *f*, rudesse *f*, grossièreté *f*; *ling.* barbarisme *m*; **bar·bar·i·ty** [~'bæriti] barbarie *f*, cruauté *f*; **bar·ba·rize** ['~bəraiz] barbariser; **'bar·ba·rous** □ barbare; cruel(le *f*), inhumain.

bar·be·cue ['baːbikjuː] **1.** grand châssis *m* pour le rôtissage; animal *m* rôti tout entier; *Am.* grande fête *f* (*en plein air*) où on rôtit des animaux tout entiers; **2.** griller au charbon de bois (*de la viande*); rôtir tout entier (*un animal*).

barbed barbelé; ⚜ aristé, hameçonné; ~ *wire* fil *m* de fer barbelé; ~*wire fence* haie *f* barbelée, haie *f* de barbelés.

bar·bel *icht.* ['baːbl] barbeau *m*.

bar·bell *sp.* ['baːbel] barre *f* à sphères *ou* à boules.

bar·ber ['baːbə] coiffeur *m*; barbier

m; *surt. Am.* ~ *shop* salon *m* de coiffure.

bar·bi·tu·rate [ba:'bitjuərət] barbiturique *m*.

bard [ba:d] barde *m*; F poète *m*.

bare [bɛə] **1.** nu; dénudé; vide; dégarni; sec (sèche *f*) (*as, valet, etc.*); *the* ~ *idea* la seule pensée; **2.** mettre à nu, découvrir; '~**back(ed)** à nu, à poil; '~·**faced** □ F éhonté, cynique; '~·**fac·ed·ness** effronterie *f*, cynisme *m*; '~'**foot·ed** aux pieds nus; nu-pieds; '~-'**head·ed** nu-tête, (la) tête nue; '**bare·ly** à peine, tout juste; '**bare·ness** nudité *f*, dénuement *m*; *style:* pauvreté *f*.

bar·gain ['ba:gin] **1.** marché *m*, affaire *f*; emplette *f*; occasion *f*; *une* véritable occasion; *a good* (*bad*) ~ une bonne (mauvaise) affaire; *a* ~ *is a* ~ marché conclu reste conclu; F *it's a* ~! entendu!, convenu!; *into the* ~ en plus, pardessus le marché; *make* (*ou strike*) *a* ~ conclure un marché (avec, *with*); ~ *basement* coin *m ou* sous-sol *m* des bonnes affaires; ~ *price* prix *m* de solde; ~ *sale* soldes *m/pl.*; **2.** négocier; traiter (de, *for*); marchander (qch., *about* s.th.); ~ *for* F s'attendre à.

barge [ba:dʒ] **1.** chaland *m*, péniche *f*; gabare *f* (*à voiles*); barge *f* de parade; ⚓ deuxième canot *m*; **2.** F se heurter (contre, *into*); bousculer (*q.*); ~ *in* faire irruption; ~ *into the* *conversation* se mêler à la conversation; **barg'ee**, '**barge·man** chalandier *m*; gabarier *m*; F batelier *m*.

bar·i·ron ['ba:aiən] fer *m* en barres.

bar·i·tone ♪ ['bæritoun] baryton *m*.

bar·i·um ⚗ ['bɛəriəm] baryum *m*.

bark¹ [ba:k] **1.** écorce *f*; *inner* ~ liber *m*; ⊕ tan *m*; **2.** écorcer, décortiquer; F écorcher (*la peau*).

bark² [~] **1.** aboyer (après, contre at); glapir (*renard*); F tousser; F be ~*ing up the wrong tree* faire fausse route; **2.** aboiement *m*, aboi *m*; glapissement *m*; F toux *f*.

bark³ [~] ⚓ *see* barque; *poét.* barque *f*.

bar·keep(·er) ['ba:ki:p(ə)] cabaretier *m*; tenancier *m* d'un bar.

bark·er ['ba:kə] aboyeur (-euse *f*) *m* (*a. fig.*); F revolver *m*.

bar·ley ['ba:li] orge *f*.

barm [ba:m] levure *f*, levain *m* de bière.

bar·maid ['ba:meid] barmaid *f*.

bar·man ['ba:mən] *see* bartender.

barm·y ['ba:mi] en fermentation; *sl.* toqué.

barn [ba:n] grange *f*; *Am.* étable *f*, écurie *f*.

bar·na·cle¹ ['ba:nəkl] *orn.* bernacle *f*; oie *f* marine; *zo.* bernache *f*; anatife *m*; *fig.* individu *m* cramponnant.

bar·na·cle² [~] *vét. usu.* ~*s pl.* morailles *f/pl.*; *iro.* ~*s pl.* besicles *f/pl.*

barn·storm *Am. pol.* ['~] faire une tournée de discours électoraux.

ba·rom·e·ter [bə'rɔmitə] baromètre *m*; **bar·o·met·ric**, **bar·o·met·ri·cal** □ [bærə'metrik(l)] barométrique.

bar·on ['bærən] baron *m*; ~ *of beef* selle *f* de bœuf; *coal etc.* ~ (haut) baron *m* du charbon *etc.*; '**bar·on·age** baronnage *m*; barons *m/pl.*; annuaire *m* de la noblesse; '**bar·on·ess** baronne *f*; **bar·on·et** ['~it] baronnet; **bar·on·et·cy** ['~si] dignité *f* de baronnet; **ba·ro·ni·al** [bə'rouniəl] de baron; F seigneurial (-aux *m/pl.*); **bar·o·ny** ['bærəni] baronnie *f*.

ba·roque [bə'rouk] baroque (*a. su./m*), rococo (*a. su./m*).

barque ⚓ [ba:k] trois-mâts barque *m*.

bar·rack ['bærək] **1.** *usu.* ~*s pl.* caserne *f*; ~ *room* chambrée *f*; **2.** *v/t. sl.* conspuer (*q.*); *v/i.* chahuter; '~**square**, '~-**yard** cour *f* du quartier.

bar·rage ['bæra:ʒ] barrage *m*; ⚔ tir *m* de barrage *ou* sur zone; *creeping* ~ barrage *m* rampant.

bar·rel ['bærl] **1.** tonneau *m*, futaille *f*, *vin etc.:* fût *m*; *fusil etc.:* canon *m*; *serrure:* cylindre *m*; *montre:* barillet *m*; ♪ cylindre *m* noté; *anat.* caisse *f* (du tympan); *harengs:* caque *f*; **2.** mettre (*qch.*) en fût; enfûtailler; (*souv.* ~ *off*, ~*up*) encaquer; '**bar·relled** en tonneau(x); en caque (*harengs*); bombé; '**bar·rel·or·gan** ♪ orgue *m* mécanique *ou* de Barbarie; piano *m* mécanique.

bar·ren □ ['bærən] stérile; aride (*a. fig.*); peu fertile (*a. fig.*); ✝ improductif (-ive *f*) (*argent*); '**bar·ren·ness** stérilité *f*; *fig.* aridité *f*.

bar·ri·cade [bæri'keid] **1.** barricade *f*; **2.** barricader.

bar·ri·er ['bæriə] barrière *f*; obstacle *m* (*a. fig.*); muraille *f* (*de glace*); 🚇 portillon *m* d'accès.

bar·ring ['bɑːriŋ] *prp.* excepté, sauf; à part.

bar·ris·ter ['bæristə] (*a.* ~-*at-law*) avocat *m*.

bar·row¹ ['bærou] tumulus *m*; tertre *m* funéraire.

bar·row² [~] *see* hand-~, wheel-~; **~·man** marchand *m* des quatre saisons.

bar·tend·er ['bɑːtendə] buvetier *m*; garçon *m* de comptoir, barman *m*.

bar·ter ['bɑːtə] **1.** échange *m*; troc *m*; ~ *shop* boutique *f* pour l'échange de marchandises; **2.** échanger, troquer (contre, *for*); *péj.* faire trafic de; *a. fig.* ~ *away* vendre.

bar·y·tone ♪ ['bæritoun] baryton *m*.

ba·salt ['bæsɔːlt] basalte *m*.

base¹ □ [beis] bas(se *f*), vil; indigne, ignoble; faux (fausse *f*) (*monnaie*).

base² [~] **1.** base *f* (*a.* ♣, ♚); fondement *m*; ⚛ soubassement *m*; ⊕ socle *m*; *phot.* support *m*; *lampe, cartouche*: culot *m*; **2.** *fig.* baser, fonder (sur, [up]on); ♚ baser; ~ *o.s. on* se baser *ou* fonder sur; *be* ~*d* (*up*)on dépendre de; être fondé sur.

base...: '~**-ball** *Am.* base-ball *m*; '~**-less** sans base *ou* fondement; '~**-line** ♚ base *f* d'approvisionnement; *sp.* ligne *f* de fond; *surv.* base *f*; **'base·ment** soubassement *m*; sous-sol *m*. [*fig.*).]

base·ness ['beisnis] bassesse *f* (*a.*

bash·ful □ ['bæʃful] timide, modeste.

bash F [bæʃ] **1.** frapper *ou* cogner dur *ou* fort; **2.** coup *m* violent; *have a* ~ *at s.th.* essayer qch., s'essayer à qch.; *have a* ~ *at it* essayer le coup.

bas·ic ['beisik] (~*ally*) fondamental (-aux *m*/*pl.*); de base; 🜹 basique; ♀ *English* (= *British, American, Scientific, International, Commercial English*) l'anglais *m* basique, le basic *m*; ~ *iron* fer *m* basique; **bas·ics** *pl.*: *the* ~ l'essentiel *m*, les éléments *m*/*pl.*

ba·sil·i·ca △ [bəˈzilikə] basilique *f*.

bas·i·lisk ['bæzilisk] **1.** basilic *m*; **2.** de basilic.

ba·sin ['beisn] bassin *m*; *soupe*: écuelle *f*, bol *m*; *lait*: jatte *f*; cuvette *f*; lavabo *m*; ⚓, *géog.* bassin *m*.

ba·sis ['beisis], *pl.* **-ses** ['~siːz] base *f*; fondement *m*; *impôt*: assiette *f*; ♚ base *f*; ⚓ station *f*; *take as* ~ se baser sur.

bask [bɑːsk] se chauffer au soleil, prendre un bain de soleil; F jouir (de, *in*).

bas·ket ['bɑːskit] corbeille *f*; panier *m*; '~**-ball** basket-ball *m*; '~**-din·ner**, ~ **sup·per** *Am.* souper *m* en piquenique; '**bas·ket·ful** plein panier *m*; '**bas·ket-work** vannerie *f*.

bass¹ ♪ [beis] basse *f*.

bass² [bæs] liber *m*; tille *f*, filasse *f*; '~**-broom** balai *m*.

bas·si·net ['bæsi'net] berceau *m*; voiture *f* d'enfant.

bas·so ♪ ['bæsou] basse *f*.

bas·soon ♪ [bə'suːn] basson *m*.

bast [bæst] liber *m*; tille *f*.

bas·tard ['bæstəd] **1.** □ bâtard; faux (fausse *f*), corrompu; **2.** bâtard(e *f*) *m*; enfant *mf* naturel(le *f*); '**bas·tar·dy** bâtardise *f*.

baste¹ [beist] arroser (*de graisse*) (*un rôti*); F bâtonner (*q.*).

baste² [~] bâtir, bâguer.

bas·ti·na·do [bæsti'neidou] **1.** bastonnade *f*; **2.** donner la bastonnade à (*q.*).

bas·tion ♚ ['bæstiən] bastion *m*.

bat¹ [bæt] chauve-souris (*pl.* chauves-souris) *f*; *be blind as a* ~ ne pas y voir plus clair qu'une taupe.

bat² [~] **1.** *cricket*: batte *f*; *ping-pong*: raquette *f*; *baseball*: *at* ~ (être) à la batte; *Am.* F *come* (*go*) *to* ~ *for* porter secours à; *off one's own* ~ *fig.* de sa propre initiative; **2.** manier la batte; être au guichet.

batch [bætʃ] pain, *a. fig.*: fournée *f*; *papiers*: paquet *m*; lot *m*.

bate [beit] diminuer; rabattre (*le prix*); baisser (*la voix*); *with* ~*d breath* en retenant son souffle.

Bath¹ [bɑːθ]: ~ *brick* brique *f* anglaise; ~ *chair* fauteuil *m* roulant.

bath² [~] **1.** (*pl.* **baths** [bɑːðz]) bain *m* (*de boue, de pieds, de soleil, de trempe, de vapeur,* ~ *douche*); ~ *foam* mousse *f* de bain; ~ *house* cabines *f*/*pl.* de bains; **2.** se baigner.

bathe [beið] **1.** (se) baigner; **2.** bain *m* (*de mer etc.*); baignade *f*.

bath·ing ['beiθiŋ] bains *m*/*pl.* (*de mer etc.*); baignades *f*/*pl.*; *attr.* de bain(s); ~ **beau·ty** belle baigneuse *f*; '~**-cap** bonnet *m* de bain; '~**-cos-**

'tume maillot *m* de bain; '~-**hut** cabine *f* de bains (de plage); ~ **re'sort** station *f* balnéaire, plage *f*; '~-**suit** maillot *m* de bain; '~-**trunks** *pl.* caleçon *m* de bain.

ba·thos ['beiθɔs] ampoulé *m*; enflure *f*; anticlimax *m*.

bath...: '~-**robe** *Am.* peignoir *m* de bain; '~-**tow·el** serviette *f* de bain; '~-**tub** baignoire *f*; '~-**wa·ter** eau *f* de bain.

ba·tiste † [bæ'ti:st] batiste *f*.

bat·man ['bætmən] brosseur *m*; ordonnance *mf*.

ba·ton ['bætən] *maréchal, chef d'orchestre, police:* bâton *m*; *police:* matraque *f*.

ba·tra·chi·an [bə'treikjən] batracien *m*.

bats·man ['bætsmən] *cricket etc.:* batteur *m*.

bat·tal·ion [bə'tæljən] bataillon *m*.

bat·ten ['bætn] 1. couvre-joint *m*; latte *f* (*a.* ⚓); 2. *v/t.* latter; (⚓ ~down) assujettir; *v/i.* repaître (de, [up]on).

bat·ter ['bætə] 1. *cricket:* batteur *m*; *cuis.* pâte *f* lisse; 2. battre; (*a.* ~ at) frapper avec violence; bossuer (*un chapeau etc.*); rouer (*q.*) de coups; ✗ battre en brèche; *fig. critique:* démolir (*q.*); '**bat·ter·ed** délabré, bossué; maltraité; ~ *babies* enfants *m/pl.* martyrs; '**bat·ter·ing·ram** bélier *m*; '**bat·ter·y** batterie *f*; *Am. baseball: the* ~ *le lanceur et le batteur;* ✗ *a.* ⊕ batterie *f*; ⚡ pile *f*; accumulateur *m*; ⚡ voie *f* de fait; rixe *f*; *assault and* ~ (menaces *f/pl.* et) voies *f/pl.* de fait; '**bat·ter·y-charging 'sta·tion** *f* station *f* de charge; '**bat·ter·y-'op·er·at·ed** ⚡ à piles.

bat·tle ['bætl] 1. bataille *f*, combat *m*; ~ *royal* bataille *f* en règle; mêlée *f* générale; 2. se battre, lutter (pour, for; avec, with; contre, against); '~-**axe** hache *f* d'armes; *Am. fig.* mégère *f*.

bat·tle·dore ['bætldɔ:] *lessive:* battoir *m*; raquette *f*.

bat·tle-field ['bætlfi:ld], **bat·tle-ground** ['~graund] champ *m* de bataille.

bat·tle·ments ['bætlmənts] *pl.* créneaux *m/pl.*; parapet *m*.

bat·tle...: '~-**plane** ✗ avion *m* de combat; '~-**ship** ✗ cuirassé *m* (de ligne).

bat·tue [bæ'tu:] battue *f*; F carnage *m*.

bau·ble ['bɔ:bl] babiole *f*; fanfreluche *f*.

baulk [bɔ:k] *see* balk.

baux·ite *min.* ['bɔ:ksait] bauxite *f*.

baw·bee *écoss.* [bɔ:'bi:] *see* half-penny.

bawd [bɔ:d] procureuse *f*; '**bawd·y** obscène; ordurier (-ère *f*) (*propos*).

bawl [bɔ:l] brailler; hurler; crier à tue-tête; F beugler; ~*out* brailler *etc.*; gueuler; *Am. sl.* injurier; F engueuler (*q.*).

bay[1] [bei] 1. bai (*cheval*); isabelle; 2. cheval *m* bai; isabelle *m*.

bay[2] [~] baie *f*; golfe *m*; anse *f*; échancrure *f*; ~ *salt* sel *m* de mer; *cuis.* gros sel *m*.

bay[3] △ [~] travée *f*; claire-voie (*pl.* claires-voies) *f*; enfoncement *m*; ⚓ quai *m* subsidiaire.

bay[4] [~] laurier *m*.

bay[5] [~] 1. aboyer; hurler (*chien*); ~ *at* hurler *etc.* à; 2. *stand at* s'acculer à *ou* contre (*qch.*); être aux abois; *bring to* ~, *keep* (*ou hold*) *at* ~ acculer (*un cerf*).

bay·o·net ✗ ['beiənit] 1. baïonnette *f*; 2. percer d'un coup de baïonnette; passer (*des gens*) à la baïonnette; '~-**catch** ⊕ encliquetage *m*.

bay·ou *géog. Am.* ['baiu:] bras *m* marécageux (*de rivière*).

bay win·dow ['bei'windou] fenêtre *f* en saillie; *Am. sl.* bedaine *f*.

ba·zaar [bə'zɑ:] bazar *m*; vente *f* de charité.

be [bi:; bi] (*irr.*) 1. être; se trouver; *there, there are* il y a; *here's to you(r health)*! à votre santé!; *here you are again!* vous revoilà!; ~ *about* (*gér.*) être occupé à (*inf.*), de (*qch.*); ~ *after* venir après (*q.*); F être en quête de (q.); ~ *at* s'occuper de (*qch.*); ~ *off* s'en aller; partir; finir; couper (*courant*); ~ *off with you!* allez-vous-en!; filez!; ~ *on at s.o.* harceler q.; ~ *on to* être en contact avec; être sur la piste de; être aux trousses de (*q.*); 2. *v/aux. et p.pr. pour exprimer la durée ou une action incomplète:* ~ *reading* (être en train de) lire; 3. *v/aux. et inf. pour exprimer le devoir, l'intention ou la possibilité: I am to inform you* je suis chargé de vous faire savoir; *it is* (*not*) *to* ~ *seen* on (ne) peut (pas) le voir *ou* visiter; *if* he were to die s'il mourait; **4.** *v/aux. et p.p. à la voix passive:* se rend ordinairement par on *et la voix active, ou par la voix passive, ou par un verbe réfléchi; I am asked on me demande.*

beach [biːtʃ] **1.** plage *f*, grève *f*; **2.** ⚓ échouer; tirer à sec; '**~-ball** ballon *m* de plage; '**~-comb·er** F rôdeur *m* (*de grève*); *sl.* propre *m* à rien; '**~-head** ⚔ tête *f* de pont.

bea·con ['biːkn] **1.** † feu *m* d'alarme; feu *m* de joie; ⚓ phare *m*, fanal *m*; balise *f*; **2.** baliser; éclairer.

bead [biːd] **1.** perle *f* (*d'émail etc.*); goutte *f* (*de sueur etc.*); *pneu:* talon *m*; *chapelet:* grain *m*; *fusil:* guidon *m*; ~**s** *pl. a.* chapelet *m*; **2.** *v/t.* couvrir *ou* orner de perles; ⊕ appliquer une baguette sur; *v/i.* perler; '**bead·ing** ⊕, △ baguette *f*.

bea·dle ['biːdl] bedeau *m*; *univ.* appariteur *m*.

bead·y ['biːdi] qui perle; percé en vrille (*yeux*).

beak [biːk] bec *m*; F nez *m* crochu; '**beaked** à bec; crochu (*nez*).

beak·er ['biːkə] gobelet *m*; coupe *f*.

beam [biːm] **1.** *bois:* poutre *f*; solive *f*; *charrue:* flèche *f*; *fig.* rayon *m*; éclat *m*; ⊕ balancier *m*; ⚓ bau *m*, barrot *m* de pont; *chasse:* merrain *m* (*bois de cerf*); *radio:* (wireless ~) faisceau *m* hertzien; *phare:* faisceau *m*; F *fig.* be off (the) ~ faire fausse route, faire erreur; F *fig.* be on (the) ~ être sur la bonne voie; **2.** *v/i. a. fig.* rayonner (*fig.* de with); *v/t.* émettre (*des ondes etc.*); transmettre (*par ondes dirigées*); '**~-'ends** *pl.:* the ship is on her ~ le navire est engagé; F *fig.* be on one's ~ F être à la côte.

bean [biːn] fève *f*; grain *m* (*de café*); *Am. sl.* tête *f*, caboche *f*; F full of ~s plein d'entrain; *sl.* give s.o. ~s laver la tête à q.; '**~-feast**, **bean·o** *sl.* ['biːnou] régal *m*; *sl.* bombe *f*.

bear[1] [bɛə] **1.** ours(e *f*) *m*; *fig.* homme *m* maussade; † *sl.* baissier *m*; **2.** † spéculer à la baisse; prendre position à la baisse.

bear[2] [~] (*irr.*) **1.** *v/t.* porter (*qch., épée, nom, date, amour etc.*); jouir de (*une réputation*); supporter (*poids, frais, conséquences*); soutenir (*un poids*); souffrir (*une douleur etc.*); tolérer, supporter, souffrir; ~ *away* (r)emporter, enlever; ~ *down* vaincre; accabler; ~ *out* emporter;

confirmer (*une assertion*); ~ *up* soutenir; résister à; **2.** *v/i.* endurer; avoir rapport (à, upon); porter; ⚓ (*avec adv.*) faire route; ⚓ ~ *down upon* courir sur (*qch.*); ~ *to the right* prendre à droite; ~ *up* tenir bon; ~ *up!* courage!; ~ (*up*)*on* porter sur; peser sur; ~ *with* se montrer indulgent pour; supporter; *bring to* ~ mettre (*qch.*) en action; braquer (*une lunette*) (sur, [up]on); '**bear·a·ble** ['bɛərəbl] supportable.

beard [biəd] **1.** barbe *f*; ♀ arête *f*; **2.** *v/t.* braver, défier, narguer (*q.*); '**beard·ed** barbu; '**beard·less** imberbe; sans barbe.

bear·er ['bɛərə] porteur (-euse *f*) *m*; *passeport:* titulaire *mf*; † *chèque:* porteur *m*; ⊕ support *m*.

bear·ing ['bɛəriŋ] port *m* (d'armes, de nouvelles; *a.* = *maintien*); allure *f*, maintien *m*; capacité *f* de supporter; appui *m*; ⚓ relèvement *m*; ⊕ *souv.* ~**s** *pl.* palier *m*; coussinet *m*, -s *m/pl.*; ~**s** *pl.* ☒ armoiries *f/pl.*, blason *m*; *lose one's* ~**s** perdre le nord, être désorienté; *take one's* ~**s** s'orienter, se repérer.

bear·ish ['bɛəriʃ] d'ours; bourru (*personne*); à la baisse (*tendance*).

beast [biːst] bête *f*; *fig. a.* animal *m*, brute *f*; ~**s** *pl.* bétail *m*; '**beast·li·ness** bestialité *f*, brutalité *f*; F saleté *f*; '**beast·ly** bestial (-aux *m/pl.*), brutal (-aux *m/pl.*); F sale, dégoûtant; *fig. adv.* terriblement.

beat [biːt] **1.** [*irr.*] *v/t.* battre (*a. chasse:* un bois; *a.* ♩ *la mesure*); donner des coups de bâton à; cogner à (*une porte*); *oiseau:* battre de (*l'aile*); dépasser (*q.*); (*a.* ~ *out*) aplatir; marteler (*un métal*); frayer, battre (*un chemin*); F assommer; F devancer (*q.*); *Am.* F rouler, refaire (*q.*); *Am. sl.* ~ *it!* filez!; ~ *the air* F taper dans le vide; *Am.* F *it* ~**s** the band ça c'est le comble; ~ *one's brains* se creuser la cervelle; ⚔ ~ *a retreat* battre en retraite; *Am.* F ~ *one's way to* gagner (*un endroit, souv. sans payer*); ~ *down* (r)abattre; donner à plomb (sur, [up]on); † faire baisser le prix à (*q.*); marchander (avec) ~ *up* fouetter (*œufs, crème etc.*); recruter (*des partisans*); *Am.* F rosser (*q.*); *v/i.* battre; ~ *about the bush* tourner autour du pot; **2.** battement *m* (*a. phys.*); pulsation *f*; *tambour:* batterie *f*; ♪ mesure *f*, temps *m*; *police*: ronde *f*; *chasse*: battue *f*; *radio*: battement *m*; *Am*. reportage *m* sensationnel que l'on est le premier à publier; *fig*. domaine *m*; **3.** F battu, confondu; F ~ out épuisé; **'beat·en** *p.p.* de beat 1; *adj*. battu (*chemin, métal*); **'beat·er** batteur (-euse *f*) *m*; battoir *m* (de laveuse); *chasse*: rabatteur *m*, traqueur *m*.

be·a·tif·ic [biə'tifik] béatifique; *wear a ~ smile* rire aux anges; **be·at·i·fi·ca·tion** *eccl.* [biːætifi'keiʃn] béatification *f*; **be'at·i·fy** *eccl.* béatifier; **be'at·i·tude** [~tjuːd] béatitude *f*.

beau [bou], *pl.* **beaux** [bouz] galant *m*, prétendant *m*; dandy *m*, élégant *m*; ~ *ideal* idéal *m*.

beau·ti·cian [bju'tiʃən] esthéticien(ne *f*)*m*, visagiste *mf*.

beau·ti·ful □ ['bjuːtəful] beau (bel *devant une voyelle ou un h muet*; belle *f*; beaux *m/pl.*); *the ~ people* les gens chic; *the ~ people of Paris* le Tout-Paris.

beau·ti·fy ['bjuːtifai] embellir.

beau·ty ['bjuːti] beauté *f* (*a. = belle femme*); F drôle de type; *Sleeping* ♀ *Belle* F au bois dormant; ~ *par-lo(u)r*, ~ *shop* institut *m* de beauté; ~ *spot* mouche *f* (*collée sur le visage*); *lieu*: coin *m* pittoresque.

bea·ver ['biːvə] *zo.* castor *m*; † chapeau *m* de castor; F barbu *m*; *casque*: visière *f*.

be·calm [bi'kɑːm] abriter, déventer (*un navire*); *poét.* calmer; ⚓ ~ed accalminé.

be·came [bi'keim] *prét.* de become.

be·cause [bi'kɔz] parce que; ~ of à cause de.

beck [bek] signe *m* (*de tête etc.*).

beck·on ['bekn] faire signe (à *q.*).

be·cloud [bi'klaud] ennuager, voiler.

be·come [bi'kʌm] [*irr.* (come)] *v/i.* devenir; se faire; advenir (de *q.*, *of s.o.*); *v/t.* convenir à, aller (bien) à; **be'com·ing** □ convenable, bienséant; seyant (*costume etc.*).

bed [bed] **1.** lit *m* (*a. d'un fleuve etc.*); banc *m* (*d'huîtres*); tanière *f* (*d'un animal*); ✿ *fleurs*: parterre *m*; *légumes*: planche *f*; ⊕ sommier *m*; assise *f*; *chaussée etc.*: assiette *f*; ~ *and breakfast* chambre(s *pl.*)*f* (avec petit déjeuner); **2.** mettre au lit; faire la litière à (*un cheval etc.*); ✿ ~ (*out*) dépoter.

42*

be·daub [bi'dɔːb] barbouiller (de peinture).

be·daz·zle [bi'dæzl] aveugler, éblouir.

bed-clothes ['bedklouðz] *pl.* draps *m/pl.* de lit.

bed·ding ['bedin] literie *f*; litière *f*; ~(-*out*) *plantes*: dépotage *m*.

be·deck [bi'dek] parer, orner.

be·dev·il [bi'devl] ensorceler; *fig.* tourmenter, lutiner; **be'dev·il·ment** ensorcellement *m*; vexation *f*.

be·dew [bi'djuː] humecter de rosée; *poét.* baigner.

bed·fel·low ['bedfelou] compagnon *m* de lit.

be·dim [bi'dim] obscurcir.

be·diz·en [bi'daizn] attifer; chamarrer (*a. fig.*).

bed·lam ['bedləm] F maison *f* de fous; **bed·lam·ite** ['~mait] F fou *m*, folle *f*.

bed·lin·en ['bedlinin] draps *m/pl.* de lit et taies *f/pl.*

bed·ou·in ['beduin] **1.** bédouin(e *f*); **2.** Bédouin(e *f*) *m*.

bed-pan ['bedpæn] bassin *m* de lit.

be·drag·gle [bi'drægl] tacher de boue; crotter.

bed...: '~**rid**(·**den**) cloué au lit; '~**rock** *géol.* roche *f* de fond; tuf *m*; *fig.* fondement *m*, fond *m*; '~**room** chambre *f* (à coucher); '~**side**: *at the ~* au chevet (*de q.*); ⚕ *good ~ manner* bonne manière *f* professionnelle; ~ *lamp* lampe *f* de chevet; ~ *rug* descente *f* de lit; '~**sit·ting-room** pièce *f* unique avec lit *ou* divan; '~**sore** ⚕ escarre *f*; '~**space** *hôtel etc.*: lits *m/pl.*; '~**spread** dessus *m* de lit; '~**stead** châlit *m*; '~**straw** ❦ gaillet *m*; '~**tick** toile *f* à matelas; '~**time** heure *f* du coucher.

bee [biː] abeille *f*; *Am.* réunion *f* pour travaux en commun; F *have a ~ in one's bonnet* avoir une araignée au plafond.

beech ❦ [biːtʃ] hêtre *m*; '~**nut** faîne *f*.

beef [biːf] **1.** bœuf *m*; F muscle *m*; **2.** *Am.* F grommeler, se plaindre; '~**eat·er** hallebardier *m* (*à la Tour de Londres*); ~**steak** ['biːf'steik] bifteck *m*; ~ *tea* *cuis.* jus *m* de viande de bœuf; consommé *m*; **'beef·y** F musculeux (-euse *f*).

bee...: '**~·hive** ruche *f*; '**~·keep·er** apiculteur *m*; '**~·keep·ing** apiculture *f*; '**~·line** ligne *f* à vol d'oiseau; *Am.* make a ~ for aller droit vers (*qch.*); '**~·mas·ter** apiculteur *m*.

been [bi:n, bin] *p.p. de* be.

beer [biə] bière *f*; ~ on tap bière *f* à la pression; *small* ~ petite bière *f*; F détail *m*, petite affaire *f*; ~ can boîte *f* de bière; ~ **en·gine** pompe *f* à bière; '**beer·y** F un peu gris.

bees·wax ['bi:zwæks] cire *f* d'abeilles.

beet ♀ [bi:t] betterave *f*; white ~ bette *f*, betterave *f* à sucre; red ~ betterave *f* rouge.

bee·tle[1] ['bi:tl] **1.** mailloche *f*; maillet *m*; **2.** damer.

bee·tle[2] [~] coléoptère *m*.

bee·tle[3] [~] **1.** bombé (*front*); touffu (*sourcils*); **2.** *v/i.* surplomber.

beet·root ['bi:tru:t] *Brit.* betterave *f*.

beet-sug·ar ['bi:tʃugə] sucre *m* de betterave.

be·fall [bi'fɔ:l] [*irr.* (*fall*)] arriver *ou* survenir à (*q.*).

be·fit [bi'fit] convenir *ou* seoir à (*q.*, *qch.*).

be·fog [bi'fɔg] envelopper de brouillard; *fig.* obscurcir.

be·fool [bi'fu:l] duper, mystifier.

be·fore [bi'fɔ:] **1.** *adv.* lieu: en avant; devant; *temps*: auparavant; avant; **2.** *cj.* avant que; **3.** *prp.* lieu: devant; *temps*: avant; *be* ~ *one's time* être en avance; *be* ~ *s.o.* être en présence de q.; *fig.* attendre q.; devancer q.; ~ *long* avant longtemps; ~ *now* déjà; **be·fore·hand** préalablement; d'avance.

be·foul [bi'faul] souiller, salir.

be·friend [bi'frend] venir en aide à (*q.*); secourir (*q.*).

beg [beg] *v/t.* mendier; solliciter; prier; supplier (*q. de faire qch.*); *I* ~ *your pardon* je vous demande pardon; plaît-il?; ~ *the question* supposer vrai ce qui est en question; *v/i.* mendier (*qch. à q.*; *for s.th. of s.o.*); demander, prier; faire le beau (*chien*); ✝ *I* ~ *to inform you* j'ai l'honneur de vous faire savoir.

be·gan [bi'gæn] *prét. de* begin.

be·get [bi'get] [*irr.* (*get*)] engendrer; **be·get·ter** père *m*; F auteur *m* (de, of).

beg·gar ['begə] **1.** mendiant(e *f*) *m*; F individu *m*; diable *m*; **2.** de men-

diant; **3.** réduire (*q.*) à la mendicité; *it* ~*s all description* cela ne peut pas se décrire, cela défie toute description; '**beg·gar·ly** chétif (-ive *f*); mesquin; '**beg·gar·y** mendicité *f*, misère *f*; *reduce to* ~ réduire à la mendicité.

be·gin [bi'gin] [*irr.*] *v/i.* commencer (à, de to; par, à at); se mettre (à *inf.*, to *inf.*); ~ (*up*)*on s.th.* entamer qch.; *to* ~ *with* pour commencer; (tout) d'abord; *to* ~ *by* (*gér.*) commencer par (*inf.*); *v/t.* commencer; **be·gin·ner** commençant(e *f*) *m*; **be·gin·ning** commencement *m*; début *m*; *from the* ~ dès le commencement.

be·gird [bi'gə:d] [*irr.* (*gird*)] ceindre, entourer (de, with).

be·gone [bi'gɔn] partez!, hors d'ici!

be·go·ni·a ♀ [bi'gounjə] bégonia *m*.

be·got, be·got·ten [bi'gɔt(n)] *prét. et p.p. de* beget.

be·grime [bi'graim] noircir, salir.

be·grudge [bi'grʌdʒ] envier, mesurer (qch. à q., s.o. s.th.).

be·guile [bi'gail] enjôler, tromper; distraire; soutirer (qch. à q., s.o. out of s.th.); faire passer (*le temps*); ~ *s.o. into* (*gér.*) induire q. à (*inf.*).

be·gun [bi'gʌn] *p.p. de* begin.

be·half [bi'hɑ:f]: on (ou in) ~ of au nom de; de la part de; en faveur de; ✝ au compte de.

be·have [bi'heiv] se conduire, se comporter (bien, mal, etc.); ~ *yourself* (*yourselves*)! sois (soyez) sage(s)!; **be·hav·io(u)r** [~jə] conduite *f* (avec, envers to[wards]); tenue *f* (a. d'une voiture); *machine*: allure *f*, fonctionnement *m*; be on one's best ~ se surveiller; **be·hav·io(u)r·al** [~jərəl] de comportement; behavioriste; ~ *pattern* type *m* de comportement; ~ *psychology* psychologie *f* du comportement.

be·head [bi'hed] décapiter; **be·head·ing** décapitation *f*.

be·hest [bi'hest] *poét.* ordre *m*.

be·hind [bi'haind] **1.** *adv.* (par) derrière; en arrière; en retard; *be* ~ *with s.th.* être en retard dans qch.; **2.** *prp.* derrière; en arrière de; en retard sur; *see time*; **3.** F derrière *m*, postérieur *m*.

be·hold [bi'hould] [*irr.* (*hold*)] voir, apercevoir; ~! voyez!; **be·hold·en** redevable (à, to); **be·hold·er** témoin *m*; spectateur (-trice *f*) *m*.

bend

be·hoof [bi'hu:f]: *to (for, on) (the)* ~ *of* au profit de, à l'avantage de.

be·hove [bi'houv]: *it* ~*s s.o. to* (*inf.*) il appartient à q. de (*inf.*).

beige [beiʒ] **1.** *tex.* beige *f*; **2.** beige; blond.

be·ing ['bi:iŋ] être *m*; existence *f*; *in* ~ vivant; existant; *come into* ~ prendre naissance; se produire.

be·la·bo(u)r F [bi'leibə] rouer (*q.*) de coups.

be·laid [bi'leid] *prét. et p.p. de belay.*

be·lat·ed [bi'leitid] attardé (*personne*); tardif (-ive *f*) (*regret, heure, etc.*).

be·laud [bi'lɔ:d] combler (*q.*) de louanges.

be·lay [bi'lei] [*irr.*] ⚓ tourner, amarrer; *alp.* assurer; **be'lay·ing** tournage *m*.

belch [beltʃ] éructer; *sl.* roter; ~ *forth* (*ou* out) vomir (*des flammes etc.*).

bel·dam ['beldəm] mégère *f*; vieille sorcière *f*.

be·lea·guer [bi'li:gə] assiéger.

bel·fry ['belfri] beffroi *m*, clocher *m*.

Bel·gian ['beldʒən] **1.** belge, de Belgique; **2.** Belge *mf*.

be·lie [bi'lai] démentir; donner un démenti à; faire mentir.

be·lief [bi'li:f] croyance *f* (à, *in*; en Dieu, *in God*); *fig.* confiance *f*; *past all* ~ incroyable; *to the best of my* ~ autant que je sache.

be·liev·a·ble [bi'li:vəbl] croyable.

be·lieve [bi'li:v] *v/i.* croire (à, en *in*); F (*not*) ~ *in* (ne pas) être partisan de (*qch.*); (ne pas) avoir confiance dans (*qch.*); *v/t.* croire; **be'liev·er** croyant(e *f*) *m*.

Be·li·sha bea·con [bə'li:ʃə'bi:kən] globe *m* orange (*indiquant un passage clouté*).

be·lit·tle [bi'litl] *fig.* décrier, amoindrir.

bell[1] [bel] **1.** cloche *f*; sonnette *f*; timbre *m*; sonnerie *f* (*électrique*); ♀ clochette *f*; ⚓ campane *f*; vase *m*; ⚓ coup *m*; ♪ *trompette:* pavillon *m*; **2.** *v/t.* ~ *the cat* attacher le grelot.

bell[2] *chasse:* [~] **1.** bramer; **2.** bramement *m*.

bell·boy *Am.* ['belbɔi] *see bellhop.*

belle [bel] beauté *f*.

bell...: '~**-flow·er** campanule *f*; '~**found·er** fondeur *m* de cloches; '~**-hop** *Am. sl.* chasseur *m*.

bel·li·cose ['belikous] belliqueux (-euse *f*); **bel·li·cos·i·ty** [~'kɔsiti] bellicosité *f*; humeur *f* belliqueuse.

bel·lied ['belid] ventru.

bel·lig·er·ent [bi'lidʒərənt] belligérant(e *f*) (*a. su./mf*).

bel·low ['belou] **1.** beugler; mugir (*a.* F); **2.** beuglement *m*; F hurlement *m*.

bel·lows ['belouz] *pl.:* (*a pair of*) ~ (un) soufflet *m*; *sg. phot.* soufflet *m*.

bell...: '~**-pull** cordon *m* de sonnette; '~**-push** *poussoir:* bouton *m*; '~**-weth·er** sonnailler *m*; '~**-wire** fil *m* à sonnerie.

bel·ly ['beli] **1.** ventre *m*; ~ *button* F nombril *m*; ~ *flop* plat-ventre *m*/*inv.*; ⚐ *landing* atterrissage *m* sur le ventre; ~ *laugh* gros rire *m*; **2.** (s')enfler, (se) gonfler.

be·long [bi'lɔŋ] appartenir (à, *to*); faire partie (de, *to*); être (à, de *to a place*); *Am.* ~ *with* aller avec; **be-'long·ings** [~iŋz] *pl.* affaires *f*/*pl.*; effets *m*/*pl.*

be·lov·ed [bi'lʌvd] **1.** aimé; **2.** chéri (-e *f*) *m*; bien-aimé(e *f*) *m*.

be·low [bi'lou] **1.** *adv.* en bas, (au-)dessous; *poét.* ici-bas; **2.** *prp.* au-dessous de; *fig.* ~ *me* indigne de moi (*de inf.*, *to inf.*).

belt [belt] **1.** ceinture *f*; porte-jarretelles *m*; *fig.* zone *f*, bande *f*; ✂ ceinturon *m*; ⊕ courroie *f*; ⚓ ceinture *f* cuirassée; *box. below the* ~ déloyal (-aux *m*/*pl.*) (*coup*); *green* ~ ceinture *f* verte; *mot. seat* ~ ceinture *f* de sécurité; **2.** ceindre; entourer (*qch.*) d'une ceinture; *Am.* F ~ *out* faire retentir *ou* éclater.

bel·ve·dere ['belvidiə] △ belvédère *m*; mirador *m*; pavillon *m*.

be·moan [bi'moun] pleurer, déplorer (*qch.*).

be·mused □ [bi'mju:zd] confus, embrouillé; rêveur(-euse *f*).

bench [bentʃ] banc *m*; banquette *f*; siège *m* (*du juge*); magistrature *f*; *menuiserie:* établi *m*; *see treasury*; '**bench·er** membre *m* du conseil d'une École de droit.

bend [bend] **1.** tournant *m*; *chemin:* coude *m*; courbure *f*; courbe *f*; *fleuve:* sinuosité *f*; ∅ bande *f*; ⚓ nœud *m*; **2.** [*irr.*] (se) courber; *v/i.* tourner (*route*); *v/t.* plier; fléchir; baisser (*la tête*); tendre (*un arc*); fixer (*les regards*); porter (*les pas* *vers qch.*); appliquer (*l'esprit*); ⚓ enverguer.

be·neath [bi'ni:θ] *see below.*

ben·e·dick ['benidik] nouveau marié *m* (*surt. vieux garçon*).

Ben·e·dic·tine [beni'diktin] *eccl.* Bénédictin(e *f*) *m*; [⌂ti:n] *liqueur:* Bénédictine *f*.

ben·e·dic·tion *eccl.* [beni'dikʃn] bénédiction *f*; bénédicité *m* (*avant les repas*).

ben·e·fac·tion [beni'fækʃn] bienfait *m*; donation *f*; œuvre *f* de charité; **'ben·e·fac·tor** bienfaiteur *m*; **ben·e·fac·tress** ['⌂tris] bienfaitrice *f*.

ben·e·fice ['benifis] bénéfice *m*; **be·nef·i·cence** [bi'nefisns] bienfaisance *f*; **be'nef·i·cent** □ bienfaisant; salutaire.

ben·e·fi·cial □ [beni'fiʃl] avantageux (-euse *f*), salutaire, utile; ⌂ *interest* usufruit *m*; ⚖ ⌂ *owner* usufruitier (-ère *f*) *m*; **ben·e'fi·ci·ar·y** ⚖, *eccl.* bénéficier (-ère *f*) *m*; bénéficiaire *mf*; ayant droit (*pl.* ayants droit) *m*.

ben·e·fit ['benifit] **1.** avantage *m*, profit *m*; *théâ.* représentation *f* au bénéfice (*de q.*); indemnité *f* (*de chômage*); ⌂ *of the doubt* bénéfice *m* du doute; *for the* ⌂ à l'intention de; au bénéfice de; **2.** *v/t.* profiter à; être avantageux (-euse *f*) à; faire du bien à; *v/i.* profiter (*de by, from*).

be·nev·o·lence [bi'nevəlans] bienveillance *f*, bonté *f*; **be'nev·o·lent** □ (*envers, to*) bienveillant; charitable; ⌂ *society* association *f* de bienfaisance.

Ben·gal [beŋ'gɔ:l] du Bengale; **Ben'gal·i** [⌂li] **1.** bengali; **2.** *ling.* bengali *m*; Bengali *mf*.

be·night·ed [bi'naitid] anuité; surpris par la nuit; *fig.* aveugle; plongé dans l'ignorance.

be·nign □ [bi'nain] bénin (-igne *f*) (*a.* ✝); doux (douce *f*); favorable; **be·nig·nant** □ [bi'nignənt] bénin (-igne *f*); bienveillant; **be'nig·ni·ty** bienveillance *f*, bonté *f*; ✝, *a. climat:* bénignité *f*.

bent¹ [bent] **1.** *prét. et p.p. de* bend 2; ⌂ *on* acharné à; **2.** penchant *m*, disposition *f* (*pour, for*); *to the top of one's* ⌂ tant qu'on peut.

bent² ♀ [⌂] jonc *m*; agrostide *f*; prairie *f*.

be·numb [bi'nʌm] engourdir (*a.* ✝); transir.

ben·zine ✿ ['benzi:n] benzine *f*.

ben·zol(e) ✿ ['benzɔl] benzol *m*.

be·queath [bi'kwi:ð] léguer.

be·quest [bi'kwest] legs *m*.

be·rate [bi'reit] réprimander.

be·reave [bi'ri:v] [*irr.*] priver; *be* ⌂*d of* perdre (*q. par la mort*); ⌂*d* affligé; **be'reave·ment** perte *f* (*d'un père etc.*); deuil *m*.

be·reft [bi'reft] *prét. et p.p. de* bereave.

be·ret ['berei] béret *m*.

Ber·lin [bə:'lin] **1.** de Berlin; ⌂ *black* vernis *m*; **2.** *voiture:* berline *f*; (*usu.* ⌂ *glove*) gant *m* de laine de Berlin; (*usu.* ⌂ *wool*) laine *f* de Berlin.

ber·ry ['beri] ♀ baie *f*.

berth [bə:θ] **1.** ⚓ évitée *f*; couchette *f*; *fig.* place *f*; emploi *m*; *give s.o. a wide* ⌂ éviter q.; **2.** *v/t.* accoster (*un navire*) le long du quai; *v/i.* mouiller; aborder à quai.

ber·yl *min.* ['beril] béryl *m*.

be·seech [bi'si:tʃ] [*irr.*] supplier (*q. de inf., s.o. to inf.*); implorer; **be'seech·ing** □ suppliant.

be·seem [bi'si:m]: *it* ⌂*s* il sied (à q. *de inf., s.o. to inf.*).

be·set [bi'set] [*irr.* (*set*)] assaillir; serrer de près; assiéger; ⌂*ting sin* péché *m* d'habitude.

be·side [bi'said] **1.** *adv. see besides;* **2.** *prp.* à côté de (*a. fig.*); auprès de; ⌂ *o.s.* transporté (*de joie etc., with*); *be* ⌂ *the purpose* ne pas entrer dans les intentions (*de q.*); ⌂ *the question* en dehors du sujet; **be'sides** [⌂dz] **1.** *adv.* en plus, en outre; d'ailleurs; **2.** *prp. fig.* sans compter; en plus de; excepté.

be·siege [bi'si:dʒ] assiéger (*a. fig.*); faire le siège de; *fig.* entourer; **be'sieg·er** assiégeant *m*.

be·slav·er [bi'slævə] baver sur; *fig.* flagorner.

be·slob·ber [bi'slɔbə] prodiguer des baisers à (*q.*).

be·smear [bi'smiə] barbouiller.

be·smirch [bi'smə:tʃ] salir.

be·som ['bi:zm] balai *m*.

be·sot·ted [bi'sɔtid] assoté; abruti (*par, with*) (*a. fig.*). [*beseech.*]

be·sought [bi'sɔ:t] *prét. et p.p. de*

be·spat·ter [bi'spætə] éclabousser; *fig.* salir le nom de; accabler (*de, with*).

be·speak [bi'spi:k] [*irr. (speak)*] commander; retenir; *fig.* annoncer; *usu. poét.* s'adresser à, parler à.

be·spoke [bi'spouk] **1.** *prét. de bespeak*; **2.** *adj.*: ~ *tailor* tailleur *m* à façon; ~ *work* travail *m* sur commande; **be'spoken** *p.p. de bespeak*.

be·sprin·kle [bi'spriŋkl] arroser.

best [best] **1.** *adj.* meilleur; F *la crème de*; ~ *man* garçon *m* d'honneur; *at* ~ au mieux; *see seller*; **2.** *adv.* le mieux; **3.** *su.* meilleur *m*; mieux *m*; *all the* ~! bonne chance!; *Sunday* ~ habits *m/pl.* du dimanche; *for the* ~ pour le mieux; *to the* ~ *of my knowledge* autant que je sache; *make the* ~ *of* s'accommoder de; *make the* ~ *of a bad job* faire bonne mine à mauvais jeu; *the* ~ *of the way* la plus grande partie du chemin; *at* ~ pour dire le mieux; **4.** *v/t.* F l'emporter sur (*q.*).

be·stead [bi'sted] [*irr.*] aider.

be·ste(a)d [~]: *hard* ~ serré de près; *ill* ~ F en mauvaise passe.

bes·tial □ ['bestjəl] bestial (-aux *m/pl.*); **bes·ti·al·i·ty** [besti'æliti] bestialité *f*.

be·stir [bi'stə:]: ~ *o.s.* se remuer.

be·stow [bi'stou] accorder, octroyer (à, [*up*]*on*); † déposer; **be'stow·al**, **be'stow·ment** don *m*, octroi *m*.

be·strew [bi'stru:] [*irr.*] joncher, parsemer (de, *with*).

be·strid·den [bi'stridn] *p.p. de bestride*.

be·stride [bi'straid] [*irr.*] être à cheval sur; enjamber (*un endroit*); enfourcher (*un cheval*).

be·strode [bi'stroud] *prét. de bestride*.

bet [bet] **1.** pari *m*; **2.** [*irr.*] parier; F *you* ~ pour sûr; *I* ~ *you a shilling* F je vous parie 50 francs.

be·take [bi'teik] [*irr. (take)*]: ~ *o.s. to* se rendre à; *fig.* se livrer à.

be·think [bi'θiŋk] [*irr. (think)*]: ~ *o.s.* se rappeler (qch. *of s.th.*); ~ *o.s. to* (*inf.*) s'aviser de (*inf.*).

be·tide [bi'taid]: *whate'er* ~ advienne que pourra; *woe* ~ *him!* gare à lui!

be·times [bi'taimz] de bonne heure.

be·to·ken [bi'toukn] être signe de, révéler; présager.

be·tray [bi'trei] trahir (*a. fig. = laisser voir*); séduire (*une femme*); **be'tray·al** trahison *f*; ~ *of trust* abus

m de confiance; **be'tray·er** traître(sse *f*) *m*; trompeur (-euse *f*) *m*.

be·troth [bi'trouð] fiancer (à, avec *to*); *the* ~*ed* le fiancé *m*; la fiancée *f*; *pl.* les fiancés *m/pl.*; **be'troth·al** fiançailles *f/pl.*

bet·ter[1] ['betə] **1.** *adj.* meilleur; mieux; *he is* ~ il va mieux; *get* ~ s'améliorer; se remettre; *for* ~ *or* (*for*) *worse* pour le meilleur ou pour le pire; **2.** *su.* meilleur *m*; mieux *m*; ~*s pl.* supérieurs *m/pl.*; *get the* ~ *of* l'emporter sur (*q.*); rouler (*q.*) (= *duper*); surmonter (*un obstacle*); maîtriser (*une émotion*); *he is my* ~ il est plus fort que moi; **3.** *adv.* mieux; *be* ~ *off* être plus à son aise (*matériellement*); *so much the* ~ tant mieux; *you had* ~ *go* vous feriez mieux de vous en aller *ou* de partir; *I know* ~ j'en sais plus long; *think* ~ *of it* se raviser; revenir de; **4.** *v/t.* améliorer; surpasser; ~ *o.s.* améliorer sa position (*etc.*); *v/i.* s'améliorer.

bet·ter[2] [~] parieur (-euse *f*) *m*.

bet·ter·ment ['betəmənt] amélioration *f*.

bet·ting ['betiŋ] paris *m/pl.*; cote *f*; mise *f*; ~*-debt* dette *f* d'honneur.

be·tween [bi'twi:n] (*poét. et prov. a.* **be·twixt** [bi'twikst]) **1.** *adv.* entre les deux; *betwixt and between* entre les deux; **2.** *prp.* entre; ~ *ourselves* entre nous, de vous à moi; *they bought it* ~ *them* ils l'ont acheté à eux deux (trois *etc.*); **be'tween-decks** ⚓ entrepont *m*; *adv.* sous barrots; **be'tween-maid** aide *f* de maison.

bev·el ['bevl] **1.** oblique; **2.** ⊕ biseau *m*, biais *m*; conicité *f*; **3.** *v/t.* biseauter; *v/i.* biaiser; aller de biais; aller en biseau; ~*-wheel* ⊕ roue *f* dentée conique; pignon *m* conique.

bev·er·age ['bevəridʒ] boisson *f*.

bev·y ['bevi] bande *f*, troupe *f*.

be·wail [bi'weil] *v/t.* pleurer (qch.); *v/i.* se lamenter.

be·ware [bi'wɛə] se méfier (de q., *of s.o.*); se garder (de qch., *of s.th.*); ~ *of the dog!* chien méchant!

be·wil·der [bi'wildə] égarer, désorienter; F ahurir; abasourdir; **be'wil·der·ment** trouble *m*, confusion *f*; ahurissement *m*; abasourdissement *m*.

be·witch F [bi'witʃ] ensorceler; F

enchanter; be'witch·ment ensorcellement m; charme m.

be·yond [bi'jɔnd] 1. adv. au-delà, par-delà, plus loin; 2. prp. au-delà de; par-delà; au-dessus de; excepté; en dehors de; autre ... que; ~ endurance intolérable; ~ measure outre mesure; ~ dispute incontestable; ~ words au-delà de toute expression; get ~ s.o. dépasser q.; go ~ one's depth ne pas avoir pied; it is ~ me cela me dépasse; je n'y comprends rien.

bi... [bai] bi(s)-; di(s)-; semi-.

bi·an·nu·al □ [bai'ænjuəl] semestriel; biennal (-aux m/pl.).

bi·as ['baiəs] 1. adj. et adv. oblique (-ment); en biais; de biais; coupé de biais, en biais; 2. couture: biais m; boules: décentrement m; déviation f; radio: polarisation f; fig. parti m pris; penchant m; 3. décentrer (une boule); fig. rendre partial; prévenir (contre, against; en faveur de, towards); ~sed partial (-aux m/pl.).

bib [bib] bavette f (d'enfant); tablier: baverette f.

bib·cock ['bibkɔk] robinet m coudé.

Bi·ble ['baibl] Bible f.

bib·li·cal □ ['biblikl] biblique.

bib·li·og·ra·pher [bibli'ɔgrəfə] bibliographe m; bib·li·o·graph·ic, bib·li·o·graph·i·cal [~o'græfik(l)] bibliographique; bib·li·og·ra·phy [~'ɔgrəfi] bibliographie f; bib·li·o·ma·ni·a [~o'meinjə] bibliomanie f; bib·li·o·ma·ni·ac [~niæk] bibliomane m; bib·li·o·phile ['~ofail] bibliophile m.

bib·u·lous □ ['bibjuləs] adonné à la boisson; absorbant (chose).

bi·car·bon·ate [bai'kɑːbənit] bicarbonate m.

bi·ceps anat. ['baiseps] biceps m.

bick·er ['bikə] se quereller; être toujours en zizanie; trembloter (lumière); murmurer (ruisseau etc.); 'bick·er·ing(s pl.) querelles f/pl.; bisbille f.

bi·cy·cle ['baisikl] 1. bicyclette f, F vélo m; folding ~ bicyclette f pliante; ~ bell timbre m ou sonnette f de bicyclette; ~ rack porte-vélos m/inv., râtelier m à bicyclettes; ~ track piste f cyclable; 2. faire de la bicyclette ou du vélo; aller à bicyclette; 'bi·cy·clist (bi)cycliste mf.

bid [bid] 1. [irr.] v/t. commander, ordonner; inviter (à dîner); cartes: appeler; fig. ~ fair promettre de; s'annoncer; ~ farewell faire ses adieux; ~ up surenchérir; ~ welcome souhaiter la bienvenue; v/i. (prét. et p.p. bid) faire une offre (pour, for); 2. offre f, mise f, enchère f; cartes: appel m; a ~ to (inf.) un effort pour (inf.); cartes: no ~ Parole!; 'bid·den p.p. de bid 1; 'bid·der enchérisseur m; cartes: demandeur (-euse f) m; see high 1, low 1; 'bid·ding ordre m; invitation f; enchères f/pl.; cartes: enchère f.

bide [baid] attendre (le moment).

bi·en·ni·al [bai'enjəl] 1. biennal (-aux m/pl.); 2. ♀ plante f bisannuelle.

bier [biə] civière f (pour un cercueil).

bi·fo·cals [bai'foukəlz] pl. lunettes f/pl. bifocales.

bi·fur·cate ['baifəːkeit] (se) bifurquer; bi·fur·ca·tion bifurcation f.

big [big] grand; gros(se f); fig. lourd, gros(se f) (de, with); enceinte f (grosse d'enfant); fig. hautain, fanfaron (-ne f); ♀ Apple surnom de New York City; F ♀ Ben grosse cloche du Palais du Parlement à Londres; ~ business grosses affaires f/pl.; F fig. ~ shot chef m de file; personnage m important, sl. grosse légume f; Am. ~ stick fig. F trique f; hit ou make the ~ time réussir, arriver; Am. ~ top cirque: chapiteau m, a. fig. cirque m; talk ~ faire l'important; fanfaronner.

big·a·mous ['bigəməs] bigame; 'big·a·my bigamie f.

bight ♪ [bait] crique f; golfe m.

big·mouth F ['bigmauθ] gueulard(e f) m.

big·ness ['bignis] grandeur f; grosseur f.

big·ot ['bigət] bigot(e f) m; fig. fanatique mf; sectaire mf; 'big·ot·ed fanatique; fig. à l'esprit sectaire; 'big·ot·ry fanatisme m; zèle m outré.

'big-time ['bigtaim] de première catégorie, important; de grande envergure; extraordinaire; magnifique.

big·wig F ['bigwig] gros bonnet m; sl. grosse légume f.

bike F [baik] vélo m.

bi·lat·er·al □ [bai'lætərl] bilatéral (-aux m/pl.).

bil·ber·ry ♀ ['bilbəri] airelle *f*, myrtille *f*.

bile [bail] bile *f* (*fig.* = *colère*).

bilge [bildʒ] bouge *m* (*de barrique*); ⚓ fond *m* de cale; bouchain *m*; *sl.* bêtises *f/pl.*

bi·lin·gual [bai'lingwəl] bilingue.

bil·ious ☐ ['biljəs] bilieux (-euse *f*); *fig.* colérique.

bilk [bilk] F tromper, escroquer.

bill¹ [bil] 1. *oiseau, ancre, géog.*: bec *m*; serpette *f* (*pour tailler*); 2. (*a. fig.* ~ *and coo*) se becqueter.

bill² [~] 1. note *f*, facture *f*; *restaurant*: addition *f*; † bill *m*; † ~ (*a.* ~ *of exchange*) traite *f*; *Am.* billet *m* (*de banque*); *théâ. etc.* affiche *f*; *parl.* projet *m* de loi; ~ *of costs* compte *m* de frais; ~ *of expenses* note *f* de(s) frais; ~ *of fare* carte *f* du jour; ⚓ ~ *of health* patente *f* de santé; ~ *of lading* connaissement *m*, police *f* de chargement; ⚖ ~ *of sale* acte *m* de vente; † ~ *of sight* déclaration *f* d'entrée; ♀ *of Rights Brit.* Déclaration *f* des Droits du citoyen (*1689*); *Am. les* amendements *m/pl.* (*1791*) à la constitution des É.-U.; 2. facturer (*des marchandises*); afficher.

bill·board *Am.* ['bil'bɔːd] panneau *m* d'affichage.

bil·let ['bilit] 1. ⚔ (billet *m* de) logement *m*; bûche *f*; billette *f* (*a. métall.*); 2. ⚔ loger (*des troupes*) (*chez on, with*).

bill·fold ['bilfould] porte-billets *m/inv.*

bil·liard ['biljəd] *attr.* de billard; '~-**cue** queue *f* de billard; '**billiards** *sg. ou pl.* (jeu *m* de) billard *m*.

bil·lion ['biljən] billion *m*; *Am.* milliard *m*.

bil·low ['bilou] 1. lame *f* (*de mer*), grande vague *f*; 2. se soulever en vagues; ondoyer (*foule etc.*); '**billow·y** houleux (-euse *f*).

bill-stick·er ['bilstikə] afficheur *m*; placardeur *m*.

bil·ly *Am.* ['bili] bâton *m* (*de police*); '~-**cock** chapeau *m* melon; '~-**goat** F bouc *m*.

bi-mo·tored ⚡ ['baimoutəd] bimoteur.

bin [bin] coffre *m*; casier *m*; F poubelle *f*.

bi·na·ry ['bainəri] binaire; *biol.* ~ *fission* division *f* binaire *ou* cellulaire.

bin·au·ral [bain'ɔːrəl] binauriculaire; stéréophonique.

bind [baind] [*irr.*] *v/t.* lier, attacher; (res)serrer; garrotter; rendre constipé; ratifier, confirmer (*un marché*); border (*une étoffe*); relier (*des livres*); fixer (*un ski*); bander (*une blessure*); lier, agglutiner (*le sable*); ~ *over* (*q.*) d'observer une bonne conduite; *fig.* be bound with être engagé (à *to*, with); ~ *s.o.* apprentice to mettre q. en apprentissage chez; *I'll be bound* je m'engagerai (à, to); F j'en suis sûr!; *v/i.* se lier; durcir; '**bind·er** lieur (-euse *f*) *m*; lien *m*; ceinture *f*; ⊕ liant *m*; relieur *m* (*de livres*); '**bind·ing** 1. obligatoire (pour, on); agglomé: ratif (-ive *f*); 2. agglutination *f*; serrage *m*; lien *m*; *étoffe*: bordure *f*; *livres*: reliure *f*; '**bind·weed** ♀ liseron *m*.

binge *sl.* [bindʒ] bombe *f*, ribote *f*.

bin·na·cle ⚓ ['binəkl] habitacle *m*.

bin·o·cle ['binɔkl] binoculaire *m*; **bin·oc·u·lar** 1. [bai'nɔkjulə] binoculaire; 2. [bi'nɔkjulə] jumelle *f*, -s *f/pl.*

bi·o·chem·i·cal ['baio'kemikl] biochimique; '**bi·o'chem·is·try** biochimie *f*.

bi·og·ra·pher [bai'ɔgrəfə] biographe *m*; **bi·o·graph·ic, bi·o·graph·i·cal** ☐ [~o'græfik(l)] biographique; **bi·og·ra·phy** [~'ɔgrəfi] biographie *f*.

bi·o·log·ic, bi·o·log·i·cal ☐ [baio-'lɔdʒik(l)] biologique; **bi·ol·o·gist** [~'ɔlədʒist] biologiste *mf*; **bi·ol·o·gy** biologie *f*.

bi·par·tite [bai'pɑːtait] biparti(te *f*); ⚖ rédigé en double. [*su./m*).]

bi·ped *zo.* ['baiped] bipède (*a.*]

bi·plane ⚡ ['baiplein] biplan *m*.

birch [bəːtʃ] 1. ♀ (*ou* ~-*tree*) bouleau *m*; (*a.* ~-*rod*) verge *f*; 2. de bouleau; '**birch·en** de bouleau.

bird [bəːd] oiseau *m*; ~ *of passage* oiseau *m* de passage; ~ *of prey* oiseau *m* de proie; F *that's for the* ~*s* ça ne vaut rien; *tell a child about the* ~*s and the bees* expliquer à un enfant comment font les petits oiseaux; *kill two* ~*s with one stone* faire d'une pierre deux coups; '~-**cage** cage *f* à oiseaux; '~-**fan·ci·er** oiselier *m*; marchand(e *f*) *m* d'oiseaux; connaisseur (-euse *f*) *m* en oiseaux; '~-**lime** glu *f*; '~-**nest** 1. *see* bird's nest; 2.

dénicher des oiseaux; **'bird's-eye view** perspective *f* à vol d'oiseau; **'bird's nest** nid *m* d'oiseaux; ~ soup soupe *f* aux nids d'hirondelles; ~ **sanc·tu·ar·y** refuge *m* d'oiseaux.

bi·ro (*TM*) ['baiərou] stylo *m* (à bille).

birth [bə:θ] naissance *f*; accouchement; *animaux*: mise *f* bas; **bring to** ~ faire naître, engendrer; *come to* ~ naître, prendre naissance; **'~con-trol** limitation *f* des naissances; **'~day** anniversaire *m*; jour *m* natal; ~ *cake* gâteau *m* d'anniversaire; *Brit.* ~ *honours pl.* distinctions *f/pl.* honorifiques accordées à l'occasion de l'anniversaire du monarque; ~ *present* cadeau *m* d'anniversaire; **'~place** lieu *m* de naissance; **'~rate** natalité *f*; **'~right** droit *m* de naissance; droit *m* d'aînesse.

bis·cuit ['biskit] biscuit *m* (*a. poterie*).

bi·sect ⚹ [bai'sekt] bissecter (*un angle*); couper en deux parties égales (*une ligne, un angle*); **bi'sec·tion** bissection *f*.

bish·op ['biʃəp] évêque *m*; *échecs*: fou *m*; **'bish·op·ric** évêché *m*.

bis·muth ♎ ['bizməθ] bismuth *m*.

bi·son *zo.* ['baisn] bison *m*.

bis·sex·tile [bi'sekstail] **1.** bissextil; ~ *year* = **2.** année *f* bissextile.

bit [bit] **1.** morceau *m*; bout *m* (*de papier etc.*); *monnaie*: pièce *f*; *cheval, tenaille*: mors *m*; ⊕ mèche *f*; perçoir *m*; *ordinateur*: bit *m*; ~ *by* ~ peu à peu; F *be a* ~ *of a coward* être plutôt lâche; **2.** mettre le mors à, brider; **3.** *prét. de* bite 2.

bitch [bitʃ] **1.** chienne *f*; *sl.* garce *f*; renarde *f*; louve *f*; **2.** F gâcher.

bite [hait] **1.** coup *m* de dent; morsure *f*; *sauce*: piquant *m*; *poisson*: touche *f*; ⊕ mordant *m*; **2.** [*irr.*] mordre (*a. poisson, ancre, outil, acide, etc.*); piquer (*insecte, poivre*); ronger (*rouille*); F *fig.* ~ *the dust* mordre la poussière (= *mourir*); ~ *one's nails* se ronger les ongles; *v/i.* adhérer (*roues*); ♎ crocher (*ancre*); ~ *at* rembarrer (*q.*); **'bit·er** animal *etc.* qui mord; *the* ~ *bit* le trompeur trompé.

bit·ing □ ['baitiŋ] mordant; perçant (*froid*); cinglant (*vent*).

bit·ten ['bitn] *p.p. de* bite 2; *be* ~ *fig.* se faire attraper; F *be* ~ *with* s'en-

ticher de; *once* ~ *twice shy* chat échaudé craint l'eau froide.

bit·ter ['bitə] **1.** □ amer (-ère *f*); aigre; glacial (-als *m/pl.*) (*vent*); ~-*sweet* aigre-doux (-douce *f*); **2.** bière *f* amère.

bit·tern *orn.* ['bitə:n] butor *m*.

bit·ter·ness ['bitənis] amertume *f*; âpreté *f*; rancune *f*.

bit·ters ['bitəz] *pl.* bitter *m*, -s *m/pl.*, amer *m*, -s *m/pl.*

bitts ♎ [bits] *pl.* bittes *f/pl.*

bi·tu·men ['bitjumin] bitume *m*; **bi-tu·mi·nous** [~'tju:minəs] bitumineux (-euse *f*); gras(se *f*) (*houille*).

biv·ouac ['bivuæk] **1.** bivouac *m*; **2.** bivouaquer.

biz F [biz] affaire *f*, -s *f/pl.*

bi·zarre [bi'za:] bizarre.

blab F [blæb] **1.** (*a.* **'blab·ber**) jaseur (-euse *f*) *m*; indiscret (-ète *f*) *m*; **2.** *v/i.* jaser, bavarder; *v/t.* divulguer (*un secret*).

black [blæk] **1.** □ noir; *fig.* sombre, triste; ~ *cattle* bœufs *m/pl.* de race écossaise ou galloise; ~ *eye* œil *m* poché; *see frost*; ~ *ice* verglas *m*; ~ *market* marché *m* noir; ~ *marketeer* profiteur (-euse *f*) *m*; ~ *marketing* vente *f* ou achats *m/pl.* au marché noir; ~ *sheep fig.* brebis *f* galeuse; **2.** noircir; *v/t.* cirer (*des bottes*); F pocher (*l'œil*); ~ *out v/t.* obscurcir; *v/i.* couper la lumière; **3.** noir *m* (*a. vêtements*); noir(e *f*) *m* (= *nègre*); flocon *m* de suie.

black...: **~·a·moor** † ['~əmuə] nègre *m*, négresse *f*; **'~·ball** blackbouler; **'~·ber·ry** ♀ mûre *f* (sauvage); **'~·bird** merle *m*; **'~·board** tableau *m* noir; **'~·coat·ed** vêtu de noir; **'~·cock** *orn.* tétras *m*; **'black·en** *v/t.* noircir (*a. fig.*); *fig.* calomnier; *v/i.* (se) noircir; s'assombrir.

black...: **~·guard** ['blægɑːd] **1.** vaurien *m*; ignoble personnage *m*; **2.** (*a.* **'~·guard·ly**) □ ignoble, canaille; **3.** adjectiver(*q.*); **~·head** ⚶ ['blækhed] comédon *m*; **'black·ing** cirage *m*; **'black·ish** □ noirâtre, tirant sur le noir.

black...: **'~·jack 1.** *surt. Am.* assommoir *m*; **2.** assener un coup d'assommoir à (*q.*); **'~·lead 1.** plombagine *f*; crayon *m* (de mine de plomb); **2.** passer à la mine de plomb; **'~·leg** renard *m*; jaune *m*; **'~·let·ter** *typ.* caractères *m/pl.* go-

thiques; '~·**list** 1. liste *f* noire; 2.
mettre sur la liste noire; '~·**mail** 1.
extorsion *f* sous menace; chantage
m; 2. faire chanter (*q.*); '~·**mail·er**
maître *m* chanteur; '**black·ness**
noirceur *f*; obscurité *f*.

black...: '~-**out** black-out *m*; *fig.*
syncope *f*, amnésie *f* passagère; '~-
smith forgeron *m*; '~·**thorn** ♀ épine
f noire; '**black·y** F nègre *m*; moricaud *m*.

blad·der ['blædə] *anat.*, *a. foot.*
vessie *f*; *anat.*, ♀ vésicule *f*.

blade [bleid] *herbe*: brin *m*; *couteau*,
rasoir, *scie*, *épée*: lame *f*; *langue*:
plat *m*; *aviron*: pale *f*; *hélice*: aile *f*;
ventilateur: vanne *f*; F gaillard *m*;
(*a. ~-bone*) *anat.* omoplate *f*.

blain [blein] pustule *f*.

blam·a·ble □ ['bleiməbl] blâmable;
répréhensible; '**blam·a·ble·ness**
caractère *m* répréhensible.

blame [bleim] 1. reproches *m/pl.*;
blâme *m*; faute *f*; 2. blâmer; *he is
not to ~ for* il n'y a pas de faute de sa
part; *he is to ~ for* il y a de sa faute;
il est responsable de; *~ s.th. on s.o.*
imputer (la faute de) qch. à q.

blame·ful ['bleimful] blâmable; répréhensible; '**blame·less** □ innocent; irréprochable; '**blame·less-
ness** innocence *f*; irréprochabilité *f*;
'**blame·wor·thi·ness** caractère *m*
blâmable *ou* répréhensible; '**blame-
wor·thy** blâmable; répréhensible.

blanch [blɑːntʃ] blanchir; pâlir; *~
over* pallier; F blanchir.

blanc-mange *cuis.* [bləˈmɔnʒ] blanc-
manger (*pl.* blancs-mangers) *m*.

bland □ [blænd] doux (douce *f*);
débonnaire; narquois (*sourire*);
'**blan·dish** cajoler, flatter; '**blan-
dish·ment** flatterie *f*.

blank [blæŋk] 1. □ blanc(he *f*);
vierge (*page*); sans expression;
étonné (*regard*); ✂ ~ *cartridge* cartouche *f* à blanc; ✝ ~ *cheque* (*Am.
check*) cheque *m* en blanc; *fig.* give
s.o. a ~ cheque donner carte blanche à
q. (pour faire, *to do*); ✂ *fire ~* tirer à
blanc; 2. blanc *m*; vide *m*; lacune *f*;
mémoire: trou *m*; *loterie*: billet *m*
blanc; ⊕ flan *m*; F *fig. draw a ~*
échouer.

blan·ket ['blæŋkit] 1. *lit*, *cheval*:
couverture *f*; F *neige*, *fumée*: manteau *m*; *typ.* blanchet *m*; *fig.* wet ~
trouble-fête *m/inv.*; rabat-joie

m/inv.; 2. mettre une couverture à;
⚓ déventer; F étouffer, supprimer;
Am. éclipser; 3. *Am.* général (-aux
m/pl.), d'une portée générale.

blank·ness ['blæŋknis] vide *m*; air *m*
confus.

blare [blɛə] *v/i.* sonner, cuivrer
(*trompette*); F faire retentir.

blar·ney ['blɑːni] 1. patelinage *n*;
2. cajoler, enjôler.

blas·pheme [blæsˈfiːm] blasphémer; ~ *against* outrager; **blas-
'phem·er** blasphémateur (-trice *f*)
m; **blas·phe·mous** □ ['blæsfiməs]
blasphémateur (-trice *f*) (*personne*);
blasphématoire (*propos*); '**blas·phe-
my** blasphème *m*.

blast [blɑːst] 1. *vent*: rafale *f*; *vent*,
explosion: souffle *m*; *trompette*:
sonnerie *f*; *sifflet*, *sirène*, *mot.* coup
m; explosion *f*; ⊕ soufflerie *f*; ♀
cloque *f*; *at full* ~ en pleine activité;
2. *v/t.* faire sauter, pétarder; flétrir;
fig. ruiner, briser; *v/i.* cuivrer; ~ (*it*)*!*
sacrebleu!; '~-**fur·nace** ⊕ haut
fourneau *m*; '**blast·ing** abattage *m*
à la poudre; travail *m* aux explosifs;
'**blast-off** *espace*: lancement *m*,
mise *f* à feu (*d'une fusée*).

bla·tan·cy ['bleitənsi] vulgarité *f*
criarde; '**bla·tant** □, ⊕ souffleur *m*;
rité criarde; criant (*tort etc.*).

blath·er *Am.* ['blæðə] 1. bêtises
f/pl.; 2. débiter des inepties.

blaze [bleiz] 1. flamme *f*; feu *m*; conflagration *f*; éclat *m*; étoile *f* (*au
front d'un cheval*); *arbre*: griffe *f*;
pl. F enfer *m*; 2. *v/i.* flamber; flamboyer (*soleil*, *couleurs*); étinceler; F
~ *away* tirer sans désemparer (sur,
at); *chasse*: *blazing scent* piste *f*
toute fraîche; *v/t.* (*usu.* ~ *abroad*)
répandre, publier; griffer (*un arbre*); '**blaz·er** blazer *m*.

bla·zon ['bleizn] 1. blason *m*; armoiries *f/pl.*; 2. ⧄ blasonner; marquer (*qch.*) aux armoires (*de q.*); *fig.*
célébrer, exalter; F publier; '**bla-
zon·ry** blasonnement *m*; science *f*
héraldique; *fig.* ornementation *f*.

bleach [bliːtʃ] 1. blanchir; *v/i.* blon-
dir (*cheveux*); 2. décolorant *m*;
'**bleach·er** blanchisseur (-euse *f*)
m; *Am.* ~*s pl.* places *f/pl.* découvertes
d'un terrain de baseball; '**bleach·ing**
blanchiment *m*; '**bleach·ing-
pow·der** poudre *f* à blanchir.

bleak □ [bliːk] sans abri, exposé au

vent; *fig.* froid; triste, morne; 'bleak·ness froidure *f*; aspect *m* morne.

blear [bliə] **1.** chassieux (-euse *f*) (*surt. des yeux*); **2.** rendre trouble; estomper (*des couleurs*); ~-eyed ['bliəraid], 'blear·y aux yeux chassieux.

bleat [bli:t] **1.** bêlement *m*; **2.** bêler.

bleb [bleb] bouton *m*, (petite) ampoule *f*.

bled [bled] *prét. et p.p. de bleed.*

bleed [bli:d] [*irr.*] *v/i.* saigner, perdre du sang; *v/t.* saigner; ~ white saigner (*q.*) à blanc; 'bleed·ing écoulement *m* de sang; ✷ saignée *f*.

blem·ish ['blemiʃ] **1.** défaut *m*, imperfection *f*; tache *f*; **2.** tacher, souiller; abîmer.

blench [blentʃ] blêmir, pâlir.

blend [blend] **1.** (se) mêler (à, avec *with*); (se) mélanger (*thé*, *café*); *v/t.* couper (*le vin*); *fig. v/i.* s'allier, se marier (*voix*, *couleurs*); **2.** mélange *m*.

blende *min.* [blend] blende *f*.

bless [bles] bénir; consacrer; ~ *s.o.* with accorder à q. le bonheur de; F ~ me!, ~ my soul! tiens, tiens!; ~ you! à vos souhaits!; bless·ed □ [*p.p.* blest; *adj.* 'blesid] bienheureux (-euse *f*); saint; *sl.* fichu; be ~ with jouir de; ~ event heureux événement *m* (= *naissance*); bless·ed·ness ['~sidnis] félicité *f*, béatitude *f*; live in single ~ vivre dans le bonheur du célibat; 'bless·ing bénédiction *f*; bienfait *m*; aux repas: bénédicité *m*.

blest *poét.* [blest] *see blessed.*

bleth·er ['bleðə] *see blather.*

blew [blu:] *prét. de blow[2] et blow[3].*

blight [blait] **1.** ✿ nielle *f* (*des céréales*); cloque *f* (*du fruit*); *fig.* influence *f* néfaste; **2.** nieller; brouir; *fig.* flétrir; 'blight·er *sl.* bon *m* à rien; individu *m*; poor ~ pauvre hère *m*; lucky ~ veinard *m*.

Blight·y ✗ *sl.* ['blaiti] la patrie (*usu. l'Angleterre*); a ~ (one) la bonne blessure.

blind □ [blaind] **1.** aveugle; sans issue (*chemin*); faux (fausse *f*) (*porte*); be ~ to ne pas voir (*qch.*); the ~ pl. les aveugles *m/pl.*; ~ alley impasse *f* (*a. fig.*); ~ corner tournant *m* encaissé; virage *m* masqué; ✗ ~ flying vol *m* sans visibilité, vol *m* en P.S.V.; *anat.* ~ gut cæcum *m*; ⚓,

✗ ~ shell obus *m* qui a raté; ~ spot *anat.* point *m* aveugle, papille *f* optique; *radar etc.*: angle *m* mort; *fig.* côté *m* faible (*d'une personne*); that's your ~ spot c'est là où vous n'y voyez pas clair; c'est là où vous refusez de voir clair; ~ story conte *m* en l'air; ~ly *fig.* aveuglément; à l'aveuglette; **2.** store *m*; jalousie *f*; abat-jour *m/inv.*; banne *f*; ✗ blinde *f*; *Am. cheval:* œillère *f*; masque *m*, prétexte *m*; **3.** aveugler (sur, to); *fig.* éblouir; *min.* blinder.

blind...: '~·fold **1.** aveuglément; **2.** bander les yeux (à ou de q., *s.o.*); '~-man's-'buff colin-maillard *m*; 'blind·ness cécité *f*.

blink [bliŋk] **1.** clignotement *m* des paupières; lueur *f* momentanée; signal *m* optique; F *fig.* on the ~ abîmé, détraqué; **2.** *v/i.* ⚓ battre *ou* cligner des paupières; papilloter (*lumière*); *v/t. fig.* fermer les yeux sur; dissimuler; 'blink·er clignotant *m*; *cheval:* œillère *f*; 'blink·ing F sacré.

bliss [blis] félicité *f*, béatitude *f*.

bliss·ful □ ['blisful] bienheureux (-euse *f*); serein; 'bliss·ful·ness félicité *f*, béatitude *f*; bonheur *m*.

blis·ter ['blistə] **1.** ampoule *f*; *peint.*, *peau:* cloque *f*; ✷ vésicatoire *m*; **2.** (se) couvrir d'ampoules; (se) cloquer (*peinture*).

blithe □ [blaið], ~·some ['blaiðsəm] *surt. poét.* joyeux (-euse *f*), gai.

blith·er *sl.* ['bliðə] dire des bêtises; ~ing F sacré.

blitz [blits] **1.** F bombardement *m* aérien; **2.** détruire par un bombardement.

bliz·zard ['blizəd] tempête *f* de neige.

bloat [blout] gonfler; boursoufler; bouffir (*a. fig.*), saurer (*des harengs*); ~ed boursouflé, gonflé; bouffi (*a. fig.*); 'bloat·er hareng *m* bouffi.

blob [blɔb] tache *f*; pâté *m*; goutte *f* d'eau.

block [blɔk] **1.** *marbre*, *fer*, *papier*, *etc.*: bloc *m*; *bois:* tronçon *m*; *roche:* quartier *m*; *mot.* tin *m*; sabot *m* (*de frein*); (*a. ~ of flats*) pâté *m* (*de maisons*); (*a. dead ~*) embouteillage *m*; blocus *m*; ~ letter *typ.* caractère *m* gras; majuscule *f*; **2.** bloquer; entraver; fermer (*une voie*, *un jeu*); ~ in esquisser à grands traits; (*usu. ~ up*)

blowy

bloquer, obstruer; murer (*une porte*); ♣ bâcler (*un port*); ~ out caviarder (*une censure*).

block·ade [blɔ'keid] **1.** blocus *m*; **2.** bloquer; faire le blocus de; **block'ade-run·ner** forceur *m* de blocus.

block...: '~**·bust·er** F ✗ bombe *f* de très gros calibre; *fig.* succès *m* fou; *fig.* personne *f ou* chose *f* d'une efficacité à tout casser; '~**·head** sot *m*; tête *f* de bois; '~**·house** blockhaus *m*.

bloke F [blouk] type *m*, individu *m*.

blond(e *f*) [blɔnd] **1.** blond; **2.** blondin(e *f*) *m*; ✝ (*a.* blonde lace) blonde *f*.

blood [blʌd] sang *m* (*a.* = descendance); race *f*; ✝ dandy *m*; *in cold* ~ de sang-froid; *see run*.

blood...: ~ **bank** banque *f* du sang; ~ **bath** *fig.* bain *f* de sang; ~ **clot** caillot *m* de sang; '~**·cur·dling** à (vous) figer le sang (*histoire etc.*); ~**do·nor** donneur (-euse *f*) *m* sang; ~ **group** groupe *m* sanguin; '~**·guilt·i·ness** culpabilité *f* d'avoir versé du sang; '~**·heat** température *f* du sang; '~**·horse** cheval *m* de race, pur-sang *m/inv.*; '~**·hound** limier *m*; '**blood·i·ness** état *m* sanglant; disposition *f* sanguinaire; '**blood·less** □ exsangue, anémié; sans effusion de sang; *fig.* pâle; sans énergie; sans courage.

blood...: '~**·let·ting** saignée *f*; '~**·poi·son·ing** ☣ empoisonnement *m* du sang; '~**·pres·sure** pression *f* vasculaire; ~ **sam·ple** prélèvement *m* de sang; '~**·shed** carnage *m*; '~**·shot** éraillé (*œil*); ~ **sports** *pl.* sports *m/pl.* sanguinaires; '~**·stanch·ing** styptique; ~ **test** analyse *f* de sang; '~**·thirst·y** avide de sang; ~ **trans·fu·sion** transfusion *f* de sang; '~**·ves·sel** vaisseau *m* sanguin; '**blood·y 1.** □ ensanglanté, sanguinaire; *sl.* sacré; **2.** *sl.* vachement; '**blood·y·mind·ed** *sl.* mauvais coucheur (-euse *f*); *she's just being* ~ elle le fait rien que pour nous emmerder.

bloom¹ [blu:m] **1.** fleur *f* (*a. fig.*); épanouissement *m*; duvet *m* (*d'un fruit*); *fig.* incarnat *m*; **2.** fleurir.

bloom² *métall.* [~] loupe *f*.

bloom·er *sl.* ['blu:mə] gaffe *f*, bévue *f*; *usu.* ~s *pl.* culotte *f* bouffante.

bloom·ing □ ['blu:miŋ] fleurissant, en fleur; florissant, prospère; *sl.* sacré; *souv.* ne se traduit pas.

blos·som ['blɔsəm] **1.** fleur *f* (*surt. des arbres*); **2.** fleurir; ~ *into* devenir.

blot [blɔt] **1.** tache *f* (*a. fig.*); pâté *m* (*d'encre*); **2.** *v/t.* tacher; ternir (*a. fig.*); sécher, passer le buvard sur (*l'encre*); (*usu.* ~ out) effacer, *fig.* masquer; *v/i.* faire des pâtés (*plume*); boire l'encre (*buvard*).

blotch [blɔtʃ] tache *f*; pustule *f*; *peau:* tache *f* rouge.

blot·ter ['blɔtə] buvard *m*; *Am.* registre *m* d'arrestations *etc.*

blot·ting...: '~**·book** bloc *m* buvard; '~**·pad** bloc *m* buvard, sous-main *m/inv.*; '~**·pa·per** papier *m* buvard.

blot·to *sl.* ['blɔtou] soûl perdu.

blouse [blauz] blouse *f*; ✗, *a. Am.* vareuse *f*.

blow¹ [blou] coup *m* (*de poing, de bâton, etc.*); *at one* ~ d'un (seul) coup; *come to* ~s en venir aux coups.

blow² [~] [*irr.*] s'épanouir.

blow³ [~] **1.** [*irr.*] *v/i.* souffler; faire du vent; claquer (*ampoule*); sauter (*plomb*); ~ *in* entrer; ~ *over* se calmer; ~ *up* éclater, sauter; *Am.* F entrer en colère; *v/t.* souffler (*a. un verre*); *vent:* pousser; vider (*un œuf*); sonner (*un instrument*); mouches: gâter (*la viande*); évacuer (*une chaudière*); ⚡ faire sauter (*les plombs*); *sl.* manger (*son argent*); F louper (*une chance*); *sl.* ~ *me!*, *I'm* ~*ed!* zut alors!; F ~ *s.o. a kiss* envoyer un baiser à q.; ~ *one's nose* se moucher; F ~ *one's top* sortir de ses gonds; ~ *up* faire sauter; gonfler (*un pneu*); *sl.* semoncer, tancer; *phot.* agrandir; **2.** coup *m* de vent, souffle *m*; '~**·dry** sécher (au sèche-cheveux); '**blow·er** souffleur (-euse *f*) *m*; rideau *m* (*de cheminée*); ⊕ machine *f* à vent; *sl.* téléphone *m*.

blow...: '~**·fly** mouche *f* à viande; '~**·hole** évent *m* (*de baleine*; *a.* ⊕); ventilateur *m*.

blown [bloun] *p.p. de* blow³ 1.

'**blow·lamp** lampe *f* à souder, chalumeau *m*; **blow-out** mot. éclatement *m* (*de pneu*); *sl.* gueuleton *m*; '**blow·pipe** sarbacane *f*; *métall.* chalumeau *m*; '**blow·torch** *see* blowlamp; '**blow·up** explosion *f*; *phot.* agrandissement *m*; F accès *m* de colère; *sl.* engueulade *m*; '**blow·y** venteux (-euse *f*); tempétueux (-euse *f*).

blowz·y [ˈblauzi] rougeaud; ébouriffé.

blub·ber [ˈblʌbə] 1. graisse *f* de baleine; 2. *v/i.* pleurnicher; *v/t.* dire en pleurant; barbouiller de larmes.

bludg·eon [ˈblʌdʒn] 1. matraque *f*; 2. assener un coup de matraque à.

blue [blu:] 1. □ bleu; F triste, sombre; 2. bleu (*pl.* -s); azur *m*; *pol.* conservateur (-trice *f*) *m*; *out of the* ~ à l'improviste, sans crier gare; 3. bleuir; azurer (*le linge*); ~ **ba·by** ⚓ enfant *mf* bleu(e); '~**ber·ry** myrtille *f*, airelle *f*; '~**book** *Am.* registre *m* des employés de l'État; '~**bot·tle** ⚓ bl(e)uet *m*; *zo.* mouche *f* à viande; ~ **dev·ils** F *pl.* cafard *m*; '~**jack·et** col-bleu (*pl.* cols-bleus) *m* (= matelot); ~ **jeans** *sg. ou pl.* blue-jean(s) *m(pl.)*; ~ **laws** *Am.* lois *f/pl.* inspirées par le puritanisme; '**blue·ness** couleur *f* bleue; '**blue·print** dessin *m* négatif; *fig.* projet *m*; **blues** *pl., a. sg.* humeur *f* noire, cafard *m*; ♩ *Am.* blues *m*; '**blue·stock·ing** *fig.* bas-bleu *m*.

bluff [blʌf] 1. □ escarpé (*falaise etc.*); brusque (*personne*); 2. bluff *m*; menaces *f/pl.* exagérées; *géog.* cap *m* à pic; 3. bluffer; *v/i.* faire du bluff.

blu·ish [ˈbluːiʃ] bleuâtre; bleuté.

blun·der [ˈblʌndə] 1. bévue *f*; erreur *f*; faux pas *m*; 2. faire une bévue *ou* une gaffe; ~ *into* heurter (*q.*), se heurter contre (*q.*); F ~ *out* laisser échapper (*un secret*) par maladresse; '**blun·der·er**, '**blun·der·head** maladroit(e *f*) *m*; lourdaud (-e *f*) *m*.

blunt [blʌnt] 1. □ émoussé; épointé; obtus (*angle*); brusque, carré; 2. émousser (*un couteau*); épointer (*un crayon*); '**blunt·ness** état *m* épointé; manque *m* de tranchant; *fig.* franchise *f*.

blur [blə:] 1. tache *f*; *fig.* brouillard *m*; apparence *f* confuse; 2. *v/t.* barbouiller; brouiller; troubler; estomper (*les lignes*); ~*red surt. phot.* mal réussi, flou.

blurb [blə:b] *livre*: bande *f* de publicité.

blurt [blə:t]: ~ *out* trahir (*qch.*) par maladresse.

blush [blʌʃ] 1. rougeur *f*; incarnat *m* (*d'une rose*); prémices *f/pl.* (*de la jeunesse*); *at the first* ~ à l'abord; 2. rougir (*de for, with, at*); ~ *to*

(*inf.*) avoir honte de (*inf.*); '**blush·ing** □ rougissant.

blus·ter [ˈblʌstə] 1. fureur *f*, fracas *m*; rodomontades *f/pl.*; 2. souffler en rafales (*vent*); faire du fracas; faire le rodomont; '**blus·ter·er** rodomont *m*, bravache *m*.

bo·a *zo.*, ✝ [ˈbouə] boa *m*.

boar [bɔ:] verrat *m*; sanglier *m*.

board [bɔ:d] 1. planche *f*; madrier *m*; tableau *m* (*d'annonces etc.*); carton *m*; *reliure*: emboîtage *m*; table *f*; pension *f*; *admin.* commission *f*; ✝ conseil *m*; *pol.* ministère *m*; ⚓ bord *m*; ~s *pl. box.* canevas *m*; *théâ.* scène *f*, tréteaux *m/pl.*; *see director*; ♀ *of Trade* Ministère *m* du Commerce; *on* ~ *a ship* (*a train etc.*) à bord d'un navire (dans un train, en wagon, *etc.*); *above* ~ dans les règles; *across the* ~ général; 2. *v/t.* planchéier; cartonner (*un livre*); nourrir (*des élèves*); (*a.* ~ *out*) mettre en pension; ⚓ aller à bord de (*un navire*); ⚓ accoster; *surt. Am.* monter (en, dans); ~ *up* boucher (*une fenêtre*); couvrir *ou* entourer de planches; *v/i.* être en pension (chez, with); '**board·er** pensionnaire *mf*.

board·ing [ˈbɔ:diŋ] planchéiage *m*; cartonnage *m*; planches *f/pl.*; pension *f*; ⚓ accostage *m*; '~**house** pension *f* de famille; '~**school** pensionnat *m*, internat *m*.

board…: '~**wag·es** *pl.* indemnité *f* de logement *ou* de nourriture; '~**walk** *surt. Am.* trottoir *m* (en planches), caillebotis *m*.

boast [boust] 1. vanterie *f*; *fig.* orgueil *m*; 2. *v/i.* (*of, about* de) se vanter, se faire gloire; *v/t. fig.* (se glorifier de) posséder (*qch.*); '**boast·er** vantard(e *f*) *m*, fanfaron(ne *f*) *m*; **boast·ful** □ [ˈ͜ful] vantard.

boat [bout] 1. bateau *m*; embarcation *f*; navire *m* (*marchand*); *be in the same* ~ être logé(s) à la même enseigne; 2. aller en bateau; faire du canotage; '**boat-hook** gaffe *f*; '**boat-house** hangar *m* à bateaux; '**boat·ing** canotage *m*; '**boat-race** régate *f*, -s *f/pl.*; **boat·swain** [ˈbousn] maître *m* d'équipage.

bob [bɔb] 1. *pendule*: lentille *f*; plomb *m*; *pêche*: bouchon *m*; *cheval*: queue *f* écourtée; *sl.* shilling *m*; *Am. traîneau*: patin *m*; chignon *m*; petite révérence *f*; *see* ~*bed hair*; 2.

bomb-proof

v/t. écourter; couper (*les cheveux*); ~bed hair cheveux *m/pl.* à la Jeanne d'Arc; *v/i.* s'agiter, danser; faire une petite révérence; *fig.* ~ *for* chercher à saisir avec les dents.

bob·bin ['bɔbin] bobine *f*; ✄ corps *m* de bobine; fuseau *m* pour dentelles; '~-**lace** dentelle *f* aux fuseaux.

bob·ble *Am.* ['bɔbl] gaffe *f*.

bob·by *Brit. sl.* ['bɔbi] agent *m* de police; '~-**pin** pince *f* à cheveux; '~-**socks** *pl.* socquettes *f/pl.*; '~-**sox·er** *Am. sl.* adolescente *f*.

bob·sled ['bɔbsled], **bob·sleigh** ['bɔbslei] bobsleigh *m*.

bob·tail ['bɔbteil] queue *f* écourtée; cheval *m ou* chien *m* à queue écourtée; F canaille *f*.

bode [boud] présager; ~ *well* (*ill*) être de bon (mauvais) augure.

bod·ice ['bɔdis] corsage *m*; brassière *f* (*d'enfant*).

bod·i·less ['bɔdilis] sans corps.

bod·i·ly ['bɔdili] corporel(le *f*), physique; ☙ ~ *harm* lésion *f* corporelle.

bod·kin ['bɔdkin] passe-lacet *m*; poinçon *m*; grande épingle *f*; F *sit* ~ être un lapin.

bod·y ['bɔdi] **1.** corps *m*; consistance *f*; *vin:* sève *f*; foule *f*; *église:* vaisseau *m*; fond *m* (*de chapeau*); (*a. dead* ~) cadavre *m*; ✈ fuselage *m*; ⊕ bâti *m*, corps *m*; *mot.* (*a.* ~-work) carrosserie *f*; ✖ troupe *f*, bande *f*; *astr.* astre *m*; F personne *f*, type *m*; ~ *odo(u)r* odeur *f* corporelle; *in a* ~ en masse, en corps; **2.** ~ *forth* donner une forme à; '~-**guard** garde *f* du corps.

Boer [buə] **1.** Boer *mf*; **2.** boer.

bog [bɔg] **1.** marécage *m*; **2.** embourber; *be* ~ged s'embourber.

bog·gle ['bɔgl] rechigner (devant *at*, *over*; à *inf. at*, *about gér.*).

bog·gy ['bɔgi] marécageux (-euse *f*).

bo·gie ['bougi] ☙ bog(g)ie *m*; *a. see bogy.*

bo·gus ['bougəs] faux (fausse *f*); feint.

bo·gy ['bougi] épouvantail *m*; croque-mitaine *m*.

bo(h) [bou] bou.

Bo·he·mi·an [bou'hi:mjən] **1.** bohémien(ne *f*); **2.** Bohémien(ne *f*) *m*; *fig.* bohème *m*.

boil [bɔil] **1.** *v/i.* bouillir (*a. fig.*); *v/t.* faire bouillir; cuire à l'eau; ~ed egg œuf *m* à la coque; **2.** ébullition *f*;

furoncle *m*, F clou *m*; '**boil·er** chaudière *f*; bain-marie (*pl.* bainsmarie) *m*; ~ *suit* bleu(s) *m(pl.)* (de travail); '**boil·ing** ébullition *f*; *sl. the whole* ~ tout le bazar.

bois·ter·ous ☐ ['bɔistərəs] bruyant; violent; tumultueux (-euse *f*); tempétueux (-euse *f*); '**bois·ter·ous·ness** violence *f*; turbulence *f*.

bold ☐ [bould] hardi, courageux (-euse *f*); assuré; à pic, escarpé (*côte etc.*); *péj.* effronté; *typ.* en vedette; *make* (*so*) ~ (*as*) *to* (*inf.*) s'enhardir jusqu'à (*inf.*); '**bold·face** *typ.* charactères *m/pl.* gras; '**bold·ness** hardiesse *f etc.*; *péj.* effronterie *f*.

bole [boul] fût *m*, tronc *m* (*d'arbre*).

boll ♀ [boul] capsule *f*.

bol·lard ⚓ ['bɔləd] pieu *m* d'amarrage; *à bord:* bitte *f*.

bo·lo·ney [bə'louni] *see baloney.*

Bol·she·vism ['bɔlʃivizm] bolchevisme; '**Bol·she·vist** bolchevik (*a. su./mf*), bolcheviste (*a. su./mf*).

bol·ster ['boulstə] **1.** traversin *m*; ⊕ matrice *f*; coussinet *m*; **2.** (*usu.* ~ *up*) soutenir; F appuyer.

bolt[1] [boult] **1.** *arbalète:* carreau *m*; *porte:* verrou *m*; *serrure:* pêne *m*; *fig., a. poét.* coup *m* de foudre; *fig.* élan *m* soudain, fuite *f*; ~ *upright* tout droit; **2.** *v/t.* verrouiller; bâcler; F gober; *Am. pol.* abandonner (*son parti, q.*); *v/i.* partir au plus vite; F s'emballer (*cheval*); filer, décamper (*personne*).

bolt[2] [~] tamiser.

bolt·er[1] ['boultə] cheval *m* porté à s'emballer; déserteur *m*.

bolt·er[2] [~] blutoir *m*.

bolt·hole ['boulthoul] *animal:* trou *m* de refuge; *fig.* échappée *f*.

bomb [bɔm] **1.** *surt.* ✖ bombe *f*; F grenade *f* à main; *hydrogen* ~ bombe *f* H; *incendiary* ~ bombe *f* incendiaire; **2.** lancer des bombes sur; ~ed *out* sinistré par suite des bombardements.

bom·bard [bɔm'bɑ:d] bombarder (*a. fig.*); **bom'bard·ment** bombardement *m*.

bom·bast ['bɔmbæst] emphase *f*, enflure *f*; **bom'bas·tic, bom'bas·ti·cal** ☐ enflé, ampoulé (*style*).

bomb·er ✖ ['bɔmə] bombardier *m* (*a. personne*).

bomb-proof ['bɔmpru:f] à l'épreuve des bombes; blindé (*abri*).

bo·na fi·de [ˈbəunəˈfaidi] **1.** de bonne foi; sérieux (-euse f) (*offre etc.*); **2.** de bonne foi.

bo·nan·za F [boˈnænzə] **1.** *fig.* vraie mine f d'or; **2.** prospère, favorable.

bon-bon [ˈbɔnbɔn] bonbon m.

bond [bɔnd] **1.** lien m (*a. fig.*); attache f (*a. fig.*); contrat m; ⊕ joint m; ✝ bon m; ✝ in ~ entreposé; **2.** liaisonner; appareiller (*un mur*); ✝ entreposer, mettre en dépôt; ~ed warehouse entrepôt m de la douane; **ˈbond·age** esclavage m, servitude f; ✝ servage m; *fig.* in ~ to s.o. sous la férule de q.; **ˈbond(s)·man** *hist.* serf m; F esclave m; **ˈbond(s)·wom·an** *hist.* serve f; F esclave f.

bone [bəun] **1.** os m; arête f (*de poisson*); ~s *pl. a.* ossements m/pl. (*des morts*); ~ of contention pomme f de discorde; feel in one's ~s en avoir le pressentiment; frozen to the ~ glacé jusqu'à la moelle, transi de froid; F have a ~ to pick with avoir maille à partir avec (q.); F make no ~s about (*gér.*) ne pas se gêner pour (*inf.*); **2.** désosser; ôter les arêtes de; garnir de baleines (*un corset*); *Am.* F (*a. ~ up*) potasser; **3.** d'os; **boned** à (aux) os ...; désossé *etc.*; **ˈ~·i·dle**, **ˈ~·la·zy** paresseux (-euse f) comme une couleuvre; **ˈbone-meal** engrais m d'os; **ˈbon·er** *Am. sl.* bourde f; **ˈbone·set·ter** rebouteur m; F renoueur m.

bon·fire [ˈbɔnfaiə] feu m de joie; feu m (de jardin); F conflagration f.

bon·kers *Brit. sl.* [ˈbɔŋkəz] cinglé, dingue.

bon·net [ˈbɔnit] **1.** bonnet m; béret m; chapeau m à brides (*de femme*); béguin m (*d'enfant*); capote f de cheminée; ⊕ capot m; *fig.* compère m, complice mf; ⚓ bonnette f maillée; **2.** mettre un béret ou chapeau à; F enfoncer le chapeau sur la tête à (q.).

bon·ny *surt. écoss.* [ˈbɔni] joli, gentil(le f).

bo·nus ✝ [ˈbəunəs] prime f; boni m; *actions:* bonus m.

bon·y [ˈbəuni] osseux (-euse f); anguleux (-euse f), décharné (*personne*); plein d'os *ou* d'arêtes.

boo [bu:] huer, conspuer (q.).

boob *Am.* [bu:b] rigaud(e f) m, benêt m.

boo·by [ˈbu:bi] *orn.* fou m; *a. see* boob; ~ prize prix m décerné à celui qui vient en dernier; ~ trap attrape-niais m/inv.; ✕ mine-piège f.

boo·hoo F [buˈhu:] pleurnicher.

book [buk] **1.** livre m; volume m; tome m; registre m; carnet m (*de billets etc.*); cahier m (*d'écolier*); ✝ stand in the ~s at ... être porté pour ... dans les livres; *fig.* be in s.o.'s good (bad) ~s être bien (mal) dans les papiers de q.; **2.** v/t. inscrire (*une commande, un voyageur à l'hôtel*); délivrer un billet à (q.); prendre (*un billet*); retenir (*une chambre, une place*); louer (*une place*); enregistrer; v/i. s'inscrire; prendre un billet; ~ through prendre un billet direct (pour, to); **ˈ~·bind·er** relieur (-euse f) m; **ˈ~·burn·er** *Am.* F fanatique mf; zélateur (-trice f) m; **ˈ~·case** bibliothèque f; ~ end serre-livres m/inv.; **book·ie** F *sp.* [ˈbuki] bookmaker m; **ˈbook·ing-clerk** employé(e f) m du guichet; **ˈbook·ing-of·fice** 🚂, *théâ.* guichet m; guichets m/pl.; **ˈbook·ish** ☐ studieux (-euse f); livresque (*style*); **ˈbook-keep·er** comptable m, teneur m de livres; **ˈbook-keep·ing** tenue f des livres; comptabilité f; **book·let** [ˈ~lit] livret m; opuscule m.

book...: **ˈ~·mak·er** faiseur m de livres; *sp.* bookmaker m; **ˈ~·mark** signet m; **ˈ~·plate** ex-libris m; **ˈ~·sell·er** libraire m; wholesale ~ libraire-éditeur (*pl.* libraires-éditeurs*) m; **ˈ~·worm** *zo.* gerce f, teigne f; *fig.* rat m de bibliothèque.

boom[1] ⚓ [bu:m] bout-dehors (*pl.* bouts-dehors) m; gui m; *port:* barrage m.

boom[2] [~] **1.** ✝ hausse f rapide; boom m; vogue f; ~ and bust prospérité f économique suivie d'une crise sévère; **2.** v/i. être en hausse; *fig.* aller très fort; v/t. faire du battage autour de (q., qch.).

boom[3] [~] gronder, mugir; bourdonner (*insectes*).

boon[1] [bu:n] faveur f; bienfait m.

boon[2] [~] gai, joyeux (-euse f); ~ companion bon vivant m.

boor *fig.* [buə] rustre m, rustaud m; butor m.

boor·ish ☐ [ˈbuəriʃ] rustre, rustaud, grossier (-ère f); malappris; **ˈboor-**

ish·ness grossièreté *f*; manque *m* de savoir-vivre.

boost [buːst] faire de la réclame pour; F chauffer; ⚡ survolter; ~ *business* augmenter les affaires; **'boost·er** ⚡ survolteur *m*; *radio*: amplificateur *m*; ⊕ (*a.* ~ *rocket*) fusée *f* de lancement; 🚀 ~ *shot* injection *f ou* piqûre *f* de rappel, rappel *m* (de vaccination).

boot[1] [buːt]: *to* ~ en sus, de plus.

boot[2] [~] chaussure *f*; *mot.* caisson *m*; F *get the* ~ se faire flanquer à la porte; *give s.o. the* ~ flanquer q. à la porte; **'~·black** *Am. see* shoeblack; **'boot·ed** chaussé; **boot·ee** ['buːtiː] bottine *f* (d'intérieur) (*de dame*); bottine *f* d'enfant.

booth [buːð] baraque *f*, tente *f* (*de marché etc.*).

boot...: **'~·jack** tire-botte *m*; **'~·lace** lacet *m*; **'~·leg** *surt. Am.* **1.** de contrebande (*alcool*); **2.** faire la contrebande de l'alcool; **'~·leg·ger** contrebandier *m* de boissons alcooliques; *p.ext.* profiteur *m*.

boots [buːts] *sg. hôtel*: garçon *m* d'étage.

boot-tree ['buːttriː] tendeur *m*.

boo·ty ['buːti] butin *m*.

booze *sl.* [buːz] **1.** faire ribote; **2.** boisson *f* alcoolique; **'booz·y** *sl.* soûlard; pompette.

bo·rax 🜍 ['boːræks] borax *m*.

bor·der ['boːdə] **1.** bord *m*; *bois*: lisière *f*; *chemin*: marge *f*; *région*: frontière *f*, confins *m/pl.*; *tableau*: bordure *f*; platebande *f* (*de gazon*); ~ *state* état *m* limitrophe; **2.** *v/t.* border; encadrer; *v/i.* confiner (à, [*up*] *on*); **'bor·der·er** frontalier (-ère *f*) *m*; **'bor·der·land** *usu. fig.* pays *m* limitrophe *ou* frontière.

bore[1] [boː] **1.** *tuyau, arme à feu*: calibre *m*; *min.* trou *m* de sonde *ou* de mine; **2.** creuser.

bore[2] [~] **1.** importun(e *f*) *m*; ennui *m*; **2.** ennuyer, F raser, assommer.

bore[3] [~] mascaret *m*; raz *m* de marée.

bore[4] [~] *prét. de* bear[2].   [*m/pl.*).\

bo·re·al ['boːriəl] boréal (-aux*f*\

bore·dom ['boːdəm] ennui *m*.

bor·er ['boːrə] perceur *m*; outil *m* de perforation.

bo·ric 🜍 ['boːrik] borique.

bor·ing ['boːriŋ] d'alésage; de perçage; à aléser.

born [boːn] *p.p. de* bear[2] naître.

borne [boːn] *p.p. de* bear[2] porter.

bo·ron 🜍 ['boːrɔn] bore *m*.

bor·ough ['bʌrə] bourg *m*; commune *f*; *Am. a.* quartier *m de New York City*; *municipal* ~ ville *f* (avec municipalité).

bor·row ['bɔrou] emprunter (à, *from*); **'bor·row·er** emprunteur (-euse *f*) *m*; **'bor·row·ing** emprunts *m/pl.*; *ling.*: emprunt *m*.

Bor·stal in·sti·tu·tion ['bɔːstl in·sti'tjuːʃn] maison *f* de redressement, école *f* de réforme.

bos·cage ['bɔskidʒ] *poét.* bocage *m*.

bosh F [bɔʃ] bêtises *f/pl.*; blague *f*.

bos·om ['buzəm] sein *m*, giron *m*; poitrine *f*; *fig.* cœur *m*; **~-friend** ami(e *f*) *m* de cœur; intime *mf*.

boss[1] [bɔs] **1.** protubérance *f*; ▲ bosse *f*; ⊕ mamelon *m*; moyeu *m* de l'hélice; **2.** relever en bosse.

boss[2] [~] **1.** F patron *m*, chef *m*; *pol. Am.* grand manitou *m* (*d'un parti*); **2.** mener; *sl.* commander, régenter.

boss·y ['bɔsi] F autoritaire, tyrannique.

Bos·ton ['bɔstən] *cartes, danse*: boston *m*.

bo·tan·ic, bo·tan·i·cal □ [bo'tænik(l)] botanique; **bot·a·nist** ['bɔtənist] botaniste *mf*; **bot·a·nize** ['~naiz] botaniser, herboriser; **'bot·a·ny** botanique *f*.

botch [bɔtʃ] **1.** F travail *m* mal fait; travail *m* bousillé; **2.** bousiller, saboter; rafistoler (*des souliers*); **'botch·er** bousilleur (-euse *f*) *m*; *fig.* savetier *m*.

both [bouθ] tous (toutes *f*) (les) deux; l'un(e) et l'autre; ~ ... *and* ... et ... et ...; ~ *of them* tous (toutes) (les) deux.

both·er F ['bɔðə] **1.** ennui *m*; tracas *m*; **2.** *v/t.* gêner, tracasser; *v/i.* s'inquiéter (de, *about*); ~ *it!* zut!; quelle scie!; **both·er'a·tion** F ennui *m*, vexation *f*; **~!** zut!

bot·tle ['bɔtl] **1.** bouteille *f*; flacon *m*; botte *f* (*de foin*); **2.** mettre en bouteille(s); *fig.* ~ *up* embouteiller (*une flotte etc.*); F étouffer (*des sentiments*); **~d** *beer* bière *f* en canette; **'~-neck** *fig.* circulation: embouteillage *m*; 🍾 col *m* de bouteille; **'~-o·pen·er** ouvre-bouteilles *m/inv.*

bot·tom ['bɔtəm] **1.** *colline, escalier*,

page: bas *m; boîte, mer, cœur, na-vire, jardin*: fond *m; chaussée*: assiette *f; verre, assiette*: dessous *m; classe*: queue *f; chaise*: siège *m; terrain*: creux *m;* F derrière *m,* postérieur *m; at the ~ (of)* au fond (de); au bas bout (de); *fig. (a. at ~)* au fond; *get to the ~ of a matter* aller au fond d'une chose; examiner une chose à fond; *jealousy is at the ~ of it* c'est la jalousie qui en est la cause; **2.** inférieur; en bas; du bas; dernier (-ère *f); ~ drawer* trousseau *m* (de mariage), F trésor *m,* cache *f;* **3.** (re)mettre au fond à fonder (sur, upon); ⚓ toucher le fond; '**bot-tomed** à fond ..., à siège (de)...; '**bot·tom·less** sans fond; *fig.* insondable; '**bot·tom·ry** ⚓ (emprunt *m* à la) grosse aventure *f.*

bough [bau] branche *f,* rameau *m.*

bought [bɔːt] *prét. et p.p.* de buy.

bou·gie ['buːʒiː] bougie *f (a. ✴).*

boul·der ['bouldə] bloc *m* de pierre roulé; *géol.* bloc *m* erratique.

bounce [bauns] **1.** rebond *m;* bond *m;* rebondissement *m;* F jactance *f,* vantardise *f;* bluff *m;* **2.** *v/i.* rebondir; F faire de l'épate; *v/t.* faire rebondir; *~ in (out)* entrer (sortir) en coup de vent; *~ s.o. out of s.th.* obtenir qch. de q. à force de bluff *ou* d'intimidation; **3.** boum!, v(')lan!; '**bounc·er** F vantard *m,* épateur *m;* mensonge *m* effronté; *sl.* chèque *m* sans provision; *Am. sl.* agent *m* du service d'ordre; *Am. sl.* videur *m;* '**bounc·ing** F plein de vie, plein de santé.

bound[1] [baund] **1.** *prét. et p.p.* de bind; **2.** *adj.* obligé; *be ~ to do* être obligé de faire, devoir faire; *I will be ~* je vous le promets.

bound[2] [~] en partance, en route (pour, *for*).

bound[3] [~] **1.** limite *f,* borne *f; in ~s* accès permis (à, *to); out of ~s* accès interdit (à, *to), sp.* hors du jeu; **2.** borner, limiter.

bound[4] [~] **1.** bond *m,* saut *m;* **2.** bondir, sauter; *fig.* sursauter.

bound·a·ry ['baundəri] limite *f;* frontière *f; ~ line* ligne *f* frontière.

bound·less □ ['baundlis] sans bornes; illimité.

boun·te·ous □ ['bauntiəs], **boun-ti·ful** □ ['~tiful] généreux (-euse *f);* libéral (-aux *m/pl.*).

boun·ty ['baunti] générosité *f;* libéralité *f;* don *m;* ✝ indemnité *f;* prime *f (a. ✕, ⚓).*

bou·quet ['bukei] *fleurs etc.,* vin: bouquet *m.*

bour·geois[1] *péj.* ['buəʒwɑː] bourgeois(e *f) (a. su./mf).*

bour·geois[2] *typ.* [bəː'dʒɔis] petit romain *m.* [geoisie *f.*\
bour·geoi·sie [buəʒwɑː'ziː] bour-\
bout [baut] tour *m,* jeux: reprise *f; lutte*: assaut *m; maladie*: accès *m,* attaque *f,* crise *f.*

bo·vine ['bouvain] **1.** bovin; F lourd; **2.** *~s pl.* bovidés *m/pl.*

bov·ver *sl.* ['bɔvə] bagarre *f, sl.* rififi *m.*

bow[1] [bau] **1.** révérence *f;* salut *m;* inclination *f* de tête; **2.** *v/i.* s'incliner (devant, *to*); saluer (q., *to s.o.); fig.* se plier (à, *to); have a ~ing acquaintance* connaître (q.) pour lui dire bonjour; *v/t.* incliner, baisser (*la tête);* fléchir (*le genou);* voûter (*le dos).*

bow[2] [~] ⚓ avant *m; poét.* proue *f;* dirigeable: nez *m.*

bow[3] [bou] arc *m; ruban*: nœud *m;* ♪ archet *m;* **2.** ♪ gouverner l'archet; faire des coups d'archet.

bowd·ler·ize ['baudləraiz] expurger (*un texte*).

bow·els ['bauəlz] *pl.* intestins *m/pl.;* entrailles *f/pl. (a. fig.); fig.* sein *m.*

bow·er ['bauə] tonnelle *f; poét.* boudoir *m;* ⚓ ancre *f* de bossoir.

bow·ie·knife ['bouinaif] couteau *m* de chasse.

bow·ing ♪ ['bouiŋ] manière *f* de gouverner l'archet *m.*

bowl[1] [boul] bol *m,* jatte *f;* sébile *f (de mendiant);* coupe *f; pipe*: fourneau *m; lampe*: culot *m.*

bowl[2] [~] **1.** boule *f; ~s pl.* (jeu *m* de) boules *f/pl.; Am.* (jeu *m* de) quilles *f/pl.;* **2.** *v/t.* rouler; *cricket*: bôler; *~ out* renverser (q., *le guichet de q.); v/i.* rouler rapidement; servir la balle; rouler la boule.

bow-legged ['boulegd] bancal (-als *m/pl.*), aux jambes arquées.

'**bowl·er** *cricket*: bôleur *m;* joueur *m* de boules; (chapeau *m)* melon *m.*

bowl·ing ['boulin] bowling *m;* jeu *m* de boules; *~ al·ley* bowling *m.*

bow-wow ['bau'wau] ouâ-ouâ!

box[1] [bɔks] **1.** boîte *f (a. d'essieu);* coffret *m;* caisse *f; voyage*: malle *f;*

chapeaux: carton *m*; siège *m* (*de cocher*); 🚂 cabine *f* (*de signaleur*), wagon *m* à chevaux; ⊕ moyeu *m* de roue; *mot.* carter *m*; *théâ.* loge *f*; 🚂 banc *m* (*du jury*), barre *f* (*des témoins*); *écurie*: stalle *f*; **2.** emboîter, encaisser; mettre en boîte; *fig.* (*a. ~up*) serrer, renfermer.

box² [~] **1.** *sp.* boxe; ~ *s.o.'s ear* gifler q.; **2.** ~ *on the ear* gifle *f*, claque *f*; '~'calf ⊕, ✝ veau *m* chromé; '**box·er** boxeur *m*, pugiliste *m*.

box·ing ['bɔksiŋ] boxe *f*; ~ *gloves* gants *m*/*pl.* de boxe; ~ *match* match *m* de boxe; ~ *ring* ring *m*.

Box·ing-day ['bɔksiŋdei] lendemain *m* de Noël.

box...: '~-keep·er ouvreuse *f* de loges; '~-of·fice bureau *m* de location; caisse *f*; ~ *hit* (spectacle *m etc.* à) succès *m*; *be a* ~ *hit a.* faire recette; ~ *room Brit.* (cabinet *m* de) débarras *m.*

box(·wood) ['bɔkswud] (bois *m*) [de] buis *m.*)

boy [bɔi] **1.** garçon *m*; *école*: élève *m*; domestique *m*; **2.** garçon ...; *jeune*; ~ *scout* boy-scout *m.*

boy·cott ['bɔikɔt] **1.** boycotter; **2.** mise *f* en interdit; boycottage *m.*

boy·hood ['bɔihud] enfance *f*, (première) jeunesse *f.*

boy·ish □ ['bɔiiʃ] puéril, enfantin, d'enfant, de garçon.

bra F [brɑ:] *see* brassière.

brace [breis] **1.** ⊕ vilebrequin *m*; armature *f*; *mur*: bracon *m*; ancre *f*; ♩, *typ.* accolade *f*; *chasse*: couple *f* (*de perdrix etc.*); laisse *f* (*de lévriers*); paire *f* (*de pistolets*); ⚓ bras *m* (*de vergue*); ~*s pl.* pantalon: bretelles *f*/*pl.*; *tambour*: corde *f*; **2.** ancrer; accolader; tendre (*les jarrets*); ⚓ brasser; *fig.* fortifier.

brace·let ['breislit] bracelet *m.*

brack·en ♣ ['brækn] fougère *f* arborescente.

brack·et ['brækit] **1.** ⚒ corbeau *m*; console *f*; support *m*; *typ.* [ ] crochet *m*; ( ) parenthèse *f*; applique *f* (*électrique, à gaz, etc.*); ⚓ courbaton *m*; support *m*; **2.** mettre entre crochets *etc.*; *fig.* placer ex aequo.

brack·ish ['brækiʃ] saumâtre.

bract ♣ [brækt] bractée *f.*

brad [bræd] pointe *f*, clou *m* étêté.

brag [bræg] **1.** vanterie *f*; **2.** se vanter (de *of*, *about*).

brag·gart ['brægət] fanfaron (*a. su./m*); vantard (*a. su./m*).

Brah·man ['brɑ:mən], *usu.* **Brahmin** ['~min] brahmane *m*, brame *m.*

braid [breid] **1.** *cheveux*: tresse *f*; galon *m* (*a.* ✂); ganse *f*; **2.** tresser; galonner; passementer.

brail ⚓ [breil] cargue *f.*

braille [breil] alphabet *m* des aveugles; système *m* Braille.

brain [brein] **1.** *anat.* cerveau *m*; F cervelle *f* (*a. cuis.*); *p.ext. usu.* ~*s pl.* tête *f*, intelligence *f*, esprit *m*; *have s.th. on the* ~ être hanté par qch.; avoir l'obsession de qch.; F *pick* (*ou suck*) *s.o.'s* ~ exploiter les connaissances de q.; **2.** défoncer le crâne à (*q.*); '~·**child** F idée *f*; invention *f*; ~ *drain* exode *m* des cerveaux; **brained**: *dull-*~ à l'esprit lourd.

brain...: '~-fag épuisement *m* cérébral; ~ *fe·ver* fièvre *f* cérébrale; '~·less sans cervelle, stupide; *fig.* irréfléchi; '~-pan (boîte *f* du) crâne *m*; '~-storm transport *m* au cerveau; **brain's trust** braintrust *m.*

brain...: '~-twist·er problème *m* à faire casser la tête à q.; '~-wash faire (subir) un lavage de cerveau à (*q.*); '~-wash·ing lavage *m* de cerveau; *media etc.*: bourrage *m* de crâne; '~-wave F idée *f* lumineuse; '~-work travail *m* cérébral; '**brain·y** intelligent.

braise [breiz] *cuis.* braiser; **braised** *cuis.* en daube, en casserole.

brake¹ [breik] fougère *f* arborescente *ou* impériale; fourré *m.*

brake² [~] **1.** *lin. etc.*: brisoir *m*; ⊕ frein *m* (*a. fig.*); ~ *fluid* liquide *m* pour freins; ~ *lining* garniture *f* de frein; ~ *pedal* pédale *f* de frein; **2.** briser, broyer (*le lin etc.*); *mot.* serrer le frein; '**brake(s)·man** 🚂 serrefreins *m*/*inv.*; *Am.* chef *m* de train; **brak·ing**: ~ *distance* distance *f* de freinage; ~ *power* puissance *f* de freinage.

bram·ble ♣ ['bræmbl] ronce *f* sauvage; mûrier *m* sauvage.

bran [bræn] son *m.*

branch [brɑ:ntʃ] **1.** *arbre, famille, fleuve*: branche *f*; *arbre, montagnes*: rameau *m*; *fleuve*: bras *m*; 🚂, *route*: embranchement *m*; (*ou local* ~) succursale *f*, filiale *f*; *chief of* ~ chef *m* de service; **2.** (*a.* ~ *out*) se ramifier; (a. ~ off) (se) bifurquer (sur, from), se partager (à, at); **'branch-line** embranchement m; **branch of·fice** agence f; bureau m de quartier; **'branch·y** branchu; rameux (-euse f).

brand [brænd] **1.** brandon m, tison m; fer m chaud; marque f; stigmate m; ⚕ rouille f; poét. flambeau m; poét. glaive m; ~ name marque f (de fabrique); **2.** marquer au fer chaud; fig. flétrir, stigmatiser (q.).

bran·dish ['brændiʃ] brandir.

bran(d)-new ['bræn(d)'nju:] tout (battant) neuf (neuve f).

bran·dy ['brændi] cognac m, eau-de-vie (pl. eaux-de-vie) f.

brash □ ['bræʃ] impertinent, éffronté; présomptueux (-euse f); impétueux (-euse f); indiscret (-ète f).

brass [brɑːs] cuivre m jaune; laiton m; fig. impertinence f, sl. toupet m; F argent m, galette f; ♪ les cuivres m/pl.; ~ band fanfare f; ~ hat ✗ sl. officier m d'état-major; Am. ~ knuckles pl. coup-de-poing (pl. coups-de-poing) m américain; sl. ~ tacks pl. les faits m/pl.; get down to ~ tacks en venir au fait.

bras·sière ['bræsiɛə] soutien-gorge (pl. soutiens-gorge) m.

bras·sy ['brɑːsi] qui ressemble au cuivre; usu. fig. cuivré; sl. effronté.

brat F [bræt] marmot m, mioche mf.

bra·va·do [brə'vɑːdou], pl. -dos, does [‿douz] bravade f.

brave [breiv] **1.** courageux (-euse f), brave; **2.** braver; défier (q.); **'brav·er·y** courage m, bravoure f; vaillance f.

bra·vo ['brɑː'vou] **1.** (pl. -vos, -voes ['‿vouz]) bravo m; spadassin m; **2.** bravo!

brawl [brɔːl] **1.** rixe f, bagarre f, querelle f; **2.** brailler; se chamailler; **'brawl·er** braillard(e f) m; tapageur (-euse f) m.

brawn [brɔːn] cuis. fromage m de cochon; muscles m/pl.; fig. force f corporelle; **'brawn·i·ness** carrure f musclée; force f; **'brawn·y** musculeux (-euse f); musclé (personne).

bray[1] [brei] **1.** âne: braiment m; fanfare f; trompette: son m strident; **2.** braire (âne); émettre un son strident.

bray[2] [‿] broyer, piler.

braze ⊕ [breiz] souder au laiton.

bra·zen □ ['breizn] d'airain; fig. (a. ~-faced) effronté.

bra·zier ['breiziə] personne: chaudronnier m; brasero m (à charbon de bois).

Bra·zil·ian [brə'ziljən] **1.** brésilien (-ne f); **2.** Brésilien(ne f) m.

Bra·zil-nut [brə'zil'nʌt] noix f du Brésil.

breach [briːtʃ] **1.** rupture f; fig. infraction f (à, of); ✗ brèche f; ~ of contract rupture f de contrat; ~ of duty violation f des devoirs; ~ of peace attentat m contre l'ordre public; **2.** v/t. ouvrir une brèche dans; v/i. se rompre.

bread [bred] pain m (a. = subsistance); sl. fric m; ~ and butter pain m beurré; take the ~ out of s.o.'s mouth ôter le pain à q.; know which side one's ~ is buttered savoir d'où vient le vent; **'~-bas·ket** corbeille f à pain; sl. estomac m; **'~-bin, '~-box** boîte f à pain; **'~-crumb** cuis. **1.** paner (une escalope etc.), gratiner (une sole etc.); **2.** miette f; **'~-knife** couteau m à pain.

breadth [bredθ] largeur f (a. de pensées, d'esprit); style: ampleur f; étoffe: lé m.

bread-win·ner ['bredwinə] gagne-pain m/inv.; chef m de famille.

break [breik] **1.** rupture f; fracture f; percée f, brèche f; éclaircie f (à travers les nuages); lacune f; ♱ Am. baisse f (de prix); voitures: break m; voiture f de dressage (des chevaux); billard: série f de carambolages; ⚡ rupture f (du circuit); école: récréation f; voix: mue f (dans la puberté), émotion: altération f; temps: changement m; répit m; ~ of day point m du jour; see brake[2] 1; F a bad ~ une sottise f; F give s.o. a ~ agir loyalement avec q.; mettre q. à l'essai; **2.** [irr.] v/t. briser, casser; enfoncer (une porte); rompre (chose, pain, rangs, cheval); entamer (la peau); résilier (un contrat); faire sauter (la banque); s'évader de (la prison); ⚡ interrompre (le courant), rompre (un circuit); ⚘ défricher; ✗ casser (un officier); violer (une loi, une trêve); ~ down abattre, démolir; ⛏ décomposer; ~ in enfoncer; défoncer (un tonneau); dresser (un cheval); rompre (à, to); ~ up mettre (qch.) en morceaux; disperser (une foule); rompre; démolir; **3.** [irr.] v/i. (se) casser, se briser, se rompre; déferler (vagues); crever (abcès); se dissiper (nuages); se briser, se fendre (cœur); changer (temps); s'altérer (voix); ~ away se détacher (de, from); s'évader (de prison); ~ down échouer (projet); fondre en larmes; mot. avoir une panne; ~ up entrer en vacances; see a. broken; '**break·a·ble** fragile; '**break·age** rupture f; verre: fracture f; ✝ a. ~s pl. casse f; '**break-down** rupture f; service: arrêt m complet; insuccès m; débâcle f de la santé; mot. panne f; ~ lorry dépanneuse f; ~ service service m de dépannage; ~ truck dépanneuse f; '**break·er** casseur (-euse f) m; ♟ brisant m.

break...: ~·**fast** ['brekfəst] **1.** petit déjeuner m; **2.** déjeuner; ~·**neck** ['breiknek] à se casser le cou; '~-**out** évasion f; '~-**through** ✕, a. fig. percée f; fig. a. bond m en avant; découverte f; solution f; réussite f; '~-'**up** dissolution f, fin f; affaissement m; école: entrée f en vacances; temps: changement m; '~-'**wa·ter** brise-lames m/inv.; môle m.

bream icht. [bri:m] brème f.

breast [brest] **1.** sein m; mamelle f; poitrine f; make a clean ~ of it dire ce qu'on a sur la conscience; **2.** affronter; lutter contre, faire front à; '**breast·ed** à poitrine ...

breast...: '~-'**feed** donner le sein à (un bébé); élever au sein; '~-**pin** épingle f de cravate; '~-**stroke** brasse f sur le ventre; '~-'**work** ✕ parapet m.

breath [breθ] haleine f, souffle m, respiration f; bad ~ mauvaise haleine f; under (ou below) one's ~ à voix basse, à mi-voix; '**breath·a·lyse** mot. [~əlaiz] faire subir l'alcootest à (q.); **breath·a·lys·er** ['~əlaizə] alcootest m; **breathe** [bri:ð] v/i. respirer, souffler; fig. vivre; v/t. respirer, exhaler (un soupir); murmurer (une prière); aspirer (l'air, un son); '**breath·er** F moment m de repos; brin m d'air; répit m.

breath·ing ['bri:ðiŋ] **1.** vivant (portrait); **2.** respiration f; souffle m; '~-**space**, '~-**time** répit m; intervalle m de repos.

breath·less ☐ ['breθlis] essoufflé;

fig. fiévreux (-euse f); '**breath·less-ness** essoufflement m.

breath-tak·ing ['breðteikiŋ] F ahurissant.

bred [bred] prét. et p.p. de breed 2.

breech ⊕ [bri:tʃ] fusil, canon: culasse f, tonnerre m; **breech·es** ['~iz] pl.: (a pair of)~ (une) culotte f; F (un) pantalon m; '**breech-load·er** ⊕ fusil m se chargeant par la culasse.

breed [bri:d] **1.** race f; péj. espèce f; Am. métis(se f) m; **2.** [irr.] v/t. produire, engendrer; élever (du bétail); v/i. se reproduire; multiplier; '**breed·er** reproducteur (-trice f) m; éleveur m (d'animaux); '**breed·ing** reproduction f; élevage m (d'animaux); bonnes manières f/pl.

breeze[1] [bri:z] **1.** brise f; F querelle f; altercation f; **2.** Am. F s'en aller (à la hâte).

breeze[2] zo. [~] œstre m.

breeze[3] ⊕ [~] braise f de houille; fraisil m.

breez·y ['bri:zi] venteux (-euse f); jovial (-als, -aux m/pl.) (personne).

breth·ren eccl. ['breðrin] pl. frères m/pl.; my ~ mes très chers frères.

breve [bri:v] syllabe: brève f.

bre·vet ✕ ['brevit] brevet m (avancement d'un officier sans augmentation de solde); ~ rank grade m honoraire; ~ colonel lieutenant-colonel m faisant fonction de colonel.

bre·vi·ar·y eccl. ['bri:vjəri] bréviaire m.

brev·i·ty ['breviti] brièveté f.

brew [bru:] **1.** v/t./i. brasser; fig. (se) tramer; v/i. s'infuser; couver (orage, tempête); **2.** brassage m; brassin m; infusion f; '**brew·age** poét. see brew 2; '**brew·er** brasseur m; '**brew·er·y** brasserie f.

bri·ar ['braiə] see brier[1] et brier[2].

bribe [braib] **1.** paiement m illicite; **2.** corrompre, acheter (pour que, to); '**brib·er** corrupteur (-trice f) m; '**brib·er·y** corruption f; ⚖ subornation f (d'un témoin); ⚖ ~ and corruption corruption f; be open to ~ être corruptible.

bric-a-brac ['brikəbræk] bric-à-brac m.

brick [brik] **1.** brique f; F a regular ~ un chic type; sl. drop a ~ faire une gaffe; **2.** briqueter; ~ up murer (une fenêtre etc.); '~-**bat** briqueton m; '~-**kiln** four m à briques; '~-'**lay·er**

maçon *m*; '**~-works** *usu. sg.* briqueterie *f*; '**brick·y** de *ou* en brique; comme une brique.

brid·al ['braidl] **1.** □ nuptial (-aux *m/pl.*), de noce(s); **2.** *usu. poét.* noce *f*, -s *f/pl.*

bride [braid] future *f* (*sur le point de se marier*); (nouvelle) mariée *f*; '**~-groom** futur *m* (*sur le point de se marier*); (nouveau) marié *m*; '**brides·maid** demoiselle *f* d'honneur; '**brides·man** garçon *m* d'honneur; **bride-to-'be** future fiancée *f ou* épouse *f*.

bride·well *Brit.* ['braidwəl] maison *f* de correction.

bridge[1] [bridʒ] **1.** pont *m*; ♱ passerelle *f*; **2.** jeter un pont sur; *fig.* relier, combler.

bridge[2] [~] *cartes*: bridge *m*.

bridge...: '**~-head** tête *f* de pont; '**~-work** bridge-work *m* (*dentaire*).

bri·dle ['braidl] **1.** bride *f*; *fig.* frein *m*; **2.** *v/t.* brider (*a. fig.*); *v/i.* (*a. ~ up*) redresser la tête; se rebiffer; '**~-path** piste *f* cavalière.

bri·doon [bri'du:n] bridon *m*.

brief [bri:f] **1.** □ bref (brève *f*); court; passager (-ère *f*); **2.** dossier *m* (*d'avocat*); abrégé *m*; *p.ext.* ordres *m/pl.*; *eccl.* bref *m*; hold a ~ for défendre; prendre le parti de; ᵗᵗ take a ~ for accepter de représenter (*q.*) en justice; **3.** ᵗᵗ confier une cause à (*un avocat*); ⚔ munir d'instructions; fournir des directives à; '**~-bag**, '**~-case** serviette *f*; '**brief·ing** instructions *f/pl.*; séance *f* d'information; '**brief·ness** brièveté *f*.

bri·er[1] ♀ ['braiə] bruyère *f* arborescente; églantier *m*.

bri·er[2] [~] (*a. ~ pipe*) pipe *f* en bruyère.

brig ♱ [brig] brick *m*.

bri·gade ⚔ [bri'geid] **1.** brigade *f*; **2.** embrigader; **brig·a·dier** [brigə-'diə] général *m* de brigade.

brig·and ['brigənd] brigand *m*, bandit *m*; '**brig·and·age** brigandage *m*; briganderie *f*.

bright □ [brait] brillant; éclatant; vif (vive *f*); clair; animé; F intelligent; '**bright·en** *v/t.* faire briller; fourbir (*un métal*); *fig.* égayer; *v/i.* s'éclaircir; *yeux*: s'allumer; '**bright·ness** éclat *m*; clarté *f*; vivacité *f*; intensité *f*; intelligence *f*; *télév.* ~

control (dispositif *m* de) réglage *m* de la luminosité.

brill *icht.* [bril] barbue *f*.

bril·lian·cy ['briljənsi] brillant *m*; éclat *m*; '**bril·liant 1.** □ brillant, éclatant; lumineux (-euse *f*) (*idée*); **2.** brillant *m*.

brim [brim] **1.** bord *m*; **2.** *v/t.* remplir jusqu'au bord; *v/i.* déborder (de, with); '**~-ful**, '**~-full** plein jusqu'aux bords; débordant (de, of).

brim·stone ['brimstən] 🜍 soufre *m* (brut); *zo.* (*ou ~ butterfly*) papillon *m* citrin.

brin·dle(d) ['brindl(d)] tacheté, tavelé.

brine [brain] **1.** saumure *f*; eau *f* salée; *poét.* mer *f*, océan *m*; **2.** saumurer.

bring [briŋ] [*irr.*] amener; apporter; intenter (*un procès*); avancer (*des arguments*); ~ *about* amener, occasionner; (*a. ~ to pass*) entraîner; ~ *along* amener (*q.*), apporter (*qch.*); ~ *down* faire baisser (*le prix*); avilir (*les prix*); *théâ.* ~ *down the house* faire crouler la salle; ~ *forth* produire; mettre au monde; mettre bas (*des petits*); ~ *forward* (faire) avancer; produire; ✝ reporter; ~ *s.th. home to s.o.* faire sentir qch. à q.; prouver qch. contre q.; ~ *in* introduire; rapporter (*une somme*); ~ *in guilty* déclarer coupable; ~ *off* ramener à terre *ou* à bord; réussir; ~ *on* occasionner; faire pousser (*une plante*); ~ *out* apporter dehors; publier; mettre en relief; faire valoir; lancer (*une actrice etc.*); ~ *round* ramener à la vie; convertir (*q.*); ~ *s.o. to* (*inf.*) amener q. à (*inf.*); ♱ ~ *to* mettre en panne; *s.o. to himself* faire reprendre connaissance à q.; ranimer q.; ~ *under* assujettir; ~ *up* approcher; élever (*un enfant*); citer en justice; vomir; (faire) monter; ♱ mouiller.

bring·er ['briŋə] porteur (-euse *f*) *m*.

brink [briŋk] bord *m*; '**~-man·ship** politique *f* du bord du gouffre.

brin·y ['braini] **1.** saumâtre, salé; **2.** F mer *f*.

bri·quette [bri'ket], **bri·quet** ['bri-kit] briquette *f*; aggloméré *m*.

brisk [brisk] **1.** □ vif (vive *f*), alerte, plein d'entrain, animé; *feu:* vif (vive *f*), ⚔ nourri; *air:* vivifiant; **2.** (*usu. ~ up*) (s')animer.

bris·ket ['briskit] poitrine *f* (*de bœuf*).

brisk·ness ['brisknis] vivacité *f*, entrain *m*; *air*: fraîcheur *f*.

bris·tle ['brisl] **1.** soie *f*; *barbe*: poil *m* raide; **2.** (*souv.* ~ *up*) se hérisser; F se rebiffer (*personne*); *fig.* ~ *with* être hérissé de; '**bris·tled**, '**bris·tly** hérissé; poilu; garni de soies.

Bri·tan·nic [bri'tænik] britannique.

Brit·ish ['britiʃ] **1.** anglais; britannique; **2.** *the* ~ *pl.* les Britanniques *m/pl.*; '**Brit·ish·er** *surt. Am.* natif (-ive *f*) *m* de la Grande-Bretagne.

Brit·on *hist., poét.* ['britən] Anglais(e *f*) *m*.

brit·tle ['britl] fragile, cassant; cendreux (-euse *f*) (*acier*); '**brit·tle·ness** fragilité *f etc.*

broach [broutʃ] **1.** broche *f*; △ flèche *f*, aiguille *f*; **2.** percer, entamer (*un fût*); aborder (*un sujet*); entrer en (*matière*).

broad □ [brɔːd] large; plein, grand (*jour*); peu voilé (*avis, allusion*); hardi, risqué (*histoire*); épanoui (*sourire*); prononcé (*accent*); ~*ly speaking* généralement parlant; '~-**axe** ⊕ doloire *f*; '~-**cast 1.** ✗ semé à la volée, *fig.* (radio)diffusé; répandu; **2.** (*irr.* [*cast*]) *v/t.* ✗ semer à la volée; *fig.* répandre; radiodiffuser; transmettre; *v/i.* parler *etc.* à la radio; ~(*ing*) *station* poste *m* émetteur; station *f* de radio-diffusion; **3.** émission *f*; '~-**cloth** drap *m* noir fin; *Am.* popeline *f*; '**broad·en** (s')élargir; '**broad-'mind·ed** tolérant; à l'esprit large; '**broad·ness** largeur *f*; grossièreté *f*; ~ *of speech* accent *m* prononcé. **broad...**: '~-**sheet** placard *m*; *hist.* canard *m*; '~-**side** ⚓ flanc *m*, travers *m*; bordée *f*, feu *m* de travers; *a. see* broadsheet; '~-**sword** latte *f*; sabre *m*.

bro·cade ✝ [bro'keid] brocart *m*; **bro'cad·ed** broché; de brocart.

broc·co·li ♣ ['brɔkəli] brocoli *m*.

bro·chure [brou'ʃjuə] brochure *f*.

brock *zo.* [brɔk] blaireau *m*.

brogue [broug] soulier *m* de golf; accent *m* (*surt.* irlandais).

broil [brɔil] **1.** querelle *f*, bagarre *f*; **2.** griller (*a. fig.*); (faire) cuire sur le gril; ~*ing* brûlant; torride; '**broil·er** gril *m*; poulet *m* à rôtir.

broke [brouk] *prét. de* break 2.

bro·ken ['broukn] *p.p. de* break 2; ~ *health* santé *f* délabrée *ou* ruinée; ~ *stones pl.* pierraille *f*, cailloutis *m*; ~ *weather* temps *m* variable; *speak* ~ *English* écorcher l'anglais; '~-'**heart·ed** navré de douleur; au cœur brisé; '**bro·ken·ly** par saccades; sans suite; à mots entre-coupés; '**bro·ken-'wind·ed** *vét.* poussif (-ive *f*).

bro·ker ['broukə] ✝ courtier *m*; agent *m* de change; '**bro·ker·age** ✝ courtage *m*; frais *m/pl.* de courtage.

bro·mide ⚗ ['broumaid] bromure *m*; *sl.* banalité *f*; **bro·mine** ⚗ ['~miːn] brome *m*.

bron·chi·al *anat.* ['brɔŋkjəl] bronchial (-aux *m/pl.*); des bronches.

bron·chi·tis ⚕ [brɔŋ'kaitis] bronchite *f*.

Bronx cheer *Am. sl.* ['brɔŋks'tʃiə] sifflement *m* (*de mépris*).

bronze [brɔnz] **1.** bronze *m*; **2.** de *ou* en bronze; **3.** (se) bronzer; (se) brunir.

brooch [broutʃ] broche *f*, épingle *f*.

brood [bruːd] **1.** couvée *f*; volée *f*; F enfants *m/pl.*; ~-*hen* couveuse *f*; ~-*mare* poulinière *f*; **2.** couver; *v/i.* F broyer du noir; *v/t.* F ruminer (*une idée*); *fig.* planer sur; '**brood·er** couveuse *f* (*Am.* artificielle).

brook[1] [bruk] ruisseau *m*.

brook[2] [~] *usu. au nég.* souffrir.

brook·let ['bruklit] ruisselet *m*.

broom ♣ [bruːm] genêt *m*; [brum] balai *m*; ~-*stick* ['brumstik] manche *m* à balai.

broth [brɔθ] bouillon *m*.

broth·el ['brɔθl] bordel *m*, maison *f* de tolérance.

broth·er ['brʌðə] frère *m*; *younger* ~ cadet *m*; ~*hood* ['~hud] fraternité *f*; confraternité *f*; *eccl.* confrérie *f*; '~-*in-law* beau-frère (*pl.* beaux-frères) *m*; '**broth·er·ly** fraternel(le *f*).

brougham ['bruːəm] coupé *m*; *mot.* coupé *m* (de ville).

brought [brɔːt] *prét. et p.p. de* bring; ~-*in capital* capital *m* d'apport.

brow [brau] sourcil *m*; arcade *f* sourcilière; front *m*; *précipice*: bord *m*; *colline*: croupe *f*; '~-*beat* [*irr* (*beat*)] rabrouer; rudoyer.

brown [braun] **1.** brun, marron(ne

f); châtain (*cheveux*); jaune (*chaussures*); ~ *bread* pain *m* bis; ~ *paper* papier *m* gris; *be in a ~ study* être plongé dans ses réflexions; **2.** brun *m*, marron *m*; **3.** (se) brunir; **brown·ie** ['ˌᵻi] farfadet *m*; '**brown·ish** brunâtre; '**brown·ness** couleur *f* brune; '**brown·stone** *Am.* **1.** grès *m* de construction; **2.** ... des gens prospères.

browse [brauz] **1.** jeunes pousses *f/pl.*; **2.** (*a. ~ on*) brouter, paître; *fig.* feuilleter (*des livres*).

bruise [bruːz] **1.** bleu *m*, meurtrissure *f*; *fruit:* talure *f*; **2.** (se) meurtrir; *v/t.* broyer (*une substance*); '**bruis·er** *sl.* boxeur *m* (brutal).

Brum·ma·gem ['brʌmədʒəm] de camelote, en toc.

bru·nette [bruːˈnet] brunette *f*.

brunt [brʌnt] choc *m*; attaque *f*; violence *f*; *the ~* of le plus fort de.

brush [brʌʃ] **1.** brosse *f*; pinceau *m*; *renard:* queue *f*; coup *m* de brosse (*aux vêtements*); échauffourée *f* (*avec un ennemi*); ⚡ faisceau *m* de rayons; *commutateur:* balai *m*; *Am. see ~wood; see backwoods; give s.o. a ~* brosser q.; *have a ~ with s.o.* froisser les opinions de q.; **2.** *v/t.* brosser; balayer (*un tapis etc.*); frôler, brosser légèrement; ~ *away* (*ou off*) enlever (*qch.*) d'un coup de brosse *ou* de balai; essuyer (*des larmes*); écarter (*un avis, une pensée*); ~ *down* donner un coup de brosse à (*q.*); ~ *up* donner un coup de brosse à (*qch.*); *fig.* se remettre à, dérouiller; *v/i.* ~ *against* frôler *ou* froisser (*q.*) en passant; ~ *by* (*ou past*) passer rapidement auprès de (*q.*); frôler (*q.*) en passant; '**~·off** *sl.:* *give s.o. the ~* envoyer promener q.; '**~·wood** broussailles *f/pl.*; bois *m* taillis; menu bois *m*.

brusque ☐ [brusk] brusque; *ton:* bourru.

Brus·sels ['brʌslz]: ⚘ ~ *sprouts pl.* choux *m/pl.* de Bruxelles.

bru·tal ☐ ['bruːtl] brutal (-aux *m/pl.*); de brute; *animal* (-aux *m/pl.*); **bru·tal·i·ty** [bruːˈtæliti] brutalité *f*; **bru·tal·ize** ['bruːtəlaiz] abrutir; animaliser; **brute** [bruːt] **1.** brut; vif (vive *f*), brutal (-aux *m/pl.*) (*force*); **2.** bête *f* brute; brute *f* (*a. fig.* = *homme brutal*); F animal *m*; *a ~ of a ... un(e) ... de chien*; '**brut-**

ish ☐ *see brute 1*; '**brut·ish·ness** bestialité *f*; abrutissement *m*.

bub·ble ['bʌbl] **1.** bulle *f*; *fig.* projet *m* chimérique; tromperie *f*; **2.** bouillonner; glouglouter (*en versant*).

buc·ca·neer [bʌkəˈniə] **1.** F pirate *m*; flibustier *m* (*a. hist*); **2.** faire le boucanier; flibuster.

buck [bʌk] **1.** *zo.* daim *m*; chevreuil *m*; mâle (*du lapin etc.*); *Am. sl.* dollar *m*; *Am.* F *pass the ~* passer la décision (à, to); se débrouiller sur le voisin; **2.** *Am.* F résister, opposer; *Am.* F chercher à prendre le dessus de; *Am.* ~ *for* viser; F ~ *up* (se) ragaillardir.

buck·et ['bʌkit] seau *m*; *a mere drop in the ~* une goutte d'eau dans la mer; *sl. kick the ~* casser sa pipe (= *mourir*); **2.** surmener (*un cheval*); '**~·ful** plein seau *m*; '**~-shop** bureau *m* d'un courtier marron.

buck·le ['bʌkl] **1.** boucle *f*, agrafe *f*; **2.** *v/t.* boucler; attacher; ceindre (*l'épée*); *v/i.* ⊕ (se) gondoler, arquer; se voiler (*tôle*); ~ *to v/t.* s'appliquer à (*un travail*); *v/i.* s'y atteler; '**buck·ler** bouclier *m*.

buck·ram ['bʌkrəm] bougran *m*; *fig.* raideur *f*.

buck...: '**~·skin** (peau *f* de) daim *m*; '**~·wheat** ⚘ blé *m* noir.

bud [bʌd] **1.** ⚘ bourgeon *m*; œil (*pl.* yeux) *m*; bouton *m*; *fig.* germe *m*; *Am.* débutante *f*; *sl.* jeune fille *f*; *in ~* qui bourgeonne; *fig. in the ~* en germe, en herbe; **2.** *v/t.* écussonner; *v/i.* bourgeonner; boutonner (*fleur*); ~*ding lawyer* juriste *m* en herbe.

bud·dy *Am.* F ['bʌdi] ami *m*; copain *m*.

budge [bʌdʒ] *v/i.* bouger, céder, reculer; *v/t.* bouger. [*che f.*\]

bud·ger·i·gar ['bʌdʒərigɑː] perru- [*che f.*]

budg·et ['bʌdʒit] collection *f*; recueil *m*; budget *m*; *usu. fig.* plein sac *m*; *draft ~* budget *m* du ménage; *open the ~* présenter le budget; '**budg·et·ar·y** budgétaire.

buff[1] [bʌf] **1.** (peau *f* de) buffle *m*; cuir *m* épais; couleur *f* chamois; *in (one's) ~* tout nu; **2.** jaune clair; **3.** polir (au buffle).

buff[2] F [~] enthousiaste *m/f*, mordu(e *f*) *m*.

buf·fa·lo *zo.* ['bʌfələu], *pl.* **-loes** ['~louz] buffle *m*; *Am.* F bison *m*.

buff·er ['bʌfə] 🔧 tampon *m*; (*a.* ~ *stop*) butoir *m*; tampon *m* d'arrêt; *sl.* vieux bonze *m*; ~ *state* état *m* tampon.

buf·fet¹ ['bʌfit] **1.** coup *m* (de poing); *poét.* soufflet *m*; **2.** flanquer une torgn(i)ole à (*q.*); bourrer (*q.*) de coups.

buf·fet² [*meuble*: 'bʌfit; *autres sens*: 'bufei] buffet *m*.

buf·foon [bʌ'fu:n] bouffon *m*, paillasse *m*; **buf'foon·er·y** bouffonneries *f/pl.*

bug [bʌg] punaise *f*; *Am.* insecte *m*; bacille *m*; loup *m* (de fabrication); *Am. sl.* fou *m*, folle (*e f*) *m*; F appareil *m* d'écoute; microphone *m* clandestin; **bug·a·boo** ['~əbu:], **'bug·bear** objet *m* d'épouvante; F cauchemar *m*; F bête *f* noire; **'bug·ger** *sl.* pédéraste *m*; con *m*, salaud *m*; bougre *m*; *poor* ~! pauvre bougre!; *a* ~ *of a job* un boulot infernal; *little* ~ petit bonhomme; **'bug·ging de·vice** appareil *m* d'écoute (clandestine); **bug·gy** ['bʌgi] boghei *m*.   [*m*.]

bu·gle¹ ['bju:gl] (*a.* ~-*horn*) clairon⌡

bu·gle² [~] verroterie *f* noire.

bu·gler 🪖 ['bju:glə] (sonneur *m* de) clairon *m*.

buhl [bu:l] *meubles*: boul(l)e *m*.

build [bild] **1.** [*irr.*] bâtir; édifier; construire; *fig.* fonder (sur, [*up*]on); faire construire; ~ *in* murer, boucher; ~ *up* affermir (*la santé*); bâtir; *be* ~*ing* être en construction; **2.** construction *f*; taille *f*; **'build·er** entrepreneur *m* en bâtiments; constructeur *m*; **'build·ing** construction *f*; bâtiment *m*; maison *f*; édifice *m*; *attr.* de construction; ~ *contractor* entrepreneur *m* en *ou* de bâtiment(s); ~ *site* chantier *m*; ~ (*p*)*lot* terrain *m* à bâtir; ~-*society* *Brit.* coopérative *f* de construction; ~ *trade* industrie *f* du bâtiment; **'build-up** construction *f*; échafaudage *m*.

built [bilt] **1.** *prét. et p.p.* de **build** 1; **2.** *adj.* ... bâti; de construction ...; **'built-'up** **'a·re·a** agglomération *f* urbaine.

bulb [bʌlb] 🌱 bulbe *m*, oignon *m*; *thermomètre, a.* 💡 ampoule *f*; **'bulb·ous** 🌱 bulbeux (-euse *f*).

Bul·gar ['bʌlgɑ:] Bulgare *mf*; **Bul·gar·i·an** [bʌl'gɛəriən] **1.** bulgare; **2.** *ling.* bulgare *m*; Bulgare *mf*.

bulge [bʌldʒ] **1.** bombement *m*; saillie *f*; 🔱, *a.fig.* hausse *f*; **2.** bomber; faire saillie; se déjeter (*mur etc.*).

bulk [bʌlk] masse *f*, grosseur *f*, volume *m*; *fig.* gros *m* (*a.* 🔱); 🔱 charge *f*; chargement *m* arrimé; *in* ~ en bloc, en vrac; *in the* ~ en bloc, en gros; ~ *goods* marchandise *f ou* marchandises *f/pl.* en masse; **'~·head** 🔱 cloison *f*; **'bulk·i·ness** grosseur *f*; volume *m* (excessif); **'bulk·y** gros(se *f*); volumineux (-euse *f*), encombrant.

bull¹ [bul] **1.** taureau *m*; 🔱 *sl.* haussier *m*; F ~ *session* réunion *f* d'hommes; **2.** 🔱 *sl.* spéculer à la hausse; chercher à faire hausser (*les cours*).

bull² *eccl.* [~] bulle *f*.

bull³ [~] bévue *f*; F, *a. Am.* bêtises *f/pl.*; *Irish* ~ inconséquence *f*.

bull·dog ['buldɔg] bouledogue *m*; chienne *f* de bouledogue; F *univ.* appariteur *m*.

bull·doze *Am.* F ['buldouz] intimider; **'bull·doz·er** ⊕ machine *f* à cintrer; bulldozer *m*.

bul·let ['bulit] *fusil, revolver*: balle *f*.

bul·le·tin ['bulitin] bulletin *m*, communiqué *m*; *radio*: informations *f/pl.*; *Am.* ~ *board* tableau *m* d'affichage (*des nouvelles du jour*).

bul·let-proof ['bulitpru:f] blindé, pare-balles *inv.*

bull...: '~-**fight** course *f* de taureaux; '~-**finch** *orn.* bouvreuil *m*; haie *f* (*avec fossé*); '~-**frog** *zo.* grenouille *f* mugissante; '~-**head·ed** F entêté.

bul·lion ['buljən] or *m* en barres; or *m* *ou* argent *m* en lingot; 🪖 franges *f/pl.*

bull·ock ['bulək] bœuf *m*.

bull·pen *Am.* ['bul'pen] F salle *f* de détention.

bull's-eye ['bulzai] 🔱 (verre *m* de) hublot *m*; *cible*: noir *m*, centre *m*, blanc *m*; ~ *pane* carreau *m* à boudine.

bull·shit V ['bulʃit] merde *f*.

bul·ly¹ ['buli] **1.** brute *f*, brutal *m*, tyran *m*; *école*: brimeur *m*; bravache *m*; **2.** bravache; *surt. Am.* F fameux (-euse *f*); *a. int.* bravo; **3.** brutaliser, rudoyer, intimider.

bul·ly² [~] (*a.* ~ *beef*) bœuf *m* en conserve; F singe *m*.

bul·rush 🌱 ['bulrʌʃ] jonc *m*.

bul·wark ['bulwək] *usu. fig.* rempart *m*; ~s *pl.* ⚓ pavois *m*.

bum[1] *sl.* [bʌm] derrière *m*, cul *m*.

bum[2] *Am.* F [~] **1.** fainéant *m*; chemineau *m*; (*be*) *go on the* ~ fainéanter; vagabonder; **2.** *v/t.* mendier; resquiller (*le trajet*); **3.** misérable.

bum·ble-bee ['bʌmblbi:] bourdon *m*.

bum·boat ['bʌmbout] bateau *m* à provisions.

bump [bʌmp] **1.** choc *m*; coup *m*, heurt *m*; *fig.* bosse *f* (de, of); **2.** (se) cogner; (se) heurter; *v/t.* entrer en collision avec (*qch.*); *Am. sl.* ~ *off* assassiner, supprimer (*q.*); *v/i.* ~ *against* buter contre; F ~ *into s.o.* rencontrer q. par hasard.

bump·er ['bʌmpə] **1.** verre *m* plein; rasade *f*, *mot.* pare-chocs *m/inv.*; *théâ.* (*a.* ~ *house*) salle *f* comble *ou* bondée; ~ *sticker* autocollant *m*; **2.** plein ...; magnifique; F exceptionnel(le *f*) (*récolte*).

bump·kin ['bʌmpkin] rustre *m*.

bump·tious □ F ['bʌmpʃəs] arrogant, présomptueux (-euse *f*), suffisant.

bump·y ['bʌmpi] cahoteux (-euse *f*); couvert de bosses; 🟰 chahuté.

bun [bʌn] petit pain *m* au lait; *cheveux*: chignon *m*.

bunch [bʌntʃ] **1.** botte *f*; *fleurs*: bouquet *m*; *personnes*: groupe *m*; ~ *of grapes* grappe *f* de raisin; **2.** (se) grouper; *v/t.* lier.

bun·combe *Am.* ['bʌnkəm] blague *f*; paroles *f/pl.* vides.

bun·dle ['bʌndl] **1.** paquet *m*; ballot *m*; *bois*: fagot *m*; **2.** *v/t.* (*a.* ~ *up*) empaqueter; F ~ *away ou off* se débarrasser de (*q.*); *v/i.* ~ *off* s'en aller sans cérémonie.

bung [bʌŋ] **1.** *fût*: bondon *m*; **2.** bondonner (*un fût*); boucher (*un trou*); F ~ *ed up* poché (*œil*).

bun·ga·low ['bʌŋgəlou] bungalow *m*.

bung-hole ['bʌŋhoul] bonde *f*.

bun·gle ['bʌŋgl] **1.** gâchis *m*; maladresse *f*; **2.** bousiller; *sl.* rater; '**bun·gler** bousilleur (-euse *f*) *m*; maladroit(e *f*) *m*; '**bun·gling 1.** □ maladroit(e *f*); **2.** *see* bungle 1.

bun·ion 🟰 ['bʌnjən] oignon *m* (*callosité au gros orteil*).

bunk[1] *surt. Am. sl.* [bʌŋk] blague *f*; balivernes *f/pl.*

bunk[2] [~] ⚓, 🚂 couchette *f*.

bunk·er ⚓ ['bʌŋkə] **1.** soute *f* (*à charbon*); **2.** mettre en soute; F *fig.* *be* ~*ed* se trouver dans une impasse.

bun·kum ['bʌŋkəm] *see* buncombe.

bun·ny ['bʌni] F Jeannot lapin *m*.

bunt *Am.* [bʌnt] *baseball*: coup *m* qui arrête la balle.

bun·ting[1] *orn.* ['bʌntiŋ] bruant *m*.

bun·ting[2] [~] *tex.* étamine *f*; *p.ext.* pavillons *m/pl.*

buoy ⚓ [bɔi] **1.** bouée *f*; **2.** baliser (*le chenal*); (*usu.* ~ *up*) faire flotter; *fig.* soutenir, appuyer.

buoy·an·cy ['bɔiənsi] flottabilité *f*; *fig.* élasticité *f* de caractère; *fig.* entrain *m*; '**buoy·ant** □ flottable; léger (-ère *f*); *fig.* allègre, optimiste; *fig.* élastique (*pas*); ♵ soutenu.

bur 🟰 [bə:] capsule *f* épineuse; teigne *f* (*de bardane*); *personne*: crampon *m*.

Bur·ber·ry ['bə:bəri] imperméable *m* (*marque Burberry*).

bur·bot *icht.* ['bə:bət] lotte *f*, barbot *m*.

bur·den[1] ['bə:dn] refrain *m*.

bur·den[2] ['bə:dn] **1.** fardeau *m*, charge *f* (*a.* 🔧); ⚓ charge *f*, contenance *f*; *discours*: substance *f*; **2.** charger; *fig.* accabler; '**bur·den·some** onéreux (-euse *f*); fâcheux (-euse *f*).

bur·dock 🟰 ['bə:dɔk] bardane *f*.

bu·reau [bjuə'rou], *pl.* **-reaux** [~'rouz] *surt. Am.* bureau *m*; service *m* (*du gouvernement*); *meuble*: secrétaire *m*, bureau *m*; *Am.* commode *f*; **bu·reauc·ra·cy** [~'rɔkrəsi] bureaucratie *f*; **bu·reau·crat** ['bjuərokræt] bureaucrate *mf*; **bu·reau-'crat·ic** (~*ally*) bureaucratique; **bu·reauc·ra·tize** [bjuə'rɔkrətaiz] bureaucratiser.

bur·gee ⚓ [bə:'dʒi:] guidon *m*.

bur·geon *poét.* ['bə:dʒən] **1.** bourgeon *m*; bouton *m*; **2.** bourgeonner; commencer à éclore.

bur·gess ['bə:dʒis] bourgeois *m*, citoyen *m*; *hist.* représentant *m* d'un bourg (*au Parlement*).

burgh *écos.* ['bʌrə] bourg *m*.

bur·glar ['bə:glə] cambrioleur *m* (*nocturne*); ~ *alarm* sonnerie *f* d'alarme *ou* antivol; **bur·glar·i·ous** □ [bə:'glɛəriəs] de cambriolage; '**bur·glar-proof** à l'épreuve de l'infraction; incrochetable (*serrure*); **bur-**

gla·ry [ˈ∖əri] vol *m* nocturne avec effraction; **bur·gle** [ˈbəːgl] cambrioler.

bur·gun·dy [ˈbəːgəndi] (vin *m* de) bourgogne *m*.

bur·i·al [ˈberiəl] enterrement *m*; '∖**ground** cimetière *m*.

bu·rin ⊕ [ˈbjuərin] burin *m*.

burke [bəːk] étouffer (*un scandale*); escamoter (*une question*).

burl *tex.* [bəːl] nope *f*.

bur·lap [ˈbəːləp] toile *f* d'emballage.

bur·lesque [bəːˈlesk] **1.** burlesque; **2.** burlesque *m*; parodie *f*; **3.** travestir, parodier; tourner (*qch.*) en ridicule.   [dement bâti.⟩

bur·ly [ˈbəːli] de forte carrure; soli-⟩

Bur·mese [bəːˈmiːz] **1.** birman; **2.** Birman(e *f*) *m*.

burn [bəːn] **1.** brûlure *f*; **2.** [*irr.*] brûler; '**burn·er** brûleur (-euse *f*) *m*; bec *m* de gaz; '**burning** □ brûlant, ardent.

bur·nish [ˈbəːniʃ] brunir, (se) polir; '**bur·nish·er** *personne*: brunisseur (-euse *f*) *m*; ⊕ brunissoir *m*.

burnt [bəːnt] *prét. et p.p. de burn* 2; ∖ *almond* amande *f* griilée; praline *f*; *mot.* ∖ *gas* gaz *m* d'échappement; ∖ *offering* holocauste *m*.

burr [bəː] **1.** r *m* de la gorge; **2.** prononcer l'r de la gorge.

bur·row [ˈbʌrou] **1.** terrier *m* (*de lapin, de renard*); **2.** *v/t.* creuser; *v/i.* se terrer; *fig.* fouiller.

bur·sa·ry [ˈbəːsəri] bourse *f* (*d'études*).

burst [bəːst] **1.** éclat(ement) *m*; jaillissement *m*; coup *m*; *fig.* poussée *f*; rafale *f*; emballage *m* (*de vitesse*); **2.** [*irr.*] *v/i.* éclater, exploser; crever (*abcès, pneu, rire, boîte, etc.*); *fig.* déborder (de, with); ♀ éclore (*bouton*); s'épanouir (*fleur*); ∖ *from* s'affranchir de; ∖ *forth* (*ou* out) jaillir; s'exclamer; apparaître (*soleil*); ∖ *into a gallop* prendre le galop; ∖ *into flame* s'enflammer brusquement; ∖ *into leaf* (se) feuiller; ∖ *into tears* fondre en larmes; ∖ *out laughing* éclater de rire; *v/t.* faire éclater; enfoncer (*une porte*).   [tenance *f*.⟩

bur·then ⚓ [ˈbəːðn] charge *f*, con-⟩

bur·y [ˈberi] enterrer, ensevelir; inhumer; ⚓ immerger; *fig.* plonger.

bus F [bʌs] **1.** autobus *m*; *sl.* bagnole *f*; *sl. fig.* miss the ∖ laisser échapper l'occasion; *Am.* ∖ *boy*

garçon *m* de restaurant qui débarrasse la table après le repas; ∖ *driver* conducteur *m* d'autobus; **2.** ∖ *it* aller *ou* venir *ou* voyager en autobus.

bus·by ⚔ [ˈbʌzbi] colback *m*.

bush [buʃ] buisson *m*; fourré *m*; ⊕ fourrure *f* métallique; **bush·el** [ˈbuʃl] boisseau *m* (*a. mesure*); F (grande) quantité *f*; **bush league** *Am. baseball*: ligue *f* de second ordre; '**bush-rang·er** broussard *m*.

bush·y [ˈbuʃi] touffu; broussailleux (-euse *f*); buissonnant (*arbrisseau*).

busi·ness [ˈbiznis] affaire *f*, besogne *f*; occupation *f*; devoir *m*; affaires *f/pl.* (*a.* ✝); ✝ entreprise *f*; maison *f* (de commerce); fonds *m* de commerce; ∖ *address* adresse *f* du bureau (de q.); ∖ *of the day* ordre *m* du jour; agenda *m*; ∖ *end* côté *m* opérant (*d'un outil etc.*), tranchant *m* (*d'un couteau etc.*); ∖ *hours pl.* heures *f/pl.* d'ouverture; ∖*man* homme *m* d'affaires; ∖ *quarter* quartier *m* commerçant; ∖ *research* étude *f* du mouvement des prix *ou* des cycles économiques; *surt. Am.* ∖ *suit see lounge suit*; ∖ *tour*, ∖ *trip* voyage *m* d'affaires; on ∖ pour affaires; *have no* ∖ *to* (*inf.*) ne pas avoir le droit de (*inf.*); *get down to* ∖ en venir au fait; *mind one's own* ∖ s'occuper de ses affaires; *send s.o. about his* ∖ F envoyer promener q.; *that's none of your* ∖ cela ne vous regarde pas; '∖**-like** pratique; sérieux (-euse *f*) (*manière*); capable.

bus·kin [ˈbʌskin] *antiquité, théâ.*: cothurne *m*; *fig.* tragédie *f*.

bus·man [ˈbʌsmən] conducteur *m* *ou* receveur *m* d'autobus; ∖*'s holiday* congé *m* passé à exercer son métier.   [trine *f*.⟩

bust¹ [bʌst] buste *m*, gorge *f*, poi-⟩

bust² *sl.* [bʌst] **1.** fiasco *m*, four *m* (noir), faillite *f*; coup *m* (violent); bringue *f*, bombe *f*; *go on the* ∖, *have a* ∖ faire la bombe; **2.** casser; (faire) crever; abîmer; arrêter, choper (*un criminel etc.*); **3.** foutu; fauché; abîmé; *go* ∖ faire faillite; s'abîmer.

bus·tard *orn.* [ˈbʌstəd] outarde *f*.

bus·tle [ˈbʌsl] **1.** mouvement *m*, confusion *f*, remue-ménage *m/inv.*; va-et-vient *m/inv.*; *cost.* tournure *f*; **2.** *v/i.* s'affairer; s'activer; faire l'empressé; se dépêcher; *v/t.* faire dépêcher (*q.*); bousculer; '**bus·tler** personne *f* très active; homme *m* expéditif; **'bus·tling** □ affairé; empressé.

bust-up *sl.* [ˈbʌstˈʌp] grabuge *f*; engueulade *f*; débâcle *f*; faillite *f*; *surt. Am.* rupture *f* (*d'un mariage etc.*).

bus·y □ [ˈbizi] **1.** occupé (à, de *at*, *with*); affairé; actif (-ive *f*) mouvementé (*rue*); diligent; ~ *packing* occupé à faire ses malles; ~*body* officieux (-euse *f*) *m*; **2.** (*usu.* ~ *o.s.*) s'occuper (à *with*, *in*, *about*; à, de *inf. with gér.*); **'bus·y·ness** affairement *m*; activité *f*.

but [bʌt] **1.** *cj.* mais; or; sauf que; (*a.* ~ *that*) sans que; et cependant; toutefois; **2.** *prp.* sans; *the last* ~ *one* l'avant-dernier (-ère *f*); *the next* ~ *one* le (la) deuxième; ~ *for* sans; ne fût-ce pour; **3.** *après négation:* que (*sbj.*); qui (*sbj.*); *there is no one* ~ *knows* il n'y a personne qui ne sache (*qch.*); **4.** *adv.* ne … que; seulement; ~ *just* tout à l'heure; tout récemment; ~ *now* à l'instant; il n'y a qu'un instant que; *all* ~ presque; *nothing* ~ rien que; *I cannot* ~ (*inf.*) il m'est impossible de ne pas (*inf.*); je ne peux m'empêcher de (*inf.*).

bu·tane [ˈbjuːtein] butane *m*.

butch·er [ˈbutʃə] **1.** boucher *m* (*a. fig.*); *fig.* massacreur *m*; 🐟 *Am.* F vendeur *m* de fruits *etc.*; **2.** égorger; massacrer (*a. fig.*); ~'*s (shop* boucherie *f*; **'butch·er·y** (*a.* ~ *business*) boucherie *f* (*a. fig.*); F massacre *m*; abattoir *m*.

but·ler [ˈbʌtlə] maître *m* d'hôtel; † sommelier *m*.

butt¹ [bʌt] **1.** coup *m* de corne (*d'un bélier*); (*a.* ~*-end*) gros bout *m*; *arbre*, *chèque:* souche *f*; *fusil:* couche *f*, crosse *f*; ✗ butte *f*; *fig.* souffre-douleur *m/inv.*; F mégot *m*; ⊕ bout *m*; *about m*; ~*s pl.* butte *f*; but *m*; *fig.* objectif *m*; **2.** *v/t.* donner un coup de corne *ou* de tête à; *v/i.* F *in* intervenir sans façon.

butt² [~] futaille *f*; (*gros*) tonneau *m*.

but·ter [ˈbʌtə] **1.** beurre *m*; *fig.* flatterie *f*, F pommade *f*; F *he looks as if* ~ *would not melt in his mouth* il fait la sainte nitouche; **2.** beurrer; (*a.* ~ *up*) F flatter; '~*·cup* bouton-d'or (*pl.* boutons-d'or) *m*; '~*·dish* beurrier *m*; '~*·fin·gered* maladroit, empoté; '~*·fly* papillon *m* (*a. fig.*); F *have butterflies in one's stomach* avoir

le trac; avoir l'estomac serré; **'but·ter·y** **1.** de beurre; butyreux (-euse *f*); graisseux (-euse *f*); **2.** *univ.* dépense *f*.

but·tock [ˈbʌtək] fesse *f*; *usu.* ~*s pl.* fesses *f/pl.*, derrière *m*.

but·ton [ˈbʌtn] **1.** bouton *m* (*a.* ✿); **2.** (*se*) boutonner; (*usu.* ~ *up*) *fig.* renfermer; mettre les boutons à; '~*·hole* **1.** boutonnière *f*; (*fleur f* portée à la) boutonnière *f*; **2.** fessonner; F accrocher (*q.*) au passage; '~*·hook* tire-bouton *m*.

but·tress [ˈbʌtris] contrefort *m*; butoir *m* (*d'une chaîne de montagnes*); *fig.* pilier *m*.

bux·om [ˈbʌksəm] dodu; rondelet(te *f*) (*femme*); grassouillet(te *f*).

buy [bai] [*irr.*] *v/t.* acheter (à, *from*); prendre (*un billet*); *fig.* payer, F suborner; ~ *back* racheter; *v/i.* (*a. and sell*) brocanter; *order to* ~ ordre *m* d'achat; **'buy·er** acheteur (-euse *f*) *m*; acquéreur *m*; † acquisiteur *m*, acheteur *m*, chef *m* de rayon.

buzz [bʌz] **1.** bourdonnement *m*; *conversation:* brouhaha *m*; ⚡ ronflement *m*; *Am.* ~ *saw* scie *f* circulaire; F *give s.o. a* ~ donner un coup de fil à q. (*téléphoner*); *fig.* payer, *v/i.* bourdonner, vrombir; *v/t.* lancer, jeter.

buz·zard *orn.* [ˈbʌzəd] buse *f*, busard *m*.

buzz·er ⚡ [ˈbʌzə] appel *m*; sonnerie *f*.

by [bai] **1.** *prp. lieu:* (au)près de, à côté de; au bord de (*la mer*); *direction:* par; *temps:* avant, pour; *moyen:* par, de; à (*la main, la machine, bicyclette, cheval, etc.*); en (*auto, tramway*); *auteur:* de; *serment:* au nom de; par (*qch.*); *mesures:* sur; selon; *North* ~ *East* nord quart nord-est; *side* ~ *side* côte à côte; ~ *day* de jour, le jour; ~ *name* de nom; (*connu*) sous le nom de; ~ *now* déjà, à l'heure qu'il est; ~ *the time* (*that*) quand; avant que (*sbj.*); *a play* ~ *Shaw* une pièce de Shaw; ~ *lamplight* à (la lumière de) la lampe; ~ *the dozen* à la douzaine; ~ *far* de beaucoup; *50 feet* ~ *20* cinquante pieds sur vingt; ~ *half* de moitié; F beaucoup; ~ *o.s.* seul; à l'écart; *land* par terre; ~ *rail* par le chemin de fer; *day* ~ *day* de jour en jour; ~ *twos* deux par deux; **2.** *adv.* près;

de côté; ~ *and* ~ tout à l'heure, tantôt, bientôt, par la suite; ~ *the* ~ à
propos ...; *close* ~ tout près; *go* ~
passer; ~ *and large* à tout prendre;
3. *adj.* latéral (-aux *m/pl.*); écarté;
supplémentaire.

bye [bai] *cricket*: balle *f* passée;
tennis: exemption *f* (*d'un match
dans un tournoi, accordée à un joueur
qui ne tire pas d'adversaire*); *be
a* ~ se trouver exempt d'un match.
bye-bye F ['bai'bai] au revoir!;
adieu!; *go to* ~ F aller faire dodo.

by...: '~·e·**lec·tion** élection *f* par-
tielle; '~·**gone 1.** écoulé, d'autrefois; **2.** ~*s pl.* passé *m*; *let* ~*s be* ~*s*
oublions le passé!; sans rancune!;
'~-**law** arrêté *m* municipal; '~-**line**
Am. rubrique *f* d'un article qui en

nomme l'auteur; '~-**name** sobriquet *m*; '~·**pass 1.** *gaz*: veilleuse *f*;
route *f* de contournement; **2.** F éviter; dévier (*la circulation*); '~·**path**
sentier *m* écarté; '~·**play** *théâ.* jeu *m*
accessoire; aparté *m* mimé; '~·
prod·uct dérivé *m*; '~-**road** chemin
m détourné; chemin *m* vicinal.

By·ron·ic [bai'rɔnik] (~*ally*) byro-
nien.

by...: '~·**stand·er** assistant *m*; spec-
tateur(-trice *f*) *m*; '~·**street** ruelle *f*;
rue *f* écartée; '~-**way** chemin *m* détourné; détour *m* (*a. péj.*); *fig.* à-côté
m; '~·**word** proverbe *m*; *be a* ~ *for*
être passé en proverbe pour; *be the*
~ *of* être la fable de.

By·zan·tine [bi'zæntain] **1.** byzantin; **2.** Byzantin(e *f*) *m*.

C

C, c [siː] C *m*, c *m*.

cab [kæb] 1. taxi *m*; fiacre *m*; camion, grue, *etc.*: guérite *f*; ⚓ poste *m* de conduite; 2. de fiacres, de taxis; 3. F ~ *it* aller *ou* venir en taxi.

ca·bal [kə'bæl] 1. cabale *f*, brigue *f*; 2. cabaler; comploter.

cab·a·ret ['kæbərei] cabaret *m*; concert *m* genre music-hall.

cab·bage ['kæbidʒ] chou *m*; ~ *butterfly* piéride *f* du chou; ~ *lettuce* laitue *f* pommée.

cab·by F ['kæbi] cocher *m*.

cab·in ['kæbin] 1. cabane *f*; ⚓ cabine *f*; ⚓ guérite *f*; 2. enfermer; '~-boy mousse *m*.

cab·i·net ['kæbinit] meuble *m* à tiroirs; *étalage etc.*: vitrine *f*; *radio*: coffret *m*; *phot.* format *m* album; *pol.* cabinet *m*, ministère *m*; ♀ *Council* conseil *m* des ministres; '~-mak·er ébéniste *m*.

ca·ble ['keibl] 1. ⚓, *a. tél.* câble *m*; ⚓ chaîne *f*; câble-chaîne (*pl.* câbles--chaînes) *m*; *buried* ~ câble *m* souterrain; 2. *tél.* câbler; '~-car téléphérique *m*; *sur rail*: funiculaire *m*; '~-gram câblogramme *m*; ~ rail·way funiculaire *m*; ~ tel·e·vi·sion télédistribution *f*, télévision *f* par câble(s).

cab·man ['kæbmən] cocher *m* de fiacre.

ca·boo·dle *sl.* [kə'buːdl]: *the whole* ~ tout le bazar.

ca·boose [kə'buːs] ⚓ cuisine *f*; 🚂 *Am.* fourgon *m*.

cab·ri·o·let *surt. mot.* [kæbrio'lei] cabriolet *m*.

cab·stand ['kæbstænd] station *f* de voitures.   [perlée.)

ca'can·ny [kɔː'kæni] faire la grève)

ca·ca·o [kə'kɑːou] cacao *m*; *arbre*: cacaotier *m*.

cache [kæʃ] cache *f*, cachette *f*.

cack·le ['kækl] 1. caquet *m* (*a. fig.*); ricanement *m*; 2. caqueter (*a. fig.*); ricaner; cacarder (*oie*); '**cack·ler** poule *f* qui caquette; *fig.* caqueteur (-euse *f*) *m*; ricaneur (-euse *f*) *m*.

cac·tus ♣ ['kæktəs] cactus *m*.

cad F [kæd] goujat *m*; canaille *f*.

ca·das·tre [kə'dæstə] cadastre *m*.

ca·dav·er·ous [kə'dævərəs] cadavéreux (-euse *f*); *fig.* exsangue.

cad·die ['kædi] golf: cadet *m*.

cad·dish F □ ['kædiʃ] voyou; digne d'un goujat.

cad·dy ['kædi] boîte *f* à thé.

ca·dence ['keidəns] ♪ cadence *f*; intonation *f*; rythme *m*.

ca·det [kə'det] cadet *m*; ~ *corps* bataillon *m* scolaire.

cadge [kædʒ] colporter; mendier; chiner (*qch.*); '**cadg·er** colporteur *m*; mendiant(e *f*) *m*; chineur (-euse *f*) *m*.

ca·du·cous ♣, *a. zo.* [kə'djuːkəs] caduc (-uque *f*).

cae·cum *anat.* ['siːkəm] cæcum *m*.

Cae·sar ['siːzə] César *m*; C(a)e·sar·i·an (sec·tion) ♂ [siːˈzɛəriən ('sekʃən)] césarienne *f*.

cae·su·ra [si'zjuərə] césure *f*.

ca·fé ['kæfei] café(-restaurant) *m*.

caf·e·te·ri·a Am. [kæfi'tiəriə] cafeteria *f*, restaurant *m* de libre service.

caf·e·to·ri·um Am. [kæfi'tɔːriəm] salle *f* des festins, restaurant *m*.

caf·fe·ine 🜊 ['kæfiːn] caféine *f*.

cage [keidʒ] 1. cage *f*; *oiseau*: cage *f*, volière *f*; ⛏ cage *f* (de puits); 2. encager (*a. fig.*); mettre en cage.

cage·y □ F ['keidʒi] peu communicatif (-ive *f*); prudent; *be* ~ *about a.* ne pas vouloir parler de, cacher.

cairn [kɛən] cairn *m*.

cais·son [kə'suːn] ✖ caisson *m* (à munitions); *hydraulique*: caisson *m*, batardeau *m*.

ca·jole [kə'dʒoul] enjôler; cajoler; persuader (à *q.* de *inf.*, *s.o. into gér.*); **ca'jol·er** cajoleur (-euse *f*) *m*; **ca'jol·er·y** cajolerie *f*, -s *f/pl.*; enjôlement *m*.

cake [keik] 1. gâteau *m*; pâtisserie *f*; *chocolat*: tablette *f*; *savon*: pain *m*; 2. faire croûte; se coller; se cailler (*sang*).

cal·a·bash ['kæləbæʃ] calebasse *f*.

cal·a·mine *min*. ['kæləmain] calamine *f*.

ca·lam·i·tous □ [kə'læmitəs] calamiteux (-euse *f*), désastreux (-euse *f*); **ca'lam·i·ty** calamité *f*, infortune *f*; désastre *m*; catastrophe *f*; **ca'lam·i·ty-howl·er** *surt. Am.* pessimiste *mf*; prophète *m* de malheur; **ca'lam·i·ty-howl·ing** *surt. Am.* défaitisme *m*; prophéties *f/pl.* de malheur.

ca·lash [kə'læʃ] calèche *f*.

cal·car·e·ous *min*. [kæl'kɛəriəs] calcaire.

cal·ci·fi·ca·tion [kælsifi'keiʃn] calcification *f*; **cal·ci·fy** ['⁓fai] (se) calcifier; **cal·ci·na·tion** ⚗ [kælsi'neiʃn] calcination *f*; cuisson *f*; **cal·cine** ['kælsain] *v/t.* ⚗ calciner; cuire; *v/i.* se calciner; **'cal·cite** *min*. calcite *f*; **cal·ci·um** ⚗ ['⁓siəm] calcium *m*.

cal·cu·la·ble ['kælkjuləbl] calculable; **cal·cu·late** ['⁓leit] *v/t.* calculer; estimer; faire le compte de; **⁓d** propre (à, to), fait (pour, to); *v/i.* compter (sur, on); *Am.* F supposer; *calculating-machine* machine *f* à calculer; **cal·cu·la·tion** calcul *m*; **'cal·cu·la·tor** calculateur (-trice *f*) *m*; machine *f* à calculer, calculatrice *f*; **'cal·cu·lus** ✍, ⚕ [⁓ləs] calcul *m*.

cal·dron ['kɔːldrən] *see* cauldron.

cal·en·dar ['kælində] **1.** calendrier *m*; ✍ rôle *m* des assises; *univ.* annuaire *m*; **2.** inscrire sur un calendrier *ou* sur une liste.

cal·en·der ⊕ [⁓] **1.** calandre *f*; laminoir *m*; **2.** calandrer; laminer.

calf [kɑːf], *pl.* **calves** [kɑːvz] veau *m*; *fig.* petit(e *f*) *m*; (*a. ⁓-leather*) veau *m*, vachette *f*; ⊕ reliure *f* en veau; *anat.* mollet *m*; *in* ⁓, *with* ⁓ pleine (*vache*); F *⁓-love* amours *f/pl.* enfantines; '**⁓·skin** (cuir *m* de) veau *m*.

cal·i·brate ⊕ ['kælibreit] étalonner; calibrer (*un tube*); **cal·i·bre** ['⁓bə] calibre *m* (*a. fig.*); alésage *m*.

cal·i·co ✝ ['kælikou] calicot *m*; *surt. Am.* indienne *f*.

Cal·i·for·nian [kæli'fɔːnjən] **1.** californien(ne *f*); de Californie; **2.** Californien(ne *f*) *m*.

ca·liph ['kælif] calife *m*; **cal·iph·ate** ['⁓eit] califat *m*.

calk¹ [kɔːk] *peint.* décalquer.

calk² [⁓] *see* caulk.

calk³ [⁓] **1.** *a.* calk·in ['kælkin] crampon *m*, clou *m* à glace; **2.** ferrer (*un cheval*) à glace.

call [kɔːl] **1.** appel *m* (*a. téléph.*, *bridge*, *etc.*); cri *m* (*a. oiseau*); *téléph.*, *clairon*, *etc.*: coup *m*; *théâ.* rappel *m*; *bridge*: annonce *f*; visite *f*; demande *f* (de, for); vocation *f*; invitation *f*, nomination *f* (*à un poste*, *à une chaire*, *etc.*); *Bourse*: appel *m* de fonds; option *f*; ✝ *⁓-money* prêts *m/pl.* au jour le jour; *port of* ⁓ port *m* d'escale; ✝ *on* ⁓ sur demande; au jour le jour; *give* s.o. *a* ⁓ donner un coup de fil à q.; **2.** *v/t.* appeler (*a. ⚡*), crier; convoquer (*une réunion*); héler (*un taxi*); faire venir (*un médecin*); appeler, attirer (*l'attention*) (sur, to); *théâ.* rappeler; réveiller; *cartes*: déclarer; décréter (*une grève*); qualifier de (*un titre*); injurier; *fig.* nommer (à, to); *be* ⁓*ed* s'appeler; ⁓ s.o. *names* injurier q.; *Am.* F ⁓ *down* injurier; reprendre (*q.*); ⁓ *forth* produire, évoquer; faire appel à (*le courage*); ⁓ *in* retirer (*une monnaie*) de la circulation; faire (r)entrer (*q.*); ⁓ *over* faire l'appel de (*les noms*); ⁓ *up* évoquer; ✄ mobiliser, appeler sous les drapeaux; appeler au téléphone; **3.** *v/i.* téléphoner; faire une visite, passer (chez *at*, on); ⁓ *at a port* faire escale; ⁓ *for* faire venir (*q.*) *ou* apporter (*qch.*); commander; *théâ.* rappeler, réclamer; venir chercher (*q.*, *qch.*); *to be* (*left till*) *⁓ed for* à remettre au messager; *poste restante*; ⁓ *on* invoquer; réclamer (*qch.* à q., s.o. *for* s.th.) requérir (*q.*) (de, *to inf.*) ⁓ *to* crier à (*q.*); ⁓ *upon see* ⁓ on; **'call·a·ble** ✝ au jour le jour (*prêt*); **'call·box** cabine *f* téléphonique; **'call·er** personne *f* qui appelle; visiteur (-euse *f*) *m*; *téléph.* demandeur (-euse *f*) *m*.

cal·li·graph·ic [kæli'græfik] (*⁓ally*) calligraphique; **cal·lig·ra·phy** [kə'ligrəfi] calligraphie *f*, belle écriture *f*.

call-in ['kɔːlin] *radio*, *télév.* programme *m ou* émission *f* avec participation des assistants, programme *m* à ligne ouverte.

call·ing ['kɔːliŋ] appel *m*; convocation *f*; métier *m*; visite *f* (à, on); *Am.* ⁓ *card* carte *f* de visite.

cal·(l)i·pers *pl.* ['kælipəz] compas *m* d'épaisseur.

cal·lis·then·ics [kælis'θeniks] *usu. sg.* callisthénie *f.*

call-of·fice ['kɔːlɔfis] bureau *m* téléphonique.

cal·los·i·ty [kæ'lɔsiti] callosité *f*; cal (*pl.* -s) *m*; *fig.* dureté *f*; '**cal·lous** □ calleux (-euse *f*); *fig.* insensible, dur.

cal·low ['kælou] sans plumes; *fig.* imberbe, sans expérience.

call-up [kɔl'ʌp] appel *m* (✕ sous les drapeaux).

cal·lus ['kaləs] callosité *f.*

calm [kɑːm] **1.** □ calme, tranquille (*a. fig.*); **2.** tranquillité *f*; calme *m* (*a. fig.*, *a.* ♁); sérénité *f*; **3.** (~ *down* se) calmer; apaiser; adoucir; '**calm·ness** tranquillité *f*; calme *m*; sérénité *f.*

ca·lor·ic *phys.* [kə'lɔrik] calorique *m*; **cal·o·rie** *phys.* ['kæləri] calorie *f*; **cal·o·rif·ic** [kælə'rifik] calorifique, calorifiant.

cal·trop ['kæltrəp] ♣ chardon *m* étoilé; ✕ *hist.* chausse-trape *f.*

ca·lum·ni·ate [kə'lʌmnieit] calomnier; **ca·lum·ni·a·tion** calomnie *f*; **ca·lum·ni·a·tor** calomniateur (-trice *f*) *m*; **ca·lum·ni·ous** □ calomnieux (-euse *f*); **cal·um·ny** ['kæləmni] calomnie *f.*

Cal·va·ry ['kælvəri] *le* Calvaire *m.*

calve [kɑːv] vêler (*a. géol.*); **calves** [kɑːvz] *see* calf. [nisme *m.*]

Cal·vin·ism ['kælvinizm] calvi-ƒ

ca·lyx ['keiliks], *pl. a.* **ca·ly·ces** ['~lisiːz] ♣, *a. zo.* calice *m.*

cam [kæm] came *f*; ~ *gear* distribution *f* à came(s).

cam·ber ⊕ ['kæmbə] **1.** *poutre:* cambrure *f*; *chaussée:* bombement *m*; **2.** (se) cambrer; bomber.

cam·bric ✝ ['keimbrik] batiste *f.*

came [keim] *prét. de* come.

cam·el *zo.*, *a.* ♁ ['kæml] chameau *m.*

ca·mel·li·a ♣ [kə'miːljə] camélia *m.*

cam·e·o ['kæmiou] camée *m.*

cam·er·a ['kæmərə] *phot.* appareil *m*; ⚖ *in* ~ à huis clos; '~·man caméraman *m*; preneur *m* de vues.

cam·i-knick·ers [kæmi'nikəz] *pl.* chemise-culotte (*pl.* chemises-culottes) *f.*

cam·o·mile ♣ ['kæməmail] camomille *f*; ~ *tea* (tisane *f* de) camomille *f.*

cam·ou·flage ✕ ['kæmuflɑːʒ] **1.** camouflage *m*; **2.** camoufler.

camp [kæmp] **1.** camp *m*; campement *m*; ~-*bed* lit *m* de camp; ~-*chair*, ~-*stool* chaise *f* pliante; pliant *m*; **2.** camper; ~ *out* camper, faire du camping.

cam·paign [kæm'pein] **1.** campagne *f* (*a. pol.*, *a. fig.*); *election* ~ campagne *f* électorale; **2.** faire une (des) campagne(s); **cam'paign·er** F *old* ~ vieux routier *m*; vétéran *m.*

camp·er ['kæmpə] campeur (-euse ƒ) *m*; *Am. a.* caravane *f.*

cam·phor ['kæmfə] camphre *m*; **cam·phor·at·ed** ['~reitid] camphré.

camp·ing ['kæmpiŋ] camping *m*; ✕ campement *m.*

camp·site ['kæmpsait] (terrain *m* de) camping *m.*

cam·pus *Am.* ['kæmpəs] terrains *m/pl.* (*d'une université*).

cam·shaft ⊕ ['kæmʃɑːft] arbre *m* à cames.

can¹ [kæn] [*irr.*] *v/aux.* (*défectif*) je peux *etc.*, je suis *etc.* capable de (*inf.*).

can² [~] **1.** bidon *m*, broc *m*, pot *m*; *Am. conserves:* boîte *f*; canette *f* en métal; ~ *opener* ouvre-boîtes *m/inv.*; F *carry the* ~ rester avec l'affaire sur les bras; **2.** *Am.* conserver (*qch.*) en boîte; *Am. sl.* ~ *it!* la ferme!

Ca·na·di·an [kə'neidjən] **1.** canadien(ne *f*); **2.** Canadien(ne *f*) *m.*

ca·nal [kə'næl] canal *m* (*a.* ✱); **ca·nal·i·za·tion** [kænəlai'zeiʃn] canalisation *f*; '**ca·nal·ize** (se) canaliser.

ca·nard [kæ'nɑːd] canard *m*, fausse nouvelle *f.*

ca·nar·y [kə'neəri] (*a.* ~ *bird*) serin *m.*

can·cel ['kænsl] biffer; annuler; *fig.* (*a.* ~ *out*) éliminer; **can·cel·la·tion** [kænse'leiʃn] annulation *f*; résiliation *f*; révocation *f.*

can·cer ['kænsə] *astr. le* Cancer *m*; ✱ cancer *m*; *attr.* cancéreux (-euse *f*); '**can·cer·ous** cancéreux (-euse *f*).

can·did □ ['kændid] franc(he *f*); sincère; impartial (-aux *m/pl.*).

can·di·date ['kændidit] candidat *m*, aspirant *m* (à, for); **can·di·da·ture** ['~ʃə] candidature *f.*

can·died ['kændid] candi; confit.

can·dle ['kændl] bougie *f*; chandelle *f*; cierge *m*; ~-*power* bougie *f*, -s *f/pl.*; 2·*mas eccl.* ['~məs] la Chandeleur *f*; '~·**stick** chandelier *m*; bougeoir *m.*

can·do(u)r ['kændə] franchise *f*, sincérité *f*; impartialité *f*.

can·dy ['kændi] **1.** sucre *m* candi; *Am.* bonbons *m/pl.*; confiseries *f/pl.*; ~ *floss* barbe *f* à papa; **2.** *v/t.* faire candir (*du sucre*); glacer (*des fruits*); *v/i.* se cristalliser.

cane [kein] **1.** ♀ jonc *m*; canne *f*; *pour sièges*: rotin *m*; **2.** battre à coups de canne; canner (*une chaise*).

ca·nine ['keinain] **1.** de chien, canin; **2.** ['kænain] *a.* ~ *tooth* canine *f*.

can·is·ter ['kænistə] boîte *f* (*en fer blanc*).

can·ker ['kæŋkə] **1.** ✻, *a.* ♀ chancre *m* (*a. fig.* = *influence corruptrice*); **2.** ronger; *fig.* corrompre; '**can·kered** *fig.* plein d'amertume; '**can·ker·ous** chancreux (-euse *f*).

can·na·bis ['kænəbis] chanvre *m*; cannabis *m*.

canned *Am.* [kænd] (conservé) en boîte; ~ *music* musique enregistrée *ou* en conserve.

can·ner·y *Am.* ['kænəri] conserverie *f*.

can·ni·bal ['kænibl] cannibale (*a. su./mf*).

can·non ['kænən] **1.** ✗ canon *m*; pièce *f* d'artillerie; *billard*: carambolage *m*; **2.** caramboler; *fig.* ~ *against* (*ou with*) se heurter contre; **can·non·ade** [~'neid] canonnade *f*; '**can·non·ball** boulet *m* de canon.

can·not ['kænɔt] *je ne peux pas etc.*

can·ny □ *écoss.* ['kæni] prudent, finaud.

ca·noe [kə'nu:] **1.** canoë *m*; pirogue *f*; périssoire *f*; *paddle one's own* ~ se débrouiller tout seul, diriger seul sa barque; **2.** faire du canoë *ou* de la périssoire; aller en canoë.

can·on ['kænən] *eccl.*, *a.* ♩ canon *m*; F règle *f*, critère *m*; canon *m*; *eccl. personne*: chanoine *m*; *typ.* gros canon *m*; ⚖ ~ *law* droit *m* canon; **can·on·i·za·tion** [~nai'zeiʃn] canonisation *f*; '**can·on·ize** canoniser (*q.*); sanctionner (*un usage*); '**can·on·ry** canonicat *m*.

can·o·py ['kænəpi] **1.** dais *m*; baldaquin *m*; marquise *f*; *fig.* voûte *f*; △ gable *m*; **2.** couvrir d'un dais *etc.*

cant¹ [kænt] **1.** inclinaison *f*, dévers *m*; △ pan *m* coupé; **2.** (s')incliner; pencher; *v/i.* ♣ éviter; ~ *over* se renverser.

cant² [~] **1.** jargon *m*, argot *m* (*des*

mendiants, criminels, etc.); langage *m* hypocrite; boniments *m/pl.*; **2.** faire le cafard; parler avec hypocrisie (*de, about*).

can't F [kɑːnt] *see* cannot.

can·ta·loup ♀ ['kæntəlu:p] cantaloup *m*.

can·tan·ker·ous F □ [kən'tæŋkərəs] revêche, acariâtre.

can·teen [kæn'ti:n] cantine *f*; *coutellerie*: service *m* de table en coffre; ✗ bidon *m*; ✗ gamelle *f*.

can·ter ['kæntə] **1.** petit galop *m*; **2.** aller au petit galop.

can·ter·bur·y ['kæntəbəri] casier *m* à musique; ♀ *bell* ♀ campanule *f*.

can·tha·ris *zo.* ['kænθəris], *pl.* **-thar·i·des** [~'θæridi:z] cantharide *f*.

can·ti·cle ['kæntikl] cantique *m*; *bibl.* ♀*s pl.* le Cantique des Cantiques.

can·ti·le·ver △ ['kæntili:və] encorbellement *m*; cantilever *m*.

can·to ['kæntou] chant *m* (*d'un poème*).

can·ton **1.** ['kæntən] canton *m*; **2.** ✗ [kən'tu:n] cantonner; '**can·ton·ment** ✗ cantonnement *m*.

can·vas ['kænvəs] (grosse) toile *f*; toile *f* de tente; *navire*: voiles *f/pl.*; *peint.* toile *f*; *p.ext.* tableau *m*.

can·vass [~] **1.** sollicitation *f* de suffrages; tournée *f* électorale; *Am. a.* dépouillement *m* (*des voix*); **2.** *v/t.* discuter; solliciter (*des suffrages*, ✚ *des commandes*); *v/i. pol.* faire une tournée électorale; ✚ faire la place; '**can·vass·er** solliciteur (-euse *f*); ✚ placier *m*; *pol.* courtier *m* électoral; *Am. a.* scrutateur *m* (*du scrutin*).

caou·tchouc ['kautʃuk] caoutchouc *m*.

cap [kæp] **1.** casquette *f*; béret *m*; *univ.* toque *f*, mortier *m*; ⊕ *etc.* chapeau *m*, capuchon *m*; ⊕ *pompe*: calotte *f*; ~ *and gown* toque *f* et toge *f*, costume *m* académique; ~ *in hand* le bonnet à la main; *set one's* ~ *at s.o.* entreprendre la conquête de q.; **2.** *v/t.* coiffer; choisir comme membre de la première équipe; capsuler (*une bouteille etc.*); *fig.* couronner; F surpasser; *sp. be* ~*ped* être admis *ou* jouer dans l'équipe nationale; *v/i.* F se découvrir (*devant* q., [*to*] *s.o.*).

ca·pa·bil·i·ty [keipə'biliti] capacité f (pour *inf.*, of *gér.*); faculté f (de *inf.*, of *gér.*); '**ca·pa·ble** capable, susceptible (de, of).

ca·pa·cious □ [kə'peiʃəs] vaste; ample; **ca·pac·i·tate** [⁓'pæsiteit] rendre capable (de, for); **ca'pac·i·ty** capacité f (pour *inf.*; for *gér.*); volume m, contenance f; *locomotive*: rendement m; *rivière*: débit m; qualité f (*professionnelle*); *disposing* (*ou legal*) ⁓ capacité f juridique; *in my* ⁓ *as* en ma qualité de.

cap-à-pie [kæpə'pi:] de pied en cap.

ca·par·i·son [kə'pærisn] caparaçon m; *fig.* parure f somptueuse.

cape[1] [keip] cap m, promontoire m.

cape[2] [⁓] pèlerine f, cape f.

ca·per[1] ⚲ ['keipə] câpre f; *plante*: câprier m.

ca·per[2] [⁓] **1.** cabriole f, entrechat m (*a. fig.*); *cut* ⁓*s* = **2.** faire des entrechats *ou* des cabrioles; gambader.

ca·pi·as ⚖ ['keipiæs]: *writ of* ⁓ mandat m d'arrêt.

cap·il·lar·i·ty [kæpi'læriti] capillarité f; **cap·il·lar·y** [kə'piləri] **1.** capillaire; **2.** *anat.* (vaisseau m) capillaire m.

cap·i·tal ['kæpitl] **1.** □ capital (-aux m/pl.) (*lettre, peine, crime, ville*); le plus haut; F excellent, fameux (-euse f); **2.** capitale f; ♰ capital m, fonds m/pl.; *typ.* (*ou* ⁓ *letter*) majuscule f, capitale f; ♰ ⁓ *assets pl.* actif m immobilisé; ♰ ⁓ *gains* (*tax*) (impôt m sur les) plus-values f/pl. (en capital); **3.** △ chapiteau m; '**cap·i·tal·ism** capitalisme m; '**cap·i·tal·ist** capitaliste mf; **cap·i·tal·is·tic** capitaliste; **cap·i·tal·i·za·tion** [kəpitəlai'zeiʃn] capitalisation f; '**cap·i·tal·ize** capitaliser; écrire avec une majuscule.

cap·i·ta·tion [kæpi'teiʃn] capitation f (*a.* ⚖); *attr.* par tête.

Cap·i·tol ['kæpitl] Capitole m.

ca·pit·u·late [kə'pitjuleit] capituler; **ca·pit·u·la·tion** capitulation f, reddition f.

ca·pon ['keipən] chapon m, poulet m.

ca·price [kə'pri:s] caprice m (*a.* ♪), lubie f; **ca·pri·cious** [kə'priʃəs] capricieux (-euse f); **ca'pri·cious·ness** humeur f capricieuse.

Cap·ri·corn *astr.* ['kæprikɔːn] le Capricorne m.

cap·ri·ole ['kæprioul] cabriole f.

cap·size ⚓ [kæp'saiz] *v/i.* chavirer; *fig.* se renverser; *v/t.* faire chavirer.

cap·stan ⚓ ['kæpstən] cabestan m.

cap·su·lar ['kæpsjulə] capsulaire; **cap·sule** ⚲, ⚛ ['⁓sju:l] capsule f.

cap·tain ['kæptin] capitaine m, chef m; *sp.* chef m d'équipe; ✕, ⚓ capitaine m; ✠ *group* ⁓ colonel m; ⁓ *of horse* capitaine m de cavalerie; ⁓ *of industry* chef m de l'industrie; '**cap·tain·cy**, '**cap·tain·ship** grade m de capitaine; *sp.* commandement m de l'équipe; *entreprise*: conduite f.

cap·tion ['kæpʃn] **1.** en-tête m; légende f; *journal*: rubrique f; *cin.* sous-titre m; **2.** *v/t.* Am. fournir d'en-têtes *etc.*

cap·tious □ ['kæpʃəs] captieux (-euse f); pointilleux (-euse f) (*personne*).

cap·ti·vate ['kæptiveit] *fig.* captiver, charmer; **cap·ti·va·tion** séduction f; '**cap·tive 1.** captif (-ive f); ⁓ *balloon* ballon m captif; **2.** captif (-ive f) m; prisonnier (-ère f) m; **cap·tiv·i·ty** [⁓'tiviti] captivité f.

cap·tor ['kæptə] preneur m; ⚓ capteur m; **cap·ture** ['⁓tʃə] **1.** capture f; prise f (*a.* ⚓); **2.** capturer, s'emparer de (*un malfaiteur*); prendre (*une ville*); ⚓ capturer.

Cap·u·chin *eccl.* ['kæpjuʃin] capucin m.

car [kɑ:] *mot.* automobile f, voiture f; 🚋 Am. voiture f, wagon m; Am. *ascenseur*: cabine f; *poét.* char m; *ballon*: nacelle f; ⁓ *park* parking m, parc m de stationnement; ⁓ *port* auvent m *ou* abri m pour voitures; ⁓ *wash* lave-auto m, tunnel m de lavage.

car·a·cole ['kærəkoul] *équit.* **1.** caracole f; **2.** caracoler.

ca·rafe [kɑ'rɑːf] carafe f.

car·a·mel ['kærəmel] caramel m; bonbon m au caramel.

car·at ['kærət] *mesure*: carat m.

car·a·van [kærə'væn] caravane f (*a. mot.*); roulotte f; ⁓ *site* camping m pour caravanes; **car·a·van·se·rai** [⁓serai] caravansérail m.

car·a·way ⚲ ['kærəwei] carvi m.

car·bide 🜍 ['kɑ:baid] carbure m.

car·bine ['kɑ:bain] carabine f.

car·bo·hy·drate 🜍 ['kɑ:bou'haidreit] hydrate m de carbone.

car·bol·ic ac·id 🜍 [kɑ:'bɔlik'æsid] phénol m.

car·bon ['kɑːbən] 🔥 carbone *m*; ✦ charbon *m*; ~ *copy* copie *f ou* double *m* au carbone; (*ou* ~ *paper*) papier *m* carbone; **car·bo·na·ceous** [~- 'neiʃəs] *géol.* charbonneux (-euse *f*); **car·bon·ate** ['~bənit] carbonate *m*; **car·bon·ic** [~'bɒnik] carbonique; ~ *acid* anhydride *m* carbonique; **car· bon·i·za·tion** [~bənai'zeiʃn] carbonisation *f*; '**car·bon·ize** carboniser.

car·boy ['kɑːbɔi] bonbonne *f*.

car·bun·cle ['kɑːbʌŋkl] *min.* escarboucle *f*; 🩸 anthrax *m*.

car·bu·ret ['kɑːbjuret] carburer; '**car·bu·ret·ter**, *usu.* '**car·bu·rettor** *mot.* carburateur *m*.

car·case, **car·cass** ['kɑːkəs] *homme, animal:* cadavre *m*; *animal, maison:* carcasse *f*; *fig.* squelette *m*, carcasse *f*.

car·ci·no·ma 🩸 [kɑːsinoumə] carcinome *m*; **car·cin·o·gen·ic** [~nə- 'dʒenik] cancérigène.

card[1] ⊕ [kɑːd] **1.** carde *f*, peigne *m*; **2.** carder, peigner (*la laine*).

card[2] [~] carte *f*; ~ *catalogue* fichier *m*; F *house of* ~*s* château *m* de cartes; *sl.* queer ~ drôle *m* de type *ou* de numéro.

car·dan ⊕ ['kɑːdən]: ~ *joint* joint *m* de cardan, joint *m* universel; ~ *shaft* arbre *m* à cardan.

card...: '~**·board** carton *m*; cartonnage *m*; ~ *box* carton *m*; '~**·case** porte-cartes *m/inv.*

car·di·ac 🩸 ['kɑːdiæk] **1.** cardiaque, cardiaire; ~ *arrest* arrêt *m* du coeur; ~ *stimulant* stimulant *m* cardiaque; **2.** cordial *m*.

car·di·gan ['kɑːdigən] cardigan *m*.

car·di·nal □ ['kɑːdinl] **1.** cardinal (-aux *m/pl.*); principal (-aux *m/pl.*); ~ *number* nombre *m* cardinal; **2.** *eccl.* cardinal *m* (*a. orn.*); **car·dinal·ate** ['~eit] cardinalat *m*.

card...: '~**·in·dex** fichier *m*, classeur *m*; '~**·sharp·er** tricheur *m*, escroc *m*.

care [kɛə] **1.** souci *m*; soin *m*, attention *f*; charge *f*; tenue *f*; medical ~ soins *m/pl.* médicaux; ~ *of the mouth* hygiène *f* orale; ~ *of the nails* soin *m* des ongles; ~ *of* (*abbr.* c/o) aux bons soins de; chez; *take* ~ faire attention; *take* ~ (*of yourself*)! fais bien attention (à toi); *take* ~ *to do* faire attention *ou* prendre soin de faire; *take* ~ *of* s'occuper de;

garder; *with* ~! fragile!; **2.** se soucier; s'inquiéter; ~ *for* soigner; aimer; se soucier de; *usu. au nég.*: tenir à; être important à (*q.*); F *I don't* ~ (*if I do*)! ça m'est égal; *I don't* ~ *what he said* peu m'importe ce qu'il a dit.

ca·reen ⚓ [kə'riːn] *v/t.* caréner; *v/i.* donner de la bande.

ca·reer [kə'riə] **1.** carrière *f*; *fig.* course *f* précipitée; ~ *diplomat* diplomate *m* de carrière; **2.** *fig.* courir rapidement; **ca·reer·ist** [kə'riərist] arriviste *mf*.

care-free ['kɛəfriː] insouciant; exempt de soucis.

care·ful □ ['kɛəful] soigneux (-euse *f*) (de *of, for*); attentif (-ive *f*) (à, of); prudent; soigné; *be* ~ *to* (*inf.*) avoir soin de (*inf.*); *be* ~ *not to fall!* prenez garde de tomber; '**care·ful·ness** soin *m*, attention *f*; prudence *f*.

care·less □ ['kɛəlis] sans soin; négligent; inconsidéré; nonchalant; insouciant (de *of, about*); '**care· less·ness** inattention *f*; insouciance *f*; manque *m* de soin.

ca·ress [kə'res] **1.** caresse *f*; **2.** caresser; *fig.* mignoter.

care·tak·er ['kɛəteikə] concierge *mf*; gardien(ne *f*) *m*; *école:* dépensier (-ère *f*) *m*.

care-worn ['kɛəwɔːn] usé par le chagrin.

car·fare *Am.* ['kɑːfɛə] prix *m* du voyage.

car·go ⚓ ['kɑːgou] cargaison *f*; *mixed* (*ou general*) ~ cargaison *f* mixte; *shifting* ~ cargaison *f* volante.

car·i·ca·ture [kærikə'tjuə] **1.** caricature *f*; **2.** caricaturer; **car·i·catur·ist** [kærikə'tjuərist] caricaturiste *m*.

car·i·es 🩸 ['kɛəriiːz] carie *f*; '**car·ious** carié; gâté (*dent etc.*).

car·man ['kɑːmən] charretier *m*.

car·mine ['kɑːmain] **1.** carmin *m*; **2.** carmin *adj./inv.*, carminé.

car·nage ['kɑːnidʒ] carnage *m*; '**carnal** □ charnel(le *f*); de la chair; sensuel(le *f*); sexuel(le *f*); mondain; **car·nal·i·ty** [~'næliti] sensualité *f*; **car·na·tion** [~'neiʃn] **1.** incarnat *m*; ✿ oeillet *m*; **2.** incarnat.

car·ni·val ['kɑːnivl] carnaval (*pl.* -s) *m*; *fig.* réjouissances *f/pl.*

car·ni·vore ['kɑːnivɔː] carnassier *m*;

car·niv·o·rous [_'nivərəs] carnassier (-ère f) (animal); carnivore (plante, personne).

car·ol ['kærl] 1. chant m, chanson f; noël m; 2. chanter joyeusement.

ca·rot·id anat. [kə'rɔtid] (a. ~artery) carotide f.

ca·rouse [kə'rauz] 1. a. **ca'rous·al** buverie f; F bombe f; 2. faire la fête.

carp[1] [kɑːp] carpe f.

carp[2] [_] gloser, épiloguer; ~ at trouver à redire à.

car·pen·ter ['kɑːpintə] 1. charpentier m; menuisier m; 2. v/i. faire de la charpenterie; v/t. charpenter; **'car·pen·try** charpente(rie) f.

car·pet ['kɑːpit] 1. tapis m (a. fig.); bring on the ~ soulever (une question); F ~-dance sauterie f; 2. recouvrir d'un tapis; F mettre (q.) sur la sellette; '~-bag·ger parl. candidat m étranger à la circonscription; '~-beat·er tapette f.

car·pet·ing ['kɑːpitiŋ] tapis m/pl. en pièce; pose f de tapis.

car·pet-sweep·er ['kɑːpitswiːpə] balai m mécanique.

car·riage ['kæridʒ] port m; transport m; (a. ⊕) voiture f, wagon m; ✕ affût m; personne: allure f; machine à écrire: chariot m; voiture: train m; **'car·riage·a·ble** charriable (objet); praticable (chemin).

car·riage...: '~-and-'pair voiture f à deux chevaux; '~-door porte f cochère; '~-drive allée f; avenue f pour voitures; '~-free, ~-'paid franc(he f) ou franco de port, envoi franco; '~-road, '~-way chaussée f; route f carrossable.

car·ri·er ['kæriə] porteur (-euse f) m (a. 𝒮); ✕ ravitailleur m; ✝ camionneur m, voiturier m; bicyclette: porte-bagages m/inv.; '~-bag sac m (en plastique); '~-pi·geon pigeon m voyageur.

car·ri·on ['kæriən] 1. charogne f; 2. pourri.

car·rot ['kærət] carotte f; **'car·rot·y** F roux (rousse f).

car·ry ['kæri] 1. v/t. porter; transporter; conduire (q.); mener (q.); mener à bonne fin (une entreprise); (rap)porter (intérêt); remporter (un prix); élever (un mur); (sup)porter (une poutre); faire adopter (une proposition); ♉ retenir (un chiffre); bien supporter (du vin); avoir en magasin (des marchandises); ✕ enlever (une forteresse); be carried être voté; être adopté; univ. ~ a course suivre un cours; ~away emmener (q.); emporter (a. fig.); ~ everything before one triompher sur toute la ligne; ✝ ~ forward (ou over) reporter (une somme); transporter (un solde); ~ on continuer; entretenir; exercer (un métier); poursuivre (un procès); ~ out porter dehors; exécuter; mener à bonne fin; ~ through exécuter, réaliser; 2. v/i. porter (son, fusil); faire une trajectoire (balle); ~ on persister; F faire des scènes; F se comporter; F ~ on with flirter avec (q.); ~ing capacity charge f utile; 3. fusil: portée f; trajet m.

cart [kɑːt] 1. charrette f; ✕ fourgon m; ~ grease cambouis m; fig. put the ~ before the horse mettre la charrue devant les bœufs; sl. in the ~ dans le pétrin; 2. charrier, charroyer; **'cart·age** charroi m; (prix m du) charriage m.

car·tel [kɑː'tel] cartel m; ✝ syndicat m de producteurs; ✕ convention f pour l'échange de prisonniers.

car·ter ['kɑːtə] charretier m, camionneur m.

car·ti·lage ['kɑːtilidʒ] cartilage m; **car·ti·lag·i·nous** [_'lædʒinəs] cartilagineux (-euse f).

cart-load ['kɑːtloud] charretée f; charbon: tombereau m.

car·tog·ra·pher [kɑː'tɔgrəfə] cartographe m; **car'tog·ra·phy** cartographie f.

car·ton ['kɑːtən] carton m; a ~ of cigarettes une cartouche de cigarettes.

car·toon [kɑː'tuːn] 1. peint. carton m; ⊕ dessin m (sur page entière), surt. portrait m caricaturé; cin. dessin m animé; 2. faire la caricature de.

car·touche [kɑː'tuːʃ] cartouche m.

car·tridge ['kɑːtridʒ] cartouche f; '~-belt ceinture: cartouchière f.

cart-wheel ['kɑːtwiːl] roue f de charrette; gymn. roue f; co. Am. dollar m d'argent.

cart·wright ['kɑːtrait] charron m.

carve [kɑːv] v/t. découper (de la viande), tailler; se frayer (un chemin); vt./i. sculpter (dans, in); graver (sur, in); **'carv·er** couteau m à découper; personne: découpeur m;

serveur *m*; ciseleur *m*; ⁓s *pl.* service *m* à découper.

carv·ing [ˈkɑːviŋ] **1.** sculpture *f*, gravure *f*; découpage *m* de la viande; **2.** à découper; à sculpter.

cas·cade [kæsˈkeid] chute *f* d'eau; cascade *f*.

case[1] [keis] **1.** caisse *f*; colis *m*; (*a. cartridge-⁓*) étui *m*; *instruments*: trousse *f*; *violon*: boîte *f*; *montre*: boîtier *m*; *magasin*: vitrine *f*; *livre*: couverture *f*; *typ.* casse *f*; **2.** encaisser; cartonner (*un livre*); ⊕ chemiser (*une chaudière*); envelopper (de, with).

case[2] [⁓] cas *m* (*a.* ⚕, ⚖, *gramm.*); ⚕ *a.* malade *mf*; *Am.* F original *m*; ⚖ *a.* cause *f*, affaire *f*; exposé *m* des faits; réclamation *f*; *a* ⁓ *for* (*gér.*) des raisons de (*inf.*); *have a strong* ⁓ être dans son droit; avoir des raisons sérieuses (*pour, for*); *as the* ⁓ *may be* selon le cas; *in* ⁓ au cas où; à tout hasard; *in any* ⁓ en tout cas; '⁓·**book** dossier *m* médical; rapports *m/pl.* de cas sociaux.

case-hard·en ⊕ [ˈkeishɑːdn] aciérer; *fig.* ⁓ed endurci.

ca·se·in ⚕ [ˈkeisiiːn] caséine *f*.

case-knife [ˈkeisnaif] couteau *m* à gaine.

case·mate ⚔ [ˈkeismeit] casemate *f*.

case·ment [ˈkeismənt] fenêtre *f* à deux battants; croisée *f*; ⁓ *cloth* tissu *m* de rideaux.

case-shot [ˈkeisʃɔt] mitraille *f*.

cash [kæʃ] **1.** espèces *f/pl.*; argent *m* comptant; ⁓ *down, for* ⁓ argent comptant; *in* ⁓ en espèces; *be in* (*out of*) ⁓ (ne pas) être en fonds; ⁓ *payment* paiement *m* (au) comptant; ⁓ *on delivery* livraison *f* contre remboursement; ⁓ *dispenser* changeur *m* de monnaie; ⁓ *price* prix *m* au comptant; ⁓ *register* caisse *f* enregistreuse; **2.** encaisser (*un coupon*); toucher (*un chèque*); '⁓·**book** livre *m* de caisse; sommier *m*; '⁓·**cheque** chèque *m* ouvert; '⁓·**desk** caisse *f*; *théâ. etc.* guichet; **cash·ier** [kæˈʃiə] **1.** caissier (-ère *f*) *m*; **2.** ⚔ casser (*un officier*); '**cash·less** sans argent; F à sec.   [*m.*⟩

cash·mere [kæʃˈmiə] *tex.* cachemire *m.*⟩

cas·ing [ˈkeisiŋ] encaissement *m*; enveloppe *f*; *livre*: cartonnage *m*; *cylindre*: chemise *f*; *turbine*: bâche *f*; ⚠ revêtement *m*.

ca·si·no [kəˈsiːnou] casino *m*.

cask [kɑːsk] fût *m*, tonneau *m*.

cas·ket [ˈkɑːskit] cassette *f*, coffret *m*; *Am.* cercueil *m* (de luxe).

cas·sa·tion ⚖ [kæˈseiʃn] cassation *f*.

cas·se·role [ˈkæsəroul] *cuis.* daubière *f*; ⚕ casserole *f*; ⁓ *of chicken* poulet *m* en cocotte.

cas·sette [kəˈset] cassette *f*; ⁓ **deck** platine *f* à cassettes; ⁓ **play·er** lecteur *m* de cassettes; ⁓ **re·cord·er** magnétophone *m* à cassettes.

cas·si·a ⚕ [ˈkæsiə] casse *f* (*a. pharm.*); *arbre*: cassier *m*.

cas·sock [ˈkæsɔk] soutane *f*.

cas·so·war·y *orn.* [ˈkæsəwɛəri] casoar *m*; *New Holland* ⁓ émeu *m*.

cast [kɑːst] **1.** jet *m*; coup *m*; ⊕ *metall.* coulée *f*; moulage *m*; ⚓ coup *m* (de sonde); bas *m* de ligne; *théâ.* troupe *f*; distribution *f* des rôles; ✝ additon *f*; *fig.* trempe *f*, tournure *f* (*d'esprit*); **2.** [*irr.*] *v/t.* jeter (*a.* ⚓ *l'ancre*), lancer; donner (*son suffrage*); *zo.* jeter (*sa dépouille*); *orn.* (*usu.* ⁓ *its feathers*) muer; perdre (*les dents*); jeter (*un regard*); projeter (*une lumière, une ombre, etc.*); *métall.* couler; *typ.* clicher (*une page*); *théâ.* distribuer les rôles de (*une pièce*), assigner (*un rôle* à q., *s.o. for a part*); ✝, Ⱥ (*a.* ⁓ *up*) additionner, faire le total; ⁓ *iron* fonte *f* (de fer); ⁓ *steel* fonte *f* d'acier; ⚖ *in costs* être condamné aux frais; ⚖ *be* ⁓ *in a lawsuit* perdre un procès, être débouté; ⁓ *lots* tirer au sort (*pour, for*); ⁓ *one's skin* se dépouiller; ⁓ *s.th. in s.o.'s teeth* reprocher qch. à q.; ⁓ *away* rejeter; ⚓ *be* ⁓ *away* faire naufrage; ⁓ *down* jeter bas; baisser (*les yeux*); *be* ⁓ *down* être découragé; ⁓ *up* lever au ciel; ⚕ rejeter; ✝ ⁓ *up* (*accounts*) additionner, faire le total; **3.** *v/i.* se voiler; ⊕ se couler; ⁓ *about for* chercher; briguer; ⚓ ⁓ *off* abattre sous le vent; démarrer.

cas·ta·net [kæstəˈnet] castagnette *f*.

cast·a·way [ˈkɑːstəwei] **1.** rejeté; ⚓ naufragé; **2.** naufragé(e *f*) *m*; *fig.* proscrit(e *f*) *m*; exilé(e *f*) *m*.

caste [kɑːst] caste *f*; *fig.* rang *m*, classe *f*; ⁓ *feeling* esprit *m* de caste.

cas·tel·lan [ˈkæstələn] châtelain *m*; **cas·tel·lat·ed** [ˈkæsteleitid] crénelé; bâti dans le style féodal.

cas·ter [ˈkɑːstə] *see* castor[2].

cas·ti·gate ['kæstigeit] châtier; *fig.* critiquer sévèrement; **cas·ti'ga·tion** châtiment *m*, correction *f*; *fig.* critique *f* sévère.

cast·ing ['kɑ:stiŋ] **1.** ~ vote voix *f* prépondérante; **2.** jet *m*; moulage *m*, fonte *f*; *théâ.* distribution *f* des rôles; ✝ addition *f*; ~s *pl.* pièces *f/pl.*

cast-i·ron ['kɑ:st'aiən] en fonte; *fig.* de fer, rigide; ~ *alibi* alibi *m* de fer.

cas·tle ['kɑ:sl] **1.** château *m* (fort); *échecs:* tour *f*; **2.** *échecs:* roquer.

cas·tor¹ ['kɑ:stə] *pharm.* castoréum *m*; F chapeau *m* castor; ~ *oil* huile *f* de ricin.

cas·tor² [~] roulette *f* (*de meuble*); *sucre etc.:* saupoudroir *m*; ~s *pl.* huilier *m*; ✝ ~ *sugar* sucre *m* en poudre.

cas·trate [kæs'treit] châtrer; **cas'tra·tion** castration *f*; éviration *f*; *fig.* émasculation *f*.

cas·u·al ['kæʒjuəl] **1.** □ fortuit, accidentel(le *f*); F insouciant; ~ *labo(u)rer* homme *m* à l'heure, manœuvre *m* d'emploi intermittent; ~ *pauper* = **2.** indigent(e *f*) *m* de passage; **'cas·u·al·ty** accident *m*; ✗ *casualties pl.* pertes *f/pl.*

cas·u·ist ['kæzjuist] casuiste *m* (*a. péj.*); **'cas·u·ist·ry** casuistique *f* (*a. péj.*).

cat [kæt] **1.** chat(te *f*) *m*; *Am. sl.* fanatique *mf* du jazz; **2.** *sl.* renarder.

cat·a·clysm ['kætəklizm] cataclysme *m*.

cat·a·comb ['kætəkoum] catacombe *f*.

cat·a·logue, *Am. a.* **cat·a·log** ['kætəlɔg] **1.** catalogue *m*, répertoire *m*; *univ. Am.* annuaire *m*; prospectus *m*; **2.** cataloguer.

ca·tal·y·sis [kə'tælisis], *pl.* **ca'tal·y·ses** [~si:z] catalyse *f*; **cat·a·lyst** ['kætəlist] catalyseur *m*.

cat·a·pult ['kætəpʌlt] catapulte *f* (*a.* ✕); ~ *launching* catapultage *m*.

cat·a·ract ['kætərækt] cataracte *f* (*a. fig., a.* 𝕘).

ca·tarrh [kə'tɑ:] catarrhe *m*; F *surt.* rhume *m* de cerveau; **ca·tarrh·al** [kə'tɑ:rəl] catarrhal (-aux *m/pl.*).

ca·tas·tro·phe [kə'tæstrəfi] catastrophe *f*, désastre *m*; **cat·a·stroph·ic** [kætə'strɔfik] (~ally) désastreux (-euse *f*).

cat...: '~**bur·glar** cambrioleur *m*

par escalade; '~**call 1.** *théâ.* etc. sifflet *m*; **2.** siffler; chahuter.

catch [kætʃ] **1.** prise *f*; *porte, fenêtre:* loqueteau *m*; attrape *f*, tromperie *f*; *fig.* aubaine *f*; F bon parti *m* (*à épouser*); ♪ chant *m* à reprises, canon *m*; ⊕ crochet *m* d'arrêt; cliquet *m*; *cricket:* prise *f* au vol; see ~ *word*; **2.** [*irr.*] *v/t.* attraper, prendre; saisir; F obtenir, gagner; rencontrer (*un regard*); *son:* frapper (*l'oreille*); recueillir (*de l'eau*); prendre; ne pas manquer (*le train etc.*); attraper, être atteint de (*une maladie*); flanquer (*un coup*) à (*q.*); prendre (*un poisson*); accrocher (*sa robe*); attirer (*l'attention*); contracter (*une habitude*); *orage etc.:* surprendre (*q.*); *fig.* entendre, comprendre; F ~ *it* se faire attraper (par, *from*); ~ *in the act* prendre (*q.*) en flagrant délit; prendre (*q.*) sur le fait; ~ *me!* F pas si bête!; ~ *cold* prendre froid; s'enrhumer; ~ *one's breath* avoir un sursaut; ~ *s.o.'s eye* attirer l'attention de *q.*; *parl.* ~ *the Speaker's eye* obtenir la parole; ~ *up* ramasser vivement; F couper la parole à (*q.*), interrompre; rattraper (*q.*); **3.** [*irr.*] *v/i.* prendre; ⊕ mordre; s'engager (*verrou etc.*); *cuis.* attacher; ~ *at* s'accrocher à; saisir; F ~ *on* avoir du succès, prendre; *Am.* F comprendre; ~ *up with* rattraper (*q.*) '~**all** *Am.* fourre-tout *m/inv.*; '~**as-catch-can** *sp.* catch *m*; **'catch·er** *baseball:* rattrapeur *m*; **'catch·ing** ♪ entraînant; ✗ contagieux (-euse *f*); infectieux (-euse *f*); **'catch-ment ba·sin** bassin *m* de réception.

catch...: '~**pen·ny** ✝ **1.** d'attrape; **2.** camelote *f* de réclame; attrape-nigaud *m*; '~**phrase** F scie *f*, rengaine *f*; devise *f*; '~**pole** huissier *m*; F scie *f*, réplique *f*; *typ.* mot-souche (*pl.* mots-souches) *m*; '~**word** *pol.* mot *m* de ralliement; F scie *f*, réplique *f*; *typ.* mot-souche (*pl.* mots-souches) *m*; **'catch·y** *fig.* F entraînant; insidieux (-euse *f*) (*question etc.*).

cat·e·chism ['kætikizm] catéchisme *m*; **cat·e·chize** ['~kaiz] catéchiser; **cat·e·chu·men** [~'kju:mən] catéchumène *mf*.

cat·e·gor·i·cal □ [kæti'gɔrikl] catégorique; **cat·e·go·ry** ['~gəri] catégorie *f*.

cat·e·nar·y [kə'ti:nəri] **1.** caténaire;

Ą ~ *curve* funiculaire *f*; **2.** caténaire *f*; chaînette *f*.

ca·ter ['keitə]: ~ *for* approvisionner; *fig.* pourvoir à; **'ca·ter·er** approvisionneur (-euse *f*) *m*; fournisseur *m*; *banquet*: traiteur *m*; **'ca·ter·ing** approvisionnement *m*.

cat·er·pil·lar ['kætəpilə] chenille *f*; ~ *wheel* roue *f* à chenille.

cat·er·waul ['kætəwɔ:l] miauler.

cat·gut ['kætgʌt] corde *f* à boyau.

ca·the·dral [kə'θi:drl] **1.** *su.* cathédrale *f*; **2.** *adj.* cathédral (-aux *m/pl.*).

Cath·er·ine-wheel △ ['kæθərin-wi:l] rosace *f* rayonnante; *pièce d'artifice*: soleil *m*; roue *f* à feu.

cath·e·ter ['kæθitə] sonde *f* creuse, cathéter *m*.

cath·ode ⚡ ['kæθoud] **1.** cathode *f*; **2.** cathodique.

cath·o·lic ['kæθəlik] **1.** (~[*al*]*ly*) universel(le *f*); catholique; **2.** catholique *mf*; **ca·thol·i·cism** [kə'θɔlisizm] catholicisme *m*.

cat·kin ♀ ['kætkin] chaton *m*.

cat·nap ['kætnæp] **1.** petit somme *m*; **2.** faire un petit somme.

cat's...: ~ **eye** cataphote *m*; **'~-paw** ['kætspɔ:] *fig.* dupe *f*; *be s.o.'s* ~ tirer les marrons du feu pour q.

cat·sup ['kætsəp] *Am. see* ketchup.

cat·tle ['kætl] bétail *m*; bestiaux *m/pl.*; **'~-plague** peste *f* bovine; **'~-rus·tler** *Am.* voleur *m* de bétail; **'~-show** comice *m* agricole; concours *m* d'élevage.

cat·walk ['kætwɔ:k] passerelle *f*.

Cau·ca·sian [kɔ:'keiziən] **1.** caucasien(ne *f*); du Caucase; **2.** Caucasien(ne *f*) *m*.

cau·cus ['kɔ:kəs] comité *m* électoral; *usu. péj.* clique *f* politique; *pol. Am.* réunion *f* préliminaire (*d'un comité électoral*).

cau·dal *zo.* ['kɔ:dl] caudal (-aux *m/pl.*); **cau·date** ['~deit] caudifère.

cau·dle ['kɔ:dl] chaudeau *f*.

caught [kɔ:t] *prét. et p.p. de catch* 2, 3.

ca(u)l·dron ['kɔ:ldrən] chaudron *m*; ⊕ chaudière *f*.

cau·li·flow·er ♀ ['kɔliflauə] chou-fleur (*pl.* choux-fleurs) *m*.

caulk ⚓ [kɔ:k] calfater; **'caulk·er** calfat *m*.

caus·al □ ['kɔ:zl] causal (*sg. seulement*); causatif (-ive *f*); **cau·sal·i·ty** [~'zæliti] causalité *f*; **'caus·a·tive**

causatif (-ive *f*); **cause** [kɔ:z] **1.** cause *f*; raison *f*, motif *m*; ⚖ cause *f*; procès *m*; *fig.* querelle *f*; *with good* ~ pour cause; **2.** occasionner, causer; faire (faire qch. à q., *s.o. to do s.th.*); **'cause·less** □ sans cause, sans motif.

cause·way ['kɔ:zwei], *a.* **cau·sey** ['~zei] chaussée *f*, digue *f* (*à travers des marécages*).

caus·tic ['kɔ:stik] **1.** caustique *m*; *phys.* caustique *f*; **2.** (~*ally*) caustique; *fig. a.* mordant.

cau·ter·i·za·tion ⚕ [kɔ:tərai'zeiʃn] cautérisation *f*; **'cau·ter·ize** cautériser; **'cau·ter·y** cautère *m*.

cau·tion ['kɔ:ʃn] **1.** précaution *f*; prudence *f*; avertissement *m*; réprimande *f*; F drôle *m* de pistolet; ⚖ caution *f*, garant *m*; ~ *money* cautionnement *m*; **2.** avertir (contre, *against*); **'cau·tion·ar·y** d'avertissement, avertisseur (-euse *f*).

cau·tious □ ['kɔ:ʃəs] prudent, circonspect; **'cau·tious·ness** prudence *f*, circonspection *f*.

cav·al·cade [kævl'keid] cavalcade *f*.

cav·a·lier [kævə'liə] **1.** cavalier *m*; F galant *m*; **2.** □ désinvolte, cavalier (-ère *f*).

cav·al·ry ⚔ ['kævlri] cavalerie *f*.

cave [keiv] **1.** caverne *f*, antre *m*; grotte *f*; **2.** des cavernes; **3.**: ~ *in* *v/i.* s'effondrer; F céder (*personne*); *v/t.* F aplatir.

ca·ve·at ⚖ ['keiviæt] opposition *f*.

cave-man ['keivmən] troglodyte *m*; F homme *m* à la manière forte.

cav·en·dish ['kævəndiʃ] tabac *m* foncé édulcoré.

cav·ern ['kævən] caverne *f* (*a.* ⚕); souterrain *m*; **'cav·ern·ous** caverneux (-euse *f*) (*a. fig.*).

cav·i·ar(e) ['kæviɑ:] caviar *m*.

cav·il ['kævil] **1.** argutie *f*; **2.** pointiller (sur *at*, *about*); **'cav·il·ler** chicaneur (-euse *f*) *m*.

cav·i·ty ['kæviti] cavité *f*; creux *m*; trou *m*.

ca·vort *Am.* F [kə'vɔ:t] cabrioler; faire des galopades.

ca·vy *zo.* ['keivi] cobaye *m*, cochon *m* d'Inde. [ment *m*.)

caw [kɔ:] **1.** croasser; **2.** croasse-)

cay·enne [kei'en], **cay·enne pep·per** ['keien] poivre *m* de Cayenne.

cay·man *zo.* ['keimən], *pl.* **-mans** caïman *m*.

cay·use Am. ['kaiju:s] petit cheval m (indien).

cease [si:s] v/i. cesser (de, from); v/t. cesser (a. ✕ le feu); arrêter; '~·'fire ✕ cessez-le-feu m/inv.; '**cease·less** □ incessant; sans arrêt.

ce·dar ♀ ['si:də] cèdre m.

cede [si:d] céder.

ceil [si:l] plafonner (une pièce); † lambrisser; '**ceil·ing** plafond m (a. fig.); ⚓ vaigrage m; ~ lighting illumination f de plafond; ~ price prix m maximum.

cel·an·dine ♀ ['seləndain] éclaire f.

cel·e·brate ['selibreit] célébrer (a. eccl., a. fig. = glorifier); '**cel·e·brat·ed** célèbre (par, for); renommé (pour, for); **cel·e·'bra·tion** célébration f (a. eccl.); in ~ of pour commémorer ou fêter (qch.); ~ of May-day fête f du premier mai; '**cel·e·bra·tor** célébrateur m.

ce·leb·ri·ty [si'lebriti] célébrité f (a. personne).

ce·ler·i·ty [si'leriti] célérité f.

cel·er·y ♀ ['seləri] céleri m.

ce·les·tial □ [si'lestjəl] céleste.

cel·i·ba·cy ['selibəsi] célibat m; **cel·i·bate** ['~bit] 1. célibataire, de célibataire; 2. célibataire mf.

cell [sel] cellule f; ⚡ élément m de pile.

cel·lar ['selə] 1. cave f; 2. mettre en cave ou en chai; '**cel·lar·age** emmagasinage m; caves f/pl.; '**cel·lar·et** cave f à liqueurs.

celled [seld] à cellule(s); ⚡ à pile(s).

cel·list ♪ ['tʃelist] violoncelliste mf; **cel·lo** ['tʃelou] violoncelle m.

cel·lo·phane ['selofein] cellophane f.

cel·lu·lar ['seljulə] cellulaire; **cel·lule** ['~ju:l] cellule f; **cel·lu·loid** ['~julɔid] celluloïd m; **cel·lu·lose** ['~lous] cellulose f.

Celt [kelt] Celte mf; '**Celt·ic** celte; celtique.

ce·ment [si'ment] 1. ciment m; anat., a. métall. cément m; 2. cimenter (a. fig.); coller; métall. cémenter; ~ mixer bétonnière f; **ce·men·ta·tion** [si:men'teiʃn] cimentage m; collage m; métall. cémentation f.

cem·e·ter·y ['semitri] cimetière m.

cen·o·taph ['senətɑ:f] cénotaphe m.

cense [sens] encenser; '**cen·ser** encensoir m.

cen·sor ['sensə] 1. censeur m; 2. interdire; expurger; **cen·so·ri·ous** □ [sen'sɔ:riəs] porté à censurer; sévère; **cen·sor·ship** ['~səʃip] censure f; contrôle m.

cen·sur·a·ble □ ['senʃərəbl] censurable, blâmable; **cen·sure** ['senʃə] 1. censure f, blâme m; réprimande f; 2. censurer; blâmer publiquement.

cen·sus ['sensəs] recensement m.

cent [sent] Am. cent m (= ¹/₁₀₀ dollar); F sou m; per ~ pour cent.

cen·taur myth. ['sentɔ:] centaure m.

cen·tau·ry ♀ ['sentɔ:ri] centaurée f.

cen·te·nar·i·an [senti'nɛəriən] centenaire (a. su./mf); **cen·te·nar·y** [sen'ti:nəri] centenaire m.

cen·ten·ni·al [sen'tenjəl] centennal (-aux m/pl.); Am. see centenary.

cen·tes·i·mal □ [sen'tesiml] centésimal (-aux m/pl.).

centi... [senti]: '~·grade centigrade; '~·gramme centigramme m; '~·me·tre centimètre m; ~·pede zo. ['~pi:d] centipède m; F mille-pattes m/inv.

cen·tral ['sentrəl] □ central (-aux m/pl.); ~ heating chauffage m central; ~ office, ⚡ ~ station centrale f; téléph. Am. central m; **cen·tral·i·za·tion** [~lai'zeiʃn] centralisation f; '**cen·tral·ize** (se) centraliser.

cen·tre, Am. **cen·ter** ['sentə] 1. centre m (a. ✕, pol.), milieu m; foot. ~ forward avant-centre m; foot. ~ half demi-centre m; 2. central (-aux m/pl.), du centre; 3. v/t. placer au centre; centrer (a. foot.); concentrer; v/i. se concentrer (dans, in; sur, on; autour de, round); '~·bit ⊕ mèche f anglaise.

cen·tric, **cen·tri·cal** □ ['sentrik(l)] central (-aux m/pl.), du centre; **cen·trif·u·gal** □ [sen'trifjugl] centrifuge; **cen·trip·e·tal** □ [~pitl] centripète.

cen·tu·ple ['sentjupl] 1. □ centuple (a. su./m); 2. centupler.

cen·tu·ry ['sentʃuri] siècle m; cricket: centaine f.

ce·ram·ic [si'ræmik] céramique; **ce·ram·ics** pl. céramique f.

ce·re·al ['siəriəl] 1. céréale; 2. céréale f; usu. ~s pl. céréales f/pl. en flocons.

cer·e·bel·lum anat. [seri'beləm] cervelet m; **cer·e·bral** ['seribrəl] céré-

bral (-aux *m/pl.*); **ce·re·brum** ['seribrəm] cerveau *m*.
cere·cloth ['siəklɔθ] toile *f* d'embaumement.
cer·e·mo·ni·al [seri'mounjəl] **1.** □ (*a.* **cer·e'mo·ni·ous** □) cérémonieux (-euse *f*), de cérémonie; **2.** cérémonial (*pl.* -s) *m*; **cer·e·mo·ny** ['serimǝni] cérémonie *f*; formalité *f*; *Master of Ceremonies* maître *m* des cérémonies; *without* ~ sans cérémonie, sans façon; *stand on* ~ faire des façons.
cer·tain □ ['sǝ:tn] certain, sûr; infaillible; *see some* 2; **'cer·tain·ty** certitude *f*; chose *f* certaine; conviction *f*.
cer·tif·i·cate 1. [sǝ'tifikit] certificat *m*, attestation *f*; diplôme *m*; brevet *m*; ~ *of birth* (*death, marriage*) acte *m* de naissance (de décès, de mariage); ~ *of employment* certificat *m* de travail; *medical* ~ certificat *m* médical; **2.** [~keit] diplômer, breveter; délivrer un certificat *etc.* à (*q.*); ~*ed* diplômé; **cer·ti·fi·a·ble** ['sǝ:tifaiǝbl] qu'on peut certifier; bon(ne *f*) à enfermer, fou (folle *f*); **cer·ti·fi·ca·tion** certification *f*; **cer·ti·fy** ['~fai] certifier, attester; diplômer; authentiquer; *this is to* ~ je soussigné certifie; **cer·ti·tude** ['~tju:d] certitude *f*.   [*m/pl.*).\
cer·vi·cal ['sǝ:vikl] cervical (-aux
ces·sa·tion [se'seiʃn] cessation *f*, arrêt *m*.
ces·sion ['seʃn] cession *f*; abandon *m*.
cess·pool ['sespu:l] fosse *f* d'aisance.
ce·ta·cean zo. [si'teiʃiǝn] **1.** cétacé *m*; **2.** *a.* **ce'ta·ceous**) cétacé.
chafe [tʃeif] *v/t.* frictionner; user par le frottement; écorcher (*la peau*); irriter; *v/i.* s'user par le frottement; s'écorcher; s'irriter (*contre, against*), s'érailler (*corde*); *chafing dish* réchaud *m* (*de table*).
chaff [tʃɑ:f] **1.** balle *f* (*de grain*); menue paille *f*; paille *f* hachée; *fig.* vétilles *f/pl.*; F raillerie *f*; **2.** hacher (*de la paille*); F railler, plaisanter (*q.*); **'~-cut·ter** hache-paille *m/inv.*
chaf·fer ['tʃæfǝ] marchander (*q., with s.o.*).
chaf·finch zo. ['tʃæfintʃ] pinson *m*.
cha·grin ['ʃægrin] **1.** chagrin *m*; **2.** chagriner.
chain [tʃein] **1.** chaîne *f* (*a. fig.*);

suite *f* (*des événements*); chaînette *f*; *surt. Am.* ~-*store* succursale *f* de grand magasin; *mot.* ~ *drive* transmission *f* par chaînes; **2.** attacher par des chaînes; enchaîner; ~ **re·ac·tion** *phys.* réaction *f* en chaîne; **'~-smoke** fumer une cigarette après l'autre; **'~-smok·er** fumeur (-euse *f*) *m* invétéré(e) (qui fume sans arrêt).
chair [tʃɛǝ] **1.** chaise *f*, siège *m*; fauteuil *m*; (*a. professorial* ~) chaire *f*; ⊞ coussinet *m*; ⚡ *Am.* fauteuil *m* électrique; *see chair(wo)man*; ~! ~! à l'ordre! à l'ordre!; *be in the* ~ présider; **2.** *v/i.* prendre la présidence; *v/t.* porter (*q.*) en triomphe; **'~-man** président *m*; **'~-wom·an** présidente *f*.
chaise [ʃeiz] cabriolet *m*, chaise *f*.
chal·dron ['tʃɔ:ldrǝn] *mesure à charbon de 36 boisseaux (72 à Newcastle) anglais.*
chal·ice ['tʃælis] calice *m*.
chalk [tʃɔ:k] **1.** craie *f*; *billard:* blanc *m*; *red* ~ sanguine *f*; F *by a long* ~ de beaucoup; **2.** marquer à la craie; talquer; (*usu.* ~ *up*) écrire à la craie; ~ *out* tracer (*un plan*); **'chalk·y** crayeux (-euse *f*), crétacé; terreux (-euse *f*) (*teint*).
chal·lenge ['tʃælindʒ] **1.** défi *m*; provocation *f* (en duel, *to a duel*); ⚖ interpellation *f*; récusation *f*; **2.** défier, provoquer (*q.*); *sp.* porter un défi à; ⚖ interpeller; récuser; disputer; mettre en doute; **'challeng·er** provocateur (-trice *f*) *m*; *sp.* lanceur *m* d'un challenge.
cha·lyb·e·ate ⚕ [kǝ'libiit] ferrugineux (-euse *f*).
cham·ber ['tʃeimbǝ] ⚘, ⊕, *poét., parl., zo., Am.* chambre *f*; ~*s pl.* appartement *m* de garçon; cabinet *m*, étude *f*; *see* ~-*pot*; **cham·ber·lain** ['~lin] chambellan *m*; **'cham·ber·maid** *hôtel:* femme *f* de chambre; **'cham·ber·pot** vase *m* de nuit.
cha·me·le·on zo. [kǝ'mi:ljǝn] caméléon *m*.
cham·fer △ ['tʃæmfǝ] **1.** biseau *m*; **2.** biseauter; canneler (*une colonne*).
cham·ois ['ʃæmwɑ:; *pl.* -wɑ:z] zo. chamois *m*; ⊕ (*ou* ~ *leather*) [*souv.* 'ʃæmi] (peau *f* de) chamois *m*.
champ¹ [tʃæmp] (*at*) mâcher bruyamment; ronger (*le mors*).
champ² *Am. sl.* [~] *see champion 1.*

cham·pagne [ʃæmˈpein] champagne *m*.

cham·paign [ˈtʃæmpein] campagne *f* ouverte.

cham·pi·on [ˈtʃæmpjən] 1. champion *m* (*a. sp.*); *sp.* recordman (*pl.* recordmen) *m*; 2. soutenir, défendre; **'cham·pi·on·ship** défense *f*; *sp.* championnat *m*.

chance [tʃɑːns] 1. chance *f*, hasard *m*; occasion *f* (de, of); *surt. Am.* risque *m*; *by* ~ par hasard; *take a* (*ou* one's) ~ encourir un risque; 2. fortuit, accidentel(le *f*); de rencontre; 3. *v/i.*: ~ *to see* voir par hasard; avoir l'occasion de voir; ~ *upon* rencontrer par hasard; *v/t.* F risquer.

chan·cel [ˈtʃɑːnsəl] chœur *m*; sanctuaire *m*; **'chan·cel·ler·y** chancellerie *f*; **'chan·cel·lor** chancelier *m*; *see* exchequer; **'chan·cel·lor·ship** dignité *f* de chancelier.

chan·cer·y 🏛 [ˈtʃɑːnsəri] cour *f* de la chancellerie; *fig. in* ~ en danger; dans une situation difficile.

chanc·y F [ˈtʃɑːnsi] risqué.

chan·de·lier [ʃændiˈliə] lustre *m*.

chan·dler [ˈtʃɑːndlə] marchand *m* (de couleurs), droguiste *m*; **'chandler·y** épicerie-droguerie *f*.

change [tʃeindʒ] 1. changement *m*; revirement *m* (*d'opinion etc.*); monnaie *f*; *Bourse:* change *m*; 2. *v/t.* changer (de) (*qch.*); échanger; modifier; relever (*la garde*); échanger (contre, *for*); ~*one's mind* changer d'avis; *v/i.* (se) changer (en, *into*); varier; changer de vêtements; 👕 (*ou* ~ *trains*) changer de **'Change** [~] *Bourse f*. [train.]

change·a·bil·i·ty [tʃeindʒəˈbiliti] *temps:* variabilité *f*; versatilité *f*; *caractère:* mobilité *f*; **'change·a·ble** ☐ changeant; variable; mobile; **'change·less** ☐ immuable; fixe; **'change·ling** enfant *m* changé en nourrice; **'change-'o·ver** changement *m*; *pol.* renversement *m*.

chan·nel [ˈtʃænl] 1. *géog.* canal *m*; conduit *m*; *rivière:* lit *m*; *port:* passe *f*; *irrigation:* rigole *f*; *télév.* chaîne *f*; *fig.* voie *f* (*diplomatique*); artère *f*; *by the official* ~*s* par (la) voie hiérarchique; 2. creuser des rigoles dans; canneler.

chant *eccl.* [tʃɑːnt] 1. plain-chant (*pl.* plains-chants) *m*; psalmodie *f*;

chant *m* monotone; 2. psalmodier; *fig.* chanter (*des louanges*); **'chan·try** *eccl.* chapelle *f*, chantrerie *f*.

cha·os [ˈkeiɔs] chaos *m*; **cha'ot·ic** (~*ally*) chaotique, sans ordre.

chap¹ [tʃæp] 1. gerçure *f*, crevasse *f*; 2. gercer, crevasser.

chap² [~] bajoue *f* (*d'un animal,* F *d'une personne*).

chap³ F [~] garçon *m*, type *m*, individu *m*.

chap-book [ˈtʃæpbuk] livre *m* de colportage.

chap·el [ˈtʃæpl] chapelle *f*; oratoire *m*; *typ.* atelier *m* (syndiqué).

chap·er·on [ˈʃæpəroun] 1. chaperon *m*; 2. chaperonner.

chap-fall·en [ˈtʃæpfɔːlən] abattu.

chap·lain [ˈtʃæplin] aumônier *m*; **'chap·lain·cy** aumônerie *f*.

chap·let [ˈtʃæplit] guirlande *f*; *eccl.* chapelet *m*.

chap·ter [ˈtʃæptə] chapitre *m* (*a. eccl.*); *Am.* filiale *f* (*d'une société*); régionale *f*; *Brit.* ~ *of accidents* suite *f* de malheurs, serie *f* noire; *give* (*ou quote*) ~ *and verse* citer ses autorités; fournir des preuves.

char¹ *icht.* [tʃɑː] ombre *m*.

char² [~] (se) carboniser.

char-à-banc [ˈʃærəbæŋ] autocar *m*; F car *m*.

char·ac·ter [ˈkæriktə] caractère *m* (*a. typ.*); marque *f* distinctive; réputation *f*; genre *m*; *domestique:* certificat *m* de moralité; *métier:* qualité *f*; *typ. a.* lettre *f*; *théâ.,* *roman:* personnage *m*; *théâ. a.* rôle *m*; F personnalité *f*; F type *m*, original *m*; F mauvais sujet *m*; ~ *assassination* assassinat *m* moral; *that's in* (*out of*) ~ *for him* cela (ne) lui ressemble (pas); **char·ac·ter'is·tic** 1. (~*ally*) caractéristique (de, of); particulier(-ère *f*) (*signe*); ✠ diacritique; ♪ de genre; 2. trait *m* caractéristique *ou* de caractère; propre *m*; **char·ac·ter·i·za·tion** [~raiˈzeiʃn] caractérisation *f*; **'char·ac·ter·ize** caractériser; être caractéristique de.

cha·rade [ʃəˈrɑːd] charade *f*.

char·coal [ˈtʃɑːkoul] charbon *m* (de bois); *peint.* fusain *m*; **'~-burn·er** charbonnier *m*.

chare [tʃɛə] 1. faire des ménages en ville; travailler à la journée; 2. *usu.* ~*s pl.* travaux *m/pl.* domestiques.

charge [tʃɑːdʒ] 1. ✗, 🏛, ⚒, ✈, *foot.,*

wagon, cartouche: charge *f* (*a. fig.*) (*de, of*); emploi *m*, fonction *f*; *eccl.* cure *f*; devoir *m*; soin *m*, garde *f*; recommandation *f*; *arme à feu*: décharge *f*; ✕ *a.* attaque *f*; *foot. a.* choc *m*; ⚖ plainte *f*, chef *m* d'accusation, réquisitoire *m*; *fig.* privilège *m* (sur, on); prix *m*; *admin.* droits *m/pl.*; ✝ ~s *pl.* frais *m/pl.*; tarif *m*; ✝ ~ *account* compte *m* crédit d'achats; *be in* ~ *of* être préposé à la garde de (*qch.*); *take* ~ *of* se charger de; *free of* ~ exempt de frais; franco; à titre gratuit; 2. *v/t.* charger (*a.* ✕); passer (à, to) (*dépense*); débiter (*des marchandises à un client, goods to a customer*); accuser, inculper (q. de qch., s.o. with s.th.); ⚖ ~ *the jury* faire le résumé des débats; ~ *on, upon* foncer sur (*q.*); porter sur (*la note*); ~ *s.o. a price* demander un prix à q. (pour qch., *for s.th.*); 'charge·a·ble □ inculpable (de, with); imputable (à, to); à la charge (de, to, on).

char·gé d'af·faires *pol.* ['ʃɑːʒei dæˈfɛə] chargé *m* d'affaires.

charg·er ✕, *poét.* ['ʃɑːdʒə] cheval *m* de bataille, cheval *m* d'armes.

char·i·ot *poét., hist.* ['tʃæriət] char *m*; char·i·ot·eer [~ˈtiə] conducteur *m* de char.

char·i·ta·ble □ ['tʃæritəbl] charitable; indulgent (*personne*); de charité (*œuvre*); ~ *society* société *f* de bienfaisance.

char·i·ty ['tʃæriti] charité *f*; bienfaisance *f*, aumônes *f/pl.*; œuvre *f* de bienfaisance; fondation *f* pieuse; *sister of* ~ fille *f* de la Charité, sœur *f* de charité; ~ *begins at home* charité bien ordonnée commence par soi-même; '~-'child enfant *mf* élevé(e) dans un orphelinat; '~-'school orphelinat *m*.

char·la·tan ['ʃɑːlətən] charlatan *m*; 'char·la·tan·ry charlatanerie *f*.

char·lotte *cuis.* ['ʃɑːlət] charlotte *f*.

charm [tʃɑːm] 1. charme *m* (*a. fig.*); porte-bonheur *m/inv.*; sortilège *m*; 2. jeter un sort sur; *fig.* charmer; ~ *away etc.* charmer (*les ennuis etc.*); *bear a* ~*ed life* F être verni; 'charm·er *fig.* charmeur (-euse *f*) *m*; F jolie femme *f*; 'charm·ing □ charmant, ravissant.

char·nel-house ['tʃɑːnlhaus] charnier *m*, ossuaire *m*.

chart [tʃɑːt] 1. ⚓ carte *f* marine; ⊕

graphique *m*; tableau *m*; 2. dresser la carte de; porter sur une carte.

char·ter ['tʃɑːtə] 1. charte *f*; privilège *m* (*a. fig.*); ⚓ affrètement *m*; (*usu.* ~-*party*) charte-partie (*pl.* chartes-parties) *f*; *Am.* ~ *member* membre *m* fondateur; 2. instituer (*une compagnie*) par charte; ~*ed accountant* expert *m* comptable.

char·wom·an ['tʃɑːwumən] femme *f* de journée *ou* de ménage.

char·y □ ['tʃɛəri] (*of*) circonspect; chiche (de); sobre (de).

chase¹ [tʃeis] 1. chasse *f* (*a.* = *proie*), poursuite *f* (*a. fig.*); *beasts of* ~ bêtes *f/pl.* fauves; 2. chasser; poursuivre (*a. fig.*); *fig.* donner la chasse à (*q.*); *v/i.* (*usu.* ~ *off*) partir à la hâte.

chase² [~] ciseler; sertir (*un bijou*).

chase³ *typ.* [~] châssis *m*.

chas·er¹ ['tʃeisə] chasseur (-euse *f*) *m* (*a.* ✕); ⚓ (*navire m*) chasseur *m*.

chas·er² [~] ciseleur *m*.

chasm ['kæzm] gouffre *m* béant; gorge *f*; fissure *f*; abîme *m* (*a. fig.*); *fig.* immense lacune *f*.

chas·sis ['ʃæsi], *pl.* -sis [-siz] châssis *m*.

chaste □ [tʃeist] chaste, pudique; pur (*a. style*).

chas·ten ['tʃeisn] châtier (*q., son style, ses passions*); assagir (*q.*).

chas·tise [tʃæsˈtaiz] corriger; chas·tise·ment ['~tizmənt] châtiment *m*.

chas·ti·ty ['tʃæstiti] chasteté *f*; *fig.* pureté *f*.

chas·u·ble *eccl.* ['tʃæzjubl] chasuble *f*.

chat [tʃæt] 1. causerie *f*; *télév.* ~ *show* causerie *f* télévisée; 2. causer, bavarder.

chat·tels ['tʃætlz] *pl.* (*usu.* goods and ~) biens *m/pl.* et effets *m/pl.*; meubles *m/pl.*

chat·ter ['tʃætə] 1. bavarder; caqueter (*personne, a. oiseau*); jaser (*oiseau, a. personne*); claquer (*dents*); 2. caquet(age) *m*; bavardage *m*; '~·box F babillard(e *f*) *m*; 'chat·ter·er bavard(e *f*) *m*.

chat·ty ['tʃæti] causeur (-euse *f*) (*personne*); sur le ton de la conversation (*article*).

chauf·feur ['ʃoufə] chauffeur *m*; chauf·feuse [~ˈfɜːz] chauffeuse *f*.

chau·vin·ism ['ʃouvinizm] chauvinisme *m*; 'chau·vin·ist chauvin(e *f*) *m*; **'chau·vin·is·tic** (~*ally*) chauvin, chauviniste.

chaw *sl.* [tʃɔ:] mâcher; *Am. sl.* ~ *up usu. fig.* démolir; massacrer.

cheap □ [tʃi:p] bon marché, pas cher (chère *f*); à prix réduits; *fig.* trivial (-aux *m/pl.*), vulgaire; F feel ~ ne pas être dans son assiette; hold ~ faire peu de cas de; F on the ~ à peu de frais; ⚲ *jack* camelot *m*; ✝ ~ *money policy* politique *f* de facilités d'escompte; **'cheap·en** *v/t.* baisser le prix de; *v/i.* diminuer de prix; **'cheap·skate** *Am. sl.* radin *m*.

cheat [tʃi:t] **1.** trompeur (-euse *f*) *m*; escroc *m*; *jeux*: tricheur (-euse *f*) *m*; **2.** tromper; frauder; frustrer (*q. de qch.,s.o.* [out] of *s.th.*); *fig.* échapper à; **'cheat·ing** tromperie *f*; *jeux*: tricherie *f*.

check [tʃek] **1.** échec *m* (*a. jeu, a.* ⚔); revers *m* (*a.* ⚔); arrêt *m*; frein *m*; contrôle *m*; billet *m*, ticket *m*; *Am.* bulletin *m* (de bagages); ✝ *Am. see* cheque; *Am. restaurant*: addition *f*; *tex.* étoffe *m* en damier; carreau *m*; ~ *pattern* damier *m*; *Am.* F *pass (ou hand) in one's* ~s mourir, avaler sa chique; keep *s.o. in* ~ tenir q. en échec; **2.** faire échec à (*a. jeu*); contenir; arrêter; retenir; refréner (*un compte*); pointer (*des noms*); (*souv.* ~ *up on*) contrôler, vérifier; (faire) enregistrer (*ses bagages*); *Am.* déposer (*son chapeau au vestiaire*); *v/i.* s'arrêter (devant, *at*); refuser (*cheval*); ~ *in* arriver; descendre à un hôtel; s'inscrire sur le registre d'un hôtel; *aéroport*: se présenter à l'enregistrement; ~ *off* cocher, pointer; ~ *out v/i.* partir; régler son compte *ou* la note en quittant un hôtel; *v/t.* retirer (*ses bagages etc.*); *surt. Am.* vérifier, contrôler; ~ *up v/t.* contrôler (*des renseignements*); *v/i.* faire la vérification; ~ **ac·count** *Am.* compte *m* courant; **'~·book** *Am.* carnet *m* de chèques, chéquier *m*; **'check·er** contrôleur *m*; ~s *pl. Am.* jeu *m* de dames; *see* chequer; **'check·er·board** *Am.* damier *m*; équiquier *m*; **'check·er·ed** *Am. see* chequered; **check-'in** *aéroport*: enregistrement *m*; ~ *counter* (guichet *m* d')enregistrement *m*; ~ *desk hôtel*: réception *f*; your ~ *time is at ...* présentez-vous à l'enregistrement à ...; **'check·ing** répression *f*;

contrôle *m*; enregistrement *m*; **'check(·ing)·room** vestiaire *m*; 🛄 *Am.* consigne *f*; **'check·list** liste *f* de contrôle, checklist *f*; **'check'mate 1.** échec et mat *m*; **2.** mater; faire échec et mat à (*a. fig.*); check-'out (*a.* ~ *counter*) caisse *f* (*à la sortie d'un self-service etc.*); **'check·up** vérification *f*; F visite *f* médicale.

cheek [tʃi:k] **1.** joue *f*; F toupet *m*; ⊕ *poulie*: joue *f*; *manivelle*: bras *m*; *étau*: mâchoire *f*; *see* jowl; **2.** F faire l'insolent avec; **'cheek·y** □ insolent, effronté.

cheep [tʃi:p] piauler.

cheer [tʃiə] **1.** (bonne) disposition *f*; encouragement *m*; bonne chère *f*; hourra *m*; bravos *m/pl.*; applaudissements *m/pl.*; be of good ~ prendre courage; three ~s! un ban (pour, for)!; vive (*q.*)!; **2.** *v/t.* applaudir (*q.*); (*a.* ~ *up*) égayer, relever le moral de; (*a.* ~ *on*) encourager; *v/i.* applaudir; pousser des vivats; (*a.* ~ *up*) reprendre sa gaieté; **cheer·ful** □ ['~ful] gai; allègre; riant; **'cheer·ful·ness**, **'cheer·i·ness** gaieté *f*; **cheer·i·o** ['~ri'ou] F à bientôt!; à la vôtre!; □ **'cheer·less** triste, sombre; **'cheer·y** □ gai, joyeux (-euse *f*).

cheese [tʃi:z] fromage *m*; hard ~ *sl.* ça, c'est de la déveine; **'~·cake** talmouse *f*; **'~·mon·ger** marchand(e *f*) *m* de fromage; **'~·par·ing** pelure *f* de fromage; *fig.* lésine *f*. **chees·y** ['tʃi:zi] caséeux (-euse *f*); de fromage.

chef [ʃef] chef *m* de cuisine.

chem·i·cal ['kemikl] **1.** □ chimique; **2.** ~s *pl.* produits *m/pl.* chimiques. **che·mise** [ʃi'mi:z] chemise *f* (*de femme*).

chem·ist ['kemist] chimiste *mf*; (*ou pharmaceutical* ~) pharmacien (-ne *f*) *m*; **'chem·is·try** chimie *f*. **chem·o·ther·a·py** 🞼 [kemo'θerəpi] chimiothérapie *f*.

cheque ✝ [tʃek] chèque *m*; not negotiable (*ou crossed*) ~ chèque *m* barré; ~ **ac·count** compte *m* courant; **'~·book** carnet *m* de chèques, chéquier *m*.

chequ·er ['tʃekə] **1.** *usu.* ~s *pl.* quadrillage *m*; **2.** quadriller; **'chequered** à carreaux, en échiquier; diapré; *fig.* accidenté (*vie*).

cher·ish ['tʃeriʃ] chérir; *fig.* caresser.

che·root [ʃə'ruːt] manille *m*.

cher·ry ['tʃeri] **1.** cerise *f*; *arbre*: cerisier *m*; **2.** cerise *adj./inv.*; vermeil(le *f*) (*lèvres*).

cher·ub ['tʃerəb], *pl.* **-ubs, -u·bim** ['ˌ⁓əbim] chérubin *m*; **che·ru·bic** [tʃə'ruːbik] chérubique; de chérubin.

cher·vil ♥ ['tʃəːvil] cerfeuil *m*.

chess [tʃes] (jeu *m* d')échecs *m/pl.*; '⁓·board échiquier *m*; '⁓·man jeu d'échecs: pièce *f*.

chest [tʃest] caisse *f*, coffre *m*; *anat.* poitrine *f*; ⁓ *of drawers* commode *f*; ♪ ⁓ *note* note *f* de poitrine; *get it off one's* ⁓ dire ce qu'on a sur le cœur.

chest·nut ['tʃesnʌt] **1.** châtaigne *f*; marron *m*; *arbre*: châtaignier *m* (commun); marronnier *m*; *fig.* vieille histoire *f*; **2.** châtain (-aine *f*).

chest·y F ['tʃesti] de poitrine (*toux etc.*); qui a la poitrine bien développée.

che·val-glass [ʃə'vælglɑːs] psyché *f*.

chev·a·lier [ʃevə'liə] chevalier *m*.

chev·i·ot *tex.* ['tʃeviət] cheviotte *f*.

chev·ron ✂ ['ʃevrən] chevron *m* (*d'ancienneté de service*); galon *m* (*de grade*).

chev·y F ['tʃevi] **1.** poursuite *f*; *sp.* (jeu *m* de) barres *f/pl.*; **2.** poursuivre; relancer (*q.*).

chew [tʃuː] *v/t.* mâcher; F ⁓ *the fat* bavarder; F ⁓ *the rag Brit.* ronchonner, *Am.* bavarder; *v/i. fig.* méditer (sur [*up*]on, over); **'chew·ing-gum** chewing-gum *m*.

chi·cane [ʃi'kein] **1.** chicane *f*; **2.** chicaner; **chi'can·er·y** chicanerie *f*; *fig.* arguties *f/pl.*

chick, chick·en ['tʃik(in)] **1.** poussin *m*, poulet *m*; **2.** *sl. chicken out* se dégonfler, flancher, caner.

chicken...: '⁓·feed *Am.* mangeaille *f*; *sl.* petite monnaie *f*; '⁓·heart·ed, '⁓·liv·ered F froussard; '⁓·pox ♥ varicelle *f*; ⁓ **run**, *Am.* ⁓ **yard** poulailler *m*.

chick...: '⁓·pea ♥ pois *m* chiche; '⁓·weed ♥ mouron *m* des oiseaux.

chic·o·ry ['tʃikəri] chicorée *f*.

chid [tʃid] *prét. et p.p.*, **'chid·den** *p.p.* de *chide*.

chide *poét.* [tʃaid] [*irr.*] gronder.

chief [tʃiːf] **1.** □ principal (-aux *m/pl.*); premier (-ère *f*); en chef; ⁓ *clerk* chef *m* de bureau; premier

clerc *m*; **2.** chef *m*; F patron *m*; ...-in-⁓ ... en chef; **chief·tain** ['ˌ⁓tən] chef *m* de clan.

chil·blain ['tʃilblein] engelure *f*.

child [tʃaild] enfant *mf*; *be a good* ⁓ être sage; *from a* ⁓ dès mon *etc.* enfance; *with* ⁓ enceinte; '⁓·bed couches *f/pl.*; '⁓·birth accouchement *m*; '⁓·hood enfance *f*; '⁓·ish □ enfantin; *péj.* puéril; '⁓·ish·ness *péj.* enfantillage *m*; puérilité *f*; '⁓·less sans enfant(s); '⁓·like enfantin; *fig.* naïf (-ïve *f*); **chil·dren** ['tʃildrən] *pl. de child*; **child's play** *fig.* jeu *m* d'enfant.

chill [tʃil] **1.** froid, glacé; **2.** froideur *f*; froid *m* (*a. fig.*); ♥ coup *m* de froid; *take the* ⁓ *off* dégourdir (*un liquide*), chambrer (*le vin*); **3.** *v/t.* refroidir, glacer; *fig.* donner le frisson à (*q.*); *métall.* tremper en coquille; '⁓ed *meat* viande *f* frigorifiée; *v/i.* se refroidir, se glacer; '**chill·ness**, '**chill·i·ness** froid *m*, fraîcheur *f*; (*a. fig.*) froideur *f*; '**chill·y** froid; frais (fraîche *f*).

chime [tʃaim] **1.** carillon *m*; *fig.* harmonie *f*; **2.** carillonner; *v/i. fig.* s'accorder, s'harmoniser (avec, with); ⁓ *in* intervenir.

chi·me·ra [kai'miərə] chimère *f*; **chi·mer·i·cal** □ [⁓'merikl] chimérique, imaginaire.

chim·ney ['tʃimni] cheminée *f* (*a. alp.*); *lampe*: verre *m*; '⁓·piece (chambranle *m* de) cheminée *f*; '⁓·pot mitre *f* ou pot *m* de cheminée; F *fig. chapeau*: tuyau *m* de poêle; '⁓·stack, '⁓·stalk souche *f*; (corps *m* de) cheminée *f*; cheminée *f* d'usine; '⁓·sweep(·er) ramoneur *m*.

chim·pan·zee *zo.* [tʃimpən'ziː] chimpanzé *m*.

chin¹ [tʃin] **1.** menton *m*; **2.** *gymn. Am.* (*usu.* ⁓ *o.s.*) faire une traction à la barre fixe.

chin² *sl.* [⁓] discourir, jaboter.

chi·na ['tʃainə] porcelaine *f*; ⁓·**man** Chinois *m*.

chine [tʃain] *anat.* échine *f*; *cuis.* échinée *f*; *géog.* arête *f*.

Chi·nese ['tʃai'niːz] **1.** chinois; **2.** *ling.* chinois *m*; Chinois(e *f*) *m*.

chink¹ [tʃiŋk] fente *f*; *mur*: lézarde *f*; *porte*: entrebâillement *m*.

chink² [⁓] **1.** *métal, verre*: tintement *m*; **2.** (faire) sonner (*son argent*); (faire) tinter.

chink³ *sl.* [~] Chinois *m.*

chintz *tex.* [tʃints] perse *f*, indienne *f.*

chin·wag *sl.* ['tʃinwæg] causerie *f.*

chip [tʃip] **1.** éclat *m*; *bois*: copeau *m*; *jeu*: jeton *m*; *ordinateur*: chip *m*; *cuis.* (*potato*) ~s *pl. Brit.* (pommes *f/pl.* de terre) frites *f/pl.*, *Am.* chips *m/pl.*; **I have a ~ on one's shoulder** chercher noise à tout le monde; **2.** *v/t.* tailler par éclats; doler (*du bois*); ébrécher (*un couteau*); enlever un morceau à (*qch.*); *v/i.* s'écailler, s'ébrécher; F ~ *in*(*to*) intervenir dans; se mêler à; **chip·muck** ['tʃipmʌk], **chip·munk** ['tʃipmʌŋk] tamias *m*; **'chip·pan** friteuse *f*; **'chip·py** sec (sèche *f*); sans saveur.

chi·rop·o·dist [ki'rɔpədist] pédicure *mf*; **chi'rop·o·dy** chirurgie *f* pédicure.

chirp [tʃɜːp] **1.** gazouiller, pépier, ramager; grésiller (*grillon*); **2.** gazouillement *m*; *grillon*: grésillement *m*; **'chirp·y** F d'humeur gaie.

chirr [tʃɜː] grésiller.

chir·rup ['tʃirəp] **1.** gazouillement *m etc.*; **2.** gazouiller *etc.*

chis·el [tʃizl] **1.** ciseau *m*; burin *m*; **2.** ciseler; buriner (*du métal*); *sl.* filouter; **'chis·el·er** ciseleur *m*; *sl.* escroc *m.*

chit [tʃit] mioche *mf*; **a ~ of a girl** une simple gosse *f.*

chit-chat ['tʃitʃæt] bavardages *m/pl.*

chiv·al·rous □ ['ʃivlrəs] chevaleresque; courtois; **'chiv·al·ry** chevalerie *f*; courtoisie *f.*

chive ♀ [tʃaiv] ciboulette *f.*

chiv·y F ['tʃivi] *see* chevy.

chlo·ral ⚗ ['klɔːrl] chloral *m*; **chlo·ride** ['~aid] chlorure *m*; **chlo·rine** ['~iːn] chlore *m*; **chlo·ro·form** ['~əfɔːm] **1.** chloroforme *m*; **2.** chloroformer.

chock ⊕ [tʃɔk] **1.** cale *f*; **2.** caler; **'~-a-'block** F bondé (de, *with*); **'~-'full** comble.

choc·o·late ['tʃɔkəlit] chocolat *m*; ~ **cream** chocolat *m* fourré à la crème.

choice [tʃɔis] **1.** choix *m*; **for ~** de préférence; **leave s.o. no ~** ôter à q. toute alternative; **make** (*ou* **take**) **one's ~** faire son choix; **2.** □ (*bien*) choisi; d'élite; de choix; surfin; † surchoix; † ~ **quality** première qualité *f.*

choir ⚘, ♪ ['kwaiə] chœur *m*; '~-

mas·ter chef *m* de chœur; ~ **stalls** *pl.* stalles *f/pl.* (de chœur).

choke [tʃouk] **1.** *v/t.* étouffer; suffoquer (*a. fig.*); étrangler; ⊕ engorger; (*usu.* ~ **up**) obstruer, boucher; ~ **down** étouffer, ravaler; fermer (*le gaz*); ~ **off** se débarrasser de; décourager; *v/i.* étouffer, se boucher; **2.** étranglement *m*; ⊕ étrangleur *m*; starter *m*; ⚡ ~ **coil** bobine *f* de réactance; self *f*; '~-**bore** ⊕ (fusil *m* de chasse à) choke-bore *m*; '~-**damp** ⚒ mofette *f*; **'chok·er** F *co.* foulard *m* (*d'ouvrier*); cravate *f* de fourrure; col *m* montant; *perles*: collier *m* court.

chol·er·a ⚕ ['kɔlərə] choléra *m*; **'chol·er·ic** colérique; irascible.

cho·les·te·rol [kə'lestərəl] cholestérol *m.*

choose [tʃuːz] [*irr.*] choisir; *v/t.* opter pour; *v/i.* ~ **to** (*inf.*) vouloir que (*sbj.*), aimer mieux (*inf.*); **'choos·y** F difficile.

chop¹ [tʃɔp] **1.** coup *m* de hache; *cuis.* côtelette *f*; ~s *pl.* bajoues *f/pl.*; babines *f/pl.*; ⊕ mâchoires *f/pl.*; ~s **and changes** vicissitudes *f/pl.*; girouetteries *f/pl.*; **2.** *v/t.* couper, fendre, hacher; (*souv.* ~ **up**) couper en morceaux; ~ **down** abattre; *v/i.* clapoter (*mer*); ~ **about** changer; ~ **and change** girouetter; tergiverser; '~**ping sea** mer *f* clapoteuse.

chop² ✝ [~] marque *f*; **first ~** (de) première qualité *f.*

chop-house ['tʃɔphaus] restaurant *m* populaire; **'chop·per** couperet *m*; *sl.* moulin *m*, banane *f* (*hélicoptère*); **'chop·ping-block** hachoir *m*; **'chop·py** variable; clapoteux (-euse *f*) (*mer*); **'chop·stick** baguette *f* (*des Chinois*).

cho·ral □ ['kɔːrl] choral (-als *ou* -aux *m/pl.*); chanté en chœur; **cho·ral**(**e**) ♪ [kɔ'rɑːl] choral (*pl.* -als) *m.*

chord [kɔːd] ♪, ♬, *poét.*, *fig.* corde *f*; ♪ accord *m*; *anat.* corde *f* (vocale), cordon *m.*

chore *surt. Am.* [tʃɔː] *see* chare.

chor·e·og·ra·phy [kɔri'ɔgrəfi] chorégraphie *f.*

chor·is·ter ['kɔristə] choriste *mf*; *eccl.* enfant *m* de chœur; *Am. a.* chef *m* de chœur.

cho·rus ['kɔːrəs] **1.** chœur *m*; refrain *m*; **2.** répéter en chœur; ~ **girl** girl *f.*

chose [tʃouz] *prét.*, **'cho·sen** *p.p. de* choose.

chough *orn.* [tʃʌf] crave *m.*

chouse F [tʃaus] **1.** filouterie *f*; **2.** filouter.

chow *Am. sl.* [tʃau] mangeaille *f.*

chrism ['krizm] chrême *m.*

Christ [kraist] le Christ *m*, Jésus-Christ *m*; *for* ~'s sake pour l'amour de Dieu; *F for* ~'s sake!, ~! Bon Dieu de Bon Dieu!

chris·ten ['krisn] baptiser; **Christen·dom** ['~dəm] chrétienté *f*; **'chris·ten·ing 1.** de baptême; **2.** baptême *m.*

Chris·tian ['kristjən] **1.** □ chrétien(ne *f*); ~ *name* prénom *m*, nom *m* de baptême; **2.** chrétien (ne *f*) *m*; **Chris·ti·an·i·ty** [~ti'æniti] christianisme *m*; **Chris·tian·ize** ['~tjənaiz] convertir au christianisme; christianiser.

Christ·mas ['krisməs] **1.** Noël *m*, (fête *f* de) Noël *f*; **2.** de Noël; ~ étrennes *f/pl.*; gratification *f*; ~ **Day** le jour de Noël; ~ **Eve** la veille de Noël; ~ **pres·ent** cadeau *m* de Noël; ~ **tide**, ~ **time** (saison *f* de) Noël; ~ **tree** arbre *m* de Noël.

chro·mat·ic ♪, *phys.* [krə'mætik] **1.** (~ally) chromatique; **2.** ~s *sg.* chromatique *f.*

chrome 🜍 [kroum] *teinture*: bichromate de potasse; **chro·mi·um** ['~jəm] chrome *m*; **'chro·mi·um-plat·ed** chromé; **chro·mo·lith·o·graph** ['kroumou'liθəgraːf] chromolithographie *f.*

chron·ic ['krɔnik] (~ally) (*usu.* ✎) chronique, constant; *sl.* insupportable; **chron·i·cle** ['~kl] **1.** chronique *f*; **2.** enregistrer, faire la chronique de; **'chron·i·cler** chroniqueur *m.*

chron·o·log·i·cal □ [krɔnə'lɔdʒikl] chronologique; ~*ly* par ordre de dates; **chro·nol·o·gy** [krə'nɔlədʒi] chronologie *f.*

chro·nom·e·ter [krə'nɔmitə] chro-

chrys·a·lis *zo.* ['krisəlis], *pl. a.* **chrys·al·i·des** [~'sælidiːz] chrysalide *f.*

chrys·an·the·mum ♣ [kri'sænθə-məm] chrysanthème *m.*

chub *icht.* [tʃʌb] chabot *m* de rivière; **'chub·by** F potelé; joufflu (*visage*); rebondi (*joues*).

chuck[1] [tʃʌk] **1.** gloussement *m*; *my* ~! mon petit chou!; **2.** glousser; **3.** petit!, petit! (*appel aux poules*).

chuck[2] F [~] **1.** lancer; ~ *out* flanquer (*q.*) à la porte; ~ *under the chin* donner une tape sous le menton; **2.** congé *m*; lancement *m.*

chuck[3] ⊕ [~] mandrin *m.*

chuck·le ['tʃʌkl] rire tout bas.

chum F [tʃʌm] **1.** camarade *mf*; copain *m*, copine *f*; *be great* ~*s* être (amis) intimes; **2.** se lier d'amitié (avec, *with*).

chump F [tʃʌmp] tronçon *m* de bois; tête *f*; nigaud(e *f*) *m*; *Brit. sl.* off one's ~ timbré; fou (fol *devant une voyelle ou un h muet*; folle *f*); déboussolé.

chunk F [tʃʌŋk] gros morceau *m*; *pain a.* quignon *m.*

church [tʃəːtʃ] **1.** église *f*; *protestantisme:* temple *m*; *attr.* d'église; de l'Église; ♀ *of England* Église *f* anglicane; ~ *rate* dîme *f*; ~ *service* office *m*; **2.** *be* ~*ed* faire ses relevailles (*femme après ses couches*); '~-go·er pratiquant(e *f*) *m*; **'church·ing** relevailles *f/pl.* (*d'une femme après ses couches*); **'church·ward·en** marguillier *m*; pipe *f* hollandaise; **'church·y** F bigot; **'church-'yard** cimetière *m.*

churl [tʃəːl] manant *m*; *fig.* rustre *m*; F grincheux (-euse *f*) *m*; **'churl·ish** □ mal élevé; grincheux (-euse *f*), hargneux (-euse *f*).

churn [tʃəːn] **1.** baratte *f*; **2.** *v/t.* baratter; *fig.* agiter (*qch.*); *v/i.* faire du beurre.

chute [ʃuːt] chute *f* d'eau; *sp.* glissière *f*; ✝ couloir *m.*

chut·ney ['tʃʌtni] chutney *m.*

chyle *physiol.* [kail] chyle *m.*

chyme ✎ [kaim] chyme *m.*

ci·ca·da *zo.* [si'kaːdə] cigale *f.*

cic·a·trice ['sikətris] cicatrice *f*; **'cic·a·trize** (se) cicatriser.

ci·ce·ro·ne [tʃitʃə'rouni], *pl.* **-ni** [~niː] cicérone *m.*

ci·der ['saidə] cidre *m.*

ci·gar [si'gaː] cigare *m*; **ci'gar-case** étui *m* à cigares; **ci'gar-cut·ter** coupe-cigares *m/inv.*

cig·a·rette [sigə'ret] cigarette *f*; **cig·a'rette-case** étui *m* à cigarettes; **cig·a'rette-end** mégot *m*; **cig·a'rette-hold·er** fume-cigarette *m/inv.*; **cig·a'rette-pa·per** papier *m* à cigarettes.

ci·gar-hold·er [si'gaːhouldə] fume-cigare *m/inv.*

cil·i·ar·y ['siliəri] ciliaire.

cinch *Am. sl.* [sintʃ] certitude *f*; chose *f* certaine.

cinc·ture ['siŋktʃə] ceinture *f*.

cin·der ['sində] cendre *f*; ~s *pl. a.* escarbilles *f/pl.*; **Cin·der·el·la** [ˌ~ə'relə] Cendrillon *f* (*a. fig.*); '**cin·der-track** *sp.* piste *f* cendrée.

cin·e·cam·er·a ['sini'kæmərə] caméra *f*; **cin·e·film** ['sinifilm] film *m* de format réduit.

cin·e·ma ['sinimə] cinéma *m*; F ciné *m*; '~**go·er** amateur *m* de cinéma, cinéphile *mf*; **cin·e·mat·o·graph** [ˌ~'mætəgrɑːf] 1. cinématographe *m*, F cinéma *m*; 2. filmer; **cin·e·mat·o·graph·ic** [ˌ~mætə'græfik] (~ally) cinématographique.

cin·er·ar·y ['sinərəri] cinéraire.

cin·na·bar ['sinəbɑː] cinabre *m*; vermillon *m*.

cin·na·mon ['sinəmən] 1. cannelle *f*; *arbre:* cannelier *m*; 2. cannelle *adj./inv.* (*couleur*).

cinque [siŋk] *dés:* cinq *m*.

ci·pher ['saifə] 1. zéro *m* (*a. fig.*); *fig.* nullité *f*; *code secret:* chiffre *m*; message *m* chiffré; 2. chiffrer.

cir·cle ['səːkl] 1. cercle *m* (*a. fig.*); *fig.* milieu *m*, monde *m*, coterie *f*; *théât.* galerie *f*; ⚙ ceinture *f*; 2. *v/t.* ceindre; *v/i.* tournoyer, tourner, circuler; **cir·clet** ['~klit] petit cercle *m*; anneau *m*.

circs F [səːks] *see* circumstances.

cir·cuit ['səːkit] ⚡, *sp.* circuit *m*; ⚖ tournée *f*, circonscription *f*; *soleil:* révolution *f*; *ville:* pourtour *m*; ⚔ parcours *m*; ⚡ *integrated* ~ circuit *m* intégré; *radio:* ⚡ *short* ~ courtcircuit (*pl. courts-circuits*) *m*; ⚡ ~ *breaker* coupe-circuit *m/inv.*; **cir·cu·i·tous** □ [sə'kjuitəs] détourné, sinueux (-euse *f*).

cir·cu·lar ['səːkjulə] 1. □ circulaire; de cercle; ~ *letter* (lettre *f*) circulaire *f*; ✝ ~ *note* lettre *f* de crédit circulaire; ~ *railway* chemin *m* de fer de ceinture; ~ *saw* scie *f* circulaire; 2. (lettre *f*) circulaire *f*.

cir·cu·late ['səːkjuleit] *v/i.* circuler; *v/t.* faire circuler (*un bruit, l'air, le vin*); mettre en circulation; ✝ transmettre par voie d'endossement; '**cir·cu·lat·ing:** ~ *decimal* fraction *f* périodique; ~ *library* bibliothèque *f* circulante; **cir·cu·la·tion** circulation *f*; *fonds:* roulement *m*; *journal:* tirage *m*; '**cir·cu·la·to·ry** circulatoire; ⚕ ~ *system* appareil *m* circulatoire; ~ *troubles pl.* troubles *m/pl.* de la circulation.

circum... [səːkəm] circon..., circum...; **cir·cum·cise** ['~saiz] circoncire (*le prépuce*); **cir·cum·ci·sion** [ˌ~'siʒn] circoncision *f*; **cir·cum·fer·ence** [sə'kʌmfərəns] circonférence *f*; périphérie *f*; **cir·cum·flex** *gramm.* ['səːkəmfleks] accent *m* circonflexe; **cir·cum·ja·cent** [ˌ~'dʒeisnt] circonjacent; **cir·cum·lo·cu·tion** [ˌ~lə'kjuːʃn] circonlocution *f*; ambages *f/pl.*; **cir·cum·nav·i·gate** [ˌ~'nævigeit] faire le tour de; **cir·cum·nav·i·ga·tor** circumnavigateur *m*; **cir·cum·scribe** ⚖ [ˌ~'skraib] circonscrire; *fig.* limiter; **cir·cum·scrip·tion** [ˌ~'skripʃn] ⚖ circonscription *f*; *fig.* restriction *f*; **cir·cum·spect** □ [ˌ~spekt] circonspect; prudent; **cir·cum·spec·tion** [ˌ~'spekʃn] circonspection *f*; prudence *f*; **cir·cum·stance** ['~stəns] circonstance *f*; détail *m*; *in* (*ou under*) *the* ~s puisqu'il en est ainsi; ~d dans une ... situation; **cir·cum·stan·tial** [ˌ~'stænʃl] circonstanciel(le *f*); détaillé; ⚖ ~ *evidence* preuves *f/pl.* indirectes; **cir·cum·stan·ti·al·i·ty** [ˌ~stænʃi'æliti] abondance *f* de détails; détail *m*; **cir·cum·val·la·tion** [ˌ~və'leiʃn] retranchements *m/pl.*; **cir·cum·vent** [ˌ~'vent] circonvenir.

cir·cus ['səːkəs] cirque *m*; *place:* rond-point (*pl. ronds-points*) *m*.

cir·rho·sis ⚕ [si'rousis] cirrhose *f*.

cir·rous ['sirəs] cirreux (-euse *f*).

cir·rus ['~rəs], *pl.* -**ri** ['~rai] *nuages* cirrus *m*; ⚘ vrille *f*.

cis·tern ['sistən] réservoir *m* à eau; citerne *f* (*souterraine*).

cit·a·del ['sitədl] citadelle *f*.

ci·ta·tion [sai'teiʃn] citation *f* (*a.* ⚖); *Am. souv.* citation *f* à l'ordre du jour; **cite** [sait] citer; assigner (*un témoin*).

cit·i·zen ['sitizn] citoyen(ne *f*) *m*; bourgeois(e *f*) *m*; *a. Am.* civil *m*; *attr.* civique; '**cit·i·zen·ship** droit *m* de cité; nationalité *f*.

cit·ric ac·id ['sitrik'æsid] acide *m* citrique; **cit·ron** ['~rən] cédrat *m*; *arbre:* cédratier *m*; **cit·rus** ['~rəs] agrumes *m/pl.*

cit·y ['siti] 1. ville *f*; *Londres:* the ♀

la Cité; *fig.* les affaires *f/pl.*; **2.** urbain, municipal (-aux *m/pl.*); *Am.* ~ *editor* rédacteur *m* chargé des nouvelles locales; *Am.* ~ *father* conseiller *m* municipal; ~ *hall* hôtel *m* de ville; *Am.* ~ *manager* chef *m* des services municipaux.

civ·ic ['sivik] **1.** civique; municipal (-aux *m/pl.*); ~ *rights pl.* droits *m/pl.* de citoyen, droits *m/pl.* civiques; **2.** ~s *pl.* instruction *f* civique.

civ·il □ ['sivl] civil (*a.* 🖩); poli, courtois; civique (*droits*); ~ *engineering* travaux *m/pl.* publics; ~ *rights movement* mouvement *m* de défense des droits du citoyen; ♀ *Servant* fonctionnaire *mf*; ♀ *Service* Administration *f*; **ci·vil·ian** ⚔ [si'viljən] civil *m*; ~ *population* civils *m/pl.*; **ci·vil·i·ty** civilité *f*; politesse *f*; **civ·i·li·za·tion** [ˌlai'zeiʃn] civilisation *f*; *fig.* culture *f*; **civ·i·lize** civiliser.

clack [klæk] **1.** claquement *m*; *fig.* caquet *m*; ⊕ (soupape *f* à) clapet *m*; **2.** claquer; *fig.* caqueter.

clad [klæd] *prét. et p.p. de clothe.*

claim [kleim] **1.** demande *f*; revendication *f*; droit *m*, titre *m* (à, to); 🖩 réclamation *f*; *dette*: créance *f*; ⚒ concession *f*; *surt. Am.* terrain *m* revendiqué par un chercheur d'or *etc.*; *lay* ~ *to* prétendre à; **2.** réclamer; revendiquer; prétendre à; ~ *to be* se prétendre (*qch.*); **'claim·a·ble** revendicable, exigible; **'claim·ant** prétendant(e *f*) *m*; réclamant(e *f*) *m.*

clair·voy·ance [kleə'vɔiəns] voyance *f*; *fig.* clairvoyance *f*; **clair'voy·ant** voyant(e *f*) *m.*

clam *zo.* [klæm] peigne *m.*

cla·mant *poét.* ['kleimənt] criant; urgent.

clam·ber ['klæmbə] grimper.

clam·mi·ness ['klæminis] moiteur *f* froide; **'clam·my** □ moite; froid et humide; collant.

clam·or·ous □ ['klæmərəs] bruyant; vociférant (*foule etc.*); **'clam·o(u)r 1.** clameur *f*; cris *m/pl.*; **2.** vociférer; réclamer à grands cris (qch., for *s.th.*).

clamp ⊕ [klæmp] **1.** crampon *m*; *étau*: mordache *f*; **2.** agrafer; cramponner; *fig.* fixer.

clan [klæn] clan *m*; *p.ext.* tribu *f*; *fig.* coterie *f.*

clan·des·tine □ [klæn'destin] clandestin.

clang [klæŋ] **1.** bruit *m* métallique *ou* retentissant; **2.** (faire) retentir; (faire) résonner; **clang·or·ous** ['klæŋgərəs] retentissant, strident; **'clang·o(u)r** *see clang* 1.

clank [klæŋk] **1.** bruit *m* sec; cliquetis *m*; **2.** *v/i.* rendre un bruit métallique; *v/t.* faire sonner.

clan·nish *péj.* ['klæniʃ] imbu de l'esprit de coterie; exclusif (-ive *f*).

clap [klæp] **1.** battement *m* de mains; applaudissements *m/pl.*; 🖤 *sl.* chaude-pisse *f*; **2.** *vt/i.* applaudir; *v/t.* donner à (*q.*) une tape (dans le dos, on the back); ~ *one's hands* battre des mains; **'~·net** *chasse*: tirasse *f*; **'clap·per** claquet *m*; *cloche*: battant *m*; **'clap·trap 1.** boniment *m*; phrases *f/pl.* à effet; **2.** sans sincérité; creux (creuse *f*).

clar·et ['klærət] bordeaux *m* (rouge); *sl.* sang *m* (*usu. du nez*).

clar·i·fi·ca·tion [klærifi'keiʃn] clarification *f*; *fig.* mise *f* au point; **clar·i·fy** ['ˌfai] *v/t.* clarifier; *fig.* éclaircir; *v/i.* s'éclaircir.

clar·i·(o·)net [klæri(o)'net] clarinette *f.*

clar·i·ty ['klæriti] clarté *f.*

clash [klæʃ] **1.** choc *m*; fracas *m*; *couleurs*: disparate *f*; **2.** (faire) résonner; (se) heurter; (s')entrechoquer; *v/i.* faire disparate (*couleurs*).

clasp [klɑ:sp] **1.** *médaille, broche*: agrafe *f*; *livre, bourse*: fermoir *m*; *collier*: fermeture *f*; *fig.* étreinte *f*; serrement *m* de mains; **2.** *vt.* agrafer; *fig.* étreindre; serrer (*les mains*); ~ *s.o.'s hand* serrer la main à q.; *v/i.* s'agrafer; **'~·'knife** couteau *m* pliant; F eustache *m.*

class [klɑ:s] **1.** classe *f*; cours *m*; genre *m*, sorte *f*, catégorie *f*; *univ. Am.* année *f*; **2.** classer; ranger par classes; ~ *with* assimiler à; **'~·'conscious** conscient de sa classe; imbu de l'esprit de caste.

clas·sic ['klæsik] **1.** classique *m*; humaniste *mf*; ~s *pl.* études *f/pl.* classiques, humanités *f/pl.*; **2.** = **'clas·si·cal** □ classique.

clas·si·fi·ca·tion [klæsifi'keiʃn] *plantes etc.*: classification *f*; codification *f*; *navire*: cote *f*; *papiers*:

classement *m*; **clas·si·fied** [ˈ‿faid] classifié; secret (-ète *f*); ~ ads *pl.* petites annonces *f/pl.*; **clas·si·fy** [ˈ‿fai] classifier; classer; ranger par classes.

class...: 'ᴖ**mate** camarade *mf* de classe; 'ᴖ**room** salle *f* de classe; ~ **strug·gle**, ~ **war(fare)** lutte *f* des classes.

clas·sy F [ˈklæsi] chic *inv.*

clat·ter [ˈklætə] **1.** vacarme *m*; bruit *m* (*de tasses etc.*); *fig.* brouhaha *m*; **2.** *v/i.* faire du bruit; retentir; *fig.* bavarder; *v/t.* faire retentir.

clause [klɔːz] clause *f*, article *m*; *gramm.* membre *m* de phrase; proposition *f*.

claus·tral [ˈklɔːstrəl] claustral (-aux *m/pl.*).

claus·tro·pho·bi·a *psych.* [klɔːstrəˈfoubiə] claustrophobie *f*.

clav·i·cle *anat.* [ˈklævikl] clavicule *f*.

claw [klɔː] **1.** griffe *f*; *aigle etc.*: serre *f*; *écrevisse*: pince *f*; ⊕ étau: mordache *f*; coup *m* de griffe *etc.*; **2.** griffer; s'accrocher à (*qch.*); **clawed** [‿d] armé de griffes *etc.*

clay [klei] argile *f*; glaise *f*; *sp.* ~ *pigeon* pigeon *m* artificiel; **clay·ey** [ˈkleii] argileux (-euse *f*), glaiseux (-euse *f*).

clean [kliːn] **1.** *adj.* □ propre; net (-te *f*) (*assiette, cassure, a. fig.*); **2.** *adv.* tout à fait, absolument; **3.** *v/t.* nettoyer; balayer; faire (*une chambre*); cirer (*les souliers*); ~ *up* nettoyer; *v/i.* faire le nettoyage; F se débarbouiller; 'ᴖ'**cut** net (-te *f*), bien défini; '**clean·er** nettoyeur *m* (-euse *f*); femme *f* de ménage; ᴖ's (*shop*) ᴖs *pl.* teinturerie *f*; *take to the* ᴖs donner (*qch.*) à la teinturerie; F nettoyer (*q.*), mettre (*q.*) à sec; '**clean·ing** nettoyage *m*; dégraissage *m*; ~ *woman* femme *f* de ménage; **clean·li·ness** [ˈklenlinis] propreté *f*; netteté *f*; **clean·ly 1.** *adv.* [ˈkliːnli] proprement, nettement; **2.** *adj.* [ˈklenli] propre; **clean·ness** [ˈkliːnnis] propreté *f*; netteté *f*; **cleanse** [klenz] nettoyer (*a.* 🏹); assainir; purifier; '**cleans·er** détergent *m*; démaquillant *m*; **clean·shav·en** [ˈkliːnˈʃeivən] rasé de près; **clean-up** [ˈkliːnˈʌp] nettoyage *m*; *pol.* épuration *f* (*de personnel etc.*).

clear [kliə] **1.** □ *usu.* clair; net (-te *f*) (*idée, vision, conscience*); évident;

dégagé; lucide; certain (de, *about*); *fig.* libre (de, *of*); débarrassé (de, *of*); disculpé (de, *of*) (*un soupçon*); ♱ net(te *f*); ~ *of* libre de; exempt de; *as* ~ *as day* clair comme le jour; *get* ~ *of* quitter, sortir de; se dégager de; *steer* ~ *of* éviter, s'écarter de; **2.** △ *in the* ~ en terrain découvert; **3.** *v/t.* éclaircir (*a. fig.*); nettoyer; *fig.* dépeupler; déblayer (*le terrain*) (*a. fig.*); rafraîchir (*l'air*); écarter (*un obstacle*); désencombrer (*une salle*); défricher (*un terrain*); dégager (*une route, une voie*); acquitter (*une dette*); clarifier (*un liquide*); (*a.* ~ *away*) enlever, ôter; disculper (de, *of*, *from*); ♱ *see* ~ *off*; ♱ faire (*un bénéfice net*); arrêter (*un compte*); ⚖ innocenter (de, *of*, *from*); ♱ ~ *off* solder (*des marchandises*); ~ *a port* sortir d'un port; ~ *a ship for action* faire le branle-bas de combat; ~ *one's throat* s'éclaircir la voix; se racler la gorge; *v/i.* (*a.* ~ *up*) s'éclaircir; (*a.* ~ *off*) se dissiper (*nuages, brouillard*); '**clear·ance** dégagement *m*; déblaiement *m*; *boîte à lettres*: levée *f*; ♱ compensation *f* (*d'un chèque*); ⚓, ♱ dédouanement *m*; ⚓ départ *m*; ♱ solde *m*; ⊕ jeu *m*, espace *m* libre; ~ *sale* vente *f* de soldes; '**clear·'cut** net(te *f*); '**clear·ing** éclaircissement *m etc.* (*see clear 3*); *forêt*: clairière *f*; ♱ *see clearance*; ~ *procedure* voie *f* de compensation; ~ *bank* banque *f* de virement; ♀ *House* chambre *f* de compensation.

cleat ⚓ [kliːt] agrafe *f*; taquet *m*.

cleav·age [ˈkliːvidʒ] fendage *m*; *fig.* scission *f*; *min.* clivage *m*.

cleave¹ [kliːv] [*irr.*] (se) fendre (*a. eau, air*).

cleave² [kliːv] *fig.* [‿] adhérer, être fidèle (à, *to*); ~ *together* rester fidèles l'un à l'autre. [ret *m* (*de viande*).\

cleav·er [ˈkliːvə] fendoir *m*; coupe-\

cleek *sp.* [kliːk] cleek *m*.

clef ♩ [klef] clef *f*, clé *f*.

cleft [kleft] **1.** fente *f*, fissure *f*, crevasse *f*; **2.** *prét. et p.p.* de *cleave¹*.

clem·en·cy [ˈklemənsi] clémence *f*; '**clem·ent** □ clément.

clench [klentʃ] (se) serrer (*lèvres, dents, poings*); (se) crisper (*mains*).

cler·gy [ˈkləːdʒi] (membres *m/pl.* du) clergé *m*; 'ᴖ**man** ecclésiastique *m*; *protestantisme*: pasteur *m*.

cler·i·cal [ˈklerikl] **1.** □ *eccl.* clérical (-aux *m/pl.*); de bureau; ~ error faute *f* de copiste; **2.** *pol.* clérical *m.*

clerk [klɑːk] employé(e *f*) *m* de bureau; ✝ commis *m*, employé(e *f*) *m* de magasin; *surt. Am.* vendeur (-euse *f*) *m* (*de magasin*); *eccl.* clerc *m.*

clev·er □ [ˈklevə] habile, adroit; intelligent; ~ **dick** *Brit. sl.* gros malin *m*, je-sais-tout *m*; **ˈclev·er·ness** habileté *f*, adresse *f*; intelligence *f.*

clew [kluː] *see* **clue.**

cli·ché [ˈkliːʃei] cliché *m.*

click [klik] **1.** cliquetis *m*, bruit *m* sec; ⊕ cliquet *m*; déclic *m*; **2.** *v/i.* cliqueter; faire tic tac; se plaire du premier coup; *v/t.* (faire) claquer (*les talons*).

cli·ent [ˈklaiənt] client(e *f*) *m*; **cli·en·tele** [kliːɑ̃ːnˈteil] clientèle *f.*

cliff [klif] falaise *f*; escarpement *m.*

cli·mac·ter·ic [klaiˈmæktərik] **1.** climatérique; **2.** ménopause *f*, retour d'âge *m*; *fig.* tournant *m.*

cli·mate [ˈklaimit] climat *m*; **cli·mat·ic** [klaiˈmætik] (~*ally*) climat(ér)ique.

cli·max [ˈklaimæks] gradation *f*; *fig.* apogée *m*, plus haut point *m.*

climb [klaim] monter; gravir, grimper à; escalader; **ˈclimb·er** ascensionniste *mf*; *fig.* arriviste *mf*; ♀ plante *f* grimpante; **ˈclimb·ing** montée *f*, escalade *f*; **ˈclimb·ing·i·ron** crampon *m.*

clinch [klintʃ] **1.** ⊕ rivet *m*, accrochage *m*; *fig.* étreinte *f*; *box.* corps-à-corps *m*; **2.** *v/t.* river; confirmer (*un argument etc.*); conclure (*un marché*); *see* **clench**; *v/i.* s'accrocher; **ˈclinch·er** ⊕ crampon *m*; *fig.* argument *m* sans réplique.

cling [kliŋ] [*irr.*] (à, **to**) s'accrocher, se cramponner, s'attacher; adhérer; coller (*robe*); **ˈcling·ing** qui s'accroche *etc.*; collant (*robe*).

clin·ic [ˈklinik] **1.** clinique *f*; **2.** = **ˈclin·i·cal** □ clinique; ~ **thermometer** thermomètre *m* médical.

clink [kliŋk] **1.** tintement *m*, choc *m*; *épées*: cliquetis *m*; **2.** *v/i.* tinter (*verres*); *v/t.* faire tinter, faire résonner; ~ **glasses with** trinquer avec; **ˈclink·er** escarbilles *f/pl.*; *sl.* personne *f* ou chose *f* épatante; **ˈclink·ing** *Brit. sl.* **1.** *adj.* épatant; **2.** *adv. sl.* très.
45*

clip[1] [klip] **1.** tonte; *Am.* F **at one** ~ d'un seul coup; **2.** tondre; rogner; tailler; écourter (*un mot*).

clip[2] [~] attache *f*, pince *f*; **paper-**~ agrafe *f* de bureau; trombone *m.*

clip·per [ˈklipə] tondeur (-euse *f*) *m*; (**a pair of**) ~**s** *pl.* (une) tondeuse *f*; F cheval *m* qui va comme le vent; ⚓ fin voilier *m*; ✈ (*flying* ~) clipper *m*; *sl.* type *m* épatant; **ˈclip·pings** *pl.* tonte *f*; *ongles etc.*: rognures *f/pl.*; *Am. presse*: coupures *f/pl.*

clique [kliːk] coterie *f*; F clan *m.*

cloak [klouk] **1.** manteau *m* (*a. fig.*); *fig.* voile *m*; **2.** revêtir d'un manteau; *fig.* masquer, voiler; **ˈ~-room** vestiaire *m*; ⛟ consigne *f.*

clob·ber *sl.* [ˈklɔbə] **1.** battre; rosser; **2.** *Brit.* frusques *f/pl.*, barda *m.*

clock [klɔk] **1.** horloge *f*; *moins grand*: pendule *f*; *bas*: coin *m*; *sp. sl.* chronomètre *m* à déclic; **2.** *v/t. sp. sl.* chronométrer; *v/i.*: ~ **in** (out) pointer à l'arrivée (au départ) (*ouvrier etc.*); **ˈ~-face** cadran *m*; ~ **ra·di·o** radio-réveil *m* (*pl.* radios-réveils); **ˈ~-wise** à droite; dans le sens des aiguilles d'une montre.

clod [klɔd] motte *f* (de terre); *fig.* terre *f*; (*a.* ~**-hopper**) lourdaud *m.*

clog [klɔg] **1.** entrave *f*; *fig.* empêchement *m*; galoche *f*; sabot *m*; **2.** entraver; *fig.* (se) boucher, (s')obstruer; **ˈclog·gy** collant.

clois·ter [ˈklɔistə] **1.** cloître *m*; **2.** cloîtrer.

close 1. [klouz] fin *f*, conclusion *f*; clôture *f*; [klous] clos *m*, enclos *m*; *cathédrale*: enceinte *f*; **2.** [klouz] *v/t.* fermer; barrer; terminer; arrêter (*un compte*); ~**d shop** atelier *etc.* qui n'admet pas de travailleurs non syndiqués; ~ **down** fermer (*une usine etc.*); ~ **one's eyes to** fermer les yeux sur; *v/i.* (se) fermer; se terminer, finir; se prendre corps à corps (avec, **with**); ✝ ~ **with** conclure le marché avec; ~ **in** cerner de près; tomber (*nuit*); ~ **on** (*prp.*) se (re)fermer sur; **3.** □ [klous] bien fermé; clos; avare; peu communicatif (-ive *f*); étroit (*vêtement etc.*); exclusif (-ive *f*) (*société*); serré (*style, rangs, lutte*); *typ.* compact; soutenu (*attention*); minutieux (-euse *f*) (*étude*); vivement contesté (*lutte*); lourd (*temps*); impénétrable (*secret*); intime (*ami*); fidèle (*traduction*); ~ **by**

(ou to) tout près *(de)*; ~ *fight (ou combat ou quarters)* combat *m* corps à corps; *have a* ~ *call (ou shave)* l'échapper belle, y échapper de justesse; *that was a* ~ *call (ou shave ou thing)* il était moins une; *at* ~ *quarters* de près; ~*(d) season (ou time) chasse:* chasse *f* fermée; *shave* ~*ly* (se) raser de près; '~-**knit** étroitement lié, très uni; '~-**meshed** à petites mailles; '**close·ness** proximité *f*; exactitude *f*; *temps:* lourdeur *f*; manque *m* d'air; réserve *f*.

clos·et ['klɔzit] **1.** cabinet *m*, armoire *f*, placard *m*; *see water-*~; **2.** *be* ~*ed with* être enfermé avec *(q.)*, être en tête avec *(q.)*.

close-up *cin.* ['klousʌp] premier plan *m*; gros plan *m*.

clos·ing ['klouziŋ] **1.** fermeture *f*; clôture *f*; **2.** dernier *(-ère f)*; final; de fermeture; *the* ~ *days* les derniers jours *m/pl.*; ~ *time* heure *f* de fermeture; ~ *time!* on ferme!

clo·sure ['klouʒə] **1.** fermeture *f*; clôture *f*; *parl. move the* ~ voter la clôture; *apply the* ~ clôturer le débat; **2.** clôturer *(un débat etc.)*.

clot [klɔt] **1.** *sang:* caillot *m*; *encre:* bourbillon *m*; **2.** figer *(le sang)*; cailler *(le lait)*.

cloth [klɔθ], *pl.* **cloths** [klɔθs] étoffe *f* de laine; drap *m*; toile *f*; linge *m*; tapis *m*; *(a. table-*~*)* nappe *f*; habit *m* *(surt.* ecclésiastique)*; F *the* ~ le clergé; *lay the* ~ mettre la nappe *ou* le couvert; *bound in* ~ relié toile; ~*-binding* reliure *f* en toile.

clothe [klouð] *[irr.]* vêtir, habiller *(de in, with)*; revêtir *(de, with) (a. fig.)*.

clothes [klouðz] *pl.* vêtements *m/pl.*, habits *m/pl.*; *(a. suit of* ~*)* complet *m*; linge *m* *(propre, sale, etc.)*; '~-**bas·ket** panier *m* à linge; '~-**brush** brosse *f* à habits; ~ **hang·er** cintre *m*; ~ **horse** séchoir *m* (à linge); '~-**line** corde *f* à linge; '~-**peg** pince *f*; fichoir *m*; '~-**pin** *surt. Am.* pince *f*; '~-**press** armoire *f* à linge.

cloth·ier ['klouðiə] drapier *m*; marchand *m* de confections.

cloth·ing ['klouðiŋ] vêtements *m/pl.*

cloud [klaud] **1.** nuage *m* *(a. fig.)*; *fig.* voile *m*; *liquide:* turbidité *f*; *poét., a. sauterelle:* nuée *f*; *be under a* ~ être l'objet de soupçons; **2.** (se)

couvrir, (se) voiler; *fig.* s'assombrir; ⊕ ~*ed* nuageux *(-euse f) (joyau)*; nuagé *(poil)*; tacheté *(marbre)*; '~-**burst** rafale *f* de pluie; trombe *f*; ~-'**cuck·oo-land** pays *m* utopique *ou* imaginaire; *live in* ~ être *ou* planer dans les nuages; '**cloud·less** ☐ sans nuages; '**cloud·let** ['~lit] petit nuage *m*; '**cloud·y** ☐ nuageux *(-euse f)*, assombri; couvert *(temps)*; trouble *(liquide)*; *fig.* fumeur *(-euse f)*.

clout [klaut] **1.** rapiécer; F flanquer une taloche à *(q.)*; **2.** chiffon *m*, torchon *m*; F taloche *f*, claque *f*.

clove[1] [klouv] clou *m* de girofle; gousse *f* (d'ail).

clove[2] [~] *prét. de* **cleave**[1]; '**clo·ven 1.** *p.p. de* **cleave**[1]; **2.** *adj.* fendu, fourchu.

clo·ver ♣ ['klouvə] trèfle *m*; '~-**leaf** ♣ feuille *f* de trèfle; *mot. (a.* ~ *crossing)* croisement *m* en trèfle.

clown [klaun] *théâ.* bouffon *m*; *cirque:* clown *m*; rustre *m*; *poét.* paysan *m*; '**clown·ish** ☐ de bouffon; de clown; gauche; grossier *(-ère f)*.

cloy [klɔi] rassasier *(de, with) (a. fig.)*; affadir.

club [klʌb] **1.** massue *f*, assommoir *m*; *sp.* crosse *f*; cercle *m*, club *m*; ~*s pl. cartes:* trèfle *m*; **2.** *v/t.* frapper avec une massue; ~ *together* mettre en commun; *v/i. (usu.* ~ *together)* s'associer *(pour faire qch.)*; '**club·ba·ble** sociable; '**club-'foot** ⚕ pied-bot *(pl.* pieds-bots) *m*; '**club-law** la loi du plus fort.

cluck [klʌk] glousser *(poule)*.

clue [klu:] *fig.* indication *f*, indice *m*; *mots croisés:* définition *f*.

clump [klʌmp] **1.** bloc *m*; *arbres:* groupe *m*; *fleurs:* massif *m*; F taloche *f*; *(a.* ~*-sole)* semelle *f* supplémentaire; **2.** marcher lourdement; ajouter des patins à *(des chaussures)*.

clum·si·ness ['klʌmzinis] gaucherie *f*, maladresse *f*; '**clum·sy** ☐ gauche, maladroit; informe.

clung [klʌŋ] *prét. et p.p. de* **cling**.

clus·ter ['klʌstə] **1.** ♣ *fleurs:* massif *m*, bouquet *m*; *arbres:* groupe *m*; *raisins:* grappe *f*; **2.** (se) grouper; (se) rassembler.

clutch [klʌtʃ] **1.** griffe *f*; *aigle etc.:* serre *f*; ⊕ embrayage *m*; *in his* ~*es* dans ses griffes, sous sa patte; *mot.* ~ *pedal* pédale *f* d'embrayage; **2.** *v/t.*

cockerel

saisir, empoigner; *v/i.* se raccrocher (à, *at*).

clut·ter ['klʌtə] **1.** méli-mélo (*pl.* mélis-mélos) *m*, encombrement *m*; désordre *m*; **2.** (*a.* ~ *up*) encombrer (de, *with*); mettre le désordre dans.

clys·ter ['klistə] clystère *m*.

coach [koutʃ] **1.** carrosse *m*; 🚋 voiture *f*, wagon *m*; *Am.* autocar *m*; *univ.* répétiteur *m*; *sp.* entraîneur *m*; **2.** *v/i.* aller en carrosse; *v/t. univ.* donner des leçons particulières à; *sp.* entraîner; '~**·box** siège *m* (du cocher); '~**·build·er** carrossier *m*; '~**·house** remise *f*; '~**·man** cocher *m*; '~**·work** carrosserie *f*.

co·ad·ju·tor *surt. eccl.* [kou'ædʒutə] coadjuteur *m*.

co·ag·u·late [kou'ægjuleit] (se) figer; (se) cailler (*lait*); **co·ag·u·la·tion** coagulation *f*, figement *m*.

coal [koul] **1.** charbon *m*; houille *f*; morceau *m* de charbon; *carry* ~*s to Newcastle* porter de l'eau à la mer; *haul* (*ou call*) *s.o. over the* ~*s fig.* semoncer q.; **2.** ⚓ (s')approvisionner de charbon; ~*ing station* port *m* à charbon; '~**·bed** couche *f* de houille, couche *f* carbonifère; '~**·dust** charbon *m* en poussière.

co·a·lesce [kouə'les] se fondre; se combiner; fusionner; **co·a·les·cence** coalescence *f*; fusion *f*; combinaison *f*.

co·a·li·tion [kouə'liʃn] coalition *f*; *pol.* cartel *m*.

coal-field ['koulfi:ld] bassin *m* houiller.

coal...: '~**·pit** houillère *f*; '~**·scut·tle** seau *m* à charbon.

coarse ☐ [kɔ:s] grossier (-ère *f*) (*a. fig.*); gros(se *f*); rude; '**coarse·ness** grossièreté *f*, rudesse *f*.

coast [koust] **1.** côte *f*, rivage *m*; plage *f*; littoral *m*; *cycl.* descente *f* en roue libre; *surt. Am.* piste *f* (*de toboggan*); **2.** suivre la côte, descendre (en toboggan, en roue libre, *mot.* le moteur débrayé); '**coast·er** *Am.* bobsleigh *m*; ⚓ caboteur *m*; **coast·er brake** *Am.* frein *m* à contre-pédalage; '**coast-guard** garde-côte (*pl.* gardes-côtes) *m*; '**coast·ing** navigation *f* côtière; cabotage *m*; ~ *trade* commerce *m* caboteur; cabotage *m*.

coat [kout] **1.** *hommes*: habit *m*; *femmes*: manteau *m*, jaquette *f*

(*courte*); robe *f*, poil *m*; *animaux*: peau *f*, fourrure *f*; *peinture*: couche *f*; ~ *of arms* armoiries *f/pl.*; écusson *m*; ~ *of mail* cotte *f* de mailles; *cut the* ~ *according to the cloth* subordonner ses dépenses à son revenu; **2.** enduire (de, *with*); revêtir, couvrir (de, *with*); '~**·hang·er** cintre *m*; '**coat·ing** enduit *m*, revêtement *m*; enveloppe *f*; couche *f*; *tex.* étoffe *f* pour habits; '**coat·rack** portemanteau *m*.

coax [kouks] cajoler, enjôler; encourager (q.) à force de cajoleries (à *inf., into gér.*); ~ *s.th. out of s.o.* soutirer qch. à q. en le cajolant.

cob [kɔb] cob *m*, bidet *m*; cygne *m* mâle; △ pisé *m*; *Am.* épi *m* de maïs; *see* ~*nut*; ~*s pl. charbon:* gaillette *f*; ~*-loaf* miche *f*.

co·balt *min.* [kə'bɔ:lt] cobalt *m*.

cob·ble ['kɔbl] **1.** galet *m*; ~*s pl.* gaillette *f*, -s *f/pl.*; **2.** paver en cailloutis; carreler (*des chaussures*); '**cob·bler** cordonnier *m*; *fig.* rapetasseur *m*; *Am.* boisson *f* rafraîchissante.

cob·nut ♀ ['kɔbnʌt] grosse noisette *f*.

cob·web ['kɔbweb] toile *f* d'araignée.

co·caine ⚕ [kə'kein] cocaïne *f*.

coch·i·neal ['kɔtʃini:l] cochenille *f*.

cock [kɔk] **1.** coq *m* (*a. fig.*); oiseau *m* mâle; chien *m* (*de fusil*); meulon *m* (*de foin*); robinet *m*; **2.** (*souv.* ~ *up*) (re)lever; dresser (*les oreilles*); armer le chien de (*un fusil*); retrousser (*le chapeau*); mettre (*le chapeau*) de travers; ~ *one's eye at s.o.* lancer une œillade à q.; ~ *one's nose at s.o.* toiser q.; ~*ed hat* tricorne *m*.

cock·ade [kɔ'keid] cocarde *f*.

Cock·aigne [kɔ'kein] pays *m* de cocagne.

cock-and-bull sto·ry ['kɔkənd'bulstɔ:ri] histoire *f* de pure invention.

cock·a·too [kɔkə'tu:] cacatoès *m*.

cock·a·trice ['kɔkətrais] basilic *m*.

cock·boat ⚓ ['kɔkbout] petit canot *m*.

cock·chaf·er ['kɔktʃeifə] hanneton *m*.

cock-crow(·ing) ['kɔkkrou(iŋ)] (premier) chant *m* du coq; aube *f*.

cock·er[1] ['kɔkə]: ~ *up* câliner.

cock·er[2] [~] (épagneul *m*) cocker *m*.

cock·er·el ['kɔkərəl] jeune coq *m*.

cock...: '~-eyed ['kɔkaid] sl. qui louche; de biais; Am. gris (ivre); '~-fight(·ing) combat, -s m/pl. de coqs; '~-'horse cheval m de bois.

cock·le¹ ⚓ ['kɔkl] nielle f des blés.

cock·le² [~] **1.** zo. bucarde f; pli m; **2.** v/t. recoquiller (les pages d'un livre); faire goder (une étoffe); v/i. se recroqueviller; goder.

cock·ney ['kɔkni] londonien(ne f) (a. su./mf); 'cock·ney·ism locution f ou prononciation f londonienne.

cock·pit ['kɔkpit] arène f de combats de coqs; ⚓ poste m des blessés; ✈ baquet m, carlingue f; poste m du pilote. [f; F cafard m.]

cock·roach zo. ['kɔkroutʃ] blatte.

cocks·comb ['kɔkskoum] crête f de coq; ♣ crête-de-coq (pl. crêtes-de-coq) f; 'cock-'sure F outrecuidant; 'cock·tail demi-sang m/inv. †; parvenu m; cocktail m; 'cock-up sl. pagaille f; make a ~ of saloper, gâcher; 'cock·y □ F outrecuidant, suffisant, effronté.

co·co ['koukou] cocotier m.

co·coa ['koukou] cacao m.

co·co·nut ['koukənʌt] noix f de coco.

co·coon zo. [kə'ku:n] cocon m.

cod icht. [kɔd] morue f; dried ~ merluche f; cured ~ morue f salée.

cod·dle ['kɔdl] gâter, câliner, douilletter; ~ up élever dans la ouate.

code [koud] **1.** code m; secret: chiffre m; **2.** tél. codifier; chiffrer.

co·de·ine 🜍 ['koudi:n] codéine f.

cod·fish ['kɔdfiʃ] see cod.

codg·er F ['kɔdʒə] vieux bonhomme m.

cod·i·cil ['kɔdisil] codicille m; **cod·i·fi·ca·tion** [~fi'keiʃn] codification f; **cod·i·fy** ['~fai] codifier (des lois).

cod·ling ['kɔdliŋ] ♣ pomme f à cuire; icht. petite morue f.

cod-liv·er oil ['kɔdlivər'ɔil] huile f de foie de morue.

co·ed Am. ['kou'ed] élève f d'une école coéducationelle.

co·ed·u·ca·tion [kouedju'keiʃn] école mixte; coéducation f.

co·ef·fi·cient [koui'fiʃnt] coefficient m; facteur m (de sûreté).

co·erce [kou'ə:s] contraindre; forcer; **co'er·ci·ble** contraignable, coercible (gaz); **co'er·cion** [~ʃn] contrainte f; under ~ par contrainte; à son corps défendant; **co'er·cive** □ [~siv] coercitif (-ive f).

co·e·val □ [kou'i:vəl] (with) de l'âge (de); contemporain (de).

co·ex·ist ['kouig'zist] coexister (avec, with); 'co·ex'ist·ence coexistence f; 'co·ex'ist·ent coexistant.

cof·fee ['kɔfi] café m; ~ bar café m, cafétéria f; '~-bean grain m de café; '~-grounds pl. marc m de café; '~-pot cafetière f; '~-room hôtel: salle f à manger; ~ shop Am. café m, cafétéria f; ~ ta·ble table f basse.

cof·fer ['kɔfə] coffre m; ⚓ caisson m; ~s pl. coffres m/pl.; fonds m/pl.

cof·fin ['kɔfin] **1.** cercueil m; **2.** mettre en bière.

cog ⊕ [kɔg] dent f (d'une roue).

co·gen·cy ['koudʒənsi] force f; 'co·gent □ valable, incontestable.

cogged ⊕ [kɔgd] à dents, denté.

cog·i·tate ['kɔdʒiteit] v/i. réfléchir, méditer (sur, [up]on); v/t. méditer (qch.); **cog·i'ta·tion** réflexion f.

co·gnac ['kounjæk] cognac m.

cog·nate ['kɔgneit] **1.** (with) parent (de), analogue (à); **2.** cognat m.

cog·ni·tion [kɔg'niʃn] connaissance f.

cog·ni·za·ble ['kɔgnizəbl] (re)connaissable; 🜪 du ressort du tribunal; 'cog·ni·zance connaissance f (a. 🜪); 🜪 compétence f, ressort m (de la cour); 'cog·ni·zant (of) ayant connaissance (de); instruit (de).

cog·no·men [kɔg'noumen] nom m de famille; sobriquet m, surnom m.

cog-wheel ⊕ ['kɔgwi:l] roue f dentée.

co·hab·it [kou'hæbit] cohabiter; **co·hab·i'ta·tion** cohabitation f.

co·heir ['kou'ɛə] cohéritier m; **co·heir·ess** ['kou'ɛəris] cohéritière f.

co·here [kou'hiə] se tenir (ensemble); **co'her·en·cy** cohérence f; **co'her·ent** □ cohérent; conséquent; **co'her·er** cohéreur m.

co·he·sion [kou'hi:ʒn] cohésion f; **co'he·sive** cohésif (-ive f).

coif·feur [kwa:'fə:] coiffeur m; **coif·fure** [~'fjuə] **1.** coiffure f; **2.** coiffer.

coign of van·tage [kɔinəv'vɑ:ntidʒ] position f avantageuse.

coil [kɔil] **1.** corde f, fil métallique, cheveux: rouleau m; câble: roue f; ⚡ bobine f; serpent: repli m; ⊕ tube: serpentin m; ~ spring ressort m en spirale; **2.** (souv. ~ up) v/t.

(en)rouler; *v/i.* serpenter; s'enrouler.

coin [kɔin] **1.** (pièce *f* de) monnaie *f; false ~* fausse monnaie *f; small ~* monnaie *f* divisionnaire; **2.** frapper (*de la monnaie*); *fig.* inventer; *fig. ~ money* faire des affaires d'or; *~ed money* argent *m* monnayé; '**coinage** monnayage *m;* monnaie *f, -s f/pl.; fig.* invention *f.*

co·in·cide [kouin'said] (*with*) coïncider (avec); *fig.* s'accorder (avec); **co·in·ci·dence** [kou'insidəns] coïncidence *f; fig.* rencontre *f,* concours *m;* **co'in·ci·dent** □ coïncident; *fig.* d'accord.

coin·er [kɔinə] monnayeur *m; souv.* faux-monnayeur; *fig.* inventeur (-trice *f*) *m.*

coir ['kɔiə] fibre *f* de coco; coir *m.*

coke [kouk] **1.** coke *m* (*a. sl. =* cocaïne); *Am.* F Coca-Cola *f;* **2.** (se) cokéfier.

col·an·der ['kʌləndə] *cuis.* passoire *f.*

cold [kould] **1.** □ froid (*a. fig.*); *~ meat* viande *f* froide; *give s.o. the ~ shoulder see ~-shoulder;* F *have ~ feet* avoir le trac (*= avoir peur*); **2.** froid *m;* froideur *f; fig. ~ in the head)* rhume *m;* '*~-'blood·ed zo.* à sang froid; *fig.* insensible, sans pitié (*personne*); accompli de sang-froid (*action*); *~ cream* crème *f* de beauté, cold-cream *m;* '*~-'heart·ed* au cœur froid, sans pitié; '**cold·ness** froideur *f; climat:* froidure *f.*

cold...: '*~-'shoul·der* battre froid à (*q.*); tourner le dos à (*q.*); *~ storage* conservation *f* par le froid; glacière *f;* '*~-'stor·age* frigorifique; *~ store* entrepôt *m* frigorifique.

cole ♀ [koul] chou-marin (*pl.* choux-marins) *m.*

cole-seed ♀ ['koulsi:d] (graine *f* de) colza *m.*

cole-slaw ['koulslɔ:] *Am.* salade *f* de choux.

col·ic ♣ ['kɔlik] colique *f.*

col·lab·o·rate [kə'læbəreit] collaborer; **col·lab·o·ra·tion** collaboration *f;* **col·lab·o·ra·tor** collaborateur (-trice *f*) *m.*

col·lapse [kə'læps] **1.** s'affaisser; s'écrouler; s'effondrer (*prix, a. personne*); **2.** affaissement *m* etc.; **col'laps·i·ble** pliant, démontable; *~ boat* canot *m* pliant, berthon *m.*

col·lar ['kɔlə] **1.** *robe:* col *m; manteau:* collet *m; chemise:* (faux) col *m; ordre:* collier *m;* ⊕ anneau *m,* collet *m;* **2.** saisir au collet; ⊕ baguer; *cuis.* rouler (*de la viande*) pour la ficeler; '*~-bone anat.* clavicule *f.*

col·late [kɔ'leit] collationner (*des textes*).

col·lat·er·al [kɔ'lætərəl] **1.** □ collatéral (-aux *m/pl.*); accessoire; additionnel(le *f*); concomitant; **2.** garantie *f* accessoire.

col·la·tion [kɔ'leiʃn] *textes, cuis., a. eccl.* collation *f.*

col·league ['kɔli:g] collègue *mf.*

col·lect 1. ['kɔlekt] *prière:* collecte *f;* **2.** [kə'lekt] *v/t.* (r)assembler; amasser; collectionner (*des timbres*); percevoir (*des impôts*); faire rentrer (*une créance*); quêter (*pour les pauvres*); *~ one's thoughts* se reprendre; se recueillir; *~ing business* service *m* d'encaissement; *v/i.* s'assembler; *~ call Am. téléph.* PCV (*= Per-Ce-Voir*), communication *f* téléphonique payable par le destinateur; **col'lect·ed** □ *fig.* plein de sang-froid; **col'lect·ed·ness** *fig.* sang-froid *m;* **col'lec·tion** rassemblement *m;* recouvrement *m;* perception *f; billet:* encaissement *m; eccl.* quête *f; forcible ~* réquisition *f;* **col'lec·tive** collectif (-ive *f*); multiple (*fruit*); ⚏ *~ ownership* possession *f* en commun; *~ bargaining* convention *f* collective; **col'lec·tive·ly** collectivement; en commun; **col'lec·tiv·ism** collectivisme *m;* **col'lec·tor** quêteur (-euse *f*) *m;* encaisseur *m;* collectionneur (-euse *f*) *m; contributions indirectes:* receveur *m, directes:* percepteur *m;* ⚙ contrôleur *m* de billets; ⚡ prise *f* de courant; *~'s item* pièce *f* de collection.

col·leen *Ir.* ['kɔli:n; *Ir.* kɔ'li:n] jeune fille *f.*

col·lege ['kɔlidʒ] collège *m; souv.* université *f;* école *f* secondaire, lycée *m;* école *f* (*militaire ou navale*); **col·le·gi·an** [kə'li:dʒiən] étudiant(e *f*) *m;* lycéen(ne *f*) *m;* élève *mf;* **col'le·gi·ate** [~dʒiit] collégial (-aux *m/pl.*); de collège.

col·lide [kə'laid] se heurter; entrer en collision (avec, *with*); *~ with* heurter (*qch.*) (*a. fig.*).

col·lie ['kɔli] colley *m.*

col·lier ['kɔliə] houilleur *m*, mineur *m*; ⚓ charbonnier *m*; **col·lier·y** ['kɔljəri] houillère *f*; mine *f* de charbon.

col·li·sion [kə'liʒn] collision *f* (*a. fig.*); rencontre *f*; *fig.* conflit *m*.

col·lo·ca·tion [kɔlo'keiʃn] collocation *f*, arrangement *m*.

col·lo·di·on [kə'loudiən] collodion *m*.

col·lo·qui·al □ [kə'loukwiəl] familier (-ère *f*); de (la) conversation; **col'lo·qui·al·ism** expression *f* familière.

col·lo·quy ['kɔləkwi] colloque *m*.

col·lude [kə'lju:d] s'entendre (avec, *with*); **col'lu·sion** [kə'lu:ʒn] collusion *f*; ⚖ complicité *f*, connivence *f*.

col·ly·wob·bles F ['kɔliwɔblz]: *have the* ∼ se sentir mal; avoir le trac.

col·o·cynth ♣ ['kɔlɔsinθ] coloquinte *f*.

co·lon ['koulən] *typ.* deux-points *m*/*inv.*; *anat.* côlon *m*.

colo·nel ⚔ ['kə:nl] colonel *m*; **'colo·nel·cy** grade *m* de colonel.

co·lo·ni·al [kə'lounjəl] colonial (-aux *m*/*pl.*) (*a. su./m*); **col·o·nist** ['kɔlənist] colon *m*; **col·o·ni·za·tion** colonisation *f*; **'col·o·nize** *v/t.* coloniser; *v/i.* former une colonie.

col·on·nade [kɔlə'neid] colonnade *f*.

col·o·ny ['kɔləni] colonie *f* (*a. fig.*).

col·o·pho·ny [kɔ'lɔfəni] colophane *f*.

col·or see colo(u)r.

Col·o·ra·do bee·tle [kɔlə'rɑ:dou'bi:tl] doryphore *m*.

co·los·sal □ [kə'lɔsl] colossal (-aux *m*/*pl.*).

col·o(u)r ['kʌlə] **1.** couleur *f*; pigment *m*; *visage*: teint *m*; *nuance*: teinte *f*; *fig.* couleur *f*, prétexte *m*; ⚔ ∼s *pl.* drapeau *m*; ∼ *bar*, ∼ *line* discrimination *f* raciale; ∼ *problem* problème *m* racial; ∼ *supplement* supplément illustré (*d'un journal*); ∼ *television* télévision *f* (en) couleur; ∼ *television set* téléviseur *m* couleur; *local* ∼ couleur *f* locale; **2.** *v/t.* colorer; colorier; teindre; *fig.* imager (*son style*); présenter sous un faux jour; *v/i.* se colorer; rougir (*personne*); **'col·o(u)r·a·ble** □ plausible; trompeur; **col·o(u)r-blind** daltonien(ne *f*); **col·o(u)r blind·ness** daltonisme *m*; **'col·o(u)red** coloré; de couleur; en couleurs; ∼ *film* film *m* en couleurs; ∼ *pencil* crayon *m* de cou-

leur; ∼ (*wo*)*man* homme *m* (femme *f*) de couleur; **'col·o(u)r·fast** bon teint; **col·o(u)r·ful** ['∼ful] coloré; **'col·o(u)r·ing 1.** colorant; ∼ *matter* colorant *m*; **2.** coloration *f*; *peint.* coloris *m*; *visage*: teint *m*; *nuance*: teinte *f*; *fig.* apparence *f*; **'col·o(u)r·ist** coloriste *m*; **'col·o(u)r·less** □ sans couleur; terne; pâle.

colt [koult] poulain *m*, pouliche *f*; *fig.* débutant(e *f*) *m*; **'colts·foot** ♣ tussilage *m*.

col·um·bine ♣ ['kɔləmbain] ancolie *f*.

col·umn ['kɔləm] colonne *f* (*a. typ., a.* ⚔); *journ. a.* rubrique *f*; **co·lum·nar** [kə'lʌmnə] en forme de colonne; en colonnes; **col·um·nist** ['kɔləmnist] *Am. journ.* collaborateur *m* régulier d'un journal.

col·za ♣ ['kɔlzə] colza *m*.

co·ma[1] ♪ ['koumə] coma *m*.

co·ma[2] [∼], *pl.* **-mae** ['∼mi:] ♣ barbe *f*, *astr.* chevelure *f*.

comb [koum] **1.** peigne *m*; *coq, vague, colline*: crête *f*; ⊕ peigne *m*, carde *f*; *curry-*∼ *see honey* ∼; **2.** *v/t.* peigner; *a.* carder (*la laine*); ∼ *out fig.* F éplucher; *v/i.* déferler (*vague*).

com·bat ['kɔmbət] **1.** combat *m*; **2.** combattre (contre, *with*; pour, *for*); **'com·bat·ant** combattant *m*; **'com·bat·ive** □ combattif (-ive *f*); agressif (-ive *f*).

comb·er ['koumə] ⊕ peigneuse *f*; ⚓ vague *f* déferlante.

com·bi·na·tion [kɔmbi'neiʃn] combinaison *f*; association *f*; ♫ combiné *m*; *fig.* mélange *m*; *usu.* ∼s *pl.* *cost.* combinaison *f*; ∼ *lock* serrure *f* à combinaison; **com·bine 1.** [∼'bain] (se) réunir; (s')allier; **2.** ['∼bain] ✝ entente *f* industrielle; cartel *m*; *surt. Am.* moissonneuse-batteuse (*pl.* moissonneuses-batteuses) *f*.

comb·ings ['koumiŋz] *pl.* peignures *f*/*pl.*

com·bus·ti·ble [kəm'bʌstəbl] **1.** combustible, comburable; inflammable (*foule etc.*); **2.** ∼s *pl.* matière *f* inflammable; *mot.* combustibles *m*/*pl.*; **com·bus·tion** [kəm'bʌstʃn] combustion *f*.

come [kʌm] [*irr.*] venir, arriver; ∼! allons!; voyons!; *to* ∼ futur, à venir, qui vient; F *how* ∼? comment ça?; ∼ *about* arriver, se passer; ∼ *across* *s.o.* tomber sur q.; ~ *along* se dépêcher; arriver; ~ *at* se jeter sur; parvenir à (*la vérité*); ~ *by* passer par; obtenir; ~ *down* descendre; *fig.* s'abaisser; déchoir; ~ *down upon s.o.* blâmer q. sévèrement; ~ *down with* F se fendre de (*une somme*); *Am.* F être frappé par (*une maladie*); ~ *for* venir chercher; ~ *in* entrer; ⚓ arriver; être de saison; devenir la mode; ~ *in!* entrez!; ~ *off* tomber (de); se détacher (*bouton*); s'enlever (*tache*); avoir lieu; réussir; tomber (*cheveux*); ~ *on* s'avancer; survenir; ~ *on!* allons-y!; ~ *out* sortir (de, *of*); se développer; débuter; ~ *out right* donner la solution juste; ~ *round fig.* reprendre connaissance; ~ *to adv. see* ~ *to o.s.*; ⚓ venir sur bâbord *ou* tribord; *prp.* arriver à; ~ *to o.s.* (*ou to one's senses*) revenir à soi; reprendre ses sens; ~ *to anchor* s'ancrer, mouiller; ~ *to know* en venir à connaître *ou* savoir; ~ *up* monter; surgir; pousser (*plante*); paraître; ~ *up to* répondre à (*une attente*); s'élever jusqu'à; s'approcher (*q.*); égaler; ~ *up with* rattraper, rejoindre (*q.*); ~ *upon* tomber sur (*q.*); rencontrer par hasard; venir à l'esprit de (*q.*); ~-**'at·a·ble** F accessible; '~-**back** rentrée *f*; retour *m* en vogue *ou* au pouvoir; *Am.* revanche *f*; *Am. sl.* réplique *f*.

co·me·di·an [kə'mi:djən] comédien(ne *f*) *m*; *music-hall:* comique *m*.

com·e·dy ['kɔmidi] comédie *f*.

come·li·ness ['kʌmlinis] mine *f* avenante; '**come·ly** avenant.

come-off F ['kʌmɔːf] résultat *m*; issue *f*.

com·er ['kʌmə] arrivant(e *f*) *m*; venant(e *f*) *m*.

co·mes·ti·ble [kə'mestibl] *usu.* ~*s pl.* comestible *m*, -s *m/pl.*

com·et ['kɔmit] comète *f*.

com·fort ['kʌmfət] **1.** soulagement *m*; consolation *f*; bien-être *m*; confort *m*; aisance *f*; agrément *m*; *fig.* réconfort *m*; **2.** soulager; consoler; réconforter; '**com·fort·a·ble** □ confortable; à son aise (*personne*); tranquille; *I am* ~ je suis à mon aise; je suis bien; '**com·fort·er** consolateur (-trice *f*) *m*; *fig.* cache-nez *m/inv.*; *Am.* couvre-pied *m*

piqué; *Brit.* sucette *f*; '**com·fort·less** □ incommode; dépourvu de confort.

com·frey ♧ ['kʌmfri] consoude *f*.

com·fy □ F ['kʌmfi] *see* **comfortable**.

com·ic ['kɔmik] (~*ally*) comique; *fig.* (*usu.* '**com·i·cal** □) ~ *journal* (*ou* *paper*) journal *m* pour rire; *journ. Am.* comic strip bande *f* dessinée; '**com·ics** *pl. journ. Am.* bandes *f/pl.* dessinées (*souvent humoristiques*).

com·ing ['kʌmiŋ] **1.** futur, qui vient; ~, *Sir!* tout de suite, monsieur!; **2.** venue *f*; approche *f*.

com·i·ty ['kɔmiti]: ~ *of nations* bon accord *m* entre les nations; courtoisie *f* internationale.

com·ma ['kɔmə] virgule *f*; *inverted* ~*s pl.* guillemets *m/pl.*

com·mand [kə'mɑːnd] **1.** ordre *m*; maîtrise *f* (*d'une langue*); ✕ commandement *m* (*souv.* ⚲, *p.ex.* *Southern* ⚲); *at* (*ou by*) ~ *of* d'après les ordres de, suivant l'ordre de; *have* ~ *of* commander; dominer; *be* (*have*) *at* ~ être à la (avoir à sa) disposition; ✕ *be in* ~ *of* commander; **2.** ordonner; commander; inspirer (*un sentiment*); forcer (*l'attention*); dominer (*une vallée*); commander; *fig.* être maître de, maîtriser; disposer de; **com·man·dant** ✕ [kɔmən'dænt] commandant *m*; **com·man·deer** [~'diə] ✕ réquisitionner; **com·mand·er** [kə'mɑːndə] commandant *m*; chef *m* de corps; ⚓ capitaine *m* de frégate; *ordres:* commandeur *m*; **com'mand·er-in-'chief** commandant *m* en chef; **com'mand·ing** commandant; en chef; *fig.* d'autorité; imposant; éminent (*lieu*); ~ *point* point *m* stratégique; **com'mand·ment** commandement *m*.

com·mem·o·rate [kə'meməreit] commémorer; célébrer le souvenir de; **com·mem·o'ra·tion** commémoration *f*; **com'mem·o·ra·tive** [~rətiv] □ commémoratif (-ive *f*) (de, *of*).

com·mence [kə'mens] commencer; initier; entamer; ⚖ intenter (*un procès*); **com'mence·ment** commencement *m*, début *m*.

com·mend [kə'mend] recommander; confier; louer; F ~ *me to* ...

saluez ... de ma part; com'**mend·a·ble** □ louable; digne d'éloges; **com·men·da·tion** [kɔmen'deiʃn] éloge *m*, louange *f*; com'**mend·a·to·ry** [‿ətəri] élogieux (-euse *f*).

com·men·su·ra·ble □ [kə'menʃərəbl] commensurable (avec *m*, to); see *commensurate*; com'**men·su·rate** □ [‿rit] proportionné (à with, to); coétendu (à, with).

com·ment ['kɔmənt] **1.** commentaire *m*; critique *f*, glose *f*, observation *f* (sur, on); **2.** (*upon*) commenter, critiquer (*qch.*); faire le commentaire (de); **com·men·tar·y** ['‿təri] commentaire *m*, glose *f*; radioreportage *m*; '**com·men·ta·tor** ['‿teitə] commentateur (-trice *f*) *m*; radioreporter *m*.

com·merce ['kɔmə:s] commerce *m*; affaires *f/pl.*; *Chamber of* ♀ Chambre *f* de Commerce; **com·mer·cial** □ [kə'mə:ʃəl] **1.** commercial (-aux *m/pl.*); mercantile; marchand; de (du) commerce; ‿ *traveller* commis *m* voyageur; représentant(e *f*) *m*; **2.** *Brit.* F *see* ‿ *traveller*; *surt. Am. radio*: réclame *f*; com'**mer·cial·ism** esprit *m* commercial; com'**mer·cial·ize** commercialiser.

com·mis·er·ate [kə'mizəreit] s'apitoyer sur le sort de (*q.*); **com·mis·er'a·tion** compassion *f* (pour, with).

com·mis·sar·i·at ✕ [kɔmi'sɛəriət] intendance *f*; **com·mis·sar·y** ['‿səri] commissaire *m*; ✕ intendant *m* général d'armée.

com·mis·sion [kə'miʃn] **1.** commission *f*; ordre *m*, mandat *m*; délégation *f* (*d'autorité, de devoirs*); *crime*: perpétration *f*; ✕ brevet *m* (*d'officier*), grade *m* d'officier; ♣ *navire*: armement *m*; commission *f*, pourcentage *m*; ŏn ‿ à la commission; **2.** commissionner; déléguer; charger; ✕ nommer (*un officier*); ♣ armer; **com·mis·sion·aire** [‿ʃə-'nɛə] commissionnaire *m*; *hôtel*: chasseur *m*; com'**mis·sion·er** [‿ʃnə] commissaire *m*; délégué *m* d'une commission.

com·mit [kə'mit] commettre (*a. un crime, une erreur*); confier; engager (*sa parole*); coucher (*par écrit*); *pol.* renvoyer à une commission; ‿ (*o.s. s'*)engager (à, to); se compromettre; ‿ (*to prison*) envoyer en prison,

écrouer (*q.*); ‿ *for trial* renvoyer aux assises; com'**mit·ment** délégation *f*; *pol.* renvoi *m* à une commission; mise *f* en prison; renvoi *m* aux assises; engagement *m* financier; com'**mit·tal** *see* commitment; mise *f* en terre (*d'un cadavre*); *crime*: perpétration *f*; ‿ *order* mandat *m* de dépôt; com'**mit·tee** comité *m*, commission *f*.

com·mode [kə'moud] commode *f*; chaise *f* percée; com'**mo·di·ous** □ [‿djəs] spacieux (-euse *f*); com'**mod·i·ty** [kə'mɔditi] (*usu.* ‿*s pl.*) marchandise *f*, -s *f/pl.*; denrée *f*, -s *f/pl.*; ‿ *value* valeur *f* vénale.

com·mo·dore ♣ ['kɔmədɔ:] chef *m* de division; commodore *m*.

com·mon ['kɔmən] **1.** □ commun; public (-ique *f*); courant; ordinaire; vulgaire; trivial (-aux *m/pl.*); *gramm.* ‿ *noun* nom *m* commun; ♀ *Council* conseil *m* municipal; *Book of* ♀ *Prayer* rituel *m* de l'Église anglicane; ‿ *law* droit *m* commun *ou* coutumier; ‿ *room* salle *f* commune; salle *f* des professeurs; ‿ *sense* sens *m* commun, bon sens *m*; ♱ ‿ *stock* actions *f/pl.* ordinaires; ‿ *weal* bien *m* public; *in* ‿ en commun (avec, with); **2.** pâtis *m*; terrain *m* communal; **com·mon·al·ty** ['‿nlti] le commun des hommes; '**com·mon·er** bourgeois *m*; homme *m* du peuple; *qqfois* membre *m* de la Chambre des Communes; *univ.* étudiant *m* ordinaire; '**com·mon·place 1.** lieu *m* commun; **2.** banal (-aux *m/pl.*); terre à terre; médiocre; **com·mons** ['‿z] *pl.* le peuple *m*; le tiers état *m*; ordinaire *m* (*de la table*); *short* ‿ maigre chère *f*; (*usu. House of*) ♀ Chambre *f* des Communes; '**com·mon·sense** sensé, raisonnable; '**com·mon·wealth** État *m*; *souv.* republique *f*; chose *f* publique; *the British* ♀ l'Empire *m* Britannique; *the* ♀ *of Australia* le Commonwealth *m* d'Australie.

com·mo·tion [kə'mouʃn] agitation *f*; troubles *m/pl.*; brouhaha *m*.

com·mu·nal □ ['kɔmjunl] communal (-aux *m/pl.*); ‿ *estate* ⅟ⅈ communauté *f* de biens; **com·mu·nal·ize** ['‿nəlaiz] mettre en commun.

com·mu·ni·ca·bil·i·ty [kəmju:nikə-'biliti] communicabilité *f*; **com-**

compensation

'mu·ni·ca·ble □ communicable; 🗲 contagieux (-euse *f*); **com'mu·ni·cant** *eccl.* communiant(e *f*) *m*; **com'mu·ni·cate** [ˌkeit] *v/t.* communiquer (à, *to*); *v/i.* communiquer (avec, *with*); par, *by*); *eccl.* recevoir la communion; **com·mu·ni'ca·tion** communication *f* (a. ✗, *téléph., voie*); voie *f* d'accès; 🖦 ~ *cord* signal *m* d'alarme; *be in* ~ *with* être en relation avec; **com'mu·ni·ca·tive** □ communicatif (-ive *f*); expansif (-ive *f*); **com'mu·ni·ca·tor** débiteur (-euse *f*) *m* (*de nouvelles*); ⊕ communicateur *m*.
com·mun·ion [kəm'juːnjən] rapport *m*; relations *f/pl.*; *eccl.* communion *f*.
com·mu·ni·qué [kəm'juːnikei] communiqué *m*.
com·mu·nism ['kɔmjunizm] communisme *m*; **'com·mu·nist 1.** communiste *mf*; **2.** = **com·mu'nis·tic** (ˌally) *ally*).
com·mu·ni·ty [kəm'juːniti] communauté *f* (a. *eccl.*); solidarité *f*; *the* ~ l'État *m*; *le public m*; ~ *ownership* collectivité *f*; ~ *service* service *m* public; ~ *spirit* sens *m* du groupe; ~ *work* travail *m* en commun.
com·mu·nize ['kɔmjunaiz] collectiviser; rendre communiste.
com·mut·a·ble [kəm'juːtəbl] permutable; commuable (*peine*); **com·mu·ta·tion** [kɔmjuːˈteiʃn] commutation *f* (en *into*, *for*); *Am.* ~ *ticket* carte *f* d'abonnement; **com·mu·ta·tive** [kəˈmjuːtətiv] commutatif (-ive *f*); **com·mu·ta·tor** ⚡ ['kɔmjuːteitə] commutateur *m*; **commute** [kəˈmjuːt] *v/t.* échanger (pour, contre *for*, *into*); commuer (*une peine*) (en, *into*); racheter (*qch.*) (par, *into*) (*une rente, une servitude*); *v/i. Am.* prendre un abonnement; **com'mut·er** *Am.* abonné(e *f*) *m*.
com·pact 1. ['kɔmpækt] convention *f*; poudrier *m*; **2.** [kəm'pækt] compact; serré; formé (de, *of*); **3.** [ˌ] *v/t.* rendre compact; **com'pact·ness** compacité *f*; *style:* concision *f*.
com·pan·ion [kəm'pænjən] compagnon *m*, compagne *f*; manuel *m*; pendant *m*; *ordre:* compagnon *m*; 🖦 capot *m* (d'échelle); ~ *in arms* compagnon *m* d'armes; **com'pan·ion·a·ble** □ sociable; **com'pan-**

ion·ship camaraderie *f*; compagnie *f*.
com·pa·ny ['kʌmpəni] compagnie *f* (a. ✝, a. ✗); assemblée *f*; bande *f*; *invités:* monde *m*; ✝ a. société *f*; 🖦 équipage *m*; *théâ.* troupe *f*; *good* (*bad*) ~ bonne (mauvaise) compagnie *f*; *bear* ~ tenir compagnie à q.; *have* ~ avoir du monde; *keep* ~ *with* sortir avec.
com·pa·ra·ble □ ['kɔmpərəbl] comparable (avec, □ *with*, *to*); **com·par·a·tive** [kəmˈpærətiv] **1.** □ comparatif (-ive *f*); comparé; relatif (-ive *f*); ~ *degree* = **2.** *gramm.* comparatif *m*; **com·pare** [ˌ'pɛə] **1.**: *beyond* (*ou without ou past*) ~ sans pareil(le *f*) *m*; **2.** *v/t.* comparer (avec, à *with*, *to*); confronter (avec, *with*); *gramm.* former les degrés de comparaison de; (*as*) ~ *d with* en comparaison de; *v/i.* être comparable (à, *with*); **com·par·i·son** [ˌ'pærisn] comparaison *f* (a. *gramm.*); confrontation *f*; *in* ~ *with* en comparaison de; auprès de.
com·part·ment [kəmˈpɑːtmənt] compartiment *m* (a. 🛆, a. 🖦); *tiroir:* case *f*; *bagages:* soute *f*.
com·pass ['kʌmpəs] **1.** boussole *f*; limite *f*, *-s f/pl.*; ♩ registre *m*; (*a pair of*) ~*es pl.* (un) compas *m*; **2.** faire le tour de; entourer; comploter (*la mort, la ruine*); atteindre (*un but*).
com·pas·sion [kəmˈpæʃn] compassion *f*; *have* ~ *on* avoir compassion de; **com'pas·sion·ate** □ [ˌ'ʃənit] compatissant (à, pour *to*[*wards*]).
com·pat·i·bil·i·ty [kəmpætəˈbiliti] compatibilité *f*; **com'pat·i·ble** □ compatible (avec, *with*).
com·pa·tri·ot [kəm'pætriət] compatriote *mf*.
com·peer [kɔm'piə] égal *m*, pair *m*; compagnon *m*.
com·pel [kəm'pel] contraindre, forcer, obliger (q. à *inf.*, *s.o. to inf.*).
com·pen·di·ous □ [kəm'pendiəs] abrégé, concis; **com'pen·di·ous·ness** concision *f*; forme *f* succincte.
com·pen·di·um [kəm'pendiəm] abrégé *m*; recueil *m*.
com·pen·sate ['kɔmpenseit] *v/t.* dédommager (de, *for*); compenser (a. ⊕) (avec *with*, *by*); *v/i.* ~ *for* racheter (*qch.*); compenser (*qch.*); **com·pen'sa·tion** compensation *f*; dédommagement *m*; indemnité *f*;

réparation *f*; *Am.* appointements *m/pl.*; ⊕ compensation *f*, rattrapage *m*; '**com·pen·sa·tive**, '**com·pen·sa·to·ry** compensatoire, -teur (-trice *f*).

com·pete [kəm'piːt] concourir (pour qch., *for s.th.*); disputer (qch. à q., *with s.o. for s.th.*); rivaliser (avec q. de qch., *with s.o. in s.th.*); faire concurrence (à q., *with s.o.*).

com·pe·tence, **com·pe·ten·cy** ['kɔmpitəns(i)] compétence *f* (en *in, at*) (*a.* ⚖); moyens *m/pl.* (*d'existence*); attributions *f/pl.*; '**com·pe·tent** □ capable; compétent (*a.* ⚖); suffisant (*connaissances*).

com·pe·ti·tion [kɔmpi'tiʃn] rivalité *f*; concurrence *f* (*a.* ✝); concours *m*; échecs: tournoi *m*; *sp.* meeting *m*; *rifle* ~ concours *m* de tir; **com·pet·i·tive** □ [kəm'petitiv] de concurrence; de concours; **com·pet·i·tor** concurrent(e *f*) *m*; rival(e *f*) *m*; compétiteur (-trice *f*) *m*.

com·pi·la·tion [kɔmpi'leiʃn] compilation *f*; recueil *m*; **com·pile** [kəm'pail] compiler; composer, établir (de, *from*); recueillir.

com·pla·cence, **com·pla·cen·cy** [kəm'pleisns(i)] satisfaction *f*; contentement *m* de soi-même; **com·pla·cent** □ content de soi-même; suffisant.

com·plain [kəm'plein] se plaindre (de *of, about*; à, *to*; que, *that*); porter plainte (contre *against, about*); *poét.* se lamenter; **com·plain·ant** plaignant(e *f*) *m*; **com·plain·er** réclamant(e *f*) *m*; mécontent(e *f*) *m*; **com·plaint** grief *m*; plainte *f*; doléances *f/pl.*; maladie *f*, mal *m*.

com·plai·sance [kəm'pleizns] complaisance *f*, obligeance *f*; **com·plai·sant** □ complaisant, obligeant.

com·ple·ment 1. ['kɔmplimənt] effectif *m* (complet); plein *m*; *gramm.* attribut *m*; *livre, a.* ♫ complément *m*; **2.** ['~ment] compléter; **com·ple·men·tal**, **com·ple·men·ta·ry** complémentaire; *be* ~ (*to*) compléter.

com·plete [kəm'pliːt] **1.** □ complet (-ète *f*); entier (-ère *f*); total (-aux *m/pl.*); achevé, parfait (*~e* *f*); **2.** compléter; achever; remplir (*un bulletin*); **com·ple·tion** achèvement *m*; *contrat:* signature *f*; réalisation *f*; accomplissement *m*.

com·plex ['kɔmpleks] **1.** □ complexe; *fig.* compliqué; **2.** tout *m*, ensemble *m*; *psych.* complexe *m*; **com·plex·ion** [kəm'plekʃn] teint *m*; aspect *m*, caractère *m*, jour *m*; **com·plex·i·ty** complexité *f*.

com·pli·ance [kəm'plaiəns] acquiescement *m* (à, *with*); obéissance *f*; *péj.* basse complaisance *f*; *in* ~ *with* en conformité de; suivant; **com·pli·ant** □ accommodant, obligeant.

com·pli·cate ['kɔmplikeit] compliquer; **com·pli·ca·tion** complication *f* (*a.* ⚘).

com·plic·i·ty [kəm'plisiti] complicité *f* (à, *in*).

com·pli·ment 1. ['kɔmplimənt] compliment *m*; honneur *m*; ~*s* *pl. a.* hommages *m/pl.*, amitiés *f/pl.*; galanteries *f/pl.*; **2.** ['~ment] *v/t.* féliciter, complimenter (de, *on*); **com·pli'men·ta·ry** flatteur (-euse *f*); ✝ à titre gracieux, en hommage; ~ *copy* livre *m* offert en hommage; *give s.o. a* ~ *dinner* donner un dîner *m* en l'honneur de q.; ~ *ticket* billet *m* de faveur.

com·ply [kəm'plai] *v/i.* ~ *with* se conformer à; se soumettre à; accéder à; accomplir (*une condition*); observer (*une règle*).

com·po·nent [kəm'pounənt] **1.** partie *f* constituante; composant *m*; **2.** constituant; composant; ~ *part see* ~ **1.**

com·port [kəm'pɔːt] *v/i.* convenir (à, *with*); *v/t.*: ~ *o.s.* se comporter.

com·pose [kəm'pouz] composer (*a. typ.*); arranger; disposer; régler (*un différend*); calmer (*l'esprit*); rasseoir; **com'posed**, *adv.* **com'pos·ed·ly** [~zidli] calme, tranquille; composé (*visage*); **com'pos·er** auteur *m*; ♪ compositeur (-trice *f*) *m*; **com'pos·ing 1.** calmant; **2.** composition *f*; ~*machine* composeuse *f*; ~*room* atelier *m* de composition; **com·pos·ite** ['kɔmpɔzit] **1.** composé; mixte; △ composite; **2.** (corps *m*) composé *m*; ♀ composée *f*; **com·po·si·tion** composition *f* (*a.* ♪, *peint.*, ♫); mélange *m*; *exercice:* dissertation *f*, rédaction *f*; thème *m*; *fig.* caractère *m*; ✝ arrangement *m*; **com·pos·i·tor** [kəm'pɔzitə] compositeur *m*, typographe *m*; **com·post** ['kɔmpɔst] compost *m*; **com·po·sure** [kəm'pouʒə] sang-froid *m*, calme *m*.

com·pote ['kɔmpout] compote *f*.

com·pound¹ 1. ['kɔmpaund] com-posé; ⚒ ~ *fracture* fracture *f* compliquée; ~ *interest* intérêts *m/pl.* composés; **2.** composé *m* (*a.* ♏); ⊕ mastic *m*; *gramm.* (*a.* ~ *word*) mot *m* composé; **3.** [kəm'paund] *v/t.* mé-langer; arranger (*un différend*); *v/i.* s'arranger; transiger (*avec q.*, *avec sa conscience*); ♱ se rédimer (de, *for*); s'accommoder.

com·pound² ['kɔmpaund] enceinte *f*; ✗ camp *m* de concentration.

com·pre·hend [kɔmpri'hend] com-prendre; se rendre compte de.

com·pre·hen·si·ble ☐ [kɔmpri-'hensəbl] compréhensible; **com·pre'hen·sion** compréhension *f*; entendement *m*; **com·pre'hen·sive** ☐ compréhensif (-ive *f*); ~ *insurance* assurance *f* tous risques; **com·pre'hen·sive·ness** étendue *f*.

com·press 1. [kəm'pres] compri-mer; condenser (*un discours*); **2.** ['kɔmpres] ✚ compresse *f*; **com·press·i·bil·i·ty** [kɔmpresi'biliti] compressibilité *f*; **com'press·i·ble** [~'presəbl] compressible; **com·pres·sion** [~'preʃn] compression *f* (*a. phys.*); **com·pres·sor** [~'presə] ⊕ compresseur *m*.   [dre, contenir.\

com·prise [kəm'praiz] compren-\

com·pro·mise ['kɔmprəmaiz] **1.** compromis *m*; *fig.* accommodement *m*; **2.** *v/t.* compromettre; arranger (*un différend*); *v/i.* aboutir à un compromis; transiger (sur, *on*); s'accommoder.

com·pul·sion [kəm'pʌlʃn] con-trainte *f*; **com'pul·sive** [~siv] compulsif (-ive *f*); **com'pul·so·ry** [~səri] obligatoire; forcé; par con-trainte.

com·punc·tion [kəm'pʌŋkʃn] re-mords *m*; componction *f*.

com·put·a·ble [kəm'pju:təbl] cal-culable; **com·pu·ta·tion** [kɔmpju:-'teiʃn] calcul *m*, estimation *f*; **com·pute** [kəm'pju:t] calculer, com-puter, estimer (à, *at*); **com·put·er** ⊕ [kəm'pju:tə] ordinateur *m*; ~ *age* ère *f* de l'ordinateur *ou* de l'infor-matique; ~-*controlled* commandé par ordinateur; ~ *language* langage *m* machine; ~ *science* informatique *f*; ~ *scientist* informaticien(ne *f*) *m*.

com·rade ['kɔmrid] camarade *m*, compagnon *m*.   [*leçon*).\

con¹ [kɔn] étudier; répéter (*une*\

con² ⚓ [~] gouverner (*un navire*); diriger la manœuvre.

con³ [~] *abr. de* contra; *pro and* ~ pour et contre; *the pros and* ~*s* le pour et le contre.

con⁴ *Am. sl.* [~] **1.** *mots composés*: *abr. de* confidence; **2.** duper, tromper.

con·cat·e·nate [kɔn'kætineit] *usu. fig.* enchaîner; **con·cat·e'na·tion** enchaînement *m*; *circonstances*: concours *m*.

con·cave ☐ ['kɔn'keiv] concave, in-curvé; **con·cav·i·ty** [~'kæviti] con-cavité *f*; *qqfois* creux *m*.

con·ceal [kɔn'si:l] cacher (*a. fig.*); celer; taire (à, *from*); masquer; voiler; **con'ceal·ment** dissimula-tion *f*; action *f* de (se) cacher; (*a. place of* ~) cachette *f*, retraite *f*.

con·cede [kɔn'si:d] concéder; ad-mettre; **con'ced·ed·ly** [~idly] *Am.* reconnu (pour, comme).

con·ceit [kɔn'si:t] vanité *f*, suffisance *f*; (*ou self-*~) amour-propre (*pl.* amours-propres) *m*, infatuation *f*; *out of* ~ *with* dégoûté de; **con'ceit·ed** ☐ vaniteux (-euse *f*), prétentieux (-euse *f*); **con'ceit·ed·ness** vanité *f*, suffisance *f*.

con·ceiv·a·ble ☐ [kɔn'si:vəbl] ima-ginable, concevable; **con'ceive** *v/i.* devenir enceinte; ~ *of s.th.* (s')ima-giner qch.; *v/t.* concevoir (*un en-fant, un projet, de l'amour*); rédiger.

con·cen·trate 1. ['kɔnsentreit] *v/t.* concentrer (*a. fig.*); ✗ faire conver-ger (*les feux*); *v/i.* se concentrer; **2.** ['~trit] concentré *m*; **con·cen·'tra·tion** concentration *f* (*a.* ♏); ✗ convergence *f* (*des feux*); **con·cen·tre, con·cen·ter** [~tə] (se) réunir; (se) con-centrer; **con'cen·tric** (~*ally*) con-centrique.

con·cep·tion [kɔn'sepʃn] *biol.* en-fant, *idée*: conception *f*; idée *f*, imagination *f*; **con·cep·tu·al** ☐ [kɔn'septjuəl] conceptuel(le *f*).

con·cern [kɔn'sə:n] **1.** rapport *m*; affaire *f*; intérêt *m* (dans, *in*); souci *m*, inquiétude *f* (à l'égard de, *about*); ♱ entreprise *f*; maison *f* de commerce; F appareil *m*; **2.** con-cerner, regarder, intéresser (*q.*, *qch.*); ~ *o.s. with* s'occuper de; ~

o.s. about (*ou* for) s'intéresser à, s'inquiéter de; **con'cerned** □ inquiet (-ète *f*) (de *at*, *about*; au sujet de *about*, *for*); soucieux (-euse *f*); impliqué (dans, *in*); *those* ~ les intéressés; *be* ~ être en cause; *be* ~ *that* s'inquiéter que (*sbj.*); *be* ~ *to* (*inf.*) tâcher de (*inf.*), chercher à (*inf.*); *be* ~ *with* s'occuper de; s'intéresser à; **con'cern·ing** *prp.* au sujet de, concernant, touchant, en ce qui concerne.

con·cert 1. [ˈkɔnsət] concert *m* (*a.* ♪); accord *m*; **2.** [kənˈsəːt] *v/t.* concerter; *fig.* arranger; *v/i.* se concerter (avec, *with*); ♪ ~ed concertant, d'ensemble; **con·cer·ti·na** ♪ [kɔnsəˈtiːnə] accordéon *m* hexagonal, concertina *f*; **'con·certpitch** ♪ diapason *m* de concert.

con·ces·sion [kənˈseʃn] *opinion, terrain*: concession *f*; *make* ~s to sacrifier à; **con·ces·sion·aire** [kənseʃəˈnɛə] concessionnaire *m*.

con·ces·sive □ [kənˈsesiv] concessif.

conch [kɔŋk] conque *f*. [(-ive *f*).]

con·cil·i·ate [kənˈsilieit] (ré)concilier; gagner (*q.*) à son parti; se concilier (*la faveur de q.*); **con·cil·i·ˈa·tion** conciliation *f*; arbitrage *m*; **con'cil·i·a·tor** conciliateur (-trice *f*) *m*; **con'cil·i·a·to·ry** [~ətəri] conciliant, conciliatoire; ~ *proposal* offre *f* de conciliation.

con·cin·ni·ty [kənˈsiniti] élégance *f* (*de style*).

con·cise □ [kənˈsais] concis; bref (brève *f*); serré (*style*); **con'ciseness** concision *f*.

con·clave [ˈkɔnkleiv] *eccl.* conclave *m*; *fig.* conseil *m*; assemblée *f*.

con·clude [kənˈkluːd] *v/t.* conclure; terminer, achever; arranger, régler (*une affaire*); *to be* ~*d in our next* la fin au prochain numéro; *v/i.* conclure, estimer; *Am.* ~ *to* (*inf.*) décider de (*inf.*); **con'clud·ing** final (-als *m/pl.*).

con·clu·sion [kənˈkluːʒn] conclusion *f*, fin *f*; *séance*: clôture *f*; conclusion *f*, décision *f*; *try* ~s *with* se mesurer contre *ou* avec; **con'clusive** □ concluant, décisif (-ive *f*).

con·coct [kənˈkɔkt] confectionner; *fig.* imaginer; tramer; **con'coc·tion** confection *f*; mixtion *f*; *fig. plan etc.*: élaboration *f*.

con·com·i·tance, con·com·i·tan·cy [kənˈkɔmitəns(i)] concomitance *f* (*a. eccl.*); **con'com·i·tant 1.** □ concomitant (de, *with*); **2.** accessoire *m*, accompagnement *m*.

con·cord 1. [ˈkɔŋkɔːd] concorde *f*; harmonie *f* (*a.* ♪); *gramm.* concordance *f*; *fig.* accord *m*; **2.** [kənˈkɔːd] concorder, s'accorder; être d'accord; **con'cord·ance** accord *m* (avec, *with*); concordance *f* (*a. eccl.*); **con'cord·ant** □ concordant (avec, *with*); qui s'accorde (avec, *with*); ♪ consonant; **con'cor·dat** *eccl.* [~dæt] concordat *m*.

con·course [ˈkɔŋkɔːs] foule *f*; rassemblement *m*; carrefour *m*; concours *m*; *Am.* hall *m* (*de gare*).

con·crete [ˈkɔŋkriːt] **1.** □ concret (-ète *f*); de *ou* en béton; **2.** △ béton *m*, ciment *m*; *phls., gramm.* concret *m*; *in the* ~ sous forme concrète; **3.** [kənˈkriːt] (se) concréter; (se) solidifier; [ˈkɔnkriːt] *v/t.* bétonner; **con·cre·tion** [kənˈkriːʃn] concrétion *f*.

con·cu·bi·nage [kɔnˈkjuːbinidʒ] concubinage *m*; **con·cu·bine** [ˈkɔŋkjubain] concubine *f*.

con·cu·pis·cence [kənˈkjuːpisns] concupiscence *f*; **con·cu·pis·cent** libidineux (-euse *f*), lascif (-ive *f*).

con·cur [kənˈkəː] coïncider; être d'accord (avec, *with*); concourir (à, *in*); contribuer (à, *to*); **con·currence** [~ˈkʌrəns] concours *m*; coopération *f*; simultanéité *f*; accord *m*; approbation *f*; *in* ~ *with* en commun avec; d'accord avec; **con'cur·rent** □ concourant; simultané; unanime.

con·cus·sion [kənˈkʌʃn] secousse *f*; commotion *f* (*cérébrale*).

con·demn [kənˈdem] condamner (*a. fig.*); condamner à mort; déclarer coupable; *fig.* blâmer; ~*ed cell* cellule *f* des condamnés; **con'dem·na·ble** condamnable, blâmable; **con·dem·na·tion** [kɔndemˈneiʃn] condamnation *f*; censure *f*; blâme *m*; **con·dem·nato·ry** □ [kənˈdemnətəri] condamnatoire.

con·den·sa·ble [kənˈdensəbl] condensable; **con·den·sa·tion** [kɔndenˈseiʃn] condensation *f*; liquide *m* condensé; **con·dense** [kənˈdens] (se) condenser; *v/t.* concentrer; **con-**

'**dens·er** condenseur *m* (*a.* ⊕); ⊕, *a.* ⚡ condensateur *m.*

con·de·scend [kɔndi'send] s'abaisser; condescendre; **con·de'scend·ing** □ condescendant (envers, *to*); **con·de'scen·sion** condescendance *f*; complaisance *f.*

con·dign □ [kən'dain] mérité; exemplaire.

con·di·ment ['kɔndimənt] condiment *m.*

con·di·tion [kən'diʃn] **1.** condition *f*; stipulation *f*; état *m*, situation *f*; on ~ *that* à condition que; **2.** soumettre à une condition; stipuler; conditionner (*l'air, la laine*; *a.* psych.); **con'di·tion·al** [~ʃənl] **1.** □ conditionnel(le *f*); dépendant (de, [up]on); ~ *mood* = **2.** gramm. conditionnel *m*; *in the* ~ au conditionnel; **con·di·tion·al·i·ty** [~'æliti] état *m* conditionnel; **con'di·tion·al·ly** [~ʃnəli] sous certaines conditions; **con'di·tioned** conditionné; *en* ... état.

con·dole [kən'doul] (*with s.o.*) partager la douleur (de q.); exprimer ses condoléances (à q.); **con'do·lence** condoléance *f.*

con·do·min·i·um [kɔndə'miniəm] condominium *m*; *Am.* immeuble *m* en copropriété.

con·do·na·tion [kɔndou'neiʃn] pardon *m*; indulgence *f* (pour, *of*); **con·done** [kən'doun] pardonner; *action*: racheter (*une offense*).

con·duce [kən'djuːs] contribuer (à, *to*); favoriser (qch., *to s.th.*); **con'du·cive** (*to*) favorable (à); qui contribue (à).

con·duct 1. ['kɔndʌkt] conduite *f*; *affaire*: gestion *f*; manière *f* de se conduire; **2.** [kən'dʌkt] conduire; (a)mener (*q.*); accompagner (*une excursion*); diriger (♪, *une opération*); mener, gérer (*une affaire*); phys. être conducteur (-trice *f*) de; ~ *o.s.* se comporter (*bien, mal, etc.*); **con·duct·i·bil·i·ty** [kəndʌkti'biliti] phys. conductibilité *f*; **con'duct·i·ble** [~təbl] phys. conductible; **con'duct·ing** conducteur (-trice *f*); **con'duc·tion** conduction *f*; **con'duc·tive** □ phys. conducteur (-trice *f*); **con·duc·tiv·i·ty** [kəndʌk'tiviti] phys. conductivité *f*; conductibilité *f*; **con·duc·tor** [kən'dʌktə] conducteur *m* (*a.* phys.);

accompagnateur *m*; *tramway etc.*: receveur; *Am.* 🚂 chef *m* de train; ♪ chef *m* d'orchestre; ⚡ (conducteur *m* de) paratonnerre *m*; **con'duc·tress** conductrice *f*; *tramway etc.*: receveuse *f.*

con·duit ['kɔndit] conduit *m*; tuyau *m* conducteur.

cone [koun] cône *m*; ⊕ cloche *f*; ♀ pomme *f*, cône *m*; *glace*: cornet *m.*

co·ney ['kouni] (peau *f* de) lapin *m.*

con·fab F ['kɔnfæb] **1.** (= **con·fab·u·late** [kən'fæbjuleit]) causer (*entre intimes*); **2.** (= **con·fab·u'la·tion**) causerie *f* intime.

con·fec·tion [kən'fekʃn] confection *f* (*de qch., a.* pharm.); *cost.* (vêtement *m* de) confection *f*; friandise *f*; **con'fec·tion·er** confiseur (-euse *f*) *m*; **con'fec·tion·er·y** confiserie *f*; bonbons *m/pl.*

con·fed·er·a·cy [kən'fedərəsi] confédération *f*; *fig.* entente *f*; *surt. Am. the* ♀ les Confédérés *m/pl.* (= *les sudistes pendant la guerre de Sécession 1860—65*); ⚖ conspiration *f*; **con'fed·er·ate** [~rit] **1.** confédéré; **2.** confédéré *m*; complice *m*; **3.** [~reit] (se) confédérer; **confed·er'a·tion** confédération *f*; *surt. Am. the* ♀ la Confédération *f* des 11 États sécessionnistes.

con·fer [kən'fəː] *v/t.* (à, on) conférer; accorder (*une faveur*); décerner (*un honneur*); *v/i.* conférer; entrer en consultation (avec, *with*); sur *about, on*); **con'fer·ence** ['kɔnfərəns] conférence *f*; consultation *f*; entretien *m*; congrès *m.*

con·fess [kən'fes] *v/t.* confesser; avouer (*qch.*; que, *that*; *inf.*, *to* gér.); *v/i.* eccl. se confesser; **con'fess·ed·ly** [~idli] de l'aveu général; franchement; **con·fes·sion** [~'feʃn] confession *f* (*a.* eccl.); aveu *m*; *go to* ~ aller à confesse; **con'fes·sion·al** **1.** confessionnel(le *f*); **2.** confessionnal *m*; **con'fes·sor** [~sə] celui (celle) qui avoue; confesseur *m.*

con·fi·dant [kɔnfi'dænt] confident *m*; **con·fi'dante** [~] confidente *f.*

con·fide [kən'faid] confier; se (con)fier (à q., *in s.o.*); avouer (*qch.*) en confidence (à q., *to s.o.*); **con·fi·dence** ['kɔnfidəns] confiance *f* (en, *in*); assurance *f*, hardiesse *f*; confidence *f*; ~ *man* escroc *m*; ~ *trick* vol *m* à l'américaine; *man of* ~

homme *m* de confiance; **'con·fi·dent** □ assuré, sûr (de, of); *péj.* effronté; **con·fi·den·tial** [‿'denʃl] □ confidentiel(le *f*); ～ *clerk* clerc *m* de confiance; ～ *agent* homme *m* de confiance.

con·fig·u·ra·tion [kənfigju'reiʃn] configuration *f*.

con·fine 1. ['kɔnfain] *usu.* ～*s pl.* confins *m/pl.*; **2.** [kən'fain] (r)enfermer (dans, *to*); borner, limiter (à, *to*); be ～*d to bed* être alité, garder le lit; be ～*d* faire ses couches; accoucher (*d'un fils etc.*); **con'fine·ment** emprisonnement *m*, réclusion *f*; alitement *m*; restriction *f*; *femme*: couches *f/pl.*, accouchement *m*.

con·firm [kən'fə:m] confirmer (*a. eccl.*); affermir (*un pouvoir*); ⚖ entériner; **con·fir·ma·tion** [kɔnfə'meiʃn] confirmation *f*; affermissement *m*; **con·firm·a·tive** □ [kən'fə:mətiv], **con'firm·a·to·ry** [‿təri] confirmatif (-ive *f*); confirmatoire; **con'firmed** invétéré; endurci; incorrigible; (*surt.* 🐾) chronique.

con·fis·cate ['kɔnfiskeit] confisquer; F voler; **con·fis'ca·tion** confiscation *f*; F *fig.* vol *m*; **con'fis·ca·to·ry** [‿kətəri] de confiscation.

con·fla·gra·tion [kɔnflə'greiʃn] conflagration *f*; incendie *m*.

con·flict 1. ['kɔnflikt] conflit *m*, lutte *f*; *intérêts*: antagonisme *m*; **2.** [kən'flikt] (*with*) être en conflit *ou* désaccord *ou* contradiction (avec); se heurter (à).

con·flu·ence ['kɔnfluəns], **con·flux** ['‿flʌks] *voies, rivières, etc.*: confluent *m*; concours *m* (*d'hommes etc.*); **con·flu·ent** ['‿fluənt] **1.** qui confluent; qui se confondent; **2.** *fleuve*: affluent *m*.

con·form [kən'fɔ:m] *v/t.* conformer; *v/i.*: ～ *to* se conformer à; obéir à; s'adapter à; ～ *with* se soumettre à; **con'form·a·ble** □ (*to*) conforme (à); docile, soumis (à); **con·for·ma·tion** [kɔnfɔ:'meiʃn] conformation *f*, structure *f*; **con'form·ist** [kən'fɔ:mist] conformiste *m*; adhérent *m* de l'Église anglicane; **con'form·i·ty** conformité *f* (à *with*, *to*); *in* ～ *with* conformément à.

con·found [kən'faund] confondre (*q., un plan*); déconcerter; bouleverser; F ～ *it!* zut!; **con'found·ed** □ F maudit, sacré.

con·fra·ter·ni·ty [kɔnfrə'tə:niti] confrérie *f*; confraternité *f*.

con·front [kən'frʌnt] être en face de; faire face à; confronter (avec, *with*); *find o.s.* ～*ed with* se trouver en présence de; **con·fron·ta·tion** [kɔnfrʌn'teiʃn] confrontation *f*.

con·fuse [kən'fju:z] confondre (*a. fig.*); mêler, brouiller; embrouiller; troubler; **con'fus·ed** □ embrouillé; bouleversé; confus; interdit; **con'fu·sion** confusion *f*; désordre *m*; *poét.* déconfiture *f*.

con·fut·a·ble [kən'fju:təbl] réfutable; **con·fu·ta·tion** [kɔnfju:'teiʃn] réfutation *f*; **con·fute** [kən'fju:t] réfuter; convaincre (*q.*) d'erreur.

con·gé ['kɔ̃:nʒei] congé *m*.

con·geal [kən'dʒi:l] (se) congeler; (se) cailler; (se) figer; geler; **con'geal·a·ble** congelable.

con·ge·la·tion [kɔndʒi'leiʃn] congélation *f*.

con·ge·ner ['kɔndʒinə] congénère (*a. su./mf*) (de, *to*).

con·gen·ial □ [kən'dʒi:njəl] sympathique (*esprit*); agréable; convenable (à, *to*); ～ *with* du même caractère que; **con·ge·ni·al·i·ty** [‿ni'æliti] communauté *f* de goûts; accord *m* d'humeur *etc.*

con·gen·i·tal [kən'dʒenitl] congénital (-aux *m/pl.*), de naissance; **con'gen·i·tal·ly** de naissance.

con·ge·ri·es [kɔn'dʒiəri:z] *sg. et pl.* amas *m*, accumulation *f*.

con·gest [kən'dʒest] 🐾 (se) congestionner; *v/t.* encombrer; **con'ges·tion** encombrement *m*; 🐾 congestion *f*; ～ *of population* surpeuplement *m*; ～ *of traffic* encombrement *m* de circulation.

con·glo·bate ['kɔŋglobeit] **1.** (se) conglober; **2.** conglobé.

con·glom·er·ate [kən'glɔmərit] **1.** congloméré; **2.** conglomérat *m*; aggloméré *m*; **3.** [‿reit] (se) conglomérer; **con·glom·er'a·tion** conglomération *f*; *roches*: agrégation *f*.

con·grat·u·late [kən'grætjuleit] féliciter (*q.* de qch., *s.o.* [*up*]*on s.th.*); **con·grat·u·la·tion** félicitation *f*; **con'grat·u·la·tor** congratulateur (-trice *f*) *m*; **con'grat·u·la·to·ry** [‿lətəri] de félicitation(s).

con·gre·gate ['kɔŋgrigeit] (se) rassembler; **con·gre'ga·tion** *eccl.* assistance *f*, paroissiens *m/pl.*; **con-**

gre·ga·tion·al en assemblée; *eccl.* congrégationaliste.

con·gress ['kɔŋgres] réunion *f*; congrès *m*; ♀ Congrès *m* (*assemblée des représentants aux É.-U.*); **con·gres·sion·al** [‿'greʃənl] du congrès; congressionnel(le *f*); **'Con·gress·man**, **'Con·gress·wo·man** *Am.* membre *m* du Congrès.

con·gru·ence, con·gru·en·cy ['kɔŋgruəns(i)] *see* congruity; Å con·gruence *f*; **'con·gru·ent** *see* congruous; Å congruent; **con'gru·i·ty** conformité *f*, convenance *f*; **'con·gru·ous** □ conforme (à *to, usu.* with).

con·ic ['kɔnik] conique; Å ~ section section *f* conique; **'con·i·cal** □ *see* conic.

co·ni·fer ['kounifə] conifère *m*; **co'nif·er·ous** conifère.

con·jec·tur·al □ [kən'dʒektʃərəl] conjectural (-aux *m/pl.*); **con'jec·ture 1.** hypothèse *f*, supposition *f*; conjecture *f*; **2.** conjecturer; supposer.

con·join [kən'dʒɔin] *v/t.* conjoindre; *v/i.* s'unir; **con'joint** conjoint, associé; **con'joint·ly** conjointement, ensemble.

con·ju·gal □ ['kɔndʒugl] conjugal (-aux *m/pl.*); **con·ju·gate 1.** ['‿geit] *v/t.* conjuguer; *v/i. biol.* se conjuguer; **2.** ['‿git] ♀ conjugué; **con·ju·ga·tion** [‿'geiʃn] conjugaison *f*.

con·junct □ [kən'dʒʌŋkt] conjoint, associé; **con'junc·tion** conjonction *f* (*a. astr., a. gramm.*); **con·junc·ti·va** *anat.* [kɔndʒʌŋk'taivə] conjonctive *f*; **con·junc·tive** [kən'dʒʌŋk·tiv] conjonctif (-ive *f*); ~ *mood gramm.* (mode *m*) conjonctif *m*; **con'junc·tive·ly** conjointement, ensemble; **con·junc·ti·vi·tis** [‿'vaitis] conjonctivite *f*; **con'junc·ture** [‿tʃə] conjoncture *f*, circonstance *f*, occasion *f*, rencontre *f*.

con·ju·ra·tion [kɔndʒuə'reiʃn] conjuration *f*; **con·jure** [kən'dʒuə] *v/t.* conjurer (q. de *inf.*, s.o. to *inf.*); ['kʌndʒə] *v/t.* conjurer (*un démon*); ~ *up* évoquer (*a. fig.*); *v/i.* faire des tours de passe-passe; **'con·jur·er**, **'con·jur·or** ♱ conjurateur *m*; prestidigitateur *m*, illusionniste *mf*; **con·jur·ing trick** tour *m* de passe-passe.

conk F [kɔŋk] avoir des ratés; flancher (*moteur*); ~ *out* (se) caler.

con·ker F *Brit.* ['kɔŋkə] marron *m*.

con man F ['kɔnmæn] escroc *m*.

con·nate ['kɔneit] ♯ inné; ♀, *a. anat.* conné, coadné; **con·nat·u·ral** [kə'nætʃrl] de la même nature (que, to).

con·nect [kə'nekt] (se) (re)lier, (se) joindre; *v/t.* ⚡ (inter)connecter; brancher (*une lampe*); **con'nect·ed** □ connexe; apparenté (*personne*); suivi (*discours*); be ~ with être allié à *ou* avec; se rattacher à; avoir des rapports avec; be well ~ être de bonne famille; **con'nect·ing** mode de connexion (*fil*), de communication; qui relie; ~ *rod* bielle *f* (motrice); **con'nec·tion** *see* connexion; **con'nec·tive** □ connectif (-ive *f*); *anat.* ~ *tissue* tissu *m* cellulaire connectif.

con·nex·ion [kə'nekʃn] rapport *m*, liaison *f*; *idées:* suite *f*; ⚡ connexion *f*; ⚡ contact *m*; prise *f* de courant; ⊕ raccord *m*; ☎ correspondance *f*; *eccl.* secte *f*; *famille:* parenté *f*, parent(e *f*) *m*; allié(e *f*) *m*; *personne:* relations *f/pl.*; ♱ clientèle *f*; relation *f* (entre, between); ~s *pl.* belles relations *f/pl.*; amis *m/pl.* influents.

conn·ing-tow·er ⚓ ['kɔniŋtauə] sous-marin: capot *m*; *cuirassé:* tourelle *f* de commandement.

con·niv·ance [kə'naivəns] complicité *f* (dans *at, in*); connivence *f* (avec, with); **con'nive:** ~ *at* fermer les yeux sur; être fauteur de (*un crime*).

con·nois·seur [kɔni'sə:] connaisseur (-euse *f*) *m* (en of, in).

con·no·ta·tion [kɔnou'teiʃn] signification *f*; *phls.* compréhension *f*; **'con·not·a·tive** □ compréhensif (-ive *f*); **con'note** *phls.* comporter; F signifier.

con·nu·bi·al □ [kə'nju:bjəl] conjugal (-aux *m/pl.*).

con·quer ['kɔŋkə] vaincre; *v/t.* conquérir; *fig.* subjuguer; **'con·quer·a·ble** qui peut être vaincu *ou* conquis; **'con·quer·or** conquérant(e *f*) *m*; vainqueur *m*; *cartes:* la belle *f*.

con·quest ['kɔŋkwest] conquête *f*.

con·san·guin·e·ous [kɔnsæŋ'gwiniəs] consanguin; F parent; **con·san·guin·i·ty** consanguinité *f*; parenté *f* (du côté du père).

con·science ['kɔnʃns] conscience *f*;

F in all ~ certes, en vérité; have the ~ to (inf.) avoir l'audace de (inf.); ~ money restitution f anonyme au fisc; '**con·science·less** sans conscience.

con·sci·en·tious □ [kɔnʃi'enʃəs] consciencieux (-euse f); de conscience; ~ objector objecteur m de conscience; **con·sci'en·tious·ness** conscience f; droiture f.

con·scious □ ['kɔnʃəs] conscient; be ~ of avoir conscience de; be ~ that sentir que; '**con·scious·ness** conscience f; ⚕ connaissance f.

con·script 1. ✗ [kɔn'skript] (ou **con·scribe** [~'skraib]) enrôler par la conscription; **2.** ['kɔnskript] conscrit (a. ✗ su./m); **con·scrip·tion** ✗ [kɔn'skripʃn] conscription f; industrial ~ conscription f industrielle.

con·se·crate ['kɔnsikreit] consacrer (a. fig.); bénir; sacrer (un évêque, un roi); **con·se'cra·tion** consécration f; fig. dévouement m; roi: sacre m; '**con·se·cra·tor** consacrant m.

con·sec·u·tive [kɔn'sekjutiv] consécutif (-ive f) (a. ♪, a. gramm.); de suite; qui se suivent; **con'sec·u·tive·ly** de suite; consécutivement.

con·sen·sus [kɔn'sensəs] consensus m; unanimité f.

con·sent [kɔn'sent] **1.** consentement m, assentiment m (à, to); accord m; with one ~ d'un commun accord; **2.** consentir (à, to); accepter (qch. to, in s.th.); **con·sen·ta·ne·ous** □ [kɔnsen'teiniəs] (to) d'accord (avec); en harmonie (avec); **con·sen·tient** [kɔn'senʃnt] unanime (sur, in); consentant (à, to).

con·se·quence ['kɔnsikwəns] (to) conséquence f; suites f/pl.; importance f (pour q., à qch.); in ~ of par suite de; en conséquence de; '**con·se·quent 1.** résultant; logique; be ~ on résulter de; **2.** Ⱥ conséquent m; phls. conclusion f; **con·se·quen·tial** □ [~'kwenʃl] conséquent (à to, [up]on); consécutif (-ive f) (à, to); personne: suffisant; **con·se·quent·ly** ['~kwəntli] par conséquent; donc.

con·ser·va·tion [kɔnsə'veiʃn] conservation f; **con·ser'va·tion·ist** partisan(e f) m de la défense de l'environnement; **con·serv·a·tism** [kɔn'sə:vətizm] conservatisme m;

con'serv·a·tive □ **1.** conservateur (-trice f) (a. pol.) (de, of); préservateur (-trice f) (de, from); prudent (évaluation); **2.** conservateur (-trice f) m; **con'ser·va·toire** [~twa:] ♪ conservatoire m; **con'ser·va·tor** conservateur (-trice f) m; **con·serv·a·to·ry** [~tri] serre f; conservatoire m; **con'serve** conserver; préserver.

con·sid·er [kɔn'sidə] v/t. considérer (une question); envisager (une possibilité); étudier, examiner (une proposition); estimer, regarder (= penser); prendre en considération; avoir égard à; v/i. réfléchir; **con'sid·er·a·ble** □ considérable, important; **con'sid·er·ate** [~rit] □ plein d'égards (pour, envers to[wards]); **con·sid·er·a·tion** [~'reiʃn] considération f; égard m, -s m/pl.; compensation f, rémunération f; pourboire m; fig. importance f; ✝ prix m; cause f (d'un billet); be under ~ être en délibération ou à l'examen; take into ~ prendre en considération; tenir compte de; money is no ~ l'argent n'est rien; l'argent n'entre pas en ligne de compte; on no ~ sous aucun prétexte; **con'sid·er·ing** □ **1.** prp. en égard à, étant donné ...; **2.** F adv. somme toute, malgré tout.

con·sign [kɔn'sain] remettre, livrer; reléguer; déposer (de l'argent); **con·sig·na·tion** [kɔnsai'neiʃn], **con·sign·ment** [kɔn'sainmənt] ✝ expédition f; envoi m; consignation f; **con·sign·ee** [kɔnsai'ni:] destinataire m; **con·sign·er, con·sign·or** [kɔn'sainə] consignateur m, expéditeur m.

con·sist [kɔn'sist] consister (en, dans of; à inf., in gén.); se composer (de, of); '**con'sist·ence, con'sist·en·cy** sirop, esprit: consistance f; sol: compacité f; conduite: uniformité f; logique f; **con'sist·ent** □ conséquent; logique; compatible (avec, with); ~ly a. uniformément; **con'sis·to·ry** [~təri] eccl. consistoire m.

con·sol·a·ble [kɔn'souləbl] consolable; **con·so·la·tion** [kɔnsə'leiʃn] consolation f; sp. ~ goal but m qui sauve l'honneur; **con·sol·a·to·ry** [kɔn'sɔlətəri] consolateur (-trice f); consolant; de consolation; **con·sole 1.** ['kɔnsoul] console f (a.

consult

⚠); ~·*table* (table *f*) console *f*; **2.**
[kən'soul] consoler; **con'sol·er** consolateur (-trice *f*) *m*.
con·sol·i·date [kən'sɔlideit] (se)
consolider (*a. fig.*); (se) tasser
(*chaussée*); *v/t.* affermir; solidifier;
unir (*des entreprises, des propriétés,
etc.*); **con·sol·i'da·tion** consoli-
dation *f*; affermissement *m*; tassement *m*; unification *f*.
con·sols [kən'sɔlz] *pl.* fonds *m/pl.*
consolidés; *3 per cent* ~ consolidés
m/pl. trois pour cent.
con·so·nance ['kɔnsənəns] consonance *f*; accord *m* (*a.* ♪); **'con·so-
nant 1.** □ ♪ harmonieux (-euse *f*);
consonant; conforme (à with, to);
2. consonne *f*; ~ *shift* mutation *f*
consonantique.
con·sort 1. ['kɔnsɔːt] époux *m*,
épouse *f*; *reine*: consort *m*; ⚓
conserve *f*; **2.** [kən'sɔːt] (*with*)
fréquenter (*q.*); frayer (avec).
con·spic·u·ous □ [kən'spikjuəs] apparent, bien visible, manifeste; *fig.*
frappant; insigne; *be* ~ *by one's
absence* briller par son absence.
con·spir·a·cy [kən'spirəsi] conspiration *f*; **con'spir·a·tor** [~tə] conspirateur (-trice *f*) *m*; **con'spir·a-
tress** [~tris] conspiratrice *f*; **conspire** [~'spaiə] conspirer (contre,
against); comploter (de, *to*); *fig.*
concourir (à, *to*).
con·sta·ble ['kʌnstəbl] gardien *m* de
la paix; *château*: gouverneur *m*;
hist. connétable *m*; *chief* ~ commissaire *m* de police; **con'stab·u·lar·y**
[kən'stæbjuləri] police *f*; *county* ~
gendarmerie *f*.
con·stan·cy ['kɔnstənsi] constance *f*,
fermeté *f*; fidélité *f*; régularité *f*;
'con·stant 1. □ constant; ferme;
fidèle; invariable; continuel(le *f*);
assidu; **2.** Å constante *f*.
con·stel·la·tion *astr.* [kɔnstə'leiʃn]
constellation *f* (*a. fig.*).
con·ster·na·tion [kɔnstə'neiʃn] consternation *f*; atterrement *m*.
con·sti·pate ♣ ['kɔnstipeit] constiper; **con·sti'pa·tion** ♣ constipation *f*.
con·stit·u·en·cy [kən'stitjuənsi] circonscription *f* électorale; électeurs
m/pl.; **con'stit·u·ent 1.** constituant,
constitutif (-ive *f*); composant; ~
body see constituency; **2.** élément *m*
(constitutif); ⚖ constituant *m*; *pol.*

électeur (-trice *f*) *m*; ~*s pl.* com-
mettants *m/pl.*, électeurs *m/pl.*
con·sti·tute ['kɔnstitjuːt] constituer;
faire (*le bonheur de q.*); constituer,
nommer (q. arbitre, *s.o. judge*);
con·sti'tu·tion constitution *f* (*de
qch., a. = santé, a. pol.*); *chose*: composition *f*; ♀*s pl. hist.* arrêts *m/pl.*;
con·sti'tu·tion·al 1. □ con-
stitutionnel(le *f*) (*a.* ♣); *fig.*
hygiénique; naturel(le *f*); ~ *law*
droit *m* constitutionnel; **2.** F promenade *f* hygiénique *ou* quotidienne; **con·sti'tu·tion·al·ist** historien
m des constitutions politiques; *pol.*
constitutionnel *m*; **con·sti·tu·tive**
□ [kən'stitjutiv] constitutif (-ive *f*).
con·strain [kən'strein] contraindre
(à, de *inf. to inf.*); retenir de force;
con'straint contrainte *f* (*a.* ⚖);
retenue *f*.
con·strict [kən'strikt] (res)serrer;
rétrécir; gêner; **con'stric·tion** resserrement *m*; ♣ *artères*: strangulation *f*; **con'stric·tor** *anat.* constricteur *m*; *zo.* (*a. boa* ~) boa *m* constricteur.
con·strin·gent [kən'strindʒnt] constringent; ♣ astringent.
con·struct [kən'strʌkt] construire;
bâtir; établir (*un chemin de fer*); *fig.*
confectionner; **con'struc·tion** construction *f*; *machine*: établissement
m; édifice *m*, bâtiment *m*; *fig.* interprétation *f*; ~ *site* chantier *m*; *under* ~
en construction; **con'struc·tive** □
constructif (-ive *f*); *esprit*: créateur;
de construction; ⚖ implicite; *par
interprétation*; **con'struc·tor** constructeur *m*; *constructions navales*:
ingénieur *m*.
con·strue [kən'struː] *gramm.* analyser; décomposer (*une phrase*); faire
le mot à mot de (*un texte*); interprè-
ter (*une conduite, des paroles, etc.*).
con·sue·tu·di·nar·y [kɔnswi'tjuːdi-
nəri] coutumier (-ère *f*).
con·sul ['kɔnsl] consul *m*; ~ *general*
consul *m* général; **con·su·lar** ['kɔn-
sjulə] consulaire; de *ou* du consul;
con·su·late ['~lit] consulat *m* (*a.
bâtiment*); ~ *general* consulat *m*
général; **con·sul·ship** ['kɔnslʃip]
consulat *m*.
con·sult [kən'sʌlt] *v/t.* consulter
(*a. fig.*); avoir égard à (*la sensibilité*);
~*ing engineer* ingénieur-conseil (*pl.*
ingénieurs-conseils) *m*; *v/i.* con-

sulter (avec q., s.o.); (a. ~ together) délibérer; **con'sult·ant** médecin m etc. consultant; ⊕ expert-conseil (pl. experts-conseils) m; **con·sul·ta·tion** [kɔnsəl'teiʃn] ⚕, ⚖, livre: consultation f; délibération f; **con'sult·a·tive** [kən'sʌltətiv] consultatif (-ive f); **con'sult·ing** consultant; ~-hours heures f/pl. de consultation; ~ physician médecin m consultant; ~ room cabinet m de consultation.

con·sum·a·ble [kən'sju:məbl] consumable (feu); consommable; **con'sume** v/t. consumer (a. feu), dévorer; consommer (des vivres); fig. absorber, brûler; dévorer; v/i. se consumer; **con'sum·er** consommateur (-trice f) m; abonné(e f) m (au gaz etc.); ~ association association f des consommateurs; ~ demand demande f; ~ durables pl. biens m/pl. de consommation durables; ~(s') goods pl. biens m/pl. de consommation; ~ resistance résistance f du consommateur; ~ society société f de consommation.

con·sum·mate 1. □ [kən'sʌmit] achevé; **2.** ['kɔnsʌmeit] consommer (un sacrifice, le mariage); **con·sum·ma·tion** [ˌ~'meiʃn] mariage, crime: consommation f; achèvement m; fin f; fig. but m, comble m.

con·sump·tion [kən'sʌmpʃn] vivres, charbon: consommation f; charbon, chaleur: dépense f; ⚕ phtisie f; tuberculose f; **con'sump·tive** □ poitrinaire (a. su./mf); tuberculeux (-euse f); phtisique (a. su./mf).

con·tact 1. ['kɔntækt] contact m (a. ⚡); ⚡ ~ breaker interrupteur m; opt. ~ lenses pl. lentilles f/pl. cornéennes, verres m/pl. de contact; phot. ~ print négatif m contact; ⚡ make (break) ~ établir (rompre) le contact; **2.** [kən'tækt] contacter (q.).

con·ta·gion ⚕ [kən'teidʒn] contagion f; maladie f contagieuse; **con'ta·gious** □ contagieux (-euse f).

con·tain [kən'tein] contenir; renfermer; ✗ maintenir, contenir (l'ennemi); fig. retenir, maîtriser; ~ o.s. se contenir; **con'tain·er** récipient m, boîte f; ⊕ conteneur m; **con'tain·er·ize** conteneuriser; **con'tain·ment** conduite: retenue f; ✗ échec m.

con·tam·i·nate [kən'tæmineit] contaminer; fig. corrompre; vicier;

con·tam·i·na·tion textes, a. ling.: contamination f; souillure f.

con·tan·go ✝ [kən'tæŋgou] intérêt m de report.

con·tem·plate ['kɔntempleit] v/t. contempler, considérer; v/i. méditer; **con·tem·pla·tion** contemplation f; méditation f; have in ~ projeter; in ~ of au ou en contemplation de; **con·tem·pla·tive** □ [kən'templətiv] contemplatif (-ive f); recueilli; songeur (-euse f).

con·tem·po·ra·ne·ous □ [kɔntempə'reinjəs] contemporain; ⚖ ~ performance exécution f simultanée; **con'tem·po·rar·y 1.** contemporain (de, with); **2.** contemporain(e f) m; confrère m.

con·tempt [kən'tempt] mépris m, dédain m; ~ of court contumace f, outrage m à la Cour; hold in ~ mépriser; in ~ of au ou en mépris de; **con'tempt·i·ble** □ méprisable; bas(se f); indigne; **con'temp·tu·ous** □ [ˌ~juəs] dédaigneux (-euse f) (de, of); méprisant, de mépris.

con·tend [kən'tend] v/i. lutter; contester (qch., for s.th.; à q., with s.o.); v/t. soutenir (que, that).

con·tent¹ ['kɔntent] vase etc: contenance f; min. teneur f; ~s pl. contenu m.

con·tent² [kən'tent] **1.** satisfait (de, with); parl. pour; oui; not ~ contre; non; **2.** contenter, satisfaire; ~ o.s. se contenter (de, with); se borner à; **3.** contentement m; to one's heart's ~ à souhait; **con'tent·ed** □ content, satisfait (de, with); be ~ to (inf.) se contenter de (inf.).

con·ten·tion [kən'tenʃn] dispute f, débat m; affirmation f, prétention f; **con'ten·tious** □ contentieux (-euse f); disputeur (-euse f) (personne).

con·tent·ment [kən'tentmənt] contentement m (de son sort).

con·ter·mi·nous [kɔn'tə:minəs] limitrophe (de, with); de même étendue ou durée (que, with).

con·test 1. ['kɔntest] lutte f; concours m; sp. match (pl. matches, matches) m; **2.** [kən'test] (se) disputer; contester, débattre; pol. ~ a seat se poser candidat pour un siège; **con'test·a·ble** contestable; débattable; **con'test·ant** contestant(e f) m; concurrent(e f) m; **con'test·ed** disputé.

con·text ['kɔntekst] texte: contexte

m; **con·tex·tu·al** □ [kɔn'tekstjuəl] d'après le contexte; **con'tex·ture** [ˌtʃə] *os, tissu*: texture *f*; *poème, discours*: facture *f*.

con·ti·gu·i·ty [kɔnti'gjuiti] contiguïté *f*; **con·tig·u·ous** □ [kɔn'tigjuəs] contigu(ë *f*), attenant (à, to).

con·ti·nence ['kɔntinəns] continence *f*, chasteté *f*; **'con·ti·nent 1.** □ continent, chaste; **2.** continent *m*; the ♀ l'Europe *f* (continentale); **con·ti·nen·tal** □ [ˌ'nentl] continental (-aux *m/pl.*); F de l'Europe; ~ quilt duvet *m*; **con·ti'nen·tal·ize** continentaliser.

con·tin·gen·cy [kɔn'tindʒənsi] éventualité *f*; cas *m* imprévu; **con'tin·gen·cies** *pl.* imprévu *m*; ✝ faux frais *m/pl.*; **con'tin·gent 1.** □ éventuel(le *f*); accidentel(le *f*); aléatoire; conditionnel(le *f*); be ~ on dépendre de; **2.** ✗ contingent *m*.

con·tin·u·al □ [kɔn'tinjuəl] continuel(le *f*), incessant; **con'tin·u·ance** continuation *f*; durée *f*; **con·tin·u'a·tion** continuation *f*; suite *f*; prolongement *m*; ✝ report *m*; *sl.* ~s *pl.* pantalon *m*; guêtres *f/pl.*; ~ school école *f* du soir, cours *m* complémentaire; **con'tin·ue** *v/t.* continuer; prolonger; reprendre; maintenir; ~ *reading* continuer à *ou* de lire; *to be* ~*d* à suivre; *v/i.* (se) continuer; se prolonger; persévérer; se poursuivre; ~ (*in*) *a business* continuer dans une affaire; **con·ti·nu·i·ty** [kɔnti'njuiti] continuité *f*; ~-*girl* script-girl *f*; **con·tin·u·ous** □ [kɔn'tinjuəs] continu; suivi; ⚡ ~ *current* courant *m* continu.

con·tort [kɔn'tɔːt] tordre; contourner; **con'tor·tion** contorsion *f*; **con'tor·tion·ist** contorsionniste *m*.

con·tour ['kɔntuə] contour *m*, profil *m*; *plan*: tracé *m*; ~ *line* courbe *f* de niveau.

con·tra ['kɔntrə] contre; ✝ *per* ~ par contre.

con·tra·band ['kɔntrəbænd] **1.** de contrebande; **2.** contrebande *f*.

con·tract 1. [kɔn'trækt] *v/t.* contracter (*habitudes, maladie, dettes, mariage, muscles*); prendre (*des habitudes, un goût*); *v/i.* se resserrer, se contracter (*a. ling.*); traiter (pour, *for*); entreprendre (de, *to*); ~ *for* entreprendre (*qch.*); ~*ing party* con-

tractant(e *f*) *m*; **2.** ['kɔntrækt] pacte *m*, contrat *m*; entreprise *f*; by ~ par contrat; *under* ~ engagé par contrat; ~ *work* travail *m* à forfait; **con·tract·ed** □ [kɔn'træktid] contracté; *fig.* rétréci; **con·tract·i·'bil·i·ty** contractilité *f*; **con'tract·i·ble** contractile; **con'trac·tile** ⚕ [ˌtail] contractile; de contraction; **con'trac·tion** contraction *f* (*a. gramm.*), rétrécissement *m*; *crédit*: amoindrissement *m*; *habitudes*: prise *f*; **con'trac·tor** *bâtiments*: entrepreneur *m*; *armée, gouvernement*: fournisseur *m*; *anat.* (muscle *m*) fléchisseur *m*; **con'trac·tu·al** [ˌtjuəl] contractuel(le *f*).

con·tra·dict [kɔntrə'dikt] contredire (*q., qch.*); **con·tra'dic·tion** contradiction *f*; **con·tra·dic·tious** contredisant; ergoteur (-euse *f*); **con·tra'dic·to·ri·ness** nature *f* contradictoire; esprit *m* de contradiction; **con·tra'dic·to·ry** □ contradictoire; opposé (à, *to*).

con·tral·to ♩ [kɔn'træltəu] **1.** contralto *m*; **2.** (de) contralto.

con·tra·dis·tinc·tion [kɔntrədis-'tiŋkʃn] opposition *f*, contraste *m*.

con·trap·tion *sl.* [kɔn'træpʃn] dispositif *m*, machin *m*; invention *f* baroque.

con·tra·ri·e·ty [kɔntrə'raiəti] contrariété *f*; **con·tra·ri·ly** ['ˌrili] contrairement; **'con·tra·ri·ness** esprit *m* contrariant *ou* de contradiction; contrariété *f*; **con·tra·ri·wise** ['ˌwaiz] au contraire; d'autre part; en sens opposé; **'con·tra·ry 1.** contraire, opposé; F [*a.* kɔn'trɛəri] indocile, revêche; ~ *to* contraire à, contre, à l'encontre de; **2.** contraire *m*; *on* (*ou to*) *the* ~ au contraire; *to the* ~ *a.* à l'encontre.

con·trast 1. ['kɔntræst] contraste *m* (avec *to*, *with*); *in* ~ *to* par contraste avec; *by* ~ en opposition; comme contraste; **2.** [kɔn'træst] *v/t.* faire contraster (avec, *with*); opposer; mettre en contraste (avec, *with*); *v/i.* contraster, faire contraste (avec, *with*).

con·tra·vene [kɔntrə'viːn] enfreindre, transgresser; contrevenir à; aller à l'encontre de; **con·tra·ven·tion** [ˌ'venʃn] contravention *f*, infraction *f* (à, *of*); violation *f* (de, *of*).

con·trib·ute [kɔn'tribjuːt] *v/t.* contribuer pour (une somme); payer; écrire (des articles); v/i. contribuer, aider (à, to); collaborer (à un journal); **con·tri·bu·tion** [kɔntri'bju:ʃn] contribution f; cotisation f; ✝ apport m (de capitaux), versement m; journal: article m; ⚔ contribution f, réquisition f; **con'trib·u·tor** [kən-'tribjutə] contribuant(e f) m; collaborateur (-trice f) m (d'un journal, to a newspaper); **con'trib·u·to·ry** contribuant.

con·trite □ ['kɔntrait] contrit, pénitent; **con·tri·tion** [kən'triʃn] contrition f, pénitence f.

con·triv·ance [kən'traivəns] invention f; combinaison f; artifice m; appareil m, dispositif m; F truc m; **con'trive** v/t. inventer, imaginer, combiner; pratiquer; v/i. se débrouiller; se tirer d'affaire; s'arranger; trouver moyen (de inf., to inf.); **con'triv·er** inventeur (-trice f) m; péj. machinateur (-trice f) m.

con·trol [kən'troul] **1.** autorité f; maîtrise f, contrainte f; empire m; contrôle m; train, navire: manœuvre f; mot. (a. ~ lever) manette f de commande; surveillance f; ⊕ commande f; contrôleur (-euse f) m (d'un médium); exchange ~ contrôle m des changes; attr. de commande, de contrôle; ⚔ ~ surfaces pl. empennage m; remote (ou distant) ~ commande f à distance; ✈ ~ board commutateur m; ⚔ ~ column levier m de commande; ⊕ ~ desk pupitre m de commande; ~ knob bouton m de réglage; ⚔ ~ panel tableau m de bord; ⚔ ~ tower tour f de contrôle; be in ~ commander (qch., of s.th.); avoir de l'autorité (sur, of); put s.o. in ~ charger q. du contrôle ou de la direction (de, of); **2.** diriger; régler; tenir (ses élèves); maîtriser; gouverner (a. fig.); dompter (ses passions); réglementer (la circulation); retenir (ses larmes); ⊕ commander (a. ⚔); ✝ ~ling interest participation majoritaire; **con'trol·la·ble** contrôlable; maniable, manœuvrable; maîtrisable; **con'trol·ler** contrôleur (-euse f) m; appareil, a. ✈ contrôleur m; affaire: gérant m.

con·tro·ver·sial □ [kɔntrə'və:ʃl] controversable; polémique; personne: disputailleur (-euse f) m; **con·tro·ver·sy** ['kɔntrə,və:si] controverse f;

polémique f; **con·tro·vert** ['kɔntrə,və:t] controverser (une question); disputer (qch.); **con·tro'vert·i·ble** □ controversable.

con·tu·ma·cious □ [kɔntju:'meiʃəs] rebelle, récalcitrant; ⚖ contumace; **con·tu·ma·cy** ['kɔntjuməsi] obstination f, entêtement m; ⚖ contumace f.

con·tu·me·li·ous [kɔntju:'mi:liəs] insolent, dédaigneux (-euse f); **con·tu·me·ly** ['kɔntjumli] insolence f; mépris m; honte f.

con·tuse ⚕ [kən'tju:z] contusionner; **con'tu·sion** contusion f.

co·nun·drum [kə'nʌndrəm] devinette f; fig. énigme f.

con·va·lesce [kɔnvə'les] être en convalescence; **con·va·les·cence** convalescence f; **con·va·les·cent** □ convalescent(e f) (a. su./mf).

con·vec·tion [kən'vekʃn] phys. convection f.

con·vene [kən'vi:n] (s')assembler, (se) réunir; v/t. convoquer (une assemblée); ⚖ citer (devant, before).

con·ven·ience [kən'vi:njəns] commodité f, convenance f; plaisir m; (a. public ~) cabinets m/pl. d'aisance, commodités f/pl.; at your earliest ~ au premier moment favorable; make a ~ of s.o. abuser de la bonté de q.; marriage of ~ mariage m de convenance; **con'ven·ient** □ commode; à proximité (de to, for).

con·vent ['kɔnvənt] couvent m (surt. de femmes); **con·ven·ti·cle** [kən'ventikl] conciliabule m; conventicule m (surt. de dissidents); **con'ven·tion** convention f; accord m; usu. ~s pl. bienséances f/pl.; **con·ven·tion·al** conventionnel(le f); de convention; courant (a. ⚔ armes); **con·ven·tion·al·ism** respect m des convenances; art: formalisme m; **con·ven·tion·al·i·ty** [ˌnæliti] convention f; conventions f/pl. sociales; **con·ven·tu·al** [ˌtjuəl] □ conventuel(le f) (a. su./mf).

con·verge [kən'və:dʒ] v/i. converger (sur, on); v/t. faire converger; **con'ver·gence, con'ver·gen·cy** convergence f; **con'ver·gent, con'verg·ing** convergent.

con·vers·able [kən'və:səbl] sociable; de commerce agréable; **con'ver·sant** familier (-ère f) (avec q., *with s.o.*); versé (dans *with, in*); compétent (en *with, in*); **con·ver·sa·tion** [ˌvəˈseiʃn] conversation *f*, entretien *m*; **con·ver'sa·tion·al** de (la) conversation; **con·verse** [ˈkɔnvəːs] **1.** contraire; **2.** conversation *f*; relations *f/pl.*, commerce *m*; Ⱥ proposition *f* réciproque; *phls.* proposition *f* converse; **3.** [kənˈvəːs] causer; s'entretenir (avec, *with*); **con'ver·sion** ⊕, *phls., eccl., pol.*, ⸙ *rentes*: conversion *f* (à, *to*; en *into*); transformation *f* (*a.* ♪); ⸓ détournement *m* (*de fonds*); ⸙ accommodation *f* (*d'une usine aux usages de qch.*).

con·vert 1. [ˈkɔnvəːt] converti(e *f*) *m*; **2.** [kənˈvəːt] transformer (*a.* ♪); changer; convertir (*a.* ⊕, *eccl., pol., phls.*); *sp.* transformer (*un essai*); ⸙ affecter (*des fonds*); ⸓ détourner (*des fonds*); ⸙ accommoder (*une usine etc.*); **con'vert·er** convertisseur (*a. personne f*) *m*; ⊕, *a.* ⚡ convertisseur *m*; *radio:* adaptateur *m*; **con·vert·i·bil·i·ty** [ˌvəˈbiliti] convertibilité *f*; **con'vert·i·ble** □ convertissable (*personne*); convertible (en, *into*) (*chose*); interchangeable (*termes*), réciproque; *mot.* décapotable, transformable.

con·vex □ [ˈkɔnˈveks] convexe; **con'vex·i·ty** convexité *f*.

con·vey [kənˈvei] (trans)porter; conduire; (a)mener (*q.*); communiquer (*une pensée, une nouvelle, etc.*); transmettre (*phys., a. odeur, son, ordre, remerciements, etc.*); ⸓ faire cession de; dresser l'acte translatif de propriété de; **con'vey·ance** transport *m*; moyen(s) *m(pl.)* de transport; transmission *f* (*a.* ⸓, *a. phys.*); communication *f*; voiture *f*; véhicule *m*; ⸓ transfert *m*, cession *f*; ⸓ acte *m* translatif de propriété; ♫ transmission *f*; transport *m* (*d'énergie*); *public* ~ voiture *f* publique; **con'vey·anc·er** notaire *m* (*qui dresse des actes translatifs de propriété*); **con'vey·or** ⊕ (*a.* ~ *belt*) bande *f* transporteuse.

con·vict 1. [ˈkɔnvikt] forçat *m*; **2.** [kənˈvikt] convaincre (de, *of*); **con'vic·tion** conviction *f*; ⸓ condamnation *f*; *previous* ~s dossier *m* du prévenu.

con·vince [kənˈvins] persuader,

convaincre (q. de qch., *s.o. of s.th.*).

con·viv·i·al [kənˈviviəl] joyeux(-euse *f*), jovial (-als *ou* -aux *m/pl.*), bon vivant; **con·viv·i·al·i·ty** [ˌviˈæliti] franche gaieté *f*; sociabilité *f*.

con·vo·ca·tion [kɔnvəˈkeiʃn] convocation *f*; *eccl.* assemblée *f*.

con·voke [kənˈvouk] convoquer.

con·vo·lu·tion [kɔnvəˈluːʃn] ⚕ circonvolution *f*; *fig.* repli *m*, sinuosité *f*.   [volubilis *m.*\
con·vol·vu·lus ⚘ [kənˈvɔlvjuləs]⎰

con·voy 1. [ˈkɔnvɔi] convoi *m*; escorte *f*; **2.** [kənˈvɔi] convoyer, escorter.

con·vulse [kənˈvʌls] *fig.* bouleverser; *be* ~*d with laughter* se tordre de rire; **con'vul·sion** *usu.* ~*s pl.* convulsion *f*, -s *f/pl.*; *fig.* bouleversement *m*; *go off in* ~*s of laughter* se tordre de rire; **con'vul·sive** □ convulsif (-ive *f*).

coo [kuː] **1.** roucouler; **2.** roucoulement *m*.

cook [kuk] **1.** cuisinier (-ère *f*) *m*; (*a. head* ~) chef *m*; **2.** *v/t.* (faire) cuire; F cuisiner (*les comptes etc.*); *v/i.* faire la cuisine; '~·book *Am.* livre *m* de cuisine; '**cook·er** cuisinière *f*; pomme *f* *ou* fruit *m* à cuire; F falsificateur (-trice *f*) *m* des comptes; *pressure-*~ marmite *f* express; '**cook·er·y** cuisine *f*; **cook·ie** [ˈ~i] *Am.* galette *f*; '**cook·ing** cuisson *f*; cuisine *f*; *attr.* de cuisine.

cool [kuːl] **1.** □ frais (fraîche *f*); froid, tiède (*sentiments*); *fig.* calme, de sang-froid; *péj.* sans gêne, peu gêné; F *a* ~ *thousand pounds* mille livres bien comptées; **2.** frais *m*; **3.** (se) rafraîchir; '**cool·er** rafraîchisseur *m*; *vin:* glacière *f*; *sl.* prison *f*; '**cool-'head·ed** à l'esprit calme; de sang-froid; imperturbable.

coo·lie [ˈkuːli] coolie *m*.

cool·ing ⊕ [ˈkuːliŋ] refroidissement *m*; *attr.* de réfrigération; '**cool·ness** fraîcheur *f*; *fig. personne:* froideur *f*; sang-froid *m*; flegme *m*; **coolth** F *ou co. Brit.* [kuːlθ] frais *m*.

coomb(e) *géog.* [kuːm] combe *f*.

coon *Am.* F [kuːn] *zo. abr. de rac(c)oon*; nègre *m*; type *m*; *he is a gone* ~ c'en est fait de lui; ~ *song* chanson *f* nègre.

coop [kuːp] **1.** cage *f* à poules;

poussinière *f*; **2.** ~ up (*ou* in) enfermer; tenir enfermé.

co-op F [kou'ɔp] *see* co(-)operative store; co(-)operative society.

coop·er ['ku:pə] tonnelier *m*; dry ~ boisselier *m*; *vins*: embouteilleur *m*; **'coop·er·age** tonnellerie *f*.

co(-)op·er·ate [kou'ɔpəreit]coopérer (avec, with); concourir (à, in); *ready to* ~ prêt à aider; **co(-)op·er·'a·tion** coopération *f*, concours *m* (à, in); **co(-)op·er·a·tive** [~pərətiv] **1.** coopératif (-ive *f*); ~ society société *f* coopérative; ~ store société *f* coopérative de consommation; F coopérative *f*; **2.** see ~ store; **co·'op·er·a·tor** [~reitə] coopérateur (-trice *f*) *m*.

co-opt [kou'ɔpt] coopter; **co-op'ta·tion** cooptation *f*.

co-or·di·nate [kou'ɔːdinit] **1.** □ coordonné; **2.** A coordonnée *f*; **3.** [~neit] coordonner (à, with); **co-or·di'na·tion** coordination *f*.

coot [ku:t] *orn.* foulque *f* noire; F niais(e *f*) *m*; **coot·ie** ['~i] *sl.* pou (*pl.* poux) *m*.

cop *sl.* [kɔp] **1.** pincer (=attraper); ~ it (se faire) attiger; recevoir un savon; **2.** sergot *m*, flic *m*.

co·par·ce·nar·y ['kou'pɑːsinəri] copartage *m*; copropriété *f*; **'co'parce·ner** indivisaire *mf*.

co·part·ner ['kou'pɑːtnə] coassocié(e *f*) *m*; **'co'part·ner·ship** coassociation *f*; coparticipation *f*; actionnariat *m* ouvrier.

cope¹ [koup] **1.** *eccl.* chape *f*; *fig.* voile *m*, manteau *m*; voûte *f* (*céleste*); **2.** recouvrir d'une voûte, chaperonner (*un mur*).

cope² [~] se débrouiller, s'en tirer; ~ with tenir tête à, faire face à; s'occuper de; venir à bout de.

cop·i·er ['kɔpiə] machine *f* à photocopier.

cope·stone ['koupstoun] *usu. fig.* couronnement *m*.

cop·ing A ['koupiŋ] chaperon *m* (*d'un mur*).

co·pi·ous □ ['koupjəs] copieux (-euse *f*), abondant; **'co·pi·ous·ness** profusion *f*, abondance *f*.

cop·per¹ ['kɔpə] **1.** cuivre *m* (rouge); pièce *f* de deux sous; lessiveuse *f*; ~s *pl.* petite monnaie *f*; **2.** de *ou* en cuivre; **3.** cuivrer; doubler (*un navire*).

cop·per² [~] *Brit. sl. see* cop 2.

cop·per·as ['kɔpərəs] couperose *f* verte.

cop·per...: '~**plate** plaque *f* de cuivre; ~ writing écriture *f* moulée; '~**works** *usu. sg.* fonderie *f* de cuivre; **'cop·per·y** cuivreux (-euse *f*).

cop·pice ['kɔpis], **copse** [kɔps] taillis *m*, hallier *m*.

cop·u·late *zo.* ['kɔpjuleit] s'accoupler; **cop·u'la·tion** coït *m*; *zo.* accouplement *m*; **cop·u·la·tive** ['~lətiv] **1.** *anat., physiol.* copulateur (-trice *f*); *gramm.* copulatif (-ive *f*); **2.** copulative *f*.

cop·y ['kɔpi] **1.** copie *f*; reproduction *f*; transcription *f*; *livre*: exemplaire *m*; *journal*: numéro *m*; *écriture*: modèle *m*; *imprimerie*: manuscrit *m*; *journ.* matière *f* à reportage; (*a.* carbon ~) double *m*; fair (*ou* clean) ~ copie *f* au net; *fig.* corrigé *m*; rough (*ou* foul) ~ brouillon *m*; **2.** copier; reproduire; transcrire; ~ fair mettre au net; *phot.* ~ing stand porte-copie *m/inv.*; '~**book** cahier *m* d'écriture; '~**cat** F imitateur *m* (-trice *f*); ~ **ed·i·tor** secrétaire *mf* de rédaction; '~**hold** ‡‡ tenure *f* censitaire; **'cop·y·ing-ink** encre *f* à copier; **'cop·y·ing-press** presse *f* à copier; **'cop·y·ist** copiste *mf*; scribe *m*; **'cop·y·right** propriété *f* littéraire; droit *m* d'auteur; *attr.* protégé par des droits d'auteur; qui n'est pas dans le domaine public (*livre*); **'cop·y·writ·er** rédacteur (-trice *f*) *m* publicitaire.

co·quet [kou'ket] faire la coquette; **co·quet·ry** [~kitri] coquetterie *f*; **co·quette** [~'ket] coquette *f*; **co·'quet·tish** □ provocant; coquet(te *f*) (*chapeau etc.*); flirteur (-euse *f*) (*femme*).

cor·al ['kɔrəl] **1.** corail (*pl.* -aux) *m*; anneau *m* de corail (*pour bébé*); **2.** (*a.* **cor·al·line** ['~lain]) corallien (-ne *f*); corallin (*couleur*).

cor·bel A ['kɔːbl] corbeau *m*, console *f*.

cord [kɔːd] **1.** corde *f*; cordon *m* (*a.* ♪); ficelle *f*; bois *m* de chauffage: corde *f*; *fig.* lien *m*; *anat.* corde *f* (*vocale*); cordon *m* (*médullaire, ombilical*); see corduroy; **2.** corder; attacher *ou* lier avec une corde; **'cord·ed** *tex.* côtelé; **'cord·age** cordages *m/pl.*

cor·dial [ˈkɔːdjəl] **1.** □ cordial (-aux *m/pl.*); chaleureux (-euse *f*); **2.** cordial *m*; **cor·dial·i·ty** [ˌdi-ˈæliti] cordialité *f*.

cord-mak·er [ˈkɔːdmeikə] cordier *m*.

cor·don [ˈkɔːdən] **1.** △, ✗, etc. cordon *m*; **2.** ~ off isoler par un cordon (*de police etc.*).

cor·do·van [ˈkɔːdəvən] (cuir *m*) de Cordoue.

cor·du·roy [ˈkɔːdərɔi] *tex.* velours *m* côtelé; ~s *pl.* pantalon *m ou* culotte *f* de velours à côtes; ~ road *Am.* chemin *m* de rondins.

core [kɔː] **1.** ♀ pomme: trognon *m*; *bois*: cœur *m*; *fig.* cœur *m*; intérieur *m*; *abcès*: bourbillon *m*; ✗ carotte *f*; ⊕ noyau *m*; ~ time temps *m* de présence obligatoire; **2.** enlever le cœur de (*une pomme*); **'cor·er** (*a. apple-*~) vide-pomme *m/inv.*

co·re·li·gion·ist [ˈkouriˈlidʒənist] coreligionnaire *mf*.

Co·rin·thi·an [kəˈrinθiən] **1.** corinthien(ne *f*); **2.** Corinthien(ne *f*) *m*.

cork [kɔːk] **1.** liège *m*; *bouteille*: bouchon *m*; **2.** boucher; *fig.* (*a.* ~ up) étouffer; **'cork·age** bouchage *m*; débouchage *m*; *restaurant*: droit *m* de débouchage; **'corked** qui sent le bouchon (*vin*); **'cork·er** *sl.* dernier cri *m*; type *m* etc. épatant; mensonge *m* un peu fort; **'cork·ing** *Am.* F fameux (-euse *f*); bath.

cork...: ~ jack·et gilet *m* de sauvetage; **'~-screw 1.** tire-bouchon *m*; ~ curl *cheveux*: tire-bouchon *m*; **2.** *v/i.* vriller (*fil*); tourner en vrille (*escalier*); **'~-tree** ♀ chêne-liège (*pl.* chênes-lièges) *m*; **'cork·y** semblable au liège; *fig.* enjoué.

cor·mo·rant *orn.* [ˈkɔːmərənt] cormoran *m*, F corbeau *m* de mer.

corn[1] [kɔːn] **1.** grain *m*; blé *m*; *Am.* (*a.* Indian ~) maïs *m*; *Am.* ~ bread pain *m* de maïs; *Am.* ~-flakes paillettes *f/pl.* de maïs; **2.** saler; ~ed beef bœuf *m* de conserve.

corn[2] ♣ [~] *orteil*: cor *m*; *pied*: oignon *m*.

corn...: **'~-chan·dler** *Brit.* marchand *m* de grains; **'~-cob** *Am.* épi *m* de maïs.

cor·ne·a *anat.* [ˈkɔːniə] *œil*: cornée *f*.

cor·nel ♀ [ˈkɔːnl] cornouille *f*; *arbre*: cornouiller *m*.

cor·nel·ian *min.* [kɔːˈniːljən] cornaline *f*.

cor·ne·ous [ˈkɔːniəs] corné.

cor·ner [ˈkɔːnə] **1.** coin *m*, angle *m*; tournant *m*; *mot.* virage *m*; *fig.* dilemme *m*, impasse *f*; ♣ monopole *m*; ♣ trust *m* d'accapareurs; *foot.* (*a.* ~ kick) corner *m*; **2.** mettre dans un coin (*fig.* une impasse); acculer (*q.*); mettre (*un animal*) à l'accul; ♣ accaparer; **'cor·nered** à angles, à coins.

corner...: **'~-house** maison *f* du coin; **'~-stone** pierre *f* angulaire (*a. fig.*).

cor·net [ˈkɔːnit] ♪ cornet *m* à pistons; *papier*: cornet *m*; *glaces*: plaisir *m*.

corn...: **'~-ex·change** bourse *f* des céréales; halle *f* aux blés; **'~-flow·er** bl(e)uet *m*; ~ blue bleu barbeau.

cor·nice [ˈkɔːnis] △, *alp.* corniche *f*; chapiteau *m* d'armoire.

Cor·nish [ˈkɔːniʃ] cornouaillais, de Cornouailles.

corn...: ~ meal *Am.* farine *f* de maïs; **'~-pop·py** ♀ coquelicot *m*; pavot *m* rouge.

cor·nu·co·pi·a [kɔːnjuˈkoupjə] corne *f* d'abondance.

corn·y [ˈkɔːni] abondant en blé; *sl.* suranné, rebattu; *surt. Am.* ♪ sentimental (-aux *m/pl.*); gnangnan *inv.*

co·rol·la ♀ [kəˈrɔlə] corolle *f*; **cor·'ol·la·ry** corollaire *m*; *fig.* conséquence *f*.

co·ro·na [kəˈrounə], *pl.* **-nae** [~niː] *astr.* couronne *f*; △ larmier *m*; **co·ro·nal** [ˈkɔrənl] *anat.* coronal (-aux *m/pl.*); **cor·o·nar·y** [ˈkɔrənəri] **1.** coronaire *m*; ~ thrombosis infarctus *m* du myocarde; **2.** infarctus *m*; **cor·o·na·tion** couronnement *m*, sacre *m*; **'cor·o·ner** ⚖ coroner *m*; **cor·o·net** [ˈ~nit] cercle *m*, couronne *f*; *dame*: diadème *m*.

cor·po·ral [ˈkɔːpərəl] **1.** □ corporel (-le *f*); **2.** ✗ *infanterie*: caporal *m*; *artillerie, cavalerie*: brigadier *m*; **cor·po·rate** [ˈ~rit] □ constitué; ~ body corps *m* constitué; personne *f* civile; **cor·po·'ra·tion** corporation *f*, corps *m* constitué; personne *f* civile; municipalité *f*; *Am.* société *f* par actions; F gros ventre *m*; **cor·po·ra·tive** [ˈ~rətiv] corporatif (-ive *f*); **cor·po·re·al** □ [~-

'pɔːriəl] corporel(le f); matériel(le f) (a. ⚡); **cor‧po‧re‧i‧ty** [‿pə'riːiti] corporéité f.

corps [kɔː], pl. **corps** [kɔːz] corps m.

corpse [kɔːps] cadavre m; corps m.

cor‧pu‧lence ['kɔːpjuləns(i)] corpulence f; '**cor‧pu‧lent** corpulent.

cor‧pus ['kɔːpəs], pl. **-po‧ra** ['‿pərə] corpus m, recueil m; ♀ **Christi** ['kɔːpəs'kristi] la Fête-Dieu f; **cor‧pus‧cle** ['kɔːpʌsl] corpuscule m; sanguin: globule m; fig. atome m.

cor‧ral surt. Am. [kɔ'rɑːl] **1.** corral (pl. -als) m; **2.** renfermer dans un corral; fig. s'emparer de; parquer (des chariots) en rond.

cor‧rect [kə'rekt] **1.** adj. □ correct; juste; bienséant; be ‿ avoir raison; fig. être en règle; **2.** v/t. corriger; rectifier (une erreur); neutraliser (une influence); reprendre (un enfant); **cor‧rec‧tion** correction f; rectification f; châtiment m, punition f; house of ‿ maison f de correction; I speak under ‿ je le dis sous toutes réserves, sauf correction; **cor‧rec‧ti‧tude** [‿itju:d] correction f; **cor‧rec‧tive 1.** correctif (-ive f), rectificatif (-ive f); punitif (-ive f); **2.** correctif m; **cor‧rec‧tor** correcteur (-trice f) m; typ. corrigeur (-euse f) m; ⊕ appareil m etc. correcteur.

cor‧re‧late ['kɔrileit] **1.** v/t. mettre en corrélation (avec, with); v/i. correspondre (à with, to); **2.** corrélatif m; **cor‧re‧la‧tion** corrélation f; **cor‧rel‧a‧tive** □ ['‿relətiv] corrélatif (-ive f); en corrélation (avec, with).

cor‧re‧spond [kɔris'pɔnd] (with, to) correspondre (avec, à); être conforme (à); (s')écrire (à); **cor‧re‧spond‧ence** correspondance f; courrier m; **cor‧re‧spond‧ent 1.** □ conforme; **2.** correspondant(e f) m (a. ✝); journ. envoyé(e f) m.

cor‧ri‧dor ['kɔridɔː] couloir m, corridor m; 🚂 ‿ train train m à intercirculation.

cor‧ri‧gi‧ble □ ['kɔridʒəbl] corrigible.

cor‧rob‧o‧rant [kə'rɔbərənt] **1.** corroborant; corroboratif (-ive f); **2.** corroborant m; fortifiant m; **cor‧rob‧o‧rate** [‿reit] corroborer, confirmer; **cor‧rob‧o‧ra‧tion** corrobo-

ration f, confirmation f; **cor‧rob‧o‧ra‧tive** [‿rətiv] corroboratif (-ive f); corroborant.

cor‧rode [kə'roud] corroder, ronger (un métal, a. fig.); **cor‧ro‧dent** corrodant (a. su./m); **cor‧ro‧sion** corrosion f; qqfois rouille f; ⚡ sulfatage m (des bornes); **cor‧ro‧sive** [‿siv] **1.** □ corrosif (-ive f) (a. fig.); corrodant; **2.** corrosif m, corrodant m; **cor‧ro‧sive‧ness** corrosivité f; mordant m.

cor‧ru‧gate ['kɔrugeit] ⊕ strier de nervures; ‿d cardboard carton m ondulé; ‿d iron tôle f ondulée.

cor‧rupt [kə'rʌpt] **1.** □ corrompu, altéré (a. texte); fig. dépravé; vénal (-aux m/pl.) (presse); pol. ‿ practices brigues f/pl.; abus m; trafic m d'influence; **2.** v/t. corrompre, altérer (a. texte); fig. dépraver, dévoyer; v/i. se corrompre; s'altérer; **cor‧rupt‧er** corrupteur (-trice f) m; démoralisateur (-trice f) m; **cor‧rupt‧i‧bil‧i‧ty** [‿'biliti] corruptibilité f; vénalité f; **cor‧rupt‧i‧ble** □ corruptible; vénal (-aux m/pl.); **cor‧rup‧tion** corruption f (a. fig.); dépravation f; subornation f (d'un témoin); **cor‧rup‧tive** □ corruptif (-ive f).

cor‧sage [kɔː'sɑːʒ] corsage m; Am. bouquet m.

cor‧sair ['kɔːsɛə] homme, vaisseau: corsaire m; pirate m.

cors(e)‧let ['kɔːslit] corselet m.

cor‧set ['kɔːsit] corset m; '**cor‧set‧ed** corseté.

cor‧ti‧cal ['kɔːtikl] cortical (-aux m/pl.); fig. extérieur.

cor‧ti‧sone ['kɔːtizoun] cortisone f.

co‧run‧dum min. [kə'rʌndəm] corindon m.

cor‧us‧cate ['kɔrəskeit] scintiller; briller; **cor‧us‧ca‧tion** vif éclat m; fig. ‿s of wit paillettes f/pl. d'esprit.

cor‧vette ⚓ [kɔː'vet] corvette f.

cor‧vine ['kɔːvain] orn. corvin.

cor‧y‧phae‧us [kɔri'fiːəs], pl. **-phae‧i** [‿'fiːai] coryphée m (a. fig.); fig. chef m de secte etc.; **co‧ry‧phée** [‿'fei] ballet: première danseuse f.

cosh‧er ['kɔʃə] dorloter, gâter.

co‧sig‧na‧to‧ry ['kou'signətəri] cosignataire (a. su.).

co‧sine ⚹ ['kousain] cosinus m.

co‧si‧ness ['kouzinis] confortable m; chaleur f agréable.

cos·met·ic [kɔzˈmetik] (ˌ~ally) cosmétique (a. su./m).

cos·mic, cos·mi·cal □ [ˈkɔzmik(l)] cosmique.

cos·mo·naut [ˈkɔzmənɔːt] cosmonaute m.

cos·mo·pol·i·tan [kɔzməˈpɔlitən], **cos·mop·o·lite** [ˌ~ˈmɔpəlait] cosmopolite (a. su./mf).

Cos·sack [ˈkɔsæk] cosaque (a. su.).

cos·set [ˈkɔsit] **1.** (agneau m) favori m; **2.** dorloter, gâter.

cost [kɔst] **1.** coût m; frais m/pl.; dépens m/pl.; prix m; ⚖ ~s pl. frais m/pl. d'instance; les frais m/pl. et dépens m/pl.; first (ou prime) ~ prix m coûtant; prix m de revient; ~ of living coût m de la vie; to my ~ à mes dépens; as I know to my ~ (comme) je l'ai appris pour mon malheur; **2.** [irr.] coûter; ⚖ établir le prix de revient de (un article); ~ dear coûter cher (à q., s.o.).

co-star cin. [ˈkouˈstɑː] **1.** partenaire mf, acteur m (actrice f) qui partage la vedette; **2.** partager la vedette.

cos·ter F [ˈkɔstə], **~mon·ger** marchand m des quatre-saisons.

cost·ing [ˈkɔstiŋ] établissement m du prix de revient.

cos·tive □ [ˈkɔstiv] constipé.

cost·li·ness [ˈkɔstlinis] prix m élevé; meubles: somptuosité f; **cost·ly** de grand prix; riche (meubles); coûteux (-euse f).

cost-price ⚖ [ˈkɔstprais] prix m coûtant, prix m de revient, prix m de fabrique.

cos·tume [ˈkɔstjuːm] **1.** costume m (pour dames: tailleur); ~ play pièce f historique; **2.** costumer; **cos·tum·i·er** [ˌ~miə] costumier m.

co·sy [ˈkouzi] **1.** □ chaud, commode, confortable; **2.** cosy m (pour œufs à la coque); couvre-théière m; molleton m.

cot [kɔt] lit m d'enfants; lit m de camp; ⚓ hamac m à cadre.

co·te·rie [ˈkoutəri] coterie f; cénacle m (littéraire etc.).

cot·tage [ˈkɔtidʒ] chaumière f; petite maison f de campagne; Am. résidence f d'été; Am. ~ cheese fromage m blanc; ~ industry industrie f à domicile; ~ piano petit piano m droit; **cot·tag·er** paysan(ne f) m; habitant(e f) m d'une chaumière; Am. estivant(e f) m.

cot·ter ⊕ [ˈkɔtə] clavette f, goupille f.

cot·ton [ˈkɔtn] **1.** coton m; arbre: cotonnier m; toile f ou fil m de coton; fil m à coudre; **2.** de coton; Am. ~ candy barbe f à papa; ~ wool ouate f; **3.** F s'accorder, faire bon ménage (avec, with); se sentir attiré (par, to); F ~ on (to s.th.) piger (qch.); ~ to s.th. s'accommoder à qch.; ~ up faire des avances (à to, with); **~-grass** linaigrette f; **cot·ton·y** cotonneux (-euse f).

couch [kautʃ] **1.** canapé m, divan m; chaise f longue; poét. lit m; **2.** v/t. coucher; mettre (sa lance) en arrêt; envelopper (sa pensée); rédiger (une lettre, une réclamation); abaisser (une cataracte); v/i. se coucher; se tapir; **~-grass** ♣ chiendent m.

cou·gar zo. [ˈkuːgɑː] couguar m, puma m.

cough [kɔf] **1.** toux f; ~ drop pastille f pour la toux; ~ mixture sirop m pour la toux; **2.** v/i. tousser; v/t. ~ down réduire (q.) au silence à force de tousser; ~ up cracher (a. sl. = payer).

could [kud] prét. de can[1].

couldn't [ˈkudnt] = could not.

coul·ter [ˈkoultə] coutre m (de charrue).

coun·cil [ˈkaunsl] conseil m; eccl. concile m; **coun·ci(l)·lor** [ˈ~ilə] conseiller m; membre m du conseil.

coun·sel [ˈkaunsəl] **1.** consultation f; conseil m; dessein m; ⚖ avocat m; conseil m; ~ for the defence défenseur m; avocat m du défendeur; ~ for the prosecution avocat m de la partie publique; keep o.'s (own) ~ observer le silence; take ~ with consulter avec; **2.** conseiller, recommander (à q. de inf., s.o. to inf.); **coun·se(l)·lor** [ˈ~lə] conseiller m.

count[1] [kaunt] **1.** compte m, calcul m; votes: dépouillement m; dénombrement m; ⚖ chef m (d'accusation); box. compte m; parl. (a. ~-out) ajournement m; lose ~ perdre le compte (de, of); **2.** v/t. compter; dénombrer; fig. tenir (q.) pour; box. be ~ed out rester sur le plancher pour le compte; F être compté dehors; v/i. compter (sur, on; pour as, for); au nombre de, among); avoir de l'importance; ~ for little compter pour peu, ne compter guère.

count² [⌐] *titre étranger*: comte *m*.

count·down [ˈkauntdaun] *fusée*: compte *m* à rebours.

coun·te·nance [ˈkauntinəns] **1.** visage *m*, figure *f*, mine *f*; expression *f* (du visage); faveur *f*; **2.** approuver; encourager, appuyer.

count·er¹ [ˈkauntə] compteur (-euse *f*) *m*; ⊕ compteur *m*; *jeux*: fiche *f* (*carrée*), jeton *m* (*rond*); *boutique*: comptoir *m*; *banque etc.*: guichets *m/pl.*; caisse *f*; *phys.* Geiger ~ compteur *m* Geiger.

count·er² [⌐] **1.** *adj.* contraire, opposé (à, *to*); **2.** *adv.* à contresens; contrairement; **3.** *su.* contre *m*; *box.* coup *m* d'arrêt; **4.** *v/t.* aller à l'encontre de; contrecarrer (*des desseins*); *box.* parer.

coun·ter·act [kauntəˈrækt] neutraliser; parer à; **coun·ter'ac·tion** action *f* contraire; neutralisation *f*; contre-mesure *f*.

coun·ter-at·tack [ˈkauntərətæk] contre-attaque *f*.

coun·ter·bal·ance 1. [ˈkauntəbæ-ləns] contrepoids *m*; **2.** [⌐'bæləns] contrebalancer; compenser; ✝ équilibrer.

coun·ter·blast [ˈkauntəblɑːst] riposte *f*.

coun·ter·change [kauntəˈtʃeindʒ] échanger (pour, contre *for*).

coun·ter·charge [ˈkauntətʃɑːdʒ] contre-accusation *f*.

coun·ter·check [ˈkauntətʃek] force *f* opposée *ou* antagoniste; riposte *f*.

coun·ter-clock·wise [ˈkauntəˈklɔk-waiz] en sens inverse des aiguilles d'une montre.

coun·ter·cur·rent [ˈkauntəˈkʌrənt] contre-courant *m*.

coun·ter·es·pi·onage [ˈkauntərespiəˈnɑːʒ] contre-espionnage *m*.

coun·ter·feit [ˈkauntəfit] **1.** □ contrefait; faux (fausse *f*); simulé; ~ *money* fausse monnaie *f*; **2.** contrefaçon *f*; *document*: faux *m*; F fausse monnaie *f*; **3.** contrefaire; simuler, feindre (*une émotion*); **'coun·ter·feit·er** contrefacteur *m*; faux-monnayeur *m*; simulateur (-trice *f*) *m*.

coun·ter·foil [ˈkauntəfɔil] souche *f*, *chèque*: talon *m*.

coun·ter·fort △ [ˈkauntəfɔːt] contrefort *m*.

coun·ter-in·tel·li·gence [ˈkauntərintelidʒəns] *see counter-espionage*.

coun·ter·jump·er F [ˈkauntə-dʒʌmpə] commis *m*; calicot *m*.

coun·ter·mand [kauntəˈmɑːnd] **1.** contrordre *m*, contremandement *m*; **2.** contremander; révoquer; ✝ décommander.

coun·ter·march [ˈkauntəmɑːtʃ] **1.** contremarche *f*; **2.** (faire) contremarcher.

coun·ter·mark [ˈkauntəmɑːk] contremarque *f*.

coun·ter·meas·ure [ˈkauntəmeʒə] contre-mesure *f*.

coun·ter·mine [ˈkauntəmain] **1.** contre-mine *f*; **2.** contre-miner (*a. fig.*).

coun·ter·or·der [ˈkauntərɔːdə] contrordre *m*.

coun·ter·pane [ˈkauntəpein] couvre-lit *m*; courtepointe *f*.

coun·ter·part [ˈkauntəpɑːt] contrepartie *f*; double *m*.

coun·ter·point ♪ [ˈkauntəpoint] contrepoint *m*.

coun·ter·poise [ˈkauntəpoiz] **1.** contrepoids *m*; équilibre *m*; **2.** contrebalancer; faire contrepoids à (*a. fig.*).

coun·ter·pro·duc·tive [ˈkauntəprəˈdʌktiv] improductif (-ive *f*); inutile; absurde; *be* ~ *a.* n'aboutir à rien.

coun·ter·scarp ✕ [ˈkauntəskɑːp] contrescarpe *f*.

coun·ter·sign [ˈkauntəsain] **1.** contreseing *m*; mot *m* d'ordre; **2.** contresigner.

coun·ter·sink ⊕ [kauntəˈsiŋk] [*irr.*] fraiser; noyer (*la tête d'une vis*); encastrer (*la tête d'un rivet*).

coun·ter·stroke [ˈkauntəstrouk] retour *m* offensif.

coun·ter·ten·or ♪ [ˈkauntəˈtenə] haute-contre (*pl.* hautes-contre) *f*; alto *m*.

coun·ter·vail [ˈkauntəveil] *v/t.* compenser; *v/t.* prévaloir (contre, *against*).

coun·ter·weight [ˈkauntəweit] contrepoids *m* (à, *to*).

coun·ter·work [ˈkauntəwəːk] contrarier; contrecarrer.

count·ess [ˈkauntis] comtesse *f*.

count·ing-house [ˈkauntiŋhaus] (bureau *m* de la) comptabilité *f*.

count·less [ˈkauntlis] innombrable.

coun·tri·fied ['kʌntrifaid] aux allures agrestes; province *inv.* (*personne*).

coun·try ['kʌntri] **1.** pays *m*; région *f*; patrie *f*; campagne *f*; province *f*; *appeal* (*ou go*) *to the* ~ en appeler au pays; **2.** campagnard; *de ou* à la campagne; ~ *policeman* garde *m* champêtre; ~ **dance** dance *f* rustique; '~**man** campagnard *m*, paysan *m*; compatriote *m*; '~**side** campagnes *f/pl.*; (population *f* de la) région *f*; '~**wom·an** campagnarde *f*, paysanne *f*; compatriote *f*.

coun·ty ['kaunti] comté *m*; ~ **town**, *Am.* ~ **seat** chef-lieu (*pl.* chefslieux) *m* de comté.

coup [kuː] coup *m* (audacieux).

cou·ple ['kʌpl] **1.** couple *m*, deux ...; couple *f* (*a. d'œufs, de pigeons*); **2.** *v/t.* coupler; associer; ⊕ engrener; 🚗 atteler, accrocher; ⚡ brancher (sur, *to*), interconnecter; *v/i.* s'accoupler (*personne*); ~ *back* coupler à réaction; '**cou·pler** *radio*: accouplement *m*; **cou·plet** ['~lit] distique *m*.

cou·pling ⊕ ['kʌpliŋ] accouplement *m*; 🚗 accrochage *m*; ⚡ couplage *m*; *radio*: accouplement *m*; *attr.* d'accouplement.

cou·pon ['kuːpɔn] coupon *m* (*a.* 🌱); ticket *m* (*de carte alimentaire*).

cour·age ['kʌridʒ] courage *m*; **cou·ra·geous** □ [kə'reidʒəs] courageux (-euse *f*).

cour·gette [kuə'ʒet] courgette *f*.

cour·i·er ['kuriə] courrier *m*, messager *m*.

course [kɔːs] **1.** *événements, fleuve, temps, univ.*: cours *m*; *événements*: marche *f*; *direction f*, route *f* (*a.* ⚓); *affaires*: courant *m*; *balle*: trajet *m*; *repas*: plat *m*, service *m*; *fig.* chemin *m*; *fig.* parti *m*; *sp.* piste *f*; *sp.* champ *m* de course(s); *golf*: parcours *m*; ⚓ cap *m*; ⚓ basse voile *f*; 🌱 cote *f* (*des changes*); 🩺 traitement *m*; ⊕ *piston*: course *f*; △ assise *f*; *cours d'eau*: lit *m*; ~ *of action* ligne *f* de conduite; *in due* ~ en temps utile; *of* ~ (bien) entendu, naturellement; *be a matter of* ~ aller de soi; ~ *of exchange* cote *f* des changes; **2.** *v/t. chasse*: (faire) courir; *v/i.* courir, couler (*liquide, surt. sang*).

cours·ing ['kɔːsiŋ] chasse *f* (à courre) au lièvre.

court [kɔːt] **1.** cour *f* (*royale, a.* ⚖); ⚖ tribunal *m*; ruelle *f*; ✗, ⚓ commission *f* (*d'enquête*); *sp.* court *m* (*de tennis*), terrain *m*; *Am. General* ♀ Parlement *m* (*des États de Vermont et New Hampshire*); *at* ~ à la cour; *pay* (*one's*) ~ faire la cour (à, *to*); **2.** courtiser; faire la cour à (*une femme*); solliciter (*qch.*); rechercher (*qch.*); aller au-devant de (*un échec, un danger*); '~**card** *cartes*: figure *f*, carte *f* peinte; '~**day** jour *m* d'audience; **cour·te·ous** □ ['kɔːtjəs] courtois, poli (envers, *to*); **cour·te·san**, *a.* **cour·te·zan** [kɔːti-'zæn] courtisane *f*; **cour·te·sy** ['kɔːtisi] courtoisie *f*, politesse *f*; ~ *call* visite *f* de politesse; *mot.* ~ *light* plafonnier *m*; **court-house** ['kɔːt-'haus] palais *m* de justice; *Am. a.* administration *f* (*d'un département*); **cour·ti·er** ['~jə] courtisan *m*; '**court·li·ness** courtoisie *f*; élégance *f*; '**court·ly** courtois; élégant.

court...: ~ *mar·tial*, *pl.* ~*s mar·tial* ✗ conseil *m* de guerre; '~**'mar·tial** faire passer en conseil de guerre; '~**'plas·ter** taffetas *m* gommé; '~**ship** cour *f* (*faite à une femme*); '~**yard** cour *f* (*d'une maison*).

cous·in ['kʌzn] cousin(e *f*) *m*; *first* ~, ~ *german* cousin(e *f*) *m* germain(e *f*); '**cous·in·ly** de bon cousinage; **cous·in·hood** ['~hud], '**cous·in·ship** cousinage *m*; parenté *f*.

cove[1] [kouv] **1.** anse *f*; petite baie *f*; △ grande gorge *f*; voûte *f* (*de plafond*); **2.** voûter.

cove[2] *sl.* [~] type *m*, individu *m*.

cov·e·nant ['kʌvinənt] **1.** ⚖ convention *f*, contrat *m*; *bibl.* alliance *f*; *pol.* pacte *m*; **2.** *v/t.* accorder par contrat; stipuler (*de l'argent*); *v/i.* convenir (de qch. avec q., *with s.o. for s.th.*).

Cov·en·try ['kɔvəntri]: *send s.o. to* ~ mettre q. en quarantaine.

cov·er ['kʌvə] **1.** couverture *f*; *table*: tapis *m*; *buffet*: dessus *m*; couvercle *m*; abri *m*; *poste*: enveloppe *f*; *fig.* masque *m*, voile *m*; *mot., bicyclette, etc.*: bâche *f*; 🌱 provision *f*, marge *f*; *repas*: couvert *m*; (*ou* ~ *address*) adresse *f* de convenance; *Am.* ~ *charge* couvert *m*; *journ.* ~ *story* article *m* principal; **2.** recouvrir; couvrir (de, *with*) (q., qch., 🌱 *risque,*

⚔ *retraite, dépenses*); envelopper; revêtir; dominer (*une vue, un terrain*); parcourir (*une distance*); tapisser (*un mur*); combler (*un déficit*); ⚡ guiper (*un fil*); assurer le compte-rendu de (*un journal*); F couvrir, dissimuler; *fig.* tenir compte de, comprendre; ⁓ed button bouton *m* d'étoffe; ⁓ed court *tennis*: court *m* couvert; ⁓ed wire fil *m* guipé; '**cover·ing** recouvrement *m*; couverture *f* (*a. de lit*); enveloppe *f*; ⚡ fil *etc.*: guipage *m*; *meubles*: housse *f*; ⚓ bâche *f*; *floor* ⁓ linoléum *m*; **cov·er·let** ['⁓lit] couvre-lit *m*; dessus *m* de lit.

cov·ert ['kʌvət] **1.** □ voilé, caché; secret (-ète *f*); ⁂ en puissance de mari; **2.** *chasse*: abri *m*, couvert *m*, fourré *m*; retraite *f*; **cov·er·ture** ['⁓tjuə] abri *m*; ⁂ condition *f* de la femme mariée.

cov·er-up ['kʌvərʌp] dissimulation *f*; tentatives *f/pl.* pour étouffer *ou* dissimuler un scandale.

cov·et ['kʌvit] convoiter; aspirer à; '**cov·et·ous** □ avide (de, *of*); avare; cupide; '**cov·et·ous·ness** convoitise *f*; cupidité *f*.

cov·ey ['kʌvi] vol *m ou* couvée *f* (*de perdrix etc.*).

cov·ing △ ['kouviŋ] *plafond etc.*: voussure *f*; saillie *f*.

cow[1] [kau] vache *f*.

cow[2] [⁓] intimider, dompter.

cow·ard ['kauəd] **1.** □ lâche; **2.** lâche *mf*; '**cow·ard·ice**, '**cow·ard·li·ness** lâcheté *f*; '**cow·ard·ly 1.** lâche; **2.** lâchement.

cow·boy ['kaubɔi] jeune vacher *m*; *Am.* cow-boy *m*; '**cow-catch·er** 🚂 *Am.* chasse-pierres *m/inv.*

cow·er ['kauə] se blottir, se tapir; *fig.* trembler (*devant, before*).

cow·herd ['kauhə:d] vacher *m*; bouvier *m*; '**cow·hide 1.** (peau *f* de) vache *f*; **2.** *Am.* donner le fouet à (*q.*).

cowl [kaul] moine, *cheminée*: capuchon *m*; *cheminée*: mitre *f*; ⚔, ⚓ capot *m*.

cow...: '⁓**man** *Am.* éleveur *m* de bétail; '⁓-'**pars·ley** □ cerfeuil *m* sauvage; '⁓-'**pars·nip** ⚘ berce *f*; '⁓-**pox** variole *f* des vaches; '⁓-**punch·er** *Am.* F cow-boy *m*.

cow·rie ['kauri] porcelaine *f*; *argent*: cauris *m*.

cow...: '⁓-**shed** étable *f*; '⁓-**slip** ⚘ (fleur *f* de) coucou *m*.

cox F [kɔks] **1.** *see* coxswain; **2.** diriger, gouverner.

cox·comb ['kɔkskoum] petit-maître (*pl.* petits-maîtres) *m*; fat *m*; **cox-'comb·i·cal** □ fat.

cox·swain ['kɔkswein; 'kɔksn] barreur *m*; ⚓ patron *m* (*d'une chaloupe*).

coy [kɔi] □ modeste, farouche, réservé; '**coy·ness** modestie *f*, réserve *f*.

coz·en ['kʌzn] tromper; '**coz·en·age** tromperie *f*.

co·zy ['kouzi] *see* cosy.

crab[1] [kræb] crabe *m*, cancre *m*; *astr.* le Cancer *m*; ⊕ treuil *m*; chèvre *f*; *sl. see* crab-louse; *catch a* ⁓ faire fausse rame; F *turn out* ⁓s échouer.

crab[2] [⁓] **1.** pomme *f* sauvage; F personne *f* revêche; critique *f*; grognon(ne *f*) *m*; **2.** *v/t.* dénigrer; *v/i.* trouver à redire (à, *about*); **crab·bed** ['kræbid] □ maussade, grognon(ne *f*); pénible (*style*); illisible (*écriture*); **crab-louse** ['kræb-laus] pou *m* du pubis.

crack [kræk] **1.** craquement *m*; fente *f*; fissure *f*; lézarde *f*; *cloche, verre, porcelaine, etc.*: fêlure *f*; F coup *m* sec; *écoss.* F cousette *f*; *sp. sl.* crack *m*, as *m*; *sl.* cambriolage *m*; *sl.* toqué(e *f*) *m*; *surt. Am. sl.* remarque *f* mordante, observation *f* satirique; plaisanterie *f*; *in a* ⁓ in un clin d'œil; **2.** F fameux (-euse *f*), de premier ordre; **3.** clac!; pan!; **4.** *v/t.* faire claquer (*un fouet*); fêler; crevasser; fendre; casser (*une noisette*); 🔧 fractionner (*une huile lourde*); ⁓ *a bottle* déboucher *ou* entamer *ou* boire une bouteille; ⁓ *a joke* faire une plaisanterie; F ⁓ *up* vanter (*q., qch.*); *v/i.* craquer; claquer; se fêler; se crevasser; se lézarder; se gercer (*peau*); se casser (*voix etc.*); *Am. sl.* ⁓ *down on s.o.* F laver la tête à q.; prendre des mesures sévères contre q.; '⁓-**brained** (au cerveau) timbré; '⁓-**down** *Am. sl.* razzia *f*; '**cracked** fêlé, fendu *etc.*; F timbré, toqué; '**crack·er** papillote *f* à pétard; pétard *m*; F mensonge *m*; *Am.* craquelin *m*, croquet *m*; biscuit *m* dur; '**crack·er·jack** *Am.*

F as *m*, expert *m*; '**crack-jaw** F (mot *m*) à vous décrocher la mâchoire; '**crack·le** craqueter; crépiter; pétiller (*feu*); (se) fendiller; '**crack·ling** *porc rôti*: peau *f* croquante; couenne *f*; **crack·nel** ['nl] craquelin *m*; '**crack·pot 1.** type *m* cinglé; **2.** cinglé; '**crack-up** collision *f*; ✈ crash *m*; '**crack·y** *see* **cracked.**

cra·dle ['kreidl] **1.** berceau *m* (*a. fig.*); *fig.* première enfance *f*; ⚓ ber *m* (de lancement); chantier *m*; *téléph.* étrier *m* du récepteur; **2.** mettre dans un berceau *etc.*

craft [krɑːft] habileté *f*; ruse *f*, artifice *m*; métier *m* manuel; profession *f*; corps *m* de métier; *coll. pl.* embarcations *f/pl.*, petits navires *m/pl.*; *the gentle* ~ la pêche à la ligne, *fig. co.* le noble art; '**craft·i·ness** ruse *f*, astuce *f*; '**crafts·man** artisan *m*, ouvrier *m*; artiste *m* dans son métier; '**crafts·man·ship** exécution *f* merveilleuse; dextérité *f* manuelle; '**craft·y** □ astucieux (-euse *f*), rusé.

crag [kræg] rocher *m* à pic; *alp.* varappe *f*; '**crag·gy** rocailleux (-euse *f*); escarpé; '**crags·man** varappeur *m*.

crake *orn.* [kreik] (cri *m* du) râle *m*.

cram [kræm] **1.** fourrer; bourrer; empâter (*de la volaille*); *fig.* empiffrer; F bûcher (*un sujet*), bourrer; *v/i.* s'entasser; se gorger de nourriture; préparer un examen; **2.** F chauffage *m* (*pour un examen*); F mensonge *m*; '~-'**full** regorgeant (de, *of*), bondé; '**cram·mer** chauffeur *m*; F mensonge *m*.

cramp [kræmp] **1.** ✸ crampe *f*; ⊕ crampon *m*; presse *f* à vis; *fig.* contrainte *f*; **2.** ⊕ cramponner, agrafer; serrer (à l'*étau*); *fig.* gêner; '**cramped** gêné; à l'étroit; '**cramp-frame** ⊕ serre-joint *m*; presse *f* à main; '**cramp-i·ron** crampon *m*, agrafe *f*.

cram·pon ['kræmpən] crampon *m* à glace.

cran·ber·ry ❀ ['krænbəri] airelle *f*; canneberge *f*.

crane [krein] **1.** grue *f* (*a.* ⊕); **2.** tendre *ou* allonger (*le cou*); ⊕ hisser *ou* descendre au moyen d'une grue; ~ *at* refuser *ou* reculer devant; **crane-fly** *zo.* ['~flai] tipule *f*;

crane's-bill ❀ bec-de-grue (*pl.* becs-de-grue) *m*.

cra·ni·um *anat.* ['kreiniəm] crâne *m*.

crank [kræŋk] **1.** ⊕ détraqué, délabré; ⚓ instable, mal équilibré; **2.** manivelle *f*; *meule à aiguiser*: cigogne *f*; coude *m*; *cloche*: bascule *f*; *starting* ~ *mot.* (manivelle *f* de) mise *f* en marche; **3.** *v/t.* ~ *off* bobiner (*un film*); *mot.* ~ *up* lancer (*une auto, un moteur*); '**crank·i·ness** humeur *f* difficile; excentricité *f*; '**crank-shaft** ⊕ vilebrequin *m*; '**crank·y** d'humeur difficile; excentrique; capricieux (-euse *f*).

cran·nied ['krænid] lézardé, crevassé; '**cran·ny** fente *f*, crevasse *f*; niche *f*.

crape [kreip] **1.** crêpe *m* noir; **2.** draper de crêpe.

craps *Am.* [kræps] *pl.* dés *m/pl.*

crap·u·lence ['kræpjuləns] crapule *f*; F débauche *f*.

crash¹ [kræʃ] **1.** fracas *m*; catastrophe *f*; ✝ krach *m*; ✈ crash *m*; ~-*helmet* casque *m* protecteur; ~-*landing* atterrissage *m* brutal, crash *m*; **2.** *v/i.* retentir; éclater avec fracas; ✈ s'écraser, atterrir brutalement; *v/t.* jeter avec fracas; **3.** F à exécuter rapidement; ~ *course* cours *m* intensif; ~ *diet* régime *m* radical (*pour maigrir*).

crash² [~] toile *f* à serviettes.

crass [kræs] grossier (-ère *f*); stupide.

crate [kreit] caisse *f* à claire-voie.

cra·ter ['kreitə] volcan, *a.* ✸ cratère *m*; ✕ entonnoir *m*.

cra·vat [krə'væt] foulard *m*; † cravate *f*.

crave [kreiv] *v/t.* implorer avec instance (de, *from*), solliciter; *v/i.* (*for*) désirer avidement (*qch.*).

cra·ven ['kreivn] **1.** poltron(ne *f*), lâche; **2.** poltron(ne *f*) *m*, lâche *mf*.

crav·ing ['kreiviŋ] désir *m* ardent, besoin *m*, passion *f*, appétit *m* insatiable (de, *for*).

craw [krɔː] jabot *m* (*d'oiseau*).

craw·fish ['krɔːfiʃ] **1.** *eau douce*: écrevisse *f*; *mer*: langouste *f*; **2.** *Am.* F se dérober; *sl.* caner.

crawl [krɔːl] **1.** rampement *m*; *personne*: mouvement *m* traînant; *nage*: crawl *m*; **2.** ramper; se traîner; grouiller (de, *with*); marauder; '**crawl·er** reptile *m*; *personne*:

traînard(e *f*) *m*; *fig.* plat valet *m*;
taxi *m* en maraude; *nage:* crawleur
m; *vêtement pour enfants:* barboteuse *f*.

cray·fish ['kreifiʃ] *eau douce:* écrevisse *f*; *mer:* langouste *f*.

cray·on ['kreiən] **1.** craie *f* à dessiner; *surt.* (crayon *m* de) pastel *m*;
fusain *m*; *blue* (*red*) ~ crayon *m*
bleu (rouge); **2.** dessiner au pastel;
crayonner.

craze [kreiz] manie *f* (de, *for*); *fig.*
fureur *f* (de); *be the* ~ faire fureur;
'crazed affolé (de, with); **'cra·zi-
ness** folie *f*, démence *f*; *maison:*
délabrement *m*; **'cra·zy** □ fou
(fol *devant une voyelle ou un h muet*;
folle *f*) (de with, about, for); affolé
(de, with); branlant; délabré (*maison*); irrégulier (-ère *f*); en pièces
rapportées.

creak [kri:k] **1.** grincement *m*;
2. grincer, crier; **'creak·y** □ qui
crie, qui grince.

cream [kri:m] **1.** crème *f* (*a. fig.*);
fig. le plus beau (*de l'histoire*);
cold ~ crème *f*, cold-cream *m*;
~ *of tartar* crème *f* de tartre;
2. (*souv.* ~-*colo(u)red*) crème *inv.*;
3. *v/t.* écrémer; ajouter de la crème
à; battre (*du beurre*) en crème; *v/i.*
se couvrir de crème; mousser;
'cream·er·y crémerie *f*; **'cream·y**
□ crémeux (-euse *f*); *fig.* velouté.

crease [kri:s] **1.** (faux) pli *m*; *tex.*
ancrure *f*; *papier:* fronce *f*; *cricket:*
ligne *f* de limite; **2.** (se) plisser; (se)
froisser.

cre·ate [kri'eit] *v/t.* créer (*qch.*, *q.
chevalier*, *théâ. rôle*, *difficulté*, *mode*);
faire; produire; faire naître; *v/i. sl.*
faire une scène (à propos de, *about*);
cre'a·tion création *f* (*a. mode*);
cre'a·tive créateur (-trice *f*); **cre-
'a·tor** créateur (-trice *f*) *m*; **cre'a-
tress** créatrice *f*; **crea·ture** ['kri:tʃə]
créature *f* (*a. péj.*); être *m* (vivant);
animal *m*, bête *f*; ~ *comforts pl.* l'aisance *f* matérielle.

cre·dence ['kri:dəns] foi *f*, croyance
f; *give* ~ *to* ajouter foi à; *letter of* ~
lettre *f* de créance; **cre·den·tials**
[kri'denʃlz] *pl.* lettres *f/pl.* de
créance; *domestique:* certificat *m*;
papiers *m/pl.* d'identité.

cred·i·bil·i·ty [kredi'biliti] crédibilité *f*; **cred·i·ble** □ ['kredəbl]
croyable; digne de foi.

cred·it ['kredit] **1.** foi *f*, croyance *f*,
créance *f*; réputation *f*, crédit *m*
(*a.* ✝); mérite *m*; honneur *m*;
banque: crédit *m*, actif *m*; *Am. école:*
unité *f* de valeur, U.V. *f*; ✝ *on* ~ à
crédit, à terme; ✝ ~ *balance* solde *m*
créditeur; ✝ ~ *card* carte *f* de crédit;
✝ ~ *note f ou* facture *f* d'avoir; ✝ ~
rate degré *m* de solvabilité; ✝ ~ *rating*
limite *f* de crédit; *do s.o.* ~ honorer q.,
faire honneur à q.; *get* ~ *for s.th.*
voir attribuer le mérite de qch.; *give
s.o.* ~ *for s.th.* attribuer (le mérite de)
qch. à q.; *put* (*ou place ou pass*) *to
s.o.'s* ~ porter (*qch.*) au crédit de q.; **2.**
ajouter foi à; attribuer, prêter (*une
qualité* à q., s.o. *with a quality*); ✝
créditer (q. d'une somme *s.o. with a
sum, a sum to s.o.*); porter (*une somme*)
au crédit; ~ *s.o. with s.th.* prêter qch.
à q.; **'cred·it·a·ble** □ honorable,
estimable; *be* ~ *to* faire honneur à;
'cred·i·tor 1. créancier (-ère *f*) *m*; **2.**
créditeur (-trice *f*).

cre·du·li·ty [kri'dju:liti] crédulité *f*;
cred·u·lous □ ['kredjuləs] crédule.

creed [kri:d] credo *m* (*a. pol.*);
croyance *f*. [*m*; petite vallée *f*.]

creek [kri:k] crique *f*; *Am.* ruisseau

creel [kri:l] panier *m* de pêche;
casier *m* à homards; ⊕ râtelier *m*
(à bobines).

creep [kri:p] **1.** [*irr.*] ramper; se
traîner; se glisser (*a. fig.*); *fig.* entrer
doucement; ⊕ glisser; **2.** glissement *m*; ~*s pl.* chair *f* de poule;
'creep·er F homme *m* rampant;
femme *f* rampante; ♀ plante *f*
rampante *ou* grimpante; **'creep·y**
rampant; qui donne la chair de
poule.

creese [kri:s] criss *m* (= *poignard
malais*).

cre·mate [kri'meit] incinérer (*un
mort*); **cre'ma·tion** incinération *f*;
crémation *f*; **crem·a·to·ri·um**
[kremə'tɔ:riəm], *pl.* -**ums**, -**ri·a**
[~riə], **cre·ma·to·ry** ['~təri] cré-
matorium *m*; four *m* crématoire.

cren·el·(l)at·ed ['krenileitid] crénelé.

cre·ole ['kri:oul] créole (*a. su.*).

cre·o·sote ['kriəsout] créosote *f*.

crep·i·tate ['krepiteit] crépiter;
crep·i·ta·tion crépitation *f*.

crept [krept] *prét. et p.p. de* **creep 1.**

cre·pus·cu·lar [kri'pʌskjulə] crépusculaire, du crépuscule.

crock

cres·cent [ˈkresnt] **1.** (en forme de) croissant; **2.** croissant *m* (*a. pâtisserie*); rue *f* en arc de cercle; ♋ *City* la Nouvelle-Orléans *f*.

cress ♎ [kres] cresson *m*.

cres·set [ˈkresit] *tour, phare*: fanal *m*.

crest [krest] △, *casque, coq, montagne, vague*: crête *f*; arête *f, colline*: sommet *m*; *alouette*: huppe *f*; *paon*: aigrette *f*; *blason*: timbre *m*; *sceau*: armoiries *f/pl.*; *casque*: cimier *m*; **ˈcrest·ed** à crête *etc.*; *casque*: orné d'un cimier; ~ **lark** cochevis *m*; **ˈcrest·fall·en** abattu, découragé; penaud (*air*).

cre·ta·ceous [kriˈteiʃəs] crétacé, crayeux (-euse *f*).

cre·tin [ˈkretin] crétin(e *f*) *m*.

cre·vasse [kriˈvæs] crevasse *f* (*glaciaire*); *Am*. fissure *f*.

crev·ice [ˈkrevis] fente *f*; lézarde *f*; fissure *f*.

crew[1] [kruː] ⚓ équipage *m*; *ouvriers*: équipe *f*; *péj*. bande *f*; ~ **cut** cheveux *m/pl.* en brosse.

crew[2] [~] *prét. de* crow 2.

crew·el ♱ [ˈkruːil] laine *f* à broder *ou* à tapisserie.

crib [krib] **1.** mangeoire *f*; lit *m* d'enfant; *eccl*. crèche *f*; F *école*: clef *f*; F plagiat *m*; sl. emploi *m*; surt. *Am*. huche *f* (*pour le maïs etc.*); *sl*. *crack a* ~ cambrioler une maison; **2.** † enfermer; F plagier (*qch*.); F copier; F tuyauter; **ˈcrib·bage** cribbage *m*; **ˈcrib·ble** crible *m*; **crib-bit·er** [ˈ~baitə] tiqueur (-euse *f*) *m*.

crick [krik] **1.** crampe *f*; ~ *in the neck* torticolis *m*; **2.** se donner un torticolis *ou* un tour de reins.

crick·et[1] *zo*. [ˈkrikit] grillon *m*.

crick·et[2] [~] **1.** *sp*. cricket *m*; F *not* ~ déloyal (-aux *m/pl.*); *ne* pas (*être*) de jeu; **2.** jouer au cricket; **ˈcrick·et·er** joueur *m* de cricket, cricketeur *m*.

cri·er [ˈkraiə] crieur *m* (public).

crime [kraim] crime *m*, délit *m*.

Cri·me·an War [kraiˈmiən wɔː] guerre *f* de Crimée.

crim·i·nal [ˈkriminl] criminel(le *f*) (*a. su./mf*); **crim·i·nal·i·ty** [~ˈnæliti] criminalité *f*; **crim·i·nate** [ˈ~neit] incriminer, accuser, convaincre d'un crime; **crim·i·na·tion** incrimination *f*.

crimp[1] ⚓, ✂ [krimp] **1.** racoleur *m*,

embaucheur *m*; **2.** racoler, embaucher.

crimp[2] [~] gaufrer, friser.

crim·son [ˈkrimzn] **1.** cramoisi (*a. su./m*); **2.** *v/t*. teindre en cramoisi; *v/i*. s'empourprer.

cringe [krindʒ] **1.** se faire tout petit, se blottir; *fig*. s'humilier, ramper (*devant to, before*); **2.** *fig*. courbette *f* servile.

crin·kle [ˈkriŋkl] **1.** pli *m*, ride *f*; **2.** (se) froisser; onduler (*a. cheveux*).

crin·o·line [ˈkrinəliːn] crinoline *f*.

crip·ple [ˈkripl] **1.** boiteux (-euse *f*) *m*, estropié(e *f*) *m*; **2.** estropier; *fig*. disloquer.

cri·sis [ˈkraisis], *pl*. **-ses** [ˈ~siːz] crise *f*.

crisp [krisp] **1.** crêpé, frisé (*cheveux etc.*); croquant (*biscuit*); vif (vive *f*), froid (*air, vent*); net(te *f*) (*profil*); tranchant (*ton*); nerveux (-euse *f*) (*style*); **2.** (se) crêper (*cheveux*); (se) froncer; *v/t*. donner du croustillant à.

criss-cross [ˈkriskrɔs] **1.** entrecroisement *m*; enchevêtrement *m*; **2.** entrecroisé; **3.** (s')entrecroiser.

cri·te·ri·on [kraiˈtiəriən], *pl*. **-ri·a** [~riə] critérium *m*, critère *m*.

crit·ic [ˈkritik] critique (*littéraire etc.*) *m*; censeur *m* (*de conduite*); critiqueur *m*; **ˈcrit·i·cal** □ critique; ⚕ dangereux (-euse *f*); *be* ~ *of* critiquer; regarder d'un œil sévère; ⚕ *in* ~ *condition* dans un état critique; **crit·i·cism** [ˈ~sizm], **cri·tique** [kriˈtiːk] critique *f* (de, sur of); **crit·i·cize** [ˈ~saiz] critiquer, faire la critique de; censurer.

croak [krouk] **1.** *v/i*. coasser (*grenouille*); croasser (*corbeau*); *fig*. grogner; *sl*. casser sa pipe (= *mourir*); *v/t*. *sl*. descendre (= *tuer*); **2.** c(r)oassement *m*; **ˈcroak·er** *fig*. prophète *m* de malheur; **ˈcroak·y** □ rauque, enroué (*voix*).

Cro·at [ˈkrouət] **1.** croate; **2.** Croate *mf*.

cro·chet [ˈkrouʃei] **1.** crochet *m*; **2.** *v/t*. faire (*qch*.) au crochet; *v/i*. faire du crochet.

crock [krɔk] **1.** pot *m* de terre; cruche *f*; F cheval *m* claqué; F *auto*: tacot *m*; F bonhomme *m* fini; F patraque *f* (= *personne maladive*); **2.** *sl*. (*usu*. ~ *up*) tomber malade, se faire abîmer; '**crock·er·y** faïence *f*, poterie *f*.

croc·o·dile zo. ['krɔkədail] crocodile *m*; *fig.* ~ *tears* pl larmes *f/pl.* de crocodile.

cro·cus ♀ ['kroukəs] crocus *m*.

croft·er *Brit.* ['krɔftə] petit fermier *m*.

crom·lech ['krɔmlek] dolmen *m*.

crone F [kroun] commère *f*, vieille *f*.

cro·ny F ['krouni] copain *m*; ami(e *f*) *m* intime.

crook [kruk] **1.** croc *m*, crochet *m*; *berger*: houlette *f*; *eccl.* crosse *f*; *fig.* angle *m*; *chemin etc.*: détour *m*, coude *m*; *sl.* escroc *m*; *sl.* fraude *f*; *on the* ~ malhonnête(ment); **2.** (se) recourber; **crooked** ['⌣kt] (re-)courbé; à béquille (*canne*); ['⌣kid] □ *fig.* tordu; tortueux (-euse *f*) (*chemin*); contourné (*jambe, arbre*); F déshonnête; oblique (*moyen*).

croon [kruːn] fredonner, chanter à demi-voix; '**croon·er** chanteur (-euse *f*) *m* de charme.

crop [krɔp] **1.** *oiseau*: jabot *m*; *fouet*: manche *m*; *stick m* (de chasse); récolte *f*, moisson *f*; *fruits*: cueillette *f*; *fig.* tas *m*; *cheveux*: coupe *f*; ~ *failure* mauvaise récolte *f*; F ~ *of hair* chevelure *f*; **2.** *v/t.* tondre, tailler, couper; brouter, paître (*l'herbe*); *v/i.* donner une récolte; ~ *up* géol. affleurer; F surgir; '**·eared** essorillé (*chien*); *hist.* aux cheveux coupés ras; '**crop·per** tondeur *m etc.* (*see crop* 2); (pigeon *m*) boulant *m*; F plante *f* qui donne bien ou mal; F culbute *f*; *Am. sl.* métayer *m*.

cro·quet ['kroukei] **1.** (jeu *m* de) croquet *m*; **2.** (*a. tight-*) croquer; (*a. loose-*~) roquer.

cro·sier eccl. ['krouʒə] crosse *f*.

cross [krɔs] **1.** croix *f* (*a. médaille, a. fig.*); croisement *m* (*de races*); métis(se *f*) *m*; *sl.* escroquerie *f*; **2.** □ (entre)croisé; mis en travers; oblique; contraire; maussade (*personne*); fâché (de qch., *at s.th.*; contre q., *with s.o.*); de mauvaise humeur; *sl.* illicite, déshonnête; *be at* ~ *purposes* y avoir malentendu; **3.** *v/t.* croiser (*deux choses, -aces, q. dans la rue*); traverser; passer (*la mer*); franchir (*le seuil*); barrer (*un chèque*); mettre les

barres à (*ses t*); *fig.* contrarier, contrebarrer (*q., un projet*); ~ *o.s.* se signer, faire le signe de la croix; ~ *out* biffer, rayer (*un mot etc.*); *v/i.* se croiser; passer; faire la traversée; '**·bar** foot. barre *f*; '**·beam** ⚟ sommier *m*; '**·bench** parl. Centre *m*; '**·bow** arbalète *f*; '**·breed** race *f* croisée; F métis(se *f*) *m*; '**·check 1.** contre-épreuve *f*; **2.** vérifier par contre-épreuve; '**·coun·try** à travers champs; ~ *running* le cross-country *m*; ~ *runner* crossman (*pl.* -men) *m*; ~ *skiing* ski *m* de randonnée; '**·cut saw** scie *f* de travers; '**·ex·am·i'na·tion** interrogatoire *m* contradictoire; ~**ex·am·ine** ['krɔsig'zæmin] contreinterroger; '**·fer·ti·li'za·tion** ♀ fécondation *f* croisée; *fig.* fécondation *f* mutuelle; '**·grained** tortillard (*bois*); *fig.* revêche; bourru; '**cross·ing** passage *m* (pour piétons); intersection *f* (*de voies*); 🚉 passage *m* à niveau; croisement *m* (*de lignes*); traversée *f*; '**cross·legged** les jambes croisées; '**cross·ness** mauvaise humeur *f*.

cross...: '**·patch** F grincheux (-euse *f*) *m*; grognon *mf*; ~ *ref·er·ence* renvoi *m*, référence *f*; '**·road** chemin *m* de traverse; ~s *pl. ou sg.* carrefour *m* (*a. fig.*); croisement *m* de routes; '**·sec·tion** coupe *f* en travers; ~ *talk* répliques *f/pl.*, échange *m* de propos; *radio etc.*: interférence *f*; '**·walk** *Am.* passage *m* clouté; '**·wind** vent *m* de travers; '**·wise** en croix, en travers; '**·word puz·zle** mots *m/pl.* croisés.

crotch [krɔtʃ] fourche *f*; **crotch·et** ['⌣it] crochet *m*; ♪ noire *f*; F lubie *f*; '**crotch·et·y** F capricieux (-euse *f*); (à l'humeur) difficile.

crouch [krautʃ] se blottir, s'accroupir (devant, *to*).

croup[1] [kruːp] croupe *f* (*de cheval*).

croup[2] 🩺 [⌣] croup *m*.

crou·pi·er ['kruːpiə] croupier *m*.

crow [krou] **1.** corneille *f*; chant *m* du coq; *Am.* F *eat* ~ avaler des couleuvres; *have a* ~ *to pick with* avoir maille à partir avec; *as the* ~ *flies* à vol d'oiseau; **2.** [*irr.*] chanter; *fig.* chanter victoire (sur, *over*); gazouiller (*enfant*); '**·bar** levier *m*, pied-de-biche (*pl.* pieds-de-biche) *m*.

crowd [kraud] **1.** foule *f*, rassemblement *m*, affluence *f*; F tas *m*; F bande *f*; *péj.* monde *m*; **2.** *v/t.* serrer; remplir (de, *with*); *v/i.* se presser (en foule); s'attrouper; ~ **out** *v/t.* ne pas laisser de place à; *v/i.* sortir en foule; ♣ ~ **sail** (on) faire force de voiles; ~ed **hours** *pl.* heures *f/pl.* de pointe.

crow·foot ⚘ ['kroufut] renoncule *f*.

crown [kraun] **1.** *roi, dent, fleurs, monnaie, etc.*: couronne *f*; *bonheur etc.*: comble *m*; *carrière*: couronnement *m*; *chapeau*: forme *f*; *tête*: sommet *m*; *arbre*: cime *f*; *mot.* axe *m* (de la chaussée); **2.** couronner; sacrer (*roi*); F mettre le comble à; '**crown·ing** *fig.* suprême; final (-als *m/pl.*).

crow's... [krouz]: '~**-foot** patte *f* d'oie (*au coin de l'œil*); '~**-nest** ♣ nid *m* de pie.

cru·cial □ ['kru:ʃəl] décisif (-ive *f*); critique; **cru·ci·ble** ['kru:sibl] creuset *m* (*a. fig.*); **cru·ci·fix** ['~fiks] crucifix *m*; **cru·ci·fix·ion** [~'fikʃn] crucifixion *f*; mise *f* en croix; '**cru·ci·form** cruciforme; **cru·ci·fy** ['~fai] crucifier (*a. fig.*).

crude □ [kru:d] **1.** (à l'état) brut (*métal, matériel, huile, etc.*); cru (*a. lumière, couleur*); vert, aigre (*fruit*); brutal (-aux *m/pl.*); grossier (-ère *f*) (*style*); fruste (*manières*); 𝄞 non encore développé (*maladie*), non assimilé (*aliment*); '**crude·ness**, **cru·di·ty** ['~iti] crudité *f* (*a. fig.*).

cru·el □ ['kruəl] cruel(le *f*) (*a. fig.*); '**cru·el·ty** cruauté *f*.

cru·et ['kru:it] burette *f*; '~**-stand** ménagère *f*.

cruise ♣ [kru:z] **1.** croisière *f*; voyage *m* d'agrément; ✕ ~ **missile** engin *m* atmosphérique; **2.** ♣ croiser; **cruising speed** vitesse *f* économique; '**cruis·er** ♣ croiseur *m*; **light** ~ contre-torpilleur *m*; *Am.* voiture *f* cellulaire; *box.* ~ **weight** poids *m* milourd.

crul·ler *Am.* ['krʌlə] *cuis.* roussette *f*.

crumb [krʌm] **1.** *pain*: miette *f*; *fig.* brin *m*; **2.** *cuis.* paner (*la viande etc.*); *a.* = **crum·ble** ['~bl] (s')émietter (*pain*); *v/t. fig.* réduire en miettes; *v/i.* s'écrouler (*maison etc.*); s'ébouler (*sol*); '**crum·bling**, '**crum·bly** friable, ébouleux (-euse

f); **crumb·y** ['krʌmi] qui s'émiette; couvert de miettes.

crum·my *sl.* ['krʌmi] minable, moche.

crump *sl.* [krʌmp] chute *f*; coup *m* violent; ✕ obus *m* qui éclate.

crum·pet ['krʌmpit] sorte de brioche grillée (*plate et poreuse*); *sl.* caboche *f* (= *tête*); **be off one's** ~ être maboul (= *fou*).

crum·ple ['krʌmpl] *v/t.* froisser, friper; *v/i.* se froisser; se recroqueviller (*parchemin, feuilles*); *fig.* s'effondrer.

crunch [krʌntʃ] *v/t.* croquer, broyer (*avec les dents*); écraser; *v/i.* craquer; s'écraser.

cru·ral ['kruərəl] *anat.* crural (-aux *m/pl.*).

cru·sade [kru:'seid] **1.** croisade *f*; (*a. fig.*); **2.** aller *ou* être en croisade; *fig.* mener une campagne (*contre qch.*); **cru·sad·er** croisé *m*.

crush [krʌʃ] **1.** écrasement *m*; F presse *f*, foule *f*; *sl.* **have a** ~ avoir un béguin (pour, *on*); ~ **hat** claque *m*; *Am.* chapeau *m* mou; **2.** *v/t.* écraser, aplatir; froisser (*une robe*); *fig.* anéantir; accabler (*de douleur etc.*); † vider (*une bouteille*); ~ **out** *v/t.* étouffer; *v/i.* se presser en foule; *Am. sl.* flirter; '**crush·er** broyeur *m*; F malheur *m etc.* accablant; coup *m* d'assommoir; '**crush-room** *théâ.* foyer *m*.

crust [krʌst] **1.** croûte *f*; *Am. sl.* toupet *m*; **2.** (se) couvrir d'une croûte; '**crust·ed** qui a du dépôt (*vin*); *fig.* invétéré; '**crust·y** □ qui a une forte croûte; *fig.* bourru.

crutch [krʌtʃ] béquille *f*; '**crutched** à béquille; à poignée à croisillon.

crux [krʌks] *fig.* nœud *m*; point *m* capital.

cry [krai] **1.** cri *m*; plainte *f*; pleurs *m/pl.*; **it is a far** ~ **from ... to** il y a loin de ... à (*a. fig.*); **within** ~ à portée de voix; **2.** crier; *v/i.* s'écrier, pousser un cri *ou* des cris; pleurer; ~ **for** demander en pleurant; crier à (*le secours*); réclamer; ~ **off** se dédire; s'excuser; annuler (*une affaire*); ~ **out** *v/t.* crier; *v/i.* s'écrier, pousser des cris; se récrier (contre, *against*); ~ **up** prôner, vanter; '~**-ba·by** pleurard(e *f*) *m*; '**cry·ing** *fig.* criant, urgent; scandaleux (-euse *f*).

crypt [kript] crypte *f*; **'cryp·tic** occulte, secret (-ète *f*); énigmatique.

crys·tal ['kristl] **1.** cristal *m*; *surt. Am.* verre *m* de montre; **2.** cristallin, limpide; **'~-clear** clair comme le jour *ou* comme de l'eau de roche; **crys·tal·line** ['~təlain] cristallin, de cristal; **crys·tal·i·za·tion** cristallisation *f*; **'crys·tal·lize** cristalliser; **~d** candi (*fruits*).

cub [kʌb] **1.** petit *m* (*d'un animal*); *ours*: ourson *m*; lionceau *m*, louveteau *m*, renardeau *m*, *etc.*; **2.** *v/t.* mettre bas (*des petits*); *v/i.* faire des petits.

cu·bage ['kju:bidʒ] cubage *m*.

cub·by-hole ['kʌbihoul] retraite *f*; placard *m*.

cube ⚥ ['kju:b] **1.** cube *m*; ~ **root** racine *f* cubique; **2.** cuber.

cub·hood ['kʌbhud] adolescence *f*.

cu·bic, **cu·bi·cal** □ ['kju:bik(l)] cubique.

cu·bi·cle ['kju:bikl] *dortoir*: alcôve *f*; *piscine etc.*: cabine *f*.

cuck·old ['kʌkəld] **1.** cocu *m*; **2.** cocufier (*son mari*).

cuck·oo ['kuku:] **1.** coucou *m*; **2.** *sl.* maboul, loufoque (= *fou*).

cu·cum·ber ['kju:kəmbə] concombre *m*.

cu·cur·bit [kju'kə:bit] ⚥ courge *f*; *alambic*: cucurbite *f*.

cud [kʌd] bol *m* alimentaire; *chew the ~* ruminer (*a. fig.*).

cud·dle ['kʌdl] **1.** F embrassade *f*; **2.** *v/t.* serrer doucement dans ses bras; *v/i.* se peloter.

cudg·el ['kʌdʒl] **1.** gourdin *m*; *take up the ~s for* prendre fait et cause pour; **2.** bâtonner; ~ *one's brains* se creuser la cervelle (pour *inf.*, *for gér.*; *pour*, *about*).

cue [kju:] *billard*: queue *f*; *surt. théâ.* réplique *f*; avis *m*, mot *m*; *take the ~ from s.o.* prendre exemple sur q.

cuff[1] [kʌf] **1.** calotte *f*, taloche *f*; **2.** calotter, flanquer une taloche à (*q.*).

cuff[2] [~] *chemise*: poignet *m*; manchette *f* (*empesée*); *jaquette etc.*: parement *m*; *Am.* pantalon: bord *m* relevé.

cui·rass [kwi'ræs] cuirasse *f*.

cui·sine [kwi'zi:n] cuisine *f*.

cu·li·nar·y ['kʌlinəri] culinaire.

cull [kʌl] (re)cueillir; choisir (dans, *from*).

cul·ly *sl.* ['kʌli] copain *m*, camaro *m*.

culm [kʌlm] ⚥ chaume *m*, tige *f*.

cul·mi·nate ['kʌlmineit] *astr.* culminer; *fig.* atteindre son apogée; *fig.* terminer (par, *in*); **cul·mi·na·tion** *astr.* culmination *f*; *fig.* point *m* culminant.

cu·lottes [kju:'lɔts] *pl.* (*a pair of ~* une) jupe-culotte *f* (*pl.* jupes-culottes).

cul·pa·bil·i·ty [kʌlpə'biliti] culpabilité *f*; **'cul·pa·ble** □ coupable; digne de blâme.

cul·prit ['kʌlprit] coupable *mf*; prévenu(e *f*) *m*.

cult [kʌlt] culte *m*.

cul·ti·va·ble ['kʌltivəbl] cultivable.

cul·ti·vate ['kʌltiveit] *usu.* cultiver; *biol.* faire une culture de (*un bacille*); **cul·ti·va·tion** culture *f*; **'cul·ti·va·tor** *personne*: cultivateur (-trice *f*) *m*; *machine*: cultivateur *m*, extirpateur *m*; *fig.* ami *m*.

cul·tur·al □ ['kʌltʃərəl] culturel (-le *f*); ✔ cultural (-aux *m/pl.*).

cul·ture ['kʌltʃə] culture *f*; **'cul·tured** cultivé, lettré; **cul·ture me·di·um**, *pl.* **-di·a** *biol.* bouillon *m* de culture; **'cul·ture-pearl** perle *f* japonaise.

cul·vert ['kʌlvət] ponceau *m*, canal *m*; ⚡ conduit *m* souterrain.

cum·ber ['kʌmbə] encombrer, gêner (de, *with*); **~·some** ['~səm], **cum·brous** □ ['~brəs] encombrant, gênant; difficile à remuer; lourd; entravant.

cum·in ⚥ ['kʌmin] cumin *m*.

cu·mu·la·tive □ ['kju:mjulətiv] cumulatif (-ive *f*); **cu·mu·lus** ['~ləs], *pl.* **-li** ['~lai] cumulus *m*.

cu·ne·i·form ['kju:niifɔ:m] cunéiforme.

cun·ning ['kʌniŋ] **1.** □ rusé; astucieux (-euse *f*); malin (-igne *f*); *Am.* mignon(ne *f*); **2.** ruse *f*; *péj.* astuce *f*.

cup [kʌp] **1.** tasse *f*; *métal*: gobelet *m*; *soutien-gorge*: bonnet *m*; *Am. cuis.* demi-pinte *f*; calice *m* (*a.* ⚥, *a. fig.*); *sp.* coupe *f*; *sp.* ~ *final* finale *f* de la coupe; *sp.* ~ *tie* match *m* de coupe; **2.** ✿ ventouser; mettre (*la main*) en cornet *ou* en porte-voix; **~·board** ['kʌbəd] armoire *f*; *mur*: placard *m*; F ~ *love* amour *m* intéressé.

Cu·pid ['kju:pid] Cupidon *m*, Amour *m*.

cu·pid·i·ty [kju'piditi] cupidité *f*.

cu·po·la ['kju:pələ] coupole *f* (*a.* ✕, ⚓); dôme *m*.

cup·ping-glass ✗ ['kʌpiŋgla:s] ventouse *f*.

cu·pre·ous ['kju:priəs] cuivreux (-euse *f*).

cur [kə:] roquet *m*; chien *m* sans race; F cuistre *m*.

cur·a·bil·i·ty [kjuərə'biliti] curabilité *f*; '**cur·a·ble** guérissable.

cu·ra·cy ['kjuərəsi] vicariat *m*; **cu·rate** ['⁓rit] vicaire *m*; **cu·ra·tor** [⁓'reitə] *musée:* conservateur *m*.

curb [kə:b] **1.** gourmette *f*; *fig.* frein *m*; (*a.* ⁓stone) bordure *f* (*de trottoir*); margelle *f* (*de puits*); **2.** gourmer (*un cheval*); *fig.* contenir, refréner; ⁓ **mar·ket** *Am. Bourse:* coulisse *f*; ⁓ **roof** toit *m* en mansarde.

curd [kə:d] **1.** (lait *m*) caillé *m*; **2.** (*usu.* **cur·dle** ['⁓dl]) se cailler (*lait*); F se figer (*sang*).

cure [kjuə] **1.** guérison *f*; cure *f* (*de raisins, de lait, etc.*); remède *m*; ⁓ *of souls* cure *f* d'âmes; **2.** guérir; saurer (*des harengs*); saler (*les peaux, la viande*); fumer (*la viande*); '⁓-**all** panacée *f*.

cur·few ['kə:fju:] couvre-feu *m* (*a. pol.*); *ring the* ⁓(-*bell*) sonner le couvre-feu.

cu·ri·o ['kjuəriou] curiosité *f*; bibelot *m*; **cu·ri·os·i·ty** [⁓'ɔsiti] curiosité *f*; F excentrique *m*; '**cu·ri·ous** ☐ curieux (-euse *f*); singulier (-ère *f*); *péj.* indiscret (-ète *f*).

curl [kə:l] **1.** *cheveux:* boucle *f*, fumée, *vague:* spirale *f*; **2.** boucler; *v/t.* friser; ⁓ *one's lip* faire la moue; *v/i.* s'élever en spirales (*fumée*); ⁓ *up* (*ou s. os. up*) se mettre en boule (*chat etc.*); '**curl·er** bigoudi *m*, rouleau *m*.

curl·ing ['kə:liŋ] *sp.* curling *m*; '⁓-**i·ron**, '⁓-**tongs** *pl.* fer *m* à friser, frisoir *m*; '**curl·y** bouclé, frisé; en spirale.

cur·mudg·eon [kə:'mʌdʒn] bourru *m*; grippe-sou (*pl.* grippe-sou[s]) *m*.

cur·rant ['kʌrənt] groseille *f*; (*a. dried* ⁓) raisin *m* de Corinthe.

cur·ren·cy ['kʌrənsi] circulation *f*, cours *m*; ✝ (terme *m* d')échéance *f*; ✝ espèces *f/pl.* de cours; monnaie *f*; *fig.* vogue *f*, idées: crédit *m*; '**cur·**rent 1. ☐ en cours, courant (*argent, compte, mois, prix, opinion, etc.*); reçu (*opinion*); qui court (*bruit*); ⁓ *events pl.* actualités *f/pl.*; ⁓ *hand* (-*writing*) (écriture *f*) courante *f*; ⁓ *pass* ⁓ avoir cours, être accepté *ou* en vogue; ⁓ *issue* dernier numéro *m* (*d'une publication*); ⁓ *problem* question *f* d'actualité; **2.** courant *m* (*a.* ⚡, *a.* d'air); fil *m* de l'eau; *fig.* cours *m*, marche *f*; ⊕ *jet m* (*d'air*); ⚡ ⁓ *impulse* impulsion *f* de courant; ⁓ *junction* prise *f* de courant.

cur·ric·u·lum [kə'rikjuləm], *pl.* -**la** [⁓lə] programme *m ou* plan *m* d'études.

cur·ri·er ['kʌriə] corroyeur *m*.

cur·rish ☐ ['kə:riʃ] *fig.* chien *m* de; qui ne vaut pas mieux qu'un roquet.

cur·ry[1] ['kʌri] **1.** *poudre, plat:* cari *m*, curry *m*; **2.** apprêter au cari; *curried eggs pl.* œufs *m/pl.* à l'indienne.

cur·ry[2] [⁓] corroyer (*le cuir*); étriller (*un cheval*); ⁓ *favo(u)r with* s'insinuer dans les bonnes grâces de (*q.*); '⁓-**comb** étrille *f*.

curse [kə:s] **1.** malédiction *f*, anathème *m*; juron *m*; *fig.* fléau *m*; **2.** *v/i.* blasphémer, jurer; *v/t.* maudire; **curs·ed** ☐ ['kə:sid] maudit; F sacré.

cur·sive ['kə:siv] cursif (-ive *f*); ⁓ *handwriting* cursive *f*.

cur·so·ry ☐ ['kə:səri] rapide; superficiel(le *f*).

curt ☐ [kə:t] brusque; sec (sèche *f*); cassant.

cur·tail [kə:'teil] raccourcir; tronquer; *fig.* restreindre; *fig.* enlever (de, *of*); **cur·tail·ment** raccourcissement *m*; restriction *f*.

cur·tain ['kə:tn] **1.** rideau *m* (*a. fig.*); *fig.* voile *m*; ✕ courtine *f*; rideau *m* (*de feu*); **2.** garnir de rideaux; ⁓ *off* séparer *ou* dissimuler par des rideaux; '⁓-**fire** ✕ (tir *m* de) barrage *m*; ⁓ **lec·ture** F semonce *f* conjugale; '⁓-**rais·er** théâ., *a. fig.* lever *m* de rideau.

curt·s(e)y ['kə:tsi] **1.** révérence *f*; *drop a* ⁓ = **2.** faire une révérence (à, *to*).

cur·va·ture ['kə:vətʃə] courbure *f*; ⁓ *of the spine* déviation *f* de la colonne vertébrale.

curve [kə:v] **1.** courbe *f*; *rue:* tournant *m*; *mot.* virage *m*; *Am. base-*

ball: balle *f* qui a de l'effet; **2.** (se) courber; *v/i.* décrire une courbe.

cush·ion ['kuʃn] **1.** coussin *m*; bourrelet *m*; *billard*: bande *f*; *mot.* ~ *tyre* bandage *m* plein avec canal à air; **2.** garnir de coussins; rembourrer; *fig.* amortir (*des coups*); ⊕ matelasser.

cush·y *sl.* ['kuʃi] facile; F pépère.

cusp [kʌsp] pointe *f*; *lune*: corne *f*; ♀ cuspide *f*; ♈ point *m* de rebroussement, sommet *m*.

cuss *Am.* F [kʌs] **1.** juron *m*; *co.* type *m*; *it's not worth a* ~ ça ne vaut pas chipette; **2.** jurer; **'cuss·ed** ['kʌsid] sacré; têtu.

cus·tard ['kʌstəd] crème *f*; œufs *m/pl.* au lait.

cus·to·di·an [kʌs'toudjən] gardien (-ne *f*) *m*; *musée*: conservateur *m*; **cus·to·dy** ['kʌstədi] garde *f*; emprisonnement *m*, détention *f*.

cus·tom ['kʌstəm] coutume *f*, usage *m*, habitude *f*; ⁇ droit *m* coutumier; ♀ clientèle *f*; patronage *m* (*du client*); **cus·tom·ar·y** ['~əri] □ habituel(le *f*); d'usage; coutumier (-ère *f*) (*droit*); **'cus·tom·er** client(e *f*) *m*; *boutique*: chaland(e *f*) *m*; F type *m*; **'cus·tom-house** (bureau *m* de la) douane *f*; ~ *officer* douanier *m*; **'cus·tom-made** *Am.* fait sur commande; **'cus·toms** *pl.* douane *f*; ~ *clearance* dédouanement *m*, expédition *f* douanière; ~ *duty* droits *m/pl.* de douane; ~ *inspection* visite *f* douanière; ~ *officer* douanier *m*.

cut [kʌt] **1.** coupe *f* (*a. vêtements*); coupure *f* (*théâ., a. blessure*); *sp.*, *épée, fouet*: coup *m*; *pierre*, ⊕ *lime*: taille *f*; *réduction f* (*de salaire*); gravure *f* (sur bois); *cuis.* morceau *m*; *unkindest* ~ *of all* coup *m* de pied de l'âne; (*a. short*-~) raccourci *m*; *cheveux*: taille *f*, coupe *f*; ⚡ coupure *f* (*de courant*); 🛤 tranchée *f*; ⚒ havage *m*; ⚔ incision *f*; ♫ enture *f*; *cartes*: tirage *m* (*pour les places*); F revers *m*; F absence *f* sans permission; *iro.* sarcasme *m* blessant; *fig.* refus *m* de saluer; *cuis.* cold ~s *pl.* tranches *f/pl.* de viande froide; F *give s.o. the* ~ (*direct*) passer près de q.; tourner le dos à q.; **2.** [*irr.*] *v/t.* couper (*a. cartes*), tailler; (*a.* ~ *in slices*) trancher; hacher (*le tabac*); ⚓ filer (*le câble*); réduire (*le prix*); *mot.* prendre (*un virage*); F

manquer exprès à; F sécher (*une classe*); F abandonner; ~ *s.o. dead* passer q. sans le saluer, tourner le dos à q.; ~ *one's finger* se couper le *ou* au doigt; *he is* ~*ting his teeth* ses dents percent; F ~ *a figure* faire figure; ~ *short* couper la parole à (*q.*); *to* ~ *a long story short* pour abréger, en fin de compte; *v/i.* (se) couper; percer (*dent*); ~ *and come again* revenir au plat; F ~ *and run* déguerpir, filer; ~ *back* rabattre (*un arbre*); F rebrousser chemin; ~ *down* abattre; couper (*un arbre, le blé*); réduire (*une distance, le prix*); (ra)baisser (*le prix*); restreindre (*la production*); raccourcir (*une jupe*); abréger (*un livre etc.*); ~ *in* v/i. intervenir; *mot.* couper; ~ *off* couper (*a. fig., a. téléph.*) (de, *from*); trancher; *fig.* priver; *fig.* déshériter; ~ *out* couper; découper (*des images*); tailler (*une robe, une statue*); *Am.* détacher (*des bêtes*) d'un troupeau; *fig.* supplanter (q.); évincer (auprès de, *with*); *fig.* cesser; supprimer; abandonner; ⚡ mettre hors circuit; faire taire (*la radio*), supprimer; ⚔ exciser; *be* ~ *out for* être taillé pour (*qch.*); *have one's work* ~ *out* avoir de quoi faire; *he had his work* ~ *out for him* on lui avait taillé de la besogne; *sl.* ~ *it out!* pas de ça!; ça suffit!; ~ *up* (dé)couper; tailler (*par morceaux, en pièces*); *fig.* affliger; critiquer sévèrement; ~ *up rough* se fâcher; **3.** coupé *etc.*; *sl.* ivre; ~ *flowers pl.* fleurs *f/pl.* coupées; ~ *glass* cristal *m* taillé; ~ *and dry* (*ou* dried) tout fait; tout taillé (*travail*).

cu·ta·ne·ous [kju'teinjəs] cutané.

cut·a·way ['kʌtəwei] (*a.* ~ *coat*) jaquette *f*.

cut·back ['kʌtbæk] *cin.* retour *m* en arrière.

cute □ F [kju:t] malin (-igne *f*); *Am.* F gentil(le *f*), coquet(te *f*).

cu·ti·cle ['kju:tikl] *anat.* épiderme *m*; ♀ cuticule *f*; ~ *scissors pl.* ciseaux *m/pl.* de manucure.

cut·in ['kʌt'in] *cin.* scène *f* raccord; ⚡ conjoncteur *m*.

cut·lass ['kʌtləs] ⚓ sabre *m* d'abordage; *Am.* couteau *m* de chasse.

cut·ler ['kʌtlə] coutelier *m*; **'cut·ler·y** coutellerie *f* (♀ et argenterie *f* de table); *canteen of* ~ ménagère *f*.

cut·let ['kʌtlit] *mouton, agneau:* côtelette *f; veau:* escalope *f.*

cut...: '~-**off** *Am.* raccourci *m; attr.* ⊕ de détente; *cin.* de sûreté; d'obscuration; '~-**out** *mot.* clapet *m* d'échappement libre; ⚡ coupe-circuit *m/inv.; cin.* déchet *m* de film; *Am.* décor *m etc.* découpé; '~-**price,** '~-**rate** ✝ à prix réduit; '**cut·ter** coupeur *m (a. de vêtements); pierre etc.:* tailleur *m; cin.* monteur (-euse *f) m;* ✂ *personne:* abatteur *m (de charbon);* haveur *m; machine:* haveuse *f;* ⊕ coupoir *m,* couteau *m;* ⚓ canot *m;* patache *f (de la douane); Am.* traîneau *m;* '**cut-throat 1.** coupe-jarret *m;* F rasoir *m* à manche; **2.** de coupe-jarret; *fig.* acharné; ~ **bridge** bridge *m* à trois; '**cut·ting 1.** ▢ tranchant; cinglant *(vent);* ⊕ *a.* de coupe, à couper; ~ **edge** coupant *m; outil:* fil *m;* ~ **nippers** *pl.* pinces *f/pl.* coupantes; **2.** coupe *f;* ⊕ cisaillage *m; bijou, vêtement:* taille *f;* 🌿 déblai *m;* tranchée *f;* 🌿 bouture *f; journal:* coupure *f;* ~**s** *pl.* bouts *m/pl.;* ⊕ copeaux *m/pl.;* rognures *f/pl.*

cut·tle *zo.* ['kʌtl] *(usu.* ~-**fish**) seiche *f,* sépia *f;* '~-**bone** os *m* de seiche; biscuit *m* de mer.

cy·a·nide 🜍 ['saiənaid] cyanure *m;* ~ **of** *potassium* prussiate *m* de potasse.

cyc·la·men ['sikləmən] cyclamen *m.*

cy·cle ['saikl] **1.** cycle *m;* période *f;* ⊕ cycle *m* (d'opérations); ✝ *a.* ~**s** *pl.* (periode *f* de) vogue *f;* bicyclette *f; mot. four-*~ engine moteur *m* à quatre temps; **2.** faire de la *ou* aller à bicyclette; **cy·clic, cy·cli·cal** ▢ ['siklik(l)] cyclique; **cy·cling** ['saiklin] **1.** cycliste; de cyclisme; **2.** cyclisme *m;* '**cy·clist** cycliste *mf.*

cy·clone ['saikloun] cyclone *m.*

cy·clo·p(a)e·di·a [saiklə'pi:djə] encyclopédie *f.*

cyg·net ['signit] jeune cygne *m.*

cyl·in·der ['silində] cylindre *m; revolver:* barillet *m; machine à écrire:* rouleau *m* porte-papier; **cy'lin·dric, cy'lin·dri·cal** ▢ cylindrique.

cym·bal ♪ ['simbl] cymbale *f.*

cyn·ic ['sinik] **1.** (*a.* '**cyn·i·cal** ▢) cynique; sceptique; **2.** *phls.* cynique *m;* sceptique *m;* **cyn·i·cism** ['~sizm] *phls.* cynisme *m;* scepticisme *m* railleur.

cy·no·sure *fig.* ['sinəsjuə] point *m* de mire.

cy·press 🌿 ['saipris] cyprès *m.*

cyst [sist] sac *m;* ⚕, *a.* 🌿 kyste *m;* '**cyst·ic** kystique, cystique; **cys·ti·tis** [sis'taitis] cystite *f.*

Czar [za:] tsar *m.*

Czech [tʃek] **1.** tchèque; **2.** *ling.* tchèque *m;* Tchèque *mf.*

Czech·o-Slo·vak ['tʃekou'slouvæk] **1.** tchécoslovaque; **2.** Tchécoslovaque *mf.*

D

D, d [di:] D *m*, d *m*.
'd F *see* had; would.
dab [dæb] **1.** coup *m* léger; tape *f*; tache *f*; petit morceau *m* (*de beurre*); *icht.* limande *f*; F expert *m*; *sl.* ~s *pl.* empreintes *f/pl.* digitales; *be a* ~ (*hand*) *at* être passé maître en (*qch.*); **2.** lancer une tape à; tapoter; appliquer légèrement (*des couleurs*); *typ.* clicher.
dab·ble ['dæbl] *v/t.* humecter; mouiller; *v/i.* ~ *in* barboter dans; *fig.* s'occuper un peu de; **'dab·bler** dilettante *mf.*
dac·ty·lo·gram [dæk'tilogræm] dactylogramme *m*.
dad(·dy) F ['dæd(i)] papa *m*.
dad·dy-long-legs *zo.* F ['dædi'loŋlegz] tipule *f*.
daf·fo·dil ♀ ['dæfədil] narcisse *m* sauvage *ou* des bois.
dag·ger ['dægə] poignard *m*; *be at* ~s *drawn* être à couteaux tirés; *look* ~s *at s.o.* foudroyer q. du regard.
dag·gle ['dægl] (se) mouiller.
da·go *Am. sl. péj.* ['deigou] Espagnol *m*, Portugais *m*, *surt.* Italien *m*.
dahl·ia ♀ ['deiljə] dahlia *m*.
Dail Eir·eann ['dail'ɛərən] *Chambre des députés de l'État libre d'Irlande.*
dai·ly ['deili] **1.** quotidien(ne *f*); F ~ *dozen* gymnastique *f* quotidienne; **2.** quotidien *m*, journal *m*; domestique *f* à la journée.
dain·ti·ness ['deintinis] délicatesse *f*, raffinement *m*; *taille*: mignonncsse *f*; **'dain·ty** □ **1.** délicat (*personne, a. chose*); friand (*mets*); exquis (*personne*); F mignon(ne *f*); **2.** friandise *f*; morceau *m* de choix.
dair·y ['dɛəri] laiterie *f* (*a. boutique*); crémerie *f*; '~-**farm** vacherie *f*; '~-**maid** fille *f* de laiterie; '~-**man** nourrisseur *m*; † laitier *m*, crémier *m*.
da·is ['deiis] estrade *f*; dais *m*.
dai·sy ['deizi] ♀ marguerite *f*; F pâquerette *f*; F personne *f ou* chose *f* épatante; (*as*) *fresh as a* ~ frais (fraîche *f*) comme une rose; F *push up*

the daisies manger les pissenlits par la racine (= *être mort*).
dale [deil] vallée *f*, vallon *m*.
dal·li·ance ['dæliəns] échange *m* de tendresses; flirtage *m*; badinage *m*; tarder.
dal·ly ['ʌli] flirter (avec, *with*); caresser (qch., *with s.th.*); badiner; *fig.* tarder.
dam[1] [dæm] mère *f* (*d'animaux*).
dam[2] [~] **1.** barrage *m* de retenue; digue *f*; ✗ serrement *m*; *rivière*: décharge *f*; **2.** (*a.* ~ *up*) contenir, endiguer; obstruer.
dam·age ['dæmidʒ] **1.** dégâts *m/pl.*; ✗✗ ~s *pl.* dommages-intérêts *m/pl.*; **2.** endommager; abîmer; *fig.* nuire à (*q.*); **'dam·age·a·ble** avariable.
dam·a·scene ['dæməsi:n] damasquiner; **dam·ask** ['dæməsk] **1.** damas *m*; *couleur*: incarnat *m*; **2.** rose foncé *adj./inv.*; vermeil(le *f*); **3.** damasquiner (*l'acier*); damasser (*une étoffe*).
dame [deim] dame *f* (*a. titre*); *sl.* femme *f*; madame *f*.
damn [dæm] **1.** condamner; ruiner; *eccl.* damner; *théâ.* éreinter (*une pièce*); ~ *it!* zut!, sapristi!; **2.** juron *m*, gros mot *m*; *I don't care a* ~! je m'en moque pas mal!, je m'en fiche!; **dam·na·ble** □ ['~nəbl] damnable, F maudit; **dam·na·tion** [~'neiʃn] damnation *f*; *théâ.* éreintement *m*; ~! sacrebleu!; **dam·na·to·ry** ['~nətəri] □ qui condamne; **damned** ['dæmd] *adj. et adv.* damné, F sacré (*a.* = *très, bigrement*); **damn·ing** ['dæmiŋ] accablant (*fait*).
damp [dæmp] **1.** humide; moite; **2.** humidité *f*; *peau*: moiteur *f*; *fig.* froid *m*; nuage *m* de tristesse; ✗ (*a.* choke-~) mofette *f*; ⚡, ⊕ ~ *course* couche *f* isolante; **3.** (*a.* '**damp·en**) mouiller; humecter; assourdir (*un son*); étouffer (*le feu*); refroidir (*le courage etc.*); décourager; '**damp·er** rabat-joie *m/inv.*; *fig.* froid *m*; *mot.* amortisseur *m*; ♪ étouffoir *m*; *foyer*: registre *m*; '**damp·ish**

un peu humide *ou* moite; **'damp-proof** imperméable.

dam·son ♀ ['dæmzn] prune *f* de Damas.

dance [dɑːns] **1.** danse *f*; bal (*pl.* -s) *m*; F sauterie *f*; *lead s.o. a* ~ donner du fil à retordre à q.; faire danser q.; **2.** danser; **'danc·er** danseur (-euse *f*) *m*.

danc·ing ['dɑːnsiŋ] danse *f*; *attr.* de danse; '~**-girl** bayadère *f*; '~**-les-son** leçon *f* de danse; '~**-room** dancing *m*.

dan·de·li·on ♀ [dændi'laiən] pissen-lit *m*.

dan·der *sl.* ['dændə]: *get s.o.'s* ~ *up* mettre q. en colère; *get one's* ~ *up* prendre la mouche.

dan·dle ['dændl] dodeliner (*un en-fant*); faire sauter (*un enfant sur ses genoux*).

dan·driff ['dændrif], **dan·druff** ['dændrəf] pellicules *f/pl.*

dan·dy ['dændi] **1.** dandy *m*, gom-meux *m*; **2.** *int. surt. Am.* F chic *inv. en genre*, chouette, *sl.* bath; **dan·dy·ish** ['~diiʃ] élégant, gom-meux (-euse *f*); **'dan·dy·ism** dan-dysme *m*.   [danois *m.*]

Dane [dein] Danois(e *f*) *m*; *chien*:]

dan·ger ['deindʒə] danger *m*, péril *m*; ~ *list*: F *be on the* ~ être dans un état grave; **'dan·ger·ous** □ dange-reux (-euse *f*); **dan·ger sig·nal** 🚩 (signal *m* à l')arrêt *m*.

dan·gle ['dæŋgl] (faire) pendiller, pendre; balancer; ~ *about* (*ou after ou round*) tourner autour de (*q.*); **'dan·gler** (*ou* ~ *after women*) soupi-rant *m*.

Dan·ish ['deiniʃ] **1.** danois; **2.** *ling.* danois *m*; *the* ~ *pl.* les Danois *m/pl.*

dank [dæŋk] humide.

dap·per □ F ['dæpə] pimpant, co-quet(te *f*), correct; sémillant.

dap·ple ['dæpl] **1.** (se) tacheter; *v/i.* se pommeler (*ciel*); **2.** tache(ture) *f*; **'dap·pled** tacheté, pommelé; **'dap·ple-'grey** (cheval *m*) gris pommelé.

dare [dɛə] *v/i.* oser; *I* ~ *say* je (le) crois bien; sans doute; peut-être bien; *v/t.* oser faire; braver, risquer (*la mort*); défier (*q.*); '~**-dev·il** casse-cou *m/inv.*; **'dar·ing** □ **1.** audacieux (-euse *f*); **2.** audace *f*, hardiesse *f*.

dark [dɑːk] **1.** □ *usu.* sombre; ob-scur; triste; foncé (*couleur*); basané

(*teint*); ténébreux (-euse *f*); *the* ~ *ages* l'âge *m* des ténèbres; ~ *horse* cheval *m* dont on ne sait rien; *fig.* concurrent *m* que l'on ne croyait pas dangereux; ~ *lantern* lanterne *f* sourde; ~ *room* chambre *f* noire; **2.** obscurité *f*, ténèbres *f/pl.*; *fig.* ignorance *f*; *leap in the* ~ saut *m* dans l'inconnu; **'dark·en** (s')ob-scurcir; (s')assombrir; *v/t.* attrister; embrumer; *never* ~ *s.o.'s door* ne plus remettre les pieds chez q.; **'dark·ish** un peu sombre; **'dark-ness** obscurité *f*, ténèbres *f/pl.*; **dark·some** *poét.* ['~səm] *see* dark 1; **'dark·y** F moricaud(e *f*) *m*.

dar·ling ['dɑːliŋ] **1.** bien-aimé(e *f*) *m*; chéri(e *f*) *m*; **2.** bien-aimé; favo-ri(te *f*).

darn[1] *sl.* [dɑːn] *see* damn 1; *a. int.* sacré.

darn[2] [~] **1.** reprise *f*; **2.** repriser, raccommoder; (*a. fine-*~) stopper; **'darn·er** repriseur (-euse *f*) *m etc.*

darn·ing ['dɑːniŋ] reprise *f*; '~**-nee-dle** aiguille *f* à repriser; '~**-wool** laine *f* à repriser.

dart [dɑːt] **1.** dard *m*, trait *m* (*a. fig.*); *couture*: pince *f*, suçon *m*; élan *m*, mouvement *m* soudain en avant; **2.** *v/t.* darder; lancer; *v/i. fig.* se précipiter, foncer (sur *at*, [up]on).

Dar·win·ism ['dɑːwinizm] darwi-nisme *m*.

dash [dæʃ] **1.** coup *m*, heurt *m*; at-taque *f* soudaine; trait *m* (*de plume, a. tél.*); ♪ brio *m*; *typ.* tiret *m*; ☿ prime; *couleur*: touche *f*, tache *f*; *fig.* brillante figure *f*; *fig.* entrain *m*, fougue *f*; élan *m* (vers for, to); *fig.* sel etc.: soupçon *m*, *liquide*: goutte *f*; *cut a* ~ faire de l'effet; *at first* ~ du premier coup; **2.** *v/t.* lancer violem-ment; éclabousser (de boue, *with mud*); (*usu.* ~ *to pieces*) fracasser; anéantir (*une espérance*); jeter, fla-quer; déconcerter, confondre; abat-tre (*le courage, l'entrain*); ~ *down* (*ou off*) enlever, exécuter à la va-vite (*une lettre etc.*); *sl.* ~ *it!* zut!; *v/i.* se précipiter, s'élancer (sur, *at*); courir; se jeter (con-tre, *against*); ~ *off* partir en vitesse; ~ *through* traverser (*une pièce etc.*) en toute hâte; ~ *up* monter à toute vitesse; '~**-board** garde-boue *m/inv.*; 🚗, *mot.* tableau *m* de bord; **'dash·er** F élégant *m*, *péj.* épateur *m*; **'dash·ing** □ plein d'élan; fougueux (**-euse** *f*) (*cheval*); *fig.* brillant, beau (**bel** *devant une voyelle ou un h muet*; belle *f*; beaux *m/pl.*).

das·tard ['dæstəd] **1.** □ (*a.* **'dastard·ly**) lâche, ignoble; **2.** lâche *m*; personnage *m* ignoble.

da·ta ['deitə] *pl.*, *Am. a. sg.* donnée *f*, -s *f/pl.*; éléments *m/pl.* d'information; ~ *bank* banque *f* de données; ~ *file* fichier *m* de données; *personal* ~ détails *m/pl.* personnels.

date[1] [deit] ♀ datte *f*; *arbre:* dattier *m*.

date[2] [~] **1.** date *f*; jour *m*, temps *m*; ✝ terme *m*, échéance *f*; *surt. Am.* F rendez-vous *m*; celui *m* ou celle *f* avec qui on a rendez-vous; *make a* ~ fixer un rendez-vous; *out of* ~ démodé; *to* ~ à ce jour; *up to* ~ au courant, à jour; F à la page; **2.** dater; assigner une date à; *surt. Am.* F fixer un rendez-vous avec; ~ *back* antidater; dater, être démodé; ~*d* démodé; ~ *from*, ~ *back to* remonter à; **'~-block** calendrier *m* à effeuiller; **'~-less** sans date; **'~-line** ligne *f* de changement de date; **'~-stamp** (timbre *m*) dateur *m*.

da·tive *gramm.* ['deitiv] (*ou* ~ *case*) datif *m*.

da·tum ['deitəm], *pl.* **-ta** ['~tə] donnée *f*; **~-*point*** point *m* de repère.

daub [dɔːb] **1.** enduit *m*; *peint.* croûte *f*; **2.** barbouiller (de, *with*) (*a. peint.*); **'daub·(st)er** barbouilleur (**-euse** *f*) *m*.

daugh·ter ['dɔːtə] fille *f*; ✝ ~ *company* société *f* filiale; **~-in-law** ['dɔːtərinlɔː] belle-fille (*pl.* **belles-filles**) *f*; **'daugh·ter·ly** filial (**-aux** *m/pl.*).

daunt [dɔːnt] intimider, décourager; **'~-less** intrépide.

dav·it ⚓ ['dævit] bossoir *m*, davier *m*.

da·vy[1] ⚒ ['deivi] (*a.* ~-*lamp*) lampe *f* Davy (= *lampe de sûreté*).

da·vy[2] *sl.* [~] *see* affidavit; *take one's* ~ donner sa parole *ou* son billet.

daw *orn.* [dɔː] choucas *m*.

daw·dle F ['dɔːdl] *v/i.* flâner; *v/t.* gaspiller (*son temps*); **'daw·dler** F flâneur (**-euse** *f*) *m*; *fig.* lambin(e *f*) *m*.

dawn [dɔːn] **1.** aube *f* (*a. fig.*), aurore *f*; point *m* du jour; **2.** poindre; se lever (*jour*); *fig.* venir à l'esprit (de, *upon*).

day [dei] jour *m* (*a.* = *aube*); journée *f*; *souv.* ~*s pl.* temps *m*; vivant *m*; âge *m*; ~ *off* jour *m* de congé; *carry* (*ou win*) *the* ~ remporter la victoire; *this* ~ aujourd'hui; *the other* ~ l'autre jour; *this* ~ *week* (d')aujourd'hui en huit; *the next* ~ le lendemain; *the* ~ *before* la veille (de qch., *s.th.*); **'~-book** ✝ journal *m*; **'~-break** point *m* du jour; aube *f*; **'~-care cen·ter** *Am.* crèche *f*; **'~-dream** rêverie *f*; **'~-fly** éphémère *m*; **'~-la·bo(u)r·er** journalier *m*; **'~-light** (lumière *f* du) jour *m*; ~-*saving time* heure *f* d'été; *sl. beat the living* ~*s out of* tabasser, rosser; **'~-nur·se·ry** garderie *f*, crèche *f*; **'~-star** étoile *f* du matin; soleil *m*; **'~-time** jour *m*, journée *f*; **'~-times** de jour.

daze [deiz] **1.** étourdir (*coup*); stupéfier (*narcotique*); **2.** étourdissement *m*, stupéfaction *f*.

daz·zle ['dæzl] éblouir, aveugler.

dea·con ['diːkn] diacre *m*; **dea·con·ess** ['diːkənis] diaconesse *f*; **'dea·con·ry** diaconat *m*.

dead [ded] **1.** *adj. usu.* mort; de mort (*silence*, *sommeil*); sourd (*douleur*, *son*); engourdi (*par le froid*); subit (*halte*); profond (*secret*); perdu (*puits*); terne (*couleur*); mat (*or*); aveugle (*fenêtre*); sans éclat (*yeux*); éventé (*boissons*); éteint (*charbon*); *sl.* vide (*bouteille*); ⊕ fixe (*essieu*); sourd (à, *to*), mort (à, *to*); ⚡ hors courant; sans courant; épuisé (*pile etc.*); ~ *bargain* véritable occasion *f*; *at a* ~ *bargain* à un prix risible; ~ *calm* calme *m* plat; *fig.* silence *m* de mort; ⊕ ~ *centre* (*ou point*) point *m* mort; centre *m* fixe; ~ *heat* manche *f* nulle; course *f* à égalité; ~ *letter* lettre *f* de rebut; *fig.* lettre morte (*loi etc.*); ~*-letter office* bureau *m* des rebuts; ~ *level* niveau *m* parfait; ~ *lift* effort *m* extrême; ~ *load* poids *m* mort; charge *f* constante; ~ *loss* perte *f* sèche; *sl. un* bon à rien *m*; ~ *man* mort *m*; *sl.* bouteille *f* vide; ~ *march* marche *f* funèbre; *play* ~ faire le mort; ~ *set fig.* attaque *f* furieuse; F *make a* ~ *set at* se jeter à la tête de (*q.*); *a* ~ *shot* tireur *m* sûr de son coup, tireur *m* qui ne rate jamais son coup; ✝ ~ *stock* fonds *m/pl.* de boutique; ~ *wall* mur *m* orbe; ~ *water* remous *m* de sillage; ~ *weight* poids *m* mort; *fig.* poids *m* inutile; *cut out the* ∼ *wood* élaguer le personnel; **2.** *adv.* absolument; complètement; ∼ *against* absolument opposé à; ∼ *asleep* profondément endormi; ∼ *broke* fauché; ∼ *drunk* ivre mort; ∼ *sure* absolument certain; ∼ *tired* mort de fatigue; **3.** *su. the* ∼ *pl.* les morts *m/pl.*; les trépassés *m/pl.*; *in the* ∼ *of winter* au cœur de l'hiver; *in the* ∼ *of night* au plus profond de la nuit; '∼-**a'live** (à moitié) mort; sans animation; '∼-'**beat 1.** épuisé; ≠ apériodique (*instrument*); **2.** *Am. sl.* chemineau *m*; quémandeur *m*; filou *m*; chevalier *m* d'industrie; '**dead·en** amortir (*un coup*); assourdir (*un son*); *fig.* feutrer (*le pas*); émousser (*les sens*); ⊕ hourder (*le plancher etc.*); '**dead·'end:** ∼ (*street*) cul-de-sac (*pl.* culs-de-sac) *m*; *Am.* ∼ *kids pl.* gavroches *m/pl.*; '**dead·'end·ed sid·ing** voie *f* (de garage) à bout fermé.

dead...: '∼-**head** personne *f* munie d'un billet de faveur; *métall.* masselotte *f*; ⊕ contre-pointe *f*; '∼-**line** *Am.* limites *f/pl.* (*d'une prison pour forçats etc.*); date *f* limite; délai *m* de rigueur; '∼-**lock** impasse *f* (*a. fig.*); situation *f* insoluble; '**dead·ly** mortel(le *f*); ∼ *pale* d'une pâleur mortelle; '**dead·ness** torpeur *f*; membres: engourdissement *m*; indifférence *f* (envers, *to*); † stagnation *f*.

dead...: '∼-**net·tle** ortie *f* blanche; ∼ **pan** *Am. sl.* acteur *m etc.* sans expression.

deaf □ [def] sourd (à, *to*); *turn a* ∼ *ear* faire la sourde oreille (à, *to*); ∼ **aid** appareil *m* acoustique, audiophone *m*; '**deaf·en** rendre sourd; assourdir; '**deaf·'mute** sourd(e *f*)-muet(te *f*) *m*.

deal[1] [di:l] madrier *m*; planche *f*; (bois *m* de) sapin *m*.

deal[2] [∼] **1.** *cartes*: donne *f*, main *f*; *fig.* marché *m*, affaire *f*, † coup *m* (*de Bourse*); *Am. usu. péj.* tractation *f*; *a good* ∼ quantité *f*, beaucoup; *a great* ∼ (grande) quantité *f*, beaucoup; *give a square* ∼ *to* agir loyalement envers; **2.** [*irr.*] *v/t.* distribuer, répartir, partager (entre *to*, *among*); *cartes*: donner, distribuer; porter, donner (*un coup*) (à, *to*); *v/i.* faire le commerce (de,

in); *cartes*: donner; en user (*bien ou mal*) (avec q., *by s.o.*); ∼ *with* avoir affaire à *ou* avec (*q.*); s'occuper de; conclure (*une affaire*); faire justice à, négocier avec; *have* ∼*t with* avoir pris des mesures à l'égard de (*q.*); '**deal·er** *cartes*: donneur *m*; ♣ négociant(e *f*) *m* (en, *in*); marchand(e *f*) *m* (de, *in*); *plain* ∼ homme *m* franc et loyal; *sharp* ∼ un fin matois; '**deal·ing** *usu.* ∼*s pl.* distribution *f*; commerce *m*; conduite *f*; relations *f/pl.*; *péj.* tractations *f/pl.*

dealt [delt] *prét. et p.p. de deal*[2] 2.

dean [di:n] doyen *m*; '**dean·er·y** doyenné *m*; résidence *f* du doyen.

dear [diə] **1.** □ cher (chère *f*); coûteux (-euse *f*); **2.** F o(h) ∼! oh là là!; hélas; ∼ *me!* mon Dieu!; vraiment?; '**dear·ness** cherté *f*; tendresse *f*; **dearth** [də:θ] disette *f*; *fig.* dénuement *m*; **dear·y** ['diəri] F mon chéri *m*, ma chérie *f*.

death [deθ] mort *f*; décès *m*; *journ.* ∼*s pl.* nécrologie *f*; ∼ *penalty* peine *f* capitale; *tired to* ∼ mort de fatigue; épuisé; '∼-**bed** lit *m* de mort; '∼-**blow** coup *m* fatal *ou* mortel; '∼-**du·ty** droit *m* de succession; '∼-**less** □ immortel(le *f*); '∼-**like** de mort; semblable à la mort; '**death·ly 1.** *adj. see* deathlike; **2.** *adv.* comme la mort; '**death-rate** (taux *m* de la) mortalité *f*; '**death-roll** liste *f* des morts; '**death's-head** tête *f* de mort; '**death-war·rant** ⚖ ordre *m* d'exécution.

dé·bâ·cle [dei'bɑ:kl] débâcle *f*.

de·bar [di'bɑ:] exclure, priver (q. de qch., *s.o. from s.th.*); défendre (à q. de *inf.*, *s.o. from gér.*).

de·bar·ka·tion [di:bɑ:'keiʃn] débarquement *m*.

de·base [di'beis] avilir; rabaisser (*son style*); altérer (*la monnaie*); **de·'base·ment** avilissement *m*, dégradation *f*; *monnaie*: altération *f*.

de·bat·a·ble □ [di'beitəbl] discutable; contestable; **de'bate 1.** débat *m*, discussion *f*; **2.** discuter, disputer (sur qch., [*on*] *s.th.*; avec q., *with s.o.*); **de'bat·er** orateur *m*.

de·bauch [di'bɔ:tʃ] **1.** débauche *f*; **2.** débaucher; *fig.* corrompre; **deb·au'chee** débauché(e *f*) *m*; **de·'bauch·er·y** débauche *f*.

de·ben·ture [di'bentʃə] obligation *f*; certificat *m* de drawback.

de·bil·i·tate [di'biliteit] débiliter; **de·bil·i'ta·tion** débilitation *f*; **de·'bil·i·ty** débilité *f*.

deb·it ✝ ['debit] **1.** débit *m*, doit *m*; ~ *balance* solde *m* débiteur; **2.** débiter; porter (*une somme*) au débit (de q. *to, against s.o.*).

de·bouch [di'bautʃ] déboucher (*dans, into*).

de·bris ['debri:] débris *m/pl.*; *géol.* détritus *m/pl.*

debt [det] dette *f*; créance *f*; ~ *collector* agent *m* de recouvrement; *active* ~ dette *f* active; *pay the* ~ *of nature* payer le tribut à l'humanité (= *mourir*); **'debt·or** débiteur (-trice *f*) *m*.

de·bug F [di:'bʌg] remettre en ordre, réparer.

de·bunk F *surt. Am.* [di:'bʌŋk] débronzer; déboulonner.

de·bus [di:'bʌs] (faire) débarquer d'un autobus; (faire) descendre.

dé·but ['deibu:] début *m*; entrée *f* dans le monde.

dec·ade ['dekəd] décade *f*; (période *f* de) dix ans *m/pl. ou* jours *m/pl.*

de·ca·dence ['dekədəns] décadence *f*; **'de·ca·dent** décadent; en décadence.

de·caf·fei·nat·ed [di'kæfineitid] décaféiné.

dec·a·log(ue) ['dekələg] décalogue *m*; *les* dix commandements *m/pl.*

de·camp [di'kæmp] ✗ lever le camp; F décamper, filer.

de·cant [di'kænt] décanter, transvaser; tirer au clair; **de'cant·er** carafe *f*; carafon *m*. [*obus*).\

de·cap [di:'kæp] désamorcer (*un*) **de·cap·i·tate** [di'kæpiteit] décapiter; *Am.* congédier, F liquider; **de·cap·i'ta·tion** décapitation *f*.

de·cath·lon *sp.* [di'kæθlɔn] décathlon *m*.

de·cay [di'kei] **1.** décadence *f*; délabrement *m*; déclin *m*; pourriture *f*; *dents*: carie *f*; **2.** tomber en décadence; pourrir; se carier (*dents*); *fig.* décliner, se perdre; ~*ed with age* rongé par le temps.

de·cease *surt.* ✝✝ [di'si:s] **1.** décès *m*; **2.** décéder; *the* ~*d* le défunt *m*, la défunte *f*; *les* défunts *m/pl.*

de·ceit [di'si:t] tromperie *f*; fourberie *f*; **de'ceit·ful** □ trompeur (-euse *f*); faux (fausse *f*); mensonger (-ère *f*) (*regard etc.*); de-

'ceit·ful·ness fausseté *f*; nature *f* trompeuse.

de·ceiv·a·ble [di'si:vəbl] facile à tromper; **de·ceive** [di'si:v] tromper; en imposer à (q.); amener (q.) par supercherie (à *inf.*, *into gér.*); *be* ~*d* se tromper; **de'ceiv·er** trompeur (-euse *f*) *m*; fourbe *m*.

de·cel·er·ate [di:'seləreit] ralentir; **de·cel·er'a·tion** ralentissement *m*; *mot. a.* décélération *f*.

De·cem·ber [di'sembə] décembre *m*.

de·cen·cy ['di:snsi] bienséance *f*; pudeur *f*; *decencies pl.* les convenances *f/pl.*

de·cen·ni·al [di'senjəl] décennal (-aux *m/pl.*); **de'cen·ni·um** [~jəm] décennie *f*, période *f* de dix ans.

de·cent □ ['di:snt] convenable; honnête; assez bon(ne *f*); *sl.* très bon(ne *f*), brave.

de·cen·tral·i·za·tion [di:sentrəlai-'zeiʃn] décentralisation *f*; **de'central·ize** décentraliser.

de·cep·tion [di'sepʃn] tromperie *f*; fraude *f*; supercherie *f*; **de'cep·tive** □ trompeur (-euse *f*); mensonger (-ère *f*).

de·cide [di'said] *v/i.* décider (de, *to*); se décider (pour *in favour of, for*; à *inf.*, *on gér.*); prendre son parti; *v/t.* trancher (*une question*); (*a.* ~ *on*) déterminer (qch.); **de'cid·ed** □ décidé; arrêté (*opinion*); résolu; **de'cid·er** *sp.* course *f ou* match *m* de décision; *la* belle *f*.

de·cid·u·ous ♀, *zo.* □ [di'sidjuəs] caduc (-uque *f*); ~ *tree* arbre *m* à feuilles caduques.

dec·i·mal ['desiml] **1.** décimal (-aux *m/pl.*); & ~ *point* virgule *f*; **2.** décimale *f*; **dec·i·mate** ['~meit] décimer; **dec·i'ma·tion** décimation *f*.

de·ci·pher [di'saifə] déchiffrer; transcrire en clair; **de'ci·pher·a·ble** [~rəbl] déchiffrable; **de'ci·pher·ment** déchiffrement *m*.

de·ci·sion [di'siʒn] décision *f* (*a.* ✝✝); ✝✝ jugement *m*, arrêt *m*; *fig. caractère*: fermeté *f*, résolution *f*; *take a* ~ prendre une décision *ou* un parti; **de·ci·sive** [di'saisiv] □ décisif (-ive *f*); tranchant (*ton*).

deck [dek] **1.** ♫ pont *m*; tillac *m*; *top* ~ impériale *f*; *surt. Am.* paquet *m* de cartes; *Am.* F *on* ~ prêt; **2.** parer, orner; ♫ ponter; **'~-'chair**

chaise *f* longue; F transat(lantique) *m*; **'deck·er:** *double-* (single-)~ autobus *m etc.* à (sans) impériale.

de·claim [di'kleim] déclamer (contre, *against*).

dec·la·ma·tion [deklə'meiʃn] déclamation *f*; **de·clam·a·to·ry** [di-'klæmətəri] déclamatoire.

de·clar·a·ble [di'klɛərəbl] déclarable; à déclarer; **dec·la·ra·tion** [deklə'reiʃn] déclaration *f* (en douane); *make a* ~ déclarer, proclamer; émettre une déclaration; **de·clar·a·tive** [di'klærətiv] qui déclare, qui annonce (*qch.*); **de·'clar·a·to·ry** [ˌtəri] déclaratoire; **de·clare** [di'klɛə] *v/t.* déclarer (*qch. à q., la guerre, qch. en douane, q. coupable, etc.*); annoncer; ~ *o.s.* prendre parti; faire sa déclaration (*amant*); ~ *off* rompre (*un marché*); *v/i.* se déclarer, se prononcer (pour, *for*; contre, *against*); F *well, I* ~! par exemple!; eh bien, alors!; **de·'clared** □ ouvert, avoué, déclaré.

de·clen·sion [di'klenʃn] déclin *m*, décadence *f*; *caractère etc.*: altération *f*; *gramm.* déclinaison *f*.

de·clin·a·ble [di'klainəbl] déclinable; **dec·li·na·tion** [dekli'neiʃn] † pente *f*, déclin *m*; *Am.* refus *m*; *astr., phys.* déclinaison *f*; **de·cline** [di'klain] **1.** déclin *m* (*a. fig.*); *prix:* baisse *f*; ⚕ consommation *f*; **2.** *v/t.* refuser (*courtoisement*); *gramm.* décliner; *v/i.* décliner (*santé, soleil*); baisser; s'incliner (*terrain*); tomber en décadence; s'excuser.

de·cliv·i·ty [di'kliviti] pente *f*, déclivité *f*; **de·'cliv·i·tous** [ˌtəs] escarpé.

de·clutch ['di:'klʌtʃ] *mot.* débrayer.

de·coct [di'kɔkt] faire bouillir; **de·'coc·tion** décoction *f*; *pharm.* décocté *m*.

de·code ['di:'koud] déchiffrer.

dé·col·le·té [dei'kɔltei] **1.** décolletage *m*; **2.** décolleté.

de·col·o(u)r·ize [di:'kʌləraiz] décolorer.

de·com·pose [di:kəm'pouz] (se) décomposer; *v/t.* analyser; *v/i.* pourrir; **de·com·po·si·tion** [di:kɔmpə-'ziʃn] décomposition *f*; désintégration *f*; putréfaction *f*.

de·com·pres·sor *mot.* [di:kəm'presə] décompresseur *m*.

de·con·tam·i·nate [di:kən'tæmi-neit] désinfecter; **de·con·tam·i·'na·tion** désinfection *f*.

de·con·trol ['di:kən'troul] libérer (*qch.*) des contraintes du gouvernement; ~ *the price of* détaxer (*qch.*).

dec·o·rate ['dekəreit] décorer (*a. d'une médaille*); orner; pavoiser (*une rue*); remettre une décoration à (*q.*); **dec·o·'ra·tion** décoration *f*; remise *f* d'une décoration (*à q.*); *appartement etc.*: décor *m*; *Am.* ♀ *Day* le 30 mai; **dec·o·ra·tive** ['dekərətiv] décoratif (-ive *f*); **dec·o·ra·tor** ['ˌreitə] décorateur (-trice *f*) *m*; (*a. house* ~) peintre *m* décorateur.

dec·o·rous □ ['dekərəs] bienséant; **de·co·rum** [di'kɔ:rəm] bienséance *f*.

de·cor·ti·cate [di'kɔ:tikeit] décortiquer.

de·coy [di'kɔi] **1.** leurre *m*, appât *m*; (*a.* ~*-duck*) oiseau *m* de leurre; moquette *f*; canard *m* privé; *fig.* compère *m* (*d'un escroc*); **2.** piper; leurrer (*a. fig.*).

de·crease 1. ['di:kri:s] diminution *f*; **2.** [di:'kri:s] diminuer; (s')amoindrir.

de·cree [di'kri:] **1.** *admin., a. eccl.:* décret *m*; arrêté *m*; ordonnance *f* (*royale*); ⚖ jugement *m*; **2.** décréter, ordonner.

dec·re·ment ['dekrimənt] décroissement *m*; perte *f*.

de·crep·it [di'krepit] décrépit (*personne*); qui tombe en ruine (*chose*); **de·'crep·i·tude** [ˌtju:d] décrépitude *f*; vermoulure *f*.

de·cres·cent [di'kresnt] en décroissance *f*.

de·cry [di'krai] dénigrer, décrier.

dec·u·ple ['dekjupl] **1.** décuple (*a. su./m*); **2.** (se) décupler.

ded·i·cate ['dedikeit] dédier (*a. fig.*); **ded·i·ca·tion** dédicace *f*; **'ded·i·ca·tor** dédicateur (-trice *f*) *m*; **'ded·i·ca·to·ry** dédicatoire.

de·duce [di'dju:s] déduire, conclure (de, *from*); **de·'duc·i·ble** que l'on peut déduire.

de·duct [di'dʌkt] retrancher (de, *from*); **de·'duc·tion** déduction *f*; *salaire:* retenue *f*; imputation *f* (sur, *from*); **de·'duc·tive** déductif (-ive *f*).

deed [di:d] **1.** action *f*, acte *m*; fait *m*; ⚖ acte *m* (notarié); **2.** *Am.* transférer par un acte.

dee·jay F ['di:'dʒei] disc-jockey *m*; animateur *m*.

deem [di:m] *v/t.* juger, considérer, estimer.

deep [di:p] **1.** □ profond (*a. fig.*); foncé, sombre (*couleur*); *fig.* vif (vive *f*); difficile à pénétrer; malin (-igne *f*) (*personne*); plongé (dans, in); *box.* ~ hit coup *m* bas; **2.** abîme *m*; *poét.* océan *m*; '~·'**breath·ing** respiration *f* à pleins poumons; '**deep·en** (s')approfondir; rendre *ou* devenir plus profond; rendre *ou* devenir plus intense (*sentiment*); *v/t.* foncer; *v/i.* devenir plus foncé (*couleur*); '~·'**freeze 1.** surgeler; **2.** *a.* '~·'**freez·er** congélateur *m*; '~·'**fro·zen** surgelé; '~·**fry** faire frire *ou* cuire dans la friture; ~*ing pan* friteuse *f*; '**deep·ness** profondeur *f*; '**deep·'root·ed** profondément enraciné; '**deep·'seat·ed** enraciné.

deer [diə] cerf *m*; *coll.* cervidés *m/pl.*; '~·**lick** *Am.* roches *f/pl.* couvertes de sel; '~·**skin** *cuir*: daim *m*; '~·**stalk·er** chasseur *m* à l'affût.

de·es·ca·late [di:'eskəleit] réduire, limiter; **de·es·ca'la·tion** reduction *f*; limitation *f*; déescalade *f*.

de·face [di'feis] défigurer; mutiler; oblitérer (*un timbre*); **de'face·ment** défiguration *f etc.*

de·fal·cate [di:'fælkeit] détourner des fonds; **de·fal'ca·tion** détournement *m* de fonds; fonds *m/pl.* manquants; '**de·fal·ca·tor** détourneur *m* de fonds.

def·a·ma·tion [defə'meiʃn] diffamation *f*; **de·fam·a·to·ry** [di-'fæmətəri] diffamatoire; diffamant; **de·fame** [di'feim] diffamer; **de-'fam·er** diffamateur (-trice *f*) *m*.

de·fault [di'fɔ:lt] **1.** manquement *m*, ♰, ⚖ défaut *m*; *droit criminel*: contumace *f*; *sp.* forfait *m*; ⚖ *judgement by* ~ jugement *m* par défaut; *in* ~ *of which* faute de quoi; au défaut duquel *etc.*; *make* ~ faire défaut; être en état de contumace; **2.** *v/i.* manquer à ses engagements; ⚖ faire défaut; être en état de contumace; *v/t.* condamner (*q.*) par défaut; '**de'fault·er** délinquant(e *f*) *m*; ♰ défaillant(e *f*) *m*; auteur *m* de détournements de fonds; ⚖ contumace *mf*; ⚔ retardataire *m*; consigné *m*.

de·fea·sance [di'fi:zns] annulation *f*.

de·feat [di'fi:t] **1.** défaite *f*; insuccès *m*; *suffer a* ~ essuyer une défaite; **2.** ⚔ battre, vaincre; faire échouer; *parl. qqfois* renverser; mettre en minorité; **de'feat·ist** défaitiste *mf*.

def·e·cate ['defikeit] déféquer, aller à la selle; **def·e'ca·tion** défécation *f*.

de·fect [di'fekt] défaut *m*; manque *m*; imperfection *f*; **de'fec·tion** défection *f*; *eccl.* apostasie *f*; **de'fec·tive** □ défectueux (-euse *f*); imparfait; anormal (-aux *m/pl.*); en mauvais état; *gramm.* défectif (-ive *f*); *be* ~ *in* manquer de; **de'fec·tor** transfuge *m*.

de·fence [di'fens] défense *f*; protection *f*; ~ *mechanism physiol.* mécanisme *m* de défense; *psych.* défenses *f/pl.*; ⚔ ~ *spending* dépenses *f/pl.* pour la défense; *witness for the* ~ témoin *m* à décharge; **de'fence·less** sans défense; désarmé.

de·fend [di'fend] défendre, protéger (contre *against*, *from*); justifier (*une opinion*); **de'fen·dant** défendeur (-eresse *f*) *m*; accusé(e *f*) *m*; **de'fend·er** défenseur *m*.

de·fense(·less) [di'fens(lis)] *Am. see* defence(less).

de·fen·si·ble [di'fensəbl] défendable; soutenable (*opinion*); **de-'fen·sive 1.** □ défensif (-ive *f*); de défense; **2.** défensive *f*; *be* (*ou stand*) *on the* ~ se tenir sur la défensive.

de·fer[1] [di'fə:] différer; *v/t. a.* remettre; ajourner; ⚔ mettre en sursis; ~*red annuity* rente *f* à paiement différé; ~*red payment* paiement *m* par versements échelonnés.

de·fer[2] [~] (*to*) déférer (à); se soumettre (à); s'incliner (devant); **de·fer·ence** ['defərəns] déférence *f*; respect *m*; *in* ~ *to*, *out of* ~ *to* par déférence pour; **def·er·en·tial** □ [~'renʃl] de déférence.

de·fer·ment [di'fə:mənt] ajournement *m* (*a.* ⚔); remise *f*; ⚔ *be on* ~ être en sursis.

de·fi·ance [di'faiəns] défi *m*; *bid* ~ *to* porter un défi à; *in* ~ *of* en dépit de (*q.*); **de'fi·ant** □ provocant; intraitable; *be* ~ *of* braver (*qch.*).

de·fi·cien·cy [di'fiʃənsi] manque *m*, défaut *m*; insuffisance *f*; *a. see* deficit; **de'fi·cient** défectueux

(-euse *f*); insuffisant; à petite mentalité (*personne*); be ~ in manquer de; être au-dessous de.

def·i·cit ['defisit] déficit *m*.

de·fi·er [di'faiə] provocateur (-trice *f*) *m*.

de·file¹ 1. ['di:fail] défilé *m*; gorge *f*; **2.** [di'fail] défiler (*troupes etc.*).

de·file² [di'fail] souiller, salir; polluer (*une église, les mœurs*); **de'file·ment** souillure *f*; pollution *f*.

de·fin·a·ble [di'fainəbl] définissable; **de'fine** définir; délimiter (*un territoire*); **def·i·nite** ['definit] □ défini; bien déterminé; **def·i'ni·tion** définition *f*; † délimitation *f*; opt. netteté *f*; by ~ par définition; **de·fin·i·tive** □ [di'finitiv] définitif (-ive *f*).

de·flate [di:'fleit] dégonfler (*un ballon, fig. une personne*); † amener la déflation de (*la monnaie*); **de'fla·tion** dégonflement *m*; † déflation *f*; **de'fla·tion·a·ry** de déflation.

de·flect [di'flekt] dévier, défléchir; **de'flec·tion**, *souv.* **de·flexion** [di'flekʃn] *lumière*: déflexion *f*; *compas*: déviation *f*; déformation *f*; ⊕ flèche *f*.

de·flow·er [di:'flauə] défleurir (*une plante*); *fig.* déflorer (*un paysage, un sujet, une jeune fille*).

de·fo·li·ate [di:'foulieit] (se) défeuiller.

de·form [di'fɔ:m] déformer; ~ed contrefait, difforme; **de·for·ma·tion** [di:fɔ:'meiʃn] déformation *f*; **de·form·i·ty** [di'fɔ:miti] difformité *f*; † *caractère etc.*: laideur *f*.

de·fraud [di'frɔ:d] frustrer (q. de qch., s.o. of s.th.); ⚖, † frauder.

de·fray [di'frei] couvrir (*les frais de q.*); défrayer (*q.*); [givreur *m*.]

de·freez·er mot. [di:'fri:zə] dé-]

de·frost ['di:'frɔst] dégivrer; décongeler; **de'frost·er** dégivreur *m*.

deft □ [deft] adroit, habile.

de·funct [di'fʌŋkt] **1.** défunt; décédé; *fig.* désuet (-ète *f*); **2.** défunt(e *f*) *m*.

de·fy [di'fai] défier; mettre (*q.*) au défi.

de·gen·er·a·cy [di'dʒenərəsi] dégénération *f*; **de'gen·er·ate 1.** [~reit] dégénérer (en, *into*); **2.** □ [~rit] dégénéré; **de·gen·er·a·tion** [~'reiʃn] dégénération *f*; dégénérescence *f*.

deg·ra·da·tion [degrə'deiʃn] dégradation *f*; avilissement *m*; ⚖ cassation *f*; **de·grade** [di'greid] *v/t.* dégrader (*a. fig.*, ⚔, *géol.*); ⚖ casser (*un officier*); *géol.* effriter; *fig.* avilir; *v/i.* dégénérer; *géol.* se dégrader.

de·gree [di'gri:] degré *m* (*a.* ♈, *géog.*, *gramm.*, *phys.*); ♪ *gamme*: échelon *m*; *autel*: marche *f*; *univ.* grade *m*; *fig.* rang *m*, condition *f*; by ~s petit à petit; par degrés; in no ~ pas le moins du monde; in some ~ dans une certaine mesure; F to a ~ éminemment; take one's ~ prendre ses grades.

de·hy·drat·ed [di:'haidreitid] déshydraté (*pommes de terre, légumes, etc.*); en poudre (*œufs*).

de·ice ✈ ['di:'ais] dégivrer; **de'ic·er** dégivreur *m*.

de·i·fi·ca·tion [di:ifi'keiʃn] déification *f*; **de·i·fy** ['di:ifai] déifier.

deign [dein] daigner (à, to).

de·ism ['di:izm] déisme *m*; **'de·ist** déiste *mf*; **de'is·tic, de'is·ti·cal** □ déiste.

de·i·ty ['di:iti] divinité *f*; dieu *m*, déesse *f*.

de·ject [di'dʒekt] décourager; **de'ject·ed** □ abattu, déprimé; **de'ject·ed·ness, de'jec·tion** découragement *m*, tristesse *f*.

dek·ko *Brit. sl.* ['dekou] (petit) coup d'œil; have a ~ jeter un (coup d')œil.

de·la·tion [di'leiʃn] dénonciation *f*.

de·lay [di'lei] **1.** délai *m*, retard *m*; arrêt *m*; sursis *m*; **2.** *v/t.* retarder, différer; retenir; arrêter; ~ing tactics *pl.* moyens *m/pl.* dilatoires; ~ed-action... ... à retardement; *v/i.* tarder (à *inf.*, in *gér.*); s'attarder.

de·lec·ta·ble *co.* □ [di'lektəbl] délicieux (-euse *f*); **de·lec·ta·tion** [di:lek'teiʃn] délectation *f*.

del·e·ga·cy ['deligəsi] délégation *f*; **del·e·gate 1.** ['~geit] déléguer; **2.** ['~git] délégué(e *f*) *m*; **del·e·ga·tion** [~'geiʃn] délégation *f* (*a. parl. Am.*); députation *f*.

de·lete [di'li:t] rayer, supprimer; **del·e·te·ri·ous** □ [deli'tiəriəs] nuisible (à la santé); **de·le·tion** [di'li:ʃn] suppression *f*; passage *m* supprimé.

delf(t) † [delf(t)] faïence *f* de Delft.

de·lib·er·ate 1. [di'libəreit] *v/i.* délibérer (de, sur on); *v/t.* délibérer au sujet de; **2.** □ [‿rit] prémédité, voulu; réfléchi, avisé (*personne*); lent, mesuré (*pas etc.*); **de'lib·er·ate·ness** intention f marquée; mesure f; **de·lib·er·a·tion** [‿'reiʃn] délibération f; circonspection f; lenteur f réfléchie; **de-'lib·er·a·tive** □ [‿rətiv] de réflexion; délibératif (-ive f); délibérant.

del·i·ca·cy ['delikəsi] délicatesse f (a. fig.); sensibilité f; santé: faiblesse f; friandise f; fig. scrupule m; touche: légèreté f; **del·i·cate** ['‿kit] □ délicat (a. fig.); fin (esprit); raffiné (sentiment); léger (-ère f) (touche); épineux (-euse f) (question); faible (santé); **del·i·ca·tes·sen** Am. [delikə'tesn] pl. charcuterie f. [(-euse f).\
de·li·cious [di'liʃəs] délicieux \
de·light [di'lait] **1.** délices f/pl., délice m; joie f; **2.** v/t. enchanter, ravir; v/i. se délecter (à, in); se complaire (à inf., in gér.); ~ to (inf.) mettre son bonheur à (inf.); **de'light·ful** [‿ful] ravissant; charmant; délicieux (-euse f); **de-'light·ful·ness** délices f/pl.; charme m.

de·lim·it [di:'limit], **de'lim·i·tate** [‿teit] délimiter; **de·lim·i'ta·tion** délimitation f.

de·lin·e·ate [di'linieit] tracer; dessiner; délinéer; **de·lin·e'a·tion** tracé m; délinéation f; **de'lin·e·a·tor** dessinateur m; instrument m traceur.

de·lin·quen·cy [di'liŋkwənsi] culpabilité f; délit m; délinquance f; **de-'lin·quent 1.** délinquant; coupable; **2.** délinquant(e f) m.

del·i·quesce [deli'kwes] fondre; ⌒ se liquéfier; fig. tomber en déliquescence.

de·lir·i·ous □ [di'liriəs] en délire; délirant; F fou (fol devant une voyelle ou un h muet; folle f) (de, with); **de'lir·i·ous·ness** délire m; **de'lir·i·um** [‿əm] délire m; fièvre f délirante; ~ tremens [‿'tri:menz] delirium m tremens.

de·liv·er [di'livə] délivrer (de, from); (a. ~ up) restituer, rendre, livrer; faire (une commission, une conférence); exprimer (une opinion); prononcer (un discours); livrer (un assaut, des marchandises); ✶ (faire)

accoucher (de, of); distribuer (des lettres), remettre (un paquet); porter, donner (un coup); lancer (une attaque, une balle); ✶ be ‿ed of accoucher de; **de'liv·er·a·ble** [‿rəbl] livrable; **de'liv·er·ance** délivrance f; libération f; expression f; **de-'liv·er·er** libérateur (-trice f) m; ✝ livreur (-euse f) m; **de'liv·er·y** remise f; discours: prononciation f; orateur: diction f; ✶ accouchement m; lettres: distribution f; colis, a. ✝ livraison f; ✝✝ signification f (d'un acte); cricket: envoi m (de la balle); ✕ ville, prisonnier: reddition f; ✝ ~ charge frais m/pl. de livraison; ~ man livreur m; ✶ ~ room salle f d'accouchement; ~ truck, ~ van voiture f de livraison; special ~ envoi m par exprès; on ~ of au reçu de; **de'liv·er·y-note** bulletin m de livraison; **de'liv·er·y-truck,** **de'liv·er·y-van** voiture f de livraison.

dell [del] vallon m, combe f.

de·louse [di:'laus] épouiller.

del·ta ['deltə] delta m.

de·lude [di'lu:d] abuser (au point de inf., into gér.); tromper; duper.

de·luge ['delju:dʒ] **1.** déluge m (a. fig.); ⌒ le Déluge m; **2.** inonder (de, with) (a. fig.).

de·lu·sion [di'lu:ʒn] illusion f, erreur f; action f de duper; **de'lu·sive** [‿siv] □, **de'lu·so·ry** [‿səri] illusoire; trompeur (-euse f).

dem·a·gog·ic, **dem·a·gog·i·cal** [demə'gɔgik(l)] démagogique; **dem·a·gogue** ['‿gɔg] démagogue m; **'dem·a·gog·y** démagogie f.

de·mand [di'ma:nd] **1.** demande f, réclamation f; ✝✝ requête f (a on, to); ✝ in ~ très demandé; on ~ à vue, sur demande; make ~s faire des demandes (à q., on s.o.); ~ note avertissement m; **2.** demander (formellement); exiger (de, from); insister (pour inf., to inf.); ✝✝ réclamer (à, from).

de·mar·cate ['di:ma:keit] délimiter; **de·mar'ca·tion** démarcation f; (usu. line of ~) ligne f de démarcation; délimitation f. [baisser.\
de·mean¹ [di'mi:n] (usu. ~ o.s. o.s. s')a-\
de·mean² [‿]: ~ o.s. se comporter; **de'mean·o(u)r** [‿ə] air m, tenue f.

de·ment·ed [di'mentid] fou (fol devant une voyelle ou un h muet; folle f).

de·mer·it [di:'merit] démérite *m*.
de·mesne [di'mein] possession *f*; domaine *m* (*a. fig.*).
demi... [demi] demi-.
dem·i·john ['demidʒɔn] dame-jeanne (*pl.* dames-jeannes) *f*; bouteille *f* clissée; bac *m* à acide.
de·mil·i·ta·ri·za·tion ['di:militərai-'zeiʃn] démilitarisation *f*; **de·mil·i·ta·rize** démilitariser.
de·mise [di'maiz] **1.** F décès *m*; ⚖ cession *f*; transfert *m*; *terrain*: affermage *m*; **2.** céder, transmettre.
de·mob *sl.* [di:'mɔb] *see* demobilize;
de·mo·bi·li·za·tion ['di:moubilai-'zeiʃn] démobilisation *f*; **de·mo·bi·lize** démobiliser.
de·moc·ra·cy [di'mɔkrəsi] démocratie *f*; **dem·o·crat** ['demokræt] démocrate *mf*; **dem·o·crat·ic**, **dem·o·crat·i·cal** □ démocratique; **de·moc·ra·tize** [di'mɔkrətaiz] (se) démocratiser.
de·mol·ish [di'mɔliʃ] démolir (*a. fig.*); F dévorer, avaler; **dem·o·li·tion** [demo'liʃn] démolition *f*.
de·mon ['di:mən] démon *m*; diable *m*; **de·mo·ni·ac** [di'mouniæk] **1.** (*a.* **de·mo·ni·a·cal** □ [di:mə'naiəkl]) démoniaque; diabolique; **2.** démoniaque *mf*; **de·mon·ic** [di:-'mɔnik] diabolique; du Démon.
de·mon·stra·ble □ ['demənstrəbl] démontrable; **dem·on·strate** ['ᴧ-streit] *v/t.* démontrer; expliquer; décrire (*un système*); *v/i.* manifester; ✕ faire une démonstration; **dem·on·stra·tion** démonstration *f* (✕); *sentiments*: témoignage *m*, démonstration *f*, effusion *f*; *pol.* manifestation *f*; ✝ *mot.* ~ car voiture *f* de démonstration; **de·mon·stra·tive** [di'mɔnstrətiv] **1.** □ démonstratif (-ive *f*) (*a. gramm.*); *a.* expansif (-ive *f*) (*personne*); démontrable (*vérité etc.*); **2.** *gramm.* pronom *m* etc. démonstratif; **dem·on·stra·tor** ['demənstreitə] démonstrateur *m* (*a. anat.*); *univ.* préparateur *m*; *pol.* manifestant *m*.
de·mor·al·i·za·tion [dimɔrəlai-'zeiʃn] démoralisation *f*; **de·mor·al·ize** corrompre; démoraliser.
de·mote *Am.* [di:'mout] réduire à un grade inférieur *ou* à une classe inférieure; *école*: faire descendre d'une classe; **de·mo·tion** réduction *f* à un grade inférieur *etc*.

de·mur [di'mə:] **1.** hésitation *f*; objection *f*; **2.** hésiter; soulever des objections (contre *to, at*).
de·mure [di'mjuə] grave; réservé; d'une modestie affectée; F (*air*) de sainte nitouche; **de·mure·ness** gravité *f*; modestie *f* (affectée); air *m* de sainte nitouche.
de·mur·rage [di'mᴧridʒ] ⚓ surestarie *f*, -s *f/pl.*; 🚃 magasinage *m*; **de·mur·rer** ⚖ fin *f* de non-recevoir.
de·my ✝ [di'mai] *papier*: coquille *f*.
den [den] tanière *f*, antre *m*; *fig.* retraite *f*; F cabinet *m* de travail; F bouge *m*. [dénationaliser.]
de·na·tion·al·ize [di:'næʃnəlaiz]⟩
de·na·ture 🜔 [di'neitʃə] dénaturer.
de·ni·a·ble [di'naiəbl] niable; **de·ni·al** déni *m*, refus *m*; dénégation *f*, démenti *m*; **de·ni·er** dénégateur (-trice *f*) *m*.
den·i·grate ['denigreit] diffamer (*q.*); noircir (*la réputation*); dénigrer (*q., un projet*).
den·im ['denim] *tex.* étoffe *f* croisée de coton (*pour salopette*); F ~s *pl.* bleus *m/pl.*
den·i·zen ['denizn] habitant(e *f*) *m*.
de·nom·i·nate [di'nɔmineit] dénommer; **de·nom·i·na·tion** dénomination *f*; catégorie *f*; *eccl.* secte *f*, culte *m*; **de·nom·i·na·tion·al** confessionnel(le *f*), sectaire; **de·nom·i·na·tive** [ᴧnətiv] dénominatif (-ive *f*); **de·nom·i·na·tor** A̸ [ᴧneitə] dénominateur *m*; *common* ~ dénominateur *m* commun.
de·no·ta·tion [di:nou'teiʃn] désignation *f*; signification *f*; *fig.* indication *f*; **de·no·ta·tive** [di'noutətiv] indicatif (-ive *f*) (de, of); **de·note** dénoter; signifier; indiquer.
de·nounce [di'nauns] dénoncer (*q., un traité, etc.*); démasquer (*un imposteur*); s'élever contre (*un abus*); ✝ prononcer (*un jugement*); **de·nounce·ment** dénonciation *f*.
dense □ [dens] épais(se *f*); profond (*obscurité etc.*); lourd (*esprit*); *fig.* stupide; *phot.* opaque; **dense·ness** épaisseur *f*; *population*: densité *f*; *fig.* stupidité *f*; **den·si·ty** *phys.* densité *f*; *a. see* denseness.
dent [dent] **1.** bosselure *f*; *lame*: brèche *f*; **2.** bosseler, bossuer; ébrécher (*une lame*).

den·tal ['dentl] **1.** dentaire; *gramm.* dental (-aux *m/pl.*); ~ *science* chirurgie *f* dentaire; **2.** *gramm.* dentale *f*; **den·tate** ['~teit] ♀ denté, dentelé; **den·ti·frice** ['~tifris] dentifrice *m*; **'den·tist** dentiste *mf*; **'den·tist·ry** art *m* dentaire; **den·ti·tion** dentition *f*; **den·ture** ['~tʃə] dentier *m*; *zo.* denture *f*.

den·u·da·tion [di:nju:'deiʃn] dénudation *f*; *géol.* érosion *f*; **de'nude** (*of*) dénuder; dépouiller (de); *fig.* dégarnir (de).

de·nun·ci·a·tion [dinʌnsi'eiʃn] dénonciation *f*; condamnation *f*; accusation *f* publique; **de'nun·ci·a·tor** dénonciateur (-trice *f*) *m*.

de·ny [di'nai] nier; dénier (*un crime*); repousser (*une accusation*); démentir (*une nouvelle*); renier (*sa foi*); refuser (*qch.* à q. *s.o. s.th.*, *s.th.* to *s.o.*); ~ *o.s. s.th.* se refuser qch.; ~ *o.s.* fermer sa porte (à q., to *s.o.*).

de·o·dor·ant [di:'oudərant] désodorisant *m*; **de·o·dor·ize** [di:'oudəraiz] désodoriser; **de'o·dor·iz·er** désodorisateur *m*.

de·part [di'pɑ:t] *v/i.* partir (pour, for), s'en aller (à, for); quitter (un lieu, *from a place*); F sortir (de, from); s'écarter (de, from); démordre (de, from); mourir; *the* ~ed le défunt *m*, la défunte *f*; *pl.* les morts *m/pl.*; *v/t.* ~ *this life* quitter ce monde; **de'part·ment** département *m* (*a. géog.*); service *m*; ♱ rayon *m*, comptoir *m*; *Am.* ministère *m*, ♀ *of Education (and Science)* Ministère *m* de l'Éducation nationale *ou* de l'Instruction publique; ♀ *of the Environment* Ministère *m* de l'Environnement; *State* ♀ Ministère *m* des Affaires étrangères; ~ *store* grand magasin *m*; **de'part·men·tal** [~'mentl] départemental (-aux *m/pl.*); **de'par·ture** [~tʃə] départ *m* (*a.* 🚢, ✈); déviation (de, from); *a new* ~ une nouvelle tendance *f*; une nouveauté *f*; une nouvelle orientation *f*; *aéroport*: ~ *lounge* salle *f* de départ; ~ *platform* (quai *m* de) départ *m*; embarcadère *m*.

de·pend [di'pend] † pendre (à, from); ⅟ être pendant; ~ (*up*)*on* dépendre de; se trouver à la charge de; compter sur; se fier à (*qch.*); F *it* ~*s* cela dépend, F c'est selon; **de'pend·a·ble** bien fondé; digne de confiance (*personne*); **de'pend·ant** protégé(e *f*) *m*; pensionnaire *mf*; ~*s pl.* charges *f/pl.* de famille; **de'pend·ence** dépendance *f* (de, [up]on); confiance *f* (en, on); **de'pend·en·cy**, *souv. dependencies pl.* dépendance *f*; **de'pend·ent 1.** □ (*on*) dépendant (de); à la charge (de); be ~ *on charity* subsister d'aumônes; **2.** *see dependant*; **de'pend·ing** ⅟ be ~ être pendant.

de·pict [di'pikt] (dé)peindre.

de·pil·a·to·ry [de'pilətəri] **1.** (d)épilatoire; **2.** dépilatoire *m*.

de·plane [di'plein] descendre d'avion.

de·plete [di'pli:t] épuiser (*a. fig.*); ✗ dégarnir (*une garnison*); **de'ple·tion** épuisement *m*; ✗ dégarnissement *m*; **de'ple·tive** épuisant, qui épuise.

de·plor·a·ble □ [di'plɔ:rəbl] déplorable; lamentable; **de·plore** [di'plɔ:] déplorer; regretter vivement.

de·ploy ✗ [di'plɔi] (se) déployer; **de'ploy·ment** ✗ déploiement *m*.

de·plume [di'plu:m] déplumer.

de·po·nent [di'pounənt] ⅟ déposant *m*; *gramm.* (verbe *m*) déponent *m*.

de·pop·u·late [di:'pɔpjuleit] (se) dépeupler; **'de·pop·u'la·tion** *pays*: dépopulation *f*; *forêt*: dépeuplement *m*.

de·port [di'pɔ:t] expulser (*un étranger*); ~ *o.s.* se conduire; **de·por'ta·tion** expulsion *f*; **de·por·tee** [di:pɔ:'ti:] détenu(e *f*) *m*; **de'port·ment** tenue *f*; conduite *f*.

de·pos·a·ble [di'pouzəbl] capable d'être déposé; **de'pose** déposer; ⅟ témoigner (que, *that*; de qch., to *s.th.*).

de·pos·it [di'pɔzit] **1.** *géol.* gisement *m*, couche *f*; ✳ encroûtement *m*; 🜂 précipité *m*, sédiment *m*; ♱ acompte *m*, somme *f* en gage, arrhes *f/pl.*; dépôt *m* (*en banque*); ♱ ~ *account* compte *m* d'épargne (à terme); **2.** de dépôts; **3.** déposer (*qch. sur qch.*, *des œufs*, *de l'argent*, *a.* 🜂); consigner (*de l'argent*); cautionner (*des droits de douane*); **de'pos·i·ta·ry** dépositaire *m*; **dep·o·si·tion** [depə'ziʃn] déposition *f*; témoignage *m*; 🜂 dépôt *m*; *eccl.* Descente *f* de Croix; **de·pos·i·tor** [di'pɔzitə] déposant *m*; **de'pos·i·to·ry** dépôt *m*, entrepôt *m*;

garde-meuble (*pl.* garde-meuble[s]) *m*; *fig.* mine *f*, trésor *m*.

de·pot ['depou] ⚔, ⚓, ✝ dépôt *m*; ✝ entrepôt *m*; *Am.* gare *f*.

dep·ra·va·tion [deprə'veiʃn] dépravation *f*; *see* depravity; **de·prave** [di'preiv] dépraver; **de'praved** dépravé (*a. goût*); **de·prav·i·ty** [di-'præviti] perversité *f*; dépravation *f*.

dep·re·cate ['deprikeit] désapprouver, désavouer, déconseiller (*une action*); **dep·re'ca·tion** désapprobation *f*; désaveu *m*; *eccl.* ✝ déprécation *f*; **dep·re·ca·to·ry** ['⌐ˌkətəri] déprécatif (-ive *f*).

de·pre·ci·ate [di'priːʃieit] *v/t.* déprécier (*a. fig.*); avilir; *fig.* dénigrer; *v/i.* se déprécier; diminuer de valeur; **de·pre·ci'a·tion** dépréciation *f* (*a.* ✝); dénigrement *m*; ✝ amortissement *m*; **de'pre·ci·a·to·ry** [ˌ⌐ətəri] dépréciateur (-trice *f*).

dep·re·da·tion [depri'deiʃn] déprédation *f*; pillage *m*; **'dep·re·da·tor** déprédateur (-trice *f*) *m*; **dep·re·da·to·ry** [di'predətəri] de déprédation.

de·press [di'pres] abaisser (*a.* ⚥); baisser; abattre (*les forces*); faire languir (*le commerce*); faire baisser (*le prix*); baisser le ton de (*la voix*); appuyer sur (*la pédale*); *fig.* attrister, décourager; **de'press·ing** *fig.* déprimant; **de'pressed** *fig.* triste; abattu; **de·pres·sion** [di'preʃn] abaissement *m* (*a. phys.*); ✝, *astr.*, *géog.*, *météor.* dépression *f*; ⚓ abattement *m*; ⚒ affaissement *m* (*a.* ✝); ⊕ trou *m*, godet *m*; *géog.* creux *m*; *météor.* baisse *f*; *tir:* pointage *m* négatif; *fig.* découragement *m*.

dep·ri·va·tion [depri'veiʃn] privation *f*; ⚔, *admin.* retrait *m* (*d'emploi*); *eccl.* révocation *f*, destitution *f*; **de·prive** [di'praiv] priver (q. de qch., *s.o. of s.th.*); déposséder (*q.*) d'une charge; *eccl.* destituer; **de·prived** déshérité.

depth [depθ] profondeur *f*; *forêt, eau:* fond *m*; *couche:* épaisseur *f*; *couleur:* intensité *f*; *son:* gravité *f*; *intelligence:* portée *f*; ~ *bomb* (*ou charge*) grenade *f* sous-marine; *phot.* ~ *of field*, ~ *of focus* profondeur *f* de foyer; *go beyond one's* ~ perdre fond; *a. be out of one's* ~ avoir perdu pied; *fig.* sortir de sa compétence; *fig. in* ~ profond, en profondeur.

dep·u·ta·tion [depju'teiʃn] délégation *f*, députation *f*; **de·pute** [di-'pjuːt] déléguer, députer; **dep·u·tize** ['depjutaiz] remplacer (*q.*); ~ *for* faire l'intérim de; **'dep·u·ty 1.** remplaçant(e *f*) *m*; ⚖ fondé *m* de pouvoir; substitut *m* (*d'un juge*); suppléant(e *f*) *m*; délégué(e *f*) *m*; **2.** sous-; suppléant.

de·rac·i·nate [di'ræsineit] déraciner.

de·rail 🚂 [di'reil] (faire) dérailler; **de'rail·ment** déraillement *m*.

de·range [di'reindʒ] déranger; désorganiser; ⊕ fausser (*une machine*); aliéner (*l'esprit*); **de'ranged** détraqué (*cerveau*); dérangé (*estomac*); **de'range·ment** dérèglement *m* (*de l'esprit*); dérangement *m*; troubles *m/pl.* (*de digestion*).

de·rate [di:'reit] dégrever.

Der·by *sp.* ['dɑːbi] le Derby *m*; **'der·by** *Am.* chapeau *m* melon.

der·e·lict ['derilikt] **1.** abandonné, délaissé; *surt. Am.* négligent; **2.** objet *m* abandonné; épave *f*; **der·e·lic·tion** [deri'likʃn] abandon *m*, délaissement *m*; ~ *of duty* manquement *m* au devoir.

de·ride [di'raid] tourner en dérision; se moquer de; railler.

de·ri·sion [di'riʒn] dérision *f*; ridicule *m*; **de·ri·sive** [di'raisiv] ☐, **de'ri·so·ry** [ˌ⌐səri] moqueur (-euse *f*); *fig.* dérisoire (*offre*).

de·riv·a·ble ☐ [di'raivəbl] dérivable; que l'on peut tirer (de, *from*); **der·i·va·tion** [deri'veiʃn] dérivation *f* (*a.* ⚥, ⚒); **de·riv·a·tive** [di-'rivətiv] **1.** ☐ dérivé; **2.** dérivé *m*; ⚥ dérivée *f*; **de·rive** [di'raiv] (*from*) tirer (de); prendre (*du plaisir etc.*) (à); devoir (*qch.*) (à); *be* ~*ed from* dériver de. [matite *f.*]

der·ma·ti·tis [dəːmə'taitis] der-⌐

der·ma·tol·o·gy [dəːmə'tɔlədʒi] dermatologie *f*.

der·o·gate ['derəgeit] déroger (à sa dignité, *from one's dignity*); diminuer (qch., *from s.th.*); **der·o'ga·tion** dérogation *f* (à une loi, *of a law*); atteinte *f* (portée à qch., *from s.th.*); **de·rog·a·to·ry** ☐ [di'rɔgətəri] (*to*) dérogatoire (à); attentatoire (à); qui déroge (à).

der·rick ['derik] ⊕ chevalement *m*; ⚓ mât *m* de charge; ⚒ chevalement *m* de sondage.

de·sal·i·nate ['diːˈsælineit] dessaler;
de·sal·i·na·tion dessalage *m*.

des·cant [disˈkænt] discourir, s'é-
tendre (sur, [up]on).

de·scend [diˈsend] descendre; *v/i.*
tomber (*pluie*); s'abaisser; tirer son
origine (de, *from*); ∼ (up)on s'abattre
sur, tomber sur, descendre sur; ∼
to passer à (*q. par héritage*); descendre jusqu'à (*bassesse etc.*); ∼ (*a.*
be ∼ed) *from* descendre de; **de-**
'scend·ant descendant(e *f*) *m*.

de·scent [diˈsent] *usu.* descente *f*;
pente *f*; chute *f*; abaissement *m*;
déchéance *f*; descendance *f*; ⚜
transmission *f* par héritage; atterrissage *m* (*p.ex. forcé, d'un avion*).

de·scrib·a·ble [disˈkraibəbl] des-
criptible; **de'scribe** décrire, dépeindre.

de·scrip·tion [disˈkripʃn] description *f*; *police etc.*: signalement *m*;
✝ désignation *f*; espèce *f*, sorte *f*;
de'scrip·tive □ descriptif (-ive *f*);
raisonné (*catalogue*).

de·scry [disˈkrai] apercevoir, aviser.

des·e·crate ['desikreit] profaner;
des·e'cra·tion profanation *f*.

de·seg·re·gate *Am.* [diˈsegrigeit]
abolir les distinctions légales *ou*
sociales entre les blancs et les races
de couleur dans (*une école etc.*); **'de-**
seg·re'ga·tion déségrégation *f*.

de·sen·si·tize ['diːˈsensitaiz] désensibiliser.

des·ert[1] ['dezət] **1.** désert; désertique (*flore*); aride (*sujet*); **2.** désert
m; **3.** [diˈzəːt] *v/t.* déserter; *fig.*
abandonner, délaisser (*q.*); *v/i.* faire
défection; ✗ déserter.

de·sert[2] [diˈzəːt], *a.* ∼s *pl.* mérite *m*,
-s *m/pl.*; dû *m*; ce qu'on mérite.

de·sert·er [diˈzəːtə] déserteur *m*; *pol.*
F saxon (*m*); **de'ser·tion** abandon *m*;
⚖ abandon *m* criminel; ✗ désertion *f*; *pol.* défection *f*.

de·serve [diˈzəːv] mériter (de, *of*);
être digne de; **de'serv·ed·ly** [∼vid-
li] à juste titre; **de'serv·ing** méritant (qch., *of* s.th.); méritoire
(*action*).

des·ic·cate ['desikeit] dessécher;
des·ic'ca·tion dessèchement *m*;
'des·ic·ca·tor dessiccateur *m*.

de·sid·er·ate [diˈzidəreit] soupirer
après; sentir le besoin de; **de·sid-**
er·a·tum [∼'reitəm], *pl.* -ta [∼tə]
desiderata *m/pl.*

de·sign [diˈzain] **1.** dessein *m* (*péj. a.*
∼s *pl.*); projet *m*; intention *f*; dessin
m d'ornement; plan *m*; modèle *m*
(*a. mot.*, ⊕); ⊕ dessin *m*, étude *f*;
by ∼ à dessein; with the ∼ dans le
dessein (de *inf.*, *of gér.*); **2.** préparer;
construire; étudier (*une machine*);
destiner (à, *for*); projeter (de *inf.*,
to *inf.*); créer (*des modes*); ∼ed to
(*inf.*) conçu pour, fait pour (*inf.*).

des·ig·nate 1. ['dezigneit] nommer;
désigner (pour, comme *as*, for);
qualifier (de, *as*); indiquer (qch.);
2. ['∼nit] *après la su.* (*p.ex. bishop* ∼);
désigné; **des·ig'na·tion** désigna-
tion *f*; nomination *f*; nom *m*.

de·sign·ed·ly [diˈzainidli] à dessein;
de'sign·er dessinateur (-trice *f*) *m*;
inventeur (-trice *f*) *m*; concepteur-
projeteur *m* (*pl.* concepteurs-proje-
teurs); *théa.* décorateur *m*; *fig.* intri-
gant(e *f*) *m*; **de'sign·ing** □ artificieux (-euse *f*).

de·sir·a·ble □ [diˈzaiərəbl] désirable; avantageux (-euse *f*); attrayant; **de·sire** [diˈzaiə] **1.** désir *m*
(de, *for*; de *inf.*, to *inf.*); souhait
m; envie *f* (de *inf.*, to *inf.*); at s.o.'s
∼ selon le désir de q.; **2.** désirer;
avoir envie de; vouloir (que q. *sbj.*,
s.o. to *inf.*); ∼ to (*inf.*) désirer (*inf.*);
de·sir·ous □ [diˈzaiərəs] désireux
(-euse *f*) (de *inf. of gér*, to *inf.*).

de·sist [diˈzist] cesser (de *inf.*, *from*
gér.); renoncer (à qch., *from* s.th.).

desk [desk] pupitre *m*; bureau *m*; ✝
caisse *f*; ∼ *pad* sous-main *m* (*pl.* sous-
mains); bloc-notes *m* (*pl.* blocs-notes).

des·o·late 1. ['desəleit] ravager; affliger (*q.*); **2.** □ ['∼lit] désert, morne;
affligé (*personne*); **des·o·la·tor**
['∼leitə] dévastateur (-trice *f*) *m*;
des·o'la·tion désolation *f* (*a. fig.*).

de·spair [disˈpɛə] **1.** désespoir *m*;
2. désespérer (de, *of*); **de·spair·ing**
□ [disˈpɛəriŋ] désespéré.

des·patch *see* dispatch.

des·per·a·do [despəˈrɑːdou] risque-
tout *m/inv.*; tête *f* brûlée; bandit *m*.

des·per·ate □ ['despərit] *adj.* désespéré; *fig.* acharné; *fig.* épouvantable; **des·per·a·tion** [despəˈreiʃn]
désespoir *m*.

des·pi·ca·ble □ ['despikəbl] méprisable.

de·spise [disˈpaiz] mépriser; dédaigner.

de·spite [dis'pait] **1.** *poét.* dépit *m*; in ~ of en dépit de; **2.** *prp.* (*a.* ~ of) en dépit de; **de'spite·ful** □ [~ful] *poét.* dédaigneux (-euse *f*).

de·spoil [dis'poil] dépouiller (de, of); **de'spoil·ment** spoliation *f*.

de·spond [dis'pond] perdre courage; ~ of envisager (*qch.*) sans espoir; **de'spond·en·cy** [~dənsi] découragement *m*, abattement *m*; **de·'spond·ent** □, **de'spond·ing** □ découragé, abattu.

des·pot ['despot] despote *m*; tyran *m*; **des'pot·ic** (~ally) despotique; **des·pot·ism** ['~pətizm] despotisme *m*.

des·qua·ma·tion [deskwə'meiʃn] exfoliation *f*.

des·sert [di'zə:t] dessert *m*; *Am.* [entremets *m*].

des·ti·na·tion [desti'neiʃn] destination *f*; **des·tine** ['~tin] destiner (à for, to); be ~d to (*inf.*) être destiné à (*inf.*); **'des·ti·ny** destin *m*, destinée *f*; sort *m*.

des·ti·tute □ ['destitju:t] dépourvu, dénué (de, of); sans ressources; **des·ti'tu·tion** dénuement *m*; misère *f*.

de·stroy [dis'troi] détruire; anéantir; tuer; **de'stroy·er** destructeur (-trice *f*) *m*; ⚓ torpilleur *m*.

de·struc·ti·bil·i·ty [distrʌkti'biliti] destructibilité *f*; **de'struc·ti·ble** [~əbl] destructible; **de'struc·tion** destruction *f*; anéantissement *m*; *feu, tempête:* ravages *m/pl.*; *fig.* perte *f*; **de'struc·tive** □ destructeur (-trice *f*); destructif (-ive *f*); fatal (à, of); **de'struc·tive·ness** effet *m* destructeur; penchant *m* à tout briser; **de'struc·tor** incinérateur *m* (*d'ordures*).

des·ue·tude [di'sju:itju:d] désuétude *f*.

des·ul·to·ri·ness ['desəltərinis] manque *m* de méthode *ou* de suite; décousu *m*; **'des·ul·to·ry** □ décousu, sans suite.

de·tach [di'tætʃ] détacher (*a.* ✕); séparer; dételer (*des wagons*); **de·'tach·a·ble** détachable; amovible; mobile; **de'tached** détaché (*a. maison*); à part; séparé; désintéressé (*personne*); désinvolte (*manière*); ✕ isolé (*poste*); **de'tach·ment** séparation *f* (de, from); indifférence *f* (envers, from); détachement *m* (*d'esprit; a.* ✕).

de·tail ['di:teil] **1.** détail *m*; particularité *f*; ⊕ organe *m*; ✕ détachement *m* (*de corvée*); ~s *pl.* détails *m/pl.*; accessoires *m/pl.*; in ~ de point en point, en détail; go into ~ entrer dans tous les détails; **2.** détailler; raconter en détail; ✕ affecter (à un service, for a duty); **'de·tailed** détaillé.

de·tain [di'tein] retenir; arrêter; empêcher de partir; consigner (*un élève*); ⚖ détenir; **de·tain·ee** [~'ni:] détenu(e *f*) *m*; **de'tain·er** détention *f*; ⚖ ordre *m* d'incarcération.

de·tect [di'tekt] découvrir; apercevoir; détecter (*radio*); **de'tect·a·ble** discernable; **de'tec·tion** découverte *f*; *radio:* détection *f*; **de·'tec·tive 1.** révélateur (-trice *f*); de détective; policier (-ère *f*) (*roman etc.*); **2.** agent *m* de la sûreté; policier *m*; **de'tec·tor** découvreur (-euse *f*) *m*; signal *m* d'alarme; ⊕, *a. radio:* détecteur *m*.

de·tent ⊕ [di'tent] détente *f*, arrêt *m*.

dé·tente [dei'tɑ̃:nt] *pol.* détente *f*.

de·ten·tion [di'tenʃn] détention *f*; arrêt *m*; retenue *f* (*d'un élève*); retard *m*; ~ camp camp *m* d'internement; house of ~ maison *f* d'arrêt.

de·ter [di'tə:] détourner (de, from).

de·ter·gent [di'tə:dʒənt] **1.** détersif (-ive *f*), détergent; **2.** détersif *m*, détergent *m*.

de·te·ri·o·rate [di'tiəriəreit] (se) détériorer; *v/i.* diminuer de valeur; dégénérer (*race*); **de·te·ri·o'ra·tion** détérioration *f*; diminution *f* de valeur; *race:* dégénération *f*.

de·ter·ment [di'tə:mənt] action *f* de détourner.

de·ter·mi·na·ble □ [di'tə:minəbl] déterminable; ⚖ résoluble; **de·'ter·mi·nant** déterminant (*a. su./m*); **de'ter·mi·nate** □ [~nit] déterminé; défini; définitif (-ive *f*); **de·ter·mi'na·tion** détermination *f*, résolution *f* (*a. d'un contrat etc.*); décision *f*; délimitation *f*; **de'ter·mi·na·tive** [~nətiv] **1.** déterminant; *gramm.* déterminatif (-ive *f*); **2.** *gramm.* déterminatif *m*; **de'ter·mine** [~min] *v/t.* déterminer, fixer; décider (de, to); *surt.* ⚖ décider (*une question*), résoudre (*un contrat*); *v/i.* décider (de *inf.* on gér., to *inf.*); se décider (à *inf.* on gér., to *inf.*);

de'ter·mined déterminé; résolu (*personne*); **de'ter·min·er** *gramm.* déterminant *m.*

de·ter·rent [di'terənt] **1.** préventif (-ive *f*); ✗ ~*weapon* arme *f* de dissuasion; **2.** préventif *m.*

de·test [di'test] détester; **de'test·a·ble** □ détestable; **de·tes'ta·tion** détestation *f* (de, *of*); horreur *f*; *he is my* ~ c'est ma bête noire.

de·throne [di'θroun] détrôner; **de·'throne·ment** détrônement *m.*

det·o·nate ['detouneit] (faire) détoner; **'det·o·nat·ing** détonant, explosif (-ive *f*); **det·o'na·tion** détonation *f*; explosion *f*; **det·o·na·tor** ['~tə] 💥 pétard *m*; ✗ détonateur *m*; amorce *f.*

de·tour [di'tuə], **dé·tour** ['deituə] détour *m*; *Am.* déviation *f* (*d'itinéraire*).

de·tract [di'trækt] diminuer, amoindrir (qch., *from* s.th.); **de'trac·tion** détraction *f*, dénigrement *m*; **de·'trac·tive** détracteur (-trice *f*); **de·'trac·tor** détracteur (-trice *f*) *m.*

de·train [di:'trein] débarquer.

det·ri·ment ['detrimənt] détriment *m*, dommage *m*; préjudice *m* (de, *to*); **det·ri·men·tal** □ [detri'mentl] nuisible (à, *to*). [*m.*⟩

de·tri·tus géol. [di:'traitəs] détritus⟩

deuce [dju:s] *jeu:* deux *m*; *tennis:* égalité *f*; F diable *m*; *the* ~*!* diable!; (*the*) ~ *a one* personne, pas un; **'deu·ced** F satané, fichu.

de·val·u·ate [di:'væljueit] dévaluer; **de·val·u·a·tion** [di:'vælju'eiʃn] dévaluation *f*; **de'val·ue** [~ju:] dévaluer.

dev·as·tate ['devəsteit] dévaster, ravager; **'dev·as·tat·ing** dévastateur (-trice *f*), écrasant (*critique etc.*); irrésistible (*charme etc.*); **dev·as'ta·tion** dévastation *f.*

de·vel·op [di'veləp] (se) développer; *v/t.* manifester; exploiter (*une région*); contracter (*une habitude, une maladie*); *Am.* mettre à jour; *v/i.* prendre une nouvelle tournure; apprendre (que, *that*); **de'vel·op·er** *phot.* révélateur *m*; **de'vel·op·ing** *phot.* développement *m*; *attr.* de ou à développement; **de'vel·op·ment** développement *m*; exploitation *f*; événement *m*, fait *m* nouveau; déroulement *m* (*des événements*).

de·vi·ate ['di:vieit] (*from*) s'écarter (de); dévier (de); **de·vi'a·tion** déviation *f* (*a. boussole*); écart *m.*

de·vice [di'vais] expédient *m*, moyen *m*; ruse *f*, stratagème *m*; plan *m*; appareil *m*; emblème *m*, devise *f*; *leave s.o. to his own* ~*s* livrer q. à lui-même.

dev·il ['devl] **1.** diable *m* (*a. fig.*); démon *m*; F mauvaise passion *f*, élan *m*; bruit *m* infernal; *fig.* nègre *m*; ⊕ dispositif *m* à dents ou à pointes; *cuis.* plat *m* grillé et poivré; *the* ~*!* diable!; *play the* ~ *with* ruiner; **2.** *v/t.* faire griller et poivrer fortement; ⊕ effilocher; *Am.* harceler (de, *with*); *v/i.* F servir de nègre (à, *for*); **'dev·il·ish** □ diabolique; F maudit; **'dev·il-may-'care 1.** F insouciant; téméraire (*a. su./m*); **2.** tête *f* brûlée; **'dev·il·(t)ry** diablerie *f*; magie *f* (noire); *fig.* mauvais coup *m.*

de·vi·ous □ ['di:viəs] tortueux (-euse *f*); détourné (*a. fig.*); ~ *path* détour *m*; chemin *m* tortueux.

de·vis·a·ble [di'vaizəbl] imaginable; **de'vise 1.** ⚖ legs *m* (immobilier); dispositions *f/pl.* testamentaires de biens immobiliers; **2.** imaginer; combiner; ⚖ disposer par testament de (*biens immobiliers*); **dev·i·see** ⚖ [devi'zi:] légataire *mf*; **de·vis·er** [di'vaizə] inventeur (-trice *f*) *m*; **de·vi·sor** ⚖ [devi'zɔ:] testateur (-trice *f*) *m.* [ser.⟩

de·vi·tal·ize [di:'vaitəlaiz] dévitali-⟩

de·void [di'vɔid] dénué, dépourvu, exempt (de, *of*).

dev·o·lu·tion [di:və'lu:ʃn] ⚖ dévolution *f*; transmission *f*; *parl.* délégation *f*; décentralisation *f* administrative; *biol.* dégénération *f*; **de·volve** [di'vɔlv] (*upon, to*) *v/t.* déléguer, transmettre (*qch.* à *q.*); *v/i.* incomber (à); ⚖ être dévolu (à).

de·vote [di'vout] consacrer, vouer; **de'vot·ed** □ dévoué, attaché; **dev·o·tee** [devou'ti:] fervent(e *f*) *m*; fanatique *m* (de, *of*); **de·vo·tion** [di'vouʃn] dévouement *m* (à, pour q., *to s.o.*); dévotion *f* (*à Dieu*); assiduité *f* (*au travail*); ~*s pl.* dévotions *f/pl.*, prières *f/pl.*; **de'vo·tion·al** □ de dévotion, de prière.

de·vour [di'vauə] dévorer (*a. fig.*); ~*ed with* dévoré de, rongé de; **de·'vour·ing** □ dévorateur (-trice *f*).

de·vout ☐ [di'vaut] dévot, pieux (-euse *f*); fervent; **de'vout·ness** dévotion *f*, piété *f*.

dew [dju:] **1.** rosée *f*; **2.** humecter de rosée; *fig.* mouiller (de, *with*); **'~-drop** goutte *f* de rosée; **'~·lap** fanon *m* (*de la vache*); **'dew·y** humecté *ou* couvert de rosée.

dex·ter·i·ty [deks'teriti] dextérité *f*; **dex·ter·ous** ☐ ['~tərəs] adroit, habile (à *inf.*, *in gér.*).

di·a·be·tes ✳ [daiə'bi:ti:z] diabète *m*; glycosurie *f*; **di·a·bet·ic** [~'betik] diabétique (*adj.*, *mf*).

di·a·bol·ic, di·a·bol·i·cal ☐ [daiə-'bɔlik(l)] diabolique; infernal (-aux *m/pl.*).

di·a·dem ['daiədem] diadème *m*.

di·ag·nose ✳ ['daiəgnouz] diagnostiquer; **di·ag'no·sis** [~sis], *pl.* **-ses** [~si:z] diagnostic *m*.

di·ag·o·nal [dai'ægənl] **1.** ☐ diagonal (-aux *m/pl.*); **2.** diagonale *f* (*a. tex.*).

di·a·gram ['daiəgræm] diagramme *m*, tracé *m*, schéma *m*; graphique *m*; **di·a·gram·mat·ic** [daiəgrə'mætik] (~ally) schématique.

di·al ['daiəl] **1.** *usu.* cadran *m*; *téléph.* tabulateur *m*; *sl.* visage *m*; ⚓ rose *f* (*des vents*); ~ light lampe *f* de cadran; **2.** *téléph. v/i.* composer un numéro; *v/t.* appeler.

di·a·lect ['daiəlekt] dialecte *m*, parler *m*, idiome *m*; **di·a'lec·tic, di·a-'lec·ti·cal** ☐ de dialecte, dialectal (-aux *m/pl.*); **di·a'lec·tics** *usu. sg.* dialectique *f*.

di·a·logue, *Am. a.* **di·a·log** ['daiə-lɔg] dialogue *m*.

di·al...: '**~-plate** *téléph.* tabulateur *m*; *montre:* cadran *m*; '**~-sys·tem** téléphone *m* automatique; '**~-tone** *téléph.* signal *m* de numérotage.

di·am·e·ter [dai'æmitə] diamètre *m*; **di·a·met·ri·cal** ☐ [daiə'metrikl] diamétral (-aux *m/pl.*).

di·a·mond ['daiəmənd] **1.** diamant *m*; losange *m*; *Am. baseball:* terrain *m* (de baseball); *cartes:* carreau *m*; ~ cut ~ à malin malin et demi; **2.** de diamant; à diamants; en losange; '**~-cut·ter** tailleur *m* de diamants.

di·a·pa·son ♪ [daiə'peisn] voix, ton: diapason *m*; *orgue:* principaux jeux *m/pl.* de fond; *poét.* harmonie *f*.

di·a·per ['daiəpə] **1.** toile *f* gaufrée; serviette *f* ouvrée; couche *f*, maillot

m (*des bébés*); **2.** ouvrer (*le linge*); gaufrer (*la toile*); emmailloter (*un bébé*).

di·aph·a·nous [dai'æfənəs] diaphane.

di·a·phragm ['daiəfræm] diaphragme *m* (*a.* ⊕, *a. opt.*); *téléph.* membrane *f*.

di·a·rist ['daiərist] personne *f* qui tient un journal; **'di·a·rize** *v/i.* tenir son journal; *v/t.* noter (*qch.*) dans son journal.

di·ar·rhoe·a ✳ [daiə'riə] diarrhée *f*.

di·a·ry ['daiəri] journal *m* intime; agenda *m*.

di·a·ther·my ✳ ['daiəθə:mi] diathermie *f*.

di·a·tribe ['daiətraib] diatribe *f*.

dib·ble ['dibl] **1.** plantoir *m*; **2.** repiquer au plantoir.

dibs *sl.* [dibz] *pl.* argent *m*; *sl.* pépette *f*.

dice [dais] **1.** *pl. de* die²; F no ~ rien à faire; **2.** *v/i.* jouer aux dés; *v/t. cuis.* couper en cubes; **dic·ey** F ['daisi] risqué.

dick *Am. sl.* [dik] agent *m* de la sûreté; policier *m*; *take one's* ~ jurer.

dick·ens F ['dikinz] diable *m*.

dick·er *Am.* ['dikə] marchander.

dick·(e)y ['diki] âne *m*; (*a.* ~-*bird*) F petit oiseau *m*; siège *m* de derrière; *mot.* spider *m*; *chemise:* faux plastron *m*.

dic·ta·phone ['diktəfoun] dictaphone *m* (*marque*); machine *f* à dicter.

dic·tate 1. ['dikteit] commandement *m*, ordre *m*; dictamen *m*; **2.** [dik'teit] dicter; *fig.* prescrire; **dic'ta·tion** dictée *f*; ordres *m/pl.*; **dic'ta·tor** celui *m ou* celle *f* qui dicte; *pol.* dictateur *m*; **dic·ta·to·ri·al** ☐ [diktə'tɔ:riəl] dictatorial (-aux *m/pl.*); impérieux (-euse *f*) (*ton etc.*); **dic·ta·tor·ship** [dik'teitəʃip] dictature *f*.

dic·tion ['dikʃn] style *m*; diction *f*; **dic·tion·ar·y** ['dikʃənri] dictionnaire *m*; glossaire *m*.

dic·tum ['diktəm], *pl.* **-ta** ['~tə] affirmation *f*; maxime *f*, dicton *m*.

did [did] *prét. de* do 1, 2, 3.

di·dac·tic [di'dæktik] (~ally) didactique.

did·dle ['didl] duper; rouler (q. de qch, *s.o. out of s.th.*).

didn't ['didnt] = did not.

die[1] [dai] (*p.pr. dying*) mourir (de *of*, *from*); périr; crever (*animal*); brûler (de, *of*); ~ away s'éteindre (*voix*); s'affaiblir (*son*); s'effacer (*couleur*); disparaître (*lumières*); ~ down s'éteindre; se calmer; baisser; ~ out s'éteindre; disparaître; F ~ hard vendre chèrement sa vie; être dur à tuer (*abus*); F *never say* ~! il ne faut pas jeter le manche après la cognée.

die[2] [~] (*pl. dice*) dé *m*.

die[3] [~], *pl.* **dies** [daiz] matrice *f*; étampe *f*; *monnaie*: coin *m*; *lower* ~ matrice *f*; *as straight as a* ~ d'une droiture absolue.

die...: '~-a'way langoureux (-euse *f*); '~-cast·ing ⊕ moulage *m* sous pression; '~-hard conservateur *m* à outrance; jusqu'au-boutiste *m*.

di·e·lec·tric [daii'lektrik] diélectrique (*a. su./m*).

Die·sel en·gine ['diːzl'endʒin] moteur *m* Diesel.   [d'étampes.]

die-sink·er ['daisiŋkə] graveur *m*

di·et[1] ['daiət] 1. nourriture *f*; régime *m*; *be on a* ~ être au régime; *put on a* ~ mettre (*q.*) au régime; 2. *v/t.* mettre (*q.*) au régime; *v/i.* être au régime.

diet[2] [~] diète *f*.

di·e·tar·y ['daiətəri] 1. régime *m*; 2. diététique; alimentaire.

dif·fer ['difə] différer (de *in*, *from*); être différent (de); ne pas s'accorder (sur, *about*); **dif·fer·ence** ['difrəns] différence *f* (*a. ℞*), écart *m* (entre, *between*); dispute *f*; différend *m* (*a. ✝*); ⚙, *théâ., etc.* supplément *m*; *split the* ~ partager la différend; '**dif·fer·ent** ~ différent (de *from*, *to*); divers; autre (que, *from*); **dif·fer·en·ti·a** [ˌdifə'renʃiə], *pl.* **-ti·ae** [ˌ~ʃiiː] attribut *m* distinctif; **dif·fer·'en·tial** [ˌ~ʃl] 1. différentiel(le *f*); distinctif (-ive *f*); ~ *calculus* calcul *m* différentiel; 2. *mot.* différentiel *m*; ℞ différentielle *f*; **dif·fer·'en·ti·ate** [ˌ~ʃieit] (se) différencier; ℞ différentier.

dif·fi·cult □ ['difikəlt] difficile (*a. caractère etc.*); malaisé; **dif·fi·cul·ty** difficulté *f*; obstacle *m*; ennui *m*; embarras *m*.

dif·fi·dence ['difidəns] manque *m* d'assurance; '**dif·fi·dent** □ qui manque d'assurance.

dif·fract *phys.* [di'frækt] diffracter; **dif·frac·tion** diffraction *f*.

dif·fuse 1. [di'fjuːz] *fig.* (se) répandre; (se) diffuser; 2. □ [~s] diffus (*lumière, style, etc.*); prolixe (*style*); **dif·fu·sion** [ˌ~ʒn] diffusion *f* (*a. ⚛*); *phys.* dispersion *f*; **dif·fu·sive** □ [~siv] diffusif (-ive *f*); diffus (*style*).

dig [dig] 1. [*irr.*] *vt/i.* creuser; *v/t.* bêcher; creuser; enfoncer; F cogner; F loger en garni; ~ *in* enterrer; ~ *into* creuser (*qch.*); mordre dans; ~ *up* déraciner, arracher; (*fig. a.* ~ *out*) mettre à jour; *v/i.* travailler la terre; ~ *for* fouiller pour trouver (*qch.*); ~ *in* ⚔ se terrer; *fig.* s'assurer; 2. F coup *m* (*de coude etc.*); sarcasme *m*.

di·gest 1. [di'dʒest] *v/t.* mettre en ordre; faire un résumé de; digérer; élaborer (*un projet*); ⚕ digérer (*a. une insulte*); *v/i.* se digérer; 2. ['daidʒest] abrégé *m*, résumé *m*, sommaire *m*; ⚖ recueil *m* de lois, digeste *m*; **di·gest·er** [di'dʒestə] rédacteur *m* d'un résumé *etc.*; marmite *f* (*de Papin*); **di·gest·i·bil·i·ty** [ˌ~ə'biliti] digestibilité *f*; **di·gest·i·ble** digestible; **di·ges·tion** digestion *f*; **di·ges·tive** digestif *m*.

dig·ger ['digə] bêcheur *m*; *Am. sl.* exploiteuse *f* d'hommes riches; **dig·gings** F ['~iŋz] *pl.* logement *m*, garni *m*; *Am.* placer *m*.

dig·it ['didʒit] doigt *m* (*a. de pied*); ℞ chiffre *m*; '**dig·it·al** digital (-aux *m/pl.*); numérique (*ordinateur, montre etc.*).

dig·ni·fied ['dignifaid] digne; plein de dignité; **dig·ni·fy** ['~fai] revêtir d'un air de majesté; donner de la dignité à; *fig.* décorer (d'un titre). **dig·ni·tar·y** *usu. eccl.* ['dignitəri] dignitaire *m*; '**dig·ni·ty** dignité *f*.

di·gress [dai'gres] faire une digression (de, *from*); **di·gres·sion** [ˌ~ʃn] digression *f*, écart *m*; **di·gres·sive** □ digressif (-ive *f*).

dike[1] [daik] 1. digue *f*, levée *f*; chaussée *f* surélevée; 2. protéger par des digues.

dike[2] *sl.* [~] gouine *f*.

di·lap·i·date [di'læpideit] (se) délabrer; **di·lap·i·dat·ed** délabré, décrépit; **di·lap·i·da·tion** délabrement *m*; ~s *pl.* ⚖ détériorations *f/pl.*

di·lat·a·bil·i·ty *phys.* [daileitə'biliti]
dilatabilité *f*; **di'lat·a·ble** dilatable;
dil·a'ta·tion dilatation *f*; **di'late**
(se) dilater; ～ *upon* s'étendre sur
(*qch.*); **di'la·tion** *see dilatation*;
dil·a·to·ri·ness ['dilətərinis] lenteur *f* (à agir); **'dil·a·to·ry** □ lent
(à agir); tardif (-ive *f*) (*action*).
di·lem·ma *phls.* [di'lemə] dilemme
m; *fig.* embarras *m*.
dil·et·tan·te [dili'tænti], *pl.* **-ti**
[～ti:] dilettante *mf*.
dil·i·gence ['dilidʒəns] assiduité *f*;
'dil·i·gent □ assidu, diligent, appliqué.
dill ♀ [dil] aneth *m*.
dil·ly-dal·ly ['dilidæli] traînasser.
dil·u·ent ['diljuənt] délayant (*a.
su./m*); **di·lute** [dai'lju:t] **1.** diluer;
arroser; délayer; *fig.* atténuer; couper avec de l'eau; **2.** dilué; délayé;
fig. atténué; **di'lu·tion** dilution *f*;
délayage *m*; *fig.* atténuation *f*;
mouillage *m*.
di·lu·vi·al [dai'lu:vjəl], **di'lu·vi·an**
géol. diluvien(ne *f*); diluvial (-aux
m/pl.).
dim [dim] **1.** □ faible; effacé (*couleur*); vague (*mémoire*); **2.** *v/t.* obscurcir; réduire (*la lumière*); ternir
(*un miroir*, *a. fig.*); *mot.* baisser (*les
phares*); *Am. mot.* ～ *the headlights a.*
se mettre en code; *v/i.* s'obscurcir;
baisser.
dime *Am.* [daim] dime *f*; ～ *novel*
roman *m* à quatre sous; ～ *store* magasin *m* uniprix.
di·men·sion [di'menʃn] dimension
f; ⊕ cote *f*; ～s *pl. a.* encombrement
m hors tout.
di·min·ish [di'miniʃ] (se) réduire;
vt/i. diminuer; **dim·i·nu·tion**
[dimi'nju:ʃn] diminution *f*; amoindrissement *m* (de, *in*); **di'min·u·
tive** [～jutiv] **1.** □ *gramm.* diminutif
(-ive *f*); *fig.* minuscule; **2.** *gramm.*
diminutif *m*.
dim·mer ['dimə] ⚡ rhéostat *m*,
interrupteur *m* à gradation de
lumière; *Am. mot.* ～s *pl.* phares *m/pl.*
code; feux *m/pl.* de position.
dim·ple ['dimpl] **1.** fossette *f*; ride *f*
(*dans l'eau*); **2.** *v/t.* former des fos-
settes dans; *v/i.* se former en fosset-
tes; onduler (*eau*); **'dim·pled** à fos-
sette(s).
din [din] **1.** fracas *m*, vacarme *m*;
2. *v/i.* retentir; *v/t.* ～ *s.th. into s.o.*

(*'s ears*) corner qch. aux oreilles à q.
dine [dain] dîner; ～ *out* dîner en
ville; **'din·er** dîneur (-euse *f*) *m*; 🚃
surt. Am. wagon-restaurant (*pl.*
wagons-restaurants) *m*; **di·nette**
[dai'net] aire *f* de repas.
ding [diŋ] retentir, résonner; ～-
dong ['～'dɔŋ] **1.** digue-dong;
2. digue-don *m/inv.*; **3.** *sp.* durement disputé.
din·gey, **din·ghy** ['diŋgi] canot *m*,
youyou *m*; *rubber* ～ berthon *m*.
din·gle ['diŋgl] vallon *m* (boisé).
din·gus *Am. sl.* ['diŋgəs] machin *m*,
truc *m*.
din·gy □ ['dindʒi] qui manque d'é-
clat; terne; sale; défraîchi (*meubles*).
din·ing... ['dainiŋ]: '～-**car** 🚃 wagon-
restaurant (*pl.* wagons-restaurants)
m; '～-**room** salle *f* à manger.
dink·ey *Am.* ['diŋki] locomotive *f* de
manœuvres.
dink·y ['diŋki] F coquet(te *f*), mi-
gnon(ne *f*).
din·ner ['dinə] dîner *m*; banquet *m*;
F déjeuner *m*; '～-**jack·et** smoking
m; '～-**pail** *Am.* potager *m* (*d'ouvrier*); '～-**par·ty** dîner *m* (par invi-
tations); '～-**set** service *m* de table;
'～-**suit** smoking *m*; ～ **ta·ble** table *f*
de salle à manger; '～-**wag·(g)on**
fourniture; servante *f*.
dint [dint] **1.** marque *f* de coup;
creux *m*; *by* ～ *of* à force de; **2.** bosseler; ébrécher (*une lame*).
di·o·ce·san *eccl.* [dai'ɔsisn] diocé-
sain (*a. su./m*); **di·o·cese** ['daiəsis]
diocèse *m*.
di·ode ⚡ ['daioud] diode *f*; *light-
emitting* ～ diode *f* lumineuse.
di·op·tric *opt.* [dai'ɔptrik] **1.** diop-
trique; **2.** dioptrie *f*; ～s *pl.* dioptri-
que *f*.
di·o·ra·ma [daiə'rɑːmə] diorama *m*.
dip [dip] **1.** *v/t.* plonger; tremper;
immerger; baisser subitement; écoper (*dans from, out of*); teindre (*une
étoffe*); baigner (*les moutons*); ⚓
saluer avec (*son pavillon*); *mot.* baisser (*les phares*); *mot.* ～ *the headlights
a.* se mettre en code; *v/i.* plonger;
baisser (*soleil*); incliner; s'abaisser
(*terrain*); *géol.* s'incliner; ～ *into*
puiser dans (*une bourse*); effleurer
(*un sujet*); feuilleter (*un livre*); **2.**
plongement *m*, immersion *f*; pente *f*,
déclivité *f*; chandelle *f* plongée; ⚓
salut *m*; *géol.* pendage *m*; dépression

f (de l'horizon); bain *m* parasiticide (*pour moutons*); *aiguille aimantée:* inclinaison *f*; F coup *m* d'œil; F baignade *f*; F *have ou take a* ~ prendre un bain rapide, faire trempette; ♣ *at the* ~ à mi-drisse.

diph·the·ri·a [dif'θiəriə] diphtérie *f*.

diph·thong ['difθɔŋ] diphtongue *f*.

di·plo·ma [di'ploumə] diplôme *m*; **di'plo·ma·cy** diplomatie *f*; **di'plo·maed** [~məd] diplômé; **dip·lo·mat** ['dipləmæt] diplomate *m*; **dip·lo'mat·ic, dip·lo'mat·i·cal** □ diplomatique; **dip·lo'mat·ics** *pl.* diplomatique; **di·plo·ma·tist** [di'ploumətist] diplomate *m*.

dip·per ['dipə] plongeur (-euse *f*) *m*; *orn.* merle *m* d'eau; *mot.* basculeur *m*; *Am.* cuiller *f* à pot; *Am.* Great (*ou* Big) ♀ *astr.* la Grande Ourse; **'dip·py** *sl.* maboul.

dip·so·ma·ni·a [dipsou'meinjə] dipsomanie *f*; **dip·so'ma·ni·ac** [~niæk] dipsomane *mf*.

dip...: '~**rod** *Am.*, '~**stick** *mot.* jauge *f* (de niveau d'huile); '~**switch** *mot.* alternateur *m* pharescode.

dire ['daiə] néfaste; affreux (-euse *f*).

di·rect [di'rekt] **1.** □ direct; absolu; franc(he *f*) (*personne*); catégorique (*réponse*); ⚔ de plein fouet (*tir*); ⚡ ~ *current* courant *m* continu; *téléph.* ~ *dial(l)ing* (numéro *m* interurbain) automatique *m*; *gramm.* ~ *speech* discours *m ou* style *m* direct; ~ *train* train *m* direct; **2.** tout droit; *see* ~*ly* 1; **3.** diriger (*vers ât, to*[*wards*]); conduire (*les affaires, un orchestre*); gérer, régir, administrer; adresser (*une lettre* à q., *to* s.o.); ordonner (à q. de *inf.*, *s.o. to inf.*); indiquer (qch. à q., *s.th. to* s.o.); **di'rec·tion** direction *f*; administration *f*; sens *m*; adresse *f*; instruction *f*; **di'rec·tion·al** dirigeable (*radio*); radiogoniométrique; **di'rec·tion-find·er** *radio:* radiogoniomètre *m*; **di'rec·tion-find·ing** *radio:* radiogoniométrie *f*; *attr.* radiogoniométrique; ~ *set* radiogoniomètre *m*; **di'rec·tion-in·di·ca·tor** *mot.* clignotant *m*; flèche *f* lumineuse; signalisateur *m* de direction; ⚔ indicateur *m* de direction; **di'rec·tive** [~tiv] directif (-ive *f*); **di'rect·ly 1.** *adv.* directement, tout droit; tout de suite; tout à fait; **2.** *cj.* aussitôt que;

di'rect·ness direction *f ou* mouvement *m* en droite ligne; *fig.* franchise *f*.

di·rec·tor [di'rektə] directeur *m*, administrateur *m*; membre *m* d'un conseil d'administration; *théâ., cin.* metteur *m* en scène; *cin.* réalisateur *m*; **di'rec·to·rate** [~rit] (conseil *m* d')administration *f*; (*a.* **di'rec·tor·ship**) directorat *m*; **di'rec·to·ry** répertoire *m* d'adresses; *téléph.* annuaire *m* (des téléphones); *en France: le* Bottin *m*; *téléph. Am.* ~ *assistance*, *Brit.* ~ *enquiries* (service *m* des) renseignements *m*/*pl.*

di·rec·tress [di'rektris] directrice *f*.

dire·ful □ ['daiəful] néfaste.

dirge [də:dʒ] hymne *m* funèbre.

dir·i·gi·ble ['diridʒəbl] dirigeable *m* (*a. adj.*).

dirk [də:k] **1.** poignard *m*; **2.** poignarder.

dirt [də:t] saleté *f*; boue *f* (*surt. fig. péj.*); langage *m* ordurier; terre *f*, sol *m*; *Am. sl. do* (one) ~ jouer un vilain tour (à q.); donné; '~'**cheap** F à vil prix; donné; ~ *road Am.* chemin *m ou* route *f* non macadamisé(e); '~**track** *sp.* (piste *f* en)cendrée *f*; **'dirt·y 1.** □ sale (*a. fig.*); **2.** (se) salir.

dis·a·bil·i·ty [disə'biliti] incapacité *f*; infirmité *f*; ⚖ inhabilité *f*; *admin.* invalidité *f*.

dis·a·ble [dis'eibl] mettre hors de service *ou* de combat; mettre (*q.*) hors d'état (de *inf. from, for gér.*); **dis'a·bled** estropié, mutilé; hors de service *ou* de combat *ou* d'état; **dis'a·ble·ment** mise *f* hors de combat; incapacité *f*; invalidité *f*.

dis·a·buse [disə'bju:z] désabuser (de, *of*).

dis·ac·cord [disə'kɔ:d] être en désaccord (avec, *with*).

dis·ac·cus·tom ['disə'kʌstəm] déshabituer (q. de qch., *s.o. to s.th.*).

dis·ad·van·tage [disəd'va:ntidʒ] désavantage *m*, inconvénient *m*; *sell to* ~ vendre à perte; **dis·ad·van·ta·geous** □ [disædvəˈn'teidʒəs] défavorable.

dis·af·fect·ed □ [disə'fektid] désaffectionné, mal disposé (à l'égard de, envers *to, towards*); **dis·af·fec·tion** désaffection *f*.

dis·af·firm ⚖ [disə'fə:m] annuler.

dis·a·gree [disə'gri:] (*with*) ne pas être d'accord, être en désaccord (avec); donner tort (à); ne pas convenir (à *q.*); se brouiller (avec); **dis·a'gree·a·ble** □ désagréable (*a. fig.*); **dis·a'gree·ment** différence *f*; désaccord *m* (avec q. sur qch., *with s.o. in s.th.*); querelle *f*, différend *m*; mésentente *f*.

dis·al·low ['disə'lau] ne pas admettre; ne pas permettre; interdire.

dis·ap·pear [disə'piə] disparaître; **dis·ap'pear·ance** [~'piərəns] disparition *f*.

dis·ap·point [disə'pɔint] décevoir; désappointer; manquer de parole à; **dis·ap'point·ment** déception *f*; mécompte *m*.

dis·ap·pro·ba·tion [disæpro'beiʃn], **dis·ap·prov·al** [disə'pru:vl] désapprobation *f*; **dis·ap'prove** désapprouver (qch., *of s.th.*).

dis·arm [dis'ɑ:m] *vt/i.* désarmer (*a. fig.*); **dis'ar·ma·ment** [~məmənt] désarmement *m*.

dis·ar·range ['disə'reindʒ] mettre en désordre; déranger; **dis·ar'range·ment** désordre *m*; dérangement *m*.

dis·as·sem·bly ⊕ [disə'sembli] démontage *m*.

dis·as·ter [di'zɑ:stə] désastre *m*; sinistre *m*; catastrophe *f*; **dis'as·trous** □ désastreux (-euse *f*).

dis·a·vow ['disə'vau] désavouer; renier; **dis·a'vow·al** désaveu *m*; reniement *m*.

dis·band [dis'bænd] ✕ *v/t.* licencier; *v/i.* se débander; être licencié; **dis'band·ment** licenciement *m*.

dis·bar [dis'bɑ:] rayer (*un avocat*) du tableau de l'ordre.

dis·be·lief ['disbi'li:f] incrédulité *f* (à l'égard de, *in*); refus *m* de croire (à, *in*); **dis·be·lieve** ['disbi'li:v] *v/i.* ne pas croire (à, *in*); *v/t.* refuser créance à (*q.*); **'dis·be'liev·er** incrédule *mf*.

dis·bur·den [dis'bə:dn] décharger (d'un fardeau, *of a burden*); déposer (*un fardeau*); ouvrir (*son cœur*); *fig.* décharger.

dis·burse [dis'bə:s] débourser; **dis'burse·ment** déboursement *m*; ~s *pl.* débours *m/pl.*

disc [disk] *see* disk.

dis·card [dis'kɑ:d] **1.** se défaire de; abandonner (*une théorie etc.*); laisser de côté, mettre au rebut (*des vêtements*); *bridge*: défausser (de

qch., *s.th.*); **2.** *bridge*: défausse *f*; *surt. Am.* (pièce *f* de) rebut *m*.

dis·cern [di'sə:n] discerner; distinguer; apercevoir; **dis'cern·i·ble** □ perceptible; **dis'cern·ing 1.** □ pénétrant; judicieux (-euse *f*) (*personne*); **2.** discernement *m*; pénétration *f*; **dis'cern·ment** discernement *m*; jugement *m*.

dis·charge [dis'tʃɑ:dʒ] **1.** *v/t.* décharger (a. ⚓ *un navire*, ⚡, ⚔ *un fusil*); ⚓ débarquer (*un équipage*); lancer (*un projectile*); jeter (*du pus*); renvoyer (*un malade*); congédier (*un employé*), débaucher (*un ouvrier*); s'acquitter de (*un devoir*); verser (*du chagrin*); déverser (*du mépris*); acquitter (*un accusé, une dette, etc.*); libérer (*q. d'une obligation*); payer, apurer (*un compte*); *v/i.* se dégorger; suppurer; se déverser; partir (*fusil*); **2.** décharge *f* (*a.* ⚡); ⚓ déchargement *m*; *cargaison*: débardage *m*; *employé*: renvoi *m*; ✕ libération *f*; *prisonnier*: élargissement *m*; *accusé*: acquittement *m*; *dette*: paiement *m*; *devoir*: accomplissement *m*; *fonctions*: exercice *m*; ✿ écoulement *m*; **dis'charg·er** ⚡ excitateur *m*.

dis·ci·ple [di'saipl] disciple *mf*; élève *mf*; **dis'ci·ple·ship** qualité *f* de disciple.

dis·ci·plin·a·ble ['disiplinəbl] disciplinable; docile; **'dis·ci·pli·nal** disciplinaire; **dis·ci·pli·nar·i·an** [~'neəriən] **1.** (*a.* **dis·ci·pli·nar·y** ['~əri]) disciplinaire; de discipline; **2.** disciplinaire *mf*; **dis·ci·pline** ['~plin] **1.** discipline *f* (*a.* = *sujet d'étude*); **2.** discipliner; former, élever; dresser (*un animal*).

dis·claim [dis'kleim] renoncer à; renier; désavouer; **dis'claim·er** renonciation *f*; déni *m*; désaveu *m*.

dis·close [dis'klouz] révéler, découvrir; divulguer; **dis'clo·sure** [~ʒə] révélation *f*; divulgation *f*.

dis·col·o(u)r·a·tion [diskʌlə'reiʃn] décoloration *f*; **dis'col·o(u)r** (se) décolorer; (se) ternir.

dis·com·fit [dis'kʌmfit] déconfire; F déconcerter; **dis'com·fi·ture** [~tʃə] déconfiture *f* (*d'une armée*); *personne*: déconvenue *f*.

dis·com·fort [dis'kʌmfət] **1.** inconfort *m*; malaise *m*, gêne *f*; **2.** incommoder.

dis·com·pose [diskəm'pouz] troubler; **dis·com'po·sure** [~ʒə] trouble *m*; perturbation *f*.

dis·con·cert [diskən'sə:t] déconcerter; troubler.

dis·con·nect ['diskə'nekt] disjoindre (de *from*, *with*); ⊕ débrayer; ⨎ déconnecter; couper; **'dis·con'nect·ed** □ détaché; décousu (*style etc.*); **'dis·con'nec·tion** séparation *f*; ⊕ débrayage *m*.

dis·con·so·late □ [dis'kɔnsəlit] désolé; triste.

dis·con·tent ['diskən'tent] **1.** † *see* ~ed; **2.** mécontentement *m*; **'dis·con'tent·ed** □ mécontent (de, *with*); peu satisfait.

dis·con·tin·u·ance ['diskən'tinjuəns] discontinuation *f*; abandon *m*; **'dis·con'tin·ue** [~nju:] discontinuer; cesser (*a. v/i.*); se désabonner à (*un journal*); **'dis·con'tin·u·ous** □ discontinu; ⅄ discret (-ète *f*).

dis·cord ['diskɔ:d], **dis'cord·ance** discorde *f*; ♪ dissonance *f*, accord *m* dissonant; **dis'cord·ant** □ discordant; en désaccord (avec *to*, *from*, *with*); ♪ dissonant.

dis·co·theque ['diskoutek] discothèque *f*.

dis·count ['diskaunt] **1.** ✝ remise *f*, rabais *m*; *banque etc.*: escompte *m*; ~ *rate* taux *m* de l'escompte; ~ *store* magasin *m* à demi-gros; *at a* ~ *en* perte; *fig.* en défaveur, peu estimé; **2.** ✝ escompter; faire l'escompte de; *fig.* ne pas tenir compte de; faire peu de cas de; envisager (*un événement*); **dis'count·a·ble** escomptable; à négliger.

dis·coun·te·nance [dis'kauntinəns] déconcerter; désapprouver; **dis'coun·te·nanced** décontenancé.

dis·cour·age [dis'kʌridʒ] décourager (de, *from*); abattre; détourner (de, *from*); **dis'cour·age·ment** découragement *m*; désapprobation *f*.

dis·course [dis'kɔ:s] **1.** allocution *f*; discours *m*; dissertation *f*; **2.** (*on*, *upon*, *about*) discourir (sur); s'entretenir (de).

dis·cour·te·ous □ [dis'kə:tiəs] impoli; **dis'cour·te·sy** [~tisi] impolitesse *f*.

dis·cov·er [dis'kʌvə] trouver, découvrir; *poét.* révéler; **dis'cov·er·a·ble** □ que l'on peut découvrir; **dis'cov·er·er** découvreur (-euse *f*)

m; **dis'cov·er·y** découverte *f*; *poét.* révélation *f*.

dis·cred·it [dis'kredit] **1.** discrédit *m*; doute *m*; **2.** mettre en doute; ne pas croire; discréditer; **dis'cred·it·a·ble** □ (*to*) indigne, peu digne (de); qui ne fait pas honneur (à).

dis·creet □ [dis'kri:t] discret (~ète *f*); avisé.

dis·crep·an·cy [dis'krepənsi] divergence *f*; désaccord *m*; écart *m*.

dis·crete □ † [dis'kri:t] discret (-ète *f*); distinct; *phls.* abstrait.

dis·cre·tion [dis'kreʃn] discrétion *f*; sagesse *f*, jugement *m*, prudence *f*; silence *m* judicieux; *at s.o.'s* ~ à la discrétion de q.; *age* (*ou years*) *of* ~ âge *m* de raison; *surrender at* ~ se rendre à discrétion; **dis'cre·tion·al** □, **dis'cre·tion·ar·y** discrétionnaire.

dis·crim·i·nate [dis'krimineit] distinguer; ~ *against* faire des distinctions contre (q.); **dis'crim·i·nat·ing** □ avisé; plein de discernement; différentiel(le *f*) (*tarif*); **dis·crim·i'na·tion** discernement *m*; jugement *m*; distinction *f*; **dis'crim·i·na·tive** [~nətiv] □ avisé; plein de discernement; différentiel(le *f*); **dis'crim·i·na·to·ry** ɛ̃ʒ̃, † [dis'kriminətəri] qui fait la distinction des personnes.

dis·cur·sive □ [dis'kə:siv] décousu, sans suite; *phls.* discursif (-ive *f*).

dis·cus ['diskəs] *sp.* disque *m*.

dis·cuss [dis'kʌs] discuter; délibérer; *co.* expédier (*un plat*), vider (*une bouteille*); **dis'cuss·i·ble** [~əbl] discutable; **dis'cus·sion** discussion *f*; débat *m*.

dis·dain [dis'dein] **1.** dédain *m* (de, *of*); mépris *m*; **2.** dédaigner; **dis'dain·ful** □ [~ful] dédaigneux (-euse *f*) (de, *of*).

dis·ease [di'zi:z] maladie *f*; mal *m*; **dis'eased** malade; morbide.

dis·em·bark ['disim'ba:k] débarquer; **dis·em·bar·ka·tion** [disemba:'keiʃn] débarquement *m*.

dis·em·bar·rass ['disim'bærəs] débarrasser (de, *of*); dégager (de, *from*).

dis·em·bod·y ['disim'bɔdi] désincorporer; ✕ licencier (*des troupes*).

dis·em·bogue [disim'boug] *v/t.* verser; *v/i.* déboucher (*rivière*); débouquer (*navire*).   [cérer.]

dis·em·bow·el [disim'bauəl] évis-⌡

dis·en·chant ['disin't∫ɑːnt] désenchanter; désabuser.

dis·en·cum·ber ['disin'kʌmbə] débarrasser (de *of*, *from*); désencombrer (*q.*).

dis·en·gage ['disin'geidʒ] (se) dégager; ⊕ (se) déclencher; *v/t.* débrayer; **'dis·en'gaged** libre; **disen'gage·ment** dégagement *m*; rupture *f* de fiançailles.

dis·en·tan·gle ['disin'tæŋgl] (se) démêler; *fig.* dépêtrer (de, *from*); **disen'tan·gle·ment** débrouillement *m*.

dis·en·tomb [disin'tuːm] exhumer.

dis·es·tab·lish ['disis'tæbli∫] séparer (*l'Église*) de l'État; **dis·es'tablish·ment** séparation *f* de l'Église et de l'État.

dis·fa·vo(u)r ['dis'feivə] 1. défaveur *f*; disgrâce *f*; désapprobation *f*; 2. voir avec défaveur; désapprouver.

dis·fig·ure [dis'figə] défigurer; gâter; **dis'fig·ure·ment** défiguration *f*.

dis·fran·chise ['dis'frænt∫aiz] priver (*q.*) du droit électoral; priver (*un bourg*) de ses droits de représentation; **dis'fran·chise·ment** [dis'frænt∫izmənt] privation *f* du droit de vote *ou* des droits civiques.

dis·gorge [dis'gɔːdʒ] rendre (= *vomir*); (*a.* ~ *o.s.*) dégorger; décharger (*rivière*).

dis·grace [dis'greis] 1. disgrâce *f*; honte *f*; déshonneur *m*; 2. déshonorer; disgracier (*q.*); *be* ~*ed* être disgracié; **dis'grace·ful** □ [~ful] honteux (-euse *f*); scandaleux (-euse *f*).

dis·grun·tled [dis'grʌntld] maussade; mécontent (de, *at*).

dis·guise [dis'gaiz] 1. déguiser; masquer (*une odeur*); dissimuler (*une émotion*); 2. déguisement *m*; fausse apparence *f*; feinte *f*; *blessing in* ~ bienfait *m* insoupçonné.

dis·gust [dis'gʌst] 1. (*at*, *for*) dégoût *m* (pour); répugnance *f* (pour); *fig.* *in* ~ dégoûté (*q.*); 2. dégoûter, écœurer; ~*ed* with profondément mécontent de; **dis'gust·ing** □ dégoûtant.

dish [di∫] 1. plat *m*; récipient *m*; *cuis.* plat *m* (*de viande etc.*), mets *m*; *fig.* *standing* ~ plat *m* de tous les jours; 2. (*usu.* ~ *up*) servir (*a. fig.*), dresser; *sl.* enfoncer, rouler (*q.*).

dis·ha·bille [disæ'biːl] négligé *m*, déshabillé *m*; *in* ~ en déshabillé.

dis·har·mo·ny [dis'hɑːməni] dissonance *f*; désaccord *m*.

dish-cloth ['di∫klɔθ] torchon *m*; lavette *f*.

dis·heart·en [dis'hɑːtn] décourager.

di·shev·el(l)ed [di'∫evld] échevelé; ébouriffé; en désordre.

dis·hon·est □ [dis'ɔnist] malhonnête; déloyal (-aux *m/pl.*); **dis'hones·ty** malhonnêteté *f*.

dis·hon·o(u)r [dis'ɔnə] 1. déshonneur *m*; honte *f*; 2. déshonorer; manquer à (*sa parole*); ✝ ne pas honorer; **dis'hon·o(u)r·a·ble** □ déshonorant, honteux (-euse *f*); sans honneur (*personne*).

dish...: **'~·pan** *Am.* cuvette *f*; **'~rag** *Am. see* dish-cloth; **'~·wa·ter** eau *f* de vaisselle; *sl.* lavasse *f*.

dish·y F ['di∫i] appétisant.

dis·il·lu·sion [disi'luːʒn] 1. désillusion *f*, désabusement *m*; 2. *a.* **disil'lu·sion·ize** désillusionner, désabuser; **dis·il'lu·sion·ment** *see* disillusion 1.

dis·in·cli·na·tion [disinkli'nei∫n] répugnance *f* (pour *for*, *to*); manque *m* d'empressement (à, *to*); **dis·incline** ['~'klain] détourner (de *for*, *to*); **'dis·in'clined** peu disposé (à *for*, *to*).

dis·in·fect ['disin'fekt] désinfecter; **dis·in'fect·ant** désinfectant (*a. su./m*); **dis·in'fec·tion** désinfection *f*.

dis·in·gen·u·ous □ [disin'dʒenjuəs] sans franchise; faux (fausse *f*).

dis·in·her·it ['disin'herit] déshériter; **dis·in'her·it·ance** déshéritement *m*; ⚖ exhérédation *f*.

dis·in·te·grate [dis'intigreit] (se) désagréger; (se) désintégrer (*minerai*); **dis·in·te'gra·tion** désagrégation *f*; effritement *m*.

dis·in·ter ['disin'tə:] déterrer, exhumer.

dis·in·ter·est·ed □ [dis'intristid] désintéressé.

dis·join [dis'dʒɔin] disjoindre; **dis'joint** [~t] démembrer, disjoindre; désassembler; ⚕ désarticuler; **dis'joint·ed** disjoint, disloqué; *fig.* décousu.

dis·junc·tion [dis'dʒʌŋk∫n] disjonction *f*; **dis'junc·tive** □ 1. disjonctif (-ive *f*) (*a. gramm.*); 2. *gramm.* disjonctive *f*.

disk [disk] disque *m*; plaque *f* (*d'i-dentité*); *mot*. ~ **brakes** freins *m/pl.* à disque; *mot*. ~ **clutch** embrayage *m* par disque unique; *✠ slipped* ~ hernie *f* discale; *Am. sl.* ~ **jockey** *radio*: présenteur *m ou* présentatrice *f* du disque des auditeurs.

dis·like [dis'laik] **1.** aversion *f*, répugnance *f* (pour *for, of, to*); **2.** ne pas aimer; détester; trouver mauvais; ~*d* mal vu.

dis·lo·cate ['dislokeit] disloquer; déboîter (*un membre*); *fig.* désorganiser; **dis·lo·ca·tion** dislocation *f* (*a. géol., a. anat.*); *fig.* désorganisation *f*. [tacher.]

dis·lodge [dis'lɔdʒ] déloger; dé-᷏

dis·loy·al ['dis'lɔiəl] infidèle; déloyal (-aux *m/pl.*); **'dis'loy·al·ty** infidélité *f*; déloyauté *f*.

dis·mal □ ['dizməl] **1.** *fig.* sombre, triste; morne; lugubre; **2.**: *the* ~*s* *pl.* le cafard *m*.

dis·man·tle [dis'mæntl] dégarnir, dépouiller (de, *of*); démanteler (*une forteresse*, *✠ un vaisseau de guerre*); *✠* dégréer (*un navire*); *⊕* démonter (*une machine*), déséquiper (*une grue etc.*); **dis'man·tling** dégarnissement *m etc.*; *⊕* démontage *m*.

dis·mast *✠* [dis'mɑːst] démâter.

dis·may [dis'mei] **1.** consternation *f*; épouvante *f*; **2.** consterner; épouvanter.

dis·mem·ber [dis'membə] démembrer; écarteler (*un corps*); **dis'mem·ber·ment** démembrement *m*.

dis·miss [dis'mis] *v/t.* congédier; renvoyer; éconduire (*un importun etc.*); relever (*q.*) de ses fonctions; quitter (*un sujet*); *cricket*: mettre hors jeu; *✝✝* acquitter (*un accusé*), rejeter (*une demande*); *be* ~*ed* du service être renvoyé du service; *v/i.* *✗* ~! rompez (les rangs)!; **dis'miss·al** congédiement *m*; renvoi *m*; *✝✝* acquittement *m* (*d'un accusé*); fin *f* de non-recevoir.

dis·mount ['dis'maunt] *v/t.* faire descendre (*q.*) de cheval; *⊕* démonter (*a. un canon*); *v/i.* descendre (de cheval, de voiture).

dis·o·be·di·ence [disə'biːdjəns] désobéissance *f* (à *to, of*); **dis·o'be·di·ent** □ désobéissant; **'dis·o'bey** désobéir à; enfreindre; *I will not be* ~*ed* je ne veux pas qu'on me désobéisse.

dis·o·blige ['disə'blaidʒ] désobliger (*q.*); **'dis·o'blig·ing** □ désobligeant, peu complaisant (envers, *to*); **'dis·o'blig·ing·ness** désobligeance *f*.

dis·or·der [dis'ɔːdə] **1.** désordre *m* (*a. ✠*); confusion *f*; tumulte *m*; *✠* affection *f*; *mental* ~ dérangement *m* d'esprit; **2.** déranger (*a. ✠*); mettre le désordre dans; **dis'or·dered** □ en désordre; désordonné; *✠* dérangé (*estomac etc.*); **dis'or·der·ly** en désordre; désordonné (*a. personne*); qui manque d'ordre; turbulent (*foule etc.*).

dis·or·gan·i·za·tion [disɔːgənai'zeiʃn] désorganisation *f*; **dis'or·gan·ize** désorganiser.

dis·own [dis'oun] désavouer; renier.

dis·par·age [dis'pæridʒ] déprécier, dénigrer; discréditer; **dis'par·age·ment** dénigrement *m*, dépréciation *f*; déshonneur *m*; **dis'par·ag·ing** □ dépréciateur (-trice *f*); peu flatteur (-euse *f*).

dis·pa·rate □ ['dispərit] **1.** disparate; **2.** ~*s* *pl.* disparates *f/pl.*; **dis·par·i·ty** [dis'pæriti] inégalité *f*; différence *f*.

dis·part [dis'pɑːt] *poét. ou* † (se) fendre; (se) séparer; *v/t.* *⊕* distribuer.

dis·pas·sion·ate □ [dis'pæʃnit] impartial (-aux *m/pl.*); calme; sans passion.

dis·patch [dis'pætʃ] **1.** expédition *f*; envoi *m*; promptitude *f*, diligence *f*; dépêche *f*; mise *f* à mort; *bearer of* ~*es* messager *m*; *mentioned in* ~*es* cité à l'ordre du jour; *by* ~ par exprès; **2.** expédier (*a.* = *mettre à mort*); envoyer; dépêcher (*un courrier*); ~**-box** valise *f* diplomatique; ~ **note** bulletin *m ou* bordereau *m* d'expédition; ~**-rid·er** *✗* estafette *f*.

dis·pel [dis'pel] dissiper, chasser (*a. fig.*).

dis·pen·sa·ble [dis'pensəbl] dont on peut se passer; *eccl.* dispensable; **dis'pen·sa·ry** pharmacie *f*; policlinique *f*; *hôpital*: dépense *f*; **dis·pen·sa·tion** [dispen'seiʃn] distribution *f*; décret *m*; *eccl.* dispense *f*; fait *m* d'être dispensé (de, *from*).

dis·pense [dis'pens] *v/t.* dispenser, distribuer; administrer (*la loi*); préparer (*un médicament*); exécuter (*une ordonnance*); ~ *from* dispenser de; *v/i.* ~ with se passer de; supprimer (*une main-d'œuvre*); ne pas exiger; **dis'pens·er** dispensateur (-trice *f*) *m*; pharmacien(ne *f*) *m*. **dis·perse** [dis'pə:s] (se) disperser; *v/t.* dissiper; répandre; *⚕* résoudre; **dis'per·sion, dis'per·sal** dispersion *f* (*a. opt.*); **dis'per·sive** □ dispersif (-ive *f*) (*a. opt.*).

dis·pir·it [dis'pirit] décourager; **dis'pir·it·ed** □ découragé, abattu. **dis·place** [dis'pleis] déplacer; évincer (*q.*); supplanter, remplacer; ~d person (*abr. D.P.*) personne *f* déplacée; **dis'place·ment** déplacement *m* (*a. ⚓*); changement *m* de place; remplacement *m*; *géol.* dislocation *f*.

dis·play [dis'plei] 1. étalage *m* (*a. ✝*); manifestation *f*; exposition *f*; parade *f*, apparat *m*; 2. étaler, exposer; afficher; montrer; faire preuve de; révéler; ~ **case** vitrine *f* (*d'exposition*); ~ **stand** présentoir *m*.

dis·please [dis'pli:z] déplaire (à *q.*, *s.o.*); *fig.* contrarier; **dis'pleased** □ mécontent (*de at, with*); **dis'pleas·ing** □ désagréable, déplaisant (à, *to*); **dis·pleas·ure** [~'pleʒə] mécontentement *m* (*de at, over*); déplaisir *m*. [*tir*; s'ébattre.]

dis·port [dis'pɔ:t]: ~ *o.s.* se diver-) **dis·pos·a·ble** [dis'pouzəbl] disponible; **dis'pos·al** disposition *f*; action *f* de disposer (*de, of*); expédition *f* (*d'une affaire*); résolution *f* (*d'une question*); ✝ délivrance *f*; *at s.o.'s* ~ à la disposition de q.; **dis'pose** *v/t.* disposer (*a. q. à, s.o. to*); arranger; incliner (*q. à, s.o. to; q. à qch., s.o. for s.th.*); *v/i.* ~ *of* disposer de; se défaire de; vaincre; expédier; ✝ vendre, écouler; trancher (*une question*); résoudre (*un problème*); **dis'posed** □ porté, enclin (à *to, for*); disposé (à, *to*); (*bien, mal*) intentionné (*envers, pour,* à l'égard de *towards*); **dis'pos·er** dispensateur (-trice *f*) *m*; ordonnateur (-trice *f*) *m*; vendeur (-euse *f*) *m*; **dis·po·si·tion** [~pə'ziʃn] disposition *f* (*a. testamentaire*); arrangement *m*; humeur *f*, naturel *m*, caractère *m*; tendance *f* (à, *to*); *at my* ~ à ma disposition, à mon service; *make* ~*s* prendre des dispositions (*pour, to*).

dis·pos·sess ['dispə'zes] (*of*) déposséder (de); exproprier; ✝ délivrer (de); ☆ dessaisir (de); **dis·pos·ses·sion** [~'zeʃn] dépossession *f*; expropriation *f*; ☆ dessaisissement *m*.

dis·praise [dis'preiz] 1. blâme *m*; dépréciation *f*; 2. blâmer; dénigrer. **dis·proof** ['dis'pru:f] réfutation *f*. **dis·pro·por·tion** ['disprə'pɔ:ʃn] disproportion *f*; **dis·pro'por·tion·ate** □ [~it] disproportionné (à, *to*); hors de proportion (*avec, to*); **dis·pro'por·tion·ate·ness** disproportion *f*. **dis·prove** ['dis'pru:v] réfuter. **dis·pu·ta·ble** [dis'pju:təbl] contestable; **dis'pu·tant** discuteur (-euse *f*) *m*; *écoles:* disputant *m*; **dis·pu·ta·tion** [~'teiʃn] débat *m*; discussion *f*; **dis·pu'ta·tious** □ chicanier (-ère *f*); **dis'pute** 1. contestation *f*, controverse *f*; querelle *f*; *beyond* ~ incontestable; *in* ~ contesté; 2. *v/t.* contester; débattre; disputer (*qch. à q., s.th. with s.o.*); *v/i.* se disputer (*sur, au sujet de about*).

dis·qual·i·fi·ca·tion [diskwɔlifi'keiʃn] incapacité *f*; mise *f* en état *ou* cause *f* d'incapacité; *sp.* disqualification *f*; ☆ inhabilité *f*; **dis·'qual·i·fy** [~fai] rendre incapable (*de inf., for gér.*); *sp.* disqualifier. **dis·qui·et** [dis'kwaiət] 1. inquiétude *f*; agitation *f*; 2. inquiéter; troubler; ~*ing* alarmant; **dis·qui·e·tude** [~'kwaiitju:d] inquétude *f*; agitation *f*. [*tation f* (*sur, on*).] **dis·qui·si·tion** [diskwi'ziʃn] disser-) **dis·re·gard** ['disri'gɑ:d] 1. indifférence *f* (à l'égard de *of, for*); inobservation *f* (*de la loi*); 2. ne tenir aucun compte de; négliger. **dis·rel·ish** [dis'reliʃ] 1. dégoût *m*, aversion *f* (*pour, for*); 2. éprouver du dégoût pour; trouver mauvais. **dis·re·pair** ['disri'pɛə] délabrement *m*; *fall into* ~ tomber en ruines; *in* ~ en mauvais état. **dis·rep·u·ta·ble** □ [dis'repjutəbl] honteux (-euse *f*); minable; de mauvaise réputation (*personne*); **dis·re·pute** ['~ri'pju:t] discrédit *m*, mépris *m*. **dis·re·spect** ['disris'pekt] manque *m* de respect *ou* d'égards (*envers, for*); **dis·re·spect·ful** [~'pektful] □ irrespectueux (-euse *f*), irrévérencieux (-euse *f*).

dis·robe ['dis'roub] (aider à) se dévêtir de sa robe; (se) déshabiller.
dis·root [dis'ru:t] déraciner.
dis·rupt [dis'rʌpt] rompre, disloquer; démembrer; **dis'rup·tion**
rupture *f*; dislocation *f*; démembrement *m*; **dis'rup·tive** perturbateur
(-trice *f*).
dis·sat·is·fac·tion ['dissætis'fækʃn]
mécontentement *m* (de *with, at*);
dissatisfaction *f*; **'dis·sat·is'fac-
to·ry** [⸝təri] peu satisfaisant; **dis-
'sat·is·fy** [⸝fai] mécontenter; ne
pas satisfaire (*q.*).
dis·sect [di'sekt] disséquer (*a. anat.*);
découper; ⚕ exciser (*une tumeur
etc.*); **dis·sec·tion** [di'sekʃn] dissection *f*; découpage *m*.
dis·sem·ble [di'sembl] *v/t.* dissimuler; passer sous silence; feindre;
v/i. déguiser sa pensée; user de
dissimulation.
dis·sem·i·nate [di'semineit] disséminer; **dis·sem·i'na·tion** dissémination *f*.   [désaccord *m.*]
dis·sen·sion [di'senʃn] dissension *f*,|
dis·sent [di'sent] 1. dissentiment *m*;
avis *m* contraire; *eccl.* dissidence *f*;
2. différer (de, *from*); *eccl.* être
dissident; **dis'sent·er** dissident(e *f*)
m; **dis'sent·ient** [di'senʃiənt] dissi-
dent(e *f*) *m* (*a. adj.*).
dis·ser·ta·tion [disə'teiʃn] dissertation *f* (sur, on).
dis·serv·ice ['dis'sə:vis] mauvais
service *m* (rendu à, to).
dis·sev·er [dis'sevə] (se) séparer,
(se) désunir; **dis'sev·er·ance** [⸝-
ərəns] séparation *f*.
dis·si·dence ['disidəns] dissidence *f*;
'dis·si·dent 1. dissident; 2. membre *m* dissident; dissident(e *f*) *m*.
dis·sim·i·lar □ ['di'similə] (to)
différent (de); dissemblable (à);
dis·sim·i·lar·i·ty [⸝'læriti] dissemblance *f*, dissimilitude *f* (de, to).
dis·sim·u·late [di'simjuleit] *see* dis-
semble; **dis·sim·u'la·tion** dissimulation *f*.
dis·si·pate ['disipeit] (se) dissiper;
v/i. F mener une vie dissipée; **'dis·si·
pat·ed** dissipé; **dis·si'pa·tion** dissipation *f*; gaspillage *m*; divertissement *m*; F vie *f* désordonnée.
dis·so·ci·ate [di'souʃieit] désasso-
cier; ⚕ dissocier; ⁓ *o.s.* se désintéresser (de, *from*); **dis·so·ci'a·tion**
désassociation *f*; ⚕ dissociation *f*;

psych. dédoublement *m* de la
personnalité.
dis·sol·u·bil·i·ty [disɔlju'biliti] dis-
solubilité *f*; **dis·sol·u·ble** [di-
'sɔljubl] dissoluble (dans, in).
dis·so·lute □ ['disəlu:t] dissolu, débauché; **dis·so'lu·tion** dissolution
f; fonte *f*; mort *f*.
dis·solv·a·ble [di'zɔlvəbl] dissoluble; **dis'solve** 1. *v/t.* (faire) dissoudre (*a. fig.*); *v/i.* se dissoudre;
fondre (*a. fig.*); se dissiper; 2. *Am.
cin.* fondu *m*; **dis'solv·ent** 1. † dissolvant; 2. dissolvant *m*.
dis·so·nance ['disənəns] ♪ dissonance *f*; désaccord *m*; **'dis·so·nant**
♪ dissonant; en désaccord (avec,
from, to).
dis·suade [di'sweid] dissuader, détourner (de, *from*); **dis·sua·sion**
[di'sweiʒn] dissuasion *f*; **dis·sua-
sive** [di'sweisiv] □ dissuasif (-ive *f*).
dis·taff ['dista:f] quenouille *f*; *attr.
fig.* du côté féminin.
dis·tance ['distəns] 1. *lieu, temps*:
distance *f*; éloignement *m*; lointain
m; intervalle *m*; *fig.* réserve *f*; at *a* ⁓
de loin; à une distance (de, of);
dans le lointain; *in the* ⁓ au loin,
dans le lointain; de loin; *a great* ⁓
away très loin, à une grande distance; *striking* ⁓ portée *f* (de la
main); 2. éloigner; *fig.* reculer;
'⁓-con'trolled commandé à distance; **'dis·tant** □ éloigné; lointain; à distance; réservé, distant
(*personne*); *two miles* ⁓ à deux
milles de distance; ⁓ *control* commande *f* à distance; ⁓ *relative* cousin
m (cousine *f*) éloigné(e).
dis·taste ['dis'teist] dégoût *m* (de,
for); aversion *f* (pour, *for*); **dis-
'taste·ful** □ [⸝ful] désagréable,
antipathique (à).
dis·tem·per[1] [dis'tempə] 1. détrempe *f*; badigeon *m*; 2. peindre
(*un tableau, un mur*) en détrempe;
badigeonner (*un mur*) en couleur.
dis·tem·per[2] [⸝] † maladie *f*; *vét.*
maladie *f* des chiens; *pol.* † désordre *m*; **dis'tem·pered** troublé,
dérangé (*esprit*).
dis·tend [dis'tend] (se) dilater; (se)
distendre; *v/t.* gonfler; *v/i.* enfler;
dis'ten·sion dilatation *f*.
dis·tich ['distik] distique *m*.
dis·til(l) [dis'til] *usu.* (se) distiller;
(laisser) tomber goutte à goutte;

v/t. raffiner (*le pétrole*); *fig.* faire couler; **dis·til·late** ['ˌit] distillat *m*; **dis·til·la·tion** [ˌ'leiʃn] distillation *f*; **dis'till·er** distillateur *m*; **dis'till·er·y** distillerie *f*.

dis·tinct □ [dis'tiŋkt] distinct (de, *from*); net(te *f*); clair; marqué; **dis'tinc·tion** distinction *f*; *draw a ~ between* faire une distinction entre; *have the ~ of* (*gér.*) avoir l'honneur de (*inf.*); **dis'tinc·tive** □ distinctif (-ive *f*); d'identification; **dis'tinct·ness** clarté *f*, netteté *f*; différence *f* totale.

dis·tin·guish [dis'tiŋgwiʃ] *v/t.* distinguer; différencier (de, *from*); *v/i.* faire une *ou* la distinction (entre, *between*); **dis'tin·guish·a·ble** que l'on peut distinguer; perceptible; **dis'tin·guished** distingué; de distinction *ou* marque; remarquable (par, *for*); *~ by* connu pour; reconnu à (*sa marche etc.*).

dis·tort [dis'tɔːt] tordre; déformer; *fig.* fausser, défigurer; *~ing mirror* miroir *m* déformant; **dis'tor·tion** distorsion *f*; déformation *f* (*a. opt., a. tél.*).

dis·tract [dis'trækt] distraire, détourner (*q.*); brouiller (*l'esprit*); **dis'tract·ed** □ affolé, éperdu (de, *with*); **dis'tract·ing** □ affolant; tourmentant; **dis'trac·tion** distraction *f*; confusion *f*; affolement *m*, folie *f*.

dis·train [dis'trein]: *~ upon* saisir; exécuter (*q.*); **dis'train·a·ble** saisissable; **dis'traint** saisie *f*.

dis·tress [dis'tres] 1. détresse *f*, angoisse *f*; embarras *m*; gêne *f*; *see distraint*; ⚓ *~ rocket* signal *m* de détresse; 2. affliger, chagriner; épuiser; **dis'tressed** affligé, désolé; épuisé; *fig.* ruiné, réduit à la misère; **dis'tress·ing** □, *poét.* **dis'tress·ful** □ [ˌful] angoissant, affligeant.

dis·trib·ut·a·ble [dis'tribjutəbl] répartissable, partageable; **dis'trib·ute** [ˌjuːt] distribuer (*a. typ.*); répartir; **dis·tri'bu·tion** (mise *f* en) distribution *f*; répartition *f* (*a. des dettes*); *typ.* mise *f* en casse; **dis'trib·u·tive** 1. □ distributif (-ive *f*) (*a. gramm.*); 2. *gramm.* distributif *m*; **dis'trib·u·tor** distributeur *m* (*a.* ⊕); ✝ concessionnaire *m*.

dis·trict ['distrikt] région *f*, contrée *f*; district *m* (*a. admin.*); quartier *m*

(*de ville*); circonscription *f* (*électorale*); *~ council* conseil *m* départemental; *Am.* ⚖ *~ court* cour *f* fédérale; ✝ *~ manager* directeur (-trice *f*) *m* régional(e).

dis·trust [dis'trʌst] 1. méfiance *f*, défiance *f* (de, *of*); 2. se méfier *ou* défier de; **dis'trust·ful** □ [ˌful] méfiant, défiant; soupçonneux (-euse *f*); *~ of o.s.* timide.

dis·turb [dis'təːb] déranger; troubler; agiter; inquiéter; **dis'turb·ance** trouble *m*; agitation *f*; tapage *m*; émeute *f*; ⚖ trouble *m* de jouissance; **dis'tur·bed** *psych.* inadapté.

dis·un·ion ['dis'juːnjən] désunion *f*; séparation *f*; **dis·u·nite** ['disjuː-'nait] (se) désunir; (se) séparer; **dis·u·ni·ty** [dis'juːniti] désunion *f*.

dis·use 1. ['dis'juːs] désuétude *f*; *fall into ~* tomber en désuétude; F être mis au rancart; 2. ['dis'juːz] cesser d'employer; abandonner.

di·syl·lab·ic ['disi'læbik] (*~ally*) dissyllabe (*mot*); dissyllabique (*vers*); **di·syl·la·ble** [di'siləbl] dissyllabe *m*.

ditch [ditʃ] 1. fossé *m*; *Am.* Canal *m* de Panama; *die in the last ~* résister jusqu'à la dernière extrémité; 2. *v/t.* entourer de fossés; *sl.* se débarrasser de, plaquer; *mot.* verser dans le fossé; *v/i.* curer les fossés; *sl.* faire un amerrissage forcé; **'ditch·er** cureur *m* de fossés.

dith·er F ['diðə] trembloter; s'agiter sans but.

dith·y·ramb ['diθiræmb] dithyrambe *m*.

dit·to ['ditou] 1. idem; de même; 2. ✝ dito *m*/*inv.*; (*suit of*) *~s pl.* complet *m*.

dit·ty ['diti] chanson(nette *f*) *f*.

di·ur·nal □ [dai'əːnl] diurne.

di·va·gate ['daivəgeit] diverger, divaguer, s'éloigner du sujet; **di·va·ga·tion** [daivə'geiʃn] divagation *f*.

di·van [di'væn] divan *m*.

di·var·i·cate [dai'værikeit] diverger; bifurquer.

dive [daiv] 1. plonger (dans, *into*); ✈, *a. fig.* piquer (du nez); F *~ into* s'enfoncer dans, entrer précipitamment dans; plonger (la main) dans (*la poche*); 2. plongeon *m*; *sous-marin:* plongée *f*; ✈ (vol *m*) piqué *m*; *Am.* F cabaret *m* borgne;

gargote f; boîte f; **'div·er** plongeur m; scaphandrier m; orn. plongeon m.

di·verge [dai'vɔ:dʒ] diverger, s'écarter; **di'ver·gence, di'ver·gen·cy** divergence f; écart m; biol. variation f; **di'ver·gent** □ divergent.

di·verse □ [dai'vɔ:s] divers, différent; varié; **di·ver·si·fi·ca·tion** [ˌsifi'keiʃn] variation f; **di'ver·si·fy** [ˌfai] diversifier, varier; **di·'ver·sion** [ˌʃn] détournement m; ✗ diversion f (a. de l'esprit); fig. divertissement m, distraction f; **di·'ver·si·ty** [ˌsiti] diversité f.

di·vert [dai'vɔ:t] détourner; écarter; divertir; distraire.

di·vest [dai'vest] dévêtir; fig. dépouiller, priver; ~ o.s. of renoncer à; **di'vest·ment** dévêtement m; fig. privation f.

di·vide [di'vaid] **1.** v/t. diviser (a. Ⱥ); (souv. ~ up) démembrer; partager, répartir (entre, among); séparer (de, from); parl. ~ the house aller aux voix; v/i. se diviser, se partager (en, into); se séparer; Ⱥ être divisible (par, by); fourcher (chemin); parl. aller aux voix; **2.** Am. ligne f de partage des eaux; **div·i·dend** ['dividend] ✦, a. Ⱥ dividende m; **di·vid·er** [di'vaidə] Am. mot. bande f médiane; Ⱥ~s pl. compas m à pointes sèches; **di·vid·ing** [di'vaidiŋ] de démarcation; mitoyen(ne f) (mur).

div·i·na·tion [divi'neiʃn] divination f; **di·vine** [di'vain] **1.** □ divin (a. fig.); ~ service office m divin; **2.** théologien m; **3.** deviner, prédire (l'avenir); **di'vin·er** devin(eresse f) m; divinateur (-trice f) m.

div·ing ['daiviŋ] action f de plonger; attr. à ou de plongeurs; à plonger; **'~·bell** cloche f à ou de plongeur.

di·vin·ing-rod [di'vainiŋrɔd] baguette f divinatoire.

di·vin·i·ty [di'viniti] divinité f (a. = dieu); théologie f.

di·vis·i·bil·i·ty [divizi'biliti] divisibilité f; **di'vis·i·ble** □ [ˌzəbl] divisible; **di'vi·sion** [ˌʒn] division f (a. = désunion, a. ✗, Ⱥ); partage m (en, into); biol. classe f; parl. vote m; parl. circonscription f (électorale); **di'vi·sion·al** ✗ etc. divisionnaire; **di·vi·sive** [di'vaisiv] qui désunit; qui sème la discorde; **di'vi·sor** Ⱥ [ˌzə] diviseur m.

di·vorce [di'vɔ:s] **1.** divorce m (a. fig.); **2.** divorcer d'avec (sa femme, son mari); F a. fig. séparer (de, from), détacher (de, from); **di·vor·cee** divorcé(e f) m.

di·vulge [dai'vʌldʒ] divulguer; révéler.

dix·ie ✗ sl. ['diksi] gamelle f; Am. ♀ États m/pl. du Sud; ♀crat Am. pol. démocrate m dissident des États du Sud.

diz·zi·ness ['dizinis] vertige m; **'diz·zy 1.** □ pris de vertige (personne); sl. étourdi; (chose); ~ spell étourdissement m; **2.** étourdir.

do [du:] (see a. done) **1.** v/t. [irr.] usu. faire; (faire) cuire; s'acquitter de; finir; jouer (une pièce); F duper, refaire (q.); sl. ~ London visiter Londres; sl. ~ s.o. traiter, soigner q.; fêter q.; what is to be done? que faire?; ~ the polite etc. faire l'aimable etc.; have done reading avoir fini de lire; ~ (over) again refaire; F ~ down rouler, enfoncer (q.); F ~ in tuer; ~ into traduire en (une langue); ~ out nettoyer; ~ over couvrir (de peinture etc.); ~ up envelopper, ficeler; emballer; boutonner; décorer, réparer; F éreinter (q.); F ~ o.s. up faire toilette; **2.** v/i. [irr.] faire l'affaire; aller; suffire; convenir; that will ~ c'est bien; cela va; cela suffira; that won't ~ cela ne va ou n'ira pas; how ~ you ~? comment allez-vous?; comment vous portez-vous?; F ça va?; ~ well aller bien; réussir; ~ badly aller mal; ne pas réussir; have done! finissez donc!; cela suffit!; ~ away with abolir; détruire; F tuer; ~ for faire le ménage de (q.); tuer (q.); ~ with s'accommoder de; I could ~ with some coffee je prendrais volontiers du café; I have done with him j'ai rompu avec lui; ~ without se passer de; **3.** v/aux. [irr.] interr.: ~ you know him? le connaissez-vous?; avec not: I ~ not know him je ne le connais pas; accentué: I ~ feel better je me sens vraiment mieux; ~ come and see me venez me voir, je vous en prie; ~ be quick dépêchez-vous donc; remplaçant un verbe déjà exprimé: do you like London? — I ~ aimez-vous Londres?

dole

— Oui; *you write better than I* ~ vous écrivez mieux que moi; *I take a bath every day.* — So ~ I je prends un bain tous les jours. — Moi aussi; **4.** F *su.* attrape *f*; réception *f*, dîner *m*; *make* ~ *with* s'accommoder de.

doc F [dɔk] *abr. de doctor 1.*

doc·ile [ˈdousail] docile; **do·cil·i·ty** [douˈsiliti] docilité *f*.

dock¹ [dɔk] écourter; *fig.* diminuer; retrancher (*qch.* à q., *s.o. of s.th.*).

dock² [~] **1.** ⚓ bassin *m*; *surt. Am.* quai *m*; ⚖ banc *m* des prévenus; ⚓ ~s *pl.* docks *m/pl.*; *dry* ~ cale *f* sèche; *floating* ~ dock *m* flottant; *wet* ~ bassin *m* à flot; **2.** ⚓ (faire) entrer au bassin; *espace:* (s')amarrer; ~ **hand**, **'dock·er** travailleur *m* aux docks.

dock·et [ˈdɔkit] **1.** fiche *f*; étiquette *f*; ⚖ registre *m* des jugements rendus, *Am.* rôle *m* des causes; ⊕ bordereau *m*; **2.** étiqueter; classer.

dock·yard [ˈdɔkjɑːd] chantier *m* de construction de navires; arsenal *m* maritime.

doc·tor [ˈdɔktə] **1.** docteur *m*; médecin *m*; ~'s *certificate* certificat *m* médical; **2.** F soigner; F droguer; (*a.* ~ *up*) réparer; fausser; frelater (*du vin*); **doc·tor·ate** [ˈ~rit] doctorat *m*.

doc·tri·naire [dɔktriˈnɛə] **1.** idéologue *m*; **2.** pédant; de théoriciens; **doc·tri·nal** □ [~ˈtrainl] doctrinal (-aux *m/pl.*); **doc·trine** [ˈ~trin] doctrine *f*; dogme *m*.

doc·u·ment 1. [ˈdɔkjumənt] document *m*; pièce *f*; **2.** [ˈ~ment] documenter; **doc·u·men·tal** *see documentary 1;* **doc·u·men·ta·ry 1.** □ documentaire; **2.** (*a.* ~ *film*) documentaire *m*; **doc·u·men'ta·tion** documentation *f*.

dod·der [ˈdɔdə] **1.** ♃ cuscute *f*; **2.** trembloter; branler.

dodge [dɔdʒ] **1.** mouvement *m* de côté; *sp.* esquive *f*; ruse *f*, F truc *m*; **2.** *v/t.* esquiver; éviter; éluder (*une question*); *v/i.* se jeter de côté; *sp.* éviter; *fig.* user d'artifices; **'dodg·er** malin *m*; *Am.* prospectus *m*; *Am.* (*sorte de*) biscuit *m* dur; **dodg·y** F [ˈdɔdʒi] épineux (-euse *f*); délicat; difficile; risqué; louche.

doe [dou] daine *f*; lapine *f*; hase *f*.

do·er [ˈduːə] faiseur (-euse *f*) *m*; auteur *m*.

does [dʌz] (*il, elle*) fait.

doe·skin [ˈdouskin] (peau *f* de) daim *m*.

dog [dɔg] **1.** chien *m* (*qqfois a.* chienne *f*); renard *m* etc. mâle; ⊕ cliquet *m*; agrafe *f*, serre *f*; (*a. fire-*~) chenet *m*; 🎿 (*landing-*~) taquets *m/pl.*; (*safety* ~) chambrière *f*; F type *m*; *Am.* F épate *f*; *Am.* F 🕆 billet *m* à ordre; ~ *show* exposition *f* canine; *go to the* ~*s* marcher à la ruine; se débaucher; 🕆 aller à vau-l'eau; *lead a* ~'*s life* mener une vie de chien; *lead s.o. a* ~'*s life* faire une vie de chien à q.; **2.** filer (*q.*); suivre (*q.*) à la piste; '~**·cart** charrette *f* anglaise; '~**-cheap** à vil prix; '~**-col·lar** collier *m* de chien; F col *m* de pasteur; '~**-days** *pl.* canicule *f*.

doge [doudʒ] doge *m*.

dogged □ [ˈdɔgid] tenace.

dog·ger·el [ˈdɔgərəl] **1.** (*a.* ~ *rhymes pl.*) vers *m/pl.* de mirliton; **2.** de mirliton.

dog·gie [ˈdɔgi] *see doggy.*

dog·gish [ˈdɔgiʃ] qui ressemble à un chien; qui a un air de chien; **dog·go** *sl.* [ˈdɔgou]: *lie* ~ se tenir coi; '**dog·gy 1.** toutou *m*; **2.** de chien; canin; *Am.* F affichant; à effet; **dog lat·in** latin *m* de cuisine.

dog·ma [ˈdɔgmə] dogme *m*; **dog·mat·ic, dog·mat·i·cal** □ [dɔgˈmætik(l)] dogmatique; *fig.* autoritaire, tranchant; **dog'mat·ics** *sg.* dogmatique *f*; **dog·ma·tism** [ˈ~mətizm] dogmatisme *m*; *fig.* ton *m ou* esprit *m* autoritaire; '**dog·ma·tist** dogmatiste *m*; *fig.* individu *m* positif; **dog·ma·tize** [ˈ~taiz] dogmatiser.

dog('s)-ear F [ˈdɔg(z)iə] corne *f* (*dans un livre*).

dog-tired [ˈdɔgˈtaiəd] éreinté.

doi·ly [ˈdɔili] dessus *m* d'assiette; petit napperon *m*.

do·ing [ˈduːiŋ] **1.** *p.pr. de do 1, 2; nothing* ~ rien à faire; 🕆 le marché est mort; **2.** action *f* de faire; fait *m*; ~*s* faits *m/pl.*; événements *m/pl.*; conduite *f*; *péj.* agissements *m/pl.*; *sl.* machin *m*, truc *m*.

doit [dɔit] F sou *m*, liard *m*; bagatelle *f*.

dol·drums [ˈdɔldrəmz] *pl.* cafard *m*; 🕆 marasme *m*; ⚓ zone *f* des calmes.

dole [doul] **1.** aumône *f*; † portion *f*; F allocation *f* de chômage; *be* (*ou* go) *on the* ~ ne vivre que des allocations de chômage; **2.** (*usu.* ~ *out*) distribuer avec parcimonie.

dole·ful □ ['doulful] lugubre; douloureux (-euse *f*); triste; '**dole·ful·ness** tristesse *f*, chagrin *m*; caractère *m* contristant.

doll [dɔl] **1.** poupée *f*; *Am.* jeune fille *f*; **2.** F ~*ed up* en grand tralala.

dol·lar ['dɔlə] dollar *m*; *Am.* F ~*s to doughnuts* très probable.

dol·lop F ['dɔləp] morceau *m* informe.

doll·y ['dɔli] poupée *f*.

dol·o·mite *min.* ['dɔləmait] dolomi(t)e *f*.

dol·o·rous □ ['dɔlərəs] *usu. poét., co.* douloureux (-euse *f*); plaintif (-ive *f*); triste.

dol·phin *icht.* ['dɔlfin] dauphin *m*.

dolt [doult] benêt *m*; *sl.* cruche *f*; '**dolt·ish** □ lourdaud, sot(te *f*).

do·main [də'mein] domaine *m* (*a. fig.*); propriété *f*; terres *f/pl.*

dome [doum] dôme *m* (*a. fig.*); ⊕ couronne *f*, dôme *m*.

do·mes·tic [də'mestik] **1.** (~*ally*) domestique; de ménage; de famille; intérieur (*commerce etc.*); casanier (-ère *f*); ~ *appliance* appareil *m* ménager; ~ *bliss* bonheur *m* familial *ou* de ménage; ~ *coal* houille *f* de ménage; 🦅 ~ *flight* vol *m* intérieur; ~ *science* enseignement *m* ménager; **2.** domestique *mf*; **do'mes·ti·cate** [~keit] apprivoiser, domestiquer (*un animal*); 🌱 *zo.* acclimater; rendre (*q.*) casanier (-ère *f*); **do·mes·ti'ca·tion** domestication *f*; acclimatation *f*; **do·mes·tic·i·ty** [doumes'tisiti] vie *f* de famille; goûts *m/pl.* domestiques.

dom·i·cile ['dɔmisail] **1.** *surt.* 🏛 domicile *m*; **2.** 🏛 domicilier (*un effet*); F résider, s'établir (dans); '**dom·i·ciled** domicilié, demeurant (à, *at*); **dom·i·cil·i·ar·y** [dɔmi-'siljəri] domiciliaire (*visite etc.*).

dom·i·nance ['dɔminəns] (pré-) dominance *f*; '**dom·i·nant 1.** dominant; **2.** ♩ dominante *f*.

dom·i·nate ['dɔmineit] dominer; **dom·i'na·tion** domination *f*; '**dom·i·na·tor** dominateur (-trice *f*) *m*; **dom·i·neer** [dɔmi'niə] se montrer autoritaire; ~ *over* tyranniser; **dom·i'neer·ing** □ autoritaire; tyrannique.

do·min·i·cal [də'minikl] dominical (-aux *m/pl.*) (*oraison*).

Do·min·i·can [də'minikən] dominicain(e *f*) *m* (*a. adj.*).

do·min·ion [də'minjən] domination *f*, maîtrise *f*; *souv.* ~*s pl.* dominion *m*, -s *m/pl.*; possessions *f/pl.*; colonie *f*, -s *f/pl.*; ♀ Dominion *m*.

dom·i·no ['dɔminou], *pl.* -**noes** ['~nouz] domino *m*; ~*s sg.* jeu: dominos *m/pl.*

don [dɔn] professeur *m* d'université.

do·nate *Am.* [dou'neit] donner; faire un don à; **do'na·tion, don·a·tive** ['dounətiv] don *m*, donation *f*.

done [dʌn] **1.** *p.p. de do* 1, 2; *be* ~ *souv.* se faire; **2.** *adj.* fait; cuit; (*ou* ~ *up*) éreinté, fourbu; *well* ~ bien cuit; *he is* ~ *for* c'est un homme coulé; **3.** *int.* d'accord!

do·nee 🏛 [dou'ni:] donataire *mf*.

don·jon ['dɔndʒən] cachot *m*.

don·key ['dɔŋki] âne(sse *f*) *m*; *attr.* qqfois auxiliaire; '~·**work** F *le* gros (du) travail.

do·nor ['dounə] donateur (-trice *f*) *m*; 🩸 donneur (-euse *f*) *m* de sang.

do-noth·ing F ['du:nʌθiŋ] fainéant(e *f*) (*a. su./mf*).

don't [dount] **1.** = *do not*; *impér.* ne fai(te)s pas ça!; **2.** défense *f*.

doo·dle ['du:dl] **1.** griffonnage *m*; griffonner.

doom [du:m] **1.** *surt. péj.* sort *m*, destin *m*; mort *f*; ruine *f*; **2.** condamner; **dooms·day** ['du:mzdei] (*jour m du*) jugement *m* dernier.

door [dɔ:] porte *f*; *auto, wagon, etc.*: portière *f*; *next* ~ (*to*) à côté (de); *fig.* approchant (de); *two* ~*s off* deux portes plus loin; (*with*)*in* ~*s* chez soi; *out of* ~*s* dehors; en plein air; *turn s.o. out of* ~*s* mettre q. à la porte; *lay s.th. to* (*ou at*) *s.o.'s* ~ imputer qch. à q.; '~·**bell** sonnette *f*; '~·**han·dle** poignée *f* de port(ièr)e); '~·**keep·er** concierge *mf*; portier *m*; ~ **knob** poignée *f ou* bouton *m* de porte; '~·**man** concierge *m*; portier *m*; '~·**way** porte *f*; portail *m*.

dope [doup] **1.** liquide *m* visqueux; 🦅 enduit *m*; *mot.* laque *f*; F stupéfiant *m*; narcotique *m*; *Am. sl.* tuyau *m*; renseignement *m*; imbécile *mf*; idiot(e *f*) *m*; type *m*; ~ *fiend* toxicomane *mf*, drogué(e *f*) *m*; ~ *peddler*, ~ *pusher* revendeur (-euse *f*) *m* de stupéfiants; **2.** *v/t.*

enduire; administrer un narcotique à; *sp.* doper (*a. un combustible*); narcotiser (*une cigarette*); *v/i.* F prendre des stupéfiants; **'dope·y** *Am. sl.* stupide; hébété.

dor·mant ['dɔ:mənt] *usu. fig.* endormi, assoupi; en repos; tombé en désuétude; ♀, ∅ dormant; ⚓ ~ *partner* commandataire *m.*

dor·mer ['dɔ:mə] (*a.* ~*-window*) lucarne *f*; (fenêtre *f* en) mansarde *f.*

dor·mi·to·ry ['dɔ:mitri] dortoir *m*; *surt. Am.* maison *f* d'étudiants.

dor·mouse ['dɔ:maus], *pl.* **-mice** [~mais] loir *m*; lérot *m.*

dor·sal □ ['dɔ:sl] dorsal (-aux *m/pl.*); **'dor·ser** hotte *f.*

dose [dous] **1.** dose *f*; **2.** médicamenter (q. avec qch., s.o. with s.th.); doser (*le vin etc.*).

doss *Brit. sl.* [dɔs] **1.** pieu *m* (*lit*); roupillon *m* (*sommeil*); somme *m*; **2.** ~ *down* se pieuter (*se coucher*); crécher (*coucher, loger*); **'~·house** asile *m* de nuit.

dos·si·er ['dɔsiei] dossier *m*, documents *m/pl.*

dot [dɔt] **1.** point *m*; mioche *mf*; *on the* ~ F à l'heure tapante; *argent comptant*; **2.** mettre un point sur; pointiller; (*a.* ~ *about*) *fig.* (par-) semer (de, with); ♪ pointer; marquer (*une surface*) avec des points.

dot·age ['doutidʒ] seconde enfance *f*; radotage *m*; **do·tard** ['~təd] radoteur (-euse *f*) *m*; gâteux (-euse *f*) *m*; **dote** [dout] radoter; tomber dans la sénilité; ~ [[up]on] aimer (q.) à la folie; **'dot·ing** sénile; qui aime follement (q., on *s.o.*).

dot·ty *sl.* ['dɔti] toqué, maboul.

dou·ble □ ['dʌbl] **1.** double; à deux personnes *ou* lits (*chambre*); deux (*lettres*); ~ *tooth* grosse dent *f*; **2.** double *m* (*a.* tennis); deux fois autant; *fleuve, lièvre*: détour *m*; ✗ pas *m* de course; **3.** *v/t.* doubler (*a.* ♫); serrer (*le poing*); bridge: contrer; plier en deux (*un papier*); *théâ.* jouer deux (*rôles*); ~ *up* replier; faire plier (q.) en deux; ~*d up* ployé; *v/i.* (se) doubler; ✗ prendre le pas de course; (*a.* ~ *back*) faire un brusque crochet (*animal*); *cartes:* contrer; **'~·bar· relled** à deux coups (*fusil*); *fig.* (*nom*) à charnière; ~ **bass** ♪ contrebasse *f*; ~ **bend** virage *m* en S;

'~·'breast·ed croisé (*gilet etc.*); **'~· check** revérifier; **'~·'cross** *Am. sl.* tomper, duper; **'~·'deal·er** homme *m* à deux visages; fourbe *m*; **'~· 'deal·ing** duplicité *f*, fourberie *f*; **'~· 'deck·er** autobus *m* à impériale; *cuis.* sandwich *m* double; **'~·'edged** à deux tranchants; ~ **en·try** ⚓ comptabilité *f* en partie double; **fea·ture** *cin. Am.* programme *m* double; **'~·'glaz·ing** doubles fenêtres *f/pl.*; double vitrage *m*; **'~· 'head·er** *Am. baseball:* deux parties *f/pl.* de suite; **'~·'joint·ed** désarticulé; ~ **line** 🚊 ligne *f* à voie double; **'dou·ble·ness** état *m* double; duplicité *f* (*a. fig.*); *fig.* mauvaise foi *f*, fausseté *f*; **'dou·ble'park** *Am.* stationner contrairement à la loi; **'dou·ble-'quick** ✗ (au) pas *m* gymnastique.

dou·blet ['dʌblit] pourpoint *m*; doublet *m* (*a. gramm.*); ~*s pl.* doublet *m* (*aux dés*).

dou·ble...: **'~·'talk** paroles *f/pl.* trompeuses *ou* ambiguës; ~ **take** F *do a* ~ y regarder à deux fois; ~ **time** ✗ pas *m* gymnastique; **'~·'track** à voie double.

doub·ling ['dʌbliŋ] doublement *m*; doublage *m*; détour *m*, crochet *m.*

doubt [daut] **1.** *v/i.* hésiter; douter; *v/t.* douter de (q., qch.); révoquer (*qch.*) en doute; **2.** doute *m*; incertitude *f*; *no* ~ sans (aucun) doute; **'doubt·er** sceptique *mf*, douteur (-euse *f*) *m*; **doubt·ful** □ ['~ful] douteux (-euse *f*); incertain; équivoque; suspect; **'doubt·ful· ness** incertitude *f*; ambiguïté *f*; irrésolution *f*; **'doubt·less** sans doute.

douche [du:ʃ] **1.** douche *f* (*a.* ✗); **2.** (se) doucher.

dough [dou] pâte *f* (*à pain*); *Am. sl.* argent *m*; **'~·boy** *Am.* F simple soldat *m*; **'~·nut** pet *m* de nonne; **'dough·y** pâteux (-euse *f*); *fig.* terreux (-euse *f*).

dour *écoss.* ['duə] austère; obstiné.

douse [daus] tremper; arroser; doucher.

dove [dʌv] colombe *f* (*a. fig.*); **'~·cot** colombier *m*; **'~·tail** ⊕ **1.** queue-d'aronde (*pl.* queues-d'a-ronde) *f*; **2.** *v/t.* adenter; *fig.* opérer le raccord entre; *v/i.* se raccorder.

dow·a·ger ['dauədʒə] douairière *f.*

dow·dy F ['daudi] 1. sans élégance; 2. femme *f* mal habillée.

dow·el ⊕ ['dauəl] goujon *m*; cheville *f* (en bois).

dow·er ['dauə] 1. douaire *m*; *fig.* don *m*, apanage *m*; 2. assigner un douaire à (*une veuve*); doter (*une jeune fille*).

dow·las ['dauləs] toile *f* commune.

down¹ [daun] duvet *m*; oreiller: plume *f*.

down² [∼] *see* dune; ∼*s pl.* hautes plaines *f/pl.* du Sussex *etc.*

down³ [∼] 1. *adv.* vers le bas; en bas; (*vu*) d'en haut; par terre; ∼ *and out fig.* ruiné, à bout de ressources; be ∼ être en baisse (*prix*); être de chute (*cartes*); F be ∼ *upon* en vouloir à (*q.*); être toujours sur le dos de (*q.*); ∼ *in the country* à la campagne; 2. *prp.* vers le bas de; en bas de; au fond de; en descendant; le long de; ∼ *the river* en aval; ∼ *the wind* à vau-vent; 3. *int.* à bas!; 4. *adj.* ♣ ∼ *payment* acompte *m*, arrhes *f/pl.*; ∼ *platform* quai *m* montant; ∼ *train* train *m* montant; 5. F *v/t.* abattre; terrasser; ∼ *tools* se mettre en grève; 6. *su. see up 5*; '∼-**and**-'**out** clochard *m*; sans-le-sou *m/inv.*; '∼-**cast** abattu; baissé (*regard*); ⦵-'**East·er** *Am.* habitant(e *f*) *m* de la Nouvelle-Angleterre, *surt.* du Maine; '∼-**fall** chute *f* (*a. fig.*); *fig.* ruine *f*; écroulement *m*; '∼-**grade** *Am.* déprécier; dégrader; '∼-'**heart·ed** déprimé, découragé; '∼-'**hill** 1. en descendant; 2. incliné; en pente; '∼-**pour** grosse averse *f*; déluge *m*; '∼-**right** □ 1. *adv.* tout à fait; carrément; nettement; 2. *adj.* franc(he *f*); direct; carré; éclatant (*mensonge*); pur (*bêtises*); véritable; '∼-**right·ness** franchise *f*; droiture *f*; '∼-**stairs** 1. d'en bas, du rez-de-chaussée (*pièce*); 2. en bas (de l'escalier); '∼-**stream** en aval, à l'aval; '∼-**stroke** *écriture*: jambage *m*; ⊕ mouvement *m* de descente; '∼-**to**-'**earth** terre-à-terre; '∼-**town** *surt. Am.* centre *m* des affaires municipales; '∼-**ward** 1. de haut en bas; descendant; *fig.* fatal, vers la ruine; dirigé en bas (*regard*); 2. (*a.* '∼-**wards**) de haut en bas; '∼-**wash** ✈ *etc.* remous *m* d'air descendant.

down·y ['dauni] duveteux (-euse *f*); velouté (*fruit*); *sl.* rusé.

dow·ry ['dauəri] dot *f* (*a. fig.*).

dowse ['daus] 1. *see* douse; 2. faire de l'hydroscopie; '**dows·er** hydroscope *m*; homme *m* à baguette; radiesthésiste *mf*; '**dows·ing-rod** baguette *f* divinatoire.

doze [douz] 1. sommeiller; ∼ *away* passer (*le temps*) à sommeiller; 2. petit somme *m*.

doz·en [dʌzn] douzaine *f*.

doz·y ['douzi] somnolent; F gourde.

drab [dræb] 1. gris brunâtre; beige; *fig.* terne; 2. drap *m* beige; toile *f* bise; *couleur*: gris *m* brunâtre; *fig.* monotonie *f*.

drachm [dræm] (*poids*), **drach·ma** ['drækmə] (*monnaie*) drachme *f*.

draff [dræf] † lie *f* de vin; † lavure *f*; drêche *f*.

draft [drɑːft] 1. *see* draught; ♣ traite *f*; lettre *f* de change; ✗ détachement *m*; *Am.* conscription *f*; ∼ *agreement* projet *m* de contract; *Am.* ✗ dodger insoumis *m*; 2. rédiger; faire le brouillon de; désigner (à, pour to); ✗ détacher; envoyer (*des troupes*) en détachement; *Am.* appeler sous les armes; **draft·ee** ✗ [drɑːf'tiː] *Am.* conscrit *m*; '**drafts·man** dessinateur *m*, traceur *m*.

drag [dræg] 1. filet *m* à la trôle, drague *f*; traîneau *m*; herse *f*; sabot *m*; drag *m*; résistance *f*; *fig.* obstacle *m*, entrave *f*; *fig.* corvée *f*; F casse-pieds *m*; *sl.* travesti *m* (*vêtements de femme*); 2. *v/t.* (en)traîner, tirer; ⚓ chasser sur (*ses ancres*); draguer; ✎ herser; enrayer (*une roue*); *see* dredge¹ 2; ∼ *along* (en)traîner; ∼ *out one's life* traîner sa vie (jusqu'à sa fin); *v/i.* traîner; draguer (à la recherche de, *for*); pêcher à la drague; † languir.

drag·gle ['drægl] traîner dans la boue; '∼-**tail** F souillon *f*.

drag·on ['drægən] dragon *m*; '∼-**fly** libellule *f*.

dra·goon [drə'guːn] 1. dragon *m*; 2. dragonner; *fig.* tyranniser.

drain [drein] 1. tranchée *f*; caniveau *m*; égout *m*; F saignée *f*, fuite *f*; 2. *v/t.* assécher, dessécher; vider (*un étang, un verre, etc.*); égoutter (*des légumes*); *fig.* épuiser; (*a.* ∼ *off*) faire écouler; évacuer (de, *of*); *v/i.* s'écouler; '**drain·age** écoulement *m*; ✎ drainage *m*; '**drain·ing**

1. d'écoulement; **2.** *see* drainage; ~s *pl.* égoutture *f*; '**drain·pipe** tuyau *m* d'écoulement; gouttière *f*; ~ *trousers* pantalon-cigarette *m* (*pl.* pantalons-cigarette).

drake [dreik] canard *m*, malard *m*.

dram [dræm] *poids:* drachme *f*; goutte *f*; petit verre *m*.

dra·ma ['drɑːmə] drame *m*; **dra·mat·ic** [drə'mætik] (~ally) dramatique; **dram·a·tist** ['dræmətist] auteur *m* dramatique; '**dram·a·tize** dramatiser; adapter (*qch.*) à la scène; **dram·a·tur·gy** ['~təːdʒi] dramaturgie *f*.

drank [dræŋk] *prét. de* drink 2.

drape [dreip] *v/t.* draper, tendre (de *with, of*); *v/i.* se draper; '**drap·er** marchand *m* d'étoffes; '**dra·per·y** draperie *f*; nouveautés *f/pl.*

dras·tic ['dræstik] (~ally) énergique.

draught [drɑːft] tirage *m*; pêche *f*; courant *m* d'air; plan *m*, tracé *m*, ébauche *f*; *boisson:* coup *m*, trait *m*; ♣ potion *f*; ♒ tirant *m* d'eau; ~s *pl.* dames *f/pl.*; *see* draft; ~ *beer* bière *f* au tonneau; *at a* ~ d'un seul trait; '**~·board** damier *m*; '**~·horse** cheval *m* de trait; '**draughts·man** dessinateur *m*, traceur *m*; '**draught·y** exposé; plein de courants d'air.

draw [drɔː] **1.** [*irr.*] *v/t.* souv. tirer; attirer (*une foule*); tracer; dessiner; établir (*une distinction*); faire infuser (*le thé*); *chasse:* battre (*le couvert*); vider (*un poulet*); toucher (*de l'argent*); dresser, rédiger (*un contrat, un acte*); aspirer (*l'air*); arracher (*des larmes*) (à, *from*); *sp.* faire partie nulle; *v/i.* s'approcher de; ♒ tirer; *the battle was* ~*n* la bataille resta indécise; ~ *away* entraîner; détourner; ~ *down* baisser; faire descendre; ~ *forth* faire paraître; susciter; ~ *near* s'approcher (de); ~ *on* mettre; *fig.* attirer; ~ *out* tirer; allonger; prolonger; ~ *up* tirer en haut; faire monter; ⚔ ranger; ⚖ dresser, rédiger; ~ (*up*)*on* fournir (*une traite*) sur (*q.*); tirer (*un chèque*); *fig.* faire appel à; **2.** tirage *m*; loterie *f*, tombola *f*; *sp.* partie *f* nulle; F attraction *f*; '**~·back** désavantage *m*, inconvénient *m*; ♣ drawback *m*; *Am.* remboursement *m*; '**~·bridge** pont-levis (*pl.* ponts-levis) *m*; **draw'ee** ♣ tiré *m*; payeur *m*; '**draw·er** dessinateur *m*; tireur

m (*a.* ♣); tiroir *m*; (*a pair of*) ~s *pl.* (un) pantalon *m* (*de femme*); (un) caleçon *m* (*d'homme*); (*usu.* chest of ~s) commode *f*.

draw·ing ['drɔːiŋ] tirage *m*; puisement *m*; attraction *f*; tirage *m* au sort, loterie *f*; dessin *m*; ébauche *f*; ♣ *effets:* traite *f*; *chèque:* tirage *m*; *out of* ~ mal dessiné; ~ *instruments pl.* instruments *m/pl.* de dessin; '**~·ac'count** compte *m* en banque; '**~·board** planche *f* à dessin; '**~·pen** tire-ligne *m*; '**~·pin** punaise *f*; '**~·room** salon *m*; réception *f*.

drawl [drɔːl] **1.** *v/t.* (*souv.* ~ *out*) dire (*qch.*) avec une nonchalance affectée; *v/i.* parler d'une voix traînante; **2.** voix *f* traînante; débit *m* traînant.

drawn [drɔːn] **1.** *p.p. de* draw 1; **2.** *adj.* tiré; ⊕ étiré; *sp.* égal; *cuis. Am.* ~ *butter* beurre *m* fondu (aux fines herbes).

draw·well ['drɔːwel] puits *m* à poulie.

dray [drei] (*a.* ~-*cart*) camion *m* (*surt.* de brasseur); '**~·man** livreur *m* de brasserie.

dread [dred] **1.** terreur *f*, épouvante *f*; **2.** redouter; **dread·ful** □ ['~ful] **1.** redoutable; terrible; atroce; **2.** *penny* ~ roman *m* à sensation; **dread·nought** ['~nɔːt] *tex.* frise *f*; ♒ dreadnought *m*.

dream [driːm] **1.** rêve *m*; songe *m*; **2.** [*irr.*] rêver (de, *of*); ~ *away* passer à rêver; '**dream·er** rêveur (-euse *f*) *m*; '**dream·read·er** interprète *m* des rêves; **dreamt** [dremt] *prét. et p.p. de* dream 2; **dream·y** ['driːmi] □ rêveur (-euse *f*); langoureux (-euse *f*).

drear·i·ness ['driərinis] tristesse *f*; aspect *m* morne; **drear·y** □ triste; morne.

dredge[1] [dredʒ] **1.** (filet *m* de) drague *f*; **2.** draguer (*fig.* à la recherche de); (*a.* ~ *up*, ~ *out*) dévaser.

dredge[2] [~] *cuis.* saupoudrer.

dredg·er[1] ['dredʒə] drague *f*; *personne:* dragueur *m*.

dredg·er[2] [~] saupoudroir *m*.

dregs [dregz] *pl.* lie *f*.

drench [drentʃ] **1.** *vét.* breuvage *m*, purge *f*; F *see* drencher; **2.** tremper, mouiller (de, *with*); *vét.* donner un breuvage à; '**drench·er** F pluie *f* battante.

dress [dres] **1.** robe *f*, toilette *f*, costume *m*; *fig.* habillement *m*, habits *m/pl.*; *théâ.* ~ *rehearsal* répétition *f* générale; *full* ~ grande tenue *f*; **2.** (s')habiller, (se) vêtir; ✕ (s')aligner; *v/t.* orner; panser (*une blessure*); tailler (*une vigne*); ⊕ dresser, parer (*des pierres*); *cuis.* apprêter; ✔ donner une façon à (*un champ*); *théâ.* costumer; *v/i.* faire sa toilette; ~ **circle** *théâ.* (premier) balcon *m*; '~**coat** frac *m*; '**dress·er** ⊕, *cuis.* apprêteur (-euse *f*) *m*; buffet *m* de cuisine; panseur (-euse *f*) *m*; *théâ.* habilleur (-euse *f*) *m*; *Am.* dressoir *m*.

dress·ing ['dresiŋ] habillement *m*, toilette *f*; pansement *m* (*d'une blessure*); ✕ alignement *m*; *cuis.* sauce *f* mayonnaise; ⊕ apprêt *m*; dressage *m* (*de pierres*); ✔ façon *f*; fumages *m/pl.*; ~**s** *pl.* △ moulures *f/pl.*; 💉 pansements *m/pl.*; ~ **down** F semonce *f*; '~**case** mallette *f* garnie; sac *m* de toilette; 💉 trousse *f* de pansement; '~**down** F réprimande *f*; F enguelade *f*; *get a* ~ se faire passer un savon; *give s.o. a (good)* ~ passer un savon à q.; '~**glass** miroir *m* de toilette; psyché *f*; '~**gown** robe *f* de chambre; '~**jack·et** camisole *f*; '~**ta·ble** (table *f* de) toilette *f*.

dress...: '~**mak·er** couturier (-ère *f*) *m*; '~**mak·ing** couture *f*; '~**shield** dessous-de-bras *m/inv.*; '~**suit** habit *m* (de soirée); '**dress·y** F élégant; chic *inv.* en genre; coquet(te *f*) (*femme*).

drew [dru:] *prét. de* draw 1.

drib·ble ['dribl] dégoutter; baver (*enfant etc.*); *foot.* dribbler.

drib·(b)let ['driblit] chiquet *m*; *in* ~**s** petit à petit.

dribs and drabs F ['dribzən'dræbz] *pl.*: *in* ~ petit à petit, peu à peu.

dried [draid] (des)séché; ~ *fruit* fruits *m/pl.* secs; ~ *vegetables pl.* légumes *m/pl.* déshydratés.

drift [drift] **1.** mouvement *m*; direction *f*, sens *m*; ⚓ dérive *f*; *fig.* cours *m*; *fig.* portée *f*, tendance *f*; *neige:* amoncellement *m*; *pluie:* rafale *f*; ⊕ poinçon *m*; *géol.* apport *m*, -s *m/pl.*; ✕ galerie *f* (chassante); ~ *from the land* dépeuplement *m* des campagnes; **2.** *v/t.* flotter; entasser;

v/i. flotter; être entraîné; ⚓ dériver; se laisser aller (*a. fig.*); '**drift·er** ⚓ chalutier *m*; *fig.* vagabond(e *f*) *m*; '**drift-ice** glaces *f/pl.* flottantes.

drill¹ [dril] **1.** foret *m*; perçoir *m*; vilebrequin *m*; ✔ rayon *m*; semeuse *f*; ✕ manœuvre *f*, -s *f/pl.*; exercice *m*, -s *m/pl.* (*a. fig.*); ~ *ground* terrain *m* d'exercice; **2.** ✕ (faire) faire l'exercice (*a. fig.*); *v/t.* forer; percer; buriner (*une dent*); ✔ semer en rayons.

drill² [~], **drill·ing** ['driliŋ] *tex.* coutil *m*, treillis *m*.

drink [driŋk] **1.** boire *m*; boisson *f*; consommation *f*; *in* ~ ivre; **2.** [*irr.*] *vt/i.* boire; *v/i.* être adonné à la boisson; ~ *s.o.'s health* boire à la santé de q.; ~ *away* boire; ~ *in* absorber; ~ *to* boire à; ~ *off*, ~ *out*, ~ *up* vider; achever de boire; avaler; '**drink·a·ble** buvable; potable (*eau*).

drink·ing ['driŋkiŋ] boire *m*; *fig.* boisson *f*; ivrognerie *f*; '~**bout** ribote *f*; '~**foun·tain** borne-fontaine (*pl.* bornes-fontaines) *f*; poste *m* d'eau potable; '~**song** chanson *f* à boire; '~**wa·ter** eau *f* potable.

drip [drip] **1.** (d)égouttement *m*; goutte *f*; F nouille *f* (*personne*); 💉 (*be on the* ~ avoir le) goutte-à-goutte *m/inv.*; **2.** (laisser) tomber goutte à goutte; *v/i.* dégoutter; ~*ping wet* trempé; '**drip·ping** (d)égouttement *m*; *cuis.* ~**s** *pl.* graisse *f* (de rôti).

drive [draiv] **1.** promenade *f* en voiture; course *f*; avenue *f*; *tennis:* drive *m*; *cartes:* tournoi *f*; *sp.* coup *m* droit; *mot.* prise *f*; traction *f*; ⊕ attaque *f*; commande *f*; propulsion *f*; *chasse:* battue *f*; *fig.* énergie *f*; urgence *f*; *Am.* campagne *f* de propagande; **2.** [*irr.*] *v/t.* chasser, passer; conduire; faire marcher; surmener; exercer (*un métier*); contraindre (à, [*in*]to); (*a.* ~ *away*) éloigner; *v/i.* chasser; ⚓ dériver; *chasse:* battre un bois; *mot.* rouler; ~ *at* viser (*qch.*); travailler à (*qch.*); sans relâche; ~ *on v/t.* pousser; *v/i.* continuer sa route; ~ *up* to s'approcher de (*qch.*) en voiture.

drive-in *Am.* ['draiv'in] *usu. attr.* (restaurant *m* ou cinéma *m*) où l'on accède en voiture.

driv·el ['drivl] **1.** baver; **2.** bave *f*; F balivernes *f/pl.*

driv·en ['drivn] *p.p. de* drive 2.

driv·er ['draivə] conducteur (-trice *f*) *m* (*a. mot.*); 🚋 mécanicien *m*; *tramway*: wattman (*pl.* -men) *m*; ⊕ poinçon *m*; heurtoir *m* (*d'une soupape*); *Am.* ∼'s *license* permis *m* de conduire.

drive·way ['draivwei] allée *f*; entrée *f* (pour voitures).

driv·ing ['draiviŋ] conduite *f* etc.; *attr.* de transmission; conducteur (-trice *f*); *a. fig.* ∼ *force* force *f* motrice *ou* agissante; *fig. a.* moteur *m*; ∼ *instructor* moniteur *m* de conduite; ∼ *licence* permis *m* de conduire; ∼ *mirror* rétroviseur *m*; ∼ *school* auto-école *f*; '∼-**belt** courroie *f* de commande; '∼-**gear** transmission *f*; '∼-**wheel** roue *f* motrice.

driz·zle ['drizl] 1. bruine *f*; 2. bruiner.

droll [droul] (*adv. drolly*) drôle; '**droll·er·y** drôlerie *f*.

drom·e·dar·y *zo.* ['drʌmədəri] dromadaire *m*.

drone¹ [droun] 1. *zo.* faux bourdon *m*; *fig.* fainéant *m*; 2. fainéanter.

drone² [∼] 1. bourdonnement *m*; ♪ bourdon *m*; 2. bourdonner; parler d'un ton monotone.

drool [dru:l] 1. baver; F radoter; 2. *Am.* F radotage *m*.

droop [dru:p] *v/t.* baisser; laisser pendre; *v/i.* pendre; languir; s'affaisser; (se) pencher; '**droop·ing** □ (re)tombant; (a)baissé; languissant.

drop [drɔp] 1. goutte *f*; bonbon: pastille *f*; chute *f*; pendant *m*; *échafaud*: trappe *f*; *théâ.* rideau *m* d'entracte; 🌱 baisse *f*; *Am.* F *get* (*ou have*) *the* ∼ *on* prendre (*q.*) au dépourvu; ∼ *light* lampe *f* suspendue; 2. *v/t.* lâcher; laisser tomber (*qch., une question, la voix*); mouiller (*l'ancre*); lancer (*une bombe*); jeter à la poste (*une lettre*); verser (*des larmes*); laisser (*un sujet*); glisser (*un mot à q.*); laisser échapper (*une remarque*); déposer (*un passager*); baisser (*la voix, les yeux, le rideau*); supprimer (*une lettre, une syllabe*); abattre (*le gibier*); tirer (*une révérence*); perdre (*de l'argent*); ∼ *s.o. a line* écrire un mot à q.; F ∼ *it!* assez! *v/i.* tomber; dégoutter; s'égoutter; s'abaisser (*terrain*); se laisser tomber (*dans un fauteuil*); baisser (*prix, température*); se calmer; ∼ *in* entrer en passant (à, chez *at*, [*up*]*on*); attraper (*q.*, [*up*]*on s.o.*); ∼ *off* tomber, se détacher; F s'endormir; ∼ *out v/t.* omettre; *v/i.* tomber dehors; renoncer; rester en arrière; **drop·let** ['drɔplit] gouttelette *f*; '**drop·ping** dégouttement *m*; abandon *m*; ∼*s pl.* fiente *f* (*d'animaux*); '**drop-scene** *théâ.* toile *f* de fond; rideau *m* d'entracte; *fig.* dernier acte *m*.

drop·si·cal □ ['drɔpsikl] hydropique; '**drop·sy** hydropisie *f*.

dross [drɔs] scories *f/pl.*; déchet *m*; *fig.* rebut *m*.

drought [draut] sécheresse *f*; '**drought·y** aride, sec (sèche *f*).

drove [drouv] 1. troupeau *m* (*de bœufs*) (en marche); *fig.* bande *f*, foule *f*; 2. *prét. de drive* 2; '**dro·ver** conducteur *m ou* marchand *m* de bestiaux.

drown [draun] *v/t.* noyer (*a. fig.*); submerger; étouffer, couvrir (*un son*); *v/i.* (*ou be* ∼*ed*) se noyer; être noyé.

drowse [drauz] *v/i.* somnoler, s'assoupir; *v/t.* assoupir; '**drow·si·ness** somnolence *f*; '**drow·sy** somnolent, assoupi; soporifique.

drub [drʌb] battre, rosser; '**drub·bing** volée *f* de coups; F tripotée *f*.

drudge [drʌdʒ] 1. *fig.* cheval *m* de bât; esclave *mf*; 2. peiner; mener une vie d'esclave; '**drudg·er·y** travail *m* ingrat; *fig.* esclavage *m*.

drug [drʌg] 1. drogue *f*; stupéfiant *m*; *be a* ∼ *in the market* être invendable; ∼ *abuse* abus *m* des drogues; ∼ *pusher* (*ou peddler*) revendeur (-euse *f*) *m* de stupéfiants; ∼ *traffic(king)* trafic *m* des stupéfiants; 2. *v/t.* donner *ou* administrer des stupéfiants à (*q.*); *v/i.* s'adonner aux stupéfiants; **drug·gist** ['drʌgist] *Am., a. écoss.* pharmacien *m*; **drug·gist's shop**, *Am.* '**drug·store** pharmacie *f*; *Am. p.ext.* débit *m* de boissons non alcoolisés et de casse-croûte.

drum [drʌm] 1. tambour *m* (*a.* ⊕); tonneau *m*; *anat.* tympan *m*; 2. battre du tambour; tambouriner (*a. fig.*); '**∼-fire** ⚔ tir *m* de barrage; '**∼-head** peau *f* de tambour; '**drum·mer** tambour *m*; *Am.* F commis *m* voyageur; '**drum·stick** baguette *f* de tambour; *cuis.* pilon *m*.

drunk [drʌŋk] 1. *p.p. de drink* 2;

2. ivre, soûl (de, *with*); get ∼ s'enivrer, se soûler; **drunk·ard** ['∼əd]
ivrogne(sse *f*) *m*; '**drunk·en** ivre; ∼
driving conduite *f* en état d'ivresse;
'**drunk·en·ness** ivresse *f*; ivrognerie *f*.

drupe ⚕ [dru:p] drupe *m*.

dry [drai] **1.** □ *usu.* sec (sèche *f*)
(F a. = *prohibitionniste*); aride (*sujet,
terrain*); tari; à sec (*maçonnerie,
puits, etc.*); mordant, caustique
(*esprit*); be ∼ F avoir le gosier sec; ⚡
∼ *cell* pile *f* sèche; ∼ *goods pl.* F *Am.*
tissus *m/pl.*; articles *m/pl.* de nouveauté; **2.** *Am.* F prohibitionniste*m*;
3. *vt/i.* sécher; *v/t.* faire sécher; essuyer (*les yeux*); *v/i.* (*a.* ∼ *up*), tarir,
se dessécher; F ∼*up!* taisez-vous!

dry·ad ['draiəd] dryade *f*.

dry-clean ['drai'kli:n] nettoyer à
sec; '**dry-'clean·ing** nettoyage *m*
à sec.

dry...: '∼**-nurse 1.** nourrice *f* sèche;
2. élever au biberon; '∼-'**rot** carie
f sèche; *fig.* désintégration *f*; '∼-
'**shod** à pied sec.

du·al □ ['dju:əl] **1.** double; jumelé
(*pneus*); **2.** *gramm.* duel *m*; '**du·al·
ism** dualité *f*; *phls.* dualisme *m*.

dub [dʌb] adouber (*q.*) chevalier;
donner l'accolade à; F qualifier (*q.*)
de (*qch.*); préparer (*le cuir*) avec le
dégras; *cin.* doubler; **dub·bing**
['∼in] *hist.* adoubement *m*; (*a.* **dub·
bin** ['∼in]) dégras *m*.

du·bi·ous □ ['dju:bjəs] douteux
(-euse *f*); incertain (de *of, about,
over*); '**du·bi·ous·ness**incertitude*f*.

du·cal ['dju:kl] de duc, ducal (-aux
m/pl.).

duc·at ['dʌkət] ducat *m*.

duch·ess ['dʌtʃis] duchesse *f*.

duch·y ['dʌtʃi] duché *m*.

duck¹ [dʌk] canard *m*; cane *f*; *Am.
sl.* type *m*, individu *m*; *cricket*: zéro
m; ⚔ camion *m* amphibie.

duck² [∼] **1.** plongeon *m*; courbette*f*;
box. esquive *f*; **2.** plonger dans
l'eau; faire (faire) une courbette;
v/t. Am. éviter; *v/i.* F partir, quitter.

duck³ F [∼] (mon) petit chou *m*;
poulet(te *f*) *m*; chat(te *f*) *m*.

duck⁴ [∼] toile *f* fine (*pour voiles*).

duck·ling ['dʌkliŋ] caneton *m*.

duck·y F ['dʌki] **1.** *see* duck³;
2. mignon(ne *f*); chic *inv. en genre.*

duct [dʌkt] conduit *m*; ⚕, *anat.*
canal *m*.

duc·tile □ ['dʌktail] malléable; *fig.
a.* docile; **duc·til·i·ty** [∼'tiliti] malléabilité *f*; *fig.* souplesse *f*.

dud *sl.* [dʌd] **1.** ⚔ obus *m* non éclaté;
type *m* nul; raté *m*; chèque *m* sans
provision; fausse monnaie *f*; crétin
m; ∼*s pl.* frusques *f/pl.*; **2.** faux
(fausse *f*); *sl.* moche.

dude *Am.* [dju:d] gommeux *m*; *Am.*
∼ *ranch* ranch *m* d'opérette.

dudg·eon ['dʌdʒn] colère *f*.

due [dju:] **1.** échu; exigible; mérité;
in ∼ *time* en temps utile; *the train is*
∼ *at* le train arrive *ou* doit arriver à; *in* ∼ *course* en temps et
lieu; *be* ∼ *to* être dû (due *f*) à, être
causé par; *be* ∼ *to* (*inf.*) devoir
(*inf.*); *Am.* être sur le point de (*inf.*);
✝ *fall* ∼ échoir, venir à échéance; ∼
date échéance *f*; **2.** *adv.* ⚓ droit;
∼ *east* est franc, droit vers l'est;
3. dû *m*; droit *m*; *usu.* ∼*s pl.* droits
m/pl.; frais *m/pl.*; cotisation *f*.

du·el ['dju:əl] **1.** duel *m*; **2.** se battre
en duel; '**du·el·list** duelliste *m*.

du·et(t) [dju'et] duo *m*.

duf·fel ['dʌfəl]: ∼ *bag* sac *m* marin; ∼
coat duffel-coat *m*.

duff·er F ['dʌfə] cancre *m*; *sp.* mala-
droit(e *f*) *m*.

dug [dʌg] **1.** *prét. et p.p. de* dig 1;
2. mamelle *f*; '∼-**out** ⚔ abri *m*
(blindé); *canot:* piroque *f*; *Am.
baseball:* (*sorte de*) fosse *f* où se tiennent les joueurs en attendant leur
tour.   [duché *m*; titre *m* de duc.)

duke [dju:k] duc *m*; '**duke·dom**

dull [dʌl] **1.** □ terne (*a. style*), mat
(*couleur*); sans éclat (*œil*); atone
(*regard*); dur (*oreille*); peu sensible
(*ouïe*); sourd (*bruit, douleur*); lourd
(*esprit, temps*); sombre (*temps*);
émoussé (*ciseau*); ✝ inactif (-ive *f*)
(*marché*); triste, ennuyeux (-euse*f*);
⚓ calme; **2.** *v/t.* émousser; assourdir; ternir; amortir (*une douleur*);
engourdir (*l'esprit*); hébéter (*q.*);
v/i. se ternir; s'engourdir; **dull·ard**
['∼əd] lourdaud(e *f*) *m*; '**dull·ness**
manque *m* d'éclat *ou* de tranchant;
lenteur *f* de l'esprit; dureté *f* (*d'o-
reille*); tristesse *f*, ennui *m*; bruit *m*
sourd; ✝ marasme *m*, inactivité *f*.

du·ly ['dju:li] *see* due 1; dûment;
convenablement; en temps voulu.

dumb □ [dʌm] muet(te *f*); interdit;
Am. F sot(te *f*); bête; *deaf and* ∼
sourd(e *f*)-muet(te *f*); *see* show 2;

strike ~ rendre muet; ~-*waiter* meu-
ble: servante *f*; *Am.* monte-plats
m/*inv*.; '~-**bell** haltère *m*; *Am. sl.* imbécile *mf*; ~'**found** F interdire; abasourdir; '**dumb·ness** mutisme *m*;
silence *m*.

dum·my ['dʌmi] chose *f* factice;
mannequin *m*; *fig.* muet(te *f*) *m*;
fig. homme *m* de paille; *fig.* sot(te *f*)
m; *cartes*: mort *m*; sucette *f* (*de
bébé*); *attr.* faux (fausse *f*); factice; ~
whist whist *m* avec un mort.

dump [dʌmp] **1.** déposer (*a. fig.*);
jeter (*des ordures*); décharger, vider;
♱ écouler à perte, faire du dumping; *fig.* laisser lourdement; **2.**
coup *m* sourd; tas *m*; ✗ *etc.*: halde *f*;
chantier *m*; décharge *f*; dépôt *m* (*de
vivres, a.* ✗ *de munitions*); (*a. refuse
~*) voirie *f*; *see* ~*ing*; *fig.* ~*s pl.* cafard
m; '**dump·ing** basculage *m*; dépôt
m; ♱ dumping *m*; '**dump·ing-
ground** (lieu *m* de) décharge *f*;
dépotoir *m* (*a. fig.*); '**dump·ling**
boulette *f*; '**dump·y** trapu, replet
(-ète *f*).

dun¹ [dʌn] **1.** brun foncé; **2.** (*cheval
m*) gris louvet *m*.

dun² [~] **1.** demande *f* pressante;
créancier *m* importun; **2.** importuner, harceler (*un débiteur*); ~*ning
letter* demande *f* pressante.

dunce [dʌns], **dun·der·head** ['dʌn-
dəhed] F crétin(e *f*) *m*; lourdaud(e
f) *m*.

dune [dju:n] dune *f*; ~ *buggy* buggy
m.

dung [dʌŋ] **1.** fiente *f*; ✔ engrais *m*;
2. fumer (*un champ*).

dun·geon ['dʌndʒn] cachot *m*.

dung·hill ['dʌŋhil] fumier *m*.

dunk *Am.* F [dʌŋk] *v*/*t*. tremper (dans
son café *etc.*); *v*/*i*. faire la trempette.

du·o ['dju:ou] duo *m*.

du·o·dec·i·mal [dju:ou'desiml] duo-
décimal (-aux *m*/*pl.*); **du·o'dec·i-
mo** [~mou] *typ.* in-douze *m*/*inv*.

dupe [dju:p] **1.** dupe *f*; **2.** duper,
tromper; '**dup·er·y** duperie *f*.

du·plex ⊕ ['dju:pleks] double; *tél.*
duplex; *Am.* maison *f* comprenant
deux appartements indépendants.

du·pli·cate ['dju:plikit] **1.** double;
en double; **2.** double *m*; *cin.*, *phot.*
contretype *m*; **3.** ['~keit] reproduire; copier; **du·pli·ca·tion** [~-
'keiʃn] reproduction *f*; dédoublement *m*; '**du·pli·ca·tor** duplicateur

m; **du·plic·i·ty** [dju:'plisiti] duplicité *f*; mauvaise foi *f*.

du·ra·bil·i·ty [djuərə'biliti] durabilité *f*; stabilité *f*; ⊕ résistance *f*;
'**du·ra·ble** □ durable; résistant;
'**dur·ance** *poét.* captivité *f*; **du·ra-
tion** [~'reiʃn] durée *f*.

du·ress(e) ⚖ [djuə'res] contrainte *f*,
violence *f*; captivité *f*.

dur·ing ['djuəriŋ] *prp.* pendant.

durst [dəːst] *prét.* de *dare*.

dusk [dʌsk] demi-jour *m*/*inv*.; crépuscule *m*; (*a.* '**dusk·i·ness**) obscurité *f*;
'**dusk·y** □ obscur, sombre; noirâ-
tre; brun foncé (*teint*); moricaud.

dust [dʌst] **1.** poussière *f*; **2.** épousseter (*la table, une pièce*); saupoudrer (de, with); '~-**bin** boîte *f* à ordures; poubelle *f*; ~ *liner* sac *m* à
poussière; '~-**bowl** *Am.* étendue *f*
désertique et inculte (*États de la
Prairie*); '~-**cart** tombereau *m* aux
ordures; '~-**cloak**, '~-**coat** cache-
poussière *m*/*inv*.; '**dust·er** torchon
m; chiffon *m*; ⚓ F pavillon *m*; *Am.*
cache-poussière *m*/*inv*.; '**dust·i-
ness** état *m* poudreux *ou* poussiéreux; '**dust·ing** *sl.* raclée *f*, frottée *f*;
'**dust·jack·et** *Am. livre*: jaquette *f*;
'**dust·man** boueur *m*; F marchand
m de sable; '**dust·pan** pelle *f* à
ordures *ou* à poussière; '**dust·up** F
querelle *f*; scène *f*; '**dust·y** □ poussiéreux (-euse *f*); poudreux (-euse *f*).

Dutch [dʌtʃ] **1.** hollandais, de Hollande ~ *courage* courage *m* puisé
dans la bouteille; *Am.* F ~ *treat* repas *m* où chacun paie sa part; *go* ~
(with s.o.) partager les frais (avec q.);
Am. F *in* ~ (with s.o.) en défaveur
(auprès de q.); **2.** *ling.* hollandais *m*;
the ~ *pl.* les Hollandais *m*/*pl.*; *double* ~
baragouin *m*; F hébreu *m*; '**Dutchman** Hollandais *m*; '**Dutch·wom-
an** Hollandaise *f*.

du·ti·a·ble ['dju:tjəbl] taxable; F
déclarable; **du·ti·ful** □ ['~tiful] respectueux (-euse *f*); soumis; obéissant; '**du·ti·ful·ness** soumission *f*,
obéissance *f*.

du·ty ['dju:ti] devoir *m* (envers, to);
respect *m*; obéissance *f*; fonction *f*,
~*s f*/*pl.*; *douane etc.*: droit *m*, ~*s m*/*pl.*;
service *m*; on ~ de service; *off* ~
libre; ~ *call* visite *f* obligée *ou* de
politesse; *in* ~ *bound* de (mon) devoir; *do* ~ *for* remplacer; *fig.* servir
de; '~-'**free** exempt de droits.

du·vet ['dju:vei] édredon *m*.

dwarf [dwɔːf] **1.** nain(e *f*) *m*; **2.** rabougrir; *fig.* rapetisser; '**dwarf·ish** □ (de) nain; chétif (-ive *f*); '**dwarf·ish·ness** nanisme *m*; petite taille *f*.

dwell [dwel] [*irr.*] habiter; demeurer (dans, à); se fixer; ~ (*up*)on s'étendre sur, insister sur; '**dwell·ing** demeure *f*; '**dwell·ing-house** maison *f* d'habitation.

dwelt [dwelt] *prét. et p.p de* dwell.

dwin·dle ['dwindl] diminuer; dépérir; se réduire (à, [*in*]to); '**dwin·dling** diminution *f*.

dye [dai] **1.** teint(ure *f*) *m*; *fig. of deepest* ~ fieffé; endurci; **2.** teindre; '**dy·er** teinturier *m*; '**dye-stuff** matière *f* colorante; '**dye-works** *usu. sg.* teinturerie *f*.

dy·ing ['daiiŋ] (*see die*[1]) **1.** mourant, moribond; **2.** mort *f*.

dy·nam·ic [dai'næmik] **1.** (*a.* **dy·'nam·i·cal** □) dynamique; **2.** force *f* dynamique; **dy'nam·ics** *usu. sg.* dynamique *f*; **dy·na·mite** ['dainəmait] **1.** dynamite *f*; **2.** faire sauter à la dynamite; '**dy·na·mit·er** dynamiteur *m*; **dy·na·mo** ['dainəmou] dynamo *f*.

dy·nas·tic [di'næstik] (~*ally*) dynastique; **dy·nas·ty** ['dinəsti] dynastie *f*.

dyne *phys.* [dain] dyne *f*.

dys·en·ter·y ✻ ['disntri] dysenterie *f*.

dys·lex·i·a [dis'leksiə] dyslexie *f*.

dys·pep·sia ✻ [dis'pepsiə] dyspepsie *f*; **dys'pep·tic** (~*ally*) dyspepsique, dyspeptique (*a. su./mf*).

E

E, e [i:] E *m*, e *m*.

each [i:tʃ] *adj.* chaque; *pron.* chacun (-e *f*); ~ *other* l'un(e) l'autre, les un(e)s les autres; *devant verbe*: se; *they cost a shilling* ~ ils coûtent un shilling chacun.

ea·ger □ ['i:gə] passionné; avide (de *after, for*); *fig.* vif (vive *f*); acharné; **'ea·ger·ness** ardeur *f*; vif désir *m*; empressement *m*.

ea·gle ['i:gl] aigle *mf*; pièce *f* de 10 dollars; **ea·glet** ['i:glit] aiglon *m*.

ea·gre ['eigə] mascaret *m*.

ear¹ [iə] blé: épi *m*.

ear² [~] oreille *f*; *sens:* ouïe *f*; ⊕ anse *f*; *be all* ~s être tout oreilles; *surt. Am. keep an* ~ *to the ground* se tenir aux écoutes; *play by* ~ ♪ jouer à l'oreille; *fig.* décider quoi faire le moment venu; *turn a deaf* ~ *to* faire la sourde oreille à; ~**ache** ['iəreik] mal *m ou* maux *m/pl.* d'oreille; ~**deaf·en·ing** ['~defniŋ] assourdissant; '~**drum** *anat.* tympan *m*.

earl [ə:l] comte *m* (*d'Angleterre*); ⚥ *Marshal* grand maréchal *m*; **earl·dom** ['~dəm] comté *m*.

ear·li·ness ['ə:linis] heure *f* peu avancée; précocité *f*.

ear·lobe ['iəloub] lobe *m*.

ear·ly ['ə:li] **1.** *adj.* matinal (-aux *m/pl.*); premier (-ère *f*); précoce; *be an* ~ *bird* être matinal, se lever de bonne heure; *Brit. it's* ~ *closing (day) today* aujourd'hui les magasins sont fermés l'après-midi; ~ *life* jeunesse *f*; ⚔ ~ *warning system* système *m* de pré-alerte; **2.** *adv.* de bonne heure; tôt; *as* ~ *as* dès; pas plus tard que.

ear...: '~**mark 1.** *bétail:* marque *f* à l'oreille; *fig.* marque *f* distinctive; **2.** marquer (*les bestiaux*) à l'oreille; *fig.* faire une marque distinctive à; affecter (*qch. à une entreprise*); réserver (*une somme*); '~**muffs** *pl.* protège-oreilles *m/inv.*, cache-oreilles *m/inv.*

earn [ə:n] gagner; acquérir (de, *for*); ~**ed** *income* revenu *m* du travail.

ear·nest¹ ['ə:nist] (*a.* ~*-money*) arrhes *f/pl.*; garantie *f*, gage *m*.

ear·nest² [~] **1.** sérieux (-euse *f*); sincère; délibéré; **2.** sérieux *m*; *be in* ~ être sérieux; '**ear·nest·ness** (caractère *m*) sérieux *m*; ardeur *f*.

earn·ings ['ə:niŋz] *pl.* gages *m/pl.*, salaire *m*; gain *m*; profits *m/pl.*

ear...: '~**phones** *pl. radio:* casques *m/pl.* (d'écoute); '~**pick** cure-oreille *m*; '~**piece** *téléph.* écouteur *m*; '~**pierc·ing** qui vous perce les oreilles; '~**plugs** *pl.* boules *f/pl.* Quiès (*TM*); '~**ring** boucle *f* d'oreille; '~**shot** portée *f* de la voix; *within* ~ à portée de voix; '~**split·ting** assourdissant, à vous fendre les oreilles.

earth [ə:θ] **1.** terre *f* (*a.* ⚡); sol *m*; monde *m*; *renard etc.:* terrier *m*; *radio:* (*a.* earth-connection) contact *m* à la terre; **2.** *v/t.* ⚡ relier à la terre *ou* mot. à la masse; ~ *up* butter, terrer; *v/i.* se terrer; '**earth·en** de *ou* en terre; '**earth·en·ware** poterie *f*; '**earth·i·ness** nature *f* terreuse; '**earth·ing** ⚡ mise *f* à la terre (*mot.* à la masse); '**earth·li·ness** nature *f* terrestre; mondanité *f*; '**earth·ly** terrestre; *F imaginable*; *no* ~ *pas le ou* le moindre; '**earth·quake** tremblement *m* de terre; '**earth·worm** lombric *m*; *fig.* piètre personnage *m*; '**earth·y** terreux (-euse *f*); de terre; *fig.* grossier (-ère *f*); terre à terre *inv.*

ear...: '~**trum·pet** cornet *m* acoustique; '~**wax** cérumen *m*.

ease [i:z] **1.** repos *m*, bien-être *m*, aise *f*; tranquillité *f* (*d'esprit*); soulagement *m*; loisir *m*; oisiveté *f*; *manières:* aisance *f*; facilité *f*; simplicité *f*; *at* ~ tranquille; à son *etc.* aise; *ill at* ~ mal à l'aise; ⚔ *stand at* ~! repos!; *take one's* ~ prendre ses aises; *with* ~ facilement; *live at* ~ vivre à l'aise; **2.** adoucir, soulager (*la douleur*); calmer; ⚓ larguer (*une amarre*), mollir (*une barre*); débarrasser (de, *of*); *it* ~*d the situation* la

situation se détendit; ~ *nature* faire ses besoins; **ease·ful** □ ['ˌful] tranquille; calmant; doux (douce *f*).
ea·sel ['iːzl] chevalet *m*.
ease·ment ⚖ ['iːzmənt] *charges:* servitude *f*.
eas·i·ness ['iːzinis] commodité *f*, bien-être *m*; aisance *f*; facilité *f*; douceur *f*; complaisance *f*; ~ *of belief* facilité *f* à croire.
east [iːst] **1.** *su.* est *m*, orient *m*; the ♀ *Am.* les États *m/pl.* de l'Est (*des É.-U.*); **2.** *adj.* d'est, de l'est; oriental (-aux *m/pl.*); **3.** *adv.* à *ou* vers l'est; **'~·bound** (allant) en direction de l'est.
East·er ['iːstə] Pâques *m/pl.*; *attr.* de Pâques; ~ *egg* œuf *m* de Pâques.
east·er·ly ['iːstəli] de *ou* à l'est; **east·ern** ['ˌtən] de l'est; oriental (-aux *m/pl.*); **'east·ern·er** oriental(e *f*) *m*; habitant(e *f*) *m* de l'est; **east·ern·most** ['iːstənmoust] *le* plus à l'est.
east·ing ⚓ ['iːstiŋ] chemin *m* est; route *f* vers l'est.
east·ward ['iːstwəd] **1.** *adj.* à *ou* de l'est; **2.** *adv. a.* **east·wards** ['ˌdz] vers l'est.
eas·y □ ['iːzi] **1.** à l'aise; tranquille; aisé (*air, style, tâche*); libre; facile (*personne, style, tâche*); doux (douce *f*); ample (*vêtement*); ✝ calme; *in ~ circumstances* dans l'aisance; *Am. on ~ street* très à l'aise, F bien renté; ✝ *on ~ terms* avec facilités de paiement; *make o.s. ~* se rassurer (sur, *about*); *take it ~* F se la couler douce; *take it ~!* doucement!; ✕ *Brit.* stand ~ repos!; **2.** halte *f*; ~ **chair** fauteuil *m*; bergère *f*; ~**·go·ing** *fig.* accommodant; insouciant; d'humeur facile.
eat [iːt] **1.** [*irr.*] *v/t.* manger; déjeuner, dîner, souper; prendre (*un plat*); ~ *up* manger jusqu'à la dernière miette; consumer; dévorer (*a. fig.*); *v/i.* manger; déjeuner *etc.*; ~ *out* manger au restaurant; **2.** *Am. sl.* ~*s pl.* manger *m*; mangeaille *f*; **'eat·a·ble 1.** mangeable; **2.** ~*s pl.* comestibles *m/pl.*; **'eat·en** *p.p.* de eat 1; **'eat·er** mangeur (-euse *f*) *m*; *be a great (poor)* ~ être gros (petit) mangeur; **'eat·ing** manger *m*; **'eat·ing-house** restaurant *m*.
eaves [iːvz] *pl.* avance *f*; gouttières *f/pl.*; **'~·drop** écouter à la porte;

être aux écoutes; **'~·drop·per** écouteur (-euse *f*) *m* aux portes.
ebb [eb] **1.** (*a.* ~*-tide*) reflux *m*; *fig.* déclin *m*; *at a low* ~ très bas; **2.** baisser (*a. fig.*); refluer; *fig.* décroître; être sur le déclin.
eb·on·ite ['ebənait] ébonite *f*; **'eb·on·y** (bois *m* d')ébène *f*.
e·bri·e·ty [iː'braiəti] ivresse *f*.
e·bul·li·ent [i'bʌljənt] bouillonnant; *fig.* débordant (de, *with*); **eb·ul·li·tion** [ebə'liʃn] ébullition *f*; *surt. fig.* débordement *m*; insurrection *f*.
ec·cen·tric [ik'sentrik] **1.** (*a.* **ec·cen·tri·cal** □) excentrique (*a. fig.*); *fig.* original (-aux *m/pl.*); **2.** ⊕ excentrique *m*; original(e *f*) *m*; **ec·cen·tric·i·ty** [eksen'trisiti] excentricité *f*.
ec·cle·si·as·tic [ikliːzi'æstik] **1.** †, *usu.* **ec·cle·si·as·ti·cal** □ ecclésiastique; **2.** ecclésiastique *m*.
ech·e·lon ✕ ['eʃələn] **1.** échelon *m*; **2.** échelonner.
e·chi·nus *zo.* [e'kainəs] oursin *m*.
ech·o ['ekou] **1.** écho *m*; **2.** *v/t.* répéter; *fig.* se faire l'écho de; *v/i.* faire écho; retentir; **~·sound·er** ['ˌsaundə] sondeur *m* acoustique.
é·clat ['eiklɑː] éclat *m*, gloire *f*.
ec·lec·tic [ek'lektik] éclectique (*a. su./mf*); **ec'lec·ti·cism** [ˌtisizm] éclectisme *m*.
e·clipse [i'klips] **1.** éclipse *f* (*a. fig.*); *fig.* ombre *f*; *in* ~ éclipsé; *orn.* dans son plumage d'hiver; **2.** *v/t.* éclipser; *v/i.* être éclipsé; **e'clip·tic** *astr.* écliptique (*a. su./f*).
ec·logue ['eklɔg] églogue *f*.
e·co·cid·al ['iːkou'saidl] nuisible à l'environnement; **e·co·cide** ['ˌsaid] destruction de l'environnement.
e·co·log·i·cal [iːkə'lɔdʒikl] écologique; **e·col·o·gist** [iː'kɔlədʒist] écologiste *mf*; **e·col·o·gy** écologie *f*; ~ *movement* mouvement *m* écologique, écologisme *m*.
e·co·nom·ic, e·co·nom·i·cal □ [iːkə'nɔmik(l)] économique; économe (*personne*); *economic aid* aide *f* économique; ~ *growth* croissance *f* économique; ~ *summit* sommet *m* économique; **e·co'nom·ics** *sg.* économie *f* politique; **e·con·o·mist** [i'kɔnəmist] économiste *m*; personne *f* économe (de, *of*); **e'con·o·mize** économiser (qch. *in, on, with* s.th.); **e'con·o·my** économie *f*; *economies*

pl. économies *f/pl.*; épargnes *f/pl.*; *political* ~ économie *f* politique; ~ *class* classe *f* touriste; ~ *drive* (mesures *f/pl. ou* campagne *f* de) restrictions *f/pl.*; ~ *pack* paquet *m* économique.

e·co·sys·tem ['iːkousistəm] écosystème *m*.

ec·sta·size ['ekstəsaiz] *v/t.* ravir; *v/i.* s'extasier (devant, *over*); **'ec·sta·sy** transport *m*; extase *f* (*religieuse etc.*); *go into ecstasies* s'extasier (devant, *over*); **ec·stat·ic** [eks'tætik] (~*ally*) extatique.

e·cu·men·i·cal [iːkjuː'menikl] œcuménique.

ec·ze·ma ⚕ ['eksimə] eczéma *m*.

e·da·cious [i'deiʃəs] vorace.

ed·dy ['edi] **1.** remous *m*; tourbillon *m*; **2.** faire des remous; tourbillonner.

e·den·tate *zo.* [i'denteit] édenté (*a. su./m*).

edge [edʒ] **1.** tranchant *m*; angle *m*; crête *f*; *livre, shilling:* tranche *f*; *forêt:* lisière *f*, orée *f*; *étoffe, table, lac, etc.:* bord *m*; be on ~ être nerveux (-euse *f*); *surt. Am.* F *have the* ~ *on* être avantagé par rapport à; *put an* ~ *on* aiguiser; *lay on* ~ mettre de champ; *set s.o.'s teeth on* ~ faire grincer les dents à q.; énerver q.; *stand on* ~ mettre de champ; **2.** *v/t.* aiguiser; border; *v/i.* (se) faufiler; ~ *in* (se) glisser dans; ~ *forward* avancer tout doucement; ~ *off* *v/t.* amincir; *v/i. fig.* s'écarter tout doucement; **edged** [edʒd] tranchant, acéré; à ... tranchant(s).

edge ...: **'~·less** dépourvu de bords; émoussé; **~-tool** outil *m* tranchant; **'~·ways**, **'~·wise** de côté; de *ou* sur champ.

edg·ing ['edʒiŋ] bordure *f*; *robe:* liséré *m*, ganse *f*.

edg·y ['edʒi] anguleux (-euse *f*); F énervé, agacé.

ed·i·ble ['edibl] **1.** bon(ne *f*) à manger; **2.** ~*s pl.* comestibles *m/pl.*

e·dict ['iːdikt] édit *m*.

ed·i·fi·ca·tion [edifi'keiʃn] édification *f*; **ed·i·fice** ['~fis] édifice *m*; **ed·i·fy** ['~fai] édifier; **'ed·i·fy·ing** □ édifiant.

ed·it ['edit] éditer (*un livre*); diriger (*un journal, une série*); **e·di·tion** [i'diʃn] édition *f*; *fig.* double *m*; **ed·i·tor** ['editə] éditeur *m*; direc-

teur *m*; rédacteur *m* en chef; *letters pl. to the* ~ courrier *m* des lecteurs; **ed·i·to·ri·al** [~'tɔːriəl] **1.** éditorial (-aux *m/pl.*) (*a. su./m*); ~ *office* (bureau *m* de) rédaction *f*; ~ *staff la* rédaction; **2.** article *m* de fond; **ed·i·tor·ship** ['~təʃip] direction *f*; travail *m* d'éditeur.

ed·u·cate ['edjukeit] instruire; pourvoir à l'instruction de; former; éduquer (*un animal*); **ed·u·ca·tion** éducation *f*; enseignement *m*; instruction *f*; *elementary* ~ enseignement *m* primaire; *secondary* ~ enseignement *m* secondaire; *Ministry of* ~ Ministère *m* de l'Éducation nationale; **ed·u·ca·tion·al** □ d'enseignement; pédagogique; ~ *film* film *m* éducatif; ~ *policy* politique *f* d'enseignement; **ed·u·ca·tion(·al)·ist** [~'keiʃn(ə)list] pédagogue *mf*; spécialiste *mf* de pédagogie; **ed·u·ca·tive** ['~kətiv] *see educational*; **ed·u·ca·tor** ['~keitə] éducateur (-trice *f*) *m*.

e·duce [i'djuːs] dégager (*a.* 🜋); déduire; évoquer.

e·duc·tion [i'dʌkʃn] extraction *f*; déduction *f*; ⊕ échappement *m*.

eel [iːl] anguille *f*.

e'en [iːn] *see even*[1] **2.**

e'er [ɛə] *see ever*.

ee·rie, ee·ry ['iəri] mystérieux (-euse *f*); étrange; qui donne le frisson.

ef·face [i'feis] effacer (*a. fig.*); *fig.* éclipser; **ef'face·a·ble** effaçable; **ef'face·ment** effacement *m*.

ef·fect [i'fekt] **1.** effet *m*; action *f* (*a.* ⊕); conséquence *f*; vigueur *f* (👁 *d'une loi*); réalisation *f*; sens *m*, teneur *f*; ~*s pl.* effets *m/pl.* (*théâ., a. d'un mort*); 🕂 provision *f*; *bring to* ~ exécuter; *take* ~, *be of* ~ produire un effet; entrer en vigueur; *deprive of* ~ rendre ineffectif (-ive *f*); *of no* ~ sans effet, inefficace; *in* ~ en effet; en réalité; *to the* ~ portant (*que, that*); *to this* ~ dans ce sens; **2.** réaliser, effectuer; *be* ~*ed* s'opérer, intervenir; **ef'fec·tive 1.** □ efficace; utile; effectif (-ive *f*) (*a.* ⊕); 👁 en vigueur; *fig.* frappant; ✗, ♠ valide; ⊕ *capacity* rendement *m*; ~ *date* date *f* d'entrée en vigueur; ~ *range* portée *f* utile; **2.** ✗ *usu.* ~*s pl.* effectifs *m/pl.*; **ef'fec·tu·al** [~juəl] efficace; valide;

en vigueur; **ef'fec·tu·ate** [‿jueit] effectuer; réaliser.

ef·fem·i·na·cy [i'feminəsi] caractère *m* efféminé; **ef'fem·i·nate** [‿nit] □ efféminé.

ef·fer·vesce [efə'ves] entrer en effervescence, mousser; **ef·fer'ves·cence** effervescence *f*; **ef·fer'ves·cent** effervescent; ∼ *drink* boisson *f* gazeuse.

ef·fete [e'fi:t] caduc (-uque *f*); épuisé.

ef·fi·ca·cious □ [efi'keiʃəs] efficace; **ef·fi·ca·cy** ['‿kəsi] efficacité *f*.

ef·fi·cien·cy [e'fiʃnsi] efficacité *f*; capacité *f*; valeur *f*; ⊕ rendement *m*; bon fonctionnement *m*; *Am.* ∼ *expert* expert *m* de l'organisation rationnelle (*de l'industrie*); **ef'fi·cient** [‿ʃnt] □ efficace; effectif (-ive *f*); à bon rendement.

ef·fi·gy ['efidʒi] effigie *f*.

ef·flo·resce [eflɔ:'res] ♀ fleurir (*a. fig.*); 🜍 (s')effleurir; **ef·flo'res·cence** efflorescence *f* (*a.* 🜍); fleuraison *f*; **ef·flo'res·cent** efflorescent; ♀ en fleur.

ef·flu·ence ['efluəns] émanation *f*, effluence *f*; **'ef·flu·ent 1.** effluent (*a. su./m.*); **2.** cours *m* d'eau dérivé; **ef·flu·vi·um** [e'flu:vjəm], *pl.* **-vi·a** [‿vjə] effluve *m*; exhalaison *f*; **ef·flux** ['eflʌks] flux *m*, écoulement *m*.

ef·fort ['efət] effort *m* (pour *inf.*, at *gér.*); *fig.* œuvre *f*; **'ef·fort·less** □ sans effort; facile.

ef·fron·ter·y [e'frʌntəri] effronterie *f*; *fig.* toupet *m*.

ef·ful·gence [e'fʌldʒns] splendeur *f*; éclat *m*; **ef'ful·gent** □ resplendissant.

ef·fuse [e'fju:z] (se) répandre; **ef·fu·sion** [i'fju:ʒn] effusion *f*, épanchement *m* (*a. fig.*); **ef'fu·sive** □ [‿siv] expansif (-ive *f*); **ef'fu·sive·ness** effusion *f*; volubilité *f*.

eft [eft] *see* newt.

egg¹ [eg] (*usu.* ∼ *on*) pousser, inciter.

egg² [‿] œuf *m*; *buttered* (*ou scrambled*) ∼*s pl.* œufs *m/pl.* brouillés; *boiled* ∼*s pl.* œufs *m/pl.*à la coque; *fried* ∼*s pl.* œufs *m/pl.* sur le plat; *sl. bad* ∼ vaurien *m*, bon *m* à rien; *as sure as* ∼*s* aussi sûr que deux et deux font quatre; **'∼-beat·er** batteur *m* à œufs; **'∼-cup** coquetier *m*; **'∼-flip**, **'∼-nog** flip *m*; **'∼-head** *Am. sl.* intellectuel *m*; **'∼-plant**

aubergine *f*; **'∼-shell** coquille *f*; **'∼-whisk** fouet *m* (à œufs).

eg·lan·tine ♀ ['egləntain] églantine *f*; *buisson:* églantier *m*.

e·go ['egou] *le* moi; **e·go·cen·tric** [‿'sentrik] égocentrique; **'e·go·ism** égotisme *m*; culte *m* du moi; *phls.* égoïsme *m*; **'e·go·ist** égotiste *mf*; égoïste *mf*; **e·go'is·tic, e·go'is·ti·cal** □ égotiste; *fig.* vaniteux (-euse *f*); **e·go·tism** ['egoutizm] égotisme *m*; **'e·go·tist** égotiste *mf*; **e·go'tis·tic, e·go'tis·ti·cal** □ égotiste.

e·gre·gious *iro.* □ [i'gri:dʒəs] insigne; fameux (-euse *f*).

e·gress ['i:gres] sortie *f*, issue *f*; ⊕ échappement *m*.

e·gret ['i:gret] *orn.* aigrette *f* (*a.* ♀); héron *m* argenté.

E·gyp·tian [i'dʒipʃn] **1.** égyptien(ne *f*); **2.** Égyptien(ne *f*) *m*.

eh [ei] eh!; hé!; hein?

ei·der ['aidə] (*a.* ∼*-duck*) eider *m*; **'∼-down** duvet *m* d'eider; (*a.* ∼ *quilt*) édredon *m* piqué.

eight [eit] **1.** huit; **2.** huit *m*; ⚓ équipe *f* de huit rameurs; huit *m* de pointe; *Am. fig. behind the* ∼ *ball* dans une position précaire; **eight·een** ['ei'ti:n] dix-huit; **'eight·eenth** [‿θ] dix-huitième; **'eight·fold** octuple; *adv.* huit fois autant; **eighth** [eitθ] huitième (*a. su./m*); **'eighth·ly** en huitième lieu; **eighthour day** ['‿'auədei] journée *f* de huit heures; **eight·i·eth** ['‿iiθ] quatre-vingtième; **'eight·y** quatre-vingt(s); ∼*-two* quatre-vingt-deux; ∼*-first* quatre-vingt-unième.

ei·ther ['aiðə, 'i:ðə] **1.** *adj.* chaque; l'un(e *f*) et l'autre de; l'un(e *f*) ou l'autre de; **2.** *pron.* chacun(e *f*); l'un(e) et *ou* ou l'autre; **3.** *cj.* ∼ ... *or* ... ou ... ou ...; soit ... soit ...; *not* (...) ∼ ne ... non plus.

e·jac·u·late [i'dʒækjuleit] éjaculer; lancer; proférer; **e·jac·u'la·tion** ⚕, *eccl.* éjaculation *f*; exclamation *f*.

e·ject [i'dʒekt] émettre; expulser (*un agitateur, un locataire*); **e'jec·tion** *flammes:* jet *m*; expulsion *f*; éviction *f*; **e'ject·ment** ⚖ réintégrande *f*; expulsion *f*; **e'jec·tor** ⊕ éjecteur *m*.

eke [i:k]: ∼ *out* suppléer à l'insuffisance de (en y ajoutant, *with*); allonger (*un liquide*); faire du remplissage (avec, *with*); ∼ *out a* *miserable existence* gagner une maigre pitance.

el *Am.* F [el] *abr. de* elevated 2.

e·lab·o·rate 1. [i'læbərit] □ compliqué; travaillé (*style*); recherché; soigné; **2.** [ˌreit] élaborer (*a. physiol.*) (en, *into*); travailler (*son style*); **e'lab·o·rate·ness** [ˌritnis] soin *m*, minutie *f*; **e·lab·o·ra·tion** [ˌ'reiʃn] élaboration *f*.

e·lapse [i'læps] (se) passer; s'écouler.

e·las·tic [i'læstik] **1.** (ˌally) élastique (*a. fig.*); flexible; *he is* ˌ il a du ressort; **2.** élastique *m*; **e·las·tic·i·ty** [ˌ'tisiti] élasticité *f*; souplesse *f*; *fig.* ressort *m*.

e·late [i'leit] **1.** □ élevé; (*usu.* ˌed) transporté (de, *with*); **2.** exalter, transporter; **e'la·tion** exaltation *f*; gaieté *f*.

el·bow ['elbou] **1.** coude *m* (*a.* ⊕); *route:* tournant *m*; ⊕ genou *m*, jarret *m*; *at one's* ˌ tout à côté; tout près; *out at* ˌs troué aux coudes; *fig.* déguenillé; **2.** coudoyer; pousser du coude; ˌ *one's way through* se frayer un passage à travers; ˌ *out* évincer (de, *of*); 'ˌ-'**chair** fauteuil *m*; 'ˌ-**grease** F huile *f* de bras (= *travail, énergie*); 'ˌ-**room:** *have* ˌ avoir du champ.

eld·er¹ ['eldə] **1.** plus âgé, aîné; *cartes:* ˌ *hand* premier *m* en main; ˌ *statesman* vétéran *m* de la politique, homme *m* d'État chevronné; **2.** plus âgé(e*f*) *m*; aîné(e*f*) *m*; *eccl.* ancien *m*; *my* ˌs *pl.* mes aînés *m/pl.*

el·der² ♀ [ˌ] sureau *m*; 'ˌ-**ber·ry** baie *f* de sureau.

eld·er·ly ['eldəli] assez âgé.

eld·est ['eldist] aîné.

e·lect [i'lekt] **1.** élu (*a. eccl.*); futur; *bride* ˌ la future *f*; **2.** élire; *eccl.* mettre parmi les élus; choisir (de *inf., to inf.*); **e'lec·tion** élection *f*; ˌ *address ou* speech discours *m* électoral; **e·lec·tion·eer** [ˌʃə'niə] solliciter des voix; **e·lec'tion'eer·ing** propagande *f* électorale; **e'lec·tive 1.** □ électif (-ive*f*); électoral (-aux *m/pl.*); *Am. univ. etc.* facultatif (-ive *f*); **2.** *Am.* cours *m ou* sujet *m* facultatif; **e'lec·tive·ly** par choix; **e'lec·tor** électeur *m*; *Am.* membre *m* du Collège électoral; **e'lec·tor·al** électoral (-aux *m/pl.*); ˌ *address ou* speech discours *m* électoral, ˌ *campaign*

campagne *f* électorale; ˌ *district ou* division circonscription *f* électorale; ˌ *roll* liste *f* électorale; **e'lec·tor·ate** [ˌrit] corps *m* électoral; votants *m/pl.*; **e'lec·tress** électrice *f*.

e·lec·tric [i'lektrik] électrique; *fig.* électrisant; ⚡ ˌ *arc* arc *m* voltaïque; ˌ *blue* bleu électrique; ˌ *circuit* circuit *m*; *zo.* ˌ *eel* anguille *f* électrique; ˌ *eye* cellule *f* photoélectrique; **e'lec·tri·cal** □ électrique; ˌ *engineer* ingénieur *m* électricien; ˌ *engineering* technique *f* électrique; **e·lec·tri·cian** [ˌ'triʃn] (monteur-) électricien *m*; **e·lec'tric·i·ty** [ˌsiti] électricité *f*; ˌ *works* centrale *f* électrique; **e·lec·tri·fi·ca·tion** [ˌfi'keiʃn] électrisation *f*; ⚡ électrification *f*; **e'lec·tri·fy** [ˌfai], **e'lec·trize** électriser (*a. fig.*); ⚡ électrifier.

electro... [ilektrou] électro-; **e'lec·tro·cute** [ˌtrəkjuːt] électrocuter; **e·lec·tro'cu·tion** électrocution *f*; **e'lec·trode** [ˌtroud] électrode *f*; **e·lec·tro·dy'nam·ics** *usu. sg.* électrodynamique *f*; **e·lec·tro·lier** [ˌ'liə] lustre *m* électrique; **e'lec·tro·lyse** [ˌtrolaiz] électrolyser; **e·lec·trol·y·sis** [ˌ'trɔlisis] électrolyse *f*; **e·lec·tro'mag·net** électro-aimant *m*; **e·lec·tro'met·al·lur·gy** électrométallurgie *f*; **e'lec·tro'mo·tor** électromoteur *m*.

e·lec·tron [i'lektrɔn] électron *m*; *attr.* à électrons, électronique; ˌ *ray tube* oscillographe *m* cathodique; **e·lec'tron·ic 1.** électronique; ˌ *data processing* traitement électronique de(s) données; **2.** ˌs *sg.* électronique *f*.

e·lec·tro·plate [i'lektroupleit] **1.** plaquer; argenter; **2.** articles *m/pl.* argentés *ou* plaqués; **e·lec·tro·type** [i'lektrotaip] électrotype *m*; (cliché *m*) galvano *m*.

e·lec·tu·ar·y ♀ [i'lektjuəri] électuaire *m*.

el·e·gance ['eligəns] élégance *f*; **'el·e·gant** □ élégant; *Am.* excellent.

el·e·gi·ac [eli'dʒaiæk] élégiaque.

el·e·gy ['elidʒi] élégie *f*.

el·e·ment ['elimənt] élément *m* (*a.* ⚡, *eccl., temps, fig.*); partie *f*; ♈ corps *m* simple; ˌs *pl.* rudiments *m/pl.*, éléments *m/pl.*; **el·e·men·tal** [ˌ'mentl] □ élémentaire; des éléments; *fig.* premier (-ère *f*); **el·e-**

'**men·ta·ry** [~təri] □ élémentaire; simple; ~ *school* école *f* primaire.

el·e·phant ['elifənt] éléphant *m* (*mâle, femelle*); *white* ~ objet *m* inutile qui occupe trop de place; **el·e·phan·tine** [~'fæntain] éléphantin; éléphantesque; *fig.* lourd.

el·e·vate ['eliveit] élever; lever; relever; '**el·e·vat·ed 1.** élevé, haut; F un peu ivre; **2.** (*a.* ~ *railroad ou train*) *Am.* F chemin *m* de fer aérien; **el·e-'va·tion** élévation *f* (*a.* ⊕, △, *astr., eccl., colline*); altitude *f*, hauteur *f*; noblesse *f*; '**el·e·va·tor** ⊕ élévateur *m*; *Am.* ascenseur *m*; ⚓ gouvernail *m* d'altitude; *Am.* (*grain*) ~ silo *m* à élévateur pneumatique; *Am.* ~ *shaft* cage *f* d'ascenseur.

e·lev·en [i'levn] onze (*a. su./m*); **e'lev·en·ses** *Brit.* F [~ziz] pausecafé *f*, (*pl.* pauses-café), casse-croûte *m*/*inv.* dans la matinée; **e'lev·enth** [~θ] onzième.

elf [elf], *pl.* **elves** [elvz] elfe *m*; lutin(e *f*) *m*; **elf·in** ['~in] d'elfe, de lutin; '**elf·ish** des elfes, de lutin; espiègle (*enfant*). [tir; obtenir.)

e·lic·it [i'lisit] faire jaillir, faire sor-)

e·lide *gramm.* [i'laid] élider.

el·i·gi·bil·i·ty [elidʒə'biliti] acceptabilité *f*; éligibilité *f*; '**el·i·gi·ble** □ admissible; éligible; F bon(ne *f*) (*parti*), acceptable; *be* ~ *for a.* avoir droit à (*qch.*).

e·lim·i·nate [i'limineit] éliminer (*surt.* ?ₒ, Aᵥ, ♂); supprimer; **e·lim·i'na·tion** élimination *f*.

e·li·sion [i'liʒn] *gramm.* élision *f*.

é·lite [ei'li:t] élite *f*, (fine) fleur *f*, choix *m*; **é'lit·ist** [~ist] élitiste, élitaire.

e·lix·ir [i'liksə] élixir *m*.

E·liz·a·be·than [iliza'bi:θn] élisabéthain.

elk *zo.* [elk] élan *m*.

ell *hist.* [el] aune *f*; aunée *f* (*de drap*).

el·lipse Aᵥ [i'lips] ellipse *f*; *gramm.* **el'lip·sis** [~sis], *pl.* **-ses** [~si:z] ellipse *f*; **el'lip·tic, el'lip·ti·cal** □ elliptique.

elm ♀ [elm] orme *m*.

el·o·cu·tion [elə'kju:ʃn] élocution *f*, diction *f*; **el·o'cu·tion·a·ry** de diction; oratoire; **el·o'cu·tion·ist** déclamateur *m*; professeur *m* d'élocution.

e·lon·gate ['i:lɔŋgeit] (s')allonger; **e·lon'ga·tion** allongement *m*; prolongement *m*; *astr.* élongation *f*.

e·lope [i'loup] s'enfuir (avec un amant); ~ *with* se faire enlever par; **e'lope·ment** fuite *f* amoureuse; enlèvement *m* (consenti).

el·o·quence ['eləkwəns] éloquence *f*; '**el·o·quent** □ éloquent.

else [els] **1.** *adv.* autrement; ou bien; **2.** *adj.* autre; encore; *all* ~ tout le reste; *anyone* ~ quelqu'un d'autre; *what* ~? quoi encore?; *or* ~ ou bien; '**else'where** ailleurs.

e·lu·ci·date [i'lu:sideit] éclaircir, élucider; **e·lu·ci'da·tion** éclaircissement *m*, élucidation *f*; **e'lu·ci·da·to·ry** [~təri] éclaircissant.

e·lude [i'lu:d] éviter; échapper à; éluder (*une question*).

e·lu·sion [i'lu:ʒn] esquive *f*; évasion *f*; **e'lu·sive** [~siv] insaisissable; évasif (-ive *f*) (*réponse*); **e'lu·sive·ness** nature *f* insaisissable; caractère *m* évasif; **e'lu·so·ry** [~səri] évasif (-ive *f*).

elves [elvz] *pl.* de **elf**.

E·ly·si·um [i'liziəm] l'Élysée *m*.

em *typ.* [em] cadratin *m*.

e·ma·ci·ate [i'meiʃieit] amaigrir; émacier; **e·ma·ci·a·tion** [imeisi'eiʃn] amaigrissement *m*, émaciation *f*.

em·a·nate ['eməneit] émaner (de, from); **em·a'na·tion** émanation *f* (*a. phys., a. fig.*); effluve *m*.

e·man·ci·pate [i'mænsipeit] émanciper; affranchir; **e·man·ci'pa·tion** émancipation *f*; affranchissement *m*; **e'man·ci·pa·tor** émancipateur (-trice *f*) *m*; affranchisseur *m*.

e·mas·cu·late 1. [i'mæskjuleit] émasculer, châtrer (*a. un texte*); efféminer (*le style*); **2.** [~lit] émasculé, châtré; énervé; **e·mas·cu·la·tion** [~'leiʃn] émasculation *f*.

em·balm [im'ba:m] embaumer (*a. fig.*); *fig.* parfumer; *be* ~*ed in fig.* être perpétué par *ou* dans.

em·bank [im'bæŋk] endiguer; remblayer (*une route*); **em'bank·ment** endiguement *m*; remblayage *m*; digue *f*; talus *m*; remblai *m*; quai *m*.

em·bar·go [em'ba:gou] **1.** *pl.* -**goes** [~gouz] embargo *m*, séquestre *m*, arrêt *m*; *put an* ~ *on fig.* interdire; **2.** mettre l'embargo sur, séquestrer (*un navire etc.*); réquisitionner.

em·bark [im'bɑːk] (s')embarquer (*a. fig.* dans, [up]on); *v/t.* prendre (*qch.*) à bord; *v/i.*: ~ (up)on *s.th.* entreprendre qch.; **em·bar·ka·tion** [embɑː'keiʃn] embarquement *m*.

em·bar·rass [im'bærəs] embarrasser, gêner; déconcerter; ~ed embarrassé, gêné; dans l'embarras; **em·'bar·rass·ing** □ embarrassant; gênant; **em·'bar·rass·ment** embarras *m*, gêne *f*.

em·bas·sy ['embəsi] ambassade *f*.

em·bat·tle ✗ [im'bætl] ranger en bataille; ~d crénelé.   [châsser.)

em·bed [im'bed] enfoncer; en-)

em·bel·lish [im'beliʃ] embellir, orner; enjoliver (*un conte*); **em·'bel·lish·ment** embellissement *m*, ornement *m*; enjolivure *f*.

em·ber-days ['embədeiz] *pl.* les Quatre-Temps *m/pl.*

em·bers ['embəz] *pl.* cendres *f/pl.* ardentes; *fig.* cendres *f/pl.*

em·bez·zle [im'bezl] détourner, s'approprier; **em·'bez·zle·ment** détournement *m* de fonds; **em·'bezzler** détourneur *m* de fonds.

em·bit·ter [im'bitə] remplir d'amertume; envenimer (*une querelle etc.*).

em·bla·zon(·ry) [im'bleizn(ri)] *see* blazon(ry).

em·blem ['embləm] emblème *m*; *sp.* insigne *m*; ✍ devise *f*; **em·blem·at·ic, em·blem·at·i·cal** □ [embli'mætik(l)] emblématique.

em·bod·i·ment [im'bɔdimənt] incorporation *f*; personnification *f*; incarnation *f*; **em·'bod·y** incarner; personnifier; incorporer (dans, *in*); réaliser; ✗ rassembler.   [*in*).)

em·bog [im'bɔg] embourber (dans,)

em·bold·en [im'bouldn] enhardir.

em·bo·lism ⚕ ['embəlizm] embolie *f*.

em·bos·om [im'buzəm] cacher dans son sein; serrer contre son sein.

em·boss [im'bɔs] graver en relief; repousser (*du métal, du cuir*); **em·'bossed** gravé en relief; repoussé, estampé.

em·bow·el [im'bauəl] éventrer.

em·brace [im'breis] **1.** *v/t.* embrasser (*a. une carrière*); saisir, profiter de (*une occasion*); adopter (*une cause, une philosophie*); contenir (dans, *in*); comprendre; envisager tous les aspects de; *v/i.* s'embrasser; **2.** étreinte *f*.

em·bra·sure [im'breiʒə] embrasure *f*.

em·bro·cate ['embrokeit] frictionner (à, *with*); **em·bro'ca·tion** embrocation *f*.

em·broi·der [im'brɔidə] broder (*a. fig.*); **em·'broi·der·y** broderie *f* (*a. fig.*).

em·broil [im'brɔil] brouiller; embrouiller; **em·'broil·ment** brouillement *m*; embrouillement *m*; brouille *f* (*entre personnes*).

em·bry·o ['embriou] **1.** embryon *m*; in ~ embryonnaire; F en herbe; **2.** (*ou* **em·bry·on·ic** [~'ɔnik]) *fig.* F en germe.

em·bus [im'bʌs] *v/t.* embarquer en autobus; *v/i.* s'embarquer dans un autobus.

em·cee F [em'siː] animateur (-trice *f*) *m*, présentateur (-trice *f*) *m*.

e·men·da·tion [iːmen'deiʃn] émendation *f*; correction *f*; **'e·men·da·tor** correcteur *m*; **e·mend·a·to·ry** [~dətəri] rectificatif (-ive *f*).

em·er·ald ['emərəld] **1.** émeraude *f*; **2.** vert d'émeraude.

e·merge [i'məːdʒ] émerger, surgir; déboucher (de, *from*); *fig.* apparaître, surgir; **e·'mer·gence** émergence *f*; **e·'mer·gen·cy** urgence *f*; cas *m* imprévu; circonstance *f* critique; ~ *brake* frein *m* de secours; *téléph.* ~ *call* appel *m* urgent; ~ *exit* sortie *f* de secours; ~ *fund* masse *f* de secours; ~ *house* habitation *f* provisoire; ✈ ~ *landing* atterrissage *m* forcé; ~ *man* ouvrier *m* supplémentaire; remplaçant *m*; ~ *measure* mesure *f* extraordinaire; ~ *number* police-secours *f*; ~ *service* service *m* des urgences; **e·'mer·gent 1.** émergent; surgissant; **2.** résultat *m*.

e·mer·sion [i'məːʃn] émersion *f*.

em·er·y ['eməri] émeri *m*; ~ *board* lime *f* émeri; **'~-pa·per** papier *m* d'émeri.

e·met·ic [i'metik] émétique (*a. su./m*).

em·i·grant ['emigrənt] émigrant(e *f*) (*a. su./mf*); **em·i·grate** ['~greit] (faire) émigrer; **em·i'gra·tion** émigration *f*; **em·i·gra·to·ry** ['~grətəri] émigrant.

em·i·nence ['eminəns] éminence *f* (*titre*: ♕); grandeur *f*; élévation *f*; monticule *m*; saillie *f*; **'em·i·nent**

□ *fig.* éminent, célèbre (pour *in*, for); '**em·i·nent·ly** par excellence.

em·is·sar·y ['emisəri] émissaire *m*; **e·mis·sion** [i'miʃn] émission *f* (*a. phys.,* ✝); lancement *m*.

e·mit [i'mit] dégager; lancer; laisser échapper; émettre (*une opinion, a.* ✝). [(*a. su./m*.).]

e·mol·li·ent [i'mɔliənt] émollient)

e·mol·u·ment [i'mɔljumənt] émolument *m*; ~s *pl.* appointements *m/pl.*

e·mo·tion [i'mouʃn] émotion *f*; émoi *m*; **e·mo·tion·al** □ émotionnable; facile à émouvoir; ✗ émotif (-ive *f*); **e·mo·tion·al·i·ty** [~'næliti] émotivité *f*; **e·mo·tive** émotif (-ive *f*); émouvant.

em·pan·el [im'pænl] inscrire (*q.*) sur la liste du jury.

em·per·or ['empərə] empereur *m*.

em·pha·sis ['emfəsis], *pl.* -ses [~si:z] force *f*; accentuation *f*; insistance *f*; accent *m* (*a. gramm.*); **em·pha·size** ['~saiz] accentuer; appuyer sur; souligner; faire ressortir; **em·phat·ic** [im'fætik] (~ally) énergique; positif (-ive *f*); autoritaire; *be* ~ *that* faire valoir que.

em·pire ['empaiə] empire *m*.

em·pir·ic [em'pirik] **1.** empirique *m*, empiriste *m*; *péj.* charlatan *m*; **2.** (*usu.* **em'pir·i·cal** □) empirique.

em·place·ment ✗ [im'pleismənt] emplacement *m*. [en avion.)

em·plane [im'plein] (faire) monter)

em·ploy [im'plɔi] **1.** employer; faire usage de; ~ *oneself* s'occuper (à *in, on, for*); **2.** emploi *m*; *in the* ~ *of* au service de; **em·ploy·é** [ɔm'plɔiei] employé *m*; **em·ploy·ée** [~] employée *f*; **em·ploy·ee** [em-plɔi'i:] employé(e *f*) *m*; ~*s' spokesman* porte-parole *m* des employés; **em·ploy·er** [im'plɔiə] patron(ne *f*) *m*; maître(sse *f*) *m*; employeur *m*; **em'ploy·ment** emploi *m*; occupation *f*; situation *f*, place *f*; travail *m*; ~ *agency* bureau *m* de placement; *full* ~ plein(-)emploi *m*; *place of* ~ emploi *m*; bureau *m*, atelier *m etc.*; ☿ *Exchange* Bourse *f* du Travail.

em·po·ri·um [em'pɔ:riəm] entrepôt *m*; marché *m*; F grand magasin *m*.

em·pow·er [im'pauə] autoriser; donner (plein) pouvoir à (*q.*) (pour *inf., to inf.*); rendre capable (de *inf., to inf.*).

em·press ['empris] impératrice *f*.

emp·ti·er ['emptiə] videur *m*; '**emp·ti·ness** vide *m*; *fig.* néant *m*, vanité *f*; **emp·ty** □ **1.** vide; *fig.* vain; F creux (creuse *f*), affamé; **2.** (se) vider; (se) décharger; **3.** bouteille *f ou* caisse *f ou* ✝ emballage *m* vide; '**emp·ty-hand·ed** les mains vides; *return* ~ *a.* revenir bredouille.

em·pur·ple [im'pə:pl] empourprer.

e·mu *orn.* ['i:mju:] émeu *m*.

em·u·late ['emjuleit] imiter; rivaliser avec; **em·u·la·tion** émulation *f*; '**em·u·la·tive** [~'leitiv] qui tente de rivaliser (avec, *of*); **em·u·la·tor** ['~leitə] émule *m/f*; '**em·u·lous** □ émulateur (-trice *f*) (de, *of*).

e·mul·sion ⚗ [i'mʌlʃn] émulsion *f*.

en·a·ble [i'neibl] rendre capable, mettre à même (de, *to*); donner pouvoir à (*q.*) (de *inf., to inf.*).

en·act [i'nækt] décréter (*une loi, une mesure*); *théâ.* jouer, représenter; *be* ~*ed* se dérouler; **en'ac·tive** décrétant; représentant; **en'act·ment** promulgation *f*; loi *f*; décret *m*.

en·am·el [i'næml] **1.** émail (*pl.* -aux) *m*; (peinture *f* au) vernis *m*; F ripolin *m*; **2.** émailler; peindre au ripolin; *poét.* embellir, orner.

en·am·o(u)r [i'næmə] rendre amoureux (-euse *f*); ~*d* épris, amoureux (-euse *f*) (de, *of*).

en·cage [in'keidʒ] mettre en cage.

en·camp ✗ [in'kæmp] camper; **en'camp·ment** camp(ement) *m*.

en·case [in'keis] enfermer (dans, *in*); F revêtir (de, *with*); **en'case·ment** revêtement *m*; enveloppe *f*.

en·cash·ment ✝ [in'kæʃmənt] recette *f*; encaissement *m*.

en·caus·tic [en'kɔ:stik] encaustique (*a. su./f*).

en·chain [in'tʃein] enchaîner.

en·chant [in'tʃɑ:nt] ensorceler; *fig.* enchanter, ravir; **en'chant·er** enchanteur *m*; **en'chant·ing** ravissant; **en'chant·ment** enchantement *m*; **en'chant·ress** enchanteresse *f*.

en·chase [in'tʃeis] enchâsser (*a. fig.*); sertir (*une pierre précieuse*); graver; incruster.

en·ci·pher [in'saifə] chiffrer.

en·cir·cle [in'sə:kl] ceindre; entourer; *surt.* ✗ envelopper; **en'cir·cle·ment** *pol.* encerclement *m*.

en·close [in'klouz] enclore; entourer; renfermer; joindre (à une lettre, *in a letter*); *eccl.* cloîtrer; ~d herewith sous ce pli, ci-joint; **en'clo·sure** [~ʒə] clôture *f* (*a. eccl.*); (en)clos *m*; ✝ pièce *f* annexée *ou* jointe.

en·code [in'koud] chiffrer.

en·co·mi·ast [en'koumiæst] panégyriste *m*; **en'co·mi·um** [~mjən] panégyrique *m*, éloge *m*.

en·com·pass [in'kʌmpəs] entourer; renfermer.

en·core [ɔŋ'kɔː] 1. bis!; 2. bisser; crier bis; 3. bis *m*.

en·coun·ter [in'kauntə] 1. rencontre *f*; duel *m*; combat *m*; *fig.* assaut *m* (*d'esprit*); 2. rencontrer; éprouver (*des difficultés*) affronter.

en·cour·age [in'kʌridʒ] encourager; inciter, aider, soutenir; favoriser; **en'cour·age·ment** encouragement *m*; **en'cour·ag·er** celui (celle *f*) qui encourage.

en·croach [in'kroutʃ] empiéter (sur, [*up*]on), léser (les droits de *q.*); ~ upon s.o.'s kindness abuser de la bonté de q.; **en'croach·ment** ([*up*]on) empiétement *m* (sur); anticipation *f* (sur), usurpation *f* (de).

en·crust [in'krʌst] (s')incruster.

en·cum·ber [in'kʌmbə] encombrer (de, *with*); gêner; grever (*une propriété*); **en'cum·brance** embarras *m*; charge *f* (*a. fig.*); servitude *f*; *without* ~ sans charges de famille.

en·cy·clo·p(a)e·di·a [ensaiklo'piːdiə] encyclopédie *f*; **en·cy·clo·'p(a)e·dic** encyclopédique.

end [end] 1. bout *m*, extrémité *f*; fin *f*; limite *f*; but *m*, dessein *m*; be at an ~ être au bout (de qch., *of s.th.*); être fini; no ~ of une infinité de, infiniment de, ... sans nombre; have s.th. at one's fingers' ~s savoir qch. sur le bout du doigt; in the ~ à la fin, enfin; à la longue; on ~ de suite; debout; stand on ~ se dresser (sur la tête); to the ~ that afin que (sbj.), afin de (inf.); to no ~ en vain; to this ~ dans ce but; make an ~ of, put an ~ to mettre fin à, achever; make both ~s meet joindre les deux bouts; s'en tirer; 2. finir, (se) terminer, (s')achever.

en·dan·ger [in'deindʒə] mettre en danger.

en·dear [in'diə] rendre cher; **en'dear·ing** qui rend sympathique; attirant; **en'dear·ment** (*ou term of* ~) mot *m* tendre; attrait *m*.

en·deav·o(u)r [in'devə] 1. effort *m*, tentative *f*; 2. (*to inf.*) essayer (de *inf.*); chercher (à *inf.*); s'efforcer (de *inf.*).

en·dem·ic ⚕ [en'demik] 1. (*a.* **en·'dem·i·cal** □) endémique; 2. maladie *f* endémique.

end·ing ['endiŋ] fin *f*; achèvement *m*; *gramm.* terminaison *f*.

en·dive ♀ ['endiv] chicorée *f*; *a.* endive *f*.

end·less □ ['endlis] sans fin (*a.* ⊕); infini; continuel(le *f*).

end-of-term [endəv'təːm] *école:* de fin de semestre.

en·dorse ✝ [in'dɔːs] endosser (*un document*); mentionner (*qch.*) au verso de qch.; avaliser (*un effet*); viser (*un passeport*); *fig.* appuyer; **endorsing ink** encre *f* à tampon; **en·dor·see** ✝ [endɔː'siː] endossataire *mf*; **en·dorse·ment** [in'dɔːsmənt] ✝ endos(sement) *m*; *fig.* approbation *f*; adhésion *f*; **en'dors·er** ✝ endosseur *m*.

en·dow [in'dau] doter (*une église etc.*); fonder; *fig.* douer; **en'dow·ment** dotation *f*; fondation *f*; *fig.* don *m* (= *qualité*); ~ assurance assurance *f* à terme fixe.

en·due [in'djuː] revêtir (*un vêtement*; *q.* de, *with*); *usu. fig.* investir; douer.

en·dur·a·ble [in'djuərəbl] supportable; **en'dur·ance** endurance *f*, résistance *f*; patience *f*; *past* ~ insupportable; ~ *flight* vol *m* d'endurance; ~ *run* course *f* d'endurance; **en·dure** [in'djuə] *v/t.* supporter, souffrir (*qch.*); *v/i.* durer, rester, persister.

end·way(s) ['endwei(z)], **end·wise** ['~waiz] debout; bout à bout.

en·e·ma ⚕ ['enimə] lavement *m*; irrigateur *m*.

en·e·my ['enimi] 1. ennemi(e *f*) *m*; the ♀ le diable *m*; *sl.* how goes the ~? quelle heure est-il?; 2. ennemi(e *f*).

en·er·get·ic [enə'dʒetik] (~ally) énergique; **'en·er·gize** stimuler; ⚡ aimanter; amorcer (*un dynamo*); **'en·er·gy** énergie *f* (*a. phys.*); force *f*; vigueur *f*; ~ *crisis* crise *f* de l'énergie; **'en·er·gy-sav·ing** qui économise de l'énergie, à faible consommation d'énergie.

en·er·vate ['enə:veit] énerver, affaiblir; **en·er·va·tion** affaiblissement *m*; mollesse *f*.

en·fee·ble [in'fi:bl] affaiblir; **en·'fee·ble·ment** affaiblissement *m*.

en·feoff [in'fef] investir d'un fief; inféoder (*une terre*); **en'feoff·ment** inféodation *f*.

en·fi·lade ⚔ [enfi'leid] **1.** enfilade *f*; **2.** battre d'enfilade.

en·fold [in'fould] envelopper.

en·force [in'fɔ:s] faire valoir (*un argument*); exécuter (*une loi*); rendre effectif (-ive *f*); faire observer; imposer (à q., *upon s.o.*); **en'force·ment** application *f*; exécution *f*; contrainte *f*; mise *f* en force.

en·fran·chise [in'fræntʃaiz] donner le droit de vote à (*q.*) *ou* de cité à (*une ville*); affranchir (*un esclave*); **en'fran·chise·ment** [~tʃizmənt] admission *f* au suffrage; affranchissement *m*.

en·gage [in'geidʒ] *v/t.* engager (*l'honneur, la parole, un domestique*); embaucher (*un ouvrier*); retenir, réserver, louer (*une place*); mettre en prise (*un engrenage*); fixer (*l'attention*); attaquer (*l'ennemi*); attirer (*l'affection*); be ~*d* être fiancé; être pris; être occupé (*a. téléph.*); be ~*d in* être occupé à; prendre part à; lier (*une conversation*); *v/i.* s'engager; s'obliger (à, to); s'embarquer (dans, in); ⚔ livrer combat, en venir aux mains; **en'gaged sig·nal** *ou* **tone** *téléph.* signal *m* d'occupé *ou* pas libre; **en·gage·ment** engagement *m*; promesse *f*; poste *m*, situation *f*; rendez-vous *m*; invitation *f*; fiançailles *f/pl.*; ⊕ mise *f* en prise; ⚔ action *f*, combat *m*.

en·gag·ing □ [in'geidʒiŋ] *fig.* attrayant, séduisant.

en·gen·der [in'dʒendə] *fig.* faire naître; engendrer; produire.

en·gine ['endʒin] machine *f*, appareil *m*; ⊕ locomotive *f*; moteur *m*; *fig.* engin *m*, instrument *m*; **'en·gined** ⚒ à ... moteurs.

en·gine-...: '~driv·er ⚒ mécanicien *m*; **'~fit·ter** ajusteur *m* mécanicien.

en·gi·neer [endʒi'niə] **1.** ingénieur *m*; *fig.* agenceur (-euse *f*) *m*, *péj.* machinateur (-trice *f*) *m*; ⚔ soldat

m du génie, ~*s pl.* le génie *m*; ⚓ ingénieur *m* maritime; ⚒ *Am.* mécanicien *m*; **2.** construire; F machiner, manigancer; **en·gi'neer·ing** art *m* de l'ingénieur; génie *m*; technique *f*; construction *f* mécanique; F manœuvres *f/pl.*; *attr.* du génie; ~ *college* école *f* des arts et métiers.

en·gine·man ['endʒinmən] machiniste *m*; ⚒ mécanicien *m*; **en·gine·ry** ['~nəri] machines *f/pl.*; *fig.* machinations *f/pl.*

en·gird [in'gə:d] [*irr.* (*gird*)] ceindre (de, with).

Eng·lish ['iŋgliʃ] **1.** anglais; *the* ~ *Channel* la Manche; **2.** *ling.* anglais *m*; *the* ~ *pl.* les Anglais *m/pl.*; ~*-speaking* anglophone (*pays etc.*); qui parle anglais (*personne*); **'Eng·lish·man** Anglais *m*; **'Eng·lish·wom·an** Anglaise *f*. [tir.)

en·gorge [in'gɔ:dʒ] dévorer, englou-∫

en·graft ↙ [in'grɑ:ft] greffer (sur in[to], [up]on); *fig.* inculquer (à, in).

en·grain [in'grein] teindre grand teint; *fig.* enraciner; **en'grained** encrassé; enraciné.

en·grave [in'greiv] graver (*a. fig.*); **en'grav·er** *personne:* graveur *m*; *outil:* burin *m*; ~ *on copper* chalcographe *m*; **en'grav·ing** gravure *f* (*sur bois, acier*); estampe *f*.

en·gross [in'grous] écrire en grosse; rédiger; absorber (*l'attention, q.*); s'emparer de; ~*ing hand* écriture *f* en grosse; **en'gross·ment** ⚖ (rédaction *f* de la) grosse *f*; absorption *f* (dans, in).

en·gulf [in'gʌlf] *fig.* engloutir, engouffrer; be ~*ed a.* être sombré.

en·hance [in'hɑ:ns] rehausser; augmenter; relever; **en'hance·ment** rehaussement *m*; augmentation *f*; ✝ *prix:* hausse *f*.

e·nig·ma [i'nigmə] énigme *f*; **e·nig·mat·ic, e·nig·mat·i·cal** □ [enig'mætik(l)] énigmatique.

en·join [in'dʒɔin] enjoindre, imposer; recommander (à q., [up]on s.o.); ~ *s.o. from* (*gér.*) interdire à q. de (*inf.*).

en·joy [in'dʒɔi] prendre plaisir à; goûter; jouir de; ~ *o.s.* s'amuser; se divertir; *I* ~ *my dinner* je trouve le dîner bon; **en'joy·a·ble** agréable; excellent; **en'joy·ment** plaisir *m*; ⚖ jouissance *f*.

en·kin·dle [in'kindl] allumer; *fig.* enflammer.

en·lace [in'leis] enlacer.

en·large [in'lɑːdʒ] *v/t.* agrandir (*a. phot.*); élargir; augmenter; *v/i.* s'agrandir, s'élargir, s'étendre (sur, [*up*]on); **en'large·ment** agrandissement *m* (*a. phot.*); élargissement *m*; accroissement *m*; **en'larg·er** *phot.* agrandisseur *m.*

en·light·en [in'laitn] *fig.* éclairer (q. sur qch., *s.o. on s.th.*); **en'light·en·ment** éclaircissements *m/pl.*

en·list [in'list] *v/t.* enrôler (*un soldat*); engager, rattacher (à, *in*); ✕ ⁓ed man (simple) soldat *m*; *v/i.* s'enrôler; s'engager (dans *in*).

en·liv·en [in'laivn] animer; *fig.* égayer, stimuler (*surt.* ✝).

en·mesh [in'meʃ] prendre dans un piège; empêtrer.

en·mi·ty ['enmiti] inimitié *f.*

en·no·ble [i'noubl] anoblir; *fig.* ennoblir.

e·nor·mi·ty [i'nɔːmiti] énormité *f*; **e'nor·mous** □ énorme.

e·nough [i'nʌf] assez; *sure* ⁓! assurément!; c'est bien vrai!; *well* ⁓ passablement; très bien; *be kind* ⁓ *to* (*inf.*) avoir la bonté de (*inf.*).

e·nounce [i'nauns] *see* enunciate.

en·quire [in'kwaiə] *see* inquire.

en·rage [in'reidʒ] enrager, rendre furieux (-euse *f*); **en'raged** furieux (-euse *f*) (contre, *at*).

en·rap·ture [in'ræptʃə] ravir.

en·rich [in'ritʃ] enrichir; ✕ fertiliser (*le sol*); **en'rich·ment** enrichissement *m.*

en·rol(l) [in'roul] *v/t.* immatriculer (*un étudiant*); inscrire (*dans une liste*); engager (*des ouvriers*); ✕ enrôler, encadrer; *v/i.* (*ou* ⁓ *o.s.*) ✕ s'engager; s'inscrire (à une société, *in a society*); se faire inscrire; **en·'rol(l)·ment** enrôlement *m*; engagement *m.*

en route [ɑ̃ːn'ruːt] en route.

en·sconce [in'skɔns] cacher; ⁓ *o.s.* se camper, se blottir (dans, *in*).

en·shrine [in'ʃrain] enchâsser (*a. fig.*) (dans, *in*).   [ensevelir.\]

en·shroud [in'ʃraud] envelopper,\]

en·sign ['ensain] étendard *m*, drapeau *m*; ⚓ ['ensn] pavillon *m*; *Am.* enseigne *m.*

en·si·lage ['ensilidʒ] **1.** ensil(ot)age *m*; **2.** (*a.* **en·sile** [in'sail]) ensil(ot)er.

en·slave [in'sleiv] réduire à l'esclavage; asservir; **en'slave·ment** asservissement *m*; **en'slav·er** *surt. fig.* ensorceleuse *f.*

en·snare [in'snɛə] prendre au piège (*a. fig.*); *fig.* séduire (*une femme*).

en·sue [in'sjuː] s'ensuivre (de *from, on*).

en·sure [in'ʃuə] (*against, from*) garantir (de), assurer (contre).

en·tab·la·ture △ [en'tæblətʃə] entablement *m.*

en·tail [in'teil] **1.** substitution *f*; bien *m* substitué; **2.** (*on*) substituer (*un bien*) (au profit de); entraîner (*des conséquences*) (pour); comporter (*des difficultés*) (pour).

en·tan·gle [in'tæŋgl] emmêler; enchevêtrer (*a. fig.*); *fig.* empêtrer; **en'tan·gle·ment** embrouillement *m*, enchevêtrement *m*; embarras *m*; ✕ barbelé *m*, -s *m/pl.*

en·ter ['entə] *v/t.* entrer dans, pénétrer dans; monter dans (*un taxi etc.*); inscrire, porter (*un nom*) dans une liste; entrer à (*l'armée, une école*); s'inscrire à (*une université etc.*); prendre part à (*une discussion, une querelle*); ✝ déclarer en douane, ✝ inscrire (*au grand livre*); faire (*des protestations*); dresser (*un animal*); ✝ ⁓ *up v/t.* inscrire (à un compte); *v/i.* entrer, s'inscrire, *sp.* s'engager (pour, *for*); entrer (à, *at school etc.*); ⁓ *into* entrer dans (*les affaires, les détails*); entrer en (*conversation*); prendre part à; partager (*des idées, des sentiments*); *fig.* contracter (*un mariage*), conclure (*un marché*), fournir (*des explications*); ⁓ (*up*)on entrer en (*fonctions*); entreprendre; embrasser (*une carrière*); entrer dans (*une année*); entamer (*un sujet*); s'engager dans (*qch.*); ⚖ entrer en possession de (*qch.*); *théâ.* ⁓ *Macbeth* entre Macbeth; **'en·ter·a·ble** ✝ importable; **'en·ter·ing** entrée *f*; inscription *f*; *attr.* d'entrée, d'attaque, de pénétration.

en·ter·ic ⚕ [en'terik] entérique; **en·ter·i·tis** [ˌentə'raitis] entérite *f.*

en·ter·prise ['entəpraiz] entreprise *f*; *fig.* initiative *f*; ✝ *private* ⁓ entreprise *f* privée; le secteur privé; **'en·ter·pris·ing** □ entreprenant.

en·ter·tain [entə'tein] *v/t.* amuser, divertir; recevoir (*des invités*); fêter; accepter, accueillir (*une proposition* *etc.*); entretenir (*la correspondance*); avoir (*des doutes, une opinion*); être animé de (*un sentiment*); *v/i.* recevoir, donner une réception; **en·ter'tain·er** hôte(sse *f*) *m*; comique *m*; diseur (-euse *f*) *m*; **en·ter·'tain·ing** □ amusant, divertissant; **en·ter'tain·ment** hospitalité *f*; soirée *f*; spectacle *m*; divertissement *m*, *a.* accueil *m*; ~ **tax** taxe *f* sur les spectacles.

en·thral(l) [in'θrɔːl] asservir; *fig.* captiver, charmer.

en·throne [in'θroun] mettre sur le trône; introniser (*un roi, un évêque*); **en'throne·ment**, **en·thron·i·za·tion** [enθronai'zeiʃn] intronisation *f*.

en·thuse F [in'θjuːz] s'enthousiasmer (de, pour *about, over*).

en·thu·si·asm [in'θjuːziæzm] enthousiasme *m*; **en'thu·si·ast** [~æst] enthousiaste *mf* (de, *for*); **en·thu·si·as·tic** (~ally) enthousiaste (de *at, about*); passionné.

en·tice [in'tais] séduire, attirer; **en·'tice·ment** séduction *f*; attrait *m*; **en'tic·er** séducteur (-trice *f*) *m*; **en'tic·ing** □ séduisant; attrayant.

en·tire [in'taiə] **1.** □ entier (-ère *f*) (*a. cheval*), complet (-ète *f*), tout; intact; **2.** entier *m*; totalité *f*; **en·'tire·ly** entièrement, tout entier; du tout au tout; **en'tire·ness** intégralité *f*; **en'tire·ty** intégr(al)ité *f*.

en·ti·tle [in'taitl] intituler; donner à (*q.*) le droit (à, *to*).

en·ti·ty *phls.* ['entiti] entité *f*; *legal* ~ personne *f* juridique.

en·tomb [in'tuːm] ensevelir; **en·'tomb·ment** ensevelissement *m*.

en·to·mol·o·gy *zo.* [entə'mɔlədʒi] entomologie *f*.

en·trails ['entreilz] *pl.* entrailles *f/pl.*

en·train ✕ [in'trein] (s')embarquer en chemin de fer.

en·trance¹ ['entrəns] entrée *f* (dans, *into*; *a.* en fonctions, *into* [*ou upon*] *office*); accès *m*; pénétration *f*; (*a.* ~ *fee*) prix *m* d'entrée; *théâ.* entrée *f* en scène; ~ *examination* examen *m* d'entrée.

en·trance² [in'trɑːns] ravir, extasier.

en·trant ['entrənt] débutant(e *f*) *m*; *sp.* inscrit(e *f*) *m*.

en·trap [in'træp] prendre au piège;

amener (*q.*) par ruse (à *inf.*, *into gér.*).

en·treat [in'triːt] supplier, prier; demander instamment (à, *of*); **en·'treat·y** prière *f*, supplication *f*.

en·trench ✕ [in'trentʃ] retrancher; ~ *upon* empiéter sur; **en'trench·ment** retranchement *m*.

en·tre·pre·neur [ɔntrəprə'nəː] entrepreneur (-euse *f*) *m*; **en·tre·pre·neur·i·al** [~'nəːriəl] des entrepreneurs.

en·trust [in'trʌst] confier (qch. à q., *s.th.* to *s.o.*); charger (q. de qch., *s.o.* with *s.th.*).

en·try ['entri] entrée *f*; inscription *f*; ⚖ prise *f* de possession, entrée *f* en jouissance (de, [*up*]*on*); ✝ *comptabilité:* partie *f*, *compte:* article *m*; *sp.* liste *f* des inscrits; *sp.* inscription *f*; ⚓ élément *m* (*du journal*); *Am.* commencement *m*; *no* ~ entrée interdite; *rue:* sens interdit; ~ *permit* permis *m* d'entrée; ~ *visa* visa *m* d'entrée; *make an* ~ *of s.th.* passer qch. en écriture; *bookkeeping by double (single)* ~ tenue *f* des livres *ou* comptabilité *f* en partie double (simple).

en·twine [in'twain], **en·twist** [in·'twist] (s')entrelacer.

e·nu·mer·ate [i'njuːməreit] énumérer; **e·nu·mer·a·tion** énumération *f*.

e·nun·ci·ate [i'nʌnsieit] prononcer, articuler; énoncer, exprimer (*une opinion*); **e·nun·ci·a·tion** prononciation *f*, articulation *f*; *opinion:* énonciation *f*; *problème:* énoncé *m*.

en·vel·op [in'veləp] envelopper (*a.* ✕); *fig.* voiler; **en·ve·lope** ['envi·loup], *Am. a.* **en·vel·op** [in'veləp] enveloppe *f*; ⚕, *biol.* tunique *f*; *in an* ~ sous enveloppe; **en·vel·op·ment** [in'veləpmənt] enveloppement *m*; *biol.* enveloppe *f*.

en·ven·om [in'venəm] empoisonner; *fig.* envenimer.

en·vi·a·ble □ ['enviəbl] enviable, digne d'envie; **'en·vi·er** envieux (-euse *f*) *m*; **'en·vi·ous** envieux (-euse *f*) (de, *of*).

en·vi·ron [in'vaiərən] entourer, environner (de *with*); **en'vi·ron·ment** environnement *m*; milieu *m*; ambiance *f*; **en·vi·ron·men·tal** [~'mentl] du milieu; de l'environnement; écologiste; **en·vi·ron'men·**

tal·ist environnementaliste *mf*; **en·vi·rons** ['environz] *pl.* environs *m/pl.*, alentours *m/pl.*; voisinage *m.*

en·vis·age [in'vizidʒ] envisager (*un danger*); faire face à; se proposer (*un but*).

en·vi·sion [in'viʒən] prévoir.

en·voy ['envɔi] envoyé *m.*

en·vy ['envi] **1.** envie *f* (au sujet de qch. *of*, *at s.th.*; de q., *of s.o.*); **2.** envier (qch. à q., *s.o. s.th.*); porter envie à (*q.*).

en·wrap [in'ræp] envelopper, enrouler.

en·zyme *biol.* ['enzaim] enzyme *m.*

e·pergne [i'pəːn] surtout *m* (*de table*).

e·phem·er·a *zo.* [i'femərə], **e·phem·er·on** [‿rɔn], *pl. a.* **-er·a** [‿ərə] éphémère *m*; *fig.* chose *f* éphémère; **e·phem·er·al** éphémère; passager (-ère *f*).

ep·ic ['epik] **1.** (*a.* **'ep·i·cal** □) épique; **2.** épopée *f.*

ep·i·cure ['epikjuə] gourmet *m*, gastronome *m*; **ep·i·cu·re·an** [‿-'riən] épicurien(ne *f*) (*a. su./mf*).

ep·i·dem·ic ♂ [epi'demik] **1.** (‿*ally*) épidémique; ‿ *disease* = **2.** épidémie *f.*   [derme *m.*]

ep·i·der·mis *anat.* [epi'dəːmis] épi-}

ep·i·gram ['epigræm] épigramme *f*; **ep·i·gram·mat·ic**, **ep·i·gram·mat·i·cal** □ [‿grə'mætik(l)] épigrammatique.

ep·i·lep·sy ♂ ['epilepsi] épilepsie *f*; **ep·i·lep·tic** ♂ épileptique (*a. su./mf*).

ep·i·logue ['epilɔg] épilogue *m.*

E·piph·a·ny [i'pifəni] Épiphanie *f*; F jour *m* des Rois.

e·pis·co·pa·cy [i'piskəpəsi] épiscopat *m*; gouvernement *m* par les évêques; **e·pis·co·pal** épiscopal (-aux *m/pl.*); **e·pis·co·pa·li·an** [‿-'peiljən] membre *m* de l'Église épiscopale; **e·pis·co·pate** [‿pit] épiscopat *m*; évêques *m/pl.*; évêché *m.*

ep·i·sode ['episoud] épisode *m*; **ep·i·sod·ic**, **ep·i·sod·i·cal** □ [‿'sɔd-ik(l)] épisodique.

e·pis·tle [i'pisl] épître *f*; *fig.* lettre *f*; **e·pis·to·lar·y** [‿tələri] épistolaire.

ep·i·taph ['epita:f] épitaphe *f.*

ep·i·thet ['epiθet] épithète *f.*

e·pit·o·me [i'pitəmi] abrégé *m*, résumé *m*; **e·pit·o·mize** abréger, résumer.

ep·och ['iːpɔk] époque *f.*

Ep·som salts ['epsəm'sɔːlts] *pl.* sulfate *m* de magnésie; sels *m/pl.* anglais.

eq·ua·bil·i·ty [ekwə'biliti] uniformité *f*, égalité *f*; **'eq·ua·ble** □ uniforme; égal (-aux *m/pl.*) (*a. fig.*).

e·qual ['iːkwl] **1.** □ égal (-aux *m/pl.*); ‿ *to* à la hauteur de; égal à; ‿ *opportunities pl.* égalité *f* des chances, chances *f/pl.* égales; ‿ *rights pl.* égalité *f* des droits; **2.** égal (-e *f*) *m*; my ‿s *pl.* mes pareil(le)s; **3.** égaler; *not to be* ‿*led* sans égal; **e·qual·i·ty** [i'kwɔliti] égalité *f*; **e·qual·i·za·tion** [iːkwəlai'zeiʃn] égalisation *f*; compensation *f*; **'e·qual·ize** *v/t.* égaliser (avec *to, with*); *v/i. sp.* marquer égalité de points; **'e·qual·i·zer** *sp.* but *m* égalisateur.

e·qua·nim·i·ty [iːkwə'nimiti] sérénité *f*; tranquillité *f* d'esprit.

e·quate [i'kweit] égaler (à *to, with*); ⅍ mettre en équation; **e·qua·tion** égalisation *f*; ⅍, *astr.* équation *f*; **e·qua·tor** équateur *m*; *at the* ‿ sous l'équateur; **e·qua·to·ri·al** □ [ekwə-'tɔːriəl] équatorial (-aux *m/pl.*).

eq·uer·ry [i'kweri] écuyer *m.*

e·ques·tri·an [i'kwestriən] **1.** équestre; d'équitation; **2.** cavalier (-ère *f*) *m.*   [équilatéral (-aux *m/pl.*).}

e·qui·lat·er·al □ ['iːkwi'lætərəl]}

e·qui·li·brate [i'kwi'laibreit] *v/t.* mettre en équilibre; contrebalancer; *v/i.* être en équilibre; **e·quil·i·brist** [i'kwilibrist] équilibriste *mf*; danseur (-euse *f*) *m* de corde; **e·qui·lib·ri·um** [‿əm] équilibre *m.*

e·quine ['iːkwain] équin; du cheval; chevalin (*race*).

e·qui·noc·tial [iːkwi'nɔkʃl] équinoxial (-aux *m/pl.*); **e·qui·nox** ['‿nɔks] équinoxe *m.*

e·quip [i'kwip] équiper; monter (*une maison, une usine*); **eq·ui·page** ['ekwipidʒ] équipement *m*; *véhicule*: équipage *m*; † suite *f*; **e·quip·ment** [i'kwipmənt] équipement *m*; *maison*: aménagement *m*; ⊕ outillage *m.*

e·qui·poise ['ekwipɔiz] **1.** équilibre *m*; poids *m* égal; **2.** équilibrer.

eq·ui·ta·ble □ ['ekwitəbl] équitable; **'eq·ui·ty** justice *f*; ⚖ équité *f*, droit *m* équitable.

e·quiv·a·lence [i'kwivələns] équivalence *f*; **e·quiv·a·lent** équivalent (à, *to*) (*a. su./m*).

e·quiv·o·cal □ [i'kwivəkl] équivoque; ambigu(ë f); **e·quiv·o·cal·i·ty** [‿'kæliti] caractère m ou expression f équivoque; **e'quiv·o·cate** [‿keit] équivoquer; tergiverser; **e·quiv·o'ca·tion** équivocation f, tergiversation f.

eq·ui·voque, eq·ui·voke ['ekwivouk] équivoque f; jeu m de mots.

e·ra ['iərə] ère f; époque f; âge m.

e·rad·i·cate [i'rædikeit] déraciner; **e·rad·i'ca·tion** déracinement m; fig. extirpation f.

e·rase [i'reiz] effacer (a. fig.), gratter, raturer; fig. oblitérer; **e'ras·er** grattoir m; gomme f; **e'ra·sure** [‿ʒə] rature f; suppression f.

ere † [ɛə] 1. cj. avant que (sbj.); 2. prp. avant; ~ this déjà; ~ long sous peu; ~ now déjà, auparavant.

e·rect [i'rekt] 1. □ droit; debout; 2. dresser; ériger; élever (une statue); édifier (une théorie etc.); **e'rec·tion** dressage m; construction f; érection f; édifice m; **e'rect·ness** attitude f droite; position f perpendiculaire; **e'rec·tor** constructeur m; ⊕ monteur m; anat. érecteur m.

er·e·mite ['erimait] ermite m; **er·e·mit·ic** [‿'mitik] érémitique.

erg phys. [ə:g] mesure: erg m.

er·go·nom·ics [ə:gou'nɔmiks] sg. ergonomie f.

er·got ♀ ['ə:gət] ergot m.

er·mine zo. ['ə:min] hermine f (a. fourrure); fig. (dignité f de) juge m.

e·rode [i'roud] éroder; ronger.

e·rog·e·nous [i'rɔdʒinəs] érogène.

e·ro·sion [i'rouʒn] érosion f; mer etc.: affouillement m; chaudière: usure f; **e'ro·sive** [‿siv] érosif (-ive f).

e·rot·ic [i'rɔtik] (poème m) érotique; **e'rot·i·cism** [‿sizm] érotisme m.

err [ə:] errer, se tromper; s'égarer (de, from).

er·rand ['erənd] commission f, course f, message m; go (on) ~s faire des commissions; '~-boy garçon m de courses; hôtel: chasseur m.

er·rant □ ['erənt] errant; see knight-~; **'er·rant·ry** vie f errante (des chevaliers).

er·rat·ic [i'rætik] (‿ally) capricieux (-euse f); irrégulier (-ère f); géol., ❀ erratique; ~ fever fièvre f inter-

mittente; **er·ra·tum** [i'reitəm], pl. -ta [‿tə] erratum m (pl. -ta).

er·ro·ne·ous □ [i'rounjəs] erroné.

er·ror ['erə] erreur f, faute f; ~ of judgement erreur f de jugement; ~ rate pourcentage m de fautes; ~s and omissions excepted sauf erreur ou omission.

e·ruc·ta·tion [i:rʌk'teiʃn] éructation f, renvoi m.

er·u·dite ['erudait] érudit, savant; **er·u·di·tion** [‿'diʃn] érudition f.

e·rupt [i'rʌpt] entrer en éruption (volcan etc.); percer (dent); **e'rup·tion** volcan, a. fig., a. ❀ éruption f; fig. éclat m, accès m; **e'rup·tive** éruptif (-ive f).

er·y·sip·e·las ❀ [eri'sipiləs] érysipèle m, érésipèle m.

es·ca·lade ✕ [eskə'leid] escalade f.

es·ca·late ['eskəleit] (s')intensifier; monter (en flèche); **es·ca·la·tion** intensification f; montée f (en flèche).

es·ca·la·tor ['eskəleitə] escalier m roulant, escalator m.

es·ca·pade [eskə'peid] escapade f; **es·cape** [is'keip] 1. v/t. échapper à, éviter; faillir (inf., gér.); v/i. s'échapper, s'évader (de, from); se dégager (gaz etc.); 2. évasion f, fuite f; vapeur: échappement m; attr. d'échappement; ~ hatch trappe f de secours; have a narrow ~ l'échapper belle; **es'cape·ment** ⊕ pendule etc.: échappement m.

es·carp [is'ka:p] 1. (a. es'carp·ment) talus m; escarpement m; 2. escarper; taluter.

es·cheat ⚖ [is'tʃi:t] 1. déshérence f; dévolution f d'héritage à l'État; 2. v/i. tomber en déshérence; v/t. confisquer.

es·chew [is'tʃu:] éviter, renoncer à.

es·cort 1. ['eskɔ:t] escorte f; bal: cavalier m; 2. [is'kɔ:t] escorter; accompagner.

es·cri·toire [eskri'twa:] secrétaire m.

es·cu·lent ['eskjulənt] comestible (a. su./m). [(a. ⊕, ♣).]

es·cutch·eon [is'kʌtʃn] écusson m]

Es·ki·mo ['eskimou] Esquimau (pl. -aux) m, Esquimaude f.

es·pal·ier ↗ [is'pæljə] espalier m.

es·pe·cial [is'peʃl] spécial (-aux m/pl.); particulier (-ère f); **es'pe·cial·ly** particulièrement, surtout; spécialement.

es·pi·al [is'paiəl] espionnage *m*; vue *f*. [nage *m*.]

es·pi·o·nage [espiə'na:ʒ] espion-

es·pous·al [is'pauzl] *fig.* adoption *f* (de, of); **es'pouse** [.z] † donner en mariage; épouser (*a. fig.*); *fig.* embrasser.

es·py [is'pai] apercevoir, entrevoir.

es·quire [is'kwaiə] † écuyer *m*; *adresse*: Monsieur.

es·say 1. [e'sei] essayer; mettre à l'épreuve; **2.** ['esei] essai *m*; tentative *f* (de, at); *école*: composition *f*, dissertation *f*; **'es·say·ist** essayiste *mf*.

es·sence ['esns] essence *f*; extrait *m*; *fig.* fond *m*; **es·sen·tial** [i'senʃl] **1.** □ essentiel(le *f*), indispensable; ~ likeness ressemblance *f* fondamentale; ~ oil huile *f* essentielle; **2.** essentiel *m*; qualité *f* indispensable.

es·tab·lish [is'tæbliʃ] établir; fonder; créer; confirmer (*dans un emploi*); ratifier; démontrer; ~ o.s. s'établir; Ↄed Church Église *f* Établie; Ↄed merchant marchand *m* patenté; **es'tab·lish·ment** établissement *m* (*a.* ✝); création *f*; fondation *f*; ✝ maison *f*; confirmation *f*; ménage *m*; ✂, ⚓ effectif *m*.

es·tate [is'teit] état *m* (*a. pol.*), condition *f*; terre *f*, propriété *f*; ⚑ immeuble *m*, bien *m*, domaine *m*; ⚑ succession *f*; rang *m*; *personal* ~ biens *m/pl.*; *real* ~ biensfonds *m/pl.*, propriété *f* immobilière; ~ agent agent *m* de location; administrateur *m* foncier; ~ duty droits *m/pl.* de succession.

es·teem [is'ti:m] **1.** estime *f*, considération *f*; **2.** estimer; priser; considérer (comme, *as*).

Es·tho·ni·an [es'tounjən] **1.** Estonien(ne *f*) *m*; **2.** estonien(ne *f*).

es·ti·ma·ble ['estiməbl] estimable, digne d'estime.

es·ti·mate 1. ['estimeit] estimer; évaluer (à, *at*); **2.** ['~mit] calcul *m*, estimation *f*; évaluation *f*; appréciation *f*; ✝ devis *m*; *parl.* Ↄs *pl.* prévisions *f/pl.* budgétaires; **es·ti·ma·tion** [~'meiʃn] jugement *m*; opinion *f*; considération *f*; **'es·ti·ma·tor** appréciateur *m*; estimateur *m*.

es·trange [is'treindʒ] aliéner l'estime (de q., *from s.o.*); Ↄd *couple* époux *m/pl.* séparés; **es'trange·ment** aliénation *f*; brouille *f*.

es·tro·gen *biol.* ['estrədʒen] œstrogène *m*.

es·tu·ar·y ['estjuəri] estuaire *m*.

et·cet·er·as [it'setrəz] *pl.* extra *m/inv.*

etch [etʃ] *v/t.* graver à l'eau-forte; *v/i.* faire de la gravure à l'eau-forte; **'etch·ing** (gravure *f* à l')eau-forte (*pl.* eaux-fortes) *f*; art *m* de graver à l'eau-forte.

e·ter·nal □ [i'tə:nl] éternel(le *f*); *fig.* sans fin; **e'ter·nal·ize** [~nəlaiz] éterniser; **e'ter·ni·ty** éternité *f*; **e·ter·nize** [i:'tə:naiz] éterniser.

e·ther ['i:θə] éther *m* (*a.* 🜍); **e·the·re·al** □ [i:'θiəriəl] éthéré; *fig.* impalpable; **'e·ther·ize** éthériser; endormir.

eth·i·cal □ ['eθikl] éthique; moral (-aux *m/pl.*); **'eth·ics** *usu. sg.* morale *f*, éthique *f*.

E·thi·o·pi·an [i:θi'oupjən] **1.** éthiopien(ne *f*); **2.** Éthiopien(ne *f*) *m*.

eth·nog·ra·phy [eθ'nɔgrəfi] ethnographie *f*; **eth·nol·o·gy** [~'lɔdʒi] ethnologie *f*.

e·ti·o·late ['i:tioleit] (s')étioler.

et·i·quette [eti'ket] étiquette *f*; protocole *m*; cérémonial *m* (*souv.* de cour).

E·ton crop ['i:tn'krɔp] cheveux *m/pl.* à la garçonne; cheveux *m/pl.* garçon.

et·y·mo·log·i·cal □ [etimə'lɔdʒikl] étymologique; **et·y·mol·o·gy** [~'mɔlədʒi] étymologie *f*.

eu·cha·rist ['ju:kərist] eucharistie *f*.

Eu·clid ♣ ['ju:klid] géométrie *f*.

eu·gen·ic *biol.* ['ju:'dʒenik] **1.** (~ally) eugénésique; **2.** ~s *sg.* eugénique *f*; eugénisme *m*.

eu·lo·gist ['ju:lədʒist] panégyriste *m*; **eu·lo·gize** ['~dʒaiz] faire l'éloge de, louer; **eu·lo·gy** ['~dʒi] éloge *m*.

eu·nuch ['ju:nək] eunuque *m*, castrat *m*.

eu·phe·mism ['ju:fimizm] euphémisme *m*; **eu·phe'mis·tic, eu·phe'mis·ti·cal** □ euphémique.

eu·phon·ic, eu·phon·i·cal □ [ju:-'fɔnik(l)] euphonique; **eu·pho·ny** ['ju:fəni] euphonie *f*.

eu·phu·ism ['ju:fjuizm] euphuisme *m*; *fig.* préciosité *f*.

Eu·ro·cheque ['juərətʃek] eurochèque *m*; **Eu·ro·crat** [~'kræt] eurocrate *mf*.

Eu·ro·pe·an [juərə'pi:ən] **1.** européen(ne *f*); ~ Community Communauté *f* Économique Européenne; ~ Parliament Assemblée *f* européenne; **2.** Européen(ne *f*) *m*.

Eu·ro·pol·i·tics ['juərəpɔlitiks] *sg.* politique *f* européenne.

eu·tha·na·si·a [ju:θə'neizjə] euthanasie *f*.

e·vac·u·ate [i'vækjueit] évacuer (*région, ville, blessés, ventre*); *mot.* expulser (*des gaz brûlés*); **e·vac·u·a·tion** évacuation *f*; **e·vac·u·ee** évacué(e *f*) *m*.

e·vade [i'veid] éviter, échapper à; éluder (*question, justice, obstacle*).

e·val·u·ate *surt.* Å [i'væljueit] évaluer; arrêter; **e·val·u·a·tion** évaluation *f*.

ev·a·nesce [i:və'nes] s'effacer; **ev·a'nes·cence** évanouissement *m*; nature *f* éphémère; **ev·a'nes·cent** évanescent.

e·van·gel·ic, e·van·gel·i·cal □ [i:-væn'dʒelik(l)] évangélique; **e·van·ge·list** [i'vændʒilist] évangéliste *m*; **e'van·ge·lize** prêcher l'évangile (à *q.*).

e·vap·o·rate [i'væpəreit] *v/t.* (faire) évaporer; *v/i.* s'évaporer (*a. fig.*); ~d fruit fruits *m/pl.* secs; ~d milk lait *m* concentré; **e·vap·o'ra·tion** évaporation *f*, vaporisation *f*.

e·va·sion [i'veiʒn] évasion *f*, évitement *m*; subterfuge *m*; **e'va·sive** □ [~siv] évasif (-ive *f*); *fig.* be ~ faire une réponse évasive.

eve [i:v] veille *f*; *poét.* soir *m*; on the ~ of sur le point de; à la veille de.

e·ven[1] ['i:vn] **1.** *adj.* □ égal (-aux *m/pl.*); uni; plat, uniforme; régulier (-ère *f*); calme; pair (*nombre*); ~ with the ground au ras du sol, à fleur de terre; be ~ with être quitte avec (*q.*); odd or ~ pair ou impair; ✝ of ~ date de même date; **2.** *adv.* même; *devant comp.*: encore; *avec négation*: seulement, même; ~ not ~ pas même; ~ though, ~ if quand même; **3.** *v/t.* égaliser, rendre égal.

e·ven[2] *poét.* [~] soir *m*.

e·ven...: '~**hand·ed** impartial (-aux *m/pl.*); '~**tem·pered** d'humeur égale.

eve·ning ['i:vniŋ] soir *m*; soirée *f*; ~ class cours *m* du soir; ~ dress tenue *f* ou toilette *f* de soirée; habit *m* (à queue); ~ star étoile *f* du berger.

e·ven·ness ['i:vənnis] égalité *f*; ré-

gularité *f*; sérénité *f*; impartialité *f*.

e·ven·song ['i:vənsɔŋ] office *m* du soir; vêpres *f/pl.*

e·vent [i'vent] événement *m*; cas *m*; *fig.* résultat *m*, issue *f*; *sp.* réunion *f* sportive; *sp.* épreuve *f*; *box.* rencontre *f*; *athletic* ~s *pl.* concours *m* athlétique; *table of* ~s programme *m*; *at all* ~s en tout cas; quoi qu'il arrive; *in any* ~ en tout cas; *in the* ~ of dans le cas où (*cond.*); **e'vent·ful** [~ful] mémorable.

e·ven·tu·al □ [i'ventjuəl] éventuel (-le *f*); définitif (-ive *f*); ~ly à la fin, en fin de compte; par la suite; **e·ven·tu·al·i·ty** [~'æliti] éventualité *f*; **e'ven·tu·ate** [~eit] se terminer (par, *in*); aboutir (à, *in*).

ev·er ['evə] jamais; toujours; ~ so très, infiniment; ... as possible; *as soon as* ~ *I can* aussitôt que je pourrai; le plus vite possible; ~ *after*, ~ *since* depuis lors; depuis le jour où ...; ~ *and anon* de temps en temps; *for* ~, *a. for* ~ *and* ~, *for* ~ *and a day* à tout jamais; *liberty for* ~! vive la liberté!; F ~ *so much* infiniment; *for* ~ *so much* pour rien au monde; *I wonder who* ~ je me demande qui donc ou diable; F *the best* ~ le meilleur *etc.* du monde; *formule finale d'une lettre*: ~ *yours* bien cordialement; '~**glade** *Am.* région *f* marécageuse; '~**green** (arbre *m*) toujours vert; ~'**last·ing** **1.** □ éternel(le *f*); inusable; **2.** éternité *f*; 🙚 immortelle *f*; '~'**more** toujours; éternellement.

ev·er·y ['evri] chaque; tous (toutes *f/pl.*) *m/pl.* les; ~ *bit as much* tout autant que; ~ *now and then* de temps à autre; par moments; ~*one* chacun(e *f*); ~ *other day* tous les deux jours; un jour sur deux; ~ *twenty years* tous les vingt ans; *her* ~ *movement* son moindre mouvement; '~**bod·y**, '~**one** chacun; tout le monde; '~**day** de tous les jours; '~**thing** tout; '~**way** sous tous les rapports; de toutes les manières; '~**where** partout.

e·vict [i'vikt] évincer, expulser; **e'vic·tion** éviction *f*, expulsion *f*.

ev·i·dence ['evidəns] **1.** évidence *f*; preuve *f*; témoignage *m*; *fig.* signe *m*; *in* ~ présent, en évidence; *furnish* ~ *of* fournir des preuves de;

give ~ témoigner (de, *of*); en faveur de, *for*; contre, *against*); 2. *v/t.* manifester, prouver (*qch.*); *v/i.* porter témoignage; **'ev·i·dent** □ évident, clair; patent; **ev·i·den·tial** □ [~-'denʃl] indicateur (-trice *f*) (de, *of*).

e·vil ['iːvl] 1. □ mauvais; méchant; sinistre; malfaisant; *the* ~ *eye* le mauvais œil *m*; *the* ♀ *One* le Malin *m*, le Mauvais *m*, le diable *m*; 2. mal *m*; malheur *m*; **'~·'do·er** malfaiteur (-trice *f*) *m*.   [moigner.∖

e·vince [i'vins] manifester, té-∫

e·vis·cer·ate [i'visəreit] éviscérer.

ev·o·ca·tion [evo'keiʃn] évocation *f*; **e·voc·a·tive** [i'vɔkətiv] évocateur (-trice *f*).

e·voke [i'vouk] évoquer.

ev·o·lu·tion [iːvə'luːʃn] développement *m*; évolution *f* (*a.* ✕); ⚓ extraction *f* (*d'une racine*).

e·volve [i'vɔlv] (se) développer; (se) dérouler; (se) dégager (*gaz*).

ewe [juː] brebis *f*.

ew·er ['juːə] pot *m* à eau; broc *m*.

ex [eks] 1. ♣ dégagé de, hors de; ~ *store* en magasin; *bourse*: ex-; ~ *officio* de droit, (à titre) d'office; 2. *devant su.*: ancien(ne *f*); *ex-minister* ex-ministre *m*.

ex·ac·er·bate [eks'æsəbeit] exaspérer, irriter; aggraver.

ex·act [ig'zækt] 1. □ exact; précis; juste; 2. exiger (*un impôt*); extorquer; réclamer; **ex'act·ing** exigeant; astreignant (*travail*); **ex'action** exaction *f*; **ex'act·i·tude** [~tjuːd] exactitude *f*; **ex'act·ly** exactement; à vrai dire; *~!* précisément!; *not* ~ ne ... pas à proprement parler; **ex'act·ness** *see* exactitude.

ex·ag·ger·ate [ig'zædʒəreit] exagérer; **ex·ag·ger'a·tion** exagération *f*; **ex'ag·ger·a·tive** □ [~ətiv] exagératif (-ive *f*); exagéré (*personne*).

ex·alt [ig'zɔːlt] élever; louer; **ex·al·ta·tion** [egzɔːl'teiʃn] élévation *f*; exaltation *f*; émotion *f* passionnée; **ex·alt·ed** [ig'zɔːltid] élevé; haut; exalté.

ex·am F [ig'zæm] *école*: examen *m*.

ex·am·i·na·tion [igzæmi'neiʃn] examen *m*; *douane*: visite *f*; interrogatoire *m*; inspection *f*; épreuve *f* (*écrite, orale*); *competitive* ~ *examen*: concours *m*; **ex'am·ine** [~min] examiner (*q., qch.*); faire une enquête sur (*qch.*); visiter; contrôler; interroger; **ex·am·i'nee** candidat(e *f*) *m*; **ex'am·in·er** examinateur (-trice *f*) *m*; **ex'am·in·ing 'bod·y** jury *m* d'examen.

ex·am·ple [ig'zɑːmpl] exemple *m*; précédent *m*; *beyond* ~ sans précédent; *for* ~ par exemple; *make an* ~ *of* faire un exemple de (*q.*).

ex·as·per·ate [ig'zɑːspəreit] exaspérer; irriter; aggraver (*la douleur etc.*); **ex·as·per'a·tion** exaspération *f*; aggravation *f* (de, *of*).

ex·ca·vate ['ekskəveit] *v/t.* creuser; approfondir; *v/i.* faire des fouilles; **ex·ca'va·tion** excavation *f*; fouille *f*; **'ex·ca·va·tor** excavateur *m*; fouilleuse *f*.

ex·ceed [ik'siːd] *v/t.* excéder, dépasser, outrepasser; surpasser (en, *in*), *v/i.* prédominer; **ex'ceed·ing** excessif (-ive *f*); **ex'ceed·ing·ly** extrêmement, excessivement.

ex·cel [ik'sel] *v/t.* surpasser; *v/i.* exceller (à *in, at*); **ex·cel·lence** ['eksələns] excellence *f*; perfection *f*; mérite *m*; **'Ex·cel·len·cy** Excellence *f*; **'ex·cel·lent** □ excellent, parfait.

ex·cept [ik'sept] 1. *v/t.* excepter, exclure; *v/i.* faire des objections; 2. *cj.* à moins que; excepté que; 3. *prp.* excepté, à l'exception de, sauf; ~ *for* à part; **ex'cept·ing** *prp.* à l'exception de; **ex'cep·tion** exception *f*; objection *f* (à, *to*); *take* ~ *to* s'offenser de; objecter (*qch.*) (à q., *in s.o.*); **ex'cep·tion·a·ble** récusable; blâmable; **ex'cep·tion·al** □ exceptionnel(le *f*); *~ly* par exception.

ex·cerpt 1. [ek'səːpt] extraire (*un passage*) (de, *from*); 2. ['eksəːpt] extrait *m* (de, *from*); emprunt *m* (à).

ex·cess [ik'ses] excès *m*; excédent *m*; surpoids *m*; *attr.* en surpoids; en excédent; *in* ~ *of* au-dessus de; *carry to* ~ pousser (*qch.*) trop loin; ~ *charge* supplément *m*; ~ *fare* supplément *m*; ~ *luggage* excédent *m* de bagages; ~ *money* argent *m* en surplus; ~ *postage* surtaxe *f* postale; ~ *profit* surplus *m* des bénéfices; **ex'ces·sive** □ excessif (-ive *f*); immodéré; *~ly* à l'excès.

ex·change [iks'tʃeindʒ] 1. échanger (contre, *for*); faire un échange de; 2. échange *m*; ♣ change *m*; (*bill of* ~) traite *f*; (*a.* ♀) Bourse *f*; *téléph.*

central *m; foreign* ~*(s pl.)* devises *f/pl.* étrangères *ou* sur l'étranger; *in* ~ *for* en échange de; ~ *control* contrôle *m* des changes; ~ *list* bulletin *m* des changes; ~ *market* marché *m* des changes; ~ *office* bureau *m* de change; *free* ~ libre-échange *m; par of* ~ pair *m* du change; *(rate of)* ~ cours *m ou* taux *m* du change; **ex·'change·able** échangeable (contre, pour *for);* ~ *value* valeur *f* d'échange; ✝ contre-valeur *f.*

ex·cheq·uer [iks'tʃekə] Trésor *m* public; F budget *m;* Ministère *m* des Finances; *Chancellor of the* ♀ Ministre *m* des Finances *(britannique);* ~ *bill* bon *m* du Trésor.

ex·cise¹ [ek'saiz] **1.** régie *f;* contributions *f/pl.* indirectes; **2.** imposer; frapper d'une imposition.

ex·cise² [~] retrancher; **ex·ci·sion** [ek'siʒn] excision *f;* incision *f.*

ex·cit·a·bil·i·ty [iksaitə'biliti] émotivité *f;* **ex·cit·a·ble** émotionnable; mobile *(foule);* **ex·cit·ant** ['eksitənt] stimulant *m;* **ex·ci·ta·tion** [eksi'teiʃn] excitation *f;* **ex·cite** [ik'sait] provoquer, soulever, exciter; animer; **ex'cite·ment** agitation *f;* émotion *f;* excitation *f;* **ex·'cit·er** instigateur (-trice *f) m;* ⚡ excitant *m;* ⚡ excitateur *m.*

ex·claim [iks'kleim] *v/i.* s'exclamer; s'écrier; ~ *against* se récrier contre; *v/t.* crier.

ex·cla·ma·tion [eksklə'meiʃn] exclamation *f;* note (*ou mark ou point) of* ~, ~ *mark* point *m* d'exclamation; **ex·clam·a·to·ry** □ [~-'klæmətəri] exclamatif (-ive *f).*

ex·clude [iks'klu:d] exclure; *fig.* écarter.

ex·clu·sion [iks'klu:ʒn] exclusion *f;* refus *m* d'admission (à, *from);* **ex·'clu·sive** □ [~siv] exclusif (-ive *f);* en exclusivité *(film);* seul, unique; très fermé *(cercle);* ~ *of* non compris; *be mutually* ~ s'exclure mutuellement.

ex·cog·i·tate [eks'kɔdʒiteit] combiner; *péj.* machiner; **ex·cog·i·'ta·tion** excogitation *f;* méditation *f.*

ex·com·mu·ni·cate [ekskə'mju:nikeit] excommunier; **ex·com·mu·ni'ca·tion** excommunication *f.*

ex·co·ri·ate [eks'kɔ:rieit] excorier, écorcher *(la peau).*

ex·cre·ment ['ekskrimənt] excrément *m;* **ex·cre·men·tal** [~'mentl], **ex·cre·men·ti·tious** [~'tiʃəs] excrémen(ti)tiel(le *f).*

ex·cres·cence [iks'kresns] excroissance *f;* excrescence *f;* **ex·'crescent** qui forme une excroissance; superflu.

ex·crete [eks'kri:t] excréter; sécréter; **ex·'cre·tion** excrétion *f;* sécrétion *f;* **ex·'cre·tive, ex·'cre·to·ry** [~təri] excréteur (-trice *f),* excrétoire.

ex·cru·ci·ate [iks'kru:ʃieit] torturer; **ex·'cru·ci·at·ing** □ atroce; **ex·cru·ci·'a·tion** torture *f,* supplice *m.*

ex·cul·pate ['eksk∧lpeit] disculper, exonérer; justifier *(q.);* **ex·cul·'pa·tion** exonération *f;* justification *f;* **ex·'cul·pa·to·ry** [~pətəri] justificatif (-ive *f).*

ex·cur·sion [iks'kə:ʃn] excursion *f;* partie *f* de plaisir; *mot.* randonnée *f;* ~ *train* train *m* de plaisir; **ex·'cur·sion·ist** excursionniste *mf.*

ex·cur·sive □ [eks'kə:siv] digressif (-ive *f);* vagabond.

ex·cus·a·ble □ [iks'kju:zəbl] excusable; **ex·cuse** [~'kju:z] **1.** excuser; pardonner (qch. à q., *s.o. s.th.);* **2.** [~'kju:s] excuse *f,* prétexte *m.*

ex·di·rec·to·ry [eksdi'rektəri] qui n'est pas dans l'annuaire téléphonique.

ex·e·cra·ble □ ['eksikrəbl] exécrable; **ex·e·crate** ['~kreit] exécrer, détester; **ex·e·'cra·tion** exécration *f;* malédiction *f.*

ex·e·cu·tant ♪ [ig'zekjutənt] exécutant(e *f) m;* **ex·e·cute** ['eksikju:t] exécuter *(projet, ordre, testament,* ♪, ⚖); ✝ effectuer *(un transfert);* ⚖ souscrire *(un acte);* **ex·e·'cu·tion** exécution *f (see execute);* ⚖ souscription *f (d'un acte),* saisie-exécution *(pl.* saisies-exécutions) *f;* jeu *m (d'un musicien); fig.* carnage *m; a man of* ~ un homme *m* énergique; *take out an* ~ *against* faire une exécution sur; ✂, *a. fig.* do ~ causer des ravages; **ex·e·'cu·tion·er** bourreau *m;* **ex·ec·u·tive** [ig'zekjutiv] **1.** □ exécutif (-ive *f);* ~ *committee* bureau *m (d'une société),* commission *f* exécutive *(d'un parti);* ~ *editor* rédacteur *m* en chef; ~ *suite* bureaux *m/pl.* de la direction;

2. (pouvoir *m*) exécutif *m*; bureau *m*; *Am.* président *m*; *pol.* gouverneur *m*; ✝ directeur *m* (*commercial*); **ex'ec·u·tor** [ₓtə] exécuteur *m* testamentaire; **ex'ec·u·to·ry** exécutif (-ive *f*); ⚖ exécutoire, en vigueur; non encore exécuté.

ex·em·plar [ig'zemplə] exemplaire *m*; **ex'em·pla·ri·ness** exemplarité *f*; **ex'em·pla·ry** exemplaire; typique.

ex·em·pli·fi·ca·tion [igzemplifi-'keiʃn] démonstration *f*; exemple *m*; ⚖ copie *f* authentique; **ex'em·pli·fy** [ₓfai] démontrer, expliquer; servir d'exemple; donner un exemple de; ⚖ faire une ampliation de.

ex·empt [ig'zempt] **1.** exempt, franc(he *f*), dispensé (de, *from*); **2.** exempter, dispenser (de, *from*); **ex'emp·tion** exemption *f*, dispense *f* (de, *from*).

ex·e·quies ['eksikwiz] *pl.* convoi *m* funèbre; obsèques *f/pl.*

ex·er·cise ['eksəsaiz] **1.** exercice *m* (*d'une faculté, a. école, ♪, etc.*); ✕, ⚓ évolution *f*; *école:* devoir *m*, thème *m*; ∼ *book école:* cahier *m*; *take* ∼ prendre de l'exercice; *Am.* ∼*s pl.* cérémonies *f/pl.*; **2.** *v/t.* exercer (*corps, esprit, influence, métier, faculté*); pratiquer; user de; promener (*un cheval*); tracasser; *v/i.* s'entraîner; ✕ faire l'exercice; **'ex·er·cis·er** exerciseur *m*.

ex·ert [ig'zəːt] exercer (*de l'influence etc.*); employer (*de la force*); ∼ *o.s.* s'employer; s'efforcer (de, *to*); **ex'er·tion** effort *m*; emploi *m*.

ex·e·unt *théâ.* ['eksiʌnt] ... sortent.

ex·fo·li·ate [eks'foulieit] (s')exfolier; (se) déliter (*pierre*).

ex·ha·la·tion [ekshə'leiʃn] exhalaison *f*; *souffle:* expiration *f*; **ex·hale** [ₓ'heil] *v/t.* exhaler (*odeur, souffle, prière, rage*); *fig.* respirer; *v/i.* s'exhaler.

ex·haust [ig'zɔːst] **1.** épuiser (*a. fig.*); vider (de, *of*); aspirer (*l'air, du gaz, etc.*); ∼ *the air* faire le vide (dans, *in*); **2.** ⊕ échappement *m*; ∼ *box* pot *m* d'échappement; silencieux *m*; ∼ *cut-out* (*ou muffler*) soupape *f* d'échappement libre; silencieux *m*; ∼ *fumes pl.*, ∼ *gas* gaz *m* d'échappement; ∼ *pipe* tuyau *m* d'échappement; ∼ *steam* vapeur *f* d'échappement; ∼ *valve* soupape *f* d'échappement; épuisé (*a. fig.*), usé; vide d'air; **ex'haust·i·ble** épuisable; **ex·'haust·ing** □ épuisant; ⊕ d'épuisement; **ex'haus·tion** épuisement *m*; **ex'haus·tive** □ *see exhausting*; approfondi.

ex·hib·it [ig'zibit] **1.** exhiber (*a. ⚖*); montrer; offrir; exposer; **2.** objet *m* exposé; exposition *f*; ⚖ pièce *f* à l'appui; *on* ∼ exposé; **ex·hi·bi·tion** [eksi'biʃn] exposition *f*; étalage *m*; démonstration *f*; *cin.* présentation *f*; ⚖ exhibition *f*; *make an* ∼ *of o.s.* faire spectacle; *on* ∼ exposé; **ex·hi-'bi·tion·er** boursier (-ère *f*) *m*; **ex·hib·i·tor** [ig'zibitə] exposant(e *f*) *m*; *cin.* exploitant *m* d'un cinéma.

ex·hil·a·rate [ig'ziləreit] égayer; ranimer; **ex·hil·a'ra·tion** gaieté *f*, joie *f* de vivre.

ex·hort [ig'zɔːt] exhorter; **ex·hor-ta·tion** [egzɔː'teiʃn] exhortation *f*; **ex·hor·ta·tive** [ig'zɔːtətiv], **ex-'hor·ta·to·ry** [ₓtəri] exhortatif (-ive *f*), exhortatoire.

ex·hu·ma·tion [ekshju:'meiʃn] exhumation *f*; **ex'hume** déterrer.

ex·i·gence, ex·i·gen·cy ['eksidʒən-s(i)] exigence *f*; nécessité *f*; situation *f* critique; **'ex·i·gent** urgent, pressant; exigeant; *be* ∼ *of* exiger. **ex·ig·u·ous** [eg'zigjuəs] exigu (-üe *f*); modique (*revenu etc.*).

ex·ile ['eksail] **1.** exil *m*; *personne:* exilé(e *f*) *m*; **2.** exiler, bannir.

ex·ist [ig'zist] exister; être; se trouver; vivre; **ex'ist·ence** existence *f*; vie *f*; *phls.* être *m*; *in* ∼ = **ex'ist·ent** existant; actuel(le *f*).

ex·it ['eksit] **1.** sortie *f*; *fig.* fin *f*, mort *f*; ∼ *permit* permis *m* de sortie; ∼ *visa* visa *m* de sortie; **2.** *théâ.* ... sort.   [*fig.* sortie *f*.⟩

ex·o·dus ['eksədəs] *bibl.* exode *m*;⟩

ex·on·er·ate [ig'zɔnəreit] exonérer, disculper; dispenser (de, *from*); **ex·on·er'a·tion** exonération *f*, décharge *f*.

ex·or·bi·tance, ex·or·bi·tan·cy [ig-'zɔːbitəns(i)] énormité *f*; **ex'or·bi·tant** □ exorbitant, excessif (-ive *f*).

ex·or·cism ['eksɔːsizm] exorcisme *m*; **'ex·or·cist** exorciste *m*; **ex·or·cize** ['ₓsaiz] exorciser (*un démon, un possédé*); chasser (de, *from*).   [que.⟩

ex·ot·ic [eg'zɔtik] (plante *f*) exoti-⟩

ex·pand [iks'pænd] (s')étendre; (se) déployer (*ailes*); (se) dilater (*yeux, gaz, solide*); (se) développer (*abrégé, poitrine, formule*); amplifier; (s')élargir; **ex'pand·er** extenseur *m*; ⊕ mécanisme *m* d'expansion; **ex·panse** [ʌ'pæns] étendue *f*; **ex·pan·si·bil·i·ty** [ʌsə'biliti] expansibilité *f*; *phys.* dilatabilité *f*; **ex'pan·si·ble** expansible; *phys.* dilatable; **ex'pan·sion** expansion *f* (*a. pol.*); ⊕ détente *f*; **ex'pan·sive** □ expansif (-ive *f*) (*a. fig.*); dilatable; étendu; **ex'pan·sive·ness** expansibilité *f* (*a. d'une personne*); dilatabilité *f*.

ex·pa·ti·ate [eks'peiʃieit] s'étendre (sur, *on*); **ex·pa·ti·a·tion** long discours *m*; prolixité *f*.

ex·pa·tri·ate [eks'pætrieit] expatrier, bannir; **ex·pa·tri·a·tion** expatriation *f*.

ex·pect [iks'pekt] attendre (de *of*, *from*); compter sur; s'attendre à; F penser, croire; **ex'pect·an·cy** attente *f*, espoir *m*; **ex'pect·ant 1.** qui attend; be ~ of attendre (*qch.*); be ~ attendre un bébé; ~ *mother* future maman *f*; **2.** aspirant (-e *f*) *m*; **ex·pec'ta·tion** attente *f*; espérance *f*; probabilité *f*; expectative *f* d'héritage; *beyond* ~ audelà de mes *etc.* espérances; *on* (*ou in*) ~ of dans l'attente de; **ex'pect·ing** *see* expectant 1.

ex·pec·to·rate [eks'pektəreit] *v/t.* expectorer; *v/i.* cracher; **ex·pec·to·'ra·tion** expectoration *f*; crachat *m*.

ex·pe·di·ence, ex·pe·di·en·cy [iks-'pi:djəns(i)] convenance *f*, à-propos *m*; *péj.* opportunisme *m*; **ex'pe·di·ent 1.** □ expédient, avantageux (-euse *f*); pratique; **2.** expédient *m*, moyen *m*, ressource *f*; **ex·pe·dite** ['ekspidait] expédier; accélérer; hâter; **ex·pe·di·tion**[ʌ'diʃn] promptitude *f*; diligence *f*; ✕ *etc.*: expédition *f*; **ex·pe'di·tion·ar·y** expéditionnaire; **ex·pe'di·tious** □ prompt; rapide; expéditif (-ive *f*).

ex·pel [iks'pel] expulser, chasser; renvoyer (q. de l'école, *s.o.* [*from*] *the school*).

ex·pend [iks'pend] dépenser (de *l'argent*); consacrer (*le temps*) (à *on s.th.*, *in inf.*); épuiser (*les forces, les ressources*); **ex'pend·a·ble** dépensable; **ex'pend·i·ture** [ʌitʃə] dé-

pense *f* (*d'argent etc.*); consommation *f*; dépense *f*, -s *f/pl.*; **ex·pense** [ʌ'pens] dépense *f*; frais *m/pl.*; F prix *m*; dépens *m/pl.*; ~s *pl.* dépenses *f/pl.*, frais *m/pl.*; indemnité *f*; *at my* ~ à mes frais; à mes dépens; *at the* ~ *of* aux dépens de; *at great* ~ à grands frais; **ex'pen·sive** □ coûteux (-euse *f*), cher (chère *f*).

ex·pe·ri·ence [iks'piəriəns] **1.** expérience *f*; aventure *f*; **2.** éprouver; essuyer (*des insultes*); **ex'pe·ri·enced** éprouvé; averti; expérimenté; exercé (à, *in*); consommé.

ex·per·i·ment 1. [iks'perimənt] expérience *f*; épreuve *f*; **2.** [ʌment] expérimenter (sur, avec *on, with*); faire des expériences; **ex·per·i·men·tal** □ [eksperi'mentl] expérimental (-aux *m/pl.*); d'expérience; d'essai; d'épreuve; **ex·per·i'men·tal·ist** [ʌtəlist], **ex·per·i·ment·er** [iks'perimentə] expérimentaliste *m/f*; expérimentateur (-trice *f*) *m*.

ex·pert ['ekspə:t] **1.** □ [*préd.* eks-'pə:t] expert (en *at, in*), adroit, habile; ~ *opinion* avis *m* d'expert; expertise *f*; ~ *worker* ouvrier *m* spécialisé; homme *m* du métier; **2.** expert *m*; spécialiste *m*; **'ex·pert·ness** adresse *f* (à, *in*); expertise *f*.

ex·pi·a·ble ['ekspiəbl] expiable; **ex·pi·ate** ['ʌpieit] expier; **ex·pi·'a·tion** expiation *f*; **ex·pi·a·to·ry** ['ʌpiətəri] expiatoire.

ex·pi·ra·tion [ekspaiə'reiʃn] expiration *f*; cessation *f*; fin *f*; † échéance *f*; **ex·pir·a·to·ry** [iks'paiərətəri] expirateur; **ex'pire** *v/t.* expirer; *v/i.* expirer (*a. temps, contrat, etc.*); mourir; s'éteindre (*feu*); *fig.* s'évanouir.

ex·plain [iks'plein] expliquer; éclaircir; élucider; justifier (*une conduite*); **ex'plain·a·ble** explicable; justifiable (*conduite*).

ex·pla·na·tion [eksplə'neiʃn] explication *f*, éclaircissement *m*; **ex·plan·a·to·ry** □ [iks'plænətəri] explicatif (-ive *f*).

ex·ple·tive [eks'pli:tiv] **1.** □ explétif (-ive *f*); **2.** *gramm.* explétif *m*; *fig.* juron *m*.

ex·pli·ca·ble ['eksplikəbl] explicable; justifiable (*conduite*); **ex·pli·cate** ['ʌkeit] développer; **ex·pli·ca-**

extension

tive ['‿kətiv], **ex·pli·ca·to·ry** ['‿tə-ri] explicatif (-ive f).

ex·plic·it □ [iks'plisit] explicite; formel(le f), clair; fig. franc(he f).

ex·plode [iks'ploud] (faire) sauter; (faire) éclater (de, with); v/t. discréditer; **ex'plod·ed** éclaté; discrédité (théorie).

ex·ploit 1. [iks'plɔit] exploiter (a. fig.); **2.** ['eksplɔit] exploit m; **ex·ploi'ta·tion** exploitation f.

ex·plo·ra·tion [eksplɔː'reiʃn] exploration f (a. ⚕); reconnaissance f (du terrain); **ex'plor·a·to·ry** ['‿rətəri] d'exploration; de découverte; **ex·plore** [iks'plɔː] explorer; aller à la découverte dans (un pays); reconnaître (un terrain); **ex'plor·er** explorateur (-trice f) m.

ex·plo·sion [iks'plouʒn] explosion f (a. fig.); détonation f; **ex'plo·sive** ['‿siv] **1.** □ explosif (-ive f); explosible (arme etc.); **2.** explosif m.

ex·po·nent [eks'pounənt] interprète mf; explicateur (-trice f) m; ⚕ exposant m.

ex·port 1. [eks'pɔːt] exporter; **2.** ['ekspɔːt] marchandise f exportée; exportation f; **‿s** pl. articles m/pl. d'exportation; exportation f; **ex'port·a·ble** exportable; **ex·por·ta·tion** ['‿'teiʃn] exportation f; **ex'port·er** exportateur (-trice f) m.

ex·pose [iks'pouz] exposer (a. phot.); étaler; démasquer; mettre à découvert; dévoiler; **ex·po·si·tion** [ekspə'ziʃn] exposition f; exposé m; **ex·pos·i·tive** ['‿pozitiv] expositoire; **ex'pos·i·tor** interprète mf; commentateur (-trice f) m.

ex·pos·tu·late [iks'pɔstjuleit] reprocher (amicalement) (qch. à q., with s.o. for s.th.); sermonner (sur, [up]on); **ex·pos·tu'la·tion** remontrance f, -s f/pl.

ex·po·sure [iks'pouʒə] exposition f (au danger, au froid, d'un bébé); étalage m (d'articles); fig. dévoilement m, mise f à nu; phot. pose f; **‿ meter** photomètre m; **‿ time** temps m de pose; **‿ table** tableau m de temps de pose; death from **‿** mort f de froid.

ex·pound [iks'paund] expliquer; exposer (une doctrine).

ex·press [iks'pres] **1.** □ exprès (-esse f); formel(le f); 🚂 rapide; **‿ company** Am. compagnie f de

messageries; Am. **‿way** autostrade f; **2.** exprès m; (a **‿ train**) rapide m, express m; by **‿** = **3.** adv. en toute hâte; sans arrêt; send s.th. **‿ poste**: envoyer qch. exprès; **4.** exprimer (un sentiment, du jus, etc.); énoncer (un principe); émettre (une opinion); not **‿ed** sous-entendu; **ex'press·i·ble** exprimable; **ex'pres·sion** [‿preʃn] ♩, ♪, gramm., peint., visage: expression f; **ex'pres·sive** □ [‿siv] expressif (-ive f); be **‿ of** exprimer (qch.); **ex'press·ly** expressément; exprès.

ex·pro·pri·ate [eks'prouprieit] exproprier (q. de qch., s.o. from s.th.); **ex·pro·pri'a·tion** expropriation f.

ex·pul·sion [iks'pʌlʃn] expulsion f; **ex'pul·sive** expulsif (-ive f).

ex·punge [eks'pʌndʒ] effacer, biffer.

ex·pur·gate ['ekspəːgeit] expurger (un livre); épurer (un texte); supprimer (un passage); **ex·pur'ga·tion** expurgation f; épuration f.

ex·qui·site ['ekskwizit] **1.** □ exquis; ravissant; délicieux (-euse f); délicat; vif (vive f), atroce (douleur etc.); **2.** dandy m; '**ex·qui·site·ness** perfection f; exquisité f; finesse f; douleur etc.: acuité f.

ex-serv·ice·man ⚔ ['eks'səːvismən] ancien combattant m.

ex·tant [eks'tænt] existant, qui existe.

ex·tem·po·ra·ne·ous □ [ekstempə-'reinjəs], **ex·tem·po·rar·y** [iks-'tempərəri], **ex·tem·po·re** [eks-'tempəri] impromptu, improvisé; **ex·tem·po·rize** [iks'tempəraiz] improviser; **ex·tem·po·riz·er** improvisateur (-trice f) m.

ex·tend [iks'tend] v/t. étendre (a. fig., la bonté, etc.); tendre (la main); agrandir (un territoire); reculer (des frontières); prolonger (une ligne, un billet, une période); transcrire (de la sténographie); ✝ proroger; ⚔ déployer; in **‿ed order** en fourrageurs; v/i. s'étendre, se prolonger; continuer.

ex·ten·si·bil·i·ty [ikstensə'biliti] extensibilité f; **ex'ten·si·ble** extensible; **ex'ten·sion** extension f; prolongation f; table: (r)allonge f; gramm. complément m; annexe f; téléph. poste m; ⚡ cord allonge f de câble; **‿ ladder** échelle f coulissante; University ♀ cours m populaire organisé par une université; **ex'ten·sive** □ [~siv] étendu, vaste; **ex·'ten·sive·ness** étendue *f*.

ex·tent [iks'tent] étendue *f*; importance *f*; *to the* ~ *of* au point de; *prêt d'argent etc.*: jusqu'à concurrence de; *to a certain* ~ jusqu'à un certain point; *to some* ~ dans une certaine mesure; *to that* ~ à ce point-là; *grant* ~ *for* atermoyer.

ex·ten·u·ate [eks'tenjueit] atténuer; † amaigrir; **ex·ten·u'a·tion** atténuation *f*; affaiblissement *m* extrême.

ex·te·ri·or [eks'tiəriə] **1.** □ extérieur (à, *to*); en dehors (de, *to*); ⚓ externe; **2.** extérieur *m* (*a. cin.*).

ex·ter·mi·nate [eks'tə:mineit] exterminer; **ex·ter·mi'na·tion** extermination *f*; **ex'ter·mi·na·tor** exterminateur (-trice *f*) *m*.

ex·ter·nal [eks'tə:nl] **1.** □ extérieur (à, *to*); du dehors; ⚓, ⚓ externe; ~ *to* en dehors de; **2.** ~*s pl.* dehors *m* (*a. pl.*); *fig.* apparence *f*; **ex'ter·nal·ize** extérioriser.

ex·tinct [iks'tiŋkt] éteint (*a. fig.*); **ex'tinc·tion** extinction *f* (*a. fig.*).

ex·tin·guish [iks'tiŋgwiʃ] éteindre (*a. fig.*); abolir (*un office, une loi, etc.*); exterminer; réduire (*q.*) au silence; **ex'tin·guish·er** *lampe etc.*: éteignoir *m*; *personne*: éteigneur (-euse *f*) *m*; *see fire-*~; **ex'tin·guish·ment** extinction *f*.

ex·tir·pate ['ekstə:peit] extirper, déraciner (*a.* ⚓); **ex·tir'pa·tion** extirpation *f*, éradication *f*; **'ex·tir·pa·tor** extirpateur (-trice *f*) *m*.

ex·tol [iks'tɔl] louer, vanter.

ex·tort [iks'tɔ:t] extorquer, arracher (à, *from*); **ex'tor·tion** extorsion *f*; **ex'tor·tion·ate** [~ʃnit] exorbitant; **ex'tor·tion·er** extorqueur (-euse *f*) *m*; exacteur *m*.

ex·tra ['ekstrə] **1.** *adj.* en plus, à part; supplémentaire; ~ *pay* salaire *m etc.* supplémentaire; *sp.* ~ *time* prolongation *f*; **2.** *adv.* extra-; plus que d'ordinaire; **3.** *su.* supplément *m*; numéro *m etc.* supplémentaire; *cin.* figurant(e *f*) *m*; *journ.* édition *f* spéciale; ~*s pl.* frais *m/pl. ou* dépenses *f/pl.* supplémentaires; ~ *special* deuxième édition *f* spéciale (*d'un journal du soir*); ~*special* F d'extra; supérieur.

ex·tract 1. ['ekstrækt] extrait *m*;

concentré *m* (*a.* 🜍); **2.** [iks'trækt] extraire (*a.* 🜍, ⚓, *une dent, un passage*); tirer (*argent, aveu, doctrine, plaisir, sons*) (de, *from*); arracher (*argent, aveu, dent*) (à, *from*); **ex'trac·tion** extraction *f*; origine *f*; **ex'trac·tive 1.** extractif (-ive *f*); **2.** extractif *m*; **ex'trac·tor** arracheur (-euse *f*) *m*; ⊕ pince *f*; extracteur *m*.

ex·tra·cur·ric·u·lar ['ekstrəkə'ri-kjulə] hors programme.

ex·tra·dit·a·ble ['ekstrədaitəbl] qui justifie l'extradition; passible d'extradition (*personne*); **ex·tra·dite** ['~dait] extrader; obtenir l'extradition de; **ex·tra·di·tion** [~'diʃn] extradition *f*.

extra...: '~**ju'di·cial** officieux (-euse *f*); extra-légal (-aux *m/pl.*); '~'**mar·i·tal** extra-conjugal (-aux *m/pl.*); '~'**mu·ral** en dehors de la ville; *univ.* hors faculté (*professeur, cours, etc.*).

ex·tra·ne·ous [eks'treinjəs] étranger (-ère *f*) (à, *to*).

ex·tra·or·di·nar·y [iks'trɔ:dnri] extraordinaire; remarquable; F prodigieux (-euse *f*). [trapoler.\]

ex·trap·o·late [ek'stræpouleit] ex-\ **ex·tra·ter·res·tri·al** ['ekstrəti'restriəl] extraterrestre.

ex·trav·a·gance [iks'trævigəns] extravagance *f*, exagération *f*; prodigalité *f*, gaspillage *m* (*d'argent*); **ex'trav·a·gant** □ extravagant, exagéré; prodigue (*personne*); exorbitant (*prix*); **ex·trav·a·gan·za** *théâ.* [ekstrævə'gænzə] œuvre *f* (musicale) fantaisiste.

ex·treme [iks'tri:m] **1.** □ extrême; très grand *ou* haut; dernier (-ère *f*) (*point, supplice*); *eccl.* ~ *unction* extrême onction *f*; **2.** extrême *m*; *in the* ~ au dernier degré; **ex'trem·ist** extrémiste *mf*, ultra *m*; **ex'trem·i·ty** [~'tremiti] extrémité *f*, bout *m*, point *m* extrême; gêne *f*; *extremities pl.* extrémités *f/pl.* (*du corps*); *be reduced to extremities* être dans la plus grande gêne.

ex·tri·cate ['ekstrikeit] dégager, tirer; 🜍 libérer; **ex·tri'ca·tion** dégagement *m*, délivrance *f*; 🜍 libération *f*.

ex·trin·sic [eks'trinsik] (~*ally*) extrinsèque; ~ *to* en dehors de.

ex·tro·vert ['ekstrouvə:t] extroverti(e *f*) *m*.

ex·trude [eks'tru:d] *v/t.* expulser; ⊕ refouler; *v/i. géol.* s'épancher.

ex·u·ber·ance [ig'zju:bərəns] exubérance *f*; richesse *f*; surabondance *f* (*en idées*); **ex·u·ber·ant** exubérant; débordant, surabondant; riche.

ex·u·da·tion [eksju:'deiʃn] exsudation *f*; écoulement *m*; **ex·ude** [ig'zju:d] exsuder; s'écouler (*sève*).

ex·ult [ig'zʌlt] exulter, se réjouir (de qch. *at, in* s.th.); triompher (de qch., *at* s.th.; sur q., *over* s.o.); **ex·'ult·ant** exultant; triomphant; **ex·ul·ta·tion** [egzʌl'teiʃn] exultation *f*; triomphe *m*.

ex·u·vi·ate [ig'zju:vieit] (se) dépouiller (*peau etc.*).

eye [ai] **1.** œil (*pl.* yeux) *m* (*a.* ⚙, *outil*); regard *m*; aiguille: trou *m*; have an ~ for s'y connaître en; *sl.* my ~(s)! mince alors!; *sl.* it's all my ~! c'est de la blague!; *mind your* ~! gare à vous!; *with an* ~ *to* en vue de; **2.** observer, regarder; suivre des yeux; mesurer (*q.*) des yeux; '~**ball** prunelle *f*; globe *m* de l'œil; '~**brow** sourcil *m*; '~-**catch·er** F attraction *f*; **eyed** [aid] aux yeux ...; ocellé (*plume, aile*).

eye ...: '~-**drops** *pl.* gouttes *f/pl.* pour les yeux; '~**ful** F coup *m* d'œil; *be (quite) an* ~ *a.* valoir le coup d'œil; *get an* ~ *se* rincer l'œil; *get an* ~ *of* viser (= *regarder*); '~-**glass** monocle *m*; (*a pair of*) ~*es pl.* (un) pince-nez *m/inv.*, (un) binocle *m*, (un) lorgnon *m*; '~-**hole** œillet *m*; △ judas *m*; ⚕ cavité *f* de l'œil; '~-**lash** cil *m*; **eye·let** ['ailit] œillet *m*; petit trou *m*; *aile:* ocelle *m*.

eye ...: '~-**lid** paupière *f*; '~-o·**pen·er** révélation *f*; surprise *f*; '~-**piece** *opt.* oculaire *m*; ~ **shad·ow** fard *m* à paupières; '~-**shot** portée *f* de (la) vue; '~-**sight** vue *f*; portée *f* de la vue; '~-**sore** *fig.* chose *f* qui offense le regard; horreur *f*; '~-**tooth** dent *f* œillère; '~-**wash 1.** collyre *m*; *sl.* boniment *m*, bourrage *m* de crâne; **2.** *sl.* jeter de la poudre aux yeux de (*q.*); '~-'**wit·ness** témoin *m* oculaire.

eye·ot [eit] îlot *m*.

eyre *hist.* [εə]: *justices in* ~ juges *m/pl.* en tournée.

ey·rie, ey·ry ['aiəri] *see* aerie.

F

F, f [ef] F *m*, f *m*.

fa·ble [ˈfeibl] **1.** fable *m*, conte *m*; *fig.* mythe *m*, invention *f*.

fab·ric [ˈfæbrik] édifice *m*, bâtiment *m*; *eccl.* fabrique *f*; étoffe *f*, tissu *m*; **fab·ri·cate** [ˈ‿keit] fabriquer (*usu. fig.*); inventer; **fab·ri·ca·tion** fabrication *f*; *fig.* invention *f*; contrefaçon *f*; **ˈfab·ri·ca·tor** inventeur *m*; *mensonge*: forgeur *m*; *document*: contrefacteur *m*.

fab·u·list [ˈfæbjulist] fabuliste *m*; *fig.* menteur (-euse *f*) *m*; **ˈfab·u·lous** □ légendaire.

fa·çade △ [faˈsɑːd] façade *f*.

face [feis] **1.** face *f*; visage *m*, figure *f*; air *m*, mine *f*; *horloge*: cadran *m*; *étoffe*: endroit *m*; aspect *m*; *fig.* impudence *f*, front *m*; *in* (the) ‿ *of* devant; en présence de; ‿ *to* ‿ *with* vis-à-vis de; *save one's* ‿ sauver la face; *on the* ‿ *of it* à première vue; *set one's* ‿ *against* s'opposer à, s'élever contre; † ‿ *value* valeur *f* nominale; **2.** *v/t.* affronter, braver; donner sur (*la cour etc.*); parer (*un habit*); envisager (*les faits*); revêtir (*un mur*); faire face à (*q.*); *be* ‿*d with* être menacé de, se heurter à; *v/i.* être exposé *ou* tourné *ou* orienté; ‿ *about* faire demi-tour; ✗ *left* ‿*l* à gauche, gauche!; *about* ‿*l* volte-face!; ‿ *up* affronter (*un danger etc.*); **face card** *cartes*: figure *f*; **faced** (*with*) à revers (de *qch.*); contre-plaqué (de *bois*); **ˈface·down** épreuve *f* de force; **ˈface·less** *fig.* anonyme; **ˈface-lift·ing** remontée *f* du visage; lifting *m*; **ˈfac·er** gifle *f*, F tuile *f*.

fac·et ⊕ [ˈfæsit] facette *f*; **ˈfac·et·ed** à facettes.

fa·ce·tious □ [fəˈsiːʃəs] facétieux (-euse *f*), plaisant. [*visage.*⟩

fa·cial [ˈfeiʃl] facial (-aux *m/pl.*); du⟩

fac·ile [ˈfæsail] facile; complaisant (*personne*); **fa·cil·i·tate** [fəˈsiliteit] faciliter; **fa·cil·i·ta·tion** action *f* de faciliter; **fa·cil·i·ty** facilité *f*; souplesse *f* de caractère.

fac·ing [ˈfeisiŋ] ⊕ revêtement *m*; *moule*: poncif *m*; ✗ conversion *f* (à droite *etc.*); ‿*s pl.* ✗ parement *m*.

fac·sim·i·le [fækˈsimili] fac-similé *m*; ⚖ copie *f* figurée; ‿ *broadcast* (*-ing*) téléphotographie *f*.

fact [fækt] fait *m*, action *f*; réalité *f*; ‿*s pl.* (*of the case*) faits *m/pl.* (de la cause), vérité *f*; *after the* ‿ par assistance; *before the* ‿ par instigation; *in* (*point of*) ‿ au fait, en vérité; *tell s.o. about the* ‿*s of life* apprendre à q. les choses de la vie; **ˈ‿-find·ing** pour établir les faits.

fac·tion [ˈfækʃn] *péj.* cabale *f*, faction *f*; dissension *f*; **ˈfac·tion·ist** factieux (-euse *f*) *m*, partisan *m*.

fac·tious □ [ˈfækʃəs] factieux (-euse *f*); **ˈfac·tious·ness** esprit *m* factieux.

fac·ti·tious □ [fækˈtiʃəs] factice, contrefait; faux (fausse *f*).

fac·tor [ˈfæktə] Ⱥ, *fig.* facteur *m*; † agent *m*, commissionnaire *m* en gros; **ˈfac·to·ry** fabrique *f*, usine *f*.

fac·to·tum [fækˈtoutəm] factotum *m*, homme *m* à tout faire.

fac·tu·al [ˈfæktjuəl] effectif (-ive *f*), positif (-ive *f*), réel(le *f*); ‿ *knowledge* connaissance *f* des faits.

fac·ul·ty [ˈfækəlti] pouvoir *m*; faculté *f* (*a. univ.*); *fig.* talent *m*; *eccl.* autorisation *f*; ⚖ droit *m*; *Am.* corps *m* enseignant.

fad F [fæd] lubie *f*, marotte *f*, dada *m*; **ˈfad·dish**, **ˈfad·dy** maniaque; capricieux (-euse *f*); **ˈfad·dist** maniaque *mf*.

fade [feid] (se) faner, flétrir; (se) décolorer (*tissu*); s'affaiblir; (*a.* ‿ *out*) s'évanouir, s'éteindre; ‿ *down* (*ou out*) *cin.* faire fondre dans le lointain; *radio*: faire fondre dans le lointain; ‿ *in* (faire) arriver dans un fondu; **ˈfade·less** ineffaçable; *tex.* bon teint; **ˈfad·ing 1.** □ qui se fane *etc.*; **2.** *radio*: fading *m*, évanouissement *m*; *cin.* fondu *m.n.*

fae·ces [ˈfiːsiːz] fèces *f/pl.*; matières *f/pl.* fécales.

fag F [fæg] **1.** corvée *f*, travail *m* pénible; *école*: petit *m* (*élève*) qui fait les corvées d'un grand; *sl.* sèche *f*, cigarette *f*; **2.** *v/i.* travailler dur; faire les corvées d'un grand élève; *v/t.* éreinter, fatiguer; '~-'**end** F bout *m*; queue *f*; *sl.* mégot *m.*

fag·ot, fag·got ['fægət] fagot *m*; ⊕ faisceau *m*, paquet *m*; *Am.* F pédé *m.*

Fahr·en·heit ['færənhait]: ~ thermo-meter thermomètre *m* Fahrenheit.

fail [feil] **1.** *v/i.* faire défaut, faillir; manquer (*cœur, force, pluie, voix, etc.*); diminuer; être refusé, échouer (*à un examen*); faire faillite; *mot.* rester en panne; baisser (*jour, lumière, santé*); he ~ed to do (*a. in doing*) manquer de faire; omettre de faire; he *cannot* ~ to il ne peut manquer de; *v/t.* manquer (à); abandonner; manquer à ses engagements envers (*q.*); refuser (*un candidat*); his heart ~ed him le cœur lui manqua; **2.** *without* ~ sans faute; à coup sûr; '**fail·ing 1.** *su.* défaut *m*; faiblesse *f*; **2.** *prp.* faute de, à défaut de; ~ which faute de quoi; **fail·ure** ['feiljə] manque *m*; défaut *m*; insuccès *m*; *mot.* panne *f*; affaiblissement *m*; fiasco *m*; faillite *f*; *personne*: raté(e *f*) *m.*

fain [fein] **1.** *adj.* bien disposé; trop heureux (-euse *f*) (de, to); **2.** *adv.* avec plaisir.

faint [feint] **1.** □ faible; léger (-ère *f*); feel ~ se sentir mal; **2.** s'évanouir; *fig.* mourir (de, with); **3.** évanouissement *m*; ~-**heart·ed** □ ['~'hɑːtid] timide; lâche; '~-'**heart·ed·ness** pusillanimité *f*; '**faint·ness** faiblesse *f.*

fair[1] [fɛə] **1.** *adj.* beau (*bel devant une voyelle ou un h muet*); belle *f*; beaux *m/pl.*); juste; blond; ✝ loyal; assez bon(ne *f*); **2.** *adj.*, *a. adv.* poli(ment); doux (douce *f*), *adv.* doucement; favorable(ment); loyal(ement); *école*: passable, assez bien (*mention*); passablement; ~ *copy* copie *f* au net; corrigé *m*; ~ *dealing* probité *f*, loyauté *f*; ~ *play* jeu *m* loyal, franc jeu *m*; traitement *m* juste; our ~ *readers* nos aimables lectrices *f/pl.*; the ~ pl. (*a.* the ~ *sex*) le beau sexe; ~ *and softly* tout doucement; ✝ ~ *trade* système réciproque de libre échange; bid ~ to promettre de; speak

s.o. ~ parler poliment à q.; *strike* ~ frapper carrément.

fair[2] [~] foire *f*; grand marché *m*; '~-**ground** champ *m* de foire; '**fair·ing** ✝ cadeau *m* acheté à la foire; 🎣 entoilage *m*; profilage *m.*

fair·ly ['fɛəli] *adv. de fair*[1]; honnête-ment, loyalement; avec impartialité; passablement, assez; '**fair·ness** beauté *f*; *cheveux*: couleur *f* blonde; teint *m* blond; blancheur *f*; loyauté *f*; probité *f*; *sp.* franc jeu *m*; '**fair-spo·ken** à la parole courtoise; '**fair·way** passage *m*, chenal *m*; '**fair-weath·er friend** ami *m* jusqu'à la bourse.

fair·y ['fɛəri] **1.** féerique; des fées; ~ *lamp*, ~ *light* lampion *m*; **2.** fée *f*; '**fair·y·land** pays *m* ou royaume *m* des fées; *fig.* pays *m* enchanté; '**fair·y·like** féerique; de fée; '**fair-y-tale** conte *m* de fées; *fig.* conte *m* bleu.

faith [feiθ] foi *f* (*à qch., en Dieu*); confiance *f* (en, in); croyance *f*; religion *f*; parole *f*; in good ~ de bonne foi; '~-**cure** guérison *f* par (auto)suggestion; **faith·ful** □ ['~-ful] fidèle; loyal (-aux *m/pl.*); exact; the ~ *pl.* les fidèles *m/pl.*; yours ~ly Agréez l'expression de mes sentiments distingués; '**faith·ful·ness** loyauté *f* (envers, to), fidélité *f*; exactitude *f*; '**faith·less** □ infidèle; perfide; incrédule; '**faith·less·ness** infidélité *f*; déloyauté *f*; perfidie *f.*

fake *sl.* [feik] **1.** chose *f* truquée; article *m* faux; (*Am. a.* '**fak·er** *personne*: simulateur (-trice *f*) *m*; **2.** (*a.* ~ *up*) truquer.

fal·con ['fɔːlkən] faucon *m*; '**fal·con·er** fauconnier *m*; '**fal·con·ry** fauconnerie *f.*

fald·stool ['fɔːldstuːl] prie-dieu *m/inv.*; siège *m* d'évêque; pliant *m.*

fall [fɔːl] **1.** chute *f* (*a. d'eau, du jour, d'une ville*); baromètre, eaux, théâ., rideau, température: baisse *f*; *nuit*: tombée *f*; pente *f*; descente *f*; *arbres*: abattis *m*; *surt. Am.* automne *m*; *pluie, neige, etc.*: quantité *f*; *usu.* ~s *pl.* chute *f* d'eau, cascade *f*; *voix*: cadence *f*; perte *f*, ruine *f*; ⚓ *usu.* ~s *pl.* garants *m/pl.*; the ♀ (*of Man*) la chute de l'homme; have a ~ tomber; **2.** [*irr.*] tomber (*a. gou-vernement, nuit, vent*); baisser (*jour, prix, etc.*); arriver; capituler (*ville*);

(*avec adj.*) devenir, tomber; naître (*animal*); (se) calmer (*mer*); retomber (*blâme, responsabilité, etc.*); s'effondrer (*bâtiment*); aller en pente, descendre; se projeter (*ombre*); *his countenance fell* sa figure s'allongea; *his spirits fell* il perdit courage; ~ *asleep* s'endormir; ~ *away* s'abaisser; déserter; ~ *back* tomber en arrière; reculer; se rabattre (sur, *upon*); ~ *behind* rester en arrière; se laisser devancer; ~ *between two stools* demeurer entre deux selles; ~ *down* tomber (par terre); s'écrouler; F échouer; ~ *due* venir à échéance; *surt. Am.* F ~ *for* tomber amoureux de/ adopter (*qch.*) avec enthousiasme; ~ *from* (re)tomber de; ~ *ill* (*ou* ~ *sick*) tomber malade; ~ *in* s'effondrer; ⚔ former les rangs; ⚓ expirer (*bail*); arriver à échéance (*dette*); ~ *in with* se prêter à (*un projet*); rencontrer (*q.*); s'accorder avec; ~ *in love with* tomber amoureux de; ~ *into* tomber dans (*l'eau*); contracter (*une habitude*); être induit en (*erreur*); dégénérer en; ~ *into line* se mettre en rangs; rentrer dans les rangs; ~ *off* tomber; faire défection; *fig.* décliner, diminuer; ~ *on* ⚔ attaquer; fondre sur; se jeter sur; tomber sur (*q.*); ~ *out* se brouiller (avec, *with*); se passer, arriver; ⚔ quitter les rangs; ~ *short* tomber en deçà (de, *of*); ~ *short of* ne pas atteindre, être au-dessous de; ~ *to see* voir; *a.* se mettre au travail; commencer; ~ *under* entrer dans (*une catégorie*).

fal·la·cious □ [fə'leiʃəs] illusoire; trompeur (-euse *f*); **fal'la·cious·ness** fausseté *f*.

fal·la·cy ['fæləsi] sophisme *m*; erreur *f*; faux raisonnement *m*.

fall·en ['fɔːlən] *p.p. de* fall 2.

fall guy *Am. sl.* ['fɔːl'gai] bouc *m* émissaire.

fal·li·bil·i·ty [fæli'biliti] faillibilité *f*; **fal·li·ble** □ ['fæləbl] faillible.

fall·ing ['fɔːliŋ] baisse *f*; chute *f etc.*; '~·'off chute *f*; défection *f*; décroissement *m*; déclin *m*; ~ *star* étoile *f* filante. [radioactives.]

fall·out ['fɔːlaut] retombées *f/pl.*]

fal·low ['fælou] 1. *zo.* fauve; ✔ en friche; 2. ✔ jachère *f*, friche *f*; 3. ✔ jachérer, défricher; '~·**deer** *zo.* daim *m*.

false □ [fɔːls] 1. *adj.* faux (fausse *f*); artificiel(le *f*); erroné; infidèle (à, to); *be* ~ *to* trahir; tromper; ~ *imprisonment* détention *f* illégale; ~ *key* crochet *m*, rossignol *m*; ~ *teeth pl.* dentier *m*; 2. *adv. play s.o.* ~ trahir q.; **false·hood** ['~hud] mensonge *m*; fausseté *f*; faux *m*; '**false·ness** fausseté *f*; *femme etc.*: infidélité *f*.

fal·set·to ♪ [fɔːl'setou] fausset *m*.

fal·si·fi·ca·tion ['fɔːlsifi'keiʃn] falsification *f*; altération *f*; **fal·si·fi·er** ['~faiə] falsificateur (-trice *f*) *m*; **fal·si·fy** ['~fai] falsifier; altérer; rendre vain; tromper; **fal·si·ty** ['~ti] fausseté *f*.

fal·ter ['fɔːltə] *v/i.* chanceler; *fig.* hésiter, trembler (*voix*); défaillir (*courage, personne*); *v/t.* balbutier.

fame [feim] renom(mée *f*) *m*; **famed** célèbre, renommé (pour, for).

fa·mil·iar [fə'miljə] 1. □ familier (-ère *f*) (à, to); intime; bien connu (de, to); au courant (de, with); 2. ami(e *f*) *m* intime; (*a.* ~ *spirit*) démon *m* familier; **fa·mil·i·ar·i·ty** [~li'æriti] familiarité *f*; connaissance *f* (de, with); **fa·mil·iar·i·za·tion** [~ljərai'zeiʃn] accoutumance *f* (à, with), habitude *f* (de, with); **fa'mil·iar·ize** rendre familier.

fam·i·ly ['fæmili] 1. famille *f*; 2. de famille, familial (-aux *m/pl.*); *in the* ~ *way* enceinte (*f*); ~ *allowance* allocation *f* familiale; ~ *doctor* médecin *m* de famille; ~ *man* père *m* de famille; ~ *tree* arbre *m* généalogique.

fam·ine ['fæmin] famine *f*; disette *f*.

fam·ish ['fæmiʃ] *v/t.* affamer; réduire à la famine; *v/i.* être affamé.

fa·mous □ ['feiməs] célèbre (pour, for); F fameux (-euse *f*), parfait.

fan[1] [fæn] 1. éventail *m* (*a.* ♣); ventilateur *m*; ✈ van *m*; *mot.* ~ *belt* courroie *f* de ventilateur; 2. éventer; ✈ vanner; souffler (*le feu*); *fig.* exciter.

fan[2] F [~] *sp. etc.* fervent(e *f*) *m*; *cin.* fanatique *mf*; *radio:* sans-filiste *mf*; *mots composés:* -ophile *mf*.

fa·nat·ic [fə'nætik] 1. (*a.* **fa'nat·i·cal** □ [~kl]) fanatique; 2. fanatique *mf*; **fa'nat·i·cism** [~isizm] fanatisme *m*.

fan·ci·er ['fænsiə] amateur (-trice *f*) *m* (d'oiseaux *etc.*).

fan·ci·ful □ [ˈfænsiful] fantastique; fantasque, imaginaire (*personne*).

fan·cy [ˈfænsi] **1.** fantaisie *f*, imagination *f*; idée *f*; caprice *m*, goût *m*; lubie *f*; the ~ les amateurs *m/pl.* de boxe; *take a* ~ *to* prendre goût à (*qch.*); s'éprendre de (*q.*); **2.** de fantaisie; de luxe; de pure imagination; ~ *apron* tablier *m* de fantaisie; ~ *ball* bal *m* travesti; ~ *dress* travesti *m*, costume *m*; ~ *fair* vente *f* de charité; ~ *goods pl.* nouveautés *f/pl.*, articles *m/pl.* de fantaisie; *sl.* ~ *man* souteneur *m*; ~ *price* prix *m* exagéré *ou* de fantaisie; **3.** s'imaginer, se figurer; croire, penser; avoir envie de (*qch.*); se sentir attiré vers (*q.*); *just* ~! figurez-vous (ça)!; '~**-free** libre comme l'air; '~**-work** broderie *f*; ouvrages *m/pl.* de dames.

fan·fare [ˈfænfɛə] fanfare *f*; sonnerie *f*; **fan·fa·ron·ade** [ˌfænrə-ˈnɑːd] fanfaronnade *f*, vanterie *f*.

fang [fæŋ] *chien*: croc *m*; *vipère*: crochet *m*; ⊕ soie *f*.

fan·ner [ˈfænə] ✎ van *m* mécanique; ⊕ ventilateur *m*.

fan·ta·sia ♩ [fænˈteizjə] fantaisie *f*; **fan·tas·tic** [~ˈtæstik] (~*ally*) fantastique, bizarre; **fan·tas·ti·cal·ness** [ˌklnis] bizarrerie *f*; **fan·ta·sy** [ˈ~təsi] fantaisie *f*, caprice *m*.

far [fɑː] *adj.* lointain, éloigné; *adv.* loin, au loin; beaucoup, fort, bien; ~ *better* beaucoup mieux; ~ *the best* de beaucoup le meilleur; *as* ~ *as* jusqu'à; *by* ~ de beaucoup; ~ *from* (*gér.*) loin de (*inf.*); *in* *so* ~ *as* dans la mesure où; ~**-a·way** [ˈfɑːrəwei] lointain; *fig.* vague.

farce *théâ.* [fɑːs] farce *f* (*a. cuis.*); **far·ci·cal** □ [ˈ~ikl] burlesque; *fig.* grotesque.

fare [fɛə] **1.** prix *m* (du voyage, de la place, *etc.*); chère *f*, manger *m*; *personne*: client(e *f*) *m*; **2.** voyager; aller (*bien ou mal*); ~ *well* adieu!; '~**-in·di·ca·tor** tarif *m*; '~**·well** **1.** adieu!; **2.** adieu *m*, -x *m/pl.*; **3.** d'adieu; ~ *party* soirée *f* d'adieu.

far... [fɑː]: '~**-fetched** *fig.* tiré par les cheveux, recherché, forcé; '~**-flung** *fig.* vaste, très étendu; ~ *gone* F (dans un état) avancé.

far·i·na·ceous [færiˈneiʃəs] farinacé; ~ *food* (aliment *m*) farineux *m*.

farm [fɑːm] **1.** ferme *f*; *see* ~ *house*; élevage *m* de volaille en grand; **2.**

v/t. cultiver; (*a.* ~ *out*) donner à ferme, affermer; exploiter (*un terrain*); mettre en nourrice (*des enfants*); *v/i.* être fermier, cultiver la terre; '**farm·er** fermier *m*; '**farm-hand** ouvrier (-ère *f*) *m* agricole; '**farm'house** (maison *f* de) ferme *f*; '**farm·ing** **1.** cultivateur (-trice *f*); à ferme; aratoire; **2.** agriculture *f*; exploitation *f*; culture *f*; **farm-stead** [ˈ~sted] ferme *f*; '**farm'yard** basse-cour (*pl.* basses-cours) *f*; cour *f* de ferme.

far·o [ˈfɛərou] *cartes*: pharaon *m*.

far...: ~**-off** [ˈfɑːˈɔːf] lointain, éloigné; ~**-out** F [ˈfɑːˈaut] insolite; extravagant; super.

far·ra·go [fəˈreigou] méli-mélo (*pl.* mélis-mélos) *m*; fatras *m*.

far·ri·er [ˈfæriə] vétérinaire *m*; ✗ maréchal-ferrant (*pl.* maréchaux-ferrants) *m*; '**far·ri·er·y** art *m* vétérinaire; ✗ maréchalerie *f*.

far·row [ˈfærou] **1.** cochonnée *f*; **2.** *vt/i.* mettre bas; *v/i.* cochonner.

far-sight·ed [ˈfɑːˈsaitid] ✗ presbyte; *fig.* prévoyant.

fart V [fɑːt] **1.** pet *m*; **2.** péter.

far·ther [ˈfɑːðə], **far·thest** [ˈ~ðist] *comp.*, *a. sup.* de far.

far·thing [ˈfɑːðiŋ] F sou *m* (¹⁄₄ penny).

fas·ci·a [ˈfæʃiə], *pl.* **fas·ci·ae** [ˈ~ii] *anat.* fascia *m*; △ fasce *f*, bande (-lette) *f*.

fas·ci·nate [ˈfæsineit] fasciner, charmer; **fas·ci·na·tion** fascination *f*; charme *m*, attrait *m*.

fas·cine [fæˈsiːn] fascine *f*.

Fas·cism *pol.* [ˈfæʃizm] fascisme *m*; '**Fas·cist** fasciste (*a. su./mf*).

fash·ion [ˈfæʃn] **1.** mode *f*; vogue *f*; façon *f*, manière *f*; forme *f*; habitude *f*; *sl. rank and* ~ le gratin *m*; *in* ~ à la mode; *out of* ~ démodé; *set the* ~ mener la mode; donner le ton; **2.** façonner, former, confectionner (*une robe*); '**fash·ion·a·ble** □ à la mode, de bon ton; élégant; '**fash·ion·a·ble·ness** vogue *f*; élégance *f*; '**fash·ion·pa·rade** présentation *f* de collections; '**fash-ion-plate** gravure *f* de modes.

fast¹ [fɑːst] **1.** *adj.* rapide; résistant, bon teint (*drap etc.*); en avance (*montre etc.*); fidèle, constant (*ami*); dissolu (*vie*); ~ *to light* résistant; *phys.* ~ *breeder* surrégénérateur *m*

rapide; 🚂 ~ *train* rapide *m*, train *m*
express; **2.** *adv.* ferme; vite.
fast² [~] **1.** jeûne *m*; **2.** jeûner;
'~**day** jour *m* maigre.
fas·ten ['fɑːsn] *v/t.* attacher (à, to);
amarrer (*un bateau*); fermer (*la
porte*); assurer; fixer (*a.* les yeux
sur, one's eyes [*up*]on); *v/i.* s'attacher; se fixer; se fermer; ~ *upon*
fig. saisir (*qch.*); s'arrêter sur; '**fas-
ten·er** (*a.* '**fas·ten·ing**) attache *f*;
robe: agrafe *f*; *bourse, livre:* fermoir
m; *fenêtre etc.:* fermeture *f*; *patent* ~
bouton-pression (*pl.* boutons-pression) *m*.
fas·tid·i·ous □ [fæs'tidiəs] difficile;
délicat; exigeant; blasé; **fas'tid·i-
ous·ness** délicatesse *f*; goût *m*
difficile.
fast·ness ['fɑːstnis] fermeté *f*;
couleurs: solidité *f*; vitesse *f*; légèreté *f* de conduite; ⚔ forteresse *f*.
fat [fæt] **1.** □ gras(se *f*); gros(se *f*);
2. graisse *f*; *viande:* gras *m*;
3. (s')engraisser.
fa·tal □ ['feitl] fatal (-als *m/pl.*);
mortel(le *f*); funeste (*a.* to); **fa·tal-
ism** ['~əlizm] fatalisme *m*; '**fa·tal-
ist** fataliste *mf*; **fa·tal·i·ty** [fə'tæliti]
fatalité *f*; mort *f*; destin *m*; accident
m mortel, sinistre *m*.
fate [feit] destin *m*; sort *m*; fatalité *f*;
the ♀*s* les Parques *f/pl.*; **fat·ed**
['~id] destiné; fatal (-als *m/pl.*);
infortuné; **fate·ful** □ ['~ful] décisif (-ive *f*).
fat·head *sl.* ['fæthed] idiot(e *f*) *m*.
fa·ther ['fɑːðə] **1.** père *m*; **2.** engendrer; adopter; avouer la pa-
ternité de; servir de père à; ~ *s.th.
upon s.o.* imputer qch. à q.; **fa-
ther·hood** ['~hud] paternité *f*;
'**fa·ther-in-law** beau-père (*pl.*
beaux-pères) *m*; '**fa·ther·land** patrie *f*; '**fa·ther·less** sans père;
'**fa·ther·ly** paternel(le *f*).
fath·om ['fæðəm] **1.** *mes.* toise *f*; ⚓
brasse *f*; ♀ 216 pieds *m/pl.* cubes;
2. ⚓ (*a. fig.*) sonder; *fig.* approfondir;
'**fath·om·less** sans fond.
fa·tigue [fə'tiːg] **1.** fatigue *f*; ⚔
corvée *f*; ~*s pl.* ⚔ tenue *f* de
corvée; **2.** fatiguer, lasser; **fa'tigue-
par·ty** ⚔ (détachement *m* de)
corvée *f*.
fat·ling ['fætliŋ] jeune bête *f* en-
graissée; '**fat·ness** graisse *f*; *personne:* embonpoint *m*; *sol:* fertilité *f*;

'**fat·ten** (s')engraisser; devenir *ou*
rendre gras; *v/t.* fertiliser (*le sol*);
'**fat·ty 1.** graisseux (-euse *f*);
gras(se *f*) (*sol*); ~ *degeneration*
stéatose *f*; **2.** F gros (bonhomme) *m*.
fa·tu·i·ty [fə'tjuiti] sottise *f*; imbécillité *f*; **fat·u·ous** □ ['fætjuəs]
sot(te *f*), imbécile.
fau·cet ⊕ *surt. Am.* ['fɔːsit] robinet
m.
faugh [fɔː] pouah!
fault [fɔːlt] faute *f* (*a. tennis*); imperfection *f*; défaut *m* (*a.* ⚡, ⊕);
⊕ *métal:* paille *f*; *géol.* faille *f*; *to
a* ~ à l'excès; *find* ~ *with* trouver à redire à; *be at* ~ être en défaut; *be
his* ~ être (de) sa faute; '~**find·er**
épilogueur (-euse *f*); censeur
(-euse *f*); '~**find·ing 1.** sermonneur (-euse *f*); grondeur (-euse *f*);
2. censure *f*, critique *f*; disposition
f à critiquer; '**fault·i·ness** imperfection *f*; '**fault·less** □ sans défaut; sans faute; parfait; '**faults-
man** *tel., téléph.* surveillant *m* de
ligne (*qui recherche les dérangements*);
'**fault·y** □ défectueux (-euse *f*)
imparfait.
fa·vo(u)r ['feivə] **1.** faveur *f*; permission *f*; bonté *f*; nœud *m* de
rubans, couleurs *f/pl.*; ✝ *your* ~
votre honorée *f ou* estimée *f*; ✝
in great ~ très recherché; *in* ~ *of* en
faveur de; *I am (not) in* ~ *of it* moi
je suis pour (contre); *under* ~ *of
night* à la faveur de la nuit; **2.** être
en faveur de; approuver; honorer
(de, *with*); **fa·vo(u)r·a·ble** □
['~vərəbl] (*to*) favorable (à); propice
(à); bon(ne *f*); '**fa·vo(u)r·a·ble-
ness** caractère *m* favorable; **fa-
vo(u)red** ['~vəd] favorisé; *well-*~
beau (bel *devant une voyelle ou un
h muet*); belle *f*; beaux *m/pl.*); **fa-
vo(u)r·ite** ['~vərit] **1.** favori(te *f*),
préféré; **2.** favori(te *f*) *m*; *sp.* favori
m; '**fa·vo(u)r·it·ism** favoritisme *m*;
sl. piston *m*.
fawn¹ [fɔːn] **1.** *zo.* faon *m*; (couleur
f) fauve *m*; **2.** mettre bas (un faon).
fawn² [~] *chien:* caresser (q.,
[*up*]on *s.o.*); *personne:* aduler (*q.*);
'**fawn·er** adulateur (-trice *f*) *m*;
'**fawn·ing** caressant; servile.
faze *surt. Am.* F [feiz] bouleverser.
fe·al·ty ['fiːəlti] féauté *f*; fidélité *f*.
fear [fiə] **1.** peur *f*, crainte *f*; *through
(ou from)* ~ *of* de peur de; *for* ~ *of*

(*gér.*) de crainte de (*inf.*); *go in* ~ *of one's life* craindre pour sa vie; **2.** craindre; *v/t.* redouter, avoir peur de; *v/i.* avoir peur; **fear·ful** □ ['~ful] craintif (-ive *f*); timide; affreux (-euse *f*); **'fear·ful·ness** caractère *m* épouvantable; timidité *f*; **'fear·less** □ intrépide; sans peur (de, *of*); **'fear·less·ness** intrépidité *f*, courage *m*.

fea·si·bil·i·ty [fi:zə'biliti] possibilité *f*; **'fea·si·ble** possible, faisable.

feast [fi:st] **1.** fête *f* (*a. eccl.*); festin *m*; *fig.* régal *m*; **2.** *v/t.* fêter; ~ *one's eyes on* assouvir ses yeux de; *v/i.* faire bonne chère; se régaler (de, [*up*]*on*).

feat [fi:t] exploit *m*, haut fait *m*.

feath·er ['feðə] **1.** plume *f*; *aile, queue*: penne *f*; *chasse*: gibier *m* à plumes; ✂ plumet *m*; F *show the white* ~ caner, manquer de courage; *that is a* ~ *in his cap* c'est une perle à sa couronne; *in high* ~ d'excellente humeur; **2.** *v/t.* emplumer; empenner (*une flèche*); ⚓ ramener à plat (*l'aviron*); *v/i.* nager plat; ~ *one's nest* faire sa pelote; **'~-brained**, **'~-head·ed** étourdi, écervelé; **'feath·ered** emplumé; empenné (*flèche*); **'feath·er-edge** ⊕ biseau *m*; morfil *m* (*d'un outil*); **'feath·er·ing** plumage *m*; empennage *m*; biseautage *m*; nage *f* plate; **'feath·er-stitch** point *m* d'arêtes; **'feath·er-weight** box. poids *m* plume; **'feath·er·y** plumeux (-euse *f*); léger (-ère *f*.)

fea·ture ['fi:tʃə] **1.** trait *m* (*a. du visage*); caractéristique *f*; spécialité *f*; *cin.* film *m*; *journ. Am.* article *m*; ~*s pl.* physionomie *f*; *pays:* topographie *f*; *œuvre:* caractère *m*; **2.** marquer, caractériser; dépeindre; *journ.* mettre en manchette; *cin.* tourner (*un rôle*), représenter (*q.*); mettre en vedette; *a film featuring N.N.* un film avec N.N. en vedette; ~ *film* grand film *m* du programme; **'fea·ture·less** sans traits bien marqués; peu intéressant.

feb·ri·fuge ['febrifju:dʒ] fébrifuge *m*.

fe·brile ['fi:brail] fiévreux (-euse *f*).

Feb·ru·ar·y ['februəri] février *m*.

feck·less ['feklis] propre à rien, incapable.

fec·u·lence ['fekjuləns] féculence

f; saleté *f*; **'fec·u·lent** féculent; sale.

fe·cun·date ['fi:kʌndeit] féconder; **fe·cun·da·tion** fécondation *f*; **fe·cun·di·ty** [fi'kʌnditi] fécondité *f*.

fed [fed] *prét. et p.p. de* feed 2; *be* ~ *up with* en avoir assez de; *well* ~ bien nourri.

fed·er·al ['fedərəl] fédéral (-aux *m*/*pl.*); **'fed·er·al·ism** fédéralisme *m*; **'fed·er·al·ist** fédéraliste *mf*; **'fed·er·al·ize** (se) fédérer; **fed·er·ate 1.** ['~reit] (se) fédérer; **2.** ['~rit] fédéré; allié; **fed·er·a·tion** fédération *f*; *ouvriers etc.:* syndicat *m*; **fed·er·a·tive** ['~rətiv] fédératif (-ive *f*).

fee [fi:] **1.** honoraires *m*/*pl.*; *école:* frais *m*/*pl.*; droit *m*; taxe *f*; *hist.* fief *m*; pourboire *m*; ~ *simple* propriété *f* libre; **2.** payer des honoraires (à q., *s.o.*); donner un pourboire à (*q.*).

fee·ble □ ['fi:bl] faible; **'~·'mind·ed** à l'esprit faible; **'fee·ble·ness** faiblesse *f*.

feed [fi:d] **1.** alimentation *f* (*a.* ⊕); pâturage *m*; *cheval:* fourrage *m*; *avoine etc.:* picotin *m*; nourriture *f*; F repas *m*; ⊕ entraînement *m*; *attr.* d'alimentation *etc.*; auxiliaire; **2.** [*irr.*] *v/t.* nourrir (*q., l'esprit*); alimenter (⊕, *sp., machine, chaudière, feu, famille*); faire paître (*les vaches etc.*); manger (*a. q. des yeux, one's eyes on s.o.*); introduire (*des matières premières dans une machine*); *théâ.* donner la réplique à; ~ *off* (*ou down*) pâturer (*un pré*); ~ *up* engraisser; *see fed; v/i.* manger, paître, se nourrir (de, [*up*]*on*); **'~·back 1.** ⚡ réaction *f*; **2.** ⊕ alimenter en retour; **'feed·er** mangeur (-euse *f*) *m*; *surt. Am.* nourrisseur *m* de bestiaux; *enfant:* bavette *f*; *bébé:* biberon *m*; canal *m* d'alimentation; ⊕ alimentateur *m*; ⚡ artère *f ou* conducteur *m* alimentaire; **feed·er line** 🚂 embranchement *m*; **'feed·ing** alimentation *f*; pâture *f*; ⊕, ⚡ avance *f*; *attr.* du repas; alimentateur (-trice *f*); *high* ~ vie *f* de luxe; **'feed·ing-bot·tle** biberon *m*; **'feed·ing-stuff** fourrage *m*.

fee-faw-fum ['fi:fɔ:'fʌm] pouah!

feel [fi:l] **1.** [*irr.*] *v/t.* sentir; tâter (*a.* ✂); ressentir (*une douleur, une émotion*); éprouver; penser; être sensible à; avoir conscience de; v/i. être ... au toucher (*chose*); sembler, paraître; se sentir (*personne*); se trouver; ~ *cold* avoir froid (*personne*), être froid (au toucher) (*chose*); *I* ~ *like* (*gér.*) j'ai envie de (*inf.*); je me sens d'humeur à (*inf.*); ~ *for* avoir de la sympathie pour; **2.** toucher *m*; sensation *f*; '**feel·er** *fig.* ballon *m* d'essai; *zo.* antenne *f*; *escargot:* corne *f*; *mollusque etc.:* tentacule *m*; *chat:* moustache *f*; ✕ éclaireur *m*; '**feel·ing 1.** □ sensible; ému; **2.** toucher *m*; émotion *f*; sentiment *m*; sensibilité *f*; *good* ~ bonne entente *f*; sympathie *f*.

feet [fi:t] *pl. de* **foot 1.**

feign [fein] feindre, faire semblant (de *inf.*, *to inf.*); ~ *mad* faire semblant d'être fou; '**feigned** feint, simulé; contrefait; déguisé; **feign·ed·ly** ['~idli] avec feinte.

feint [feint] **1.** feinte *f*; ✕ fausse attaque *f*; **2.** feinter; ✕ faire une fausse attaque.

fe·lic·i·tate [fi'lisiteit] féliciter (de, sur *on*); **fe·lic·i·ta·tion** félicitation *f*; **fe·lic·i·tous** □ heureux (-euse *f*); à propos; **fe'lic·i·ty** félicité *f*, bonheur *m*; à-propos *m*.

fe·line ['fi:lain] félin, de chat.

fell¹ [fel] **1.** *prét. de* **fall 2**; **2.** abattre; assommer.

fell² *poét.* [~] cruel(le *f*); funeste.

fell³ [~] peau *f*; toison *f*.

fell⁴ [~] colline *f* rocheuse.

fel·loe ['felou] jante *f*.

fel·low ['felou] personne *f*; camarade *m*; compagnon, compagne *f*; collègue *m*; semblable *m*, pareil *m*; *univ.* agrégé(e *f*) *m*; *société:* membre *m*; F homme *m*, type *m*; *péj.* individu *m*; *attr.* compagnon de; co(n)-; F *a* ~ *on*; F *old* ~ mon vieux *m*; *the* ~ *of a glove* l'autre gant *m*; *he has not his* ~ il n'a pas son pareil *ou* de rival; '~-'**be·ings** *pl.* semblables *m/pl.*; '~-'**cit·i·zen** concitoyen(ne *f*) *m*; '~-'**coun·try·man** compatriote *mf*; '~-'**crea·ture** semblable *m*; prochain *m*; '~-'**feel·ing** sympathie *f*; ~**ship** ['~ʃip] communauté *f*; association *f*; (*a. good* ~) camaraderie *f*, solidarité *f*; association *f*, société *f*; fraternité *f*; *univ.* dignité *f* d'agrégé (*d'un collège universitaire*); titre *m* de membre (*d'une société savante*); ~ **sol·dier**

compagnon *m* d'armes; '~-'**stu·dent** camarade *mf* d'études; '~-'**trav·el·ler** compagnon *m* (compagne *f*) de voyage; *pol.* communisant(e *f*) *m*.

fel·ly ['feli] jante *f*.

fel·on ['felən] ⚖ criminel(le *f*) *m*; ⚕ panaris *m*; **fe·lo·ni·ous** □ ⚖ [fi'lounjəs] criminel(le *f*); délictueux (-euse *f*); **fel·o·ny** ⚖ ['feləni] crime *m*.

felt¹ [felt] *prét. et p.p. de* **feel 1.**

felt² [~] **1.** feutre *m*; **2.** (se) feutrer; ~**-tip(ped) pen** ['~tip(t) pen] crayon *m* feutre.

fe·male ['fi:meil] **1.** féminin (*personne*); femelle (*animal*); ~ *child* enfant *m* du sexe féminin; ~ *screw* vis *f* femelle; **2.** femme *f*; *animal:* femelle *f*.

fem·i·nine □ ['feminin] féminin; *gramm.* du féminin; *souv. péj.* de femme; **fem·i'nin·i·ty** féminité *f*; *péj.* caractère *m* féminin; '**fem·i·nism** féminisme *m*; '**fem·i·nist** féministe (*a. su. mf*); **fem·i·nize** ['~naiz] (se) féminiser.

fen [fen] marais *m*, marécage *m*.

fence [fens] **1.** clôture *f*; palissade *f*; ⊕ guide *m*; garde *f*; *sp.* haie *f*; *Am.* mur *m* de clôture; *sl.* receleur (-euse *f*) *m*; *sit on the* ~ attendre d'où vient le vent; **2.** *v/t.* (*a.* ~ *in*) enclore, entourer; protéger (contre, *from*); *sl.* receler; *v/i.* faire de l'escrime; *fig.* parer (qch., *with s.th.*); *sp.* sauter les haies; *sl.* faire le recel; '**fence·less** ouvert, sans clôture.

fenc·ing ['fensiŋ] clôture *f*, palissade *f*; escrime *f*; ⊕ garde *f*; *attr.* d'armes; '~-'**foil** fleuret *m*; '~-**mas·ter** maître *m* d'armes.

fend [fend]: ~ *off* détourner; F ~ *for* pourvoir à; ~ *for o.s.* se débrouiller; '**fend·er** △ bouteroue *f*; garde-feu *m/inv.*; *mot. Am.* aile *f*; *mot.* pare-chocs *m/inv.*; ⚓ défense *f*.

Fe·ni·an ['fi:niən] **1.** fénian; **2.** fénian *m* (*membre d'une association d'Irlandais aux É.-U. partisans de l'Indépendance de l'Irlande*).

fen·nel ♀ ['fenl] fenouil *m*.

fen·ny ['feni] marécageux (-euse *f*).

feoff [fef] fief *m*; **feoff·ee** [fe'fi:] fieffataire *m*; '**feoff·ment** inféodation *f*; don *m* en fief; **feof·for** [fe'fɔ:] fieffant(e *f*) *m*.

fer·ment 1. ['fə:ment] ferment *m*; *fig.* agitation *f*; **2.** [fə'ment] (faire) fermenter; *fig.* (s')échauffer; **fer-'ment·a·ble** fermentable; **fer-men·ta·tion** [fə:men'teiʃn] fermentation *f*; *fig.* effervescence *f*; **fer-'ment·a·tive** [‿‿tətiv] fermentatif (-ive *f*).

fern ♀ [fə:n] fougère *f*.

fe·ro·cious □ [fə'rouʃəs] féroce; **fe·roc·i·ty** [fə'rɔsiti] férocité *f*.

fer·ret ['ferit] **1.** *zo.* furet *m* (*a. fig.*); **2.** *v/t.* fureter (*un terrier*); prendre au furet; ~ *out* découvrir, dénicher; *fig.* déterrer; *v/i.* chasser au furet.

fer·ric ↗ ['ferik] ferrique; **fer·rif-er·ous** [fe'rifərəs] ferrifère.

Fer·ris wheel ['feriswi:l] *foire:* grande roue *f*.

fer·ru·gi·nous [fe'ru:dʒinəs] ferrifère; **fer·ro·con·crete** ⊕ ['ferou-'kɔnkri:t] béton *m* armé; **fer·rous** ↗ ['ferəs] ferreux (-euse *f*).

fer·rule ['feru:l] bout *m* ferré; ⊕ virole *f*.

fer·ry ['feri] **1.** passage *m*; bac *m*; **2.** passer la rivière en bac; '~-**boat** bac *m*; '**fer·ry·man** passeur *m*.

fer·tile □ ['fə:tail] (*a. fig.*) fertile, fécond (en *of*, *in*); **fer·til·i·ty** [fə:'tiliti] fertilité *f* (*a. fig.*); **fer·ti-li·za·tion** [‿tilai'zeiʃn] fertilisation *f*; ♀ pollinisation *f*; '**fer·ti·lize** (*a.* ♀) fertiliser, féconder; amender (*la terre*); '**fer·ti·liz·er** engrais *m*.

fer·ule † ['feru:l] férule *f* (*a.* ♀).

fer·ven·cy ['fə:vənsi] (*usu. fig.*) ferveur *f*; ardeur *f*; '**fer·vent** □ ardent (*a. fig.*); *fig.* fervent, vif (vive *f*).

fer·vid □ ['fə:vid] *see* fervent.

fer·vo(u)r ['fə:və] *see* fervency.

fes·tal □ ['festl] de fête; joyeux (-euse *f*).

fes·ter ['festə] **1.** (faire) suppurer; (s')ulcérer; *fig.* couver; **2.** inflammation *f* avec suppuration.

fes·ti·val ['festəvl] fête *f*; ♪, *théâ.* festival *m*; **fes·tive** □ ['‿iv] de fête, joyeux (-euse *f*); **fes·'tiv·i·ty** fête *f*, réjouissance *f*, festivité *f*.

fes·toon [fes'tu:n] **1.** feston *m*; **2.** festonner.

fetch [fetʃ] *v/t.* apporter (*qch.*); amener (*q.*); aller chercher; rapporter (*un prix*); F captiver; F flanquer (*un coup*); pousser (*un soupir*); tirer (*des larmes*); ~ *up* faire monter; vomir; *v/i.:* ~ *and carry* être aux ordres (de *q.*, *for* s.o.); ~ *up* s'arrêter; *usu. Am.* aboutir (à, *at*); '**fetch·ing** F □ ravissant, séduisant.

fête [feit] **1.** fête *f* (*a. eccl.*); **2.** fêter.

fet·id □ ['fetid] fétide, puant.

fe·tish ['fi:tiʃ] fétiche *m*.

fet·lock ['fetlɔk] fanon *m*.

fet·ter ['fetə] **1.** chaîne *f*; **2.** enchaîner.   [dition *f*.]

fet·tle ['fetl] forme *f*; bonne con-)

fe·tus ['fi:təs] *see* foetus.

feud [fju:d] inimitié *f*; fief *m*; **feu·dal** □ ['‿dl] féodal (-aux *m/pl.*); **feu·dal·ism** ['‿dəlizm] féodalité *f*; **feu·dal·i·ty** [‿'dæliti] féodalité *f*; fief *m*; **feu·da·to·ry** ['‿dətəri] feudataire (*a. su./m*), vassal (-aux *m/pl.*) (*a. su./m*).

fe·ver ['fi:və] fièvre *f*; **fe·vered** ['fi:vəd] *surt. fig.* fiévreux (-euse *f*); '**fe·ver·ish** □ fiévreux (-euse *f*) (*a. fig.*).

few [fju:] **1.** *adj.* peu de; quelques; **2.** *pron.: a* ~ quelques-uns (-unes *f*); *a good* ~ pas mal (de); **3.** *su.* petit nombre *m*; *the* ~ la minorité.

fi·at ['faiæt] décret *m*; consentement *m*; *Am.* ~ *money* monnaie *f* fiduciaire (*billets de banque*).

fib [fib] **1.** petit mensonge *m*; blague *f*; **2.** mentir; blaguer; '**fib·ber** menteur (-euse *f*) *m*; blagueur (-euse *f*) *m*.

fi·bre, *Am.* **fi·ber** ['faibə] fibre *f* (*a.* ⊕); ♀ radicelle *f*; *fig.* nature *f*, trempe *f*; '**fi·brin** ['‿brin] ↗, *physiol.* fibrine *f*; **fi·bro·si·tis** ['‿brou'saitis] cellulite *f*; '**fi·brous** □ fibreux (-euse *f*).

fib·u·la *anat.* ['fibjulə], *pl.* **-lae** [‿li:], **-las** péroné *m*.

fick·le ['fikl] inconstant, volage; changeant; '**fick·le·ness** inconstance *f*; humeur *f* volage.

fic·tile ['fiktail] plastique, céramique (*argile*).

fic·tion ['fikʃn] fiction *f* (*a.* ⚖); (*a. works of* ~) romans *m/pl.*, littérature *f* d'imagination; '**fic·tion·al** □ de romans; d'imagination.

fic·ti·tious □ [fik'tiʃəs] fictif (-ive *f*); imaginaire; inventé; feint; '**fic·tive** fictif (-ive *f*), imaginaire.

fid·dle ['fidl] **1.** violon *m*; **2.** *v/i.* jouer du violon; tripoter; *v/t.* jouer (*un air*) sur le violon; *souv. Am.* truquer; ~ *away* perdre (*son temps*);

fid·dle·de·dee [ˈ⸾di'diː] quelle blague!; **fid·dle·fad·dle** F [ˈ⸾fædl]
1. fadaises f/pl.; ⸾! quelle blague!;
2. musard; **3.** baguenauder; **'fiddler** joueur m du violon; **'fid·dle-
stick** archet m; ⸾s! quelle bêtise!

fi·del·i·ty [fi'deliti] fidélité f, loyauté
f (à, envers to, towards).

fidg·et F ['fidʒit] **1.** usu. ⸾s pl.
agitation f, énervement m; personne: énervé(e f) m; have the ⸾s
ne pas tenir en place; **2.** (s')énerver,
(se) tourmenter; v/i. s'agiter; **'fidg-
et·y** agité, nerveux (-euse f), impatient.

fi·du·ci·a·ry [fi'djuːʃiəri] **1.** fiduciaire; **2.** héritier (-ère f) m
fiduciaire; dépositaire mf.

fie [fai] fi (donc)!

fief [fiːf] fief m.

field [fiːld] **1.** champ m; pré m; sp.
terrain m; course: champ m; fig.
domaine m; ✝ marché m; ✕ champ
m de bataille; glace: banc m; hold
the ⸾ ✕ se maintenir sur ses posi-
tions; fig. être toujours en faveur;
2. cricket: v/i. tenir le champ; v/t.
arrêter et relancer (la balle); **'⸾-day**
✕ jour m de grandes manœuvres ou
de revue; fig. grande occasion f,
grand jour m; Am. réunion f athlétique; Am. journée f d'expédition
en pleine campagne; **'field·er**
cricket: chasseur m.

field ...: **'⸾-fare** litorne f; **'⸾-glass**
jumelle f, -s f/pl.; **'⸾-jack·et** anorak
m; **'⸾-Mar·shal** feld-maréchal m;
'⸾-sports pl. chasse f et pêche f;
'⸾-work travaux m/pl. ou recherches
f/pl. sur le terrain ou sur les lieux; ✝
démarchage m auprès de la clientèle;
sociologie: travail m avec des cas
sociaux.

fiend [fiːnd] démon m, esprit m
malin; diable mf; fig. monstre m;
fig. fanatique mf (de); **'fiend·ish** □
diabolique; infernal (-aux m/pl.).

fierce □ [fiəs] féroce; violent;
furieux (-euse f); **'fierce·ness** férocité f; violence f; fureur f.

fi·er·i·ness ['faiərinis] ardeur f (a.
fig.); **'fi·er·y** □ de feu; enflammé;
ardent; emporté (personne).

fife [faif] **1.** fifre m; **2.** v/t. fifrer; v/i.
jouer du fifre; **'fif·er** (joueur m de)
fifre m.

fif·teen ['fif'tiːn] quinze; **'fif'teenth**

[⸾θ] quinzième (a. su./m); **fifth** [fifθ]
cinquième (a. su./m); **'fifth·ly** en
cinquième lieu; **fif·ti·eth** ['⸾tiiθ]
cinquantième (a. su./m); **'fif·ty**
cinquante; **'fif·ty-'fif·ty** chacun(e f)
la moitié; go ⸾ être de moitié.

fig¹ [fig] figue f; arbre: figuier m;
a ⸾ for ...! zut pour ...!; I don't care
a ⸾ for him je m'en fiche (de
lui).

fig² F [⸾] **1.** forme f; gala f; in full ⸾
en grande toilette ou tenue; in good
⸾ en bonne forme; **2.** ⸾ out attifer.

fight [fait] **1.** combat m, bataille f;
box. assaut m; (a. free ⸾) bagarre f;
fig. lutte f; make a ⸾ for lutter pour;
put up a good ⸾ se bien acquitter;
show ⸾ offrir de la résistance;
2. [irr.] v/t. se battre avec ou
contre; combattre; lutter contre;
⸾ off repousser, résister à; v/i. se
battre; combattre; lutter; ⸾ against
combattre (q., qch.); ⸾ back résister à, repousser; ⸾ for se battre
pour; ⸾ shy of éviter; ⸾ing fit frais
et dispos; en parfaite santé;
'fight·er combattant m, guerroyeur
m; ⸾ plane avion m de chasse,
chasseur m; **'fight·ing** combat m;
attr. de combat.   [vention f.)

fig·ment ['figmənt] fiction f, in-⸾
fig-tree ['figtriː] figuier m.

fig·u·rant ['figjurənt] figurant m.

fig·u·ra·tion [figju'reiʃn] (con-)
figuration f; ♪ embellissement m;
fig·ur·a·tive □ ['⸾rətiv] figuratif
(-ive f); figuré; en images.

fig·ure ['figə] **1.** figure f (a. ♪,
danse, géométrie, livre); taille f,
forme f; A chiffre m; image f;
tissu: dessin m; F what's the ⸾? ça
coûte combien?; at a high ⸾ à un
prix élevé; **2.** v/t. écrire en chiffres;
♪ chiffrer; brocher (un tissu); (a.
⸾ to o.s., se) figurer, représenter;
Am. estimer; ⸾ up (ou out) calculer;
⸾ out résoudre (un problème); v/i.
chiffrer, calculer; ⸾ as représenter;
⸾ on se trouver sur; Am. compter
sur; ⸾ out at (se) monter à; **'⸾-head**
⚓ figure f de proue; fig. personnage
m purement décoratif; prête-nom
m; **'⸾-skat·ing** tracé m des figures
sur la glace.

fig·u·rine ['figjuriːn] figurine f.

fil·a·ment ['filəmənt] filament m
(a. ⚡); ⚢, zo., phys. filet m; attr. ⚡,
radio: de chauffage.

fil·bert ♀ ['filbə:t] aveline f; *arbre*: avelinier m.

filch [filtʃ] chiper (à, *from*).

file¹ [fail] **1.** dossier m (*a.* ⚖ǁ), *lettres*: classeur m; *papiers*: liasse f; crochet m à papiers; fichier m; ✗ file f; *in single* ∼ en file indienne; *Am.* ∼ *case* classeur m; fichier m; *Am.* ∼ *clerk* documentaliste mf; ∼*leader* chef m de file; **2.** ✗ (faire) marcher en ligne de file;✗ ∼ *off* (faire) défiler; v/t. enfiler; classer; ranger; joindre au dossier; enregistrer (*une enquête*); *Am.* déposer (*une plainte*); *filing cabinet* fichier m; classeur m; *filing clerk* documentaliste mf.

file² [∼] **1.** lime f; *sl. deep* ∼ fin matois m; **2.** limer; '∼*-cut·ter* tailleur m de limes.

fil·i·al □ ['filjəl] filial (-aux m/pl.).

fil·i·a·tion [fili'eiʃn] filiation f.

fil·i·bus·ter ['filibʌstə] **1.** (*ou* **fil·i·'bus·ter·er**) flibustier m; *Am.* obstructionniste m; **2.** flibuster; *Am.* faire de l'obstruction.

fil·i·gree ['filigri:] filigrane m.

fil·ings *pl.* ['failiŋz] limaille f.

fill [fil] **1.** (se) remplir (de, *with*); (se) combler; v/t. plomber (*une dent*); occuper (*un poste*); charger, satisfaire (*un besoin, un désir*); *Am.* ♀, *pharm.* exécuter; *Am.* répondre à; ∼ *s.o.'s glass* verser à boire à q.; ∼ *in* combler (*un trou etc.*); remplir (*un bulletin, une formule*); libeller (*un chèque*); ∼ *out* (s')enfler; grossir; ∼ *up* (se) remplir, (se) combler; libeller (*un chèque*); **2.** suffisance f; soûl m; plein m de pipe; plumée f; *eat* (*drink*) one's ∼ manger à sa faim (boire à sa soif).

fill·er ['filə] remplisseur (-euse f) m; remplissage m.

fil·let ['filit] **1.** △, *cheveux*: filet m; *cuis.* filet m (*de bœuf etc.*); ⚜ bandelette f; ruban m; *veau*: rouelle f; △ fasce f; **2.** orner d'un filet; *cuis.* détacher les filets de.

fill·ing ['filiŋ] remplissage m; charge f; *dent*: plombage m; *mot.* ∼ *station* poste m d'essence.

fil·lip ['filip] **1.** *doigt*: chiquenaude f; encouragement m, stimulant m; **2.** donner une chiquenaude à; stimuler.

fil·ly ['fili] pouliche f; F jeune fille f.

film [film] **1.** pellicule f (*a. phot.*); voile m; peau f (*du lait chaud*); *cin.*

film m, bande f; *œil*: taie f; ∼ *cartoon* dessin m animé; ∼ *cartridge* phot. (pellicule f en) bobine f; *take a* ∼ tourner un film; **2.** (se) couvrir d'une pellicule *ou* d'un voile; v/t. phot., cin. filmer; v/i. fig. se voiler; 'film·y □ fig. voilé; transparent.

fil·ter ['filtə] **1.** filtre m; ∼ *tip* bout m filtre; cigarette f à bout filtre; **2.** v/t. filtrer; v/i. fig. s'infiltrer; ∼ *in* changer de file; '**fil·ter·ing** filtrage m; **fil·ter-tipped** ['filtətipt] à bout filtre.

filth [filθ] saleté f; '**filth·y** □ sale, dégoûtant; crapuleux (-euse f).

fil·trate ['filtreit] **1.** (s'in)filtrer; **2.** ⚗ filtrat m; **fil'tra·tion** filtration f; *pharm.* colature f.

fin [fin] nageoire f; *sl.* main f; ✈ plan m fixe; *mot.* ailette f.

fi·nal ['fainl] **1.** □ final (-als m/pl.) (*a. gramm.*); dernier (-ère f); définitif (-ive f); sans appel; *sp.* ∼ *whistle* coup m de sifflet final; **2.** *a.* ∼*s pl.* examen m final; *sp.* finale f; **fi·nal·ist** ['∼nəlist] *sp.* finaliste mf; **fi·nal·i·ty** [∼'næliti] caractère m définitif; décision f; **fi·nal·ize** ['∼nəlaiz] terminer, mener (*qch.*) à bonne fin; mettre la dernière main à; rendre (*qch.*) définitif (-ive f).

fi·nance [fai'næns] **1.** finance f; **2.** v/t. financer; v/i. être dans la finance; **fi'nan·cial** □ [∼ʃl] financier (-ère f); ∼ *year* année f budgétaire; **fin'an·cier** [∼siə] financier m; *fig.* bailleur m de fonds.

finch orn. [fintʃ] pinson m.

find [faind] **1.** [*irr.*] trouver; découvrir; constater; retrouver; croire; fournir, procurer; ⚖ déclarer, prononcer (*coupable etc.*); ∼ *o.s.* se trouver; se pourvoir soi-même; *all found* tout fourni; ∼ *out* découvrir; se renseigner (sur, *about*); inventer; *I cannot* ∼ *it in my heart* je n'ai pas le cœur (de *inf.*, to *inf.*); **2.** trouvaille f, découverte f; '**find·er** trouveur (-euse f) m; *phot.* viseur m; *opt.* chercheur m; '**find·ing** découverte f; *a.* ∼*s pl.* trouvaille f; ⚖ conclusion f; verdict m.

fine¹ □ [fain] **1.** fin, pur; raffiné, subtil; bon(ne f); excellent; petit; beau (bel *devant une voyelle ou un h muet*; belle f; beaux m/pl.) (*a. temps*); joli; élégant; *you are a* ∼ *fellow!* iro. vous êtes joli, vous!; ∼

arts *pl.* beaux arts *m/pl.*; **2.** *adv.*
finement; admirablement; *cut* ~
tout juste (*temps*); au plus bas
(*prix*); **3.** *météor.* beau temps *m*;
4. (se) clarifier (*bière*); ~ *away* (*ou
down ou off*) (s')amincir; rendre *ou*
devenir effilé.

fine² [~] **1.** amende *f*; *in* ~ bref; enfin; **2.** mettre (*q.*) à l'amende; frapper
(*q.*) d'une amende (d'une livre, *a
pound*).

fine-draw ['fain'drɔ:] rentraire; ~*n*
fig. amaigri; subtil.

fine·ness ['fainnis] finesse *f*; pureté
f; subtilité *f*; beauté *f*; élégance *f*.

fin·er·y ['fainəri] parure *f*; atours
m/pl.; ⊕ (af)finerie *f*.

fi·nesse [fi'nes] finesse *f*; ruse *f*;
cartes: impasse *f*.

fine-tooth(ed) comb ['fain'tu:θ(t)
koum] peigne *m* fin; *go through ou
over s.th. with a* ~ passer qch. au
peigne fin.

fin·ger ['fiŋgə] **1.** doigt *m*; *have a* ~
in the pie être mêlé à *ou* se mêler
de l'affaire; *see end 1*; **2.** manier,
toucher; tâter; ♪ doigter; tapoter
sur (*un piano*); '~**board** ♪ *piano
etc.*: clavier *m*; *violon etc.*: touche *f*;
'~**bowl** rince-doigts *m*; '**fin·gered**
aux doigts ...; '**fin·ger·ing** maniement *m*; ♪ doigté *m*; grosse laine *f* à
tricoter.

fin·ger...: '~**lan·guage** langage *m*
mimique; '~**nail** ongle *m*; ~ **pol·ish**
vernis *m* à ongles; '~**post** poteau *m*
indicateur; '~**print** **1.** empreinte *f*
digitale; **2.** prendre les empreintes
digitales de (*q.*); '~**stall** doigtier *m*.

fin·i·cal □ ['finikl], **fin·ick·ing**
['~kiŋ], **fin·ick·y** ['~ki], **fin·i·kin**
['~kin] difficile; méticuleux (-euse
f) (*personne*).

fin·ish ['finiʃ] **1.** *v/t.* finir; terminer;
casser; (*a.* ~ *off, up*) achever, mener
à terme; ⊕ usiner; *tex.* apprêter;
~*ed goods pl.* articles *m/pl.* apprêtés;
sp. ~*ing line* ligne *f* d'arrivée; ~*ing
touch* dernière main *f*; *v/i.* finir; se
terminer; prendre fin; **2.** achèvement *m*; ⊕ apprêtage *m*; ⊕ finissage
m; ✝ fini *m*, apprêt *m*; '**fin·ish·er** ⊕
finisseur (-euse *f*) *m*, apprêteur
(-euse *f*) *m*; F coup *m* de grâce.

fi·nite □ ['fainait] borné, limité; fini
(*a.* ⚤); *gramm.* ~ *verb* verbe *m* à un
mode fini; '**fi·nite·ness** nature *f*
limitée.

fink *Am. sl.* [fiŋk] jaune *m*.

Fin·land·er ['finləndə], **Finn** [fin]
Finlandais(e *f*) *m*; Finnois(e *f*) *m*.

Finn·ish ['finiʃ] finlandais; *ling.* finnois *m*.

fin·ny ['fini] à nageoires.

fir [fə:] sapin *m*; *Scotch* ~ pin *m*
rouge; '~**cone** pomme *f* de sapin.

fire ['faiə] **1.** feu *m*; incendie *m*; ✗
tir *m*; *fig.* ardeur *f*; radiateur *m* (*à
gaz, électrique*); ~! au feu!; *come
under* ~ (*from*) ✗ essuyer le feu (de
l'ennemi etc.); *fig.* être vivement
attaqué (par *q.*); *on* ~ en flammes, en
feu; **2.** *v/t.* mettre le feu à; (*a.* ~ *off*) ✗
tirer; cuire (*des briques etc.*); *fig.*
enflammer; F congédier, renvoyer;
⊕ chauffer (*le four etc.*); ~ *up*
allumer; chauffer; *v/i.* prendre feu;
s'enflammer (*a. fig.*); partir; tirer
(*sur at*, [*up*]*on*); F ~ *away!* allez-y!; ~
up s'emporter (contre, *at*); '~
a·larm signal *m* d'incendie; '~
arms *pl.* armes *f/pl.* à feu; '~**ball**
météor. aérolithe *m*; éclair *m* en
boule; ✗ balle *f* à feu; '~**box** ⊕ boîte
f à feu; '~**brand** F brandon *m* (de
discorde); '~**bri·gade** sapeurs-
pompiers *m/pl.*; '~**bug** *Am.* F incendiaire *m*; '~**crack·er** pétard *m*; '~
cur·tain *théâ.* rideau *m* métallique;
'~**damp** ⚒ grisou *m*; '~**de·part-
ment** *Am.* sapeurs-pompiers *m/pl.*;
'~**dog** chenet *m*; landier *m*; '~**door**
porte *f* anti-incendie *ou* coupe-feu; ~
drill exercice *f* anti-incendie; '~
en·gine ⊕ pompe *f* à incendie; '~
es·cape échelle *f ou* escalier *m* de
sauvetage; '~**ex·tin·guish·er** extincteur *m* (d'incendie); '~**fight·er**
pompier *m* (volontaire); lutteur
(-euse *f*) *m* contre l'incendie; '~**fly**
luciole *f*; F mouche *f* à feu; '~
gre·nade grenade *f* extinctrice; '~
in·sur·ance assurance *f* contre
l'incendie; '~**i·rons** *pl.* garniture *f*
de foyer; '~**light·er** allume-feu
m/inv.; '~**man** (sapeur-)pompier
m; ⊕ chauffeur *m*; '~**of·fice** bureau
m d'assurance contre l'incendie; '~
place cheminée *f*; foyer *m*; '~**plug**
bouche *f* d'incendie; '~**proof**
ignifuge; '~**rais·ing** incendie *f*
volontaire; pyromanie *f*; '~**screen**
devant *m* de cheminée; '~**side 1.**
cheminée *f*, foyer *m*; coin *m* du feu;
2. de *ou* au coin du feu; '~**sta·tion**
poste *m* de pompiers; '~**wall**

cloison *m* pare-feu; '~-**war·den** responsable *mf* de la lutte anti-incendie; guetteur *m* d'incendies; '~-**wood** bois *m* à brûler; '~-**work(s** *pl. fig.*) feu *m* d'artifice; '~-**work** pièce *f* d'artifice.

fir·ing ['faiəriŋ] chauffage *m*; ⊕ chauffe *f*; *brisques etc.*: cuite *f*; ✕ tir *m*; ~ *squad* peleton *m* d'exécution.

fir·kin ['fə:kin] *mesure*: quartaut *m* (45,5 *litres*); tonnelet *m*.

firm [fə:m] **1.** □ ferme; solide; inébranlable; **2.** maison *f* (de commerce); raison *f* sociale.

fir·ma·ment ['fə:məmənt] firmament *m*. [solidité *f*.\

firm·ness ['fə:mnis] fermeté *f*;∫

first [fə:st] **1.** *adj.* premier (-ère *f*); ~ *aid* premiers secours *m/pl. ou* soins *m/pl.* d'urgence; ✝ ~ *cost* prix *m* coûtant *ou* initial *ou* de revient; *Am.* ~ *floor see ground floor*;~ *name* prénom *m*; ~ *night théâ.* première*f*; *Am.* ~ *papers pl.* déclaration*f* de naturalisation; **2.** *adv.* premièrement, d'abord; pour la première fois; plutôt; *at* ~, *of all* pour commencer; tout d'abord; ~ *and last* en tout et pour tout; **3.** *su.* premier (-ère *f*) *m*; ✝ ~ *of exchange* première *f* de change; *from the* ~ dès le premier jour; *go* ~ passer devant; prendre le devant; ~ voyager en première; '~-'**aid box** *ou* **kit** trousse *f* de premiers secours *ou* à pharmacie; '~-'**aid post** poste *m* de secours; '~-**born** premier-né (premier-née *ou* première-née *f*); '~-'**class** de première classe; de première qualité; '~-**fruits** *pl.*,

first·lings *pl.* ['~liŋz] prémices *f/pl.*; '**first·ly** premièrement; d'abord; *see first-class.*

firth [fə:θ] estuaire *m*, golfe *m*.

fis·cal ['fiskl] fiscal (-aux *m/pl.*); financier (-ère *f*).

fish [fiʃ] **1.** poisson *m*; *coll.* poissons *m/pl.*; ⚙ éclisse *f*; F type *m*; *odd* ~ drôle *m* de type; *have other* ~ *to fry* avoir d'autres chats à fouetter; **2.** *v/i.* pêcher (qch., *for s.th.*); aller à la pêche (de, *for*); *v/t.* pêcher; ⚙ éclisser; ~ *out* tirer; sortir; '~-**bone** arête *f*; '~-**cake** *cuis.* croquette *f* de poisson.

fish·er·man ['fiʃəmən] pêcheur *m*; '**fish·er·y** pêche *f*; *lieu*: pêcherie *f*.

fish...: ~ **fin·gers** *pl. cuis.* bâtonnets *m/pl.* de poisson; ~ **hook** hameçon *m*.

fish·ing ['fiʃiŋ] pêche *f*; '~-**line** ligne *f* de pêche; '~-**rod** canne *f* à pêche; '~-**tack·le** attirail *m* de pêche.

fish...: ~ **line** *Am.* ligne *f* de pêche; '~-**mon·ger** marchand(e *f*) *m* de poisson; ~ **pole** *Am.* canne *f* à pêche; ~ **pond** étang *m* à poissons; ~ **sticks** *pl. Am. see fish fingers*; ~ **sto·ry** *Am.* F histoire *f* incroyable; '~-**wife** marchande *f* de poisson; '**fish·y** de poisson; vitreux (-euse *f*) (*œil*); louche; véreux (-euse *f*).

fis·sion ['fiʃn] fission *f*; *see atomic*; **fis·sion·a·ble** *phys.* ['~əbl] fissile; **fis·sure** ['fiʃə] **1.** fissure *f*, fente *f*; **2.** fendre.

fist [fist] poing *m*; F main *f*; F écriture *f*; **fist·i·cuffs** ['~ikʌfs] *pl.* coups *m/pl.* de poing.

fis·tu·la 🩹 ['fistjulə] fistule *f*.

fit¹ [fit] **1.** □ bon, propre, convenable (à, *for*); digne (de); en bonne santé; capable; F prêt (à, *for*); *sp.* en forme, en bonne santé; *it is not* ~ il ne convient pas; F ~ *as a fiddle* en parfaite santé; **2.** *v/t.* adapter, ajuster, accommoder (à *to*, *for*); préparer; s'accorder avec; aller à (q.), (a. ~ *together*) assembler (*des pièces*); ⊕ (a. ~ *in*) emboîter; pourvoir (de, *with*); ~ *out* équiper (de, *with*); ~ *up* monter; établir; appareiller; *v/i.* s'ajuster; aller (*robe etc*); convenir; **3.** coupe *f*, costume *etc.*: ajustement *m*; *it is a bad* ~ il est mal ajusté.

fit² [~] 🩹 attaque *f*, crise *f*, *colère*; accès *m*; *by* ~*s and starts* par boutades, à bâtons rompus; *give s.o. a* ~ F donner un coup de sang à q.

fitch·ew *zo.* ['fitʃu:] putois *m*.

fit·ful □ ['fitful] irrégulier (-ère *f*); capricieux (-euse *f*); d'humeur changeante; '**fit·ment** meuble *m*; ⊕ montage *m*; '**fit·ness** convenance*f*; aptitude *f*; justesse *f*; santé *f*; '**fit·out** équipement *m*; '**fit·ted**: ~ *carpet* tapis *m* ajusté, moquette *f*; ~ *sheet* drap-housse *m*; '**fit·ter** monteur *m*; appareilleur *m*; *cost. etc.* essayeur (-euse *f*) *m*; '**fit·ting 1.** □ convenable, propre; **2.** montage *m*; *cost. etc.* essayage *m*;~*s pl. chambre*: garniture *f*; installations *f/pl.*; *gaz, électri-*

cité: appareillage *m*; **'fit-up** F scène *f* démontable; accessoires *m/pl*.

five [faiv] **1.** cinq (*a. su./m*); **2.** ~s *sg.* (jeu *m* de) balle *f* au mur; **'five-fold** quintuple.

fix [fiks] **1.** *v/t.* fixer (*a. phot., a. les yeux sur q.*); attacher (*a. un regard sur q.*); nommer (*un jour*); régler; déterminer; *surt. Am.* F arranger, faire (*le lit etc.*); réduire à quia; graisser la patte à; ~ *o.s.* s'établir; ~ *up* arranger; installer; *Am.* réparer; *v/i.* s'installer; se fixer; se décider (pour, *on*); **2.** F embarras *m*, difficulté *f*; **fix'a·tion** fixation *f*; *phot.* fixage *m*; **fix·a·tive** ['~ətiv], **fix·a·ture** ['~ətʃə] fixatif *m*; **fixed** ['~t] (*adv.* **fix·ed·ly** ['~idli]) fixe; arrêté; permanent; invariable; figé (*sourire*); ~ *quota* contingent *m* (déterminé); ~ *star* étoile *f* fixe; **fixed-in·ter·est** ✝ à intérêt fixe; **fix·ed·ness** ['~idnis] fixité *f*; constance *f*; **'fix·er** *phot.* fixateur *m*; bain *m* de fixage; **'fix·ing** fixage *m*; *tex.* bousage *m*; *Am.* ~s *pl.* équipement *m*; garniture *f*; **'fix·i·ty** fixité *f*; fermeté *f*; **fix·ture** ['~tʃə] meuble *m* fixe; appareil *m* fixe; *sp.* engagement *m*; ~s *pl.* meubles *m/pl.* fixes; appareil *m* (*à gaz etc.*).

fizz [fiz] **1.** pétiller; cracher (*vapeur*); **2.** pétillement *m*; F champagne *m*; mousseux *m*; **'fiz·zle 1.** pétiller; siffler; (*usu.* ~ *out*) faire fiasco; avorter; **2.** pétillement *m*; fiasco *m*; **'fiz·zy** ☐ pétillant; gazeux (*-euse f*).

flab·ber·gast F ['flæbəgɑ:st] abasourdir; *be* ~*ed* (*en*) rester interdit.

flab·by ☐ ['flæbi] flasque, mou (mol *devant une voyelle ou un h muet*; molle *f*).

flac·cid ☐ ['flæksid] flasque, mou (mol *devant une voyelle ou un h muet*; molle *f*).

flag[1] [flæg] **1.** drapeau *m*; ✪ pavillon *m*; ~ *of truce* drapeau *m* parlementaire; *black* ~ pavillon *m* noir; **2.** pavoiser; transmettre par signaux; *sp.* ~ *out* jalonner.

flag[2] [~] carreau *m*; dalle *f*.

flag[3] ♣ [~] iris *m*.

flag[4] [~] languir; traîner.

flag-day ['flægdei] jour *m* de quête; *Am. Flag Day* le quatorze juin (*anniversaire de l'adoption du drapeau national*).

flag·el·late ['flædʒeleit] flageller; **flag·el'la·tion** flagellation *f*.

fla·gi·tious ☐ [flə'dʒiʃəs] infâme, abominable.

flag·on ['flægən] flacon *m*; ✝ vin: pot *m* à anse; *bière*: grosse bouteille *f*.

flag·pole ['flægpoul] *see* flagstaff.

fla·grant ☐ ['fleigrənt] infâme; flagrant, énorme.

flag...: '~**ship** vaisseau *m* amiral; '~**staff** mât *m ou* hampe *f* de drapeau; ✪ mât *m* de pavillon; '~**stone** pierre *f* à paver; dalle *f*; '~**wag·ging** ✕, ✪ signalisation *f*; *sl.* chauvinisme *m*.

flail ✔ [fleil] fléau *m*. [*for*).\
flair [flɛə] flair *m*; F aptitude *f* (à,\
flake [fleik] **1.** flocon *m*; *savon*: paillette *f*; *métal*: écaille *f*; **2.** (s')écailler; (s')épaufrer (*pierre*); **'flak·y** floconneux (*-euse f*); écailleux (*-euse f*); feuilleté (*pâte*).

flam F [flæm] blague *f*; charlatanerie *f*.

flam·boy·ant [flæm'bɔiənt] flamboyant; éclatant; voyant.

flame [fleim] **1.** flamme *f*; feu *m*; *fig.* passion *f*; F béguin *m*; **2.** flamber (*a. fig.*); s'enflammer; ~ *out* (*ou up*) jeter des flammes; s'enflammer.

flam·ma·ble *surt. Am.* ['flæməbl] inflammable.

flan *Brit.* [flæn] tarte *f*.

flange ⊕ [flændʒ] *roue*: boudin *m*; *pneu*: talon *m*; *poutre*: semelle *f*.

flank [flæŋk] **1.** flanc *m* (*a.* ✕, *a. fig.*); **2.** flanquer (de *by*, with); ✕ prendre de flanc.

flan·nel ['flænl] *tex.* flanelle *f*; *attr.* de flanelle; ~s *pl.* flanelles *f/pl.*; pantalon *m* de flanelle; *face-*~ gant *m* de toilette.

flap [flæp] **1.** patte *f*; pan *m*; *table*: battant *m*; *chaussure*: oreille *f*; léger coup *m*; clapotement *m*; F affolement *m*, panique *f*; F *be ou get in a* ~ s'affoler, paniquer; **2.** *v/t.* frapper légèrement; battre de (*les ailes, les bras, etc.*); *v/i.* battre; claquer; ballotter; **'flap·per** battoir *m*; claquette *f*; *sl.* jeune fille *f*; *see flap* 1.

flare [flɛə] **1.** flamboyer; brûler avec une lumière inégale; s'évaser (*jupe, tube, etc.*); ~ *up* s'enflammer; s'emporter (*personne*); **2.** flamme *f* vacillante; ✕ fusée *f* éclairante; ✈ feu *m*; *jupe*: godet *m*.

flash [flæʃ] **1.** voyant; contrefait, faux (fausse *f*); **2.** éclair *m*; éclat *m*; *fig.* saillie *f*; rayon *m*; *surt. Am.* dernière nouvelle *f*; nouvelle *f* brève; *in a* ~ en un clin d'œil; ~ *of wit* boutade *f*; ~ *in the pan* feu *m* de paille; **3.** *v/i.* lancer des étincelles; briller; étinceler; *v/t.* faire étinceler; faire parade de; diriger, projeter (*un rayon de lumière*); darder (*un regard*); télégraphier; riposter; *it* ~*ed on me* l'idée me vint tout d'un coup; '~·**back** *cin.* scène *f* de rappel; '~·**bulb** *phot.* ampoule *f* (de) flash; '~·**cube** *phot.* cube-flash *m* (*pl.* cubes-flash); '~·**gun** *phot.* flash *m*; '~·**light** *phot.* lumière-éclair *f*; *Am.* lampe *f* de poche; '~·**point** point *m* d'inflammabilité; '**flash·y** □ voyant; superficiel(le *f*); tapageur (-euse *f*).

flask [flɑːsk] flacon *m*; poire *f* à poudre; *vacuum* ~ thermos *m*.

flat [flæt] **1.** □ plat, uni; étendu; insipide; catégorique; ♩ net(te *f*); languissant; mat (*peinture*); ♩ faux (fausse *f*); ♩ bémol *inv.*; calme (*bourse*); ~ *price* prix *m* unique; *fall* ~ rater, manquer; *sing* ~ chanter faux; **2.** pays *m* plat; plaine *f*; *théâ.* ferme *f*; paroi *f*; appartement *m*; ♩ bas-fond *m*; ♩ bémol *m*; F benêt *m*, niais(e *f*) *m*; *mot. sl.* pneu *m* à plat; '~·**foot** pied *m* plat; *souv. Am.* agent *m*, flic *m*; '~-'**foot·ed** à pieds plats; *Am.* F formel(le *f*); franc(he *f*); '~-**i·ron** fer *m* à repasser; **flat·let** ['~lit] studio *m*; '**flat·ness** nature *f* plate; égalité *f*; *fig.* monotonie *f*; franchise *f*; ♩ langueur *f*, marasme *m*; **flat out** F **1.** toute allure; work ~ travailler d'arrache-pied; **2.** épuisé, à plat, vidé; '**flat·ten** (s')aplatir; ✈ ~ *out* se redresser; allonger le vol.

flat·ter ['flætə] flatter; '**flat·ter·er** flatteur (-euse *f*) *m*; '**flat·ter·y** flatterie *f*.

flat·u·lence, flat·u·len·cy ['flætjuləns(i)] flatuosité *f*, flatulence *f*; '**flat·u·lent** □ flatulent.

flaunt [flɔːnt] faire étalage (de).

flau·tist ['flɔːtist] flûtiste *mf*.

fla·vo(u)r ['fleivə] **1.** saveur *f*; goût *m*; arome *m*; *vin:* bouquet *m*; *fig.* atmosphère *f*; **2.** assaisonner (de, *with*); parfumer; '**fla·vo(u)red**: *vanilla-*~ (parfumé) à la vanille; '**fla·vo(u)r·less** insipide, fade.

flaw [flɔː] **1.** défaut *m*, défectuosité *f*; imperfection *f*; ⊕ paille *f*; ⚖ vice *m* de forme; *fig.* tache *f*; ⚓ grain *m*; **2.** (se) fêler; *fig.* (s')endommager; '**flaw·less** □ sans défaut; parfait.

flax ♀ [flæks] lin *m* (*a. tex.*); '**flax·en, 'flax·y** de lin; F blond.

flay [flei] écorcher; *fig.* rosser; '**flay·er** écorcheur *m*.

flea [fliː] puce *f*; '~·**bane** ♀ érigéron *m*; '~·**bite** morsure *f* de puce; '~·**pit** F ciné(ma) de quartier.

fleck [flek] **1.** petite tache *f*; **2.** tacheter (de, *with*).

flec·tion ['flekʃn] *see* flexion.

fled [fled] *prét. et p.p. de* flee.

fledge [fledʒ] *v/i.* s'emplumer; *v/t.* pourvoir de plumes; **fledg(e)·ling** ['~liŋ] oisillon *m*; *fig.* novice *mf*.

flee [fliː] [*irr.*] *v/i.* s'enfuir (de, *from*); *v/t.* (*a.* ~ *from*) fuir.

fleece [fliːs] **1.** toison *f*; *tex.* nappe *f*; ⊕ molleton *m*; **2.** tondre; écorcher; '**fleec·y** floconneux (-euse *f*); moutonné (*nuage, vagues*).

fleer [fliə] **1.** † ricanement *m*; **2.** se moquer (de, *at*), railler (q., *at s.o.*).

fleet [fliːt] **1.** □ *poét.* rapide; léger (-ère *f*); **2.** flotte *f*; *fig.* série *f*; ♀ *Street* la presse *f* (*à Londres*); **3.** passer rapidement; '**fleet·ing** □ fugitif (-ive *f*); passager (-ère *f*).

Flem·ing ['flemiŋ] Flamand(e *f*) *m*; '**Flem·ish 1.** flamand; **2.** *ling.* flamand *m*; Flamand(e *f*) *m*.

flesh [fleʃ] **1.** chair *f* (*a. eccl.*, *a. des fruits*); viande *f*; *make s.o.'s* ~ *creep* donner la chair de poule à q.; **2.** donner le goût (*fig.* le baptême) du sang à; '~·**brush** brosse *f* à friction; **flesh·ings** ['~iŋz] *pl. théâ.* maillot chair *m*/*inv.*; '**flesh·ly** charnel(le *f*); sensuel(le *f*); '**flesh·y** charnu; gras(se *f*).

flew [fluː] *prét. de* fly 2.

flex ⚡ [fleks] flexible *m*, cordon *m* souple; **flex·i·bil·i·ty** [~ə'biliti] souplesse *f* (*a. fig.*); '**flex·i·ble** □ flexible; souple; pliant; ~ *working hours pl.* horaire *m* souple; **flex·ion** ['flekʃn] flexion *f*; courb(ur)e *f*; *gramm.* (in)flexion *f*; **flex·or** ['~ksə] *anat.* (muscle *m*) fléchisseur *m*; **flex·u·ous** ['fleksjuəs] flexueux (-euse *f*); **flex·ure** ['flekʃə] flexion *f*; *géol.* pli *m*.

flick [flik] **1.** effleurer (*un cheval etc.*); (*a.* ~ *at*) donner une chique-

naude à; **2.** petit coup *m*; chiquenaude *f*; ~s *pl. sl.* ciné *m*.

flick·er ['flikə] **1.** trembler, vaciller;
clignoter; **2.** tremblement *m*; battement *m*; *Am.* évanouissement *m*.

fli·er ['flaiə] *see* flyer.

flight [flait] vol *m* (*a.* ⚡); essor *m*
(*a. fig.*); *abeilles:* essaim *m*; *oiseaux:*
volée *f*; fuite *f* (*a.* ⚔); ⚡ ligne *f*;
(~ *of stairs*) escalier *m*, perron *m*;
put to ~ mettre (*q.*) en déroute; *take*
(*to*) ~ prendre la fuite; '~-**com·**
'**mand·er** commandant *m* de
groupe; '~-**lieu'ten·ant** capitaine
m aviateur; '~-**re'cord·er** enregistreur *m* de vol; '**flight·y** □ frivole,
étourdi; volage; inconstant.

flim·flam *Am.* F ['flimflæm] **1.** boniments *m/pl.*, baratin *m*; **2.** tromper,
duper, F rouler.

flim·sy ['flimzi] **1.** tenu; fragile;
léger (-ère *f*); frivole; **2.** papier *m*
pelure; F fafiot *m* (=*billet de ban-*
que); télégramme *m*; *journ.* copie *f*.

flinch [flintʃ] broncher; reculer (devant, *from*); tressaillir.

fling [fliŋ] **1.** coup *m*, jet *m*; *cheval:*
ruade *f*; *fig.* essai *m*; *have one's* ~
jeter sa gourme; **2.** [*irr.*] *v/i.*
s'élancer, se précipiter; (*a.* ~ *out*)
ruer (*cheval*); étendre; *v/t.* jeter, lancer; ~ *o.s.* se précipiter; ~ *away* jeter
de côté; gaspiller (*l'argent*); ~ *forth*
jeter dehors; F flanquer à la porte;
~ *open* ouvrir tout grand; ~ *out* étendre (*les bras*).

flint [flint] caillou (*pl.* -x) *m*; *géol.*
silex *m*; pierre *f* à briquet; '**flint·y**
caillouteux (-euse *f*); *fig.* insensible.

flip [flip] **1.** chiquenaude *f*; petite
secousse *f* vive; ⚡ *sl.* petit tour *m*
de vol; *boisson:* flip *m*; *the* ~ *side* (*of a*
record) l'autre face *ou* le revers (d'un
disque); **2.** donner une chiquenaude
à; donner une petite secousse à;
claquer (*le fouet*).

flip-flap ['flipflæp] **1.** *su.* saut *m*
périlleux; **2.** *adv.* flic flac.

flip-flops ['flipflɔps] *pl.* tongs *f/pl.*
(*TM*).

flip·pan·cy ['flipənsi] légèreté *f*;
'**flip·pant** □ léger (-ère *f*); irrévérencieux (-euse *f*). [main *f*.]

flip·per ['flipə] *zo.* nageoire *f*; *sl.*]

flirt [flə:t] **1.** coquette *f*; flirteur *m*;
2. *v/i.* flirter; faire la coquette; *v/t.*
see flip 2; **flir'ta·tion** flirt *m*; coquetterie *f*.

flit [flit] voltiger; s'en aller; passer
rapidement; déménager.

flitch [flitʃ] flèche *f* de lard.

flit·ter ['flitə] voltiger.

fliv·ver *Am.* F ['flivə] **1.** voiture *f*
bon marché, F tacot *m*; **2.** subir un
échec.

float [flout] **1.** ⊕, *pêche:* flotteur *m*;
filet: galet *m*; masse *f* flottante; *théâ.*
paroi *f* mobile; *théâ.* rampe *f*;
radeau *m*; wagon *m* en plate-
forme; char *m* de cortège; **2.** *v/t.*
flotter; transporter dans les airs;
inonder (*un terrain*); *fig.* émettre,
faire circuler; ⚓ lancer, fonder,
monter; *v/i.* flotter, nager; ⚓ être
à flot; *nage:* faire la planche; '**float·**
a·ble flottable; '**float·age** flotte-
ment *m*; **float'a·tion** *see* flotation;
'**float·ing** flottant; à flot; sur mer;
⚓ courant (*dette*); ~ *bridge* pont
flottant; ⚓ ~ *capital* capital disponible; ~ *ice* glace *f* flottante; ~ *kidney*
rein *m* mobile; ~ *light* bateau-feu
(*pl.* bateaux-feux) *m*; ⚓ ~ *rate* taux *m*
de change flottant; *pol.* ~ *voter* électeur *m* (-trice *f*) non engagé(e).

flock¹ [flɔk] **1.** bande *f* (*a. fig.*);
troupeau *m*; *oiseaux:* volée *f*; *eccl.*
ouailles *f/pl.*; *fig.* foule *f*; **2.** s'attrouper; aller (entrer *etc.*) en foule.

flock² [~] flocon *m*; *coussin etc.:*
bourre *f* de laine.

floe [flou] glaçon *m* (flottant).

flog [flɔg] fouetter; battre à coups
de verge; '**flog·ging** (coups *m/pl.*
de) fouet *m*; F bastonnade *f*.

flood [flʌd] **1.** (*a.* ~-*tide*) marée *f*
montante; flux *m*; déluge *m*; inondation *f*; *rivière:* débordement *m*;
the ♀ le Déluge; **2.** *v/t.* inonder (*a.*
with); noyer (*a. mot.*); *v/i.* déborder;
'~-**dis·as·ter** inondation *f*; '~-**gate**
écluse *f*; vanne *f*; '~-**light** **1.** lumière *f* à grands flots; illumination
f par projecteurs; **2.** [*irr.* (*light*)]
illuminer par projecteurs.

floor [flɔ:] **1.** plancher *m*; parquet *m*
(*a. parl., a. sl.* Bourse); ✓ blé: airée *f*;
maison: étage *m*; ~ *lamp* lampadaire
m; *Am.* ~ *leader* chef *m* de parti (*qui*
dirige les votes dans l'hémicycle); ~
manager ⚡ chef *m* de rayon; *télév.*
régisseur *m*; ~ *price* prix *m* minimum; *restaurant etc.:* ~ *show* attractions *f/pl.*; *hold the* ~ *parl.* avoir la
parole; F accaparer la conversation;
take the ~ prendre la parole; se

joindre aux danseurs; 2. planchéier; terrasser; F réduire à quia; '~**-cloth** linoléum *m*; torchon *m* à laver; '**floor·er** F coup *m* qui (*vous etc.*) terrasse; '**floor·ing** planchéiage *m*; plancher *m*; dallage *m*; renversement *m*; '**floor-walk·er** *Am. see* shopwalker; '**floor-wax** cire *f* (à parquet), encaustique *f*.

floo·zy *sl.* ['flu:zi] poule *f*, pouffiasse *f*.

flop F [flɔp] 1. faire floc; se laisser tomber; pendre (*bords d'un chapeau*); *sl.* échouer; *Am. pol.* tourner casaque; 2. bruit *m* sourd; coup *m* mat; fiasco *m*; *Am. sl.* lit *m*; *Am. sl.* ~ *house see* doss-house; hôtel *m* borgne; 3. patapouf!; '**flop·py** pendant, flasque; lâche; F veule.

flo·ral ['flɔ:rəl] floral (-aux *m*/*pl.*).

flo·res·cence [flɔ:'resns] floraison *f*.

flor·id □ ['flɔrid] fleuri; flamboyant; rubicond (*visage*); '**flor·id·ness** style *m* fleuri; flamboyant *m*; teint: rougeur *f*.   [deux shillings.]

flor·in ['flɔrin] florin *m*; pièce *f* de]

flo·rist ['flɔrist] fleuriste *mf*.

floss [flɔs] (*a.* ~ *silk*) bourre *f* de soie; soie *f* floche; '**floss·y** soyeux (-euse *f*).

flo·ta·tion [flou'teiʃn] ♨ flottaison *f*; flottage *m*; ✝ lancement *m*.

flot·sam ['flɔtsəm] épave(s) *f*(*pl.*) flottante(s).

flounce[1] [flauns] 1. *cost. etc.* volant *m*; 2. garnir de volants.

flounce[2] [~] s'élancer; se débattre; ~ *in* (*out*) entrer (sortir) brusquement.

floun·der[1] *icht.* ['flaundə] flet *m*.

floun·der[2] [~] patauger (*a. fig.*).

flour ['flauə] 1. farine *f*; 2. saupoudrer de farine.

flour·ish ['flʌriʃ] 1. geste *m*; *discours*: fleurs *f*/*pl.*; brandissement *m*; trait *m* de plume; ♪ fanfare *f*; ornement *m*; 2. *v*/*i*. fleurir; prospérer; *v*/*t*. brandir; agiter; *fig.* faire parade de.

flout [flaut] *v*/*t*. narguer; se moquer de; *v*/*i*. se railler (de, *at*).

flow [flou] 1. (é)coulement *m*; courant *m*, cours *m*; passage *m*; flux *m*; ~ *chart* organigramme *m*; ~ *of spirits* fonds *m* de gaieté; 2. couler; s'écouler; monter (*marée*); circuler; flotter (*cheveux*); découler (de, *with*); ~ *from* dériver de.

flow·er ['flauə] 1. fleur *f*; élite *f*; *plantes*: fleuraison *f*; ~ *girl* marchande *f* de fleurs, bouquetière *f*; ~ *shop* (boutique *f* de) fleuriste *m*; *say it with* ~*s* exprimez vos sentiments avec des fleurs; 2. fleurir; '**flow·er·i·ness** style *m* fleuri; fleurs *f*/*pl*. de rhétorique; '**flow·er·pot** pot *m* à fleurs; '**flow·er·y** fleuri, de fleurs.

flown [floun] *p.p. de* fly 2.

flu F [flu:] *see* influenza.

flub-dub *Am.* ['flʌbdʌb] 1. radotage *m*; 2. ridicule.

fluc·tu·ate ['flʌktjueit] varier; **fluc·tu'a·tion** fluctuation *f*.

flue[1] [flu:] conduite *f*; tuyau *m*; cheminée *f*; ♪ *tuyau d'orgue*: bouche *f*.

flue[2] [~] duvet *m*, peluches *f*/*pl*.

flu·en·cy ['fluənsi] *parole etc.*: facilité *f*; '**flu·ent** □ courant, facile.

fluff [flʌf] peluche *f*; duvet *m*; '**fluff·y** pelucheux (-euse *f*); duveteux (-euse *f*); *sl.* pompette (= *ivre*); ~ *hair* cheveux *m*/*pl*. flous.

flu·id ['flu:id] 1. fluide; liquide; 2. liquide *m*, fluide *m*; **flu'id·i·ty** fluidité *f*.

fluke[1] [flu:k] *ancre*: patte *f*.

fluke[2] F [~] coup *m* de veine.

flum·mer·y ['flʌməri] *cuis.* crème *f* aux œufs; F flagornerie *f*.

flung [flʌŋ] *prét. et p.p. de* fling 2.

flunk *Am.* F [flʌŋk] *v*/*i*. échouer (à *un examen*); *v*/*t*. recaler (*q.*).

flunk·(e)y ['flʌŋki] laquais *m*; '**flunk·ey·ism** servilité *f*; flagornerie *f*.

flu·o·res·cence *phys.* [fluə'resns] fluorescence *f*.

flur·ry ['flʌri] 1. agitation *f*; ♨ brise *f* folle; *Am.* rafale *f* (de neige); averse *f*; 2. agiter; bouleverser.

flush [flʌʃ] 1. ⊕ de niveau, affleuré; très plein; abondant; F en fonds; 2. rougeur *f*; abondance *f*; *W.-C.*: chasse *f* d'eau; *fig.* fraîcheur *f*; transport *m*; *cartes*: flush *m*; 3. *v*/*t*. inonder; laver à grande eau; lever (*le gibier*); donner une chasse à; rincer; *v*/*i*. rougir; jaillir.

flus·ter ['flʌstə] 1. confusion *f*; 2. *v*/*t*. agiter, ahurir; ✝ griser; *v*/*i*. s'agiter; s'énerver.

flute [flu:t] 1. ♪ flûte *f*; ▲ cannelure *f*; *linge*: tuyau *m*; 2. jouer de la flûte; flûter; jouer (*qch.*) sur la flûte; parler d'une voix flûtée; '**flut·ist** flûtiste *mf*.

flut·ter ['flʌtə] 1. *ailes*: battement *m*; palpitation *f*; agitation *f*; F petit pari *m*; spéculation *f*; 2. *v/t.* agiter; *v/i.* battre des ailes; s'agiter; palpiter.

flux [flʌks] *fig.* flux *m* (*a.* ⚕*ᵏ*); *fig.* changement *m* continuel; ~ *and reflux* flux *m* et reflux *m*.

fly [flai] 1. mouche *f*; voiture *f* de place; *pantalon*: braguette *f*; *Am. mot.* volant *m*; *Am. baseball*: balle *f* lancée en chandelle; *théâ.* flies *pl.* cintres *m/pl.*; 2. [*irr.*] *v/i.* voler; voyager en avion; flotter (*pavillon*); passer rapidement (*temps*); courir; ~ *at* s'élancer sur; ~ *in s.o.'s face* défier q.; ~ *into a passion* se mettre en colère; ~ *off* s'envoler; ~ *on instruments* piloter sans visibilité; ~ *out at* s'emporter contre; ~ *open* s'ouvrir subitement; *v/t.* battre (*un pavillon*); *see* flee; ~ *the Atlantic* survoler l'Atlantique.

fly-blow ['flaiblou] 1. *fig.* souillures *f/pl.*; œufs *m/pl.* de mouche; 2. couvrir d'œufs de mouche; *fig.* souiller.

fly·er ['flaiə] *surt.* ✈ aviateur (-trice *f*) *m*; bon coureur *m*; oiseau *m* qui vole; *Am.* express *m*; *take a* ~ être projeté; *Am. sl.* s'engager dans une opération risquée à la Bourse.

fly-flap ['flaiflæp] tue-mouches *m/inv.*

fly·ing ['flaiiŋ] volant; d'aviation; rapide; ~ *boat* hydravion *m* (à coque); ⚓ ~ *buttress* arc-boutant (*pl.* arcs-boutants) *m*; ~ *deck* pont *m* d'atterrissage; ~ *field* champ *m* d'aviation; ~ *jump* saut *m* avec élan; ~ *machine* avion *m*; ~ *school* école *f* de pilotage; *police*: ~ *squad* brigade *f* mobile; ~ *start* départ *m* lancé; ~ *visit* courte visite *f*; *come off with* ~ *colo(u)rs* s'en tirer brillamment; remporter une victoire magnifique; ⚲ **Of·fi·cer** lieutenant *m* aviateur.

fly...: '~-**leaf** *typ.* feuille *f* de garde; '~-**sheet** feuille *f* volante; *camping*: double toit *m*; '~-**weight** *box.* poids *m* mouche; '~-**wheel** volant *m* (de commande).

foal [foul] 1. poulain *m*, pouliche *f*; 2. *v/t.* mettre bas (*un poulain*); *v/i.* pouliner.

foam [foum] 1. écume *f*; mousse *f*; 2. écumer; mousser; ~ **bath** bain *m* moussant; ~ **rub·ber** caoutchouc *m*

mousse; '**foam·y** écumeux (-euse *f*); mousseux (-euse *f*).

fob¹ [fɔb] *pantalon*: gousset *m*; (*ou* ~-**seal**) breloque *f*; (*ou* ~-**chain**) régence *f*. [*s.th. on s.o.*).]

fob² [~]: ~ *off fig.* refiler (qch. à q.,]

fo·cal ['foukl] focal (-aux *m/pl.*); *phot.* ~ *distance* distance *f* focale; *phot.* ~ *plane shutter* obturateur *m* à rideau.

fo·cus ['foukəs] 1. foyer *m*; *fig. a.* siège *m*; 2. (faire) converger; *v/t.* concentrer (*des rayons, a. l'attention*); *opt.* mettre au point.

fod·der ['fɔdə] 1. fourrage *m*; 2. donner le fourrage à.

foe *poét.* [fou] ennemi(e *f*) *m*, adversaire *m*.

foe·tus *biol.* ['fiːtəs] fœtus *m*.

fog [fɔg] 1. brouillard *m* (*a. fig.*); ⚓ brume *f*; *phot.* voile *m*; 2. *v/t.* embrumer; *fig.* embrouiller; *phot.* voiler; *v/i.* se voiler.

fo·g(e)y F ['fougi]: *old* ~ ganache *f*; vieille baderne *f*.

fog·gy □ ['fɔgi] brumeux (-euse *f*); *phot.* voilé; *fig.* confus; '**fog-horn** corne *f* de brume. [marotte *f*.]

foi·ble ['fɔibl] *fig.* faible *m*; F]

foil¹ [fɔil] feuille *f*; lame *f*; *glace*: tain *m*; *escrime*: fleuret *m*; *fig.* repoussoir *m*.

foil² [~] faire échouer; déjouer.

foist [fɔist] imposer (à, on); refiler (qch. à q., *s.th. on s.o.*).

fold¹ [fould] 1. enclos *m*; *fig.* sein *m*; (*a.* sheep-~) parc *m* à moutons; 2. (em)parquer.

fold² [~] 1. pli *m*, repli *m*; *porte*: battant *m*; 2. -uple; 3. *v/t.* plier; plisser; croiser (*les bras*); serrer (dans, in); ~ *in three* plier en trois doubles; ~ *down* retourner; plier; ~ *up* plier; fermer; *v/i.* se (re)plier; *Am.* F fermer boutique; '**fold·er** plieur (-euse *f*) *m*; plioir *m*; dépliant *m*; chemise *f*; (*a pair of*) ~*s* *pl.* (un) pince-nez *m/inv.* pliant.

fold·ing ['fouldiŋ] pliant; repliable; '~-**bed** lit *m* pliant; '~-**boat** canot *m* pliable; '~-**cam·er·a** *phot.* appareil *m* pliant; '~-**chair** pliant *m*; '~-**cot** lit *m* pliant; '~-**door(s** *pl.*) porte *f* à deux battants; '~-**hat** (chapeau *m*) claque *m*; '~-**screen** paravent *m*; '~-**seat** pliant *m*; *théâ. etc.* strapontin *m*; '~-**ta·ble** table *f* pliante.

fo·li·age ['fouliidʒ] feuillage *m*; **fo·li·at·ed** ['ˌeitid] feuilleté, folié; lamellaire, lamelleux (-euse *f*); **fo·li'a·tion** *plante*: frondaison *f*; *miroir*: étamage *m*; *métal*: laminage *m*.

fo·li·o ['fouliou] folio *m*; feuille *f*; *volume*: in-folio *m/inv.*

folk [fouk] peuple *m*; gens *mf/pl.*; F ⁓s *pl.* famille *f*.

folk·lore ['fouklɔ:] folklore *m*; légendes *f/pl.* populaires; '**folk-song** chanson *f* populaire.

fol·low ['folou] *v/t.* suivre; poursuivre (*a. les plaisirs*); succéder à; exercer (*un métier*); être partisan de; comprendre; *it* ⁓s *that* il s'ensuit que; ⁓ *out* poursuivre (*qch.*) jusqu'à sa conclusion; *cartes*: ⁓ *suit* jouer dans la couleur; *fig.* en faire autant; ⁓ *up* (pour)suivre; *v/i.* (s'en)suivre; *to* ⁓ à suivre; '**fol·low·er** serviteur *m*; disciple *m*; sectateur (-trice *f*) *m*; ⊕ plateau *m*; F amoureux (-euse *f*) *m*; '**fol·low·ing** suite *f*; partisans *m/pl.*; *the* ⁓ *pl.* les suivant(e)s *mf/pl.*; ⁓ *wind* vent *m* arrière; '**fol·low-up** poursuite *f*; rappel *m*, contrôle *m*; ✚ soins *m/pl.* post-hospitaliers.

fol·ly ['foli] folie *f*, sottise *f*.

fo·ment [fou'ment] ✚ fomenter (*a. une discorde*); *fig.* exciter; **fo·men·'ta·tion** fomentation *f*; stimulation *f*; **fo'ment·er** *fig.* fauteur (-trice *f*) *m*.

fond □ [fond] affectueux (-euse *f*); amateur (de, of); *be* ⁓ *of* aimer; *be* ⁓ *of dancing* aimer danser.

fon·dle ['fondl] caresser, câliner.

fond·ness ['fondnis] (pour, for) tendresse *f*; penchant *m*; goût *m*.

font *eccl.* [font] fonts *m/pl.* baptismaux.

food [fu:d] nourriture *f* (*a. fig.*); vivres *m/pl.*; aliment(s) *m(pl.)*; manger *m*; *fig.* matière *f*; ⁓ *hall* magasin *m* rayon *m* d'alimentation; '⁓-**stuffs** *pl.* produits *m/pl.* alimentaires; '⁓-**val·ue** valeur *f* nutritive.

fool¹ [fu:l] **1.** fou (folle *f*) *m*; sot(te *f*) *m*; imbécile *mf*; idiot(e *f*) *m*; *make a* ⁓ *of s.o.* se moquer de q.; duper q.; *make a* ⁓ *of o.s.* se rendre ridicule; *live in a* ⁓*'s paradise* se bercer d'un bonheur illusoire; *on a* ⁓*'s errand* pour des prunes; **2.** *Am.* F stupide; imbécile de; **3.** *v/t.* duper, berner; escamoter (qch. à

q., *s.o. out of s.th.*); F ⁓ *away* gaspiller; *v/i.* faire la bête; ⁓ *about*, *surt. Am.* ⁓ *(a)round* baguenauder; gâcher son temps.

fool² [⁓] marmelade *f* à la crème.

fool·er·y ['fu:ləri] bêtise *f*; '**fool-hard·y** □ téméraire; '**fool·ish** □ insensé, étourdi; '**fool·ish·ness** folie *f*, sottise *f*; '**fool-proof** ⊕ indétraquable; à toute épreuve; **fool's-cap** ['ˌkæp] bonnet *m* de fou; **fools·cap** ['ˌskæp] papier *m* ministre.

foot [fut] **1.** (*pl.* feet) homme, bas, échelle, lit, arbre: pied *m* (*a. mesure 30,48 cm*); chat, chien, insecte, oiseau: patte *f*; marche *f*; ⚔ infanterie *f*; *page*: bas *m*; on ⁓ à pied; sur pied, en train (*affaire*); *put one's* ⁓ *down* faire acte d'autorité; opposer son veto (à, upon); F *I have put my* ⁓ *into it* j'ai mis le pied dans le plat; j'ai dit *ou* fait une sottise; *set on* ⁓ mettre en train; *set* ⁓ *on* mettre pied sur; **2.** *v/t.* mettre un pied à; (*usu.* ⁓ *up*) additionner (*le compte*); F ⁓ *the bill* payer la note; *v/i.* ⁓ *it* danser; marcher; '**foot·age** longueur *f* en pieds; métrage *m*; '**foot-and-'mouth dis·ease** fièvre *f* aphteuse; '**foot·ball** ballon *m*; football *m*; *Am.* rugby *m*; '**foot-board** *mot.* marchepied *m*; '**foot-boy** *hôtel*: chasseur *m*; '**foot-brake** frein *m* à pied; '**foot-bridge** passerelle *f*; '**foot·ed** swift-⁓ aux pieds légers; '**foot·fall** (bruit *m* de) pas *m*; '**foot-gear** chaussures *f/pl.*; '**foot-guards** ⚔ *pl.* gardes *m/pl.* à pied; '**foot-hills** *pl.* collines *f/pl.* avancées; '**foot·hold** prise *f* pour le pied; *fig.* pied *m*.

foot·ing ['futiŋ] place *f* pour le pied; point *m* d'appui; situation *f* sûre; condition *f*; △ base *f*; *fig.* entrée *f*; ✝ addition *f*; *upon the same* ⁓ *as* sur un pied d'égalité avec; *get a* ⁓ prendre pied; *lose one's* ⁓ perdre pied; *pay (for) one's* ⁓ payer sa bienvenue.

foo·tle F ['fu:tl] **1.** *v/t.* gâcher (*le temps*); *v/i.* s'occuper à des futilités; **2.** bêtise *f*, niaiserie *f*.

foot ...: '⁓-**lights** *pl. théâ.* rampe *f*; '⁓-**loose** (*and fancy-free*) libre comme l'air; '⁓-**man** laquais *m*; '⁓-**note** note *f* au bas d'une page; '⁓-**pace** pas *m*; '⁓-**pas·sen·ger** piéton *m*; '⁓-

path sentier *m*; *ville*: trottoir *m*; '~-**print** empreinte *f* de pas; pas *m*; '~--**race** course *f* à pied; '~-**rule** règle *f*.

foot·sie F ['futsi]: *play ~ (with)* faire du pied (à, avec); *fig.* s'entendre.

foot...: '~-**slog** *sl.* marcher; '~-**sore** aux pieds endoloris; '~-**stalk** ♀ pétiole *m*; pédoncule *m*; '~-**step** pas *m*; trace *f*; ⊕ butée *f*; '~-**stool** tabouret *m*; '~-**wear** *see* foot-gear; '~-**work** *sp.* jeu *m* de pieds *ou* de jambes.

fop [fɔp] fat *m*, dandy *m*; '**fop·per·y** dandysme *m*; '**fop·pish** □ fat; affecté.

for [fɔː; fə] **1.** *prp. usu.* pour (*a. destination*); comme; à cause de; de (*peur, joie, etc.*); par (*exemple, charité, etc.*); avant (*3 jours*), d'ici (à) (*2 mois*); pendant (*une semaine*); depuis, il y a (*un an*); *distance*: jusqu'(à), pendant (*10 km*); contre, en échange de; en, dans; malgré, en dépit de; *destination*: à (*Londres*); vers, envers, ⚓ allant à; *he is ~ London* il va à Londres; *~ example* (*ou instance*) par exemple; *were it not ~ that* sans cela; *he is a fool ~ doing that* il est sot de faire cela; *I walked ~ a mile* j'ai fait un mille; *~ 3 days* pour *ou* pendant 3 jours; *~ all that* en dépit de *ou* malgré tout; *come ~ dinner* venir dîner; *I ~ one* moi entre autres; *go ~* aller chercher (*q.*); *it is good ~ us to* (*inf.*) il est bon que nous (*sbj.*); *the snow was too deep ~ them to come* la neige était trop profonde pour qu'ils viennent; *it is ~ you to decide* c'est à vous à décider; *~ sure!* bien sûr! *pour for après verbe voir le verbe simple*; **2.** *cj.* car.

for·age ['fɔridʒ] **1.** fourrage *m*; **2.** fourrager (pour, *for*).

for·as·much [fərəz'mʌtʃ]: *~ as* puisque, vu que, d'autant que.

for·ay ['fɔrei] incursion *f*; raid *m*.

for·bade [fə'beid] *prét. de* forbid.

for·bear[1] ['fɔː·bɛə] ancêtre *m*.

for·bear[2] [fɔː'bɛə] [*irr.*] *v/t.* s'abstenir de; *v/i.* s'abstenir (de, *from*); montrer de la patience; **for'bear·ance** patience *f*, indulgence *f*; abstention *f*.

for·bid [fə'bid] [*irr.*] défendre (*qch.* à *q.*, *s.o. s.th.*); interdire (*qch.* à *q.*, *s.o. s.th.*); *God ~!* à Dieu ne plaise!; **for'bid·den** *p.p. de* forbid; **for'bid·ding** □ sinistre; menaçant.

for·bore, **for·borne** [fɔː'bɔː(n)] *prét. et p.p. de* forbear[2].

force [fɔːs] **1.** force *f*, violence *f*; puissance *f*, autorité *f*; intensité *f*; effort *m*; énergie *f*; *the ~* la police; *armed ~s pl.* forces *f/pl.* armées; *by ~* de vive force; *come (put) in ~* entrer (mettre) en vigueur; **2.** *usu.* forcer; contraindre, obliger; prendre par force; violer (*une femme*); faire avancer; pousser (*a. F un élève*); imposer (*qch.* à *q.*, *s.th.* [*up*]*on s.o.*); *~ one's way* se frayer un chemin; *~ back* repousser; ✈ *~ down* forcer à atterrir; *~ on* forcer à avancer; *~ open* enfoncer; ouvrir de force; **'forced** (*adv.* **forc·ed·ly** ['~idli]) forcé; obligatoire; contraint; *~ loan* emprunt *m* forcé; *~ landing* atterrissage *m* forcé; *~ march* marche *f* forcée; *~ sale* vente *f* forcée; '**force-feed** alimenter (*q.*) de force; **force·ful** □ ['~ful] énergique; plein de force; vigoureux (-euse *f*); violent.

'**force-meat** ['fɔːsmiːt] *cuis.* farce *f*.

for·ceps ⚕, *zo.* ['fɔːseps] *sg. ou pl.* pince *f*; *dentiste*: davier *m*.

force-pump ['fɔːspʌmp] pompe *f* foulante.

forc·er ⊕ ['fɔːsə] plongeur *m*.

for·ci·ble □ ['fɔːsəbl] de force, forcé; vigoureux (-euse *f*); énergique.

forc·ing-house ['fɔːsiŋhaus] forcerie *f*.

ford [fɔːd] **1.** gué *m*; **2.** passer à gué; '**ford·a·ble** guéable.

fore [fɔː] **1.** *adv.* ⚓ *~ and aft* de l'avant à l'arrière; *to the ~* en évidence; présent; *bring (come) to the ~* (se) mettre en évidence; **2.** *adj.* de devant; antérieur; pré-; '~-**arm** avant-bras *m*; ~'**bode** présager; pressentir (*personne*); ~'**bod·ing** présage *m*; pressentiment *m*; '~-**cast** **1.** prévision *f*; *weather ~* prévisions *f/pl.* météorologiques; **2.** [*irr.* (*cast*)] prédire; prévoir; '~-**cas·tle** ⚓ ['fouksl] gaillard *m* d'avant; poste *m* de l'équipage; ~'**close** exclure (de, *from*), empêcher (de *from*, to); saisir (*un immeuble hypothéqué*); ~'**date** antidater; ~'**doom** condamner d'avance; présager; '~-**fa·ther** aïeul (*pl.* -eux) *m*; '~-**fin·ger** index *m*; '~-**foot** pied *m* antérieur; '~-**front** F premier rang *m*; ~'**go** [*irr.* (go)] aller devant; ~*ing* précédent; ~'**gone** passé; ~

conclusion chose *f* prévue; '**~‑ground** premier plan *m*; '**~‑hand** avant-main *f*; **~‑head** ['fɔrid] front *m*.

for·eign ['fɔrin] étranger (-ère *f*) (*a. fig.*); **~** *affairs pl.* Affaires *f*/*pl.* étrangères; **~** *exchange* devises *f*/*pl.* étrangères; *the* ⩲ *Office* le Ministère des Affaires étrangères; **~** *policy* politique *f* extérieure; ⩲ *Secretary* Ministre *m* des Affaires étrangères;**~** *trade* commerce *m* extérieur; '**for·eign·er** étranger (-ère *f*) *m*; '**for·eign·ness** caractère *m ou* air *m* étranger.

fore...: **~'judge** préjuger; **~'know** [*irr.* (*know*)] prévoir; savoir d'avance; '**~‑land** promontoire *m*; '**~‑leg** patte *f ou* jambe *f* de devant; '**~‑lock** mèche *f* sur le front; *take time by the* **~** saisir l'occasion aux cheveux; '**~‑man** 🔨 chef *m* du jury; ⊕ chef *m* d'équipe; contremaître *m*; '**~‑mast** ⚓ mât *m* de misaine; '**~‑most 1.** *adj.* premier (-ère *f*), le plus avancé; **2.** *adv.* tout d'abord; '**~‑noon** matinée *f*.

fo·ren·sic [fə'rensik] judiciaire; légal (-aux *m*/*pl.*); **~** *medicine* médecine *f* légale.

fore...: '**~‑run·ner** avant-courrier (-ère *f*) *m*, -coureur *m*, précurseur *m*; **~‑sail** ['~seil, ⚓ '~sl] (voile *f* de) misaine *f*; **~'see** [*irr.* (*see*)] prévoir; **~‑see·a·ble** qu'on peut prévoir; prévisible *f*; **~'shad·ow** présager, laisser prévoir; '**~‑shore** plage *f*; **~‑short·en** dessiner en raccourci; **~'show** [*irr.* (*show*)] préfigurer; '**~‑sight** prévoyance *f*; prévision *f*; *arme à feu*: guidon *m*; '**~‑skin** prépuce *m*.

for·est ['fɔrist] **1.** forêt *f*; **2.** boiser. **fore·stall** [fɔː'stɔːl] anticiper, prévenir.

for·est·er ['fɔristə] (garde-)forestier *m*; habitant(e *f*) *m* d'une forêt; '**for·est·ry** sylviculture *f*.

fore...: '**~‑taste** avant-goût *m*; **~‑tell** [*irr.* (*tell*)] prédire, présager; '**~‑thought** prévoyance *f*; préméditation *f*; '**~‑top** ⚓ hune *f* de misaine; **~‑warn** avertir, prévenir; '**~‑wom·an** première ouvrière *f*; contremaîtresse *f*; '**~‑word** avant-propos *m*/*inv.*; préface *f*.

for·feit ['fɔːfit] **1.** confisqué; **2.** confiscation *f*; amende *f*; gage *m*;

punition *f*; ✝ dédit *m*; *sp.* forfait *m*; *jeu*: **~***s pl.* gages *m*/*pl.*; **3.** confisquer, perdre; forfaire à (*l'honneur*); '**for·feit·a·ble** confiscable; **for·fei·ture** ['~tʃə] confiscation *f*, perte *f*.

for·gath·er [fɔː'gæðə] s'assembler. **for·gave** [fə'geiv] *prét. de forgive.* **forge**[1] [fɔːdʒ] (*usu.* **~** *ahead*) avancer à toute vitesse *ou* à travers les obstacles.

forge[2] [fɔːdʒ] **1.** forge *f*; **2.** forger (*a. fig. une excuse etc.*); contrefaire (*une signature etc.*); inventer; '**forg·er** forgeron *m*; faussaire *mf*; faux-monnayeur *m*; '**for·ger·y** falsification *f*; contrefaçon *f*; faux *m*.

for·get [fə'get] [*irr.*] oublier; F *I* **~** j'ai oublié, ça m'échappe; **for'get·ful** □ [~ful] oublieux (-euse *f*); **for'get·ful·ness** oubli *m*; négligence *f*; **for'get‑me‑not** ♀ myosotis *m*, F ne-m'oubliez-pas *m*.

for·give [fə'giv] [*irr.*] pardonner (à q., s.o.); faire remise de (*une dette*); **for'giv·en** *p.p. de forgive*; **for'give·ness** pardon *m*; clémence *f*; **for'giv·ing** □ clément; peu rancunier (-ère *f*).

for·go [fɔː'gou] [*irr.* (*go*)] renoncer à; s'abstenir de.

for·got [fə'gɔt], **for'got·ten** [~n] *prét. et p.p. de forget.*

fork [fɔːk] **1.** *table*: fourchette *f*; ✔, *routes*: fourche *f*; *tuning* **~** diapason *m*; **2.** fourcher; F **~** *out* *v*/*t.* allonger (*de l'argent*); *v*/*i.* casquer, cracher; '**forked** fourchu; en fourche.

for·lorn [fə'lɔːn] abandonné, perdu, désespéré; **~** *hope* ✗ enfants *m*/*pl.* perdus; troupe *f* sacrifiée; *fig.* tentative *f* désespérée.

form [fɔːm] **1.** forme *f*; taille *f*; formule *f*, bulletin *m*, feuille *f* (*d'impôts*); *école*: classe *f*; banc *m*; *lièvre*: gîte *m*; *sp. in* **~** en forme; *in good* **~** en haleine; *that is bad* **~** c'est de mauvais ton; cela ne se fait pas; **2.** *v*/*t.* former, faire; organiser; établir; contracter (*une alliance, une habitude*); arrêter (*un plan*); ✗ se mettre en; *v*/*i.* se former; prendre forme; ✗ se ranger; **~** *up* se former en rang.

for·mal □ ['fɔːml] cérémonieux (-euse *f*); formel(le *f*); en règle; régulier (-ère *f*) (*jardin*); '**for·mal·ist** formaliste *mf*; **for·mal·i·ty**

[fɔ:'mæliti] formalité *f*; *maintien*: raideur *f*; cérémonie *f*; **for·mal·ize** ['fɔ:məlaiz] donner une forme (conventionnelle) à.

for·ma·tion [fɔ:'meiʃn] formation *f* (*a.* ✕, *a. géol.*); disposition *f*, ordre *m*; ✕ vol *m* de groupe; **form·a·tive** ['fɔ:mətiv] formateur (-trice *f*).

form·er[1] ['fɔ:mə] façonneur (-euse *f*) *m*; ⊕ gabarit *m*.

for·mer[2] [~] précédent; ancien(ne *f*); antérieur; premier (-ère *f*); '**for·mer·ly** autrefois, jadis.

for·mic ['fɔ:mik]: ~ *acid* acide *m* formique.

for·mi·da·ble □ ['fɔ:midəbl] formidable (*a. fig.*), redoutable.

form·less □ ['fɔ:mlis] informe.

for·mu·la ['fɔ:mjulə], *pl.* **-lae** ['~li:], **-las** formule *f*; **for·mu·lar·y** ['~ləri] 1. rituel(le *f*); prescrit; 2. formulaire *m*; **for·mu·late** ['~leit] formuler; **for·mu·la·tion** formulation *f*.

for·ni·cate ['fɔ:nikeit] forniquer; **for·ni·ca·tion** fornication *f*.

for·sake [fə'seik] [*irr.*] abandonner, délaisser; renoncer à; **for'sak·en** *p.p. de* forsake.

for·sook [fə'suk] *prét. de* forsake.

for·sooth *iro.* [fə'su:θ] ma foi!

for·swear [fɔ:'swɛə] [*irr.* (*swear*)] renier, répudier; ~ *o.s.* se parjurer; **for'sworn** parjure.

fort [fɔ:t] ✕ fort *m*; forteresse *f*.

forte [~] *fig.* fort *m*.

forth [fɔ:θ] *lieu*: en avant; *temps*: désormais; *and so* ~ et ainsi de suite; *from this day* ~ à partir de ce jour; dès maintenant; ~'**com·ing** qui arrive; futur; prochain; prêt à paraître; *be* ~ paraître; ne pas se faire attendre; '~**right** 1. *adj.* franc(he *f*); 2. *adv.* carrément; '~'**with** tout de suite.

for·ti·eth ['fɔ:tiiθ] quarantième (*a. su./m*).

for·ti·fi·ca·tion [fɔ:tifi'keiʃn] fortification *f* (*a.* ✕); **for·ti·fi·er** ['~faiə] fortificateur *m*; *boisson etc.*: fortifiant *m*; **for·ti·fy** ['~fai] ✕ fortifier (*a. fig.*); **for·ti·tude** ['~tju:d] courage *m*, fortitude *f*.

fort·night ['fɔ:tnait] quinze jours *m/pl.*; quinzaine *f*; *this day* ~ d'aujourd'hui en quinze; '**fort·night·ly** 1. *adj.* bimensuel(le *f*); 2. *adv.* tous les quinze jours.

for·tress ['fɔ:tris] forteresse *f*.

for·tu·i·tous □ [fɔ:'tjuitəs] fortuit; **for'tu·i·tous·ness, for'tu·i·ty** fortuité *f*; casualité *f*.

for·tu·nate ['fɔ:tʃnit] heureux (-euse *f*); ~*ly usu.* par bonheur, heureusement.

for·tune ['fɔ:tʃn] fortune *f*; sort *m*, destinée *f*; chance *f*; richesses *f/pl.*; ♀ ['fɔ:tju:n] Fortune *f*, Destin *m*; *good* ~ bonheur *m*; *bad* ~, *ill* ~ malheur *m*, mauvaise chance *f*; *marry a* ~ faire un riche mariage; '~**hunt·er** coureur *m* de dots; '~**tel·ler** diseur (-euse *f*) *m* de bonne aventure.

for·ty ['fɔ:ti] quarante (*a. su./m*). *Am.* ~**-niner** chercheur *m* d'or de 1849; F ~ *winks pl.* petit somme *m*.

fo·rum ['fɔ:rəm] forum *m*; F tribunal *m*.

for·ward ['fɔ:wəd] 1. *adj.* de devant, d'avant; avancé; précoce; effronté; impatient; ♦ à terme; 2. *adv.* en avant; sur l'avant; ♦ *carried* ~ à reporter; *from this time* ~ désormais, à l'avenir; 3. *su.* foot. avant *m*; 4. *v/t.* avancer, favoriser; expédier; faire suivre; *poste*: *please* ~ prière de faire suivre; '**for·ward·er** expéditeur (-trice *f*) *m*.

for·ward·ing ['fɔ:wədiŋ] expédition *f*, avancement *m*; ~ *address* adresse *f* (pour faire suivre le courrier); ~ *agent* expéditeur *m*; entrepreneur *m* de transports.

for·ward·ness ['fɔ:wədnis] empressement *m*; précocité *f*; hardiesse *f*; présomption *f*; **for·wards** ['fɔ:wədz] en avant.

fosse [fɔs] ✕ fossé *m*; *anat.* fosse *f*.

fos·sil ['fɔsl] fossile (*a. su./m*.).

fos·ter ['fɔstə] 1. *fig.* nourrir, encourager; ~ *up* élever; 2. adoptif (-ive *f*) (*p.ex.* ~-*brother*); ~ *home* famille *f* adoptive *ou* nourricière; '**fos·ter·age** mise *f* en nourrice; fonctions *f/pl.* de nourrice; '**fos·ter·er** parent *m* adoptif; *fig.* promoteur (-trice *f*) *m*; '**fos·ter·ling** nourrison(ne *f*) *m*.

fought [fɔ:t] *prét. et p.p. de* fight.

foul [faul] 1. □ infect (*a.* haleine); sale (*a. temps*, *a.* ♦ carène); *fig.* dégoûtant; ♦ engagé (*ancre etc.*); ♦ gros(se *f*) (*temps*); ♦ contraire (*vent*); *box.* bas(se *f*) (*coup*); encrassé (*fusil*); déloyal (-aux *m/pl.*)

(*jeu*); bourbeux (-euse *f*) (*eau*); atroce, infâme (*action*); impur (*pensée*); grossier (-ère *f*) (*mot. etc.*); ⁓ tongue langage *m* ordurier; *fall* (*ou run*) ⁓ *of* ⚓ entrer en collision avec; *fig.* se brouiller avec; **2.** ⚓ collision *f*; *sp.* faute *f*; *box.* coup *m* bas; *foot.* poussée *f* irrégulière; **3.** (s')engager; (s')encrasser; *v/t.* salir; souiller; *sp.* commettre une faute contre; ⚓ entrer en collision avec; ⁓**-mouthed** ['⁓'mauðd] mal embouché; au langage ordurier.

found[1] [faund] *prét. et p.p. de* **find** 1.

found[2] [⁓] fonder (*a. fig.*); établir.

found[3] ⊕ [⁓] fondre; mouler (*la fonte*).

foun·da·tion [faun'deiʃn] fondation *f*; ⚠, *a. fig.* fondement *m*; base *f*; établissement *m*; **foun'da·tion-school** école *f* dotée; **foun'da·tion-stone** première pierre *f*.

found·er[1] ['faundə] fondateur *m*; auteur *m*; fondeur *m*; ⁓ **member** membre *m* fondateur.

found·er[2] [⁓] *v/i.* ⚓ sombrer, couler à fond; *fig.* échouer; s'effondrer (*cheval, maison, etc.*); s'enfoncer; *v/t.* ⚓ couler; outrer (*un cheval*).

found·ling ['faundliŋ] enfant *mf* trouvé(e).

found·ress ['faundris] fondatrice *f*.

found·ry ⊕ ['faundri] fonderie *f*.

fount [faunt] *poét.* source *f*; *typ.* [*usu.* fɔnt] fonte *f*.

foun·tain ['fauntin] fontaine *f*; jet *m* d'eau; *fig.* source *f*; ⊕ distributeur *m*; '⁓**head** source *f* (*a. fig.*); '⁓**-'pen** stylographe *m*, F stylo *m*.

four [fɔ:] quatre (*a. su./m*); '**four-eyes** *sg.* F binoclard(e *f*) *m*; '**four-'flush·er** *Am. sl.* bluffeur *m*, vantard *m*; '**four-fold** quadruple; '**four-in-hand** voiture *f* à quatre chevaux; '**four-'let·ter word** mot *m* obscène, obscénité *f*; '**four-'square** carré (-ment *adv.*); *fig.* inébranlable (*devant, to*); '**four-'stroke** *mot.* à quatre temps; **four·teen** ['⁓'ti:n] quatorze (*a. su./m*); **four·teenth** ['⁓'ti:nθ] quatorzième (*a. su./m*); **fourth** [fɔ:θ] quatrième (*a. su./m*); ♩ quart *m*; '**fourth·ly** en quatrième lieu; '**four'wheel·er** fiacre *m*.

fowl [faul] **1.** poule *f*; volaille *f* (*a. cuis.*); **2.** faire la chasse au gibier; oiseler (*au filet*); '**fowl·er** oiseleur *m*.

fowl·ing ['fauliŋ] chasse *f* aux oiseaux; '⁓**-piece** fusil *m* de chasse.

fox [fɔks] **1.** renard *m*; **2.** *sl.* tromper; '⁓**-brush** queue *f* de renard; '⁓**earth** terrier *m*; **foxed** ['⁓t] piqué (*papier, bière, etc.*).

fox···: '⁓**glove** ♀ digitale *f*; F gantelée *f*; '⁓**hole** ⚔ nid *m* d'embusqués; '⁓**hound** chien *m* courant; fox-hound *m*; '⁓**hunt** chasse *f* au renard; '⁓**trot** fox-trot *m/inv.*; '**fox·y** rusé; astucieux (-euse *f*); roux (rousse *f*); piqué.

fra·cas ['fræka:] fracas *m*; *sl.* bagarre *f*.

frac·tion ♣ ['frækʃn] fraction *f*; *fig.* fragment *m*; '**frac·tion·al** □ fractionnaire; ⌒ fractionné.

frac·tious □ ['frækʃəs] revêche; difficile; maussade.

frac·ture ['fræktʃə] **1.** fracture *f* (*souv.* ⚕); **2.** briser; ⚕ fracturer.

frag·ile □ ['frædʒail] fragile; *fig.* faible; **fra·gil·i·ty** [frə'dʒiliti] fragilité *f*; faiblesse *f*.

frag·ment ['frægmənt] fragment *m*; morceau *m*; '**frag·men·tar·y** □ fragmentaire; *géol.* clastique.

fra·grance ['freigrəns] parfum *m*; bonne odeur *f*; '**fra·grant** □ parfumé, odoriférant.

frail[1] □ ['freil] peu solide; fragile; frêle (*personne*), délicat; '**frail·ty** *fig.* faiblesse *f* morale; défaut *m*.

frail[2] [⁓] cabas *m*.

frame [freim] **1.** construction *f*, forme *f*; cadre *m* (*a.* ⚓ *de l'hélice*); ⊕ charpente *f*; métier *m*; ⚔ fuselage *m*; ⚓ carcasse *f* (*d'un navire*); ⚓ couple *m*; *fenêtre:* chambranle *m*; ⚘ châssis *m*; *télév.* trame *f*; ⁓ aerial antenne *f* en cadre; ⁓ house maison *f* à charpente de bois; ⁓ *of mind* état *m* d'esprit; **2.** former; construire; encadrer (*a. fig.*); ⊕ faire la charpente de (*un toit*); *fig.* imaginer; fabriquer; *surt. Am. sl.* ⁓ *up* monter une accusation contre (*q.*); truquer (*qch.*); '**fram·er** auteur *m*; encadreur *m*; '**frame-up** *surt. Am.* F coup *m* monté; '**frame·work** ⊕ squelette *m*; ⚠ bâti *m*; charpente *f*; *fig.* cadre *m*.

fran·chise 🏛 ['fræntʃaiz] franchise *f*, privilège *m*; *pol.* droit *m* de vote; *admin.* droit *m* de cité.

Fran·cis·can *eccl.* [fræn'siskən] franciscain(e *f*) *m* (*a. adj.*).

fran·gi·ble ['frændʒibl] frangible, fragile.

Frank¹ [fræŋk] Franc (Franque *f*) *m*; *npr.* François *m*.

frank² □ [~] franc(he *f*); sincère; ouvert.

frank·furt·er *Am.* ['fræŋkfətə] saucisse *f* de Francfort.

frank·in·cense ['fræŋkinsens] encens *m*. [sincérité *f*.]

frank·ness ['fræŋknis] franchise *f*,)

fran·tic ['fræntik] (~ally) frénétique; fou (fol *devant une voyelle ou un h muet*; folle *f*) (de, with).

fra·ter·nal □ [frə'tə:nl] fraternel(le *f*); **fra'ter·ni·ty** fraternité *f*; confrérie *f*; *Am. univ.* association *f* estudiantine; **frat·er·ni·za·tion** [frætənai'zeiʃn] fraternisation *f*; **'frat·er·nize** fraterniser (avec, with).

frat·ri·cide ['freitrisaid] fratricide *m*; *personne*: fratricide *mf*.

fraud [frɔ:d] fraude *f*; F déception *f*, duperie *f*; imposteur *m*; **fraud·u·lence** ['~juləns] caractère *m* frauduleux; **'fraud·u·lent** □ frauduleux (-euse *f*).

fraught *poét.* [frɔ:t]: ~ with plein de; gros(se *f*) de; fertile en.

fray¹ [frei] (s')érailler; (s')effiler; s'effranger (*faux col*).

fray² [~] bagarre *f*.

fraz·zle *surt. Am.* F ['fræzl] **1.** état *m* usé; *beat to a* ~ battre (*q.*) à plates coutures; **2.** (s')érailler.

freak [fri:k] caprice *m*; tour *m*; F excentrique *mf*, *un* drôle de type; F mordu *m*, fana *mf*; *a film* ~ un mordu du film; ~ *of nature* monstre *m*; phénomène *m*; **'freak·ish** □ capricieux (-euse *f*); fantasque; **freak out** *sl.* se défoncer.

freck·le ['frekl] **1.** tache *f* de rousseur; *fig.* point *m*; **2.** marquer *ou* se couvrir de taches de rousseur.

free [fri:] **1.** □ libre; en liberté; franc(he *f*); gratuit; exempt, débarrassé, affranchi (*de from, of*); prodigue (de, with); ✝ franco; ~ *of debt etc.* exempt ou quitte de dettes etc.; *he is* ~ *to* (*inf.*) il lui est permis de (*inf.*); ~ *and easy* sans gêne; ✝ ~ *enterprise* libre entreprise *f*; ~ *fight* mêlée *f* générale; bagarre *f*; ~ *port* port *m* franc; ~ *trade* libre échange *m*; ~ *wheel* roue *f* libre; *make* ~ prendre

des libertés (avec q., with s.o.); *make* ~ *to* (*inf.*) se permettre de (*inf.*); *make* ~ *with s.th.* se servir de qch. sans se gêner; *make s.o.* ~ *of a city* créer q. citoyen d'honneur; ⊕ *run* ~ marcher à vide; *set* ~ libérer; **2.** (from, of) libérer (de); dégager (de); débarrasser (de); exempter (de); affranchir (*un esclave*); **'~·boot·er** flibustier; F maraudeur *m*; **'free·dom** liberté *f*; indépendance *f*; franchise *f*; facilité *f*; familiarité *f*; ~ *of a city* citoyenneté *f* d'honneur d'une ville; ~ *of a company* maîtrise *f* d'une corporation; ~ *of the press* liberté *f* de la presse; ~ *of speech* franc-parler *m*; ~ *of worship* liberté *f* religieuse.

free...: **'~·hold** ⚏ propriété *f* foncière (perpétuelle et libre); **'~·hold·er** propriétaire *m* foncier; **'~·kick** *foot.* coup *m* franc; **'~·man** homme *m* libre; citoyen *m* (d'honneur); **'~·ma·son** franc-maçon (*pl.* francs-maçons) *m*; **'~·ma·son·ry** franc-maçonnerie *f*; **'~·stone** grès *m*; **'~·style** nage *f* libre; **'~·'think·er** libre penseur (-euse *f*) *m*; **'~·'think·ing**, **'~·'thought** libre pensée *f*; **'~·way** *Am.* mot. autoroute *f*.

freeze [fri:z] [*irr.*] **1.** *v/i.* (se) geler; se figer; ~ *to death* mourir de froid; *v/t.* (con)geler; glacer; bloquer (*les prix, les fonds*); geler (*des capitaux*); *sl.* ~ *out* évincer; **2.** gel *m* (*a. fig.*, *a.* ✝ *des crédits*); gelée *f*; ✝ *etc. a.* blocage *m*; *price* (*wage*) ~ blocage *m* des prix (*des salaires*); **'~·dry** lyophiliser; **'freez·er** congélateur *m*; sorbetière *f*; **'freez·ing** □ réfrigérant; glacial (-als *m/pl.*); ~ *of prices* blocage *m* des prix; ~ *compartment* congélateur *m*, compartiment *m* de congélation; ~-*mixture phys.* mélange *m* réfrigérant; ~-*point* point *m* de congélation.

freight [freit] **1.** fret *m* (*a. prix*); cargaison *f*; *attr. Am.* de marchandises; ~ *out* (*home*) fret *m* de sortie (de retour); ~ *plane* avion-cargo *m* (*pl.* avions-cargo); *Am.* ~ *train* train *m* de marchandises; ~ *yard* dépôt des marchandises; **2.** (af)fréter; **'freight·age** *see* freight 1; **'freight-car** *Am.* 🚃 wagon *m* de marchandises; **'freight·er** affréteur *m*; navire *m* de charge; *Am.* consignateur (-trice *f*) *m*; *Am.* convoi *m*; *Am. see* freight-car.

French [frentʃ] **1.** français; ~ *beans*

haricots *m*/*pl.* verts; *cuis.* ~ *dressing* vinaigrette *f*; *cuis.* ~ *fried potatoes,* *Am. a.* ~ *fries* (pommes *f*/*pl.* [de terre] frites *f*/*pl.*; *take* ~ *leave* filer à l'anglaise; ~ *window* portefenêtre (*pl.* portes-fenêtres) *f*; 2. *ling.* français *m*, langue *f* française; *the* ~ *pl.* les Français *m*/*pl.*; '~·**man** Français *m*; '~·**wom·an** Française *f*.

fren·zied ['frenzid] forcené; fou (fol *devant une voyelle ou un h muet*; folle *f*); '**fren·zy** frénésie *f*; *fig.* transport *m*; $\cancel{s}$ délire *m*.

fre·quen·cy ['fri:kwənsi] fréquence *f* (*a.* $\cancel{f}$); **fre·quent 1.** □ ['~kwənt] fréquent; très répandu; 2. [~'kwent] fréquenter; hanter; **fre·quen'ta·tion** fréquentation *f* (de, *of*); **fre·'quent·er** habitué(e *f*) *m*; familier (-ère *f*) *m*.

fres·co ['freskou], *pl.* -**co**(**e**)**s** ['~kouz] (peinture *f* à) fresque *f*.

fresh [freʃ] **1.** □ frais (fraîche *f*); récent; nouveau (-el *devant une voyelle ou un h muet*; -elle *f*; -eaux *m*/*pl.*); éveillé; *Am. sl.* effronté; ~ *water* eau *f* fraîche; eau *f* douce (= *non salée*); 2. fraîcheur *f* (*du matin etc.*); crue *f*; '**fresh·en** *vt*/*i.* rafraîchir; '**fresh·er** *Brit. sl. pour* *freshman*; **fresh·et** ['~it] courant *m* d'eau douce; inondation *f*; '**fresh-fro·zen** frais (fraîche *f*) frigorifié; '**fresh·man** *univ.* étudiant(e *f*) *m* de première année; '**fresh·ness** fraîcheur *f*; nouveauté *f*; '**fresh-wa·ter** d'eau douce; *Am.* ~ *college* petit collège *m* de province.

fret[1] [fret] **1.** agitation *f*; irritation *f*; **2.** (se) ronger; (se) frotter; (s')irriter; (s')inquiéter; *v*/*i.* s'agiter (*eau*); *v*/*t.* érailler (*un cordage*); ~ *away*, ~ *out* éroder.

fret[2] [~] **1.** $\triangle$ frette *f*; **2.** sculpter; *fig.* bigarrer.

fret[3] [~] ♪ touche(tte) *f*; ~*ted in-strument* instrument *m* à touchettes.

fret·ful □ ['fretful] chagrin.

fret-saw ['fretsɔ:] scie *f* à découper.

fret·work ['fretwɔ:k] ouvrage *m* à claire-voie; découpage *m*.

Freud·i·an ['frɔidjən] freudien(ne *f*); ~ *slip* lapsus *m*.

fri·a·bil·i·ty [fraiə'biliti] friabilité *f*; '**fri·a·ble** friable.

fri·ar ['fraiə] moine *m*, frère *m*; '**fri·ar·y** monastère *m*; couvent *m*.

frib·ble ['fribl] **1.** baguenauder; gaspiller (*de l'argent*); **2.** frivolité *f*; *personne*: baguenaudier *m*.

fric·as·see [frikə'si:] **1.** fricassée *f*; **2.** fricasser.

fric·tion ['frikʃn] friction *f* ($\cancel{s}$, *a.* *fig.*); frottement *m*; *Am.* ~ *tape* chatterton *m*, ruban *m* isolant; '**fric·tion·al** à *ou* de frottement *ou* friction; '**fric·tion·less** □ sans frottement.

Fri·day ['fraidi] vendredi *m*.

fridge *Brit.* F [fridʒ] frigo *m*.

friend [frend] ami(e *f*) *m*; connais-sance *f*; ♀ Quaker(esse *f*) *m*; *his* ~*s* *pl. souv.* ses connaissances *f*/*pl.*; *make* ~*s with* se lier d'amitié avec; '**friend·less** sans ami(s); abandon-né; '**friend·ly** amical (-aux *m*/*pl.*); ami; bienveillant; *fig.* intime; ♀ *Society Brit.* société *f* de secours mutuel; '**friend·ship** amitié *f*.

frieze [fri:z] frise *f* (*tex., a.* $\triangle$).

frig·ate ⚓ ['frigit] frégate *f*.

fright [frait] peur *f*, effroi *m*, épou-vante *f*; F épouvantail *m*; '**fright·en** effrayer, faire peur à; *be* ~*ed at* (*ou of*) avoir peur de; **fright·ful** □ ['~ful] affreux (-euse *f*); '**fright-ful·ness** horreur *f*.

frig·id □ ['fridʒid] glacial (-als *m*/*pl.*); froid (*a. fig.*); **fri·gid·i·ty** frigidité *f*; (grande) froideur *f*.

frill [fril] **1.** ruche *f*; jabot *m*; F *fig.* *put on* ~*s* faire des façons; **2.** plisser, rucher.

fringe [frindʒ] **1.** frange *f*; bord (-ure *f*) *m*; *forêt*: lisière *f*; *a.* ~*s pl.* cheveux *m*/*pl.* à la chien; ~ *benefits pl.* avantages *m*/*pl.* supplémentaires; ~ *group* groupe *m* marginal; **2.** franger; border.

frip·per·y ['fripəri] **1.** camelote *f*; faste *m*; **2.** sans valeur; de camelote.

frisk [frisk] **1.** gambade *f*, cabriole *f*; **2.** gambader; '**frisk·i·ness** vivacité *f*; '**frisk·y** □ vif (vive *f*); fringant (*cheval*); animé.

frith [friθ] *see firth*.

frit·ter ['fritə] **1.** beignet *m*; **2.** ~ *away* gaspiller.

fri·vol·i·ty [fri'vɔliti] frivolité *f*; légèreté *f* d'esprit; **friv·o·lous** □ ['frivələs] frivole; léger (-ère *f*); futile, vain; évaporé (*personne*).

frizz [friz] frisotter; *cuis.* faire frire; *a. see frizzle 2*; **friz·zle** ['~l] **1.** cheveux *m*/*pl.* crêpelés; **2.** (*a.* ~ *up*) frisotter; v/t. cuis. griller (qch.); v/i. grésiller; **'friz·z(l)y** crêpelé, frisotté.

fro [frou]: to and ~ çà et là, de long en large.

frock [frɔk] moine: froc m; (usu. ~-coat) femme, enfant: robe f; redingote f; ✗ tunique f de petite tenue.

frog [frɔg] grenouille f; cost. soutache f; ♥ (cœur m de) croisement m; ✗ porte-épée m/inv.; **'~·man** homme-grenouille (pl. hommesgrenouilles) m.

frol·ic ['frɔlik] 1. gambades f/pl.; ébats m/pl., jeu m; escapade f; divertissement m; 2. folâtrer, gambader; **frol·ic·some** □ ['~səm] folâtre, gai, joyeux (-euse f) m.

from [frɔm; frəm] prp. de; depuis; à partir de; par suite de; de la part de; par; defend ~ protéger contre; draw ~ nature dessiner d'après nature; drink ~ boire dans; hide ~ cacher à; remove ~ enlever à; ~ above d'en haut; ~ amidst d'entre; ~ before dès avant.

front [frʌnt] 1. devant m; premier rang m; façade f; boutique: devanture f; promenade f (au bord de la mer); ✗ front m; chemise: plastron m; F prête-nom m (pl. prête-noms), façade f; in ~ of devant, en face de; two-pair ~ chambre f sur le devant au deuxième; fig. come to the ~ se faire connaître; arriver au premier rang; 2. antérieur, de devant; ✗ u. fig. ~ line front m, première ligne f, ligne f de contact; mot. ~ wheel drive traction f avant; ~ yard Am. jardin m de devant; 3. v/t. (a. ~ on, towards) faire face à; donner sur; braver; Am. F prêter son nom à, agir en homme de paille pour; v/i. regarder front; **'front·age** △ façade f; **'fron·tal** 1. frontal (-aux m/pl.); de face; de front; 2. △ façade f; eccl. devant m d'autel; **fron·tier** ['~jə] frontière f; surt. Am. hist. frontière f des États occidentaux; **'fron·tier·run·ner** passeur m de frontière; **fron·tiers·man** ['~jezmən] frontalier m; hist. Am. broussard m; **fron·tis·piece** ['~ispi:s] △, a. typ. frontispice m; **front·let** ['~lit] cost. bandeau m; **front page** journ. première page f; **'front-page** en première page.

frost [frɔst] 1. (a. hoar ~, white ~) gelée f blanche, givre m; F fiasco m, déception f; black ~ froid m noir; 2. geler; saupoudrer; givrer; dépolir (un verre); ⊕ glacer (le métal); ~ed glass verre m dépoli; **'~-bite** gelure f; **'frost-bit·ten** gelé; ✗ brûlé par le froid; **'frost·i·ness** froid m glacial; fig. froideur f; **'frost·y** □ gelé; glacial (-als m/pl.) (a. fig.); couvert de givre.

froth [frɔθ] 1. écume f; mousse f; fig. paroles f/pl. creuses; 2. écumer, mousser; moutonner (mer); **'froth-i·ness** état m écumeux etc.; fig. manque m de substance; **'froth·y** □ écumeux (-euse f); moutonneux (-euse f) (mer); vide, creux (creuse f).

frown [fraun] 1. froncement m de sourcils; air m désapprobateur; 2. v/t. ~ down imposer le silence à (q.) d'un regard sévère; v/i. froncer les sourcils; se renfrogner; avoir l'air menaçant (montagne etc.); ~ at, ~ (up)on regarder en fronçant les sourcils; fig. désapprouver.

frowst F [fraust] odeur f de renfermé; atmosphère f qui sent le renfermé; **'frowst·y** □, **frowz·y** ['frauzi] qui sent le renfermé; mal tenu, sale.

froze [frouz] prét. de freeze; **'frozen** 1. p.p. de freeze; 2. a. adj. gelé; frigorifié; bloqué (capital); ~ locker Am. chambre f frigorifique; ~ meat viande f frigorifiée.

fruc·ti·fi·ca·tion [frʌktifi'keiʃn] fructification f; **fruc·ti·fy** ['~fai] v/t. féconder; v/i. fructifier (a. fig.).

fru·gal □ ['fru:gəl] frugal (-aux m/pl.); économe; simple; **fru·gal·i·ty** [fru'gæliti] frugalité f; sobriété f.

fruit [fru:t] 1. fruit m (a. fig. = résultat); coll. fruits m/pl.; ~ cocktail macedoine f de fruits; ~ cup coupe f de fruits rafraîchis; ~ knife couteau m à fruits; 2. porter des fruits; **'fruit·age** fructification f; coll. fruits m/pl.; **frui·ta·ri·an** [fru:'tɛərjən] fruitarien(ne f) m; **'fruit·cake** cake m, gâteau m de fruits confits; **'fruit·er** arbre m fruitier; **'fruit·er·er** fruitier (-ère f) m; **fruit·ful** □ ['~ful] fructueux (-euse f); (a. fig. = profitable); fécond, fertile (en of, in); **fru·i·tion** [fru'iʃn] projet etc.: réalisation f;

come to ~ porter fruit; **'fruit·less** ☐
stérile; *fig.* vain; **'fruit·y** de fruit;
fruité; *fig.* corsé.

frump [frʌmp] *fig.* femme *f* fagotée;
'frump·ish, **'frump·y** mal attifée
(*femme*).

frus·trate [frʌs'treit] frustrer; déjouer; **frus'tra·tion** frustration *f*;
anéantissement *m*.

fry [frai] **1.** *cuis.* friture *f*; **2.** frai *m*,
fretin *m*; F *small* ~ petites gens *f/pl.*;
gosses *m/pl.*; **3.** (faire) frire; *see egg*;
fried potatoes (pommes *f/pl.* de
terre) frites *f/pl.*; **'fry·ing-pan**
poêle *f*; *get out of the* ~ *into the fire*
sauter de la poêle sur la braise.

fuch·sia ♀ ['fju:ʃə] fuchsia *m*.

fuck V [fʌk] **1.** baiser; **2.** merde (de la
merde)!, putain!

fud·dle ['fʌdl] **1.** *v/t.* griser; hébéter;
v/i. riboter; F se pocharder; **2.** ribote *f*.

fudge F [fʌdʒ] **1.** bousiller; cuisiner
(*les comptes*); **2.** bousillage *m*; *bonbon*: fondant *m*; ~! quelle bla-
gue!

fu·el ['fjuəl] **1.** combustible *m*; carburant *m*; *mot.* essence *f*; *mot.* ~
ga(u)ge jauge *f* d'essence; ~ *oil* fueloil
m; mazout *m*; ~ *tank* réservoir *m*
d'essence; **2.** *v/t.* pourvoir de combustibles; *v/i.* obtenir du combustible; *mot.* s'approvisionner en
essence.

fug [fʌg] **1.** touffeur *f*; forte odeur *f*
de renfermé; **2.** rester enfermé.

fu·ga·cious [fju:'geiʃəs] fugace;
éphémère.

fu·gi·tive ['fju:dʒitiv] **1.** fugitif
(-ive *f*) (*a. fig.*); **2.** fugitif (-ive *f*) *m*;
exilé(e *f*) *m*.

fu·gle·man ✗ ['fju:glmæn] chef *m*
de file; *fig.* chef *m*; porte-parole
m/inv.

fugue ♪ [fju:g] fugue *f*.

ful·crum ['fʌlkrəm], *pl.* -**cra** ['~krə]
⊕ pivot *m*; *fig.* point *m* d'appui.

ful·fil [ful'fil] remplir; accomplir;
s'acquitter de; réaliser; **ful'fill·er**
celui (celle *f*) *m* qui remplit *etc.*;
ful'fil·ment accomplissement *m*.

ful·gent *poét.* ['fʌldʒənt] resplendissant.

full¹ [ful] **1.** *adj.* ☐ plein; rempli;
entier (-ère *f*); complet (-ète *f*); comble; *cost.* large, ample; *at* ~ *length*
tout au long; ~ *employment* plein-
emploi *m*; *of* ~ *age* majeur; ~ *stop*

gramm. point *m*; **2.** *adv.* tout à fait;
en plein; précisément; parfaite-
ment; bien; ~ *nigh* tout près; F ~ *up*
au complet, comble; **3.** *su.* plein *m*;
cœur *m*, fort *m*; apogée *f*; *in* ~ intégralement; in extenso; *en toutes
lettres*; *pay in* ~ payer intégralement; *to the* ~ complètement, tout
à fait.

full² ⊕ [~] (re)fouler.

full...: '~-'**blown** épanoui; '~-'**bod-
ied** corsé (*vin*); ~ **dress** grande
tenue *f*; '~-**dress** de cérémonie;
solennel(le *f*); ~ *rehearsal* répétition *f* générale *ou* des couturières.

full·er ⊕ ['fulə] fouleur (-euse *f*)
m.

full-fledged ['ful'fledʒd] qui a
toutes ses plumes (*oiseau*); *fig.*
qualifié, achevé.

full·ing-mill ['fuliŋmil] foulon *m*.

full-length ['ful'leŋθ] (portrait *m*)
en pied; ~ *film* film *m* principal.

ful(l)·ness ['fulnis] plénitude *f*.

full...: '~-**orbed** dans son plein
(*lune*); '~-**time** de toute la journée;
à pleines journées; à temps plein.

ful·mi·nate ['fʌlmineit] fulminer
(*a. fig.* contre, *against*); faire explosion; **ful·mi·na·tion** fulmination *f*
(*a. fig.*); **ful·mi·na·to·ry** ['~ətəri]
fulminatoire.

ful·some ☐ ['fulsəm] excessif (-ive
f); répugnant (*flatterie*).

fum·ble ['fʌmbl] fouiller, tâtonner;
'fum·bler maladroit(e *f*) *m*.

fume [fju:m] **1.** fumée *f*, vapeur *f*;
in a ~ en rage, furieux (-euse *f*);
2. *v/i.* fumer (*a. fig.*); s'exhaler; *v/t.*
exposer à la fumée.

fu·mi·gate ['fju:migeit] fumiger;
désinfecter; **fu·mi·ga·tion** fumiga-
tion *f*.

fum·ing ☐ ['fju:miŋ] *fig.* enragé,
bouillonnant de colère.

fun [fʌn] amusement *m*, gaieté *f*;
have ~ s'amuser; *make* ~ *of* se moquer
de; *for* ~, *in* ~ pour rire, par plaisanterie, pour s'amuser.

func·tion ['fʌŋkʃn] **1.** fonction *f* (*a.
physiol.*, *a.* ♣); réception *f*, soirée *f*;
cérémonie *f*; **2.** fonctionner; **'func-
tion·al** ☐ fonctionnel(le *f*); **'func-
tion·ar·y** fonctionnaire *m*.

fund [fʌnd] **1.** fonds *m*; *fig.* trésors
m/pl.; ~*s pl.* fonds *m(pl.)*; capital *m*;
ressources *f/pl.* pécuniaires; *banque*:
provision *f*; **2.** consolider (*une dette*);

placer (*de l'argent*) dans les fonds publics.

fun·da·ment ['fʌndəmənt] fondement *m*; **fun·da·men·tal 1.** □ [~'mentl] fondamental (-aux *m/pl.*); essentiel(le *f*); **2.** ~*s pl.* principe *m*; premiers principes *m/pl.*

fu·ner·al ['fju:nərəl] **1.** funérailles *f/pl.*, obsèques *f/pl.*; **2.** funèbre; des morts; ~ **pile** bûcher *m* funéraire; **fu·ne·re·al** □ [~'niəriəl] funéraire; *fig.* lugubre, funèbre.

fun-fair ['fʌnfɛə] foire *f* aux plaisirs; parc *m* d'attractions.

fun·gous ['fʌŋgəs] fongueux (-euse *f*); **fun·gus** [~], *pl.* **-gi** ['~gai] ♧ champignon *m* mycète; ⚕ fongus *m*.

fu·nic·u·lar [fju'nikjulə] **1.** funiculaire; ~ *railway* = **2.** funiculaire *m*.

funk *sl.* [fʌŋk] **1.** frousse *f*, trac *m*; *personne*: caneur (-euse *f*) *m*; *blue* ~ peur *f* bleue; **2.** caner; avoir peur de (*qch.*); **'funk·y** *sl.* froussard.

fun·nel ['fʌnl] entonnoir *m*; ⊕ trémie *f*; ⚓, 🚂 cheminée *f*.

fun·ny □ ['fʌni] **1.** drôle, comique; curieux (-euse *f*); **2.** *funnies pl. see comics*; '~**-bone** ⚙ F petit juif *m*.

fur [fə:] **1.** fourrure *f*; *lapin*: pelage *m*; *bouilloire*: dépôt *m*; *langue*: enduit *m*; ~*s pl.* peaux *f/pl.*; ~ *coat* manteau *m* de fourrure; **3.** ⊕ (s')incruster; *v/t.* fourrer, garnir de fourrure; ~*red tongue* langue *f* chargée.

fur·be·low ['fə:bilou] falbala *m*; *usu.* ~*s pl. iro.* fanfreluches *f/pl.*

fur·bish ['fə:biʃ] polir, nettoyer; mettre à neuf.

fur·ca·tion [fə:'keiʃn] bifurcation *f*.

fu·ri·ous □ ['fjuəriəs] furieux (-euse *f*).

furl [fə:l] *v/t.* ferler (*une voile*); rouler (*un parapluie*); replier (*les ailes*); *v/i.* se rouler.

fur·long ['fə:lɔŋ] *mesure*: furlong *m* (*201 mètres*).

fur·lough ['fə:lou] **1.** permission *f*, congé *m*; **2.** ✕ envoyer (*q.*) en permission; *Am.* accorder un congé à.

fur·nace ['fə:nis] four(neau) *m*; *chaudière*: foyer *m*; *fig.* brasier *m*.

fur·nish ['fə:niʃ] fournir, munir, pourvoir (de, *with*); meubler, garnir (*une maison*); ~*ed rooms* meublé *m*; **'fur·nish·er** fournisseur *m*; marchand *m* d'ameublement; **'fur**

nish·ing fourniture *f*; provision *f*; ~*s pl.* ameublement *m*.

fur·ni·ture ['fə:nitʃə] meubles *m/pl.*; ameublement *m*; mobilier *m*; *typ.* garniture *f*; ⚓ matériel *m*.

fur·ri·er ['fʌriə] pelletier *m*; '**furri·er·y** pelleterie *f*.

fur·row ['fʌrou] **1.** sillon *m* (*a. fig.*); ⊕ cannelure *f*; **2.** labourer; sillonner; ⊕ canneler; rider profondément.

fur·ry ['fə:ri] qui ressemble à (de) la fourrure.

fur·ther ['fə:ðə] **1.** *adj. et adv.* plus éloigné; *see furthermore*; **2.** avancer; servir; '**fur·ther·ance** avancement *m*; appui *m*; '**fur·ther·er** celui (celle *f*) *m* qui aide à l'avancement (*de qch.*); '**fur·ther·more** en outre, de plus, d'autre part; '**further·most** le plus lointain, le plus éloigné.

fur·thest ['fə:ðist] *see furthermost*; *at* (*the*) ~ au plus tard.

fur·tive □ ['fə:tiv] furtif (-ive *f*).

fu·ry ['fjuəri] furie *f*, fureur *f*; acharnement *m*.

furze ♧ [fə:z] ajonc *m*, genêt *m* épineux.

fuse [fju:z] **1.** (se) fondre; (se) réunir par fusion; *v/t.* pourvoir d'une fusée; *v/i.* ⚡ sauter (*plombs*); **2.** ⚡ plomb *m*; fusible *m*; ✕ fusée *f*.

fu·see [fju:'zi:] montre *etc.*: fusée *f*; tison *m*.

fu·se·lage ['fju:zila:ʒ] ✈ fuselage *m*.

fu·si·bil·i·ty [fju:zə'biliti] fusibilité *f*.

fu·si·ble ['fju:zəbl] fusible.

fu·sil·ier ✕ [fju:zi'liə] fusilier *m*.

fu·sil·lade [fju:zi'leid] fusillade *f*.

fu·sion ['fju:ʒn] fusion *f*; fonte *f*.

fuss F [fʌs] **1.** agitation *f*, F potin *m*; façons *f/pl.*; *kick up a* ~ faire un tas d'histoires; **2.** *v/t.* tracasser, agiter; *v/i.* se tracasser (de, *over*); faire des histoires; faire l'empressé; '~**-pot** F enquiquineur (-euse *f*) *m*; coupeur (-euse *f*) *m* de cheveux en quatre; '**fuss·y** □ F tracassier (-ère *f*) tatillon(ne *f*).

fus·tian ['fʌstiən] ♧ futaine *f*; *fig.* emphase *f*.

fust·i·ness ['fʌstinis] odeur *f* de renfermé; *fig.* caractère *m* démodé; '**fust·y** □ qui sent le renfermé *ou* moisi; *fig.* démodé.

fu·tile □ ['fju:tail] futile; vain; pué

ril; **fu·til·i·ty** [fju'tiliti] futilité *f*; vanité *f*; puérilité *f*.

fu·ture ['fju:tʃə] **1.** futur; à venir; **2.** avenir *m*; *in the* ~ à l'avenir; † ~*s pl.* livraisons *f/pl.* à terme; **'fu·tur·ism** *peint.* futurisme *m*;

fu·tu·ri·ty [fju'tjuəriti] avenir *m*. **fuzz** [fʌz] **1.** duvet *m*; *a* ~ *of hair* des cheveux bouffants; *sl. the* ~ les flics *m/pl.*, la flicaille; **2.** (faire) bouffer; (faire) frisotter; **'fuzz·y** □ bouffant; frisotté; flou (*a. phot.*).

G

G, g [dʒiː] G *m*, g *m*.

gab F [gæb] faconde *f*; *the gift of the* ~ la langue bien pendue.

gab·ble ['gæbl] 1. bredouillement *m*; caquet *m*; 2. bredouiller; caqueter; **'gab·bler** bredouilleur (-euse *f*) *m*; caquetage *m*.

gab·by ['gæbi] bavard.

gab·er·dine ['gæbədiːn] *tex.* gabardine *f*.

ga·ble ['geibl] (*a.* ~-end) pignon *m*.

ga·by ['geibi] nigaud *m*, benêt *m*.

gad [gæd]: ~ *about* courir (le monde *etc.*); ♀ *poét.* errer; **'gad·a·bout** F coureur (-euse *f*) *m*.

gad·fly *zo.* ['gædflai] taon *m*; œstre *m*.

gadg·et F ['gædʒit] dispositif *m*; machin *m*, truc *m*.

Gael·ic ['geilik] gaélique (*a.* *ling.* *su./m*).

gaff [gæf] gaffe *f*; ♆ corne *f*; *sl.* théâtre *m* de bas étage; *blow the* ~ *sl.* vendre la mèche.

gaffe F [gæf] bêtise *f*; faux pas *m*.

gaf·fer F ['gæfə] † ancien *m*; contremaître *m*; patron *m*.

gag [gæg] 1. bâillon *m* (*a. fig.*); *parl.* clôture *f*; *théá.* improvisation *f*; plaisanterie *f*; F blague *f*; *sl. what's the* ~? à quoi vise tout cela?; 2. *v/t.* bâillonner (*a. fig. la presse*); *pol.* clôturer (*un débat*); *v/i. théá.* improviser; plaisanter.

gage [geidʒ] gage *m*, garantie *f*; F défi *m*.

gai·e·ty ['geiəti] gaieté *f*; réjouissances *f/pl*.

gai·ly ['geili] *adv. de gay*.

gain [gein] 1. gain *m*; *surt.* ✝ ~s *pl.* profit *m*; 2. gagner, profiter; ~ *on* gagner sur; ~ *s.o. over* gagner q. à sa cause; **'gain·er** gagnant(e *f*) *m*; gagneur (-euse *f*) *m* (*d'argent*); **gain·ful** □ ['~ful] profitable; ~ *employment* travail *m* rémunéré; *be* ~ly *occupied* avoir un travail rémunéré; **gain·ings** ['~iŋz] *pl.* gain *m*, -s *m/pl.*; profit *m.* [nier (*qch.*).)

gain·say † [gein'sei] contredire;}

gait [geit] allure *f*; *cheval*: train *m*.

gai·ter ['geitə] guêtre *f*.

gal *Am. sl.* [gæl] jeune fille *f*.

ga·la ['gɑːlə] fête *f*, gala *m*.

gal·ax·y ['gæləksi] *astr.* voie *f* lactée; *fig.* essaim *m*; constellation *f*.

gale [geil] grand vent *m*; tempête *f*.

gall[1] [gɔːl] fiel *m* (*a. fig.*); *surt. Am. sl.* audace *f*; toupet *m*; ~ *bladder* vésicule *f* biliaire; ~ *stone* calcul *m* biliaire.

gall[2] ♀ [~] galle *f*.

gall[3] [~] 1. écorchure *f*; *fig.* blessure *f*; 2. écorcher; *fig.* froisser, blesser; irriter.

gal·lant ['gælənt] 1. □ vaillant; superbe; galant; 2. galant *m*; *péj.* coureur *m* de femmes; 3. faire le galant; **'gal·lant·ry** vaillance *f*; galanterie *f* (*auprès des femmes*).

gal·ler·y ['gæləri] galerie *f* (*a.* ⚒).

gal·ley ['gæli] ♆ † galère *f*; ♆ cuisine *f*; *typ.* galée *f*; **'~-proof** *typ.* placard *m*.

Gal·lic ['gælik] gaulois; **Gal·li·can** ['~kən] *eccl.* gallican.

gal·li·vant ['gæliˌvænt] courailler.

gall·nut ♀ ['gɔːlnʌt] noix *f* de galle.

gal·lon ['gælən] gallon *m* (*4,54 litres, Am. 3,78 litres*).

gal·loon [gəˈluːn] galon *m*.

gal·lop ['gæləp] 1. galop *m*; 2. (faire) aller au galop.

gal·lows ['gælouz] *usu. sg.* potence *f*.

ga·lore [gəˈlɔː] à foison.

ga·losh [gəˈlɔʃ] galoche *f*; ~s *pl.* caoutchoucs *m/pl*.

gal·van·ic [gælˈvænik] (~ally) galvanique; **gal·va·nism** ['gælvənizm] galvanisme *m*; **'gal·va·nize** galvaniser (*a. fig.*); **gal·va·no·plas·tic** [gælvənoˈplæstik] galvanoplastique.

gam·ble ['gæmbl] 1. *v/i.* jouer de l'argent; *v/t.* ~ *away* perdre (*qch.*) au jeu; 2. F jeu *m* de hasard; *fig.* affaire *f* de chance; **'gam·bler** joueur (-euse *f*) *m*; ✝ spéculateur (-trice *f*) *m*; **'gam·bling-house** maison *f* de jeu. [gutte (*pl.* gommes-guttes) *f*.)

gam·boge ♀ [gæmˈbuːʒ] gomme-}

gam·bol ['gæmbl] 1. cabriole *f*; 2. cabrioler; s'ébattre.

game [geim] 1. jeu *m*; amusement *m*; *cartes*: partie *f*; *péj.* manège *m*; *cuis. etc.* gibier *m*; *play the* ~ jouer franc jeu; *fig.* agir loyalement; 2. F courageux (-euse *f*); *die* ~ mourir crânement; 3. jouer; '~**cock** coq *m* de combat; '~**keep·er** garde-chasse (*pl.* gardes-chasse[s]) *m*; '~**li·cence** permis *m* de chasse; **game·ster** ['~stə] joueur (-euse *f*) *m*.

gam·mer ['gæmə] vieille *f*.

gam·mon¹ ['gæmən] 1. quartier *m* de lard fumé; jambon *m* fumé; 2. saler et fumer.

gam·mon² [~] 1. bredouille *f* (*au jeu*); blague *f*; *sl.* ~! quelle bêtise!; 2. blaguer.

gam·my F ['gæmi] estropié; boiteux (-euse *f*).

gam·ut ♪ ['gæmət] gamme *f* (*a. fig.*).

gam·y ['geimi] giboyeux (-euse *f*); *cuis.* faisandé.

gan·der ['gændə] jars *m*; *Am. sl.* coup *m* d'œil.

gang [gæŋ] 1. groupe *m*; troupe *f*; bande *f*; équipe *f*; *péj.* clique *f*; 2. ~ *up* se liguer (contre *against, on*); '~**board** ⚓ planche *f* à débarquer; **gang·er** ['gæŋə] chef *m* d'équipe.

gan·grene 🌿 ['gæŋgriːn] gangrène *f*, mortification *f*.

gang·ster *Am.* ['gæŋstə] bandit *m*, gangster *m*.

gang·way ['gæŋwei] passage *m*, couloir *m*; ⚓ passerelle *f* de service; ⚓ coupée *f*.

gaol [dʒeil] *see* jail.

gap [gæp] trou *m* (*a. fig.*); ouverture *f*; brèche *f*; interstice *m*.

gape [geip] rester bouche bée (de- vant, *at*); s'ouvrir tout grand (*abîme*). [rage *m*; 2. *mot.* garer.]

ga·rage ['gæraːʒ; 'gæridʒ] 1. ga-]

garb [gaːb] costume *m*, vêtement *m*.

gar·bage *surt. Am.* ['gaːbidʒ] ordu- res *f/pl.*; immondices *f/pl.*; ~ *can* boîte *f* aux ordures; ~ *collector* (é)boueur *m*, boueux *m*; ~ *pail* poubelle *f*.

gar·ble ['gaːbl] fausser; tronquer.

gar·den ['gaːdn] 1. jardin *m*; 2. *v/i.* jardiner, faire du jardinage; *v/t.* entretenir; '**gar·den·er** jardinier *m*; '**gar·den·ing** jardinage *m*; horticul- ture *f*.

gar·gan·tu·an [gaː'gæntjuən] gar- gantuesque.

gar·gle ['gaːgl] 1. se gargariser; 2. gargarisme *m*.

gar·goyle 🔺 ['gaːgɔil] gargouille *f*.

gar·ish □ ['gɛəriʃ] voyant; cru (*lu- mière*).

gar·land ['gaːlənd] 1. guirlande *f*, couronne *f*; 2. (en)guirlander.

gar·lic ♀ ['gaːlik] ail (*pl.* aulx, ails) *m*.

gar·ment ['gaːmənt] vêtement *m*.

gar·ner ['gaːnə] 1. grenier *m*; *fig.* recueil *m*; 2. mettre en grenier.

gar·net *min.* ['gaːnit] grenat *m*.

gar·nish ['gaːniʃ] garnir, orner, em- bellir (de, *with*); '**gar·nish·ing** gar- nissage *m*; *cuis.* garniture *f*.

gar·ni·ture ['gaːnitʃə] garniture *f*.

gar·ret ['gærit] mansarde *f*.

gar·ri·son ✖ ['gærisn] 1. garnison *f*; 2. mettre une garnison dans; mettre (*des troupes*) en garnison; garnir; *be* ~*ed* être en garnison.

gar·ru·li·ty [gæ'ruːliti] loquacité *f*; *style*: verbosité *f*; **gar·ru·lous** □ ['gæruləs] loquace; verbeux (-euse *f*).

gar·ter ['gaːtə] jarretière *f*; *Am.* jar- retelles *f/pl.*; *Order of the* ♀ Ordre *m* de la jarretière.

gas [gæs] 1. gaz *m*; F bavardage *m*; *Am. see* gasoline; *mot. step on the* ~ appuyer sur le champignon; *fig.* se dépêcher; 2. asphyxier; ✖ gazer; F jaser; '~**bag** ♐ enveloppe *f* à gaz; F grand parleur *m*; phraseur *m*; ~ **brack·et** applique *f* à gaz; '~**burn- er** bec *m* de gaz; '~**cook·er** cuisi- nière *f* à gaz; **gas·e·lier** [~ə'liə] lustre *m* à gaz; '**gas-en·gine** moteur *m* à gaz; **gas·e·ous** ['geiziəs] gazeux (-euse *f*); '**gas-fit·ter** gazier *m*; poseur *m* d'appareils à gaz; '**gas- fit·tings** *pl.* appareillage *m* pour le gaz.

gash [gæʃ] 1. entaille *f* (*dans la chair*); taillade *f*; balafre *f* (*dans la figure*); coup *m* de couteau *etc.*; 2. entailler.

gas·ket ['gæskit] ⚓ garcette *f*; ⊕ joint *m* en étoupe *etc.*

gas...: '~**light** lumière *f* du gaz; '~**light·er** allume-gaz *m/inv.*; '~**man·tle** manchon *m*; '~**mask** masque *m* à gaz; '~**me·ter** comp- teur *m* à gaz; **gas·o·line** *Am. mot.* ['gæsəliːn] essence *f*; **gas·om·e·ter** [gæ'sɔmitə] gazomètre *m*, réservoir

m à gaz; **'gas·ov·en** four *m* à gaz.
gasp [gɑːsp] **1.** sursaut *m*; *fig.* souffle *m*; **2.** sursauter; (*ou* ~ for breath) suffoquer.

gas-proof ['gæs'pruːf] à l'épreuve du *ou* des gaz; **'gas-range** cuisinière *f* à gaz; **gassed** [gæst] asphyxié; ✖ gazé; **'gas-sta·tion** *Am.* poste *m* d'essence, station *f* service; **'gas-stove** four *m ou* réchaud *m* à gaz; F radiateur *m* à gaz; **'gas·sy** gazeux (-euse *f*); mousseux (-euse *f*) (*vin*); *fig.* bavard.

gas·tric ☞ ['gæstrik] gastrique; **gas·tri·tis** [gæs'traitis] gastrite *f*.

gas·tron·o·mist [gæs'trɔnəmist] gastronome *m*; **gas'tron·o·my** gastronomie *f*.

gas-works ['gæswəːks] *usu. sg.* usine *f* à gaz.

gate [geit] porte *f* (*a. fig.*); barrière *f*; grille *f*; *sp.* public *m*; *see* ~-money; **'~-crash·er** *sl.* intrus(e *f*) *m*; **'~-keep·er** portier *m* (-ière *f*); **'~-leg(ged) ta·ble** table *f* à abattants; **'~-man** 🚂 garde-barrière [*pl.* gardes-barrière[s]] *m*; **'~-mon·ey** *sp.* recette *f*; **'~-way** entrée *f*, porte *f*.

gath·er 'gæðə] **1.** *v/t.* (r)assembler; ramasser; (re)cueillir; retrousser (*ses jupes*); percevoir (*des impôts*); conclure; *cost.* froncer; *see* information; ~ speed prendre de la vitesse; *v/i.* se rassembler; se réunir; s'accumuler; se préparer (*orage*); 🩺 abcéder; (🩺 *a.* ~ to a head) mûrir (*a. fig.*); **2.** ~s *pl.* fronces *f/pl.*; **'gath·er·ing** rassemblement *m*; cueillette *f*; accumulation *f*; froncement *m*; assemblée *f*.

gaud·y ['gɔːdi] **1.** □ voyant, criard; fastueux (-euse *f*); **2.** *univ.* banquet *m* anniversaire.

gauge [geidʒ] **1.** calibre *m*; jauge *f*; vérificateur *m*; indicateur *m*; 🚂 largeur *f* de la voie; ⚓ tirant *m* d'eau; **2.** calibrer; mesurer; *fig.* mesurer; **'gaug·er** jaugeur *m*, mesureur *m*.

Gaul [gɔːl] Gaulois(e *f*) *m*; *pays:* la Gaule *f*.

gaunt □ [gɔːnt] décharné; désolé.

gaunt·let ['gɔːntlit] gant *m* à crispins; *fig.* gant *m*; run the ~ ✖ passer les bretelles, *fig.* soutenir un feu roulant (de, of).

gauze [gɔːz] gaze *f*; wire ~ tissu *m* métallique; **'gauz·y** diaphane.

gave [geiv] *prét. de* give 1, 2.

gav·el *Am.* ['gævl] marteau *m* (*du commissaire-priseur*).

gawk F [gɔːk] godiche *mf*; personne *f* gauche; **'gawk·y** gauche; godiche.

gay □ [gei] gai, allègre; brillant; F homo; *Am. sl.* effronté.

gaze [geiz] **1.** regard *m* (fixe); **2.** regarder fixement; ~ at (*ou* on) contempler, considérer.

ga·zelle *zo.* [gə'zel] gazelle *f*.

gaz·er ['geizə] contemplateur (-trice *f*) *m*; curieux (-euse *f*) *m*.

ga·zette [gə'zet] **1.** journal *m* officiel; **2.** publier dans un journal officiel; be ~d être publié à l'Officiel; **gaz·et·teer** [gæzi'tiə] répertoire *m* géographique.

gear [giə] **1.** accoutrement *m*; effets *m/pl.* personnels; ustensiles *m/pl.*; attirail *m*, appareil *m*; harnais *m*; ⊕ transmission *f*, commande *f*; *mot.* (low première, high grande) vitesse *f*; top ~ prise *f* directe; in ~ en jeu; *mot.* engrené; out of ~ hors d'action; *mot.* débrayé, désengrené; **2.** *v/t.* gréer; engrener; ⊕ ~ up (down) multiplier (démultiplier); ~ into engrener (*qch.*) dans; *v/i.* s'engrener; ~ with (s')engrener dans; **'~-box**, **'~-case** ⊕ carter *m*; *mot.* boîte *f* de vitesses; **'gear·ing** ⊕ engrenage *m*; transmission *f*; *cycl.* développement *m*; **'gear-le·ver**, *surt. Am.* **'gear-shift** levier *m* de(s) vitesse(s).

gee [dʒiː] hue!, huhau!; *Am.* sapristi!; sans blague!

geese [giːs] *pl. de* goose.

gee·zer *sl.* ['giːzə] bonhomme *m*; vieille taupe *f*.

gei·sha ['geiʃə] geisha *f*.

gel·a·tin(e) ['dʒelətiːn] gélatine *f*; **ge·lat·i·nize** [dʒi'lætinaiz] (se) gélatiniser; **ge'lat·i·nous** gélatineux (-euse *f*).

geld [geld] [*irr.*] hongrer (*un cheval*); châtrer; **'geld·ing** (cheval *m*) hongre *m*.

gel·id ['dʒelid] glacial (-als *m/pl.*).

gelt [gelt] *prét. et p.p. de* geld.

gem [dʒem] **1.** pierre *f* précieuse; gemme *f*; joyau *m* (*a. fig.*); **2.** orner de pierres précieuses.

Gem·i·ni *astr.* ['dʒeminai] *pl.* les Gémaux *m/pl.*

gen *Brit. sl.* [dʒen] **1.** informations *f/pl.*, renseignements *m/pl.*; **2.** ~ up renseigner, F rancarder.

gen·der gramm. ['dʒendə] genre m; F sexe m.

gen·e·a·log·i·cal □ [dʒi:niə'lɔdʒikl] généalogique; **gen·e·al·o·gy** [dʒi:ni'ælədʒi] généalogie f.

gen·er·a ['dʒenərə] pl. de genus.

gen·er·al ['dʒenərəl] **1.** □ général (-aux m/pl.); commun; grand (public etc.); en chef; ♣ ~ an(a)esthetic anesthésie f générale; ~ election élections f/pl. générales; ~ practitioner médecin m de médecine générale, (médecin m) généraliste; médecin m de famille; ✕ ~ staff état-major m (pl. états-majors); Am. ~ store magasin m qui vend de tout; **2.** ✕ général m; **gen·er·al·i·ty** [~'ræliti] généralité f; la plupart; **gen·er·al·i·za·tion** [~rəlai'zeiʃn] généralisation f; **'gen·er·al·ize** généraliser; populariser; **'gen·er·al·ly** généralement; universellement; F pour la plupart; **'gen·er·al·'pur·pose** universel(le f); **'gen·er·al·ship** ✕ généralat m; stratégie f.

gen·er·ate ['dʒenəreit] engendrer; produire; generating station station f génératrice; **gen·er·a·tion** génération f; ⚛ engendrement m; **'gen·er·a·tive** [~ətiv] générateur (-trice f); productèur (-trice f); **'gen·er·a·tor** ['~eitə] générateur (-trice f) m; ⊕ générateur m; surt. mot. Am. dynamo f d'éclairage.

ge·ner·ic [dʒi'nerik] générique.

gen·er·os·i·ty [dʒenə'rɔsiti] générosité f; libéralité f; **'gen·er·ous** □ généreux (-euse f) (a. vin); libéral (-aux m/pl.); magnanime; riche.

gen·e·sis ['dʒenisis] genèse f; origine f; bibl. ♀ (la) Genèse; **ge·net·ic** [dʒi'netik] **1.** (~ally) génétique; génésique (instinct); F see generative; **2.** ~s sg. génétique f.

gen·ial □ ['dʒi:njəl] doux (douce f) (climat); propice; génial (-aux m/pl.) (talent); jovial (-als ou -aux m/pl.) (personne); **ge·ni·al·i·ty** [~ni-'æliti] douceur f; bienveillance f.

gen·i·tals anat. ['dʒenitlz] pl. organes m/pl. génitaux. [case) génitif m.]

gen·i·tive gramm. ['dʒenitiv] (ou ~ſ)

gen·ius ['dʒi:njəs] génie m; pl. **gen·i·i** ['~niai] démon m, esprit m; pl. **~ius·es** ['~jəsiz] génie m; F don m, aptitudes f/pl. naturelles.

gen·o·cide ['dʒenousaid] extermination f d'une race.

53*

gent F [dʒent] homme m, monsieur m.

gen·teel □ sl. ou iro. [dʒen'ti:l] comme il faut; maniéré.

gen·tian ♀ ['dʒenʃiən] gentiane f.

gen·tile ['dʒentail] **1.** gentil m; **2.** païen(ne f); Am. non mormon.

gen·til·i·ty souv. iro. [dʒen'tiliti] prétention f au bon ton; haute bourgeoisie f.

gen·tle □ ['dʒentl] usu. doux (douce f); modéré; léger (-ère f); cher (chère f) (lecteur); co. noble; † bien né; bon(ne f) (naissance); '~·folk(s) personnes f/pl. de bonne famille; '~·man monsieur (pl. messieurs) m; homme m comme il faut; ♞ rentier m; sp. amateur m; bal: cavalier m; † gentilhomme (pl. gentils-hommes) m; gentlemen! messieurs!; ~'s agreement convention f verbale (qui n'engage que la parole d'honneur des partis); '~·man·like, '~·man·ly comme il faut; bien élevé; '**gen·tle·ness** douceur f; '**gen·tle·wom·an** dame f ou demoiselle f bien née.

gen·try ['dʒentri] petite noblesse f; péj. individus m/pl.

gen·u·flec·tion, gen·u·flex·ion [dʒenju'flekʃn] génuflexion f.

gen·u·ine □ ['dʒenjuin] authentique; véritable; franc(he f); sincère.

ge·nus ['dʒi:nəs] (pl. genera) genre m (a. fig.).

ge·od·e·sy [dʒi'ɔdisi] géodésie f.

ge·og·ra·pher [dʒi'ɔgrəfə] géographe m; **ge·o·graph·i·cal** □ [dʒiə-'græfikl] géographique; **ge·og·ra·phy** [~'ɔgrəfi] géographie f.

ge·o·log·ic, ge·o·log·i·cal □ [dʒiə-'lɔdʒik(l)] géologique; **ge·ol·o·gist** [dʒi'ɔlədʒist] géologue m f; **ge·ol·o·gy** géologie f.

ge·om·e·ter [dʒi'ɔmitə] géomètre m; **ge·o·met·ric, ge·o·met·ri·cal** □ [dʒiə'metrik(l)] géométrique; **ge·om·e·try** [~'ɔmitri] géométrie f.

ge·o·phys·ics [dʒiə'fiziks] usu. sg. géophysique f.

ge·ra·ni·um ♀ [dʒi'reinjəm] géranium m.

germ [dʒə:m] **1.** germe m; **2.** germer.

Ger·man[1] ['dʒə:mən] **1.** allemand; ♣ ~ measles rubéole f; ~ Ocean mer f du Nord; ⊕ ~ silver argentan m, maillechort m; ~ steel acier m brut; ~ text caractères m/pl. gothiques; ~ *toys* pl. jouets m/pl. de Nuremberg; **2.** *ling.* allemand m; Allemand(e f) m.

ger·man² [~]: *brother etc.* ~ frère m etc. germain; **ger·mane** [dʒəː'mein] (*to*) approprié (à); se rapportant (à). **Ger·man·ic** [dʒəː'mænik] allemand; *hist.* germanique.

germ-car·ri·er ['dʒəːmkæriə] porteur m de bacilles.

ger·mi·nal ['dʒəːminl] germinal (-aux m/pl.); *fig.* en germe; **ger·mi·nate** ['~neit] (faire) germer; **ger·mi'na·tion** germination f.

germ-proof ['dʒəːmpruːf] aseptique.

ger·ry·man·der *pol.* ['dʒerimændə] truquage m électoral.

ger·und *gramm.* ['dʒerənd] gérondif m.

ges·ta·tion ⚕, *vet.* [dʒes'teiʃn] gestation f.

ges·tic·u·late [dʒes'tikjuleit] v/i. gesticuler; v/t. exprimer par des gestes; **ges·tic·u'la·tion** gesticulation f.

ges·ture ['dʒestʃə] geste m; signe m.

get [get] [*irr.*] **1.** v/t. obtenir, procurer; gagner; prendre; se faire (*une réputation etc.*); recevoir; aller chercher; attraper (*un coup, une maladie*); faire parvenir; faire (*inf., p.p.*); *Am.* F saisir; ~ *a wife* prendre femme; *have got to* avoir; F *you have got to obey* il faut que vous obéissiez; ~ *one's hair cut* se faire couper les cheveux; ~ *me the book!* allez me chercher le livre!; ~ *by heart* apprendre par cœur; ~ *with child* faire un enfant à; ~ *away* arracher, éloigner; ~ *down* descendre (*qch.*); avaler (*une pilule etc.*); mettre (*qch.*) par écrit; ~ *in* rentrer; placer (*un mot*); donner (*un coup*); ~ *off* ôter (*un vêtement*); expédier (*une lettre*); ~ *on* mettre (*qch.*); ~ *out* arracher, tirer; (faire) sortir; ~ *over* faire passer (*qch.*) par-dessus; en finir avec (*qch.*); ~ *through* terminer; assurer le succès de; *parl.* faire adopter; ~ *up* faire monter; organiser; préparer; F (*se*) faire beau (belle); ~ *up steam* faire monter la pression; chauffer. **2.** v/i. devenir, se faire; aller, se rendre (à, *to*); en arriver (à *inf.*, *to inf.*); se mettre; ~ *ready* se préparer; ~ *about* circuler; être sur pied; ~ *abroad* se

répandre; ~ *ahead* prendre de l'avance; ~ *along* s'avancer; faire du chemin; ~ *along with* s'accorder avec, s'entendre bien avec; ~ *around* to en venir à, trouver le temps de; ~ *at* atteindre; parvenir à; ~ *away* partir; s'échapper; ~ *away with it* réussir; faire accepter la chose; ~ *down to* descendre jusqu'à; *fig.* en venir à; F se mettre à; ~ *in* rentrer; placer (*un coup*); ~ *into* entrer ou monter dans; mettre (*une robe etc.*); ~ *off* descendre (*de qch.*); se tirer d'affaire; F entreprendre un mari; 🐎 décoller; ~ *off with* faire la conquête de; ~ *on* monter sur; s'avancer (vers *qch.*); ~ *to* s'approcher (de, *to*); prendre de l'âge; s'entendre (bien), s'accommoder (avec, *with*); ~ *out* (*of, from*) sortir (de); s'échapper (de); se soustraire (à); ~ *over* franchir; passer par-dessus; *fig.* guérir de (*une maladie*); ~ *it over with* en finir avec; ~ *through* passer; obtenir la communication; ~ *to hear* (*ou know ou learn*) apprendre; ~ *up* se lever; grossir (*mer*); monter; s'élever (*prix etc.*); **get-at-a·ble** [get'ætəbl] accessible; d'accès facile; **get-a·way** ['getəwei] *sp.* départ m; démarrage m; *Am.* fuite f; *make one's* ~ s'échapper; **'get·ter** acquéreur m; *zo.* reproducteur m; **'get·ting** acquisition f; mise f; 🔨 extraction f; **'get-to·geth·er** F réunion f; **get-'up** tenue f; ✝ habillage m; *Am.* F entrain m; esprit m entreprenant.

gew·gaw ['gjuːgɔː] babiole f, bagatelle f; ~s pl. afféteries m/pl.

gey·ser (*mer*) géog. geyser m; ['giːzə] chauffe-bain m; chauffe-eau m/inv. à gaz.

ghast·li·ness ['gɑːstlinis] horreur f; pâleur f mortelle; **'ghast·ly** horrible; affreux (-euse f); blême.

gher·kin ['gəːkin] cornichon m.

ghost [goust] fantôme m, spectre m, revenant m; F nègre m (*d'un auteur*); *Holy* ♀ Saint-Esprit m; **'ghost·like**, **'ghost·ly** spectral (-aux m/pl.); **'ghost-write** *Am.* écrire un article *etc.* qui paraîtra sous la signature d'autrui.

gi·ant ['dʒaiənt] géant m (*a. su./m*).

gib·ber ['dʒibə] baragouiner; **'gib·ber·ish** baragouin m, charabia m.

gib·bet ['dʒibit] **1.** gibet m; ⊕

flèche *f* de grue; **2.** pendre; *fig.* clouer au pilori.

gib·bos·i·ty [gi'bɔsiti] gibbosité *f*, bosse *f*; **gib·bous** ['gibəs] gibbeux (-euse *f*); bossu (*personne*).

gibe [dʒaib] **1.** railler (q., *at s.o.*); se moquer (de q., *at s.o.*); **2.** raillerie *f*; moquerie *f*; brocard *m*.

gib·lets ['dʒiblits] *pl.* abatis *m*.

gid·di·ness ['gidinis] vertige *m*; *fig.* étourderie *f*; frivolité *f*; **'gid·dy** □ pris de vertige (*personne*); étourdi (*a. fig.*); *fig.* frivole; vertigineux (-euse *f*), qui donne le vertige.

gift [gift] **1.** don *m*; cadeau *m*, présent *m*; † prime *f* (*à un acheteur*); *deed of* ~ (acte *m* de) donation *f* entre vifs; ~ *shop surt. Am.* magasin *m* de nouveautés; *never look a* ~ *horse in the mouth* à cheval donné on ne regarde pas la bride; **2.** douer (de, with); donner en présent; **'gift·ed** bien doué; de talent.

gig [gig] cabriolet *m*; ♣ petit canot *m*.

gi·gan·tic [dʒai'gæntik] (~*ally*) géant, gigantesque.

gig·gle ['gigl] **1.** rire nerveusement; **2.** petit rire *m* nerveux.

gild [gild] [*irr.*] dorer; **'gild·er** doreur (-euse *f*) *m*; **'gild·ing** dorure *f*.

gill¹ [dʒil] (*approx.*) huitième *m* de litre.

gill² [gil] *icht.* ouie *f*; *fig. usu.* ~*s pl.* bajoue *f*, -s *f/pl.*; *champignon:* lame *f*; *tex.* peigne *m*; ⊕ ailette *f*.

gill³ [dʒil] jeune fille *f*; bonne amie *f*.

gilt [gilt] **1.** *prét. et p.p. de* gild; **2.** dorure *f*; doré *m*; **'~·edged** doré sur tranche; † de premier ordre; *†* ~ *securities* (*ou* shares *ou* stock) valeurs *f/pl.* de tout repos.

gim·crack ['dʒimkræk] **1.** article *m* de pacotille *ou* en toc; **2.** de pacotille (*meuble*); en toc (*bijou*); de carton (*maison*).

gim·let ⊕ ['gimlit] vrille *f*.

gim·mick *Am. sl.* ['gimik] truc *m*; tour *m*.

gin¹ [dʒin] genièvre *m*.

gin² [◡] **1.** piège *m*, trébuchet *m*; ⊕ chèvre *f*; ⊕ égrener.

gin·ger ['dʒindʒə] **1.** gingembre *m*; F entrain *m*, énergie *f*; **2.** F (*souv.* ~ *up*) secouer; mettre du cœur au ventre de; **3.** roux (rousse *f*) (*cheveux*); **~ ale**, **~ beer** boisson *f*

gazeuse au gingembre; **'~·bread** pain *m* d'épice; ~ **group** *pol.* groupe *m* de pression; **'gin·ger·ly 1.** *adj.* délicat; **2.** *adv.* délicatement; **'gin·ger-nut** biscuit *m* au gingembre.

gip·sy ['dʒipsi] bohémien(ne *f*) *m*.

gi·raffe *zo.* [dʒi'rɑ:f] girafe *f*.

gir·an·dole ['dʒirəndoul] girandole *f*.

gird¹ [gə:d] **1.** raillerie *f*; brocard *m*; **2.** railler (q., *at s.o.*); se moquer (de, at).

gird² [◡] [*irr.*] ceindre (de, with); encercler (de, with).

gird·er ⊕ ['gə:də] poutre *f*.

gir·dle ['gə:dl] **1.** ceinture *f*; gaine *f*; **2.** entourer, ceindre.

girl [gə:l] jeune fille *f*; F employée *f*; domestique *f*; ~ *Friday* aide *f* de bureau; *Brit.* ~ *guide*, *Am.* ~ *scout* éclaireuse *f*; **girl·hood** ['◡hud] jeunesse *f*; adolescence *f*; **'girl·ish** □ de jeune *ou* petite fille; **'girl·ish-ness** air *m* de petite fille; **'girl·y** *Am.* F magazine *m* (*de beautés légèrement vêtues*).

girt [gə:t] **1.** *prét. et p.p. de* gird²; **2.** ⊕ circonférence *f*.

girth [gə:θ] **1.** sangle *f* (de selle); circonférence *f*; **2.** sangler (*un cheval*).

gist [dʒist] *ᵗᵗᵗ* principal motif *m*; F essence *f*; point *m* essentiel; fond *m*.

give [giv] **1.** [*irr.*] *v/t. usu.* donner; remettre; causer; faire (*attention, aumône, peine, plaisir, saut, etc.*); pousser (*un soupir etc.*); présenter (*des compliments*) porter (*un coup*); prononcer (*un arrêt*); céder (*une place*); ~ *attention* to faire attention à; ~ *battle* donner bataille; ~ *birth to* donner le jour à; donner naissance à (*a. fig.*); ~ *chase to* donner la chasse à; ~ *credit to* ajouter foi à; ~ *ear to* prêter l'oreille à; ~ *one's mind to* s'appliquer à; ~ *it to s.o.* rosser q.; semoncer vertement q.; ~ *away* donner; F trahir; ~ *away the bride* conduire la mariée à l'autel; ~ *back* rendre; ~ *forth* émettre; dégager; ~ *in* donner; remettre; ~ *out* distribuer; annoncer; exhaler (*une odeur etc.*); émettre; ~ *over* abandonner; remettre; ~ *up* rendre (*une proie*); abandonner (*affaire, malade, prétention*); ~ *o.s. up* se livrer (à, to); se constituer prisonnier; **2.** [*irr.*] *v/i.* ~ (*in*) céder;

se rendre; ~ *into*, ~ (*up*)*on* donner sur (*la rue etc.*); ~ *out* manquer; faire défaut; être à bout; s'épuiser; ~ *over finir*; **give-and-take** ['givən'teik] concessions *f/pl.* mutuelles; **give·a·way** ['givə'wei] F trahison *f*; *radio*, *télév.*, *surt. Am.* ~ *show* (*ou program*) audition *f* où on décerne des prix à des concurrents; '**giv·en** *p.p. de give*; ~ *name Am.* nom *m* de baptême; ~ *to* adonné à; ~ (*that*) étant donné (que); '**giv·er** donneur (-euse *f*) *m*; ✝ *lettre de change*: tireur *m*.

giz·zard ['gizəd] gésier *m*.

gla·cé ['glæsei] glacé.

gla·ci·al □ ['gleisiəl] glacial (-als *m/pl.*); *géol.* glaciaire; ⌖ cristallisé; **gla·cier** ['glæsjə] glacier *m*; **gla·cis** ⚔ ['glæsis] glacis *m*.

glad □ [glæd] heureux (-euse *f*), content, bien aise (de *of*, *at*, to); joyeux (-euse *f*); ~*ly* volontiers, avec plaisir; F *give s.o. the* ~ *eye* lancer des œillades à q.; **glad·den** ['~dn] réjouir.

glade [gleid] clairière *f*; *Am.* région *f* marécageuse.

glad·i·a·tor ['glædieitə] gladiateur *m*.

glad·ness ['glædnis] joie *f*; **glad·some** ['~səm] heureux (-euse *f*), joyeux (-euse *f*).

Glad·stone ['glædstən] (*a.* ~ *bag*) sac *m* américain.

glair [glɛə] 1. glaire *f*; 2. glairer.

glam·or·ize ['glæməraiz] faire apparaître sous de belles couleurs; glorifier, magnifier; embellir; **glam·or·ous** ['~əs] magnifique; brillant; enchanteur (-eresse *f*); *fig.* éblouissant; **glam·o(u)r** ['~mə] 1. charme *m*, enchantement *m*; ~ *girl* jeune beauté *f* fascinante; 2. fasciner.

glance [glɑːns] 1. ricochet *m*; regard *m*; coup *m* d'œil; 2. jeter un regard (sur, *at*); lancer un coup d'œil (à, *at*); refléter; ~ *aside* (*ou off*) ricocher, dévier; ~ *over* parcourir, examiner rapidement.

gland *anat.*, ♀ [glænd] glande *f*; **glan·dered** *vét.* ['~əd] morveux (-euse *f*); **glan·ders** *vét.* ['~əz] *pl.* morve *f*; **glan·du·lar** ['~julə] glandulaire.

glare [glɛə] 1. éclat *m*, clarté *f*; éblouissement *m*; regard *m* fixe et furieux; 2. briller d'un éclat éblouissant; lancer un regard furieux (à, *at*); **glar·ing** □ ['~riŋ] éblouissant, aveuglant; *fig.* manifeste; flagrant.

glass [glɑːs] 1. verre *m*; miroir *m*, glace *f*; (*a. reading-*~) loupe *f*; baromètre *m*; *coll.* verrerie *f*; (*a pair of*) ~*es pl.* (*des*) lunettes *f/pl.*; 2. de *ou* en verre; 3. vitrer; '~**-blow·er** souffleur *m* de verre; verrier *m*; **glass·ful** ['~ful] (plein) verre *m*; '**glass·i·ness** aspect *m* vitreux.

glass...: '~**-roofed court** cour *f* vitrée; '~**-shade** cloche *f*; '~**works** ⊕ *usu. sg.* verrerie *f*; '**glass·y** □ vitreux (-euse *f*).

glaze [gleiz] 1. vernis *m*; *cuis.* glace *f*; *peint.* glacis *m*; 2. (se) glacer; *v/t.* vitrer; vernir; lisser; *v/i.* devenir vitreux (*œil*); ~*d paper* papier *m* brillant; ~*d veranda* véranda *f* vitrée; **gla·zier** ['~iə] vitrier *m*; '**glaz·ing** pose *f* des vitres; vernissage *m*; vitrerie *f*; '**glaz·y** glacé.

gleam [gliːm] 1. lueur *f* (*a. fig.*); reflet *m*; 2. (re)luire; miroiter (*eau*).

glean [gliːn] *v/t.* glaner; *v/i.* faire la glane; '**glean·er** glaneur (-euse *f*) *m*; **glean·ings** ['~iŋz] *pl.* glanure *f*, ~*s f/pl.*

glebe [gliːb] terre *f* assignée à un bénéfice; *poét.* terrain *m*, glèbe *f*.

glee [gliː] joie *f*, allégresse *f*; ♪ petit chant *m* (à 3 *ou* 4 parties) sans accompagnement; (*male*) ~ *club* chorale *f*; **glee·ful** □ ['~ful] allègre, joyeux (-euse *f*).

glen [glen] vallon *m*.

glib □ [glib] ✝ glissant; *péj.* spécieux (-euse *f*); beau parleur (*personne*); '**glib·ness** spéciosité *f*; faconde *f*.

glide [glaid] 1. glissement *m*; *danse*: glissade *f*; ✈ vol *m* plané; *gramm.* son *m* transitoire; 2. (faire) glisser; couler; *v/i.* ✈ faire du vol plané; '**glid·er** planeur *m*, glisseur *m*; ~ *pilot* pilote *m* de planeur; '**glid·ing** glissement *m*; ✈ vol *m* plané.

glim·mer ['glimə] 1. faible lueur *f*; miroitement *m*; *min.* mica *m*; 2. entreluire, jeter une faible lueur; miroiter (*eau*).

glimpse [glimps] 1. vision *f* momentanée; 2. entrevoir; ~ *at* avoir la vision fugitive de; jeter un rapide coup d'œil sur.

glint [glint] **1.** étinceler, entreluire; **2.** éclair *m*, reflet *m*.

glis·sade *alp.* [gli'sɑːd] **1.** faire une descente en glissade; **2.** glissade *f*.

glis·ten ['glisn], **glit·ter** ['glitə] étinceler, (re)luire; scintiller; *fig.* briller.

gloam·ing ['gloumiŋ] crépuscule *m*.

gloat [glout] ([up]on, over) savourer (*qch.*); se réjouir (de); triompher (de).

glob·al ['gloubl] global (-aux *m/pl.*); mondial (-aux *m/pl.*); universel(le *f*); **globe** [gloub] globe *m* (*a. anat.*); sphère *f*; terre *f*; **'globe-trot·ter** globe-trotter *m*; **glo·bose** ['‿ous] ⚘ globeux (-euse *f*); **glo·bos·i·ty** [‿'bositi] caractère *m* globuleux *etc.*; **glob·u·lar** □ ['globjulə] globuleux (-euse *f*); globulaire; **glob·ule** ['‿juːl] globule *m*.

gloom [gluːm] **1.** obscurité *f*, ténèbres *f/pl.*; mélancolie *f*; **2.** *v/i.* se renfrogner; s'assombrir; *v/t.* obscurcir; assombrir; **'gloom·i·ness** obscurité *f*; mélancolie *f*, tristesse *f*; **'gloom·y** □ sombre, obscur, ténébreux (-euse *f*); morne.

glo·ri·fi·ca·tion [glɔːrifi'keiʃn] glorification *f*; **glo·ri·fy** ['‿fai] glorifier; **'glo·ri·ous** □ glorieux (-euse *f*); resplendissant; *fig.* magnifique.

glo·ry ['glɔːri] **1.** gloire *f*; renommée *f*; splendeur *f*, éclat *m*; *Am.* F Old ♀ drapeau *m* des É.-U.; **2.** (*in*) se glorifier (de); être fier (-ère *f*) (de); F se réjouir (de).

gloss[1] [glɔs] **1.** glose *f*; commentaire *m*; **2.** gloser sur; F expliquer.

gloss[2] [‿] **1.** vernis *m*, lustre *m*; high ‿ painting ripolin *m*; **2.** lustrer, glacer; ‿ over glisser sur, farder.

glos·sa·ry ['glɔsəri] glossaire *m*, lexique *m*.

gloss·i·ness ['glɔsinis] vernis *m*, lustre *m*; **'gloss·y** □ lustré, brillant, glacé.

glot·tis *anat.* ['glɔtis] glotte *f*.

glove [glʌv] gant *m*; *see* hand 1; *mot.* ‿ *compartment* boîte *f* à gants; **'glov·er** gantier (-ère *f*) *m*.

glow [glou] **1.** lueur *f*; chaleur *f*; **2.** rayonner; rougir; **'‿-worm** ver *m* luisant; luciole *f*.

gloze [glouz] (*usu.* ‿ over) glisser sur, pallier.

glu·cose ⚘ ['gluːkous] glucose *m*.

glue [gluː] **1.** colle *f*; **2.** coller (*a. fig.*); ‿ one's eyes on ne pas quitter (*qch.*) des yeux; **'glue·y** gluant, poisseux (-euse *f*).

glum □ [glʌm] renfrogné, maussade, morne.

glut [glʌt] **1.** excès *m*; surabondance *f*; ✝ encombrement *m* (du marché); **2.** inonder, encombrer; ‿ o.s. se rassasier.

glu·ten ⚘ ['gluːtən] gluten *m*; **glu·ti·nous** □ ['gluːtinəs] glutineux (-euse *f*).

glut·ton ['glʌtn] gourmand(e *f*) *m*; glouton(ne *f*) *m*, goulu(e *f*) *m*; *zo.* glouton *m*; ‿ *for work* bourreau *m* de travail; **'glut·ton·ous** □ glouton(ne *f*); **'glut·ton·y** gourmandise *f*.

G-man *Am.* ['dʒiːmæn] agent *m* armé du F.B.I.

gnarl [nɑːl] nœud *m*, loupe *f*; **gnarled**, *a.* **'gnarl·y** noueux (-euse *f*); tordu.

gnash [næʃ] grincer (*les dents*).

gnat [næt] moustique *m*, moucheron *m*. [geur *m*.⎞

gnaw [nɔː] ronger; **'gnaw·er** ron-⎭

gnome[1] ['noumiː] maxime *f*, aphorisme *m*.

gnome[2] [noum] gnome *m*; gobelin *m*; **'gnom·ish** de gnome.

go [gou] **1.** [*irr.*] aller; se rendre; faire une promenade *ou* un voyage; marcher (*machine, cœur, affaire*); visiter (*qch., to s.th.*); sonner (*cloche*); passer (*temps*); aboutir (*affaire, guerre*); partir (de, *from*); s'en aller; disparaître; se casser; s'épuiser; *avec adj.:* devenir; se rendre; s'étendre (jusqu'à, *to*); adjuger (à, *for*) (*lot*); ‿ *bad* se gâter; *see* mad, sick; (*this dog etc.*) *must* ‿ il faut absolument qu'on se débarrasse de (*ce chien etc.*); *the story* ‿es *that* on dit que; *sl.* here ‿es! allons-y!; *sl.* ‿ it! vas-y!; allez-y!; *as men etc.* ‿ étant donné les hommes *etc.*; *let* ‿ lâcher; laisser aller; ‿ *shares* partager; ‿ *to* (*ou and*) *see* aller voir; *just* ‿ *and try!* essayez toujours!; ‿ *about* circuler, aller çà et là; se mettre à (*une tâche*); ‿ *abroad* voyager à l'étranger; émigrer; ‿ *ahead* avancer; faire des progrès; persister; ‿ *at* s'attaquer à; ‿ *back* rentrer; retourner; ~ *back from* (*ou* F *on*) revenir sur (*une promesse*); ~ *before* *fig.* devancer; ~ *behind* revenir sur (*qch.*); ~ *between* servir de médiateur entre (... *et* ...); passer entre; ~ *by* (*adv.*) passer; (*prp.*) se régler sur; ~ *by the name of* être connu sous le nom de; ~ *down* descendre; F prendre (avec, *with*), être (*bien ou mal*) reçu (de, *with*); ~ *for* aller chercher; F tomber sur; F s'en prendre à (*q.*); ~ *for* (aller) faire (*une promenade, un voyage, etc.*); ~ *in* entrer, rentrer; se cacher (*soleil*); ~ *in for* se mêler de, s'adonner à; ~ *in for an examination* se présenter à *ou* passer un examen; ~ *into* entrer dans; examiner (*une question*); ♣ diviser; ~ *off* partir (*a. fusil etc.*), s'en aller; s'écarter; se passer; se détériorer; passer (*beauté*); tourner (*lait*); ~ *on* continuer sa route; continuer (de *inf., gér.*); marcher; passer (à, *to*); F se passer; F se conduire; ~ *on!* avancez!; *iro.* allons donc!; ~ *out* sortir; disparaître; baisser (*marée*); s'éteindre (*feu*); *pol.* quitter le pouvoir; ~ *over* passer (à, *to*) (*un parti etc.*); traverser; ~ *through* passer par; traverser; remplir; subir (*une épreuve*); examiner; ~ *through with* aller jusqu'au bout de; ~ *to* aller à; ~ *to* *expense* se mettre en dépense; ~ *up* monter; sauter; ✝ subir une hausse; ~ *up to town* aller à la ville; ~ *with* accompagner; s'accorder avec; ~ *without* se passer de; 2. F aller *m*; entrain *m*, coup *m*, essai *m*; F accès *m*; *sl.* dernier cri *m*; *sl.* affaire *f*; *univ. sl.* little ~ premier examen *m*; great ~ examen *m* final; on the ~ à courir, remuant; *it is no* ~ ça ne prend pas; *is it a* ~? entendu?; *in one* ~ d'un seul coup; *have a* ~ essayer (de *inf., at gér.*).

goad [goud] 1. aiguillon *m* (*a. fig.*); 2. aiguillonner, piquer (*a. fig.*).

go-a·head F ['gouəhed] 1. entreprenant; actif (-ive *f*); 2. *surt. Am.* F esprit *m* entreprenant; *Am. sl.* voie *f* libre.

goal [goul] but *m* (*a. sp., a. foot.*); '~-ar·e·a *foot.* surface *f* de but; **goal·ie** F ['gouli] = '~-keep·er *foot.* gardien de but; F goal *m*; ~ kick *foot.* coup *m* de pied de but.

goat [gout] *zo.* chèvre *f*; he-~ bouc *m*; *fig.* imbécile *m*; *sl.* get s.o.'s ~ irriter q.; **goat·ee** barbiche *f*; bouc *m*; '**goat·ish** de bouc; lascif.

gob [gɔb] *sl.* crachat *m*; ⚒ remblai *m*; *Am.* F marin *m*; **gob·bet** ['~it] grosse bouchée *f*.

gob·ble ['gɔbl] dévorer; glouglouter (*dindon*); **gob·ble·dy·gook** *Am. sl.* ['gɔbldiguk] style *m* ampoulé; jargon *m* (*des fonctionnaires*); '**gob·bler** avaleur (-euse *f*) *m*; dindon *m*.

go-be·tween ['goubitwi:n] intermédiaire *mf*.

gob·lin ['gɔblin] gobelin *m*, lutin *m*.

go-by ['goubai]: *give s.o. the* ~ éviter q.; se dérober à q.

go-cart ['gouka:t] poussette *f*, charrette *f* (*pour bébés*).

god [gɔd] *eccl.* ♀ dieu *m*; *fig.* idole *f*; '**god·child** filleul(e *f*) *m*; '**god·dess** déesse *f*; '**god·fa·ther** parrain *m*; '**god·for·sak·en** perdu (*endroit*); '**god·head** divinité *f*; '**god·less** impie; athée; '**god·like** de dieu; divin; '**god·li·ness** piété *f*; '**god·ly** saint; pieux (-euse *f*), dévot; '**god·moth·er** marraine *f*; '**god·send** aubaine *f*; bienfait *m* du ciel; '**god·speed** bon voyage *m*, adieu *m*.

go·er ['gouə] passant *m*; *play*~ habitué(e *f*) *m* du cinéma *ou* théâtre; *cheval*: marcheur *m*; F homme *m* énergique.

gof·fer ['goufə] gaufrer; tuyauter.

go-get·ter *Am. sl.* ['gou'getə] arriviste *mf*; homme *m* d'affaires etc. énergique.

gog·gle ['gɔgl] 1. (*a.* ~ *one's eyes*) rouler de gros yeux; 2. (*a pair of*) ~s *pl.* lunettes *f/pl.*; '~-box *sl.* télé *f*.

go·ing ['gouiŋ] 1. qui marche; qui va (*sur*); qui soit; F actuel(le *f*); *be* ~ *to* (*inf.*) être sur le point de (*inf.*); aller (*inf.*); avoir l'intention de (*inf.*); *keep* ~ aller toujours; *set* (*a-*)~ mettre en train; *a* ~ *concern* une affaire etc. en pleine activité; ~, ~, *gone!* une fois, deux fois, adjugé!; 2. allée *f*; départ *m*; recours *m*; *sp.* état *m* du sol; *be heavy* ~ être difficile; '**go·ings-on** *pl.* F conduite *f*.

goi·tre ☞ ['gɔitə] goitre *m*; **goi·trous** ['gɔitrəs] goitreux (-euse *f*).

gold [gould] 1. or *m*; 2. d'or; *sl.* ~ brick escroquerie *f*; attrapenigaud *m*; *Am. sl.* ~brick se défiler,

tirer au flanc; '~-**dig·ger** *Am.*
chercheur *m* d'or; *sl.* maîtresse *f*
coûteuse; '**gold·en** † d'or; *fig.* précieux (-euse *f*); '**gold·finch** *orn.*
chardonneret *m*; '**gold-plat·ed**
plaqué or; '**gold·smith** orfèvre *m*.
golf [gɔlf] *sp.* golf *m*; '~-**ball** balle *f* de
golf; '~-**club** club *m* de golf; crosse *f*
de golf; '**golf·er** golfeur (-euse *f*) *m*;
joueur (-euse *f*) *m* de golf; '**golf-
links** *pl.* terrain *m* de golf.
gol·li·wog(g) ['gɔliwɔg] poupée *f*
grotesque; *fig.* objet *m* d'épouvante.
go·losh [gə'lɔʃ] caoutchouc *m*.
gon·do·la ⚓, ✈ ['gɔndələ] gondole *f*.
gone [gɔn] **1.** *p.p. de* go **1**; **2.** *adj.* absent; mort; F épris, amoureux (-euse
f) (de, on); F désespéré; *be*~! *get you
*~! allez-vous-en!; *sl.* filez!; *sl.* ~ *on*
épris de (*q.*), emballé sur (*q.*);
'**gon·er** *sl.* homme *m* fichu *ou*
mort.
gong [gɔŋ] gong *m*.
good [gud] **1.** *usu.* bon(ne *f*);
valable (*excuse*); excellent; avantageux (-euse *f*) (*mariage, prix, etc.*);
~ *and* *Am.* très, tout à fait; ♀ *Friday*
(le) Vendredi *m* saint; *the* ~
Samaritan le bon Samaritain; ~ *at*
bon *ou* fort en; *in* ~ *earnest* pour
(tout) de bon; ~ *afternoon* bonjour!;
plus tard: bonsoir!; ~ *evening* bonsoir!; ~ *morning* bonjour!; ~ *night*
bonne nuit!; **2.** bien *m*; ~*s pl.* articles
m/pl.; marchandises *f/pl.*; ⚖ biens
m/pl.; *Am.* F avantage *m* (sur, on);
that's no ~ cela ne vaut rien; *it is no* ~
talking inutile de parler; *for* ~ pour de
bon; ~*s station* (*train*) gare *f* (*train m*)
de marchandises; ~*s in process* produits *m/pl.* semi-fabriqués; ~*s in*
short supply marchandises *f/pl.* qui
manquent; ~-**bye 1.** [gud'bai] adieu
m; **2.** ['gud'bai] au revoir!, adieu!;
'~-**for-noth·ing 1.** bon(ne *f*) à rien;
sans valeur; **2.** bon(ne *f*) à rien;
vaurien(ne *f*) *m*; '**good-hu·mo(u)red**
de bonne humeur; jovial, bon-
homme; '**good·li·ness** beauté *f*;
'**good-look·ing** joli; '**good·ly** beau
(bel *devant une voyelle ou un h muet*);
belle *f*; beaux *m/pl.*); ample; considérable; '**good·'na·tured** bon(ne
f); au bon naturel; '**good·ness**
bonté *f*; bonne qualité *f*; *int.* dieu *m*!;
see gracious; '**good·sized** assez
grand; '**good·wife** maîtresse *f* de la

maison; '**good'will** bonne volonté
f; bienveillance *f* (envers, pour
towards); ♥ clientèle *f*; ♥ achalandage *m*.
good·y¹ ['gudi] bonbon *m*.
good·y² [~] **1.** *adj.* édifiant; d'une
piété affectée; **2.** *int. Am.* F chouette!
goo·ey F ['gu:i] gluant; sentimental.
goof F [gu:f] **1.** idiot(e *f*) *m*; gaffe *f*; **2.**
a. ~ *up* saloper, gâcher, bousiller;
'**goof·y** F idiot, toqué.
goon *Am. sl.* [gu:n] voyou *m*.
goose [gu:s] (*pl.* geese) oie *f*; *fig.*
sot(te *f*) *m*; (*pl.* gooses) carreau *m*
(*à repasser*).
goose·ber·ry ['guzbəri] groseille *f*
verte; *buisson:* groseillier *m*; F
play ~ se trouver en tiers; *sl.* faire
sandwich.
goose...: '~-**flesh**, *surt. Am.* '~-
pim·ples *pl. fig.* chair *f* de poule;
'~-**step** pas *m* de l'oie; '**goos·ey**,
'**goos·ie** F oison *m*.
go·pher *surt. Am.* ['goufə] sacco-
phore *m*; chien *m* de prairie.
Gor·di·an ['gɔ:diən] gordien; *fig.*
difficile, compliqué.
gore¹ [gɔ:] sang *m* coagulé.
gore² [~] **1.** *cost.* godet *m*; soufflet *m*;
⚓ pointe *f*; **2.** blesser avec les
cornes; découdre; *cost.* faire goder.
gorge [gɔ:dʒ] **1.** gorge *f* (*a. géog.*);
gosier *m*; *my* ~ *rises at it* j'en ai des
nausées; **2.** (se) rassasier; (se)
gorger.
gor·geous □ ['gɔ:dʒəs] magnifique;
superbe; '**gor·geous·ness** splendeur *f*.
gor·get ⚔ ['gɔ:dʒit] hausse-col *m*.
gor·mand·ize ['gɔ:məndaiz] *vt/i.*
bâfrer; *v/i.* goinfrer.
gorm·less *Brit.* F ['gɔ:mlis] bête;
lourdaud; bouché.
gorse ⚘ [gɔ:s] genêt *m* épineux.
gor·y □ ['gɔ:ri] ensanglanté.
gosh F [gɔʃ] sapristi!
gos·hawk *orn.* ['gɔshɔ:k] autour *m*.
gos·ling ['gɔzliŋ] oison *m*.
gos·pel ['gɔspl] évangile *m*.
go-slow [gou'slou] grève *f* perlée;
travail *m* au ralenti.
gos·sa·mer ['gɔsəmə] filandres *f/pl.*;
♥ gaze *f* légère.
gos·sip ['gɔsip] **1.** causerie *f*; *péj.*
cancans *m/pl.*; *personne:* bavard(e *f*)
m; *journ.* ~ *column* échos *m/pl.*; **2.**

bavarder; faire des cancans (sur, *about*).

got [gɔt] *prét. et p.p. de* get.

Goth [gɔθ] *hist.* Goth *m* (*a. fig.*); *fig.* vandale *m*; **'Goth·ic** gothique.

got·ten † *ou Am.* ['gɔtn] *p.p. de* get.

gouge [gaudʒ] **1.** ⊕ gouge *f*; **2.** (*usu.* ～ out) creuser à la gouge; *fig.* faire sauter (un œil à *q.*); *Am.* F duper, refaire.

gourd ♀ ['guəd] courge *f*; gourde *f* (*a. bouteille*).

gout ✠ [gaut] goutte *f*; podagre *f*; **'gout·y** □ goutteux (-euse *f*); podagre.

gov·ern ['gʌvən] *v/t.* gouverner, régir (*a. gramm.*); *fig.* maîtriser; *v/i.* gouverner; ～*ing body* conseil *m* d'administration; **'gov·ern·a·ble** □ gouvernable; **'gov·ern·ess** gouvernante *f*; institutrice *f*; **'gov·ern·ment** gouvernement *m*; régime *m*; ministère *m*; *Am.* conseil *m* municipal; *attr.* public, d'État, gouvernemental (-aux *m/pl.*); **gov·ern·men·tal** [～'mentl] gouvernemental(-aux *m/pl.*); **'gov·er·nor** gouverneur *m* (*Am. d'un État des É.-U.*); F patron *m*; F vieux *m*; ⊕ régulateur *m*.

gown [gaun] **1.** robe *f*; *univ.*, 📕 toge *f*; **2.** *v/t.* revêtir d'une robe; *v/i.* revêtir sa robe; **gowns·man** ['～zmən] étudiant *m*; civil *m*.

grab F [græb] **1.** *v/t.* saisir, empoigner; *v/i.* ～ *at* s'agripper à; **2.** mouvement *m* vif de la main (*pour saisir q. etc.*); ⊕ benne f preneuse; *surt. Am.* ～*-bag* sac *m* à surprise; **'grab·ber** accapareur (-euse *f*) *m*.

grace [greis] **1.** grâce *f*; bénédicité *m*; ✝ délai *m*; *style*: aménité *f*; ～*s pl.* † agréments *m/pl.*; ♪ ～*-note* note *f* d'agrément; *myth.* the ♀*s pl.* les Grâces *f/pl.*; *act of* ～ faveur *f*; *with (a) good (bad)* ～ avec bonne (mauvaise) grâce; *Your* ♀ votre Grandeur *f*; *good* ～*s pl.* bonnes grâces *f/pl.*; **2.** embellir, orner; honorer (*de, with*); **grace·ful** □ ['～ful] gracieux (-euse *f*); **'grace·ful·ness** élégance *f*, grâce *f*; **'grace·less** □ impie; F effronté; inélégant.

gra·cious □ ['greiʃəs] gracieux (-euse *f*); bienveillant; miséricordieux (-euse *f*); *good(ness)* ～! bonté

divine!; mon Dieu!; **'gra·cious·ness** grâce *f*; bienveillance *f*.

gra·da·tion [grə'deiʃn] gradation *f*.

grade [greid] **1.** grade *m*, rang *m*, degré *m*; qualité *f*; *surt. Am. see* gradient; *Am.* classe *f*; *Am.* make the ～ arriver; surmonter les difficultés; *surt. Am.* ～ crossing passage *m* à niveau; *surt. Am.* ～(d) school école *f* primaire; **2.** classer; graduer; 🐂 ménager la pente de; améliorer (*le bétail*) par le métissage.

gra·di·ent ['greidiənt] 🐂 *etc.* rampe *f*, pente *f*.

grad·u·al □ ['grædjuəl] progressif (-ive *f*); graduel(le *f*); doux (douce *f*); **grad·u·ate 1.** ['～eit] *v/t.* graduer; *v/i. Am.* recevoir son diplôme; *univ.* passer sa licence; prendre ses grades; **2.** ['～it] *univ.* gradué(e *f*) *m*; **grad·u·a·tion** [～'eiʃn] gradation *f*; 🐂, ✠ graduation *f*; *Am.* remise *f* d'un diplôme; *univ.* réception *f* d'un grade.

graft¹ [grɑːft] **1.** 🌱 greffe *f*; **2.** 🌱 greffer (*a.* ✠), enter (*a. fig.*) (sur *in, upon*).

graft² *Am.* [～] **1.** corruption *f*, gratte *f*; rabiot *m*; **2.** F rabioter, gratter; **'graft·er** F *surt. pol.* rapineur *m*, F tripoteur *m*.

grail, *a.* ♀ [greil] (Saint-)Graal *m*.

grain [grein] grain *m* (*a. fig., a. mesure, a. bois*); *coll.* grains *m/pl.*; céréales *f/pl.*; *fig.* brin *m*; *in* ～ invétéré, fieffé; *dyed in the* ～ (teint) grand teint; *against the* ～ contre le fil; *fig.* à contrecœur.

gram·i·na·ceous ♀ [greimi'neiʃəs] graminé.

gram·ma·logue ['græmələg] sténogramme *m*.

gram·mar ['græmə] grammaire *f* (*a. livre*); ～*-school* école *f* secondaire; collège *m*, lycée *m*; *Am.* école *f* primaire; **gram·mar·i·an** [grə'meəriən] grammairien *m*; **gram·mat·i·cal** □ [grə'mætikl] grammatical (-aux *m/pl.*).

gram(me) [græm] gramme *m*.

gram·o·phone ['græməfoun] phonographe *m*; ～ pick-up pick-up *m/inv.*; ～ record disque *m*.

gran·a·ry ['grænəri] grenier *m*.

grand □ [grænd] **1.** *fig.* grand; grandiose, magnifique; principal (-aux *m/pl.*); F excellent; ♀ *Duchess* grande-duchesse (*pl.* grandes-duchesses) *f*; ♀ *Duke* grand-duc (*pl.* grands-ducs) *m*; *Am.* ♀ *Old Party* parti *m* républicain; *sp.* ~ *stand* grande *f* tribune; **2.** ♪ (*a.* ~ *piano*) piano *m* à queue; *Am. sl.* mille dollars *m/pl.*; *miniature* ~ piano *m* demi-queue; **gran·dam(e)** ['~dæm] † grand-mère (*pl.* grand[s]-mères) *f*; '**grand·child** petit-fils (*pl.* petits-fils) *m*; petite-fille (*pl.* petites-filles) *f*; ~**ren** *pl.* petits-enfants *m/pl.*; **gran(d)·dad** F ['grændæd] bon-papa (*pl.* bons-papas) *m*, grand-papa (*pl.* grands-papas) *m*; '**grand·daugh·ter** petite-fille (*pl.* petites-filles) *f*; **gran·dee** [græn'di:] grand *m* (*d'Espagne*); *fig.* grand personnage *m*.

gran·deur ['grændʒə] grandeur *f*; noblesse *f*; splendeur *f*; '**grand·fa·ther** grand-père (*pl.* grands-pères) *m*; ~'**s clock** horloge *f* de parquet.

gran·dil·o·quence [græn'dıləkwəns] emphase *f*; **gran·dil·o·quent** □ grandiloquent; emphatique.

gran·di·ose □ ['grændıous] grandiose, magnifique; pompeux (-euse *f*); **gran·di·os·i·ty** [~'ositi] grandiose *m*; caractère *m* pompeux.

grand·moth·er ['grænmʌðə] grand-mère (*pl.* grand[s]-mères) *f*; '**grand·ness** *see* grandeur.

grand...: '~**par·ents** *pl.* grands-parents *m/pl.*; ~**sire** ['~saiə] † *ou animal:* grand-père (*pl.* grands-pères) *m*; aïeul (*pl.* -eux) *m*; '~**son** petit-fils (*pl.* petits-fils) *m*; '~**stand** tribune *f*.

grange [greindʒ] manoir *m*, château *m*; *Am.* fédération *f* agricole.

gran·ite ['grænit] granit *m*; **gra·nit·ic** [græ'nitik] granitique, graniteux (-euse *f*).

gran·ny F ['græni] bonne-maman (*pl.* bonnes-mamans) *f*.

grant [grɑ:nt] **1.** concession *f*; subvention *f* (*pécuniaire*); ⚖ don *m*, cession *f*; **2.** accorder; céder; admettre; ⚖ faire cession de; *take for* ~**ed** prendre pour avéré, présupposer; ~**ing** *this* (*to*) *be so* admettant qu'il en soit ainsi; ceci posé; *God* ~...! Dieu veuille ...!; **gran'tee** ⚖ cessionnaire *mf*; donataire *mf*; **grant-in-aid** ['grɑ:ntin'eid] subvention *f* de l'État; **grant·or** ⚖ [~'tɔ:] donateur (-trice *f*) *m*.

gran·u·lar ['grænjulə] granuleux (-euse *f*); **gran·u·late** ['leit] (se) cristalliser; (se) grenailler; **gran·u·la·tion** granulation *f*; **gran·ule** ['~ju:l] granule *m*; **gran·u·lous** ['~julǝs] granuleux (-euse *f*), granulaire.

grape [greip] (grain *m* de) raisin *m*; *unfermented* ~ *juice* jus *m* de raisin (*infermenté*); '~**fruit** ♀ pamplemousse *m ou f*; ♀ grape-fruit *m*; '~**sug·ar** sucre *m* de raisin; '~**vine** vigne *f*; rumeur *f* publique; *hear s.th. through ou on the* ~ apprendre qch. par le téléphone arabe.

graph [grɑːf] graphique *m*, courbe *f*; '**graph·ic**, '**graph·i·cal** □ graphique; *fig.* pittoresque, vivant; ~ *arts pl.* graphique *f*; **graph·ite** *min.* ['~fait] graphite *m*; **graph·ol·o·gy** [~'fɔlədʒi] graphologie *f*.

grap·nel ['græpnəl] ⚓ grappin *m*; ⚔ ancre *f*.

grap·ple ['græpl] **1.** ⚓ grappin *m*; ⊕ araignée *f*; **2.** *v/t.* accrocher; *v/i. fig.* en venir aux prises (avec, *with*), s'attaquer (à, *with*).

grasp [grɑ:sp] **1.** poigne *f*; prise *f*; étreinte *f*; *fig.* compréhension *f*; **2.** *v/t.* saisir; empoigner; *fig.* comprendre; *v/i.:* ~ *at* chercher à saisir (*qch.*); saisir avidement (*une offre etc.*); '**grasp·ing** □ tenace; F avare.

grass [grɑ:s] herbe *f*; pâture *f*; gazon *m*; *sl.* herbe *f* (*marijuana*); *at* ~ *au vert* (*a. fig. = en congé*); *send to* ~ F étendre (*q.*) par terre; '~**hop·per** sauterelle *f*; '~**plot** pelouse *f*; '~**roots** **1.** émanant du peuple, populaire; **2.** *pol. etc.* base *f*; *fig.* les faits *m/pl.* fondamentaux; '~**wid·ow** veuve *f* temporaire; femme *f* séparée (de son mari); '~**wid·ow·er** F veuf *m* temporaire; homme *m* séparé (de sa femme); '**grass·y** herbeux (-euse *f*), herbu.

grate[1] [greit] grille *f* (*du foyer, a.* ⊕); âtre *m*; *fig.* foyer *m*.

grate[2] [~] *v/t.* râper; grincer de (*ses dents*); *v/i.* grincer, crier; ~ (*up*)*on fig.* choquer (*les oreilles*), agacer (*les nerfs*).

grate·ful □ ['greitful] reconnaissant; agréable (*chose*); bienfaisant.

grat·er ['greitǝ] râpe *f*.

grat·i·fi·ca·tion [grætifi'keiʃn] satisfaction *f*, plaisir *m*; **grat·i·fy** ['~fai] satisfaire; faire plaisir à;

gratifying 844

'**grat·i·fy·ing** flatteur (-euse *f*), agréable.

grat·ing ['greitiŋ] **1.** □ grinçant, discordant; **2.** treillis *m*; grillage *m*; grincement *m*.

gra·tis ['greitis] gratuit, gratis.

grat·i·tude ['grætitju:d] reconnaissance *f*, gratitude *f* (envers, to).

gra·tu·i·tous □ [grə'tju:itəs] gratuit; sans motif; bénévole; injustifié; **gra·tu·i·ty** gratification *f*; F pourboire *m*. [*m*, fondement *m*.]

gra·va·men ɪ̃ː [grə'veimen] fond⟩

grave[1] □ [greiv] grave; sérieux (-euse *f*); *gramm.* ~ *accent* accent *m* grave.

grave[2] [⸜] **1.** tombe(au *m*) *f*; **2.** [*irr.*] *usu. fig.* graver; '⸜**-dig·ger** fossoyeur *m*.

grav·el ['grævl] **1.** gravier *m*; ⚕ gravelle *f*; **2.** graveler; sabler; F réduire (*q.*) à quia; '**grav·el·ly** graveleux (-euse *f*).

grav·en ['greivən] *p.p. de* grave[2].

grav·er ⊕ ['greivə] échoppe *f*.

grave...: '⸜**-side**: *at his* ~ au bord de son tombeau; '⸜**-stone** pierre *f* tombale; '⸜**-yard** cimetière *m*.

grav·ing dock ⚓ ['greiviŋ'dɔk] cale *f* sèche; bassin *m* de radoub.

grav·i·tate ['græviteit] graviter (vers, to[wards]); **grav·i·ta·tion** gravitation *f*; **grav·i·ta·tion·al** [⸜ʃənl] de gravitation (*force etc.*); *phys.* ~ *pull* gravitation *f*.

grav·i·ty ['græviti] gravité *f* (*phys.*, *a. fig.*); *fig.* sérieux *m*; centre *of* ~ centre *m* de gravité; *phys. specific* ~ poids *m* spécifique.

gra·vy ['greivi] jus *m*; sauce *f* au jus; '⸜**-boat** saucière *f*.

gray [grei] gris; blême (*teint*); *Am.* F moyen(ne *f*); *a.* **grey**.

graze[1] [greiz] **1.** *vt/i.* paître; *v/t.* *vaches:* pâturer (*un champ*).

graze[2] [⸜] **1.** écorcher; *fig.* raser; **2.** écorchure *f*.

gra·zier ['greiziə] éleveur *m*.

grease 1. [gri:z] graisser; **2.** [gri:s] graisse *f*; *wool* ~ suint *m*; '⸜**-cup** *mot.* graisseur *m*; '⸜**-gun** *mot.* pompe *f* à graisse; '⸜**-pa·per** papier *m* parcheminé; papier *m* jambon; '⸜**-proof** parchemin *f*; **greas·er** *Am. sl.* ['gri:zə] Mexicain *m*, Américain *m* du Sud; **greas·y** □ ['gri:zi] graisseux (-euse *f*); taché de graisse; gras(se *f*).

great □ [greit] **1.** *usu.* grand; *qqfois* magnifique; important; F fameux (-euse *f*); ~ *grandchild* arrière-petit-fils *m*, arrière-petite-fille *f* (*pl.* ⸜*grandchildren* arrière-petits-enfants *m/pl.*). ~ *grandfather* arrière-grand-père (*pl.* arrière-grands-pères) *m*; *see deal,many*; **2.** the ~ *pl.* les grands (hommes) *m/pl.*, les célébrités *f/pl.*; *Am.* no ~ nullement; '⸜**coat** pardessus *m*; '**great·ly** beaucoup, fortement; '**great·ness** grandeur *f*; importance *f*.

greave [gri:v] jambière *f*. [*m/pl.*]

greaves [gri:vz] *pl. cuis.* cretons⟩

Gre·cian ['gri:ʃn] grec(que *f*).

greed [gri:d], '**greed·i·ness** cupidité *f*; gourmandise *f*; '**greed·y** □ avide (de *of*, *for*); gourmand.

Greek [gri:k] **1.** grec(que *f*); **2.** *ling.* grec *m*; Grec(que *f*); *that is* ~ *to me* c'est de l'hébreu pour moi.

green [gri:n] **1.** □ vert (*a.* ⊕); inexpérimenté, jeune; naïf (-ïve *f*); frais (fraîche *f*); blême (*teint*); **2.** vert *m*; gazon *m*, pelouse *f*; *fig.* première jeunesse *f*; ⸜*s pl.* légumes *m/pl.* verts; '⸜**back** *Am.* billet *m* d'un dollar *m*; '⸜**baize ta·ble** tapis *m* vert, table *f* de jeu; '**green·er·y** verdure *f*, feuillage *m*.

green...: '⸜**gage** ⚘ reine-claude (*pl.* reines-claudes) *f*; '⸜**gro·cer** marchand(e *f*) *m* de légumes; fruitier (-ère *f*) *m*; '⸜**gro·cer·y** commerce *m* de légumes; légumes *m/pl.* et fruits *m/pl.*; '⸜**horn** F blanc-bec (*pl.* blancs-becs) *m*, bleu *m*; '⸜**house** serre *f* (chaude); '**green·ish** verdâtre.

Green·land·er ['gri:nləndə] Groenlandais(e *f*) *m*; **Green·land·man** ⚓ ['⸜ləndmən] baleinière *f* (*des pêcheries du Groenland*).

green light F voie *f* libre; *fig.* permission *f*; '**green·ness** verdeur *f*; verdure *f*; immaturité *f*; naïveté *f*.

green...: '⸜**room** *théâ.* foyer *m* des artistes; '⸜**sick·ness** ⚕ chlorose *f*; '⸜**sward** gazon *m*.

greet [gri:t] saluer; accueillir; '**greet·ing** salut(ation *f*) *m*; accueil *m*; ~*s card* carte *f* de vœux.

gre·gar·i·ous □ [gre'gɛəriəs] grégaire.

gre·nade ⚔ [gri'neid] grenade *f* (à main, extinctrice); **gren·a·dier** [grenə'diə] grenadier *m*.

grew [gru:] *prét. de* grow.

grey □ [grei] **1.** gris; *fig.* ~ *area* zone *f* sombre; ♀ *Friar* frère *m* mineur; Franciscain *m*; ~ *matter* anat. substance *f* grise (du cerveau); *fig.* intelligence *f*; **2.** gris *m*; cheval *m* gris; **3.** grisailler; *v/i.* grisonner (*cheveux*); '~·**haired** aux cheveux gris, grisonnant; '~·**hound** lévrier *m*, levrette *f*; '**grey·ish** grisâtre; grisonnant (*cheveux*).

grid [grid] grille *f*, grillage *m*; réseau *m*; treillis *m*; *national* ~ caisse *f* nationale de l'énergie; *foot. Am.* (*a.* ~ *iron*) terrain *m* de rugby; *see a.* **gridiron**; '**grid·i·ron** *cuis.* gril *m*; *cycl.* F bicyclette *f*.

grief [gri:f] douleur *f*, chagrin *m*; *fig.* accident *m*.

griev·ance ['gri:vəns] grief *m*; injustice *f*; **grieve** [gri:v] (s')affliger; (se) chagriner; '**griev·ous** □ pénible; cruel(le *f*); grave; '**griev·ous·ness** gravité *f*.

grif·fin ['grifin] *myth.* griffon *m* (*a. chien*).

grig [grig] petite anguille *f*; grillon *m*.

grill [gril] **1.** griller; *v/t. sl.* cuisiner (*q.*); **2.** gril *m*; *cuis.* grillade *f*; '~·**room** grill-room *m*.

grim □ [grim] sinistre; sévère; farouche; ~ *facts* faits *m/pl.* brutaux; ~ *humo(u)r* humour *m* macabre.

gri·mace [gri'meis] **1.** grimace *f*; **2.** grimacer.

gri·mal·kin [gri'mælkin] mistigri *m*; *femme:* mégère *f*.

grime [graim] **1.** saleté *f*; poussière *f* de charbon *etc.*; **2.** noircir, salir; '**grim·y** □ noirci, sale; barbouillé.

grin [grin] **1.** large sourire *m*; **2.** sourire d'une oreille à l'autre; ~ *at* adresser un large sourire à (*q.*).

grind [graind] **1.** [*irr.*] *v/t.* moudre; broyer; dépolir (*un verre*); ⊕ meuler; aiguiser (*une lame*); *fig.* opprimer; *Am. sl.* faire enrager; *sl.* faire travailler; ~ *one's teeth* grincer des dents; ~ *out* tourner (*un air*); dire entre les dents; *v/i.* grincer, crisser; *sl.* potasser; bûcher; **2.** grincement *m*; *sl.* turbin *m*; '**grind·er** pileur (-euse *f*) *m*; (*dent f*) molaire *f*; moulin *m* (à café); ~ *rectifieuse f*; *sl.* joueur *m* d'orgue de Barbarie; '**grind·ing** *fig.* déchirant, rongeur (-euse *f*); ⊕ à roder; '**grind·stone** meule *f* à

aiguiser; *keep s.o.'s nose to the* ~ faire travailler q. sans relâche.

grip [grip] **1.** empoigner; saisir (*a. fig.*); *fig.* ~*ping* passionnant; **2.** prise *f*, serrement *m*; poignée *f* (*a. cycl.*); *Am. see* **gripsack**; *get to* ~*s with* en venir aux prises avec.

gripe [graip] **1.** saisissement *m*; étreinte *f*; poignée *f*; ~*s pl.* colique *f*; *surt. Am.* plaintes *f/pl.*; **2.** *v/t.* saisir, empoigner; donner la colique à; *v/i. surt. Am.* F rouspéter, se plaindre.

grip·sack *Am.* ['gripsæk] petite valise *f* à main. [frayant.\
gris·ly ['grizli] affreux (-euse *f*); effgrist** [grist] blé *m* moulu *ou* à moudre; *fig. bring* ~ *to the mill* faire venir l'eau au moulin.

gris·tle ['grisl] cartilage *m*; '**gris·tly** cartilagineux (-euse *f*).

grit [grit] **1.** grès *m*; sable *m*; *pierre:* grain *m*; ⊕ impuretés *f/pl.*; F courage *m*; **2.** ~ *one's teeth* grincer des dents; '**grit·ty** sablonneux (-euse *f*); graveleux (-euse *f*) (*a. poire*); *Am. sl.* qui a du cran.

griz·zle F ['grizl] grognonner; pleurnicher; '**griz·zled** *see* grizzly 1; '**griz·zly 1.** grisonnant (*cheveux etc.*); ~ *bear* = **2.** ours *m* grizzlé.

groan [groun] **1.** gémissement *m*, plainte *f*; **2.** gémir; pousser des gémissements; † ~ *for* languir après.

groat [grout]: *not worth a* ~ qui ne vaut pas un liard.

groats [grouts] *pl.* gruau *m* d'avoine *ou* de froment.

gro·cer ['grousə] épicier (-ère *f*) *m*; '**gro·cer·y** épicerie *f*; *Am.* boutique *f* d'épicier; *Am.* débit *m* de boissons; *groceries pl.* (articles *m/pl.* d')épicerie *f*. [celant; soûl.\
grog [grɔg] grog *m*; '**grog·gy** changroin** [grɔin] **1.** *anat.* aine *f*; △ arête *f*; nervure *f*; **2.** △ fournir d'arêtes; tailler les nervures sur.

groom [grum] **1.** valet *m* (*du roi etc*); valet *m* d'écurie; laquais *m*; *see* bridegroom; **2.** panser (*un cheval*); *Am. pol.* dresser (*un candidat*); *well* ~*ed* bien entretenu; élégant, bien soigné (*personne*); **grooms·man** ['~zmən] garçon *m* d'honneur.

groove [gru:v] **1.** rainure *f*; cannelure *f*; *vis:* creux *m*; *disque:* sillon *m*; *fig.* routine *f*; ~*s pl. canon etc.:* rayures *f/pl.*; *fig. in the* ~ rangé;

dans la bonne voie; **2.** rainer, canneler; rayer.

grope [group] tâtonner.

gross [grous] **1.** □ gros(se *f*); gras (-se *f*); grossier (-ère *f*); global (-aux *m/pl.*); † brut; † ~ *national product* revenu *m* national brut; **2.** grosse *f* (*12 douzaines*); *Am.* recette *f* brute; *in the* ~ à tout prendre; **'gross·ness** grossièreté *f*; énormité *f*.

gro·tesque □ [grou'tesk] grotesque.

grot·to ['grɔtou] grotte *f*.

grouch *Am.* F [grautʃ] **1.** rouspéter; ronchonner; **2.** maussaderie *f*; plainte *f*; *personne:* grogneur (-euse *f*) *m*; **'grouch·y** grognon(ne *f*).

ground¹ [graund] *prét. et p.p. de* grind¹; ~ *glass* verre *m* dépoli; *phot.* (châssis *m* à) glace *f* dépolie.

ground² [~] **1.** fond *m*; terre *f*; terrain *m* (*a. sp.*); raison *f*, cause *f*; base *f*; sol *m*; ⚡ terre *f*, masse *f*; ~s *pl.* parc *m*, terrains *m/pl.*; motifs *m/pl.*; raisons *f/pl.*; marc *m* de café; *on the* ~(*s*) *of* pour *ou* en raison de; *fall to the* ~ tomber par *ou* à terre; *fig.* ne pas aboutir; *give* ~ lâcher pied; *stand one's* ~ tenir bon; **2.** *v/t.* fonder, baser; enseigner à fond; ⊕ donner la première couche de peinture à, préparer; ⚡ mettre à la terre *ou* masse; ⚓ jeter à la côte; *v/i.* ⚓ (s')échouer; *well* ~*ed* bien fondé; **'ground·age** ⚓ droits *m/pl.* de mouillage *ou* d'ancrage.

ground...: **'~-con·nex·ion** ⚡ prise *f* de terre; *mot.* mise *f* à la masse; **'~-floor** rez-de-chaussée *m/inv.*; **'~-hog** *surt. Am.* marmotte *f* d'Amérique; **'~-less** □ sans fondement; **'~-nut** arachide *f*; **'~-'plan** plan *m* de fondation.

ground·sel ['graunsl] séneçon *m*.

ground...: **'~-sheet** tapis *m* de sol; **'~s·man** gardien *m* de stade; ~ **staff** ✈ personnel *m* rampant *ou* non-navigant; ~ **swell** houle *f* de fond; ~ **wire** ⚡ fil *m* de terre *ou* masse; **'~-work** fond(ement) *m*; *poét.* canevas *m*.

group [group] **1.** groupe *m*; peloton *m*; *psych.* ~ *therapy* thérapie *f* de groupe; **2.** (se) grouper.

grouse¹ *orn.* [graus] tétras *m*; lagopède *m* rouge.

grouse² F [~] ronchonner, grogner (*contre at, about*).

grout [graut] **1.** ⚒ coulis *m*; **2.** jointoyer (avec du mortier liquide).

grove [grouv] bosquet *m*, bocage *m*.

grov·el ['grɔvl] *usu. fig.* ramper; **'grov·el·(l)er** *usu. fig.* flagorneur (-euse *f*) *m*; **'grov·el·(l)ing 1.** rampant (*usu. fig.*); *fig.* abject; **2.** rampement *m*; *fig.* aplatissement *m*.

grow [grou] [*irr.*] *v/i.* croître, pousser; devenir; grandir (*personne*); ~ *in* s'incarner (*ongle*); ~ *into fashion* devenir de mode; ~ *out of use* se perdre; être abandonné; ~ (*up*)*on s.o.* plaire à q. de plus en plus; ~ *up* grandir; *fig.* naître, se répandre; *v/t.* cultiver; faire venir; laisser pousser; **'grow·er** cultivateur (-trice *f*) *m*; planteur *m*.

growl [graul] **1.** grondement *m*, grognement *m*; **2.** gronder, grogner.

growl·er ['graulə] *fig.* grognon(ne *f*) *m*; *Am. sl.* cruche *f* à bière.

grown [groun] **1.** *p.p. de grow*; **2.** *adj.* (*a.* ~*-up*) grand, fait; (*a.* ~*-over*) (re)couvert; **growth** [grouθ] croissance *f*; accroissement *m*; augmentation *f*; extension *f*; poussée *f*; ⚕ tumeur *f*; *of one's own* ~ indigène; qu'on a cultivé soi-même.

grub [grʌb] **1.** larve *f*; ver *m*; *péj.* gratte-papier *m/inv.*; *sl.* mangeaille *f*; **2.** *v/i.* (*a.* ~ *away*) fouiller (pour trouver qch., *for s.th.*); *sl.* bouffer (= *manger*); *v/t.* ~ *up* essarter; déraciner; (*usu.* ~ *out*) arracher; **'grub·by** malpropre; **'grub·stake** *Am.* avances *f/pl.*; équipement *m* (*que fournit un commandataire à un prospecteur*); fonds *m/pl.* (*fournis à un entrepreneur*).

grudge [grʌdʒ] **1.** rancune *f*; *bear s.o. a* ~ garder rancune à q.; avoir une dent contre q.; **2.** accorder à contrecœur; voir d'un mauvais œil; ~ *no pains* ne pas marchander sa peine; **'grudg·er** envieux (-euse *f*) *m*; **'grudg·ing·ly** ['~iŋli] à contrecœur, en rechignant.

gru·el ['gruəl] gruau *m* (*d'avoine*); *sl.* **get** (*ou have*) *one's* ~ avaler sa médecine; **'gru·el·(l)ing** éreintant.

grue·some □ ['gru:səm] macabre.

gruff □ [grʌf] bourru, revêche, rude.

grum·ble ['grʌmbl] grommeler; grogner; gronder (*tonnerre*); **'grumbler** *fig.* mécontent(e *f*) *m*.

gunman

grump·y □ F ['grʌmpi] maussade; grincheux (-euse f).

grunt [grʌnt] **1.** grognement m; **2.** grogner; **'grunt·er** porc m.

guar·an·tee [gærən'ti:] **1.** garant(e f) m, caution f; garanti(e f) m; see *guaranty*; **2.** garantir; se porter caution pour; **guar·an·tor** [‿'tɔ:] garant(e f) m; **'guar·an·ty** garantie f; caution f, gage m.

guard [gɑ:d] **1.** garde f (a. ⚔); ⊕ protecteur m (*d'une machine*), carter m (*d'engrenages*); 🚃 chef m de train; ⚔ ⌀s pl. Garde f; *be off* ⌀ être pris au dépourvu; ⌀ *of honour* haie f d'honneur; ⚔ *mount* ⌀ monter la garde; ⚔ *relieve* ⌀ relever la garde; **2.** v/t. protéger (a. ⊕); garder (de *from, against*); v/i. se garder (de, *against*); **'guard·ed** □ prudent, réservé, mesuré; **'guard·i·an** gardien(ne f) m; ⚖ tuteur (-trice f) m; *attr.* tutélaire; ⌀ *of the poor* administrateur (-trice f) m de l'Assistance publique; **'guard·i·an·ship** garde f; tutelle f; **'guard·rail** barrière f de sécurité; **guards·man** ⚔ ['gɑ:dzmən] officier m *ou* soldat m de la Garde.

gudg·eon ['gʌdʒən] *icht.*, ⊕ goujon m; *fig.* benêt m.

guer·don *poét.* ['gə:dən] **1.** récompense f; **2.** récompenser.

gue(r)·ril·la [gə'rilə] (*souv.* ⌀ *war*) guerre f d'embuscades *ou* de partisans.

guess [ges] **1.** conjecture f; **2.** v/t. deviner; *surt. Am.* croire, supposer; v/i. deviner; estimer (qch., *at* s.th.); **'guess·work** conjecture f, estime f.

guest [gest] invité(e f) m; pensionnaire mf; **'⌀·house** pension f de famille; **'⌀·room** chambre f d'amis.

guf·faw [gʌ'fɔ:] **1.** gros rire m; **2.** pouffer de rire.

guid·a·ble ['gaidəbl] dirigeable; **guid·ance** ['gaidəns] conduite f; gouverne f; direction f; orientation f.

guide [gaid] **1.** guide m (a. ⊕); see ⌀*book*; *attr.* directeur (-trice f); **2.** guider; conduire; diriger; *guiding principle* principe m directeur, gouverne f; **'⌀·book** guide m; **'⌀·dog** chien m d'aveugle; **'⌀·lines** pl. directives f/pl.; **'⌀·post** poteau m indicateur; **'⌀·rope** ✠ guiderope m.

gui·don ⚔ ['gaidən] guidon m.

guild [gild] association f; corps m (*de métier*); *hist.* corporation f; **'Guild'hall** hôtel m de ville.

guile [gail] ruse f, astuce f; **'guile·ful** □ ['‿ful] rusé; **'guile·less** □ candide; franc(he f); **'guile·less·ness** candeur f; franchise f.

guil·lo·tine [gilə'ti:n] guillotine f; ⊕ presse f à rogner.

guilt [gilt], *a.* **'guilt·i·ness** culpabilité f; **'guilt·less** □ innocent (de, *of*); *fig.* vierge (de, *of*); **'guilt·y** □ coupable; *plead* ⌀ s'avouer coupable.

guin·ea ['gini] guinée f (*21 shillings*); **'⌀·fowl** pintade f; **'⌀·pig** cobaye m, cochon m d'Inde.

guise [gaiz] † costume m; forme f; apparence f (a. fig.).

gui·tar ♪ [gi'tɑ:] guitare f.

gulch *Am.* [gʌltʃ] ravin m étroit.

gulf [gʌlf] *géog.* golfe m; abysse m (*de la mer*); abîme m, gouffre m.

gull¹ *orn.* [gʌl] mouette f, goéland m.

gull² [‿] **1.** jobard m, dupe f; **2.** jobarder, duper; amener (q.) par ruse (à *inf.*, *into gér.*).

gul·let ['gʌlit] œsophage m; F gosier m; † ravin m.

gul·li·bil·i·ty [gʌli'biliti] crédulité f; **gul·li·ble** □ ['‿əbl] crédule; facile à duper.

gul·ly ['gʌli] ravine f; ruisseau: ru m; ⊕ caniveau m; (a. ⌀*·hole*) bouche f d'égout.

gulp [gʌlp] **1.** coup m (de gosier); **2.** avaler (à pleine gorge).

gum¹ [gʌm] *usu.* ⌀s pl. gencive f.

gum² [‿] **1.** gomme f; colle f; *Am.* gomme f à mâcher; ⌀s pl. *Am.* caoutchouc m/pl., bottes f/pl. de caoutchouc; **2.** gommer; coller.

gum·boil ['gʌmbɔil] abcès m à la gencive, 🐾 parulie f.

gum·my ['gʌmi] gommeux (-euse f); gluant; chassieux (-euse f) (*yeux*).

gump·tion ['gʌmpʃn] jugeotte f; sens m pratique.

gun [gʌn] **1.** canon m; fusil m (de chasse); ⊕ injecteur m (à graisse); *peint.* pistolet m; *surt. Am.* revolver m, pistolet m; *Am. mot. sl.* accélérateur m; F *big* (*ou great*) ⌀ grand personnage m; **2.** Am. chasser au tir; *fig.* pourchasser; **'⌀·boat** (chaloupe f) canonnière f; **'⌀·carriage** ⚔ affût m; **'⌀·cot·ton** coton m azotique; **'⌀·li·cence** *Am.* permis m de port d'armes; **'⌀·man** *surt. Am.*

bandit *m*, gangster *m*, terroriste *m*; '**gun·ner** ✕, ⚓ canonnier *m*.

gun...: '~**pow·der** poudre *f* (*à canon*); '~**run·ning** contrebande *f* d'armes; '~**shot** coup *m* de fusil *ou* de feu; portée *f* de fusil; '~**shy** qui a peur du coup de fusil; '~**smith** armurier *m*; *Am. sl.* professeur *m* de vol à la tire; '~**stock** fût *m* (*de fusil*); '~**tur·ret** tourelle *f*.

gur·gle ['gəːgl] glouglouter.

gush [gʌʃ] **1.** jaillissement *m*; jet *m*; débordement *m* (sentimental); **2.** jaillir (de, from); bouillonner; *fig.* sortir à flots; *fig.* faire de la sensiblerie; '**gush·er** *fig.* personne *f* expansive; puits *m* jaillissant; '**gush·ing**, **gush·y** □ exubérant, expansif (-ive *f*).

gus·set ['gʌsit] *cost.* soufflet *m*; gousset *m*.

gust [gʌst] rafale *f*, bourrasque *f*, coup *m* de vent; bouffée *f* (*de colère*).

gus·ta·to·ry ['gʌstətəri] gustatif (-ive *f*).

gus·to ['gʌstou] délectation *f*; entrain *m*.

gus·ty ['gʌsti] à rafales; venteux (-euse *f*).

gut [gʌt] **1.** boyau *m*, intestin *m*; ♪ corde *f* de boyau; *fig.* passage *m* étroit; ~*s pl. sl.* cran *m* (= *courage*); **2.** vider (*un poisson*); *fig.* résumer; *incendie*: ne laisser que les murs de (*une maison*); piller; '**gut·less** F mou (molle *f*), lâche, qui manque de cran; '**guts·y** F qui a du cran; qui a du punch.

gut·ter ['gʌtə] **1.** gouttière *f* (*d'un toit*); *rue*: ruisseau *m*; *chaussee*: caniveau *m*; **2.** *v/t.* sillonner, raviner; rainer (*une tôle etc.*); *v/i.* couler (*bougie*); ~ **press** bas-fonds

m/pl. du journalisme; '~**snipe** gavroche *m*; gamin(e *f*) *m* des rues.

gut·tur·al *anat., a. gramm.* ['gʌtərəl] **1.** □ guttural (-aux *m/pl.*); **2.** gutturale *f*.

guy¹ [gai] **1.** F épouvantail *m*; *surt. Am.* F type *m*, individu *m*; **2.** se moquer de; travestir.

guy² [~] retenue *f*; ⚓ étai *m*, hauban *m*.

guz·zle ['gʌzl] boire avidement; *v/t.* bouffer; *v/i.* goinfrer.

gym *sl.* [dʒim] *abr. de* gymnasium, gymnastics.

gym·kha·na [dʒim'kɑːnə] gymkhana *m*.

gym·na·si·um [dʒim'neizjəm] gymnase *m*; **gym·nast** ['dʒimnæst] gymnaste *m*; **gym'nas·tic 1.** (~*ally*) gymnastique; ~ *competition* concours *m* de gymnastique; **2.** ~*s pl.* gymnastique *f*; éducation *f* physique; *heavy* ~*s pl.* gymnastique *f* aux agrès; *light* ~*s* callisthénie *f*.

gyn·ae·col·o·gist ⚕ [gaini'kɔlədʒist] gynécologiste *m*; **gyn·ae'col·o·gy** gynécologie *f*.

gyp *sl.* [dʒip] *Am.* voler; tromper.

gyp·se·ous ['dʒipsiəs] gypseux (-euse *f*).

gyp·sum *min.* ['dʒipsəm] gypse *m*.

gy·rate [dʒaiə'reit] tourn(oy)er; **gy'ra·tion** giration *f*, révolution *f*; **gy·ra·to·ry** ['dʒaiərətəri] giratoire.

gy·ro·com·pass *phys.* ['gaiəro-'kʌmpəs] gyrocompas *m*; **gy·ro·scope** ['gaiərəskoup] gyroscope *m*; **gy·ro·scop·ic sta·bi·liz·er** [gaiə-rəs'kɔpik'steibilaizə] gyrostat *m* (*de bateau*); toupie *f* gyroscopique.

gyve *poét.* [dʒaiv] **1.**: ~*s pl.* fers *m/pl.*, chaînes *f/pl.*; **2.** enchaîner, mettre les fers à.

H

H, h [eitʃ] H *m*, h *m*; *drop one's hs* ne pas aspirer les h.

ha [hɑː] ha!; ah!

ha·be·as cor·pus 🕇 ['heibjəs-ˈkɔːpəs] (*a. writ of* ~) habeas corpus *m*.

hab·er·dash·er ['hæbədæʃə] mercier (-ère *f*) *m*; *surt. Am.* chemisier *m*; **'hab·er·dash·er·y** mercerie *f*; *surt. Am.* chemiserie *f*.

ha·bil·i·ments [hə'bilimənts] *pl.* vêtements *m/pl.* de cérémonie.

hab·it ['hæbit] **1.** habitude *f*; disposition *f* (*d'esprit*); habit *m* (*de moine*); *be in the* ~ *of* (*gér.*) avoir l'habitude de (*inf.*); *see riding-*~; **2.** vêtir; **'hab·it·a·ble** habitable; **hab·i·tat** 🕂, *zo.* [ˈ~tæt] habitat *m*; aire *f* d'habitation; **hab·i'ta·tion** habitation *f*; demeure *f*.

ha·bit·u·al □ [hə'bitjuəl] habituel(le *f*); invétéré; **ha'bit·u·ate** [~eit] habituer (à, *to*); **hab·i·tude** ['hæbitjuːd] habitude *f*.

hack¹ [hæk] **1.** ⊕ pic *m*, pioche *f*; taillade *f*; *foot.* coup *m* de pied; **2.** hacher; couper; *foot.* (*ou v/i.* ~ *at*) donner à (*q.*) un coup de pied sur le tibia; ~*ing cough* toux *f* sèche.

hack² [~] **1.** cheval *m* de louage *ou* de selle à toutes fins; *fig.* homme *m* de peine; (*souv.* ~ *writer*) nègre *m*; **2.** à la tâche; *fig.* banal (-als *m/pl.*); **3.** banaliser.

hack·le ['hækl] **1.** ⊕ peigne *m*; *orn.* plume *f* de cou *ou* de dos; **2.** (se) taillader; *v/t.* peigner.

hack·ney ['hækni] *see hack²*; ~ *coach* voiture *f* de louage; **'hack·neyed** banal (-als *m/pl.*).

hack·saw ['hæksɔː] scie *f* à métaux.

had [hæd, həd] *prét. et p.p. de have 1, 2.*

had·dock *icht.* ['hædək] aiglefin *m*; *finnan* ~ haddock *m*.

hae·mal 𝔯 ['hiːml] hémal (-aux *m/pl.*); **haemo...** [hiːmo] hém(o)-.

haem·or·rhage ['hemɔridʒ] hémorragie *f*; **haem·or·rhoids** [ˈ~rɔidz] *pl.* hémorroïdes *f/pl.*

haft [hɑːft] manche *m*, poignée *f*.

hag [hæg] sorcière *f*; *fig. sl.* vieille taupe *f*.

hag·gard □ ['hægəd] hagard; hâve.

hag·gle ['hægl] marchander; chicaner (sur, *over*).

hag·rid·den ['hægridn] tourmenté par les cauchemars.

hail¹ [heil] **1.** grêle *f*; **2.** *v/impers.* grêler; *v/t. fig.* faire pleuvoir.

hail² [~] **1.** *v/t.* saluer; héler; *v/i.*: ~ *from* venir de; être originaire de; **2.** appel *m*; ~! salut!; *within* ~ à portée de (la) voix.

hail-fel·low ['heilfelou] très gentil pour *ou* avec tous.

hail·stone ['heilstoun] grêlon *m*; **'hail·storm** abat *m* de grêle.

hair [hɛə] cheveu *m*, -x *m/pl.* (*sur la tête*); poil *m*; *sl.* keep your ~ *on!* calmez-vous!; ~*'s breadth* = **'~-breadth** épaisseur *f* d'un cheveu; *by* (*ou within*) *a* ~ à un cheveu (de), à deux doigts (de); ~ **cream** crème *f* à coiffer; '~**cut** taille *f* (de cheveux); *have a* ~ se faire couper les cheveux; '~-**do** F coiffure *f*; '~-**dress·er** coiffeur (-euse *f*) *m*; '~-**dry·er** sèche-cheveux *m/inv.*; séchoir *m*; '~-**dye** teinture *f* pour les cheveux; '**haired** aux cheveux ...; à pelage ...; '**hair·i·ness** aspect *m* hirsute.

hair...: '~-**less** sans cheveux, chauve; '~**line** naissance *f* des cheveux; *écriture*: délié *m*; ~ *crack* fissure *f* fine; '~-**piece** postiche *m*; '~-**pin** épingle *f* à cheveux; ~ *bend* lacet *m*; '~-**rais·ing** horripilant, horrifique; '~-**re·mov·er** dépilatoire *m*; '~-**re·stor·er** régénérateur *m* des cheveux; '~-**split·ting** ergotage *m*; '~**spray** laque *f* (en aérosol); '~**style** coiffure *f*; ~ **styl·ist** coiffeur *m* (-euse *f*); '**hair·y** chevelu; poilu, velu.   [colin *m*.]

hake [heik] *icht.* merluche *f*; F]

ha·la·tion *phot.* [hə'leiʃn] halo *m*.

hal·berd ⚔ *hist.* ['hælbəd] hallebarde *f*.

hal·cy·on [ˈhælsiən] **1.** orn. alcyon m; martin-pêcheur (pl. martins-pêcheurs) m; **2.** fig. calme, serein.

hale [heil] vigoureux (-euse f); robuste; ~ and hearty frais et gaillard.

half [hɑːf] **1.** demi; adv. à moitié; ~ a crown une demi-couronne f; à pound and a ~ une livre et demie; F not ~ et comment!; it isn't ~ bad ce n'est pas mauvais du tout; **2.** moitié f; ᴁ demi m; see ~-year; ᴁ parti m; too clever by ~ beaucoup trop malin; by halves à demi; go halves se mettre de moitié (avec q., with s.o.), partager; ~-back [ˈ~ˈbæk] foot. demi(-arrière) m; ~-baked [ˈ~ˈbeikt] fig. inexpérimenté; niais; incomplet (-ète f); '~-bind·ing demi-reliure f à petits coins; '~-blood parenté f d'un seul côté; '~-'bound en demi-reliure à petits coins; '~-bred demi-sang m/inv.; '~-breed métis(se f) m; '~-broth·er demi-frère m; '~-caste métis(se f) m; '~-court line tennis: ligne f médiane; '~-crown demi-couronne f; '~-'fare **1.** demi-tarif m; **2.** à demi-tarif; '~-'heart·ed □ tiède; hésitant; '~-'length (a. ~ portrait) portrait m en buste; '~-'mast: (at) ~ à mi-mât; en berne (pavillon); '~-'moon demi-lune f; '~-'mourn·ing demi-deuil m; ~ note ♪ blanche f; '~-'pay demi-solde f; ~ pen·ny [ˈheipni] **1.** demi-penny m; F sou m; **2.** à un sou; '~-'price: at ~ à moitié prix; ~seas·o·ver F [ˈhɑːfsiːzˈouvə] à moitié ivre; '~-'time sp. mi-temps f; '~-tone proc·ess ⊕ simili(gravure) f (tramée); '~-truth demi-vérité f; '~-'way à mi-chemin; ~ house maison f à demi-étape; fig. compromis m; '~-'wit simple mf, faible mf d'esprit; '~-'wit·ted simple; niais; '~-'year semestre m.

hal·i·but icht. [ˈhælibət] flétan m.

hal·i·to·sis [hæliˈtəusis] mauvaise haleine f.

hall [hɔːl] grande salle f; vestibule m; hall m (hôtel); château m; univ. maison f estudiantine, foyer m; réfectoire m; see guild-~, music-~.

hal·le·lu·jah [hæliˈluːjə] alléluia m.

hall...: '~-'mark **1.** contrôle m; fig. cachet m, empreinte f; **2.** contrôler; '~-'stand porte-parapluies m/inv.

hal·loo [həˈluː] **1.** holà!; **2.** ohé m;

chasse: huée f; **3.** v/i. crier (taïaut); v/t. encourager.

hal·low [ˈhælou] sanctifier, consacrer; **Hal·low·mas** [ˈ~mæs] la Toussaint f.

hal·lu·ci·na·tion [həluːsiˈneiʃn] hallucination f, illusion f.

halm [hɑːm] see haulm.

ha·lo [ˈheilou] astr., anat. halo m; auréole f (a. eccl., a. fig.).

halt [hɔːlt] **1.** halte f (a. ⚙), arrêt m; **2.** faire halte; s'arrêter; fig. hésiter, balancer; **3.** boiteux (-euse f).

hal·ter [ˈhɔːltə] cheval: licou m; corde f (au cou).

halve [hɑːv] diviser en deux; **halves** [~z] pl. de half.

hal·yard ⚓ [ˈhæljəd] drisse f.

ham [hæm] jambon m; Am. sl. (a. ~ actor ou fatter) cabotin m; (souv. radio) amateur m.

ham·burg·er [ˈhæmbəːgə] hamburger m, bifteck m haché; viande f de bœuf hachée.

ham-fist·ed [ˈhæmfistid], **ham-hand·ed** [ˈ~hændid] gauche, maladroit.

ham·let [ˈhæmlit] hameau m.

ham·mer [ˈhæmə] **1.** marteau m; armes à feu: chien m; F ~ and tongs tant qu'on peut; **2.** v/t. marteler, battre au marteau; bourse: exécuter (un agent); F critiquer; ~ out gironner; F forger; v/i. ~ at heurter à; s'acharner à.

ham·mock [ˈhæmək] hamac m; ~ chair transatlantique m.

ham·per [ˈhæmpə] **1.** panier m, banne f; **2.** embarrasser, gêner; entraver.

ham·string [ˈhæmstriŋ] **1.** anat. tendon m du jarret; **2.** couper le jarret à; fig. couper les moyens à.

hand [hænd] **1.** main f (a. zo., a. fig. = aide, autorité, possession, protection); montre: aiguille f; ouvrier (-ère f) m; ⚓ matelot m; côté m; cartes: joueur (-euse f) m; cartes: jeu m; mesure: paume f; écriture f; signature f; typ. index m; baromètre etc.: indicateur m; ⚘ régime m (de fruits); at ~ sous la main; à portée de la main; tout près; at first ~ de première main; a good (poor) ~ at bon (piètre) joueur de; fort à (faible en); be ~ and glove être d'intelligence (avec, with); être comme les deux doigts de la main;

by ~ à la main; *change* ~*s* changer de propriétaire *ou* de mains; *get out of* ~ s'indiscipliner, devenir impossible; *have a* ~ *in* prendre part à; *in* ~ en main; au poing; à la main; en question; en préparation; *sp.* de retard; ✝ en caisse; en magasin; *lay* ~*s on* faire violence à; s'emparer de; mettre les mains sur; *lend a* ~ aider; donner un coup de main (à); *off* ~ brusque; tout de suite; ~*s off!* n'y touchez pas!; *on* ~ en main; ✝ en magasin; *surt. Am.* tout près; prêt; *on one's* ~*s* à sa charge; *on all* ~*s* de tous les côtés; de toutes parts; *on the one* ~ d'une part; *on the other* ~ d'autre part; par contre; *have one's* ~ *out* avoir perdu l'habitude; *out of* ~ sur-le-champ; indiscipliné; ~ *over fist* main sur main; rapidement; *take a* ~ *at* faire une partie de (*bridge etc.*); *to* (*one's*) ~ sous la main; ~ *to* ~ corps à corps; *come to* ~ parvenir, arriver; *put one's* ~ *to* entreprendre; *he can turn his* ~ *to anything* c'est un homme à toute main; ~*s up!* haut les mains!; *see high* 1; **2.** passer; ~ *about* faire circuler; ~ *down* descendre (*qch.*); transmettre; ~ *in* remettre; présenter (*une demande*); ~ *out* distribuer; tendre; ~ *over* remettre; céder; '~**-bag** sac *m* à main; '~**-bar·row** brancard *m*, civière *f*; '~**-bell** sonnette *f*; '~**-bill** affiche *f* à la main; ✝ prospectus *m*; '~**-brake** ⊕ frein *m* à main; '~**-cuff 1.**: ~*s pl.* menottes *f/pl.*; **2.** mettre les menottes à (*q.*); '**hand·ed** à ... mains; aux mains ...; **hand·ful** ['~ful] poignée *f*; F enfant *mf* terrible; '**hand-glass** loupe *f* à main; miroir *m* à main.

hand·i·cap ['hændikæp] **1.** *sp.* handicap *m*; *fig.* désavantage *m*; **2.** *sp.* handicaper; *fig.* gêner; *fig.* désavantager; '**hand·i·capped 1.** handicapé; **2.**: *the* (*mentally ou physically*) ~ les handicapés (mentaux *ou* physiques); '**hand·i·cap·per** *sp.* handicapeur *m*.

hand·i·craft ['hændikrɑːft] travail *m* manuel *f*; métier *m* manuel; '**hand·i·crafts·man** artisan *m*, ouvrier *m*; '**hand·i·ness** commodité *f*; adresse *f*, dextérité *f*; '**hand·i·work** travail *m* manuel; ouvrage *m* (*a. fig.*).

hand·ker·chief ['hæŋkətʃif] mouchoir *m*; foulard *m* (*pour le cou*).

han·dle ['hændl] **1.** *épée, porte*: poignée *f*; *outil*: manche *m*; *seau, cruche*: anse *f*; *pompe*: balancier *m*; *Am.* F *fly off the* ~ s'emporter; *sl.* sortir de ses gonds; **2.** manier; manœuvrer (*un navire*); traiter; prendre en main; '~**-bar** *cycl.* guidon *m*; *dropped* ~ guidon *m* course.

hand...: '~**-'made pa·per** papier *m* à la cuve; '~**-maid** *fig.* servante *f*; '~**-me-downs** *Am.* F *pl.* costume *m* de confection; décrochez-moi-ça *m/inv.*; '~**-out** *Am.* F aumône *f*; '~**-rail** main *f* courante; garde-fou *m*; '~**-saw** scie *f* à main; égoïne *f*; **hand·sel** ['hænsl] **1.** étrenne *f*; ✝ première vente *f*; arrhes *f/pl.*; **2.** donner des étrennes; ✝ donner des arrhes à; inaugurer; '**hand-shake** poignée *f* de main; **hand·some** □ ['hænsəm] beau (bel *devant une voyelle ou un h muet*; belle *f*; beaux *m/pl.*); élégant; noble; riche.

hand...: '~**-spike** ⊕ levier *m* de manœuvre; '~**-work** travail *m* à la main; '~**-writ·ing** écriture *f*; '**hand·y** □ adroit; habile; commode (*chose*); maniable; ~**man** homme *m* à tout faire; factotum *m*, bricoleur *m*; F débrouillard *m*.

hang [hæŋ] **1.** [*irr.*] *v/t.* (sus)pendre (à *from, on*); tapisser (de, *with*); accrocher (à *from, on*); coller (*un papier à tapisser*); (*usu. prét. et p.p.* ~*ed*) pendre; F *I'll be* ~*ed if* ... que le diable m'emporte si ...; F ~ *it!* zut alors!; F ~ *fire* traîner; ~ *out vt/i.* pendre au dehors; ~ *up* accrocher, pendre; *téléph.* raccrocher (*le récepteur*); *fig.* ajourner; *v/i.* pendre, être suspendu (à, *on*); *fig.* planer (sur, *over*); ~ *about* flâner; rôder; ~ *back* rester en arrière; *fig.* hésiter; ~ *on* s'accrocher, se cramponner (à, *to*); *fig.* tenir bon; *téléph.* ~ *up* raccrocher; **2.** pente *f*; *cost.* ajustement *m*; F façon *f*; F *get the* ~ *of* comprendre, saisir le truc de (*qch.*); *sl. I don't care a* ~ je m'en moque pas mal.

hang·ar ['hæŋə] hangar *m*.

hang-dog ['hæŋdɔg] **1.** F gibier *m* de potence; **2.** patibulaire (*mine*).

hang·er ['hæŋə] *personne*: tendeur *m*; crochet *m*; porte-vêtements *m/inv.*; ⊕ suspenseur *m*; *Am.*

pancarte *f*; ~**-on** [ˈɑːrˈɔn], *pl.* ˈ~**s-**ˈ**on** *fig.* parasite *m*; dépendant *m*.

hang-glid·ing [ˈhæŋglaidiŋ] vol *m* libre.

hang·ing [ˈhæŋiŋ] **1.** suspendu; tombant; *peint.* ~ *committee* jury *m* d'admission (des tableaux); **2.**: ~**s** *pl.* tenture *f*, tapisserie *f*; rideaux *m/pl.*

hang·man [ˈhæŋmən] bourreau *m*.

hang·nail ⚓ [ˈhæŋneil] envie *f*.

hang·out *Am. sl.* [ˈhæŋˈaut] repaire *m*, nid *m* (*de gangsters etc.*).

hang·over *sl.* [ˈhæŋouvə] gueule *f* de bois.

hang·up *sl.* [ˈhæŋʌp] problème *m*; complexe *m*. [neau *m.*]

hank [hæŋk] écheveau *m*; ⚓ an-

han·ker [ˈhæŋkə]: ~ *after* soupirer après, désirer vivement; être assoiffé de; ˈ**han·ker·ing** vif désir *m*, soif *f*.

Han·o·ve·ri·an [hænoˈviəriən] **1.** hanovrien(ne *f*); **2.** Hanovrien(ne *f*) *m*.

Han·sard [ˈhænsəd] compte *m* rendu officiel des débats parlementaires.

han·som [ˈhænsəm] (*a.* ~**-cab**) cab *m*; hansom *m*.

hap † [hæp] hasard *m* (*malencontreux*); destin *m*; ˈ**hap·haz·ard** **1.** hasard *m*; *at* ~ au petit bonheur; **2.** fortuit; ~ *chaos* tohu-bohu *m*; ˈ**hap·less** □ infortuné, malheureux (-euse *f*).

ha'p'orth F [ˈheipəθ] (valeur *f* d')un sou *m*; *a* ~ *of* ... ... pour un sou.

hap·pen [ˈhæpən] arriver, se passer; *he* ~*ed to be at home* il se trouvait chez lui; ~ (*up*)*on* tomber sur; rencontrer par hasard; *Am.* F ~, ~ *in*(*to*) entrer en passant; ˈ**hap·pen·ing** événement *m*.

hap·pi·ness [ˈhæpinis] bonheur *m*; félicité *f* (*a. d'expression*).

hap·py □ [ˈhæpi] *usu.* heureux (-euse *f*); content; joyeux (-euse *f*); F un peu parti *ou* gris; ˈ~**-go-luck·y** F insouciant.

ha·rangue [həˈræŋ] **1.** harangue *f*; **2.** *v/t.* haranguer; *v/i.* prononcer une harangue.

har·ass [ˈhærəs] harceler; tourmenter (de, *with*); tracasser; accabler (de dettes, *with debt*); ˈ**har·ass·ment** harcèlement *m*; tracassement *m*.

har·bin·ger [ˈhɑːbindʒə] **1.** *fig.* avant-coureur *m*; **2.** annoncer.

har·bo(u)r [ˈhɑːbə] **1.** port *m*; *fig.* asile *m*; **2.** *v/t.* héberger; receler (*un criminel*); entretenir (*un soupçon*); garder (*une rancune etc.*); *v/i.* se réfugier; ˈ**har·bo(u)r·age** abri *m*, asile *m*; ⚓ mouillage *m*.

hard [hɑːd] **1.** *adj. usu.* dur; sévère; fort (*gelée*); rigoureux (-euse *f*) (*temps*); pénible; cruel(le *f*); rude; difficile; *surt. Am.* incorrigible; *surt. Am.* riche (en alcool); ferme (*rendez-vous*); ~ *cash* espèces *f/pl.* sonnantes; ~ *coal* anthracite *m*; ~ *core* noyau *m* dur; *tennis:* ~ *courts pl.* terrains *m/pl.* de tennis; ~ *currency* devises *f/pl.* fortes; ~ *drink* (*ou liquor*) alcool *m* fort; *the* ~ *facts* les faits brutaux; ~ *hat* casque *m*; *pol.* ~ *line* ligne *f* dure; F ~ *luck* déveine *f*, malchance *f*; ~ *sell* promotion *f* de vente agressive; *mot.* ~ *shoulder* accotement *m* stabilisé; ~ *of hearing* dur d'oreille; ~ *to deal with* peu commode; intraitable; *be* ~ (*up*)*on s.o.* être sévère envers q.; traiter q. sévèrement; *give s.o. a* ~ *time* donner du mal à q.; faire passer un mauvais quart d'heure à q.; faire la vie dure à q.; **2.** *adv.* fort; durement; avec peine; ~ *by* tout près; ~ *up* sans moyens; dans la gêne; à court (de, *for*); *be* ~ *put to it* avoir beaucoup de mal (à *to*); *ride* ~ chevaucher à toute vitesse; **3.** F travaux *m/pl.* forcés; ~**s** *pl.* gêne *f*; ˈ~**-ˈbit·ten** F tenace; dur à cuire; ˈ~**-ˈboiled** dur (*œuf*); tenace; *surt. Am.* expérimenté, dur à cuire; ˈ**hard·en** (se) durcir; (s')endurcir; rendre *ou* devenir dur; *v/i.* ♥, *bourse:* se raffermir; *v/t.* ⊕ tremper (*l'acier*); ˈ**hard·en·ing** durcissement *m*.

hard...: ˈ~**-ˈfea·tured** aux traits durs *ou* sévères; ˈ~**-ˈfist·ed** dur à la détente; ˈ~**-ˈhead·ed** pratique; positif (-ive *f*); ˈ~**-ˈheart·ed** □ au cœur dur; **har·di·hood** [ˈhɑːdihud] hardiesse *f*; ˈ**har·di·ness** vigueur *f*, robustesse *f*; ˈ**hard·lin·er** partisan *m* d'une ligne dure; ˈ**hard·ˈluck·stor·y** F récit *m* de misères; ˈ**hard·ly** durement; avec difficulté; à peine; ne ... guère; ˈ**hard·ˈmouthed** dur de bouche; ˈ**hard·ness** dureté *f*, difficulté *f* (*a. fig.*); rudesse *f*; *temps:* rigueur *f*; *acier:* trempe *f*.

hard...: ˈ~**-pan** *Am.* sol *m* résistant;

'⁓-'**set** fort gêné; affamé; durci;
'⁓-**shell** à carapace dure; à coque
dure; *fig.* dur à cuire; '**hard·ship**
privation *f*; gêne *f*; épreuve *f*, tribulation *f*; '**hard·ware** quincaillerie *f*; *ordinateur*: hardware *m*,
matériel *m*; '**har·dy** □ robuste,
endurci; hardi; ♀ de pleine terre.

hare [hɛə] lièvre *m*; '⁓-**bell** jacinthe
f des prés; clochette *f*; '⁓-**brained**
étourdi, écervelé; '⁓'**lip** *anat.* bec-
de-lièvre (*pl.* becs-de-lièvre) *m*.

ha·rem ['hɛərem] harem *m*.

har·i·cot ['hærikou] *cuis.* haricot *m*
(*de mouton*); ♀ (*a.* ⁓ *bean*) haricot
m.

hark [hɑːk] (*to*) écouter; prêter
l'oreille (à); ⁓! écoutez!; ⁓ *back*
chasse: prendre le contre-pied; *fig.*
en revenir (à, sur *to*).

har·lot ['hɑːlət] prostituée *f*; '**har·**
lot·ry prostitution *f*.

harm [hɑːm] **1.** mal *m*; tort *m*;
danger *m*; **2.** faire du mal *ou* tort
à; nuire à; '**harm·ful** □ ['⁓ful]
nuisible; '**harm·less** □ inoffensif
(-ive *f*); innocent.

har·mon·ic [hɑːˈmɔnik] (⁓*ally*) harmonique; **har**'**mon·i·ca** [⁓ikə]
harmonica *m*; **har·mo·ni·ous** □
[hɑːˈmounjəs] harmonieux (-euse *f*)
(*a. fig.*); **har·mo·nize** ['hɑːmənaiz]
v/t. harmoniser (*a.* ♪); faire accorder; *v/i.* s'harmoniser; s'assortir;
'**har·mo·ny** harmonie *f*.

har·ness ['hɑːnis] **1.** harnais *m*;
attelage *m*; die in ⁓ mourir à la
besogne; **2.** harnacher; atteler; *fig.*
aménager; '⁓-**mak·er** sellier *m*,
bourrelier *m*.

harp ♪ [hɑːp] **1.** harpe *f*; **2.** jouer de
la harpe; ⁓ (*up*)*on* rabâcher (*qch.*);
be always ⁓*ing on the same string*
réciter toujours la même litanie;
'**harp·er**, '**harp·ist** harpiste *mf*.

har·poon [hɑːˈpuːn] **1.** harpon *m*;
2. harponner.

har·py ['hɑːpi] *myth.* harpie *f* (*a.*
fig. = *vieille mégère*); *fig.* personne *f*
rapace.

har·ri·dan ['hæridən] vieille mégère *f*.

har·ri·er ['hæriə] *chasse*: braque *m*;
sp. coureur *m*.

har·row ✗ ['hærou] **1.** herse *f*;
2. herser; *fig.* ravager, piller.

har·ry ['hæri] ravager, piller, mettre
à sac; *fig.* harceler, tourmenter.

harsh □ [hɑːʃ] rude; âpre (*goût*);
rauque; discordant (*son*); rigoureux
(-euse *f*); dur; '**harsh·ness** rudesse
f; âpreté *f*; rigueur *f*; sévérité *f*.

hart *zo.* [hɑːt] cerf *m*.

har·um-scar·um F ['hɛərəm'skɛə-
rəm] **1.** étourdi, écervelé (*a. su.*/*mf*);
2. étourneau *m*; hurluberlu *m*.

har·vest ['hɑːvist] **1.** moisson *f* (*a.*
fig.); récolte *f*; ⁓ *festival* actions
f/*pl.* de grâces pour la récolte;
2. *v/t.* moissonner; récolter; *v/i.*
rentrer la moisson; '**har·vest·er**
moissonneur (-euse *f*, *a. machine*) *m*;
har·vest-home ['⁓'houm] fête *f*
de la moisson.

has [hæz, həz] (*il, elle*) a; '⁓-**been** F
vieux ramolli *m*; homme *m* etc.
fini.

hash[1] [hæʃ] **1.** hachis *m*; *Am.* F
mangeaille *f*, boulot *m*; *fig.* gâchis
m; *fig.* réchauffé *m*; F *make a* ⁓ *of*
faire un joli gâchis de; **2.** hacher (*de*
la viande).

hash[2] *sl.* [⁓] hachich *m*, hash *m*.

hash·ish ['hæʃiːʃ] hachich *m*.

hasp [hɑːsp] **1.** moraillon *m*; loquet
m; fermoir *m*; **2.** cadenasser.

has·sle F ['hæsl] chamaillerie *f*; affaire *f*, histoire *f*.   [*eccl.* coussin *m.*⟩

has·sock ['hæsək] touffe *f* d'herbe;⟩

hast † [hæst] (*tu*) as.

haste [heist] hâte *f*; diligence *f*;
make ⁓ se dépêcher, se hâter; *more*
⁓ *less speed*, *make* ⁓ *slowly* hâtez-
vous lentement; **has·ten** ['heisn]
(se) hâter, (se) presser; *v/t.* avancer (*qch.*); '**hast·i·ness** ['heistinis]
précipitation *f*, hâte *f*; emportement *m* (*de colère etc.*); '**hast·y**
□ précipité; fait à la hâte; irréfléchi; emporté; rapide.

hat [hæt] chapeau *m*; *sl.* my ⁓!
pigez-moi ça!; F *hang up one's* ⁓
with s.o. s'introniser chez q.; *talk*
through one's ⁓ extravaguer; exagérer.

hatch[1] [hætʃ] **1.** *poussins*: couvée *f*;
demi-porte *f*; ⚓, ⚔ panneau *m*,
écoutille *f*; *serving* ⁓ passe-plats
m; *under* ⁓*es* dans la cale; *fig.*
mort et enterré; **2.** (faire) éclore;
v/t. fig. tramer, ourdir.

hatch[2] [⁓] hach(ur)er.

hatch·back *mot.* ['hætʃbæk] (voiture
f à) hayon *m* arrière.

hat·check girl *Am.* ['hætʃek'gəːl]
dame *f* du vestiaire.

hatch·et ['hætʃit] hachette *f*; *bury the ~* enterrer la hache de guerre; **'~-face** visage *m* en lame de couteau.

hatch·way ♣ ['hætʃwei] écoutille *f*.

hate [heit] 1. *poét.* haine *f* (de, contre *to*[*wards*]); 2. détester, haïr; **hate·ful** □ ['~ful] odieux (-euse *f*), détestable; **'hat·er** haïsseur (-euse *f*) *m*; **ha·tred** ['heitrid] haine *f* (de, contre *of*).

hat·ter ['hætə] chapelier (-ère *f*) *m*.

haugh·ti·ness ['hɔːtinis] arrogance *f*, morgue *f*; **'haugh·ty** □ arrogant, hautain.

haul [hɔːl] 1. amenée *f*; effort *m*; *pêche*: coup *m* de filet; prise *f*; *Am.* trajet *m*; *a. fig. long ~* long voyage *m*, longue route *f*; 2. *v/t.* tirer (sur, *at*); traîner; ♣ haler sur; transporter par camion(s); ⚒ hercher; ♣ repiquer dans (*le vent*); *v/i.* haler (*vent*); **'haul·age** traction *f*; (frais *m/pl.* de) roulage *m*, (frais *m/pl.* de) transport *m*; ⚒ herchage *m*; *~ contractor* entrepreneur *m* de transports.

haulm [hɔːm] fane *f* (*de légume*); *coll.* chaume *m*.

haunch [hɔːnʃ] hanche *f*; *cuis.* cuissot *m*, quartier *m*; △ *voûte*: rein *m*.

haunt [hɔːnt] 1. lieu *m* fréquenté; repaire *m*; 2. fréquenter; hanter (*a. revenants*); *fig.* obséder, troubler; *the house is ~ed* il y a des revenants dans la maison; *~ed house* maison *f* hantée; **'haunt·er** *fig.* habitué(e *f*) *m*.

haut·boy ♪ ['oubɔi] hautbois *m*.

Ha·van·a [hə'vænə] (*ou ~ cigar*) havane *m*.

have [hæv, həv] 1. [*irr.*] *v/t.* avoir, posséder; tenir; prendre (*un bain, un repas*); faire (*une promenade etc.*); obtenir; affirmer; F rouler; *~ to* (*inf.*) être obligé de (*inf.*); *I ~ my hair cut* je me fais couper les cheveux; *he had his leg broken* il s'est cassé la jambe; *I would ~ you know that* ... sachez que ...; *he will ~ it that* ... il soutient que ...; *I had as well* (*inf.*) j'aurais pu aussi bien (*inf.*); *I had better* (*best*) (*inf.*) je ferai(s) mieux de (*inf.*); *I had rather* (*inf.*) j'aime(rais) mieux (*inf.*); *let s.o. ~ s.th.* céder qch. à q.; *~ about one* avoir sur soi; *~ on* porter; *~ it out with* s'expliquer avec; F

~ s.o. up citer q. en justice (pour, *for*); *v/i. ~ at him!* à l'attaque; 2. [*irr.*] *v/aux.* avoir; *qqfois* être; *~ come* être venu; 3. riche *m*.

ha·ven ['heivn] havre *m*, port *m*; *fig.* asile *m*, abri *m*.

have-not ['hævnɔt] pauvre *m*.

haven't ['hævnt] = *have not*.

hav·er·sack ['hævəsæk] ⚔ musette *f*; *touriste etc.*: havresac *m*.

hav·ing ['hæviŋ] (*souv. ~s pl.*) possession *f*; *pl. a.* biens *m/pl.*

hav·oc ['hævək] dévastation *f*, dégâts *m/pl.*, ravage *m*; *make ~ of, play ~ with* (*ou among*) faire de grands dégâts dans; massacrer.

haw¹ ♀ [hɔː] cenelle *f*.

haw² [~] 1. toussoter, bredouiller; 2. hem *m* (*a. int.*).

haw-haw ['hɔː'hɔː] rire bruyamment.

hawk¹ [hɔːk] 1. *orn.* faucon *m*; *fig.* vautour *m*; *attr. fig.* d'aigle (*yeux*); 2. chasser au faucon; *~ at* fondre sur.

hawk² [~] graillonner.

hawk³ [~] colporter, cameloter; **hawk·er** ['hɔːkə] colporteur *m*; marchand(e *f*) *m* ambulant(e *f*).

hawk·ing ['hɔːkiŋ] chasse *f* au faucon.

hawse ♣ [hɔːz] (*a. ~-hole*) écubier *m*.

haw·ser ♣ ['hɔːzə] (h)aussière *f*; amarre *f*.

haw·thorn ♀ ['hɔːθɔːn] aubépine *f*.

hay [hei] 1. foin *m*; *~ fever* rhume *m* des foins; *make ~ of* faire un gâchis de; démolir; 2. faire les foins; **'~-box** (*ou ~ cooker*) marmite *f* norvégienne; **'~-cock** meulon *m* ou meule *f* de foin; **'~-fe·ver** rhume *m* des foins; **'~-loft** grenier *m* à foin; **'~-mak·er** *sl.* coup *m* de poing balancé; **'~-mak·ing** fenaison *f*; **'~-rick** *see ~cock*; **'~-seed** graine *f* de foin; *fig. Am.* paysan *m*; **'~-stack** *see ~cock*; **'~-wire** *Am. sl.*: *go ~* ne tourner plus rond; avorter (*projet*).

haz·ard ['hæzəd] 1. hasard *m*; risque *m*; *golf*: accident *m* de terrain; *tennis*: trou *m* gagnant; jeu *m* de hasard; *run a ~* courir un risque; 2. hasarder; risquer; **'haz·ard·ous** □ risqué; hasardeux (-euse *f*). [obscurité *f*.]

haze¹ [heiz] brume *f* légère; *fig.*]

haze² [~] ♣ harasser (*q.*) de corvées; *Am.* brimer.

ha·zel ['heizl] **1.** ♀ noisetier *m*; **2.** couleur noisette; '**~-nut** noisette *f*.

ha·zy □ ['heizi] brumeux (-euse *f*), embrumé; estompé (*contour etc.*); *fig.* vague, nébuleux (-euse *f*).

H-bomb ['eitʃbɔm] bombe *f* H.

he [hi:] **1.** il, *accentué*: lui; ~ (*who*) celui qui; **2.** *attr.* mâle.

head [hed] **1.** *anat.*, *cuis.*, *sp.*, *arbre*, *chasse*, *cortège*, *fleur*, *furoncle*, *humérus*, *intelligence*, *légume*, *liste*, *sculpture*, *violon*, *volcan*, *etc.*: tête *f*; *chasse*: bois *m*; ⚓ *voile*: envergure *f*; *torpille*: cône *m*; nez *m*, avant *m*, *navire*: cap *m*; ✗, *mine*: carreau *m*; *puits de mine*: gueule *f*; *mot.* capote *f*; ⊕ *eau*: charge *f*, *vapeur*: volant *m*; ⊕ culasse *f*; *asperge*: pointe *f*; *céleri*: pied *m*; *blé*: épi *m*; *chou*: pomme *f*; *escalier*, *page*: haut *m*; *lit*: chevet *m*; *table*: haut bout *m*; *bière*: mousse *f*; *rivière*: source *f*; *tambour*: peau *f*; *géog.* cap *m*; *personne*: chef *m*; ✝, *école*: directeur (-trice *f*) *m*; *patron(ne f) m*; *fig.* cervelle *f*, esprit *m*, entendement *m*, mémoire *f*; *fig.* crise *f*; *fig.* point *m*, rubrique *f*; ~ *restraint mot.* appui-tête *m* (*pl.* appuis-tête); ~ *and shoulders above the rest* dépassant les autres de la tête; *bring to a* ~ faire aboutir (*a. fig.*); *come to a* ~ aboutir (*abcès*); mûrir; *gather* ~ monter en pression; augmenter; prendre de l'importance; *get it into one's* ~ *that* se mettre dans la ~ en tête que; ~(*s*) *or tail(s)?* pile ou face?; ~ *over heels* à la renverse; *over* ~ *and ears* surchargé, débordé; *make* ~, *against* faire tête à; *I can't make* ~ *or tail of it* je n'y comprends rien, je m'y perds; *take the* ~ prendre la tête; **2.** premier (-ère *f*); principal (-aux *m/pl.*); ... en chef; ~ *office* bureau *m ou* siège *m* central; ~ *start sp.* avance *f*; ~ *waiter* maître *m* d'hôtel; **3.** *v/t.* mener, être en tête de; être à la tête de; conduire; mettre une tête à; mettre *ou* porter en tête (de); *foot.* jouer de la tête; *be* ~*ed* se diriger (vers, *for*); ~ *off* intercepter; *v/i.* ⚓ avoir le cap (sur, *for*); *Am.* prendre sa source (à, *at*); *fig.* ~ *for* se diriger vers; '**head·ache** mal *m ou* maux *m/pl.* de tête; '**head·ach·y** sujet(te *f*) aux maux de tête, migraineux (-euse *f*); '**head-dress** coiffure *f*; garniture *f* de tête; '**head·ed** à

... tête(s); aux cheveux; '**head·er** ⚓ boutisse *f*; F plongeon *m*; *foot.* coup *m* de tête; '**head-gear** garniture *f* de tête; coiffure *f*; chapeau *m*; '**head-hunt·er** chasseur *m* de têtes; '**head-i-ness** emportement *m*, impétuosité *f*; *vin*: qualité *f* capiteuse; '**head·ing** entête *m*; rubrique *f*; manchette *f*; titre *m*; ✗ (galerie *f* d')avancement *m*; *sp.* (jeu *m* de) tête *f*; '**head-land** cap *m*, promontoire *m*; '**head·less** sans tête; *fig.* sans chef.

head...: '**~·light** 🚗 feu *m* d'avant; *mot.* phare *m*; '**~-line** titre *m*; manchette *f*; *typ.* titre *m* courant, entête *m*; F *he hits the* ~*s* il est en vedette; il défraye la chronique; '**~-long** *adj.* précipité; impétueux (-euse *f*); *adv.* la tête la première; '**~·man** chef *m*; '**~·mas·ter** directeur *m*; *lycée*: proviseur *m*; '**~'mistress** directrice *f*; '**~·most** au premier rang; '**~-'on** de front; frontal (-aux *m/pl.*); '**~-phone** *radio*: écouteur *m*; casque *m*; '**~-piece** casque *m* (*a. radio*); F tête *f*; *typ.* fleuron *m* de tête; en-tête *m*; '**~-quar·ters** *pl.* ✗ quartier *m* général; ✝ *etc.* siège *m* (social); '**~·rest** appui-tête *m* (*pl.* appuis-tête); '**~·set** *radio*: casque *m*; '**head·ship** première place *f*; direction *f*; '**head-shrink·er** F psy(chiatre) *m*; '**heads·man** bourreau *m*; ⚓ patron *m*.

head...: '**~·strong** entêté; obstiné; '**~·wa·ters** *pl.* cours *m* supérieur d'une rivière; '**~·way** progrès *m*; *make* ~ avancer, faire des progrès; '**~·wind** vent *m* contraire; '**~·work** travail *m* intellectuel; *foot.* jeu *m* de tête; '**head·y** □ capiteux (-euse *f*) (*vin etc.*); emporté (*personne*).

heal [hi:l] guérir (de, *of*); ~ *up* (se) guérir, se cicatriser; '**~-all** panacée *f*; '**heal·ing 1.** □ curatif (-ive *f*); cicatrisant; *fig.* calmant; **2.** guérison *f*; cicatrisation *f*.

health [helθ] santé *f* (*a. toast*); *Board of* ♀ Ministère *m* de la santé publique; ~ *certificate* certificat *m* médical; ~ *food(s pl.)* aliments *m/pl.* naturels; ~ *food shop ou store* magasin *m* diététique; ~ *hazard* risque *m* pour la santé; ~ *service* (Service *m* de Santé de la) Sécurité *f* Sociale; **health·ful** □ ['~ful] salubre; salutaire; '**health-i-ness** salubrité *f*; '**health-re-sort** station *f* estivale *ou* thermale;

'**health·y** ☐ en bonne santé; *see* healthful.

heap [hiːp] **1.** tas *m* (*a. fig.*), monceau *m*; F ~s *pl.* beaucoup (de, of); *sl.* F *struck all of a* ~ stupéfait; **2.** (*a.* ~ *up*) entasser, mettre en tas; accabler (de, with); ~ed spoon cuiller *f* à dos d'âne.

hear [hiə] [*irr.*] entendre; écouter; recevoir des nouvelles (de, from); apprendre; faire répéter (*une leçon etc.*); ~ *of* entendre parler de; ~ *that* entendre dire que; **heard** [hɔːd] prét. et p.p. de hear; '**hear·er** ['hiərə] auditeur (-trice *f*) *m*; '**hear·ing** sens: ouïe *f*; audition *f* (*a. ♪♫, a. ♪*); ♪♫ audience *f*; ~ *aid* appareil *m* acoustique, audiophone *m*; **heark·en** ['haːkən] écouter (qch., to s.th.); '**hear·say** ['hiəsei] ouï-dire *m*/*inv.*

hearse [hɔːs] corbillard *m*.

heart [haːt] cœur *m* (*fig. = courage, enthousiasme, etc.*); fond *m*; cartes: ~s *pl.* cœur *m*; (*a. dear* ~) *see* sweetheart; ~ *and soul* corps et âme, de tout son cœur; *I have a matter at* ~ j'ai qch. à cœur; *by* ~ par cœur; *in good* ~ bien entretenu (*sol*); en train (*personne*); *in his* ~ (*of* ~s) au plus profond de son cœur; *out of* ~ effrité (*sol*); découragé (*personne*); *with all my* ~ de tout mon cœur; *lose* ~ perdre courage; *take* ~ prendre courage; *take* (*ou lay*) *to* ~ prendre (qch.) à cœur; '**~·ache** chagrin *m*; '**~·beat** battement *m* du cœur; '**~·break** déchirement *m* de cœur; '**~·break·ing** ☐ navrant; '**~·bro·ken** le cœur brisé, navré; '**~·burn** ♥ aigreurs *f*/*pl.*; '**~·burn·ing** rancune *f*; jalousie *f*; '**~·com·plaint**, '**~·dis·ease** maladie *f* de cœur; ...; '**heart·ed** au cœur (/); '**heart·en** *v*/*t.* encourager; *v*/*i.* reprendre courage; '**heart-fail·ure** arrêt *m* du cœur; '**heart·felt** sincère; profond.

hearth [haːθ] foyer *m*, âtre *m*; '**~·rug** tapis *m* de foyer; '**~·stone** foyer *m*; pierre *f* de la cheminée.

heart·i·ness ['haːtinis] cordialité *f*; chaleur *f*; vigueur *f*; '**heart·less** ☐ insensible; cruel(le *f*); '**heart-rend·ing** navrant.

heart...: '**~·sick** *fig.* découragé, désolé; '**~·strings** *pl. fig.* sensibilité *f*, cœur *m*; '**~·throb** F idole *f*; ~·**trans·plant** ♥ greffe *f* du cœur; ~·**troub·le** troubles *m*/*pl.* cardiaques;

have ~ *a.* être cardiaque, souffrir du cœur; '**~-whole** au cœur libre; *fig.* sincère; *fig.* aucunement ébranlé; '**heart·y 1.** ☐ cordial (-aux *m*/*pl.*); sincère; vigoureux (-euse *f*), robuste; gaillard; ~ *eater* gros mangeur *m*, belle fourchette *f*; **2.** ♣ brave *m*; *univ.* sportif *m*.

heat [hiːt] **1.** chaleur *f*; *phys. a.* calorique *m*; ardeur *f*; *fig.* colère *f*; *animal*: rut *m*; *sp.* épreuve *f*, manche *f*; *dead* ~ manche *f* nulle; *course f à égalité*; **2.** (s')échauffer (*a. fig.*); *v*/*t.* chauffer (*de l'eau etc.*); '**heat·ed** ☐ chauffé; chaud (*a. fig.*); '**heat·er** ⊕ bouilleur *m*; four *m*; radiateur *m*; *Am. sl.* revolver *m*.

heath [hiːθ] bruyère *f*, brande *f* (*a.* ♀); '**~-cock** petit coq *m* de bruyère.

hea·then ['hiːðən] païen(ne *f*) (*a. su.*/*mf*); '**hea·then·dom** paganisme *m*; '**hea·then·ish** ☐ *usu. fig.* barbare, grossier (-ère *f*); '**hea·then·ism** paganisme *m*; barbarie *f*.

heath·er ♀ ['heðə] bruyère *f*, brande *f*; '**~-bell** ♀ cloche *f* de bruyère.

heat·ing ['hiːtiŋ] chauffage *m*; *attr.* de chaleur; ~ *battery* batterie *f* de four *etc.*; ~ *cushion*, ~ *pad* coussin *m* chauffant *ou* électrique.

heat...: ~ *light·ning Am.* éclairs *m*/*pl.* de chaleur; '**~-re·sist·ant** résistant à la chaleur; '**~-stroke** coup *m* de chaleur; ~ *treat·ment* ⚙ thermothérapie *f*; '**~-val·ue** pouvoir *m* calorifique; *météor.* onde *f* calorifique; ~ *wave phys.* onde *f* de chaleur; *météor.* vague *f* de chaleur.

heave [hiːv] **1.** soulèvement *m*; effort *m*; palpitation *f* (*du sein*); ♣ houle *f*; **2.** [*irr.*] *v*/*t.* (sou)lever; lancer, jeter; pousser (*un soupir*); ~ *the anchor* déraper; ♣ ~ *down* caréner; ♣ ~ *out* déferler; *v*/*i.* se soulever (*a. vagues, poitrine*); haleter; s'agiter (*mer*); palpiter (*sein*); avoir des haut-le-cœur; ~ *for breath* panteler; ♣ ~ *at* haler sur; ♣ ~ *in sight* paraître; ♣ ~ *to* se mettre à la cape.

heav·en ['hevn] ciel *m*, cieux *m*/*pl.*; ~s *pl.* ciel *m*; ~! juste ciel!; '**heav·en·ly** céleste; divin; **heav·en·ward(s)** ['~wəd(z)] vers le ciel.

heav·er ['hiːvə] (dé)chargeur *m*; ⊕ levier *m* de manœuvre.

heav·i·ness ['hevinis] pesanteur *f*, lourdeur *f*; *fig.* tristesse *f*, abattement *m*; *mot.* mauvais état *m* (*des routes*).

heav·y □ ['hevi] *usu.* lourd; pesant; gros(se *f*) (*cœur, pluie, rhume, etc.*); triste; violent; pénible; profond; gras(se *f*) (*sol*); ✕ lourd, de gros calibre, gros(se *f*); ✌ ～ *current* courant *m* fort; '～-**du·ty** ⊕ à grande puissance; très résistant; '～-**handed** qui a la main lourde; gauche, maladroit; '～-**heart·ed** qui a le cœur gros, accablé; '～-**lad·en** lourdement chargé; *fig.* chargé de soucis; '～-**weight** *box.* poids *m* lourd.

heb·dom·a·dal □ [heb'dɔmədl], **heb·dom·a·da·ry** hebdomadaire.

He·bra·ic [hi'breiik] (～*ally*) hébraïque.

He·brew ['hi:bru:] 1. hébraïque, israélite; 2. *ling.* hébreu *m*; *bibl.* Hébreu(e *f*) *m*; Israélite *mf*.

hec·a·tomb ['hekətoum] hécatombe *f*.

heck·le ['hekl] *see* hackle; *pol.* interrompre par des questions embarrassantes.

hec·tic ✍ ['hektik] 1. hectique; *fig.* fiévreux (-euse *f*); 2. rougeur *f*; (*usu.* ～ *fever*) fièvre *f* hectique.

hec·tor ['hektə] *v/t.* rudoyer, dragonner; *v/i.* prendre un ton autoritaire; faire de l'esbroufe.

hedge [hedʒ] 1. haie *f*; *attr. souv.* ignorant, interlope (*p.ex.* ～-*priest*); 2. *v/t.* entourer d'une haie; enfermer; ～ *off* séparer par une haie; ～ *up* clore d'une haie; ～ *a bet* parier pour et contre; *v/i.* éviter de se compromettre; '～-**bill** serpe *f*; '～-**hog** *zo.* hérisson *m*; *Am.* porc-épic *m*; '～-**hop** *sl.* ☡ voler en rase-mottes; '～-**row** bordure *f* de haies; haie *f*; '～-**spar·row** *orn.* fauvette *f*.

heed [hi:d] 1. attention *f* (à, to), soin *m*; compte *m* (de, to); *take* ～ *of* tenir compte de, prendre garde à; *take no* ～ *of* ne tenir aucun compte de; 2. faire attention à, observer; tenir compte de; **heed·ful** □ ['～ful] attentif (-ive *f*) (à, of); '**heed·less** □ insouciant.

hee-haw ['hi:'hɔ:] 1. hi-han *m*; *fig.* ricanement *m*; 2. braire; *fig.* ricaner.

heel¹ ⚓ [hi:l] *v/i.* se coucher sur le flanc; avoir de la bande.

heel² [～] 1. talon *m*; *surt. Am. sl.* gouape *f*; *be at* (*on*) *s.o.'s* ～*s* être

aux trousses de q.; marcher sur les talons de q.; *down at* ～ éculé; *fig.* minable, de pauvre apparence; *take to one's* ～*s* prendre ses jambes à son cou; s'enfuir; 2. mettre un talon à; *foot.* ～ *out* talonner le ballon (*pour le sortir de la mêlée*); '**heeled** *Am.* pourvu d'argent; muni d'un revolver; '**heel·er** *pol. Am. sl.* partisan *m* servile.

heel-tap ['hi:ltæp] ⊕ rondelle *f* de hausse; ～*s pl.* fonds *m/pl.* de verre; *no* ～*!* vidons les verres.

heft [heft] 1. poids *m*; effort *m*; *Am.* F gros *m* (de la récolte); 2. *Am.* soupeser; '**heft·y** F solide; *Am.* lourd.

he·gem·o·ny [hi:'geməni] hégémonie *f*.

he-goat ['hi:gout] bouc *m*.

heif·er ['hefə] génisse *f*.

heigh-ho [hei'hou] ah!

height [hait] hauteur *f*, élévation *f*; comble *m*, apogée *m*; *personne:* taille *f*; altitude *f*; cœur *m* (d'été); '**height·en** augmenter (*a. fig.*); rehausser; *fig.* relever.

hei·nous □ ['heinəs] atroce; odieux (-euse *f*); '**hei·nous·ness** énormité *f*.

heir [ɛə] héritier (-ère *f*) *m* (de, to); ～ *apparent* héritier *m* présomptif; ～-*at-law* héritier *m* légitime; '**heir·dom** droit *m* de succession; † héritage *m*; '**heir·ess** héritière *f*; '**heir·less** sans héritier; **heir·loom** ['～lu:m] meuble *m* ou bijou *m* de famille; *fig.* apanage *m*; '**heir·ship** qualité *f* d'héritier.

held [held] *prét. et p.p. de* hold 2.

hel·i·bus *Am.* F ['helibʌs] hélicoptère *m qui fait le service de communication entre l'aéroport et la ville.*

hel·i·cal ⊕ ['helikl] en spirale.

hel·i·cop·ter ['helikɔptə] hélicoptère *m*.

helio... ['hi:liou] hélio-; **he·li·ograph** ['～ogrɑ:f] héliographe *m* (*a. phot.*); héliographier *v/i.*; **he·li·ograph·ic** [～'græfik] héliographique; ～ *calking* (reproduction *f* par) héliogravure *f*; **he·li·o·gra·vure** ['hi:liougrəvjuə] héliogravure *f*; **he·li·o·trope** ['heljətroup] ⚘ héliotrope *m* (*a. couleur*).

hel·i·port ['helipɔ:t] héliport *m*.

he·lix ['hi:liks], *pl. usu.* **hel·i·ces** ['helisi:z] ⅍, ⊕, *zo.* hélice *f*; △ spirale *f*, volute *f*; *anat.* hélix *m*, ourlet *m*.

hell [hel] enfer *m*; *attr.* de l'enfer; *like* ~ infernal (-aux *m/pl.*); *oh* ~! diable!; sapristi!; *go to* ~ aller en enfer; F *what the* ~ ...? que diable...?; *a* ~ *of a noise* un bruit infernal; *raise* ~ faire un bruit infernal; faire une scène; *ride* ~ *for leather* aller au triple galop; '~-'bent *Am. sl.* résolu; acharné; '~-cat *fig.* mégère *f*. [*m.*]

hel·le·bore ♀ ['helibɔ:] ellébore ⌡

Hel·lene ['heli:n] Hellène *mf*.

hell·ish □ ['heliʃ] infernal (-aux *m/pl.*); diabolique.

hel·lo [he'lou] holà!; *téléph.* allô!

helm ⚓ [helm] (barre *f* du) gouvernail *m*; timon *m* (*a. fig.* de l'État); *fig.* direction *f*.

hel·met ['helmit] casque *m*; '**hel·met·ed** casqué.

helms·man ⚓ ['helmzmən] homme *m* de barre; timonier *m*.

hel·ot *hist.* ['helət] ilote *m*; *fig.* esclave *m*.

help [help] **1.** aide *f*; secours *m*; remède *m*; *surt. Am.* domestique *mf*; *lady* ~ dame *f* (de bonne maison) qui aide aux soins du ménage; *mother's* ~ jeune fille *f* qui aide dans le soin des enfants; *by the* ~ *of* à l'aide de; **2.** *v/t.* aider; secourir; prêter son concours à; faciliter; *à table*: servir (q., *s.o.*; qch., *s.th.*; qch. à q., *s.o. to s.th.*); ~ *o.s.* se servir (de, *to*); s'aider; *I could not* ~ *laughing* je ne pouvais m'empêcher de rire; *v/i.* aider, servir, contribuer (à, *to*); '**help·er** aide *mf*; assistant(e *f*) *m*; ⚙ machine *f* de secours; **help·ful** □ ['~ful] utile; salutaire; serviable (*personne*); '**help·ing** portion *f*; '**help·less** □ ~ sans ressource; impuissant; '**help·less·ness** faiblesse *f*; '**help·mate**, '**help·meet** aide *mf*; compagnon *m*, compagne *f*.

hel·ter-skel·ter ['heltə'skeltə] *adv.* pêle-mêle; à la débandade.

helve [helv] manche *m*.

Hel·ve·tian [hel'vi:ʃiən] **1.** helvétien (-ne *f*), suisse; **2.** Helvétien(ne *f*) *m*, Suisse *mf*.

hem¹ [hem] **1.** *cost.* bord *m*; ourlet *m*; **2.** border; ourler; ~ *in* entourer.

hem² [~] **1.** toussoter; **2.** hem!

he-man *Am. sl.* ['hi:mæn] homme *m* viril.

hem·i·sphere ['hemisfiə] hémisphère *m*.

hem·lock ♀ ['hemlɔk] ciguë *f*.

hemo... [hi:mo] *see haemo...*

hemp [hemp] chanvre *m*; '**hemp·en** de chanvre.

hem·stitch ['hemstitʃ] **1.** ourlet *m* à jour; **2.** ourler à jour.

hen [hen] poule *f*; femelle *f* (*d'oiseau*); ~'s *egg* œuf *m* de poule.

hen·bane ['henbein] jusquiame *f*.

hence [hens] (*souv. from* ~) d'ici; à partir d'aujourd'hui, désormais; de là, ce qui explique...; ~! hors d'ici!; va-t'en d'ici!; *a year* ~ dans un an; '~'forth, '~'for·ward désormais, à l'avenir.

hench·man ['hentʃmən] F partisan *m*; homme *m* de confiance.

hen...: '~'par·ty F assemblée *f* de jupes; '~-pecked dominé par sa femme; '~-roost juchoir *m*.

hep *Am. sl.* [hep]: *be* ~ être dans le vent; '~-cat *Am. sl.* fanatique *mf* du jazz.

he·pat·ic *anat.* [hi'pætik] hépatique.

hepta... [heptə] hepta-; **hep·ta·gon** ['~gən] heptagone *m*.

her [hə:; hə] **1.** *accusatif*: la; *datif*: lui; à elle; se, soi; celle; **2.** son, sa, ses.

her·ald ['herəld] **1.** héraut *m*; *fig.* avant-coureur *m*; **2.** annoncer; ~ *in* introduire; **he·ral·dic** [he-'rældik] (~*ally*) héraldique; **her·ald·ry** ['herəldri] blason *m*.

herb [hə:b] herbe *f*; **her·ba·ceous** [~'beiʃəs] herbacé; '**herb·age** herbage *m*; herbes *f/pl.*; ♃ droit *m* de pacage; '**herb·al 1.** d'herbes; **2.** herbier *m*; '**herb·al·ist** botaniste *m*; guérisseur *m*; ♣ herboriste *mf*; **her·bar·i·um** [~'bɛəriəm] herbier *m*; **her·biv·o·rous** [~'bivərəs] herbivore; **her·bo·rize** ['~bəraiz] herboriser; [léen(ne *f*); d'Hercule ⌡

Her·cu·le·an [hə:kju'li:ən] hercu-⌡

herd [hə:d] **1.** troupeau *m* (*a. fig.*); **2.** *v/t.* assembler; *v/i.* (*a.* ~ *together*) s'assembler en troupeau; s'attrouper; '**herds·man** bouvier *m*.

here [hiə] ici; ~ *is* voici; ~'s *to* ...! à la santé de ...!

here-a·bout(s) ['hiərəbaut(s)] près d'ici; **here·aft·er** [hiər'ɑ:ftə] **1.** dorénavant; **2.** avenir *m*; *l'*au-delà *m*, *la* vie *f* à venir; '**here·by** par là; ♃ par les présentes.

her·e·dit·a·ment ⚷ [heri'ditəmənt] bien *m* transmissible par héritage; *fig.* patrimoine *m*; **he·red·i·tar·y** [hi'reditəri] héréditaire; **he'red·i·ty** hérédité *f*.

here·in ['hiər'in] ici; en ceci; **here·in·be'fore** ci-dessus; **here·of** [hiər-'ɔv] de ceci.

her·e·sy ['herəsi] hérésie *f*.

her·e·tic ['herətik] **1.** (*usu.* **he·ret·i·cal** □ [hi'retikl]) hérétique; **2.** hérétique *mf*.

here·to·fore ['hiətu'fɔ:] jusqu'ici; **here·up·on** ['hiərə'pɔn] là-dessus; sur ce; '**here'with** avec ceci; ci-joint.

her·it·a·ble ['heritəbl] héréditaire; héritable (*propriété*); '**her·it·age** héritage *m*, patrimoine *m*.

her·maph·ro·dite ⚷, *zo.* [hə:'mæfrədait] hermaphrodite (*a. su./m*).

her·met·ic, **her·met·i·cal** □ [hə:-'metik(l)] hermétique.

her·mit ['hə:mit] ermite *m*; '**her·mit·age** ermitage *m*.

her·ni·a ⚷ ['hə:njə] hernie *f*; '**her·ni·al** herniaire.

he·ro ['hiərou], *pl.* **-roes** ['⌄z] héros *m*; **he·ro·ic** [hi'rouik] (⌄*ally*) héroïque; épique; **her·o·ine** ['herouin] héroïne *f*; '**her·o·ism** héroïsme *m*.

her·on *orn.* ['herən] héron *m*.

her·ring *icht.* ['heriŋ] hareng *m*; '**her·ing·bone** arête *f* de hareng; point *m* de chausson.

hers [hə:z] le sien, la sienne, les siens, les siennes; à elle.

her·self [hə:'self] elle-même; réfléchi: se, *accentué*: soi.

hes·i·tance, **hes·i·tan·cy** ['hezitəns(i)] hésitation *f*, irrésolution *f*; **hes·i·tate** ['⌄teit] hésiter (à, *to*; sur *about*, *over*; entre, *between*); **hes·i'ta·tion** hésitation *f*.

het·er·o·dox ['hetərədɔks] hétérodoxe; '**het·er·o·dox·y** hétérodoxie *f*; **het·er·o·dyne** ['⌄dain] *radio*: hétérodyne (*a. su./m*); **het·er·o·ge·ne·i·ty** [⌄rodʒi'ni:iti] hétérogénéité *f*; **het·er·o·ge·ne·ous** □ ['⌄ro'dʒi:njəs] hétérogène; ⟁ disparate.

het up F [het'ʌp] excité, agité, nerveux (-euse *f*).

hew [hju:] [*irr.*] couper; tailler (*a.* ⊕); ⊕ abattre; ⊕ dresser; '**hew·er** tailleur *m*; abatteur *m* (*d'arbres*); ⚒

piqueur *m*; **hewn** [hju:n] *p.p. de* hew.

hexa... [heksə] hex(a)-; **hex·a·gon** ['⌄gən] hexagone *m*; **hex·ag·o·nal** □ [hek'sægənl] hexagonal (-aux *m/pl.*); **hex·am·e·ter** [hek'sæmitə] hexamètre *m*.

hey [hei] hé!; holà!; hein?

hey·day ['heidei] **1.** tiens!; **2.** *fig.* apogée *m*; fleur *f* de l'âge; beaux jours *m/pl.*

hi [hai] hé!; holà!; ohé!

hi·a·tus [hai'eitəs] ⚷, *gramm.* hiatus *m*; lacune *f*.

hi·ber·nate ['haibə:neit] hiberner; hiverner (*a. personne*); **hi·ber'na·tion** hibernation *f*.

hic·cup, *a.* **hic·cough** ['hikʌp] **1.** hoquet *m*; **2.** avoir le hoquet; hoqueter.

hick F [hik] paysan *m*, rustaud *m*; *attr.* de province.

hick·o·ry ['hikəri] noyer *m* d'Amérique.

hid [hid] *prét. et p.p. de* hide[2]; **hid·den** ['hidn] *p.p. de* hide[2].

hide[1] [haid] **1.** peau *f*; ✝ cuir *m*; **2.** F tanner le cuir à (*q.*).

hide[2] [⌄] [*irr.*] (se) cacher (à, *from*); (se) dérober (à, *from*); '**hide-and-'seek** cache-cache *m*; *play* (*at*) ⌄ jouer au cache-cache; '**hide·a·way** F cachette *f*, F planque *f*.

hide·bound *fig.* ['haidbaund] aux vues étroites; rigide.

hid·e·ous □ ['hidiəs] affreux (-euse *f*); horrible; '**hid·e·ous·ness** laideur *f*, horreur *f*.

hide·out ['haidaut] cachette *f*.

hid·ing[1] F ['haidiŋ] rossée *f*; tripotée *f*.

hid·ing[2] [⌄]: *go into* ⌄ se cacher; *in* ⌄ caché; '**⌄-place** cachette *f*.

hie *poét.* [hai] (*p.pr.* hying) se rendre (à la hâte).

hi·er·arch·y ['haiəra:ki] *admin.*, *eccl.*, *etc.* hiérarchie *f*.

hi·er·o·glyph ['haiəroglif] hiéroglyphe *m*; **hi·er·o'glyph·ic** (*a.* **hi·er·o'glyph·i·cal** □) hiéroglyphique; **hi·er·o'glyph·ics** *pl.* hiéroglyphes *m/pl.*

hi-fi *Am.* ['hai'fai] (*abr. de* high fidelity) de haute fidélité (*reproduction*).

hig·gle ['higl] marchander.

hig·gle·dy-pig·gle·dy F ['higldi-'pigldi] en pagaïe, sans ordre.

high [hai] **1.** *adj.* □ (*see a.* ~**ly**) *usu.*
haut; élevé; fort, violent (*vent*);
grand (*vitesse*); faisandé (*gibier*);
avancé (*viande*); fort (*beurre*); *attr.*
de fête; solennel(le *f*); F *ivre*: parti,
par la drogue: drogué, camé; F *get* ~
se défoncer; ~*est bidder le* plus
offrant *m*; *with a* ~ *hand* arbitraire-
ment; tyranniquement; de façon
cavalière; ~ *spirits pl.* gaieté *f*, entrain
m; ♀ *Church* haute Église *f* (anglicane); ~ *colo(u)r* vivacité *f* de teint
(*d'une personne*); couleur *f* vive; ~
dive plongeon *m* de haut vol; ♂ ~
frequency haute fréquence *f*; *surt.*
Am. sl. ~*hat* gommeux *m*; *v/t.* traiter
d'une manière hautaine; *v/i.* se
donner de grands airs; ~ *life la* vie *f*
mondaine; ~ *noon* plein midi; ~ *street*
grand-rue *f*, rue *f* principale; *see tea*;
♂ ~ *tension* haute tension *f*; *it is* ~ *time*
il est grand temps; ~ *treason* lèse-
majesté *f*; haute trahison *f*; ~ *water*
marée *f* haute; ~ *wind* gros vent *m*; ~
words paroles *f/pl.* dures; **2.** *su.*
météor. aire *f* anticyclonique; *surt.*
Am. ♀ *see* High School; ~ *and low* les
grands et les petits; *on* ~ *en* haut; **3.**
adv. haut; en haut; fort(ement); '~**backed** à grand dossier; '~**ball**
Am. whisky *m* et soda *m*; '~**born** de
haute naissance; '~**boy** *Am.* commode *f*; '~**bred** de race; '~**brow** F
1. intellectuel(le *f*) *m*; **2.** *iro.* préten-
du intellectuel(le *f*); '~**class** de première classe *ou* qualité; '~**day** jour
m de fête; '~**ex'plo·sive** brisant; à
haut explosif; ~ **fa·lu·tin(g)** [ˌ~fəˈluː-
tin, -iŋ] **1.** prétentieux (-euse *f*); **2.**
discours *m* pompeux; '~**flown**
ampoulé; ambitieux (-euse *f*); '~**grade** de qualité supérieure; '~**hand·ed** arbitraire; ~ **jump** saut *m*
en hauteur; '~**land·er** montagnard
m écossais; soldat *m* d'un régiment
écossais; '~**lands** hautes terres *f/pl.*;
'~**lev·el** *adj.*: *alp.* ~ *climb* ascension *f*
à haute altitude; '~**light 1.** *peinture*:
rehaut; reflet *m*; *fig.* point *m* marquant, F clou *m*; **2.** mettre en
lumière, mettre en vedette; souligner; '~**liv·ing** bonne chère *f*;
'**high·ly** fort(ement); très; bien; extrêmement; *speak* ~ *of* parler en termes très flatteurs de; vanter; ~ *de-
scended* de haute naissance; '**high-mind·ed** magnanime; généreux
(-euse *f*); '**high·ness** élévation

f; *fig.* grandeur *f*; ♀ *titre*: Altesse *f*.
high...: '~ **oc·tane pet·rol** essence *f*
à haut indice d'octane; '~**pitched**
aigu('ë *f*) (*ton etc.*); à forte inclinaison
(*toit etc.*); '~**pow·er**: ~ *station* station *f* génératrice de haute puissance; ~ *radio station* poste *m* de
grande portée; '~**priced** coûteux
(-euse *f*), chèr; '~**rank·ing** haut, de
haut rang; '~**rise** tour *f* d'habitation; '~**road** grand-route *f*; grand
chemin *m*; '~**speed** à grande vitesse; ⊕ à marche rapide; '~**spir·it-
ed** plein d'ardeur, fougueux (-euse
f); '~**step·ping** qui trousse (*che-
val*); *Am. sl.* noceur (-euse *f*); '~**strung** (au tempérament) nerveux;
'~**toned** *surt. Am.* F chic, élégant; '~**wa·ter** marée *f* haute; '~**way**
grand-route *f*; grand chemin *m*; *fig.*
bonne voie *f*; chemin *m*; '~**way-
man** voleur *m* de grand chemin.
hi·jack ['haidʒæk] **1.** détourner (*un
avion*); **2.** détournement (*d'un
avion*); '**hi·jack·er** pirate *m* de
l'air).
hike F [haik] **1.** faire du footing;
2. excursion *f* à pied; *surt. Am.* F
hausse *f* (*des prix*); '**hik·er** excursionniste *mf* à pied.
hi·lar·i·ous □ [hiˈlɛəriəs] joyeux
(-euse *f*).
hi·lar·i·ty [hiˈlæriti] hilarité *f*.
Hil·a·ry ['hiləri]: ♀, *a. univ.* ~
Term session *f* de la Saint-Hilaire
(*janvier à mars*).
hill [hil] colline *f*, coteau *m*; côte *f*;
~**bil·ly** *Am.* F ['~bili] montagnard
m; '~**climb·ing** *mot.* montée *f* des
côtes; ~ *contest* course *f* de côte;
'**hill·i·ness** nature *f* accidentée
(*d'une région*); **hill·ock** ['~ək] petite
colline *f*; '**hill·y** montueux (-euse
f); accidenté (*terrain*).
hilt [hilt] épée: poignée *f*; *up to the* ~
jusqu'à la garde; *fig.* complètement,
sans réserve.
him [him] *accusatif*: le; *datif*: lui;
se, soi; celui.
him·self [him'self] lui-même; *réfléchi*: se, *accentué*: soi; *of* ~ de lui-
même; de son propre choix; *by* ~
tout seul.
hind[1] *zo.* [haind] biche *f*.
hind[2] [~] valet *m* de ferme; paysan *m*.
hind[3] [~]: ~ *leg* jambe *f* *ou* patte *f*
derrière; = '**hind·er** de derrière;
postérieur; arrière-...

hin·der [ˈhində] v/t. empêcher (q.) (de, from); gêner; retarder.

hind·most [ˈhaindmoust] dernier (-ère f); **hind·quar·ters** [ˈhaindkwɔːtəz] pl. arrière-train m (pl. arrière-trains).

hin·drance [ˈhindrəns] empêchement m; obstacle m.

hind·sight [ˈhaindsait] sagesse f (d')après coup; with ~ (en réfléchissant) après coup.

Hin·du, a. **Hin·doo** [ˈhinˈduː] 1. hindou; 2. Hindou(e f) m.

Hin·du·sta·ni ling. [hinduˈstæni] hindoustani m.

hinge [hindʒ] 1. gond m; charnière f; fig. pivot m; off the ~s hors de ses gonds; 2. ~ upon fig. dépendre de; ~d lid couvercle m à charnière(s).

hin·ny zo. [ˈhini] bardot m.

hint [hint] 1. avis m; allusion f; signe m; 2. suggérer, insinuer; faire allusion (à, at).

hip[1] [hip] 1. hanche f; ~ bath bain m de siège; ~ flask flacon m plat; 2. coxal (-aux m/pl.); de la hanche; sur les hanches.

hip[2] ♀ [~] cynorrhodon m; F gratte-cul m/inv.

hip[3] [~] 1. mélancolie f; 2. attrister; F donner le cafard à.

hip[4] [~]: int. ~, ~, hurra(h)! hip! hip! hourra!

hipped F [hipt] mélancolique; Am. sl. obsédé.

hip·po F [ˈhipou] = **hip·po·pot·a·mus** [hipəˈpɔtəməs], pl. a. ~mi [~mai] hippopotame m.

hip-roof △ [ˈhipruːf] toit m en croupe.

hip-shot [ˈhipʃɔt] (d)éhanché.

hire [ˈhaiə] 1. louage m; maison: location f; gages m/pl.; ~ charge prix m de (la) location; on ~ en location; à louer; à louage; for ~ libre (taxi); 2. louer; arrêter; engager (un domestique); ~ out louer; Am. entrer en service; **hire·ling** péj. [ˈ~liŋ] mercenaire (a. su./m); **'hire-'pur·chase** vente f à tempérament; on the ~ system à tempérament.

hir·sute [ˈhəːsjuːt] hirsute, velu; fig. grossier (-ère f).

his [hiz] 1. son, sa, ses; 2. le sien, la sienne, les siens, les siennes; à lui.

hiss [his] 1. sifflement m; 2. v/i. siffler; chuinter (vapeur etc.); v/t. sif-

fler; ~ off chasser à coups de sifflets.

hist [s:t] chut; pour attirer l'attention: pst!

his·to·ri·an [hisˈtɔːriən] historien m; **his·tor·ic, his·tor·i·cal** □ [~ˈtɔrik(l)] historique; de l'histoire; **his·to·ri·og·ra·pher** [~ˌtɔːriˈɔgrəfə] historiographe m; **his·to·ry** [ˈ~təri] histoire f; manuel m d'histoire; *théâ.* drame m historique.

his·tri·on·ic [histriˈɔnik] théâtral (-aux m/pl.); *péj.* histrionique.

hit [hit] 1. coup m; touche f; trait m satirique, coup m de patte; *théâ.* (pièce f à) succès m; ♪ succès m; 2. [irr.] v/t. frapper; heurter; atteindre (un but); porter (un coup); trouver (le mot juste); *Am.* F arriver à; ~ it off with s'accorder avec; ~ off imiter exactement; ~ one's head against se cogner la tête contre; ~ s.o. a blow porter un coup à q.; v/i. ~ at décocher un coup à; ~ or miss à tout hasard; ~ out détacher des coups (à, at); ~ (up)on découvrir; trouver; tomber sur; '~-and-'run driv·er mot. chauffard m.

hitch [hitʃ] 1. saccade f; ⚓ nœud m, clef f; fig. empêchement m soudain; accroc m; radio etc.: technical ~ incident m technique; 2. remuer par saccades; accrocher; nouer; attacher (un cheval etc.); ⚓ amarrer; ~ up remonter (le pantalon); *Am.* atteler (des chevaux); *Am. sl.* get ~ed se marier; '~-hike *Am.* F faire de l'auto-stop; '~-hik·ing *Am.* F auto-stop m.

hith·er poét. [ˈhiðə] ici; le plus rapproché; **hith·er·to** [ˈ~tuː] jusqu'ici.

hive [haiv] 1. ruche f (a. fig.); essaim m; fig. fourmilière f; ✳ ~s pl. urticaire f; varicelle f pustuleuse; croup m; 2. v/t. mettre dans une ruche; ~ up accumuler; v/i. entrer dans la ruche; fig. vivre ensemble.

ho [hou] ho!; hé!; ⚓ en vue!

hoar [hɔː] 1. see hoarfrost; 2. chenu (personne).

hoard [hɔːd] 1. amas m; accumulation f secrète; F argent: magot m; 2. (a. ~ up) amasser; accumuler; thésauriser (de l'argent).

hoard·ing[1] [ˈhɔːdiŋ] resserre f; accumulation f; thésaurisation f.

hoard·ing[2] [~] clôture f de bois; panneau m d'affichage.

hoar·frost ['hɔːˈfrɔst] gelée *f* blanche, givre *m*.

hoar·i·ness ['hɔːrinis] blancheur *f*; vieillesse *f*.

hoarse □ [hɔːs] rauque, enroué; **'hoarse·ness** enrouement *m*.

hoar·y ['hɔːri] blanchi (*cheveux*); chenu (*personne*); *fig.* séculaire.

hoax [houks] 1. tour *m*, mystification *f*, farce *f*; supercherie *f*; *journ.* canard *m*; 2. attraper, jouer un tour à, mystifier.

hob¹ [hɔb] *cheminée:* plaque *f* de côté; fiche *f* de but (*au jeu de palets*).

hob² [⌣] see hobgoblin; *surt. Am.* F *raise* ⌣ faire du raffut; rouspéter fort.

hob·ble ['hɔbl] 1. clochement *m*, boitillement *m*; F embarras *m*; 2. *v/i.* clocher, boitiller, clopiner; *v/t.* entraver; F embarrasser.

hob·ble·de·hoy F ['hɔbldiˈhɔi] jeune homme *m* gauche; F grand dadais *m*.

hob·by ['hɔbi] *fig.* marotte *f*, dada *m*; '⌣-**horse** † petit cheval *m* de selle; cheval *m* de bois; dada *m*.

hob·gob·lin ['hɔbgɔblin] lutin *m*.

hob·nail ['hɔbneil] clou *m* à ferrer; caboche *f*.

hob·nob ['hɔbnɔb]: ⌣ *with* être à tu et à toi avec (*q.*); fréquenter (*q.*).

ho·bo *Am.* ['houbou] ouvrier *m* ambulant; F chemineau *m*.

hock¹ [hɔk] 1. *zo.* jarret *m*; 2. couper le jarret à.

hock² [⌣] vin *m* du Rhin.

hock³ *sl.* [⌣] 1. gage *m*; prison *f*; 2. engager.

hock·ey *sp.* ['hɔki] hockey *m*.

hock-shop ['hɔkʃɔp] mont *m* de piété; F ma tante *f*.

ho·cus ['houkəs] duper; droguer (*q., qch.*); narcotiser (*une boisson*); ⌣-**po·cus** ['⌣'poukəs] 1. (tour *m* de) passe-passe *m/inv.*; tromperie *f*; 2. *v/i.* faire des tours de passe-passe; *v/t.* mystifier; escamoter (*qch.*).

hod [hɔd] oiseau *m* (*de maçon*); seau *m* à charbon.

hodge-podge ['hɔdʒpɔdʒ] see hotchpotch.

hod·man ['hɔdmən] aide-maçon (*pl.* aides-maçons) *m*.

hoe ↗ [hou] 1. houe *f*; 2. houer.

hog [hɔg] 1. porc *m* (châtré); *fig.* goinfre *m*; *sl.* go the whole ⌣ aller jusqu'au bout; 2. F accaparer, monopoliser; *mot.* ⌣ *the road* tenir toute la

route; **hogged** [hɔgd] fortement bombé; en brosse; **hog·get** ['hɔgit] agneau *m* antenais; **hog·gish** □ ['⌣iʃ] de cochon; grossier (*-ère f*); **'hog·gish·ness** grossièreté *f*; gloutonnerie *f*; **hogs·head** ['⌣zhed] tonneau *m*; *mesure:* fût *m* (240 *litres*); *Am.* grosse balle *f* de tabac (*de 750 à 1200 livres*); **'hog·skin** peau *f* de porc; **'hog·wash** eaux *f/pl.* grasses; F lavasse *f*.

hoi(c)k [hɔik] ✈ (faire) monter en chandelle; F lever d'un coup sec.

hoist [hɔist] 1. (coup *m* de) treuil *m*; 2. hisser; guinder.

hoi·ty-toi·ty ['hɔitiˈtɔiti] 1. susceptible; qui fait l'important; 2. taratata!

ho·kum *Am. sl.* ['houkəm] balivernes *f/pl.*; absurdité *f*, fumisterie *f*.

hold [hould] 1. *su.* prise *f*; appui *m*; empire *m*, pouvoir *m*; influence *f*; *box.* tenu *m*; tanière *f* (*d'une bête fauve*); ♪ cale *f*; *catch* (*ou get ou lay ou take*) ⌣ *of* saisir, s'emparer de; *have a* ⌣ *of* (*ou on*) tenir; *keep* ⌣ *of* ne pas lâcher (*qch.*); 2. [*irr.*] *v/t. usu.* tenir; retenir (*l'attention, l'haleine, dans la mémoire*); contenir; maintenir; détenir; tenir pour; professer (*une opinion*); avoir (*une idée*); arrêter; célébrer (*une fête*); tenir (*une séance*); faire (*une enquête*); ⚖ décider (*que, that*); *surt. Am.* ⌣ *down a job* occuper un emploi; se montrer à la hauteur d'un emploi; ⌣ *one's own* tenir bon; défendre sa position; *téléph.* ⌣ *the line* ne pas quitter; ⌣ *water* être étanche; *fig.* tenir debout; ⌣ *off* tenir à distance; ✈ intercepter; ⌣ *on* maintenir; tenir (*qch.*) en place; ⌣ *out* tendre; offrir; ⌣ *over* remettre à plus tard; ⌣ *up* lever en l'air; soutenir; relever (*la tête*); offrir (*comme modèle*); arrêter; entraver; tourner (*en ridicule*); exposer; 3. [*irr.*] *v/i.* tenir (*bon*); se maintenir; persister; être vrai; ⌣ *forth* pérorer, disserter (*sur, on*); ⌣ *good* (*ou true*) être valable; ne pas se démentir; ⌣ *hard!* arrêtez!; halte là!; ♪ baste!; ⌣ *in* se maîtriser; ⌣ *off* se tenir à distance; ♪ tenir le large; ⌣ *on* se cramponner (à, *to*); ne pas lâcher; F ⌣ *on!* tenez ferme!; attendez un instant!; *téléph.* ne quittez pas!; ~ to s'en tenir à; ~ up se maintenir; se soutenir; 'hold-all fourre-tout *m/inv.*; 'hold·er *maison*: possesseur *m*; locataire *mf*; *médaille, poste*: titulaire *mf*; *sp.*, ✝ détenteur (-trice *f*) *m*; ~ of shares actionnaire *mf*; 'hold·fast crampon *m* (*a.* ⚓); serre-joint *m*; 'hold·ing tenue *f*; possession *f*; ⊕ serrage *m*; ✝ portefeuille *m* effets, dossier *m*; small ~ petite propriété *f*; ~ company société *f* de portefeuille; 'hold-o·ver *Am.* survivance *f*, restant *m*; 'hold-up *Am.* F coup *m* à main armée; hold-up *m*; *mot.* embouteillage *m*, bouchon *m*.

hole [houl] **1.** trou *m* (*a. fig.*); ouverture *f*; F *fig.* embarras *m*, difficulté *f*; pick ~s in critiquer; **2.** trouer, percer, faire un trou dans; *golf*: poter; *billard*: blouser; '~-and-'cor·ner clandestin, secret (-ète *f*); obscur.

hol·i·day ['hɔlədi] jour *m* de fête; congé *m*; ~s *pl.* vancances *f/pl.*; on ~ vacances; '~-mak·er vacancier (-ère *f*) *m*.

ho·li·ness ['houlinis] sainteté *f*.

hol·la ['hɔlə], hol·lo(a) ['hɔlou] **1.** holà!; tiens!; *souv.* bonjour!; **2.** crier holà.

hol·land ['hɔlənd] (*a.* brown ~) toile *f* de Hollande, toile *f* écrue.

hol·ler *Am.* F ['hɔlə] **1.** crier (à tuetête); **2.** grand cri *m*.

hol·low ['hɔlou] **1.** *adj.* □ creux (creuse *f*); vide; faux (fausse *f*); sourd (*bruit*); **2.** F *adv.* (*a.* all ~) complètement (*sonner*) creux; **3.** *su.* creux *m*, cavité *f*; *terrain*: dénivellation *f*, enfoncement *m*; ⊕ évidure *f*; **4.** *v/t.* creuser, évider; 'hol·low·ness creux *m*; *fig.* fausseté *f*.

hol·ly ⚘ ['hɔli] houx *m*.

hol·ly·hock ⚘ ['hɔlihɔk] rose *f* trémière.

holm [houm] îlot *m*; rive *f* plate; ⚘ yeuse *f*.

hol·o·caust ['hɔləkɔːst] holocauste *m*; *fig.* massacre *m*.   [volver.\

hol·ster ['houlstə] étui *m* de re-/

ho·ly ['houli] saint; pieux (-euse *f*); ♀ of Holies le saint *m* des saints; ♀ Thursday le jeudi *m* saint; ~ water eau *f* bénite; ♀ Week la semaine *f* sainte.

hom·age ['hɔmidʒ] hommage *m*; do (*ou* pay *ou* render) ~ rendre hommage (à, to).

home [houm] **1.** *su.* foyer *m*; maison *f*, demeure *f*; asile *m*; patrie *f*; at ~ chez moi (lui, elle, *etc.*); **2.** *adj.* domestique, maison; qui porte (*coup*); bien senti (*vérité*); ~ affairs *pl.* affaires *f/pl.* intérieures; ~ help aide *f* ménagère; ♀ Office Ministère *m* de l'Intérieur; ~ rule autonomie *f*; ♀ Secretary Ministre *m* de l'Intérieur; ~ straight, ~ stretch *sp.* dernière ligne droite *f*; *fig.* phase *f* finale; ~ trade commerce *m* intérieur; F tell s.o. a few ~ truths dire ses quatre verités à q.; **3.** *adv.* à la maison, chez moi *etc.*; à son pays; à la patrie; à fond; ~ delivery livraison *f* à domicile; be ~ être chez soi; être de retour; bring (*ou* press) s.th. ~ to s.o. faire sentir qch. à q.; convaincre q. de qch.; come ~ retourner au pays; rentrer; it came ~ to her *fig.* elle s'en rendit compte; hit (*ou* strike) ~ frapper juste; **4.** *v/i.* revenir au foyer (*pigeon*: au colombier); '~-'baked de ménage; fait à la maison; '~-'bred indigène; *fig.* naturel(le *f*); '~-'com·ing retour *m* (au foyer *ou* au pays), rentrée *f*; '~-'croft petite ferme *f*; ~ e·co'nom·ics *sg. Am.* économie *f* domestique; '~-'felt dans son for intérieur; profond; '~-'grown indigène, du cru (*vin*); 'home·less sans foyer, sans asile; 'home·like qui rappelle le foyer; intime; 'home·li·ness simplicité *f*; *Am.* manque *m* de beauté; 'home·ly □ *fig.* simple, modeste, ordinaire; *Am.* sans beauté.

home... : '~-'made fait à la maison; du pays; '~-mak·er mère *f* de famille, ménagère *f*; '~-'sick nostalgique; '~-'sick·ness nostalgie *f*; '~-'spun **1.** filé à la maison; *fig.* simple, rude; **2.** gros drap *m*; '~-'stead ferme *f* avec dépendances; *Am.* bien *m* de famille; '~-'town ville *f* natale; '~-'ward **1.** *adv.* (*ou* '~-'wards) vers la maison; vers son pays; **2.** *adj.* de retour; '~-'work travail *m* fait à la maison; *école*: devoirs *m/pl.*; do one's ~ faire ses devoirs; *fig.* se bien préparer.

hom·i·cide ['hɔmisaid] homicide *m*; meurtre *m*; *personne*: homicide *mf*.

hom·i·ly ['hɔmili] homélie *f*.

hom·ing ['houmiŋ] retour *m* à la maison; 📡 retour *m* par radio-guidage; ~ *instinct* instinct *m* qui ramène au foyer; ~ *pigeon* pigeon *m* voyageur. [maïs.⟩

hom·i·ny ['hɔmini] semoule *f* de⟩

ho·mo F ['houmou] homo *m*, pédé *m*.

ho·moe·o·path ['houmiopæθ] homéopathe *mf*; **ho·moe·o'path·ic** (~*ally*) homéopathique; homéopathe (*médecin*); **ho·moe·op·a·thist** [~'ɔpəθist] homéopathe *mf*; **ho·moe'op·a·thy** homéopathie *f*.

ho·mo·ge·ne·i·ty [hɔmodʒe'niːiti] homogénéité *f*; **ho·mo·ge·ne·ous** □ [~'dʒiːnjəs] homogène; **ho·mog·en·ized** [hə'mɔdʒənaizd] homogénéisé; **ho·mol·o·gous** [hɔ'mɔləgəs] homologue; **ho'mol·o·gy** [~dʒi] homologie *f*; **hom·o·nym** ['hɔmənim] homonyme *m*; **ho·mo·sex·u·al** ['houmou'seksjuəl] homosexuel(le *f*).

hom·y F ['houmi] *see* homelike.

hone ⊕ [houn] **1.** pierre *f* à aiguiser; **2.** aiguiser; repasser (*un rasoir*).

hon·est □ ['ɔnist] honnête, sincère, loyal (-aux *m/pl.*); intègre; ~ *truth* exacte vérité *f*; **'hon·es·ty** honnêteté *f*, probité *f*, loyauté *f*.

hon·ey ['hʌni] miel *m*; *my* ~! chéri(e *f*)!; **'~·comb** rayon *m* de miel; **'~·combed** alvéolé; criblé; **hon·eyed** ['hʌnid] emmiellé; *fig.* mielleux (-euse *f*); **'hon·ey·moon** **1.** lune *f* de miel; **2.** passer la lune de miel; **hon·ey·suck·le** ⚘ ['~sʌkl] chèvrefeuille *m*.

honk mot. [hɔŋk] **1.** cornement *m*; **2.** corner, klaxonner.

honk·y-tonk Am. sl. ['hɔŋkitɔŋk] beuglant *m*.

hon·o·rar·i·um [ɔnə'rɛəriəm] honoraires *m/pl.*; **hon·or·ar·y** ['ɔnərəri] honoraire, d'honneur.

hon·o(u)r ['ɔnə] **1.** honneur *m*; distinction *f* honorifique; *fig.* gloire *f*; ~*s* *pl.* honneurs *m/pl.*; distinctions *f/pl.*; *your* ♀ Monsieur le juge; *in* ~ *of s.o.* en honneur de q., à la gloire de q.; *do the* ~*s of the house* faire les honneurs de sa (*etc.*) maison; **2.** honorer; faire honneur à (*a.* ♱).

hon·o(u)r·a·ble □ ['ɔnərəbl] honorable; *Right* ♀ (le) très honorable; **'hon·o(u)r·a·ble·ness** honorabilité *f*; caractère *m* honorable.

hooch Am. sl. [huːtʃ] gnôle *f*.

hood [hud] capuchon *m*; ✀ cloche *f*; ⊕ *forge etc.*: hotte *f*; *univ.* chaperon *m*; mot. capote *f*; Am. mot. capot *m* (*du moteur*); **'hood·ed** encapuchonné (*personne*), ♀ capuchonné; *cost.* à capuchon; *fig.* couvert.

hood·lum Am. F ['huːdləm] voyou *m*; gangster *m*; galapiat *m*.

hoo·doo *surt.* Am. ['huːduː] **1.** déveine *f*, guigne *f*; porte-malheur *m/inv.*; **2.** porter la guigne à; jeter un sort sur.

hood·wink ['hudwiŋk] † bander les yeux à; *fig.* tromper.

hoo·ey Am. sl. ['huːi] bêtise *f*.

hoof [huːf] sabot *m*; F pied *m*; **hoofed** [huːft] à sabots.

hook [huk] **1.** croc(het) *m*; *robe:* agrafe *f*; *vestiaire:* patère *f*; *pêche:* hameçon *m*; ~*s and eyes* agrafes et œillets; *by* ~ *or by crook* coûte que coûte; Am. F ~, *line and sinker* sans exception, totalement; sans réserve; **2.** *v/t.* accrocher; agrafer (*une robe*); prendre (*un poisson*); courber (*le doigt*); *fig.* crocher (*le bras*); *sl.* voler à la tire; attraper; *sl.* ~ *it* attraper; ficher le camp; ~ *up* agrafer (*une robe*); suspendre; *v/i.* (*a.* ~ *on*) s'accrocher; **hooked** [~t] crochu (*a. nez*); muni de crochets *etc.*; *sl.* toxicomane; **'hook·er** ⚓ hourque *f*; Am. sl. pouffiasse *f* (= *prostituée*); **'hook-up** combinaison *f*, alliance *f*; *radio:* relais *m* radiophonique; postes *m/pl.* conjugués; **'hook·y:** Am. *play* ~ faire l'école buissonnière.

hoo·li·gan ['huːligən] gouape *f*, voyou *m*.

hoop [huːp] **1.** *tonneau:* cercle *m*; ⊕ *roue:* jante *f*; *cost.* panier *m*; cerceau *m* (*d'enfant*); Am. sl. bague *f*; **2.** cercler; garnir de jantes; **'hoop·er** tonnelier *m*, cerclier *m*.

hoop·ing-cough ['huːpiŋkɔf] coqueluche *f*.

hoo·poe orn. ['huːpuː] huppe *f*.

hoose·gow Am. sl. ['huːsgau] prison *f*; cabinets *m/pl.*

hoot [huːt] **1.** *su.* hibou: ululement *m*; *personne:* huée *f*; mot. cornement *m*; coup *m* de sifflet; **2.** *v/i.* ululer; huer; mot. klaxonner; *théâ.* siffler; *v/t.* huer; (*a.* ~ *at*, ~ *out*, ~ *away*) chasser (*q.*) par des huées; **'hoot·er**

sirène *f*; avertisseur *m*; *mot.* klaxon *m*.

hop[1] [hɔp] **1.** *su.* ♀ houblon *m*; ⁓*s pl.* houblon *m*; **2.** *v/t.* houblonner (*la bière*); *v/i.* cueillir le houblon.

hop[2] [⁓] **1.** saut *m*; gambade *f*; 🎖 étape *f*; *sl.* sauterie *f* (= *bal*); **2.** sauter; *v/t. sl.* ⁓ it ficher le camp, filer; se débiner; *v/i.* sautiller; 🎖 ⁓ off décoller, partir.

hope [houp] **1.** espoir *m* (de, of); espérance *f*; of great ⁓s qui promet; **2.** espérer (qch., for s.th.); ⁓ in mettre son espoir en; **hope·ful** □ ['⁓ful] plein d'espoir; qui promet; be ⁓ that avoir bon espoir que; '**hope·ful·ly** *surt. Am.* on espère (que); '**hope·less** □ désespéré; sans espoir; incorrigible; inutile.

hop-o'-my-thumb ['hɔpəmi'θʌm] le Petit Poucet; *fig.* petit bout *m* d'homme.

hop·per ['hɔpə] ⊕ *moulin:* trémie *f*, huche *f*; 🏏 semoir *m*; ⚕ marie-salope (*pl.* maries-salopes) *f*.

horde [hɔ:d] horde *f*.

ho·ri·zon [hə'raizn] horizon *m*; on the ⁓ à l'horizon; **hor·i·zon·tal** □ [hɔri'zɔntl] horizontal (-aux *m/pl.*).

hor·mone *biol.* ['hɔ:moun] hormone *f*.

horn [hɔ:n] *usu.* corne *f*; *zo.* antenne *f*; *hibou:* aigrette *f*; ♪ cor *m*; ♪ instrument *m* à vent; *radio etc.:* pavillon *m*; † corne *f* à boire; *mot.* klaxon *m*; trompe *f*; (*stag's*) ⁓s *pl.* bois *m*; ⁓ of plenty corne *f* d'abondance; **horned** ['⁓id; hɔ:nd] à ... cornes, cornu.

hor·net *zo.* ['hɔ:nit] frelon *m*.

horn·less ['hɔ:nlis] sans cornes; '**horn·pipe** (*a.* sailor's ⁓) *danse:* matelote *f*; **horn·swog·gle** *Am. sl.* ['⁓swɔgl] escroquer, tromper (*q.*); '**horn·y** □ corné; de *ou* en corne; calleux (-euse *f*) (*main*); ∨ excité, en chaleur.

hor·o·loge ['hɔrəlɔdʒ] horloge *f*; **hor·o·scope** ['⁓skoup] horoscope *m*; cast s.o's ⁓s ⁓ dresser l'horoscope de q.

hor·ren·dous [hə'rendəs] terrible, horrible.

hor·ri·ble □ ['hɔrəbl] horrible, affreux (-euse *f*); **hor·rid** □ ['hɔrid] horrible, affreux (-euse *f*); **hor·rif·ic** [hɔ'rifik] horrifique; **hor·ri·fy** ['⁓fai] horrifier; *fig.*

scandaliser; **hor·ror** ['hɔrə] horreur *f* (de, of); čhose *f* horrible; F the ⁓s *pl.* delirium *m* tremens.

horse [hɔ:s] **1.** *su.* cheval *m*; *coll.* cavalerie *f*; séchoir *m*; take ⁓ monter à cheval; ⁓ artillery artillerie *f* montée; **2.** *v/t.* fournir des chevaux à; mettre des chevaux à; *v/i.* chevaucher; '⁓·back: on ⁓ à cheval; sur un cheval; be (*ou* go) on ⁓ aller à cheval; get on ⁓ monter à cheval; '⁓·bean féverole *f*; '⁓·box 🚂 wagon *m* à chevaux; fourgon *m* pour le transport des chevaux; '⁓·break·er dresseur *m* de chevaux; '⁓·deal·er marchand *m* de chevaux; ♀ **Guards** *pl. la* cavalerie de la Garde; '⁓·hair crin *m* (de cheval); '⁓·laugh F gros rire *m* bruyant; '⁓·man cavalier *m*; '⁓·man·ship manège *m*, équitation *f*; ⁓ op·er·a *Am.* Western *m*; '⁓·play jeu *m* de main(s), jeu *m* brutal; '⁓·pond abreuvoir *m*; '⁓·pow·er *mesure:* cheval-vapeur (*pl.* chevaux-vapeur) *m*; '⁓·race course *f* de chevaux; '⁓·rad·ish ♀ raifort *m*; '⁓·sense gros bon sens *m*; '⁓·shoe fer *m* à cheval; '⁓·whip cravache *f*; '⁓·wom·an amazone *f*, cavalière *f*.

hors·y ['hɔ:si] chevalin; hippomane (*personne*).

hor·ta·tive □ ['hɔ:tətiv], **hor·ta·to·ry** ['⁓təri] exhortatif (-ive *f*).

hor·ti·cul·tur·al [hɔːti'kʌltʃərəl] d'horticulture; '**hor·ti·cul·ture** horticulture *f*; **hor·ti'cul·tur·ist** horticulteur *m*.

hose [houz] **1.** 🧦 bas *m/pl.*; *jardin:* tuyau *m*; manche *f* à eau; **2.** *v/t.* arroser au tuyau.

ho·sier † ['houʒə] bonnetier (-ère *f*) *m*; '**ho·sier·y** † bonneterie *f*.

hos·pice ['hɔspis] hospice *m*.

hos·pi·ta·ble □ ['hɔspitəbl] hospitalier (-ère *f*).

hos·pi·tal ['hɔspitl] hôpital *m*; hospice *m*; ♀ Sunday dimanche *m* de quête pour les hôpitaux; **hos·pi·tal·i·ty** [⁓'tæliti] hospitalité *f*; **hos·pi·tal·ize** ['⁓təlaiz] hospitaliser; envoyer à l'hôpital; **hos·pi·tal·(l)er** ['⁓tlə] hospitalier *m*; *qqfois* aumônier *m*; '**hos·pi·tal·train** 🚂 train *m* sanitaire.

host[1] [houst] hôte *m* (*a. zo.*, ♀); hôtelier *m*, aubergiste *m*; *radio, télév.* présentateur (-trice *f*) *m*.

host² [⌐] *fig.* foule *f*, multitude *f*;
bibl. Lord of ⌐s le Dieu des armées.

host³ *eccl.* [⌐] hostie *f*.

hos·tage ['hɔstidʒ] otage *m*.

hos·tel ['hɔstəl] † hôtellerie *f*; *univ.*
foyer *m*; *youth* ⌐ auberge *f* de la
jeunesse.

host·ess ['houstis] hôtesse *f*.

hos·tile ['hɔstail] hostile, ennemi;
hos·til·i·ty [hɔs'tiliti] hostilité *f*
(contre, to); animosité *f*.

hos·tler ['ɔslə] valet *m* d'écurie.

hot [hɔt] **1.** chaud; brûlant, cuisant;
violent (*colère*); piquant (*sauce*); *sl.*
volé; *Am.* remarquable; *Am. sl.* radio-actif (-ive *f*); F ⌐ *air* discours
m/pl. vides; *Am.* F ⌐ *dog* petit pain
m fourré d'une saucisse chaude; *go*
(*ou sell*) *like* ⌐ *cakes* se vendre comme
des petits pains; *pol.* ⌐ *line* téléphone
m rouge; ⌐ *spot* point *m* névralgique;
boîte *f* de nuit; *sl.* ⌐ *stuff* as *m*; viveur
m; marchandise *f* récemment volée;
2. F chauffer; '**hot·bed** couche *f* à *ou*
de fumier; *fig.* foyer *m*.

hotch·potch ['hɔtʃpɔtʃ] salmigondis
m; hochepot *m*; *fig.* méli-mélo (*pl.*
mélis-mélos) *m*.

ho·tel [hou'tel] hôtel *m*.

hot...: '⌐**foot** **1.** à toute vitesse; **2.** F
se dépêcher; '⌐**head** tête *f* chaude,
impétueux (-euse *f*) *m*; '⌐**house**
serre *f* chaude; '**hot·ness** chaleur *f*;
violence *f*; *moutarde etc.*: force *f*.

hot...: '⌐**plate** chauffe-assiettes
m/inv., réchaud *m*; '⌐**pot** hochepot
m, (*sorte de*) ragoût *m*; '⌐**press** satiner (*le papier*), *tex.* calandrer; ⌐ *rod*
mot. Am. sl. bolide *m*; '⌐**spur**
cerveau *m* brûlé; tête *f* chaude;
'⌐'**wa·ter:** ⌐ *bottle* bouillotte *f*.

hough [hɔk] *see* hock¹.

hound [haund] **1.** chien *m* (*usu.* de
chasse); *fig.* (sale) type *m*; **2.** chasser; *fig.* s'acharner après; exciter
(contre *at*, on *s.th.*).

hour ['auə] heure *f*; *fig. a.* moment
m; ⌐s *pl.* heures *f/pl.* de bureau *etc.*;
eccl. heures *f/pl.*; '⌐**glass** sablier
m; '⌐**hand** petite aiguille *f*; '**hour·**
ly (*adj.*) de) toutes les heures;
d'heure en heure.

house 1. *su.* [haus], *pl.* **hous·es**
['hauziz] maison *f*, habitation *f*,
demeure *f*; † maison *f* (de commerce); *parl.* Chambre *f*; *théâ.* salle
f; *fig.* ⌐ *of cards* château *m* de cartes;
fig. put ones ⌐ *in order* mettre de

l'ordre dans ses affaires; **2.** [hauz]
v/t. loger; mettre à l'abri; *v/i.*
habiter, loger; '⌐**a·gent** ['haus⌐]
agent *m* de location; ⌐ **ar·rest** assignation *f* à domicile; *put s.o. under* ⌐
assigner q. à domicile; '⌐**boat** barge
f de parade; '⌐**break·er** voleur *m*
avec effraction, cambrioleur *m*;
démolisseur *m*; '⌐**bro·ken** *Am.*
propre (*animal*); docile, obéissant
(*personne*); '⌐**check** perquisition *f* à
domicile; '⌐**fly** mouche *f* commune; '⌐**hold** ménage *m*, famille *f*;
domestiques *m/pl.*; *attr.* domestique, de *ou* du ménage; *King's* ⌐
Maison *f* du roi; ⌐ *troops pl.* la Garde
f; ⌐ *word* mot *m* d'usage courant;
'⌐**hold·er** propriétaire *f*, locataire
m; chef *m* de famille; '⌐**hunt·ing** F
recherche *f* d'un appartement *ou*
d'une maison; '⌐**keep·er** ménagère
f; gouvernante *f*; '⌐**keep·ing 1.**
ménage *m*; **2.** du ménage; '⌐**less**
sans domicile *ou* abri; '⌐**maid**
bonne *f*; fille *f* de service; '⌐**mas·**
ter *école:* professeur *m* directeur
(*d'une pension officielle*); '⌐**paint·er**
peintre *m* décorateur; '⌐**proud:** *be* ⌐
être (une) ménagère très méticu-
leuse; '⌐**room** logement *m*, place *f*;
give s.o. ⌐ loger q.; '⌐**to'house:**
collection *etc.* quête *f etc.* à domicile;
'⌐**trained** *Brit. see* housebroken; '⌐**
warm·ing** (*ou* ⌐*party*) pendaison *f*
de la crémaillère; ⌐ *wife* ['⌐waif]
ménagère *f*, maîtresse *f* de maison;
['hʌzif] trousse *f* de couture; '⌐**wife·**
ly ['⌐waifli] ménager (-ère *f*); de *ou*
du ménage; '⌐**wif·er·y** [⌐'wifəri]
économie *f* domestique; travaux
m/pl. domestiques; '⌐**wreck·er**
démolisseur *m*.

hous·ing¹ ['hauziŋ] logement *m*;
récolte, moutons, etc.: rentrée *f*; †
emmagasinage *m*; ⌐ *conditions pl.* état
m du logement; '⌐ *estate* (*ou project ou
scheme*) cité *f*, grand ensemble *m*; ⌐
shortage crise *f* du logement.

hous·ing² [⌐] caparaçon *m*.

hove [houv] *prét. et p.p. de* heave 2.

hov·el ['hɔvl] taudis *m*, masure *f*.

hov·er ['hɔvə] planer, se balancer;
fig. hésiter.

how [hau] comment; ⌐ *much* (*ou
many*) combien (de); ⌐ *large a
room!* que la pièce est grande!;
⌐ *about* ...? et ...?; si on ...?;
'⌐**d'ye-do** *sl.* ['⌐djə'du:] affaire *f*;

humbug

pétrin *m*; ~-'**ev·er 1.** *adv.* de quelque manière que (*sbj.*); *devant adj. ou adv.*: quelque ... que (*sbj.*), tout ... que (*ind.*); F comment diable?; **2.** *conj.* cependant, toutefois, pourtant.

how·itz·er ✕ ['hauitsə] obusier *m*.

howl [haul] **1.** hurler; **2.** hurlement *m*; mugissement *m*; huée *f*; *radio*: réaction *f* dans l'antenne; '**howl·er** hurleur (-euse *f*) *m*; *sl.* gaffe *f*, perle *f*; '**howl·ing 1.** hurlant; F énorme; **2.** hurlement *m*.

hoy [hɔi] **1.** hé!; holà!; **2.** ⚓ bugalet *m* (= *petit vaisseau côtier*).

hoy·den ['hɔidn] jeune fille *f* garçonnière.

hub [hʌb] moyeu *m*; *fig.* centre *m*.

hub·ble-bub·ble ['hʌblbʌbl] glouglou *m*; bruit *m* confus de voix, brouhaha *m*.

hub·bub ['hʌbʌb] brouhaha *m*, vacarme *m*, tohu-bohu *m*.

hub(·by) F ['hʌb(i)] mari *m*.

huck·a·back ⬧ ['hʌkəbæk] toile *f* grain d'orge; toile *f* ouvrée.

huck·le ['hʌkl] hanche *f*; '~·**ber·ry** ♀ airelle *f* myrtille; '~·**bone** os *m* de la hanche; jointure *f* du doigt.

huck·ster ['hʌkstə] **1.** *su.* regrattier (-ère *f*) *m*; **2.** *v/t.* colporter; *v/i.* marchander; trafiquer; regratter.

hud·dle ['hʌdl] **1.** *v/t.* entasser (pêle-mêle); *v/i.* (*a.* ~ *together,* ~ *up*) s'entasser, s'empiler; ~ *on* mettre à la hâte; **2.** *su.* tas *m* confus; méli-mélo (*pl.* mélis-mélos) *m*; *Am.* conclave *m*, conférence *f* confidentielle.

hue¹ [hju:] teinte *f*, couleur *f*.

hue² [~]: ~ *and* cry clameur *f* de haro; clameur *f* publique.

huff [hʌf] **1.** *su.*: *take* (*the*) ~ se froisser; **2.** *v/t.* froisser; *dames*: souffler (*un pion*); *v/i.* † haleter; se fâcher; *dames*: souffler; '**huff·ish** □ irascible; susceptible; '**huff·i·ness**, '**huff·ish·ness** mauvaise humeur *f*; susceptibilité *f*; '**huff·y** □ irascible; susceptible; fâché.

hug [hʌg] **1.** étreinte *f*; **2.** étreindre, embrasser; serrer dans ses bras; tenir à, ne pas démordre de; chérir; serrer (*le trottoir, un mur*); ~ *o.s.* se féliciter (de *inf.,* on *gér.*).

huge □ [hju:dʒ] immense, énorme, vaste; '**huge·ness** immensité *f*.

hug·ger-mug·ger F ['hʌgəmʌgə] **1.** *adj.* sans ordre; en désordre (*a.*

adv.); **2.** *v/t.* (*a.* ~ *up*) étouffer, supprimer; *v/i.* patauger; agir sans méthode; vivre sans ordre; **3.** *su.* confusion *f*, pagaïe *f*.

Hu·gue·not *hist.* ['hju:gənɔt] huguenot(e *f*) *m* (*a. adj.*).

hulk ⚓ [hʌlk] ponton *m* (*carcasse de navire*); *fig.* lourdaud *m*, gros pataud *m*; '**hulk·ing** lourd, gros(se *f*).

hull [hʌl] **1.** ♀ cosse *f*; *fig.* enveloppe *f*; ⚓, ✈ coque *f*; **2.** écosser (*des pois*), décortiquer (*de l'orge, du riz*); monder (*de l'orge*); ⚓ percer la coque de.

hul·la·ba·loo [hʌləbə'lu:] vacarme *m*, brouhaha *m*.

hul·lo ['hʌ'lou] ohé!; tiens!; *téléph.* allô!

hum [hʌm] **1.** bourdonnement *m* (*des abeilles ou fig.*); ronflement *m*; murmure *m*; F supercherie *f*; **2.** hmm!; **3.** *v/i.* bourdonner; ronfler; fredonner; ~ *and ha* bredouiller; tourner autour du pot; F *make things* ~ faire ronfler les choses; *v/t.* fredonner (*un air*).

hu·man ['hju:mən] **1.** □ humain; ~*ly* en être humain; ~*ly possible* possible à l'homme; ~*ly speaking* humainement parlant; ~ *rights* pl. droits *m/pl.* de l'homme; **2.** F être *m* humain; **hu·mane** □ [hju:'mein] humain, compatissant; humanitaire; ~ *learning* humanités *f/pl.*; '**hu·man·ism** ['hju:mənizm] humanisme *m*; '**hu·man·ist** humaniste (*a. su./m*); **hu·man·i·tar·i·an** [hju:mæni'tɛəriən] humanitaire (*a. su./mf*); **hu·man·i·ty** humanité *f*; nature *f* humaine; genre *m* humain, hommes *m/pl.*; *humanities pl.* humanités *f/pl.*, lettres *f/pl.*; **hu·man·i·za·tion** [hju:mənai'zeiʃn] humanisation *f*; '**hu·man·ize** (s')humaniser; **hu·man·kind** ['hju:mən'kaind] le genre *m* humain, les hommes *m/pl.*

hum·ble ['hʌmbl] **1.** □ humble; modeste; *in my* ~ *opinion* à mon humble avis; *your* ~ *servant* votre humble serviteur *m*; *eat* ~ *pie* s'humilier, se rétracter; **2.** humilier; rabaisser.

hum·ble-bee ['hʌmblbi:] bourdon *m*.

hum·ble·ness ['hʌmblnis] humilité *f*.

hum·bug ['hʌmbʌg] **1.** charlatan

(-isme) *m*; blagues *f/pl.*; *personne*: blagueur (-euse *f*) *m*; bonbon *m* glacé à la menthe; **2.** mystifier; conter des blagues à; enjôler (*q.*).

hum·drum ['hʌmdrʌm] **1.** monotone; banal (-aux *m/pl.*); ennuyeux (-euse *f*); **2.** monotonie *f*.

hu·mer·al *anat.* ['hju:mərəl] huméral (-aux *m/pl.*).

hu·mid ['hju:mid] humide; moite (*peau, chaleur*); **hu'mid·i·ty** humidité *f*.

hu·mil·i·ate [hju'milieit] humilier; mortifier; **hu·mil·i'a·tion** humiliation *f*; affront *m*.

hu·mil·i·ty [hju'militi] humilité *f*.

hum·mer ['hʌmə] *surt. téléph.* appel *m* vibré; sonnerie *f*; *sl.* brasseur *m* d'affaires; personne *f* très active.

hum·ming F ['hʌmiŋ] bourdonnant; vrombissant; '**~-bird** *orn.* colibri *m*, oiseau-mouche (*pl.* oiseaux-mouches) *m*; '**~-top** toupie *f* d'Allemagne.

hum·mock ['hʌmək] mamelon *m*, coteau *m*; *glace*: monticule *m*.

hu·mor·ist ['hju:mərist] humoriste *m*; comique *m*; farceur (-euse *f*) *m*.

hu·mor·ous □ ['hju:mərəs] comique, drôle; facétieux (-euse *f*); '**hu·mor·ous·ness** drôlerie *f*; humeur *f* facétieuse.

hu·mo(u)r ['hju:mə] **1.** *usu.* humeur *f*; plaisanterie *f*; caractère *m*; out of ~ mécontent (de, *with*); **2.** complaire à (*q.*); laisser faire (*q.*); flatter les caprices de; '**hu·mo(u)r·less** froid, austère; **hu·mo(u)r·some** □ ['~səm] capricieux (-euse *f*).

hump [hʌmp] **1.** bosse *f*; *sl.* cafard *m*; give s.o. the ~ embêter *q.*; **2.** courber, arquer; F embêter (*q.*); *Am. sl.* ~ o.s. se fouler; '**hump·back(ed)** *see* hunchback(ed).

humph [mm] hmm!

Hum·phrey ['hʌmfri]: *dine with Duke ~* dîner par cœur.

hump·ty-dump·ty F ['hʌmpti-'dʌmpti] petite personne *f* boulotte.

hump·y ['hʌmpi] couvert de protubérances.

hunch [hʌntʃ] **1.** *see* hump; gros morceau *m*; *pain*: quignon *m*; *Am.* F pressentiment *m*; **2.** (*a.* ~ out, ~ up) voûter; '**hunch·back** bossu(e *f*) *m*; '**hunch·backed** bossu.

hun·dred ['hʌndrəd] **1.** cent; **2.** cent *m*; centaine *f* (de); *admin.* canton *m*; '**hun·dred·fold** centuple; **hun·dredth** ['~θ] centième (*a. su./m*); '**hun·dred·weight** quintal *m* (*50,802 kg, Am. 45,359 kg*).

hung [hʌŋ] **1.** *prét. et p.p. de* hang 1; **2.** *adj.* faisandé (*gibier, viande*).

Hun·gar·i·an [hʌŋ'gɛəriən] **1.** hongrois; **2.** Hongrois(e *f*) *m*; *ling.* hongrois *m*.

hun·ger ['hʌŋgə] **1.** *su.* faim *f*; *fig.* ardent désir *m* (de, *for*); **2.** *v/i.* avoir faim; *fig.* avoir soif (de *for*, *after*); *v/t.* affamer; contraindre par la faim (à *inf.*, *into gér.*); ~ **strike** grève *f* de la faim; go on (*a*) ~ faire la grève de la faim.

hun·gry □ ['hʌŋgri] affamé (de *for*, *after*); avide (*œil*); maigre (*sol*).

hunk F [hʌŋk] gros morceau *m*; *pain*: quignon *m*; '**hun·kers** *pl.*: on one's ~ à croupetons.

hunks F [hʌŋks] grippe-sou *m*, avare *m*.

hunk·y(-do·ry) *Am. sl.* ['hʌŋki (-'dɔːri)] parfait; d'accord.

hunt [hʌnt] **1.** *su.* chasse *f*; terrain *m* de chasse; recherche *f* (de, *for*); vénerie *f*; **2.** *v/t.* chasser; poursuivre; ~ out, ~ up déterrer; découvrir; *v/i.* chasser (au chien courant *ou* à courre); aller à la recherche (de *for*, *after*); '**hunt·er** chasseur *m*; tueur *m* (*de lions etc.*); chien *m* de chasse; '**hunt·ing** **1.** chasse *f*; poursuite *f*; vénerie *f*; **2.** de chasse; '**hunt·ing-box** pavillon *m* de chasse; muette *f*; '**hunt·ing-ground** terrain *m* de chasse; '**hunt·ress** chasseuse *f*; '**hunts·man** chasseur *m* (à courre).

hur·dle ['hə:dl] claie *f*, clôture *f*; *sp.* haie *f*; '**hur·dler** *sp.* sauteur *m* de haies; '**hur·dle-race** *sp.*, *turf*: course *f* de haies; steeple-chase *m*.

hur·dy-gur·dy ['hə:digə:di] † vielle *f*.

hurl [hə:l] **1.** lancement *m*; **2.** lancer (*a. fig.*), jeter.

hurl·y-burl·y ['hə:libə:li] brouhaha *m*, tintamarre *m*.

hur·ra(h) *int.* [hu'rɑ:] hourra! (*a. su./m*).   [♣ tempête *f*.)

hur·ri·cane ['hʌrikən] ouragan *m*;)

hur·ried □ ['hʌrid] pressé, précipité.

hur·ry ['hʌri] **1.** hâte *f*; précipitation *f*; empressement *m*; *in a* ~ à la hâte; *be in a* ~ être pressé; *is there any* ~? est-ce que cela presse?; F *not ... in a* ~ ne ... pas de sitôt; **2.** *v/t.* hâter, presser; ~ *on*, ~ *up* faire hâter le pas à; pousser; *v/i.* (*a.* ~ *up*) se hâter, se dépêcher; presser le pas; ~ *over s.th.* expédier qch.; faire qch. à la hâte; '~**-scur·ry 1.** désordre *m*; débandade *f*; **2.** à la débandade; pêle-mêle.

hurt [həːt] **1.** *su.* mal *m*; blessure *f*; tort *m*; **2.** [*irr.*] *v/t.* faire du mal à; *fig.* nuire à; blesser (*a. les sentiments*); faire de la peine à; gâter, abîmer; *v/i.* faire mal; offenser; F s'abîmer; **hurt·ful** □ ['~ful] (to) nuisible (à); préjudiciable (à).

hur·tle ['həːtl] *v/t.* heurter; *v/i.* se précipiter.

hus·band ['hʌzbənd] **1.** mari *m*, époux *m*; **2.** ménager; ✍ cultiver; '**hus·band·man** cultivateur *m*; laboureur *m*; '**hus·band·ry** agronomie *f*; industrie *f* agricole; *good* ~ bonne gestion *f*; *bad* ~ gaspillage *m*.

hush [hʌʃ] **1.** *int.* silence!; chut!; **2.** *su.* silence *m*; **3.** *v/t.* calmer; faire taire; étouffer (*un bruit*); ~ *up* étouffer; *v/i.* se taire; '~**-mon·ey** prix *m* du silence (*de q.*).

husk [hʌsk] **1.** ✿ cosse *f*, gousse *f*; brou *m*; *fig.* carcasse *f*; **2.** écosser (*des pois*); décortiquer; '**husk·i·ness** enrouement *m*, raucité *f*.

husk·y¹ □ ['hʌski] cossu (*pois*); enroué (*voix*); altéré par l'émotion (*voix*); F fort, costaud.

hus·ky² [~] Esquimau *mf*; chien *m* esquimau.

hus·sar ✗ [hu'zaː] hussard *m*.

hus·sy ['hʌsi] coquine *f*; garce *f*.

hus·tings *hist.* ['hʌstiŋz] *pl.* estrade *f*, tribune *f*; élection *f*.

hus·tle ['hʌsl] **1.** *v/t.* bousculer; pousser; *v/i.* se dépêcher, se presser; **2.** *su.* bousculade *f*; hâte *f*; activité *f* énergique; ~ *and bustle* animation *f*; remue-ménage *m/inv.*; '**hus·tler** homme *m* d'expédition.

hut [hʌt] **1.** hutte *f*, cabane *f*; ✗ baraquement *m*; **2.** (se) baraquer; loger.

hutch [hʌtʃ] coffre *m*, huche *f*; cage *f* (*à lapins*); *fig.* logis *m* étroit; pétrin *m*.

hut·ment ✗ ['hʌtmənt] (camp *m* de) baraques *f/pl.*; baraquements *m/pl.*

huz·za *int.* [hu'zaː] hourra!; vivat! (*a. su./m*).

hy·a·cinth ✿ ['haiəsinθ] jacinthe *f*.

hy·a(e)·na *zo.* [hai'iːnə] hyène *f*.

hy·brid ['haibrid] **1.** *biol.* hybride *m*; *personne:* métis(se *f*) *m*; **2.** hybride; hétérogène; '**hy·brid·ism** hybridité *f*; '**hy·brid·ize** (s')hybrider.

hy·drant ['haidrənt] prise *f* d'eau; **hy·drate** ⚗ ['haidreit] hydrate *m*.

hy·drau·lic [hai'drɔːlik] **1.** (~*ally*) hydraulique; **2.** ~*s pl.* hydraulique *f*, hydromécanique *f*.

hydro... [haidro] hydr(o)-; '~**'a·er·o·plane** hydravion *m*; '~**'car·bon** ⚗ hydrocarbure *m*; '~**'chlo·ric ac·id** *m* chlorhydrique; '~**-dy'nam·ics** *pl.* hydrodynamique *f*; '~**-e'lec·tric** hydroélectrique; ~ *generating station* centrale *f* hydroélectrique; '~**-foil** hydrofoil *m*; **hy·dro·gen** ⚗ ['haidridʒən] hydrogène *m*; **hy·dro·gen·at·ed** [hai'drɔdʒineitid] hydrogéné; **hy·drog·e·nous** hydrogénique; **hy·drog·ra·phy** [~grəfi] hydrographie *f*; **hy·dro·path·ic** ['haidro'pæθik] **1.** hydrothérapique; hydropathe (*personne*); **2.** (*a.* ~ *establishment*) établissement *m* hydrothérapique; **hy·drop·a·thy** [hai'drɔpəθi] hydropathie *f*.

hydro...: ~'**pho·bi·a** hydrophobie *f*; '~**plane** hydravion *m*; bateau *m* glisseur; ~'**stat·ic 1.** hydrostatique; ~ *press* presse *f* hydraulique; **2.** ~*s pl.* hydrostatique *f*.

hy·giene ['haidʒiːn] hygiène *f*; **hy·gien·ic 1.** (~*ally*) hygiénique; **2.** ~*s pl. see* hygiene.

hy·grom·e·ter *phys.* [hai'grɔmitə] hygromètre *m*.

Hy·men ['haimen] *myth.* Hymen *m*.

hymn [him] **1.** *eccl.* hymne *f*, cantique *m*; hymne *m* (*national, de guerre, etc.*); **2.** glorifier, louer; **hym·nal** ['~nəl] **1.** qui se rapporte à un cantique; **2.** (*ou* '**hymn-book**) recueil *m* d'hymnes.

hy·per·bo·la Å [hai'pəːbələ] hyperbole *f*; **hy·per·bo·le** [~li] *rhétorique*: hyperbole *f*; **hy·per·bol·ic** Å [~'bɔlik] hyperbolique; **hy·per·bol·i·cal** □ hyperbolique; **hy·per·crit·i·cal** □ ['~'kritikl] hypercritique; difficile; **hy·per·tro·phy** [~trəfi] hypertrophie *f*.

hy·phen ['haifən] **1.** trait *m* d'union;

typ. division *f*; **2.** écrire avec un trait d'union; **hy·phen·ate** ['~eit] mettre un trait d'union à; ~d *Americans pl.* étrangers *m/pl.* naturalisés (*qui conservent leur sympathie pour leur pays d'origine*).

hyp·no·sis [hip'nousis], *pl.* **-ses** [~si:z] hypnose *f*.

hyp·not·ic [hip'nɔtik] **1.** (~ally) hypnotique; **2.** narcotique *m*; **hyp·no·tism** ['~nətizm] hypnotisme *m*; **'hyp·no·tist** hypnotiste *mf*; **hyp·no·tize** ['~taiz] hypnotiser.

hy·po·chon·dri·a [haipo'kɔndriə] hypocondrie *f*; F spleen *m*; **hy·po-'chon·dri·ac** [~driæk] **1.** hypocondriaque; **2.** hypocondre *mf*; **hy·poc·ri·sy** [hi'pɔkrəsi] hypocrisie *f*; **hyp·o·crite** ['hipokrit]

hypocrite *mf*; F *homme:* tartufe *m*, *femme:* sainte nitouche *f*; **hyp·o-'crit·i·cal** □ hypocrite; **hy·po·der·mic** [haipo'də:mik] **1.** sous-cutané (*injection*); ~ needle canule *f*; **2.** seringue *f* hypodermique; **hy·pot·e·nuse** ♣ [hai'pɔtinju:z] hypoténuse *f*; **hy'poth·e·car·y** [~θikəri] ⚖ hypothécaire; **hy'poth·e·cate** [~θikeit] hypothéquer; **hy-'poth·e·sis** [~θisis], *pl.* **-ses** [~si:z] hypothèse *f*; **hy·po'thet·ic, hy·po·thet·i·cal** □ [~po'θetik(l)] hypothétique, supposé.

hys·te·ri·a ♣ [his'tiəriə] hystérie *f*; F crise *f* de nerfs; **hys·ter·ic,** *usu.* **hys·ter·i·cal** □ [his'terik(l)] hystérique; **hys'ter·ics** *pl.* crise *f ou* attaque *f* de nerfs; **go into** ~ avoir une crise de nerfs.

I

I, i [ai] I *m*, i *m*.

I [ai] je; *accentué:* moi.

i·am·bic [ai'æmbik] **1.** iambique; **2.** (*ou* **'i·amb, i'am·bus** [ˌˈbəs]) iambe *m*.

i·bex *zo.* ['aibeks] bouquetin *m*.

ice [ais] **1.** glace *f* (*a. cuis.*); F *cut no* ˌ ne faire aucune impression (sur, *with*); F ne pas compter; *fig.* skate *on thin* ˌ être *ou* s'engager dans une situation dangereuse; **2.** (con)geler; *v/i.* être pris dans les glaces; *v/t.* ⚡️ (*a.* ˌ *up*) givrer; *cuis.* glacer (*un gâteau*); frapper (*le vin*); **'ˌ-age** période *f* glaciaire; **'ˌ-axe** piolet *m*; **ice·berg** ['ˌbəːg] iceberg *m*.

ice...: **'ˌ-bound** fermé *ou* retenu par les glaces; **'ˌ-box**, *surt. Am.* **'ˌ-chest** glacière *f*; sorbetière *f*; **'ˌ-cream** (crème *f* à la) glace *f*; **'ˌ-cube** glaçon *m*, cube *m* de glace; **'ˌ-hock·ey** hockey *m* sur glace.

Ice·land·er ['aisləndə] Islandais(e *f*) *m*.

ice...: **'ˌ-pack** embâcle *m* (de glaçons); **'ˌ-rink** patinoire *f*; **'ˌ-show** spectacle *m* sur glace; **'ˌ-skate 1.** patinage *m* (sur glace); **2.** patiner, faire du patinage (sur glace).

ich·thy·ol·o·gy [ikθi'ɔlədʒi] ichtyologie *f*.

i·ci·cle ['aisikl] glaçon *m*.

i·ci·ness ['aisinis] froid *m* glacial; *fig.* froideur *f* glaciale.

ic·ing ['aisiŋ] glaçage *m*; glacé *m* (*de sucre*); ⚡️ givrage *m*; ˌ *sugar* sucre *m* glace.

i·con·o·clast [ai'kɔnəklæst] iconoclaste *mf*.

i·cy □ ['aisi] glacial (-als *m/pl.*).

i·de·a [ai'diə] idée *f*; notion *f*; intention *f*; *form an* ˌ *of* se faire une idée de; **i'de·al 1.** □ idéal (-als, -aux *m/pl.*); optimum; *le* meilleur; F parfait; **2.** idéal (*pl.* -als, -aux) *m*; **i'de·al·ism** idéalisme *m*; **i'de·al·ist** idéaliste *mf*; **i·de·al'is·tic** (ˌally) idéaliste; **i'de·al·ize** [ˌaiz] idéaliser.

i·den·ti·cal □ [ai'dentikl] identique (à, *with*), même; **i'den·ti·cal·ness** *see identity;* **i·den·ti·fi·ca·tion** [ˌfi-'keiʃn] identification *f*; ˌ *card* carte *f* d'identité; ˌ *mark* ✝ estampille *f*; **i'den·ti·fy** [ˌfai] identifier; établir *ou* constater l'identité de; reconnaître (pour, *as*); F découvrir; **i'den·ti·kit** [ˌkit] portrait-robot *m* (*pl.* portraits-robots); **i'den·ti·ty** identité *f*; ˌ *card* carte *f* d'identité; ⚔ ˌ *disk* plaque *f* d'identité.

id·e·o·log·i·cal □ [aidiə'lɔdʒikl] idéologique; **id·e·ol·o·gy** [ˌ'ɔlədʒi] idéologie *f*.

id·i·o·cy ['idiəsi] idiotie *f*; idiotisme *m*; *fig.* bêtise *f*.

id·i·om ['idiəm] idiotisme *m*; *région:* idiome *m*; locution *f*; style *m*; ♪, *peint.* manière *f* de s'exprimer; **id·i·o·mat·ic** [idiə'mætik] (ˌally) idiomatique.

id·i·o·syn·cra·sy [idiə'siŋkrəsi] 🏥 idiosyncrasie *f*; *fig.* petite manie *f*.

id·i·ot ['idiət] 🏥 idiot(e *f*) *m*, imbécile *mf* (*a.* F); **id·i·ot·ic** [idi'ɔtik] (ˌally) idiot; inepte; stupide, bête.

i·dle ['aidl] **1.** □ paresseux (-euse *f*); inoccupé; en chômâge; *fig.* inutile, vain, sans fondement; dormant (*capital, fonds*); ⊕ arrêté (*machine*), parasite (*roue*); ˌ *hours pl.* heures *f/pl.* perdues; ˌ *motion* mot. mouvement *m* perdu; ⊕ *run* ˌ marcher à vide; **2.** *v/t.* (*usu.* ˌ *away*) perdre; *v/i.* fainéanter; muser; **'i·dle·ness** paresse *f*; oisiveté *f*; chômage *m*; *fig.* inutilité *f*; **'i·dler** fainéant(e *f*) *m*; flâneur (-euse *f*) *m*.

i·dol ['aidl] idole *f* (*a. fig.*); **i·dol·a·ter** [ai'dɔlətə] idolâtre *m*; **i'dol·a·tress** idolâtre *f*; **i'dol·a·trous** □ idolâtre; **i'dol·a·try** idolâtrie *f*; **i·dol·ize** ['aidəlaiz] idolâtrer.

i·dyl(l) ['idil] idylle *f*; **i'dyl·lic** (ˌally) idyllique.

if [if] **1.** si; *even* ˌ quand même; ˌ *not* sinon; ˌ *so* s'il en est ainsi; *as* ˌ *to say* comme pour dire; **2.** si *m/inv.*; **'if·fy** *Am.* F plein de si, douteux (-euse *f*).

ig·ne·ous ['ignɪəs] igné.

ig·nis fat·u·us ['ignɪs'fætjuəs] feu *m* follet.

ig·nit·a·ble [ig'naɪtəbl] inflammable; **ig'nite** *v/t.* mettre le feu à, allumer; 🔥 enflammer; *v/i.* prendre feu; **ig·ni·tion** [ʌ'nɪʃn] ignition *f*; ⚡, *mot.* allumage *m*; *attr.* d'allumage; *mot.* ~ **key** clef *f* de contact.

ig·no·ble □ [ig'noubl] ignoble; vil, infâme; de basse naissance.

ig·no·min·i·ous □ [ignə'minɪəs] ignominieux (-euse *f*); méprisable; **'ig·no·min·y** ignominie *f*, honte *f*; infamie *f*.

ig·no·ra·mus F [ignə'reiməs] ignorant(e *f*) *m*; F bourrique *f*; **ig·no·rance** ['ignərəns] ignorance *f*; **'ig·no·rant** ignorant (de, of); étranger (à, of); **ig·nore** [ig'nɔː] ne tenir aucun compte de; feindre de ne pas voir; ⚖ rejeter (*une plainte*).

Il·i·ad ['ilɪəd] Iliade *f* (*a. fig.*).

ill [il] **1.** *adj.* mauvais; malade; souffrant; *see* **ease**; **2.** *adv.* mal; **3.** *su.* mal (*pl.* maux) *m*; malheur *m*; dommage *m*; tort *m*.

I'll [ail] = *I will, shall.*

ill...: '~-ad'vised impolitique; malavisé (*personne*); **'~-'bred** mal élevé; **'~-con'di·tioned** en mauvais état; de mauvaise mine (*personne*); méchant; **'~-dis'posed** malintentionné; mal disposé (envers, to).

il·le·gal □ [i'liːgəl] illégal (-aux *m/pl.*); **il·le·gal·i·ty** [ili'gæliti] illégalité *f*.

il·leg·i·ble □ [i'ledʒəbl] illisible.

il·le·git·i·ma·cy [ili'dʒitiməsi] illégitimité *f*; **il·le·git·i·mate** □ [ʌmit] illégitime (*a. enfant*); non autorisé; bâtard (*enfant*).

ill...: '~-'fat·ed malheureux (-euse *f*); infortuné; **'~-'fa·vo(u)red** laid; **'~-'feel·ing** ressentiment *m*, rancune *f*; **'~-'got·ten** mal acquis; **'~-'hu·mo(u)red** de mauvaise humeur; maussade.

il·lib·er·al □ [i'libərəl] grossier (-ère *f*); illibéral (-aux *m/pl.*); borné (*esprit*); **il·lib·er·al·i·ty** [iliba'ræliti] illibéralité *f*; petitesse *f*; manque *m* de générosité.

il·lic·it □ [i'lisit] illicite; clandestin.

il·lim·it·a·ble □ [i'limitəbl] illimité; illimitable.

il·lit·er·ate □ [i'litərit] **1.** illettré; ignorant; **2.** analphabète *mf*.

ill...: '~-'judged malavisé; peu sage; **'~-'man·nered** malappris, mal élevé; **'~-'na·tured** □ méchant; désagréable.

ill·ness ['ilnis] maladie *f*.

il·log·i·cal □ [i'lɔdʒikl] illogique.

ill...: ~-o·mened ['il'oumend] de mauvais augure; **'~-'starred** malheureux (-euse *f*); **'~-'tem·pered** de mauvaise humeur; de méchant caractère (*a. animal*); **'~-'timed** mal à propos; **'~-'treat** maltraiter.

il·lu·mi·nant [i'ljuːminənt] illuminant, éclairant (*a. su./m*); **il'lu·mi·nate** [ʌneit] éclairer (*a. fig.*); illuminer (*de dehors*); enluminer (*un manuscrit etc.*); *fig.* embellir (*une action*); ~d advertising enseigne *f* lumineuse, enseignes *f/pl.* lumineuses; **il'lu·mi·nat·ing** lumineux (-euse *f*); qui éclaire (*a. fig.*); **il·lu·mi·na·tion** éclairage *m*; illumination *f* (*de dehors*); *manuscrit:* enluminure *f*; **il'lu·mi·na·tive** [ʌnətiv] éclairant; d'éclairage; **il'lu·mi·na·tor** [ʌneitə] illuminateur (-trice *f*) *m*; enlumineur (-euse *f*) *m*; dispositif *m* d'éclairage; **il'lu·mine** [ʌmin] *see* illuminate.

ill-use ['il'juːz] maltraiter.

il·lu·sion [i'luːʒn] illusion *f*, tromperie *f*; **il'lu·sive** □ [ʌsiv], **il'lu·so·ry** □ [ʌsəri] illusoire, trompeur (-euse *f*).

il·lus·trate ['iləstreit] expliquer; éclairer; illustrer; **il·lus'tra·tion** exemple *m*; explication *f*; **'il·lus·tra·tive** □ qui sert d'exemple; *be* ~ *of* expliquer; éclaircir; **'il·lus·tra·tor** illustrateur *m*.

il·lus·tri·ous □ [i'lʌstrɪəs] illustre; célèbre.

ill will ['il'wil] rancune *f*, malveillance *f*.

I'm [aim] = *I am.*

im·age ['imidʒ] **1.** *tous les sens:* image *f*; idole *f*; portrait *m*; idée *f*; **2.** représenter par une image; tracer le portrait de; *be* ~d se refléter; **'im·age·ry** idoles *f/pl.*; images *f/pl.*; langage *m* figuré.

im·ag·i·na·ble □ [i'mædʒinəbl] imaginable; **im'ag·i·nar·y** imaginaire, de pure fantaisie; **im·ag·i·na·tion** [ʌ'neiʃn] imagination *f*; **im'ag·i·na·tive** □ [ʌnətiv] d'ima-

impasse

gination; imaginatif (-ive *f*) (*personne*); im'ag·ine [ˌˈdʒin] imaginer; concevoir; se figurer.

im·be·cile □ [ˈimbisiːl] imbécile (*a. su./mf*); im·be·cil·i·ty [ˌˈsiliti] imbécillité *f*; faiblesse *f* (d'esprit).

im·bibe [imˈbaib] boire; absorber (*a. fig.*); *fig.* s'imprégner de.

im·bro·glio [imˈbrouliou] imbroglio *m*.   [*in, with*).]

im·brue [imˈbruː] tremper (dans)

im·bue [imˈbjuː] imbiber; imprégner; *fig.* pénétrer (de, *with*).

im·i·ta·ble [ˈimitəbl] imitable; im·i·tate [ˈɪˌteit] imiter; copier (*a.* ⊕); singer (*q.*); im·i·ta·tion imitation *f*; copie *f*; ⊕ contrefaçon *f*; *attr.* simili-; factice; artificiel(le *f*); ~ *leather* similicuir *m*; im·i·ta·tive □ [ˈˌtətiv] imitatif (-ive *f*); imitateur (-trice *f*) (*personne*); ~ *of* qui imite; im·i·ta·tor [ˈˌteitə] imitateur (-trice *f*) *m*; † contrefacteur *m*.

im·mac·u·late □ [iˈmækjulit] immaculé; impeccable.

im·ma·nent [ˈimənənt] immanent.

im·ma·te·ri·al □ [iməˈtiəriəl] immatériel(le *f*); peu important; sans conséquence; indifférent (à, *to*).

im·ma·ture [iməˈtjuə] pas mûr(i); im·ma·tu·ri·ty immaturité *f*.

im·meas·ur·a·ble □ [iˈmeʒərəbl] immesurable; infini.

im·me·di·ate □ [iˈmiːdjət] immédiat; sans intermédiaire; instantané; urgent; im'me·di·ate·ly 1. *adv.* tout de suite, immédiatement; 2. *cj.* dès que.

im·me·mo·ri·al □ [imiˈmɔːriəl] immémorial (-aux *m/pl.*).

im·mense □ [iˈmens] immense; vaste; *sl.* magnifique; im'men·si·ty immensité *f*.

im·merse [iˈməːs] immerger, plonger; *fig.* ~ *o.s. in* se plonger dans; ~*d in* plongé dans (*un livre*); accablé de (*dettes*); im'mer·sion immersion *f*; submersion *f*; *fig.* absorption *f*; ~ *heater* thermo-plongeur *m*.

im·mi·grant [ˈimigrənt] immigrant(e *f*) *m*, -gré(e *f*) *m*; im·mi·grate [ˈˌgreit] *v/i.* immigrer; *v/t.* introduire des étrangers (dans, [*in*]to); im·mi'gra·tion immigration *f*.

im·mi·nence [ˈiminəns] imminence *f*, proximité *f*; 'im·mi·nent □ imminent, proche.

im·mit·i·ga·ble □ [iˈmitigəbl] que l'on ne saurait adoucir; implacable.

im·mo·bile [iˈmoubail] immobile; fixe; im·mo·bil·i·ty [imoˈbiliti] immobilité *f*; fixité *f*; im·mo·bi·lize [iˈmoubilaiz] immobiliser (*a. des espèces monnayées*); rendre indisponible (*un capital*).

im·mod·er·ate □ [iˈmɔdərit] immodéré, excessif (-ive *f*).

im·mod·est □ [iˈmɔdist] immodeste; † impudent; im'mod·es·ty immodestie *f*; † impudence *f*.

im·mo·late [ˈimoleit] immoler; im·mo'la·tion immolation *f*; 'im·mo·la·tor immolateur *m*.

im·mor·al □ [iˈmɔrəl] immoral (-aux *m/pl.*); im·mo·ral·i·ty [imoˈræliti] immoralité *f*.

im·mor·tal □ [iˈmɔːtl] immortel(le *f*); im·mor·tal·i·ty [ˌˈtæliti] immortalité *f*; im'mor·tal·ize [ˌˈtəlaiz] immortaliser; perpétuer.

im·mov·a·ble [iˈmuːvəbl] 1. □ immobile; inébranlable; 2. ~*s pl.* biens *m/pl.* immeubles.

im·mune [iˈmjuːn] à l'abri (de) (*a.* 🎖); inaccessible (à, *from*); 🎖 immunisé (contre *from*, *against*); im'mu·ni·ty exemption *f* (de, *from*); 🎖 immunité *f* (contre); im·mu·nize [ˈˌaiz] 🎖 immuniser.

im·mure [iˈmjuə] enfermer.

im·mu·ta·bil·i·ty [imjuːtəˈbiliti] immu(t)abilité *f*; im'mu·ta·ble □ immuable; inaltérable.

imp [imp] diablotin *m*; petit démon *m*; lutin *m*; petit(e *f*) espiègle *m(f*).

im·pact [ˈimpækt] choc *m*; impact *m*; collision *f*.

im·pair [imˈpɛə] altérer; endommager; diminuer; affaiblir (*la santé*).

im·pale [imˈpeil] empaler (*un criminel*); enclore d'une palissade; *fig.* fixer.

im·pal·pa·ble □ [imˈpælpəbl] impalpable; *fig.* insaisissable; subtil.

im·pan·(n)el [imˈpænl] *see empanel.*

im·part [imˈpɑːt] communiquer; annoncer; donner.

im·par·tial □ [imˈpɑːʃl] impartial (-aux *m/pl.*); im·par·ti·al·i·ty [ˌˈʃiˈæliti] impartialité *f* (envers, *to*).

im·pass·a·ble □ [imˈpɑːsəbl] infranchissable (*rivière*); impraticable (*chemin*).

im·passe [æmˈpɑːs] impasse *f*.

im·pas·si·ble □ [im'pæsibl] impassible; insensible (à, *to*).

im·pas·sion [im'pæʃn] passionner; exalter; enivrer (*de passion*).

im·pas·sive □ [im'pæsiv] impassible; insensible (aux émotions); **im'pas·sive·ness** impassibilité *f*; insensibilité *f*.

im·pa·tience [im'peiʃns] impatience *f*; intolérance *f* (*de of, with*); **im'pa·tient** □ impatient; intolérant (*de at, of, with*); avide (*de, for*); *be* ~ *of* (*inf.*) être impatient de (*inf.*); F brûler de (*inf.*).

im·peach [im'pi:tʃ] accuser (*de of, with*); attaquer; dénoncer; mettre (*qch.*) en doute; **im'peach·a·ble** accusable; blâmable; récusable (*témoin*); **im'peach·ment** accusation *f*; dénigrement *m*; ⚖ mise *f* en accusation.

im·pec·ca·bil·i·ty [impekə'biliti] impeccabilité *f*; **im'pec·ca·ble** □ impeccable, irréprochable.

im·pe·cu·ni·ous [impi'kju:njəs] impécunieux (-euse *f*), besogneux (-euse *f*).

im·pede [im'pi:d] empêcher, entraver.

im·ped·i·ment [im'pedimənt] empêchement *m* (à, *to*); ~ *in one's speech* empêchement *m* de la langue; **im·ped·i·men·ta** ✗ [~'mentə] *pl.* impedimenta *m/pl.*; attirail *m*; F bagages *m/pl.*

im·pel [im'pel] pousser (à, *to*); **im'pel·lent** 1. moteur (-trice *f*); impulsif (-ive *f*); 2. moteur *m*; force *f* motrice.

im·pend [im'pend] être suspendu (sur, *over*); *fig.* menacer (q., *over s.o.*); être imminent; **im'pend·ence** imminence *f*; proximité *f*; **im'pend·ent** imminent; menaçant.

im·pen·e·tra·bil·i·ty [impenitrə'biliti] impénétrabilité *f* (*a. fig.*); **im'pen·e·tra·ble** □ impénétrable (à *to, by*); *fig.* insondable.

im·pen·i·tence [im'penitəns] impénitence *f*; **im'pen·i·tent** □ impénitent.

im·per·a·tive [im'perətiv] 1. □ péremptoire; impérieux (-euse *f*); urgent; impératif (-ive *f*); ~ *mood* = 2. *gramm.* (mode *m*) impératif *m*.

im·per·cep·ti·ble □ [impə'septəbl] imperceptible; *fig.* insensible.

im·per·fect [im'pə:fikt] 1. □ imparfait, défectueux (-euse *f*); ⚠ surbaissé; ~ *tense* = 2. *gramm.* (temps *m*) imparfait *m*; *in the* ~ à l'imparfait; **im·per·fec·tion** *f*; *fig. a.* faiblesse *f*.

im·pe·ri·al [im'piəriəl] 1. □ impérial (-aux *m/pl.*); *fig.* majestueux (-euse *f*); 2. impériale *f*; *papier:* grand jésus *m*; **im'pe·ri·al·ism** impérialisme *m*; césarisme *m*; *pol.* colonialisme *m*; **im'pe·ri·al·ist** impérialiste *m*; césariste *m*; *pol.* colonialiste *m*; **im·pe·ri·al'is·tic** impérialiste.

im·per·il [im'peril] mettre en péril.

im·pe·ri·ous □ [im'piəriəs] impérieux (-euse *f*); arrogant; péremptoire.

im·per·ish·a·ble □ [im'periʃəbl] impérissable.

im·per·me·a·ble □ [im'pə:mjəbl] imperméable.

im·per·son·al □ [im'pə:snl] impersonnel(le *f*); **im·per·son·al·i·ty** [~sə'næliti] impersonnalité *f*.

im·per·son·ate [im'pə:səneit] personnifier; se faire passer pour; *théâ.* représenter; **im·per·son·a·tion** personnification *f*; *théâ.* interprétation *f*; ⚖ supposition *f* de personne.

im·per·ti·nence [im'pə:tinəns] impertinence *f*; insolence *f*; **im'per·ti·nent** □ impertinent (*a.* ⚖); insolent.

im·per·turb·a·bil·i·ty ['impətə:bə'biliti] imperturbabilité *f*; flegme *m*; **im·per'turb·a·ble** □ imperturbable, flegmatique.

im·per·vi·ous □ [im'pə:vjəs] inaccessible (à, *to*) (*a. fig.*); imperméable (à).

im·pet·u·os·i·ty [impetju'ɔsiti] impétuosité *f*; **im'pet·u·ous** □ impétueux (-euse *f*); emporté; **im·pe·tus** ['~pitəs] élan *m*, poussée *f*; *fig.* impulsion *f*.

im·pi·e·ty [im'paiəti] impiété *f*.

im·pinge [im'pindʒ] entrer en collision (avec [*up*]*on, against*); empiéter (sur, *on*) (*a.* ⚖); **im'pinge·ment** heurt *m*; collision *f* (avec [*up*]*on, against*); empiètement *m* (sur, *on*) (*a. fig., a.* ⚖).

im·pi·ous □ ['impiəs] impie.

imp·ish □ ['impiʃ] de démon; (d')espiègle.

im·pla·ca·bil·i·ty [implækə'biliti]

im·pla·ca·ble □ [ˌ'plækəbl] implacable (à, pour *towards*).

im·plant [im'plɑːnt] *usu. fig.* implanter (dans, *in*); inculquer (à, *in*).

im·plau·si·ble [im'plɔːzəbl] peu plausible.

im·ple·ment 1. ['implimənt] instrument *m*, outil *m*; **2.** [ˌment] exécuter (*un contrat, une promesse*); accomplir; suppléer à; **im·ple·men'ta·tion** [ˌ'teiʃn] exécution *f*; mise *f* en œuvre.

im·pli·cate ['implikeit] impliquer, mêler (dans, *in*); compromettre; **im·pli'ca·tion** implication *f*; insinuation *f*; ~s *pl.* portée *f*.

im·plic·it □ [im'plisit] implicite; tacite; *fig.* aveugle, parfait.

im·plied □ [im'plaid] implicite; sous-entendu.

im·plore [im'plɔː] implorer; supplier; **im'plor·ing** [ˌriŋ] suppliant.

im·ply [im'plai] impliquer; emporter; signifier, vouloir dire.

im·pol·i·cy [im'pɔlisi] mauvaise politique *f*; *fig.* maladresse *f*.

im·po·lite □ [impə'lait] impoli.

im·pol·i·tic □ [im'pɔlitik] impolitique.

im·pon·der·a·ble [im'pɔndərəbl] **1.** impondérable; **2.** ~s *pl.* impondérables *m/pl.*

im·port 1. ['impɔːt] ✝ importation *f*; signification *f*, sens *m*; portée *f*; importance *f*; ✝ ~s *pl.* marchandises *f/pl.* ou articles *m/pl.* d'importation, importations *f/pl.*; ~ duty droits *m/pl.* d'importation; **2.** [im'pɔːt] importer (*des marchandises*); signifier, indiquer; déclarer; **im'por·tance** importance *f*; F conséquence; **im'por·tant** □ important; **im·por·ta·tion** [ˌ'teiʃn] importation *f*; **im'port·er** importateur (-trice *f*) *m*.

im·por·tu·nate □ [im'pɔːtjunit] importun; ennuyeux (-euse *f*); **im·por·tune** [ˌ'pɔːtjuːn] importuner; presser; **im·por'tu·ni·ty** importunité *f*.

im·pose [im'pouz] *v/t.* imposer (à, [up]on); *v/i.* ~ *upon* en imposer à; tromper; abuser de; **im'pos·ing** □ imposant; grandiose; **im·po·si·tion** [ˌpə'ziʃn] *eccl., typ.* imposition *f*; impôt *m*; tromperie *f*, imposture *f*; *école:* pensum *m*.

im·pos·si·bil·i·ty [impɔsə'biliti] im-possibilité *f*; **im'pos·si·ble** □ impossible.

im·post ['impoust] impôt *m*; taxe *f*; tribut *m*; **im·pos·tor** [im'pɔstə] imposteur *m*; **im'pos·ture** [ˌtʃə] imposture *f*, supercherie *f*.

im·po·tence ['impətəns] impuissance *f* (*a. physiol.*); faiblesse *f*; **'im·po·tent** impuissant; faible.

im·pound [im'paund] confisquer; enfermer; mettre en fourrière (*une auto, un animal*).

im·pov·er·ish [im'pɔvəriʃ] appauvrir; dégraisser (*le sol*).

im·prac·ti·ca·bil·i·ty [impræktikə'biliti] impraticabilité *f*, impossibilité *f*; **im'prac·ti·ca·ble** □ impraticable; infaisable; intraitable (*personne*).

im·pre·cate ['imprikeit] lancer des imprécations (contre, *upon*); **im·pre'ca·tion** imprécation *f*, malédiction *f*; **im·pre·ca·to·ry** [ˌ'keitəri] imprécatoire.

im·preg·na·bil·i·ty [impregnə'biliti] caractère *m* imprenable *ou* F invincible; **im'preg·na·ble** □ imprenable; F invincible; **im·preg·nate** ['ˌneit] **1.** ♀, ⚒, *biol.* imprégner; imbiber, saturer; pénétrer (*a. fig.*); **2.** [im'pregnit] imprégné, fécondé; **im·preg'na·tion** fécondation *f*; imprégnation *f*; ⊕ injection *f*.

im·pre·sa·ri·o [impre'sɑːriou] imprésario *m*.

im·pre·scrip·ti·ble [impris'kriptəbl] imprescriptible.

im·press 1. ['impres] impression *f*; empreinte *f*; *fig.* marque *f*, cachet *m*; **2.** [im'pres] imprimer (à, *on*); graver (dans la mémoire, *on the memory*); inculquer (*une idée*) (à, *on*); faire bien comprendre (qch. à q. *s.th. on s.o., s.o. with s.th.*); ⊕ empreindre (qch. sur qch. *s.th. on s.th., s.th. with s.th.*); *fig.* impressionner, en imposer à; ⚓ ✝ presser (*les marins*); *fig.* réquisitionner; **im'press·i·ble** susceptible de recevoir une empreinte; *a. see impressionable*; **im'pres·sion** [ˌʃn] impression *f* (*a. fig.*); ⊕, *a. typ. caractères:* empreinte *f*; *livre:* impression *f*; *be under the* ~ *that* avoir l'impression que; **im'pres·sion·a·ble** impressionnable, susceptible, sensible; **im'pres·sive** □

impressionnant; **im'press·ment** ♏
† *marines*: presse *f.*

im·print 1. [im'print] imprimer (sur, on); *fig.* graver (dans on, in); **2.** ['imprint] empreinte *f* (*a. fig.*); *typ.* nom *m* (*de l'imprimeur*); rubrique *f* (*de l'éditeur*).

im·pris·on [im'prizn] emprisonner; mettre en prison; enfermer; **im'pris·on·ment** emprisonnement *m.*

im·prob·a·bil·i·ty [improbə'biliti] improbabilité *f*; invraisemblance *f*; **im'prob·a·ble** □ improbable; invraisemblable.

im·pro·bi·ty [im'proubiti] improbité *f*; manque *m* d'honnêteté.

im·promp·tu [im'promtju:] **1.** *adv.* (à l')impromptu; **2.** *adj.* impromptu; **3.** *su.* (discours *m etc.*) impromptu *m.*

im·prop·er □ [im'propə] incorrect; malséant, malhonnête, indécent; déplacé; ⅍ ~ *fraction* expression *f* fractionnaire; **im·pro·pri·e·ty** [imprə'praiəti] impropriété *f*; inexactitude *f*; inconvenance *f*, indécence *f.*

im·prov·a·ble □ [im'pru:vəbl] améliorable; bonifiable (*sol*).

im·prove [im'pru:v] *v/t.* améliorer; perfectionner; cultiver (*l'esprit*); bonifier (*le sol*); *v/i.* s'améliorer; faire des progrès; ~ *upon* surpasser; enchérir sur; **im'prove·ment** amélioration *f*; perfectionnement *m*; culture *f* (*de l'esprit*); progrès *m* (*pl.*); supériorité *f* (à, [up]on); **im'prov·er** réformateur (-trice *f*) *m*; ⊕ apprenti(e *f*) *m*; *cost.* petite main *f.*

im·prov·i·dence [im'providəns] imprévoyance *f*; **im'prov·i·dent** □ imprévoyant; prodigue.

im·pro·vi·sa·tion [imprəvai'zeiʃn] improvisation *f*; **im·pro·vise** ['~vaiz] improviser; **'im·pro·vised** improvisé; impromptu *inv.*

im·pru·dence [im'pru:dəns] imprudence *f*; **im'pru·dent** □ imprudent.

im·pu·dence ['impjudəns] impudence *f*, insolence *f*; **'im·pu·dent** □ effronté, insolent.

im·pugn [im'pju:n] attaquer, contester; **im'pugn·a·ble** contestable.

im·pulse ['impʌls], **im'pul·sion** impulsion *f*; choc *m* propulsif; *fig.* mouvement *m* (spontané); **im-**

'pul·sive □ impulsif (-ive *f*); *fig.* irréfléchi, spontané, involontaire.

im·pu·ni·ty [im'pju:niti] impunité *f*; *with* ~ impunément.

im·pure □ [im'pjuə] impur (*a. fig.*); **im'pu·ri·ty** [~riti] impureté *f.*

im·put·a·ble [im'pju:təbl] imputable, attribuable (à, to); **im·pu·ta·tion** [~'teiʃn] imputation *f*; **im·pute** [~'pju:t] imputer, attribuer.

in [in] **1.** *prp.* dans (*les circonstances, la foule, la maison, la rue, l'eau*); en (*un mot, soie, anglais, Europe, juin, été, réponse*); à (*l'église, la main de q., la campagne, le crayon*); au (*lit, Canada, désespoir, soleil, printemps*); de (*cette manière*); par (*groupes, soi-même, ce temps, écrit*); sur (*un ton*); sous (*le règne de*); chez (*les Anglais, Corneille*); pendant (*l'hiver de 1812, la journée*); comme; ~ *a few words* en peu de mots; ~ *all probability* selon toutes probabilités; ~ *crossing the road* en traversant la rue; *the thing* ~ *itself* la chose en elle-même *ou phls.* en soi; *trust* ~ *s.o.* avoir confiance en q., se fier à q.; *professor* ~ *the university* professeur à l'université; *wound* ~ *the head* blessure à la tête; *engaged* ~ (*gér.*) occupé à (*inf.*); ~ *a ... voice* d'une voix ...; *blind* ~ *one eye* borgne; ~ *length* de long; ~ *our time* de nos jours; *at two* (*o'clock*) ~ *the morning* à deux heures du matin; ~ *the rain* à *ou* sous la pluie; ~ *the paper* dans le journal; *one* ~ *ten* un sur dix; ~ *the firm of* sous firme de; ~ *the press* sous presse; ~ *excuse of* comme excuse de; ~ *1966* en 1966; *two days* ~ *three* deux jours sur trois; *there is nothing* ~ *it* il est sans fondement; F cela n'a pas d'importance; l'un vaut l'autre; *it is not* ~ *her to* (*inf.*) il n'est pas de sa nature de (*inf.*); *he hasn't it* ~ *him* il n'en est pas capable; ~ *that* puisque, vu que; **2.** *adv.* dedans; au dedans; rentré; au pouvoir; *be* ~ être chez soi, être à la maison, y être; être élu; être au pouvoir; *sport, train*: être arrivé; brûler encore (*feu*); *be* ~ *for* en avoir pour (*qch.*); être inscrit pour (*un examen etc.*); F *be* ~ *with* avoir de belles relations avec, être en bons termes avec; **3.** *adj.* intérieur; F en vogue, à la mode, dans le vent; **4.** *su. parl. the*

~s *pl.* le parti au pouvoir; ~s *and outs* méandres *m/pl.*, coins *m/pl.* et recoins *m/pl.*; tous les détails *m/pl.*

in·a·bil·i·ty [inə'biliti] impuissance *f* (à, *to*), incapacité *f* (de, *to*).

in·ac·ces·si·bil·i·ty ['inæksesə'biliti] inaccessibilité *f*; **in·ac'ces·si·ble** □ inaccessible.

in·ac·cu·ra·cy [in'ækjurəsi] inexactitude *f*; **in'ac·cu·rate** □ [~rit] inexact; incorrect.

in·ac·tion [in'ækʃn] inaction *f*.

in·ac·tive □ [in'æktiv] inactif (-ive*f*); ✝ en chômage; ⚙ inerte; **in·ac'tiv·i·ty** inactivité *f*; inertie *f*.

in·ad·e·qua·cy [in'ædikwəsi] insuffisance *f*; imperfection *f*; **in'ad·e·quate** □ [~kwit] insuffisant; incomplet (-ète *f*).

in·ad·mis·si·bil·i·ty ['inədmisə'biliti] inadmissibilité *f*; **in·ad'mis·si·ble** □ inadmissible; ⚖ irrecevable.

in·ad·vert·ence, **in·ad·vert·en·cy** [inəd'və:təns(i)] inadvertance *f*; étourderie *f*; mégarde *f*; **in·ad'vert·ent** inattentif (-ive *f*); négligent; involontaire; ~*ly* par inadvertance. [inaliénable; indisponible.]

in·al·ien·a·ble □ [in'eiljənəbl]⌡

in·al·ter·a·ble □ [in'ɔːltərəbl] immuable; inaltérable (*couleur*).

in·am·o·ra·ta [inæmə'raːtə] amante *f*; amoureuse *f*; **in·a·mo'ra·to** [~tou] amant *m*, amoureux *m*.

in·ane □ [i'nein] *usu. fig.* stupide, inepte, bête, niais.

in·an·i·mate □ [in'ænimit] inanimé, sans vie (*a. fig.*).

in·a·ni·tion [inə'niʃn] ⚕ inanition *f*.

in·an·i·ty [i'næniti] inanité *f*, niaiserie *f*.

in·ap·pli·ca·bil·i·ty ['inæplikə'biliti] inapplicabilité *f*; **in'ap·pli·ca·ble** inapplicable (à, *to*); étranger (-ère *f*) (à).

in·ap·po·site □ [in'æpəsit] sans rapport (avec, *to*); hors de propos; inapplicable (à, *to*).

in·ap·pre·ci·a·ble □ [inə'priːʃəbl] inappréciable.

in·ap·pre·hen·si·ble □ [inæpri'hensəbl] insaisissable, incompréhensible.

in·ap·proach·a·ble [inə'proutʃəbl] inabordable; incomparable.

in·ap·pro·pri·ate □ [inə'proupriit] peu approprié; déplacé.

in·apt □ [in'æpt] inapte; incapable; inhabile; peu approprié; **in'apt·i·tude** [~itjuːd], **in'apt·ness** inaptitude *f* (à, *for*); incapacité *f*.

in·ar·tic·u·late □ [inaː'tikjulit] muet(te *f*); bégayant (de, *with*); *zo.* inarticulé; **in·ar'tic·u·late·ness** mutisme *m*; défaut *m* d'articulation.

in·as·much [inəz'mʌtʃ] *adv.*: ~ *as* vu que, puisque; ✝ dans la mesure que.

in·at·ten·tion [inə'tenʃn] inattention *f*; **in·at'ten·tive** □ inattentif (-ive *f*) (à, *to*); négligent (de); peu attentionné (pour, *to*[*wards*]).

in·au·di·ble □ [in'ɔːdəbl] imperceptible; faible (*voix*).

in·au·gu·ral [i'nɔːgjurəl] inaugural (-aux *m/pl.*); **in'au·gu·rate** [~reit] inaugurer; commencer; mettre en vigueur; **in·au·gu'ra·tion** inauguration *f*; commencement *m*; ♀ *Day Am.* entrée *f* en fonction du nouveau président des É.-U.

in·aus·pi·cious □ [inɔːs'piʃəs] peu propice; fâcheux (-euse *f*).

in·board ⚓ ['inbɔːd] **1.** *adj.* intérieur; **2.** *adv.* en abord; **3.** *prp.* en abord de.

in·born ['in'bɔːn] inné.

in·breathe ['in'briːð] inspirer (à, *into*).

in·bred [in'bred] inné; consanguin (*chevaux etc.*).

in·breed·ing ['in'briːdiŋ] consanguinité *f*.

in·cal·cu·la·ble □ [in'kælkjuləbl] incalculable.

in·can·des·cence [inkæn'desns] incandescence *f*; *métall.* chaleur *f* blanche; **in·can'des·cent** incandescent; ~ *light* lumière *f* à incandescence; ~ *mantle* manchon *m* (à incandescence).

in·can·ta·tion [inkæn'teiʃn] incantation *f*; charme *m*.

in·ca·pa·bil·i·ty [inkeipə'biliti] incapacité *f*; ⚖ inéligibilité *f*; **in'ca·pa·ble** □ incapable (de, *of*); non susceptible (de, *of*); ⚖ inéligible; en état d'ivresse manifeste; **in·ca·pac·i·tate** [inkə'pæsiteit] rendre incapable (de *for*, *from*); ⚖ frapper d'incapacité; **in·ca'pac·i·ty** incapacité *f* (de *for*, *to*).

in·car·cer·ate [in'kaːsəreit] incarcérer; **in·car·cer'a·tion** incarcération *f*.

in·car·nate 1. [in'kɑːnit] fait chair; incarné (*a. fig.*); **2.** ['inkɑːneit] incarner; **in·car'na·tion** incarnation *f* (*a. fig.*).

in·case [in'keis] *see* encase.

in·cau·tious □ [in'kɔːʃəs] imprudent; inconsidéré.

in·cen·di·ar·y [in'sendjəri] **1.** incendiaire (*a. fig.*); ∼ *bomb* bombe *f* incendiaire; **2.** incendiaire *m*; auteur *m* d'un incendie; F *see* ∼ *bomb*.

in·cense¹ ['insens] **1.** encens *m*; **2.** encenser; *fig.* embaumer.

in·cense² [in'sens] exaspérer, courroucer, irriter (contre, with).

in·cen·tive [in'sentiv] **1.** provocant; stimulant; **2.** stimulant *m*, encouragement *m*.

in·cep·tion [in'sepʃn] commencement *m*; **in'cep·tive** initial (-aux *m/pl.*); *gramm.* inchoatif (-ive *f*) (*a. su./m*). [titude *f.*⟩

in·cer·ti·tude [in'səːtitjuːd] incer-⟩

in·ces·sant □ [in'sesnt] incessant, continuel(le *f*).

in·cest ['insest] inceste *m*; **in·ces·tu·ous** □ [in'sestjuəs] incestueux (-euse *f*).

inch [intʃ] pouce *m* (*2,54 cm*); *fig.* pas *m*; ∼*es pl. a.* taille *f*; *by* ∼*es* peu à peu, petit à petit; **inched** [∼t] de ... pouces.

in·cho·a·tive ['inkoueitiv] initial (-aux *m/pl.*); *gramm.* inchoatif (-ive *f*).

in·ci·dence ['insidəns] incidence *f*; *angle of* ∼ angle *m* d'incidence; '**in·ci·dent 1.** (à, to) qui arrive; qui appartient; qui tient; **2.** incident *m*; événement *m*; *pièce, roman:* épisode *m*; ⚖ servitude *f* ou privilège *m* attachés à une tenure; **in·ci·den·tal** □ [∼'dentl] accidentel(le *f*), fortuit; inséparable (de, to); *be* ∼ *to* résulter de, appartenir à; ∼*ly* ci-incidemment.

in·cin·er·ate [in'sinəreit] incinérer (*a. Am. un mort*); réduire en cendres; **in·cin·er'a·tion** incinération *f*; **in'cin·er·a·tor** incinérateur *m*; *Am.* four *m* crématoire.

in·cip·i·ence [in'sipiəns] commencement *m*; **in'cip·i·ent** naissant, qui commence.

in·cise [in'saiz] inciser (*a.* ⚕), faire une incision dans; **in·ci·sion** [∼'siʒn] incision *f* (*a.* ⚕); ✗ enture *f*; **in·ci·sive** □ [∼'saisiv] incisif (-ive

f); mordant; pénétrant; **in'ci·sor** [∼zə] (*dent f*) incisive *f*.

in·ci·ta·tion [insai'teiʃn] *see* incitement; **in'cite** inciter; pousser; animer (à, to); **in'cite·ment** incitation *f*, encouragement *m*; stimulant *m*, aiguillon *m*; mobile *m*.

in·ci·vil·i·ty [insi'viliti] incivilité *f*.

in·clem·en·cy [in'klemənsi] inclémence *f*, rigueur *f*; *temps:* intempérie *f*; **in'clem·ent** inclément; rigoureux (-euse *f*).

in·cli·na·tion [inkli'neiʃn] tête, *a. fig.:* inclination *f*; inclinaison *f*, pente *f*; *fig.* penchant *m*; **in·cline** [∼'klain] **1.** *v/i.* s'incliner, se pencher (*personne*); incliner, pencher (*chose*); *fig.* avoir un penchant (pour qch., *to s.th.*; à *inf.*, *to inf.*); être disposé (à, to); incliner (à, to); *v/t.* (faire) pencher; *fig.* disposer; ∼*d plane* plan *m* incliné; **2.** pente *f*, déclivité *f*; ✗ oblique *f*.

in·close [in'klouz] *see* enclose.

in·clude [in'kluːd] renfermer; comprendre.

in·clu·sion [in'kluːʒn] inclusion *f*; **in'clu·sive** □ qui renferme, qui comprend; tout compris; *be* ∼ *of* comprendre, renfermer (*qch.*); ∼ *terms* prix tout compris.

in·cog F [in'kɔg], **in'cog·ni·to** [∼ni·tou] **1.** incognito, sous un autre nom; **2.** incognito *m*.

in·co·her·ence, **in·co·her·en·cy** [inkou'hiərəns(i)] incohérence *f*; manque *m* de suite; **in·co'her·ent** □ incohérent; sans suite; décousu.

in·com·bus·ti·ble □ [inkəm'bʌstəbl] incombustible.

in·come ['inkəm] revenu *m*; **in·com·er** ['inkʌmə] entrant *m*; immigrant(e *f*) *m*; ⚖ successeur *m*; **in·come-tax** ['inkəmtæks] impôt *m* sur le revenu; ∼ *form* feuille *f* d'impôts.

in·com·ing ['inkʌmiŋ] **1.** entrée *f*; ∼*s pl.* recettes *f/pl.*, revenus *m/pl.*; † rentrées *f/pl.*; **2.** qui entre, qui arrive.

in·com·men·su·ra·bil·i·ty ['inkəmenʃərə'biliti] incommensurabilité *f*; **in·com'men·su·ra·ble** □ incommensurable.

in·com·mode [inkə'moud] incommoder, gêner, déranger; **in·com·'mo·di·ous** □ [∼jəs] incommode; peu confortable.

in·com·mu·ni·ca·bil·i·ty ['inkə-mju:nikə'biliti] incommunicabilité *f*; **in·com'mu·ni·ca·ble** □ incommunicable; **in·com·mu·ni·ca·do** *surt. Am.* [inkəmjuni'ka:dou] sans contact avec l'extérieur; **in·com'mu·ni·ca·tive** □ [‿kətiv] taciturne; peu communicatif (-ive *f*).

in·com·mut·a·ble □ [inkə'mju:-təbl] non-interchangeable; immuable.

in·com·pa·ra·ble □ [in'kɔmpərəbl] incomparable.

in·com·pat·i·bil·i·ty ['inkəmpætə-'biliti] incompatibilité *f*; inconciliabilité *f*; **in·com'pat·i·ble** □ incompatible, inconciliable.

in·com·pe·tence, in·com·pe·ten·cy [in'kɔmpitəns(i)] incompétence *f* (*a.* ⚖️); insuffisance *f*; **in'com·pe·tent** □ incompétent (*a.* ⚖️); incapable; ⚖️ inhabile.

in·com·plete □ [inkəm'pli:t] incomplet (-ète *f*); inachevé; imparfait.

in·com·pre·hen·si·bil·i·ty [inkəm-prihensə'biliti] incompréhensibilité *f*; **in·com·pre'hen·si·ble** □ incompréhensible.

in·com·press·i·bil·i·ty ['inkəm-presə'biliti] incompressibilité *f*; **in·com'press·i·ble** incompressible.

in·con·ceiv·a·ble □ [inkən'si:vəbl] inconcevable.

in·con·clu·sive □ [inkən'klu:siv] peu *ou* non concluant.

in·con·gru·i·ty [inkɔŋ'gruiti] incongruité *f*, absurdité *f*; désaccord *m*; inconséquence *f*; inconvenance *f*; **in'con·gru·ous** □ incongru, absurde; qui ne s'accorde pas (avec, *with*); sans rapport (avec *to*, *with*).

in·con·se·quence [in'kɔnsikwəns] inconséquence *f*; manque *m* de logique; **in·con·se·quen·tial** [‿-'kwenʃl] sans importance; illogique.

in·con·sid·er·a·ble □ [inkən'sidə-rəbl] insignifiant; **in·con'sid·er·ate** □ [‿rit] irréfléchi, inconsidéré; sans égards (pour, *towards*); **in·con'sid·er·ate·ness** irréflexion *f*, imprudence *f*; manque *m* d'égards.

in·con·sist·en·cy [inkən'sistənsi] inconséquence *f*; inconsistance *f*; incompatibilité *f*; **in·con'sist·ent** □ incompatible; contradictoire (avec,

with); en désaccord (avec, *with*); illogique, inconséquent (*personne*).

in·con·sol·a·ble □ [inkən'souləbl] inconsolable (de, *for*).

in·con·so·nant [in'kɔnsənənt] en désaccord (avec, *with*).

in·con·spic·u·ous □ [inkən'spi-kjuəs] discret (-ète *f*); insignifiant; peu frappant.

in·con·stan·cy [in'kɔnstənsi] inconstance *f*; instabilité *f*; **in'con·stant** □ inconstant, variable.

in·con·test·a·ble □ [inkən'testəbl] incontestable; irrécusable.

in·con·ti·nence [in'kɔntinəns] incontinence *f*; ⚕️ ~ *of urine* incontinence *f* d'urine; **in'con·ti·nent** □ incontinent; ⚕️ qui ne peut retenir son urine; ~ *of speech* bavard; ~*ly* sur-le-champ, incontinent; incontinemment.

in·con·tro·vert·i·ble □ ['inkɔntrə-'və:təbl] indisputable.

in·con·ven·ience [inkən'vi:njəns] **1.** inconvénient *m*; embarras *m*; incommodité *f*; **2.** incommoder, gêner, déranger; **in·con'ven·ient** □ incommode; inopportun; gênant.

in·con·vert·i·bil·i·ty ['inkənvə:tə-'biliti] (*a.* ✝) non-convertibilité *f*; **in·con'vert·i·ble** □ inconvertible; ✝ *a.* non convertible.

in·con·vin·ci·ble □ [inkən'vinsəbl] impossible à convaincre.

in·cor·po·rate 1. [in'kɔ:pəreit] *v/t.* incorporer (à *in*[to], *with*; avec, *with*); mêler, unir (à, avec *with*); ériger (*une ville*) en municipalité; ⚖️ constituer en société commerciale; *v/i.* s'incorporer (en, *in*; à, avec *with*); **2.** [‿rit] incorporé; faisant corps; **in'cor·po·rat·ed** [‿-reitid] *see incorporate* 2; ~ *company* société *f* constituée, *Am.* société *f* anonyme (*abbr.* S.A.); **in·cor·po-'ra·tion** incorporation *f* (à, avec, dans *in*[to], *with*); incorporation *f* communale; constitution *f* en société commerciale.

in·cor·po·re·al □ [inkɔ:'pɔ:riəl] incorporel(le *f*).

in·cor·rect □ [inkə'rekt] incorrect; inexact; défectueux (-euse *f*); **in·cor'rect·ness** incorrection *f*; inexactitude *f*.

in·cor·ri·gi·bil·i·ty [inkɔridʒə'biliti] incorrigibilité *f*; **in'cor·ri·gi·ble** □ incorrigible.

in·cor·rupt·i·bil·i·ty [ˈinkərʌptəˈbiliti] incorruptibilité *f*; **in·corˈrupt·i·ble** □ incorruptible; **inˈcorˈrupt·ness** incorruption *f*.

in·crease 1. [inˈkriːs] *v/i.* augmenter (de, *in*); s'augmenter; grandir; croître, s'accroître; grossir; se multiplier; *v/t.* augmenter; agrandir; accroître; grossir; **2.** [ˈinkriːs] augmentation *f*; accroissement *m*; *effort:* redoublement *m*; multiplication *f*.

in·cred·i·bil·i·ty [inkrediˈbiliti] incrédibilité *f*; **inˈcred·i·ble** □ incroyable.

in·cre·du·li·ty [inkriˈdjuːliti] incrédulité *f*; **inˈcred·u·lous** □ [inˈkredjuləs] incrédule.

in·cre·ment [ˈinkrimənt] *see increase 2;* profit *m*; ~ **value** plus-value *f*.

in·crim·i·nate [inˈkrimineit] incriminer; impliquer; **inˈcrim·i·na·to·ry** [~əri] tendant à incriminer.

in·crust [inˈkrʌst] *see encrust;* **inˈcrusˈta·tion** incrustation *f*; ⊕ *chaudière:* entartrage *m*, tartre *m*.

in·cu·bate [ˈinkjubeit] *v/t.* couver (*a. fig.*); *v/i.* être soumis à l'incubation; ⚕ couver; **inˈcuˈba·tion** incubation *f* (*a. biol., a.* ⚕); ~ **period** période *f* d'incubation; **ˈin·cu·ba·tor** incubateur *m*, couveuse *f*; **inˈcu·bus** [ˈ~bəs] *myth.* incube *m*; F fardeau *m*; cauchemar *m*.

in·cul·cate [ˈinkʌlkeit] inculquer (à q., *upon s.o.*; dans l'esprit, *in the mind*); **inˈculˈca·tion** inculcation *f*.

in·cul·pate [ˈinkʌlpeit] inculper, incriminer; mêler à une affaire; **inˈculˈpa·tion** inculpation *f*; **inˈcul·pa·to·ry** [~pətəri] tendant à inculper; accusateur (-trice *f*).

in·cum·ben·cy [inˈkʌmbənsi] *eccl.* charge *f*; période *f* d'exercice d'une charge; **inˈcum·bent 1.** étendu, appuyé; *be* ~ *on s.o.* incomber à q.; **2.** *eccl.* titulaire *m* d'une charge.

in·cu·nab·u·la [inkjuˈnæbjulə] *pl.* incunables *m/pl.*

in·cur [inˈkəː] encourir, s'attirer; contracter (*une dette*); courir (*un risque*); faire (*des dépenses*).

in·cur·a·bil·i·ty [inkjuərəˈbiliti] incurabilité *f*; **inˈcur·a·ble 1.** □ inguérissable; **2.** incurable *mf*.

in·cu·ri·ous □ [inˈkjuəriəs] sans curiosité, indifférent.

in·cur·sion [inˈkəːʃn] incursion *f*; descente *f* (dans, *into*).

in·cur·va·tion [inkəːˈveiʃn] incurvation *f*; courbure *f*; **ˈin·curve** s'incurver, se courber en dedans.

in·debt·ed [inˈdetid] endetté; *fig.* redevable (à q. de qch., *to s.o. for s.th.*); **inˈdebt·ed·ness** dette *f* (*a. fig.*), dettes *f/pl.*

in·de·cen·cy [inˈdiːsnsi] indécence *f*; ⚖ attentat *m* aux mœurs; **inˈde·cent** □ indécent, peu décent; ~ *assault* attentat *m* à la pudeur.

in·de·ci·pher·a·ble [indiˈsaifərəbl] indéchiffrable.

in·de·ci·sion [indiˈsiʒn] indécision *f*, irrésolution *f*; **inˈde·ci·sive** □ [~ˈsaisiv] peu concluant; indécis (*personne, a. bataille*), irrésolu.

in·de·clin·a·ble *gramm.* [indiˈklainəbl] indéclinable.

in·dec·o·rous □ [inˈdekərəs] malséant; inconvenant; **inˈdec·o·rousˈness,** *a.* **in·de·co·rum** [indiˈkɔːrəm] inconvenance *f*; manque *m* de maintien.

in·deed [inˈdiːd] **1.** *adv.* en effet; en vérité; même; à vrai dire; **2.** *int.* effectivement!; vraiment?

in·de·fat·i·ga·ble □ [indiˈfætigəbl] infatigable, inlassable.

in·de·fea·si·ble □ [indiˈfiːzəbl] irrévocable; ⚖ indestructible (*intérêt*).

in·de·fect·i·ble □ [indiˈfektəbl] indéfectible; impeccable.

in·de·fen·si·ble □ [indiˈfensəbl] indéfendable; *fig.* insoutenable.

in·de·fin·a·ble □ [indiˈfainəbl] indéfinissable; *fig.* vague.

in·def·i·nite □ [inˈdefinit] indéfini (*a. gramm.*); imprécis.

in·del·i·ble □ [inˈdelibl] ineffaçable, indélébile; ~ *ink* encre *f* indélébile; ~ *pencil* crayon *m* à copier.

in·del·i·ca·cy [inˈdelikəsi] indélicatesse *f*; manque *m* de délicatesse; grossièreté *f*, inconvenance *f*; **inˈdel·i·cate** □ [~kit] peu délicat; indélicat; inconvenant; risqué; qui manque de tact.

in·dem·ni·fi·ca·tion [indemnifiˈkeiʃn] indemnisation *f*; indemnité *f*; **inˈdem·ni·fy** [~fai] indemniser, dédommager (de, *for*); garantir (contre *against, from*); compenser; **inˈdem·ni·ty** garantie *f*, assurance *f*; indemnité *f*, dédommagement *m*; *act of* ~ bill *m* d'indemnité.

in·dent [in'dent] **1.** denteler; découper; ⊕ adenter; *typ.* faire un alinéa; ⚒ passer (*un contrat etc.*) en partie double; ✝ passer une commande pour; ~ *upon s.o. for s.th.* réquisitionner qch. de q.; **2.** dentelure *f*; découpure *f*; *littoral:* échancrure *f*; ✝ ordre *m* d'achat; ⚒ ordre *m* de réquisition; *see* indenture; **in·den-'ta·tion** découpage *m*; impression *f*; dentelure *f*; découpure *f*; *littoral:* échancrure *f*; **in·den·tion** *typ.* renfoncement *m*; **in·den·ture** [~tʃə] **1.** contrat *m* bilatéral; ~s *pl.* contrat *m* d'apprentissage; **2.** lier par contrat; engager par un contrat d'apprentissage.

in·de·pend·ence [indi'pendəns] indépendance *f* (à l'égard de, *of*); *État:* autonomie *f*; *Am.* ♀ *Day* le 4 juillet; **in·de'pend·ent** □ **1.** indépendant; autonome (*État*); ~ *fortune f* personnelle; *rentes f/pl.*; **2.** indépendant *m.*

in-depth [in'depθ] en profondeur.

in·de·scrib·a·ble □ [indis'kraibəbl] indescriptible; indicible.

in·de·struct·i·ble □ [indis'trʌktəbl] indestructible.

in·de·ter·mi·na·ble □ [indi'tə:minəbl] indéterminable; interminable (*dispute*); **in·de'ter·mi·nate** [~nit] indéterminé; *fig.* imprécis; **in·de'ter·mi·nate·ness, in·de·ter·mi·na·tion** ['~'neiʃn] indétermination *f*; *fig.* irrésolution *f.*

in·dex ['indeks] **1.** (*pl. a. indices*) *eccl., volume:* index *m*; *cadran etc.:* aiguille *f*; indice *m*, signe *m*; ✋ exposant *m*; *opt.* indice *m*; (*ou* ~ *finger*) index *m*; (*ou* ~ *number*) coefficient *m*; ~ *card* fiche *f*; ~ *figure* indice *m*; **2.** dresser l'index de (*un volume*); classer; répertorier.

In·di·a ['indjə] Inde *f*; ~ *paper* papier *m* indien, papier *m* bible; ~ *rubber* gomme *f* (à effacer); caoutchouc *m*; '**In·di·a·man** ⚓ long-courrier *m* des Indes.

In·di·an ['indjən] **1.** indien(ne *f*); de l'Inde; des Indes; *gymn.* ~ *club* bouteille *f* en bois; ~ *corn* maïs *m*; *in* ~ *file* en file indienne; *Am.* F ~ *giver* personne *f* qui fait un cadeau dans l'intention d'en demander à son tour; ~ *ink* encre *f* de Chine; *surt. Am.* ~ *summer* été *m* de la Saint-

Martin; **2.** Indien(ne *f*) *m*; F Hindou(e *f*) *m*; (*usu.* Red ~) *a.* Peau-Rouge (*pl.* Peaux-Rouges) *m.*

in·di·cate ['indikeit] indiquer; signaler; montrer; témoigner; faire savoir; **in·di'ca·tion** indication *f*; indice *m*, signe *m*; **in·dic·a·tive** [in-'dikətiv] **1.** □ indicatif (-ive *f*) (de, *of*); *be* ~ *of* dénoter; ~ *mood* = **2.** *gramm.* indicatif *m*; **in·di·ca·tor** ['~keitə] indicateur (-trice *f*) *m* (*a.* ⊕, *tél. su./m*); aiguille *f*; **in·di·ca·to·ry** [~kətəri] indicateur (-trice *f*) (de, *of*).

in·di·ces ['indisi:z] *pl. de* index **1.**

in·dict [in'dait] inculper (de for, on a charge of); **in·dict·a·ble** inculpable; ~ *offence* délit *m*; **in·dict·ment** inculpation ₀ *f*; document: acte *m* d'accusation.

in·dif·fer·ence [in'difrəns] indifférence *f* (pour, à l'égard de to, towards); **in·dif·fer·ent** □ indifférent (à, to); médiocre, passable; ✝ impartial (-aux *m/pl.*); ♎ neutre.

in·di·gence ['indidʒəns] indigence *f*; F misère *f.*

in·di·gene ['indidʒi:n] indigène *mf*; **in·dig·e·nous** [in'didʒinəs] indigène (à, to); du pays.

in·di·gent □ ['indidʒənt] indigent; nécessiteux (-euse *f*).

in·di·gest·ed [indi'dʒestid] mal digéré *e*; **in·di'gest·i·ble** □ indigeste (*a. fig.*); **in·di'ges·tion** dyspepsie *f*; indigestion *f.*

in·dig·nant □ [in'dignənt] indigné (de, at); d'indignation; **in·dig-'na·tion** indignation *f* (contre with, against); ~ *meeting* meeting *m* de protestation; **in'dig·ni·ty** [~niti] indignité *f*; affront *m*; honte *f.*

in·di·rect □ [indi'rekt] indirect (*a. gramm.*); détourné (*moyen*).

in·dis·cern·i·ble [indi'sə:nəbl] indiscernable; imperceptible.

in·dis·creet □ [indis'kri:t] indiscret (-ète *f*); imprudent, peu judicieux (-euse *f*); inconsidéré; **in·dis·cre·tion** [~'kreʃn] indiscrétion *f*; manque *m* de discrétion; imprudence *f*; F faux pas *m.*

in·dis·crim·i·nate □ [indis'kriminit] au hasard, à tort et à travers; (*a.* **in·dis'crim·i·nat·ing** □ [~nei-tiŋ], **in·dis'crim·i·na·tive** [~nətiv]) sans discernement; *fig.* aveugle;

'**in·dis·crim·i·na·tion** manque *m* de discernement.

in·dis·pen·sa·ble □ [indis'pensəbl] obligatoire; indispensable (à, *to*).

in·dis·pose [indis'pouz] indisposer; prévenir (contre, *towards*); détourner (de, *from*); rendre peu propre (à qch., *for s.*th.); rendre incapable (de *inf.*, *for gér.*); rendre peu disposé (à *inf.*, *to inf.*); **in·dis·po·si·tion** [indispə'ziʃn] indisposition *f* (à l'égard de, *to[wards]*); aversion *f* (pour); malaise *f*, indisposition *f*.

in·dis·pu·ta·ble □ ['indis'pju:təbl] incontestable; hors de controverse.

in·dis·so·lu·bil·i·ty ['indisɔlju'biliti] indissolubilité *f*; ⚗ insolubilité *f*; **in·dis·so·lu·ble** □ [ˌ'sɔljubl] indissoluble.

in·dis·tinct □ [indis'tiŋkt] indistinct, vague, confus; **in·dis'tinct·ness** indistinction *f*, vague *m*.

in·dis·tin·guish·a·ble □ [indis·'tiŋgwiʃəbl] indistinguible; imperceptible; insaisissable.

in·dite [in'dait] composer (*un poème*); rédiger (*une lettre*).

in·di·vid·u·al [indi'vidjuəl] **1.** □ individuel(le *f*); particulier (-ère *f*); ~ **drive** commande *f* séparée; **2.** individu *m*; **in·di·vid·u·al·i·ty** [ˌ'æliti] individualité *f*; personnalité *f*; **in·di'vid·u·al·ize** [ˌəlaiz] individualiser.

in·di·vis·i·bil·i·ty ['indivizi'biliti] indivisibilité *f*; **in·di'vis·i·ble** □ indivisible; ⅍ insécable.

Indo... [indou] indo-; Indo-.

in·doc·ile [in'dousail] indocile; **in·do·cil·i·ty** [ˌdo'siliti] indocilité *f*.

in·doc·tri·nate [in'dɔktrineit] instruire; endoctriner; ~ *s.o.* with *s.*th. inculquer qch. à q.

in·do·lence ['indoləns] indolence *f* (*a.* ⚕); paresse *f*; '**in·do·lent** □ indolent (*a.* ⚕); paresseux (-euse *f*).

in·dom·i·ta·ble □ [in'dɔmitəbl] indomptable.

in·door ['indɔ:] de maison; d'intérieur; intérieur; *sp.* de salle, de salon; ~ *aerial* antenne *f* d'appartement; ~ *game* jeu *m* de salle *ou* de salon *ou* de société; ~ *plant* plante *f* d'appartement; ~ *relief* assistance *f* des pauvres hospitalisés; ~ *swimming-bath* piscine *f*; **in·doors**

['in'dɔ:z] à la maison; à l'intérieur.

in·dorse *etc.* [in'dɔ:s] *see* endorse.

in·du·bi·ta·ble □ [in'dju:bitəbl] indubitable, incontestable.

in·duce [in'dju:s] persuader (à q., *s.o.*); amener; occasionner, produire; ⚡ amorcer, induire; ⚡ ~*d current* courant *m* induit *ou* d'induction; **in'duce·ment** motif *m*; attrait *m*; raison *f*.

in·duct *eccl.* [in'dʌkt] installer; **in'duct·ance** ⚡ inductance *f*; ~*-coil* (bobine *f* de) self *f*; bobine *f* d'inductance; **in'duc·tion** *eccl.*, *fonctionnaire*: installation *f*; ⚡, *phls.*, *phys.* induction *f*; ⚕ production *f*; **in'duc·tive** □ qui induit (à, *to*); ⚡, *phls.* inductif (-ive *f*) (*a.* ⚡ *charge*); ⚡ inducteur (-trice *f*).

in·dulge [in'dʌldʒ] *v/t.* gâter (*q.*), avoir de l'indulgence pour (*q.*); se livrer à, s'adonner à; donner libre cours à (*ses passions, ses caprices*); F boire; ~ *s.o.* with *s.*th. accorder qch. à q.; ~ *o.s. in* se livrer à, s'adonner à (*qch.*); *v/i.* se permettre (à, *in*); se livrer, s'adonner (à, *in*); **in'dul·gence** indulgence *f* (*a.* *eccl.*); complaisance *f* (envers, *to*); assouvissement *m* (de of, *in*); abandon *m* (à, *in*); † délai *m* de paiement; **in'dul·gent** □ indulgent (envers, à, pour *to*); faible.

in·du·rate ['indjuəreit] (s')endurcir; durcir; ⚕ (s')indurer; **in·du'ra·tion** (*fig.* en)durcissement *m*; ⚕ induration *f*.

in·dus·tri·al [in'dʌstriəl] **1.** □ industriel(le *f*); professionnel(le *f*); de l'industrie; ~ *art* art *m* mécanique; ~ *court* tribunal *m* industriel; ~ *disease* maladie *f* professionnelle; ~ *espionage* espionnage *m* industriel; ~ *school* école *f* des arts et métiers; école *f* professionnelle de rééducation; ~ *tribunal* conseil *m* de prud'hommes; **2.** *see* industrialist; ~*s pl.* † valeurs *f/pl.* industrielles; **in'dus·tri·al·ist** industriel *m*, industrialiste *m*; **in'dus·tri·al·ize** [ˌaiz] industrialiser; *become* ~*d* s'industrialiser; **in'dus·tri·ous** □ travailleur (-euse *f*), laborieux (-euse *f*), assidu.

in·dus·try ['indəstri] assiduité *f* au travail, diligence *f*; travail *m*; ⊕ industrie *f*; *heavy industries pl.* industries *f/pl.* lourdes.

in·dwell ['in'dwel] [*irr. (dwell)*] demeurer dans; habiter (*un lieu*); *fig.* reposer dans.

in·e·bri·ate 1. [i'ni:brieit] enivrer; **2.** [i'ni:briit] ivre, enivré; **3.** ivrogne *mf*; **in·e·bri'a·tion**, **in·e·bri·e·ty** [ini:'braiəti] ivresse *f*; alcoolisme *m*; enivrement *m*.

in·ed·i·ble [in'edibl] immangeable.

in·ed·it·ed [in'editid] inédit; publié sans notes.

in·ef·fa·ble □ [in'efəbl] ineffable, indicible.

in·ef·face·a·ble □ [ini'feisəbl] ineffaçable.

in·ef·fec·tive [ini'fektiv], **in·ef'fec·tu·al** □ [ˌˌtjuəl] inefficace, sans effet, sans résultat; ✗ inapte au service.

in·ef·fi·ca·cious □ [inefi'keiʃəs] inefficace; **in'ef·fi·ca·cy** [ˌˌkəsi] inefficacité *f*.

in·ef·fi·cien·cy [ini'fiʃənsi] incapacité *f*; incompétence *f*; inefficacité *f*; **in·ef'fi·cient** incapable; incompétent; inefficace.

in·el·e·gance [in'eligəns] inélégance *f*; **in'el·e·gant** □ sans élégance (*personne*); inélégant (*style*).

in·el·i·gi·bil·i·ty [inelidʒə'biliti] inéligibilité *f*; caractère *m* peu acceptable; **in'el·i·gi·ble** □ inéligible; indigne d'être choisi; *fig.* peu acceptable; ✗ inapte.

in·ept □ [in'ept] inepte; déplacé; mal à propos; ⚖ de nul effet; **in'ept·i·tude** [ˌˌitju:d], **in'ept·ness** manque *m* d'à-propos *ou* de justesse; inaptitude *f*; sottise *f*.

in·e·qual·i·ty [ini'kwɔliti] inégalité *f*; *sol, bois*: rugosité *f*; irrégularité *f*.

in·eq·ui·ta·ble □ [in'ekwitəbl] inéquitable, injuste; **in'eq·ui·ty** injustice *f*.

in·e·rad·i·ca·ble □ [ini'rædikəbl] indéracinable.

in·ert □ [i'nə:t] inerte; **in·er·tia** [i'nə:ʃiə], **in'ert·ness** inertie *f*.

in·es·cap·a·ble [inis'keipəbl] inévitable, inéluctable.

in·es·sen·tial ['ini'senʃl] négligeable; non essentiel(le *f*) (à, *to*).

in·es·ti·ma·ble □ [in'estiməbl] inestimable; incalculable.

in·ev·i·ta·ble □ [in'evitəbl] inévitable, inéluctable; immanquable; fatal (-als *m/pl.*); **in'ev·i·ta·ble·ness** inévitabilité *f*.

in·ex·act □ [inig'zækt] inexact; **in·ex'act·i·tude** [ˌˌitju:d], **in·ex'act·ness** inexactitude *f*.

in·ex·cus·a·ble □ [iniks'kju:zbl] inexcusable, sans excuse.

in·ex·haust·i·bil·i·ty ['inigzɔ:stə'biliti] nature *f* inépuisable; **in·ex·'haust·i·ble** □ inépuisable; intarissable (*source*).

in·ex·o·ra·bil·i·ty [ineksərə'biliti] inexorabilité *f*; caractère *m* implacable; **in'ex·o·ra·ble** □ inexorable, implacable.

in·ex·pe·di·en·cy [iniks'pi:diənsi] inopportunité *f*; **in·ex'pe·di·ent** □ inopportun, malavisé.

in·ex·pen·sive □ [iniks'pensiv] bon marché; peu coûteux (-euse *f*); pas cher (chère *f*).

in·ex·pe·ri·ence [iniks'piəriəns] inexpérience *f*; **in·ex'pe·ri·enced** inexpérimenté, sans expérience.

in·ex·pert □ [ineks'pə:t] inexpert; peu habile (à, *in*).

in·ex·pi·a·ble □ [in'ekspiəbl] inexpiable; † impitoyable.

in·ex·pli·ca·ble □ [in'eksplikəbl] inexplicable; inconcevable.

in·ex·press·i·ble [iniks'presəbl] **1.** □ inexprimable; indicible; **2.** *co. ou* † ~*s pl.* pantalon *m*, culotte *f*.

in·ex·pres·sive □ [iniks'presiv] inexpressif (-ive *f*); sans expression.

in·ex·pug·na·ble □ [iniks'pʌgnəbl] inexpugnable; *fig.* inattaquable.

in·ex·tin·guish·a·ble □ [iniks'tiŋgwiʃəbl] inextinguible.

in·ex·tri·ca·ble □ [in'ekstrikəbl] inextricable.

in·fal·li·bil·i·ty [infælə'biliti] infaillibilité *f*; **in'fal·li·ble** □ infaillible; sûr.

in·fa·mous □ ['infəməs] infâme; mal famé; abominable; **in·fa·my** ['ˌˌmi] (note *f* d')infamie *f*.

in·fan·cy ['infənsi] première enfance *f*; ⚖ minorité *f*; **in·fant** ['ˌˌfənt] **1.** enfant *mf*; ⚖ mineur(e *f*) *m*; ~ *school* école *f* maternelle *ou* enfantine; ~, *welfare* puériculture *f* sociale; **2.** d'enfance; enfantin.

in·fan·ta [in'fæntə] infante *f*; **in'fan·te** [ˌˌti] infant *m*.

in·fan·ti·cide [in'fæntisaid] infanticide *m*; *personne*: infanticide *mf*; **in·fan·tile** ['infəntail] d'enfant; 🩺 infantile; *péj.* enfantin; ~ *paralysis* poliomyélite *f*; **in·fan·tine** ['‿tain] *see infantile.*

in·fan·try ✕ ['infəntri] infanterie *f*; **'in·fan·try·man** soldat *m* d'infanterie; fantassin *m*.

in·fat·u·ate [in'fætjueit] infatuer, affoler; enticher; **in·fat·u'a·tion** infatuation *f*, engouement *m*; béguin *m* (pour, *for*).

in·fect [in'fekt] infecter; ⚕ contaminer; *fig.* inculquer (qch. à q., s.o. with s.th.); become ‿ed se contagionner; **in'fec·tion** ⚕, *fig.* infection *f*, contagion *f*; **in'fec·tious** □, **in'fec·tive** ⚕ infectieux (-euse *f*); *fig.* contagieux (-euse *f*).

in·fe·lic·i·tous [infi'lisitəs] malheureux (-euse *f*); mal trouvé; **in·fe'lic·i·ty** infélicité *f*; manque *m* de justesse; gaffe *f*.

in·fer [in'fəː] déduire, conclure (de, *from*); impliquer; **in'fer·a·ble** qu'on peut inférer; qu'on peut déduire; **in·fer·ence** ['infərəns] inférence *f*, conclusion *f*; **in·fer·en·tial** □ [‿'renʃl] déductif (-ive *f*); obtenu par déduction; ‿ly par déduction.

in·fe·ri·or [in'fiəriə] **1.** inférieur (à, *to*); ⚕ infère; **2.** inférieur *m*; subordonné(e *f*) *m*; **in·fe·ri·or·i·ty** [‿ri'ɔriti] infériorité *f* (par rapport à, *to*); ‿ complex complexe *m* d'infériorité.

in·fer·nal □ [in'fəːnl] infernal (-aux *m/pl.*); des enfers; de l'enfer; F diabolique, infernal (-aux *m/pl.*); ‿ machine machine *f* infernale.

in·fer·tile [in'fəːtail] stérile; **in·fer·til·i·ty** [‿'tiliti] stérilité *f*, infertilité *f*.

in·fest [in'fest] infester (de, with) (*fig.*); **in·fes'ta·tion** infestation *f*.

in·fi·del ['infidəl] infidèle (a. su./*mf*); *péj.* incroyant(e *f*) (a. su.); **in·fi·del·i·ty** [‿'deliti] infidélité *f*.

in·fight(·ing) ['infait(iŋ)] box. corps à corps *m*; *fig.* guerre *f* intestine.

in·fil·trate ['infiltreit] *v/t.* infiltrer; imprégner; pénétrer dans; *v/i.* s'infiltrer (dans, *into*; à travers, *through*); **in·fil'tra·tion** infiltration *f*.

in·fi·nite □ ['infinit] infini; illimité; *astr.* sans nombre; **in'fin·i·tive** (a. ‿ mood) *gramm.* infinitif *m*; **in·fin·i·tude** [‿tju:d], **in'fin·i·ty** in-

finité *f*, infinitude *f*; ∡ infini *m*.

in·firm □ [in'fəːm] débile, infirme, faible; (a. ‿ of purpose) irrésolu, flottant; **in'fir·ma·ry** infirmerie *f*; hôpital *m*; **in'fir·mi·ty** [‿iti] infirmité *f*; faiblesse *f* (a. *fig.*).

in·fix [in'fiks] implanter; *gramm.* infixer; *fig.* inculquer.

in·flame [in'fleim] (s')enflammer (a. *fig.*, a. ⚕); (s')allumer (a. *fig.*); *v/t.* mettre le feu à; *v/i.* prendre feu.

in·flam·ma·bil·i·ty [inflæmə'biliti] inflammabilité *f*; **in'flam·ma·ble 1.** □ inflammable *f*; **2.** ‿s *pl.* substances *f/pl.* inflammables; **in·flam·ma·tion** [inflə'meiʃn] inflammation *f*; **in·flam·ma·to·ry** [in'flæmətəri] incendiaire; ⚕ inflammatoire.

in·flate [in'fleit] gonfler (a. *fig.*); ✝ grossir; ✝ hausser (le prix); **in'flat·ed** gonflé, enflé; ✝ exagéré; ampoulé (style); **in'fla·tion** gonflement *m*; ⚕, ✝ inflation *f*; ✝ prix: hausse *f*; *fig.* enflure *f*; **in'fla·tion·ar·y** d'inflation, inflationniste.

in·flect [in'flekt] fléchir; moduler (la voix); ♪ altérer; *gramm.* conjuguer (un verbe), décliner (un substantif); **in'flec·tion** see inflexion.

in·flex·i·bil·i·ty [infleksə'biliti] inflexibilité *f* (a. *fig.*); **in'flex·i·ble** □ inflexible (a. *fig.*); **in'flex·ion** [‿ʃn] inflexion *f*; voix: modulation *f*; *gramm.* flexion *f*.

in·flict [in'flikt] donner (un coup) (à, on); infliger (une punition) (à, on); ‿ o.s. (ou one's company) on imposer sa compagnie à; **in'flic·tion** infliction *f*; châtiment *m*, peine *f*; *fig.* vexation *f*.

in·flo·res·cence ♀ [inflo'resns] inflorescence *f*; floraison *f*.

in·flow ['inflou] see influx.

in·flu·ence ['influəns] **1.** influence *f* (sur, [up]on; auprès de, with); **2.** influencer; influer sur; **in·flu·en·tial** □ [‿'enʃl] influent.

in·flu·en·za ⚕ [influ'enzə] grippe *f*.

in·flux ['inflʌks] affluence *f*, entrée *f*; *fig.* invasion *f*, inondation *f*.

in·form [in'fɔːm] *v/t.* informer (de, of); renseigner (sur, about); avertir; faire part à; mettre au courant; well ‿ed bien renseigné; keep s.o. ‿ed tenir q. au courant (de, of); *v/i.* dénoncer (q., against s.o.).

in'for·mal □ [in'fɔːml] sans cérémonie; officieux (-euse *f*); irrégulier(-ère f); **in·for·mal·i·ty**[ˌ͜'mæliti] absence f de cérémonie; irrégularité f.

in·form·ant [in'fɔːmənt] informateur (-trice f) m; ⚥ déclarant(e f) m; see informer; **in·for·ma·tion** [infə'meiʃn] renseignements m/pl., informations f/pl.; instruction f; ⚥ dénonciation f (contre, against); ~ film documentaire m; ~ science informatique f; gather ~ recueillir des renseignements (sur, about); **in·form·a·tive** [in'fɔːmətiv] instructif (-ive f); **in'form·er** dénonciateur (-trice f), F mouchard m.

in·frac·tion [in'frækʃn] infraction f; contravention f.

in·fra...: ~ dig F au-dessous de la dignité (de q.), déshonorant; '~·red phys. infrarouge; '~·struc·ture infrastructure f.

in·fre·quen·cy [in'friːkwənsi] rareté f; **in'fre·quent** □ rare, infréquent.

in·fringe [in'frindʒ] v/t. enfreindre, violer (la loi, un serment); v/i. empiéter (sur, upon) (un brevet etc.); **in'fringe·ment** infraction f; contrefaçon f.

in·fu·ri·ate [in'fjuərieit] rendre furieux (-euse f).

in·fuse [in'fjuːz] infuser (du thé) (à, into); faire infuser (le thé); inspirer (qch. à q., s.o. with s.th.); pharm. macérer; **in'fu·sion** [ˌ͜ʒn] infusion f (a. fig.); **in·fu·so·ri·a** zo. [infjuː'sɔːriə] pl. infusoires m/pl.

in·gath·er·ing ['ingæðəriŋ] rentrée f; récolte f.

in·gen·ious □ [in'dʒiːnjəs] ingénieux (-euse f); **in·ge·nu·i·ty** [indʒi'njuiti] ingéniosité f; **in·gen·u·ous** □ [in'dʒenjuəs] ingénu, naïf (-ïve f); franc(he f).

in·gle ['iŋgl] foyer m; feu m.

in·glo·ri·ous □ [in'glɔːriəs] honteux (-euse f); ignominieux (-euse f); humble, obscur.

in·go·ing ['ingouiŋ] **1.** entrée f; **2.** qui entre, entrant; nouveau (nouvel devant une voyelle ou un h muet; -elle f; -eaux m/pl.) (locataire).

in·got ['iŋgət] lingot m; étain: saumon m; '~·steel acier m en lingots.

in·grain ['in'grein] teindre grand teint; '**in'grained** fig. imprégné; invétéré (personne).

in·gra·ti·ate [in'greiʃieit]: ~ o.s.

s'insinuer (dans les bonnes grâces de, with); **in·grat·i·tude** [ˌ͜'græti·tjuːd] ingratitude f.

in·gre·di·ent [in'griːdiənt] ingrédient m; 🜛 principe m.

in·gress ['ingres] entrée f; droit m d'accès.

in·gui·nal anat. ['iŋgwinl] inguinal (-aux m/pl.).

in·gur·gi·tate [in'gəːdʒiteit] ingurgiter, avaler.

in·hab·it [in'hæbit] habiter;**in'hab·it·a·ble** habitable; **in'hab·it·an·cy** habitation f; résidence f; **in'hab·it·ant** habitant(e f) m.

in·ha·la·tion [inhə'leiʃn] aspiration f; 🜂 inhalation f; **in·hale** [ˌ͜'heil] aspirer; respirer; 🜂 inhaler; **in·'hal·er** 🜂 inhalateur m.

in·har·mo·ni·ous □ [inhɑː'mounjəs] inharmonieux (-euse f).

in·here [in'hiə] (in) être inhérent (à); appartenir (à); exister (dans); **in·'her·ence, in'her·en·cy** [ˌ͜rəns(i)] inhérence f (à, in); **in'her·ent** □ inhérent, propre (à, in).

in·her·it [in'herit] hériter de (qch.); succéder à; tenir (de, from); **in·'her·it·a·ble** □ dont on peut hériter; transmissible (a. 🜂); **in'her·it·ance** succession f; héritage m; biol. hérédité f;**in'her·i·tor** héritier m; **in'her·i·tress** héritière f.

in·hib·it [in'hibit] empêcher (q. de, s.o. from); défendre (à q. de inf., s.o. from gér.); psych. inhiber; **in·hi·bi·tion** [ˌ͜'biʃn] défense f (expresse); eccl. interdit m; psych. inhibition f; **in'hib·i·to·ry** [ˌ͜təri] prohibitif (-ive f); physiol., psych. inhibiteur (-trice f).

in·hos·pi·ta·ble □ [in'hɔspitəbl] inhospitalier (-ère f); **in·hos·pi·tal·i·ty** ['ˌ͜'tæliti] inhospitalité f.

in·hu·man □ [in'hjuːmən] inhumain; barbare; **in·hu·mane** □ [ˌ͜'mein] inhumain, cruel(le f); **in·hu·man·i·ty** [ˌ͜'mæniti] inhumanité f; cruauté f.

in·hu·ma·tion [inhjuː'meiʃn] inhumation f; enterrement m; **in·hume**[in'hjuːm] inhumer, enterrer.

in·im·i·cal □ [i'nimikl] ennemi, hostile; contraire (à, to).

in·im·i·ta·ble □ [i'nimitəbl] inimitable.

in·iq·ui·tous □ [i'nikwitəs] inique; **in'iq·ui·ty** iniquité f.

in·i·tial [i'niʃl] 1. □ initial (-aux *m/pl.*); premier (-ère *f*); du début; ~ *payment* acompte *m*; ~ *salary* salaire *m* initial *ou* du début; 2. initiale *f*; paraphe *m*; 3. parafer; viser; **in·i·ti·ate** 1. [i'niʃiit] initié(e *f*) (*a. su.*); 2. [i'niʃieit] commencer; lancer (*une entreprise etc.*); inaugurer; initier (à, *into*); **in·i·ti·a'tion** début *m*; commencement *m*; inauguration *f*; initiation *f*; *surt. Am. société:* ~ *fee* droits *m/pl.* d'admission; **in·i·ti·a·tive** [~ətiv] 1. préliminaire, préparatoire; 2. initiative *f*; *on one's own* ~ de sa propre initiative; *take the* ~ prendre l'initiative (pour *inf.*, in *gér.*); **in'i·ti·a·tor** [~eitə] initiateur (-trice *f*) *m*; lanceur *m* (*d'une mode etc.*); **in'i·ti·a·to·ry** [~ətəri] préliminaire, préparatoire, premier (-ère *f*).

in·ject [in'dʒekt] injecter (dans, *into*; de, *with*); **in'jec·tion** injection *f*.

in·ju·di·cious □ [indʒu'diʃəs] malavisé, peu judicieux (-euse *f*).

in·junc·tion [in'dʒʌŋkʃn] injonction *f*, ordre *m*.

in·jure ['indʒə] nuire à, faire du mal à, faire du tort à; gâter; endommager; **in·ju·ri·ous** □ [in'dʒuəriəs] nuisible, préjudiciable (à, *to*); injurieux (-euse *f*) (*langage*); **in·ju·ry** ['indʒəri] tort *m*; mal *m*; dommage *m*; blessure *f*.

in·jus·tice [in'dʒʌstis] injustice *f*.

ink [iŋk] 1. encre *f*; (*usu. printer's* ~) noir *m* d'imprimerie; *attr.* à encre, d'encre; 2. noircir d'encre; *typ.* encrer.

ink·ling ['iŋkliŋ] soupçon *m* (*a. fig.*).

ink...: '~·pot encrier *m*; '~·stand grand encrier *m*; '**ink·y** taché *ou* barbouillé d'encre.

in·land ['inlənd] 1. du pays, intérieur (*commerce etc.*); ♀ Revenue fisc *m*; 2. intérieur *m*; 3. [in'lænd] dans les terres; vers l'intérieur; **in·land·er** ['inləndə] habitant(e *f*) *m* de l'intérieur.

in-laws ['inlɔːz] *pl.* parents *m/pl.* par alliance; beaux-parents *m/pl.*

in·lay ['in'lei] 1. [*irr.* (*lay*)] incruster (de, *with*); marqueter (*une table*); parqueter (*un plancher*) en mosaïque; 2. incrustation *f*; marqueterie *f*; *livre:* encartage *m*.

in·let ['inlet] entrée *f*; bras *m* de mer; crique *f*; ⊕ arrivée *f*, admission *f*.

in·mate ['inmeit] habitant(e *f*) *m*; *aliéné:* pensionnaire *mf*; *hospice etc.:* hôte *m*.

in·most ['inmoust] le plus profond.

inn [in] auberge *f*; *ville:* hôtellerie *f*; ♀s *pl. of Court* écoles *f/pl.* de droit (*Londres*).

in·nate □ ['i'neit] inné.

in·ner ['inə] intérieur; interne, de dedans; intime; *cycl., mot.* ~ *tube* chambre *f* à air, boudin *m* d'air; '**in·ner·most** le plus profond *ou* intime.

in·ner·vate ['inəːveit] *physiol.* innerver.

in·nings ['iniŋz] *pl. ou sg. sp.* tour *m* de batte; tournée *f*; *have one's* ~ être au guichet, *fig.* être au pouvoir, prendre son tour.

inn·keep·er ['inkiːpə] aubergiste *mf*; hôtelier (-ère *f*) *m*.

in·no·cence ['inəsns] innocence *f*; naïveté *f*, candeur *f*; '**in·no·cent** 1. □ innocent(e *f*); dépourvu (de); pur, sans péché; F ~ *of* sans; 2. innocent(e *f*); naïf (-ïve *f*) *m*; idiot(e *f*) *m*.

in·noc·u·ous □ [i'nɔkjuəs] inoffensif (-ive *f*).

in·nom·i·nate [i'nɔminit] *anat.* innominé; ♀♀ innomé.

in·no·vate ['inoveit] innover; **in·no·'va·tion** innovation *f*; nouveauté *f*; '**in·no·va·tor** (in)novateur (-trice *f*) *m*.

in·nox·ious □ [i'nɔkʃəs] inoffensif (-ive *f*).

in·nu·en·do [inju'endou] insinuation *f*; allusion *f*.

in·nu·mer·a·ble □ [i'njuːmərəbl] innombrable.

in·nu·tri·tious [inju'triʃəs] peu nourrissant; peu nutritif (-ive *f*).

in·ob·serv·ance [inəb'zəːvəns] (*of*) inobservance *f* (de); *promesse:* inobservation *f* (de); inattention *f* (à).

in·oc·u·late [i'nɔkjuleit] ✗ greffer; ✗ inoculer (qch. à q. *s.o. with s.th.*, *s.th. into s.o.*); contre, *against*); **in·oc·u·la·tion** ✗ greffe *f*; ✗ inoculation *f*; **in'oc·u·la·tor** inoculateur (-trice *f*) *m*. [odeur, inodore.]

in·o·dor·ous [in'oudərəs] sans)

in·of·fen·sive □ [inə'fensiv] inoffensif (-ive *f*).

in·of·fi·cial [inə'fiʃl] inofficieux (-euse *f*).

in·op·er·a·tive [in'ɔpərətiv] inopérant.

in·op·por·tune □ [in'ɔpətju:n] inopportun; hors de saison.

in·or·di·nate □ [i'nɔ:dinit] démesuré, immodéré; effréné.

in·or·gan·ic [inɔ:'gænik] inorganique.

in·pa·tient ['inpeiʃənt] hospitalisé(e *f*) *m*.

in·put ⊕, *surt.* ⚡ ['input] puissance *f*; entrée *f* de courant.

in·quest ⚖ ['inkwest] enquête *f* (sur, *on*); *coroner's* ~ enquête *f* judiciaire après mort d'homme.

in·qui·e·tude [in'kwaiitju:d] agitation *f*, inquiétude *f*.

in·quire [in'kwaiə] demander (qch., *for s.th.*); se renseigner (sur *about*, *after*), s'informer (de qch.); ~ *into* faire des recherches *ou* une enquête sur; **in'quir·er** investigateur (-trice *f*) *m*; **in'quir·ing** □ curieux (-euse *f*); interrogateur (-trice *f*); **in'quir·y** enquête *f*, investigation *f*; demande *f* (*a.* ✝); *make inquiries* prendre des renseignements (sur *about*, *on*); s'informer (auprès de, *of*); **in'quir·y-of·fice** bureau *m* de renseignements; Service *m* des renseignements.

in·qui·si·tion [inkwi'ziʃn] investigation *f*; ⚖ enquête *f*; *hist.* ♀ Inquisition *f*; **in'quis·i·tive** □ questionneur (-euse *f*); curieux (-euse *f*); **in'quis·i·tive·ness** curiosité *f* (indiscrète); **in'quis·i·tor** enquêteur *m*; *hist.* Inquisiteur *m*; **in·quis·i·to·ri·al** □ [~'tɔ:riəl] inquisitorial (-aux *m/pl.*).

in·road ['inroud] ✕ incursion *f*, irruption *f*; *fig.* empiétement *m* (sur, *upon*); *make* ~*s upon* (*ou in*) ébrécher, harceler.

in·sa·lu·bri·ous [insə'lu:briəs] malsain; insalubre.

in·sane [in'sein] fou (fol *devant une voyelle ou un h muet*; folle *f*); insensé; **in·san·i·tar·y** □ [~'sænitəri] insalubre; malsain; **in'san·i·ty** folie *f*, démence *f*.

in·sa·ti·a·bil·i·ty [inseiʃjə'biliti] insatiabilité *f*; **in'sa·ti·a·ble** □, **in'sa·ti·ate** [~ʃiit] inassouvissable; insatiable (de, *of*).

in·scribe [in'skraib] inscrire (*a.* ◬, *a.* ✝ *actions*); graver (un nom sur qch., *s.th. with a name*); *fig.*

inscrire (sur, *on*; dans, *in*); dédier.

in·scrip·tion [in'skripʃn] inscription *f* (✝ au grand livre); *fig.* dédicace *f*.

in·scru·ta·bil·i·ty [inskru:tə'biliti] inscrutabilité *f*; **in'scru·ta·ble** □ inscrutable, impénétrable; fermé (*visage*).

in·sect ['insekt] insecte *m*; **in'sec·ti·cide** [~isaid] insecticide (*a. su./m*); **in·sec·tiv·o·rous** [~'tivərəs] insectivore.

in·se·cure □ [insi'kjuə] peu sûr; incertain; **in·se'cu·ri·ty** [~riti] insécurité *f*; danger *m*.

in·sen·sate [in'senseit] insensé; insensible (*matière*); **in·sen·si·bil·i·ty** [~sə'biliti] défaillance *f*; insensibilité *f* (à, *to*); indifférence *f* (pour, *to*); **in'sen·si·ble** □ insensible (à *of*, *to*); indifférent (à *of*, *to*); évanoui, sans connaissance; **in'sen·si·tive** insensible (à, *to*).

in·sen·ti·ent [in'senʃiənt] insensible.

in·sep·a·ra·bil·i·ty [insepərə'biliti] inséparabilité *f*; **in'sep·a·ra·ble** □ inséparable.

in·sert 1. [in'sə:t] *usu.* insérer (dans, *in*[to]); introduire; intercaler (*une ligne, un mot*); **2.** ['insə:t] insertion *f*; pièce *f* rapportée; **in'ser·tion** insertion *f*, introduction *f*; *cost.* incrustation *f*; *dentelle*: entre-deux *m/inv.*

in·set ['inset] *typ.* encart *m*; feuillet *m*; hors-texte *m/inv.*; médaillon *m*; *attr.* en médaillon.

in·shore ⚓ ['in'ʃɔ:] **1.** *adj.* côtier (-ère *f*); **2.** *adv.* près de terre.

in·side ['in'said] **1.** *su.* dedans *m*, intérieur *m*; F entrailles *f/pl.*; **2.** *adj.* (d')intérieur; interne; *mot.* ~ *drive* conduite *f* intérieure; *sp.* ~ *lane* piste *f* intérieure; *foot.* ~ *left* intérieur *m* gauche; **3.** *adv.* en dedans; *Am. a.* ~ *of* en moins de (*temps*); **4.** *prp.* à l'intérieur de; **'in'sid·er** initié(e *f*) *m*. [(-euse *f*).]

in·sid·i·ous □ [in'sidiəs] insidieux.✗

in·sight ['insait] perspicacité *f*; *fig.* aperçu *m* (de, *into*).

in·sig·ni·a [in'signiə] *pl.* insignes *m/pl.*; signes *m/pl. etc.* distinctifs.

in·sig·nif·i·cance, *a.* **in·sig·nif·i·can·cy** [insig'nifikəns(i)] insignifiance *f*; **in·sig'nif·i·cant** insignifiant; sans importance.

in·sin·cere □ [insin'siə] peu sincère; faux (fausse *f*); **in·sin'cer·i·ty** [‿'seriti] manque *m* de sincérité; fausseté *f*.

in·sin·u·ate [in'sinjueit] insinuer; laisser entendre; donner à entendre; glisser (dans, *into*); ‿ *o.s. into* s'insinuer dans; **in'sin·u·at·ing** □ insinuant; suggestif (-ive *f*) (*propos etc.*); **in·sin·u'a·tion** insinuation *f* (*a. fig.*); introduction *f*.

in·sip·id □ [in'sipid] insipide, fade; **in·si'pid·i·ty** insipidité *f*; fadeur *f*.

in·sist [in'sist] insister; ‿ (*up*)on insister sur, appuyer sur; revendiquer (*un droit*); insister pour (*inf.*); vouloir (*qch.*) absolument; ‿ that insister pour que (*sbj.*), exiger que (*sbj.*); **in'sist·ence** insistance *f*; protestations *f/pl.* (de, on); at his ‿ devant son insistance; puisqu'il insistait; **in'sist·ent** □ qui insiste (sur, [*up*]on); instant; importun.

in·so·bri·e·ty [inso'braiəti] intempérance *f*.

in·(·)so(·)far as [insə'fɑːrəz] tant que, dans la mesure où.

in·so·la·tion [inso'leiʃn] insolation *f* (✼, *a. phot.*); ✼ coup *m* de soleil.

in·so·lence ['insələns] insolence *f*, effronterie *f* (envers, *to*); **'in·so·lent** □ insolent (envers, *to*).

in·sol·u·bil·i·ty [insɔlju'biliti] insolubilité *f*; **in'sol·u·ble** □ [‿jubl] insoluble (*a. fig.*).

in·sol·ven·cy [in'sɔlvənsi] insolvabilité *f*; faillite *f*; **in'sol·vent** **1.** insolvable; en faillite; **2.** débiteur *m* insolvable; failli *m*.

in·som·ni·a [in'sɔmniə] insomnie *f*.

in·so·much [insou'mʌtʃ]: ‿ that au point que; tellement que.

in·spect [in'spekt] examiner; contrôler; **in'spec·tion** inspection *f*; examen *m*; contrôle *m*; visite *f*; ✝ for ‿ à l'essai; **in'spec·tor** inspecteur *m*; surveillant *m*; **in'spec·tor·ate** [‿tərit] *office*: inspectorat *m*; corps *m* d'inspecteurs.

in·spi·ra·tion [inspə'reiʃn] inspiration *f*; **in·spire** [‿'spaiə] aspirer, inspirer; *fig.* inspirer (qch. à q. *s.th. in[to]* s.o., *s.o. with s.th.*); aiguillonner (*q.*); **in·spir·it** [‿'spirit] animer, encourager.

in·spis·sate [in'spiseit] (s')épaissir.

in·sta·bil·i·ty [instə'biliti] instabi-

lité *f*; manque *m* de solidité; *fig.* inconstance *f*.

in·stall [in'stɔːl] installer (dans, *in*) (*a.* ⊕); ⊕ monter (*un atelier, une machine*); **in·stal·la·tion** [instə'leiʃn] installation *f* (*a.* ⚡); ⊕, *radio*: montage *m*; poste *m* (*de T.S.F.*).

in·stal(l)·ment [in'stɔːlmənt] ✝ fraction *f*; acompte *m*; versement *m*; *ouvrage*: fascicule *m*; *monthly* ‿ mensualité *f*; *by* ‿s par paiements à termes; *fig.* peu à peu; ‿ **plan** ✝ système *m* de crédit; *buy s.th. on the* ‿ acheter qch. à tempérament.

in·stance ['instəns] **1.** instance *f* (*a.* ⚖); exemple *m*, cas *m*; *for* ‿ par exemple; *in the first* ‿ en premier lieu; *at the* ‿ *of* à la demande de; *sur l'instance de*; **2.** citer (*qch.*) en exemple.

in·stant □ ['instənt] **1.** instant, urgent; pressant; immédiat; *on the 10th* ‿ le 10 courant; **2.** instant *m*, moment *m*; *in an* ‿, *on the* ‿ sur-le-champ, tout de suite; *the* ‿ *you come* dès que vous viendrez; **in·stan·ta·ne·ous** □ [‿'teinjəs] instantané; **in·stan·ter** [in'stæntə], **in·stant·ly** ['instəntli] immédiatement, sur-le-champ.

in·state [in'steit] établir (dans, *in*).

in·stead [in'sted] au lieu de cela; ‿ *of* (*gér.*) au lieu de (*inf.*).

in·step ['instep] cou-de-pied (*pl.* cous-de-pied) *m*; *soulier*: cambrure *f*.

in·sti·gate ['instigeit] exciter, inciter, provoquer (à, *to*); **in·sti·ga·tion** instigation *f*; **in·sti·ga·tor** instigateur (-trice *f*) *m*; auteur *m* (*d'une révolte*).

in·stil(l) [in'stil] instiller; *fig.* inculquer (à, *into*), inspirer (à, *into*); **in·stil·la·tion** [insti'leiʃn], **in·stil(l)·ment** ['instilmənt] instillation *f*; inspiration *f*; inculcation *f*.

in·stinct 1. ['instiŋkt] instinct *m*; **2.** [in'stiŋkt] plein; ‿ *with life* plein ou doué de vie; **in'stinc·tive** □ instinctif (-ive *f*).

in·sti·tute ['institjuːt] **1.** institut *m*; cercle *m*; ✝ institution *f*; ♈ *of Justinian Institutes f/pl.* de Justinien; **2.** instituer, établir (*q.*); fonder; intenter (*un procès*); investir (*q.*) (de, [*in*]to), ⚖ instituer (*q.*) (héritier, *as heir*); **in·sti'tu·tion** institution *f*, établissement *m* (*a. édifice*); commencement *m*; association *f* (*d'ingénieurs etc.*); hospice *m* (*de charité*); *eccl.* investiture *f*; ⚖ institution *f*; **in·sti'tu·tion·al·ize** [~əlaiz] faire une institution de (*qch.*); **'in·sti·tu·tor** fondateur (-trice *f*) *m*; auteur *m*.

in·struct [in'strʌkt] instruire; enseigner (*qch. à q., s.o. in s.th.*); charger (de, *to*); **in'struc·tion** instruction *f*, enseignement *m*; ordre *m*; **in'struc·tion·al** d'instruction; ⚔ *~ school* école *f* d'application; **in'struc·tive** □ instructif (-ive *f*); **in'struc·tor** maître *m*; précepteur *m*; ✈ moniteur *m*; *Am. univ.* chargé *m* de cours; **in'struc·tress** maîtresse *f*, préceptrice *f*.

in·stru·ment ['instrumənt] (⚕, ♪, ⚖, *a. fig.*) instrument *m*; appareil *m*; ⚖ *a.* acte *m* juridique; ✈, *mot.* *~ board ou panel* tablier *m* des instruments; ✈ *fly on ~s* voler en P.S.V.; **in·stru·men·tal** □ [~'mentl] contributif (-ive *f*), qui contribue (à, *in*); *gramm.*, *a.* ♪ instrumental (-aux *m/pl.*); *be ~ to* contribuer à (*qch. ou inf.*); **in·stru·men·tal·i·ty** [~'tæliti] moyen *m*, concours *m*, intermédiaire *m*.

in·sub·or·di·nate [insə'bɔːdnit] insubordonné; mutin; **'in·sub·or·di·'na·tion** insubordination *f*, insoumission *f*.

in·suf·fer·a·ble □ [in'sʌfərəbl] insupportable, intolérable.

in·suf·fi·cien·cy [insə'fiʃənsi] insuffisance *f*; **in·suf'fi·cient** □ insuffisant.

in·su·lar □ ['insjulə] insulaire; *fig.* borné, étroit; **in·su·lar·i·ty** [~'læriti] insularité *f*; *fig.* esprit *m* borné, étroitesse *f* de vues; **in·su·late** ['~leit] faire une île de; ⚡, *a. fig.* isoler; *phys.* calorifuger, protéger (contre, *against*); **'in·su·lat·ing** isolant; *~ tape* chatterton *m*; **in·su'la·tion** isolement *m* (*a. phys.*); *a.* = **'in·su·la·tor** *phys.* isolant *m*.

in·sult 1. ['insʌlt] insulte *f*, affront *m*; **2.** [in'sʌlt] insulter, affronter.

in·su·per·a·bil·i·ty [insjuːpərə'biliti] caractère *m ou* nature *f* insurmontable; **in'su·per·a·ble** □ insurmontable; infranchissable.

in·sup·port·a·ble □ [insə'pɔːtəbl] insupportable, intolérable.

in·sup·press·i·ble [insə'presəbl] irrépressible.

in·sur·ance [in'ʃuərəns] assurance *f*; *attr.* d'assurance; *~ fraud* escroquerie *f* à l'assurance; **in'sur·ant** assuré(e *f*) *m*; **in·sure** [in'ʃuə] (faire) assurer; *fig. a.* garantir; **in'sured** assuré(e *f*) *m*; **in'sur·er** assureur *m*.

in·sur·gent [in'səːdʒənt] insurgé, révolté (*a. su./mf*).

in·sur·mount·a·ble □ [insə'mauntəbl] insurmontable (*a. fig.*).

in·sur·rec·tion [insə'rekʃn] insurrection *f*, soulèvement *m*; **in·sur'rec·tion·al** insurrectionnel(le *f*); **in·sur'rec·tion·ist** [~ʃnist] insurgé(e *f*) *m*.

in·sus·cep·ti·ble [insə'septəbl] non susceptible (de, *of*), inaccessible (à, *of*); insensible (à, *to*).

in·tact [in'tækt] intact, indemne.

in·take ['inteik] prise *f* (*d'eau etc.*); ⊕ *~ valve* soupape *f* d'admission.

in·tan·gi·bil·i·ty [intændʒə'biliti] intangibilité *f*; *traité*: inviolabilité *f*; **in'tan·gi·ble** □ [~dʒəbl] intangible; immatériel(le *f*); *fig.* impondérable.

in·te·ger ['intidʒə] totalité *f*; 𝔄 nombre *m* entier; **in·te·gral** ['~grəl] **1.** □ intégrant; total; entier (-ère *f*); 𝔄 intégral; **2.** 𝔄 intégrale *f*; **in·te·grant** ['~grənt] intégrant; **in·te·grate** ['~greit] rendre entier; 𝔄 intégrer; *be ~d into* s'intégrer dans; ⚡ *~d circuit* circuit *m* intégré; **in·te'gra·tion** intégration *f*; **in·teg·ri·ty** [~'tegriti] intégrité *f*; probité *f*; totalité *f*.

in·teg·u·ment [in'tegjumənt] (in)tégument *m*, enveloppe *f* (*a.* ♀).

in·tel·lect ['intilekt] intelligence *f*, esprit *m*, intellect *m*; **in·tel'lec·tu·al** [~tjuəl] **1.** □ intellectuel(le *f*); **2.** intellectuel(le *f*) *m*; **in·tel·lec·tu·al·i·ty** ['~'æliti] intellectualité *f*.

in·tel·li·gence [in'telidʒəns] intelligence *f*; esprit *m*; renseignements *m/pl.*, nouvelles *f/pl.*; informations *f/pl.*; *~ department*, ⚔, ⚓ *a. ~ service* service *m* des renseignements; **in'tel·li·genc·er** informateur (-trice *f*) *m*; espion *m*.

in·tel·li·gent □ [in'telidʒənt] intelligent; avisé; † *~ of* au courant de; **in·tel·li·gent·si·a** [~'dʒentsiə] *la* classe *f* des intellectuels *m/pl.*; élite *f* intellectuelle; **in·tel·li·gi·bil·i·ty**

[~dʒə'biliti] intelligibilité *f*; **in'tel·li·gi·ble** □ intelligible.

in·tem·per·ance [in'tempərəns] intempérance *f*; alcoolisme *m*; **in-'tem·per·ate** □ [~rit] immodéré, intempérant; adonné à la boisson.

in·tend [in'tend] avoir l'intention de, se proposer de, compter; entendre (par, *by*); ~ *for* destiner à; **in-'tend·ant** intendant *m*; **in'tend·ed 1.** projeté; intentionnel(le *f*); ~ *husband* fiancé *m*, prétendu *m*; **2.** F fiancé(e *f*) *m*, prétendu(e *f*) *m*, futur(e *f*) *m*.

in·tense □ [in'tens] intense; vif (vive *f*) (*a. couleur*); fort; **in'tense·ness** intensité *f*; violence *f*; force *f*.

in·ten·si·fi·ca·tion [intensifi'keiʃn] renforcement *m* (*a. phot.*); **in'ten·si·fy** [~fai] (s')augmenter; (s')intensifier; *v/t. phot.* renforcer.

in·ten·sion [in'tenʃn] tension *f* (*d'esprit*); *phls.* compréhension *f*; **in-'ten·si·ty** *see intenseness*; **in'ten·sive** □ *see intense*; intensif (-ive *f*); ~ *care unit* service *m* de réanimation *ou* de soins intensifs.

in·tent [in'tent] **1.** □ tout entier (-ère *f*) (à, *on*); acharné (à, *on*); fixe (*regard*); **2.** intention *f*, but *m*, dessein *m*; *to all* ~*s and purpose* à toutes fins utiles; *with* ~ *to kill* dans l'intention de tuer; **in'ten·tion** intention *f*; dessein *m*; but *m*; **in'ten·tion·al** □ [~ʃnl] voulu, intentionnel (-le *f*); fait exprès; **in'ten·tioned** (*bien ou mal*) intentionné; **in'tent·ness** application *f*; tension *f* d'esprit; attention *f* soutenue (*du regard*).

in·ter [in'tə:] enterrer, ensevelir.

inter... [intə] entre-; inter-; réciproque.

in·ter·act 1. ['intərækt] *théâ.* entracte *m*; intermède *m*; **2.** [~'ækt] agir l'un sur l'autre; **in·ter'ac·tion** action *f* réciproque.

in·ter·breed ['intə'bri:d] [*irr.* (*breed*)] (s')entrecroiser; *v/t.* accoupler (*des animaux*).

in·ter·ca·lar·y [in'tə:kələri] intercalaire; *géol.* intercalé (*couche*); **in-'ter·ca·late** [~leit] intercaler; **in·ter·ca'la·tion** intercalation *f*.

in·ter·cede [intə'si:d] intercéder, plaider (auprès de, *with*); **in·ter-'ced·er** intercesseur *m*; médiateur (-trice *f*) *m*.

in·ter·cept [intə'sept] intercepter (*une lettre, un navire, un message*); couper (*la retraite*); ⚔ comprendre (*un espace*); **in·ter'cep·tion** interception *f*; *téléph. etc.* captation *f*; **inter'cep·tor** celui (celle *f*) *m* qui intercepte; ⚔ ~ *fighter* intercepteur *m*.

in·ter·ces·sion [intə'seʃn] intercession *f*; médiation *f*; **in·ter·ces·sor** [~'sesə] intercesseur *m*; médiateur (-trice *f*) *m*.

in·ter·change 1. [intə'tʃeindʒ] *v/t.* échanger; mettre (*qch.*) à la place de (*qch. d'autre*); *v/i.* s'interchanger; **2.** ['~'tʃeindʒ] échange *m*; alternance *f*; ⚡ interversion *f*; **in·ter-'change·a·ble** interchangeable, permutable.

in·ter·com·mu·ni·cate [intəkə-'mju:nikeit] communiquer (entre eux *ou* elles); **'in·ter·com·mu·ni-'ca·tion** communication *f* réciproque; rapports *m/pl.*; 🚭 intercirculation *f*; **in·ter·com'mun·ion** [~jən] rapports *m/pl.* intimes; *eccl.* intercommunion *f*.

in·ter·con·nect ['intəkə'nekt] communiquer (réciproquement).

in·ter·con·ti·nen·tal ['intəkɔnti-'nentl] intercontinental (-aux *m/pl.*).

in·ter·course ['intəkɔ:s] commerce *m*, relations *f/pl.*

in·ter·de·nom·i·na·tion·al [intədi-nɔmi'neiʃənl] interconfessionnel(le *f*).

in·ter·de·pend·ent [intədi'pendənt] solidaire (de, *with*).

in·ter·dict 1. [intə'dikt] interdire (*qch.* à q., *s.th.* to *s.o.*; à q. de *inf.*, *s.o.* from *gér.*); prohiber; **2.** ['intədikt]. **in·ter'dic·tion** interdiction *f*, défense *f*; *eccl.* interdit *m*.

in·ter·est ['intrist] **1.** *usu.* intérêt *m*; participation *f* (à, *in*); *fig.* groupe *m*, parti *m*, monde *m*; profit *m*, avantage *m*; † influence *f*, crédit *m* (auprès de, *with*); ⬆ intérêt *m*; revenu *m*; *be of* ~ *to* intéresser (*q.*); *take an* ~ *in* s'intéresser à; **2.** *usu.* intéresser (dans, *in*); éveiller l'intérêt de (*q.*); *be* ~*ed in* s'intéresser à; s'occuper de; ⬆ être intéressé dans; ~ *o.s.* s'intéresser (à, *in*); **'in·ter·est·ed** □ intéressé; d'intérêt (*regard*); **'in·ter·est-free** ⬆ sans intérêts; **'in·ter-est·ing** □ intéressant.

in·ter·fere [intə'fiə] se mêler (de,

with); toucher (à, with); intervenir (dans, in); gêner, déranger (qch., with s.th.); **in·ter·fer·ence** intervention f, ingérence f (dans, in); *phys.* interférence f; *radio*: interférences f/pl.; ~ *elimination radio*: filtrage m à interférences; ~ *suppressor* antiparasite m.

in·ter·flow [intə'flou] se mélanger.

in·ter·flu·ent [in'tə:fluənt] se mélangeant; mêlant leurs eaux.

in·ter·fuse [intə'fju:z] (se) mélanger, (se) confondre.

in·ter·im ['intərim] **1.** *su.* intérim m; *ad* ~ par intérim; *in the* ~ sur ces entrefaites; **2.** *adv.* en attendant, entretemps; **3.** *adj.* intérimaire.

in·te·ri·or [in'tiəriə] **1.** □ (de l')intérieur; *fig.* intime; ♣ interne; **2.** intérieur m (*tous les sens*); ~ *decorator* ensemblier m, artiste mf décorateur (-trice f).

in·ter·ja·cent [intə'dʒeisənt] intermédiaire, interjacent.

in·ter·ject [intə'dʒekt] interrompre; faire (*une remarque*); **in·ter'jec·tion** interjection f; **in·ter'jec·tion·al** □ interjectionnel(le f).

in·ter·lace [intə'leis] (s')entrelacer, (s')entrecroiser, (s')entremêler.

in·ter·lard [intə'lɑ:d] *fig.* piquer (de, with).

in·ter·leave [intə'li:v] interfolier (*un livre*).

in·ter·line [intə'lain] écrire (qch.) entre les lignes; *typ.* interligner; **in·ter·lin·e·ar** [intə'liniə] (à traduction) interlinéaire; **in·ter·lin·e·a·tion** ['‿lini'eiʃn] interlinéation f, entre-ligne m; intercalation f de mots etc. dans un texte.

in·ter·lock [intə'lɔk] (s')emboîter; ⚙ (s')enclencher; (s')engrener.

in·ter·lo·cu·tion [intələ'kju:ʃn] interlocution f; **in·ter·loc·u·tor** [‿'lɔkjutə] interlocuteur m; **in·ter'loc·u·to·ry** en forme de dialogue; ⚖ interlocutoire.

in·ter·lope [intə'loup] faire intrusion; ♱ vendre sans autorisation; **'in·ter·lop·er** intrus(e f) m; ♱ commerçant m marron.

in·ter·lude ['intəlu:d] intermède m.

in·ter·mar·riage [intə'mæridʒ] intermariage m; **'in·ter'mar·ry** se marier entre parents ou entre membres de races etc. différentes.

in·ter·med·dle [intə'medl] s'ingérer

(dans with, in); **in·ter'med·dler** fig. officieux (-euse f) m.

in·ter·me·di·ar·y [intə'mi:diəri] intermédiaire (a. su./m); **in·ter·me·di·ate** □ [‿'mi:diət] intermédiaire; intermédiat; moyen(ne f); ✈ ~ *landing* escale f; *Am.* ~ *school* école f secondaire; ~ *trade* commerce m intermédiaire.   [ment m.]

in·ter·ment [in'tə:mənt] enterre-)

in·ter·mi·na·ble □ [in'tə:minəbl] sans fin, interminable.

in·ter·min·gle [intə'miŋgl] (s')entremêler.

in·ter·mis·sion [intə'miʃn] interruption f, intervalle m; pause f; *Am. théâ.* entracte m.

in·ter·mit [intə'mit] (s')interrompre; *v/t.* suspendre; **in·ter'mit·tent 1.** □ intermittent; ~ *fever* = **2.** ♣ fièvre f intermittente; **in·ter'mit·ting·ly** par intervalles.

in·ter·mix [intə'miks] (s')entremêler, (se) mélanger; **in·ter'mix·ture** [‿tʃə] mélange m; mixtion f.

in·tern [in'tə:n] interner.

in·tern(e) ['intə:n] interne m (*des hôpitaux*).

in·ter·nal □ [in'tə:nl] interne; intérieur; intime, secret (-ète f); *Am.* ♱ ~ *revenue* revenu m fiscal; *le* fisc m; ~-**com'bus·tion en·gine** moteur m à combustion interne.

in·ter·na·tion·al [intə'næʃnəl] **1.** □ international (-aux m/pl.); ~ *data line* ligne f de changement de date; ✈ ~ *departures pl.* départ m vols internationaux; ~ *exhibition* exposition f internationale; ✈ ~ *flight* vol m international; ~ *law* droit m international ou des gens; **2.** *pol.* F Internationale f; *sp.* international(e f) m; **in·ter·na·tion·al·i·ty** [‿'næliti] internationalité f; **in·ter'na·tion·al·ize** [‿əlaiz] internationaliser.

in·ter·ne·cine war [intə'ni:sain'wɔ:] guerre f d'extermination réciproque.

in·ter·nee [intə:'ni:] interné(e f) m; **in'tern·ment** internement m; ~ *camp* camp m d'internement.

in·ter·pel·late [in'tə:peleit] interpeller; **in·ter·pel·la·tion** interpellation f.

in·ter·phone ['intəfoun] téléphone m privé; ✈ téléphonie f de bord.

in·ter·plan·e·tar·y [intə'plænitəri] interplanétaire.

in·ter·play ['intə'plei] effet *m* réciproque; jeu *m*.

in·ter·po·late [in'tə:poleit] interpoler; intercaler; **in·ter·po·la·tion** interpolation *f*.

in·ter·pose [intə'pouz] *v/t.* interposer; faire (*une observation*); *v/i.* s'interposer, intervenir; **in·ter·po·si·tion** [intə:pə'ziʃn] interposition *f*; intervention *f*.

in·ter·pret [in'tə:prit] interpréter; **in·ter·pre·ta·tion** interprétation *f*; **in·ter·pre·ta·tive** [ˌtətiv] interprétatif (-ive *f*); qui explique (qch., of s.th.); **in'ter·pret·er** interprète *mf*.

in·ter·ro·gate [in'terogeit] interroger, questionner; **in·ter·ro·ga·tion** interrogation *f*; *police:* interrogatoire *m*; question *f*; *note* (*ou mark ou point*) of ∼ point *m* d'interrogation; **in·ter·rog·a·tive** [ˌtə'rɔgətiv] **1.** □ interrogateur (-trice *f*); *gramm.* interrogatif (-ive *f*); **2.** *gramm.* pronom *m* interrogatif; **in·ter·rog·a·to·ry** [ˌtəri] **1.** interrogateur (-trice *f*); **2.** ⚖ question *f*; interrogatoire *m*.

in·ter·rupt [intə'rʌpt] interrompre; **in·ter'rupt·ed·ly** de façon interrompue; **in·ter'rupt·er** interrupteur (-trice *f*) *m*; ⚡ interrupteur *m*, *a.* coupe-circuit *m/inv.*; **in·ter'rup·tion** interruption *f*.

in·ter·sect [intə'sekt] (s')entrecouper, (s')entrecroiser; ⚕ (se) couper; **in·ter'sec·tion** intersection *f* (🚉 *de voies*); *chemins:* carrefour *m*.

in·ter·space ['intə'speis] espacement *m*; *temps:* intervalle *m*.

in·ter·sperse [intə'spə:s] entremêler (de, *with*); parsemer (de, *with*).

in·ter·state *Am.* ['intə'steit] entre États.

in·ter·stel·lar [intə'stelə] interstellaire.

in·ter·stice [in'tə:stis] interstice *m*; **in·ter·sti·tial** □ [intə'stiʃl] interstitiel(le *f*).

in·ter·twine [intə'twain], **in·ter·twist** [intə'twist] (s')entrelacer.

in·ter·val ['intəvəl] intervalle *m* (*a. de temps, a.* ♪); distance *f*; *sp.* mitemps *f*; *théâ.* entracte *m*; *école:* récréation *f*.

in·ter·vene [intə'vi:n] intervenir, s'interposer; s'écouler (*années*); séparer; arriver, survenir; **in·ter·ven·tion** [ˌ'venʃn] intervention *f*; interposition *f*.

in·ter·view ['intəvju:] **1.** entrevue *f*; *journ.* interview *f*; **2.** avoir une entrevue avec; *journ.* interviewer; **in·ter·view·ee** [ˌi:] personne *f* interviewée, interviewé(e *f*) *m*; **'in·ter·view·er** interviewer *m*.

in·ter·weave [intə'wi:v] [*irr.* (*weave*)] (s')entrelacer; *fig.* (s')entremêler.

in·tes·ta·cy ⚖ [in'testəsi] absence *f* de testament; **in·tes·tate** ⚖ [ˌtit] intestat (*usu. su./m*); ∼ *succession* succession *f* ab intestat.

in·tes·ti·nal *anat.* [in'testinl] intestinal (-aux *m/pl.*); **in'tes·tine** [ˌtin] intestin (*a. su./m*).

in·ti·ma·cy ['intiməsi] intimité *f*; *péj.* accointances *f/pl.*; ⚖ relations *f/pl.* charnelles; **in·ti·mate 1.** ['ˌmeit] signifier; indiquer, suggérer; intimer (*un ordre*); **2.** ['ˌmit] □ intime; *fig.* approfondi; **3.** ['ˌmit] intime *mf*; **in·ti·ma·tion** [ˌ'meiʃn] avis *m*; indication *f*; suggestion *f*.

in·tim·i·date [in'timideit] intimider; **in·tim·i·da·tion** intimidation *f*; ⚖ menaces *f/pl.*

in·tim·i·ty [in'timiti] intimité *f*.

in·to ['intu; 'intə] *prp.* dans, en; à; entre (*les mains*).

in·tol·er·a·ble □ [in'tɔlərəbl] intolérable, insupportable; **in·tol·er·ance** intolérance *f*; **in'tol·er·ant** □ intolérant.

in·to·na·tion [into'neiʃn] ♪, *voix:* intonation *f*; *eccl.* psalmodie *f*; cadence *f*, *voix:* ton *m*; **in·to·nate** ['ˌneit], **in·tone** [in'toun] psalmodier; entonner.

in·tox·i·cant [in'tɔksikənt] **1.** enivrant; **2.** boisson *f* alcoolique; **in·'tox·i·cate** [ˌkeit] enivrer; **in·tox·i·ca·tion** ivresse *f*; *fig.* enivrement *m*; 🗡 *poison:* intoxication *f*.

in·trac·ta·bil·i·ty [intræktə'biliti] indocilité *f*; *terrain:* nature *f* incultivable; **in'trac·ta·ble** □ intraitable, obstiné, difficile; incultivable; ingrat. [l'intérieur de la ville.)

in·tra·mu·ral ['intrə'mjuərəl] dans]

in·tran·si·gent *pol.* [in'trænsidʒənt] intransigeant(e *f*) (*a. su.*).

in·tran·si·tive □ [in'trænsitiv] intransitif (-ive *f*).

in·tra·state *Am.* [intrə'steit] intérieur de l'État; qui ne concerne que l'État.

in·tra·ve·nous 🗡 [intrəvi:nəs] intraveineux (-euse *f*).

in·trep·id □ [in'trepid] intrépide, courageux (-euse *f*); **in·tre·pid·i·ty** [intri'piditi] intrépidité *f*, courage *m*.

in·tri·ca·cy ['intrikəsi] complication *f*; complexité *f*; **in·tri·cate** □ ['ˌkit] compliqué; confus; embrouillé.

in·trigue [in'tri:g] **1.** intrigue *f* (*a. théâ.*); liaison *f* (*amoureuse*); cabale *f*; **2.** *v/i.* intriguer (*a. v/t.*); mener des intrigues; *v/t. fig.* piquer la curiosité de (*q.*); **in·tri·guer** intrigant(e *f*) *m*.

in·trin·sic, in·trin·si·cal □ [in·'trinsik(l)] intrinsèque.

in·tro·duce [intrə'dju:s] introduire, faire entrer; présenter (q. à q., s.o. to s.o.; *a. parl. un projet de loi*); faire connaître (*un livre*); initier (q. à qch., s.o. to s.th.); établir; commencer (*une phrase*); **in·tro·duc·tion** [ˌˈdʌkʃn] introduction *f*; présentation *f*; avant-propos *m/inv.*; *letter of* ~ lettre *f* de recommandation; **in·tro'duc·to·ry** [ˌtəri] préliminaire; de recommandation (*lettre*); ✝ ~ *price* prix *m* de lancement.

in·tro·spec·tion [intro'spekʃn] introspection *f*; **in·tro'spec·tive** □ introspectif (-ive *f*).

in·tro·vert 1. [intro'və:t] ✍ retourner, introvertir (*a. psych.*); **2.** ['introvə:t] caractère *m* introverti.

in·trude [in'tru:d] *v/t.* introduire de force (dans, *into*); imposer (à, [*up*]on); *v/i.* faire intrusion (auprès de, [*up*]on); empiéter (sur, on); être importun; **in'trud·er** intrus(e *f*) *m*; importun(e *f*) *m*; F resquilleur (-euse *f*) *m* (*à une soirée*).

in·tru·sion [in'tru:ʒn] intrusion *f*, empiétement *m*.

in·tru·sive □ [in'tru:siv] importun (*personne*); *géol.* d'intrusion; *gramm.* intrusif (-ive *f*).

in·trust [in'trʌst] *see* entrust.

in·tu·it [in'tju:it] savoir intuitivement; **in·tu·i·tion** [intju'iʃn] intuition *f*; **in·tu·i·tive** □ [ˌ'tjuitiv] intuitif (-ive *f*).

in·un·date ['inʌndeit] inonder (de, with); **in·un'da·tion** inondation *f*.

in·ure [i'njuə] habituer (à, to); **in·'ure·ment** habitude *f* (de, to); endurcissement *m* (à, to).

in·u·til·i·ty [inju'tiliti] inutilité *f*.

in·vade [in'veid] envahir; faire une invasion dans (*un pays*); *fig.* violer; empiéter sur (*un droit*); **in'vad·er** envahisseur *m*; *fig.* intrus(e *f*) *m*; transgresseur *m* (*d'un droit*).

in·val·id¹ [in'vælid] invalide; nul (-le *f*).

in·val·id² ['invəli:d] **1.** malade (*a. su./mf*); infirme (*a. su./mf*); **2.** ✕, ⚓ invalide *m*; **3.** *v/t.* rendre malade *ou* infirme; ✕, ⚓ réformer; *v/i.* être réformé.

in·val·i·date [in'vælideit] rendre nul, invalider; ✍ casser (*un jugement*); **in·val·i'da·tion** invalidation *f*; cassation *f*.

in·va·lid·i·ty [invə'liditi] invalidité *f*.

in·val·u·a·ble □ [in'væljuəbl] inestimable.

in·var·i·a·ble □ [in'vɛəriəbl] invariable.

in·va·sion [in'veiʒn] invasion *f* (*a. ✍*), envahissement *m*; *fig.* violation *f* (*a. ✍*), empiétement *m* (sur, of); **in'va·sive** [ˌsiv] envahissant; d'invasion.

in·vec·tive [in'vektiv] invective *f*, injures *f/pl.*

in·veigh [in'vei]: ~ *against* déclamer *ou* fulminer contre, maudire (*qch.*).

in·vei·gle [in'vi:gl] séduire; attirer (dans, *into*); **in'vei·gle·ment** séduction *f*; leurre *m*.

in·vent [in'vent] inventer; **in'ven·tion** invention *f* (*a. fig.*); *fig.* mensonge *m*; **in'ven·tive** □ inventif (-ive *f*); **in'ven·tive·ness** fécondité *f* d'invention; imagination *f*; **in'ven·tor** inventeur (-trice *f*) *m*; **in·ven·to·ry** ['invəntri] **1.** inventaire *m*; **2.** inventorier; dresser l'inventaire de.

in·verse □ ['in'və:s] inverse; **in·ver·sion** [in'və:ʃn] renversement *m*; *gramm.*, ♪, ♫, etc. inversion *f*.

in·vert 1. [in'və:t] renverser; invertir; ♫ intervertir; *ed commas pl.* guillemets *m/pl.*; ✈ *ed flight* vol *m* renversé *ou* sur le dos; **2.** ['invə:t] inverti(e *f*) *m*.

in·ver·te·brate [in'və:tibrit] **1.** invertébré; *fig.* flasque, faible; **2.** *zo.* invertébré *m*; *fig.* personne *f* qui manque de caractère.

in·vest [in'vest] *v/t.* revêtir (de with, in); *fig.* investir (q. de qch., s.o. with s.th.; *a. de l'argent*); prêter (qch. à q., s.o. with s.th.); ✕ investir, cerner; ✝ investir, placer (*des fonds*) (dans, *in*); *v/i.* ✝ placer de l'argent (dans, *in*); F ~ *in s.th.* acheter qch., se payer qch.

in·ves·ti·gate [in'vestigeit] examiner, étudier, rechercher; *investigating committee* commission *f* d'enquête; **in·ves·ti'ga·tion** investigation *f*, recherches *f/pl.*; **in'ves·ti·ga·tor** [~tə] investigateur (-trice *f*) *m.*

in·ves·ti·ture [in'vestitʃə] remise *f* de décorations; *eccl.* investiture *f*; *poét.* (re)vêtement *m*; **in'vest·ment** placement *m* (*de fonds*); ✕ investissement *m*; **in'vest·or** capitaliste *mf*; spéculateur *m*; *small* ~ petit rentier *m.*

in·vet·er·a·cy [in'vetərəsi] caractère *m* invétéré; **in'vet·er·ate** □ [~rit] invétéré, enraciné (*chose*); acharné (*personne*).

in·vid·i·ous □ [in'vidiəs] odieux (-euse *f*), haïssable; qui excite la haine *ou* l'envie *ou* la jalousie.

in·vig·or·ate [in'vigəreit] *v/t.* fortifier, donner de la vigueur à; **in·vig·or'a·tion** invigoration *f.*

in·vin·ci·bil·i·ty [invinsi'biliti] invincibilité *f*; **in'vin·ci·ble** □ invincible.

in·vi·o·la·bil·i·ty [invaiələ'biliti] inviolabilité *f*; **in'vi·o·la·ble** □ inviolable; **in'vi·o·late** [~lit] inviolé.

in·vis·i·bil·i·ty [invizə'biliti] invisibilité *f*; **in'vis·i·ble** □ invisible.

in·vi·ta·tion [invi'teiʃn] invitation *f*; **in·vite** [in'vait] 1. inviter (*q. à inf.*, *s.o. to inf.*); convier (*a. à dîner*); solliciter (*qch.*); provoquer (*une critique*, *un danger*, etc.); 2. F invitation *f.*

in·vo·ca·tion [invo'keiʃn] invocation *f*; **in·voc·a·to·ry** [in'vɔkətəri] invocatoire.

in·voice ✝ ['invɔis] 1. facture *f*; 2. facturer.

in·voke [in'vouk] invoquer (*Dieu*, *la mémoire*, *un esprit*); appeler.

in·vol·un·tar·y □ [in'vɔləntəri] involontaire.

in·vo·lute ['invəlu:t] 1. ⚕ involuté; A, de *ou* à développante; 2. A développante *f*; **in·vo'lu·tion** complication *f*; enchevêtrement *m*; ⚕, A, *biol.* involution *f.*

in·volve [in'vɔlv] envelopper (dans, *in*); embarrasser; impliquer (dans, *in*); engager (dans, *in*); entraîner; comprendre; **in'volve·ment** impli-

cation *f*; confusion *f*; embarras *m/pl.* pécuniaires.

in·vul·ner·a·bil·i·ty [invʌlnərə'biliti] invulnérabilité *f*; **in'vul·ner·a·ble** □ invulnérable.

in·ward ['inwəd] 1. *adj.* intérieur (*a. fig.*); interne; vers l'intérieur; 2. *adv.* (*usu.* **inwards** ['~z]) vers l'intérieur; ✝ pour l'importation; *fig.* dans l'âme; 3. *su. fig.* ~*s pl.* entrailles *f/pl.*, ventre *m*; **'in·ward·ly** intérieurement (*a. fig.*); dans *ou* vers l'intérieur; **'in·ward·ness** essence *f*, signification *f* intime; spiritualité *f.*

in·weave ['in'wi:v] [*irr.* (*weave*)] brocher (de, *with*); tisser (dans, *into*).

in·wrought ['in'rɔ:t] broché, ouvragé (de, *with*; dans, *into*).

i·od·ic 🜍 [ai'ɔdik] iodique; **i·o·dide** ['aiədaid] iodure *m*; **i·o·dine** ['~di:n] iode *m*; **i·o·do·form** 🜍 [ai'ɔdəfɔ:m] iodoforme *m.*

i·on *phys.* ['aiən] ion *m.*

I·o·ni·an [ai'ounjən] 1. ionien(ne *f*); 2. Ionien(ne *f*) *m.*

I·on·ic[1] [ai'ɔnik] △ ionique; ♪, *ling.* ionien(ne *f*).

i·on·ic[2] *phys.* [~] ionique; **i·on·ize** *phys.* ['aiənaiz] (s')ioniser.

i·o·ta [ai'outə] iota *m* (*a. fig.*).

I O U ['aiou'ju:] (*abr. de I owe you*) reconnaissance *f* de dette.

ip·e·cac·u·an·ha ⚕ [ipikækju'ænə] ipécacuana *m*, *abr.* ipéca *m.*

I·ra·ni·an [ai'reinjən] 1. iranien(ne *f*); 2. Iranien(ne *f*) *m.*

i·ras·ci·bil·i·ty [iræsi'biliti] irascibilité *f*; tempérament *m* colérique; **i'ras·ci·ble** □ [~sibl] irascible; colérique (*tempérament*).

i·rate [ai'reit] en colère, furieux (-euse *f*).

ire *poét.* ['aiə] colère *f*; courroux *m.*

ire·ful □ ['aiəful] plein de colère.

ir·i·des·cence [iri'desns] irisation *f*; *plumage etc.*: chatoiement *m*; **ir·i·des·cent** irisé; chatoyant.

I·ris ['aiəris] *myth.* Iris *f*; ♀ ⚕, *anat.*, *cin.*, *opt.* iris *m*; *phot.* ~ *diaphragm* diaphragme *m* iris.

I·rish ['aiəriʃ] 1. irlandais; d'Irlande; 2. *ling.* irlandais *m*; *the* ~ les Irlandais *m/pl.*; **'I·rish·ism** locution *f* irlandaise; **'I·rish·man** Irlandais *m*; **'I·rish·wom·an** Irlandaise *f.*

irk ✝ [ə:k] ennuyer; en coûter à (*q.*).

irk·some □ ['ə:ksəm] ennuyeux (-euse *f*); ingrat; **'irk·some·ness** caractère *m* ingrat; ennui *m*.
i·ron ['aiən] **1.** fer *m* (*a. fig.*); *fig. souv.* airain *m*; cast ⁓ fonte *f*; (*qqfois* flat-⁓) fer *m* à repasser; ⁓s *pl.* fers *m/pl.*; **2.** de fer (*a. fig.*); en fer; ⊕ de fonte; **3.** repasser; donner un coup de fer à; garnir de fer; mettre (*q.*) aux fers; '⁓-**bound** cerclé de fer; *fig.* sévère, inflexible; à pic (*côte*); '⁓-**clad** cuirassé (*a. su./m*); **'i·ron·er** repasseur (-euse *f*) *m*; **'i·ron-found·ry** fonderie *f* de fonte; **'i·ron-heart·ed** *fig.* dur, sans pitié.
i·ron·ic, i·ron·i·cal □ [ai'rɔnik(l)] ironique.
i·ron·ing ['aiəniŋ] **1.** repassage *m*; **2.** à repasser.
i·ron...: ⁓ **lung** ⚕ poumon *m* d'acier; '⁓-**mas·ter** maître *m* de forges; '⁓-**mon·ger** quincaillier (-ère*f*) *m*; '⁓-**mon·ger·y** quincaillerie *f*; '⁓-**mould** tache *f* de rouille; '⁓-**willed** à la volonté de fer; '⁓-**work** construction *f* en fer; serrurerie *f*; ⁓s *usu. sg.* ⊕ fonderie *f* (de fonte).
i·ro·ny¹ ['aiəni] de *ou* en fer; qui ressemble au fer.
i·ro·ny² ['aiərəni] ironie *f*.
ir·ra·di·ance, ir·ra·di·an·cy [i'reidiəns(i)] rayonnement *m*; éclat *m* (*a. fig.*); **ir'ra·di·ant** rayonnant (de, with).
ir·ra·di·ate [i'reidieit] irradier; *v/i.* rayonner (de, with); *v/t.* rayonner sur; *a.* éclairer; illuminer; faire rayonner; **ir·ra·di·a·tion** rayonnement *m*, éclat *m* (*a. fig.*); *phys.* irradiation *f*; *fig.* illumination *f*.
ir·ra·tion·al □ [i'ræʃnəl] déraisonnable; dépourvu de raison; ⅋ irrationnel(le *f*); **ir·ra·tion·al·i·ty** [⁓ʃə'næliti] déraison *f*; absurdité *f*.
ir·re·claim·a·ble □ [iri'kleiməbl] incorrigible; ✍ incultivable.
ir·rec·og·niz·a·ble □ [i'rekəgnaizəbl] méconnaissable.
ir·rec·on·cil·a·ble □ [i'rekənsailəbl] incompatible (avec, with); implacable (*haine etc.*).
ir·re·cov·er·a·ble □ [iri'kʌvərəbl] irrécouvrable; irréparable (*perte*).
ir·re·deem·a·ble □ [iri'di:məbl] irrachetable (*faute, fonds*); irrémédiable (*désastre etc.*); ✝ non amortissable; incorrigible (*coquin*).

ir·re·duc·i·ble [iri'dju:səbl] irréductible.
ir·ref·ra·ga·bil·i·ty [irefrəgə'biliti] caractère *m* irréfragable *etc.*; **ir'ref·ra·ga·ble** □ irréfragable; irréfutable.
ir·ref·u·ta·ble □ [i'refjutəbl] irréfutable; irrécusable.
ir·reg·u·lar [i'regjulə] **1.** □ irrégulier (-ère *f*); anormal (-aux *m/pl.*); inégal (-aux *m/pl.*); saccadé (*mouvement etc.*); **2.** ⁓s *pl.* troupes *f/pl.* irrégulières, irréguliers *m/pl.*; **ir·reg·u·lar·i·ty** [⁓'læriti] irrégularité *f*.
ir·rel·a·tive [i'relətiv] sans rapport (avec, to), étranger (-ère *f*) (à, to).
ir·rel·e·vance, ir·rel·e·van·cy [i'relivəns(i)] inconséquence *f*; inapplicabilité *f*; **ir'rel·e·vant** □ hors de propos; étranger (-ère *f*) (à, to).
ir·re·li·gion [iri'lidʒn] irréligion *f*, indévotion *f*; **ir·re'li·gious** □ [⁓dʒəs] irréligieux (-euse *f*).
ir·re·me·di·a·ble □ [iri'mi:djəbl] irrémédiable; sans remède.
ir·re·mis·si·ble □ [iri'misəbl] impardonnable; irrémissible.
ir·re·mov·a·ble □ [iri'mu:vəbl] inébranlable; bien ancré; inamovible (*juge etc.*).
ir·rep·a·ra·ble □ [i'repərəbl] irréparable; irrémédiable.
ir·re·press·i·ble □ [iri'presəbl] irrésistible; irrépressible.
ir·re·proach·a·ble □ [iri'proutʃəbl] irréprochable; **ir·re'proach·a·ble·ness** caractère *m* irréprochable.
ir·re·sist·i·bil·i·ty ['irizistə'biliti] irrésistibilité *f*; **ir·re'sist·i·ble** □ irrésistible.
ir·res·o·lute □ [i'rezəlu:t] irrésolu; indécis; hésitant; **ir·res·o·lute·ness, ir·res·o'lu·tion** irrésolution*f*; indécision *f*.
ir·re·solv·a·ble [iri'zɔlvəbl] insoluble; indécomposable.
ir·re·spec·tive □ [iris'pektiv] (*of*) indépendant (de); *adv.* sans tenir compte (de).
ir·re·spon·si·bil·i·ty ['irispɔnsə'biliti] étourderie *f*; ⚖ irresponsabilité *f*; **ir·re'spon·si·ble** □ étourdi, irréfléchi; ⚖ irresponsable.
ir·re·triev·a·ble □ [iri'tri:vəbl] irréparable, irrémédiable.
ir·rev·er·ence [i'revərəns] irrévérence *f*; manque *m* de respect (pour,

envers *towards*); **ir'rev·er·ent** □ irrévérent; irrévérencieux (-euse *f*).
ir·re·vers·i·ble □ [iri'və:səbl] irrévocable; *mot.* irréversible.
ir·rev·o·ca·bil·i·ty [irevəkə'biliti] irrévocabilité *f*; **ir'rev·o·ca·ble** □ irrévocable.
ir·ri·gate ['irigeit] arroser; ✍, ⚕ irriguer; **ir·ri'ga·tion** arrosage *m*; ✍, ⚕ irrigation *f*.
ir·ri·ta·bil·i·ty [irita'biliti] irritabilité *f*; **'ir·ri·ta·ble** □ irritable; **'ir·ri·tant** irritant (*a. su./m*); **ir·ri·tate** ['iriteit] irriter; agacer; **'ir·ri·tat·ing** □ irritant; agaçant; **ir·ri·ta·tion** irritation *f*; *biol.* stimulation *f*.
ir·rup·tion [i'rʌpʃn] irruption *f*.
is [iz] *il, elle, etc.* est.
i·sin·glass ['aizingla:s] ichtyocolle *f*; gélatine *f*.
Is·lam ['izla:m] Islam *m*.
is·land ['ailənd] île *f*; îlot *m* (*a. fig.*); (*a. traffic-~*) refuge *m*; **'is·land·er** insulaire *mf*.
isle [ail] *poét. ou géogr. devant npr.* île *f*; **is·let** ['ailit] îlot *m*.
ism *usu. péj.* [izm] théorie *f*, doctrine *f*.
isn't ['iznt] = *is not*.
iso... [aiso] *préf.* is(o)-.
i·so·late ['aisəleit] isoler; ⚗, ⚙ dégager; **i·so'la·tion** isolement *m*; ~ *hospital* hôpital *m* de contagieux; **i·so'la·tion·ist** *Am. pol.* isolationniste (*a. su./mf*).
i·so·met·rics [aisou'metriks] *pl.* exercices *f/pl.* isométriques.
i·so·tope ⚙ ['aisotoup] isotope *m*.
Is·ra·el·ite ['izriəlait] Israélite *mf*; **'Is·ra·el·it·ish** israélite.
is·sue ['isju:, 'iʃu:] **1.** sortie *f*; *fleuve*: embouchure *f*; résultat *m*, dénouement *m*, fin *f*; perte *f*, *sang*: épanchement *m*; ⚮ progéniture *f*, postérité *f*; ⚖ cause *f*; question *f*; distribution *f* (*de vivres etc.*); ✝ émission *f* (*des billets de banque etc.*); publication *f* (*d'un livre*; *a.* ✕, ⚓ *d'ordres*); numéro *m*, *journal*: édition *f*; *prospectus*: lancement *m*; *passeport etc.*: délivrance *f*; ~ *of fact* question *f* de fait; ~ *of law* question *f* de droit; *force an* ~ forcer une décision; amener une crise; *join* (*the*) ~ différer d'opinion; F relever le gant; *join* ~ *with s.o.* contredire q., discuter l'opinion de q.; *be at* ~ être en débat (*sur, on*); être en question;

2. *v/i.* sortir, jaillir (*de, from*); provenir (*de, from*); se terminer (*par, in*); *v/t.* publier (*a. des livres*); distribuer (*qch. à q., s.o. with s.th.*); lancer (*un mandat d'arrêt*); donner (*un ordre*); ✝ émettre (*des billets de banque*); **'~-de·part·ment** section *f* émettrice (*de la Banque d'Angleterre*); **'is·sue·less** sans enfants.
isth·mus ['isməs] isthme *m*.
it [it] **1.** *pron.* il, *accentué*: lui; elle (*a. accentué*); ce, *accentué*: cela; *accusatif*: le, la; *datif*: lui; *of* (*ou from*) ~ en; *to* (*ou at*) ~ y; *how is* ~ *with* ~ comment va *etc.*?; *see lord* 2, *foot* 2; F *go* ~ aller grand train; *sl. go* ~! vas-y!; allez-y!; *we had a very good time of* ~ nous nous sommes bien amusés; **2.** *adj. préd.* F épatant; **3.** *su.* F quelque chose; F *abr. de Italian* vermouth.
I·tal·ian [i'tæljən] **1.** italien(ne *f*); ~ *warehouse* magasin *m* de comestibles, épicerie *f*; **2.** *ling.* italien *m*; Italien(ne *f*) *m*.
i·tal·ics *typ.* [i'tæliks] italiques *m/pl.*
itch [itʃ] **1.** ⚕ gale *f*; démangeaison *f* (*a. fig.*, *de inf. for, to inf.*); **2.** démanger; *personne*: éprouver des démangeaisons; *fig.* avoir une démangeaison (*de inf. for, to inf.*); *be ~ing to* (*inf.*) brûler de (*inf.*); **'itch·ing** ⚕ prurit *m*; démangeaison *f* (*a. fig.*); *fig.* grande envie *f*; **'itch·y** ⚕ galeux (-euse *f*).
i·tem ['aitem] **1.** item; de plus; **2.** article *m*, détail *m*; question *f*; *journ.* fait *m* divers; ✝ poste *m*; **3.** noter; **i·tem·ize** ['aitəmaiz] *surt. Am.* détailler, donner les détails de.
it·er·ate ['itəreit] réitérer; **it·er'a·tion** réitération *f*, répétition *f*; **it·er·a·tive** □ ['itərətiv] itératif (-ive *f*).
i·tin·er·ant □ [i'tinərənt] ambulant; **i·tin·er·a·ry** [ai'tinərəri] itinéraire (*a. su./m*); **i·tin·er·ate** [i'tinəreit] voyager de lieu en lieu.
its [its] son, sa; ses.
it's F [its] = *it is*; *it has*.
it·self [it'self] lui-même, elle-même; *réfléchi*: se, *accentué*: soi; *of* ~ tout seul; de lui-même, d'elle-même; *in* ~ en lui-même *etc.*; en soi, de soi; *by* ~ à part; tout seul.
I've F [aiv] = *I have*.

i·vied ['aivid] couvert de lierre.

i·vo·ry ['aivəri] **1.** ivoire *m*; F *ivories pl.* touches *f/pl.* de piano; ♪ *tickle the ivories* jouer du piano; **2.** en ivoire; d'ivoire; *fig.* ~ *tower* tour *f* d'ivoire.

i·vy ♀ ['aivi] lierre *m*.

J

J, j [dʒei] J *m*, j *m*.

jab F [dʒæb] **1.** piquer (*q., qch.*) du bout (de qch., *with* s.th.); *box.* lancer un coup sec à; **2.** coup *m* de pointe; *box.* coup *m* sec.

jab·ber ['dʒæbə] **1.** *vt/i.* baragouiner; *v/i.* jacasser; **2.** baragouinage *m*; jacasserie *f*.

Jack [dʒæk] Jean *m*; ∼ *Frost* bonhomme *m* Hiver; ∼ *and Jill* Jeannot et Colette; ∼ *Ketch* le bourreau; ∼ *Pudding* bouffon *m*; ∼ *Rake* noceur *m*, roué *m*; ∼ *Sprat* nabot *m*; ♣ ∼ *Tar* matelot *m*; F mathurin *m*.

jack [dʒæk] **1.** *cartes:* valet *m*; ♣ pavillon *m* de beaupré; *mot.* cric *m*; tournebroche *m*; *icht.* brocheton *m*; *boules:* cochonnet *m*; *horloge:* jaquemart *m*; tire-botte *m*; *Am. sl.* argent *m, sl.* fric *m*; *zo.* ∼ *rabbit* gros lièvre *m*; **2.** soulever (avec un cric); *sl.* ∼ *up* abandonner; *surt. Am.* F augmenter rapidement (*les prix*).

jack·al ['dʒækɔːl] *zo.* chacal (*pl.* -als) *m* (*a. fig.*).

jack·a·napes ['dʒækəneips] petit(*e f*) vaurien(ne *f*) *m*; impertinent *m*; '**jack·ass** baudet *m*; *fig.* imbécile *m*; '**jack·boots** bottes *f/pl.* de cavalier; '**jack·daw** *orn.* choucas *m*.

jack·et ['dʒækit] veston *m* (*d'homme*); jaquette *f* (*de femme*); veste *f* (*d'un garçon de café*); ⊕ chemise *f* (*a. de documents*); *livre:* couverture *f*; *potatoes in their* ∼*s* pommes *f/pl.* de terre en robe de chambre.

jack...: '∼**-in-of·fice** bureaucrate *m*; '∼**-in-the-box** diable *m* à ressort; '∼**-knife** couteau *m* pliant; '∼**-of-** '**all-trades** maître Jacques *m*; '∼**-of-**'**all-work** factotum *m*; '∼**-o'-** '**lan·tern** feu *m* follet; '∼**pot** *poker:* pot *m*; *Am.* F *hit the* ∼ décrocher la timbale; '∼**-'tow·el** essuie-mains *m/inv.* à rouleau.

Jac·o·bin *hist.* ['dʒækəbin] jacobin(e *f*) *m*; **Jac·o·bite** *hist.* ['∼bait] jacobite *mf*.

jade¹ [dʒeid] **1.** rosse *f*, haridelle *f*; *péj.* drôlesse *f*; *fickle* ∼ oiseau *m* volage; **2.** *v/t.* éreinter; fatiguer; *v/i.* languir.

jade² *min.* [∼] jade *m*.

jag [dʒæg] **1.** pointe *f*, saillie *f*; *sl.* bombe *f*, noce *f*, ivresse *f*; **2.** déchiqueter; **jag·ged** □ ['∼id] *surt. Am. sl.* soûl, gris; '**jag·gy** déchiqueté, ébréché.

jail [dʒeil] **1.** prison *f*; **2.** mettre en prison; '∼**-bird** F gibier *m* de potence; '∼**-break** évasion *f* de prison; **jail·er** ['dʒeilə] gardien *m* de prison.

ja·lop·(p)y *mot. surt. Am.* F [dʒə'lɔpi] bagnole *f*; ✈ avion *m* de transport.

jam¹ [dʒæm] confiture *f*.

jam² [∼] **1.** presse *f*, foule *f*; ⊕ arrêt *m* (de fonctionnement); *radio:* brouillage *m*; *traffic* ∼ embouteillage *m*; *sl. be in a* ∼ être en difficulté; ∼ *session* séance *f* de jazz improvisé; **2.** *v/t.* serrer, presser; enfoncer de force; obstruer (*un passage*); *radio:* brouiller; ⊕ coincer; ∼ *the brakes* freiner brusquement; *v/i.* s'enrayer (*fusil*); se caler (*roue*); ⊕ se coincer.

Ja·mai·ca [dʒə'meikə] (*a.* ∼ *rum*) rhum *m* de la Jamaïque.

jamb [dʒæm] chambranle *m*.

jam·bo·ree [dʒæmbə'ri] *sl.* bombance *f*; congrès *m* bruyant; *boy-scouts:* jamboree *m*.

jam·my *Brt. sl.* ['dʒæmi] facile comme tout; veinard, verni; ∼ *fellow* veinard *m*.

jam-packed F ['dʒæmpækt] plein à craquer, bondé.

jan·gle ['dʒæŋgl] **1.** (faire) rendre des sons discordants (à qch.); *v/i.* s'entrechoquer; *v/t.* (faire) entrechoquer; (*a.* ∼ *upon*) agacer; **2.** sons *m/pl.* discordants; cliquetis *m*; '**jan·gling** cacophonique, discordant.

jan·i·tor ['dʒænitə] concierge *m*.

Jan·u·ar·y ['dʒænjuəri] janvier *m*.

Jap F *péj.* [dʒæp] Japonais(e *f*) *m*.

ja·pan [dʒə'pæn] **1.** laque *m*; vernis *m* japonais; **2.** du Japon; **3.** laquer; vernir (*du cuir*).

Jap·a·nese [dʒæpə'niːz] **1.** japonais; **2.** *ling.* japonais *m*; Japonais(e *f*) *m*; the ~ *pl.* les Japonais *m/pl.*

ja·pan·ner [dʒə'pænə] vernisseur *m*.

jar[1] [dʒɑː] pot *m* (*pour la moutarde etc.*); bocal *m*; récipient *m*; ⚡ verre *m*; *phys.* Leyden ~ bouteille *f* de Leyde.

jar[2] [~] **1.** choc *m*; secousse *f*; discorde *f*; **2.** heurter, cogner; vibrer; être en désaccord; ♩ détonner (*note*); ~ *upon* choquer, agacer; taper sur (*les nerfs*); ~ *with* jurer avec.

jar[3] F [~]: *on the* ~ *see* ajar.

jar·gon ['dʒɑːgən] jargon *m*; *péj.* charabia *m*.

jas·min(e) ♧ ['dʒæsmin] jasmin *m*.

jas·per *min.* ['dʒæspə] jaspe *m*.

jaun·dice ['dʒɔːndis] jaunisse *f*; *fig.* prévention *f*; **'jaun·diced** ictérique; *fig.* prévenu; *fig.* ~ *eye* regard *m* envieux.

jaunt [dʒɔːnt] **1.** balade *f*, randonnée *f*, sortie *f*; **2.** faire une petite excursion; **'jaun·ti·ness** désinvolture *f*; air *m* effronté; **'jaun·ty** □ désinvolte, insouciant; vif (vive *f*); effronté.

jave·lin ['dʒævlin] javeline *f*; javelot *m* (*a. sp.*); *throwing the* ~ lancement *m* du javelot.

jaw [dʒɔː] **1.** mâchoire *f*; F caquet *m*; F sermon *m*; ~*s pl.* mâchoire *f*, -s *f/pl.*; *fig.* bras *m/pl.* (*de la mort*); ⊕ étau: mors *m*; *clef anglaise*: bec *m*; **2.** *v/i.* F caqueter; *v/t.* F chapitrer (*q.*); **'~·bone** os *m* maxillaire; mâchoire *f*; **'~·break·er** F mot *m* à vous décrocher la mâchoire.

jay [dʒei] *orn.* geai *m*; F jobard *m*; gogo *m*; **'~·walk** traverser (la rue) sans regarder; **'~·walk·er** badaud *m*; piéton *m* imprudent.

jazz [dʒæz] **1.** ♩ jazz *m*; **2.** F bariolé; discordant; tapageur (-euse *f*); **3.** jouer *ou* danser le jazz; F ~ *up* animer, égayer, mettre de l'animation dans (*qch.*); rajeunir (*une robe etc.*); **'~-'band** jazz-band *m*.

jeal·ous □ ['dʒeləs] jaloux (-ouse *f*) (de, of); **'jeal·ous·y** jalousie *f*.

jeep ✗, *mot. Am.* [dʒiːp] jeep *f*.

jeer [dʒiə] **1.** huée *f*; raillerie *f*; **2.** se moquer (de, *at*), se railler (de qch., *at s.th.*); railler (q., *at s.o.*); huer; **'jeer·er** railleur (-euse *f*) *m*, mo-

queur (-euse *f*) *m*; **'jeer·ing** □ railleur (-euse *f*), moqueur (-euse *f*).

je·june □ [dʒi'dʒuːn] stérile, aride; *a.* maigre (*sol*).

jell [dʒel] *cuis.* épaissir, prendre; F *fig.* prendre forme, se réaliser, réussir.

jel·ly ['dʒeli] **1.** gelée *f*; **2.** *v/t.* faire prendre en gelée; *v/i.* se prendre en gelée; **'~-fish** *zo.* méduse *f*.

jem·my ['dʒemi] pince-monseigneur (*pl.* pinces-monseigneur) *f* (*du cambrioleur*), rossignol *m*.

jen·ny ⊕ ['dʒeni] machine *f* à filer; chariot *m* de roulement.

jeop·ard·ize ['dʒepədaiz] mettre en péril, exposer au danger; **'jeop·ard·y** danger *m*, péril *m*.

jer·e·mi·ad [dʒeri'maiəd] jérémiade *f*.

jerk [dʒəːk] **1.** *su.* saccade *f*, secousse *f*; ✗ réflexe *m* tendineux; tic *m*; *Am. sl.* nigaud *m*; *by* ~*s* par à-coups; *sl. put a* ~ *in it!* mets-y-en!; dépêchez-vous!; **2.** *v/t.* donner une secousse *ou* une saccade à; tirer d'un coup sec; *v/i.* se mouvoir brusquement; *avec adv. ou prp.*: lever, arracher; **'~·wa·ter** *Am.* **1.** petit train *m*, tortillard *m*; **2.** F petit, de province, sans importance; **'jerk·y** **1.** □ saccadé; **2.** *Am.* viande *f* conservée; charqui *f*; *sl.* singe *m*.

jer·ry-build·ing ['dʒeribildiŋ] construction *f* de maisons de pacotille; **'jer·ry-built** de pacotille, de boue et de crachat (*maison*).

jer·sey ['dʒəːzi] jersey *m*; chandail *m*; *foot.* maillot *m*.

jes·sa·mine ♧ ['dʒesəmin] jasmin *m*.

jest [dʒest] **1.** plaisanterie *f*, badinage *m*; **2.** plaisanter (sur, *about*); badiner; **'jest·er** railleur (-euse *f*) *m*; *hist.* bouffon *m*.

Jes·u·it ['dʒezjuit] jésuite *m*; **Jes·u-'it·ic**, **Jes·u'it·i·cal** □ *péj.* jésuitique.

jet[1] *min.* [dʒet] jais *m*.

jet[2] [~] **1.** jet *m* (*d'eau etc.*); bec *m* (*de gaz*); ⊕ gicleur *m*; ⊕ brûleur *m*; ~ *age* époque *f* des avions à réaction; ✗ ~ *fighter* chasseur *m* à réaction; ~ *lag* (troubles *m/pl.* dus au) décalage *m* horaire; ~ *propulsion* propulsion *f* par réaction; ~ *set* jet-set *m*; **2.** (faire) s'élancer en jet.

jet-black ['dʒet'blæk] noir comme du jais.

jet...: '**~-plane** avion *m* à réaction, jet *m*; '**~-pro·pelled** à réaction.

jet·sam ['dʒetsəm] épaves *f/pl.* jetées à la côte; marchandise *f* jetée à la mer.

jet·ti·son ['dʒetisn] **1.** jet *m* (de marchandises) à la mer; **2.** jeter à la mer; se délester de (*a. fig.*).

jet·ty ⚓ ['dʒeti] jetée *f*, digue *f*; estacade *f*.

Jew [dʒuː] juif *m*; *attr.* juif (-ive *f*), des juifs; ~'s *harp* guimbarde *f*.

jew·el ['dʒuːəl] **1.** bijou (*pl.* -x) *m*, joyau (*pl.* -x) *m*; *horloge*: rubis *m*; *fig. personne*: perle *f*; **2.** orner de bijoux; monter (*un horloge*) sur rubis; '**jew·el·(l)er** bijoutier *m*; '**jew·el·ry**, '**jew·el·ler·y** bijouterie *f*.

Jew·ess ['dʒuːis] juive *f*; '**Jew·ish** juif (-ive *f*); **Jew·ry** ['dʒuəri] Juiverie *f*.

jib [dʒib] **1.** ⚓ foc *m*; ⊕ volée *f* (de grue); ~ *door* porte *f* dérobée; **2.** *vt/i.* gambier, coiffer (*voile*); regimber (devant, *at*); '**jib·ber** cheval *m* rétif; *fig.* récalcitrant(e *f*) *m*; '**jib-'boom** ⚓ bout-dehors (*pl.* bouts-dehors) *m* de foc.

jibe *Am.* F [dʒaib] s'accorder, F coller.

jif·fy F ['dʒifi] instant *m*, clin *m* d'œil; *in a* ~ en un clin d'œil; F en cinq sec.

jig [dʒig] **1.** ♪ gigue *f*; **2.** danser la gigue; *fig.* se trémousser.

jig·ger *Am.* ['dʒigə] **1.** machin *m*, truc *m*; petite mesure *f* (*pour spiritueux*); **2.** *sl.* sautiller (= *danser*).

jig·gered F ['dʒigəd]: *I'm* ~ *if* ... du diable si ...

jig·gle F ['dʒigl] *v/t.* secouer légèrement; *v/i.* sautiller.

jig-saw ['dʒigsɔː] scie *f* à chantourner; ~ *puzzle* puzzle *m*.

jilt [dʒilt] **1.** coquette *f*; **2.** laisser là (*un amoureux*).

Jim Crow [dʒim'krou] *Am. sl.* nègre *m* (*a. attr.*); discrimination *f* (entre races blanche et noire).

jim·my *sl.* ['dʒimi] *see* jemmy.

jimp *sl.* [dʒimp] diable *m*.

jin·gle ['dʒiŋgl] **1.** cliquetis *m*; *grelot*: tintement *m*; **2.** (faire) tinter *ou* cliqueter.

jin·go ['dʒiŋgou], *pl.* -goes ['~z] chauvin(e *f*) *m*; patriotard *m*; F *by* ~! nom de nom!; '**jin·go·ism** chauvinisme *m*.

jinks [dʒiŋks] *pl.*: F *high* ~ ébats *m/pl.* bruyants.

jinx *Am. sl.* [~] porte-malheur *m/inv.*

jit·ney *Am. sl.* ['dʒitni] pièce *f* de 5 cents; tacot *m*.

jit·ter F ['dʒitə] **1.** frétiller (de nervosité), être nerveux (-euse *f*); **2.** *sl.* ~s *pl.* nervosité *f*, crise *f* nerveuse; ~·**bug** ['~bʌg] **1.** fanatique *m* du swing; *danse*: swing *m*; paniquard *m*; **2.** faire du jitterbug; '**jit·ter·y** *sl.* nerveux (-euse *f*) à l'excès.

jiu-jit·su [dʒuː'dʒitsu] jiu-jitsu *m*.

jive *Am. sl.* [dʒaiv] hot jazz *m*; jargon *m* des musiciens swing.

Job¹ [dʒoub]: ~'s *comforter* consolateur *m* pessimiste, ami *m* de Job; ~'s *news* nouvelle *f* fatale.

job² [dʒɔb] **1.** tâche *f*, travail (*pl.* -aux) *m*, besogne *f*; F emploi *m*; *sl.* chose *f*, article *m*; ✝ soldes *m/pl.*, marchandise *f* d'occasion; *péj.* intrigue *f*; *typ.* travail (*pl.* -aux) *m* de ville; ~ *analysis* analyse *f* des tâches *ou* des postes de travail; *by the* ~ à la pièce, à forfait; *make a* (*good*) ~ *of s.th.* bien faire qch., réussir à qch.; *a bad* ~ une mauvaise *ou* triste affaire, un malheur; *odd* ~s *pl.* petits travaux *m/pl.*; métiers *m/pl.* à part; ~ *horse* cheval *m* loué; ~ *lot* soldes *m/pl.*; *on the* ~ *training* apprentissage *m ou* formation *f* sur le tas; ~ *printer* imprimeur *m* à façon, imprimeur *m* de travaux de ville; ~ *work* travail (*pl.* -aux) *m* à la pièce *ou* tâche; **2.** *v/t.* louer (*un cheval etc.*); ✝ marchander; donner *ou* prendre à forfait (*un travail*); *v/i.* faire des petits travaux, bricoler; travailler à la tâche; ✝ agioter.

job·ber ['dʒɔbə] ouvrier (-ère *f*) *m* à la tâche; intermédiaire *m* revendeur; *péj.* tripoteur (-euse *f*) *m*; ✝ marchand *m* de titres; '**job·ber·y** tripotages *m/pl.*; ✝ agiotage *m*; *a piece of* ~ une affaire maquignonnée; '**job·bing** ouvrage *m* à la tâche; ✝ courtage *m*; ✝ vente *f* en demi-gros; *see* jobbery; '**job-hunting** chasse *f* à l'emploi; '**job·less** sans emploi, en chômage, chômeur (-euse *f*).

jock·ey ['dʒɔki] **1.** *su.* jockey *m*; **2.** *v/t.* tromper, duper; *v/i.* manœuvrer; intriguer.

jock·strap ['dʒɔkstræp] suspensoir *m*.

jo·cose □ [dʒə'kous] facétieux (-euse *f*); jovial (-aux *m/pl.*); **jo'cose·ness** jocosité *f*; humeur *f* joviale.

joc·u·lar ['dʒɔkjulə], **joc·u·lar·i·ty** [~'læriti] *see* jocose(ness).

joc·und □ ['dʒɔkənd] gai; jovial (-als *ou* -aux *m/pl.*).

Joe [dʒou]: ~ *Miller* vieille plaisanterie *f*; plaisanterie *f* usée.

jog [dʒɔg] **1.** *su.* secousse *f*, cahot *m*; coup *m* de coude; petit trot *m*; **2.** *v/t.* pousser le coude à; donner un coup de coude à; *fig.* rafraîchir (*la mémoire à q.*); secouer; *v/i.* (*usu.* ~ *along*, ~ *on*) aller son petit train; aller au petit trot; *be* ~ging se (re)mettre en route.

jog·gle ['dʒɔgl] **1.** secouer (*qch.*); branler; ⊕ goujonner; **2.** petite secousse *f*; ⊕ (joint *m* à) goujon *m*.

jog-trot ['dʒɔg'trɔt] **1.** petit trot *m*, *fig.* train-train *m*; **2.** routinier (-ère *f*); monotone.

John [dʒɔːn]: ~ *Bull l'Anglais*; *Am.* ~ *Hancock* signature *f* (*de q.*); ♀ *Am.* F cabinets *m/pl.*, toilette *f*.

john·ny F ['dʒɔni] type *m*, individu *m*; *surt. Am.* ~ *cake* galette *f* de farine de maïs.

join [dʒɔin] **1.** *v/t.* joindre (*a.* ⊕), (ré)unir; (re)nouer; se joindre à, rejoindre; ajouter; ⊕ raboutir; ✕, ⚓ rallier; s'affilier à; s'enrôler dans; *v/i.* s'unir, se (re)joindre (à, *with*); (*a.* ~ *together*) se réunir; ~ *battle* livrer bataille (à, *with*); ~ *company* se joindre (à, *with*); ~ *hands* se donner la main; *fig.* se joindre (à, *with*); ~ *a ship* rallier le bord; ~ *in* prendre part à; se mettre de la partie; s'associer à; ~ *up* s'engager dans l'armée; *I* ~ *with you* je me joins avec *ou* à vous (pour *inf.*, *in gér.*); **2.** *su.* joint *m*, jointure *f*; ligne *f* de jonction.

join·er ['dʒɔinə] menuisier *m*; **'join·er·y** menuiserie *f* (*travail, a.* endroit).

joint [dʒɔint] **1.** joint *m* (*a. du genou*), jointure *f*; ⊕ assemblage *m*; *livre:* mors *m*; *anat.* articulation *f*; *doigt:* phalange *f*; *cuis.* quartier *m*, rôti *m*; ♀ nœud *m*; *Am. sl.* boîte *f*, bistrot *m*; *put out of* ~ disloquer; *fig. out of* ~ détraqué;

2. □ (*en*) commun; combiné; collectif (-ive *f*); co-; ~ *heir* cohéritier *m*; ~ *ownership* copropriété *f*; ~ *production* coproduction *f*; ~ *venture* entreprise *f* commune; **3.** joindre, assembler (*a.* ⊕); *cuis.* découper; *anat.* (s')articuler; '**joint·ed** articulé (*a. zo.*, *a.* ♀); ~ *doll* poupée *f* articulée; '**joint-stock**: ~ *company* société *f* par actions; **join·ture** ['~tʃe] douaire *m*.

joist [dʒɔist] **1.** solive *f*, poutre *f*; **2.** poser le solivage de; assujettir (*les ais*) sur le solivage.

joke [dʒouk] **1.** *su.* plaisanterie *f*; farce *f*; **2.** *v/i.* plaisanter, badiner; *v/t.* railler; '**jok·er** farceur (-euse *f*) *m*; *cartes:* joker *m*; F type *m*; *Am. sl.* clause *f* ambiguë; '**jok·y** □ facétieux (-euse *f*).

jol·li·fi·ca·tion F [dʒɔlifi'keiʃn] partie *f* de plaisir; '**jol·li·ness**, '**jol·li·ty** gaieté *f*.

jol·ly ['dʒɔli] **1.** □ gai, joyeux (-euse *f*); F fameux (-euse *f*); **2.** F *adv.* rudement; **3.** F railler; flatter.

jol·ly-boat ⚓ ['dʒɔlibout] canot *m*.

jolt [dʒoult] **1.** cahoter; *v/t.* secouer. **2.** cahot *m*; secousse *f*; '**jolt·y** cahotant; cahoteux (-euse *f*) (*chemin*).

Jon·a·than ['dʒɔnəθən]: *Brother* ~ *l'Américain*.

jon·quil ♀ ['dʒɔŋkwil] jonquille *f*.

jo·rum ['dʒɔːrəm] bol(ée *f*) *m*.

josh *Am. sl.* [dʒɔʃ] **1.** blague *f*; **2.** blaguer; taquiner.

joss [dʒɔs] idole *f* chinoise; ~ *stick* bâton *m* d'encens.

jos·tle ['dʒɔsl] **1.** *v/t.* coudoyer; *v/i.* jouer des coudes; **2.** *su.* bousculade *f*; coudoiement *m*.

jot [dʒɔt] **1.** iota *m*; atome *m*; **2.** ~ *down* prendre note de; '**jot·ting** note *f*.

jour·nal ['dʒəːnl] journal *m*; revue *f*; ✝ (*livre m*) journal *m*; ⚓ journal *m* de bord; ⊕ tourillon *m*; ⊕ fusée *f*; **jour·nal·ese** F [~nə'liːz] style *m* de journaliste; '**jour·nal·ism** journalisme *m*; '**jour·nal·ist** journaliste *mf*; **jour·nal·is·tic** (~ally) journalistique; '**jour·nal·ize** tenir un journal de; ✝ porter au journal.

jour·ney ['dʒəːni] **1.** voyage *m*; trajet *m* (*d'autobus etc.*); parcours *m*; **2.** voyager; '**~·man** compagnon *m*; ouvrier *m*; '**~-work** travail (*pl.* -aux) *m* à la journée; *fig.* dure besogne *f*.

joust [dʒaust] **1.** joute *f*; **2.** jouter.

Jove [dʒouv]: *by* ~! parbleu!

jo·vi·al □ ['dʒouviəl] jovial (-als *ou* -aux *m/pl.*); enjoué; **jo·vi·al·i·ty** [∼'æliti] jovialité *f*; bonne humeur *f*.

jowl [dʒaul] mâchoire *f*; joue *f*; *cheek by* ~ côte à côte.

joy [dʒɔi] joie *f*, allégresse *f*; **joy·ful** □ ['∼ful] joyeux (-euse *f*); heureux (-euse *f*); enjoué; **joy·ful·ness** joie *f*; **joy·less** □ triste, sans joie; **joy·ous** □ joyeux (-euse *f*), heureux (-euse *f*); **joy-ride** *mot.* F balade *f* en auto (*souv.* à l'insu du propriétaire); **joy·rid·er** baladeur (-euse *f*) *m*; **joy-stick** ✈ *sl.* manche *m* à balai.

ju·bi·lant ['dʒuːbilənt] joyeux (-euse *f*); réjoui, exultant (*personne*); **ju·bi·late** ['∼leit] se réjouir, exulter; **ju·bi·la·tion** allégresse *f*; **ju·bi·lee** ['∼liː] jubilé *m*; cinquantenaire *m*.

Ju·da·ism ['dʒuːdeiizm] judaïsme *m*.

Ju·das ['dʒuːdəs] *fig.* Judas *m*; traître *m*; '**ʘ(-hole)** judas *m*.

judge [dʒʌdʒ] **1.** *su.* juge *m* (*a. fig.*, *a. sp.*); président *m* du tribunal; *fig.* connaisseur (-euse *f*) *m*; *Am.* magistrat *m*; *sp.* arbitre *m*; *commercial* ~ juge *m* préposé au tribunal commercial; **2.** *v/i.* juger (d'après, par *from*, *by*; de, *of*); estimer; *v/t.* juger (par, *by*); estimer; arbitrer (à qch., *s.th.*).

judg(e)·ment ['dʒʌdʒmənt] jugement *m*; arrêt *m*, décision *f* judiciaire; *fig.* avis *m*; *fig.* discernement *m*; *in my* ~ à mon avis; *pronounce* ~ rendre un arrêt; *sit in* ~ juger; *eccl.* ~*-day* jugement *m* dernier.

judge·ship ['dʒʌdʒʃip] fonctions *f/pl.* de juge.

ju·di·ca·ture ['dʒuːdikətʃə] judicature *f*; (cour *f* de) justice *f*; *coll.* magistrature *f*.

ju·di·cial □ [dʒuː'diʃl] judiciaire; de juge; de bonne justice; légal (-aux *m/pl.*); *fig.* impartial (-aux *m/pl.*); ~ *murder* assassinat *m* judiciaire; ~ *system* système *m* judiciaire.

ju·di·cious □ [dʒuː'diʃəs] judicieux (-euse *f*), sensé; **ju·di·cious·ness** discernement *m*.

jug [dʒʌg] **1.** cruche *f*; pot *m*; *sl.* prison *f*; **2.** étuver; ~*ged hare* civet *m* de lièvre.

Jug·ger·naut ['dʒʌgənɔːt] *fig.* poids *m* écrasant; roues *f/pl.* meurtrières.

jug·gins F ['dʒʌginz] niais *m*.

jug·gle ['dʒʌgl] **1.** jonglerie *f*; tour *m* de passe-passe; *fig.* supercherie *f*; **2.** jongler; faire des tours de passe-passe; escamoter (à q., *out of s.o.*); '**jug·gler** jongleur (-euse *f*) *m*; prestidigitateur *m*; escamoteur (-euse *f*) *m*; '**jug·gler·y** jonglerie *f*; prestidigitation *f*; *fig.* supercherie *f*.

Ju·go·slav ['juːgou'slaːv] **1.** Yougoslave *mf*; **2.** yougoslave.

jug·u·lar *anat.* ['dʒʌgjulə] jugulaire; ~ *vein* (veine *f*) jugulaire *f*; **ju·gu·late** ['∼leit] *fig.* étrangler; supprimer.

juice [dʒuːs] jus *m* (*a. mot. sl.*, *a.* ⚡ F); *mot. sl.* essence *f*; ⚡ courant *m*; **juic·i·ness** ['∼inis] succulence *f*; '**juic·y** □ succulent; F savoureux (-euse *f*).

ju·jube ['dʒuː'dʒuːb] ♀ jujube *f*; *pharm.* boule *f* de gomme.

juke-box *Am.* F ['dʒuːkbɔks] pick-up *m/inv.* à sous.

ju·lep ['dʒuːlep] ⚗ julep *m*; *surt. Am.* boisson *f* alcoolique glacée.

Ju·ly [dʒuː'lai] juillet *m*.

jum·ble ['dʒʌmbl] **1.** *su.* méli-mélo (*pl.* mélis-mélos) *m*; fatras *m*; **2.** *v/t.* (*a.* ~ *up*) brouiller, mêler; *v/i.* se brouiller; ~ *along* avancer en cahotant; '**~-sale** vente *f* d'objets usagés.

jum·bo ['dʒʌmbou] *fig.* éléphant *m*; *attr.* (*a.* ~*-sized*) géant.

jump [dʒʌmp] **1.** *su.* saut *m* (*a. sp.*); bond *m*; sursaut *m*; *sp.* obstacle *m*; *surt. Am.* F *get* (*ou have*) *the* ~ *on* devancer; *give a* ~ sursauter (*q.*); faire un saut; **2.** *v/i.* sauter, bondir; sursauter; *poét.* être d'accord; ~ *at fig.* saisir, sauter sur; ~ *to conclusions* conclure à la légère, juger trop vite; *v/t.* franchir, sauter; faire sauter (*un cheval etc.*); saisir à l'improviste; ⚅ quitter (*les rails*); *Am.* F usurper; voler; ~ *the gun sp.* partir avant le départ; F *fig.* (ré)agir prématurément; *mot.* ~ *the lights* brûler le feu (rouge), passer au rouge; ~ *the queue* (*Am.* line) passer avant son tour; ~ *a train* sauter dans un train en marche;

'jump·er sauteur (-euse *f*) *m* (*a.* = *cheval*, *insecte*); ⚓ chemise *f*; (*a. knitted* ⁓) casaque *f*, jumper *m* (*de femme*); barre *f* à mine; **'jump·ing-board** tremplin *m*; **'jump·ing-'off** *fig.* départ *m*; **'jump-seat** strapontin *m*; **'jump·y** nerveux (-euse *f*), agité.

junc·tion ['dʒʌŋkʃn] jonction *f*; bifurcation *f*; *rivières:* confluent *m*; 🚂 gare *f* d'embranchement; ⚡ ⁓ box boîte *f* de dérivation; **junc·ture** ['⁓tʃə] jointure *f*; jonction *f* (*de rivières*); conjoncture *f* (*de circonstances*); *at this* ⁓ *of things* à ce moment critique.

June [dʒuːn] juin *m*.

jun·gle ['dʒʌŋgl] jungle *f*; *fig.* confusion *f*.

jun·ior ['dʒuːnjə] **1.** cadet(te *f*); plus jeune (que, *to*); second; *univ. Am.* de troisième année (*étudiant*); *Am.* ⁓ *high school* (*sorte d'*)école *f* secondaire (*moyennes classes*); ⁓ *partner* second associé *m*, associé *m* en second; **2.** cadet(te *f*) *m*; *rang:* subalterne *m*, second associé *m*; *Am.* élève *mf* de troisième année dans un *collège*; F le jeune *m*; *he is my* ⁓ *by four years, he is four years my* ⁓ il est plus jeune que moi de quatre ans; **jun·ior·i·ty** [dʒuːni-'ɔriti] infériorité *f* d'âge; position *f* moins élevée.

ju·ni·per ♀ ['dʒuːnipə] genièvre *m*; *arbuste:* genévrier *m*.

junk¹ ⚓ ['dʒʌŋk] jonque *f*.

junk² [⁓] ⚓ vieux cordages *m/pl.*; ⚓ bœuf *m* salé; 🐟 rossignol *m*, camelote *f*; déchets *m/pl.*; *fig.* bêtises *f/pl.*; *pej.* pacotille *f*; *sl.* came *f*, drogue *f*; ⁓ *heap* dépotoir *m*.

jun·ket ['dʒʌŋkit] **1.** lait *m* caillé; festin *m*, banquet *m*; *Am.* partie *f* de plaisir; voyage *m* d'agrément aux frais de l'État *ou* du gouvernement; **2.** faire bombance; festoyer; F ⁓*ing party* pique-nique *m*.

junk·ie *sl.* ['dʒʌŋki] camé(e *f*) *m*, drogué(e *f*) *m*.

junk·yard ['dʒʌŋkjɑːd] dépotoir *m*.

jun·ta ['dʒʌntə] junte *f*; (*a.* **jun·to** ['⁓tou]) cabale *f*.

ju·rid·i·cal □ [dʒuə'ridikl] juridique, judiciaire.

ju·ris·dic·tion [dʒuəris'dikʃn] juridiction *f*; compétence *f*, ressort *m*;

ju·ris·pru·dence ['⁓pruːdəns] jurisprudence *f*; **'ju·ris·pru·dent** légiste *m*.

ju·rist ['dʒuːrist] juriste *m*; *Am.* avocat *m*.

ju·ror ⚖ ['dʒuːrə] membre *m* du jury.

ju·ry ⚖ ['dʒuːri] jury *m*; jurés *m/pl.*; ⁓**-box** banc *m* du jury; '⁓**-man** membre *m* du jury.

ju·ry-mast ⚓ ['dʒuːrimɑːst] mât *m* de fortune.

just □ [dʒʌst] **1.** *adj.* juste, équitable; légitime; impartial (-aux *m/pl.*); exact; **2.** *adv.* précisément, justement; tout près (de, *by*); tout à fait; seulement; ⁓ *as* au moment où; ⁓ *as ... so ...* de même que ... de même ...; *be* ⁓ (*p.pr.*) être en train de (*inf.*); *have* ⁓ (*p.p.*) venir de (*inf.*); ⁓ *now* actuellement; tout à l'heure; ⁓ *over* (*below*) juste au-dessus (au-dessous) (*de qch., s.th.*); ⁓ *let me see!* faites(-moi) voir!; *it's* ⁓ *splendid!* c'est vraiment magnifique!

jus·tice ['dʒʌstis] justice *f*; *personne:* juge *m*; magistrat *m*; ⁒ *of the Peace* juge *m* de paix; *court of* ⁓ tribunal *m*, cour *f* de justice; *do* ⁓ *to* rendre justice à (*q.*); **'jus·tice·ship** fonctions *f/pl.* de juge; magistrature *f*.

jus·ti·fi·a·bil·i·ty [dʒʌstifaiə'biliti] caractère *m* justifiable; justice *f*; **'jus·ti·fi·a·ble** □ justifiable; légitime.

jus·ti·fi·ca·tion [dʒʌstifi'keiʃn] justification *f*; **jus·ti·fi·ca·to·ry** ['⁓-təri] justificatif (-ive *f*); justificateur (-trice *f*).

jus·ti·fi·er *typ.* ['dʒʌstifaiə] justificateur *m*; **jus·ti·fy** ['⁓fai] justifier (*a. typ. une ligne*); *typ.* parangonner (*les caractères*).

just·ly ['dʒʌstli] avec justice *ou* justesse.

just·ness ['dʒʌstnis] justice *f* (*d'une cause*); justesse *f* (*d'une observation*).

jut [dʒʌt] **1.** (*a.* ⁓*out*) être en *ou* faire saillie; **2.** saillie *f*.

Jute¹ [dʒuːt] Jute *mf*.

jute² ♀, 🌿 [⁓] jute *m*.

ju·ve·nes·cence [dʒuːvi'nesns] adolescence *f*; jeunesse *f*; **ju·ve'nes·cent** adolescent; **ju·ve·nile** ['⁓nail] **1.** juvénile; de (la) jeunesse; pour enfants; ♀ *Court* tribunal *m* pour enfants; ~ *delinquent* mineur(e *f*) *m* délinquant(e); *théâ.* ~ *lead* jeune premier *m*; 2. jeune *mf*; ~*s pl.* livres *m/pl.* pour enfants *ou* pour la jeunesse; **ju·ve·nil·i·ty** [~'niliti] jeunesse *f*, juvénilité *f*.

jux·ta·pose [dʒʌkstə'pouz] juxtaposer; **jux·ta·po·si·tion** [~pə'ziʃən] juxtaposition *f*.

K

K, k [kei] K *m*, k *m*.

Kaf·(f)ir ['kæfə] Cafre *mf*.

kale [keil] chou (*pl.* -x) *m* (frisé); *Am. sl.* argent *m*, pognon *m*; *Scotch* ~ chou *m* rouge.

ka·lei·do·scope *opt.* [kə'leidəskoup] kaléidoscope *m*.

kan·ga·roo *zo.* [kæŋgə'ru:] kangourou *m*.

ka·o·lin *min.* ['keiəlin] kaolin *m*.

ka·put *sl.* [kə'put] fichu, foutu.

keck [kek] avoir des haut-le-cœur; ~ *at* F rejeter avec dégoût.

kedge ⚓ [kedʒ] 1. ancre *f* de touée; ancre *f* à jet; 2. haler sur une ancre à jet.

keel ⚓ [ki:l] 1. quille *f*; *on an even* ~ sans différence de calaison; *fig.* symétrique(ment); 2. ~ *over* chavirer; F s'évanouir; '**keel·age** ⚓ droits *m/pl.* de mouillage; '**keeled** ⚓ caréné; **keel·haul** ⚓ ['~hɔ:l] † donner la grande cale à; **keel·son** ⚓ ['kelsn] carlingue *f*.

keen □ [ki:n] aiguisé; perçant (*froid, œil, vent, etc.*); vif (vive *f*) (*froid, plaisir, vent, etc.*); mordant (*satire*); zélé, ardent; vorace (*appétit*); *be* ~ *on hunting* être chasseur enthousiaste, avoir la passion de la chasse; ~**-edged** ['~edʒd] tranchant, bien affilé; '**keen·ness** acuité *f*, finesse *f*; *froid*: âpreté *f*; *fig.* zèle *m*, ardeur *f*.

keep [ki:p] 1. *su.* frais *m/pl.* de subsistance; nourriture *f*; *hist.* donjon *m*, réduit *m*; F surt. *Am.* for ~*s* pour de bon; 2. [*irr.*] *v/t. usu.* tenir (*p.ex. boutique, comptes, école, journal, promesse, scène, a. devant adj.*); garder (*sp. but, lit, provisions, qch. pour q.*); avoir (*une auto*); (*a.* ~ *up*) maintenir (*la discipline, l'ordre*); contenir; conserver (*sa sveltesse etc.*); préserver (*de, from*); retenir (*q. à dîner, en prison; l'attention*); suivre (*une règle*); célébrer, observer (*une fête*); subvenir aux besoins de; cacher (*qch. à q., s.th. from s.o.*); ~ *s.o. company* tenir compagnie à q.; ~ *company with* sortir avec; ~ *silence*

garder le silence; ~ *one's temper* se contenir; ~ *time* être exact (*montre*); ♩ suivre la mesure; ⚔ être au pas; ~ *watch* monter la garde, veiller; ~ *s.o. waiting* faire attendre q.; ~ *away* tenir éloigné; ~ *down* empêcher de monter; réprimer; maintenir (*les prix*) bas; ~ *s.o. from* (*gér.*) empêcher q. de (*inf.*); préserver q. de; ~ *in* retenir; contenir (*la colère*); consigner, mettre en retenue (*un élève*); entretenir (*un feu*); ~ *s.o. in money* fournir de l'argent à q.; ~ *in view* ne pas perdre de vue; ~ *off* éloigner; ~ *on* garder; ~ *out* empêcher d'entrer; se garantir de (*le froid, la pluie*); ~ *up* soutenir; tenir haut; maintenir (*un prix etc.*); entretenir (*la correspondance*); sauver (*les apparences*); 3. [*irr.*] *v/i.* rester, se tenir; se conserver (*fruit etc.*); continuer; F ne rien perdre (*pour attendre*); ~ *clear of* éviter, rester à distance de; ~ *doing* ne pas cesser de faire, continuer de faire; ~ *away* se tenir éloigné *ou* à l'écart; ~ *from* s'abstenir de; ~ *in with* rester bien avec, cultiver; ~ *off* se tenir éloigné; ~ *on* (*gér.*) continuer de (*inf.*), s'obstiner à (*inf.*); ~ *to* s'en tenir à; observer; suivre; ~ *up* se maintenir; ~ *up with* aller de pair avec; *fig.* se maintenir au niveau de.

keep·er ['ki:pə] garde *m*, gardien (-ne *f*) *m*, surveillant(e *f*) *m*; *musée:* conservateur *m*; *troupeaux:* gardeur (-euse *f*) *m*; '**keep·ing** observation *f*; célébration *f*; garde *f*; *be in* (*out of*) ~ *with* (ne pas) être en accord avec; **keep·sake** ['~seik] souvenir *m* (*cadeau etc.*).

keg [keg] *harengs:* caque *f*; *alcool:* barillet *m*.

kel·son ⚓ ['kelsn] *see* keelson.

ken [ken] connaissance *f*, -s *f/pl.*

ken·nel[1] ['kenl] ruisseau *m* (*de rue*).

ken·nel[2] [~] 1. niche *f* (*de chien*); *chien de chasse:* chenil *m*; *chasse:* la meute *f*; 2. *fig.* enfermer.

kept [kept] *prét. et p.p.* de *keep* 2.

kerb(·stone) ['kəːb(stoun)] *see* **curb (-stone).**

ker·chief ['kəːtʃif] fanchon *f*, mouchoir *m* de tête; fichu *m*.

kerf [kəːf] trait *m ou* voie *f* de scie; bout *m* coupé (*d'un arbre abattu*).

ker·nel ['kəːnl] noisette *etc.*: amande *f*; *céréales:* grain *m*; *fig.* fond *m*, essentiel *m*.

ker·o·sene ['kerəsiːn] kérosène *m*, pétrole *m* lampant.

kes·trel *orn.* ['kestrəl] émouchet *m*.

ketch·up ['ketʃəp] sauce *f* tomate très relevée.

ket·tle ['ketl] bouilloire *f*; '**~-drum** ♩ timbale *f*; *Am.* F thé *m ou* réception *f* sans cérémonie.

key [kiː] **1.** clé *f*, clef *f* (*a. fig.*); ⊕ clavette *f*, coin *m*, cale *f*; *machine à écrire, piano:* touche *f*; *flûte etc.:* clef *f*; ♯ fiche *f*; ♩ ton *m* (*a. fig.*); *école:* corrigé *m*; *pendule etc.:* remontoir *m*; ♩~s *pl.* instruments *m/pl.* à clavier ou à touches; ~ *industry* industrie *f* clef; ~ *money* pas *m* de porte; ~ *punch* poinçonneuse *f*; ♩ ~ *signature* armature *f*; *fig.* ~ *saw* scie *f* à guichet; **2.** claveter; coincer; adenter (*une planche*); ♩ accorder; ~ *up* ↑ hausser; *fig.* stimuler; *be* ~*ed up* être tendu; '**~-bit** panneton *m* de clef; '**~-board** clavier *m*; porte-clefs *m/inv.*; '**~-bu·gle** ♩ bugle *m*; '**~-hole** trou *m* de serrure; '**~-less** sans clef; ~ *watch* montre *f* à remontoir; '**~-man** pivot *m*; '**~-note** tonique *f*; *fig.* note *f* dominante; '**~-stone** clef *f* de voûte.

khak·i ['kɑːki] *tex., a. couleur:* kaki *m* (*a. adj./inv.*).

kib·butz [ki'buts], *pl.* **-but·zim** [ˌ'butsim] kibboutz (*pl.* kibboutzim) *m*.

kibe [kaib] gerçure *f*.

kib·itz·er *Am.* F ['kibitsə] je sais tout *m* (*qui donne des conseils à des joueurs aux cartes sans qu'on les lui demande*).

ki·bosh *sl.* ['kaibɔʃ] bêtises *f/pl.*; *put the* ~ *on* faire son affaire à (*q.*); bousiller (*qch.*).

kick [kik] **1.** coup *m* de pied; *arme à feu:* recul *m*, réaction *f*; F vigueur *f*, énergie *f*; résistance *f*; *surt. Am.* F plaintes *f/pl.*, protestation *f*; *foot. see* ~*er*; F *do s.th. for* ~*s* faire qch. pour le plaisir *ou* pour s'amuser; F *get a* ~ *out of* éprouver du plaisir à; *sl. it's got a* ~ *to it* ça vous remonte; **2.** *v/t.* donner des coups *ou* un coup de pied à; F congédier (*q.*); F ~ *s.o. around* maltraiter q.; *sl.* ~ *the bucket* casser sa pipe (= *mourir*); ~ *s.o. downstairs* faire dégringoler l'escalier à q.; F ~ *one's heels* faire le pied de grue (= *attendre*); F ~ *out* ficher à la porte; *sl.* ~ *up a row* faire du chahut; *fig.* faire un scandale; *v/i.* donner un coup de pied; reculer (*arme à feu*); ruer (*animal*); rechigner (*à against, at*); *sl.* rouspéter; F ~ *around ou about* traîner (*quelque part*); *Am. sl.* ~ *in with* contribuer (*de l'argent*); '**kick-back** *surt. Am.* F réaction *f* violente; *Am. sl.* ristourne *f*; '**kick·er** cheval *m* qui rue; *sp.* joueur *m*; *Am. sl.* rouspéteur (-euse *f*) *m*; '**kick-'off** *foot.* coup *m* d'envoi; commencement *m*; **kick-shaw** ['kikʃɔː] bagatelle *f*; *cuis.* friandise *f*; '**kick-'up** *sl.* boucan *m*.

kid [kid] **1.** chevreau (-ette *f*) *m*; (peau *f* de) chevreau *m*; *sl.* gosse *mf*; ~ *glove* gant *m* de chevreau; gant *m* glacé; **2.** mettre bas (*v/t. un chevreau*); *v/i. sl.* plaisanter, taquiner; *v/t.* en conter à; tromper; '**kid·dy** F gosse *m/f*, petit(e *f*) *m*.

kid·nap ['kidnæp] kidnapper, enlever (*surt. un enfant*); ✗, ⚓ prendre par la presse; enlever; '**kid·nap·(p)er** ravisseur (-euse *f*) *m* (*d'enfant*), kidnappeur *m*.

kid·ney ['kidni] *anat.* rein *m*; *cuis.* rognon *m*; F genre *m*; ~ *bean* ♧ haricot *m* nain; ✺ ~ *machine* rein *m* artificiel.

kike *Am. sl. péj.* [kaik] juif *m*.

kill [kil] tuer, faire mourir; abattre (*une bête*); amortir (*un son*); *fig.* supprimer; *parl.* couler (*un projet de loi*); ~ *off* exterminer; ~ *time* tuer le temps; '**kill·er** tueur (-euse *f*) *m*; meurtrier (-ère *f*) *m*; '**kill·ing 1.** meurtrier (-ère *f*); écrasant (*travail etc.*); F tordant; **2.** *Am.* F opération *f* lucrative; succès *m* (*financier*); '**kill-joy** rabat-joie *m/inv.*

kiln [kiln] four *m*; séchoir *m*, étuve *f*; meule *f* (*de charbon de bois*); '**~-dry** sécher (*qch.*) au four *etc.*

kil·o·cy·cle *phys.* ['kilosaikl] kilocycle *m*; **kil·o·gram(me)** ['~əɡræm] kilogramme *m*; F kilo *m*; **kil·o·me·ter, kil·o·me·tre** ['~miːtə] kilomètre *m*.

kilt [kilt] **1.** *écoss.* kilt *m* (*jupe courte*

et plissée); **2.** plisser; retrousser (*ses jupes*).

kin [kin] **1.** parents *m/pl.*; *the next of ~* le parent le plus proche; F la famille; **2.** apparenté (avec, *to*).

kind [kaind] **1.** □ bon(ne *f*) (pour, *to*); aimable (à, *of*); **2.** espèce *f*; sorte *f*; genre *m*; nature *f*; *people of all ~s* monde *m* de tous les genres; des gens de toutes sortes; *different in ~* qui diffère(nt) en nature; *pay in ~* payer en nature; *fig.* payer de la même monnaie; *F I ~ of expected it* je m'en doutais presque.

kin·der·gar·ten ['kindəgɑːtn] jardin *m* d'enfants; école *f* maternelle; ~ *teacher* jardinière *f* d'enfants; institutrice *f* d'école maternelle.

kind-heart·ed ['kaind'hɑːtid] bienveillant, bon(ne *f*).

kin·dle ['kindl] (s')allumer; (s')enflammer; *fig.* susciter.

kind·li·ness ['kaindlinis] bonté *f*, bienveillance *f*.

kin·dling ['kindliŋ], *a.* ~s *pl.* petit bois *m*; bois *m* d'allumage.

kind·ly ['kaindli] **1.** *adj.* bienveillant, bon(ne *f*); doux (douce *f*) (*climat*); **2.** *adv.* avec bonté; ~ *do s.th.* avoir la bonté de faire qch.

kind·ness ['kaindnis] bonté *f* (pour, *to*); bienveillance *f*; amabilité *f* (envers, *to*).

kin·dred ['kindrid] **1.** analogue; de la même nature; **2.** parenté *f*; *coll.* parents *m/pl.*; affinité *f* (avec, *with*).

ki·net·ic *phys.* [kai'netik] **1.** cinétique; **2.** ~s *pl.* cinétique *f*.

king [kiŋ] roi *m*; *jeu de dames*: dame *f*; ♀'s *English* anglais *m* correct; ♂ ~'s *evil* scrofule *f*; écrouelles *f/pl.*; '**king·craft** art *m* de régner; '**king·cup** ♀ bouton *m* d'or; '**king·dom** royaume *m*; *surt.* ♀, *zo.* règne *m*; '**king·fish·er** martin-pêcheur (*pl.* martins-pêcheurs) *m*; **king·let** ['~lit] roitelet *m*; '**king·like** royal (-aux *m/pl.*), de roi; '**king·li·ness** prestance *f* royale; noblesse *f*; '**king·ly** royal (-aux *m/pl.*), de roi; '**king·post** △ poinçon *m*, aiguille *f*; '**king·ship** royauté *f*; '**king-size** F de taille *etc.* exceptionnelle.

kink [kiŋk] **1.** *corde etc.*: tortillement *m*, nœud *m*; *fil de fer*: faux pli *m*; *tex.* boucle *f*; *fig.* lubie *f*, point *m* faible; F *have a ~* être un peu toqué;

2. (se) nouer, tortiller; '**kink·y** crépu (*cheveux*); F bizarre, excentrique.

kins·folk ['kinzfouk] *pl.* parenté *f*, famille *f*; '**kin·ship** parenté *f*; '**kins·man** ['~zmən] parent *m*; allié *m*; '**kins·wom·an** parente *f*; alliée *f*.

ki·osk [ki'ɔsk] kiosque *m*.

kip F [kip] **1.** roupillon *m* (= *sommeil*); pieu *m* (= *lit*); *have a ~* piquer un roupillon; **2.** coucher; roupiller (*dormir*); ~ *down* se pieuter (= *se coucher*).

kip·per ['kipə] **1.** hareng *m* fumé *ou* doux; *sl.* jeune personne *f*; **2.** saurer, saler et fumer (*des harengs*).

kirk [kəːk] *écoss.* église *f*.

kiss [kis] **1.** baiser *m*; *fig.* frôlement *m*; **2.** (s')embrasser; '**~-proof** indélébile.

kit [kit] seau *m*; ✂, ⚓ petit équipement *m*; ✂ bagage *m*; ⚓ sac *m*; ⊕ trousse(au *m*) *f*; F effets *m/pl.*; '**~-bag** ✂ musette *f*; sac *m* (de voyage); ⊕ trousse *f* d'outils.

kitch·en ['kitʃin] cuisine *f*; '**kitch·en·er** cuisinière *f*; **kitch·en·ette** [~'net] cuisine *f* miniature.

kitch·en...: ~ gar·den (jardin *m*) potager *m*; '**~-maid** fille *f* de cuisine; '**~-range** cuisinière *f* anglaise; '**~-sink** évier *m*.

kite [kait] *orn.* milan *m*; *fig.* vautour *m*; cerf-volant (*pl.* cerfs-volants) *m*; *fig.* ballon *m* d'essai; ✈ *sl.* traite *f* de complaisance; ✂ ~ *balloon* ballon *m* captif. [rents.]

kith [kiθ]: ~ *and kin* amis et pa-}

kit·ten ['kitn] **1.** chaton *m*, petit(e *f*) chat(te *f*) *m*; **2.** *chatte*: mettre bas (*v/t. des petits*); '**kit·ten·ish** coquet(te *f*); enjoué.

kit·tle ['kitl] *fig.* difficile (à manier); ~ *cattle* gens *m/pl.* difficiles à manier.

Klans·man *Am.* ['klænzmən] membre *m* du Ku-Klux-Klan.

klax·on *mot.* ['klæksn] klaxon *m*.

klep·to·ma·ni·a [klepto'meinjə] kleptomanie *f*; **klep·to'ma·ni·ac** [~niæk] kleptomane (*a. su./mf*).

knack [næk] tour *m* de main; F truc *m*; *get the ~ of (gér.*) attraper le chic pour (*inf.*).

knack·er ['nækə] *Brit.* équarrisseur *m*; entrepreneur *m* de démolitions; '**knack·ered** *Brit. sl.* éreinté; '**knack·er·y** *Brit.* abattoir *m* de chevaux.

knack·y ['næki] adroit, habile.

knag [næg] nœud m; **'knag·gy** noueux (-euse f).

knap·sack ['næpsæk] (havre)sac m; ✕ sac m d'ordonnance.

knar [nɑ:] nœud m saillant.

knave [neiv] fripon m; cartes: valet m; **knav·er·y** ['-əri] friponnerie f, fourberie f; **'knav·ish** □ fourbe; **'knav·ish·ness** fourberie f.

knead [ni:d] pétrir (a. ⚙); travailler (la pâte etc.).

knee [ni:] **1.** genou (pl. -x) m (a. ⊕); **2.** pousser du genou; F fatiguer (un pantalon) aux genoux; **'~-cap**, **'~-pan** rotule f; **'~-joint** articulation f du genou; ⊕ rotule f; **kneel** [ni:l] [irr.] s'agenouiller, se mettre à genoux (devant, to); **'kneel·er** personne f à genoux.

knell [nel] glas m.

knelt [nelt] prét. et p.p. de kneel.

knew [nju:] prét. de know 1.

knick·er·bock·ers ['nikəbɔkəz] pl. culotte f (bouffante); **'knick·ers** F pl. culotte f, pantalon m (de femme); see knickerbockers.

knick·knack ['niknæk] babiole f, bibelot m; **~s** pl. afféteries f/pl.

knife [naif] **1.** (pl. knives) couteau m; **2.** poignarder; **'~-bat·tle** rixe f entre gens armés de poignards; **'~-grind·er** repasseur m de couteaux.

knight [nait] **1.** chevalier m; échecs: cavalier m; **2.** créer chevalier; **'knight·age** corps m des chevaliers; **knight er·rant** ['nait'erənt], pl. **knights er·rant** chevalier m errant; **knight·hood** ['-hud] chevalerie f; titre m de chevalier; **'knight·li·ness** caractère m chevaleresque; air m de chevalier; **'knight·ly** chevaleresque, de chevalier.

knit [nit] [irr.] v/t. tricoter; joindre; v/i. se nouer; **~** the brows froncer les sourcils; **'knit·ter** tricoteur (-euse f) m; **'knit·ting 1.** tricot m; action: tricotage m; soudure f (d'os); **2.** à tricoter; **~-needle** aiguille f à tricoter; **'knit·wear** tricot m.

knives [naivz] pl. de knife 1.

knob [nɔb] bosse f; tiroir, porte: bouton m; canne: pomme f; charbon, sucre, etc.: morceau m; **'knob·by** plein de bosses; loupeux (-euse f) (arbre); **'knob·stick** canne f à

pommeau; gourdin m; ✝ F jaune m.

knock [nɔk] **1.** coup m, heurt m, choc m; **2.** v/i. frapper; taper (sur, at); mot. cogner, taper; F se heurter (à, against); **~** off sl. cesser le travail; **~** under se rendre; v/t. frapper, cogner, heurter; Am. sl. critiquer; **~** down renverser, abattre; vente aux enchères: adjuger; ⊕ démonter; be ~ed down être renversé par une auto; **~** off faire tomber de; rabattre (qch. du prix); F voler, chiper; box. **~** out knockouter; F endormir; **~** up faire sauter (en l'air); construire à la hâte; réveiller; fig. éreinter, épuiser; **'~-a·bout 1.** violent; vagabond; de tous les genres (habits); théâ. de bateleur, de clown; **2.** Am. rixe m; **'~-down** de réclame, minimum (prix); **'knock·er** frappeur (-euse f) m; marteau m (de porte); Am. sl. critique m impitoyable; Brit. sl. **~s** pl. nénés f/pl. (= seins); **'knock·kneed** cagneux (-euse f); panard (cheval); **'knock·out** box. (a. **~** blow) knock-out m; sl. chose f ou personne f épatante.

knoll¹ [noul] tertre m, butte f.

knoll² [~] ✝ sonner; tinter.

knot [nɔt] **1.** nœud m (a. fig., a. ⚓); gens: groupe m; cheveux: chignon m; sailor's **~** nœud m régate; F be tied up in **~s** ne savoir plus que faire ou dire; **2.** (se) nouer; v/t. froncer (les sourcils); **'~-hole** trou m (provenant d'un nœud d'arbre); **'knot·ti·ness** nodosité f; bois: caractère m noueux; fig. complexité f; **'knot·ty** plein de nœuds; noueux (-euse f) (bois); fig. épineux (-euse f); **'knot·work** couture: macramé m.

knout [naut] **1.** knout m; **2.** knouter.

know [nou] **1.** [irr.] savoir (un fait); connaître (q., un endroit); reconnaître; distinguer (de, d'avec from); **~** French connaître ou parler le français; come to **~** apprendre; **2.** F be in the **~** être au courant (de l'affaire); être dans le secret; **know·a·ble** ['nouəbl] (re)connaissable; **'know-all 1.** omniscient; **2.** je sais tout m; **'know-how** savoir-faire m/inv.; connaissances f/pl. techniques; **'know·ing 1.** □ instruit; intelligent; habile; rusé, malin (-igne f); F chic inv. en genre; **2.** connaissance f, compréhension f; **knowl·edge**

['nɔlidʒ] connaissance *f*; savoir *m*, connaissances *f/pl.*; *to my* ~ autant que je sache; à mon vu et su; **known** [noun] *p.p. de know* 1; *come to be* ~ se répandre (*bruit*); se faire connaître; se savoir; *make* ~ faire connaître; signaler.

knuck·le ['nʌkl] 1. (*a.* ~-*bone*) articulation *f* du doigt; *veau*: jarret *m*; 2. ~ *down* (*ou* under) se soumettre; céder; '~-**dust·er** coup-de-poing (*pl.* coups-de-poing) *m* américain.

knur [nə:] nœud *m*.

knut F [(k)nʌt] gommeux *m*.

ko·dak *phot.* ['koudæk] 1. kodak *m*; 2. photographier avec un kodak.

Ko·ran [kɔ'rɑ:n] Koran *m*, Coran *m*.

ko·tow ['kou'tau] 1. prosternation *f* (à la chinoise); 2. saluer à la chinoise; *fig.* faire des courbettes (devant, *to*).

krem·lin ['kremlin] Kremlin *m*.

ku·dos *co.* ['kju:dɔs] gloriole *f*.

Ku-Klux-Klan *Am.* ['kju:'klʌks-'klæn] *association secrète de l'Amérique du Nord, hostile aux Noirs.*

L

L, l [el] L *m*, l *m*.

lab F [læb] laboratoire *m*.

la·bel ['leibl] **1.** étiquette *f*; *fig.* désignation *f*, titre *m*; ⚓ queue *f*; △ larmier *m*; **2.** étiqueter; adresser; attacher une étiquette à; ✝ marquer le prix de; *fig.* qualifier (du nom de, *as*). [*m/pl.*); 2. labiale *f*.\

la·bi·al ['leibjəl] **1.** labial (-aux)\

lab·o·ra·to·ry [lə'bɔrətəri] laboratoire *m*; ~ *assistant* préparateur (-trice *f*) *m*.

la·bo·ri·ous □ [lə'bɔːriəs] laborieux (-euse *f*); pénible; travailleur (-euse *f*).

la·bo(u)r ['leibə] **1.** travail (*pl.* -aux) *m*, peine *f*, labeur *m*; main-d'œuvre (*pl.* mains-d'œuvre) *f*, travailleurs *m/pl.*; *pol.* les travaillistes *m/pl.*; ✻ couches *f/pl.*; *Ministry of* ♀ Ministère *m* du Travail; *hard* ~ travail *m* forcé; travaux *m/pl.* forcés; **2.** travailliste (*parti*); du travail; ♀ *Day* fête *f* du travail; ~ *dispute* conflit *m* social *ou* du travail; ~ *Exchange* Bourse *f* du Travail; ~ *force* les employés *m/pl.*, le personnel *m*; ♀ *Office* bureau *m* de placement; *surt. Am.* ~ *union* syndicat *m* ouvrier; **3.** *v/i.* travailler; peiner (*a. fig.*); ~ *under* être courbé sous; avoir à lutter contre; ~ *under a delusion* être victime d'une illusion; *v/t.* travailler; '**la·bo(u)r·age** paie *f*; '**la·bo(u)r·cre·a·tion** création *f* des emplois; '**la·bo(u)red** travaillé (*style*); pénible (*respiration*); '**la·bo(u)r·er** travailleur *m*; manœuvre *m*; *heavy manual* ~ travailleur *m* de force; '**la·bo(u)r·ing** ouvrier (*-ère f*); haletant (*poitrine*); palpitant (*cœur*); ~ *force* effectif *m* de la main-d'œuvre; **la·bo(u)r·ist** ['~rist], **la·bo(u)r·ite** ['~rait] membre *m* du parti travailliste.

la·bur·num ♀ [lə'bəːnəm] cytise *m*.

lab·y·rinth ['læbərinθ] labyrinthe *m*, dédale *m*; **lab·y·rin·thi·an** [~'rin-θiən], *usu.* **lab·y·rin·thine** [~'rin-θain] labyrinthique.

lac [læk] (gomme *f*) laque *f*; (*souv.* ~ *of rupees*) lack *m*; 100 000 de roupies.

lace [leis] **1.** lacet *m*; cordon *m*; *tex.* dentelle *f*; **2.** lacer (*un soulier*); entrelacer (de, *avec with*); arroser (*une boisson*) (à, *with*); garnir de dentelle(s); *fig.* (*a.* ~ *into s.o.*) rosser, battre; '~-'**pil·low** coussin(et) *m* à dentelle.

lac·er·ate 1. ['læsəreit] lacérer; *fig.* déchirer; **2.** ['~rit] lacéré; **lac·er'a·tion** lacération *f*; déchirement *m* (*a. fig.*); ✻ déchirure *f*.

lach·ry·mal *anat.* ['lækriml] lacrymal (-aux *m/pl.*); **lach·ry·ma·to·ry** ['~mətəri] lacrymatoire; lacrymogène (*gaz*); **lach·ry·mose** ['~mous] larmoyant.

lack [læk] **1.** *su.* manque *m*, défaut *m*, absence *f*; **2.** *v/t.* manquer de; ne pas avoir; *he* ~*s money* il n'a pas d'argent, l'argent lui fait défaut; *v/i.* be ~*ing* manquer, faire défaut; *be* ~*ing in* ... manquer de ...

lack·a·dai·si·cal □ [lækə'deizikl] apathique; affecté.

lack·ey ['læki] **1.** laquais *m*; **2.** *fig.* faire le plat valet auprès de (*q.*).

lack...: '~**land** sans terre (*a. su./m/ inv.*); '~**lus·ter**, '~**lus·tre** terne.

la·con·ic [lə'kɔnik] (~*ally*) laconique, bref (brève *f*).

lac·quer ['lækə] **1.** vernis *m* du Japon; laque *m*; **2.** laquer, F vernir.

lac·ta·tion [læk'teiʃn] lactation *f*.

lac·te·al ['læktiəl] lacté; laiteux (-euse *f*) (*suc*).

la·cu·na [lə'kjuːnə] lacune *f*, hiatus *m*.

lac·y ['leisi] de dentelle; fin comme de la dentelle.

lad [læd] garçon *m*; jeune homme *m*.

lad·der ['lædə] **1.** échelle *f* (*a. fig.*, *a.* ⚓); *bas:* maille *f* qui file, éraillure *f*; **2.** se démailler; '~**proof** indémaillable (*bas etc.*).

lade [leid] [*irr.*] charger (de, *with*); puiser de l'eau (à, *from*); '**lad·en** chargé.

lad·ing ['leidiŋ] chargement *m*; embarquement *m*.

la·dle ['leidl] **1.** cuiller *f* à pot; poche *f* (*a. métall.*); ⊕ puisoir *m*; **2.** servir (avec une louche); *métall.* couler; ⊕ (*a. ⁓ out*) pucher.

la·dy ['leidi] dame *f*; *titre*: Lady, F milady, madame *f* de ...; *my ⁓* madame; *ladies!* mesdames!; *young ⁓* demoiselle *f*; jeune dame *f* (*mariée*); ♀ *Day* (fête *f* de) l'Annonciation *f* (*le 25 mars*); *⁓* doctor femme *f* docteur, doctoresse *f*; *⁓'s maid* femme *f* de chambre; *⁓'s* (*ou ladies'*) *man* galant *m*; '*⁓-bird* coccinelle *f*, F bête *f* à bon Dieu; '*⁓-kill·er* bourreau *m* des cœurs; don Juan *m*; '*⁓-like* distingué; *péj.* efféminé; '*⁓-love* bien-aimée *f*; '*⁓-ship*: *her ⁓*, *Your* ♀ madame (la comtesse *etc.*).

lag¹ [læg] traîner; (*a. ⁓ behind*) rester en arrière; retard *m*.

lag² *sl.* [⁓] **1.** forçat *m*; **2.** condamner aux travaux forcés.

lag³ [⁓] garnir d'un calorifuge.

la·ger (**beer**) ['lɑːgə (biə)] bière *f* blonde.

lag·gard ['lægəd] **1.** lent, paresseux (-euse *f*); **2.** traînard *m*.

la·goon [lə'guːn] atoll: lagon *m*; *Adriatique*: lagune *f*.

la·ic ['leiik] **1.** *a.* 'la·i·cal □ laïque; **2.** laïque *mf*; **la·i·cize** ['leiisaiz] laïciser.

laid [leid] *prét. et p.p. de lay⁴* 2; *⁓ up* alité, au lit; *⁓ paper* papier *m* vergé.

lain [lein] *p.p de lie²* 1.

lair [lɛə] tanière *f*, repaire *m* (*d'une bête fauve*).

laird *écoss.* [lɛəd] propriétaire *m* foncier; F châtelain *m*.

la·i·ty ['leiiti] laïques *m/pl.*

lake¹ [leik] lac *m*; *ornamental ⁓* bassin *m*.

lake² [⁓] *peint.* laque *f*.

lake-dwel·lings ['leikdweliŋz] *pl.* habitations *f* lacustres.

lam *sl.* [læm] *v/t.* (*a. ⁓ into*) rosser, étriller; *v/i.* s'évader, s'enfuir.

lamb [læm] **1.** agneau *m*; *⁓ chop* côtelette *f* d'agneau; **2.** agneler.

lam·baste *sl.* [læm'beist] donner une râclée à.

lam·bent ['læmbənt] blafard (*yeux*, *étoile*); chatoyant (*style*, *esprit*).

lamb·kin ['læmkin] agnelet *m*; '**lamb·like** doux (douce *f*) comme un agneau; '**lamb·skin** peau *f* d'a-

gneau; *fourrure*: agnelin *m*; '**lambs-wool** laine *f* d'agneau.

lame [leim] **1.** □ boiteux (-euse *f*); estropié; *fig.* faible, piètre (*excuse etc.*); *⁓ duck fig.* faible *mf*; ♱ failli *m*; *Am. ⁓* député *m* non réélu; **2.** rendre boiteux (-euse *f*); estropier; '**lame-ness** boitement *m*; *cheval*: boiterie *f*; *fig.* faiblesse *f*.

la·ment [lə'mənt] **1.** lamentation *f*; **2.** se lamenter (sur, *for*), pleurer (*q.*, *for s.o.*); **lam·en·ta·ble** □ ['læməntəbl] lamentable, déplorable; **lam-en·ta·tion** lamentation *f*.

lam·i·na ['læminə], *pl.* **-nae** ['⁓niː] lam(ell)e *f*; ⚡ feuillet *m*; ♀ limbe *m*; '**lam·i·nar** laminaire; **lam·i·nate** ['⁓nit], **lam·i·nat·ed** ['⁓neitid] à feuilles; contre-plaqué (*bois*).

lamp [læmp] lampe *f*; *mot.* lanterne *f*; *head ⁓* phare *m*; '**⁓-chim·ney** verre *m* de lampe; '**⁓-light** lumière *f* de la (*ou* d'une) lampe; '**⁓-light·er** allumeur *m* de réverbères, lampiste *m*.

lam·poon [læm'puːn] **1.** satire *f*, libelle *m*, brocard *m*; **2.** lancer des libelles *etc.* contre; chansonner (*q.*); **lam'poon·er**, **lam'poon·ist** libelliste *m*, satiriste *m*.

lamp-post ['læmppoust] (poteau *m* de) réverbère *m*.

lam·prey *icht.* ['læmpri] lamproie *f*.

lamp·shade ['læmpʃeid] abat-jour *m/inv.*

lance [lɑːns] **1.** lance *f*; ⚔ bistouri *m*; *free ⁓* soldat *m* mercenaire; *parl.* politique *m* indépendant; *journ.* journaliste *m* indépendant; *couch a ⁓* mettre une lance en arrêt; **2.** percer (*a. ⚔*); '**⁓-'cor·po·ral** ⚔ caporal *m*; **lan·ce·o·late** *surt.* ♀ ['lænsialit] lancéolé; **lanc·er** ['lɑːnsə] ⚔ lancier *m*; *⁓s pl. danse anglaise*: lanciers *m/pl.*

lan·cet ['lɑːnsit] bistouri *m*, lancette *f*; *⁓ arch* △ arc *m* à lancette.

land [lænd] **1.** terre *f*; sol *m*; terrain *m*; pays *m*; propriété *f* foncière; *⁓s pl.* terres *f/pl.*, terrains *m/pl.*; *⁓ reclamation* mise *f* en valeur (*des marais*); défrichement *m* (*d'un terrain*); *⁓ reform* réforme *f* agraire; *⁓ register* cadastre *m*; *fig. see how the ⁓ lies* prendre le vent, tâter le terrain; **2.** *v/t.* mettre à terre; ⚓ débarquer (*a. v/t.*); ✈ atterrir (*a. v/i.*); F porter (*un coup*); F remporter (*un* *prix*); amener à terre (*un poisson*); '**~-a·gent** intendant *m* (*d'un domaine*); courtier *m* en immeubles; '**land·ed** foncier (-ère *f*) (*propriété*); terrien(ne *f*) (*personne*).

land...: '**~·fall** ⚓ atterrissage *m*; '**~·forc·es** *pl.* armée *f* de terre; '**~·grab·ber** accapareur *m* de terre; '**~·grave** landgrave *m*; '**~·hold·er** propriétaire *m* foncier.

land·ing ['lændiŋ] débarquement *m*; ✕, ⚓ descente *f*; ✈ atterrissage *m*; amerrissage *m*; ✈ ~ *gear* train *m* d'atterrissage; ~ *ground* terrain *m* d'atterrissage; ✈ ~ *run* distance *f* d'atterrissage; '**~·net** épuisette *f*; '**~·stage** débarcadère *m*, embarcadère *m*.

land...: '**~·la·dy** propriétaire *f*; *pension etc.*: logeuse *f*; aubergiste *f*, F patronne *f*; '**~·locked** entouré de terre; intérieur (*lac etc.*); '**~·lop·er** vagabond *m*; '**~·lord** propriétaire *m*; *pension etc.*: logeur *m*; aubergiste *m*, F patron *m*; '**~·lord·ism** landlordisme *m*; '**~·lub·ber** ⚓ *péj.* marin *m* d'eau douce; terrien *m*; '**~·mark** *surt.* ⚓ indice *m*; point *m* coté (*sur une carte*); borne *f* limite; *fig.* point *m* de repère; *fig.* événement *m* marquant; '**~·own·er** propriétaire *mf* foncier (-ère *f*); **~·scape** ['lænskeip] paysage *m*; ~ *architecture ou design* architecture *f* de paysage; ~ *gardener* jardinier *m* paysagiste; ~ *gardening* jardinage *m* paysagiste; '**~·slide** éboulement *m* (de terrain); *fig.* catastrophe *f*; *pol.* débâcle *f*, *Am.* victoire *f* écrasante; '**~·slip** éboulement *m* (de terrain); **~s·man** ⚓ ['~zmən] terrien *m*; '**~·sur·vey·or** arpenteur *m*; '**~·tax** impôt *m* foncier; '**~·ward** ['~wəd] vers la terre; du côté de la terre.

lane [lein] chemin *m* (vicinal); *ville*: ruelle *f*, passage *m*; ⚓ route *f* de navigation; *mot.* voie *f*.

lang syne *écoss.* ['læŋ'sain] **1.** jadis; **2.** le temps *m* jadis; les jours *m/pl.* d'autrefois.

lan·guage ['læŋgwidʒ] langue *f*; langage *m*; ~ *laboratory* laboratoire *m* de langues; *bad* ~ langage *m* grossier; *strong* ~ langage *m* violent; injures *f/pl.*

lan·guid □ ['læŋgwid] languissant, langoureux (-euse *f*); mou (mol *devant une voyelle ou un h muet*; molle

f); faible; '**lan·guid·ness** langueur *f*, faiblesse *f*.

lan·guish ['læŋgwiʃ] languir (après, pour *for*); dépérir; ⚕ s'étioler; ✝ traîner (*affaires*); '**lan·guish·ing** □ languissant, langoureux (-euse *f*); ✝ faible.

lan·guor ['læŋgə] langueur *f*; '**lan·guor·ous** langoureux (-euse *f*).

lank □ [læŋk] maigre; sec (sèche *f*); efflanqué (*personne*, *a.* bête); plat (*cheveux*); '**lank·y** □ grand et maigre.

lans·que·net ✕ ['lænskinet] lansquenet *m* (*a. cartes*).

lan·tern ['læntən] lanterne *f*; ⚓ fanal *m*; △ lanterne (au *m*) *f*; *dark* ~ lanterne *f* sourde; '**~·jawed** aux joues creuses; '**~·slide** (diapositive *f* de) projection *f*; ~ *lecture* conférence *f* avec projections.

lan·yard ⚓ ['lænjəd] aiguillette *f*.

lap¹ [læp] **1.** *su. cost.* pan *m*; genoux *m/pl.*; ⊕ recouvrement *m*; *corde etc.*: tour *m*; *sp.* tour *m*, circuit *m*; ⚡ guipage *m*; *sp.* ~ *of hono(u)r* tour *m* d'honneur; **2.** *v/t.* enrouler; entourer, envelopper (q. de qch. *s.o. about with s.th.*, *s.th. round s.o.*); ⊕ enchevaucher (*des planches*); ⚡ guiper; *v/i.* (*usu.* ~ *over*) dépasser, chevaucher.

lap² [~] **1.** gorgée *f*; coup *m* de langue; *vagues*: clapotis *m*; **2.** laper; *fig.* avaler; clapoter (*vagues*).

lap-dog ['læpdɔg] chien *m* de manchon.

la·pel *cost.* [lə'pel] revers *m*.

lap·i·dar·y ['læpidəri] lapidaire (*a. su./m.*).

lap·pet ['læpit] *cost.* pan *m*; revers *m*; *oreille*: lobe *m*.

lapse [læps] **1.** erreur *f*; faux pas *m*; laps *m* (de temps); délai *m* (*de temps*); défaillance *f* (*de la mémoire*); ⚖ déchéance *f*; *eccl.* apostasie *f*; chute *f*; **2.** déchoir; *au sens moral*: tomber (dans, *into*); manquer à ses devoirs; ✝ cesser d'être en vigueur; *fig.* rentrer (dans le silence, *into silence*); ⚖ tomber en désuétude; s'abroger (*loi*).

lap·wing *orn.* ['læpwiŋ] vanneau *m*.

lar·ce·ny ⚖ ['lɑːsni] larcin *m*, vol *m* insignifiant; *grand* ~ vol *m*; *petty* ~ vol *m* simple.

larch ♣ [lɑːtʃ] mélèze *m*.

lard [lɑːd] **1.** saindoux *m*, graisse *f* de porc; **2.** larder (de, *with*) (*a.*

fig.); **'lard·er** garde-manger *m/inv.*;
'lard·ing-nee·dle, **'lard·ing-pin**
lardoire *f*; **'lard·y** lardeux (-euse *f*).
large □ [lɑːdʒ] grand; gros(se *f*);
fort; nombreux (-euse *f*); large;
~ *farmer* gros fermier *m*; *at* ~ en
liberté, libre; en général; en détail;
talk at ~ parler au hasard; parler
longuement (sur qch.); *in* ~ en
grand; **'large·ly** en grande partie;
pour la plupart; pour une grande
part; **'large·ness** grandeur *f*;
grosseur *f*; *fig.* largeur *f*; **'large-**
'mind·ed à l'esprit large; tolérant;
'large-'scale de grande envergure;
'large-'sized de grandes dimensions.
lar·gess(e) *poét.* ['lɑːdʒes] largesse *f*.
lark[1] *orn.* [lɑːk] alouette *f*.
lark[2] [~] **1.** farce *f*, blaque *f*; **2.** rigoler, faire des farces; **lark·some**
['~səm] *see* larky.
lark·spur ♀ ['lɑːkspəː] pied *m*
d'alouette.
lark·y F ['lɑːki] espiègle; foli-
chon(ne *f*).
lar·va *zo.* ['lɑːvə], *pl.* -**vae** ['~viː]
larve *f*; **lar·val** ['~vl] larvaire; ✶
latent.
lar·ynx ['lærɪŋks] larynx *m*.
las·civ·i·ous □ [ləˈsɪvɪəs] lascif
(-ive *f*).
la·ser ['leizə] laser *m*; ~ *beam* rayon *m*
laser.
lash [læʃ] **1.** coup *m* de fouet; lanière
f; *fig.* supplice *m* du fouet; *œil:* cil
m; **2.** fouailler; cingler (*a. pluie*);
fouetter; *fig.* flageller, cingler; attacher, lier (à, *to*); ⚓ amarrer; ~ *out*
ruer (*cheval*); *fig.* se livrer (à, *into*);
~ *out at* lâcher un coup à.
lass [læs] jeune fille *f*; **las·sie** ['~i]
fillette *f*.
las·si·tude ['læsitjuːd] lassitude *f*.
last[1] [lɑːst] **1.** *adj.* dernier (-ère *f*);
~ *but one* avant-dernier (-ère *f*);
~ *night* hier soir; la nuit dernière;
the ~ *two* les deux derniers (-ères *f*);
2. *su.* dernier (-ère *f*) *m*; bout *m*;
fin *f* (= *mort*); *my* ~ ma dernière
lettre; *mon dernier m*, ma dernière
f (*enfant*); *at* ~ enfin; à la fin; *at long*
~ enfin; à la fin (des fins); *breathe*
one's ~ rendre le dernier soupir;
3. *adv.* la dernière fois; le (la)
dernier (-ère *f*); ~, *but not least* et
mieux encore ..., le dernier, mais
non le moindre.

last[2] [~] durer, se maintenir; (*a.*
~ *out*) aller (*comestibles etc.*); faire
(*robe etc.*); soutenir (*une allure*).
last[3] [~] forme *f* (*à chaussures*).
last[4] ✝ [~] *mesure:* last(e) *m*.
last-ditch [lɑːstˈdɪtʃ] ultime, désespéré (*efforts etc.*); **last-ditch·er**
jusqu'auboutiste *mf*.
last·ing ['lɑːstɪŋ] **1.** □ durable; résistant; **2.** *tex.* lasting *m*; **'last·ing-**
ness durabilité *f*, permanence *f*.
last·ly ['lɑːstli] en dernier lieu; pour
finir.
last-min·ute [lɑːstˈmɪnɪt] de dernière minute *ou* heure.
latch [lætʃ] **1.** loquet *m*; serrure *f* de
sûreté; *on the* ~ au loquet; fermé
à demi-tour; **2.** fermer au loquet
ou à demi-tour; **'~-key** clef *f* de
maison; passe-partout *m/inv.*
late [leit] en retard; retardé; tard;
tardif (-ive *f*) (*fruit etc.*); ancien(ne
f), ex-; feu (= *mort*); récent; *at*
(*the*) ~*st* au plus tard; tout au plus;
as ~ *as* pas plus tard que; *of* ~
récemment; *of* ~ *years* ces dernières années; depuis quelques
années; ~*r on* plus tard; *be* ~ être
en retard; 🕰 avoir du retard *ou* un
retard de ...; *keep* ~ *hours* se coucher tard; rentrer tard; **'~-com·er**
retardataire *mf*; tard-venu(e *f*) *m*;
'late·ly dernièrement, récemment;
depuis peu.
la·ten·cy ['leitənsi] état *m* latent.
late·ness ['leitnis] arrivée *f* tardive;
date *f* récente; heure *f* avancée;
fruit etc.: tardiveté *f*.
la·tent □ ['leitənt] caché; latent.
lat·er·al □ ['lætərəl] latéral (-aux
m/pl.).
lath [lɑːθ] **1.** latte *f*; *toit:* volige *f*;
jalousie: lame *f*; **2.** latter; voliger
(*un toit*).
lathe [leið] ⊕ tour *m*; *tex., métier*
battant *m*.
lath·er ['lɑːðə] **1.** *su.* mousse *f* de
savon; écume *f*; **2.** *v/t.* savonner; F
rosser (*q.*), fouailler (*un cheval*); *v/i.*
mousser (*savon*); jeter de l'écume
(*cheval*).
lath·y ['lɑːθi] latté; *fig.* long et
mince.
Lat·in ['lætɪn] **1.** latin; **2.** Latin(e *f*)
m; *ling.* latin *m*; ~ **A·mer·i·ca**
Amérique *f* latine; **'Lat·in·ism**
latinisme m, tournure *f* latine.
lat·i·tude ['lætitjuːd] latitude *f* (*a.*

fig., *géog.*, *astr.*); *fig. a.* étendue *f*; liberté *f* d'action; ~*s pl.* latitudes *f*/*pl.*, F parages *m*; **lat·i'tu·di·nal** [~inl] latitudinal (-aux *m*/*pl.*); **lat·i·tu·di·nar·i·an** [ˈ~ˈneəriən] **1.** latitudinaire (*a. su.*/*mf*); **2.** partisan(e *f*) *m* du tolérantisme.

lat·ter [ˈlætə]: *the* ~ le dernier *m*, la dernière *f*; celui-ci *m* (celle-ci *f*, ceux-ci *m*/*pl.*, celles-ci *f*/*pl.*); ~ *end* fin *f*; ˈ~-**day** récent, moderne; **'lat·ter·ly** dans les derniers temps; dans la suite; récemment.

lat·tice [ˈlætis] **1.** (*a.* ~-*work*) treillage *m*, treillis *m*; **2.** treillager, treillisser.

Lat·vi·an [ˈlætviən] **1.** lettonien(ne *f*); **2.** Lettonien(ne *f*) *m*.

laud [lɔːd] louer, chanter les louanges de; **laud·a'bil·i·ty** caractère *m* louable; **'laud·a·ble** □ louable, digne d'éloges; **lau'da·tion** louange *f*; **laud·a·to·ry** □ [ˈ~ətəri] élogieux (-euse *f*).

laugh [lɑːf] **1.** rire *m*; **2.** (*at*) rire (de); se moquer (de); ~ *off* traiter (*qch.*) en plaisanterie; ~ *out of* faire renoncer à force de plaisanteries; *see sleeve*; **'laugh·a·ble** □ risible, ridicule; **'laugh·er** rieur (-euse *f*) *m*; **'laugh·ing** rires *m*/*pl.*; **2.** □ riant; rieur (-euse *f*); **'laugh·ing-stock** objet *m* de risée; **'laugh·ter** rire *m*, -s *m*/*pl.*

launch [lɔːntʃ] **1.** ⚓ lancement *m*; chaloupe *f*; *motor* ~ vedette *f*; **2.** *v*/*t.* lancer (*a. un navire, une fusée*); débarquer (*un canot*); ✗ déclencher; *fig.* mettre en train, lancer; *v*/*i.* ~ *out* lancer un coup (à *at*, *against*); ⚓ mettre à la mer; ~ (*out*) *into* se lancer dans; **'launch·ing** **1.** lancement *m*; **2.** ~ *pad* (*site etc.*) rampe *f* (aire *f* *etc.*) de lancement.

laun·dress [ˈlɔːndris] blanchisseuse *f*; **'laun·dry** blanchisserie *f*; lessive *f*.

lau·re·ate [ˈlɔːriit] **1.** lauréat; *poet* ~ = **2.** poète *m* lauréat.

lau·rel ♀ [ˈlɔrl] laurier *m*; *fig.* win ~*s* cueillir des lauriers; **'lau·relled** couronné (de lauriers).

la·va [ˈlɑːvə] lave *f*.

lav·a·to·ry [ˈlævətəri] lavabo *m*; cabinet *m* de toilette; *public* ~ cabinets *m*/*pl.*

lave [leiv] *usu. poét.* laver; ✗ bassiner.

lav·en·der ♀ [ˈlævində] lavande *f*.

lav·ish [ˈlæviʃ] **1.** □ prodigue (de *in*, *of*); abondant; **2.** prodiguer; **'lav·ish·ness** prodigalité *f*.

law [lɔː] loi *f*; droit *m*; code *m*; législation *f*; justice *f*; règle *f*; *at* ~ en justice, en procès; *go to* ~ avoir recours à la justice; *have the* ~ *of s.o.* faire un procès à q., poursuivre q. en justice; *necessity knows no* ~ nécessité n'a point de loi; *lay down the* ~ expliquer la loi; F dogmatiser; *practise* ~ exercer le droit; **'~-a·bid·ing** 🏛 ami de l'ordre; **'~-court** cour *f* de justice; tribunal *m*; **'law·ful** □ légal (-aux *m*/*pl.*); licite, permis; légitime; juste; valide (*contrat etc.*); **'law·giv·er** législateur *m*; **'law·less** □ sans loi; désordonné.

lawn[1] [lɔːn] *tex.* batiste *f*; linon *m*.

lawn[2] [~] pelouse *f*; gazon *m*; **'~-mow·er** tondeuse *f*; **'~-'sprin·kler** arrosoir *m* de pelouse; ~ *ten·nis* (lawn-)tennis *m*.

law·suit [ˈlɔːsjuːt] procès *m*; **law·yer** [ˈ~jə] homme *m* de loi; juriste *m*; jurisconsulte *m*; *see a. solicitor*, *barrister*.

lax □ [læks] mou (mol *devant une voyelle ou un h muet*; molle *f*); flasque; relâché; négligent; facile (*morale*); **lax·a·tive** [ˈ~ətiv] **1.** laxatif (-ive *f*); **2.** laxatif *m*; **'lax·i·ty**, **'lax·ness** mollesse *f*; relâchement *m*; inexactitude *f*.

lay[1] [lei] *prét. de lie*[2] **2.**

lay[2] [~] lai *m*, chanson *f*; *poét.* poème *m*.

lay[3] [~] laïque, lai.

lay[4] [lei] **1.** *su. cordage*: commettage *m*; *terrain*: configuration *f*; *sl.* spécialité *f*; **2.** [*irr.*] *v*/*t.* coucher; abattre (*q., la poussière*); exorciser (*un fantôme*); mettre (*couvert*, *nappe*, *sur qch.*, *enjeu*, *impôt*, *nappe*); parier (*une somme*, *fig.* que, *that*); faire (*un pari*); pondre (*un œuf*); porter (*une plainte*); poser (*des fondements*, *un tapis*, *qch. sur qch.*); ~ *bare* mettre à nu; dévoiler; découvrir; ~ *before* exposer, présenter à (*q.*); ~ *by* mettre de côté; ~ *down* déposer; rendre (*les armes*); résigner (*un office*); donner (*la vie* *etc.*); étaler (*les cartes*); poser (*qch., voie, câble, principe*); imposer (*une condition*); formuler (*un principe*); ~ *in* s'approvisionner de; ♁ emmagasiner; ~

in stock s'approvisionner; ~ *low* étendre, abattre; ~ *off* congédier; *peint.* lisser avec la brisse; faire la contre-partie de (*un pari*); *Am. sl.* en finir avec (*q., qch.*), laisser (*tranquille*); ~ *on* imposer; étendre (*un enduit*); ne pas ménager (*des couleurs*); appliquer; porter (*des coups*); amener (*de l'eau*); installer (*le gaz etc.*); *fig.* ~ *it on* (thick) flatter (grossièrement); ~ *open* exposer; ~ (*o.s.*) *open to* (s')exposer à (*qch.*); ~ *out* arranger, étaler (*devant les yeux*); disposer (*le jardin*); dépenser (*l'argent*); F aplatir (*q.*); ~ *o.s. out* faire de son mieux (pour *for, to*); ~ *up* accumuler, amasser (*de l'argent, des provisions*); amasser (*des connaissances*); mettre (*qch.*) en réserve; mettre (*la terre*) en jachère; ⚓ mettre en rade; ⚓ désarmer; ~ *with* coucher avec; **3.** [*irr.*] *v/i.* pondre (des œufs); (*a.* ~ *a wager*) parier; ⚓ être (à l'ancre); mettre la table (pour, *for*); ~ *about one* frapper de tous côtés; *sl.* ~ *into* rosser (*q.*); F ~ (*it*) *on* porter des coups.

lay...: '~·**a·bout** *Brit.* F fainéant(e *f*) *m*, paresseux (-euse *f*) *m*; '~·**by** *Brit. mot.* petite aire *f* de stationnement.

lay·er 1. *su.* ['leiə] poseur *m*; parieur *m*; *poule*: pondeuse *f*; *peint. etc.* couche *f*; *géol.* assise *f*, strate *f*; **2.** *v/t.* [ˈlɛə] marcotter; *v/i.* se coucher (*blé*).

lay·ette [lei'et] layette *f*.

lay fig·ure mannequin *m*.

lay·ing ['leiiŋ] *câble, rail, tuyau, etc.*: pose *f*; *fondements*: assise *f*; *œufs*: ponte *f*.   [laïque *m*.]

lay·man ['leimən] profane *m*; *eccl.*

lay...: '~·**off** *Am.* période *f* de chômage; vacances *f/pl.* (*d'un ouvrier*); '~·**out** disposition *f*; tracé *m*.

laz·a·ret, *usu.* **laz·a·ret·to** [læzəˈret(ou)] léproserie *f*; ⚓ lazaret *m*.

laze F [leiz] fainéanter; baguenauder; '**la·zy 1.** paresseux (-euse *f*), fainéant; **2.** = '**la·zy-bones** fainéant(e *f*) *m*, F flémard(e *f*) *m*.

lea *poét.* [li:] prairie *f*.

leach [li:tʃ] *vt/i.* filtrer.

lead¹ [led] **1.** plomb *m*; ⚓ (plomb *m* de) sonde *f*; *typ.* interligne *f*; *crayon*: mine *f*; ~*s pl.* plombs *m/pl.*; ~ *pencil* crayon *m* (à la mine de

plomb); **2.** plomber; garnir de plomb; *typ.* interligner.

lead² [li:d] **1.** *su.* conduite *f*, exemple *m*; tête *f*; *théâ.* premier rôle *m*, vedette *f*; *cartes*: main *f*, couleur *f*; ⚡ câble *m*, connexion *f*; *chien*: laisse *f*; *journ.* ~ *story* article *m* de tête; *cartes*: *it's my* ~ à moi de jouer; *take the* ~ prendre la tête; *fig.* gagner les devants (sur *of*, over); **2.** [*irr.*] *v/t.* mener, conduire (à, *to*); amener; induire (en, *into*); guider; entamer de (*cartes*); ~ *on* entraîner; *fig.* encourager (à parler); *v/i.* mener, conduire; ~ *to* produire; ~ *off* commencer (par, *with*); *sp.* jouer le premier; ~ *up to* donner accès à; *fig.* introduire, amener.

lead·en ['ledn] de plomb (*a. fig.*).

lead·er ['li:də] chef *m* (*a.* ⚔); conducteur (-trice *f*) *m*; guide *m*; ♩ chef *m* d'attaque; *journ.* article *m* de fond; *cin.* bande *f* amorce; '**lead·er·ette** [~'ret] article *m* de fond succinct; '**lead·er·ship** conduite *f*; ⚔ commandement *m*; direction *f*.

lead·ing ['li:diŋ] **1.** premier (-ère *f*), principal (-aux *m/pl.*); de tête; ~ *article* article *f* de fond; ✝ spécialité *f* de réclame; ⚖ ~ *case* cas *m* d'espèce qui fait autorité; *théâ.* ~ *man* (*lady*) vedette *f*, premier rôle *m*; ⚖ ~ *question* question *f* tendancieuse; **2.** conduite *f*, direction *f*; ⚔ commandement *m*; '~-**strings** *pl.* lisière *f*.

leaf [li:f] (*pl. leaves*) ⚘ feuille *f* (*a. or etc., papier*); *fleur*: F pétale *m*; *livre*: feuillet *m*; *porte, table*: battant *m*; *table*: rallonge *f*; '**leaf·age** feuillage *m*; '**leaf·less** sans ou dépourvu de feuilles; '**leaf·let** [~'lit] feuillet *m*; feuille *f* volante; papillon *m* (*de publicité*); ⚘ foliole *f*; '**leaf·y** feuillu; couvert de feuilles; de feuillage.

league¹ [li:g] lieue *f* (marine) (= 4,8 km.).

league² [~] **1.** ligue *f*; *sp.* ♀ *match* match *m* de championnat; ♀ *of Nations* Société *f* des Nations; **2.** se liguer; '**lea·guer** ligueur (-euse *f*) *m*.

leak [li:k] **1.** écoulement *m*; ⚓ voie *f* d'eau; **2.** couler, fuir; se perdre; ⚓ faire eau; ~ *out* couler; *fig.* s'ébruiter; transpirer; '**leak·age** fuite *f*, perte *f*; ✝ coulage *m*; *fig. secrets*:

fuite *f*; **'leak·y** qui coule; qui prend l'eau; *fig.* peu fidèle, peu discret (-ète *f*).

lean¹ [liːn] maigre (*a. su./m*).

lean² [~] **1.** [*irr.*] *v/t.* appuyer (contre, *against*); *v/i.* s'appuyer (sur, *on*; contre, *against*); s'adosser (à, contre *against*); s'accouder (à, contre *against*); se pencher (sur, *over*; vers, *towards*); pencher (*mur etc.*), incliner (*a. fig.*); **2.** inclinaison *f*; *fig.* (*a.* **'lean·ing** penchant *m* (pour, *to* [*wards*]); tendance *f* (à, to[*wards*]).

lean·ness ['liːnnis] maigreur *f*.

leant [lent] *prét. et p.p. de lean²* 1.

lean-to ['liːn'tuː] appentis *m*.

leap [liːp] **1.** *su.* saut *m*, bond *m*; *by ~s and bounds* par bonds et par sauts; **2.** [*irr.*] *v/i.* sauter (*a. fig.*); jaillir (*flamme etc.*); *v/t.* franchir d'un saut; sauter; **'~-frog 1.** saute-mouton *m*; **2.** sauter comme à saute-mouton; **leapt** [lept] *prét. et p.p. de leap* 2; **'leap-year** année *f* bissextile.

learn [ləːn] [*irr.*] apprendre; *~ from* mettre (*qch.*) à profit; **learn·ed** □ ['~id] instruit, savant; **'learn·er-driv·er** conducteur *m* novice; **'learn·ing** étude *f*; action *f* d'apprendre; érudition *f*; **learnt** [ləːnt] *prét. et p.p. de learn.*

lease [liːs] **1.** bail (*pl.* baux) *m*; *terre*: bail *m* à ferme; *fig.* concession *f*; *let (out) on ~* louer à bail; *a new ~ of life* un renouveau *m* de vie; **2.** donner *ou* prendre à bail; louer; affermer (*une terre*); louer; **'~-hold** tenure *f ou* propriété *f* à bail; *attr.* tenu à bail; **'~-hold·er** bailleur *m*.

leash [liːʃ] **1.** laisse *f*, attache *f*; *chasse*: harde *f* (= 3 *chiens*); **2.** mettre à l'attache.

least [liːst] **1.** *adj.* le (*la*) moindre; le (*la*) plus petit(e); **2.** *adv.* (le) moins; *not ~* pas le moindre; **3.** *su.*: *at* (*the*) *~* au moins; du moins; *at the very ~* tout au moins; *not in the ~* pas du tout; *to say the ~* pour ne pas dire plus.

leath·er ['leðə] **1.** cuir *m*; F *foot.* ballon *m*; *~s pl.* culotte *f ou* guêtres *f/pl.* de cuir; **2.** de *ou* en cuir; **3.** garnir de cuir; F tanner le cuir à, rosser; **leath·er·ette** [~'ret] similicuir *m*; **leath·ern** ['leðən] de cuir, en cuir; **'leath·er·y** qui ressemble au cuir; coriace (*viande*).

leave [liːv] **1.** permission *f*, autorisation *f*; (*a. ~ of absence*) mois: congé *m*, jours: permission *f*; *by your ~* si vous le voulez bien; **2.** [*irr.*] *v/t.* laisser; abandonner; déposer (à la consigne); léguer (*une fortune etc.*); quitter (*un endroit*); sortir de; F *~ it at that* en demeurer là; *see call*; *~ behind* laisser (*a. des traces*), oublier; devancer, distancer; *~ off* cesser; renoncer à (*une habitude*); cesser de porter (*un vêtement*); *v/i.* partir (pour, *for*).

leaved [liːvd] aux feuilles ...; feuillu; à ... battants (*porte*); à ... rallonges (*table*).

leav·en ['levn] **1.** levain *m*; **2.** faire lever; *fig.* modifier (par, *with*); **'leav·en·ing** ferment *m*; *fig.* addition *f*, nombre *m*.

leaves [liːvz] *pl. de leaf.*

leav·ings ['liːviŋz] *pl.* restes *m/pl.*

lec·tern *eccl.* ['lektən] lutrin *m*.

lec·ture ['lektʃə] **1.** conférence *f* (sur, *on*); leçon *f* (de, *on*); *give a ~* faire une conférence; *attend ~s* suivre un cours; *see curtain ~*; *read s.o. a ~* faire une semonce à q.; **2.** *v/i.* faire une conférence (sur, *on*); faire un cours (de, *on*); *v/t.* F semoncer, sermonner; **'lec·tur·er** conférencier (-ère *f*) *m*; *univ.* maître *m* de conférences; chargé *m* de cours; professeur *m*; **'lec·ture·ship** poste *m* de conférencier (-ère *f*); *univ.* maîtrise *f* de conférences.

led [led] *prét. et p.p. de lead²* 2.

ledge [ledʒ] rebord *m*; saillie *f*; corniche *f*; banc *m* de récifs.

ledg·er ['ledʒə] ✝ grand livre *m*; *Am.* registre *m*; ⊕ échafaudage; filière *f*.

lee ⚓ [liː] côté *m* sous le vent.

leech [liːtʃ] *zo.* sangsue *f* (*a. fig.*); *fig.* crampon *m*.

leek ⚘ [liːk] poireau *m*.

leer [liə] **1.** œillade *f* en dessous; regard *m* paillard; **2.** *~ at* lorgner d'un air méchant; lancer des œillades à; **'leer·y** □ *sl.* malin(-igne *f*), rusé; soupçonneux (-euse *f*).

lees [liːz] *pl.* lie *f* (*a. fig.*). [*vent.*]

lee·ward ⚓ ['liːwəd] sous le]

lee·way ⚓ ['liːweɪ] dérive *f*; *make ~* dériver; *fig.* traîner; *fig. make up ~* rattraper le temps/ perdu.

left¹ [left] *prét. et p.p. de leave* 2; *be ~* rester.

left² [ʌ] *adj.* gauche; 2. *adv.* à gauche; 3. *su.* gauche *f*; '~-'**hand** de ou à gauche; *mot.* ~ drive conduite *f* à gauche; '~-'**hand·ed** □ gaucher (-ère *f*) (*personne*); *fig.* gauche; douteux (-euse *f*) (*compliment*); ⊕ à gauche. [*mf*).]

left·ist *pol.* ['leftist] gauchiste (*adj.,*)

left...: '~-'**lug·gage lock·er** casier *m* à consigne automatique; '~-'**luggage of·fice** consigne *f*; '~-o·vers** *pl.* restes *m*/*pl.*

Left-Wing *pol.* ['left'wiŋ] de gauche.

leg [leg] jambe *f*; *chien, oiseau, etc.*: patte *f*; *table*: pied *m*; & branche *f*; *course*: étape *f*; ~ of mutton gigot *m*; give s.o. a ~ up faire la courte échelle à q.; F donner un coup d'épaule à q.; F be on one's last ~s être à bout de ses ressources; pull s.o.'s ~ se payer la tête de q., faire marcher q.

leg·a·cy ['legəsi] legs *m*; '~-'**hunt·er** coureur (-euse *f*) *m* d'héritages.

le·gal ['li:gəl] légal (-aux *m*/*pl.*); juridique; judiciaire; de droit; de loi; ~ adviser conseiller *m* juridique; ~ aid assistance *f* judiciaire; ~ capacity capacité *f* de contracter; ~ costs *pl.* dépens *m*/*pl.*, frais *m*/*pl.* de justice; ✝ ~ department service *m* du contentieux; ~ dispute litige *m*, procès *m*; ~ entity personne *f* morale; ~ remedy voie *f* de recours; ~ status capacité *f* juridique; see tender² 1; **le·gal·i·ty** [li'gæliti] légalité *f*; **le·gal·i·za·tion** [li:gəlai'zeiʃn] légalisation *f*; '**le·gal·ize** rendre légal; autoriser; authentiquer (*un document*).

leg·ate ['legit] légat *m* (*du pape*).

leg·a·tee ⚖ [legə'ti:] légataire *mf*.

le·ga·tion [li'geiʃn] légation *f*.

leg-bail ['leg'beil]: give ~ F s'évader; filer à l'anglaise.

leg·end ['ledʒənd] légende *f* (*a.* = inscription); explication *f*; '**leg·end·ar·y** légendaire.

leg·er·de·main ['ledʒədə'mein] passe-passe *m*/*inv.*; prestidigitation *f*.

legged [legd] à ou aux jambes; short-~ aux jambes courtes; **leg·gings** ['~z] *pl.* guêtres *f*/*pl.*; '**leg·gy** aux longues jambes.

leg·horn [le'gɔ:n] chapeau *m* de paille d'Italie; *poule*: leghorn *f*.

leg·i·bil·i·ty [ledʒi'biliti] lisibilité *f*; **leg·i·ble** ['ledʒəbl] □ lisible.

le·gion ['li:dʒən] légion *f* (*a. fig.*); '**le·gion·ar·y** légionnaire (*a. su.*/*m*).

leg·is·late ['ledʒisleit] faire des lois; **leg·is·la·tion** législation *f*; '**leg·is·la·tive** □ législatif (-ive *f*); '**leg·is·la·tor** législateur *m*; **leg·is·la·ture** ['~tʃə] législature *f*; corps *m* législatif.

le·git·i·ma·cy [li'dʒitiməsi] *enfant, opinion, etc.*: légitimité *f*; **le·git·i·mate** 1. [~mit] □ légitime; F vrai; 2. [~meit] (*a.* **le·git·i·mize**) légitimer; **le·git·i·ma·tion** légitimation *f*; légalisation *f*.

leg·room ['legrum] place *f* pour les jambes.

leg·ume ['legju:m] fruit *m* d'une légumineuse; **le·gu·mi·nous** légumineux (-euse *f*).

lei·sure ['leʒə] loisir *m*, -s *m*/*pl.*; ~ activities *pl.* loisirs *m*/*pl.*; ~ time temps *m* libre, loisir *m*; ~ wear tenue *f* de détente; be at ~ être de loisir; at your ~ à (votre) loisir; '**lei·sured** de loisir; désœuvré; '**lei·sure·ly** 1. *adj.* posé, tranquille; qui n'est pas pressé; 2. *adv.* posément; à loisir.

lem·on ['lemən] 1. citron *m*; *sl.* saloperie *f*; 2. jaune citron *adj.*/*inv.*; **lem·on·ade** [~'neid] limonade *f*; **lem·on squash** citron *m* pressé; citronnade *f*; '**lem·on-squeez·er** presse-citron *m*/*inv.*

lend [lend] [*irr.*] prêter (*a. secours*); ~ out louer; ~ o.s. to se prêter à; ~ing library bibliothèque *f* de prêt; '⊙- -'**Lease Act** loi *f* prêt-bail (*américaine*); '**lend·er** prêteur (-euse *f*) *m*.

length [leŋθ] longueur *f*; morceau *m*; pièce *f*; *temps*: durée *f*; at ~ enfin, à la fin; at (great) ~ d'un bout à l'autre; go all ~s aller jusqu'au bout; go (to) great ~s se donner bien de la peine (pour, to); he goes the ~ of saying il va jusqu'à dire; '**length·en** (s')allonger; (se) prolonger; *v*/*i.* augmenter; '**length·ways**, '**length·wise** □ en longueur, en long; '**length·y** assez long; plein de longueurs (*discours etc.*).

le·ni·ence, le·ni·en·cy ['li:njəns(i)], **len·i·ty** ['leniti] clémence *f*; douceur *f*; **le·ni·ent** □ ['li:njənt] clément, indulgent (pour, envers to [-wards]); '**len·i·tive** ✚ 1. lénitif (-ive *f*); 2. lénitif *m*.

lens [lenz] loupe *f*; *opt.* lentille *f*,

verre *m*; *phot.* objectif *m*; *phot.*
~ system objectif *m*.
lent¹ [lent] *prét. et p.p.* de lend.
Lent² [~] carême *m*.
Lent·en ['lentən] de carême (*a. fig.*).
len·tic·u·lar □ [len'tikjulə] lenti-
forme, lenticulaire.
len·til ♀ ['lentil] lentille *f*.
Leo *astr.* ['li:ou] le Lion.
leop·ard ['lepəd] léopard *m*.
le·o·tard ['li:ətɑːd] collant *m*, maillot
m.
lep·er ['lepə] lépreux (-euse *f*) *m*.
lep·ro·sy ♣ ['leprəsi] lèpre *f*; **'lep·**
rous lépreux (-euse *f*).
les·bi·an ['lezbiən] 1. lesbien; 2. lesbienne *f*; **'les·bi·an·ism** lesbianis-
me *m*.
lese-maj·es·ty ⚖ ['li:z'mædʒisti]
lèse-majesté *f*.
le·sion ⚖, ♣ ['li:ʒən] lésion *f*.
less [les] 1. *adj.* moindre; plus petit;
moins de; inférieur; † moins important, mineur; *no* ~ *a person than*
ne ... rien moins que; 2. *adv.*
moins; 3. *prp.* Å moins; † sans;
4. *su.* moins *m*; *no* ~ *than* ne ... rien
moins que; autant que.
les·see [le'si:] locataire *mf*; concessionnaire *mf*.
less·en ['lesn] *v/t.* amoindrir, diminuer; ralentir; raccourcir; *fig.*
atténuer; *v/i.* diminuer, s'amoindrir; *fig.* s'atténuer.
less·er ['lesə] petit; moindre.
les·son ['lesn] 1. leçon *f* (*a. eccl., a.*
fig.); exemple *m*; ~s *pl.* leçons *f/pl.*;
cours *m*; 2. faire la leçon à, enseigner.
les·sor ⚖ [le'sɔ:] bailleur (-eresse
f) *m*.
lest [lest] de peur *ou* de crainte que
... ne (*sbj.*) *ou* de (*inf.*).
let¹ [let] [*irr.*] *v/t.* permettre, laisser;
faire (*inf.*); louer (*une maison etc.*);
~ *alone* laisser tranquille *ou* en
paix; laisser (*q.*) faire; ne pas se
mêler de (*qch.*); *adv.* sans parler
de ...; ~ *down* baisser; F laisser (*q.*)
en panne; ~ *s.o. down gently* refuser
qch. à *q. ou* corriger q. avec tact;
~ *fly* lancer; lâcher; ~ *go* lâcher; ⚓
mouiller (*l'ancre*); ~ *into* laisser
entrer; *cost.* incruster; mettre (*dans*
un secret, into a secret); ~ *loose*
lâcher; ~ *off* tirer; décocher (*a. fig.*
une épigramme); *fig.* dispenser (*de*
inf., from gér.); *see* steam; ~ *out*

laisser sortir; laisser échapper; *cost.*
rélargir; (*a.* ~ *on hire*) louer; *v/i.* se
louer (à *at, for*); ~ *on* rapporter,
trahir; ~ *up* diminuer; cesser.
let² [~] *tennis:* (*a.* ~ *ball*) balle *f* de
filet; *without* ~ *or hindrance* sans
entrave, en toute liberté.
let-down F ['letdaun] déception *f*.
le·thal □ ['li:θl] mortel(le *f*).
le·thar·gic, le·thar·gi·cal □ [le-
'θɑːdʒik(l)] léthargique (*a. fig.*).
leth·ar·gy ['leθədʒi] léthargie *f*;
fig. inaction *f*, inertie *f*.
let·ter ['letə] 1. lettre *f*; caractère *m*;
missive *f*; ~s *pl.* (belles-)lettres
f/pl.; littérature *f*; *by* ~ par lettre,
par correspondance; *man of* ~s
homme *m* de lettres, littérateur *m*;
to the ~ au pied de la lettre;
2. marquer avec des lettres; ⚖, †
coter; mettre le titre à (*un livre*);
'~-bal·ance pèse-lettre *m*; **'~-box**
boîte *f* aux lettres; **'~-car·ri·er**
Am. facteur *m*; **'~-case** portefeuille
m; **'~-cov·er** enveloppe *f*; **'let·**
tered marqué avec des lettres; *fig.*
lettré; **'let·ter-file** classeur *m* de
lettres; relieur *m f*; **'let·ter-found·er**
fondeur *m* typographe; **let·ter·**
gram *Am.* ['~græm] télégramme *m*
à tarif réduit; **'let·ter-head** en-tête
m (*pl.* en-têtes); **'let·ter·ing** lettrage
m; inscription *f*.
let·ter...: **'~-'o·pen·er** ouvre-lettres
m/inv.; **'~-pa·per** papier *m* à lettres; **'~'per·fect** *théâ.*: *be* ~ savoir
son rôle par cœur; **'~-press** *typ.*
impression *f* typographique; texte
m; ~ *printing* typographie *f*; **'~-**
press presse *f* à copier; **'~-weight**
presse-papiers *m/inv.*
let·tuce ♀ ['letis] laitue *f*.
let-up F ['letʌp] relâchement *m*, diminution *f*; arrêt *m*; *without* (*a*) ~ *a.*
sans s'arrêter, d'affilé.
leuco... [lju:ko] leuco-; **leu·co·cyte**
['~sait] leucocyte *m*.
le·vant [li'vænt] F décamper sans
payer.
lev·ee¹ ['levi] réception *f* royale;
hist. lever *m*.
lev·ee² *Am.* [~] digue *f*, endiguement *m*, levée *f* (*d'une rivière*).
lev·el ['levl] 1. *adj.* égal (-aux *m/pl.*);
à *ou* de niveau; *fig.* équilibré; ~ *with*
à fleur de; *my* ~ *best* tout mon possible; 🚂 ~ *crossing* passage *m* à
niveau; *cuis. a* ~ *spoonful* une cuille-

919   licence

rée rase; **2.** *su.* niveau *m* (*a.* ⊕, *a. fig.*);
terrain *m* ou surface *f* de niveau;
hauteur *f*; 🚢, *mot.* palier *m*; ⚔
galerie *f* (de niveau); ~ *of the sea*
niveau *m* de la mer; *on a* ~ *with* de
niveau avec, à la hauteur de; *fig.* au
niveau de (*q.*); *dead* ~ franc niveau *m*,
🚢 palier *m* absolu; *fig.* uniformité *f*;
on the ~ loyal (-aux *m/pl.*); tout à fait
sincère; **3.** *v/t.* niveler, aplatir, égaliser; *surv.* déniveler; pointer (*un fusil*); braquer (*un canon*); *fig.* raser
(*une ville*); *fig.* lancer (contre, *at*); ~
with (*ou to*) *the ground* raser (*qch.*); ~
down araser; *fig.* abaisser à son niveau; ~ *up* élever (*qch.*) au niveau de
qch., *to s.th.*); *v/i.* ~ *at* (*ou against*)
viser; ~ *off* cesser de monter, se
raffermir (*prix*); '~-'**head·ed** à la
tête bien équilibrée; (à l'esprit) rassis; '**lev·el·(l)er** *surv.* niveleuse *f* de
route; *personne:* niveleur (-euse *f*) *m*;
pol. égalitaire *mf*; '**lev·el·(l)ing** de
nivellement.
le·ver ['liːvə] **1.** *su.* levier *m*; **2.** *v/t.*
soulever au moyen d'un levier; *v/i.*
manœuvrer un levier; '**le·ver·age**
force *f* de levier; *fig.* prise *f*.
lev·er·et ['levərit] levraut *m*.
le·vi·a·than [li'vaiəθən] *bibl.* Lé-
viathan *m*; *fig.* navire *m* monstre.
lev·i·gate *pharm.* ['levigeit] réduire
en poudre; délayer (avec, *with*).
lev·i·tate ['leviteit] *spiritisme:* (se)
soulever (par lévitation).
lev·i·ty ['leviti] légèreté *f*, manque
m de sérieux.
lev·y ['levi] **1.** impôt, *a.* ⚔ *troupes:*
levée *f*; ⚔ *chevaux:* réquisition *f*;
impôt *m*, contribution *f*; *capital* ~
prélèvement *m* sur le capital;
2. lever, percevoir (*un impôt*); imposer (*une amende*); ⚔ lever (*des
troupes*); réquisitionner; faire (*la
guerre, du chantage*).
lewd □ [luːd] lascif (-ive *f*); impudique; '**lewd·ness** impudicité *f*;
débauche *f*.
lex·i·cal □ ['leksikl] lexicologi-
que.
lex·i·cog·ra·pher [leksi'kɔgrəfə]
lexicographe *mf*; **lex·i·co·graph·i-
cal** □ [~ko'græfikl] lexicographi-
que; **lex·i·cog·ra·phy** [~'kɔgrəfi]
lexicographie *f*.
li·a·bil·i·ty [laiə'biliti] responsabilité
f (*a.* ⚖); risque *m* (de, *to*); *fig.*
disposition *f*, tendance *f* (à, *to*);

liabilities pl. engagements *m/pl.*; ✝
ensemble *m* des dettes; passif *m*.
li·a·ble □ ['laiəbl] ⚖ responsable
(de, *for*); passible (de, *for*) (*une
amende, un impôt*); sujet(te *f*), apte
(à, *to*); susceptible (de *inf.*, *to inf.*);
Am. probable; *be* ~ *to* avoir une
disposition à; être sujet(te *f*) à;
~ *to duty* assujetti à un impôt; ~ *to
punishment* punissable.
li·aise F [li'eiz] entrer *ou* rester en
liaison; **li·ai·son** [li'eizɔ̃ːŋ] liaison *f*
(*a.* ⚔); *attr.* de liaison.
li·ar ['laiə] menteur (-euse *f*) *m*.
li·bel ['laibl] **1.** diffamation *f*,
calomnie *f* (contre, *on*); ⚖ écrit *m*
diffamatoire; **2.** calomnier; ⚖ diffamer (par écrit); '**li·bel·(l)ous** □
diffamatoire; *fig.* peu flatteur
(-euse *f*).
lib·er·al ['libərəl] **1.** □ libéral (-aux
m/pl.) (*a. pol.*); généreux (-euse *f*);
prodigue (de, *of*); abondant; **2.** *pol.*
libéral (-aux *pl.*) *m*; '**lib·er·al·ism**
libéralisme *m*; **lib·er·al·i·ty** [~-
'ræliti] libéralité *f*; générosité *f*.
lib·er·ate ['libəreit] libérer (*a.* ⚗);
mettre en liberté; délivrer (de,
from); affranchir (*un esclave*); **liber'a·tion** libération *f*; '**lib·er·a·tor**
libérateur (-trice *f*) *m*; '**lib·er·a-
to·ry** libératoire.
lib·er·tar·i·an [libə'tɛəriən] libertaire *mf*.
lib·er·tine ['libətain] **1.** libertin, débauché (*a. su./m*); **2.** libre penseur
m; '**lib·er·tin·ism** ['~tinizm] libertinage *m*, débauche *f*.
lib·er·ty ['libəti] liberté *f*; permission *f*; *take liberties* prendre des
libertés (avec, *with*); *be at* ~ être
libre (de, *to*).
li·bid·i·nous □ [li'bidinəs] libidineux (-euse *f*), lascif (-ive *f*); **li·bi-
do** [li'biːdou] libido *f*.
li·brar·i·an [lai'brɛəriən] bibliothé-
caire *m*; **li'brar·y** ['laibrəri] bibliothèque *f*; ~ *science* bibliothéconomie
f.
lice [lais] *pl.* de *louse* 1.
li·cence ['laisəns] *admin.* permis *m*,
autorisation *f*, patente *f*; permission *f*; *fig.* licence *f* (*a. morale, a.
univ.*); *driving* ~ permis *m* de conduire; *mot.* ~ *number* numéro *m* d'immatriculation; *mot.* ~ *plate* plaque *f*
d'immatriculation *ou* minéralogique.

li·cense [~] **1.** *see* licence; **2.** accorder un permis à; ✝ patenter (*q.*); autoriser la parution de (*un livre, une pièce de théâtre, etc.*); *Brit.* (fully) ~d autorisé à vendre des boissons alcooliques; **li·cen·see** [~'siː] patenté(e *f*) *m*; concessionnaire *mf*; **'li·cens·er** concesseur *m*; *théâ. etc.*: censeur *m*.

li·cen·ti·ate *univ.* [lai'senʃiit] licence *f*; *personne*: licencié(e *f*) *m*.

li·cen·tious □ [lai'senʃəs] licencieux (-euse *f*); dévergondé.

li·chen ♀, *a.* ✿ ['laiken] lichen *m*.

lich-gate ['litʃgeit] porche *m* (couvert) de cimetière.

lick [lik] **1.** coup *m* de langue; *Am.* terrain *m* salifère; *sl.* ✝ coup *m*; F vitesse *f*; **2.** lécher; F battre, rosser; ~ the dust mordre la poussière; ~ into shape façonner; mettre au point; **'lick·er** celui *m* (celle *f*) qui lèche; ⊕ lécheur *m*; **'lick·er·ish** friand; gourmand, avide (de, *after*); **'lick·ing** lèchement *m*; F raclée *f*; F défaite *f*; **'lick·spit·tle** flagorneur *m*.

lic·o·rice ['likəris] *Am.* ['likəris] réglisse *f*.

lid [lid] couvercle *m*; *sl.* chapeau *m*; paupière *f*.

lie¹ [lai] **1.** mensonge *m*; give s.o. the ~ donner un démenti à q.; *tell a* ~ mentir; *white* ~ mensonge *m* innocent; **2.** mentir.

lie² [~] **1.** (dis)position *f*; ♐, *géol.* gisement *m*; **2.** [*irr.*] être couché; se tenir, rester; se trouver; ♐ être recevable;~ by rester inactif (-ive *f*); être en réserve; se tenir à l'écart; ~ down se coucher; take it lying down se laisser faire, ne pas dire mot; ~ in (*adv.*) être en couches; (*prp.*) être situé dans; ~ in wait for se tenir à l'affût de (*q.*); ✝ ~ over différer l'échéance de; ♐ ~ to être à la cape; ~ under être dominé par; encourir (*un déplaisir*); être sous le coup de (*une accusation*); ~ up rentrer dans l'inactivité; garder le lit; it ~s with you il vous incombe (de *inf.*, *to inf.*).

lie-a·bed ['laiəbed] grand(e *f*) dormeur (-euse *f*) *m*; paresseux (-euse *f*) *m*.

liege [liːdʒ] *hist.* **1.** lige (*f*); **2.** (*a.* ~lord) suzerain *m*; (*a.* ~man) vassal *m*.

li·en ♐ ['liːən] privilège *m*.

lieu [ljuː]: in ~ of au lieu de.

lieu·ten·an·cy [lef'tenənsi; ♐ le't-; *Am.* luː'tenənsi] grade *m* de lieutenant (♐ de vaisseau); *hist.* lieutenance *f*.

lieu·ten·ant [lef'tenənt; ♐ le't-; *Am.* luː'tenənt] lieutenant *m* (♐ de vaisseau); *fig.* délégué *m*, premier adjoint *m*; '~-**colo·nel** lieutenant-colonel (*pl.* lieutenants-colonels) *m*; '~-**com·mand·er** capitaine *m* de corvette; lieutenant de vaisseau; '~-**gen·er·al** général *m* de division; *Am.* ✝ commandant *m* en chef; '~-**gov·er·nor** sous-gouverneur *m*; vice-gouverneur *m* (*d'un État des É.-U.*).

life [laif] (*pl. lives*) vie *f*; vivant *m*; biographie *f*; ~ and limb corps et âme; for ~ à vie, à perpétuité; for one's ~ (*ou* for dear) ~ de toutes ses (*etc.*) forces; to the ~ naturel(le *f*); '~-**an·nu·i·ty** rente *f* viagère; '~-**as·sur·ance** assurance *f* sur la vie, assurance-vie (*pl.* assurances-vie) *f*; '~-**belt** ceinture *f* de sauvetage; '~-**blood** sang *m*; *fig.* âme *f*; '~-**boat** canot *m* de sauvetage; '~-**buoy** bouée *f* de sauvetage; ~ **ex·pect·an·cy** espérance *f* de vie; '~-**guard** garde *f* du corps; '~-**guard** *Am.* sauveteur *m* (*à la plage*); ~ **in·sur·ance** see life assurance; ~ **in·ter·est** usufruit *m* (de, *in*); '~-**'jack·et** ♐ brassière *f* de sauvetage; '~-**less** □ sans vie; mort; *fig.* sans vigueur, inanimé; '~-**less·ness** absence *f* de vie; manque *m* d'animation; '~-**like** vivant; '~-**line** ligne *f* de sauvetage; *à bord*: sauvegarde *f*; '~-**long** de toute la vie; '~-**pre·serv·er** ♐ appareil *m* de sauvetage; canne *f* plombée; casse-tête *m/inv.*; ~ **raft** radeau *m* de sauvetage; ~ **sen·tence** ✝ condamnation *f* à vie; '~-**size** de grandeur naturelle; '~-**span** (durée *f* de) vie *f*; '~-**strings** *pl.* ce qui est nécessaire à l'existence; '~-**time** vie *f*, vivant *m*.

lift [lift] **1.** *su.* haussement *m*; levée *f* (*a.* ⊕); ⊕ hauteur *f* de levage; ⚡ poussée *f*; *fig.* élévation *f*; ascenseur *m*; give s.o. a ~ donner un coup de main à q.; *mot.* conduire q. un bout; **2.** *v/t.* (*souv.* ~ up) *usu.* lever, soulever; redresser; relever; élever (*la voix*); *sl.* plagier; *sl.* voler; *v/i.* s'élever; ⚡ décoller; '~-**at·tend·ant** liftier (-ère *f*) *m*; '**lift·er**

souleveur *m*; ⊕ came *f*; **'lift·ing** ⊕ de levée; de levage; de suspension; **'lift-off** décollage *m*.

lig·a·ment *anat.* ['ligəmənt] ligament *m*.

lig·a·ture ['ligətʃuə] **1.** ♫, *typ.* ligature *f*; ♪ liaison *f*; **2.** ♫ ligaturer; lier.

light¹ [lait] **1.** *su.* lumière *f*; jour *m* (*a. fig.*); lampe *f*; feu *m*, phare *m*; fenêtre *f*; éclairage *m*; *fig.* ~s *pl.* lumières *f/pl.*; *phot.* ~ meter photomètre *m*; ~ wave onde *f* lumineuse; ~ year année-lumière *f* (*pl.* années-lumière); *in the* ~ *of* à la lumière de (*a. fig.*); *bring to* ~ mettre à jour; *come to* ~ se révéler; *will you give me a* ~ voudriez-vous bien me donner du feu?; *put a* ~ *to* allumer; *see the* ~ voir le jour (= *naître*); *fig.* comprendre, *Am.* être convaincu; **2.** *adj.* clair; éclairé; blond; ~ *blue* bleu clair *inv.*; **3.** [*irr.*] *v/t.* (*souv.* ~ *up*) allumer; éclairer; illuminer (*la rue, un visage, etc.*); ~ *up* éclairer (*q.*) jusqu'à (en); *v/i.* (*usu.* ~ *up*) s'allumer; s'éclairer; *Am. sl.* ~ *out* détaler, ficher le camp.

light² [~] **1.** □ *usu.* léger (-ère *f*); frivole; amusant; facile; ~ *car* voiturette *f*; ~ *reading* lecture *f* distrayante; *make* ~ *of* faire peu de cas de; *prendre à la légère*; **2.** *see lights*; **3.** ~ *on* s'abattre sur (*a. oiseau*); tomber sur (*a. fig.*); rencontrer; trouver par hasard. [faire des éclairs.\

light·en¹ ['laitn] (s')éclairer; *v/i.*\

light·en² [~] *v/t.* alléger (*a. fig.*); réduire le poids de; *v/i.* être soulagé.

light·er¹ ['laitə] *personne*: allumeur (-euse *f*) *m*; (*a. petrol-*~) briquet *m*.

light·er² ⚓ [~] péniche *f*, chaland *m*.

light...: **'~-'fin·gered** aux doigts agiles; **'~-fit·ting** plafonnier *m*; *mur*: applique *f*; **'~-'foot·ed** au pied léger, leste; **'~-'head·ed** étourdi; *feel* ~ avoir le cerveau vide; **'~-'heart·ed** □ allègre; au cœur léger; **~-'heav·y·weight** *sp.* (poids *m*) milourd *m*; **'~-house** phare *m*.

light·ing ['laitiŋ] *mot.* (*a.* ~-*up*), *a.* *bâtiment*: éclairage *m*; ⚡ ~ *point* prise *f* de courant (d'éclairage).

light·less ['laitlis] sans lumière.

light·ly ['laitli] *adv.* légèrement; à la légère; à bon marché; **'light-'mind·ed** frivole, étourdi; **'light-ness** légèreté *f*.

light·ning ['laitniŋ] **1.** éclairs *m/pl.*, foudre *f*; **2.** de paratonnerre; *fig.* foudroyant, rapide; **'~-ar'rest·er** parafoudre *m*; **'~-con·duc·tor**, **'~-rod** (tige *f* de) paratonnerre *m*; **'~-strike** grève *f* surprise.

lights [laits] *pl.* mou *m* (*de veau etc.*).

light-ship ['laitʃip] bateau-feu (*pl.* bateaux-feux) *m*; **'light-treat-ment** ♫ photothérapie *f*.

light weight *sp.* ['lait'weit] poids *m* léger; **'light-weight** *sp.* léger (-ère *f*).

lig·ne·ous ['ligniəs] ligneux (-euse *f*); **lig·nite** ['lignait] lignite *m*.

like [laik] **1.** *adj., adv.* pareil(le *f*), semblable, tel(le *f*); ~ *a man* digne de l'homme; qui ressemble à un homme; F *he is* ~ *to die* il est en cas de mourir; *such* ~ similaire, de la sorte; F *feel* ~ (*gér.*) se sentir d'humeur à (*inf.*); avoir envie de (*inf.*); *s.th.* ~ qch. d'approchant à; environ (*2 mois, 100 francs*); ~ *that* de la sorte; *what is he* ~? comment est-il?; *that's more* ~ *it* à la bonne heure!; *cela en approche plus*; *cela laisse moins à désirer*; **2.** *su.* semblable *mf*, pareil(le *f*) *m*; ~s *pl.* préférences *f/pl.*; sympathies *f/pl.*; *his* ~ ses congénères; *the* ~ chose *f* pareille; F *the* ~(*s*) *of* des personnes *ou* choses comme; **3.** *v/t.* aimer; avoir de la sympathie pour; souhaiter, vouloir; *how do you* ~ *London?* comment trouvez-vous Londres?, vous vous plaisez à Londres?; *I should* ~ *time* il me faut du temps; *I should* ~ *to know* je voudrais bien savoir.

lik(e)·a·ble ['laikəbl] sympathique, agréable.

like·li·hood ['laiklihud] probabilité *f*; **'like·ly** probable; susceptible (*de, to*); *be* ~ *to* (*inf.*) être en cas de (*inf.*).

like...: **'~-'mind·ed** du même avis; **'lik·en** comparer (à, avec *to*); **'like·ness** ressemblance *f*; apparence *f*; image *f*, portrait *m*; *have one's* ~ *taken* se faire peindre *ou* photographier; **'like·wise** de plus, aussi.

lik·ing ['laikiŋ] (*for*) goût *m* (de), penchant *m* (pour); *to one's* ~ à souhait; à son gré.

li·lac ['lailək] **1.** lilas *adj./inv.*; **2.** ♀ lilas *m*.

lilt [lilt] **1.** chanter gaiement; **2.** rythme *m*, cadence *f*; chant *m* gai.

lil·y ♀ ['lili] lis *m*; ~ *of the valley* muguet *m*; *gild the* ~ orner la beauté même.

limb[1] [lim] membre *m* (*du corps*); ♀ branche *f*; F suppôt *m*.

limb[2] astr., ♀ [~] limbe *m*, bord *m*; *fig.* go out on a ~ aller jusqu'au bout.

limbed [limd] aux membres ...

lim·ber[1] ['limbə] souple, agile.

lim·ber[2] ✗ [~] 1. avant-train *m*; 2. atteler à l'avant-train; ~ *up* mettre l'avant-train.

lim·bo ['limbou] limbes *m/pl.*; *sl.* prison *f*; *fig.* oubli *m*.

lime[1] [laim] 1. chaux *f*; (*a. bird* ~) glu *f*; 2. ✗ chauler; gluer (*des rameaux*).

lime[2] ♀ [~] lime *f*; (*a.* ~*-tree*) tilleul *m*. [*m* de limon.]

lime[3] ♀ [~] limon *m*; '~*-juice* jus⌡

lime...: '~*·kiln* four *m* à chaux; '~*-light* lumière *f* oxhydrique; *théâ.* rampe *f*; *fig.* in the ~ très en vue.

lim·er·ick ['limərik] (*sorte de*) petit poème *m* comique (*en 5 vers*).

lime·stone géol. ['laimstoun] calcaire *m*.

lim·it ['limit] 1. limite *f*, borne *f*; in (*off*) ~s accès *m* permis (interdit); F *that is the* ~! ça, c'est le comble!; ça, c'est trop fort!; *Am.* F go the ~ aller jusqu'au bout; risquer le tout; 2. limiter, borner (à, *to*); '**lim·i·tar·y** ['limitar·y qui sert de limite à; **lim·i·ta·tion** restriction *f*, limitation *f*; entrave *f*; ⟐ prescription *f*; '**lim·it·ed** limité, restreint (à, *to*); ~ (*liability*) *company* (*abbr.* Co.Ltd.) société *f* à responsabilité limitée; société *f* anonyme; ~ *in time* à terme; de durée restreinte; *surt. Am.* ~ (*express train*) rapide *m*; train *m* de luxe; '**lim·it·less** □ illimité, sans bornes.

limn [lim] dessiner, peindre.

lim·ou·sine ['limu(:)zi:n] limousine *f*.

limp[1] [limp] 1. boiter (*a. fig.*); 2. boitement *m*, clochement *m*.

limp[2] [~] flasque; mou (mol *devant une voyelle ou un h muet*; molle *f*); *fig.* sans énergie.

lim·pet ['limpit] zo. patelle *f*; *fig.* crampon *m*; fonctionnaire *m* ancré dans son poste.

lim·pid □ ['limpid] limpide, clair; **lim·pid·i·ty**, '**lim·pid·ness** limpidité *f*, clarté *f*.

lim·y ['laimi] gluant; ⚲ calcaire.

lin·age journ. ['lainidʒ] nombre *m* de lignes; paiement *m* à la ligne.

linch·pin ['lintʃpin] esse *f*; cheville *f* d'essieu.

lin·den ♀ ['lindən] (*a.* ~*-tree*) tilleul *m*.

line[1] [lain] 1. *su.* ⚓, ⚗, 🕮, *armes*, *démarcation*, *dessin*, *pêche*, *personne*, *téléph.*, *télév.*, *tennis*, *typ.*, *phys.* (*de force*): ligne *f*; ⚠ alignement *m*; ♥ articles *m/pl.*; ✗, ⚓ ligne *f* de bataille; 🕮 voie *f*; *téléph.* fil *m*; *peint.* cimaise *f*; *surv.* cordeau *m*; *dessin*, *phys.* (*du spectre*): raie *f*; *dessin*, *visage*: trait *m*; *front*: ride *f*; *véhicules*: file *f*, colonne *f*; *objets*, *personnes*: rangée *f*; *fig.* emploi *m*; *fig.* mot *m*; *Am. fig.* tuyaux *m/pl.*; F mesure *f*; ~s *pl.* modèle *m*; (*bonne*, *mauvaise*) voie *f*; formes *f/pl.*; F acte *m* de mariage; ✗ rangs *m/pl.*; ~ *of battle* ligne *f* de bataille; ~ *of business* genre *m* d'affaires; ~ *of conduct* ligne *f* de conduite; ~ *of danger* zone *f* dangereuse; *ship of the* ~ vaisseau *m* de ligne; *hard* ~s *pl.* mauvaise chance *f*; *all down the* ~ sur toute la ligne; *in* ~ *with* d'accord avec; *position*: de pair avec; *that is not in my* ~ ce n'est pas mon métier; *stand in* ~ se tenir en ligne; *fall into* ~ s'aligner; *fig.* se conformer (à, *with*); 2. *v/t.* ligner, régler; rayer; border (*allée*, *chemin*, *rive*, *etc.*); ~ *the streets* faire la haie; ~ *out* ⚲ repiquer; tracer; ~ *through* biffer, rayer; *v/i. sp.* ~ *out* se mettre en lignes parallèles pour la touche; ~ *up* s'aligner; faire la queue.

line[2] [~] cost. etc. doubler; *fig.* ~ *one's pocket* faire sa pelote.

lin·e·age ['liniidʒ] lignée *f*; F famille *f*; **lin·e·al** □ ['liniəl] linéal (-aux *m/pl.*); direct; **lin·e·a·ment** ['~iəmənt] trait *m*, linéament *m*; **lin·e·ar** ['~iə] linéaire.

lin·en ['linin] 1. toile *f* (*de lin*); linge *m*; 2. de *ou* en toile; de lin (*fil*); '~*-bas·ket* panier *m* à linge; '~*-clos·et*, '~*-cup·board* lingerie *f*; armoire *f* à linge; '~*-drap·er* marchand(e *f*) *m* de toiles.

lin·er ['lainə] paquebot *m* (de ligne); grand avion *m* de transport; *personne*: traceur *m* de filets; *cost.* doubleur (-euse *f*) *m*; **lines·man** ['lainzmən] ✗ soldat *m* de la ligne; 🕮

literati

garde-ligne *m*; *sp.* arbitre *m* de ligne; **'line-'up** mise *f* en rang; *sp.* rassemblement *m*; *sp. Am.* composition *f* d'une équipe.

ling[1] *icht.* [liŋ] morue *f* longue.

ling[2] ♀ [⌣] bruyère *f* commune.

lin·ger ['liŋgə] tarder; s'attarder (sur, over [up]on); traîner (*a. malade*); flâner (*dans la rue*); subsister (*doute*); ⁓ at (*ou* about) s'attarder sur *ou* à (*qch.*) *ou* dans (*un endroit*).

lin·ge·rie ✝ ['lɛ̃:nʒəri] lingerie *f* (de dame).

lin·ger·ing □ ['liŋgəriŋ] prolongé; persistent (*espoir*); qui traîne (*a. maladie*).

lin·go ['liŋgou] jargon m. [*m*/*pl.*).]

lin·gual ['liŋgwəl] lingual (-aux)

lin·guist ['liŋgwist] linguiste *mf*; **lin'guis·tic** (⌣ally) linguistique; **lin'guis·tics** *usu. sg.* linguistique *f*.

lin·i·ment ✻ ['linimənt] liniment *m*.

lin·ing ['lainiŋ] *vêtement*: doublage *m*; *robe*: doublure *f*; *mur*: incrustation *f*; ⊕ *fourneau, cylindre*: chemise *f*.

link [liŋk] **1.** *su.* chaînon *m*; *chaîne*: anneau *m*; *fig.* lien *m*; *cuff*-⁓ bouton *m* de manchette; **2.** (se) joindre; *v*/*t. a.* relier, enchaîner.

links [liŋks] *pl.* dunes *f*/*pl.*; lande *f* sablonneuse; (*a.* golf-⁓) terrain *m* de golf.

link·up ['liŋkʌp] connexion *f*; lien *m*, rapport *m*; jonction *f*.

lin·net *orn.* ['linit] linot(te *f*) m.

lin·o·type *typ.* ['lainotaip] linotype *f*.

lin·seed ['linsi:d] graine *f* de lin; ⁓ *oil* huile *f* de lin.

lin·sey-wool·sey ✝ ['linzi'wulzi] tiretaine *f*.

lint ✻ [lint] charpie *f* anglaise; lint *m*.

lin·tel ⌂ ['lintl] linteau *m*.

lin·y ['laini] strié de lignes; ridé.

li·on ['laiən] lion *m* (*zo., astr. a. fig.*); F ⁓s *pl. of a place* curiosités *f*/*pl.* d'un endroit; **'li·on·ess** lionne *f*; **'li·on·ize** visiter les curiosités de (*un endroit*); faire une célébrité de (*q.*).

lip [lip] lèvre *f* (*a.* ♀, *a. plaie*); *animal*: babine *f*; *tasse*: (re)bord *m*, saillie *f*; F insolence *f*; **'⁓-read** lire sur les lèvres; **'⁓-serv·ice** hommages *m*/*pl.* peu sincères; **'⁓-stick** rouge *m* à lèvres, bâton *m* de rouge.

liq·ue·fac·tion [likwi'fækʃn] liquéfaction *f*; **liq·ue·fi·a·ble** [⁓'faiəbl]

liquéfiable; **liq·ue·fy** ['⁓fai] (se) liquéfier.

li·queur [li'kjuə] liqueur *f*; **'⁓-choc·o·late** chocolat *m* aux liqueurs.

liq·uid ['likwid] **1.** □ liquide (*a. gramm.*); doux (douce *f*) (*son*); ✝ disponible; limpide (*œil etc.*); **2.** liquide *m*; *gramm.* liquide *f*.

liq·ui·date ['likwideit] ✝ liquider (*une dette*); mobiliser (*des capitaux*); **liq·ui'da·tion** liquidation *f*; **'liq·ui·da·tor** liquidateur *m*; **'liq·uid·iz·er** *cuis.* centrifugeuse *f*.

liq·uor ['likə] **1.** ⌂, *pharm.* solution *f*; boisson *f* alcoolique; *in* ⁓ ivre; **2.** *sl. v*/*i.* chopiner; *v*/*t.* (*a.* ⁓ *up*) enivrer.

liq·uo·rice ♀ ['likəris] réglisse *f*.

lisp [lisp] **1.** zézayement *m*; **2.** zézayer.

lis·som(e) ['lisəm] souple, agile.

list[1] [list] **1.** *su.* ⌂ lisière *f* (*a. tex.*); liste *f*, répertoire *m*; carte *f* (*des vins*); **2.** enregistrer; inscrire (*des noms*); dresser la liste de; cataloguer; ⁓ed *a.* classé, historique (*édifice*).

list[2] ♎ [⌣] **1.** bande *f*, gîte *f*; **2.** donner de la bande; prendre de la gîte.

lis·ten ['lisn] (*to*) écouter; prêter l'oreille (à); faire attention (à); ⁓ *in radio*: se mettre à l'écoute; écouter (qch., *to* s.th.); **'lis·ten·er** auditeur (-trice *f*) *m*; ✕ *a. péj.* écouteur *m*; *radio*: ⁓s' requests disques *m*/*pl.* des auditeurs; **'lis·ten·er-'in** (*pl.* **'lis·ten·ers-'in**) *radio*: auditeur (-trice *f*) *m*.

lis·ten·ing ['lisniŋ] d'écoute; ⁓ *apparatus* appareil *m* d'écoute; **'⁓-'in** *radio*: écoute *f*; **'⁓-post** poste *m* d'écoute.

list·less □ ['listlis] apathique, sans énergie; indifférent; **'list·less·ness** apathie *f*, manque *m* d'énergie; indifférence *f*.

lists [lists] *pl.* lice *f*.

lit [lit] *prét. et p.p. de* light[1] 3; ⁓ *up sl.* ivre, soûl.

lit·a·ny *eccl.* ['litəni] litanie *f*.

lit·er·al □ ['litərəl] littéral (-aux *m*/*pl.*) (*a.* A₊); propre (*sens*); sans imagination (*personne*); **'lit·er·al·ism**, **'lit·er·al·ness** littéralité *f*.

lit·er·ar·y □ ['litərəri] littéraire; de lettres; **lit·er·ate** [⌣it] **1.** qui sait lire et écrire; lettré; **2.** lettré *m*; *eccl.* prêtre *m* sans grade universitaire; **lit·e·ra·ti** [litə'rɑ:ti] *pl.* hommes *m/pl.* de lettres, littérateurs *m/pl.*; **lit·e·ra·tim** [⁓'rɑ:tim] mot à mot; **lit·er·a·ture** ['litǝritʃǝ] littérature *f*; écrits *m/pl.*; ✝ prospectus *m/pl.*

lithe(·some) ['laið(sǝm)] souple, agile, leste.

lith·o·graph ['liθǝgrɑ:f] 1. lithographie *f*; 2. lithographier; **li·thog·ra·pher** [li'θɔgrǝfǝ] lithographe *m*; **lith·o·graph·ic** [liθǝ'græfik] (⁓ally) lithographique; **li·thog·ra·phy** [li'θɔgrǝfi] lithographie *f*, procédés *m/pl.* lithographiques.

Lith·u·a·ni·an [liθju'einjǝn] 1. lituanien(ne *f*); 2. Lituanien(ne *f*) *m*.

lit·i·gant ⚖ ['litigǝnt] 1. plaidant; 2. plaideur (-euse *f*) *m*; **lit·i·gate** ['⁓geit] *v/i.* plaider; être en procès; *v/t.* contester; **lit·i·ga·tion** litige *m*, procès *m*; **li·ti·gious** □ [li'tidʒǝs] litigieux (-euse *f*) (*cas, a. personne*).

lit·mus 🜊 ['litmǝs] tournesol *m*.

lit·ter ['litǝ] 1. litière *f* (*véhicule, a. de paille*); civière *f*; désordre *m*; ordures *f/pl.*; *zo.* portée *f*; 2. mettre en désordre; joncher (de, *with*); *zo.* mettre bas; (*a. ⁓ down*) faire la litière à; joncher (*qch.*) de paille; '⁓bag *Am.*, '⁓bas·ket, '⁓bin boîte *f* à ordures.

lit·tle ['litl] 1. *adj.* petit; peu de ...; mesquin (*esprit*); *a ⁓ one* un(e *f*) petit(e *f*) (*enfant*); F *my ⁓ Mary* mon estomac *m*; *his ⁓ ways* ses petites manies *f/pl.*; *⁓ people* les fées *f/pl.*; 2. *adv.* peu; *a ⁓ red* un *ou* quelque peu rouge; 3. *su.* peu *m* (de chose); *⁓ by ⁓, by ⁓ and ⁓* peu à peu; petit à petit; *for a ⁓* pendant un certain temps; *not a ⁓* beaucoup; '**lit·tle·ness** petitesse *f*.

lit·to·ral ['litǝrǝl] 1. du littoral; 2. littoral *m*.

lit·ur·gy *eccl.* ['litǝ(:)dʒi] liturgie *f*.

liv·a·ble ['livǝbl] F habitable (*maison etc.*); supportable (*vie*); F (*usu. ⁓ with*) accommodant, sociable (*personne*).

live 1. [liv] vivre (de, *on*); se nourrir (de, [*up*]*on*); demeurer, habiter; durer; *v/t.* mener (*une vie*); *⁓ to see* vivre assez longtemps pour voir (*qch.*); *⁓ down* faire oublier; surmonter; *⁓ off one's capital* manger son capital; *⁓ out* passer; durer (jusqu'à la fin de); *⁓ up to one's promise* remplir sa promesse; *⁓ up*

to a standard atteindre un niveau *etc.*; 2. [laiv] vivant, en vie; ardent (*charbon*); *fig.* actuel(le *f*); utile (*poids*); ⚡ chargé (*cartouche etc.*); ⚡ sous tension; *télév., radio:* en direct; *fig. ⁓ wire* homme *m etc.* très entreprenant; '**live·a·ble** *see* livable; **lived** [livd]: *short-⁓* éphémère; **live·li·hood** ['laivlihud] vie *f*; gagne-pain *m/inv.*; **live·li·ness** ['⁓linis] vivacité *f*, entrain *m*; **live·long** *poét.* ['livlɔŋ]: *⁓ day* toute la (sainte) journée; **live·ly** ['laivli] vif (vive *f*); animé; vivant.

liv·en ['laivn] *souv. ⁓ up v/t.* animer, égayer; *v/i.* s'animer; s'activer.

liv·er[1] ['livǝ] vivant *m*; celui *m* (celle *f*) qui vit; *fast ⁓* viveur (-euse *f*) *m*; débauché(e *f*) *m*; *good ⁓* amateur *m* de bonne chère.

liv·er[2] [⁓] foie *m*.

liv·er·y ['livǝri] ⚖ mise *f* en possession; (*a. ⁓ company*) corporation *f* d'un corps de métier; *cost.* livrée *f*; *at ⁓* en pension (*cheval*); '**⁓·man** membre *m* d'une corporation (*see livery company*); *⁓ sta·ble* écuries *f/pl.* de louage.

lives [laivz] *pl. de* life; '**live·stock** bétail *m*, bestiaux *m/pl.*; '**live·weight** poids *m* utile.

liv·id ['livid] blême, livide, plombé (*ciel*); **li'vid·i·ty** lividité *f*.

liv·ing ['liviŋ] 1. □ vivant; vif (vive *f*); ardent (*charbon*); *within ⁓ memory* de mémoire d'homme; 2. vie *f*; séjour *m*; train *m ou* niveau *m* de vie; *eccl.* bénéfice *m*, cure *f*; '**⁓-room** salle *f* de séjour; *⁓ space* espace *m* vital; *⁓ 'stan·dard* niveau *m* de vie.

Li·vo·ni·an [li'vounjǝn] 1. livonien (-ne *f*); 2. Livonien(ne *f*) *m*.

liz·ard ['lizǝd] lézard *m*.

Liz·zie *Am. co.* ['lizi] (*a. tin ⁓*) vieille Ford *f*.

lla·ma *zo.* ['lɑ:mǝ] lama *m*.

Lloyd's [lɔidz] la Société *f* Lloyd; *approx.* le Véritas *m*.

load [loud] 1. *su.* fardeau *m* (*a. fig.*); ⊕, *a. armes:* charge *f*; *test ⁓* charge *f* d'essai; 2. *v/t.* charger (de, *with*); *fig.* combler (de, *with*); *v/i. (a. ⁓ up)* prendre charge; '**load·ed** plombé (*canne etc.*); *⁓ dice pl.* dés *m/pl.* pipés; *fig. ⁓ question* question-piège *f* (*pl.* questions-piège); '**load·er** chargeuse *f*; *personne:* chargeur *m*; '**load·ing**

1. de chargement; **2.** chargement *m*; **'load·line** ⚓ ligne *f* de charge; **'load·star** étoile *f* polaire; *fig.* point *m* de mire; **'load·stone** pierre *f* d'aimant; aimant *m* naturel.

loaf¹ [louf] (*pl.* **loaves**) pain *m* (*a. de sucre*); miche *f* (*de pain*).

loaf² [~] fainéanter, flâner.

loaf·er ['loufə] flâneur *m*; voyou *m*.

loaf·sug·ar ['loufʃugə] sucre *m* en pain.

loam [loum] 🖉 terre *f* grasse; *métall.* glaise *f*; **'loam·y** 🖉 gras(se *f*); *métall.* argileux (-euse *f*).

loan [loun] **1.** prêt *m*; avance *f*; emprunt *m*; on ~ à titre d'emprunt; détaché (auprès de, to) (*personne*); ask *s.o.* for the ~ of *s.th.* demander à emprunter qch. à q.; *put out to* ~ prêter; **2.** *surt. Am.* prêter; **'~·word** mot *m* d'emprunt.

loath □ [louθ] peu disposé; be ~ for *s.o.* to do *s.th.* ne pas vouloir que q. fasse qch.; nothing ~ très volontiers; **loathe** [louð] détester; abhorrer; **loath·ing** ['~ðiŋ] aversion *f*, répugnance *f* (pour for, of); **loath·some** ['~səm] dégoûtant; **'loath·some·ness** caractère *m ou* nature *f* dégoûtant(e).

loaves [louvz] *pl.* de **loaf¹**.

lob [lɔb] *tennis:* **1.** lob *m*; **2.** lober (*la balle*).

lob·by ['lɔbi] **1.** vestibule *m* (*a. parl.*); *parl.* salle *f* des pas perdus; *théâ.* foyer *m*, entrée *f*; *parl. Am.* groupe *m* d'intrigants; **2.** *surt. Am. parl.* faire les couloirs; influencer certains députés *etc.*; **'lob·by·ist** *parl. surt. Am.* faiseur *m* des couloirs.

lobe *anat.*, ♀ [loub] lobe *m*; ⊕ nez *m*; F oreille *f*.

lob·ster ['lɔbstə] homard *m*.

lo·cal □ ['loukəl] **1.** local (-aux *m/pl.*), régional (-aux *m/pl.*); de la localité, du pays; *see* branch; 🖉 ~ an(a)esthetic anesthésie *m* local; *téléph.* ~ call communication *f* interurbaine *ou* locale; ~ colour couleur *f* locale; ~ elections (élections *f/pl.*) municipales *f/pl.*; ~ government administration *f* décentralisée; **2.** *journ.* nouvelles *f/pl.* de la région; 🚆 (a. ~ train) train *m* d'intérêt local; F tortillard *m*; ~s *pl.* habitants *m/pl.* de l'endroit; **lo·cale** [lou'kɑːl] scène *f* (*des événements*); **lo·cal·i·ty** [~'kæli-

ti] localité *f*; région *f*; **lo·cal·ize** ['~kəlaiz] localiser.

lo·cate [lou'keit] *v/t.* localiser; déterminer la situation de; établir; repérer (*une épave etc.*); *Am.* fixer l'emplacement de; be ~d être situé; it was ~d on le trouva; *v/i. Am.* s'établir; **lo·ca·tion** situation *f*, emplacement *m*; établissement *m*; 🎬 location *f*; *Am.* concession *f* minière; *cin.* extérieurs *m/pl.*

loch *écoss.* [lɔx] lac *m*; bras *m* de mer.

lock¹ [lɔk] **1.** *su.* porte *etc.*: serrure *f*, fermeture *f*; *fusil:* platine *f*; écluse *f*; ⊕ roue: enrayure *f*; verrou *m* (*a. fig.*); *sp. lutte:* clef *f*; *mot.* (*a.* steering ~) angle *m* de braquage; **2.** *v/t.* fermer à clef; (*a.* ~ up) enfermer; ⊕ enrayer (*une roue*); écluser (*un bateau*); verrouiller (*des armes*); *fig.* serrer; ~ the door against fermer sa porte à (*q.*); ~ in enfermer à clef; mettre sous clef; ~ out fermer la porte à *ou* sur; ⊕ lock-outer; ~ up bloquer, immobiliser (*des capitaux*); *v/i.* se fermer à clef; s'enrayer (*roues*); s'enclencher (*pièces d'un mécanisme*).

lock² [~] *cheveux:* boucle *f*; *laine:* flocon *m*.

lock·age ['lɔkidʒ] éclusage *m*; droit *m* d'écluse; **'lock·er** armoire *f*, coffre *m* (*fermant à clef*); ⚓ caisson *m*; ⚓ soute *f*; **lock·et** ['~it] médaillon *m*.

lock...: '~·gate porte *f* d'écluse; '~·jaw 🖉 trisme *m*; F tétanos *m*; '~·keep·er gardien *m* d'écluse, éclusier *m*; '~·nut ⊕ contre-écrou *m*; '~·out lock-out *m/inv.*; '~·smith serrurier *m*; '~·stitch point *m* de navette; '~·up **1.** *su. surt. école:* fermeture *f* des portes; hangar *m ou* magasin *m etc.* fermant à clef; F poste *m* de police; 🖉 immobilisation *f* (*de capital*); **2.** *adj.* fermant à clef.

lo·co *Am. sl.* ['loukou] toqué, fou (fol *devant une voyelle ou un h muet*); folle *f*).

lo·co·mo·tion [loukə'mouʃn] locomotion *f*; **lo·co·mo·tive** ['~tiv] **1.** locomotif (-ive *f*); *co.* voyageur (-euse *f*); **2.** 🚆 (*ou* ~ engine) locomotive *f*.

lo·cum-ten·ens ['loukəm'tiːnenz] remplaçant(e *f*) *m*; **lo·cus** ['loukəs], *pl.* **-ci** [~sai] Å lieu *m* géométrique.

lo·cust ['loukəst] *zo.* grande saute- relle *f*; ♀ caroube *f*; ~-*tree* carou- bier *m*; faux acacia *m*.

lo·cu·tion [loˈkjuːʃn] locution *f*.

lode ⚒ [loud] veine *f*.

lodge [lɔdʒ] **1.** *su.* pavillon (*de chasse, d'entrée*); *concierge, francs-maçons*: loge *f*; maison *f* (*de garde-chasse*); **2.** *v/t.* loger (*q., une balle*); avoir (*q.*) comme locataire; *v/i.* (*usu.* se) loger; demeurer (chez, *with*); être en pen- sion (chez, *with*); **'lodge·ment** *see* **lodgment**; **'lodg·er** locataire *mf*; pensionnaire *mf*; **'lodg·ing** héber- gement *m*; argent *etc.*: dépôt *m*; ~*s pl.* logement *m*, logis *m*, apparte- ment *m* meublé; *souv.* chambre *f*; **'lodg·ing-house** hôtel *m* garni; pension *f*; **'lodg·ment** prise *f*; ✕ logement *m*, ⚙ dépôt *m*, remise *f*.

loft [lɔft] grenier *m*; *église etc.*: gale- rie *f*; ⊕ atelier *m*; colombier *m*; **loft·i·ness** ['~inis] hauteur *f* (*a. fig.*); élévation *f* (*a. du style, des sen- timents, etc.*); **'loft·y** □ haut, élevé; hautain (*personne, a. air*).

log [lɔg] (*grosse*) bûche *f*; ⚓ loch *m*; *see a. log-book.* [rithme *m*.]

log·a·rithm ⚛ [ˈlɔgəriθm] loga-

log...: **'~-book** ⚓ livre *m* de loch; journal *m* de bord; *mot.* carnet *m* de route; ≋ livre *m* de vol; ~ **cab·in** cabane *f* de bois; **logged** [lɔgd] im- bibé (*d'eau*); **log·ger** [ˈlɔgə] bûche- ron *m*; **log·ger·head** [ˈlɔgəhed]: *be at* ~*s* être en bisbille (avec, *with*); **'log-house, 'log-hut** cabane *f* de bois.

log·ic [ˈlɔdʒik] logique *f*; **'log·i·cal** □ logique; **lo·gi·cian** [loˈdʒiʃən] logicien(ne *f*) *m*.

lo·gom·a·chy *poét.* [lɔˈgɔməki] logo- machie *f*, dispute *f* de mots.

log·roll *pol. surt. Am.* [ˈlɔgroul] échanger des faveurs, se prêter une entraide intéressée; **log·roll·ing** échange *m* de faveurs mutuelles.

log·wood [ˈlɔgwud] bois *m* de cam- pêche.

loin [lɔin] *cuis.* filet *m* (*de mouton ou de veau*), aloyau *m* (*de bœuf*), longe *f* (*de veau*); ~*s pl.* reins *m/pl.*; *anat.* lombes *m/pl.*

loi·ter [ˈlɔitə] traîner, flâner; ⚖ rôder; ~ *away one's time* perdre son temps à flâner; **'loi·ter·er** flâneur (-euse *f*) *m*; ⚖ rôdeur *m*.

loll [lɔl] *v/t.* pencher; laisser pendre;

v/i. pendre; être étendu (*personne*); se renverser nonchalamment; ~ *about* fainéanter, flâner; ~ *out* (*v/t.* laisser) pendre (*langue*).

lol·li·pop ⏚ [ˈlɔlipɔp] sucette *f*; *usu.* ~*s pl.* bonbons *m/pl.*; sucreries *f/pl.*

lol·lop ⏚ [ˈlɔləp] se traîner; marcher lourdement; [(= *argent*).]

lol·ly *Brit.* ⏚ *see* **lollipop**; *sl.* fric *m*]

Lom·bard [ˈlɔmbəd] Lombard(e *f*) *m*; ~ *Street* centre des opérations de banque à Londres.

Lon·don [ˈlʌndən] de Londres; **'Lon·don·er** Londonien(ne *f*) *m*, habitant(e *f*) *m* de Londres.

lone *poét.* [loun] solitaire, seul; ~ *wolf* solitaire *mf*; **'lone·li·ness** soli- tude *f*, isolement *m*; **'lone·ly** □ *see* **lonesome**; **'lon·er** solitaire *mf*; **lone- some** □ [ˈ~səm] solitaire, isolé.

long¹ [lɔŋ] **1.** *su.* longueur *f*; ⏚ ~*s pl. les grandes vacances f/pl.*; *before* ~ sous peu; avant peu; *for* ~ pendant longtemps; *take* ~ = *be* ~ (*see* ~ 2); *the* ~ *and the short of it* le tort et le fin de l'affaire; en un mot comme en mille; **2.** *adj.* long(ue *f*); ⏚ *see* tall; ⚘ ~ *figure* gros chiffre *m*; ⚘ *firm* bande *f* noire; ⏚ *johns* caleçon *m* long; *sp.* ~ *jump* saut *m* en longueur; ~ *price* prix *m* élevé; *radio:* ~ *waves* grandes ondes *f/pl.*; ⚘ *at* ~ *date* à longue échéance; *in the* ~ *run* à la longue; avec le temps; en fin de compte; *be* ~ prendre du temps (*chose*); tarder (à *inf.*, *to inf.*) [*in*] *gér.*) (*personne*); **3.** *adv.* longtemps; depuis longtemps; *as* ~ *ago as 1900* dès 1900; *I have* ~ *sought* je cherche depuis longtemps, voilà longtemps que je cherche; ~*er plus longtemps; no* ~*er ne* ... plus; *no* ~*er ago than* ... pas plus tard que ...

long² [~] désirer ardemment (qch., *for s.th.*); brûler (de, *to*).

long...: **'~-chair** chaise *f* longue; **'~-dat·ed** à longue échéance; **'~- 'dis·tance** à longue distance; *sp.* raid de fond (*coureur, course*); ~ *flight* raid *m*; *radio:* ~ *reception* réception *f* à longue distance; **lon·gev·i·ty** [lɔnˈdʒeviti] longévité *f*; **'long-hair** *Am.* ⏚ amateur *m* de la musique classique; adversaire *mf* du jazz *etc.*; intellectuel(le *f*) *m*; **'long- hand** écriture *f* courante.

long·ing [ˈlɔŋiŋ] **1.** □ impatient, avide; **2.** désir *m* ardent, grande envie *f* (de, *for*).

long·ish [ˈlɔŋiʃ] assez *ou* plutôt long.
lon·gi·tude *géog.* [ˈlɔndʒitjuːd] longitude *f*; **lon·gi·tu·di·nal** □ [ˌ~inl] en long; longitudinal (-aux *m/pl.*).
long...: 'ˌ~'**range** à longue *ou* grande portée (*a.* ✕); ✕ à grand rayon d'action; '~**shore·man** débardeur *m*; docker *m*; '~ **shot** *cin.* plan *m* lointain; '~'**sight·ed** presbyte; *fig.* prévoyant; '~'**suf·fer·ing** 1. patient; longanime; 2. patience *f*; longanimité *f*; '~'**term** à long terme; ~ *memory* mémoire *f* à long terme; '~'**ways** en long(ueur); '~**wind·ed** □ interminable; diffus, intarissable (*personne*).
loo [luː] *cartes*: mouche *f*.
loo·by [ˈluːbi] nigaud *m*.
look [luk] 1. *su.* regard *m*; air *m*, aspect *m*; (*usu.* ~s *pl.*) mine *f*; new ~ nouvelle mode *f*; have a ~ at s.th. jeter un coup d'œil sur qch., regarder qch.; *I like the* ~ *of him* sa figure me revient; 2. *v/i.* regarder (qch., at s.th.); par, out of); avoir l'air (*malade etc.*); sembler (*que ...*); paraître; porter la mine (de qch., [*like*] s.th.); *it* ~s *like rain* on dirait qu'il va pleuvoir; *he* ~s *like winning* on dirait qu'il va gagner; ~ *about* chercher (*qch., for* s.o.) des yeux; regarder autour de soi; ~ *after* soigner; s'occuper de; ~ *at* regarder; examiner; ~ *for* chercher; ~ *forward to* s'attendre à, attendre; ~ *in* faire une petite visite (à, on), entrer en passant (chez, on); *télév.* recevoir une émission, regarder; ~ *into* examiner, étudier; ~ *out!* attention!; ~ *out for* être à la recherche de; guetter; ~ *over* jeter un coup d'œil sur (*qch.*); ~ *to* voir à, s'occuper de; compter sur; ~ *to* s.o. *to* (*inf.*) compter sur q. pour (*inf.*); ~ *up* regarder en haut, lever les yeux, s'améliorer (*affaires, prix, etc.*); F ~ *up to* respecter; *fig.* (*up*)on regarder, envisager (comme, *as*); 3. *v/t.*: ~ s.o. *in the face* regarder q. en face; ~ *one's age* paraître *ou* accuser son âge; ~ *disdain* lancer un regard dédaigneux; ~ *over* revoir (*qch.*); jeter un coup d'œil sur; parcourir; ~ *up* (re)chercher; consulter; F aller voir (*q.*).
look-a·like [ˈlukəlaik] double *m*.
look·er-on [ˈlukərˈɔn] spectateur (-trice *f*) *m* (de, at); assistant *m* (à, at).

look·ing-glass [ˈlukiŋglɑːs] miroir *m*, glace *f*.
look...: 'ˌ~'**out** guet *m*, surveillance *f*; ✕ guetteur *m*; ⚓ vigie *f*; *fig.* qui-vive *m/inv.*; ⚓ *keep a* ~ être en vigie; *be on the* ~ ⚓ être de veille; *fig.* être sur ses gardes; *that is my* ~ ça c'est mon affaire; 'ˌ~-o'**ver** examen *m* superficiel; coup *m* d'œil; *give* s.th. *a* ~ examiner qch. rapidement; jeter un coup d'œil à qch.
loom[1] [luːm] métier *m* (à tisser).
loom[2] [~] se dessiner, s'estomper; se dresser; surgir (*du brouillard*).
loon[1] *écoss.* [luːn] garçon *m*; vaurien *m*; lourdaud *m*.
loon[2] *orn.* [~] grand plongeon *m*.
loon·y *sl.* [ˈluːni] dingue (= *fou*) (*adj., mf*); ~ *bin* maison *f* de fous.
loop [luːp] 1. *su.* boucle *f*; œil *m*, ganse *f*; *rideau*: embrasse *f*; sinuosité *f*; ⚓ boucle *f* d'évitement; *radio*: ~ *aerial* antenne *f* en cadre; 2. *v/t.* boucler; enrouler; ~ *up* retrousser, relever (*les cheveux, la robe*); retenir (*un rideau*) avec une embrasse; ✈ ~ *the* ~ boucler la boucle; *v/i.* faire une boucle, boucler; 'ˌ~**hole** trou *m*, ouverture *f*; *fig.* échappatoire *f* (à, for); ✕ meurtrière *f*; 'ˌ~**line** ✈ voie *f* de dérivation; *tél.* ligne *f* dérivée.
loose [luːs] 1. □ branlant; détaché; défait; échappé; libre; mobile; ✈ en vrac; mou (mol *devant une voyelle ou un h muet*; molle *f*); lâche; meuble (*terre*); vague (*terme etc.*); débauché; dissolu; ⚡ ~ *connection* contact *m* intermittent; *at a* ~ *end* désœuvré; 2. *v/t.* défaire (*un nœud etc.*); dénouer (*les cheveux, une ficelle, etc.*); détacher; ⚓ larguer; (*a.* ~ *off*) décocher, tirer; lâcher (*une prise*); ~ *one's hold on* lâcher (*qch.*); *v/i.* tirer (sur q., at s.o.); 3. *su.*: *give* (*a.*) ~ *to* donner libre cours à; 'ˌ~**leaf**: ~ *book* album *m* à feuilles mobiles; **loos·en** [ˈluːsn] (se) défaire, délier; (se) relâcher; (se) desserrer; 'ˌ**loose·ness** état *m* branlant; jeu *m*; robe *etc.*: ampleur *f*; relâchement *m* (*a.* ✘); *sol*: inconsistance *f*; imprécision *f*; *morale*: licence *f*.
loot [luːt] 1. piller; voler; 2. pillage *m*; butin *m*.
lop[1] [lɔp] tailler, émonder (*un arbre*); (*usu.* ~ *away ou off*) élaguer, couper.
lop[2] [~] pendre flasque; retomber.

lope [loup]: ~ *along* courir à petits bonds.

lop...: '~-**ears** *pl.* oreilles *f*/*pl.* pendantes; '~-'**sid·ed** de guingois; déjeté; qui manque de symétrie.

lo·qua·cious [loˈkweiʃəs] loquace; **lo·quac·i·ty** [loˈkwæsiti] loquacité *f*.

lord [lɔ:d] **1.** seigneur *m*, maître *m*; *titre*: lord *m*; *the* ♀ le Seigneur (= *Dieu*); *my* ~ monsieur le baron *etc.*; *parl. the* (*House of*) ♀s la Chambre des Lords; ♀ *Mayor* maire *m*; *the* ♀'s *Prayer* l'oraison *f* dominicale, le Pater *m*; *the* ♀'s *Supper* la Cène *f*; **2.** ~ *it* faire l'important; ~ *it over* en imposer à (*q.*); '**lord·li·ness** dignité *f*; *péj.* orgueil *m*; '**lord·ling** petit seigneur *m*; '**lord·ly** de grand seigneur; magnifique; majestueux (-euse *f*); *péj.* hautain; '**lord·ship** suzeraineté *f* (*de*, *over*); *titre*: seigneurie *f*.

lore [lɔ:] science *f*, savoir *m*.

lor·ry [ˈlɔri] 🚚 lorry *m*; *motor* ~ camion *m*.

lose [lu:z] [*irr.*] *v*/*t. usu.* perdre; égarer; gaspiller (*le temps*); *montre*: retarder de (*cinq minutes*); manquer (*le train*); coûter; ~ *o.s.* s'égarer; se perdre; *fig.* s'absorber; ~ *sight of s.th.* perdre qch. de vue; *v*/*i.* subir une perte, perdre; retarder (*montre*); *Am.* ~ *out* échouer; perdre; '**los·er** battu(e *f*) *m*, vaincu(e *f*) *m*; celui *m* (celle *f*) qui perd; *sp.* perdant(e *f*) *m*; *come off a* ~ échouer; '**los·ing** perdant; de vaincu.

loss [lɔs] perte *f*; ✝ ~ *leader* article-réclame *m* (*pl.* articles-réclame); *at a* ~ désorienté; embarrassé (*pour inf.*, *to inf.*); ✝ *à perte*; *be at a* ~ ne savoir trouver (*qch.*); *be at a* ~ *what to say* ne savoir que dire.

lost [lɔst] *prét. et p.p. de lose*; *be* ~ être perdu (*a. fig.*); être désorienté; *sl. get* ~! fiche le camp!; *this won't be* ~ *on me* j'en prendrai bonne note; *je comprends*; *be* ~ *upon s.o.* être en pure perte en ce qui concerne q.; '~-**prop·er·ty of·fice** (service *m* des) objets *m*/*pl.* trouvés.

lot [lɔt] **1.** sort *m* (*a. fig.*); *fig.* destin *m*, destinée *f*, fortune *f*; ✝ lot *m*; partie *f*; ✝ quantité *f*; monde *m*; beaucoup; *Am.* terrain *m*; *cin. Am.* terrain *m* de studio; F *a* ~ (*ou* ~s *pl.*) *of* beaucoup de; bien des; *draw* ~s *for s.th.* tirer qch. au sort; *fall to*

s.o.'s ~ revenir à q. (*de*, *to*); tomber en partage à q.; *throw in one's* ~ *with* unir sa destinée à celle de; s'attacher à la fortune de; **2.** (*usu.* ~ *out*) lotir; *Am.* ~ *upon* compter sur.

lo·tion [ˈlouʃn] lotion *f*.

lot·ter·y [ˈlɔtəri] loterie *f*.

loud 🔲 [laud] bruyant; retentissant; criard (*couleur*); haut (*a. adv.*); '~-**mouth** gueulard(e *f*) *m*, grande gueule *f*; '**loud·ness** caractère *m* bruyant; grand bruit *m*; force *f*; *radio*: volume *m*; '**loud·speak·er** *radio*: haut-parleur *m* (*pl.* haut-parleurs).

lounge [laundʒ] **1.** flâner; s'étendre à son aise; s'étaler; **2.** flânerie *f*; *maison*: salon *m*; *hôtel*: hall *m*; *théá.* foyer *m*; promenoir *m*; (*a.* ~ *chair*) chaise *f* longue; *sl.* ~-*lizard* gigolo *m*, greluchon *m*; ~ *suit* complet *m* veston; ~ *coat* veston *m*; '**loung·er** flâneur (-euse *f*) *m*.

lour [ˈlauə] se renfrogner (*personne*); menacer (*orage*); s'assombrir (*ciel*); '**lour·ing** 🔲 renfrogné; menaçant.

louse 1. [laus] (*pl. lice*) pou (*pl.* -x) *m*; **2.** [lauz] † épouiller; **lous·y** [ˈlauzi] pouilleux (-euse *f*); plein de poux; F sale.

lout [laut] rustre *m*, lourdaud *m*; '**lout·ish** rustre, lourdaud.

lou·vre, *Am.* **lou·ver** [ˈluːvə] persienne *f*.

lov·a·ble 🔲 [ˈlʌvəbl] aimable; digne d'être aimé.

love [lʌv] **1.** amour *m* (*de*, *pour*, *envers of*, *for*, *to*[*wards*]); tendresse *f*; *personne*: ami(e *f*) *m*; Amour *m*, Cupidon *m*; *sp.* rien *m*, zéro *m*; *attr.* d'amour; F *a* ~ *of a dress* un amour de robe; *for the* ~ *of God* pour l'amour de Dieu; *play for* ~ jouer pour l'honneur; *sp. four* (*to*) ~ quatre à zéro; *give* (*ou send*) *one's* ~ *to* envoyer son affectueux souvenir *ou* ses meilleures amitiés à (*q.*); *in* ~ *with* amoureux (-euse *f*) de; *make* ~ *to* faire la cour à; *neither for* ~ *nor money* à aucun prix; **2.** aimer (*d'amour*), affectionner; ~ *to do* aimer à faire; '~-**af·fair** affaire *f* de cœur; intrigue *f* galante; '~-**bird** psittacule *m*, inséparable *m*; '~-**child** enfant *m* naturel; ~ *game sp.* jeu *m* blanc; '**love·less** sans amour; '**love-let·ter** billet *m* doux; '**love·li·ness** beauté *f*; '**love·lock** accroche-cœur *m*; '**love·ly** beau

(bel *devant une voyelle ou un h muet*;
belle *f*; beaux *m/pl.*); ravissant; F
charmant; '**love-mak·ing** cour *f*
(amoureuse); '**love-match** mariage
m d'amour; '**love-po·tion** philtre *m*;
'**lov·er** amoureux *m*; fiancé *m*;
amant *m*; *fig.* ami(e *f*) *m*; *pair of*
~s deux amoureux *m/pl.*; '**love·set**
sp. six jeux *m/pl.* à zéro; '**love·sick**
féru d'amour; qui languit d'amour;
'**love·to·ken** gage *m* d'amour.

lov·ing □ ['lʌviŋ] affectueux (-eu-
se *f*).

low¹ (□ †) [lou] **1.** bas(se *f*), peu
élevé; petit (*classe, vitesse, etc.*);
lent (*fièvre*); grave (*son*); décolleté
(*robe*); (*a. in* ~ *spirits*) abattu; *fig.*
bas(se *f*), vil; *adv.* bas; ~*est bidder*
le moins disant *m*; *in a* ~ *voice* à voix
basse, doucement; *bring* ~ abattre;
humilier; *lie* ~ se tapir; se tenir coi; **2.**
météor. aire *f* de basses pressions;
surt. Am. niveau *m* le plus bas.

low² [~] **1.** meugler (*vache*); **2.**
meuglement *m*.

low...: '~**-brow 1.** peu intellectuel
(-le *f*), terre à terre; **2.** homme
m etc. terre à terre; *péj.* philis-
tin(e *f*) *m*; '~**-cost** (à) bon marché;
'~**-'down** *sl.* **1.** bas(se *f*); ignoble; **2.**
['~] tuyau *m*, renseignement *m*; substance *f*, fond *m*.

low·er¹ ['louə] **1.** *adj.* plus bas(se *f*)
etc. (*see low*¹ *1*); inférieur; d'en bas
inv.; **2.** *v/t.* baisser; abaisser (*chapeau, paupières, voile, etc.*); rabaisser
(*le prix, q.*); diminuer; (*faire*) descendre; *v/i.* descendre, s'abaisser;
baisser (*prix etc.*).

low·er² ['lauə] *see lour*.

low·er·most ['louəmoust] le (la) plus
bas(se *f*); '**low-in·come** à revenus
modérés; '**low-key(ed)** discret (-ète
f), retenu, modéré; '**low·land** plaine *f* basse; pays *m* plat; '**low·li·ness**
humilité *f*; '**low·ly** *adj.*, † *adv.*
humble, sans prétention, modeste;
'**low-'necked** décolleté (*robe*);
'**low·ness** manque *m* de hauteur;
petitesse *f*; *son:* gravité *f*; *conduite:*
bassesse *f*; ~ *of spirits* abattement *m*,
découragement *m*; '**low-'pres·sure**
basse pression *f*; '**low-shoe** soulier
m; '**low-spir·it·ed** abattu, découragé; '**low-'wa·ter** basse mer *f ou*
marée *f*.

loy·al □ ['lɔiəl] (*to*) loyal (-aux
m/pl.); fidèle (à); '**loy·al**-

ist loyaliste *mf*; '**loy·al·ty** fidélité *f*;
loyauté *f*.

loz·enge ['lɔzindʒ] losange *m*;
pharm. pastille *f*, tablette *f*.

lub·ber ['lʌbə] lourdaud *m*; ⚓ maladroit *m*; '**lub·ber·ly** lourdaud;
gauche.

lu·bri·cant ['lu:brikənt] lubrifiant
(*a. su./m*); **lu·bri·cate** ['~keit]
graisser; **lu·bri·ca·tion** lubrification *f*, ⊕ graissage *m*; '**lu·bri·ca-
tor** ⊕ graisseur *m*; **lu·bric·i·ty**
[lu:'brisiti] onctuosité *f*; *fig.* lubricité *f*.

lu·cid □ ['lu:sid] lucide, clair; ♀ luisant; *poét.* brillant; *poét.* transparent; ✴ ~ *interval* intervalle *m* de
lucidité; **lu'cid·i·ty**, '**lu·cid·ness**
lucidité *f*.

Lu·ci·fer ['lu:sifə] Lucifer *m* (*a.
bibl.*); *astr. a.* Vénus *f*; ♀ allumette *f*.

luck [lʌk] hasard *m*, fortune *f*,
chance *f*; *good* ~ bonne chance *f*;
bad (*ou hard ou ill*) ~ mauvaise fortune *f*, malheur *m*; *be down on one's*
~ avoir de la déveine; '**luck·i·ly** par
bonheur; '**luck·i·ness** bonheur *m*;
chance *f*; '**luck·less** infortuné;
malencontreux (-euse *f*) (*jour etc.*).

'**luck·y** □ fortuné; heureux (-euse
f); ~ *hit* (*ou break*) coup *m* de bonheur; '**luck·y-bag**, '**luck·y-dip**
boîte *f* à surprises.

lu·cra·tive □ ['lu:krətiv] lucratif
(-ive *f*); **lu·cre** ['lu:kə] lucre *m*.

lu·cu·bra·tion [lu:kju'breiʃn] *usu.* ~s
pl. élucubration *f*, -s *f/pl.*

lu·di·crous □ ['lu:dikrəs] grotesque,
risible.

lu·do ['lu:dou] jeu *m* des petits chevaux.

luff ⚓ [lʌf] **1.** *su.* lof *m*; ralingue *f*
du vent; **2.** *v/i.* lofer; *v/t.* (*a.* ~ *up*)
faire lofer.

lug [lʌg] **1.** traîner, tirer; *fig.* ~ *in*
amener (*qch.*) à toute force; **2.** ⊕
a. F oreille *f*; *casquette:* oreillette *f*.

luge [lu:ʒ] **1.** luge *f*; **2.** luger; faire de
la luge.

lug·gage ['lʌgidʒ] bagage *m*, -s
m/pl.; '~**-car·ri·er** *cycl.*, *mot.* porte-
bagages *m/inv.*; '~**-grid** *mot.* porte-
bagages *m/inv.*; '~**-of·fice** 🚆 consigne *f*; '~**-rack** filet *m* (à bagages);
'~**-van** 🚆 fourgon *m* aux bagages.

lug·ger ⚓ ['lʌgə] lougre *m*.

lu·gu·bri·ous □ [lu:'gju:briəs] lugubre.

luke·warm ['luːkwɔːm] tiède (*a. fig.*); '**luke·warm·ness** tiédeur *f.*
lull [lʌl] **1.** *v/t.* endormir (*a. fig.*); calmer; bercer; *v/i.* se calmer; s'apaiser; tomber (*vent etc.*); **2.** *su.* moment *m* de calme; ⏚ accalmie *f.*
lull·a·by ['lʌləbai] berceuse *f.*
lum·ba·go ⚕ [lʌm'beigou] lumbago *m.*
lum·ber ['lʌmbə] **1.** *su.* fatras *m*; vieux meubles *m/pl.*; *surt. Am.* bois *m* de charpente; **2.** *v/t.* (*usu.* ~ *up*) encombrer; *v/i.* aller lourdement *ou* à pas pesants; *Am.* débiter (le bois); '**lum·ber·er**, '**lum·ber·man** bûcheron *m*; '**lum·ber·ing** lourd; '**lum·ber·jack** bûcheron *m*; '**lumber·room** fourre-tout *m/inv.*
lu·mi·nar·y ['luːminəri] corps *m* lumineux; astre *m*; *fig.* lumière *f*; '**lu·mi·nous** □ lumineux (-euse *f*) (*a. fig.*); *fig.* illuminant; ~ **clock** horloge *f* à cadran lumineux; ~ **dial** cadran *m* lumineux; ~ **paint** peinture *f* lumineuse.
lump [lʌmp] **1.** *su. pierre, sucre, etc.*: morceau *m*; bloc *m*; masse *f*; bosse *f* (*au front etc.*); *fig. personne*: lourdaud *m*, empoté *m*; *in the* ~ en bloc; en gros; ~ **sugar** sucre *m* en morceaux; ~ **sum** somme *f* globale; **2.** *v/t.* mettre en bloc *ou* en tas; *fig.* réunir; ~ *together* réunir, considérer en bloc; *v/i.* former des mottes; *sl.* ~ *it* s'arranger; '**lump·er** ⏚ déchargeur *m*, débardeur *m*; '**lump·ing** F énorme; gros(se *f*); '**lump·ish** (ba)lourd; à l'esprit lent; '**lump·y** □ rempli de mottes; couvert de bosses; grumeleux (-euse *f*) (*sauce*); houleux (-euse *f*) (*mer*).
lu·na·cy ['luːnəsi] folie *f*; ⚖ démence *f.*
lu·nar ['luːnə] de (la) lune; lunaire; ⚗ ~ *caustic* caustique *m* lunaire; ~ *landing* alunissage *m*; ~ *module* module *m* lunaire.
lu·na·tic ['luːnətik] **1.** de fou(s); fou (fol *devant une voyelle ou un h muet*; folle *f*); ~ *asylum* maison *f* d'aliénés; F *pol.* ~ *fringe les* outranciers *m/pl.*, *les* ultras *m/pl.*; **2.** fou (folle *f*) *m*; aliéné(e *f*) *m.*
lunch [lʌntʃ] **1.** (*abr. de* **lunch·eon** ['~ən]) *su.* déjeuner *m*; *Am. a.* cassecroûte *m/inv.*; ~ *basket*, *packed* ~ panier-repas *m* (*pl.* paniers-repas); **2.** *v/i.* déjeuner; *Am.* prendre un

petit repas; *v/t.* offrir un déjeuner à (*q.*); ~ **hour**, '~ **time** heure *f* du déjeuner.
lung [lʌŋ] poumon *m*; *animal tué*: mou *m*; ⚙ *iron* ~ poumon *m* d'acier.
lunge [lʌndʒ] **1.** *su. escrime*: botte *f*; *fig.* mouvement *m* en avant; **2.** *v/i.* lancer un coup (à, *at*); *escrime*: porter une botte (à, *at*), se fendre; *fig.* se précipiter; *v/t.* darder, lancer.
lung·er *sl.* ['lʌŋə] tuberculeux (-euse *f*) *m.*
lu·pin(e) ♀ ['luːpin] lupin *m.*
lurch[1] [ləːtʃ] **1.** ⏚ embardée *f*; *fig.* pas *m* titubant; **2.** ⏚ embarder (*a. F*); *fig.* marcher en titubant.
lurch[2] [~]: *leave in the* ~ laisser (*q.*) dans l'embarras; planter là (*q.*).
lurch·er ['ləːtʃə] chien *m* croisé d'un lévrier avec un chien de berger.
lure [ljuə] **1.** leurre *m*; *fig.* piège *m*; *fig.* attrait *m*; **2.** leurrer; *fig.* séduire.
lu·rid ['ljuərid] blafard; *fig.* corsé; haut en couleur (*langage*).
lurk [ləːk] se cacher; rester tapi; '**lurk·ing·place** cachette *f.*
lus·cious □ [~]: *leave in the* succulent; *péj.* trop sucré *ou* fleuri; '**lus·cious·ness** succulence *f*; douceur *f* extrême.
lush [lʌʃ] plein de sève; luxuriant.
lust *poét.* [lʌst] **1.** appétit *m*; luxure *f*; *fig.* soif *f*; **2.** ~ *after* convoiter; avoir soif de; '**lust·ful** □ lubrique, lascif (-ive *f*); plein de convoitise.
lust·i·ness ['lʌstinis] vigueur *f.*
lus·tra·tion *eccl.* [lʌs'treiʃn] lustration *f.*
lus·tre, *Am.* **lus·ter** ['lʌstə] éclat *m*, brillant *m*; lustre *m* (*a. fig.*); '**lus·tre·less** terne (*a. fig.*); *fig.* sans éclat.
lus·trine ['lʌstrin] lustrine *f.*
lus·trous □ ['lʌstrəs] brillant *m*; *tex.* lustré.
lust·y □ ['lʌsti] vigoureux (-euse *f*), robuste; *fig.* puissant.
lu·ta·nist, lut·ist ['luːt(ə)nist] joueur (-euse *f*) *m* de luth, luthiste *mf.*
lute[1] ♪ [luːt] luth *m.*
lute[2] [~] **1.** lut *m*, mastic *m*; **2.** luter, mastiquer; *métall.* brasquer.
lute·string ['luːtstriŋ] *see* lustrine.
Lu·ther·an ['luːθərən] luthérien(ne *f*) (*a. su./mf*); '**Lu·ther·an·ism** luthéranisme *m.*
lux·ate ⚕ ['lʌkseit] luxer; déboîter

lux·u·ri·ance [lʌgˈzjuəriəns] exubérance *f*; **lux'u·ri·ant** □ exubérant; **lux'u·ri·ate** [⁓rieit] croître avec exubérance; *fig.* jouir avec délices (de, *in*); vivre (dans, *in*); **lux'u·ri·ous** □ [⁓riəs] luxueux (-euse *f*); F voluptueux (-euse *f*); **lux'u·ri·ous·ness** somptuosité *f*; luxe *m*; **lux·u·ry** [ˈlʌkʃəri] luxe *m*; objet *m* de luxe.

ly·ce·um [laiˈsiəm] Lycée *m*.

lye 🜍 [lai] lessive *f*.

ly·ing [ˈlaiiŋ] **1.** *p.pr.* de *lie*[1] et *lie*[2]; **2.** *adj.* menteur (-euse *f*); '⁓-'in couches *f/pl.*, accouche-

ment *m*; ⁓ *hospital* maternité *f*.

lymph ⚕ [limf] vaccin *m*; lymphe *f*; **lym·phat·ic** [⁓ˈfætik] **1.** (⁓*ally*) lymphatique; **2.** ⁓*s pl.* (vaisseaux *m/pl.*) lymphatiques *m/pl.*

lynch [lintʃ] lyncher; ⁓ **law** loi *f* de Lynch; lynchage *m*.

lynx *zo.* [liŋks] lynx *m*; loup-cervier (*pl.* loups-cerviers) *m*.

lyre [laiə] lyre *f*; *orn.* ⁓-*bird* ménure *m*.

lyr·ic [ˈlirik] **1.** lyrique; **2.** poème *m* lyrique; chanson *f*; ⁓*s pl.* lyrisme *m*; 'lyr·i·cal □ lyrique.

ly·sol *pharm.* [ˈlaisɔl] lysol *m*.

M

M, m [em] M *m*, m *m*.
ma F [mɑ:] maman *f*.
ma'am [mæm; *sl.* məm] *see madam.*
mac·ad·am [mə'kædəm] macadam *m*; **mac'ad·am·ize** macadamiser.
mac·a·ro·ni [mækə'rouni] macaroni *m*/*inv.*
mac·a·roon [mækə'ru:n] macaron *m*.
mace[1] [meis] *hist.* masse *f* d'armes; masse *f* (*portée devant un fonctionnaire*).
mace[2] [~] ♣ fleur *f* de muscade.
mac·er·ate ['mæsəreit] (faire) macérer; **mac·er'a·tion** macération *f*.
mach·i·na·tion [mæki'neiʃn] complot *m*, intrigue *f*; *~s pl.* agissements *m*/*pl.*, intrigues *f*/*pl.*; **mach·i·na·tor** ['~tə] machinateur (-trice *f*) *m*; intrigant(e *f*) *m*; **ma·chine** [mə-'ʃi:n] **1.** machine *f*; appareil *m* (*a.* = *avion*); bicyclette *f*; *fig.* automate *m*; *pol.* organisation *f*; *attr.* des machines, à la machine; ~ *fitter* assembleur *m*, ajusteur *m*; ✗ *~-gun* mitrailleuse *f*; ~ *translation* traduction *f* automatique; **2.** façonner; usiner; coudre à la machine; **ma·'chine·made** fait à la machine; **ma'chin·er·y** mécanisme *m*; machines *f*/*pl.*; appareil *m*, -s *m*/*pl.*; **ma'chine-shop** atelier *m* de construction mécanique; atelier *m* d'usinage; **ma'chine-tool** machine-outil *f* (*pl.* machines-outils) *f*; **ma·'chine-wash·a·ble** lavable en machine; **ma'chin·ist** machiniste *m*; mécanicien(ne *f*) *m*.
mack·er·el *icht.* ['mækrəl] maquereau *m*; ~ *sky* ciel *m* pommelé.
mack·i·naw *Am.* ['mækinɔ:] couverture *f* épaisse.
mack·in·tosh ['mækintɔʃ] imperméable *m*; caoutchouc *m*.
macro... [mækro] macro-; *~·bi·ot·ic* [~bai'ɔtik] macrobiotique; *~·bi'ot·ics* *sg.* macrobiotisme *m*; *~·cosm* ['~kɔzəm] macrocosme *m*.
mac·u·lat·ed ['mækjuleitid] maculé.
mad □ [mæd] fou (fol *devant une*

voyelle ou un h muet; folle *f*) (*a. fig.*), aliéné; enragé (*a.* chiens *etc.*); *fig.* éperdu, affolé, ivre (de *about, with, on*); *Am.* fâché (contre, *with*); F furieux (-euse *f*), furibond; *go* ~ devenir fou; *drive* ~ rendre fou; affoler (*a. fig.*).
mad·am ['mædəm] madame *f*; mademoiselle *f*.
mad·cap ['mædkæp] écervelé (*a. su./mf*); **mad·den** ['mædn] rendre fou, exaspérer; *it is* ~*ing* c'est exaspérant.
mad·der ♀, ⊕ ['mædə] garance *f*.
made [meid] *prét. et p.p. de* make *1, 2.*
made-to-meas·ure ['meidtə'meʒə] fait sur mesure; **made-to-ord·er** ['~'ɔ:də] fait sur commande.
made-up ['meidʌp] assemblé; artificiel(le *f*); tout fait (*vêtement*); maquillé (*femme*); faux (fausse *f*), inventé (*histoire etc.*).
mad·house ['mædhaus] maison *f* de fous; asile *m* d'aliénés; **'mad·man** fou *m*, aliéné *m*, insensé *m*; **'mad·ness** folie *f*; démence *f*; *vét.* rage *f*; hydrophobie *f*; *Am.* colère *f*; rage *f*; **'mad·wom·an** folle *f*, aliénée *f*, insensée *f*.
mael·strom ['meilstroum] *géog.* le Malstrom *m*; *fig.* tourbillon *m*.
mag·a·zine [mægə'zi:n] *fusil:* magasin *m*; ✗ magasin *m* d'armes, de vivres, *etc.*; ✗ dépôt *m* de munitions; (*revue f*) périodique *m*; magazine *m* (*illustré*).
mag·da·len ['mægdəlin] fille *f* repentie.
mag·got ['mægɔt] asticot *m*; *fig.* lubie *f*; F ver *m*; **'mag·got·y** plein de vers; *fig.* capricieux (-euse *f*).
Ma·gi ['meidʒai] *pl.:* the ~ les Rois *m*/*pl.* Mages.
mag·ic ['mædʒik] **1.** (*a.* **'mag·i·cal** □) magique, enchanté; **2.** magie *f*, enchantement *m*; **ma·gi·cian** [mə-'dʒiʃn] magicien(ne *f*) *m*.
mag·is·te·ri·al □ [mædʒis'tiəriəl] magistral (-aux *m*/*pl.*); *a. péj. de*

maître; de magistrat; **mag·is·tra·cy** ['⁓trəsi] magistrature *f*; les magistrats *m/pl.*; **mag·is·trate** ['⁓trit] magistrat *m*, juge *m*; *usu.* juge *m* de paix.

mag·na·nim·i·ty [mægnə'nimiti] magnanimité *f*; **mag·nan·i·mous** □ [⁓'næniməs] magnanime.

mag·nate ['mægneit] magnat *m*.

mag·ne·sia ♩ [mæg'ni:ʃə] magnésie *f*.

mag·net ['mægnit] aimant *m*; **mag·net·ic** [⁓'netik] (⁓*ally*) magnétique; aimanté; ⁓ *field* (*pole*) champ *m* (pôle *m*) magnétique; **mag·net·ism** ['⁓nitizm] magnétisme *m*; **mag·net·i·za·tion** [⁓tai'zeiʃn] aimantation *f*; **'mag·net·ize** aimanter; F magnétiser; **'mag·net·iz·er** *phys.* dispositif *m* d'aimantation; *personne*: magnétiseur *m*; **mag·ne·to** [mæg'ni:tou] ⊕ *etc.* magnéto *m*.

mag·nif·i·cence [mæg'nifisns] magnificence *f*; **mag'nif·i·cent** magnifique; somptueux (-euse *f*); **mag·ni·fi·er** ['mægnifaiə] loupe *f*, verre *m* grossissant; **mag·ni·fy** ['⁓fai] *v/t.* grossir (*a. fig.*); ⁓*ing glass* loupe *f*, verre *m* grossissant; **mag·nil·o·quence** [mæg'niləkwəns] emphase *f*, grandiloquence *f*; **mag'nil·o·quent** □ emphatique, grandiloquent; **mag·ni·tude** ['⁓tju:d] grandeur *f*; *star of the first* ⁓ étoile *f* de première magnitude.

mag·pie *orn.* ['mægpai] pie *f*; *a. fig.* bavard(e *f*) *m*.

mahl·stick *peint.* ['mɔ:lstik] appui(e)-main (*pl.* appuis-main, appuie-main) *m*.

ma·hog·a·ny [mə'hɔgəni] acajou *m*; *attr.* en acajou.

maid [meid] †, *co.* pucelle *f*; † demoiselle *f*; † jeune fille *f* (*ou* ⁓*servant*) bonne *f*, domestique *f*, servante *f*; *old* ⁓ vieille fille *f*; ⁓ *of all work* bonne *f* à tout faire; ⁓ *of* hono(u)*r* fille *f* d'honneur; *Am.* première demoiselle *f* d'honneur.

maid·en ['meidn] **1.** *prov.*, *co. see* *maid*; **2.** de jeune fille; non mariée; *fig.* premier; de début; ⁓ *name* nom *m* de jeune fille; ⁓ *speech* discours *m* de début; ⁓ *voyage* ♩ premier voyage *m*; ⁓ premier vol *m*; **'⁓-hair** ♧ capillaire *m*; **'⁓-head**, **'⁓-hood** virginité *f*; célibat *m* (*de fille*); **'⁓-like**,

'maid·en·ly virginal (-aux *m/pl.*); modeste.

mail¹ [meil] mailles *f/pl.*

mail² [meil] **1.** *poste*: courrier *m*; poste *f*; départ *m* du courrier; **2.** envoyer par la poste; expédier; ⁓*ing list* liste *f* d'adresses; **'mail·a·ble** *Am.* transmissible par la poste.

mail...: **'⁓-bag** sac *m* de dépêches *ou* de poste; **'⁓-boat** courrier *m* postal; paquebot *m*; **'⁓-box** *surt. Am.* boîte *f* aux lettres; **'⁓-car·ri·er** *Am.* facteur *m*; **'⁓-clad** revêtu de mailles; **'⁓-coach**, *Brit.* **'⁓-cart** wagon-poste (*pl.* wagons-poste) *m*; **'⁓-man** *Am.* facteur *m*; ⁓ *or·der·firm*, *surt. Am.* **'⁓-or·der house** maison *f* qui vend par correspondance; **'⁓-train** train-poste (*pl.* trains-poste[s]) *m*. [(*a. fig.*).]

maim [meim] estropier, mutiler.

main [mein] **1.** principal (-aux *m/pl.*); premier (-ère *f*), essentiel(le *f*); grand (*route*); ⁓ *chance* son propre intérêt; *téléph.* ⁓ *station* table *f* (principale); *by* ⁓ *force* de vive force; ⁓ *plane* voilure *f*; **2.** vigueur *f*; ⊕ canalisation *f* maîtresse; ⚡ conducteur *m* principal; *poét.* océan *m*; ⁓*s pl.* ⚡ secteur *m*; ⚡ *rising* ⁓ conducteur *m* principal montant; ⁓*s aerial* antenne *f* secteur; ⁓*s receiving set* poste *m* secteur; *in the* ⁓ en général, à tout prendre; **'⁓-land** terre *f* ferme; continent *m*; **'main·ly** surtout.

main...: ⁓*mast* ['⁓mɑ:st; ♩ '⁓məst] grand mât *m*; ⁓*sail* ['⁓seil; ♩ '⁓sl] grand-voile *f*; **'⁓-spring** ressort *m* moteur; *fig.* mobile *m* essentiel; **'⁓-stay** ♩ étai *m* de grand mât; *fig.* soutien *m* principal; **'⁓-stream** *fig.* tendance *f* principale; ♄-*Street* *Am.* grand-rue *f*; habitants *m/pl.* d'une petite ville.

main·tain [men'tein] maintenir; soutenir (*opinion, famille, conversation, cause, guerre*); entretenir (*famille, correspondance, route, relations*); défendre (*ses droits, une cause*); conserver (*l'allure, la santé*); garder (*l'attitude, l'avantage*); ⁓ *that* affirmer *ou* maintenir que; **main'tain·a·ble** (sou)tenable.

main·te·nance ['meintinəns] maintien *m*; entretien *m*; défense *f*; appui *m*; subsistance *f*; ⁓ *costs pl.* frais *m/pl.* d'entretien.

main·top ⚓ ['meintɔp] grand-hune f.

maize ♀ [meiz] maïs m.

ma·jes·tic [mə'dʒestik] (~ally) majestueux (-euse f); **ma·jes·ty** ['mædʒisti] majesté f.

ma·jor ['meidʒə] 1. majeur(e f); le plus grand; *mot.* de priorité (route); principal (-aux m/pl.) (a. *couleurs aux cartes*); ♪ A ~ la m majeur; ♪ ~ third tierce f majeure; ♪ ~ key ton m majeur; *Am.* baseball: ~ league ligue f majeure; 2. ✗ commandant m; ✗ chef m de bataillon (*infanterie*) ou d'escadron (*cavalerie*); *personne*: majeur(e f) m; *phls.* majeure f; *Am. univ.* sujet m principal; 3. *Am.* (in) se spécialiser (en) (*un sujet*); être reçu à l'examen supérieur (de); '~·'gen·er·al général m de brigade; **ma·jor·i·ty** [mə'dʒɔriti] majorité f (a. *âge*); le plus grand nombre; la plus grande partie; ✗ (a. **ma·jor·ship** ['meidʒəʃip]) grade m de commandant; ~ decision décision f prise à la majorité; *pol.* ~ rule gouvernement m majoritaire ou de la majorité; *join the* ~ mourir, s'en aller ad patres.

make [meik] 1. [*irr.*] v/t. faire (*qch., distinction, amis, paix, guerre, discours, testament, thé, bruit, faute, fortune, etc.*); construire; fabriquer; confectionner (*des vêtements*); conclure (*un marché*); fixer (*les conditions*); établir (*une règle*); subir (*une perte*); conclure (*la paix, un traité*); battre (*les cartes*); ⚡ fermer (*le circuit*); nommer (*un juge, un professeur, etc.*); ~ the best of it en prendre son parti; ~ capital out of tirer parti de; ~ good réparer (*un tort*), tenir (*sa parole*), établir (*son droit à qch.*); *Am.* F ~ it réussir (à qch.); arriver à temps; ⚓ ~ the land atterrir; ~ or mar s.o. faire la fortune ou la ruine de q.; ~ one joindre, unir; do you ~ one of us? êtes-vous des nôtres?; ⚓ ~ a port arriver à un port; ~ shift s'accommoder (*de qch.*); ~ sure of s'assurer de (*un fait*); s'assurer (*une place etc.*); ~ sure that s'assurer que; F être persuadé que; ~ way faire du chemin; ~ way for faire place à (q.) (a. fig.); ~ into transformer en; ~ out dresser (*une liste, un compte*); faire (*un chèque*); prouver; discerner;

démêler (*les raisons de q.*); déchiffrer (*une écriture*); F feindre; ~ over céder; transférer; ~ up compléter; combler (*un déficit*); faire (*un paquet*); préparer; façonner (*une robe etc.*); dresser (*une liste, un compte*); établir (*un compte*); inventer (*une excuse, une histoire*); composer (*un ensemble*); accommoder (*un différend*); *made up of* composé de; *see* ~ up for (v/i.); ~ up one's mind se décider (à, to; pour for, in favo[u]r of); prendre son parti; 2. [*irr.*] v/i. ⚡ se fermer (*circuit*); monter (*marée*); ~ as if faire mine de; faire semblant de; ~ after s'élancer sur ou après; ~ against s'opposer à; ~ at ruer sur (q.); ~ away with enlever; détruire; dérober (*de l'argent*); ~ for se diriger vers; s'élancer sur, ⚓; ⚓ mettre le cap sur; favoriser; ~ off se sauver; décamper; ~ up compenser; se réconcilier; se maquiller; ~ up for réparer; se rattraper de (*une perte*); suppléer à (*un manque*); compenser; ~ up to s'approcher de; F faire la cour à; 3. fabrication f; façon f; taille f (*de q.*); ✝ marque f; ⚡ circuit: fermeture f; *our own* ~ de notre marque; *of poor* ~ de qualité inférieure; '~·be·lieve 1. semblant m; feinte f; trompe-l'œil m/inv.; 2. fictif (-ive f), imaginaire, feint; '**mak·er** faiseur (-euse f) m; ✝ fabricant m; constructeur m; *the* ♀ ~ Créateur m (= *Dieu*).

make...: '~·shift 1. pis-aller m/inv.; 2. de fortune; '~·up *see* make 3; composition f; maquillage m; invention f; ~ charge façon f; '~·weight complément m de poids; *fig.* supplément m.

mak·ing ['meikiŋ] fabrication f; création f; F ~s pl. recettes f/pl.; petits profits m/pl.; *in the* ~ en train de se faire; *have the* ~s *of* avoir ce qu'il faut pour.

mal·a·chite *min.* ['mæləkait] malachite f; cendre f verte.

mal·ad·just·ment ['mælə'dʒʌstmənt] ajustement m défectueux; dérèglement m.

mal·ad·min·is·tra·tion ['mæləd-minis'treiʃn] mauvaise administration f ou gestion f.

mal·a·droit ['mælə'drɔit] maladroit.

mal·a·dy ['mælədi] maladie f.

mal·ap·ro·pos ['mæl'æprəpou] 1.

adv. mal à propos; **2.** *adj.* inopportun.

ma·lar·i·a ⚕ [mə'lɛəriə] malaria *f*, paludisme *m*; **ma'lar·i·al** paludéen(ne *f*).

ma·lar·key *Am.* F [mə'lɑːki] baliverne(s) *f*/(*pl.*), blague(s) *f*/(*pl.*), baratin *m*.

mal·con·tent ['mælkəntent] mécontent (*a. su./mf*).

male [meil] **1.** mâle; ~ *child* enfant *m* mâle; ~ *screw* vis *f* mâle *ou* pleine; **2.** mâle *m*; homme *m*.

mal·e·dic·tion [mæli'dikʃn] malédiction *f*; anathème *m*.

mal·e·fac·tor ['mælifæktə] malfaiteur (-trice *f*) *m*.

ma·lef·i·cence [mə'lefisns] malfaisance *f*; **ma'lef·i·cent** malfaisant (envers, *to*); criminel(le *f*).

ma·lev·o·lence [mə'levələns] malveillance *f* (envers, *to*[*wards*]); **ma'lev·o·lent** □ malveillant (envers, *to*[*wards*]).

mal·for·ma·tion ['mælfɔː'meiʃn] malformation *f*; défaut *m* de conformation.

mal·func·tion [mæl'fʌŋkʃən] **1.** fonctionnement *m* défectueux, dérèglement *m*; **2.** fonctionner mal.

mal·ice ['mælis] malice *f*; malveillance *f*; méchanceté *f*; 🕱 intention *f* criminelle; *bear s.o.* ~ vouloir du mal à q., en vouloir à q.; 🕱 *with* ~ *aforethought* avec intention criminelle.

ma·li·cious □ [mə'liʃəs] méchant; malveillant; 🕱 avec intention criminelle; **ma'li·cious·ness** malice *f* etc.

ma·lign [mə'lain] **1.** □ pernicieux (-euse *f*), nuisible; ⚕ malin (-igne *f*); **2.** calomnier, diffamer; **ma·lig·nan·cy** [mə'lignənsi] malignité *f* (*a.* ⚕); virulence *f*; **ma'lig·nant** □ **1.** malin (-igne *f*) (*a.* ⚕); méchant; **2.** *hist.* ~s *pl.* dissidents *m*/*pl.*; **ma'lig·ni·ty** malignité *f*; méchanceté *f*; *souv.* ⚕ malignité *f*.

ma·lin·ger [mə'liŋgə] faire le malade; **ma'lin·ger·er** faux malade *m*, fausse malade *f*.

mall *Am.* [mɔːl] centre *m* commercial.

mal·lard *orn.* ['mæləd] malard *m*; canard *m* sauvage.

mal·le·a·bil·i·ty [mæliə'biliti] malléabilité *f*; *fig.* souplesse *f*; '**mal-**

le·a·ble malléable; *fig.* complaisant.

mal·let ['mælit] maillet *m*.

mal·low ♧ ['mælou] mauve *f*.

malm·sey ['mɑːmzi] Malvoisie *f*.

mal·nu·tri·tion ['mælnjuː'triʃn] sous-alimentation *f*; alimentation *f* défectueuse.

mal·o·dor·ous □ [mæ'loudərəs] malodorant.

mal·prac·tice ['mæl'præktis] méfait *m*; ⚕ négligence *f*; 🕱 malversation *f*.

malt [mɔːlt] **1.** malt *m*; ~ *liquor* bière *f*; **2.** (se) convertir en malt; *v/t.* malter.

Mal·tese ['mɔːl'tiːz] **1.** maltais; **2.** Maltais(e *f*) *m*.

malt·ing ['mɔːltiŋ] maltage *m*.

mal·treat [mæl'triːt] maltraiter, malmener; **mal'treat·ment** mauvais traitement *m*.

malt·ster ['mɔːltstə] malteur *m*.

mal·ver·sa·tion [mælvə'seiʃn] malversation *f*; mauvaise administration *f*.

ma(m)·ma [mə'mɑː] maman *f*.

mam·mal ['mæməl] mammifère *m*; **mam·ma·li·an** [mə'meiljən] mammifère (*a. su./m*).

mam·mon ['mæmən] Mammon *m*.

mam·moth ['mæməθ] **1.** *zo.* mammouth *m*; **2.** géant, monstre.

mam·my F ['mæmi] maman *f*; *Am.* nourrice *f* noire.

man [mæn; *mots composés:* -mən] **1.** (*pl. men*) homme *m* (*a.* ⚔); domestique *m*, valet *m*; ouvrier *m*; F mari *m*; *échecs:* pièce *f*; *dames:* pion *m*; *attr.* d'homme(s); *to a* ~ jusqu'au dernier; ⚔ ~ *on leave* permissionnaire *m*; **2.** ⚔, ⚓ garnir d'hommes; armer, équiper; ~ *o.s.* faire appel à tout son courage.

man·a·cle ['mænəkl] **1.** menotte *f*; **2.** mettre les menottes à (*q.*).

man·age ['mænidʒ] *v/t.* manier (*un outil*); conduire (*une auto, une entreprise*); régir (*une propriété*); gérer (*une banque, une affaire*); manœuvrer (*un navire*); gouverner (*une banque*); maîtriser (*un animal*); venir à bout de (*qch.*); *v/i.* s'arranger; se débrouiller; ~ *to* (*inf.*) venir à bout de (*inf.*); réussir à (*inf.*); ~ *without s.th.* se passer de qch.; '**man·age·a·ble** □ maniable; traitable (*personne*); '**man·age·ment** maniement *m*; direction *f*; conduite *f*; gestion *f*; savoir-faire *m/inv.*; administrateurs *m/pl.*; '**man·ag·er** directeur *m*; régisseur *m*; gérant *m*; chef *m* (*du service etc.*); *journal:* administrateur *m*; *théâ.* imprésario *m*; *departmental* ~ chef *m* de rayon; chef *m* de service; *sales* ~ directeur *m* commercial; *she is a good* (*bad*) ~ elle est bonne (mauvaise) ménagère *f*; '**man·ag·er·ess** directrice *f*, gérante *f*; **man·a·ge·ri·al** ☐ [~ə'dʒɪərɪəl] directorial (-aux *m/pl.*).

man·ag·ing ['mænɪdʒɪŋ] 1. directeur (-trice *f*); gérant; *fig.* entreprenant; F autoritaire; ~ *clerk* chef *m* de bureau; ⚖ premier clerc *m*; 2. direction *f*; conduite *f*; gestion *f*.

man·da·mus ⚖ [mæn'deɪməs] commandement *m* (*à une cour inférieure*).

man·da·rin ['mændərɪn] mandarin *m*; ♀ (*ou* '**man·da·rine** [~]) mandarine *f*.

man·da·ta·ry ⚖ [mændətəri] mandataire *mf*; **man·date** ['~deɪt] 1. *pol.* mandat *m*; *poét.* commandement *m*, ordre *m*; 2. attribuer sous mandat; **man'da·tor** mandant *m*; **man·da·to·ry** ['~dətəri] 1. mandataire; 2. état *m* mandataire.

man·di·ble ['mændɪbl] mandibule *f*; *anat.* mâchoire *f* inférieure.

man·do·lin(e) ♪ ['mændəlɪn] mandoline *f*.   [dragore *f*.⟍

man·drake ♀ ['mændreɪk] man-⟍

man·drel ⊕ ['mændrɪl] mandrin *m*.

man·drill *zo.* ['mændrɪl] mandrill *m*.

mane [meɪn] crinière *f*.

man·eat·er ['mæniːtə] mangeur *m* d'hommes; *personne:* cannibale *m*.

ma·nes ['meɪniːz] *pl.* antiquité romaine: mânes *m/pl.*

ma·neu·ver [mə'nuːvə] *Am. see manœuvre.*

man·ful ☐ ['mænful] viril; hardi; '**man·ful·ness** virilité *f*; vaillance *f*.

man·ga·nese ⚗ [mæŋgə'niːz] manganèse *m*; **man·gan·ic** [~'gænɪk] manganique.   [rogne *f*.⟍

mange *vét.* [meɪndʒ] gale *f*; F⟍

man·ger ['meɪndʒə] crèche *f*; F *dog in the* ~ chien *m* du jardinier.

man·gle¹ ['mæŋgl] 1. calandre *f*; 2. calandrer; cylindre.

man·gle² [~] déchirer; mutiler (*a. fig.*); *fig.* massacrer.

man·gler ['mæŋglə] machine *f* à calandrer.

man·gy ['meɪndʒɪ] galeux (-euse *f*); *fig.* minable.

man...: '**~·han·dle** manutentionner, transporter à force de bras; *sl.* malmener; bousculer; '**~·hat·er** misanthrope *m*; '**~·hole** ⊕ trou *m* de regard; bouche *f* d'accès; '**~·hood** humanité *f*; âge *m* viril, âge *m* d'homme; '**~·hours** *pl.* heures *f/pl.* de travail (par homme).

ma·ni·a ['meɪnjə] manie *f*; folie *f*; F passion *f*; *suffixe:* -manie *f*; **ma·ni·ac** ['~ɪæk] 1. fou (folle *f*) *m* enragé(e *f*) *m*; 2. (*a.* **ma·ni·a·cal** ☐ [mə'naɪəkl]) de fou (folle *f*); furieux (-euse *f*).

man·i·cure ['mænɪkjuə] 1. soin *m* des mains; toilette *f* des ongles; 2. soigner les mains; '**~·case** trousse *f* de manucure.

man·i·cur·ist ['mænɪkjuərɪst] *personne:* manucure *mf*.

man·i·fest ['mænɪfest] 1. ☐ manifeste, évident, clair; 2. ♦ manifeste *m* (de sortie); 3. *v/t.* manifester, témoigner; ♠ déclarer (*qch.*) en douane; *v/i.* manifester; **man·i·fes'ta·tion** manifestation *f*; **man·i·fes·to** [~'festou] *pol. etc.* manifeste *m*.

man·i·fold ☐ ['mænɪfould] 1. divers, varié; nombreux (-euse *f*); 2. *mot. intake ou inlet* (*exhaust*) ~ collecteur *m* d'admission (d'échappement); 3. polycopier; ~ *writ·er* appareil *m* à polycopier.

man·i·kin ['mænɪkɪn] petit homme *m*; homoncule *m*.

ma·nip·u·late [mə'nɪpjuleɪt] manipuler (*qch.*); ⊕ manœuvrer; agir sur (*une pédale*, ♦ *le marché*); **ma·nip·u'la·tion** manipulation *f*; ⊕ manœuvre *f*; tripotages *m/pl.* en Bourse; ♣ exploration *f*; **ma·nip·u·la·tive** [~] de manipulation; **ma·nip·u·la·tor** manipulateur *m*; ♣ agioteur *m*.

man·kind [mæn'kaɪnd] le genre humain; ['mænkaɪnd] les hommes *m/pl.*; '**man·like** *see* **manly**; **mannish**; '**man·li·ness** caractère *m* viril, virilité *f*; '**man·ly** viril, d'homme; '**man-made** artificiel(le *f*); ~ *fibre* fibre *f* synthétique.

man·ne·quin ['mænɪkɪn] mannequin *m*; ~ *parade* défilé *m* de mannequins.

man·ner ['mænə] manière *f* (*a. art*,

a. littérature); façon *f*; *peinture*: style *m*; ~s *pl.* mœurs *f/pl.*, usages *m/pl.*; manières *f/pl.*; tenue *f*; *no* ~ *of doubt* aucune espèce de doute; *in a* ~ *d'une* façon; *in such a* ~ *that* de manière que, de sorte que; ¹**man·nered** aux manières ...; *littérature, art*: maniéré; recherché; ¹**man·ner·ism** maniérisme *m*; particularité *f*; ¹**man·ner·li·ness** courtoisie *f*, politesse *f*; ¹**man·ner·ly** courtois, poli.   [masse (*femme*).]
man·nish [ˈmæniʃ] d'homme; hom-⟩
ma·neu·vra·ble, *Am. a.* **ma·neu·ver·a·ble** [məˈnuːvrəbl] manœuvrable, maniable; **maˈnœu·vre**, *Am. a.* **maˈneu·ver** [~və] **1.** manœuvre *f* (*a. fig.*); *fig.* ~s *pl.* F intrigues *f/pl.*; **2.** (faire) manœuvrer.
man-of-war [ˈmænəvˈwɔː] vaisseau *m* de guerre *ou* de ligne.
ma·nom·e·ter ⊕, *phys.* [məˈnɔmitə] manomètre *m*.
man·or [ˈmænə] seigneurie *f*; *see* ~**-house**; *lord of the* ~ seigneur *m*; châtelain *m*; ¹**~-house** château *m* seigneurial; manoir *m*; **ma·no·ri·al** [məˈnɔːriəl] seigneurial (-aux *m/pl.*); de seigneur.
man·pow·er [ˈmænpauə] ⊕ force *f* des bras; main-d'œuvre (*pl.* mains-d'œuvre) *f*; ✗ effectifs *m/pl.*
manse *écoss.* [mæns] presbytère *m*.
man·serv·ant [ˈmænsəːvənt] domestique *m*, valet *m*.
man·sion [ˈmænʃn] château *m*; hôtel *m* particulier (*en ville*); ~s *pl.* maison *f* de rapport.
man·slaugh·ter [ˈmænslɔːtə] homicide *m* par imprudence.
man·tel [ˈmæntl] manteau *m* de cheminée; ~*piece*, ~*shelf* dessus *m* de cheminée; F cheminée *f*.
man·tel·et [ˈmæntlit] mantelet *m*; ✗ pare-balles *m/inv.*
man·til·la [mænˈtilə] mantille *f*.
man·tle [ˈmæntl] **1.** manteau *m* (*a.* △, *anat.*, *zo.*); △ parement *m* (*d'un mur*); *fig.* voile *m*, manteau *m* (*a. incandescent* ~) manchon *m*; **2.** *v/t.* vêtir d'un manteau; *fig.* couvrir; revêtir; ~ *on* recouvrir; *v/i.* rougir (*joues*); se couvrir (de, *with*).
mant·let [ˈmæntlit] *see mantelet*.
man·trap [ˈmæntræp] piège *m* à hommes *ou* à loups.
man·u·al [ˈmænjuəl] **1.** □ manuel

(-le *f*); fait à la main; ✗ ~ *exercise* maniement *m* des armes; *sign* ~ seing *m*; **2.** manuel *m*; aide-mémoire *m/inv.*; *orgue*: clavier *m*; *instruction* ~ manuel *m* d'entretien.
man·u·fac·to·ry [mænjuˈfæktəri] fabrique *f*, usine *f*.
man·u·fac·ture [mænjuˈfæktʃə] **1.** fabrication *f*; confection *f*; *p.ext.* industrie *f*; **2.** fabriquer; confectionner; ~*d article* produit *m* industriel; ~*d goods pl.* produits *m/pl.* fabriqués; **man·uˈfac·tur·er** fabricant *m*; industriel *m*; **man·uˈfac·tur·ing** manufacturier (-ère *f*); industriel(le *f*).
ma·nure [məˈnjuə] **1.** engrais *m*; **2.** fumer, engraisser.
man·u·script [ˈmænjuskript] **1.** manuscrit *m*; **2.** manuscrit, écrit à la main.
Manx [mæŋks] **1.** manxois, mannois; **2.** *ling.* mannois *m*; Mannois(e *f*) *m*; *the Manx pl.* les Mannois *m/pl.*
man·y [ˈmeni] **1.** beaucoup de; bien des; plusieurs; ~ *a* maint(e *f*); bien des; ~ *a one* bien des gens; *one too* ~ un(e) de trop; **2.** beaucoup (de gens); un grand nombre; *a good* ~ pas mal de; un assez grand nombre (de gens); *a great* ~ un grand nombre (*de personnes*); ~**-**¹**sid·ed** *fig.* complexe, divers.
map [mæp] **1.** *géog.* carte *f*; *ville*: plan *m*; F *off the* ~ ne plus de saison; *on the* ~ d'actualité; **2.** dresser une carte *etc.* (de qch., *s.th.*); ~ *out* dresser.
ma·ple ♀ [ˈmeipl] érable *m*.
map·per [ˈmæpə] cartographe *m*.
mar [mɑː] gâter; déparer; troubler (*la joie*); ruiner.
mar·a·bou *orn.* [ˈmærəbuː] marabout *m*.
Mar·a·thon [ˈmærəθən] *sp.* (*a.* ~ *race*) marathon *m*.
ma·raud [məˈrɔːd] marauder; **maˈraud·er** maraudeur *m*.
mar·ble [ˈmɑːbl] **1.** marbre *m*; *jeu*: bille *f*; **2.** de marbre; *fig.* dur; **3.** marbrer.
March¹ [mɑːtʃ] mars *m*.
march² [~] **1.** marche *f* (*a.* ♩, *événements*); *civilisation, événements*: progrès *m*; ✗ ~ *past* défilé *m*; **2.** *v/i.* marcher; *fig.* avancer; faire des progrès; *v/t.* faire marcher; ✗ ~ *off*

v/t. emmener (*un prisonnier*); *v/i.* se mettre en marche; ~ *past* défiler.

march³ [~] **1.** *hist.* marche *f*; *usu.* ~es *pl.* pays *m* limitrophe; **2.** confiner (à, *with*).

march·ing ['mɑ:tʃiŋ] **1.** marche *f*; ~ *order* tenue *f* de route; ~ *orders pl.* feuille *f* de route; *fig.* congé *m*; *in heavy* ~ *order* en tenue de campagne; **2.** ~ *past* défilé *m*.

mar·chion·ess ['mɑ:ʃənis] marquise *f*.

march·pane ['mɑ:tʃpein] massepain *m*.

mare [mɛə] jument *f*; *fig.* ~'s nest canard *m*, découverte *f* illusoire.

mar·ga·rine [mɑ:dʒə'ri:n] margarine *f*.

mar·gin ['mɑ:dʒin] marge *f*; *bois:* lisière *f*; *rivière:* rive *f*; écart *m*; ~ *of error* tolérance *f*; ~ *of profit* bénéfice *m*, marge *f*; *safety* ~, ~ *of safety* marge *f* de sécurité; '**mar·gin·al** □ marginal (-aux *m/pl.*); en marge.

mar·grave ['mɑ:greiv] margrave *m*; **mar·gra·vine** ['~grəvi:n] margrave *f*, margravine *f*.

Ma·ri·a [mə'raiə]: *F Black* ~ panier *m* à salade (= *voiture cellulaire*).

mar·i·gold ♀ ['mærigould] souci *m*.

mar·i·jua·na [mɑ:ri'hwɑ:nə] marihuana *f*.

mar·i·nade [mæri'neid] **1.** marinade *f*; **2.** mariner.

ma·rine [mə'ri:n] **1.** marin; de mer; de (la) marine; **2.** soldat *m* de l'infanterie de marine; marine *f* (*a. peint.*); *tell that to the* ~s! allez conter ça ailleurs!; **mar·i·ner** *usu.* ⚓ ['mærinə] marin *m*.

mar·i·o·nette [mæriə'net] marionnette *f*.

mar·i·tal □ [mə'raitl] marital (-aux *m/pl.*); matrimonial (-aux *m/pl.*); ~ *status* état *m* familial.

mar·i·time ['mæritaim] maritime; naval (-als *m/pl.*); ~ *affairs pl.* affaires *f/pl.* maritimes.

mar·jo·ram ♀ ['mɑ:dʒərəm] origan *m*, marjolaine *f*.

mark¹ [mɑ:k] *monnaie:* mark *m*.

mark² [~] **1.** marque *f*; but *m*; signe *m*; *école:* note *f*; *école:* point *m* (*a. ponctuation*); *sp.* ligne *f* de départ; croix *f* (*au lieu de signature*); ☩ cote *f* (*d'une valeur*); marque *f* (*d'un produit*); *vét.* marque *f*; *a man*

of ~ un homme *m* marquant; *fig. up to the* ~ à la hauteur; dans son assiette (*santé*); *hit the* ~ frapper juste; *make one's* ~ se faire une réputation; *miss the* ~ manquer le but; *we are not far from the* ~ *in saying that* nous ne sommes pas loin de compte en disant que; **2.** *v/t.* (*a.* ~ *out*) tracer; estampiller (*des marchandises*); marquer ([*les points de*] *un jeu*); ☩ marquer; chiffrer; mettre le prix à; piquer (*les cartes*); coter (*un devoir*); indiquer; témoigner (*son approbation etc.*); guetter; observer; ~ *down* baisser de prix; repérer (*le gibier, un point*); ~ *off* séparer; mesurer (*une distance*); ~ *out* délimiter, tracer; borner (*un champ*); jalonner; ⚔ ~ *time* marquer le pas; **marked** [mɑ:kt], **mark·ed·ly** adv. ['mɑ:kidli] marqué; *fig.* sensible; accusé (*accent*); '**mark·er** *billard:* marqueur *m*; pointeur *m*.

mar·ket ['mɑ:kit] **1.** marché *m*; place *f* du marché; halle *f*, -s *f/pl.*; débouché *m* (*pour, for*); *Bourse:* cours *m/pl.*; *be in the* ~ être au marché; *come into the* ~ être mis en vente; *condition of the* ~ le marché; ~ *gardener* maraîcher (-ère *f*) *m*; *Am. sl. play the* ~ spéculer (*à la Bourse*); **2.** *v/t.* lancer (*qch.*) sur le marché; trouver des débouchés pour (*qch.*); *v/i.* faire son marché *ou* ses emplettes; '**mar·ket·a·ble** □ vendable; marchand (*valeur etc.*); **mar·ket·eer** [~'tiə] *see black* **1**; '**mar·ket·ing** achat *m* *ou* vente *f* au marché; '**mar·ket·val·ue** valeur *f* marchande; cours *m*.

mark·ing ['mɑ:kiŋ] marquage *m*; *usu.* -s *pl.* marque *f*, tache *f*; rayure *f*; '~-ink encre *f* à marquer.

marks·man ['mɑ:ksmən] bon tireur *m*; '**marks·man·ship** adresse *f* au tir.

marl [mɑ:l] **1.** *géol.* caillasse *f*; ⚒ marne *f*; **2.** ⚒ marner.

mar·ma·lade ['mɑ:məleid] confiture *f* d'oranges.

mar·mo·re·al □ *poét.* [mɑ:'mɔ:riəl] marmoréen(ne *f*).

mar·mot *zo.* ['mɑ:mət] marmotte *f*.

ma·roon¹ [mə'ru:n] marron pourpré *inv.*; châtain.

ma·roon² [~] **1.** nègre *m* marron, négresse *f* marronne; **2.** abandonner (*q.*) sur une île déserte.

mar·plot ['mɑ:plɒt] brouille-tout *m*/*inv*.   [quise *f*.\

mar·quee [mɑ:'ki:] (tente-)mar-⌐
mar·quess ['mɑ:kwis], *usu.* **marquis** ['mɑ:kwis] marquis *m*.

mar·que·try ['mɑ:kitri] marqueterie *f*.

mar·riage ['mæridʒ] mariage *m*; *fig.* union *f*; *civil* ~ mariage *m* civil; *by* ~ par alliance; *related by* ~ allié de près; *take in* ~ épouser (*q*.); prendre (*q*.) en mariage; ~*-guidance* guidance *f* de mariage; ~ *counsellor* raccommodeur *m* de ménages; **'marriage·a·ble** nubile; à marier; d'âge à se marier; ~ *person* parti *m*.

mar·riage...: '~*-lines pl.* acte *m* de mariage; '~*-'mar·ket: in the* ~ mariable; '~*-'por·tion* dot *f* (*de la femme*).

mar·ried ['mærid] marié (*personne*); conjugal (-aux *m*/*pl.*) (*vie*); ~ *couple* ménage *m*.

mar·row ['mærou] moelle *f* (*a. fig.*); *fig.* essence *f*; ⚥ *vegetable* ~ courge *f* à la moelle; '~*-bone* os *m* à moelle; ~*s pl. co.* genoux *m*/*pl.*; **'mar·row·y** plein de moelle (*a. fig.*).

mar·ry ['mæri] *v*/*t.* marier (*q.* à *q.*, *s.o.* to *s.o.*); se marier avec, épouser (*q.*); *v*/*i.* se marier (à, *to*).

marsh [mɑ:ʃ] **1.** marais *m*, marécage *m*; **2.** des marais; ~*-fever* paludisme *m*, fièvre *f* paludéenne; ~ *gas* gaz *m* des marais.

mar·shal ['mɑ:ʃəl] **1.** maréchal *m*; ✠ général *m*; maître *m* des cérémonies; *Am.* chef *m* de (la) police (*d'un comté*); **2.** placer en ordre; ranger (*les troupes*); 🚂 classer, trier (*des wagons*); **'mar·shal·ship** maréchalat *m*.

marsh·i·ness ['mɑ:ʃinis] état *m* marécageux (*du terrain*); **marsh mal·low** ⚘ guimauve *f*, althée *f*; bonbon *m* à la guimauve; **marsh mar·i·gold** souci *m* d'eau; **'marsh·y** marécageux (-euse *f*).

mar·su·pi·al *zo.* [mɑ:'sju:piəl] marsupial (-aux *m*/*pl.*) (*a. su.*/*m.*).

mart [mɑ:t] marché *m*; salle *f* de vente; centre *m* de commerce.

mar·ten *zo.* ['mɑ:tin] mart(r)e *f*.

mar·tial □ ['mɑ:ʃəl] martial (-aux *m*/*pl.*); guerrier (-ère *f*); ~ *law* loi *f* martiale; *state of* ~ *law* état *m* de siège; ~ *music* musique *f* militaire.

mar·tin¹ *zo.* ['mɑ:tin] martinet *m*.

Mar·tin² [~] St. ~'s *summer* été *m* de la Saint-Martin.

mar·ti·net [mɑ:ti'net] F exploiteur *m*; F gendarme *m*; garde-chiourme (*pl.* gardes-chiourme) *m*.

Mar·tin·mas ['mɑ:tinməs] la Saint-Martin *f* (*le 11 novembre*).

mar·tyr ['mɑ:tə] **1.** martyr(e *f*) *m*; **2.** martyriser; **'mar·tyr·dom** martyre *m*; **'mar·tyr·ize** martyriser.

mar·vel ['mɑ:vəl] **1.** merveille *f*; **2.** ~ *at* s'émerveiller de; s'étonner de.

mar·vel·(l)ous □ ['mɑ:viləs] merveilleux (-euse *f*), étonnant; **'marvel·(l)ous·ness** merveilleux *m*.

Marx·ism ['mɑ:ksizm] marxisme *m*; **Marx·ist** marxiste (*adj.*, *fm*).

mas·cot ['mæskət] mascotte *f*; porte-bonheur *m*/*inv*.

mas·cu·line ['mæskjulin] **1.** □ masculin; mâle; **2.** *gramm.* masculin. masculin. masculin *m*.

mash [mæʃ] **1.** mélange *m*; pâte *f*; *brassage*: fardeau *m*; ⚞ *chevaux*: mâche *f*; *chiens, volaille*: pâtée *f*; **2.** écraser; brasser; démêler (*le moût*); F faire infuser (*le thé*); ~*ed potatoes pl.* purée *f* (*de pommes de terre*); *sl.* be ~*ed* on avoir un béguin pour (*q.*); **'mash·er** broyeur *m*; *pommes de terre*: presse-purée *m*/*inv*.; *sl.* dandy *m*; gommeux *m*; **'mash(·ing)-tub** cuve-matière (*pl.* cuves-matière) *f*; ⚞ barbotière *f*.

mask [mɑ:sk] **1.** masque *m*; *renard*: face *f*; *see* **masque**; **2.** masquer; *fig.* cacher, déguiser; **masked** masqué; caché; ~ *ball* bal *m* masqué; **'mask·er** *personne*: masque *m*.

ma·son ['meisn] maçon *m*; franc-maçon (*pl.* francs-maçons) *m*; **ma·son·ic** [mə'sɒnik] des francs-maçons; **'ma·son·ry** maçonnerie *f*.

masque [mɑ:sk] † masque *m*; **masquer·ade** [mæskə'reid] **1.** mascarade *f*; bal *m* masqué; F déguisement *m*; **2.** *fig.* se déguiser (en, *as*).

mass¹ *eccl.* [mæs] messe *f*; *High* ♀ grand-messe *f*; *Low* ♀ messe *f* basse.

mass² [~] **1.** masse *f*, amas *m*; ~ *meeting* réunion *f* en masse; ~ *production* fabrication *f* en série; **2.** (se) masser.   [*m*; **2.** massacrer.\

mas·sa·cre ['mæsəkə] **1.** massacre\

mas·sage ['mæsɑ:ʒ] **1.** massage *m*; **2.** masser (*le corps*); malaxer (*les muscles*).

mas·seur [mæ'sə:] masseur *m*; **masseuse** [~'sə:z] masseuse *f*.

mas·sive □ ['mæsiv] massif (-ive *f*); énorme; solide; '**mas·sive·ness** massiveté *f*; aspect *m* massif.

mass...: ~ **me·dia** *pl.* media *m/pl.*; ~ **psy·chol·o·gy** psychologie *f* des foules; ~ **so·ci·e·ty** société *f* de masse.

mas·sy ['mæsi] massif (-ive *f*); solide; lourd.

mast¹ ♃ [mɑːst] **1.** mât *m*; *radio:* pylône *m*; **2.** mâter.

mast² [~] faines *f/pl.*; glands *m/pl.*

mas·ter¹ ['mɑːstə] **1.** maître *m* (*a. art, propriété, a. peint., a. fig.*); patron *m* (*d'employés, d'un navire de commerce*); *école:* instituteur *m*; *lycée:* professeur *m*; *univ.* (di)recteur *m*; *titre:* monsieur *m*; ♀ of Arts maître *m* ès arts, agrégé *m* des lettres; ♀ of Ceremonies maître *m* des cérémonies; ~ copy original *m*; be one's own ~ ne dépendre que de soi; **2.** maître; de maître; *fig.* magistral (-aux *m/pl.*), supérieur, dominant; **3.** dompter, maîtriser; régir (*une maison etc.*).

mas·ter² ♃ [~] à mât(s); three-~ trois-mâts *m/inv.*

mas·ter-at-arms ♃ ['mɑːstərət-'ɑːmz] capitaine *m* d'armes; '**master-'build·er** entrepreneur *m* de bâtiments; **mas·ter·ful** □ ['~ful] impérieux (-euse *f*); autoritaire; '**mas·ter-key** passe-partout *m/inv.*; '**mas·ter·less** sans maître; indiscipliné; '**mas·ter·li·ness** domination *f*, autorité *f*; caractère *m* magistral; '**mas·ter·ly** magistral (-aux *m/pl.*), de maître; '~-**mind 1.** *fig.* cerveau *m* (*d'une entreprise etc.*); **2.** organiser, diriger.

mas·ter...: '~-**piece** chef-d'œuvre (*pl.* chefs-d'œuvre) *m*; '~-**ship** maîtrise *f* (de over, of); poste *m* de professeur *ou* de maître; '~-**stroke** coup *m* de maître; '**mas·ter·y** maîtrise *f* (de over, of); domination *f* (sur over, of); dessus *m*; connaissance *f* approfondie (*d'une langue etc.*).

mas·tic ['mæstik] mastic *m*; ♃ lentisque *m*.

mas·ti·cate ['mæstikeit] mastiquer; **mas·ti·ca·tion** mastication *f*; **mas·ti·ca·to·ry** ['~təri] masticateur (-trice *f*).

mas·tiff ['mæstif] mâtin *m*; dogue *m* anglais.

mat¹ [mæt] **1.** *paille:* natte *f*; *laine etc.:* tapis *m*; **2.** (s')emmêler (*cheveux*); *v/t.* natter.

mat² ⊕ [~] mat; mati.

mat³ ⊕ *sl.* [~] matrice *f*.

match¹ [mætʃ] allumette *f*; *min.* canette *f*; mèche *f*.

match² [~] **1.** égal(e *f*) *m*, pareil(le *f*) *m*; *couleurs:* assortiment *m*; mariage *m*, alliance *f*; *sp.* partie *f*, match (*pl.* matchs, matches) *m*; *personne:* parti *m*; be a ~ for pouvoir le disputer à (*q.*); meet one's ~ trouver à qui parler; trouver son homme; **2.** *v/t.* égaler (*q.*); rivaliser avec (*q.*); assortir (*des couleurs*); apparier (*des gants*); unir (à, with); *sp.* matcher (*des adversaires*); ⊕ bouveter (*des planches*); ~ s.o. against opposer q. à (*q.*); well ~ed bien assorti; *v/i.* s'assortir, s'harmoniser; ~ with aller avec; to ~ à l'avenir; assorti.

match-box ['mætʃbɔks] boîte *f* à *ou* d'allumettes.

match·less □ ['mætʃlis] incomparable; sans pareil; '**match-mak·er** marieur (-euse *f*) *m*.

match·wood ['mætʃwud] bois *m* d'allumettes; *fig.* miettes *f/pl.*

mate¹ [meit] faire échec et mat (*échecs*); mater.

mate² [~] **1.** camarade *mf*; compagnon *m*, compagne *f*; *oiseau:* mâle *m*, femelle *f*; *personne:* époux *m*, épouse *f*; *école:* condisciple *m*, camarade *mf*; ♃ second maître *m*; *marine marchande:* officier *m*; **2.** (s')accoupler; (s')unir (*personne*); '**mate·less** seul, sans compagnon.

ma·te·ri·al □ [məˈtiəriəl] **1.** matériel(le *f*); grossier (-ère *f*); essentiel(le *f*) (pour, to); pertinent (*fait*); sensible (*service*); **2.** matière *f*; étoffe *f*, tissu *m*; matériaux *m/pl.* (*a. fig.*); ✗ matériel *m*; ~s *pl.* fournitures *f/pl.*; working ~ matière *f* première de base; writing ~s *pl.* de quoi écrire; **ma·te·ri·al·ism** matérialisme *m*; **ma·te·ri·al·ist** matérialiste *mf*; **ma·te·ri·al·is·tic** (~ally) matérialiste; matériel(le *f*) (*plaisirs*); **ma·te·ri·al·i·ty** [~ri'æliti] matérialité *f*; ✍ pertinence *f*; **ma·te·ri·al·i·za·tion** [~riəlai'zeiʃn] matérialisation *f*; *projet etc.:* aboutissement *m*; **ma·te·ri·al·ize** (se) matérialiser; *v/i.* F se réaliser; aboutir (*projet etc.*).

ma·ter·nal □ [mə'təːnl] maternel

(-le *f*); de mère; d'une mère; **ma·
'ter·ni·ty** [‿niti] maternité *f*; (*a.
~ hospital*) maternité *f*; *~ benefit* allocation *f* de maternité; *~ dress* robe *f*
pour futures mamans; *~ ward* salle *f*
des accouchées.

math·e·mat·i·cal □ [mæθi'mætikl]
mathématique; **math·e·ma·ti·cian**
[‿mə'tiʃn] mathématicien(ne *f*) *m*;
math·e·mat·ics [‿'mætiks] *usu.
sg.* mathématiques *f/pl.*

mat·in ['mætin] **1.** *poét.* matinal (-aux
m/pl.), de grand matin; **2.** *eccl. ~s
pl.* matines *f/pl.*; *poét. a. ~s pl.* chant
m des oiseaux au point du jour.

mat·i·née ['mætinei] matinée *f*.

mat·ing *biol.* ['meitiŋ] accouplement
m; *~ season* saison *f* des amours.

ma·tri·cide ['meitrisaid] matricide
m; *personne:* matricide *mf*.

ma·tric·u·late [mə'trikjuleit] *v/t.*
immatriculer; *v/i.* prendre ses
inscriptions; **ma·tric·u'la·tion** inscription *f*.

mat·ri·mo·ni·al □ [mætri'mounjəl]
matrimonial (-aux *m/pl.*); conjugal
(-aux *m/pl.*); **mat·ri·mo·ny** ['mæt-
riməni] mariage *m*; vie *f* conjugale.

ma·trix ['meitriks] *anat.*, *géol.* matrice *f*; ⊕ (*a.* ['mætriks]) matrice *f*,
moule *m*.

ma·tron ['meitrən] matrone *f*; mère
f de famille; *institution:* intendante
f; *hôpital:* infirmière *f* en chef;
'ma·tron·ly matronal (-aux *m/pl.*);
de matrone; domestique; *fig.* brave;
ma·tron-of-hon·o(u)r dame *f*
d'honneur.

mat·ter ['mætə] **1.** matière *f*; substance *f*; sujet *m*; chose *f*, affaire *f*;
✇ matière *f* purulente; *typ.* copie *f*;
printed ~ imprimés *m/pl.*; *in the ~ of*
quant à; *what's the ~?* qu'est-ce
qu'il y a? *what's the ~ with you?*
qu'est-ce que vous avez?; *no ~* n'importe; cela ne fait rien; *no ~ who* qui
que ce soit; *as a ~ of course* comme
de raison; *for that ~* quant à cela,
d'ailleurs; *~ of fact* question *f* de(s)
fait(s); *as a ~ of fact* en effet; à vrai
dire; *~ in hand* chose *f* en question;
2. avoir de l'importance; importer
(à, *to*); *it does not ~* n'importe; cela
ne fait rien; **'~-of-'course** de raison, naturel(le *f*); **'~-of-'fact** pratique; prosaïque.

mat·ting ['mætiŋ] natte *f*, -s *f/pl.*;
paillassons *m/pl.*

mat·tock ['mætək] hoyau *m*;
pioche *f*.

mat·tress ['mætris] matelas *m*.

ma·ture [mə'tjuə] **1.** □ mûr; d'âge
mûr; ✝ échu (*traite etc.*); **2.** mûrir;
affiner (*vin, fromage*); ✝ échoir;
ma'tu·ri·ty maturité *f*; ✝ échéance *f*.

ma·tu·ti·nal □ [mætju'tainl] ma-
(tu)tinal (-aux *m/pl.*); du matin.

maud·lin □ ['mɔ:dlin] larmoyant,
pleurard (*souv. état d'ivresse*).

maul [mɔ:l] meurtrir, malmener;
usu. ~ about tirer de ci de là.

maul·stick ['mɔ:lstik] *see* mahlstick.

maun·der ['mɔ:ndə] radoter, divaguer; flâner; se trimbaler.

Maun·dy Thurs·day ['mɔ:ndi-
'θə:zdi] jeudi *m* saint.

mau·so·le·um [mɔ:sə'li:əm] mausolée *m*.

mauve [mouv] **1.** mauve *m*;
2. mauve.

mav·er·ick *Am.* ['mævərik] bouvillon *m* errant sans marque de propriétaire; *pol.* indépendant(e *f*) *m*.

maw [mɔ:] caillette *f* (*de ruminant*);
jabot *m* (*d'oiseau*); gueule *f* (*de lion*);
co. panse *f*.

mawk·ish □ ['mɔ:kiʃ] insipide; sentimental(-aux*m/pl.*); **'mawk·ish·ness**
fadeur *f*; fausse sentimentalité *f*.

maw·worm ['mɔ:wə:m] ver *m* intestinal, ascaride *m*.

max·il·lar·y [mæk'siləri] maxillaire.

max·im ['mæksim] maxime *f*, dicton *m*; **'max·i·mal** □ ['‿əl] maximal; **'max·i·mize** ['‿aiz] maxim(al)iser, porter (*qch.*) ou maximum; **max·i·mum** ['‿əm] **1.** *pl.
usu.* **-ma** [‿mə] maximum (*pl. a.*
-ma) *m*; **2.** maximum; limite; *~ wages*
salaire *m* maximum.

May[1] [mei] **1.** mai *m*; ♀ ♣ aubépine
f; **2.** *go ~ing* fêter le premier mai.

may[2] [‿] [*irr.*] *v/aux.* (*défectif*) je
peux *etc.*; il se peut que.

may·be ['meibi:] peut-être.

May·day ['meidei] le premier mai;
♀ mayday *m*, S.O.S. *m*.

may·hem ['meihem] *Am.* ⚖ mutilation *f*; F chaos *m*, tohu-bohu *m*,
grabuge *m*.

may·or [mεə] maire *m*; **'may·or·al**
de maire, du maire; **'may·or·al·ty**
mairie *f*; (temps *m* d')exercice *m*
des fonctions de maire; **'may·or-
ess** femme *f* du maire; mairesse *f*.

may·pole ['meipoul] mai *m*.

maze [meiz] **1.** labyrinthe *m*, dédale *m*; *fig.* enchevêtrement *m*; *be in a ~* ne savoir où donner de la tête; **2.** embarasser, désorienter; *be ~d* être désorienté; **'ma·zy** labyrinthique; sinueux (-euse *f*); *fig.* compliqué.

Mc Coy *Am. sl.* [mə'kɔi]: *the real ~* authentique. [moi.)

me [mi:; mi] *accusatif*: me; *datif*:∫

mead[1] [mi:d] hydromel *m*.

mead[2] [~] *poét. see meadow.*

mead·ow ['medou] pré *m*, prairie *f*; **'~-'saf·fron** ♀ safran *m* des prés; **'mead·ow·y** de prairie; herbu; herbeux (-euse *f*).

mea·ger, mea·gre □ ['mi:gə] maigre (*a. fig.*); peu copieux (-euse *f*); *fig.* pauvre; **'mea·ger·ness, 'mea·gre·ness** maigreur *f*; pauvreté *f*.

meal[1] [mi:l] repas *m*; *~s pl.* on wheels repas *m/pl.* livrés à domicile.

meal[2] [~] farine *f* d'avoine, d'orge *etc.*; **meal·ies** ['~iz] *usu. pl.* maïs *m*.

meal-time ['mi:ltaim] heure *f* du repas.

meal·y ['mi:li] farineux (-euse *f*); **~-mouthed** doucereux (-euse *f*), patelin.

mean[1] □ [mi:n] misérable; mesquin, bas(se *f*), méprisable; méchant; avare; pauvre.

mean[2] [~] **1.** moyen(ne *f*); *in the ~ time see ~time;* **2.** milieu *m*; moyen terme *m*; ⅍ moyenne *f*; *~s pl.* moyens *m/pl.*, ressources *f/pl.*; *~s sg.* voie *f*, moyen *m*, -s *m/pl.* (*de faire qch.*); *a ~s of* (*gér.*) *ou to* (*inf.*) un moyen (*de inf.*); *by all* (*manner of*) *~s* par tous les moyens; mais certainement!; *by no* (*manner of*) *~s* en aucune façon; *by this ~s sg.* par ce moyen; ainsi; *by ~s of* au moyen de.

mean[3] [~] (*irr.*) avoir l'intention (de *inf., to inf.*); se proposer (de *inf., to inf.*); vouloir; vouloir dire; entendre (par, *by*); destiner (pour, *for*); *~ well* (*ill*) vouloir du bien (mal) (à, *by*).

me·an·der [mi'ændə] **1.** méandre *m*, repli *m*; sinuosité *f*; **2.** serpenter.

mean·ing ['mi:niŋ] **1.** □ significatif (-ive *f*); d'intelligence (*sourire*); *well-~* bien intentionné; **2.** sens *m*, acception *f*; *astr.* signification *f*; **'mean·ing·less** dénué de sens; qui ne signifie rien.

mean·ness ['mi:nnis] médiocrité *f*, pauvreté *f*, bassesse *f*; avarice *f*; *see mean*[1].

meant [ment] *prét. et p.p. de mean*[3].

mean·time ['mi:ntaim], **mean·while** ['min:wail] en attendant, dans l'intervalle.

mea·sle F ['mi:zl] être atteint de rougeole; **'mea·sled** *vét.* ladre; **'mea·sles** *pl.* ⅍ rougeole *f*; *vét.* ladrerie *f*; *German* ⅍ rubéole *f*; **'mea·sly** rougeoleux (-euse *f*); *vét.* ladre; *sl.* misérable.

meas·ur·a·ble □['meʒərəbl] me(n)-surable.

meas·ure ['meʒə] **1.** mesure *f* (*a. ♪, a. fig.*); *fig.* limite *f*; *~ of capacity* mesure *f* de capacité; *beyond ~* outre mesure; *in some ~* jusqu'à un certain point; *in a great ~* en grande partie; *made to ~* fait sur mesure; *take s.o.'s ~* prendre les mesures de q.; *fig.* prendre la mesure de q. **2.** mesurer (pour, *for*); métrer (*un mur*); faire l'arpentage de (*un terrain*); *Am. ~ up to s.th.* se montrer à la hauteur de qch.; **'meas·ure·less** □ infini, illimité; **'meas·ure·ment** mesurage *m*; mesure *f*; tour *m* (*de tête, de hanches*); ⚓ tonnage *m*.

meas·ur·ing ['meʒəriŋ] de mesure; d'arpentage.

meat [mi:t] viande *f*; †, *prov.* nourriture *f*; *fig.* moelle *f*; *butcher's ~* grosse viande *f*; *cold ~* rôti *m* froid; *fresh-killed ~* viande *f* fraîche; *preserved ~* viande *f* de conserve; *green ~* fourrages *m/pl.* verts; *roast ~* viande *f* rôtie; rôti *m*; *~ tea* thé *m* de viande; bouillon *m*; **'~-ball** boulette *f* de viande; **'~-fly** mouche *f* à viande; **'~-head** *Am. sl.* idiot(e *f*) *m*; **'~-safe** garde-manger *m/inv.*; **'meat·y** charnu; *fig.* étoffé.

mec·ca·no [me'kɑ:nou] jeu *m* mécanique (*pour enfants*).

me·chan·ic [mi'kænik] artisan *m*, ouvrier *m*; ⊕ mécanicien *m*; **me·chan·i·cal** □ mécanique; *fig.* machinal (-aux *m/pl.*), automatique; *~ engineering* construction *f* mécanique; **me·chan·i·cal·ness** caractère *m* machinal; **mech·a·ni·cian** [mekə-'niʃn] mécanicien *m*; **me·chan·ics** [mi'kæniks] *usu. sg.* mécanique *f*.

mech·a·nism ['mekənizm] mécanisme *m*; *biol., pol.* machinisme *m*;

mech·a·nize [ˈ⌣naiz] mécaniser (a. ✕); ✕ motoriser.

med·al [ˈmedl] médaille f; décoration f; **'med·al(l)ed** medaillé; décoré; **me·dal·lion** [miˈdæljən] médaillon m; **med·al·(l)ist** [ˈmedlist] médailliste mf; graveur: médailleur m; médaillé(e f) (m).

med·dle [ˈmedl] (with, in) se mêler (de); s'immiscer (dans); toucher (à); **'med·dler** officieux (-euse f) m; intrigant(e f) m; touche-à-tout m/inv.; **med·dle·some** [ˈ⌣səm] □ officieux (-euse f), intrigant; qui touche à tout; **'med·dle·some·ness** tendance f à se mêler des affaires d'autrui.

me·di·a [ˈmiːdjə] pl. les media m/pl.

me·di·ae·val [mediˈiːvəl] see medieval.

me·di·al □ [ˈmiːdjəl], **'me·di·an** 1. médial (-als, -aux m/pl.); médian; 2. médiale f; médiane f.

me·di·an strip Am. mot. [ˈmiːdjən-ˈstrip] bande f médiane.

me·di·ate 1. □ [ˈmiːdiit] intermédiaire; 2. [ˈ⌣eit] s'interposer; agir en médiateur; **me·di·a·tion** médiation f; **me·di·a·tor** [ˈ⌣tə] médiateur (-trice f) m (a. école); **me·di·a·to·ri·al** □ [⌣ˈtɔːriəl], **me·di·a·to·ry** [ˈ⌣təri] médiateur (-trice f); **me·di·a·trix** [ˈ⌣eitriks] médiatrice f.

med·ic F [ˈmedik] étudiant: carabin m; médecin: toubib m.

Med·ic·aid Am. [ˈmedikeid] assistance f medicale aux économiquement faibles.

med·i·cal □ [ˈmedikəl] médical (-aux m/pl.); de médecine; ~ board conseil m de santé; ~ certificate attestation f de médicin; ~ evidence témoignage m des médecins; ~ jurisprudence médecine f légale; ~ man médecin m; ~ officer médecin m militaire; ~ specialist spécialiste mf; ~ student étudiant m en médecine; ♀ Superintendent médecin m en chef; **me·dic·a·ment** médicament m.

Med·i·care Am. [ˈmedikεə] assistance f medicale aux personnes agées.

med·i·cate [ˈmedikeit] médicamenter; traiter; rendre médicamenteux (du vin); **med·i·ca·tion** médication f; emploi m de medicaments; **med·i·ca·tive** [ˈmedikətiv] médicateur (-trice f).

me·dic·i·nal □ [meˈdisinl] médicinal (-aux m/pl.) (bains etc.); médicamenteux (-euse f) (vin etc.); **med·i·cine** [ˈmedsin] art, profession, médicament: médecine f; médicament m, remède m; F drogue f; ~-chest (coffret m de) pharmacie f.

me·di·e·val □ [mediˈiːvəl] médiéval (-aux m/pl.); du Moyen Âge; **me·di·'e·val·ism** médiévisme m; culture f médiévale; **me·di·e·val·ist** médiéviste mf.

me·di·o·cre [ˈmiːdioukə] médiocre; **me·di·oc·ri·ty** [⌣ˈɔkriti] médiocrité f.

med·i·tate [ˈmediteit] v/i. méditer (sur, [up]on); se recueillir; v/t. méditer (qch.; de faire qch., doing s.th.); projeter; avoir l'intention (de faire qch., doing s.th.); **med·i·'ta·tion** méditation f; recueillement m; (profondes) pensées f/pl.; **med·i·ta·tive** □ [ˈ⌣tativ] méditatif (-ive f).

me·di·um [ˈmiːdiəm] 1. pl. -di·a [⌣djə], -di·ums milieu m; ambiance f (sociale); intermédiaire m; moyen m; phys. milieu m, véhicule m; 🜨 agent m; biol. bouillon m; spiritisme: médium m; élément: milieu m; 2. moyen(ne f); radio: ~ wave onde f moyenne; '~-'sized de grandeur ou de taille moyenne.

med·lar ♀ [ˈmedlə] nèfle f; arbre: néflier m.

med·ley [ˈmedli] mélange m; couleurs etc.: bigarrure f; péj. idées etc.: bariolage m; ♪ pot-pourri (pl. pots-pourris) m.

me·dul·la [meˈdʌlə] épinière: moelle f; **med·ul·lar·y** médullaire.

meed poét. [miːd] récompense f.

meek □ [miːk] doux (douce f); humble; soumis; **'meek·ness** humilité f; soumission f.

meer·schaum [ˈmiəʃəm] (pipe f en) écume f de mer.

meet[1] [miːt] † convenable; séant.

meet[2] [⌣] 1. [irr.] v/t. rencontrer, aller à la rencontre de; faire la connaissance de; fréquenter; croiser (dans la rue); aller chercher (q. à la gare); se conformer à (des opinions); satisfaire à, répondre à (des désirs, des besoins); faire face à (des demandes, des besoins, la mort); trouver (la mort); faire honneur à (ses engagements); prévenir (une objection); subvenir à (des frais);

rivières: confluer avec; *fig.* ~ *s.o.* half-way faire la moitié des avances; come (go, run) to ~ *s.o.* venir (aller, courir) à la rencontre de q.; *they are well met* ils sont bien assortis; ils font la paire; *v/i.* se rencontrer; se voir; se réunir (*société, gens*); se joindre; confluer (*rivières*); ~ *with* rencontrer, éprouver (*des difficultés*); essuyer (*un refus*); faire (*des pertes*); trouver (*un accueil*); être victime de (*un accident*); *make both ends* ~ joindre les deux bouts, arriver à boucler son budget; **2.** *sp.* réunion *f*; assemblée *f* de chasseurs.

meet·ing ['miːtiŋ] rencontre *f*; réunion *f*; assemblée *f*; *rivières*: confluent *m*; *pol., sp.* meeting *m*; '~**place** rendez-vous *m*; lieu *m* de réunion.

meg·a·fog ['megəfɔg] très fort signal *m* de brume; **meg·a·lo·ma·ni·a** ['͟louˈmeinjə] *⚕* mégalomanie *f*; **meg·a·lop·o·lis** [͟ˈlɔpəlis] conurbation *f*; **meg·a·phone** ['͟foun] portevoix *m/inv.*; *sp.* mégaphone *m*; **meg·a·ton** ['͟tʌn] mégatonne *f*.

me·grim ['miːgrim] migraine *f*; ~**s** *pl.* vapeurs *f/pl.*; spleen *m*.

mel·an·chol·ic [melənˈkɔlik] mélancolique; **mel·an·chol·y** ['͟kɔli] **1.** mélancolie *f*; tristesse *f*; **2.** mélancolique; triste.

mê·lée ['melei] mêlée *f*; bagarre *f*.

mel·io·rate ['miːljəreit] (s')améliorer.

mel·lif·lu·ent [meˈliflʊənt], *usu.* **mel'lif·lu·ous** mielleux (-euse *f*); mellifluu (*éloquence*).

mel·low ['melou] **1.** □ mûr (*a. esprit, caractère*); moelleux (-euse *f*); doux (douce *f*) (*ton, lumière, vin*); velouté (*vin*); *fig.* doux (douce *f*), tendre (*couleur*); débonnaire (*personne*); *sl.* un peu gris *ou* ivre; **2.** (faire) mûrir; (s')adoucir (*personne*); *v/i.* prendre de la patine; '**mel·low·ness** *fruit, sol:* maturité *f*; *vin, voix:* moelleux *m*; *caractère:* douceur *f*.

me·lo·di·ous □ [miˈloudjəs] mélodieux (-euse *f*), harmonieux (-euse *f*); **me'lo·di·ous·ness** mélodie *f*; **mel·o·dist** ['melədist] mélodiste *mf*; '**mel·o·dize** rendre mélodieux (-euse *f*); mettre en musique; *v/i.* chanter; faire des mélo-

dies; **mel·o·dra·ma** ['͟draːmə] mélodrame *m*; '**mel·o·dy** mélodie *f*, chant *m*, air *m*.

mel·on ♀ ['melən] melon *m*; *water-*~ melon *m* d'eau; pastèque *f*.

melt [melt] fondre; *fig.* (se) dissoudre; *v/t.* attendrir (*le cœur*); *v/i.:* ~ *away* fondre complètement; *fig.* se dissiper; ~ *down* fondre; ~ *into tears* fondre en larmes.

melt·ing □ ['meltiŋ] fondant; *fig.* attendri (*voix*); '~**point** point *m* de fusion; '~**pot** creuset *m*; *be in the* ~ tout remettre en question.

mem·ber ['membə] membre *m* (*a. gramm.*); organe *m*; ⊕ pièce *f*; député *m*; membre *m* de la Chambre des Communes; *make s.o. a* ~ élire q. membre (de, of); '**mem·ber·ship** qualité *f* de membre; nombre *m* des membres; ~ *card* carte *f* de membre; ~ *fee* cotisation *f*.

mem·brane ['membrein] membrane *f*; enveloppe *f* (*d'un organe*); **mem'bra·nous**, **mem'bra·ne·ous** [͟jəs] membraneux (-euse *f*).

me·men·to [miˈmentou] souvenir *m*, mémento *m*.

mem·oir ['memwaː] mémoire *m*; notice *f* biographique; ~**s** *pl.* mémoires *m/pl.*; mémorial *m*; autobiographie *f*.

mem·o·ra·ble □ ['memərəbl] mémorable.

mem·o·ran·dum [meməˈrændəm] mémorandum *m* (*a. pol.*); acte *m* (*de société*); *pol.* note *f* (diplomatique).

me·mo·ri·al [miˈmɔːriəl] **1.** mémoratif (-ive *f*); commémoratif (-ive *f*) (*monument*); *Am.* ♀ *Day* jour *m* des morts au champ d'honneur; **2.** monument *m* (*commémoratif*); pétition *f*; **me'mo·ri·al·ist** pétitionnaire *mf*; auteur *m* de mémoires; **me'mo·ri·al·ize** commémorer; pétitionner.

mem·o·rize ['meməraiz] apprendre par cœur.

mem·o·ry ['meməri] mémoire *f* (*a. ordinateur*); souvenir *m*; *commit to* ~ apprendre par cœur; se mettre dans la mémoire; *beyond the* ~ *of man* de temps immémorial; *within the* ~ *of man* de mémoire d'homme; *in* ~ *of* à la mémoire de; en souvenir de.

men [men] (*pl. de* man) hommes *m/pl.*; l'homme *m*, le genre *m* hu-

mere

main, l'humanité *f*; *sp*. ~'s *doubles pl.*
double *m* messieurs.

men·ace ['menəs] **1.** menacer;
2. *póet.* menace *f*.

me·nag·er·ie [mi'nædʒəri] ménagerie *f*.

mend [mend] **1.** *v/t.* raccommoder
(*un vêtement*); réparer (*un outil, une
machine*); rectifier, corriger; hâter
(*le pas*); ~ the fire arranger le feu;
~ one's ways changer de conduite,
se corriger; *v/i.* se corriger; s'améliorer; **2.** raccommodage *m*; amélioration *f*; on the ~ en voie de
guérison, en train de se remettre.

men·da·cious □ [men'deiʃəs] menteur (-euse *f*), mensonger (-ère *f*);
men·dac·i·ty [~'dæsiti] penchant
m au mensonge; fausseté *f*.

mend·er ['mendə] raccommodeur
(-euse *f*) *m*; *invisible* ~ stoppeur
(-euse *f*) *m*.

men·di·can·cy ['mendikənsi] mendicité *f*; **'men·di·cant** mendiant
(*a. su./m*); **men'dic·i·ty** [~siti]
mendicité *f*.

men·folk F ['menfouk] hommes
m/pl. (*de la famille*).

men·hir ['menhiə] menhir *m*.

me·ni·al *usu. péj.* ['mi:njəl] **1.** □
servile, bas(se *f*); **2.** domestique
mf; laquais *m*.

men·in·gi·tis ⚕ [menin'dʒaitis] méningite *f*.

men·o·pause ['menoupɔ:z] ménopause *f*.

men·ses ['mensi:z] *pl.* menstrues
f/pl., époques *f/pl.*; *see menstruation*;
men·stru·al ['~struəl] menstruel(le
f); **'men·stru·ate** ['~strueit] avoir
ses règles; **men·stru'a·tion** menstruation *f*; règles *f/pl.*, époques *f/pl.*

men·su·ra·tion [mensjuə'reiʃn]
mesurage *m*; ⚕ mensuration *f*.

men·tal □ ['mentl] mental (-aux
m/pl.); de l'esprit; ~ *arithmetic* calcul
m de tête; ~ *home* (*ou hospital ou
institution*) hôpital *m ou* clinique *f*
psychiatrique; *maison f* de santé; ~*ly
ill* aliéné; **men·tal·i·ty** [~'tæliti]
mentalité *f*; esprit *m*.

men·thol *pharm.* ['menθɔl] men-
thol *m*.

men·tion ['menʃn] **1.** mention *f*;
allusion *f*; **2.** mentionner, faire
allusion à, citer; *don't* ~ *it!* je vous
en prie!; il n'y a pas de quoi!; *not
to* ~ sans parler de; sans compter;

'men·tion·a·ble digne de mention; dont on peut parler.

men·tor ['mentɔ:] mentor *m*,
guide *m*.

men·u ['menju:] menu *m*; carte *f*.

me·phit·ic [me'fitik] méphitique;
me·phi·tis [~'faitis] méphitisme *m*.

mer·can·tile ['mə:kəntail] mercantile, marchand; commercial (-aux
m/pl.), de commerce; commerçant.

mer·ce·nar·y ['mə:sinəri] **1.** □
mercenaire, intéressé; **2.** ✕ mercenaire *m*.

mer·cer ['mə:sə] marchand(e *f*) *m*
de soieries; † mercier (-ère *f*) *m*;
'mer·cer·ize merceriser; **'mer-
cer·y** (commerce *m* des) soieries
f/pl.; † mercerie *f*.

mer·chan·dise ['mə:tʃəndaiz] **1.**
marchandise *f*, -s *f/pl.*; **2.** *Am.*
commercer.

mer·chant ['mə:tʃənt] **1.** négociant
m; commerçant *m*; *Am.* mar-
chand(e *f*) *m*; boutiquier (-ère *f*)
m; **2.** marchand; de *ou* du commerce; ~ *bank* banque *f* de commerce; *law* ~ droit *m* commercial; *Am.* ~
marine, *Brit.* ~ *navy* marine *f* marchande; **'mer·chant·a·ble** vendable; négociable; **'mer·chant·man**
navire *m* marchand *ou* de commerce.

mer·ci·ful □ ['mə:siful] miséricordieux (-euse *f*) (pour, to); clément (envers, to); **'mer·ci·ful-
ness** miséricorde *f*; clémence *f*;
pitié *f*.

mer·ci·less □ ['mə:silis] impitoyable, sans pitié; **'mer·ci·less·ness**
caractère *m* impitoyable; manque *m*
de pitié.

mer·cu·ri·al [mə:'kjuəriəl] *astr.* de
Mercure; ♍ mercuriel(le *f*); *fig.*
vif (vive *f*); inconstant, changeant.

Mer·cu·ry ['mə:kjuri] *astr.* Mercure; *fig.* messager *m*; ♍ ☿ mercure *m*.

mer·cy ['mə:si] miséricorde *f*; clémence *f*; pitié *f*; *be at s.o.'s* ~ être
à la merci de q.; *at the* ~ *of the
waves* au gré des flots; *it is a* ~ *that*
c'est un bonheur que; *for* ~'s *sake*
par pitié; *poét., co.* have ~ (*up*)on
avoir pitié de; ~ *killing* euthanasie *f*.

mere □ [miə] simple, seul, pur;
~(*st*) *nonsense* extravagance *f* pure
et simple; ~ *words* vaines paroles
f/pl.; rien que des mots; ~*ly* simplement; tout bonnement.

mer·e·tri·cious □ [meri'triʃəs] de courtisane; *fig.* factice; d'un éclat criard.

merge [mə:dʒ] (*in*) *v/t.* fondre (dans); amalgamer (avec); *v/i.* se fondre, se perdre (dans); s'amalgamer; *mot.* s'enfiler; **'merg·er** fusion *f*.

me·rid·i·an [mə'ridiən] **1.** méridien(ne *f*); *fig.* culminant, le plus haut; **2.** *géog.* méridien *m*; *fig.* point *m* culminant, apogée *m*; **me'rid·i·o·nal** □ [⌣iənl] méridional(-aux *m/pl.*); du midi.

me·ringue [mə'ræŋ] meringue *f*.

mer·it ['merit] **1.** mérite *m*; valeur *f*; *usu.* ⚖ ⌣s *pl.* bien-fondé *m*; le pour et le contre (*de qch.*); *on the* ⌣s *of the case* (*juger qch.*) au fond; *on its* (*own*) ⌣s selon ses mérites; *make a* ⌣ *of* se faire un mérite de; **2.** *fig.* mériter; **mer·i·to·ri·ous** □ [⌣'tɔːriəs] méritoire; méritant (*personne*).

mer·maid ['mə:meid] sirène *f*.

mer·ri·ment ['merimənt] gaieté *f*, réjouissance *f*.

mer·ry □ ['meri] joyeux (-euse *f*), gai; jovial (-als, -aux *m/pl.*); *make* ⌣ se réjouir; se divertir; ⌣ **an·drew** paillasse *m*, bouffon *m*; '⌣**-go-round** carrousel *m*; chevaux *m/pl.* de bois; '⌣**-mak·ing** réjouissances *f/pl.*, fête *f*; '⌣**thought** lunette *f* (*d'une volaille*).

mes·en·ter·y *anat.* ['mesəntəri] mésentère *m*.

mesh [meʃ] **1.** maille *f*; *fig. usu.* ⌣es *pl.* réseau *m*; ⊕ *be in* ⌣ être en prise (avec, with); ⊕ *fig.* (s')engrener; **meshed** [⌣t] à ... mailles; **'mesh-work** réseau *m*; treillis *m*.

mes·mer·ism ['mezmərizm] mesmérisme *m*, hypnotisme *m*; **'mes·mer·ize** hypnotiser; magnétiser.

mess¹ [mes] **1.** désordre *m*; gâchis *m*, fouillis *m*; saleté *f*; F *a fine* ⌣ *of things* du joli, une belle équipée, un chef-d'œuvre; F *look a* ⌣ être dans un état épouvantable; *make a* ⌣ *of* gâcher, bousiller; **2.** *v/t. a.* ⌣ *up* gâcher, galvauder, abîmer; salir; *v/i.* F ⌣ *about* patauger (*dans la boue*); gaspiller son temps.

mess² [⌣] **1.** † plat *m*, mets *m*; ✕, ⚓ *officiers:* mess *m*, table *f*; ✕ *hommes:* ordinaire *m*, ⚓ plat *m*; **2.** manger à la même table.

mes·sage ['mesidʒ] message *m*;

commission *f*; F *get the* ⌣ comprendre, F piger; *give s.o. the* ⌣ faire la commission à q.; *take a* ⌣ faire la commission.

mes·sen·ger ['mesindʒə] messager (-ère *f*) *m*; ⌣ *boy hôtel:* chasseur *m*, *télégraphes:* facteur *m*.

Mes·si·ah [mi'saiə] Messie *m*.

Mes·sieurs, *usu.* **Messrs.** ['mesəz] ✝ Messieurs *m/pl.*; maison *f*.

mess-room ['mesrum] ✕ salle *f* de mess; ⚓ carré *m* (des officiers); **'mess-tin** ✕ gamelle *f*, ⚓ quart *m*.

mess-up F ['mesʌp] gâchis *m*; pagaille; embrouillement *m*, embrouillamini *m*; malentendu *m*; **mess·y** ['mesi] embrouillé, en désordre; sale, malpropre.

met [met] *prét. et p.p. de* meet² 1.

met·a·bol·ic [metə'bɔlik] métabolique; **me·tab·o·lism** *physiol.* [me'tæbəlizm] métabolisme *m*.

met·age ['mi:tidʒ] mesurage *m*.

met·al ['metl] **1.** métal *m*; ⊕ empierrement *m*; *route:* cailloutis *m*, pierraille *f*; 🚂 F ⌣s *pl.* rails *m/pl.*; **2.** empierrer, caillouter; **me·tal·lic** [mi'tælik] (⌣*ally*) métallique; métallin; de métal; **met·al·lif·er·ous** [metə'lifərəs] métallifère; **met·al·line** ['metəlain] métallin; **'met·al·lize** métalliser; vulcaniser (*le caoutchouc*); **met·al·log·ra·phy** [⌣'lɔgrəfi] métallographie *f*; **met·al·lur·gic**, **met·al·lur·gi·cal** □ [⌣'lə:dʒik(l)] métallurgique; **'met·al·lur·gy** métallurgie *f*.

met·a·mor·phose [metə'mɔ:fouz] métamorphoser, transformer (en, [in]to); **met·a·mor·pho·sis** [⌣fə-sis], *pl.* -ses [⌣si:z] métamorphose *f*.

met·a·phor ['metəfə] métaphore *f*; image *f*; **met·a·phor·ic**, *usu.* **met·a·phor·i·cal** □ [⌣'fɔrik(l)] métaphorique.

met·a·phys·ic [metə'fizik] **1.** (*usu.* **met·a·phys·i·cal** □) métaphysique; **2.** ⌣s *souv. sg.* métaphysique *f*; ontologie *f*.

mete [mi:t] *litt.* mesurer; (*usu.* ⌣ *out*) assigner; décerner, distribuer.

me·te·or ['mi:tjə] météore *m* (*a. fig.*); **me·te·or·ic** [mi:ti'ɔrik] météorique; *fig.* rapide; **me·te·or·ite** ['mi:tjərait] météorite *mf*; aérolithe *m*; **me·te·or·o·log·i·cal** □ [mi:-tjərə'lɔdʒikl] météorologique; aérologique; **me·te·or·ol·o·gist** [⌣'rɔlədʒist] météorologiste *mf*, -logue *mf*; **me·te·or'ol·o·gy** météorologie *f*, aérologie *f*.

me·ter ['miːtə] (*a.* gas ~) compteur *m*; jaugeur *m*; '~·**maid** *Am.* F contractuelle *f*.

me·thinks [mi'θiŋks] (*prét.* methought) il me semble.

meth·od ['meθəd] méthode *f*; système *m*; manière *f*; procédé *m* (pour *for*, of); **me·thod·ic, me·thod·i·cal** □ [mi'θɔdik(l)] méthodique; **Meth·od·ism** *eccl.* ['meθədizm] méthodisme *m*; '**meth·od·ist** *péj.* qui a le souci exagéré de la méthode; *eccl.* ♀ méthodiste *mf*; '**meth·od·ize** ordonner, régler.

meth·yl ♫ ['meθil] méthyle *m*; **meth·yl·at·ed spir·it** ['meθileitid 'spirit] alcool *m* à brûler.

me·tic·u·lous □ [mi'tikjuləs] méticuleux (-euse *f*).

me·tre ['miːtə] mètre *m*, mesure *f*; mètre *m* (*39,37 inches*).

met·ric ['metrik] (~*ally*) métrique; '**met·ri·cal** □ métrique; en vers; '**met·rics** *sg.* métrique *f*.

me·trop·o·lis [mi'trɔpəlis] métropole *f*; **me·tro·pol·i·tan** [metrə-'pɔlitən] 1. métropolitain; ♀ *Railway* chemin *m* de fer métropolitain; 2. métropolitain *m*, archevêque *m*.

met·tle ['metl] *personne*: ardeur *f*, courage *m*, feu *m*; tempérament *m*, caractère *m*; *cheval*: fougue *f*; be on one's ~ se piquer d'honneur; faire de son mieux; *put s.o. on his* ~ piquer q. d'honneur; stimuler le zèle de q.; *horse of* ~ cheval *m* fougueux; '**met·tled, met·tle·some** ['~səm] fougueux (-euse *f*) (*cheval*); ardent (*personne*).

mew¹ *poét.* [mjuː] mouette *f*.

mew² [~] 1. miaulement *m*; 2. miauler.

mew³ [~] 1. mue *f*, cage *f* (*pour les faucons*); 2. *v/i.* se cloîtrer; *v/t.* (*usu.* ~ *up*) renfermer. [miauler.]

mewl [mjuːl] vagir, piailler; F♩

mews [mjuːz] *sg.*, † *pl.* écuries *f/pl.*; *Londres*: impasse *f*, ruelle *f*.

Mex·i·can ['meksikən] 1. mexicain; 2. Mexicain(e *f*) *m*.

mi·aow [mi'au] 1. miaulement *m*, miaou *m*; 2. miauler.

mi·as·ma [mi'æzmə], *pl.* -ma·ta [~mətə], -mas miasme *m*; **mi'as·mal** □ miasmatique.

mi·aul [mi'ɔːl] miauler.

mi·ca *min.* ['maikə] mica *m*; **mi·ca·ce·ous** [~'keiʃəs] micacé.

mice [mais] *pl. de* mouse 1.

Mich·ael·mas ['miklməs] la Saint-Michel *f* (*le 29 septembre*).

mick·ey *sl.* ['miki] (*a.* ~ finn) boisson *f* droguée; *take the* ~ *out of s.o.* se payer la tête de q.

micro... [maikro] micro-.

mi·crobe ['maikroub] microbe *m*; **mi'cro·bi·al** [~iəl] microbien(ne *f*).

mi·cro·cosm ['maikrəkɔzəm] microcosme *m*; **mi·crom·e·ter** [mai-'krɔmitə] micromètre *m*; **mi·cro·phone** ['maikrəfoun] microphone *m*; F micro *m*; **mi·cro·pro·ces·sor** ['~prə'sesə] microprocesseur *m*, chip *m*; **mi·cro·scope** ['~skoup] microscope *m*; **mi·cro·scop·ic, mi·cro·scop·i·cal** □ [~s'kɔpik(l)] microscopique; au microscope (*examen*); F minuscule, très petit; **mi·cro·wave** ♩ ['maikrəweiv] micro-onde *f*.

mid [mid] *see* middle 2; mi-; *poét. see* amid; ~-'air: *in* ~ entre ciel et terre; '~-**course**: *in* ~ en pleine carrière; '~-**day** 1. midi *m*; 2. de midi, méridien(ne *f*).

mid·den ['midn] (tas *m* de) fumier *m*.

mid·dle ['midl] 1. milieu *m*, centre *m*; *fig.* taille *f*, ceinture *f*; ♄ ~*s pl.* qualité *f* moyenne; 2. ordinaire; bon(ne *f*); du milieu, central (-aux *m/pl.*); moyen(ne *f*), intermédiaire; ♀ *Ages pl.* Moyen Âge *m*; ~ *class(es pl.)* classe *f* moyenne; bourgeoisie *f*; '~-'**aged** F entre deux âges; '~-'**class** bourgeois; '~-**man** F entremetteur *m*; † intermédiaire *m*; '~-**most** central (-aux *m/pl.*); le plus au milieu; '~-**sized** de grandeur *ou* taille moyenne; '~-**weight** *box.* poids *m* moyen.

mid·dling ['midliŋ] 1. *adj.* médiocre; passable, assez bon(ne *f*); moyen(ne *f*); † de qualité moyenne; 2. *adv.* (*a.* ~*ly*) passablement, assez bien; 3. *su.* † ~*s pl.* marchandises *f/pl.* de qualité moyenne.

mid·dy F ['midi] *see* midshipman.

midge [midʒ] moucheron *m*; **midg·et** ['~it] nain(e *f*) *m*; nabot(e *f*) *m*.

mid·land ['midlənd] 1. entouré de terre; intérieur (*mer*); 2. *the* ♀*s pl.*

les Midlands *m/pl.*; '**mid·most** central (-aux *m/pl.*); le plus près du milieu; '**mid·night 1.** minuit *m*; **2.** de minuit; **mid·riff** ['⌣rif] diaphragme *m*; '**mid·ship·man** ⚓ aspirant *m*; *Am.* enseigne *m*; '**mid·ships** ⚓ par le travers; **midst** [midst] **1.** *su.* milieu *m*; *in the* ⌣ *of* au milieu de; parmi; *in our* ⌣ au milieu de nous, parmi nous; **2.** *prp. poét.* *see amidst*; '**mid·sum·mer** milieu *m* de l'été; solstice *m* d'été; ⚹ *Day* la Saint-Jean *f*; ⌣ *holidays pl.* vacances *f/pl.* d'été; '**mid·way 1.** *su. Am.* allée *f* centrale (*d'une exposition*); **2.** *adj.* du milieu, central (-aux *m/pl.*), intermédiaire; **3.** *adv.* à michemin; '**mid·wife** sage-femme (*pl.* sages-femmes) *f*; **mid·wife·ry** ['midwifri] obstétrique *f*; '**mid·win·ter** milieu *m* de l'hiver; solstice *m* d'hiver.

mien *poét.* [mi:n] mine *f*, air *m*.

miff F [mif] boutade *f*; accès *m* d'humeur.

might [mait] **1.** puissance *f*, force *f*, -s *f/pl.*; *with* ⌣ *and main* de toutes mes (*etc.*) forces; **2.** *prét. de may*[2]; '**might·i·ness** ['⌣inis] puissance *f*, force *f*, grandeur *f*; '**might·y** (□ †) **1.** *adj.* puissant, fort; vaste; F considérable; **2.** F *adv.* très, extrêmement.

mi·grant ['maigrənt] **1.** *see migratory*; **2.** (*ou* ⌣ *bird*) migrateur (-trice *f*) *m*.

mi·grate [mai'greit] émigrer; passer; **mi'gra·tion** migration *f*, émigration *f*; **mi·gra·to·ry** ['⌣grətəri] migrateur (-trice *f*) (*personne*, *a. oiseau*); nomade (*personne*); de passage (*oiseau*).

mike *sl.* [maik] microphone *m*, F micro *m*.

Mil·an·ese [milə'ni:z] **1.** milanais; **2.** Milanais(e *f*) *m*.

milch [miltʃ] à lait, laitière (*vache*).

mild □ [maild] doux (douce *f*); tempéré (*climat*); peu sévère; peu rigoureux (-euse *f*); bénin (-igne *f*); *to put it* ⌣*ly* pour m'exprimer avec modération.

mil·dew ['mildju:] **1.** *pain etc.*: chancissure *f*; *froment etc.*: rouille *f*; *vignes etc.*: mildiou *m*; moisissure *f*; **2.** chancir (*le pain*); rouiller, moisir (*la plante etc.*); piquer (*le papier etc.*).

mild·ness ['maildnis] douceur *f*; *maladie*: bénignité *f*.

mile [mail] mille *m* (*anglais*) (1609,33 *m*).

mil(e)·age ['mailidʒ] distance *f ou* vitesse *f* en milles; *fig.* parcours *m*.

mile·stone ['mailstoun] borne *f* milliaire *ou* kilométrique.

mil·foil ⚘ ['milfoil] mille-feuille *f*.

mil·i·tan·cy ['militənsi] esprit *m* militant; *pol.* activisme *m*; '**mil·i·tant** □ militant; activiste; **mil·i·tar·i·ness** ['militərinis] caractère *m* militaire; **mil·i·ta·rism** ['⌣rizəm] militarisme *m*; '**mil·i·ta·ry 1.** □ militaire; de guerre; de soldat; ⌣ *college* école *f* militaire; ⚹ *Government* gouvernement *m* militaire; ⌣ *map* carte *f* d'état-major; ⌣ *service* service *m* militaire; *of* ⌣ *age* en âge de servir; **2.** *les militaires m/pl.*; l'armée *f*; **mil·i·tate** ['⌣teit]: ⌣ *in favo(u)r of* (*against*) militer en faveur de (contre); **mi·li·tia** [mi'liʃə] milice *f*; garde *f* nationale.

milk [milk] **1.** lait *m*; *powdered* (*whole*) ⌣ lait *m* en poudre (non écrémé); *Brit.* ⌣ *float* voiture *f* de laitier; ⌣ *tooth* dent *f* de lait; **2.** traire; *fig.* dépouiller; ⚡, *a. tél.* capter; '**milk-and-'wa·ter** F insipide, fade; '**milk·er** *personne*: trayeur (-euse *f*) *m*; *vache*: laitière *f*; *machine*: trayeuse *f*; **milk·i·ness** ['⌣inis] lactescence *f*; couleur *f* laiteuse; *fig.* douceur *f*.

milk...: '⌣**·maid** laitière *f*, crémière *f*; trayeuse *f*; '⌣**·man** laitier *m*, crémier *m*; '⌣**·shake** shake *m* (*mélange de lait, crème glacée et sirop battus ensemble*); '⌣**·sop** F poule *f* mouillée; peureux (-euse *f*) *m*; '**milk·y** laiteux (-euse *f*), lactescent; *fig.* blanchâtre; *astr.* ⚹ *Way* Voie *f* lactée.

mill[1] [mil] **1.** moulin *m*; usine *f*; fabrique *f*; filature *f*; *sl.* combat *m* à coups de poings; **2.** *v/t.* moudre; ⊕ fraiser; créneler (*la monnaie*); fouler (*un drap*); mousser (*une crème*); broyer (*le minerai*); *sl.* rouer de coups; *F* fourmiller.

mill[2] *Am.* [⌣] millième *m* (*de dollar*).

mill·board ['milbɔ:d] carton-pâte (*pl.* cartons-pâtes) *m*; carton *m* épais; '**mill-dam** barrage *m* de moulin.

mil·le·nar·i·an [mili'nɛəriən], **mil-**

len·ni·al [mi'leniəl] millénaire;
mil·le·nar·y ['⁓əri] millénaire (*a.
su./m*); **mil'len·ni·um** [⁓iəm] *eccl.*
millénium *m*; mille ans *m/pl.*
mil·le·pede *zo.* ['milipi:d] mille-
pieds *m/inv.*; mille-pattes *m/inv.*
mill·er ['milə] meunier *m*; ⊕
fraiseur *m*; *machine*: fraiseuse *f.*
mil·les·i·mal [mi'lesiməl] millième
(*a. su./mf*).
mil·let ♀ ['milit] millet *m.*
mill-hand ['milhænd] ouvrier (-ère
f) *m* d'usine.
mil·li·ard ['miljɑ:d] milliard *m.*
mil·li·gram ['miligræm] milligramme *m.*
mil·li·me·tre ['milimi:tə] millimètre *m.*
mil·li·ner ['milinə] modiste *f*; **'mil-
li·ner·y** (articles *m/pl.* de) modes
f/pl.
mill·ing ['miliŋ] meunerie *f*;
moulage *m*; broyage *m*; foulage *m*;
⊕ ⁓ *cutter* fraise *f*, fraiseuse *f*; ⁓
plant moulin *m*; laminerie *f*; ⁓
machine machine *f* à fraiser; ⁓
product produit *m* de moulin.
mil·lion ['miljən] million *m*; **mil-
lion·aire** [⁓'neə] millionnaire *mf*;
mil·lionth ['miljənθ] millionième
(*a. su./m*).
mill...: '⁓**-pond** réservoir *m* de
moulin; '⁓**-race** bief *m* de moulin;
'⁓**-stone** meule *f*; F *see through a* ⁓
voir à travers les murs; '⁓**-wright**
constructeur *m* de moulins.
milt[1] [milt] laitance *f* (*des poissons*).
milt[2] [⁓] rate *f.*   [laité.\
milt·er *icht.* ['miltə] poisson *m*|
mime [maim] **1.** mime *m*; **2.** mimer.
mim·e·o·graph ['mimiəgrɑ:f] **1.**
autocopiste *m*, machine *f* à polycopier; **2.** polycopier.
mim·ic ['mimik] **1.** mimique; imitateur (-trice *f*); **2.** mime *m*; imitateur (-trice *f*) *m*; **3.** imiter;
contrefaire; F singer (*q.*); **'mim-
ic·ry** mimique *f*, imitation *f*; *zo.*
mimétisme *m.*
min·a·to·ry ['minətəri] menaçant.
mince [mins] **1.** *v/t.* hacher; *he does
not* ⁓ *matters* il ne mâche pas ses
mots; ⁓ *one's words* minauder, parler du bout des lèvres; ⁓*d meat*
hachis *m*; *v/i.* marcher *etc.* d'un air
affecté; **2.** hachis *m*; '⁓**-meat** com-
pôte *f* de raisins secs, de pommes,
d'amandes *etc.*; *make* ⁓ *of* F rédu-

ire (*q.*) en chair à pâté; ⁓ *pie* petite
tarte *f* au *mincemeat*; **'minc·er**
hachoir *m.*
minc·ing □ ['minsiŋ] affecté, minaudier (-ère *f*); '⁓**-ma·chine**
hachoir *m.*
mind [maind] **1.** esprit *m*, âme *f*;
pensée *f*, idée *f*, avis *m*; mémoire *f*,
souvenir *m*; raison *f*; *to my* ⁓ à mon
avis, selon moi, à ce que je pense;
⁓*'s eye* idée *f*, imagination *f*; *out of
one's* ⁓ hors de son bon sens; insensé; *time out of* ⁓ de temps immémorial; *change one's* ⁓ changer d'a-
vis; se raviser; *bear s.th. in* ⁓ se rappeler qch.; tenir compte de qch.;
F *blow s.o.'s* ⁓ bouleverser q., renverser q.; *have (half) a* ⁓ *to* avoir (bonne)
envie de; *have s.th. on one's* ⁓ avoir
qch. sur sa conscience; *have in* ⁓ avoir
(*qch.*) en vue; (*not*) *know one's own* ⁓
(ne pas) savoir ce qu'on veut; *make
up one's* ⁓ se décider, prendre son
parti; *put s.o. in* ⁓ *of* rappeler (*qch. ou
q.*) à q.; **2.** faire attention à; s'occuper
de; ne pas manquer de (*inf.*); prendre garde à (*qch.*); soigner (*un
enfant*), garder (*un chien etc.*); ⁓*!*
attention!; *never* ⁓*!* n'importe!; ne
vous inquiétez pas!; ⁓ *the step!* attention à la marche!; *I don't* ⁓ (*it*) cela
m'est égal; peu (m')importe; *do you* ⁓
smoking? la fumée ne vous gêne pas?;
would you ⁓ *taking off your hat?* voudriez-vous bien ôter votre chapeau?;
⁓ *your own business!* mêlez-vous de ce
qui vous regarde!; '⁓**-bend·ing** F
halluzinant; '⁓**-blow·ing** F renversant, bouleversant; halluzinant;
'⁓**-bog·gling** F inimaginable, inconcevable; **'mind·ed** disposé, enclin
à l'esprit...; sensibilisé à *ou* sur ...;
'mind·er surveillant(e *f*) *m*; gardeur (-euse *f*) *m* (*d'animaux*);
'mind·ful □ (*of*) attentif (-ive *f*) (à);
soigneux (-euse *f*) (de); **'mind·ful-
ness** attention *f* (à, *of*); soin *m* (de,
of); **'mind·less** □ sans esprit; in-
soucient (de, *of*); indifférent (à, *of*);
oublieux (-euse *f*) (de, *of*); **'mind-
read·er** liseur (-euse *f*) *m* de pensées.
mine[1] [main] **1.** le mien, la mienne,
les miens, les miennes; à moi;
2. les miens *m/pl.*
mine[2] [⁓] ⚒, *a.* ⚔ mine *f*;
fig. trésor *m*, bureau *m*; **2.** *v/i.*
fouiller (sous) la terre; *v/t.* miner,

saper; ⚒ exploiter (*le charbon*); creuser; ⚒ miner, saper; ⚓ miner, semer des mines dans; '**lay·er** ⚓, ⚒ poseur *m ou* mouilleur *m* de mines; '**min·er** mineur *m* (*a.* ⚒).

min·er·al ['minərəl] **1.** minerai *m*; ⁓s *pl.* minérales; F boissons *f/pl.* gazeuses; **2.** minéral (-aux *m/pl.*); ⁓ *jelly* vaseline *f*; '**min·er·al·ize** minéraliser; **min·er·al·o·gist** [⁓'rælədʒist] minéralogiste *m*; **min·er·al·o·gy** minéralogie *f*.

mine·sweep·er ⚓ ['mainswiːpə] dragueur *m* de mines.

min·gle ['miŋgl] (se) mêler (avec, à *with*); (se) mélanger (avec, *with*).

min·i... [mini] mini-.

min·i·a·ture ['minjətʃə] **1.** miniature *f*; **2.** en miniature, en raccourci; petit modèle; minuscule; ⁓ *camera* appareil *m* de petit format; ⁓ *grand piano m* à queue écourtée; ⁓ *rifle shooting* tir *m* au fusil de petit calibre.

min·i·bus ['minibʌs] minibus *m*.

min·i·kin ['minikin] **1.** mignon(ne *f*); affecté; **2.** homuncule *m*.

min·im ['minim] ♩ blanche *f*; *mesure*: goutte *f*; F bout *m* d'homme; '**min·i·mize** réduire au minimum; *fig.* mettre au minimum l'importance de (*qch.*); **min·i·mum** ['⁓məm] **1.** *pl.* **-ma** [⁓mə] minimum (*pl.* -s, -ma) *m*; **2.** minimum (*qqfois* -ma *f*).

min·ing ['mainiŋ] **1.** minier (-ère *f*); de mine(s); ✝ de mine; ⚒, ⚓ de mouilleur de mines; **2.** exploitation *f* des mines, travaux *m/pl.* de mines; ⚒ sape *f*; ⚓ pose *f* de mines.

min·ion ['minjən] favori(te *f*) *m*; *typ.* mignonne *f*; F ⁓ *of the law* sbire *m*.

mini-skirt ['miniskəːt] mini-jupe *f*.

min·is·ter ['ministə] **1.** ministre *m* (*a. pol., a. eccl.*); *eccl.* pasteur *m* (*protestant*); **2.** *v/t.* ✝ fournir; *v/i.* ⁓ *to* soigner (*q.*); subvenir aux besoins de (*q.*); aider à (*qch.*); **min·is·te·ri·al** □ [⁓'tiəriəl] accessoire; *pol.* ministériel(le *f*); exécutif (-ive *f*); gouvernemental (-aux *m/pl.*); *eccl.* sacerdotal (-aux *m/pl.*); **min·is·te·ri·al·ist** ministériel *m*.

min·is·trant ['ministrənt] **1.** qui subvient à (*q.*); **2.** *eccl.* officiant *m*; **min·is'tra·tion** service *m*; ministère *m*; *eccl.* saint ministère *m*, sacerdoce *m*; '**min·is·try** ministère *m*; *pol. a.* gouvernement *m*.

min·i·ver ['minivə] petit-gris (*pl.* petits-gris) *m* (*a. fourrure*).

mink *zo.* [miŋk] vison *m*.

min·now *icht.* ['minou] vairon *m*.

mi·nor ['mainə] **1.** petit, mineur; peu important; d'importance secondaire; ♩ mineur; A ⁓ *la m* mineur; ⁓ *third* tierce *f* mineure; ⁓ *key* mineur *m*; **2.** mineur(e *f*) *m*; le plus jeune (*de deux frères*); *phls.* mineure *f*, petit terme *m*; *Am. univ.* sujet *m* (*d'étude*) secondaire; **mi·nor·i·ty** [mai'nɔriti] minorité *f* (*a.* ⚖); ⁓ *government* gouvernement *m* minoritaire.

min·ster ['minstə] cathédrale *f*; église *f* abbatiale.

min·strel ['minstrəl] ménestrel *m*; F musicien *m*; ⁓s *pl.* (troupe *f* de) chanteurs *m/pl.* déguisés en nègres; **min·strel·sy** ['⁓si] chants *m/pl. ou* art *m* des ménestrels.

mint[1] ♃ [mint] menthe *f*; ⁓ *sauce* vinaigrette *f* à la menthe.

mint[2] [⁓] **1.** Hôtel *m* de la Monnaie; source *f*; *a* ⁓ *of money* une somme *f* fabuleuse; **2.** (à l'état) neuf (neuve *f*) (*volume etc.*); *fig.* intrinsèque; **3.** monnayer; battre monnaie; '**mint·age** monnayage *m*; fabrication *f*; espèces *f/pl.* monnayées; empreinte *f*.

min·u·et ♩ [minju'et] menuet *m*.

mi·nus ['mainəs] **1.** *prp.* moins; F sans; **2.** *adj.* négatif (-ive *f*).

min·ute[1] ['minit] **1.** minute *f*; *fig.* moment *m*; instant *m*; projet *m*; note *f*; ⁓s *pl.* procès-verbal (*pl.* procès-verbaux) *m*; ⁓-*hand* grande aiguille *f*; *just a* ⁓! minute!; **2.** faire la minute de (*un contrat*); prendre note de; dresser le procès-verbal de.

mi·nute[2] □ [mai'njuːt] tout petit; minuscule; détaillé; *fig.* dans ses moindres détails; **mi'nute·ness** petitesse *f*; exactitude *f* minutieuse.

mi·nu·ti·a [mai'njuːʃiə], *pl.* **-ti·ae** [⁓ʃiiː] petits détails *m/pl.*

minx [miŋks] friponne *f*, coquine *f*.

mir·a·cle ['mirəkl] miracle *m*; F prodige *m*; *to a* ⁓ à merveille; **mi·rac·u·lous** □ [mi'rækjuləs] miraculeux (-euse *f*); F merveilleux (-euse *f*); **mi'rac·u·lous·ness** miraculeux *m*.

mi·rage ['miraːʒ] mirage *m*.

miser

mire [ˈmaiə] **1.** boue *f*, fange *f*; bourbier *m*; vase *f* (*de fleuve*); **2.** be ~d s'embourber; F s'avilir.

mir·ror [ˈmirə] **1.** miroir *m*, glace *f*; **2.** refléter (*a. fig.*).

mirth [məːθ] gaieté *f*; hilarité *f*; **mirth·ful** □ [ˈ~ful] gai, joyeux (-euse *f*); **'mirth·less** □ triste.

mir·y [ˈmaiəri] bourbeux (-euse *f*), fangeux (-euse *f*); vaseux (-euse *f*).

mis... [mis] mé-, més-, mal-, mauvais ...; faux (fausse *f*).

mis·ad·ven·ture [ˈmisədˈventʃə] mésaventure *f*, contretemps *m*; ⚖ accident *m*.   [liance *f*.]

mis·al·li·ance [misəˈlaiəns] mésal-

mis·an·thrope [ˈmizənθroup] misanthrope *m*; **mis·an·throp·ic, mis·an·throp·i·cal** □ [~ˈθrɔpik(l)] misanthrope (*personne*), misanthropique (*humeur*); **mis·an·thro·pist** [miˈzænθrəpist] misanthrope *m*; **mis·an·thro·py** misanthropie *f*.

mis·ap·pli·ca·tion [ˈmisæpliˈkeiʃn] mauvaise application *f*; mauvais usage *m*; détournement *m* (*de fonds*); **mis·ap·ply** [ˈ~əˈplai] mal appliquer; détourner (*des fonds*).

mis·ap·pre·hend [ˈmisæpriˈhend] mal comprendre; **'mis·ap·pre·'hen·sion** malentendu *m*, méprise *f*.

mis·ap·pro·pri·ate [ˈmisəˈproupri-eit] détourner, distraire (*des fonds*); **'mis·ap·pro·pri·'a·tion** détournement *m*, distraction *f* (*de fonds*).

mis·be·come [ˈmisbiˈkʌm] messeoir à (*q.*), mal convenir à (*q.*); **'mis·be·'com·ing** malséant.

mis·be·got·(ten) [ˈmisbiˈɡɔt(n)] illégitime, bâtard; F misérable.

mis·be·have [ˈmisbiˈheiv] se conduire mal; **'mis·be·'hav·io(u)r** [~jə] mauvaise conduite *f*, inconduite *f*.

mis·be·lief [ˈmisbiˈliːf] fausse croyance *f*; opinion *f* erronée; **mis·be·lieve** [ˈ~ˈliːv] être infidèle; **'mis·be·'liev·er** infidèle *mf*.

mis·cal·cu·late [ˈmisˈkælkjuleit] *v/t.* mal calculer; *v/i.* se tromper (sur, *about*); **'mis·cal·cu·'la·tion** faux calcul *m*; mécompte *m*.

mis·car·riage [misˈkæridʒ] *lettre*: perte *f*; avortement *m*; ⚕ fausse couche *f*; ~ of justice erreur *f* judiciaire; **mis·car·ry** avorter; échouer; s'égarer (*lettre*); ⚕ faire une fausse couche.

mis·cel·la·ne·ous □ [misiˈleinjəs] mélangé, varié, divers; **mis·cel·la·ne·ous·ness** variété *f*, diversité *f*.

mis·cel·la·ny [miˈselani] mélange *m*; collection *f* d'objets variés; *miscellanies pl.* mélanges *m/pl.*

mis·chance [misˈtʃɑːns] malchance *f*; malheur *m*, accident *m*.

mis·chief [ˈmistʃif] mal *m*, dommage *m*, dégât *m*; F discorde *f*, trouble *m*; malice *f*; bêtises *f/pl.* (*d'un enfant*); *personne*: fripon(ne *f*) *m* what *etc.* the ~ ...? que *etc.* diantre ...?; **'~-mak·er** brandon *m* de discorde.

mis·chie·vous □ [ˈmistʃivəs] méchant, espiègle, malin (-igne *f*) (*personne*); mauvais, nuisible; **'mis·chie·vous·ness** méchanceté *f*; espièglerie *f*, malice *f*; caractère *m* nuisible (*de qch.*).

mis·con·ceive [ˈmiskənˈsiːv] mal concevoir; mal comprendre; **mis·con·cep·tion** [ˈ~ˈsepʃn] idée *f* fausse; malentendu *m*.

mis·con·duct **1.** [ˈmisˈkɔndəkt] mauvaise conduite *f* (*d'une personne*); mauvaise gestion *f* ou administration *f* (*d'une affaire*); **2.** [ˈ~kənˈdʌkt] mal diriger *ou* gérer; ~ o.s. se conduire mal.

mis·con·struc·tion [ˈmiskənˈstrʌkʃn] fausse interprétation *f*; **mis·con·strue** [ˈ~ˈstruː] mal interpréter.

mis·count [ˈmisˈkaunt] **1.** mal compter; se tromper; **2.** faux calcul *m*; erreur *f* d'addition.

mis·cre·ant [ˈmiskriənt] scélérat (*a. su./m*); misérable (*a. su./mf*).

mis·date [ˈmisˈdeit] **1.** erreur *f* de date; **2.** mal dater.

mis·deal [ˈmisˈdiːl] *cartes* **1.** [*irr.* (*deal*)] faire maldonne; **2.** maldonne *f*.

mis·deed [ˈmisˈdiːd] méfait *m*.

mis·de·mean·ant ⚖ [ˈmisdiːˈmiːnənt] délinquant(e *f*) *m*; **mis·de·mean·o(u)r** ⚖ [~nə] délit *m* correctionnel.

mis·di·rect [ˈmisdiˈrekt] mal diriger; mal adresser (*une lettre*); **'mis·di·rec·tion** renseignement *m* erronné; fausse adresse *f*.

mis·do·ing [ˈmisˈduːiŋ] méfait *m*.

mis·doubt [ˈmisˈdaut] se douter de (*qch.*, *q.*); soupçonner.

mi·ser [ˈmaizə] avare *mf*.

mis·er·a·ble □ ['mizərəbl] malheureux (-euse *f*); triste; misérable; déplorable; '**mis·er·a·ble·ness** état *m* malheureux *ou* misérable.

mi·ser·ly ['maizəli] avare; sordide.

mis·er·y ['mizəri] souffrance *f*; misère *f*, détresse *f*.

mis·fea·sance ⚖ ['mis'fi:zəns] infraction *f* à la loi; abus *m* d'autorité.

mis·fire ['mis'faiə] **1.** *fusil*: raté *m*; *mot.* raté *m* d'allumage; **2.** rater (*a. mot.*).

mis·fit ['mis'fit] vêtement *m* ou soulier *m* manqué; F inapte *mf*.

mis·for·tune [mis'fɔ:tʃn] malheur *m*, infortune *f*, calamité *f*.

mis·give [mis'giv] [*irr.* (*give*)] avoir des inquiétudes; *my heart misgave me* j'avais de mauvais pressentiments; '**mis·giv·ing** pressentiment *m*, doute *m*, crainte *f*.

mis·gov·ern ['mis'gʌvən] mal gouverner; '**mis·gov·ern·ment** mauvais gouvernement *m*; mauvaise administration *f*.

mis·guide ['mis'gaid] mal guider *ou* conseiller.

mis·han·dle ['mis'hændl] malmener, maltraiter (*q.*); traiter mal (*un sujet*).

mis·hap ['mishæp] mésaventure *f*; *mot.* panne *f*.

mis·hear [mis'hiə] [*irr.* (*hear*)] mal entendre; mal comprendre.

mish·mash ['miʃmæʃ] fatras *m*.

mis·in·form ['misin'fɔ:m] mal renseigner; '**mis·in·for'ma·tion** faux renseignement *m*, -s *m/pl.*

mis·in·ter·pret ['misin'tə:prit] mal interpréter; mal comprendre; '**mis·in·ter·pre'ta·tion** fausse interprétation *f*.

mis·judge ['mis'dʒʌdʒ] mal juger; se tromper sur; '**mis'judg(e)·ment** jugement *m* erroné.

mis·lay [mis'lei] [*irr.* (*lay*)] égarer.

mis·lead [mis'li:d] [*irr.* (*lead*)] tromper, induire en erreur; fourvoyer.

mis·man·age ['mis'mænidʒ] mal administrer; mal conduire; '**mis·man·age·ment** mauvaise administration *f ou* gestion *f*.

mis·no·mer ['mis'noumə] faux nom *m*; erreur *f* de nom.

mi·sog·y·nist [mai'sɔdʒinist] misogyne *m*; **mi'sog·y·ny** misogynie *f*.

mis·place ['mis'pleis] déplacer (*qch.*); mal placer (*sa confiance*); '**mis'place·ment** déplacement *m*.

mis·print 1. [mis'print] imprimer incorrectement; **2.** ['mis'print] faute *f* d'impression.

mis·pri·sion ⚖ [mis'priʒn] non-révélation *f* (*d'un crime*); négligence *f* (coupable).

mis·pro·nounce ['misprə'nauns] mal prononcer; **mis·pro·nun·ci·a·tion** ['‿prənʌnsi'eiʃn] mauvaise prononciation *f*.

mis·quo·ta·tion ['miskwou'teiʃn] citation *f* inexacte; fausse citation *f*; '**mis'quote** citer inexactement.

mis·read [mis'ri:d] [*irr.* (*read*)] mal lire *ou* interpréter.

mis·rep·re·sent ['misrepri'zent] mal représenter; dénaturer (*les faits*); '**mis·rep·re·sen'ta·tion** faux rapport *m*; ⚖ fausse déclaration *f*; ⚖ réticence *f*.

mis·rule ['mis'ru:l] **1.** confusion *f*, désordre *m*; mauvaise administration *f*; **2.** mal gouverner.

miss¹ [mis] mademoiselle (*pl.* mesdemoiselles) *f*; co. demoiselle *f*; adolescente *f*.

miss² [‿] **1.** coup *m* manqué, perdu *ou* raté; **2.** *v/t.* manquer; F rater (*le but, une occasion, le train*); ne pas trouver; ne pas saisir; se tromper de (*chemin*); ne pas avoir; sauter; remarquer *ou* regretter l'absence de; (*gér.*) faillir (*inf.*); ~ *one's footing* poser le pied à faux; ~ *one's hold* lâcher prise; ne pas saisir; *v/i.* manquer le coup; frapper à vide; ~ *out on s.th.* louper qch., rater qch.

mis·sal *eccl.* ['misəl] missel *m*.

mis·shap·en ['mis'ʃeipən] difforme, contrefait; déformé (*chapeau etc.*).

mis·sile ['misail] projectile *m*; ~ *site* base *f* de lancement; *ballistic* ~ engin *m* balistique.

miss·ing ['misiŋ] absent, perdu; *surt.* ⚔ disparu; *be* ~ manquer; être égaré *ou* perdu.

mis·sion ['miʃn] mission *f* (*a. eccl., a. fig.*); '**mis·sion·ar·y 1.** missionnaire *m*; **2.** missionnaire; de missionnaires; des missions.

mis·sis F ['misiz] femme *f*, dame *f*.

mis·sive ['misiv] lettre *f*, missive *f*.

mis·spell ['mis'spel] [*irr.* (*spell*)] mal épeler *ou* écrire (*un mot*).

mis·spend ['mis'spend] [*irr.* (*spend*)]

mal employer (*son temps, son argent*).

mis·state [ˈmisˈsteit] exposer incorrectement; altérer (*des faits*); **ˈmisˈstate·ment** exposé *m* inexact; erreur *f* de fait.

mis·sus F [ˈmisəz] femme *f*, dame *f*.

miss·y F [ˈmisi] mademoiselle (*pl.* mesdemoiselles) *f*.

mist [mist] **1.** brume *f*; buée *f* (*sur une glace*); *fig.* in a ~ désorienté, perdu; **2.** (se) couvrir de buée (*glace*); *v/i.* disparaître sous la brume.

mis·tak·a·ble [misˈteikəbl] sujet(te *f*) à méprise; facile à confondre; **mis·take** [~ˈteik] **1.** [*irr.* (take)] *v/t.* se tromper de; se méprendre sur; mal comprendre; confondre (avec, for); be ~n se tromper; *v/i.* se tromper; **2.** erreur *f*, méprise *f*, faute *f*; by ~ par méprise; and no ~ décidément; **misˈtak·en** □ erroné; mal compris; ~ identity erreur *f* sur la personne.

mis·ter [ˈmistə] (*abr.* **Mr.**) monsieur (*pl.* messieurs) *m*.

mis·time [ˈmisˈtaim] mal calculer; faire (*qch.*) mal à propos; **ˈmisˈtimed** inopportun.

mist·i·ness [ˈmistinis] état *m* brumeux; brouillard *m*; obscurité *f* (*a. fig.*).

mis·tle·toe ♀ [ˈmisltou] gui *m*.

mis·trans·late [ˈmistrænsˈleit] mal traduire; **ˈmisˈtransˈla·tion** traduction *f* inexacte; contresens *m*.

mis·tress [ˈmistris] maîtresse *f*; patronne *f*; *lycée:* professeur *m*; *école primaire:* institutrice *f*; (*abr.* **Mrs.** [ˈmisiz]) madame (*pl.* mesdames) *f*.

mis·trust [ˈmisˈtrʌst] **1.** se méfier de; **2.** méfiance *f*, défiance *f* (de in, of); **ˈmisˈtrustˈful** □ [~ful] méfiant, soupçonneux (-euse *f*) (à l'endroit de, of).

mist·y □ [ˈmisti] brumeux (-euse *f*); *fig.* vague, confus.

mis·un·der·stand [ˈmisʌndəˈstænd] [*irr.* (stand)] mal comprendre *ou* interpréter; **ˈmisˈunˈderˈstand·ing** malentendu *m*; mésentente *f*.

mis·use 1. [ˈmisˈjuːz] faire mauvais emploi *ou* usage de; maltraiter; **2.** [ˈ~ˈjuːs] abus *m*; mauvais emploi *m ou* usage *m*.

mite¹ *zo.* [mait] mite *f*; acarien *m*.

mite² [~] denier *m*, obole *f*; *personne:* mioche *mf*; petit(e *f*) *m*; a ~

of a child un(e *f*) enfant haut(e *f*) comme ma botte.

mit·i·gate [ˈmitigeit] adoucir, atténuer (*a. fig.*); **mit·iˈga·tion** adoucissement *m*, atténuation *f*.

mi·tre, mi·ter [ˈmaitə] **1.** *eccl.* mitre *f*; ⊕ onglet *m*; **2.** *eccl.* mitrer; ⊕ tailler *ou* assembler à onglet; **ˈ~ˈwheel** ⊕ roue *f* dentée conique.

mitt [mit] mitaine *f*; *baseball:* gant *m*; *sl.* patte *f* (= *main*).

mit·ten [ˈmitn] mitaine *f*; F get the ~ recevoir son congé.

mix [miks] (se) mêler (à, avec with); (se) mélanger; (s')allier (*couleurs*); *v/i.:* ~ in society fréquenter la société; ~ed mêlé, mélangé, mixte; confus (*a. fig.*); ~ed bathing bains *m/pl.* mixtes; ~ed marriage mariage *m* mixte; ~ed mathematics mathématiques *f/pl.* appliquées; ~ed pickles *pl.* variantes *f/pl.*; pickles *m/pl.* assortis; ~ up mêler; confondre; embrouiller; ~ed up with mêlé à, engagé dans (*une affaire*); ~ed with accointé avec; impliqué dans; **ˈmixˈer** ⊕ brasseur *m*; garçon *m* de bar (*qui prépare des cocktails*), F barman *m*; *cuis.* mixe(u)r *m*; *radio:* opérateur *m* des sons, *machine:* mélangeur *m* des sons; be a good (bad) ~ (ne pas) savoir s'adapter à son entourage; **mix·ture** [ˈ~tʃə] mélange *m* (*a. fig.*), *pharm.* mixtion *f*, mixture *f*; **ˈmixˈup** confusion *f*; embrouillement *m*.

miz·(z)en ⚓ [ˈmizn] artimon *m*; *attr.* d'artimon; de fougue (*perroquet*).

miz·zle [ˈmizl] bruiner, crachiner.

mne·mon·ic [niˈmɔnik] **1.** (~ally) mnémonique; **2.** ~s *pl.* mnémonique *f*, mnémotechnie *f*.

moan [moun] **1.** gémissement *m*; **2.** gémir; se lamenter.

moat [mout] fossé *m*, douve *f*; **ˈmoat·ed** entouré d'un fossé.

mob [mɔb] **1.** foule *f*, ameutement *m*; populace *f*; **2.** *v/t.* assiéger; *v/i.* s'attrouper; **ˈmobˈbish** de la populace; canaille; tumultueux (-euse *f*).

mob-cap [ˈmɔbkæp] petite coiffe *f*; cornette *f*; F charlotte *f*.

mo·bile [ˈmoubail] mobile (*a.* ✕); changeant; ~ police (policiers *m/pl.* de la) brigade *f* mobile; *télév.* ~ unit motard *m*; **mo·bil·i·ty** [moˈbiliti] mobilité *f*; **mo·bi·li·za·tion** [moubilai'zeiʃn] mobilisation f; '**mo·bi·lize** ⚔ mobiliser.

mob-law ['mɔblɔ:] loi f de la populace; loi f de Lynch.

mob·oc·ra·cy [mɔ'bɔkrəsi] F voyoucratie f.

moc·ca·sin ['mɔkəsin] mocassin m.

mock [mɔk] **1.** dérision f; (sujet m de) moquerie f; **2.** faux (fausse f); contrefait; d'imitation; ~ fight simulacre m de combat; **3.** v/t. imiter, singer; tromper; v/i. se moquer (de, at); '**mock·er** moqueur (-euse f) m; '**mock·er·y** raillerie f; (sujet m de) moquerie f; objet m de risée; simulacre m; '**mock-he·ro·ic** héroï-comique; burlesque.

mock·ing ['mɔkiŋ] **1.** raillerie f, moquerie f; **2.** □ moqueur (-euse f); '**~-bird** orn. moqueur m.

mock...: '**~-king** roi m pour rire; '**~-'tur·tle soup** potage m (à la) fausse tortue; '**~-up** ⊕ maquette f.

mod·al □ ['moudl] modal (-aux m/pl.); ⚖ conditionnel(le f); **mo·dal·i·ty** [mou'dæliti] modalité f.

mode [moud] méthode f, manière f, façon f, mode m (a. ♪, gramm., phls.); mode f (= coutume).

mod·el ['mɔdl] **1.** modèle m (a.fig.); maquette f; figurine f (de cire); personne: mannequin m, modèle mf; attr. modèle; act as a ~ servir de modèle; **2.** modeler (sur after, [up]on) (a. fig.); **mod·el·(l)er** ['mɔdlə] modeleur (-euse f) m.

mod·er·ate 1. □ ['mɔdərit] modéré; raisonnable; moyen(ne f); médiocre; **2.** ['~reit] (se) modérer; v/t. tempérer; **mod·er·ate·ness** ['~ritnis] modération f; prix: modicité f; médiocrité f; **mod·er·a·tion** [~'reiʃn] modération f, mesure f; langage: sobriété f; in ~ modérément; frugalement; univ. ⓢs pl. premier examen m pour le B.A. (Oxford); '**mod·er·a·tor** assemblée, jury, etc.: président m; univ. examinateur m (Oxford); phys. modérateur m.

mod·ern ['mɔdən] **1.** moderne; **2.** the ~s pl. les modernes m/pl.; '**mod·ern·ism** modernité f; goût m du moderne; eccl. modernisme m; gramm. néologisme m; **mo·der·ni·ty** [mɔ'də:niti] modernité f; '**mod·ern·ize** moderniser.

mod·est □ ['mɔdist] modeste; sans prétentions; honnête, chaste;

'**mod·es·ty** modestie f; modération f; simplicité f; honnêteté f.

mod·i·cum ['mɔdikəm] faible quantité f.

mod·i·fi·a·ble ['mɔdifaiəbl] modifiable; **mod·i·fi·ca·tion** [~fi'keiʃn] modification f; atténuation f; **mod·i·fy** ['~fai] modifier (a. gramm.); apporter des modifications à; atténuer.

mod·u·late ['mɔdjuleit] moduler (v/i. a. ♪); ajuster; **mod·u·la·tion** modulation f; **'mod·u·la·tor** modulateur (-trice f) m; ~ of tonality cin. modulateur m de tonalité.

Mo·gul [mo'gʌl]: the Great (ou Grand) ~ le Grand Mogol m.

mo·hair ['mouhɛə] mohair m.

Mo·ham·med·an [mo'hæmidən] **1.** Mahométan(e f) m; **2.** mahométan.

moi·e·ty ['mɔiəti] moitié f; part f.

moil [mɔil] peiner.

moire [mwɑ:] moire f; ~ crêpe crêpe m ondé.

moi·ré ['mwɑrei] moiré (a. su./m.)

moist [mɔist] humide; moite; **mois·ten** ['mɔisn] (se) mouiller, (s')humecter; '**moist·ness, mois·ture** ['~tʃə] humidité f; peau: moiteur f; **mois·tur·ize** ['~tʃəraiz] humidifier (air); hydrater (peau); **mois·tur·iz·ing cream** crème f hydratante.

moke sl. [mouk] âne m; bourrique f.

mo·lar ['moulə] (ou ~ tooth) molaire f.

mold [mould] see mould etc.

mo·las·ses [mə'læsiz] mélasse f.

mole¹ zo. [moul] taupe f.

mole² [~] grain m de beauté; nævus (pl. -vi) m.

mole³ [~] mole m; brise-lames m/inv.

mo·lec·u·lar [mo'lekjulə] moléculaire; **mol·e·cule** phys. ['mɔlikju:l] molécule f.

mole·hill ['moulhil] taupinière f; '**mole·skin** (peau f de) taupe f; ⊕ velours m de coton.

mo·lest [mo'lest] rudoyer; ⚖ molester; **mo·les·ta·tion** [moules'teiʃn] molestation f; voies f/pl. de fait.

moll F [mɔl] catin f.

mol·li·fy ['mɔlifai] adoucir; apaiser.

mol·lusc zo. ['mɔləsk] mollusque m; **mol·lus·cous** [mɔ'lʌskəs] de(s) mollusque(s); fig. mollasse.

mol·ly·cod·dle ['mɔlikɔdl] **1.** douillet *m*; petit chéri *m* à sa maman; **2.** dorloter.

mol·ten ['moultən] en fusion; fondu.

mom *Am.* F [mɔm] maman *f*; *~-and-pop store* épicerie *f* du coin.

mo·ment ['moumənt] moment *m*; instant *m*; *see momentum*; *at (ou for) the ~* pour le moment; *en ce moment*; *of ~* important; **'mo·men·tar·y** □ momentané, passager (-ère *f*); **'mo·ment·ly** *adv.* d'un moment à l'autre; momentanément; **mo·men·tous** □ [~'mentəs] important; grave; **mo'men·tum** *phys.* [~təm] force *f* vive; vitesse *f* acquise.   [chisme *m*.]

mon·a·chism ['mɔnəkizm] mona-

mon·arch ['mɔnək] monarque *m*; **mo·nar·chic, mo·nar·chi·cal** □ [mɔ'nɑːkik(l)] monarchique; **mon·arch·y** ['mɔnəki] monarchie *f*.

mon·as·ter·y ['mɔnəstri] monastère *m*; **mo·nas·tic, mo·nas·ti·cal** □ [mɔ'næstik(l)] monastique; monacal (-aux *m/pl.*).

Mon·day ['mʌndi] lundi *m*.

mon·e·tar·y ['mʌnitəri] monétaire.

mon·ey ['mʌni] argent *m*; monnaie *f*; *~ matters pl.* affaires *f/pl.* financières; *ready ~* argent *m* comptant; F *out of ~* à sec; *keep s.o. out of his ~* frustrer q. de son argent; *make ~* faire de l'argent; **'~-box** caisse *f*, cassette *f*; **'~-chang·er** changeur *m*, cambiste *m*; **mon·eyed** ['mʌnid] riche; qui a de l'argent.

mon·ey...: **'~-grub·ber** gripppe-sou (*pl.* grippe-sou[s]) *m*; **'~-of·fice** caisse *f*; **'~-or·der** mandat-poste (*pl.* mandats-poste) *m*; **'~'s-worth**: *get one's ~* en avoir pour son argent.

mon·ger ['mʌngə] marchand(e *f*) *m* (de).

Mon·gol ['mɔŋgɔl], **Mon·go·lian** [~'goulian] **1.** mongol; mongolique; ♂ idiot; **2.** Mongol(e *f*) *m*.

mon·grel ['mʌŋgrəl] **1.** métis(se *f*) *m*; bâtard(e *f*) *m*; **2.** métis(se *f*).

mo·ni·tion [mo'niʃn] avertissement *m*; **mon·i·tor** ['mɔnitə] moniteur (-trice *f*) *m*; ♻ monitor *m*; *radio*: contrôleur *m* d'enregistrement; *télév.* moniteur *m*, écran *m* de contrôle; **'mon·i·tor·ing** monitoring *m*; service *m* d'écoute; **'mon·i·to·ry** d'avertissement, d'admonition; monitoire.

monk [mʌŋk] moine *m*, religieux *m*; **'monk·er·y** *usu. péj.* moinerie *f*.

mon·key ['mʌŋki] **1.** singe *m*; *fig.* polisson *m*, espiègle *mf*; ⊕ mouton *m*; *sl.* monnaie: cinq cents livres *f/pl.* ou *Am.* dollars *m/pl.*; *sl. ~'s allowance* plus de coups que de pain; F *put s.o.'s ~ up* mettre q. en colère; F *~ business*, *~ tricks pl.* affaire *f* peu loyale; procédé *m* irrégulier; fumisterie *f*; **2.** F faire des tours de singe; *~ about with* tripoter (*qch.*); **'~-en·gine** ⊕ (*sorte de*) sonnette *f* (à mouton); **'~-puz·zle** araucaria *m*; **'~-wrench** ⊕ clé *f* anglaise; *Am. sl. throw a ~ in s.th.* saboter une affaire.

monk·hood ['mʌŋkhud] monachisme *m*; moinerie *f*; **'monk·ish** *usu. péj.* de moine, monacal (-aux *m/pl.*).

mon·o F ['mɔnou] **1.** mono(phonique); **2.** (*in ~ en*) monophonie *f*; F disque *m* mono.

mono- [mɔno] mon(o)-; **mon·o·cle** ['mɔnɔkl] monocle *m*; **mo'noc·u·lar** [~kjulə] monoculaire; **mo'nog·a·my** [~gəmi] monogamie *f*; **mon·o·gram** ['mɔnəgræm] monogramme *m*; **mon·o·graph** ['~grɑːf] monographie *f*; **mon·o·lith** ['mɔnoliθ] monolithe *m*; **mon·o·lith·ic** monolithe; *a. fig.* monolithique; gigantesque; **mon·o·logue** ['mɔnəlɔg] monologue *m*; **mon·o·ma·ni·a** ['mɔno'meiniə] monomanie *f*; **mon·o'ma·ni·ac** [~niæk] monomane *mf*; **mon·o·plane** ✈ ['mɔnəplein] monoplan *m*; **mo·nop·o·list** [mɔ'nɔpəlist] accapareur (-euse *f*) *m*; **mo'nop·o·lize** [~laiz] monopoliser; *fig.* s'emparer de; **mo'nop·o·ly** monopole *m* (de, *of*); **mon·o·syl·lab·ic** ['mɔnəsi'læbik] (~*ally*) monosyllabe, monosyllabique; **mon·o·syl·la·ble** ['~ləbl] monosyllabe *m*; **mon·o·the·ism** ['mɔnoθi:izm] monothéisme *m*; **mon·o·tone** ['mɔnətoun] **1.** débit *m* monotone; *in ~* d'une voix uniforme *ou* monotone; **2.** chanter sur le même ton; **mo·not·o·nous** □ [mə'nɔtənəs] monotone; *fig.* fastidieux (-euse *f*); **mo'not·o·ny** [~təni] monotonie *f*; **mon·o·type** *typ.* ['mɔnətaip] monotype *f*.

mon·soon [mɔn'suːn] mousson *f*.

mon·ster ['mɔnstə] **1.** monstre *m* (*a. fig.*); monstruosité *f*; avorton *m*; F géant(e f) m; **2.** F monstre; colossal (-aux m/pl.).

mon·strance eccl. ['mɔnstrəns] ostensoir m.

mon·stros·i·ty [mɔns'trɔsiti] monstruosité f; **'mon·strous** □ monstrueux (-euse f); colossal (-aux m/pl.).

mon·tage cin., phot. [mɔn'tɑːʒ] montage m.

month [mʌnθ] mois m; **'month·ly 1.** mensuel(le f); ~ season ticket (carte f d')abonnement m (valable pour un mois); **2.** revue f mensuelle.

mon·u·ment ['mɔnjumənt] monument m; pierre f tombale; **mon·u·men·tal** □ [~'mentl] monumental (-aux m/pl.); F colossal (-aux m/pl.), prodigieux (-euse f).

moo [muː] **1.** meuglement m, beuglement m; **2.** meugler, beugler.

mooch F [muːtʃ]: v/i. ~ about flâner; ~ along traîner.

mood¹ gramm., a. ♪ [muːd] mode m.

mood² [~] humeur f, disposition f.

mood·i·ness ['muːdinis] morosité f; humeur f changeante; **'mood·y** □ maussade; mal luné.

moon [muːn] **1.** lune f; poét. mois m; F once in a blue ~ tous les trente-six du mois; F be over the ~ être aux anges; cry for the ~ demander la lune; promise s.o. the ~ promettre la lune et monts et merveilles à q.; **2.** (usu. ~ about) F muser; **'moon·less** sans lune; **'moon·light** clair m de lune; clarté f de la lune; **'moon·light·ing** travail m noir; **'moon·lit** éclairé par la lune;

moon...: **'~·shine** clair m de lune; F balivernes f/pl.; alcool m de contrebande; **'~·shin·er** Am. F contrebandier m de boissons alcooliques; bouilleur m de contrebande; **'~·struck** halluciné; F hébété; **moon·y** □ de ou dans la lune; F rêveur (-euse f); vague.

Moor¹ [muə] Maure m, Mauresque f.

moor² [~] lande f, bruyère f; † ou prov. terrain m marécageux.

moor³ ⚓ [~] (s')amarrer; **moor·age** ['muərɪdʒ] amarrage m, mouillage m.

moor-game ['muəgeim] lagopède m rouge d'Écosse.

moor·ing-mast ['muərɪŋmɑːst] mât m d'amarrage.

moor·ings ⚓ ['muərɪŋz] pl. amarres f/pl.; corps-morts m/pl.

Moor·ish ['muərɪʃ] mauresque.

moose zo. [muːs] (a. ~-deer) élan m, orignal m.

moot [muːt] **1.** hist. assemblée f du peuple; **2.** ~ case (ou point) point m litigieux; **3.** soulever (une question).

mop [mɔp] **1.** balai m à franges; cheveux: tignasse f; **2.** essuyer, (a. ~up) éponger (de l'eau); engloutir (les bénéfices); ✗ F nettoyer; sl. aplatir (q.).

mope [moup] **1.** fig. cafardeux (-euse f) m; ~s pl. idées f/pl. noires; F cafard m; **2.** v/i. voir tout en noir, s'ennuyer; v/t. ~ o.s., be ~d languir.

mo·ped ['mouped] cyclomoteur m, mobylette f (TM).

mop·ing □ ['moupiŋ], **'mop·ish** □ morose, mélancolique, triste.

mo·raine géol. [mɔ'rein] moraine f.

mor·al ['mɔrəl] **1.** □ moral (-aux m/pl.); conforme aux bonnes mœurs; **2.** morale f; moralité f (d'un conte); ~s pl. mœurs f/pl.; conduite f; **mo·rale** [mɔ'rɑːl] usu. ✗ moral m; **mor·al·ist** ['mɔrəlist] moraliste mf; **mo·ral·i·ty** [mə'ræliti] moralité f; sens m moral; probité f; bonnes mœurs f/pl.; péj. sermon m; théâ. hist. moralité f; **mor·al·ize** ['mɔrəlaiz] v/i. faire de la morale (sur, [up]on); v/t. moraliser (q.); indiquer la morale de.

mo·rass □ ['mɔ'ræs] marais m, marécage m; fig. bourbier m.

mor·bid □ ['mɔːbid] morbide; malsain; **'mor·bid·i·ty, 'mor·bid·ness** morbidité f; état m maladif.

mor·dant ['mɔːdənt] **1.** mordant; **2.** mordant m.

more [mɔː] **1.** adj. plus (de); **2.** adv. plus, davantage; once ~ encore une fois; de nouveau; two ~ deux de plus; so much (ou all) the ~ d'autant plus; à plus forte raison; no ~ ne ... plus; ~ and ~ de plus en plus; **3.** su. plus m.

mo·rel ♣ [mɔ'rel] morelle f.

more·o·ver [mɔː'ouvə] d'ailleurs, du reste.

Mo·resque [mɔ'resk] **1.** mauresque; **2.** Mauresque f; arabesque f.

mor·ga·nat·ic [mɔːgə'nætik] (~ally) morganatique.

morgue [mɔːg] morgue f; dépôt m mortuaire.

mor·i·bund [ˈmɔribʌnd] moribond.

Mor·mon [ˈmɔ:mən] mormon(e f)
m.

morn poét. [mɔ:n] matin m.

morn·ing [ˈmɔ:niŋ] **1.** matin m;
matinée f; in the ~ le matin; du
matin; tomorrow ~ demain matin;
2. du matin; matinal (-aux m/pl.);
~ coat jaquette f; ~ dress tenue f de
ville; femmes: négligé m; ~ performance matinée f.

Mo·roc·can [məˈrɔkən] marocain.

mo·roc·co [məˈrɔkou] (ou ~ leather)
maroquin m.

mo·ron [ˈmɔ:rɔn] faible mf d'esprit;
F idiot(e f) m.

mo·rose □ [məˈrous] morose,
chagrin; **mo'rose·ness** morosité f.

mor·phi·a [ˈmɔ:fjə], **mor·phine**
[ˈmɔ:fi:n] morphine f.

mor·pho·log·i·cal [mɔ:fəˈlɔdʒikl]
morphologique.

mor·row [ˈmɔrou] usu. poét. lendemain m; good ~! bonjour!

mor·sel [ˈmɔ:səl] (petit) morceau m;
terre: lopin m.

mor·tal [ˈmɔ:tl] **1.** adj. □ mortel(le
f); fig. funeste, fatal (-s m/pl.); à outrance (combat); **2.** adv. F très; **3.** su.
mortel(le f) m, être m humain;
mor·tal·i·ty [mɔ:ˈtæliti] mortalité
f; les mortels m/pl.

mor·tar [ˈmɔ:tə] mortier m (a. ⚔);
enduit m.

mort·gage [ˈmɔ:gidʒ] **1.** hypothèque f; (a. ~-deed) contrat m hypothécaire; **2.** hypothéquer; **mort-
ga·gee** [ˌmɔ:gəˈdʒi:] créancier m hypothécaire; **mort·ga·gor** [ˌ~ˈdʒɔ:]
débiteur m hypothécaire.

mor·tice [ˈmɔ:tis] see mortise.

mor·ti·cian Am. [mɔ:ˈtiʃn] entrepreneur m de pompes funèbres.

mor·ti·fi·ca·tion [mɔ:tifiˈkeiʃn] ⚕
mortification f; gangrène f; déconvenue f, mortification f; humiliation f; **mor·ti·fy** [ˈ~fai] v/t.
mortifier; humilier; ⚕ gangrener;
v/i. se gangrener.

mor·tise ⊕ [ˈmɔ:tis] **1.** mortaise f;
serrure f encastrée; **2.** mortaiser.

mort·main ⚏ [ˈmɔ:tmein] main-
morte f.

mor·tu·ar·y [ˈmɔ:tjuəri] **1.** mortuaire; **2.** dépôt m mortuaire;
morgue f.

mo·sa·ic¹ [məˈzeiik] mosaïque f.

Mo·sa·ic² [~] mosaïque, de Moïse.

Mo·selle [məˈzel] vin m de Moselle,
moselle m.

Mos·lem [ˈmɔzlem] musulman (a.
su.); mahométan (a. su.).

mosque [mɔsk] mosquée f.

mos·qui·to zo. [məsˈki:tou], pl.
-toes [ˌ~touz] moustique m.

moss [mɔs] ♧ mousse f; tourbière f;
'moss·y moussu.

most [moust] **1.** adj. □ le plus de;
la plupart de; for the ~ part pour la
plupart; **2.** adv. le plus; surtout;
très, fort, bien; **3.** su. le plus; la plupart d'entre eux (elles); at (the) ~
tout au plus; make the ~ of tirer le
meilleur parti possible de; faire
valoir.

most·ly [ˈmoustli] pour la plupart;
le plus souvent.

mote [mout] atome m de poussière;
bibl. paille f.

mo·tel [ˈmoutel] motel m.

mo·tet ♪ [mouˈtet] motet m.

moth [mɔθ] mite f, teigne f des
draps; papillon m de nuit; '~-eat·en
rongé des mites.

moth·er [ˈmʌðə] **1.** mère f; ♀'s Day
la fête des Mères; **2.** servir de mère
à; fig. dorloter; **moth·er·hood**
[ˈ~hud] maternité f; **'moth·er-in-
law** belle-mère f (pl. belles-mères);
'moth·er·less sans mère; **'moth-
er·li·ness** affection f maternelle;
'moth·er·ly maternel(le f).

moth·er...: ~ of pearl nacre f;
'~-of-pearl en ou de nacre; '~-ship
Brit. ravitailleur m; navire-atelier
(pl. navires-ateliers) m; '~-tongue
langue f maternelle.

moth·y [ˈmɔθi] mangé aux mites.

mo·tif [mouˈti:f] motif m.

mo·tion [ˈmouʃn] **1.** mouvement m,
marche f (a. ⊕); signe m; parl. proposition f, motion f; ⚕ selle f; parl.
bring forward (agree upon) a ~
présenter (adopter) une motion;
set in ~ mettre en train; **2.** v/t.
faire signe à (q.) (de inf., to inf.);
v/i. faire un signe ou geste; '**mo-
tion·less** immobile; '**mo·tion-
pic·ture** Am. film m; ~s pl. films
m/pl.; projection f animée; attr.
ciné...

mo·ti·vate [ˈmoutiveit] motiver;
mo·ti'va·tion motivation f.

mo·tive [ˈmoutiv] **1.** moteur (-trice
f); **2.** motif m; mobile m; **3.** motiver; '**mo·tive·less** immotivé.

mo·tiv·i·ty [moˈtiviti] motilité *f*.

mot·ley [ˈmɔtli] bariolé; bigarré.

mo·tor [ˈmoutə] **1.** moteur *m*; mécanisme *m*; *see* ~-*car*; **2.** moteur (-trice *f*); à *ou* par moteur; d'automobile; ~ *ambulance* auto-ambulance *f*; *Am.* ~ *court see* ~ *park*; ~ *goggles pl.* lunettes *f*/*pl.* d'automobiliste; ~ *mechanic* (*ou fitter*) mécanicien *m* automobiliste; ~ *park Am. usu.* stationnement *m*; garage *m* pour autos; ~ *school* auto-école *f*; **3.** *v*/*i.* voyager *ou* aller en auto; *v*/*t.* conduire (*q.*) en auto; ~ **bi·cy·cle** motocyclette *f*; '~·**boat** canot *m* automobile; vedette *f* à moteur; '~·**bus** autobus *m*; ~ **cab** autotaxi *m*; '~·**cade** *Am.* [ˈˌkeid] défilé *m* d'automobiles; '~·**car** auto(mobile) *f*; ~ **cy·cle** motocyclette *f*; ~ **cy·clist** motocycliste *mf*; **mo·to·ri·al** [moˈtɔːriəl] moteur (-trice *f*); **mo·tor·ing** [ˈmoutəriŋ] automobilisme *m*; tourisme *m* en auto; '**mo·tor·ist** automobiliste *mf*; **mo·tor·i·za·tion** [ˌraiˈzeiʃn] motorisation *f*; '**mo·tor·ize** motoriser; '**mo·tor·launch** vedette *f*; bateau *m* automobile; '**mo·tor·less** sans moteur. **mo·tor...**: '~·**lor·ry** (auto-)camion *m*; '~·**man** *Am.* wattman (*pl.* -men) *m*; '~·**plough** charrue *f* automobile; '~·**pool** autos *f*/*pl.* communes; '~·**road** autostrade *f*; ~ **scoot·er** scooter *m*; '~·**truck** *Am.* (auto-)camion *m*; '~·**way** autoroute *f*.

mot·tled [ˈmɔtld] marbré; pommelé; madré (*bois, savon*).

mot·to [ˈmɔtou], *pl.* **-toes** [ˈˌtouz] devise *f*; ⊠ mot *m*.

mo(u)ld¹ [mould] terre *f* végétale; terreau *m*.

mo(u)ld² [~] **1.** moule *m* (*a. fig.*); *typ.* matrice *f*; *cuis.* crème *f* renversée; △ moulure *f*; **2.** mouler, façonner (sur, [*up*]on); pétrir (*le pain*).

mo(u)ld·er¹ [ˈmouldə] mouleur *m*; façonneur *m*.

mo(u)ld·er² [~] s'effriter; (*a.* ~ *away*) tomber en poussière.

mo(u)ld·i·ness [ˈmouldinis] (état *m*) moisi *m*.

mo(u)ld·ing [ˈmouldiŋ] moulage *m*; moulure *f*; F formation *f*; △ *square* ~ baguette *f*; *plain* ~ bandeau *m*;

grooved ~ moulure *f* à gorge; *attr.* de mouleur; à moulurer *etc.*

mo(u)ld·y [ˈmouldi] moisi; chanci (*pain, confiture*).

moult [moult] **1.** mue *f*; **2.** *v*/*i.* muer; *vt*/*i. fig.* perdre (ses cheveux).

mound [maund] tertre *m*; monceau *m*, tas *m*.

mount [maunt] **1.** montagne *f*; *poét.*, *a. géog.* mont *m*; (carton *m* de) montage *m*; monture *f* (= *cheval*); ⊕ *machine*: armement *m*; **2.** *v*/*i.* monter; monter à cheval, se mettre en selle; s'élever (à, to); (*usu.* ~ *up*) augmenter; *v*/*t.* monter sur (*un banc, un cheval*); monter, gravir (*une colline etc.*); ✗ affûter (*une pièce*); ⊕ installer; entoiler, coller (*un tableau*); monter (*un bijou*); *théâ.* mettre à la scène; *see guard 1*.

moun·tain [ˈmauntin] **1.** montagne *f*; *make a* ~ *out of a molehill* (se) faire d'une mouche un éléphant; **2.** des montagnes; montagneux (-euse *f*); **moun·tain·eer** [ˌˈniə] montagnard(e *f*) *m*; alpiniste *mf*; **moun·tain·eer·ing 1.** alpinisme *m*; **2.** alpin; '**moun·tain·ous** montagneux (-euse *f*); **moun·tain rail·way** chemin *m* de fer de montagne; **moun·tain range** chaîne *f* de montagnes; **moun·tain sick·ness** mal *m* des montagnes.

mount·e·bank [ˈmauntibæŋk] saltimbanque *m*; *fig.* charlatan *m*.

mount·ing ⊕ [ˈmauntiŋ] montage *m*; entoilage *m*.

mourn [mɔːn] (se) lamenter; *v*/*i.* porter le deuil; *v*/*t.* (*ou* ~ *for, over*) pleurer (*q.*), déplorer (*qch.*); '**mourn·er** affligé(e *f*) *m*; **mourn·ful** □ [ˈˌful] lugubre; mélancolique; '**mourn·ful·ness** aspect *m* lugubre; air *m* désolé; tristesse *f*.

mourn·ing [ˈmɔːniŋ] **1.** □ de deuil; en deuil; qui pleure; **2.** deuil *m*, affliction *f*; '~·**bor·der**, '~·**edge** bordure *f* noire; '~·**pa·per** papier *m* deuil.

mouse 1. [maus] (*pl.* **mice**) souris *f*; **2.** [mauz] chasser les souris.

mous·tache [məsˈtɑːʃ] moustache *f*, -s *f*/*pl.*

mous·y [ˈmausi] gris souris; de souris; effacé, timide (*personne*); *péj.* peu distingué.

mouth [mauθ] **1.** *pl.* **mouths** [mauðz] bouche *f*; *chien, four, sac*:

gueule *f*; *fleuve, clarinette*: embouchure *f*; *bouteille*: goulot *m*; *port, tunnel, trou*: entrée *f*; *entonnoir*: pavillon *m*; *fig.* grimace *f*; *by word of* ~ de vive voix; *down in the* ~ déprimé; *keep one's* ~ *shut* ne pas souffler mot, rester bouche cousue; *shut your* ~!, *keep your* ~ *shut!* ferme ta bouche!, F la ferme!; *stop s.o.'s* ~ faire taire q.; fermer la bouche à q.; 2. [mauð] *vt/i.* déclamer (*des phrases*); *v/i.* faire des grimaces; **mouthed** [mauðd] embouché (*cheval*); *clean-*~ au langage honnête; **mouth·ful** ['~ful] bouchée *f*; F mot *m* long d'une aune.

mouth...: '~-**or·gan** harmonica *m*; '~-**piece** ♪ bec *m*, embouchure *f*; *porte-voix*: embout *m*; *fig.* porteparole *m/inv.*; '~-**wash** (eau *f*) dentifrice *m*; '~-**wa·ter·ing** qui fait venir l'eau à la bouche, appétissant.

move [mu:v] 1. *v/t.* déplacer (*qch.*); bouger (*qch.*); remuer (*la tête etc.*); émouvoir (*q.*); toucher (*q.*); exciter (*la pitié*); faire changer d'avis à (*q.*); proposer (*une motion*); mouvoir; ~ *on* faire circuler; *v/i.* se déplacer, se mouvoir; circuler; faire un mouvement, bouger; s'avancer; déménager; marcher (*échecs*); ~ *for s.th.* demander qch.; ~ *in* entrer; emménager; ~ *on* avancer, continuer son chemin; 2. mouvement *m*; déménagement *m*; échecs: coup *m*; *fig.* démarche *f*, pas *m*; *on the* ~ en marche; F *get a* ~ *on* se dépêcher, se presser; *make a* ~ faire un mouvement (*vers qch.*); F partir, prendre congé; **mov(e)·a·ble** ['mu:vəbl] 1. mobile; 2. ~*s pl.* mobilier *m*; biens *m/pl.* mobiliers; '**mov(e)·a·ble·ness** mobilité *f*; '**move·ment** mouvement *m* (*a.* ♪); geste *m*; ⊕ mécanisme *m*; ✗ selle *f*; '**mov·er** moteur *m*; mobile *m*; inspirateur (-trice *f*) *m*; auteur *m*.

mov·ie F ['mu:vi] 1. de ciné(ma); de vues; 2. ~*s pl.* ciné(ma) *m*; films *m/pl.*; '~-**go·er** amateur *m* de cinéma, cinéphile *mf*.

mov·ing □ ['mu:viŋ] en mouvement; en marche; mobile; moteur (-trice *f*); *fig.* émouvant; ~-*band production* travail *m* à la chaîne; ~ *pictures pl. see* motion-pictures; ~ *staircase* escalier *m* roulant.

mow[1] [mau] meule *f* (*de foin*); tas *m* (*de blé*) (*en grange*).

mow[2] [mou] [*irr.*] faucher; '**mow·er** faucheur (-euse *f*) *m*; tondeuse *f* (*de gazon*); '**mow·ing** fauchage *m*; *gazon*: tondaison *f*, fauchée *f*; '**mow·ing-ma·chine** faucheuse *f*; *gazon*: tondeuse *f*; **mown** *p.p. de* mow[2].

much [mʌtʃ] 1. *adj.* beaucoup de, bien du (*etc.*); 2. *adv.* beaucoup, bien, fort; *as* ~ *more* (*ou again*) encore autant; *as* ~ *as* autant que; *not so* ~ *as* ne ... pas (au)tant que; *ne* ... *pas même*; *nothing* ~ peu de chose; F pas fameux; ~ *less* moins encore; *bien moins*; ~ *as I would like* pour autant que je désire *ou* veuille; *I thought as* ~ je m'y attendais; *make* ~ *of* faire grand cas de; *I am not* ~ *of a dancer* F je ne suis pas fameux comme danseur; '**much·ness** F grandeur *f*; *much of a* ~ c'est bonnet blanc et blanc bonnet.

mu·ci·lage ['mju:silidʒ] mucilage *m*; *surt. Am.* colle *f*, gomme *f*; **mu·ci·lag·i·nous** [~'lædʒinəs] mucilagineux (-euse *f*).

muck *sl.* [mʌk] 1. fange *f*; fumier *m*; saletés *f/pl.* (*a. fig.*); 2. souiller; (*usu.* ~ *up*) F gâcher; '**muck·er** *sl.* culbute *f*; *come* (*ou go*) *a* ~ faire la culbute; **muck-rake** ['~reik] râteau *m* à fumier; racloir *m* à boue; '**muck-rake** *Am.* déterrer des scandales; '**muck-rak·er** *Am.* déterreur *m* de scandales; '**muck·y** sale, crotté.

mu·cous ✗ ['mju:kəs] muqueux (-euse *f*); ~ *membrane* ✗ muqueuse *f*.

mu·cus [~] mucus *m*, glaire *f*.

mud [mʌd] boue *f*, bourbe *f*; *fleuve*: vase *f*; '**mud·di·ness** saleté *f*; *liquide*: turbidité *f*; **mud·dle** ['mʌdl] 1. *v/t.* brouiller; emmêler (*a.* ~ *up, together*) embrouiller; *v/i.* s'embrouiller; F lambiner; 2. confusion *f*, embrouillement *m*; F pagaille *f*; *get into a* ~ s'embrouiller; '**mud·dle-head·ed** à l'esprit confus; brouillon(ne *f*); '**mud·dy** 1. □ boueux (-euse *f*); fangeux (-euse *f*); vaseux (-euse *f*) (*fleuve*); trouble (*liquide*); brouillé (*teint*); 2. crotter; troubler; (em)brouiller (*l'esprit*).

mud...: '~**-guard** garde-boue *m/inv.*; pare-boue *m/inv.*; '~**·lark** F gamin *m* des rues; '~**·sling·er** F médisant(e *f*) *m*, calomniateur (-trice *f*) *m*; '~**-sling·ing** F médisance *f*; calomnies *f/pl.*

muff[1] [mʌf] **1.** F empoté *m*; *sl.* andouille *f*; *sp.* coup *m* raté; **2.** F rater, manquer.

muff[2] [~] manchon *m*; **muf·fe·tee** [mʌfi'tiː] miton *m*.

muf·fin ['mʌfin] *petit pain mollet qui se mange beurré à l'heure du thé*; **muf·fin·eer** [~'niə] saupoudroir *m*.

muf·fle ['mʌfl] **1.** ⊕ moufle *m*; **2.** (*souv.* ~ *up*) (s')emmitoufler; amortir (*un son*); assourdir (*les avirons, un tambour*); *tapis*: étouffer (*le bruit*); '**muf·fler** cache-nez *m/inv.*; F moufle *f*; ♪ étouffoir *m*; *mot.* pot *m* d'échappement, silencieux *m*.

muf·ti ['mʌfti] costume *m* de ville; *in* ~ en civil.

mug [mʌg] **1.** chope *f*, pot *m*; *sl.* binette *f* (= *visage*); *sl.* nigaud *m*, dupe *f*; **2.** agresser; '**mug·ger** agresseur *m*; '**mug·ging** (vol *m* avec) agression *f*.

mug·gy ['mʌgi] chaud et humide, lourd.

mug·wump *Am. iro.* ['mʌgwʌmp] personnage *m* important, gros bonnet *m*; *pol.* indépendant *m*; *sl.* rouspéteur *m*.

mu·lat·to [mju'lætou] mulâtre(sse *f*) *m*.

mul·ber·ry ['mʌlbəri] mûre *f*; *arbre*: mûrier *m*.

mulct [mʌlkt] **1.** amende *f*; **2.** frapper d'une amende; imposer une amende (de, *in*); priver (de, *of*).

mule [mjuːl] mulet *m*, mule *f*; métis(se *f*) *m*; (*a.* ~*-jenny*) mule-jenny *f*; **mu·le·teer** [~li'tiə] muletier *m*; '**mule-track** piste *f* muletière.

mul·ish □ ['mjuːliʃ] de mulet; *fig.* têtu, entêté.

mull[1] ✝ [mʌl] mousseline *f*.

mull[2] F [~] **1.** F bousiller; rater; *Am.* ~ *over* ruminer; **2.** gâchis *m*; *make a* ~ *of* gâcher, F bousiller.

mulled [mʌld] chaud (et) épicé (*bière, vin*).

mul·le(i)n ⚘ ['mʌlin] molène *f*.

mul·let *icht.* ['mʌlit] muge *m*; *grey* ~ mulet *m*; *red* ~ rouget *m*.

mul·li·gan *Am.* F ['mʌligən] ratatouille *f*; **mul·li·ga·taw·ny** [mʌligə'tɔːni] potage *m* au curry.

mul·li·grubs *sl.* ['mʌligrʌbz] *pl.* cafard *m*; colique *f*.

mul·lion △ ['mʌljən] meneau *m*; '**mul·lioned** à meneau(x).

mul·ti·far·i·ous □ [mʌlti'fɛəriəs] varié; multiple; **mul·ti·form** ['~fɔːm] multiforme; **mul·ti·lat·er·al** □ [~'lætərəl] multilatéral (-aux *m/pl.*); complexe; **mul·ti-mil·lion·aire** ['~miljə'nɛə] milliardaire *mf*; **mul·ti·na·tion·al** ['~'næʃənl] multinationale *f*; **mul·ti·ple** ['mʌltipl] **1.** multiple; ~ *firm* maison *f* à succursales multiples; ~ *shop* succursale *f*; ⚡ ~ *switchboard* commutateur *m* (multiple); **2.** multiple *m*; **mul·ti·plex** ['~pleks] multiplex; **mul·ti·pli·cand** ⅍ [~'kænd] multiplicande *m*; **mul·ti·pli'ca·tion** multiplication *f*; *compound* (*simple*) ~ multiplication *f* de nombres complexes (de chiffres); ~ *table* table *f* de multiplication; **mul·ti·plic·i·ty** [~'plisiti] multiplicité *f*; **mul·ti·pli·er** ['~plaiə] multiplicateur *m*; **mul·ti·pur·pose** ['~'pəːpəs] universel(le *f*), à usages multiples, multi-usages *inv.*; **mul·ti·ply** ['~plai] (se) multiplier; **mul·ti-ra·cial** ['~'reiʃəl] multiracial; **mul·ti·tude** ['~tjuːd] multitude *f*; foule *f*; multiplicité *f*; **mul·ti'tu·di·nous** [~dinəs] □ innombrable; de toutes sortes.

mum[1] [mʌm] **1.** silencieux (-euse *f*); **2.** chut!; **3.** mimer.

mum[2] F [~] maman *f*.

mum·ble ['mʌmbl] *v/t.* marmotter; *v/i.* manger ses mots.

mum·mer *péj.* ['mʌmə] cabotin(e *f*) *m*; '**mum·mer·y** *péj.* momerie *f*; † pantomime *f*.

mum·mied ['mʌmid] momifié.

mum·mi·fi·ca·tion [mʌmifi'keiʃn] momification *f*; **mum·mi·fy** ['~fai] momifier.

mum·my[1] ['mʌmi] momie *f*; F *beat to a* ~ battre (*q.*) comme plâtre.

mum·my[2] F [~] maman *f*.

mump [mʌmp] mendier; '**mump·ish** maussade; **mumps** [mʌmps] *sg.* ⚕ oreillons *m/pl.*; parotidite *f* épidémique.

munch [mʌntʃ] mâcher, mâchonner.

mun·dane □ ['mʌndein] mondain; terrestre.

mustiness

mu·nic·i·pal □ [mju:'nisipl] municipal (-aux *m/pl.*); de (la) ville; interne (*droit*); **mu·nic·i·pal·i·ty** [ˌ~'pæliti] municipalité *f*; administration *f* municipale; **mu'nic·i·pal·ize** [ˌ~pəlaiz] municipaliser.

mu·nif·i·cence [mju:'nifisns] munificence *f*; **mu'nif·i·cent** □ munificent, généreux (-euse *f*).

mu·ni·ments ['mju:nimənts] *pl.* titres *m/pl.*; chartes *f/pl.*

mu·ni·tion [mju:'niʃn] **1.** de munitions de guerre; **2.** ~s *pl.* munitions *f/pl.*; armements *m/pl.*

mu·ral ['mjuərəl] **1.** mural (-aux *m/pl.*); **2.** peinture *f* murale.

mur·der ['mə:də] **1.** assassinat *m*, meurtre *m*; F *fig.* get away with (*blue*) ~ pouvoir faire n'importe quoi impunément; **2.** assassiner; *fig.* massacrer; écorcher; **'mur·der·er** assassin *m*, meurtrier *m*; **'mur·der·ess** assassine *f*, meurtrière *f*; **'mur·der·ous** meurtrier (-ère *f*); *fig.* sanguinaire.

mure [mjuə] (*usu.* ~ up) murer.

mu·ri·at·ic ac·id 🜄 [mjuəri'ætik·'æsid] acide *m* chlorhydrique.

murk·y □ ['mə:ki] ténébreux (-euse *f*); obscur.

mur·mur ['mə:mə] **1.** murmure *m* (*a.* 🜨); bruissement *m*; **2.** murmurer (contre *at*, *against*); bruire (*ruisseau*); **'mur·mur·ous** □ murmurant. [épizootie *f.*)

mur·rain ['mʌrin] † peste *f*; *vét.*)

mus·ca·dine ['mʌskədin], **mus·cat** ['ˌ~kət], **mus·ca·tel** [ˌ~'tel] muscat *m*.

mus·cle ['mʌsl] **1.** muscle *m*; **2.** Am. sl. ~ in s'immiscer dans (*usu.* dans la spécialité d'un escroc); **mus·cu·lar** ['mʌskjulə] musculaire; musculeux (-euse *f*), musclé (*personne*).

Muse¹ [mju:z] Muse *f*.

muse² [~] méditer (sur, [*up*]on); **'mus·er** rêveur (-euse *f*) *m*; rêvasseur (-euse *f*) *m*.

mu·se·um [mju:'ziəm] musée *m*.

mush *surt.* Am. [mʌʃ] bouillie *f* de farine de maïs; *fig.* sottises *f/pl.*

mush·room ['mʌʃrum] **1.** champignon *m*; *fig.* parvenu(e *f*) *m*; **2.** de champignons, à champignon, à tête de champignon; *fig.* parvenu; champignon *inv.* (*ville*); **3.** F (s')aplatir (*balle de fusil, cigarette, etc.*); *v/i.* faire champignon; se répandre (*flammes etc.*).

mu·sic ['mju:zik] musique *f*, harmonie *f* (*a. fig.*); set to ~ mettre en musique; F face the ~ affronter la tempête; **'mu·si·cal 1.** □ musical (-aux *m/pl.*); musicien(ne *f*) (*personne*); *fig.* harmonieux (-euse *f*); ~ box boîte *f* à musique; ~ clock horloge *f* à carillon; ~ instrument instrument *m* de musique; **2.** (*ou* ~ comedy*) comédie *f* musicale.

mu·sic...: '~-book cahier *m* de musique; '~-box boîte *f* à musique; '~-hall music-hall *m*.

mu·si·cian [mju:'ziʃn] musicien(ne *f*) *m*; ~·ship sens *m* de la musique.

mu·si·col·o·gy [mju:zi'kɔlədʒi] musicologie *f*.

mu·sic...: '~-pa·per papier *m* à *ou* de musique; '~-stand pupitre *m* à musique; '~-stool tabouret *m* de piano.

musk [mʌsk] musc *m* (*a.* ♀); (*a.* ~-deer*) zo. porte-musc *m/inv.*

mus·ket ['mʌskit] mousquet *m*; **mus·ket·eer** *hist.* [ˌ~'tiə] mousquetaire *m*; **'mus·ket·ry** ⚔ mousqueterie *f*; tir *m*; mousquets *m/pl.*

musk·y ['mʌski] musqué, de musc.

Mus·lim ['mʌzlim] see Moslem.

mus·lin 🕂 ['mʌzlin] mousseline *f*.

mus·quash ['mʌskwɔʃ] zo. rat *m* musqué; 🕂 castor *m* du Canada.

muss *surt.* Am. F [mʌs] **1.** désordre *m*; **2.** déranger; *fig.* confondre.

mus·sel ['mʌsl] moule *f*.

Mus·sul·man ['mʌslmən] musulman (*a. su.*).

must¹ [mʌst, məst] **1.** *v/aux.* (*défectif*): I ~ (*inf.*) je dois *etc.*, il faut que je (*sbj.*), il est nécessaire que je (*sbj.*); I ~ not (*inf.*) il ne faut pas que je (*sbj.*); **2.** impératif *m*; nécessité *f* absolue.

must² [~] moût *m*, vin *m* doux.

must³ [~] moisi *m*; moisissure *f*.

mus·tache Am. [məs'tæʃ] see moustache.

mus·tard ['mʌstəd] moutarde *f*.

mus·ter ['mʌstə] **1.** ⚔ revue *f*; ⚓ appel *m*; rassemblement *m*; inspection *f*; ⚔ (*usu.* ~-roll*) contrôles *m/pl.*; *fig.* assemblée *f*, réunion *f*; pass ~ être passable, passer; **2.** *v/t.* ⚔ passer en revue; ⚓ faire l'appel de; (*fig. usu.* ~ up*) rassembler; ~ in compter; *v/i.* se rassembler.

mus·ti·ness ['mʌstinis] goût *m* ou odeur *f* de moisi; moisi *m*; relent *m*;

'**mus·ty** de moisi; *be* ~ sentir le renfermé.

mu·ta·bil·i·ty [mjuːtəˈbiliti] mutabilité *f*; inconstance *f*; '**mu·ta·ble** □ muable, variable; **mu'ta·tion** mutation *f* (*a*. *gramm*.).

mute [mjuːt] **1.** □ muet(te *f*); **2.** muet(te *f*) *m*; *théâ*. personnage *m* muet; ♪ sourdine *f*; *gramm*. consonne *f* sourde; **3.** *surt*. ♪ assourdir.

mu·ti·late [ˈmjuːtileit] mutiler (*a*. *fig*.); **mu·ti·la·tion** mutilation *f*.

mu·ti·neer [mjuːtiˈniə] révolté; '**mu·ti·nous** □ rebelle, mutin; '**mu·ti·ny** **1.** révolte *f*; **2.** se révolter.

mutt *sl*. [mʌt] nigaud *m*.

mut·ter [ˈmʌtə] **1.** murmure *m*; **2.** marmotter; murmurer (contre, *against*).

mut·ton [ˈmʌtn] mouton *m*; *leg of* ~ gigot *m*; '~'**chop** côtelette *f* de mouton; ~*s pl*., ~ *whiskers pl*. favoris *m*/*pl*. en côtelette.

mu·tu·al □ [ˈmjuːtjuəl] mutuel(le *f*), réciproque; commun; ~ *insurance company* (compagnie *f* d'assurance) mutuelle *f*; *Am*. ~ *fund* société *f* d'investissement; *by* ~ *consent* par consentement mutuel; **mu·tu·al·i·ty** [~ˈæliti] mutualité *f*, réciprocité *f*.

muz·zle [ˈmʌzl] **1.** *animal*: museau *m*; *chien*: muselière *f*; *arme à feu*: bouche *f*; **2.** museler (*a*. *fig*.); '~-**load·er** ⚔ pièce *f* se chargeant par la bouche.

muz·zy □ [ˈmʌzi] estompé; confus

(*idées*); brumeux (-euse *f*) (*temps*).

my [mai; *a*. mi] mon, ma, mes.

my·ope ⚓ [ˈmaioup] myope *mf*; **my·op·ic** [~ˈɔpik] (~*ally*) (de) myope; **my·o·pi·a** [~ˈoupjə], **my·o·py** [ˈ~əpi] myopie *f*.

myr·i·ad [ˈmiriəd] **1.** myriade *f*; **2.** innombrable.

myr·mi·don [ˈməːmidən] myrmidon *m*; *F* assassin *m* à gages; ~*s pl*. *of the law* sbires *m*/*pl*.

myrrh ⚘ [məː] myrrhe *f*.

myr·tle ⚘ [ˈməːtl] myrte *m*.

my·self [maiˈself] moi-même; *réfléchi*: me, *accentué*: moi.

mys·te·ri·ous □ [misˈtiəriəs] mystérieux (-euse *f*); *fig*. *a*. incompréhensible; **mys'te·ri·ous·ness** mystère *m*; caractère *m* mystérieux.

mys·ter·y [ˈmistəri] mystère *m* (*a*. *eccl*.); *hist*. (*a*. ~-*play*) mystère *m*; *Am*. (*ou* ~ *story*) roman *m* policier; *mysteries pl*. arcanes *m*/*pl*.; '~-**ship** piège *m* à sous-marin(s).

mys·tic [ˈmistik] **1.** (*a*. '**mys·ti·cal** □) mystique; ésotérique (*rite*); occulte; **2.** *eccl*. mystique *mf*; initié(e *f*) *m*; **mys·ti·cism** [ˈ~sizm] mysticisme *m*; **mys·ti·fi·ca·tion** [~fiˈkeiʃn] mystification *f*; embrouillement *m*; **mys·ti·fy** [ˈ~fai] mystifier; désorienter; *fig*. intriguer.

myth [miθ] mythe *m*; **myth·ic**, **myth·i·cal** □ [ˈ~ik(l)] mythique.

myth·o·log·ic, **myth·o·log·i·cal** □ [miθəˈlɔdʒik(l)] mythologique; **my·thol·o·gy** [~ˈθɔlədʒi] mythologie *f*.

N

N, n [en] N *m*, n *m*.
nab *sl.* [næb] saisir, arrêter.
na·bob [ˈneibɔb] nabab *m*; *fig.*
richard *m*.
na·celle ✈ [nəˈsel] nacelle *f*.
na·cre [ˈneikə] nacre *f*; **na·cre·ous**
[ˈ↲kriəs] nacré.
na·dir [ˈneidiə] *astr.* nadir *m*; *fig.*
stade *m* le plus bas.
nag¹ F [næg] petit cheval *m*,
bidet *m*.
nag² [↲] *v/i.* chamailler; criailler
(contre, *at*); *v/t.* harceler (*q.*); ˈ↲-
ging criailleries *f/pl.*; harcèlement
m.
nail [neil] **1.** *doigt*, *orteil*: ongle *m*;
⊕ clou *m*; ∼ *clippers pl.* pince *f* à
ongles; ∼ *file* lime *f* à ongles; *Am.* ∼
polish vernis *m* à ongles; ∼ *scissors pl.*
ciseaux *m/pl.* à ongles; ∼ *varnish*
vernis *m* à ongles; *fig.* hit the ∼ on the
head frapper juste; **2.** clouer (*a. les
yeux sur q.*); clouter (*la porte*, *les
chaussures*); *fig.* attraper; ∼ *down*
clouer; *fig.* ∼ *s.o. down to* ne pas
laisser à *q.* le moyen d'échapper à
(*qch.*); ∼ *to the counter* démontrer la
fausseté de; ˈ**nail·er** cloutier *m*; *sl.*
bon type *m*; passé maître *m* (en, *at*);
ˈ**nail·er·y** clouterie *f*; ˈ**nail·ing 1.**
clou(t)age *m*; **2.** *sl.* (*souv.* ∼ *good*)
épatant.
na·ive □ [nɑːˈiːv], **na·ive** □ [neiv]
naïf (-ïve *f*); ingénu; **na·ive·té**
[nɑːˈiːvtei], **na·ive·ty** [ˈneivti] naïveté *f*.
na·ked □ [ˈneikid] nu; sans vêtements; dénudé (*pays etc.*); dépouillé (*arbre*); *fig.* découvert;
poét. sans protection; ∼ *facts pl.* faits
m/pl. bruts; *with the* ∼ *eye* à l'œil nu;
ˈ**na·ked·ness** nudité *f*; F pauvreté *f*.
nam·by-pam·by [ˈnæmbiˈpæmbi]
1. maniéré; fade; **2.** F pouille *f*
mouillée.
name [neim] **1.** nom *m*; *navire*:
devise *f*; *fig.* réputation *f*; *of* (*ou* F
by) the ∼ of du nom de, nommé;
Christian ∼ prénom *m*; *call s.o.* ∼*s*
injurier *q.*; *know s.o. by* ∼ connaître

q. de nom; **2.** nommer; désigner
par son nom; dénommer; citer;
fixer (*un jour*); ˈ**name-day** fête *m*;
ˈ**name·less** □ sans nom; inconnu;
anonyme; *fig.* indicible; ˈ**name·ly**
(*abr.* *viz.*) c'est-à-dire; ˈ**name-
plate** plaque *f*; écusson *m*; ˈ**name-
sake** homonyme *m*.
nan·keen [nænˈkiːn] nankin *m*; ∼*s*
pl. pantalon *m* de nankin.
nan·ny [ˈnæni] nounou *f*; bonne *f*
(d'enfant); ˈ∼-**goat** chèvre *f*, bique *f*.
nap¹ [næp] *velours etc.*: poil *m*.
nap² [↲] **1.** petit somme *m*; **2.** sommeiller; *catch s.o.* ↲*ping* surprendre
la vigilance de *q.*; surprendre *q.* en
faute.
nap³ [↲] *cartes*: go ∼ jouer son va-
tout.
nape [neip] (*usu.* ∼ *of the neck*)
nuque *f*.
naph·tha ⚗ [ˈnæfθə] naphte *m*.
nap·kin [ˈnæpkin] (*souv.* table-∼)
serviette *f*; (*a. baby's* ∼) couche *f*;
ˈ∼-**ring** rond *m* de serviette.
na·poo(h) *sl.* [nɑːˈpuː] épuisé; inutile; mort; fini; *sl.* fichu.
nar·co·sis ⚕ [nɑːˈkousis] narcose *f*.
nar·cot·ic [nɑːˈkɔtik] **1.** (∼*ally*) narcotique; **2.** stupéfiant *m*; narcotique
m; **nar·co·tize** [ˈnɑːkətaiz] narcotiser.
nard [nɑːd] nard *m*.
nar·rate [næˈreit] raconter; **nar-
ra·tion** narration *f*; récit *m*; **nar-
ra·tive** [ˈ↲rətiv] **1.** □ narratif (-ive
f); **2.** récit *m*; **nar·ra·tor** [↲ˈreitə]
narrateur (-trice *f*).
nar·row [ˈnærou] **1.** □ étroit; encaissé (*vallon*); borné (*esprit*); faible (*majorité*); *see escape*; **2.** ∼*s pl.*
passe *f* étroite; *port*: goulet *m*;
3. *v/t.* resserrer; rétrécir; restreindre; limiter; *v/i.* devenir plus étroit;
se resserrer; se rétrécir; ˈ∼-ˈ**chest-
ed** à poitrine étroite; ˈ∼-ˈ**gauge** 🚂 à
voie étroite; ˈ∼-ˈ**mind·ed** □ borné;
ˈ**nar·row·ness** étroitesse *f* (*a. fig.*);
petitesse *f*; limitation *f*.

nar·whal zo. [ˈnɑːwəl] narwal (pl. -s) m.

na·sal [ˈneizl] **1.** □ nasal (-aux m/pl.); nasillard (accent); **2.** gramm. nasale f; **na·sal·i·ty** [ˌ~ˈzæliti] nasalité f; **na·sal·ize** [ˈ~zəlaiz] nasaliser; v/i. parler du nez; nasiller.

nas·cent [ˈnæsnt] naissant.

nas·ti·ness [ˈnɑːstinis] goût m ou odeur f désagréable; méchanceté f (d'une personne); fig. saleté f; '**nas·ty** □ désagréable; dégoûtant; sale; méchant, désagréable (personne); fig. malpropre.

na·tal [ˈneitl] natal (-als m/pl.); **na·tal·i·ty** [nəˈtæliti] natalité f.

na·ta·tion [neiˈteiʃn] natation f.

na·tion [ˈneiʃn] nation f, peuple m; member ~ État m membre.

na·tion·al [ˈnæʃənl] **1.** □ national (-aux m/pl.); de l'État; ~ grid caisse f nationale de l'énergie; **2.** national (-e f) m; '**na·tion·al·ism** nationalisme m; '**na·tion·al·ist** nationaliste mf; **na·tion·al·i·ty** [næʃəˈnæliti] nationalité f; caractère m ou esprit m national; **na·tion·al·ize** [ˈnæʃnəlaiz] nationaliser; naturaliser; ~d undertakings entreprises f/pl. nationalisées.

na·tion-wide [ˈneiʃnwaid] répandu par tout le pays; souv. général (-aux m/pl.).

na·tive [ˈneitiv] **1.** □ indigène, originaire (de, to) (personne, plante); naturel(le f), inné (qualité); de naissance, natal (-als m/pl.) (lieu); à l'état natif (métaux); ~ language langue f maternelle; **2.** natif (-ive f) m; indigène mf; a ~ of Ireland Irlandais m de naissance.

na·tiv·i·ty [nəˈtiviti] nativité f; horoscope m.

na·tron [ˈneitrən] natron m.

nat·ty □ [ˈnæti] coquet(te f); pimpant; bien ménagé.

na·tu·ral [ˈnætʃrəl] **1.** □ naturel(le f); de la nature; inné, natif (-ive f); illégitime, naturel(le f) (enfant); ~ disaster catastrophe f naturelle; ~ gas gaz m naturel; ~ history histoire f naturelle; ♪ ~ note note f naturelle; ~ philosopher physicien m; ~ philosophy physique f; ~ reserve réserve f naturelle; ~ science sciences f/pl. naturelles; **2.** idiot(e f) m; ♪ bécarre m; '**nat·u·ral·ism** naturalisme m; arts: naturisme m; '**nat·u·ral·ist** natura-

liste mf; naturiste mf; **nat·u·ral·i·za·tion** [ˌ~lai'zeiʃn] naturalisation f; '**nat·u·ral·ize** naturaliser; ♀, zo. acclimater; '**nat·u·ral·ness** naturel m.

na·ture [ˈneitʃə] nature f; caractère m, essence f; naturel m, tempérament m; espèce f, genre m; by ~ de ou par nature; '**na·tured** au cœur ...; de caractère ...

na·tur·ism [ˈneitʃərizəm] naturisme m; '**na·tur·ist** naturiste mf.

naught [nɔːt] rien m, néant m; bring to ~ faire échouer; come to ~ échouer, n'aboutir à rien; set at ~ ne tenir aucun compte de; '**naugh·ti·ness** [ˈ~tinis] mauvaise tenue f; désobéissance f; '**naugh·ty** □ méchant, vilain.

nau·se·a [ˈnɔːsiə] nausée f; mal m de mer; fig. dégoût m; **nau·se·ate** [ˈ~sieit] v/i. avoir la nausée (de, at); v/t. dégoûter; donner des nausées à (q.); **nau·se·ous** □ [ˈ~siəs] dégoûtant.

nau·ti·cal □ [ˈnɔːtikl] nautique, marin; de marine; ~ mile mille m marin.

na·val [ˈneivəl] naval (-als m/pl.); de marine; ~ architect ingénieur m des constructions navales; ~ base port m de guerre; base f navale; ~ staff officiers m/pl. de l'état-major; '**na·val·ly** au point de vue naval.

nave[1] △ [neiv] nef f, vaisseau m.

nave[2] [~] roue: moyeu m.

na·vel [ˈneivəl] nombril m; fig. centre m; ~ orange (orange f) navel f; anat. ~ string cordon m ombilical.

nav·i·ga·ble □ [ˈnævigəbl] navigable; ~ balloon ballon m dirigeable; **nav·i·gate** [ˈ~geit] v/i. naviguer; v/t. naviguer sur (la mer); gouverner (un navire); **nav·i·ga·tion** navigation f; ballon, navire: conduite f; '**nav·i·ga·tor** navigateur m.

nav·vy [ˈnævi] terrassier m; (a. steam-~) piocheuse f.

na·vy [ˈneivi] marine f de guerre; marine f de l'État; '~-'blue bleu m marine inv.

nay [nei] **1.** † ou prov. non; pour mieux dire; **2.** non m; refus m.

Naz·a·rene [næzəˈriːn] Nazaréen (-ne f) [m.]

naze [neiz] cap m, promontoire

neap [niːp] (a. ~-tide) marée f de morte-eau; '**neaped** ⚓: be ~ être amorti.

Ne·a·pol·i·tan [niə'pɔlitən] **1.** napolitain; **2.** Napolitain(e f) m.

near [niə] **1.** adj. proche; voisin; à peu près juste; intime (ami); (le plus) court (chemin); chiche (personne); serré (traduction); mot. gauche (côté); montoir (cheval); have (ou be) a ~ escape l'échapper belle; ~ at hand tout près; ~ beer bière f faible; ~ horse cheval m de gauche (Am. de droite); it was a ~ miss (ou thing) il s'en est fallu de peu, le coup est passé très près; **2.** adv. près, proche; **3.** prp. (a.~ to) (au)près de; **4.** v/t. (s')approcher de; **near·by** ['~bai] tout près (de), tout proche (de); **'near·ly** (de) près; presque; à peu près; près de; **'near·ness** proximité f; fidélité f; parcimonie f; **'near-'sight·ed** myope.

neat¹ □ [ni:t] bien rangé ou tenu; soigné; élégant; pur, sans eau, sec (sèche f) (boisson); net(te f) (écriture).

neat² † [~] bête f bovine; **'~'s-foot** de pied de bœuf; **'~'s-leath·er** cuir m de vache; **'~'s-tongue** langue f de bœuf.

neat·ness ['ni:tnis] bon ordre m; simplicité f; bon goût m; adresse f.

neb·u·la astr. ['nebjulə], pl. -lae ['~li:] nébuleuse f; **'neb·u·lar** nébulaire; **neb·u·los·i·ty** [~'lɔsiti] nébulosité f; **'neb·u·lous** nébuleux (-euse f) (a. fig.).

nec·es·sar·y □ ['nesisəri] **1.** nécessaire, indispensable (à, for); inévitable (résultat); **2.** nécessaire m; usu. necessaries pl. nécessités f/pl.; **ne·ces·si·tate** [ni'sesiteit] nécessiter (qch.); rendre (qch.) nécessaire; **ne'ces·si·tous** nécessiteux (-euse f); **ne'ces·si·ty** nécessité f; obligation f; besoin m; usu. necessities pl. nécessaire m; nécessités f/pl.; the bare necessities pl. (of life) les choses f/pl. essentielles à la vie; of ~ de toute nécessité.

neck [nek] **1.** cou m; cuis. collier m (de bœuf), collet m (de mouton); bouteille: goulot m; robe: encolure f; ~ of land langue f de terre; ~ and ~ à égalité; F ~ and crop tout entier; F ~ or nothing à corps perdu; (jouer) le tout pour le tout; F be up to one's ~ in s.th. être dans qch. jusqu'au cou; be up to one's ~ in work a. avoir du travail par-dessus la tête;

sl. get it in the ~ en prendre pour son compte; F stick one's ~ out prendre des risques, s'avancer; se compromettre; **2.** Am. sl. (se) caresser; v/t. peloter; **'~·band** col m; encolure f; **neck·er·chief** ['nekət∫if] foulard m; **neck·lace** ['~lis] collier m; **neck·let** ['~lit] see necklace; tour m de cou (en fourrure); **'neck·line** encolure f; **'neck·tie** cravate f.

ne·crol·o·gy [ne'krɔlədʒi] nécrologe m (d'une église etc.); nécrologie f; **nec·ro·man·cy** ['nekrəmænsi] nécromancie f.

nec·tar ['nektə] nectar m.

née [nei]: Mrs. X, ~ Y Mme X, née Y.

need [ni:d] **1.** besoin m, nécessité f (de of, for); adversité f; indigence f; one's own ~s pl. son (propre) compte m; if ~ be au besoin; le cas échéant; be (ou stand) in ~ of avoir besoin de; **2.** avoir besoin de; réclamer, demander (qch.); être obligé de; **need·ful** ['~ful] **1.** □ nécessaire; **2.** F nécessaire m, souv. argent m nécessaire; **'need·i·ness** indigence f, nécessité f.

nee·dle ['ni:dl] **1.** aiguille f; **2.** surt. Am. irriter, agacer; F ajouter de l'alcool à, renforcer (une consommation); **'~·case** étui m à aiguilles; **'~·craft** couture f; **'~·gun** fusil m à aiguille; **'~·mak·ing** aiguillerie f.

need·less □ ['ni:dlis] inutile; ~ly inutilement, sans raison; **'need·less·ness** inutilité f.

nee·dle...: **'~·tel·e·graph** télégraphe m à cadran; **'~·wom·an** couturière f; **'~·work** travail (pl. -aux) m à l'aiguille.

needs [ni:dz] adv. de nécessité; I must ~ (inf.) force m'est de (inf.); **'need·y** □ nécessiteux (-euse f).

ne'er [nɛə] = never; **~-do-well** ['~du:wel] propre-à-rien mf (pl. propres-à-rien), vaurien(ne f) m.

ne·far·i·ous □ [ni'fɛəriəs] infâme, scélérat.

ne·gate [ni'geit] nier; **ne·ga·tion** négation f; **neg·a·tive** ['negətiv] **1.** □ négatif (-ive f); **2.** négative f; gramm. négation f; phot. négatif m, cliché m; answer in the ~ répondre par la négative; **3.** rejeter, s'opposer à; nier; annuler; neutraliser.

neg·lect [ni'glekt] **1.** manque m de soin; mauvais entretien m; négligence *f*; 2. négliger; manquer de soins pour; laisser échapper (*une occasion*); **neg·lect·ful** ☐ [~ful] négligent; insoucieux (-euse *f*) (de, of).

neg·li·gence ['neglidʒəns] incurie *f*; négligence *f*; **'neg·li·gent** ☐ négligent; ~ of insoucieux (-euse *f*) de; ~ *attire* tenue *f* négligée.

neg·li·gi·ble ['neglidʒəbl] négligeable.

ne·go·ti·a·bil·i·ty [nigouʃiə'biliti] négociabilité *f*, commercialité *f*; **ne'go·ti·a·ble** ☐ négociable, commerciable; franchissable (*montagne*); praticable (*chemin*); not ~ *cheque* chèque *m* barré; **ne'go·ti·ate** *v/t.* négocier (*affaire, effet, traité*); prendre (*un virage*); franchir (*une montagne*); *fig.* surmonter; *v/i.* traiter (avec q. de *ou* pour, with s.o. for); **ne'go·ti·at·ing ta·ble** table *f* de conférence; at the ~ par des négociations, par voie de négociations; **ne·go·ti·a·tion** *effets, traite:* négociation *f*; pourparlers *m/pl.*; *fig.* franchissement *m*; under ~ en négociation; **ne'go·ti·a·tor** négociateur (-trice *f*) *m*.

ne·gress ['ni:gris] négresse *f*; **ne·gro** ['ni:grou], *pl.* -groes [~z] nègre *m*; **ne·groid** ['ni:grɔid] négroïde.

ne·gus ['ni:gəs] vin *m* chaud et épicé.

neigh [nei] 1. hennissement *m*; 2. hennir.

neigh·bo(u)r ['neibə] 1. voisin(e *f*) *m*; *bibl.* prochain *m*; 2. être le voisin de (*personne*); avoisiner (*terrain*); **'neigh·bo(u)r·hood** voisinage *m*; **'neigh·bo(u)r·ing** avoisinant, voisin, proche; **'neigh·bo(u)r·ly** de bon voisinage; obligeant.

nei·ther ['naiðə] 1. *adj. ou pron.* ni l'un(e) ni l'autre; aucun(e *f*); 2. *adv.* ~ ... nor ... ni ... ni ...; not ... ~ (ne ... pas) ... ne ... pas non plus. [gisme *m*.]

ne·ol·o·gism [ni'ɔlədʒism] néolo-

ne·on ['ni:ən] néon *m*; ~ *lamp* lampe *f* au néon; ~ *light(ing)* éclairage *m* au néon; ~ *sign* enseigne *m* au néon.

ne·o·phyte ['ni:(:)oufait] néophyte *mf*; *fig.* débutant(e *f*) *m*.

neph·ew ['nevju(:)] neveu *m*.

nep·o·tism ['nepətizm] népotisme *m*.

nerve [nə:v] 1. nerf *m*; ⚕, ⚕ nervure *f*; *fig.* courage *m*, sang-froid *m*; *fig.* vigueur *f*; F audace *f*, aplomb *m*; F *be all ~s* être un paquet de nerfs; F *have the ~ do to s.th.* avoir le toupet de faire qch.; *lose one's ~s* perdre son sang-froid *ou* son calme; 2. fortifier; donner du courage à (q.); ~ *o.s.* s'armer de courage (pour, to); **'nerved** ⚕ nervé; **'nerve·less** ☐ inerte, sans force; **'nerve'rack·ing** énervant.

nerv·ine ⚕ ['nə:vain] nervin (*a. su./m.*).

nerv·ous ☐ ['nə:vəs] timide, peureux (-euse *f*); inquiet (-ète *f*); excitable; *anat.* nerveux (-euse *f*), des nerfs; ⚕ ~ *breakdown* dépression *f* nerveuse; ~ *system* système *m* nerveux; **'nerv·ous·ness** timidité *f*; état *m* nerveux.

nerv·y *sl.* ['nə:vi] irritable; énervé; nerveux (-euse *f*), saccadé (*mouvement*).

nes·ci·ence ['nesiəns] ignorance *f*; **'nes·ci·ent** ignorant.

ness [nes] promontoire *m*, cap *m*.

nest [nest] 1. nid *m* (*a. fig.*); nichée *f* (*d'oiseaux*); *fig.* série *f*; 2. (se) nicher; **'nest·ed** niché; emboîté (*caisses etc.*); **'nest-egg** nichet *m*; argent *m* mis de côté; gentille petite somme *f*; **nes·tle** ['nesl] *v/i.* se nicher; *fig.* se blottir; se serrer (contre, [up] to); *v/t.* serrer; **nest·ling** ['neslin] oisillon *m*.

net¹ [net] 1. filet *m* (*a. fig.*); *tex.* tulle *m*; mousseline *f*; ~ *courtains pl.* voilage *m*; 2. prendre (*qch.*) au filet.

net² [~] 1. net(te *f*); sans déduction; 2. rapporter *ou* toucher net.

neth·er ['neðə] inférieur; **'~·most** le plus profond, le plus bas.

net·ting ['netin] pêche *f* au filet; pose *f* de filets; *tex.* tulle *m*; *fig.* réseau *m*.

net·tle ['netl] 1. ⚕ ortie *f*; 2. † fustiger avec des orties; *fig.* piquer, irriter; **'~-rash** ⚕ urticaire *f*.

net·work ['netwə:k] réseau *m* (*a. fig.*); ouvrage *m* en filet; *national* ~ réseau *m* national.

neu·ral·gia ⚕ [njuə'rældʒə] névralgie *f*; *facial* ~ tic *m* douloureux; **neu·ras·the·ni·a** [njuərəs'θi:njə] ⚕ neurasthénie *f*; **neu·ras·then·ic** [~'θenik] neurasthénique (*a. su/mf*); **neu·ri·tis** ⚕ [njuə'raitis] névrite *f*;

neu·rol·o·gy ☞ [~'rɔlədʒi] neurologie *f*, névrologie *f*; **neu·ron** ['nju̇ərɔn] neurone *m*; **neu·ro·path·ic** [nju̇əro'pæθik] **1.** névropathique; **2.** névropathe *mf*; **neu·ro·sis** ☞ [~'rousis] névrose *f*; **neu·rot·ic** [~'rɔtik] névrosé (*a. su./mf.*).

neu·ter ['nju̇:tə] **1.** neutre; **2.** animal *m* châtré; abeille *f etc.* asexuée; *gramm.* neutre *m*.

neu·tral ['nju̇:trəl] **1.** □ neutre (*a.* 🎵); indéterminé, moyen(ne *f*); **2.** neutre *m*; **neu·tral·i·ty** [nju(:)-'træliti] neutralité *f*; **neu·tral·i·za·tion** [nju̇:trəlai'zeiʃn] neutralisation *f* (*a.* 🎵); **'neu·tral·ize** neutraliser (*a.* 🎵); rendre inutile *ou* inoffensif (-ive *f*).

neu·tron *phys.* ['nju̇:trɔn] neutron *m*; ✗ ~ **bomb** bombe *f* à neutrons.

né·vé *géol.* ['neivei] névé *m*.

nev·er ['nevə] ne ... jamais; jamais (de la vie); ~ **so** quelque (*adj.*) que (*sbj.*); '~**more** (ne ...) plus jamais; (ne ...) jamais plus; ~**the·less** [~ðə'les] néanmoins, quand même, pourtant.

new [nju̇:] nouveau (-el *devant une voyelle ou un h muet*); -elle *f*; -eaux *m/pl.*); neuf (neuve *f*); frais (fraîche *f*); **'new·com·er** nouveau venu *m*; nouvel arrivé *m*; **new·fan·gled** ['~fæŋgld] *péj.* d'une modernité outrée; **'new·ly** récemment, nouvellement; **'new·ness** nouveauté *f*; état *m* neuf; inexpérience *f*.

news *pl. ou sg.* [nju̇:z] nouvelle *f*, -s *f/pl.*; *what's the* ~? quelles nouvelles?; F quoi de neuf?; *break the (bad)* ~ *to s.o.* annoncer les nouvelles à q. (avec ménagement); F *he is much in the* ~ il défraye la chronique; '~**a·gen·cy** agence *f* d'informations; '~**a·gent** marchand *m* de journaux; '~**boy** vendeur *m* de journaux; '~**butch·er** 📞 *Am.* vendeur *m* ambulant de journaux; '~**cast** (bulletin *m* d')informations *f/pl.*; '~**cast·er** speaker(ine *f*) *m*; ~ **flash** *radio:* flash *m*; ~ **let·ter** bulletin *m*, circulaire *m*; ~ **mag·a·zine** revue *f*; ~ **mon·ger** débiteur (-euse *f*) *m* de nouvelles; '~**pa·per** journal *m*; *attr.* de journaux; '~**print** papier *m* de journal; *Brit.* ~ **read·er** speaker(ine *f*) *m*; '~**reel** film *m* d'actualité; actualités *f/pl.*; '~**room** salle *f* des journaux; *journ.*

Am. salle *f* de rédaction; '~**-stall,** *Am.* '~**-stand** étalage *m* de marchand de journaux; *France*: kiosque *m* (à journaux); '~**-ven·dor** vendeur *m* de journaux; **news·y** ['nju̇:zi] F plein de nouvelles.

newt *zo.* [nju̇:t] triton *m*, F lézard *m* d'eau.

new-year, *usu.* **New year** ['nju̇:'jə:] nouvel an *m*; nouvelle année *f*; ~'s **day** le jour de l'an; ~'s **eve** la Saint-Sylvestre *f*; ~'s **gift** étrennes *f/pl.*

next [nekst] **1.** *adj.* prochain; voisin; *le* plus proche; suivant; ~ **but one** *le* deuxième; ~**-door** voisin; ~ **door** maison *f* d'à côté; *fig.* ~ **door to** approchant de; *the* ~ *of kin* la famille; ⚖ *le(s)* parent(s) *le(s)* plus proche(s); ~ *to* contigu(ë *f*) à *ou* avec; à côté de; ~ *to nothing* ne ... presque rien; *what* ~? et ensuite?; F *par exemple!*; **2.** *adv.* ensuite, après.

nex·us ['neksəs] lien *m*, rapport *m*.

nib [nib] **1.** bec *m* (de plume); **2.** mettre une plume à (*un porteplume*).

nib·ble ['nibl] *v/t.* grignoter (*qch.*); mordiller; *mouton:* brouter; *v/i.* ~ *at* grignoter (*qch.*); mordre à (*a. fig.*); *fig.* être attiré par.

nice □ [nais] aimable, gentil(le *f*), sympathique (*naturel*); délicat (*question, oreille*); juste, sensible (*oreille, œil*); fin, subtil (*distinction*); joli (*repas, montre, etc.*); difficile (*pour, about*); scrupuleux (-euse *f*) (*quant à, about*); ~ *and warm* bien (au) chaud; '**nice·ness** gentillesse *f*, amabilité *f*; délicatesse *f*; finesse *f*; justesse *f*; **nice·ty** ['~iti] exactitude *f*; subtilité *f*; délicatesse *f* exagérée; méticulosité *f*; *to a* ~ à merveille; exactement; *stand upon niceties* faire des façons.

niche [nitʃ] niche *f*.

Nick¹ [nik] F *Old* ~ le diable *m*.

nick² [~] **1.** entaille *f*; fente *f*; *in the (very)* ~ *of time* juste à temps; à pic; **2.** entailler; *sl.* choper.

nick·el ['nikl] **1.** *min.* nickel *m* (*Am. a. pièce de 5 cents*); *Am.* ~**-in-the-slot machine** distributeur *m* automatique; **2.** nickeler.

nick·el·o·de·on *Am.* [nikl'oudiən] pick-up machine *f*, juke-box *m*.

nick-nack ['niknæk] *see knickknack.*

nick·name ['nikneim] **1.** surnom *m*;

sobriquet *m*; 2. surnommer; donner un sobriquet à.

nic·o·tine ['nikəti:n] nicotine *f*.

nid-nod ['nidnɔd] dodeliner ⟨de la⟩ tête.

niece [ni:s] nièce *f*.

niffed F [nift] offensé.

nif·ty *Am.* ['nifti] 1. élégant; pimpant; 2. remarque *f* bien à propos.

nig·gard ['nigəd] 1. grippe-sou *m*; pingre *m*, avare *mf*; 2. avare, parcimonieux (-euse *f*); '**nig·gard·li·ness** pingrerie *f*; parcimonie *f*; '**nig·gard·ly** *adj. (a. adv.)* chiche (-ment); mesquin(ement).

nig·ger F *usu. péj.* ['nigə] nègre *m*, négresse *f*; *Am. sl. that's the ~ in the woodpile* il y a anguille sous roche!

nig·gle ['nigl] vétiller; '**nig·gling** insignifiant; fignolé (*travail*); tatillon(ne *f*) (*personne*).

nigh † *ou prov.* [nai] *see near 1, 2, 3*.

night [nait] nuit *f*, soir *m*; obscurité *f*; *by ~* de nuit; *in the ~* (pendant) la nuit; *at ~* la nuit; *~ out* soir *m* de sortie; *make a ~ of it* faire la noce toute la nuit; *be on ~* être (au poste) de nuit; *fig.* grog *m* (avant de se coucher); '**~-club** boîte *f* de nuit; '**~-dress** chemise *f* de nuit (*de femme*); '**~-fall** tombée *f* de la nuit; '**~-gown** *see night-dress*; **night·in·gale** *orn.* ['~iŋgeil] rossignol *m*; '**night·ly** de nuit, nocturne; (de) tous les soirs.

night...: '**~-mare** cauchemar *m*; '**~-school** classe *f* du soir; '**~-shade** ♀ morelle *f* noire; *deadly ~* belladone *f*; *~ shift* équipe *f* de nuit; poste *m* de nuit; '**~-shirt** chemise *f* de nuit (*d'homme*); '**~-spot** *Am.* F boîte *f* de nuit; '**~-time** nuit *f*; *~ watch·man* gardien *m* de nuit.

ni·hil·ism ['naiilizm] nihilisme *m*; '**ni·hil·ist** nihiliste *mf*.

nil [nil] rien *m*; *sp.* zéro *m*; *~ return* état *m* néant.

nim·ble □ ['nimbl] agile, leste; délié (*esprit*); '**nim·ble·ness** agilité *f*; vivacité *f* (*d'esprit*); '**nim·ble-wit·ted** à l'esprit vif; qui a la réplique facile, qui a de la repartie.

nim·bus ['nimbəs], *pl.* -**bi** [~bai], -**bus·es** nimbe *m*, auréole *f*; *météor.* nimbus *m*.

nim·i·ny-pim·i·ny ['nimini'pimini] maniéré; mignard.

nin·com·poop F ['ninkəmpu:p] nigaud *m*, benêt *m*, niais *m*.

nine [nain] 1. neuf; *~ days' wonder* merveille *f* d'un jour; 2. neuf *m*; '**~-fold** nonuple, neuf fois; '**~-pins** *pl.* quilles *f/pl.*; **nine·teen** ['~'ti:n] dix-neuf (*a. su./m*); '**nine'teenth** [~θ] dix-neuvième; **nine·tieth** ['~tiiθ] quatre-vingt-dixième(*a. su./m*); '**nine·ty** quatre-vingt-dix.

nin·ny F ['nini] niais(e *f*) *m*.

ninth [nainθ] 1. neuvième; 2. neuvième *m*; ♩ neuvième *f*; '**ninth·ly** en neuvième lieu.

nip¹ [nip] 1. pincement *m*; morsure *f*; ⚓ coup *m* de gelée; 2. pincer; piquer, mordre (*froid*); brûler (*gelée*); *~ in the bud* tuer dans l'œuf; faire avorter (*un complot*).

nip² [~] 1. goutte *f*, doigt *m* (*d'alcool*); 2. boire la *ou* une goutte.

nip³ *sl.* [~] chiper, choper, refaire.

nip·per ['nipə] F gamin *m*, gosse *m*; homard *etc.*: pince *f*; (*a pair of*) *~s pl.* (une) pince *f*; (des) tenailles *f/pl.*

nip·ple ['nipl] mamelon *m*; bout *m* de sein; ⊕ raccord *m*.

nip·py F ['nipi] vif (vive *f*); âpre; piquant.

Ni·sei *Am.* ['ni'sei] (*a. pl.*) japonais *m* (*né aux É.-U.*).

nit [nit] œuf *m* de pou; '**~-pick·ing** F qui coupe les cheveux en quatre.

ni·tre, ni·ter ⚗ ['naitə] nitre *m*, salpêtre *m*.

ni·tric ac·id ⚗ ['naitrik'æsid] acide *m* nitrique *ou* azotique.

ni·tro·gen ⚗ ['naitrədʒən] azote *m*; **ni·trog·e·nous** [~'trɔdʒinəs] azoté.

ni·tro·glyc·er·in(e) ['naitrouglisə'ri:n] nitroglycérine *f*.

ni·trous ⚗ ['naitrəs] azoteux (-euse *f*).

nit·ty-grit·ty *sl.* ['niti'griti]: *the ~* l'essentiel; *come (ou get down) to the ~* en venir au fait; en venir au fond.

nit·wit F [nitwit] imbécile *mf*.

nix *sl.* [niks] 1. rien *m* (du tout), F peau *f* de balle; 2. non!; rien à faire!; 3. dire non à (*qch.*).

no [nou] 1. *adj.* aucun, pas de; *in ~ time* en un clin d'œil; *~ man's land* zone *f* neutre; *~ one* personne (... ne); 2. *adv.* peu; non; *avec comp.*: pas (plus); 3. *su. m/inv.*: non; **noes** [nouz] *pl.* les non *m/pl.*; voix *f/pl.* contre.

nob[1] *sl.* [nɔb] caboche *f* (= *tête*); ⊕ bouton *m.*   [rupins *m*/*pl.*]

nob[2] *sl.* [⌣] aristo *m*; the ⌣s *pl.* les |

nob·ble *sl.* ['nɔbl] écloper (*un cheval*); soudoyer (*q.*); pincer (*un criminel*); filouter (*de l'argent*).

nob·by *sl.* ['nɔbi] élégant, chic.

No·bel prize [nou'bel'praiz] Prix *m* Nobel; *Nobel peace prize* Prix *m* Nobel de la paix; ⌣ *winner* (lauréat *m* du) Prix Nobel *m.*

no·bil·i·ar·y [nou'biliəri] nobiliaire.

no·bil·i·ty [nou'biliti] noblesse *f* (*a. fig.*).

no·ble ['noubl] 1. □ noble (*a. sentiment, métal, joyau*); sublime; grand (*vin, âme, etc.*); admirable; 2. noble *mf*, aristocrate *mf*; '⌣·man noble *m*, gentilhomme (*pl.* gentilshommes) *m*; '⌣·'mind·ed à l'âme noble; généreux (-euse *f*); '**no·ble·ness** noblesse *f* (*a. fig.*); '**no·ble·wom·an** noble *f*, aristocrate *f.*

no·bod·y ['noubədi] 1. personne, aucun (... ne); 2. zéro *m*, nullité *f.*

nock [nɔk] (en)coche *f.*

no-claims bo·nus ['nou'kleimz bounəs] *assurance:* bonification *f* pour non-sinistre.

noc·tur·nal [nɔk'tə:nl] nocturne.

nod [nɔd] 1. *v/i.* faire signe que oui; incliner la tête; dodeliner de la tête; somnoler; *fig.* danser; *have a* ⌣*ding acquaintance* se connaître vaguement; ⌣ *off* somnoler; *v/t.* incliner (*la tête*);⌣ *s.o. out* faire sortir q. d'un signe de la tête; 2. signe *m* de (la) tête; penchement *m* de tête (*au sommeil*).

nod·dle F ['nɔdl] caboche *f* (= *tête*).

nod·dy F ['nɔdi] niais(e *f*) *m.*

node [noud] nœud *m* (*a.* ♀, *a. astr.*); ♂ nodosité *f.*

nod·u·lar ['nɔdjulə] nodulaire.

nod·ule ['nɔdju:l] nodule *m.*

nog [nɔg] cheville *f* de bois; **nog·gin** ['⌣in] (petit) pot *m* (*en étain etc.*); **nog·ging** △ ['⌣in] hourdage *m.*

no·how F ['nouhau] en aucune façon.

noil [nɔil] *tex.* blousse *f.*

noise [nɔiz] 1. bruit *m*, tapage *m*, fracas *m*, vacarme *m*; son *m*; ⌣ *abatement* lutte *f* anti-bruit *ou* contre le bruit; ⌣ *level* niveau *m* des bruits; *surt. Am.* F *big* ⌣ gros bonnet *m*; 2.⌣ *about*, ⌣ *abroad* ébruiter; crier sur les toits.

noise·less □ ['⌣lis] sans bruit; silencieux (-euse *f*); '**noise·less·ness** silence *m*, absence *f* de bruit.

nois·i·ness ['nɔizinis] caractère *m* bruyant; tintamarre *m.*

noi·some ['nɔisəm] fétide, infect; *fig.* désagréable; '**noi·some·ness** fétidité *f*, puanteur *f.*

nois·y □ ['nɔizi] bruyant, tapageur (-euse *f*); turbulent (*enfant*).

no·mad ['nɔməd] nomade *mf*; **no·mad·ic** [no'mædik] (⌣*ally*) nomade; **no·mad·ize** ['nɔmədaiz] *v/t.* nomadiser; *v/i.* vivre en nomade(s).

no·men·cla·ture [nou'menklətʃə] nomenclature *f*; recueil *m* de noms propres.

nom·i·nal □ ['nɔminl] nominal (-aux *m*/*pl.*); fictif (-ive *f*) (*prix, valeur*); ✗ nominatif (-ive *f*); ⌣ *value* valeur *f* fictive *ou* nominale; **nom·i·nate** ['⌣neit] nommer, désigner; proposer; **nom·i·na·tion** nomination *f*; présentation *f* (*d'un candidat*); *in* ⌣ nommé; proposé; **nom·i·na·tive** *gramm.* ['⌣nətiv] (*a.* ⌣ *case*) nominatif *m*, cas *m* sujet; **nom·i·na·tor** ['⌣neitə] présentateur *m*; **nom·i·nee** [⌣'ni:] candidat *m* désigné *ou* choisi.

non ... [nɔn] non-; in-; sans ...

non-ac·cept·ance ['nɔnək'septəns] non-acceptation *f.*

non·age ['nounidʒ] minorité *f.*

non·a·ge·nar·i·an [nounədʒi'neəriən] nonagénaire (*a. su.*/*mf*).

non-ag·gres·sion ['nɔnə'greʃn]: ⌣ *pact* pacte *m* de non-agression.

non-al·co·hol·ic ['nɔnælkə'hɔlik] sans alcool; non alcoolique.

non·a·ligned ['nɔnə'laind] neutraliste, non aligné; '**non·a·lign·ment** neutralisme *m*, non-alignement *m.*

non-ap·pear·ance ⚖ ['nɔnə'piərəns] non-comparution *f*; *souv.* défaut *m.*

non-at·tend·ance ⚖ ['nɔnə'tendəns] absence *f.*

nonce [nɔns]: *for the* ⌣ pour l'occasion; ⌣ *word* mot *m* de circonstance.

non·cha·lance ['nɔnʃələns] nonchalance *f*, indifférence *f*; '**non·cha·lant** □ nonchalant, indifférent.

non-com·mis·sioned ['nɔnkə'miʃənd] sans brevet; ✗ ⌣ *officer* sous-officier *m* gradé.

non-com·mit·tal ['nɔnkə'mitl] diplomatique; qui n'engage à rien.

non-com·pli·ance ['nɔnkəm'plaiəns] refus *m* d'obéissance (à, *with*).

non com·pos men·tis ɪ⚖ [nɔn 'kɔmpɔs 'mentis] aliéné, fou (fol *devant une voyelle ou un h muet*; folle *f*).

non-con·duc·tor ⚡ ['nɔnkən'dʌktə] inconducteur *m*; *phys.* non-conducteur *m*.

non-con·form·ist ['nɔnkən'fɔ:mist] non-conformiste *mf*; dissident(e *f*) *m*;'**non·con'form·i·ty** non-conformisme *m* (*a. eccl.*). [sable.⟩

non-creas·ing ['nɔn'kri:siŋ]infrois-⟩

non-de·nom·i·na·tion·al ['nɔndinɔmi'neiʃnl] laïque (*école*).

non-de·script ['nɔndiskript] 1. inclassable; 2. *fig.* personne *f ou* chose *f* indéfinissable.

none [nʌn] 1. aucun; pas de; 2. aucunement; ~ *the less* cependant, pourtant, quand même.

non·en·ti·ty ['nɔn'nentiti] personne *f* insignifiante; *fig.* non-valeur *f*; nullité *f*.

non-es·sen·tial ['nɔni'senʃəl] 1. non essentiel(le *f*); 2. accessoire *m*.

non-ex·ist·ence ['nɔnig'zistəns] non-être *m*.

non-fic·tion ['nɔn'fikʃn] ouvrages *m/pl.* autres que les romans.

non-in·ter·ven·tion ['nɔnintə(:)-'venʃn] non-intervention *f*.

non-i·ron ['nɔn'aiən] ne pas repasser.

non-lad·der·ing ['nɔn'lædəriŋ] indémaillable.

non-ob·serv·ance ['nɔnəb'zə:vəns] inobservance *f*.

non-pa·reil ['nɔnpərel] 1. nonpareil(le *f*); 2. personne *f ou* chose *f* sans pareille; *typ.* nonpareille *f*.

non-par·ti·san [nɔn'pɑ:tizæn] impartial.

non-par·ty *pol.* ['nɔn'pɑ:ti] non partisan; impartial (-aux *m/pl.*).

non-pay·ment ['nɔn'peimənt] non-paiement *m*; défaut *m* de paiement.

non-per·form·ance ɪ⚖ ['nɔnpə'fɔ:məns] non-exécution *f*.

non-plus ['nɔn'plʌs] 1. embarras *m*, perplexité *f*; *at a* ~ à quia; 2. confondre, réduire à quia; ~*sed* désemparé; interdit.

non-prof·it-mak·ing ['nɔn'prɔfitmeikiŋ] sans but lucratif.

non-pro·lif·er·a·tion ['nɔnprɔulifə-'reiʃən] non-prolifération *f* (des armes nucléaires); ~ *treaty* traité *m* de non-prolifération.

non-res·i·dent ['nɔn'rezidənt] externe; forain; non-résident (*a. su./mf*).

non·sense ['nɔnsəns] absurdité *f*; bêtise *f*, -s *f/pl.*; **non·sen·si·cal** □ [~'sensikl] absurde; bête.

non-skid ['nɔn'skid] antidérapant.

non-smok·er ['nɔn'smoukə] non-fumeur *m*.

non-start·er ['nɔn'stɑ:tə] nonvaleur *f*; projet *m* sans d'avance.

non-stick ['nɔn'stik] qui n'attache pas (*casserole etc.*).

non-stop ['nɔn'stɔp] 🚌, ✈ direct; sans arrêt; 🚄 sans escale.

non-such ['nʌnsʌtʃ] personne *f ou* chose *f* sans pareille.

non-suit ɪ⚖ ['nɔn'sju:t] débouté *m*, rejet *m* de la demande.

non-un·ion [nɔn'ju:njən] non-syndiqué (*ouvrier*).

noo·dle[1] ['nu:dl] F niais(e *f*) *m*.

noo·dle[2] [~] *usu.* ~s *pl.* nouilles *f/pl.*

nook [nuk] (re)coin *m*.

noon [nu:n] 1. (*a.* '~·**day**, '~·**tide**) midi *m*; 2. de midi.

noose [nu:s] 1. nœud *m* coulant; corde *f* (de potence); *fig.* piège *m*; 2. prendre au lacet; attraper au⟩

nope *Am.* F [noup] non! [lasso.⟩

nor [nɔ:] *précédé de neither*: ni; *début de la phrase*: ne ... pas non plus; ~ *do I* (ni) moi non plus.

norm [nɔ:m] norme *f*; règle *f*; '**nor·mal** □ 1. normal (-aux *m/pl.*) (*a.* Ⓐ); Ⓐ perpendiculaire; ~ *school* école *f* normale; 2. condition *f* normale; Ⓐ normale *f*, perpendiculaire *f*; '**nor·mal·ize** rendre normal; régulariser. [2. Normand(e *f*) *m*.⟩

Nor·man ['nɔ:mən] 1. normand; ⟩

north [nɔ:θ] 1. *su.* nord *m*; 2. *adj.* du nord; septentrional (-aux *m/pl.*); '~·**bound** en direction du nord, allant vers le nord; '~·'**east** 1. nord-est *m*; 2. (*a.* '~·'**east·ern**) du nord-est; **north·er·ly** ['~ðəli] du *ou* au nord; **north·ern** ['~ən] du nord; septentrional (-aux *m/pl.*); '**north·ern·er** habitant(e *f*) *m* du nord; *Am.* ♀ nordiste *mf*; '**north·ern·most** le plus au nord; **north·ing** ⚓ ['~θiŋ] chemin *m* nord; *astr.* mouvement *m* vers le nord; **north·ward** ['~wəd] 1. *adj.* au *ou* du nord; 2. *adv.* (*a.* **north·wards** ['~dz]) vers le nord.

north...: '~-**west 1.** nord-ouest *m*; ⚓ *a.* norois *m*; **2.** (*a.* '~-'**west·ern,** '~-'**west·er·ly**) (du) nord-ouest *inv.*

Nor·we·gian [nɔː'wiːdʒən] **1.** norvégien(ne *f*); **2.** Norvégien(ne *f*) *m.*

nose [nouz] **1.** nez *m* (*a.* = *flair*); odorat *m*; *outil:* bec *m*; *tuyau:* ajutage *m*; ⚔ *balle:* pointe *f*; ⚓ *torpille:* cône *m* de choc; **2.** *v/t.* (*a.* ~ *out*) sentir, flairer; ~ *out* découvrir; ~ *one's way* s'avancer avec précautions; *v/i.* chercher (qch., *after* [*ou for*] *s.th.*); ~ *ahead of* aller un peu en avant de (*qch.*); '~-**bag** musette *f*; '~-**band** muserolle *f*; **nosed** au nez ...

nose...: '~-**dive** ✈ (vol *m*) piqué *m*; '~-**gay** bouquet *m* de fleurs; '~-**heav·y** ✈ lourd de l'avant.

no-show F ['nou'ʃou] personne qui ne se présente pas à l'heure convenue.

nos·ing ⩜ ['nouziŋ] arête *f* (de moulure); *marche d'escalier:* nez *m.*

nos·tal·gi·a [nɔs'tældʒiə] nostalgie *f*; **nos·tal·gic** [⌣dʒik] nostalgique.

nos·tril ['nɔstril] narine *f*; *cheval, bœuf:* naseau *m.*

nos·trum ['nɔstrəm] panacée *f*; remède *m* de charlatan.

nos·y ['nouzi] parfumé; *péj.* curieux (-euse *f*); F fouinard, indiscret (-ète *f*); ♀ *Parker* indiscret *m*; F fouinard *m.*

not [nɔt] (ne) pas, (ne) point.

no·ta·bil·i·ty [noutə'biliti] notabilité *f*; caractère *m* notable (*d'un événement*); *see notable 2*; **no·ta·ble** ['noutəbl] **1.** □ notable, insigne, considérable; sensible, perceptible (*quantité*); éminent (*personne*); **2.** *personne:* notable *m*, notabilité *f*; '**no·ta·bly 1.** remarquablement; **2.** notamment.

no·tar·i·al □ [nou'tɛəriəl] de notaire; notarié (*document*); notarial (-aux *m/pl.*) (*sceau*); **no·ta·ry** ['noutəri] (*a.* ~ *public*) notaire *m.*

no·ta·tion [nou'teiʃn] *surt.* ♫, *a.* ♪ notation *f.*

notch [nɔtʃ] **1.** encoche *f*; ⊕ cran *m*; *Am.* défilé *m*, gorge *f*; **2.** entailler, encocher; denteler (*une roue*).

note [nout] **1.** note *f* (*a.* ♯, ♪, *pol.*); F ton *m* (*de la voix*); ♪ son *m*, ♪ *piano:* touche *f*; marque *f*, signe *m*; *pol.* mémorandum *m*; ♱ billet *m*, lettre *f*; *banque:* billet *m*; *texte:*

annotation *f*; renom *m*; *take* ~s *of* prendre des notes de; **2.** noter; constater, remarquer; relever (*une erreur*); faire attention à; (*a.* ~ *down*) inscrire, prendre note de; '~-**book** carnet *m*; *sténographie:* bloc-notes (*pl.* blocs-notes) *m*; '**not·ed** distingué, éminent (*personne*); célèbre (par, *for*), connu (pour, *for*) (*chose*); ~ly surtout; nettement; digne d'attention; '**note·wor·thy** remarquable; digne d'attention.

noth·ing ['nʌθiŋ] **1.** rien (de *adj.*) (*su./m*); ♈ zéro *m*; néant *m*; *fig.* bagatelle *f*; *for* ~ gratis; *good for* ~ bon à rien, inutile; *bring to* ~ faire échouer; *come to* ~ ne pas aboutir; *make* ~ *of* ne faire aucun cas de; *I can make* ~ *of it* je n'y comprends rien; **2.** *adv.* aucunement; pas du tout; '**noth·ing·ness** néant *m*; *fig.* nullité *f.*

no·tice ['noutis] **1.** avis *m*; avertissement *m*; convocation *f* (*d'une réunion*); ♱ délai *m*; *bourse:* terme *m*; affiche *f*; écriteau *m*; annonce *f*, *journ.* notice *f*; revue *f* (*d'un ouvrage*); *fig.* attention *f*; congé *m*; *at short* ~ à bref délai; *give* ~ *of departure* annoncer son départ; *give* ~ *that* prévenir que; *give s.o. a week's* ~ donner ses huit jours à q.; *take* ~ *of* faire attention à; *until further* ~ jusqu'à nouvel ordre; *without* ~ sans avis préalable; **2.** remarquer, observer; s'apercevoir de *ou* que; prendre garde à; faire le compte rendu de (*un ouvrage*); faire attention à; '**no·tice·a·ble** □ sensible, perceptible; digne d'attention; '**no·tice-board** écriteau *m*; porte-affiches *m/inv.*; panneau *m* indicateur.

no·ti·fi·a·ble ✺ ['noutifaiəbl] dont la déclaration est obligatoire (*maladie*); **no·ti·fi·ca·tion** [⌣fi'keiʃn] avis *m*; avertissement *f*; annonce *f*; déclaration *f*; notification *f.*

no·ti·fy ['noutifai] annoncer; avertir; déclarer; aviser, notifier.

no·tion ['nouʃn] notion *f*, idée *f*; pensée *f*; *fig.* caprice *m*; *Am.* ~s *pl.* petites inventions *f/pl.* bon marché; (*petits*) articles *m/pl.* ingénieux; '**no·tion·al** □ spéculatif (-ive *f*) (*connaissances etc.*); imaginaire; *surt. Am.* F capricieux (-euse *f*); fantasque.

no·to·ri·e·ty [noutə'raiəti] notoriété f; *personne*: notabilité f; **no·to·ri·ous** □ [nou'tɔːriəs] notoire, (re-)connu; *péj.* d'une triste notoriété; fameux (-euse f).

not·with·stand·ing [nɔtwiθ'stæn-diŋ] **1.** *prp.* malgré, en dépit de; **2.** *adv.* pourtant; tout de même; **3.** *cj.* ~ that quoique (*sbj.*), bien que (*sbj.*).

nought *surt.* ↗ [nɔːt] zéro m; F rien m; *come to* ~ échouer, tomber à l'eau.

noun *gramm.* [naun] nom m, substantif m.

nour·ish ['nʌriʃ] nourrir (*a. fig.*); alimenter; **'nour·ish·ing** nourrissant, nutritif (-ive f); **'nour·ish·ment** nourriture f; alimentation f.

nov·el ['nɔvl] **1.** nouveau (-el *devant une voyelle ou un h muet*; -elle f), original (-aux m/pl.); **2.** roman m; *short* ~ = **nov·el·ette** [nɔvə'let] nouvelle f; **'nov·el·ist** romancier (-ère f) m; **nov·el·ty** ['nɔvlti] nouveauté f (*a.* ✝).

No·vem·ber [nou'vembə] novembre m.

nov·ice ['nɔvis] novice mf (*a. eccl.*); débutant(e f) m.

no·vi·ci·ate, no·vi·ti·ate [no'viʃiit] noviciat m (*a. eccl.*); apprentissage m.

now [nau] **1.** *adv.* maintenant; en ce moment; tout de suite; *avec vbe. passé:* alors, à ce moment-là; *just* ~ tout à l'heure; *before* ~ déjà; *jusqu'ici*; ~ *and again* de temps à autre; ~ *and then* de temps en temps; **2.** *cj.* (*a.* ~ *that*) maintenant que; or; **3.** *su.* présent m.

now·a·day ['nauədei] d'aujourd'hui; **now·a·days** ['‿z] de nos jours.

no·way(s) F ['nouwei(z)] en aucune façon.

no·where ['nouwɛə] nulle part.

no·wise ['nouwaiz] *see* noway(s).

nox·ious □ ['nɔkʃəs] nuisible.

noz·zle ['nɔzl] ⊕ ajutage m; jet m.

nub [nʌb] (petit) morceau m; *Am.* F essentiel m (*d'une affaire*).

nu·cle·ar ['njuːkliə] nucléaire; ~ *deterrent* force f de dissuasion nucléaire; ~ *disintegration* désintégration f nucléaire; ~ *energy* énergie f nucléaire; ~ *physics* physique f nucléaire; ~ *pile* pile f nucléaire; ~ *power* énergie f nucléaire; ~ *power plant* centrale f (électro-)nucléaire; ~ *reactor* bouilleur m atomique; ~ *research* recherches f/pl. nucléaires; ~ *submarine* sous-marin m atomique; ~ *warfare* guerre f nucléaire *ou* atomique; ~ *warhead* ogive f nucléaire; **nu·cle·on** *phys.* ['njuːkliən] nucléon m; **nu·cle·us** ['njuːkliəs], *pl.* -i [‿ai] noyau m.

nude [njuːd] **1.** nu; **2.** *figure* f nue; *peint.* nu m; nudité f; *study from the* ~ nu m.

nudge F [nʌdʒ] **1.** pousser (*q.*) du coude; **2.** coup m de coude.

nud·ism ['njuːdizm] nudisme m; **'nud·ist** nudiste mf; **'nu·di·ty** nudité f; *figure* f nue.

nu·ga·to·ry ['njuːgətəri] futile, sans valeur; inefficace.

nug·get ['nʌgit] pépite f (*d'or*).

nui·sance ['njuːsns] dommage m; *fig. personne:* peste f, gêneur (-euse f) m; *chose:* ennui m; *what a* ~! quel ennui!; F quelle scie!; *commit no* ~! défense de déposer des immondices!; défense d'uriner; *make o.s.* (*ou be*) *a* ~ être assommant.

nuke *Am. sl.* [nuːk] **1.** arme f nucléaire; **2.** attaquer avec des armes nucléaires.

null [nʌl] ⚖, *a. fig.* nul(le f); *fig.* inefficace, insignifiant; ~ *and void* nul et sans effet; **nul·li·fi·ca·tion** annulation f, infirmation f; **nul·li·fy** ['‿ifai] annuler; nullifier; infirmer; **'nul·li·ty** nullité f, invalidité f; *fig.* homme m nul, non-valeur f.

numb [nʌm] **1.** engourdi (par, *with*); transi; **2.** engourdir (*a. fig.*).

num·ber ['nʌmbə] **1.** ↗, *gramm.*, *personnes:* nombre m; chiffre m (*écrit*); numéro m (*de maison, auto, journal, programme, etc.*); *poét.* ~s *pl.* vers m/pl.; ♩ accords m/pl.; **2.** compter; numéroter; ~ *among*, ~ *in*, ~ *with* (se) compter parmi; **'num·ber·less** sans nombre; innombrable; **'num·ber-plate** mot. plaque f matricule.

numb·ness ['nʌmnis] engourdissement m; *fig.* torpeur f.

nu·mer·a·ble ['njuːmərəbl] (dé-)nombrable; **'nu·mer·al 1.** numéral (-aux m/pl.); **2.** nombre m, chiffre m; nom m de nombre; ~s *pl.* numéraux m/pl.; **nu·mer·a·tion** numé-

nymph

ration *f*; **'nu·mer·a·tor** ＆ numérateur *m* (*d'une fraction*).

nu·mer·i·cal □ [nju'merikl] numérique.

nu·mer·ous □ ['nju:mərəs] nombreux (-euse *f*); *vers:* cadencé; **'nu·mer·ous·ness** (grand) nombre *m*; abondance *f*.

nu·mis·mat·ic [nju:miz'mætik] (*~ally*) numismatique; **nu·mis'mat·ics** *usu. sg.* numismatique *f*; **nu·mis·ma·tist** [nju(:)'mizmətist] numismat(ist)e *m*.

num·skull F ['nʌmskʌl] nigaud(e *f*) *m*; idiot(e *f*) *m*.

nun [nʌn] religieuse *f*; *orn.* mésange *f* bleue, *a.* pigeon *m* nonnain.

nun·ci·a·ture *eccl.* ['nʌnʃiətʃə] nonciature *f*; **nun·ci·o** *eccl.* ['~ʃiou] nonce *m*.

nun·ner·y ['nʌnəri] couvent *m* (de religieuses).

nup·tial ['nʌpʃəl] **1.** nuptial (-aux *m/pl.*); **2.** *~s pl.* noces *f/pl.*

nurse [nəːs] **1.** (*souv.* wet-*~*) nourrice *f*; bonne *f* d'enfants; garde-malade (*pl.* gardes-malades) *f*; *hôpital:* infirmière *f*; *at a ~* en nourrice; *put s.o. out to ~* mettre q. en nourrice; **2.** allaiter (*un bébé*); soigner (*malade, plante, popularité, rhume*); entretenir (*un espoir, un sentiment*); mijoter (*un projet*); cultiver (*des électeurs, une relation, etc.*); **'~-maid** bonne *f* d'enfants.

nurs·er·y ['nəːsri] chambre *f* des enfants; garderie *f*; ✿ pépinière *f* (*a. fig.*); *~ school* maternelle *f*; *~* **gov·ern·ess** gouvernante *f* (pour jeunes enfants); **'~-man** pépiniériste *m*; *~* **rhyme** chanson *f* de nourrice; poésie *f* enfantine.

nurs·ing ['nəːsiŋ] allaitement *m*; soins *m/pl.*; profession *f* de garde-malade; *~ home* maison *f* de santé *ou* de convalescence *ou* de repos *ou* de retraite; *Brit. a.* clinique *f* privée; *~ bottle* biberon *m*.

nurs·ling ['nəːsliŋ] nourrisson *m*.

nur·ture ['nəːtʃə] **1.** nourriture *f*; aliments *m/pl.*; soins *m/pl.*, éducation *f*; **2.** nourrir (de, *on*) (*a. fig.*); élever; instruire.

nut [nʌt] **1.** noix *f*; ⊕ écrou *m*; *sl.* problème *m ou* personne *f* difficile; *sl.* boule *f* (= *tête*); ♪ *violon:* sillet *m*, *archet:* hausse *f*; *sl.* insensé(e *f*) *m*; *~s pl. charbon:* gailletin *m*; **2.** *sl. ~s* toqué; *sl. that is ~s to* (*ou* for) *him* c'est un plaisir pour lui; *be ~s on* raffoler de; *sl. drive s.o. ~s* affoler q.; *go ~s* être toqué, déménager; **3.**: *go ~ting* aller aux noisettes.

nu·ta·tion [nju:'teiʃn] nutation *f*.

nut·crack·er ['nʌtkrækə] *usu.* (*a pair of*) *~s pl.* (des) casse-noisettes *m/inv.*; **'nut-gall** noix *f* de galle; **nut·meg** ['~meg] (noix *f* de) muscade *f*.

nu·tri·ent ['nju:triənt] **1.** nourrissant, nutritif (-ive *f*); **2.** substance *f* nutritive; **'nu·tri·ment** nourriture *f*; aliments *m/pl.* nourrissants.

nu·tri·tion [nju:'triʃn] nutrition *f*; **nu'tri·tion·al** □ [~əl] alimentaire; nutritif (-ive *f*); *~ value see nutritiousness*; **nu'tri·tious** □ nourrissant, nutritif (-ive *f*); **nu'tri·tious·ness** nutritivité *f*, valeur *f* nutritive.

nu·tri·tive □ ['nju:tritiv] *see nutritious*.

nut·shell ['nʌtʃel] coquille *f* de noix; *in a ~* en peu de mots; **nut·ty** ['nʌti] abondant en noix *ou* en noisettes; ayant un goût de noisette; plein de saveur (*conte*); *sl.* entiché (de, *on*), timbré, un peu fou (*fol devant une voyelle ou un h muet*; *folle f*).

nuz·zle ['nʌzl] (contre, *against*) fouiller avec le groin (*cochon etc.*); fourrer son nez; *personne:* se blottir, se serrer.

ny·lon ['nailɔn] *tex.* nylon *m*; *~s pl.* bas *m/pl.* nylon.

nymph [nimf] nymphe *f*.

O

O, o [ou] O *m*, o *m*.

o [ou] **1.** ♀ (= *nought*) zéro *m*; **2.** *int.* O, ô, oh; ~ *for* ...! que ne donnerais-je pas pour ...!

oaf [ouf] idiot(e *f*) *m*; lourdaud(e *f*) *m*; **'oaf·ish** lourdaud.

oak [ouk] **1.** ♀ chêne *m*; *univ.* F porte *f* extérieure; *see* sport 2; **2.** de ou en chêne; **'~-ap·ple**, **'~-gall** noix *f* de galle; **'oak·en †** de ou en chêne; **oak·let** ['~lit], **'oak·ling** chêneau *m*.

oa·kum ['oukəm] étoupe *f*.

oar [ɔ:] **1.** aviron *m*, rame *f*; *fig.* rameur (-euse *f*) *m*; *fig.* put one's ~ *in* intervenir, s'en mêler; F *rest on one's* ~*s* dormir sur ses lauriers; **2.** *v/i.* ramer; *v/t.* faire avancer à la rame; **oared** [ɔ:d] à rames; **oars·man** ['ɔ:zmən] rameur *m*; **'oars·wom·an** rameuse *f*.

o·a·sis [o'eisis], *pl.* -ses [~si:z] oasis *f* (*a. fig.*).

oast [oust] séchoir *m* (à houblon).

oat [out] *usu.* ~*s pl.* avoine *f*; F *fig. feel one's* ~*s* se sentir gaillard; *Am. a.* se donner des airs; *sow one's wild* ~*s* faire des fredaines.

oath [ouθ], *pl.* **oaths** [ouðz] serment *m*; *péj.* juron *m*, gros mot *m*; *administer* (*ou* tender) *an* ~ *to* faire prêter serment à, assermenter (*q.*); *bind s.o. by* ~ lier par serment; *on* ~ sous (la foi du) serment; *put s.o. on his* ~ assermenter q.; *take an* ~ prêter serment (sur, on); jurer (sur, on; de *inf.*, to *inf.*).

oat·meal ['outmi:l] farine *f* d'avoine.

ob·du·ra·cy ['ɔbdjurəsi] opiniâtreté *f*; inflexibilité *f*; **ob·du·rate** □ ['~rit] obstiné; inflexible.

o·be·di·ence [o'bi:djəns] obéissance *f*; *eccl.* obédience *f*; ✝ *in* ~ *to* conformément à; **o'be·di·ent** □ obéissant.

o·bei·sance [o'beisns] hommage *m*; † révérence *f*; *do* (*ou* make *ou* pay) ~ (à, to) rendre hommage, prêter obéissance (*au roi etc.*).

ob·e·lisk ['ɔbilisk] obélisque *m*; *typ.* croix *f*, obèle *m*.

o·bese □ [o'bi:s] obèse; **o'bese·ness**, **o'bes·i·ty** obésité *f*.

o·bey [o'bei] *v/t.* obéir à (*q.*, un ordre); *v/i.* obéir.

ob·fus·cate ['ɔbfʌskeit] *fig.* obscurcir; F griser.

o·bit·u·ar·y [o'bitjuəri] **1.** registre *m* des morts; nécrologe *m*; **2.** nécrologique; *journ.* ~ *column* nécrologie *f*.

ob·ject 1. ['ɔbdʒikt] objet *m* (*a. fig.*); chose *f*; *fig.* but *m*; *gramm.* complément *m*, régime *m*; *salary no* ~ les appointements importent peu; **2.** [əb'dʒekt] *v/t.* objecter (qch. à q., *s.th.* to s.o.); *v/i.* protester (contre, to); ~ *to* (*gér.*) s'opposer à (*inf.*); se refuser à (*inf.*); désapprouver (*inf.*); **~-glass** *opt.* ['ɔbdʒikt-glɑ:s] objectif *m*.

ob·jec·tion [əb'dʒekʃn] objection *f*; *fig.* aversion *f*; *there is no* ~ (*to it*) il n'y a aucun inconvénient; **ob'jec·tion·a·ble** □ répréhensible; désagréable; choquant.

ob·jec·tive [əb'dʒektiv] **1.** □ objectif (-ive *f*); **2.** objectif *m* (*a.* ✕, *opt.*); but *m*; *gramm.* régime *m*; **ob'jec·tive·ness**, **ob·jec'tiv·i·ty** objectivité *f*.

ob·ject...: '~-lens *opt.* objectif *m*; '~-less □ sans but, sans objet; '~-les·son leçon *f* de choses; *fig.* exemple *m*.

ob·jec·tor [əb'dʒektə] réclameur *m*; contradicteur *m*; *see* conscientious.

ob·jur·gate ['ɔbdʒə:geit] accabler (*q.*) de reproches; **ob·jur'ga·tion** réprimande *f*; **ob'jur·ga·to·ry** [~gətəri] objurgatoire.

ob·late □ ['ɔbleit] **1.** ♀ aplati (aux pôles); **2.** *eccl.* oblat(e *f*) *m*; **'ob·late·ness** ♀ aplatissement *m*.

ob·la·tion *eccl.* [o'bleiʃn] oblation *f*.

ob·li·ga·tion [ɔbli'geiʃn] obligation *f* (*a.* ✝); devoir *m*; ✝ engagement *m*; dette *f* de reconnaissance; *be under* (*an*) ~ *to s.o.* avoir des obligations envers q.; devoir de la reconnaissance à q.; *be under ~ to* (*inf.*) être dans l'obligation de (*inf.*), être tenu de (*inf.*); **ob·lig·a·to·ry** ['‿gətəri] obligatoire (à q., *on s.o.*); de rigueur.

o·blige [ə'blaidʒ] *v/t.* obliger (*a.* 🜨); astreindre; rendre service à (*q.*); *~ the company with a song* avoir l'amabilité de chanter; *much ~d* bien reconnaissant; *v/i.* F *~ with a song etc.* avoir l'amabilité de chanter *etc.*; *please ~ with an early reply* prière de bien vouloir répondre sous peu; **ob·li·gee** [ɔbli'dʒiː] 🜨 obligataire *m*, créancier *m*; F obligé(e *f*) *m*; **o·blig·ing** □ [ə'blaidʒiŋ] obligeant, serviable, complaisant; **o'blig·ing·ness** obligeance *f*, complaisance *f*; **ob·li·gor** 🜨 [ɔbli'gɔː] obligé(e *f*) *m*.

ob·lique □ [ə'bliːk] ♉, ♀, ♪, ♓, ⚔, *anat.*, *astr.*, *gramm.* oblique; indirect (*discours*, *a. fig.*); de biais (*regard*); **ob'lique·ness**, **ob'liq·ui·ty** [‿kwiti] obliquité *f*.

ob·lit·er·ate [o'blitəreit] effacer, faire disparaître; *fig.* passer l'éponge sur; 💰, *anat.*, *poste*: oblitérer; **ob·lit·er'a·tion** effaçage *m*; rature *f*; 💰, *anat.*, *timbre*: oblitération *f*.

ob·liv·i·on [o'bliviən] oubli *m*; *pol.* amnistie *f*; *fall* (*ou sink*) *into ~* tomber dans l'oubli; **ob'liv·i·ous** □ oublieux (-euse *f*); *be ~ of* oublier complètement; F ignorer tout à fait.

ob·long ['ɔblɔŋ] **1.** oblong(ue *f*); **2.** rectangle *m*.

ob·lo·quy ['ɔblɔkwi] blâme *m*, calomnie *f*; opprobre *m*, honte *f*.

ob·nox·ious □ [əb'nɔkʃəs] odieux (-euse *f*); désagréable; détesté (par, *to*); **ob'nox·ious·ness** caractère *m* odieux.

o·boe ♪ ['oubou] hautbois *m*; *personne*: hautboïste *mf*.

ob·scene □ [ɔb'siːn] obscène; *fig.* répugnant; **ob'scen·i·ty** [‿iti] obscénité *f*; *langage*: grossièreté *f*.

ob·scur·ant [ɔb'skjuərənt] obscurantiste *mf*; **ob·scu·ra·tion** [‿skju'reiʃn] obscurcissement *m*; *astr.* obscuration *f*, éclipse *f*; **ob·scure** [əb'skjuə] **1.** □ obscur (*a. fig.*); sombre; **2.** *v/t.* obscurcir (*a. fig.*); masquer (*la lumière*); *fig.* éclipser; **ob'scu·ri·ty** obscurité *f* (*a. fig.*).

ob·se·quies ['ɔbsikwiz] *pl.* obsèques *f/pl.*, funérailles *f/pl.*

ob·se·qui·ous □ [əb'siːkwiəs] obsé-

quieux (-euse *f*); **ob'se·qui·ous·ness** obséquiosité *f*, servilité *f*.

ob·serv·a·ble □ [əb'zəːvəbl] visible; sensible; remarquable; **ob'serv·ance** *eccl.*, *dimanche*, *loi*, *ordre*: observance *f*; pratique *f*; **ob'serv·ant** □ observateur (-trice *f*) (de, *of*); attentif (-ive *f*) (à, *of*); **ob·ser·va·tion** [ɔbzə'veiʃn] observation *f*; surveillance *f*; remarque *f*; *attr.* d'observation; 🚃 *~ car* wagon *m* d'observation; 💰 *~ ward* salle *f* des malades en observation; **ob·serv·a·to·ry** [əb'zəːvətri] observatoire *m*; **ob'serve** *v/t.* observer (*a. fig.*); regarder; remarquer, apercevoir; dire; *v/i. ~ on* commenter (*qch.*); **ob'serv·er** observateur (-trice *f*) *m*.

ob·sess [əb'ses] obséder; *~ed by* (*ou with*) obsédé par, hanté par; en proie à; **ob'ses·sion** obsession *f*.

ob·so·les·cence [ɔbsə'lesns] vieillissement *m*; *biol.* atrophie *f*; **ob·so·'les·cent** qui tombe en désuétude; *biol.* atrophié.

ob·so·lete ['ɔbsəliːt] désuet (-ète *f*); hors d'usage; démodé; *zo.* obsolète.

ob·sta·cle ['ɔbstəkl] obstacle *m*.

ob·ste·tri·cian 💰 [ɔbste'triʃn] accoucheur *m*; **ob'stet·rics** [‿riks] *usu. sg.* obstétrique *f*.

ob·sti·na·cy ['ɔbstinəsi] obstination *f*, opiniâtreté *f*; 💰 persistance *f*; **ob·sti·nate** □ ['‿nit] obstiné (*a.* 💰), opiniâtre; acharné; rebelle (*fièvre*).

ob·strep·er·ous □ [əb'strepərəs] bruyant; rebelle; indiscipliné.

ob·struct [əb'strʌkt] *v/t.* obstruer (*a.* 💰); encombrer; gêner; empêcher; **ob'struc·tion** ⊕ engorgement *m*; 💰, *parl.* obstruction *f*; obstacle *m*; *fig.* empêchement *m*; encombrement *m*; **ob'struc·tive** □ 💰 obstructif (-ive *f*); d'obstruction; *be ~ of* gêner.

ob·tain [əb'tein] *v/t.* obtenir, se procurer; gagner; *v/i.* régner, exister; **ob'tain·a·ble** procurable; trouvable; **ob'tain·ment** obtention *f*.

ob·trude [əb'truːd] (s')imposer (*on*, à); **ob'tru·sion** importunité *f*, intrusion *f*; **ob'tru·sive** □ [‿siv] importun; indiscret (-ète *f*).

ob·tu·rate ['ɔbtjuəreit] boucher, obturer; **'ob·tu·ra·tor** obturateur *m*.

ob·tuse □ [əb'tjuːs] ♉, angle, esprit, pointe: obtus; *fig.* émoussé, sourd;

fig. stupide; **ob'tuse·ness** manque *m* de pointe; *fig.* stupidité *f*.

ob·verse ['ɔbvəːs] obvers *m*; *médaille, monnaie:* face *f*; *fig.* opposé *m*.

ob·vi·ate ['ɔbvieit] *fig.* obvier à, éviter; prévenir.

ob·vi·ous □ ['ɔbviəs] évident, manifeste, clair; *fig.* voyant; **'ob·vi·ous·ness** évidence *f*.

oc·ca·sion [ə'keiʒn] **1.** occasion *f*, cause *f*; sujet *m*; besoin *m*; fois *f*; ~s *pl.* affaires *f/pl.*; on ~ de temps à autre; *on several* ~s à plusieurs reprises; *on all* ~s en toute occasion; *on the* ~ à l'occasion de; *have no* ~ *for* n'avoir aucun sujet de; *rise to the* ~ être *ou* se montrer à la hauteur de la situation; **2.** occasionner, donner lieu à; **oc·ca·sion·al** □ ... de temps en temps; épars; ~ *furniture* meuble *m* volant.

oc·ci·dent *poét.* ['ɔksidənt] occident *m*, ouest *m*; **oc·ci·den·tal** □ [~'dentl] occidental (-aux *m/pl.*); de l'ouest.

oc·cult □ [ɔ'kʌlt] occulte, secret (-ète *f*); **oc·cul'ta·tion** *astr.* occultation *f*; **oc·cult·ism** ['ɔkəltizm] occultisme *m*; **'oc·cult·ist** occultiste *mf*; **oc·cult·ness** [ɔ'kʌltnis] caractère *m* occulte.

oc·cu·pan·cy ['ɔkjupənsi] occupation *f*, habitation *f* (de, of); *emploi:* possession *f*; **'oc·cu·pant** *terre:* occupant(e *f*) *m*; *maison:* locataire *mf*; *emploi:* titulaire *mf*; **oc·cu'pa·tion** occupation *f* (a. ⚔); emploi *m*, métier *m*, profession *f*; *be in* ~ *of* occuper; *employed in an* ~ employé; **oc·cu·pa·tion·al** de métier; professionnel(le *f*); ~ *disease* maladie *f* professionnelle; ~ *hazard* risque *m* du métier; ~ *therapy* thérapeutique *f* occupationnelle; **oc·cu·pi·er** ['~paiə] *see occupant;* **oc·cu·py** ['~pai] occuper (*q., qch., a.* ⚔ *une ville*); habiter (*une maison*); remplir (*l'espace, le temps, un emploi*); occuper (*la place, le temps*); passer (*le temps*); ⚔ s'emparer de (*un point stratégique*), garnir (*une place de guerre*); donner du travail à; ~ *o.s.* (*ou be occupied*) *with* (*ou in*) être occupé à, s'occuper à.

oc·cur [ə'kəː] avoir lieu; arriver; se produire; se trouver; venir à l'esprit (à q., *to* s.o.); **oc·cur·rence**

[ə'kʌrəns] événement *m*; occurrence *f*; *min.* venue *f*.

o·cean ['ouʃn] océan *m*; mer *f*; F ~s *pl.* d'un tas *m* de; **'~-go·ing** ⚓ de haute mer (*bateau*); **o·ce·an·ic** [ouʃi'ænik] océanique; de l'océan.

o·chre *min.* ['oukə] ocre *f*.

o'clock [ə'klɔk]: *five* ~ cinq heures.

oc·ta·gon ['ɔktəgən] octogone *m*; **oc·tag·o·nal** [ɔk'tægənl] octogonal (-aux *m/pl.*).

oc·tane 🜍 ['ɔktein] octane *m*.

oc·tave ♪ ['ɔktiv] octave *f*; **oc·ta·vo** [~'teivou] in-octavo *inv.* (*a. su./m*).

Oc·to·ber [ɔk'toubə] octobre *m*.

oc·to·ge·nar·i·an ['ɔktoudʒi'nɛəriən] octogénaire (*a. su./mf*).

oc·to·pus *zo.* ['ɔktəpəs] poulpe *m*; *surt.* pieuvre *f* (*a. fig.*).

oc·u·lar □ ['ɔkjulə] oculaire, des yeux, de l'œil; ~ *demonstration* démonstration *f* oculaire; ~*ly* oculairement, des yeux; **'oc·u·list** oculiste *m*.

odd □ [ɔd] impair (*nombre*); dépareillé, déparié (*de deux*); qui ne vont pas ensemble; *fig.* quelconque; *40* ~ une quarantaine; quelque quarante ...; *12 pounds* ~ 12 livres et quelques shillings; *there is still some* ~ *money* il reste encore quelque argent (de surplus); *at* ~ *times* par-ci par-là; *be* ~ *man* rester en surnombre; ~*ly enough* curieusement, chose curieuse; *see a.* odds; **'~·ball** *Am.* F drôle de type *m*; **Odd·fel·lows** ['ɔdfelouz] *pl.* une société de secours mutuels; **'odd·i·ty** singularité *f*, bizarrerie *f*; F original(e *f*) *m*; **'odd·ments** *pl.* restes *m/pl.*; ✝ fins *f/pl.* de série; fonds *m/pl.* de boutique; **odds** [ɔdz] *pl., a. sg.* chances *f/pl.*; avantage *m*; différence *f*; *courses:* cote *f*; *Am. a.* faveurs *f/pl.*; *at* ~ brouillé, en désaccord; ~ *and ends* bribes *f/pl.* et morceaux *m/pl.*; petits bouts *m/pl.*; *nourriture:* restes *m/pl.*; *sp.* give s.o. ~ concéder des points à q.; *what's the* ~? qu'est-ce que ça fait?; *it makes no* ~ ça ne fait rien; cela n'a pas d'importance; *the* ~ *are for* (*against*) *him* les chances sont pour (contre) lui.

ode [oud] ode *f*.

o·di·ous □ ['oudiəs] odieux (-euse *f*); détestable; répugnant; **o·di·um** ['oudiəm] détestation *f*; réprobation *f*; haine *f*.

o·dom·e·ter *mot.* [oˈdɔmitə] odomètre *m*; compteur *m* enregistreur.

o·don·to·lo·gy ⚕ [ɔdɔnˈtɔlədʒi] odontologie *f*.

o·dor·if·er·ous □ [oudəˈrifərəs], **ˈo·dor·ous** □ odorant; parfumé; *péj.* puant.

o·do(u)r [ˈoudə] parfum *m*; odeur *f* (*a. fig.*); *fig.* faveur *f*; **ˈo·do(u)r·less** sans odeur, inodore.

œconom... *see* econom...

œc·u·men·i·cal *eccl.* □ [iːkjuːˈmenikl] œcuménique; F universel(le *f*).

œ·de·ma ⚕ [iːˈdiːmə] œdème *m*.

o'er [ɔə] *see* over. [œsophage *m*.]

œ·soph·a·gus *anat.* [iːˈsɔfəgəs]∫

of [ɔv; əv] *prp.* possession, dépendance: de (*mon père*); origine: de (*bonne famille*); cause: de (*joie, faim, etc.*); qualité, quantité, action, distance: de; *lieu de bataille, etc.*: de; *titre de noblesse*: de; *matière*: en (*soie, or, etc.*); *titre universitaire*: en (*philosophie, droit, etc.*), ès (*lettres, sciences*); parmi, (d')entre (*un groupe*); *après certains verbes comme priver, ôter, etc.*: de; *génitif de déscription*: a man ~ honour un homme d'honneur; *the city* ~ London la cité de Londres; *génitif subjectif*: the love ~ a mother l'amour d'une mère; *génitif objectif*: the love ~ God l'amour de Dieu; a hatred ~ cruelty une haine de la cruauté; *article partitif*: a glass ~ wine un verre de vin; *pour* ~ *après verbe ou adjectif voir le verbe simple ou l'adjectif*; die ~ cancer mourir de cancer; enough ~ assez de; loved ~ all aimé de tous; north ~ Paris au nord de Paris; Duke ~ Kent Duc de Kent; get rid ~ se débarrasser de; cheat s.o. ~ s.th. frustrer q. de qch.; rob s.o. ~ s.th. voler qch. à q.; think ~ penser à; *fig.* juger de; be afraid (ashamed) ~ avoir peur (honte) de; desirous (proud) ~ désireux (fier) de; it is very kind ~ you c'est très aimable à vous; the best ~ my friends le meilleur de mes amis; ~ late récemment; ~ old de jadis; the 2nd ~ May le 2 mai; it smells ~ roses cela sent les roses; the remedy ~ remedies le remède par excellence; this world ~ ours ce monde terrestre; he ~ all men lui entre tous; F ~ an evening le soir.

off [ɔːf; ɔf] **1.** *adv. usu. avec verbe, voir le verbe simple*; ⚓ au large; 3 miles ~ à 3 milles de distance; 5 months ~ à 5 mois d'ici *ou* de là; ~ and on par intervalles; be ~ partir, s'en aller; *fig.* être fermé (*gaz etc.*); être coupé (*allumage etc.*); être épuisé (*plat*); être abandonné (*jeu*); être avancé (*viande etc.*); ne plus pondre (*poule*); be ~ with en avoir fini avec (*q.*); have one's shoes ~ avoir ôté ses souliers; be well (badly) ~ être dans l'aisance (dans la gêne *ou* misère, mal loti); **2.** *prp. usu.* de; *après certains verbes comme prendre, ôter, emprunter, etc.*: à; *distance*: éloigné de, écarté de; dégoûté de (*la nourriture*); ⚓ au large de; a street ~ the Strand une rue aboutissant au Strand; **3.** *adj.* de dehors; extérieur; droit (*Am.* gauche); *cheval*: de sous-verge; côté hors montoir (*cheval*); latéral (-aux *m/pl.*) (*rue*); subsidiaire (*importance*); ~ chance chance *f* douteuse; possibilité *f*; on the ~ chance au cas où; à tout hasard; dans le vague espoir (de *that*, *of* gér.); be (*ou* feel) ~ colo(u)r ne pas être en forme *ou* dans son assiette; ~ day jour *m* où l'on n'est pas en train; **4.** *su. cricket*: to the ~ en avant à droite; **5.** *int.* filez!; allez-vous-en!

of·fal [ˈɔfəl] déchets *m/pl.*, rebut *m*; ~s *pl. boucherie*: déchets *m/pl.* d'abattage; abats *m/pl.*

off... | **ˈ~·beat** F excentrique; **ˈ~·cast** **1.** rebut *m*; **2.** de rebut; **ˈ~·cen·tre**, *Am.* **ˈ~·cen·ter** décentré, désaxé, en porte-à-faux; **~ˈcol·o(u)r** scabreux (-euse *f*) (*histoire*).

off-du·ty hours [ˈɔːfdjuːtiˈauəz] *pl.* loisirs *m/pl.*, (heures *f/pl.* de) liberté *f*, congé *m*.

of·fence [əˈfens] offense *f*, faute *f*; sujet *m* de déplaisir; ⚖ crime *m*, délit *m*; minor ~ contravention *f*; no ~! pardonnez-moi!; je ne veux offenser personne!; give ~ offenser, froisser, blesser (*q., to s.o.*); take ~ se froisser (de, *at*).

of·fend [əˈfend] *v/t.* offenser, froisser, blesser; *v/i.* pécher (contre, *against*); violer (la loi, *against the law*); déplaire; **ofˈfend·er** délinquant(e *f*) *m*; coupable *mf*; offenseur *m*; pécheur (-eresse *f*) *m*; first ~ délinquant(e *f*) *m* primaire.

of·fense [əˈfens] *Am. see* offence.

of·fen·sive [ə'fensiv] **1.** □ offensif
(-ive *f*); choquant, offensant; désagréable; **2.** offensive *f*.
of·fer ['ɔfə] **1.** offre *f*; demande *f*
(*en mariage*); on ~ en vente; **2.** *v/t.*
offrir (*qch., prix, ✝, occasion, etc.*);
présenter (*spectacle, difficulté, excuses*); inviter (*un combat*); faire
(*opposition, résistance, insulte*); avancer (*une opinion*); adresser (*des
prières*); essayer (*de, to*); ~ *violence*
faire violence (à, *to*); *v/i.* s'offrir,
se présenter; **'of·fer·ing** action *f*,
chose: offre *f*; *eccl.* offrande *f*.
of·fer·to·ry *eccl.* ['ɔfətəri] oblation
f; *argent*: (montant *m* de la) quête *f*.
off-hand F ['ɔːf'hænd] sans préparation; à première vue; cavalièrement; brusque(ment); improvisé;
sans gêne.
of·fice ['ɔfis] service *m*; office *m* (*a.
eccl.*); emploi *m*, charge *f*, fonctions
f/pl.; dignité *f*; bureau *m*; ♀ ministère *m*; portefeuille *m*; *good* ~*s pl.* bons
offices *m/pl.*; *in* ~ au pouvoir (*gouvernement, parti*); *Insurance* ♀ compagnie *f* d'assurance*s*; *sl. give s.o. the* ~
avertir q.; F passer la consigne à q.; ~
appliances pl. articles *m/pl.* de bureau; ~ *bearer* fonctionnaire *m*; ✝
membre *m* du comité *m* directeur; ~
boy garçon *m* de bureau; ~ *holder*
employé(e *f*) *m* de l'État; ~ *hours pl.*
heures *f/pl.* de bureau.
of·fi·cer ['ɔfisə] fonctionnaire *m*; officier *m* (*a.* ✗); **'of·fi·cered** (*by*)
commandé (par); sous le commandement (de).
of·fi·cial □ [ə'fiʃl] **1.** officiel(le *f*);
titulaire; de service; *see officinal*; ~
agency agence *f*; *poste*: ~ *business*
en franchise; service *m* de l'État; ~
channel filière *f*, voie *f* hiérarchique;
~ *clerk* employé *m*; fonctionnaire *m*;
~ *hours pl.* heures *f/pl.* de bureau;
2. fonctionnaire *m*; employé *m*;
of·fi·cial·dom, of·fi·cial·ism [~-
ʃəlizm] bureaucratie *f*, fonctionna-
risme *m*.
of·fi·ci·ate [ə'fiʃieit] officier; *fig. a.*
exercer les fonctions d'hôte.
of·fic·i·nal ⚕ [ɔfi'sainl] officinal
(-aux *m/pl.*).
of·fi·cious □ [ə'fiʃəs] trop zélé; officieux (-euse *f*); empressé.
off·ing ⚓ ['ɔfiŋ] large *m*, pleine mer
f; *in the* ~ au large, *fig.* en perspective; **'off·ish** F distant, réservé.

off...: '~-**key** ♪ faux (fausse *f*); '~-
peak: ~*charges pl.* tarif *m* réduit (aux
heures creuses); ~ *hours pl.* heures
f/pl. creuses; '~-**print** tirage *m* à
part; '~-**put·ting** peu engageant, rebutant; répugnant; '~-**scour·ings**
pl., '~-**scum** rebut *m*; *fig.* lie *f*; '~-
sea·son 1. morte-saison *f*; **2.** hors-
saison (*tarif etc.*); '~-**set 1.** compensation *f*; ⚠ saillie *f*; ⚠ retrait *m* (*d'un
mur*); ⊕ *tuyau*: double coude *m*;
piston: rebord *m*; *typ.* maculage *m*;
phot. offset *m*; *see off-shoot*; set-off; **2.**
compenser; '~-**shoot** rejeton *m*; ✝
ramification *f*; '~-**shore** côtier, littoral; '~-**side** *sp.* hors jeu; '~-**spring**
descendants *m/pl.*; progéniture *f*;
fig. produit *m*; '~-**stage** *théâ.* dans la
coulisse; *fig.* dans la vie privée; '~-
the-cuff impromptu, au pied levé;
'~-**the-peg** *cost.* de confection, prêt
à porter; '~-**the-rec·ord** confiden-
tiel(le *f*); '~-**time** temps *m* (de) libre;
loisirs *m/pl.*; ~-**white** blanc cassé
inv.
of·ten ['ɔːfn], ✝, *poét. ou mots composés* **oft** [ɔːft] souvent, fréquemment. [maise *f*.]
o·gee ⚠ ['oudʒiː] doucine *f*, ci-]
o·gi·val [ou'dʒaivəl] ogival (-aux
m/pl.); en ogive; **o·give** ['oudʒaiv]
⚠ ogive *f*.
o·gle ['ougl] lancer des œillades (à).
o·gre ['ougə] ogre *m*; '**o·gress**
ogresse *f*.
oh [ou] O!, ô!
oil [ɔil] **1.** huile *f*; *sens restreint*: pétrole *m*; F *souv.* ~*s pl. see* ~-*colo(u)r*;
~ *dash-pot* frein *m* à huile; ~ (*level*)
gauge jauge *f* de niveau d'huile;
~ *slick* nappe *f* de pétrole; **2.** graisser
(*a. fig.*); ~ *up* (s')encrasser; '~-
change *mot.* vidange *m*; '~-**cloth**
toile *f* cirée; linoléum *m* imprimé; '~-
col·o(u)r couleur *f* à l'huile; '**oil·er**
personne: graisseur *m*; *chose*: burette
f de graissage; '**oil·field** gisement *m*
ou champ *m* pétrolifère; '**oil·i·ness**
état *m ou* aspect *m* graisseux; onctuosité *f* (*a. fig.*); '**oil-paint·ing** peinture *f* à l'huile; '**oil-pro·duc·ing
coun·tries** *pl.* pays *m/pl.* producteurs de pétrole; **oil-rig** plate-for-
me *f* pétrolière; '**oil·skin** toile *f* cirée *ou*
huilée; ~*s pl.* ciré *m*; cirage *m*; '**oil·y**
□ huileux (-euse *f*); graisseux (-euse
f); gras(se *f*) (*a. voix*); *fig.* onctueux
(-euse *f*), mielleux (-euse *f*).

oint·ment [ˈɔintmənt] onguent *m*, pommade *f*.

O.K., **o·kay**, **o·keh** [ˈouˈkei] **1.** parfait!; d'accord!; *écrit:* vu et approuvé; **2.** approuver; contresigner (*un ordre*).

old [ould] vieux (vieil *devant une voyelle ou un h muet*); vieille *f*; vieux *m/pl.*) (*a.* = *expérimenté, rebattu, du temps ancien*); ancien(ne *f*) (*devant su.* = *qui n'est plus en fonctions*); du temps ancien, de jadis; F ce cher ..., ce bon vieux ...; *of* ~ d'autrefois, de jadis; depuis longtemps; *in times of* ~ jadis, autrefois; *a friend of* ~ un vieux camarade; ~ *age* vieillesse *f*; *an* ~ *boy* un ancien élève; *surt. Am.* ♀ *Glory* la bannière étoilée; F *my* ~ *man* mon homme; F *my* ~ *woman* ma femme; '~·**age**: ~ pension retraite*f*, pension *f* vieillesse; ~ **pensioner** retraité(e *f*) *m*; **'old·en** † *ou poét.* (de) jadis; vieux (vieil *devant une voyelle ou un h muet*); vieille *f*; vieux *m/pl.*); **'old-'fash·ioned** démodé; à l'ancienne mode; **'old·ish** vieillot(te *f*); **'old-'maid·ish** de vieille fille; **old·ster** [ˈ~stə] F vieillard(e *f*) *m*; **old wives' tale** conte *m* de bonne femme.

o·le·ag·i·nous [ouliˈædʒinəs] oléagineux (-euse *f*), huileux (-euse *f*).

ol·fac·to·ry *anat.* [ɔlˈfæktəri] olfactif (-ive *f*).

ol·i·garch·y [ˈɔligɑːki] oligarchie *f*.

o·li·o [ˈouliou] F pot-pourri (*pl.* pots-pourris) *m*.

ol·ive [ˈɔliv] **1.** ⊕ olive *f*; *a.* see ~-*tree*; **2.** olive *adj./inv.*); '~·**branch** (rameau *m* d')olivier *m* (*a.* *fig.*); '~·**tree** olivier *m*.

O·lym·pi·ad [oˈlimpiæd] olympiade *f*.

O·lym·pi·an [oˈlimpiən] olympien (-ne *f*); de l'Olympe; **O'lym·pic games** *pl.* jeux *m/pl.* Olympiques.

om·buds·man [ˈɔmbudzmən] médiateur *m*, protecteur *m* du citoyen.

om·e·let(te) [ˈɔmlit] omelette *f*.

o·men [ˈoumen] présage *m*, augure *m*; **om·i·nous** □ [ˈɔminəs] de mauvais augure.

o·mis·si·ble [oˈmisibl] négligeable; **o'mis·sion** omission *f*; négligence *f*; *fig.* oubli *m*; *eccl.* sin of ~ péché *m* ou faute *f* d'omission.

o·mit [oˈmit] omettre (*qch.*; de, *to*); oublier (de, *to*); passer sous silence.

om·ni·bus [ˈɔmnibəs] **1.** autobus *m*; **2.** embrassant (*des choses*) diverses; 🚋 ~ *train* train *m* omnibus.

om·nip·o·tence [ɔmˈnipətəns] toute-puissance *f*; **om'nip·o·tent** tout-puissant (toute-puissante *f*).

om·ni·pres·ence [ˈɔmniˈprezəns] omniprésence *f*; **'om·ni·pres·ent** □ omniprésent.

om·nis·cience [ɔmˈnisiəns] *eccl.* omniscience *f*; **om'nis·cient** □ omniscient.

om·niv·o·rous [ɔmˈnivərəs] omnivore; *fig.* insatiable.

on [ɔn] **1.** *prp. usu.* sur; à (*la Bourse, cheval, l'arrivée de, pied, l'occasion de*); en (*vacances, route, perce, vente*); après; avec (*une pension, un salaire de*); de (*ce côté-ci*); pour; dans (*le train*); sous (*peine de*); direction: vers; ~ *the shore* sur le rivage; ~ *shore* à terre; ~ *the death of* à la mort de; ~ *examination* après considération; ~ *both sides* des deux côtés; ~ *all sides* de tous côtés; ~ *business* pour affaires; be ~ *a committee* faire partie d'un comité; ~ *Friday* vendredi; ~ *Fridays* le(s) vendredi(s); ~ *the 5th of April* le 5 avril; ~ *the left* (*right*) à gauche (droite); *surt. Am.* get ~ *a train* monter en voiture; *turn one's back* ~ montrer le dos à (*q.*); ~ *these conditions* dans ces conditions; ~ *the model of* à l'imitation de; ~ *hearing it* lorsque je (*etc.*) l'entendis; *pour on après verbe, voir le verbe simple*; **2.** *adv.* (en) avant; *souv. ne se traduit pas* (*p.ex.* put ~ mettre) *ou s'exprime tout autrement* (*p.ex.* théâ. be ~ être en scène); *have one's shoes* ~ être chaussé *etc.*) *ou se traduit par l'idée verbale de* continuer (*qch.*; à *inf.*); *and so* ~ et ainsi de suite; ~ *and* ~ sans fin; ~ *to* sur, à; *from that day* ~ dès ce jour, à partir de ce jour; be ~ se trouver sur (*qch.*); faire partie de; se passer; être ouvert (*robinet, électricité*); *théâ.* être en scène; *sl.* be a bit ~ être quelque peu pompette (= *ivre*); F *what's* ~? qu'est-ce qui arrive?; *théâ.* qu'est-ce qui se joue?; **3.** *int.* en avant!, allez(-y)!

once [wʌns] **1.** *adv.* une (seule) fois; autrefois; jadis; *at* ~ tout de suite; sur-le-champ; à l'instant; *all at* ~ tout d'un coup, soudain; ~ *again* encore une fois, une fois de plus; ~

for *all* une fois pour toutes; *for* ~ pour une fois; ~ *in a while* (une fois) de temps en temps; *this* ~ cette fois-ci; ~ *more* une fois de plus, encore une fois; *contes etc.:* ~ *upon a time there was* ... il était une fois; **2.** *cj.* (*a.* ~ *that*) dès que; pour peu que.

once-o·ver *Am.* F ['wʌnsouvə]: *give s.o. a* ~ jeter un coup *m* d'œil rapide sur q.

on·com·ing ['ɔnkʌmiŋ] **1.** imminent; qui approche; ~ *traffic* circulation *f* en sens inverse; **2.** arrivée *f*; approche *f*.

one [wʌn] **1.** un(e *f*); unique, seul; seul et même; celui *m* (celle *f*; ceux *m/pl.*); *pron. sujet indéfini :* on; *his* ~ *care* son seul souci; ~ *day* un jour; ~ *of these days* un de ces jours; ~ *Mr. Miller* un certain M. Miller, un nommé M.; *see any*~, *every*~, *no 1*; *give* ~'s *view* donner son avis; *a large dog and a little* ~ un grand chien et un petit; *for* ~ *thing* entre autres raisons, en premier lieu; **2.** un(e *f*) *m*; ~ *o'clock* une heure; *the little* ~s les petit(e)s; ~ *another* l'un(e) l'autre, les un(e)s les autres; *at* ~ d'accord; ~ *by* ~, ~ *after another* un(e) à un(e), l'un(e) après l'autre; *it is all* ~ (*to me*) cela m'est égal; *I for* ~ ... quant à moi, je ...; pour ma part, je ...; '~'**horse** à un cheval; *fig. sl.* insignifiant; '**one·ness** unité *f*; identité *f*; accord *m*; '**one-night stand** *théâ.* soirée unique.

on·er·ous □ ['ɔnərəs] onéreux (-euse *f*); pénible.

one…: ~'**self** soi-même; *réfléchi:* se, *accentué:* soi; *by* ~ tout seul; '~-'**sid·ed** □ inégal (-aux *m/pl.*), injuste; asymétrique (*forme*); '~-'**time** ancien(ne *f*); ~-'**up·man·ship** art *m* de faire mieux que les autres; '~-**way:** ~ *street* (rue *f* à) sens *m* unique; ~ *fare* (prix *m* du) billet *m* simple.

on·fall ['ɔnfɔːl] assaut *m*.

on-go·ings ['ɔngouiŋz] *pl.* F manège *m*.

on·ion ['ʌnjən] oignon *m*.

on·look·er ['ɔnlukə] spectateur (-trice *f*) *m*.

on·ly ['ounli] **1.** *adj.* seul, unique; **2.** *adv.* seulement, ne ... que; rien que; ~ *yesterday* pas plus tard qu'hier; ~ *just* à peine; tout juste; ~ *think!* imaginez un peu!; **3.** *cj.* mais; ~ *that* si ce n'est *ou* était que.

on·rush ['ɔnrʌʃ] ruée *f*.

on·set ['ɔnset], **on·slaught** ['ɔnslɔːt] assaut *m*; attaque *f* (*a. fig.*); *fig. at the onset* de prime abord.

on·shore ['ɔn'ʃɔː] à terre; du large (*vent*).

o·nus ['ounəs] (*pas de pl.*) *fig.* responsabilité *f*, charge *f*.

on·ward ['ɔnwəd] **1.** *adj.* en avant, progressif (-ive *f*); **2.** *adv.* (*a.* **on·wards** ['~z]) en avant; plus loin.

oo·dles F ['uːdlz] *pl.* un tas *m* (de, of).

oof *sl.* [uːf] galette *f* (= *argent*).

oomph *sl.* [uːmf] énergie *f*, allant *m*, entrain *m*.

ooze [uːz] **1.** vase *f*; boue *f*; ⊕ jus(ée *f*) *m*; **2.** suinter; (*a.* ~ *out*) dégoutter; ~ *away* s'écouler, disparaître; *Am. sl.* ~ *out* (se dé)filer.

oo·zy □ ['uːzi] vaseux (-euse *f*); suintant.

o·pac·i·ty [o'pæsiti] opacité *f*; *fig. intelligence:* lourdeur *f*.

o·pal *min.* ['oupəl] opale *f*; **o·pal·es·cent** [~'lesnt] opalescent.

o·paque □ [ou'peik] opaque; *fig.* obtus, peu intelligent.

o·pen ['oupən] **1.** *adj.* □ *usu.* ouvert; plein (*air, campagne, mer*); grand (*air*); débouché (*bouteille*); courant (*compte*); non barré (*chèque*); nu (*feu*); public (-ique *f*) (*jugement*); haut (*mer*); défait (*paquet*); béant (*plaie*); discutable (*question*); déclaré (*rival*); manifeste (*sentiment*); franc(he *f*); doux (douce *f*) (*temps*); découvert (*voiture*); exposé à; ~ *to* accessible à; exposé à; ~ *to conviction* accessible à la conviction; *in the* ~ *air* en plein air, au grand air; ⚔ ~-**cast**, ~-**cut** à ciel ouvert (*exploitation*); *in* ~ *court* court en plein tribunal; *sp.* ~ *race* omnium *m*; *Am.* ~ *shop* atelier *m etc.* qui admet les ouvriers non-syndiqués; ♀ *University* (Centre *m* de) Téléenseignement *m* universitaire; *leave o.s.* ~ *to* s'exposer à; **2.** *su.* *bring into the* ~ exposer au grand jour; **3.** *v/t. usu.* ouvrir; inaugurer; écarter; révéler, exposer; commencer, entamer; ~ *up* ouvrir; *v/i.* s'ouvrir; s'épanouir; s'étendre (*vue*); commencer; ~ *into* donner dans, communiquer avec; ~ *on to* donner sur, ouvrir sur; '~-'**air** en *ou* de plein air; '~-'**end(ed)** sans limite de durée; illimité; ✝ flexible (*offre*); '**o·pen·er**

['oupnə] *personne:* ouvreur (-euse *f*) *m*; **'o·pen'hand·ed** libéral (-aux *m/pl.*); **'o·pen·ing 1.** ouverture *f*; inauguration *f*; commencement *m*, début *m*; trou *m*; éclaircie *f* (*dans les nuages*); *mur,forêt:* percée *f*; clairière *f* (*dans un bois*); **2.** d'ouverture, inaugural (-aux *m/pl.*); *théâ.* ~ *night* première *f*; ~ *time* heure *f* d'ouverture; **'o·pen'mind·ed** *fig.* impartial (-aux *m/pl.*); qui a l'esprit large; **'o·pen'mouthed** bouche *f* bée; **o·pen·ness** ['oupnnis] aspect *m* découvert, situation *f* exposée; *fig.* franchise *f*; **'o·pen-plan** sans cloisons, à aire ouverte (*bureau etc.*); **'o·pen·work 1.** ouvrage *m* ajouré; (a)jours *m/pl.*; **2.** ajouré; à claire-voie.

op·er·a ['ɔpərə] opéra *m.*

op·er·a·ble ['ɔpərəbl] *ℱ* opérable; praticable.

op·er·a...: '~-'danc·er danseur (-euse *f*) *m* d'opéra; ballerine *f*; '~-glass(es *pl.*) jumelle *f*, -s *f/pl.*; '~-hat (chapeau *m*) claque *m*; '~-house opéra *m.*

op·er·ate ['ɔpəreit] *v/t.* opérer, effectuer (*a.* ✝, *ℱ*, ✗); ✝ exploiter; *Am.* actionner; faire manœuvrer (*une machine*); gérer, diriger (*une entreprise*); *v/i. ℱ* opérer (q., on s.o.); *Am.* fonctionner; ✝ faire des opérations, spéculer; entrer en vigueur, jouer; *be operating* fonctionner; **op·er·at·ic** [~'rætik] d'opéra; ~ *singer* chanteur (-euse *f*) *m* dramatique d'opéra; **op·er·at·ing** ['ɔpəreitiŋ] qui opère; *ℱ* opérateur (*chirurgien*); d'exploitation; d'opération; ~ *expenses pl.* dépenses *f/pl.* courantes; ~ *instructions pl.* indications *f/pl.* du mode d'emploi; *ℱ* ~ *room* (*ou theatre, theater*) salle *f* d'opération; **op·er·a·tion** fonctionnement *m*, action *f*; *ℱ*, ✗, ✝ opération *f; be in* ~ fonctionner, jouer; être en vigueur; *come into* ~ entrer en vigueur; **op·er·a·tion·al** d'opération; d'exploitation; **op·er·a·tive** ['~rətiv] **1.** ☐ actif (-ive *f*), opératif (-ive *f*); pratique; *fig.* essentiel(le *f*); *ℱ* opératoire; **2.** ouvrier (-ère *f*) *m*; **op·er·a·tor** ['~reitə] opérateur (-trice *f*) *m* (*a.* ⊕); *ℱ* opérateur *m* (*a. cin., a.* ✝); téléphoniste *mf*; ✝ joueur *m*; ouvrier (-ère *f*) *m*; *Am. mot.* conducteur *m.*

op·er·et·ta [ɔpə'retə] opérette *f.*

oph·thal·mi·a *ℱ* [ɔf'θælmiə] ophtalmie *f*; **oph'thal·mic** ophtalmique; ~ *hospital* hôpital *m* ophtalmologique.

o·pi·ate *pharm.* **1.** ['oupiit] opiat *m*, opiacé *m*, narcotique *m*; **2.** ['~ieit] opiacer (*un médicament*).

o·pine [o'pain] *v/t.* être d'avis (que); *v/i.* opiner; **op·in·ion** [ə'pinjən] opinion *f*, avis *m*; *ℱ* consultation *f*; ~ *poll* sondage *m* (d'opinion); *counsel's* ~ avis *m* motivé; *be of* ~ estimer, être d'avis (que, *that*); *in my* ~ à mon avis; **o'pin·ion·at·ed** [~eitid] opiniâtre; imbu de ses opinions.

o·pi·um *pharm.* ['oupjəm] opium *m*; ~ *addict* opiomane *mf*; ~ *den* fumerie *f* d'opium.

o·pos·sum *surt. Am.* [ə'pɔsəm] opossum *m*; sarigue *f*, *a. m.*

op·po·nent [ə'pounənt] **1.** adversaire *mf*; **2.** opposé; *anat.* opposant.

op·por·tune ☐ ['ɔpətjuːn] opportun, commode; à propos; **'op·por·tun·ism** opportunisme *m*; **'op·por·tun·ist** opportuniste *mf*; **op·por'tu·ni·ty** occasion *f* (favorable) (pour *inf. of gér., to inf.*); facilités *f/pl.* (de, *for*).

op·pose [ə'pouz] opposer (*deux choses*); s'opposer à (*q., qch.*); résister à (*q., qch.*); parler contre (*une proposition*); **op'posed** opposé, contraire, hostile; *be* ~ *to* être le rebours de; aller au contraire de; **op·po·site** ['ɔpəzit] **1.** *adj.* ☐ (*to*) opposé (à); en face (de); vis-à-vis (de); contraire (à); ~ *number* correspondant *m* en grade, F similaire *m*; **2.** *prp.* en face de, vis-à-vis de; **3.** *adv.* en face, vis-à-vis; **4.** *su.* opposé *m*; contre-pied *m*; **op·po·si·tion** opposition *f* (*a. parl., a. astr.*); résistance *f*; camp *m* adverse; ✝ concurrence *f.*

op·press [ə'pres] opprimer; *fig. a.* accabler, oppresser; **op·pres·sion** [ə'preʃn] oppression *f*; *fig.* accablement *m*; ✝ abus *m* d'autorité; **op'pres·sive** ☐ [~siv] oppressif (-ive *f*), tyrannique; *fig.* lourd (*temps*); **op'pres·sive·ness** caractère *m* oppressif; *fig. temps:* lourdeur *f*; **op'pres·sor** oppresseur *m.*

op·pro·bri·ous ☐ [ə'proubriəs] outrageant, injurieux (-euse *f*); **op'pro·bri·um** [~briəm] opprobre *m.*

opt [ɔpt] opter (pour, *for*; entre, *between*).

op·tic ['ɔptik] optique, de l'œil; de vision; (*ou* **'op·ti·cal** □) optique; **op·ti·cian** [ɔp'tiʃn] opticien *m*; **'op·tics** *sg.* optique *f*.

op·ti·mism ['ɔptimizm] optimisme *m*; **'op·ti·mist** optimiste *mf*; **op·ti·mis·tic** (ˌally) optimiste; ˌally avec optimisme; **op·ti·mize** ['ˌmaiz] optimiser.

op·tion ['ɔpʃn] choix *m*, option *f*; faculté *f*; ✝ (marché *m* à) prime *f*; ∼ right option *f*; **'op·tion·al** □ facultatif (-ive *f*).

op·u·lence ['ɔpjuləns] opulence *f*, richesse *f*; **'op·u·lent** □ opulent, très riche.

o·pus ['oupəs] opus *m*; *magnum* ∼ œuvre *f* maîtresse.

or [ɔː] ou; *either* ... ∼ ou ... ou; *soit* ... soit; ∼ *else* ou bien; sinon.

or·a·cle ['ɔrəkl] oracle *m*; F *work the* ∼ arriver à ses fins; faire agir certaines influences; **o·rac·u·lar** [ɔ'rækjulə] (in style) d'oracle; *fig.* équivoque, obscur.

o·ral □ ['ɔːrəl] oral (-aux *m/pl.*); buccal (-aux *m/pl.*).

or·ange ['ɔrindʒ] **1.** orange *f*; *arbre:* oranger *m*; *couleur:* orange *m*; orangé *m*; **2.** orangé; orange *adj./inv.*; **or·ange·ade** ['ˌeid] orangeade *f*; **or·ange·ry** ['ˌəri] orangerie *f*.

o·rate *co.* [ɔː'reit] pérorer; **o·ra·tion** allocution *f*, discours *m*; *co.*, *péj.* harangue *f*; **or·a·tor** ['ɔrətə] orateur *m*; **or·a·tor·i·cal** □ [ɔrə'tɔrikl] oratoire; ampoulé (*discours*); phraseur (-euse *f*) (*personne*); **or·a·to·ri·o** ♪ [ˌ'tɔːriou] oratorio *m*; **or·a·to·ry** ['ɔrətəri] éloquence *f*; art *m* oratoire.

orb [ɔːb] orbe *m*; globe *m*; *poét.* astre *m*; **orbed** [ɔːbd; *usu. poét.* 'ɔːbid] rond, sphérique; **or·bic·u·lar** □ [ɔː'bikjulə], **or'bic·u·late** [ˌlit] orbiculaire, sphérique; **or·bit** ['ɔːbit] *anat.*, *a. astr.* orbite *f*; *put* (*go*) *into* ∼ (se) placer sur son orbite.

or·chard ['ɔːtʃəd] verger *m*; **'or·chard·ing** fructiculture *f*; *Am.* terrains *m/pl.* aménagés en vergers.

or·ches·tra ♪ ['ɔːkistrə] orchestre *m*; ∼ *fosse* théâ. fosse *f* d'orchestre; **or·ches·tral** [ɔː'kestrl] orchestral (-aux *m/pl.*); **or·ches·trate** ♪ ['ɔːkistreit] orchestrer, instrumenter.

or·chid ⚘ ['ɔːkid] orchidée *f*.

or·dain [ɔː'dein] ordonner (*a. un diacre*); conférer les ordres à (*un prêtre*); fixer, destiner; prescrire.

or·deal [ɔː'diːl] épreuve *f*; *hist.* jugement *m* de Dieu, ordalie *f*.

or·der ['ɔːdə] **1.** ordre *m* (*a. moines, chevalerie, fig.,* ✝, ▲, ✕ [*de bataille*], ⚓ [*tactique*]); ✝ commande *f*; ordonnance *f* (*de paiement*); *parl.* rappel *m* à l'ordre; *admin.* arrêt(é) *m*; ✕, ⚓ consigne *f*; *poste:* mandat *m*; ⊕ état *m* de fonctionnement; instruction *f*; suite *f*, succession *f*; classe *f* (*sociale*); ✝ ∼ *blank* (*ou form*) billet *m* de commande; ✝ ∼ *book* carnet *m* de commandes; *by* ∼ par ordre; ∼ *of the day* ordre *m* du jour (*a. fig.*); *take* (*holy*) ∼s prendre les ordres; *in* ∼ dans les règles; *put in* ∼ mettre en règle; *in* ∼ *to* (*inf.*) pour (*inf.*), afin de (*inf.*); *in* ∼ *that* pour que (*sbj.*), afin que (*sbj.*); *a. see in* ∼ *to; on the* ∼s *of* sur les ordres de; ✝ *be on* ∼ être commandé; *make to* ∼ faire sur commande; faire sur mesure (*un habit*); *parl. rise to* ∼ se lever pour demander le rappel à l'ordre; *parl. standing* ∼s *pl.* ordres *m/pl.* permanents; ✝, *pol.* règlement *m*, -s *m/pl.*; *to* (*the*) ∼ *of* ✝ à l'ordre de (*q.*); **2.** (ar)ranger; ordonner; régler; ✗ prescrire; ✝ commander; ✕ ∼ *arms!* reposez armes!; ∼ *about* faire marcher (*q.*); ∼ *s.o. down* (*up*) ordonner à q. de descendre (monter); **'or·der·er** ordonnateur (-trice *f*) *m*; **'or·der·li·ness** bon ordre *m*; discipline *f*; bonne conduite *f*; **'or·der·ly 1.** méthodique; réglé (*vie etc.*); discipliné (*foule etc.*); ✕ ∼ *officer* officier *m* de service *ou* de semaine; ∼ *room* salle *f* de rapport; **2.** ✕ planton *m*; (*medical*) ∼ infirmier *m*.

or·di·nal ['ɔːdinl] ordinal (-aux *m/pl.*) (*a. su./m*).

or·di·nance ['ɔːdinəns] ordonnance *f*, décret *m*, règlement *m*; *eccl.* rite *m*.

or·di·nar·y ['ɔːdnri] **1.** □ ordinaire; coutumier (-ère *f*); *péj.* quelconque; ✝ ∼ *debts pl.* dettes *f/pl.* compte; ⚓ ∼ *seaman* matelot *m* de troisième classe; *see share 1*; **2.** *eccl.* ordinaire *m*; table *f* d'hôte; *Am.* auberge *f*; commun *m*; *in* ∼ ordinaire; ⚓ en réserve (*navire*).

or·di·nate ⊿ ['ɔːdnit] ordonnée *f*.

or·di·na·tion [ɔːdiˈneiʃn] *eccl.* ordination *f*; arrangement *m*.

ord·nance ✕, ⚓ [ˈɔːdnəns] artillerie *f*; ✕ service *m* du matériel; ~ *map* carte *f* d'état-major; ~ *survey* service *m* cartographique.

or·dure [ˈɔːdjuə] ordure *f*; immondic· *f*.

or·e [ɔː] minerai *m*; *poét.* métal *m*.

or·gan [ˈɔːgən] ♪ orgue *m* (*f*/*pl.* -s); organe *m* (*ouïe, vue, etc., admin., a.* = *journal*); bulletin *m*, porte-parole *m*/*inv.*; '~**grind·er** joueur *m* d'orgue de Barbarie; **or·gan·ic** [ɔːˈgænik] (~*ally*) organique; organisé (*êtres, croissance*); **or·gan·ism** [ˈɔːgənizm] organisme *m*; '**or·gan·ist** organiste *mf*; **or·gan·i·za·tion** [~naiˈzeiʃn] organisation *f*; *pol.* organisme *m*; œuvre *f* (*de charité*); '**or·gan·ize** organiser; arranger; ~d constitué; *biol., pol.* organisé; '**or·gan·iz·er** organisateur (-trice *f*) *m*.

or·gasm [ˈɔːgæzəm] orgasme *m*.

or·gy [ˈɔːdʒi] orgie *f* (*a. fig.*); *fig.* profusion *f*.

o·ri·el △ [ˈɔːriəl] fenêtre *f* en saillie.

o·ri·ent 1. [ˈɔːriənt] oriental (-aux *m*/*pl.*); de l'orient; **2.** orient *m* (*a.* = *éclat d'une perle*); *Am.* Asie *f*; **3.** [ˈ~ent] orienter; **o·ri·en·tal** [~ˈentl] **1.** □ oriental (-aux *m*/*pl.*); d'Orient; **2.** Oriental(e *f*) *m*; indigène *mf* de l'Orient; **o·ri·en·tate** [ˈɔːrienteit] orienter; **o·ri·en·ta·tion** orientation *f*.   [ture *f*.]

or·i·fice [ˈɔrifis] orifice *m*, ouver-]

or·i·gin [ˈɔridʒin] origine *f*, génèse *f*; provenance *f*.

o·rig·i·nal [əˈridʒənl] **1.** □ originaire; premier (-ère *f*); original (-aux *m*/*pl.*) (*livre, style, idée, etc.*); inédit; *see share*; ~ *capital* capital *m* d'apport; ~ *sin* péché *m* original; **2.** original *m*; *personne*: original(e *f*) *m*; **o·rig·i·nal·i·ty** [~ˈnæliti] originalité *f*.

o·rig·i·nate [əˈridʒineit] *v/t.* faire naître, donner naissance à, être l'auteur de; *v/i.* (*from, in*) tirer son origine, dériver (de); avoir son origine (dans); **o·rig·i'na·tion** source *f*, origine *f*; naissance *f*; invention *f*; création *f*; **o'rig·i·na·tive** □ créateur (-trice *f*); **o'rig·i·na·tor** auteur *m*; initiateur (-trice *f*) *m*.

o·ri·ole *orn.* [ˈɔːrioul] loriot *m*.

or·mo·lu [ˈɔːmolu:] or *m* moulu; similor *m*.

or·na·ment 1. [ˈɔːnəmənt] ornement *m* (*a. fig.*); parure *f*; **2.** [ˈ~ment] orner, parer; agrémenter (*une robe*); **or·na'men·tal** ornemental (-aux *m*/*pl.*); d'ornement; d'agrément.

or·nate □ [ɔːˈneit] orné; *fig.* fleuri.

or·ni·tho·log·i·cal □ [ɔːniθəˈlɔdʒikl] ornithologique; **or·ni·thol·o·gist** [~ˈθɔlədʒist] ornithologue *mf*, -logiste *mf*; **or·ni'thol·o·gy** ornithologie *f*.

o·rog·ra·phy [ɔˈrɔgrəfi] orographie *f*.

o·ro·tund [ˈɔrotʌnd] sonore.

or·phan [ˈɔːfən] **1.** orphelin(e *f*) *m*; **2.** (*a.* '**or·phaned**) orphelin(e *f*); **or·phan·age** [ˈ~idʒ], '**or·phan·a'sy·lum** orphelinat *m*.

or·rer·y [ˈɔrəri] planétaire *m*.

or·tho·dox □ [ˈɔːθədɔks] orthodoxe; *fig.* classique; bien pensant (*personne*); '**or·tho·dox·y** orthodoxie *f*.

or·tho·graph·ic, or·tho·graph·i·cal □ [ɔːθəˈgræfik(l)] orthographique, d'orthographie; **or·thog·ra·phy** [ɔːˈθɔgrəfi] orthographe *f*; Å coupe *f* perpendiculaire.

or·tho·pae·dic [ɔːθoˈpiːdik] (~*ally*) orthopédique; **or·tho'pae·dist** orthopédiste *mf*; '**or·tho·pae·dy** orthopédie *f*.

Os·car [ˈɔskə] *surt. cin. Am.* oscar *m*; *p.ext.* récompense *f*.

os·cil·late [ˈɔsileit] osciller (*a. fig.*); *fig.* hésiter, balancer; *mot.* oscillating *axle* essieu *m* orientable; **os·cil'la·tion** oscillation *f*; **os·cil·la·to·ry** [ˈ~lətəri] oscillatoire; **os·cil·lo·graph** [ɔˈsilougrɑːf] oscillographe *m*.

os·cu·late *co.* [ˈɔskjuleit] s'embrasser.

o·sier ♀ [ˈouʒjə] osier *m*.

os·prey [ˈɔspri] *orn.* orfraie *f*; ✝ aigrette *f*.

os·se·ous [ˈɔsiəs] osseux (-euse *f*); **os·si·fi·ca·tion** [ɔsifiˈkeiʃn] ossification *f*; **os·si·fy** [ˈ~fai] (s')ossifier; **os·su·ar·y** [ˈɔsjuəri] ossuaire *m*.

os·ten·si·ble □ [ɔsˈtensəbl] prétendu.

os·ten·ta·tion [ɔstenˈteiʃn] ostentation *f*; faste *m*; parade *f*; **os·ten-**

'ta·tious □ fastueux (-euse *f*); plein d'ostentation.

os·te·ol·o·gy *anat.* [ɔsti'ɔlǝdʒi] ostéologie *f*.

ost·ler ['ɔslǝ] valet *m* d'écurie.

os·tra·cism ['ɔstrǝsizm] ostracisme *m*; **os·tra·cize** ['ˌsaiz] bannir; ostraciser (*a. fig.*).

os·trich *orn.* ['ɔstritʃ] autruche *f*.

oth·er ['ʌðǝ] autre (*than, from que*); *the* ~ *day* l'autre jour, récemment; *the* ~ *morning* l'autre matin; *every* ~ *day* tous les deux jours; *each* ~ l'un(e) l'autre, les un(e)s les autres; *somebody or* ~ je ne sais qui; *péj.* quelque individu; '~·**wise** autrement.

o·ti·ose □ ['ouʃious] superflu; oiseux (-euse *f*); **o·ti·os·i·ty** [ouʃi'ɔsiti] superfluité *f*.

ot·ter *zo.* ['ɔtǝ] loutre *f* (*a. peau*).

Ot·to·man ['ɔtǝmǝn] **1.** ottoman, turc (turque *f*); **2.** Ottoman(e *f m*); ♀ divan *m*, ottomane *f*.

ought[1] [ɔːt] *see* aught.

ought[2] [ɔːt] *v/aux.* (*défectif*): I ~ *to* (*inf.*) je dois *ou* devrais (*inf.*); *you* ~ *to have done it* vous auriez dû le faire.

ounce[1] [auns] once *f* (*28,35 g*); *by the* ~ à l'once; au poids.

ounce[2] *zo.* [~] once *f*; léopard *m* des neiges.

our ['auǝ] notre, nos; **ours** ['auǝz] le (la) nôtre, les nôtres; à nous; *a* ... *of* ~ un(e) de nos ...; **our·self** nous-même; *réfléchi*: nous (*a. accentué*); **our·selves** nous-mêmes; *réfléchi*: nous (*a. accentué*).

oust [aust] évincer; supplanter; déloger (*d'un poste*).

out [aut] **1.** *adv.* (au, en) dehors; au clair, découvert; sorti; éteint; au bout, à la fin; *be* ~ être sorti; sortir; se tromper; être bas(se *f*) (*marée*); être démodé (*vêtement*); faire la grève, être en grève (*ouvrier*); être épanoui *ou* en fleur; être paru (*livre*); être éventé (*secret*); avoir fait son entrée dans le monde (*jeune fille*); être luxé (*épaule etc.*); être sur pied (*troupes*); être achevé *ou* à bout (*patience, mois, etc.*); *pol.* n'être plus au pouvoir; être connu *ou* publié (*nouvelle etc.*); *sp.* être hors jeu *ou* éliminé *ou* knock-out; avoir perdu connaissance; *sl.* be ~ *for s.th.* être à la recherche de qch.;

be ~ *to* (*inf.*) avoir entrepris de (*inf.*); avoir pour but de (*inf.*); *be* ~ *with* être fâché avec; *hear s.th.* ~ entendre qch. jusqu'au bout; ~ *and* ~ complètement; ~-*and*-~ achevé, convaincu; ~ *and about* (de nouveau) sur pied; levé; ~ *and away* de beaucoup; *see* elbow; *come* ~ *théâ.* débuter; débuter, faire son entrée dans le monde (*jeune fille*); *have it* ~ *with* vider une querelle avec (*q.*), s'expliquer avec (*q.*); *voyage* ~ aller *m*; *way* ~ sortie *f*; *her Sunday* ~ son dimanche de sortie; *upon him!* fi de lui!; ~ *with him!* à la porte!; **2.** *su. typ.* bourdon *m*; *Am.* F excuse *f*; *parl.* the ~*s pl.* l'opposition *f*; **3.** *adj.* aller (*match*); exceptionel(le *f*) (*taille*); hors série; **4.** *prp.* ~ *of* hors de, au *ou* en dehors de; par (*la fenêtre*); *choix:* parmi, d'entre; démuni de; *drink* ~ *of* boire dans (*un verre*), à (*la bouteille*); *3* ~ *of 10* 3 sur 10; ~ *of respect* par respect; *see* date[2] 1; *laugh* 2; *money;* *box.* ~ mettre knock-out.

out...: ~-*and*-'**out·er** *sl.* outrancier (-ère *f*) *m*; intransigeant(e *f*) *m*; chef-d'œuvre *m* (*pl.* chefs-d'œuvre) *m*; ~'**bal·ance** l'emporter sur; ~'**bid** [*irr.* (bid)] renchérir sur; '~·**board** hors bord; extérieur; ~'**brave** braver; surpasser (*q.*) en bravoure; '~·**break** éruption *f*; début *m*; '~·**build·ing** bâtiment *m* extérieur; '~·**burst** explosion *f*, éruption *f*; '~·**cast** expulsé(e *f*) (*a. su.*); *fig.* réprouvé(e *f*) (*a. su.*); ~'**class** *sp.* surclasser; ~'**col·lege** externe (*étudiant[e]*); '~·**come** issue *f*, conséquence *f*; '~·**crop** ⚒, *géol.* affleurement *m*; *fig.* épidémie *f*; '~·**cry** cri *m*; clameur *f*; ~'**dat·ed** vieilli, démodé; '~·**dis·tance** dépasser, distancer; ~'**do** [*irr.* (do)] surpasser; '~·**door** *adj.*, '~·**doors** *adv.* au dehors; en plein air; au grand air.

out·er ['autǝ] extérieur; externe; '~·**most** le plus en dehors; extrême.

out...: ~'**face** dévisager (*q.*); faire baisser les yeux à (*q.*); '~·**fall** *égout:* déversoir *m*; *rivière:* embouchure *f*; '~·**fit** équipement *m*; trousse *f*; ⚓ armement *m*; *habits:* trousseau *m*; *Am.* équipe *f* d'ouvriers; ✕ compagnie *f*, bataillon *m*; '~·**fit·ter** fournisseur (-euse *f*) *m*; marchand *m* de confections; ~'**flank** ✕ déborder; '~**flow** *gaz, eau, etc.*: dépense *f*; *égout*: décharge *f*; ~'**go 1.** [*irr.* (go)] surpasser; dépasser; **2.** ['~] dépenses *f/pl.*; '~**go·ing 1.** sortant; **2.** sortie *f*; dépenses *f/pl.*; ~'**grow** [*irr.* (grow)] devenir plus grand que (*q.*); devenir trop grand pour (*qch.*); *fig.* se défaire de; '~**growth** excroissance *f*; conséquence *f* naturelle; ~'**house** dépendance *f*; appentis *m*; *Am.* water *m* extérieur.

out·ing ['autin] promenade *f*; partie *f* de plaisir; excursion *f*, sortie *f*.

out...: ~'**land·ish** baroque, bizarre; barbare (*langue*); retiré (*endroit*); ~'**last** survivre à; ~'**law 1.** hors-la-loi *m/inv.*; proscrit(e *f*) *m*); **2.** proscrire; '~**law·ry** proscription *f*; '~**lay** dépenses *f/pl.*; frais *m/pl.*; ~'**let** sortie *f*, départ *m*; issue *f*; *tuyau*, *a.* ✝ débouché *m*; *fig.* issue *f*, déversoir *m*; '~**line 1.** silhouette *f*; profil *m*; tracé *m*; *roman*, *pièce de théâ.*: canevas *m*; **2.** silhouetter; ébaucher; esquisser; ~d dessiné, profilé (sur, *against*); ~'**live** survivre à; ~'**look** guet *m*; vue *f*; perspective *f* (*a. fig.*); *pol.* horizon *m*; '~**ly·ing** éloigné, écarté; ⚓ qui déborde (*appareil*); ~**ma'nœu·vre** l'emporter sur (*q.*) en tactique; F déjouer; ~'**march** devancer; ~'**mod·ed** démodé; '~**most** le plus en dehors; extrême; ~'**num·ber** surpasser en nombre; '~**of-door**(s) *see* outdoor(s); ~'**of-the-'way** écarté (*lieu*); *fig.* insolite; '~**of-'work pay** indemnité *f* de chômage; ~'**pace** distancer; gagner de vitesse; '~**pa·tient** malade *mf* qui va consulter à la clinique; '~**post** poste *m* avancé; '~**pour·ing** épanchement *m* (*a. fig.*); '~**put** rendement *m*; *mine*: production *f*; ⊕ débit *m*; *ordinateur*: sortie *f*.

out·rage ['autreidᴣ] **1.** atteinte *f*; outrage *m* (à on, *against*); attentat *m* (à, on); *fig.* indignité *f*; **2.** outrager, faire outrage à; violenter (*une femme*); *fig.* aller à l'encontre de; **out'ra·geous** □ immodéré; outrageux (-euse *f*); atroce.

out...: ~'**reach** tendre la main plus loin que; *fig.* prendre de l'avance sur; '~**re·lief** secours *m/pl.* à domi-

cile; ~'**ride** [*irr.* (ride)] dépasser *ou* devancer à cheval; ⚓ étaler (*une tempête*); F avant-coureur *m*; '~**rig·ger** ⚓ *prao*: balancier *m*; outrigger *m*; espar *m* en saillie; ~'**right 1.** *adj.* ['autrait] à forfait; franc(he *f*); **2.** *adv.* [aut'rait] complètement; à forfait; sur le coup; carrément; ~'**ri·val** surpasser; l'emporter sur (*q.*); ~'**run** [*irr.* (run)] dépasser (*le but etc.*); distancer (*un concurrent*); *fig.* l'emporter sur; '~**run·ner** *see* outrider; ~'**sail** ⚓ dépasser (*un navire*); ~'**set** commencement *m*, début *m*; ~'**shine** [*irr.* (shine)] éclipser; surpasser en éclat; '~**side 1.** *su.* extérieur *m*, dehors *m*; *autobus*: impériale *f*; *fig.* maximum *m*; *at the* ~ tout au plus; **2.** *adj.* extérieur; du dehors; de l'impériale (*d'un autobus*); du bout (*d'une place ou chaise*); maximum (*prix*); *foot.*: ~ *right* (*left*) ailier *m* droit (gauche); **3.** *adv.* (en) dehors; à l'extérieur; **4.** *prp.* en dehors de; à l'extérieur de; hors de; '~**sid·er** F étranger (-ère *f*) *m*; profane (*personne*); ~'**sit** [*irr.* (sit)] rester plus longtemps que; '~**size** ✝ taille *f* exceptionnelle; ~'**skirts** *pl. ville*: faubourgs *m/pl.*, banlieue *f*; *forêt*: lisière *f*; abords *m/pl.*; ~'**smart** *Am.* F surpasser en finesse; déjouer; ~'**spo·ken** □ carré; franc(he *f*); ~'**stand·ing** saillant; marquant, *fig.* éminent; en suspens (*affaire*); ✝ dû (due *f*); échu (*intérêt*); ~'**stay** rester plus longtemps que; ~ *one's welcome* lasser l'amabilité de ses hôtes; ~'**step** *fig.* outrepasser; ~'**stretch** étendre, déployer; ~'**strip** dépasser, gagner de vitesse; *fig.* surpasser; '~**turn** rendement *m* net; ~'**val·ue** surpasser en valeur; '~**vote** obtenir une majorité sur; mettre (*q.*) en minorité; ~'**vot·er** électeur (-trice *f*) *m* qui ne réside pas dans la circonscription.

out·ward ['autwəd] **1.** *adj.* en dehors; extérieur, de dehors; d'aller (*billet*); ⚓ pour l'étranger; **2.** *adv.* (*usu.* **out·wards** ['~dz]) au dehors; vers l'extérieur; '**out·ward·ness** extériorité *f*; *fig.* objectivité *f*.

out...: ~'**wear** [*irr.* (wear)] user complètement; durer plus longtemps que; se défaire de (*une habitude etc.*); '~**weigh** dépasser en poids; *fig.* l'emporter sur; ~'**wit** déjouer les menées de; '~**work** ⚔ ouvrage *m* avancé; ⊕ travail (*pl. -aux*) *m* fait à domicile; '~**work·er** ouvrier (-ère *f*) *m* à domicile.

ou·zel *orn.* ['u:zl] merle *m*.

o·val ['ouvl] **1.** (en) ovale; **2.** ovale *m*.

o·va·ry ['ouvəri] *anat.*, *a.* ♀ ovaire *m*.

o·va·tion [ou'veiʃn] ovation *f*.

ov·en ['ʌvn] four *m*; ⊕ étuve *f*; ~ *cloth* poignée *f*; '~**proof** allant au four; '~**read·y** prêt à rôtir.

o·ver ['ouvə] **1.** *adv.* par-dessus (*qch.*); en plus; fini, achevé; à la renverse; *avec adj. ou adv.*: trop; *avec verbe*: sur-, trop; *avec su.*: excès *m* de; ~ *and above* en outre; (*all*) ~ *again* d'un bout à l'autre; de nouveau; ~ *against* vis-à-vis de; *all* ~ partout; ~ *and* ~ (*again*) maintes et maintes fois; à plusieurs reprises; *fifty times* ~ cinquante fois de suite; *F get it* ~ (*and done*) *with* venir à bout de qch.; en finir avec qch.; *make* ~ transférer; *Am.* refaçonner; *read* ~ lire (*qch.*) en entier; parcourir; **2.** *prp.* sur, (par-)dessus; au-dessus de; au-delà de; *all* ~ *the town* partout dans la ville, dans toute la ville; ~ *night* pendant la nuit; ~ *a glass of wine* en prenant un verre de vin; ~ *the way* en face.

over...: '~**act** exagérer; '~**all** tablier *m* blouse; *école*: blouse *f*; sarrau (*pl. -s, -x*) *m*; ~**s** *pl.* salopette *f* (*a. d'enfant*); F bleus *m/pl.*; '~**arch** former un arc au-dessus de (*qch.*); ~'**awe** intimider; ~'**bal·ance 1.** excédent *m*; **2.** (se) renverser; *v/t.* peser plus que; *v/i.* perdre l'équilibre (*personne*); ~'**bear** [*irr.* (*bear*)] l'emporter sur; ~'**bear·ing** ☐ arrogant; ~'**bid** [*irr.* (*bid*)] enchérir sur; '~**blown** trop épanoui; '~**board** ⚓ par-dessus bord; à la mer (*homme*); '~**brim** déborder; '~**build** [*irr.* (*build*)] trop construire dans (*une localité*); ~'**bur·den** surcharger (*de, with*); '~**cast 1.** [*irr.* (*cast*)] obscurcir; ~ *a seam* faire un surjet; **2.** obscurci, couvert; ~ *seam* surjet *m*; ~**charge 1.** ['ouvə'tʃɑ:dʒ] surcharger; survendre (*des marchandises*); faire payer (*qch.*) trop cher à (*q.*);

2. ['ouvətʃɑ:dʒ] surcharge *f*; prix *m* surfait; ~'**cloud** (se) couvrir de nuages; (s')assombrir; '~**coat** pardessus *m*; ~'**come** [*irr.* (*come*)] vaincre; maîtriser; '~**con·fi·dent** ☐ trop confiant; suffisant; ~'**crowd** trop remplir; ~'**do** [*irr.* (*do*)] outrer; charger (*un rôle*); *fig.* exagérer; *cuis.* trop cuire; ~**done** [ouvə'dʌn] outré, excessif (-ive *f*); F éreinté; exagéré; ['ouvə'dʌn] trop cuit; ~**dose** dose *f* trop forte *ou* excessive; '~**draft** découvert *m*; ~'**draw** [*irr.* (*draw*)] charger, exagérer; ♣ mettre à découvert; ~'**dress** faire trop de toilette; (s')habiller avec trop de recherche; '~**drink** [*irr.* (*drink*)]: ~ *o.s.* se soûler; '~**drive** *mot.* surmultiplication *f*; ~'**due** en retard (*a.* ⛟); ♣ arriéré, échu; '~**eat** [*irr.* (*eat*)]: ~ *o.s.* trop manger; '~**es·ti·mate** surestimer; '~**ex·pose** *phot.* surexposer; '~**ex·po·sure** *phot.* surexposition *f*; '~**fa·tigue 1.** surmener; **2.** surmenage *m*; '~**feed** [*irr.* (*feed*)] *v/t.* suralimenter; *v/i.* trop manger; ~'**flow 1.** [ouvə'flou] [*irr.* (*flow*)] *v/t.* déborder de; inonder; *v/i.* déborder; **2.** ['ouvəflou] débordement *m*; inondation *f*; trop-plein *m*; '~**freight** surcharge *f*; ~'**ground** (qui voyage) par voie de terre; ~'**grow** [*irr.* (*grow*)] (re)couvrir; envahir; '~**growth** surcroissance *f*; couverture *f* (*de ronces etc.*); ~**hang 1.** ['ouvə'hæn] [*irr.* (*hang*)] surplomber; faire saillie (au-dessus de qch., *s.th.*); **2.** ['ouvəhæn] saillie *f*; ~'**haul** examiner en détail; réparer; ~**head 1.** [ouvə'hed] *adv.* en haut; *works* ~! attention, travaux (en haut)!; **2.** ['ouvəhed] *adj.* ♣ général (-aux *m/pl.*) (*frais, dépenses, etc.*); ~ *railway* ⊕ pont *m* roulant; ⛟ chemin *m* de fer aérien; ⊕~ *wire* câble *m* aérien; **3.** *su.* ♣ ~**s** *pl.* frais *m/pl.* généraux; '~**hear** [*irr.* (*hear*)] surprendre (*q.*, *une conversation*); '~**heat** ⊕ surchauffer; ~ *o.s.* s'échauffer; '~**house** *radio*: d'extérieur (*antenne*); '~**in·dulge** montrer trop d'indulgence envers (*q.*), gâter (*q.*); céder trop facilement à (*un vice*); ~ *in* faire abus de (*qch.*); '~**in·dul·gence** indulgence *f* excessive; '~**is·sue** faire une surémission de (*billets de banque*); ~'**joy** ravir; *be* ~**ed** *a.* être aux anges, être au

comble (de la joie); '~·**kill** ✕ (capacité *f* de) surextermination *f*; ~'**land**
1. ['ouvəlænd] *adj.* qui voyage par
voie de terre; **2.** [ouvə'lænd] *adv.* par
voie de terre; ~'**lap** *v/t.* recouvrir
(partiellement); dépasser; faire double emploi avec; *v/i.* (se) chevaucher; ~'**lay 1.** [ouvə'lei] [*irr. (lay)*]
(re)couvrir (de, *with*); ⊕ mettre des
hausses sur; **2.** ['ouvəlei]: ~ *mattress*
matelas *m*; couvre-lit *m*; '~'**leaf** au
verso; ~'**load 1.** ['ouvəloud] surcharge *f*; **2.** [ouvə'loud] surcharger;
~'**look** avoir vue sur; dominer; surveiller (*un travail*); *fig.* oublier; négliger; fermer les yeux sur; laisser
passer; '~·**lord** suzerain *m*.

o·ver·ly ['ouvəli] trop, excessivement, à l'excès.

o·ver...: ~'**manned** ayant trop de
personnel; '~·**man·tel** étagère *f* de
cheminée; ~'**mas·ter** subjuguer;
'~'**much** (par) trop; '~'**night 1.**
(pendant) la nuit; jusqu'au lendemain; du jour au lendemain; **2.**
d'une nuit; de nuit; *fig.* soudain; ~
bag sac *m* de voyage; ~ *stay* séjour *m*
d'une nuit; ~ *stop* arrêt *m* pour la
nuit; '~'**pay** [*irr. (pay)*] trop payer;
surpayer; ~'**peo·pled** surpeuplé;
'~'**play** exagérer; *fig.* ~ *one's hand*
essayer de faire qch. au-dessus de ses
moyens; '~·**plus** surplus *m*;
~'**pow·er** maîtriser; *fig.* accabler;
'~·**pres·sure** surpression *f*; surmenage *m* (*de l'esprit*); '~'**print** *phot.*
trop pousser; '~'**rate** surestimer;
~'**reach** dépasser; ~ *o.s.* être victime
de sa propre fourberie; ~'**re'act**
réagir excessivement *ou* trop vivement (à, *to*); ~'**ride** [*irr. (ride)*] outrepasser (*un ordre*); fouler aux pieds
(*des droits*); surmener (*un cheval*);
avoir plus d'importance que; ~'**rid·ing** primordial (-aux *m/pl.*); ~'**rule**
décider contre; ⚖ annuler; rejeter;
~'**run** [*irr. (run)*] envahir; dépasser
(*les bornes*); surmener (*une machine*);
typ. reporter à la ligne ou page
suivante; '~·**seas** d'outre-mer; à l'étranger; *adj. a.* étranger (-ère *f*); ~
aid aide *f* aux pays étrangers; ~ *trade*
commerce *m* extérieur; '~'**see** [*irr.
(see)*] surveiller; '~·**se·er** surveillant(e *f*) *m*; ⊕ chef *m* d'atelier; ~ *of
the poor* directeur *m* du Bureau de
bienfaisance; ~'**set** [*irr.* (set)] *v/t.*
renverser; *fig.* bouleverser; *v/i.* se

renverser; ~·**sew** [*irr. (sew)*] surjeter; ~'**shad·ow** ombrager; éclipser
(*q.*); ~'**shoe** galoche *f*; '~'**shoot** [*irr.
(shoot)*] dépasser; dépeupler (*une
chasse*); ~ *o.s.* aller trop loin; '~'**shot** à
augets (*roue*); ~'**sight** oubli *m*; surveillance *f*; '~·**sim·pli·fi·ca·tion**
simplisme *m*; '~'**sleep** [*irr. (sleep)*]
(*a.* ~ *o.s.*) dormir trop longtemps;
'~·**sleeve** fausse manche *f*; '~·**spill**
excédent *m* (*surt.* de la population);
~'**spread** [*irr. (spread)*] couvrir (de,
with); inonder (*qch.*); s'étendre sur;
~'**staffed** avec trop de personnel;
'~·**state** exagérer; '~'**step** outrepasser; '~'**stock** constituer un cheptel
trop important pour (*une ferme*); ✝
encombrer (*le marché*); ~·**strain 1.**
['ouvə'strein] surtendre; *fig.* surmener; **2.** [ouvə'strein] tension *f* excessive; *fig.* surmenage *m*; ~·**strung**
['ouvə'strʌŋ] surexcité; ['ouvəstrʌŋ]
oblique (*piano*); ~'**sub'scribe** ✝
surpasser (*une émission*); '~·**sup'ply**
provision *f* excessive; excès *m*.

o·vert ['ouvəːt] patent, évident.

over...: ~'**take** [*irr. (take)*] dépasser
(*qch.*); doubler (*une auto*); rattraper
(*q.*); *fig.* arriver à, surprendre;
'~·**tax** pressurer (*le peuple*); *fig.* trop
exiger de (*q.*); surmener; ~·**throw**
1. [ouvə'θrou] [*irr. (throw)*] renverser (*a. fig.*); vaincre; **2.** ['ouvəθrou]
renversement *m*; défaite *f* (*a. fig.*,
a. ✕); '~·**time** heures *f/pl.* supplémentaires; '~'**tire** surmener;
'~·**tone** ♪ harmonique *m*; *fig.* sousentendu *m*, note *f*, nuance *f*, accent
m; '~'**top** dépasser en hauteur;
~'**train** (s')épuiser par un entraînement trop sévère; '~·**trump** surcouper.

o·ver·ture ['ouvətjuə] ouverture *f*
(*a.* ♪); offre *f*.

over...: ~'**turn 1.** ['ouvətəːn] renversement *m*; **2.** [ouvə'təːn] (se)
renverser; *mot.* (faire) capoter; ⚓
(faire) chavirer; '~·**val·ue** faire trop
de cas de; ✝ surestimer; ~·**ween·ing**
outrecuidant; ~·**weight 1.** ['ouvəweit] *poids, bagages, etc.*: excédent
m; **2.** [ouvə'weit] surcharger (de,
with); ~'**whelm** accabler (*a. fig.*);
submerger; combler; ~·**whelm·ing**
□ accablant; écrasant; '~·**wise** □
prétentieux (-euse *f*); ~·**work
1.** ['ouvəwəːk] travail (*pl.* -aux) *m*
en plus; ['ouvə'wəːk] *fig.* surmenage

m; **2.** [~] [*irr.* (work)] (se) surmener; '~-
'~**wrought** surmené; excédé de
fatigue *etc.*; surexcité.

o·vi·form ['ouvifɔːm] ovoïde, ovi-
forme; **o·vip·a·rous** *biol.* [ou'vipə-
rəs] ovipare.

owe [ou] devoir (*de l'argent, de l'o-
béissance, etc.*); *sp.* rendre (*des
points*); ~ *s.o. a grudge* en vouloir à q.

ow·ing ['ouiŋ] dû (due *f*); ~ *to* par
suite de; à cause de; *be* ~ *to* (pro-)
venir de.

owl *orn.* [aul] hibou (*pl.* -x) *m*;
chouette *f*; **owl·et** ['aulit] jeune
hibou *m*; '**owl·ish** □ de hibou.

own [oun] **1.** propre; à moi (toi *etc.*);
le mien (tien *etc.*); *my* ~ *self* moi-
même; ~ *brother to* frère germain de
(*q.*); **2.** *my* ~ le mien (la mienne *etc.*);
a house of one's ~ une maison à soi;
come into one's ~ entrer en possession de son bien; F *get one's* ~ *back*
se venger, prendre sa revanche (sur,
on); *hold one's* ~ tenir ferme; maintenir sa position; F *on one's* ~ (tout)
seul; **3.** posséder; avoir; (*a.* ~ *to*)
reconnaître; avouer; convenir de;
F ~ *up* (*to*) faire l'aveu (de); avouer
(*avoir fait qch.*).

own·er ['ounə] propriétaire *mf*; '~-
'**driv·er** conducteur *m* propriétaire; '~-**less** sans propriétaire;
'**own·er·ship** (droit *m* de) propriété
f; possession *f*.

ox [ɔks], *pl.* **ox·en** ['~ən] bœuf *m*.

ox·al·ic ac·id ⚗ [ɔk'sælik'æsid]
acide *m* oxalique.

Ox·ford shoes ['ɔksfəd'ʃuːz] *pl.*
souliers *m/pl.* de ville.

ox·i·da·tion [ɔksi'deiʃən] ⚗ oxydation *f*; *métall.* calcination *f*; **ox·ide**
⚗ ['ɔksaid] oxyde *m*; **ox·i·dize**
['ɔksidaiz] (s')oxyder; *v/t. métall.*
calciner.

Ox·o·ni·an [ɔk'sounjən] **1.** oxonien
(-ne *f*); **2.** membre *m* de l'Université d'Oxford. [la queue de bœuf.)

ox·tail soup ['ɔksteil'suːp] soupe *f* à)

ox·y·a·cet·y·lene [ɔksiə'setiliːn]: ~
burner (*ou lamp ou torch*) chalumeau
m oxycétylénique, oxycoupeur *m*.

ox·y·gen ⚗ ['ɔksidʒən] oxygène *m*;
ox·y·gen·ate [ɔk'sidʒineit] oxygé-
ner, oxyder.

o·yer ⚖ ['ɔiə] audition *f*.

oys·ter ['ɔistə] huître *f*; *attr.* à huîtres, d'huître(s); '~-**bed** huîtrière *f*.

o·zone ⚗ ['ouzoun] ozone *m*.

P

P, p [pi:] P *m*, p *m*; *mind one's Ps and Qs* se surveiller; faire bien attention.

pa F [pɑ:] papa *m*.

pab·u·lum ['pæbjuləm] nourriture *f*.

pace [peis] **1.** pas *m* (*a. mesure*); vitesse *f*; allure *f*; *équitation*: amble *m*; *keep ~ with* marcher de pair avec; *put s.o. through his ~s* mettre q. à l'épreuve; *sp. set the ~* donner l'allure; **2.** *v/t.* mesurer (*qch.*) au pas; arpenter; *sp.* entraîner (*q.*); *v/i.* marcher à pas mesurés; aller au pas; aller l'amble (*cheval*); **'pace-mak·er** *sp.* entraîneur *m*; meneur *m* de train; ♥ stimulateur *m* cardiaque; **'pac·er** cheval *m* ambleur; *see pace-maker.*

pach·y·derm *zo.* ['pækidə:m] pachyderme *m*.

pa·cif·ic [pə'sifik] (*~ally*) pacifique; paisible; ♀ *Ocean* l'océan *m* Pacifique, le Pacifique *m*; **pac·i·fi·ca·tion** [pæsifi'keiʃn] apaisement *m*; pacification *f*.

pac·i·fi·er ['pæsifaiə] pacificateur (-trice *f*) *m*; *Am.* sucette *f*; **'pac·i·fism** pacifisme *m*; **'pac·i·fist** pacifiste *mf*.

pac·i·fy ['pæsifai] pacifier (*la foule, un pays*); calmer, apaiser.

pack [pæk] **1.** paquet *m*; ballot *m*; bande *f*; ✕ paquetage *m*; *cartes*: jeu *m*, paquet *m*; ✗ enveloppement *m*; *sp. rugby*: pack *m*; *a. ~ of non-sense* un tas *m* de sottises; *~ animal* bête *f* de somme; *Am. ~ train* convoi *m* de bêtes de somme; **2.** *v/t.* tasser; remplir, bourrer; (*souv. ~ up*) emballer, empaqueter, envelopper (*a. ✗*); (*a. ~ off*) envoyer (au lit, promener, *etc.*); F faire (*une malle*); conserver en boîtes (*la viande etc.*); *fig.* serrer, combler; ⊕ garnir (*le piston, le gland*); *v/i.* (*usu. ~ up*) faire sa malle; plier bagage; s'attrouper (*personne*); se tasser; *~ s.o. off*, *send s.o. ~ing* envoyer q. à la balançoire; **'pack-age** empaquetage *m*, emballage *m*;

surt. *Am.* paquet *m*, colis *m*; ✝ *~ deal* marché *m* ou contrat *m* global; achat *m* forfaitaire; panier *m*; *~ holi-day* vacances *f/pl.* organisées; *~ tour* voyage *m* organisé à prix forfaitaire; **'pack·er** emballeur *m*; *Am.* fabricant *m* de conserves en boîtes; **pack·et** ['~it] paquet *m*; colis *m*; (*a. ~-boat*) paquebot *m*; **'pack·horse** cheval *m* de bât (*a. fig.*), sommier *m*.

pack·ing ['pækiŋ] emballage *m*; *viande etc.*: conservation *f*; tassement *m*; matière *f* pour emballage; ⊕ garniture *f*; *attr.* d'emballage; **'~box** ⚙ presse-étoupe *m/inv.*; *~ house Am. usu.* fabrique *f* de conserves. [d'emballage; ficelle *f*.]

pack·thread ['pækθred] fil *m* [*pacte m, contrat m.*]

pact [pækt] pacte *m*, contrat *m*.

pad¹ *sl.* [pæd] (*a. ~ it*) aller à pied, trimarder.

pad² [~] **1.** bourrelet *m*, coussinet *m*; *ouate, encreur, etc.:* tampon *m*; bloc *m*; bloc-notes (*pl.* blocs-notes) *m*; *lapin etc.:* patte *f*; *doigt etc.:* pulpe *f*; *sp.* jambière *f*; **2.** rembourrer; ouater; *fig. ~ out* délayer; ajouter du remplissage à; *~ded cell* cellule *f* matelassée; **'pad·ding** remplissage *m* (*a. fig.*); rembourrage *m*; ouate *f*; bourre *f*.

pad·dle ['pædl] **1.** aube *f*, palette *f*; *tortue etc.:* nageoire *f*; pagaie *f*; ⚓ roue *f* à aubes; **2.** pagayer; *fig.* barboter; patauger; *Am.* F fesser; **'~-box** ⚓ caisse *f* de roue; **'~-steam-er** ⚓ vapeur *m* à aubes; **'~-wheel** roue *f* à aubes.

pad·dock ['pædək] enclos *m* (*pour chevaux*); *sp.* paddock *m*, pesage *m*.

pad·dy¹ ['pædi] paddy *m* (= *riz non décortiqué*).

pad·dy² F [~] colère *f*.

pad·dy wag·on *Am. sl.* ['pædiwægən] panier *m* à salade.

pad·lock ['pædlɔk] cadenas *m*.

pa·gan ['peigən] païen(ne *f*) (*a. su.*); **'pa·gan·ism** paganisme *m*.

page¹ [peidʒ] **1.** page *m* (*d'un roi etc.*); (*a. ~-boy*) hôtel: chasseur *m*, groom *m*; *Am.* huissier *m*; 2. *Am.* envoyer chercher (*q.*) par un chasseur.

page² [~] 1. *livre:* page *f*; 2. numéroter; paginer; *typ.* mettre en pages.

pag·eant ['pædʒənt] spectacle *m* historique; fête *f*; (*a.* '**pag·eant·ry** pompe *f*; spectacle *m* pompeux.

pag·i·nate ['pædʒineit] *see* page² 2; '**pag·i'na·tion** pagination *f*; numérotage *m* (*des pages*).

paid [peid] *prét. et p.p. de* pay 2.

pail [peil] seau *m*.

pail·lasse [pæl'jæs] paillasse *f*.

pain [pein] 1. douleur *f*, souffrance *f*, peine *f* (*morale*); douleur *f* (*physique*); ~s *pl.* douleurs *f/pl.*; *fig.* peine *f*; soins *m/pl.*; (*up*)on ~ of sous peine de; F be a ~ *in the neck* être casse-pieds; *be in* ~ souffrir; *be at* ~s (*of gér., to inf.*), *take* ~s (*to inf.*) prendre *ou* se donner de la peine (pour *inf.*); 2. faire souffrir (*q.*); faire de la peine à (*q.*); '**pain·ful** □ ['~ful] douloureux (-euse *f*); *fig.* pénible; '**pain·kill·er** anodin *m*; '**pain·less** □ sans douleur; '**pains·tak·ing** 1. □ assidu; appliqué (*élève*); soigné (*travail*); 2. application *f*; assiduité *f*.

paint [peint] 1. peinture *f*; couleur *f*; *visage:* fard *m*; *wet* ~! attention à la peinture!; 2. peindre; (se) farder; *v/t.* peinturer; *⚕️, co.* badigeonner; † *fig.* dépeindre; ~ *out* effacer (au moyen d'une couche de peinture); *v/i.* faire de la peinture; '~-**brush** pinceau *m*.

paint·er¹ ['peintə] (artiste-)peintre *m*; *a.* peintre *m* en bâtiments.

paint·er² ⚓ ['peintə] amarre *f*.

paint·ing ['peintiŋ] peinture *f*; tableau *m*; '**paint·ress** femme *f* peintre; '**paint·y** de peinture.

pair [pɛə] 1. paire *f*; *a* ~ *of scissors* une paire *f* de ciseaux; *a carriage and* ~ une voiture *f* à deux chevaux; *go up three* ~ *of stairs* monter trois étages; *three* ~ *front* au troisième sur la rue; 2. (s')apparier; *v/i.* faire la paire (avec, with); (*a.* ~ *off*) s'en aller deux par deux.

pa·ja·mas *pl. usu. Am.* [pə'dʒɑːməz] *see* pyjamas.

pal *sl.* [pæl] 1. camarade *mf*; *sl.* copain *m*, copine *f*; 2. ~ *up* se lier d'amitié (avec, with).

pal·ace ['pælis] palais *m*.

pal·at·a·ble □ ['pælətəbl] agréable

(au palais); '**pal·at·a·ble·ness** goût *m* agréable; caractère *m* agréable.

pal·a·tal ⚕️ ['pælətl] 1. palatal (-aux *m/pl.*); 2. *gramm.* palatale *f*.

pal·ate ['pælit] palais *m* (*a. fig.*); *soft* ~ voile *m* du palais.

pa·la·tial □ [pə'leiʃəl] grandiose.

pa·lat·i·nate [pə'lætinit] palatinat *m*; *the* ♀ le Palatinat *m*.

pal·a·tine ['pælətain] palatin; *Count* ♀ comte *m* palatin.

pa·lav·er [pə'lɑːvə] 1. palabre *f*, conférence *f*; *sl.* flagornerie *f*, *sl.* chichis *m/pl.*; 2. palabrer.

pale¹ [peil] 1. □ pâle (*a. couleur*), blême; ~ *blue* bleu pâle; ~ *ale* bière *f* blonde, pale-ale *m*; 2. *v/t.* (faire) pâlir; *v/i.* pâlir, blêmir.

pale² [~] pieu *m*; *fig.* limites *f/pl.*

pale·face ['peilfeis] visage pâle *mf*.

pale·ness ['peilnis] pâleur *f*.

Pal·es·tin·i·an [pæles'tiniən] palestinien(ne *f*).

pal·ette *peint.* ['pælit] palette *f*; '~-**knife** couteau *m* à palette.

pal·frey ['pɔːlfri] palefroi *m*.

pal·ing ['peiliŋ] clôture *f* à claire-voie; palissade *f*.

pal·i·sade [pæli'seid] 1. palissade *f*; 2. palissader.

pall¹ [pɔːl] 1. *eccl.* poêle *m*; *fig.* manteau *m*, voile *m*; 2. couvrir d'un poêle.

pall² [~] s'affadir; devenir insipide (pour *q.*, [*up*]on *s.o.*).

pal·la·di·um ⚗️, *myth.* [pə'leidiəm] palladium *m*.

pal·let¹ ['pælit] paillasse *f*; grabat *m*.

pal·let² ⊕ [~] cliquet *m*; *horloge etc.:* palette *f*.

pal·liasse [pæl'jæs] paillasse *f*.

pal·li·ate ['pælieit] pallier; atténuer; **pal·li'a·tion** palliation *f*; atténuation *f*; **pal·li·a·tive** ['pæliətiv] 1. palliatif (-ive *f*); lénitif (-ive *f*); 2. palliatif *m*; lénitif *m*, anodin *m*.

pal·lid □ ['pælid] décoloré; blafard (*lumière*); blême (*visage*); '**pal·lid·ness**, **pal·lor** ['pælə] pâleur *f*.

pal·ly F ['pæli]: *be* ~ *with s.o.* être copain (copine *f*) avec *q*.

palm [pɑːm] 1. *main:* paume *f*; *ancre:* oreille *f*; *bois de cerf:* empaumure *f*; ♀ *arbre:* palmier *m*; *branche:* palme *f*; *eccl.* rameau *m*; 2. empalmer; cacher dans la main; ~ *off on s.o.* F refiler (*qch.*) à *q.*; **pal·mar** ['pælmə] palmaire; **pal·mate**

['pælmit], **pal·mat·ed** ['‿meitid] palmé; **pal·mer** ['pɑːmə] pèlerin *m*; **palm·is·try** ['‿istri] chiromancie *f*; **'palm-oil** huile *f* de palme; *co.* use ‿ on *s.o.* graisser la patte à q.; **Palm Sun·day** (dimanche *m* des) Rameaux *m/pl.*; **'palm-tree** palmier *m*; **'palm·y** F heureux (-euse *f*), florissant.

pal·pa·bil·i·ty [pælpə'biliti] palpabilité *f*; *fig.* évidence *f*; **'pal·pa·ble** □ palpable; *fig.* évident, manifeste; **'pal·pa·ble·ness** *see* palpability.

pal·pi·tate ['pælpiteit] palpiter; **pal·pi·ta·tion** palpitation *f*.

pal·sied ['pɔːlzid] paralysé, paralytique.

pal·sy ['pɔːlzi] 1. paralysie *f*; *fig.* évanouissement *m*; 2. paralyser.

pal·ter ['pɔːltə] *(with)* biaiser (avec); transiger (avec, sur).

pal·tri·ness ['pɔːltrinis] mesquinerie *f*; **'pal·try** □ mesquin, misérable.

pam·per ['pæmpə] choyer, dorloter.

pam·phlet ['pæmflit] brochure *f*; opuscule *m*; *péj.* pamphlet *m*; **pam·phlet·eer** [‿'tiə] auteur *m* de brochures; *péj.* pamphlétaire *m*.

pan [pæn] 1. casserole *f*; *balance:* plateau *m*; 2. *Am.* F *v/t.* décrier, rabaisser; ‿ out laver (*le gravier*); *v/i.* ‿ out réussir.

pan... [‿] pan-.

pan·a·ce·a [pænə'siə] panacée *f*; remède *m* universel.

pan·cake ['pænkeik] crêpe *f*; ✈ ‿ landing descente *f* à plat.

pan·da ['pændə] panda *m*; *Brit.* ‿ car voiture *f* pie (de la police); *Brit.* ‿ crossing passage *m* pour piétons.

pan·de·mo·ni·um [pændi-'mouniəm] *fig.* bruit *m* infernal.

pan·der ['pændə] 1. se prêter à (*un vice*); servir de proxénète à (*q.*); 2. entremetteur (-euse *f*) *m*.

pane [pein] vitre *f*, carreau *m*; ⊕ pan *m*.

pan·e·gyr·ic [pæni'dʒirik] panégyrique *m*; **pan·e'gyr·ist** panégyriste *m*.

pan·el ['pænl] 1. ⚠ entre-deux *m/inv.*; panneau *m*; *porte:* placard *m*; *plafond:* caisson *m*; panneau *m* (*de lambris, de robe*); tableau *m* (♱♱ du jury, a. mot. de manœuvre); ♱♱ le jury *m*; *peint.* panneau *m*; vantail

(pl. -aux) *m*; ‿ discussion réunion-débat *f* (*pl.* réunions-débats); ‿ doctor médecin *m* conventionné; 2. diviser en *ou* recouvrir de panneaux; lambrisser (*un paroi*); **'pan·el·ist** membre *m* d'un jury; **'pan·el·(l)ing**, *a.* **'pan·el-work** lambris(sage *m*) *m/pl.*

pang [pæŋ] angoisse *f* subite; douleur *f*; *fig.* blessure *f*, tourments *m/pl.*; ‿ of hunger tiraillement *m* d'estomac.

pan·han·dle ['pænhændl] 1. *Am.* langue de terre d'un État, encaissée entre deux autres États; 2. *Am.* F mendigoter; **'pan·han·dler** *Am.* F mendigot *m*.

pan·ic ['pænik] 1. de panique; 2. panique *f*; affolement *m*; 3. (s')affoler; remplir *ou* être pris de panique; **'pan·ick·y** F sujet à *ou* dicté par la panique; alarmiste; **'pan·ic-mon·ger** semeur (-euse *f*) *m* de panique.

pan·nier ['pæniə] panier *m*.

pan·ni·kin ['pænikin] écuelle *f ou* gobelet *m* en fer blanc.

pan·o·ply ['pænəpli] *fig.* panoplie *f*.

pan·o·ra·ma [pænə'rɑːmə] panorama *m*; **pan·o·ram·ic** [‿'ræmik] (‿ally) panoramique.

pan·sy ['pænzi] ♀ pensée *f*; *sl.* homme *m* efféminé.

pant [pænt] haleter; panteler; chercher à reprendre haleine; palpiter (*cœur*); *fig.* ‿ for (*ou* after) soupirer après; ‿ out dire (*qch.*) en haletant.

Pan·ta·loon [pæntə'luːn] Pantalon *m*; ♀s *pl.* pantalon *m* (*see* pants).

pan·tech·ni·con [pæn'teknikən] garde-meuble *m*; (*a.* ‿ van) voiture *f* de déménagement.

pan·the·ism ['pænθiizm] panthéisme *m*; **pan·the'is·tic** (‿ally) panthéiste.

pan·ther *zo.* ['pænθə] panthère *f*.

pant·ies *Am.* ['pæntiz] *pl.*: (*a pair of*) ‿ (une) culotte *f* collante (*de femme*);   [panne *f*.]

pan·tile ['pæntail] tuile *f* flamande;}

pan·to·mime ['pæntəmaim] pantomime *f*; spectacle *m* traditionnel de Noël, fondé sur un conte de fée; **pan·to·mim·ic** [‿'mimik] (‿ally) pantomimique; *a.* de féerie.

pan·try ['pæntri] garde-manger *m/inv.*; dépense *f*; (*souv.* butler's *ou* housemaid's ‿) office *f*.

pants *surt. Am.* F [pænts] *pl.*: (*a pair of*) ~ (un) pantalon *m*; (un) caleçon *m*; ~ *suit* tailleur-pantalon *m* (*pl.* tailleurs-pantalons).

pan·ty hose *Am.* ['pænti'həus] collant *m*.

pap [pæp] bouillie *f*.

pa·pa [pə'pɑː] papa *m*.

pa·pa·cy ['peipəsi] papauté *f*.

pa·pal □ ['peipəl] papal (-aux *m/pl.*); du Pape.

pa·per ['peipə] 1. papier *m*; (*ou* news.~) journal *m*; carte *f* (*d'épingles etc.*); document *m*; (*ou* wall-~) tenture *f*, papier *m* peint; étude *f*, mémoire *m*; *école:* composition *f*, épreuve *f*; † papier *m* négociable; billets *m/pl.* de banque; papiers-valeurs *m/pl.*; ~s *pl.* papiers *m/pl.*; journaux *m/pl.*; *pol., a.* ⚖ documents *m/pl.*; communiqués *m/pl.*; *read a* ~ *on* faire une conférence sur; 2. papier; en carton; papetier (-ère *f*); à papier; ~ *war* guerre *f* de plume; 3. tapisser; *sl. théâ.* remplir de billets de faveur; '~·**back** livre *m* broché; '~·**bag** sac *m* de *ou* en papier; '~·**chase** rallye-paper *m*; '~·**clip** agrafe *f*, pince *f*; '~·'**cred·it** † dettes *f/pl.* compte; '~·'**fast·en·er** attache *f* métallique; '~·**hang·er** colleur *m* de papiers peints; '~·**hang·ings** *pl.* papier *m* peint, papiers *m/pl.* peints; '~·**mill** papeterie *f*; '~·'**stain·er** imprimeur *m* de papiers peints; '~·**thin** extrêmement fin; '~·**weight** presse-papiers *m/inv.*; '~·**work** écriture(s) *f(pl.)*; paperasserie *f*; **pa·per·y** ['~ri] semblable au papier; tout mince.

pa·pier mâ·ché ['pæpjei'mɑːʃei] carton-pâte (*pl.* cartons-pâtes) *m*.

pa·pil·la *anat.* [pə'pilə], *pl.* **-lae** [~liː] papille *f*.

pa·pist ['peipist] papiste *mf*; **pa·pis·tic**, **pa·pis·ti·cal** □ [pə'pis-tik(l)] *péj.* papiste; **pa·pis·try** ['peipistri] *péj.* papisme *m*.

pap·py ['pæpi] pâteux (-euse *f*); *fig.* flasque.   [papyrus *m*.⟩

pa·py·rus [pə'pairəs], *pl.* **-ri** [~rai]⟨

par [pɑː] égalité *f*; pair *m* (*a.* †); *above,* (*below*) ~ au-dessus (*au-dessous*) du pair; *at* ~ au pair, à (la) parité; *be on a* ~ *with* être l'égal *ou* au niveau de; *put on a* ~ *with* mettre au même niveau que; ne faire aucune distinction entre.

par·a·ble ['pærəbl] parabole *f*.

pa·rab·o·la ⅍ [pə'ræbələ] parabole *f*; **par·a·bol·ic**, **par·a·bol·i·cal** □ [pærə'bɔlik(l)] parabolique (*a.* ⅍).

par·a·chute ['pærəʃuːt] parachute *m*; ~ *jump* saut *m* en parachute; parachutage *m*; '**par·a·chut·ist** parachutiste *mf*.

pa·rade [pə'reid] 1. parade *m*; *fig.* étalage *m*; ✕ défilé *m*; ✕ exercice *m*; ✕ (*ou* ~-ground) place *f* d'armes; esplanade *f*; défilé *m* (*de mannequins*); *make a* ~ *of* faire parade de; 2. *v/t.* faire parade de; ✕ faire défiler; faire l'inspection de; *v/i.* défiler; parader (*pour, for*).

par·a·digm *gramm.* ['pærədaim] paradigme *m*.

par·a·dise ['pærədais] paradis *m*.

par·a·dis·i·ac [pærə'disiæk], **par·a·di·si·a·cal** □ [pærədi'saiəkəl] paradisiaque.

par·a·dox ['pærədɔks] paradoxe *m*; **par·a·dox·i·cal** □ paradoxal (-aux *m/pl.*).

par·af·fin 🜹 ['pærəfin] paraffine *f*; F pétrole *m* (lampant).

par·a·gon ['pærəgən] parangon *m*; modèle *m* (*a. fig.*).

par·a·graph ['pærəgrɑːf] paragraphe *m*; alinéa *m*; *journal:* entrefilet *m*; *typ.* † pied *m* de mouche.

par·a·keet *orn.* ['pærəkiːt] perruche *f*.

par·al·lel ['pærəlel] 1. parallèle (à *to, with*); *fig.* pareil(le *f*), semblable; analogue; ~ *bars pl.* barres *f/pl.* parallèles; 2. ligne, *a.* tranchée: parallèle *f*; *géog.* parallèle *m*; *fig.* parallèle *m*, comparaison *f*, pareil(le *f*) *m*; cas *m* analogue; ∮ *connect* (*ou join*) *in* ~ coupler en parallèle; *have no* ~ être sans pareil(le *f*); *without* ~ incomparable, sans égal (-aux *m/pl.*); 3. égaler (*qch.*); être égal (*ou* pareil) à (*qch.*); mettre (*deux choses*) en parallèle; ∮ synchroniser; '**par·al·lel·ism** parallélisme *m*; **par·al'lel·o·gram** ⅍ [~əgræm] parallélogramme *m*.

par·a·lyse ['pærəlaiz] paralyser (*a. fig.*); *fig.* transir; **pa·ral·y·sis** 🜽 [pə'rælisis] paralysie *f*; **par·a·lyt·ic** [pærə'litik] 1. (~*ally*) paralytique; 2. paralytique *m*.

par·a·mil·i·tar·y ['pærə'militəri] paramilitaire.

par·a·mount ['pærəmaunt] 1. souverain, éminent; suprême (*impor-*

tance); be ~ (*to*) l'emporter (sur);
2. suzerain(e *f*) *m*; **'par·a·mount-cy** suzeraineté *f*; primauté *f*.

par·a·mour ['pærəmuə] amant(e *f*)
m; maîtresse *f*.

par·a·noi·a [pærə'nɔiə] paranoïa *f*;
par·a·noi·ac [~'nɔiæk] paranoïaque
mf.

par·a·pet ['pærəpit] ✖ parapet *m*;
pont: garde-corps *m/inv.*

par·a·pher·na·li·a [pærəfə'neiljə]
pl. F affaires *f/pl.*, bataclan *m*; attirail *m*, appareil *m*.

par·a·phrase ['pærəfreiz] **1.** paraphrase *f*; **2.** paraphraser, résumer.

par·a·ple·gi·a [pærə'pli:dʒə] para-
plégie *f*; **par·a'ple·gic** paraplégique
(*adj.*, *mf*).

par·a·site ['pærəsait] parasite *m*;
fig. écornifleur (-euse *f*) *m*; **par·a-
sit·ic**, **par·a·sit·i·cal** □ [~'sitik(l)]
parasite (de, on).

par·a·sol ['pærə'sɔl] ombrelle *f*.

par·a·troop·er ✖ ['pærətru:pə]
parachutiste *m*; **par·a·troops** ['~
tru:ps] *pl.* les parachutistes *m/pl.*

par·a·ty·phoid 🩺 ['pærə'taifɔid] pa-
ratyphoïde *f*.

par·boil ['pa:bɔil] faire bouillir à
demi; *fig.* étourdir (*la viande*).

par·buck·le ⚓ ['pa:bʌkl] **1.** trévire
f; **2.** trévirer.

par·cel ['pa:sl] **1.** paquet *m*, colis *m*;
✝ lot *m*, envoi *m*; *péj.* tas *m*; parcelle *f* (*de terrain*); ~s office bureau
m de(s) messageries; **2.** empaqueter;
emballer; (*usu.* ~ out) parceler, lotir,
morceler (*un terrain*); ~ **post** service
m des colis postaux.

parch [pa:tʃ] (se des)sécher; *v/t.*
rôtir, griller; ~**ing** *heat* chaleur *f*
brûlante.

parch·ment ['pa:tʃmənt] parchemin
m.

par·don ['pa:dn] **1.** pardon *m*; ⚖
grâce *f*; *eccl.* indulgence *f*; **2.** pardonner (qch. à q., s.o. s.th.); ⚖
faire grâce à; gracier; **'par·don·a-
ble** □ pardonnable; graciable;
'par·don·er *hist.* vendeur *m* d'in-
dulgences.

pare [pɛə] rogner (*les ongles etc.*);
peler (*une pomme etc.*); éplucher;
(*a.* ~ *away*, ~ *down*) *fig.* rogner.

par·ent ['pɛərənt] père *m*, mère *f*;
fig. mère *f*, source *f*; ~s *pl.* parents
m/pl., les père et mère; ~-*teacher
association* association *f* des parents

d'élèves et des professeurs; **'par-
ent·age** naissance *f*, parentage *m*;
extraction *f*; **pa·ren·tal** □ [pə-
'rentl] paternel(le *f*).

pa·ren·the·sis [pə'renθisis], *pl.* -**ses**
[~si:z] parenthèse *f* (*a. typ.*); *fig.*
intervalle *m*; **pa'ren·the·size** mettre entre parenthèses (*a. typ.*); intercaler; **par·en·thet·ic**, **par·en-
thet·i·cal** □ [pærən'θetik(l)] entre
parenthèses.

par·ent·less ['pɛərəntlis] orphelin,
sans mère ni père.

par·get ['pa:dʒit] recouvrir (*un mur*)
d'une couche de plâtre; crépir.

pa·ri·ah ['pæriə] paria *m*, réprouvé
(-e *f*) *m*.

pa·ri·e·tal [pə'raiitl] pariétal (-aux
m/pl.); *anat.* ~ *bone* pariétal *m*.

par·ing ['pɛəriŋ] rognage *m*; épluchage *m*; ~s *pl.* rognures *f/pl.*; pe-
lures *f/pl.*; *métal:* cisaille *f*; ~-*knife*
⊕ rognoir *m*; *souliers etc.:* tranchet
m.

par·ish ['pæriʃ] **1.** paroisse *f*; (*a.
civil* ~) commune *f*; go on the ~ tomber à la charge de la commune;
2. paroissial (-aux *m/pl.*); municipal
(-aux *m/pl.*); ~ *clerk* clerc *m* de paroisse; ~ *council* conseil *m* municipal; ~ *register* registre *m* paroissial;
pa·rish·ion·er [pə'riʃənə] parois-
sien(ne *f*) *m*; habitant(e *f*) *m* de la
commune.

Pa·ri·sian [pə'rizjən] **1.** parisien
(-ne *f*); de Paris; **2.** Parisien(ne *f*)
m. [(*a. Bourse*).\

par·i·ty ['pæriti] égalité *f*; parité *f*]

park [pa:k] parc *m* (*a.* ✖); *chasse:*
réserve *f*; *château:* dépendances
f/pl.; *mot.* parc *m* de(s) stationnement *m*; ~ *keeper* gardien(ne *f*) *m*
de parc; **2.** *v/t.* enfermer dans un
parc; ✖ mettre en parc; *mot.* parquer, garer; *v/i.* *mot.* stationner;
'park·ing *mot.* parcage *m*; *attr.* de
stationnement; ~ *brake* frein *m* à
main; ~ *fee* tarif *m* ou droit *m* de
stationnement; ~ *light* feu *m* de position; ~ *meter* *Am.* compteur *m* de
stationnement; ~ *place* parc *m* ou
endroit *m* de stationnement *m*; ~
space créneau *m*; ~ *ticket* *Am.* par-
cage: contravention *f*.

par·ka ['pa:kə] anorak *m*.

par·lance ['pa:ləns] langage *m*, parler *m*.

par·ley ['pa:li] **1.** conférence *f*; ✖

pourparlers *m/pl.*; **2.** *v/i.* entrer en pourparlers; parlementer; ✕ entamer des négociations; *v/t. co.* parler.

par·lia·ment ['pɑːləmənt] parlement *m*; Chambres *f/pl.* (*en France*); **par·lia·men·tar·i·an** [ˌmenˈtɛəriən] parlementaire (*a. su./mf*); **par·lia·men·ta·ry** □ [ˌˈmentəri] parlementaire; législatif (-ive *f*); 👑 ˷ train train *m* omnibus.

par·lo(u)r ['pɑːlə] petit salon *m*; *couvent:* parloir *m*; *Am.* salon *m* (*de coiffure etc.*), cabinet *m* (*de dentiste etc.*); *Am.* ˷ car 👑 wagon-salon (*pl.* wagons-salons) *m*; '˷-maid bonne *f*.

Par·me·san cheese [pɑːmiˈzænˈtʃiːz] parmesan *m*.

pa·ro·chi·al □ [pəˈroukjəl] *eccl.* paroissial (-aux *m/pl.*), de la paroisse; communal (-aux *m/pl.*); *fig.* de clocher, borné; ˷ *politics pl.* politique *f* de clocher.

par·o·dist ['pærədist] parodiste *mf*; pasticheur (-euse *f*) *m*; '**par·o·dy 1.** parodie *f*, pastiche *m*; *fig.* travestissement *m*; **2.** parodier, pasticher; *fig.* travestir.

pa·role [pəˈroul] **1.** ✕ parole *f* (*d'honneur*); *put on ˷ see 3*; **2.** ⚖ *adj.* verbal (-aux *m/pl.*); **3.** ⚖ *surt. Am.* libérer sur parole *ou* conditionnellement.

par·ox·ysm ['pærəksizm] paroxysme *m*; F crise *f*; accès *m* (*de fureur*).

par·quet ['pɑːkei] parquet(age) *m*; *Am.* théâ. orchestre *m*; **par·quet·ed** ['ˌkitid] parqueté, en parquetage; '**par·quet·ry** parquetage *m*, parqueterie *f*.

par·ri·cid·al [pæriˈsaidl] parricide; '**par·ri·cide** parricide *m*; *personne:* parricide *mf*.

par·rot ['pærət] **1.** *orn.* perroquet *m*; **2.** répéter *ou* parler comme un perroquet.

par·ry *sp.* ['pæri] **1.** parade *f*; **2.** parer (*a. fig.*).

parse *gramm.* [pɑːz] faire l'analyse de.

par·si·mo·ni·ous □ [pɑːsiˈmounjəs] parcimonieux (-euse *f*); *péj.* pingre; **par·si·mo·ni·ous·ness**, **par·si·mo·ny** ['pɑːsiməni] parcimonie *f*; *péj.* pingrerie *f*.

pars·ley ⚘ ['pɑːsli] persil *m*.

pars·nip ⚘ ['pɑːsnip] panais *m*.

par·son ['pɑːsn] curé *m* (*catholique*);

pasteur *m* (*protestant*); F ˷'s nose croupion *m*; '**par·son·age** presbytère *m*; cure *f*.

part [pɑːt] **1.** *su.* partie *f* (*a. gramm., a.* ♪) (de, of); part *f* (à, in); théâ., *fig.* rôle *m*; *fig.* comédie *f*; *publication:* fascicule *m*, livraison *f*; ⊕ pièce *f*, organe *m*, élément *m*; parti *m*; ⚔ ˷s *pl.* (*usu. private ou privy* ˷s *pl.*) parties *f/pl.*; parages *m/pl.*, pays *m/pl.*, endroit *m*; facultés *f/pl.*; *gramm.* ˷s *pl. of speech* parties *f/pl.* du discours; ˷ *and parcel of* partie *f* intégrante de; *a man of* ˷s homme *m* bien doué; *have neither* ˷ *nor lot in* n'avoir aucune part dans; *in foreign* ˷s à l'étranger *take s.o.'s* ˷ prendre parti pour q.; *take* ˷ *in s.th.* participer à qch., prendre part à qch.; *take in good (bad)* ˷ prendre en bonne (mauvaise) part; *for my (own)* ˷ pour ma part, pour ce qui est de moi, quant à moi; *for the most* ˷ pour la plupart; *in* ˷ *en partie; partiellement; do one's* ˷ faire son devoir; *on the* ˷ *of* de la part de; *on my* ˷ de ma part; **2.** *adv.* en partie, mi-, moitié ...; **3.** *v/t.* séparer (en deux); fendre; ˷ *one's hair* se faire une raie; ˷ *company* se séparer (de, with), *fig.* n'être plus d'accord (avec, with); *v/i.* se diviser; se quitter; se rompre; se séparer (de, from); ˷ *with* céder (*qch.*); se départir de; ⚖ aliéner; *fig.* dépenser (*de l'argent*).

par·take [pɑːˈteik] [*irr.* (*take*)] participer, prendre part (à *in*, *of*); ˷ *of* prendre (*un repas*); partager (*le repas*) (de, with); goûter (*un mets*); *fig.* tenir de; *eccl.* s'approcher de (*les sacrements*); **par·tak·er** participant(e *f*) *m* (à, in); partageant(e *f*) *m* (de, in).

par·terre ✔, théâ. [pɑːˈtɛə] parterre *m*.

par·tial □ ['pɑːʃl] partiel(le *f*), en partie; partial (-aux *m/pl.*) (*personne*); *be* ˷ *to* avoir un faible pour; **par·ti·al·i·ty** [pɑːʃiˈæliti] partialité *f* (*pour, envers for, to*); prédilection *f* (*pour, for*); injustice *f*.

par·tic·i·pant [pɑːˈtisipənt] participant(e *f*) *m* (à, in); **par·tic·i·pate** [ˌpeit] participer, prendre part (à, in); **par·tic·i·pa·tion** participation *f* (à, in); **par·ti·cip·i·al** □ *gramm.* [ˌˈsipiəl] participial (-aux *m/pl.*);

pass

par·ti·ci·ple _gramm._ ['pɑːtsipl] participe _m._
par·ti·cle ['pɑːtikl] particule _f_ (_a. gramm._); _métal:_ paillette _f_; _fig._ ombre _f_, trace _f_, grain _m_; _nobiliary_ ~ particule _f_ nobiliaire.
par·ti·col·oured ['pɑːtikʌləd] mi-parti; bigarré.
par·tic·u·lar [pə'tikjulə] **1.** □ particulier (-ère _f_); spécial (-aux _m/pl._); détaillé; méticuleux (-euse _f_); pointilleux (-euse _f_); exigeant (sur _about, as to_); délicat (sur _on, about_); ~ly en particulier; **2.** détail _m_, particularité _f_; ~s _pl._ détails _m/pl._; plus amples renseignements _m/pl._; in ~ en particulier; **par·tic·u·lar·i·ty** [~'læriti] particularité _f_; méticulosité _f_; minutie _f_; **par·tic·u·lar·ize** [~ləraiz] particulariser; entrer dans les détails.
part·ing ['pɑːtiŋ] séparation _f_; départ _m_; rupture _f_; _cheveux:_ raie _f_; ~ of the ways _fig._ carrefour _m._
par·ti·san[1] _hist._ ['pɑːtizn] pertuisane _f._
par·ti·san[2] [pɑːti'zæn] **1.** partisan _m_ (_a._ ✕); **2.** de parti; sectaire; **par·ti·san·ship** esprit _m_ de parti; partialité _f_; appartenance _f_ à un parti.
par·ti·tion [pɑː'tiʃn] **1.** partage _m_; _terre:_ morcellement _m_; cloison(nage _m_) _f_; ~ wall paroi _f_, cloison _f_; mur _m_ de refend; **2.** morceler; démembrer; cloisonner (_une pièce_).
par·ti·tive _gramm._ ['pɑːtitiv] □ partitif (-ive _f_) (_a. su./m_).
part·ly ['pɑːtli] en partie, partiellement.
part·ner ['pɑːtnə] **1.** associé(e _f_) _m_ (_a._ ♱); _sp._ partenaire _mf_; danseur (-euse _f_) _m_, cavalier _m_, dame _f_; **2.** s'associer à, être associé à; _sp._ être le partenaire de; _danse:_ mener (_une dame_); be ~ed by s.o. avoir q. pour associé _etc._; **part·ner·ship** association _f_ (_a._ ♱); ♱ société _f_; limited ~ société _f_ en commandite; enter into ~ with s'associer avec.
part…: '~-own·er copropriétaire _mf_; '~-pay·ment versement _m_ à compte; acompte _m._
par·tridge _orn._ ['pɑːtridʒ] perdrix _f._
part…: '~-song chant _m_ à plusieurs voix _ou_ parties; '~-time chômage _m_ partiel; _attr._ pour une partie de la journée _ou_ de la semaine; ~ school école _f_ du soir; ~ worker employé(e

_f_) _m_ à l'heure; travailleur (-euse _f_) _m_ pour une partie de la journée _etc._; have a ~ job, work ~ travailler à temps partiel.
par·ty ['pɑːti] partie _f_ (_de plaisir, a._ ⚖); ⚖ personne _f_; _pol._ parti _m_; soirée _f_, réception _f_; bande _f_, groupe _m_; équipe _f_; ✕ détachement _m_; _fig._ complice _mf_; F individu _m_, monsieur _m_, dame _f_; be a ~ to prendre part à; ~ boss chef _m_ de parti; ~ line _téléph._ poste _m_ groupé; _Am. parl._ directive _f_ du parti; follow the ~ line _parl._ observer (à la lettre) les directives de son parti; ~ liner _Am. péj._ politicien _m_ qui observe à la lettre les directives de son parti; ~ meeting (_ou_ ~ rally) rassemblement _m_ politique (_organisé par un parti_); ~ status qualité _f_ de membre d'un parti politique; ~ ticket _Am._ liste _f_ des candidats (_d'un parti politique_); ~-wall mur _m_ mitoyen.
par·ve·nu ['pɑːvənjuː] parvenu _m_; nouveau riche _m._
pas·chal ['pɑːskəl] pascal (-als, -aux _m/pl._); de Pâques _ou_ Pâque.
pass [pɑːs] **1.** _su. géog._ col _m_, défilé _m_; ⚓, _sp._, escrime; prestidigitation: passe _f_; _univ._ mention _f_ passable; diplôme _m_ sans spécialisation; _théâ._ (_usu. free_ ~) billet _m_ de faveur; 🚃 carte _f_ de circulation; coupe-file _m/inv._; **2.** _v/i._ passer (de … à _ou_ en, _from_ … _to_); s'écouler, passer (_temps_); disparaître; avoir lieu, arriver; avoir cours (_monnaie_); être voté (_loi etc._); être reçu (_à un examen_); _escrime, a. foot._ faire une passe; _cartes:_ passer (parole); être approuvé (_action_); bring to ~ amener, faire arriver; come to ~ avoir lieu, arriver; ~ as passer pour; ~ away disparaître; trépasser (= mourir); ~ by passer, défiler (devant); ~ by the name of G. être connu sous le nom de G.; ~ for passer pour; ~ into entrer dans; devenir; ~ into law passer en loi; ~ off disparaître; (se) passer; _surt. Am._ passer pour (un) blanc (_nègre à peau blanche_); ~ on continuer sa route; passer (à, to); F trépasser; ~ out sortir; _sl._ s'évanouir; ~ through s.th. passer par qch. (_a. fig._); _fig._ traverser (_une crise_); ~ under s.o.'s control être soumis au contrôle _ou_

à la direction de q.; **3.** *v/t.* passer devant *ou* près de; dépasser; croiser; ne pas s'arrêter à; franchir (*le seuil, la frontière*); outrepasser (*les bornes*); surpasser (*q.*); rattraper (*q.*); *sp.* devancer; refiler (*de la fausse monnaie*); passer (*qch. en revue, le temps, l'été, sa main entre qch., d'un endroit à un autre*); laisser passer (*q.*); transmettre, faire circuler; subir (*une épreuve*) avec succès; réussir à, être reçu à (*un examen*); recevoir (*un candidat*); approuver (*une facture etc.*); voter (*une loi*); prononcer (*un jugement*); ~ one's hand over passer sa main sur; the bill has not yet ~ed the house le projet (*de loi*) n'a pas encore été adopté *ou* voté; ~ one's opinion upon dire *ou* émettre son opinion sur; ✝ ~ to account porter en compte; ~ water uriner, F faire de l'eau; ~ one's word donner sa parole; ~ by (*ou* over) s.th. franchir qch.; passer sur qch. (*a. fig.*); ~ off as faire passer pour; ~ on transmettre, (faire) passer; ~ round faire circuler; ~ a rope round s.th. passer une corde autour de qch.; ~ s.th. through s.th. passer qch. à travers qch.; ~ s.th. up dépenser, monter qch.; ~ s.o. up négliger q.; surt. Am. ~ up négliger; refuser; 'pass·a·ble traversable; praticable (*chemin*); passable, assez bon; ayant cours (*monnaie*); 'pass·a·bly passablement, assez; F plutôt.

pas·sage ['pæsidʒ] passage *m* (*a. d'un texte*); ruelle *f*, passage *m*; couloir *m*, corridor *m*; ⊕ conduit *m*; adoption *f* (*d'un projet de loi*); ♪ trait *m*; ~s *pl.* texte: morceaux *m/pl.*; *fig.* relations *f/pl.* intimes; ~ of (*ou* at) arms passe *f* d'armes; échange *m* de mots vifs; bird of ~ oiseau *m* passager; '~-boat paquebot *m*; '~-mon·ey prix *m* du passage *ou* de la traversée; '~way passage *m*, ruelle *f*; Am. couloir *m*, corridor *m*.

pass...: '~-book ✝ carnet *m* de banque; *mot.* carnet *m* de passage en douane; '~-check *théâ.* contremarque *f*.

pas·sen·ger ['pæsindʒə] ⚓, ✈ passager (-ère *f*) *m*; voyageur (-euse *f*) *m*; '~ coach wagon *m* à voyageurs; '~ train 🚂 train *m* de voyageurs *ou* de grande vitesse.

passe-par·tout ['pæspa:'tu:] (clef *f*) passe-partout *m/inv.*; *phot.* bande *f* gommée.

pass·er-by ['pa:sə'bai], *pl.* pass·ers-by passant(e *f*) *m*.

pass·ing ['pa:siŋ] **1.** passage *m*; oiseaux: passe *f*; *mot.* doublement *m*; *loi:* adoption *f*; *fig.* mort *f*, trépas *m*; *in* ~ en passant; **2.** passant; passager (-ère *f*); éphémère; '~-bell glas *m*; 'pass·ing·ly en passant; fugitivement.

pas·sion ['pæʃn] passion *f*, amour *m*; colère *f*; crise *f* (*de larmes*); ♀ Passion *f*; be in a ~ être furieux (-euse *f*); ✝✝ in ~ dans la chaleur du moment; ♀ Week semaine *f* de la Passion; semaine *f* sainte; 'pas·sion·ate □ ['~ʃənit] passionné; véhément; 'pas·sion·ate·ness passion *f*, ardeur *f*; véhémence *f*; 'pas·sion-flow·er ♀ fleur *f* de la Passion, passiflore *f*; 'pas·sion·less □ impassible; sans passion; 'pas·sion-play mystère *m* de la Passion.

pas·sive □ ['pæsiv] **1.** passif (-ive *f*); ~ voice = **2.** gramm. passif *m*; 'pas·sive·ness, pas·siv·i·ty [~'siviti] passivité *f*, inertie *f*.

pass-key ['pa:ski:] (clef *f*) passe-partout *m/inv.*; ♀ agneau *m* pascal.}

Pass·o·ver ['pa:souvə] Pâque *f*;}

pass·port ['pa:spɔ:t] passeport *m*.

pass·word ✗ ['pa:swə:d] mot *m* de passe.

past [pa:st] **1.** *adj.* passé (*a. gramm.*); ancien(ne *f*); de jadis; *fig.* ~ master expert *m* (dans, at), maître *m* passé (en, at; dans l'art de *inf.*, at gér.); *for some time* ~ depuis quelque temps; **2.** *adv. see* verbe simple; rush ~ passer en courant; **3.** *prp.* au-delà de; plus de; half ~ two deux heures et demie; be ~ comprehension être hors de toute compréhension; ~ cure inguérissable; ~ endurance insupportable; ~ hope perdu sans retour; I would not put it ~ her je ne l'en crois pas incapable; **4.** *su.* passé *m*.

paste [peist] **1.** pâte *f* (*a. cuis.*); colle *f*; faux brillants *m/pl.*; **2.** coller; *sl.* battre; '~-board planche *f* à pâte; carton *m*: *sl.* carte *f*; *attr.* de *ou* en carton.

pas·tel ['pæstəl] ♀ pastel *m*, guède *f*; *peint.* (crayon *m*) pastel *m*; 'pas·tel·(l)ist pastelliste *mf*.

pas·tern *vét.* ['pæstə:n] paturon *m*;
'**∼-joint** boulet *m*.

pas·teur·ize ['pæstəraiz] pasteuriser;
stériliser.

pas·tille [pæs'ti:l] pastille *f*.

pas·time ['pɑ:staim] passe-temps
m/inv.; distraction *f*.

pas·tor ['pɑ:stə] pasteur *m*, ministre *m*; *Am.* prêtre *m*; '**pas·to·ral**
1. □ pastoral (-aux *m/pl.*); ∼ *staff*
bâton *m* pastoral; crosse *f*; **2.** poème
m pastoral; *peint.* scène *f* pastorale;
poésie, a. ♪ pastourelle *f*; *eccl.* lettre
f pastorale.

pas·try ['peistri] pâtisserie *f*; pâte *f*
(*non cuite*); '∼-**cook** pâtissier (-ère
f) *m*.

pas·tur·age ['pɑ:stjuridʒ] pâturage
m, pacage *m*.

pas·ture ['pɑ:stʃə] **1.** (lieu *m* de)
pâture *f*; pré *m*; pâturage *m*; ∼
ground lieu *m* de pâturage; **2.** *v/t.*
(faire) paître; *v/i.* paître.

past·y 1. ['peisti] pâteux (-euse *f*);
fig. terreux (-euse *f*) (*visage*);
2. ['pæsti] pâté *m* (*sans terrine*).

pat [pæt] **1.** coup *m* léger; petite tape
f; caresse *f*; *beurre*: rondelle *f*;
2. tap(ot)er; caresser; **3.** apte; à
propos (*a. adv.*); prêt; ∼ *answer* réponse *f* toute prête; *answer* ∼ répondre sur-le-champ; *have* (*ou know*)
s.th. (*off*) ∼ savoir qch. sur le bout du
doigt.

patch [pætʃ] **1.** pièce *f*; *mot. boudin
d'air*: pastille *f*, *pneu*: guêtre *f*;
couleur: tache *f*; *fig.* plaque *f*; *mot.*
légumes: carré *m*; *terre*: parcelle *f*;
∼ *pocket cost.* poche *f* appliquée;
2. rapiécer, raccommoder; poser
une pastille à; mettre une pièce à
(*un pneu*); ∼ *up* rapetasser; ⊕ rafistoler; *fig.* arranger, ajuster;
'**patch·er** raccommodeur (-euse *f*)
m; *fig.* rapetasseur (-euse *f*) *m*.

patch·ou·li ['pætʃuli] patchouli *m*.

patch·work ['pætʃwə:k] rapiéçage
m; '**patch·y** inégal (-aux *m/pl.*)
(*a. fig.*).

pate *sl.* [peit] tête *f*, caboche *f*.

pat·en *eccl.* ['pætən] patène *f*.

pat·ent 1. ['peitnt]; ᵗᵗ *Am.*
'pætnt] manifeste, patent; *letters* ∼
['pætnt] *pl.* lettres *f/pl.* patentes; ∼
article article *m* breveté; ∼ *fastener*
bouton-pression (*pl.* boutons-pression) *m*; attache *f* à fermoir; ∼ *fuel*
boulets *m/pl.*, briquettes *f/pl.*; ∼

leather cuir *m* verni; ∼ *leather shoes*
souliers *m/pl.* vernis; **2.** ['pætnt]
brevet *m* d'invention; lettres *f/pl.*
patentes; ᵗᵗ ∼ *pending* brevet *m*
pendant; ∼ *agent* agent *m* en
brevets; ∼ *office* bureau *m* des
brevets; **3.** [∼] faire breveter; **pat-
ent·ee** [peitən'ti:] breveté *m*; concessionnaire *m* du brevet.

pa·ter·nal □ [pə'tə:nl] paternel(le
f); **pa·ter·ni·ty** paternité *f*; *fig. a.*
origine *f*.

path [pɑ:θ], *pl.* **paths** [pɑ:ðz]
chemin *m*; sentier *m*; *jardin*: allée
f; *fig.* route *f*; *sp.* piste *f*.

pa·thet·ic [pə'θetik] (∼*ally*) pathétique; attendrissant.

path·less ['pɑ:θlis] sans chemin
frayé.

path·o·log·i·cal □ [pæθə'lɔdʒikl]
pathologique; **pa·thol·o·gist** [pə-
'θɔlədʒist] pathologiste *mf*; **pa·thol-
o·gy** [pə'θɔlədʒi] pathologie *f*.

pa·thos ['peiθɔs] pathétique *m*.

path·way ['pɑ:θwei] sentier *m*;
rue: trottoir *m*.

path·y ⚕ *Am. co., a. péj.* ['pæθi]
système *m* de traitement.

pa·tience ['peiʃns] patience *f*;
cartes: réussite *f*, -s *f/pl.*; *be out of*
∼ (*ou have no* ∼) *with* être à bout de
patience avec; '**pa·tient 1.** □
patient, endurant; *be* ∼ *o f* avoir de
la patience avec; *fig.* savoir supporter (*qch.*); **2.** malade *mf*.

pa·ti·o *Am.* ['pætiou] patio *m*.

pa·tri·arch ['peitriɑ:k] patriarche
m; **pa·tri·ar·chal** □ patriarcal
(-aux *m/pl.*).

pa·tri·cian [pə'triʃn] patricien(ne *f*)
m (*a. su.*).

pat·ri·mo·ny ['pætriməni] patrimoine *m*; *eccl.* biens-fonds *m/pl.*

pat·ri·ot ['pætriət] patriote *mf*;
pa·tri·ot·eer *Am. sl.* [∼'tiə] faux
patriote *m*; **pa·tri·ot·ic** [∼'ɔtik]
(∼*ally*) patriotique (*discours etc.*);
patriote (*personne*); **pa·tri·ot·ism**
['∼ətizm] patriotisme *m*.

pa·trol ⚔ [pə'troul] **1.** patrouille *f*;
ronde *f*; *police*: secteur *m*; *Am.* ∼
wagon voiture *f* de police; ⊦ panier
m à salade; **2.** *v/t.* faire la patrouille
dans; *v/i.* patrouiller; ∼**man** *Am.*
['∼mæn] patrouilleur *m*; agent *m* de
police.

pa·tron ['peitrən] protecteur *m*;
eccl. patron(ne *f*) *m*; ✝ client(e *f*)

m; *charité*: patron *m*; **pa·tron·age** ['pætrənidʒ] protection *f*; patronage *m*; clientèle *f*; *eccl.* droit *m* de présentation; *péj.* air *m* protecteur; **pa·tron·ess** ['peitrənis] protectrice *f*; *charité*: patronnesse *f*; **pa·tron·ize** ['pætrənaiz] protéger; patronner; ✝ accorder sa clientèle à; *péj.* traiter d'un air protecteur; **'pa·tron·iz·er** protecteur (-trice *f*) *m*; client(e *f*) *m*.

pat·ten ['pætn] socque *m*.

pat·ter ['pætə] **1.** *v/i.* sonner par petits coups; crépiter (*pluie etc.*); caqueter; *v/t.* bredouiller; parler tant bien que mal; **2.** petit bruit *m*; fouettement *m*; boniment *m*.

pat·tern ['pætən] **1.** modèle *m*, exemple *m* (*a. fig.*); type *m*; dessin *m*; patron *m* (*en papier*); échantillon *m*; **by ~** échantillon sans valeur; *télév.* test *~* mire *f*; **2.** modeler (sur *after*, *on*); **'~-mak·er** ⊕ modeleur *m* (-euse *f*) *m*.

pat·ty ['pæti] petit pâté *m*; bouchée *f* à la reine.

pau·ci·ty ['pɔ:siti] disette *f*, manque *m*.

Paul·ine ['pɔ:lain] paulinien(ne *f*).

paunch [pɔ:ntʃ] panse *f*, ventre *m*; **'paunch·y** pansu.

pau·per ['pɔ:pə] **1.** indigent(e *f*) *m*; pauvre(sse *f*) *m*; **2.** assisté, pauvre; **'pau·per·ism** paupérisme *m*; **'pau·per·ize** réduire à l'indigence.

pause [pɔ:z] **1.** pause *f*, arrêt *m*; hésitation *f*; ♩ point d'orgue; **2.** faire une pause; hésiter; s'arrêter (sur, [*up*]*on*).

pave [peiv] paver; *fig.* préparer; **'pave·ment** pavé *m*; dallage *m*; trottoir *m*; *~* *artist* artiste *mf* de trottoir.

pa·vil·ion [pə'viljən] pavillon *m*.

pav·ing-stone ['peiviŋstoun] pavé *m*; pierre *f* à paver.

pav·io(u)r ['peivjə] paveur *m*; dalleur *m*; carreleur *m*.

paw [pɔ:] **1.** patte *f* (*sl. a.* = main); **2.** donner des coups de patte à; piaffer (*cheval*); F tripoter.

pawn¹ [pɔ:n] *échecs*: pion *m*; *fig.* jouet *m*.

pawn² [~] **1.** gage *m*; **in** (*ou* **at**) *~* en gage; **2.** mettre en gage, engager; **'~-bro·ker** prêteur (-euse *f*) *m* sur gage(s); **pawn·ee** [~'ni:] créancier (-ère *f*) *m* sur gage; **'pawn-**

er emprunteur (-euse *f*) *m* sur gage; **'pawn·shop** maison *f* de prêt; **'pawn-tick·et** reconnaissance *f* (de prêt sur gage).

pay [pei] **1.** salaire *m*; gages *m/pl.*; traitement *m*; ✗, ♣ solde *f*; **2.** [*irr.*] *v/t.* payer; régler (*un compte*); acquitter (*des droits*); présenter (*ses respects à q.*); faire (*honneur à q., une visite à q.*); **~-as-you-earn** *Am.* retenue *f* des impôts à la source; **~** *attention* (*ou* *heed*) *to* faire attention à; tenir compte de; **~** *away* dépenser; ♣ laisser filer (*un câble*); **~** *down* payer comptant; **~** *in* donner (*qch.*) à l'encaissement; **~** *off* régler (*qch.*); rembourser (*un créancier*); congédier (*un employé*); **~** *out* payer, débourser; F se venger sur (*q.*); ♣ (laisser) filer; **~** *up* se libérer de (*dettes*); rembourser intégralement; *v/i.* payer; rapporter; *fig.* expier; **'pay·a·ble** payable (*a.* ✝); acquittable; ✗ exploitable; **'pay-day** jour *m* de paye; **pay-dirt** *Am.* alluvion *f* exploitable; *fig.* source *f* d'argent; **pay-ee** ✝ [~'i:] preneur (-euse *f*) *m*; porteur *m* (*d'un effet*); **'pay-en·ve·lope** sachet *m* de paie; **'pay·er** payant(e *f*) *m*; ✝ tiré *m*, accepteur *m*; **pay freeze** blocage *m* des salaires; **'pay·ing** payant; profitable; rémunérateur (-trice *f*); avantageux (-euse *f*); **'pay·ing-'in slip** bordereau *m* de versement; **'pay-load** charge *f* payante; ✈ poids *m* utile; **'pay·mas·ter** trésorier *m* (*a.* ✗); ♣ commissaire *m*; **'pay·ment** paiement *m*, versement *m*; rémunération *f*; *additional* *~* supplément *m*; *on* *~* *of* moyennant paiement de.

pay...: **'~-off** règlement *m*; remboursement *m*; *Am.* F comble *m*; F bakchich *m*; **'~-of·fice** caisse *f*, guichet *m*; **'~-pack·et** sachet *m* de paie; **'~-roll** feuille *f* de paie; **~** *sta·tion* *Am.* téléphone *m* public.

pea ♦ [pi:] (petit) pois *m*; *attr.* de pois; aux petits pois.

peace [pi:s] paix *f*; tranquillité *f*; ordre *m*; traité *m* de paix; *~* *movement* mouvement *m* pacifiste; *~* *offering* cadeau *m* de réconciliation; *~* *pipe* calumet *m* de la paix; *~* *talks* *pl.* pourparlers *m/pl.* de paix; *~* *treaty* traité *m* de paix; *the* (*King's*) *~* l'ordre *m* public; *at* *~* en paix, paisible; *break* the ~ troubler l'ordre public; *keep the* ~ veiller à *ou* ne pas troubler l'ordre public; **'peace·a·ble** □ pacifique; en paix; paisible; **'peace-break·er** violateur (-trice *f*) *m* de l'ordre public; **peace·ful** □ ['~ful] paisible, tranquille; pacifique; **'peace-keep·ing force** forces *f/pl.* de maintien de la paix; **'peace·mak·er** conciliateur (-trice *f*) *m*; **'peace of·fi·cer** agent *m* de la sûreté.

peach[1] ♀ [pi:tʃ] pêche *f*; *arbre:* pêcher *m*; F vrai bijou *m*.

peach[2] *sl.* [~]: ~ (*up*)on moucharder; dénoncer.

pea-chick ['pi:tʃik] paonneau *m*.

peach·y ['pi:tʃi] velouté (*peau etc.*); *couleur:* fleur de pêcher *adj./inv.*; *sl.* épatant; délicieux (-euse *f*).

pea·cock ['pi:kɔk] paon *m*; **'pea-fowl** paon(ne *f*) *m*; **'pea'hen** paonne *f*. [reuse *f*.\

pea-jack·et ⚓ ['pi:dʒækit] va-\

peak [pi:k] **1.** pic *m*, cime *f*, sommet *m*; casquette: visière *f*; *attr.* de pic; de pointe; maximum; ~ *load* charge *f* maximum; ~ *power* débit *m* maximum; ~ *season* pleine saison *f*; **2.** F dépérir; tomber en langueur; **peaked** [pi:kt] en pointe; ~ *cap* casquette *f* à visière; **'peak·y** F pâlot, malingre; hâve.

peal [pi:l] **1.** carillon *m*; *tonnerre:* grondement *m*; retentissement *m*; ~ *of laughter* éclat *m* de rire; **2.** *v/t.* sonner à toute volée; carillonner; *v/i.* carillonner; retentir; gronder (*tonnerre*).

pea·nut ['pi:nʌt] ♀ arachide *f*, ♣ cacahouette *f*; *fig.* gnognote *f*; *Am. sl.* ~ *politics* politicailleries *f/pl.*

pear ♀ [pɛə] poire *f*; *arbre:* poirier *m*.

pearl [pɜ:l] **1.** perle *f* (*a. fig.*); *typ.* parisienne *f*; *attr.* de perles; **2.** perler; **'pearl·y** perlé, nacré.

pear-tree ['pɛətri:] poirier *m*.

peas·ant ['pezənt] **1.** paysan(ne *f*) *m*; **2.** campagnard; **'peas·ant·ry** paysannerie *f*; paysannat *m*.

pea-shoot·er ['pi:ʃu:tə] petite sarbacane *f* de poche.

pea-soup ['pi:'su:p] potage *m* aux pois, potage *m* St.-Germain; **'pea-'soup·y** jaune et épais (*brouillard*).

peat [pi:t] tourbe *f*; **'~-moss** tourbière *f*.

peb·ble ['pebl] caillou (*pl.* -x) *m*; *plage:* galet *m*; agate *f*; **'peb·bly** caillouteux (-euse *f*); à galets (*plage*).

pec·ca·ble ['pekəbl] peccable; **peccant** ♣ ['pekənt] peccant.

peck[1] [pek] (*approx.*) boisseau *m* (*9,087 litres*); *fig.* grande quantité *f*; *a* ~ *of* beaucoup de.

peck[2] [~] picoter (*qch.*, *at s.th.*); picorer; ~ *at* chipoter (*un plat*); ~ *at one's food* manger son repas du bout des dents; **'peck·er** *sl.* courage *m*; nez *m*; **'peck·ish** F: *be* ~ avoir faim.

pec·to·ral ['pektərəl] pectoral (-aux *m/pl.*) (*a. su./m.*).

pec·u·late ['pekjuleit] détourner des fonds; **pec·u'la·tion** détournement *m* de fonds; péculat *m*; **'pec·u·la·tor** dilapidateur *m* des deniers publics.

pe·cu·li·ar □ [pi'kju:ljə] bizarre, singulier (-ère *f*); étrange; particulier (-ère *f*); **pe·cu·li·ar·i·ty** [~li'æriti] particularité *f*; trait *m* distinctif; singularité *f*.

pe·cu·ni·ar·y [pi'kju:njəri] pécuniaire; d'argent.

ped·a·gog·ic, **ped·a·gog·i·cal** □ [pedə'gɔdʒik(l)] pédagogique; **ped·a'gog·ics** *usu. sg.* pédagogie *f*; **ped·a·gogue** ['~gɔg] pédagogue *m*; **ped·a·go·gy** ['~gi] pédagogie *f*.

ped·al ['pedl] **1.** pédale *f*; **2.** du pied; **3.** *cycl.* pédaler; ♪ mettre la pédale.

ped·ant ['pedənt] pédant(e *f*) *m*; **pe·dan·tic** [pi'dæntik] (~*ally*) pédant(esque); **ped·ant·ry** ['pedəntri] pédantisme *m*.

ped·dle ['pedl] *v/t.* colporter; *v/i.* faire le colportage; **'ped·dling** colportage *m*; **'ped·dler** *Am. see pedlar.*

ped·es·tal ['pedistl] piédestal *m* (*a. fig.*); socle *m*.

pe·des·tri·an [pi'destriən] **1.** pédestre; à pied; prosaïque; **2.** piéton *m*; voyageur (-euse *f*) *m* à pied.

ped·i·cure ['pedikjuə] chirurgie *f* pédicure; *personne:* pédicure *mf*; **ped·i·cur·ist** ['~kjuərist] pédicure *mf*.

ped·i·gree ['pedigri:] **1.** arbre *m* généalogique; généalogie *f*; **2.** (*a.* **ped·i·greed** ['~d]) de race, de bonne souche. [ton *m*.\

ped·i·ment △ ['pedimənt] fron-\

ped·lar [ˈpedlə] colporteur *m*; **'ped-lar·y** colportage *m*; marchandise *f* de balle.

pe·dom·e·ter [piˈdɔmitə] compte-pas *m/inv.*

pee F [piː] faire pipi, pisser.

peek [piːk] **1.** jeter un coup d'œil furtif (sur, at); **2.** coup *m* d'œil rapide *ou* furtif; **peek·a·boo** *Am.* [ˈpiːkəbuː] **1.** en dentelle; **2.** *Am.* cache-cache *m*.

peel [piːl] **1.** pelure *f*; peau *f*; *citron:* zeste *m*; **2.** (*a.* ~ *off*) *v/t.* peler; se dépouiller de (*les vête-ments*); *v/i.* peler; s'écailler; *sl.* se déshabiller.

peel·er *sl.* [ˈpiːlə] agent *m* de police; F flic *m*.

peel·ing [ˈpiːliŋ] épluchure *f*; *action:* épluchage *m*; (*a.* ~ *off*) écaillement *m*.   [2. pépier.]

peep¹ *orn.* [piːp] **1.** pépiement *m*;⌉

peep² [~] **1.** coup *m* d'œil rapide *ou* furtif; point *m* (*du jour*); **2.** regarder à la dérobée; jeter un coup *m* d'œil rapide (sur, at); *fig.* (*a.* ~ *out*) percer; se laisser entrevoir; **'peep·er** curieux (-euse *f*) *m*; indiscret (-ète *f*) *m*; *sl.* œil; **'peep-hole** judas *m*; **'peep·ing Tom** voyeur *m*; **'peep-show** optique *f*.

peer¹ [piə] risquer un coup d'œil; ~ *at* scruter du regard; ~ *into s.o.'s face* dévisager q.

peer² [~] pair *m*; **'peer·age** pairie *f*; pairs *m/pl.*; **'peer·ess** pairesse *f*; **'peer·less** □ sans pair; sans pareil(le *f*).

peeved F [piːvd] irrité.

pee·vish □ [ˈpiːviʃ] irritable; maussade; **'pee·vish·ness** mauvaise humeur *f*; humeur *f* maussade.

peg [peg] **1.** cheville *f* (*a.* ♪); fiche *f*; toupie: pointe *f*; *whisky:* doigt *m*; (*a. clothes-~*) vêtements: patère *f*; pince *f*; *fig.* take s.o. down a ~ or two remettre q. à sa place; be a round ~ in a square hole ne pas être dans son emploi; **2.** cheviller; (*a.* ~ *out*) piqueter (*une concession*); stabiliser, maintenir (*le prix, les gages, etc.*); F ~ *away* (*a.* ~ *along*) travailler ferme (à, at); *sl.* ~ *out sl.* casser sa pipe (= *mourir*).

peg-top [ˈpegtɔp] toupie *f*.

peign·oir [ˈpeinwaː] peignoir *m*.

pe·jo·ra·tive [ˈpiːdʒərətiv] péjoratif (-ive *f*).

pe·kin·ese [piːkiˈniːz] pékinois *m*.

pelf *péj.* [pelf] richesses *f/pl.*

pel·i·can *orn.* [ˈpelikən] pélican *m*.

pe·lisse [peˈliːs] pelisse *f*.

pel·let [ˈpelit] boulette *f*; *pharm.* pilule *f*; grain *m* de plomb.

pel·li·cle [ˈpelikl] pellicule *f*; membrane *f*.

pell-mell [ˈpelˈmel] **1.** pêle-mêle; en désordre; **2.** confusion *f*.

pel·lu·cid [peˈljuːsid] transparent; clair.

pelt¹ † [pelt] fourrure *f*, peau *f*.

pelt² [~] **1.** *v/t.* (*a.* ~ *at*) lancer (*une volée de pierres*) à; *v/i.* tomber à verse; F courir à toutes jambes; **2.** grêle *f*.   [terie *f*.]

pelt·ry [ˈpeltri] peaux *f/pl.*; pelle-⌋

pel·vis *anat.* [ˈpelvis] bassin *m*.

pen¹ [pen] **1.** plume *f*; *Brit.* ~ *friend, Am.* ~ *pal* correspondant(e *f*) *m*; ~ *pusher* gratte-papier *m/inv.*; **2.** écrire; composer.

pen² [~] **1.** enclos *m*; **2.** [*irr.*] parquer; (*usu.* ~ *up*, ~ *in*) renfermer.

pe·nal □ [ˈpiːnl] pénal (-aux *m/pl.*) (*loi, code*); qui entraîne une pénalité; ~ *servitude* travaux *m/pl.* forcés; **pe·nal·ize** [ˈpiːnəlaiz] sanctionner (*qch.*) d'une peine; *sp.* pénaliser; *fig.* punir; **pen·al·ty** [ˈpenlti] peine *f*; pénalité *f* (*a. sp.*); *foot.* ~ *area* surface *f* de réparation; ~ *kick* penalty *m*; *under* ~ *of* sous peine de.

pen·ance [ˈpenəns] pénitence *f*.

pen...: '~-and-'ink draw·ing dessin *m* à la plume; '~-case plumier *m*.

pence [pens] *pl.* de penny.

pen·cil [ˈpensl] **1.** crayon *m*; *sl.* pinceau *m*; *opt.* faisceau *m*; **2.** marquer (*ou* dessiner) au crayon; crayonner (*une lettre*); se faire (*les sourcils*) au crayon; **'pen·cil(l)ed** écrit *ou* tracé au crayon; *opt.* en faisceau lumineux; **'pen·cil-sharp-en·er** taille-crayon *m/inv.*

pend·ant [ˈpendənt] *collier:* pendentif *m*; *lustre:* pendeloque *f*; *tableau:* pendant *m*; ♨ *drapeau:* flamme *f*; △ cul-de-lampe (*pl.* culs-de-lampe) *m*.

pend·ent [~] pendant; retombant.

pend·ing [ˈpendiŋ] **1.** *adj.* ⚖ pendant; en instance; **2.** *prp.* pendant; en attendant.

pen·du·lous [ˈpendjuləs] pendant; oscillant; **pen·du·lum** [ˈ~ləm] pendule *m*, balancier *m*.

pen·e·tra·bil·i·ty [penitrə'biliti] pénétrabilité *f*; **pen·e·tra·ble** □ ['⁓trəbl] pénétrable; **pen·e·tra·li·a** F [peni'treiliə] *pl.* sanctuaire *m*; **pen·e·trate** ['⁓treit] *v/t.* percer; pénétrer (de, with) (*a. fig., un secret etc.*); *v/i.* pénétrer (jusqu'à to, as far as); **pen·e'tra·tion** pénétration *f* (*a. fig.* = *perspicacité*); '**pen·e·tra·tive** □ pénétrant; perçant (*a. fig.*); ⁓ effect effet *m* marqué.

pen-feath·er ['penfeðə] penne *f*.

pen·guin *orn.* ['peŋgwin] pingouin *m*; manchot *m*.

pen·hold·er ['penhouldə] porteplume *m/inv.*

pen·i·cil·lin *pharm.* [peni'silin] pénicilline *f*.

pen·in·su·la [pi'ninsjulə] presqu'île *f*; péninsule *f*; **pen'in·su·lar** péninsulaire.

pen·i·tence ['penitəns] pénitence *f*; contrition *f*; '**pen·i·tent 1.** □ pénitent, contrit; **2.** pénitent(e *f*) *m*; **pen·i·ten·tial** □ [⁓'tenʃl] pénitentiel(le *f*); de pénitent; **pen·i·ten·tia·ry** [⁓'tenʃəri] maison *f* de correction; *Am.* prison *f*; *eccl.* (*ou* ⁓ *priest*) pénitencier *m*.

pen·man ['penmən] écrivain *m*; auteur *m*; '**pen·man·ship** art *m* d'écrire; calligraphie *f*.

pen-name ['penneim] nom *m* de plume; *journ.* nom *m* de guerre.

pen·nant ['penənt] ⚓ flamme *f*; *surt. Am.* fanion *m* (*usu. de championnat, sp.*).

pen·ni·less □ ['penilis] sans ressources; sans le sou.

pen·non ['penən] ✗ flamme *f*, banderole *f*; *sp.* fanion *m*.

pen·ny ['peni], *pl. valeur:* **pence** [pens], *pièces:* **pen·nies** penny *m* (¹/₁₀₀ *pound*); gros sou *m*; *Am.* cent *m*, F sou *m*; '⁓-a-'lin·er journaliste *m* à deux sous la ligne; écrivaillon *m*; '⁓-'dread·ful roman *m* à deux sous; feuilleton *m* à gros effets; '⁓-in-the-'slot automatique; ⁓ *machine* distributeur *m* automatique; '⁓-wise lésineur (-euse *f*); ⁓**worth** ['penəθ] valeur *f* de deux sous; *fig.* miette *f*; *a* ⁓ *of tobacco* deux sous de tabac.

pen·sion 1. ['penʃn] pension *f*; retraite *f* de vieillesse; ✗ (solde *f* de) retraite *f*; ⁓ *scheme* caisse *f* de retraite; ['pɑ̃:ŋsiɔ̃:ŋ] pension *f* de famille;

2. ['penʃn] *usu.* ⁓ *off* mettre (*q.*) à la retraite; pensionner (*q.*); **pen·sion·ar·y** ['penʃənəri] '**pen·sion·er** titulaire *mf* d'une pension; pensionnaire *mf* (*de l'État*); ✗ retraité *m*; invalide *m*; *be s.o.'s* ⁓ *péj.* être à la solde de q.

pen·sive □ ['pensiv] pensif (-ive *f*); songeur (-euse *f*); rêveur (-euse *f*); '**pen·sive·ness** air *m* pensif.

pent [pent] *prét. et p.p. de* pen² 2; ⁓-*up* contenu, refoulé (*colère etc.*).

pen·ta·gon ['pentəgən] pentagone *m*; *Am. the* ♀ Ministère *m* de la Défense Nationale (*à Washington*); **pen·tag·o·nal** [⁓'tægənl] pentagonal (-aux *m/pl.*), pentagone.

pen·tath·lon *sp.* [pen'tæθlɔn] pentathlon *m*.

Pen·te·cost ['pentikɔst] la Pentecôte *f*; **pen·te'cos·tal** de la Pentecôte.

pent·house ['penthaus] appentis *m*; auvent *m*; *Am.* appartement *m* (*construit sur le toit d'un bâtiment élevé*).

pent-up ['pent'ʌp] enfermé; refoulé (*sentiment etc.*), réprimé.

pe·nul·ti·mate [pi'nʌltimit] pénultième, avant-dernier (-ière *f*).

pe·num·bra [pi'nʌmbrə] pénombre *f*.

pe·nu·ri·ous □ [pi'njuəriəs] pauvre; mesquin; parcimonieux (-euse *f*); **pe'nu·ri·ous·ness** avarice *f*; mesquinerie *f*.

pen·u·ry ['penjuri] pénurie *f*; indigence *f*; manque *m* (de, of).

pen-wip·er ['penwaipə] essuieplume *m*.

pe·o·ny ♦ ['piəni] pivoine *f*.

peo·ple ['pi:pl] **1.** *sg.* peuple *m*; nation *f*; *pl. coll.* peuple *m*, habitants *m/pl.*; *pol.* citoyens *m/pl.*; gens *m/pl.*; les gens *m/pl.*, on; ⁓ *say* on dit; *English* ⁓ *pl.* des *ou* les Anglais *m/pl.*; *many* ⁓ *pl.* beaucoup de monde; F *my* ⁓ *pl.* mes parents *m/pl.*; *ma famille*; *the* ⁓ *pl.* le grand public *m*, le peuple *m*; *pol.* ⁓*'s republic* république *f* populaire; **2.** peupler (de, with).

pep *Am. sl.* [pep] **1.** vigueur *f*, vitalité *f*; entrain *m*; F ⁓ *pill* excitant *m*; F ⁓ *talk* mots *m/pl.* d'encouragement; **2.** ⁓ *up* ragaillardir (*q.*); donner de l'entrain à (*qch.*).

pep·per ['pepə] **1.** poivre *m*; ⁓ *pot* poivrière *f*; **2.** poivrer; F cribler; '⁓-

and-'salt poivre et sel (*cheveux*); *cost.* marengo *inv.*; '**~·corn** grain *m* de poivre; '**~·mint** ♀ menthe *f* poivrée; (*a.* ~ *lozenge*) pastille *f* de menthe; '**pep·per·y** □ poivré; *fig.* irascible.

pep·tic ['peptik] gastrique, digestif (-ive *f*); ~ *ulcer* ulcère *m* de l'estomac.

per [pəː] par; suivant; d'après; par l'entremise de; ~ *cent* pour cent (%).

per·ad·ven·ture [pərəd'ventʃə] **1.** peut-être; par hasard; **2.** doute *m*; *beyond* (*ou without*) ~ à n'en pas douter.

per·am·bu·late [pə'ræmbjuleit] se promener dans (*qch.*); parcourir (*qch.*); **per·am·bu·la·tion** promenade *f*; inspection *f*; **per·am·bu·la·tor** ['præmbjuleitə] voiture *f* d'enfant.

per·ceive [pə'siːv] (a)percevoir; s'apercevoir de; voir; comprendre.

per·cent·age [pə'sentidʒ] pourcentage *m*; proportion *f*; guelte *f*; tantième *m*, -s *m/pl.*

per·cep·ti·ble □ [pə'septəbl] perceptible; sensible; **per·cep·tion** perception *f*; sensibilité *f*; **per·cep·tive** □ perceptif (-ive *f*); **per·cep·tive·ness**, **per·cep·tiv·i·ty** perceptivité *f*.

perch¹ *icht.* [pəːtʃ] perche *f*.

perch² [~] **1.** perche *f* (= *5,029 m*); oiseau: perchoir *m*; F *fig.* trône *m*; *carrosse:* flèche *f*; **2.** (se) percher; (se) jucher; ~*ed fig.* perché; '**perch·er** *orn.* percheur *m*.

per·cip·i·ent [pə'sipiənt] **1.** percepteur (-trice *f*); conscient; **2.** sujet *m* télépathique.

per·co·late ['pəːkəleit] *v/t.* passer (*le café*); *v/i.* s'infiltrer; filtrer (*café*); '**per·co·la·tor** filtre *m*.

per·cus·sion [pəː'kʌʃn] choc *m*; percussion *f* (*a.* ♪); ~ *cap* capsule *f* de fulminate; ♪ ~ *instruments pl.* instruments *m/pl.* 'de *ou* à percussion; **per·cus·sive** [pəː'kʌsiv] percutant.

per·di·tion [pəː'diʃn] perte *f*, ruine *f*.

per·du(e) ⚔ [pəː'djuː] caché.

per·e·gri·nate ['perigrineit] voyager, pérégriner; **per·e·gri·na·tion** voyage *m*, pérégrination *f*.

per·emp·to·ri·ness [pə'remtərinis] intransigeance *f*; ton *m ou* caractère *m* absolu; **per'emp·to·ry** □

péremptoire; décisif (-ive *f*); absolu; tranchant (*ton*).

per·en·ni·al [pə'renjəl] **1.** □ éternel (-le *f*); ♀ vivace, persistant; **2.** ♀ plante *f* vivace.

per·fect ['pəːfikt] **1.** □ parfait; achevé (*ouvrage*); complet (-ète *f*); ♪ juste; ♪ ~ *pitch* l'oreille *f* absolue; **2.** *gramm.* (*ou* ~ *tense*) parfait *m*; **3.** [pə'fekt] (par)achever; rendre parfait, parfaire; **per·fect·i·bil·i·ty** [~i'biliti] perfectibilité *f*; **per'fect·i·ble** [~təbl] perfectible; **per'fec·tion** perfection *f*, *a.* **per·fect·ness** ['pəːfiktnis] achèvement *m*, accomplissement *m*; perfectionnement *m*; *fig. be the* ~ *of* ... être ... même.

per·fid·i·ous □ [pə'fidiəs] perfide; traître(sse *f*); **per'fid·i·ous·ness**, **per·fi·dy** ['pəːfidi] perfidie *f*, traîtrise *f*.

per·fo·rate ['pəːfəreit] *v/t.* perforer, percer; *v/i.* pénétrer (dans, *into*); **per·fo·ra·tion** perforation *f* (*a. coll.*); percement *m*; (petit) trou *m*; '**per·fo·ra·tor** perforateur *m*; ⚒ perforatrice *f*.

per·force [pə'fɔːs] forcément.

per·form [pə'fɔːm] *v/t.* accomplir; célébrer (*un rite*); s'acquitter de (*un devoir*); exécuter (*un mouvement, a.* ♪ *un morceau*); ♪, *théâ.* jouer; *théâ.* représenter; *v/i.* jouer; ♪ ~ *on* jouer de; **per'form·ance** exécution *f*; exploit *m*; *théâ.* représentation *f*; *sp., mot.* performance *f*; *cin.* séance *f*; ⊕ fonctionnement *m*, marche *f*; **per'form·er** artiste *mf*; *théâ.* acteur (-trice *f*) *m*; ♪ exécutant(e *f*) *m*; **per'form·ing** savant (*animal*).

per·fume 1. ['pəːfjuːm] parfum *m*; odeur *f*; **2.** [pə'fjuːm] parfumer; **per'fum·er** parfumeur (-euse *f*) *m*; **per'fum·er·y** parfumerie *f*; parfums *m/pl.*

per·func·to·ry □ [pə'fʌŋktəri] superficiel(le *f*); peu zélé; négligent.

per·haps [pə'hæps; præps] peut-être.

per·i·car·di·um *anat.* [peri'kaːdjəm] péricarde *m*.

per·i·gee *astr.* ['peridʒiː] périgée *m*.

per·il ['peril] **1.** péril *m*; danger *m*; *at my* ~ à mes risques et périls; **2.** mettre en péril; '**per·il·ous** □ périlleux (-euse *f*).

pe·ri·od ['piəriəd] période *f*; durée *f*; délai *m*; époque *f*, âge *m*; *école:*

leçon *f*; *rhétorique*: période *f*; *gramm.* point *m*; ⚓ *~s pl.* règles *f*/*pl.*; *a girl of the ~* une jeune fille moderne; *~ furniture* mobilier *m* de style; **per·i·od·ic** [⌣'ɔdik] périodique; **pe·ri'od·i·cal 1.** □ périodique; 2. (publication *f*) périodique *m*.

per·i·pa·tet·ic [peripə'tetik] (*~ally*) F ambulant.

pe·riph·er·y [pə'rifəri] pourtour *m*.

pe·riph·ra·sis [pə'rifrəsis], *pl.* **-ses** [⌣si:z] périphrase *f*; circonlocution *f*; **per·i·phras·tic** [peri'fræstik] (*~ally*) périphrastique. [riscope *m.*⧵

per·i·scope ⚓, ✕ ['periskoup] pé-⧸

per·ish ['periʃ] (faire) périr *ou* mourir; (se) détériorer; *be ~ed with* mourir de (*froid etc.*); **'per·ish·a·ble 1.** □ périssable; *fig.* éphémère; 2. *~s pl.* marchandises *f*/*pl.* périssables; **'per·ish·ing** □ transitoire; destructif (-ive *f*); F sacré.

per·i·style ['peristail] péristyle *m*.

per·i·to·ne·um *anat.* [peritou'ni:əm] péritoine *m*.

per·i·wig ['periwig] perruque *f*.

per·i·win·kle ['periwiŋkl] **1.** ♀ pervenche *f*; 2. *zo.* bigorneau *m*.

per·jure ['pə:dʒə] *~ o.s.* se parjurer; **'per·jured** parjure; **'per·jur·er** parjure *mf*; **'per·ju·ry** parjure *m*; ⚖ faux témoignage *m*.

perk F [pə:k] **1.** (*usu. ~ up*) *v/i.* se ranimer; redresser la tête; *v/t.* se redresser; requinquer (*q.*); 2. *see ~y*; **perk·i·ness** ['⌣inis] air *m* alerte *ou* éveillé.

perks F [pə:ks] *pl. see* perquisites.

perk·y □ ['pə:ki] alerte, éveillé; désinvolte.

perm F [pə:m] (ondulation *f*) permanente *f*, indéfrisable *f*; *have a ~* se faire faire une permanente.

per·ma·nence ['pə:mənəns] permanence *f*; stabilité *f*; **'per·ma·nen·cy** *see* permanence; emploi *m* permanent; **'perma·nent** □ permanent; fixe; inamovible (*place*); ~ *wave* ondulation *f* permanente; ⚓ *~ way* voie *f* ferrée.

per·me·a·bil·i·ty [pə:miə'biliti] perméabilité *f*; **'per·me·a·ble** □ perméable; **per·me·ate** ['⌣mieit] *v/t.* filtrer à travers; *v/i.* pénétrer; s'infiltrer (dans *into, among*).

permed F [pə:md] ondulé; *have one's hair ~* se faire faire une permanente.

per·mis·si·ble □ [pə'misəbl] permis, tolérable; **per·mis·sion** [⌣'miʃn] permission *f*; autorisation *f*; **per·mis·sive** □ [⌣'misiv] qui permet; facultatif (-ive *f*); permis.

per·mit 1. [pə'mit] (*a. ~ of*) permettre; souffrir; *weather ~ting* si le temps s'y prête; 2. ['pə:mit] autorisation *f*, permis *m*; ✝ passavant *m*.

per·ni·cious □ [pə:'niʃəs] pernicieux (-euse *f*); délétère.

per·nick·et·y F [pə'nikiti] pointilleux (-euse *f*); difficile.

per·o·ra·tion [perə'reiʃn] péroraison *f*.

per·ox·ide ⚗ [pə'rɔksaid] peroxyde *m*; ~ *of hydrogen* eau *f* oxygénée.

per·pen·dic·u·lar [pə:pən'dikjulə] **1.** □ vertical (-aux *m*/*pl.*); perpendiculaire (*a.* △ *style*); 2. perpendiculaire *m*; aplomb *m*; fil *m* à plomb.

per·pe·trate ['pə:pitreit] perpétrer; commettre (F *a. un jeu de mots etc.*); **per·pe'tra·tion** perpétration *f*; péché *m*; **'per·pe·tra·tor** auteur *m*.

per·pet·u·al □ [pə'petjuəl] perpétuel(le *f*), éternel(le *f*); F sans fin; **per'pet·u·ate** [⌣eit] perpétuer; **per·pet·u'a·tion** perpétuation *f*; préservation *f*; **per·pe·tu·i·ty** [pə:pi'tjuiti] perpétuité *f*; rente *f* perpétuelle; *in ~* à perpétuité.

per·plex [pə'pleks] embarrasser; troubler l'esprit de; **per'plexed** □ perplexe; confus; **per'plex·i·ty** perplexité *f*; embarras *m*; confusion *f*.

per·qui·sites ['pə:kwizits] *pl.* petits profits *m*/*pl.*; *sl.* gratte *f*.

per·se·cute ['pə:sikju:t] persécuter; *fig.* tourmenter; **per·se'cu·tion** persécution *f*; ~ *mania* délire *m* de (la) persécution; **per·se·cu·tor** ['⌣tə] persécuteur (-trice *f*) *m*.

per·se·ver·ance [pə:si'viərəns] persévérance *f*; constance *f*; **per·se·vere** [⌣'viə] persévérer (dans *in, with*; à *inf.*, *in gér.*); **per·se'ver·ing** □ assidu (à, *in*), constant (dans, *in*).

Per·sian ['pə:ʃn] **1.** persan; de Perse; 2. *ling.* persan *m*; Persan(e *f*) *m*.

per·sist [pə'sist] persister, s'obstiner (dans, *in*; à *inf.*, *in gér.*); **per·sist·ence, per·sist·en·cy** [pə'sistəns(i)] persistance *f*; obstination *f*; **per'sist·ent** □ persistant; continu.

per·son ['pə:sn] personne *f*; individu *m*; *théâ.* personnage *m*; *a* ~ quelqu'un(e); *no* ~ personne ... ne; *in* ~ en (propre) personne; *téléph.* ~-*to*-~ *call* communication *f* (téléphonique) avec préavis; **'per·son·a·ble** bien de sa personne; beau (bel *devant une voyelle ou un h muet*; belle *f*); **'per·son·age** personnage *m* (*a. théâ.*); personnalité *f*; **'per·son·al 1.** ☐ personnel(le *f*) (*a. gramm.*); individuel(le *f*); particulier (-ère *f*); *be* ~ faire des personnalités; ⚹~ *property* (*ou estate*) *see personalty*; **2.** ~*s pl. Am. F journ.* chronique *f* mondaine; échos *m/pl.*; **per·son·al·i·ty** [~sə-'næliti] personnalité *f*; caractère *m* propre; **per·son·al·ty** ⚹ ['~snlti] biens *m/pl.* meubles; fortune *f* mobilière; **per·son·ate** ['~səneit] se faire passer pour; *théâ.* jouer; **per·son·a·tion** usurpation *f* de nom *etc.*; *théâ.* représentation *f*; **per·son·i·fi·ca·tion** [~sɔnifi'keiʃn] personnification *f*; **per·son·i·fy** [~'sɔnifai] personnifier; **per·son·nel** [~sə'nel] personnel *m*.

per·spec·tive [pə'spektiv] **1.** ☐ perspectif (-ive *f*), en perspective; **2.** perspective *f*.

per·spi·ca·cious ☐ [pə:spi'keiʃəs] perspicace; **per·spi·cac·i·ty** [~'kæsiti] perspicacité *f*; **per·spi·cu·i·ty** [~'kjuiti] clarté *f*, netteté *f*; **per·spic·u·ous** [pə'spikjuəs] ☐ clair, lucide.

per·spi·ra·tion [pə:spə'reiʃn] transpiration *f*; sueur *f*; **per·spire** [pəs'paiə] transpirer; suer.

per·suade [pə'sweid] persuader (de, *of*; que, *that*; à q. de *inf. s.o. into gér.*, *s.o. to inf.*); convaincre; **per·'suad·er** *sl.* éperon *m*; arrosage *m* (= *paiement illicite*).

per·sua·sion [pə'sweiʒən] persuasion *f*; religion *f*; F *co.* race *f*, genre *m*; *powers pl.* of ~ force *f* persuasive; art *m* de persuader.

per·sua·sive ☐ [pə'sweisiv] persuasif (-ive *f*); persuadant; **per·'sua·sive·ness** (force *f* de) persuasion *f*.

pert ☐ [pə:t] effronté; mutin; *Am.* gaillard.

per·tain [pə:'tein] (*to*) appartenir (à); avoir rapport (à); être le propre (de).

per·ti·na·cious ☐ [pə:ti'neiʃəs] obstiné, entêté; **per·ti·nac·i·ty** [~'næ-

siti] obstination *f*; opiniâtreté *f* (à, *in*).

per·ti·nence, per·ti·nen·cy ['pə:ti-nəns(i)] pertinence *f*; justesse *f*, à-propos *m*; **'per·ti·nent** ☐ pertinent, juste, à propos; ~ *to* ayant rapport à.

pert·ness ['pə:tnis] effronterie *f*.

per·turb [pə'tə:b] troubler; agiter; **per·tur·ba·tion** [pə:tə:'beiʃn] trouble *m*; agitation *f*; inquiétude *f*.

pe·ruke † [pə'ru:k] perruque *f*.

pe·rus·al [pə'ru:zl] lecture *f*; examen *m*; **pe·ruse** [pə'ru:z] lire attentivement; *fig.* examiner.

Pe·ru·vi·an [pə'ru:viən] **1.** péruvien (-ne *f*); ⚘ ~ *bark* quinquina *m*; **2.** Péruvien(ne *f*) *m*.

per·vade [pə:'veid] s'infiltrer dans; *fig.* animer; **per·va·sion** [~ʒn] infiltration *f*, pénétration *f*; **per·va·sive** [~siv] pénétrant.

per·verse ☐ [pə'və:s] pervers; méchant; revêche; contrariant; entêté dans le mal; ⚓ rebelle; **per·'verse·ness** *see perversity*; **per·'ver·sion** perversion *f*; *fig.* travestissement *m*; **per·'ver·si·ty** perversité *f*; esprit *m* contraire; caractère *m* revêche; ⚓ dépravation *f*; **per·'ver·sive** malsain, dépravant.

per·vert 1. [pə'və:t] pervertir; dépraver; fausser; détourner; **2.** ['pə:-və:t] apostat *m*; ⚓ perverti(e *f*) *m*; (*a. sexual* ~) inverti(e *f*) *m*; **per·'vert·er** pervertisseur (-euse *f*) *m*.

per·vi·ous ['pə:viəs] perméable (à, *to*); *fig.* accessible (à, *to*).

pes·ky ☐ *surt. Am.* F ['peski] maudit, sacré.

pes·sa·ry ['pesəri] passaire *m*.

pes·si·mism ['pesimizm] pessimisme *m*; **'pes·si·mist** pessimiste *mf*; **pes·si·mis·tic** (~ally) pessimiste.

pest [pest] animal *m ou* insecte *m* nuisible; *fig.* fléau *m*; peste *f*; ~ *control* lutte *f* antiparasitaire; **'pes·ter** importuner; tourmenter; *fig.* infester.

pest·i·cide ['pestisaid] pesticide *m*; insecticide *m*.

pes·tif·er·ous ☐ [pes'tifərəs] pestifère; nuisible; **pes·ti·lence** ['pesti-ləns] peste *f*; **'pes·ti·lent** *co.* assommant; **pes·ti·len·tial** ☐ [~'lenʃl] pestilentiel(le *f*); contagieux (-euse *f*); infecte.

pes·tle ['pesl] pilon *m*.
pet¹ [pet] accès *m* de mauvaise humeur; *in a* ~ de mauvaise humeur.
pet² [~] **1.** animal *m* favori; *fig.* enfant *mf* gâté(e), benjamin(e *f*) *m*, F chouchou(te *f*) *m*; **2.** favori(te *f*); de prédilection; ~ *dog* chien *m* favori *ou* de salon; ~ *name* diminutif *m*; ~ *subject* dada *m*; *co. it is my* ~ *aversion* il est mon cauchemar; **3.** choyer, F chouchouter; câliner; F (se) peloter; *Am.* F *petting party* réunion *f* intime (*entre jeunes gens des deux sexes*).
pet·al ♀ ['petl] pétale *m*.
pe·tard [pi'ta:d] † pétard *m* (*a. pyrotechnie*).
pe·ter F ['pi:tə]: ~ *out* s'épuiser; disparaître; *mot.* s'arrêter.
pe·ti·tion [pi'tiʃn] **1.** pétition *f*; supplique *f*; requête *f*; *eccl.* prière *f*; ⚖ ~ *in bankruptcy* demande *f* d'ouverture de la faillite; ~ *for divorce* demande *f* en divorce; **2.** adresser une pétition *etc.* à; réclamer (qch. à q., *s.o. for s.th.*); **pe'ti·tion·er** solliciteur (-euse *f*) *m*; ⚖ requérant(e *f*) *m*.
pet·rel *orn.* ['petrəl] pétrel *m*; *stormy* ~ oiseau *m* des tempêtes; *fig.* émissaire *m* de discorde.
pet·ri·fac·tion [petri'fækʃn] pétrifaction *f*.
pet·ri·fy ['petrifai] (se) pétrifier.
pet·rol *mot. Brit.* ['petrəl] essence *f*; ~ *engine* moteur *m* à essence; ~ *station* poste *m* d'essence; ~ *tank* réservoir *m* à essence.
pe·tro·le·um [pi'trouljəm] pétrole *m*, huile *f* minérale *ou* de roche; ~ *jelly* vaseline *f*.
pe·trol·o·gy [pe'trɔlədʒi] pétrologie *f*.
pet·ti·coat ['petikout] jupon *m* (*a. fig.*), jupe *f* de dessous; *attr. fig.* de cotillons; ~ *government* régime *m* de cotillons.
pet·ti·fog·ger ['petifɔgə] avocassier *m*; chicaner *m*; **'pet·ti·fog·ging** chicanier (-ère *f*).
pet·ti·ness ['petinis] mesquinerie *f*, petitesse *f*.
pet·ting F ['petin] pelotage *m*; *heavy* ~ pelotage *m* poussé.
pet·tish □ ['petiʃ] irritable; de mauvaise humeur; **'pet·tish·ness** irritabilité *f*; mauvaise humeur *f*.
pet·ty □ ['peti] insignifiant, petit; mesquin; ~ *bourgeoisie les* petits

bourgeois; ✝ ~ *cash* petite caisse *f*; ⚓ ~ *officer* contremaître *m*; ⚖ ~ *sessions pl.* session *f* de juges de paix.
pet·u·lance ['petjuləns] *see pettishness*; **pet·u·lant** ['~lənt] *see pettish*.
pew [pju:] banc *m* d'église; *sl.* siège *m*, place *f*.
pe·wit *orn.* ['pi:wit] vanneau *m* (huppé).
pew·ter ['pju:tə] **1.** étain *m*, potin *m*; **2.** d'étain; **'pew·ter·er** potier *m* d'étain.
pha·e·ton ['feitn] phaéton *m*; *mot. Am.* torpédo *f*.
pha·lanx ['fælæŋks] phalange *f*.
phan·tasm ['fæntæzm] chimère *f*; ⚕ phantasme *m*; **phan·tas·ma·go·ri·a** [~mə'gɔ:riə] fantasmagorie *f*.
phan·tom ['fæntəm] **1.** fantôme *m*, spectre *m*; **2.** fantôme.
Phar·i·sa·ic,   Phar·i·sa·i·cal □ [færi'seiik(l)] pharisaïque.
Phar·i·see ['færisi:] pharisien *m* (*a. fig.*).
phar·ma·ceu·ti·cal □ [fɑ:mə'sju:tikl] pharmaceutique; **phar·ma'ceu·tics** *sg.* pharmacie *f*; **phar·ma·cist** ['fɑ:məsist] pharmacien(ne *f*) *m*; **phar·ma·col·o·gy** [~'kɔlədʒi] pharmacologie *f*; **'phar·ma·cy** pharmacie *f*.
phar·ynx *anat.* ['færinks] pharynx *m*.
phase [feiz] phase *f*.
pheas·ant *orn.* ['feznt] faisan([d]e *f*) *m*; **'pheas·ant·ry** faisanderie *f*.
phe·nom·e·nal □ [fi'nɔminl] phénoménal (-aux *m/pl.*); *fig.* prodigieux (-euse *f*); **phe'nom·e·non** [~nən], *pl.* **-na** [~nə] phénomène *m* (*a. fig.*); *fig. personne:* prodige *m*.
phew [fju:] pouf!; pouah! (*dégoût*).
phi·al ['faiəl] flacon *m*, fiole *f*.
Phi Be·ta Kap·pa *Am.* ['fai 'bi:tə 'kæpə] *la plus ancienne association d'étudiants universitaires*.
phi·lan·der [fi'lændə] flirter; **phi·lan·der·er** coureur *m* de jupons.
phil·an·throp·ic [filən'θrɔpik] (~-*ally*) philanthropique; philanthrope (*personne*); **phi·lan·thro·pist** [fi-'lænθrəpist] philanthrope *mf*; **phi-'lan·thro·py** philanthropie *f*.
phi·lat·e·list [fi'lætəlist] philatéliste *mf*; **phi'lat·e·ly** philatélie *f*.
phi·lip·pic [fi'lipik] philippique *f*.
Phi·lis·tine ['filistain] philistin *m* (*a. fig.*).

phil·o·log·i·cal □ [filə'lɔdʒikl] philologique; **phi·lol·o·gist** [fi'lɔlədʒist] philologue *mf*; **phi'lol·o·gy** philologie *f*.

phi·los·o·pher [fi'lɔsəfə] philosophe *mf*; ~*s'* stone pierre *f* philosophale; **phil·o·soph·ic, phil·o·soph·i·cal** □ [filə'sɔfik(l)] philosophique; **phi·los·o·phize** [fi'lɔsəfaiz] philosopher; **phi'los·o·phy** philosophie *f*; ~ of life conception *f* de la vie.

phil·tre, phil·ter ['filtə] philtre *m*.

phiz F *co.* [fiz] visage *m*, F binette *f*.

phle·bi·tis ✛ [fli'baitis] phlébite *f*.

phlegm [flem] flegme *m* (a. ✛), calme *m*; **phleg·mat·ic** [fleg'mætik] (~*ally*) flegmatique.

pho·bi·a ['foubiə] phobie *f*.

Phoe·ni·cian [fi'niʃiən] 1. phénicien(ne *f*) *m*; 2. *ling.* phénicien *m*; Phénicien(ne *f*) *m*.

ph(o)e·nix ['fi:niks] phénix *m*.

phone F [foun] *see telephone*; ~ *call* coup *m* de fil; '~-in radio, télév. programme *m* à ligne ouverte.

pho·net·ic [fo'netik] 1. (~*ally*) phonétique; ~ *spelling* écriture *f* phonétique; 2. ~*s pl.* phonétique *f*; **pho·ne·ti·cian** [founi'tiʃn] phonéticien *m*.

pho·no·graph ['founəgrɑ:f] phonographe *m*; **pho·no·graph·ic** [~'græfik] (~*ally*) phonographique.

pho·nol·o·gy [fo'nɔlədʒi] phonologie *f*.

pho·n(e)y ['founi] 1. *Am. sl.* escroc *m*; 2. *Am.* F faux (fausse *f*); factice; en toc; ~ *flash* renseignement *m* inexact; nouvelle *f* inexacte; ~ *war* drôle de guerre.

phos·phate ⚗ ['fɔsfeit] phosphate *m*.

phos·pho·resce [fɔsfə'res] être phosphorescent; **phos·pho'res·cent** phosphorescent; **phos·phor·ic** ⚗ [~'fɔrik] phosphorique; **phos·pho·rous** ⚗ ['~fərəs] phosphoreux (-euse *f*); **phos·pho·rus** ⚗ ['~rəs] phosphore *m*.

pho·to F ['foutou] *see ~graph*; '~-cop·i·er machine *f* à photocopier, photocopieur *m*; '~-cop·y 1. photocopie *f*; 2. photocopier; ~·e'lec·tric cell cellule *f* photoélectrique; ~-en·grav·ing [~in'greivin] photogravure *f* industrielle; '~-'fin·ish décision *f* par photo, photo *f* à l'arrivée; '~-flash flash (*pl.* flashes) *m* (à ampoule);

~·'gram·me·try [~'græmitri] photogrammétrie *f*.

pho·to·graph ['foutəgrɑ:f] 1. photographie *f*; 2. photographier; prendre une photographie de; **pho·tog·ra·pher** [fə'tɔgrəfə] photographe *m*; **pho·to·graph·ic** [foutə'græfik] (~*ally*) photographique; ~ *library* archives *f/pl.* photographiques, photothèque *f*; **pho·tog·ra·phy** [fə'tɔgrəfi] photographie *f*; prise *f* de vues.

pho·to·gra·vure [foutəgrə'vjuə] photogravure *f*, héliogravure *f*; **pho·tom·e·ter** [fo'tɔmitə] photomètre *m*; **pho·to·play** ['foutəplei] film *m* dramatique; **pho·to·sen·si·tive** ['foutou'sensitiv] photosensible; **pho·to·stat** ['foutəstæt], **pho·to·stat·ic** [~'stætik] ~ *copy* photocopie *f*; **pho·to·te·leg·ra·phy** [foutəti'legrəfi] téléphotographie *f*; **pho·to·type** ['~taip] prototype *m*.

phrase [freiz] 1. locution *f*; tour *m* de phrase; expression *f*; *gramm.* membre *m* de phrase; ♪ phrase *f*, période *f*; 2. exprimer (*une pensée*), rédiger; ♪ phraser; '~-book recueil *m* d'expressions; '~-mon·ger phraseur (-euse *f*) *m*; **phra·se·ol·o·gy** [~zi'ɔlədʒi] phraséologie *f*.

phre·net·ic [fri'netik] (~*ally*) affolé; frénétique.

phre·nol·o·gy [fri'nɔlədʒi] phrénologie *f*.

phthis·i·cal ['θaisikl] phtisique; **phthi·sis** ['~sis] phtisie *f*.

phut *sl.* [fʌt]: *go* ~ claquer.

phys·ic [fizik] 1. médecine *f*; F drogues *f/pl.*; ~*s sg.* physique *f*; 2. *sl.* médicamenter (*q.*); '**phys·i·cal** □ physique; corporel(le *f*); matériel(le *f*); ~ *condition* état *m* physique; ~ *culture* culture *f* physique; ~ *test* visite *f* médicale; **phy·si·cian** [fi'ziʃn] médecin *m*; **phys·i·cist** ['~sist] physicien(ne *f*) *m*.

phys·i·og·no·my [fizi'ɔnəmi] physionomie *f*; **phys·i·og·ra·phy** [~'ɔgrəfi] physiographie *f*; géographie *f* physique; **phys·i·ol·o·gy** [~'ɔlədʒi] physiologie *f*.

phys·i·o·ther·a·pist [fiziou'θerəpist] kinésithérapeute *mf*; **phys·i·o·ther·a·py** [~'θerəpi] kinésithérapie *f*.

phy·sique [fi'zi:k] physique *m*.

pi·an·ist ['pjænist; ♪ 'piənist] pianiste *mf*.

pi·a·no¹ ♪ ['pjɑ:nou] *adv.* piano.

pi·an·o² ['pjænou; ♪ 'pjɑːnou] piano *m*; *cottage* ~ petit droit *m*; *grand* ~ piano *m* à queue.

pi·an·o·for·te [pjæno'fɔːti] *see* piano².

pi·az·za [pi'ædzə] place *f*; *Am.* véranda *f*.

pi·broch ['piːbrɔk] pibroch *m* (= *air de cornemuse*).

pic·a·roon [pikə'ruːn] corsaire *m*.

pic·a·yune *Am.* [pikə'juːn] **1.** *usu. fig.* sou *m*; bagatelle *f*; **2.** mesquin.

pic·ca·nin·ny *co.* ['pikənini] **1.** négrillon(ne *f*) *m*; *Am.* F mioche *mf*; **2.** enfantin.

pick [pik] **1.** pic *m*, pioche *f*; ✗ rivelaine *f*; (*ou tooth*~) cure-dent *m*; élite *f*, choix *m*; **2.** *v/t.* piocher (*la terre*); se curer (*les dents*); ronger (*un os*); plumer (*la volaille*); cueillir (*une fleur, un fruit*); trier (*du minerai*); effilocher (*des chiffons*); éplucher (*de la laine*); *Am.* jouer de (*le banjo*); crocheter (*la serrure*); choisir; F (*a.* ~ *at*) pignocher (*sa nourriture*); ~ one's way marcher avec précaution; ~ pockets voler à la tire; ~ *a quarrel with* chercher querelle à; *see* bone 1; crow 1; ~ out choisir; enlever; trouver; reconnaître; *peint.* échampir; *v/i.* picoter, picorer (*oiseau*); F manger du bout des dents; *surt. Am.* F ~ *at* (*ou on*) chercher noise à (*q.*); critiquer; ~ up *v/t.* prendre; ramasser, relever; (re)trouver; apprendre; aller chercher (*q.*); repérer (*un avion*); faire la connaissance de (*q.*); capter (⚡ *le courant*); *un message*); *radio:* avoir (*un poste*); *v/i.* se rétablir; *mot.* reprendre; ~-**back** ['~əbæk] sur le dos; '~-**axe** pioche *f*; **picked** choisi, de choix; '**pick·er** cueilleur (-euse *f*) *m etc.*; ⊕ machine *f* à éplucher.

pick·et ['pikit] **1.** piquet *m* (*a.* ✗, *a. de grève*); **2.** *v/t.* mettre (*un cheval*) au(x) piquet(s); palissader; ✗ détacher en grand-garde; ⊕ installer des piquets de grève; *v/i.* être gréviste en faction.

pick·ing ['pikiŋ] piochage *m etc.* (*see* pick); choix *m*; ~s *pl.* restes *m/pl.*, *fig. sl.* gratte *f*.

pick·le ['pikl] **1.** marinade *f*; saumure *f*; conserve *f* au vinaigre; F enfant *mf* terrible; F pétrin *m*; *see* mix; **2.** mariner, conserver; ~d herring hareng *m* salé.

pick...: '~-**lock** crochet *m*; *personne:* crocheteur *m* de serrures; '~-**me-up** F cordial *m*; remontant *m*; '~-**pock·et** voleur (-euse *f*) *m* à la tire; '~-**up 1.** ramassement *m*; *chose f* ramassée; *phonographe:* pick-up *m/inv.*; ✝ (*ou* ~ *in prices*) hausse *f*; *Am.* radio, télév. pick-up *m/inv.*; **2.** F hâtivement rassemblé (*équipe, formation, etc.*); improvisé; ~ *dinner* repas *m* fait de restes.

pick·y ['piki] difficile, délicat.

pic·nic ['piknik] **1.** pique-nique *m*; partie *f* de plaisir; dînette *f* sur l'herbe; **2.** faire un pique-nique; dîner sur l'herbe.

pic·to·ri·al [pik'tɔːriəl] **1.** ☐ en images; pittoresque; illustré; **2.** périodique *m ou* journal *m* illustré.

pic·ture ['piktʃə] **1.** tableau *m*; image *f*; peinture *f*; gravure *f*; portrait *m*; ~s *pl.* cinéma *m*; films *m/pl.*; *attr.* d'images; du cinéma; ~-*palace* cinéma *m*; ~ (*post*)*card* carte *f* postale illustrée; ~ *puzzle* rébus *m*; **2.** dépeindre; représenter; se figurer (*qch.*); s'imaginer (*qch.*); '~-**book** album *m*; livre *m* d'images; '~-**go·er** *Brit.* habitué(e *f*) *m* du cinéma.

pic·tur·esque ☐ [piktʃə'resk] pittoresque.

pidg·in Eng·lish ['pidʒin'iŋgliʃ] jargon *m* commercial anglo-chinois; *fig.* F petit nègre *m*.

pie¹ [pai] *viande etc.:* pâté *m*; *fruits:* tourte *f*; *typ.* pâte *f*, pâté *m*; *see* finger 1.   [*fig.* bigarré.]

pie² *orn.* [~] pie *f*; '~-**bald** pie;]

piece [piːs] **1.** pièce *f* (*a. théâ., échecs, monnaie,* ♪); fragment *m*; morceau *m* (*a.* ♪); partie *f*; ~ *of advice* conseil *m*; ~ *of jewellery* bijou (*pl.* -x) *m*; ~ *of news* nouvelle *f*; *by the* ~ à la pièce; *in* ~s en morceaux; *of a* ~ uniforme; *all of a* ~ tout d'une pièce; *break* (*ou go*) *to* ~s se désagréger; tomber en lambeaux (*robe etc.*); *give s.o. a* ~ *of one's mind* parler carrément à q.; *take to* ~s défaire; ⊕ démonter; **2.** raccommoder, rapiécer; ~ *out* rallonger; augmenter; ~ *together* joindre, unir; coordonner; ~ *up* raccommoder; '~-**goods** *pl.* marchandises *f/pl.* à la pièce; '~-**meal** pièce à pièce, peu à peu; '~-**work** travail (*pl.* -aux) *m* à la tâche.

pied [paid] mi-parti; bigarré.

pie-eyed *sl.* ['paiaid] soûl, rond, plein.

pie-plant *Am.* ['paiplɑ:nt] rhubarbe *f*.

pier [piə] jetée *f*, digue *f*; quai *m*; △ pilastre *m*; pilier *m*; '**pier·age** ⚓ droits *m/pl.* de jetée.

pierce [piəs] *v/t.* percer (*a. fig.*); transpercer (*le cœur*); *v/i.* percer; *fig.* pénétrer; '**pierc·er** ⊕ perçoir *m*, poinçon *m*; '**pierc·ing** □ pénétrant (*a. fig.*).

pier-glass ['piəglɑ:s] trumeau *m*.

pi·e·tism ['paiətizm] piétisme *m*.

pi·e·ty ['paiəti] piété *f*.

pif·fle *sl.* ['pifl] **1.** balivernes *f/pl.*; futilités *f/pl.*; ⚡ dire des sottises.

pig [pig] **1.** porc *m*, cochon *m*; *métall.* gueuse *f* (*de fonte*); saumon *m* (*de plomb*); buy a ~ in a poke acheter chat en poche; **2.** cochonner; ⚡ vivre comme dans une étable.

pi·geon ['pidʒin] *zo.* pigeon *m*; ⚡ pigeon *m*, dupe *f*; *sl.* affaire *f*; '~**hole 1.** case *f*; **2.** caser (*des papiers*); *admin.* classer; ⚡ faire rester dans les cartons; '**pi·geon·ry** colombier *m*.

pig·ger·y ['pigəri] porcherie *f*.

pig·gish □ ['pigiʃ] malpropre; entêté. [gueuse.]

pig·head·ed ['pig'hedid] obstiné, têtu.

pig·i·ron ['pigaiən] fonte *f* en]

pig·let ['piglit] petit cochon *m*.

pig·ment ['pigmənt] pigment *m*, colorant *m*.

pig·my *see* **pygmy**.

pig...: '~**nut** gland *m* de terre; '~**skin** peau *f* de porc; *Am. sl.* ballon *m* de football; ~**sty** ['~stai] porcherie *f*; *fig.* taudis *m*; '~**tail** queue *f* (*de cheveux*); '~**wash** pâtée *f* pour les porcs.

pike [paik] ⚔ pique *f*; *géog.* pic *m*; *icht.* brochet *m*; '**pik·er** *Am. sl.* boursicoteur *m*; lâcheur *m*; '**pike·staff**: *as plain as a* ~ clair comme le jour.

pil·chard *icht.* ['piltʃəd] sardine *f*.

pile[1] [pail] **1.** tas *m*; ⚔ *armes*: faisceau *m*; △ masse *f*; édifice *m*; *fig.* fortune *f*; ⚡ pile *f* de Volta; *phys.* (*ou* atomic ~) pile *f* atomique; **2.** *v/i.* (*a.* ~ up) s'entasser, s'amonceler; *v/t.* (*a.* ~ up) entasser, empiler; amasser (*une fortune*); ⚔ ~

arms former les faisceaux; *fig.* ~ *it on* exagérer.

pile[2] [~] pieu *m*.

pile[3] [~] *tex.* poil *m*.

pile-driv·er ⊕ ['paildraivə] sonnette *f*; '**pile-dwell·ing** habitation *f* lacustre *ou* sur pilotis.

piles ⚕ [pailz] *pl.* hémorroïdes *f/pl.*

pile-up F ['pailʌp] carambolage *m ou* télescopage *m* (*en série*).

pil·fer ['pilfə] *v/t.* chiper; *v/i.* faire de petits vols.

pil·grim ['pilgrim] pèlerin(e *f*) *m*; ☿ Père *m* pèlerin; '**pil·grim·age** pèlerinage *m*.

pill [pil] pilule *f*; F personne *f* embêtante, casse-pieds *mf inv.*

pil·lage ['pilidʒ] **1.** pillage *m*; **2.** piller, saccager.

pil·lar ['pilə] pilier *m*, colonne *f*; '~**box** boîte *f* aux lettres; borne *f* postale; **pil·lared** ['~ləd] à piliers, à colonnes; en pilier *etc.*

pil·lion ['piljən] coussinet *m* de cheval; *mot.* siège *m* arrière; *ride* ~ monter derrière.

pil·lo·ry ['piləri] **1.** pilori *m*; *in the* ~ au pilori; **2.** mettre au pilori; *fig.* exposer au ridicule.

pil·low ['pilou] **1.** oreiller *m*; coussin *m*; ⊕ coussinet *m*; **2.** reposer sa tête (*sur, on*); '~**case**, ✝ '~**slip** taie *f* d'oreiller.

pi·lot ['pailət] **1.** pilote *m* (*a.* ⚓, ✈); *fig.* guide *m*; ~ *instructor* professeur *m* de pilotage; ☿ *Officer* sous-lieutenant *m* aviateur; ~ *plant* installation *f* d'essai; ~ *project* projet *m* d'essai, projet-pilote *m* (*pl.* projets-pilotes); **2.** piloter; conduire; '**pi·lot·age** (*frais m/pl.* de) pilotage *m*; '**pi·lot-bal'loon** ballon *m* d'essai.

pil·ule ['pilju:l] petite pilule *f*.

pi·men·to [pi'mentou] piment *m*.

pimp [pimp] **1.** entremetteur (-euse *f*) *m*; **2.** exercer le métier de proxénète.

pim·ple ['pimpl] bouton *m*, bourgeon *m*; '**pim·pled**, '**pim·ply** boutonneux (-euse *f*); pustuleux (-euse *f*).

pin [pin] **1.** épingle *f*; ⊕ goupille *f*, cheville *f*; *jeu*: quille *f*; clou *m*; *cuis.* rouleau *m* (*à pâte*); *Am.* insigne *m* (*d'une association estudiantine etc.*); ~s *pl. sl.* quilles *f/pl.* (= *jambes*); **2.** épingler; attacher avec des épingles; clouer; *sl. fig.*

obliger (q.) à reconnaître les faits;
(souv. ~ down) obliger (à, to); ~
one's hopes on mettre toutes ses
espérances dans.

pin·a·fore ['pinəfɔ:] tablier m.

pin·ball ma·chine ['pinbɔ:lmaˈʃi:n]
flipper m.

pin·cers ['pinsəz] pl.: (a pair of) ~
(une) pince f, (des) tenailles f/pl.

pinch [pintʃ] **1.** pinçade f; tabac:
prise f; sel etc.: pincée f; fig.
morsure f; fig. besoin m; **2.** v/t.
pincer; gêner; sl. chiper (=voler);
arrêter (q.); v/i. (se res)serrer; faire
des petites économies; se priver;
pinched étroit; gêné; fig. hâve.

pinch·beck ['pintʃbek] **1.** ⊕ chryso-
cale m, similor m; fig. trompe-l'œil
m/inv.; **2.** d'occasion.

pinch-hit Am. ['pintʃhit] suppléer,
remplacer (q., for s.o.).

pin·cush·ion ['pinkuʃin] pelote f à
aiguilles.   [pin.\

pine¹ ♀ [pain] pin m; bois m de⌡

pine² [⁓] languir (après, pour for);
~ away dépérir; mourir de langueur.

pine...: '~**ap·ple** ♀ ananas m;
'~**cone** pomme f de pin.

pin·er·y ['painəri] serre f à ananas;
(a. '**pine·wood**) pineraie f.

pin-feath·er ['pinfeðə] plume f
naissante.

pin·fold ['pinfould] parc m (à
moutons etc.); fourrière f.

ping [piŋ] cingler, fouetter.

ping-pong ['piŋpɔŋ] ping-pong m.

pin·ion ['pinjən] **1.** aileron m; poét.
aile f; (a. ~-feather) penne f; ⊕
pignon m; **2.** rogner les ailes à; fig.
lier les bras à.

pink¹ [piŋk] **1.** ♀ œillet m; couleur:
rose m; chasse: rouge m; fig. modèle
m; comble m; sl. in the ~ florissant,
en parfaite santé. **2.** v/t. teindre en
rose; v/i. rougir.

pink² [⁓] toucher; denteler les
bords de (une robe); fig. orner; ~ing
shears pl. ciseaux m/pl. à denteler.

pink³ mot. [⁓] cliqueter.

pink·ish ['piŋkiʃ] rosâtre.

pin-mon·ey ['pinmʌni] argent m de
poche (d'une femme ou jeune fille).

pin·nace ⊕ ['pinis] grand canot m,
pinasse f.

pin·na·cle ['pinəkl] ⚠ pinacle m;
montagne: cime f; fig. faîte m,
apogée f.

pi·noc(h)·le Am. ['pi:nʌkl] (sorte de)
belote f.

pin...: '~**point** localiser précisément; bien définir; mettre le doigt
sur (un problème); '~**prick** piqûre f
d'épingle; '~**stripe** tex. filet m.

pint [paint] pinte f (0,57, Am.
0,47 litre).

pin·tle ⊕ ['pintl] pivot m central;
mot. cheville f ouvrière.

pin·to Am. ['pintou] **1.** pl. -tos
cheval m pie; **2.** pie.

pin-up (girl ['pinʌp('gə:l)]) pin-up
f/inv.; beauté f.

pi·o·neer [paiəˈniə] **1.** ⚔, fig. pionnier m; fig. défricheur (-euse f) m;
2. frayer (un chemin).

pi·ous □ ['paiəs] pieux (-euse f);
pie (œuvre).

pip¹ [pip] vét. pépie f; sl. have the ~
avoir le cafard.

pip² [⁓] fruit: pépin m; carte, dé,
etc.: point m; ⚔ grades: étoile f.

pip³ sl. [⁓] v/t. refuser (un candidat);
vaincre; v/i. ~ out mourir.

pipe [paip] **1.** tuyau m (a. gaz);
tube m (a. anat.); pipe f (tabac,
a. mesure de vin: 572,4 litres); ♪
chalumeau m; oiseau etc.: chant m;
2. canaliser; amener etc. par un
pipe-line; jouer (un air); lisérer
(une robe etc.); ⚓ siffler, donner un
coup de sifflet; F ~ one's eye(s)
pleurnicher; ~d music musique f
de fond enregistrée; '~**clay 1.** terre f
de pipe; blanc m de terre à pipe; **2.**
astiquer au blanc de terre à pipe;
dream fig. château m en Espagne;
'~**lay·er** poseur m de tuyaux; Am.
pol. intrigant m; '~**line** pipeline m;
'**pip·er** joueur m de chalumeau etc.;
F pay the ~ payer les violons.

pip·ing ['paipiŋ] **1.** sifflant; heureux
(-euse f) (époque); ~ hot tout chaud;
2. canalisation f; tuyauterie f;
oiseaux: gazouillement m; robe:
lisérage m; cost. passepoil m.

pip·it orn. ['pipit] pipit m.

pip·kin ['pipkin] poêlon m.

pip·pin ♀ ['pipin] reinette f; sl.
it's a ~ il est remarquable.

pip·squeak F ['pipskwi:k] rien du
tout m/ (pl. riens du tout ou inv.).

pi·quan·cy ['pi:kənsi] (goût m)
piquant m.

pi·quant □ ['pi:kənt] piquant.

pique [pi:k] **1.** pique f, ressentiment

m; 2. piquer; exciter (*la curiosité*); ~ *o.s. upon* se piquer de.

pi·ra·cy ['paiərəsi] piraterie *f*; contrefaçon *f* (*d'un livre*); plagiat *m*; **pi·rate** ['~rit] 1. *homme ou navire*: pirate *m*; contrefacteur *m*; plagiaire *m*; *radio* ~, ~ *listener* auditeur (-trice *f*) *m* illicite; ~ *station* radio *f* pirate; 2. pirater; contrefaire; plagier; **pi·rat·i·cal** □ [pai'rætikl] de pirate *etc.*

Pis·ces *astr.* ['paisi:z] les Poissons *m/pl.* [culture *f*.]

pis·ci·cul·ture ['pisikʌltʃə] pisci-

pish [piʃ] bah!; pouah!

piss ∨ [pis] 1. pisse *f*, urine *f*; 2. pisser, uriner; ~ *off!* fous le camp!; ~*ed* soûl, plein; *be* ~*ed off* en avoir marre, en avoir ras le bol.

pis·ta·chi·o [pi'sta:ʃiou] pistache *f*.

pis·til ♀ ['pistil] pistil *m*.

pis·tol ['pistl] pistolet *m*; '~-**whip** *Am.* F frapper d'un pistolet.

pis·ton ⊕ ['pistən] piston *m*; *pompe*: sabot *m*; ~ *displacement* cylindrée *f*; ~ *ring* segment *m* de piston; ~ *rod* tige *f* de piston; ~ *stroke* coup *m* de *ou* course *f* du piston.

pit [pit] 1. fosse *f*, trou *m*; *anat.* creux *m*; *théâ.* parterre *m*; *Am.* bourse *f* de commerce, parquet *m*; *mot.* fosse *f*; mine *f* (*de charbon*); *petite vérole*: cicatrice *f*; piège *m* (*à animaux*); 2. piquer, trouer; marquer; ⚓ ~ *against* ensiler; ~ *against* mettre (*q.*) aux prises avec; ~*ted with smallpox* marqué de la petite vérole.

pit-(a-)pat ['pit(ə)'pæt] tic-tac.

pitch¹ [pitʃ] 1. poix *f*; brai *m*; 2. enduire de brai; ⚓ calfater.

pitch² [~] 1. lancement *m*; ♪ *son*: hauteur *f*; *instrument*: diapason *m*; ⊕ pas *m*; *scie*: angle *m* des dents; ⚓ tangage *m*; ♥ *marché*: place *f*, *camelot*: place *f* habituelle; *cricket*: terrain *m*; *fig.* degré *m*; ~ *and toss* jeu *m* de pile ou face; 2. *v/t.* lancer; mettre; paver (*la chaussée*); charger (*le foin etc.*); dresser (*une tente*); établir (*un camp*); poser (*une échelle*); ♪ ~ *higher* (*lower*) hausser (baisser) (*le ton*); ♪ jouer dans une clef donnée; *fig.* arrêter, déterminer; ~*ed battle* bataille *f* rangée; ~ *one's hope too high* viser trop haut; *v/i.* ⚒ camper; tomber; ⚓ tanguer; ~ *upon* arrêter son choix sur; F ~ *into* taper sur; dire son fait à.

pitch·er¹ ['pitʃə] lanceur *m* (*de la balle*).

pitch·er² [~] cruche *f*; broc *m*.

pitch·fork ['pitʃfɔːk] 1. fourche *f* à foin *etc.*; ♪ diapason *m*; 2. lancer avec la fourche; *fig.* bombarder (*q.* dans un poste, *s.o. into a job*).

pitch-pine ♀ ['pitʃpain] faux sapin *m*.

pitch·y ['pitʃi] poisseux (-euse *f*); noir comme poix.

pit-coal ⚒ ['pitkoul] houille *f*.

pit·e·ous □ ['pitiəs] pitoyable, piteux (-euse *f*).

pit·fall ['pitfɔːl] trappe *f*; piège *m*.

pith [piθ] moelle *f* (*a. fig.*); *orange*: peau *f* blanche; sève *f*, ardeur *f*.

pit-head ⚒ ['pithed] carreau *m*.

pith·i·ness ['piθinis] concision *f*; **'pith·less** □ mou (mol *devant une voyelle ou un h muet*; molle *f*).

pith·y □ ['piθi] moelleux (-euse *f*); concis.

pit·i·a·ble □ ['pitiəbl] pitoyable.

pit·i·ful □ ['pitiful] compatissant; pitoyable; lamentable (*a. péj.*).

pit·i·less □ ['pitilis] impitoyable.

pit·man ['pitmən] mineur *m*; houilleur *m*.

pit-props ⚒ ['pitprɔps] *pl.* bois *m* de soutènement.

pit·tance ['pitəns] maigre salaire *m*; gages *m/pl.* dérisoires; † aumône *f*.

pi·tu·i·tar·y *anat.* [pi'tju:itəri] pituitaire. [mine.]

pit·wood ⚒ ['pitwud] bois *m* de

pit·y ['piti] 1. pitié *f*, compassion *f* (*de on, for*); *for* ~*'s sake!* par pitié!; *de grâce!*; *it is a* ~ c'est dommage; *it is a thousand pities* c'est mille fois *ou* bien dommage; 2. plaindre; avoir pitié de; *I* ~ *him* il me fait pitié.

piv·ot ['pivət] 1. ⊕, ✕ pivot *m*; ⊕ tourillon *m*; *fig.* axe *m*, pivot *m*; 2. *v/i.* pivoter (*sur*, ~ *[up]on*); *v/t.* faire pivoter; **'piv·o·tal** pivotal (-aux *m/pl.*); à pivot.

pix·ie ['piksi] lutin *m*; fée *f*.

pix·i·lat·ed *Am.* ['piksəleitid] loufoque; dingo *inv.*

pix·y ['piksi] *see* **pixie**.

pla·ca·bil·i·ty [pleikə'biliti] douceur *f*; **'pla·ca·ble** doux (douce *f*); facile à apaiser.

pla·card ['plækɑːd] 1. écriteau *m*, affiche *f*; 2. afficher; couvrir (*qch.*) d'affiches.

pla·cate [plə'keit] apaiser, calmer.

place [pleis] **1.** lieu *m*, endroit *m*, localité *f*; station *f*; place *f*; rang *m*; emploi *m*, poste *m*, situation *f*; ~ *of delivery* destination *f*; ~ *of employment usu.* travail (*pl.* -aux) *m*, emploi *m*, bureau *m etc.*; *give* ~ *to* faire place à (*qch.*); *in* ~ *en* place; *in* ~ *of* au lieu de; *in his* ~ à sa place; *in the first* ~ d'abord; *out of* ~ déplacé; **2.** placer (*a. de l'argent*); (re)mettre; ⚔ mettre en faction (*la sentinelle*); ✝ passer (*une commande*), mettre en vente; faire accepter (*un article à un éditeur etc.*); ~ *a child under s.o.'s care* mettre un enfant sous la garde de q.; ~ **mat** set *m*, napperon *m* individuel; '~**name** nom *m* de lieu.

plac·id □ ['plæsid] calme; serein; **pla·cid·i·ty** calme *m*, tranquillité *f*.

plack·et ['plækit] fente *f* (*de jupe*).

pla·gi·a·rism ['pleidʒiərizm] plagiat *m*; '**pla·gi·a·rist** plagiaire *m*; démarqueur *m*; '**pla·gi·a·rize** plagier.

plague [pleig] **1.** peste *f*; fléau *m*; **2.** tourmenter, harceler; '~**spot** *usu. fig.* foyer *m* d'infection.

pla·guy F ['pleigi] assommant; *adv.* rudement.

plaice *icht.* [pleis] plie *f*.

plaid [plæd] *tex.* tartan *m*; plaid *m* (*écossais*).

plain [plein] **1.** *adj.* □ évident, clair, simple; *tricot:* endroit *inv.*; lisse; carré, franc(he *f*); sans beauté; *cuis.* au naturel, bourgeois; *in* ~ *English* en bon anglais; ~ *chocolate* chocolat *m* à craquer; ~ *fare* cuisine *f* bourgeoise; ~ *knitting* tricot *m* à l'endroit; ~ *paper* papier *m* non réglé; ~ *sewing* couture *f* simple; **2.** *adv.* clairement; carrément; **3.** *su.* plaine *f*; *surt. Am. attr.* des champs; '~**clothes man** agent *m* en civil; agent *m* de la sûreté; ~ **deal·ing 1.** franchise *f*, loyauté *f*; **2.** franc(he *f*) et loyal(e *f*); '**plain·ness** simplicité *f*; franchise *f*; clarté *f*; netteté *f*; manque *m* de beauté.

plaint ⚖ [pleint] plainte *f*; **plain·tiff** ⚖ ['~if] demandeur (-eresse *f*) *m*; '**plain·tive** □ plaintif (-ive *f*).

plait [plæt] **1.** *chevaux:* tresse *f*, natte *f*; *see pleat 1*; **2.** tresser; *see pleat 2.*

plan [plæn] **1.** plan *m*; projet *m*,

dessein *m*; levé *m* (*d'un terrain*); **2.** tracer le plan de; *fig.* projeter, se proposer (*qch., s.th.*; de *inf.*, to *inf.*); méditer; ~*ned economy* économie *f* planifiée; ~*ning board* conseil *m* de planification.

plane[1] [plein] **1.** uni; plat; égal (-aux *m/pl.*); **2.** ⚙ plan *m*, aile *f*; *fig.* niveau *m*; F avion *m*; ⊕ rabot *m*; *elevating (depressing)* ~ ✈ gouvernail *m* d'altitude (de profondeur); **3.** planer, dresser; aplanir; raboter; ✈ voyager en avion; planer.

plane[2] ♀ [~] (*a. ~tree*) platane *m*.

plan·et *astr.* ['plænit] planète *f*.

plane-ta·ble *surv.* ['pleinteibl] planchette *f*.

plan·e·tar·i·um [plæni'tɛəriəm] planétaire *m*; **plan·e·tar·y** ['~təri] planétaire; terrestre; *fig.* errant.

pla·nim·e·try ♀ [plæ'nimitri] planimétrie *f*.

plan·ish ⊕ ['plæniʃ] aplanir; polir.

plank [plæŋk] **1.** planche *f*; madrier *m*; *Am. parl.* point *m* d'un programme électoral; **2.** planchéier; couvrir de planches; *sl., Am.* F ~ *down (out)* payer, allonger (*l'argent*); ~ *bed* lit *m* de camp; couchette *f* en bois; '**plank·ing** planchéiage *m*; revêtement *m*.

plant [plɑːnt] **1.** plante *f*; pose *f*; installation *f*; machines *f/pl.*; *sl.* coup *m* monté, escroquerie *f*; *Am. sl. a.* cachette *f*; **2.** planter (*a.* ✍, *a. fig.*); implanter (*une idée*) (dans l'esprit de q., *into s.o.'s. mind*); loger; poser; enterrer (*des légumes*); F appliquer (*un coup de poing*); *sl.* monter (*un coup*) (contre, on); ~ *o.s.* se planter (devant, *in front of*).

plan·tain[1] ♀ ['plæntin] plantain *m*.

plan·tain[2] ♀ [~] banane *f* (des Antilles).

plan·ta·tion [plæn'teiʃn] plantation *f*; bosquet *m*; '**plant·er** ['plɑːntə] planteur *m*; '**plant·louse** puceron *m*, aphis *m*. [~ plaque *f*.]

plaque [plɑːk] plaque *f*; ⚕ *dental*]

plash[1] ['plæʃ] **1.** clapotis *m*; flac *m*; flaque *f* d'eau; **2.** flac! floc!; **3.** *v/t.* plonger en faisant flac; *v/i.* clapoter; faire flac.

plash[2] [~] entrelacer (*les branches d'une haie*).

plash·y ['plæʃi] bourbeux (-euse *f*); couvert de flaques d'eau.

plasm, plas·ma *biol.* ['plæzm(ə)] (proto)plasma *m.*

plas·ter ['plɑːstə] 1. *pharm.* emplâtre *m;* sparadrap *m;* ⊕ plâtre *m;* enduit *m; (usu.* ~ *of Paris)* plâtre *m* de moulage; ~ *cast* moulage *m* au plâtre; 2. ✠ mettre un emplâtre sur; plâtrer; enduire; *fig.* recouvrir (de, *with*); '**plas·ter·er** plâtrier *m.*

plas·tic ['plæstik] 1. *(~ally)* plastique; *(synthetic)* ~ *material* = 2. (matière *f*) plastique *m;* **plas·ti·cine** ['~tisiːn] plasticine *f;* **plas·tic·i·ty** [~'tisiti] plasticité *f.*

plas·tron ['plæstrən] plastron *m.*

plat [plæt] *see* plait; plot¹.

plate [pleit] 1. *usu.* plaque *f (a. mot., photo, radio, a.* de *porte); métal:* lame *f; typ.* cliché *m; livre:* planche *f,* gravure *f;* assiette *f; course:* coupe *f; (a.* ~ *iron)* tôle *f; Am. baseball:* point *m* de départ du batteur; limite *f* du batteur; *(a. dental* ~*)* dentier *m; radio:* anode *f;* ⊕ *machine:* plateau *m;* 2. plaquer; métalliser; ✕ blinder; ♣ border en acier *etc.*

pla·teau *géog.* ['plætou] plateau *m.*

plate-bas·ket ['pleitbɑːskit] ramasse-couverts *m/inv.;* **plate·ful** ['~ful] assiettée *f.*

plate...: '~**glass** glace *f* de vitrage; '~**hold·er** *phot.* châssis *m;* '~**lay·er** ⊕ poseur *m* de rails; ouvrier *m* de la voie.

plat·en ['plætn] *typ.* platine *f; machine* à écrire: cylindre *m.*

plat·er ['pleitə] ⊕ plaqueur *m; sp.* cheval *m* à réclamer.

plat·form ['plætfɔːm] terrasse *f;* estrade *f; géog.* plate-forme *(pl.* plates-formes) *f;* ⛴ quai *m,* trottoir *m; Am. surt.* plate-forme *(pl.* plates-formes) *f* de wagon; *pol.* programme *m (Am. souv.* électoral).

plat·i·num *min.* ['plætinəm] platine *m.* [tude *f.*]

plat·i·tude *fig.* ['plætitjuːd] plati-]

pla·toon ✕ [plə'tuːn] section *f.*

plat·ter ['plætə] écuelle *f.*

plau·dit ['plɔːdit] *usu.* ~*s pl.* applaudissements *m/pl.*

plau·si·bil·i·ty [plɔːzə'biliti] plausibilité *f;* vraisemblance *f.*

plau·si·ble ☐ ['plɔːzəbl] plausible; vraisemblable; spécieux (-euse *f*).

play [plei] 1. jeu *m (a.* ⊕, *lumière, amusement); théâ.* pièce *f;* spectacle

m; ⊕ liberté *f;* ⊕ fonctionnement *m; fair (foul)* ~ jeu *m* loyal (déloyal); ~ *on words* jeu *m* de mots; calembour *m; bring into* ~ mettre en jeu *ou* en œuvre; *make great* ~ *with* attacher beaucoup d'importance à; souligner; 2. *v/i.* jouer *(a. fig.);* s'amuser; folâtrer; ⊕ fonctionner librement, jouer; ~ *fast and loose with* jouer double jeu avec; *sp.* ~ *at football (at cards)* jouer au football (aux cartes); ~ *for time* temporiser; *théâ.* ~ *to the gallery* jouer pour la galerie; ~ *up* jouer de son mieux; F ~ *up to* flatter; ~ *upon* abuser de; agir sur; *v/t. sp.* jouer à; ♪ jouer de *(un instrument); théâ.* jouer *(un rôle); fig.* se conduire en; ~ *the deuce with* ruiner; faire un mal du diable à; ~ *down* minimiser; ~ *off* opposer (q. à q., *s.o. against s.o.);* ~*ed out* à bout de forces; épuisé; F ~ *up* chahuter (q.); '~**act** *fig.* faire du théâtre, jouer la comédie; '~**ing** *fig.* (pure) comédie *f,* cinéma *m;* '~**back** lecture *f* sonore; play-back *m;* '~**bill** affiche *f* de théâtre; '~**book** *théâ.* recueil *m* de pièces; '~**boy** viveur *m;* '**play·er** joueur (-euse *f) m;* acteur (-trice *f) m; ♪* exécutant(e *f) m; sp.* équipier *m;* '**play·er-pi·an·o** piano *m* mécanique; '**play·fel·low** camarade *mf* de jeu; **play·ful** ☐ ['~ful] badin, enjoué; '**play·ful·ness** badinage *m;* enjouement *m.*

play...: '~**go·er** amateur (-trice *f) m* du théâtre; '~**ground** terrain *m* de jeu(x); cour *f* de récréation; '~**house** théâtre *m; Am.* maison *f* de poupée.

play·ing...: '~**card** carte *f* (à jouer); '~**field** terrain *m* de jeu(x) *ou* de sports.

play...: '~**mate** *see* playfellow; '~**off** match *m* décisif *(après match nul);* '~**pen** parc *m* pour bébés; '~**thing** jouet *m;* '~**wright** auteur *m* dramatique; '~**writ·er** auteur *m* de pièces.

plea [pliː] ✠ défense *f;* excuse *f,* prétexte *m;* F prière *f; make a* ~ alléguer; *on the* ~ *of (ou that)* sous prétexte de *ou* que.

plead [pliːd] *v/i.* plaider (pour, en faveur de *for) (q., qch.);* ~ *for mercy* demander grâce; *see guilty; v/t.* plaider; alléguer, invoquer *(une excuse);* prétexter *(qch.);*

'**plead·a·ble** plaidable; invocable;
'**plead·er** ⚖ avocat *m*; défenseur
m; '**plead·ing** ⚖ plaidoirie *f*; *fig.*
intercession *f*; *special* ~ F argument *m* spécieux; ~s *pl.* dossier *m*;
débats *m*/*pl.*

pleas·ant □ ['pleznt] agréable,
charmant, doux (douce *f*); affable;
'**pleas·ant·ness** charme *m*; affabilité *f*; '**pleas·ant·ry** plaisanterie *f*;
gaieté *f*.

please [pli:z] *v/i.* plaire; être agréable; *if you* ~ s'il vous plaît; je vous
en prie; ~ *come in!* veuillez entrer;
v/t. plaire à, faire plaisir à; ~ *o.s.*
agir à sa guise; *be* ~*d to do s.th.*
faire qch. avec plaisir; *be* ~*d with*
être (très) content de; '**pleased**
content, satisfait.

pleas·ing □ ['pli:ziŋ] agréable;
doux (douce *f*).

pleas·ur·a·ble □ ['pleʒərəbl] agréable.

pleas·ure ['pleʒə] **1.** plaisir *m*;
volonté *f*; *attr.* d'agrément; ~ *boat*
bateau *m* de plaisance; *at* ~ à
volonté *f*; *give s.o.* ~ faire plaisir à
q.; *take* (*a*) ~ éprouver du plaisir
(à *inf.*, *in gér.*) prendre (du) plaisir
(à qch. *in s.th.*); **2.** *v/i.* prendre
plaisir (à *inf.*, *in gér.*); *v/t.* † faire
plaisir à; '~**ground** jardin *m* ou
parc *m* d'agrément.

pleat [pli:t] **1.** pli *m*; *unpressed* ~s
pl. plis *m*/*pl.* non repassés; **2.** plisser.

ple·be·ian [pli'bi:ən] **1.** du peuple;
plébéien(ne *f*); **2.** plébéien(ne *f*) *m*.

pleb·i·scite ['plebisit] plébiscite *m*.

pledge [pledʒ] **1.** gage *m*, nantissement *m*; promesse *f*, vœu *m*; toast
m; *put in* ~ engager; *take out of* ~
dégager; **2.** engager, mettre en
gage; porter un toast à (*q.*); *he* ~*d
himself* il promit, il engagea sa
parole; **pledg'ee** gagiste *m*; '**pledg-
er** gageur *m*.

Ple·iad *ou pl.* **Ple·ia·des** ['plaiəd
(-i:z)] Pléiade *f*.

ple·na·ry ['pli:nəri] complet (-ète *f*),
entier (-ère *f*); plénier (-ère *f*).

plen·i·po·ten·ti·ar·y [plenipə'ten-
ʃəri] plénipotentiaire (*a. su./m*).

plen·i·tude ['plenitju:d] plénitude *f*.

plen·te·ous □ *poét.* ['plentjəs]
abondant; riche (en, *in*); '**plen·te-
ous·ness** abondance *f*.

plen·ti·ful □ ['plentiful] abondant.

plen·ty ['plenti] **1.** abondance *f*; ~ *of*
beaucoup de; *en* abondance; assez
de; *horn of* ~ corne *f* d'abondance;
2. F beaucoup de; *Am.* F très.

ple·o·nasm ['pli:ənæzm] pléonasme
m.

pleth·o·ra ['pleθərə] pléthore *f*; *fig.*
surabondance *f*; **ple·thor·ic** [ple-
'θɔrik] (~*ally*) pléthorique.

pleu·ri·sy ⚕ ['pluərisi] pleurésie *f*.

pli·a·bil·i·ty [plaiə'biliti] souplesse *f*.

pli·a·ble □ ['plaiəbl] pliant; souple
(*a. fig.*); *fig.* docile.

pli·an·cy ['plaiənsi] souplesse *f*.

pli·ant □ ['plaiənt] *see* pliable.

pli·ers ['plaiəz] *pl.*: (*a pair of*) ~
(une) pince *f*, (des) tenailles *f*/*pl.*

plight[1] [plait] **1.** engager (*sa foi, sa
parole*); **2.** *poét.* engagement *m*.

plight[2] [~] condition *f*, état *m*.

plim·soll ['plimsəl] (chaussure *f* de)
tennis *m*.

plinth △ [plinθ] socle *m*.

plod [plɔd] (*a.* ~ *along, on*) marcher
lourdement *ou* péniblement; '**plod-
ding** □ persévérant; lourd, pesant
(*pas*).

plonk F [plɔŋk] vin *m* ordinaire;
pinard *m*.

plop [plɔp] **1.** flac (*a. su./m*);
2. faire flac; tomber en faisant flac
ou pouf.

plot[1] [plɔt] (*parcelle f ou lot m* de)
terrain *m*.

plot[2] [~] **1.** complot *m*, conspiration
f; action *f*, intrigue *f*, *roman etc.*:
plan *m*; **2.** *v/t.* (*a.* ~ *down*) tracer;
relever, dresser le plan de (*un
terrain, un diagramme, etc.*); *péj.*
combiner, comploter; *v/i.* comploter, conspirer; '**plot·ter** traceur
m; conspirateur (-trice *f*) *m*.

plough [plau] **1.** charrue *f*; ⊕
guimbarde *f*; *astr. the* ⚹ le Chariot;
univ. sl. retoquage *m*; **2.** labourer;
creuser (*un sillon*); *fig.* sillonner;
univ. sl. be ~*ed* être refusé *ou*
collé; '~**man** laboureur *m*; '~**-
share** soc *m* de charrue; '~**-tail**
mancheron *m* de charrue.

plov·er ['plʌvə] *orn.* pluvier *m*; *a.
cuis.* F vanneau *m*.

plow *surt. Am.* [plau] *see* plough.

ploy F [plɔi] stratagème *m*, truc *m*.

pluck [plʌk] **1.** arrachage *m*; *poulet
etc.*: plumage *m*; *guitare*: pincement *m*; F courage *m*, cran *m*; **2.** arracher; plumer (*un poulet etc., a.*

fig.); épiler (*les sourcils*); détacher (de, *from*); pincer (*la guitare*); *univ. sl.* refuser, recaler; ~ *at* tirer; ~ *up courage* s'armer de courage.

pluck·y □ ['plʌki] courageux (-euse *f*); F crâne.

plug [plʌg] **1.** tampon *m* (⚡ d'ouate); bouchon *m*; ⚡ fiche *f*; ⚡ prise *f*; *tabac*: chique *f*; *W.-C.*: chasse *f* d'eau; *W.-C.*: chaînette *f*; bouche *f* d'incendie; *radio Am.* publicité *f*; réclame *f*; *Am.* vieux cheval *m*; ~ *socket* douille *f*; prise *f*; **2.** *v/t.* boucher; tamponner; plomber (*une dent*); *sl.* flanquer un coup à; *Am.* F faire de la publicité en faveur de; ⚡ ~ *in* brancher; *v/i. sl.* ~ *away* turbiner (= *travailler dur*); **'plug-'ug·ly** *Am. sl.* pugiliste *m*; voyou *m*.

plum [plʌm] prune *f*; † raisin *m* sec; *fig.* morceau *m* de choix; *fig.* la meilleure situation *f*; ✝ £ 100.000.

plum·age ['pluːmidʒ] plumage *m*.

plumb [plʌm] **1.** d'aplomb; vertical (-aux *m/pl.*); droit; **2.** plomb *m*; ⚓ sonde *f*; aplomb *m*; **3.** *v/t.* sonder (*la mer*); plomber (*la canalisation*); vérifier l'aplomb de; *fig.* sonder; F installer les tuyaux dans (*une maison*); *v/i.* F être plombier; **plum·ba·go** [~'beigou] plombagine *f*; **plumb·er** ['~mə] plombier *m*; **plum·bic** ['~mbik] ⚗ plombique; **plumb·ing** ['~miŋ] plomberie *f*; tuyauterie *f*; **'plumb-line** ⊕ fil *m* à plomb; ⚓ ligne *f* de sonde; **'plumb-rule** niveau *m* vertical.

plume [pluːm] **1.** panache *m*; *poét.* plume *f*; **2.** orner (*qch.*) de plumes; ~ *itself* se lisser les plumes (*oiseau*); ~ *o.s.* on se glorifier de.

plum·met ['plʌmit] plomb *m*; ⚓ sonde *f*.

plum·my F ['plʌmi] délicieux (-euse *f*); excellent.

plu·mose ♃, *zo.* ['pluːmous] plumeux (-euse *f*).

plump[1] [plʌmp] **1.** rebondi, dodu, grassouillet(te *f*); **2.** rendre *ou* devenir dodu; engraisser.

plump[2] [~] **1.** *v/i.* tomber lourdement; *v/t.* flanquer; *parl.* donner tous ses votes (à, *for*); **2.** *su.* plouf *m*; **3.** F *adv.* plouf; avec un floc; carrément; **4.** F *adj.* □ catégorique.

plump·er ['plʌmpə] *sl.* gros men-

songe *m*; *parl.* vote *m* donné à un seul candidat; électeur *m* qui donne tous ses votes à un seul candidat.

plump·ness ['plʌmpnis] rondeur *f* (*a.* F *d'une réponse*), embonpoint *m*.

plum-pud·ding ['plʌm'pudiŋ] plum-pudding *m*.

plum·y ['pluːmi] plumeux (-euse *f*); empanaché (*casque*).

plun·der ['plʌndə] **1.** pillage *m* (*d'une ville*); butin *m*; **2.** piller, dépouiller; **'plun·der·er** pillard *m*; pilleur *m*.

plunge [plʌndʒ] **1.** plongeon *m*; *cheval etc.*: course *f* précipitée; F risque *m*; F *make* (*ou take*) *the* ~ sauter le pas; **2.** *v/t.* plonger, immerger (dans, *in*[*to*]); *v/i.* plonger, s'enfoncer (dans, *into*); ruer (*cheval*); ⚓ tanguer; risquer de grosses sommes (*à la Bourse*).

plung·er ['plʌndʒə] plongeur *m*; *sl.* risque-tout *m/inv.*

plunk [plʌŋk] *v/t.* pincer (*la guitare etc.*); *v/i.* tomber raide; *Am.* F lancer, tirer (*sur, at*).

plu·per·fect *gramm.* ['pluː'pəːfikt] plus-que-parfait *m.*

plu·ral *gramm.* ['pluərəl] (**1.** ~ *number*) pluriel *m*; *in the* ~ au pluriel; **plu·ral·i·ty** [~'ræliti] pluralité *f*; cumul *m*; ~ *of wives* polygamie *f*.

plus [plʌs] **1.** *prp.* plus; **2.** *adj.* positif (-ive *f*); **3.** *su.* plus *m*; **~-fours** F ['~'fɔːz] *pl.* culotte *f* de golf.

plush [plʌʃ] peluche *f*.

plush·y ['plʌʃi] pelucheux (-euse *f*).

plu·toc·ra·cy [pluː'tɔkrəsi] ploutocratie *f*; **plu·to·crat** ['~təkræt] ploutocrate *m*; [plutonium *m.*]

plu·to·ni·um ☢ [pluː'touniəm]

plu·vi·al ['pluːviəl], **'plu·vi·ous** pluvial (-aux *m/pl.*); **plu·vi·om·e·ter** [~'ɔmitə] pluviomètre *m.*

ply [plai] **1.** pli *m* (*a. fig.*); *three-~* laine *f* trois fils; *bois:* contre-plaqué *m* à trois épaisseurs; **2.** *v/t.* manier vigoureusement; exercer (*un métier*); faire courir (*l'aiguille*); presser (*q. de questions*); ~ *with drink* faire boire (*q.*) sans arrêt; *v/i.* faire le service; ~ *for hire* prendre des voyageurs.

ply-wood ['plaiwud] contre-plaqué *m.*

pneu·mat·ic [njuː'mætik] **1.** (~*ally*) pneumatique; ~ *hammer* frappeur

m pneumatique; ~ *post* tube *m*
pneumatique; ~ *tire* = **2.** pneu *m*.

pneu·mo·ni·a ✻ [nju'mounjə] pneumonie *f*.

poach[1] [poutʃ] braconner.

poach[2] [~] (*a*. ~ *up*) labourer (*la terre*).

poach[3] [~]: ~*ed eggs* œufs *m*/*pl*. pochés.

poach·er ['poutʃə] braconnier *m*.

PO Box [pi:'ou'bɔks] boîte *f* postale.

po·chette [po'ʃet] pochette *f*.

pock ✻ [pɔk] pustule *f*.

pock·et ['pɔkit] **1.** poche *f* (*a*. *géol*.); laine, houblon, *a*. géol. minerai: sac *m*; ✈ trou *m* d'air; **2.** mettre dans sa poche (*a*. *orgueil*); *péj*. chiper; refouler (*la colère*); avaler (*un affront*); *Am*. *pol*. ne pas signer, mettre un veto à (*une loi*); **3.** de poche; ~ *calculator* calculatrice *f* de poche; ~ *edition* édition *f* de poche; ~ *lighter* briquet *m*; ~ *lamp* torche *f*; '~·**book** carnet *m* de poche, calepin *m*; *Am*. sac *m* à main; *Am*. livre *m* de poche; *surt*. *Am*. porte-billets *m*/*inv*.

pod [pɔd] **1.** ❧ cosse *f*; *pois*: écale *f*; *sl*. ventre *m*; **2.** *v*/*t*. écosser, écaler; *v*/*i*. former des cosses.

po·dag·ra ✻ [pə'dægrə] podagre *f*, goutte *f*.

podg·y F ['pɔdʒi] boulot(te *f*); rondelet(te *f*).

po·di·um ['poudiəm] podium *m*.

po·em ['pouim] poème *m*.

po·e·sy ['pouizi] poésie *f*.

po·et ['pouit] poète *m*; **po·et·as·ter** [~'tæstə] rimailleur *m*; '**po·et·ess** femme *f* poète, poétesse *f*; **po·et·ic**, **po·et·i·cal** □ [pou'etik(l)] poétique; **po·et·ics** *sg*. art *m* poétique; **po·et·ize** ['~itaiz] *v*/*i*. faire des vers; *v*/*t*. poétiser; '**po·et·ry** poésie *f*; vers *m*/*pl*.

poign·an·cy ['pɔinənsi] piquant *m*; âpreté *f*; *fig*. violence *f*; acuité *f*; '**poign·ant** □ piquant, âpre; *fig*. vif (vive *f*).

point [pɔint] **1.** point *m* (*a*. ♟, ✞, *astr*., *sp*., *typ*., *cartes*, *dés*); détail *m* (*a*. *fig*.); question *f* (*a*. *gramm*.); ⊕, *couteau*, *barbe*, *géog*. pointe *f*; extrémité *f*; aire *f* (*de vent*); *plume* à *écrire*: bec *m*; piquant *m* (*d'une plaisanterie*); *gramm*. point *m* (*de ponctuation*); ♟ (*a*. *decimal* ~) virgule *f*; *phys*. *thermomètre*: division *f*; *chien*: arrêt *m*; ⚡ contact *m*; ⚡ prise

f de courant; ⚓ quart *m*; *fig*. cas *m* (*de conscience*), point *m* (*d'honneur*); *fig*. caractère *m*; *see* ~-*lace*; 🚂 ~*s* *pl*. aiguillage *m*; ~*s* *pl*. *chasse*: cors *m*/*pl*. (*cerf*); ~ *of view* point *m* de vue; *the* ~ *is that* ce dont il s'agit c'est que; *there is no* ~ *in* (*gér*.) il est inutile de (*inf*.); *make a* ~ faire ressortir un argument; *make a* ~ *of* ne pas manquer de (*inf*.); tenir à; *make the* ~ *that* faire remarquer que; *stretch a* ~ faire une concession; *in* ~ *of* sous le rapport de; *in* ~ *of fact* au *ou* en fait; *off* (*ou beyond*) *the* ~ hors de propos; *differ on many* ~*s* ne pas être d'accord sur bien des détails; *be on the* ~ *of* (*gér*.) être sur le point de (*inf*.); *win on* ~*s* gagner aux points; *to the* ~ à propos, bien dit; *stick to the* ~ ne pas s'écarter de la question; **2.** *v*/*t*. marquer de points; aiguiser; *opt*. braquer (*une jumelle etc*.); △ jointoyer; (*souv*. ~ *out*) indiquer; inculquer (*la morale*); ~ *at* braquer (*une arme*) sur; *v*/*i*. *chasse*: tomber en arrêt; ~ *at* montrer du doigt; ~ *to* faire ressortir; marquer (*l'heure*); signaler; '~-**blank** **1.** *adj*. direct; net(te *f*) (*refus*); de but en blanc (*question*); **2.** *adv*. à bout portant; *fig*. carrément; ~ *shot* coup *m* de feu à bout portant; '~-**du·ty** service *m* à poste fixe; *policeman* on ~ agent-vigie (*pl*. *agents-vigies*) *m*; '**point·ed** □ pointu, à pointe; *fig*. mordant, peu voilé; '**point·ed·ness** mordant *m*; caractère *m* peu voilé; '**point·er** aiguille *f*, index *m*; baguette *f*; *chasse*: chien *m* d'arrêt; F tuyau *m*; '**point·lace** guipure *f*; '**point·less** émoussé; *fig*. sans sel; *fig*. inutile; '**points·man** 🚂 aiguilleur *m*; '**point-to-'point race** course *f* au clocher.

poise [pɔiz] **1.** équilibre *m*, aplomb *m*; port *m* (*du corps etc*.); **2.** *v*/*t*. équilibrer, balancer; tenir (*la tête etc*.); *v*/*i*. (*a*. *be* ~*d*) être en équilibre.

poi·son ['pɔizn] **1.** poison *m*; ~-*pen letter* lettre *f* anonyme venimeuse; **2.** empoisonner; *fig*. corrompre; '**poi·son·er** empoisonneur (-euse *f*) *m*; '**poi·son·ous** □ toxique; vénimeux (-euse *f*) (*animal*); vénéneux (-euse *f*) (*plante*); *fig*. pernicieux (-euse *f*); F empoisonnant.

poke [pouk] **1.** poussée *f*; coup *m* de

coude; 2. *v/t.* pousser du coude *etc.*; (*a.* ~ *up*) attiser (*le feu*); fourrer (*a. fig.* son nez); passer, avancer (*la tête*); ~ *fun at* se moquer de; *v/i.* (*a.* ~ *about*) fouiller; fourrer (dans, *in*[to]).

pok·er[1] ['poukə] tisonnier *m*.

po·ker[2] [~] *cartes:* poker *m; fig.* ~-**face** visage *m* impassible.

pok·er-work ['poukəwəːk] pyrogravure *f*.

pok·y ['pouki] misérable; mesquin.

po·lar ['poulə] polaire; du pôle; ~ **bear** ours *m* blanc; **po·lar·i·ty** *phys.* [po'læriti] polarité *f*; **po·lar·i·za·tion** *phys.* [pouləraiˈzeiʃn] polarisation *f; phot.* ~ *filter* filtre *m* de polarisation; **'po·lar·ize** *phys.* (se) polariser.

Pole[1] [poul] Polonais(e *f*) *m*.

pole[2] [~] *géog., astr., fig.* pôle *m; ⚡* électrode *f*.

pole[3] [~] 1. perche *f* (*a. sp.*); mât *m*; hampe *f* (*de drapeau*); *voiture:* timon *m; mesure:* perche *f* (5,029 *m*); 2. pousser *ou* conduire à la perche; '~-**ax(e)** ⚔ hache *f* d'armes; ⚓ hache *f* d'abordage; assommoir *m*; '~-**cat** *zo.* putois *m; Am.* putois *m* d'Amérique; '~-**jump**, '~-**vault** saut *m* à la perche.

po·lem·ic [poˈlemik] 1. (*a.* **poˈlem·i·cal** □) polémique; 2. polémique *f*; **poˈlem·ics** *sg.* polémique *f*.

pole-star ['poulstɑː] (étoile *f*) polaire *f; fig.* point *m* de mire.

po·lice [pəˈliːs] 1. police *f; two* ~ deux agents *m/pl.* de (police); ~ *force la* police, *les* forces *f/pl.* de l'ordre; ~ *record* casier *m* judiciaire; 2. policer; **poˈlice·man** agent *m* de police; gardien *m* de la paix; **poˈlice-of·fice** préfecture *f* de police; **poˈlice-sta·tion** poste *m* de police; **poˈlice-sur·veil·lance** surveillance *f* de police; **poˈlice-trap** zone *f* de contrôle de vitesse.

pol·i·cy[1] ['polisi] politique *f*; diplomatique *f*.

pol·i·cy[2] [~] police *f; Am.* loterie *f* clandestine.

po·li·o·my·e·li·tis [ˈpoliou(maiə-ˈlaitis)] poliomyélite *f*.

Pol·ish[1] ['pouliʃ] polonais.

pol·ish[2] ['poliʃ] 1. poli *m*; brillant *m; fig.* vernis *m; floor* ~ encaustique *f; boot* ~ cirage *m*; 2. *v/t.* polir (*a. fig.*); brunir (*le métal*); cirer; F ~ *off* expé-

dier; ~ *up* polir; *v/i.* prendre bien le poli, la cire *etc.*; 'pol·ish·ing 1. polissage *m*; cirage *m*; 2. à polir.

po·lite □ [pəˈlait] poli, courtois, civil; cultivé; **poˈlite·ness** politesse *f*.

pol·i·tic □ ['politik] politique; adroit; *body* ~ corps *m* politique; **po·lit·i·cal** □ [pəˈlitikl] politique; ~ *science* sciences *f/pl.* politiques; ~ *scientist* politologue *mf*; **pol·i·ti·cian** [poliˈtiʃn] homme *m* politique; *péj.* politicien *m*; **pol·i·tics** ['politiks] *pl.,* souv. *sg.* politique *f*.

pol·i·ty ['politi] administration *f* politique; état *m*; régime *m*.

pol·ka-dot *Am.* *tex.* ['polkəˈdot] pois *m*.

poll[1] [poul] 1. *prov. ou co.* tête *f*; sommet *m*, haut *m*; vote *m* (par bulletins); scrutin *m; go to the* ~s prendre part au vote; se rendre aux urnes; 2. *v/t.* † tondre; étêter (*un arbre*); réunir (*tant de voix*); *v/i.* voter (pour, *for*).

poll[2] [pol] perroquet *m; npr.* Tacquot *m*.

pol·lard ['poləd] arbre *m* étêté; animal *m* sans cornes; *farine:* repasse *f*.

poll-book ['poulbuk] liste *f* électorale.

pol·len ⚘ ['polin] pollen *m*.

poll·ing...: '~-**booth** bureau *m* de scrutin; isoloir *m*; '~-**dis·trict** section *f* de vote; '~-**place**, '~-**sta·tion** poste *m* (de section de vote).

poll·ster ['poulstə] sondeur (-euse *f*) *m*.

poll-tax ['poultæks] capitation *f*.

pol·lut·ant [pəˈluːtənt] agent *m* de pollution; **polˈlute** [pəˈluːt] polluer; souiller; corrompre (*a. fig.*); profaner; **polˈlu·tion** pollution *f*; profanation *f*.

po·lo *sp.* ['poulou] polo *m*; ~ *neck* (chandail *m* à) col *m* roulé.

po·lo·ny [pəˈlouni] cervelas *m*.

pol·troon [polˈtruːn] poltron *m*; **polˈtroon·er·y** poltronnerie *f*.

po·lyg·a·my [pɔˈligəmi] polygamie *f*; **pol·y·glot** ['poliglot] polyglotte (*a. su./mf*); **pol·y·gon** ['~gən] polygone *m*; **po·lyg·o·nal** [pɔˈligənl] polygonal (-aux *m/pl.*); **pol·y·phon·ic** ♪ [~ˈfonik] polyphonique; **pol·yp** *zo.* ['~ip], **pol·y·pus** ⚕ ['~pəs], *pl.* -**pi** [~pai] polype *m*; **pol·y·sty·rene** [poliˈstaiəriːn] polystyrène *m*; **pol-**

y·syl·lab·ic [ˈpɔlisiˈlæbik] polysyllab(iqu)e; **pol·y·syl·la·ble** [ˈↄsiləbl] polysyllabe *m*; **pol·y·tech·nic** [ↄˈteknik] 1. polytechnique; 2. école *f* des arts et métiers; **pol·y·the·ism** [ˈↄθiizm] polythéisme *m*; **pol·ythene** [ˈↄθiːn] polyéthylène *m*; ~ *bag* sac *m* en plastique.

po·made [pəˈmɑːd], **po·ma·tum** [pəˈmeitəm] pommade *f*.

pome·gran·ate ⚘ [ˈpɔmgrænit] grenade *f*; *arbre*: grenadier *m*.

Pom·er·a·nian [pɔməˈreinjən] poméranien(ne *f*); ~ (*dog*) loulou *m* de Poméranie.

pom·mel [ˈpʌml] 1. *épée, selle*: pommeau *m*; 2. bourrer (*q.*) de coups.

pomp [pɔmp] pompe *f*, apparat *m*.

pom-pom [ˈpɔmpɔm] canon-revolver (*pl.* canons-revolvers) *m*.

pom·pos·i·ty [pɔmˈpɔsiti] emphase *f*, suffisance *f*; **pomp·ous** □ pompeux (-euse *f*); suffisant (*personne*).

ponce *Brit. sl.* [pɔns] souteneur *m*, maquereau *m*; pédé *m*, tapette *f*.

pond [pɔnd] étang *m*; mare *f*; réservoir *m*; **pond·age** accumulation *f* de l'eau; capacité *f*.

pon·der [ˈpɔndə] méditer (sur *on, over*); **pon·der·a·bil·i·ty** [ↄrəˈbiliti] pondérabilité *f*; **pon·der·a·ble** pondérable; **pon·der·os·i·ty** [ↄˈrↄsiti] lourdeur *f* (*a. de style*); *fig.* importance *f*; **pon·der·ous** □ lourd; massif (-ive *f*); laborieux (-euse *f*); *fig.* important; **pon·der·ous·ness** *see* ponderosity.

pone *Am.* [poun] pain *m* de maïs.

pong *Brit. sl.* [pɔŋ] 1. puanteur *f*; 2. puer.

pon·iard [ˈpɔnjəd] 1. poignard *m*; 2. poignarder.

pon·tiff [ˈpɔntif] pontife *m*; prélat *m*; **pon·tif·i·cal** pontifical (-aux *m/pl.*); épiscopal (-aux *m/pl.*); **pon·tif·icate** 1. [ↄkit] pontificat *m*; 2. [ↄkeit] pontifier.

pon·toon ⚒ [pɔnˈtuːn] ponton *m*; **pon·toon-bridge** pont *m* de bateaux.

po·ny [ˈpouni] poney *m*; F *fig.* baudet *m*; *Am.* F traduction *f*; *sl.* 25 livres sterling; *Am.* F petit verre *m* d'alcool; *Am. attr.* petit; '~-'en·gine 🚂 locomotive *f* de manœuvre.

pooch *Am. sl.* [puːtʃ] cabot *m*, chien *m*.

poo·dle [ˈpuːdl] caniche *mf*.

poof *Brit. sl.* [puːf] tapette *f*, tante *f*.

pooh [puː] bah!; peuh!

pooh-pooh [puːˈpuː] ridiculiser; faire peu de cas de (*qch.*); faire fi de (*conseils etc.*).

pool¹ [puːl] flaque *f* d'eau; mare *f*; fontaine *f*.

pool² [~] 1. cagnotte *f*; poule *f* (*a. billard*); concours *m* de pronostics; (*sorte de*) jeu *m* de billard; ⚓ syndicat *m*; fonds *m/pl.* communs; *Brit.* the ~s les pronostics *m/pl.* (sur les matchs de football); *Am.* ~ *room* salle *f* de billard; *Am.* ~ *table* billard *m*; 2. mettre en commun; ⚓ mettre en syndicat.

poop ⚓ [puːp] 1. poupe *f*; dunette *f*; 2. balayer la poupe de; embarquer par l'arrière; *Am.* ~ed exténué.

poor □ [puə] *usu.* pauvre; malheureux (-euse *f*); médiocre; de piètre qualité; maigre (*sol*); ~ *me!* pauvre de moi!; *make but a* ~ *shift's* accommoder mal de (*qch.*); *a* ~ *dinner* un mauvais dîner; ~ *health* santé *f* débile; '~-box tronc *m* pour les pauvres; '~-house asile *m* de pauvres; '~-law assistance *f* judiciaire; 'poor·ly 1. *adj. prédicatif* souffrant; 2. *adv.* pauvrement; 'poor·ness pauvreté *f*, insuffisance *f*; infériorité *f*; 'poor-rate taxe *f* des pauvres; 'poor-'spir·it·ed pusillanime.

pop¹ [pɔp] 1. bruit *m* sec; F boisson *f* pétillante; limonade *f* gazeuse; 2. *v/t.* crever; faire sauter; F mettre en gage; *Am.* faire éclater (*le maïs*); F fourrer vite; F ~ *the question* faire la demande en mariage; *v/i.* éclater, sauter; crever; ~ *in* entrer pour un instant (*chez q.*); ~ *up* se lever vivement; apparaître; 3. inattendu; 4. crac!; pan!

pop² F [~] concert *m* populaire; chanson *f* populaire.

pop³ *Am.* F [~] papa *m*; pépère *m*, pépé *m*.

pop·corn *usu. Am.* [ˈpɔpkɔːn] maïs *m* grillé et éclaté.

pope [poup] pape *m*; Saint-Père *m*; **pope·dom** [ˈↄdəm] papauté *f*; **pop·er·y** *péj.* [ˈↄəri] papisme *m*.

pop-eyed [ˈpɔpaid] aux yeux en boules de loto.

pop-gun [ˈpɔpɡʌn] pétoire *f*.

pop·in·jay *fig.* [ˈpɔpindʒei] fat *m*.

pop·ish □ *péj.* [ˈpoupiʃ] papiste.

pop·lar ⚘ [ˈpɔplə] peuplier *m*.

pop·lin *tex.* ['pɔplin] popeline *f*.

pop·per *surt. Brt.* ['pɔpə] bouton-pression *m* (*pl.* boutons-pression).

pop·pet ['pɔpit] ⚓ colombier *m*; ⊕ poupée *f*; *see* **puppet**.

pop·py ♀ ['pɔpi] pavot *m*; '**~·cock** *Am.* F fadaises *f/pl.*, bêtises *f/pl.*

pop·u·lace ['pɔpjuləs] peuple *m*; *péj.* populace *f*.

pop·u·lar □ ['pɔpjulə] populaire; du peuple; goûté du public; ⚓ à la portée de tous; **pop·u·lar·i·ty** [~-'læriti] popularité *f*; **pop·u·lar·ize** ['~ləraiz] populariser, vulgariser; rendre populaire; '**pop·u·lar·ly** populairement; communément.

pop·u·late ['pɔpjuleit] peupler; **pop·u·la·tion** population *f*; **~ explosion** explosion *f* démographique.

pop·u·lous □ ['pɔpjuləs] très peuplé; '**pop·u·lous·ness** densité *f* de (la) population.

por·ce·lain ['pɔːslin] porcelaine *f*.

porch [pɔːtʃ] porche *m*; portique *m*; *Am.* véranda *f*.

por·cu·pine *zo.* ['pɔːkjupain] porc-épic (*pl.* porcs-épics) *m*.

pore[1] [pɔː] pore *m*.

pore[2] [~] être plongé (dans *over*, *on*), méditer (qch. *over*, *on s.th.*).

pork [pɔːk] porc *m*; *Am.* F **~ barrel** fonds *m/pl.* publics; trésor *m* public; **~ butcher** charcutier *m*; **~ chop** côtelette *f* de porc; '**pork·er** goret *m*; porc *m*; '**pork·y** 1. F gras(se *f*), obèse; 2. *Am.* F *see* **porcupine**.

por·nog·ra·phy [pɔː'nɔgrəfi] pornographie *f*.

po·ros·i·ty [pɔː'rɔsiti], **po·rous·ness** ['pɔːrəsnis] porosité *f*.

po·rous □ ['pɔːrəs] poreux (-euse *f*).

por·phy·ry *min.* ['pɔːfiri] porphyre *m*.

por·poise *zo.* ['pɔːpəs] marsouin *m*; phocène *f*.

por·ridge ['pɔridʒ] bouillie *f* d'avoine; **por·rin·ger** ['pɔrindʒə] écuelle *f*.

port[1] [pɔːt] port *m*; **~ of call** port *m* d'escale; **~ of destination** port *m* de destination; **~ of transhipment** port *m* de transbordement.

port[2] ⚓ [~] sabord *m*.

port[3] [~] 1. ✗ présenter (*les armes*); 2. maintien *m*, port *m*.

port[4] ⚓ [~] 1. *côté*: bâbord *m*; 2. *v/t.* mettre à bâbord; *v/i.* venir sur bâbord.

port[5] [~] porto *m*.

port·a·ble ['pɔːtəbl] portatif (-ive *f*); mobile; **~ gramophone** (*typewriter*, *radio*) phonographe *m* (machine *f* à écrire, poste *m*) transportable; **~ railway** chemin *m* de fer à voie démontable.

por·tage ['pɔːtidʒ] portage *m*; *see* **porterage**.

por·tal ['pɔːtl] portail *m*; portique *m*; *fig.* (porte *f* d')entrée *f*; '**portal-to-'por·tal pay** paye *f* pour le temps d'aller de la porte (*de l'usine etc.*) à son travail et retour.

port·cul·lis ✗ *hist.* [pɔːt'kʌlis] herse *f*.

por·tend [pɔː'tend] présager.

por·tent ['pɔːtent] présage *m* de malheur; prodige *m*; **por·ten·tous** □ sinistre; de mauvais augure; prodigieux (-euse *f*); *co.* lugubre.

por·ter[1] ['pɔːtə] concierge *m*.

por·ter[2] [~] portefaix *m*; *hôtel*: garçon *m*; 🍺 porteur *m*; bière *f* brune; **por·ter·age** ['~ridʒ] (prix *m* de) transport *m*; factage *m*; '**por·terhouse** taverne *f*; *Am.* **~ steak** aloyau *m*, châteaubriant *m*.

port·fire ['pɔːtfaiə] boutefeu *m*; étoupille *f*.

port·fo·li·o [pɔːt'fouljou] serviette *f*; chemise *f* (*de carton*); portefeuille *m* (*d'un ministre*).

port·hole ⚓ ['pɔːthoul] sabord *m*.

por·ti·co △ ['pɔːtikou] portique *m*.

por·tion ['pɔːʃn] 1. part *f*, partie *f*; portion *f*; *viande*: ration *f*; *gâteau*: quartier *m*; *terre*: lot *m*; *mariage*: dot *m*; *fig.* sort *m*; 2. partager, répartir; doter; '**por·tion·less** sans dot.

port·li·ness ['pɔːtlinis] prestance *f*; embonpoint *m*; '**port·ly** majestueux (-euse *f*); corpulent.

port·man·teau [pɔːt'mæntou] valise *f*; *gramm.* **~ word** mot *m* fantaisiste (*fait de mots télescopés*).

por·trait ['pɔːtrit] portrait *m*; '**portrait·ist** portraitiste *mf*; **por·traiture** ['~tʃə] portrait *m*; l'art *m* du portrait; *fig.* description *f*.

por·tray [pɔː'trei] (dé)peindre; décrire; **por·tray·al** peinture *f*, représentation *f*.

Por·tu·guese [pɔːtju'giːz] 1. portugais; 2. *ling.* portugais *m*; Portugais (-e *f*) *m*.

pose [pouz] 1. pose *f*; 2. *v/i.* se

poser; se faire passer (pour, *as*); *v/t.* poser (*une question*); énoncer; **'pos·er** question *f* embarrassante; F colle *f*.

posh *sl.* [pɔʃ] chic *inv.* en genre, chouette.

po·si·tion [pə'ziʃn] position *f* (*a. fig.*, ⚔, *posture*); situation *f*; place *f*; emploi *m*; état *m*; *fig.* attitude *f*; *fig.* point *m* de vue; ⚓ lieu *m*, point *m*; ⚓ poste *m*; ~ light feu *m* de position; *be in a ~ to do* être à même de faire.

pos·i·tive ['pɔzətiv] **1.** □ positif (-ive *f*); formel(le *f*); vrai; sûr, certain, convaincu; A̸, ⚡, *phls.*, *phys.*, *phot.* positif (-ive *f*); **2.** positif *m*; **'pos·i·tive·ness** certitude *f*; ton *m* décisif.

pos·se ['pɔsi] troupe *f*, foule *f*; ~ **co·mi·ta·tus** [~ kɔmi'teitəs] détachement *m* de police.

pos·sess [pə'zes] avoir, posséder (*fig.* de, *with*); *fig.* pénétrer (de, *with*); ~*ed* possédé; *be* ~*ed of* posséder; ~ *o.s. of* s'emparer de (*qch.*); **pos·ses·sion** [pə'zeʃn] possession *f* (*a. fig.*); jouissance *f* (de, *of*); colonie *f*; *in* ~ en possession de; **pos·ses·sive** *gramm.* [pə'zesiv] **1.** □ possessif (-ive *f*); ~ *case* (cas *m*) possessif *m*; **2.** possessif *m*; **pos-'ses·sor** possesseur *m*; **pos'ses·so·ry** possessoire.

pos·set ['pɔsit] posset *m*.

pos·si·bil·i·ty [pɔsə'biliti] possibilité *f*; **'pos·si·ble 1.** possible; **2.** *sp.* maximum *m*; **'pos·si·bly** peut-être; *if I* ~ *can* s'il y a moyen; *how can I* ~ *do it?* comment pourrais-je le faire?; *I cannot* ~ *do it* il m'est impossible de le faire.

pos·sum F ['pɔsəm] *see* opossum.

post¹ [poust] **1.** poteau *m*; pieu *m*; **2.** (*usu.* ~ *up*) afficher, placarder.

post² [~] **1.** ⚔ *sentinelle etc.*: poste *m*, garnison *f*; ✝ station *f* (de commerce); situation *f*, poste *m*; † malle-poste (*pl.* malles-poste) *f*; *poste*: courrier *m*, poste *f*; papier *m* écu; ⚔ *at one's* ~ à son poste; *by* (*the*) ~ par la poste; ⚔ *last* ~ sonnerie *f* aux morts; retraite *f*; *Am.* ~ *exchange* magasin *m*, cantine *f*; **2.** *v/t.* ⚔ poster, mettre en faction (*une sentinelle*); ⚓ nommer (*q. capitaine*); ✝ (*souv.* ~ *up*) mettre au courant (*le grand-livre*); mettre à la

poste; envoyer par la poste; F (*souv.* ~ *up ou keep s.o.* ~*ed*) mettre (*q.*) au courant, documenter (*q.*); *well* ~*ed* bien renseigné; ✝ ~ *an entry* passer écriture d'un article; *v/i.* F aller un train de poste.

post·age ['poustidʒ] port *m*, affranchissement *m*; ... ~ ... *pour* frais d'envoi; ~ *due* surtaxe *f* postale; ~ **stamp** timbre-poste (*pl.* timbres-poste) *m*.

post·al □ ['poustəl] postal (-aux *m/pl.*); *Am.* ~ (*card*) carte *f* postale; ~ *cheque* chèque *m* postal; ~ *order* mandat-poste (*pl.* mandats-poste) *m*, mandat *m* postal; ♀ *Union* Union *f* postale.

post...: **'~·card** carte *f* postale; **'~·code** code *m* postal.

post·date ['poust'deit] postdater; **post·er** ['poustə] affiche *f*; placard *m*.

pos·te·ri·or F [pɔs'tiəriə] **1.** □ postérieur (à, *to*); derrière; **2.** (*a.* ~*s pl.*) postérieur *m*, derrière *m*.

pos·ter·i·ty [pɔs'teriti] postérité *f*.

pos·tern ['poustə:n] porte *f* de derrière.

post-free ['poust'fri:] franco *inv.*

post-grad·u·ate ['poust'grædjuit] **1.** postscolaire; **2.** candidat *m* à un diplôme supérieur (*doctorat etc.*).

post-haste ['poust'heist] en toute hâte.

post·hu·mous □ ['pɔstjuməs] posthume.

pos·til·(l)ion [pəs'tiljən] postillon *m*.

post...: **'~·man** facteur *m*; **'~·mark 1.** cachet *m* de la poste; timbre *m* (d'oblitération); **2.** timbrer; **'~·mas·ter** receveur *m* des postes; ♀ *General* ministre *m* des Postes et Télécommunications.

post·me·rid·i·an ['poustmə'ridiən] de l'après-midi; du soir; **post-mor·tem** ['~'mɔ:təm] **1.** après décès; **2.** (*a.* ~ *examination*) autopsie *f*; **post-o·bit** [~'ɔbit] exécutoire après le décès d'un tiers.

post...: **'~·of·fice**, *surt.* ~ **of·fice** bureau *m* de poste; *Am.* (*sorte de*) jeu *m* avec embrassades; *general* ~ bureau *m* central; ~ *box* boîte *f* postale; ~ *clerk* employé(e *f*) *m* des postes; ~ *counter* (*ou window*) guichet *m*; ~ *order* mandat *m* postal; ~ *savings-bank* caisse *f* d'épargne postale; **'~·paid** franco *inv.*, affranchi.

post·pone [poust'poun] ajourner,

remettre, renvoyer à plus tard; **post'pone·ment** ajournement *m*; remise *f* à plus tard.

post·pran·di·al □ *co.* [poust'prændiəl] après dîner, après le repas.

post·script ['pousskript] post-scriptum *m/inv.* (*abbr.* P.-S.); postface *f* (*d'un livre*).

pos·tu·lant ['postjulənt] postulant (-e *f*) *m*; **pos·tu·late 1.** ['⌣lit] postulat *m*; **2.** ['⌣leit] postuler (*a. v/i.*); poser (*qch.*) en postulat; **pos·tu·la·tion** sollicitation *f*; *phls.* supposition *f*, postulat *m*.

pos·ture ['postʃə] **1.** posture *f*, *corps:* attitude *f*; position *f*; **2.** *v/t.* poser; *v/i.* prendre une pose; se poser en.

post-war ['poust'wɔ:] d'après-guerre.

po·sy[1] ['pouzi] devise *f*.

po·sy[2] [⌣] bouquet *m* (de fleurs).

pot [pot] **1.** pot *m*; marmite *f*; *sp.* coupe *f*; F a ⌣ of money des tas *m/pl.* d'argent; **2.** *v/t.* mettre en pot (*cuis. a. des plantes*); blouser (*au billard*); abattre (*du gibier*); *v/i.*: ⌣ at lâcher un coup de fusil à (*q.*); tirer sur.

po·ta·ble ['poutəbl] potable, buvable.

pot·ash 🜩 ['potæʃ] potasse *f*.

po·tas·si·um 🜩 [pə'tæsiəm] potassium *m*.

po·ta·tion [pou'teiʃn] gorgée *f*; (*usu. pl.* ⌣s) libation *f*.

po·ta·to [pə'teitou], *pl.* **po'ta·toes** [⌣z] pomme *f* de terre; ⌣ bug doryphore *m*; *Am.* ⌣ chips *pl.*, *Brit.* ⌣ crisps *pl.* pommes *f/pl.* chips; ⌣ masher presse-purée *m/inv.*; ⌣ omelette omelette *f* parmentière; *fig.* hot ⌣ sujet *m* brûlant, affaire *f* épineuse; *cuis.* mashed ⌣s purée *f* (de pommes de terre), pommes *f/pl.* mousseline.

pot...: '⌣-bel·ly panse *f*; '⌣-boil·er littérature *f* alimentaire; besognes *f/pl.* alimentaires; écrivain *m* etc. qui travaille pour faire bouillir sa marmite; '⌣-boy garçon *m* de cabaret.

po·ten·cy ['poutənsi] puissance *f*; force *f*; '**po·tent** □ puissant; fort; **po·ten·tate** ['⌣teit] potentat *m*; **po·ten·tial** [pə'tenʃl] **1.** latent, virtuel (-le *f*); potentiel(le *f*) (*a. phys.*); **2.** *gramm.* (*a.* ⌣ mood) potentiel *m*; *phys.* (*souv.* ⌣ function) fonction *f* potentielle; *p.ext.* rendement *m*

maximum; **po·ten·ti·al·i·ty** [⌣ʃi'æliti] potentialité *f*; potentiel *m* (*militaire etc.*); *fig.* promesse *f*.

poth·er ['poðə] **1.** nuage *m* de fumée *etc.*; confusion *f*; tumulte *m*; **2.** (se) tourmenter; *v/i.* faire des histoires (à propos de, *about*).

pot...: '⌣-herb herbe *f* potagère; '⌣-hole mot. nid-de-poule (*pl.* nids-de-poule) *m*; *géol.* marmite *f* torrentielle; '⌣-hol·er spéléologue *mf*; '⌣-hook crémaillère *f*; ⌣s *pl.* bâtons *m/pl.*; '⌣-house cabaret *m*, taverne *f*.

po·tion ['pouʃn] potion *f*; 🝆 dose *f*.

pot-luck ['pot'lʌk]: take ⌣ with s.o. manger chez q. à la fortune du pot.

pot·ter[1] ['potə] s'amuser (à, *at*); s'occuper en amateur (de, *at*); flâner.

pot·ter[2] [⌣] potier *m*; ⌣'s wheel tour *m* de potier; disque *m*; '**pot·ter·y** poterie *f*.

pot·ty *sl.* ['poti] insignifiant; simple; toqué.

pouch [pautʃ] **1.** petit sac *m*; bourse *f*; *yeux:* poche *f*; blague *f*; *zo.* poche *f* ventrale; *singe:* abajoue *f*; **2.** *v/t.* empocher; faire bouffer (*une robe*); avaler (*un poisson*); *v/i.* bouffer; **pouched** à poche; à abajoue.

poul·ter·er ['poultərə] marchand *m* de volaille.

poul·tice 🝆 ['poultis] cataplasme *m*.

poul·try ['poultri] volaille *f*.

pounce[1] [pauns] **1.** (poudre *f* de) sandaraque *f*; ponce *f*; **2.** polir à la ponce; poncer (*un dessin*).

pounce[2] [⌣] **1.** *oiseau:* serre *f*; saut *m*; **2.** *v/t.* (*ou* ⌣ upon) *oiseau:* s'abattre sur (*sa proie*); *v/i.* *fig.* ⌣ [up]on se jeter sur.

pound[1] [paund] livre *f* (*abr.* lb.) (453,6 g); ⌣ (sterling) livre *f* (sterling) (*abr.* £).

pound[2] [⌣] **1.** parc *m* (à moutons *etc.*); fourrière *f*; **2.** mettre en fourrière.

pound[3] [⌣] *v/t.* broyer, piler; bourrer de coups de poing; ⚒ pilonner; *sl. Bourse:* faire baisser (*les prix*); *v/i.*: ⌣ along avancer d'un pas lourd; ⌣ away frapper *ou* cogner dur (sur, *at*).

pound·age ['paundidʒ] remise *f* ou taux *m* de tant par livre.

pound·er ['paundə] de ... livres.

pour [pɔ:] *v/t.* (*a.* ⌣ out) verser; ⌣ out répandre; décharger (*son cœur*); *v/i.*

tomber à verse (*pluie*); sortir à flots *ou* en foule.

pout [paut] **1.** moue *f*; **2.** (*a. ~ the lips*) faire la moue; bouder.

pov·er·ty ['pɔvəti] pauvreté *f*; pénurie *f*.

pow·der ['paudə] **1.** poudre *f*; **2.** pulvériser; poudrer (*le visage*); saupoudrer (de, with); '**~·box** boîte *f* à poudre; **~ keg** *fig.* poudrière *f*; '**~·puff** houpette *f* (à poudre); **~ room** toilettes *f/pl.* pour dames; '**pow·der·y** poudreux (-euse *f*); friable.

pow·er ['pauə] *m* pouvoir (*a.* ⚖ *pol.* exécutif etc.); puissance *f* (*a.* ⊕, ♉, *pol.* = *pays, influence*); vigueur *f*; ⚡ énergie *f* (*électrique*); aimant: force *f*; *admin.* autorité *f*; ⚖ mandat *m*; F quantité *f*, foule *f*; be in ~ être au pouvoir; *Western* ~*s pl. pol.* puissances *f/pl.* occidentales; '**~·as·sist·ed** ⊕ assisté; **~ break** servofrein *m*; '**~·cur·rent** courant *m* à haute intensité; **~ cut** ⚡ coupure *f* de courant; **~ fail·ure** panne *f* de courant; **pow·er·ful** ['~ful] □ puissant, fort; '**pow·er·house** centrale *f* électrique; '**pow·er·less** impuissant; inefficace; '**pow·er line** ligne *f* à haute tension; '**pow·er·plant** groupe *m* générateur; *Am.* centrale *f* électrique; **~ point** *Brit.* prise *f* de courant; **~ saw** scie *f* à moteur; '**pow·er sta·tion** centrale *f* électrique; *long-distance* ~ centrale *f* interurbaine; **~ steer·ing** servodirection *f*; **~ strug·gle** *pol. etc.* lutte *f* pour le pouvoir.

pow·wow ['pau'wau] sorcier *m* guérisseur; *Am.* F conférence *f* (politique); palabre *f*.

pox V [pɔks] syphilis *f*.

pra(a)m ⚓ [prɑːm] prame *f*.

prac·ti·ca·bil·i·ty [præktikə'biliti] praticabilité *f*; '**prac·ti·ca·ble** □ praticable; faisable; '**prac·ti·cal** □ pratique; appliqué (*science*); quasi; ~ **joke** mystification *f*; mauvais tour *m*; brimade *f*; attrape *f*; ~ **chemistry** chimie *f* appliquée; **prac·ti·cal·i·ty** [~'kæliti] caractère *m* pratique; esprit *m* pratique; **prac·ti·cal·ly** ['~kli] pratiquement; en pratique; presque.

prac·tice ['præktis] **1.** pratique *f*; exercice *m* (*d'un métier*); habitude *f*, coutume *f*, usage *m*; *sp.* entraîne-

ment *m*; clientèle *f*; *usu.* ~*s pl.* menés *f/pl.*, intrigue *f*; *be out of* ~ avoir perdu l'habitude; *put into* ~ mettre en pratique *ou* en action; **2.** *Am. see* practise.

prac·tise [~] *v/t.* mettre en pratique *ou* en action; pratiquer; exercer (*une profession*); s'exercer (*au piano etc., sur la flûte*); entraîner (*q.*); *v/i.* exercer (*médecin*); *sp.*, ♩ s'exercer; répéter; ~ [up]on exploiter (*q.*), abuser de (*la faiblesse de q.*); '**prac·tised** expérimenté; versé (dans *at, in*).

prac·ti·tion·er [præk'tiʃnə] praticien *m*; *qqfois* médecin *m*; *general* ~ médecin *m* ordinaire, médecin *m* de médecine générale.

prag·mat·ic [præg'mætik] (~*ally*) pragmatique; (*souv.* **prag'mat·i·cal**) suffisant; dogmatique.

prai·rie *Am.* ['prɛəri] prairie *f*; savane *f*; *Am.* ~ **schooner** voiture *f* couverte (*des pionniers*).

praise [preiz] **1.** éloge *m*; louange *f*; **2.** louer, faire l'éloge de; F vanter. **praise·wor·thi·ness** ['preizwə:ðinis] caractère *m* estimable; mérite *m*; '**praise·wor·thy** □ digne d'éloges; méritoire.

pra·line ['prɑːliːn] praline *f*.

pram F [præm] *see* perambulator.

prance [prɑːns] piaffer (*cheval*); se pavaner (*personne*); *fig.* trépigner (de, with).

pran·di·al □ ['prændiəl] *co.* de *ou* du dîner; de table.

prang ✕ *Brit. sl.* [præŋ] raid *m* sévère.

prank [præŋk] **1.** escapade *f*; tour *m*; **2.** (*a.* ~ up) parer (de, with).

prate [preit] **1.** riens *m/pl.*; jaserie *f*; **2.** dire des riens; jaser; '**prat·er** babillard(e *f*) *m*; '**prat·ing 1.** □ babillard, jaseur (-euse *f*); **2.** jaserie *f*.

prat·tle ['prætl] *see* prate.

prawn *zo.* [prɔːn] crevette *f* rouge.

pray [prei] *v/i.* prier (*q., to s.o.*; de *inf., to inf.*; pour *q., for s.o.*); ~ *for s.th.* prier Dieu qu'il (nous) accorde qch.; ~ je vous en prie, veuillez (*inf.*); ~ *for s.o.'s soul* prier pour l'âme de *q.*; *v/t.* prier, implorer; demander.

pray·er ['prɛə] prière *f*, oraison *f*; demande *f*; *souv.* ~*s pl.* dévotions *f/pl.*; *Lord's* ♀ oraison *f* dominicale;

pater *m*; *Book of Common* ♀ rituel *m* de l'Église anglicane; '~-book livre *m* de prières; **pray·er·ful** □ ['~ful] pieux (-euse *f*).

pre… [pri:; pri] pré-; avant; antérieur à.

preach [pri:tʃ] prêcher; '**preach·er** prédicateur (-trice *f*) *m*; '**preach·ing** prédication *f*, sermon *m*; '**preach·ment** *péj.* sermon *m*.

pre·am·ble [pri:'æmbl] préambule *m*.

preb·end *eccl.* ['prebənd] prébende *f*; '**preb·en·dar·y** prébendier *m*, chanoine *m*.

pre·car·i·ous □ [pri'kɛəriəs] précaire, incertain; **pre'car·i·ous·ness** incertitude *f*; situation *f* précaire.

pre·cau·tion [pri'kɔ:ʃn] précaution *f*; **pre'cau·tion·ar·y** de précaution; d'avertissement.

pre·cede [pri'si:d] (faire) précéder; préfacer; *fig.* avoir le pas sur; **pre'ced·ence, pre'ced·en·cy** [~dəns(i)] priorité *f*; préséance *f*; **prec·e·dent** ['presidənt] précédent *m* (*a.* ⚖).

pre·cen·tor *eccl.* [pri'sentə] premier chantre *m*; maître *m* de chapelle.

pre·cept ['pri:sept] précepte *m*; règle *f*; ⚖ mandat *m*; **pre·cep·tor** [pri'septə] précepteur *m*; **pre'cep·tress** [~tris] préceptrice *f*.

pre·cinct ['pri:siŋkt] enceinte *f*, enclos *m*; *surt. Am.* circonscription *f* électorale; *Am.* poste *m* de police d'une circonscription; *a.* ~s *pl.* pourtour *m*.

pre·cious ['preʃəs] **1.** *adj.* □ précieux (-euse *f*); F *a. iro.* fameux (-euse *f*); **2.** F *adv.* particulièrement, joliment; '**pre·cious·ness** haute valeur *f*.

prec·i·pice ['presipis] précipice *m*; **pre·cip·i·tance, pre·cip·i·tan·cy** [pri'sipitəns(i)] précipitation *f*; empressement *m*; **pre'cip·i·tate 1.** [~teit] *v/t.* précipiter (*a.* ⚗); accélérer; *météor.* condenser; *v/i.* se précipiter; **2.** [~tit] □ précipité (⚗ *a. su./m*); fait à la hâte; irréfléchi; **pre·cip·i·ta·tion** [~'teiʃn] précipitation *f* (*a.* ⚗); **pre'cip·i·tous** □ à pic; escarpé; abrupt.

pré·cis ['preisi:], *pl.* -cis [~si:z] précis *m*, résumé *m*, abrégé *m*.

pre·cise □ [pri'sais] exact; précis; méticuleux (-euse *f*); ~ly! précisément!; **pre'cise·ness** précision *f*; méticulosité *f*.

pre·ci·sion [pri'siʒn] précision *f*; *attr.* de précision.

pre·clude [pri'klu:d] prévenir, empêcher; ~ *s.o. from* (*gér.*) mettre q. dans l'impossibilité de (*inf.*).

pre·co·cious □ [pri'kouʃəs] précoce; **pre'co·cious·ness, pre·coc·i·ty** [pri'kɔsiti] précocité *f*.

pre·con·ceive ['pri:kən'si:v] préconcevoir; ~d préconçu (*idée*).

pre·con·cep·tion ['pri:kən'sepʃn] préconception *f*; préjugé *m*.

pre·con·cert·ed ['pri:kən'sə:tid] convenu *ou* arrangé d'avance.

pre·con·di·tion ['pri:kən'diʃn] condition *f* préliminaire.

pre·cool ⊕ ['pri:'ku:l] préréfrigérer.

pre·cur·sor [pri:'kə:sə] précurseur *m*, avant-coureur *m*; **pre'cur·so·ry** précurseur; préliminaire.

pre·date ['pri:'deit] antidater; venir avant.

pred·a·to·ry ['predətəri] rapace; de proie (*bête*).

pre·de·cease ['pri:di'si:s] mourir avant (*q.*).

pre·de·ces·sor ['pri:disesə] prédécesseur *m*.

pre·des·ti·nate [pri'destineit] prédestiner; **pre·des·ti·na·tion** *eccl.* prédestination *f*; **pre'des·tined** prédestiné.

pre·de·ter·mine ['pri:di'tə:min] déterminer d'avance; *eccl.* préordonner. [cable.\

pred·i·ca·ble ['predikəbl] prédi-\
pre·dic·a·ment [pri'dikəmənt] *phls.* catégorie *f*; *fig.* situation *f* difficile.

pred·i·cate 1. ['predikeit] affirmer; **2.** ['~kit] *gramm.* attribut *m*; *phls.* prédicat *m*; **pred·i·ca·tion** assertion *f*; **pred·i·ca·tive** [pri'dikətiv] □ affirmatif (-ive *f*); *gramm.* prédicatif (-ive *f*).

pre·dict [pri'dikt] prédire; **pre·dic·tion** [~'dikʃn] prédiction *f*.

pre·di·lec·tion [pri:di'lekʃn] prédilection *f* (*pour, for*).

pre·dis·pose ['pri:dis'pouz] prédisposer (à, *to*); **pre·dis·po·si·tion** ['~dispə'ziʃn] prédisposition *f* (à, *to*).

pre·dom·i·nance [pri'dɔminəns] prédominance *f*; ascendant *m* (sur, *over*); **pre'dom·i·nant** □ prédominant; **pre'dom·i·nate** [~neit] prédominer; l'emporter par le nombre *etc.* (sur, *over*).

pre·em·i·nence [priː'eminəns] pré-éminence *f*; primat *m*; **pre·'em·i·nent** □ prééminent; remarquable (par, *in*).

pre·emp·tion [priː'empʃn] (droit *m* de) préemption *f*; **pre·'emp·tive** [‿tiv] ✝ de préemption (*droit*); *fig.* préventif (-ive); ✗ ~ first strike attaque *f* préventive.

preen [priːn] lisser (*les plumes*).

pre·en·gage [priːin'geidʒ] retenir *ou* engager d'avance; **pre·en·'gage·ment** engagement *m* préalable.

pre·ex·ist [priːig'zist] préexister; **'pre·ex·'ist·ence** préexistence *f*; **'pre·ex·'ist·ent** préexistant.

pre·fab [priː'fæb] 1. préfabriqué; 2. maison *f* préfabriquée; **'pre·fab·ri·cate** [‿rikeit] préfabriquer.

pref·ace ['prefis] 1. préface *f*; avant-propos *m/inv.*; 2. préfacer; préluder à.   [liminaire.\
pref·a·to·ry □ ['prefətəri] pré-⌋
pre·fect ['priːfekt] préfet *m*; *école*: élève *mf* surveillant(e *f*).

pre·fer [pri'fəː] préférer (à, to), aimer mieux (que *sbj.*, to *inf.*); nommer (*q. à un emploi*); déposer (*une plainte*); intenter (*une action*); émettre (*une prétention*); *see* share 1; **pre·fer·a·ble** □ ['prefərəbl] préférable (à, to); **'pref·er·a·bly** de préférence (à, to); préférablement; **'pref·er·ence** préférence *f* (pour, for); (*surt.* ✝) droit *m* de priorité; *douane*: tarif *m* de préférence; *see* share 1; **pref·er·en·tial** □ [‿'renʃl] préférentiel(le *f*); de préférence; **pref·er'en·tial·ly** de préférence; **pre·fer·ment** [pri'fəːmənt] avancement *m*; promotion *f*.

pre·fix 1. ['priːfiks] préfixe *m*; titre *m*; 2. [priː'fiks] mettre comme introduction; *gramm.* préfixer.

preg·nan·cy ['pregnənsi] grossesse *f*; *animal*: gestation *f*; *fig.* grande portée *f*; fécondité *f*; **'preg·nant** □ ⚥ enceinte (*femme*); gravide (*animal*); *fig.* gros(se *f*), fertile (en, with).

pre·heat ⊕ ['priː'hiːt] réchauffer d'avance.

pre·hen·sile [pri'hensail] préhensile.

pre·his·tor·ic ['priːhis'tɔrik] préhistorique.

pre·ig·ni·tion *mot.* ['priːig'niʃn] auto-allumage *m*; allumage *m* prématuré.

pre·judge ['priː'dʒʌdʒ] préjuger.

prej·u·dice ['predʒudis] 1. préjugé *m*, prévention *f*; préjudice *m*, dommage *m*; *without* ~ to réservation faite de; 2. prévenir, prédisposer; porter préjudice à; ~d prévenu; to préjugés.

prej·u·di·cial □ [predʒu'diʃl] préjudiciable, nuisible (à, to).

prel·a·cy ['preləsi] épiscopat *m*; prélats *m/pl.*

prel·ate ['prelit] prélat *m*.

pre·lec·tion [pri'lekʃn] conférence *f*; **pre·'lec·tor** conférencier *m*; *univ.* maître *m* de conférences.

pre·lim·i·nar·y [pri'liminəri] 1. □ préliminaire; préalable; 2. prélude *m*; *preliminaries pl.* préliminaires *m/pl.*

prel·ude ['preljuːd] 1. prélude *m* (*a.* ♪); 2. *v/i.* ♪ préluder; *v/t.* précéder; préluder à.

pre·mar·i·tal [priː'mæritl] prématrimonial (-aux *m/pl.*), avant le mariage.

pre·ma·ture [premə'tjuə] *fig.* prématuré; ~ *delivery* accouchement *m* avant terme; **pre·ma·'ture·ness**, **pre·ma'tu·ri·ty** [‿riti] *fig.* prématurité *f*.

pre·med·i·tate [priː'mediteit] préméditer; **pre·med·i·'ta·tion** préméditation *f*.

pre·mi·er ['premjə] 1. premier (-ère *f*); 2. premier ministre *m*; président *m* du conseil; *Am.* ministre *m* des Affaires étrangères; **'pre·mi·er·ship** fonctions *f/pl.* de premier ministre; *Am.* Ministère *m* des Affaires étrangères.

pre·mise 1. ['premis] prémisse *f*; ~s *pl.* local *m*; immeuble *m*; ⚖ intitulé *m*; *licensed* ~s *pl.* débit *m* de boissons; *on the* ~s sur les lieux; dans l'établissement; 2. [pri'maiz] poser en prémisse; faire remarquer.

pre·mi·um ['priːmjəm] *m*; prime *f* (*a.* ✝); indemnité *f*; *au début d'un bail*: droit *m*; ✝ agio *m*; *at* a ~ à prime.

pre·mo·ni·tion [priːmə'niʃn] prémonition *f*; pressentiment *m*; **pre·mon·i·to·ry** □ [pri'mɔnitəri] prémonitoire; précurseur.

pre·na·tal ['priː'neitl] prénatal (-als, -aux *m/pl.*).

pre·oc·cu·pan·cy [priː'ɔkjupənsi] *fig.* absorption *f* (par, in); **pre·oc·**

cu·pa·tion [priːɔkjuˈpeiʃn] préoccupation *f*; absorption *f* (par, with); souci *m*; préjugé *m*; **pre·oc·cu·pied** [ˌ.ˈɔkjupaid] préoccupé; absorbé; **preˈoc·cu·py** [ˌ.pai] préoccuper, absorber; occuper par avance.

pre·or·dain [priːɔːˈdein] régler d'avance; préordonner.

prep F [prep] *see* preparation; preparatory school.

prep·a·ra·tion [prepəˈreiʃn] préparation *f*; préparatifs *m/pl.*; *école*: étude *f* (du soir); **pre·par·a·tive** [priˈpærətiv] *usu.* ˌ.s *pl.* préparatifs *m/pl.*; **preˈpar·a·to·ry** [ˌ.təri] 1. □ préparatoire; ˌ school école *f* préparatoire à; 2. *adv.* ˌ to préalablement à.

pre·pare [priˈpɛə] *v/t.* préparer; dresser; confectionner (*un mets*); *v/i.* se préparer, s'apprêter (à, for; à *inf.*, to *inf.*); **preˈpared** □ préparé; sur le qui-vive; ˌ for prêt à (*qch.*) *ou* pour (*inf.*).

pre·pay [ˈpriːˈpei] [*irr.* (pay)] payer d'avance; affranchir (*une lettre*); **ˈpreˈpay·ment** paiement *m* d'avance; *lettre*: affranchissement *m*.

pre·pense □ [priˈpens] prémédité; with malice ˌ avec intention criminelle.

pre·pon·der·ance [priˈpɔndərəns] prépondérance *f*; **preˈpon·der·ant** □ prépondérant; **preˈpon·der·ate** [ˌ.reit] peser davantage; *fig.* l'emporter (sur, over).

prep·o·si·tion *gramm.* [prepəˈziʃn] préposition *f*; **prep·o·si·tion·al** □ prépositionnel(le *f*).

pre·pos·sess [priːpəˈzes] imprégner, pénétrer (*l'esprit*) (de, with); prévenir (*q.*) (en faveur de, in favour of; contre, against); **preˈpos·sess·ing** □ prévenant; agréable; **pre·pos·ses·sion** [ˌ.ˈzeʃn] prévention *f*, préjugé *m*.

pre·pos·ter·ous [priˈpɔstərəs] absurde; déraisonnable; contraire au bon sens.

pre·puce *anat.* [ˈpriːpjuːs] prépuce *m*.

pre·req·ui·site [ˈpriːˈrekwizit] nécessité *f* préalable; condition *f* préalable.

pre·rog·a·tive [priˈrɔgətiv] prérogative *f*; privilège *m*.

pres·age [ˈpresidʒ] 1. présage *m*;

pressentiment *m*; 2. présager, annoncer; prédire.

pres·by·ter [ˈprezbitə] prêtre *m*; ancien *m*; **Pres·by·te·ri·an** [ˌ.ˈtiəriən] 1. presbytérien(ne *f*); 2. Presbytérien(ne *f*) *m*; **pres·by·ter·y** [ˈˌ.təri] 🔺 sanctuaire *m*; *eccl.* presbytère *m*, consistoire *m*.

pre·sci·ence [ˈpresiəns] prescience *f*, prévision *f*; **ˈpre·sci·ent** prescient, prévoyant.

pre·scribe [prisˈkraib] *v/t.* prescrire, ordonner (*a.* ⚕); *v/i.*: ˌ for prescrire à, ordonner à (*q.*); ⚕ indiquer un traitement pour (*q.*); ⚖ (*ou* ˌ to) prescrire, acquérir (*un droit*) par prescription.

pre·script [ˈpriːskript] prescription *f*, précepte *m*; **pre·scrip·tion** [prisˈkripʃn] prescription *f* (*a.* ⚖); ordre *m*; ⚕ ordonnance *f*; ⚖ coutume *f*; droit *m* consacré par l'usage; *Brit.* ˌ charge somme *f* fixe à payer lors de l'exécution d'une ordonnance; **preˈscrip·tive** □ consacré par l'usage; ordonnateur (-trice *f*).

pres·ence [ˈprezns] présence *f*; mine *f*, air *m*, maintien *m*; in the ˌ of en présence de (*q.*); ˌ of mind présence *f* d'esprit; **ˈˌ-cham·ber** salle *f* d'audience.

pres·ent[1] [ˈpreznt] 1. □ présent; actuel(le *f*); courant (*année etc.*); ˌ record holder recordman *m* de l'heure; *gramm.* ˌ tense (temps *m*) présent *m*; ˌ value valeur *f* actuelle; ˌ! présent! 2. présent *m* (*a. gramm.*); temps *m* présent; ✝ the ˌ, ⚖ by these ˌs par la présente; at ˌ à présent, actuellement; for the ˌ pour le moment.

pre·sent[2] [priˈzent] présenter (*a.* qch. à q., s.o. with s.th.); donner; offrir; faire cadeau de (*qch.*); ˌ o.s. se présenter; s'offrir; ˌ one's compliments to s.o. présenter ses compliments à q.

pres·ent[3] [ˈpreznt] cadeau *m*; make s.o. a ˌ of s.th. faire cadeau de qch. à q.

pre·sent·a·ble [priˈzentəbl] présentable; portable (*robe etc.*).

pres·en·ta·tion [prezənˈteiʃn] présentation *f*; ✝ remise *f*; *théâ.* (re)présentation *f*; souvenir *m*; ˌ copy spécimen *m* gratuit; exemplaire *m* offert à titre d'hommage.

pres·ent-day ['prezntdei] d'aujourd'hui, actuel(le f).

pre·sen·ti·ment [pri'zentimənt] pressentiment m.

pres·ent·ly ['prezntli] bientôt; tout à l'heure; F actuellement.

pre·sent·ment [pri'zentmənt] see presentation; ♓ déclaration f émanant du jury; théâ. représentation f.

pres·er·va·tion [prezə'veiʃn] conservation f; préservation f (de, from); maintien m; ~ of natural beauty préservation f des beautés de la nature; in good ~ en bon état de conservation f; **pre·serv·a·tive** [pri'zə:vətiv] 1. préservateur (-trice f); 2. préservatif m; antiseptique m.

pre·serve [pri'zə:v] 1. préserver, garantir (de, from); conserver; mettre en conserve; maintenir; garder (le silence, la chasse); ♓ naturaliser; élever (du gibier) dans une réserve; 2. chasse f gardée; réserve f; poisson: vivier m; confiture f; **pre'serv·er** préservateur (-trice f) m; sauveur m; propriétaire m d'une chasse gardée ou d'un vivier; conservateur (-trice f) m; agent m de conservation.

pre·side [pri'zaid] présider (qch., à qch. over s.th.); occuper le fauteuil présidentiel; ~ over an assembly présider une assemblée.

pres·i·den·cy ['prezidənsi] présidence f; école: directorat m, rectorat m; **'pres·i·dent** président(e f) m; école: (di)recteur m; ✝ Am. directeur m général; **pres·i·den·tial** [~'denʃl] présidentiel(le f).

press [pres] 1. pression f (sur qch.); presse f (hydraulique, à copier, de journaux, fig. des affaires, a. typ.); typ. imprimerie f; 2. v/t. presser; appuyer sur; serrer (a.✕); donner un coup de fer à (une robe etc.); fig. poursuivre (un avantage); forcer à accepter; réclamer (une dette, une réponse); imposer (une opinion); ~ the button appuyer sur le bouton; ~ the point that insister sur le fait que; be ~ed for time être très pressé ou à court de temps; v/i. se serrer, se presser; ~ for insister pour obtenir ou pour que (sbj.); ~ on presser le pas, forcer le pas, se dépêcher; ~ (up)on peser à (q.); ~ **a·gen·cy** agence f d'informa-

tions; ~ **a·gent** agent m de publicité; ~ **bar·on** magnat m de la presse; ~ **but·ton** bouton m à pression; gant: bouton m fermoir; ~ **clip·ping** see press cutting; ~ **con·fer·ence** conférence f de presse; ~ **cor·rec·tor** typ. correcteur m (-trice f); ~ **cut·ting** coupure f de journal; **'press·er** presse f (à viande); pressoir m (aux raisins); presseur (-euse f) m (personne); **'press-gal·le·ry** tribune f de la presse; **'press-gang**: F ~ s.o. into doing s.th. faire pression sur q. pour qu'il fasse qch.; **'press·ing** □ pressant; urgent, pressé; ~ **lord** see press baron; **'press·man** ⊕ presseur m; journaliste m; **'press-mark** bibliothèque: numéro m de classement; **press re·lease** communiqué m de presse; **'press-stud** bouton-pression m (pl. boutons-pression), pression f; **'press-up**: do ~s faire des tractions ou des pompes; **pres·sure** ['preʃə] pression f (a. fig.); ⚡, ✈ tension f; ~ group groupe m de pression; **pres·sure-cook·er** marmite f à pression; **'pres·sure-gauge** ⊕ manomètre m; **pres·sur·ize** ['~raiz] ✈ pressuriser; **'press-work** typ. impression f.

pres·ti·dig·i·ta·tion ['prestididʒi'teiʃn] prestidigitation f.

pres·tige [pres'ti:ʒ] prestige m; crédit m; **pres·ti·gious** [~'tidʒəs] prestigieux.

pre·sum·a·ble □ [pri'zju:məbl] présumable (de la part de q., of s.o.); **pre'sum·a·bly** [~i] probablement; **pre'sume** v/t. présumer, supporter; v/i. présumer; prendre des libertés; se permettre (de, to); prendre la liberté (de, to); ~ (up)on abuser de; se prévaloir de; **pre'sum·ed·ly** [~idli] probablement; **pre'sum·ing** □ présomptueux (-euse f); indiscret (-ète f).

pre·sump·tion [pri'zʌmpʃn] présomption f; arrogance f; préjugé m; qqfois conclusion f; **pre'sump·tive** □ par présomption; heir ~ héritier m présomptif; **pre'sump·tu·ous** □ [~tjuəs] présomptueux (-euse f), outrecuidant.

pre·sup·pose [pri:sə'pouz] présupposer; **pre·sup·po·si·tion** [pri:-sʌpə'ziʃn] présupposition f.

pre·tence, Am. **pre·tense** [pri-'tens] (faux) semblant m; prétexte *m*; prétention *f* (à, to); *false* ~ fraude *f*; faux semblant *m*.

pre·tend [pri'tend] feindre, simuler; prétendre (*inf.*, to *inf.*; à qch., to *s.th.*); faire semblant (de *inf.*, to *inf.*); **pre'tend·ed** □ feint, faux (fausse *f*); soi-disant (*personne*); prétendu; **pre'tend·er** simulateur (-trice *f*) *m*; prétendant *m* (*au trône*).

pre·ten·sion [pri'tenʃn] prétention *f*; droit *m*, titre *m*.

pre·ten·tious [pri'tenʃəs] prétentieux (-euse *f*); **pre'ten·tious·ness** prétention *f*.

pret·er·it(e) *gramm.* ['preterit] prétérit *m*, passé *m*.

pre·ter·mis·sion [pri:tə'miʃn] omission *f*; interruption *f*.

pre·ter·mit [pri:tə'mit] omettre; interrompre; négliger (de *inf.*).

pre·ter·nat·u·ral □ [pri:tə'nætʃrəl] surnaturel(le *f*).

pre·text ['pri:tekst] prétexte *m*, excuse *f*.

pret·ti·ness ['pritinis] gentillesse *f* (*a. style*).

pret·ty ['priti] **1.** *adj.* □ joli, beau (bel *devant une voyelle ou un h muet*; belle *f*); gentil(le *f*); *my* ~! ma mignonne! **2.** *adv.* assez, passablement; ~ *near* à peu près; ~ *close to perfect* presque parfait; ~ *much the same thing* à peu près la même chose; *a* ~ *large number* un assez grand nombre.

pre·vail [pri'veil] prédominer; régner; prévaloir (sur, over; contre, *against*); l'emporter (sur *over*, *against*); ~ (*up*)*on s.o.* à (*inf.*) amener *ou* déterminer q. à (*inf.*); **pre'vail·ing** □ courant; en vogue; dominant.

prev·a·lence ['prevələns] prédominance *f*; généralité *f*; fréquence *f*; **'prev·a·lent** □ (pré)dominant; répandu, général (-aux *m/pl.*).

pre·var·i·cate [pri'værikeit] équivoquer; mentir; **pre·var·i·ca·tion** équivoques *f/pl.*; mensonge *m*; **pre'var·i·ca·tor** barguigneur (-euse *f*) *m*; menteur (-euse *f*) *m*.

pre·vent [pri'vent] empêcher (de, from); mettre obstacle à (qch.); prévenir (*un malheur etc.*); **pre'vent·a·ble** évitable; **pre'vent·a·tive** [~tətiv] *see* preventive; **pre'vent·er** empêcheur (-euse *f*) *m*; ⚓ faux

étai *m*; **pre'ven·tion** empêchement *m*; protection *f* (contre, of); **pre'ven·tive 1.** □ préventif (-ive *f*); ~ *custody* détention *f* préventive; ~ *detention* emprisonnement *m* à titre préventif; ~ *medicine* médecine *f* préventive; **2.** empêchement *m*; médicament *m* préventif; mesure *f* préventive (contre, of).

pre·view ['pri:vju:] exhibition *f* préalable; *cin.* avant-première *f*.

pre·vi·ous □ ['pri:viəs] antérieur, antécédent (à, to); préalable; F trop pressé; ~ *conviction* condamnation *f* antérieure; ~ *to a.* avant; ~*ly* auparavant; préalablement.

pre·vi·sion [pri:'viʒn] prévision *f*.

pre·vo·ca·tion·al train·ing [pri:vo'keiʃnl'treiniŋ] enseignement *m* professionnel.

pre·war ['pri:'wɔ:] d'avant-guerre.

prey [prei] **1.** proie *f*; *beast* (*bird*) *of* ~ bête *f* (oiseau *m*) de proie; **2.**: ~ (*up*)*on* faire sa proie de; piller, ravager; *fig.* ronger.

price [prais] **1.** prix *m*; *course:* cote *f*; *bourse:* cours *m*; *at any* ~ coûte que coûte; **2.** mettre un prix à; estimer, évaluer; demander le prix de; ~ *s.o. out* chasser q. du marché en demandant des prix plus bas que celui-ci; ~ *o.s. out* (*of the market*) perdre un marché en demandant des prix trop élevés; ~ *brack·et see price range*; **'pric·ey** F coûteux (-euse *f*), F cherot; **'price·less** inestimable; *sl.* impayable; **price range** éventail *m ou* gamme *f* des prix; *within my* ~ dans mes prix; *in the medium* ~ dans les prix moyens; **price tick·et, price tag** étiquette *f* (de prix); *fig.* prix *m*; *have a heavy* ~ coûter cher.

prick [prik] **1.** piqûre *f*; *fig.* picoterie *f*; *conscience:* remords *m*; **2.** *v/t.* piquer; crever (*une ampoule*); pointer (*une carte*); (*a.* ~ *out*) tracer un dessin en le piquant; ✗ ~ *out* repiquer; ~ *up one's ears* dresser l'oreille; *v/i.* picoter; fourmiller (*membre*); ~ *up* se dresser; **'prick·er** poinçon *m*, pointe *f*; **prick·le** ['~] piquant *m*, épine *f*; **'prick·ly** épineux (-euse *f*); ✗ ~ *heat* bouton *m* de chaleur; ♀ ~ *pear* figuier *m ou* figue *f* de Barbarie.

pride [praid] **1.** orgueil *m*; *péj.* vanité *f*; faste *m*; *saison etc.:* apogée *m*; ~ *of place* priorité *f*;

take ~ *in* être fier (fière *f*) de; 2.: ~ *o.s.* se piquer, se faire gloire, tirer vanité (de, [up]on).

pri·er ['praiə] curieux (-euse *f*) *m*.

priest [pri:st] prêtre *m*; '~·craft *péj.* cléricalisme *m*; intrigues *f/pl.* sacerdotales; '**priest·ess** prêtresse *f*; **priest·hood** ['~hud] le clergé *m*; sacerdoce *m*; '**priest·ly** sacerdotal (-aux *m/pl.*).

prig [prig] 1. poseur *m* à la vertu; *sl.* chipeur (-euse *f*) *m*; 2. *sl.* chiper; '**prig·gish** □ suffisant; collet monté *adj./inv.*

prim □ [prim] guindé, compassé; collet monté *adj./inv.* (*personne*).

pri·ma·cy ['praiməsi] primauté *f*; *eccl.* primatie *f*; **pri·ma·ri·ly** ['~rili] principalement; '**pri·ma·ry** □ principal (-aux *m/pl.*); primitif (-ive *f*); premier (-ère *f*) (*a. importance*); ⚡, ☀, *astr.*, *couleur*, *école*: primaire; *Am.* ~ (*meeting*) élection *f* primaire directe; *see* *share*; **pri·mate** *eccl.* ['~mit] primat *m*.

prime [praim] 1. □ premier (-ère *f*); de premier ordre; principal (-aux *m/pl.*); de surchoix (*viande*); ♱ ~ *cost* prix *m* coûtant, prix *m* d'achat; ♀ *Minister* président *m* du Conseil; premier ministre *m*; ~ *number* nombre *m* premier; *radio, télév.* ~ *time* heure(s) *f(pl.)* d'écoute maximum; 2. *fig.* perfection *f*; fleur *f* de l'âge; choix *m*; premiers jours *m/pl.*; *eccl.* prime *f*; 3. *v/t.* amorcer (*une arme, un obus, une pompe*); *peint.* apprêter; *fig.* faire la leçon à; abreuver (*q. d'alcool*); *v/i.* primer.

prim·er[1] ['praimə] premier cours *m* ou livre *m* de lecture; premiers éléments *m/pl.*; *typ.* ['primə]: *great* ~ gros romain *m*; corps 16; *long* ~ philosophie *f*; corps 10.

prim·er[2] ['praimə] amorceur *m*; apprêteur *m*; *peint.* couche *f* d'impression.

pri·me·val [prai'mi:vəl] primordial (-aux *m/pl.*).

prim·ing ['praimiŋ] *peint.* apprêtage *m*; couche *f* d'impression; ⚔ amorce *f*; amorçage *m*.

prim·i·tive ['primitiv] 1. □ primitif (-ive *f*), primaire; rude, grossier (-ère *f*); 2. *gramm.* mot *m* primitif; *peint.* primitif *m*; '**prim·i·tive·ness**

caractère *m* primitif; *peuple*: rudesse *f*.

prim·ness ['primnis] air *m* collet monté; *chambre etc.*: ordre *m* parfait.

pri·mo·gen·i·ture[praimo'dʒenitʃə] primogéniture *f*; droit *m* d'aînesse.

pri·mor·di·al □ [prai'mɔ:diəl] primordial (-aux *m/pl.*).

prim·rose ⚜ ['primrouz] primevère *f* (à grandes fleurs); *fig.* ~ *path* chemin *m* de velours.

prince [prins] prince *m*; '**prince·like** princier (-ère *f*); '**prince·ly** princier (-ère *f*); royal (-aux *m/pl.*) (*a. fig.*); *fig.* magnifique; **prin·cess** [prin'ses; *devant npr.* 'prinses] princesse *f*.

prin·ci·pal ['prinsəpəl] 1. □ principal (-aux *m/pl.*); en chef; premier (-ère *f*); *gramm.* ~ *parts pl.* temps *m/pl.* principaux (*du verbe.*); 2. directeur *m*; chef *m*; patron *m*; employeur *m*; ⚖ *crime*: auteur *m*; ♱ capital *m*; *univ.* recteur *m*; **prin·ci·pal·i·ty** [prinsi'pæliti] principauté *f*.

prin·ci·ple ['prinsəpl] principe *m* (*a.* ⚗); *in* ~ en principe; *on* ~ par principe; *on a* ~ d'après un principe.

prink F [priŋk] (s')attifer.

print [print] 1. empreinte *f (digitale)*; impression *f*; moule *m*; trace *f*; gravure *f*, estampe *f*; *typ.* matière *f* imprimée; caractères *m/pl.*; *phot.* copie *f*, épreuve *f*; ⊕ dessin; *usu. Am.* journal *m*; feuille *f* imprimée; ♱ *tex.* indienne *f*, cotonnade *f*; *out of* ~ épuisé; *in cold* ~ à la lecture, par écrit; *please* ~ écrire en lettres d'imprimerie; 2. *v/t.* imprimer; marquer d'une empreinte; *phot.* tirer une épreuve de; *fig.* ~ *o.s.* se graver (dans, on); ~*ed form* imprimé; ~*ed matter* imprimés *m/pl.*; *v/i.* être à l'impression; '**print·er** imprimeur *m*; ouvrier *m* typographe; ~'*s devil* apprenti *m* imprimeur; ~'*s flower* fleuron *m*; ~'*s ink* encre *f* d'impression.

print·ing ['printiŋ] impression *f*; *art:* imprimerie *f*; *phot.* tirage *m*; *attr.* à imprimer; d'impression; '~**-frame** châssis *m* (*positif*); '~**-ink** noir *m* d'imprimerie; '~**-of·fice** imprimerie *f*; '~**-pa·per** *phot.*

papier *m* photographique; papier *m* sensible; '∼-**press** presse *f* d'imprimerie.

print-out ['printaut] ordinateur: listage *m*.

pri·or ['praiə] 1. adj. préalable; antérieur (à, to); 2. adv.: ∼ to antérieurement à; 3. su. eccl. prieur *m*; '**pri·or·ess** eccl. prieure *f*; **pri·or·i·ty** ['∼riti] priorité *f* (sur, over); antériorité *f*; give s.th. (top) ∼ donner la priorité (absolue) à qch.; have (ou take) ∼ over s.th. avoir la priorité sur qch., primer qch.; get one's priorities right décider de ce qui est le plus important pour q.; see share; **pri·or·ry** eccl. ['∼əri] prieuré *m*.

prism ['prizm] prisme *m*; ∼ binoculars pl. jumelles *f/pl.* à prismes; **pris·mat·ic** [priz'mætik] (∼ally) prismatique.

pris·on ['prizn] 1. prison *f*; 2. poét. emprisonner; '**pris·on·er** prisonnier (-ère *f*) *m*; 🎗 accusé(e *f*) *m*, prévenu(e *f*) *m*; détenu(e *f*) *m*; fig. be a ∼ to être cloué à; take s.o. ∼ faire q. prisonnier (-ère *f*); ∼'s bars (ou base) (jeu *m* de) barres *f/pl.*

pris·sy Am. F ['prisi] chichiteux (-euse *f*).

pris·tine ['pristain] premier (-ère *f*), primitif (-ive *f*).

pri·va·cy ['praivəsi] intimité *f*; secret *m*; in the ∼ of retiré dans.

pri·vate ['praivit] 1. □ privé; particulier (-ère *f*); personnel(le *f*); secret (-ète *f*); réservé; retiré (*droit*); ∼ company société *f* en nom collectif; ∼ gentleman rentier *m*; parl. ∼ member simple député *m*; ∼ lessons pl. leçons *f/pl.* particulières; ∼ theatricals comédie *f* de salon; ∼ view exposition: avant-première *f*; ∼ sale vente *f* à l'amiable; 2. ⚔ (ou ∼ soldier) simple soldat *m*; ∼s pl. (usu. parts pl.) parties *f/pl.* sexuelles; in ∼ en séance privée; sans témoins; dans l'intimité; en famille.

pri·va·teer ⚓ [praivi'tiə] vaisseau, a. personne: corsaire *m*; **pri·va'teer·ing** course *f*; attr. de course.

pri·va·tion [prai'veiʃn] privation *f* (a. fig.).

pri·va·tive □ ['privətiv] négatif (-ive *f*); gramm. privatif (-ive *f*).

priv·et ♣ ['privit] troène *m*.

priv·i·lege ['privilidʒ] 1. privilège *m*, prérogative *f*; 2. privilégier (*q.*),

accorder le privilège à (*q.*) (de inf., to inf.); ∼d privilégié.

priv·i·ty 🎗 ['priviti] obligation *f*; lien *m* de droit.

priv·y ['privi] 1. □: ∼ to instruit de; 🎗 intéressé dans, trempé dans; ♀ Council Conseil *m* privé; ♀ Councillor conseiller *m* privé; ∼ parts pl. parties *f/pl.* sexuelles; ∼ purse cassette *f* du roi; ♀ Seal petit Sceau *m*; Lord ♀ Seal Garde *m* du petit Sceau; 2. 🎗 partie *f* intéressée; complice *mf*; F lieux *m/pl.* d'aisance.

prize[1] [praiz] 1. prix *m*; loterie: lot *m*; ⚓ prise *f*, capture *f*; first ∼ loterie: le gros lot; 2. couronné; médaillé; de prix; ⚓ de prise; ∼ competition concours *m* pour un prix; 3. estimer, priser; ⚓ capturer.

prize[2] [∼] 1. (a. ∼ open) forcer avec un levier; 2. force *f* de levier.

prize...: '∼-**fight·er** boxeur *m* professionnel; '∼-**list** palmarès *m*; '∼-**man**, '∼-**win·ner** lauréat(e *f*) *m*; gagnant(e *f*) *m* du prix.

pro[1] [prou] pour; see con[3].

pro[2] [∼] professionnel(le *f*) *m*, F pro *mf*.

prob·a·bil·i·ty [prɔbə'biliti] probabilité *f*; '**prob·a·ble** □ probable.

pro·bate 🎗 ['proubit] homologation *f* (d'un testament).

pro·ba·tion [prə'beiʃn] épreuve *f*, stage *m*; eccl. probation *f*; 🎗 liberté *f* surveillée; on ∼ en stage; 🎗 en liberté sous surveillance; **pro'ba·tion·ar·y** 🎗 ∼ period période *f* de liberté surveillée; **pro'ba·tion·er** stagiaire *mf*; eccl. novice *mf*; 🎗 condamné(e *f*) *m* mis(e *f*) en liberté sous surveillance.

pro·ba·tive 🎗 ['proubətiv] probant, probatoire.

probe ♣ [proub] 1. sonde *f*, poinçon *m*; surt. Am. parl., pol. enquête *f*; 2. (a. ∼ into) sonder; '∼-**scis·sors** pl. (sorte de) ciseaux *m/pl.* de chirurgie, ciseaux *m/pl.* boutonnés.

pro·bi·ty ['prɔbiti] probité *f*.

prob·lem ['prɔbləm] problème *m* (a. ♣); question *f*; ∼ child enfant *mf* difficile; ∼ play pièce *f* à thèse; **prob·lem·at·ic**, **prob·lem·at·i·cal** □ [∼bli'mætik(l)] problématique; fig. douteux (-euse *f*).

pro·bos·cis zo. [prə'bɔsis] trompe *f*.

pro·ce·dur·al [prə'siːdʒərəl] de procédure; **pro'ce·dure** [‿dʒə] procédure *f*; procédé *m*.

pro·ceed [prə'siːd] continuer son chemin; aller (*a. fig.*); marcher (*a. fig.*); continuer (qch., *with s.th.*); agir; se mettre (à *inf.*, *to inf.*); se poursuivre (q., *against s.o.*); *univ.* prendre le grade de; ~ *from* sortir de; ~ *on one's journey* poursuivre sa route; **pro'ceed·ing** procédé *m*; façon *f* d'agir; ~s *pl.* ⚖ procès *m*, poursuites *f/pl.* judiciaires; *société:* transactions *f/pl.*, débats *m/pl.*; cérémonie *f*, séance *f*; ⚖ *take* ~s *against* intenter un procès à; **proceeds** ['prousiːdz] *pl.* produit *m*, montant *m* (de, *from*); net ~ produit *m* net.

pro·cess¹ [prə'ses] aller en procession.

proc·ess² ['prouses] 1. processus *m* (*a. anat.*); procédé *m*; progrès *m*, marche *f*, cours *m*; méthode *f*; ⚖, *a. anat.* procès *m*; 🜂 réaction *f*, mode *m* (*humide, sec*); ♀ proéminence *f*; *in* ~ en voie; en train; *in* ~ *of construction* en voie *ou* cours de construction; *in the* ~ *of* au cours de; 2. ⊕ faire subir une opération à; apprêter; ~ *into* transformer en; **pro'cess·ing** ⊕ traitement *m* (*d'une matière première*).

pro·ces·sion [prə'seʃn] cortège *m*; défilé *m*; procession *f*.

pro·claim [prə'kleim] proclamer; déclarer (*a. la guerre*); publier (*les bans*); faire annoncer; *fig.* crier.

proc·la·ma·tion [prɔklə'meiʃn] proclamation *f*; déclaration *f*; publication *f*.

pro·cliv·i·ty [prə'kliviti] penchant (à, *to*).

pro·cras·ti·nate [prou'kræstineit] remettre (qch.) à plus tard; temporiser; **pro·cras·ti'na·tion** remise *f* à plus tard; temporisation *f*.

pro·cre·ate ['proukrieit] engendrer; **pro·cre'a·tion** procréation *f*; **'pro·cre·a·tive** procréateur (-trice *f*).

proc·tor ['prɔktə] ⚖ procureur *m* (*devant une cour*); *univ.* censeur *m*; *sl.* ~'s (*bull*)dog appariteur *m* du censeur; **'proc·tor·ize** *univ.* réprimander; infliger une amende à.

pro·cum·bent [prou'kʌmbənt] couché sur le ventre; ♀ rampant.

pro·cur·a·ble [prə'kjuərəbl] procurable.

proc·u·ra·tion [prɔkju'reiʃn] procuration *f*; ✝ commandement *m*; *by* ~ en vertu d'un commandement; **'proc·u·ra·tor** fondé *m* de pouvoir; procureur *m*.

pro·cure [prə'kjuə] *v/t.* obtenir; procurer (qch. à q. *s.o. s.th.*, *s.th. for s.o.*); *v/i.* faire le métier de proxénète; **pro'cure·ment** obtention *f*; proxénétisme *m*; **pro'cur·er** acquéreur (-euse *f*) *m*; entremetteur *m*; **pro'cur·ess** entremetteuse *f*, procureuse *f*.

prod [prɔd] 1. coup *m* de coude *etc.*; *fig.* aiguillon *m*; 2. pousser (*du bout d'un bâton etc.*); *fig.* aiguillonner.

prod·i·gal ☐ ['prɔdigəl] 1. prodigue (de, *of*); *the* ♌ *Son* l'enfant prodigue; 2. prodigue *mf*; **prod·i·gal·i·ty** [‿'gæliti] prodigalité *f*.

pro·di·gious ☐ [prə'didʒəs] prodigieux (-euse *f*); **prod·i·gy** ['prɔdidʒi] prodige *m*; *fig.* merveille *f*; (*souv. infant* ~) enfant *m* prodige.

prod·uce¹ ['prɔdjuːs] *champ:* rendement *m*; produit *m*; *coll.* denrées *f/pl.*, produits *m/pl.*

pro·duce² [prə'djuːs] produire; créer; ⚖, *théâ.* représenter; ✝ engendrer (*du courant*); causer, provoquer; ⊕ fabriquer; *théâ.* mettre en scène; ♪ prolonger; *cin.* éditer, diriger; **pro'duc·er** producteur (-trice *f*) *m*; *théâ.* metteur *m* en scène; *cin.* directeur *m* de productions; *surt. Am.* tenancier *m* d'un théâtre; *gas-*~ gazogène *m*; **pro'duc·i·ble** productible; **pro'duc·ing** producteur (-trice *f*); productif (-ive *f*).

prod·uct ['prɔdəkt] produit *m* (*a. ♪*), résultat *m*; **pro·duc·tion** [prə'dʌkʃn] production *f* (*a. d'un livre*); *théâ.* mise *f* en scène; ⚖, *théâ.* représentation *f*; ⊕ fabrication *f*, fabrique *f*; produit *m*, -s *m/pl.*; ♪ prolongement *m*; *be in good* ~ être fabriqué en grand nombre; ⊕ *flow* ~ travail (*pl.* -aux) *m* à la chaîne; **pro'duc·tive** ☐ productif (-ive *f*), générateur (-trice *f*) (de, *of*); fécond (*sol*); en rapport (*capital, arbre, usine, etc.*); **pro'duc·tive·ness**, **pro·duc·tiv·i·ty** [prɔdʌk'tiviti] productivité *f*.   [*prof m.*]

prof *Am.* ℉ [prɔf] professeur *m*, ℉

prof·a·na·tion [prɔfə'neiʃn] profanation f; **pro·fane** [prə'fein] **1.** □
profane; impie; blasphématoire;
non initié; **2.** profaner; polluer;
fig. violer; **pro·fan·i·ty** [prə-
'fæniti] impiété f; blasphème m,
-s m/pl.

pro·fess [prə'fes] déclarer; professer (la foi, école: un sujet); faire
profession de; exercer (un métier);
prétendre; ~ to be s.th. passer pour
qch.; **pro'fessed** □ prétendu; soi-
disant; fig. déclaré; eccl. profès
(-esse f); **pro'fess·ed·ly** [~idli] de
son propre aveu.

pro·fes·sion [prə'feʃn] profession f,
métier m; déclaration f; **pro'fes·
sion·al 1.** □ professionnel(le f);
expert; du ou de métier; the ~
classes les membres m/pl. des professions libérales; **2.** expert m; sp.
professionnel(le f) m; **pro'fes·
sion·al·ism** [~əlizm] profession-
nalisme m.

pro·fes·sor [prə'fesə] professeur m;
pro'fes·sor·ship professorat m;
chaire f.

prof·fer ['prɔfə] **1.** offrir; **2.** offre f.

pro·fi·cien·cy [prə'fiʃənsi] compétence f, capacité f (en, in); **pro'fi·
cient 1.** □ compétent; versé (dans
in, at); **2.** expert m (en, in).

pro·file ['proufail] profil m (a. △);
silhouette f; △ coupe f perpendiculaire.

prof·it ['prɔfit] **1.** profit m; avantage
m; † souv. ~s pl. bénéfice m; † ~
margin marge f bénéficiaire; excess ~
bénéfices m/pl. extraordinaires; **2.**
v/t. profiter à (q.); v/i.: ~ by profiter
de; mettre (qch.) à profit; **prof·it·a·
'bil·i·ty** rentabilité f; **'prof·it·a·
ble** □ profitable; avantageux (-euse
f); rémunérateur (-trice f), rentable;
'prof·it·a·ble·ness nature f avantageuse; profit m, avantage m; **prof·
it·eer** [~'tiə] **1.** faire des bénéfices
excessifs; **2.** profiteur (-euse f) m,
mercanti m (surt. de guerre); **prof·it·
'eer·ing** mercantilisme m; **'prof·
it·less** □ sans profit; **prof·it·shar·
ing** ['~ʃɛəriŋ] participation f aux bénéfices.

prof·li·ga·cy ['prɔfligəsi] débauche
f; prodigalité f; **prof·li·gate** ['~git]
1. □ débauché, libertin; prodigue;
2. débauché(e f) m, libertin(e f) m.

pro·found □ [prə'faund] profond

(a. fig.); fig. absolu; **pro'found·
ness**, **pro·fun·di·ty** [~'fʌnditi]
profondeur f (a. fig.).

pro·fuse □ [prə'fju:s] prodigue (de
in, of); abondant, excessif (-ive f);
pro'fuse·ness, **pro·fu·sion** [~-
'fju:ʒn] profusion f, abondance f.

prog sl. [prɔg] boustifaille f.

pro·gen·i·tor [prou'dʒenitə] aïeul
m, ancêtre m; **pro'gen·i·tress** aïeule
f; **prog·e·ny** ['prɔdʒini] progéniture f; descendants m/pl.; fig. conséquence f.

prog·no·sis ⚕ [prɔg'nousis], pl.
-ses [~si:z] pronostic m; science:
prognose f.

prog·nos·tic [prəg'nɔstik] **1.** pronostique; be ~ of prédire (qch.);
2. pronostique m; symptôme m;
prog'nos·ti·cate [~keit] pronostiquer; prédire; **prog·nos·ti·ca·tion**
pronostication f.

pro·gram(me) ['prougræm] **1.** programme m (a. traitement de l'information); **2.** programmer; **'pro·
gram·mer** radio: programmateur
m; traitement de l'information: personne: programmeur (-euse f) m,
machine: programmateur m; **'pro·
gram·ming** radio, traitement de
l'information: programmation f.

prog·ress[1] ['prougres] progrès m;
avancement m; marche f (a. ⚙);
étapes f/pl. successives; in ~ en
cours (d'exécution).

pro·gress[2] [prə'gres] s'avancer;
faire des progrès; **pro'gres·sion**
[~ʃn] progression f (a. ♪); ♪
marche f; **pro'gres·sist** pol. progressiste (a. su./mf); **pro'gres·sive**
□ progressif (-ive f); du progrès;
pol. progressiste (a. su./mf).

pro·hib·it [prə'hibit] défendre, interdire (qch., s.th.; à q. de inf., s.o.
from gér.); empêcher (q. de inf.,
s.o. from gér.); **pro·hi·bi·tion**
[proui'biʃn] prohibition f, défense f;
Am. régime m sec; **pro·hi'bi·tion·
ist** prohibitionniste mf; surt. Am.
partisan m du régime sec; **pro·hib·
i·tive** □ [prə'hibitiv]; **pro'hib·i·
to·ry** □ [~təri] prohibitif (-ive f);
prohibitive duty droits m/pl. prohi-
bitifs.

proj·ect[1] ['prɔdʒekt] projet m.

pro·ject[2] [prə'dʒekt] v/t. projeter (a.
⚙); lancer; avancer; ~ o.s. into se
transporter dans; v/i. faire saillie;

pro·jec·tile [prə'dʒektail] projectile (*a. su./m*); **pro'jec·tion** ⚡, *cin.*, *lumière, cartes*: projection *f*; lancement *m*; △ (partie *f* qui fait) saillie *f*; *fig.* image *f*; prolongement *m*; **pro'jec·tor** projecteur (-euse *f*) *m*; ✝ fondateur (-trice *f*) *m*; *opt.* projecteur *m*, appareil *m* de projection.

pro·le·tar·i·an [proule'tɛəriən] prolétaire (*a. su./mf*); prolétarien(ne *f*); **pro·le'tar·i·at(e)** [˷riət] prolétariat *m*.

pro·lif·e·rate [prou'lifəreit] proliférer; se multiplier; **pro·lif·e'ra·tion** prolifération *f*; **pro·lif·ic** [prə'lifik] (˷ally) prolifique; fécond (en *of*, *in*).

pro·lix ☐ ['prouliks] prolixe, diffus; **pro'lix·i·ty** prolixité *f*.

pro·logue, *Am. a.* **pro·log** ['proulɔg] prologue *m* (de, *to*).

pro·long [prə'lɔŋ] prolonger; ✝ proroger; ♪ allonger (*un coup d'archet*); **pro·lon·ga·tion** [proulɔŋ'geiʃn] prolongation *f*, prolongement *m*.

prom·e·nade [prɔmi'nɑːd] **1.** promenade *f*; esplanade *f*; *théâ.* promenoir *m*; **2.** *v/i.* se promener (dans, *in*); parader; *v/t.* promener (*q.*).

prom·i·nence ['prɔminəns] éminence *f*; importance *f*; protubérance *f*, saillie *f*; relief *m*; **'prom·i·nent** ☐ éminent; remarquable; saillant, prononcé.

prom·is·cu·i·ty [prɔmis'kjuːiti] promiscuité *f*; **pro·mis·cu·ous** ☐ [prə'miskjuəs] mêlé, confus; mixte; sans distinction de sexe; F dévergondé.

prom·ise ['prɔmis] **1.** promesse *f*; *fig.* espérance *f*; *of great* ˷ plein de promesses, d'un grand avenir; **2.** *v/t.* promettre; *fig.* annoncer, laisser prévoir; F *I* ˷ *you* je vous le promets; *v/i.* promettre; s'annoncer (*bien*, *mal*); **'prom·is·ing** ☐ plein de promesses, encourageant; **prom·is·so·ry** ['˷səri] promissoire; ✝ ˷ *note* billet *m* à ordre.

prom·on·to·ry ♻, *géog.* ['prɔmən-tri] promontoire *m*.

pro·mote [prə'mout] promouvoir (*q.*); nommer (*q.*); *surt. Am. école:* faire passer; *parl.* prendre l'initiative de (*un projet de loi*); ✝ fonder, lancer (*une compagnie*); *surt. Am.*

faire de la réclame pour (*un produit*); **pro'mot·er** instigateur (-trice *f*) *m*; ✝ fondateur *m*; monteur *m* (*d'affaires*); **pro'mo·tion** avancement *m*, promotion *f*; ✝ lancement *m* (*d'un article*); ✝ (*a. sales* ˷) promotion *f* de la vente; ˷ *prospects pl.* possibilités *f/pl.* d'avancement *ou* de développement.

prompt [prɔmpt] **1.** ☐ prompt; rapide; immédiat; **2.** promptement; **3.** inciter, pousser (à, *to*); suggérer (qch. à q., *s.o. to s.th.*); inspirer (*un sentiment*), donner (*une idée*); *théâ.* souffler; **4.** ✝ délai *m* de paiement; '˷-box *théâ.* trou *m* du souffleur; **'prompt·er** instigateur (-trice *f*) *m*; *théâ.* souffleur (-euse *f*) *m*; **promp·ti·tude**['˷itjuːd],**'prompt·ness** promptitude *f*, empressement *m*.

pro·mul·gate ['prɔməlgeit] promulguer (*une loi*); répandre; **pro·mul'ga·tion** *loi:* promulgation *f*; *idee:* dissémination *f*; proclamation *f*.

prone ☐ [proun] couché sur le ventre; en pente (*terrain*); escarpé; *fig.* ˷ *to* porté à; prédisposé à; **'prone·ness** disposition *f* (à, *to*).

prong [prɔŋ] fourchon *m*, *fourche:* dent *f*; pointe *f*; *Am. rivière:* embranchement *m*; **pronged** à fourchons, à dents.

pro·nom·i·nal ☐ *gramm.* [prə'nɔminl] pronominal (-aux *m/pl.*).

pro·noun *gramm.* ['prounaun] pronom *m*.

pro·nounce [prə'nauns] *v/t.* déclarer; prononcer, articuler; *v/i.* se déclarer (pour, *in favour of*); **pro'nounced** ☐ prononcé; marqué; **pro'nounc·ed·ly** [˷idli] de façon prononcée; **pro'nounce·ment** déclaration *f*.

pro·nounc·ing [prə'naunsiŋ] qui indique la prononciation.

pron·to *Am.* F ['prɔntou] sur-le-champ.

pro·nun·ci·a·tion [prənʌnsi'eiʃn] prononciation *f*.

proof [pruːf] **1.** preuve *f* (*a. fig.*, *a.* 🜕 *alcool*); *typ.*, *phot.* épreuve *f*; *a. see* test *f*; confirmation *f*; *in* ˷ *of* pour *ou* en preuve de; **2.** résistant (à *against*, *to*); à l'abri (de, *against*); '˷-read *typ.* corriger les épreuves (de); '˷-read·er *typ.* correcteur

(-trice *f*) *m*; '~**-sheet** *typ.* épreuve *f*; '~**-spir·it** 🜋 trois-six *m*.

prop [prɔp] **1.** appui *m* (*a. fig.*); *théâ. sl.* accessoire *m*; *Am. sl.* épingle *f* de cravate; **2.** (*ou* ~ *up*) appuyer, soutenir.

prop·a·gan·da [prɔpə'gændə] propagande *f*; **prop·a'gan·dist** propagandiste *mf*; **prop·a·gate** ['prɔpəgeit] (se) propager (*a. fig.*); *fig.* (se) répandre; **prop·a'ga·tion** propagation *f*; dissémination *f*; '**prop·a·ga·tor** propagateur (-trice *f*) *m*; semeur (-euse *f*) *m*.

pro·pel [prə'pel] pousser en avant; mouvoir (*une machine*); **pro'pel·lant** propulseur *m*; **pro'pel·lent** propulsif (*a. su./m*); propulsif (-ive *f*); **pro'pel·ler** propulseur *m*; ⚓, 🖅 hélice *f*; ~*-shaft* ⚓ arbre *m* porte-hélice; 🖅 arbre *m* à cardan; *mot.* arbre *m* de transmission; **pro'pel·ling** moteur (-trice *f*); ~ *pencil* porte-mine *m/inv.*

pro·pen·si·ty [prə'pensiti] penchant *m*, tendance *f* (à, vers *to, for*).

prop·er ☐ ['prɔpə] propre; (*souv. après le su.*) proprement dit; particulier (-ère *f*) (à, *to*); juste, vrai; convenable (à, *for*); comme il faut; *F* parfait, dans toute l'acception du mot; ~ *name* nom *m* propre; '**prop·er·ty** (droit *m* de) propriété *f* (*a. ⚖, a. fig.*); biens *m/pl.*; immeuble *m*, -s *m/pl.*; *fig. a.* qualité *f*; *théâ.* accessoire *m*; *théâ. properties pl. a.* réserve *f* de décors *etc.*; '**prop·er·ty tax** impôt *m* foncier.

proph·e·cy ['prɔfisi] prophétie *f*; **proph·e·sy** ['~sai] *vt/i.* prophétiser; *v/t. a.* prédire.

proph·et ['prɔfit] prophète *m*; '**proph·et·ess** prophétesse *f*; **pro·phet·ic, pro·phet·i·cal** ☐ [prə'fetik(l)] prophétique.

pro·phy·lac·tic [prɔfi'læktik] (~*ally*) prophylactique (*a. su./m*).

pro·pin·qui·ty [prə'piŋkwiti] proximité *f*; voisinage *m*; parenté *f*.

pro·pi·ti·ate [prə'piʃieit] apaiser; rendre favorable; **pro·pi·ti'a·tion** apaisement *m*; propitiation *f*; expiation *f*; **pro'pi·ti·a·tor** [~tə] propitiateur (-trice *f*) *m*; **pro'pi·ti·a·to·ry** ☐ [~ʃiətəri] propitiatoire; expiatoire.

pro·pi·tious ☐ [prə'piʃəs] propice, favorable; **pro'pi·tious·ness** na-

ture *f* propice *ou* favorable (*a. fig.*).

pro·po·nent [prə'pounənt] partisan(e *f*) *m*, défenseur (-euse *f*) *m*.

pro·por·tion [prə'pɔːʃn] **1.** partie *f*; part *f*; portion *f*; proportion *f* (*a. △, 🜨, 🜋*); 🜨 proportionnalité *f*; ~*s pl.* dimensions *f/pl.*, proportions *f/pl.*; **2.** proportionner (à, *to*); ⊕ déterminer les dimensions de; coter (*un dessin*); **pro'por·tion·al 1.** ☐ proportionnel(le *f*); en proportion (de, *to*); *see proportionate*; **2.** 🜨 proportionnelle *f*; **pro'por·tion·ate** ☐ [~it] proportionné (à, *to*).

pro·pos·al [prə'pouzəl] proposition *f*, offre *f*; demande *f* en mariage; projet *m*; **pro'pose** *v/t.* proposer; suggérer; porter (*un toast*); ~ *s.o.'s health* boire à la santé de q., porter un toast à q.; ~ *to o.s.* se proposer; *v/i.* faire la demande en mariage; demander sa main (à, *to*); **pro'pos·er** proposeur (-euse *f*) *m*; **prop·o·si·tion** [prɔpə'ziʃn] proposition *f* (*a. phls., 🜨*); *sl.* affaire *f*.

pro·pound [prə'paund] (pro)poser (*une question etc.*); exposer (*un programme*).

pro·pri·e·tar·y [prə'praiətəri] **1.** de propriété; de propriétaire; privé; possédant (*classe etc.*); ~ *article* spécialité *f*; **2.** (droit *m* de) propriété *f*; **pro'pri·e·tor** propriétaire *mf*; patron(ne *f*) *m*; **pro'pri·e·tress** propriétaire *f*; patronne *f*; **pro'pri·e·ty** propriété *f*, justesse *f*; bienséance *f*; *the proprieties pl.* les convenances *f/pl.*, la décence *f*.

pro·pul·sion ⊕ [prə'pʌlʃn] propulsion *f*; **pro'pul·sive** [~siv] propulsif (-ive *f*); de propulsion.

pro·rate *Am.* [prou'reit] évaluer au pro rata.

pro·ro·ga·tion *parl.* [prourə'geiʃn] prorogation *f*; **pro·rogue** *parl.* [prə'roug] proroger.

pro·sa·ic [prou'zeiik] (~*ally*) *fig.* prosaïque (= *banal*).

pro·scribe [pro'skraib] proscrire.

pro·scrip·tion [pros'kripʃn] proscription *f*; interdiction *f*.

prose [prouz] **1.** prose *f*; **2.** en prose; **3.** *v/t.* mettre en prose; *v/i. F* tenir des discours ennuyeux.

pros·e·cute ['prɔsikjuːt] poursuivre (*a. en justice*); ⚖ intenter (*une action*); exercer (*un métier*); effectuer (*un voyage*); **pros·e'cu·tion** continuation *f*; exercice *m*; ⚖ poursuites *f/pl.* (judiciaires); accusation *f*; *in* ~ *of* conformément à; ⚖ *the* ♀ *le Ministère public*; *witness for the* ~ témoin *m* à charge; **'prose·cu·tor** ⚖ plaignant *m*; poursuivant *m*; *public* ~ Ministère *m* public; procureur *m*.

pros·e·lyte *eccl.* ['prɔsilait] prosélyte *mf*; **pros·e·lyt·ism** ['ᴗlitizm] prosélytisme *m*; **'pros·e·lyt·ize** *v/t.* convertir; *v/i.* faire des prosélytes.

pros·er ['prouzə] conteur *m* ennuyeux; F raseur *m*.

pros·o·dy ['prɔsədi] prosodie *f*, métrique *f*.

pros·pect 1. ['prɔspekt] vue *f*; perspective *f* (*a. fig.*); paysage *m*; ~*s pl.* espérances *f/pl.*, avenir *m*; ✝ *Am.* client *m* possible; ⚒ prélèvement *m* d'essai; *have in* ~ avoir (*qch.*) en vue; *hold out a* ~ *of* offrir des espérances de (*qch.*); **2.** [prɔs'pekt] *v/t.* prospecter; ~ *for* chercher; **pro'spec·tive** □ à venir; futur; ~ *buyer* client *m* éventuel; **pro'spec·tor** ⚒ chercheur *m* (*d'or*); **pro'spec·tus** [ᴗtəs] prospectus *m*.

pros·per ['prɔspə] (faire) réussir; *v/t.* prospérer; **pros·per·i·ty** [prɔs'periti] prospérité *f*; **pros·per·ous** □ ['ᴗpərəs] prospère, florissant; *fig.* propice; favorable (*vent etc.*).

pros·tate *anat.* ['prɔsteit] (*a.* ~ *gland*) prostate *f*.

pros·ti·tute ['prɔstitju:t] **1.** prostituée *f*; *sl.* poule *f*; **2.** prostituer (*a. fig.*); **pros·ti'tu·tion** prostitution *f* (*a. fig.*).

pros·trate 1. ['prɔstreit] prosterné, étendu; ⚕ prostré; *fig.* accablé, abattu; **2.** [prɔs'treit] ⚕ abattre; *fig.* ~ *o.s.* se prosterner (*devant*, *before*); **pros'tra·tion** prosternation *f*; ⚕ prostration *f*; *fig.* abattement *m*.

pros·y □ *fig.* ['prouzi] prosaïque; verbeux (-euse *f*) (*personne*); ennuyeux (-euse *f*).

pro·tag·o·nist *théâ., a. fig.* [prou'tægənist] protagoniste *m*.

pro·tect [prə'tekt] protéger (contre, *from*); abriter (de, *from*); ✝ faire provision pour; **pro'tec·tion** protection *f*; défense *f*; sauvegarde *f*; patronage *m*; abri *m*; **pro'tec·tion·ist** protectionniste (*a. su./mf*); **pro'tec·tive** protecteur (-trice *f*); de

sûreté; ~ *custody* détention *f* préventive; ~ *duty* droit *m* protecteur; **pro'tec·tor** protecteur *m* (*a.* ⊕); *fig.* patron *m*; -~ protège- *m*; **pro'tec·tor·ate** [ᴗtərit] protectorat *m*; **pro'tec·to·ry** asile *m* des enfants abandonnés; **pro'tec·tress** protectrice *f*; *fig.* patronne *f*.

pro·te·in 🜛 ['prouti:n] protéine *f*.

pro·test 1. ['proutest] protestation *f*; ✝ protêt *m*; *in* ~ *against* pour protester contre; *enter* (*ou make*) *a* ~ élever des protestations, faire une protestation; **2.** [prə'test] *v/t.* protester (*a.* ✝); *Am.* protester contre; *v/i.* protester, réclamer (contre, *against*).

Prot·es·tant ['prɔtistənt] protestant (*a. su.*); **'Prot·es·tant·ism** protestantisme *m*.

prot·es·ta·tion [proutes'teiʃn] protestation *f*; **pro·test·er** [prə'testə] protestateur (-trice *f*) *m*; protestataire *mf*; ✝ débiteur *m* qui a fait protester un effet.

pro·to·col ['proutəkɔl] **1.** protocole *m*; **2.** dresser un protocole.

pro·ton *phys.* ['proutɔn] proton *m*.

pro·to·plasm *biol.* ['proutəplæzm] protoplasme *m*, protoplasma *m*.

pro·to·type ['proutətaip] prototype *m*, archétype *m*.

pro·tract [prə'trækt] prolonger; traîner (*qch.*) en longueur; *surv.* relever (*un terrain*); **pro'trac·tion** prolongation *f*; *surv.* relevé *m*; **pro'trac·tor** 𝐀 rapporteur *m*.

pro·trude [prə'tru:d] *v/t.* faire sortir; *v/i.* faire saillie, s'avancer; **pro'tru·sion** [ᴗʒn] saillie *f*; protubérance *f*.

pro·tu·ber·ance [prə'tju:bərəns] protubérance *f*; **pro'tu·ber·ant** protubérant.

proud □ [praud] fier (fière *f*) (de of, *to*); orgueilleux (-euse *f*); ⚕ fongueux (-euse *f*) (*chair*). ⎮

prov·a·ble □ ['pru:vəbl] démontrable, prouvable; **prove** [pru:v] *v/t.* prouver, démontrer; vérifier (*un calcul*); ⊕ éprouver (*a. fig.*), essayer; *v/i.* se montrer, être, se trouver; ~ *true* (*false*) se révéler comme étant vrai (faux).

prov·e·nance ['prɔvinəns] origine *f*, provenance *f*.

prov·en·der ['prɔvində] *bêtes:* fourrage *m*, provende *f*; F, *a. co.* nourriture *f*.

prov·erb ['prɔvəb] proverbe *m*; *be a ~* être proverbial (-aux *m/pl.*); *péj.* être d'une triste notoriété; *he is a ~ for generosity* sa générosité est passée en proverbe; **pro·ver·bi·al** □ [prə'və:bjəl] proverbial (-aux *m/pl.*).

pro·vide [prə'vaid] *v/t.* pourvoir, fournir, munir (*q.*) (*de, with*); fournir (qch. à q., *s.o. with s.th.*); stipuler (que, *that*); *~d school* école *f* communale; *v/i.* venir en aide (à q., *for s.o.*); *~ against* parer à; se pourvoir contre; *~ for* pourvoir aux besoins de; prévoir; ✝ faire provision pour; *~d that* pourvu que (*sbj.*); à condition que (*ind. ou sbj.*).

prov·i·dence ['prɔvidəns] prévoyance *f*; prudence *f*; providence *f* (*divine*); épargne *f*; **'prov·i·dent** □ prévoyant; économe; frugal (-aux *m/pl.*); *~ society* société *f* de prévoyance; **prov·i·den·tial** □ [~'denʃl] providentiel(le *f*); F heureux (-euse *f*).

pro·vid·er [prə'vaidə] pourvoyeur (-euse *f*) *m*; fournisseur (-euse *f*) *m*.

prov·ince ['prɔvins] province *f*; ⚖, *a. fig.* juridiction *f*, ressort *m*, compétence *f*.

pro·vin·cial [prə'vinʃl] 1. provincial (-aux *m/pl.*); de province; 2. provincial(e *f*) *m*; *péj.* rustre *m*; **pro·'vin·cial·ism** provincialisme *m* (*souv. = locution provinciale*); esprit *m* de clocher.

pro·vi·sion [prə'viʒn] 1. disposition *f*; fourniture *f*; ✝ réserve *f*, provision *f*; *fig.* stipulation *f*, clause *f*; *~s pl.* comestibles *m/pl.*, vivres *m/pl.*; *make ~ for* pourvoir aux besoins de; prévoir; pourvoir à; *~-merchant* marchand *m* de comestibles; 2. approvisionner, ravitailler; **pro·'vi·sion·al** □ provisoire.

pro·vi·so [prə'vaizou] condition *f*; *with the ~ that* à condition que; **pro·'vi·so·ry** [~zəri] conditionnel (-le *f*); provisoire (*gouvernement etc.*).

prov·o·ca·tion [prɔvə'keiʃn] provocation *f*; **pro·voc·a·tive** [prə'vɔkətiv] 1. provocateur (-trice *f*); provocant; 2. stimulant *m*.

pro·voke [prə'vouk] provoquer, inciter (à, *to*); exaspérer, irriter; faire naître, exciter; **pro'vok·ing** □ exaspérant, irritant, agaçant.

prov·ost ['prɔvəst] prévôt *m*; *écoss.* maire *m*; *univ.* principal *m*; ✗ [prə-'vou]: *~ marshal* grand prévôt *m*.

prow ⚓ [prau] proue *f*.

prow·ess ['prauis] prouesse *f*, vaillance *f*; exploit *m*, *-s m/pl.*

prowl [praul] 1. *v/i.* rôder (en quête de proie); *v/t.* rôder; 2. action *f* de rôder; *fig.* be on the *~* rôder; *Am.* *~ car police:* voiture *f* de patrouille; **'prowl·er** rôdeur (-euse *f*) *m*.

prox·i·mate □ ['prɔksimit] proche, prochain, immédiat; approximatif (-ive *f*); **prox'im·i·ty** proximité *f*; *in the ~ of* à proximité de; **prox·i·mo** ✝ ['~mou] (du mois) prochain.

prox·y ['prɔksi] procuration *f*; mandat *m*, pouvoir *m*; *personne:* mandataire *mf*, fondé *m* de pouvoir(s); délégué(e *f*) *m*; *by ~* par procuration.

prude [pru:d] prude *f*, F bégueule *f*.

pru·dence ['pru:dəns] prudence *f*, sagesse *f*; **'pru·dent** □ prudent, sage, judicieux (-euse *f*); **pru·den·tial** □ [pru'denʃl] prudent; dicté par la prudence.

prud·er·y ['pru:dəri] pruderie *f*; F pudibonderie *f*; **'prud·ish** □ prude; F pudibond.

prune¹ [pru:n] pruneau *m*.

prune² [~] émonder (*un arbre*); tailler (*un rosier etc.*); (*a. ~ away, off*) élaguer (*a. fig.*).

prun·ing...: **'~-hook** émondoir *m*; **'~-knife** serpette *f*.

pru·ri·ence, pru·ri·en·cy ['pruə-riəns(i)] lasciveté *f*; curiosité *f* (de, *after*); **'pru·ri·ent** □ lascif (-ive *f*).

Prus·sian ['prʌʃn] 1. prussien(ne *f*); *~ blue* bleu *m* de Prusse; 2. Prussien (-ne *f*) *m*.

prus·sic ac·id 🜍 ['prʌsik'æsid] acide *m* prussique.

pry¹ [prai] fureter; fouiller; *~ into* chercher à pénétrer (*qch.*); F fourrer le nez dans; **'pry·ing** □ curieux (-euse *f*).

pry² [~] 1.: *~ open* forcer la serrure de; forcer avec un levier; *~ up* soulever à l'aide d'un levier; 2. levier *m*.

psalm [sɑ:m] psaume *m*; **'psalm·ist** psalmiste *m*; **psal·mody** ['sælmədi] psalmodie *f*.

Psal·ter ['sɔːltə] psautier *m*.

pse·phol·o·gy [pse'fɔlədʒi] étude *f* des élections.

pseudo... [psju:dou] pseud(o)-; faux (fausse *f*); **pseu·do·nym** ['ˌdənim] pseudonyme *m*; **pseu·don·y·mous** □ [ˌˈdɔniməs] pseudonyme.

pshaw [pʃɔ:] peuh!; allons donc!

pso·ri·a·sis 𝒔 [psɔˈraiəsis] psoriasis *m*.

psy·chi·a·trist [sai'kaiətrist] psychiatre *m*; **psy'chi·a·try** psychiatrie *f*.

psy·chic ['saikik] **1.** (*ou* **'psy·chi·cal** □) psychique; **2.** ～*s sg.* métapsychique *f*; métapsychisme *m*.

psy·cho·a·nal·y·sis [saikouəˈnæləsis] psychanalyse *f*; **psy·cho·an·a·lyst** [ˌˈænəlist] psychanalyste *m*.

psy·cho·log·i·cal □ [saikəˈlɔdʒikl] psychologique; **psy·chol·o·gist** [sai'kɔlədʒist] psychologue *m*; **psy·'chol·o·gy** psychologie *f*.

psy·cho·sis [sai'kousis] psychose *f*.

pto·maine ⚛ ['toumein] ptomaïne *f*.

pub F [pʌb] cabaret *m*; *sl.* bistrot *m*.

pu·ber·ty ['pju:bəti] puberté *f*.

pu·bes·cence [pju'besns] puberté *f*; ♀ pubescence *f*; **pu'bes·cent** pubère; ♀ pubescent; velu.

pub·lic ['pʌblik] **1.** □ public (-ique *f*); ～ *address system* (batterie *f* de) haut-parleurs *m/pl.*; ～ *enemy* ennemi *m* universel *ou* F public; ♀ *Health* hygiène *f*; santé *f* publique; ～ *holiday* jour *m* férié; ～ *house* cabaret *m*; bistrot *m*; ～ *law* droit *m* public; ～ *library* bibliothèque *f* municipale *ou* communale; ～ *man* homme *m* public *ou* très en vue; ✝～ *relations pl.* relations *f/pl.* publiques; ～ *spirit* civisme *m*, patriotisme *m*; *see school, utility, works*; **2.** *sg.*, *a. pl.* (grand) public *m*; F cabaret *m*; bistrot *m*; *in* ～ en public, publiquement; **pub·li·can** ['ˌkən] aubergiste *m*; débitant *m* de boissons; *hist.* publicain *m*; **pub·li'ca·tion** publication *f*; apparition *f* (*d'un livre*); *loi:* promulgation *f*; ouvrage *m* (publié); *monthly* ～ revue *f* etc. mensuelle; **pub·li·cist** ['ˌsist] publiciste *m*; journaliste *m*; **pub'lic·i·ty** [ˌsiti] publicité *f*; réclame *f*; propagande *f*; service *m* de presse; ～ *agent* agent *m* de publicité; **pub·li·cize** ['ˌsaiz] faire connaître au public; **'pub·lic·'pri·vate** mixte (*éco-*

nomie); **'pub·lic·'spir·it·ed** □ dévoué au bien public, soucieux (-euse *f*) du bien public.

pub·lish ['pʌbliʃ] *usu.* publier; éditer; promulguer (*une loi*); révéler, répandre; **'pub·lish·er** éditeur *m*; libraire-éditeur (*pl.* libraires-éditeurs) *m*; *Am.* propriétaire *m* d'un journal; **'pub·lish·ing** publication *f*; mise *f* en vente; *attr.* d'édition; ～ *house* maison *f* d'édition.

puck [pʌk] puck *m*; lutin *m*; *hockey sur glace:* palet *m* en caoutchouc.

puck·er ['pʌkə] **1.** godet *m*, faux pli *m*; *visage:* ride *f*; F embarras *m*; **2.** *v/t.* froncer; faire goder, rider (*le visage*); *v/i.* (*a.* ～ *up*) se crisper; froncer, goder, grigner; se contracter. [cieux (-euse *f*).\

puck·ish □ ['pʌkiʃ] de lutin; mali-\

pud·ding ['pudiŋ] pudding *m*, pouding *m*; *black* ～ boudin *m*; *white* ～ boudin *m* blanc.

pud·dle ['pʌdl] **1.** flaque *f* (d'eau); ⊕ braye *f* (d'argile); **2.** *v/t.* ⊕ corroyer (*l'argile, le fer*); puddler (*le fer*); damer (*la terre*); *v/i.* barboter; **'pud·dler** ⊕ brasseur *m* mécanique; *personne:* puddleur *m*; **'pud·dling-fur·nace** ⊕ four *m* à puddler.

pu·den·cy ['pju:dənsi] pudicité *f*; **pu·den·da** [pju:'dendə] *pl.* parties *f/pl.* génitales; **'pu·dent** pudique.

pudg·y F ['pʌdʒi] boulot(te *f*).

pu·er·ile □ ['pjuərail] puéril; *péj. a.* enfantin; **pu·er·il·i·ty** [ˌˈriliti] puérilité *f*.

puff [pʌf] **1.** *air, respiration:* souffle *m*; *vapeur:* échappement *m* soudain; *fumée, tabac:* bouffée *f*; *robe:* bouillon *m*, *manche:* bouffant *m*; houppe(tte) *f* (*à poudre*); *fig.* (gâteau *m*) feuilleté *m*; tourtelet *m*; réclame *f*; F haleine *f*; **2.** *v/t.* lancer, émettre (*une bouffée de fumée etc.*); (*a.* ～ *out, up*) gonfler (*les joues etc.*); faire balloner (*une manche*); (*a.* ～ *at*) tirer sur (*une pipe*), fumer; (*a.* ～ *up*) vanter; ～ *up* augmenter (*le prix*); ～*ed eyes* yeux *m/pl.* gonflés; ～*ed sleeve* manche *f* bouffante; *v/i.* souffler, lancer des bouffées (*de fumée*); ～ *out* bouffer (*jupe*); **'puff·er** ✝ renchérisseur *m*, allumeur *m*; ✝ réclamiste *m*; **'puff·er·y** art *m* du puffisme; réclame *f* tapageuse; **puff·i·ness** ['ˌinis] boursouflure *f*; **'puff-**

ing ✝ puffisme *m*; réclame *f* tapageuse; '**puff-'paste** pâte *f* feuilletée; '**puff-y** qui souffle par bouffées (*vent*); à l'haleine courte; gonflé; boursouflé; bouffant (*manche*).

pug[1] [pʌg] (*ou* ~-dog) carlin *m*; petit dogue *m*.

pug[2] ⊕ [~] corroyer (*a. un bassin*); pétrir (*l'argile*).

pu·gil·ism ['pju:dʒilizm] pugilat *m*, boxe *f*; '**pu·gil·ist** pugiliste *m*, boxeur *m*.

pug·na·cious [pʌg'neiʃəs] batailleur (-euse *f*); querelleur (-euse *f*); **pug·nac·i·ty** [~'næsiti] caractère *m* batailleur *ou* querelleur; attitude *f* batailleuse *ou* querelleuse.

pug-nose ['pʌgnouz] nez *m* troussé.

puis·ne ⚮ ['pju:ni] subalterne (*juge*).

puke *sl.* [pju:k] dégobiller (= *vomir*).

pule [pju:l] piauler, piailler.

pull [pul] **1.** (effort *m* de) traction *f*; tirage *m*; force *f* d'attraction (*d'un aimant*); *fig.* attrait *m*; *golf:* coup *m* tiré; *rame:* coup *m* d'aviron; *typ.* première épreuve *f*; F gorgée *f* (*de bière etc.*); *sl.* avantage *m*, *sl.* piston *m*; *sl.* ~ at the bottle coup *m* à même la bouteille; ~-*fastener* fermeture *f* éclair; **2.** *v/t.* tirer (*a. typ., a. sp. un cheval*); traîner; cueillir (*un fruit*); *fig.* attirer; ⚓ manier (*un aviron*); ⚓ ramer; ⚓ souquer; ~ *the trigger* presser la détente; F ~ one's weight y mettre du sien; ~ *down* faire descendre; baisser; démolir; ~ *in* retenir (*un cheval*); ~ *off* arracher, ôter; remporter (*un prix*); ~ *through* tirer (*q.*) d'affaire; ~ *up* (re)monter; relever; arracher (*une plante*); arrêter (*un cheval, une voiture, etc.*); *fig.* réprimander; *v/i.* tirer (sur, *at*); *mot.* peiner; ⚓ ramer; 🚂 ~ *out* sortir de la gare; partir; ~ *through* se tirer d'affaire; ~ *up* s'arrêter.

pul·let ['pulit] poulette *f*; *fattened* ~ poularde *f*.

pul·ley ⊕ ['puli] poulie *f*; *set of* ~s *pl.* palan *m*, moufle *f*.

Pull·man car 🚂 ['pulmən'kɑː] voiture *f* Pullman; *Am.* wagon-salon (*pl.* wagons-salons) *m*.

pull...: '~-out **1.** supplément *m* détachable; **2.** détachable; rétractable; '~-o·ver pull-over *m*, F pull *m*; '~-'up arrêt *m*; auberge *f* (*etc. pour automobilistes*).

pul·mo·nar·y 𝄋 ['pʌlmənəri] pulmonaire, des poumons; poitrinaire (*personne*).

pulp [pʌlp] **1.** *dents etc.:* pulpe *f*; *fruits:* chair *f*; ⊕ pâte *f* à papier; *Am.* (*a.* ~ *magazine*) revue *f etc.* à bon marché; **2.** réduire en pulpe *ou* pâte; mettre (*des livres*) au pilon.

pul·pit ['pulpit] chaire *f*.

pulp·y □ ['pʌlpi] pulpeux (-euse *f*), charnu; F flasque.

pul·sate [pʌl'seit] palpiter; vibrer; battre (*cœur*); **pul·sa·tile** ♪ ['~sətail] de percussion; **pul'sa·tion** pulsation *f*; battement *m*.

pulse[1] [pʌls] **1.** pouls *m*; battement *m*; **2.** palpiter; vibrer; battre.

pulse[2] [~] légumineuses *f/pl.*

pul·ver·i·za·tion [pʌlvərai'zeiʃn] pulvérisation *f*; '**pul·ver·ize** *v/t.* pulvériser; réduire en poudre; *fig.* démolir; atomiser; *v/i.* tomber en poussière; se vaporiser; '**pul·ver·iz·er** pulvérisateur *m*; vaporisateur *m*.

pum·ice ['pʌmis] (*a.* ~-stone) (pierre *f*) ponce *f*.

pum·mel ['pʌml] bourrer de coups de poings.

pump[1] [pʌmp] **1.** pompe *f*; *attr.* de pompe; **2.** *v/t.* pomper de l'eau; refouler (*dans, into*); F sonder (*q.*), faire parler (*q.*); *sl.* épuiser; *v/i.* pomper.

pump[2] [~] escarpin *m*; soulier *m* de bal.

pump·kin 𝄋 ['pʌmpkin] citrouille *f*; potiron *m*.

pump-room ['pʌmprum] *station thermale:* buvette *f*; Pavillon *m*.

pun [pʌn] **1.** jeu *m* de mots, calembour *m*; **2.** faire des jeux de mots *etc.*

Punch[1] ['pʌntʃ] polichinelle *m*; guignol *m*; *as pleased as* ~ heureux (-euse *f*) comme un roi; ~ *and Judy* ['dʒu:di] *show* guignol *m*.

punch[2] ⊕ [~] **1.** pointeau *m*; chasse-clou *m*; perçoir *m*; poinçon *m* (*a.* 🔨); emporte-pièce *m/inv.*; **2.** percer; poinçonner; découper; estamper; ~ed card *see* punch card.

punch[3] F [~] **1.** coup *m* de poing; F force *f*; **2.** donner un coup de poing à; cogner sur; *Am.* conduire *ou* garder (*des bœufs*).

punch[4] [~] *boisson:* punch *m*.

punch[5] F [~] *cheval, homme:* trapu

m; sl. **pull no** ⤳**es** parler carrément; ne faire de quartier à personne.

punch card ['pʌntʃkɑ:d] carte *f* perforée.

punch-drunk ['pʌntʃdrʌŋk] abruti (par les coups).

punch·er ['pʌntʃə] poinçonneur *m*; perceur *m*; estampeur *m*; *outil:* poinçonneuse *f*; découpeuse *f*; F pugiliste *m*; *Am.* cowboy *m*; '**punch(·ing)-ball** *boxe:* punchingball *m*.

punch line ['pʌntʃlain] pointe *f* (*d'une plaisanterie*).

punch-up F ['pʌntʃʌp] bagarre *f*.

punc·til·i·o [pʌŋk'tiliou] point *m* d'étiquette; *see* punctiliousness.

punc·til·i·ous [pʌŋk'tiliəs] méticuleux (-euse *f*), pointilleux (-euse *f*); très soucieux (-euse *f*) du protocole; **punc'til·i·ous·ness** souci *m* du protocole; formalisme *m*; scrupule *m* des détails.

punc·tu·al □ ['pʌŋktjuəl] exact; **punc·tu·al·i·ty** [⤳'æliti] exactitude *f*, ponctualité *f*.

punc·tu·ate ['pʌŋktjueit] ponctuer (*a. fig.*); **punc·tu·a·tion** ponctuation *f*.

punc·ture ['pʌŋktʃə] **1.** crevaison *f*; 𝒳 ponction *f*; *mot. etc.* piqûre *f* de clou, crevaison *f*; **2.** *v/t.* 𝒳 ponctionner; *mot.* crever (*a. v/i.*).

pun·dit ['pʌndit] pandit *m*; F pontife *m*.

pun·gen·cy ['pʌndʒənsi] goût *m* piquant; odeur *f* piquante; *fig.* aigreur *f*; mordant *m*; saveur *f*; '**pun·gent** aigu (-uë *f*); poignant (*chagrin*); âcre (*odeur*); mordant (*paroles etc.*).

pu·ni·ness ['pju:ninis] chétiveté *f*.

pun·ish ['pʌniʃ] punir, châtier; F *fig.* taper dur sur (*q.*); ne pas épargner; '**pun·ish·a·ble** □ punissable; 𝔱𝔱 délictueux (-euse *f*); '**pun·ish·er** punisseur (-euse *f*) *m*; '**pun·ish·ment** punition *f*; châtiment *m*.

pu·ni·tive ['pju:nitiv] punitif (-ive *f*), répressif (-ive *f*).

punk *Am.* [pʌŋk] **1.** amadou *m*; *fig.* sottises *f/pl.*; **2.** mauvais, sans valeur.   [lembours.]

pun·ster ['pʌnstə] faiseur *m* de ca-]

punt[1] ⚓ [pʌnt] **1.** bateau *m* plat (*conduit à la perche*); bachot *m*; **2.** conduire à la perche; transporter dans un bateau plat.

punt[2] [⤳] *turf:* parier; *cartes:* ponter.

pu·ny □ ['pju:ni] menu; mesquin; chétif (-ive *f*).   [bas (des petits).]

pup [pʌp] **1.** *see* puppy; **2.** *zo.* mettre]

pu·pil ['pju:pl] *anat.* pupille *f* (*a.* 𝔱𝔱 *mf*); élève *mf*, écolier (-ère *f*) *m*; **pu·pil·(l)age** ['⤳pilidʒ] état *m* d'élève; 𝔱𝔱 minorité *f*.

pup·pet ['pʌpit] marionnette *f*; *fig.* pantin *m*; '⤳-**show** théâtre *m ou* spectacle *m* de marionnettes.

pup·py ['pʌpi] jeune chien(ne *f*) *m*; *fig.* freluquet *m*.

pur·blind ['pə:blaind] presque aveugle; *fig.* obtus.

pur·chase ['pə:tʃəs] **1.** achat *m*; emplette *f*; acquisition *f*; ⊕ force *f* mécanique; ⊕ prise *f*; 𝔱𝔱 loyer *m*; *fig.* (point *m* d')appui *m*; **make** ⤳**s** faire des emplettes; *at twenty years'* ⤳ moyennant vingt années de loyer; *his life is not worth an hour's* ⤳ on ne lui donne(rait) pas une heure à vivre; ✝ ⤳ permit ordre *m* d'achat; **2.** acheter, acquérir (*a. fig.*); ⚓ lever à l'aide du cabestan; '**pur·chas·er** acheteur (-euse *f*) *m*; ✝ preneur (-euse *f*) *m*.

pure □ [pjuə] pur; '⤳-**bred** *Am.* de race pure; '**pure·ness** pureté *f*.

pur·ga·tion [pə:'geiʃn] purgation *f* (*a.* 𝒳); **pur·ga·tive** 𝒳 ['⤳gətiv] purgatif (-ive *f*) (*a. su./m*); '**pur·ga·to·ry** *eccl.* purgatoire *m* (*a. fig.*).

purge [pə:dʒ] **1.** 𝒳 purgatif *m*; purgation *f*; *pol.* épuration *f*; **2.** *fig.* nettoyer; épurer; purger (de *of, from*) (*a.* 𝔱𝔱); 𝔱𝔱 faire amende honorable pour; *pol.* épurer, purger.

pu·ri·fi·ca·tion [pjuərifi'keiʃn] purification *f*; épuration *f*; **pu·ri·fi·er** ['⤳faiə] épurateur *m* (*de gaz etc.*); *personne:* purificateur (-trice *f*) *m*; **pu·ri·fy** ['⤳fai] purifier; ⊕, *a. fig.* épurer.

Pu·ri·tan ['pjuəritən] puritain(e *f*) (*a. su.*); **pu·ri·tan·ic** [⤳'tænik] (⤳**ally**) (de) puritain; **Pu·ri·tan·ism** ['⤳tənizm] puritanisme *m*.

pu·ri·ty ['pjuəriti] pureté *f* (*a. fig.*).

purl[1] [pə:l] cannetille *f* (*à broder*); picot *m* (*de dentelle*); (*a.* ⤳ *stitch*) maille *f* à l'envers.

purl[2] [⤳] **1.** *ruisseau:* (*doux*) murmure *m*; **2.** murmurer.

purl·er F ['pə:lə] chute *f* la tête la première; *sl.* billet *m* de parterre.

pur·lieus ['pəːljuːz] *pl.* bornes *f/pl.*; alentours *m/pl.*

pur·loin [pəːˈlɔin] détourner; voler; **pur·loin·er** détourneur *m*; voleur (-euse *f*) *m*; *fig.* plagiaire *m*.

pur·ple ['pəːpl] **1.** violet(te *f*); **2.** pourpre *f*; violet *m*; **3.** (s')empourprer.

pur·port ['pəːpət] **1.** sens *m*, signification *f*; portée *f* (d'un mot); **2.** avoir la prétention (de *inf.*, to *inf.*); † indiquer, vouloir dire.

pur·pose ['pəːpəs] **1.** dessein *m*; but *m*, intention *f*; fin *f*; résolution *f*; for the ~ of pour; dans le but de; on ~ exprès, de propos délibéré; to the ~ à propos; to no ~ en vain, inutilement; *novel with a* ~ roman *m* à thèse; *strenght of* ~ détermination *f*; résolution *f*; **2.** avoir l'intention (de *inf.*, *gér.* ou to *inf.*), se proposer (qch., s.th.; de *inf.*, *gér.* ou to *inf.*); '~-**built** construit spécialement; fonctionnalisé; **pur·pose·ful** □ ['~ful] réfléchi; tenace, avisé (*personne*); '**pur·pose·less** □ inutile, sans but; '**pur·pose·ly** *adv.* à dessein; exprès.

purr [pəː] **1.** ronronner (*chat*, *moteur*); **2.** ronron *m*.

purse [pəːs] **1.** bourse *f*, portemonnaie *m/inv.*; *fig.* bourse *f*; *sp.* prix *m* (d'argent); *public* ~ Trésor *m*; *finances f/pl.* de l'État; **2.** (*souv.* ~ up) pincer (*les lèvres*); plisser (*le front*); froncer (*les sourcils*); '~-**proud** orgueilleux (-euse *f* de sa fortune; '**purs·er** ⚓ commissaire *m*; '**purse-strings** *pl.*: hold the ~ tenir les cordons de la bourse.

pur·si·ness ['pəːsinis] peine *f* à respirer; essoufflement *m*.

purs·lane ♀ ['pəːslin] pourpier *m*.

pur·su·ance [pəˈsjuːəns] poursuite *f*; *in* ~ of par suite de, en vertu de, conformément à; **pur·su·ant** □: ~ to conformément à, par suite de.

pur·sue [pəˈsjuː] *v/t.* poursuivre; *fig.* rechercher (*le plaisir*); *fig.* courir après; suivre (*le chemin, une ligne de conduite, une profession, etc.*); *v/i.* suivre, continuer; ~ *after* poursuivre; **pur·su·er** poursuivant(e *f*) *m*; **pur·suit** [~ˈsjuːt] poursuite *f*; recherche *f* (de, of); occupation *f*; *usu.* ~s *pl.* travaux *m/pl.*; carrière *f*; *qqfois* passe-temps *m/inv.*; ~ *plane* chasseur *m*.

pur·sy¹ ['pəːsi] à l'haleine courte; gros(se *f*), corpulent.

pur·sy² [~] pincé (*bouche, lèvres*); riche; orgueilleux (-euse *f*) de sa fortune.

pu·ru·lent □ ✎ ['pjuərulənt] purulent.

pur·vey [pəːˈvei] *v/t.* fournir (*des provisions*); *v/i.* être (to fournisseur (de, for); **pur·vey·ance** fourniture *f* de provisions; approvisionnement *m*; **pur·vey·or** fournisseur (-euse *f*) *m* (*surt. de provisions*).

pur·view ['pəːvjuː] portée *f*, limites *f/pl.*; ✦✦ *statut:* corps *m*. [boue *f.*]

pus ✎ [pʌs] pus *m*; sanie *f*; abcès *m*.]

push [puʃ] **1.** poussée *f*, impulsion *f*; coup *m*; effort *m*; ✗ attaque *f* en masse; F énergie *f*; F hardiesse *f*; *last* ~ effort *m* suprême; *sl.* get the ~ se faire dégommer (= *recevoir son congé*); give s.o. the ~ flanquer q. à la porte; donner son congé à q.; **2.** *v/t.* pousser; bousculer; appuyer sur (*un bouton*); enfoncer (dans, in[to]); pousser la vente de; importuner; (*a.* ~ through) faire accepter; faire passer (à travers, through); revendiquer (*un droit*); (*a.* ~ ahead *ou* forward *ou* on) (faire) avancer *ou* pousser (en avant); ~ s.th. (up)on s.o. imposer qch. à q.; ~ one's way se frayer un chemin (à travers, through); ~ed pressé; à court (d'argent, for money); fort embarrassé; *v/i.* avancer; pousser; ~ on se presser, se hâter; se remettre en route; ~ off ⚓ pousser au large; F *fig.* se mettre en route; '~-**ball** *sp.* (*sorte de*) jeu *m* de ballon; '~-**bike** bicyclette *f*; '~-**but·ton** ⚡ bouton *m* à pression; poussoir *m*; '~-**cart** charrette *f* à bras; '~-**chair** poussette *f*; '**push·er** personne *f* qui pousse; arriviste *mf*; avion *m* à hélice propulsive; ✈ *Am.* locomotive *f* de renfort; **push·ful** □ ['~ful], '**push·ing** □ débrouillard, entreprenant; *péj.* ambitieux (-euse *f*), trop accostant; '**push·off** ⚓ poussée *f* au large; *fig.* impulsion *f*; '**push·o·ver** *surt. Am.* chose *f* facile à obtenir; tâche *f* facile à faire; victoire *f* facile; personne *f* crédule; *a* ~ la facilité même; *be a* ~ *for* ne pas pouvoir résister à; '**push-up**: do ~s faire des tractions *ou* des pompes; **push·y** arriviste, qui se met trop en avant.

pu·sil·la·nim·i·ty [pjuːsiləˈnimiti]

pusillanimité *f*; **pu·sil·lan·i·mous**
□ [ˌ~ˈlænɪməs] pusillanime.

puss(·y) [ˈpʊs(i)] minet(te *f*) *m*; *fig.*
coquine *f*; *fig.* chipie *f*; *Am. sl.*
visage *m*; ♣ bouleau: chaton *m*;
'puss·y-foot *Am.* F **1.** personne *f*
furtive; fin Normand *m*; **2.** F aller
furtivement; ne pas se compromettre.

pus·tule ⚕ [ˈpʌstjuːl] pustule *f*.

put [pʊt] [*irr.*] **1.** *v/t.* mettre, poser
(*a. une question*), placer; présenter
(à, to); lancer (*un cheval*) (sur, at);
exposer (*une condition, la situation,
etc.*); exprimer; parler; estimer (à,
at); ~ it s'exprimer; ~ about faire
circuler, répandre; ⚓ virer de bord;
F mettre (*q.*) en émoi, inquiéter;
déranger; ~ across réussir dans (*une
entreprise*); ~ away serrer; remiser
(*son auto*); écarter; mettre de côté;
fig. tuer; ~ back remettre; retarder
(*une horloge, l'arrivée, etc.*); ~ by
mettre de côté; mettre en réserve;
~ down (dé)poser; noter; supprimer;
mettre fin à; fermer (*le parapluie*);
juger; attribuer (à, to); inscrire (q.
pour, s.o. for); débarquer (*les voyageurs*); ~ forth émettre; avancer; publier (*un livre etc.*); déployer, exercer; pousser (*des feuilles etc.*); ~ forward avancer (*l'heure, la montre,
une opinion, etc.*); émettre; faire valoir (*une proposition, une théorie,
etc.*); ~ o.s. forward se mettre en
avant; s'imposer; se donner (pour,
as); ~ in introduire dans; mettre,
insérer dans (*un journal*); placer (*un
mot*); ✐ planter; présenter (*un
document, un témoin*; à q. à un
examen*); ⚖ installer (*un huissier*);
F faire (*des heures de travail*), passer
(*le temps*); ~ off enlever, ôter, retirer
(*un vêtement, le chapeau*); remettre
(*un rendez-vous, l'heure, une tâche*);
ajourner; renvoyer (*q.*); déconcerter, dérouter (*q.*); décourager (*q.*)
(de, from); ~ on mettre (a. la lumière, la vapeur, des vêtements*);
prendre (*un air, du poids, de la
vitesse*); gagner (*du poids*); ✝ augmenter (*le prix*); ajouter à; allumer
(*le gaz etc.*); avancer (*la pendule*);
théâ. monter (*une pièce*); confier
(*une tâche*) (à q., to s.o.); *école:* dé-
mander à (*un élève*) (de, to); 🚆 mettre en service; ajouter (*des voitures
à un train*); *mot.* serrer (*le frein*);

sp. miser (*un pari*); *sp.* ~ on (a score
of) thirty marquer trente points; F
~ the screw on s.o. forcer la main à
q.; he is ~ting it on il fait l'important;
il fait du chiqué; *fig.* ~ it on thick
exagérer; flatter grossièrement; ~
on airs se donner des airs; ~ s.o. on
(*gér.*) mettre q. à (*inf.*); ~ out mettre
dehors; tendre (*la main*); étendre
(*les bras*); tirer (*la langue*); sortir (*la
tête*); mettre à l'eau (*un canot*); placer (*de l'argent*) (à intérêt, to interest); émettre (*un document etc.*);
publier (*une revue etc.*); crever
(*l'œil à q., s.o.'s eye*); éteindre (*le
feu, le gaz, etc.*); lancer (*une histoire*);
fig. déconcerter; *fig.* contrarier; *fig.*
gêner; ~ s.o. out expulser q., chasser
q. (de, of); ~ out of action mettre hors
de combat; ⊕ détraquer; ~ over
faire réussir; ~ s.th. over on s.o. faire
accepter qch. à q.; ~ through téléph.
mettre en communication (avec,
to); F mener à bien; ~ to attacher;
atteler (*un cheval*); ~ s.o. to it donner du mal à q.; contraindre q. (à,
to); ~ to expense faire faire des dépenses à (*q.*); ~ to death mettre (*q.*)
à mort; exécuter (*q.*); ~ to the rack
(*ou torture*) mettre (*q.*) à la question
ou torture; ~ up construire; ériger;
installer; lever (*la fenêtre, une glace
de wagon*); accrocher (*un tableau*);
ouvrir (*le parapluie, a. qqfois la
fenêtre*); augmenter, hausser (*le
prix*); (faire) lever (*du gibier*); mettre (*en vente, aux enchères*); regainer
(*l'épée*); relever (*les cheveux, le col*);
afficher (*un avis*), coller (*une affiche*); poser (*le rideau*); fournir
(*de l'argent*); faire, offrir (*une prière,
une résistance*); proposer (*un candidat*); faire un paquet de (*sandwiches
etc.*); loger (*q.*), donner à coucher à
(*q.*); ✝ présenter (en, in); *sp.* F faire
courir; *jeu:* se caver de; ~ s.o. up to
mettre q. au courant de; inciter q.
à; ~ upon en imposer à; ~ it upon
laisser (à *q.*) le soin de; **2.** *v/i.* ⚓ ~
in entrer dans; faire escale dans (*un
port*); ⚓ ~ off (*ou* out *ou* to sea)
démarrer, pousser au large, quitter
la côte etc.; ~ up at loger à *ou* chez
(*q.*); descendre à *ou* chez (*q.*); ~ up
for poser sa candidature à; ~ up with
s'arranger de; tolérer; se résigner
à; F ~ upon exploiter (*q.*); abuser de
(*q.*); be ~ upon s'en laisser imposer.

pu·ta·tive [ˈpjuːtətiv] putatif (-ive f).

put·lock, put·log ⊕ [ˈpʌtlɔk; ˈ⁓lɔg] boulin m.

put-on F [ˈpʊtɔn] **1.** affecté, feint, simulé, faux (fausse f); **2.** manière(s) f(pl.) affectée(s); mystification f, farce f.

pu·tre·fac·tion [pjuːtriˈfækʃn] putréfaction f; **pu·treˈfac·tive** putréfactif (-ive f); putride; de putréfaction.

pu·tre·fy [ˈpjuːtrifai] v/i. se putréfier; pourrir; ⚕ suppurer; v/t. putréfier, pourrir.

pu·tres·cence [pjuːˈtresns] putrescence f; **puˈtres·cent** putrescent; en putréfaction.

pu·trid ☐ [ˈpjuːtrid] putride; en putréfaction; infect; sl. moche; **puˈtrid·i·ty** pourriture f.

put·tee [ˈpʌti] bande f molletière.

put·ty [ˈpʌti] **1.** (a. glaziers' ⁓) mastic m (à vitres); (a. plasterers' ⁓) pâte f de chaux; (a. jewellers' ⁓) potée f (d'étain); **2.** mastiquer.

put-up job [ˈpʊtʌpˈdʒɔb] coup m monté; affaire f machinée à l'avance.

puz·zle [ˈpʌzl] **1.** énigme m; problème m; devinette f; picture ⁓ rébus m; **2.** v/t. intriguer; embarrasser; ⁓ out débrouiller; déchiffrer; v/i. (souv. ⁓ one's brains) se creuser la tête (pour comprendre qch., over

s.th.); ˈ⁓-head·ed confus; ˈ⁓-lock serrure f à combinaisons; cadenas m à secret; **ˈpuz·zler** question f embarrassante; F colle f.

pyg·m(a)e·an [pigˈmiːən] pygméen (-ne f); **pyg·my** [ˈpigmi] pygmée m; attr. pygméen(ne f). [m.]

py·ja·mas [pəˈdʒɑːməz] pl. pyjama

py·lo·rus anat. [paiˈlɔːrəs] pylore m.

py·or·rh(o)e·a [paiəˈriə] pyorrhée f.

pyr·a·mid [ˈpirəmid] pyramide f; **py·ram·i·dal** ☐ [piˈræmidl] pyramidal (-aux m/pl.).

pyre [ˈpaiə] bûcher m (funéraire).

py·ret·ic [paiˈretik] pyrétique.

pyro... [ˈpairou] pyr(o)-; **py·rog·ra·phy** [paiˈrɔgrəfi] pyrogravure f; **ˈpy·ro·scope** pyroscope m; **py·ro·tech·nic, py·ro·tech·ni·cal** [pairouˈteknik(l)] pyrotechnique; **py·roˈtech·nics** pl. pyrotechnique f; **py·roˈtech·nist** pyrotechnicien m; artificier m.

Pyr·rhic vic·to·ry [ˈpirikˈviktəri] victoire f à la Pyrrhus.

Py·thag·o·re·an [paiθægəˈriːən] **1.** pythagoricien(ne f); de Pythagore; **2.** pythagoricien m.

Pyth·i·an [ˈpiθiən] pythien(ne f).

py·thon [ˈpaiθən] python m.

pyx [piks] **1.** eccl. ciboire m; **2.** boîte f des monnaies destinées au contrôle; trial of the ⁓ essai m des monnaies.

Q

Q, q [kju:] Q *m*, q *m*.
Q-boat ⚓ ['kju:bout] piège *m* à sous-marins.
quack¹ [kwæk] **1.** coin-coin *m*; **2.** crier, faire coin-coin.
quack² [∼] **1.** charlatan *m*; † guérisseur *m*; **2.** de charlatan; **3.** F faire le charlatan; ∼ *up* vanter; rafistoler (*qch. d'usagé*); **quack·er·y** ['∼əri] charlatanisme *m*; hâblerie *f*.
quad [kwɔd] *see* quadrangle; quadrat.
quad·ra·ge·nar·i·an [kwɔdrədʒi-'neəriən] quadragénaire (*a. su./mf*).
quad·ran·gle ['kwɔdræŋgl] 𝔸 quadrilatère *m*; *école etc.*: cour *f*.
quad·rant ['kwɔdrənt] ⚓, ⊕ secteur *m*; 𝔸 quart *m* de cercle.
quad·ra·phon·ic [kwɔdrə'fɔnik] quadriphonique; *in* ∼ *sound* en quadriphonie.
quad·rat *typ.* ['kwɔdrit] cadrat *m*; **quad·rat·ic** 𝔸 [kwɔ'drætik] **1.** du second degré; **2.** (*a.* ∼ *equation*) équation *f* du second degré; **quad·ra·ture** ['kwɔdrətʃə] quadrature *f*.
quad·ren·ni·al □ [kwɔ'drenjəl] quadriennal (-aux *m/pl.*); qui a lieu tous les quatre ans.
quad·ri·lat·er·al 𝔸 [kwɔdri'lætərəl] **1.** quadrilatéral (-aux *m/pl.*); **2.** quadrilatère *m*.
qua·drille [kwə'dril] quadrille *m*.
quad·ri·par·tite [kwɔdri'pɑːtait] quadripartite.
quad·ru·ped ['kwɔdruped] **1.** quadrupède *m*; **2.** (*a.* **quad·ru·pe·dal** [kwɔ'druːpidl]) quadrupède; **quad·ru·ple** ['kwɔdrupl] **1.** □ quadruple; (*a.* ∼ *to ou of*) au quadruple de; **2.** quadruple *m*; **3.** (se) quadrupler; **quad·ru·plet** ['∼plit] quadruplé(e *f*) *m*; **quad·ru·pli·cate** [kwɔ'druːplikit] **1.** quadruplé, quadruple; **2.** quatre exemplaires *m/pl.*; **3.** [∼keit] quadrupler.
quaff [kwɑːf] boire à plein verre; ∼ *off* vider d'un trait.
quag [kwæg] *see* ∼mire; **'quag·gy**

marécageux (-euse *f*); **quag·mire** ['∼maiə] marécage *m*; fondrière *f*; *fig.* embarras *m*.
quail¹ *orn.* [kweil] caille *f*.
quail² [∼] fléchir, faiblir (devant, *before*).
quaint □ [kweint] bizarre; singulier (-ère *f*); pittoresque; **'quaint·ness** bizarrerie *f*; pittoresque *m*.
quake [kweik] trembler (de, *with*; pour, *for*); frémir (de, *with*).
Quak·er ['kweikə] quaker *m*; **'Quak·er·ism** quakerisme *m*.
qual·i·fi·ca·tion [kwɔlifi'keiʃn] titre *m* (à un emploi, *for a post*); aptitude *f*, capacité *f*; réserve *f*; **qual·i·fied** ['∼faid] qui a les qualités requises *ou* titres requis; diplômé; compétent; autorisé; restreint, modéré; sous condition; **qual·i·fy** ['∼fai] *v/t.* qualifier (*a. gramm.*) (de, *as*); rendre apte à; modifier; apporter des réserves à; couper (*une boisson*); *v/i.* se qualifier (pour, *for*), acquérir les titres requis *ou* connaissances requises; être reçu; ∼*ing examination* examen *m* pour certificat d'aptitude; examen *m* d'entrée; **qual·i·ta·tive** □ ['∼tətiv] qualitatif (-ive *f*); **'qual·i·ty** *usu.* qualité *f*; valeur *f*; pouvoir *m*; caractère *m*; *son:* timbre *m*.
qualm [kwɔːm] nausée *f*; scrupule *m*, remords *m*; pressentiment *m* de malheur; hésitation *f*; **'qualm·ish** □ sujet(te *f*) aux nausées; mal à l'aise.   [*m*; impasse *f*.\
quan·da·ry ['kwɔndəri] embarras⌡
quan·ti·ta·tive □ ['kwɔntitətiv] quantitatif (-ive *f*); **'quan·ti·ty** quantité *f* (*a.* ♫, 𝔸, *prosodie*); somme *f*; *bill of quantities* devis *m*; 𝔸 *unknown* ∼ inconnue *f* (*a. fig.*).
quan·tum ['kwɔntəm], *pl.* -ta [∼tə] quantum *m*; part *f*; *phys.* ∼ *theory* théorie *f* des quanta.
quar·an·tine ['kwɔrənti:n] **1.** quarantaine *f*; *place in* ∼ = **2.** mettre en quarantaine.
quar·rel ['kwɔrəl] **1.** querelle *f*,

dispute *f*; 2. se quereller, se disputer (avec, *with*; à propos de *about*, *over*); *fig.* se plaindre (de, *with*); **quar·rel·some** ['∼səm] □ querelleur (-euse *f*), batailleur (-euse *f*).

quar·ry¹ ['kwɔri] 1. carrière *f*; *fig.* mine *f*; 2. *v/t.* extraire (*des pierres*) de la carrière; creuser une carrière dans; *v/i.* exploiter une carrière; *fig.* puiser (qch., *for s.th.*).

quar·ry² [∼] *chasse*: proie *f*.

quar·ry·man ['kwɔrimən], *a.* **quar·ri·er** ['∼iə] carrier *m*.

quart [kwɔːt] quart *m* (*de gallon*, = *approx.* 1 *litre*); *escrime*: [kɑːt] quarte *f*.

quar·tan ⚕ ['kwɔːtn] (fièvre *f*) quarte.

quar·ter ['kwɔːtə] 1. quart *m* (*a. cercle*, *heure*, *pomme*, *siècle*, *etc.*); terme *m* de loyer; région *f*, partie *f*; *ciel*: coin *m*; *Am.* quart *m* de dollar (25 *cents*); ⊘, *cuis.*, *lune*, *ville*: quartier *m*; ⚓ hanche *f*; ⚓ quart *m* de brasse; ⚓ (quart *m* d')aire *f* de vent; côté *m*, direction *f*; *orange*: tranche *f*; *mesure*: quart *m* de livre), quarter *m* (2,909 *hl*); ⚔, *a. fig.* cantonnement, quartier *m*; ∼s *pl.* appartements *m/pl.*; résidence *f*; ⚔ quartier *m*, -s *m/pl.*; logement *m*; in this ∼ ici, de ce côté-ci; *from all* ∼s de toutes parts, de tous côtés; *free* ∼s droit *m* au logement; 2. diviser en quatre; équarrir (*un bœuf*); *hist.* écarteler (*un condamné*, *a.* ⊘); ⚔ cantonner; *be* ∼ed (*up)on* (*ou at*) loger chez; '∼-day jour *m* du terme; '∼-deck ⚓ plage *f* arrière; *coll.* officiers *m/pl.*; '**quar·ter·ly** 1. trimestriel(le *f*); 2. publication *f* trimestrielle; '**quar·ter·mas·ter** ⚔ intendant *m* militaire; ⚓ second maître *m*; **quar·tern** ['∼ən] quart *m* (*de pinte*); (*a.* ∼ *loaf*) pain *m* de quatre livres.

quar·tet(·te) ♪ [kwɔːˈtet] quatuor *m*.

quar·to ['kwɔːtou] in-quarto *m/inv.* (*a. adj.*).

quartz *min.* [kwɔːts] quarts *m*.

quash [kwɔʃ] ᵗᵗᵇ casser, annuler; *fig.* étouffer.

qua·si ['kwɑːzi] quasi-, presque.

qua·ter·na·ry ⚗, ♑, *géol.* [kwəˈtəːnəri] quaternaire *f*.

qua·ver ['kweivə] 1. tremblement

m; ♪ croche *f*; ♪ trille *m*; 2. chevroter, (*a.* ∼ *out*) trembloter (*voix*); ♪ faire des trilles; '**qua·ver·y** tremblotant.

quay [kiː] quai *m*; **quay·age** ['∼idʒ] droit *m*, -s *m/pl.* de quai; quais *m/pl.*

quea·si·ness ['kwiːzinis] malaise *f*; nausées *f/pl.*; scrupules *m/pl.* de conscience; '**quea·sy** □ sujet(te *f*) à des nausées; délicat (*estomac*); scrupuleux (-euse *f*); dégoûtant (*mets*); *I feel* ∼ j'ai mal au cœur; F j'ai le cœur fade.

queen [kwiːn] 1. reine *f*; *cartes*: dame *f*; *échecs*: dame *f*, reine *f*; *sl.* (*homosexuel*) tante *f*, tapette *f*; ∼ *bee* reine *f*, abeille *f* mère; ∼'s *metal* métal *m* blanc; ∼'s-ware faïence *f* crème; 2. *échecs*: *v/t.* damer; *v/i.* aller à dame; ∼ *it* faire la reine; '**queen·like**, '**queen·ly** de reine, digne d'une reine; majestueux (-euse *f*).

queer [kwiə] 1. bizarre; singulier (-ère *f*); étrange; suspect; F tout patraque (*malade*); 2. *Am. sl.* homosexuel *m*; 3. *vb.*: *sl.* ∼ *the pitch for* contrecarrer (*q.*); faire échouer les projets de (*q.*).

quell *poét.* [kwel] apaiser; étouffer.

quench [kwentʃ] *fig.* apaiser (*la soif etc.*); étouffer, réprimer (*un désir*, *a.* ⚔); éteindre; '**quench·er** F boisson *f*, consommation *f*; '**quench·less** □ inextinguible; inassouvissable.

que·rist ['kwiərist] questionneur (-euse *f*) *m*.

quern [kwəːn] moulin *m* à bras.

quer·u·lous ['kweruləs] plaintif (-ive *f*); grognon(ne *f*).

que·ry ['kwiəri] 1. reste à savoir (si, *if*); 2. question *f*; *typ.* point *m* d'interrogation; 3. *v/t.* mettre *ou* révoquer en doute; *v/i.* s'informer (si, *whether*).

quest [kwest] 1. recherche *f*; *chasse*: quête *f*; *in* ∼ *of* à la recherche de; en quête de; 2. rechercher; *chasse*: quêter.

ques·tion ['kwestʃn] 1. question *f*; (mise *f* en) doute *m*; affaire *f*; sujet *m*; ∼ *mark* point *m* d'interrogation; *radio*, *télév.* ∼ *master* animateur *m*; *parl.* ∼ *time* heure *f* réservée aux questions orales; *parl.* ∼! au fait!; *beyond* (*all*) ∼ sans aucun doute; incontestable(ment); *in* ∼ en question, dont il s'agit; en doute; *come into* ~ arriver sur le tapis; *call in* ~ révoquer en doute; *beg the* ~ faire une pétition de principe, supposer vrai ce qui est en question; *the* ~ *is whether* il s'agit de savoir si; *that is out of the* ~ c'est impossible; *there is no* ~ il n'est pas question (de qch., *of s.th.*; *que sbj.*, *of ger.*); **2.** interroger; révoquer en doute; **'ques·tion·a·ble** □ contestable, discutable; *péj.* équivoque; **'ques·tion·a·ble·ness** caractère *m* douteux *ou* équivoque (de, *of*); **ques·tion·naire** [kwestiə'nɛə] questionnaire *m*; **'ques·tion·er** interrogateur (-trice *f*) *m*.

queue [kju:] **1.** queue *f* (*de personnes, de voitures, de cheveux, etc.*); **2.** (*usu.* ~ *up*) prendre la file (*voitures*); faire la queue; ~ *on* s'attacher à la queue.

quib·ble ['kwibl] **1.** chicane *f* (de mots); argutie *f*; † calembour *m*; **2.** *fig.* chicaner (sur les mots); **'quib·bler** chicaneur (-euse *f*) *m*; ergoteur (-euse *f*) *m*.

quick [kwik] **1.** vif (vive *f*) (*a. esprit, haie, œil*); fin (*oreille etc.*); † vivant; rapide, prompt; éveillé (*enfant, esprit, a.* ♪); ~ *to prompt* à; ⚔ ~ *march* pas *m* cadencé *ou* accéléré, ~ *step* pas *m* rapide *ou* pressé; *double* ~ *step* pas *m* gymnastique; **2.** vif *m*, chair *f* vive; *the* ~ les vivants *m/pl.*; *to the* ~ jusqu'au vif; *fig.* au vif, au cœur; jusqu'à la moelle des os; *cut s.o. to the* ~ piquer q. au vif; **3.** *see* ~*ly*; **'~change ac·tor** acteur *m* à transformations rapides; **'quick·en** *v/t.* (r)animer; accélérer (*a.* ♫); presser; *v/i.* s'animer, se ranimer; devenir plus rapide; **'quick-fir·ing** ⚔ à tir rapide; **'quick·fro·zen** surgelé; **quick·ie** F ['~i] chose *f* faite à la va-vite; **'quick·lime** chaux *f* vive; **'quick·ly** vite; vivement; rapidement; **'quick·match** mèche *f* d'artilleur; **'quick·mo·tion pic·ture** *cin.* accéléré *m*; **'quick·ness** vitesse *f*, rapidité *f*; vivacité *f*, promptitude *f* (*d'esprit*); finesse *f* (*d'oreille*); acuité *f* (*de vision*).

quick...: **'~·sand** sable *m* mouvant; lise *f*; **'~·set** ♂ aubépine *etc.*: bouture *f*; (*a.* ~ *hedge*) haie *f* vive; **'~-'sight·ed** aux yeux vifs; perspicace; **'~-'sil·ver** *min.* vif-argent *m* (*a. fig.*), mercure *m*; **'~-·tem·pered** irascible; **'~-'wit·ted** éveillé; à l'esprit prompt; adroit.

quid¹ [kwid] *tabac:* chique *f*.

quid² *sl.* [~] livre *f* (sterling).

quid·di·ty ['kwiditi] *phls.* quiddité *f*, essence *f*; F chicane *f*.

quid·nunc F ['kwidnʌŋk] nouvelliste *mf*; curieux (-euse *f*) *m*.

quid pro quo ['kwid prou 'kwou] pareille *f*, équivalent *m*, compensation *f*.

qui·es·cence [kwai'esns] repos *m*; tranquillité *f*; **qui·es·cent** □ en repos; tranquille (*a. fig.*).

qui·et ['kwaiət] **1.** □ tranquille, calme; silencieux (-euse *f*); paisible; discret (-ète *f*) (*couleur etc.*); simple; voilé; **2.** repos *m*; tranquillité *f*; calme *m*; F *on the* ~ en douce; **3.** (s')apaiser; **'qui·et·en:** ~ *down* (s')apaiser; **'qui·et·ism** *eccl.* quiétisme *m*; **'qui·et·ist** quiétiste *mf*; **'qui·et·ness**, **qui·e·tude** ['~tju:d] tranquillité *f*, calme *m*; *fig.* sobriété *f*.   [grâce.\

qui·e·tus F [kwai'i:təs] coup *m* de]

quill [kwil] **1.** *orn.* tuyau *m* (de plume); *porc-épic:* piquant *m*; (*a.* ~*-feather*) penne *f*; (*a.* ~ *pen*) plume *f* d'oie; **2.** tuyauter, rucher; **'~-driv·er** F gratte-papier *m/inv.*; **'quill·ing** tuyautage *m*; ruche *f*; **quill pen** plume *f* d'oie (*pour écrire*).

quilt [kwilt] **1.** édredon *m* piqué; **2.** piquer; ouater (*une robe*); **'quilt·ing** piquage *m*; piqué *m*.

quince ♀ [kwins] coing *m*; *arbre:* cognassier *m*.

qui·nine *pharm.* [kwi'ni:n; *Am.* 'kwainain] quinine *f*; ~ *wine* quinquina *m*.

quin·qua·ge·nar·i·an [kwiŋkwədʒi'nɛəriən] quinquagénaire (*a. su./mf*).

quin·quen·ni·al □ [kwiŋ'kwenjəl] quinquennal (-aux *m/pl.*).

quins F [kwinz] *pl.* quintuplés *m/pl.*

quin·sy ♀ ['kwinzi] esquinancie *f*.

quin·tal ['kwintl] quintal *m* (métrique).

quint·es·sence [kwin'tesns] quintessence *f*; F moelle *f* (*d'un livre*).

quin·tu·ple ['kwintjupl] **1.** quintuple (*a. su./m*); **2.** *vt/i.* quintupler; **quin·tu·plets** ['~plits] *pl.* quintuplés *m/pl.*

quip [kwip] mot *m* piquant; bon mot *m*; sarcasme *m*; raillerie *f*.

quire ['kwaiə] main *f* (*de papier*); *in* ~s en feuilles.

quirk [kwəːk] sarcasme *m*; bon mot *m*; repartie *f*; équivoque *f*; △ gorge *f*.

quis·ling *pol.* F ['kwizliŋ] collaborateur *m*.

quit [kwit] **1.** *v/t.* quitter; lâcher (*la prise*); déménager; *Am.* cesser; † récompenser; † ~ *o.s.* se comporter; *v/i. usu. Am.* démissionner; céder; **2.** quitte, libéré; débarrassé (de, *of*).

quite [kwait] tout à fait; entièrement; parfaitement; véritable; bien; ~ *a hero* un véritable *ou* vrai héros; F ~ *a* pas mal de; ~ (so)! (*ou that!*) parfaitement!; ~ *the go* le dernier cri; le grand chic.

quits [kwits] quitte (with, avec); *let's call it* ~ restons-en là; *we'll cry* ~ nous voilà quittes.

quit·tance ['kwitəns] acquit *m*; quittance *f*.

quit·ter *Am.* F ['kwitə] lâcheur (-euse *f*) *m*; *he is no* ~ *a.* il n'abandonne pas facilement la partie.

quiv·er[1] ['kwivə] **1.** tremblement *m*; frémissement *m*; frisson *m*; *paupière*: battement *m*; *cœur*: palpitation *f*; **2.** trembl(ot)er; tressaillir; frémir.

quiv·er[2] [~] carquois *m*.

quix·ot·ic [kwik'sɔtik] (~*ally*) de Don Quichotte; visionnaire; par trop chevaleresque.

quiz [kwiz] **1.** plaisanterie *f*, farce *f*; attrape *f*; *souv. Am.* F colle *f*; examen *m* oral; ~ *program(me)*, ~ *show* quiz *m*; **2.** railler; lorgner; *souv. Am.* examiner; poser des colles à; **'quiz·zi·cal** ☐ railleur (-euse *f*), moqueur (-euse *f*); risible.

quod *sl.* [kwɔd] boîte *f*, bloc *m* (= *prison*).

quoin [kɔin] pierre *f* d'angle; ⊕, *a. typ.* coin *m*.

quoit [kɔit] (*a. jeu*: ~*s sg.*) palet *m*.

quon·dam ['kwɔndæm] d'autrefois.

quo·rum *parl.* ['kwɔːrəm] quorum *m*; nombre *m* suffisant; *be a* ~ être en nombre.

quo·ta ['kwoutə] quote-part *f*; contingent *m*.

quo·ta·tion [kwou'teiʃn] citation *f*; *typ.* cadrat *m* creux; ✝ cours *m*, prix *m*; *familiar* ~*s pl.* citations *f/pl.* très connues; **quo'ta·tion-marks** *pl.* guillemets *m/pl.*

quote [kwout] *v/t.* citer; *typ.* guillemeter; *à la Bourse:* coter (à, *at*); ✝ faire un prix (pour, *for*; à, *to*); *v/i.* citer; faire un prix (pour, *for*; à, *to*).

quoth † [kwouθ]: ~ *I* dis-je; ~ *he* dit-il.

quo·tid·i·an [kwɔ'tidiən] quotidien(ne *f*); de tous les jours; banal (-als *m/pl.*). [*m.*]

quo·tient ℛ ['kwouʃənt] quotient

R

R, r [ɑ:] R *m*, r *m*.

rab·bet ⊕ ['ræbit] **1.** feuillure *f*, rainure *f*; **2.** faire une feuillure *ou* rainure à.

rab·bi ['ræbai] rabbin *m*; *titre:* rabbi *m*.

rab·bit ['ræbit] lapin *m*; *Welsh* ~ toast *m* au fromage fondu.

rab·ble ['ræbl] cohue *f*; *the* ~ la canaille *f*; '~**-rous·er** agitateur *m*; '~**-rous·ing** qui incite à la violence.

rab·id □ ['ræbid] féroce, acharné; *fig.* à outrance; *vét.* enragé (*chien etc.*); '**rab·id·ness** violence *f*; rage *f*.

ra·bies *vét.* ['reibi:z] rage *f*, hydrophobie *f*.

ra(c)·coon *zo.* [rə'ku:n] raton *m* laveur.

race[1] [reis] race *f*; lignée *f*; sang *m*; ~ *riot* bagarre *f* raciale.

race[2] [~] course *f* (*a. fig.*); *soleil:* cours *m*; *courant:* ras *m*; *fig.* carrière *f*; ~ *against the clock* course *f* contre la montre; ~s *pl.* course *f*, -s *f/pl.* (*de bateaux, de chevaux*); **2.** lutter de vitesse (avec, with); courir à toute vitesse; ⊕ s'emballer; battre la fièvre (*pouls*); *v/t.* ⊕ emballer à vide (*le moteur*); *sl.* faire la noce; '~**course** champ *m* de courses; piste *f*; '~**-crew** course à l'aviron: équipe *f* de canot.

race-ha·tred ['reis'heitrid] racisme *m*.

race·horse ['reishɔːs] cheval *m* de course.

rac·er ['reisə] coureur (-euse *f*) *m*; cheval *m* de course; *mot.* coureur *m*; yacht *m* *ou* bicyclette *f* *etc.* de course.

ra·cial ['reiʃl] de (la) race; ~ *discrimination* discrimination *f* raciale; **ra·cial·ism** ['~ʃəlizm] racisme *m*.

rac·i·ness ['reisinis] verve *f*, piquant *m*; *vin etc.*: goût *m* de terroir.

rac·ing ['reisiŋ] courses *f/pl.*; *attr.* de course(s), de piste; ~ (*bi*)*cyclist* routier *m*; ~ *motorist* coureur *m*, racer *m*; ~ *car* automobile *f* de course.

ra·cism ['reisizəm] racisme *m*; '**ra·cist** raciste (*adj.*, *mf*).

rack[1] [ræk] **1.** *écurie, armes, etc.:* râtelier *m*; portemanteau *m*; ♪ classeur *m* (à musique); ⊕ crémaillère *f*; ✈ bomb ~ lance-bombes *m/inv.*; 🚂 luggage ~ porte-bagages *m/inv.*; filet *m* (à bagages); **2.** *hist.* faire subir le supplice du chevalet à; *fig.* tourmenter, torturer; extorquer (*un loyer*); pressurer (*un locataire*); étirer (*les peaux*); épuiser (*le sol*); détraquer (*une machine*); ~ *one's brains* se creuser la cervelle.

rack[2] [~] **1.** légers nuages *m/pl.* traînants; cumulus *m*; **2.** se traîner (*nuages*).

rack[3] [~]: *go to* ~ *and ruin* tomber en ruine; se délabrer (*maison*).

rack[4] [~] (*a.* ~ *off*) soutirer (*le vin etc.*).

rack·et[1] ['rækit] *tennis etc.:* raquette *f*; *jeu:* ~s *souv. sg.* la raquette *f*.

rack·et[2] [~] **1.** vacarme *m*, tapage *m*; *fig.* epreuve *f*; *fig.* dépenses *f/pl.*; gaieté *f*; F spécialité *f*; entreprise *f* (*de gangster*); chantage *m*; **2.** faire du tapage; *sl.* faire la noce; **rack·et·eer** *surt. Am. sl.* [~'tiə] gangster *m*; combinard *m*; bandit *m*; **rack·et·eer·ing** *surt. Am.* banditisme *m* au chantage; '**rack·et·y** tapageur (-euse *f*); *fig.* noceur (-euse *f*).

rack-rail·way ['ræk'reilwei] chemin *m* de fer à crémaillère.

rack-rent ['rækrent] **1.** loyer *m* exorbitant; **2.** imposer un loyer exorbitant à (*q.*).

rac·y □ ['reisi] qui sent le terroir (*vin*); vif (vive *f*), piquant (*personne*); *fig.* plein de verve; *fig.* savoureux (-euse *f*) (*histoire*); *be* ~ *of the soil* sentir le terroir.

rad *pol.* F [ræd] radical *m*.

ra·dar ['reidɑ:] radar *m*; ~ *set* (appareil *m* de) radar *m*.

rad·dle ['rædl] **1.** ocre *f* rouge; **2.** marquer à l'ocre; *fig.* farder.

ra·di·al □ ['reidjəl] ⊕, *a. anat.*

radial (-aux *m/pl.*); centrifuge (*force*); ☢ du radium; ~ *engine* moteur *m* en étoile; ~ *tyre*, *Am.* ~ *tire* pneu *m* à carcasse radiale.

ra·di·ance, ra·di·an·cy ['reidjəns(i)] rayonnement *m*; splendeur *f*; '**ra·di·ant** □ rayonnant (*a. fig.*); radieux (-euse *f*) (*a. fig.*).

ra·di·ate 1. ['reidieit] *v/i.* rayonner; émettre des rayons; *v/t.* émettre; répandre; **2.** ['~it] *zo. etc.* radié, rayonné; **ra·di·a·tion** rayonnement *m*; *radium etc.*: radiation *f*; **ra·di·a·tor** ['~eitə] radiateur *m* (*a. mot.*); ~ *mascot* bouchon *m* enjoliveur.

rad·i·cal ['rædikəl] **1.** □ radical (-aux *m/pl.*) (*a. pol.*); fondamental (-aux *m/pl.*); A ~ *sign* (signe *m*) radical (-aux *m/pl.*); **2.** ♫, A, *gramm.* radical *m*; *pol.* radical(e *f*) *m*; '**rad·i·cal·ism** radicalisme *m*.

ra·di·o ['reidiou] **1.** radio *f*, télégraphie *f* sans fil, T.S.F. *f*; ☢ radiographie *f*; ☢ radiologie *f*; (*a. ~-telegram*) radio *m*; ~ *drama* (*ou play*) pièce *f* radiophonique; ~ *engineer* ingénieur *m* radio; ~ *fan* sans-filiste *mf*; ~ *operator* (opérateur *m*) radio *m*; ~ *set* poste *m* (récepteur); ~ *studio* studio *m* d'émission; auditorium *m*; **2.** envoyer (*qch.*) par la radio; radiotélégraphier; ☢ radiographier; ☢ traiter au radium; '**~ac·tive** radioactif (-ive *f*); rayonnant (*matière*); ~ *waste* déchets *m/pl.* radioactifs; '**~ac·tiv·i·ty** radio-activité *f*; **ra·di·o·gram** ['~græm] radiogramme *m*; radiographie *f*; *a. abr.* de '**ra·di·o·gram·o·phone** radiophono *m*; **ra·di·o·graph** ☢ ['~grɑːf] **1.** radiographie *f*, radiogramme *m*; **2.** radiographier; '**ra·di·o·lo·ca·tion** radiorepérage *m*; **ra·di·ol·o·gist** [reidi'ɔlədʒist] radiologue *mf*; **ra·di·ol·o·gy** *phys.* [reidi'ɔlədʒi] radiologie *f*; **ra·di·os·co·py** [~'ɔskəpi] radioscopie *f*; '**ra·di·o·tel·e·gram** radiotélégramme *m*; '**ra·di·o·tel·e·scope** radiotélescope *m*; '**ra·di·o·ther·a·py** ☢ radiothérapie *f*.

rad·ish ♣ ['rædiʃ] radis *m*.

ra·di·um ['reidjəm] radium *m*.

ra·di·us ['reidjəs], *pl.* **~di·i** ['~diai] A, ♣, *mot.*, *a. fig.* rayon *m*; *anat.* radius *m*; ⊕ *grue*: portée *f*; *fig. a.* circonscription *f*. [(*air*).⟩

raff·ish ['ræfiʃ] bravache; canaille⟩

raf·fle ['ræfl] **1.** *v/t.* mettre en tombola; *v/i.* prendre part à une tombola; prendre un billet (pour, *for*); **2.** tombola *f*, loterie *f*.

raft [rɑːft] **1.** radeau *m*; **2.** transporter *etc.* sur un radeau; '**raft·er** (*a.* rafts·man ['~smən]) flotteur *m*; △ chevron *m*.

rag¹ [ræg] chiffon *m*; lambeau *m*; *journ. péj.* feuille *f* de chou; ~*s pl.* haillons *m/pl.*, guenilles *f/pl.*; F *chew the* ~ tailler une bavette;

rag² *min.* [~] calcaire *m* oolithique.

rag³ *sl.* [~] **1.** *v/t.* chahuter; brimer; *v/i.* faire du chahut, chahuter; **2.** brimade *f*; chahut *m*.

rag·a·muf·fin ['rægəmʌfin] gueux *m*; gamin *m* des rues; '**rag-and-bone man** chiffonnier *m*; '**rag-bag** sac *m* aux chiffons; '**rag-book** livre *m* d'images sur toile.

rage [reidʒ] **1.** rage *f*, fureur *f* (*a. du vent*), emportement *m*; manie *f* (de, *for*); *it is all the* ~ cela fait fureur, c'est le grand chic; **2.** être furieux (-euse *f*) (*personne*); faire rage (*vent*); *fig.* tempêter (contre, *against*); sévir (*peste*).

rag-fair ['rægfɛə] marché *m* aux vieux habits; F marché *m* aux puces.

rag·ged □ ['rægid] déguenillé, en haillons (*personne*); en lambeaux, ébréché (*rocher*); désordonné (☓, *feu*); déchiqueté (*contour*).

rag·man ['rægmən] chiffonnier *m*.

ra·gout ['ræguː] ragoût *m*.

rag...: '**~tag** canaille *f*; '**~time** ♪ musique *f* de jazz (nègre).

raid [reid] **1.** descente *f* (*inattendue*); ☓, ✈ raid *m*; *police:* rafle *f*; *bandits:* razzia *f*; **2.** *v/i.* faire une descente *ou* une rafle *etc.*; *v/t. a.* marauder, razzier.

rail¹ [reil] **1.** barre(au *m*) *f*; *chaise:* bâton *m*; *charrette:* ridelle *f*; (*a.* ~*s pl.*) palissade *f* (*en bois*), grille *f* (*en fer*); ⚓ rail *m*; F chemin *m* de fer, train *m*; ⚓ lisse *f*; ✝ ~*s pl.* les chemins *m/pl.* de fer; ~ *strike* grève *f* des cheminots; *get* (*ou run*) *off the* ~*s* dérailler (*a. fig.*); **2.** (*a.* ~ *in ou off*) entourer d'une grille, griller, palissader; envoyer *ou* transporter par (le) chemin de fer.

rail² [~] crier, se répandre en invectives (contre *at*, *against*).

rail³ *orn.* [~] râle *m*.

rail·er ['reilə] criailleur (-euse *f*) *m*; mauvaise langue *f*.

rail·ing ['reiliŋ] (*a.* ⁓*s pl.*) palissade *f* (*en bois*), grille *f* (*en fer*).

rail·ler·y ['reiləri] raillerie *f*.

rail·mo·tor ['reil'moutə] autorail *m*.

rail·road ['reilroud] **1.** *surt. Am.*, (*Brit.* = **rail·way** ['reilwei]) chemin *m* de fer; ⁓ *carriage* voiture *f*, wagon *m*; **2.** *v/t. pol. Am.* faire voter avec vitesse; *Am. sl.* emprisonner après un jugement précipité.

rail·way·man ['reilweimən] employé *m* de chemin de fer, cheminot *m*.

rai·ment *poét.* ['reimənt] habillement *m*, vêtement *m*, -s *m/pl.*

rain [rein] **1.** pluie *f*; **2.** pleuvoir; '⁓**bow** arc-en-ciel (*pl.* arcs-en-ciel) *m*; '⁓**coat** imperméable *m*; '⁓**fall** averse *f*; chute *f* de pluie; pluviosité *f*; ⁓**gauge** ['⁓geidʒ] pluviomètre *m*; **rain·i·ness** ['⁓inis] pluviosité *f*; temps *m* pluvieux; '**rain-lack·ing** dépourvu de pluie, sans pluie; sec (sèche *f*); '**rainproof** imperméable (*a. su./m*); '**rain·y** ☐ pluvieux (-euse *f*); de pluie.

raise [reiz] (*souv.* ⁓ *up*) dresser, mettre debout; *fig.* exciter (*la foule, le peuple*); relever (*courage, navire, store, tarif*); lever (*armée, bras, camp, gibier, impôt, siège, verre, yeux, etc.*); (re)hausser (*le prix*); bâtir; élever (*bétail, édifice, famille, prix, q., voix, etc.*); ériger (*une statue*); cultiver (*des plantes*); produire (*un sourire, de la vapeur, etc.*); faire naître (*une espérance*); soulever (*objection, peuple, poids, question*); mettre sur pied (*une armée*); se procurer, emprunter (*de l'argent*); évoquer (*un esprit, le souvenir*); ressusciter (*un mort*); pousser (*un cri*); augmenter (*le salaire*); revendiquer (*des droits*); '**rais·er** souleveur *m*; éleveur *m*.

rai·sin ['reizn] raisin *m* sec.

ra·ja(h) ['rɑːdʒə] rajah *m*.

rake¹ [reik] **1.** râteau *m*; (*a.* fire-⁓) fourgon *m*; **2.** *v/t.* (*usu.* ⁓ *together*) râteler, ratisser; gratter (*la surface*); *fig.* fouiller; (*a.* ⁓ *up ou over*) revenir sur; ✕, ⚓ enfiler; *fig.* dominer, embrasser du regard; ⁓ *off* (*ou away*) enlever au râteau; *v/i.* scruter; fouiller (*pour trouver qch., for*

s.th.); '⁓**off** *Am. sl.* gratte *f*, ristourne *f*.

rake² ⚓ [⁓] **1.** inclinaison *f*; **2.** *v/i.* être incliné; *v/t.* incliner vers l'arrière.

rake³ [⁓] roué *m*, noceur *m*.

rak·ish¹ ⚓ *etc.* ['reikiʃ] élancé; en pente.   [bravache (*air*).\
rak·ish² ☐ [⁓] libertin, dissolu; *fig.*\
ral·ly¹ ['ræli] **1.** ralliement *m*; réunion *f*; *sp. fig.* retour *m* d'énergie; reprise *f* des forces *ou* ✕ en main; ✝ reprise *f*; *tennis*: échange *m* de balles; **2.** *v/i.* se rallier; se reprendre; se grouper; *v/t.* rassembler, réunir; ranimer.

ral·ly² [⁓] se gausser de (*q.*); railler (*q.*) (de, on).

ram [ræm] **1.** ✕, *zo., astr.* bélier *m*; ⊕ piston *m* plongeur; ⚓ éperon *m*; **2.** battre, tasser (*le sol*); heurter; *mot.* tamponner (*une voiture*); ⚓ éperonner; ⁓ *up* boucher (*un trou*); bourrer.

ram·ble ['ræmbl] **1.** promenade *f*, F balade *f*; **2.** errer à l'aventure; faire une excursion à pied; *fig.* parler sans suite; '**ram·bler** excursionniste *mf*; promeneur *m*; *fig.* radoteur *m*; ♀ rosier *m* grimpant; '**ram·bling 1.** ☐ vagabond; *fig.* décousu, sans suite; ♀ grimpant, rampant; *fig.* tortueux (-euse *f*); **2.** vagabondage *m*; excursions *f/pl.* à pied; *fig.* radotages *m/pl.*

ram·i·fi·ca·tion [ræmifi'keiʃn] ramification *f*; **ram·i·fy** ['⁓fai] (se) ramifier.

ram·jet ['ræmdʒet] (*a.* ⁓ *engine*) statoréacteur *m*.

ram·mer ⊕ ['ræmə] pilon *m*.

ramp¹ *sl.* [ræmp] supercherie *f*.

ramp² [⁓] **1.** rampe *f*; pont *m* élévateur; **2.** *v/t.* construire (*qch.*) en rampe; *v/i.* ⚓ ramper; *fig.* rager; **ram'page** *co.* **1.** rager, tempêter; se conduire comme un fou furieux; **2.**: *be on the* ⁓ en avoir après tout le monde; '**ramp·an·cy** violence *f*; exubérance *f*; *fig.* extension *f*; '**ramp·ant** ☐ violent; exubérant; *fig.* effréné; ▨, *a.* ▲ rampant.

ram·part ['ræmpɑːt] rempart *m*.

ram·rod ['ræmrɔd] fusil: baguette *f*; *straight as a* ⁓ droit comme un i.

ram·shack·le ['ræmʃækl] délabré.

ran [ræn] *prét. de* run 1, 2.

ranch [rɑːntʃ; *surt. Am.* ræntʃ]

ferme *f* *ou* prairie *f* d'élevage; ranch *m*.

ran·cid □ ['rænsid] rance, ranci; **ran'cid·i·ty**, **'ran·cid·ness** rancidité *f*. [nier (-ère *f*).]

ran·cor·ous □ ['ræŋkərəs] rancu-

ran·co(u)r ['ræŋkə] rancune *f*, ressentiment *m*.

ran·dom ['rændəm] **1.**: *at* ~ au hasard; à l'aveuglette; **2.** fait au hasard; de passage; ~ *sample* échantillon *m* prélevé au hasard; ~ *shot* coup *m* tiré au hasard; coup *m* perdu.

rand·y *sl.* ['rændi] excité, aguiché.

rang [ræŋ] *prét. de ring²* **2.**

range [reindʒ] **1.** rangée *f*; chaîne *f* (*de montagnes*); ✝ assortiment *m*; série *f*; étendue *f*, portée *f* (*a. d'une arme à feu*); direction *f*; champ *m* libre; *sp.* distance *f*; *Am.* prairie *f*; fourneau *m* (de cuisine); (*a. shoot-ing-*~) champ *m* de tir; *fig.* libre essor *m*; *fig.* variété *f*; take the ~ estimer *ou* régler le tir; **2.** *v/t.* aligner, ranger; disposer; parcourir (*une région*); braquer (*un télescope*); ⚓ longer (*la côte*); *v/i.* errer, courir; s'étendre (*a. fig.*); varier; ✕ régler le tir; ~ *along* longer; ~ *over* parcourir; *canon*: avoir une portée (de six milles, *over six miles*); '~**-find·er** télémètre *m*; **'rang·er** ✝ vagabond(e *f*) *m*; grand maître *m* des parcs royaux; *Indes*: garde-général (*pl.* gardes-généraux) *m* adjoint; ♀s *pl.* gendarmes *m/pl.* à cheval; ✕ *Am.* soldats *m/pl.* de commando spécial.

rank¹ [ræŋk] **1.** rang *m* (*social*, ✕, *a. fig.*); ligne *f*; classe *f*; ✕, ⚓ grade *m*; stationnement *m* (*pour taxis*); the ~s *pl.* (*ou and file*) (les hommes *m/pl.* de) troupe *f*; *fig.* le commun *m* des hommes; *join the* ~s devenir soldat; entrer dans les rangs; *rise from the* ~s de simple soldat passer officier, sortir du rang; **2.** *v/t.* ranger, compter; classer (avec, *with*); *v/i.* se ranger, être classé (avec, *with*; parmi, *among*); compter (parmi, *among*); occuper un rang (supérieur à, *above*); ~ *next to* occuper le premier rang après; ~ *as* avoir qualité de; compter pour.

rank² □ [~] luxuriant; exubérant (*plante*); riche, gras(se *f*) (*sol, terrain*); rance, fort, fétide; *fig.* péj. complet (-ète *f*), pur, parfait.

rank·er ✕ ['ræŋkə] simple soldat *m*; officier *m* sorti des rangs.

ran·kle *fig.* ['ræŋkl] rester sur le cœur (de q., *with s.o.*).

rank·ness ['ræŋknis] luxuriance *f*; odeur *f* etc. forte; *fig.* grossièreté *f*.

ran·sack ['rænsæk] fouiller (dans); saccager.

ran·som ['rænsəm] **1.** rançon *f*; rachat *m* (*eccl.*, *a. d'un captif*); **2.** mettre à rançon, rançonner; racheter.

rant [rænt] **1.** rodomontades *f/pl.*; **2.** déclamer avec extravagance; ✝ tempêter; **'rant·er** déclamateur (-trice *f*) *m*; énergumène *mf*.

ra·nun·cu·lus ♀ [rə'nʌŋkjuləs], *pl.* **-lus·es**, **-li** [~lai] renoncule *f*.

rap¹ [ræp] **1.** petit coup *m* (sec); **2.** frapper (à, *at*); *fig.* ~ *s.o.'s fingers* (*ou knuckles*) donner sur les doigts à q.; F remettre q. à sa place; ~ *out* lâcher; dire (*qch.*) d'un ton sec.

rap² *fig.* [~] sou *m*, liard *m*; *not care a* ~ s'en ficher.

ra·pa·cious □ [rə'peiʃəs] rapace; **ra·pac·i·ty** [rə'pæsiti] rapacité *f*.

rape¹ [reip] **1.** rapt *m*; enlèvement *m*; ⚖ viol *m*; **2.** ravir; ⚖ violer.

rape² ♀ [~] colza *m*; navette *f*; '~**-oil** huile *f* de colza *ou* de navette; '~**-seed** graine *f* de colza.

rap·id ['ræpid] **1.** □ rapide; ~ *fire* feu *m* continu *ou* accéléré; **2.** ~s *pl.* rapide *m*; **ra·pid·i·ty** [rə'piditi] rapidité *f*.

ra·pi·er ['reipjə] *escrime*: rapière *f*.

rap·ine *poét.* ['ræpain] rapine *f*.

rap·ist ['reipist] violeur *m*.

rap·proche·ment *pol.* [ræ'prɔʃmãːŋ] rapprochement *m*.

rapt *fig.* [ræpt] ravi, extasié (par *by*, *with*); absorbé (dans, *in*); profond.

rap·to·ri·al *zo.* [ræp'tɔːriəl] de proie.

rap·ture ['ræptʃə] (*a.* ~s *pl.*) extase *m*, ravissement *m*; *in* ~s ravi, enchanté; *go into* ~s s'extasier (sur, *over*); **'rap·tur·ous** □ d'extase, de ravissement; enthousiaste.

rare □ [rɛə] rare (*a. phys. etc.*, *a. fig.*); F fameux (-euse *f*), riche; *surt. Am.* saignant (*bifteck*).

rare·bit ['rɛəbit] toast *m*: Welsh ~ toast *m* au fromage fondu.

rar·e·fac·tion *phys.* [rɛəri'fækʃn] raréfaction *f*; **rar·e·fy** ['~fai] *v/t.* raréfier; affiner (*le goût*); subtiliser (*une idée*); *v/i.* se raréfier;

'rare·ness, 'rar·i·ty rareté *f*; F excellence *f*.

ras·cal ['rɑːskəl] coquin(e *f*) *m* (*a. fig.*); fripon *m*; gredin *m*; **ras·cal·i·ty** [ˌˈkæliti] coquinerie *f*, gredinerie *f*; **ras·cal·ly** *adj. a. adv.* ['ˌkəli] de coquin; méchant; retors; ignoble.

rase † [reiz] raser (*une ville etc.*).

rash[1] □ [ræʃ] irréfléchi, inconsidéré; téméraire; impétueux (-euse *f*).

rash[2] ⚕ [ˌ] éruption *f*.

rash·er ['ræʃə] tranche *f* de lard.

rash·ness ['ræʃnis] témérité *f*; étourderie *f*.

rasp [rɑːsp] **1.** râpe *f*; grincement *m*; **2.** *v/t.* râper; racler (*le gosier, une surface, etc.*); *v/i.* grincer, crisser.

rasp·ber·ry ♀ ['rɑːzbəri] framboise *f*; *sl.* get the ~ se faire rabrouer.

rasp·er ['rɑːspə] râpeur (-euse *f*) *m*; râpe *f*.

rasp·ing ['rɑːspiŋ] râpage *m*; grincement *m*; ~s *pl.* râpure *f*, -s *f*/*pl.*

rat [ræt] **1.** *zo.* rat *m*; *pol.* renégat *m*, transfuge *m*; *sl.* jaune *m*, faux frère *m*; *fig.* ~ race foire *f* d'empoigne; smell a ~ soupçonner anguille sous roche; **2.** attraper des rats; *pol.* tourner casaque; *sl.* faire le jaune; F ~ on trahir (*q.*), vendre (*q.*).

rat·a·bil·i·ty [reitəˈbiliti] caractère *m* imposable; **'rat·a·ble** □ évaluable; imposable.

ratch ⊕ [rætʃ] encliquetage *m* à dents; *horloge*: cliquet *m*.

ratch·et ⊕ ['rætʃit] encliquetage *m* à dents; cliquet *m*; '~**-wheel** roue *f* à cliquet.

rate[1] [reit] **1.** quantité *f* proportionnelle; taux *m*; raison *f*, degré *m*; tarif *m*, cours *m*; droit *m*; prix *m*; impôt *m* local; taxe *f* municipale; *fig.* évaluation *f*; vitesse *f*, allure *f*, train *m*; † classe *f*, rang *m*; at the ~ of au taux de, à raison de; sur le pied de; *mot.* à la vitesse de; ✝ at a cheap ~ à un prix *ou* taux réduit; at any ~ de toute façon, en tout cas; ✝ à n'importe quel prix; ~ of exchange cours *m* du change; ~ of interest taux *m* d'intérêt; ~ of taxation taux *m* de l'imposition; ~ of wages taux *m* du salaire; **2.** *v/t.* estimer; *Am.* mériter; considérer; classer (*a.* ⚓); taxer (à raison de, *at*); *v/i.* être classé.

rate[2] [ˌ] *v/t.* semoncer (de *for,*
about); *v/i.* gronder, crier (contre, *at*).

rate-pay·er ['reitpeiə] contribuable *mf.*

rath·er ['rɑːðə] plutôt; quelque *ou* un peu; assez; pour mieux dire; F ~! bien sûr!, pour sûr!; I had (*ou* would) ~ (*inf.*) j'aime mieux (*inf.*); I ~ expected it je m'en doutais, je m'y attendais.

rat·i·fi·ca·tion [rætifiˈkeiʃn] ratification *f*; **rat·i·fy** ['ˌfai] ratifier, approuver.

rat·ing[1] ['reitiŋ] évaluation *f*; répartition *f* des impôts locaux; ⚓ classe *f* (*d'un homme*); ⚓ classement *m* (*d'un navire*); ⚓ matelot *m*; *télév.* (*a. popularity* ~) indice *m* de popularité, taux *m* d'écoute.

rat·ing[2] [ˌ] semonce *f*.

ra·tio ['reiʃiou] raison *f*, rapport *m*.

ra·tion ['ræʃn] **1.** ration *f*; ~ card carte *f* alimentaire; ~ tickets tickets *m*/*pl.* (*de pain etc.*); off the ~ see ~-free; **2.** rationner; mettre (*q.*) à la ration.

ra·tion·al □ ['ræʃnəl] raisonnable; doué de raison; raisonné; ⚕ rationnel(le *f*) (*a. croyance*); **ra·tion·al·ism** ['ˌnəlizm] rationalisme *m*; **'ra·tion·al·ist** rationaliste (*a. su.*/*mf*); **ra·tion·al·i·ty** [ˌˈnæliti] rationalité *f*; faculté *f* de raisonner; **ra·tion·al·i·za·tion** ['ˌlaiˈzeiʃn] rationalisation *f* (*a.* ✝); **'ra·tion·al·ize** rationaliser; organiser de façon rationnelle.

ra·tion-free ['ræʃnfriː] sans tickets, en vente libre.   [rats *f.*

rats·bane † ['rætsbein] mort-aux-

rat-tat ['rætˈtæt] toc-toc *m*.

rat·ten ⊕ ['rætn] *v/t.* saboter; *v/i.* saboter l'outillage *ou* le matériel; **'rat·ten·ing** sabotage *m*.

rat·tle ['rætl] **1.** bruit *m*; *fusillade*: crépitement *m*; *machine à écrire*: tapotis *m*; crécelle *f*; *enfant*: hochet *m*; *fig.* caquetage *m*; ⚕ râle *m*; ~s *pl. serpent*: sonnettes *f*/*pl.*); **2.** *v/i.* branler; crépiter; cliqueter; faire du bruit; ⚕ râler; *v/t.* faire sonner; faire cliqueter; agiter; F consterner; ~ off (*ou* out) expédier; réciter rapidement; '~**-brained**, '~**-pat·ed** écervelé, étourdi; **'rat·tler** ⚓ klaxon *m* d'alarme; F coup *m* dur; *sl.* personne *f ou* chose *f* épatante; *Am. sl.* tramway *m*; *Am. sl.* tacot *m*; *Am.*

rattlesnake

F = **'rat·tle·snake** serpent *m* à sonnettes; **'rat·tle·trap 1.** délabré; **2.** guimbarde *f*, tapecul *m*.

rat·tling ['rætliŋ] **1.** □ bruyant; crépitant; F vif (vive *f*); **2.** *adv.* rudement; *at a* ～ *pace* au grand trot, très rapidement.

rat·ty ['ræti] infesté de rats; en queue de rat (*natte*); *sl.* grincheux (-euse *f*); fâché.

rau·cous □ ['rɔ:kəs] rauque.

rav·age ['rævidʒ] **1.** ravage *m*, -s *m/pl.*, dévastation *f*; **2.** *v/t.* ravager, dévaster; *v/i.* faire des ravages.

rave [reiv] être en délire; *fig.* pester (contre, *at*); s'extasier (sur *about*, *of*).

rav·el ['rævl] *v/t.* embrouiller; (*a.* ～ *out*) effilocher; *v/i.* s'embrouiller, s'enchevêtrer; (*a.* ～ *out*) s'effilocher.

rav·en¹ ['reivn] (grand) corbeau *m*.

rav·en² ['rævn] **1.** *see* ravin; **2.** faire des ravages; chercher sa proie; être affamé (de, *for*); **'rav·en·ous** □ vorace; affamé; **'rav·en·ous·ness** voracité *f*; faim *f* de loup.

rav·in ['rævin] rapine *f*; butin *m*.

ra·vine [rə'vi:n] ravin *m*.

rav·ings *pl.* ['reiviŋz] délires *m/pl.*; paroles *f/pl.* incohérentes.

rav·ish ['ræviʃ] violer (*une femme*); *fig.* enchanter, ravir; † enlever de force, ravir; **'rav·ish·er** ravisseur *m*; **'rav·ish·ing** □ ravissant; **'rav·ish·ment** rapt *m*; enlèvement *m*; viol *m* (*d'une femme*); *fig.* ravissement *m*.

raw □ [rɔ:] **1.** cru (= *pas cuit*; *a.* couleur, peau); brut; premier (-ère *f*); vert (*cuir*); inexpérimenté (*personne*); âpre (*temps*); vif (vive *f*) (*plaie*); ～ *material* matériaux *m/pl.* bruts; matières *f/pl.* premières; F *he got a* ～ *deal* on le traita avec peu de générosité; **2.** vif *m*; endroit *m* sensible; **'~-boned** décharné; efflanqué (*cheval*); **'~-hide** cuir *m* vert; **'raw·ness** crudité *f*; écorchure *f*; *temps:* âpreté *f*; *fig.* inexpérience *f*.

ray¹ *icht.* [rei] raie *f*.

ray² [～] **1.** ♀, *phys., zo., etc.* rayon *m*; *fig.* lueur *f* (*d'espoir*); ☢ ～ *treatment* radiothérapie *f*; **2.** (*v/t.* faire) rayonner; **'~-less** sans rayons.

ray·on *tex.* ['reiɔn] rayonne *f*, soie *f* artificielle.

raze [reiz] (*a.* ～ *to the ground*) raser; ⚔ receper (*un mur*); *fig.* effacer.

ra·zor ['reizə] rasoir *m*; **'~-blade** lame *f* de rasoir; *be on the* ～'*s edge* être sur la corde raide; **'~-strop** cuir *m* à rasoir.

razz *Am. sl.* [ræz] **1.** ridicule *m*; **2.** taquiner, se moquer de, se payer la tête de.

raz·zi·a ['ræziə] *police:* razzia *f*.

re [ri:] ⚖ (en l')affaire; ✝ relativement à; *en-tête d'une lettre:* objet ...

re... [～] re-, r-, ré-; de nouveau; à nouveau.

reach [ri:tʃ] **1.** extension *f* (*de la main*), *box.* allonge *f*; portée *f*; étendue *f* (*a. fig.*); partie *f* droite (*d'un fleuve*) entre deux coudes; *beyond* ～, *out of* ～ hors de portée; *within easy* ～ à proximité (de, *of*); tout près; à peu de distance; **2.** *v/i.* (*a.* ～ *out*) tendre la main (pour, *for*); s'étendre ([jusqu']à, *to*); (*a.* ～ *to*) atteindre; *v/t.* arriver à, parvenir à; (*souv.* ～ *out*) (é)tendre; atteindre.

reach-me-down F ['ri:tʃmi'daun] costume *m* de confection, F décroche-moi-ça *m/inv.*

re·act [ri'ækt] réagir (sur, *upon*; contre, *against*); réactionner (*prix*).

re·ac·tion [ri'ækʃn] réaction *f* (*a.* ⚡, ♠, *physiol., pol.*); contrecoup *m*; **re'ac·tion·ar·y** *surt. pol.* **1.** réactionnaire; **2.** (*a.* **re'ac·tion·ist**) réactionnaire *mf*.

re·ac·tive □ [ri'æktiv] réactif (-ive *f*); de réaction (*a. pol.*); **re'ac·tor** *phys.* réacteur *m*; ⚡ bobine *f* de réactance.

read 1. [ri:d] [*irr.*] *v/t.* (*un livre, un thermomètre, etc.*); (*a.* ～ *up*) étudier; déchiffrer; *fig.* interpréter; ～ *off* lire sans hésiter; ～ *out* lire à haute voix; donner lecture (de); ～ *to* faire la lecture à (*q.*); *v/i.* lire; être conçu; marquer (*thermomètre*); ～ *for* préparer (*un examen*); ～ *like* faire l'effet de; ～ *well* se laisser lire; **2.** [red] *prét. et p.p. de* 1; **3.** [red] *adj.* instruit (en, *in*); versé (dans, *in*).

read·a·ble □ ['ri:dəbl] lisible.

read·er ['ri:də] lecteur (-trice *f*) *m* (*a. eccl.*); *typ.* correcteur *m* d'épreuves; lecteur *m* de manuscrits; *univ.*

maître m de conférences, chargé(e f) m de cours; livre m de lecture; **'read·er·ship** journal etc.: (nombre m de) lecteurs m/pl.; univ. maîtrise f de conférences; charge f de cours.

read·i·ly ['redili] adv. volontiers, avec empressement; **'read·i·ness** alacrité f, empressement m; bonne volonté f; facilité f; ~ of mind (ou wit) vivacité f d'esprit.

read·ing ['ri:diŋ] 1. lecture f (a. d'un instrument de précision); compteur: relevé m; observation f; cote f; hauteur f (barométrique); interprétation f; leçon f, variante f, parl. second ~ prise f en considération; 2. lecture; ~ matter lecture(s) f (pl.), de quoi lire.

re·ad·just ['ri:ə'dʒʌst] rajuster; remettre à point (un instrument); **'re·ad'just·ment** rajustement m, rectification f; ⚓ régulation f.

re·ad·mis·sion ['ri:əd'miʃn] réadmission f.

re·ad·mit ['ri:əd'mit] réadmettre; réintégrer; **'re·ad'mit·tance** réadmission f.

read·y ['redi] 1. adj. ☐ prêt (à inf., to inf.); sous la main; disposé, sur le point (de inf., to inf.); facile; prompt (à, with); ✝ comptant (argent); ⚓ paré; ~ reckoner barème m (de comptes); ✕ ~ for action prêt au combat; ~ for use prêt à l'usage; make (ou get) ~ (se) préparer; (s')apprêter; 2. adv. tout, toute; readier plus promptement; readiest le plus promptement; 3. su.: at the ~ paré à faire feu; **'~-made** tout fait; de confection (vêtement); **'~-to-'wear** prêt à porter.

re·af·firm ['ri:ə'fə:m] réaffirmer.

re·a·gent ⚗ [ri'eidʒənt] réactif m.

re·al ☐ [riəl] 1. vrai; véritable; réel (-le f); ~ property (ou estate) propriété f immobilière; biens-fonds m/pl.; 2. surt. Am. F vraiment; très, F rudement, vachement; 3. surt. Am. F for ~ sérieusement, F pour de vrai; sérieux (-euse f); **'re·al·ism** réalisme m; **re·al'is·tic** (~ally) réaliste; ~ally avec réalisme; **re·al·i·ty** [ri'æliti] réalité f; réel m; fig. vérité f, réalisme m; **re·al·iz·a·ble** ☐ ['riəlaizəbl] réalisable; imaginable; **re·al·i'za·tion** réalisation f (projet, a. ✝ placement); fig. perception f; idée f; ✝ conversion f en espèces; **'re·al·ize** réaliser

(un projet, a. ✝ un placement); concevoir nettement, bien comprendre; se rendre compte de; rapporter (un prix); ✝ convertir en espèces; gagner (une fortune); **'re·al·ly** vraiment, en effet; à vrai dire; réellement.

realm [relm] royaume m; fig. domaine m; peer of the ~ pair m du Royaume.

re·al·tor Am. ['riəltə] agent m immobilier; courtier m en immeubles; **'re·al·ty** 🏛 biens m/pl. immobiliers.

ream¹ [ri:m] papier: rame f; papier à lettres: ramette f.

ream² ⊕ [~] fraiser (un trou); (usu. ~ out) aléser; **'ream·er** alésoir m.

re·an·i·mate [ri'ænimeit] ranimer; **re·an·i'ma·tion** retour m à la vie; fig. reprise f (des affaires).

reap [ri:p] moissonner (le blé, un champ); (re)cueillir (un fruit, a. fig.); fig. récolter; **'reap·er** moissonneuse (-euse f) m; personne: moissonneur (-euse f) m; **'reap·ing** moisson f; **'reap·ing-hook** faucille f.

re·ap·pear ['ri:ə'piə] reparaître; **'re·ap'pear·ance** réapparition f; théâ. rentrée f.

re·ap·pli·ca·tion ['ri:æpli'keiʃn] nouvelle application f.

re·ap·point ['ri:ə'point] réintégrer (dans ses fonctions); renommer.

rear¹ [riə] v/t. élever; ériger; dresser; ✿ cultiver; v/i. se dresser; se cabrer (cheval).

rear² [~] 1. arrière m (a. ✕), derrière m; queue f; dernier rang m; ✕ arrière-garde f; bring up the ~ venir en queue, ✕ fermer la marche; at the ~ of, in (the) ~ of derrière, en queue de; 2. (d')arrière; de derrière; dernier (-ère f); ~ exit sortie f de derrière; mot. ~-vision (ou ~-view) mirror rétroviseur m; ~ wheel roue f arrière; mot. ~-wheel drive traction f arrière; mot. ~ window glace f arrière; **'~-'ad·mi·ral** ⚓ contre-amiral m; **'~-guard** ✕ arrière-garde f; **'~-lamp** mot. feu m arrière.

re·arm ['ri:'ɑ:m] réarmer; **'re·'arma·ment** [~məmənt] réarmement m.

rear·most ['riəmoust] dernier (-ère f).

re·ar·range ['ri:ə'reindʒ] rarranger; remettre en ordre.

rear·ward ['riəwəd] 1. adj. à l'arrière; en arrière; 2. adv. (a. **'rear-**

wards [⌄z]) à *ou* vers l'arrière; (par) derrière.

re·as·cend ['riːə'send] remonter.

rea·son ['riːzn] **1.** raison *f*, cause *f*; motif *m*; bon sens *m*; *by ~ of* à cause de, en raison de; *for this ~* pour cette raison; *listen to ~* entendre raison; *it stands to ~ that* il est de toute évidence que; **2.** *v/i.* raisonner (sur, *about*); *~ whether* discuter pour savoir si; *v/t.* (*a. ~ out*) arguer, déduire; *~ away* prouver le contraire de (*qch.*) par le raisonnement; *~ s.o. into (out of)* doing *s.th.* amener q. à (dissuader q. de) faire qch.; *~ed* raisonné; logique; **'rea·son·a·ble** □ raisonnable (*a. fig.*); équitable; juste; bien fondé; **'rea·son·a·bly** raisonnablement; **'rea·son·er** raisonneur (-euse *f*) *m*; **'rea·son·ing** raisonnement *m*; dialectique *f*; *attr.* doué de raison.

re·as·sem·ble ['riːə'sembl] (se) rassembler; remonter (*une machine*).

re·as·sert ['riːə'səːt] réaffirmer; insister.

re·as·sur·ance ['riːə'ʃuərəns] action *f* de rassurer; nouvelle affirmation*f*; *give s.o. a ~ about* rassurer q. sur; ✝ réassurer; **re·as·sure** ['~'ʃuə] tranquilliser (sur, *about*); ✝ réassurer.

re·bap·tize ['riːbæp'taiz] rebaptiser.

re·bate¹ ✝ ['riːbeit] rabais *m*, escompte *m*; remboursement *m*.

re·bate² ⊕ ['ræbit] **1.** feuillure *f*; **2.** faire une feuillure à; assembler (*deux planches*) à feuillure.

reb·el ['rebl] **1.** rebelle *mf*, insurgé(e *f*) *m*, révolté(e *f*) *m*; **2.** insurgé; *fig.* (*a.* **re·bel·lious** [ri'beljəs]) rebelle; **3.** [ri'bel] se révolter, se soulever (contre, *against*); **re·bel·lion** [~jən] rébellion *f*, révolte *f*.

re·birth ['riː'bəːθ] renaissance *f*.

re·bound [ri'baund] **1.** rebondir; **2.** rebondissement *m*; balle *etc.*: ricochet *m*; *fig.* moment *m* de détente.

re·buff [ri'bʌf] **1.** échec *m*; refus *m*; **2.** repousser, rebuter.

re·build ['riː'bild] [*irr.* (*build*)] rebâtir, reconstruire.

re·buke [ri'bjuːk] **1.** réprimande *f*, blâme *m*; **2.** réprimander; reprocher (qch. à q., *s.o. for s.th.*).

re·bus ['riːbəs] rébus *m*.

re·but [ri'bʌt] réfuter; repousser; **re'but·tal** réfutation *f*.

re·cal·ci·trant [ri'kælsitrənt] récalcitrant, rebelle.

re·call [ri'kɔːl] **1.** rappel *m*; révocation *f*; rappel *m* d'un souvenir, évocation *f*; *total ~* capacité *f* de se souvenir de tout détail; *théâ.* *give a ~* rappeler (*un acteur*); *beyond* (*ou past*) *~* irrémédiable; irrévocable; **2.** rappeler (*un ambassadeur etc.*; *fig.* qch. à q., *s.th. to s.o.*['*s mind*]); se rappeler, se souvenir de; revoir; retirer (*une parole*); rétracter, revenir sur (*une promesse*); ⚖ annuler; révoquer (*un décret*, ✝ *un ordre*); *~ that* se rappeler que; *until ~ed* jusqu'à nouvel ordre.

re·cant [ri'kænt] (se) rétracter; abjurer; **re·can·ta·tion** [riːkæn'teiʃn] rétractation *f*, abjuration *f*.

re·cap¹ F ['riːkæp] **1.** récapituler; résumer; **2.** récapitulation *f*; résumé *m*.

re·cap² [~] **1.** rechaper (*un pneu*); **2.** pneu *m* rechapé.

re·ca·pit·u·late [riːkə'pitjuleit] récapituler; résumer; **'re·ca·pit·u·la·tion** récapitulation *f*; résumé *m*.

re·cap·ture ['riː'kæptʃə] **1.** reprise *f*; **2.** reprendre; *fig.* revivre (*le passé*).

re·cast ['riː'kɑːst] **1.** [*irr.* (*cast*)] ⊕ refondre; remanier (*un roman etc.*); reconstruire; refaire le calcul de; *théâ.* faire une nouvelle distribution des rôles de; **2.** refonte *f*; nouveau calcul *m* etc.

re·cede [ri'siːd] s'éloigner, reculer (de, *from*); fuir (*front*); ⚒ se retirer (de, *from*); *fig.* *~ from* abandonner (*une opinion*).

re·ceipt [ri'siːt] **1.** réception *f*; reçu *m*; accusé *m* de réception; ✝ récépissé *m*, quittance *f*; ✝ recette *f* (*a. cuis.*); **2.** acquitter.

re·ceiv·a·ble [ri'siːvəbl] recevable; ✝ à recevoir; **re·ceive** *v/t. usu.* recevoir; accepter; accueillir; essuyer (*un refus*), subir (*une défaite*); toucher (*un salaire*); *radio:* capter; ⚖ receler (*des objets volés*); ⚖ être condamné à; *v/i.* recevoir; **re'ceived** reçu; admis; ✝ *sur facture:* pour acquit; **re'ceiv·er** personne *f* qui reçoit; *lettre:* destinataire *mf*; *tél.*, *téléph.* récepteur *m*; *radio:* poste *m* (récepteur); ✝ réceptionnaire *m*; (*a. ~ of stolen goods*) receleur (-euse *f*) *m*; ⚖ (*official ~*) administrateur *m* judiciaire, (*en France*) syndic *m* de faillite; ⚒, *phys.* récipient *m,* ballon *m*; *téléph.* lift the ~ décrocher; **re'ceiv·ing 1.** réception *f*; ⚖ recel *m*; **2.** récepteur (-trice *f*); ~ set poste *m* récepteur.

re·cen·cy ['ri:snsi] caractère *m* récent.

re·cen·sion [ri'senʃn] révision *f*; texte *m* révisé.

re·cent □ ['ri:snt] récent; de fraîche date; nouveau (-el *devant une voyelle ou un h muet*; -elle *f*; -eaux *m/pl.*); **'re·cent·ly** récemment, dernièrement; **'re·cent·ness** caractère *m* récent.

re·cep·ta·cle [ri'septəkl] récipient *m*; ♀ (*a. floral* ~) réceptacle *m* (*a. fig.*).

re·cep·tion [ri'sepʃn] réception *f* (*a. radio*); accueil *m*; acceptation *f* (*d'une théorie*); **re'cep·tion·ist** réceptionniste *mf*; **re'cep·tion-room** salle *f* de réception, salon *m*.

re·cep·tive □ [ri'septiv] réceptif (-ive *f*); sensible (à, of); **re·cep-'tiv·i·ty** réceptivité *f*.

re·cess [ri'ses] vacances *f/pl.* (*a.* ⚖, *a. parl.*); *Am.* école: récréation *f*; recoin *m*; enfoncement *m*; niche *f*; embrasure *f*; ~es *pl. fig.* replis *m/pl.*

re·ces·sion [ri'seʃn] retraite *f*, recul *m*; ✝ récession *f*; **re'ces·sion·al 1.** *eccl.* de sortie; *parl.* pendant les vacances; **2.** *eccl.* (*a.* ~ hymn) hymne *m* de sortie du clergé.

re·chris·ten ['ri:'krisn] rebaptiser.

rec·i·pe ['resipi] *cuis.* recette *f* (*a. fig.*); ✚ ordonnance *f*; *pharm.* formule *f*; ~ book livre *m* de cuisine.

re·cip·i·ent [ri'sipiənt] personne *f* qui reçoit; destinataire *mf*; ⚒ récipient *m*.

re·cip·ro·cal [ri'siprəkəl] **1.** □ réciproque (*a. gramm., phls., a.* ⅄ figure); ⅄ inverse (*fonction, raison*); mutuel(le *f*); **2.** ⅄ réciproque *f,* inverse *m*; **re'cip·ro·cate** [~keit] *v/i.* retourner le compliment; ⊕ avoir un mouvement alternatif; *v/t.* échanger; répondre à; **re·cip·ro-'ca·tion** (action *f* de payer de) retour *m*; ⊕ va-et-vient *m/inv.*; **rec·i·proc·i·ty** [resi'prɔsiti] réciprocité *f*.

re·cit·al [ri'saitl] récit *m,* narration *f*; ♫ exposé *m* (*des faits*); ♩ récital (*pl.* -s) *m*; audition *f*; **rec·i·ta·tion** [resi'teiʃn] récitation *f*; **rec·i·ta-**

tive ♩ [ˌrɛtə'ti:v] récitatif *m*; **re·cite** [ri'sait] réciter (*un poème*); déclamer; énumérer; ⚖ exposer (*les faits*); **re'cit·er** récitateur (-trice *f*) *m*; livre *m* de récitations.

reck·less □ ['reklis] téméraire; ~ of insouciant de; **'reck·less·ness** témérité *f*, imprudence *f*; insouciance *f*.

reck·on ['rekn] *v/t.* compter (parmi among, with); calculer; juger; estimer; considérer (comme for, as); ~ up calculer, additionner; *v/i.* compter (sur, [up]on), calculer; ~ with faire rendre compte à; compter avec (*q., a. des difficultés etc.*); **'reck·on·er** calculateur (-trice *f*) *m*; barème *m*; **'reck·on·ing** compte *m,* calcul *m*; estimation *f*; ✝ règlement *m*; note *f*; addition *f*; *fig.* be out in (*ou of*) one's ~ s'être trompé dans son calcul; être loin de compte.

re·claim [ri'kleim] *fig.* tirer (de, from); corriger (*q.*), réformer (*q.*); civiliser; ramener (à, to); défricher, rendre cultivable, gagner sur l'eau (*du terrain*); assécher (*un marais*); ⊕ récupérer; régénérer(*l'huile etc.*); **re'claim·a·ble** corrigible (*personne*); amendable (*terrain*); asséchable (*marais*); ⊕ récupérable.

rec·la·ma·tion [reklə'meiʃn] réforme *f*; défrichement *m*, mise *f* en valeur; récupération *f*; réclamation *f*.

re·cline [ri'klain] *v/t.* reposer; coucher; *v/i.* être couché; se reposer; ~ upon s'étendre sur; *fig.* être appuyé sur; **re'clin·ing chair** confortable *m*; fauteuil *m*.

re·cluse [ri'klu:s] **1.** retiré du monde; reclus; **2.** reclus(e *f*) *m*; anachorète *m*; solitaire *mf*.

rec·og·ni·tion [rekəg'niʃn] reconnaissance *f*; **rec·og·niz·a·ble** □ ['~naizəbl] reconnaissable; **re·cog-ni·zance** ⚖ [ri'kɔgnizəns] caution *f* personnelle; engagement *m*; **rec·og·nize** ['rekəgnaiz] reconnaître (*a. fig.*) (à, by); saluer (*dans la rue*).

re·coil [ri'kɔil] **1.** se détendre; reculer (devant, from) (*personne, arme à feu*); *fig.* rejaillir (sur, on); **2.** rebondissement *m*; détente *f*; ✗ recul *m*; mouvement *m* de dégout.

re·coin [ri:'kɔin] refrapper.

rec·ol·lect 1. [rekə'lekt] se souvenir de; se rappeler (*qch.*); **2.** ['ri:kə-**

'lekt] réunir de nouveau; **rec·ol·lec·tion** [rekə'lekʃn] souvenir *m*, mémoire *f*; *fig.* recueillement *m* (*de l'âme*).

re·com·mence ['ri:kə'mens] recommencer.

rec·om·mend [rekə'mend] recommander; **rec·om'mend·a·ble** recommandable; **rec·om·men'da·tion** recommandation *f*; **rec·om'mend·a·to·ry** [~ətəri] de recommandation.

re·com·mis·sion ['ri:kə'miʃn] réarmer (*un navire*); réintégrer dans les cadres (*un officier*).

re·com·mit ['ri:kə'mit] *parl.* renvoyer à une commission; commettre de nouveau; ~ *to prison* renvoyer en prison.

rec·om·pense ['rekəmpens] **1.** récompense *f* (de, *for*); compensation *f* (de, *pour for*); dédommagement *m* (de, *for*); **2.** récompenser (q. de qch., s.o. *for s.th.*); réparer (*un mal*); dédommager (q. de qch., s.o. *for s.th.*).

re·com·pose ['ri:kəm'pouz] rarranger; calmer de nouveau; 🎜 recomposer; ~ *o.s. to* se disposer de nouveau à.

rec·on·cil·a·ble ['rekənsailəbl] conciliable, accordable (avec, *with*); **'rec·on·cile** réconcilier (avec *with*, to); faire accorder; faire accepter (qch. à q., s.o. *to s.th.*); ajuster (*une querelle*); ~ *o.s. to* se résigner à; **'rec·on·cil·er** réconciliateur (-trice *f*) *m*; **rec·on·cil·i·a·tion** [~sili-'eiʃn] réconciliation *f*; conciliation *f* (*d'opinions contraires*).

rec·on·dite □ *fig.* ['ri'kəndait] abstrus; obscur.

re·con·di·tion ['ri:kən'diʃn] rénover, remettre à neuf.

re·con·nais·sance ✕ [ri'kɔnisəns] reconnaissance *f*.

rec·on·noi·ter, rec·on·noi·tre ✕ [rekə'nɔitə] *v/t.* reconnaître; *v/i.* faire une reconnaissance.

re·con·quer ['ri:'kɔŋkə] reconquérir; **'re'con·quest** ✕ [~kwest] reprise *f*.

re·con·sid·er ['ri:kən'sidə] examiner de nouveau; revoir; revenir sur (*une décision*); **'re·con·sid·er'a·tion** examen *m* de nouveau; révision *f*.

re·con·sti·tute ['ri:'kɔnstitju:t] re-

constituer; **'re·con·sti'tu·tion** reconstitution *f*.

re·con·struct ['ri:kəns'trʌkt] reconstruire; reconstituer (*un crime*); **'re·con'struc·tion** reconstruction *f*; *crime:* reconstitution *f*.

re·con·ver·sion ✝ ['ri:kən'və:ʃn] reconversion *f* (*en industries de paix*); **'re·con'vert** reconvertir; transformer.

rec·ord 1. ['rekɔ:d] mémoire *m*; ⚖ enregistrement *m*; ⚖ feuille *f* d'audience; ⚖ procès-verbal *m* de témoignage; minute *f*; note *f*; dossier *m*; (*a. police-*~) casier *m* judiciaire; registre *m*; monument *m*; ♪ disque *m*, *a.* enregistrement *m*; *sp. etc.* record *m*; ~ *breaker* personne *f* ou chose *f* qui bat le record; ~ *holder* recordman (*pl.* -men) *m*, recordwoman (*pl.* -men) *f*; ~ *time* temps *m* record; *it is left* (*ou stands*) *on* ~ *that* il est rapporté que; *place on* ~ prendre acte de; consigner par écrit; *beat* (*ou break*) *the* ~ battre le record; *set up* (*ou establish*) *a* ~ établir un record; ⚖ *Office* les Archives *f/pl.*; *surt. Am.* off *the* ~ non officiel(le *f*); confidentiel(le *f*); *on the* ~ authentique; **2.** [ri'kɔ:d] enregistrer; consigner par écrit; rapporter, relater; *by* ~ed *delivery* en recommandé; ~ing *apparatus* appareil *m* enregistreur; (*a. tape-*~) magnétophone *m*; **re'cord·er** personne *f* qui enregistre; ⚖ (*sorte de*) juge *m* municipal (= *avocat chargé de remplir certaines fonctions de juge*); appareil *m* enregistreur; ♪ flûte *f* à bec.

re·count¹ [ri'kaunt] raconter.

re·count² ['ri:'kaunt] recompter.

re·coup [ri'ku:p] (se) dédommager; indemniser; ⚖ défalquer.

re·course [ri'kɔ:s] recours *m*; expédient *m*; *have* ~ *to* avoir recours à, recourir à.

re·cov·er¹ [ri'kʌvə] *v/t.* retrouver, recouvrer (*a. la santé*); regagner; rentrer en possession de; reprendre (*haleine*); rattraper (*de l'argent, le temps perdu*); obtenir; ⊕ récupérer; *be* ~ed être remis (*malade*); *v/i.* guérir; (*a.* ~ *o.s.*) se remettre; ⚖ se faire dédommager (*par q.*).

re·cov·er² ['ri:'kʌvə] recouvrir; regarnir (*un fauteuil*).

re·cov·er·a·ble [ri'kʌvərəbl] recouvrable, récupérable; guérissable (*personne*); **re'cov·er·y** recouvrement *m*; ⊕ récupération *f*; rétablissement *m* (*a. fig.*), guérison *f*; ✝ reprise *f*; redressement *m* (*économique*); ⚖ obtention *f* (*de dommages-intérêts*); *mot.* ~ *vehicle* dépanneuse *f*.

rec·re·an·cy ['rekriənsi] lâcheté *f*; apostasie *f*; **'rec·re·ant 1.** □ lâche; infidèle, apostat; **2.** lâche *m*; renégat *m*.

re·cre·ate[1] ['ri:kri'eit] recréer.

rec·re·ate[2] ['rekrieit] *v/t.* divertir; *v/i.* (*a.* ~ *o.s.*) se divertir; **rec·re·'a·tion** récréation *f*, divertissement *m*; délassement *m*; ~ *centre* (*Am. center*) centre *m* de loisirs; ~ *ground* terrain *m* de jeux; *école:* cour *f* de récréation; **'rec·re·a·tive** divertissant, récréatif (-ive *f*).

re·crim·i·nate [ri'krimineit] récriminer; **re·crim·i·na·tion** récrimination *f*.

re·cru·desce [ri:kru:'des] s'enflammer de nouveau (*plaie*); reprendre (*maladie, a. fig.*); **re·cru·'des·cence** recrudescence *f* (*a. fig.*).

re·cruit [ri'kru:t] **1.** recrue *f* (*a. fig.*); **2.** *v/t.* ✕ recruter (*a. pol.*); ✕ *hist.* racoler (*des hommes pour l'armée*); *fig.* apporter *ou* faire des recrues; *fig.* restaurer (*la santé*); *v/i.* faire des recrues; se remettre (*malade*); **re·'cruit·ment** recrutement *m*; racolage *m*; *santé:* rétablissement *m*.

rec·tan·gle ['rektæŋgl] rectangle *m*; **rec·'tan·gu·lar** □ [~gjulə] rectangulaire.

rec·ti·fi·a·ble ['rektifaiəbl] rectifiable; **rec·ti·fi·ca·tion** [~fi'keiʃn] rectification *f* (*a.* ⚗, ⚛, ⚡); ⚡ redressement *m*; **rec·ti·fi·er** ['~faiə] rectificateur (-trice *f*) *m*; ⚛ rectificateur *m*; ⚡, *radio:* redresseur *m*; **rec·ti·fy** ['~fai] rectifier (*a.* ⚗, ⚛); corriger (*a.* ⚗); ⚡, *radio:* redresser; **rec·ti·lin·e·al** [rekti-'linjəl], **rec·ti·lin·e·ar** □ [~njə] rectiligne; **rec·ti·tude** ['~tju:d] rectitude *f*; *caractère:* droiture *f*.

rec·tor ['rektə] curé *m*; *univ.* recteur *m*; *écoss.* directeur *m* (*d'une école*); **rec·tor·ate** ['~rit], **'rec·tor·ship** rectorat *m*; **'rec·to·ry** presbytère *m*; cure *f*.

rec·tum *anat.* ['rektəm] rectum *m*.

re·cum·bent □ [ri'kʌmbənt] couché, étendu.

re·cu·per·ate [ri'kju:pəreit] *v/i.* se remettre, se rétablir; *v/t.* ⊕ récupérer; **re·cu·per'a·tion** rétablissement *m*; ⊕ récupération *f*; *power of* ~ = **re'cu·per·a·tive pow·er** [~rətiv 'pauə] pouvoir *m* de rétablissement.

re·cur [ri'kə:] revenir (*à la memoire, sur un sujet*); se renouveler; se reproduire (*a.* ♑); ~ *to s.o.'s mind* revenir à la mémoire de q.; ♑ ~*ring decimal* fraction *f* décimale périodique; **re·cur·rence** [ri'kʌrəns] renouvellement *m*, réapparition *f*; ♑ récidive *f*; ~ *to* retour *m* à; **re'cur·rent** □ périodique (*a.* ♑ *fièvre*); *anat.* récurrent.

re·curve [ri:'kə:v] (se) recourber.

rec·u·sant ['rekjuzənt] **1.** réfractaire (à, *against*); dissident; **2.** réfractaire *mf*; *eccl.* récusant(e *f*) *m*.

re·cy·cle [ri:'saikl] recycler, retraiter; **re'cy·cling** recyclage *m*, retraitement *m*.

red [red] **1.** rouge (*a. pol.*); roux (rousse *f*) (*cheveux, feuille*); ♀ *Cross* Croix-Rouge *f*; ♀ ~ *currant* groseille *f* rouge; *zo.* ~ *deer* cerf *m* commun; ⊕ ~ *heat* chaude *f* rouge; ~ *herring* hareng *m* saur; *fig.* draw ~ *herrings* brouiller la piste; *min.* ~ *lead* minium *m*; ~ *man see* redskin; *sl.* paint the town ~ faire la nouba, faire la bringue; **2.** rouge *m* (*a. pol. mf*); *billard:* bille *f* rouge; *surt. Am.* F sou *m* (de bronze); see ~ voir rouge; *Am.* F be in the ~ avoir débit en banque; F in the ~ en déficit.

re·dact [ri'dækt] rédiger, mettre au point; **re'dac·tion** rédaction *f*; mise *f* au point; révision *f*.

red·breast ['redbrest] (*souv. robin* ~) see robin; **'red·cap** 🎖 *Am.* porteur *m*; *Angl.* soldat *m* de la police militaire; **red·den** ['redn] *vt/i.* rougir; *v/i.* roussir (*feuille*); rougeoyer (*ciel*); **'red·dish** rougeâtre; roussâtre; **red·dle** ['~l] ocre *f* rouge.

re·dec·o·rate [ri:'dekəreit] peindre (et tapisser) à nouveau (*une chambre etc.*); **'re·dec·o'ra·tion** nouvelle décoration *f*; nouveau décor *m*.

re·deem [ri'di:m] racheter (*eccl., obligation, défaut, esclave, temps, etc.*); amortir (*une dette*); purger (*une hypothèque*); dégager, retirer (*une montre etc.*); honorer (*une traite*); libérer (*un esclave*); tenir (*une* *promesse*); F réparer (*le temps perdu*); *fig.* arracher (à, *from*); *fig.* ~*ing feature* qualité *f* qui rachète les défauts (*de q.*), *le seul bon côté* (*de q.*); **re'deem·a·ble ✝** rachetable, amortissable; **Re'deem·er** Rédempteur *m*, Sauveur *m*.

re·de·liv·er ['riːdi'livə] remettre de nouveau (*une lettre*); répéter.

re·demp·tion [ri'dempʃn] *eccl.* rédemption *f*; *crime, esclave, etc., a.* ✝: rachat *m*; ✝ amortissement *m*; dégagement *m*; purge *f*; **re'demp·tive** rédempteur (-trice *f*).

re·de·ploy ['riːdi:plɔi] réorganiser; ⚔ redéployer; **re·de'ploy·ment** réorganisation *f*; ⚔ redéploiement *m*.

re·de·vel·op ['riːdi:veləp] *urbanisme:* (re)mettre en valeur; **re·de'vel·op·ment** (re)mise *f* en valeur.

red...: '~**faced** rougeaud, rubicond; rougissant (*de colère, gêne etc.*); '~**haired** roux (rousse *f*), rouquin; '~**hand·ed** *fig. catch s.o. (be caught)* ~ prendre q. (être pris) en flagrant délit *ou* les mains dans le sac; '~**head** F rouquin(e*f*) *m*; '~**head·ed** rouquin; '~**hot** (chauffé au) rouge; *fig.* ardent, enthousiaste; *fig.* tout chaud, (de) denière heure.

red·in·te·grate [re'dintigreit] rétablir (*qch.*) dans son intégrité; réintégrer (*q.*) dans ses possessions; **red·in·te'gra·tion** rétablissement *m* intégral; réintégration *f*.

re·di·rect ['riːdi'rekt] faire suivre, adresser de nouveau (*une lettre etc.*).

re·dis·cov·er ['riːdis'kʌvə] retrouver; redécouvrir.

re·dis·trib·ute [riːdis'tribjuːt] redistribuer; répartir de nouveau.

red-let·ter day ['redletə'dei] jour *m* de fête; *fig.* jour *m* de bonheur.

red-light dis·trict *Am.* ['redlait-'distrikt] quartier *m* réservé *ou* malfamé.

red·ness ['rednis] rougeur *f*; *cheveux, feuille:* rousseur *f*.

re·do ['riː'duː] [*irr.* (do)] refaire.

red·o·lence ['redoləns] odeur *f*; parfum *m*; '**red·o·lent** parfumé; qui a une forte odeur (de, *of*); *fig.* *be* ~ *of* sentir (*qch.*).

re·dou·ble [ri'dʌbl] redoubler.

re·doubt ⚔ [ri'daut] réduit *m*, redoute *f*; **re'doubt·a·ble** *poét.* redoutable.

re·dound [ri'daund]: ~ *to* contribuer à; résulter (*de qch.*) pour; ~ (*up*)*on* rejaillir sur.

re·draft ['riː'drɑːft] **1.** nouvelle rédaction *f*; ✝ retraite *f*; **2.** (*ou* **re·draw** ['riː'drɔː] [*irr.* (*draw*)] rédiger; ✝ faire retraite *bis*.

re·dress [ri'dres] **1.** redressement *m*; remède *m*; réforme *f*; réparation *f* (*a.* ⚖); **2.** redresser; réparer; rétablir (*l'équilibre*).

red...: '~**skin** Peau-Rouge (*pl.* Peaux-Rouges) *m*; '~**start** *orn.* rouge-queue (*pl.* rouges-queues) *m*; ~ **tape** ['~'teip], ~**tap·ism** ['~'teipizm] bureaucratie *f*, F paperasserie *f*; '~'**tap·ist** bureaucrate *m*; paperassier (-ère *f*) *m*.

re·duce [ri'djuːs] *fig.* réduire (*a.* ⚗, ⚕, ♪, ⚔ *une ville*) (en, *to*); ⚕, *a.* *fig.* ramener (à, *to*); abaisser (⚡, *la tension, la température*); (ra)baisser, diminuer (*le prix*); affaiblir (*a. phot.*; *q.*); ⚔ casser; amincir (*une planche*); ralentir (*la marche*); atténuer (*un contraste*); *fig.* ~ *to* ériger en; ~ *to writing* coucher ou consigner par écrit; **re'duc·i·ble** réductible (à, *to*); **re·duc·tion** [ri'dʌkʃn] réduction *f* (*a.* ✝, ⚕ *une ville*, ⚗, ♪); diminution *f*; ⚔ rétrogradation *f* (*d'un sous-officier*), cassation *f*; ✝ rabais *m*; ✝ remise *f* (*sur, on*); baisse *f* (*de température*); rapetissement *m* (*d'un dessin etc.*); *phot.* atténuation *f*; ⚖ relaxation *f*.

re·dun·dance, re·dun·dan·cy [ri'dʌndəns(i)] surplus *m*; surabondance *f*; **re'dun·dant** □ superflu; surabondant; *poét.* redondant.

re·du·pli·cate [riː'djuː·plikeit] redoubler; répéter; **re·du·pli'ca·tion** redoublement *m*.

re·dye ['riː'dai] (faire) reteindre.

re-ech·o [riː'ekou] *v/t.* répéter; *v/i.* résonner.

reed [riːd] roseau *m*; *poét.* chalumeau *m*; ♪ hautbois etc.: anche *f*.

re-ed·it ['riː'edit] rééditer.

re-ed·u·ca·tion ['riː·edju'keiʃn] rééducation *f*.

reed·y ['riːdi] couvert de *ou* abondant en roseaux; grinçant (*voix*); nasillard (*timbre*).

reef¹ [riːf] récif *m* (*de corail etc.*).

reef² ⚓ [~] **1.** ris *m*; ~*-knot* nœud *m* plat; **2.** prendre un ris dans (*la voile*); rentrer (*le beaupré etc.*).

reef·er[1] ['ri:fə] veste *f* quartier-maître, caban *m*.
reef·er[2] *Am. sl.* [~] cigarette *f* à marijuana.
reek [ri:k] **1.** odeur *f* forte; atmosphère *f* fétide; *écoss.* vapeur *f*; fumée *f*; **2.** exhaler une mauvaise odeur *ou* des vapeurs; *fig.* puer (qch., *of s.th.*); *écoss.* fumer; '**reek·y** enfumé.
reel [ri:l] **1.** *tex., papier, cin. a. film* ~: bobine *f*; *tél.* moulinet *m* (*a. canne à pêche*); *phot., a.* ⊕ rouleau *m*; *cin.* bande *f*; titubation *f*, chancellement *m*; *danse*: branle *m* écossais; **2.** *v/t.* bobiner; dévider; ~ *in* remonter; ~ *off* dévider; *fig.* réciter d'un trait; *v/i.* tournoyer; chanceler; tituber.
re-e·lect ['ri:i'lekt] réélire.
re-el·i·gi·ble ['ri:'elidʒəbl] rééligible.
re-en·act ['ri:i'nækt] remettre en vigueur; *théâ.* reproduire.
re-en·gage ['ri:in'geidʒ] ⚔ rengager; réintégrer (*un employé*); rengrener (*une roue dentée*); *mot.* ~ *the clutch* rembrayer.
re-en·list ⚔ ['ri:in'list] (se) rengager.
re-en·ter ['ri:'entə] *v/t.* rentrer dans; ⚕ inscrire de nouveau; *v/i.* rentrer; se présenter de nouveau (*à un examen*); '**re-'ent·er·ing, re-en·trant** [ri:'entrənt] rentrant; '**re-'en·try** rentrée *f*.
re-es·tab·lish ['ri:is'tæbliʃ] rétablir; '**re-es'tab·lish·ment** rétablissement *m*.
reeve ⚓ [ri:v] [*irr.*] passer (*un cordage dans une poulie*).
re-ex·am·i·na·tion ['ri:igzæmi'neiʃn] nouvel examen *m ou* ⚖ interrogatoire *m*; '**re-ex'am·ine** [~min] examiner *ou* ⚖ interroger de nouveau.
re-ex·change ['ri:iks'tʃeindʒ] nouvel échange *m*; ⚕ rechange *m*; ⚕ retraite *f*.
re·fec·tion [ri'fekʃn] rafraîchissement *m*; **re'fec·to·ry** [~təri] réfectoire *m*.
re·fer [ri'fə:] *v/t.* rapporter; rattacher (*a. une plante à sa famille*); soumettre (*à un tribunal*); s'en référer (à q. de qch., *s.th. to s.o.*); renvoyer (q. à q., *s.o. to s.o.*); *fig.* attribuer; *école*: ajourner (*un candidat*); ⚕ refuser d'honorer (*un chèque*); *v/i.* (*to*) se rapporter (à); se reporter (à) (*un document*); se référer (à) (*une autorité*); faire allusion (à), faire mention (de); reparler (de);
ref'er·a·ble: ~ *to* attribuable à; qui relève de; **ref·er·ee** [refə'ri:] **1.** répondant *m*; *sp.* arbitre *m*; ⚖ arbitre *m* expert; **2.** *sp.* arbitrer;
ref·er·ence ['refrəns] renvoi *m*, référence *f* (*à une autorité*); rapport *m*; mention *f*, allusion *f*; ⚖ compétence *f*; *cartographie*: point *m* coté; (*a. foot-note* ~) appel *m* de note; *typ.* (*ou* ~ *mark*) renvoi *m*; *accompagnant une demande d'emploi*: référence *f*; *in* (*ou with*) ~ *to* comme suite à, me (*etc.*) référant à; *terms pl. of* ~ mandat *m*, compétence *f*; *work of* ~, ~ *book* ouvrage *m* à consulter; ~ *library* bibliothèque *f* de consultation sur place; ~ *number* cote *f*; ⚕ numéro *m* de commande; ~ *point* point *m* de repère; *make* ~ *to* signaler, faire mention de.
ref·er·en·dum [refə'rendəm] (*a. people's ou national* ~) référendum *m*, plébiscite *m*.
re·fill ['ri:'fil] **1.** objet *m* de remplacement; pile *f ou* feuilles *f/pl. ou* mine *f* de rechange; **2.** *v/t.* remplir (de nouveau); *v/i. mot.* faire le plein.
re·fine [ri'fain] *v/t. fig.* épurer; raffiner; *v/i.* se raffiner (*a.* ⊕, *a. fig.*); ~ (*up*)*on* renchérir sur; **re'fine·ment** (r)affinage *m*; *fig. cruauté, goût, pensée*: raffinement *m*; **re'fin·er** raffineur *m* (*a. fig.*); ⊕ affineur *m*; **re'fin·er·y** ⊕ (r)affinerie *f*; *fer*: finerie *f*.
re·fit ['ri:'fit] **1.** *v/t.* ⚓ radouber; réarmer; ⊕ rajuster; remonter (*une usine*); *v/i.* réparer ses avaries; réarmer; **2.** (*a.* '**re'fit·ment**) ⚓ radoub *m*, réparation *f*; réarmement *m*; ⊕ rajustement *m*; remontage *m*.
re·flect [ri'flekt] *v/t.* réfléchir, refléter; renvoyer; *fig.* être le reflet de; *v/i.* ~ (*up*)*on* réfléchir sur *ou* à; méditer sur; *fig.* faire du tort à; *fig.* critiquer; **re'flec·tion** réflexion *f* (*a. fig.*); reflet *m* (*a. fig.*), image *f*; pensée *f*; blâme *m* (de, *on*); **re'flec·tive** □ réfléchissant; de réflexion; réfléchi (*esprit, personne*); **re'flec·tor** réflecteur *m*; *cycl. rear* ~ catadioptre *m*.
re·flex ['ri:fleks] **1.** reflété; réfléchi (*a.* ⚘); *physiol.* réflexe; *fig.* indirect; *physiol.* ~ *action* (mouvement *m*)

réflexe *m*; *phot.* ~ *camera* (appareil *m*) reflex *m*; 2. reflet *m*; *physiol.* réflexe *m*; **re·flex·ive** □ [ri'fleksiv] réfléchi (*a. gramm.*).

ref·lu·ent ['refluənt] qui reflue.

re·flux ['ri:flʌks] reflux *m*; jusant *m* (*marée*). [boisement *m*.)

ref·or·est·a·tion ['ri:fɔris'teiʃn] re-)

re·form[1] [ri'fɔ:m] 1. réforme *f*; 2. (se) réformer, corriger; apporter des réformes à.

re·form[2] ['ri:fɔ:m] (se) reformer.

ref·or·ma·tion [refə'meiʃn] réformation *f*; réforme *f* (*a. eccl.* ♎); **re·form·a·to·ry** [ri'fɔ:mətəri] 1. de réforme; de correction; 2. maison *f* de correction; **re'formed** réformé (*a. eccl.*); **re'form·er** réformateur (-trice *f*) *m*; **re'form·ist** réformiste.

re·found [ri:'faund] refondre.

re·fract [ri'frækt] réfracter, briser (*un rayon de lumière*); ~*ing telescope* lunette *f* d'approche; **re'frac·tion** réfraction *f*; **re'frac·tive** *opt.* réfractif (-ive *f*); à réfraction; **re'frac·tor** *opt.* milieu *m* ou dispositif *m* réfringent; **re'frac·to·ri·ness** indocilité *f*; ⚕ *fièvre etc.*: opiniâtreté *f*; ⚕ nature *f* réfractaire; **re'frac·to·ry** 1. □ réfractaire (*a.* ⚒, ⊕ à l'épreuve du feu); indocile, récalcitrant; ⊕ rebelle (*minerai*); ⚕ opiniâtre (*fièvre etc.*); 2. ⊕ substance *f* réfractaire.

re·frain[1] [ri'frein] *v/t.* † refréner (*ses passions*); *v/i.* se retenir, s'abstenir (de, *from*).

re·frain[2] [~] refrain *m*.

re·fran·gi·ble *phys.* [ri'frændʒəbl] réfrangible.

re·fresh [ri'freʃ] (se) rafraîchir; (se) reposer; ranimer; **re'fresh·er** F rafraîchissement *m*; ⚖ honoraires *m/pl.* supplémentaires; **re'fresh·ment** rafraîchissement *m* (*a. cuis.*); délassement *m*; ~ *room* buffet *m*.

re·frig·er·ant [ri'fridʒərənt] ⚕, ⊕ réfrigérant (*a. su./m*); **re'frig·er·ate** [~reit] réfrigérer; *v/t. a.* frigorifier; **re'frig·er·at·ing** réfrigérant, frigorifique; **re'frig·er'a·tion** réfrigération *f*, frigorification *f*; **re'frig·er·a·tor** réfrigérateur *m*, glacière *f*, chambre *f* frigorifique; ~ *van* wagon *m* frigorifique.

re·fu·el ⚒, *mot.* [ri:'fjuəl] faire le plein (d'essence).

ref·uge ['refju:dʒ] refuge *m*, abri *m*; (lieu *m* d')asile *m*; *alp.* refuge *m*; *take* ~ *in* se réfugier dans (*a. fig.*); **ref·u·gee** [~'dʒi:] réfugié(e *f*) *m*.

re·ful·gence [ri'fʌldʒəns] splendeur *f*; **re'ful·gent** □ resplendissant.

re·fund [ri:'fʌnd] rembourser.

re·fur·bish ['ri:'fə:biʃ] remettre à neuf. [neuf.)

re·fur·nish ['ri:'fə:niʃ] meubler de)

re·fus·al [ri'fju:zl] refus *m*; droit *m* de refuser.

re·fuse[1] [ri'fju:z] refuser; *sp.* refuser de sauter (*cheval*); repousser, rejeter.

ref·use[2] ['refju:s] 1. de rebut; à ordures; de décharge; ⊕ ~ *water* eaux *f/pl.* vannes; 2. rebut *m*; déchets *m/pl.*; ordures *f/pl.* (*a. fig.*).

ref·u·ta·ble □ ['refjutəbl] réfutable; **ref·u·ta·tion** réfutation *f*; **re·fute** [ri'fju:t] réfuter.

re·gain [ri'gein] regagner, reprendre.

re·gal □ ['ri:gəl] royal (-aux *m/pl.*).

re·gale [ri'geil] *v/t.* régaler (de, *with*); *v/i.* se régaler (de *on*, *with*).

re·ga·li·a [ri'geiljə] *pl.* insignes *m/pl.*; joyaux *m/pl.* de la Couronne.

re·gard [ri'gɑ:d] 1. † regard *m*; égard *m*; attention *f*; estime *f*, respect *m*; *have* ~ *to* tenir compte de; avoir égard à, faire attention à; *with* ~ *to* quant à; pour ce qui concerne; *with kind* ~*s* avec les sincères amitiés (de, *from*); 2. regarder (comme, *as*); prendre garde à; concerner; *as* ~*s* en ce qui concerne; **re'gard·ful** □ [~ful] plein d'égards (pour q., *of s.o.*); attentif (-ive *f*) (à, *of*), soigneux (-euse *f*) (de, *of*); **re'gard·ing** à l'égard de; quant à, en ce qui concerne; **re'gard·less** □ inattentif (-ive *f*) (à, *of*); peu soigneux (-euse *f*) (de, *of*); ~ *of* sans regarder à.

re·gat·ta [ri'gætə] régate *f*, -s *f/pl.*

re·ge·late ['ri:dʒəleit] se regeler.

re·gen·cy ['ri:dʒənsi] régence *f*.

re·gen·er·ate 1. [ri'dʒenəreit] (se) régénérer; 2. [~rit] régénéré; **re·gen·er'a·tion** régénération *f* (*a. fig.*); *fig.* amélioration *f*; ⊕ *huile*: épuration *f*; **re'gen·er·a·tive** [~rətiv] régénérateur (-trice *f*).

re·gent ['ri:dʒənt] 1. régent; 2. régent(e *f*) *m*; *Am.* membre *m* du

conseil d'administration; 're·gent-
ship régence f.
reg·i·cide ['redʒisaid] régicide mf;
crime: régicide m.
reg·i·men ['redʒimen] ♃, *gramm.,
etc.* régime m.
reg·i·ment ✗ **1.** ['redʒimənt] régiment m; *fig.* légion f; **2.** ['⁀mənt]
enrégimenter; organiser; **reg·i-
'men·tal** ✗ de *ou* du régiment;
reg·i'men·tal·ly [⁀təli] par régiment; **reg·i'men·tals** ✗ [⁀tlz] *pl.*
(grand) uniforme m; **reg·i·men'tation** enrégimentation f.
re·gion ['ri:dʒən] région f; *fig.* domaine m; '**re·gion·al** □ régional
(-aux m/pl.); *radio:* (*a.* ⁀ station)
poste m régional.
reg·is·ter ['redʒistə] **1.** registre m
(*a.* ✝, ♪, *⁂ fourneau*); matricule f;
liste f (*électorale*); ⊕ *cheminée:*
rideau m; ⚓ lettre f de mer; ♪ *voix:*
étendue f; compteur m (*kilométrique*); ⁀ office bureau m d'enregistrement *ou* de l'état civil *ou* de placement; ⚓ net ⁀ ton tonne f de jauge
nette; **2.** *v/t.* enregistrer (*a. bagages,
a. Am. émotion*); inscrire; immatriculer (*une auto, un étudiant*); *thermomètre:* marquer (*les degrés*); ✝
déposer (*une marque*), recommander
(*une lettre etc.*); *typ.* mettre en registre; *v/i.* ⊕ coïncider exactement;
typ. être en registre; s'inscrire (*personne*); '**reg·is·tered** enregistré,
inscrit, immatriculé; recommandé
(*lettre etc.*); ⁀ design modèle m déposé; ✝ ⁀ share (*ou Am.* stock)
action f nominative.
reg·is·trar [redʒis'trɑ:] teneur m des
registres; officier m de l'état civil;
⚖ greffier m; *univ.* secrétaire m; get
married before the ⁀ se marier ci-
vilement; **reg·is·tra·tion** [⁀'treiʃn]
enregistrement m, inscription f;
auto etc.: immatriculation f; *marque:*
dépôt m; ⁀ fee droit m d'inscription; *lettre etc.:* taxe f de recommandation; '**reg·is·try** enregistrement m; *admin.* greffe m; (*a.* ⁀ of-
fice) bureau m d'enregistrement *ou*
de l'état civil *ou* de placement; *servants'* ⁀ agence f de placement.
reg·nant ['regnənt] régnant.
re·gress 1. ['ri:gres] retour m en
arrière; *fig.* déclin m; **2.** [ri'gres]
retourner en arrière, reculer; *biol.
etc.* rétrograder; **re·gres·sion** [ri-

'greʃn] rétrogression f; *biol.* régression f; ⚕ rebroussement m; **re·gres-
sive** □ [ri'gresiv] régressif (-ive f).
re·gret [ri'gret] **1.** regret m (de at,
for); **2.** regretter (de *inf., gér. ou to
inf.*); **re'gret·ful** □ [⁀ful] plein de
regrets; ⁀ly avec *ou* à regret; **re-
'gret·ta·ble** □ regrettable; à regretter.
re·group ['ri:'gru:p] (se) regrouper;
re'group·ment regroupement m.
reg·u·lar ['regjulə] **1.** □ régulier
(-ère f) (*a.* ✗, *eccl., etc.*); habituel
(-le f); ordinaire, normal (-aux
m/pl.); réglé; réglementaire, dans
les règles; *Am.* ⁀ gas, *Brit.* ⁀ petrol
essence f ordinaire; **2.** *eccl.* régulier
m, religieux m; ✗ soldat m de carrière; **reg·u·lar·i·ty** [⁀'læriti] régularité f.
reg·u·late ['regjuleit] régler (*a.* ⊕,
a. fig.); diriger; ⊕ ajuster; '**reg·u-
lat·ing** ⊕ régulateur (-trice f); ré-
glant; **reg·u'la·tion 1.** règlement
m; ⊕ réglage m; ✝ direction f;
2. réglementaire; d'ordonnance (*revolver*); '**reg·u·la·tive** □ régulateur (-trice f); '**reg·u·la·tor** régulateur (-trice f) m; ⊕ régulateur m;
⊕ ⁀ lever registre m.
re·gur·gi·tate [ri'gə:dʒiteit] *v/t.*
régurgiter, regorger; *v/i.* refluer,
regorger.
re·ha·bil·i·tate [ri:ə'biliteit] réhabiliter; **re·ha·bil·i'ta·tion** réhabilitation f; *finances:* assainissement m.
re·hash *fig.* ['ri:'hæʃ] réchauffer.
re·hears·al [ri'hə:sl] récit m détaillé;
♪, *théâ.* répétition f; **re·hearse**
[ri'hə:s] énumérer; raconter (tout
au long); ♪, *théâ.* répéter.
re·heat ['ri:'hi:t] réchauffer.
reign [rein] **1.** règne m (*a. fig.*); in
the ⁀ *of* sous le règne de; **2.** régner
(*sur, over*) (*a. fig.*).
re·im·burse ['ri:im'bə:s] rembourser (*a.* ✝) (q. de qch., s.o. [for]
s.th.); '**re·im'burse·ment** remboursement m.
rein [rein] **1.** rêne f; guide f; *fig.*
give ⁀ to lâcher la bride à; **2.**: ⁀ in
ou up ou back retenir.
rein·deer *zo.* ['reindiə] renne m.
re·in·force [ri:in'fɔ:s] **1.** renforcer;
affermir (*la santé*); ⊕ ⁀d concrete
béton m armé; **2.** ⊕ armature f;
canon: renfort m; '**re·in'force-
ments** ✗ *pl.* renfort m, -s m/pl.

re·in·sert ['riːin'səːt] réinsérer; remettre en place.
re·in·stall ['riːin'stɔːl] réinstaller;
'**re·in'stal(l)·ment** réinstallation f.
re·in·state ['riːin'steit] réintégrer
(*dans ses fonctions*); rétablir; '**re·in-**
'**state·ment** réintégration f; rétablissement m.
re·in·sur·ance ['riːin'ʃuərəns] réass-
urance f; contre-assurance f; **re-**
in·sure ['~'ʃuə] réassurer.
re·in·vest ['riːin'vest] investir *etc.* de
nouveau (*see* invest).
re·is·sue ['riː'iʃjuː; *surt.* Am. 'riː'iʃuː]
1. rééditer (*un livre*); ✝ émettre de
nouveau; **2.** nouvelle édition f *ou*
✝ émission f.
re·it·er·ate [riː'itəreit] réitérer, répéter; **re·it·er'a·tion** réitération f,
répétition f.
re·ject [ri'dʒekt] rejeter; refuser;
repousser; ⊕ mettre au rebut; **re-**
'**jec·tion** rejet m; refus m; repous-
sement m; **~s** *pl.* rebuts *m/pl.*,
pièces *f/pl.* de rebut; **re'jec·tor**
cir·cuit *radio:* filtre m.
re·joice [ri'dʒɔis] *v/t.* réjouir (*q.*); **~d**
heureux (-euse f) (de *at, by*); *v/i.*
se réjouir (de *at, in*); **re'joic·ing**
1. □ réjouissant; plein de joie (*personne*); **2.** (*souv.* **~s** *pl.*) réjouissances
f/pl., fête f. [réunir (à *to*, *with*).\
re·join¹ ['riː'dʒɔin] (se) rejoindre;⌡
re·join² [ri'dʒɔin] répliquer; **re-**
'**join·der** ⚖ réplique f; repartie f.
re·ju·ve·nate [ri'dʒuːvineit] *vt/i.*
rajeunir; **re·ju·ve'na·tion**, **re·ju-**
ve·nes·cence [~'nesns] rajeunissement m.
re·kin·dle ['riː'kindl] (se) rallumer.
re·lapse [ri'læps] **1.** ⚕, *a.* fig. rechute f; **2.** retomber; ⚕ faire une
rechute.
re·late [ri'leit] *v/t.* (ra)conter; rattacher (à *to*, *with*); *v/i.* se rapporter,
avoir rapport (à, *to*); **re'lat·ed** ayant
rapport (à, *to*); apparenté (à, *to*)
(*personne*); allié (à, *to*); ○**re'lat·er**
conteur (-euse f) m, narrateur
(-trice f) m.
re·la·tion [ri'leiʃn] récit m, relation f; rapport m (à *to*, *with*); pa-
rent(e f) m; in **~** to par rapport à; **re-**
'**la·tion·ship** rapport m; lien m; relations *f/pl.*, rapports *m/pl.*; (liens
m/pl. de) parenté f; have a good **~** with
s.o. être en bons rapports avec q.;
s'entendre bien avec q.

rel·a·tive ['relətiv] **1.** □ relatif
(-ive f) (*a.* gramm.); qui se rapporte
(à, *to*); **2.** *adv.:* **~** to au sujet de;
3. *su.* gramm. pronom m relatif;
rel·a'tiv·i·ty relativité f.
re·lax [ri'læks] *v/t.* relâcher; détendre; desserrer (*une étreinte*); mitiger
(*un jugement etc.*); ⚕ enflammer (*la
gorge*); ⚕ relâcher (*le ventre*); *v/i.*
se relâcher; se détendre; diminuer;
se délasser; **re·lax'a·tion** relâchement m; détente f, repos m, délassement m; mitigation f.
re·lay¹ [ri'lei] **1.** relais m (*a.* ⚡);
⚡ contacteur m; relève f (*d'ouvriers*); radiodiffusion f relayée; *sp.*
~-race course f de ou à relais;
2. *radio:* relayer; **~ed by** (*ou* from)
en relais de.
re·lay² ['riː'lei] poser de nouveau;
remettre.
re·lease [ri'liːs] **1.** délivrance f; *fig.*
libération f; élargissement m; ✝
mise f en vente; ✝ acquit m; *cin.*
(*souv. first* **~**) mise f en circulation;
⚖ relaxation f (*d'un prisonnier*); ⚖
cession f (*de terres*); ⊕ mise f en
marche; ⊕ dégagement m; *phot.* déclencheur m; **2.** relâcher; libérer
(de *from*); lâcher; renoncer à (*un
droit*); faire la remise de (*une dette*);
céder (*des terres*); ✝ mettre en
vente; *cin.* mettre en circulation;
émettre, dégager (*la fumée etc.*); ⊕,
phot. déclencher; ⊕ décliquer; ⊕
mettre en marche.
rel·e·gate ['religeit] reléguer (à, *to*);
renvoyer (à, *to*); bannir (*q.*); *sp.* be **~d**
être relégué (à la division inférieure);
rel·e'ga·tion relégation f; mise f à
l'écart; renvoi m (*sp. à la division
inférieure*).
re·lent [ri'lent] s'adoucir; se laisser
attendrir; **re'lent·less** □ implacable; impitoyable.
rel·e·vance, **rel·e·van·cy** ['reli-
vəns(i)] pertinence f; applicabilité f
(à, *to*); rapport m (avec, *to*); '**rel·e-**
vant (à, *to*) pertinent; applicable;
qui se rapporte.
re·li·a·bil·i·ty [rilaiə'biliti] sûreté f;
véracité f; **re'li·a·ble** □ sûr; digne
de foi (*source*) *ou* de confiance (*personne*).
re·li·ance [ri'laiəns] confiance f;
place **~** on se fier à; **re'li·ant:** be **~**
on compter sur; se fier à.
rel·ic ['relik] relique f (*a. eccl.*); *fig.*

vestige *m*; ~s *pl.* restes *m/pl.*; **rel·ict** † [',\kt] veuve *f*.

re·lief [ri'li:f] soulagement *m*; décharge *f*; *détresse*: allégement *m*; ⚔ *endroit*: délivrance *f*; *garde etc.*: relève *f*; ⚖ *tort*: réparation *f*, redressement *m* (*a.* aux pauvres), aide *f*; △ relief *m*; *fig.* agrément *m*; *fig.* détente *f*; ⊕ dégagement *m*; *be on* ~ être un pauvre assisté; *poor* ~ secours *m* aux pauvres; ~ *work* secours *m* aux sinistrés; ~ *works pl.* travaux *m/pl.* publics organisés pour aider les chômeurs; *in* ~ *against* découpé sur; qui se détache sur.

re·lieve [ri'li:v] soulager (*a.* △ *une poutre*); alléger (*la détresse*); secourir, aider (*les pauvres etc.*); ⚔ dégager (*un endroit*, *a.* ⊕); ⚔ relever (*les troupes etc.*); *peint. etc.* mettre en relief, donner du relief à; *fig.* faire ressortir; *cost.* agrémenter (*de* *with*, *by*); débarrasser (*de*, *of*); *fig.* tranquilliser (*l'esprit*), dissiper (*l'ennui*); F ~ *nature* faire ses besoins.

re·lie·vo [ri'li:vou] relief *m*.

re·li·gion [ri'lidʒən] religion *f*.

re·li·gious □ [ri'lidʒəs] religieux (-euse *f*) (*a. fig.*, *a. eccl.*); dévot; pieux (-euse *f*); de piété; **re'li·gious·ness** piété *f*; F *fig.* religiosité *f*.

re·lin·quish [ri'liŋkwiʃ] renoncer à (*une idée, un projet, etc.*); abandonner; ⚖ délaisser; lâcher (*qch.*); **re'lin·quish·ment** abandon *m* (*de*, *of*); renonciation *f* (*à*, *of*). [*m*.]

rel·i·quar·y ['relikwəri] reliquaire

rel·ish ['reliʃ] **1.** goût *m*, saveur *f*; *fig.* attrait *m*; *cuis.* piment: soupçon *m*, pointe *f*; assaisonnement *m*; *with* ~ très volontiers; **2.** *v/t.* relever le goût de; savourer, goûter; *fig.* trouver du plaisir à, avoir le goût de; *did you* ~ *your dinner?* votre dîner vous a-t-il plu?; *v/i.* sentir (*qch.*, *of s.th.*), avoir un léger goût (*de*, *of*).

re·lo·cate ['ri:lou'keit] transférer, déplacer; **'re·lo'ca·tion** transfert *m*, déplacement *m*.

re·luc·tance [ri'lʌktəns] répugnance *f* (*à inf.*, *to inf.*); *phys.* reluctance *f*; **re'luc·tant** □ qui résiste; fait *ou* donné à contrecœur; *be* ~ *to* (*inf.*) être peu disposé à (*inf.*), hésiter à (*inf.*).

re·ly [ri'lai]: ~ (*up*)*on* compter sur, s'en rapporter à.

re·main [ri'mein] **1.** rester; demeurer; persister; **2.** ~*s pl.* restes *m/pl.*; vestiges *m/pl.*; **re'main·der** reste *m*, restant *m*; *livres*: solde *m* d'édition; ⚖ réversion *f* (*sur*, *to*).

re·make ['ri:'meik] *film*: nouvelle version *f* *ou* réalisation *f*, remake *m*.

re·mand [ri'mɑ:nd] **1.** ⚖ renvoyer (*un prévenu*) à une autre audience; **2.**: *on* ~ renvoyé à une autre audience; *prisoner on* ~ préventionnaire *mf*.

re·mark [ri'mɑ:k] **1.** remarque *f*; observation *f*; **2.** *v/t.* remarquer, observer; faire la remarque (*que*, *that*); *v/i.* (*sur*, [*up*]*on*) faire des remarques; commenter; **re'mark·a·ble** □ remarquable (*par*, *for*); frappant; singulier (-ère *f*); **re'mark·a·ble·ness** ce qu'il y a de remarquable (*dans*, *of*); mérite *m*.

re·mar·ry ['ri:'mæri] *v/t.* se remarier à (*q.*); remarier (*des divorcés*); *v/i.* se remarier.

re·me·di·a·ble □ [ri'mi:djəbl] réparable; remédiable; **re·me·di·al** □ [ri'mi:djəl] réparateur (-trice *f*); ⚕ curatif (-ive *f*); ~ *teaching* cours *m/pl.* de rattrapage.

rem·e·dy ['remidi] **1.** remède *m*; ⚖ réparation *f*; **2.** porter remède à, remédier.

re·mem·ber [ri'membə] se rappeler (*qch.*), se souvenir de (*qch.*); ne pas oublier (*a.* = *donner qch. à* [*q.*]); ~ *me to him!* dites-lui bien des choses de ma part!; *rappelez-moi à son bon souvenir!*; **re'mem·brance** souvenir *m*, mémoire *f*; *give my kind* ~*s to him!* dites-lui bien des choses de ma part!

re·mind [ri'maind] rappeler (*qch.* à *q.*, *s.o. of s.th.*); ~ *o.s. that* se rappeler que; **re'mind·er** mémento *m*; † rappel *m* de compte.

rem·i·nisce [remi'nis] remonter dans le passé, parler de *ou* évoquer ses souvenirs; **rem·i·nis·cence** [~'nisns] réminiscence *f*; souvenir *m*; **rem·i·nis·cent** □ qui se souvient (*de*, *of*); *be* ~ rappeler, faire penser à (*qch.*).

re·miss □ [ri'mis] négligent, insouciant; nonchalant; **re'mis·si·ble** [~əbl] rémissible; **re·mis·sion** [~'miʃn] dette, *peine*: remise *f*; ⚕, *eccl.* rémission *f*; *eccl.* pardon *m*;

relâchement *m*; re'miss·ness négligence *f*.

re·mit [ri'mit] *v/t.* remettre (*une dette, une peine*, ♰, *a. eccl.*); *eccl.* pardonner; relâcher; ⚖ renvoyer; *v/i.* diminuer d'intensité; *please* ⌐ prière de nous couvrir; re'mit·tance ♰ remise *f*; ♰ envoi *m* de fonds; re·mit'tee destinataire *mf*; re'mit·tent ⚕ rémittent; re'mit·ter ♰ remetteur (-euse *f*) *m*; envoyeur (-euse *f*) *m* (de fonds).

rem·nant ['remnənt] reste *m*, restant *m*; ♰ coupon *m* (*d'étoffe*); ⌐*s* *pl.* soldes *m/pl.*

re·mod·el ['ri:'mɔdl] remodeler; remanier; ⊕ transformer.

re·mon·strance [ri'mɔnstrəns] remontrance *f*; re'mon·strant 1. de remontrance; qui proteste (*personne*); 2. remontreur (-euse *f*) *m*; re'mon·strate [⌐streit] faire des représentations (à q., *with s.o.*; au sujet de, [*up*]*on*); protester (que, *that*).

re·morse [ri'mɔːs] remords *m* (pour, *for*; de, *at*); re'morse·ful □ [⌐ful] plein de remords; re'morse·less □ sans remords; impitoyable.

re·mote □ [ri'mout] écarté; éloigné; reculé; lointain; *fig.* vague; ⌐ con·trol ⊕ 1. commande *f* à distance; 2. télécommandé; re'mote·ness éloignement *m*; degré *m* éloigné; *fig.* faible degré (*de ressemblance*).

re·mount 1. [ri:'maunt] *v/t.* remonter (*a.* ✕); *v/i.* remonter (*a.* à cheval); 2. ✕ ['ri:maunt] (cheval *m* de) remonte *f*; *army* ⌐*s* *pl.* chevaux *m/pl.* de troupe.

re·mov·a·ble [ri'mu:vəbl] détachable; extirpable (*mal*); transportable; révocable; re'mov·al [⌐vəl] *tache etc.*: enlèvement *m*; *mot. pneu.*: démontage *m*; ⚕ *pansement*: levée *f*; déplacement *m*; transport *m*; *fonctionnaire*: révocation *f*; *abus, mal*: suppression *f*; déménagement *m*; ⌐ *expenses* frais *m/pl.* de déplacement; ⌐ *service* entreprise *f* de déménagements; ⌐ *van* voiture *f* de déménagement; re·move [⌐'mu:v] 1. *v/t.* enlever, ôter; écarter; chasser; déplacer; éloigner; révoquer (*un fonctionnaire*); assassiner; supprimer; ⌐ *furniture* déménager; *v/i.* se déplacer; déménager; 2. distance *f*; degré *m*; *école anglaise*: classe *f*

intermédiaire; *école:* passage *m* à une classe supérieure; re'mov·er déménageur *m*; 🜩 dissolvant *m*; *pour taches:* détachant *m*; *pour vernis etc.:* décapant *m*.

re·mu·ner·ate [ri'mju:nəreit] rémunérer (de, *for*); re·mu·ner·a·tion rémunération *f*; re'mu·ner·a·tive □ [⌐rətiv] rémunérateur (-trice *f*).

ren·ais·sance [rə'neisəns] Renaissance *f*.

re·nal *anat.* ['ri:nl] des reins, rénal (-aux *m/pl.*).

re·nas·cence [ri'næsns] retour *m* à la vie; Renaissance *f*; re'nas·cent renaissant.

rend [rend] [*irr.*] déchirer; *fig. a.* fendre.

ren·der ['rendə] rendre (*a. compte, forteresse, grâce, hommage, service*, ♪ *phrase, a. = faire devenir*); faire (*honneur*); traduire (en, *into*); ♰ remettre (un compte à q., *s.o. an account*); 🜩 enduire (de, *with*); ♪ interpréter (*un morceau*); *cuis.* clarifier, fondre; 'ren·der·ing ✕ reddition *f*; ♪ interprétation *f*; traduction *f*; *cuis.* clarification *f*, fonte *f*; 🜂 enduit *m*.

ren·dez·vous ['rɔndivu:] rendezvous *m*.

ren·di·tion [ren'diʃn] ✕ reddition *f*; *Am.* interprétation *f*; traduction *f*.

ren·e·gade ['renigeid] renégat(e *f*) *m*.

re·new [ri'nju:] renouveler; re'new·al [⌐əl] renouvellement *m*; remplacement *m*.

ren·net ['renit] présure *f*; *pomme:* reinette *f*.

re·nounce [ri'nauns] *v/t.* renoncer à, abandonner; répudier; *v/i. cartes:* renoncer.

ren·o·vate ['renoveit] renouveler; remettre à neuf; ren·o·va·tion renouvellement *m*; rénovation *f*; 'ren·o·va·tor rénovateur (-trice *f*) *m*.

re·nown [ri'naun] renom(mée *f*) *m*; re'nowned (*for*) renommé (pour), célèbre (par).

rent¹ [rent] 1. *prét. et p.p. de* rend; 2. déchirure *f*; *terrain:* fissure *f*.

rent² [⌐] 1. loyer *m*; location *f*; 2. louer; affermer (*une terre*); 'rent·a·ble qui peut se louer; affermable (*terre*); 'rent-a-'car (serv·ice) location *f* de voitures; 'rent·al (montant *m* du) loyer *m*; *Am.* location *f* (*d'une auto etc.*); ~ *value* valeur *f* locative; **ˈrent-charge** servitude *f* de rente (*à faire à un tiers*); **ˈrent·er** locataire *mf*; *cin.* distributeur *m*; **ˈrentˈfree 1.** *adj.* exempt de loyer; **2.** *adv.* sans payer de loyer.

re·num·ber [riˈnʌmbə] renuméroter, numéroter de nouveau; **reˈnum·ber·ing** renumérotage *m*.

re·nun·ci·a·tion [rinʌnsiˈeiʃn] (*of*) renoncement *m* (à); reniement *m* (de); ⚖ répudiation *f* (de).

re·oc·cu·pa·tion [riɔkjuˈpeiʃn] réoccupation *f* (*d'un pays, d'un territoire, etc.*); **reˈoc·cu·py** réoccuper (*un pays, un territoire, etc.*).

re·o·pen [ˈriːˈoupn] *v/t.* rouvrir; recommencer; *v/i.* se rouvrir (*plaie*); rentrer (*école*); *théâ.* rouvrir; **reˈo·pen·ing** réouverture *f*.

re·or·ga·ni·za·tion [ˈriːɔːgənaiˈzeiʃn] réorganisation *f*; ⚕ assainissement *m*; **reˈor·gan·ize** (se) réorganiser; ⚕ assainir.

rep ⚕ [rep] reps *m*. [*se*); remballer.

re·pack [ˈriːˈpæk] refaire (*une vali-*

re·paint [ˈriːˈpeint] repeindre.

re·pair[1] [riˈpɛə] **1.** réparation *f*; rétablissement *m* (*d'une maison etc.*); ⚓ radoub *m*; ~*s pl.* réparations *f/pl.*; réfection *f* (*d'une route*); ~ *kit* trousse *f* de réparation; ~ *man* réparateur *m*; ~ *shop* atelier *m* de réparations; (*damaged*) *beyond* ~ irréparable; *in* (*good*) ~ en bon état; *out of* ~ en mauvais état; '*road* ~*s*' 'chantier' *m*; *under* ~ en réparation; **2.** réparer (*a. fig.*); raccommoder (*un vêtement*); remettre en état (*une machine*); ⚓ radouber; rétablir (*la santé*).

re·pair[2] [~] se rendre (à, *to*).

re·pa·ra·ble [ˈrepərəbl] réparable; **rep·aˈra·tion** réparation *f* (*a. pol., a. fig.*); *pol. make* ~*s* réparer.

rep·ar·tee [repɑːˈtiː] repartie *f*, réplique *f* spirituelle; *be good at* ~ avoir de la repartie; avoir la repartie facile; savoir répondre du tac au tac.

re·par·ti·tion [riːpɑːˈtiʃn] répartition *f*; nouveau partage *m*.

re·pass [ˈriːˈpɑːs] *v/i.* passer de nouveau; repasser; *v/i.* repasser (devant); *parl.* voter de nouveau.

re·past [riˈpɑːst] repas *m*.

re·pa·tri·ate 1. [riːˈpætrieit] rapatrier; **2.** [~iit] rapatrié(e *f*) *m*; **ˈre·pa·triˈa·tion** rapatriement *m*.

re·pay [riːˈpei] [*irr.* (*pay*)] rembourser; récompenser; rendre (*de l'argent*); *fig.* se venger de; s'acquitter (de qch., *s.th.*; envers q., *s.o.*); *fig.* payer (de, *with*); **reˈpay·a·ble** remboursable; **reˈpay·ment** remboursement *m*; récompense *f*.

re·peal [riˈpiːl] **1.** abrogation *f*; ⚖ annulation *f*; **2.** abroger; révoquer; annuler.

re·peat [riˈpiːt] **1.** *v/t.* répéter; réitérer; recommencer; ⚕ ~ *an order* renouveler une commande (de qch., *for s.th.*); *v/i.* (*a.* ~ *o.s.*) se répéter; revenir (*nourriture*); être à répétition (*montre, fusil*); **2.** ♪ reprise *f*; renvoi *m*; ⚕ (*souv.* ~ *order*) commande *f* renouvelée; **reˈpeat·ed** □ réitéré; **reˈpeat·er** rediseur (-euse *f*) *m*; ⅍ fraction *f* périodique; montre *f ou* fusil *m* à répétition; *tél.* répétiteur *m*.

re·pel [riˈpel] repousser (*a. fig.*); rebuter; inspirer de la répulsion à; **reˈpel·lent** répulsif (-ive *f*).

re·pent [riˈpent] (*a.* ~ *of*) se repentir de.

re·pent·ance [riˈpentəns] repentir *m*; **reˈpent·ant** repenti.

re·peo·ple [ˈriːˈpiːpl] repeupler.

re·per·cus·sion [riːpəːˈkʌʃn] répercussion *f* (*a. fig.*); contre-coup *m*.

rep·er·to·ry ♪, *théâ., a. fig.* [ˈrepətəri] répertoire *m*.

rep·e·ti·tion [repiˈtiʃn] répétition *f*; recommencement *m*; *tél.* collationnement *m*; ♪ reprise *f*; ⚕ ~ *order* commande *f* renouvelée.

re·pine [riˈpain] se chagriner, se plaindre (de, *at*); **reˈpin·ing** □ mécontent; chagrin.

re·place [riːˈpleis] replacer, remettre en place; remplacer (par, *by*); *téléph.* raccrocher (*le récepteur*); **reˈplace·ment** remise *f* en place; remplacement *m*; ⊕ pièce *f* de rechange.

re·plant [ˈriːˈplɑːnt] replanter.

re·play *sp.* [ˈriːplei] match *m* rejoué.

re·plen·ish [riˈpleniʃ] remplir; se réapprovisionner (de, en *with*); **reˈplen·ish·ment** remplissage *m*; ravitaillement *m*.

re·plete [riˈpliːt] rempli, plein (de, *with*); **reˈple·tion** réplétion *f*; *eat to* ~ manger jusqu'à satiété.

rep·li·ca [ˈreplikə] *peint. etc.* réplique *f*, double *m* (*a. fig.*); *fig.* copie *f*.

rep·li·ca·tion [repli'keiʃn] ⚏ réplique *f*; repartie *f*; *fig.* copie *f*; répercussion *f*.

re·ply [ri'plai] **1.** (à, to) répondre; répliquer (*a.* ⚏); **2.** réponse *f*; ⚏ réplique *f*; ~ *postcard* carte *f* postale avec réponse payée.

re·port [ri'pɔːt] **1.** rapport *m* (sur, on); *journ.* reportage *m*; *école*, *a. météor.* bulletin *m*; *fig.* nouvelle *f*; rumeur *f*; *arme à feu*: détonation *f*; *fusil*: coup *m*; réputation *f*; *école*: ~ *card* bulletin *m* (scolaire); **2.** *v/t.* rapporter (*a. parl.*); faire un rapport sur; faire le compte rendu de; dire; signaler; *v/i. journ.* faire des reportages; faire un rapport (sur, [up]on); (*a. ~ o.s.*) se présenter (à, devant to); *gramm.* ~*ed speech* discours *m ou* style *m* indirect; **re'port·er** journaliste *m*, reporter *m*.

re·pose [ri'pouz] **1.** repos *m*; sommeil *m*; calme *m*; **2.** *v/t.* reposer (*q., sa tête, etc.*); ~ *trust etc.* in mettre sa confiance *etc.* en; *v/i.* se reposer; dormir; se délasser; *fig.* reposer (sur, [up]on); **re·pos·i·to·ry** [ri'pɔzitəri] dépôt *m*, entrepôt *m*; dépositaire *mf* (*personne*); *fig.* répertoire *m*.

re·pos·sess [ˈriːpəˈzes]: ~ *o.s. of* reprendre possession de (*qch.*).

rep·re·hend [repri'hend] blâmer, réprimander; **rep·re'hen·si·ble** □ répréhensible; **rep·re'hen·sion** réprimande *f*.

rep·re·sent [repri'zent] représenter (*a.* ♱, *a. théâ. une pièce*); *théâ.* jouer (*un personnage*); symboliser; signaler (qch. à q., *s.th.* to *s.o.*); **rep·re·sen'ta·tion** représentation *f* (*a.* ♱, ⚏, *pol., fig., théâ. pièce*); *théâ.* interprétation *f* (*d'un rôle*); *coll.* représentants *m/pl.*; *fig.* ~*s pl.* remontrance *f* courtoise; **rep·re'sent·a·tive** □ [~tətiv] **1.** représentatif (-ive *f*); *parl. a.* par députés; typique; *be* ~ *of* représenter (*qch.*); ~ *of* représentant (*qch.*); **2.** représentant(e *f*) *m*; *pol.* député *m*; *parl. Am.* House of ~s Chambre *f* des Représentants.

re·press [ri'pres] réprimer; retenir; étouffer; *psych.* refouler; **re·pres·sion** [ri'preʃn] (*a. psych. conscious* ~) répression *f*; *psych.* (*a. un-*

conscious ~) refoulement *m*; **re'pres·sive** □ répressif (-ive *f*), réprimant.

re·prieve [ri'priːv] **1.** surséance *f* (à, from); ⚏ commutation *f* de la peine capitale; **2.** accorder un délai à; ⚏ accorder une commutation de la peine capitale à (*q.*).

rep·ri·mand ['reprimaːnd] **1.** réprimande *f*; ⚏ blâme *m*; **2.** réprimander; ⚏ blâmer publiquement.

re·print ['riːˈprint] **1.** réimprimer; **2.** nouveau tirage *m*; réimpression*f*.

re·pris·als [ri'praizls] *pl.* représailles *f/pl.*

re·proach [ri'proutʃ] **1.** reproche *m*, blâme *m*; **2.** reprocher (qch. à q., *s.o. with s.th.*); faire des reproches (à q. au sujet de qch., *s.o. with s.th.*); **re'proach·ful** □ [~ful] réprobateur (-trice *f*).

rep·ro·bate ['reprobeit] **1.** vil, bas(se *f*); **2.** *eccl.* réprouvé(e *f*) *m*; F vaurien *m*; **3.** réprouver; **rep·ro·ba·tion** réprobation *f*.

re·pro·cess ['riːˈprouses] retraiter, recycler; ~*ing plant* usine *f* de retraitement *ou* de recyclage.

re·pro·duce [riːprə'djuːs] (se) reproduire; (se) multiplier; **re·pro·duc·tion** [~'dʌkʃn] reproduction *f* (*a. physiol., cin.,* ♱); copie *f*, imitation *f*; **re·pro'duc·tive** □ reproducteur (-trice *f*).

re·proof [ri'pruːf] reproche *m*, blâme *m*; réprimande *f*.

re·prov·al [ri'pruːvl] reproche *m*, blâme *m*; **re·prove** [~'pruːv] condamner; réprimander, reprendre.

rep·tile ['reptail] **1.** reptile *m* (*a. fig.*); *fig. a.* chien *m* couchant; **2.** rampant.

re·pub·lic [ri'pʌblik] république *f*; **re'pub·li·can** républicain (*a. su./mf*); **re'pub·li·can·ism** républicanisme *m*.

re·pub·li·ca·tion ['riːpʌbli'keiʃn] nouvelle publication *f, livre*: nouvelle édition *f*. [(*une loi*); rééditer.]

re·pub·lish ['riːˈpʌbliʃ] republier/

re·pu·di·ate [ri'pjuːdieit] répudier (*femme, dette, doctrine, etc.*); **re·pu·di·a·tion** répudiation *f*; *dette*: reniement *m*.

re·pug·nance [ri'pʌgnəns] répugnance *f*, antipathie *f* (pour to, against); **re'pug·nant** □ répugnant (à, *to*); incompatible (avec *to*, *with*); contraire (à *to*, *with*).

re·pulse [ri'pʌls] **1.** échec *m*; défaite *f*; rebuffade *f*; **2.** repousser (*a. fig.*); **re'pul·sion** *phys., a. fig.* répulsion *f*; *fig. a.* aversion *f*; **re'pul·sive** □ *phys., a. fig.* répulsif (-ive *f*); *fig.* froid, distant (*personne*).

re·pur·chase [ri'pəːtʃəs] **1.** rachat *m*; ₮₮ réméré *m*; **2.** racheter.

rep·u·ta·ble □ ['repjutəbl] honorable (*personne, a. emploi*); estimé; **rep·u·ta·tion** [ˌ'teiʃn] réputation *f*, renom *m*; **re·pute** [ri-'pjuːt] **1.** réputation *f*; *by* ~ de réputation; **2.** tenir pour; *be* ~*d to be* (*ou as*) passer pour; *be well (ill)* ~*d* avoir une belle (mauvaise) réputation; **re'put·ed** réputé; supposé; ₮₮ putatif (-ive *f*); **re'put·ed·ly** suivant l'opinion commune.

re·quest [ri'kwest] **1.** demande *f* (*a.* ✝); requête *f*; recherche *f*; *at s.o.'s* ~ à *ou* sur la demande de q.; *by* ~ sur demande; facultatif (-ive *f*) (*arrêt*); *in* (*great*) ~ (très) recherché, demandé; ~ *stop* arrêt *m* facultatif; (*musical*) ~ *programme* disques *m/pl. etc. ou* programme *m* des auditeurs; **2.** demander (qch. à q., *s.th. of s.o.*); à q. de *inf.*, *s.o. to inf.*); prier (q. de *inf.*, *s.o. to inf.*).

re·qui·em ['rekwiem] requiem *m/inv.*, messe *f* pour les morts.

re·quire [ri'kwaiə] exiger (qch. de q., *s.th. of s.o.*); réclamer (qch. à q., *s.th. of s.o.*); avoir besoin de (*qch.*); ~ (*of*) *s.o. to* (*inf.*) *a.* vouloir que q. (*sbj.*); **re'quired** exigé; voulu; **re'quire·ment** demande *f*; *fig.* exigence *f*; condition *f* requise.

req·ui·site ['rekwizit] **1.** requis (pour, *to*); nécessaire (à, *to*); voulu; **2.** condition *f* requise (pour, *for*); chose *f* nécessaire; *toilet* ~*s pl.* accessoires *m/pl.* de toilette; **req·ui·si·tion 1.** demande *f*; ✕ réquisition *f*; **2.** avoir recours à; ✕ réquisitionner; mettre (*qch.*) en réquisition; faire des réquisitions dans (*un endroit*).

re·quit·al [ri'kwaitl] récompense *f*; revanche *f*; **re'quite** [ˌ'kwait] récompenser; ~ *s.o.'s love* répondre à l'amour de q.

re·read ['riː'riːd] [*irr.* (*read*)] relire.

re·run 1. ['riː'rʌn] repasser, passer

(*un film*) de nouveau; **2.** ['riːrʌn] reprise *f*.

re·sale ['riː'seil] revente *f*; ~ *price* prix *m* de revente; ~ *value* valeur *f* à la revente.

re·scind [ri'sind] abroger (*une loi*); rétracter (*un arrêt*); annuler (*un contrat, une décision, un vote, etc.*); casser (*un jugement*).

re·scis·sion [ri'siʒn] rescision *f*, abrogation *f etc., see* rescind.

re·script ['riːskript] rescrit *m*; transcription *f*.

res·cue ['reskjuː] **1.** sauvetage *m*; secours *m*; délivrance *f*; ~ *operation* opérations *f/pl.* de sauvetage; ~ *party* équipe *f* de sauvetage *ou* de secours; *come* (*ou go*) *to s.o.'s* ~ venir en aide à q., aller à la rescousse de q.; **2.** sauver; secourir, porter secours à; délivrer; ~ *s.o. from danger* arracher q. à un danger; **'res·cu·er** sauveteur (-euse *f*) *m*; secoureur (-euse *f*) *m*; libérateur (-euse *f*) *m*.

re·search [ri'səːtʃ] recherche *f* (de *for, after*); recherches *f/pl.* (*savantes*); ~ *establishment* institut *m* de recherches (*scientifiques etc.*); *marketing* (*motivation*) ~ étude *f* du marché (de motivation); ~ *work* recherches *f/pl.*; ~ *worker* chercheur (-euse *f*) *m*; **re'search·er** chercheur (-euse *f*) *m*.

re·seat ['riː'siːt] (faire) rasseoir; remettre un fond à (*une chaise*); ⊕ roder le siège de.

re·se·da [ri'siːdə] réséda *m*.

re·sell ['riː'sel] [*irr.* (sell)] revendre; **'re'sell·er** revendeur (-euse *f*) *m*.

re·sem·blance [ri'zembləns] ressemblance *f* (à, avec *to*; entre, *between*); **re'sem·ble** [ˌbl] ressembler à.

re·sent [ri'zent] s'offenser de; être froissé de; **re'sent·ful** □ [ˌful] rancunier (-ère *f*); plein de ressentiment; froissé, irrité (de, *of*); **re'sent·ment** ressentiment *m*; rancune *f*.

res·er·va·tion [rezə'veiʃn] ₮₮ réservation *f*; *Am.* terrain *m* réservé, réserves *f/pl.* indiennes; *fig. a. places*: réserve *f*; *Am.* place *f* retenue.

re·serve [ri'zəːv] **1.** *usu.* réserve *f*; terrain *m* réservé; restriction *f*; ~ *price* prix *m* minimum; *in* ~ en réserve; *with certain* ~*s* avec quel-

ques réserves; **2.** réserver; retenir
(*une chambre, une place, etc.*); mettre
(*qch.*) en réserve; **re'served** □
renfermé, réservé; *fig.* froid; ~ seat
place *f* réservée.
re·serv·ist ✕ [ri'sə:vist] réserviste *m*.
res·er·voir ['rezɜvwɑ:] réservoir *m*
(*a. fig.*); (bassin *m* de) retenue *f*.
re·set ['ri:'set] [*irr.* (set)] remettre en
place; ⊕ raffûter (*un outil*); *typ.*
recomposer.
re·set·tle ['ri:'setl] (se) réinstaller;
(se) rasseoir; se reposer (*vin*); **'re-
'set·tle·ment** nouvelle colonisation
f; *vin etc.*: nouveau dépôt *m*.
re·ship ['ri:'ʃip] rembarquer; remonter (*l'hélice etc.*).
re·shuf·fle ['ri:'ʃʌfl] **1.** rebattre (*des
cartes*); *fig.* remanier; **2.** nouveau
battement *m*; *fig.* remaniement *m*.
re·side [ri'zaid] résider (à, at; dans,
in) (*a. fig.*); demeurer; **res·i·dence**
['rezidəns] résidence *f*; demeure *f*;
séjour *m*; maison *f*; habitation *f*; ~
permit permis *m ou* carte *f* de
séjour; **'res·i·dent 1.** résidant, qui
réside; à demeure (*maître d'école
etc.*); en résidence; ✆ ~ *physician*
interne *m*; **2.** habitant(e *f*) *m*; (ministre) résident *m*; **res·i·den·tial**
[~'denʃl] d'habitation; résidentiel(le
f).
re·sid·u·al [ri'zidjuəl] résiduel(le *f*);
re'sid·u·ar·y résiduaire; qui reste;
ᵗᵗ₁ ~ *legatee* légataire *m* universel;
res·i·due ['rezidju:] 🔥, 🜂 résidu
m; reste *m*, -s *m/pl.*; ᵗᵗ₁ reliquat *m*;
re·sid·u·um [ri'zidjuəm] *surt.* 🔥
résidu *m*; reste *m*.
re·sign [ri'zain] *v/t.* résigner; donner sa démission de (*son emploi*);
abandonner; ~ *o.s.* to se résigner à;
s'abandonner à; *v/i.* démissionner;
res·ig·na·tion [rezig'neiʃn] démission *f*; abandon *m*; résignation
f (à, to); **re·signed** □ [ri'zaind]
résigné.
re·sil·i·ence [ri'ziliəns] ⊕ résilience
f; *personne, a. peau:* élasticité *f*;
rebondissement *m*; **re'sil·i·ent** re-
bondissant, élastique; *fig.* plein de
ressort.
res·in ['rezin] **1.** résine *f*; colophane
f; **2.** résiner; **'res·in·ous** résineux
(-euse *f*).
re·sist [ri'zist] *v/t.* résister à (*qch.,
q.*); s'opposer à; repousser; *v/i.*
résister; **re'sist·ance** résistance *f*

(*a. phys.*, ⚡) (à, to); **re'sist·ant**
résistant; **re'sis·tor** ⚡ résistance *f*,
rhéostat *m*.
re·sole ['ri:'soul] ressemeler.
re·sol·u·ble ['ri:'zɔljubl] qu'on peut
résoudre; résoluble (*problème*); 🔥
décomposable.
res·o·lute □ ['rezəlu:t] résolu;
ferme; **'res·o·lute·ness** résolution *f*.
res·o·lu·tion [rezə'lu:ʃn] 🔥, 🜂, ♪,
parl., phys., fig. résolution *f*;
détermination *f*; *fig. a.* fermeté *f*.
re·solv·a·ble [ri'zɔlvəbl] résoluble;
réductible.
re·solve [ri'zɔlv] **1.** *v/t.* 🔥, ♪, 🜂,
admin., fig. résoudre; ⊕ décomposer; *personne:* se résoudre à
(*qch.*); *fig.* dissiper (*un doute*); *parl.*
the House ~s itself into a committee
la Chambre se constitue en commission; *v/i.* (*a.* ~ *o.s.*) se résoudre;
~ (*up*)on se résoudre à; **2.** résolution
f; **re'solved** □ résolu, décidé.
res·o·nance ['reznəns] résonance *f*;
'res·o·nant □ résonnant; sonore
(*voix*).
re·sorp·tion *physiol.* [ri'sɔ:pʃn] résorption *f*.
re·sort [ri'zɔ:t] **1.** recours *m*; ressource *f*; affluence *f*; lieu *m* de
séjour; *health* ~ station *f* thermale;
seaside ~ plage *f*; station *f* balnéaire; *summer* ~ station *f* d'été; *in
the last* ~ en dernier ressort; en fin
de compte; **2.**: ~ to avoir recours à;
fréquenter (*un lieu*); se rendre
à (*un endroit*).
re·sound [ri'zaund] (faire) résonner,
retentir (de, with).
re·source [ri'sɔ:s] ressource *f*; expédient *m*; distraction *f*; **re'source-
ful** □ [~ful] fertile en ressources; F
débrouillard.
re·spect [ris'pekt] **1.** rapport *m* (à,
to; de, of); égard *m*; respect *m*
(pour, for); considération *f* (pour,
envers for); ~s *pl.* hommages *m/pl.*;
with ~ *to* quant à; *en ou* pour ce qui
concerne; *out of* ~ *for* pour respect
de; † au compte de; *pay one's* ~s *to*
présenter ses hommages à, rendre
ses respects à (*q.*); **2.** *v/t.* respecter
honorer; avoir égard à; concerner;
avoir rapport à; **re·spect·a·bil·i·ty**
respectabilité *f*; † *a.* solidité *f*;
re'spect·a·ble □ respectable; convenable; honorable; passable; †

solide; **re'spect·ful** □ [⌣ful] respectueux (-euse *f*) (envers, pour to[wards]); *Yours* ⌣*ly* je vous prie d'agréer mes salutations très respectueuses; **re'spect·ful·ness** respect *m*; **re'spect·ing** en ce qui concerne; touchant; quant à; **re'spec·tive** □ respectif (-ive *f*); *we went to our* ⌣ *places* nous sommes allés chacun à notre place.

res·pi·ra·tion [respə'reiʃn] respiration *f*.

res·pi·ra·tor ['respəreitə] respirateur *m* (*a.* ⚓); ⚔ masque *m* à gaz; **re·spir·a·to·ry** [ris'paiərətəri] respiratoire.

re·spire [ris'paiə] respirer.

res·pite ['respait] **1.** ⚖ sursis *m*, délai *m*; répit *m*; **2.** accorder un sursis à; remettre.

re·splend·ence, re·splend·en·cy [ris'plendəns(i)] splendeur *f*, éclat *m* (*a. fig.*); **re'splend·ent** □ resplendissant.

re·spond [ris'pɔnd] répondre (*a. fig.*); *eccl.* réciter les répons; ⌣ *to* obéir à; être sensible à; **re'spond·ent 1.** ⚖ défendeur (-eresse *f*); ⌣ *to* sensible à, qui réagit à; **2.** ⚖ défendeur (-eresse *f*) *m*; *cour de cassation:* intimé(e *f*) *m*.

re·sponse [ris'pɔns] réponse *f* (*a. fig.*), réplique *f*; *eccl.* répons *m*.

re·spon·si·bil·i·ty [rispɔnsə'biliti] responsabilité *f* (de *for*, of); ✝ solidité *f*; **re'spon·si·ble** responsable (de, *for*; envers, to); chargé (de, *for*); capable; qui comporte des responsabilités (*poste*); sérieux (-euse *f*) (*personne*); *be* ⌣ *for* être maître de; être comptable de; être coupable de; **re'spon·sive** □ sensible (à, to); impressionnable; *be* ⌣ *to* répondre à, obéir à.

rest[1] [rest] **1.** repos *m* (*a. fig.*); sommeil *m*; *fig.* mort *f*; ♪ silence *m*; abri *m*; support *m*; ⚓⌣ *cure* cure *f* de repos; ⌣ *home* maison *f* de repos; *Am.* ⌣ *room* toilettes *f/pl.*; *at* ⌣ en repos; *set at* ⌣ calmer; régler; **2.** *v/i.* se reposer; avoir *ou* prendre du repos; s'appuyer (sur, on); *fig.* ⌣ (*up*)*on* reposer sur; peser sur (*q.*) (*responsabilité*); ⌣ *with s.o. fig.* dépendre de (*q.*); *v/t.* (faire) reposer; appuyer; déposer (*un fardeau*).

rest[2] [⌣] **1.** reste *m*, restant *m*; *les autres m/pl.*; ✝ (fonds *m* de) réserve

f; for the ⌣ quant au reste; **2.** rester, demeurer; ⌣ *assured* être assuré (que, *that*).

re·state·ment ['ri:'steitmənt] révision *f* (*d'un texte*); nouvel énoncé *m*.

res·tau·rant ['restərɔ̃:ŋ] restaurant *m*.

rest·ing-place ['restiŋpleis] abri *m*; (lieu *m* de) repos *m*; *last* ⌣ dernière demeure *f*.

res·ti·tu·tion [resti'tju:ʃn] restitution *f*; réintégration *f* (*du domicile conjugal*); *make* ⌣ *of* restituer qch.

res·tive □ ['restiv] nerveux (-euse *f*); rétif (-ive *f*) (*cheval*, F *personne*); **'res·tive·ness** humeur *f* rétive *ou* inquiète; nervosité *f*.

rest·less ['restlis] sans repos; agité; inquiet (-ète *f*); **'rest·less·ness** agitation *f*; turbulence *f*; mouvement *m* incessant; nervosité *f*.

re·stock ['ri:'stɔk] ✝ réapprovisionner (en, *with*); repeupler (*un étang*).

res·to·ra·tion [resto'reiʃn] restitution *f*; restauration *f* (*d'un bâtiment, a. pol.*); réintégration *f* (dans une fonction, *to a post*); **re·stor·a·tive** □ [ris'tɔrətiv] fortifiant (*a. su./m*); cordial (-aux *m/pl.*) (*a. su./m*).

re·store [ris'tɔ:] restituer, rendre; restaurer; réintégrer; rétablir; ramener (à la vie, to *life*); ⌣ *s.th. to its place* remettre qch. en place; ⌣ *s.o. to liberty* rendre q. à la liberté; mettre q. en liberté; ⌣ *to health* rétablir la santé de q.; **re'stor·er** restaurateur (-trice *f*) *m*; *meubles:* rénovateur *m*; *hair* ⌣ régénérateur *m* des cheveux.

re·strain [ris'trein] retenir, empêcher (de, *from*); refréner; contenir; **re'strained** tempéré; contenu (*colère*); sobre; **re'strain·ed·ly** [⌣idli] avec retenue *ou* contrainte; **re'straint** contrainte *f* (*a. fig.*); frein *m*; *fig.* réserve *f*; sobriété *f*; internement *m* (*d'un aliéné*).

re·strict [ris'trikt] restreindre; réduire; **re'stric·tion** restriction *f*; réduction *f* (de *of*, on); **re'stric·tive** □ restrictif (-ive *f*).

re·sult [ri'zʌlt] **1.** résultat *m*; aboutissement *m*; **2.** résulter, provenir (de, *from*); ⌣ *in* mener à, produire; avoir pour résultat; **re'sult·ant 1.** résultant; **2.** Å, *phys.* (force *f*) résultante *f*.

ré·su·mé ['rezju:mei] résumé *m*.

re·sume [ri'zju:m] reprendre, regagner; se remettre à; **re·sump·tion** [ri'zʌmpʃn] reprise *f*.

re·sur·gence [ri'sə:dʒəns] résurrection *f*; **re'sur·gent** qui resurgit.

res·ur·rect [rezə'rekt] *vt/i*. ressusciter; **res·ur'rec·tion** résurrection *f*; **res·ur'rec·tion·ist**, *a*. **res·ur·rec·tion man** déterreur *m* de cadavres.

re·sus·ci·tate [ri'sʌsiteit] *vt/i*. ressusciter; *v/t*. rappeler à la vie; *v/i*. revenir à la vie; **re·sus·ci'ta·tion** ressuscitation *f*.

re·tail ['ri:teil] 1. *su*. (vente *f* au) détail *m*; by ~ au détail; ~ *bookseller* libraire *m*; ~ *price* prix *m* de détail; 2. *adj*. au détail; de détail; 3. *adv*. au détail; 4. [ri:'teil] (se) vendre au détail; (se) détailler; *v/t*. *fig*. colporter (*des nouvelles*); be ~ed se vendre au détail (à, *at*); **re'tail·er** marchand(e *f*) *m* au détail; *fig*. colporteur *m*.

re·tain [ri'tein] retenir (*un avocat, qch., fig. a. dans son souvenir*); maintenir (*en position*); conserver (*qch., coutume, faculté, etc.*); engager (*un domestique etc.*); **re'tain·er** *hist*. serviteur *m*, suivant *m*; (*usu. retaining fee*) avance *f*; honoraires *m/pl*. (*versés à un avocat pour retenir ses services*); *old* ~ vieux serviteur *m*.

re·take ['ri:'teik] [*irr*. (take)] reprendre; *cin*. tourner à nouveau.

re·tal·i·ate [ri'tælieit] *v/t*. user de représailles (envers, *on*); retourner (*une accusation*) (contre, *upon*); *v/i*. rendre la pareille (à, *on*); **re·tal·i'a·tion** représailles *f/pl*.; **re'tal·i·a·to·ry** [~iətəri] de représailles.

re·tard [ri'tɑ:d] *v/t*. retarder; *v/i*. tarder (*personne*); retarder (*chose*); *mot*. ~ed *ignition* retard *m* à l'allumage; ~ed *child* enfant *m* arriéré; **re·tar·da·tion** [ri:tɑ:'deiʃn] retard(ement) *m*; *phys*. retardation *f*; ♪ *mesure*: ralentissement *m*.

retch ⅋ [ri:tʃ] avoir des haut-le-cœur.

re·tell ['ri:'tel] [*irr*. (tell)] répéter; raconter de nouveau.

re·ten·tion [ri'tenʃn] conservation *f*; maintien *m*; ⅋, *a. psych*. rétention *f*; **re'ten·tive** □ gardeur (-euse *f*) (de, *of*); fidèle, tenace (*mémoire*); *anat*. rétentif (-ive *f*); contentif (-ive *f*) (*bandage*).

re·think ['ri:'θiŋk] [*irr*. (think)] réfléchir encore sur; repenser à.

ret·i·cence ['retisəns] réticence *f*; *fig*. réserve *f*; **'ret·i·cent** taciturne; réservé; peu communicatif (-ive *f*).

re·tic·u·late □ [ri'tikjulit], **re'tic·u·lat·ed** □ [~leitid] réticulé; réti-forme; **ret·i·cule** ['retikju:l] réticule *m* (*a. opt.*); sac *m* à main.

ret·i·na *anat*. ['retinə] rétine *f*.

ret·i·nue ['retinju:] suite *f* (*d'un noble*).

re·tire [ri'taiə] *v/t*. mettre à la retraite; ✝ retirer (*un effet*); *v/i*. se retirer (dans, *to*); s'éloigner; se coucher; se démettre; prendre sa retraite; ⚔ se replier; *sp*. se retirer (de, *from*); **re'tired** □ retiré (*endroit, vie*); retraité; mis à la retraite; ~ *pay* pension *f* de retraite; **re'tire·ment** retraite *f* (*a*. ⚔); ✝ retrait *m* (*d'un effet*); ⚔ repliement *m*; *sp*. abandon *m* (de la partie); *early* ~ préretraite *f*; **re'tir·ing** □ sortant; réservé; farouche; ~ *pension* pension *f* de retraite.

re·tort [ri'tɔ:t] 1. réplique *f*; riposte *f*; 🜊 cornue *f*; 2. *vt./i*. répliquer, riposter; relancer (à, [*up*]*on*).

re·touch ['ri:'tʌtʃ] retoucher (*a. phot.*).

re·trace [ri'treis] retracer (*un dessin*); remonter à l'origine de; *fig*. ~ *one's steps* revenir sur ses pas.

re·tract [ri'trækt] (se) rétracter; *vt/i*. rentrer; ⊕ (se) contracter; ⚔ escamoter, rentrer; **re'tract·a·ble** *zo*. rétractile; ⚔ rentrant, escamotable; **re·trac'ta·tion** rétractation *f*; **re'trac·tion** retrait *m*; rétraction *f* (*a*. ⚔); *gramm*. recul *m*.

re·train ['ri:'trein] (se) recycler.

re·trans·late ['ri:træns'leit] retraduire; **'re·trans'la·tion** nouvelle traduction *f*.

re·trans·mit ['ri:trænz'mit] *télév.*, *a. radio*: retransmettre.

re·tread ['ri:'tred] 1. rechaper (*un pneu*); 2. pneu *m* rechapé.

re·treat [ri'tri:t] 1. retraite *f* (*a*. ⚔, *a. fig.*); *glacier*: décrue *f*; *fig*. asile *m*; repaire *m* (*de brigands*); 2. *v/t*. ramener; *v/i*. se retirer, s'éloigner; ⚔ battre en retraite; *box. etc.* rompre.

re·trench [ri'trentʃ] v/t. restreindre; réformer; supprimer (un mot etc.); ✗ retrancher; v/i. faire des économies; restreindre sa dépense; **re'trench·ment** réduction f; économies f/pl.; suppression f; ✗ retranchement m.

re·tri·al ⅍ ['ri:'traiəl] procédure f de révision.

ret·ri·bu·tion [retri'bju:ʃn] châtiment m; **re·trib·u·tive** □ [ri-'tribjutiv] vengeur (-eresse f).

re·triev·a·ble [ri'tri:vəbl] recouvrable (argent); réparable (erreur etc.); récupérable (matière etc.); **re'triev·al** recouvrement m; réparation f; récupération f; beyond (ou past) ~ irréparable, irrémédiable; (definitivement) perdu; **re·trieve** [ri'tri:v] recouvrer; retrouver; rétablir; récupérer; arracher (à, from); réparer; chasse: rapporter; **re'triev·er** chasse: chien m rapporteur; race: retriever m.

retro- [retrou] rétro...; ~'ac·tive rétroactif (-ive f); ~'cede reculer; ~'ces·sion recul m; mouvement m rétrograde; ~·gra'da·tion astr. rétrogradation f; biol. régression f; '~·grade **1.** rétrograde; **2.** rétrograder (a. fig.); fig. a. dégénérer.

ret·ro·gres·sion [retrou'greʃn] rétrogression f; fig. dégénérescence f; **ret·ro·spect** ['~spekt] coup m d'œil rétrospectif; consider in ~ jeter un coup d'œil rétrospectif sur; **ret·ro'spec·tion** examen m rétrospectif; **ret·ro'spec·tive** □ rétrospectif (-ive f) (vue etc.); vers l'arrière; ⅍ à effet rétroactif (loi).

re·try ⅍ ['ri:'trai] juger à nouveau (q., un procès).

re·turn [ri'tə:n] **1.** retour m (a. ⚔, ✝, marchandises, ⚠ mur); recrudescence f (a. ⚔); ⚡ circuit m de retour; parl. élection f; ✝ (souv. ~s pl.) recettes f/pl., rendement m, profit m; remboursement m (d'un capital); déclaration f (de revenu); Banque: situation f; rapport m, relevé m (officiel); balle, son, etc.: renvoi m; ⊕ rappel m; ✝ ~s pl. rendus m/pl.; restitution f; fig. récompense f; fig. échangé m; ~s pl. relevé m; statistique f; attr. de retour; many happy ~s of the day mes meilleurs vœux pour votre anniversaire, joyeux anniversaire; in ~ en retour;

en échange (de, for); by ~ (of post) par retour de courrier; ~ match match m retour; ~ ticket billet m d'aller et retour; pay a ~ visit rendre une visite (à q.); **2.** v/i. revenir; rentrer; retourner; fig. ~ to revenir à (un sujet etc.); v/t. rendre; renvoyer (accusation, balle, lumière); adresser (des remerciements); fig. répliquer, répondre; ✝ rapporter (un bénéfice, a. admin.); faire une déclaration de (revenu); ⅍ déclarer (q. coupable), rendre, prononcer (un verdict); parl. élire; cartes: rejouer; **re'turn-a·ble** restituable; **re'turn·er** personne f qui revient ou qui rend; **re·turn·ing of·fi·cer** directeur m du scrutin; deputy ~ scrutateur m.

re·un·ion ['ri:'ju:njən] réunion f; assemblée f; **re·u·nite** ['ri:ju:'nait] (se) réunir; (se) réconcilier.

rev mot. F [rev] **1.** tour m; **2.** (a. ~ up) (faire) s'emballer.

re·val·or·i·za·tion [ri:vælərai'zeiʃn] revalorisation f; **re'val·or·ize** [~-aiz] revaloriser; **re·val·u·a·tion** [~vælju'eiʃn] réévaluation f; réestimation f; **re·val·ue** [~'vælju:] réévaluer; réestimer.

re·vamp ⊕ ['ri:'væmp] remplacer l'empeigne de (un soulier); Am. rafraîchir, renflouer.

re·veal [ri'vi:l] révéler, découvrir; faire connaître ou voir; dévoiler (un mystère); **re'veal·ing** révélateur (-trice f).

re·veil·le ✗ [ri'væli] réveil m.

rev·el ['revl] **1.** réjouissances f/pl.; divertissement m, ~s m/pl.; péj. orgie f; **2.** se divertir; faire bombance; se délecter (à, in).

rev·e·la·tion [revi'leiʃn] révélation f; bibl. ♀ l'Apocalypse f.

rev·el·(l)er ['revlə] noceur (-euse f) m; joyeux convive m; **'rev·el·ry** divertissements m/pl.; péj. orgie f.

re·venge [ri'vendʒ] **1.** vengeance f; jeux: revanche f; **2.** v/i. se venger (de qch., sur q. on); v/t. venger (q., qch.); ~ o.s. (ou be ~d) on se venger de (qch.) ou sur (q.); **re'venge·ful** □ [~ful] vindicatif (-ive f); vengeur (-eresse f); **re'venge·ful·ness** esprit m de vengeance; caractère m vindicatif; **re'veng·er** vengeur (-eresse f) m.

rev·e·nue ['revinju:] (*a.* ~*s pl.*) revenu *m*; rapport *m*; rentes *f/pl.*; ~ *board* (*ou office*) (bureau *m* de) perception *f*; ~ *cutter* cotre *m* de la douane; ~ *officer* employé *m* de la douane; ~ *stamp* timbre *m* fiscal.

re·ver·ber·ate [ri'və:bəreit] *v/t.* renvoyer (*un son*); réfléchir (*la lumière etc.*); *v/i.* résonner (*son*); réverbérer (*chaleur, lumière*); **re·ver·ber'a·tion** renvoi *m*; réverbération *f*; **re'ver·ber·a·tor** réflecteur *m*; **re'ver·ber·a·to·ry fur·nace** *métall.* [~ətəri] four *m* à réverbère.

re·vere [ri'viə] vénérer; **rev·er·ence** ['revərəns] **1.** vénération *f*; révérence *f*; respect *m* (religieux); F *Your* ♀ monsieur l'abbé; *co. saving your* ~ sauf révérence; **2.** révérer; **'rev·er·end 1.** vénérable; *eccl.* révérend; *Right* ♀ très révérend; **2.** *the Right* ~ *X* le révérend *m* X.

rev·er·ent □ ['revərənt], **rev·er·en·tial** □ [~'renʃl] révérenciel(le *f*); plein de vénération.

rev·er·ie ['revəri] rêverie *f*.

re·ver·sal [ri'və:səl] renversement *m* (*a.* ⊕, *a. opt.*); revirement *m* (*d'une opinion*); ⚖ réforme *f*, annulation *f*; ⊕ ~ *of stroke* changement *m* de course; **re·verse** [~'və:s] **1.** contraire *m*, inverse *m*; ⚔, *a. fig.* revers *m*; *mot.* (*a.* ~ *gear*) marche *f* arrière; *feuillet*: verso *m*; *in* ~ en ordre inverse; en marche arrière; ⚔ à revers; **2.** □ contraire, inverse; ~ *side tissu*: envers *m*; **3.** renverser (*a.* ⚔); invertir (*un ordre, a. phot.*); *cost.* retourner; ⚖ réformer, révoquer; *mot. a. v/i.* faire (marche arrière); **re'vers·i·ble** réversible (*procès*); *phot.* inversible; à deux endroits (*tissu*); à double face (*manteau*); **re'vers·ing** ⊕ de renvoi.

re·ver·sion [ri'və:ʃn] ⚖ retour *m* (*a. fig.*), réversion *f* (*a. biol.*); substitution *f*; survivance *f*; *phot.* inversion *f*; *in* ~ grevé d'une réversion; réversible (*rente*); **re'ver·sion·ar·y** ⚖ de réversion; réversible; **re'ver·sion·er** ⚖ détenteur (-trice *f*) *m* d'un droit de réversion *ou* substitution.

re·vert [ri'və:t] (*to*) revenir (à) (*a.* ⚖, *biol., fig.*); *a. biens*: faire retour (à *q.*).

rev·er·y *see reverie.*

re·vet·ment ⊕ [ri'vetmənt] revêtement *m*.

re·view [ri'vju:] **1.** ⚖ révision *f*; ⚔, ⚓, *périodique, fig.*: revue *f*; examen *m*; compte rendu *m*; *year under* ~ année *f* de rapport; **2.** *v/t.* ⚖ réviser; ⚔, ⚓, *fig.* passer en revue; *fig.* revoir, examiner; faire le compte rendu de; *v/i.* faire de la critique littéraire *etc.*; **re'view·er** critique *m* (littéraire); ~*'s copy* exemplaire *m* de service de presse.

re·vile [ri'vail] injurier (*q.*).

re·vis·al [ri'vaizl] révision *f*.

re·vise [ri'vaiz] **1.** revoir, relire (*un livre etc.*); corriger (*des épreuves*); réviser (*une loi*); **2.** *typ.* épreuve *f* de révision; seconde *f*; **re'vis·er** réviseur *m*; *typ.* correcteur *m*.

re·vi·sion [ri'viʒn] révision *f*; **re'vi·sion·ism** [~izəm] révisionisme *m*.

re·vis·it ['ri:'vizit] visiter de nouveau.

re·vi·so·ry [ri'vaizəri] de révision.

re·vi·tal·ize ['ri:'vaitəlaiz] revivifier.

re·viv·al [ri'vaivl] ⚕ retour *m* des forces, retour *m* à la vie; reprise *f* des sens; *théâ., a.* ✝ reprise *f*; *fig.* renaissance *f*; renouveau *m*; **re·vive** [~'vaiv] *v/t.* ressusciter; rappeler à la vie; ranimer; réveiller; renouveler; *v/i.* reprendre connaissance; se ranimer; ✝ *etc.* reprendre; **re'viv·er** ressusciteur *m*; personne *f* qui ranime; F verre *m* (*de cognac etc.*); **re·viv·i·fy** [~'vivifai] revivifier.

rev·o·ca·ble □ ['revəkəbl] révocable; **rev·o·ca·tion** [~'keiʃn] révocation *f*; abrogation *f*.

re·voke [ri'vouk] *v/t.* révoquer; retirer; *v/i. cartes*: renoncer à faux.

re·volt [ri'voult] **1.** révolte *f*; **2.** *v/i.* se révolter (*a. fig.*), se soulever (contre *against, from*); *v/t. fig.* dégoûter; indigner (*q.*).

rev·o·lu·tion [revə'lu:ʃn] ⊕, *pol., astr., fig.* révolution *f*; ⊕ tour *m*; rotation *f*; ~*s per minute* tours *m/pl.* à la minute; **rev·o'lu·tion·ar·y 1.** révolutionnaire; **2.** (*a.* **rev·o'lu·tion·ist**) révolutionnaire *mf*; **rev·o'lu·tion·ize** révolutionner.

re·volve [ri'vɔlv] *v/i.* tourner (sur, *on*; autour de, *round*); revenir (*saisons*); *v/t.* faire tourner; *fig.* ruminer, retourner; **re'volv·er** revolver *m*; **re'volv·ing** tournant; ~

stage scène *f* tournante; ~ *door* porte *f* tournante *ou* pivotante; ~ *pencil* porte-mine *m*/*inv.*

re·vue *théâ.* [ri'vjuː] revue *f.*

re·vul·sion [ri'vʌlʃn] *fig.* revirement *m* (*des sentiments*); nausée *f*; ✴ révulsion *f*; **re·vul·sive** □ ✴ révulsif (-ive *f*) (*a. su.*/*m*).

re·ward [ri'wɔːd] **1.** récompense *f*; **2.** récompenser, rémunérer (de, *for*); *fig.* payer (qch., *for s.th.*).

re·word ['riː'wɔːd] rédiger à nouveau.

re·write ['riː'rait] [*irr.* (*write*)] récrire; remanier, recomposer.

rhap·so·dist ['ræpsədist] rhapsodiste *m*; **'rhap·so·dize** s'extasier (sur, *over*); **'rhap·so·dy** rhapsodie *f*; *fig.* transports *m*/*pl.*

rhe·o·stat ⚡ ['riːostæt] rhéostat *m.*

rhet·o·ric ['retərik] rhétorique *f* (*a. péj.*); éloquence *f*; **rhe·tor·i·cal** □ [ri'tɔrikl] de rhétorique; *péj.* ampoulé; **rhet·o·ri·cian** [retə'riʃn] rhétoricien *m*; *hist.*,*a. péj.* rhéteur *m.*

rheu·mat·ic ✴ [ruː'mætik] (~*ally*) rhumatismal (-aux *m*/*pl.*); rhumatisant (*a. su.*/*mf*) (*personne*); **rheu·'mat·ics** F *pl.*, **rheu·ma·tism** ✴ ['ruːmətizm] rhumatisme *m.*

rhi·no¹ *sl.* ['rainou] galette *f* (= *argent*).

rhi·no² [~], **rhi·noc·er·os** *zo.* [rai-'nɔsərəs] rhinocéros *m.*

rhomb, rhom·bus ♔ ['rɔm(bəs)], *pl.* **-bus·es, -bi** [~bai] losange *m*, † rhombe *m.*

rhu·barb ♣ ['ruːbɑːb] rhubarbe *f.*

rhumb ⚓ [rʌm] rhumb *m.*

rhyme [raim] **1.** rime *f* (à, *to*); poésie *f*, vers *m*/*pl.*; *without ~ or reason* sans rime ni raison; **2.** (faire) rimer (avec, *with*); **'rhyme·less** sans rime; **'rhym·er, rhyme·ster** ['~stə] versificateur *m*; *péj.* rimailleur *m.*

rhythm [riðm] rythme *m*; **'rhyth·mic, 'rhyth·mi·cal** □ rythmique, cadencé.

Ri·al·to *Am.* [ri'æltou] quartier *m* des théâtres (*de Broadway*).

rib [rib] **1.** côte *f*; ♀, ⧌ nervure *f*; *parapluie*: baleine *f*; ~ *cage* cage *f* thoracique; **2.** garnir de côtes *ou* de nervures; *Am. sl.* taquiner (*q.*).

rib·ald ['ribəld] **1.** paillard; licencieux (-euse *f*); **2.** paillard(e *f*) *m*;

homme *m* éhonté; **'rib·ald·ry** paillardises *f*/*pl.*; propos *m*/*pl.* grossiers.

rib·and ⊕ ['ribənd] ruban *m.*

ribbed [ribd] ♀ à nervures (*a. plafond*); *tex.* à côtes.

rib·bon ['ribən] ruban *m* (*a. décoration, machine à écrire*, ⊕ *etc.*); *ordre*: cordon *m*; bande *f*; ~*s pl.* lambeaux *m*/*pl.*; *sl.* guides *f*/*pl.*; ~ *building ou development* alignement *m* de maisons en bordure de route; ⊕ ~*work* travail (*pl.* -aux) *m* à la chaîne; **'rib·boned** orné de rubans; *zo.* rubané.

rice [rais] riz *m*; ~ *pudding* riz *m* au lait; *ground* ~ farine *f* de riz.

rich □ [ritʃ] riche (en, *in*) (*personne, terre, couleur, style, a. fig.*); fertile; gras(se *f*); somptueux (-euse *f*); de luxe; superbe; corsé (*vin*); ample, plein (*voix etc.*); F impayable, épatant; ~ *in meaning* significatif (-ive *f*); *gramm.* ayant beaucoup d'acceptions; ~ *milk* lait *m* non écrémé; **rich·es** ['~iz] *pl.* richesses *f*/*pl.*; **'rich·ness** richesse *f*; abondance *f*; luxe *m*; couleur: éclat *m*; voix: ampleur *f.*

rick¹ ✎ [rik] **1.** meule *f* (*de foin*); **2.** mettre en meule(s).

rick² [~] *see* **wrick.**

rick·ets ✴ ['rikits] *sg. ou pl.* rachitisme *m*; **'rick·et·y** rachitique; F branlant, bancal (*m*/*pl.* -als), chancelant.

rid [rid] [*irr.*] débarrasser (de, *of*); *get* ~ *of* se débarrasser de; ♔ éliminer; **'rid·dance** débarras *m*; *he is a good* ~ bon débarras!

rid·den ['ridn] *p.p. de* **ride 2**; *gang-*~ infesté de gangsters; *family-*~ tyrannisé par sa famille.

rid·dle¹ ['ridl] **1.** énigme *f* (*a. fig.*), devinette *f*; **2.** *v/t.* trouver la clef de; *v/i.* parler par énigmes; ~ *me donnez-moi le mot de* (*cette énigme*).

rid·dle² [~] **1.** crible *m*, claie *f*; **2.** cribler (*a. fig.*) (de, *with*); passer au crible.

rid·dling □ ['ridliŋ] énigmatique.

ride [raid] **1.** promenade *f*; voyage *m*; course *f*; *autobus etc.*: trajet *m*; **2.** [*irr.*] *v/i.* se promener, aller (à cheval, en auto, à bicyclette); voyager; chevaucher; *fig.* voguer; remonter; ⚓ ~ *at anchor* être mouillé; ~ *for a fall* aller en casse-cou; *fig.*

courir à un échec, aller au-devant de la défaite; *v/t.* monter (*un cheval etc.*); aller à (*une bicyclette etc.*); parcourir (*le pays*) (à cheval); diriger (*son cheval*); opprimer; voguer sur (*les vagues*); ~ (*on*) *a bicycle* aller à bicyclette; ⚓ *out* étaler (*une tempête*); *fig.* surmonter (*une crise*); '**rid·er** cavalier (-ère *f*) *m*; *course:* jockey *m*; *cirque:* écuyer (-ère *f*) *m*; clause *f* additionnelle; annexe *f*; ⚕ exercice *m* d'application (*d'un théorème*); ⊕ cavalier *m*.

ridge [ridȝ] **1.** *montagne:* arête *f*, crête *f*; faîte *m* (*a.* △); *sable:* ride *f*; *rochers:* banc *m*; *coteaux:* chaîne *f*; ⚹ billon *m*, butte *f*; **2.** *v/t.* △ enfaîter; ⚹ disposer en billons, sillonner; *v/i.* former des crêtes; se rider; ~ **way** route *f* des crêtes, chemin *m* de faîte.

rid·i·cule ['ridikjuːl] **1.** moquerie *f*, raillerie *f*; dérision *f*; ridicule *m*; **2.** se moquer de; ridiculiser; **ri·'dic·u·lous** □ [~juləs] ridicule; **ri·'dic·u·lous·ness** ridicule *m*.

rid·ing ['raidiŋ] **1.** équitation *f*; **2.** d'équitation; de cavalier (-ère *f*); '~-**breech·es** *pl.* culotte *f* de cheval; '~-**hab·it** *cost.* amazone *f*; ~ **mas·ter** professeur *m* d'équitation; ~ **school** manège *m*, école *f* d'équitation; ~ **sta·ble(s** *pl.*) centre *m* d'équitation, manège *m*; écurie *f*; ~ **whip** cravache *f*.

rife □ [raif] abondant (en, *with*); nombreux (-euse *f*); *be* ~ régner; abonder (en, *with*).

riff-raff ['rifræf] canaille *f*.

ri·fle¹ ['raifl] piller.

ri·fle² [~] **1.** fusil *m* (*rayé*); rayure *f* (*d'un fusil*); ⚔ ~*s pl.* fusiliers *m/pl.*; **2.** rayer (*un fusil*); '~**man** ⚔ fusilier *m*; chasseur *m* à pied; ~ **range** stand *m ou* champ *m* de tir; *within* ~ à portée de fusil; ~ **shot** coup *m* de fusil; *within* ~ à portée de fusil.

ri·fling ⊕ ['raifliŋ] rayage *m*; *coll.* rayure *f*, -s *f/pl.* [fêlure *f*.]

rift [rift] fente *f*, fissure *f*; *fig.*)

rig¹ F [rig] **1.** farce *f*; coup *m* monté; **2.** travailler (*le marché*); tripoter sur; truquer.

rig² [~] **1.** ⚓ gréement *m*; F *fig.* équipement *m*; F toilette *f*; *Am.* F attelage *m*; **2.** (*a.* ~ *out ou up*) gréer; F *fig.* accoutrer; ~ *up* monter; '~**ger** ⚓ gréeur *m*; ⊕ monteur-régleur (*pl.* monteurs-régleurs) *m*;

'**rig·ging** ⚓ gréage *m*; ⚔ gréement *m*.

right [rait] **1.** □ droit (*a.* = *contraire de gauche*); bon(ne *f*); honnête; correct, exact, juste; bien placé; ⚕ ~ *angle* angle *m* droit; *pol.* ~ *wing* (aile *f*) droite *f*; *be* ~ avoir raison; être à l'heure (*montre*); convenir (à, *for*); *be* ~ *to* (*inf.*) avoir raison de (*inf.*); bien faire de (*inf.*); être fondé à (*inf.*); *all* ~! entendu!; parfait!; très bien!; allez-y!; c'est bon!; *be on the* ~ *side of* 40 avoir moins de 40 ans; *put* (*ou* set) ~ ajuster; réparer; corriger; désabuser (*q.*); réconcilier (avec, *with*); **2.** *adv.* droit; tout ...; bien; fort, très; correctement; à droite; *dans un titre:* très; F *send to the* ~*about* envoyer promener (*q.*); ~ *away* tout de suite; sur-le-champ; ~ *in the middle* au beau milieu; ~ *on* tout droit; **3.** *su.* droit *m*, titre *m*; bien *m*; justice *f*; côté *m* droit, droite *f* (*a. pol.*); *box.* coup *m* du droit; ~ *of way* priorité *f*; *in his* (*ou her*) *own* ~ de son propre chef; *en propre*; *the* ~*s pl. of a story* la vraie histoire; *by* ~(*s*) en toute justice; *by* ~ *of* par droit de; à titre de; à cause de; *set* (*ou put*) *to* ~*s* mettre en ordre; arranger; *on* (*ou to*) *the* ~ à droite; **4.** *v/t.* redresser (*qch.*, *un tort*); rendre justice à; corriger; ⚓ (*v/i. se*) redresser; ~-**an·gled** ⚕ ['~'æŋgld] à angle droit; rectangle (*triangle*); '**right·eous** □ ['~ȝəs] juste (*a.* = *justifié*); vertueux (-euse *f*); '**right·eous·ness** droiture *f*, vertu *f*; **right·ful** □ ['~ful] légitime; équitable (*conduite*); '**right-hand** à *ou* de droite; *mot.* ~ *drive* conduite *f* à droite; *fig.* ~ *man* le bras droit (*de q.*); '**right-'hand·ed** droitier (-ère *f*) (*personne*); ⊕ pour la main droite; à droite (*vis etc.*); '**right·ist** *pol.* **1.** homme *m* de droite; **2.** de droite; '**right-'mind·ed** bien pensant; '**right·ness** droiture *f*; décision *etc.:* justesse *f*; '**right-'wing** *pol.* de droite; '**right-'wing·er** *pol.* homme *m* de droite; *sp.* ailier *m* droit.

rig·id □ ['ridȝid] raide, rigide; *fig.* strict, sévère; **ri·'gid·i·ty** raideur *f*, rigidité *f*; *fig.* sévérité *f*; intransigeance *f*.

rig·ma·role ['rigmərəul] discours *m* sans suite; F litanie *f*.

rig·or ⚕ ['raigɔː] frissons *m/pl.*; ~ **mor·tis** [~'mɔːtis] rigidité *f* cadavé-

rique; **rig·or·ous** □ ['rigərəs] rigoureux (-euse *f*).

rig·o(u)r ['rigə] rigueur *f*, sévérité *f*;
fig. austérité *f*; *preuve*: exactitude *f*;
~s *pl. a.* âpreté *f* du temps.

rile F [rail] agacer, exaspérer.

rill [ril] petit ruisseau *m*.

rim [rim] bord *m*; *lunettes*: monture *f*; *roue*: jante *f*.

rime¹ [raim] rime *f*.

rime² *poét.* [~] givre *m*, gelée *f*
blanche; **'rim·y** couvert de givre;
givré.

rind [raind] écorce *f*, peau *f* (*a. d'un
fruit*); *fromage*: croûte *f*; *lard*:
couenne *f*.

ring¹ [riŋ] **1.** anneau *m*; bague *f*;
rond *m* (*de serviette*); ⊕ segment *m*;
personnes: groupe *m*, cercle *m*; ✝
cartel *m*; *cirque*: arène *f*; box. ring
m; *lune*: auréole *f*; ~ binder classeur *m*
à anneaux; ~ road route *f* de ceinture;
(boulevard *m*) périphérique *m*; **2.**
boucler (*un taureau*); baguer (*un
pigeon*); (*usu.* ~ in *ou* round *ou* about)
entourer, encercler.

ring² [~] **1.** son(nerie *f*) *m*; tintement *m*; coup *m* de sonnette; F coup
m de téléphone; **2.** [*irr.*] *v/i.* sonner;
tinter (*a. oreilles*); (*souv.* ~ out) résonner, retentir (de, *with*); ~ again
sonner de nouveau; *téléph.* ~ off raccrocher; *the bell is* ~*ing* on sonne;
v/t. (faire) sonner; ~ *the bell* agiter
la sonnette; sonner; *fig.* réussir le
coup; ~ *up* sonner pour faire lever
(*qch.*); *téléph.* donner un coup de
téléphone à (*q.*); **'ring·er** sonneur
m; **'ring·ing** □ qui résonne; retentissant; **'ring·lead·er** □ meneur *m*;
chef *m* de bande; **ring·let** ['~lit]
cheveux: boucle *f*; **'ring·worm** ✿
teigne *f* tonsurante.

rink [riŋk] patinoire *f*; skating
m.

rinse [rins] **1.** (*souv.* ~ out) rincer;
2. = **'rins·ing** rinçage *m*; ~s *pl.*
rinçure *f*, -s *f/pl.*

ri·ot ['raiət] **1.** émeute *f*, F bagarre *f*;
fig. orgie *f*; ~ squad police *f* secours;
run ~ pulluler; se déchaîner; **2.** provoquer une émeute; s'ameuter; faire
du vacarme; *fig.* se livrer sans frein
(à, *in*); **'ri·ot·er** émeutier *m*; séditieux *m*; *fig.* noceur *m*; **'ri·ot·ous** □
tumultueux (-euse *f*); séditieux
(-euse *f*); tapageur (-euse *f*) (*personne*); dissolu (*vie*).

rip¹ [rip] **1.** déchirure *f*; fente *f*;
✂ ~ cord corde *f* de déchirure (*d'un
ballon*), tirette *f* (*d'un parachute*);
2. *v/t.* déchirer; fendre; ~ off arracher; *sl.* estamper; *sl.* voler, chiper; ~ up découdre; déchirer; *v/i.* se
déchirer; se fendre; *mot.* F filer.

rip² F [~] mauvais garnement *m*;
personne: gaillard *m*.

ri·par·i·an [rai'pɛəriən] riverain(e *f*)
m, adj.

ripe □ [raip] mûr; fait (*fromage*);
'rip·en *vt/i.* mûrir; **'ripe·ness** maturité *f*.

rip-off *sl.* ['ripɔf] estampage *m*; vol
m.

ri·poste [ri'poust] **1.** *escrime*: riposte *f* (*a. fig.*); **2.** riposter.

rip·per ['ripə] fendoir *m* (*pour ardoises*); burin *m* à défoncer; scie *f* à
refendre; *sl.* type *m* épatant; chose
f épatante; **'rip·ping** □ *sl.* fameux (-euse *f*), épatant.

rip·ple ['ripl] **1.** ride *f*; *cheveux*: ondulation *f*; *ruisseau*: gazouillement
m; murmure *m*; **2.** (se) rider; *v/i.*
onduler; murmurer.

rise [raiz] **1.** *eau*, *route*: montée *f*;
côte *f*; rampe *f*; *terrain*: éminence *f*;
ascension *f*; hausse *f* (*a.* ✝, ‰);
soleil, *théâ.* rideau: lever *m*; *eaux*:
crue *f*; △ flèche *f*; *prix etc.*: augmentation *f*; *emploi*, *rang*: avancement *m*; *fleuve*, *a. fig.*: source *f*;
give ~ *to* engendrer; provoquer; *take* (*one's*) ~ prendre sa
source, avoir son origine (dans, *in*);
2. [*irr.*] se lever (*gibier*, *personne*,
soleil, etc.); se dresser (*cheval*, *montagne*, *monument*); se relever (*personne*); s'élever (*bâtiment*, *terrain*);
monter (*mer*, *terrain*, *à la surface*, *à
un rang*); lever (*pain*); se révolter,
se soulever (contre, *against*); ressusciter (*des morts*); *parl.* s'ajourner; ✝
être à la hausse (*a. baromètre*); ‰
sortir (*du rang*); prendre sa source
(dans, *in*; à, *at*); ~ *to the occasion* se
montrer à la hauteur de la situation;
~ *to the bait* monter à la mouche;
mordre; **ris·en** ['rizn] *p.p. de* **rise 2**;
'ris·er △ contremarche *f*; *early* ~
personne *f* matinale.

ris·i·bil·i·ty [rizi'biliti] faculté *f* de
rire; **'ris·i·ble** □ risible, dérisoire;
✝ rieur (-euse *f*) (*personne*).

ris·ing ['raiziŋ] **1.** lever *m*; *chasse*:
envol *m*; *prix*, *baromètre*: hausse *f*;

eaux: crue *f*; soulèvement *m*, ameutement *m*; résurrection *f*; **2.** d'avenir; nouveau (-el *devant une voyelle ou un h muet*); -elle *f*; -eaux *m/pl*.); ~ **ground** élévation *f* de terrain.

risk [risk] **1.** risque *m* (*a.* ✝); péril *m*; *at the* ~ *of* (*gér.*) au risque de (*inf.*); *run a* (*ou the*) ~ courir un *ou* le risque; **2.** risquer; **'risk·y** □ hasardeux (-euse *f*); scabreux (-euse *f*).

ris·sole *cuis.* ['risoul] rissole *f*.

rite [rait] rite *m*; **rit·u·al** ['ritjuəl] **1.** □ rituel(le *f*); **2.** rites *m/pl.*; *livre*: rituel *m*.

ri·val ['raivl] **1.** rival(e *f*) *m*; émule *mf*; concurrent(e *f*) *m*; **2.** rival(e *f*, -aux *m/pl.*); ✝ concurrent; **3.** *vt/i.* rivaliser (avec); *v/t.* être l'émule de; **'ri·val·ry** rivalité *f*; concurrence *f*; émulation *f*.

rive [raiv] [*irr.*] (se) fendre.

riv·en ['rivn] *p.p* de rive.

riv·er ['rivə] fleuve *m*; rivière *f*; *fig.* flot *m*; ~ *basin* bassin *m* fluvial; **'~·bank** rive *f*; **'~·bed** lit *m* de rivière; **'~·horse** hippopotame *m*; **'~·side** rive *f*; bord *m* de l'eau; *attr.* situé au bord de la rivière.

riv·et ['rivit] **1.** ⊕ rivet *m*; **2.** rive(te)r; *fig.* fixer, river (à, *to*; sur, [*up*]on); **'riv·et·ing** à river.

riv·u·let ['rivjulit] ruisseau *m*.

roach *icht.* [routʃ] gardon *m*.

road [roud] route *f*; rue *f*; chemin *m* (*a. fig.*); voie *f* (*a. fig.*); *Am. see* railroad 1; ~ *map* carte *f* routière; ~ *works* travaux *m/pl.*; *by* ~ par route; *en auto* (*personne*); ♣ *usu.* ~*s pl.* (*a.* **'~·stead**) rade *f*; *on the* ~ en route; *hit the* ~ se mettre en route; **'~·house** relais *m*, hostellerie *f*; ~ **hog** *mot.* chauffard *m*; **'~·man,** **'~·mend·er** cantonnier *m*; **'~·race** course *f* sur route; **'~·sense** *surt. mot.* sens *m* pratique de la conduite sur route; **'road·ster** ['~·stə] cheval *m* de fatigue; *mot. etc.* voiture *f ou* bicyclette *f* de route; **'road·way** chaussée *f*; voie *f*; **'road·wor·thy** en état de marche (*voiture*).

roam [roum] *v/i.* errer, rôder; *v/t.* parcourir; **'roam·er** vagabond *m*; nomade *m*.

roan [roun] **1.** rouan(e *f*); **2.** (-cheval *m*) rouan *m*; vache *f* rouanne; ⊕ basane *f*.

roar [rɔ:] **1.** *vt/i.* hurler, vociférer; *v/i.* rugir; mugir (*mer, taureau*);

tonner, gronder; ronfler (*auto, feu*); *v/t.* beugler (*un refrain*); **2.** hurlement *m*; rugissement *m*; éclat *m* (*de rires*); mugissement *m*; grondement *m*; **roar·ing** ['~·riŋ] **1.** *see* roar 2; **2.** □ rugissant; mugissant; grondant; ✝ gros(se *f*); F superbe.

roast [roust] **1.** *v/t.* (faire) rôtir; *sl.* passer un savon à (*q.*); *v/i.* rôtir; *vt/i.* griller; **2.** rôti; ~ *beef* rôti *m* de bœuf, rosbif *m*; ~ *meat* viande *f* rôtie; *see* rule 2; **'roast·er** *personne*: rôtisseur *m* (-euse *f*) *m*); *cuis.* rôtissoire *f*; volaille *f* à rôtir; **'roast·ing-jack** tournebroche *m*.

rob [rɔb] voler; **'rob·ber** voleur (-euse *f*) *m*; **'rob·ber·y** vol *m*.

robe [roub] **1.** robe *f* (*d'office, de cérémonie,* 🜨) vêtement *m*; maillot *m* anglais (*pour bébés*); ~*s pl.* robe *f*, -s *f/pl.*; *gentlemen of the* ~ gens *m/pl.* de robe; **2.** *v/t.* revêtir (*q.*) d'une robe (*ou univ.* de sa toge); *fig.* recouvrir; *v/i.* revêtir sa robe *ou* toge.

rob·in *orn.* ['rɔbin] rouge-gorge (*pl.* rouges-gorges) *m*).

ro·bot ['roubɔt] automate *m*; *attr.* automatique.

ro·bust □ [rə'bʌst] robuste; vigoureux (-euse *f*); **ro'bust·ness** nature *f ou* caractère *m* robuste; vigueur *f*.

rock[1] [rɔk] rocher *m*; roc *m*; roche *f*; *Am.* pierre *f*, diamant *m*; *get down to* ~ *bottom* être au plus bas; *toucher le fin fond*; **~·crystal** cristal *m* de roche; **~·salt** sel *m* gemme.

rock[2] [~] *v/t.* bercer; basculer; *v/i.* osciller; *vt/i.* balancer.

rock-bot·tom F ['rɔk'bɔtəm] le plus bas (*prix*).

rock·er ['rɔkə] berceau *etc.*: bascule *f*; *see* rocking-chair; *sl. be off one's* ~ être un peu toqué. [rocaille.]

rock·er·y ['rɔkəri] jardin *m* de\

rock·et[1] ['rɔkit] **1.** fusée *f*; ~ *plane* avion-fusée (*pl.* avions-fusées) *m*); ~ *propulsion* propulsion *f* par fusée; **2.** passer en trombe; (*a.* ~ *up*) monter en flèche.

rock·et[2] ♀ [~] roquette *f*.

rock·et...: '~**·launch·ing site** base *f* de lancement (de fusées); '~**·powered** propulsé par réaction.

rock...: '~**·fall** éboulement *m* de rocher; '~**·gar·den** jardin *m* de rocaille.

rock·ing... ['rɔkiŋ]: '~-**chair** rock-ing-chair *m*; '~-**horse** cheval *m* à bascule.

rock·y ['rɔki] rocailleux (-euse *f*); rocheux (-euse *f*); de roche.

ro·co·co [rə'koukou] rococo *inv.* (*a. su./m*).

rod [rɔd] verge *f*; baguette *f*; *rideau, escalier*: tringle *f*; ⊕ tige *f*; *surv.* mire *f*; *mesure*: perche *f* (5½ yards); *Am. sl.* revolver *m*, pistolet *m*; *Black* ♀ Huissier *m* de la Verge noire (*haut fonctionnaire de la Chambre des Lords et de l'Ordre de la Jarretière*).

rode [roud] *prét. de* ride 2.

ro·dent [roudənt] rongeur *m*.

ro·de·o *Am.* [rou'deiou] rassemble-ment *m* du bétail; concours *m* d'é-quitation (*des cowboys*).

rod·o·mon·tade [rɔdəmɔn'teid] ro-domontade *f*.

roe¹ [rou] (*a.* hard ~) œufs *m/pl.* (*de poisson*); *soft* ~ laite *f*, laitance *f*.

roe² [~] chevreuil *m*, chevrette *f*; '~-**buck** chevreuil *m* (mâle).

ro·ga·tion *eccl.* [rou'geiʃn] Roga-tion *f*; ♀ *Sunday* dimanche *m* des Rogations.

rogue [roug] fripon(ne *f*) *m*; coquin (-e *f*) *m*; *éléphant*: solitaire *m*; ~s' *gallery* musée *m ou* album *m* de portraits *ou* photos de criminels; '**ro·guer·y** fourberie *f*; coquinerie*f*; '**ro·guish** □ coquin; fripon(ne *f*) (*a. fig.*).

roist·er ['rɔistə] faire du tapage; '**roist·er·er** tapageur (-euse *f*) *m*; fêtard(e *f*) *m*.

role *théâ.* [roul] rôle *m* (*a. fig.*).

roll [roul] 1. ⊕, *tex., étoffe, papier, tabac*: rouleau *m*; ⊕ *a.* cylindre *m*; † *étoffe*: pièce *f*; *Am. billets*: liasse*f*; *typ., phot.* bobine *f*; *admin.* con-trôle *m*; *beurre*: coquille *f*; petit pain *m*; *tambour, tonnerre*: roulement *m*; ♂ (coup *m* de) roulis *m*; 2. *v/t.* rouler; cylindrer; ⊕ laminer; ~ *out* étendre (au rouleau); ~ *up* (en)rou-ler; ⊕ ~*ed gold* doublé *m*; *v/i.* rou-ler; couler (*larmes*); gronder (*ton-nerre*); ♂ rouler, avoir du roulis; ~ *up* s'enrouler; F arriver; '~-**call** ap-pel *m* (nominal) (*a.* ✕); '**roll·er** rouleau *m*; cylindre *m*; *tex., papier*: calandre *f*; ✂ (*usu.* ~ *bandage*) bande *f* roulée; ♂ lame *f* de houle; *Am.* ~ *coaster* montagnes *f/pl.* russes; ~

towel essuie-mains *m/inv.* à rou-leau; '**roll·er-skate** 1. patiner sur roulettes; 2. patin *m* à roulettes; '**roll·film** *phot.* pellicule *f* en bo-bine.

rol·lick ['rɔlik] faire la bombe; rigo-ler; '**rol·lick·ing** joyeux (-euse *f*); rigoleur (-euse *f*).

roll·ing ['rouliŋ] 1. roulant; ♂ hou-leux (-euse *f*); ondulé; ⊕ de lami-nage; 2. roulement *m*; ⊕ laminage *m*; ~ *pin* rouleau *m* (à pâtisserie); ⊕ ~ *mill* usine *f* de laminage; laminoir *m*; *typ.* ~ *press* presse *f* à cylindres; '~-**stock** ♒ matériel *m* roulant.

roll...: '~-**neck** col *m* roulé; '~-**top** *desk* bureau *m* américain *ou* à cy-lindre.

ro·ly-po·ly ['rouli'pouli] 1. pouding *m* en rouleau aux confitures; 2. F boulot(te *f*).

Ro·man ['roumən] 1. romain; 2. Romain(e *f*) *m*; *typ.* (*usu.* ♀) (caractère *m*) romain *m*; ~-'**Cath·o·lic** catholique *mf*, *adj.*

ro·mance [rə'mæns] 1. † roman *m*; conte *m* bleu; *fig.* fable *f*; ♪ romance *f*; *fig.* affaire *f*, amour *m*; romanes-que *m*; *ling.* ♀ roman *m*, langue *f* ro-mane; 2. *fig.* inventer à plaisir; 3. *ling.* ♀ roman; **ro·'manc·er** † ro-mancier (-ère *f*) *m*; brodeur (-euse *f*) *m*; menteur (-euse *f*) *m*.

Ro·man·esque [roumə'nesk] roman (*a. su./m*).

Ro·man·ic [rou'mænik] romain; *ling.* roman; *surt.* ~ *peoples pl.* Ro-mains *m/pl.*

ro·man·tic [rə'mæntik] 1. (~ally) romantique; 2. (*usu.* **ro'man·ti·cist** [~tisist]) romantique *mf*; **ro·'man·ti·cism** romantisme *m*; idées *f/pl.* romanesques.

Ro·ma·ny ['rouməni] 1. romani-chel(le *f*) *m*; *ling.* le romanichel; 2. de bohémien.

Rom·ish *usu. péj.* ['roumiʃ] catholi-que.

romp [rɔmp] 1. gambades *f/pl.*; enfant *mf* turbulent(e *f*); gamine *f*; 2. s'ébattre; F *home* gagner haut la main; '**romp·ers** *pl.* barboteuse *f* (*pour enfants*).

rönt·gen·ize ['rɔntgənaiz] radio-graphier.

rönt·gen·o·gram [rɔnt'genəgræm] radiogramme *m*; **rönt·gen·og·ra·phy** [~gə'nɔgrəfi] radiographie *f*;

rönt·gen·ol·o·gist [‿'ɔlədʒist] radiographe *m*; **rönt·gen'ol·o·gy** [‿dʒi] radiologie *f*; **rönt·gen'os·co·py** [‿skəpi] radioscopie *f*.

rood [ru:d] crucifix *m*; *mesure*: quart *m* d'arpent (*10,117 ares*); '**∼-screen** ⚠ jubé *m*.

roof [ru:f] **1.** toit(ure *f*) *m*; voûte *f*; *mot.* ∼ **rack** galerie *f*; ∼ **of the mouth** (dôme *m* du) palais *m*; **2.** (*souv.* ∼ *in ou over*) recouvrir d'un toit; '**roof·ing** toiture *f*; pose *f* de la toiture; *attr.* de toits; ∼ **felt** carton-pierre (*pl.* cartons-pierres) *m*.

rook[1] [ruk] **1.** *orn.* freux *m*; *fig.* escroc *m*; **2.** refaire (*q.*); filouter (son argent à *q.*, *s.o. of his money*).

rook[2] [∼] *échecs*: tour *f*.

rook·er·y ['rukəri] colonie *f* de freux; *fig.* colonie *f*, rookerie *f*.

rook·ie *sl.* ['ruki] ✕ recrue *f*, bleu *m*; *fig.* débutant *m*.

room [rum] place *f*; salle *f*; (*a.* **bed**∼) chambre *f*; place *f*, espace *m*; *fig.* lieu *m*; ∼**s** *pl.* appartement *m*; ∼ **and board** pension *f* (complète); *in my* ∼ à ma place; *make* ∼ faire place (à, *for*); **-roomed** [rumd] de ... pièces; '**room·er** *surt. Am.* sous-locataire *mf*; '**room·ing-house** *surt. Am.* hôtel *m* garni, maison *f* meublée; '**room-mate** compagnon *m* (compagne *f*) de chambre; '**room·y** ☐ spacieux (-euse *f*); ample.

roor·back *Am.* ['ru:rbæk] fausse nouvelle *f* (*répandue pour nuire à un parti politique*).

roost [ru:st] **1.** juchoir *m*, perchoir *m*; *see* **rule 2**; **2.** se jucher, se percher pour la nuit; '**roost·er** coq *m*.

root[1] [ru:t] racine *f* (*a.* ✗, *anat.*, *ling.*); *fig.* source *f*; ♪ base *f*; *take* ∼, *strike* ∼ prendre racine; ∼**idea** idée *f* fondamentale; **2.** (s')enraciner; ∼ *out* arracher; *fig.* extirper; '**root·ed** enraciné (*a. fig.*); *fig.* (*a.* ∼ *in*) fondé sur.

root[2] [∼] *v/t.* fouiller; (*a.* ∼ *up*) trouver en fouillant; *fig.* ∼ *out*, ∼ *up* dénicher; *v/i.* fouiller avec le groin; *Am. sl.* ∼ *for* appuyer; encourager par des cris; '**root·er** *Am. sl.* spectateur *m etc.* qui encourage par des cris; fanatique *mf* (de, *for*).

root·let ['ru:tlit] petite racine *f*.

rope [roup] **1.** corde *f* (*a. à pendre un criminel*); cordage *m*; câble *m* (*mé* tallique); *perles*: grand collier *m*; *sonnette*: cordon *m*; *Am. sl.* cigare *m* bon marché; *alp. on the* ∼ en cordée; *alp.* ∼ **team** cordée *f*; F *be at the end of one's* ∼ être à *ou* au bout de ses ressources; *know the* ∼**s** connaître son affaire; *show s.o. the* ∼**s** mettre q. au courant; **2.** *v/t.* corder; (*usu.* ∼ *in ou off ou out*) entourer de cordes; *Am.* prendre au lasso; *alp.* encorder; ∼ *down* immobiliser au moyen d'une corde; *v/i.* devenir graisseux (-euse *f*); '**∼-danc·er** funambule *mf*; '**∼-lad·der** échelle *f* de corde; '**∼-maker** cordier *m*; '**rop·er·y** corderie *f*; '**rope-walk** corderie *f*.

rop·i·ness ['roupinis] viscosité *f*; graisse *f*; '**rop·y** visqueux (-euse *f*); gras(se *f*), graisseux (-euse *f*).

ro·sa·ry ['rouzəri] *eccl.* rosaire *m*; chapelet *m*; ✗ roseraie *f*.

rose[1] [rouz] ❀ rose *f*; *couleur*: rose *m* (*a. adj.*); rosette *f* (*chapeau etc.*); ⚠, ⚡, *fenêtre*: rosace *f*; *arrosoir*: pomme *f*.

rose[2] [∼] *prét. de* **rise 2**.

ro·se·ate ['rouziit] rosé.

rose ...: '**∼-bud** bouton *m* de rose; '**∼-bush** rosier *m*; '**∼'col·o(u)red** rose, couleur de rose *inv.*; *see things (ou the world) through* ∼ *glasses (ou spectacles)* voir tout *ou* la vie en rose; '**∼-hip** gratte-cul *inv.*; ∼ **mar·y** ['rouzməri] romarin *m*.

ro·se·ry ['rouzəri] roseraie *f*.

ro·sette [rou'zet] rosette *f*; *ruban*: chou (*pl.* -x) *m*.

ros·in ['rɔzin] **1.** colophane *f*; **2.** frotter de colophane.

ros·ter ✕ ['rɔstə] tableau *m* de service; liste *f*.

ros·trum ['rɔstrəm] tribune *f*.

ros·y ☐ ['rouzi] (de) rose; vermeil (-le *f*) (*teint*).

rot [rɔt] **1.** pourriture *f*; ⚕ carie *f*; *fig.* démoralisation *f*; *sl.* blague *f*; **2.** *v/t.* (faire) pourrir; *sl.* railler, blaguer (*q.*); gâcher (*un projet*); *v/i.* (se) pourrir; se décomposer.

ro·ta·ry ['routəri] rotatoire, rotatif (-ive *f*); de rotation; ⊕ ∼ **press** rotative *f*; ⚡ ∼ **switch** commutateur *m* rotatif; **ro·tate** [rou'teit] (faire) tourner; (faire) basculer; *v/t.* alterner (*les cultures*); **ro'ta·tion** rotation *f*; basculage *m*; *fig.* succession *f* tour à tour; *fig.* roulement *m*; ✎ ~ *of crops* assolement *m*; **ro‧ta‧to‧ry** ['ˌʌtətəri] *see rotary*; ~ *door* (*ou gate*) porte *f* tournante; ~ *stage* plateau *m* tournant.

rote [rout] routine *f*; *by* ~ par cœur, mécaniquement.

ro‧tor ['routə] ⊕, ✈, ✈ *hélicoptère*: rotor *m*.

rot‧ten □ ['rɔtn] pourri (*a. fig.*); gâté; 🐛 carié; *sl.* moche, sale, mauvais; **'rot‧ten‧ness** (état *m* de) pourriture *f*.

rot‧ter *sl.* ['rɔtə] sale type *m*.

ro‧tund □ [rou'tʌnd] rond, arrondi; ampoulé (*style*); **ro'tun‧da** 🏛 [ˌdə] rotonde *f*; **ro'tun‧di‧ty** rondeur *f*; *style*: grandiloquence *f*.

rou‧ble ['ruːbl] rouble *m*.

rouge [ruːʒ] 1. rouge *m*, fard *m*; 2. (se) farder; mettre du rouge.

rough [rʌf] 1. □ rude (*chemin, parler, peau, surface, vin, voix*); rêche, rugueux (-euse *f*) (*peau, surface, voix*); grossier (-ère *f*); dépoli (*verre*); inégal (-aux *m/pl.*) (*terrain*); brutal (-aux *m/pl.*), violent; fruste (*conduite, style*); agité (*mer*); âpre (*vin*); ⊕ brut; approximatif (-ive *f*); ~ *draft* brouillon *m*; ~ *and ready* exécuté grossièrement; *fig.* de fortune; *fig.* primitif (-ive *f*); sans façon (*personne*); *be* ~ *on s.o. évènement etc.*: être un coup dur pour q.; *be* ~ *with s.o.,* give *s.o. a* ~ *time* (*of it*) être dur ave q.; *cut up* ~ réagir avec violence; 2. état *m* brut; terrain *m* accidenté; *golf:* herbe *f* longue; *personne:* voyou *m*; 3. ébouriffer; (faire) aciérer les fers (*d'un cheval*); ~ *it* vivre à la dure; **'rough‧age** détritus *m/pl.*; **'rough‧cast** 1. ⊕ pièce *f* brute de fonderie; 2. 🏛 crépi; ⊕ brut de fonte; 3. ⊕ crépir (*un mur*); *fig.* ébaucher (*un plan*); **'rough‧en** rendre ou devenir rude *etc.*

rough...: ~**hewn** ['ˌ'hjuːn] taillé à coups de hache; dégrossi; *fig.* ébauché; ~ **house** *sl.* chahut *m*; '~**house** *v/i.* chahuter; *v/t.* malmener; '~**neck** *Am. sl.* canaille *f*, voyou *m*; **'rough‧ness** rudesse *f*, rugosité *f*; grossièreté *f*; **'rough‧rid‧er** dresseur *m* de chevaux; F casse-cou *m/inv.*; ✗ *hist.* cavalier *m* d'un corps irrégulier; **'rough‧shod**: *ride* ~ *over* fouler (*q.*) aux pieds; traiter cavalièrement.

Rou‧ma‧ni‧a(n) *see Rumania(n)*.

round [raund] 1. □ rond (*a. fig.*); circulaire; plein; gros(se *f*) (*juron etc.*); voûté (*épaules*); ~ *game* jeu *m* en commun; ~ *hand* (écriture *f*) ronde *f*; ~ *trip* aller *m* et retour *m*; 2. *adv.* (tout) autour; (*souv.* ~ *about*) à l'entour; *all* ~ tout autour; tout à l'entour; *fig.* dans l'ensemble; sans exception; *all the year* ~ (pendant) toute l'année; *10 inches* ~ dix pouces de tour; 3. *prp.* (*souv.* ~ *about*) autour de; vers (*trois heures*); environ; *go* ~ *the shops* faire le tour des magasins; 4. *su.* cercle *m*, rond *m* (*a.* 🏛); *cartes, tennis, voyage, etc.*: tour *m*; *bière, facteur, médecin:* tournée *f*; ✗ ronde *f* (*d'un officier*); *sp.* circuit *m*; *box.* round *m*; *fig.* train *m*; ✗ fusillade, *fig.* applaudissements: salve *f*; ✗ *munitions:* cartouche *f*; ♩ canon *m*; ✗ *100* ~*s* cent cartouches; 5. (s')arrondir; contourner (*une colline, un obstacle*); ⚓ doubler (*un cap*); ~ *off* arrondir; *fig.* achever; F ~ *on* dénoncer (*q.*); ~ *up* rassembler; rafler (*des voleurs*).

round‧a‧bout ['raundəbaut] 1. indirect, détourné; ~ *system* (*of traffic*) sens *m* giratoire; 2. détour *m*; clôture *f* circulaire; carrousel *m*; *mot.* F sens *m* gyro.

roun‧del ['raundl] rondeau *m*; ♩ ronde *f*; **roun‧de‧lay** ['ˌdilei] chanson *f* à refrain; *danse:* ronde *f*.

round‧ers ['raundəz] *pl.* balle *f* au camp; **'round‧head** *hist.* tête *f* ronde; **'round‧ish** presque rond; **'round‧ness** rondeur *f*; **rounds‧man** ✝ ['ˌzmən] livreur *m*; **'round‧ta‧ble con‧fer‧ence** *f* paritaire; **'round-'up** rassemblement *m*; rafle *f* (*de voleurs etc.*).

roup *vét.* [ruːp] diphtérie *f* des poules.

rouse [rauz] *v/t.* (*a.* ~ *up*) (r)éveiller; faire lever (*le gibier*); susciter; mettre en colère; remuer; *v/i.* se réveiller; (*a.* ~ *o.s.*) se secouer; **'rous‧ing** qui excite; enlevant (*discours*); chaleureux (-euse *f*) (*applaudissements*).

roust‧a‧bout *Am.* ['raustəbaut] débardeur *m*; manœuvre *m*.

rout[1] [raut] bande *f*; ⚖ attroupement *m*; *a. see riot 1*; † soirée *f*.

rout² [~] 1. ⚔ déroute f; débandade f; put to ~ = 2. mettre en déroute.
rout³ [~] see root².

route [ru:t; ⚔ raut] route f (a. ⚔); itinéraire m; '~-march marche f d'entraînement.

rou·tine [ru:'ti:n] 1. routine f; ⚔, ⚓ emploi m du temps; fig. train-train m (journalier); 2. courant; ordinaire.

rove [rouv] v/i. rôder; vagabonder, errer; v/t. parcourir; '**rov·er** coureur m, vagabond m; éclaireur m.

row¹ [rou] rang m (a. théâ.), rangée f; file f (de voitures); ligne f (de maisons etc.); Am. a hard ~ to hoe une tâche f difficile.

row² [~] 1. ramer; faire du canotage; 2. promenade f en canot.

row³ F [rau] 1. vacarme m, tapage m; chahut m; dispute f, rixe f; F réprimande f; what's the ~? qu'est-ce qui se passe?; 2. v/t. semoncer (q.); v/i. se quereller (avec, with).

row·an ♀ ['rauən] sorbier m commun; '~-ber·ry sorbe f.

row-boat ['roubout] bateau m à rames, canot m.

row·dy ['raudi] 1. chahuteur m; voyou m; 2. tapageur (-euse f).

row·el ['rauəl] 1. molette f (d'éperon); 2. éperonner.

row·er ['rouə] rameur (-euse f) m.

row·house Am. ['rouhaus] maison f attenante aux maisons voisines.

row·ing-boat ['rouiŋbout] see row-boat.

row·lock ⚓ ['rɔlək] tolet m, dame f.

roy·al ['rɔiəl] 1. □ royal (-aux m/pl.); fig. princier (-ère f); 2. ⚓ cacatois m; (a. ~ stag) cerf m à douze andouillers; F the ~s pl. la famille f royale; '**roy·al·ism** royalisme m; '**roy·al·ist** royaliste (a. su./mf); '**roy·al·ty** royauté f; personnage m royal; royalties pl. droits m/pl. d'auteur; redevance f (à un inventeur).

rub [rʌb] 1. frottement m; friction f; coup m de torchon; F there is the ~ c'est là le diable; 2. v/t. frotter; frictionner; ~ down frictionner; ⊕ adoucir; panser (un cheval); ~ in frictionner (q. à qch.); F don't ~ it in! n'insiste(z) pas!; ~ off enlever par le frottement; ~ out effacer; ~ up astiquer; faire reluire; rafraîchir sa mémoire de; v/i. (personne: se)

frotter (contre against, on); fig. ~ along (ou on ou through) se débrouiller.

rub-a-dub ['rʌbədʌb] tambour: rataplan m.

rub·ber ['rʌbə] caoutchouc m; gomme f à effacer; personne: frotteur (-euse f) m; ⊕ frottoir m; torchon m; ⊕ (a. ~ file) carreau m; cartes: robre m; Am. ~s pl. caoutchoucs m/pl.; attr. de ou en caoutchouc; à gomme (arbre); Am. sl. ~ check chèque m sans provision; ~ solution dissolution f de caoutchouc; '~-neck Am. sl. 1. badaud(e f) m; touriste mf; 2. badauder; ~ stamp timbre m (en) caoutchouc; tampon m; fig. Am. F fonctionnaire m qui exécute aveuglément les ordres de ses supérieurs.

rub·bish ['rʌbiʃ] Brit. ordures f/pl., immondices f/pl., détritus m/pl.; ⊕ rebuts m/pl.; fig. fatras m; fig. camelote f; fig. bêtises f/pl.; Brit. ~ bin poubelle f; Brit. ~ chute vide-ordures m/inv.; Brit. ~ dump décharge f, dépotoir m; Brit. ~ heap monceau m de détritus, tas m d'ordures. '**rub·bish·y** sans valeur; de camelote.

rub·ble ['rʌbl] moellons m/pl. (bruts); (a. ~-work) moellonage m.

rube Am. sl. [ru:b] croquant m; nigaud m.

ru·be·fa·cient ✣ [ru:bi'feiʃjənt] rubéfiant (a. su./m).

ru·bi·cund ['ru:bikənd] rubicond, rougeaud.

ru·bric typ., eccl. ['ru:brik] rubrique f; **ru·bri·cate** ['~keit] rubriquer.

ru·by ['ru:bi] 1. min. rubis m; couleur f de rubis; typ. corps m 5½; 2. rouge, vermeil(le f).

ruck [rʌk] courses: the ~ les coureurs m/pl.; fig. le commun m (du peuple); cost. fronçure f.

ruck(·le) ['rʌk(l)] (se) froisser; v/i. se rider; plisser.

ruck·sack ['ruksæk] sac m à dos.

ruc·tion sl. ['rʌkʃn] bagarre f, scène f.

rud·der ⚓, a. ✈ ['rʌdə] gouvernail m.

rud·di·ness ['rʌdinis] rougeur f; coloration f du teint; **rud·dle** ['rʌdl] 1. ocre f rouge; 2. frotter d'ocre rouge; marquer ou passer (qch.) à l'ocre rouge; '**rud·dy** rouge; rougeâtre; coloré (teint); sl. sacré.

rude □ [ru:d] primitif (-ive *f*) (*dessin, outil, peuple, temps, etc.*); grossier (-ère *f*) (*langage, méthode, outil, personne*); rudimentaire; fruste (*style etc.*); *fig.* violent; mal élevé, impoli (*personne*); ⊕ brut (*minerai*); robuste (*santé*).

ru·di·ment *biol.* ['ru:dimənt] rudiment *m* (de, of) (*a. fig.*); **~s** *pl. a.* éléments *m/pl.*; **ru·di·men·ta·ry** [~'mentəri] rudimentaire.

rue[1] ♀ [ru:] rue *f*.

rue[2] [~] se repentir de, regretter amèrement.

rue·ful □ ['ru:ful] triste, lugubre; **'rue·ful·ness** tristesse *f*; air *m* triste *ou* lugubre; ton *m* triste.

ruff[1] [rʌf] fraise *f*, collerette *f*; *orn., zo.* collier *m*, cravate *f*; *orn.* pigeon *m* à cravate; *orn.* paon *m* de mer.

ruff[2] [~] *whist*: 1. coupe *f*; 2. couper (*avec un atout*).

ruf·fi·an ['rʌfjən] bandit *m*, apache *m*; F enfant: polisson *m*; **'ruf·fi·an·ly** de bandit, de brute; brutal (-aux *m/pl.*).

ruf·fle ['rʌfl] 1. manchette *f* en dentelle; rides *f/pl.* (*sur l'eau*); *fig.* ennui *m*; agitation *f*; **~ collar** fraise *f*; 2. *v/t.* ébouriffer; agiter; hérisser (*les plumes*); irriter, froisser (*q.*); *cost.* rucher; plisser; froisser (*une robe*); *v/i.* s'ébouriffer; s'agiter; se hérisser (*oiseau*).

rug [rʌg] couverture *f*; (*a. floor ~*) carpette *f*; descente *f* de lit.

Rug·by (**foot·ball**) ['rʌgbi ('futbɔ:l)] *le* rugby *m*.

rug·ged □ ['rʌgid] raboteux (-euse *f*) (*terrain, style*); rugueux (-euse *f*); rude (*traits, tempérament*); **'rugged·ness** nature *f* raboteuse; rudesse *f*.

ru·in ['ru:in] 1. ruine *f*; *usu.* **~s** *pl.* ruine *f*, -s *f/pl.*; *lay in* **~s** détruire de fond en comble; 2. ruiner; abîmer; gâcher; séduire (*une femme*); **ru·in·a·tion** F ruine *f*, perte *f*; **'ru·in·ous** □ délabré, en ruines; *fig.* ruineux (-euse *f*) (*dépenses etc.*).

rule [ru:l] 1. règle *f* (*a. eccl.*); règlement *m*; (*a. standing ~*) règle *f* fixe; empire *m*, autorité *f*; 𝔱𝔱 ordonnance *f*, décision *f*; ⊕ mètre *m*; *typ.* filet *m*; *as a ~* en règle générale; 𝔱𝔱 **~(s)** *of court* directive *f* de procédure; décision *f* du tribunal;

mot. **~** *of the road* code *m* de la route; ⚓ règles *f/pl.* de route; ✠ **~** *of three* règle *f* de trois; **~** *of thumb* méthode *f* empirique; procédé *m* mécanique; *make it a* **~** se faire une règle (de *inf.*, to *inf.*); *work to* **~** faire la grève du règlement; **2.** *v/t.* gouverner; (*a.* **~** *over*) régner sur; commander à; 𝔱𝔱 décider, déclarer; régler (*du papier*); tracer à la règle (*une ligne*); **~** *the roost* (*ou roast*) être le maître; **~** *out* rayer; éliminer; *v/i.* régner; ✝ rester, se pratiquer (*prix*); **'rul·er** souverain(e *f*) *m*; règle *f*, mètre *m*; **'rul·ing** **1.** *surt.* 𝔱𝔱 ordonnance *f*, décision *f*; **2.** ✝ *price* prix *m* du jour.

rum[1] [rʌm] rhum *m*; *Am.* spiritueux *m*.

rum[2] *sl.* [~] □ bizarre.

Ru·ma·nian [ru:'meinjən] **1.** roumain; **2.** *ling.* roumain *m*; Roumain(e *f*) *m*.

rum·ble[1] ['rʌmbl] **1.** roulement *m*; *tonnerre:* grondement *m*; grouillement *m*; *surt. mot.* siège *m* de derrière; (*Am.* **~-seat**) spider *m*; *Am.* F bagarre *f* entre deux bandes d'adolescents; **2.** rouler; gronder (*tonnerre*); grouiller (*ventre*).

rum·ble[2] *sl.* [~] pénétrer les intentions de (*q.*) *ou* le secret de (*qch.*).

rum·bus·tious □ F [rʌm'bʌstiəs] exubérant.

ru·mi·nant ['ru:minənt] ruminant (*a. su./m*); **ru·mi·nate** ['~neit] ruminer (*a. fig.*); *fig. a.* méditer; **ru·mi·na·tion** rumination *f*; méditation *f*.

rum·mage ['rʌmidʒ] **1.** fouille *f*, recherches *f/pl.*; ✝ (*usu.* **~** *goods pl.*) choses *f/pl.* de rebut; **~** *sale* vente *f* d'objets usagés; **2.** *v/t.* (far)fouiller; *v/i.* fouiller (pour trouver, for).   [Rhin.]

rum·mer ['rʌmə] verre *m* à vin du }

rum·my[1] *sl.* □ ['rʌmi] bizarre.

rum·my[2] [~] *sorte de jeu de cartes*.

ru·mo(u)r ['ru:mə] **1.** rumeur *f*, bruit *m*; **2.** répandre (*une nouvelle*); *it is* **~ed** *that* le bruit court que; **'~-mon·ger** colporteur *m* de faux bruits.

rump *anat.* [rʌmp] croupe *f*, *orn.* croupion *m* (*a.* F *co. d'un homme*); *cuis.* culotte *f* (*de bœuf*).

rum·ple ['rʌmpl] *v/t.* froisser; chiffonner; *fig.* contrarier, vexer.

rump·steak [ˈrʌmpsteik] romsteck *m.*

rum·pus F [ˈrʌmpəs] chahut *m*; fracas *m*; *Am.* ~ room salle *f* de jeux.

rum-run·ner *Am.* [ˈrʌmrʌnə] contrebandier *m* de spiritueux.

run [rʌn] **1.** [*irr.*] *v/i.* courir (*personne, animal, bruit, sp.,* ♣, *fig., etc.*); *mot.* aller, rouler, marcher (*a.* ⊕); ♣ faire route; ♣ faire la traversée; 🚢 faire le service (entre Londres et la côte, *between London and the coast*); ⊕ fonctionner, être en marche; ⊕ tourner (*roue*); remonter les rivières (*saumon*); (s'en)fuir, se sauver; s'écouler (*temps*); couler (*rivière, plume,* ⊕ *pièce, a. couleur au lavage*); s'étendre (*encre, tache*); 🩸 suppurer (*ulcère*); *théâ.* tenir l'affiche; se jouer; se démailler (*bas*); *journ. Am.* paraître (*annonce*); ~ *across s.o.* rencontrer q. par hasard; ~ *after* courir après; ~ *away* s'enfuir; *fig.* enlever (q., *with s.o.*); ~ *down* descendre en courant; s'arrêter (*montre etc.*); *fig.* décliner; ~ *dry* se dessécher, s'épuiser; F ~ *for* courir après; *parl.* se porter candidat à *ou* pour; ~ *high* gros(se *f*) (*mer*); s'échauffer (*sentiments*); *that* ~*s in the blood* (*ou family*) cela tient de famille; ~ *into* tomber dans; entrer en collision avec; rencontrer (q.) par hasard; s'élever à; ~ *low* s'abaisser; ~ *mad* perdre la tête; ~ *off* (s'en)fuir; ~ *on* continuer sa course; s'écouler (*temps*); suivre son cours; continuer à parler; ~ *out* sortir en courant; couler; s'épuiser; *I have* ~ *out of tobacco* je n'ai plus de tabac; ~ *over* parcourir; passer en revue; écraser (q.); ~ *short of* venir à bout de (*qch.*); ~ *through* traverser (en courant); parcourir du regard; dissiper (*une fortune*); ~ *to* se monter à, s'élever à; être de l'ordre de; F durer; F être suffisant pour (*inf.*); ~ *up* monter en courant; accourir; s'élever (*somme*); ~ *up to* s'élever à; ~ (*up*)*on* se ruer sur; rencontrer par hasard; ~ *with* ruisseler de; **2.** [*irr.*] *v/t.* courir (*une distance, une course*); mettre au galop (*un cheval*); *équit.* faire courir; chasser (*un renard*); diriger (*un navire, un train*) (sur, *to*); assurer le service de (*un navire, un autobus*); ⊕ faire fonc-

tionner; ⊕ couler, jeter (*du métal*); *fig.* entretenir (*une auto*); avoir (*une auto, la fièvre*); diriger (*affaire, ferme, hôtel, magasin, théâtre, etc.*); tenir (*hôtel, magasin, ménage*); éditer (*un journal etc.*); exploiter (*une usine*); (faire) passer; tracer (*une ligne*); 🌱 vendre; F appuyer (*un candidat*); ~ *the blockade* forcer le blocus; ~ *down* renverser (q.); *mot.* écraser (q.); ♣ couler; *fig.* dénigrer, éreinter; F attraper, dépister; *be* ~ *down* être à plat; être épuisé; ~ *errands* faire des courses *ou* commissions; ~ *s.o. hard* presser q.; ~ *in mot. etc.* roder; F arrêter (*un criminel*), conduire au poste (*de police*); *mot.* s'embou-tir contre; ~ *off* faire écouler (*un liquide*); réciter tout d'une haleine; faire (*qch.*) en moins de rien *ou* à la hâte; ~ *out* chasser; filer (*une corde*); ~ *over* passer sur le corps à, écraser (q.); parcourir (*un texte*); ~ *s.o. through* transpercer q.; ~ *up* hisser (*un pavillon*); faire monter (*le prix*); bâtir à la va-vite (*un bâtiment*); confectionner à la hâte (*une robe*); laisser grossir (*un compte*); laisser monter (*une dette*); **3.** action *f* de courir; course *f*; *mot.* tour *m*, promenade *f*; ♣ traversée *f*, parcours *m*; ⊕ trajet *m*; ⊕ marche *f*; *fig.* cours *m*, marche *f*; suite *f*; *théâ.* durée *f*; ♪ roulade *f*; 🌱 ruée *f*, descente *f* (sur, [*up*]*on*); *Am.* petit ruisseau *m*; *surt. Am.* bas de dames: échelle *f*; 🌱 catégorie *f*; *cartes:* séquence *f*; *fig.* libre accès *m*; élan *m*; *the common* ~ le commun, l'ordinaire; *théâ. a* ~ *of 50 nights* 50 représentations; ~ (*up*)*on a bank* descente *f* sur une banque; *be in the* ~(*ning*) avoir des chances (d'arriver); *in the long* ~ à la longue, en fin de compte; *in the short* ~ ne songeant qu'au présent; *on the* ~ sans le temps de s'asseoir; en fuite.

run···: ~·**a·bout** *mot.* [ˈrʌnəbaut] voiturette *f*; (*a.* ~ *car*) petite auto *f*; ~·**a·way** [ˈrʌnəwei] fugitif (-ive *f*) *m*; cheval *m* emballé.

run-down 1. [rʌnˈdaun] épuisé; surmené; ruiné; délabré; **2.** F [ˈrʌndaun] compte *m* rendu minutieux.

rune [ruːn] rune *f.*

rung¹ [rʌŋ] *p.p.* de *ring²* 2.

rung² [⌣] échelon *m*; *échelle:* traverse *f.*

run·ic ['ruːnik] runique.

run-in F ['rʌn'in] querelle *f*, altercation *f.*

run·let ['rʌnlit], **run·nel** ['rʌnl] ruisseau *m*; rigole *f.*

run·ner ['rʌnə] coureur (-euse *f*) *m*; ✗ courrier *m*; *traîneau:* patin *m*; *lit, tiroir, etc.:* coulisseau *m*; ♀ coulant *m*; ♀ traînée *f* (*du fraisier*); *courses:* partant *m*; ⊕ poulie *f* fixe; ⊕ roue *f* mobile; chariot *m* ou galet *m* de roulement; *métall.* jet *m* (de coulée); **~-up** *sp.* ['⌣ər'ʌp] bon second *m*; deuxième *m.*

run·ning ['rʌniŋ] **1.** courant; *two days* ~ deux jours de suite; ✗ ~ *fight* combat *m* de retraite; ✗ ~ *fire* feu *m* roulant *ou* continu; ~ *hand* écriture *f* cursive; *sp.* ~ *start* départ *m* lancé; ~ *stitch* point *m* devant; **2.** course *f*, -s *f/pl.*; '**~-board** mot., 🚂 marchepied *m*; 🚂 tablier *m.*

run-of-the-mill [rʌnɔvðə'mil] ordinaire; banal (-als *m/pl.*); médiocre.

runt [rʌnt] *zo.* bœuf *m* ou vache *f* de petite race; *fig.* nain *m.*

run-up ['rʌnʌp] période *f* préparatoire.

run·way ['rʌnwei] ✈ piste *f* d'envol; *chasse:* coulée *f*; ⊕ chemin *m* de roulement.

ru·pee [ruː'piː] roupie *f.*

rup·ture ['rʌptʃə] **1.** rupture *f*; ⚕ *a.* hernie *f*; **2.** (se) rompre; *be* ~*d* avoir une hernie.

ru·ral [ː] ['ruərəl] rural (-aux *m/pl.*); champêtre; *des champs;* '**ru·ral·ize** *v/t.* rendre rural; *v/i.* vivre à la campagne.

rush¹ ♀ [rʌʃ] jonc *m.*

rush² [⌣] **1.** course *f* précipitée; élan *m*, bond *m*; hâte *f*; bouffée *f* (*d'air*); ✗ bond *m*; ✗, ✝ demande *f* considérable; torrent *m* (*d'eau*); ~ *hours pl.* heures *f/pl.* d'affluence; ✝ coup *m* de feu; ✝ ~ *order* commande *f* urgente; **2.** *v/i.* se précipiter, s'élancer (sur, *at*); se jeter; ~ *into extremes* se porter aux dernières extrémités; ~ *into print*

publier à la légère; F ~ *to conclusions* conclure trop hâtivement; *v/t.* pousser *etc.* violemment; chasser; faire faire au galop; ✗ prendre d'assaut; *fig.* envahir; dépêcher (*un travail*); exécuter à la hâte *ou* d'urgence; *sl.* faire payer (*qch.* à *q.*); *parl.* ~ *through* faire passer à la hâte; '**rush·ing** ☐ tumultueux (-euse *f*).

rush·y ['rʌʃi] plein de joncs; fait de jonc.

rusk [rʌsk] biscotte *f.*

rus·set ['rʌsit] **1.** roussâtre; **2.** couleur *f* roussâtre; † drap *m* de bure.

Rus·sia leath·er ['rʌʃə'leðə] cuir *m* de Russie; '**Rus·sian 1.** russe; **2.** *ling.* russe *m*; Russe *mf.*

rust [rʌst] **1.** rouille *f*; **2.** (se) rouiller (*a. fig.*).

rus·tic ['rʌstik] **1.** (~*ally*) rustique; agreste; paysan(ne *f*); **2.** paysan(ne *f*) *m*, campagnard(e *f*) *m*; rustaud(e *f*) *m*; **rus·ti·cate** ['⌣keit] *v/t. univ.* renvoyer pendant un temps; *v/i.* habiter la campagne; **rus·ti·ca·tion** vie *f* à la campagne; *univ.* renvoi *m* temporaire; **rus·tic·i·ty** [⌣'tisiti] rusticité *f.*

rus·tle ['rʌsl] **1.** (faire) bruire, froufrouter; *v/t. a.* froisser; *Am.* F ramasser, réunir; voler (*du bétail*); **2.** bruissement *m*; frou-frou *m*; froissement *m.*

rust...: '**~·less** sans rouille; ✝ inoxydable; '**~-'proof,** '**~-re·sist·ant** antirouille; inoxydable; '**rust·y** rouillé (*a. fig.*); couleur de rouille; rouilleux (-euse *f*).

rut¹ *zo.* [rʌt] **1.** rut *m*; **2.** être en rut.

rut² [⌣] ornière *f* (*a. fig.*); *fig. a.* routine *f.*

ruth·less ☐ ['ruːθlis] impitoyable; brutal (-aux *m/pl.*) (*acte, vérité*); '**ruth·less·ness** nature *f* *ou* caractère *m* impitoyable.   [(*chemin*).\

rut·ted ['rʌtid] coupé d'ornières∫

rut·ting *zo.* ['rʌtiŋ] du rut; en rut; ~ *season* saison *f* du rut.

rut·ty ['rʌti] coupé d'ornières (*chemin*).

rye [rai] ♀ seigle *m*; *Am. sorte de whisky.*

S

S, s [es] S *m*, s *m*.

sab·bath ['sæbəθ] *bibl.* sabbat *m*; *eccl.* dimanche *m*.

sab·bat·ic, sab·bat·i·cal □ [sə-'bætik(l)] sabbatique; *univ.* sab-batical year année *f* de congé.

sa·ble ['seibl] **1.** *zo.* zibeline *f* (*a. fourrure*); noir *m*; ▨ sable *m*; **2.** noir; *poét.* de deuil.

sab·o·tage ['sæbətɑːʒ] **1.** sabotage *m*; **2.** saboter (*a. fig.*).

sa·bre ['seibə] **1.** sabre *m*; **2.** sabrer; **sa·bre·tache** ✗ ['sæbətæʃ] sabre-tache *f*.

sac·cha·rin(e) 🜛 ['sækərin] saccha-rine *f*; **sac·cha·rine** ['⁓rain] saccha-rin.

sac·er·do·tal □ [sæsə'doutl] sacer-dotal (-aux *m/pl.*); de prêtre.

sack[1] [sæk] **1.** sac *m*; (*a. ⁓ coat*) vareuse *f* de sport, *p*ardessus *m* sac; F get the ⁓ recevoir son congé; give s.o. the ⁓ donner son congé à q.; F hit the ⁓ se pieuter, aller au pieu (= *se coucher*); **2.** mettre en sac; F congédier (*q.*), mettre (*q.*) à pied.

sack[2] [⁓] **1.** sac *m*, pillage *m*; **2.** (*a. put to ⁓*) mettre à sac *ou* au pil-lage.

sack·cloth ['sækklɔθ], **'sack·ing** toile *f* à sacs; *sackcloth and ashes* le sac et la cendre; **sack·ful** ['⁓ful] plein sac *m*, sachée *f*.

sac·ra·ment *eccl.* ['sækrəmənt] sa-crement *m*; **sac·ra·men·tal** □ [⁓'mentl] sacramentel(le *f*).

sa·cred □ ['seikrid] sacré; saint (*histoire*); religieux (-euse *f*) (*musi-que etc.*); **'sa·cred·ness** caractère *m* sacré; *serment*: inviolabilité *f*.

sac·ri·fice ['sækrifais] **1.** sacrifice *m*; ✝ at a ⁓ à perte; **2.** sacrifier; ✝ a. vendre à perte; **'sac·ri·fic·er** sacrificateur (-trice *f*) *m*.

sac·ri·fi·cial [sækri'fiʃl] sacrifica-toire; ✝ à perte (*vente*).

sac·ri·lege ['sækrilidʒ] sacrilège *m*; **sac·ri·le·gious** □ [⁓'lidʒəs] sacri-lège.

sa·crist ['seikrist], **sac·ris·tan** *eccl.* ['sækristən] sacristain *m*.

sac·ris·ty *eccl.* ['sækristi] sacristie *f*.

sad □ [sæd] triste; déplorable; malheureux (-euse *f*); cruel(le *f*); fâcheux (-euse *f*); terne (*couleur*).

sad·den ['sædn] (s')affliger; *v/t.* at-trister.

sad·dle ['sædl] **1.** selle *f*; **2.** (*a. ⁓ up*) seller; *fig.* charger (q. de qch. *s.o. with s.th.*, *s.th. on s.o.*); F encombrer (de, *with*); **'⁓·backed** ensellé (*che-val*); **'⁓·bag** sacoche *f* de selle; **'⁓·cloth** tapis *m* de selle; housse *f* de cheval; **'sad·dler** sellier *m*; *Am.* cheval *m* de selle; **'sad·dler·y** sel-lerie *f*.

sad·ism ['sædizm] sadisme *m*; **'sad·ist** sadique *mf*; **sa·dis·tic** [sæ'distik] sadique; ⁓ally avec sadisme.

sad·ness ['sædnis] tristesse *f*, mélan-colie *f*.

sa·fa·ri [sə'fɑːri] expédition *f* de chasse.

safe [seif] **1.** □ en sûreté (contre, *from*), à l'abri (de, *from*); sûr; sans risque; hors de danger; ⁓ and sound sain et sauf; be on the ⁓ side être du bon côté; **2.** coffre-fort (*pl.* coffres-forts) *m*; ♣ caisse *f* du bord; *cuis.* garde-manger *m/inv.*; *théâ.* ⁓ deposit dépôt *m* en coffre-fort; **'⁓·break·er**, **'⁓·crack·er** *Am.* crocheteur *m* de cof-fres-forts; **'⁓·con·duct** sauf-con-duit *m*; **'⁓·guard 1.** sauvegarde *f*; **2.** sauvegarder, protéger; ⁓ing duty tarif *m* de sauvegarde; **'safe·ness** sûreté *f*; sécurité *f*.

safe·ty ['seifti] **1.** sûreté *f*; sécurité *f*; **2.** de sûreté; ⁓ belt ceinture *f* de sécurité; *théâ.* ⁓ curtain rideau *m* de fer; ⁓ glass verre *m* Sécurit (*TM*); ⁓ island refuge *m*; ⁓ lamp lampe *f* de mineur; ⁓ match allumette *f* de sûreté; ⁓ lock serrure *f* de sûreté; ⁓ pin épingle *f* de nourrice; ⁓ razor rasoir *m* de sûreté.

saf·fron ['sæfrən] **1.** safran *m* (*a. couleur*); **2.** safran *inv.*

sag [sæg] **1.** fléchir (*a.* ✝); s'affaisser; ⊕ pencher d'un côté; se relâcher (*corde*); pendre; **2.** affaissement *m* (*a.* ⊕); ♣ dérive *f*; ✝ baisse *f*.

sa·ga ['sɑːgə] saga *f*.

sa·ga·cious □ [sə'geiʃəs] sagace, avisé, rusé.

sa·gac·i·ty [sə'gæsiti] sagacité *f*.

sage[1] [seidʒ] **1.** □ sage, prudent; **2.** sage *m*.

sage[2] ♀ [~] sauge *f*.

Sa·git·tar·i·us *astr.* [sædʒi'tɛəriəs] le Sagittaire *m*.

sa·go ['seigou] sagou *m*.

said [sed] *prét. et p.p. de* say 1.

sail [seil] **1.** voile *f*; *coll.* toile *f*; promenade *f* à voile; *10* ~ dix navires *m/pl.*; **2.** *v/i.* naviguer; faire route; partir; *fig.* planer, voler; *v/t.* naviguer sur; conduire (*un vaisseau*); '~**boat** canot *m* à voiles; '~**cloth** toile *f* à voile, canevas *m*; '**sail·er** bateau: voilier *m*; '**sail·ing-ship**, '**sail·ing-vessel** voilier *m*; navire *m* à voiles; '**sail·or** marin *m*; matelot *m*; *cost.* ~ *blouse* marinière *f*; ~'*s knot* nœud *m* régate; *be a good* (*bad*) ~ (*ne pas*) avoir le pied marin; '**sail-plane** planeur *m*.

sain-foin ♀ ['seinfɔin] sainfoin *m*; F éparcette *f*.

saint [seint; *devant npr.* sənt] **1.** saint(e *f*) *m*; *the* ~*s pl.* les fidèles *m/pl.* trépassés; **2.** *v/t.* canoniser; *v/i.* F ~ (*it*) faire le saint; '**saint·ed** saint; '**saint·li·ness** sainteté *f*; '**saint·ly** *adj.* (de) saint.

sake [seik]: *for the* ~ *of* à cause de; pour l'amour de; dans l'intérêt de; *for my* ~ pour moi, pour me faire plaisir; *for God's* ~ pour l'amour de Dieu.

sal 🜔 [sæl] sel *m*; ~ *ammoniac* sel *m* ammoniac; ~ *volatile* sels *m/pl.* (volatils).

sal·a·ble ['seiləbl] vendable.

sa·la·cious □ [sə'leiʃəs] lubrique.

sal·ad ['sæləd] salade *f*.

sal·a·man·der ['sæləmændə] *zo.* salamandre *f*; *cuis.* couvercle *m* à braiser.

sa·la·me, sa·la·mi [sə'lɑːmi] salami *m*.

sal·a·ried ['sælərid] rétribué; aux appointements (*personne*); '**sal·a·ry** **1.** traitement *m*, appointements *m/pl.*; **2.** payer des appointements

à; '**sal·a·ry-earn·er** salarié(e *f*) *m*.

sale [seil] vente *f* (✝ *de réclame*); (*a. public* ~) vente *f* aux enchères; *for* (*ou on*) ~ en vente; à vendre; *private* ~ vente *f* à l'amiable; '**sale·a·ble** vendable; de vente facile.

sale...: '~**-note** bordereau *m* de vente; '~**-room** salle *f* de(s) vente(s).

sales... [seilz]: ~ *clerk* Am. vendeur (-euse *f*)*m*; ~ **com·mis·sion** commission *f* (pour la vente); '~**man** vendeur *m*; '~**-girl**, '~**-wom·an** vendeuse *f*; ~ **room** salle *f* des ventes; ~ **talk** Am. boniment *m*.

sa·li·ence ['seiliəns] projection *f*; saillie *f*; '**sa·li·ent** □ saillant (*a. fig.*); en saillie; *fig.* frappant.

sa·line 1. ['seilain] salin (*a.* 🜊), salé; **2.** [sə'lain] salin *m*; 🜊 sel *m* purgatif.

sa·li·va [sə'laivə] salive *f*; '**sal·i·var·y** ['sælivəri] salivaire; **sal·i·'va·tion** salivation *f*.

sal·low[1] ♀ ['sælou] saule *m*.

sal·low[2] [~] jaunâtre, olivâtre; '**sal·low·ness** teint: ton *m* jaunâtre.

sal·ly ['sæli] **1.** ⚔ sortie *f* (*a. fig.*), *esprit, etc.:* saillie *f*; **2.** ⚔ (*a.* ~ *out*) faire une sortie; ~ *forth* (*ou out*) se mettre en route; '~**-port** ⚔ poterne *f* (de sortie).

sal·ma·gun·di [sælmə'gʌndi] salmigondis *m*; *fig.* méli-mélo (*pl.* mélismélos) *m*.

salm·on ['sæmən] **1.** saumon *m* (*a. couleur*); **2.** saumon *inv.*

sa·loon [sə'luːn] salon *m* (*a. de paquebot*); salle *f*; première classe *f* (*en bateau*); *Am.* cabaret *m*; **sa·'loon-car** 🚆 wagon-salon (*pl.* wagonssalons) *m*); *mot.* (voiture *f* à) conduite *f* intérieure, limousine *f*.

salt [sɔːlt] sel *m* (*a. fig.*); *fig.* piquant *m*; *old* ~ loup *m* de mer (= *vieux matelot*); *above* (*below*) *the* ~ au haut (bas) bout de la table; **2.** salé (*a. fig.*); salin; salifère; **3.** saler; *sl.* ~ *away* mettre de côté, économiser.

sal·ta·tion [sæl'teiʃn] saltation *f*; *biol.* mutation *f*.

salt...: '~**-cel·lar** salière *f*; '**salt·ed** F immunisé; *fig.* endurci; '**salt·er** saleur (-euse *f*) *m*; saunier *m*; fabricant *m* de sel; '**salt-free** sans sel; '**salt·ness** salure *f*, salinité *f*; **salt·pe·tre** ['~-piːtə] salpêtre *m*, nitre *m*; '**salt-shak·er** Am. salière *f*; '**salt·works**

saunerie *f*, saline *f*; **'salt·y** salé (*a. fig.*); de sel.

sa·lu·bri·ous □ [sə'lu:briəs] salubre, sain; **sa'lu·bri·ty** salubrité *f*; **sal·u·tar·i·ness** ['sæljutərinis] caractère *m* salutaire; **'sal·u·tar·y** □ salutaire (à, *to*).

sal·u·ta·tion [sælju'teiʃn] salutation *f*; **sa·lu·ta·to·ry** [sə'ju:tətəri] de salutation; de bienvenue; **sa·lute** [sə'lu:t] **1.** salut(ation *f*) *m*; *co.* baiser *m*; ✕, ⚓ salut *m*; **2.** saluer (*a.* ✕, ⚓).

sal·vage ['sælvidʒ] **1.** (indemnité *f* de) sauvetage *m*; objets *m/pl.* sauvés; **2.** récupérer; ⚓ effectuer le sauvetage de.

sal·va·tion [sæl'veiʃn] salut *m* (*a. fig.*); ♀ *Army* Armée *f* du Salut; **sal'va·tion·ist** salutiste *mf*.

salve[1] [sælv] sauver; effectuer le sauvetage de.

salve[2] [sɑ:v] **1.** *usu. fig.* baume *m*; **2.** *usu. fig.* adoucir; calmer.

sal·ver ['sælvə] plateau *m*.

sal·vo ['sælvou], *pl.* **-voes** ['~vouz] ✕ salve *f* (*a. fig.*); ✕ ~ *release* bombardement *m* en traînée; lâchage *m* par salves; **sal·vor** ⚓ ['~və] sauveteur *m*.

Sa·mar·i·tan [sə'mæritn] **1.** samaritain; **2.** Samaritain(e *f*) *m*.

sam·ba ['sæmbə] samba *f*.

same [seim] the ~ le (la) même; les mêmes *pl.*; *all the* ~ tout de même; *it is all the* ~ *to me* ça m'est égal; cela ne me fait rien; **'same·ness** identité *f* (avec, *with*); ressemblance *f* (à, *with*); monotonie *f*. [maïs.]

samp *Am.* [sæmp] gruau *m* de⌡ **sam·ple** ['sɑ:mpl] **1.** *surt.* ♰ échantillon *m*; *sang, minerai, etc.*: prélèvement *m*; **2.** échantillonner; *fig.* essayer, goûter; **'sam·pler** modèle *m* de broderie; **'sam·pling** échantillonnage *m*.

san·a·tive ['sænətiv] guérisseur (-euse *f*); **san·a·to·ri·um** [~'tɔ:riəm] sanatorium *m*; *école:* infirmerie *f*; **san·a·to·ry** ['~təri] guérisseur (-euse *f*), curatif (-ive *f*).

sanc·ti·fi·ca·tion [sæŋktifi'keiʃn] sanctification *f*; **sanc·ti·fy** ['~fai] sanctifier; consacrer; **sanc·ti·mo·ni·ous** □ [~'mounjəs] bigot(te *f*), papelard; **sanc·tion** ['sæŋkʃn] **1.** sanction *f*; autorisation *f*; **2.** sanction-

ner; *fig.* approuver; **sanc·ti·ty** ['~titi] sainteté *f*; caractère *m* sacré; **sanc·tu·ar·y** ['~tjuəri] sanctuaire *m*; asile *m*; **sanc·tum** ['~təm] sanctuaire *m*; *fig.* F turne *f*.

sand [sænd] **1.** sable *m*; *Am. sl.* cran *m*, étoffe *f*; *fig.* rope of ~ de vagues liens *m/pl.*; **2.** sabler; répandre du sable sur.

san·dal[1] ['sændl] sandale *f*. [-s) *m*.⌡ **san·dal[2]** [~] (*ou* ~-*wood*) santal (*pl.*⌡ **sand...:** '~-**bag** ✕ sac *m* à terre; *porte, fenêtre:* boudin *m*; '~-**blast** ⊕ jet *m* de sable; *appareil:* sableuse *f*; '~-**glass** sablier *m*; horloge *f* de sable; '~-**pit** tas *m* de sable (*pour enfants*); *carrière:* sablonnière *f*; '~-**shoes** espadrilles *f/pl.*

sand·wich ['sænwidʒ] **1.** sandwich *m*; *Brit.* ~ *course* cours *m* intercalaire (de promotion professionnelle); **2.** (*a.* ~ *in*) serrer; '~-**man** homme-sandwich (*pl.* hommes-sandwichs) *m*.

sand·y ['sændi] sabl(onn)eux (-euse *f*); sablé (*allée etc.*); blond roux (*cheveux*) *inv.*

sane [sein] sain d'esprit; sensé; sain (*jugement*).

San·for·ize *Am.* ['sænfəraiz] rendre irrétrécissable.

sang [sæŋ] *prét. de sing*.

san·gui·nary □ ['sæŋgwinəri] sanguinaire; altéré de sang; **san·guine** ['~gwin] sanguin; confiant, optimiste; d'un rouge sanguin; **san·guin·e·ous** [~niəs] de sang; *see* sanguine.

san·i·tar·i·an [sæni'tɛəriən] hygiéniste (*a. su.*); **san·i·tar·y** □ ['~təri] hygiénique (*a.* ⊕); sanitaire (*a.* ✕, ⚓); ~ *towel*, *Am.* ~ *napkin* serviette *f* hygiénique.

san·i·ta·tion [sæni'teiʃn] hygiène *f*; système *m* sanitaire; salubrité *f* publique; **'san·i·ty** santé *f* d'esprit; jugement *m* sain; bon sens *m*; modération *f*.

sank [sæŋk] *prét. de sink* 1.

San·skrit ['sænskrit] sanscrit *m*.

San·ta Claus [sæntə'klɔ:z] Père *m ou* bonhomme *m* Noël.

sap[1] [sæp] ♀ sève *f* (*a. fig.*); *sl.* niais *m*.

sap[2] [~] **1.** ✕ sape *f*; F piocheur (-euse *f*) *m*; *sl.* boulot *m*; **2.** *v/i.* saper; *sl.* piocher, bûcher; *v/t.* saper, miner (*a. fig.*).

sap·id ['sæpid] savoureux (-euse *f*); **sa·pid·i·ty** [sə'piditi] sapidité *f*.

sa·pi·ence *usu. iro.* ['seipjəns] sagesse *f*; **'sa·pi·ent** *usu. iro.* □ savant, sage.

sap·less ['sæplis] sans sève; sans vigueur (*personne*).

sap·ling ['sæpliŋ] jeune arbre *m*; *fig.* jeune homme *m*.

sap·o·na·ceous [sæpo'neiʃəs] saponacé; *fig.* onctueux (-euse *f*).

sap·per ✕ ['sæpə] sapeur *m*.

sap·phire *min.* ['sæfaiə] saphir *m*.

sap·pi·ness ['sæpinis] abondance *f* de sève.

sap·py ['sæpi] plein de sève (*a. fig.*); vert (*arbre*); *sl.* nigaud.

Sar·a·cen ['særəsn] Sarrasin(e *f*) *m*.

sar·casm ['sɑːkæzm] ironie *f*; sarcasme *m*; **sar'cas·tic, sar'cas·ti·cal** □ sarcastique, mordant.

sar·coph·a·gus [sɑː'kɔfəgəs], *pl.* **-gi** [‿dʒai] sarcophage *m*.

sar·dine *icht.* [sɑː'diːn] sardine *f*.

Sar·din·i·an [sɑː'dinjən] **1.** sarde; **2.** *ling.* sarde *m*; Sarde *mf*.

sar·don·ic [sɑː'dɔnik] (‿ally) sardonique (*rire*); ⚕ sardonien(ne *f*).

sar·to·ri·al [sɑː'tɔːriəl] de tailleur; vestimentaire.

sash¹ [sæʃ] châssis *m* (*de fenêtre à guillotine*).

sash² [‿] ceinture *f*; ✕ *a.* écharpe *f*.

sa·shay *Am.* F [sæ'ʃei] marcher d'un pas vif; danser.

sash-win·dow fenêtre *f* à guillotine.

sas·sy *Am.* ['sæsi] *see* saucy.

sat [sæt] *prét. et p.p. de* sit.

Sa·tan ['seitən] Satan *m*.

sa·tan·ic [sə'tænik] (‿ally) satanique, diabolique.

satch·el ['sætʃl] sacoche *f*; *école:* carton *m*.

sate [seit] *see* satiate.

sa·teen [sæ'tiːn] satinette *f*.

sat·el·lite ['sætəlait] satellite *m* (*a. fig.*); (*a.* ~ *town*) ville *f* satellite; ~ *country* pays *m* satellite.

sa·ti·ate ['seiʃieit] rassasier (de, with); **sa·ti'a·tion** rassasiement *m*; satiété *f*; **sa·ti·e·ty** [sə'taiəti] satiété *f*.

sat·in ['sætin] *tex.* satin *m*; **sat·i·net** ['sætinet], *usu.* **sat·i·nette** [‿'net] satinette *f*; *soie:* satinade *f*.

sat·ire ['sætaiə] satire *f* (contre, [up]on); **sa·tir·ic, sa·tir·i·cal** □

sa·tir·i·cal [sə'tirik(l)] satirique; ironique; **sat·i·rist** ['sætərist] satiriste *m*; **'sat·i·rize** satiriser.

sat·is·fac·tion [sætis'fækʃn] satisfaction *f*, contentement *m* (de at, with); acquittement *m*, paiement *m*; *promesse:* exécution *f*; réparation *f* (*d'une offense*).

sat·is·fac·to·ri·ness [sætis'fæktərinis] caractère *m* satisfaisant; **sat·is'fac·to·ry** □ satisfaisant; *eccl.* expiatoire.

sat·is·fied □ ['sætisfaid] satisfait, content (de, with; que, that); **sat·is·fy** ['‿fai] satisfaire; contenter; payer, liquider (*une dette*); exécuter (*une promesse*); remplir (*une condition*); éclaircir (*un doute*).

sa·trap ['sætrəp] satrape *m*.

sat·u·rate ⌐ℳ, *a. fig.* ['sætʃəreit] saturer (de, with); **sat·u'ra·tion** saturation *f*; imprégnation *f*; ~ *point* point *m* de saturation.

Sat·ur·day ['sætədi] samedi *m*.

sat·ur·nine ['sætənain] taciturne; sombre.

sat·yr ['sætə] satyre *m*.

sauce [sɔːs] **1.** sauce *f*; *fig.* assaisonnement *m*; F impertinence *f*; **2.** assaisonner; F dire des impertinences à (*q.*); '~**·boat** saucière *f*; '~**·pan** casserole *f*; **'sauc·er** soucoupe *f*.

sau·ci·ness F ['sɔːsinis] impertinence *f*; chic *m* (*d'un chapeau*).

sau·cy □ F ['sɔːsi] gamin; effronté, impertinent; chic *inv. en genre*, coquet(te *f*).

sau·na ['sɔːnə] sauna *m* ou *f*.

saun·ter ['sɔːntə] **1.** flânerie *f*; promenade *f* (faite à loisir); **2.** flâner; se balader; **'saun·ter·er** flâneur (-euse *f*) *m*.

sau·ri·an *zo.* ['sɔːriən] saurien *m*.

sau·sage ['sɔsidʒ] saucisse *f*; saucisson *m*.

sav·age ['sævidʒ] **1.** □ sauvage; féroce; brutal (-aux *m/pl.*) (*coup*); F furieux (-euse *f*); **2.** sauvage *mf*; *fig.* barbare *mf*; **3.** attaquer, mordre (*chien*); **'sav·age·ness, 'sav·age·ry** sauvagerie *f*, barbarie *f*; férocité *f*.

sa·van·na(h) [sə'vænə] savane *f*.

save [seiv] **1.** *v/t.* sauver; économiser, épargner; gagner (*du temps*); mettre de côté; garder; éviter; *v/i.* faire des économies, économiser; **2.** *prp.* excepté, sauf; **3.** *cj.* ~ *that* excepté que, hormis que; ~ *for* sauf; si ce n'était ...

sav·e·loy ['sævilɔi] cervelas *m.*

sav·er ['seivə] libérateur (-trice *f*) *m*; sauveteur *m*; ⊕ économiseur *m*; personne *f* économe.

sav·ing ['seiviŋ] **1.** □ économique; économe (*personne*); ⊥⊥ ~ **clause** clause *f* de sauvegarde; réservation *f*; **2.** épargne *f*; *fig.* salut *m*; sauvetage *m*; ~*s pl.* économies *f/pl.*

sav·ings... ['seiviŋz]: ~ **ac·count** compte *m* d'épargne; '~**-bank** caisse *f* d'épargne; '~**-de·pos·it** dépôt *m* à la caisse d'épargne.

sav·io(u)r ['seivjə] sauveur *m*; *eccl. the* ♀ *le* Sauveur *m.*

sa·vor·y ♀ ['seivəri] sarriette *f.*

sa·vo(u)r ['seivə] **1.** saveur *f*; goût *m* (*a. fig.*); *fig.* trace *f*; **2.** *v/i. fig.* ~ *of* sentir (*qch.*), tenir de (*qch.*); *v/t. fig.* savourer; **sa·vo(u)r·i·ness** ['~rinis] saveur *f*, succulence *f*; '**sa·vo(u)r·less** fade, insipide; sans saveur; '**sa·vo(u)r·y** □ savoureux (-euse *f*), succulent, appétissant; piquant, salé.

sa·voy [sə'vɔi] chou *m* frisé *ou* de Milan.

sav·vy *sl.* ['sævi] **1.** jugeote *f*; **2.** comprendre.

saw¹ [sɔ:] *prét. de* see.

saw² [~] adage *m*; dicton *m.*

saw³ [~] **1.** scie *f*; **2.** [*irr.*] scier; '~**-buck** *Am. sl.* billet *m* de dix dollars; '~**-dust** sciure *f*; '~**-horse** chevalet *m* de scieur; '~**-mill** scierie *f*; **sawn** [sɔ:n] *p.p. de* saw³ 2; **saw·yer** ['~jə] scieur *m* (de long).

Sax·on ['sæksn] **1.** saxon(ne *f*); **2.** *ling.* saxon *m*; Saxon(ne *f*) *m.*

sax·o·phone ♪ ['sæksəfoun] saxophone *m.*

say [sei] **1.** [*irr.*] dire; avouer; affirmer; réciter; ~ *no* refuser; ~ *grace* dire le bénédicité; ~ *mass* dire la messe; *that is to* ~ c'est-à-dire; *do you* ~ *so?* vous croyez?, vous trouvez?; *you don't* ~ *so!* pas possible!, vraiment!; *I* ~! dites donc!; pas possible!; *he is said to be rich* on dit qu'il est riche; on le dit riche; *no sooner said than done* sitôt dit, sitôt fait; **2.** dire *m*, mot *m*, parole *f*; *it is my* ~ *now* maintenant c'est à moi la parole; *let him have his* ~ laissez-le parler; F *have a* (*no*) ~ *in s.th.* (ne pas) avoir voix au chapitre;

'**say·ing** dicton *m*, proverbe *m*; dit *m*; récitation *f*; *it goes without* ~ cela va sans dire.

scab [skæb] *plaie:* croûte *f*; *vét. etc.* gale *f*; *sl.* jaune *m*; *sl.* sale type *m.*

scab·bard ['skæbəd] *épée:* fourreau *m*; *poignard:* gaine *f.*

scab·by □ ['skæbi] croûteux (-euse *f*); galeux (-euse *f*); ⊕ dartreux (-euse *f*); *sl.* méprisable.

sca·bi·es ♂ ['skeibii:z] gale *f.*

sca·bi·ous ♀ ['skeibiəs] scabieuse *f.*

sca·brous ['skeibrəs] rugueux (-euse *f*); scabreux (-euse *f*) (*conte etc.*).

scaf·fold ['skæfəld] ⊥⊥ échafaud *m*; ⚠ échafaudage *m*; '**scaf·fold·ing** échafaudage *m*; ~ *pole* écorperche *f.*

scald [skɔ:ld] **1.** échaudure *f*; **2.** (*a. ~ out*) échauder; faire chauffer (*le lait*) sans qu'il entre en ébullition.

scale¹ [skeil] **1.** ♂, *peau, poisson, reptile; a. de fer:* écaille *f*; ⊕, ♂ dartre *f*; ⊕, ♂ *dents:* tartre *m*; **2.** *v/t.* écailler; ⊕ piquer; ⊕ détarter (*a. dents*); ⊕ entartrer (= *incruster*); *v/i.* s'écailler; s'exfolier (*arbre*); se déplâtrer (*mur etc.*); ♂ se desquamer; ⊕ (*souv.* ~ *off*) s'entartrer.

scale² [~] **1.** plat(eau) *m*; (*a pair of*) ~*s pl.* (une) balance *f*; *astr.* Balance *f*; **2.** peser.

scale³ [~] **1.** échelle *f*; ♪, ♀ gamme *f*; ♀ tarif *m*; *fig.* étendue *f*, envergure *f*; *on a large* (*small*) ~ en grand (petit); ~ *model* maquette *f*; *on a national* ~ à l'échelon national; **2.** escalader (*un mur etc.*); tracer (*q.*) à l'échelle; ~ *up* (*down*) augmenter (réduire) (*les gages etc.*) à l'échelle.

scaled [skeild] écaillé; écailleux (-euse *f*).

scale·less ['skeillis] sans écailles.

scal·ing-lad·der ['skeiliŋlædə] ⚔ † échelle *f* d'escalade.

scal·lion ♀ ['skæljən] ciboule *f.*

scal·lop ['skɔləp] **1.** *zo.* pétoncle *m*; *cuis.* coquille *f*; *cost.* feston *m*; dentelure *f*; **2.** découper, denteler; festonner; faire cuire en coquille(s).

scalp [skælp] **1.** épicrâne *m*; cuir *m* chevelu; *Peaux-Rouges:* scalpe *m*; **2.** scalper; ♂ ruginer.

scal·pel ♂ ['skælpəl] scalpel *m.*

scal·y [skeili] écailleux (-euse *f*); squameux (-euse *f*); *sl.* mesquin.

scamp [skæmp] **1.** vaurien *m*; *enfant:* coquin *m*; **2.** bâcler; '**scamp·er 1.** courir allégrement; ~ *off* détaler; **2.** *fig.* course *f* folâtre *ou* rapide.

scan [skæn] *v/t.* scander (*des vers*); examiner, scruter; *v/i.* se scander.

scan·dal ['skændl] scandale *m*; honte *f*; médisance *f*; ⚖ diffamation *f*; **'scan·dal·ize** scandaliser; *be ⌐d at (ou by)* être choqué de *ou* scandalisé par; **'scan·dal·monger** médisant(e *f*) *m*; cancanier (-ère *f*) *m*; **'scan·dal·ous** □ scandaleux (-euse *f*), infâme; honteux (-euse *f*); diffamatoire; **'scan·dal·ous·ness** infamie *f*; caractère *m* scandaleux *etc.*

Scan·di·na·vi·an [skændi'neivjən] **1.** scandinave; **2.** Scandinave *mf.*

scant [skænt] rare, insuffisant.

scant·i·ness ['skæntinis] rareté *f*, insuffisance *f.*

scant·ling ['skæntliŋ] volige *f*; bois *m* équarri; échantillon *m* (*de construction*); équarrissage *m*; *fig.* très petite quantité *f.*

scant·y □ ['skænti] rare, insuffisant, peu abondant; maigre.

scape·goat ['skeipgout] souffre-douleur *m/inv.*

scape·grace ['skeipgreis] polisson *m*; petit(e) écervelé(e) *m*(*f*).

scap·u·lar ['skæpjulə] **1.** *anat.* scapulaire; **2.** *eccl.* scapulaire *m.*

scar¹ [skɑ:] **1.** cicatrice *f* (*a.* ⚕, *a. fig.*); balafre *f* (*le long de la figure*); **2.** *v/t.* balafrer; *v/i.* se cicatriser.

scar² [⌐] rocher *m* escarpé.

scar·ab *zo.* ['skærəb] scarabée *m.*

scarce [skɛəs] rare; peu abondant; F *make o.s. ⌐* s'éclipser, déguerpir; **'scarce·ly** à peine; (ne) guère; **'scar·ci·ty** rareté *f*; manque *m*, disette *f* (de, *of*).

scare [skɛə] **1.** effrayer; faire peur à (*q.*); épouvanter; *⌐d* épouvanté, apeuré; *be ⌐d (of)* avoir peur (de); *be ⌐d to death* avoir une peur bleue; **2.** panique *f*); '**⌐·crow** épouvantail *m* (*a. fig.*); '**⌐·head** *journ. Am.* manchette *f* sensationnelle; '**⌐·mon·ger** alarmiste *mf*; *sl.* paniquard *m.*

scarf¹ [skɑ:f] ✂, *a. femme:* écharpe *f*; *homme:* cache-nez *m/inv.*; *soie:* foulard *m*; *eccl.* étole *f*; † cravate *f.*

scarf² ⊕ [⌐] **1.** assemblage *m* à mi-bois; enture *f*; *métal:* chanfrein *m* de soudure; **2.** ⚓ enter; ⊕ amorcer.

scarf...: '**⌐·pin** épingle *f* de cravate; '**⌐·skin** épiderme *m.*

scar·i·fi·ca·tion [skɛərifi'keiʃn] ⚚ scarification *f*; **scar·i·fy** ['⌐fai] scarifier (*a.* ⚘); *fig.* éreinter (*un auteur*). [scarlatine *f.*\]

scar·la·ti·na [skɑ:lə'ti:nə] (fièvre *f*)\]

scar·let ['skɑ:lit] écarlate (*a. su./f*); *⌐ fever* (fièvre *f*) scarlatine *f*; ⚕ *⌐ runner* haricot *m* d'Espagne.

scarp [skɑ:p] **1.** escarper; *⌐ed* à pic; **2.** escarpement *m*; versant *m* abrupt.

scarred [skɑ:d] balafré; portant des cicatrices.

scarves [skɑ:vz] *pl.* de *scarf¹.*

scar·y F ['skɛəri] timide; épouvantable.

scathe [skeið]: *without ⌐* indemne; **'scath·ing** *fig.* mordant, cinglant, caustique.

scat·ter ['skætə] (se) disperser, (s')éparpiller; (se) répandre; *v/t.* dissiper; *⌐ed a.* épars, clairsemé; '**⌐·brain** écervelé(e *f*) *m*, étourdi(e *f*) *m.*

scav·enge ['skævindʒ] balayer, nettoyer; **'scav·en·ger** éboueur *m*, balayeur *m* (des rues); **'scav·eng·ing** balayage *m* (des rues); ébouage *m.*

sce·nar·i·o *cin., théâ.* [si'nɑ:riou] scénario *m*; '**⌐·writ·er**, *a.* **sce·nar·ist** ['si:nərist] scénariste *m.*

scene [si:n] scène *f* (*a. théâ.*); *fig. a.* théâtre *m*, lieu *m*; vue *f*, paysage *m*; spectacle *m*; *see ⌐ry*, *⌐s pl.* coulisse *f*, -s *f/pl.*; '**⌐·paint·er** peintre *m* de *ou* en décors; **scen·er·y** ['⌐əri] décors *m/pl.*, (mise *f* en) scène *f*; paysage *m*, vue *f.*

sce·nic, sce·ni·cal ['si:nik(l)] scénique; théâtral (-aux *m/pl.*) (*a. fig.*); *scenic railway* montagnes *f/pl.* russes; *⌐ road* route *f* pittoresque.

scent [sent] **1.** parfum *m*; odeur *f* (agréable); *chasse:* vent *m*; voie *f*, piste *f*; *chien:* flair *m*, nez *m*; **2.** parfumer, embaumer; *chasse:* (*souv. ⌐ out*) flairer (*a. fig.*), sentir; '**scent·ed** parfumé (de, *with*); odorant; **'scent·less** inodore, sans odeur; *chasse:* sans fumet.

scep·tic ['skeptik] sceptique *mf*; **'scep·ti·cal** □ sceptique; *be ⌐ about* douter (de, *of*); **scep·ti·cism** ['⌐sizm] scepticisme *m.*

scep·tre ['septə] sceptre *m.*

sched·ule ['ʃedju:l; *Am.* 'skedju:l] **1.** inventaire *m*; cahier *m*; liste *f*;

scheme 1088

impôts: cédule *f*; ₮₮₮ annexe *f*; *surt. Am.* horaire *m*; *surt. Am.* plan *m*; on ~ à l'heure; *fig.* selon les prévisions; **2.** inscrire sur l'inventaire *etc.*; ₮₮₮ ajouter comme annexe; *Am.* dresser un plan de; *Am.* marquer sur l'horaire; *be* ~*d for* devoir arriver *ou* partir *etc.* à; ~*d flight* vol *m* de ligne, vol *m* régulier.

scheme [ski:m] **1.** plan *m*, projet *m*; arrangement *m*; *péj.* intrigue *f*; **2.** *v/t.* projeter; *v/i. péj.* intriguer (pour, *to*); comploter; combiner (de, *to*); **'schem·er** faiseur (-euse *f*) *m* de projets; *péj.* intrigant(e *f*) *m*.

schism ['sizm] schisme *m*; *fig.* division *f*; **schis·mat·ic** [siz'mætik] **1.** (*a.* **schis'mat·i·cal** □) schismatique; **2.** schismatique *mf*.

schist *min.* [ʃist] schiste *m*.

schol·ar ['skɔlə] élève *mf*; écolier (-ère *f*) *m*; érudit(e *f*) *m*; *univ.* boursier (-ère *f*) *m*; *he is an apt* ~ il apprend vite; **'schol·ar·ly** *adj.* savant; érudit; **'schol·ar·ship** érudition *f*, science *f*; *univ.* humanisme *m*; *univ.* bourse *f* (d'études).

scho·las·tic [skə'læstik] (~*ally*) scolaire; *fig.* pédant; *phls.* scolastique (*a. su./m*).

school[1] [sku:l] *see* **shoal**[1].

school[2] [~] **1.** école *f* (*a. fig. de pensée etc.*); académie *f*; *at* ~ à l'école; *grammar* ~ lycée *m*, collège *m*; *high* ~ *Angl.* lycée *m* (*souv. de jeunes filles*); *Am. et écoss.* collège *m*, école *f* secondaire; *primary* ~ école *f* primaire; *public* ~ *Angl.* grande école *f* d'enseignement secondaire; *Am. et écoss.* école *f* communale; *secondary modern* ~ collège *m* moderne; *technical* ~ école *f* des arts et métiers; *see a.* **board-**~; *put to* ~ envoyer à l'école; **2.** instruire; habituer; discipliner; **'~·boy** écolier *m*, élève *m*; **'~·fel·low**, **'~·mate** camarade *mf* de classe; **'~·girl** élève *f*, écolière *f*; **'school·ing** instruction *f*, éducation *f*.

school...: **'~·leav·er** jeune *mf* qui a terminé ses études scolaires; **'~·man** scolastique *m*; *Am.* professeur *m*; **'~·mas·ter** *école primaire*: instituteur *m*; *lycée, collège*: professeur *m*; **'~·mis·tress** institutrice *f*; professeur *m*; **'~·room** (salle *f* de) classe *f*.

schoon·er ['sku:nə] schooner *m*;

goélette *f*; *Am.* chope *f*, verre *m* de bière.

sci·at·i·ca ℣ [sai'ætikə] sciatique *f*.

sci·ence ['saiəns] science *f*, -s *f/pl.* (*a.* † = *savoir*); **'~·fic·tion** science-fiction *f*.

sci·en·tif·ic [saiən'tifik] (~*ally*) scientifique; *box.* qui possède la science du combat; ~ *man* homme *m* de science.

sci·en·tist ['saiəntist] homme *m* de science; scientifique *mf*; ♀ *Am.* Scientiste *m* (chrétien).

scin·til·late ['sintileit] scintiller, étinceler; **scin·til'la·tion** scintillement *m*.

sci·on ['saiən] ✗ scion *m*; *fig.* rejeton *m*, descendant *m*.

scis·sion ['siʒn] cisaillage *m*; *fig.* scission *f*, division *f*; **scis·sors** ['sizəz] *pl.*: (*a pair of*) ~ (des) ciseaux *m/pl.*; **'scis·sor-tooth** *zo.* dent *f* carnassière.

scle·ro·sis ℣ [skliə'rousis] sclérose *f*.

scoff [skɔf] **1.** sarcasme *m*; **2.** se moquer; ~ *at s.o.* railler q., se moquer de q.; **'scoff·er** moqueur (-euse *f*) *m*, gausseur (-euse *f*) *m*.

scold [skould] **1.** mégère *f*; **2.** gronder, crier (contre, *at*); **'scold·ing** réprimande *f*, semonce *f*.

scol·lop ['skɔləp] *see* **scallop**.

sconce[1] [skɔns] tête *f*; jugeote *f*.

sconce[2] [~] bougeoir *m*; bobèche *f*; applique *f*; flambeau *m* (*de piano*).

sconce[3] *univ.* [~] mettre à l'amende.

scon(e) *cuis.* [skɔn] galette *f* au lait.

scoop [sku:p] **1.** pelle *f* à main; ⚓ épuisette *f*; ⊕, 🥄 cuiller *f*; ℣ curette *f*; *sl.* rafle *f*, coup *m*; *sl.* (*primeur f d'une*) nouvelle *f* sensationnelle; **2.** (*usu.* ~ *out*) écoper (*l'eau*); excaver; évider; *sl.* publier une nouvelle à sensation avant (*un autre journal etc.*); *sl.* ~ *a large profit* faire une belle rafle.

scoot·er ['sku:tə] *enfants*: trottinette *f*, patinette *f*; *mot.* scooter *m*; motoscooter *m*.

scope [skoup] étendue *f*, portée *f*; liberté *f*, jeu *m*; espace *m*; but *m*; *have free* ~ avoir toute liberté (pour, *to*).

scorch [skɔ:tʃ] *v/t.* roussir, brûler; *v/i.* F *mot.* brûler le pavé; **'scorch·er** F journée *f* torride; *mot.* chauffard *m*; *cycl.* cycliste *m* casse-cou.

score [skɔ:] **1.** (en)coche *f*; *peau*:

éraflure f; (trait m de) repère m; vingtaine f; sp. points m/pl., total m; foot. score m; fig. sujet m, point m, raison f; ♪ partition f; sl. aubaine f, coup m de fortune; three ~ soixante; run up a ~ contracter une dette; on the ~ of pour cause de; à titre de; what's the ~? où en est le jeu?; get the ~ faire le nombre de points voulu; **2.** v/t. entailler; (a. ~ up) inscrire, enregistrer; sp. compter, marquer (les points); gagner (une partie, a. fig.); remporter (un succès); ♪ noter (un air), orchestrer, arranger; souligner (une erreur, un passage); Am. F réprimander (q.), laver la tête à (q.); ~ out rayer; v/i. gagner; sp., a. cartes: faire ou marquer des points; foot. enregistrer un but; sl. remporter un succès; sl. ~ off s.o. faire pièce à q.; '**scor·er** sp. marqueur (-euse f) m (foot. d'un but).

sco·ri·a ['skɔːriə], pl. **-ri·ae** ['~riiː] scorie f.

scorn [skɔːn] **1.** mépris m, dédain m; **2.** mépriser, dédaigner; '**scorn·er** contempteur (-trice f) m; **scorn·ful** □ ['~ful] méprisant.

Scor·pi·o astr. ['skɔːpiou] le Scorpion m.

scor·pi·on zo. ['skɔːpjən] scorpion m. [Scot m.]

Scot[1] [skɔt] Écossais(e f) m; hist.]

scot[2] [~] hist. écot m; compte m; ~ and lot taxes f/pl. communales.

Scotch[1] [skɔtʃ] **1.** écossais; **2.** ling. écossais m; F whisky m; the ~ pl. les Écossais m/pl.

scotch[2] [~] **1.** entaille f; sp. ligne f de limite; **2.** mettre hors de combat ou hors d'état de nuire.

scotch[3] [~] **1.** cale f; taquet m d'arrêt; **2.** caler (une roue); fig. faire casser.

Scotch·man ['skɔtʃmən] Écossais m.

scot-free ['skɔt'friː] indemne.

Scots ecoss. [skɔts], '**Scots·man** see Scotch(man).

Scot·tish ['skɔtiʃ] écossais.

scoun·drel ['skaundrəl] scélérat m; vaurien m; '**scoun·drel·ly** adj. scélérat, vil.

scour[1] ['skauə] nettoyer; frotter; curer (un fossé, un port); décaper (une surface métallique).

scour[2] [~] v/i. ~ about battre la campagne; v/t. parcourir; écumer (les mers).

scourge [skəːdʒ] **1.** fléau m (a. fig.); eccl. discipline f; **2.** fouetter; fig. affliger.

scout[1] [skaut] **1.** éclaireur m, avant-coureur m; ✕ reconnaissance f; ⚓ vedette f, croiseur m, éclaireur m; ✈ avion m de reconnaissance; univ. garçon m de service; Boy ~s pl. (boys-)scouts m/pl.; ✕ ~ party reconnaissance f; **2.** aller en reconnaissance.

scout[2] [~] repousser avec mépris.

scow ⚓ [skau] chaland m; (a. ferry-~) toue f.

scowl [skaul] **1.** air m renfrogné; **2.** se renfrogner, F regarder noir.

scrab·ble ['skræbl] jouer des pieds et des mains; chercher à quatre pattes (qch., for s.th.); gratter çà et là.

scrag [skræg] **1.** fig. personne f ou bête f décharnée; ~(-end) (of mutton) collet m (de mouton); **2.** sl. garrotter; **scrag·gi·ness** ['~inis] maigreur f; '**scrag·gy** □ maigre, décharné. [le camp.]

scram Am. sl. [skræm] fiche-moi]

scram·ble ['skræmbl] **1.** monter etc. à quatre pattes; se bousculer (pour avoir qch., for s.th.); jouer des pieds et des mains (a. fig.); ~d eggs pl. œufs m/pl. brouillés; **2.** marche f etc. difficile; lutte f, mêlée f.

scrap [skræp] **1.** petit morceau m; bout m; terrain: parcelle f (a. fig.); journal: coupure f; pain, étoffe: bribe f; ⊕ déchets m/pl.; sl. rixe f, querelle f; box. match (pl. match[e]s) m; ~s pl. restes m/pl.; débris m/pl.; péj. ~ of paper chiffon m de papier; **2.** mettre au rebut; mettre hors service; fig. mettre au rancart; '~-book album m (de découpures).

scrape [skreip] **1.** coup m de grattoir; grincement m; fig. mince couche f; F embarras m, mauvais pas m; **2.** v/t. gratter, racler; écorcher (la peau); décrotter (les souliers); ~ together (ou up) amasser peu à peu; ~ acquaintance with faire connaissance casuellement avec (q.); v/i. gratter; s'érafler; grincer (violon); '**scrap·er** grattoir m, racloir m; souliers: décrottoir m; personne: racleur m; '**scrap·ing** raclage m; ~s pl. raclures f/pl.; grattures f/pl.; bribes f/pl., restes m/pl.; fig. sous m/pl. amassés un à un.

scrap...: '**~-heap** (tas *m* de) ferraille *f*; *a. fig.* throw on the ~ mettre au rancart, jeter au rebut; '**~-i·ron** ferraille *f*; débris *m/pl.* de fer; '**scrap·py** F □ hétérogène; *fig.* décousu; *Am. a.* batailleur (-euse *f*), querelleur (-euse *f*); '**scrap·yard** chantier *m* de ferraille; *pour voitures*: cimetière *m* de voitures.

scratch [skrætʃ] **1.** coup *m* d'ongle *ou* de griffe; égratignure *f*; grattement *m*; *surface polie*: rayure *f*; *sp.* zéro *m*; *sp.* scratch *m*; *plume etc.*: grincement *m*; come up to the ~ se mettre en ligne; *fig.* se montrer à la hauteur de l'occasion; **2.** improvisé; *sp.* mixte, sans homogénéité (*équipe*); *parl.* par surprise; **3.** *v/t.* gratter, égratigner; donner un coup de griffe à; *sp.* scratcher; *sp.* décommander; ~ out rayer, biffer; gratter; *v/i.* gratter; grincer; *sp.* déclarer forfait; griffer (*chat*); '**scratch·y** qui gratte; grinçant; inégal (-aux *m/pl.*), peu assuré; *see scratch* 2.

scrawl [skrɔːl] **1.** griffonner; **2.** (*a.* '**scrawl·ing**) griffonnage *m*.

scraw·ny *Am.* F ['skrɔːni] décharné.

scream [skriːm] **1.** cri *m* perçant; F he is a ~ il est tordant; **2.** (*souv.* ~ out) pousser un cri perçant *ou* d'angoisse; '**scream·ing** □ perçant; sifflant; criard (*personne*, *a.* *couleur*); F tordant; à mourir de rire; '**scream·y** F aigu(ë *f*); criard.

scree [skriː] éboulis *m*, pierraille *f*.

screech [skriːtʃ] *see* scream; '**~-owl** *orn.* chouette *f* (des clochers).

screed [skriːd] longue liste *f*; longue lettre *f*; jérémiade *f*.

screen [skriːn] **1.** ✗, *phot.*, *cin.*, *radar*, *a.* meuble: écran *m*; (*a.* draught-~) paravent *m*; scrible *m*; sas *m*; mot. rideaux *m/pl.* de côté; *fig.* rideau *m*; on the ~ à l'écran; ~ advertising publicité *f* à l'écran; *phot.* focussing ~ verre *m* dépoli; *cin.* ~ record film *m* de reportage; *cin.* ~ test essai *m* à l'écran; *mot.* ~ wiper essuie-glace *m*; **2.** abriter, protéger; ✗ dérober (à, from); voier (*le soleil etc.*); cacher; *cin.* mettre à l'écran; passer au crible; tamiser; *fig.* couvrir (*q.*); '**~-play** *cin.* scénario *m*.

screw [skruː] **1.** vis *f*; tour *m* de vis; *tabac*, *papier*: cornet *m*; bonbons: cornet *m*, *fig.* rigueur *f*; *sl.* paie *f*, salaire *m*, appointements *m/pl.*; ⚓ hélice *f*; F avare *m*; F he has a ~ loose il est timbré *ou* *sl.* maboul; **2.** *v/t.* visser; *fig.* tordre; *fig.* opprimer; *fig.* rappeler (*tout son courage*); *v/i.* tourner; ~ round tordre (le cou, one's head); ~ up visser; tortiller; plisser (*les yeux*); pincer (*les lèvres*); ~ up one's face faire une grimace; '**~-ball** *Am. sl.* type *m* excentrique *ou* dingo; '**~-driv·er** tournevis *m*; '**~-jack** cric *m* (*menuisier*: à vis); viole *f*; '**~-pro·pel·ler** hélice *f*; '**~-steam·er** navire *m* à hélice.

scrib·ble ['skribl] **1.** griffonnage *m*; écriture *f* illisible; **2.** *v/t.* griffonner; ~ over rendre illisible (*au moyen du griffonnage*); *v/i.* F écrivailler; '**scrib·bler** griffonneur (-euse *f*) *m*; F écrivailleur (-euse *f*) *m*, gratte-papier *m/inv.*

scribe [skraib] *bibl. ou co.* scribe *m*; *péj.* plumitif *m*; ⊕ pointe *f* à tracer.

scrim·mage ['skrimidʒ] mêlée *f* (*a. sp.*); escarmouche *f*.

scrimp [skrimp] **1.** *v/t.* être parcimonieux (-euse *f*) de, ménager (-ère *f*) outre mesure; *v/i.* lésiner sur tout; économiser outre mesure; **2.** chiche (*personne*); (*a.* '**scrimp·y**) insuffisant.

scrip ✝ [skrip] titres *m/pl.*; certificat *m ou* titre *m* provisoire.

script [skript] écriture *f*; manuscrit *m*; *cin.* scénario *m*; ~s *pl.* école *etc.*: copies *f/pl.* d'examen.

Scrip·tur·al ['skriptʃərəl] scriptural (-aux *m/pl.*); biblique; **Scrip·ture** ['~tʃə] Écriture *f* sainte.

scrof·u·la ✗ ['skrɔfjulə] scrofule *f*, strume *f*; '**scrof·u·lous** □ scrofuleux (-euse *f*), strumeux (-euse *f*).

scroll [skroul] *papier*: rouleau *m*; banderole *f* à inscription; *écriture*: arabesque *f*; ⚠ spirale *f*; volute *f* (*a. violon*). [*m.*]

scro·tum *anat.* ['skroutəm] scrotum|

scrounge [skraundʒ] chiper; écornifler (*un repas etc.*); ✗ *sl.* récupérer.

scrub¹ [skrʌb] broussailles *f/pl.*; arbuste *m* rabougri; F personne *f* rabougrie.

scrub² [~] **1.** nettoyer; récurer; **2.** *sp. Am.* équipe *f* numéro deux.

scrub·bing-brush ['skrʌbiŋbrʌʃ] brosse *f* en chiendent *ou* de cuisine.

scrub·by ['skrʌbi] rabougri; insignifiant; couvert de broussailles.

seamless

scrub·wom·an *Am.* [ˈskrʌbwumən] femme *f* de ménage.

scruff of the neck [ˈskrʌfəvðəˈnek] peau *f* de la nuque *ou* du cou.

scrum·mage [ˈskrʌmidʒ] mêlée *f* (*a. sp.*); escarmouche *f*.

scrump·tious *sl.* [ˈskrʌmpʃəs] exquis, épatant, délicieux (-euse *f*).

scrunch [skrʌntʃ] *v/t.* croquer; *v/i.* craquer.

scru·ple [skruːpl] **1.** scrupule *m* (20 *grains* = *1,296 g*) (*a.* = *conscience*); *make no* ~ *to* (*inf.*) ne pas hésiter à (*inf.*); **2.** avoir des scrupules (à *inf.*, *to inf.*); **scru·pu·lous** □ [ˈ~juləs] scrupuleux (-euse *f*) (sur *about*, *over*); *a.* méticuleux (-euse *f*) (*travail etc.*).

scru·ti·neer [skruːtiˈniə] scrutateur *m*; **ˈscru·ti·nize** scruter; pointer (*des suffrages etc.*); **ˈscru·ti·ny** examen *m* minutieux *ou* attentif *ou* rigoureux; *suffrages*: vérification *f*.

scu·ba [ˈskjuːbə] scaphandre *m* autonome; ~ *diving* plongée *f* sous-marine autonome.

scud [skʌd] **1.** fuite *f*, course *f* rapide; *nuages*: diablotins *m/pl.*; rafale *f*; embrun *m*; **2.** courir, fuir; ⚓ fuir devant le temps.

scuff [skʌf] *v/t.* effleurer; érafler; user; ~ *up* soulever; *v/i.* traîner les pieds; s'érafler (*cuir*).

scuf·fle [ˈskʌfl] **1.** rixe *f*, mêlée *f*; bagarre *f*; **2.** se bousculer; traîner les pieds.

scull ⚓ [skʌl] **1.** aviron *m* de couple; godille *f*; **2.** ramer en couple; godiller.

scul·ler·y [ˈskʌləri] arrière-cuisine *f*; ~*-maid* laveuse *f* de vaisselle.

sculp·tor [ˈskʌlptə] sculpteur *m*.

sculp·ture [ˈskʌlptʃə] **1.** sculpture *f*; **2.** sculpter; orner de sculptures; **ˈsculp·tur·ing** sculpture *f*, sculptage *m*.

scum [skʌm] écume *f*; ⊕ scories *f/pl.*; *fig.* lie *f*, rebut *m*.

scup·per ⚓ [ˈskʌpə] dalot *m*.

scurf [skəːf] pellicules *f/pl.* (*du cuir chevelu*); ⊕ instruction *f*; **ˈscurf·y** □ pelliculeux (-euse *f*); ✿ ~ *affection* dartre *f*.

scur·ril·i·ty [skʌˈriliti] goujaterie *f*; grossièreté *f*; *action*, *personne*: bassesse *f*; **ˈscur·ril·ous** grossier (-ère *f*); bas(se *f*); ignoble.

scur·ry [ˈskʌri] **1.** *v/i.* se hâter; aller

à pas précipités; ~ *through s.th.* expédier qch.; **2.** débandade *f*; bousculade *f*.

scur·vy[1] ✿ [ˈskəːvi] scorbut *m*.

scur·vy[2] [~] vil(ain), bas(se *f*).

scut [skʌt] *lapin*, *lièvre*, *etc.*: couette *f*.

scutch·eon [ˈskʌtʃn] *see* escutcheon.

scut·tle[1] [ˈskʌtl] seau *m* à charbon.

scut·tle[2] [~] **1.** écoutillon *m*; hublot *m*; *mot.* bouclier *m* avant; *Am. toit etc.*: trappe *f*; **2.** saborder (*un navire*).

scut·tle[3] [~] **1.** fuite *f*; *pol.* F lâchage *m*; **2.** décamper, filer; débouler; *pol.* F lâcher.

scythe ↗ [saið] **1.** faux *f*; **2.** faucher.

sea [siː] mer *f*; *fig.* océan *m*; lame *f*, houle *f*; *at* ~ *en* mer; *fig.* dérouté; *go to* ~ se faire marin; *see put* 2; ˈ~**board** littoral *m*; rivage *m*; ~ **captain** capitaine *m* de la marine; ˈ~**far·ing** de mer; ~ *man* marin *m*; ˈ~**food** *Am. a.* ~*s pl.* fruits *m/pl.* de mer (= *coquillages*, *crustacés et poissons*); ˈ~**front** bord *m* de (la) mer; digue *f*, esplanade *f*; ˈ~**go·ing** de haute mer; de long cours; maritime (*commerce*).

seal[1] *zo.* [siːl] phoque *m*.

seal[2] [~] **1.** *bouteille*, *distinction*, *a. lettre*: cachet *m*; *document*: sceau *m*; plomb *m*; ⊕ joint *m* étanche; *great* (*ou broad*) ~ grand sceau *m*; **2.** cacheter; sceller; (*a.* ~ *up*) fermer; *fig.* décider; *fig.* fixer; *fig.* ~ *off* boucher, fermer; ~ *up* fermer hermétiquement; ~ (*with lead*) plomber.

seal·er ⊕ [ˈsiːlə] pince *f* à plomber.

sea-lev·el [ˈsiːlevl] niveau *m* de la mer.

seal·ing [ˈsiːliŋ] scellage *m*; cachetage *m*; plombage *m*; fermeture *f*.

seal·ing-wax [ˈsiːliŋwæks] cire *f* à cacheter.

seal·skin [ˈsiːlskin] peau *f* de phoque; † phoque *f*.

seam [siːm] **1.** couture *f* (*a. métall.*); ⊕ joint *m*; *géol.* couche *f*, veine *f*; *fig. visage*: ride *f*; *fig. burst at the* ~*s* craquer, crever; **2.** faire une couture à; ⊕ agrafer; couturer (*un visage*).

sea·man [ˈsiːmən] marin *m*, matelot *m*; ˈsea·man·ship manœuvre *f*.

sea-mew [ˈsiːmjuː] mouette *f*, goéland *m*.

seam·less □ [ˈsiːmlis] sans couture; ⊕ sans soudure.

seam·stress ['semstris] (ouvrière *f*) couturière *f*.

seam·y ['si:mi] qui montre les coutures; *fig.* ~ *side* dessous *m*/*pl*., mauvais côté *m*.

sea...: '~**-piece** *peint.* marine *f*; '~**plane** hydravion *m*; '~**port** port *m* de mer; '~**pow·er** *pol.* puissance *f* navale.

sear [sia] dessécher (*a. fig.*); faner (*les feuilles*); ⚕ cautériser; *fig.* endurcir.

search [sɔ:tʃ] **1.** recherche *f* (de, for); *admin.* visite *f*; *police*: perquisition *f*; fouille *f*; *in* ~ *of* à la recherche de; **2.** *v*/*t*. chercher dans (*qch.*); fouiller dans; visiter; ⚖ faire une perquisition dans; ⚕ sonder; *fig.* scruter; ~ *out* dénicher; découvrir; *v*/*i*. faire des recherches; ~ *for* chercher (*qch.*); ~ *into* rechercher; '**search·er** (re)chercheur (-euse *f*) *m*; douanier *m*; ⚖ perquisiteur *m*; ⚕ sonde *f*; '**search·ing** □ minutieux (-euse *f*); pénétrant (*regard*, *vent*); '**search·light** projection *f* électrique; ⚓ *etc.* projecteur *m*; '**search-war·rant** ⚖ ordre *m* de perquisition.

sea...: ~**scape** ['si:skeip] *see* seapiece; '~'**ser·pent** serpent *m* de mer; '~'**shore** rivage *m*; côte *f*; plage *f*; '~**sick:** *be* ~ avoir le mal de mer; '~**sick·ness** mal *m* de mer; '~'**side** bord *m* de la mer; ~ *resort* plage *f*; *bains m*/*pl*. de mer; *go to the* ~ aller au bord de la mer.

sea·son ['si:zn] **1.** saison *f*; période *f*, temps *m*; époque *f*; *vét.* rut *m*; F abonnement *m*; *height of the* ~ (pleine) saison *f*; *in* (*good ou due*) ~ en temps voulu; *cherries are in* ~ c'est la saison des cerises; *out of* ~ hors de saison; ne pas (être) de saison; *for a* ~ pendant un *ou* quelque temps; *with the compliments of the* ~ meilleurs souhaits de nouvel an *etc.*; **2.** *v*/*t*. mûrir; dessécher (*le bois*); assaisonner (*a. fig.*), relever (de, with); *fig.* acclimater; *fig.* tempérer; *v*/*i*. se sécher (*bois*); mûrir; **sea·son·a·ble** □ de (la) saison; opportun; '**sea·son·a·ble·ness** opportunité *f*; **sea·son·al** □ ['si:znl] des saisons; ✝, ⚕ saisonnier (-ère *f*); embauché pour les travaux de saison (*ouvrier*); '**sea·son·ing** dessèchement *m*; *cuis.* assaisonnement *m*,

condiment *m*; '**sea·son-'tick·et** carte *f* d'abonnement.

seat [si:t] **1.** siège *m* (*a.* ✿, ⊕); *théâ.*, *autobus*: place *f*; chaise *f*; banc *m*; (*a. country* ~) château *m*; *pantalon*: fond *m*; assiette *f* (*à cheval*); (*a. pilot's* ~) baquet *m*; ~ *of war* théâtre *m* de la guerre; **2.** (faire) asseoir; établir (*sur un trône etc.*); placer; fournir de chaises; poser; ⚡ caler; ⊕ faire reposer sur son siège; ~ *o.s.* s'asseoir; *be* ~*ed* être assis; avoir son siège (dans, in); '~**belt** ceinture *f* de sécurité; '**seat·ed** assis; **-seat·er** *surt. mot.*, ✈: *two-*~ voiture *f* à deux places; appareil *m* biplace.

sea-ur·chin *zo.* ['si:'ə:tʃin] oursin *m*; **sea·ward** ['~wəd] **1.** *adj.* qui porte au large; du large (*brise*); **2.** *adv.* (*a.* **sea·wards** ['~z]) vers le large *ou* la mer.

sea...: '~**weed** ♀ algue *f*; varech *m*; '~**wor·thy** navigable; qui tient la mer.

se·ba·ceous ⚕ [si'beiʃəs] sébacé.

se·cant ⅍ ['si:kənt] **1.** sécant; **2.** sécante *f*.

séc·a·teur ⚒ ['sekətə:] *usu.* (*a pair of*) ~*s pl.* (un) sécateur *m*.

se·cede [si'si:d] se séparer, faire scission (de, from); **se'ced·er** séparatiste *mf*; *eccl.* dissident(e *f*) *m*.

se·ces·sion [si'seʃn] scission *f*; sécession *f*; *eccl.* dissidence *f*; **se'ces·sion·ist** sécessioniste *mf*.

se·clude [si'klu:d] tenir éloigné; **se'clu·sion** [~ʒn] solitude *f*, isolement *m*.

sec·ond ['sekənd] **1.** □ second; deuxième; autre; *he is* ~ *to none* il ne le cède à personne (pour, in); *on* ~ *thoughts* toute réflexion faite; *the* ~ *of May* le deux Mai; *Charles the* ♀ Charles Deux; **2.** *temps*: seconde *f*; le (la) second(e *f*) *m ou* deuxième *mf*; *box.* second *m*; *duel*: témoin *m*; ✝ ~*s pl.* articles *m*/*pl*. de deuxième qualité; ✝ ~ *of exchange* seconde *f* de change; **3.** seconder; appuyer (*des débats, des troupes*); ✗ [si'kɔnd] mettre (*un officier*) en disponibilité; détacher; **sec·ond·ar·i·ness** ['sekəndərinis] caractère *m* secondaire *ou* peu important; '**sec·ond·ar·y** □ secondaire; auxiliaire; peu *ou* moins important; *see school*[2] 1; '**sec·ond-'best** numéro deux; deuxième; F *come off* ~ être battu; '**sec·ond·er**

parl. deuxième parrain *m; be the* ~ *of a motion* appuyer une proposition; **sec·ond-hand 1.** ['sekənd'hænd] d'occasion; ~ *bookseller* bouquiniste *mf;* ~ *bookshop* librairie *f* d'occasion; **2.** ['sekəndhænd] aiguille *f* des secondes; trotteuse *f;* **'sec·ond·ly** en second lieu; deuxièmement; **'sec·ond·rate** inférieur(e *f*); de qualité inférieure; ✝ ~ *quality* seconde qualité *f.*

se·cre·cy ['si:krisi] discrétion *f*; secret *m*; se·cret ['⹀krit] **1.** ▢ secret (-ète *f*); caché; retiré, isolé (-ète *f*); **2.** secret *m; in* ~ en secret; *be in the* ~ être du *ou* dans le secret.   [crétariat *m.*] **sec·re·tar·i·at(e)** [sekri'tɛəriət] se-} **sec·re·tar·y** ['sekrətri] secrétaire *mf*; dactylo *f*; ♀ *of State* ministre *m; Am.* ministre *m* des Affaires étrangères; **'sec·re·tar·y·ship** secrétariat *m;* fonction *f* de secrétaire; *pol.* ministère *m.*

se·crete [si'kri:t] cacher; ⨏ recéler; *physiol.* sécréter; **se'cre·tion** *physiol.* sécrétion *f;* ⨏ recel *m;* **se'cre·tive** *fig.* réservé, F cachottier (-ère *f*).

sect [sekt] secte *f;* **sec·tar·i·an** [⹀'tɛəriən] sectaire (*a. su./m*).

sec·tion ['sekʃn] section *f* (*a.* ✴, ♈, ⚹, ⚬, *typ.*, *zo.*); ⚔ groupe *m* de combat; *microscope etc.:* lame *f* mince; ⟁ coupe *f*, profil *m; typ.* paragraphe *m*, alinéa *m*; division *f;* tranche *f* (*a.* d'oranges); 🏢 secteur *m, Am.* compartiment *m; Am. ville:* quartier *m;* **'sec·tion·al** ▢ de classe *ou* parti; en profil, en coupe; ⊕ démontable; ⊕ sectionnel(le *f*); **'sec·tion-mark** paragraphe *m.*

sec·tor ['sektə] ✕, ♈, ⊕, *admin., astr., cin.* secteur *m;* ♈ compas *m* de proportion.

sec·u·lar ▢ ['sekjulə] séculier (-ère *f*); laïque; très ancien(ne *f*); **sec·u·lar·i·ty** [⹀'læriti] mondanité *f;* laïcité *f; clergé:* sécularité *f;* **'sec·u·lar·ize** séculariser; laïciser (*une école*); désaffecter (*une église*).

se·cure [si'kjuə] **1.** ▢ sûr; assuré; en sûreté; à l'abri (de *against, from*); ferme; **2.** mettre en sûreté *ou* à l'abri (de *from, against*); assurer, fixer, retenir; se procurer; s'emparer de; garantir (*une dette*); nantir (*un prêteur*); ✕ fortifier.

se·cu·ri·ty [si'kjuəriti] sécurité *f;* sûreté *f;* solidité *f;* caution *f,* garantie *f; securities pl.* titres *m/pl.*, valeurs *f/pl.; public securities pl.* fonds *m/pl.* d'État; ♀ *Council* Conseil *m* de sécurité; ♀ *Forces* forces *f/pl.* de sécurité; *be a* ~ *risk* constituer un risque pour la sécurité, ne pas être sûr.

se·dan [si'dæn] (*voiture f à*) conduite intérieure, limousine *f;* (*a.* ~ *chair*) chaise *f* à porteur.

se·date ▢ [si'deit] (re)posé; calme; **se'date·ness** calme *m;* manière *f* posée.

se·da·tion 🜊 [si'deiʃən] sédation *f.*

sed·a·tive *usu.* 🜊 ['sedətiv] calmant (*a. su./m*).

sed·en·tar·i·ness ['sedntərinis] sédentarité *f;* vie *f* sédentaire; **'sed·en·tar·y** ▢ sédentaire (*emploi, oiseau, troupes, vie*); assis.

sedge [sedʒ] ♣ carex *m;* F joncs *m/pl.*

sed·i·ment ['sedimənt] sédiment *m; vin:* lie *f;* ⚗ résidu *m; géol.* atterrissement *m;* **sed·i·men·ta·ry** *géol.* [⹀'mentəri] sédimentaire.

se·di·tion [si'diʃn] sédition *f;* **se'di·tious** ▢ [⹀ʃəs] séditieux (-euse *f*).

se·duce [si'dju:s] séduire; **se'duc·er** [⹀'dʌkʃn] séducteur (-trice *f*) *m;* **se·duc·tion** [⹀'dʌkʃn] séduction *f;* **se'duc·tive** ▢ séduisant.

sed·u·lous ▢ ['sedjuləs] assidu.

see¹ [si:] [*irr.*] *v/t./i.* voir; *fig.* comprendre; *I* ~ je comprends; ~ *about* s'occuper de (*qch.*); ~ *through* pénétrer les intentions de (*q.*), pénétrer (*qch.*); ~ *to* s'occuper de; veiller à; *v/t.* voir; s'assurer (*que, that*); visiter; accompagner; remarquer; consulter (*le médecin*); comprendre; ~ *s.th. done* veiller à ce que qch. soit faite *ou* se fasse; *go to* ~ *s.o.* aller voir q.; rendre visite à q.; ~ *s.o. home* accompagner q. chez lui; ~ *off* reconduire, conduire (*un hôte, une visite à la gare etc.*); ~ *out* accompagner (*q.*) jusqu'à la porte; mener (*qch.*) à bonne fin; ~ *through* assister jusqu'au bout à (*qch.*); soutenir (*q.*) jusqu'au bout; *live to* ~ vivre assez longtemps pour voir.

see² [⹀] évêché *m;* archevêché *m; Holy* ♀ Saint-Siège *m.*

seed [si:d] **1.** grain(e *f*) *m; coll., a. fig.* semence *f;* † lignée *f; go* (*ou run*) *to* ~ s'affricher (*terrain*); monter en graine (*plante*); *fig.* se décatir; **2.** *v/t.* semer; enlever la graine de (*un fruit*); *sp.* trier (*les joueurs*); ~ed players têtes *f/pl.* de série; *v/i.* venir à graine; monter en graine; s'égrener; '~**bed** *see* seed-plot; **seed·i·ness** ['~inis] état *m* râpé *ou* misérable; F (état *m* de) malaise *f*; '**seed·ling** ✍ (jeune) plant *m*; '**seed-plot** ✍ germoir *m*; **seeds·man** ['~zmən] grainetier *m*; '**seed·y** râpé, usé; F indisposé, souffrant.

see·ing ['si:iŋ] **1.** *su.* vue *f*, vision *f*; worth ~ qui vaut la peine d'être vu; **2.** *cj.*: ~ *that* puisque, étant donné que.

seek [si:k] [*irr.*] (*a.* ~ *after*, *for*) (re)chercher; poursuivre; be to ~ *fig.* être peu clair; '**seek·er** chercheur (-euse *f*) *m*.

seem [si:m] sembler; paraître; '**seem·ing 1.** □ apparent; soi-disant; **2.** apparence *f*; '**seem·li·ness** bienséance *f*, décence *f*; beauté *f*; '**seem·ly** convenable; agréable à voir.

seen [si:n] *p.p. de* see[1].

seep [si:p] (s'in)filtrer; suinter; '**seep·age** suintement *m*, infiltration *f*.

seer ['si:ə] voyant(e *f*) *m*, prophète *m*.

see-saw ['si:'sɔ:] **1.** bascule *f*; balançoire *f*; **2.** basculer; *fig.* balancer (*personne*).

seethe [si:ð] bouillonner; s'agiter (*a. fig.*); *fig.* grouiller (de, with).

seg·ment ['segmənt] ⚓ *etc.* segment *m*; *orange*: tranche *f*.

seg·re·gate ['segrigeit] (se) séparer; **seg·re·ga·tion** séparation *f*; *pol.* ségrégation *f*; **seg·re·ga·tion·ist** ségrégationniste *mf*, *adj.*

seine [sein] *filet*: seine *f*.

sei·sin ⚖ ['si:zin] saisine *f*.

seis·mic ['saizmik] sismique; **seis·mo·graph** ['saizməgrɑ:f] sismographe *m*; **seis·mol·o·gy** [~'mɔlədʒi] sismologie *f*.

seize [si:z] *v/t.* saisir (*a.* = *comprendre*); s'emparer de; ⚓ amarrer (*des cordages*), velter (*un espar*); ⚖, *admin.* confisquer; *v/i.* ⊕ gripper; (se) caler; ~ upon saisir (*a. fig.*); '**seiz·ing** saisie *f*; empoignement *m*; ⚓ amarrage *m*; **sei·zure** ['~ʒə] saisie *f* (*a.* ⚖); ⚕ (attaque *f* d')apoplexie *f*.

sel·dom *adv.* ['seldəm] peu souvent, rarement.

se·lect [si'lekt] **1.** choisir; sélectionner; trier; **2.** choisi; d'élite; très fermé (*cercle*); **se'lec·tion** choix *m*; ♀, *zo.* sélection *f*; ♪ sélection *f* (sur, from); emprunté à q., from s.o.); morceaux *m/pl.* choisis (de, from); **se'lec·tive** □ de sélection; *radio*: sélecteur (-trice *f*); sélectif (-ive *f*); **se·lec·tiv·i·ty** [~'tiviti] *radio*: sélectivité *f*; **se'lect·man** *Am.* membre *m* du conseil municipal (*Nouvelle-Angleterre*); **se'lec·tor** *radio*: sélecteur *m*.

self [self] **1.** *pron.* même; ✝ *ou* F *see* myself; **2.** *adj.* automatique; de même; non mélangé; ♀ de couleur uniforme; **3.** *su.* (*pl.* **selves** [selvz]) personnalité *f*; moi *m*; my poor ~ ma pauvre (petite) personne *f*; '~-a'**base·ment** humiliation *f* de soi-même; '~-'**act·ing** automatique; '~-ad'**he·sive** auto-adhésif (-ive *f*); '~-as'**ser·tion** caractère *m* impérieux; autoritarisme *m*; '~-as'**ser·tive** impérieux (-euse *f*); autoritaire; '~-as'**sur·ance** confiance *f* en soi; assurance *f*; '~-as'**sured** sûr de soi; plein d'assurance; '~-'**cen·tred**, *Am.* '~-'**cen·tered** égocentrique; '~-com'**mand** maîtrise *f* de soi; sang-froid *m*; '~-con'**ceit** suffisance *f*, vanité *f*; '~-con'**ceit·ed** suffisant, vaniteux (-euse *f*); '~-'**con·fi·dence** confiance *f* en soi; '~-'**con·fi·dent** sûr de soi, plein de confiance en soi; '~-'**con·scious** gêné; contraint; ~-con'**tained** ['~kən'teind] indépendant; réservé (*personne*); ~ country pays *m* qui se suffit à lui-même; ~ flat appartement *m* indépendant; '~-con'**trol** maîtrise *f* de soi; possession *f* de soi-même; '~-de'**fence** défense *f* personnelle; in ~ en légitime défense; '~-'**de·ni·al** abnégation *f* (de soi); '~-de·ter·mi·'**na·tion** libre disposition *f* de soi-même; '~-'**ed·u·cat·ed** autodidacte; '~-es'**teem** respect *m* de soi; '~-'**ev·i·dent** évident en soi; '~-ex'**plan·a·to·ry** évident (en soi), qui s'explique de soi-même; '~-'**gov·ern·ing** autonome; '~-im'**port·ance** suffisance *f*, présomption *f*; '~-im'**port·ant** suffisant, présomptueux (-euse *f*); '~-'**in·ter·est** intérêt *m* personnel; '**self·ish** □ égoïste,

intéressé; **'self·ish·ness** égoïsme *m*.
self...: **'~·less** altruiste, désintéressé;
'~-'made: ~ *man* fils *m* de ses
œuvres; parvenu *m*; **'~-o'pin·ion-
at·ed** entêté, opiniâtre; **'~-'pit·y**
apitoiement *m* sur soi-même; **'~-
'por·trait** autoportrait *m*; **'~-pos-
'sessed** calme, qui a du sang-froid;
'~-pos'ses·sion aplomb *m*, sang-
froid *m*; **'~-pre·ser'va·tion** conservation *f* de soi-même; **'~-pro'pelled**
autopropulsé; **'~-re'gard** respect *m*
de soi; **'~-re'li·ance** indépendance
f; **'~-re'li·ant** indépendant; **'~-
re'spect** respect *m* de soi; **'~-
re'spect·ing** qui se respecte; **'~-
'right·eous** pharisaïque; **'~-same**
poét. identique; **'~-'seek·ing** intéressé, égoïste; **'~-'serv·ice res·tau-
rant** restaurant *m* libre-service, self-
service *m*; **'~-'start·er** *mot.* (auto-)
démarreur *m*; **'~-suf'fi·cien·cy**
indépendance *f*; suffisance *f*; **'~-
'will** obstination *f*, opiniâtreté *f*; **'~-
'willed** obstiné, opiniâtre; **'~-
'wind·ing** (à remontage) automatique.

sell [sel] [*irr.*] **1.** *v/t.* vendre (*a. fig.*); F
tromper; *Am.* F convaincre, persua-
der; F ~ (*out*) vendre tout son stock de
(*qch*); **†** ~ *off* solder; liquider; ~ *up*
vendre (*q.*); *v/i.* se vendre; être en
vente; **†** ~ *off* (*ou out*) liquider; tout
vendre; **2.** F déception *f*; *sl.* blague *f*;
'sell·er vendeur (-euse *f*) *m*; **†** *good
etc.* ~ article *m* de bonne *etc.* vente;
best ~ livre *m* à (gros) succès, best-
seller *m*; **'sell·out** F succès *m* énorme, pièce *f etc.* pour laquelle tous les
billets sont vendus; trahison *f*; capitulation *f*.

selt·zer ['seltsə] (*a.* ~ *water*) eau *f* de
Seltz.

sel·vage, sel·vedge ['selvidʒ] *tex.*
lisière *f*; *géol.* salbande *f*.

se·man·tics [si'mæntiks] *sg.* sémantique *f*.

sem·a·phore ['seməfɔ:] **1.** sémaphore *m*; signal *m* à bras; **2.** transmettre par sémaphore *ou* par signaux à bras.

sem·blance ['sembləns] semblant
m, apparence *f*.

sem·i... [semi] semi-; demi-; à
moitié; mi-; **'~·breve** ♪ ronde *f*;
'~·cir·cle demi-cercle *m*; **'~·co·lon**
point-virgule (*pl.* points-virgules)
m; **'~·con'duc·tor** ⚡ semi-conduc-

teur *m*; **'~-'fi·nal** *sp.* demi-finale *f*;
'~·man·u'fac·tured semi-ouvré.
sem·i·nal ['si:minl] séminal (-aux
m/pl.); *fig.* embryonnaire.
sem·i·nar ['semina:] *univ.* séminaire
m.
sem·i·nar·y ['seminəri] *fig.* pensionnat *m* (*de jeunes filles*); *eccl.* séminaire
m.
sem·i·of·fi·cial ['semiə'fiʃl] officieux (-euse *f*), semi-officiel(le *f*).
sem·i·prec·ious ['semi'preʃəs]: ~
stone pierre *f* fine *ou* semi-précieuse.
sem·i·qua·ver ♪ ['semikweivə]
double croche *f*.
Sem·ite ['si:mait] Sémite *mf*; **Se-
mit·ic** [si'mitik] sémitique.
sem·i·tone ♪ ['semitoun] demi-ton
m, semi-ton *m*.   [voyelle *f*.]
sem·i·vow·el ['semi'vauəl] semi-}
sem·o·li·na [semə'li:nə] semoule *f*.
sem·pi·ter·nal □ *poét.* [sempi-
'tə:nl] éternel(le *f*).
semp·stress ['sempstris] (ouvrière
f) couturière *f*.
sen·ate ['senit] sénat *m*; *univ.* conseil *m* de l'université.
sen·a·tor ['senətə] sénateur *m*; **sen-
a·to·ri·al** □ [~'tɔ:riəl] sénatorial
(-aux *m/pl.*).
send [send] [*irr.*] *v/t.* envoyer; expédier; diriger (*un coup, une balle*);
remettre (*de l'argent*); rendre (*fou
etc.*); ~ *s.o.* (*gér.*) faire q. (*inf.*); *see
pack* 2; ~ *forth* envoyer (dehors);
répandre; émettre; lancer; ♀ pousser; ~ *in* faire (r)entrer; envoyer; ~
in one's name se faire annoncer; ~
off expédier; faire partir; envoyer;
~ *up* faire monter (*a. fig.*); ~ *word to
s.o.* envoyer un mot à q.; *v/i.*: ~
for faire venir, envoyer chercher;
'send·er envoyeur (-euse *f*) *m*;
lettre, télégramme: expéditeur (-trice
f) *m*; *tél.* transmetteur *m*; **'send-
'off** fête *f* d'adieu; *sl.* recommandation *f*, début *m*.
se·nile ['si:nail] sénile; **se·nil·i·ty**
[si'niliti] sénilité *f*.
sen·ior ['si:njə] **1.** aîné; plus âgé (que,
to); supérieur (à, *to*); premier (-ère *f*)
(*commis etc.*); ~ *citizens pl.* personnes
f/pl. âgées; **†** ~ *partner* associé *m*
principal; **2.** aîné(e *f*) *m*; le (la) plus
ancien(ne *f*) *m*; supérieur(e *f*) *m*;
Am. univ. étudiant(e *f*) *m* de quatrième année; *he is my* ~ *by a year, he
is a year my* ~ il est mon aîné d'un an;

sen·ior·i·ty [siːniˈɔriti] priorité *f* d'âge; *grade*: ancienneté *f*.

sen·sa·tion [senˈseiʃn] sensation *f* (*a. fig.* = *effet sensationnel*); sentiment *m*, impression *f*; **sen·sa·tion·al** □ sensationnel(le *f*); à sensation (*roman etc.*); **sen·sa·tion·al·ism** recherche *f* du sensationnel.

sense [sens] 1. sens *m*; sentiment *m*; sensation *f*; intelligence *f*; signification *f*; ~ *of direction* sens *m* de l'orientation; ~ *of duty* sentiment *m* du devoir; ~ *of humo(u)r* (sens *m* de l')humour *m*; ~ *of time* notion *f* de l'heure; *common (ou good)* ~ sens *m* commun; *bon* sens *m*; *in one's* ~*s* sain d'esprit; *be out of one's* ~*s* avoir perdu le sens *ou* la tête; *bring s.o. to his* ~*s* remener q. à la raison; *make* ~ être compréhensible; *make* ~ *of* arriver à comprendre; *talk* ~ parler raison; 2. sentir; *Am.* comprendre.

sense·less □ [ˈsenslis] insensé, déraisonnable, stupide; sans connaissance, inanimé; **'sense·less·ness** stupidité *f*, absurdité *f*; insensibilité *f*.

sen·si·bil·i·ty [sensiˈbiliti] sensibilité *f* (à, *to*); conscience *f* (*de to, of*); ~ *to light* sensibilité *f* à la lumière.

sen·si·ble □ [ˈsensəbl] sensible, perceptible; appréciable, conscient (de, *of*); raisonnable, sensé; *fig.* pratique; *be* ~ *of* se rendre compte de (*qch.*); avoir conscience de (*qch.*); **'sen·si·ble·ness** bon sens *m*; intelligence *f*; raison *f*.

sen·si·tive □ [ˈsensitiv] sensible (à, *to*); susceptible; ombrageux (-euse *f*) (à l'endroit de, *with regard to*); ✝ instable (*marché*); *phot.* sensible (*papier*), impressionnable (*plaque*); **'sen·si·tive·ness, sen·si·tiv·i·ty** [~ˈtiviti] sensibilité *f* (à, *to*).

sen·si·tize *phot.* [ˈsensitaiz] rendre sensible.

sen·so·ri·al [senˈsɔːriəl], **sen·so·ry** [ˈ~səri] sensoriel(le *f*); des sens.

sen·su·al □ [ˈsensjuəl] sensuel(le *f*); **'sen·su·al·ism** sensualité *f*; *phls.* sensualisme *m*; **'sen·su·al·ist** sensualiste *mf*; voluptueux (-euse *f*); **sen·su·al·i·ty** [~ˈæliti] sensualité *f*.

sen·su·ous □ [ˈsensjuəs] qui provient des sens; voluptueux (-euse *f*).

sent [sent] *prét. et p.p. de send.*

sen·tence [ˈsentəns] 1. ⚖ jugement

m; condamnation *f*; peine *f*; *gramm.* phrase *f*; *serve one's* ~ subir sa peine; *see life*; 2. condamner (à, *to*).

sen·ten·tious [senˈtenʃəs] □ sentencieux (-euse *f*); **sen·ten·tious·ness** caractère *m ou* ton *m* sentencieux.

sen·tient [ˈsenʃnt] sensible.

sen·ti·ment [ˈsentimənt] sentiment *m*; opinion *f*; sentimentalité *f*; toast *m*; *see* ~*ality*; **sen·ti·men·tal** □ [~ˈmentl] sentimental (-aux *m/pl.*); ~ *value* valeur *f* affective; **sen·ti·men·tal·i·ty** [~ˈtæliti] sentimentalité *f*; sensiblerie *f*.

sen·ti·nel [ˈsentinl], **sen·try** [ˈsentri] ✗ sentinelle *f*; factionnaire *m*. **sen·try...**: **'~-box** guérite *f*; **'~-go** faction *f*.

se·pal ♀ [ˈsiːpəl] sépale *m*.

sep·a·ra·bil·i·ty [sepərəˈbiliti] séparabilité *f*; **'sep·a·ra·ble** □ séparable; **sep·a·rate** 1. □ [ˈseprit] séparé, détaché; indépendant; particulier (-ère *f*); ~ *property* biens *m/pl.* réservés; 2. [ˈ~əreit] (se) séparer; (se) détacher; (se) désunir; *v/t.*: ~ *o.s. from* se séparer de; rompre avec; **sep·a·ra·tion** séparation *f* (d'avec q., *from s.o.*); *opt. etc.* écart *m*; **sep·a·ra·tist** [ˈ~ərətist] *pol.*, *a. eccl.* séparatiste *mf*; **sep·a·ra·tor** [ˈ~reitə] séparateur *m*; classeur *m*; (*a. cream-*~) écrémeuse *f*.

se·pi·a *icht., a. peint.* [ˈsiːpjə] sépia *f*.

se·poy [ˈsiːpɔi] cipaye *m* (= *soldat de l'Inde anglaise*).

sep·sis ✄ [ˈsepsis] septicémie *f*; putréfaction *f*.

Sep·tem·ber [sepˈtembə] septembre *m*.

sep·ten·ni·al □ [sepˈtenjəl] septennal (-aux *m/pl.*); ~*ly* tous les sept ans.

sep·tic ✄ [ˈseptik] septique.

sep·tu·a·ge·nar·i·an [ˈseptjuedʒiˈnεəriən] septuagénaire (*a. su.*).

se·pul·chral [siˈpʌlkrəl] sépulcral (-aux *m/pl.*); **sep·ul·chre** *poét.* [ˈsepəlkə] 1. sépulcre *m*, tombeau *m*; 2. ensevelir; servir de tombe(au) à; **sep·ul·ture** [ˈsepəltʃə] sépulture *f*.

se·quel [ˈsiːkwəl] suite *f*; *fig. a.* conséquence *f*; *in the* ~ par la suite.

se·quence [ˈsiːkwəns] suite *f*; succession *f*; ordre *m*; ♩, *cartes*, *cin.*: séquence *f*; *cin.* F scène *f*; *gramm.* ~ *of tenses* concordance *f* des temps; **'se·quent** conséquent; consécutif (-ive *f*) (à [*up*]*on*, to); qui suit.

se·ques·ter [si'kwestə] se sequestrate; ~ *o.s.* se retirer (de, *from*); ~*ed* retiré, isolé; ♊ en séquestre.

se·ques·trate ♊ [si'kwestreit] séquestrer (*des biens*), mettre en séquestre; confisquer; **se·ques·tra·tion** [si:kwes'treiʃn] retraite *f*; confiscation *f*; ♊ séquestration *f*; **'se·ques·tra·tor** ♊ séquestre *m*.

se·quin ['si:kwin] paillette *f*.

se·quoi·a ♀ [si'kwɔiə] séquoia *m*.

se·ragl·io [se'rɑ:liou] sérail *m*.

ser·aph ['serəf], *pl. a.* **-a·phim** ['~fim] séraphin *m*; **se·raph·ic** [se'ræfik] (~*ally*) séraphique.

Serb [sə:b], **Ser·bi·an** ['~jən] **1.** serbe; **2.** *ling.* serbe *m*; Serbe *mf*.

sere *poét.* [siə] flétri, desséché.

ser·e·nade [seri'neid] **1.** ♩ sérénade *f*; **2.** donner une sérénade à.

se·rene □ [si'ri:n] serein, calme, paisible; *titre*: ♀ sérénissime; *Your* ♀ *Highness* votre Altesse *f* sérénissime; **se·ren·i·ty** [si'reniti] sérénité *f* (*a. titre*); calme *m*.

serf [sə:f] serf (serve *f*) *m*; **'serf·age**, **'serf·dom** servage *m*.

serge [sə:dʒ] serge *f*; *cotton* ~ sergé *m*.

ser·geant ⚔ ['sɑ:dʒnt] sergent *m*; (*a. police* ~) brigadier *m*; '~·**ma·jor** ⚔ adjudant *m*.

se·ri·al □ ['siəriəl] **1.** de série; en série; de reproduction en feuilleton (*droit*); ~*ly* en série, par série; en feuilleton; **2.** roman-feuilleton (*pl.* romans-feuilletons) *m*; **se·ri·al·ize** publier *ou* adapter en feuilleton *ou* épisodes (*un roman etc.*).

se·ries ['siəri:z] *sg., a. pl.* série *f*, suite *f* (*a.* ♉); ⚡ *connect* (*ou* join) *in* ~ grouper en série; ~ *connexion* montage *m* en série.

se·ri·ous □ ['siəriəs] sérieux (-euse *f*) (= *grave*; *réfléchi*; *sincère*; *gros, etc.*); *be* ~ ne pas plaisanter; **'se·ri·ous·ness** gravité *f*; sérieux *m*.

ser·jeant *hist.* ['sɑ:dʒnt] (*a.* ~ *at law*) avocat *m* (supérieur); *Common* ♀ magistrat *m* de la corporation de Londres; *parl.* ♀-*at-arms* commandant *m* militaire du Parlement.

ser·mon ['sə:mən] sermon *m* (*a.*

fig.); *catholique*: prône *m*, *protestant*: prêche *m*; **'ser·mon·ize** *v/i.* prêcher; *v/t.* chapitrer; faire la morale à.

se·rol·o·gy ⚕ [siə'rɔlədʒi] sérologie *f*.

se·rous ['siərəs] séreux (-euse *f*).

ser·pent ['sə:pənt] serpent *m*; **ser·pen·tine** ['~ain] **1.** serpentin; serpentant; tortueux (-euse *f*); **2.** *min.* serpentine *f*.

ser·rate ['serit], **ser·rat·ed** [se'reitid] dentelé; denté (en scie) **ser·ra·tion** dent(el)ure *f*; *anat.* engrenure *f*.

ser·ried ['serid] serré.

se·rum ['siərəm] sérum *m*.

serv·ant ['sə:vənt] serviteur *m*; domestique *mf*; employé(e *f*) *m*; (*a.* ~-*girl ou* ~-*maid*) servante *f*, bonne *f*; *see civil*; ~*s pl.* domestiques *m/pl.*; personnel *m*; ~*s' hall* office *f*; salle *f* commune des domestiques.

serve [sə:v] **1.** *v/t.* servir (*a.* ⚔, ♱, *eccl.*, *tennis*, [*a.* ~ *up*] *un mets*); être utile à; contenter; 🏭, *compagnie de gaz, etc.*: desservir, traiter (*q.*) (*bien ou mal*); subir, purger (*une peine*); ♊ *a writ on s.o.*, ~ *s.o. with a writ* délivrer une assignation à q.; (*it*) ~*s him right* cela lui apprendra; *see sentence 1*; ~ *out* distribuer (*qch.*); F faire payer (*qch. à q., s.o. s.th.*); *v/i.* servir (à, *for*; de, *as*); ⚔ servir dans l'armée; ⚔ faire la guerre (sous, *under*); être favorable (*temps*); ~ *at table* servir à table; ~ *on a jury* être du jury; **2.** *tennis*: service *m*; **'server** *tennis*: serveur (-euse *f*) *m*; *eccl.* acolyte *m*.

serv·ice ['sə:vis] **1.** service *m* (*a.* ⚔, 🏭, *domestique, mets, tennis, a. fig.*); *eau, électricité, gaz*: distribution *f*; entretien *m*; *mot.* entretien *m* et dépannage *m*; *fonctionnaire*: emploi *m*; disposition *f*; (*a. divine*) office *m*, *protestantisme*: service *m*, culte *m*; ⚓ *cordage*: fourrure *f*; ♊ délivrance *f*, signification *f*; 🏭 *etc.* parcours *m*, ligne *f*; *fig.* utilité *f*; garniture *f* (*de toilette*); the (*army*) ~*s pl.* l'armée *f*; *public* ~*s pl.* services *m/pl.* publics; ⚔ *Army* ♀ *Corps* service *m* de l'Intendance, F *le Train m*; *see civil*; *be at s.o.'s* ~ être à la disposition de q.; **2.** entretenir et réparer (*les automobiles etc.*); soigner l'entretien de; **'serv·ice·a·ble** □ utile, pratique; durable, avantageux (-euse *f*); en état de fonctionner; utilisable; serviable; **'serv·ice-a·ble·ness** utilité *f*; état *m* satisfaisant; solidité *f*.

serv·ice...: ~ **ar·e·a** *mot.* aire *f* de service; **'~-ball** *tennis:* balle *f* de service; ~ **charge** service *m*; **'~-line** *tennis:* ligne *f* de service *ou* fond; ~ **pipe** ⊕ branchement *m*; ~ **sta·tion** station-service (*pl.* stations-service) *f*; **'~-tree** ♀ cormier *m*.

ser·vile □ ['sə:vail] servile (*a. fig.*); d'esclave; bas(se *f*) (*personne*); vil; **ser·vil·i·ty** [~'viliti] servilité *f* (*a. d'une personne*); bassesse *f*; *copie:* exactitude *f* trop étroite.

ser·vi·tude ['sə:vitju:d] servitude *f* (*a. ⚖️*); asservissement *m*, esclavage *m*; *see penal.*

ses·a·me ♀, *a. fig.* ['sesəmi] sésame *m*.

ses·qui·pe·da·li·an ['seskwipi'deiljən] sesquipédale; *fig.* ampoulé, pédant (*personne*).

ses·sion ['seʃn] session *f* (*a. ⚖️*); séance *f*; *univ.* année *f* universitaire; *be in* ~ siéger; ⚖️ être en session; **'ses·sion·al** (de la) session; annuel(le *f*).

set [set] **1.** [*irr.*] *v/t.* mettre (*a. le couvert*), poser (*a. un problème, une question*), placer; imposer (*une tâche*); régler (*la montre, a. ⊕*); mettre (*le réveille-matin*) (*sur, for*); dresser (*un piège*); donner (*un exemple*); fixer (*un jour, la mode*); 🌱 planter; lancer (*un chien*) (*contre at, on*); ajuster; ⊕ redresser (*une lime*); affiler (*un outil*); affûter (*une scie*); monter (*une pierre précieuse*); *théâ. le décor*); déployer (*la voile*); mettre en plis (*les cheveux*); 🩹 remettre; ~ *s.o. laughing* provoquer les rires de q., faire rire q.; ~ *the fashion* lancer la mode; fixer *ou* mener la mode; ~ *sail* faire voile, prendre la mer; ~ *one's teeth* serrer les dents; ~ *against* animer *ou* prévenir contre; ~ *apart*, ~ *aside* mettre de côté; *fig.* rejeter, laisser de côté; écarter; ⚖️ casser; ~ *at defiance* défier (*q.*); ~ *at ease* mettre à son aise; ~ *at liberty* mettre en liberté; ~ *at rest* calmer; décider (*une question*); ~ *store by* attacher grand prix à; ~ *down* (dé)poser; consigner par écrit; attribuer (à,

to); prendre (*q.*) (*pour, for*); ~ *forth* énoncer; exposer; formuler; ~ *off* compenser (par, *against*); faire ressortir, rehausser; faire partir (*une fusée*); ~ *on* inciter à attaquer; acharner (contre, *on*); lancer (contre, on); mettre (à *inf.*, *to* à *inf.*); ~ *out* arranger, disposer; étaler; équiper (*q.*); orner (*q.*); mettre dehors; ~ *up* monter, dresser; fixer; relever; organiser; fonder; monter (*un magasin*); occasionner; afficher (*des prétentions*); mettre en avant; pousser (*une clameur*); rétablir (*la santé*); *typ.* ~ *up in type* composer; **2.** [*irr.*] *v/i.* se coucher (*soleil etc.*); (se) prendre; se figer (*gelée etc.*); prendre racine (*plante*); tomber (*robe etc.*); devenir fixe; 🩹 se nouer (*a. fruit*); souffler (*vent*); porter (*marée*); *chasse:* tomber en arrêt; ~ *about* se mettre à (*qch.*); attaquer (*q.*); ~ *forth* partir; ~ *forward* se mettre en route; ~ *in* commencer; ~ *off* se mettre en route; partir; ~ *out* se mettre en route; faire voile; partir; ~ *to* commencer à descendre (*marée*); ~ *to* se mettre au travail; F en venir aux coups; ~ *up* se poser (en, *as*); s'établir (*qch., as s.th.*); ~ *up for* poser pour; se donner des airs de; ~ (*up*)*on* attaquer; † se mettre à; **3.** fixe; résolu; pris; noué, immobile, assigné; prescrit; ~ (*up*)*on* déterminé à; résolu à; ~ *with* orné de; ~ *fair* (*au*) beau (fixe) (*baromètre*); *hard* ~ fort embarrassé; *peint. etc.* ~ *piece* pièce *f* montée; *théâ.* ferme *f*; ~ *speech* discours *m* étudié; **4.** ensemble *m*; collection *f*; série *f* (*a.* ♠); garniture *f* (*de boutons etc.; a. de toilette etc.*); porcelaine, linge: service *m*; lingerie, pierres précieuses: parure *f*; casseroles etc.: batterie *f*; échecs, outils, etc.: jeu *m*; coterie *f*, monde *m*, bande *f*; groupe *m* (*a.* ♠); scie: voie *f*; cheveux: mise *f* en plis; radio: poste *m*; 🌱 plaçon *m*; tennis: set *m*; ⚓ voiles: orientation *f*; poét. soleil: coucher *m*; *fig.* attaque *f*; théâ. décor *m* (monté); (*a.* ~ scene) mise *f* en scène; ~ *of teeth* denture *f*; ~ *of false teeth* dentier *m*.

set·back ['set'bæk] *fig.* échec *m*; ✝ recul *m*; mur *m* en retrait; **'set·'down** humiliation *f*; **'set·'off** contraste *m*; ✝ compensation *f*; ⚖️ reconvention *f*; △ saillie *f*; *voyage:*

départ *m*; **'set·'square** ⅄ équerre *f* à dessin.

set·tee [se'ti:] canapé *m*.

set·ter ['setə] *typ*. compositeur *m*; poseur *m*; monteur *m* etc.; *see* set 1; *chasse*: chien *m* d'arrêt, setter *m*.

set·ting ['setiŋ] mise *f* (*a*. en musique, *to music*; *a. scie*: en voie; *cheveux*: en plis); arrangement *m* (*a.* ♪); ♪ ton *m*; *astr.* coucher *m*; monture *f* (*d'une pierre précieuse*); *spécimen*: montage *m*; *fig.* encadrement *m*; *théâ*. mise *f* en scène; *typ*. composition *f*; ⊕ calage *m*; ⊕ installation *f*; ⊕ *outil*: aiguisage *m*; *ciment, gelée*: prise *f*; ⚙ *os brisé*: recollement *m*; *fracture*: réduction *f*; **'~-lo·tion** *cheveux*: fixatif *m*.

set·tle ['setl] **1.** banc *m* à dossier; **2.** *v/t*. fixer; établir; installer; calmer (*un enfant*); régler (*un compte*); arranger (*une dispute*, ♕ *un procès*); résoudre (*une question*); décider; ♕ assigner (à, *on*); clarifier (*un liquide*); coloniser (*un pays*); *v/i*. (*souv.* ~ *down*) s'établir (*p.ex. à Paris*); se calmer (*enfant, passion*); (*a.* ~ *o.s.*) s'installer; se poser (*oiseau*); se tasser (*maison, sol*); ⚓ s'enfoncer; se remettre au beau (*temps*); (*a.* ~ *up*) s'acquitter (envers, *with*); se clarifier (*liquide*); se rasseoir (*vin*); se décider (pour, *on*); se ranger (*conduite, personne*); se mettre (à, *to*); *it is settling for a frost* le temps est à la gelée.

set·tled ['setld] sûr (*a. temps*); ⚓ établi (*temps, brise*); enraciné (*idée etc.*); rangé (*personne*); ✝ réglé; ✝ ~! pour acquit.

set·tle·ment ['setlmənt] établissement *m*; installation *f*; *sol etc.*: tassement *m*; arrangement *m*; *problème*: solution *f*; colonie *f*; ♕ constitution *f* de rente (en faveur de, *on*); ♕ contrat *m*; *fig.* accord *m*; ✝ règlement *m*; liquidation *f*; ✝ *for* ~ à terme.

set·tler ['setlə] colon *m*; F coup *m* décisif.

set·tling ['setliŋ] établissement *m* etc.; *see* settle 2; ✝ règlement *m*.

set...: '~-'to dispute *f*; lutte *f*; prise *f* de bec; '~-'up organisation *f*; *Am. sl.* affaire *f* bricolée (*surt. match de boxe*).

sev·en ['sevn] sept (*a. su.*/*m*); **'sev-en·fold 1.** *adj*. septuple; **2.** *adv*. sept

fois autant; **sev·en·teen(th)** ['~-'ti:n(θ)] dix-sept(ième) (*a. su.*/*m*); **sev·enth** ['~θ] **1.** □ septième; **2.** septième *m*, ♪ *f*; **sev·en·ti·eth** ['~tiiθ] soixante-dixième (*a. su.*/*m*); **'sev·en·ty** soixante-dix (*a. su.*/*m*).

sev·er ['sevə] (se) séparer, rompre; *v/t.* couper; désunir.

sev·er·al □ ['sevrəl] plusieurs; quelques; divers; séparé, différent; individuel(le *f*) (*surt.* ♕); ♕ joint and ~ solidaire; **'sev·er·al·ly** séparément; chacun à soi.

sev·er·ance ['sevərəns] séparation *f*; disjonction *f* (*a.* ♕).

se·vere □ [si'viə] sévère (*beauté, personne, regard, style, etc.*); vif (*vive f*) (*douleur*); grave (*blessure, maladie*); intense, violent; rigoureux (-euse *f*) (*personne, sentence, climat, hiver, temps, etc.*); dur; **se·ver·i·ty** [~'veriti] sévérité *f*; violence *f*; gravité *f*; rigueur *f*.

sew [sou] [*irr.*] coudre; brocher (*un livre*); ~ *up* coudre; faire un point à (*une robe etc.*).

sew·age ['sju:idʒ] eaux *f*/*pl.* d'égouts; ~ *farm* champs *m*/*pl.* d'épandage.

sew·er¹ ['souə] couseur (-euse *f*) *m*; *livres*: brocheur (-euse *f*) *m*.

sew·er² ['sjuə] égout *m*; **'sew·er·age** système *m* d'égouts.

sew·ing ['souiŋ] couture *f*; *livres*: brochage *m*; ouvrage *m* à l'aiguille; *attr.* à coudre.

sewn [soun] *p.p. de* sew.

sex [seks] sexe *m*; *attr.* sexuel(le *f*); ~ *appeal* sex-appeal *m*; attrait *m*; ~ *education* enseignement *m* de la biologie humaine; F *have* ~ *with* coucher avec.

sex·a·ge·nar·i·an [seksədʒi'nɛəriən] sexagénaire (*a. su.*); **sex·en·ni·al** □ [sek'senjəl] sexennal (-aux *m*/*pl.*); **sex·tant** ['sekstənt] sextant *m*.

sex·ton ['sekstən] sacristain *m*; F fossoyeur *m*; F sonneur *m* (*du glas*).

sex·tu·ple ['sekstjupl] sextuple (*a. su.*/*m*).

sex·u·al □ ['seksjuəl] sexuel(le *f*); ~ *desire* désir *m* sexuel; ~ *intercourse* rapports *m*/*pl.* sexuels; ~ *urge* instinct *m* sexuel, pulsion *f* sexuelle; **sex·u·al·i·ty** [~'æliti] sexualité *f*; **sex·y** ['seksi] qui a du sex-appeal, F sexy *inv.*

shab·bi·ness ['ʃæbinis] état *m* râpé;

pauvreté *f*; mesquinerie *f*; **'shab-by** □ râpé, usé; pauvre; *fig.* mes-quin, vilain; *fig.* parcimonieux (-euse *f*).

shack *surt. Am.* [ʃæk] cabane *f*.

shack·le ['ʃækl] **1.** fer *m* (*fig. usu.* ~s *pl.*), entraves *f/pl.*, contrainte *f*; ⚓ maillon *m* (*de chaîne*); ⊕ maillon *m* de liaison; **2.** entraver (*a. fig.*); ⊕ maniller; ⚓ étalinguer (*une an-cre*).

shad *icht.* [ʃæd] alose *f*. [*cre*).

shade [ʃeid] **1.** ombre *f*; *fig.* obscu-rité *f*; *lampe*: abat-jour *m/inv.*; *yeux*: garde-vue *m/inv.*; *couleur, opi-nion*: nuance *f*; teinte *f*; *Am. fenêtre*: store *m*; *fig.* soupçon *m*, nuance *f*; **2.** *v/t.* ombrager; obscur-cir (*a. fig.*); *fig.* assombrir; voiler, masquer (*la lumière*); abriter (de, *from*); *tex. etc.* nuancer; *peint.* ombrer; *dessin etc.*: hachurer; ~ one's eyes with mettre (*qch.*) en abat-jour (sur les yeux); ~ away (*ou off*) estomper; *v/i.* (*ou* ~ off) se fon-dre (en, *qfois* dans *into*); **shades** [ʃeidz] *pl.* F lunettes *f/pl.* de soleil.

shad·i·ness ['ʃeidinis] ombre *f*, om-brage *m*; F aspect *m* louche; réputa-tion *f* louche.

shad·ow ['ʃædou] **1.** ombre *f* (*a. fig.*); *peint., phot.* noir *m*; *see* shade; *police*: filateur (-trice *f*) *m*; *fig.* mauvaise foi *f*; ~ boxing boxe *f* à vide; *pol. Brit.* ~ cabinet cabinet *m* fantôme; **2.** ombra-ger; *tex.* chiner; *police*: filer (*q.*); (*usu.* ~ forth, out) faire pressentir, symboliser; **'shad·ow·y** ombragé; obscur, ténébreux (-euse *f*); indécis, faible.

shad·y ['ʃeidi] ombragé, à l'ombre; frais (fraîche *f*); F louche; F be on the ~ side of forty avoir dépassé la quarantaine.

shaft [ʃɑ:ft] flèche *f* (*a. fig.*); manche *m*; *lance*: hampe *f*; *poét. lumière*: trait *m*; ⊕ arbre *m*; *voitures*: bran-card *m*; ⚒ puits *m*.

shag [ʃæg] **1.** ⚜ peluche *f*; tabac *m* fort coupé fin; broussaille *f*; † poil *m* touffu; **2.** ébouriffer (*les cheveux*).

shag·gy ['ʃægi] ébouriffé (*cheveux*); touffu (*barbe*); en broussailles (*sour-cils*); ⚜ poilu. [chagrin *m*).

sha·green [ʃə'gri:n] (peau *f* de).

Shah [ʃɑ:] s(c)hah *m*.

shake [ʃeik] **1.** [*irr.*] *v/t.* secouer; agiter; ébranler; *fig.* bouleverser; *fig.* effrayer; ~ down faire tomber

(*qch.*) en secouant; tasser (*qch.*) en le secouant; *Am. sl.* ~ s.o. down for faire cracher (*une somme*) à q.; ~ hands serrer la main (à, *with*); ~ up secouer (*a.* F *fig.*); agiter; *v/i.* trem-bler (de, *with*; devant, *at*); chance-ler; branler (*tête*); ♪ faire des trilles; ~ down s'habituer (à, [*in*]to); s'instal-ler; **2.** secousse *f*; tremblement *m* (*Am.* de terre); ♪ trille *m*; hochement *m* (*de tête*) F rien m de temps; ~ of the hand see ~-hands; F no great ~s bien médiocre, bien peu de chose; '~-**down** lit *m* improvisé; *Am. sl.* extorsion *f*; ⚓ *Am.* ~ cruise voyage *m* d'essai; '~-**hands** serrement *m ou* poignée *f* de main; '**shak·en** **1.** *p.p. de* shake **1**; **2.** secoué, ébran-lé; '**shak·er** secoueur (-euse *f*) *m*; ⊕ secoueur *m*; shaker *m*; *eccl.* ♀ Trembleur (-euse *f*) *m*.

shake-up *Am.* F ['ʃeik'ʌp] remanie-ment *m*; chose *f* improvisée.

shak·i·ness ['ʃeikinis] manque *m* de solidité; tremblement *m*; *voix*: chevrotement *m*; '**shak·y** □ peu solide; chancelant; tremblant; *fig.* véreux (-euse *f*) (*cas, compagnie, etc.*).

shall [ʃæl] [*irr.*] *v/aux.* (*défectif*) usité *pour former le fut.*; *qqfois* je veux *etc.*, je dois *etc.*; *promesse, menace*: se traduit par le fut.

shal·lot ♀ [ʃə'lɔt] échalote *f*.

shal·low ['ʃælou] **1.** peu profond, *fig.* superficiel(le *f*); **2.** bas-fond *m*; **3.** *v/t.* rendre *ou v/i.* devenir moins profond; '**shal·low·ness** peu *m* de profondeur; *fig.* superficialité *f*.

shalt † [ʃælt] *2e personne du sg. de* shall.

sham [ʃæm] **1.** faux (fausse *f*), simulé; feint; **2.** feinte *f*, *sl.* chiqué *m*; *personne*: imposteur *m*; **3.** *v/t.* feindre, simuler; faire; *v/i.* faire semblant; jouer une comédie; ~ ill faire le malade.

sham·ble ['ʃæmbl] aller à pas traî-nants.

sham·bles ['ʃæmblz] *sg.* abattoir *m*; *fig.* scène *f* de carnage.

sham·bling □ ['ʃæmbliŋ] traînant.

shame [ʃeim] **1.** honte *f*; (*for*) ~! quelle honte!; vous n'avez pas honte!; cry ~ upon se récrier contre; put to ~ faire honte à; **2.** faire honte à; humilier; couvrir de honte.

shame·faced □ ['ʃeimfeist] honteux

(-euse *f*); embarrassé; **'shame·faced·ness** embarras *m*; timidité *f*.

shame·ful □ ['ʃeimful] honteux (-euse *f*); **'shame·ful·ness** honte *f*, indignité *f*.

shame·less □ ['ʃeimlis] sans honte, éhonté; **'shame·less·ness** effronterie *f*; immodestie *f*.

sham·my ['ʃæmi] (peau *f* de) chamois *m*.

sham·poo [ʃæm'puː] **1.** (se) dégraisser (*les cheveux*); *v/t.* faire un shampooing à (*q.*); frictionner; **2.** *a.* = **sham'poo·ing** shampooing *m*; dry ~ friction *f*; ~ and set shampooing *m* (et) mise *f* en plis; have a ~ and set se faire faire un shampooing (et) mise en plis.

sham·rock ['ʃæmrɔk] ♀ trèfle *m* d'Irlande (*a. emblème national irlandais*).

shan·dy Brit. ['ʃændi] panaché *m*.

shang·hai ⚓ *sl.* [ʃæŋ'hai] embarquer un homme pour l'engager après l'avoir enivré.

shank [ʃæŋk] tige *f*; ⚓ verge *f* (*d'ancre*); queue *f* (*de bouton*); *cuis.* jarret *m* (*de bœuf*), manche *m* (*de gigot de mouton*); jambe *f*; ride ~s's mare (*ou pony*) prendre le train onze; **shanked:** short-~ aux jambes courtes (*personne*).

shan't [ʃɑːnt] = shall not.

shan·ty ['ʃænti] cabane *f*, hutte *f*.

shape [ʃeip] **1.** forme *f*; *cost.* coupe *f*; *personne:* taille *f*; *cuis.* moule *m*; crème *f*; in bad ~ en mauvais état; **2.** *v/t.* façonner, former; tailler; ajuster (à, *to*); ~ one's course ⚓ faire (une) route; *fig.* se diriger (vers, *for*); *v/i.* se développer; promettre; **shaped** façonné; en forme de; **'shape·less** informe; difforme; **'shape·li·ness** beauté *f* de forme; **'shape·ly** bien fait; beau (bel *devant une voyelle ou un h muet*), belle *f*; beaux *m/pl.*.

share [ʃɛə] **1.** part *f*, portion *f*; contribution *f*; ✝ action *f*, titre *m*, valeur *f*; *charrue:* soc *m*; ✝ original (*ou ordinary ou primary*) ~ action *f* ordinaire; ✝ preference (*ou preferred ou priority*) ~ action *f* privilégiée; have a ~ in avoir part à; go ~s partager (qch. avec q., *in s.th. with s.o.*); ~ and ~ alike en partageant également; **2.** *v/t.* partager (entre, *among[st]*; avec, *with*); avoir part à

(*qch.*); *v/i.* prendre part (à, *in*), participer (à, *in*); **'~·crop·per** Am. métayer (-ère *f*) *m*; **'~·hold·er** ✝ actionnaire *mf*; **'shar·er** participant(e *f*) *m*.

shark [ʃɑːk] **1.** *icht.* requin *m*; *fig. a.* escroc *m*; *Am. sl.* as *m* (= *expert*); **2.** *v/i.* écornifler.

sharp [ʃɑːp] **1.** *adj.* □ tranchant (*couteau etc.*); aigu(ë *f*) (*pointe*); vif (vive *f*) (*froid*); *fig.* éveillé; *fig.* rusé; aigre (*fruit*); violent (*douleur*); vert (*vin*, *réprimande*); perçant (*cri*, *œil*); pénétrant (*regard*); fin (*oreille*, *esprit*); net(te *f*) (*profil*); piquant (*goût*, *sauce*); saillant (*angle*); raide (*pente*); prononcé (*courbe*); fort (*averse*, *gelée*); F élégant, chic *inv.* (*vêtement*, *voiture*, *personne etc.*); *péj.* peu honnête; ♪ dièse; ♪ C ~ do *m* dièse; **2.** *adv.* ♪ trop haut, en disant; F ponctuellement; look ~! dépêchez-vous!; faites vite!; **3.** *su.* ♪ dièse *m*; F escroc *m*; *Am. sl.* as *m*; **'sharp·en** aiguiser (*a. fig. l'appétit*); tailler (*un crayon*); accentuer (*un trait*, *un contraste*); ♪ diéser; **sharp·en·er** fusil *m* (à aiguiser), taille-crayon *m/inv.*; **'sharp·er** escroc *m*; *cartes:* tricheur (-euse *f*) *m*; **'sharp-'eyed** à la vue perçante; à qui n'échappe rien; **'sharp·ness** tranchant *m*; pointe *f*; acuité *f*; violence *f*; acidité *f*; *fig.* rigueur *f*.

sharp...: **'~·'set** en grand appétit, affamé; be ~ on avoir un vif désir de; **'~·shoot·er** tirailleur *m*; **'~·'sight·ed** à la vue perçante; *fig.* perspicace; **'~·'wit·ted** éveillé.

shat·ter ['ʃætə] (se) fracasser; (se) briser (en éclats); *v/t.* détraquer (*les nerfs*, *la santé*); briser (*les espérances*); **'~·proof:** ~ glass verre *m* Sécurit (*TM*).

shave [ʃeiv] **1.** [*irr.*] *v/t.* raser; planer (*le bois*); friser, effleurer; *fig.* rogner; *v/i.* se raser; ~ through se faufiler entre (*les voitures etc.*); **2.** coup *m* à fleur de peau; give s.o. a ~ faire la barbe à q.; have a ~ se (faire) raser; by a ~ d'un iota; tout juste; to have a close (*ou narrow*) ~ l'échapper belle; **'shav·en** rasé; a ~ head une tête *f* rasée; **'shav·er** barbier *m*; rasoir *m* électrique; F young ~ gamin *m*.

Sha·vi·an ['ʃeivjən] de G.B. Shaw; à la G.B. Shaw.

shav·ing ['ʃeiviŋ] **1.** action f de (se) raser; ⁓s pl. bois: copeaux m/pl.; métal: rognures f/pl.; **2.** à barbe; ⁓ brush blaireau m; ⁓ cream crème f à raser; ⁓ mug plat m à barbe; ⁓ soap savon m à barbe; ⁓ stick bâton m de savon à barbe.

shawl [ʃɔ:l] châle m; fichu m.

shawm ♪ [ʃɔ:m] chalumeau m.

she [ʃi:] **1.** elle (a. accentué); **2.** femelle f; femme f; **she-** femelle f (d'un animal).

sheaf [ʃi:f] (pl. sheaves) blé: gerbe f; papiers: liasse f.

shear [ʃiə] **1.** [irr.] tondre; couper; métall. cisailler (une tôle); fig. dépouiller; **2.** (a pair of) ⁓s pl. (des) cisailles f/pl.; 'shear·ing coupage m; moutons: tonte f; drap: tondage m; ⁓s pl. tontes f/pl. (de laine).

sheath [ʃi:θ] gaine f (a. ⚲, a. anat.); épée: fourreau m; phot. châssis m; **sheathe** [ʃi:ð] mettre au fourreau; rengainer; ⊕, a. fig. revêtir, recouvrir (de, with); 'sheath·ing ⊕ revêtement m; enveloppe f; chemise f; câble: gaine f.

sheave ⊕ [ʃi:v] rouet m; plateau m d'excentrique.

sheaves [ʃi:vz] pl. de sheaf.

she·bang Am. sl. [ʃə'bæŋ] hutte f; cabaret m, bar m; carriole f; the whole ⁓ tout le bazar.

she-bear ['ʃi:'bɛə] ourse f.

shed[1] [ʃed] [irr.] perdre (ses feuilles, ses dents); verser (des larmes, du sang); répandre (du sang, de la lumière, a. fig.); F ⁓ light on jeter le jour dans.

shed[2] [⁓] hangar m; ⚲ tente f à marchandises.

shed·der ['ʃedə] personne f qui répand (qch.).

sheen [ʃi:n] étoffe etc.: brillant m; reflet m; chatoiement m; 'sheen·y luisant, brillant.

sheep [ʃi:p] mouton m; brebis f (a. fig.); coll. moutons m/pl.; fig. ⁓'s eyes pl. yeux m/pl. doux; '⁓-cot see sheep-fold; '⁓-dog chien m de berger; '⁓-fold parc m à moutons; 'sheep·ish ☐ timide; penaud; 'sheep·ish·ness timidité f; air m penaud.

sheep...: '⁓-man Am. éleveur m de moutons; '⁓-run see sheep-walk; '⁓-skin peau f de mouton; Am. sl. diplôme m; (a. ⁓ leather) basane f;

'⁓-walk pâturage m pour moutons.

sheer[1] [ʃiə] **1.** adj. pur, vrai, véritable; à pic (a. adv.), escarpé, abrupt; **2.** adv. tout à fait; abruptement; à plomb.

sheer[2] [⁓] **1.** ⚲ embarder; ⁓ off ⚲ prendre le large, s'écarter, s'éloigner; **2.** ⚲ embardée f.

sheet [ʃi:t] **1.** métal, papier, verre, etc.: feuille f; eau etc.: nappe f; neige: couche f; lit: drap m; ⚲ écoute f; ⁓ copper (iron) cuivre m (fer m) en feuilles; ⁓ glass verre m à vitres; ⁓ steel tôle f d'acier; **2.** couvrir d'un drap; fig. recouvrir; '⁓-an·chor ⚲ ancre f de veille (fig. de salut); 'sheet·ing tex. toile f pour draps; ⊕ tôles f/pl.; 'sheet-light·ning éclairs m/pl. en nappe ou de chaleur.

sheik(h) [ʃeik] cheik m.

shelf [ʃelf] (pl. shelves) rayon m; planche f; four, a. géog.: plateau m; rebord m; écueil m; banc m de sable; ✝ ⁓ life durée f de conservation avant vente; fig. on the ⁓ au rancart; en passe de devenir vieille fille; fig. get on the ⁓ coiffer sainte Catherine (femme).

shell [ʃel] **1.** coquille f (vide); œuf: coque f; huîtres: écaille f; homard etc.: carapace f; pois: cosse f; ⊕ paroi f; métall. manteau m; ✕ obus m; classe f intermédiaire; cercueil m; maison: carcasse f; **2.** écaler; écosser; ✕ bombarder; sl. ⁓ out débourser; payer (la note etc.).

shel·lac [ʃe'læk] gomme f laque.

shell-cra·ter ['ʃelkreitə] cratère m, entonnoir m; **shelled** [ʃeld] à coquille etc.

shell...: '⁓-fire tir m à obus; '⁓-fish coquillage m; crustacé m; '⁓-proof à l'épreuve des obus; blindé; '⁓-work coquillages m/pl.

shel·ter ['ʃeltə] **1.** abri m; asile m; fig. protection f; in the (ou under) ⁓ of à l'abri de; **2.** v/t. abriter; donner asile à; v/i. (a. ⁓ o.s.) s'abriter; 'shel·ter·less sans abri etc.

shelve[1] [ʃelv] garnir de rayons; mettre sur un rayon; fig. remettre, ajourner; fig. mettre au rancart, remiser (q.); F classer (une question).

shelve[2] [⁓] aller en pente douce.

shelves [ʃelvz] pl. de shelf.

shelv·ing ['ʃelviŋ] **1.** rayons m/pl.; **2.** en pente.

she·nan·i·gan *Am.* F [ʃiˈnænigən] mystification *f.*

shep·herd [ˈʃepəd] **1.** berger *m*; **2.** garder (*des moutons*); **'shep·herd·ess** bergère *f.*

sher·bet [ˈʃəːbət] sorbet *m* (= *sorte de boisson à demi glacée*); (*a.* ⁓-*powder*) limonade *f* (sèche).

sher·iff [ˈʃerif] *Angl.* chérif *m* (= *préfet*); *Am.* chef *m* de la police.

sher·ry [ˈʃeri] vin *m* de Xérès, cherry *m.*

shew † [ʃou] *see* show 1.

shib·bo·leth *fig.* [ˈʃibələθ] doctrine *f*; mot *m* d'ordre.

shield [ʃiːld] **1.** bouclier *m*; *fig.* défense *f*; ▨ écu *m*; **2.** protéger (contre *from*, *against*); **'shield·less** sans bouclier; *fig.* sans défense.

shift [ʃift] **1.** changement *m*; moyen *m*; expédient *m*; échappatoire *f*; ⊕ équipe *f*; ⊕ journée *f* (de travail); † chemise *f* (*de femme*); *make* ⁓ s'arranger (pour *inf.*, *to inf.*; avec, *with*); trouver moyen (de, *to*); *make* ⁓ *without* se passer de; *make* ⁓ *to live* arriver à vivre; **2.** *v/t.* changer (de place *etc.*); ⚓ changer (*une voile*); déplacer (*a.* ⚓ *la cargaison*); *v/i. Am. mot.* changer de vitesse; changer de place; bouger, se déplacer; changer (*scène*); tourner (*vent*); ⚓ se désarrimer (*cargaison*); F (*a.* ⁓ *for o.s.*) se débrouiller; **'shift·ing** □ qui se déplace; mobile; ⁓ *sands pl.* sables *m/pl.* mouvants; **'shift·less** □ sans ressources; peu débrouillard; *fig.* futile; **'shift·y** □ sournois, peu franc(he *f*); fuyant (*yeux*); louche; † peu solide.

shil·ling [ˈʃiliŋ] shilling *m*; *take the King's* ⁓ s'engager; *fig. cut s.o. off with a* ⁓ déshériter q.

shil·ly-shal·ly [ˈʃiliʃæli] **1.** barguignage *m*; **2.** barguigner.

shim·mer [ˈʃimə] miroiter, chatoyer.

shim·my¹ [ˈʃimi] **1.** *danse:* shimmy *m*; **2.** osciller, vibrer.

shim·my² F [⁓] chemise *f* (de femme).

shin [ʃin] **1.** (*ou* ⁓-*bone*) tibia *m*; **2.:** ⁓ *up* grimper à.

shin·dy F [ˈʃindi] chahut *m*, tapage *m.*

shine [ʃain] **1.** éclat *m*; brillant *m*; F *take the* ⁓ *out of* s.o. éclipser q.; *Am. sl. take a* ⁓ *to* s'enticher de; **2.** [*irr.*] *v/i.* briller (*a. fig.*); (re)luire; ⁓ *on*

éclairer; *v/t.* (*a.* ⁓ *up*) polir; cirer.

shin·er *sl.* [ˈʃainə] pièce *f* d'or; œil *m* poché.

shin·gle¹ [ˈʃiŋgl] **1.** △ bardeau *m*; *cheveux:* coupe *f* à la garçonne; *Am.* petite enseigne *f*; **2.** couvrir de bardeaux; couper à la garçonne.

shin·gle² [⁓] galets *m/pl.*; plage *f* à galets.

shin·gles ⚕ [ˈʃiŋglz] *pl.* zona *m*, F ceinture *f.*

shin·gly [ˈʃiŋgli] couvert de galets.

shin·y □ [ˈʃaini] brillant, luisant.

ship [ʃip] **1.** (*usu. f*) navire *m*; vaisseau *m*; ⁓'s company équipage *m*; **2.** *v/t.* embarquer; ⚓ (*souv.* ⁓ *off*) mettre à bord, expédier; ⚓ mettre en place, monter; ⚓ rentrer (*les avirons*); recruter (*des marins*); ⁓ *a sea* embarquer un coup de mer; *v/i.* s'embarquer; armer (sur, *on* [*board*]) (*marin*); **'⁓·board:** ⚓ *on* ⁓ à bord; **'⁓·build·er** constructeur *m* de navires; **'⁓·build·ing** construction *f* navale; **'⁓·ca·nal** canal *m* maritime; **'⁓·chan·dler** fournisseur *m* de navires; **'⁓-'chan·dler·y** fournitures *f/pl.* de navires; **'ship·ment** embarquement *m*, mise *f* à bord; envoi *m* par mer; chargement *m* (= *choses embarquées*); **'ship·own·er** armateur *m*; **'ship·per** affréteur *m*; expéditeur *m*; **'ship·ping 1.** embarquement *m*; navires *m/pl.*; marine *f* marchande. **2.** d'embarquement; maritime; de navigation; d'expédition.

ship...: **'⁓-shape** bien tenu (*a. fig.*); en bon ordre; **'⁓·wreck 1.** naufrage *m*; **2.** *v/t.* faire naufrager; *v/i. (a. be* ⁓*ed)* faire naufrage; **'⁓·wrecked** naufragé; **'⁓·wright** charpentier *m* de navires; **'⁓·yard** chantier *m* de constructions navales.

shire [ˈʃaiə; *mots composés* ʃiə] comté *m*; ⁓ *horse* cheval *m* de gros trait.

shirk [ʃəːk] *v/t.* se dérober à, négliger, esquiver; *v/i.* négliger son devoir; **'shirk·er** carotteur (-euse *f*) *m.*

shirt [ʃəːt] chemise *f* (*d'homme, a.* ⊕); (*a.* ⁓-*blouse*) chemisier *m*; *Am. sl. keep one's* ⁓ on ne pas se fâcher *ou* s'emballer; **'shirt·ing** ⚓ shirting *m* (*toile pour chemises*); **'shirt-sleeve 1.** manche *f* de chemise; **2.** en bras de chemise; *fig.* sans cérémonie; *surt. Am.* ⁓

diplomacy diplomatie *f* franche et honnête; **'shirt·y** *sl.* irritable.

shit V [ʃit] **1.** merde *f*; **2.** chier.

shiv·er¹ ['ʃivə] **1.** fragment *m*; *break to* ~*s* = **2.** (se) briser en éclats.

shiv·er² [~] **1.** frisson *m*; F *the* ~*s pl.* la tremblote *f*; *it gives me the* ~*s* ça me donne le frisson, ça me fait trembler; **2.** frissonner; grelotter; *have a* ~*ing fit* être pris de frissons; **'shiv·er·y** tremblant; fiévreux (-euse *f*).

shoal¹ [ʃoul] **1.** *poissons:* banc *m* voyageur; *fig.* multitude *f*; **2.** se réunir en *ou* aller par bancs.

shoal² [~] **1.** haut-fond (*pl.* hautsfonds) *m*; **2.** diminuer de fond; **3.** (*a.* **'shoal·y**) plein de hautsfonds.

shock¹ ✔ □ [ʃɔk] moyette *f*.

shock² [~] **1.** choc *m* (*a.* ✸, ⊕, ✕); ✕ assaut *m*; secousse *f* (*a.* ⚡); coup *m*; *mot.* road ~*s pl.* cahots *m/pl.*; **2.** *fig.* choquer, scandaliser; bouleverser; offenser; ~*ed at* choqué de; scandalisé par.

shock³ [~]: ~ *of hair* tignasse *f*.

shock-ab·sorb·er *mot.* ['ʃɔkəbsɔːbə] amortisseur *m* (de chocs); parechocs *m/inv.*

shock·er *sl.* ['ʃɔkə] (*qqfois* shilling ~) roman *m* à gros effets.

shock·ing □ ['ʃɔkiŋ] choquant; affreux (-euse *f*); abominable.

shock...: '~·**proof** anti-choc *inv.*; ~ **ther·a·py** thérapeutique *f* de choc; ~ **treat·ment** traitement *m* (de) choc; *electric* ~ traitement *m* par électrochocs; ~ **wave** onde *f* de choc.

shod [ʃɔd] *prét. et p.p. de* shoe 2.

shod·dy ['ʃɔdi] **1.** *tex.* drap *m* de laine d'effiloché; *fig.* camelote *f*; pacotille *f*; **2.** d'effiloché; de camelote; de pacotille; *surt. Am.* ~ *aristocracy* parvenus *m/pl.*

shoe [ʃuː]: **1.** chaussure *f*, soulier *m*; *cheval:* fer *m*; ⊕ sabot *m*; traîneau, *piston:* patin *m*; **2.** [*irr.*] chausser); ferrer; garnir d'un patin *etc.*; '~·**black** cireur *m* (de chaussures); '~·**black·ing** cirage *m ou* crème *f* pour chaussures; '~·**horn** chaussepied *m*; corne *f*; '~·**lace** lacet *m*; '~·**mak·er** cordonnier *m*; ~ **pol·ish** cirage *m ou* crème pour chaussures; '~·**shine** cirage *m* (de chaussures); (*a.* ~ *boy*) cireur *m* (de chaussures);

'~·**string** *Am.* lacet *m*; *surt. Am.* F minces capitaux *m/pl.*

shone [ʃɔn] *prét. et p.p. de* shine 2.

shoo [ʃuː] chasser (*des oiseaux*).

shook [ʃuk] *prét. de* shake 1.

shoot [ʃuːt] **1.** *rivière:* rapide *m*; ✔ rejeton *m*, pousse *f*; partie *f* de chasse; chasse *f* gardée; ✕ (concours *m* de) tir *m*; *tex.* duite *f*; ⚒ couloir *m*; *fig.* jaillissement *m*; **2.** [*irr.*] *v/t.* tirer (*une arme à feu, les manchettes*); fusiller; tuer; chasser (*le gibier*); *fig.* passer rapidement sous (*un pont*); darder (*des rayons, fig. un regard*); décharger; (*a.* ~ *out*) ⚡ pousser; pousser (*le verrou*); *phot.* prendre un instantané de; tourner (*un film*); *sp.* marquer (*un but*); *sp.* shooter; *mot.* brûler (*les feux*); franchir (*un rapide*); *v/i.* tirer (sur, at); viser; *fig.* se précipiter, s'élancer; élancer (*douleur*); (*a.* ~ *forth*) pousser; ~ *ahead* aller rapidement en avant; ~ *ahead of* devancer (*q.*) rapidement.

shoot·er ['ʃuːtə] tireur (-euse *f*) *m*; *sp.* marqueur *m* de but.

shoot·ing ['ʃuːtiŋ] **1.** tir *m*; chasse *f*; fusillade *f*; ~*-ground* (*ou* ~*-range*) champ *m* de tir; *go* ~ aller à la chasse; ~ *of a film* prise *f* de vue; tournage *m*; **2.** lancinant (*douleur*); ~ *star* étoile *f* filante; '~·**box** pavillon *m* de chasse; muette *f*; '~·**brake** canadienne *f*.

shoot-out F ['ʃuːtaut] échange *m* de coups de feu.

shop [ʃɔp] **1.** boutique *f*; magasin *m*; bureau *m* (*de tabac*); F métier *m*, affaires *f/pl.*; ~ *floor* les ouvriers *m/pl.*; *talk* ~ parler boutique; **2.** (*usu.* F *go* ~*ping*) faire des achats; '~·**keep·er** boutiquier (-ère *f*) *m*; marchand(e *f*) *m*; '~·**lift·er** voleur (-euse *f*) *m* à l'étalage; '~·**man** commis *m* de magasin; ⊕ homme *m* d'atelier; '**shop·ping** achats *m/pl.*; emplettes *f/pl.*; ~ *centre* quartier *m* commerçant; *Christmas* ~ emplettes *f/pl.* de Noël; '**shop·py** F qui sent la boutique; à l'esprit boutiquier.

shop...: '~·**soiled** ✝ défraîchi; '~·**stew·ard** délégué *m* (syndical) d'atelier; '~·**walk·er** chef *m* de rayon; inspecteur (-trice *f*) *m*; '~·**win·dow** vitrine *f*; devanture *f*.

shore¹ [ʃɔː] rivage *m*, bord *m*; côte *f*; ⚓ terre *f*; *on* ~ à terre.

shore² [◡] **1.** étai *m*, appui *m*; **2.**: ◡ *up* étayer; buter.

shorn [ʃɔ:n] *p.p. de shear 1*; *fig.* ◡ *of* dépouillé de (*qch.*).

short [ʃɔ:t] **1.** *adj.* court; de petite taille; bref (brève *f*); insuffisant; *fig.* brusque, cassant; *cuis.* croquant; aigre (*métal*); revêche (*fer*); *see cir-cuit*; *Brit.* ◡ *list* liste *f* des candidats sélectionnés; ◡ *time* chômage *m* partiel; ◡ *waves pl.* petites ondes *f/pl.*; *radio:* ondes *f/pl.* courtes; *by a* ◡ *head turf:* de justesse; *fig.* tout juste; *nothing* ◡ *of* ni plus ni moins; *come* (*ou fall*) ◡ *of* rester au-dessous de (*qch.*); manquer à; ne pas être à la hauteur de (*q.*); ne pas atteindre; *fall* (*ou run*) ◡ manquer; s'épuiser (*provisions*); **2.** *adv.* court; brusquement; ◡ *of* sauf; à moins de; ◡ *of London* à quelque distance de Londres; ◡ *of lying* à moins de mentir; *cut* ◡ couper la parole à (*q.*); *stop* ◡ *of* s'arrêter au seuil de; ne pas aller jusqu'à; **3.** *su. gramm.* voyelle *f* brève; *cin.* court métrage *m*; *≠* court-circuit (*pl.* courts-circuits) *m*; F ◡*s pl.* culotte *f* de sport; short *m*; *in* ◡ bref, en un mot; **4.** *v/t. see* ◡*-circuit*; **'short·age** manque *m*, insuffisance *f*; disette *f*; *admin.* crise *f*; *✝* déficit *m*.

short...: '◡-**cake** sablé *m*; '◡-'**change** tromper (*q.*) sur la monnaie; rouler (*q.*); '◡-'**cir·cuit** *≠* court-circuiter; ◡-'**com·ing** défaut *m*, imperfection *f*; manque *m*; ◡ *cut* chemin *m* de traverse; raccourci *m*; '◡-'**dat·ed** *✝* à courte échéance; '**short·en** *v/t.* rac-courcir; abréger; *v/i.* (se) raccourcir; se resserrer; diminuer; '**short·en-ing** raccourcissement *m*; abrège-ment *m*; *cuis.* matière *f* grasse.

short...: '◡-**fall** déficit *m*; '◡-**hand** sténographie *f*; ◡ *writer* sténographe *mf*; '◡-'**hand·ed** à court de person-nel; '◡-**haul** à courte distance; '◡-**list** mettre (*q.*) sur la liste des candidats sélectionnés; '◡-'**lived** qui vit peu de temps; passager (-ère *f*), éphémère; '**short·ly** *adv.* briève-ment; bientôt; brusquement; '**short·ness** brièveté *f*; *taille:* peti-tesse *f*; brusquerie *f*; manque *m*.

short...: '◡-**range** à courte portée (*fusil etc.*); à court terme (*projet etc.*); à court rayon d'action (*avion etc.*); '◡-**run** de courte durée; '◡-

'**sight·ed** myope; *fig.* imprévoyant; '◡-'**tem·pered** irascible; vif (vive *f*); '◡-**term** *✝* à court terme; ◡ *memory* mémoire *f* immediate; '◡-'**wave** radio: sur ondes courtes; '◡-'**wind·ed** à l'haleine courte.

shot¹ [ʃɔt] **1.** *prét. et p.p. de shoot 2*; **2.** chatoyant (*soie*).

shot² [◡] coup *m* (*a. fig., a. sp.*); *revolver:* coup *m* de feu; (*usu.* ◡*pl.*) plomb *m*; F tireur (-euse *f*) *m*; chasseur *m*; *sp.* shot *m*; *phot.* prise *f* de vue; *cin.* plan *m*; *✄* piqûre *f*; *sl. alcool:* goutte *f*; *fig.* essai *m*; *have a* ◡ *at* essayer (*qch.*); F *not by a long* ◡ tant s'en faut; pas à beaucoup près; *within* (*out of*) ◡ à (hors de) portée; F *like a* ◡ comme un trait; avec empressement; F *fig. big* ◡ grosse légume *f* (= *per-sonnage important*); *make a bad* ◡ rater son coup; *fig.* deviner faux; '◡-**gun** fusil *m* de chasse; F ◡ *marriage* mariage *m* forcé; '◡-**proof** à l'épreuve des balles; '◡-**put** *sp.* lancer *m* du poids.

shot·ten her·ring ['ʃɔtn'heriŋ] ha-reng *m* guais.

should [ʃud] *prét. de shall* (*a. usité pour former le cond.*).

shoul·der ['ʃouldə] **1.** épaule *f*; ⊕ épaulement *m*; *give s.o. the cold* ◡ battre froid à q., tourner le dos à q.; *put one's* ◡ *to the wheel* se mettre à l'œuvre; donner un coup d'épaule; *rub* ◡*s with* s'associer avec, côtoyer; ◡ *to* ◡ côte à côte; **2.** pousser avec ou de l'épaule; mettre sur l'épau-le; *fig.* endosser; ✗ porter (*l'arme*); '◡-**bag** sac *m* à bandoulière; '◡-**blade** *anat.* omoplate *f*; '◡-**knot** nœud *m* d'épaule (*a.* ✗); '◡-**strap** bretelle *f*; *dames, a.* ✗: patte *f* d'épaule; ✗ *uniforme:* attente *f*.

shout [ʃaut] **1.** cri *m*; clameur *f*; *rire:* éclat *m*; *sl. boisson:* tournée *f*; **2.** *v/i.* pousser des cris, crier; hurler (*de douleur*); *v/t.* ◡ *down* huer (*q.*).

shove [ʃʌv] **1.** poussée *f*, coup *m* d'épaule; **2.** pousser; bousculer; fourrer (qch. dans qch., *s.th. in*[*to*] *s.th.*).

shov·el ['ʃʌvl] **1.** pelle *f*; **2.** pelleter; '◡-**board** jeu *m* de galets.

show [ʃou] **1.** [*irr.*] *v/t.* montrer; faire voir; manifester; faire (*misé-ricorde à q.*); témoigner (de); laisser paraître; indiquer; représenter; *cin.* présenter; prouver; exposer (*des peintures, des raisons, etc.*); ~ *forth* proclamer; ~ *in* introduire; faire entrer; ~ *off* faire valoir *ou* ressortir; faire parade de; ~ *out* reconduire; ~ *up* faire monter; révéler; faire ressortir; démasquer; *v/i.* (*a.* ~ *up ou forth*) ressortir, se détacher; se montrer; se laisser voir; *sl.* faire parader; se donner des airs; *sl.* faire de l'épate; **2.** spectacle *m*; étalage *m*; exposition *f*; concours *m*; *mot.* salon *m*; parade *f*, ostentation *f*, semblant *m*; *sl.* affaire *f*; ~ *of hands* vote *m* à mains levées; *dumb* ~ pantomime *f*; jeu *m* muet; *on* ~ exposé; *sl. run the* ~ diriger l'affaire; être le manitou de l'affaire; '~·**biz** F ['ʃoubiz], ~ **busi·ness** le monde *m ou* l'industrie *f* du spectacle; '~·**card** pancarte *f*; étiquette *f*; '~·**case** montre *f*, vitrine *f*; '~·**down** *cartes*: étalement *m* de son jeu; *fig.* mise *f* au jour de ses projets *etc.*; *come to a* ~ en venir au fait et au prendre.

show·er ['ʃauə] **1.** averse *f*; ondée *f*; grêle, *neige*: giboulée *f*; *fig.* volée *f*, pluie *f*; **2.** *v/t.* verser; *fig.* accabler (de, *with*), combler (de, *with*); *v/i.* pleuvoir; '~·**bath** ['~ba:θ] bain-douche (*pl.* bains-douches) *m*; douche *f*; '**show·er·y** de giboulées; pluvieux (-euse *f*).

show·i·ness ['ʃouinis] prétention *f*; ostentation *f*; '**show·man** montreur *m* de curiosités; forain *m*; F passé maître *m* pour la mise en scène; '**show·man·ship** art *m* de la mise *f* en scène; **shown** [ʃoun] *p.p. de show* 1; '**show·piece** pièce *f ou* objet *m* exemplaire, modèle *m* du genre; '**show·room** salon *m* d'exposition; '**show·win·dow** *surt. Am.* vitrine *f*; étalage *m*; devanture *f*; '**show·y** □ fastueux (-euse *f*); prétentieux (-euse *f*); voyant.

shrank [ʃræŋk] *prét. de shrink.*
shrap·nel ⚔ ['ʃræpnl] shrapnel *m*.
shred [ʃred] **1.** brin *m*; lambeau *m*; petit morceau *m*; *fig.* parcelle *f*, grain *m*; **2.** [*irr.*] déchirer en lambeaux *ou* en morceaux.

shrew [ʃru:] *zo.* (*a.* ~*-mouse*) musaraigne *f*; *personne*: mégère *f*, femme *f* criarde.

shrewd □ [ʃru:d] pénétrant, sagace; fin; *have a* ~ *idea* être porté à croire

(que, *that*); '**shrewd·ness** perspicacité *f*; pénétration *f*.
shrew·ish □ ['ʃru:iʃ] acariâtre.
shriek [ʃri:k] **1.** cri *m* perçant; éclat *m* (*de rire*); **2.** pousser un cri aigu.
shriev·al·ty ['ʃri:vəlti] fonctions *f/pl.* de shérif.
shrift [ʃrift]: *give short* ~ expédier vite.
shrill [ʃril] **1.** □ aigu(ë *f*), perçant; **2.** *v/i.* pousser un son aigu; *v/t.* (*a.* ~ *out*) chanter *ou* crier (*qch.*) d'une voix aiguë.
shrimp [ʃrimp] *zo.* crevette *f*; *fig.* petit bout *m* d'homme.
shrine [ʃrain] châsse *f*; reliquaire *m*; tombeau *m* (de saint[e]).
shrink [ʃriŋk] [*irr.*] *v/i.* se contracter; se rétrécir (*tissu*); se rapetisser; (*a.* ~ *back*) reculer (devant qch., *from s.th.*; à *inf.*, *from gér.*); *v/t.* contracter (*un métal*); (faire) rétrécir (*un tissu*); ~ *with age* se tasser; '**shrink·age** rétrécissement *m*; contraction *f* (*a. cin.*); *fig.* diminution *f.*
shriv·el ['ʃrivl] (*a.* ~ *up*) (se) ratatiner; *fig.* (se) dessécher.
shroud[1] [ʃraud] **1.** linceul *m*; *fig.* voile *m*; ⊕ blindage *m*; ⊕ bandage *m*; **2.** ensevelir; *fig.* envelopper.
shroud[2] ⚓ [~] hauban *m*.
Shrove·tide ['ʃrouvtaid] jours *m/pl.* gras; **Shrove Tues·day** mardi *m* gras.
shrub [ʃrʌb] arbrisseau *m*; arbuste *m*; **shrub·ber·y** ['~əri] bosquet *m*; plantation *f* d'arbustes; '**shrub·by** ressemblant à un arbuste.
shrug [ʃrʌg] **1.** hausser (les épaules); **2.** haussement *m* d'épaules.
shrunk [ʃrʌŋk] *p.p. de shrink*; '**shrunk·en** *adj.* contracté; rétréci; ratatiné (*figure etc.*).
shud·der ['ʃʌdə] **1.** frissonner, frémir (de, *with*); **2.** frisson *m*, frémissement *m.*
shuf·fle ['ʃʌfl] **1.** *v/t.* traîner (*les pieds*); brouiller; battre (*les cartes*); ~ *away* faire disparaître (*qch.*); ~ *off* se débarrasser de; rejeter (*qch.*) (*sur upon, on, to*); ôter (*qch.*) à la hâte; *v/i.* traîner les pieds; avancer en traînant les pieds; *fig.* équivoquer, tergiverser; ~ *through* faire un travail tant bien que mal; **2.** pas *m/pl.* traînants; marche *f* traînante; *cartes*: battement *m*; *fig.* équivoca-

tion *f*; faux-fuyant *m*; **'shuf·fler**
personne *f* qui bat les cartes; *fig.*
tergiversateur (-trice *f*) *m*; **'shuf·**
fling □ traînant (*pas*); *fig.* équivoque; *fig.* tergiversateur (-trice *f*).
shun [ʃʌn] fuir, éviter.
shunt [ʃʌnt] **1.** 🚂 garage *m*; 🚂 changement *m* de voie; ⚡ shunt *m*; **2.** *v/t.*
🚂 manœuvrer, garer; *fig.* détour-
ner; ⚡ shunter; ~ *with care* défense
de tamponner!; *v/i.* 🚂 se garer; *fig.*
s'esquiver; **'shunt·er** 🚂 gareur *m*;
sl. pousseur (-euse *f*) *m*; **'shunt·ing**
yard 🚂 chantier *m* de voies de
garage et de triage.
shut [ʃʌt] [*irr.*] *v/t.* fermer; ~ *one's*
eyes to fermer les yeux sur; se refuser à; ~ *down* fermer (*une usine*);
couper (*la vapeur*); arrêter (*le*
moteur); ~ *in* enfermer; entourer
(de, by); se pincer (*le doigt*) dans;
~ *into* enfermer dans; ~ *out* exclure;
~ *up* enfermer; F faire taire (*q.*); ~ *up*
shop sl. fermer boutique; *v/i.* (se)
fermer; F ~ *up!* taisez-vous!, *sl.* la
ferme!; **'~-down** fermeture *f*,
chômage *m*; **~'out** *sp.* Am. victoire *f*
écrasante; **'shut·ter** volet *m*; *phot.*
obturateur *m*; *instantaneous* ~ obturateur *m* instantané; *phot.* ~ *speed*
vitesse *f* d'obturation.
shut·tle ['ʃʌtl] **1.** *tex.*, *a.* 🚂 navette *f*;
~ *service* (service *m* de) navette *f*; ~
train train *m* qui fait la navette; **2.**
faire la navette; **'~-cock** volant *m*.
shy[1] [ʃai] **1.** □ timide; farouche
(*animal*); ombrageux (-euse *f*)
(*cheval*); be (F *fight*) ~ *of* (*gér.*) hésiter
à (*inf.*); *sl.* I'm ~ *ten pounds* il me
manque dix livres; je suis en perte
de dix livres; **2.** prendre ombrage
(de, *at*) (*a. fig.*); faire un écart.
shy[2] F [~] **1.** lancer (*une pierre*);
2. jet *m*; tentative *f* (pour faire qch.,
at s.th.); *have a* ~ *at* s'essayer à.
shy·ness ['ʃainis] timidité *f*.
shy·ster *sl.*, *surt.* Am. ['ʃaistə] homme *m* d'affaires véreux; avocassier
m.
Si·a·mese [saiə'miːz] **1.** siamois;
2. *ling.* siamois *m*; Siamois(e *f*) *m*.
Si·be·ri·an [sai'biəriən] **1.** sibé-
rien(ne *f*), de Sibérie; **2.** Sibé-
rien(ne *f*) *m*.
sib·i·lant ['sibilənt] **1.** □ sifflant; ♫
sibilant; **2.** *gramm.* sifflante *f*.
sib·ling ['sibliŋ] frère *m*; sœur *f*.
sib·yl·line [si'bilain] sybillin.

Si·cil·ian [si'siljən] **1.** sicilien(ne *f*);
2. Sicilien(ne *f*) *m*.
sick [sik] malade (de *of*, *with*); *fig.*
las(se *f*), dégoûté (de, *of*); malsain;
macabre; *be* ~ vomir; *fig.* be ~ (*and*
tired) *of* (en) avoir assez de, F en avoir
marre de; *feel* ~ avoir mal au cœur; *go*
~ se faire porter malade; **'~-bed** lit *m*
de malade; **'~-cer·tif·i·cate** attestation *f* de médecin; **'sick·en** *v/i.* tomber malade; languir (*plante*); *fig.* se
lasser (de qch., *of s.th.*); ~ *at* être
écœuré à la vue de *ou* de voir; *v/t.*
rendre malade; dégoûter; **'sick·**
fund caisse *f* de maladie; **'~-in·sur·**
ance assurance-maladie *f*.
sick·le ['sikl] faucille *f*.
sick-leave ['sikliːv] congé *m* de maladie; **'sick·li·ness** mauvaise santé
f, état *m* maladif; pâleur *f*; odeur *etc.*:
caractère *m* écœurant; *climat*: insalubrité *f*; **'sick·ly** maladif (-ive *f*);
étiolé (*plante*); pâle; fade; écœurant
(*odeur etc.*); malsain, insalubre (*cli-*
mat); **'sick·ness** maladie *f*; mal *m*;
nausées *f/pl.*; *Brit.* ~ *benefit* presta-
tions *f/pl.* d'assurance maladie; ~
pay indemnité *f* de maladie.
side [said] **1.** *usu.* côté *m*; flanc *m*;
pente *f*; bord *m*; *sp.* camp *m*, équipe
f; *pol. etc.* parti *m*; ~ *by* ~ côte à côte,
⚓ bord à bord; *fig.* en plus (de, *with*);
~ *by* ~ *with* à côté de; *at* (*ou by*) *s.o.'s* ~
à côté de q.; *Am* on the ~ par-dessus le
marché; **2.** latéral (-aux *m/pl.*), de
côté; secondaire; ~ *effect* effet *m*
secondaire; ~ *street* rue *f* transversale; **3.** prendre parti (pour, *with*); se
ranger du côté (de, *with*); **'~-arms** *pl.*
⚔ armes *f/pl.*; **'~-board**
buffet *m*; *Brit.* ~s *pl.* = **'~-burns** *pl.*
Am. favoris *m/pl.*, pattes *f/pl.*; **'~-car**
mot. side-car *m*; **'sid·ed** *four-*~ à
quatre faces.
side...: **'~-face** profil *m*; *attr.* de profil; **'~-kick** *surt. Am.* F copain *m*,
copine *f*; sous-fifre *m*; **'~-light** fenêtre *f* latérale; *mot.* feu *m* de côté;
fig. aperçu *m* indirect; **'~-line** 🚂 voie
f secondaire; *fig.* occupation *f* secondaire; **'~-long 1.** *adv.* de côté; obliquement; **2.** *adj.* de côté, en coulisse
(*a. fig.*); **'~-path** sentier *m* de côté;
chemin *m* de traverse.
si·de·re·al *astr.* [sai'diəriəl] sidéral
(-aux *m/pl.*).
side...: **'~-sad·dle** selle *f* de dame;
'~-slip ✈ glisser sur l'aile; *mot.*, *a.*

cycl. déraper; **'~-split·ting** homérique (*rire*), F désopilant; **'~-step 1.** pas *m* de côté; **2.** *v/i.* faire un pas de côté; *v/t. fig.* éviter; **'~-stroke** nage *f* sur le côté; **'~-track 1.** 🚂 voie *f* secondaire *ou* de service; **2.** garer (*un train*); aiguiller (*un train*) sur une voie de service; *souv. Am. fig.* détourner; **'~-walk** *surt. Am.* trottoir *m*; **side·ward** ['~wəd] **1.** *adj.* latéral (-aux *m/pl.*), de côté; **2.** *adv.* (*a.* **side·wards** ['~z], **'side·ways** ['~weiz], **'side·wise**) de côté.

sid·ing ['saidiŋ] 🚂 voie *f* de garage *ou* de service; embranchement *m*.

si·dle ['saidl] s'avancer *etc.* de guingois *ou* de côté.

siege [si:dʒ] siège *m*; *lay ~ to* assiéger.

sieve [siv] crible *m*; tamis *m*.

sift [sift] *v/t.* passer au crible *ou* au tamis; *fig.* examiner en détail; *~ out fig.* démêler; *v/i. fig.* filtrer; **'sift·er** cribleur (-euse *f*) *m*; tamiseur (-euse *f*) *m*; crible *m*; tamis *m*.

sigh [sai] **1.** soupir *m*; **2.** soupirer (*pour, for*; *après, after*).

sight [sait] **1.** vue *f*; *fig.* spectacle *m*; portée *f* de la vue; visée *f*; bouton *m* de mire, guidon *m* (*d'une arme à feu*); ✝ vue *f*; F beaucoup; *a ~ of* énormément de; *a ~ too big de* beaucoup trop grand; *~s pl.* monuments *m/pl.*, curiosités *f/pl.* (*d'une ville*); beautés *f/pl.* naturelles; *second ~* seconde vue *f*; voyance *f*; *at* (*ou on*) *~* à vue (*a.* ✝, *a.* ♪); *du* premier coup; *by ~* de vue; *catch ~ of* apercevoir, entrevoir; *lose ~ of* perdre de vue; *out of ~* caché aux regards, hors de vue; *take ~* viser; *within ~* en vue, à portée de la vue; **2.** *v/t.* apercevoir; viser; pointer (*une arme à feu*); ✝ voir (*un effet*); *v/i.* viser; **'sight·ed** à la vue; qui voit; **'sight·ing-line** ligne *f* de visée; **'sight·less** aveugle; **'sight·li·ness** beauté *f*, grâce *f*, charme *m*; **'sight·ly** charmant, avenant.

sight...: **'~-'read** [*irr.* (*read*)] ♪ jouer *ou* chanter à première vue; **'~-see·ing** visite *f* (de la ville); tourisme *m*; **'~-se·er** excursionniste *mf*; curieux (-euse *f*) *m*; **'~-sing·ing** ♪ chant *m* à vue.

sign [sain] **1.** signe *m*; réclame *f*; *auberge etc.*: enseigne *f*; *fig.* trace *f*; indice *m*; *~ manual* signature *f*; seing

m; *in* (*ou as a*) *~ of* en signe de; **2.** *v/i.* signer; faire signe; *v/t.* signer; *~ on v/t.* embaucher, engager; *v/i.* s'embaucher.

sig·nal ['signl] **1.** signal *m*; signe *m*; ⚔ *Brit. ~s pl.* sapeurs-télégraphistes *m/pl.*; *téléph.* busy *~* signal *m* de ligne occupée; **2.** □ insigne; remarquable; **3.** *vt/i.* signaler; *v/t.* donner un signal à; *~-box* 🚂 cabine *f* à signaux *ou* d'aiguillage; **sig·nal·ize** ['~nəlaiz] signaler, marquer; *see signal 3*; **'sig·nal·man** signaleur *m*.

sig·na·to·ry ['signətəri] signataire (*a. su./mf*); *~ powers pl. to an agreement* pays *m/pl. ou* puissances *f/pl.* signataires d'une convention *ou* d'un accord.

sig·na·ture ['signitʃə] ✝, *typ.* signature *f*; *admin.* visa *m*; ♪ *~ tune radio*: indicatif *m* musical.

sign·board ['sainbɔːd] *boutique etc.*: enseigne *f*; écriteau *m* indicateur; **'sign·er** signataire *mf*.

sig·net ['signit] sceau *m*, cachet *m*; **'~-ring** chevalière *f*; † anneau *m* à cachet.

sig·nif·i·cance, **sig·nif·i·can·cy** [sig'nifikəns(i)] signification *f*; importance *f*; **sig'nif·i·cant** □ significatif (-ive *f*); *~ of* qui accuse *ou* trahit; **sig·ni·fi·ca·tion** signification *f*, sens *m*; **sig'nif·i·ca·tive** [~kətiv] significatif (-ive *f*) (de, *of*).

sig·ni·fy ['signifai] *v/t.* signifier; être (le) signe de; faire connaître; vouloir dire; *v/i.* importer; *it does not ~* cela ne fait rien.

sign...: **'~-paint·er** peintre *m* d'enseignes; **'~-post** poteau *m* indicateur.

si·lence ['sailəns] **1.** silence *m*; *~!* silence!, taisez-vous!; **2.** faire taire; réduire au silence; **'si·lenc·er** ⊕ amortisseur *m* de son; *mot.* pot *m* d'échappement.

si·lent □ ['sailənt] silencieux (-euse *f*); muet(te *f*) (*a. lettre*); *fig.* taciturne; *~ film* film *m* muet; *surt. Am.* ✝ *~ partner* commanditaire *m*.

sil·hou·ette [silu:'et] **1.** silhouette *f*; **2.**: *be ~d against* se silhouetter contre.

sil·i·cate 🔬 ['silikit] silicate *m*; **sil·i·cat·ed** ['~keitid] silicaté(is)é; **si·li·ceous** [si'liʃəs] siliceux (-euse *f*); boueux (-euse *f*) (*sources*).

single

silk [silk] **1.** soie *f*; *p.ext.* fil *m* de soie, rayonne *f*; ⚖ conseiller *m* du roi; **2.** de soie; en soie; à soie; **'silk·en** de *ou* en soie; soyeux (-euse *f*); *fig.* miellaux (-euse *f*); *see* silky; **'silk·i·ness** nature *f* soyeuse; *fig. voix*: moelleux *m*; **'silk-'stock·ing** *Am.* distingué; **'silk·worm** ver *m* à soie; **'silk·y** □ soyeux (-euse *f*); *fig. péj.* miellaux (-euse *f*).

sill [sil] seuil *m*; rebord *m* (de fenêtre).

sil·li·ness ['silinis] sottise *f*.

sil·ly □ ['sili] sot(te *f*), niais; stupide; *journ.* ~ *season* l'époque *f* où la politique chôme.

si·lo ['sailou] silo *m*.

silt [silt] **1.** vase *f*, limon *m*; **2.** (*usu.* ~ *up*) *v/t.* envaser, ensabler; *v/i.* s'ensabler.

sil·ver ['silvə] **1.** argent *m*; argenterie *f*; pièce *f* *ou* pièces *f/pl.* d'argent; **2.** d'argent, en argent; *fig.* argenté; **3.** (*ou* ⊕ ~*-plate*) argenter (*a. fig.*); étamer (*un miroir*); **'sil·ver·y** argenté (*a. zo.*, *a.* ☽); d'argent; argentin (*ton, rire, voix*).

sim·i·lar □ ['similə] pareil(le *f*), semblable; ⚕ *qqfois* similaire; **sim·i·lar·i·ty** [~'læriti] ressemblance *f*; similitude *f* (*a.* ⚕).

sim·i·le ['simili] comparaison *f*, image *f*.

si·mil·i·tude [si'militju:d] similitude *f*, ressemblance *f*; allégorie *f*.

sim·mer ['simə] *v/i.* frémir; mijoter (*a. fig.*); *fig.* fermenter, être près d'éclater; *v/t.* faire mijoter.

Si·mon ['saimən] Simon *m*; F *the real* ~ *Pure* l'objet *m* authentique; la véritable personne *f*; F *simple* ~ nicodème *m*.

si·moom [si'mu:m] simoun *m*.

sim·per ['simpə] **1.** sourire *m* minaudier; **2.** minauder; faire des grimaces.

sim·ple □ ['simpl] simple; naïf (-ïve *f*); crédule; **'~-'heart·ed,** **'~-'mind·ed** simple, naïf (-ïve *f*), ingénu; **sim·ple·ton** ['~tən] nigaud(e *f*) *m*.

sim·plic·i·ty [sim'plisiti] candeur *f*; naïveté *f*; simplicité *f*; **sim·pli·fi·ca·tion** [~fi'keiʃn] simplification *f*; **sim·pli·fy** ['~fai] simplifier.

sim·ply ['simpli] *adv.* simplement *etc.*; *see* simple; absolument; uniquement.

sim·u·late ['simjuleit] simuler, fein-

dre; se faire passer pour; **sim·u·'la·tion** simulation *f*, feinte *f*.

si·mul·ta·ne·i·ty [siməltə'niəti] simultanéité *f*.

si·mul·ta·ne·ous □ [siməl'teinjəs] simultané; qui arrive en même temps (que, *with*); **si·mul'ta·ne·ous·ness** simultanéité *f*.

sin [sin] **1.** péché *m*; **2.** pécher; *fig.* ~ *against* blesser (*qch.*).

since [sins] **1.** *prp.* depuis; **2.** *adv.* depuis; *long* ~ depuis *ou* il y a longtemps; *how long* ~? il y a combien de cela?; *a short time* ~ il y a peu de temps; **3.** *cj.* depuis que; puisque; que.

sin·cere □ [sin'siə] sincère; franc(he *f*); *yours* ~*ly* votre tout(e) dévoué(e *f*); cordialement à vous; **sin·cer·i·ty** [~'seriti] sincérité *f*, bonne foi *f*.

sine ⚕ [sain] sinus *m*.

si·ne·cure ['sainikjuə] sinécure *f*.

sin·ew ['sinju:] tendon *m*; *cuis.* croquant *m*; *fig. usu.* ~*s pl.* nerf *m*, force *f*; **'sin·ew·y** musclé, nerveux (-euse *f*); *cuis.* tendineux (-euse *f*).

sin·ful □ ['sinful] pécheur (-eresse *f*); coupable; F scandaleux (-euse *f*); **'sin·ful·ness** culpabilité *f*; péché *m*.

sing [siŋ] [*irr.*] *v/t.* chanter (*fig.* = raconter, célébrer); célébrer; *v/i.* chanter (*bouilloire*); siffler (*vent etc.*); tinter, bourdonner (*oreilles*); *Am. sl.* se mettre à table, moucharder; F ~ *out* crier; F ~ *small* déchanter; se dégonfler, filer doux; ~ *another song* (*ou tune*) chanter une autre chanson; F changer de ton.

singe [sindʒ] brûler légèrement; roussir (*le drap*); *coiffeur*: brûler (*la pointe des cheveux*).

sing·er ['siŋə] chanteur (-euse *f*) *m*; *eccl.*, *a. poét.* chantre *m*; cantatrice *f* (*de profession*).

sing·ing ['siŋiŋ] chant *m*; ~*-bird* oiseau *m* chanteur.

sin·gle ['siŋgl] **1.** □ seul; simple; unique; individuel(le *f*); célibataire, pas marié; ✝ ~ *bill* billet *m* à ordre; ~ *combat* combat *m* singulier; *bookkeeping by* ~ *entry* comptabilité *f* en partie simple; *in* ~ *file* en file indienne; **2.** ⚙ aller *m* (simple); *théâ. etc.* place *f* séparée *ou* isolée; ♪ *disque*: 45 tours *m/inv.*; (*a.* ~ *game*) *tennis*: (partie *f*) simple *m*; **3.**

(*usu.* ~ *out*) choisir; distinguer; '~-'breast·ed droit (*veston etc.*); '~-'en·gin·ed ⚓ à un moteur; '~-'hand·ed sans aide, seul; '~-'heart·ed □, '~-'mind·ed □ sincère, loyal (-aux *m/pl.*), honnête; '~-'line à voie unique; 'sin·gle·ness sincérité *f*, honnêteté *f*; célibat *m*; unicité *f*; 'sin·gle-seat·er ⚓, *mot.* monoplace *m*; 'sin·gle·stick canne *f*; sin·glet ✝ ['~it] gilet *m* de corps; *sp.* maillot *m* fin; sin·gle·ton ['~tən] *cartes:* singleton *m*; 'sin·gle-'track à une voie, à voie unique.

sing·song ['siŋsɔŋ] chant *m* monotone; *fig.* concert *m* improvisé.

sin·gu·lar ['siŋgjulə] **1.** □ seul; singulier (-ère *f*) (*a. gramm.*); remarquable, rare; bizarre; **2.** *gramm.* (*a.* ~ *number*) singulier *m*; sin·gu·lar·i·ty [~'læriti] singularité *f*.

Sin·ha·lese [sinhə'li:z] **1.** cingalais; **2.** *ling.* cingalais *m*; Cingalais(e *f*) *m*.

sin·is·ter □ ['sinistə] sinistre; menaçant; ⊘ sénestre.

sink [siŋk] **1.** [*irr.*] *v/i.* ⚓ sombrer, couler; descendre; s'enfoncer(dans, *into*); tomber (dans, *into*); se tasser (*édifice*); se renverser (*dans un fauteuil*); succomber, se plier (*sous beneath, under*); baisser; se serrer (*cœur*); *v/t.* enfoncer; baisser; ⚓ couler, faire sombrer; ⚒ mouiller; creuser, foncer (*un puits*); amortir (*une dette*); placer (*de l'argent*); renoncer provisoirement à (*un nom*); supprimer (*une objection*); **2.** évier *m* (*de cuisine*); †, *a. fig.* cloaque *m*; 'sink·er ⚒ fonceur *m* de puits, puisatier *m*; *ligne de pêche:* plomb *m*; 'sink·ing foncement *m*; ⚓ naufrage *m*, torpillage *m*; tassement *m*; *fig.* défaillance *f*; ⚓ affaiblissement *m*; ~ *fund* caisse *f* d'amortissement.

sin·less ['sinlis] sans péché, pur.

sin·ner ['sinə] pécheur (-eresse *f*) *m*.

Sinn Fein ['ʃin'fein] (= *nous-mêmes*) mouvement nationaliste irlandais.

Sino... [sino] sino...

sin·u·os·i·ty [sinju'ɔsiti] sinuosité *f*; *route:* lacet *m*; 'sin·u·ous □ sinueux (-euse *f*), tortueux (-euse *f*), onduleux (-euse *f*); agile (*personne*).

si·nus *anat.* ['sainəs] sinus *m*; si·nus·i·tis ✻ [~'saitis] sinusite *f*.

sip [sip] **1.** petite gorgée *f*, F goutte *f*; **2.** boire à petits coups, siroter.

si·phon ['saifən] **1.** siphon *m* (à eau de seltz); **2.** *v/t.* siphonner; *v/i.* se transvaser.

sir [sə:] monsieur (*pl.* messieurs) *m*; ♀ titre de chevalerie, suivi du prénom: Sir.

sire ['saiə] **1.** *poét.* père *m*; titre donné à un souverain: sire *m*; *zo.* père *m*, *souv.* étalon *m*; **2.** *zo.* engendrer.

si·ren ['saiərin] sirène *f* (*a.* = trompe d'alarme).

sir·loin ['sə:lɔin] aloyau *m*.

sis·kin *orn.* ['siskin] tarin *m*.

sis·sy *Am.* ['sisi] mollasson *m*.

sis·ter ['sistə] sœur *f* (*a. eccl.*); *eccl.* religieuse *f*; (*a. ward-*~) infirmière *f* en chef; ~ *of charity* (*ou mercy*) sœur *f* de Charité; 'sis·ter·hood ['~hud] communauté *f* religieuse; 'sis·ter-in-law belle-sœur (*pl.* belles-sœurs) *f*; 'sis·ter·ly de sœur.

sit [sit] [*irr.*] *v/i.* s'asseoir; être assis; siéger (*assemblée*); couver (*poule*); se présenter (à, *for*); poser (pour, *for*); ~ *down* s'asseoir; *fig.* ~ (*up*)*on s.o.* remettre q. à sa place; *sl.* moucher q.; ~ *up* veiller tard, se coucher tard; se redresser (*sur sa chaise*); F *make s.o.* ~ *up* étonner q.; *v/t.* asseoir; ~ *a horse well* se tenir bien à cheval; ~ *s.th. out* rester jusqu'à la fin de qch.; ~ *s.o. out* rester jusqu'après le départ de q.; '~-down strike grève *f* sur le tas.

site [sait] **1.** emplacement *m*; site *m*; terrain *m* à bâtir; **2.** situer, placer.

sit·ter ['sitə] personne *f* assise; personne *f* qui pose; *poule:* couveuse *f*; *Am. see baby-sitter*; *sl.* affaire *f* sûre.

sit·ting ['sitiŋ] séance *f*; ♣ session *f*; '~-room petit salon *m*.

sit·u·at·ed ['sitjueitid] situé; *thus* ~ dans cette situation; ainsi situé; sit·u·a·tion situation *f*, position *f*; emploi *m*, place *f*.

six [siks] six (*a. su./m*); *be at* ~*es and sevens* être sens dessus dessous; manquer d'ensemble; *two and* ~ deux shillings *m/pl.* et six pence *m/pl.*; ~ *of charity* sextuple; **2.** *adv.* six fois autant; six·teen ['~-'ti:n] seize (*a. su./m*); 'six·teenth [~θ] seizième (*a. su./m*); sixth [~θ] sixième (*a. su./m*); 'sixth·ly sixièmement; six·ti·eth ['~tiiθ]

soixantième (*a. su./m*); **'six·ty**
soixante (*a. su./m*).
size¹ [saiz] **1.** grandeur *f*; grosseur *f*;
personne: taille *f*; *papier etc.*: format *m*; *souliers etc.*: pointure *f*;
chemise: encolure *f*; numéro *m*;
2. classer par grosseur *etc.*; ~ *s.o.*
up juger q., prendre la mesure de
q.; *large-~d* de grande taille.
size² [~] **1.** colle *f*; *tex.* empois *m*;
2. apprêter, (en)coller; *tex.* parer.
siz(e)·a·ble □ ['saizəbl] assez grand;
d'une belle taille.
siz·zle ['sizl] grésillement *m*; *radio*:
friture *f*.
skate¹ [skeit] *icht.* raie *f*.
skate² [~] **1.** patin *m*; (*ou roller-~*)
patin *m* à roulettes; **2.** patiner (*a.*
sur roulettes); **'skat·er** patineur
(-euse *f*) *m*; **'skat·ing-rink** skating
m; patinoire *f*.
ske·dad·dle F [ski'dædl] se sauver;
décamper, filer.
skee·sicks *Am.* F ['ski:ziks] vaurien
m.
skein [skein] *laine etc.*: écheveau *m*.
skel·e·ton ['skelitn] **1.** squelette *m*,
homme, bâtiment, etc.: ossature *f*;
charpente *f*; carcasse *f* (*a. d'un
parapluie*); *roman etc.*: esquisse *f*;
⚔ personnel *m* réduit; ⚔ cadre *m*;
fig. ~ *in the cupboard* (*Am.* closet)
secret *m* honteux (de la famille); **2.**
réduit; esquisse *f* de; ⊕ à clairevoie,
à jour; ⚔ -cadre; ~ *crew* équipage *m*
ou personnel *m* réduit; ~ *key* passe-
partout *m/inv.*; *sl.* rossignol *m* (*de
cambrioleur*); ~ *map* carte *f* muette.
skep·tic *Am.* ['skeptik] *see* sceptic.
sketch [sketʃ] **1.** esquisse *f*, croquis
m; *théâ.* sketch *m*, saynète *f*; *fig.*
aperçu *m*, plan *m*; **2.** esquisser;
faire un *ou* des croquis de; **'sketch-
y** □ imprécis; rudimentaire.
skew [skju:] (de) biais.
skew·er ['skuə] **1.** brochette *f*;
2. brocheter.
ski [ʃi:] **1.** *pl.* ski(s) ski *m*; *attr.* de
ski; à skis; ~ *platform* plate-forme
(*pl.* plates-formes) *f*; tremplin *m*; ~
run piste *f* de ski; **2.** faire du ski.
skid [skid] **1.** sabot *m ou* patin *m*
d'enrayage; ⚔ patin *m*; *mot.* dérapage *m*, embardée *f*; *mot.* ~ *mark*
trace *f* de dérapage; **2.** *v/t.* ensaboter,
enrayer; mettre sur traîneau; *v/i.*
déraper, glisser; *mot.* faire une embardée; ⚔ glisser sur l'aile; ~ *row*

Am. quartier *m* de(s) clochards; *be on
~* être clochard.
ski·er ['ʃi:ə] skieur (-euse *f*) *m*.
skiff ⚓ [skif] esquif *m*; youyou *m*
(*de bateau de commerce*); *canotage*:
skiff *m*.
ski·ing ['ʃi:iŋ] ski *m*; **'ski-jump**
tremplin *m* de ski; (*a.* **'ski-jump-
ing**) saut *m* à skis; **'ski-lift** (re)monte-
te-pente *m*.
skil(l)·ful □ ['skilful] adroit, habile;
'skil(l)·ful·ness, skill [skil] adresse
f, habileté *f*.
skilled [skild] habile; spécialisé
(*ouvrier etc.*); expérimenté (*en at,
in*).
skim [skim] **1.** *v/t.* (*souv.* ~ *off*)
écumer; dégraisser (*la soupe*); écrémer (*le lait*); *fig.* effleurer (*la surface*); ~ *through* feuilleter, parcourir
rapidement; *v/i.* glisser (sur, over);
2.: ~ *milk* lait *m* écrémé; **'skimmer** écumoire *f*; écrémoir *m*.
skimp [skimp] ménager outre
mesure; mesurer (qch. à q., *s.o. in
s.th.*); lésiner sur tout; F bâcler (*un
ouvrage*); **'skimp·y** □ maigre,
insuffisant; chiche, parcimonieux
(-euse *f*) (*personne*).
skin [skin] **1.** peau *f* (*a. d'un animal,
d'orange*); cuir *m*; pelure *f* (*de banane*); *café, lait, raisin*: pellicule *f*;
saucisson: robe *f*; outre *f* (*à vin*);
⚓ *navire*: coque *f*, *voile*: chemise *f*;
⊕ *fonte*: croûte *f*; *by* (*ou* with) *the
~ of one's teeth* tout juste; à peine;
Am. F *have got s.o. under one's ~*
ne pouvoir oublier *ou* se débarrasser de q.; **2.** *v/t.* écorcher; peler,
éplucher (*un fruit*); *sl.* tondre (*q.*),
dépouiller (*q.*) (*au jeu*); *keep one's
eyes ~ned* avoir l'œil américain; F ~ *off*
enlever (*les bas etc.*); *v/i.* (*a.* ~ over)
recouvrir de peau; **'~-'deep** à fleur
de peau, peu profond; **'~-'dive** faire
de la plongée sous-marine; **'~-'diving** plongée *f* sous-marine; **'~-'flick**
surt. *Am. sl.* film *m* porno; **'~-'flint**
grippe-sou (*pl.* grippe-sou[s]) *m*; **'~-
'graft·ing** ✂ greffe *f* épidermique;
'skin·ner écorcheur *m*; pelletier *m*;
'skin·ny décharné, maigre; efflanqué (*cheval*); F chiche, avare.
skint *Brit. sl.* [skint] fauché, sans le
rond.
skin·tight ['skintait] collant.
skip [skip] **1.** saut *m*; gambade *f*; ⚒
benne *f*; **2.** *v/i.* sauter, gambader;

v/t. (*a.* ~ *over*) sauter (*qch.*); '~**jack** poussah *m*; *zo.* scarabée *m* à ressort.

skip·per[1] ['skipə] sauteur (-euse *f*) *m.*

skip·per[2] [~] patron *m*, capitaine *m*; *sp.* chef *m* d'équipe.

skip·ping-rope ['skipiŋroup] corde *f* à sauter.

skir·mish ✕ ['skə:miʃ] **1.** escarmouche *f*; **2.** escarmoucher; tirailler (*contre*, *with*); '**skir·mish·er** tirailleur *m.*

skirt [skə:t] **1.** *cost.* jupe *f*; *pardessus etc.*: pans *m/pl.*; *souv.* ~s *pl.* bord *m*; *forêt*: lisière *f*; **2.** *v/t.* border; *vt/i.* (*a.* ~ *along*) longer, contourner, côtoyer; '**skirt·ing-board** ⊕ plinthe *f*; bas *m* de lambris.

skit[1] [skit] *usu.* ~s *pl.* tas *m/pl.*

skit[2] [~] pièce *f* satirique; satire *f* (*de*, *on*); '**skit·tish** ☐ ombrageux (-euse *f*) (*cheval*); volage, capricieux (-euse *f*) (*personne*).

skit·tle ['skitl] quille *f*; *play* (*at*) ~s jouer aux quilles; '~**al·ley** jeu *m* de quilles.

skive *Brit. sl.* [skaiv] tirer au flanc; **skiv·er** tire-au-flanc *mf/inv.*

skiv·vy F *péj.* ['skivi] bonniche *f* (= *bonne à tout faire*).

skul·dug·ger·y *Am.* F [skʌl'dʌgəri] fourberie *f*, ruse *f.*

skulk [skʌlk] se tenir caché; se cacher; rôder furtivement; '**skulk·er** carotteur (-euse *f*) *m.*

skull [skʌl] crâne *m.*

skunk [skʌŋk] *zo.* mouffette *f*; *fourrure*: skunks *m*; F mufle *m*; ladre *m.*

sky [skai] *souv.* **skies** *pl.* ciel (*pl.* cieux, ciels) *m*; '~-'**blue** bleu ciel *adj./inv.* (*a. su./m/inv.*); '~-'**div·ing** parachutisme *m* en chute libre; '~**lark** **1.** *orn.* alouette *f* des champs; **2.** rigoler; '~**light** jour *m* d'en haut; lucarne *f*; '~**line** ligne *f* d'horizon; profil *m* (de l'horizon); ~ *advertising* publicité *f* dessinée en silhouette sur le ciel; '~**rock·et** *Am.* F augmenter rapidement; monter en flèche (*prix*); '~**scrap·er** gratte-ciel *m/inv.*; **sky·ward**(s) ['~wəd(z)] vers le ciel; '**sky-writ·ing** ✈ publicité *f* aérienne.

slab [slæb] *pierre*: dalle *f*; *ardoise*: table *f*; *métal*, *marbre*, *etc.*: plaque *f*; *chocolat*: tablette *f*; ⊕ *bois*: dosse *f.*

slack [slæk] **1.** lâche; faible (*a.* ✝); négligent (*personne*); ✝ *a.* peu vif (vive *f*); ⚓ ~ *water*, ~ *tide* mer *f* étale; **2.** ⚓ *cable etc.*: mou *m*; ✝ accalmie *f*; ⊕ jeu *m*; ~s *pl.* pantalon *m*; **3.** *see* ~*en*; *see* **slake**; F flémarder; '**slack·en** (se) relâcher; (se) ralentir; diminuer (*de*); *v/t.* détendre; ⊕ donner du jeu à; *v/i.* devenir négligent; prendre du mou (*cordage*, *câble*); ✝ s'alanguir; '**slack·er** F paresseux (-euse *f*), F flémard(e *f*) *m*; ✕ tireur *m* au flanc; '**slack·ness** relâchement *m*; négligence *f*; lenteur *f*; paresse *f*; ✝ stagnation *f.*   [scoriacé.)

slag [slæg] scories *f/pl.*; '**slag·gy**ᛃ

slain [slein] *p.p.* de **slay.**

slake [sleik] étancher (*la soif*); éteindre (*le chaux*).

slam [slæm] **1.** *porte*: claquement *m*; *bridge*: chelem *m*; **2.** *v/t.* (faire) claquer; fermer avec violence; *v/i.* claquer.

slan·der ['slɑːndə] **1.** calomnie *f*; **2.** calomnier, diffamer; '**slan·der·er** calomniateur (-trice *f*) *m*; ♈ diffamateur (-trice *f*) *m*; '**slan·der·ous** ☐ calomnieux (-euse *f*); ♈ diffamatoire.

slang [slæŋ] **1.** argot *m*; **2.** F réprimander vivement; injurier; ~*ing match* prise *f* de bec; '**slang·y** ☐ argotier (-ère *f*); argotique.

slant [slɑːnt] **1.** pente *f*, inclinaison *f*; biais *m*; *Am.* F point *m* de vue; **2.** *v/t.* incliner; *v/i.* (s')incliner, être en pente; être oblique; '**slant·ing** ☐ *adj.*, '**slant·wise** *adv.* en biais, de biais; oblique(ment *adv.*).

slap [slæp] **1.** coup *m*, tape *f*; claquement *m* (*d'un piston*); ~ *in the face* gifle *f*, soufflet *m*; *fig.* affront *m*; **2.** claquer; gifler; donner une tape à; **3.** pan!; '~-**bang** de but en blanc; '~-**dash** sans soin; à la six-quatre-deux; '~-**jack** *Am.* crêpe *f*; '~-**stick** *théâ.* batte *f* (d'Arlequin); ~ *comedy* pièce *f* etc. burlesque; arlequinades *f/pl.*; '~-**up** F fameux (-euse *f*), de premier ordre.

slash [slæʃ] **1.** balafre *f*; entaille *f*; *cost.* taillade *f*; **2.** *v/t.* balafrer; taillader; cingler (*a. fig.*); F éreinter (*un livre etc.*); *cost.* faire des taillades dans; F réduire (*le prix etc.*); *v/i.* frapper à droite et à gauche; cingler; '**slash·ing** ☐ cinglant (*a. fig.*); *fig. a.* mordant; *sl.* épatant.

slat [slæt] **1.** *jalousie*: lame(lle) *f*; *lit*: traverse *f*; **2.** battre, frapper sur.

slate [sleit] **1.** ardoise *f*; *surt. Am.* liste *f* provisoire des candidats; **2.** couvrir d'ardoises *ou* en ardoise; F tancer; F éreinter; *be* ~*d for être un candidat sérieux à* (*un poste*); '~-'**pen·cil** crayon *m* d'ardoise; '**slat·er** couvreur *m* (en ardoises).

slat·tern ['slætə:n] **1.** souillon *f*; **2.** (*a.* '**slat·tern·ly**) mal soigné (*femme*).

slat·y □ ['sleiti] ardoiseux (-euse *f*), schisteux (-euse *f*); ardoisé (*couleur*).

slaugh·ter ['slɔːtə] **1.** *bêtes*: abattage *m*; *gibier*: abattis *m*; *fig.* massacre *m*, carnage *m*; **2.** abattre; massacrer; '**slaugh·ter·er** abatteur *m*; *fig.* tueur *m*; '**slaugh·ter·house** abattoir *m*; '**slaugh·ter·ous** □ *poét.* meurtrier (-ère *f*).

Slav [slɑːv] **1.** slave; **2.** Slave *mf*.

slave [sleiv] **1.** esclave *mf*; *attr.* d'esclaves, des esclaves; *a. fig.* ~ *driver* négrier *m*; **2.** travailler comme un nègre; peiner.

slav·er[1] ['sleivə] négrier *m*; *personne*: marchand *m* d'esclaves.

slav·er[2] ['slævə] **1.** bave *f*, salive *f*; **2.** baver (sur, over).

slav·er·y ['sleivəri] esclavage *m*; *fig.* asservissement *m*.

slav·ey *sl.* ['slævi] bonniche *f*.

Slav·ic ['slɑːvik] **1.** slave; **2.** *ling.* slave *m*.

slav·ish □ ['sleivis] servile, d'esclave; '**slav·ish·ness** servilité *f*.

slaw *Am.* [slɔː] salade *f* de choux.

slay *poét.* [slei] [*irr.*] tuer, mettre à mort; assassiner; '**slay·er** meurtrier (-ère *f*) *m*; tueur (-euse *f*) *m*; assassin *m*.

slea·zy ['sliːzi] usé; miteux (-euse *f*), minable.

sled [sled] *see* sledge[1].

sledge[1] [sledʒ] **1.** traîneau *m*; **2.** *v/t.* transporter en traîneau; *v/i.* aller en traîneau.

sledge[2] [~] (*a.* ~-*hammer*) marteau *m* de forgeron; masse *f* (*de pierres*).

sleek [sliːk] **1.** □ lisse; luisant; *fig.* doucereux (-euse *f*), mielleux (-euse *f*); **2.** lisser; planer; '**sleek·ness** luisant *m*; *fig.* douceur *f*, onctuosité *f*.

sleep [sliːp] **1.** [*irr.*] *v/i.* dormir (*a. toupie*); coucher; ~ (*up*)*on* (*ou over*) *it* remettre cela jusqu'au lendemain; consulter son chevet; *v/t.* coucher (*q.*); ~ *the hours away* passer les heures en dormant; ~ *off* faire passer (*une migraine*) en dormant; **2.** sommeil *m*; *go to* ~ s'endormir; *put* (*ou send*) *to* ~ endormir; (faire) piquer (*un animal*); '**sleep·er** dormeur (-euse *f*) *m*; 🚃 wagon-lit (*pl.* wagons-lits) *m*; couchette *f*; *be a light* ~ avoir le sommeil léger; '**sleep·i·ness** assoupissement *m*.

sleep·ing ['sliːpiŋ]: ♀ *Beauty* Belle *f* au bois dormant; ♂ ~ *partner* commanditaire *m*; '~-**bag** sac *m* de couchage; '~-**car**, '~-'**car·riage** 🚃 wagon-lit (*pl.* wagons-lits) *m*; '~-**draught** narcotique *m*, somnifère *m*; ~ **pill** (comprimé *m*) somnifère *m*; '~-'**sick·ness** maladie *f* du sommeil.

sleep·less □ ['sliːplis] sans sommeil; *fig.* inlassable; '**sleep·less·ness** insomnie *f*.

sleep·walk·er ['sliːpwɔːkə] somnambule *mf*.

sleep·y □ ['sliːpi] somnolent; *fig.* endormi; blet(te *f*) (*fruit*); *be* ~ avoir sommeil; ~ *sickness* encéphalite *f* léthargique; '~-**head** F *fig.* endormi(e *f*) *m*.

sleet [sliːt] **1.** neige *f* à moitié fondue; **2.**: *it is* ~*ing* la pluie tourne à la neige; '**sleet·y** de pluie et de neige, de grésil.

sleeve [sliːv] **1.** manche *f*; ⊕ fourreau *m*; *attr.* à manches; de manchette; ⊕ de manchon, à manchon; *have something up one's* ~ avoir qch. dans son sac; *laugh up* (*ou in*) *one's* ~ rire sous cape; **2.** mettre des manches à; **sleeved** à manches; '**sleeve·less** sans manches; '**sleeve-link** bouton *m* de manchette.

sleigh [slei] **1.** traîneau *m*; **2.** *v/t.* transporter en traîneau; *v/i.* aller en traîneau.

sleight [slait] (*usu.* ~ *of hand*) adresse *f*; prestidigitation *f*.

slen·der □ ['slendə] mince, ténu; svelte (*personne*); faible (*espoir*); maigre; modeste, exigu(ë *f*); '**slen·der·ness** minceur *f*; sveltesse *f*; faiblesse *f*; exiguïté *f*.

slept [slept] *prét. et p.p. de* sleep **1.**

sleuth [sluːθ] (*a.* ~-*hound*) limier *m*; F détective *m*.

slew[1] [sluː] *prét. de* slay.

slew² [~] (a. ~ round) (faire) pivoter.
slice [slais] **1.** tranche f; tartine f (de beurre etc.); fig. part f; cuis. truelle f (à poisson); ~ of luck coup m de veine; **2.** découper en tranches; (a. ~ off) trancher, couper; tennis: choper; golf: faire dévier la balle à droite; **'slic·er** machine f à couper; coupe-jambon m/inv.
slick [slik] **1.** adj. (a. adv.) habile (-ment adv.), adroit(ement adv.); **2.** (a. ~ paper) Am. sl. magazine m de luxe.
slick·er Am. ['slikə] F escroc m (adroit); imperméable m.
slid [slid] prét. et p.p. de slide 1.
slide [slaid] **1.** [irr.] v/i. glisser (dans, into), couler; faire des glissades (personne); let things ~ laisser tout aller à vau-l'eau; v/t. faire glisser; **2.** glissade f; coulisse f; cheveux: barrette f; phot. châssis m; ⊕ glissoir m; projection f; **'slid·er** glisseur (-euse f) m; ⊕ coulisseau m; **'slide-rule** règle f à calcul.
slid·ing ['slaidiŋ] **1.** glissement m; **2.** glissant, coulant; mot. ~ roof toit m décapotable; ~ rule règle f à calcul; ~ scale échelle f mobile; ~ seat mot. siège m amovible; canot: banc m à glissières; ~ table table f à rallonges.
slight [slait] **1.** □ léger (-ère f); mince; frêle; svelte; peu important; insignifiant; **2.** affront m; manque m d'égards (pour, on); **3.** manquer d'égards pour; faire un affront à; **'slight·ing** □ de mépris; dédaigneux (-euse f); **'slight·ness** légèreté f; minceur f; insignifiance f.
slim [slim] **1.** □ svelte, mince, élancé; sl. mince, léger (-ère f); **2.** (s')amincir; v/i. suivre un régime amaigrissant; ~ming line ligne f qui amincit.
slime [slaim] limon m, vase f; limace: bave f; liquide: bitume m.
slim·i·ness ['slaiminis] état m vaseux ou boueux, fig. obséquiosité f.
slim·ness ['slimnis] sveltesse f.
slim·y □ ['slaimi] vaseux (-euse f), boueux (-euse f); fig. obséquieux (-euse f).
sling [sliŋ] **1.** fronde f; barriques: élingue f; suspenseur m (de câble); ⚕ écharpe f; **2.** [irr.] lancer (avec

une fronde); élinguer (un fardeau); F ~ over jeter sur; ~ up hisser.
slink [sliŋk] [irr.]: ~ in (out) entrer (sortir) furtivement; ~ away a. s'éclipser.
slip [slip] **1.** [irr.] v/i. glisser; couler (nœud); F aller (vite); (souv. ~ away) s'esquiver, fig. s'écouler; se tromper; v/t. glisser, couler; filer (un câble); s'échapper de; se dégager de; ~ in v/t. introduire; v/i. se faufiler, entrer discrètement; ~ into se glisser dans; ~ on enfiler, passer (une robe etc.); ~ off enlever, ôter (une robe etc.); **2.** glissade f; erreur f; écart m de conduite; faux pas m; oreiller: taie f; chien: laisse f; géol. éboulement m; (a. ~ of paper) feuille f, fiche f; ✗ bouture f; fig. rejeton m; cost. combinaison f; fond m de robe; ⚓ cale f; chantier m; ~s pl. sp. slip m; caleçon m de bain; théâ. coulisses f/pl.; F a ~ of a girl une jeune fille f fluette; ~ of the pen lapsus m calami; ~ of the tongue lapsus m linguae, faux pas m; give s.o. the ~ se dérober à q., planter q. là; **'~-knot** nœud m coulant; **'~-on** robe f etc. à enfiler; **'slip·per** pantoufle f; ⊕ patin m; **'slip·per·y** □ glissant; incertain; fig. matois; **slip·shod** ['~ʃɔd] en savates; fig. négligé, bâclé; **slip·slop** ['~slɔp] bouillons m/pl.; lavasse f; fig. sensiblerie f; **slipt** prét. et p.p. de slip 1; **'slip-up** F gaffe f; contretemps m; fiasco m.
slit [slit] **1.** fente f; ajour m; boîte aux lettres: guichet m; incision f; **2.** [irr.] (se) fendre; v/t. éventrer: faire une incision dans.
slith·er F ['sliðə] v/i. glisser; v/t. traîner (les pieds etc.).
sliv·er ['slivə] **1.** tranche f; bois: éclat m; tex. ruban m; **2.** v/t. couper en tranches; établir les rubans de; v/i. éclater.
slob F [slɔb] rustaud m, goujat m.
slob·ber ['slɔbə] **1.** bave f; boue f; fig. sentimentalité f excessive; **2.** baver; fig. s'attendrir (sur, over); **'slob·ber·y** baveux (-euse f); négligé.
sloe ⚘ [slou] prunelle f; arbre: prunellier m.
slog F [slɔg] **1.** cogner; travailler avec acharnement; **2.** coup m violent; corvée f, sl. boulot m.
slo·gan ['slougən] écoss. cri m de

guerre (*a. fig.*); *pol.* mot *m* d'ordre;
♱ devise *f*; slogan *m*; **slo·gan·eer-
ing** *Am.* F [slougə'niəriŋ] emploi
m des mots d'ordre *ou* des cris de
guerre.   [aviso *m*.]
sloop ⚓ [slu:p] sloop *m*; *marine:*
slop¹ [slɔp] **1.** gâchis *m*; ⁓*s pl.*
lavasse *f*; eaux *f/pl.* ménagères;
2. (*a.* ⁓ **over**) *v/t.* répandre; *v/i.* déborder; *fig.* faire de la sensiblerie.
slop² [⁓] blouse *f*; vêtements *m/pl.*
de confection; hardes *f/pl.*; ⚓
frusques *f/pl.*
slop-ba·sin ['slɔpbeisn] bol *m* à
rinçures (de thé).
slope [sloup] **1.** pente *f*, inclinaison
f; talus *m*; montagne: versant *m*;
2. *v/t.* couper en pente; taluter; ⊕
biseauter; ⚔ ⁓ **arms!** l'arme sur l'é-
paule droite!; *v/i.* être en pente;
incliner; aller en pente; *sl.* ⁓ **off** décamper, filer; **'slop·ing** □ en pente,
incliné.
slop-pail ['slɔppeil] seau *m* de ménage; seau *m* de toilette; **'slop·py**
□ fangeux (-euse *f*); encore mouillé; *cost.* mal ajusté, trop large; mou
(mol *devant une voyelle ou un h
muet*; molle *f*) (*personne*); *fig.* par
trop sentimental (-aux *m/pl.*).
slop-shop ['slɔpʃɔp] magasin *m* de
confections.
slosh F [slɔʃ] flanquer un coup;
'sloshed F soûl, bourré.
slot [slɔt] *chasse:* erres *f/pl.*; fente *f*
(*d'un distributeur*); ⊕ entaille *f*.
sloth [slouθ] paresse *f*; *zo.* paresseux
m; **sloth·ful** ['⁓ful] paresseux (-euse
f); indolent.
slot-ma·chine ['slɔtməʃi:n] *chocolat,
cigarettes:* distributeur *m* automatique; *jeu de hasard:* appareil *m* à
jetons.
slouch [slautʃ] **1.** *v/i.* manquer de
tenue; traîner en marchant; (*a.
⁓ about*) rôder; *v/t.* rabattre le bord
de (*un chapeau*); ⁓**ed** rabattu; mollasse (*allure*); aux épaules arrondies
(*personne*); **2.** démarche *f ou* allure
f mollasse; fainéant *m*; ⁓ **hat**
chapeau *m* rabattu.
slough¹ [slau] bourbier *m* (*a. fig.*).
slough² [slʌf] **1.** *zo.* dépouille *f*; 🩹
escarre *f*; *plaie:* croûte *f*; **2.** *v/i.* se
dépouiller; 🩹 se couvrir d'une
escarre; 🩹 se détacher (*croûte*); *v/t.*
jeter; *fig.* (*a.* ⁓ **off**) se dépouiller
de.

slough·y ['slaui] bourbeux (-euse *f*).
Slo·vak ['slouvæk] **1.** *ling.* slovaque
m; Slovaque *mf*; **2.** (*ou* **Slo'va·ki-
an** [⁓iən]) slovaque.
slov·en ['slʌvn] souillon *f*; bousilleur
(-euse *f*) *m*; **'slov·en·li·ness** négligence *f*; **'slov·en·ly** mal soigné,
malpropre; négligent; débraillé
(*style, tenue*); déhanché (*allure*).
slow [slou] **1.** □ lent (*à of, to*); en
retard (*pendule*); lourd (*esprit*); 🚌
omnibus; petit (*vitesse*); ennuyeux
(-euse *f*) (*spectacle etc.*); *sp.* qui
ne rend pas; *mot.* ⁓ **lane** voie *f* pour
véhicules lents; 🚌 ⁓ **train** train *m*
omnibus; **be** ⁓ **to** (*inf.*) être lent à
(*inf.*); my watch is ten minutes ⁓ ma
montre retarde de dix minutes; **2.**
adv. lentement; **3.** (*souv.* ⁓ **down, up,
off**) *v/t.* ralentir; *v/i.* ralentir;
diminuer de vitesse; **'⁓-coach** F
lambin(e *f*) *m*; **'⁓-match** corde *f* à
feu; **'-'mo·tion pic·ture** film *m*
tourné au ralenti; **'slow·ness** lenteur *f*; *montre:* retard *m*; **'slow-
worm** *zo.* orvet *m*.
sludge [slʌdʒ] fange *f*; ⊕ boue *f*; 🛠
schlamm *m*.
slue [slu:] (*a.* ⁓ **round**) (faire) pivoter.
slug¹ [slʌg] lingot *m* (*a. typ.*); *linotype:* ligne-bloc (*pl.* lignes-blocs) *f*.
slug² *zo.* [⁓] limace *f*.
slug³ *Am.* F [⁓] **1.** coup *m* (violent);
coup *m* (*de whisky etc.*); **2.** cogner,
frapper; ⁓ **it out** se rentrer dedans, se
taper dessus.
slug·gard ['slʌgəd] paresseux (-euse
f) *m*; fainéant(e *f*) *m*; **'slug·gish** □
paresseux (-euse *f*).
sluice [slu:s] **1.** écluse *f*; **2.** *v/t.*
vanner; (*a.* ⁓ **out**) laisser échapper;
laver à grande eau; *v/i.* ⁓ **out** couler
à flots; **'⁓-gate** porte *f* d'écluse;
vanne *f*; **'⁓-way** canal *m* à vannes.
slum [slʌm] bas quartier *m*.
slum·ber ['slʌmbə] **1.** *a.* ⁓*s pl.*
sommeil *m*; **2.** sommeiller, dormir;
slum·brous ['⁓brəs], **slum·ber-
ous** ['⁓bərəs] assoupi, somnolent.
slump [slʌmp] *à la Bourse:* **1.** baisse *f* soudaine; marasme *m*; F crise *f*;
2. baisser tout à coup; s'effondrer.
slung [slʌŋ] *prét. et p.p. de* sling 2.
slunk [slʌŋk] *prét. et p.p. de* slink.
slur [slə:] **1.** tache *f*; *fig.* affront *m*,
insulte *f*; mauvaise articulation *f*; ♪
liaison *f*; **2.** *v/t.* (*a.* ⁓ **over**) glisser
sur; ♪ lier (*deux notes*), couler (*un*

passage); bredouiller; *v/i.* s'estomper.

slush [slʌʃ] neige *f* à demi fondue; fange *f*; F lavasse *f*; F sensiblerie *f*; '**slush·y** détrempé par la neige; boueux (-euse *f*); F fadasse.

slut [slʌt] souillon *f*; F *co.* coquine *f*; '**slut·tish** malpropre.

sly □ [slai] sournois, rusé, matois; *on the* ~ en cachette; '~·**boots** F sournois(e *f*) *m*; espiègle *mf*; '**sly·ness** sournoiserie *f*, finesse *f*; espièglerie *f*.

smack¹ [smæk] **1.** léger goût *m*; soupçon *m* (*a. fig.*); *fig.* grain *m*; **2.**: ~ *of* avoir un goût de; sentir (*qch.*) (*a. fig.*).

smack² [~] **1.** *main:* claque *f*; *fouet:* claquement *m*; F gros baiser *m*; F essai *m*; **2.** *v/i.* claquer; *v/t.* faire claquer (*a. un baiser*); frapper, taper (avec, *with*); **3.** *int.* paf!, vlan!

smack³ ⚓ [~] bateau *m* de pêche.

smack·er *Am. sl.* ['smækə] dollar *m*.

small [smɔːl] **1.** *usu.* petit; de petite taille; faible (*pouls, ressources*); peu important; menu (*bétail, gibier, plomb*); court (*durée etc.*); léger (-ère *f*) (*progrès*); maigre (*récolte*); fluet(te *f*) (*voix*); bas(se *f*) (*carte*); *une* demi-mesure *f* de (*alcool*); *une* demi-tasse *f* de (*café*); *make s.o. feel* ~ humilier q., ravaler q.; ~ *fry* le menu fretin *m*; *les gosses m/pl.*; ~ *game* menu gibier *m*; ~ *holder* petit propriétaire *m*; ~ *holding* petite propriété *f*; *in the* ~ *hours pl.* fort avant dans la nuit; *surt. Am.* F *fig.* ~ *potatoes* bien peu de chose, insignifiant; ~ *print* les petits caractères *m/pl.*; *l'*important du bas de la page; ✝ ~ *wares pl.* mercerie *f*; **2.** partie *f* mince; *charbon:* menu *m*; *jambe:* bas *m*; *anat.* ~ *of the back* creux *m* des reins; '~·**arms** *pl.* armes *f/pl.* portatives; '**small·ish** assez petit; '**small·ness** petitesse *f*; mesquinerie *f*; '**small·pox** ✼ *pl.* petite vérole *f*; **small talk** banalités *f/pl.*; menus propos *m/pl.*; '**small·time** insignifiant, petit, piètre.

smalt ⊕ [smɔːlt] smalt *m*; émail (*pl. -aux*) *m* de cobalt.

smarm·y F ['smɑːmi] mielleux (-euse *f*), flagorneur (-euse *f*).

smart [smɑːt] **1.** □ vif (vive *f*) (*allure, attaque, etc.*) (à *inf.*, *in gér.*); cuisant (*douleur etc.*); vert (*réprimande*); ✕ chaud (*affaire*); habile, adroit; intelligent; éveillé, débrouillard; *péj.* malin (-igne *f*); bien entretenu, soigné; chic *inv.* *en genre*, élégant, coquet(te *f*); *Am.* ~ *aleck* finaud *m*; *un je sais tout m*; **2.** douleur *f* cuisante; **3.** cuire; souffrir (*personne*); *you shall* ~ *for it* il vous en cuira; '**smart·en** *v/t.* donner du chic à; *v/i.* prendre du chic; se faire beau; '**smart-mon·ey** pension *f* pour blessure; ✝ forfait *m*; '**smart·ness** finesse *f*; intelligence *f*; élégance *f*, chic *m*; *esprit:* vivacité *f*.

smash [smæʃ] **1.** *v/t.* briser (en morceaux), (*souv.* ~ *up*) casser; *fig.* détruire; écraser (*a. tennis*); ~ *against* (*ou on*) heurter contre; *v/i.* se briser (contre *against*, on); éclater en morceaux, *fig.* échouer; ✝ F (*a.* ~ *up*) faire faillite; **2.** mise *f* en morceaux; fracas *m*; collision *f*; 🚗 désastre *m*; ✝ débâcle *f*, faillite *f*; *tennis:* smash *m*; F ~ *hit* succès *m* fou; *all to* ~ en miettes; '~-**and-'grab raid** vol *m* après bris de devanture; '**smash·er** *sl.* coup *m* écrasant; critique *f* mordante; '**smash·ing** écrasant; F formidable; '**smash-up** destruction *f* complète; collision *f*; ✝ faillite *f*.

smat·ter·er ['smætərə] demi-savant *m*; '**smat·ter·ing** légère connaissance *f*.

smear [smiə] **1.** salir (de, *with*); barbouiller (de, *with*) (*a. une page écrite*); enduire (de graisse, *with grease*); **2.** tache *f*, macule *f*; ☤ frottis *m* (*de sang*).

smell [smel] **1.** senteur *f*, parfum *m*; (*a. sense of* ~) odorat *m*; **2.** [*irr.*] *v/i.* sentir (*qch.*, *of* s.th.); avoir un parfum; *v/t.* sentir, flairer; (*a.* ~ *at*) sentir (*une fleur*). [*smell* 2.]

smelt¹ [smelt] *prét. et p.p. de*

smelt² *icht.* [~] éperlan *m*.

smelt³ [~] fondre; extraire par fusion; '**smelt·er** ⊕ fondeur *m*; métallurgiste *m*; '**smelt·ing-'furnace** fourneau *m* de fusion *ou* de fonte.

smile [smail] **1.** sourire *m*; **2.** sourire (à *at*, on). [*souiller.*]

smirch *poét.* [smɜːtʃ] tacher; *fig.*

smirk [smɜːk] **1.** minauder, mignarder; **2.** sourire *m* affecté; minauderie *f*.

smite [smait] [*irr.*] *poét. ou co.* frapper; abattre; ~ *upon* frapper sur; *fig.* frapper (*p.ex. l'oreille*).

smith [smiθ] forgeron *m.*

smith·er·eens F ['smiðə'ri:nz] *pl.* miettes *f/pl.*; morceaux *m/pl.*; *smash to* ~ briser en mille morceaux.

smith·y ['smiði] forge *f.*

smit·ten ['smitn] **1.** *p.p. de smite;* **2.** frappé, pris (de, *with*); *fig.* épris, amoureux (-euse *f*) (de, *with*).

smock [smɔk] **1.** orner de smocks (= *fronces*); **2.** (*ou* ~-*frock*) blouse *f,* sarrau *m.*

smog [smɔg] brouillard *m* enfumé.

smoke [smouk] **1.** fumée *f*; F action *f* de fumer; F cigare *m*, cigarette *f*; ~-*consumer* (appareil *m*) fumivore *m*; *have a* ~ fumer; **2.** *v/i.* fumer; *v/t.* fumer (*du jambon, du tabac*); enfumer (*une plante*); noircir de fumée (*le plafond etc.*); ✗ enfumer; '~-**dried** fumé; '~-**hel·met** casque *m* à fumée; '**smoke·less** ☐ sans fumée; fumivore (*foyer*); '**smok·er** fumeur (-euse *f*) *m*; *see smoking-compartment*; '**smoke-screen** ✗ rideau *m* de fumée; brume *f* artificielle; '**smoke·stack** 🚂, *a.* ⚓ cheminée *f.*

smok·ing ['smoukiŋ] **1.** émission *f* de fumée; *jambon:* fumage *m*; no ~! défense *f* de fumer; **2.** fumant; '~-**com·part·ment** 🚂 compartiment *m* de fumeurs, F fumeur *m*; '~-**con·cert** concert *m* où il est permis de fumer; '~-**room** fumoir *m.*

smok·y ☐ ['smouki] fumeux (-euse *f*); plein de fumée; noirci par la fumée.

smol·der *Am.* ['smouldə] *see smoulder.*

smooth [smu:ð] **1.** ☐ lisse; uni; poli; calme (*mer*); doux (douce *f*); *fig.* doucereux (-euse *f*); *Am.* F chic *inv. en genre*; **2.** (*souv.* ~ *out, down*) lisser; (*a.* ~ *over, away*) aplanir (*le bois; fig. une difficulté*); *fig.* calmer; adoucir (*une courbe*); ~ *down* (se) calmer, (s')apaiser; '**smooth·ing 1.** lissage *m*; **2.** à repasser; '**smooth·ness** égalité *f*; douceur *f* (*fig.* feinte); calme *m*; '**smooth-tongued** mielleux (-euse *f*), enjôleur (-euse *f*).

smote [smout] *pret. de smite.*

smoth·er ['smʌðə] **1.** fumée *f* épaisse; nuage *m* épais de poussière; **2.** (*a.* ~ *up*) étouffer (*a. fig.*); *fig.* couvrir.

smoul·der ['smouldə] brûler lentement; *fig.* couver.

smudge [smʌdʒ] **1.** *v/t.* souiller; barbouiller, maculer; tacher (*plume*); s'estomper (*silhouette*); **2.** tache *f*; encre: pâté *m*; '**smudg·y** ☐ taché; barbouillé; estompé (*silhouette*); illisible.

smug [smʌg] suffisant, satisfait de soi-même; glabre (*visage*).

smug·gle ['smʌgl] *v/t.* (faire) passer (*qch.*) en contrebande; *v/i.* faire la contrebande; '**smug·gler** contrebandier *m*; fraudeur *m*; '**smug·gling** contrebande *f.*

smut [smʌt] **1.** noir *m*; flocon *m ou* tache *f* de suie; ✿ *céréales:* charbon *m*; *coll.* saletés *f/pl.*; **2.** noircir, salir; *v/i.* ✿ être atteint du charbon.

smutch [smʌtʃ] **1.** tacher; souiller; **2.** tache *f.*

smut·ty ☐ ['smʌti] noirci; sale; *fig.* malpropre; ✿ piqué.

snack [snæk] casse-croûte *m/inv.*; F *go* ~*s* partager (qch. avec q., *in s.th. with s.o.*); '~-**bar** bar *m*, casse-croûte *m/inv.*

snaf·fle¹ ['snæfl] (*a.* ~-*bit*) filet *m.*

snaf·fle² *Angl. sl.* [~] chiper (= *voler*).

sna·fu *Am. sl.* ✗ [snæ'fu:] **1.** en désarroi; en pagaille; **2.** pagaille *f.*

snag [snæg] arbre, dent: chicot *m*; saillie *f*, protubérance *f*; *fig.* obstacle *m*, F cheveu *m*, pépin *m*; *bas, robe:* accroc *m*; *Am.* chicot *m* submergé; souche *f* au ras d'eau; **snag·ged** ['~id], '**snag·gy** épineux (-euse *f*); semé d'obstacles submergés.

snail *zo.* [sneil] limaçon *m*; escargot *m* (comestible).

snake *zo.* [sneik] serpent *m*; '~-**weed** ✿ bistorte *f.*

snak·y ☐ ['sneiki] de serpent; infesté de serpents; *fig.* perfide; *fig.* serpentant (*chemin*).

snap [snæp] **1.** coup *m* de dents *ou* de ciseaux *ou* de froid; coup *m* sec, claquement *m*; *fig.* énergie *f*, entrain *m*; *collier, valise:* fermoir *m*; *gant:* fermoir *m* pression; rupture *f* soudaine; *cartes:* (sorte de) jeu enfantin; *phot.* instantané *m*; *cuis.* croquet *m* au gingembre; *cold* ~

froid *m* soudain; **2.** *v/i.* happer; tâcher de saisir (q., qch. *at* s.o., *at* s.th.); claquer (*dents, fouet, etc.*); se casser (avec un bruit sec); *fig.* ~ *at* saisir (*une occasion*); F ~ *at* s.o. parler à q. d'un ton sec; *Am.* F ~ *into* (*ou out of*) *it* secouez-vous!; grouillez-vous!; *v/t.* happer; saisir d'un coup de dents; faire claquer; casser, rompre; *phot.* prendre un instantané de, F prendre; F ~ *one's fingers at* narguer (q.); se moquer de; ~ *out* dire d'un ton sec; ~ *up* saisir (*a. fig.*); happer; enlever (vite); **3.** crac!; **'~-drag·on** ♀ gueule-de-loup (*pl.* gueules-de-loup) *f*; *a. jeu qui consiste à happer des raisins secs dans du cognac flambant*; **'~-fas·ten·er** gant, robe: fermoir (pression) *m*; **'snap·per** personne *f* hargneuse; **'snap·pish** □ hargneux (-euse *f*); irritable; **'snap·pish·ness** humeur *f* hargneuse; irritabilité *f*; mauvaise humeur *f*; **'snap·py** *see* snappish; F vif (vive *f*); F make it ~! dépêchez-vous!, grouillez-vous!; **'snap·shot 1.** coup *m* lâché sans viser; *phot.* instantané *m*; **2.** prendre un instantané de.

snare [snɛə] **1.** piège *m*; lacet *m*; **2.** prendre au lacet *ou* au piège (*a. fig.*); attraper; **'snar·er** tendeur *m* de lacets.

snarl [snɑːl] **1.** *v/i.* grogner, gronder; *tex.* vriller; *Am.* s'emmêler; *v/t.* emmêler; **2.** grognement *m*, grondement *m*; *tex.* vrillage *m*; *Am.* enchevêtrement *m*; **'~-up** pagaïe *f*; embouteillage *m* (*de voitures*).

snatch [snætʃ] **1.** mouvement *m* pour saisir; morceau *m*; courte période *f*; by ~es par boutades; par courts intervalles; **2.** saisir; se saisir de; empoigner; ~ *at* tâcher de saisir; arracher (qch. à q., *s.th. from* s.o.); ~ *up* saisir.

sneak [sniːk] **1.** *v/i.* se glisser furtivement (dans, *in[to]*; hors de, *out of*); *école:* moucharder (q., *on* s.o.); *v/t.* F chipper; **2.** pied *m* plat; *école:* mouchard *m*; **'sneak·ers** *pl. Am.* F (chaussures *m/pl.* de) tennis *m/pl.*; **'sneak·ing** □ furtif (-ive *f*); servile; dissimulé, inavoué; **sneak-'thief** chapardeur (-euse *f*) *m*; **'sneak·y** F sournois.

sneer [sniə] **1.** ricanement *m*, rire *m* moqueur; sarcasme *m*; **2.** ricaner; se moquer (de, *at*); dénigrer (qch., *at*

s.th.); **'sneer·er** moqueur (-euse *f*) *m*; **'sneer·ing** □ ricaneur (-euse *f*); sarcastique.

sneeze [sniːz] **1.** éternuer; **2.** éternuement *m*.

snib [snib] *porte:* loquet *m*; arrêt *m* de sûreté.

snick·er ['snikə] *see* snigger; hennir (*cheval*).

sniff [snif] **1.** *v/i.* renifler (sur, *at*); flairer (qch., [*at*] s.th.); *v/t.* renifler; humer; flairer; **2.** reniflement *m*; **'sniff·les** F ['sniflz] *pl.* petit rhume *m*; have the ~ être (légèrement) enrhumé; **'sniff·y** F malodorant; dédaigneux (-euse *f*); de mauvaise humeur.

snig·ger ['snigə] rire sous cape (de, *at*); ricaner tout bas.

snip [snip] **1.** coup *m* de ciseaux; petit bout *m*; petite entaille *f*; *sl.* certitude *f*; **2.** couper; détacher (*d'un coup de ciseaux*); poinçonner (*un billet*).

snipe [snaip] **1.** *orn.* bécassine *f*; *coll.* bécassines *f/pl.*; **2.** ✕ tirailler contre; **'snip·er** ✕ canardeur *m*.

snip·pets ['snipits] *pl.* bouts *m/pl.*; *livre:* extraits *m/pl.*; **'snip·py** F fragmentaire; hargneux (-euse *f*).

snitch *sl.* [snitʃ]: ~ *on* s.o. dénoncer q.

sniv·el ['snivl] avoir le nez qui coule; *fig.* pleurnicher; **'sniv·el·(l)ing** qui coule; morveux (-euse *f*) (*personne*); *fig.* pleurnicheur (-euse *f*).

snob [snob] snob *m*, parvenu(e *f*) *m*, poseur (-euse *f*) *m*; **'snob·ber·y** snobisme *m*, morgue *f*; **'snob·bish** □ poseur (-euse *f*); snob *adj./inv.*

snog F [snog] se peloter.

snoop *Am. sl.* [snuːp] **1.** *fig.* ~ *on* épier (q.); **2.** inquisiteur (-euse *f*) *m*; personne *f* indiscrète *ou* curieuse.

snoot·y *Am.* F ['snuːti] arrogant; suffisant.

snooze F [snuːz] **1.** petit somme *m*; **2.** sommeiller; faire un petit somme.

snore [snɔː] **1.** ronflement *m*; **2.** ronfler.

snort [snɔːt] **1.** reniflement *m* (*a. fig.* de dégoût); ⊕ ronflement *m*; *cheval:* ébrouement *m*; **2.** renifler; s'ébrouer (*cheval*); *v/t.* grogner (*une réponse*).

snot *sl.* [snot] morve *f*; **'snot·ty** *sl.* morveux (-euse *f*); *fig.* maussade.

snout [snaut] museau *m*; *porc:* groin *m*.

snow [snou] **1.** neige *f*; *sl.* cocaïne *f*; **2.**

v/i. neiger; *v/t.* saupoudrer (de, with); *sl.* en imposer à (*q.*), impressionner (*q.*); *surt. Am.* F *fig.* be ~ed under être accablé (de, with); ~ed in (*ou* up) pris *ou* bloqué par la neige; '~**ball** 1. boule *f* de neige; 2. lancer des boules de neige; *fig.* faire boule de neige; '~**drift** amas *m* de neige, congère *f*; '~**drop** ♀ perce-neige *f/inv.*; '~**gog·gles** *pl.* (*a pair of*) ~ (des) lunettes *f/pl.* d'alpiniste; ~**mo·bile** ['~məbiːl] autoneige *f*; '~**plough,** *Am.* '~**plow** chasse-neige *m/inv.*; '~**white** blanc(he *f*) comme la neige; '**snow·y** ☐ neigeux (-euse *f*), de neige.

snub [snʌb] 1. remettre (*q.*) à sa place; rembarrer; 2. rebuffade *f*; mortification *f*; '**snub·ber** *mot.* amortisseur *m* à courroie; '**snub-nose** nez *m* retroussé; '**snub-nosed** (au nez) camus.

snuff [snʌf] 1. *chandelle:* mouchure *f*; tabac *m* (à priser); F *up to* ~ degourdi, à la coule; F *give s.o.* ~ laver la tête à q.; 2. (*a. take* ~) priser; moucher; '~**box** tabatière *f*; '**snuff·er** priseur (-euse *f*) *m*; (*a pair of*) ~s *pl.* (des) mouchettes *f/pl.*; **snuf·fle** ['~l] renifler; nasiller; ~ *at* flairer (*qch.*); '**snuff·y** au linge tacheté de tabac; au nez barbouillé de tabac; F *fig.* peu soigné.

snug ☐ [snʌg] confortable; bien au chaud; gentil(le *f*); ⚓ paré; '**snug·ger·y** petite pièce *f* confortable; petit fumoir *m*; *sl.* turne *f*; **snug·gle** ['~l] (se) serrer; *v/i.* se pelotonner (contre *up to*, *into*); ~ *down* se blottir (dans, *in*).

so [sou] ainsi; par conséquent; si, tellement; donc; *I hope* ~ je l'espère bien; *are you tired?* ~ *I am* êtes-vous fatigué?; je le suis en effet; *you are tired,* ~ *am I* vous êtes fatigué, (et) moi aussi; *a mile or* ~ un mille à peu près; ~ *as to* pour *ou* afin de (*inf.*), pour *ou* afin que (*sbj.*); de sorte que (*sbj.*); de façon à (*inf.*); ~ *far* jusqu'ici; ~ *far as I know* autant que je sache.

soak [souk] 1. *v/t.* tremper (dans, *in*); imbiber (de, *in*); F faire payer; ~ *up* (*ou in*) absorber; *v/i.* tremper, s'imbiber (dans, *into*); F boire comme une éponge; 2. trempe *f*; F bain *m*; F ivrogne *m*, biberon(ne

f) *m*; F tombée *f*, *pluie:* arrosage *m*.

so-and-so ['souənsou] machin *m*, chose *m*; Mr. ♀ Monsieur *m* un tel.

soap [soup] 1. savon *m*; F ~ *opera* mélodrame *m* radiodiffusé *ou* télévisé; *soft* ~ savon *m* vert; F flatterie *f*, flagornerie *f*; 2. savonner; '~**boil·er** chaudière *f* à savon; *personne:* savonnier (-ère *f*) *m*; '~**box** caisse *f* à savon; ~ *orator* orateur *m* de carrefour; '~**dish** plateau *m* à savon; '~**suds** *pl.*, *a. sg.* eau *f* de savon; '**soap·y** ☐ savonneux (-euse *f*); qui sent le savon.

soar [sɔː] prendre son essor; s'élever (*a. fig.*); ✈ faire du vol à voile; '**soar·ing** 1. qui s'élève; plané (*vol*); 2. essor *m*; hausse *f*; vol *m* plané.

sob [sɔb] 1. sanglot *m*; 2. sangloter.

so·ber ['soubə] 1. ☐ sobre, modéré; grave; sérieux (-euse *f*); pas ivre; 2. (*souv.* ~ *down*) (se) dégrisser; '**so·ber·ness,** **so·bri·e·ty** [sou-'braiəti] sobriété *f*; sérieux *m*.

sob-stuff F ['sɔbstʌf] sensiblerie *f*, histoire *f* larmoyante.

so-called ['sou'kɔːld] prétendu, ce qu'on est convenu d'appeler.

soc·cer *sp.* ['sɔkə] football *m* association.

so·cia·bil·i·ty [souʃə'biliti] sociabilité *f*; '**so·cia·ble** ☐ 1. sociable; *zo.* sociétaire; 2. *véhicule:* sociable *m*; *meuble:* causeuse *f*; *Am.* soirée *f* amicale.

so·cial ['souʃl] 1. ☐ social (-aux *m/pl.*); ~ *activities pl.* mondanités *f/pl.*; ~ *insurance* assurance *f ou* prévoyance *f* sociale; ~ *insurance stamp* timbre *m* de sécurité sociale; ~ *science* science *f* sociale; ~ *security* aide *f* sociale; *be on* ~ *security* recevoir l'aide sociale; ~ *services pl.* institutions *f/pl.* sociales; 2. F soirée *f*; réunion *f*; '**so·cial·ism** socialisme *m*; '**so·cial·ist** socialiste (*a. su./mf*); **so·cial·ite** F ['souʃəlait] mondain(e *f*) *m*; '**so·cial·ize** rendre social; réunir en société; *pol.* socialiser.

so·ci·e·ty [sə'saiəti] société *f*; association *f*; beau monde *m*.

so·ci·o·log·i·cal [sousiə'lɔdʒikl] sociologique; **so·ci·ol·o·gist** [~-'ɔlədʒist] sociologue *m*; **so·ci·ol·o·gy** sociologie *f*. [intérieure.]

sock[1] [sɔk] chaussette *f*; semelle *f*

sock[2] *sl.* [~] 1. coup *m*, beigne *f*;

give s.o. ~(s pl.) = 2. flanquer une beigne à (q.).

sock·dol·a·ger Am. sl. [sɔk'dɔlədʒə] coup m violent, gnon m; argument m décisif.

sock·er F ['sɔkə] see soccer.

sock·et ['sɔkit] emboîture f (a. os); douille f (a. ⚡); œil: orbite f; dent: alvéole m; ⊕ godet m; ⚡ socle m; cavité f; chandelle: bobèche f.

so·cle ['sɔkl] socle m.

sod [sɔd] 1. gazon m; motte f; poét. terre f; 2. gazonner.

so·da ⚗ ['soudə] soude f; '~-foun-tain siphon m; Am. bar m, débit m (de boissons non alcoolisées).

sod·den ['sɔdn] détrempé; pâteux (-euse f) (pain etc.); (trop long-temps) bouilli; fig. abruti (par la boisson).

so·di·um ⚗ ['soudjəm] sodium m; attr. de soude.

so·ev·er [sou'evə] que ce soi(en)t.

so·fa ['soufə] canapé m.

sof·fit ⌂ ['sɔfit] soffite m; cintre m.

soft [sɔft] 1. □ mou (mol devant une consonne ou un h muet; molle f); doux (douce f); tendre; flasque; F facile; F nigaud; F ~ drink boisson f non alcoolisée; F a ~ thing une bonne affaire f; see soap; 2. adv. douce-ment; sans bruit; 3. F nigaud(e f) m; **soft·en** ['sɔfn] (s')amollir; (s')a-doucir (a. couleurs, a. ⊕ acier); (s')attendrir; (se) radoucir (ton, voix, etc.); v/t. atténuer (des couleurs, la lumière, a. phot. les contours); **soft·ness** ['sɔftnis] douceur f (a. fig.); caractère: mollesse f; F niaiserie f; **'soft-soap** F passer de la pommade à (q.), flatter; **'soft-'spok·en** à la voix douce; **'soft·ware** logiciel m, soft-ware m; **'soft·y** F nigaud(e f) m, niais(e f) m.

sog·gy ['sɔgi] détrempé; lourd (temps); pâteux (-euse f).

soil¹ [sɔil] sol m, terre f, terroir m.

soil² [~] 1. souillure f; tache f; 2. (se) salir; v/t. souiller; '~-pipe descente f (de W.-C.).

so·journ ['sɔdʒəːn] 1. séjour m; 2. séjourner; **'so·journ·er** personne f de passage; hôte(sse f) m.

sol·ace ['sɔləs] 1. consolation f; 2. consoler.

so·lar ['soulə] solaire; ~ battery bat-terie f solaire, photopile f; ~ cell cellule f photovoltaïque; ~ eclipse

éclipse f du soleil; anat. ~ plexus plexus m solaire; ~ system système m solaire, planétaire m.

sold [sould] prét. et p.p. de sell.

sol·der ⊕ ['sɔldə] 1. soudure f; 2. (res)souder; **sol·der·ing-i·ron** ['~riŋaiən] fer m à souder.

sol·dier ['souldʒə] 1. soldat m; 2. (a. go ~ing) faire le métier de soldat; **'sol·dier·like**, **'sol·dier·ly** de soldat; militaire; **sol·dier·ship** ['~ʃip] aptitude f militaire; **'sol·dier·y** militaires m/pl.; péj. solda-tesque f.

sole¹ □ [soul] seul, unique; ~ agent agent m exclusif.

sole² [~] 1. semelle f; pied: plante f; 2. ressemeler.

sole³ icht. [~] sole f.

sol·e·cism ['sɔlisizm] solécisme m; faute f de grammaire.

sol·emn □ ['sɔləm] solennel(le f); sérieux (-euse f); grave; **so·lem·ni-ty** [sə'lemniti] solennité f (a. = fête); gravité f; **sol·em·ni·za·tion** [sɔləmnai'zeiʃn] célébration f, solennisation f; **'sol·em·nize** célé-brer (un mariage); solenniser (une fête); rendre grave.

so·lic·it [sə'lisit] solliciter (qch. de q. s.o. for s.th., s.th. from s.o.); prostituée: raccrocher (un homme); **so·lic·i·ta·tion** sollicitation f; votes: brigue f; prostituée: racolage m; **so-lic·i·tor** ⚖ avoué m, Brit. solicitor m; Am. ♀ placier m; ♀ General conseiller m juridique de la Cou-ronne; **so·lic·it·ous** □ préoccupé (de, about); soucieux (-euse f) (de, of; de inf., to inf.); be ~ about s'inquiéter de; be ~ for avoir (qch.) à cœur; **so·lic·i·tude** [~tju:d] solli-citude f; souci m.

sol·id ['sɔlid] 1. □ solide (a. fig., ♀ angle); plein (acajou, mur, pneu, volume); vif (vive f) (argent); épais(se f); de volume (mesures); ⊕ solidaire (de, with); fig. bon(ne f); fig. ininter-rompu; fig. unanime; surt. Am. □ make o.s. ~ with être bien avec, se mettre sur un bon pied avec; a ~ hour une bonne heure, une pleine heure; ♀ ~ geometry géométrie f dans l'espace; ~ leather cuir m à semelles; ~ rubber caoutchouc m plein; 2. solide m; **sol·i·dar·i·ty** [~'dæriti] solidarité f; **so'lid·i·fy**

sophisticated

[ˌfai] (se) solidifier; v/i. se figer; **so·lid·i·ty** solidité f; ⁉ solidarité f.

so·lil·o·quize [səˈliləkwaiz] se parler à soi-même; faire un soliloque; **so·lil·o·quy** soliloque m, monologue m.

sol·i·taire [ˌsɔliˈtɛə] diamant, a. jeu: solitaire m; cartes: jeu m de patience; **sol·i·tar·y** □ [ˈˌtəri] solitaire, isolé; retiré; ~ confinement prison f cellulaire; **sol·i·tude** [ˈˌtjuːd] solitude f.

so·lo [ˈsoulou] ♩ solo m; cartes: whist m de Gand; ✠ vol m solo; **ˈso·lo·ist** ♩ soliste mf.

sol·stice [ˈsɔlstis] solstice m.

sol·u·bil·i·ty [sɔljuˈbiliti] solubilité f; problème: résolubilité f; **sol·u·ble** [ˈsɔljubl] soluble; résoluble.

so·lu·tion [səˈluːʃn] solution f (a. ⅋, ⚗, ⚘); ⊕ (dis)solution f.

solv·a·ble [ˈsɔlvəbl] soluble; ⅋ a. résoluble; **solve** [sɔlv] résoudre; trouver la solution de; éclaircir (un mystère etc.); **sol·ven·cy** [ˈˌvənsi] solvabilité f; **ˈsol·vent 1.** dissolvant; ✝ solvable; **2.** (dis)solvant m.

som·ber, som·bre □ [ˈsɔmbə] sombre; morne.

some [sʌm, səm] **1.** pron. indéf. certains; quelques-uns, quelques-unes; un peu, en; I need ~ j'en ai besoin; **2.** adj. quelque, quelconque; un certain, une certaine; du, de la, des, quelques; ~ bread du pain; ~ few quelques-uns, quelques-unes; ~ 20 miles une vingtaine de milles; in ~ degree, to ~ extent quelque peu; jusqu'à un certain point; that was ~ meal! c'était un chouette repas!; **3.** adv. quelque, environ; sl. pas mal; he was annoyed ~ il n'était pas mal fâché; **ˈ~·bod·y, ˈ~·one** quelqu'un; **ˈ~·how** de façon ou d'autre; ~ or other d'une manière ou d'une autre.

som·er·sault [ˈsʌməsɔːlt], **som·er·set** [ˈˌset] gymn. saut m périlleux; culbute f; cabriole f; turn ~s faire le saut périlleux; faire des cabrioles.

some...: ~·**thing** [ˈsʌmθiŋ] quelque chose (a. su./m); adv. quelque peu; that is ~ c'est déjà quelque chose; ~ like en forme de; F un vrai ...; **ˈ~·time 1.** adv. autrefois; jadis; **2.** adj. ancien(ne f) (devant su.); ~·**times** [ˈˌz] parfois, quelquefois;

ˈ~·what quelque peu, un peu; assez; **ˈ~·where** quelque part.

som·nam·bu·lism [sɔmˈnæmbjulizm] somnambulisme m, noctambulisme m; **som·nam·bu·list** somnambule mf, noctambule mf.

som·nif·er·ous □ [sɔmˈnifərəs] somnifère, endormant.

som·no·lence [ˈsɔmnoləns] somnolence f, assoupissement m; **ˈsom·no·lent** somnolent, assoupi.

son [sʌn] fils m.

so·nant gramm. [ˈsounənt] (consonne f) sonore.

so·na·ta ♩ [səˈnɑːtə] sonate f.

song [sɔŋ] chant m; chanson f; eccl. cantique m; F for a mere (ou an old) ~ pour une bagatelle, pour rien; **ˈ~·bird** oiseau m chanteur; **ˈ~·book** recueil m de chansons; **ˈ~·hit** succès m; **ˈsong·ster** oiseau m chanteur; chanteur m; **ˈsong·stress** chanteuse f.

son·ic [ˈsɔnik] sonique (vitesse); ~ bang (ou boom) bang m ou détonation f supersonique; ~ barrier mur m du son.

son-in-law [ˈsʌninlɔː], pl. **sons-in-law** gendre m.

son·net [ˈsɔnit] sonnet m.

son·ny F [ˈsʌni] (mon) petit m.

so·nor·i·ty [səˈnɔriti] sonorité f; **so·no·rous** □ [səˈnɔːrəs] sonore; **soˈno·rous·ness** sonorité f.

soon [suːn] bientôt; tôt; vite; de bonne heure; as (ou so) ~ as dès que, aussitôt que; **ˈsoon·er** plus tôt; plutôt; no ~ ... than à peine... que; no ~ said than done sitôt dit, sitôt fait.

soot [sut] **1.** suie f; **2.** couvrir de suie; calaminer (les bougies).

sooth [suːθ]: ✝ in ~ en vérité, vraiment; ~ to say à vrai dire; **soothe** [suːð] calmer, apaiser; **sooth·say·er** [ˈsuːθseiə] devin(eresse f) m.

soot·y □ [ˈsuti] couvert de suie; (noir) de suie; fuligineux (-euse f).

sop [sɔp] **1.** morceau m (de pain etc.) trempé; fig. don m propitiatoire; **2.** tremper; ~ up éponger.

soph·ism [ˈsɔfizm] sophisme m.

soph·ist [ˈsɔfist] sophiste m; **so·phis·tic, so·phis·ti·cal** □ [səˈfistik(l)] sophist(iqu)e; captieux (-euse f) (argument); **soˈphis·ti·cate** [ˌkeit] sophistiquer; falsifier; **soˈphis·ti·cat·ed** sophistiqué, falsifié; blasé; aux goûts compliqués; **soph·ist·ry** ['sɔfistri] sophistique *f*; sophistication *f*; sophismes *m/pl.* **soph·o·more** *Am.* ['sɔfəmɔ:] étudiant(e *f*) *m* de seconde année.

so·po·rif·ic [soupə'rifik] (~ally) soporifique (*a. su./m*), somnifère (*a. su./m*).

sop·ping ['sɔpiŋ] (*a.* ~ wet) trempé; trempé jusqu'aux os (*personne*); **'sop·py** détrempé; *fig.* mou (*mol devant une voyelle ou un h muet*; molle *f*); F fadasse.

so·pran·o ♪ [sə'prɑ:nou] soprano *m*.

sor·cer·er ['sɔ:sərə] sorcier *m*; **'sor·cer·ess** sorcière *f*; **'sor·cer·y** sorcellerie *f*.

sor·did □ ['sɔ:did] sordide (*souv. fig.* = *sale, vil*); ✍ infect; **'sor·did·ness** sordidité *f*; saleté *f*; bassesse *f*.

sore [sɔ:] 1. □ douloureux (-euse *f*); irrité, enflammé; ulcéré; *fig.* cruel(le *f*); chagriné (*personne*), *Am.* F fâché; ~ throat mal *m* de gorge; 2. plaie *f* (*a. fig.*); écorchure *f*; ulcère *m*; **'sore·head** *Am.* F *fig.* rouspéteur *m*; **'sore·ly** *adv.* gravement, vivement; **'sore·ness** sensibilité *f*; *fig.* chagrin *m*.

so·ror·i·ty [sə'rɔriti] communauté *f* religieuse; *univ. Am.* cercle *m* d'étudiantes.

sor·rel¹ ['sɔrəl] 1. saure, alezan (*cheval*); 2. alezan *m*.

sor·rel² ♣ [~] oseille *f*.

sor·row ['sɔrou] 1. douleur *f*, tristesse *f*, chagrin *m*; 2. s'attrister; être affligé; **sor·row·ful** □ ['~ful] triste, attristé; pénible.

sor·ry □ ['sɔri] désolé, fâché, peiné (*de to, at*); *fig.* misérable, pauvre; (*I am*) (*so*) ~! pardon!; *I am* ~ *for you* je vous plains; *we are* ~ *to say* nous regrettons d'avoir à dire...

sort [sɔ:t] 1. sorte *f*, genre *m*, espèce *f*; classe *f*; façon *f*; *people of all* ~s des gens de toutes sortes; *something of the* ~, *that* ~ *of thing* quelque chose de pareil(le *f*); *in some* ~, *I like it*, F *I* ~ *of like it* jusqu'à un certain point je l'aime; *out of* ~s indisposé; de mauvaise humeur; F *he is a good* ~ c'est un brave type; (*a*) ~ *of peace* une paix telle quelle; 2. trier, assortir; ✝ classifier, classer, lotir; ~ *out* séparer (*de, d'avec from*).

sor·tie ✗ ['sɔ:ti:] sortie *f*.

sot [sɔt] ivrogne(sse *f*) *m*; *sl.* soû-

lard(e *f*) *m*; **sot·tish** □ ['sɔtiʃ] d'ivrogne; abruti par l'alcool.

sough [sau] 1. murmure *m*, susurrement *m*; 2. murmurer, susurrer.

sought [sɔ:t] *prét. et p.p. de* seek; **'~-'aft·er** recherché.

soul [soul] âme *f*; F *the* ~ *of la* premier mobile (*d'une entreprise*); **'soul·less** □ sans âme; (*a.* **'soul·de·stroy·ing**) abrutissant.

sound¹ □ [saund] sain; en bon état; bon(ne *f*); *fig.*, *a.* △ solide; droit; profond (*sommeil*); ✝ bon(ne *f*); ⚖ valable, légal (-aux *m/pl.*).

sound² [~] 1. son *m*, bruit *m*; *phys.* acoustique *f*; ~ *barrier* mur *m* du son; ~ *effects pl.* bruitage *m*; ~ *film* film *m* sonore; ~ *wave* onde *f* sonore; 2. *v/i.* (ré)sonner; retentir; paraître; avoir le son de; *v/t.* sonner; faire retentir; prononcer (*les R etc.*); chanter (*des louanges*); ✍ ausculter (*la poitrine*); ✗ ~ *the retreat* sonner la retraite.

sound³ [~] *géog.* détroit *m*; bras *m* de mer; *icht.* vessie *f* natatoire; *géog. the* ♀ *le Sund m.*

sound⁴ [~] 1. ✍ sonde *f*; 2. ✍ sonder (*a. fig.*, *a.* ⚓); ~ *s.o. out* sonder q. (*relativement à, about*).

sound·ing ⚓ ['saundiŋ] sondage *m*; ~s *pl.* sondes *f/pl.*, fonds *m/pl.*

sound(·ing)-board ['saund(iŋ)bɔ:d] chaire *etc.*: abat-voix *m/inv.*; ♪ orgue: tamis *m*; *piano*: table *f* d'harmonie.

sound·less □ ['saundlis] muet(te *f*).

sound·ness ['saundnis] bon état *m*; solidité *f* (*a. fig.*).

sound...: **'~-proof** 1. insonorisé, insonore; 2. insonoriser; **'~-track** piste *f ou* bande *f* sonore.

soup¹ [su:p] potage *m*; soupe *f*.

soup² *Am. sl.* [~] 1. cheval-vapeur (*pl.* chevaux-vapeur) *m*; 2.: ~ *up* doper; *mot.* ~*ed up engine* moteur *m* comprimé.

sour ['sauə] 1. □ aigre, acide; vert (*fruit*); *fig.* revêche; aigre; acariâtre; 2. *v/t.* aigrir (*a. fig.*); *v/i.* surir; (s')aigrir (*a. fig.*).

source [sɔ:s] source *f*; *fig.* origine *f*; ~ *language* langue *f* de départ.

sour·dough *Am.* ['sauədou] vétéran *m* (*des placers d'Alaska*).

sour·ish □ ['sauəriʃ] aigrelet(te *f*); **'sour·ness** aigreur *f* (*a. fig.*); *fig.* humeur *f* revêche; **'sour·puss** ['sauəpus] grincheux (-euse *f*) *m*.

souse [saus] **1.** *v/t.* plonger; tremper (d'eau, *with water*); *cuis.* faire mariner; *v/i.* mariner; faire un plongeon; **~d** *sl.* ivre, F gris, parti; **2.** immersion *f*; plongon *m*; trempée *f*; *cuis.* marinade *f*; *Am.* ivrogne *m*; **3.** plouf!, floc!

south [sauθ] **1.** *su.* sud *m*; midi *m*; **2.** *adj.* du sud; méridional (-aux *m/pl.*); **3.** *adv.* au sud, vers le sud; '**~bound** en direction du Sud, allant vers le Sud.

south-east ['sauθ'iːst] **1.** sud-est *m*; **2.** (*a.* **south-'east-ern**) du sud-est.

south·er·ly ['sʌðəli], **south·ern** ['~ən] (du) sud; du midi; méridional (-aux *m/pl.*); '**south·ern·er** habitant(e *f*) *m* du sud; *Am.* ♀ sudiste *mf*.

south·ern·most ['sʌðənmoust] le plus au sud.

south·ing ['sauðiŋ] ♐ chemin *m* sud; *astr.* passage *m* au méridien.

south·paw *Am.* ['sauθpɔː] *baseball*: gaucher *m*.

south·ward ['sauθwəd] **1.** *adj.* au *ou* du sud; **2.** *adv.* (*a.* **south·wards** ['~dz]) vers le sud.

south...: '**~west 1.** *su.* sud-ouest *m*; **2.** *adv.* vers le sud-ouest; **3.** *adj.* (*a.* **~·'west·er·ly**, **~·'west·ern**) (du) sud-ouest; '**~·'west·er** (vent *m* du) sud-ouest *m*; ♐ suroît *m* (= *chapeau imperméable*).

sou·ve·nir ['suːvəniə] souvenir *m*, mémento *m*.

sov·er·eign ['sɔvrin] **1.** □ souverain (*a. fig.*), suprême; **2.** souverain(e *f*) *m*; monarque *m*; *monnaie anglaise*: souverain *m* (= *pièce de 20 shillings*); '**sov·er·eign·ty** souveraineté *f*.

so·vi·et ['souviət] Soviet *m*; *attr.* soviétique.

sow¹ [sau] *zo.* truie *f*; ⊕ gueuse *f* des mères; (*a.* **~·channel**) mère-gueuse (*pl.* mères-gueuses) *f*.

sow² [sou] [*irr.*] semer (de, *with*); ensemencer (*la terre*) (en blé, *with wheat*); '**sow·er** semeur (-euse *f*) *m* (*a. fig.*); **sown** [soun] *p.p.* de **sow**².

sox [sɔks] *pl. see* **sock**¹.

so·y(a) ♀ ['sɔi(ə)] (*a.* **~** *bean*) soya *m*.

spa [spɑː] source *f* minérale; ville *f* d'eau.

space [speis] **1.** espace *m*, *typ. f*; intervalle *m* (*a. temps*); étendue *f*, surface *f*; F place *f*; **2.** (*a.* **~** *out*) espacer (*a. typ*); échelonner (*des*

troupes, des versements); **3.** spatial (-aux *m/pl.*), interplanétaire; **~** *flight* vol *m* spatial; vols *m/pl.* spatiaux; **~** *lab* laboratoire *m* spatial; **~** *shuttle* navette *f*; **~** *travel* voyages *m/pl.* spatiaux *ou* dans l'espace; **~** *weapons f/pl.* armes *f/pl.* spatiales; '**~·craft**, '**~·ship** vaisseau *m* spatial.

spa·cious □ ['speiʃəs] spacieux (-euse *f*), vaste; ample.

spade [speid] **1.** bêche *f*; *call a* **~** *a* **~** appeler les choses par leur nom; *usu.* **~s** *pl. cartes*: pique *m*; **2.** bêcher; '**~·work** travaux *m/pl.* à la bêche *ou fig.* préliminaires.

span¹ [spæn] **1.** *main*: empan *m*; court espace *m* de temps; △ portée *f*, largeur *f*; *bras, ailes, a.* ✈ envergure *f*; *Am.* paire *f*; **2.** franchir, enjamber; *fig.* embrasser; mesurer à l'empan.

span² [~] *prét.* de **spin 1.**

span·gle ['spæŋgl] **1.** paillette *f*; **2.** pailleter (de, *with*); *fig.* parsemer (de, *with*).

Span·iard ['spænjəd] Espagnol(e *f*) *m*.

span·iel ['spænjəl] épagneul *m*.

Span·ish ['spæniʃ] **1.** espagnol; d'Espagne; **2.** *ling.* espagnol *m*; *the* **~** *pl.* les Espagnols *m/pl.*

spank F [spæŋk] **1.** *v/t.* fesser; *v/i.* **~** *along* aller bon train; **2.** claque *f* sur le derrière; '**spank·er** ♐ brigantine *f*; '**spank·ing 1.** □ qui va bon train; vigoureux (-euse *f*); F de premier ordre; *sl.* épatant; **2.** F fessée *f*.

span·ner ⊕ ['spænə] clef *f* (à écrous); *fig. throw a* **~** *in the works* mettre des bâtons dans les roues.

spar¹ [spɑː] ♐ espar *m*; ✈ longeron *m*.

spar² [~] faire mine de vouloir boxer (q., *at s.o.*); boxer (*coqs*); *se battre* (*coqs*); *fig.* argumenter (avec, *with*); *box.* **~·ring** *partner* sparringpartner *m*, partenaire *m* d'entraînement.

spar³ *min.* [~] spath *m*.

spare [spɛə] **1.** □ frugal (-aux *m/pl.*); maigre; sec (sèche *f*) (*personne*); disponible, de reste; de réserve, de rechange, de secours; **~** *hours* (heures *f/pl.* de) loisir *m*; **~** *room* chambre *f* d'ami; **~** *time* temps *m* disponible; **2.** ⊕ pièce *f* de rechange; **3.** *v/t.* épargner, ménager;

se passer de; prêter, donner; faire grâce à (*q.*); respecter; *enough and to* ~ plus qu'il n'en faut (de, *of*); *v/i.* épargner, faire des économies; **'spare·ness** minceur *f*; maigreur *f*; frugalité *f*; **spare·rib** *cuis.* ['~rib] côte *f* de porc.

spar·ing □ ['spɛəriŋ] ménager (-ère *f*) (de *in*, *of*); économe; frugal (-aux *m/pl.*); limité (*emploi*); **'spar·ing·ness** épargne *f*; frugalité *f*.

spark[1] [spɑːk] **1.** étincelle *f* (*a. fig.*); F ♀s radiotélégraphiste *m*; **2.** *v/i.* émettre des étincelles; cracher (*dynamo*); *v/t.* faire éclater avec une étincelle électrique.

spark[2] [~] élégant *m*; beau cavalier *m*; joyeux compagnon *m*.

spark(·ing)-plug *mot.* ['spɑːk(iŋ)-plʌg] bougie *f*.

spar·kle ['spɑːkl] **1.** étincelle *f*; éclat *m*; *fig.* vivacité *f* d'esprit; **2.** étinceler, scintiller, chatoyer (*bijou*); pétiller (*esprit*, *feu*, *yeux*, *vin*); *sparkling wine* vin *m* mousseux; **spar·klet** ['~it] petite étincelle *f*; *eau de seltz:* sparklet *m*.

spar·row *orn.* ['spærou] moineau *m*, passereau *m*; **'~-hawk** *orn.* épervier *m*.

sparse □ [spɑːs] épars, clairsemé.

spasm ♂ ['spæzm] spasme *m*; *fig.* accès *m*; **spas·mod·ic, spas·mod·i·cal** □ [~'mɔdik(l)] spasmodique; involontaire; *fig.* par saccades; **spas·tic** ['spæstik] **1.** (~*ally*) spasmodique; **2.** paraplégique (spasmodique) *mf*.

spat[1] [spæt] *huîtres:* frai *m*.

spat[2] [~] guêtre *f* de ville.

spat[3] [~] *prét. et p.p.* de *spit*[2] 2.

spatch·cock ['spætʃkɔk] *cuis.* faire cuire à la crapaudine; *fig.* faire une intervention dans (*une dépêche*) (à la dernière minute).

spate [speit] crue *f*; *fig.* déluge *m*.

spa·tial □ ['speiʃl] spatial (-aux *m/pl.*).

spat·ter ['spætə] éclabousser (de, *with*); **spat·ter·dash** † ['~dæʃ] guêtre *f*.

spat·u·la ['spætjulə] spatule *f*; *cuis.* gâche *f*.

spav·in *vét.* ['spævin] éparvin *m*.

spawn ♂ [spɔːn] **1.** frai *m*, œufs *m/pl.*; *fig. usu. péj.* progéniture *f*; **2.** *v/i.* frayer; *péj.* se multiplier; naître (de, *from*); *v/t. péj.* donner naissance à; **'spawn·er** poisson *m* qui fraye; **'spawn·ing** (acte *m* ou époque *f* du) frai *m*.

speak [spiːk] [*irr.*] *v/i.* parler (*a. fig.* = *retentir*); faire un discours; ♩ sonner; *téléph.* Brown *~ing!* ici Brown!; ~ *out* parler à haute voix; parler franchement; ~ *to* parler à *ou* avec; ~ *up* parler plus fort *ou* haut; ~ *up!* (parlez) plus fort!; *that* ~*s well for him* cela est tout à son honneur; *v/t.* dire (*qch.*); parler (*une langue*); exprimer; faire (*un éloge*); témoigner de; **'~-eas·y** *Am. sl.* bar *m* clandestin; **'speak·er** parleur (-euse *f*) *m*; interlocuteur (-trice *f*) *m*; orateur *m*; *radio:* haut-parleur *m*; *parl.* Président *m*.

speak·ing ['spiːkiŋ] parlant (*a. fig. portrait*); expressif (-ive *f*); *be on* ~ *terms with* se connaître assez pour se parler; **'~-trum·pet** porte-voix *m/inv.*

spear [spiə] **1.** lance *f*; *chasse:* épieu *m*; javelot *m*; *fig.* ~ *side* côté *m* paternel *ou* mâle; **2.** frapper *ou* tuer d'un coup de lance (*ou une bête:* d'épieu); **'~-head** pointe *f* de lance; *fig.* pointe *f*.

spec † *sl.* [spek] spéculation *f*.

spe·cial ['speʃl] **1.** □ spécial (-aux *m/pl.*); particulier (-ère *f*); *journ.* ~ *correspondent* envoyé(e *f*) *m* spécial(e); **2.** (*ou* ~ *constable*) agent *m* de police suppléant (= *citoyen assermenté*); (*ou* ~ *edition*) édition *f* spéciale; (*ou* ~ *train*) train *m* spécial; *Am. magasin:* ordre *m* exprès; *Am.* plat *m* du jour; *restaurant:* spécialité *f* de la maison; **spe·cial·ist** ['~ʃəlist] spécialiste *mf*; **spe·ci·al·i·ty** [speʃi'æliti] spécialité *f* (*a.* †); particularité *f*, caractéristique *f*; **spe·cial·ize** ['speʃəlaiz] *v/t.* particulariser; désigner *ou* adapter à un but spécial; *v/i.* se spécialiser (dans, *in*); *biol.* se différencier; **spe·cial·ty** ['~ʃlti] *see speciality*; ⚖ contrat *m* formel sous seing privé.

spe·cie ['spiːʃiː] monnaie *f* métallique; espèces *f/pl.* (sonnantes).

spe·cies ['spiːʃiːz] *sg. ou. pl.* espèce *f* (*a. eccl.*); genre *m*, sorte *f*.

spe·cif·ic [spi'sifik] **1.** (~*ally*) spécifique; précis; *phys.* ~ *gravity* pesan-

spherical

teur *f* spécifique; ⚐ ~ *performance* contrat: exécution *f* intégrale; 2. ⚙ spécifique *m* (contre, *for*).

spec·i·fi·ca·tion [spesifi'keiʃn] spécification *f*; △ cahier *m* des charges; ⚐ description *f* (*de brevet*); **spec·i·fy** ['~fai] spécifier, déterminer; préciser.

spec·i·men ['spesimin] exemple *m*, spécimen *m*; échantillon *m*.

spe·cious ☐ ['spi:ʃəs] spécieux (-euse *f*); trompeur (-euse *f*); '**spe·cious·ness** spéciosité *f*; apparence *f* trompeuse.

speck [spek] 1. graine *f*; point *m*; tache *f*; *fig.* brin *m*; 2. moucheter, tacheter; **speck·le** ['~kl] 1. moucheture *f*; *see* speck 1; 2. *see* speck 2.

specs F [speks] *pl.* lunettes *f/pl.*

spec·ta·cle ['spektəkl] spectacle *m*; (*a pair of*) ~s *pl.* (des) lunettes *f/pl.*; '**spec·ta·cled** qui porte des lunettes; à lunettes.

spec·tac·u·lar ☐ [spek'tækjulə] 1. spectaculaire; impressionnant; 2. *Am.* F revue *f* à grand spectacle.

spec·ta·tor [spek'teitə] spectateur (-trice *f*) *m*.

spec·tral ☐ ['spektrəl] spectral (-aux *m/pl.*) (*a. opt.*); spec·ter, *Brit.* **spec·tre** ['~tə] fantôme *m*, spectre *m*; **spec·trum** *opt.* ['~trəm] spectre *m*.

spec·u·late ['spekjuleit] spéculer (*a.* ♰), méditer (sur, [*up*]on); ♰ *a.* jouer; **spe·cu·la·tion** spéculation *f* (*a.* ♰), méditation *f* (sur, [*up*]on); entreprise *f* spéculative; **spec·u·la·tive** ☐ ['~lətiv] spéculatif (-ive *f*) (*a.* ♰); contemplatif (-ive *f*); théorique; '**spec·u·la·tor** penseur *m*; ♰ spéculateur *m*; ♰ agioteur *m*.

spec·u·lum ['spekjuləm] ⚙ spéculum *m*; *opt.* miroir *m*.

sped [sped] *prét. et p.p. de* speed 2.

speech [spi:tʃ] parole *f*, -s *f/pl.*; langue *f*; discours *m*; ~ *defect* défaut *m* d'élocution; '**~-day** *école:* distribution *f* des prix; **speech·i·fy** *péj.* ['~ifai] pérorer, *sl.* laïusser; '**speech·less** ☐ muet(te *f*).

speed [spi:d] 1. vitesse *f* (*a.* ⊕, *mot., etc.*); marche *f*; hâte *f*; ~ *control* réglage *m* de la vitesse; ~ *trap* piège *m* de police (pour contrôle de vitesse); *good* ~! bonne chance!; 2. [*irr.*] *v/i.* se hâter, se presser; aller *etc.* vite; † *a. poét.* réussir; *no* ~*ing!* vitesse *f* limi-

tée!; *v/t.* hâter, accélérer; † expédier, souhaiter le bon voyage à; ~ *up* accélérer; *mot.* mettre en vitesse; '**~-boat** hors-bord *m/inv.*; '**~-cop** motard *m*; '**speed·i·ness** rapidité *f*; promptitude *f*; **speed lim·it** vitesse *f* maxima; vitesse *f* limitée; '**speed-mer·chant** *mot.* chauffard *m*; **speed·om·e·ter** *mot.* [spi'dɔmitə] compteur *m*, indicateur *m* de vitesse; '**speed·way** *Am.* autostrade *f*; *Am. sp.* (piste *f* d')autodrome *m*; '**speed-well** ♀ véronique *f*; '**speed·y** ☐ rapide, prompt.

spell[1] [spel] temps *m*, période *f*; ⊕ tour *m* (de travail).

spell[2] [~] 1. charme *m*, incantation *f*; 2. [*irr.*] épeler (*de vive voix*); écrire, orthographier; *fig.* signifier; ~ *out* lire péniblement; épeler; '**~-bind·er** *Am.* beau diseur *m*; '**~-bound** *fig.* fasciné, charmé; '**spell·er:** *he is a bad* ~ il ne sait pas l'orthographe.

spell·ing ['spelin] épellation *f*; orthographe *f*; '**~-bee** *surt. Am.* concours *m* d'orthographe; '**~-book** syllabaire *m*.

spelt[1] [spelt] *prét. et p.p. de* spell[2] 2.

spelt[2] ♀ épeautre *m*.

spel·ter ['speltə] zinc *m*.

spen·cer ['spensə] *cost.* spencer *m*.

spend [spend] [*irr.*] *v/t.* dépenser (*de l'argent*) (en, à; pour on), *péj.* dissiper (pour, on); employer, passer (*le temps*), *péj.* perdre; épuiser (*des forces*); ~ *o.s.* s'épuiser; ~*ing money* argent *m* de poche; *v/i.* dépenser de l'argent; '**spend·er** personne *f* qui dépense; *péj.* dépensier (-ère *f*) *m*.

spend·thrift ['spendθrift] dépensier (-ère *f*) *m* (*a. attr.*).

spent [spent] 1. *prét. et p.p. de* spend; 2. épuisé (*personne, a.* 🐑 *acide*); mort (*balle*), vide (*cartouche*); écoulé (*jour*); apaisé (*orage*).

sperm *physiol.* [spə:m] semence *f* (*des mâles*); **sper·ma·ce·ti** [~ə'seti] spermacéti *m*; blanc *m* de baleine; **sper·ma·to·zo·on** *biol.* [~əto-'zouɔn], *pl.* **-zo·a** [~'zouə] spermatozoïde *m*.

spew *sl.* [spju:] *vt/i.* vomir.

sphere [sfiə] sphère *f* (*a. fig. d'activité, d'influence, etc.*); *fig.* domaine *m*; *fig.* milieu *m*; **spher·i·cal** ☐ ['sferikl] sphérique, en forme de sphère.

sphinc·ter *anat.* ['sfiŋktə] sphincter *m*, orbiculaire *m*.

spice [spais] **1.** épice *f*; *fig.* soupçon *m*, grain *m*, nuance *f*; **2.** épicer (*a. fig.*); **spic·er·y** ['⁓əri] épices *f/pl.* [épicé; *fig.* piquant *m*.\
spic·i·ness ['spaisinis] goût *m*\

spick and span ['spikən'spæn] propre comme un sou neuf; tiré à quatre épingles (*personne*).

spic·y □ ['spaisi] épicé (*a. fig.*); aromatique; *fig.* piquant.

spi·der *zo.* ['spaidə] araignée *f*; ⁓'s web toile *f* d'araignée.

spiel *Am. sl.* [spi:l] discours *m*, allocution *f*; *sl.* laïus *m*.

spiff·y *sl.* ['spifi] élégant; pimpant.

spig·ot ['spigət] *tonneau*: fausset *m*; *robinet*: clef *f*.

spike [spaik] **1.** pointe *f*; *fil barbelé*: piquant *m*; clou *m* à large tête; ⁊ *blé*: épi *m*; ⁊ (*a. ⁓-lavender*) spic *m*; **2.** clouer; ⚔ enclouer (*un canon*); *fig.* damer le pion à (*q.*); armer de pointes; **spike·nard** ['⁓nɑ:d] nard *m* (indien); **'spik·y** □ à pointe(s) aiguë(s); armé de pointes.

spill [spil] **1.** [*irr.*] *v/t.* répandre (*a. le sang*); renverser; F désarçonner (*un cavalier*); *Am.* dire; *v/i.* se répandre; s'écouler; **2.** F culbute *f*, chute *f* (*de cheval etc.*).

spill·way ['spilwei] passe-déversoir (*pl.* passes-déversoirs) *f*.

spilt [spilt] *prét. et p.p. de* spill *1*; *cry over* ⁓ *milk* lamenter ce qu'on ne pourrait changer.

spin [spin] **1.** [*irr.*] *v/t.* filer; faire tourner (*a. une toupie*); *fig.* raconter (*une histoire*); ⊕ centrifuger (*le métal*); *v/i.* tourner; (*a. ⁓ round*) tournoyer; ✈ faire la vrille; ⁓ *along* filer; ⁓ (*a*)*round* se retourner vivement (*personne*); *send s.o.* ⁓*ning* faire chanceler q.; **2.** tournoiement *m*, ✈ vrille *f*; *cricket*: effet *m*; F *go for a* ⁓ se balader en auto.

spin·ach ⁊ ['spinidʒ] épinard *m*; *cuis.* épinards *m/pl.*

spi·nal ['spainl] vertébral (*-aux m/pl.*); ⁓ *column* colonne *f* vertébrale; ⁓ *cord* (*ou marrow*) moelle *f* épinière; ⁓ *curvature* déviation *f* de la colonne vertébrale.

spin·dle ['spindl] fuseau *m*; ⊕ arbre *m*; **'spin·dly** long(ue *f*) et grêle.

spin·drift ['spindrift] *courant*: embruns *m/pl.*

spin-dry ['spindrai] essorer à la machine.

spine [spain] épine *f*; *homme*: épine *f* dorsale; *géog.* arête *f*; *livre*: dos *m*; **'spine·less** sans épines; *fig.* mou (mol *devant une voyelle ou h muet*; molle *f*).

spin·ner ['spinə] fileur (-euse *f*) *m*; machine *f ou* métier *m* à filer.

spin·ney ['spini] bosquet *m*, petit bois *m*.

spin·ning...: ⁓**-jen·ny** ⊕ ['spiniŋ-'dʒeni] machine *f* à filer; **'⁓-mill** filature *f*; **'⁓-wheel** rouet *m*.

spin-off ['spinɔf] sous-produit *m*; avantage *m* supplémentaire.

spin·ster ['spinstə] fille *f* (*non mariée*); *p.ext.* vieille fille *f*; *admin.* célibataire *f*.

spin·y ['spaini] épineux (-euse *f*); ⁊ spinifère.

spi·ra·cle ['spaiərəkl] évent *m*.

spi·rae·a ⁊ [spai'riə] spirée *f*.

spi·ral ['spaiərəl] **1.** □ spiral (*-aux m/pl.*); spiralé; en spirale; spiroïdal (*-aux m/pl.*) (*mouvement*); en boudin (*ressort*); *zo.* cochléaire; **2.** spirale *f*, hélice *f*; tour *m ou* ✈ montée *f* etc. en spirale; *fig. prix*: montée *f* en flèche; **3.** former une spirale; monter *ou* descendre en spirale.

spire [spaiə] *église, arbre*: flèche *f*.

spir·it ['spirit] **1.** esprit *m*, âme *f*; *fig.* élan *m*, entrain *m*, ardeur *f*; courage *m*; alcool *m*; ⚗ *hist.* esprit *m*; *mot.* essence *f*; ⁓s *pl.* spiritueux *m/pl.*; liqueurs *f/pl.* fortes; *pharm.* alcoolat *m*; ⁓ *of wine* esprit *m* de vin; *in (high)* ⁓s en train; *en verve; in low* ⁓s abattu; accablé; tout triste; **2.** : ⁓ *away* (*ou off*) enlever, faire disparaître; F escamoter; ⁓ *up* encourager.

spir·it·ed □ ['spiritid] animé, vif (vive *f*); plein d'entrain; fougueux (-euse *f*); *low-*⁓ abattu; **'spir·it·ed·ness** ardeur *f*, feu *m*; *cheval*: fougue *f*.

spir·it·ism ['spiritizm] *métapsychisme*: spiritisme *m*; **'spir·it·ist** spirite *mf* (*a. adj.*).

spir·it·less □ ['spiritlis] abattu; inanimé; sans vie (*a. fig.*); mou (mol *devant une voyelle ou un h muet*; molle *f*).

spir·it·u·al ['spiritjuəl] **1.** □ spirituel(le *f*); immatériel(le *f*); **2.** chant *m* religieux (*des nègres aux É.-U.*);

'spir·it·u·al·ism *phls.* spiritualisme *m*; *métapsychisme*: spiritisme *m*; spir·it·u·al·i·ty [ˌⁿæliti] spiritualité *f*; spir·it·u·al·ize ['ˌⁿəlaiz] spiritualiser.

spir·it·u·ous ['spiritjuəs] spiritueux (-euse *f*), alcoolique.

spirt [spəːt] 1. *v/t.* faire jaillir; *v/i.* jaillir, gicler; *see spurt 1*; 2. (re)jaillissement *m*; jet *m*; *see spurt 2.*

spit¹ [spit] 1. *cuis.* broche *f*; *géog.* langue *f* de sable, pointe *f* de terre; 2. embrocher (*a. fig.*).

spit² [ˌⁿ] 1. crachat *m*; salive *f*; F *be the very ⁿ of s.o.* être q. tout craché; 2. [*irr.*] *v/i.* cracher (*a. chat, plume*); (*a. ⁿ with rain*) crachiner; *ⁿ at* (*ou upon*) cracher sur; *v/t.* (*a. ⁿ out*) cracher.

spit³ [ˌⁿ] profondeur *f* de fer de bêche; bêche *f* pleine.

spite [spait] 1. dépit *m*, pique *f*; rancune *f*; *in ⁿ of* malgré; 2. contrarier, vexer; spite·ful □ ['ˌⁿful] rancunier (-ère *f*); méchant; 'spite·ful·ness rancune *f*; méchanceté *f*.

spit·fire ['spitfaiə] rageur (-euse *f*) *m*.

spit·tle ['spitl] salive *f*, crachat *m*.

spit·toon [spi'tuːn] crachoir *m*.

spiv *sl.* [spiv] parasite *m*; profiteur *m*.

splash [splæʃ] 1. éclaboussement *m*; éclaboussure *f*; *vague*: clapotement *m*; *sl.* esbroufe *f*; F *make a ⁿ* faire sensation; 2. *v/t.* éclabousser (de, with); tacher (de, with); *v/i.* jaillir; clapoter; barboter; cracher (*robinet*); 'ⁿ-board garde-boue *m/inv.*; *métall.* parapluie *m*; plongeur *m* (*de tête de bielle*); 'ⁿ-down amerissage *m*; 'splash-leath·er pare-boue *m/inv.*; 'splash·y □ bourbeux (-euse *f*); barbouillé (*dessin etc.*).

splay [splei] 1. évasement *m*; 2. évasé; tourné en dehors (*pied*); 3. *v/t.* évaser; ⊕ chanfreiner; tourner en dehors; *v/i.* s'évaser.

splay·foot ['spleifut] pied *m* plat.

spleen [spliːn] *anat.* rate *f*; *fig.* spleen *m*, humeur *f* noire; spleen·ful ['ˌⁿful], 'spleen·y atrabilaire; de mauvaise humeur.

splen·did □ ['splendid], splen·dif·er·ous [ˌⁿ'difərəs] splendide, magnifique; F épatant; splen·do(u)r ['ˌⁿdə] splendeur *f*; éclat *m*.

sple·net·ic [spli'netik] 1. (*a.* sple·'net·i·cal □ [ˌⁿkl]) splénique (*a.* ⁂), atrabilaire; 2. hypocondriaque *mf*.

splice [splais] 1. ligature *f*; ⊕ enture *f* (*cricket: du manche de la batte*); 2. ⊕ enter; *cin.* réparer; épisser; *sl.* marier.

splint ⁂ [splint] 1. éclisse *f*; 2. éclisser.

splin·ter ['splintə] 1. éclat *m*; *os*: esquille *f*; 2. *v/t.* briser; *v/i.* voler en éclats; se fendre; 'ⁿ-bone *anat.* péroné *m*; 'splin·ter·less se brisant sans éclats (*verre*).

split [split] 1. fente *f*, fissure *f*; *fig.* scission *f*; F *do the ⁿs* faire le grand écart; 2. fendu; 3. [*irr.*] *v/t.* fendre; déchirer; partager; couper en deux; *ⁿ hairs* couper un cheveu en quatre; *ⁿ one's sides with laughing* se tordre de rire; *ⁿ up* fractionner; *v/i.* se fendre; éclater; *fig.* se diviser; *sl.* filer, ficher le camp (= *s'en aller*); *sl.* *ⁿ on* dénoncer (*q.*); F cafarder; 'split·ting qui (se) fend; F fou (fol *devant une voyelle ou un h muet*; folle *f*), affreux (-euse *f*).

splotch [splɔtʃ] tache *f*.

splurge [spləːdʒ] *Am.* épate *f*; esbroufe *f*; grosse averse *f*.

splut·ter ['splʌtə] *see sputter*; *v/i.* bredouiller; cracher; ⚞ bafouiller (*moteur*).

spoil [spɔil] 1. *souv.* *ⁿs pl.* butin *m* (*a. fig.*); *fig.* profit *m*; *surt. Am. pol.* *ⁿs system* octroi *m* des places à ses adhérents (*en arrivant au pouvoir*); 2. [*irr.*] *v/t.* gâter (*a. un enfant*); piller; dépouiller (de, of); abîmer; couper (*l'appétit*); *v/i.* se gâter; s'altérer; *ⁿ for a fight* brûler du désir de se battre; 'spoil·er spoliateur (-trice *f*) *m*; gâcheur (-euse *f*) *m*; spoils·man *Am. pol.* ['ˌⁿzmən] chacal (*pl.* -s) *m*; 'spoil·sport trouble-fête *mf/inv.*

spoilt [spɔilt] *prét. et p.p. de spoil 2.*

spoke¹ [spouk] *prét. et p.p. de speak.*

spoke² [ˌⁿ] rayon *m*; *échelle*: échelon *m*; bâton *m* (*a. fig.*); ⚓ poignée *f*.

spo·ken ['spoukən] *p.p. de speak.*

spokes·man ['spouksmən] porteparole *m/inv.*; orateur *m*.

spo·li·a·tion [spouli'eiʃn] spoliation *f*, dépouillement *m*; pillage *m*.

spon·dee ['spɔndiː] spondée *m*.

sponge [spʌndʒ] 1. éponge *f*; *cuis.* pâte *f* molle; *throw up the ⁿ box.* jeter l'éponge; *fig.* abandonner (la partie); **2.** *v/t.* nettoyer *ou* laver avec une éponge; ~ *up* éponger; *v/i.* vivre aux crochets (de q., *on* s.o.); F écornifler; **'~-bag** sac *m* de toilette; **'~-'cake** gâteau *m* de Savoie; baba *m* (*au rhum etc.*); **'spong·er** *fig.* écornifleur (-euse *f*) *m*; parasite *m.*

spon·gi·ness ['spʌndʒinis] spongiosité *f*; **'spon·gy** spongieux (-euse *f*).

spon·sor ['spɔnsə] **1.** garant *m*, caution *f*; *eccl.*, *club*: parrain *m*, marraine *f*; *be a* ~ *to radio*: offrir (*un programme*); **2.** être le garant de; prendre en charge; *radio*: offrir (*un programme*); financer; **spon·sor·ship** ['~ʃip] parrainage *m.*

spon·ta·ne·i·ty [spɔntə'ni:iti] spontanéité *f*; **spon·ta·ne·ous** □ [~'teinjəs] spontané; volontaire; automatique; ♀ qui pousse à l'état sauvage; ~ *combustion* inflammation *f* spontanée; auto-allumage *m.*

spoof F [spu:f] **1.** mystification *f*; blague(s) *f(pl.)*; **2.** mystifier; raconter des blagues (à); faire marcher.

spook F [spu:k] **1.** revenant *m*; **2.** hanter; effrayer; **'spook·y** F de spectres, de revenants (*histoire*); qui donne le frisson; lugubre.

spool [spu:l] **1.** bobine *f*; **2.** bobiner.

spoon [spu:n] **1.** cuiller *f*, cuillère *f*; F amoureux *m* d'une sentimentalité exagérée; *golf*: spoon *m*; *sl.* be ~*s on* avoir un béguin pour (*q.*); **2.** manger *ou* ramasser *ou* servir *etc.* avec une cuiller; *sl.* faire le galant auprès de (*q.*); **'~-drift** embrun *m*; 'spoon·er·ism contrepèterie *f*; **'spoon-feed** *fig.* mâcher la besogne à; **spoon·ful** ['~ful] cuillerée *f*; **'spoon-meat** aliment *m* liquide; **'spoon·y** □ F amoureux (-euse *f*) (de, on).

spo·rad·ic [spə'rædik] (~*ally*) *fig.* isolé, rare; ♂, *zo.* sporadique.

spore ♀ [spɔ:] spore *f.*

sport [spɔ:t] **1.** sport *m*; jeu *m*; divertissement *m*; *fig.* jouet *m*; *fig.* moquerie *f*; ♀, *biol.* type *m* anormal; *sl.* (*a good* ~) chic type *m*; **2.** *v/i.* jouer; se divertir; ♀, *biol.* produire une variété anormale; *v/t.* F. porter; étaler; *univ. sl.* ~ *one's oak* défendre sa porte; s'enfermer à double porte; **'sport·ing** □ de sport; sportif (-ive *f*); amateur de la chasse; **'spor·tive** □ folâtre,

badin, enjoué; **sports-ground** ['~sgraund] terrain *m* de jeux; stade *m*; **sports·man** ['~smən] amateur *m* du sport, sportsman (*pl.* sportsmen) *m*; sportif *m*; chasseur *m*; **'sports·man·like** de sportsman; digne d'un sportsman; **'sports-wear** costume *m* de sport; **'sports·wom·an** femme *f* amateur du sport *ou* de la chasse *etc.*; sportive *f.*

spot [spɔt] **1.** tache *f*; *cravate*, *étoffe*: pois *m*; endroit *m*, lieu *m*; *figure*: bouton *m*; *sl.* vin: goutte *f*, petit verre *m*; *théâ. etc.* projecteur *m*; *radio*: spot *m*; *Am.* F ten ~ billet *m* de dix dollars; ♈ ~*s pl.* marchandises *f/pl.* payées comptant; F *a* ~ *of* un peu de; *on the* ~ sur place; *adv.* immédiatement; *be on the* ~ être là; arriver sur les lieux; **2.** ♈ (au) comptant, (du) disponible; fait au hasard; ~ *check* contrôle *m ou* vérification *f* fait(e) au hasard; sondage *m*; **3.** *v/t.* tacher; tacheter, moucheter; F apercevoir; repérer; F reconnaître; *v/i.* tacher; F commencer à pleuvoir; **'~-check** contrôler au hasard *ou* à l'improviste; **'spot·less** □ sans tache; immaculé; pur; **'spot·less·ness** netteté *f*; propreté *f*; pureté *f*; **'spot·light** *théâ.* projecteur *m*, spot *m*; *mot.* projecteur *m* orientable; *fig. in the* ~ en vedette; sous les feux de la rampe; **'spot-'on** *Brit.* F exact(ement), précis(ément), F en plein dans le mille; **'spot·ted** tacheté, moucheté; *tex.* à pois; *zo.* taché; ♂ ~ *fever* méningite *f* cérébro-spinale; *be on the* ~; **'spot·ter** ✈ avion *m* de réglage de tir; *personne*: observateur *m*; *Am.* détective *m* privé; *Am.* ♠ inspecteur *m* en civil; **spot·ti·ness** ['~inis] caractère *m* tacheté *ou* boutonneux; **'spot·ty** moucheté; couvert de boutons (*figure*).

spouse [spauz] époux (-ouse *f*) *m.*

spout [spaut] **1.** *théière etc.*: bec *m*; *arrosoir*: goulot *m*; *pompe*: jet *m*; ◬ tuyau *m* de décharge; ◭ gargouille *f*; gouttière *f*; **2.** (faire) jaillir; *v/t.* F déclamer.

sprain [sprein] **1.** entorse *f*, foulure *f*; **2.** se fouler (la cheville, *one's ankle*).

sprang [spræŋ] *prét.* de **spring** 2.

sprat *icht.* [spræt] sprat *m.*

sprawl [sprɔ:l] *v/i.* s'étendre, s'étaler (*a. fig.*); ⚓ traîner, ramper; *v/t.* étendre (*les jambes*).

spray[1] [sprei] brin *m*, brindille *f*; *fleurs*: branche *f*.

spray[2] [∼] **1.** poussière *f* d'eau; écume *f*, embrun *m*; jet *m*; (*a. ∼ can*) *see* ∼er; **2.** vaporiser (*un liquide*); arroser; passer (*un arbre*) au vaporisateur; **'spray·er** aérosol *m*, bombe *f*; atomiseur *m*, vaporisateur *m*; *foam* ∼ extincteur *m* à mousse.

spread [spred] **1.** [*irr.*] *v/t.* (*a. ∼ out*) étendre; tendre (*le filet*); répandre (*un bruit, une nouvelle, une terreur*); propager (*une maladie*); tartiner (*une tranche de pain*); faire circuler, faire connaître; ∼ *the table* mettre le couvert; *v/i.* s'étendre, s'étaler; **2.** *prét. et p.p. de 1*; 🗲 ∼ *eagle* aigle *f* éployée; **3.** étendue *f*; *ailes*: envergure *f*; diffusion *f*, propagation *f*; *Am.* dessus *m* de lit; *sandwich etc.*: pâte *f*; *sl.* régal *m*, festin *m*; **'∼-ea·gle** F grandiloquent; chauviniste; **'spread·er** étaleur (-euse *f*) *m*; semeur (-euse *f*) *m*; **'spread·ing** étendu; rameux (-euse *f*) (*arbre*).

spree F [spri:] bombe *f*, noce *f*; bringue *f*; *go on the* ∼ faire la bringue *etc.*

sprig [sprig] **1.** brin *m*, brindille *f*; petite branche *f*; *fig.* rejeton *m*; ⊕ clou *m* (*de vitrier*); pointe *f* (*de Paris*); **2.**: ∼ *on* (*ou down*) cheviller; ∼*ged* à ramages (*tissu*).

spright·li·ness ['spraitlinis] vivacité *f*, sémillance *f*; **'spright·ly** éveillé; vif (vive *f*).

spring [spriŋ] **1.** saut *m*, bond *m*; ressort *m*; *auto*: suspension *f*; source *f* (*a. fig.*); *fig.* origine *f*; *saison*: printemps *m*; **2.** [*irr.*] *v/t.* faire sauter; faire jouer (*un piège*); suspendre (*l'auto*); munir de ressorts; franchir; (faire) lever (*le gibier*); proposer *ou* présenter (*un projet etc.*) à l'improviste, faire (*une surprise*) (à q., [up]on s.o.); ⚓ ∼ *a leak* faire une voie d'eau; *v/i.* sauter, bondir; jaillir, sourdre (de, *from*); ⚓ pousser; *fig.* sortir, descendre (de, *from*); ∼ *up* sauter en l'air; ⚓ pousser; se lever; se former (*idée*); ∼ *into existence* naître, (ap)paraître; **'∼-bal·ance** balance *f ou* peson *m* à ressort; **'∼-board** tremplin *m*; **'∼-bolt** ⊕ verrou *m* à ressort; *serrure*:

pêne *m* coulant; **'∼-'clean·ing** grand nettoyage *m* de printemps.

springe [sprind3] *oiseaux*: lacet *m*; *lapins*: collet *m*.

spring-gun ['spriŋgʌn] piège *m* à fusil; **'spring·i·ness** élasticité *f*; ressort *m*.

spring...: **'∼-mat·tress** sommier *m* élastique; **'∼-tide** grande marée *f*; *poét.* printemps *m*; **'∼-time** printemps *m*; **'spring·y** □ élastique; flexible; *fig.* moelleux (-euse *f*).

sprin·kle ['spriŋkl] *v/t.* (with, de) répandre; arroser; *eccl.* asperger; saupoudrer; *fig.* semer; *v/i.* tomber en pluie fine; **'sprin·kler** arrosoir *m*; extincteur *m* (*d'incendie*); *eccl.* goupillon *m*; **'sprin·kling** aspersion *f*; légère couche *f*; *fig. a* ∼ *of* quelques bribes *f/pl.* de (*une science etc.*).

sprint [sprint] **1.** *sp.* course *f* de vitesse, sprint *m*; **2.** de vitesse; **3.** faire une course de vitesse, sprinter; **'sprint·er** *sp.* coureur (-euse *f*) *m* de vitesse; sprinter *m*.

sprit ⚓ [sprit] livarde *f*.

sprite [sprait] lutin *m*, farfadet *m*; esprit *m*.

sprock·et-wheel ⊕ ['sprɔkitwiːl] pignon *m* de chaîne.

sprout [spraut] **1.** (laisser) pousser; **2.** ⚘ pousse *f*; bourgeon *m*; *Brussels* ∼*s pl.* choux *m/pl.* de Bruxelles.

spruce[1] □ [spruːs] soigné; pimpant.

spruce[2] ⚘ [∼] (*a.* ∼ *fir*) sapin *m*, épinette *f*.

sprung [sprʌŋ] *p.p. de spring 2.*

spry [sprai] vif (vive *f*), éveillé.

spud [spʌd] sarcloir *m*; *sl.* patate *f* (= *pomme de terre*); F personne *f* trapue.

spume *poét.* [spjuːm] écume *f*; **'spu·mous**, **'spum·y** □ écumeux (∼euse *f*).

spun [spʌn] *prét. et p.p. de spin 1.*

spunk [spʌŋk] amadou *m*; *fig.* courage *m*; *Am.* irritation *f*.

spur [spəː] **1.** éperon *m* (*a. géog.*, ⚘, †, ⚓); *coq, seigle*: ergot *m*; *fig.* aiguillon *m*; *act on the* ∼ *of the moment* agir sous l'inspiration du moment; *put* (*ou set*) ∼*s to* éperonner, donner de l'éperon à (*un cheval*); *fig.* stimuler; *win one's* ∼*s* F faire ses preuves; *hist.* gagner ses éperons; ⊕ ∼*-gear* engrenage *m* droit; **2.** *v/t.* (*a.* ∼ *on*) éperonner;

fig. aiguillonner, pousser; *v/i.* *poét.* aller au galop, piquer des deux.

spurge ♀ [spə:dʒ] euphorbe *f*.

spu·ri·ous ☐ ['spjuəriəs] faux (fausse *f*); **'spu·ri·ous·ness** fausseté *f*.

spurn [spə:n] repousser du pied; rejeter *ou* traiter avec mépris.

spurred [spə:d] éperonné; ergoté (*seigle, a. orn.*); ♀ calcarifère.

spurt [spə:t] **1.** (re)jaillir; *sp.* démarrer, faire un emballage; *see* **spirt 1**; **2.** effort *m* soudain; *sp.* effort *m* de vitesse, emballage *m*, rush *m*; *see* **spirt 2**.

sput·ter ['spʌtə] **1.** bredouillement *m*; *bois, feu:* pétillement *m*; **2.** *v/i.* bredouiller (*a.* qch. à q., *s.th. at s.o.*); cracher (*plume*); *v/t.* (*a.* ~ **out**) débiter en bredouillant.

spy [spai] **1.** espion(ne *f*) *m*; mouchard *m*; **2.** *v/i.* espionner; *v/t.* apercevoir; ~ **out** explorer (*un terrain*); ~ (**up**)**on** *s.o.* épier, guetter q.; **'~-glass** lunette *f* d'approche; **'~-hole** *porte:* judas *m*; *rideau etc.:* trou *m*.

squab [skwɔb] boulot(te *f*) *m*; courtaud(e *f*) *m*; *orn.* pigeonneau *m* sans plumes; *Am. sl. jeune fille:* typesse *f*; *mot.* coussin *m*; ottomane *f*; pouf *m* (*a. adv.*).

squab·ble ['skwɔbl] **1.** querelle *f*, dispute *f*; prise *f* de bec; chamaille *f*; **2.** se chamailler (avec, *with*); **'squab·bler** chamaillard *m*; querelleur (-euse *f*) *m*.

squad [skwɔd] escouade *f*; peloton *m*; *police:* brigade *f*; *Am. sp.* équipe *f*; **squad·ron** ['~rən] ✕ escadron *m*; ✈ escadrille *f*; ♣ escadre *f*.

squal·id ☐ ['skwɔlid] sordide, crasseux (-euse *f*).

squall¹ [skwɔ:l] **1.** cri *m* rauque; **2.** *vt/i.* brailler, crier.

squall² ♣ [~] grain *m*, coup *m* de vent; **'squall·y** ♣ à grains, à rafales (*temps*); orageux (-euse *f*).

squa·lor ['skwɔlə] misère *f*; caractère *m* sordide.

squa·mous ['skweiməs] squameux (-euse *f*).

squan·der ['skwɔndə] gaspiller; **'~·ma·ni·a** prodigalité *f*.

square [skwɛə] **1.** ☐ carré; *fig.* honnête; en bon ordre; solide (*repas etc.*); catégorique (*refus*); ⊕ plat; ~ *measure* mesure *f* de surface; ~ *mile* mille *m* carré; ⚡ *take a* ~ *root* extraire la racine carrée; ♣ ~ *sail* voile *f* carrée; *Am.* F ~ *shooter* homme *m* loyal *ou* qui agit loyalement; ~ *with* (*ou* to) d'équerre avec; **2.** carré *m* (*a.* ⚡, ✕); carreau *m*; *échiquier etc.:* case *f*; *surv.* équerre *f*; place *f*; *Am.* bloc *m* de maisons; *silk* ~ foulard *m*; **3.** *v/t.* carrer; équarrir (*le bois, un bloc de marbre*); *fig.* accorder (avec, *with*); mettre en croix (*les vergues*); ✝ régler, balancer; *sl.* graisser la patte à (*q.*); F arranger; *v/i.* se carrer, se raccorder; *fig.* cadrer (avec, *with*); s'accorder (avec, *with*); **'~-built** bâti en carré; aux épaules carrées (*personne*); **'~-rigged** ♣ gréé en carré; **'~-toes** *sg.* F pédant *m*; rigoriste *m* de l'ancienne mode.

squash¹ [skwɔʃ] **1.** écrasement *m*; F cohue *f*, presse *f*; *sp.* jeu *m* de balle au mur; *lemon* ~ citronnade *f*; **2.** (s')écraser; *fig.* (se) serrer.

squash² ♀ [~] gourde *f*; *Am.* courge *f*.

squat [skwɔt] **1.** accroupi; trapu; **2.** s'accroupir, se tapir; s'approprier une maison; **'squat·ter** *surt. Am. et Australie:* squatter *m*.

squaw [skwɔ:] femme *f* peau-rouge.

squawk [skwɔ:k] **1.** pousser des cris rauques; **2.** cri *m* rauque.

squeak [skwi:k] **1.** *v/i.* pousser des cris aigus; grincer; F *v/t.* crier d'une voix aiguë; **2.** cri *m* aigu; grincement *m*; **'squeak·y** ☐ criard; aigu(ë *f*).

squeal [skwi:l] pousser des cris aigus; F ~ *on s.o.* dénoncer q.; *see* **squeak 1**.

squeam·ish ☐ ['skwi:miʃ] sujet(te *f*) aux nausées; délicat, difficile, dégoûté; **'squeam·ish·ness** disposition *f* aux nausées; délicatesse *f*.

squee·gee ['skwi:'dʒi:] rabot *m* en caoutchouc; *phot.* raclette *f*.

squeez·a·ble ['skwi:zəbl] compressible, comprimable.

squeeze [skwi:z] **1.** *v/t.* serrer; presser; exercer une pression sur; *fig.* extorquer (à, *from*); ~ *into* faire entrer (de force); ~ *out* exprimer; *v/i.:* ~ *into* s'introduire dans; ~ *together* (*ou* up) se serrer; **2.** étreinte *f*, compression *f*; *main:* serrement *m*; F exaction *f*; **'squeez·er** machine *f* à compression, presse-citron *m/inv.*; F extorqueur *m*.

squelch F [skwelt∫] v/t. aplatir; réprimer; v/i. gicler; gargouiller.

squib [skwib] pétard m; fig. brocard m.

squid zo. [skwid] calmar m.

squif·fy sl. ['skwifi] gris, pompette.

squig·gle F ['skwigl] gribouillis m.

squill ♀ [skwil] scille f.

squint [skwint] 1. loucher; 2. strabisme m; regard m louche; F coup m d'œil.

squire ['skwaiə] 1. propriétaire m terrien; seigneur m du village; Am. juge m de paix; hist. écuyer m; co. cavalier m servant; 2. escorter (une dame).

squir(e)·arch·y ['skwaiəraːki] corps m des propriétaires fonciers; tyrannie f terrienne.

squirm F [skwəːm] se tortiller; fig. se crisper (sous un reproche, under a rebuke).

squir·rel zo. ['skwirəl] écureuil m; (a. ~fur) petit-gris (pl. petits-gris) m.

squirt [skwəːt] 1. seringue f; jet m (d'eau etc.); F petit fat m; 2. (faire) jaillir; v/i. gicler.

squish F [skwi∫] giclement m.

stab [stæb] 1. coup m de poignard ou de couteau; 2. v/t. poignarder; v/i. porter un coup de poignard etc. (à, at).

sta·bil·i·ty [stə'biliti] stabilité f (a. ✎); fermeté f, constance f.

sta·bi·li·za·tion [steiblai'zei∫n] stabilisation f (a. ✈).

sta·bi·lize ['steibilaiz] stabiliser; **'sta·bi·liz·er** ✎ plan m fixe horizontal; ⚓ stabilisateur m.

sta·ble[1] □ ['steibl] stable; solide, fixe; ferme, constant.

sta·ble[2] [~] 1. écurie f; 2. mettre à l'écurie; mettre dans une écurie; **sta·ble·boy** palefrenier m.

sta·bling ['steibliŋ] logement m à l'écurie; coll. écuries f/pl.

stack [stæk] 1. ✎ foin etc.: meule f; tas m, pile f; cheminée: souche f; ✖ faisceau m; 🏭 cheminée f; ~s pl. magasin m de livres; F ~s pl. un tas m; Am. F blow one's ~ sortir de ses gonds; se mettre en rogne; 2. mettre en meule; fig. entasser; ✖ mettre en faisceaux.

sta·di·um sp. ['steidiəm], pl. -**di·a** ['~diə] stade m.

staff [staːf] 1. bâton m; mât m; ♪ (pl.

staves [steivz]) portée f; ✖ état-major (pl. états-majors) m; ✞ personnel m (école, univ.: enseignant); ecole: ~ room salle f des professeurs; 2. fournir de personnel.

stag [stæg] 1. zo. cerf m; F homme m non accompagné d'une dame; ✞ loup m; 2. ✞ acheter pour revendre à prime.

stage [steidʒ] 1. estrade f; échafaudage m; théâ. scène f; fig. théâtre m; période f; étape f; phase f; (a. landing-~) débarcadère m; go on the ~ se faire acteur (-trice f); fare ~ autobus etc.: section f itinéraire; 2. mettre sur la scène; monter; '~-'box loge f d'avant-scène; '~-coach diligence f; ~ di·rec·tion indication f scénique; ~ fright trac m; ~ hand machiniste m; ~ man·ag·er régisseur m; 'stag·er: old ~ vieux routier m; 'stage·struck fou (folle f) du théâtre; stage whis·per aparté m; 'stage·y see stagy.

stag·ger ['stægə] 1. v/i. chanceler, tituber; fig. hésiter; v/t. faire chanceler; ⊕ disposer en quinconce; étager; fig. échelonner; F confondre; 2. chancellement m; allure f chancelante; ⊕ disposition f en quinconce; fig. échelonnement m; ~s pl. vét. mouton: lourd vertige m; cheval: vertigo m; F vertige m; 'stag·ger·ing renversant.

stag·nan·cy ['stægnənsi] stagnation f; 'stag·nant □ stagnant (a. ✞); ✞ en stagnation; dormant; **stag·nate** ['~neit] être ou devenir stagnant; croupir (eau); **stag·na·tion** stagnation f; ✞ a. marasme m.

stag-par·ty F ['stægpaːti] réunion f d'hommes.

stag·y □ ['steidʒi] théâtral (-aux m/pl.).

staid □ [steid] posé, sérieux (-euse f); 'staid·ness caractère m ou air m posé ou sérieux.

stain [stein] 1. tache f (a. fig.); ⊕ couleur f (pour bois); 2. v/t. tacher (a. fig.); ⊕ teindre, mettre en couleur; v/i. se tacher; se teindre; ~ed glass verre m de couleur; ~ed glass (window) vitrail (pl. -aux) m; 'stain·less □ sans tache; immaculé; ⊕ inoxydable (acier); inrouillable.

stair [stɛə] marche f, degré m; ~s pl. escalier m; flight of ~s pl. (volée f d')escalier m; '~-car·pet tapis m d'escalier; '~·**case** (cage f d')escalier m; moving ~ escalier m roulant, escalator m; '~-**rod** tringle f d'escalier; Am. '~·**way** see staircase.

stake [steik] **1.** pieu m; poteau m; jeu: enjeu m; jeu m (a. fig.); bûcher m (d'un martyr); ~s pl. turf: prix m/pl.; surt. Am. pull up ~s partir, ficher le camp; be at ~ être en jeu; place one's ~ on parier sur; **2.** garnir de ou soutenir avec des pieux; mettre en jeu; jouer, parier; hasarder; ~ out (ou off) jalonner.

stale¹ □ [steil] **1.** vieux (vieil devant une voyelle ou un h muet); vieille f; vieux m/pl.); rassis (pain etc.); éventé (bière etc.); défraîchi (article, nouvelle); vicié (air); de renfermé (ōdeur); rance; rebattu (plaisanterie etc.); **2.** v/i. s'éventer (bière); perdre son intérêt.

stale² [~] **1.** uriner (cheval etc.); **2.** urine f.

stale·mate ['steil'meit] **1.** échecs: pat m; fig. impasse f; **2.** faire pat (q.).

stalk¹ [stɔːk] tige f; chou: trognon m; verre: pied m.

stalk² [~] **1.** v/i. marcher à grandes enjambées; se pavaner; chasser sans chiens; v/t. traquer d'affût; **2.** chasse f à l'affût; '**stalk·er** chasseur m à l'affût; '**stalk·ing-horse** fig. masque m, prétexte m.

stall [stɔːl] **1.** cheval: stalle f; bœuf: case f; porc: loge f; marché: étalage m; théâ. fauteuil m d'orchestre; eccl. stalle f; **2.** v/t. mettre à l'étable ou l'écurie; ✗ mettre en perte de vitesse; mot. caler; v/i. mot. (se) caler; ✗ s'engager; '~-**feed·ing** nourrissage m à l'étable.

stal·lion ['stæljən] étalon m.

stal·wart ['stɔːlwət] **1.** □ robuste, vigoureux (-euse f); fig. ferme; **2.** pol. tenant m; partisan m.

sta·men ♀ ['steimen] étamine f; **stam·i·na** ['stæminə] vigueur f, résistance f.

stam·mer ['stæmə] **1.** bégayer, balbutier; **2.** bégaiement m; '**stam·mer·er** bègue mf.

stamp [stæmp] **1.** battement m (a. bruit m) de pied; ⊕ estampeuse f; ⊕ emboutisseuse f; empreinte f (a. fig.); fig. trempe f; timbre (-poste) m; coin m; ✝ estampille f; ~ pad tampon m (encreur); see date-~; **2.** v/t. frapper (du pied, one's foot);

estamper; ✝ estampiller; ✝ contrôler; marquer (a. fig.); timbrer (un document); affranchir (une lettre); ~ on the memory (se) graver dans la mémoire, imprimer sur l'esprit; ~ out étouffer; ⊕ découper à la presse; v/i. frapper du pied; piétiner; '~-**al·bum** album m de timbres-poste; '~-**du·ty** droit m de timbre.

stam·pede [stæm'piːd] **1.** panique f; débandade f; ruée f; **2.** v/t. mettre en fuite; v/i. fuir en désordre; se précipiter (vers, sur for, towards).

stamp·er ['stæmpə] estampeuse f; personne: timbreur (-euse f), estampeur (-euse f) m, frappeur (-euse f) m de monnaie; '**stamp·(ing)-mill** métall. (moulin m à) bocard(s pl.) m.

stanch [stɑːntʃ] **1.** étancher (le sang); **2.** adj. see staunch 1; **stan·chion** ['stɑːnʃən] étançon m; colonnette f de soutien.

stand [stænd] **1.** [irr.] v/i. se tenir (debout); être; se trouver; rester; se maintenir; se porter candidat; (usu. ~ still) s'arrêter; se lever; ~ against s'adosser à; résister à, combattre; ~ aside se tenir à l'écart; s'écarter; fig. se désister (en faveur de q.); ~ at être à; marquer (les degrés); ~ back se tenir en arrière; (se) reculer; être écarté (de, from); ~ by se tenir prêt; ⚓ se tenir paré; ✗ être consigné; se tenir à côté de; fig. soutenir; fig. rester fidèle à; radio: ne pas quitter l'écoute; ~ for tenir lieu de; se présenter comme candidat à; soutenir; vouloir dire; représenter; F supporter, tolérer; ⚓ ~ in courir (vers, à to); ~ in with s'associer à; ~ off se tenir éloigné ou à l'écart; s'éloigner; ⊕ chômer; ⚓ courir au large; avoir le cap au large; ~ off! tenez-vous à distance!; ~ on se tenir sur (a. fig.); insister sur; ~ out être en ou faire saillie, avancer; fig. se détacher (sur, against); se profiler (sur, against); se tenir à l'écart; résister (à, against); tenir bon (contre, against); insister (sur, for); ⚓ se tenir au large; courir au large; ~ over rester en suspens; se pencher sur; Am. F ~ pat tenir ferme, ne pas en démordre; ~ to ne pas démordre de, en tenir à; ⚓ avoir le cap à; see reason 1; ✗ ~ to! aux armes!; ~ up se lever; se dresser; ~ up for soutenir, prendre le parti de; ~ up to résister à; ~ upon se tenir sur (a. fig.); insister sur; **2.** [irr.] v/t. poser, mettre; supporter, endurer; soutenir (un combat, un choc, ✗ le feu); see ground² 1; F ~ s.o. a dinner payer un dîner à q.; ~ treat régaler; **3.** position f, place f; station(nement m) f; estrade f, tribune f; étalage m; socle m, dessous m; surt. Am. barre f des témoins; arrêt m; (a. wash-~) lavabo m; fig. résistance f; composés: -~ porte- m; umbrella-~ porte-parapluies m/inv.; ✗ ~ of arms armement m (d'un soldat); make a (ou one's) ~ against s'opposer résolument à.

stand·ard ['stændəd] **1.** ✗ étendard m; ⚓ pavillon m (a. ⚘); mesure: étalon m, type m; ♱ échantillon m, modèle m, norme f; niveau m (a. école, fig.); qualité f; degré m (d'excellence); hauteur f; or, argent, a. ⚘: titre m; école primaire: classe f; ⊕ pied m; ⚲ arbre m de plein vent; above ~ au-dessus de la moyenne; ~ lamp torchère f, lampadaire m; the ~ is high le niveau est élevé; ~ of living niveau m de vie; ~ of value prix m régulateur; **2.** standard adj./inv.; -étalon; type; classique; normal (-aux m/pl.); courant; ~-gauge 🚆 ['~geidʒ] voie f normale; **stan·ard·i·za·tion** ['~ai'zeiʃn] étalonnage m; unification f; ⊕, cin. standardisation f; ⚒ titrage m; **'stand·ard·ize** étalonner, unifier; normaliser; ⊕, cin. standardiser; ⚒ titrer.

stand-by ['stændbai] **1.** expédient m; réserve f; **2.** de réserve, de secours.

stand·ee Am. F [stæn'di:] spectateur (-trice f) m debout.

stand·er-by ['stændə'bai], pl. **'stand·ers-'by** spectateur (-trice f) m; assistant(e f) m, temoin m.

stand-in cin. ['stænd'in] doublure f.

stand·ing ['stændiŋ] **1.** ☐ debout inv.; dormant (eau); permanent; ordinaire; fixe; ~ jump saut m à pieds joints; parl. ~ orders pl. règlement m, -s m/pl.; **2.** position f; rang m; importance f; durée f; date f; of long ~ d'ancienne date; '~-room place f, ~ f/pl. debout.

stand...: '~-off Am. raideur f, réserve f, morgue f; '~-'off·ish dis-

tant; raide; ~'pat·ter Am. pol. immobiliste m; '~-pipe réservoir m cylindrique; '~·point point m de vue; '~-still arrêt m; be at a ~ n'avancer plus; come to a ~ s'arrêter; '~-up: ~ collar col m droit; ~ fight bataille f rangée; combat m en règle.

stank [stæŋk] prét. de stink 2.

stan·nic ⚒ ['stænik] stannique.

stan·za ['stænzə] strophe f, stance f.

sta·ple¹ ['steipl] **1.** matière f première; fig. fond m; produit m principal; marché m aux laines; **2.** principal (-aux m/pl.).

sta·ple² [~] crampon m, crampillon m; clou m à deux pointes; serrure: gâche f.

star [sta:] **1.** étoile f (a. fig.); astre m; théâ. vedette f; Am. ♀s and Stripes pl. bannière f étoilée; **2.** étoiler; marquer d'un astérisque; théâ. figurer en vedette, tenir le premier rôle; ~ (it) briller; théâ. figurer en vedette de la semaine etc.

star·board ⚓ ['sta:bəd] **1.** tribord m; **2.** v/t. mettre la barre à tribord; v/i. venir sur tribord.

starch [sta:tʃ] **1.** amidon m; pâte: empois m; fig. raideur f; **2.** empesé; fig. ~ed guindé, raide; '**starch·i·ness** manières f/pl. empesées, raideur f; '**starch·y** ☐ **1.** féculent; fig. guindé; **2.** (ou ~ food) féculent m.

star·dom ['sta:dəm] célébrité f; rise to ~ devenir une vedette.

stare [stɛə] **1.** regard m fixe; **2.** regarder fixement (qch., at s.th.); ouvrir de grands yeux; ~ s.o. out dévisager q.

star·fish zo. ['sta:fiʃ] étoile f de mer.

star·ing ☐ ['stɛəriŋ] fixe (regard); effrayé; criard.

stark [sta:k] raide; poét. fort; ~ naked tout nu; nu comme un ver.

star·ling orn. ['sta:liŋ] étourneau m.

star·ling² [~] brise-glace m/inv.

star·lit ['sta:lit] étoilé.

star·ring théâ. ['sta:riŋ] présentant... (en vedette).

star·ry ['sta:ri] étoilé (a. ⚘); fig. brillant; '~-eyed rêveur (-euse); extasié; peu réaliste.

star-span·gled ['sta:spæŋgld] constellé d'étoiles; Am. Star-Spangled Banner bannière f étoilée.

start [sta:t] **1.** départ m (a. sp.); commencement m; sp. envolée f; sp. avance f; fig. sursaut m, tressaillement *m*; get the ~ of s.o. devancer q.; *sp.* give s.o. a ~ donner de l'avance à q.; laisser q. partir le premier; **2.** *v/i.* partir, se mettre en route; commencer (*a. qch.*, on *s.th.*; *a.* à *inf.*, on *gér.*); *mot.* démarrer; ✖ prendre son vol; *fig.* tressaillir, (sur)sauter (de, *with*; à *at*, *with*); faire un écart brusque (*cheval*); jaillir (de, *from*) (*larmes*); ~ up se lever brusquement; *v/t.* faire partir (*a. le gibier*); mettre (*une machine*) en marche; *sp.* donner le signal du départ à; lever (*un lièvre*); lancer (*une personne, une affaire, etc.*); commencer (*un travail, une lutte, etc.*); entamer (*une conversation, un sujet, etc.*); soulever (*une question*); ~ s.o. (*gér.*) mettre q. à (*inf.*).

start·er ['stɑːtə] auteur *m*; *sp.* starter *m*; *sp.* partant *m* (= *concurrent*); *mot. etc.* démarreur *m*; *fig.* lanceur (-euse *f*) *m*.

start·ing ['stɑːtiŋ] **1.** départ *m*; commencement *m* etc.; **2.** de départ; de début; initial; *sp.* ~ block bloc *m* de départ; *sp.* ~ line ligne *f* de départ; ~ phase phase *f* initiale; ~ place (*ou* point) point *m* de départ; ~ salary salaire *m* initial *ou* de début.

star·tle ['stɑːtl] effrayer; **'star·tler** F chose *f* sensationnelle; **'star·tling** ☐ effrayant; étonnant.

star·va·tion [stɑːˈveiʃn] faim *f*; ✚ inanition *f*; *attr.* de famine; (*be on a*) ~ diet (suivre un) régime *m* draconien; **starve** [stɑːv] (faire) mourir de faim; *fig. v/t.* priver (de, *of*); **starv·ling** ['~liŋ] affamé(e *f*) (*a. su./mf*); famélique (*a. su./mf*); *a.* de famine.

state [steit] **1.** état *m*, condition *f*; pompe *f*, apparat *m*; *pol. usu.* ♔ État *m*; *hist.* ♔s *pl.* États *m/pl.*, ordres *m/pl.*; ~ of life rang *m*; in ~ en grand apparat *ou* gala; lie in ~ être exposé solennellement (*mort*); F be in a ~ être très agité; **2.** d'État; national (-aux *m/pl.*); d'apparat; *see department*; ~ funeral obsèques *f/pl.* nationales; *Am.* ♔ house palais *m* du gouvernement; **3.** énoncer, déclarer, affirmer; poser (*un problème*); fixer (*une date etc.*); ✚ spécifier (*un compte*); **'state·less** sans patrie; **'state·li·ness** majesté *f*; grandeur *f*; **'state·ly** majestueux (-euse *f*); imposant; noble; **'state·ment** déclaration *f*; exposition *f*, énoncé *m*; affirmation *f*; ✚

état *m* (de compte, *of account*); ✚ bilan *m*; **'state·room** salle *f* de réception; ♣ cabine *f* de luxe; **'state·side** *Am.* aux *ou* des États-Unis; F go ~ rentrer.

states·man ['steitsmən] homme *m* d'État; **'states·man·like** d'homme d'État; F magistral (-aux *m/pl.*); **'states·man·ship** science *f* du gouvernement; politique *f*.

State(s') rights *Am.* ['steit(s)raits] droits *m/pl.* fondamentaux des États fédérés.

stat·ic ['stætik] statique; **'stat·ics** *pl. ou sg. phys.* statique *f*; *pl. radio:* parasites *m/pl.*

sta·tion ['steiʃn] **1.** position *f*, place *f*; poste *m* (*a.* ✖, ♣, *radio*); *sauvetage etc.:* station *f*; ♀, *zo.* habitat *m*; 🚂 gare *f*; *métro:* station *f*; rang *m*, situation *f* sociale; **2.** placer; poster; **'sta·tion·ar·y** ☐ immobile; stationnaire; fixe; ~ engine moteur *m* fixe; **'sta·tion·er** papetier *m*; ♔s' Hall Hôtel *m* de la Corporation des libraires (*à Londres*); **'sta·tion·er·y** papeterie *f*; **'sta·tion·mas·ter** chef *m* de gare; **sta·tion wag·on** *Am. mot.* canadienne *f*.

sta·tis·ti·cal ☐ [stəˈtistikl] statistique; **stat·is·ti·cian** [stætisˈtiʃn] statisticien(ne *f*) *m*; **sta·tis·tics** [stəˈtistiks] *pl., comme science sg.* statistique *f*.

stat·u·ar·y ['stætjuəri] **1.** statuaire; **2.** statuaire *f*, art *m* statuaire; *personne:* statuaire *mf*; *coll.* statues *f/pl.*; **stat·ue** ['~tjuː] statue *f*; **stat·u·esque** ☐ [~tjuˈesk] plastique; sculptural (-aux *m/pl.*); **stat·u·ette** [~tjuˈet] statuette *f*.

stat·ure ['stætʃə] taille *f*; stature *f*.

sta·tus ['steitəs] statut *m* légal; situation *f*; état *m* (*a.* ♪); rang *m*; ~ seeker ambitieux (-euse *f*) *m*; ~ symbol marque *f* de standing.

stat·ute ['stætjuːt] loi *f*, ordonnance *f*; ~s *pl.* statuts *m/pl.*; ~ law droit *m* écrit; **'~book** code *m* des lois,.

stat·u·to·ry ☐ ['stætjutəri] établi par la loi; statutaire.

staunch [stɔːntʃ] **1.** ☐ ferme; sûr, dévoué; étanche (*navire*); **2.** étancher.

stave [steiv] **1.** douve *f*; bâton *m*; strophe *f*; ♪ mesure *f*; **2.** [*irr.*] (*usu.* ~ in) défoncer, enfoncer; ~ off prévenir, parer à.

staves [steivz] *pl. de* staff 1.

stay [stei] 1. ⚓ *mât*: accore *m*, étai *m*; hauban *m*; *fig.* soutien *m*; séjour *m*; ⚓ suspension *f*; ⚓ sursis *m*; (*a pair of*) ⚓s *pl.* (un) corset *m*; 2. *v/t.* arrêter; remettre; étayer; ⚓ *one's stomach* tromper la faim; *v/i.* rester; demeurer; se tenir; séjourner; *sp.* soutenir l'allure; ⚓ *away* s'absenter; ⚓ *for* attendre; ⚓ *in* rester à *ou* garder la maison; ⚓ *put* rester en place; *sl.* ne plus changer; ⚓ *up* veiller; rester debout; ⚓*ing power* fond *m*, résistance *f*; '⚓*-at-home* casanier (-ère *f*) *m*; '**stay·er** *sp. personne*: stayer *m*; cheval *m* de longue haleine.

stead [sted] place *f*; *in his* ⚓ à sa place; *stand s.o. in good* ⚓ être fort utile à q.

stead·fast □ ['stedfəst] ferme, stable; solide; inébranlable; constant; '**stead·fast·ness** fermeté *f*, constance *f*.

stead·i·ness ['stedinis] persévérance *f*; ✝ stabilité *f*; *a. see* steadfastness.

stead·y ['stedi] 1. □ ferme; solide (*a.* ✝); constant; soutenu; sûr; régulier (-ère *f*); *walk a* ⚓ 2 *miles* aller deux bons milles; 2. *v/t.* (r)affermir; assurer; calmer; stabiliser; *v/i.* se raffermir; reprendre son aplomb *ou* équilibre; 3. *Am.* F ami(*e*) *m* attitré(*e* *f*); 4. F *go* ⚓ sortir ensemble, être de bons amis; F *go* ⚓ *with s.o.* sortir avec q.

steak [steik] tranche *f*; bifteck *m*; *fillet* ⚓ tournedos *m*.

steal [sti:l] 1. [*irr.*] *v/t.* voler, dérober; (*a.* ⚓ *away*) séduire (le cœur de q., *s.o.'s heart*); ⚓ *a glance* jeter un coup d'œil furtif (à, *at*); ⚓ *a march* on devancer q.; *v/i.* marcher à pas furtifs; ⚓ *into* se faufiler dans; 2. *Am.* filouterie *f*; transaction *f* malhonnête.

stealth [stelθ] *by* ⚓ à la dérobée; furtivement; '**stealth·i·ness** caractère *m* furtif; '**stealth·y** □ furtif (-ive *f*).

steam [sti:m] 1. vapeur *f*; buée *f*; *let off* ⚓ ⊕ lâcher la vapeur; *fig.* donner libre cours à ses sentiments; dépenser son superflu d'énergie; 2. de *ou* à vapeur; 3. *v/i.* fumer; jeter de la vapeur; *v/t.* cuire à la vapeur; vaporiser (*du*

drap); '⚓*-boil·er* chaudière *f* à vapeur; **steamed** couvert de buée (*fenêtre*); '**steam-en·gine** machine *f* à vapeur; '**steam·er** ⚓ vapeur *m*; *cuis.* marmite *f* à l'étuvée; '**steam·i·ness** *climat*: humidité *f*; '**steam-roll·er** rouleau *m* compresseur; **steam tug** ⚓ remorqueur *m* à vapeur; '**steam·y** □ couvert de buée (*fenêtre*); humide (*climat etc.*).

ste·a·rin ⚛ ['stiərin] stéarine *f*.

steed *poét.* [sti:d] destrier *m*.

steel [sti:l] 1. acier *m*; *poét.* épée *f*; *cuis.* affiloir *m*; 2. d'acier; ⚓*-works usu. sg.* aciérie *f*; ⚓ *engraving* gravure *f* sur acier; 3. aciérer; ⚓ *o.s.* s'endurcir; '⚓*-clad* revêtu d'acier; '**steel·y** *usu. fig.* d'acier; '**steel·yard** romaine *f*.

steep[1] [sti:p] 1. raide, escarpé; F fort, raide; incroyable; 2. *poét.* escarpement *m*.

steep[2] [⚓] 1. trempage *m*; mouillage *m*; 2. baigner, tremper; *fig.* ⚓ *o.s.* se noyer (dans, *in*).

steep·en *fig.* ['sti:pən] *vt/i.* augmenter.

stee·ple ['sti:pl] clocher *m*; '⚓*-chase* steeple(-chase) *m*.

steep·ness ['sti:pnis] raideur *f*; pente *f* rapide.

steer[1] [stiə] jeune bœuf *m*, bouvillon *m*; *Am.* bœuf *m*.

steer[2] [⚓] diriger, conduire; '**steer·a·ble** dirigeable.

steer·age ⚓ ['stiəridʒ] ✝ manœuvre *f* de la barre; entrepont *m*; troisième classe *f*; '⚓*-way* ⚓ : *have good* ⚓ sentir la barre.

steer·ing... ['stiəriŋ]: '⚓*-arm* mot. levier *m* d'attaque de (la) direction; ⚓ *com·mit·tee* comité *m* d'organisation; '⚓*-wheel* ⚓ roue *f* du gouvernail; *mot.* volant *m*.

steers·man ⚓ ['stiəzmən] timonier *m*.

stein [stain] chope *f*, pot *m*.

stel·lar ['stelə] stellaire.

stem[1] [stem] 1. *plante, fleur*: tige *f*; *fruit*: queue *f*; *arbre*: souche *f*, tronc *m*; *bananes*: régime *m*; *verre*: pied *m*; *pipe*: tuyau *m*; *mot*: radical *m*; 2. *v/t.* enlever les queues de; égrapper (*des raisins*); *v/i. Am.* être issu (de, *from*).

stem[2] [⚓] 1. ⚓ avant *m*; *poét.* proue *f*; 2. *v/t.* contenir, refouler; arrêter; résister à; *v/i. ski*: se ralentir en faisant un angle aigu; ~(ming) turn stemmbogen m.

stench [stentʃ] odeur f infecte; puanteur f.

sten·cil ['stensl] 1. patron m; machine à écrire: cliché m; 2. peindre etc. au patron; polycopier.

ste·nog·ra·pher [ste'nɔgrəfə] sténographe mf; **sten·o·graph·ic** [steno'græfik] (~ally) sténographique; **ste·nog·ra·phy** [ste'nɔgrəfi] sténographie f.

step¹ [step] 1. pas m (a. fig.); marche f (a. autel); échelon m; auto etc.: marchepied m; maison: seuil m; démarche f, mesure f; (a pair ou set of) ~s pl., (a) ~-ladder (une) échelle f double, (un) escabeau m; in ~ with au pas avec; 2. v/i. faire un pas; marcher; ~ down descendre; fig. donner sa démission, se retirer; ~ in entrer; ~ on it! sl. dépêchez-vous!; dégrouillez-vous!; ~ out sortir; allonger le pas; v/t. (a. ~ off, out) mesurer (une distance) au pas; ~ up rehausser le niveau de; ⚡ survolter.

step² [~] mots composés: beau- (belle f); '~-fa·ther beau-père (pl. beaux-pères) m.

steppe [step] steppe f.

step·ping-stone ['stepiŋstoun] pierre f de gué (dans une rivière); fig. marchepied m; tremplin m.

ster·eo... ['steriə] stéreo...

ster·eo ['steriou] 1. (a. ~ sound) stéréophonie f, F stéréo f; (a. ~ set) appareil m stéréo; phonographe m stéréo; typ. cliché m; 2. stéréophonique, F stéréo inv.; **~·scope** ['~skoup] stéréoscope m; '~·type 1. cliché m; 2. stéréotyper.

ster·ile ['sterail] stérile; ⚕ acarpe; **ster·il·i·ty** [~'riliti] stérilité f; **ster·i·lize** ['~rilaiz] stériliser.

ster·ling ['stə:liŋ] de bon aloi (a. fig.); ✝ sterling; a pound ~ une livre sterling.

stern¹ □ [stə:n] sévère, dur; austère.

stern² ⚓ [~] arrière m; derrière m.

stern·ness ['stə:nnis] sévérité f, dureté f; austérité f.

stern-post ⚓ ['stə:npoust] étambot m. [num m.]

ster·num anat. ['stə:nəm] ster-]

steth·o·scope 🩺 ['steθəskoup] stéthoscope m.

ste·ve·dore ⚓ ['sti:vidɔ:] arrimeur m; entrepreneur m d'arrimage.

stew [stju:] 1. v/t. fricasser, mettre en ragoût; faire une compote de (fruit); ~ed fruit compote f; v/i. mijoter; cuire à la casserole; 2. ragoût m; F émoi m.

stew·ard ['stjuəd] économe m; maison: maître m d'hôtel; ⚓ garçon m, steward m; sp., a. bal: commissaire m; '**stew·ard·ess** ✈ hôtesse f de l'air; ⚓ stewardess f.

stew...: '~-pan, '~-pot casserole f; cocotte f.

stick¹ [stik] 1. bâton m (a. cire à cacheter); canne f; baguette f; vigne: échalas m; balai: manche m; ✈ manche m à balai; ✈ bombes: chapelet m; sp. crosse f; fig. F type m; ~s pl. du menu bois m; 2. ⚘ ramer; mettre des tuteurs à.

stick² [~] [irr.] v/i. se piquer; tenir (à, to); se coller; se coincer (porte); hésiter (devant, at); ~ at nothing n'être retenu par rien; ~ out faire saillie; F persister; F s'obstiner (à demander qch., for s.th.); ~ up se dresser; F résister (à, to); fig. ~ to persévérer dans; rester fidèle à; F ~ up for s.o. prendre la défense de q.; v/t. piquer; attacher; fixer; coller; percer; ranger (des pois); sl. supporter (q.); ~ up afficher; sl. attaquer à main armée; '**stick·er** couteau m; colleur m; Am. affiche f; '**stick·i·ness** viscosité f; '**stick·ing-plas·ter** sparadrap m; taffetas m anglais; '**stick-in-the-mud** F mal dégourdi; routinier (-ère f) m.

stick·le ['stikl] (se) disputer; '**stick·le·back** icht. épinoche f; '**stick·ler** rigoriste mf (à l'égard de, for).

stick-up ['stikʌp] F (a. ~ collar) col m droit; Am. sl. bandit m.

stick·y □ ['stiki] collant; fig. pâteux (-euse f); sl. difficile; peu accommodant.

stiff □ [stif] 1. raide, rigide; guindé, gêné; ferme; fort (boisson, vent); difficile; 2. sl. cadavre m; Am. sl. nigaud m, bêta (-asse f) m; '**stiff·en** v/t. raidir (a. ⚕); renforcer; empeser (un plastron); lier (une sauce); corser (une boisson); v/i. (se) raidir; devenir ferme; '**stiff·en·er** renfort m; F verre m qui ravigote; '**stiff-'necked** fig. intraitable, obstiné.

sti·fle¹ vét. ['staifl] (affection f du) grasset m.

sti·fle² [~] étouffer (a. fig.).

stig·ma ['stigmə] stigmate *m*; *fig.*
a. flétrissure *f*; **'stig·ma·tize** marquer de stigmates; *fig.* stigmatiser.
stile [stail] échalier *m*, échalis *m*; ⊕
porte etc.: montant *m*.
sti·let·to [sti'letou] stylet *m*; *couture*:
poinçon *m*; ~ *heel* talon *m* aiguille.
still¹ [stil] **1.** *adj.* tranquille; silencieux (-euse *f*); calme; ~ *wine* vin *m*
non mousseux; **2.** *su. cin.* photographie *f*; **3.** *adv.* encore; **4.** *cj.* cependant, pourtant; encore; **5.** (se)
calmer; *v/t.* tranquilliser, apaiser.
still² [~] alambic *m*; appareil *m* de
distillation.
still...: '~·**birth** enfant *mf* mort-
né(e); mort *f* à la naissance; '~·**born**
mort-né(e *f*); '~·**hunt** *Am.* traquer
d'affût; '~·**hunt·ing** *Am.* chasse *f*
d'affût; ~ *life* nature *f* morte; **'still-**
ness calme *m*; silence *m*.
still-room ⌂ ['stilrum] office *f*.
still·y *poét.* ['stili] *adj.* calme, tranquille; **stil·ly** [~] *adv.* silencieuse-
ment.
stilt [stilt] échasse *f*; **'stilt·ed** *fig.*
guindé, tendu.
stim·u·lant ['stimjulənt] **1.** ⚕ stimulant; **2.** ⚕ surexcitant *m*; stimulant *m*; **stim·u·late** ['~leit] stimuler
(*a.* ⚕); *fig. a.* encourager (à *inf.*, to
inf.); **stim·u'la·tion** stimulation *f*;
stim·u·la·tive ['~lətiv] stimulateur
(-trice *f*); **stim·u·lus** ['~ləs], *pl.* **-li**
['~lai] stimulant *m*, F aiguillon *m* (de,
to); ⚕ stimule *m*; *physiol.* stimulus *m*.
sting [stiŋ] **1.** *insecte*: aiguillon *m*;
piqûre *f*; ⚕ dard *m*; *fig.* pointe *f*,
mordant *m*; **2.** [*irr.*] *v/t.* piquer (*fig.*
au vif); *v/i.* cuire; *sl. be stung for*
s.th. payer qch. un prix exorbitant; **'sting·er** F coup *m* raide *ou*
douloureux; **stin·gi·ness** ['stindʒi-
nis] mesquinerie *f*, ladrerie *f*; **sting-**
(ing)-net·tle ⚕ ['stiŋ(iŋ)netl] ortie
f brûlante; **stin·gy** □ ['stindʒi]
mesquin, chiche.
stink [stiŋk] **1.** puanteur *f*; **2.** [*irr.*]
v/i. puer (qch., of *s.th.*); *sl. a. fig.*
~ *of* trahir, accuser; *v/t.* enfumer
(*un renard*); *fig.* sentir (qch.); **stink-**
er F salaud *m*; salope *f*; vacherie *f*,
saloperie *f*; lettre *f* d'engueulade.
stint [stint] **1.** restriction *f*; besogne
f assignée; travail *m* exigé; **2.** imposer des restrictions à; priver (*q.*),
être chiche de (qch.).
sti·pend ['staipend] traitement *m*

(*surt. eccl.*); **sti'pen·di·ar·y** [~jəri]
1. appointé; **2.** *Angl.* juge *m* d'un
tribunal de simple police.
stip·ple *peint.* ['stipl] pointiller.
stip·u·late ['stipjuleit] (*a.* ~ *for*)
stipuler; convenir (de, for); **stip-**
u'la·tion ⚕⚕ stipulation *f*; condition *f*.
stir¹ [stə:] **1.** remuement *m*; mouvement *m* (*a. fig.*); *fig.* vie *f*; agitation
f; **2.** *v/t.* remuer; tourner; agiter;
fig. exciter; ~ *up* exciter; pousser;
susciter; *v/i.* remuer, bouger.
stir² *sl.* [~] prison *f*.
stir·rup ['stirəp] étrier *m*.
stitch [stitʃ] **1.** point *m*, piqûre *f*;
⚕ suture *f*; piqûre *f* au côté; *he*
has not a dry ~ *on him* il est complètement trempé; **2.** coudre; piquer
(*le cuir, deux étoffes*); brocher (*un*
livre); ⚕ suturer.
stoat *zo.* [stout] hermine *f* (d'été).
stock [stɔk] **1.** *arbre*: tronc *m*;
souche *f*; *outil*: manche *m*; *fusil*:
fût *m*; *fig.* race *f*, famille *f*; ⚘ (*a.*
~-*gilly-flower*) matthiole *f*, giroflée *f*
des jardins; ✚ marchandises *f/pl.*; provision *f*; ✚ marchandises *f/pl.*, stock
m; ✚ *a.* ~*s pl.* fonds *m/pl.*, valeurs
f/pl., *fig.* actions *f/pl.*; (*a. live* ~)
bétail *m*, bestiaux *m/pl.*; (*a. dead* ~)
matériel *m*; *cost.* cravate *f*; *eccl.*
plastron *m* en soie noire; *cuis.* consommé *m*, bouillon *m*; ~*s pl. a.*
hist. pilori *m*; ⚓ chantier *m*; ~
building ✚ stockage *m*; approvisionnement *m*; ~ *in hand* marchandises *f/pl.* en magasin; *rolling* ~
matériel *m* roulant; *take* ~ *of* ✚
dresser l'inventaire de; *fig.* scruter,
examiner attentivement; **2.** courant; de série; classique; consacré;
théâ. ~ *company* troupe *f* à demeure; ~ *play* pièce *f* de *ou* du
répertoire; **3.** *v/t.* (*a.* ~ *up*) approvisionner, fournir (de, with); ✚ avoir
en magasin, tenir; *v/i.* se monter
(en, with), s'approvisionner (de,
with).
stock·ade [stɔ'keid] **1.** palissade *f*;
Am. prison *f*; **2.** palissader.
stock...: '~·**book** livre *m* de magasin; '~·**breed·er** éleveur *m*; '~·
brok·er agent *m* de change; courtier *m* de bourse; ~ **ex·change**
bourse *f* (des valeurs); '~·**hold·er**
actionnaire *mf*; porteur *m* de titres.
stock·i·net ['stɔkinet] tricot *m*.

stock·ing ['stɔkiŋ] bas *m*; '**~-loom** métier *m* à bas.

stock·ist † ['stɔkist] stockiste *m*.

stock...: '**~·job·ber** marchand *m* de titres; '**~·job·bing** courtage *m*; *péj.* agiotage *m*; '**~-pile** *vt/i.* stocker; amonceler; '**~-pot** pot-au-feu *m/inv.*; '**~-'still** (complètement) immobile; sans bouger; '**~-'tak·ing** inventaire *m*; ~ *sale* solde *m* avant *ou* après inventaire; '**stock·y** trapu; ragot (*a. cheval*).

stodge *sl.* [stɔdʒ] se bourrer (*de nourriture*); '**stodg·y** □ lourd; qui bourre.

sto·gy, sto·gie *Am.* ['stougi] cigare *m* long et fort (à bouts coupés).

sto·ic ['stouik] stoïcien(ne *f*) (*a. su.*); stoïque; '**sto·i·cal** □ *fig.* stoïque.

stoke [stouk] charger; chauffer; '**stok·er** chauffeur *m*; chargeur *m*.

stole[1] [stoul] *cost.* écharpe *f*; étole *f* (*a. eccl.*).

stole[2] [~] *prét.*, '**sto·len** *p.p.* de steal 1.

stol·id □ ['stɔlid] impassible, lourd, lent; flegmatique; **sto·lid·i·ty** [~-'liditi] flegme *m*; impassibilité *f*.

stom·ach ['stʌmək] 1. estomac *m*; *fig.* appétit *m*; goût *m* (de, *for*); *euphémisme:* ventre *m*; 2. *fig.* supporter, tolérer, digérer; '**~-ache** mal *m* à l'estomac; **sto·mach·ic** [sto-'mækik] (~*ally*) stomachique (*a. su./m*); stomacal (-aux *m/pl.*).

stomp *Am.* [stɔmp] marcher à pas bruyants.

stone [stoun] 1. pierre *f*; *fruit:* noyau *m*; *a. mesure:* 6,348 kg; ⚕ calcul *m*; 2. de *ou* en pierre; de *ou* en grès; 3. lapider; ôter les noyaux de (*un fruit*); '**~-'blind** complètement aveugle; '**~-coal** anthracite *m*.

stoned *sl.* [stound] soûl; drogué, F défonce.

stone...: '**~-'dead** raide mort; '**~-'deaf** complètement sourd; '**~-'fruit** fruit *m* à noyau; '**~-ma·son** maçon *m*; '**~-pit** carrière *f* de pierre; '**~-'wall·ing** *fig.* jeu *m* prudent; *pol.* obstructionnisme *m*; '**~-ware** (poterie *f* de) grès *m*.

ston·i·ness ['stouninis] nature *f* pierreuse; *fig.* dureté *f*.

ston·y ['stouni] pierreux (-euse *f*); de pierre (*a. fig.*); *fig.* dur; F~-broke à sec, sans le sou, fauché.

stood [stud] *prét. et p.p. de stand* 1, 2.

stooge *Am. sl.* [stu:dʒ] *théâ.* nègre *m*; *fig.* souffre-douleur *mf/inv.*

stool [stu:l] tabouret *m*; (*a. three-legged* ~) escabeau *m*; ⚕ selle *f*; ♀ plante *f* mère; ♀ talle *f*; '**~-pi·geon** surt. *Am. sl.* mouchard *m*.

stoop [stu:p] 1. *v/i.* se pencher, se baisser; *fig.* s'abaisser, descendre ([jusqu']là, *to*); être voûté; *v/t.* incliner (*la tête*); 2. penchement *m* en avant; dos *m* voûté; *Am.* véranda *f*; *Am.* terrasse *f* surélevée.

stop [stɔp] 1. *v/t.* (*a.* ~ *up*) boucher; arrêter; bloquer (*un chèque*; *a. box.*, *foot.*); retenir (*les gages*); plomber (*une dent*); étancher (*le sang*); *mot.* stopper; interrompre (*la circulation*); fermer, barrer (*la route etc.*); couper (*l'électricité, la respiration*); suspendre (*le paiement, une procédure*, ✗ *les permissions*); cesser; mettre fin à, supprimer; parer à (*un coup*); empêcher; ♪ presser (*une corde*), flûte: boucher (*des trous*); *gramm.* ponctuer; *v/i.* s'arrêter; cesser; rester, demeurer; attendre; descendre (à, *at*) (*un hôtel*); ~ *in* faire une petite visite, s'arrêter un moment; ~ *off* faire étape; ~ *over* faire une halte, faire étape; 2. arrêt *m* (*a.* ⊕); halte *f*; interruption *f*; ⊕ butoir *m*; ⊕ crochet *m*; *porte:* butée *f*; *machine à écrire:* margeur *m*; ♪ jeu *m*, *orgue:* registre *m*, *clarinette:* clé *f*, *violon etc.:* barré *m*; *guitare:* touche *f*; *gramm.* (*a. full* ~) point *m*; *ling.* occlusive *f*; '**~-cock** ⊕ robinet *m* d'arrêt; '**~-gap** bouche-trou *m*; '**~-light** *Am.* feu *m* rouge; *auto:* stop *m*; '**~-off**, '**~-o·ver** *surt. Am.* court séjour *m*, courte visite *f*, étape *f*; faculté *f* d'arrêt; '**stop·page** obstruction *f* (*a.* ⚕); arrêt *m*; *gages:* retenue *f*; *paiements etc.:* suspension *f*; *travail:* chômage *m*; *travail:* interruption *f*; ⊕ à-coup *m*; ⚡ ~ *of current* coupure *f* du courant; '**stop·per** 1. bouchon *m*; ⊕ taquet *m*; ♣ bosse *f*; 2. boucher; ♣ bosser; '**stop·ping** *dent:* plombage *m*; bouchon *m*; *a.* stoppage; '**stop·ping train** 🚂 train *m* omnibus; '**stop-press news** *pl.* informations *f/pl.* de dernière heure; '**stop-watch** *sp.* montre *f* à arrêt.

stor·age ['stɔ:ridʒ] emmagasinage *m*; entrepôts *m/pl.*; frais *m/pl.* d'entrepôt; ~ *battery* accumulateur *m*, F accu *m*.

store [stɔː] **1.** (*fig.* bonne) provision *f*; *fig. a.* ~s *pl.* abondance *f*; *a.* ~s *pl.* magasin *m*; *fig.* fonds *m* (*de connaissances*); *fig.* prix *m*; *Am.* boutique *f*; ~s *pl.* entrepôt *m*; ✂, ⚓ magasin *m*; vivres *m/pl.*; *in* ~ en réserve; *be in* ~ *for* attendre (*q.*); *have in* ~ *for* ménager (*qch.*) à; *set great* ~ *by* faire grand cas de; **2.** (*a.* ~ *up*) amasser; emmagasiner; mettre en dépôt (*des meubles*); approvisionner (de, *with*); garnir (*la mémoire*); '~**house** magasin *m*, entrepôt *m*; *fig.* mine *f*; ✂ manutention *f*; '~**keep·er** garde-magasin (*pl.* gardes-magasin[s]) *m*; *Am.* boutiquier (-ère *f*) *m*, marchand(e *f*) *m*; '~**room** office *f*, maison: dépense *f*; ⚓ magasin *m*; ⊕ halle *f* de dépôt.

sto·rey(ed) *see* story²; storied².

sto·ried¹ ['stɔːrid] historié; † célébré dans la légende *ou* histoire.

sto·ried² [~]: *four*-~ à quatre étages.

stork [stɔːk] cigogne *f*.

storm [stɔːm] **1.** orage *m*; tempête *f* (*a. fig.*); ✂ assaut *m*; *fig.* pluie *f*; *take by* ~ emporter (*a. fig.*), prendre d'assaut; **2.** *v/i.* se déchaîner; *fig.* tempêter; s'emporter (contre, *at*); *v/t.* ✂ livrer l'assaut à; prendre d'assaut; '**storm·y** □ tempétueux (-euse *f*); orageux (-euse *f*), d'orange; ~ *petrel orn.* pétrel *m*; *fig.* enfant *m* terrible.

sto·ry¹ ['stɔːri] histoire *f*, récit *m*; conte *m* (*a.* F = *mensonge*); *pièce*, *roman*: intrigue *f*; anecdote *f*; *short* ~ nouvelle *f*.

sto·ry² [~] étage *m*.

sto·ry·tell·er ['stɔːritelə] conteur (-euse *f*) *m*; F menteur (-euse *f*) *m*.

stout [staut] **1.** □ gros(se *f*); fort, vigoureux (-euse *f*); résolu, intrépide; solide; **2.** bière *f* brune forte; '~**heart·ed** vaillant; '**stout·ness** embonpoint *m*, corpulence *f*; *sp.* persévérance *f*.

stove [stouv] **1.** poêle *m*; ⊕ four *m*; ⚘ serre *f* chaude; **2.** ⊕ étuver (*a. des vêtements*); ⚘ élever en serre chaude; **3.** *prét. et p.p. de* stave 2; '~**pipe** tuyau *m* de poêle; *Am.* F cylindre *m*, chapeau *m* haut de forme.

stow [stou] ranger, serrer; ⚓ arrimer; '**stow·age** magasinage *m*; ⚓ (frais *m/pl.* d')arrimage *m*; '**stow·a·way** ⚓ passager *m* clandestin.

stra·bis·mus [strə'bisməs] strabisme *m*.

strad·dle ['strædl] *v/t.* se mettre à califourchon sur; enfourcher; ✂ être à cheval sur; écarter (*les jambes*); *v/i.* écarter les jambes; marcher *ou* se tenir les jambes écartées; *Am.* éviter de se compromettre.

strafe [straːf] ✂ bombarder; F marmiter.

strag·gle ['strægl] marcher sans ordre; ✂ rester en arrière, traîner (*a.* ⚘); *fig.* s'éparpiller; '**strag·gler** celui (celle *f*) qui reste en arrière; ✂ traînard *m*; ⚓ retardataire *m*; '**strag·gling** □ épars, éparpillé.

straight [streit] **1.** *adj.* droit (*a. fig.*); d'aplomb; en ordre; *fig.* honnête; *Am.* sec (sèche *f*) (*whisky etc.*); *Am. pol.* bon teint, vrai; *put* ~ (r)ajuster; arranger, remettre de l'ordre dans; **2.** *su. the* ~ *turf:* la ligne droite; **3.** *adv.* droit; directement; ~ *ahead* tout droit; ~ *away*, ~ *off* immédiatement, aussitôt, tout de suite; du premier coup, d'emblée; ~ *on* tout droit; ~ *out* carrément, franchement; '**straight·en** redresser; ranger; ~ *out* mettre en ordre; arranger; **straight·for·ward** □ [~'fɔːwəd] franc(he *f*); honnête; loyal (-aux *m/pl.*); '**straight·'out** direct, franc(he *f*); droit; *Am.* F *a.* vrai, véritable, à cent pour cent.

strain¹ [strein] **1.** ⊕ tension *f* (de, on); effort *m*, fatigue *f*; ⊕ déformation *f*; *fig.* ton *m*, *discours*: sens *m*; *esprit*: surmenage *m*; ♪ entorse *f*; ♪ *usu.* ~s *pl.* accents *m/pl.*; *musique:* sons *m/pl.*; *put a great* ~ *on* beaucoup exiger de; mettre à l'épreuve; **2.** *v/t.* tendre; *fig.* forcer (*a.* ⊕), pousser trop loin; ⊕ déformer; ⊕ filtrer; *fig.* fatiguer; serrer; ♪ fouler, forcer; *cuis.* égoutter; *v/i.* faire un (grand) effort; peiner; tirer (sur, *at*); ⊕ déformer; ~ *after s.th.* faire tous ses efforts pour atteindre qch.

strain² [~] qualité *f* (héritée); tendance *f*; race *f*, lignée *f*.

strain·er ['streinə] ⊕ tendeur *m*; *cuis.* passoire *f*; tamis *m*; filtre *m*; (*a. tea*-~) passe-thé *m/inv.*

strait [streit] **1.** (*noms propres, géog.* ~s *pl.*) détroit *m*; ~s *pl.* embarras *m*, gêne *f*; **2.:** ~ *jacket* (*ou waistcoat*) camisole *f* de force; '**strait·en** † rétrécir; † resserrer; ~ed pauvre; *in*

‿ed *circumstances* dans la gêne; **strait-laced** ['‿leist] collet monté *inv.*; prude; '**strait·ness** rigueur *f*; gêne *f*, besoin *m*; † étroitesse *f*.

strand[1] [strænd] 1. plage *f*, rive *f*; 2. *v/t.* jeter à la côte; *fig.* laisser (*q.*) en plan; ‿ed échoué; *fig.* à bout de ressources; *fig.* abandonné; *mot.* resté en panne; *v/i.* (s')échouer.

strand[2] [‿] toron *m*, *cordage*: brin *m*; *tissu*, *a. fig.*: fil *m*; *cheveux*: tresse *f*.

strange □ [streindʒ] étrange; singulier (-ère *f*); curieux (-euse *f*); inconnu; † étranger (-ère *f*); '**strange·ness** singularité *f*; étrangeté *f*; '**stran·ger** inconnu(e *f*) *m*; étranger (-ère *f*) *m* (à, to); ⚓ tiers *m*.

stran·gle ['stræŋgl] étrangler (*a. la presse*); *fig.* étouffer; '‿·hold *fig.* étau *m*; *have a* ‿ *on s.o.* tenir q. par la gorge.

stran·gu·late ⚕ ['stræŋgjuleit] étrangler; **stran·gu'la·tion** étranglement *m* (*a.* ⚕).

strap [stræp] 1. courroie *f*; *cuir*, *toile*: bande *f*; *soulier*: barrette *f*; ⊕ *frein*: bande *f*; bride *f*; *soutien-gorge*: bretelle *f*; 2. attacher *ou* lier avec une courroie; boucler (*une malle*); ⚕ mettre des bandelettes *m*, maintenir au moyen de bandages; bander; '‿·hang·er F voyageur (-euse *f*) *m* debout (*dans l'autobus etc.*); '**strap·ping** 1. robuste, bien découplé; 2. ⚕ emplâtre *m* adhésif.

strat·a·gem ['strætidʒəm] ruse *f* (*de guerre*), stratagème *m*.

stra·te·gic [strə'ti:dʒik] (‿ally) stratégique; **strat·e·gist** ['strætidʒist] stratégiste *m*; stratège *m*; '**strat·e·gy** stratégie *f*.

strat·i·fy ['strætifai] (se) stratifier.

stra·to·cruis·er ['strætoukru:zə] avion *m* stratosphérique.

strat·o·sphere *phys.* ['strætousfiə] stratosphère *f*.

stra·tum ['streitəm] *pl.* **-ta** ['‿tə] *géol.* strate *f*; couche *f* (*a. fig.*); *fig.* étage *m*, rang *m* social.

straw [strɔ:] 1. paille *f*; chalumeau *m*; *fig.* brin *m* d'herbe; *fig.* indication *f*; (*usu.* ‿ *hat*) chapeau *m* de paille; *surt. Am.* ‿ *man* homme *m* de paille; F *I don't care a* ‿ je m'en fiche; *the last* ‿ le comble *m*; 2. de paille; paille *adj./inv.* (*couleur*); *Am. pol.* ‿ *vote* vote *m* d'essai; '‿·ber·ry fraise *f*;

plante: fraisier *m*; '**straw·y** de paille; paille *adj./inv.*, jaunâtre.

stray [strei] 1. s'égarer, s'écarter (de, from); errer (*a. fig.*); *fig.* sortir (d'un sujet, *from a subject*); 2. (*a.* ‿ed) égaré (*a. fig.*), errant; 3. bête *f* perdue *ou* ⚓ épave; enfant *m* abandonné; ‿s *pl. radio*: parasites *m/pl.*; crachements *m/pl.*; '**stray·er** égaré(e *f*) *m*.

streak [stri:k] 1. raie *f*, bande *f*; *fig.* trace *f*; *aube*: lueur *f*; *Am.* F *talk a blue* ‿ parler à n'en plus finir; 2. rayer (de, with); '**streak·y** □ rayé, bariolé; en raies *ou* bandes; *tex.* vergé; entrelardé (*lard etc.*).

stream [stri:m] 1. cours *m* d'eau, ruisseau *m*; courant *m*; torrent *m* (*a. fig.*); 2. *v/i.* ruisseler, couler à flots (*a. yeux*); flotter (au vent) (*cheveux*, *drapeau*, *etc.*); ‿ in (out) entrer (sortir) à flots; *v/t.* verser à flots; laisser couler; ⚓ mouiller; '**stream·er** banderole *f*; *papier*: serpentin *m*; *journ.* manchette *f*; *météor.* ‿s *pl.* lumière *f* polaire.

stream·let ['‿lit] petit ruisseau *m*, ru *m*.

stream·line ['stri:mlain] 1. fil *m* de l'eau; courant *m* naturel; *carrosserie*: ligne *f* aérodynamique; 2. (*a.* stream-lined) profilé, caréné, fuselé; 3. *v/t.* caréner (*une auto etc.*); *fig.* rénover, alléger.

street [stri:t] rue *f*; *Am.* ‿ *floor* rez-de-chaussée *m/inv.*; *the man in the* ‿ l'homme *m* moyen; F *not in the same* ‿ *as* ne pas de taille avec; '‿·car *surt. Am.* tramway *m*; '‿·walk·er fille *f* de trottoir.

strength [streŋθ] force *f* (*a. fig.*); solidité *f*; *fig.* fermeté *f*; ⊕ résistance *f*; ✗, ⚓ effectif *m*, -s *m/pl.*; contrôles *m/pl.*; *on the* ‿ *of* sur la foi de, s'appuyant sur; par que; '**strength·en** *v/t.* affermir, renforcer; fortifier (*la santé*); *v/i.* s'affermir *etc.*; (re)prendre des forces.

stren·u·ous □ ['strenjuəs] énergique, actif (-ive *f*); ardu (*travail*); tendu (*effort*); acharné (*lutte etc.*); '**stren·u·ous·ness** ardeur *f*; acharnement *m*.

stress [stres] 1. force *f*; insistance *f*; *circonstances*: pression *f*; *gramm.* accent *m*; appui *m* de la voix (sur, on); violence *f* (*du temps*); ⊕ tension *f*, effort *m*; *lay* ‿ (*up*)*on* insister sur, attacher de l'importance à; **2.** insister sur, appuyer sur; ⊕ faire travailler, fatiguer.

stretch [stretʃ] **1.** v/t. (usu. ~ out) tendre (a. la main); étendre; allonger; prolonger; déployer (les ailes); fig. exagérer; ~ one's legs se dégourdir les jambes; ~ a point faire une exception (en faveur de, for); ~ words forcer le sens des mots; v/i. (souv. ~ out) s'étendre; s'élargir; prêter (étoffe); fig. aller, suffire; **2.** étendue f; extension f; élasticité f; ⊕ tension f, effort m; sl. do a ~ faire de la prison; at a ~ (tout) d'un trait; sans arrêt; on the ~ tendu; '**stretch·er** ⊕ tendeur m (a. pour chaussures); brancard m (pour malades); tente: traverse f; ♫ panneresse f.

strew [struː] [irr.] répandre, semer (de, with); **strewn** [struːn] p.p. de strew. ['eitid] strié.｝

stri·ate ['straiit], **stri·at·ed** [strai-｝

strick·en ['strikən] frappé, fig. accablé (de, with); (well) ~ in years chargé d'années.

strict [strikt] sévère, rigoureux (-euse f); précis, exact; ~ly speaking à proprement parler; '**strict·ness** rigueur f; exactitude f; **stric·ture** ['striktʃə] ✗ rétrécissement m; intestin: étranglement m; usu. ~s pl. critique f (sur, on).

strid·den ['stridn] p.p. de stride 1.

stride [straid] **1.** [irr.] v/t. enjamber; se tenir à califourchon sur; enfourcher (un cheval); v/i. marcher à grands pas; **2.** (grand) pas m; enjambée f; get into one's ~ prendre son allure normale; être lancé.

stri·dent □ ['straidnt] strident; ~ly stridemment.

strife [straif] conflit m, lutte f.

strike [straik] **1.** coup m; grève f; Am. F fig. rencontre f; coup m de veine; Am. baseball: coup m (du batteur); ~ ballot référendum m; ~ pay salaire m de gréviste; be on ~ être en ou faire grève; go on ~ se mettre en grève, F débrayer; **2.** [irr.] v/t. frapper (a. une médaille, ♫, a. fig.) (de, with); heurter, cogner; porter (un coup); ⚓ rentrer (le pavillon); amener (la voile); plier (une tente), lever (le camp); former (une commission); faire (le marché); allumer (une allumette); faire jaillir (une étincelle); prendre (une attitude, la moyenne, la racine); ♫ toucher de (la harpe); sonner (l'heu-

re); bouturer (une plante); ⚓ donner sur (les écueils); fig. faire une impression sur; impressionner; rencontrer; découvrir, tomber sur; fig. paraître; ~ a balance établir une balance; dresser le bilan; ~ oil rencontrer le pétrole, fig. avoir du succès, trouver le filon; ~ work se mettre en grève; ~ off abattre; rayer; ~ out rayer; ouvrir (une route); ~ up commencer à jouer ou à chanter; lier (une connaissance); v/i. porter un coup, frapper (à, at); ⚓ (ou ~ [the] bottom) toucher le fond; ⚓, ✗ rentrer son pavillon; ~ se mettre en grève, F débrayer; sonner (l'heure); prendre feu (allumette); prendre racine; ~ home frapper juste; porter (coup); ~ in s'enfoncer; intervenir (personne); ~ into pénétrer dans; ♪ ~ up commencer à jouer ou à chanter; ~ upon the ear frapper l'oreille; '~-**break·er** briseur m de grève, F jaune m; '**strik·er** frappeur (-euse f) m; pendule: marteau m; fusée: rugueux m; arme à feu: percuteur m; ⊕ gréviste mf; foot. buteur m.

strik·ing □ ['straikiŋ] à sonnerie; fig. frappant; saillant; impressionnant.

string [striŋ] **1.** ficelle f (a. fig.); corde f (a. ♪, arc, raquette); cordon m; ♀ fibre f, filament m; eccl. a. oignons, outils: chapelet m; fig. condition f; Am. F prise f; fig. lisière f; fig. procession f, série f; F ✗ ligature f; ~ of horses écurie f; ~ of pearls collier m; ♪ ~s pl. instruments m/pl. à cordes; have two ~s to one's bow avoir deux cordes à son arc, avoir un pied dans deux chaussures; pull the ~s tirer les ficelles, tenir les fils; **2.** [irr.] bander (un arc); ficeler (un paquet); filer (a. ~ up) tendre (les nerfs); enfiler (des perles, a. fig.); corder (une raquette); monter (un violon), monter les cordes de (un piano); effiler (des haricots); Am. sl. faire marcher (q.); F ~ along v/t. payer (q.) de promesses, faire marcher (q.); v/i. suivre; ~ along with s.o. suivre q., accompagner q.; venir ou aller avec q.; fig. se ranger à l'avis de q.; ~ up suspendre; ~ band ♪ orchestre m à cordes; ~ **bean** Am. haricot m vert; **stringed** ♪ à cordes.

strin·gen·cy ['strindʒənsi] rigueur f; puissance f, force f; ✝ resser-

rement *m*; **'strin·gent** □ rigoureux
(-euse *f*), strict; convainant; **✝**
serré (*argent*); tendu (*marché*).

string·y ['striŋi] filandreux (-euse
f); visqueux (-euse *f*) (*liquide*).

strip [strip] **1.** *v/t.* dépouiller (de,
of) (*a.* ⚡, *a. fig.*); ⚡, *a. fig.* dénuder
(de, of); *fig.* dégarnir (*une maison*);
⊕ démonter (*une machine*); *métall.*
démouler; ⚓ déshabiller, dégréer;
(*a.* ~ off) ôter, enlever; *v/i.* F se
déshabiller; *sl.* se mettre à poil;
2. bande(lette) *f*.

stripe [straip] **1.** *couleur:* raie *f*;
pantalon: bande *f*; ✗ galon *m*;
(*a.* long-service ~) chevron *m*;
2. rayer.   [tout jeune homme *m*.\

strip·ling ['stripliŋ] adolescent *m*,\

strive [straiv] [*irr.*] s'efforcer (de,
to; d'obtenir qch. *after s.th.*, *for
s.th.*); tâcher (de, to); lutter (contre,
against); **striv·en** ['strivn] *p.p. de*
strive.

strode [stroud] *prét. de* stride 1.

stroke [strouk] **1.** *usu.* coup *m*; ✂
congestion *f* cérébrale, apoplexie *f*;
⊕ *piston:* course *f*; *peint.* coup *m* de
pinceau; *fig.* retouche *f*; trait *m*
(de plume, *a. fig.*); coup *m* (d'horloge); *canotage:* nage *f*, *personne:*
chef *m* de nage; *nage:* brassée *f*; ~
of *genius* trait *m* de génie; ~ of *luck*
coup *m* de bonheur; **2.** caresser;
être chef de nage de (*un canot*); ~ 32
nager à 32 coups par minute.

stroll [stroul] **1.** *v/i.* flâner; se promener à l'aventure; F se balader;
v/t. se promener dans (*les rues*); **2.**
petit tour *m*; flânerie *f*; F balade *f*;
'stroll·er, 'stroll·ing ac·tor co-
médien(ne) *f* *m* ambulant(e *f*).

strong □ [strɔŋ] *usu.* fort (*a.*
gramm.), solide; ferme (*a.* ✝ *marché*); vif (vive *f*) (*souvenir*); bon(ne
f) (*mémoire*); robuste (*foi, santé*);
ardent (*partisan*); sérieux (-euse *f*)
(*candidat*); énergique (*mesure*);
accusé (*trait*); *cartes:* long(ue *f*)
(*couleur*); *see* language; feel ~(ly)
about attacher une grande importance à; F *go it* ~ dépasser les bornes;
F *going* ~ vigoureux (-euse *f*); solide; 30 ~ au nombre de 30; **'~box**
coffre-fort (*pl.* coffres-forts) *m*;
'~hold forteresse *f*; *fig.* citadelle *f*;
'~mind·ed à l'esprit décidé;
'~room chambre *f* blindée; cave *f*
forte.

strop [strɔp] **1.** cuir *m* (*à rasoir*); ⚓
estrope *f*; **2.** repasser (*un rasoir*) sur
le cuir.

stro·phe ['stroufi] strophe *f*.

strop·py *Brit.* F ['strɔpi] de mauvaise
humeur.

strove [strouv] *prét. de* strive.

struck [strʌk] *prét. et p.p. de*
strike 2.

struc·tur·al □ ['strʌktʃərəl] de
structure, structural (-aux *m/pl.*);
⊕ de construction; **struc·ture**
['strʌtʃə] structure *f*; édifice *m* (*a.*
fig.); *péj.* bâtisse *f*.

strug·gle ['strʌgl] **1.** lutter (contre,
against; avec, with); se débattre;
faire de grands efforts (pour, to);
2. lutte *f* (*a. fig.*); combat *m*;
'strug·gler lutteur *m*.

strum [strʌm] tapoter (du piano);
gratter (de la guitare *etc.*); *fig.* pianoter.

strum·pet *poét.*, F ['strʌmpit] prostituée *f*; catin *f*.

strung [strʌŋ] *prét. et p.p. de*
string 2.

strut [strʌt] **1.** *v/i.* se pavaner; *v/t.*
⊕ entretoiser; contreficher; **2.** démarche *f* fière; ⊕ entretoise *f*; arc-
boutant (*pl.* arcs-boutants) *m*; ~
pilier *m*, traverse *f*; **'strut·ting-
piece** ⊕ entretoise *f*, lierne *f*.

strych·nine ♈ ['strikniːn] strychnine *f*.

stub [stʌb] **1.** *arbre:* souche *f*;
cigarette: bout *m*; *Am. chèque:*
souche *f*, talon *m*; **2.** (*usu.* ~ up)
arracher, essoucher (*un champ*);
cogner (*le pied*); ~ out éteindre (*une
cigarette*) en l' écrasant par le bout.

stub·ble ['stʌbl] chaume *m*.

stub·bly ['stʌbli] couvert de chaume; court et raide (*barbe, cheveux*).

stub·born □ ['stʌbən] ǫbstiné,
opiniâtre, entêté; rebelle, réfractaire; ingrat (*sol, terre*); **'stub·born-
ness** opiniâtreté *f*, entêtement *m*.

stub·by ['stʌbi] trapu (*personne*);
tronqué (*arbre etc.*).

stuc·co ['stʌkou] **1.** stuc *m*; **2.** stuquer; recouvrir de stuc(age).

stuck [stʌk] *prét. et p.p. de* stick²;
Am. F ~ on amoureux (-euse *f*) de
(*q.*); F **'~up** hautain; prétentieux
(-euse *f*).

stud¹ [stʌd] **1.** clou *m* à grosse tête;
clou *m* (*sur une robe, a. d'un passage
clouté*); *chemise etc.:* bouton *m*; *foot.*

crampon *m*; ⚓ poteau *m*; **2.** clouter; orner (de, *with*); *fig.* parsemer (de, *with*).

stud² [⌣] écurie *f*; (*a.* ⌣ *farm*) haras *m*; '⌣**-book** livre *m* d'origines, studbook *m*; '⌣**-horse** étalon *m*.

stud·ding ⚓ ['stʌdiŋ] lattage *m*; lattis *m*.

stu·dent ['stju:dənt] étudiant(e *f*) *m*; boursier (-ère *f*) *m*; amateur *m* de livres; investigateur (-trice *f*) *m*;⌣ *hostel* foyer *m* d'étudiants; '**student·ship** bourse *f* d'études.

stud·ied □ ['stʌdid] instruit (*personne*) (dans, *in*); étudié, recherché (*toilette etc.*); voulu, prémédité (*geste, insulte, etc.*).

stu·di·o ['stju:diou] atelier *m*; *radio*: studio *m*; ⌣ *couch* divan *m*.

stu·di·ous □ ['stju:djəs] appliqué, studieux (-euse *f*); attentif (-ive *f*) (à qch., *of* s.th.; à *inf. of* gér., *to inf.*); soigneux (-euse *f*) (de *inf.*, *to inf.*); '**stu·di·ous·ness** amour *m* de l'étude; *fig.* attention *f*, zèle *m* (à *inf.*, *in* gér.).

stud·y ['stʌdi] **1.** étude *f* (*a.* ♪, *a. peint.*); cabinet *m* de travail; bureau *m*; soins *m/pl.*; *fig.* rêverie *f*; **2.** *v/i.* préparer (un examen, *for an examination*); étudier; *v/t.* étudier; observer; s'occuper de (*a. fig.*).

stuff [stʌf] **1.** matière *f*, substance *f*; étoffe *f* (*a. fig.*), tissu *m*; *péj.* camelote *f*; *fig.* F sottises *f/pl.*; **2.** *v/t.* bourrer (de, *with*); remplir (de, *with*); fourrer (dans, *into*); gaver; *cuis.* farcir; ⌣ *up* boucher; *Am. sl.* ⌣*ed shirt* collet *m* monté; *v/i.* manger avec excès; *fig. sl.* se les caler; '**stuff·ing** (rem)bourrage *m*; *oie etc.*: gavage *m*; *cuis.* farce *f*, farcissure *f*; matelassure *f* (*de crin*); ⊕ étoupe *f*; '**stuff·y** □ mal aéré; qui sent le renfermé; F collet monté *adj./inv.*; sans goût; F *Am.* fâché.

stul·ti·fi·ca·tion [stʌltifi'keiʃn] action *f* de rendre sans effet (*un décret etc.*) *ou* ridicule (*q.*); '**stul·ti·fy** ['⌣fai] infirmer, rendre nul *ou* vain *ou* sans effet; rendre ridicule.

stum·ble ['stʌmbl] **1.** trébuchement *m*, faux pas *m*; *cheval*: bronchade *f*; **2.** trébucher; faire un faux pas; broncher (*cheval*); se heurter (contre, *against*); hésiter (*en parlant*); '**stum·bling-block** *fig.* pierre *f* d'achoppement.

stump [stʌmp] **1.** tronçon *m*, souche *f*; *crayon, cigare*: bout *m*; *dessin*: estompe *f*; *dent*: chicot *m*; *cricket*: piquet *m*; moignon *m* (*d'un membre coupé*); F propagande *f* électorale; F ⌣*s pl.* quilles *f/pl.* (= *jambes*); ⌣ *speaker* (*ou orator*) orateur *m* de carrefour; orateur *m* de réunion électorale; **2.** *v/t. cricket*: mettre hors jeu en abattant le guichet avec la balle tenue à la main; F coller, embarrasser; *Am.* F défier; *sl.* ⌣ *up* cracher (= *payer*); ⌣ *the country* faire une tournée électorale; ⌣*ed for* embarrassé pour; *v/i.* clopiner; harangueur *m*; '**stump·y** □ écourté; trapu (*personne*).

stun [stʌn] étourdir; *fig.* abasourdir.

stung [stʌŋ] *prét. et p.p.* de sting 2.

stunk [stʌŋk] *prét. et p.p.* de stink 2.

stun·ner F ['stʌnə] type *m* épatant, chose *f* épatante; '**stun·ning** □ F épatant, étourdissant.

stunt¹ [stʌnt] **1.** tour *m* de force; F coup *m* d'épate; F nouvelle *f* sensationnelle; ✈ acrobaties *f/pl.* aériennes, vol *m* de virtuosité; **2.** faire des acrobaties.

stunt² [⌣] rabougrir; empêcher de croître; '**stunt·ed** rabougri; noué (*esprit*).

stupe ✶ [stju:p] **1.** compresse *f* (pour fomentation); **2.** fomenter.

stu·pe·fac·tion [stju:pi'fækʃn] stupéfaction *f*; ahurissement *m*.

stu·pe·fy ['stju:pifai] *fig.* hébéter (par la douleur, *by grief*); stupéfier, abasourdir.

stu·pen·dous □ [stju:'pendəs] prodigieux (-euse *f*).

stu·pid □ ['stju:pid] stupide, sot(te *f*); F bête; insupportable; **stu·pid·i·ty** [stju:'piditi] stupidité *f*; lourdeur *f* d'esprit; sottise *f*, bêtise *f*.

stu·por ['stju:pə] stupeur *f*.

stur·di·ness ['stə:dinis] vigueur *f*; résolution *f*; '**stur·dy** vigoureux (-euse *f*); robuste; hardi.

stur·geon *icht.* ['stə:dʒən] esturgeon *m*.

stut·ter ['stʌtə] **1.** bégayer; **2.** bégaiement *m*; '**stut·ter·er** bègue *mf.*

sty¹ [stai] étable *f* (à porcs); porcherie *f*.

sty² [⌣] *œil*: orgelet *m*.

style [stail] **1.** style *m* (*pour écrire,*

pour graver), △, ♀, *cadran*, *peint.*, *a.* = *manière*); façon *f*, manière *f*; *cost.* mode *f*; ton *m*, chic *m*; titre *m*; élégance *f*; ✝ raison *f* sociale; *in* ~ grand train; *in the* ~ *of* dans le style *ou* goût de; ✝ *under the* ~ *of* sous la raison de; **2.** appeler, dénommer; qualifier (*q.*) de.

styl·ish □ ['stailiʃ] élégant; chic *inv.* en genre; à la mode; **'styl·ish·ness** élégance *f*, chic *m*.

styl·ist ['stailist] styliste *mf*.

sty·lo F ['stailou], **sty·lo·graph** ['stailəgrɑːf], *a.* **sty·lo·graph·ic pen** [~'græfik'pen] stylographe *m*, F stylo *m*.

styp·tic ['stiptik] styptique (*a. su./m*), astringent (*a. su./m*).

sua·sion ['sweiʒn] persuasion *f*.

suave □ [sweiv] suave; affable; doux (douce *f*) (*vin*); *péj.* doucereux (-euse *f*); **suav·i·ty** ['swæviti] suavité *f*; douceur *f*; *péj.* politesse *f* mielleuse.

sub F [sʌb] *abr. de* subordinate 2; subscription; substitute 2; submarine.

sub...: *usu.* sous-; *qqfois* sub-; presque.

sub·ac·id ['sʌb'æsid] aigrelet(te *f*); *fig.* aigre-doux (-douce *f*).

sub·al·tern ['sʌbltən] **1.** subalterne (*a. su./m*); **2.** ✕ (sous-)lieutenant *m*.

sub·com·mit·tee ['sʌbkəmiti] sous-comité *m*; sous-commission *f*.

sub·con·scious □ ['sʌb'kɔnʃəs] subconscien̄t (*psych. a. su./m*); ~*ly* inconsciemment.

sub·con·tract [sʌb'kɔntrækt] sous-traité *m*.

sub·cu·ta·ne·ous □ ['sʌbkju:'teinjəs] sous-cutané; ✆ ~ *injection* injection *f* sous-cutanée.

sub·dean ['sʌb'di:n] sous-doyen *m*.

sub·di·vide ['sʌbdi'vaid] (se) subdiviser.

sub·di·vi·sion ['sʌbdiviʒn] subdivision *f*; sectionnement *m*; sous-division *f*; *biol.* sous-classe *f*; ⚓ section *f*.

sub·due [səb'dju:] subjuguer; dompter; maîtriser; réprimer; adoucir; baisser (*la lumière*).

sub·head(·ing) ['sʌbhed(iŋ)] sous-titre *m*.

sub·ja·cent [sʌb'dʒeisənt] sous-jacent, subjacent.

sub·ject ['sʌbdʒikt] **1.** *adj.* assujetti,

soumis; sujet(te *f*), exposé; porté (à, *to*); *fig.* ~ *to* passible de (*droit*, *courtage*); sous réserve de (*une ratification*); sauf; ~ *to a fee* (*ou duty*) sujet(te *f*) à une taxe *ou* à un droit; **2.** *adv.*: ~ *to* sous (la) réserve de; ~ *to change without notice* sauf modifications sans avis préalable; **3.** *su.* sujet(te *f*) *m* (*d'un roi etc.*); ♪, ♫, *gramm.*, *conversation*, *peint.* tableau: sujet *m*; (*a.* ~*-matter*) livre *etc.*: sujet *m*, thème *m*; question *f*; ✆ malade *mf*; matière *f*; *lettre*: contenu *m*; *peint. paysage*: motif *m*; *contrat réel*, *méditation*: objet *m*; **4.** *v/t.* [səb'dʒekt] assujettir, subjuguer; ~ *to* soumettre à (*un examen etc.*); exposer à (*un danger etc.*);

sub·jec·tion sujétion *f*; asservissement *m*; **sub·jec·tive** □ [sʌb'dʒektiv] subjectif (-ive *f*).

sub·join ['sʌb'dʒɔin] adjoindre, ajouter.

sub·ju·gate ['sʌbdʒugeit] subjuguer; **sub·ju·ga·tion** subjugation *f*, assujettissement *m*.

sub·junc·tive *gramm.* [səb'dʒʌŋktiv] (*a.* ~ *mood*) subjonctif *m*; *in the* ~ au subjonctif.

sub·lease ['sʌb'li:s], **sub·let** ['~'let] [*irr.* (*let*)] donner *ou* prendre en sous-location *ou* à sous-ferme; sous-louer.

sub·li·mate ♏ **1.** ['sʌblimit] sublimé *m*; **2.** ['~meit] sublimer; **sub·li·ma·tion** sublimation *f* (*a. psych.*); **sub·lime** [sə'blaim] **1.** □ sublime; **2.**: *the* ~ le sublime; **3.** ♏ (se) sublimer; *v/t. fig.* idéaliser; **sub·lim·i·nal** □ [sʌb'liminəl] subliminal (-aux *m/pl.*); ~ *advertising* publicité *f* insidieuse; **sub·lim·i·ty** [sə'blimiti] sublimité *f*.

sub·ma·chine gun ['sʌbmə'ʃi:n-'gʌn] mitraillette *f*.

sub·ma·rine ['sʌbməri:n] sous-marin (*a.* ⚓ *su./m*).

sub·merge [səb'mə:dʒ] *v/t.* submerger; noyer, inonder; *v/i.* plonger; **sub·mers·i·bil·i·ty** [səbmə:sə-'biliti] caractère *m* submersible; **sub·mer·sion** submersion *f*, plongée *f*.

sub·mis·sion [səb'miʃn] soumission *f* (*a. fig.*), résignation *f* (à, *to*); ♎ plaidoirie *f*; thèse *f*; **sub·mis·sive** □ [~'misiv] soumis (*air etc.*); docile (*personne*).

sub·mit [sʌbˈmit] v/t. soumettre; présenter; poser en thèse (que, that); v/i. (a. ~ o.s.) se soumettre (à, to); fig. se résigner (à, to); s'astreindre (à la discipline, to discipline).

sub·nor·mal [səbˈnɔːməl] au-dessous de la normale; faible d'esprit, arriéré.

sub·or·di·nate 1. □ [səˈbɔːdnit] subordonné; inférieur; secondaire; gramm. ~ clause proposition f subordonnée; **2.** [~] subalterne mf, subordonné(e f) m; **3.** [~ˈbɔːdineit] subordonner (à, to); **sub·or·di·na·tion** subordination f (à, to); soumission f (à, to).

sub·orn 🟥 [sʌˈbɔːn] suborner, séduire; **sub·or·na·tion** subornation f, corruption f.

sub·p(o)e·na 🟥 [səbˈpiːnə] **1.** assignation f; **2.** assigner, faire une assignation à.

sub·scribe [səbˈskraib] v/t. souscrire (un nom, une obligation, etc.; pour une somme, a sum); v/i. souscrire (à, to, for; pour une somme, for a sum; a. à une opinion, to an opinion); s'abonner (à, to) (un journal); **subˈscrib·er** signataire mf (de, to); fig. adhérent(e f) m; souscripteur m, cotisant m; journal, a. téléph. abonné(e f) m.

sub·scrip·tion [səbˈskripʃn] souscription f; fig. adhésion f; société, club, etc.: cotisation f; journal: abonnement m.

sub·se·quence [ˈsʌbsikwəns] conséquence f; postériorité f; **ˈsub·se·quent** □ conséquent, ultérieur; postérieur, consécutif (-ive f) (à, to); ~ly plus tard; postérieurement (à, to); par la suite.

sub·serve [səbˈsəːv] favoriser, aider à; **subˈser·vi·ence** [~viəns] soumission f; utilité f; servilité f; **subˈser·vi·ent** □ servile, obséquieux (-euse f); utile; subordonné.

sub·side [səbˈsaid] baisser; s'affaisser, se tasser (sol, maison); s'apaiser, tomber (orage, fièvre, etc.); F se taire; ~ into se changer en; **subˈsid·i·ary** [~ˈsidjəri] **1.** □ subsidiaire (à, to), auxiliaire; ~ company filiale f; **2.** filiale f; **sub·si·dize** [ˈsʌbsidaiz] subventionner; primer (une industrie); fournir des subsides à;

ˈsub·si·dy subvention f; industrie: prime f.

sub·sist [səbˈsist] v/i. subsister; persister; vivre (de on, by); v/t. entretenir; **subˈsist·ence** existence f; subsistance f; ~ money acompte m.

sub·soil [ˈsʌbsɔil] sous-sol m.

sub·son·ic [səbˈsɔnik] subsonique.

sub·stance [ˈsʌbstəns] substance f (a. eccl., a. fig.), matière f; fig. essentiel m, fond m; corps m, solidité f; fortune f, biens m/pl.

sub·stan·dard [səbˈstændəd] de qualité inférieure; au-dessous de la moyenne.

sub·stan·tial □ [səbˈstænʃl] substantiel(le f), réel(le f); solide; riche; considérable (somme, prix, etc.); **sub·stan·ti·al·i·ty** [~ʃiˈæliti] solidité f; phls. substantialité f.

sub·stan·ti·ate [səbˈstænʃieit] justifier, établir, prouver.

sub·stan·ti·val □ gramm. [sʌbstənˈtaivl] substantival (-aux m/pl.); **ˈsub·stan·tive 1.** □ réel(le f), autonome, indépendant; positif (-ive f) (droit); formel(le f) (résolution); gramm. substantival (-aux m/pl.); **2.** gramm. substantif m, nom m.

sub·sti·tute [ˈsʌbstitjuːt] **1.** v/t. substituer (à, for); remplacer (par, by); v/i. ~ for s.o. remplacer q., suppléer q.; **2.** personne: remplaçant(e f) m (a. sp.), suppléant(e f) m; nourriture etc.: succédané m, factice m; **sub·sti·tu·tion** substitution f, remplacement m; 🟥 subrogation f; créance: novation f.

sub·stra·tum [ˈsʌbˈstrɑːtəm], pl. -ta [ˈ~tə] couche f inférieure; souscouche f; phls. substrat(um) m; fig. fond m.

sub·struc·ture [ˈsʌbstrʌktʃə] édifice: fondement m; route, pont roulant: infrastructure f.

sub·ten·ant [ˈsʌbˈtenənt] sous-locataire mf.   [fuge m.}

sub·ter·fuge [ˈsʌbtəfjuːdʒ] subter-}

sub·ter·ra·ne·an □ [sʌbtəˈreinjən] souterrain.

sub·til·ize [ˈsʌtilaiz] v/t. subtiliser; raffiner (son style), péj. alambiquer; v/i. subtiliser, raffiner.

sub·ti·tle [ˈsʌbtaitl] livre, cin.: soustitre m.

sub·tle □ [ˈsʌtl] subtil, fin; raffiné;

rusé, astucieux (-euse *f*); **'sub·tle·ty** subtilité *f*; finesse *f*; ruse *f*.

sub·tract [səb'trækt] soustraire; **sub'trac·tion** soustraction *f*.

sub·urb ['sʌbə:b] faubourg *m*; *in the* ~**s** dans la *ou* en banlieue; **sub·ur·ban** [sə'bə:bən] de banlieue (*a. péj.*); suburbain; **Sub·ur·bi·a** F [sə'bə:biə] la banlieue.

sub·ven·tion [səb'venʃn] subvention *f*; *industrie*: prime *f*; octroi *m* d'une subvention.

sub·ver·sion [sʌb'və:ʃn] subversion *f*; subvertir *f*; **sub'ver·sive** [~siv] subversif (-ve *f*) (de, of). [vertir.\
sub·vert [sʌb'və:t] renverser, sub-∫

sub·way ['sʌbwei] (passage *m ou* couloir *m*) souterrain *m*; *Am.* métro *m*; chemin *m* de fer souterrain.

sub-ze·ro ['sʌb'ziərou] au-dessous de zéro.

suc·ceed [sək'si:d] *v/t.* succéder (à q., à qch., [to] s.o., s.th.); suivre; *v/i.* réussir; arriver, aboutir; ~ *to* prendre la succession *ou* la suite de; hériter (de) (*biens etc.*); *he* ~*s in* (*gér.*) il réussit *ou* parvient à (*inf.*).

suc·cess [sək'ses] succès *m*, réussite *f*; (bonne) chance *f*; *he was a great* ~ il a eu un grand succès; **suc'cess·ful** □ [~ful] heureux (-euse *f*), réussi; couronné de succès; *be* ~ réussir; avoir du succès; **suc·ces·sion** [~'seʃn] succession *f*, suite *f*; *récoltes*: rotation *f*; héritage *m*; lignée *f*, descendants *m/pl.*; ~ *to the throne* avènement *m*; *in* ~ successivement, tour à tour; ~ *duty* droits *m/pl.* de succession; **suc'ces·sive** [~siv] □ successif (-ive *f*), consécutif (-ive *f*); **suc'ces·sor** successeur *m* (de *of*, to); ~ *to the throne* successeur *m* à la couronne.

suc·cinct □ [sək'siŋkt] succinct, concis.

suc·co·ry ♀ ['sʌkəri] chicorée *f*.

suc·co·tash *Am.* ['sʌkətæʃ] purée *f* de maïs et de fèves.

suc·co(u)r ['sʌkə] **1.** secours *m*, aide *f*; ⚔ renforts *m/pl.*; **2.** secourir; aider, venir en aide à, venir à l'aide de; ⚔ renforcer.

suc·cu·lence ['sʌkjuləns] succulence *f*; **'suc·cu·lent** □ succulent (*a. fig.*).

suc·cumb [sə'kʌm] succomber, céder.

such [sʌtʃ] **1.** *adj.* tel(le *f*); pareil(le *f*); semblable; ~ *a man* un tel homme; *see another*; *there is no* ~ *thing* cela n'existe pas; *no* ~ *thing!* il n'en est rien!; ~ *as* tel que; ~ *and* ~ *tel et tel*; F ~ *a naughty dog* un chien si méchant; ~ *is life* c'est la vie; **2.** *pron.* tel(le *f*); ceux (celles *f/pl.*) *m/pl.*; **'such·like** de ce genre, de la sorte.

suck [sʌk] **1.** (*v/t. a.* ~ *out*) sucer; **2.** action *f* de sucer; *pompe*: succion *f*; *give* ~ donner la tétée *ou* le sein; **'suck·er** suceur (-euse *f*) *m*; ⊕ *pompe*: piston *m*; ♀ *arbre*: surgeon *m*, *plante*: rejeton *m*; *Am.* blanc-bec (*pl.* blancs-becs) *m*; niais *m*; **'suck·ing** à la mamelle (*enfant*); qui tette (*animal*); ~ *pig* cochon *m* de lait; **suck·le** ['~l] allaiter, nourrir; donner le sein à; **'suck·ling** allaitement *m*; nourrisson *m*.

suc·tion ['sʌkʃn] **1.** succion *f*; aspiration *f*; **2.** aspirant, d'aspiration; à succion; ~-*cleaner* (*ou* *sweeper*) aspirateur *m*.

sud·den □ ['sʌdn] soudain, brusque; *on a* ~, (*all*) *of a* ~ soudain, tout à coup; **'sud·den·ness** soudaineté *f*; brusquerie *f*.

su·dor·if·ic [sju:də'rifik] sudorifique (*a. su./m*).

suds [sʌdz] *pl.* eau *f* de savon; lessive *f*; **'suds·y** *Am.* plein *ou* couvert d'eau de savon.

sue [sju:] *v/t.* poursuivre; (*usu.* ~ *out*) obtenir à la suite d'une requête; *v/i.* solliciter (de q., to *s.o.*; qch., *for s.th.*); demander (qch., *for s.th.*).

suède [sweid] (peau *f* de) suède *m*; *chaussures*: daim *m*.

su·et ['sjuit] graisse *f* de rognon *ou* de bœuf; **'su·et·y** graisseux (-euse *f*).

suf·fer ['sʌfə] *v/i.* souffrir (de, from); être affligé (de, from); *v/t.* souffrir, éprouver; subir (*une peine, une défaite, une dépréciation*); ressentir (*une douleur*); tolérer, supporter; **'suf·fer·ance** tolérance *f*; *on* ~ par tolérance; **'suf·fer·er** victime *f*; ✚ malade *mf*; **'suf·fer·ing** souffrance *f*.

suf·fice [sə'fais] *v/i.* suffire (à, to); *v/t.* suffire à.

suf·fi·cien·cy [sə'fiʃənsi] suffisance *f*; quantité *f* suffisante; *a* ~ *of money* l'aisance *f*; **suf'fi·cient** □

assez de; suffisant; *I am not ~ of a naturalist* je ne suis pas assez naturaliste.

suf·fix *gramm.* ['sʌfiks] **1.** suffixer; **2.** suffixe *m*.

suf·fo·cate ['sʌfəkeit] *vt/i.* étouffer, suffoquer; **suf·fo·ca·tion** suffocation *f*; étouffement *m*; **'suf·fo·ca·tive** □ qui suffoque; suffocant.

suf·fra·gan *eccl.* ['sʌfrəgən] *évêque:* suffragant *m*; **'suf·frage** suffrage *m*; (droit *m* de) vote *m*; voix *f*; **suf·fra·gette** [ˌ~'dʒet] suffragette *f*; **suf·fra·gist** ['~dʒist] partisan *m* du droit de vote (*surt.* des femmes).

suf·fuse [sə'fjuːz] inonder; se répandre sur; **suf'fu·sion** [ˌ~ʒn] épanchement *m*; rougeur *f*; ⚘ suffusion *f*.

su·gar ['ʃugə] **1.** sucre *m*; **2.** sucrer; saupoudrer (*un gâteau*) de sucre; **'~-ba·sin,** *Am.* **'~-bowl** sucrier *m*; **'~-cane** canne *f* à sucre; **'~-coat** revêtir de sucre; *fig.* sucrer; **'~-free** sans sucre; **'~-loaf** pain *m* de sucre; **'~-lump** morceau *m* de sucre; **'~-plum** dragée *f*, bonbon *m*; **'sug·ar·y** sucré (*a. fig.*); *fig.* mielleux (-euse *f*).

sug·gest [sə'dʒest] suggérer (*a.* ⚘, *a. psych.*); proposer; inspirer; évoquer, donner l'idée de *ou* que; insinuer; **sug'ges·tion** suggestion *f*; conseil *m*; *fig.* trace *f*, nuance *f*. **sug·ges·tive** □ [sə'dʒestiv] suggestif (-ive *f*); évocateur (-trice *f*); *péj.* grivois; *be ~ of s.th.* évoquer qch.; **sug'ges·tive·ness** caractère *m* suggestif.

su·i·cid·al □ [sjui'saidl] de suicide; *~ maniac* suicidomane *mf*; **su·i·cide** ['~said] **1.** suicide *m*; *personne:* suicidé(e *f*) *m*; **2.** *Am.* se suicider.

suit [sjuːt] **1.** requête *f*; demande *f*; (*a. ~ of clothes*) homme: complet *m*; *femme:* ensemble *m*; *cartes:* couleur *f*; ⚖ procès *m*; *fig. follow ~* en faire autant; **2.** *v/t.* adapter, accommoder (à *to, with*); convenir à, aller à; être l'affaire de; être fait pour; être apte à; accommoder (*q.*); *~ed* fait (pour *to, for*); satisfait; *be ~ed* avoir trouvé (*qch.*) qui convient; être satisfait; *v/i.* aller, convenir; **suit·a'bil·i·ty** convenance *f*; accord *m*; aptitude *f* (à, *for*); **'suit·a·ble** □ convenable, qui convient; bon, adapté (à *to, for*); **'suit·a·ble·ness** *see* suitability;

'suit·case mallette *f*, valise *f*; **suite** [swiːt] *prince, a.* ♪: suite *f*; *pièces:* appartement *m*; ameublement *m*; ensemble *m*; *salon:* mobilier *m*; *bedroom ~* chambre *f* à coucher; **suit·ing** ⊕ ['sjuːtiŋ] tissu *m* *ou* étoffe *f* pour complets; **'suit·or** soupirant *m*; ⚖ plaideur (-euse *f*) *m*.

sulk [sʌlk] **1.** (*a. be in the ~s*) bouder, faire la mine; **2.** *~s pl.* (*ou* **'sulk·i·ness**) bouderie *f*; **'sulk·y 1.** □ boudeur (-euse *f*), maussade; **2.** *sp.* sulky *m*.

sul·lage ['sʌlidʒ] eaux *f/pl.* d'égout; limon *m*; ⊕ scories *f/pl.*

sul·len □ ['sʌlən] maussade, morose (*personne*); morne, lugubre (*chose*); obstiné (*silence*); rétif (-ive *f*).

sul·phate 🜍 ['sʌlfeit] sulfate *m*; **sul·phide** 🜍 ['~faid] sulfure *m*; **sul·phon·a·mide** [ˌ~'fɒnəmaid] sulfamide *m*.

sul·phur 🜍 ['sʌlfə] **1.** soufre *m*; **2.** soufrer; **sul·phu·re·ous** [sʌl'fjuəriəs] sulfureux (-euse *f*); **sul·phu·ret·ted hy·dro·gen** ['sʌlfjuretid 'haidrɒdʒən] hydrogène *m* sulfuré, sulfure *m* d'hydrogène; **sul·phu·ric** [ˌ~'fjuərik] sulfurique, F vitriolique; *~ acid* acide *m* sulfurique; **'sul·phu·rize** ⊕ sulfurer (*un métal*); soufrer (*la laine*).

sul·tan ['sʌltən] sultan *m*; **sul·tan·a** [sʌl'tɑːnə] sultane *f*; [səl'tɑːnə] (*a. ~ raisin*) raisin *m* sec.

sul·tri·ness ['sʌltrinis] lourdeur *f*. **sul·try** □ ['sʌltri] étouffant, lourd; *fig.* chaud; *fig.* épicé.

sum [sʌm] **1.** somme *f*, total *m*; *fig.* fond *m*, essence *f*; F problème *m*; F *~s pl.* calcul *m*; **2.** (*usu. ~ up*) additionner, faire la somme de; *fig.* résumer, récapituler.

sum·ma·rize ['sʌməraiz] résumer; **'sum·ma·ry 1.** □ sommaire (*a.* ⚖); succinct; en peu de mots; récapitulatif (-ive *f*); **2.** résumé *m*, sommaire *m*; récapitulation *f*.

sum·mer¹ ['sʌmə] **1.** été *m*; **'~-house** pavillon *m*, kiosque *m* de jardin; *~ resort* station *f* estivale; **2.** *vt/i.* estiver; *v/i. a.* passer l'été.

sum·mer² △ [ˌ~] poutre *f* de plancher; poitrail *m*; linteau *m* de baie.

sum·mer·like ['sʌməlaik], **'sum·mer·ly, 'sum·mer·y** d'été; estival (-aux *m/pl.*).

sum·mit ['sʌmit] sommet *m* (*a. pol.*),

faîte *m* (*a. fig.*); cime *f*; *fig.* comble *m*; ~ *conference* conférence *f* au sommet.

sum·mon ['sʌmən] appeler; convoquer; sommer (ᵗᵗ de comparaître); *fig.* (*usu* ~ *up*) faire appel à; **'sum·mon·er** convocateur *m*; † huissier *m*; **sum·mons** ['~z] appel *m*; ᵗᵗ citation *f*, assignation *f*; ✝ convocation *f*; ✗ ~ *to surrender* sommation *f*.

sump *mot.* [sʌmp] (fond *m* de) carter *m*.

sump·ter ['sʌmptə] (*usu.* ~-*horse*, ~-*mule*) cheval *m ou* mulet *m* de somme.

sump·tu·ar·y ['sʌmptjuəri] somptuaire.

sump·tu·ous □ ['sʌmptjuəs] somptueux (-euse *f*), fastueux (-euse *f*); **'sump·tu·ous·ness** faste *m*; richesse *f*; somptuosité *f*.

sun [sʌn] 1. soleil *m*; 2. du *ou* au *ou* de soleil, par le soleil; 3. *v/t.* exposer au soleil; ~ *o.s.* se chauffer au soleil; prendre le soleil; **'~·baked** brûlé par le soleil; **~·beam** ['sʌnbi:m] rayon *m* de soleil.

sun·burn ['sʌnbə:n] hâle *m*; ⚕ coup *m* de soleil; **'sun·burnt** basané, brûlé par le soleil.

sun·dae *Am.* ['sʌnd(e)i] glace *f* aux fruits.

Sun·day ['sʌndi] dimanche *m*.

sun·der *poét.* ['sʌndə] (se) séparer; *v/t.* fendre en deux.

sun·di·al ['sʌndaiəl] cadran *m* solaire, gnomon *m*.

sun·down ['sʌndaun] coucher *m* du soleil; *Am.* occident *m*; *Am.* chapeau *m* à larges bords; **'sun·down·er** petit verre *m* pris au coucher du soleil.

sun·dry ['sʌndri] 1. divers; 2. *sundries pl. surt.* ✝ articles *m/pl.* divers; frais *m/pl.* divers.

sung [sʌŋ] † *prét. et p.p. de sing.*

sun...: '~·glass·es *pl.* (*a. a pair of* ~) (des) lunettes *f/pl.* fumées *ou* solaires; '~-'hel·met casque *m* colonial.

sunk [sʌŋk] *p.p.*, *a. prét. de sink* 1.

sunk·en ['sʌŋkən] sombré; *fig.* creux (creuse *f*) (*joues, yeux*); ⊕ enterré.

sun·lamp *cin.* ['sʌnlæmp] grand réflecteur *m*.

sun·lit ['sʌnlit] ensoleillé; éclairé par le soleil.

sun·ni·ness ['sʌninis] caractère *m*

ensoleillé; *fig.* gaieté *f*; **'sun·ny** □ ensoleillé; de soleil; *fig.* rayonnant; *fig.* heureux (-euse *f*).

sun...: '~·rise lever *m* du soleil; '~-**room** solarium *m*; '~·set coucher *m* du soleil; '~·shade ombrelle *f*; ⊕, *a. mot.* pare-soleil *m/inv.*; '~·shine (lumière *f* du) soleil *m*; *mot.* ~ *roof* toit *m* découvrable *ou* ouvrant; '~-**shin·y** ensoleillé, de soleil; '~·spot *astr.* tache *f* solaire; '~·stroke ✗ coup *m* de soleil; insolation *f*; '~·up lever *m* du soleil.

sup [sʌp] *v/i.* souper (de *off*, on); *v/t.* donner à souper à (*q.*).

su·per¹ ['sju:pə] 1. *théâ., a. cin.* F figurant(e *f*) *m*; 2. F *mesure:* carré; ✝ surfin.

su·per-² [~] super-; plus que; sus-.

su·per...: ~·a'bound surabonder (de, in *in*, with); foisonner (de *in*, with); ~·a'bun·dant □ surabondant; ~*ly* surabondamment; '~·add surajouter; ~·an·nu·ate [~'rænjueit] mettre à la retraite; *fig.* mettre au rancart; ~*d* suranné; démodé; en retraite (*personne*); ~·an·nu·a·tion mise *f* en retraite; ~ *fund* caisse *f* des retraites.

su·perb □ [sju:'pə:b] superbe, magnifique.

su·per·car·go ⚓ ['sju:pəka:gou] subrécargue *m*; **'su·per·charg·er** *mot.* (sur)compresseur *m*; **su·per·cil·i·ous** □ [~'siliəs] hautain, dédaigneux (-euse *f*); **su·per'cil·i·ous·ness** hauteur *f*; arrogance *f*; **super-'dread·nought** super-dreadnought *m* (= *grand cuirassé*); **su·per·e·ro·ga·tion** [~'rero'gei∫n] surérogation *f*; **su·per·e·rog·a·to·ry** □ ['~re'rɔgətəri] surérogatoire; **su·per·fi·cial** □ [~'fi∫l] superficiel(le *f*); **su·per·fi·ci·al·i·ty** [~fi∫i'æliti] superficialité *f*; **su·per·fi·ci·es** [~'fi∫i:z] superficie *f*; '**su·per'fine** superfin; ✝ surfin; *fig.* raffiné; **su·per·flu·i·ty** [~'fluiti] superfluité *f*; embarras *m* (de, of); **su·per'flu·ous** □ [sju:'pə:fluəs] superflu; **su·per'heat** ⊕ surchauffer; **su·per·het** ['~'het] *radio:* superhétérodyne *m*.

su·per...: ~·hu·man □ [~'hju:mən] surhumain; ~·in·duce ['~rin'dju:s] surajouter (à, [up]on); superposer (sur, [up]on); ~·in·tend [~prin'tend] surveiller, diriger; présider à; ~·in-

'**tend·ence** direction *f*, surveillance *f*; ~**in'tend·ent 1.** surveillant(e *f*) *m*; directeur (-trice *f*) *m*; **2.** surveillant.

su·pe·ri·or [sju:'piəriə] **1.** □ supérieur (à, *to*); *fig.* arrogant, de supériorité; *fig.* au-dessus (de, *to*); **2.** supérieur(e *f*) *m* (*a. eccl.*); (*Lady*) ♀ mère *f* abbesse; **su·pe·ri·or·i·ty** [~'ɔriti] supériorité *f*.

su·per·la·tive [sju:'pə:lətiv] **1.** □ suprême; F *a.* gramm. superlatif (-ive *f*); **2.** gramm. (*a.* ~ *degree*) superlatif *m*; '**su·per·man** surhomme *m*; '**su·per·mar·ket** supermarché *m*; '**su·per'nat·u·ral** □ surnaturel (-le *f*); **su·per·nu·mer·ar·y** [~'nju:mərəri] **1.** surnuméraire (*a. su./m*); **2.** *théâ.* figurant(e *f*) *m*; '**su·per'pose** superposer (à, [*up*]*on*); '**su·per·po'si·tion** superposition *f*; *géol.* disposition *f* en couches; stratification *f*; '**su·per'pow·er** *pol.* superpuissance *f*; '**su·per'scribe** mettre une inscription sur; mettre l'adresse sur; **su·per'scrip·tion** inscription *f*; adresse *f*; **su·per'sede** [~'si:d] remplacer; *fig.* démonter; *fig.* supplanter; **su·per'ses·sion** remplacement *m*; évincement *m*; **su·per·son·ic** *phys.* [~'sɔnik] ultrasonore; supersonique; **su·per·sti·tion** [~'stiʃn] superstition *f*; **su·per·'sti·tious** □ [~ʃəs] superstitieux (-euse *f*); **su·per·struc·ture** ['~strʌktʃə] superstructure *f*; **su·per·vene** [~'vi:n] survenir; arriver (à la suite de, [*up*]*on*); **su·per·ven·tion** [~'venʃn] survenance *f*, survenue *f*; **su·per·vise** ['~vaiz] surveiller, diriger; **su·per·vi·sion** [~'viʒn] surveillance *f*; direction *f*; **su·per·vi·sor** ['~vaizə] surveillant(e *f*) *m*; directeur (-trice *f*) *m*.

su·pine 1. gramm. ['sju:pain] supin *m*; **2.** □ [~'pain] couché *ou* étendu sur le dos; *fig.* indolent; mou (mol *devant une voyelle ou un h muet*; molle *f*); nonchalant; **su·'pine·ness** indolence *f*, mollesse *f*, inertie *f*.

sup·per ['sʌpə] souper *m*; *the* (*Lord's*) ♀ la Cène *f*.

sup·plant [sə'plɑ:nt] supplanter; remplacer; évincer (*q.*); F dégommer.

sup·ple ['sʌpl] **1.** □ souple; complaisant; **2.** assouplir.

sup·ple·ment 1. ['sʌplimənt] supplément *m*; annexe *f*, appendice *m*; **2.** ['~ment] ajouter à, compléter; **sup·ple·men·tal** □, **sup·ple·men·ta·ry** supplémentaire (de, *to*); additionnel(le *f*) (à, *to*); ~ *benefit* allocation *f* supplémentaire; ✝ ~ *order* commande *f* renouvelée; *give a* ~ *ticket* prendre un billet supplémentaire.

sup·ple·ness ['sʌplnis] souplesse *f* (*a. fig.*); *fig.* complaisance *f*.

sup·pli·ant ['sʌpliənt] **1.** □ suppliant; de supplication; **2.** suppliant(e *f*) *m*.

sup·pli·cate ['sʌplikeit] supplier (pour obtenir, *for*; de *inf.*, *to inf.*); prier avec instance; **sup·pli·ca·tion** supplication *f*; supplique *f*; **sup·pli·ca·to·ry** ['~kətəri] supplicatoire, de supplication.

sup·pli·er [sə'plaiə] fournisseur (-euse *f*) *m* (*a.* ✝); pourvoyeur (-euse *f*) *m*.

sup·ply [sə'plai] **1.** fournir, approvisionner, munir (de, *with*); combler (*une lacune*); réparer (*une omission*); remplir; répondre à (*un besoin*); remplacer (*q.*); **2.** fourniture *f*; approvisionnement *m*; ravitaillement *m* (*a. en munitions*); provision *f*; service *m* de (*gaz etc.*); ✝ offre *f*; *usu. supplies pl.* ✝ fournitures *f/pl.*; *parl.* budget *m*; crédits *m/pl.*; ✗ vivres *m/pl.*; approvisionnements *m/pl.*; ravitaillement *m* en munitions; *be in short* ~ manquer; *on* ~ par intérim; ~ *teacher* (professeur *mf*) suppléant(e *f*) *m*; *parl. Committee of* ♀ commission *f* du budget.

sup·port [sə'pɔ:t] **1.** appui *m*, soutien *m* (*a.* ⊕, *a. fig.*); ⊕ soutènement *m*; maintien *m*, entretien *m*; ressources *f/pl.*; ✗ (troupes *f/pl.* de) soutien *m*; **2.** appuyer (*a. fig.*); soutenir (*a. parl. une motion, a. théâ. un rôle*); maintenir; entretenir; subvenir aux besoins de (*une famille*); venir à l'appui de (*une opinion etc.*); tolérer (*une injure*); entourer (*un président etc.*); *théâ.* donner la réplique à (*le premier rôle*); seconder; *théâ.* ~*ing part* rôle *m* secondaire; *cin.* ~*ing programme* film *m ou* -s *m/pl.* d'importance secondaire; △ ~*ing wall* mur *m* d'appui; **sup'port·a·ble** □ tolérable, supportable; soutenable (*opinion*); **sup-port·er** adhérent(e *f*) *m*; partisan (-e *f*) *m*; *sp.* supporter *m*; défenseur *m* (*d'une opinion*); ⚡ support *m*; *appareil*: soutien *m*.

sup·pose [sə'pouz] supposer, s'imaginer; croire; he is ~d to (*inf.*) il est censé (*inf.*); ~ (*that*), supposing (*that*) admettons que (*sbj.*), supposé que (*sbj.*); F ~ we do so eh bien! et puis après?; he is rich, I ~ je suppose qu'il est riche.

sup·posed □ [sə'pouzd] supposé, prétendu; soi-disant; **sup'pos·ed·ly** [~idli] probablement.

sup·po·si·tion [sʌpə'ziʃn] supposition *f*; hypothèse *f*; **sup·pos·i·ti·tious** □ [səpɔzi'tiʃəs] faux (fausse *f*), supposé; **sup'pos·i·to·ry** 💊 [~təri] suppositoire *m*.

sup·press [sə'pres] supprimer; réprimer; **sup·pres·sion** [sə'preʃn] suppression *f*; répression *f*; étouffement *m*; **sup'pres·sive** □ [sə'presiv] suppressif (-ive *f*), répressif (-ive *f*); **sup'pres·sor** personne *f* qui supprime *ou* réprime; *radio*: grille *f* de freinage; *télév.* antiparasite *m*.

sup·pu·rate ['sʌpjureit] suppurer; **sup·pu'ra·tion** suppuration *f*.

su·prem·a·cy [sju'preməsi] suprématie *f* (sur, over); **su·preme** □ [sju'pri:m] suprême (*a. poét. heure*); souverain.

sur·charge 1. [sə:'tʃɑ:dʒ] surcharger (de, with; *a. un timbre-poste*); surtaxer; **2.** ['~] surcharge *f* (*a. timbre-poste*); charge *f* excessive; *lettre*: surtaxe *f*.

surd Ⱥ [sə:d] **1.** incommensurable; irrationnel(le *f*); **2.** quantité *f* incommensurable; racine *f* irrationnelle.

sure □ [ʃuə] sûr, certain; to be ~!, F ~ enough!, Am. ~! vraiment!, en effet!, bien sûr; Am. F ~ fire infaillible; absolument sûr; Am. F ~ thing! bien sûr!; mais oui!; it's a ~ thing c'est une certitude, c'est sûr et certain; I'm ~ I don't know je ne sais vraiment pas; he is ~ to return il reviendra sûrement *ou* à coup sûr; make ~ s'assurer (de, of); prendre les dispositions nécessaires (pour *inf.*, to *inf.*); be ~ to write ne manquez pas d'écrire; **'sure·ly** assurément; certainement; **'sure·ness** sûreté *f*; cer-

titude *f*; **'sure·ty** caution *f*, garant(e *f*) *m*; † garantie *f*.

surf [sə:f] **1.** ressac *m*; brisants *m/pl.*; **2.** (*a.* ~ride, go ~ing) surfer, faire du surfing; ~ board planche *f* de surf.

sur·face ['sə:fis] **1.** surface *f*; *fig.* dehors *m*; 🛫 supporting (*ou* lifting) ~ aile *f* voilure; 🛫 control ~ gouverne *f*; **2.** *v/i.* revenir en *ou* faire surface; **'~·man** 🚂 cheminot *m*.

sur·feit [sə:fit] **1.** excès *m*, surabondance *f*; *fig.* dégoût *m*; **2.** (se) gorger (de on, with) (*a. fig.*).

surf·rid·ing ['sə:fraidiŋ] *sp.* planking *m*; sport *m* de l'aquaplane.

surge [sə:dʒ] **1.** houle *f*; vague *f* (*a.* 𝆑 de courant); lame *f* de fond; **2.** se soulever; être *ou* devenir houleux; *fig.* se répandre en flots.

sur·geon ['sə:dʒən] chirurgien(ne *f*) *m*; ⚓, ✗ médecin *m* (militaire); **sur·ger·y** ['sə:dʒəri] chirurgie *f*; médecine *f* opératoire; *endroit*: cabinet *m* de consultation; dispensaire *m*.

sur·gi·cal □ ['sə:dʒikl] chirurgical (-aux *m/pl.*), de chirurgie.

sur·li·ness ['sə:linis] maussaderie *f*; caractère *m* hargneux; air *m* bourru; **'sur·ly** □ maussade; hargneux (-euse *f*); bourru.

sur·mise 1. ['sə:maiz] conjecture *f*, supposition *f*; **2.** [~'maiz] conjecturer; soupçonner.

sur·mount [sə:'maunt] surmonter (*a. fig.*); *fig.* triompher de (*qch.*); ~ed by (*ou* with) surmonté *ou* couronné de; **sur'mount·a·ble** surmontable.

sur·name ['sə:neim] **1.** nom *m* (de famille); **2.** donner un nom de famille à; ~d surnommé.

sur·pass *fig.* [sə:'pɑ:s] surpasser; dépasser; **sur'pass·ing** □ sans égal (-aux *m/pl.*); prééminent.

sur·plice *eccl.* ['sə:pləs] surplis *m*.

sur·plus ['sə:pləs] **1.** surplus *m*, excédent *m*; **2.** d'excédent; surplus de; **'sur·plus·age** see surplus 1; surabondance *f*; ⚖ redondance *f*.

sur·prise [sə'praiz] **1.** surprise *f*; étonnement *m*; ✗ coup *m* de main; take by ~ prendre au dépourvu, surprendre; **2.** à l'improviste; **3.** étonner; surprendre (*a.* ✗); **sur'pris·ing** □ étonnant, surprenant.

sur·re·al·ism [sə'riəlizm] *art*: surréalisme *m*; **sur're·al·ist** surréaliste (*a. su./mf*).

sur·ren·der [sə'rendə] **1.** ✗ reddition *f*; abandon *m*; **2.** *v/t.* abandonner (*a.fig.*); ✗ rendre; *v/i.* (*a. ~ o.s.*) se rendre.

sur·rep·ti·tious □ [sʌrəp'tiʃəs] clandestin, subreptice.

sur·ro·gate ['sʌrəgit] suppléant(e *f*) *m*; ⚖, *eccl.* subrogé(e *f*) *m*.

sur·round [sə'raund] entourer (*a.* ✗); cerner; investir (*une ville*); **sur'round·ing 1.** environnant, d'alentour; **2.** *~s pl.* environnement *m*; milieu *m*; entourage *m*.

sur·tax ['sə:tæks] surtaxe *f*.

sur·veil·lance [sə:'veiləns] surveillance *f*.

sur·vey 1. [sə:'vei] contempler, promener ses regards sur; examiner attentivement; *surv.* arpenter (*un terrain*); faire le levé du plan de; **2.** ['sə:vei] vue *f* générale, aperçu *m*; étude *f* (*de la situation*); inspection *f*, visite *f*; *surv. terrain*: arpentage *m*; levé *m* (*des plans*); **sur'vey·or** arpenteur *m*, géomètre *m* expert; *admin.* inspecteur (-trice *f*) *m*; contrôleur (-euse *f*) *m*.

sur·viv·al [sə'vaivl] survivance *f*; restant *m*; ⚖ survie *f*; **sur'vive** [~'vaiv] *v/t.* survivre à; *v/i.* survivre; demeurer en vie; subsister; **sur'vi·vor** survivant(e *f*) *m*.

sus·cep·ti·bil·i·ty [səseptə'biliti] prédisposition *f* (à, *to*), susceptibilité *f*; *souv.* susceptibilities *pl.* sensibilité *f*; **sus'cep·ti·ble** □, **sus'cep·tive** sensible, prédisposé (à *of*, *to*); *be ~ of* se prêter à (*qch.*); être susceptible de.

sus·pect 1. [səs'pekt] soupçonner; avoir idée (que, *that*); se douter de (*qch.*); **2.** ['sʌspekt] suspect(e *f*) *m*; **3.** [~] (*a. ~ed*) suspect.

sus·pend [səs'pend] pendre; suspendre (*fonctionnaire, jugement, paiements, poursuite, travail, etc.*); cesser; ✗ mettre (*un officier*) en non-activité; *parl.* exclure temporairement; ⚖ surseoir à (*un jugement*); *sp.* exécuter (*un joueur*), mettre (*un jockey*) à pied; *~ed* suspendu; interrompu; *~ed* animation syncope *f*; *fig.* suspens *m*; **sus'pend·er** suspensoir *m*; *surt. Am. ~s pl.* bretelles *f/pl.*; jarretelles *f/pl*; fixe-chaussettes *m/inv.*

sus·pense [səs'pens] suspens *m*; incertitude *f*; *in ~* pendant(e *f*); ✝ *~ account* compte *m* d'ordre; **sus'pen·sion** [~'penʃn] suspension *f*; ⚖ *jugement*: surséance *f*; *parl. député*: exclusion *f* temporaire; *sp.* exécution *f*; mise *f* à pied (*d'un jockey*); *~-bridge* pont *m* suspendu; *~ railway* chemin *m* de fer suspendu; **sus'pen·sive** □ suspensif (-ive *f*); **sus'pen·so·ry** [~'pensəri] **1.** suspensif (-ive *f*); **2.** *anat.* suspenseur *m*; ♂ *~ bandage* suspensoir *m*.

sus·pi·cion [səs'piʃn] soupçon *m* (*a. fig.*); *fig. sourire*: ébauche *f*.

sus·pi·cious □ [səs'piʃəs] suspect; équivoque; louche; méfiant; **sus'pi·ciuos·ness** caractère *m* suspect *etc.*; méfiance *f*.

sus·tain [səs'tein] *usu.* soutenir (*a. fig.*); entretenir (*la vie*); appuyer (*des témoignages*); essuyer (*une perte*); **sus'tain·a·ble** soutenable; **sus'tained** soutenu, nourri (*a.fig.*); continu.

sus·te·nance ['sʌstinəns] sustentation *f*; subsistance *f*; nourriture *f*.

sut·ler ✗ ['sʌtlə] cantinier (-ère *f*) *m*; *sl.* mercanti *m*.

su·ture ['sju:tʃə] **1.** ♀, ♂, *anat.* suture *f*; **2.** suturer.

su·ze·rain ['su:zərein] suzerain *m*; **'su·ze·rain·ty** suzeraineté *f*.

swab [swɔb] **1.** torchon *m*; ⚓ faubert *m*; ♂ tampon *m* d'ouate; ♂ prélèvement *m* (dans, *of*); *sl.* andouille *f*; *sl.* ⚓ marin *m* d'eau douce; **2.** (*a. ~ down*) nettoyer; ⚓ fauberter.

swad·dle ['swɔdl] **1.** emmailloter (de, *with*); *swaddling clothes pl.* maillot *m*; F *fig.* langes *m/pl.*; **2.** lange *m*; bande *f*.

swag·ger ['swægə] **1.** crâner, se pavaner, se donner des airs; fanfaronner; **2.** F ultra-chic *inv.* en genre; élégant; **3.** air *m* avantageux; rodomontades *f/pl.*; **'~-cane** ✗ jonc *m* d'officier; jonc *m* de tenue de sortie.

swain [swein] ✝ berger *m*; *poét.*, *a. co.* soupirant *m*.

swal·low¹ *orn.* ['swɔlou] hirondelle *f*.

swal·low² [~] **1.** gosier *m*; gorgée *f*; **2.** *v/t.* avaler (*a. fig. une histoire, un affront*); gober (*une huître, a. fig.* [*qqfois ~ up*] *une histoire*); *fig.*

ravaler (*ses paroles*); mettre dans sa poche (*son orgueil*); *v/i.* avaler.

swam [swæm] *prét. de swim 1.*

swamp [swɔmp] **1.** marais *m*, marécage *m*; **2.** inonder (*a. fig.*); ⚓ remplir d'eau, submerger; *fig.* déborder (de, *with*); écraser; '**swamp·y** marécageux (-euse *f*).

swan [swɔn] cygne *m*.

swank *sl.* [swæŋk] **1.** prétention *f*, épate *f*; **2.** prétentieux (-euse *f*); snob *adj./inv.*; **3.** crâner, faire de l'épate.

swan-neck ['swɔnnek] ⊕ cou *m* de cygne; ⚓ gui: aiguillot *m*; **swan-ner·y** ['∼əri] endroit *m* où l'on élève des cygnes; '**swan-song** chant *m* du cygne (*a. fig.*).

swap F [swɔp] troquer, échanger.

sward [swɔːd] gazon *m*; pelouse *f*.

swarm[1] [swɔːm] **1.** essaim *m*; *sauterelles*: vol *m*; *fig.* foule *f*, troupe *f*; **2.** essaimer; *fig.* fourmiller (de, *with*).

swarm[2] [∼] (*usu.* ∼ *up*) escalader; monter à.

swarth·i·ness ['swɔːθinis] teint *m* basané; '**swarth·y** □ basané, noiraud, brun.

swash [swɔʃ] **1.** *v/i.* clapoter; *v/t.* clapoter contre; faire jaillir; **2.** clapotis *m*, *vagues*: clapotage *m*; ∼**buck·ler** ['∼bʌklə] rodomont *m*, fanfaron *m*.

swas·ti·ka ['swɔstikə] svastika *m*; croix *f* gammée.

swat [swɔt] **1.** frapper; écraser (*une mouche*); **2.** coup *m*.

swath ⚮ [swɔːθ] andain *m*, fauchée *f*.

swathe [sweið] **1.** bandage *m*, bande *f*; *see swath*; **2.** emmailloter, envelopper; rouler.

sway [swei] **1.** balancement *m*; oscillation *f*; *mot.* roulis *m*; empire *m*, domination *f*; **2.** *v/t.* balancer; influencer; gouverner; *v/i.* osciller, se balancer; *fig.* incliner, pencher.

swear [sweə] **1.** [*irr.*] *v/i.* jurer (qch., *by s.th.*); prêter serment; sacrer, blasphémer; ∼ *to* attester (*qch.*) sous serment; ∼ *at* maudire; *fig.* ∼ *by* se fier à; *v/t.* jurer (de, *to*); faire (*un serment*); faire jurer (*q.*); ∼ *s.o.* faire prêter serment à q.; *be sworn (in)* prêter serment; ∼ *off* jurer de renoncer à; **2.** F (*a. ∼-word*) juron *m*.

sweat [swet] **1.** sueur *f*, transpira-

tion *f*; ⊕ ressuage *m*; *sl.* corvée *f*; ⚮ F *old* ∼ vieux troupier *m*; *by the* ∼ *of one's brow* à la sueur de son front; **2.** [*irr.*] *v/i.* suer, transpirer; *v/t.* (faire) suer; ⚮ faire transpirer; exploiter (*un ouvrier*); ⊕ souder (*un câble*) à l'étain; '**sweat·ed** fait à la sueur des ouvriers (-ères *f*); '**sweat·er** chandail *m*; tricot *m*; F pull *m*; ∼**shirt** sweat-shirt *m*; '∼**shop** atelier *m* où les ouvriers sont exploités; '**sweat·y** en sueur; imprégné de sueur; d'une chaleur humide.

Swede [swiːd] Suédois(e *f*) *m*; ⚮ ♀ navet *m* de Suède, chou-navet (*pl.* choux-navets) *m*.

Swedish ['swiːdiʃ] **1.** suédois; **2.** *ling.* suédois *m*; *the* ∼ *pl.* les Suédois *m/pl.*

sweep [swiːp] **1.** [*irr.*] *v/t.* balayer (*une pièce, a. fig. une robe, les mers, etc.*); *fig.* parcourir; *fig.* (*souv. avec adv.*) entraîner; ramoner (*la cheminée*); *fig.* effleurer (*les cordes d'une harpe*); ⚮ enfiler; *fig.* embrasser du regard; tracer (*une courbe*); *v/i.* s'étaler; s'étendre; *fig.* (*usu. avec adv.*) avancer rapidement; envahir, parcourir; entrer *etc.* d'un air majestueux; ∼ *for mines* draguer des mines; ∼ *in* entrer vivement ou majestueusement; **2.** coup *m* de balai *ou* de pinceau *ou* de faux; geste *m* large; mouvement *m* circulaire; courbe *f*; ligne *f* ininterrompue; *fig.* mouvement *m* majestueux; ♪ harpe: effleurement *m*; *mot.* virage *m*; *fleuve*: course *f* rapide; *maison*: allée *f*; *télév.* balayage *m*; étendue *f*, envergure *f*; ⚮ *etc.* portée *f* (*a. fig.*); ⊕ zone *f* de jeu; *formes d'un navire*: courbure *f*; *colline*: versant *m*; ramoneur *m* (*de cheminées*); *embarcation etc.*: aviron *m* de queue; *pompe etc.*: balancier *m*; F sweepstake *m*; *make a clean* ∼ faire table rase (de, *of*); *jeu*: faire rafle; *fig. at one* ∼ d'un seul coup; '**sweep·er** balayeur *m* (*de rues*); *machine*: balayeuse *f*; '**sweep·ing 1.** □ rapide; entier (-ère *f*); par trop absolu (*affirmation*); allongé, élancé (*lignes*); **2.** ∼*s pl.* ordures *f/pl.*, balayures *f/pl.*; **sweep·stake** ['∼steik] sweepstake *m*, poule *f*.

sweet [swiːt] **1.** □ doux (douce *f*); sucré; mélodieux (-euse *f*); gentil(le *f*) (*personne*); odorant; agréable; sain (*haleine, sol, etc.*); ~ oil huile *f* douce; *souv.* huile *f* d'olive; ♀ ~ pea pois *m* de senteur; ♀ ~-william œillet *m* de poète; have a ~ tooth aimer les douceurs; **2.** chérie *f*; bonbon *m*; *cuis.* entremets *m* (sucré); ~s *pl.* confiseries *f/pl.*; friandises *f/pl.*; *fig.* délices *f/pl.*; '~·**bread** ris *m* de veau *ou* qqfois d'agneau; '**sweet·en** sucrer; adoucir (*a. fig.*); assainir (*l'air, le sol, etc.*); '**sweet·en·er** édulcorant *m*; *fig.* pot-de-vin *m* (*pl.* pots-de-vin); '**sweet·heart** bien-aimé(e *f*) *m*; chéri(e *f*) *m*; '**sweet·ish** assez doux (douce *f*); '**sweet·meat** bonbon *m*; ~s *pl.* confiserie *f*, sucreries *f/pl.*; '**sweet·ness** douceur *f* (*a. fig.*); *fig.* gentillesse *f*; air etc.: fraîcheur *f*; '**sweet·shop** confiserie *f*.

swell [swel] **1.** [*irr.*] *v/i.* se gonfler (*a. voiles*); s'enfler (*a. fig.* jusqu'à devenir qch., *into* s.th.); grossir; se soulever (*mer*); *fig.* augmenter; *v/t.* gonfler, enfler; augmenter; **2.** F élégant, chic *inv.* en genre; *sl.* bath; **3.** bosse *f*; *terrain*: ondulation *f*; gonflement *m*; ♪ *orgue*: soufflet *m*, crescendo *m* (*et diminuendo m*); ♣ houle *f*; F élégant(e *f*) *m*); the ~s *pl.* le gratin *m*; '**swell·ing 1.** enflure *f*; tumeur *f*; gonflement *m*; *vagues*: soulèvement *m*; *mot. etc.* hernie *f*; **2.** □ qui s'enfle *ou* se gonfle; enflé, gonflé; boursouflé (*style*). [nage.]

swel·ter ['sweltə] étouffer; être en]

swept [swept] *prét. et p.p. de* sweep 1.

swerve [swɜːv] *v/i.* faire un écart; *mot.* faire une embardée; dévier; *foot.* crocheter; *v/t.* faire écarter; *mot.* faire faire une embardée; faire dévier (*la balle*).

swift [swift] **1.** □ rapide; prompt; **2.** *orn.* martinet *m*; '**swift·ness** vitesse *f*; promptitude *f*.

swig F [swig] **1.** gorgée *f*; grand coup *m*; **2.** boire à grands coups; lamper.

swill [swil] **1.** lavage *m* à grande eau; pâtée *f* pour les porcs; F *péj.* rinçure *f*, mauvaise boisson *f*; **2.** *v/t.* laver à grande eau; *v/i.* avaler; boire comme une éponge.

swim [swim] **1.** [*irr.*] nager; être inondé (de, *with*); my head ~s

la tête me tourne; *v/t.* traverser à la nage; faire (*une distance etc.*) à la nage; faire nager (*un cheval*); **2.** action *f* de nager; *be in the* ~ être à la page; être lancé.

swim·ming ['swimiŋ] **1.** nage *f*; natation *f*; **2.** □ de natation; ~ly F à merveille; ~ *pool* piscine *f*; ~ *trunks pl.* (a pair of ~ trunks un) caleçon de bain.

swim·suit ['swimsjuːt] maillot *m* (de bain).

swin·dle ['swindl] **1.** *v/t.* escroquer (qch. à q., s.o. out of s.th.); *v/i.* faire de l'escroquerie; **2.** escroquerie *f*, filouterie *f*; '**swin·dler** escroc *m*, filou *m*; *sl.* floueur (-euse *f*) *m*.

swine *poét.* zo., *fig. péj.* [swain], *pl.* **swine** cochon *m*; *sl.* salaud *m*; '**swine·herd** porcher *m*.

swing [swiŋ] **1.** [*irr.*] *v/i.* se balancer, osciller, tournoyer, pivoter; ♣ éviter (*sur l'ancre*); être pendu; ✗ faire une conversion (vers, *to*); ~ along avancer en scandant le pas; ~ into motion se mettre en mouvement; ~ to se refermer (*porte*); *v/t.* (faire) balancer, faire osciller; faire pivoter; pendre; brandir; **2.** balancement *m*; coup *m* balancé; va-et-vient *m/inv.*; balançoire *f* (*d'enfant*); mouvement *m* rythmé; ♣ évitage *m*; *fig.* entrain *m*, marche *f*; ♪, *a. box.* swing *m*; in full ~ en pleine marche; ~ **bridge** pont *m* tournant; ~ **door** porte *f* battante, porte *f* à bascule.

swinge·ing □ F ['swindʒiŋ] énorme; écrasant.

swing·ing □ F ['swiŋiŋ] balançant, oscillant; à bascule; *fig.* cadencé; *fig.* entraînant; *Am.* ~ door see swing door; ♫ ~ temperature température *f* variable.

swin·gle ⊕ ['swiŋgl] **1.** teiller, écanguer (*le lin, le chanvre*); **2.** écang *m*; '~·**tree** palonnier *m*.

swin·ish □ ['swainiʃ] de cochon; bestial (-aux *m/pl.*).

swipe [swaip] **1.** frapper à toute volée; F donner une taloche à; *Am. sl.* chiper; **2.** F taloche *f*; ~s *pl.* petite bière *f*, bibine *f*.

swirl [swɜːl] **1.** (faire) tournoyer *ou* tourbillonner; **2.** remous *m*; tourbillon(nement) *m*.

swish [swiʃ] **1.** *v/i.* bruire; siffler; *v/t.* fouetter; faire siffler; **2.** bruissement *m*; sifflement *m*; frou(-)frou *m*; **3.** F chic *inv. en genre*, élégant.

Swiss [swis] **1.** suisse; **2.** Suisse(sse *f*) *m*; *the* ~ *pl.* les Suisses *m/pl.*

switch [switʃ] **1.** badine *f*; houssine *f* (*a. de cavalier*); 🚂 aiguille *f*; ⚡ interrupteur *m*, commutateur *m*; *cheveux*: postiche *m*; **2.** cingler; housser; 🚂 aiguiller (*a. fig.*); manœuvrer (*un train*); ⚡ (*souv.* ~ *over*) commuter (*le courant*); ⚡ ~ *on* (*off*) allumer (éteindre); '~·**back** montagnes *f/pl.* russes; '~·**board** ⚡ panneau *m ou* tableau *m* de distribution; *telephone* ~ standard *m* téléphonique; '~·**box** caisson *m* d'interrupteur, boîte *f* de distribution; '~·**le·ver** 🚂 levier *m* d'aiguille.

swiv·el ⊕ ['swivl] émerillon *m*; pivot *m*; *attr.* tournant, pivotant; à pivot.

swol·len ['swouln] *p.p. de* swell 1.

swoon [swuːn] **1.** évanouissement *m*; ✚ syncope *f*; **2.** s'évanouir.

swoop [swuːp] **1.** (*usu.* ~ *down*) s'abattre, foncer (sur, [up]on); **2.** descente *f* rapide; attaque *f* inattendue.

swop F [swɔp] troquer.

sword [sɔːd] épée *f*; *cavalry* ~ sabre *m* de cavalerie; '~·**cane** canne *f* à épée; '~·**knot** dragonne *f*.

swords·man ['sɔːdzmən] épéiste *m*, escrimeur *m*, F lame *f*; '**swords·man·ship** escrime *f*.

swore [swɔː] *prét. de* swear 1.

sworn [swɔːn] *p.p. de* swear 1; ⚖ juré, assermenté.

swot *école sl.* [swɔt] **1.** travail *m* intense, *sl.* turbin *m*; *personne*: bûcheur (-euse *f*) *m*; **2.** bûcher, piocher, potasser.

swum [swʌm] *p.p. de* swim 1.

swung [swʌŋ] *prét. et p.p. de* swing 1.

syb·a·rite ['sibərait] sybarite (*a. su./mf*).

syc·o·phant ['sikəfənt] sycophante *m*; flagorneur (-euse *f*) *m*; adulateur (-trice *f*) *m*; **syc·o·phan·tic** [sikə'fæntik] (~*ally*) adulateur (-trice *f*); ~*ally* bassement.

syl·lab·ic [si'læbik] (~*ally*) syllabique; **syl·la·ble** ['siləbl] syllabe *f*.

syl·la·bus ['siləbəs] *cours, études*: programme *m*; *eccl.* syllabus *m*.

syl·lo·gism *phls.* ['silədʒizm] syllogisme *m*.

sylph [silf] sylphe *m*; sylphide *f* (*a. fig.*).

sym·bi·o·sis *biol.* [simbai'ousis] symbiose *f*.

sym·bol ['simbəl] symbole *m* (*a.* ⚗); signe *m*; attribut *m*; **sym·bol·ic, sym·bol·i·cal** □ [~'bɔlik(l)] symbolique; **sym·bol·ism** ['~bəlizm] symbolisme *m*; '**sym·bol·ize** symboliser.

sym·met·ri·cal □ [si'metrikl] symétrique; **sym·me·try** ['simitri] symétrie *f*.

sym·pa·thet·ic [simpə'θetik] (~*ally*) sympathique (*a. nerf, encre*); de sympathie; compatissant; bien disposé; ~ *strike* grève *f* de solidarité; **sym·pa·thize** ['~θaiz] sympathiser (avec, *with*); compatir (à, *with*); s'associer (à, *with*); **sym·pa·thy** ['~θi] sympathie *f*; compassion *f*; *in* ~ par solidarité (*grève*); par contrecoup (*hausse de prix*); *letter of* ~ lettre *f* de condoléances.

sym·phon·ic ♪ [sim'fɔnik] symphonique; **sym·pho·ny** ♪ ['simfəni] symphonie *f*.

symp·tom ['simptəm] symptôme *m*; indice *m*; **symp·to·mat·ic** [~'mætik] (~*ally*) symptomatique; *qui est un symptôme* (de, *of*); *be* ~ *of* caractériser (*qch.*).

syn·a·gogue ['sinəgɔg] synagogue *f*.

sync(h) F [siŋk] synchronisation *f*; synchronisme *m*; *out of* ~ mal synchronisé, pas en synchronisme.

syn·chro·mesh gear *mot.* ['siŋkromeʃ'giə] boîte *f* de vitesses synchronisée.

syn·chro·nism ['siŋkrənizm] synchronisme *m*; ⚡ *in* ~ en phase; *télév. irregular* ~ drapeau *m*; '**syn·chro·nize** *v/i.* marquer la même heure; arriver simultanément; *v/t.* synchroniser (*a. cin.*); ⚡ coupler en phase; *cin.* repérer; '**syn·chro·nous** □ synchrone; ⚡ *in* ~ en phase.

syn·co·pate ['siŋkəpeit] syncoper; **syn·co·pe** ✚, ♪, *a. gramm.* ['~pi] syncope *f*.

syn·dic ['sindik] syndic *m*; **syn·di·cate 1.** ['~kit] syndicat *m*; conseil *m* de syndics; **2.** ['~keit] (se) syndiquer; '**syn·di·cat·ed** publié simultanément dans plusieurs journaux.

syn·drome ['sindroum] syndrome *m*.

syn·od *eccl.* ['sinəd] synode *m*, con-

cile *m*; **syn·od·al** [ˈ‿dl], **syn·od·ic,**
syn·od·i·cal □ *eccl.* [siˈnɔdik(l)]
synodal (-aux *m/pl.*).

syn·o·nym [ˈsinənim] synonyme *m*;
syn·on·y·mous □ [siˈnɔniməs]
synonyme (de, *with*).

syn·op·sis [siˈnɔpsis], *pl.* -ses [‿siːz]
résumé *m*, abrégé *m*; tableau *m*
synoptique; *bibl.* synopse *f*; *école:*
aide-mémoire *m/inv.*

syn·op·tic, syn·op·ti·cal □ [si-
ˈnɔptik(l)] synoptique.

syn·tac·tic, syn·tac·ti·cal □
gramm. [sinˈtæktik(l)] syntaxique;
syn·tax *gramm.* [ˈsintæks] syntaxe *f*.

syn·the·sis [ˈsinθisis], *pl.* -ses [ˈ‿siːz]
synthèse *f*; **syn·the·size** ⊕ [ˈ‿saiz]
synthétiser; faire la synthèse de.

syn·thet·ic, syn·thet·i·cal □ [sin-
ˈθetik(l)] synthétique; de synthèse.

syn·to·nize [ˈsintənaiz] *radio:* syntoniser, accorder; **syn·to·ny** [ˈ‿ni]
syntonie *f*, accord *m*.

syph·i·lis ✤ [ˈsifilis] syphilis *f*.

syph·i·lit·ic ✤ [sifiˈlitik] syphiliti-
que.

sy·phon [ˈsaifən] *see* siphon.

Syr·i·an [ˈsiriən] **1.** syrien(ne *f*);
2. Syrien(ne *f*) *m*.

sy·rin·ga ♀ [siˈriŋgə] seringa(t) *m*;
jasmin *m* en arbre.

syr·inge [ˈsirindʒ] **1.** seringue *f*;
2. seringuer; ✤ laver avec une
seringue.

syr·up [ˈsirəp] sirop *m*.

sys·tem [ˈsistim] système *m*; *pol.*
régime *m*; méthode *f*; **sys·tem·**
at·ic [‿ˈmætik] (‿*ally*) systématique, méthodique.

T

T, t [ti:] T *m*, t *m*; F *to* a *T* à merveille.

tab [tæb] patte *f*; étiquette *f*; *cordon de soulier*: ferret *m*; *manteau etc.*: attache *f*; *fichier*: touche *f*; ✕ patte *f* du collet; *Am.* **pick up the** ~ payer (la note); F **keep** ~(s) on **ne pas perdre** (q.) **de vue.**

tab·ard *hist.* ['tæbəd] tabar(d) *m*.

tab·by ['tæbi] **1.** soie *f* moirée; (*usu.* ~ *cat*) chat *m* tigré; F chatte *f*; F vieille chipie *f*; **2.** *tex.* de *ou* en tabis; rayé.

tab·er·nac·le ['tæbənækl] tabernacle *m*; *Am.* temple *m*.

ta·ble ['teibl] **1.** table *f* (*a. fig.* = *bonne chère*; *a.* ♈); ⊕ plaque *f*; ♈ banc *m* (*d'une machine à percer*); ♈ table *f* de multiplication; *occasional* ~ guéridon *m*; *nest of* ~s table *f* gigogne; ~ *of contents* table *f* des matières; *turn the* ~s renverser les rôles; reprendre l'avantage (sur, on); **2.** mettre sur la table; *p.ext. parl.* saisir la Chambre de (*un projet de loi*); *Am.* ajourner (*usu. un projet de loi*); '~-**cloth** nappe *f*; '~-**lin·en** linge *m* de table; ~ **nap·kin** serviette *f*; '~-**spoon** cuiller (cuillère) *f* à bouche *ou* à soupe.

tab·let ['tæblit] tablette *f* (*de chocolat*, △, *pharm.*, *pour écrire, etc.*); plaque *f*; *savon*: pain *m*; *pharm.* comprimé *m*.

table...: ~ **ten·nis** ping-pong *m*; '~-**top** dessus *m* de table; '~-**ware** vaisselle *f*; ~ **wine** vin *m* de table.

tab·loid ['tæbloid] *pharm.* comprimé *m*; pastille *f*; petit journal *m* qui vise à la sensation.

ta·boo [tə'bu:] **1.** tabou; F interdit; **2.** tabou *m*; **3.** tabouer; F interdire.

tab·u·lar □ ['tæbjulə] tabulaire; disposé en lamelles; **tab·u·late** ['~leit] disposer en forme de tables *ou* tableaux; classifier.

tac·it □ ['tæsit] tacite; **tac·i·turn** □ ['~tə:n] taciturne; **tac·i'tur·ni·ty** taciturnité *f*.

tack [tæk] **1.** petit clou *m*; pointe *f*;

(*a. tin* ~) semence *f*; *couture*: point *m* de bâti; ♈ bord(ée *f*) *m* (en louvoyant); *fig.* voie *f*; tactique *f*; *on the wrong* ~ sur la mauvaise voie; fourvoyé; **2.** *v/t.* clouer; faufiler (*un vêtement*); *fig.* attache, annexer (à to, on); *v/i.* ♈ louvoyer; virer (*a. fig.*).

tack·le ['tækl] **1.** appareil *m*, ustensiles *m/pl.*; ♈ apparaux *m/pl.*, palan *m*; ⊕ appareil *m* de levage; *sp.* arrêt *m*; **2.** saisir à bras-le-corps; essayer, entreprendre; *sp.* plaquer.

tack·y ['tæki] collant; *Am.* F minable.

tact [tækt] tact *m*, savoir-faire *m/inv.*; **tact·ful** □ ['~ful] (plein) de tact.

tac·ti·cal □ ✕ ['tæktikl] tactique; **tac·ti·cian** [~'tiʃn] tacticien *m*; **tac·tics** *pl. ou sg.* ['~iks] tactique *f*.

tac·tile ['tæktail] tactile.

tact·less □ ['tæktlis] dépourvu de tact.

tad·pole *zo.* ['tædpoul] têtard *m*.

taf·fe·ta ['tæfitə] taffetas *m*.

taf·fy ['tæfi] caramel *m* au beurre; *Am.* F flagornerie *f*.

tag [tæg] **1.** morceau *m* qui pend, bout *m*; étiquette *f*, attache *f*; ferret *m*; *fig.* cliché *m*; **2.** ferrer; *fig.* attacher (à on, to); *Am.* attacher une fiche à; F ~ *along* suivre, traîner derrière.

tag-rag ['tægræg]: ~ (*and bobtail*) canaille *f*.

tail [teil] **1.** queue *f* (*a. de jupe*, *a. fig. d'une classe, etc.*); F *chemise*: pan *m*; (*usu.* ~s *pl.*) monnaie: pile *f*; *page*: pied *m*; *charrue*: manche *f*; *voiture*: arrière *m*; ✈ empennage *m*; adhérents *m/pl.* (*d'un parti*); F ~s *pl.* habit *m* à queue; *fig.* ~s *up* en train; de bonne humeur; ✈ ~ *unit* empennage *m*; **2.** *v/t.* mettre une queue à; *fig.* être *ou* se mettre à la queue de; couper la queue à (*un animal*); enlever les queues de (*les groseilles etc.*); *Am.* F filer (q.); *v/i.* suivre de près; ~ *off* s'espacer; s'allonger; s'éteindre (*voix*); '~-**back** bouchon *m* (de voitures), retenue *f*; '~·**board** layon *m*; '~·'**coat** habit *m* à queue; '**tailed** à queue; *zo.* caudifère; '~·**gate** *mot.* 1. hayon *m* arrière; 2. coller (*voiture*); '**tail·less** sans queue; '**tail·light** *mot.* feu *m* arrière *ou* rouge.

tai·lor ['teilə] 1. tailleur *m*; 2. *v/t.* faire (*un complet etc.*); habiller (*q.*); well ~ed bien habillé (*personne*); '~-**made** 1. tailleur (*vêtement*); 2. (*a.* ~ suit) tailleur *m*.

tail...: '~·**piece** *typ.* cul-de-lampe (*pl.* culs-de-lampe) *m*; vignette *f*; '~-**pipe** *mot.* tuyau *m* d'échappement; ~-**plane** ✈ plan *m* fixe; ~ **skid** ✈ béquille *f*; ~ **wind** vent *m* arrière.

taint [teint] 1. tache *f*; infection *f*, corruption *f*; trace *f*; tare *f* héréditaire; 2. *v/t.* infecter; (se) corrompre; (se) gâter.

take [teik] 1. [*irr.*] *v/t.* prendre (*q. livraison, maladie, nourriture, poison, repas, temps, a. bien ou mal*); saisir; s'emparer de; emprunter (à, *from*); conduire, (em)mener (à, *to*); louer (*une maison, une voiture*); faire (*phot., promenade, repas, vœu, voyage, etc.*); produire (*un effet*); tirer (*une épreuve*); passer (*un examen*); tourner (*un film*); acheter régulièrement (*un journal*); franchir (*un obstacle*); profiter de, saisir (*une occasion*); attraper (*un poisson etc.*); remporter (*le prix*); F comprendre; F tenir, prendre (*pour, for*); *the devil ~ it!* que le diable l'emporte!; *I ~ it that* je suppose que; ~ *air* se faire connaître; se répandre (*nouvelle*); ~ *the air* prendre l'air; ✈ s'envoler, prendre son vol; ~ (*a deep*) *breath* respirer (profondément); ~ *comfort* se consoler; ~ *compassion* avoir compassion *ou* pitié (de, *on*); ~ *counsel* prendre conseil (de, *with*); ~ *a drive* faire une promenade (en auto); ~ *fire* prendre feu; ~ *in hand* entreprendre; ~ *a hedge* franchir une haie; ~ *hold of* s'emparer de, saisir; ~ *an oath* prêter serment; ~ *offence* se froisser (de, *at*); ~ *pity on* prendre pitié de; ~ *place* avoir lieu; se passer; ~ *rest* se donner du repos; ~ *a rest* se reposer; ✕ faire la pause; ~ *a seat* s'asseoir; ~ *ship* (s')embarquer; ~ *a view of* envisager (*qch.*), avoir une opinion de; ~ *a walk* faire une promenade; ~ *my*

word *for it* croyez-m'en; ~ *s.o. about* faire visiter (*qch.*) à q.; ~ *down* démonter (*une machine etc.*); descendre (*qch.*); avaler; prendre note de, écrire; ~ *for* prendre pour; ~ *from* prendre, enlever à; ~ *in* faire entrer (*q.*); acheter régulièrement (*un journal*); recevoir (*un locataire etc.*); recueillir (*un réfugié etc.*); accepter (*un travail*); comprendre; F tromper; F rouler; ~ *in sail* diminuer de voile(s); ~ *off* enlever; quitter (*ses vêtements*); emmener (*q.*); rabattre (*sur un prix*); supprimer (*un train*); F imiter, singer; ~ *on* entreprendre; accepter; engager; prendre; ~ *out* sortir (*qch.*); arracher (*une dent*); ôter (*une tache*); faire sortir (*q.*), emmener (*un enfant*) en promenade; retirer (*ses bagages*); contracter (*une assurance*); obtenir (*un brevet*); F ~ *it out of* se venger de (*q.*); épuiser (*q.*); ~ *to pieces* démonter (*une machine*); défaire; *fig.* démolir; ~ *up* relever (*a. un défi*); ramasser; prendre (*les armes*); embrasser (*une carrière*); ✝ honorer (*un effet*); lever (*une prime*); occuper (*une place*); fixer (*sa résidence*); *cost.* raccourcir; 🚢 embarquer; absorber (*de l'eau, le temps*); adopter (*une idée*); faire (*une promenade, un saut, un prisonnier*); ~ *upon o.s.* prendre sur soi (de, *to*); *see* consideration; decision; effect 1; exercise 1; heart; liberty; note 1; notice 1; rise 1; 2. [*irr.*] *v/i.* prendre; réussir; avoir du succès; *phot.* he ~s *well* il est photogénique; il fait un bel effet sur une photographie; ~ *after* tenir de; ressembler à; ~ *from* diminuer (*qch.*); ~ *off* prendre son élan *ou* son essor; ✈ s'envoler; décoller; F ~ *on* laisser éclater son chagrin; avoir du succès *ou* de la vogue; F ~ *on with* s'embaucher chez; ~ *over* prendre le pouvoir; assumer la responsabilité; ~ *to* s'adonner à; prendre goût à; prendre (*la fuite*); prendre (*q.*) en amitié; ~ *to* (*ger.*) se mettre à (*inf.*); ~ *up with* se lier d'amitié avec; s'associer à; *that won't ~ with me* ça ne prend pas avec moi; 3. action *f* de prendre; prise *f*; *cin.* prise *f* de vues.

take...: '~·**a·way** 1. à emporter; 2. restaurant *m* qui vend des repas à emporter; '~-'**home pay** gages *m/pl.* nets; salaire *m* net; '~-'**in** F attrape *f*; leurre *m*; '**tak·en** *p.p.* de take 1, 2; be ~ être pris; be ~ with être épris de; be ~ ill tomber malade; F be ~ in se laisser attraper; be ~ up with être occupé de, être tout à; '**take**'**off** caricature *f*; élan *m*; ✂ décollage *m*; '**tak·er** preneur (-euse *f*) *m*; *pari*: tenant *m*.

tak·ing ['teikiŋ] 1. □ F attrayant, charmant; 2. prise *f*; † état *m* nerveux; ✝ ~s *pl.* recettes *f/pl.*

talc *min.* [tælk] talc *m.*

tale [teil] conte *m*, récit *m*, histoire *f*; *tell* ~s (*out of school*) rapporter; trahir un secret; '~-**bear·er** ['~-bɛərə] rapporteur (-euse *f*) *m*; mauvaise langue *f.*

tal·ent ['tælənt] talent *m*; aptitude *f*; don *m*; ~ *scout* (*ou spotter*) dénicheur (-euse *f*) *m* de futures vedettes; '**tal·ent·ed** doué; de talent.

ta·les 🔖 ['teili:z] *sg.* jurés *m/pl.* suppléants.

tal·is·man ['tælizmən] talisman *m.*

talk [tɔ:k] 1. conversation *f*; causerie *f*; discours *m*; bruit *m*; bavardage *m*; 2. parler (de *of*, *about*); causer (avec, to); bavarder; ~ *back* répondre d'une manière impertinente, répliquer; ~ *down* faire taire, réduire (*q.*) au silence; ~ *down to s.o.* parler à q. avec condescendance; **talk·a·tive** □ ['~ətiv] bavard; causeur (-euse *f*); **talk·ee-talk·ee** F ['tɔ:ki'tɔ:ki] pur bavardage *m*; † jargon *m* petit-nègre; '**talk·er** causeur (-euse *f*) *m*, parleur (-euse *f*) *m*; **talk·ie** F ['~i] film *m* parlant *ou* parlé; '**talk·ing** conversation *f*; bavardage *m*; **talk·ing-to** F ['~tu:] semonce *f.*

tall [tɔ:l] grand, de haute taille; haut, élevé (*bâtiment etc.*); *sl.* ~ *order* grosse affaire *f*; demande *f* exagérée; *sl.* ~ *story, Am. a.* ~ *tale* histoire *f* dure à avaler; F craque *f*; '**tall·boy** commode *f*; '**tall·ness** grandeur *f*; hauteur *f*, grande taille *f.*

tal·low ['tælou] suif *m*; '**tal·low·y** suiffeux (-euse *f*); *fig.* terreux (-euse *f*) (*teint etc.*).

tal·ly ['tæli] 1. taille *f*; pointage *m* (de, of); étiquette *f* (*plantes etc.*); contre-partie *f*; 2. s'accorder (avec, with).

tal·ly-ho ['tæli'hou] *chasse*: 1. taïaut!; 2. taïaut *m*; 3. crier taïaut.

tal·on *orn.* ['tælən] serre *f*; griffe *f.*

ta·lus[1] ['teiləs] talus *m* (*a. géol.*).

ta·lus[2] *anat.* [~] astragale *m.*

tam·a·ble ['teiməbl] apprivoisable.

tam·a·rind 🌿 ['tæmərind] (fruit *m* du) tamarinier *m.*

tam·bour ['tæmbuə] 1. *usu.* tambour *m*; ♪ grosse caisse *f*; 2. broder au tambour; **tam·bou·rine** ♪ [~bə'ri:n] tambour *m* de basque; *sans grelots*: tambourin *m.*

tame [teim] 1. □ apprivoisé; domestique; soumis, dompté (*personne*); fade, insipide (*style*); 2. apprivoiser; domestiquer; dompter; '**tame·ness** docilité *f*, soumission *f*; fadeur *f*; '**tam·er** dompteur (-euse *f*) *m*; apprivoiseur (-euse *f*) *m.*

Tam·ma·ny *Am.* ['tæməni] parti *m* démocrate de New York.

tam-o'-shan·ter [tæmə'ʃæntə] béret *m* écossais.

tamp [tæmp] ⚒ bourrer; ⊕ refouler, damer.

tam·per ['tæmpə]: ~ *with* toucher à; se mêler à; falsifier (*un registre*); suborner (*un témoin*); altérer (*un document*).

tam·pon 🎗 ['tæmpən] tampon *m.*

tan [tæn] 1. tan *m*; couleur *f* du tan; (*a. sun* ~) brunissage *m*; 2. tanné; tan *adj./inv.*; jaune (*soulier*); 3. *v/t.* tanner; *fig.* bronzer (*le teint*); rosser (*q.*).

tan·dem ['tændem] tandem *m*; ⚡ ~ *connexion* accouplement *m* en série; *drive* ~ conduire en tandem; *cycl.* se promener en tandem; *in* ~ en collaboration, en tandem.

tang[1] [tæŋ] soie *f* (*d'un ciseau, couteau, etc.*); *fig.* goût *m* vif; *épice etc.*: montant *m*; *air marin*: salure *f.*

tang[2] [~] 1. son *m* aigu; tintement *m*; 2. (faire) retentir; rendre un son aigu.

tan·gent ⚹ ['tændʒənt] tangente *f*; *go* (*ou fly*) *off at a* ~ changer brusquement de sujet, s'échapper par la tangente; **tan·gen·tial** □ ⚹ [~'dʒenʃl] tangentiel(le *f*); de tangence (*point*).

tan·gi·bil·i·ty [tændʒi'biliti] tangibilité *f*, réalité *f*; **tan·gi·ble** □ ['tændʒəbl] tangible, palpable; *fig.* réel(le *f*).

tan·gle ['tæŋgl] 1. enchevêtrement *m*; nœud *m*; *fig.* embarras *m*;

2. (s')embrouiller, emmêler; F ~ *with s.o.* se disputer avec q., avoir une prise de bec avec q.; se colleter avec q.; *be* ~*d with s.th.* se trouver impliqué dans qch.

tan·go ['tæŋgou] tango *m* (*danse*).

tank [tæŋk] **1.** réservoir *m* (*a.* ⊕); *phot.* cuve *f*; ⚔ char *m* d'assaut; ~ *car* (*ou truck*) camion-citerne (*pl.* camions-citernes) *m*; 🚃 wagon-citerne (*pl.* wagons-citernes) *m*; **2.** faire le plein d'essence; *Am. sl.* s'alcooliser; '**tank·age** capacité *f* d'un réservoir.

tank·ard ['tæŋkəd] pot *m* (*surt. de ou à bière*); *en étain*: chope *f*.

tank·er ⚓ ['tæŋkə] pétrolier *m*.

tan·ner¹ ['tænə] tanneur *m*.

tan·ner² *sl.* [~] (*pièce f de*) six pence.

tan·ner·y ['tænəri] tannerie *f*.

tan·nic ac·id 🜍 ['tænik'æsid] acide *m* tannique.

tan·nin 🜍 ['tænin] tan(n)in *m*.

tan·noy (*TM*) *Brit.* ['tænɔi] système *m* de haut-parleurs.

tan·ta·lize ['tæntəlaiz] tourmenter.

tan·ta·mount ['tæntəmaunt] équivalent (à, *to*).

tan·trum F ['tæntrəm] accès *m* de colère.

tap¹ [tæp] **1.** tape *f*, petit coup *m*; **2.** taper, toucher, frapper doucement.

tap² [~] *fût*: fausset *m*; *eau*: robinet *m*; F boisson *f*, *usu.* bière *f*; ⊕ taraud *m*; *Brit.* ~ *water* eau *f* du robinet; F *see* ~*room*; *on* ~ en perce; **2.** percer; mettre en perce; ⚡ ~ *the wire(s)* faire une prise sur un fil télégraphique; *téléph.* capter un message télégraphique.   [claquettes.)

tap-dance ['tæpdɑːns] danse *f* à∫

tape [teip] ruban *m*; *sp.* bande *f* d'arrivée; *tél.* bande *f* du récepteur; *fig.* red~ bureaucratie *f*, paperasserie *f*; '~**meas·ure** mètre *m* à ruban; centimètre *m*; '~**re·cord** enregistrer sur bande; '~**re·cord·er** magnétophone *m*; '~**re·cord·ing** enregistrement *m* sur magnétophone.

ta·per [teipə] **1.** bougie *f* filée; *eccl.* cierge *m*; ⊕ cône *m*; **2.** *adj.* effilé; ⊕ conique; **3.** *v/i.* s'effiler; diminuer; ~*ing see* ~ 2; *v/t.* effiler; tailler en pointe.

tap·es·tried ['tæpistrid] tendu de tapisseries; tapissé; '**tap·es·try** tapisserie *f*.

tape·worm ['teipwəːm] ver *m* solitaire.

tap·pet ⊕ ['tæpit] came *f*; taquet *m*.

tap·room ['tæprum] buvette *f*, estaminet *m*.

tap-root 🜍 ['tæpruːt] pivot *m*.

taps *Am.* ⚔ [tæps] *pl.* extinction *f* des feux.

tap·ster ['tæpstə] cabaretier *m*; garçon *m* de cabaret.

tar [tɑː] **1.** goudron *m*; F *Jack* ⚓ mathurin *m*; **2.** goudronner.

ta·ran·tu·la *zo.* [tə'ræntjulə] tarentule *f*.

tar-board ['tɑːbɔːd] carton *m* bitumé.

tar·di·ness ['tɑːdinis] lenteur *f*; *Am.* retard *m*; F ⚓ lent; peu empressé; tardif (-ive *f*); *Am.* en retard.

tare¹ 🜍 [tɛə] (*usu.* ~ *pl.*) vesce *f*.

tare² ✝ [~] **1.** tare *f*; **2.** tarer.

tar·get ['tɑːgit] cible *f*; but *m*, objectif *m* (*a. fig.*); *fig.* butte *f*; ~ *date* date *f* limite; ~ *language* langue *f* d'arrivée; ~ *practice* tir *m* à la cible.

tar·iff ['tærif] tarif *m* (*souv.* douanier).

tarn [tɑːn] laquet *m*.

tar·nish ['tɑːniʃ] **1.** *v/t.* ⊕ ternir (*a. fig.*); *v/i.* se ternir; se dédorer (*dorure*); **2.** ternissure *f*.

tar·pau·lin [tɑː'pɔːlin] ⚓ toile *f* goudronnée; bâche *f*; ⚓ prélart *m*.

tar·ra·gon ['tærəgən] estragon *m*.

tar·ry¹ *poét.* ['tæri] tarder; attendre; rester.   [*f*.)∫

tar·ry² ['tɑːri] goudronneux (-euse∫

tart [tɑːt] **1.** □ âpre, aigre; *fig.* mordant; **2.** tourte *f*; tarte *f*; *sl.* poule *f* (= *prostituée*).

tar·tan ['tɑːtən] tartan *m*; ⚓ tartane *f*; ~ *plaid* plaid *m* en tartan.

Tar·tar¹ ['tɑːtə] Tartare *m*; *fig.* homme *m* intraitable; *femme*: mégère *f*; *catch a* ~ trouver son maître.

tar·tar² 🜍 [~] tartre *m* (*a. dent*).

task [tɑːsk] **1.** tâche *f*; besogne *f*, ouvrage *m*; *école*: devoir *m*; *take to* ~ réprimander (*pour avoir fait, for having done*). **2.** assigner une tâche à; ⚓ mettre à l'épreuve (*les bordages etc.*); ~ *force* ⚔ *Am.* détachement *m* spécial des forces de terre, de l'air et de mer; '~**mas·ter** surveillant *m*; chef *m* de corvée; *fig.* tyran *m*.

tas·sel ['tæsl] 1. gland *m*, houppe *f*; 2. garnir de glands *etc.*

taste [teist] 1. goût *m* (de *of, for*; pour, *for*); *fig. a.* prédilection *f* (pour, *for*); *to* ∼ à volonté, selon son goût; *season to* ∼ goûtez et rectifiez l'assaisonnement; 2. *v/t.* goûter (*a. fig.*); déguster; *v/i.* sentir (qch., *of s.th.*); avoir un goût (de, *of*); **taste·ful** □ ['∼ful] de bon goût; élégant; de goût (*personne*).

taste·less □ ['teistlis] sans goût, insipide, fade; **'taste·less·ness** insipidité *f*; manque *m* de goût.

tas·ter ['teistə] dégustateur (-trice *f*) *m* (*de thé, vins, etc.*).

tast·y □ F ['teisti] savoureux (-euse *f*).

tat¹ [tæt] *see* **tit¹**.

tat² [∼] *couture:* faire de la frivolité.

ta-ta ['tæ'tɑː] *enf., a. co.* au revoir!

tat·ter ['tætə] lambeau *m*, loque *f*; **tat·ter·de·mal·ion** [∼də'meiljən] loqueteux (-euse *f*) *m*; **tat·tered** ['∼əd] en lambeaux; déguenillé (*personne*).

tat·tle ['tætl] 1. bavarder, babiller; *péj.* cancaner; 2. bavardage *m*; *péj.* cancans *m/pl.*; **'tat·tler** bavard(e *f*) *m*; *péj.* cancanier (-ère *f*) *m*.

tat·too¹ [tə'tuː] 1. ✕ retraite *f* du soir; *fig. beat the devil's* ∼ tambouriner (*sur la table*); 2. *fig.* tambouriner.

tat·too² [∼] 1. *v/t.* tatouer; 2. tatouage *m*.

tat·ty F ['tæti] défraîchi, miteux (-euse *f*).

taught [tɔːt] *prét. et p.p. de* **teach**.

taunt [tɔːnt] 1. reproche *m*; brocard *m*; sarcasme *m*; 2. accabler de sarcasmes; reprocher (qch. à q., *s.o. with s.th.*); **'taunt·ing** □ de sarcasme, sarcastique.

Tau·rus *astr.* ['tɔːrəs] le Taureau.

taut ⚓ [tɔːt] raide, tendu; étarque (*voile*); **'taut·en** (se) raidir; (s')étarquer (*voile*).

tav·ern ['tævən] taverne *f*, cabaret *m*.

taw¹ ⊕ [tɔː] mégir.

taw² [∼] grosse bille *f* de verre.

taw·dri·ness ['tɔːdrinis] clinquant *m*, faux brillant *m*; **'taw·dry** □ d'un mauvais goût; voyant.

taw·ny ['tɔːni] fauve; basané (*teint*).

tax [tæks] 1. impôt *m* (sur, *on*), contribution *f*; droit *m*, taxe *f* (sur, *on*); *fig.* charge *f* (à, *on*), fardeau *m*; ∼ allowances *pl.* sommes *f/pl.* déductibles; ∼ *bracket* catégorie *f* d'imposition; ∼ *dodger,* ∼ *evader* fraudeur (-euse *f*) *m* fiscal(e); ∼ *evasion* fraude *f* fiscale; ∼ *haven* refuge *m* fiscal; ∼ *relief* allègement *m* fiscal; ∼ *return* déclaration *f* d'impôts; 2. taxer; frapper d'un impôt; *fig.* mettre à l'épreuve; ⚖ taxer (*les dépens, q. de qch., a. fig.*); reprocher (qch. à q., *s.o. with s.th.*); ∼ *s.o. with s.th. a.* accuser q. de qch.; **'tax·a·ble** □ imposable; **tax·a·tion** imposition *f*; prélèvement *m* fiscal; impôts *m/pl.*; ⚖ taxation *f*; **'tax col·lec·tor** percepteur *m* des contributions (*directes*); receveur *m*; **'tax-de·duct·i·ble** déductible (de l'impôt); **'tax-'free** exempt d'impôts.

tax·i ['tæksi] 1. (*ou* ∼-*cab*) taxi *m*; 2. aller en taxi; ✈ rouler sur le sol; hydroplaner; **'∼-danc·er, '∼-girl** *Am.* entraîneuse *f*; **'∼-driv·er** chauffeur *m* de taxi; **'∼-me·ter** taximètre *m*; **'∼-rank, '∼-stand** station *f* de taxis.

tax·pay·er ['tækspeiə] contribuable *mf.*

tea [tiː] thé *m*; goûter *m*, five-o'clock *m*; *high* (*ou meat*) ∼ repas *m* à la fourchette; **'∼-bag** sachet *m* de thé; ∼ *break* pause-thé *f* (*pl.* pauses-thé); **'∼-cad·dy** *see* **caddy**.

teach [tiːtʃ] *(irr.)* enseigner; apprendre (qch. à q., *s.o. s.th.*); à *inf., to inf.*); **'teach·a·ble** □ enseignable; à l'intelligence ouverte (*personne*); **'teach·er** instituteur (-trice *f*) *m*; maître(sse *f*) *m*; professeur *mf*; **'teach·er-'train·ing col·lege** école *f* normale; **'teach·ing** école: enseignement *m*; *phls. etc.* doctrine *f*.

tea...: **'∼-co·sy** couvre-théière *m*; **'∼-cup** tasse *f* à thé; *fig. storm in a* ∼ tempête *f* dans un verre d'eau; **'∼-gown** déshabillé *m*, robe *f* d'intérieur.

teak ♦ [tiːk] (bois *m* de) te(c)k *m*.

team [tiːm] attelage *m*; *surt. sp.* équipe *f*; *by a* ∼ effort tous ensemble; **'∼-'spir·it** esprit *m* d'équipe; **'team·ster** ['∼stə] conducteur *m* (*d'attelage*); charretier *m*; **'team-work** ⊕, *sp.* travail *m* d'équipe, jeu *m* d'ensemble; *fig.* collaboration *f*.

tea·pot ['tiːpɔt] théière *f*.

tear¹ [tɛə] 1. *[irr.]* *v/t.* déchirer; arracher (*les cheveux*); *v/i.* se déchirer; F *avec adv. ou prp.* aller *etc.* à toute vitesse; 2. déchirure *f*; *see* wear2.

tear² [tiə] larme *f*; '**⁓‧drop** larme *f*.

tear‧ful □ ['tiəful] larmoyant, en pleurs.

tear-gas ['tiə'gæs] gaz *m* lacrymogène.

tear‧ing ['tɛəriŋ] *fig.* rapide; déchirant.

tear‧jerk‧er F ['tiədʒəːkə] film *ou* histoire *etc.* larmoyant(e).

tear‧less □ ['tiəlis] sans larmes, sec (*œil*).

tear-off cal‧en‧dar ['tɛərɔf 'kælində] éphéméride *f*.

tease [tiːz] 1. démêler (*de la laine*); carder (*la laine etc.*); effil(och)er (*un tissu*); *fig.* taquiner; 2. F taquin(e *f*) *m*; **tea‧sel** ['⁓l] ♀ cardère *f*; ⊕ carde *f*; '**teas‧er** F *fig.* colle *f* (= *problème difficile*).

teat [tiːt] bout *m* de sein; mamelon *m*; *vache*: tette *f*; *biberon*: tétine *f*; ⊕ *vis*: téton *m*.

tea...: '**⁓‧things** *pl.* F service *m* à thé; '**⁓‧time** l'heure *f* du thé; **⁓ tow‧el** *Brit.* torchon *m* à vaisselle; **⁓ tray** plateau *m* (à thé); **⁓ trol‧ley**, **⁓ wag‧on** table *f* roulante; **⁓ urn** fontaine *f* à thé.

tech‧nic ['teknik] (*a.* **⁓s** *pl. ou sg.*) *see* technique; '**tech‧ni‧cal** □ technique; ⨯ spécial (-aux *m/pl.*); ⅓ de procédure; professionnel(le *f*); **⁓ hitch** incident *m* technique; **tech‧ni‧cal‧i‧ty** [⁓'kæliti] détail *m ou* terme *m* technique; considération *f* d'ordre technique; **tech‧ni‧cian** [tek'niʃn] technicien *m*.

tech‧ni‧col‧or ['teknikʌlə] 1. en couleurs; 2. film *m* en couleurs; *cin.* technicolor *m*.

tech‧nique [tek'niːk] technique *f*; mécanique *f*.

tech‧nol‧o‧gy [tek'nɔlədʒi] technologie *f*; *school of* **⁓** école *f* de technologie, école *f* technique.

tech‧y ['tetʃi] *see* testy.

ted‧der ['tedə] faneuse *f*; *personne*: faneur (-euse *f*) *m*.

te‧di‧ous □ ['tiːdjəs] ennuyeux (-euse *f*); fatigant; assommant; '**te‧di‧ous‧ness** ennui *m*; manque *m* d'intérêt.

te‧di‧um ['tiːdiəm] ennui *m*.

tee [tiː] 1. *sp.* curling: but *m*; golf:

dé *m*, tee *m*; 2.: **⁓** off jouer sa balle; placer la balle sur le dé.

teem [tiːm] (*with*) abonder (en), fourmiller (de).

teen-ag‧er ['tiːneidʒə] adolescent(e *f*) *m* (*entre 13 et 19 ans*).

teens [tiːnz] *pl.* années *f/pl.* entre 13 et 19 ans; adolescence *f*; *in one's* **⁓** n'ayant pas encore vingt ans.

teen‧(s)y [tiːn(z)i], **teen‧(s)y-ween‧(s)y** ['tiːn(z)i'wiːn(z)i] tout petit, minuscule.   [celer.)

tee‧ter F ['tiːtə] se balancer; chan-)

teeth [tiːθ] *pl.* de tooth.

teethe [tiːð] faire ses dents; **teeth‧ing** ['⁓iŋ] dentition *f*.

tee‧to‧tal [tiː'toutl] antialcoolique; qui ne prend pas de boissons alcooliques; **tee‧to‧tal‧(l)er** néphaliste *mf*; abstinent(e *f*) *m*.

tee‧to‧tum ['tiːtou'tʌm] toton *m*.

tel‧e‧com‧mu‧ni‧ca‧tions ['telikəmjuːni'keiʃənz] *pl.* télécommunication *f*.

tel‧e‧course *Am.* ['telikɔːs] cours *m* (de leçons) télévisé.

tel‧e‧gram ['teligræm] télégramme *m*, dépêche *f*.

tel‧e‧graph ['teligrɑːf] 1. télégraphe *m*; ♣ transmetteur *m* d'ordres; 2. télégraphique, de télégramme; 3. télégraphier, envoyer un télégramme; **tel‧e‧graph‧ic** [⁓'græfik] (**⁓ally**) télégraphique (*a. style*); **te‧leg‧ra‧phist** [ti'legrəfist] télégraphiste *mf*; **te'leg‧ra‧phy** télégraphie *f*.

tel‧e‧phone ['telifoun] 1. téléphone *m*; **⁓** book (*ou directory*) annuaire *m* (des téléphones); **⁓** booth (*ou box*) cabine *f* téléphonique; **⁓** call appel *m* téléphonique, F coup de fil; **⁓** charges *pl.* taxe *f* téléphonique; **⁓** kiosk cabine *f* téléphonique; **⁓** line ligne *f* téléphonique; **⁓** number numéro *m* de téléphone; **⁓** subcriber abonné(e *f*) *m* au téléphone; *at the* **⁓** au téléphone; *by* **⁓** par téléphone; *on the* **⁓** téléphoniquement; par téléphone; *be on the* **⁓** avoir le téléphone; être à l'appareil; 2. téléphoner (à q., [*to*] s.o.); **tel‧e‧phon‧ic** [⁓'fɔnik] (**⁓ally**) téléphonique; **te‧leph‧o‧nist** [ti'lefənist] téléphoniste *mf*; standardiste *f*; **te‧leph‧o‧ny** téléphonie *f*.

tel‧e‧pho‧to *phot.* ['teli'foutou] téléphotographie *f*; **⁓** lens téléobjectif *m*.

tel‧e‧print‧er ['teliprintə] téléscripteur *m*.

tel·e·scope ['teliskoup] **1.** *opt.* télescope *m*; lunette *f*; **2.** (se) télescoper; **tel·e·scop·ic** [~'kɔpik] télescopique; à coulisse (*échelle etc.*); *phot.* ~ lens téléobjectif *m*; ~ sight lunette *f* de visée.

tel·e·type ['teli'taip] télétype *m*; *postes:* télex *m*.

tel·e·view·er ['telivjuːə] téléspectateur (-trice *f*) *m*.

tel·e·vise ['telivaiz] téléviser; **tel·e·vi·sion** ['telivi3n] télévision *f*; ~ set appareil *m* de télévision; ~ channel chaîne *f* de télévision.

tel·ex ['teleks] **1.** télex *m*; **2.** envoyer (*un message*) par télex.

tell [tel] [*irr.*] *v/t.* dire; raconter; apprendre; exprimer; savoir; reconnaître (à, *by*); compter; annoncer; ~ s.o. to do s.th. dire *ou* ordonner à q. de faire qch.; *I have been told* that on m'a dit que; j'ai appris que; *fig.* ~ a story en dire long; ~ off désigner (pour qch., *for* s.th.); F dire son fait à (*q.*); rembarrer (*q.*); *Am. sl.* ~ the world faire savoir partout; publier à son de trompe; produire son effet; porter; ~ of (*ou* about) annoncer, révéler, accuser; ~ on se faire sentir à; influer sur; peser sur; *sl.* cafarder; dénoncer (*q.*); '**tell·er** raconteur (-euse *f*) *m*; *parl. etc.* scrutateur *m*; *banque:* caissier *m*; '**tell·ing** □ efficace; impressionnant; qui porte; '**tell·ing-off:** F *give s.o. a* ~ gronder q., passer un savon à q.; **tell·tale** ['~teil] **1.** indicateur (-trice *f*); révélateur (-trice *f*); *fig.* qui en dit long; **2.** rapporteur (-euse *f*) *m*; *école:* cafard(e *f*) *m*; ⊕ indicateur *m*; ~ clock horloge *f* enregistreuse.

tel·pher ['telfə] ⊕ de téléphérage; ~ line téléphérique *m*; ligne *f* de téléphérage.

te·mer·i·ty [ti'meriti] témérité *f*, audace *f*.

temp F [temp] intérimaire *mf*.

tem·per ['tempə] **1.** tempérer; modérer; *fig.* retenir; ♪ accorder par tempérament; broyer (*les couleurs, le mortier, l'encre, etc.*); donner la trempe à (*l'acier*); adoucir (*le métal*); **2.** ⊕ trempe *f*; *métall.* coefficient *m* de dureté; humeur *f*; colère *f*; caractère *m*, tempérament *m*; *lose one's* ~ se mettre en colère; perdre son sang-froid; s'emporter; **tem-per·a·ment** ['~rəmənt] tempérament *m* (*a.* ♪); humeur *f*; **tem·per-a·men·tal** □ [~'mentl] du tempérament; capricieux (-euse *f*) (*personne*); '**tem·per·ance 1.** tempérance *f*, modération *f*; antialcoolisme *m*; **2.** antialcoolique (*hôtel*); **tem·per·ate** □ ['~rit] tempéré (*climat, a.* ♪); sobre (*personne*); modéré; **tem·per·a·ture** ['temprit∫ə] température *f*; ~ chart feuille *f* de température; **tem·pered** ['tempəd]: *bad-*~ de mauvaise humeur.

tem·pest ['tempist] tempête *f*, tourmente *f*; **tem·pes·tu·ous** □ [~'pestjuəs] de tempête; fougueux (-euse *f*), turbulent (*personne, humeur*); orageux (-euse *f*) (*réunion etc.*).

Tem·plar ['templə] *hist.* templier *m*; *univ.* étudiant(e *f*) *m* en droit du *Temple* (à *Londres*).

tem·ple¹ ['templ] temple *m*; ⚥ *deux écoles de droit* (= *Inns of Court*) à *Londres.*

tem·ple² *anat.* [~] tempe *f*.

tem·po·ral □ ['tempərəl] temporel (-le *f*); **tem·po·ral·i·ties** [~'rælitiz] *pl.* possessions *f/pl. ou* revenus *m/pl.* ecclésiastiques; **tem·po·ra·ri·ness** ['~pərərinis] caractère *m* temporaire *ou* provisoire; '**tem·po·rar·y** □ temporaire, provisoire; momentané; passager (-ère *f*); ~ bridge pont *m* provisoire; ~ work situation *f* intérimaire; '**tem·po·rize** temporiser; ~ with transiger provisoirement avec (*q.*).

tempt [tempt] tenter; induire (à *inf., s.o. to inf.*); **temp'ta·tion** tentation *f*; '**tempt·er** tentateur *m*; '**tempt·ing** □ tentant; séduisant, attrayant; '**tempt·ress** tentatrice *f*.

ten [ten] dix (*a. su./m*).

ten·a·ble ['tenəbl] tenable; *fig.* soutenable.

te·na·cious □ [ti'nei∫əs] tenace; attaché (à, *of*); obstiné, opiniâtre; **te·nac·i·ty** [ti'næsiti] ténacité *f*; sûreté *f* (*de la mémoire*); attachement *m* (à, *of*); obstination *f*.

ten·an·cy ['tenənsi] location *f*.

ten·ant ['tenənt] **1.** locataire *mf*; *fig.* habitant(e *f*) *m*; pensionnaire *mf*; ~ right droits *m/pl.* du tenancier; **2.** habiter comme locataire; occuper; '**ten·ant·ry** locataires *m/pl.*; fermiers *m/pl.*

terminal

tench *icht.* [tenʃ] tanche *f.*

tend[1] [tend] **1.** tendre, se diriger (vers, *towards*); tourner; *fig.* pencher (vers, *towards*), tirer (sur, *to*); tendre (à, *to*); être susceptible (de *inf.*, *to inf.*); être enclin (à, *to*); ~ from s'écarter de.

tend[2] [~] soigner (*un malade*); garder (*les bêtes*); surveiller (*une machine etc.*); *Am.* tenir (*une boutique*); **'tend·ance** † soin *m*; serviteurs *m/pl.*

tend·en·cy ['tendənsi] tendance *f*, disposition *f*, penchant *m* (à, *to*); **ten·den·tious** [~'denʃəs] tendanciel(le *f*), tendancieux (-euse *f*); à tendance (*livre*).

ten·der[1] □ ['tendə] *usu.* tendre; sensible (*au toucher*); délicat (*sujet*); affectueux (-euse *f*) (*lettre*); jeune; soigneux (-euse *f*) (de, *of*); of ~ years en bas âge.

ten·der[2] [~] **1.** offre *f* (*de paiement etc.*); *contrat:* soumission *f*; *legal* ~ cours *m* légal; **2.** offrir; ⊕ soumissionner ([pour], *for*); présenter.

ten·der[3] [~] gardien *m*; 🚂, ⚓ tender *m*; ⚓ bateau *m* annexe; *bar-*~ garçon *m* de comptoir.

ten·der·foot *Am.* F ['tendəfut] nouveau débarqué *m*; cow-boy *m* d'opérette; **'ten·der·ize** attendrir (*viande*); **ten·der·loin** ['~lɔin] *surt. Am.* filet *m*; *Am.* quartier *m* malfamé; **'ten·der·ness** tendresse *f*; sensibilité *f*; *fig.* douceur *f*; *cuis.* tendreté *f.*

ten·don *anat.* ['tendən] tendon *m.*

ten·dril ⊕ ['tendril] vrille *f.*

ten·e·ment ['tenimənt] † habitation *f*; appartement *m*; 🏠 fonds *m* de terre; tenure *f*; ~ house maison *f* de rapport.

ten·et ['ti:net] doctrine *f*, principe *m.*

ten·fold ['tenfould] **1.** *adj.* décuple; **2.** *adv.* dix fois (autant).

ten·nis ['tenis] tennis *m*; '~-court terrain *m* de tennis, court *m.*

ten·on ⊕ ['tenən] tenon *m*; '~-saw ⊕ scie *f* à tenon.

ten·or ['tenə] cours *m*, progrès *m*; teneur *f*; sens *m* général; ♪ ténor *m.*

tense[1] *gramm.* [tens] temps *m.*

tense[2] □ [~] tendu (*a. fig.*); raide; **'tense·ness** tension *f* (*a. fig.*); **ten·sile** ['tensail] extensible; de tension, de traction; ~ strength résistance *f* à la tension; **ten·sion** ['~ʃn]

tension *f*; ⚡ high ~ circuit *m* de haute tension; ~ test essai *m* de traction.

tent[1] [tent] tente *f.*

tent[2] 🧵 [~] mèche *f.*

ten·ta·cle *zo.* ['tentəkl] tentacule *m*; cir(r)e *m.*

ten·ta·tive ['tentətiv] **1.** □ expérimental (-aux *m/pl.*); sujet(te *f*) à révision; hésitant; ~ly à titre d'essai; **2.** tentative *f*, essai *m.*

ten·ter *tex.* ['tentə] élargisseur *m*; '~·hook crochet *m*; *fig.* be on ~s être sur des charbons ardents.

tenth [tenθ] **1.** dixième; **2.** dixième *m*, ♪ *f*; *eccl.* dîme *f*; **'tenth·ly** en dixième lieu.

tent-peg ['tentpeg] piquet *m* de tente.

ten·u·i·ty [te'njuiti] *usu.* ténuité *f*; finesse *f*; faiblesse *f*; **ten·u·ous** □ ['tenjuəs] ténu; effilé; mince; grêle (*voix*); raréfié (*gaz*).

ten·ure ['tenjuə] tenure *f*; (*période f* de) jouissance *f*; *office etc.*: occupation *f.*

tep·id □ ['tepid] tiède; dégourdi (*eau*); **te'pid·i·ty**, **'tep·id·ness** tiédeur *f.*

ter·cen·te·nar·y [tə:sen'ti:nəri], **ter·cen·ten·ni·al** [~'tenjəl] tricentenaire (*a. su./m*).

ter·gi·ver·sa·tion [tə:dʒivə:'seiʃn] tergiversation *f.*

term [tə:m] **1.** temps *m*, durée *f*, limite *f*; terme *m* (*a.* Ⱥ, *phls.*, *ling.*); *ling. a.* mot *m*, expression *f*; *gr* session *f*; *univ., école:* trimestre *m*; 📅 échéance *f*; délai *m* (*de congé*, *du droit d'auteur, de paiement, etc.*); beginning of ~ rentrée *f*; ~s *pl.* conditions *f/pl.*, termes *m/pl.*; prix *m/pl.*; relations *f/pl.*, rapports *m/pl.*; Ⱥ énoncé *m* (*d'un problème*); in ~s of en fonction de; be on good (bad) ~s être bien (mal) (avec, *with*); come to (*ou* make) ~s with s'arranger, prendre un arrangement avec; ✂ partiser; **2.** appeler, nommer; qualifier (de qch., *s.th.*).

ter·ma·gant ['tə:məgənt] **1.** □ revêche, acariâtre; **2.** mégère *f*; dragon *m* (= *femme*).

ter·mi·na·ble □ ['tə:minəbl] terminable; résiliable (*contrat*); **'ter·mi·nal 1.** □ extrême; dernier (-ère *f*); final; *école:* trimestriel(le *f*); terminal (-aux *m/pl.*); ~ly par trimestre;

2. bout *m*; ⚡ borne *f*; *gramm.* terminaison *f*; 🏛 *Am.* terminus *m*; *ordinateur*: terminal *m*; **ter·mi·nate** ['⌁neit] (se) terminer; finir; **ter·mi·na·tion** fin *f*, conclusion *f*; terminaison *f* (*a. gramm.*); ⚖ extinction *f*.

ter·mi·nol·o·gy [təːmi'nɔlədʒi] terminologie *f*.

ter·mi·nus ['təːminəs], *pl.* **-ni** [⌁nai] terminus *m*, tête *f* de ligne (*a.* 🏛).

ter·mite *zo.* ['təːmait] termite *m*.

tern *orn.* [təːn] sterne *f*, hirondelle *f* de mer.

ter·na·ry ['təːnəri] ternaire.

ter·race ['terəs] terrasse *f*; rangée *f* de maisons; **'ter·raced** en terrasse; en rangée (*maisons*).

ter·rain ['terein] terrain *m*.

ter·rene □ [te'riːn] terreux (-euse *f*); terrestre. [(tre.)]

ter·res·tri·al □ [ti'restriəl] terres-

ter·ri·ble □ ['terəbl] terrible; affreux (-euse *f*); **'ter·ri·ble·ness** horreur *f*.

ter·ri·er *zo.* ['teriə] terrier *m*.

ter·rif·ic [tə'rifik] (⌁ally) épouvantable; terrible; colossal (-aux *m/pl.*); **ter·ri·fy** ['terifai] *v/t.* épouvanter, terrifier.

ter·ri·to·ri·al [teri'tɔːriəl] **1.** □ territorial (-aux *m/pl.*); terrien(ne *f*), foncier (-ère *f*); ⌁ *waters* eaux *f/pl.* territoriales; ⚔ ♀ *Army* (*ou* F *Force*) territoriale *f*; **2.** ⚔ territorial *m*; **ter·ri·to·ry** ['⌁təri] territoire *m*; *Am.* ♀ territoire *m* des É.-U.

ter·ror ['terə] terreur *f* (*a. fig.*), effroi *m*, épouvante *f*; **'ter·ror·ism** terrorisme *m*; **'ter·ror·ist** terroriste *m*; **'ter·ror·ize** terroriser.

ter·ry(·cloth) ['teri(klɔθ)] tissu *m* éponge.

terse □ [təːs] concis, net(te *f*); **'terse·ness** concision *f*.

ter·tian 🩺 ['təːʃn] (fièvre *f*) tierce; **ter·ti·ar·y** ['⌁ʃəri] tertiaire.

tes·sel·lat·ed ['tesileitid] en mosaïque (*pavé*).

test [test] **1.** épreuve *f*, essai *m* (*a.* 🝫); *psych.*, ⊕ test *m*; 🝫 réactif *m* (*de, for*); examen *m*; *fig.* épreuve *f*, critérium *m*; *put to the* ⌁ mettre à l'épreuve *ou* l'essai; **2.** *v/t.* éprouver, mettre à l'épreuve; examiner; essayer; *v/i.* 🝫 faire la réaction (*de, for*).

tes·ta·ceous *zo.* [tes'teiʃəs] testacé.

tes·ta·ment *bibl.*, †, ⚖ ['testəmənt]

testament *m*; **tes·ta·men·ta·ry** [⌁'mentəri] testamentaire.

tes·ta·tor [tes'teitə] testateur *m*.

tes·ta·trix [tes'teitriks] testatrice *f*.

test...: ⌁ **ban** (**treat·y**) (traité *m* d')interdiction *f* d'essais nucléaires; ⌁ **case** ⚖ cas *m* qui fait jurisprudence, précédent *m*; ⌁ **drive** *mot.* essai sur *ou* de route; '⌁**drive** faire faire un essai de route à (*une voiture*).

test·er ['testə] essayeur *m*; vérificateur (-trice *f*) *m*; *outil*: vérificateur *m*.

tes·ti·cle *anat.* ['testikl] testicule *m*.

tes·ti·fi·er ['testifaiə] témoin *m* (*de, to*); **tes·ti·fy** ['⌁fai] *v/t.* témoigner (*a. fig.*); déposer; *v/i.* attester (qch., *to s.th.*), témoigner (*de, to*).

tes·ti·mo·ni·al [testi'mounjəl] certificat *m*, attestation *f*; recommandation *f*; témoignage *m* d'estime; **tes·ti·mo·ny** ['⌁məni] témoignage *m* (*de, to*); ⚖ *témoin*: déposition *f*.

tes·ti·ness ['testinis] irritabilité *f*.

test...: '⌁**pa·per** 🝫 papier *m* réactif; *école*: composition *f*, épreuve *f*; '⌁**pi·lot** ✈ pilote *m* d'essai; '⌁**print** *phot.* épreuve *f* témoin; ⌁ **run** course *f* d'essai; essai *m* (de bon fonctionnement); '⌁**tube** 🝫 éprouvette *f*; ⌁ *baby* bébé-éprouvette *m* (*pl.* bébés-éprouvettes).

tes·ty □ ['testi], **tetch·y** □ ['tetʃi] irascible, irritable; bilieux (-euse *f*).

teth·er ['teðə] **1.** attache *f*, longe *f*; *fig.* ressources *f/pl.*; **2.** mettre au piquet, attacher.

tet·ra·gon 📐 ['tetrəgən] quadrilatère *m*; **te·trag·o·nal** [⌁'træɡənl] tétragone.

tet·ter 🩺 ['tetə] dartre *f*.

Teu·ton ['tjuːtən] Teuton(ne *f*) *m*; **Teu·ton·ic** [⌁'tɔnik] teuton(ne *f*), teutonique; ⌁ *Order* l'ordre *m* Teutonique.

text [tekst] texte *m*; *fig.* sujet *m*; *typ.* ⌁ *hand* grosse (écriture) *f*; '⌁**book** manuel *m*, livre *m* de classe.

tex·tile ['tekstail] **1.** textile; **2.** ⌁s *pl.* tissus *m/pl.*; textiles *m/pl.*

tex·tu·al □ ['tekstjuəl] textuel(le *f*).

tex·ture ['tekstʃə] texture *f* (*a. fig.*); tissu *m*; *bois, peau*: grain *m*.

tha·lid·o·mide [θə'lidəmaid] thalidomide *f*; ⌁ *baby*, ⌁ *child* (bébé *m*) victime *f* de la thalidomide.

than [ðæn; ðən] *après comp.* que; *devant nombres*: de.

thank [θæŋk] **1.** remercier (de *inf.*, *for gér.*); ~ *you* merci; *I will* ~ *you for* je vous saurais bien gré de (*me donner etc.*); *iro.* ~ *you for nothing* merci de rien; **2.** ~*s pl.* remerciements *m/pl.*; ~*s to* grâce à; **thank·ful** □ ['~ful] reconnaissant; '**thank·less** □ ingrat; **thanks·giv·ing** [~s'givin] action *f* de grâce(s); *surt. Am.* ♀ (*Day*) le jour *m* d'action de grâces (*le dernier jeudi de novembre*); '**thank·wor·thy** † digne de reconnaissance.

that [ðæt] **1.** *cj.* [*usu.* ðət] que; **2.** *pron. dém.* (*pl. those*) celui-là (*pl.* ceux-là), celle-là (*pl.* celles-là); celui (*pl.* ceux), celle (*pl.* celles); cela, F ça; ce; *so* ~*'s* ~! et voilà!; *and ... at* ~ et encore ..., et ... par-dessus le marché; *with* ~ là-dessus; **3.** *pron. rel.* [*a.* ðət] qui, que; lequel, laquelle, lesquels, lesquelles; **4.** *adj.* ce (cet *devant une voyelle ou un h muet*; *pl.* ces), cette (*pl.* ces); ce (cet, cette, *pl.* ces) ...-là; **5.** *adv.* F (aus)si; ~ *far* si loin.

thatch [θætʃ] **1.** chaume *m*; **2.** couvrir de chaume.

thaw [θɔ:] **1.** dégel *m*; **2.** *v/i.* fondre (*neige etc.*); *v/t.* décongeler (*de la viande*); *mot.* dégeler (*le radiateur*).

the [ði:; *devant une voyelle* ði, *devant une consonne* ðə] **1.** *art.* le, la, les; **2.** *adv.* ~ *richer he is* ~ *more arrogant he seems* plus il est riche, plus il semble arrogant.

the·a·tre, *Am.* **the·a·ter** ['θiətə] théâtre *m* (*a. fig.*); **the·at·ric**, **the·at·ri·cal** □ [θi'ætrik(l)] théâtral (-aux *m/pl.*) (*a. fig.*); spectaculaire; d'acteur(s); **the·at·ri·cals** [~klz] *pl.* (*usu. amateur* ~) spectacle *m* d'amateurs, comédie *f* de société.

thee *bibl.*, *poét.* [ði:] *accusatif*: te; *datif*: toi.

theft [θeft] vol *m*.

their [ðɛə] leur, leurs; **theirs** [~z] le (la) leur, les leurs; à eux, à elles.

the·ism ['θi:izm] théisme *m*.

them [ðem; ðəm] *accusatif*: les; *datif*: leur; à eux, à elles.

theme [θi:m] thème *m* (*a.* ♪, *a. gramm.*); sujet *m*; *gramm.* radical (-aux *pl.*) *m*; *école*: dissertation *f*, *Am.* thème *m*; ~ *song* leitmotiv (*pl.* -ve) *m*.

them·selves [ðəm'selvz] eux-mêmes, elles-mêmes; *réfléchi*: se.

then [ðen] **1.** *adv.* alors; en ce temps-là; puis; ensuite; aussi; d'ailleurs; *every now and* ~ de temps en temps; de temps à autre; *there and* ~ sur-le-champ; *now* ~ allons, voyons; **2.** *cj.* donc, alors, en ce cas; **3.** *adj.* de ce temps-là, d'alors.

thence *poét.* [ðens] par conséquent; *temps*: dès lors; '~**forth** *poét.* depuis ce temps-là; dès lors, à partir de ce jour.

the·oc·ra·cy [θi'ɔkrəsi] théocratie *f*; **the·o·crat·ic** [θiə'krætik] (~*ally*) théocratique.

the·o·lo·gi·an [θiə'loudʒjən] théologien *m*; **the·o·log·i·cal** [~'lɔdʒikl] théologique; **the·ol·o·gy** [θi'ɔlədʒi] théologie *f*.

the·o·rem ['θiərəm] théorème *m*; **the·o·ret·ic**, **the·o·ret·i·cal** □ [~'retik(l)] théorique; '**the·o·rist** théoricien(ne *f*) *m*; théoriste *mf*; '**the·o·rize** théoriser; '**the·o·ry** théorie *f*.

the·os·o·phy [θi'ɔsəfi] théosophie *f*.

ther·a·peu·tics [θerə'pju:tiks] *usu. sg.* thérapeutique *f*; '**ther·a·py** thérapie *f*; *see occupational*; '**ther·a·pist** thérapeute *mf*; *mental* ~ psycho-thérapeute *m*.

there [ðɛə] **1.** *adv.* là; y; là-bas; F ce, cette, ces, cettes ...-là; *the man* ~ cet homme-là; ~ *is*, ~ *are* il y a; ~*'s a good fellow!* vous serez bien gentil!; ~ *you are!* vous voilà!; ça y est!; **2.** *int.* voilà!

there...: '~**a·bout(s)** près de là, par là; à peu près; '**aft·er** après cela, ensuite; '~**by** par là, de cette façon; '~**fore** donc, par conséquent; aussi (*avec inversion*); ~**'in** là-dedans; à cet égard, en cela; ~**'of** en; de cela; '~**up'on** là-dessus; ~**'with** avec cela.

ther·mal □ ['θə:məl] thermal (-aux *m/pl.*); *phys. a.* thermique, calorifique; ~ *value* pouvoir *m* calorifique; **ther·mic** ['~mik] (~*ally*) thermique; **therm·i·on·ic** [~mi'ɔnik]: ~ *valve radio*: lampe *f* thermoïonique. **ther·mo·e·lec·tric cou·ple** *phys.* ['θə:moi'lektrik 'kʌpl] élément *m* thermo-électrique; **ther·mom·e·ter** [θə'mɔmitə] thermomètre *m*; **ther·mo·met·ric**, **ther·mo·met·ri·cal** □ [θə:mə'metrik(l)] thermométrique; **ther·mo·nu·cle·ar** *phys.* ['ᷱ'nju:kliə] thermonucléaire; **ther·mo·pile** *phys.* ['ᷱmopail] thermopile *f*; **Ther·mos** ['ᷱmɔs] (*ou* ᷱ*flask*, ᷱ*bottle*) bouteille *f* Thermos; **ther·mo·stat** ['ᷱmostæt] thermostat *m*.

the·sau·rus [θi'sɔːrəs], *pl.* **-ri** [ᷱrai] thésaurus *m*; trésor *m*.

these [ðiːz] *pl. de this* 1, 2; ᷱ **three years** depuis trois ans; *in* ᷱ *days* à notre époque.

the·sis ['θiːsis], *pl.* **-ses** [ᷱsiːz] thèse *f*, dissertation *f*.

they [ðei] ils, *accentué*: eux; elles (*a. accentué*) a. on; ᷱ **who** ceux *ou* celles qui.

thick [θik] **1.** □ *usu.* épais(se *f*) (*brouillard, liquide, etc.*); dense (*brouillard, foule*); abondant, dru (*cheveux*); trouble (*eau, vin*); crème (*potage*); empâté (*voix*); serré (*foule*); profond (*ténèbres*); F (*souv. as* ᷱ *as thieves*) très lié, intime; ᷱ *with* très lié avec; *sl. that's a bit* ᷱ! ça c'est un peu fort!; **2.** partie *f* épaisse; gras *m*; fort *m*; *in the* ᷱ *of* au plus fort de; au beau milieu de; '**thick·en** *v/t.* épaissir; *cuis.* lier; *v/i.* s'épaissir; se lier; se compliquer; s'échauffer; **thick·et** ['ᷱit] fourré *m*, bosquet *m*; '**thick·head·ed** lourdaud; obtus; '**thick·ness** épaisseur *f* (*a.* ⊕); grosseur *f*; abondance *f*; état *m* trouble; empâtement *m*; ⊕ couche *f*; '**thick·set** ⊕ dru; épais(se *f*); trapu (*personne*); '**thick·skinned** *fig.* peu sensible.

thief [θiːf], *pl.* **thieves** [θiːvz] voleur (-euse *f*) *m*; F moucheron *m* (*de chandelle*); **thieve** [θiːv] voler; **thiev·er·y** ['ᷱvəri] vol(erie *f*) *m*.

thiev·ish □ ['θiːviʃ] voleur (-euse *f*); '**thiev·ish·ness** habitude *f* du vol; penchant *m* au vol.

thigh [θai] cuisse *f*; '**ᷱ·bone** fémur *m*.

thill [θil] limon *m*, brancard *m*.

thim·ble ['θimbl] dé *m*; ⊕ bague *f*; ⚓ cosse *f*; **thim·ble·ful** ['ᷱful] plein un dé (de, *of*); **thim·ble·rig** ['ᷱrig] F *vt/i.* frauder.

thin [θin] **1.** □ *usu.* mince; peu épais (-se *f*); maigre; pauvre (*sol etc.*); clair (*liquide, tissu*); grêle (*voix*); ténu; rare, clairsemé; sans corps (*vin*); *fig.* peu convaincant; *théâ. a* ᷱ *house* un auditoire peu nombreux; **2.** *v/t.* amincir; diminuer; (*a.* ᷱ *out*) éclaircir; *cuis.* délayer;

v/i. s'amincir, maigrir; s'éclaircir.

thine *bibl., poét.* [ðain] le tien, la tienne, les tiens, les tiennes; à toi.

thing [θiŋ] chose *f*, objet *m*, affaire *f*; être *m* (= *personne*); ᷱ**s** *pl.* effets *m/pl.*; vêtements *f/pl.*; affaires *f/pl.*; choses *f/pl.*; F *be the* ᷱ être l'usage *ou* correct *ou* ce qu'il faut; F *know a* ᷱ *or two* être malin (-igne *f*); *en savoir plus d'un(e)*; *above all* ᷱ**s** avant tout; ᷱ**s** *are going better* les affaires vont mieux.

thing·um(·a)·bob F ['θiŋəm(i)bɔb], **thing·um·my** F ['ᷱəmi] chose *m*; truc *m*.

think [θiŋk] [*irr.*] *v/i.* penser; réfléchir (sur *about, over*); compter (*inf.*, *to inf.*); s'attendre (à *inf.*, *to inf.*); ᷱ*of* penser à, envisager; penser (*bien, mal*) de; considérer; ᷱ*of* (*gér.*) penser à (*inf.*); *v/t.* croire; penser; s'imaginer; juger, trouver; tenir pour; ᷱ *much etc. of* avoir une bonne *etc.* opinion de; ᷱ *out* imaginer (*qch.*); arriver à la solution de (*qch.*); ᷱ *s.th. over* réfléchir sur qch.; '**think·a·ble** concevable; '**think·er** penseur (-euse *f*) *m*; '**think·ing** pensant; qui pense.

thin·ness ['θinnis] minceur *f*; peu *m* d'épaisseur; légèreté *f*; maigreur *f*.

third [θəːd] **1.** troisième *f*; *date, roi:* trois; *surt. Am.* F ᷱ *degree* passage *m* à tabac; troisième degré *m*; *the* ♀ *World* le Tiers-Monde; **2.** tiers *m*; troisième *mf*; ♪ tierce *f*; '**third·ly** en troisième lieu; '**third·'par·ty in·sur·ance** assurance *f* aux tiers; '**third·'rate** de qualité très inférieure.

thirst [θəːst] **1.** soif *f* (*a. fig.*); **2.** avoir soif (de *for, after*); '**thirst·y** □ altéré (de, *for*) (*a. fig.*); desséché (*sol*); F *it is* ᷱ *work* cela vous sèche le gosier.

thir·teen ['θəː'tiːn] treize; '**thir·teenth** [ᷱθ] treizième; **thir·ti·eth** ['ᷱtiiθ] trentième; '**thir·ty** trente.

this [ðis] **1.** *pron. dém.* (*pl.* these) celui-ci (*pl.* ceux-ci), celle-ci (*pl.* celles-ci); celui (*pl.* ceux), celle (*pl.* celles); ceci; ce; **2.** *adj. dém.* (*pl.* these) ce (cet *devant une voyelle ou un h muet*; *pl.* ces), cette (*pl.* ces) ...-ci; *in this country* chez nous; ᷱ *day week* aujourd'hui en huit; **3.** *adv.* F comme ceci; ᷱ *big* grand comme ça.

this·tle ♣ [ˈθisl] chardon *m*.

thith·er *poét*. [ˈðiðə] là; y.

thole ⚓ [θoul] (*a*. ∼-*pin*) tolet *m*.

thong [θɔŋ] lanière *f* (*souv. de fouet*).

tho·rax *anat*., *zo*. [ˈθɔːræks] thorax *m*.

thorn ♣ [θɔːn] épine *f*; **'thorn·y** épineux (-euse *f*) (*a. fig*.); ♣ spinifère.

thor·ough ☐ [ˈθʌrə] complet (-ète *f*); profond; minutieux (-euse *f*); parfait; vrai; achevé (*coquin*); ∼*ly a*. tout à fait; **'∼·bass** ♪ basse *f* continue; **'∼·bred 1**. pur sang *inv*.; de race; **2**. cheval *m* pur sang; chien *m* etc. de race; **'∼·fare** voie *f* de communication; passage *m*; **'∼·go·ing** achevé; consciencieux (-euse *f*); **'thor·ough·ness** perfection *f*; sincérité *f*; **'thor·ough-paced** achevé; parfait; enragé.

those [ðouz] **1**. *pl. de* that; are ∼ your parents? sont-ce là vos parents?; **2**. *adj*. ces (...-là).

thou *bibl*., *poét*. [ðau] tu, *accentué*: toi.

though [ðou] quoique, bien que (*sbj*.); F (*usu. à la fin de la phrase*) pourtant, cependant; *int*. vraiment!; *as* ∼ comme si.

thought [θɔːt] **1**. *prét. et p.p. de* think; **2**. pensée *f*; idée *f*; souci *m*; intention *f*; *give* ∼ *to* penser à; *on second* ∼*s* réflexion faite; *take* ∼ *for* songer à.

thought·ful ☐ [ˈθɔːtful] pensif (-ive *f*); rêveur (-euse *f*); réfléchi; soucieux (-euse *f*) (de, *of*); prévenant (pour, *of*); **'thought·ful·ness** méditation *f*; prévenance *f*, égards *m/pl*.; souci *m*.

thought·less ☐ [ˈθɔːtlis] étourdi, irréfléchi, négligent (de, *of*); **'thought·less·ness** irréflexion *f*; inattention *f*; insouciance *f*; négligence *f*.

thought-read·ing [ˈθɔːtriːdiŋ] lecture *f* de pensée.

thou·sand [ˈθauzənd] **1**. mille; *dates à* mil; **2**. mille *m/inv*.; millier *m*; **thou·sandth** [ˈ∼zənθ] millième (*a. su./m*).

thrall *poét*. [θrɔːl] esclave *m* (de *of*, to); *a*. = **thral(l)·dom** [ˈθrɔːldəm] esclavage *m*; asservissement *m* (*a. fig*.).

thrash [θræʃ] *v/t*. battre; rosser; *sl*.

vaincre; ∼ *out* débattre; *v/i*. battre, clapoter; ⊕ vibrer; ⚓ se frayer un chemin; *qqfois* bourlinguer; *see* thresh; **'thrash·ing** battage *m*; rossée *f*; F défaite *f*; *see* threshing.

thread [θred] **1**. fil *m* (*a. fig*.); filament *m*; ⊕ *vis*: filet *m*; **2**. enfiler; *fig*. s'insinuer, se faufiler; ⊕ fileter; **'∼·bare** râpé; *fig*. usé; **'thread·y** fibreux (-euse *f*); plein de fils; ténu (*voix*).

threat [θret] menace *f*; **'threaten** *vt/i*. menacer (de qch., [*with*] s.th.).

three [θriː] trois (*a. su./m*); **'∼·colo(u)r** trichrome; **'∼·fold** triple; ∼**pence** [ˈθrepəns] pièce *f* de trois pence; **'∼·pen·ny** coûtant trois pence; *fig*. mesquin; **∼·phase** cur·rent ⚡ [ˈθriːfeizˈkʌrənt] courant *m* triphasé; **'∼·piece** en trois pièces; ∼ *suit* trois-pièces *m/inv*.; **'∼·score** soixante; **'∼·valve** receiv·er *radio*: poste *m* à trois lampes.

thresh [θreʃ] battre (*le blé*); *see* thrash; *fig*. ∼ *out* discuter (*une question*) à fond.

thresh·ing [ˈθreʃiŋ] battage *m*; **'∼floor** aire *f*; **'∼·ma·chine** batteuse *f*, machine *f* à battre.

thresh·old [ˈθreʃhould] seuil *m*.

threw [θruː] *prét. de* throw **1**.

thrice † [θrais] trois fois.

thrift(·i·ness) [ˈθrift(inis)] économie *f*, épargne *f*; ♣ statice *m*; **'thrift·less** ☐ prodigue; imprévoyant; **'thrift·y** ☐ économe, ménager (-ère *f*); *poét*., *a*. *Am*. florissant.

thrill [θril] **1**. (*v/t*. faire) frissonner, frémir (de, *with*); *v/t. fig*. troubler; émotionner; **2**. frisson *m*; vive émotion *f*; **'thrill·er** F roman *m* sensationnel; pièce *f* à gros effets; **'thrill·ing** saisissant, émouvant; sensationnel(le *f*).

thrive [θraiv] [*irr*.] se développer; réussir, *fig*. prospérer; **thriv·en** [ˈθrivn] *p.p. de* thrive; **thriv·ing** ☐ [ˈθraiviŋ] vigoureux (-euse *f*); florissant.

throat [θrout] gorge *f* (*a. géog*.); ⚓ ancre: collet *m*; ⊕ rabot: lumière *f*; *fourneau*: gueulard *m*; *clear one's* ∼ s'éclaircir le gosier; **'throat·y** ☐ guttural (-aux *m/pl*.).

throb [θrɔb] **1**. battre (*cœur etc*.);

lanciner (*doigt*); **2.** battement *m*, pulsation *f*; ⊕ vrombissement *m*.

throe [θrou] convulsion *f*; ~s *pl.* douleurs *f/pl.*; affres *f/pl.*; *fig.* tourments *m/pl.*

throm·bo·sis ❀ [θrɔm'bousis] thrombose *f*.

throne [θroun] **1.** trône *m*; **2.** *v/t.* mettre sur le trône; *v/i.* trôner.

throng [θrɔŋ] **1.** foule *f*; cohue *f*; presse *f*; **2.** *v/i.* se presser, affluer; *v/t.* encombrer; presser.

throt·tle ['θrɔtl] **1.** étrangler (*a.* ⊕ *le moteur etc.*); ⊕ mettre (*une machine*) au ralenti; **2.** = '~-**valve** soupape *f* de réglage; étrangleur *m*.

through [θru:] **1.** *prp.* à travers; au travers de; au moyen de, par; à cause de; pendant (*un temps*); **2.** *adj.* direct (*train, vol etc.*); *Am.* ~ *street* rue *f* prioritaire; ~ *traffic* transit *m*; ~'**out 1.** *prp.* d'un bout à l'autre de; dans tout; pendant tout (*un temps*); **2.** *adv.* partout; d'un bout à l'autre; '~·**way** *see* thruway.

throve [θrouv] *prét.* de thrive.

throw [θrou] **1.** [*irr.*] *v/t. usu.* jeter (*a. fig.*); lancer; projeter (*de l'eau, une image, etc.*); désarçonner (*un cavalier*); *tex.* jeter, tordre (*la soie*); tournasser (*un pot*); envoyer (*un baiser*); rejeter (*une faute*); *zo.* mettre bas (*des petits*); *Am.* F terrasser (*un adversaire*); ~ *away* (re)jeter; gaspiller; ne pas profiter de; ~ *in* jeter dedans; ajouter; placer (*un mot*); ~ *off* jeter; ôter (*un vêtement*); se défaire de; se dépouiller de; *fig.* dépister; ~ *out* jeter dehors; émettre; *fig.* faire ressortir; lancer (*une insinuation etc.*); *surt. parl.* rejeter; ⊕ désaccoupler; ~ *over* abandonner; ⊕ renverser (*un levier*); ~ *up* jeter en l'air; lever; abandonner (*un poste*); vomir; construire à la hâte; ~ *up the cards* donner gagné à q.; *see* sponge 1; ~ *off fig.* débuter; ~ *up* vomir; **2.** jet *m*; coup *m*; coup *m* de dé; ⊕ déviation *f*, écart *m*; '~-'**back** *surt. biol.* régression *f*; **thrown** [θroun] *p.p.* de throw 1; '**throw-'off** *chasse:* lancé *m*; *p.ext.* mise *f* en train.

thru *Am.* [θru:] *see* through.

thrum[1] [θrʌm] *tex.* penne *f*, -s *f/pl.*; bout *m*, -s *m/pl.*; ⚓ ~s *pl.* lardage *m*.

thrum[2] [~] (*a.* ~ *on*) tapoter (*le piano*); pincer de (*la guitare*).

thrush[1] *orn.* [θrʌʃ] grive *f*.

thrush[2] [~] ❀ aphtes *m/pl.*; *vét.* teigne *f*.

thrust [θrʌst] **1.** poussée *f* (*a.* ⊕); ⚔, *a. fig.* assaut *m*; *escrime:* botte *f*; coup *m* de pointe (*d'épée*); **2.** [*irr.*] *v/t.* pousser; *v/i.* porter un coup (à, *at*); ~ *o.s. into* s'enfoncer dans; ~ *out* mettre dehors, chasser; tirer (*sa langue*); ~ *s.th. upon s.o.* forcer q. à accepter qch.; imposer qch. à q.; ~ *o.s. upon* s'imposer à.

thru·way *Am.* ['θru:wei] autoroute *f* (à péage); rue *f* prioritaire.

thud [θʌd] **1.** résonner sourdement; tomber *etc.* avec un bruit sourd; **2.** bruit *m* sourd; son *m* mat.

thug [θʌg] thug *m*; *fig.* bandit *m*.

thumb [θʌm] **1.** pouce *m*; *Tom* ♀ le petit Poucet *m*; **2.** feuilleter (*un livre*); manier; *Am.* ~ *one's nose* faire un pied de nez (à q., *to s.o.*); ~ *a lift* (*ou a ride*) faire de l'auto-stop; arrêter une voiture (pour se faire emmener); ~ **in·dex** onglets *m/pl.* (d'un livre); '~·**nail** ongle *m* du pouce; ~ *sketch* petit croquis *m* (hâtif); '~-**print** marque *f* de pouce; '~-**screw** *torture:* poucettes *f/pl.*; ⊕ vis *f* ailée; '~-**stall** poucier *m*; ❀ doigtier *m* pour pouce, F pouce *m*; '~-**tack** *Am.* punaise *f*.

thump [θʌmp] **1.** coup *m* de poing; bruit *m* sourd; **2.** *v/t.* cogner (sur, on), donner un coup de poing à; *v/i.* sonner sourdement; battre fort (*cœur*); '**thump·er** *sl.* chose *f* énorme; *sl.* mensonge *m*; '**thump·ing** *sl.* colossal (-aux *m/pl.*).

thun·der ['θʌndə] **1.** tonnerre *m* (*a. fig.*); F *steal s.o.'s* ~ anticiper q.; **2.** tonner; '~·**bolt** foudre *f* (*poét. a. m*); '~·**clap** coup *m* de tonnerre *ou fig.* de foudre; '~·**cloud** nuage *m* orageux; '~·**head** partie *f* supérieure d'un cumulus; *fig.* menace *f*; '**thun·der·ing** *sl.* **1.** *adj.* colossal (-aux *m/pl.*), formidable; **2.** *adv.* joliment, rudement; '**thun·der·ous** □ orageux (-euse *f*); *fig.* menaçant; à tout rompre; de tonnerre (*bruit etc.*); '**thun·der·storm** orage *m*; '**thun·der·struck** foudroyé, abasourdi; '**thun·der·y** orageux (-euse *f*).

Thurs·day ['θə:zdi] jeudi *m*.

thus [ðʌs] ainsi; de cette manière; donc.

thwack [θwæk] *see* whack.

thwart [θwɔːt] **1.** contrarier; frustrer, déjouer; **2.** ⚓ banc *m* de nage.

thy *bibl.*, *poét.* [ðai] ton, ta, tes.

thyme ♀ [taim] thym *m*.

thy·roid *anat.* ['θairɔid] **1.** thyroïde; ⁓ *extract* extrait *m* thyroïde; ⁓ *gland* = **2.** glande *f* thyroïde.

thy·self *bibl.*, *poét.* [ðai'self] toi-même; *réfléchi*: te.

ti·a·ra [ti'ɑːrə] tiare *f*.

tib·i·a *anat.* ['tibiə], *pl.* -ae [⁓iː] tibia *m*.

tic ✻ [tik] tic *m*.

tick¹ *zo.* [tik] tique *f*.

tick² [⁓] toile *f* à matelas.

tick³ F [⁓]: on ⁓ à crédit.

tick⁴ [⁓] **1.** tic-tac *m*/*inv.*; F instant *m*, moment *m*; marque *f*; *to the* ⁓ à l'heure sonnante; **2.** *v*/*i.* faire tic-tac; battre; *mot.* ⁓ *over* tourner au ralenti; *v*/*t.* pointer, faire une marque à; ⁓ *off* pointer; vérifier; *sl.* rembarrer (*q.*).

tick·er ['tikə] téléscripteur *m*; téléimprimeur *m*; F tocante (= *montre*); F palpitant *m* (= *cœur*); '⁓*tape* bande *f* de téléscripteur; serpentin *m*.

tick·et ['tikit] **1.** 🎭 *théâ.*, *loterie*: billet *m*; *métro*, *consigne*, *place réservée*, *etc.*: ticket *m*; coupon *m*; (*a. price-*⁓) étiquette *f*; bon *m* (*de soupe*); *mot.* *Am.* F contravention *f*; *parl. Am.* liste *f* des candidats; F programme *m*; F *the* ⁓ ce qu'il faut, correct; ⁓ *of leave* (bulletin *m* de) libération *f* conditionelle; *on* ⁓ *of leave* libéré conditionellement; **2.** étiqueter, marquer; ⁓ **a·gen·cy** agence *f* de voyages; *théâ. etc.* agence *f* de spectacles; '⁓**-col·lec·tor** 🎭 contrôleur *m* des billets; '⁓**in·spec·tor** *auto-bus*: contrôleur *m*; '⁓ **of·fice**, '⁓ **win·dow** *surt. Am.* guichet *m*; '⁓**-punch** poinçon *m* de contrôleur.

tick·ing ['tikiŋ] toile *f* à matelas.

tick·le ['tikl] chatouiller; *fig.* amuser; flatter; **tick·ler** (*ou* ⁓ *coil*) *radio*: bobine *f* de réaction; '**tick·lish** ☐ chatouilleux (-euse *f*); délicat; *fig.* susceptible (*personne*).

tid·al ☐ ['taidl] de marée; à marée; ⁓ *wave* raz *m* de marée; flot *m* de la marée; *fig.* vague *f*.

tid·bit *Am.* ['tidbit] *see* titbit.

tide [taid] **1.** marée *f*; *fig.* vague *f*; ⚓ flot *m*; *low* (*high*) ⁓ marée *f* basse (haute); *fig.* fortune *f*; † saison *f*, temps *m*; *turn of the* ⁓ étale *m*; *fig.* tournure *f* (*des affaires*); **2.** porter (*par la marée*); *fig.* ⁓ *over* venir à bout de; s'en tirer; *s.o. over* dépanner q., aider q. à s'en tirer, tirer q. d'embarras; '⁓**mark** ligne *f* de marée haute; F ligne crasse (*au cou*, *dans une baignoire etc.*).

ti·di·ness ['taidinis] (bon) ordre *m*; propreté *f*; *habillement*: bonne tenue *f*.

ti·dings *pl. ou sg.* ['taidiŋz] nouvelle *f*, -s *f*/*pl.*

ti·dy ['taidi] **1.** bien rangé; bien tenu, *fig.* passable, F joli; **2.** voile *m* (*sur un fauteuil etc.*); récipient *m* (*pour peignures*); corbeille *f* (*à ordures*); **3.** (*a.* ⁓ *up*) ranger; mettre de l'ordre dans, arranger (*une chambre etc.*).

tie [tai] **1.** lien *m* (*a. fig.*); attache *f*; (*a. neck-*⁓) cravate *f*; nœud *m*; ♩ liaison *f*; △ chaîne *f*, ancre *f*; *fig.* entrave *f*; *soulier*: cordon *m*; *sp.* match *m* à égalité, partie *f* nulle; *sp.* match *m* de championnat; *parl.* nombre *m* égal de suffrages; **2.** *v*/*t.* lier; nouer (*la cravate*); ficeler; △ chaîner; *v*/*i. sp.* être à égalité; ⁓ *down fig.* assujettir (*à une condition etc.*, *to*); asservir (*q.*) (à, *to*); ⁓ *up* attacher; ficeler; ⚓ amarrer; *fig.* immobiliser; F marier; *Am.* F gêner.

tier [tiə] rangée *f*; étage *m*; *théâ.* balcon *m*.

tierce [tiəs] *escrime*, *cartes*: tierce *f*.

tie-up ['tai'ʌp] cordon *m*; association *f*; impasse *f*; *surt. Am.* grève *f*; *Am.* arrêt *m* (*de la circulation etc.*).

tiff F [tif] **1.** petite querelle *f*; boutade *f*; **2.** bouder.

tif·fin ['tifin] *anglo-indien*: déjeuner *m* (*de midi*).

ti·ger ['taigə] tigre *m*; *fig.* as *m*; *fig.* homme *m* féroce; *Am.* F three *cheers and a* ⁓! trois hourras et encore un hourra!; '**ti·ger·ish** ☐ *fig.* cruel(le *f*); féroce; de tigre.

tight ☐ [tait] serré; tendu, raide; collant, étroit, juste (*vêtements*); bien fermé, imperméable; resserré, rare (*argent*); F ivre, gris; F *fig.* a ⁓ *place* (*ou* squeeze) on tenait tout juste; *it was a ~ squeeze to get through* il y avait à peine la place de passer; *hold ~* tenir serré; *in a ~ corner* en mauvaise passe; *in a ~ squeeze* dans l'embarras; **'tight·en** *v/t.* (res)serrer (*sa ceinture, une vis*); retendre (*une courroie*); tendre, remonter (*un ressort*); *v/i.* se (res)serrer; se bander (*ressort*); **'~-'fist·ed** F dur à la détente; **'~-'laced** serré dans son corset; *fig.* collet monté *inv.*, prude; **'~-'lipped** qui ne desserre pas les lèvres, taciturne; à l'air pincé; **'tight·ness** tension *f*; raideur *f*; étroitesse *f*; **'tight-rope** corde *f* tendue; **tights** [~s] *pl. théâ.* maillot *m*; **'tight·wad** *Am. sl.* grippe-sou *m*; pingre *m*.

ti·gress ['taigris] tigresse *f*.

tile [tail] **1.** *toit*: tuile *f*; *plancher*: carreau *m*; *sl.* chapeau *m*; **2.** couvrir de tuiles; carreler; **'~-lay·er, 'til·er** couvreur *m*; carreleur *m*.

till[1] [til] tiroir-caisse (*pl.* tiroirs-caisses) *m*; caisse *f*.

till[2] [~] **1.** *prp.* jusqu'(à); **2.** *cj.* jusqu'à ce que (*sbj.*).

till[3] 🖝 [~] labourer; cultiver; **'till·age** labour(age) *m*; (agri)culture *f*; terre *f* en labour.

till·er ⚓ ['tilə] barre *f* franche.

tilt[1] [tilt] bâche *f*, banne *f*; ⚓ tendelet *m*.

tilt[2] [~] **1.** pente *f*, inclinaison *f*; † tournoi *m*; † coup *m* de lance; *fig.* coup *m* de patte, attaque *f*; *full ~* tête baissée; *on the ~* incliné, penché; **2.** *v/t.* pencher, incliner; *v/i.* pencher, s'incliner; courir une lance (*contre, at*); *fig.* donner un coup de patte (*à, at*); *~ up* basculer; **'tilt·ing** incliné, penché; à bascule.

tilth *poét.* [til[1]] *see* tillage.

tim·ber ['timbə] **1.** bois *m* (*d'œuvre, de charpente, de construction*); pièce *f* of *~* poutre *f*; ⚓ couple *m*; *Am. fig.* qualité *f*; **2.** boiser (*sl.*); boisé (*terrain*); **'~-line** limite *f* de la végétation arborescente; **'~-work** charpente *f*; construction *f* en bois; **'~-yard** chantier *m*.

time [taim] **1.** temps *m*; fois *f*; heure *f*; moment *m*; saison *f*; époque *f*; terme *m*; *gymn. etc.*: pas *m*; ♪ mesure *f*, tempo *m*; *~, gentlemen, please!* on ferme!; *~ and again* à maintes reprises; *at ~s* de temps en temps; *parfois*; *at a (ou at the same)*

~ à la fois; *at the same ~* en même temps; *before (one's) ~* en avance; prématurément; *behind (one's) ~* en retard; *behind the ~s* arriéré; *by that ~* à l'heure qu'il était; à ce moment-là; alors; *for the ~ being* pour le moment; provisoirement; actuellement; *have a good ~* s'amuser (bien); *in ~* à temps, à l'heure; *in good ~* de bonne heure; *see mean*[2] **1**; *on ~* à temps, à l'heure; *out of ~* mal à propos; à contre-temps (*a.* ♪); *beat (the) ~* battre la mesure; *see* keep **2**; **2.** *v/t.* faire (*qch.*) à propos; fixer l'heure de; choisir le moment de; régler (sur, *by*); *sp.* chronométrer; calculer la durée de; (*a.* take the *~* of) mesurer le temps de; *the train is ~d to leave at 7* le train doit partir à 7 heures; *v/i.* faire coïncider (avec *with, to*); **'~-and-'mo·tion stud·y** † étude *f* des cadences; **'~-bar·gain** † marché *m* à terme; **'~ bomb** bombe *f* à retardement; **'~-clock** enregistreur *m* de temps; **'~-con·sum·ing** qui prend beaucoup de temps; **'~-ex·po·sure** *phot.* pose *f*; **'~-hon·o(u)red** séculaire, vénérable; **'~-keep·er** chronomètre *m*, *surt.* montre *f*; *see* timer; contrôleur *m* (de présence); *~ lag* retard *m*; **'~-'lim·it** limite *f* de temps; délai *m*; durée *f*; **'time·ly** opportun, à propos; **'time-out** *Am.* pause *f*; **'time-piece** pendule *f*; montre *f*; **'tim·er** chronométreur *m*.

time...: **~-serv·er** ['taimsə:və] opportuniste *mf*; **'~-sheet** feuille *f* de présence; semainier *m*; **'~-'sig·nal** *surt. radio:* signal *m* horaire; **'~-ta·ble** horaire *m*; 🚂 indicateur *m*; *école:* emploi *m* du temps; *~ zone* fuseau *m* horaire.

tim·id □ ['timid] timide, peureux (-euse *f*); **ti·mid·i·ty** [ti'miditi] timidité *f*.

tim·ing ['taimiŋ] ⊕ *mot.* réglage *m*; *sp.* chronométrage *m*; *fig.* choix *m* du moment.

tim·or·ous □ ['timərəs] *see* timid.

tin [tin] **1.** étain *m*; fer-blanc (*pl.* fers-blancs) *m*; boîte *f* (*de conserves*); bidon *m* (*à essence*); *sl.* galette *f* (= *argent*); *Brit. ~ opener* ouvre-boîtes *m/inv.*; **2.** en *ou* d'étain; en fer-blanc; de plomb (*soldat*); *fig. péj.* en toc; *~ can* boîte *f* (en fer-blanc); F *~ god* (faux) idole *m*; F ~ *hat* casque *m*; **3.** étamer; mettre en boîtes; ~ned *meat* viande *f* de conserve; F ~ned *music* musique *f* enregistrée.

tinc·ture ['tɪŋktʃə] **1.** teinte *f*; ⊘, *pharm.*, *a. fig.* teinture *f*; **2.** teindre, colorer.

tin·der ['tɪndə] amadou *m*.

tine [taɪn] dent *f*; fourchon *m*; *zo.* cor *m*, branche *f*.

tin·foil ['tɪn'fɔɪl] feuille *f* d'étain; papier *m* (d')étain.

ting F [tɪŋ] *see* tinkle.

tinge [tɪndʒ] **1.** teinte *f*; nuance *f* (*a. fig.*); **2.** teinter (*a. fig.*), colorer (de, *with*); *be* ~d *with* avoir une teinte de.

tin·gle ['tɪŋgl] tɪnter; picoter; cuire; *fig.* avoir grande envie (de *inf.*, *to inf.*).

tink·er ['tɪŋkə] **1.** chaudronnier *m*; **2.** *v/t.* rafistoler; *v/i.* bricoler (dans, *about*); ~ *at* rafistoler; ~ *up* faire des réparations de fortune; ~ *with* retaper.

tin·kle ['tɪŋkl] **1.** (faire) tinter; **2.** tintement *m*; F coup *m* de téléphone.

tin·man ['tɪnmən] étameur *m*; ferblantier *m*; '**tin·ny** métallique (*son*); '**tin·o·pen·er** ouvre-boîtes *m/inv.*; '**tin·plate** fer-blanc (*pl.* fers-blancs) *m*; ferblanterie *f*.

tin·sel ['tɪnsl] **1.** lamé *m*, paillettes *f/pl.*; clinquant *m* (*a. fig.*); *fig. a.* faux éclat *m*; **2.** de paillettes; *fig.* de clinquant, faux (fausse *f*); **3.** garnir de paillettes; clinquanter; *fig.* donner un faux éclat à.

tin·smith ['tɪnsmɪθ] *see* tinman.

tint [tɪnt] **1.** teinte *f*, nuance *f*; *peint.* ton *m*; **2.** teinter, colorer; ~ed *paper* papier *m* teinté.

tin·tack ['tɪntæk] broquette *f*; ~s *pl.* semence *f*.

tin·tin·nab·u·la·tion ['tɪntɪnæbjuː'leɪʃn] tintement *m*.

tin·ware ['tɪnwɛə] ferblanterie *f*.

ti·ny □ ['taɪnɪ] tout petit.

tip [tɪp] **1.** pointe *f*; *cigarette*: bout *m*; extrémité *f*; F pourboire *m*; F tuyau *m*; pente *f*; F coup *m* léger; *give s.th. a* ~ faire pencher qch.; **2.** *v/t.* mettre un bout à; ferrer, embouter (*une canne*); *fig.* dorer; F donner un pourboire à (*q.*); F (*a.* ~ *off*) tuyauter, avertir (*q.*); ~ *over* renverser; *v/i.* se renverser; '~-

cart tombereau *m* à bascule; '~·**cat** bâtonnet *m* (*sorte de jeu d'enfants*); '~-**off** tuyau *m*.

tip·pet ['tɪpɪt] pèlerine *f*; écharpe *f* en fourrure.

tip·ple ['tɪpl] **1.** se livrer à la boisson; F lever le coude; **2.** boisson *f*; '**tip·pler** ivrogne *m*; buveur (-euse *f*) *m*.

tip·si·ness ['tɪpsɪnɪs] ivresse *f*.

tip·staff ['tɪpstɑːf] huissier *m*.

tip·ster ['tɪpstə] tuyauteur *m*.

tip·sy ['tɪpsɪ] gris, ivre; F pompette.

tip·toe ['tɪptou]: *on* ~ sur la pointe des pieds.

tip·top F ['tɪp'tɔp] **1.** le plus haut point *m*; **2.** de premier ordre; extra; F chic *inv.*

tip-up seat ['tɪpʌp'siːt] strapontin *m*.

ti·rade [taɪ'reɪd] tirade *f*, diatribe *f*.

tire[1] ['taɪə] pneu(matique) *m*.

tire[2] [~] (se) lasser, ennuyer (de *of*, *with*).

tired □ ['taɪəd] fatigué (*fig.* de, *of*); '**tired·ness** lassitude *f*, fatigue *f*.

tire·less □ ['taɪəlɪs] infatigable.

tire·some □ ['taɪəsəm] ennuyeux (-euse *f*); F exaspérant.

tire-valve ['taɪəvælv] valve *f* de pneumatique.

ti·ro ['taɪərou] novice *mf*.

tis·sue ['tɪsjuː] tissu *m*; étoffe *f*; '~-'**pa·per** papier *m* de soie; ✝ papier *m* pelure.

tit[1] [tɪt]: ~ *for tat* à bon chat bon rat; un prêté pour un rendu.

tit[2] *Am.* [~] *see* teat.

tit[3] *orn.* [~] mésange *f*.

Ti·tan ['taɪtən] Titan *m*; '**Ti·tan·ess** femme *f* titanesque; **ti·ta·nic** [~'tænɪk] (~*ally*) titanique, titanesque; géant.

tit·bit ['tɪtbɪt] friandise *f*; bon morceau *m*; *fig.* quelque chose de piquant.

tithe [taɪð] **1.** dîme *f*; *usu. fig.* dixième *m*; **2.** payer la dîme sur; dîmer sur.

tit·il·late ['tɪtɪleɪt] chatouiller; **tit·il·'la·tion** chatouillement *m*.

tit·i·vate F ['tɪtɪveɪt] (se) faire beau (belle *f*).

ti·tle ['taɪtl] **1.** titre *m*; nom *m*; ⚖ droit *m* (à, *to*); **2.** intituler (*un livre*); titrer (*un film*); '~-**deed** ⚖ titre *m* de propriété; acte *m*; '~-**hold·er** *surt. sp. record, coupe*: détenteur (-trice *f*) *m*; *championnat*: tenant(e *f*) *m*; ~ **role** *théâ.* rôle *m* principal.

tit·mouse *orn.* ['titmaus], *pl.* **-mice** [~mais] mésange *f*.

ti·trate ⚗ ['taitreit] titrer, doser; **ti'tra·tion** dosage *m*; analyse *f* volumétrique.

tits ∨ [tits] nénés *m/pl.* (= *seins*).

tit·ter ['titə] **1.** avoir un petit rire étouffé; **2.** rire *m* étouffé.

tit·tle ['titl] point *m*; *fig.* la moindre partie; *to a* ~ trait pour trait; '~-**tat·tle 1.** cancans *m/pl.*; bavardage *m*; **2.** cancaner; bavarder.

tit·tup ['titəp] F aller au petit galop.

tit·u·lar □ ['titjulə] titulaire; nominal (-aux *m/pl.*).

to [tu:; tu; tə] **1.** *prp. usu.* à; *airection:* à; vers (*Paris, la maison*); en (*France*); chez (*moi, ma tante*); *sentiment:* envers, pour (*q.*); *distance:* jusqu'à; *parenté, hérédité:* de; *pour indiquer le datif:* à; ~ *my father* à mon père; ~ *me accentué:* à moi, *inaccentué:* me; *it happened* ~ *me* cela m'arriva; ~ *the United States* aux États-Unis; ~ *Japan* au Japon; *I bet 10* ~ *1* je parie 10 contre 1; *the train (road)* ~ *London* le train (la route) de Londres; *a quarter* (*ten*) ~ *six* six heures moins le quart (dix); *alive* ~ sensible à (*qch.*); *cousin* ~ cousin(e *f*) de; *heir* ~ héritier (-ère *f*) de; *secretary* ~ secrétaire de; *here's* ~ *you!* à votre santé!, F à la vôtre!; **2.** *adv.* [tu:]: ~ *and fro* de long en large; *go* ~ *and fro* aller et venir; *come* ~ revenir à soi; *pull the door* ~ fermer la porte; **3.** *pour indiquer l'inf.:* ~ *take* prendre; *I am going* ~ (*inf.*) je vais (*inf.*); *souvent on supprime l'inf.:* *I worked hard*, *I had* ~ (*sc. work hard*) je travaillais dûr, il le fallut bien; *avec inf., remplaçant une proposition subordonnée:* *I weep* ~ *think of it* quand j'y pense, je pleure.

toad *zo.* [toud] crapaud *m*; '~·**stool** champignon *m* vénéneux.

toad·y ['toudi] **1.** sycophante *m*, flagorneur (-euse *f*) *m*; **2.** lécher les bottes à (*q.*); flagorner (*q.*); '**toad·y·ism** flagornerie *f*. [venues *f/pl.*]

to-and-fro F ['tu:ən'frou] allées et

toast [toust] **1.** toast *m* (*a. fig.*); pain *m* grillé; **2.** griller, rôtir; *fig.* chauffer; *fig.* porter un toast à.

to·bac·co [tə'bækou] tabac *m*; **to·'bac·co·nist** [~kənist] marchand *m* de tabac.

to·bog·gan [tə'bɔgən] **1.** toboggan *m*; luge *f* (suisse); **2.** faire du toboggan.

to·by ['toubi] (*ou* ~ *jug*) pot *m* à bière (de fantaisie); ~ *collar* collerette *f* plissée.

to·co *sl.* ['toukou] châtiment *m* corporel; raclée *f*.

toc·sin ['tɔksin] tocsin *m*.

tod F [tɔd]: *on one's* ~ tout(e) seul(e).

to·day [tə'dei] aujourd'hui.

tod·dle ['tɔdl] **1.** marcher à petits pas; trottiner; F ~ *off* se trotter; **2.** F pas *m/pl.* (*d'un petit enfant*); F balade *f*; '**tod·dler** tout(e) petit(e) enfant *m*(*f*).

tod·dy ['tɔdi] grog *m* chaud.

to-do F [tə'du:] affaire *f*; scène *f*; façons *f/pl.*

toe [tou] **1.** *anat.* doigt *m* de pied; orteil *m*; *chaussettes:* bout *m*; **2.** botter (*a. sp.*); mettre un bout à (*un soulier*); ~ *the line* s'aligner; *fig.* ~ *the (party) line* obéir (aux ordres de son parti); s'aligner (avec son parti).

-toed [toud]: *three* ~ à trois orteils.

toff *sl.* [tɔf] rupin(e *f*) *m*; dandy *m*.

tof·fee, tof·fy ['tɔfi] caramel *m* au beurre; '**tof·fee-nosed** F bêcheur (-euse *f*).

to·geth·er [tə'geðə] ensemble; en même temps; ~ *with* avec; *all* ~ tous ensemble.

tog·ger·y F ['tɔgəri] nippes *f/pl.*, frusques *f/pl.*

tog·gle ['tɔgl] **1.** ⚓ cabillot *m*; ⊕ clef *f*; ⚡ ~ *switch* interrupteur *m* à bascule; **2.** ⚓ fixer avec *ou* munir d'un cabillot.

togs *sl.* [tɔgz] *pl.* nippes *f/pl.*, frusques *f/pl.*

toil [tɔil] **1.** travail (*pl.* -aux) *m*, peine *f*; **2.** travailler (dur); '**toil·er** travailleur (-euse *f*) *m*.

toi·let ['tɔilit] toilette *f*; ⚕ détersion *f*; *les cabinets m/pl.*; *make one's* ~ faire sa toilette; '~-**bag** trousse *f* de toilette; '~-**pa·per** papier *m* hygiénique; '~-**set** garniture *f* de toilette; '~-**ta·ble** table *f* de toilette.

toils [tɔilz] *pl.* filet *m*, lacs *m*, *a. m/pl.* (*a. fig.*).

toil·some □ ['tɔilsəm] fatigant.

toil-worn ['tɔilwɔ:n] usé par le travail; marqué par la fatigue (*visage*).

to·ken ['toukən] signe *m*, marque *f*; jeton *m*; bon *m* (*de livres*); ~ *money* monnaie *f* fiduciaire; ~ *payment* paiement *m* symbolique; ~ *strike* grève *f* d'avertissement; *in* ~ *of* en signe *ou* témoignage de.

told [tould] *prét. et p.p. de tell*; *all* ~ tout compris; tout compte fait.

tol·er·a·ble □ ['tɔlərəbl] supportable, tolérable; assez bon(ne *f*); **'tol·er·ance** tolérance *f* (*a.* ✕, ⊕); **'tol·er·ant** □ tolérant (à l'égard de, *of*); **tol·er·ate** ['ˌreit] tolérer, supporter; **tol·er·a·tion** tolérance *f*.

toll[1] [toul] droit *m* de passage; *marché*: droit *m* de place; *téléph.* (*a.* ~-*call*) conversation *f* interurbaine; ~ *of the road* la mortalité *f* sur routes; *take* ~ *of* faire payer le droit de passage à; *fig.* retrancher une bonne partie de; ~ *bar*, ~ *gate* barrière *f* (de péage); ~ *road* route *f* à péage.

toll[2] [~] **1.** tintement *m*; *souv.* glas *m*; **2.** tinter; sonner (*souv.* le glas).

tom [tɔm] mâle *m* (*animal*); ~ *cat* matou *m*.

tom·a·hawk ['tɔməhɔːk] **1.** hache *f* de guerre, tomahawk *m*; **2.** assommer; frapper avec un tomahawk.

to·ma·to ♀ [təˈmɑːtou; *Am.* təˈmeitou], *pl.* **-toes** [ˌtouz] tomate *f*.

tomb [tuːm] tombe(au *m*) *f*; ~*stone* pierre *f* tombale.

tom·boy ['tɔmbɔi] fillette *f* d'allures garçonnières; garçon *m* manqué.

tome [toum] tome *m*, livre *m*.

tom·fool ['tɔmˈfuːl] **1.** niais *m*; *attr.* insensé; stupide; **2.** faire *ou* dire des sottises; **tom'fool·er·y** niaiserie *f*, -s *f/pl.*

tom·my *sl.* ['tɔmi] simple soldat *m* anglais; mangeaille *f*; ~*gun* mitraillette *f*; ~ *rot* bêtises *f/pl.*

to·mor·row [təˈmɔrou] demain; ~ *week* de demain en huit.

tom·tom ['tɔmtɔm] tam-tam *m*.

ton [tʌn] tonne *f*; F ~*s pl.* tas *m/pl.*

to·nal·i·ty ♪, *a. peint.* [toˈnæliti] tonalité *f*.

tone [toun] **1.** ton *m* (*a. ling.*, *peint.*, *fig.*); son *m*; accent *m*; voix *f*; *fig.* atmosphère *f*; ✕ tonicité *f*; *out of* ~ désaccordé; **2.** *v/t.* teinter; ♪ accorder; *peint.* adoucir les tons de; *phot.* virer; *v/i.* s'harmoniser (avec, *with*); *phot.* virer; ~ *down* s'adoucir.

tongs [tɔŋz] *pl.*: (*a pair of*) ~ (des)

pincettes *f/pl.*; ⊕ (des) tenailles *f/pl.*

tongue [tʌŋ] *usu.* langue *f* (*a. fig.*, *ling.*); *soulier*, *bois*, *hautbois*: languette *f*; *cloche*: battant *m*; *give* ~ donner de la voix, aboyer (*chien*); *hold one's* ~ se taire; *speak with one's* ~ *in one's cheek* parler ironiquement; blaguer; **'tongue·less** sans langue; *fig.* muet(te *f*); **tongue-tied** qui a la langue liée; *fig.* interdit; muet(te *f*).

ton·ic ['tɔnik] **1.** (~*ally*) ♪, ✕, *gramm.* tonique; ♪ ~ *chord* accord *m* naturel; **2.** ♪ tonique *f*; ✕ tonique *m*, réconfortant *m*.

to·night [təˈnait] ce soir; cette nuit.

ton·ing so·lu·tion *phot.* ['touniŋ səˈluːʃn] (bain *m* de) virage *m*.

ton·nage ⚓ ['tʌnidʒ] tonnage *m*, jauge *f*; *hist.* droit *m* de tonnage.

-ton·ner ⚓ ['tʌnə]: *four-hundred* ~ vaisseau *m* de quatre cent tonneaux.

ton·sil *anat.* ['tɔnsl] amygdale *f*; **ton·sil·li·tis** [ˌsiˈlaitis] amygdalite *f*, inflammation *f* des amygdales.

ton·sure ['tɔnʃə] **1.** tonsure *f*; **2.** tonsurer.

ton·y *Am. sl.* ['touni] chic, élégant.

too [tuː] (par) trop; aussi; d'ailleurs.

took [tuk] *prét. de take* **1, 2.**

tool [tuːl] **1.** outil *m*; ustensile *m*; instrument *m* (*a. fig.*); **2.** ciseler (*le cuir*, *un livre*); bretteler (*une pierre*); ⊕ travailler; **'~-bag**, **'~-kit** sac *m* à outils; *mot.* sacoche *f*; ~ *shed* cabane *f* à outils.

toot [tuːt] **1.** sonner; *mot.* (*a.* ~ *the horn*) corner; klaxonner; **2.** cornement *m*; coup *m* de klaxon.

tooth [tuːθ] (*pl.* **teeth**) dent *f*; **'~-ache** mal *m* de dents; **'~-brush** brosse *f* à dents; **toothed** [ˌθt] à ... dents; aux dents ...; ⊕ denté; **'tooth·ing** ⊕ *scie*: taille *f* des dents; *roue*: dents *f/pl.*; **'tooth·less** □ sans dents; **'tooth-paste** (pâte *f*) dentifrice *m*; **'tooth·pick** cure-dent *m*.

tooth·some □ ['tuːθsəm] savoureux (-euse *f*); **'tooth·some·ness** succulence *f*; goût *m* agréable.

too·tle ['tuːtl] flûter; *mot.* corner; F ~ *along* aller son petit bonhomme de chemin.

toot·sie, toot·sy F ['tu(ː)tsi] peton *m* (*pied*); *surt. Am.* nana *f* (= *fille*); *surt. Am.* chéri(e *f*) *m*.

top¹ [tɔp] **1.** sommet *m*, cime *f*; *tête*: haut *m*; *arbre, toit*: faîte *m*; *maison*: toit *m*; *page*: tête *f*; *eau, terre*: surface *f*; *cheminée, table, soulier*: dessus *m*; *table*: haut bout *m*; *bas, botte*: revers *m*; *boîte*: couvercle *m*; *autobus etc.*: impériale *f*; *fig.* chef *m*, tête *f* (*de rang*); *fig.* comble *m*; *mot. Am.* capote *f*; ⚓ hune *f*; *at the ~* (*of*) au sommet (de), en haut (de); *at the ~ of one's speed* à toutes jambes, à toute vitesse; *at the ~ of one's voice* à pleine gorge, (*crier*) de toutes ses forces; *on ~* sur le dessus; en haut; *on ~ of* sur, en haut de; *et aussi*, immédiatement après; F *blow one' ~* sortir de ses gonds; se mettre en rogne; **2.** supérieur; d'en haut; *the ~ floor* le plus haut étage; *~ speed* vitesse maximum; plafond *m*; *~ coat* pardessus *m*, manteau *m*; *the ~ earners pl.* les gros salaires; *sl. ~ banana* la personne la plus importante; *sl. ~ dog* être celui qui commande; **3.** surmonter, couronner; dépasser, surpasser; atteindre le sommet de; être à la tête de (*une classe, une liste, etc.*); 🌿 écimer (*un arbre*); pincer (*l'extrémité d'une plante*); *golf*: topper; F *~ up, ~ off* remplir.

top² [~] toupie *f*.

to·paz *min.* ['toupæz] topaze *f*.

top-boots ['tɔp'buːts] *pl.* bottes *f/pl.* à revers.

to·pee ['toupi] casque *m* colonial.

to·per ['toupə] ivrogne *m*.

top...: *'~·flight* F de premier ordre; *~·gal·lant* ⚓ ['~'gælənt]; ⚓ tə-'gælənt] **1.** de perroquet; **2.** (*ou ~ sail*) voile *f* de perroquet; *'~'hat* chapeau *m* haut-de-forme (*pl.* hauts-de-forme) *m*; *'~·'heav·y* trop lourd du haut; ⚓ jaloux (-se *f*); *'~·'hole sl.* excellent, épatant.

top·ic ['tɔpik] sujet *m*, thème *m*; question *f*; matière *f*; *'top·i·cal* ☐ topique, local (-aux *m/pl.*) (*a.* 🔧); d'actualité.

top·knot ['tɔpnɔt] chignon *m*; *orn.* huppe *f*.

top·less ['tɔplis] en monokini; aux seins nus, torse nu.

top...: *'~·mast* ⚓ mât *m* de hune; *'~·most* le plus haut *ou* élevé; *'~·notch* F de premier ordre.

to·pog·ra·pher [tə'pɔgrəfə] topographe *m*; **top·o·graph·ic, top·o-**

graph·i·cal ☐ [tɔpə'græfik(l)] topographique; **to·pog·ra·phy** [tə-'pɔgrəfi] topographie *f*; anatomie *f* topographique.

top·per *sl.* ['tɔpə] type *m* épatant; *see* tophat; *'top·ping* F excellent, chouette, chic.

top·ple ['tɔpl] (*usu. ~ over ou down*) (faire) écrouler, dégringoler.

tops *sl.* [tɔps] **1.** fantastique, le (la *f*) meilleur(e); **2.** *be the ~* être champion.

top·sail ⚓ ['tɔpsl] hunier *m*.

top-se·cret ['tɔp'siːkrət] ultra-secret (-ète *f*).

top·sy·tur·vy ☐ ['tɔpsi'təːvi] sens dessus dessous; en désarroi.

tor [tɔː] pic *m*, massif *m* de roche.

torch [tɔːtʃ] torche *f*, flambeau *m*; *electric ~* lampe *f* électrique de poche; torche *f* électrique; *~ battery* pile *f*; *Am. ~ song* chanson *f* d'amour non partagé; *'~·light* lumière *f* de(s) torches; *~ procession* défilé *m* aux flambeaux.

tore [tɔː] *prét. de* tear¹ 1.

tor·ment 1. ['tɔːmənt] tourment *m*, torture *f*, supplice *m*; **2.** [tɔː'ment] tourmenter, torturer; harceler; *fig.* taquiner; **tor·men·tor** tourmenteur (-euse *f*) *m*; harceleur (-euse *f*) *m*.

torn [tɔːn] *p.p. de* tear¹ 1.

tor·na·do [tɔː'neidou], *pl.* **-does** [~douz] tornade *f*; ouragan *m* (*a. fig.*).

tor·pe·do [tɔː'piːdou], *pl.* **-does** [~douz] **1.** ⚓, ⚔, *icht.* torpille *f*; *Am. sl.* homme *m* de main; **2.** ⚓ torpiller (*a. fig. un projet*); *'~·boat* ⚓ torpilleur *m*.

tor·pid ☐ ['tɔːpid] inerte, engourdi (*a. fig.*), torpide; *fig.* lent, léthargique; **tor·pid·i·ty, tor·pid·ness, tor·por** ['tɔːpə] engourdissement *m*, torpeur *f*; *fig.* léthargie *f*.

torque ⊕ [tɔːk] moment *m* de torsion.

tor·rent ['tɔrənt] torrent *m* (*a. fig.*); *fig.* déluge *m*; *in ~s* à torrents; **tor·ren·tial** ☐ [tɔ'renʃl] torrentiel(le *f*).

tor·rid ['tɔrid] torride.

tor·sion ['tɔːʃn] torsion *f*; **tor·sion·al** de torsion.

tort ⚖ [tɔːt] acte *m* dommageable; préjudice *m*.

tor·toise *zo.* ['tɔːtəs] tortue *f*;

~-shell ['~təʃel] écaille *f* (de tortue).
tor·tu·os·i·ty [tɔːtjuˈɔsiti] tortuosité *f*; **'tor·tu·ous** ☐ tortueux (-euse *f*); sinueux (-euse *f*); tortu (*esprit*); ⅄ gauche (*courbe*).
tor·ture ['tɔːtʃə] **1.** torture *f*, question *f*; supplice *m*; **2.** mettre (*q.*) à la question; torturer; **'tor·tur·er** bourreau *m*; harceleur *m*.
To·ry ['tɔːri] tory *m* (*membre du parti conservateur anglais*) (*a. adj.*); **'To·ry·ism** torysme *m*.
tosh *sl.* [tɔʃ] bêtises *f/pl.*
toss [tɔs] **1.** jet *m*, coup *m*; mouvement *m* (*de tête*) dédaigneux; *équit.* chute *f* de cheval; (*a. ~up*) coup *m* de pile ou face; *it is a ~up* les chances sont égales; *win the ~* gagner (*à pile ou face*); **2.** *v/t.* agiter, (*a. ~ about*) secouer; démonter (*un cavalier*); *~ aside* jeter de côté; lancer; faner (*le foin*); *cuis.* sauter; (*a. ~ up*) lancer en l'air; *~* (*up*) *a coin* jouer à pile ou face; hocher (*la tête*); *~ off* (*ou down*) avaler d'un trait (*du vin etc.*); ⚓ *~ the oars* mâter les avirons; *v/i.* s'agiter; tanguer (*navire*); être ballotté; *~* (*up*) choisir à pile ou face (qch., *for s.th.*).
tot¹ F [tɔt] tout(e) petit(e) enfant *mf*; petit verre *m*.
tot² F [~] **1.** addition *f*; **2.**: *~ up v/t.* additionner; *v/i.* s'élever (à, to).
to·tal ['toutl] **1.** ☐ total (-aux *m/pl.*); entier (-ère *f*); complet (-ète *f*); **2.** total *m*, montant *m*; *grand ~* total *m* global, somme *f* globale; **3.** *v/t.* additionner; *v/i.* s'élever (à, *up to*); **to·tal·i·tar·i·an** [toutæli-ˈtɛəriən] totalitaire; **to·tal·i·tar·i·an·ism** totalitarisme *m*; **to·tal·i·ty** totalité *f*; **to·tal·i·za·tor** ['~təlaizeitə] totalisateur *m*; **to·tal·ize** ['~aiz] totaliser, additionner.
tote *Am.* [tout] (trans)porter.
tot·ter ['tɔtə] chanceler (*a. fig.*); tituber (*ivrogne*); **'tot·ter·ing** ☐, **'tot·ter·y** chancelant; titubant (*ivrogne*).
touch [tʌtʃ] **1.** *v/t.* toucher (de, with); émouvoir; effleurer (*une surface*, ♪ *les cordes de la harpe*); trinquer (*des verres*); toucher à (= déranger); *fig.* atteindre; F taper (de, for); rehausser (*un dessin*); *~ one's hat* saluer (q., *to s.o.*); porter la main à son chapeau; F *a bit* (*ou a*

little) *~ed* un peu toqué; *sl. ~ s.o. for a pound* taper q. d'une livre; *~ off* ébaucher; faire partir (*une mine*); *~ up* rafraîchir; repolir; *phot.* faire des retouches à; *v/i.* se toucher; être en contact; ⚓ *~ at* toucher à; faire escale à; *~ on* toucher (qch.) (= *traiter*, *mentionner*); **2.** toucher *m* (♪, *a. sens*); contact *m*; attouchement *m*; léger coup *m*; *cuis.*, *maladie*, *etc.*: soupçon *m* (*qch.* coup *m* de) pinceau *m*; *sp.*, *peint.* touche *f*; *dactylographe*: frappe *f*; *fig.* nuance *f*, pointe *f*; *~ of bronchitis* pointe *f* de bronchite; *get in(to) ~* (avec, with) se mettre en communication, prendre contact; **'~-and-'go 1.** affaire *f* hasardeuse; *it is ~* ça reste en balance; **2.** très incertain; hasardeux (-euse *f*); **'~-down** ✈ atterrissage *m*; amerrissage *m*; **'~-hole** *canon*: lumière *f*; **'touch·i·ness** susceptibilité *f*; **'touch·ing 1.** ☐ touchant, émouvant; **2.** *prp.* touchant, concernant; **'touch-line** *foot.* ligne *f* de touche; **'touch-stone** pierre *f* de touche (*a. fig.*); **touch-type** taper au toucher; **'touch·y** ☐ susceptible; *see testy.*
tough [tʌf] **1.** dur, résistant; *fig.* fort; rude; inflexible (*personne*); *Am.* dur; brutal (-aux *m/pl.*); de bandit; **2.** *surt. Am.* apache *m*, bandit *m*; **'tough·en** *vt/i.* durcir; (s')endurcir (*personne*); **'tough·ness** dureté *f*; résistance *f* (à la fatigue); *fig.* difficulté *f*.
tour [tuə] **1.** tour *m*; excursion *f*; tournée *f*; *~ operator* organisateur *m* de voyage; **2.** faire le tour de; voyager; visiter en touriste; **'tour·ing** en tournée; de touristes; *mot. ~ car* voiture *f* de tourisme; **'tour·ism** tourisme *m*; **'tour·ist** touriste *mf*; voyageur (-euse *f*) *m*; *~ agency* (*ou office ou bureau*) bureau *m* de tourisme; *~ industry* tourisme *m*; *~ season* la saison *f*; *~ ticket* billet *m* circulaire.
tour·na·ment ['tuənəmənt], **tourney** ['~ni] tournoi *m*.
tou·sle ['tauzl] houspiller; chiffonner (*une femme*, *une robe*); ébouriffer (*les cheveux*).
tout [taut] **1.** pisteur *m*, racoleur *m*; (*a. racing ~*) tout *m*; **2.**: *~ for* pister, racoler; *Am.* solliciter.
tow¹ ⚓ [tou] **1.** (*câble m de*) remorque *f*; *~ car* voiture *f* remorqueuse; *take*

in ~ prendre à la remorque; 2. remorquer; haler (*un chaland*).

tow² [~] étoupe *f* (blanche).

tow·age ⚓ ['touidʒ] remorquage *m*; *chaland*: halage *m*.

to·ward(s) [tə'wɔːd(z)] vers, du côté de; *sentiment*: pour, envers.

tow·el ['tauəl] 1. serviette *f*; essuie-mains *m/inv.*; 2. frotter avec une serviette; *sl.* donner une raclée à (*q.*); '~-**horse**, '~-**rack** porte-serviettes *m/inv.*

tow·er ['tauə] 1. tour *f*; ⊕ pylône *m*; *église*: clocher *m*; *fig.* a ~ *of strength* un puissant appui; *Brit.* ~ *block* immeuble-tour *m* (*pl.* immeubles-tours); 2. (*a.* ~ *over*) dominer; monter très haut; '**tow·ered** surmonté *ou* flanqué d'une tour *ou* de tours; '**tow·er·ing** □ très élevé, qui domine; *fig.* violent, sans bornes.

tow(·ing)... ['tou(in)]: '~-**line** (câble *m* de) remorque *f*; '~-**path** chemin *m* *ou* banquette *f* de halage; ~ **truck** dépanneuse *f*.

town [taun] 1. ville *f*; cité *f*; *county* ~ chef-lieu (*pl.* chefs-lieux) *m*; 2. municipal (-aux *m/pl.*); de la ville; à la ville; ~ *clerk* secrétaire *m* de mairie; ~ *council* conseil *m* municipal; ~ *hall* hôtel *m* de ville; mairie *f*; *surt. Am.* (*Nouvelle-Angleterre*): ~ *meeting* réunion *f* des électeurs de la ville; '~-'**plan·ning** urbanification *f*; ~**scape** ['~skeip] panorama *m* de la ville.

towns·folk ['taunzfouk] *pl.*, '**towns·peo·ple** *pl.* citadins *m/pl.*; bourgeois *m/pl.*; concitoyens *m/pl.*

town·ship ['taunʃip] commune *f*.

towns·man ['taunzmən] citadin *m*; bourgeois *m* (*a. univ.*); (*ou fellow* ~) concitoyen *m*.

tow-rope ⚓ ['touroup] (câble *m* de) remorque *f*; *chaland*: corde *f* de halage.

tox·ic, tox·i·cal □ ['tɔksik(l)] toxique; intoxicant; '**tox·in** toxine *f*.

toy [tɔi] 1. jouet *m*; F joujou(x *pl.*) *m*; *attr.* d'enfant; de jouets; tout petit; pour rire; 2. jouer, s'amuser (avec, *with*); *fig.* faire (*qch.*) en amateur; '~-**book** livre *m* d'images; '~-**box** boîte *f* à joujoux; '~-**shop** magasin *m* de jouets.

trace¹ [treis] 1. trace *f*; vestige *m* (*a. fig.*); *fig.* ombre *f*; 2. tracer (*a. un plan*); calquer (*un dessin*); *fig.* es-

quisser; suivre la piste de; suivre à la trace; recouvrer; retrouver les vestiges de; suivre (*un chemin*); ~ *back* faire remonter (à, *to*); ~ *out* tracer; esquisser; *surv.* faire le tracé de; ~ *to* (faire) remonter à.

trace² [~] trait *m*; ~-*horse* cheval *m* de renfort.

trace·a·ble □ ['treisəbl] que l'on peut tracer *ou* décalquer; facile à suivre; '**trac·er**: *radio-active* ~ traceur *m* radio-actif; ~ *bullet* balle *f* traçante; '**trac·er·y** △ réseau *m*; tympan *m* (*de fenêtre gothique*).

tra·che·a 🜨 [trə'kiːə] trachée-artère (*pl.* trachées-artères) *f*.

trac·ing ['treisiŋ] tracé *m*; traçage *m*; calquage *m*; calque *m*; '~-**pa·per** papier *m* à calquer.

track [træk] 1. trace *f*; piste *f* (*a. sp.*, *chasse*, ⊕); voie *f* (*a.* 🚂, *chasse*); sentier *m*; chemin *m* (*a.* ⊕); *tracteur*: chenille *f*; *Am.* 🚂 rail *m*; *surt. Am.* ~*athletics pl.* l'athlétisme *m* (sur piste); la course, le saut, et le lancement du poids; ~ *events pl.* épreuves *f/pl.* d'athlétisme; 2. *v/t.* suivre à la trace *ou* à la piste; traquer (*un malfaiteur*); ~ *down* (*ou out*) dépister; retrouver les traces de; *v/i.* être en alignement; '~-**and**-'**field sports** *pl.* l'athlétisme (sur piste); '**track·er** *usu. chasse*: traqueur *m*; '**track·less** sans traces; sans chemin; ⊕ sans rails, sans voie.

tract¹ [trækt] étendue *f*; région *f*; *anat.* appareil *m*.

tract² [~] brochure *f*.

trac·ta·bil·i·ty [træktə'biliti], '**trac·ta·ble·ness** docilité *f*; humeur *f* traitable; '**trac·ta·ble** □ docile, traitable.

trac·tion ['trækʃn] traction *f*; ~*engine* machine *f* routière; remorqueur *m*; '**trac·tive** tractif (-ive *f*); de traction; '**trac·tor** ⊕ tracteur *m*; *caterpillar* ~ autochenille *f*; *Am.* ~-*trailer* tracteur *m* à remorque.

trade [treid] 1. commerce *m*, affaires *f/pl.*; métier *m*, emploi *m*; état *m*; *Am.* marché *m*, vente *f* en reprise; *Board of* ♀ Ministère *m* du Commerce; *free* ~ libre échange *m*; *do a good* ~ faire de bonnes affaires, vendre beaucoup; 2. *v/i.* faire des affaires (avec, *with*); faire le commerce (de, *in*), trafiquer (en, *in*); ~ *in* échanger (contre, *for*); donner (*une vieille voi*-

ture) en reprise; *v/t.* échanger (con-tre, *for*); '⁓-**fair** ♱ foire *f*; '⁓-**in** reprise; objet *m* donné en reprise; ⁓ *price* (*value*) prix *m* (valeur *f*) à la reprise; *take s.th. as a* ⁓ prendre qch. en reprise; '⁓-**mark** marque *f* de fabrique; *souv.* marque *f* déposée; ⁓ **name** raison *f* de commerce; nom *m* commercial, appellation *f* (*d'un ar-ticle*); ⁓ **price** prix *m* marchand; '**trad·er** commerçant(e *f*) *m*, négo-ciant(e *f*) *m*; marchand(e *f*) *m*; **trade re·la·tions** *pl.* relations *f/pl.* com-merciales; '**trade school** école *f* industrielle; '**trades·man** mar-chand *m*; fournisseur *m*; *prov.* arti-san *m*; '**trades·peo·ple** *pl.* com-merçants *m/pl.*

trade(s)...: ⁓ **un·ion** syndicat *m* ouvrier; ⁓-'**un·ion·ism** syndicalis-me *m*; mouvement *m* syndical; ⁓-'**un-ion·ist 1.** syndiqué(e *f*) *m*; **2.** syn-dical (-aux *m/pl.*).

trade...: ⁓ **war** guerre *f* économique; ⁓ **wind** (vent *m*) alizé *m*.

trad·ing ['treidiŋ] de commerce; commercial (-aux *m/pl.*); commer-çant (*ville*).

tra·di·tion [trə'diʃn] tradition *f* (*a.* ⚖); **tra·di·tion·al** □, **tra·di·tion-ar·y** □ traditionnel(le *f*); de tradi-tion.

traf·fic ['træfik] **1.** commerce *m*, tra-fic *m* (in) (*a. péj.*); *rue*: circulation *f*; ⁓ *census* recensement *m* de la circulation; ⁓ *jam* embouteillage *m*; ⁓ *lights pl.* feux *m/pl.* (de circulation); ⁓ *news pl.* radioguidage *m*; ⁓ *sign* po-teau *m* de signalisation; ⁓ *warden* contractuel(le *f*) *m*; **2.** *v/i.* trafiquer; faire le commerce (de, in); *v/t. usu. péj.* trafiquer de; ⁓ *away* vendre; **traf·fi·ca·tor** *mot.* ['træfikeitə] flè-che *f* mobile; '**traf·fick·er** trafi-quant *m* (de, en in) (*a. péj.*).

tra·ge·di·an [trə'dʒi:djən] (auteur *m*) tragique *m*; *théâ.* tragédien(ne *f*) *m*; **trag·e·dy** ['trædʒidi] tragédie *f* (*a. fig.*); *fig.* drame *m*.

trag·ic, trag·i·cal □ ['trædʒik(l)] tragique (*a. fig.*).

trag·i·com·e·dy ['trædʒi'kɔmidi] tragi-comédie *f*; '**trag·i·com·ic** (⁓*ally*) tragi-comique.

trail [treil] **1.** *fig.* traînée *f*; sillon *m*; queue *f*; *chasse*: voie *f*, piste *f*; sen-tier *m*; **2.** *v/t.* traîner; *chasse*: suivre à la piste, traquer (*a. un criminel*);

F suivre; *v/i.* traîner; se traîner (*per-sonne*); ♀ grimper; ramper; ⁓ **blaz-er** *Am.* pionnier *m*; précurseur *m*; '**trail·er** ♀ plante *f* grimpante *ou* rampante; *chasse*: traqueur *m*; *véhicule*: remorque *f*; baladeuse *f*; *mot. Am.* roulotte *f*; *cin.* film-annonce *m*.

train [trein] **1.** suite *f*, cortège *m*; train *m* (*a.* ⚙); animaux, bateaux, wagons: file *f*; *poudre*: traînée *f*; *cost.* queue *f*; *fig.* chaîne *f*; ⚒ rame *f* (*de bennes, a. du Métro*); *by* ⁓ par le train; *in* ⁓ en train; *set in* ⁓ mettre en train; ⁓ *journey* voyage *m* en *ou* par chemin de fer; **2.** *v/t.* former; dresser (*un animal*); élever (*un en-fant*); diriger (*une plante*); *sp.* en-traîner; braquer (*une arme à feu*); *v/i.* s'exercer; *sp.* s'entraîner; F ⁓ (*it*) voyager en *ou* par chemin de fer; '⁓-**ac·ci·dent**, '⁓-**dis·as·ter** accident *m* de chemin de fer; **train'ee** apprenti *m*; *box.* poulain *m*; '**train·er** dresseur *m* (*d'ani-maux*); *sp.* entraîneur *m*; '**train-'fer·ry** bac *m* transbordeur.

train·ing ['treiniŋ] éducation *f*; ⚒ dressage *m* (*a. d'animaux*); *sp.* en-traînement *m*; ⁓ *of horses* manège *m*; *physical* ⁓ éducation *f* physique; *go into light* ⁓ effectuer un léger en-traînement; '⁓-**col·lege** école *f* nor-male; '⁓-**ship** navire-école (*pl.* navires-écoles) *m*.

train-oil ['treinɔil] huile *f* de ba-leine.

trait [treit] trait *m* (*de caractère etc.*).

trai·tor ['treitə] traître *m*; '**trai·tor-ous** □ traître(sse *f*).

trai·tress ['treitris] traîtresse *f*.

tra·jec·to·ry *phys.* ['trædʒiktəri] tra-jectoire *f*.

tram [træm] *see* ⁓*-car*, ⁓*way*; '⁓-**car** (voiture *f* de) tramway *m*.

tram·mel ['træml] **1.** ⚓ tramail *m*; *fig.* ⁓*s pl.* entraves *f/pl.*; **2.** entraver, empêtrer (de, with).

tramp [træmp] **1.** promenade *f* à pied; pas *m* lourd, bruit *m* des pas; *personne*: vagabond *m*, chemineau *m*; ⚓ (*souv. ocean* ⁓) cargo *m* sans ligne régulière; F *on the* ⁓ sur le tri-mard; *be on the* ⁓ courir les routes; **2.** *v/i.* marcher lourdement; voya-ger à pied; *v/t.* battre (*le pavé*); courir (*le pays*); **tram·ple** ['⁓l] piétiner, fouler (*qch.*) aux pieds.

tram·way ['træmwei] (voie *f* de) tramway *m*.

trance [trɑːns] transe *f*; extase *f*.

tran·ny *sl.* ['træni] transistor *m*.

tran·quil □ ['træŋkwil] tranquille, calme; **tran'quil·(l)i·ty** tranquillité *f*, calme *m*; **tran·quil·(l)i·za·tion** [ˌlai'zeiʃn] apaisement *m*; **'tran·quil·(l)ize** calmer, apaiser; **'tran·quil·(l)iz·er** *ℳ* tranquillisant *m*.

trans·act [træn'zækt] négocier; ~ *business* faire des affaires; **trans'ac·tion** conduite *f*; opération *f*; affaire *f*; ~s *pl. péj.* commerce *m*; comptes-rendus *m/pl.* (des séances); **trans'ac·tor** négociateur (-trice *f*) *m*.

trans·al·pine ['trænz'ælpain] transalpin.

trans·at·lan·tic ['trænzət'læntik] transatlantique.

tran·scend [træn'send] outrepasser; dépasser; surpasser (*q.*); **tran'scend·ence, tran'scend·en·cy** [ˌ~dəns(i)] transcendance *f* (*a. phls*); **tran'scend·ent** □ transcendant; *a.* = **tran·scen·den·tal** □ [ˌ~'dentl] *Å* transcendant; *phls.* transcendantal (-aux *m/pl.*); F vague.

tran·scribe [træns'kraib] transcrire (*a. ♪*); traduire (*des notes sténographiques*); *radio:* enregistrer.

tran·script ['trænskript] copie *f*, transcription *f*; traduction *f* (*de notes sténographiques*); **tran'scrip·tion** transcription *f* (*a. ♪*); *radio:* enregistrement *m*; *see a. transcript*.

tran·sept △ ['trænsept] transept *m*.

trans·fer 1. [træns'fəː] *v/t.* transférer; transporter; *ⱹ* transmettre, céder; (dé)calquer (*un dessin, une image*); *banque:* virer (*une somme*); *comptabilité:* contre-passer, ristourner; *☸* déclasser; *v/i.* changer de train *etc.*; **2.** ['trænsfə] transport *m*; *ⱹ* transmission *f*, acte *m* de cession; *♱* transfert *m*; déclassement *m* (*☸* de voyageurs); *ⱹ* mutation *f* (*de biens*); *banque:* virement *m*; ristourne *f*; décalque *m*; ~*-picture* décalcomanie *f*; *♱* ~ *ticket* transfert *m*; *Am.* billet *m* de correspondance; **trans'fer·a·ble** transmissible; *ⱹ* cessible; **trans·fer·ee** *ⱹ*, *♱* [ˌ~fə-'riː] cessionnaire *mf*; **trans·fer·ence** ['~fərəns] transfèrement *m*;

psych. transfert *m* affectif; **'transfer·or** *ⱹ* cédant(e *f*) *m*.

trans·fig·u·ra·tion [trænsfigjuə-'reiʃn] transfiguration *f*; **trans·fig·ure** [ˌ~'figə] transfigurer.

trans·fix [træns'fiks] transpercer; *fig.* ~ed cloué au sol (par, *with*).

trans·form [træns'fɔːm] transformer, convertir (en, *into*); **trans·for·ma·tion** [ˌ~fə'meiʃn] transformation *f*; conversion *f*; *fig.* métamorphose *f*; faux toupet *m*; **trans·form·er** *ⱹ* [ˌ~'fɔːmə] transformateur *m*.

trans·fuse [træns'fjuːz] transfuser (*a. ℳ du sang*); *ℳ* faire une transfusion de sang à (*un malade*); *fig.* pénétrer (de, *with*); *fig.* inspirer (qch. à q., *s.o. with s.th.*); **trans·fu·sion** [ˌ~ʒn] transfusion *f* (*surt. ℳ de sang*).

trans·gress [træns'gres] *v/t.* transgresser, violer, enfreindre; *v/i.* pécher; **trans·gres·sion** [ˌ~'greʃn] transgression *f*; péché *m*, faute *f*; **trans·gres·sor** [ˌ~'gresə] transgresseur *m*; pécheur (-eresse *f*) *m*.

tran·ship(·ment) [træn'ʃip(mənt)] *see transship(ment)*.

tran·sience, tran·sien·cy ['trænziəns(i)] caractère *m* passager; courte durée *f*.

tran·sient ['trænziənt] **1.** passager (-ère *f*), transitoire; éphémère; momentané; *♪* de transition; **2.** *Am.* voyageur *m ou* client *m* de passage; ~ *camp* camp *m* de passage; **'transient·ness** caractère *m* passager; courte durée *f*.

tran·sis·tor [træn'sistə] transistor *m*; **tran·sis·tor·ize** [ˌ~raiz] transistoriser.

tran·sit ['trænsit] passage *m*.

tran·si·tion [træn'siʒn] transition *f*; passage *m*; **tran·si·tion·al** □ de transition; transitionnel(le *f*).

tran·si·tive □ *gramm.* ['trænsitiv] transitif (-ive *f*).

tran·si·to·ri·ness ['trænsitərinis] caractère *m* transitoire *ou* passager; courte durée *f*; **'tran·si·to·ry** □ transitoire, passager (-ère *f*); de courte durée.

trans·lat·a·ble [træns'leitəbl] traduisible; **trans·late** [ˌ~'leit] traduire (*un livre etc.*); déchiffrer; *fig.* prendre pour; convertir (en, *into*); transférer (*un évêque*); **trans'la-**

trashy

tion traduction *f*; déchiffrement *m*; *école*: version *f*; *eccl.* translation *f*; **trans'la·tor** traducteur (-trice *f*) *m*.

trans·lu·cence, **trans·lu·cen·cy** [trænz'luːsns(i)] translucidité *f*; **trans'lu·cent** translucide; *fig.* clair.

trans·ma·rine [trænzmə'riːn] d'outre-mer.

trans·mi·grant ['trænzmigrənt] émigrant *m* de passage; **trans·mi·grate** ['trænzmaigreit] transmigrer (*a. fig.*); **trans·mi'gra·tion** transmigration *f* (*a. des âmes*); *fig.* métempsycose *f*.

trans·mis·si·ble [trænz'misəbl] transmissible; **trans·mis·sion** [~'miʃn] transmission *f* (*a.* ⊕, *biol., phys., radio*); *radio a.* émission *f*.

trans·mit [trænz'mit] transmettre (*a. biol., phys., radio*); ⚡ transporter (*la force*); *radio a.* émettre; communiquer (*un mouvement*); **trans'mit·ter** celui (celle *f*) *m* qui transmet; *tél.* transmetteur *m*; *radio:* (poste *m*) émetteur *m*; **trans'mit·ting** transmetteur (-trice *f*); *radio:* émetteur (-trice *f*); d'émission; ~ *station* poste *m* émetteur.

trans·mog·ri·fy F [trænz'mɔgrifai] transformer (en, *into*).

trans·mut·a·ble □ [trænz'mjuːtəbl] transmu(t)able (en, *into*); **trans·mu'ta·tion** transmutation *f*; 🜍 mutation *f*; **trans·mute** [~'mjuːt] transformer, convertir (en, *into*).

trans·o·ce·an·ic [ˈtrænzouʃiˈænik] transocéanien(ne *f*).

tran·som ⊕ ['trænsəm] traverse *f*; meneau *m* horizontal; *surt. Am.* vasistas *m*.

trans·par·en·cy [træns'pɛərənsi] transparence *f*; limpidité *f*; *phot.* diapositif *m*; **trans'par·ent** □ transparent; limpide; *fig.* évident.

tran·spi·ra·tion [trænspi'reiʃn] transpiration *f* (*a. fig.*); **tran·spire** [~'paiə] transpirer (*a. fig.*); V se passer.

trans·plant [træns'plɑːnt] transplanter; **trans·plan'ta·tion** transplantation *f*.

trans·port 1. [træns'pɔːt] transporter (*a. fig.*); *fig.* enlever; **2.** ['trænspɔːt] transport *m* (*a. fig.*); *coll.* ⚔ charrois *m/pl.*; *road* ~ transport *m* routier; ~ *undertaking* (*ou firm*) entreprise *f* de transport; *Minister*

of ♀ ministre *m* des transports; *in* ~*s* transporté (*de joie, de colère*); **trans'port·a·ble** transportable; **trans·por'ta·tion** transport *m*; déportation *f* (*d'un criminel*); ⚙ *Am.* billet *m*.

trans·pose [træns'pouz] transposer (*a.* ♪); **trans·po·si·tion** [~pə'ziʃn] transposition *f*; ⚘ permutation *f*.

trans·ship ⚓, ⚙ [træns'ʃip] *v/t.* transborder; *v/i.* changer de vaisseau; **trans'ship·ment** transbordement *m*.

tran·sub·stan·ti·ate [trænsəb'stænʃieit] transsubstantier; **tran·sub·stan·ti'a·tion** transsubstantiation *f*.

tran·sude *physiol.* [træn'sjuːd] *vt/i.* transsuder.

trans·ver·sal [trænz'vɔːsl] **1.** □ transversal (-aux *m/pl.*); **2.** ⚘ transversale *f*; *anat.* transversal *m*; **trans·verse** ['~vɔːs] transversal (-aux *m/pl.*); en travers; ~ *section* section *f* transversale; ⊕ ~ *strength* résistance *f* à la flexion.

trans·ves·tite [træns'vestait] travesti(e *f*) *m*.

trap[1] [træp] **1.** piège *m* (*a. fig.*); trappe *f* (*a. théâ., a. de colombier*); *sp.* ball-trap *m* (*pour pigeons artificiels*); boîte *f* de lancement (*pour pigeons vivants*); ⊕ collecteur *m* (*d'eau etc.*); *see* ~*door*; F carriole *f*; **2.** prendre au piège (*a. fig.*); *foot.* bloquer; ⊕ mettre un collecteur dans.

trap[2] *min.* [~] trapp *m*.

trap·door *théâ.* ['træp'dɔː] trappe *f*; abattant *m*.

trapes F [treips] se balader (dans).

tra·peze [trə'piːz] *cirque:* trapèze *m*; **tra'pe·zi·um** ⚘ [~ziəm] trapèze *m*; **trap·e·zoid** ⚘ ['træpizɔid] quadrilatère *m* irrégulier.

trap·per ['træpə] piégeur *m*; *Am.* trappeur *m*.

trap·pings ['træpiŋz] *pl.* *cheval:* harnachement *m*; caparaçon *m*; *fig.* apparat *m*.

trap·py F ['træpi] plein de traquenards.

traps F [træps] *pl.* effets *m/pl.* (*personnels*).

trash [træʃ] *surt. Am.* ordures *f/pl.*; déchets *m/pl.*; rebut *m*; camelote *f*; *fig.* sottises *f/pl.*; vauriens *m/pl.*; *Am.* ~ *can* poubelle *f*; **'trash·y** □ sans valeur, de rebut, de camelote.

trau·ma [ˈtrɔːmə] trauma m; **trau-mat·ic** [ˌ\mætik] traumatique; ~ *experience* traumatisme m.

trav·el [ˈtrævl] **1.** v/i. voyager; faire des voyages; ✝ être voyageur de commerce, représenter une maison de commerce; *fig.* se propager, se répandre; ⊕ se déplacer; F aller à toute vitesse; v/t. parcourir; faire (*une distance*); **2.** voyage m, -s m/pl.; ⊕ parcours m; ~ *agency,* ~ *agent's,* ~ *bureau* agence f de voyages; ~ *allow-ance* indemnité f de déplacement; **ˈtrav·el(l)ed** qui a beaucoup voyagé; **ˈtrav·el·(l)er** voyageur (-euse f) m; ✝ commis m voyageur; ⊕ grue f roulante; pont m roulant; ~'s *cheque* chèque m de voyage; **ˈtrav·el·(l)ing** voyageur (-euse f); ambulant; de voyage; ⊕ roulant; ~ *salesman* représentant m ou voyageur m de commerce.

trav·e·log(ue) Am. [ˈtrævəloug] conférence f avec projections décrivant un voyage.

trav·erse [ˈtrævəːs] **1.** traversée f (a. alp.); passage m à travers (a.), *alp.* traverse f; ⚖ dénégation f; ✕ pare-éclats m/inv.; ⊕ *chariot de tour:* translation f latérale; **2.** v/t. traverser (a. fig.), passer à travers; *fig.* passer en revue; *fig.* contrarier; ⚖ nier; ✕ pointer en direction (*un canon*); v/i. alp. prendre une traverse.

trav·es·ty [ˈtrævisti] **1.** parodie f; *fig. péj.* travestissement m; **2.** parodier; travestir.

trawl ⚓ [trɔːl] **1.** chalut m; câble m balayeur; **2.** pêcher au chalut; **ˈtrawl·er** *personne, a. bateau:* chalutier m.

tray [trei] plateau m; cuvette f; *malle, caisse:* compartiment m.

treach·er·ous □ [ˈtretʃərəs] traître (-sse f) (a. fig.); déloyal (-aux m/pl.); perfide; **ˈtreach·er·ous-ness, ˈtreach·er·y** perfidie f, trahison f; caractère m dangereux (*de la glace*).

trea·cle [ˈtriːkl] mélasse f.

tread [tred] **1.** [irr.] v/i. marcher, aller, avancer (*sur,* [up]on); v/t. marcher sur; fouler; ✝ danser; *coq:* côcher; ~ *water* nager debout; **2.** pas m; bruit m des pas; *coq:* accouplement m; *escalier:* marche f; *soulier, roue:* semelle f; **trea·dle**

[ˈ\l] **1.** pédale f; **2.** v/i. pédaler; **ˈtread·mill** ✝ moulin m de discipline; *fig.* besogne f ingrate.

trea·son [ˈtriːzn] trahison f; **ˈtrea-son·a·ble** □ traître(sse f); de trahison.

treas·ure [ˈtreʒə] **1.** trésor m; ~s *of the soil* richesses f/pl. du (sous-)sol; ~ *hunt* chasse f au trésor; ⚖ ~ *trove* trésor m; **2.** priser; (*usu.* ~ *up*) conserver précieusement; **ˈtreas·ur·er** trésorier (-ère f) m; économe m.

treas·ur·y [ˈtreʒəri] trésorerie f; caisse f centrale; Trésor m public; *Am.* ♀ *Department* ministère m des Finances; *parl.* ♀ *Bench* banc m ministériel; ~ *bill* billet m du Trésor; ~ *bond* bon m du Trésor; ~ *note* coupure f émise par le Trésor.

treat [triːt] **1.** v/t. traiter; régaler (q.); payer à voir à; v/i. traiter (*de, of;* avec q. pour avoir qch., *with s.o. for s.th.*); **2.** régal (s pl.) m, festin m, plaisir m; F *it is my* ~ c'est moi qui régale, c'est ma tournée; *see stand 2;* **ˈtreat·er** négociateur (-trice f) m; celui (celle f) m qui paye à boire; **trea·tise** [ˈ\iz] traité m; **ˈtreat·ment** traitement m; **ˈtrea·ty** traité m; convention f; contrat m; *be in* ~ *with* être en pourparlers avec; ~ *port* port m ouvert au commerce étranger.

tre·ble [ˈtrebl] **1.** □ triple; ♪ de soprano; ♪~ *clef* clef f de sol; **2.** triple m; ♪ dessus m; *personne, voix:* soprano m; **3.** *adv.* trois fois autant; **4.** vt/i. tripler.

tree [triː] **1.** arbre m; *souliers:* embauchoir m; poutre f; *see family 2;* F *up a* ~ dans le pétrin; **2.** (forcer à) se réfugier dans un arbre; F réduire à quia.

tre·foil ♧, △ [ˈtrefɔil] trèfle m.

trek [trek] *Afrique du Sud:* **1.** voyager en chariot (à bœufs); F faire route; **2.** (étape f d'un) voyage m en chariot.

trel·lis [ˈtrelis] **1.** treillis m; ✿ treille f; **2.** treillisser (*une fenêtre*); ✿ échalasser (*une vigne*).

trem·ble [ˈtrembl] **1.** trembler (de-vant, at; de, with); **2.** trembl(ot)ement m.

tre·men·dous □ [triˈmendəs] épouvantable, terrible; F énorme, immense. [frémissement m.]

trem·or [ˈtremə] tremblement m,〕

trem·u·lous □ ['tremjuləs] trembl(ot)ant; frémissant; **'trem·u·lous·ness** tremblotement *m*; timidité *f*.

trench [trentʃ] **1.** tranchée *f* (*a.* ✂); fossé *m*; ~ *warfare* guerre *f* de tranchées; **2.** *v/t.* creuser une tranchée *ou* un fossé dans; ✘ défoncer (*un terrain*); planter (*le céleri*) dans une rigole; *v/i.* ✂ creuser des tranchées; empiéter (sur, [*up*]*on*); *fig.* friser; **'trench·ant** □ tranchant (*surt. fig.*); *fig.* incisif (-ive *f*); **trench coat** (manteau *m*) imperméable *m*.

trench·er ['trentʃə] tranchoir *m*; *fig.* table *m*; ~ **cap** toque *f* universitaire.

trench...: '~**jack·et** blouson *m*; '~**plough,** *Am.* '~**plow 1.** rigoleuse*f*; **2.** rigoler.

trend [trend] **1.** direction *f*; *fig.* cours *m*; *fig.* marche *f*, tendance *f*; **2.** tendre, se diriger (vers, *to* [-*wards*]); '~**setter** lanceur (-euse *f*) *m* de modes; personne *f* qui donne le ton; **'trend·y** F à la (dernière) mode, dernier cri; dans le vent; *the trendies pl.* les gens *m/pl.* dans le vent.

tre·pan [tri'pæn] **1.** 🗡 trépan *m*; **2.** 🗡, *a.* ⊕ trépaner.

trep·i·da·tion [trepi'deiʃn] trépidation *f*; émoi *m*.

tres·pass ['trespəs] **1.** transgression *f*; délit *m*; ⚖ violation *f* (*des droits de q.*); *eccl.* offense *f*; F empiétement *m* (sur, [*up*]*on*); abus *m* (de, [*up*]*on*); **2.** violer *ou* enfreindre les droits; empiéter sans autorisation sur la propriété de q.; ~ *against* violer, enfreindre (*les droits etc.*); *fig.* ~ (*up*)*on* empiéter sur, abuser de; **'tres·pass·er** violateur *m* des droits d'autrui; intrus(e *f*) *m*; ~*s will be prosecuted* défense d'entrer sous peine d'amende.

tress [tres] tresse *f*, boucle *f* (*de cheveux*).

tres·tle ['tresl] tréteau *m*, chevalet *m*; ~**bridge** pont *m* de chevalets; ponton *m* à chevalets.

trey [trei] *cartes, a. dés:* trois *m*.

tri·ad ['traiəd] triade *f*; *phls., eccl.* unité *f* composée de trois personnes; ♪ accord *m* en tierce; 🜍 élément *m* trivalent.

tri·al ['traiəl] essai *m*, épreuve *f* (de, *of*); *fig.* adversité *f*, épreuve *f*; ⚖ procès *m*, cause *f*, jugement *m*; ~

marriage mariage *m* à l'essai; *sp.* ~ *match* match *m* de sélection; ~ *offer* offre *f* à l'essai; ~ *period* période *f* d'essai; *on* ~ à l'essai; ⚖ en jugement; *prisoner on* ~ prévenu(e *f*) *m*; ~ *of strength* essai *m* de force; *bring to* ~ mettre en jugement; *give s.th. a* ~ faire l'essai de qch.; *send s.o. for* ~ renvoyer q. en jugement; ⚖ *stand* ~ comparaître devant le tribunal; passer en jugement, être jugé (pour, *for*).

tri·an·gle ['traiæŋgl] triangle *m* (*a.* ♪); **tri·an·gu·lar** □ [~'æŋgjulə] triangulaire; en triangle; **tri'an·gu·late** *surv.* [~leit] trianguler.

trib·al □ ['traibl] de tribu; qui appartient à la tribu; tribal; **tribe** [traib] tribu *f* (*a. zo.*); 🜍, *zo.* classe *f*, genre *m*; *péj.* clan *m*; **tribes·man** ['~zmən] membre *m* d'une *ou* de la tribu.

tri·bu·nal [trai'bju:nl] tribunal (-aux *pl.*) *m*; cour *f* (de justice); **trib·une** ['tribju:n] tribun *m*; tribune *f* (*d'orateur*).

trib·u·tar·y ['tribjutəri] **1.** □ tributaire; **2.** tributaire *m* (*a. géog.*); *géog.* affluent *m*; **trib·ute** ['~bju:t] tribut *m*; *fig.* hommage *m*; (*a. floral* ~) couronne *f*.

tri·car ['traika:] tricar *m*.

trice [trais]: *in a* ~ en un clin d'œil.

tri·chi·na *zo.* [tri'kainə], *pl.* **-nae** [~ni:] trichine *f*.

trick [trik] **1.** tour *m*; tour *m* d'adresse; ruse *f*; truc *m*; espièglerie *f*; habitude *f*; *cartes:* levée *f*; ~ *film* film *m* à truquages; **2.** duper, attraper; ~ *into* (*gér.*) amener par ruse à (*inf.*); ~ *s.o. out of s.th.* escroquer qch. à q.; *fig.* ~ *out* (*ou up*) attifer (de *in*, *with*); **'trick·er, trick·ster** ['~stə] escroc *m*, fourbe *m*; **'trick·er·y** fourberie *f*, tromperie *f*; **'trick·ish** □ trompeur (-euse *f*), fourbe; compliqué.

trick·le ['trikl] **1.** couler goutte à goutte; suinter; F *fig.* se répandre peu à peu; passer un à un; **2.** filet *m* (d'eau); quelques gouttes *f/pl.*; petits groupes *m/pl.* (*d'hommes etc.*).

trick·si·ness ['triksinis] humeur *f* capricieuse; espièglerie *f*; **'trick·sy** □ capricieux (-euse *f*); espiègle; = **'trick·y** □ astucieux (-euse *f*); F délicat, compliqué.

tri·col·o·(u)r ['trikələ] **1.** tricolore; **2.** drapeau *m* tricolore.

tri·cy·cle ['traisikl] tricycle *m*.

tri·dent ['traidənt] trident *m* (*a.* Ŷ).

tri·en·ni·al □ [trai'enjəl] trisannuel (-le *f*); triennal (-aux *m/pl.*), qui dure trois ans.

tri·er ['traiə] juge *m*; F celui (celle *f*) *m* qui ne se laisse pas décourager.

tri·fle ['traifl] **1.** bagatelle *f*; *fig.* un tout petit peu *m*; *cuis.* charlotte *f* russe; **2.** *v/i.* jouer, badiner (avec, with); *v/t.* ~ away gaspiller (*son argent*); '**tri·fler** personne *f* frivole; amuseur (-euse *f*) *m*.

tri·fling ['traifliŋ] **1.** manque *m* de sérieux; badinage *m*; futilités *f/pl.*; **2.** □ insignifiant; léger (-ère *f*); '**tri·fling·ness** insignifiance *f*.

trig[1] [trig] **1.** caler; enrayer; **2.** cale *f*; sabot *m* d'enrayage.

trig[2] [~] soigné; net(te *f*).

trig·ger ['trigə] poussoir *m* à ressort; *arme à feu:* détente *f*; *phot.* déclencheur *m*; '~-'**hap·py** prêt à tirer pour un rien; *fig.* prêt à déclencher la guerre pour un rien.

trig·o·no·met·ric, trig·o·no·met·ri·cal □ Ŷ [trigənə'metrik(l)] trigonométrique; **trig·o·nom·e·try** [~'ɔmitri] trigonométrie *f*.

tri·lat·er·al □ Ŷ ['trai'lætərəl] trilatéral (-aux *m/pl.*).

tril·by ['trilbi] chapeau *m* mou.

tri·lin·gual □ ['trai'liŋgwəl] trilingue.

trill [tril] **1.** trille *m*; *oiseau:* chant *m* perlé; R *m* roulé; **2.** *v/t.* triller; rouler (*les R*); *v/i.* faire des trilles; perler son chant (*oiseau*).

tril·lion ['triljən] trillion *m*; *Am.* billion *m*.

tril·o·gy ['trilədʒi] trilogie *f*.

trim [trim] **1.** □ en bon ordre; soigné; coquet(te *f*); bien tourné; ⚓ bien voilé; étarque (*voile*); **2.** bon ordre *m*; parfait état *m*; ⚓ assiette *f*, arrimage *m*; *voiles:* orientation *f*; ✈ équilibrage *m*; *cheveux:* coupe *f*; *just a* ~! simplement rafraîchir!; **3.** *v/t.* mettre en ordre; arranger (*a. une lampe*); (*a.* ~ up) rafraîchir (*la barbe, les cheveux*); *cost.* garnir (de, with); tailler, tondre (*une haie etc.*); orner (de, with); F plumer (*q.*); *cuis.* parer (*la viande*); ⚓ redresser (*un navire*), orienter (*les voiles*); *v/i.* *fig.* tergiverser, nager entre deux eaux;

'**trim·mer** garnisseur (-euse *f*) *m*; ⊕ *personne:* pareur (-euse *f*) *m*; ⊕ machine *f* à trancher; ⚓ arrimeur *m*; *pol.* opportuniste *m*; *coal-*~ soutier *m*; '**trim·ming** ornement *m*; taille *f*; *usu.* ~*s pl.* passementerie *f*; *cuis.* garniture *f*; ⊕ rognures *f/pl.*; '**trim·ness** air *m* soigné *ou* coquet; élégance *f*.

tri·mo·tor ['traimoutə] trimoteur *m*; '**tri·mo·tored** trimoteur.

Trin·i·ty ['triniti] Trinité *f*.

trin·ket ['triŋkit] petit bijou *m*, colifichet *m*; bibelot *m*; ~*s pl.* affiquets *m/pl.*; *péj.* camelote *f*.

tri·o ♪ ['tri:ou] trio *m*.

trip [trip] **1.** excursion *f*, voyage *m* d'agrément; randonnée *f*; *fig.* faux pas *m*; croc-en-jambe (*pl.* crocs-en-jambe) *m*; ⊕ déclic *m*; déclenche *f*; ⊕ ~ *dog* (*ou* *pin*) déclic *m*; **2.** *v/i.* trébucher; faire un faux pas (*a. fig.*); ~ *along* aller d'un pas léger; *catch s.o.* ~*ping* prendre *q.* en défaut; *v/t.* (*usu.* ~ *up*) donner un croc-en-jambe à; faire trébucher (*q.*); surprendre (*un témoin etc.*) en contradiction.

tri·par·tite ['trai'pɑ:tait] tripartite; triple; trilatéral (-aux *m/pl.*).

tripe [traip] *cuis.* tripe *f*, -s *f/pl.*; *sl.* bêtises *f/pl.*, fatras *m*.

tri·phase ⚡ ['trai'feiz] triphasé (*courant*). [triple saut *m*.\
tri·ple □ ['tripl] triple; *sp.* ~ *jump*⌡

tri·plet ['triplit] trio *m*; *prosodie:* tercet *m*; ♪, ♩ triplet *m*; ♪ triolet *m*.

tri·plex ['tripleks] se brisant sans éclats (*verre*), triplex (*TM*).

trip·li·cate **1.** ['triplikit] triplé; triple (*a. su./m*); **2.** ['~keit] tripler; rédiger en triple exemplaire.

tri·pod ['traipɔd] trépied *m*; pied *m* (à trois branches).

tri·pos ['traipɔs] examen *m* supérieur (*pour honours à Cambridge*).

trip·per F ['tripə] excursionniste *mf*; '**trip·ping 1.** □ léger (-ère *f*) (*pas*), leste; **2.** pas *m* léger; faux pas *m*; ⊕ déclenchement *m*.

tri·sect [trai'sekt] diviser *ou* couper en trois.

tris·yl·lab·ic ['traisi'læbik] (~*ally*) trisyllab(iqu)e; **tri·syl·la·ble** ['~'si-ləbl] trisyllabe *m*.

trite □ [trait] banal (-als *ou* -aux *m/pl.*); rebattu.

trit·u·rate ['tritjureit] triturer.

tri·umph ['traiəmf] **1.** triomphe *m* (*a. fig.*) (sur, over); **2.** triompher (*a. fig.*) (de, over); **tri·um·phal** [ˌ⁓'ʌm-fəl] de triomphe, triomphal (-aux *m/pl.*); ⁓ *arch* arc *m* de triomphe; ⁓ *procession* cortège *m* triomphal; **tri·um·phant** □ triomphant.

tri·une ['traiju:n] d'une unité triple.

triv·et ['trivit] trépied *m* (*pour bouilloire etc.*); F *as right as a* ⁓ en excellente santé; en parfait état.

triv·i·al □ ['triviəl] insignifiant, sans importance; frivole (*personne*); banal (-als *ou* -aux *m/pl.*); † de tous les jours; **triv·i·al·i·ty** [ˌ⁓'æliti] insignifiance *f*; banalité *f*.

tro·chee ['trouki:] trochée *m*.

trod [trɔd] *prét.*, **trod·den** ['ˌ⁓n] *p.p. de* tread 1.

trog·lo·dyte ['trɔglədait] troglodyte *m*.

Tro·jan ['troudჳn] **1.** de Troie; troyen(ne *f*); **2.** Troyen(ne *f*) *m*; F *like a* ⁓ en vaillant homme; (*travailler*) comme un nègre.

troll [troul] pêcher à la cuiller.

trol·l(e)y ['trɔli] **1.** 🚋 chariot *m* à bagages; fardier *m*; diable *m*; ⊕ moufle *mf*; chariot *m* (*de pont roulant*); ⚡ trolley *m*; (*a. dinner* ⁓) serveuse *f*; *Am.* (*a.* ⁓ *car*) tramway *m* à trolley; **2.** charrier; '⁓-**bus** trolleybus *m*.

trol·lop *péj.* ['trɔləp] **1.** souillon *f*; traînée *f*; **2.** rôder; traîner la savate.   [bone *m*.]

trom·bone ♪ [trɔm'boun] trom-

troop [tru:p] **1.** troupe *f*, bande *f*; foule *f*; peloton *m* (*de cavalerie*); **2.** s'assembler; ⁓ *along* avancer en foule; ⁓ *away*, ⁓ *off* partir en bande; ✕ ⁓*ing the colo(u)r(s)* parade *f* du drapeau; '⁓-**car·ri·er** ✈ avion *m* de transport; ⚓ transport *m*; '**troop·er** cavalier *m*; soldat *m ou* F cheval *m* de cavalerie; *Am.* membre *m* de la police montée; ⚓ transport *m*; *péj.* old⁓ soudard *m*; '**troop-horse** cheval *m* de cavalerie.

trope [troup] trope *m*.

tro·phy ['troufi] trophée *m*; *sp. a.* coupe *f*.

trop·ic ['trɔpik] **1.** tropique *m*; **2.** *a.* '**trop·i·cal** □ tropique; tropical (-aux *m/pl.*).

trot [trɔt] **1.** trot *m*; F petit(e) enfant *m(f)*; *Am. sl. école:* traduction *f*

juxtalinéaire; **2.** (faire) trotter; F ⁓ *out* sortir; présenter.

trot·ter ['trɔtə] trotteur (-euse *f*) *m*; ⁓*s pl.* pieds *m/pl.* de cochon; F *co.* pieds *m/pl.*

trouble ['trʌbl] **1.** trouble *m* (*a.* ⚙, ⊕); peine *f*; chagrin *m*; ennui *m*; inquiétude *f*; ⊕ conflits *m/pl.*; difficultés *f/pl.*; ⁓ *spot* point *m* de conflit, foyer *m* de troubles; *be in* ⁓ avoir des ennuis; avoir des soucis (d'argent); *look for* ⁓ se préparer des ennuis; *make* ⁓ semer la discorde; *take* (the) ⁓ se donner de la peine (de, to); se déranger (pour, to); **2.** *v/t.* affliger, chagriner (de, with); inquiéter; déranger; ennuyer; donner de la peine à; *may I* ⁓ *you for the salt?* voudriez-vous bien me passer le sel?; *v/i.* F se déranger; '⁓-**man**, '⁓-**shoot·er** *Am.* F dépanneur *m*; **trou·ble·some** □ ['⁓səm] ennuyeux (-euse *f*); gênant.

trough [trɔf] auge *f*; (*a. drinking* ⁓) abreuvoir *m*; pétrin *m* (*pour le pain*); caniveau *m*; ⌢ cuve(tte) *f*; ⚡, *phys.*, *a. fig.* creux *m*; *météor.* dépression *f*.

trounce [trauns] rosser (*q.*).

troupe [tru:p] *théâ. etc.:* troupe *f*.

trou·sered ['trauzəd] portant un pantalon; '**trou·ser·ing** étoffe *f* pour pantalon(s); **trou·sers** ['⁓z] *pl.* (*a pair of* ⁓ un) pantalon *m*; **trou·ser suit** tailleur-pantalon *m* (*pl.* tailleurs-pantalons).

trous·seau ['tru:sou] trousseau *m*.

trout *icht.* [traut] truite *f*.

tro·ver ⚖ ['trouvə] appropriation *f* (*d'une chose perdue*); *action of* ⁓ action *f* en restitution.

trow·el ['trauəl] truelle *f*; ✔ déplantoir *m*.

troy (**weight**) [trɔi(weit)] poids *m* troy (*pour peser de l'or etc.*).

tru·an·cy ['tru:ənsi] absence *f* de l'école sans permission; '**tru·ant** **1.** absent; *fig.* vagabond; **2.** absent *m*; *fig.* vagabond *m*; *play* ⁓ faire l'école buissonnière; *fig.* vagabonder.

truce [tru:s] trêve *f* (*a. fig.*) (de, to); *political* ⁓ trêve *f* (*des partis*).

truck¹ [trʌk] **1.** *surt. Am.* camion *m*; chariot *m* (à bagages); 🚋 wagon *m* (à marchandises); (*a. bogie*⁓) boggie *m*; ⁓ *driver* camionneur *m*, routier *m*; ⁓ *stop* relais *m* des routiers; ⁓ *trailer* remorque *f*; **2.** transporter par camion, camionner.

truck² [~] **1.** *vt/i.* troquer; *v/i.* ~ *in* faire le commerce de, trafiquer en; **2.** troc *m*, échange *m*; (*usu.* ~ *system*) paiement *m* des ouvriers en nature; *fig.* relations *f/pl.*; *péj.* camelote *f*; *Am.* légumes *m/pl.*; *attr.* maraîcher (-ère *f*); *Am.* ~ *farm* jardin *m* maraîcher.

truck·le¹ ['trʌkl] s'abaisser, ramper (devant, *to*).

truck·le² [~] poulie *f*; † *meuble:* roulette *f*; **~-bed** grabat *m*, lit *m* de fortune.

truck·man ['trʌkmən] camionneur *m*, routier *m*.

truc·u·lence, truc·u·len·cy ['trʌkjuləns(i)] férocité *f*; '**truc·u·lent** féroce, farouche; brutal (-aux *m/pl.*).

trudge [trʌdʒ] marcher lourdement ou péniblement.

true [truː] (*adv.* truly) vrai; véritable; sincère, fidèle, honnête; exact; d'aplomb, juste; *be* ~ *of* en être de même pour; *it is* ~ il est vrai (que, *that*); c'est vrai; *come* ~ se réaliser; ~ *to life* (*ou nature*) tout à fait naturel; pris sur le vif; vécu (*roman*); *prove* ~ se vérifier; se réaliser; '**~·blue** *fig.* loyal (-aux *m/pl.*), fidèle; '**~-bred** pur sang *inv.*; de bonne race; '**~-love** bien-aimé(e *f*) *m*; '**true·ness** vérité *f*; sincérité *f*; justesse *f*.

truf·fle ♀ ['trʌfl] truffe *f*.

tru·ism ['truːizm] truisme *m*, axiome *m*.

tru·ly ['truːli] vraiment, véritablement, justement; sincèrement; loyalement; *yours* ~ agréez, Monsieur (Madame), l'expression de mes sentiments les plus distingués.

trump [trʌmp] **1.** *cartes:* atout *m*; F brave garçon (fille *f*) *m*; **2.** *v/i.* jouer atout; *v/t.* couper (*une carte*); ~ *up* forger, inventer; **trump·er·y** ['~əri] friperie *f*, camelote *f*; farce *f*; *attr.* de camelote; ridicule.

trum·pet ['trʌmpit] **1.** trompette *f* (*a.* ♀, ✗, *orgues*); ✗ *personne:* trompette *m*; ♫ cornet *m* acoustique; *see* ear-~, speaking-~; **2.** *v/i.* sonner de la trompette; barrir (*éléphant*); *v/t. fig.* (*a.* ~ *forth*) proclamer, publier à son de trompe; '**trum·pet·er** ♪, *orn.* trompette *m*.

trun·cate ['trʌŋkeit] tronquer; **trun'ca·tion** troncature *f*.

trun·cheon ['trʌnʃn] bâton *m* (*d'un agent de police*); casse-tête *m/inv.*, matraque *f*.

trun·dle ['trʌndl] **1.** roulette *f* (*pour meubles*); **2.** (faire) rouler; *v/t.* passer.

trunk [trʌŋk] tronc *m* (*d'arbre, a.* de corps); torse *f*; *éléphant:* trompe *f*; malle *f*; ~*s pl.* caleçon *m* de bain; slip *m*; *téléph.* ~*s, please!* l'inter, s.v.p.; *see* ~-line; '**~-call** *téléph.* communication *f* interurbaine; ~ *ex·change* *téléph.* (service *m*) interurbain *m*; '**~-line** 🚂 grande ligne *f*; *téléph.* ligne *f* interurbaine; '**~-road** route *f* nationale.

trun·nion ⊕ ['trʌnjən] tourillon *m*.

truss [trʌs] **1.** botte *f*; *fleurs:* touffe *f*; ♫ bandage *m* herniaire; △ armature *f*; ferme *f*; cintre *m*; **2.** mettre en bottes; lier; trousser (*une poule*); △ renforcer; '**~-bridge** ⊕ pont *m* à poutres en treillis métallique.

trust [trʌst] **1.** confiance *f* (en, *in*); espérance *f*, espoir *m*; charge *f*, responsabilité *f*; ♦ crédit *m*; ⚖ fidéicommis *m*; ♦ trust *m*, syndicat *m*; ~ *company* institution *f* de gestion: trust-company *f*; *in* ~ par fidéicommis; *en dépôt*; *on* ~ en dépôt; ♦ à crédit; *position of* ~ poste *m* de confiance; **2.** *v/t.* se fier à; mettre sa confiance en; confier (qch. à q. *s.o. with s.th., s.th. to s.o.*); ♦ F faire crédit à (de qch., *with s.th.*); *fig.* espérer (que, *that*); ~ *s.o. to do s.th.* se fier à q. pour qu'il fasse qch.; *v/i.* se fier (à *in, to*); se confier (en *in, to*).

trus·tee [trʌs'tiː] dépositaire *m*, consignataire *m*; ♦, *admin.* administrateur *m*; ⚖ fidéicommissaire *m*, fiduciaire *m*; curateur (-trice *f*) *m*; ~ *securities pl.* (*ou stock*) valeurs *f/pl.* de tout repos; **trus'tee·ship** fidéicommis *m*; curatelle *f*, administration *f*; *pol.* tutelle *f*. [confiant.]

trust·ful □ ['trʌstful], '**trust·ing** □
trust·wor·thi·ness ['trʌstwəːðinis] loyauté *f*, fidélité *f*; crédibilité *f* (*d'une nouvelle*); '**trust·wor·thy** digne de confiance, loyal (-aux *m/pl.*); digne de foi.

truth [truːθ, *pl.* ~ðz] vérité *f*; véracité *f*; *home* ~*s pl.* vérités *f/pl.* bien senties; ~ *to life* fidélité *f*, exactitude *f*.

truth·ful □ ['tru:θful] vrai; véridique; fidèle; **'truth·ful·ness** véracité *f*, fidélité *f*.

try [trai] **1.** *v/t.* essayer (de, to); tâcher (de, to); fatiguer (*les yeux*); *fig.* vexer; ⚖ juger, mettre en jugement, *Am.* plaider (*une cause*); éprouver, mettre à l'épreuve; ⊕ vérifier; *cuis.* goûter (*un mets*); ~ on essayer (*une robe etc.*); ~ one's hand at s'essayer à; *v/i.* faire un effort; essayer; ~ for tâcher d'obtenir (*qch.*); se porter candidat pour; F ~ and read! essayez de lire!; **2.** essai *m* (*a. rugby*); tentative *f*; have a ~ essayer; faire un effort; **'try·ing** □ difficile, vexant, ennuyeux (-euse *f*); **'try-'on** ballon *m* d'essai; tentative *f* de déception, F de bluff; **'try-'out** essai *m* à fond; *sp.* (jeu d')essai *m*; **try-sail** ⚓ ['traisl] voile *f* goélette.

tryst *écoss.* [traist] **1.** rendez-vous *m*; **2.** donner rendez-vous à (*q.*).

Tsar [za:] tsar *m*, czar *m*.

T-square ['ti:skweə] équerre *f* en T.

tub [tʌb] **1.** cuve *f*, baquet *m*; tonneau *m*; (*a. bath-~*) tub *m*; F bain *m*; ✗ benne *f*; F co. coque *f*, baille *f*; F co. ventre *m*, panse *f*; **2.** *v/t.* encaisser (*une plante*); ✗ boiser (*un puits*); donner un tub à; *v/i.* prendre un tub; s'exercer dans un canot d'entraînement; **'tub·by** rond comme un tonneau.

tube [tju:b] tube *m* (*a. radio*), tuyau *m*; *mot.* chambre *f* à air; F métro *m*, chemin *m* de fer souterrain (*à Londres*); **'tube·less** sans chambre à air (*pneu*).

tu·ber ♀ ['tju:bə] tubercule *m*; truffe *f*; **tu·ber·cle** *anat.*, *zo.*, *a.* ♒ ['tju:bə:kl] tubercule *m*; **tu·ber·cu·lo·sis** ♒ [tjubə:kju'lousis] tuberculose *f*; **tu'ber·cu·lous** ♒ tuberculeux (-euse *f*); **tu·ber·ous** ♀ ['tju:bərəs] tubéreux (-euse *f*).

tub·ing ['tju:biŋ] tuyautage *m*; tuyau *m* en caoutchouc.

tub-thump·er ['tʌbθʌmpə] orateur *m* démagogue.

tu·bu·lar □ ['tju:bjulə] tubulaire.

tuck [tʌk] **1.** petit pli *m*, rempli *m*; *sl.* mangeaille *f*; **2.** remplier; serrer; (*avec adv. ou prp.*) mettre; ~ up relever, retrousser; border (*q.*) (*dans son lit.*).

tuck·er ['tʌkə] **1.** *sl.* (*Australie*)

mangeaille *f*; **2.** *Am.* F fatiguer, lasser.

Tues·day ['tju:zdi] mardi *m*; *Shrove* ~ mardi *m* gras.

tu·fa *min.* ['tju:fə], **tuff** [tʌf] tuf *m* calcaire *ou* volcanique.

tuft [tʌft] *herbe*, *cheveux*, *plumes*: touffe *f*; *oiseau*, *laine*: houppe *f*; *brosse*: loquet *m*; *cheveux*: toupet *m*; **'~-hunt·er** sycophante *m*; **'tuft·y** □ touffu.

tug [tʌg] **1.** secousse *f*; saccade *f*; ⚓ remorqueur *m*; *fig.* effort *m*; *sp.* ~ of war lutte *f* à la corde (de traction); *fig.* course *f* au poteau; **2.** tirer (sur, at); ⚓ remorquer; *fig.* se mettre en peine; **'~·boat** remorqueur *m*.

tu·i·tion [tju'iʃn] instruction *f*.

tu·lip ♀ ['tju:lip] tulipe *f*.

tulle [tju:l] tulle *m*.

tum·ble ['tʌmbl] **1.** *v/i.* tomber; faire la culbute; *v/t.* bouleverser; déranger; chiffonner; **2.** chute *f*; culbute *f*; désordre *m*; **'~·down** en ruines, délabré; croulant; **'~-'drier** séchoir *m* (à linge) à air chaud; **'tum·bler** acrobate *mf*, jongleur *m*; *orn.* culbutant *m*; verre *m* sans pied; ⊕ gorge *f*; *serrure*: arrêt *m*; *arme à feu*: noix *f* (*de platine*).

tum·brel ['tʌmbrəl], **tum·bril** ['~·bril] tombereau *m*.

tu·mid □ ['tju:mid] ❡ enflé, gonflé; *zo.* protubérant; *fig.* boursouflé; **tu'mid·i·ty** enflure *f* (*a. fig.*).

tum·my F ['tʌmi] estomac *m*, ventre *m*; bedaine *f*.

tu·mo(u)r ❡ ['tju:mə] tumeur *f*.

tu·mult ['tju:mʌlt] tumulte *m* (*a. fig.*); fracas *m*; *fig.* trouble *m*, émoi *m*; **tu·mul·tu·ous** □ [tju'mʌltjuəs] tumultueux (-euse *f*); orageux (-euse *f*).

tun [tʌn] **1.** tonneau *m*, fût *m*; cuve *f* (*de fermentation*); **2.** mettre en tonneaux.

tu·na *icht.* ['tju:nə] thon *m*.

tune [tju:n] ♪ air *m*; harmonie *f*; accord *m*; *fig.* ton *m*; *fig.* humeur *f*; in ~ d'accord; *fig.* en bon accord (avec, with); out of ~ désaccordé; faux (fausse *f*); *fig.* en désaccord (avec, with); F to the ~ of £ *100* pour la somme de 100 livres; à la cadence de 100 livres; *fig.* change one's ~ changer de ton; **2.** accorder; *fig.* incliner; ~ in radio: accorder (sur, *to*), capter (un poste, *to a station*); ~ *out radio*: éliminer; ~ *up* ♪ *v/i.* s'accorder; *v/t. fig. mot.*, *a.* ⊕ mettre au point; *fig.* (se) tonifier; *v/t.* ♪ accorder; **tune·ful** □ ['~ful] mélodieux (-euse *f*), harmonieux (-euse *f*); **'tune·less** □ discordant; **'tun·er** ♪ accordeur *m*; *radio*: syntonisateur *m*.

tung·sten ⚗ ['tʌŋstən] tungstène *m*.

tu·nic *cost.*, ⚔, *anat.*, *eccl.*, *a.* ⚘ ['tjuːnik] tunique *f*.

tun·ing...: **'~-coil** *radio*: bobine *f* syntonisatrice; self *f* d'accord; **'~-fork** ♪ diapason *m*.

tun·nel ['tʌnl] **1.** tunnel *m* (*a.* 🚂); ⚒ galerie *f* à flanc de coteau; **2.** percer un tunnel (à travers, dans, sous).

tun·ny *icht.* ['tʌni] thon *m*.

tun·y F ['tjuːni] mélodieux (-euse *f*).

tur·ban ['təːbən] turban *m*.

tur·bid ['təːbid] trouble (*a. fig.*); bourbeux (-euse *f*); confus; **'tur·bid·ness** état *m* trouble; turbidité *f*.

tur·bine ⊕ ['təːbain] turbine *f*; **'~-'pow·ered** à turbines.

tur·bo-prop ['təːbou'prɔp] à turbopropulseur (*avion*); **tur·bo·su·per·charg·er** ['təːbou'sjupətʃaːdʒə] turbocompresseur *m* de suralimentation.

tur·bot *icht.* ['təːbət] turbot *m*.

tur·bu·lence ['təːbjuləns] turbulence *f*; tumulte *m*; indiscipline *f*; **'tur·bu·lent** □ turbulent; orageux (-euse *f*); à remous (*vent*); insubordonné.

turd V [təːd] merde *f*; salaud *m*, salope *f*.

tu·reen [təˈriːn] soupière *f*; saucière *f*.

turf [təːf] **1.** gazon *m*; pelouse *f*; tourbe *f*; turf *m*, courses *f/pl.* de chevaux; **2.** gazonner; *sl.* ~ *out* flanquer (*q.*) dehors; **turf·ite** ['~ait] turfiste *m*; **'turf·y** gazonné, couvert de gazon; tourbeux (-euse *f*); F du turf.

tur·gid □ ['təːdʒid] enflé, gonflé; *fig.* boursouflé; **tur'gid·i·ty** enflure *f* (*a. fig.*).

Turk [təːk] Turc (Turque *f*) *m*; *fig.* tyran *m*; homme *m* indiscipliné.

tur·key ['təːki]: ♀ *carpet* tapis *m* d'Orient *ou* de Turquie; *orn.* dindon *m*, dinde *f*; *cuis.* dindonneau

m; *théâ.*, *cin. Am. sl.* navet *m*; *sl.* *talk* ~ ne pas ménager ses mots.

Turk·ish ['təːkiʃ] turc (turque *f*), de ·Turquie; ~ *bath* bain *m* turc; ~ *delight* rahat-lokoum *m*; ~ *towel* serviette-éponge (*pl.* serviettes-éponges) *f*.

tur·moil ['təːmɔil] trouble *m*, agitation *f*, tumulte *m*.

turn [təːn] **1.** *v/t.* tourner; faire tourner; retourner; rendre; changer, transformer (en, *into*); traduire (en anglais, *into English*); diriger; ⊕ tourner, façonner au tour; *fig.* tourner (*une phrase*, *des vers, etc.*); F *he has* ~*ed* (*ou is* ~*ed* [*of*]) 50 il a passé la cinquantaine; il a 50 ans passés; ~ *colo(u)r* pâlir *ou* rougir; changer de couleur; ~ *a corner* tourner un coin; ~ *the enemy's flanks* tourner le flanc de l'ennemi; *he can* ~ *his hand to anything* c'est un homme à toute main; F ~ *tail* prendre la fuite; ~ *s.o.'s argument against himself* rétorquer un argument contre q.; ~ *aside* détourner; écarter; ~ *away* détourner; *théâ.* refuser; ~ *down* rabattre; retourner (*une carte*); corner (*une page*); baisser (*le gaz etc.*); faire (*la couverture d'un lit*), ouvrir (*le lit*); F refuser (*une invitation etc.*); ~ *in* tourner en dedans; replier (*le bord*); F quitter (*un emploi*); renvoyer; 🚂 garer (*des wagons*); fermer (*l'eau, le gaz*); ~ *off* (*on*) fermer, (ouvrir) (*un robinet*); ~ *out* faire sortir; mettre dehors; vider (*les poches etc.*); nettoyer à fond; fabriquer, produire (*des marchandises*); éteindre, couper (*le gaz*); ~ *over* renverser; feuilleter, tourner (*les pages*); *fig.* transférer, remettre; ✍ retourner (*le sol*); ⚕ faire; ~ *over a new leaf* revenir de ses erreurs; ~ *up* retourner (*a. des cartes, a.* ✍); relever (*un col, un pantalon*); retrousser (*les manches*); donner (*tout le gaz etc.*); remonter (*une mèche*); chercher, trouver (*dans le dictionnaire etc.*); F ~ *one's nose at* faire le dédaigneux devant; renifler sur; **2.** *v/i.* tourner; se (re)tourner; se diriger; se transformer (en, *into*); changer (*marée, temps*); tourner (*au froid etc.*); se faire, devenir (*chrétien, soldat, etc.*); se colorer en (*rouge etc.*); prendre une teinte (*bleue etc.*); (*a. ~ sour*) tourner (*lait*); ~ *about* se (re)tourner; ✗ faire demi-tour; ~ *away* se détourner (de, *from*); ~ *back* rebrousser chemin; regarder en arrière; faire demi-tour; ~ *in* se tourner en dedans; F se coucher; *his toes* ~ *in* il a les pieds tournés en dedans; ~ *off* prendre (*à gauche, à droite*); bifurquer; faire le coin avec; ~ *on* se retourner contre, attaquer; *see* ~ *upon*; ~ *out* sortir; se tourner en dehors (*pieds*); se mettre en grève; tourner (*mal, bien*); aboutir; devenir; se passer; arriver; se trouver; se mettre (*à la pluie, au beau, etc.*); F se lever, sortir du lit; ✗ sortir; ~ *over* se (re)tourner; *mot. etc.* capoter; se renverser; ~ *round* tourner; tournoyer; ~ *to* se mettre à; tourner à; devenir; F ~ *to* (*adv.*) se mettre au travail; ~ *up* se relever; se retrousser (*nez*); arriver, se présenter; ~ *upon* rouler sur (*a. fig.*); attaquer; **3.** *su.* tour *m* (*de corde, de jeu, de roue*; *théâ.*; *a. = promenade*, *a. = disposition d'esprit*; *roue:* révolution *f*; changement *m* de direction, *mot.* virage *m*, ♏ giration *f*; *chemin:* tournant *m*; *typ.* caractère *m* retourné; fin *f* (*du mois*); allure *f*, tournure *f* (*des affaires*); disposition *f* (pour, for); *théâ.* numéro *m*; *fig.* choc *m*, coup *m*; crise *f*; *fig.* service *m*; *fig.* but *m*; *at every* ~ à tout propos, à tout moment; *by* (*ou in* ~*s*) à tour de rôle, tour à tour; *in my* ~ à mon tour; *it is my* ~ c'est à moi (de, to); *take a* ~ faire un tour; *take a* ~ *at s.th.* faire qch. à son tour; *take one's* ~ prendre son tour; *take* ~*s* alterner (pour *inf. at*, *in gér.*); *to a* ~ à point; *a friendly* ~ un service *m* d'ami; *do s.o. a good* ~ rendre un service à q.; *does it serve your* ~? est-ce que cela fera votre affaire?; '~·**about** demi-tour *m*; '~·**buck·le** ⊕ lanterne *f* de serrage; '~·**coat** renégat *m*; apostat(e *f*) *m*; '~·**down 1.** refus *m*; (tendance *f* à la) baisse *f*; **2.** à rabattre; ~ *collar* col *m* rabattu; '**turn·er** tourneur *m*; '**turn·er·y** travail (*pl.* -aux) *m* au tour, tournage *m*; articles *m/pl.* tournés; atelier *m* de tourneur.

turn·ing ['təːniŋ] action *f* de tourner; giration *f*; changement *m* de direction; *mot.* virage *m*; tournant *m* (*du chemin*); retournage *m* (*d'un vêtement*); *typ.* blocage *m*; ⊕ tournage *m*; '~-**lathe** ⊕ tour *m*; '~-**point** *fig.* moment *m* critique, point *m* décisif.

tur·nip ✿ ['təːnip] navet *m*.

turn·key ['təːnkiː]   porte-clefs *m/inv.*; geôlier *m*; *admin.* fontainier *m*; '**turn-off** *Am.* sortie *f* (d'autoroute); embranchement *m*; '**turn-out** tenue *f*, uniforme *m*; équipage *m*; assemblée *f*; assistance *f*, gens *m/pl.*; grève *f*; ✝ production *f*, produits *m/pl.*; aiguillage *m*; voie *f* de garage; changement *m* de voie; '**turn·o·ver** chausson *m* (*aux pommes etc.*); ✝ chiffre *m* d'affaires; *tax* impôt *m* sur le chiffre d'affaires; '**turn·pike** (route *f* à) barrière *f* de péage; tourniquet *m* d'entrée; '**turn·screw** tournevis *m*; '**turn·spit** tournebroche *m*; '**turn·stile** tourniquet *m* (*d'entrée*); '**turn·ta·ble** plaque *f* tournante; *phonographe:* tourne-disque *m*, plateau *m*; '**turn·up 1.** pliant (*lit.*); à bords relevés; **2.** *pantalon:* revers *m*; F rixe *f*, bagarre *f*; F affaire *f* de chance.

tur·pen·tine ⌒ ['təːpəntain] térébenthine *f*.

tur·pi·tude ['təːpitjuːd] turpitude *f*.

tur·quoise *min.* ['təːkwɑːz] turquoise *f*.

tur·ret ['tʌrit] tourelle *f* (*a.* ✗, ♏, ⊕); *a.* revolver *m*; ⊕ ~ *lathe* tour *m* à revolver; '**tur·ret·ed** surmonté *ou* garni de tourelles; *zo.* turriculé (*conque*).

tur·tle[1] *zo.* ['təːtl] tortue *f* de mer; *turn* ~ chavirer; *canot, mot.:* capoter.

tur·tle[2] *orn.* [~] (*usu.* ~-*dove*) tourterelle *f*, tourtereau *m*.

tur·tle·neck *surt. Am.* ['təːtlnek] (pullover *m* à) col *m* roulé.

Tus·can ['tʌskən] **1.** toscan; **2.** *ling.* toscan *m*; Toscan(e *f*) *m*.

tusk [tʌsk] *éléphant:* défense *f*; ~*s pl.* *sanglier:* broches *f/pl.*

tus·sle ['tʌsl] **1.** mêlée *f*, lutte *f*; *fig.* passe *f* d'armes; **2.** lutter.

tus·sock ['tʌsək] touffe *f* d'herbe.

tut [tʌt] allons donc!; zut!

tu·te·lage ['tjuːtilidʒ] tutelle *f*.

tu·te·lar·y ['tjuːtiləri] tutélaire.

tu·tor ['tjuːtə] (*a. private* ~) précepteur (-trice *f*) *m*; *école, univ.* directeur (-trice *f*) *m* d'études; *univ. a.* répétiteur (-trice *f*) *m*; *Am.*

univ. chargé *m* de cours; 🔲 tuteur (-trice *f*) *m*; **2.** instruire; donner des leçons particulières à; diriger les études de; **tu·to·ri·al** [tju-'tɔːriəl] **1.** d'instruction; de répétiteur *etc.*; **2.** cours *m* individuel; travaux *m*/*pl.* pratiques; **tu·tor·ship** ['tjuːtəʃip] emploi *m* de répétiteur *etc.*; *private* ~ préceptorat *m*.

tux·e·do *Am.* [tʌk'siːdou] smoking *m*.

twad·dle ['twɔdl] **1.** fadaises *f*/*pl.*, sottises *f*/*pl.*; **2.** dire des sottises.

twang [twæŋ] **1.** bruit *m* sec; (*usu. nasal* ~) accent *m* nasillard; **2.** (faire) résonner; nasiller (*personne*).

tweak [twiːk] pincer.

tweed [twiːd] cheviote *f* écossaise; tweed *m* (=*étoffe de laine*).

'tween [twiːn] *see* between.

tween·y ['twiːni] (*a.* ~ *maid*) *see* between-maid.

tweez·ers ['twiːzəz] *pl.*: (*a pair of*) ~ (une) petite pince *f*; (des) pinces *f*/*pl.* à épiler.

twelfth [twelfθ] douzième (*a. su.*/*mf*; *a.* ⅟₁₂ *su.*/*m*); ⚹-*cake* galette *f* des Rois; ⚹-**night** veille *f* des Rois.

twelve [twelv] douze (*a. su.*/*m*); ~ *o'clock* midi *m*; minuit *m*; ~·**fold** ['~fould] douze fois autant.

twen·ti·eth ['twentiiθ] vingtième (*a. su.*/*mf*; *a.* ⚹ *su.*/*m*).

twen·ty ['twenti] vingt (*a. su.*/*m*); ~·**fold** ['~fould] **1.** *adj.* vingtuple; **2.** *adv.* vingt fois autant.

twerp *sl.* [twəːp] cruche *f* (= *imbécile*).

twice [twais] deux fois; ~ *as much* deux fois autant; ~ *as many books* deux fois plus de livres.

twid·dle ['twidl] **1.** jouer (avec); *v*/*t.* tripoter (*qch.*); **2.** enjolivure *f*; ornement *m*.

twig¹ [twig] brindille *f*; *hydroscopie:* baguette *f* (*de coudrier*).

twig² *sl.* [~] observer (*q.*); comprendre, saisir (*qch.*).

twi·light ['twailait] **1.** crépuscule *m* (*a. fig.*); **2.** crépusculaire, du crépuscule; ⚹ ~ *sleep* demi-sommeil *m* provoqué.

twin [twin] **1.** jumeau (-elle *f*); jumelé; géminé; ~ *beds pl.* lits *m*/*pl.* jumeaux; **2.** jumeau (-elle *f*) *m*; ~·**en·gined** ⚹ ['~endʒind] bimoteur; '~·**jet** biréacteur *m*.

twine [twain] **1.** ficelle *f*; fil *m*

retors; *fig.* sinuosité *f*, repli *m*; **2.** *v*/*t.* tordre, tortiller; entrelacer (*les doigts etc.*); *fig.* entourer (de, *with*); (en)rouler (autour de *about*, *round*); *v*/*i.* (*a.* ~ *o.s.*) se tordre, se tortiller, s'enrouler; serpenter.

twinge [twindʒ] élancement *m*; légère atteinte *f*; *fig.* remords *m* (*de conscience*).

twin·kle ['twiŋkl] **1.** scintiller, étinceler; pétiller (*feu, a. fig.* de, *with*); **2.** (*a.* '**twin·kling**) scintillement *m*, clignotement *m*; *in a* ~ (ou *the twinkling of an eye*) en un clin d'œil.

twirl [twəːl] **1.** tournoiement *m*; *moustache:* tortillement *m*; pirouette *f*; *fumée:* volute *f*; enjolivure *f*; **2.** (faire) tourn(oy)er; '**twirl·ing-stick** *cuis.* agitateur *m*.

twist [twist] **1.** (fil *m*) retors *m*; torsion *f*; *chemin:* coude *m*; *soie:* tordage *m*; *cheveux:* torsade *f*; *tabac:* carotte *f*, rouleau *m*; *papier:* papillote *f*; contorsion *f* (*du visage*); *sp.* tour *m* de poignet; *mot. cornet:* spire *f*; *fig.* déformation *f*; *fig.* tournure *f*, prédisposition *f* (*de l'esprit*); *fig.* repli *m* (*du serpent*); F appétit *m*; **2.** *v*/*t.* tordre (*a. le visage, le bras, etc.*), tortiller; *tex.* retordre; torquer (*le tabac*); entortiller; enrouler; dénaturer, fausser; donner de l'effet à (*une balle*); *v*/*i.* se tordre, se tortiller; *fig.* tourner, serpenter; '**twist·er** tordeur (-euse *f*) *m*; *tex.* retordeur (-euse *f*) *m*; *sp.* balle *f* qui a de l'effet; *sl.* ficelle *f* (= *ricaneur*); *Am.* tornade *f*, ouragan *m*.

twit¹ [twit]: ~ *s.o. with s.th.* railler q. de qch.; reprocher qch. à q.

twit² *sl.* [~] idiot(e *f*) *m*.

twitch [twitʃ] **1.** *v*/*t.* tirer brusquement; *v*/*i.* se crisper, se contracter (de, *with*); **2.** saccade *f*, coup *m* sec; contraction *f*, tic *m* (*de visage*); *see* twinge; *vét.* serre-nez *m*/*inv.*

twit·ter ['twitə] **1.** gazouiller; **2.** gazouillement *m*; *be in a* ~ être agité *ou* en émoi.

two [tuː] deux (*a. su.*/*m*); *in* ~ en deux; *fig. put* ~ *and* ~ *together* tirer ses conclusions; raisonner juste; '~·**bit** *Am.* F sans importance, infime; bon marché; '~·**edged** à deux tranchants (*a. fig.*); '~·'**faced** hypocrite; '~·'**fist·ed** costaud; '~·**fold** double; '~·**hand·ed** à deux mains; ambidextre;

qui se joue à deux; '~-'**job man** F cumulard *m*; ~·**pence** ['tʌpəns] deux pence *m*; ~·**pen·ny** ['tʌpni] à *ou* de deux pence; *fig.* de quatre sous; '~-**phase** ⚡ biphasé, diphasé; '~-'**pin plug** ⚡ fiche *f* à deux broches; '~-**ply** à deux brins (*cordage*); à deux épaisseurs (*contre-plaqué*); '~-'**seat·er** *mot.* voiture *f* à deux places; '~·**some** couple *m*; jeu *m ou* partie *f* à deux; '~-'**step** two-step *m* (*danse*); '~·'**sto·rey** à deux étages; '~-'**stroke** *mot.* à deux temps; '~-'**time** tromper, tricher; '~-'**valve re·ceiv·er** *radio*: poste *m* à deux lampes; '~-**way** ⊕ à deux voies; ⚡ ~ *adapter* bouchon *m* de raccord.

ty·coon *Am.* F [tai'kuːn] chef *m* de l'industrie; baron *m* de l'industrie.

tyke [taik] vilain chien *m*; rustre *m*.

tym·pa·num *anat., a.* ⚠ ['timpə-nəm], *pl.* **-na** [~nə] tympan *m*.

type [taip] **1.** type *m*; genre *m*; modèle *m*; *typ.* caractère *m*, type *m*, *coll.* caractères *m/pl.*; *typ. in* ~ composé; ~ *area* surface *f* imprimée; *true to* ~ conforme au type ancestral; *typ. set in* ~ composer; **2.** = ~*write*; '~-**found·er** fondeur *m* typographe; '~-**script** manuscrit *m* dactylographié; '~-**set·ter** *typ.* compositeur *m*; '~·**write** [*irr.* (*write*)] écrire à la machine; F taper (à la machine); '~·**writ·er** machine *f* à écrire; † dactylographe *mf*, F dactylo *mf*; ~ *ribbon* ruban *m* encreur.

ty·phoid ✗ ['taifɔid] **1.** typhoïde; ~ *fever* = **2.** (fièvre *f*) typhoïde *f*.

ty·phoon *météor.* [tai'fuːn] typhon *m*.

ty·phus ✗ ['taifəs] typhus *m*.

typ·i·cal □ ['tipikl] typique; caractéristique (de, of); *it's* ~ *of him* c'est bien lui; **typ·i·fy** ['~fai] être caractéristique de; être le type de (*l'officier militaire*); symboliser.

typ·ing ['taipiŋ] dactylo(graphie) *f*; ~ *pool* bureau *m* des dactylos, F dactylo *f*; *be good at* ~ taper bien (à la machine); **typ·ist** ['taipist] dactylographe *mf*, F dactylo *mf*; *shorthand* ~ sténodactylographe *mf*, F sténodactylo *mf*.

ty·pog·ra·pher [tai'pɔgrəfə] typographe *m*, F typo *m*; **ty·po·graph·ic, ty·po·graph·i·cal** □ [~pə-'græfik(l)] typographique; **ty·pog·ra·phy** [~'pɔgrəfi] typographie *f*.

ty·ran·nic, ty·ran·ni·cal □ [ti-'rænik(l)] tyrannique; **ty'ran·ni·cide** [~said] *personne*: tyrannicide *mf*; *crime*: tyrannicide *m*; **tyr·an·nize** ['tirənaiz] faire le tyran; ~ *over* tyranniser (*q.*); '**tyr·an·nous** □ tyrannique; *fig.* violent; '**tyr·an·ny** tyrannie *f*.

ty·rant ['taiərənt] tyran *m* (*a. orn.*).

tyre ['taiə] *see* tire[1].

ty·ro ['taiərou] *see* tiro.

Tyr·o·lese [tirə'liːz] **1.** tyrolien(ne *f*); **2.** Tyrolien(ne *f*) *m*.

Tzar [zɑː] *see* Tsar.

U

U, u [ju:] U *m*, u *m*.

u·biq·ui·tous □ [ju'bikwitəs] qui se trouve *ou* que l'on rencontre partout; **u'biq·ui·ty** ubiquité *f*.

ud·der ['ʌdə] mamelle *f*.

ugh [uh; ə:h] brrr!

ug·li·fy F ['ʌglifai] enlaidir.

ug·li·ness ['ʌglinis] laideur *f*.

ug·ly □ ['ʌgli] laid; vilain (*blessure, aspect, etc.*); mauvais (*temps*).

U·krain·i·an [ju:'kreinjən] **1.** ukrainien(ne *f*); **2.** Ukrainien(ne *f*) *m*.

u·ku·le·le ♪ [ju:kə'leili] ukulélé *m*.

ul·cer ✇ ['ʌlsə] ulcère *m*; **ul·cer·ate** ['~reit] (s')ulcérer; **ul·cer·'a·tion** ulcération *f*; **'ul·cer·ous** ulcéreux (-euse *f*).

ul·lage ✝ ['ʌlidʒ] coulage *m*; *douanes:* manquant *m*.

ul·na *anat.* ['ʌlnə], *pl.* ~nae [~ni:] cubitus *m*.

ul·ster ['ʌlstə] *manteau:* ulster *m*.

ul·te·ri·or □ [ʌl'tiəriə] ultérieur; *fig.* caché, secret (-ète *f*); ~ *motive* arrière-pensée *f*; motif *m* secret.

ul·ti·mate □ ['ʌltimit] final (-als *m/pl.*); dernier (-ère *f*); fondamental (-aux *m/pl.*); *phys.* ~ *stress* résistance *f* de rupture; ~*ly* en fin de compte, à la fin.

ul·ti·ma·tum [ʌlti'meitəm], *pl. a.* ~ta [~tə] ultimatum *m*. [dernier.]

ul·ti·mo ✝ ['ʌltimou] (du mois)

ultra- [ʌltrə] ultra-; extrêmement; **'~'fash·ion·a·ble** ultra-chic; **'~ high fre·quen·cy** *radio:* très haute fréquence; **~'ma'rine 1.** d'outre-mer; **2.** 🎨, *peint.* (bleu *m* d')outre-mer *m/inv.*; **~'mon·tane** *eccl., pol.* [~'mɔntein] ultramontain(e *f*) (*a. su.*); **'~-'red** infrarouge; **'~-'short wave** onde *f* ultracourte; **'~-'vi·o·let** ultraviolet(te *f*).

ul·u·late ['ju:ljuleit] ululer; hurler.

um·bel ♀ ['ʌmbl] ombelle *f*.

um·ber *min., peint.* ['ʌmbə] terre *f* d'ombre; *couleur:* ombre *f*.

um·bil·i·cal □ [ʌm'bilikl]; ✇ ~'laikl] ombilical (-aux *m/pl.*); ~ *cord* cordon *m* ombilical.

um·brage ['ʌmbridʒ] ressentiment *m*; ombrage *m* (*a. poét.*); **um·bra·geous** □ [~'breidʒəs] ombragé; ombrageux (-euse *f*) (*a. fig.*).

um·brel·la [ʌm'brelə] parapluie *m*; *pol.* compromis *m*; ⚔ protection *f*; ~ *organization* organisation *f* de tête; ~ *stand* porte-parapluies *m/inv.*

um·pire ['ʌmpaiə] **1.** arbitre *m*; **2.** *v/t.* arbitrer; *v/i.* servir d'arbitre.

ump·teen ['ʌmti:n], **'ump·ty** F je ne sais combien.

un- [ʌn] non; in-; dé(s)-; ne ... pas; peu; sans.

un·a·bashed ['ʌnə'bæʃt] sans se déconcerter; aucunement ébranlé.

un·a·ble ['ʌn'eibl] incapable (de, *to*); impuissant (à, *to*).

un·a·bridged ['ʌnə'bridʒd] non abrégé; intégral (-aux *m/pl.*).

un·ac·cent·ed ['ʌnæk'sentid] inaccentué; *gramm.* atone.

un·ac·cept·a·ble ['ʌnək'septəbl] inacceptable.

un·ac·com·mo·dat·ing ['ʌnə'kɔmədeitiŋ] peu commode; peu accommodant (*personne*).

un·ac·count·a·ble □ ['ʌnə'kauntəbl] inexplicable; bizarre.

un·ac·cus·tomed ['ʌnə'kʌstəmd] inaccoutumé (à, *to*) (*a. personne*); peu habitué (à, *to*) (*personne*).

un·ac·knowl·edged ['ʌnək'nɔlidʒd] non avoué; demeuré sans réponse (*lettre*).

un·ac·quaint·ed ['ʌnə'kweintid]: *be* ~ *with* ne pas connaître (*q.*); ignorer (*qch.*).

un·a·dorned ['ʌnədɔ:nd] sans ornements, naturel(le *f*); *fig.* sans fard.

un·a·dul·ter·at·ed □ ['ʌnə'dʌltəreitid] pur, sans mélange.

un·ad·vis·a·ble □ ['ʌnəd'vaizəbl] imprudent; peu sage; **'un·ad·'vised** [*adv.* ~zidli] imprudent; sans prendre conseil.

un·af·fect·ed □ ['ʌnə'fektid] qui n'est pas atteint; *fig.* sincère; sans affectation *ou* pose.

un·aid·ed ['ʌn'eidid] sans aide;

(tout) seul; inassisté (*pauvre*); nu (*œil*).

un·al·loyed ['ʌnə'lɔid] sans alliage; *fig.* pur, sans mélange.

un·al·ter·a·ble □ [ʌn'ɔːltərəbl] invariable, immuable.

un·am·big·u·ous□ ['ʌnæm'bigjuəs] non équivoque, sans ambiguïté.

un·am·bi·tious □ ['ʌnæm'biʃəs] sans prétention; sans ambition (*personne*).

un·a·me·na·ble ['ʌnə'miːnəbl] rebelle, réfractaire (à, *to*).

un·a·mi·a·ble □ [ʌn'eimjəbl] peu aimable.

u·na·nim·i·ty [juːnə'nimiti] unanimité *f*; **u·nan·i·mous** □ [ju'næniməs] unanime.

un·an·swer·a·ble [ʌn'ɑːnsərəbl] sans réplique; incontestable.

un·ap·palled ['ʌnə'pɔːld] peu effrayé. [sans appel.\

un·ap·peal·a·ble ⚖ ['ʌnə'piːləbl]/

un·ap·peas·a·ble □ ['ʌnə'piːzəbl] insatiable; implacable.

un·ap·proach·a·ble□ ['ʌnə'proutʃəbl] inaccessible; inabordable (*a. personne*); *fig.* incomparable.

un·ap·pro·pri·at·ed ['ʌnə'prouprieitid] disponible; libre.

un·apt □ ['ʌn'æpt] peu juste; mal approprié; inapte (à, *for*), peu disposé (à *inf.*, *to inf.*); *be* ~ *to* (*inf.*) avoir beaucoup de mal à (*inf.*).

un·a·shamed □ ['ʌnə'ʃeimd; *adv.* ~midli] sans honte *ou* pudeur.

un·asked ['ʌn'ɑːskt] non invité; spontané(ment *adv.*).

un·as·sail·a·ble □ [ʌnə'seiləbl] inattaquable; irréfutable.

un·as·sist·ed □ ['ʌnə'sistid] tout seul, sans aide.

un·as·sum·ing ['ʌnə'sjuːmiŋ] sans prétentions; modeste.

un·at·tached ['ʌnə'tætʃt] non attaché; indépendant (de, *to*); *univ.* qui ne dépend d'aucun collège; ✕ en disponibilité; isolé; ⚖ sans propriétaire.

un·at·tain·a·ble □ ['ʌnə'teinəbl] inaccessible (de, *by*).

un·at·tend·ed ['ʌnə'tendid] seul; sans escorte; dépourvu (de, *by*); (*usu.* ~ *to*) négligé.

un·at·trac·tive □ ['ʌnə'træktiv] peu attrayant; peu sympathique (*personne*).

un·au·thor·ized ['ʌn'ɔːθəraizd] sans

autorisation; illicite; *admin.* sans mandat.

un·a·vail·a·ble ['ʌnə'veiləbl] non disponible; inutilisable; **un·a·vail·ing** □ vain; inutile.

un·a·void·a·ble □ ['ʌnə'vɔidəbl] inévitable.

un·a·ware ['ʌnə'wɛə] ignorant; *be* ~ ignorer (qch., *of s.th.*; que, *that*); **'un·a'wares** au dépourvu; sans s'en rendre compte.

un·backed ['ʌn'bækt] *fig.* sans appui; non endossé (*a.* ✝); *turf:* sur lequel personne n'a parié.

un·bal·ance ['ʌn'bæləns] défaut *m* d'équilibrage; balourd *m*; **'un'bal·anced** mal équilibré (*a. fig.*); ⊕ non compensé; ✝ non soldé; *phys.* en équilibre instable.

un·bap·tized ['ʌnbæp'taizd] non baptisé.

un·bar ['ʌn'bɑː] débarrer, *fig.* ouvrir; dessaisir (*un sabord*).

un·bear·a·ble □ [ʌn'bɛərəbl] insupportable, intolérable.

un·beat·en ['ʌn'biːtn] invaincu; non frayé (*chemin*).

un·be·com·ing □ ['ʌnbi'kʌmiŋ] peu seyant (*robe*); peu convenable; déplacé (chez *q. of*, *to*, *for*).

un·be·friend·ed ['ʌnbi'frendid] sans amis; délaissé.

un·be·known ['ʌnbi'noun] **1.** *adj.* inconnu (de, *to*); **2.** *adv.* à l'insu (de *q.*, *to s.o.*).

un·be·lief ['ʌnbi'liːf] incrédulité *f*; *eccl.* incroyance *f*; **un·be'liev·a·ble** □ incroyable; **'un·be'liev·er** incrédule *mf*; *eccl.* incroyant(e *f*) *m*; **'un·be'liev·ing** □ incrédule.

un·be·loved ['ʌnbi'lʌvd] peu aimé.

un·bend ['ʌn'bend] [*irr.* (*bend*)] *v/t.* détendre (*a. fig.*); redresser (*q.*, *a.* ⊕); *v/i.* se détendre; *fig.* se déraidir; se détordre (*ressort*); se redresser; se déplier (*jambe*); **'un'bend·ing** □ inflexible; *fig. a.* raide.

un·bi·as(s)ed □ ['ʌn'baiəst] *fig.* impartial (-aux *m/pl.*), sans parti pris.

un·bid, **un·bid·den** ['ʌn'bid(n)] non invité; spontané.

un·bind ['ʌn'baind] [*irr.* (*bind*)] dénouer (*les cheveux*); délier (*a. fig.*).

un·bleached *tex.* ['ʌn'bliːtʃt] écru.

un·blem·ished [ʌn'blemiʃt] sans tache (*a. fig.*).

un·blush·ing □ [ʌn'blʌʃiŋ] qui ne rougit pas; sans vergogne.

un·bolt [ˈʌnˈboult] déverrouiller; dévisser (*un rail etc.*); **ˈunˈbolt·ed** déverrouillé; ⊕ déboulonné; dévissé (*rail*); non bluté (*farine*).

un·born [ˈʌnˈbɔːn] à naître; qui n'est pas encore né; *fig.* futur.

un·bos·om [ʌnˈbuzm] révéler; ∾ o.s. ouvrir son cœur (à q., *to s.o.*).

un·bound [ˈʌnˈbaund] délié; dénoué (*cheveux*); broché (*livre*).

un·bound·ed □ [ʌnˈbaundid] sans bornes; illimité; démesuré (*ambition etc.*).

un·bowed [ˈʌnˈbaud] invaincu.

un·brace [ˈʌnˈbreis] défaire; détendre (*les nerfs*); énerver (*q.*).

un·break·a·ble [ˈʌnˈbreikəbl] incassable.

un·bri·dled [ʌnˈbraidld] débridé (*a. fig.*); sans bride; *fig.* déchaîné.

un·bro·ken [ˈʌnˈbroukn] intact; non brisé; inviolé; imbattu (*record*); non dressé (*cheval*); *fig.* insoumis.

un·buck·le [ˈʌnˈbʌkl] déboucler.

un·bur·den [ʌnˈbɔːdn] décharger; *fig.* alléger; ∾ o.s. (*ou one's heart*) se délester (le cœur).

un·bur·ied [ˈʌnˈberid] déterré; sans sépulture.

un·busi·ness·like [ʌnˈbiznislaik] peu commerçant; *fig.* irrégulier (-ère *f*).

un·but·ton [ˈʌnˈbʌtn] déboutonner.

un·called [ʌnˈkɔːld] non appelé (*a.* ✝); **unˈcalled-for** injustifié; déplacé (*remarque*); spontané.

un·can·ny □ [ʌnˈkæni] sinistre; mystérieux (-euse *f*).

un·cared-for [ˈʌnˈkɛədfɔː] mal *ou* peu soigné; abandonné; négligé (*air*).

un·ceas·ing □ [ʌnˈsiːsiŋ] incessant; continu; soutenu.

un·cer·e·mo·ni·ous □ [ˈʌnseriˈmounjəs] peu cérémonieux (-euse *f*); sans gêne (*personne*).

un·cer·tain □ [ʌnˈsɔːtn] incertain; douteux (-euse *f*); irrésolu; peu sûr; be ∾ ne pas savoir au juste (si, *whether*); **unˈcer·tain·ty** incertitude *f*. [donner libre cours à.]

un·chain [ˈʌnˈtʃein] déchaîner; *fig.*)

un·chal·lenge·a·ble [ˈʌnˈtʃælindʒəbl] incontestable; **ˈunˈchal·lenged** incontesté.

un·change·a·ble □ [ʌnˈtʃeindʒəbl], **unˈchang·ing** □ immuable, invariable; éternel(le *f*).

un·char·i·ta·ble □ [ʌnˈtʃæritəbl] peu charitable.

un·chaste □ [ˈʌnˈtʃeist] impudique; **un·chas·ti·ty** [ˈʌnˈtʃæstiti] impudicité *f*; infidélité *f* (*d'une femme*).

un·checked [ˈʌnˈtʃekt] libre(ment *adv.*); ✝ non vérifié.

un·chris·tian □ [ˈʌnˈkristjən] peu chrétien(ne *f*); païen(ne *f*).

un·civ·il □ [ˈʌnˈsivl] impoli; **unˈciv·i·lized** [˷vilaizd] barbare, incivilisé.

un·claimed [ˈʌnˈkleimd] non réclamé; épave (*chien etc.*); de rebut (*lettre*).

un·clasp [ˈʌnˈklɑːsp] défaire, dégrafer; (se) desserrer (*poing*); laisser échapper.

un·clas·si·fied [ˈʌnˈklæsifaid] non classé; non secret (-ète) (*information*).

un·cle [ˈʌŋkl] oncle *m*; *sl.* at my ∾'s chez ma tante, au clou.

un·clean □ [ˈʌnˈkliːn] sale; *fig.*, *eccl.* immonde, impur.

un·clench [ˈʌnˈklentʃ] (se) desserrer.

un·cloak [ˈʌnˈklouk] ôter le manteau de; *fig.* dévoiler.

un·close [ˈʌnˈklouz] (s')ouvrir.

un·clothe [ˈʌnˈklouð] (se) déshabiller. [nuage; clair (*a. fig.*).)

un·cloud·ed [ˈʌnˈklaudid] sans)

un·coil [ˈʌnˈkɔil] (se) dérouler.

un·col·lect·ed [ˈʌnkəˈlektid] non recueilli; *fig.* confus.

un·col·o·(u)red [ˈʌnˈkʌləd] non coloré; incolore; *fig.* non influencé.

un·come·ly [ˈʌnˈkʌmli] peu gracieux (-euse *f*).

un·com·fort·a·ble □ [ʌnˈkʌmfətəbl] peu confortable; désagréable; peu à son aise (*personne*).

un·com·mon □ [ʌnˈkɔmən] (*a.* F *adv.*) peu commun; singulier (-ère *f*); rare.

un·com·mu·ni·ca·tive [ˈʌnkəˈmjuːnikeitiv] réservé, taciturne; peu communicatif (-ive *f*).

un·com·plain·ing □ [ˈʌnkəmˈpleiniŋ] patient; sans plainte; **ˈunˈcom·plain·ing·ness** patience *f*, résignation *f*.

un·com·pro·mis·ing □ [ˈʌnˈkɔmprəmaiziŋ] intransigeant; sans compromis; *fig.* raide; absolu.

un·con·cern [ˈʌnkənˈsɔːn] indifférence *f*; insouciance *f*; **ˈun·con-**

'**cerned** □ [*adv.* ⁓idli] insouciant; indifférent (à, *about*); étranger (-ère *f*) (à *with*, *in*).

un·con·di·tion·al □ ['ʌnkən'diʃnl] absolu; sans réserve.

un·con·fined □ ['ʌnkən'faind] illimité, sans bornes; libre.

un·con·firmed ['ʌnkən'fəːmd] non confirmé *ou* avéré; *eccl.* qui n'a pas reçu la confirmation.

un·con·gen·ial ['ʌnkən'dʒiːnjəl] peu agréable; peu favorable; peu sympathique (*personne*).

un·con·nect·ed □ ['ʌnkə'nektid] sans lien *ou* rapport; décousu (*idées*).

un·con·quer·a·ble □ [ʌn'kɔŋkərəbl] invincible; *fig.* insurmontable.

un·con·sci·en·tious □ ['ʌnkɔnʃi-'enʃəs] peu consciencieux (-euse *f*).

un·con·scion·a·ble □ [ʌn'kɔnʃə-nəbl] peu scrupuleux (-euse *f*); déraisonnable (*a. fig.*); exorbitant.

un·con·scious □ [ʌn'kɔnʃəs] **1.** inconscient; sans connaissance (= *évanoui*); be ⁓ of ne pas avoir conscience de; **2.** *psych.* the ⁓ l'inconscient *m*; **un'con·scious·ness** inconscience *f*; évanouissement *m*.

un·con·sid·ered ['ʌnkən'sidəd] irréfléchi, inconsidéré; sans valeur.

un·con·sti·tu·tion·al □ ['ʌnkɔnsti-'tjuːʃənl] in-, anticonstitutionnel(le *f*).

un·con·strained □ ['ʌnkən'streind] sans contrainte; aisé.

un·con·test·ed □ ['ʌnkən'testid] incontesté; *pol.* qui n'est pas disputé.

un·con·tra·dict·ed ['ʌnkɔntrə'diktid] non contredit.

un·con·trol·la·ble □ [ʌnkən'trouləbl] ingouvernable; irrésistible; absolu.

un·con·ven·tion·al □ ['ʌnkən-'venʃnl] qui va à l'encontre des conventions; original (-aux *m/pl.*).

un·con·vert·ed ['ʌnkən'vəːtid] inconverti (*a. eccl.*); ✝ *a.* non converti.

un·con·vinced ['ʌnkən'vinst] sceptique (à l'égard de, *of*).

un·cork ['ʌn'kɔːk] déboucher.

un·cor·rupt·ed □ ['ʌnkə'rʌptid] intègre; incorrompu. [comptable.)

un·count·a·ble ['ʌn'kauntəbl] in-}

un·cou·ple ['ʌn'kʌpl] découpler.

un·couth □ [ʌn'kuːθ] grossier (-ère *f*), rude; gauche, agreste.

un·cov·er [ʌn'kʌvə] découvrir (✗, *a. une partie du corps*); démasquer.

un·crit·i·cal □ ['ʌn'kritikl] sans discernement; peu difficile.

un·crowned ['ʌn'kraund] non couronné; découronné.

un·crush·a·ble *tex.* [ʌn'krʌʃəbl] infroissable.

unc·tion ['ʌŋkʃn] onction *f* (*a. fig.*); *poét.* onguent *m*; *eccl.* extreme ⁓ extrême-onction *f*; **unc·tu·ous** □ ['ʌŋktjuəs] onctueux (-euse *f*) (*a. fig.*); graisseux (-euse *f*); *péj.* patelin.

un·cul·ti·vat·ed ['ʌn'kʌltiveitid] inculte; en friche (*terre*); *fig.* sans culture; ♇ à l'état sauvage.

un·cured ['ʌn'kjuəd] ⚕ non guéri; *cuis.* frais (*hareng*).

un·curl ['ʌn'kəːl] (se) défriser (*cheveux*); (se) dérouler.

un·cut ['ʌn'kʌt] intact; sur pied (*blé etc.*); non coupé (*haie*, *livre*); non rogné (*livre*).

un·dam·aged ['ʌn'dæmidʒd] en bon état.

un·damped ['ʌn'dæmpt] sec (sèche *f*); *fig.* non découragé.

un·dat·ed ['ʌn'deitid] sans date.

un·daunt·ed □ [ʌn'dɔːntid] intrépide; non intimidé.

un·de·ceive ['ʌndi'siːv] désabuser (de, *of*); dessiller les yeux à (*q.*).

un·de·cid·ed □ ['ʌndi'saidid] indécis.

un·de·ci·pher·a·ble ['ʌndi'saifərəbl] indéchiffrable.

un·de·fend·ed ['ʌndi'fendid] sans protection.

un·de·filed ['ʌndi'faild] sans tache, pur.

un·de·fined □ ['ʌndi'faind]; *adv.* ⁓nidli] non défini; vague.

un·de·mon·stra·tive □ ['ʌndi'mɔnstrətiv] réservé.

un·de·ni·a·ble □ ['ʌndi'naiəbl] incontestable; qu'on ne peut nier.

un·de·nom·i·na·tion·al □ ['ʌndi-nɔmi'neiʃənl] non confessionnel(le *f*); laïque (*école*).

un·der ['ʌndə] **1.** *adv.* (au-)dessous; en *ou* dans la soumission; **2.** *prp.* sous; au-dessous de; *from* ⁓ de sous; de dessous; ⁓ *sentence* of condamné à; **3.** *mots composés*: trop peu; insuffisamment; inférieur; sous-; '⁓-'**age** mineur; de mineurs; '⁓'**bid** [*irr.* (*bid*)] demander moins cher que; '~'**bred** mal élevé; qui n'a pas de race (*cheval*); '~'**brush** broussailles *f/pl.*; sousbois *m*; '~-**carriage,** '~-**cart** ⚒ train *m* d'atterrissage; '~-**cloth·ing** linge *m* de corps; lingerie *f* (*pour dames*); '~-**cur·rent** courant *m* de fond *ou* sous-marin; *fig.* fond *m*; '~'**cut** [*irr.* (*cut*)] vendre moins cher que; '~-**de'vel·oped** sous-développé; '~-**dog** perdant *m*; *fig.* the ~(*s pl.*) les opprimés *m/pl.*; '~'**done** pas assez cuit; saignant (*viande*); '~'**dress** (s')habiller trop simplement; '~-**em'ploy·ment** sous-emploi *m*; '~-**es·ti·mate** sous-estimer; '~-**ex'pose** sous-exposer; '~'**fed** mal nourri; '~-**feed·ing** sous-alimentation *f*; '~-**felt** assise *f* de feutre; '~'**foot** sous les pieds; '~'**gar·ments** *pl.* sous-vêtements *m/pl.*; '~'**go** [*irr.* (*go*)] subir; supporter; '~'**grad·u·ate** *univ.* étudiant(e *f*) *m*; '~-**ground 1.** souterrain; sous terre; ~ *engineering* construction *f* souterraine; ~ *mouvement* mouvement *m* clandestin; ⚔ résistance *f*; ~ *water* eaux *f/pl.* souterraines; ~ *railway* = **2.** métro *m*; chemin *m* de fer souterrain; '~-**growth** broussailles *f/pl.*; '~-**hand** clandestin; sournois (*a. personne*); ~ *service tennis:* service *m* par en dessous; '~'**hung** ⚙ prognathe; coulissant (*porte*); ~**lay 1.** [ˌʌndəˈlei] [*irr.* (*lay*)]: ~ *s.th. with s.th.* mettre qch. sous qch.; **2.** [ˈʌndəlei] assise *f* de feutre; *géol.* inclinaison *f*; '~'**let** [*irr.* (*let*)] sous-louer; louer à trop bas prix; ⚓ sous-fréter; '~'**lie** [*irr.* (*lie*)] être en dessous *ou* au-dessous *ou fig.* à la base de; ~**line 1.** [ˌʌndəˈlain] souligner; **2.** [ˈʌndəlain] légende *f* (*d'une illustration*).

un·der·ling [ˈʌndəliŋ] subordonné (-e *f*) *m*; sous-ordre *m*; **un·der·manned** [ˈ~ˈmænd] à court de personnel *ou* ⚓ d'équipage; '**un·der·men·tioned** (cité) ci-dessous; **un·der·mine** miner, saper (*a. fig.*); '**un·der·most 1.** *adj.* le (la) plus bas(se *f*); le plus en dessous; **2.** *adv.* en dessous; **un·der·neath** [~ˈniːθ] **1.** *prp.* au-dessous de, sous; **2.** *adv.* au-dessous; par-dessous.

under...: '~'**nour·ished** mal nourri; '~-**pants** *pl.* (*a pair of* ~ un) caleçon *ou* slip; '~'**pass** *Am.* passage *m* souterrain; '~'**pay** [*irr.* (*pay*)] rétribuer

mal; ~'**pin** ⚙ étayer (*un mur*); *fig.* soutenir; ~'**pin·ning** ⚙ étayage *m*; étais *m/pl.*; soutènement *m*; '~'**play** minimiser; ~ *one's hand* dissimuler ses intentions, cacher son jeu; '~-**plot** intrigue *f* secondaire; '~'**print** *phot.* tirer (*une épreuve*) trop claire; '~-**priv·i·leged** déshérité (*a. su.*); ~'**rate** sous-estimer; mésestimer; ~'**score** souligner; '~-'**sec·re·tar·y** sous-secrétaire *mf*; '~'**sell** ⚔ [*irr.*(*sell*)] vendre moins cher que (*q.*); vendre (*qch.*) au-dessous de sa valeur; '~'**shot** en dessous, à aubes (*roue*); ~'**signed** soussigné(e *f*) *m*; '~'**sized** trop petit; rabougri; ~'**slung** *mot.* à châssis surbaissé; ~'**staffed** à court de personnel; ~'**stand** [*irr.* (*stand*)] comprendre (*a. fig.*); s'entendre à; se rendre compte de; *gramm.* sous-entendre; *fig. a.* écouter bien; *make o.s. understood* se faire comprendre; *it is understood that* il est (bien) entendu que; *that is understood* cela va sans dire; *an understood thing* chose *f* convenue; ~'**stand·a·ble** compréhensible; ~'**stand·ing 1.** entendement *m*, compréhension *f*; entente *f*, accord *m*; *on the ~ that* à condition que; **2.** intelligent; '~'**state** rester au-dessous de la vérité; amoindrir (*les faits*); '~'**state·ment** affirmation *f* qui reste au-dessous de la vérité; amoindrissement *m* (*des faits*).

under...: '~-**strap·per** *see underling*; '~-**stud·y** *théâ.* **1.** doublure *f*; **2.** doubler; ~'**take** [*irr.* (*take*)] entreprendre; se charger de; ~ *that* F promettre que; '~-**tak·er** entrepreneur *m* de pompes funèbres; '~**tak·ing** [ˌʌndəˈteikiŋ] entreprise *f* (*a.* ⚓); promesse *f*; ~-**tak·ing** [ˈʌndəˈteikiŋ] entreprise *f* de pompes funèbres; '~-**ten·ant** sous-locataire *mf*; '~-**the-coun·ter** clandestin(ement); '~-**tone** *fig.* fond *m*; *in an* ~ à demi-voix, à voix basse; '~'**val·ue** sous-estimer; mésestimer; '~-**wear** linge *m* de corps; lingerie *f* (*pour dames*); '~-**weight** manque *m* de poids; '~-**wood** broussailles *f/pl.*; sous-bois *m*; '~-**world** les enfers *m/pl.*; les basfonds *m/pl.* de la société; '~-**write** ⚔ [*irr.*(*write*)] souscrire (*une émission, un risque*); garantir; '~-**writ·er** assureur *m*; membre *m* d'un syndicat de garantie.

un·de·served □ [ˈʌndiˈzəːvd; adv. ~vidli] immérité; injuste; **ˈun·de·ˈserv·ing** peu méritoire; sans mérite (personne).

un·de·signed □ [ˈʌndiˈzaind; adv. ~nidli] imprévu; involontaire.

un·de·sir·a·ble □ [ˈʌndiˈzaiərəbl] peu désirable; indésirable (a. su./mf).

un·de·terred [ˈʌndiˈtəːd] aucunement découragé.

un·de·vel·oped [ˈʌndiˈveləpt] non développé; inexploité (terrain).

un·de·vi·a·ting □ [ʌnˈdiːvieitiŋ] constant; droit.

un·di·gest·ed [ˈʌndiˈdʒestid] mal digéré.

un·dig·ni·fied □ [ʌnˈdignifaid] qui manque de dignité; peu digne.

un·dis·cerned □ [ˈʌndiˈsəːnd] inaperçu; **ˈun·disˈcern·ing** sans discernement.

un·dis·charged [ˈʌndisˈtʃɑːdʒd] inaccompli (tâche etc.); inacquitté (dette); non réhabilité (failli).

un·dis·ci·plined [ʌnˈdisiplind] indiscipliné.

un·dis·crim·i·nat·ing □ [ˈʌndisˈkrimineitiŋ] sans discernement.

un·dis·guised □ [ˈʌndisˈgaizd] non déguisé; franc(he f).

un·dis·posed [ˈʌndisˈpouzd] peu disposé (à, to); (usu. ~of) qui reste; ✝ non vendu.

un·dis·put·ed □ [ˈʌndisˈpjuːtid] incontesté.

un·dis·turbed □ [ˈʌndisˈtəːbd] tranquille; calme; non dérangé.

un·di·vid·ed □ [ˈʌndiˈvaidid] indivisé; non partagé; tout.

un·do [ʌnˈduː] [irr. (do)] défaire (= ouvrir); dénouer; annuler; réparer (un mal); ✝ ruiner; ✝ tuer; **ˈun·doˈing** action f de défaire etc.; ruine f, perte f; **un·done** [ʌnˈdʌn] défait etc.; inachevé; non accompli; he is ~ c'en est fait de lui; come ~ se défaire. [table; incontestable.)

un·doubt·ed □ [ʌnˈdautid] indubi-∫

un·dreamt-of [ʌnˈdremtɔv] inattendu; inimaginé.

un·dress [ʌnˈdres] **1.** (se) déshabiller ou dévêtir; **2.** déshabillé m, négligé m; ✕ petite tenue f; **ˈun·ˈdressed** déshabillé; en déshabillé; brut (pierre); inapprêté (cuir etc.); non pansé (blessure); cuis. non garni ou habillé.

un·due [ʌnˈdjuː] (adv. unduly) inexigible; ✝ non échu; injuste; exagéré; illégitime.

un·du·late [ˈʌndjuleit] vt/i. onduler; v/i. ondoyer; **ˈun·du·lat·ing** □ ondulé; vallonné (terrain); ondoyant (blé); **un·duˈla·tion** ondulation f; pli m de terrain; **un·du·la·to·ry** [ˈ~lətəri] ondulatoire; ondulé.

un·dy·ing □ [ʌnˈdaiiŋ] immortel(le f); éternel(le f).

un·earned [ʌnˈəːnd] immérité; ~ income rente f, -s f/pl.

un·earth [ʌnˈəːθ] déterrer; chasse: faire sortir de son trou; fig. découvrir, F dénicher; **unˈearth·ly** sublime; surnaturel(le f); F abominable.

un·eas·i·ness [ʌnˈiːzinis] gêne f; inquiétude f; **unˈeas·y** □ gêné; mal à l'aise; inquiet (-ète f) (au sujet de, about).

un·eat·a·ble □ [ʌnˈiːtəbl] immangeable.

un·e·co·nom·ic, un·e·co·nom·i·cal □ [ˈʌniːkəˈnɔmik(l)] non économique; non rémunérateur (-trice f) (travail etc.).

un·ed·u·cat·ed [ʌnˈedjukeitid] sans éducation; ignorant; vulgaire (langage).

un·em·bar·rassed [ˈʌnimˈbærəst] peu gêné, désinvolte.

un·e·mo·tion·al □ [ˈʌniˈmouʃnl] peu émotif (-ive f); peu impressionnable.

un·em·ployed [ˈʌnimˈplɔid] **1.** désœuvré, inoccupé; sans travail; ✕ en non-activité; ✝ inemployé; **2.:** the ~ pl. les chômeurs m/pl.; Welfare Work for the ♀ assistance f sociale contre le chômage; **ˈun·emˈployment** chômage m; manque m de travail; ~ benefit secours m de chômage; allocation f de chômage.

un·end·ing □ [ʌnˈendiŋ] sans fin; interminable; éternel(le f).

un·en·dur·a·ble [ˈʌninˈdjuərəbl] insupportable.

un·en·gaged [ˈʌninˈgeidʒd] libre; disponible; non fiancé.

un-English [ˈʌnˈiŋgliʃ] peu anglais.

un·en·light·ened fig. [ˈʌninˈlaitnd] non éclairé.

un·en·ter·pris·ing [ʌnˈentəpraiziŋ] peu entreprenant.

un·en·vi·a·ble □ ['ʌn'enviəbl] peu enviable.

un·e·qual □ ['ʌn'iːkwəl] inégal (-aux *m/pl.*); irrégulier (-ère *f*); ~ to au-dessous de; be ~ to (*inf.*) ne pas être de taille à (*inf.*); '**un'e·qual(l)ed** sans égal (-aux *m/pl.*); sans pareil(le *f*).

un·e·qui·vo·cal □ ['ʌni'kwivəkl] clair; franc(he *f*); sans équivoque.

un·err·ing □ ['ʌn'əːriŋ] infaillible.

un·es·sen·tial □ ['ʌni'senʃl] non essentiel(le *f*); accessoire.

un·e·ven □ ['ʌn'iːvn] inégal (-aux *m/pl.*) (*a.* humeur, souffle); accidenté (*terrain*); raboteux (-euse *f*) (*chemin*); rugueux (-euse *f*); impair (*nombre*); irrégulier (-ère *f*).

un·e·vent·ful □ ['ʌni'ventful] calme; sans incidents.

un·ex·am·pled ['ʌnig'zɑːmpld] unique; sans pareil(le *f*).

un·ex·cep·tion·a·ble □ ['ʌnik-'sepʃənəbl] irréprochable; irrécusable (*témoignage*).

un·ex·cep·tion·al ['ʌnik'sepʃənl] ordinaire; banal (-als *m/pl.*), qui ne sort pas de l'ordinaire.

un·ex·pect·ed □ ['ʌniks'pektid] imprévu; inattendu.

un·ex·plored ['ʌniks'plɔːd] encore inconnu; ⚓ insondé.

un·ex·posed *phot.* ['ʌniks'pouzd] vierge.

un·ex·pressed ['ʌniks'prest] inexprimé; sousentendu (*a.* gramm.).

un·fad·ing □ [ʌn'feidiŋ] bon teint *inv.*; *fig.* impérissable.

un·fail·ing □ [ʌn'feiliŋ] sûr, infaillible; qui ne se dément jamais; inépuisable.

un·fair □ ['ʌn'fɛə] inéquitable; injuste, partial (-aux *m/pl.*) (*personne*); déloyal (-aux *m/pl.*) (*jeu etc.*); '**un'fair·ness** injustice *f*; partialité *f*; déloyauté *f*.

un·faith·ful □ ['ʌn'feiθful] infidèle; inexact; déloyal (-aux *m/pl.*) (envers, to); '**un'faith·ful·ness** infidélité *f*; [me; assuré.)

un·fal·ter·ing □ [ʌn'fɔːltəriŋ] fer-)

un·fa·mil·iar ['ʌnfə'miljə] étranger (-ère *f*); peu connu *ou* familier (-ère *f*).

un·fash·ion·a·ble □ ['ʌn'fæʃnəbl] démodé.

un·fas·ten ['ʌn'fɑːsn] délier; détacher; ouvrir; défaire.

un·fath·om·a·ble □ [ʌn'fæðəməbl] insondable.

un·fa·vo(u)r·a·ble □ ['ʌn'feivərəbl] défavorable.

un·feel·ing □ [ʌn'fiːliŋ] insensible.

un·feigned □ [ʌn'feind; *adv.* ~nidli] sincère, réel(le *f*), vrai.

un·felt ['ʌn'felt] insensible.

un·fer·ment·ed ['ʌnfə'mentid] non fermenté.

un·fet·ter [ʌn'fetə] désenchaîner; briser les fers de; *fig.* affranchir.

un·fil·i·al □ ['ʌn'filjəl] indigne d'un fils.

un·fin·ished ['ʌn'finiʃt] inachevé; imparfait; ⊕ brut.

un·fit 1. □ ['ʌn'fit] peu propre, qui ne convient pas (à *inf.*, to *inf.*; à qch., for *s.th.*); inapte (à, for); **2.** [ʌn'fit] rendre inapte *ou* impropre (à, for); '**un'fit·ness** inaptitude *f*; mauvaise santé *f*; **un'fit·ted** (*to*, for) impropre (à); incapable (de); indigne (de).

un·fix ['ʌn'fiks] (se) détacher, défaire; '**un'fixed** mobile; instable (*personne*); flottant; *phot.* non fixé.

un·flag·ging □ [ʌn'flægiŋ] infatigable; soutenu (*intérêt*).

un·flat·ter·ing □ [ʌn'flætəriŋ] peu flatteur (-euse *f*) (pour, to).

un·fledged ['ʌn'fledʒd] sans plumes; *fig.* sans expérience.

un·flinch·ing □ [ʌn'flintʃiŋ] ferme, qui ne bronche pas; stoïque; impassible.

un·fold ['ʌn'fould] (se) déployer; (se) dérouler; *v/t.* [~'fould] révéler; développer.

un·forced □ ['ʌn'fɔːst; *adv.* ~sidli] libre; volontaire; naturel(le *f*).

un·fore·see·a·ble ['ʌnfɔː'siːəbl] imprévisible.

un·fore·seen ['ʌnfɔː'siːn] imprévu, inattendu.

un·for·get·ta·ble □ ['ʌnfə'getəbl] inoubliable.

un·for·giv·a·ble ['ʌnfə'givəbl] impardonnable; '**un·for'giv·ing** implacable; rancunier (-ère *f*).

un·for·got·ten ['ʌnfə'gɔtn] inoublié.

un·for·ti·fied ['ʌn'fɔːtifaid] sans défenses; ouvert (*ville etc.*).

un·for·tu·nate [ʌn'fɔːtʃənit] **1.** □ malheureux (-euse *f*) (*a. su.*); défavorable; ~ly malheureusement, par malheur.

un·found·ed □ [ˈʌnˈfaundid] sans fondement; gratuit; non fondé.

un·fre·quent·ed [ˈʌnfriˈkwentid] peu fréquenté.

un·friend·ly [ˈʌnˈfrendli] inamical (-aux m/pl.); hostile.

un·fruit·ful □ [ˈʌnˈfruːtful] infécond (arbre); improductif (-ive f).

un·ful·filled [ˈʌnfulˈfild] inaccompli; inassouvi (désir); inexaucé (vœu).

un·furl [ʌnˈfɔːl] (se) déferler (voile, drapeau); (se) dérouler; (se) déplier.

un·fur·nished [ˈʌnˈfɔːniʃt] dégarni; dépourvu (de, with); non meublé (appartement etc.).

un·gain·li·ness [ʌnˈgeinlinis] gaucherie f; air m gauche; **un·gain·ly** gauche; dégingandé (marche).

un·gear ⊕ [ˈʌnˈgiə] débrayer.

un·gen·er·ous □ [ˈʌnˈdʒenərəs] peu généreux (-euse f); ingrat (sol).

un·gen·tle □ [ˈʌnˈdʒentl] rude, dur.

un·gen·tle·man·ly [ʌnˈdʒentlmənli] mal élevé; impoli.

un·glazed [ˈʌnˈgleizd] sans vitres; non glacé (papier).

un·gloved [ˈʌnˈglʌvd] déganté.

un·god·li·ness [ʌnˈgɔdlinis] impiété f; **un·god·ly** □ impie; F abominable.

un·gov·ern·a·ble □ [ʌnˈgʌvənəbl] irrésistible; effréné; ingouvernable (enfant, pays); **un·gov·erned** effréné; sans gouvernement (pays, peuple); désordonné.

un·grace·ful □ [ˈʌnˈgreisful] gauche; disgracieux (-euse f).

un·gra·cious □ [ˈʌnˈgreiʃəs] désagréable; peu aimable (personne); peu cordial (-aux m/pl.) (accueil etc.).

un·grate·ful □ [ʌnˈgreitful] ingrat; peu reconnaissant.

un·ground·ed [ˈʌnˈgraundid] sans fondement; ∉ non (relié) à la terre.

un·grudg·ing □ [ˈʌnˈgrʌdʒiŋ] accordé de bon cœur; généreux (-euse f). [(-aux m/pl.); ongulé.)

un·gual anat. [ˈʌŋgwəl] unguéal]

un·guard·ed □ [ˈʌnˈgɑːdid] non gardé; sans garde; sans défense (ville); ⊕ sans dispositif protecteur; fig. imprudent.

un·guent [ˈʌŋgwənt] onguent m.

un·guid·ed □ [ˈʌnˈgaidid] sans guide.

un·gu·late [ˈʌŋgjuleit] (ou ∼ animal) ongulé m.

un·hal·lowed [ʌnˈhæloud] profane; imbéni; fig. impie.

un·ham·pered [ˈʌnˈhæmpəd] libre.

un·hand·some □ [ʌnˈhænsəm] laid (action); vilain.

un·hand·y □ [ʌnˈhændi] incommode; maladroit, gauche (personne).

un·hap·pi·ness [ʌnˈhæpinis] chagrin m; inopportunité f; **un·hap·py** □ triste, malheureux (-euse f); fig. peu heureux (-euse f).

un·harmed [ˈʌnˈhɑːmd] sain et sauf (-ve f).

un·har·ness [ˈʌnˈhɑːnis] dételer.

un·health·y □ [ʌnˈhelθi] malsain (a. fig.); maladif (-ive f) (personne).

un·heard [ˈʌnˈhɔːd] non entendu; ∼**-of** [ʌnˈhɔːdɔv] inouï; inconnu.

un·heed·ed [ˈʌnˈhiːdid] négligé; inaperçu.

un·hes·i·tat·ing □ [ʌnˈheziteitiŋ] ferme, résolu; prompt.

un·hinge [ʌnˈhindʒ] enlever (une porte) de ses gonds; fig. déranger, détraquer.

un·his·tor·i·cal □ [ˈʌnhisˈtɔrikl] contraire à l'histoire; légendaire.

un·ho·ly [ʌnˈhouli] profane; impie (personne); F invraisemblable.

un·hon·o(u)red [ˈʌnˈɔnəd] qui n'est pas honoré; dédaigné; † impayé (chèque etc.).

un·hook [ˈʌnˈhuk] (se) décrocher; (se) dégrafer.

un·hoped·for [ʌnˈhouptfɔː] inespéré; inattendu; **un·hope·ful** [∼ful] peu optimiste; désespérant.

un·horse [ˈʌnˈhɔːs] désarçonner; dételer (une voiture).

un·house [ˈʌnˈhauz] déloger; laisser sans abri.

un·hurt [ˈʌnˈhɔːt] intact; sans blessure (personne); indemne.

u·ni·corn [ˈjuːnikɔːn] licorne f.

un·i·den·ti·fied [ˈʌnaiˈdentifaid] non identifié; ∼ flying object objet m volant non identifié.

u·ni·fi·ca·tion [juːnifiˈkeiʃn] unification f.

u·ni·form [ˈjuːnifɔːm] **1.** □ uniforme; constant; ∼ price prix m unique; **2.** uniforme m; ✗ a. habit m d'ordonnance; **3.** vêtir d'un uniforme; ∼d en uniforme; **u·ni·form·**

i·ty uniformité *f*; régularité *f*; *eccl.* conformisme *m*.

u·ni·fy ['ju:nifai] unifier.

u·ni·lat·er·al ['ju:ni'lætərəl] unilatéral (-aux *m/pl.*).

un·im·ag·i·na·ble □ [ʌni'mædʒinəbl] inconcevable; **'un·im'ag·i·na·tive** □ [‿nətiv] prosaïque.

un·im·paired ['ʌnim'pɛəd] intact; non diminué; non affaibli.

un·im·peach·a·ble □ [ʌnim'pi:tʃəbl] inattaquable; irréprochable (*conduite*).

un·im·por·tant □ ['ʌnim'pɔ:tənt] sans importance; insignifiant.

un·im·proved ['ʌnim'pru:vd] non amélioré; ✓, *fig.* inculte.

un·in·flu·enced ['ʌn'influənst] libre de toute prévention; non influencé.

un·in·formed ['ʌnin'fɔ:md] ignorant; non averti.

un·in·hab·it·a·ble ['ʌnin'hæbitəbl] inhabitable; **'un·in'hab·it·ed** inhabité; désert.

un·in·jured ['ʌn'indʒəd] intact; sain et sauf (-ve *f*) (*personne*); indemne.

un·in·struct·ed ['ʌnin'strʌktid] ignorant; sans instruction.

un·in·tel·li·gi·bil·i·ty ['ʌnintelidʒə'biliti] inintelligibilité *f*; **'un·in·'tel·li·gi·ble** inintelligible.

un·in·ten·tion·al □ ['ʌnin'tenʃənl] involontaire; non voulu.

un·in·ter·est·ing □ ['ʌn'intristiŋ] sans intérêt; peu intéressant.

un·in·ter·rupt·ed □ ['ʌnintə'rʌptid] ininterrompu; ~ *working-hours* heures *f/pl.* de travail d'affilée.

un·in·vit·ed ['ʌnin'vaitid] sans être invité; intrus; **'un·in'vit·ing** □ peu attrayant.

un·ion ['ju:njən] union *f* (*a.* ⊕, *pol.* etc.); réunion *f*; *pol.* syndicat *m*; association *f*; asile *m* des pauvres; *fig.* concorde *f*; ⚒ soudure *f*; ⊕ raccord *m*; ♀ *Jack* pavillon *m* britannique; ~ *member* syndiqué(e *f*) *m*; ~ *shop* atelier *m* d'ouvriers syndiqués; ~ *suit Am.* combinaison *f*; **'un·ion·ism** *pol. etc.* unionisme *m*; syndicalisme *m*; **'un·ion·ist** *pol. etc.* unioniste *mf*; syndiqué(e *f*) *m*; syndicaliste *mf*.

u·nique [ju:'ni:k] **1.** = unique; seul en son genre; **2.** chose *f* unique.

u·ni·son ♪, *a. fig.* ['ju:nizn] unisson

m; *in* ~ à l'unisson (de, *with*); *fig.* de concert (avec, *with*).

u·nit ['ju:nit] unité *f* (*a.* ✖, ♀, ✝, *mesure*); élément *m*; ⊕ bloc *m*; **U·ni·tar·i·an** [ju:ni'tɛəriən] **1.** unita(i)rien(ne *f*) *m*; unitaire *mf*; **2.** = **u·ni·tar·y** ['‿təri] unitaire; **u·nite** [ju:'nait] (s')unir; (se)réunir; (se) joindre (à, *with*); ♀d *Kingdom* Royaume-Uni *m*; ♀d *Nations Organisation* Organisation *f* des Nations Unies; ♀d *States pl.* États-Unis *m/pl.* (d'Amérique); **u·ni·ty** ['‿niti] unité *f*.

u·ni·ver·sal □ [ju:ni'vɔ:səl] universel(le *f*); ~ *legatee* légataire *m* universel; ⊕ ~ *joint* joint *m* brisé *ou* de cardan; ~ *language* langue *f* universelle; ♀ *Postal Union* Union *f* Postale Universelle; ~ *suffrage* suffrage *m* universel; **u·ni·ver·sal·i·ty** [‿'sæliti] universalité *f*; **u·ni·verse** ['‿vɔ:s] univers *m*; **u·ni·ver·si·ty** [‿'vɔ:siti] université *f*.

un·just □ ['ʌn'dʒʌst] injuste (avec, envers, pour *to*); **un·jus·ti·fi·a·ble** □ [ʌn'dʒʌstifaiəbl] injustifiable; inexcusable.

un·kempt ['ʌn'kempt] mal peigné; *fig.* mal *ou* peu soigné; mal tenu.

un·kind □ [ʌn'kaind] dur, cruel (-le *f*); peu aimable.

un·knot ['ʌn'nɔt] dénouer.

un·know·ing □ ['ʌn'nouiŋ] ignorant; inconscient (de, *of*); **'un·'known 1.** inconnu (de, à *to*); *adv.* ~ *to me* à mon insu; **2.** inconnu *m*; *personne:* inconnu(e *f*) *m*; ♀ inconnue *f*.

un·lace ['ʌn'leis] délacer, défaire.

un·lade ['ʌn'leid] [*irr.* (*lade*)] décharger (*a.* ⚓); *fig.* délester.

un·la·dy·like ['ʌn'leidilaik] peu distingué; vulgaire.

un·laid ['ʌn'leid] détordu (*câble*); non posé (*tapis*); non mis (*couvert, table*). [regretté.)

un·la·ment·ed ['ʌnlə'mentid] non)

un·latch ['ʌn'lætʃ] lever le loquet de; ouvrir.

un·law·ful □ ['ʌn'lɔ:ful] illégal (-aux *m/pl.*); contraire à la loi; illicite; *p.ext.* illégitime.

un·learn ['ʌn'lə:n] désapprendre; **'un·'learn·ed** □ [‿id] ignorant; illettré; peu versé (dans, *in*).

un·leash ['ʌn'li:ʃ] découpler, lâcher; *fig.* déchaîner; détacher.

un·leav·ened [ˈʌnˈlevnd] sans levain, azyme.

un·less [ənˈles] **1.** *cj.* à moins que (*sbj.*); à moins de (*inf.*); si ... ne ... pas; **2.** *prp.* sauf, excepté.

un·let·tered [ˈʌnˈletəd] illettré.

un·li·censed [ˈʌnˈlaisənst] non autorisé; sans brevet.

un·like □ [ˈʌnˈlaik] différent (de q., [*to*] s.o.); dissemblable; à la différence de; **un'like·li·hood** improbabilité *f*; **un'like·ly** invraisemblable, improbable.

un·lim·it·ed [ʌnˈlimitid] illimité; sans bornes (*a. fig.*).

un·link [ˈʌnˈliŋk] défaire, détacher; ~ *hands* se lâcher.

un·load [ˈʌnˈloud] décharger (*un bateau, une voiture, une cargaison*; *a. une arme à feu*; *a. phot.*); ✝ se décharger de; *fig.* ~ *one's heart* épancher son cœur, se soulager.

un·lock [ˈʌnˈlɔk] ouvrir; tourner la clef dans; débloquer (*une roue*); *mot.* déverrouiller (*la direction*).

un·looked-for [ʌnˈluktfɔ:] imprévu; inattendu.   [faire.

un·loose(n) [ˈʌnˈlu:s(n)] lâcher; dé-

un·lov·a·ble [ˈʌnˈlʌvəbl] peu aimable *ou* sympathique; **'un'love·ly** sans charme; laid; **'un'lov·ing** □ froid; peu affectueux (-euse *f*).

un·luck·y □ [ʌnˈlʌki] malheureux (-euse *f*).

un·make [ˈʌnˈmeik] [*irr.* (*make*)] défaire (*qch., un roi, etc.*); perdre (*q.*), causer la ruine de (*q.*).

un·man [ˈʌnˈmæn] amollir (*une nation*); attendrir; *fig.* décourager.

un·man·age·a·ble □ [ʌnˈmænidʒəbl] intraitable; indocile; difficile à manier; difficile à diriger (*entreprise*).

un·man·ly [ˈʌnˈmænli] efféminé; indigne d'un homme.

un·man·ner·ly [ʌnˈmænəli] sans savoir-vivre; impoli, mal élevé.

un·mar·ried [ˈʌnˈmærid] célibataire; non marié.

un·mask [ˈʌnˈmɑ:sk] (se) démasquer; *v/t. fig.* dévoiler.

un·matched [ˈʌnˈmætʃt] incomparable; désassorti.

un·mean·ing □ [ʌnˈmi:niŋ] vide de sens; **un·meant** [ˈʌnˈment] involontaire; fait sans intention.

un·meas·ured [ʌnˈmeʒəd] non mesuré; *fig.* infini.

un·men·tion·a·ble [ʌnˈmenʃnəbl] **1.** dont il ne faut pas parler; qu'il ne faut pas prononcer; **2.** F the ~s *pl.* le pantalon *m.*

un·mer·ci·ful □ [ʌnˈmə:siful] impitoyable.

un·mer·it·ed [ʌnˈmeritid] immérité.

un·mind·ful □ [ʌnˈmaindful] négligent (*personne*); ~ *of* oublieux (-euse *f*) de; sans penser à.

un·mis·tak·a·ble □ [ˈʌnmisˈteikəbl] clair; qui ne prête à aucune erreur; facilement reconnaissable.

un·mit·i·gat·ed [ʌnˈmitigeitid] non mitigé; *fig.* parfait; véritable.

un·mo·lest·ed [ˈʌnmoˈlestid] sans être molesté; sans empêchement.

un·moor [ˈʌnˈmuə] dé(sa)marrer; désaffourcher.

un·mort·gaged [ˈʌnˈmɔ:gidʒd] libre d'hypothèques.

un·mount·ed [ˈʌnˈmauntid] non monté; non serti (*pierre précieuse*); non encadré (*photo etc.*); ✄ à pied.

un·moved □ [ˈʌnˈmu:vd] toujours en place; *fig.* impassible.

un·mu·si·cal □ [ˈʌnˈmju:zikl] peu mélodieux (-euse *f*); peu musical (-aux *m/pl.*); qui n'aime pas la musique (*personne*).

un·muz·zle [ˈʌnˈmʌzl] démuseler (*a. fig.*); ~d *a.* sans muselière.

un·named [ˈʌnˈneimd] anonyme.

un·nat·u·ral □ [ʌnˈnætʃrl] non naturel(le *f*); anormal (-aux *m/pl.*); forcé; dénaturé (*père etc.*).

un·nec·es·sar·y □ [ʌnˈnesisəri] superflu.

un·neigh·bo(u)r·ly [ˈʌnˈneibəli] de mauvais voisin; peu obligeant.

un·nerve [ˈʌnˈnə:v] effrayer; faire perdre son courage (*etc.*) à (*q.*).

un·no·ticed [ˈʌnˈnoutist] inaperçu.

un·num·bered [ˈʌnˈnʌmbəd] non numéroté; *poét.* innombrable.

un·ob·jec·tion·a·ble □ [ˈʌnəbˈdʒekʃnəbl] irréprochable.

un·ob·serv·ant □ [ˈʌnəbˈzə:vənt] peu observateur (-trice *f*); be ~ *of* ne pas faire attention à; faire peu de cas de; **'un·ob'served** □ inaperçu, inobservé.

un·ob·tru·sive □ [ˈʌnəbˈtru:siv] modeste; discret (-ète *f*).

un·oc·cu·pied [ˈʌnˈɔkjupaid] inoccupé; oisif (-ive *f*); inhabité; libre.

un·of·fend·ing [ˈʌnəˈfendiŋ] innocent.

un·of·fi·cial □ [ˈʌnəˈfiʃl] officieux
(-euse *f*); non confirmé.

un·op·posed [ˈʌnəˈpouzd] sans opposition; *pol.* unique (*candidat*).

un·os·ten·ta·tious □ [ˈʌnɔstən-
ˈteiʃəs] simple; modeste; sans faste.

un·pack [ˈʌnˈpæk] déballer; défaire (*v*/*i.* sa valise *etc.*).

un·paid [ˈʌnˈpeid] impayé; sans
traitement; ✝ non acquitté; non
affranchi (*lettre*).

un·pal·at·a·ble [ʌnˈpælətəbl] désagréable (*au goût, a. fig.*).

un·par·al·leled [ʌnˈpærəleld] incomparable; sans égal (-aux *m*/*pl.*);
sans précédent.

un·par·don·a·ble □ [ʌnˈpɑːdnəbl]
impardonnable.

un·par·lia·men·ta·ry □ [ˈʌnpɑːlə-
ˈmentəri] antiparlementaire; F
grossier (-ère *f*).

un·pa·tri·ot·ic [ˈʌnpætriˈɔtik] (~
ally) peu patriotique; peu patriote
(*personne*).

un·paved [ˈʌnˈpeivd] non pavé.

un·peo·ple [ˈʌnˈpiːpl] dépeupler.

un·per·ceived □ [ˈʌnpəˈsiːvd] inaperçu; non ressenti.

un·per·formed [ˈʌnpəˈfɔːmd] in-
exécuté (*a.* ♪); ♪, *théâ.* non joué.

un·phil·o·soph·i·cal □ [ˈʌnfilə-
ˈsɔfikl] peu philosophique.

un·picked [ˈʌnˈpikt] non trié; non
cueilli (*fruit*).

un·pin [ˈʌnˈpin] enlever les épingles
de; défaire; ⊕ dégoupiller.

un·pit·ied [ˈʌnˈpitid] sans être
plaint; que personne ne plaint.

un·placed [ˈʌnˈpleist] sans place;
turf: non placé; non classé.

un·pleas·ant □ [ʌnˈpleznt] désagréable; fâcheux (-euse *f*); **un'pleas-
ant·ness** caractère *m* désagréable;
fig. ennui *m*.

un·plumbed [ˈʌnˈplʌmd] insondé.

un·po·et·ic, un·po·et·i·cal □ [ˈʌn-
pouˈetik(l)] peu poétique.

un·po·lished [ˈʌnˈpɔliʃt] non poli;
non verni; *fig.* fruste.

un·pol·lut·ed [ˈʌnpəˈluːtid] im-
pollué; pur.

un·pop·u·lar □ [ˈʌnˈpɔpjulə] impopulaire; mal vu; **un·pop·u·lar-
i·ty** [ˈ~ˈlæriti] impopularité *f*.

un·prac·ti·cal □ [ˈʌnˈpræktikl] impraticable; peu pratique (*personne*);

un'prac·ticed, un'prac·tised [~ˈ
tist] (*in*) inexercé (à, dans); peu
versé (dans).

un·prec·e·dent·ed □ [ʌnˈpresi-
dəntid] sans précédent; inouï.

un·prej·u·diced □ [ˈʌnˈpredʒudist]
sans préjugé; impartial (-aux
m/*pl.*).

un·pre·med·i·tat·ed □ [ˈʌnpri-
ˈmediteitid] impromptu; spontané;
ɡ'ɡ non prémédité.

un·pre·pared □ [ˈʌnpriˈpɛəd]; *adv.*
~ridli] non préparé; au dépourvu;
improvisé (*discours*).

un·pre·pos·sess·ing [ˈʌnpriːpə-
ˈzesiŋ] peu engageant.

un·pre·sent·a·ble [ˈʌnpriˈzentəbl]
peu présentable.

un·pre·tend·ing □ [ˈʌnpriˈtendiŋ],
un'pre·ten·tious □ sans prétention.

un·prin·ci·pled [ˈʌnˈprinsəpld]
sans principes; improbe.

un·pro·duc·tive □ [ˈʌnprəˈdʌktiv]
improductif (-ive *f*); stérile; ✝
dormant (*capital*); be ~ of ne pas
produire (*qch.*).

un·pro·fes·sion·al □ [ˈʌnprəˈfeʃənl]
contraire aux usages du métier;
sp. amateur.

un·prof·it·a·ble □ [ʌnˈprɔfitəbl]
improfitable; inutile; ingrat; **un-
'prof·it·a·ble·ness** inutilité *f*.

un·prom·is·ing □ [ˈʌnˈprɔmisiŋ]
qui promet peu; qui s'annonce mal
(*temps*).

un·pro·nounce·a·ble □ [ˈʌnprə-
ˈnaunsəbl] imprononçable.

un·pro·pi·tious □ [ˈʌnprəˈpiʃəs]
impropice; peu favorable (à, *to*).

un·pro·tect·ed □ [ˈʌnprəˈtektid]
sans défense; ⊕ exposé.

un·proved [ˈʌnˈpruːvd] non prouvé.

un·pro·vid·ed [ˈʌnprəˈvaidid] non
fourni; dépourvu (de, *with*); **'un-
pro'vid·ed-for** imprévu; non pré-
vu; (laissé) sans ressources (*personne*).

un·pro·voked □ [ˈʌnprəˈvoukt]
non provoqué; gratuit.

un·pub·lished [ˈʌnˈpʌbliʃt] non
publié; inédit.

un·punc·tual □ [ˈʌnˈpʌŋktjuəl]
inexact; en retard; **un·punc·tu·al-
i·ty** [ˈ~ˈæliti] inexactitude *f*.

un·pun·ished □ [ˈʌnˈpʌniʃt] impuni;
go ~ rester impuni; échapper à la
punition (*personne*).

unripe

un·qual·i·fied □ [ʌnˈkwɔlifaid] incompétent; sans diplôme; *fig.* absolu, sans réserve; F achevé, fieffé (*menteur etc.*).
un·quench·a·ble □ [ʌnˈkwentʃəbl] inextinguible; *fig.* inassouvissable.
un·ques·tion·a·ble □ [ʌnˈkwestʃənəbl] incontestable; indiscutable; un'ques·tioned incontesté; indiscuté; un'ques·tion·ing □ *fig.* aveugle.
un·quote [ˈʌnˈkwout] fermer les guillemets; un'quot·ed *Bourse:* non coté.
un·rav·el [ʌnˈrævl] (s')effiler; (se) défaire; (s')éclaircir; *v/t.* dénouer (*une intrigue*).
un·read [ˈʌnˈred] non lu; illettré (*personne*); un·read·a·ble [ˈʌnˈriːdəbl] illisible.
un·read·i·ness [ˈʌnˈredinis] manque *m* de préparation *ou* promptitude; ˈun'read·y □: be ~ ne pas être prêt *ou* prompt, être peu disposé (à qch., for s.th.; à *inf.*, to *inf.*); *attr.* hésitant.
un·re·al □ [ˈʌnˈriəl] irréel(le *f*); un·re·al·is·tic [ˈʌnriəˈlistik] peu réaliste; peu pratique.
un·rea·son [ˈʌnˈriːzn] déraison *f*; un'rea·son·a·ble □ déraisonnable; exorbitant; indu; *a.* exigeant (*personne*).
un·re·claimed [ˈʌnriˈkleimd] non réformé; indéfriché (*terrain*).
un·rec·og·niz·a·ble □ [ˈʌnˈrekəgnaizəbl] méconnaissable; ˈun'rec·og·nized non reconnu; méconnu (*génie etc.*). [réconcilié.]
un·rec·on·ciled [ˈʌnˈrekənsaild] ir-∫
un·re·cord·ed [ˈʌnriˈkɔːdid] non enregistré (*a. ♪*).
un·re·deemed □ [ˈʌnriˈdiːmd] non racheté *ou* récompensé (par, by); inaccompli (*promesse*); ✝ non remboursé *ou* amorti.
un·re·dressed [ˈʌnriˈdrest] non redressé.
un·reel [ˈʌnˈriːl] (se) découler.
un·re·fined [ˈʌnriˈfaind] non raffiné; brut; *fig.* grossier (-ère *f*); fruste.
un·re·formed [ˈʌnriˈfɔːmd] non réformé; qui ne s'est pas corrigé.
un·re·gard·ed [ˈʌnriˈɡɑːdid] négligé; ˈun're·gard·ful [~ful] (of) négligent (de); peu soigneux (-euse *f*) (de); inattentif (-ive *f*) (à).

un·reg·is·tered [ˈʌnˈredʒistəd] non enregistré, non inscrit; non déposé (*marque*); non recommandé (*lettre*).
un·re·gret·ted [ˈʌnriˈɡretid] (*mourir*) sans laisser de regrets.
un·re·lat·ed [ˈʌnriˈleitid] sans rapport (avec, to); non apparenté (*personne*).
un·re·lent·ing □ [ˈʌnriˈlentiŋ] implacable; acharné.
un·re·li·a·ble [ˈʌnriˈlaiəbl] sur lequel on ne peut pas compter.
un·re·lieved □ [ˈʌnriˈliːvd] non soulagé; sans secours; monotone.
un·re·mit·ting □ [ˈʌnriˈmitiŋ] ininterrompu; soutenu.
un·re·mu·ner·a·tive □ [ˈʌnriˈmjuː-nərətiv] peu rémunérateur (-trice *f*).
un·re·pealed [ˈʌnriˈpiːld] irrévoqué; encore en vigueur; non abrogé.
un·re·pent·ed [ˈʌnriˈpentid] non regretté.
un·re·quit·ed [ˈʌnriˈkwaitid] non récompensé; non partagé (*sentiment*).
un·re·sent·ed [ˈʌnriˈzentid] dont on ne se froisse pas.
un·re·served □ [ˈʌnriˈzəːvd] *adv.* ~vidli] sans réserve; franc(he *f*); entier (-ère *f*); non réservé (*place*).
un·re·sist·ing □ [ˈʌnriˈzistiŋ] docile; qui ne résiste pas; mou (mol *devant une voyelle ou un h muet*; molle *f*); souple.
un·re·spon·sive [ˈʌnrisˈpɔnsiv] froid; peu sensible (à, to).
un·rest [ˈʌnˈrest] inquiétude *f*; malaise *m*; *pol.* agitation *f*; *pol. etc.* mécontentement *m*.
un·re·strained □ [ˈʌnrisˈtreind] non restreint; effréné; immodéré.
un·re·strict·ed □ [ˈʌnrisˈtriktid] absolu; sans restriction.
un·re·vealed [ˈʌnriˈviːld] non divulgué; caché.
un·re·ward·ed [ˈʌnriˈwɔːdid] sans récompense; non récompensé.
un·rhymed [ˈʌnˈraimd] sans rime(s); ~ *verse vers m/pl.* blancs.
un·rid·dle [ˈʌnˈridl] résoudre.
un·rig ⚓ [ˈʌnˈrig] dégréer; dégarnir.
un·right·eous □ [ʌnˈraitʃəs] impie; injuste.
un·rip [ˈʌnˈrip] découdre; ouvrir en déchirant.
un·ripe [ˈʌnˈraip] vert; *fig.* pas encore mûr.

un·ri·val(l)ed [ʌnˈraivəld] sans pareil(le *f*); incomparable.

un·roll [ˈʌnˈroul] (se) dérouler.

un·rope *alp.* [ˈʌnˈroup] détacher la corde.

un·ruf·fled [ˈʌnˈrʌfld] calme (*personne, mer*); serein (*a. personne*).

un·ruled [ˈʌnˈruːld] non gouverné; *fig.* sans frein; sans lignes (*papier*).

un·rul·y [ʌnˈruːli] indiscipliné, mutin; *fig.* déréglé; fougueux (-euse *f*) (*cheval*).

un·sad·dle [ˈʌnˈsædl] desseller (*un cheval*); désarçonner (*un cavalier*).

un·safe □ [ˈʌnˈseif] dangereux (-euse *f*); † véreux (-euse *f*).

un·said [ʌnˈsed] non prononcé; *leave* ~ passer sous silence.

un·sal·a·ried [ˈʌnˈsælərid] non rémunéré.

un·sal(e)·a·ble [ˈʌnˈseiləbl] invendable.

un·sanc·tioned [ˈʌnˈsæŋkʃnd] non autorisé; non ratifié.

un·san·i·tar·y [ˈʌnˈsænitəri] non hygiénique; insalubre.

un·sat·is·fac·to·ry □ [ˈʌnsætisˈfæktəri], **'un·sat·is·fy·ing** □ [~faiiŋ] peu satisfaisant; défectueux (-euse *f*).

un·sa·vo(u)r·y □ [ˈʌnˈseivəri] désagréable; *fig.* répugnant; vilain.

un·say [ˈʌnˈsei] (*irr.* (*say*)) rétracter, se dédire de.

un·scathed [ˈʌnˈskeiðd] indemne; sans dommage *ou* blessure.

un·schooled [ˈʌnˈskuːld] illettré; spontané; peu habitué (à, *to*).

un·sci·en·tif·ic [ˈʌnsaiənˈtifik] (~ally) peu *ou* non scientifique.

un·screw [ˈʌnˈskruː] (se) dévisser.

un·scru·pu·lous □ [ʌnˈskruːpjuləs] sans scrupules.

un·seal [ˈʌnˈsiːl] décacheter (*une lettre*); *fig.* dessiller (les yeux à q., *s.o.'s eyes*).

un·search·a·ble □ [ʌnˈsəːtʃəbl] inscrutable.

un·sea·son·a·ble □ [ʌnˈsiːznəbl] hors de saison; *fig.* inopportun; ~ *weather* temps *m* qui n'est pas de saison; **'un·sea·soned** vert (*bois*); *cuis.* non assaisonné; *fig.* non acclimaté.

un·seat [ˈʌnˈsiːt] désarçonner (*un cavalier*); *parl.* faire perdre son siège à; invalider; **'un·seat·ed** sans chaise; *parl.* non réélu.

un·sea·wor·thy ⚓ [ˈʌnˈsiːwəːði] incapable de tenir la mer; ⚓ innavigable.

un·see·ing *fig.* [ˈʌnˈsiːiŋ] aveugle.

un·seem·li·ness [ʌnˈsiːmlinis] inconvenance *f*; **'un·seem·ly** *adj.* inconvenant; peu convenable.

un·seen [ˈʌnˈsiːn] 1. inaperçu, invisible; 2. *l'*autre monde *m*; *le* surnaturel *m*; *école:* (*a.* ~ *translation*) version *f* à livre ouvert.

un·self·ish □ [ˈʌnˈselfiʃ] sans égoïsme; désintéressé; dévoué.

un·sen·ti·men·tal [ˈʌnsentiˈmentl] peu sentimental (-aux *m/pl.*).

un·serv·ice·a·ble □ [ˈʌnˈsəːvisəbl] inutilisable; peu pratique.

un·set·tle [ˈʌnˈsetl] déranger; troubler le repos de (*q.*); ébranler (*les convictions*); **'un·set·tled** dérangé; troublé (*pays etc.*); variable (*temps*); incertain; inquiet (-ète *f*) (*esprit*); † non réglé, impayé; indécis (*question, esprit*); sans domicile fixe; non colonisé (*pays*).

un·shack·le [ˈʌnˈʃækl] ôter les fers à; ⚓ détalinguer (*l'ancre*).

un·shak(e)·a·ble [ˈʌnˈʃeikəbl] inébranlable.

un·shak·en [ˈʌnˈʃeikn] ferme; constant.

un·shape·ly [ˈʌnˈʃeipli] difforme; informe.

un·shav·en [ˈʌnˈʃeivn] non rasé.

un·sheathe [ˈʌnˈʃiːð] dégainer.

un·ship [ˈʌnˈʃip] décharger (*a.* F *fig.*).

un·shod [ˈʌnˈʃɔd] nu-pieds *adj./inv.*; sans fers, déferré (*cheval*).

un·shorn [ˈʌnˈʃɔːn] non tondu; *poét.* non coupé, non rasé.

un·shrink·a·ble *tex.* [ˈʌnˈʃriŋkəbl] irrétrécissable; **'un·shrink·ing** □ qui ne bronche pas.

un·sight·ed [ˈʌnˈsaitid] inaperçu; sans hausse (*arme à feu*); **un·sight·ly** laid.

un·signed [ˈʌnˈsaind] sans signature.

un·sized [ˈʌnˈsaizd] sans colle (*papier*).

un·skil(l)·ful □ [ˈʌnˈskilful] inhabile (à *at, in*); **'un·skilled** inexpérimenté (à, *in*); ~ *work* main-d'œuvre (*pl.* mains-d'œuvre) *f* non spécialisée; ~ *worker* manœuvre *m*.

un·skimmed [ˈʌnˈskimd] non écrémé.

un·so·cia·ble [ʌn'souʃəbl] farouche; sauvage; **un'so·cial** [~ʃl] insocial (-aux *m/pl.*); *a. see* unsociable.

un·sold [ʌn'sould] invendu.

un·sol·dier·ly [ʌn'souldʒəli] *adj.* peu militaire.

un·so·lic·it·ed [ʌnsə'lisitid] spontané; non sollicité.

un·solv·a·ble [ʌn'sɔlvəbl] insoluble; **'un'solved** non résolu.

un·so·phis·ti·cat·ed [ʌnsə'fistikeitid] pur; non adultéré; candide, ingénu (*personne*).

un·sought [ʌn'sɔːt] **1.** *adj.* non (re)cherché; **2.** *adv.* spontanément.

un·sound □ [ʌn'saund] peu solide; véreux (-euse *f*); malsain (*personne*); taré (*cheval*); gâté (*pomme etc.*); défectueux (-euse *f*); faux (fausse *f*) (*opinion, doctrine, etc.*); *of* ~ *mind* non sain d'esprit.

un·spar·ing □ [ʌn'spɛəriŋ] libéral (-aux *m/pl.*); prodigue (de *of, in*); impitoyable (pour q., *of s.o.*).

un·speak·a·ble □ [ʌn'spiːkəbl] indicible; inexprimable; F *fig.* ignoble.

un·spec·i·fied [ʌn'spesifaid] non spécifié.   [*fig.* inépuisé.⟩

un·spent [ʌn'spent] non dépensé;⟩

un·spo·ken [ʌn'spoukn] non dit; (*a.* **'un'spo·ken-of**) dont on ne fait pas mention.

un·sports·man·like [ʌn'spɔːtsmənlaik] indigne d'un sportsman; peu loyal (-aux *m/pl.*).

un·spot·ted [ʌn'spɔtid] non tacheté; *fig.* sans tache.

un·sta·ble □ [ʌn'steibl] instable; peu sûr; inconstant; ✝ peu solide.

un·stamped [ʌn'stæmpt] non estampé (*papier*); sans timbre, non affranchi (*lettre*).

un·stead·y □ [ʌn'stedi] peu stable; peu solide; irrésolu; chancelant (*pas*); mal assuré (*voix*); *fig.* déréglé (*personne*); irrégulier (-ère *f*).

un·stint·ed [ʌn'stintid] abondant; à discrétion.

un·stitch [ʌn'stitʃ] découdre.

un·stop [ʌn'stɔp] déboucher.

un·strained [ʌn'streind] non filtré (*liquide*); non tendu (*corde etc.*); *fig.* non forcé, naturel(le *f*).

un·stressed [ʌn'strest] inaccentué; *gramm.* atone.

un·string [ʌn'striŋ] [*irr.* (*string*)] déficeler; détraquer (*les nerfs*); dé-(sen)filer (*des perles etc.*).

un·stud·ied [ʌn'stʌdid] naturel(le *f*); ignorant (de, *in*).

un·sub·mis·sive □ [ʌnsəb'misiv] insoumis, indocile.

un·sub·stan·tial □ [ʌnsəb'stænʃl] insubstantiel(le *f*); immatériel(le *f*); sans substance; chimérique.

un·suc·cess·ful □ [ʌnsək'sesful] non réussi; qui n'a pas réussi (*personne*); *pol.* non élu.

un·suit·a·ble □ [ʌn'sjuːtəbl] impropre (à *for, to*); déplacé; mal assorti (*mariage*); peu fait (pour *for, to*) (*personne*); **'un'suit·ed** (*for, to*) mal adapté (à); peu fait (pour) (*personne*).

un·sul·lied [ʌn'sʌlid] immaculé.

un·sure [ʌn'ʃuə] peu sûr; peu solide.

un·sus·pect·ed [ʌnsəs'pektid] insoupçonné (de, *by*); non suspect; **'un'sus'pect·ing** qui ne se doute de rien; sans soupçons; sans défiance.

un·sus·pi·cious □ [ʌnsəs'piʃəs] qui ne suscite pas de soupçons; *be* ~ *of* ne pas se douter de.

un·swerv·ing □ [ʌn'swəːviŋ] constant.

un·sworn [ʌn'swɔːn] qui n'a pas prêté serment.

un·taint·ed □ [ʌn'teintid] pur, non corrompu (*a. fig.*); *fig.* sans tache (*réputation*).

un·tam(e)·a·ble [ʌn'teiməbl] inapprivoisable; *fig.* indomptable; **'un·tamed** inapprivoisé; *fig.* indompté.

un·tar·nished [ʌn'taːniʃt] non terni (*a. fig.*); sans tache.

un·tast·ed [ʌn'teistid] non goûté.

un·taught [ʌn'tɔːt] illettré (*personne*); naturel(le *f*); non enseigné.

un·taxed [ʌn'tækst] exempt(é) d'impôts *ou* de taxes.

un·teach·a·ble [ʌn'tiːtʃəbl] incapable d'apprendre (*personne*); non enseignable (*chose*).

un·tem·pered [ʌn'tempəd] ⊕ détrempé; *fig.* non adouci (de, *with*).

un·ten·a·ble [ʌn'tenəbl] intenable (*position*); insoutenable (*opinion etc.*).

un·ten·ant·ed [ʌn'tenəntid] inoccupé; vide; sans locataire.

un·thank·ful □ [ʌn'θæŋkful] ingrat.

un·think·a·ble [ʌn'θiŋkəbl] inconcevable; un'think·ing ☐ irréfléchi; étourdi.

un·thought ['ʌn'θɔːt], un'thought-of oublié; imprévu (*événement*).

un·thread ['ʌn'θred] dé(sen)filer; *fig.* trouver la sortie de.

un·thrift·y ☐ ['ʌn'θrifti] dépensier (-ère *f*); malvenant (*arbre*).

un·ti·dy ☐ [ʌn'taidi] en désordre; négligé; mal peigné (*cheveux*).

un·tie ['ʌn'tai] dénouer; délier (*q.*, *qch.*, *un nœud*).

un·til [ən'til] 1. *prp.* jusqu'à; 2. *cj.* jusqu'à ce que; jusqu'au moment où.

un·tilled ['ʌntild] inculte; en friche.

un·time·ly [ʌn'taimli] prématuré; inopportun; mal à propos.

un·tir·ing ☐ [ʌn'taiəriŋ] infatigable.

un·to ['ʌntu] *see to 1*.

un·told ['ʌn'tould] non raconté (*incident etc.*); non compté; *fig.* immense.

un·touched ['ʌn'tʌtʃt] non manié; *fig.* intact; *fig.* indifférent; *phot.* non retouché.

un·trained ['ʌn'treind] inexpérimenté; inexpert; non dressé (*chien etc.*); non formé.

un·trans·fer·a·ble ['ʌntræns'fəːrəbl] intransférable; strictement personnel(le *f*) (*billet*); ⚖ inaliénable.

un·trans·lat·a·ble ['ʌntræns'leitəbl] intraduisible.

un·trav·el(l)ed ['ʌn'trævld] inexploré; qui n'a jamais voyagé (*personne*).

un·tried ['ʌn'traid] inessayé; jamais mis à l'épreuve; ⚖ pas encore jugé (*cause*); pas encore passé en jugement (*détenu*).

un·trimmed ['ʌn'trimd] non arrangé; non taillé (*haie*); ⊕, *a. cuis.* non paré; sans garniture (*robe etc.*).

un·trod·den ['ʌn'trɔdn] non frayé; inexploré.

un·trou·bled ['ʌn'trʌbld] non troublé; calme.

un·true ☐ ['ʌn'truː] faux (fausse *f*); infidèle (*personne*).

un·trust·wor·thy ☐ ['ʌn'trʌstwəːði] douteux (-euse *f*); faux (fausse *f*).

un·truth ['ʌn'truːθ] fausseté *f*; mensonge *m*.

un·tu·tored ['ʌn'tjuːtəd] illettré; naturel(le *f*).

un·twine ['ʌn'twain], un·twist ['ʌn'twist] (se) détordre, détortiller.

un·used ['ʌn'juːzd] inutilisé; neuf (neuve *f*); ['ʌn'juːst] peu habitué (à, *to*); un·u·su·al ☐ [ʌn'juːʒuəl] extraordinaire; peu commun.

un·ut·ter·a·ble ☐ [ʌn'ʌtərəbl] indicible; imprononçable (*mot*).

un·val·ued ['ʌn'væljuːd] non *ou* peu estimé (*personne*).

un·var·ied [ʌn'vɛərid] peu varié; uniforme.

un·var·nished ['ʌn'vɑːniʃt] non verni; *fig.* simple.

un·var·y·ing ☐ [ʌn'vɛəriiŋ] invariable.

un·veil ['ʌn'veil] (se) dévoiler.

un·versed ['ʌn'vəːst] ignorant (de, *in*); peu versé (dans, *in*).

un·voiced ['ʌn'vɔist] non exprimé; *gramm.* sourd (*consonne etc.*), muet(te *f*).

un·vouched ['ʌn'vautʃt], *usu.* un·vouched-for [ʌn'vautʃtfɔː] non garanti.

un·want·ed ['ʌn'wɔntid] non voulu; superflu.

un·war·i·ness [ʌn'wɛərinis] imprudence *f*.

un·war·rant·a·ble ☐ [ʌn'wɔrəntəbl] inexcusable; 'un'war·rant·ed injustifié; sans garantie.

un·war·y ☐ ['ʌn'wɛəri] imprudent.

un·wa·tered ['ʌn'wɔːtəd] sans eau; non arrosé (*jardin*); non dilué (*capital*). [tant; inébranlable.\
un·wa·ver·ing [ʌn'weivəriŋ] cons-⌡
un·wea·ry·ing ☐ [ʌn'wiəriiŋ] infatigable.

un·wel·come [ʌn'welkəm] importun; *fig.* fâcheux (-euse *f*).

un·well ['ʌn'wel] indisposé.

un·whole·some ['ʌn'houlsəm] malsain (*a. fig.*); insalubre.

un·wield·y ☐ [ʌn'wiːldi] peu maniable; encombrant (*colis*).

un·will·ing ☐ ['ʌn'wiliŋ] rétif (-ive *f*); fait *etc.* à contre-cœur; *be ~ to* (*inf.*) ne pas vouloir (*inf.*); *be ~ for s.th. to be done* ne pas vouloir que qch. soit faite.

un·wind ['ʌn'waind] [*irr.* (*wind*)] (se) dérouler; ⚓ *vt/i.* dévirer.

un·wis·dom ['ʌn'wizdəm] imprudence *f*; stupidité *f*; un·wise ☐ ['ʌn'waiz] imprudent; peu sage.

un·wished ['ʌn'wiʃt], *usu.* un·wished-for [ʌn'wiʃtfɔː] peu désiré.

un·wit·ting ☐ [ʌn'witiŋ] inconscient.

                                         uppish

un·wom·an·ly [ʌnˈwumənli] peu digne d'une femme.

un·wont·ed □ [ʌnˈwountid] inaccoutumé (à *inf.*, to *inf.*); insolite.

un·work·a·ble [ˈʌnˈwɔːkəbl] impraticable; ⚓ immaniable; ⊕ rebelle; inexploitable.

un·wor·thy □ [ʌnˈwɔːði] indigne.

un·wound·ed [ˈʌnˈwuːndid] non blessé; sans blessure.

un·wrap [ˈʌnˈræp] enlever l'enveloppe de; défaire (*un paquet*).

un·wrin·kle [ˈʌnˈriŋkl] (se) dérider.

un·writ·ten [ˈʌnˈritn] non écrit; coutumier (-ère *f*), oral (-aux *m/pl.*) (*droit*); blanc(he *f*) (*page*).

un·wrought [ˈʌnˈrɔːt] non travaillé; brut.

un·yield·ing □ [ʌnˈjiːldiŋ] qui ne cède pas; ferme.

un·yoke [ˈʌnˈjouk] dételer; découpler.

un·zip [ˈʌnˈzip] ouvrir la fermeture éclair de.

up [ʌp] **1.** *adv.* vers le haut; en montant; haut; en haut; en dessus; en l'air; debout; levé (*a. soleil etc.*); fini (*temps*); fermé (*fenêtre etc.*); ouvert (*fenêtre à guillotine, stores, etc.*); *Am.* baseball: à la batte; *sl.* be hard ~ être fauché (= *être à court d'argent*); be ~ against a task être aux prises avec une tâche; ~ to jusque, jusqu'à; *see* date² 1; be ~ to s.th. être à la hauteur de qch.; être capable de qch.; être occupé à faire qch.; *it is* ~ *to me* (*inf.*) c'est à moi de (*inf.*); *see* mark² 1; what are you ~ to there? qu'est-ce que vous faites *ou* mijotez?; *sl.* what's ~? qu'est-ce qu'il y a?; qu'est-ce qui se passe?; ~ with au niveau de; it's all ~ with him c'en est fait de lui; *sl.* il est fichu; **2.** *int.* en haut!; **3.** *prp.* au haut de; sans *ou* vers le haut de; ~ the hill en montant *ou* en haut de la colline; **4.** *adj.* ~ train train *m* en direction de la capitale; F train *m* de retour; **5.** *su.*: *Am.* F on the ~ and ~ honnête, en règle, loyal (-aux *m/pl.*); en bonne voie, en train de monter *ou* de s'améliorer; ~s *pl.* and downs *pl.* ondulations *f/pl.*; *fig.* vicissitudes *f/pl.* (*de la vie*); **6.** F *v/i.* se lever; *v/t.* (*a.* ~ with) lever.

up·and·com·ing *Am.* F [ˈʌpənˈkʌmiŋ] ambitieux (-euse *f*); qui promet; qui a de l'avenir.

up·beat ♪ [ˈʌpbiːt] levé *m*.

up·braid [ʌpˈbreid] reprocher (qch. à q., *s.o.* with *ou* for s.th.).

up·bring·ing [ˈʌpbriŋiŋ] éducation *f*.

up·cast [ˈʌpkɑːst] relèvement *m*; ⚒ (*a.* ~ shaft) puits *m* de retour.

up·com·ing *Am.* [ˈʌpkʌmiŋ] imminent.

up·coun·try **1.** [ˈʌpˈkʌntri] *adj.* de l'intérieur du pays; **2.** *adv.* [ʌpˈkʌntri] à l'intérieur du pays.

up·cur·rent ⚡ [ˈʌpkʌrənt] courant *m* d'air ascendant.

up·date [ʌpˈdeit] mettre à jour; moderniser.

up·end [ʌpˈend] mettre debout; *fig.* renverser (*l'adversaire etc.*).

up·grade [ˈʌpgreid] montée *f*; on the ~ *fig.* en bonne voie; ⚑ à la hausse.

up·heav·al [ʌpˈhiːvl] *géol.* soulèvement *m*; *fig.* bouleversement *m*, agitation *f*.

up·hill [ˈʌpˈhil] montant; *fig.* ardu.

up·hold [ʌpˈhould] [*irr.* (*hold*)] soutenir, maintenir; **upˈhold·er** partisan(e *f*) *m*.

up·hol·ster [ʌpˈhoulstə] tapisser, couvrir (*un meuble*) (de in, with); garnir (*une pièce*); **upˈhol·ster·er** tapissier *m*; **upˈhol·ster·y** tapisserie *f* d'ameublement; *meuble*: capitonnage *m*; *mot.* garniture *f*; *métier*: tapisserie *f*.

up·keep [ˈʌpkiːp] (frais *m/pl.* d')entretien *m*.

up·land [ˈʌplənd] **1.** *usu.* ~s *pl.* hautes terres *f/pl.*; **2.** des montagnes.

up·lift 1. [ʌpˈlift] soulever; élever (*a. fig.*); **2.** [ˈʌplift] élévation *f* (*a. fig.*); *géol.* soulèvement *m*; ⚑ reprise *f*.

up·on [əˈpɔn] *see* on.

up·per [ˈʌpə] **1.** plus haut; supérieur; the ~ class(es *pl.*) la haute société; F the ~ crust le gratin; get the ~ hand (of) prendre le dessus (sur); get the ~ hand of a. avoir raison de, venir à bout de; have the ~ hand avoir le dessus; the ~ ten (thousand) la haute société; **2.** *usu.* ~s *pl.* empeignes *f/pl.*; *bottes*: tiges *f/pl.*; '~-ˈcase let·ter *typ.* majuscule *m*; '~-ˈclass aristocratique; '~-cut *box.* uppercut *m*; '~-most le plus haut; principal.

up·pish □ [ˈʌpiʃ] arrogant.

up·pi·ty *Am.* F [ˈʌpiti] suffisant; arrogant.

up·raise [ʌpˈreiz] (sou)lever, élever.

up·rear [ʌpˈriə] dresser.

up·right 1. □ [ˈʌpˈrait] vertical (-aux *m/pl.*); droit (*a. fig.*); debout; *fig.* [ˈʌprait] juste, intègre; **2.** [ʌ] montant *m*; piano *m* droit; *out of* ʌ hors d'aplomb.

up·ris·ing [ʌpˈraiziŋ] lever *m*; insurrection *f*.

up·roar [ˈʌprɔ:] *fig.* tapage *m*, vacarme *m*; tumulte *m*; **upˈroar·i·ous** □ tumultueux (-euse *f*); tapageur (-euse *f*).   [racher.)

up·root [ʌpˈru:t] déraciner; ar-)

up·set [ʌpˈset] **1.** [*irr.* (set)] renverser; bouleverser (*a. fig.*); déranger; *fig.* mettre (*q.*) en émoi; ⚕ indisposer, déranger; ⊕ refouler; **2.:** ʌ *price* mise *f* à prix, prix *m* de départ; **3.** renversement *m*; bouleversement *m*; désordre *m*.

up·shot [ˈʌpʃɔt] résultat *m*, dénouement *m*; *in the* ʌ à la fin.

up·side *adv.* [ˈʌpsaid]: ʌ *down* sens dessus dessous; à l'envers; *fig.* en désordre; *turn* ʌ *down* renverser; *fig.* bouleverser.

up·stage F [ˈʌpˈsteidʒ] **1.** orgueilleux (-euse *f*), arrogant, hautain; **2.** éclipser (*q.*); remettre (*q.*) à sa place.

up·stairs [ˈʌpˈstɛəz] **1.** *adv.* en haut; jusqu'en haut; **2.** *adj.* d'en haut.

up·start [ˈʌpstɑ:t] **1.** parvenu(e *f*) *m*; **2.** se lever brusquement.

up·state *Am.* [ˈʌpˈsteit] région *f* éloignée; *surt.* État *m* de New-York.

up·stream [ˈʌpˈstri:m] **1.** *adv.* en amont; en remontant le courant; **2.** *adj.* d'amont.   [*m*.)

up·stroke [ˈʌpstrouk] *écriture*: délié)

up·surge [ˈʌpˈsɜ:dʒ] soulèvement *m*; accès *m* (*de colère etc.*); poussée *f*.

up·swing [ˈʌpˈswiŋ] essor *m*; montée *f*.

up·take [ˈʌpteik] entendement *m*; F *be slow* (*quick*) *in* (*ou on*) *the* ʌ avoir la compréhension difficile (facile), saisir mal (vite).

up·throw [ˈʌpθrou] rejet *m* en haut.

up·tight F [ˈʌptait] crispé, tendu; nerveux (-euse *f*).

up-to-date [ˈʌptəˈdeit] moderne; au courant, à jour; à la page.

up-to-the-min·ute [ˈʌptəðəˈminit] le (la *f*) plus moderne; très récent; de dernière heure, dernier (-ière *f*).

up-town [ˈʌpˈtaun] **1.** *adv. Am.* dans le quartier résidentiel de la ville; **2.** *adj.* du quartier bourgeois.

up·turn [ʌpˈtə:n] **1.** lever; retourner; **2.** *Am.* reprise *f* des affaires.

up·ward [ˈʌpwəd] **1.** *adj.* montant; vers le haut; **2.** *adv.* (*ou* **up·wards** [ˈʌz]) de bas en haut; vers le haut; en dessus, au-dessus; ʌ *of* plus de.

u·ra·ni·um ⚗ [juəˈreinjəm] uranium *m*.

ur·ban [ˈə:bən] urbain; **ur·bane** □ [ə:ˈbein] courtois, poli; **ur·ban·i·ty** [ə:ˈbæniti] urbanité *f*; courtoisie *f*; politesse *f*; **ur·ban·i·za·tion** [ə:bənaiˈzeiʃn] aménagement *m* des agglomérations urbaines; **ˈur·ban·ize** urbaniser.

ur·chin [ˈə:tʃin] gamin *m*; gosse *mf*.

urge [ə:dʒ] **1.** pousser (*q.* à *inf.*, *s.o. to inf.*; *qch.*); (*souv.* ʌ *on*) encourager; hâter; *fig.* insister sur; mettre en avant; recommander (*qch.* à *q.*, *s.th. on s.o.*); **2.** impulsion *f*; forte envie *f*; **ur·gen·cy** [ˈʌɔnsi] urgence *f*; besoin *m* pressant; **ˈur·gent** □ urgent, pressant; *be* ʌ *with s.o. to* (*inf.*) insister pour que q. (*sbj.*).

u·ric ⚗ [ˈjuərik] urique.

u·ri·nal [ˈjuərinl] urinoir *m*; ⚕ urinal *m*; **ˈu·ri·nar·y** urinaire; **u·ri·nate** [ˈʌneit] uriner; **u·rine** [ˈʌrin] urine *f*.

urn [ə:n] urne *f*; (*usu. tea-*ʌ) samovar *m*.

us [ʌs; əs] *accusatif*, *datif*: nous.

us·a·ble [ˈju:zəbl] utilisable.

us·age [ˈju:zidʒ] usage *m* († de commerce); coutume *f*; emploi *m*; traitement *m*.

us·ance † [ˈju:zəns] usance *f*; *bill at* ʌ effet *m* à usance.

use 1. [ju:s] emploi *m* (*a.* ⚕); usage *m*; *fig.*, *a.* ⚖ jouissance *f*; coutume *f*, habitude *f*; utilité *f*; service *m*; *be of* ʌ être utile (à *for*, *to*); *it is* (*of*) *no* ʌ (*gér.*, *to inf.*) il est inutile (que *sbj.*); *inutile* (*de inf.*); *have no* ʌ *for* ne savoir que faire de (*qch.*); F ne pas pouvoir voir (*q.*); *put s.th. to* ʌ profiter de qch.; faire bon (mauvais) usage de qch.; **2.** [ju:z] employer; se servir de; ʌ *up* user, épuiser; *I* ʌ*d* [ˈju:s(t)] *to do* je faisais; j'avais l'habitude de faire; **used** [ˈju:st] habitué (à, to); [ˈju:zd] usé, usagé; usité; *a.* sale (*linge*); ʌ *car* auto *f* d'occasion; **useful** □ [ˈjuːsful] utile (*a.* ⊕); pratique; ~ *capacity,* ~ *efficiency* rendement *m ou* effet *m* utile; ~ *load* charge *f* utile; **ˈuse·ful·ness** utilité *f*; **ˈuse·less** □ inutile; inefficace; vain; **us·er** [ˈjuːzə] usager (-ère *f*) *m.*

ush·er [ˈʌʃə] **1.** huissier *m*; introducteur *m*; ⚖ audiencier *m*; *péj.* sous-maître *m*; maître *m* d'étude; **2.** (*usu.* ~ *in*) faire entrer, introduire; **ush·er·ette** *cin.* [~ˈret] ouvreuse *f.*

u·su·al □ [ˈjuːʒuəl] ordinaire; habituel(le *f*); ~ *in* (*the*) *trade* d'usage dans le métier.

u·su·fruct ⚖ [ˈjuːsjufrʌkt] usufruit *m*; **u·su·ˈfruc·tu·ar·y** [~juəri] **1.** usufruitier (-ère *f*) *m*; **2.** *adj.* usufructuaire (*droit*).

u·su·rer [ˈjuːʒərə] usurier *m*; **u·su·ri·ous** □ [juːˈzjuəriəs] usuraire; usurier (-ère *f*) (*personne*).

u·surp [juːˈzəːp] *vt/i.* usurper (*sur from, on*); *v/t.* voler (à, *from*); **u·sur·ˈpa·tion** usurpation *f*; **uˈsurp·ing** □ usurpateur (-trice *f*).

u·su·ry [ˈjuːʒuri] usure *f.*

u·ten·sil [juːˈtensl] ustensil *m*; outil *m*; ~*s pl.* articles *m/pl.*, ustensiles *m/pl.*

u·ter·ine [ˈjuːtərain] utérin; ~ *brother* frère *m* utérin *ou* de mère; **u·ter·us** *anat.* [ˈ~rəs], *pl.* **u·ter·i** [ˈ~tərai] utérus *m*, matrice *f.*

u·til·i·tar·i·an [juːtiliˈtɛəriən] utilitaire (*a. su./mf*); **uˈtil·i·ty 1.** utilité *f*; *public* ~ (entreprise *f* de) service *m* public; **2.** à toutes fins (*chariot etc.*).

u·ti·li·za·tion [juːtilaiˈzeiʃn] utilisation *f*; exploitation *f*; emploi *m*; **ˈu·ti·lize** utiliser, se servir de; tirer parti de, profiter de.

ut·most [ˈʌtmoust] **1.** extrême; **2.** dernier degré *m.*

U·to·pi·an [juːˈtoupjən] **1.** d'utopie; **2.** utopiste *mf*; idéaliste *mf.*

u·tri·cle *biol.* [ˈjuːtrikl] utricule *m.*

ut·ter [ˈʌtə] **1.** □ *fig.* absolu; extrême; complet (-ète *f*); **2.** dire, exprimer; pousser (*un gémissement etc.*); émettre (*de la monnaie*); **ˈut·ter·ance** expression *f*; émission *f*; prononciation *f*; ~*s pl.* propos *m/pl.*; *give* ~ *to* exprimer; **ˈut·ter·er** diseur (-euse *f*) *m*; débiteur (-euse *f*) *m* (*de nouvelles etc.*); émetteur *m* (*de monnaie*); **ut·ter·most** [ˈ~moust] extrême; dernier (-ère *f*).

U-turn [ˈjuːtəːn] *mot.* demi-tour *m*; *fig.* revirement *m*, volte-face *f/inv.*; *mot.* '*no* ~*s*' 'défense de faire demi-tour'.

u·vu·la *anat.* [ˈjuːvjulə] luette *f*; uvule *f*; **u·vu·lar** [~] uvulaire; ~ *R R m* vélaire.

ux·o·ri·ous [ʌkˈsɔːriəs] (extrêmement) dévoué à sa femme (*mari*).

V

V, v [vi:] V *m*, v *m*.

va·can·cy ['veikənsi] vide *m*; vacance *f*, poste *m* vacant; chambre *f* à louer; espace *m* vide; ~ *for* on cherche (*employé etc.*); *no vacancies travail*: pas d'embauche; *hotel*: complet; *gaze into* ~ regarder dans l'espace; **va·cant** □ ['∼kənt] vacant, libre; hébété (*air*), inoccupé (*esprit*).

va·cate [və'keit] quitter (*un emploi, un hôtel, un siège, etc.*); évacuer (*un appartement*); laisser libre; *v/i.* *Am. sl.* ficher le camp; **va·ca·tion 1.** *école, a. Am.*: vacances *f/pl.*; ⚖ vacations *f/pl.*; **2.** *surt. Am.* prendre des *ou* être en vacances; **va·ca·tion·ist** *Am.* vacancier *m*; estivant(e *f*) *m*.

vac·ci·nate ['væksineit] vacciner; **vac·ci·na·tion** vaccination *f*; **'vac·ci·na·tor** vaccinateur *m*; **vac·cine** ['∼si:n] **1.** vaccinal (-aux *m/pl.*); ~ *matter* = **2.** vaccin *m*.

vac·il·late ['væsileit] vaciller; hésiter; **vac·il·la·tion** vacillation *f*; hésitation *f*.

va·cu·i·ty [væ'kjuiti] vacuité *f*; vide *m* (*a. fig.*); **vac·u·ous** □ ['∼kjuəs] vide; *fig. usu.* bête; **vac·u·um** ['∼əm] *phys.* **1.** vide *m*, vacuum *m*; ~ *brake* frein *m* à vide; ~ *cleaner* aspirateur *m*; ~ *flask*, ~ *bottle* (bouteille *f*) Thermos *f*; ~ *tube* tube *m* à vide; *radio*: audion *m*; **2.** F nettoyer à l'aspirateur; **vac·u·um-packed** emballé sous vide.

va·de-me·cum ['veidi'mi:kəm] vade-mecum *m/inv.*

vag·a·bond ['vægəbɔnd] **1.** vagabond, errant; **2.** chemineau *m*; vagabond(e *f*) *m*; F vaurien *m*; **vag·a·bond·age** ['∼bɔndidʒ] vagabondage *m*.

va·gar·y ['veigəri] caprice *m*; fantaisie *f*.

va·gi·na *anat.* [və'dʒainə] vagin *m*.

va·gran·cy ['veigrənsi] vie *f* de vagabond; ⚖ vagabondage *m*; **'va·grant 1.** errant, vagabond (*a. fig.*); **2.** *see vagabond 2.*

vague □ [veig] vague; imprécis; estompé; indécis; *be* ~ ne rien préciser (*personne*).

vain □ [vein] vain; fier (-ère *f*) (de, *of*); inutile; mensonger (-ère *f*); vaniteux (-euse *f*); *in* ~ en vain; *do s.th. in* ~ avoir beau faire qch.; ~**glo·ri·ous** □ [∼'glɔ:riəs] vaniteux (-euse *f*); ~**glo·ry** vaine gloire *f*.

val·ance ['væləns] frange *f* *ou* tour *m* de lit.

vale [veil] *poét.*, *a. dans les noms propres*: vallée *f*, vallon *m*.

val·e·dic·tion [væli'dikʃn] adieu *m*, -x *m/pl.*; **val·e'dic·to·ry** [∼təri] **1.** d'adieu; **2.** discours *m* d'adieu.

va·lence ⚗ ['veiləns] valence *f*.

val·en·tine ['væləntain] carte *f* de salutations (envoyée à la Saint-valentin) (*le 14 février*); *fig. personne*: valentin(e *f*) *m*, amour *m*.

va·le·ri·an ⚘ [və'liəriən] valériane *f*.

val·et ['vælit] **1.** valet *m* de chambre; **2.** servir (*q.*) comme valet de chambre; remettre (*un costume*) en état.

val·e·tu·di·nar·i·an ['vælitju:di'nɛəriən] valétudinaire (*a. su./mf*).

val·iant □ ['væljənt] vaillant.

val·id □ ['vælid] valable, valide; bon (pour, *for*); irréfutable; **val·i·date** ['∼deit] rendre valable, valider; **va·lid·i·ty** [və'liditi] validité *f*; justesse *f* (*d'un argument*).

val·ley ['væli] vallée *f*; vallon *m*; △ cornière *f*.

val·or·i·za·tion [vælərai'zeiʃn] valorisation *f*; **'val·or·ize** valoriser.

val·or·ous □ *poét.* ['vælərəs] vaillant.

val·o(u)r *poét.* ['vælə] vaillance *f*.

val·u·a·ble ['væljuəbl] **1.** □ précieux (-euse *f*); **2.** ~s *pl.* objets *m/pl.* de valeur.

val·u·a·tion [vælju'eiʃn] évaluation *f*; valeur *f* estimée; inventaire *m*; **'val·u·a·tor** estimateur *m*.

val·ue ['vælju:] **1.** valeur *f*; prix *m* (*a. fig.*); ~ *judgement* jugement *m* de valeur; ♣ *get good* ~ (*for one's money*) en avoir pour son argent; **2.** évaluer;

estimer, priser (*a. fig.*); **ˈval·ue·less** sans valeur; **ˈval·u·er** estimateur (-euse *f*) *m*; expert *m*; commissaire-priseur *m* (*pl.* commissaires-priseurs).

valve [vælv] soupape *f*; *mot. pneu*: valve *f*; *anat.* valvule *f*; *radio*: lampe *f*; *radio*: ~ *amplifier, amplifying* ~ lampe *f* amplificatrice; ~ *set* poste *m* à lampes.

va·moose *Am. sl.* [vəˈmuːs] filer; ficher le camp; décamper.

vamp[1] [væmp] **1.** *souliers*: empeigne *f*; ♪ accompagnement *m* improvisé; **2.** *v/t.* remonter (*un soulier*); mettre une empeigne à; *v/i.* ♪ improviser; tapoter au piano.

vamp[2] F [~] **1.** vamp *f*; femme *f* fatale; flirteuse *f*; **2.** *v/t.* ensorceler; enjôler; *v/i.* flirter.

vam·pire [ˈvæmpaiə] vampire *m*.

van[1] [væn] fourgon *m* (de déménagement *etc.*); 🚃 wagon *m*; fourgon *m* à bagages.

van[2] ✕ *ou fig.* [~] avant-garde *f*.

Van·dal [ˈvændl] **1.** vandale *m*; **2.** (*a.* **Van·dal·ic** [~ˈdælik]) vandalique; **van·dal·ism** [ˈ~dəlizm] vandalisme *m*; **van·dal·ize** [ˈ~dəlaiz] saccager, mutiler.

van·dyke [vænˈdaik] barbe *f* à la Van Dyck; pointe *f* (*de col à la Van Dyck*); *attr.* ♀ à la Van Dyck.

vane [vein] (*a.* weather-~, wind-~) girouette *f*; ⊕ ailette *f*; *radio*: lamette *f*; *surv.* viseur *m* (*de compas*).

van·guard ✕ [ˈvænɡɑːd] (tête *f* d')avant-garde *f*.

va·nil·la ♀ [vəˈnilə] vanille *f*.

van·ish [ˈvæniʃ] disparaître; s'évanouir; ~*ing cream* crème *f* de jour.

van·i·ty [ˈvæniti] vanité *f*; orgueil *m*; ~ *bag* sac(oche *f*) *m* de dame; ~ *case* pochette-poudrier *f*.

van·quish *poét.* [ˈvæŋkwiʃ] vaincre; triompher de.

van·tage [ˈvɑːntidʒ] *tennis*: avantage *m*; **ˈ~-ground** position *f* avantageuse. [(*conversation*).]

vap·id □ [ˈvæpid] insipide; fade⟩

va·po(u)r·ize [ˈveipəraiz] (se) vaporiser; (se) pulvériser; **ˈva·po(u)r·iz·er** ⊕ vaporisateur *m* (*a.* ⚕).

va·por·ous □ [ˈveipərəs] vaporeux (-euse *f*) (*a. fig.*); *fig. a.* vague, nuageux (-euse *f*).

va·po(u)r [ˈveipə] **1.** vapeur *f* (*a. fig.*); ~ *bath* bain *m* de vapeur; ~ *trail*

traînée *f* de condensation; **2.** s'évaporer; *fig.* débiter des fadaises; **ˈva·po(u)r·y** *see vaporous*.

var·i·a·bil·i·ty [vɛəriəˈbiliti] variabilité *f*, inconstance *f*; **ˈvar·i·a·ble** □ variable, inconstant; **ˈvar·i·ance** variation *f*; divergence *f*, discorde *f*; *be at* ~ être en désaccord; avoir un différend; *set at* ~ mettre en désaccord; **ˈvar·i·ant 1.** différent (de, *from*); **2.** variante *f*; **var·i'a·tion** variation *f* (*a.* ♪); changement *m*; différence *f*, écart *m*; ⊕ ~ *of load* fluctuation *f* de charge.

var·i·cose ⚕ [ˈværikous] variqueux (-euse *f*); ~ *vein* varice *f*.

var·ied □ [ˈvɛərid] varié, divers; **var·i·e·gate** [ˈ~riɡeit] varier; barioler; **ˈvar·i·e·gat·ed** varié; bariolé, bigarré; ♀ *etc.* panaché; **var·i·e·'ga·tion** diversité *f* de couleurs; ♀ panachure *f*; **va·ri·e·ty** [vəˈraiəti] diversité *f*; variété *f* (*a. biol.*); ↑ assortiment *m*; *théâ.* F music-hall *m*; ~ *show* attractions *f/pl.*; (spectacle *m* de) music-hall *m*; ~ *theatre* théâtre *m* de variétés.

va·ri·o·la ⚕ [vəˈraiələ] variole *f*.

var·i·ous □ [ˈvɛəriəs] varié, divers; différent; plusieurs.

var·mint [ˈvɑːmint] *sl.* petit polisson *m*; *chasse*: renard *m*; vermine *f*.

var·nish [ˈvɑːniʃ] **1.** vernis *m* (*a. fig.*); vernissage *m*; **2.** vernir; vernisser; *fig.* farder, glisser sur.

var·si·ty F [ˈvɑːsiti] université *f*.

var·y [ˈvɛəri] *v/t.* (faire) varier; diversifier; ♪ varier (*un air*); *v/i.* varier, changer; être variable; s'écarter (de, *from*).

vas·cu·lar ♀, *anat.* [ˈvæskjulə] vasculaire.

vase [vɑːz] vase *m*.

vas·sal [ˈvæsl] vassal (-aux *m/pl.*) (*a. su.*); **ˈvas·sal·age** vassalité *f*, vasselage *m*; *fig.* sujétion *f*.

vast □ [vɑːst] vaste, immense; **ˈvast·ness** immensité *f*; vaste étendue *f*.

vat [væt] **1.** cuve *f*; (*petit*) cuveau *m*; bain *m*; **2.** mettre en cuve; encuver. **vat·ted** [ˈvætid] mis en cuve (*vin etc.*); en fût (*vin*).

vault[1] [vɔːlt] **1.** voûte *f* (*a. fig.*); *banque*: souterrain *m*; cave *f* (*à vin*); tombeau *m* (*de famille etc.*); **2.** (se) voûter.

vault² [~] **1.** *v/i.* sauter; *v/t.* (*ou* ~ *over*) sauter (*qch.*); **2.** saut *m.*

vault·ing △ ['vɔːltiŋ] (construction *f* de) voûtes *f/pl.*

vault·ing-horse ['vɔːltiŋhɔːs] *gymn.* cheval *m* de bois.

vaunt *poét.* [vɔːnt] **1.** (se) vanter (de); **2.** vanterie *f*; '**vaunt·ing** □ vantard.   [de veau.]

veal [viːl] veau *m*; *roast* ~ rôti *m*

ve·dette ✗ [vi'det] vedette *f.*

veer [viə] **1.** (faire) virer; *v/i.* tourner; **2.** (*a.* ~ *round*) changement *m* de direction.

veg F *Brit.* [vedʒ] légume(s) *m* (*pl.*).

veg·e·ta·ble ['vedʒitəbl] **1.** végétal (-aux *m/pl.*); ~ *garden* (jardin *m*) potager *m*; ~ *soup* soupe *f* de légumes; **2.** légume *m*; ♀ végétal (*pl.* -aux) *m*; **veg·e·tar·i·an** [~'tɛəriən] végétarien(ne *f*) (*a. su.*); **veg·e·tate** ['~teit] végéter; **veg·e·ta·tion** végétation *f*; **veg·e·ta·tive** □ ['~tətiv] végétatif (-ive *f*).

ve·he·mence ['viːiməns] véhémence *f*; impétuosité *f*; '**ve·he·ment** □ véhément; passionné; violent.

ve·hi·cle ['viːikl] voiture *f*; véhicule *m* (*a. fig., pharm., peint.*); *pharm.* excipient *m*; **ve·hic·u·lar** □ [vi'hikjulə] des voitures; véhiculaire (*a. langue*).

veil [veil] **1.** voile *m* (*a. fig.*); *phot.* voile *m* faible; **2.** (se) voiler (*a. fig.*); *v/t. fig. a.* cacher; '**veil·ing** action *f* de voiler; voile *m* faible; voile *m*, -s *m/pl.* (*a.* ✝).

vein [vein] veine *f* (*a. fig.*) (de *inf.*, *for gér.*); ♀ nervure *f* (*a. d'aile*); *in the same* ~ dans le même esprit; **veined** veiné; ♀ nervuré; '**vein·ing** veinage *m*; veines *f/pl.*; ♀ nervures *f/pl.*

vel·le·i·ty [ve'liːiti] velléité *f.*

vel·lum ['veləm] vélin *m*; ~ *paper* papier *m* vélin.

ve·loc·i·ty [vi'lɒsiti] vitesse *f.*

vel·vet ['velvit] **1.** velours *m*; *bois de cerf*: peau *f* velue; F *fig. on* ~ *sur* le velours; **2.** de velours; velouté; **vel·vet·een** [~'tiːn] velours *m* de coton; ~*s pl.* pantalon *m* en velours de chasse; '**vel·vet·y** velouté.

ve·nal ['viːnl] vénal (-aux *m/pl.*); mercenaire; **ve·nal·i·ty** [viː'næliti] vénalité *f.*

vend [vend] vendre; '**vend·er**, '**ven·dor** vendeur (-euse *f*) *m*;

marchand(e *f*) *m*; '**vend·i·ble** vendable; '**vend·ing ma·chine** distributeur *m* (automatique).

ve·neer [vi'niə] **1.** (bois *m* de) placage *m*; F vernis *m*, masque *m*; **2.** plaquer; *fig.* cacher (*qch.*) sous un vernis.

ven·er·a·ble □ ['venərəbl] vénérable; **ven·er·ate** ['~reit] vénérer; **ven·er·a·tion** vénération *f*; '**ven·er·a·tor** vénérateur (-trice *f*) *m.*

ve·ne·re·al [vi'niəriəl] vénérien(ne *f*); ~ *disease* maladie *f* vénérienne.

Ve·ne·tian [vi'niːʃn] **1.** de Venise; vénitien(ne *f*); ~ *blind* jalousie *f*; **2.** Vénitien(ne *f*) *m.*

venge·ance ['vendʒəns] vengeance *f*; F *with a* (*ou for*) ~ pas d'erreur!; pour de bon!; furieusement.

venge·ful □ ['vendʒful] vengeur (-eresse *f*).

ve·ni·al □ ['viːnjəl] pardonnable; véniel(le *f*) (*péché*).

ven·i·son ['venzn] venaison *f.*

ven·om ['venəm] venin *m* (*souv. fig.*); '**ven·om·ous** □ venimeux (-euse *f*) (*animal, a. fig.*); vénéneux (-euse *f*) (*plante*).

ve·nous ['viːnəs] veineux (-euse *f*).

vent [vent] **1.** trou *m*, orifice *m*, passage *m*; soupirail (-aux *pl.*) *m*; *orn., icht.* ouverture *f* anale; *give* ~ *to* donner libre cours à (*sa colère etc.*); *find* ~ s'échapper (*en, in*); **2.** *fig.* décharger, épancher (*sur, on*).

ven·ti·late ['ventileit] ventiler; aérer; *fig.* faire connaître, agiter (*une question*); **ven·ti·la·tion** aération *f*; ventilation *f*, aérage *m* (*a.* ✗); *fig.* mise *f* en discussion publique; '**ven·ti·la·tor** ventilateur *m*; soupirail (-aux *pl.*) *m*; *porte, fenêtre:* vasistas *m.*

vent-peg ['ventpeg] fausset *m.*

ven·tral ⚕, *zo.* ['ventrəl] ventral (-aux *m/pl.*).

ven·tri·cle *anat.* ['ventrikl] ventricule *m.*

ven·tril·o·quist [ven'triləkwist] ventriloque *mf*; **ven'tril·o·quize** [~kwaiz] faire de la ventriloquie.

ven·ture ['ventʃə] **1.** risque *m*; aventure *f*; entreprise *f*; ✝ opération *f*, affaire *f*; *at a* ~ au hasard; **2.** *v/t.* risquer, hasarder; *v/i.:* ~ *to* (*inf.*) se risquer à (*inf.*), oser (*inf.*); *I* ~ *to say* je me permets de dire; ~ (*up*)*on* s'aventurer dans (*un endroit*);

ven·ture·some □ ['⁀səm], **'ven·tur·ous** □ risqué, hasardeux (-euse *f*); aventureux (-euse *f*) (*personne*).
ven·ue ['venju:] ⚖ lieu *m* du jugement; *fig.* scène *f*; F rendez-vous *m*.
ve·ra·cious □ [vəˈreiʃəs] véridique; **ve·rac·i·ty** [⁀ˈræsiti] véracité *f*.
verb *gramm.* [vəːb] verbe *m*; **'ver·bal** □ verbal (-aux *m/pl.*); de mots; littéral (-aux *m/pl.*); (*ou* **ver·ba·tim** [⁀ˈbeitim]) mot pour mot; **'ver·bal·ize** verbaliser, rendre par des mots; **ver·bi·age** ['⁀biidʒ] verbiage *m*; **ver·bose** □ [⁀ˈbous] verbeux (-euse *f*), prolixe; **ver·bos·i·ty** [⁀ˈbɔsiti] verbosité *f*, prolixité *f*.
ver·dan·cy ['vəːdənsi] verdure *f*; F *fig.* inexpérience *f*; **'ver·dant** □ vert; F *fig.* inexpérimenté.
ver·dict ['vəːdikt] ⚖ verdict *m* (*du jury*); *fig.* jugement *m* (sur, on); *bring in* (*ou return*) *a* ⁀ (*of guilty etc.*) rendre un verdict (de culpabilité *etc.*).
ver·di·gris ['vəːdigris] vert-de-gris *m*.
ver·dure ['vəːdʒə] verdure *f*.
verge¹ [vəːdʒ] *eccl.* verge *f*.
verge² [⁀] 1. *usu. fig.* bord *m*; seuil *m*; *on the* ⁀ *au* seuil (de, of); à deux doigts (de, of); sur le point (de *inf.*, of *gér.*); 2. baisser; approcher (de, towards); ⁀ (up)on côtoyer (*qch.*); friser; être voisin de, toucher à.
ver·i·fi·a·ble ['verifaiəbl] vérifiable; facile à vérifier; **ver·i·fi·ca·tion** [⁀fiˈkeiʃn] vérification *f*, contrôle *m*; ⚖ confirmation *f*; **ver·i·fy** ['⁀fai] prouver; confirmer; contrôler, vérifier; **ver·i·si·mil·i·tude** [⁀siˈmilitjuːd] vraisemblance *f*; **'ver·i·ta·ble** □ véritable; **'ver·i·ty** vérité *f*.
ver·juice *usu. fig.* ['vəːdʒuːs] verjus *m*.
ver·mi·cel·li [vəːmiˈseli] vermicelle *m*; **ver·mi·cide** *pharm.* ['⁀said] vermicide *m*; **ver·mic·u·lar** [⁀ˈmikjulə] vermiculaire; vermoulu; **ver·mi·form** ['⁀fɔːm] vermiforme; **ver·mi·fuge** *pharm.* ['⁀fjuːdʒ] vermifuge *m*.
ver·mil·ion [vəˈmiljən] 1. vermillon *m*; 2. vermeil(le *f*); (de) vermillon *adj./inv.*
ver·min ['vəːmin] vermine *f* (*a. fig.*); *chasse:* bêtes *f/pl.* puantes; '⁀-'**kill·er** *personne:* preneur *m* de vermine; insecticide *m*; mort-aux-

rats *f*; '**ver·min·ous** couvert de vermine; ⚕ vermineux (-euse *f*).
ver·m(o)uth ['vəːməθ] vermouth *m*.
ver·nac·u·lar □ [vəˈnækjulə] 1. indigène; du pays; vulgaire (*langue*); 2. langue *f* du pays; idiome *m* national; langue *f* vulgaire; langage *m* (*d'un métier*).
ver·nal ['vəːnl] printanier (-ère *f*); ♀, *astr.* vernal (-aux *m/pl.*).
ver·ni·er ['vəːnjə] ♀, *surv.* vernier *m*; ⊕ ⁀ cal(l)iper jauge *f* micrométrique.
ver·sa·tile □ ['vəːsətail] aux talents variés; souple; ♀, *zo.* versatile; **ver·sa·til·i·ty** [⁀ˈtiliti] souplesse *f*; ♀, *zo.* versatilité *f*; adaptation *f*.
verse [vəːs] vers *m*; strophe *f*; *coll.* vers *m/pl.*, poésie *f*; ♪ *motet:* solo *m*; **versed** versé (en, dans in).
ver·si·fi·ca·tion [vəːsifiˈkeiʃn] versification *f*; métrique *f* (*d'un auteur*); **ver·si·fy** ['⁀fai] *vt/i.* versifier; *v/t.* mettre (*qch.*) en vers; *v/i.* faire des vers.
ver·sion ['vəːʃn] version *f*; traduction *f*.
ver·so ['vəːsou] verso *m*.
ver·sus *surt.* ⚖ ['vəːsəs] contre.
vert F *eccl.* [vəːt] se convertir.
ver·te·bra *anat.* ['vəːtibrə], *pl.* -**brae** [⁀briː] vertèbre *f*; **ver·te·bral** ['⁀brəl] vertébral (-aux *m/pl.*); **ver·te·brate** ['⁀brit] 1. vertébré; ⁀ *animal =* 2. vertébré *m*.
ver·tex ['vəːteks], *pl. usu.* -**ti·ces** [⁀tisiːz] sommet *m*; *astr.* zénith *m*; '**ver·ti·cal** 1. □ vertical (-aux *m/pl.*); à pic (*falaise*); ⚓ ⁀ *angles* angles *m/pl.* opposés par le sommet; ⁀ *takeoff aircraft* avion *m* à décollage vertical; 2. verticale *f*; *astr.* vertical *m*.
ver·tig·i·nous □ [vəːˈtidʒinəs] vertigineux (-euse *f*); **ver·ti·go** ['⁀tigou] vertige *m*.
verve [vɛəv] verve *f*.
ver·y ['veri] 1. *adv.* très; fort; bien; *the* ⁀ *best* tout ce qu'il y a de mieux; 2. *adj.* vrai, véritable, ⁀ même; *the* ⁀ *same* le (la *etc.*) ... même(s *pl.*); *in the* ⁀ *act* sur le fait; *to the* ⁀ *bone* jusqu'aux os; jusqu'à l'os même; *the* ⁀ *thing* ce qu'il faut; *the* ⁀ *thought* la seule pensée; *the* ⁀ *stones* les pierres mêmes; *the veriest baby* (même) le plus petit enfant; *the veriest rascal* le plus

parfait coquin; *radio:* ∼ *high frequency* très haute fréquence *f.*

ves·i·ca·to·ry ['vesikeitəri] vésicatoire (*a. su./m*); **ves·i·cle** ['∼kl] vésicule *f*; *géol.* vacuole *f.*

ves·pers *eccl.* ['vespəz] *pl.* vêpres *f/pl.*

ves·sel ['vesl] vaisseau *m* (*a.* ♀, *anat., fig.*); ⚓ *a.* navire *m*, bâtiment *m.*

vest [vest] **1.** gilet *m*; ⚓ gilet *m* de dessous; *sp.* maillot *m*; **2.** *v/t. usu. fig.* revêtir, investir (de, *with*); assigner (qch. à q., *s.th. in s.o.*); *v/i.* être dévolu (à q., *in s.o.*); ∼ed *rights pl.* droits *m/pl.* acquis.

ves·ta ['vestə] (*a.* ∼ *match, wax* ∼) allumette-bougie (*pl.* allumettes-bougies) *f*; *astr.* ♀ vesta *f.*

ves·tal ['vestl] **1.** de(s) vestale(s); **2.** vestale *f.*

ves·ti·bule ['vestibju:l] vestibule *m* (*a. anat.*); salle *f* des pas perdus; ⚏ *surt. Am.* soufflet *m* (*entre deux wagons*); ∼ *train* train *m* à soufflets.

ves·tige ['vestidʒ] vestige *m*, trace *f*; **ves·tig·i·al** à l'état rudimentaire.

vest·ment ['vestmənt] vêtement *m* (*a. eccl.*). [dimensions.\

vest·pock·et ['vest'pɔkit] de petites⌋

ves·try ['vestri] *eccl.* sacristie *f*; (réunion *f* du) conseil *m* d'administration de la paroisse; salle *f* de patronage; '∼·**man** marguillier *m.*

ves·ture ['vestʃə] **1.** vêtement *m*; **2.** revêtir.

vet [vet] **1.** vétérinaire *m*; *Am.* ancien combattant *m*; **2.** traiter (*un animal*); *fig.* examiner médicalement; revoir, corriger; *fig.* mettre au point.

vetch ♀ [vetʃ] vesce *f.*

vet·er·an ['vetərən] **1.** expérimenté; ancien(ne *f*); de(s) vétéran(s); vieux (vieil *devant une voyelle ou un h muet*; vieille *f*); *mot.* ∼ *car* vétéran *m*; **2.** vétéran *m*; ancien *m*; ancien combattant *m.*

vet·er·i·nar·i·an *Am.* [vetəri'nɛəriən] vétérinaire *mf*; **vet·er·i·nar·y** ['vetərinəri] **1.** vétérinaire; ∼ *surgeon* = **2.** vétérinaire *mf.*

ve·to ['vi:tou] **1.** *pl.* -toes [∼touz] veto *m*; *put a* (*ou* one's) ∼ (*up*)on = **2.** mettre son veto à.

vex [veks] vexer (*a.* ⚖); fâcher, contrarier; **vex·a·tion** vexation *f*; tourment *m*; désagrément *m*; dépit *m*; **vex·a·tious** □ ennuyeux (-euse

f); fâcheux (-euse *f*); ⚖ vexatoire; '**vexed** □ fâché, vexé (de qch., *at s.th.*; contre q., *with s.o.*); ∼ *question* question *f* très débattue; '**vex·ing** □ agaçant; ennuyeux (-euse *f*).

vi·a ['vaiə] par; *poste:* voie.

vi·a·ble *biol.* ['vaiəbl] viable.

vi·a·duct ['vaiədʌkt] viaduc *m.*

vi·al ['vaiəl] fiole *f.*

vi·ands *poét.* ['vaiəndz] *pl.* aliments *m/pl.*

vi·at·i·cum *eccl.* [vai'ætikəm] viatique *m.*

vibes F [vaibz] *sg.* ♪ vibraphone *m*; *pl.* vibrations *f/pl.*

vi·brant ['vaibrənt] vibrant; *fig.* palpitant (de, *with*).

vi·bra·phone ♪ ['vaibrəfoun] vibraphone *m.*

vi·brate [vai'breit] (faire) vibrer *ou* osciller; **vi·bra·tion** vibration *f*; **vi·bra·to·ry** ['∼brətəri] vibratoire.

vic·ar *eccl.* ['vikə] curé *m*; ∼ *general* vicaire *m* général; '**vic·ar·age** presbytère *m*; cure *f*; **vi·car·i·ous** □ [vai'kɛəriəs] délégué; fait *ou* souffert pour *ou* par un autre.

vice[1] [vais] vice *m*; *fig.* défaut *m.*

vice[2] ⊕ [∼] étau *m.*

vice[3] **1.** ['vaisi] *prp.* à la place de; **2.** [vais] *adj.* vice-; sous-; '∼·**ad·mi·ral** vice-amiral *m*; '∼·**chair·man** vice-président(e *f*) *m*; '∼·**chan·cel·lor** vice-chancelier *m*; *univ.* recteur *m*; '∼·**con·sul** vice-consul *m*; ∼·**ge·rent** ['∼'dʒerənt] représentant *m*; '∼·**pres·i·dent** vice-président(e *f*) *m*; '∼·**re·gal** de *ou* du vice-roi; '∼·**reine** [∼'rein] vice-reine *f*; ∼·**roy** ['∼rɔi] vice-roi *m.*

vi·ce ver·sa ['vaisi'və:sə] vice versa, réciproquement.

vic·i·nage ['visinidʒ], **vi·cin·i·ty** environs *m/pl.* (de, *of*); proximité *f* (de to, *with*); *in the* ∼ *of 40* environ 40.

vi·cious □ ['viʃəs] vicieux (-euse *f*); dépravé (*a. personne*); *fig.* méchant (*a. cheval*); *phls.* ∼ *circle* cercle *m* vicieux; ' *argument m* circulaire.

vi·cis·si·tude [vi'sisitju:d] *usu.* ∼*s pl.* vicissitudes *f/pl.*

vic·tim ['viktim] victime *f*; '**vic·tim·ize** prendre comme victime; ✗, *pol.* exercer des représailles contre; *fig.* duper.

vic·tor ['viktə] vainqueur *m*; **Vic·to·ri·an** *hist.* [vik'tɔːriən] victorien (-ne *f*) (*a. su.*); **vic'to·ri·ous** □ victorieux (-euse *f*); de victoire; **vic·to·ry** ['ˌtəri] victoire *f*.

vict·ual ['vitl] **1.** (s')approvisionner; ✕, ⚓ (se) ravitailler; *v/i.* F bâfrer (= *manger*); **2.** *usu.* ~s *pl.* provisions *f/pl.*..; vivres *m/pl.*; **vict·ual·(l)er** ['vitlə] fournisseur *m* de vivres; *licensed* ~ débitant *m* de boissons.

vi·de ['vaidi] voir.

vi·de·li·cet [vi'diːliset] (*abr.* viz.) à savoir; c'est-à-dire.

vid·e·o ['vidiou] **1.** vidéo *f*; *Am.* F télévision *f*; **2.** vidéo *inv.*; ~ **cart·ridge,** ~ **cas·sette** vidéo(-)cassette *f*; ~ **disc** vidéo(-)disque *m*; '~·**phone** vidéophone *m*; ~ **re·cord·er** magnétoscope *m*; ~ **tape** bande *f* vidéo; '~ **tape** enregistrer sur bande *f* vidéo, magnétoscoper; '~·**tel·e·phone** vidéotéléphone *m*.

vie [vai] le disputer (à, *with*); rivaliser (avec, *with*).

Vi·en·nese [vie'niːz] **1.** viennois; **2.** Viennois(e *f*) *m*.

view [vjuː] **1.** vue *f*, coup *m* d'œil; regard *m*; scène *f*; perspective *f*; aperçu *m*; *fig.* intention *f*; *fig.* idée *f*, opinion *f*, avis *m*; *field of* ~ champ *m*; *at first* ~ à première vue; *in* ~ en vue, sous les regards; *in* ~ *of* en vue de; *fig.* en raison *ou* considération de; étant donné; *in my* ~ à mon avis; *on* ~ exposé; ouvert au public; *on the long* ~ à la longue, envisageant les choses de loin; *out of* ~ hors de vue; caché aux regards; *with a* ~ *to* (*gér.*), *with the* ~ *of* (*gér.*) dans le but de (*inf.*), en vue de (*inf.*); dans l'intention de (*inf.*); *have in* ~ avoir en vue; *keep in* ~ ne pas perdre de vue; **2.** regarder (*a. télév.*); contempler; voir; apercevoir; *fig.* envisager; '**view·er** (*télév.* télé)spectateur (-trice *f*) *m*; '**view·find·er** *phot.* viseur *m*; '**view·phone** vidéophone *m*; '**view·point** point *m* de vue; belvédère *m* (*dans le paysage*); '**view·y** □ F visionnaire.

vig·il ['vidʒil] veille *f*; *eccl.* vigile *f*; '**vig·i·lance** vigilance *f*; ~ *com·mittee Am.* comité *m* de surveillance (des mœurs *ou* de l'ordre); '**vig·i·lant** □ vigilant, éveillé; **vig·i·lan·te** *Am.* ['ˌlænti] membre *m* du comité de surveillance.

vi·gnette [vi'njet] **1.** *typ.* vignette *f*; *phot.* cache *m* dégradé; **2.** *phot.* dégrader (*un portrait etc.*).

vig·or·ous □ ['vigərəs] vigoureux (-euse *f*), robuste; *phot.* à contrastes; corsé (*couleur*); '**vig·o(u)r** vigueur *f* (*a. fig.*); énergie *f*; ♪ brio *m*.

vile □ [vail] vil; infâme; F sale.

vil·i·fi·ca·tion [vilifi'keiʃn] dénigrement *m*, détraction *f*; **vil·i·fy** ['ˌfai] diffamer, dénigrer; médire de (*q.*).

vil·la ['vilə] villa *f*, maison *f* de campagne.

vil·lage ['vilidʒ] village *m*; '**vil·lag·er** villageois(e *f*) *m*.

vil·lain ['vilən] scélérat *m*; bandit *m*; misérable *m*; F *a. co.* coquin(e *f*) *m*; '**vil·lain·ous** □ infâme, vil; scélérat; F sale; '**vil·lain·y** infamie *f*; vilenie *f*.

vil·lein *hist.* ['vilin] vilain *m*; serf *m*.

vim F [vim] énergie *f*, vigueur *f*.

vin·di·cate ['vindikeit] défendre (contre, *from*); justifier; revendiquer (*ses droits*); **vin·di·ca·tion** défense *f*; revendication *f*; **vin·di·ca·to·ry** □ ['ˌkeitəri] vindicatif (-ive *f*); vengeur (-eresse *f*).

vin·dic·tive □ [vin'diktiv] vindicatif (-ive *f*); *a.* rancunier (-ère *f*) (*personne*).

vine ♀ [vain] vigne *f*; houblon *etc.*: sarment *m*; *Am.* plante *f* grimpante; '~·**dres·ser** vigneron(ne *f*) *m*; **vin·e·gar** ['vinigə] **1.** vinaigre *m*; **2.** vinaigrer; '**vine-grow·er** viticulteur *m*; vigneron(ne *f*) *m*; '**vine-grow·ing** viticulture *f*; *attr.* vignoble; '**vine-louse** phylloxéra *m*; '**vine·yard** ['vinjəd] vigne *f*; clos *m* de vigne; vignoble *m*.

vi·nous ['vainəs] vineux (-euse *f*); F ivrogne.

vin·tage ['vintidʒ] vendange *f*; cru *m*; *fig.* modèle *m*; ~ *year* grande année *f*; '**vin·tag·er** vendangeur (-euse *f*) *m*.

vi·o·la¹ ♪ [vi'oulə] alto *m*.

vi·o·la² ♀ ['vaiələ] pensée *f*.

vi·o·la·ble □ ['vaiələbl] qui peut être violé.

vi·o·late ['vaiəleit] violer (*un serment, une femme*); outrager (*une femme*); profaner (*une église*); **vi·o·la·tion** violation *f*; viol *m* (*d'une* *femme*); profanation *f*; **'vi·o·la·tor** violateur (-trice *f*) *m*.

vi·o·lence ['vaiələns] violence *f*; do (*ou offer*) ~ to faire violence à; **'vi·o·lent** □ violent; vif (vive *f*); criard (*couleur*).

vi·o·let ['vaiəlit] **1.** ♀ violette *f*; *couleur*: violet *m*; **2.** violet(te *f*).

vi·o·lin ♪ [vaiə'lin] violon *m*; **'vi·o·lin·ist** violoniste *mf*.

vi·o·lon·cel·list ♪ [vaiələn't∫elist] violoncelliste *mf*; **vi·o·lon'cel·lo** [‿lou] violoncelle *m*.

vi·per *zo.* ['vaipə] vipère *f* (*a. fig.*); ⬙ guivre *f*; **vi·per·ine** ['‿rain], **vi·per·ous** □ ['‿rəs] *usu. fig.* vipérin.

vi·ra·go [vi'rɑːgou] vrai gendarme *m*; mégère *f*.

vir·gin ['vəːdʒin] **1.** vierge *f*; **2.** vierge (*a.* ⊕, *a. fig.*); = **'vir·gin·al** □ virginal (-aux *m/pl.*); de vierge; **Vir·gin·ia** [və'dʒinjə] (*ou* ~ *tobacco*) tabac *m* de Virginie, virginie *f*; ~ *creeper* vigne *f* vierge; **vir·gin·i·ty** [vəː'dʒiniti] virginité *f*.

Vir·go *astr.* ['vəːgou] la Vierge.

vir·ile ['virail] viril, mâle; **vi·ril·i·ty** [vi'riliti] virilité *f*.

vir·tu [vəː'tuː] goût *m* des objets d'art; *article of* ~ objet *m* d'art; **vir·tu·al** □ ['‿tjuəl] de fait; véritable; ⊕ virtuel(le *f*); **vir·tue** ['‿tjuː] vertu *f*; *fig.* qualité *f*; avantage *m*; efficacité *f*; propriété *f*; *in* (*ou by*) ~ *of* en raison *ou* vertu' de; **vir·tu·os·i·ty** [‿tju'ɔsiti] ♪ *etc.* virtuosité *f*; **vir·tu·o·so** [‿'ouzou] *surt.* ♪ virtuose *mf*; amateur *m* des arts; amateur *m* de curiosités *etc.*; **'vir·tu·ous** □ vertueux (-euse *f*).

vir·u·lence ['virulans] virulence *f*; *fig.* venin *m*; **'vir·u·lent** □ virulent (*a. fig.*); *fig. a.* venimeux (-euse *f*).

vi·rus 𝕤 ['vaiərəs] virus *m*; *fig.* poison *m*.

vi·sa ['viːzə] *see* visé.

vis·age *poét.* ['vizidʒ] visage *m*.

vis·cer·a ['visərə] *pl.* viscères *m/pl.*

vis·cid □ ['visid] *see* viscous.

vis·cose ⚗ ['viskous] viscose *f*; ~ *silk* soie *f* artificielle; **vis·cos·i·ty** [‿'kɔsiti] viscosité *f*.

vis·count ['vaikaunt] vicomte *m*; **'vis·count·ess** vicomtesse *f*.

vis·cous □ ['viskəs] visqueux (-euse *f*); gluant; pâteux (-euse *f*).

vi·sé ['viːzei] **1.** visa *m*; **2.** apposer un visa à (*un passeport*); viser.

vis·i·bil·i·ty [vizi'biliti] visibilité *f*; *good* ~ vue *f* dégagée; **vis·i·ble** □ ['vizəbl] visible; *fig.* évident; *be* ~ se montrer (*chose*); être visible (*personne*).

vi·sion ['viʒn] vision *f*, vue *f*; *fig.* pénétration *f*; imagination *f*; fantôme *m*, apparition *f*.

vi·sion·ar·y ['viʒnəri] chimérique; rêveur (-euse *f*) (*personne*) (*a. su./mf*); visionnaire (*a. su./mf*).

vis·it ['vizit] **1.** *v/t.* faire (une) visite à, rendre visite à; aller voir; visiter (*un endroit*); ✝ passer chez; *fig.* causer avec; ~ *s.th. on* faire retomber qch. sur (*q.*); *v/i.* faire des visites; *Am.* F causer (avec, *with*); **2.** visite *f*; **'vis·it·ant** visiteur (-euse *f*) *m*; apparition *f*; *orn.* oiseau *m* de passage; **vis·it'a·tion** visite *f*; tournée *f* d'inspection; *fig.* affliction *f*; calamité *f*; apparition *f*; **vis·it·a·to·ri·al** [‿tə'tɔːriəl] de visite; d'inspection; **'vis·it·ing** en visite; de visite; ~ *card* carte *f* de visite; ~ *hours* heures *f/pl.* de visite; *sp.* ~ *team* les visiteurs *m/pl.*; **'vis·i·tor** visiteur (-euse *f*) *m* (*de, to*); *hôtel*: client(e *f*) *m*; *admin.* inspecteur *m*; *they have* ~s ils ont du monde; ~*s' book* livre *m ou* registre *m* des voyageurs.

vi·sor ['vaizə] visière *f* (*de casque*, *Am. de casquette*); *mot.* pare-soleil *m/inv.*

vis·ta ['vistə] perspective *f* (*a. fig.*); *forêt*: éclaircie *f*.

vis·u·al □ ['vizjuəl] visuel(le *f*); *anat.* optique; **'vis·u·al·ize** se représenter (*qch.*), se faire une image de (*qch.*).

vi·tal □ ['vaitl] **1.** vital (-aux *m/pl.*); essentiel(le *f*); mortel(le *f*) (*blessure*); ~ *parts pl.* = **2.** ~s *pl.* organes *m/pl.* vitaux; **vi·tal·i·ty** [‿'tæliti] vitalité *f*; vie *f*, vigueur *f*; **vi·tal·ize** ['‿təlaiz] vivifier, animer.

vi·ta·min ['vitəmin], **vi·ta·mine** ['‿miːn] vitamine *f*; **vi·ta·mi·nized** ['‿minaizd] enrichi de vitamines.

vi·ti·ate ['vi∫ieit] vicier (*a.* ⚖); corrompre; gâter.

vit·i·cul·ture ['vitikʌltʃə] viticulture *f.*

vit·re·ous ☐ ['vitriəs] vitreux (-euse *f*); *⚡, a. anat.* vitré.

vit·ri·fac·tion [vitri'fækʃn] vitrification *f;* **vit·ri·fy** ['⁓fai] (se) vitrifier.

vit·ri·ol ⚗ ['vitriəl] vitriol *m;* **vit·ri·ol·ic** [vitri'ɔlik] ⚗ vitriolique; *fig.* mordant.

vi·tu·per·ate [vi'tju:pəreit] injurier; outrager, insulter, vilipender; **vi·tu·per·a·tion** injures *f/pl.;* invectives *f/pl.;* **vi·tu·per·a·tive** ☐ [⁓reitiv] injurieux (-euse *f*); mal embouché.

Vi·tus ['vaitəs] *⚕* St. ⁓'(s) *dance* chorée *f;* danse *f* de Saint-Guy.

vi·va (**vo·ce**) ['vaivə ('vousi)] **1.** *adv.* de vive voix; **2.** *adj.* oral (-aux *m/pl.);* **3.** *su.* oral *m.*

vi·va·cious ☐ [vi'veiʃəs] animé, enjoué; vif (vive *f*); **vi·vac·i·ty** [⁓'væsiti] vivacité *f;* verve *f;* enjouement *m.*

viv·id ☐ ['vivid] vif (vive *f*); éclatant, frappant; **'viv·id·ness** éclat *m.*

viv·i·fy ['vivifai] (s')animer; **vi·vip·a·rous** ☐ [⁓'vipərəs] vivipare; **viv·i·sec·tion** [⁓'sekʃn] vivisection *f.*

vix·en ['viksn] renarde *f;* F mégère *f.*

vi·zor ['vaizə] *see* visor.

vo·cab·u·lar·y [və'kæbjuləri] vocabulaire *f;* glossaire *m.*

vo·cal ☐ ['voukl] vocal (-aux *m/pl.*) (♩, *son, prière*); sonore, bruyant; doué de voix; *gramm.* voisé; sonore; *anat.* ⁓ c(h)ords *pl.* cordes *ou* bandes *f/pl.* vocales; ⁓ *part* partie *f* chantée; **'vo·cal·ist** chanteur *m;* cantatrice *f;* **'vo·cal·ize** *v/t.* chanter; *gramm.* voiser, sonoriser; *v/i.* vocaliser; F chanter; **'vo·cal·ly** *adv.* à l'aide du chant; oralement.

vo·ca·tion [vou'keiʃn] vocation *f* (*a. au sacerdoce etc.*); profession *f,* métier *m;* **vo'ca·tion·al** ☐ professionnel(le *f*); ⁓ *guidance* orientation *f* professionnelle.

voc·a·tive *gramm.* ['vɔkətiv] (*a.* ⁓ *case*) vocatif *m.*

vo·cif·er·ate [vou'sifəreit] *vt/i.* vociférer, crier (contre, *against*); **vo·cif·er'a·tion** (*a.* ⁓*s pl.*) vociférations *f/pl.;* cri *m,* -s *m/pl.;* **vo'cif·er·ous** ☐ vociférant, bruyant.

vogue [voug] vogue *f,* mode *f.*

voice [vɔis] **1.** voix *f; gramm.* *active* ⁓ actif *m; passive* ⁓ passif *m;* *in* (*good*) ⁓ en voix; *give* ⁓ *to* exprimer (*qch.*); **2.** exprimer, énoncer; *gramm.* voiser, sonoriser; ♪ harmoniser; **voiced** *gramm.* voisé, sonore; *low-*⁓ à voix basse; **'voice·less** ☐ *surt. gramm.* sans voix, sourd.

void [vɔid] **1.** vide; *⚖* nul(le *f*); ⁓ *of* dépourvu *ou* libre de, sans; **2.** vide *m;* **3.** *⚖* annuler, résilier; **'void·ness** vide *m; ⚖* nullité *f.*

vol·a·tile ⚗ ['vɔlətail] volatil; *fig.* gai; *fig.* volage; **vol·a·til·i·ty** [⁓'tiliti] ⚗ volatilité *f; fig.* inconstance *f;* **'vol·a·til·ize** (se) volatiliser.

vol·can·ic [vɔl'kænik] (⁓*ally*) volcanique (*a. fig.*); **vol·ca·no** [⁓'keinou], *pl.* -noes [⁓nouz] volcan *m.*

vole *zo.* [voul] campagnol *m.*

vo·li·tion [vou'liʃn] volonté *f,* volition *f; on one's own* ⁓ de son propre gré.

vol·ley ['vɔli] **1.** volée *f,* salve *f* (*a. fig.*); *pierres, coups:* grêle *f; tennis:* volée *f;* **2.** *v/t.* lancer une volée *ou* grêle de; (*usu.* ⁓ *out*) lâcher une bordée de; reprendre (*la balle*) de volée; *v/i.* partir ensemble (*canons*); *fig.* tonner; **'vol·ley-ball** *sp.* volley-ball *m.*

vol·plane ✈ ['vɔl'plein] **1.** vol *m* plané; **2.** planer; descendre en vol plané.

volt [voult] volt *m;* **'volt·age** ⚡ voltage *m,* tension *f;* **vol·ta·ic** ⚡ [vɔl'teiik] voltaïque.

vol·u·bil·i·ty [vɔlju'biliti] volubilité *f;* **vol·u·ble** ☐ ['⁓bl] facile; grand parleur; coulant.

vol·ume ['vɔljum] livre *m;* volume *m* (*a. phys., voix, fig., etc.*); *fig. a.* ampleur *f;* ⁓ *of sound radio:* volume *m;* ⁓ *control,* ⁓ *regulator* volume-contrôle *m;* **vo·lu·mi·nous** ☐ [və'lju:minəs] volumineux (-euse *f*).

vol·un·tar·y ☐ ['vɔləntəri] **1.** volontaire (*a. physiol.*); spontané; **2.** ♪ prélude *m;* improvisation *f;* **vol-**

un·teer [ˌˈtiə] **1.** volontaire *m*; *attr.* de volontaires; **2.** *v/i.* s'offrir; ⚔ s'engager comme volontaire; *v/t.* offrir spontanément.

vo·lup·tu·ar·y [vəˈlʌptjuəri] voluptueux (-euse *f*) *m*; **vo·lup·tu·ous** ☐ sensuel(le *f*); voluptueux (-euse *f*); **vo·lup·tu·ous·ness** sensualité *f*.

vo·lute △ [vəˈljuːt] volute *f*; **vo·lut·ed** voluté; à volutes.

vom·it [ˈvɔmit] **1.** *vt/i.* vomir (*a. fig.*); *v/t.* rendre; **2.** vomissement *m*; matières *f/pl.* vomies.

voo·doo [ˈvuːduː] **1.** vaudou *m*; **2.** envoûter.

vo·ra·cious ☐ [vəˈreiʃəs] vorace, dévorant; **vo·ra·cious·ness**, **vo·rac·i·ty** [vɔˈræsiti] voracité *f*.

vor·tex [ˈvɔːteks], *pl. usu.* **-ti·ces** [ˌtisiːz] tourbillon (*a. fig.*).

vo·ta·ry [ˈvoutəri] dévot(e *f*) *m* (à, of); adorateur (-trice *f*) *m* (de, of); *fig.* suppôt *m* (de, of).

vote [vout] **1.** vote *m*; scrutin *m*; voix *f*; droit *m* de vote(r), suffrage *m*; *parl.* crédit *m*; résolution *f*; ~ of (no) confidence vote *m* de confiance (défiance); *cast a* ~ donner sa voix *ou* son vote; *put to the* ~ procéder au scrutin; mettre (*qch.*) aux voix; *take a* ~ procéder au scrutin; **2.** *v/t.* voter; F déclarer; *v/i.* voter; donner sa voix (pour, for); F être d'avis (de *inf.*, for gér.); être en faveur (de qch. for s.th.); F ~ *that* proposer que; **vot·er** votant(e *f*) *m*; électeur (-trice *f*) *m*.

vot·ing [ˈvoutiŋ] vote *m*, scrutin *m*; ~ *booth* isoloir *m*; ~ *box* urne *f* de scrutin; ~ *machine* machine *f* pour enregistrer les votes; ~ *paper* bulletin *m* de vote.

vo·tive [ˈvoutiv] votif (-ive *f*).

vouch [vautʃ] *v/t.* garantir, affirmer; *v/i.* répondre (de, for); ~ *that* affirmer que; **'vouch·er** pièce *f* justificative; † bon *m*; † fiche *f*; *théâ. etc.* contremarque *f*; *personne*: garant(e *f*) *m*; **vouch'safe** *v/t.* accorder; *v/i.:* ~ *to* (*inf.*) daigner (*inf.*). [**2.** *v/t.* vouer, jurer.↑

vow [vau] **1.** vœu *m*; serment *m*;↑ **vow·el** [ˈvauəl] voyelle *f*.

voy·age [ˈvɔidʒ] **1.** voyage *m* (sur mer; ✈ *Am.* par air); traversée *f*; **2.** *v/i.* voyager (sur *ou* par mer); *v/t.* parcourir (*la mer*).

vul·can·ite [ˈvʌlkənait] vulcanite *f*, caoutchouc *m* vulcanisé; **vul·can·i'za·tion** ⊕ vulcanisation *f*; **'vul·can·ize** ⊕ (se) vulcaniser.

vul·gar [ˈvʌlgə] **1.** ☐ du peuple; vulgaire (*a. péj.*); commun; ~ *tongue* langue *f* vulgaire; **2.** *the* ~ le vulgaire *m*; le commun *m* des hommes; **'vul·gar·ism** vulgarisme *m*; (*usu.* **vul·gar·i·ty** [ˌˈgæriti]) vulgarité *f*, trivialité *f*; **'vul·gar·ize** vulgariser.

vul·ner·a·bil·i·ty [vʌlnərəˈbiliti] vulnérabilité *f*; **'vul·ner·a·ble** ☐ vulnérable; ~ *spot fig.* défaut *m* dans la cuirasse; **'vul·ner·ar·y** vulnéraire (*a. su./m*).

vul·pine [ˈvʌlpain] de renard; qui a rapport au renard; *fig.* rusé.

vul·ture *orn.* [ˈvʌltʃə] vautour *m*; **vul·tur·ine** [ˌtʃurain] de(s) vautour(s). [lité *f*.↑

vy·ing [ˈvaiiŋ] **1.** *p.pr. de* vie; **2.** riva-↑

W

W, w ['dʌblju:] W *m*, w *m*.

wab·ble ['wɔbl] *see* **wobble**.

wack·y *Am. sl.* ['wæki] fou (fol *devant une voyelle ou un h muet*; folle *f*); toqué.

wad [wɔd] **1.** *ouate etc.*: tampon *m*, pelote *f*; ✗ cartouche *etc.*: bourre *f*; *surt. Am.* F *billets de banque*: liasse *f*; **2.** ouater; cotonner; bourrer (*une arme à feu*); *Am.* rouler en liasse; '**wad·ding** ouate *f*; bourre *f*; ouatage *m*.

wad·dle ['wɔdl] se dandiner.

wade [weid] *v/i.* marcher dans l'eau; *fig.* (s')avancer péniblement; *v/t.* (faire) passer à gué; '**wad·er** (oiseau *m*) échassier *m*; ⁓s *pl.* grandes bottes *f/pl.* imperméables.

wa·fer [weifə] **1.** gaufrette *f*; pain *m* à cacheter; *eccl. consecrated* ⁓ hostie *f*; **2.** apposer un cachet à.

waf·fle ['wɔfl] gaufre *f* (américaine).

waft [wɑːft] **1.** *v/t.* porter; faire avancer; *v/i.* flotter dans l'air; **2.** souffle *m*.

wag¹ [wæg] **1.** agiter, remuer (*le bras, la queue, etc.*) ⁓ one's tongue jacasser; **2.** agitation *f*; hochement *m* (*de la tête*).

wag² [⁓] moqueur (-euse *f*) *m*; blagueur *m*; *sl. play* ⁓ faire l'école buissonnière.

wage [weidʒ] **1.** ⁓ war faire la guerre (à on, against); **2.** *souv.* ⁓s *pl.* salaire *m*, paye *f*; gages *m/pl.*; ⁓(s) claim, ⁓ demands revendication(s) *f(pl.)* de salaire(s); ⁓ dispute conflit *m* salarial; ⁓ earner salarié(e *f*)*m*; soutien *m* de (la) famille; ⁓ increase augmentation *f* de salaire(s); ⁓ packet enveloppe *f* de paye; ⁓ scale échelle *f* des salaires; ⁓ slip fiche *f* de paye; ⁓(s) sheet feuille *f* des salaires.

wa·ger *poét.* ['weidʒə] **1.** pari *m*, gageure *f*; **2.** parier, gager (sur, on).

wag·ger·y ['wægəri] facétie *f*, -s *f/pl.*, plaisanterie *f*; '**wag·gish** □ plaisant, espiègle, blagueur (-euse *f*).

wag·gle F ['wægl] *see* **wag¹** 1; '**waggly** F qui branle; serpentant.

wag·(g)on ['wægən] charrette *f*; camion *m*; ✗ fourgon *m*; 🚃 wagon *m* (découvert); *Am.* F be (go) on the ⁓ s'abstenir de boissons alcooliques; '**wag·(g)on·er** roulier *m*; camionneur *m*; **wag·(g)on·ette** [⁓'net] wagonnette *f*.

wag·tail *orn.* ['wægteil] bergeronnette *f*.

waif [weif] ⚖, *a. fig.* épave *f*; ⁓s and strays enfants *m/pl.* abandonnés; épaves *f/pl.*

wail [weil] **1.** plainte *f*; gémissement *m*; **2.** *v/t.* lamenter sur, pleurer; *v/i.* gémir, se lamenter.

wain *poét.* [wein] *see* **wag(g)on**; *astr.* Charles's ⁓, the ⁓ le Chariot *m*.

wain·scot ['weinskət] **1.** lambris *m*; *salle*: boiserie *f*; **2.** lambrisser, boiser (de, with).

waist [weist] taille *f*, ceinture *f*; ⚓ embelle *f*; '⁓-belt ceinturon *m*; ⁓-coat ['weiskout] gilet *m*; '⁓'deep jusqu'à la ceinture; '**waist·ed** *cost.* cintré; high-⁓ (low-⁓) à taille haute (basse); slim-⁓ à la taille fine, à la taille fine; '⁓-line taille *f*; ligne *f*.

wait [weit] **1.** *v/i.* attendre; (*souv.* ⁓ at table) servir; F ⁓ about faire le pied de grue; ⁓ for attendre (qch., q.); ⁓ (up)on servir (q.); être aux ordres de (q.); être la conséquence de (qch.); keep s.o. ⁓ing faire attendre q.; ⁓ and see attendre voir; ⁓ in line faire la queue; play a ⁓ing game attendre son heure; *v/t.* attendre; différer (*un repas*) (jusqu'à l'arrivée de q., for s.o.); **2.** attente *f*; ⁓s *pl.* chanteurs *m/pl.* de noëls; have a long ⁓ devoir attendre longtemps; be in ⁓ être à l'affût (de, for); '**wait·er** *restaurant*: garçon *m*; *fig.* plateau *m*.

wait·ing ['weitiŋ] attente *f*; service *m*; in ⁓ de service; ⁓ list liste *f* d'attente; ⁓ room salle *f* d'attente; antichambre *f*.

wait·ress ['weitris] fille *f* de service; ⁓! mademoiselle!

waive [weiv] ne pas insister sur, ⚖; renoncer à; **'waiv·er** ⚖ abandon *m*.

wake[1] [weik] ⚓ sillage *m* (*a. fig.*); *fig.* suite *f*; ⚔ remous *m* d'air.

wake[2] [⁓] **1.** [*irr.*] *v/i.* veiller; (*fig.* ⁓ *up*) se réveiller, s'éveiller; *v/t.* réveiller; ⁓ *a corpse* veiller un mort; **2.** veillée *f* de corps; fête *f* annuelle; **wake·ful** □ ['⁓ful] éveillé; sans sommeil; **'wak·en** (se) réveiller; (s')éveiller (*a. fig.*).

wale [weil] marque *f*; ⊕ *drap*: côté *f*; *palplanches*: moise (*f*); ⚓ platbord (*pl.* plats-bords) *m*.

walk [wɔ:k] **1.** *v/i.* marcher, se promener; aller à pied; cheminer; aller au pas (*cheval*); revenir (*spectre*); ⁓ *about* se promener, circuler; *sl.* ⁓ *into* se heurter à (*qch.*); *Am.* ⁓ *out* se mettre en grève; *Am.* F ⁓ *out on* laisser *ou* planter là (*q.*); *v/t.* faire marcher; courir (*les rues*); faire (*une distance*); conduire *ou* mettre un cheval au pas; ⁓ *the hospitals* faire les hôpitaux; assister aux leçons cliniques; ⚔ ⁓ *the rounds* faire sa faction; ⁓ *s.o. off* emmener q.; **2.** marche *f*; promenade *f*; tour(née *f*) *m*; allée *f*, avenue *f*; démarche *f*; pas *m*; ⁓ *of life* position *f* sociale; métier *m*; **'⁓-a·bout** go on a ⁓ prendre un bain de foule; **'⁓-a·way** surt. *Am.* victoire *f* facile; **'walk·er** marcheur (-euse *f*) *m*; piéton *m*; *sp.* amateur *m* du footing; *be a good* ⁓ être bon marcheur; **'walk·er·ton** *sl.* figurant(e *f*) *m*.

walk·ie-talk·ie ['wɔ:ki'tɔ:ki] appareil *m* d'émission et réception radiophonique, walkie-talkie *m*.

walk·ing ['wɔ:kiŋ] **1.** marche *f*; promenade *f* à pied; *sp.* footing *m*; **2.** ambulant; de marche; *Am.* F ⁓ *papers pl.* congé *m*; ⁓ *tour* excursion *f* à pied; **'⁓-stick** canne *f*.

walk...: **'⁓-out** *Am.* grève *f*; **'⁓-o·ver** *sp.* walk-over *m*; *fig.* victoire *f* facile; **'⁓-up** *Am.* sans ascenseur (*appartement*).

wall [wɔ:l] **1.** mur *m*; muraille *f*; (*a. side⁓*) paroi *f* (*a.* ⊕); *give s.o. the* ⁓ donner à q. le haut du pavé; *fig. go to the* ⁓ être ruiné *ou* mis à l'écart; **2.** entourer de murs; murer; *fig.* emmurer; ⁓ *up* murer.

wal·la·by *zo.* ['wɔləbi] petit kangourou *m*, wallaby *m*. [sacoche *f*.]

wal·let ['wɔlit] portefeuille *m*; sac *m*,)

wall...: **'⁓-eye** *vét.* œil *m* vairon; **'⁓-'eyed** *vét.* vairon; qui louche, à strabisme divergent; **'⁓-flow·er** ♀ giroflée *f* (jaune); *fig. be a* ⁓ faire tapisserie; **'⁓-fruit** fruit *m* d'espalier; **'⁓-map** carte *f* murale.

Wal·loon [wɔ'lu:n] **1.** wallon(ne *f*); **2.** *ling.* wallon *m*; Wallon(ne *f*) *m*.

wal·lop F ['wɔləp] **1.** rosser (*q.*), tanner le cuir à (*q.*); **2.** gros coup *m*; *sl.* bière *f*; **'wal·lop·ing** F énorme.

wal·low ['wɔlou] **1.** se vautrer; *fig.* se plonger (*dans*, *in*), nager (*dans*, *in*); **2.** fange *f*; *chasse*: souille *f*; *have a* ⁓ se vautrer.

wall...: **'⁓-pa·per** papier *m* peint *ou* à tapisser; **'⁓-sock·et** ⚡ prise *f* de courant; **'⁓-to-wall car·pet(ing)** moquette *f*.

wal·nut ♀ ['wɔ:lnʌt] noix *f*; *arbre*: noyer *m*; (*bois m de*) noyer *m*.

wal·rus *zo.* ['wɔ:lrəs] morse *m*.

waltz [wɔ:ls] **1.** valse *f*; **2.** valser.

wan □ [wɔn] blême, pâle; blafard.

wand [wɔnd] baguette *f*; bâton *m* (*de commandement*); verge *f* (*d'huissier*).

wan·der ['wɔndə] errer (*a.* ⁓ *about*) se promener au hasard, aller à l'aventure; *fig.* s'écarter (*de*, *from*); *fig.* divaguer (*personne*); **'wan·der·er** vagabond(e *f*) *m*; **'wan·der·ing** **1.** □ errant; vagabond (*a. fig.*); *fig.* distrait; **2.** vagabondage *m*; ⚕ délire *m*; *fig.* rêverie *f*; **'wan·der·lust** envie *f* de voyager.

wane [wein] **1.** décroître (*lune*); *fig.* s'affaiblir; **2.** déclin *m*; *on the* ⁓ sur *ou* à son déclin.

wan·gle *sl.* ['wæŋgl] employer le système D; carotter (*qch.*); **'wan·gler** carotteur (-euse *f*) *m*.

wan·ness ['wɔnnis] pâleur *f*.

want [wɔnt] **1.** manque *m*, défaut *m* (*de*, *of*); besoin *m*; gêne *f*; *for* ⁓ *of* faute de; *Am.* ⁓ *ad* demande *f* d'emploi (*dans les petites annonces*); **2.** *v/i. be* ⁓*ing* faire défaut, manquer (*chose*); *be* ⁓*ing* manquer (*de*, *in*) (*personne*); *be* ⁓*ing* to ne pas être à la hauteur de (*une tâche etc.*); *he does not* ⁓ *for talent* les talents ne lui font pas défaut; *v/t.* vouloir, désirer; manquer de; avoir besoin de; falloir; *it* ⁓*s five minutes of eight o'clock* il est huit heures moins cinq; *it* ⁓*s two days to* il y a encore deux jours à; *he* ⁓*s energy* il manque d'énergie; you ~ to be careful il faut faire attention; ~ s.o. to (inf.) vouloir que q. (sbj.); ~ed recherché (par la police).

wan·ton ['wɔntən] **1.** □ impudique; licencieux (-euse f); folâtre; poét. luxuriant; gratuit; **2.** voluptueux (-euse f) m; femme f impudique; **3.** folâtre; 'wan·ton·ness libertinage m; gaieté f de cœur.

war [wɔ:] **1.** guerre f; attr. de guerre; guerrier (-ère f); ~ of nerves guerre f des nerfs; at ~ en guerre (avec, contre with); make ~ faire la guerre (à, contre [up]on); **2.** poét. lutter; mener une campagne, fig. faire la guerre (à, against).

war·ble ['wɔ:bl] **1.** vt/i. chanter (en gazouillant); v/i. gazouiller; **2.** gazouillement m; ruisseau: murmure m; 'war·bler oiseau m chanteur; fauvette f. [gle de guerre.)

war·blind·ed ['wɔ:blaindid] aveu-)

ward [wɔ:d] **1.** garde f; † tutelle f; personne: pupille mf; escrime: garde f, parade f; quartier m (d'une prison); salle f (d'hôpital); admin. arrondissement m; circonscription f électorale; ~s pl. dents f/pl., bouterolles f/pl. (d'une clef); casual ~ asile m de nuit; in ~ en tutelle; sous la tutelle (de, to); Am. F pol. ~ heeler politicien m à la manque; **2.** faire entrer (à l'hôpital etc.); ~ off écarter; 'ward·en directeur (-trice f) m; recteur m; 'ward·er gardien m de prison; 'ward·robe garde-robe f; meuble: armoire f; ~ dealer marchand(e f) m de toilette; ~ trunk malle-armoire (pl. malles-armoires) f; 'ward·room ⚓ carré m des officiers; 'ward·ship tutelle f.

ware [wɛə] marchandise f; ustensiles m/pl.

ware·house 1. ['wɛəhaus] entrepôt m; magasin m; **2.** ['~hauz] emmagasiner; douane: entreposer; ~·man ['~hausmən] emmagasineur m; douane: entreposeur m; garçon m de magasin; Italian ~ épicier m.

war...: '~·fare la guerre f; '~·grave sépulture f militaire; '~·head torpille etc.: cône m (de charge).

war·i·ness ['wɛərinis] circonspection f; prudence f; défiance f.

war...: '~·like martial (-aux m/pl.); '~·loan emprunt m de guerre.

77*

warm [wɔ:m] **1.** □ chaud (a. fig.); fig. chaleureux (-euse f), vif (vive f); F riche; be ~ avoir chaud (personne); être chaud (chose); **2.** F action f de (se) chauffer; **3.** v/t. chauffer; fig. (r)échauffer; sl. flanquer une tripotée à; ~ up (ré)chauffer; v/i. (a. ~ up) s'échauffer, se (ré)chauffer; s'animer; ~ to se sentir attiré vers (q.); '~·'heart·ed affectueux (-euse f), chaleureux (-euse f); 'warm·ing sl. rossée f.

war·mon·ger ['wɔ:mʌŋgə] belliciste m; 'war·mon·ger·ing, 'war·mon·ger·y propagande f de guerre.

warmth [wɔ:mθ] chaleur f.

warm-up ['wɔ:mʌp] mise f en train.

warn [wɔ:n] avertir (de of, against); prévenir; (ou ~ off) détourner; conseiller (de inf., to inf.); alerter; 'warn·ing avertissement m; avis m; turf: exécution f; congé m (d'un employé etc.); alerte f; take ~ from profiter de l'exemple de; tirer une leçon de.

warp [wɔ:p] **1.** tex. chaîne f; tapisserie: lisse f; ⚓ amarre f; voilure f (d'une planche); fig. perversion f; **2.** v/i. se voiler (bois); ⚓ (usu. ~ out) déhaler; v/t. (faire) voiler, déverser (du bois etc.); ⚓ gauchir (les ailes); tex. ourdir (une étoffe), empeigner (un métier); ⚓ haler, touer; fig. fausser (les sens); pervertir (l'esprit).

war...: '~·paint peinture f de guerre (des Peaux-Rouges); F fig. grande tenue f; gros maquillage m; '~·path (be on the ~ être sur le) sentier m de la guerre.

warp·ing ⚓ ['wɔ:piŋ] gauchissement m des ailes.

war...: '~·plane avion m de guerre; '~·prof·it·eer mercanti m de guerre.

war·rant ['wɔrənt] **1.** garantie f; fig. garant m; justification f; ⚖ mandat m; pouvoir m; ⚔ feuille f (de route); ⚔ ordonnance f (de paiement); ⚓ warrant m; ~ of (apprehension) mandat m d'amener; ~ of arrest mandat m d'arrêt; **2.** garantir (a. ⚓); certifier; attester; répondre de (qch.); justifier; 'war·rant·a·ble □ légitime; justifiable; que l'on peut garantir; chasse: courable; 'war·rant·ed garanti; war·ran·tee ⚖ [~ti:] receveur (-euse f) m d'une garantie; 'war·rant·of·fi·cer ⚓

premier maître *m*; ⚔ sous-officier *m* breveté; **war·ran·tor** ⚖ ['⁓tɔ:] répondant *m*; '**war·ran·ty** garantie *f*; autorisation *f*.

war·ren ['wɔrin] garenne *f*, lapinière *f*.

war·ri·or ['wɔriə] guerrier *m*; *the Unknown* ♀ le Soldat inconnu.

war·ship ['wɔːʃip] vaisseau *m* de guerre.

wart [wɔːt] verrue *f*; ♉ excroissance *f*; '**wart·y** verruqueux (-euse *f*).

war...: '**⁓·time** temps *m* de guerre.

war·y □ ['wɛəri] circonspect, prudent; défiant; précautionneux (-euse *f*).

was [wɔz; wəz] *prét. de* be; *he ⁓ to have come* il devait venir.

wash [wɔʃ] **1.** *v/t.* laver; blanchir (*le linge*); *fig.* baigner; ⁓*ed out* délavé; décoloré; F flapi; ⁓ *up* faire la vaisselle; ⚓ rejeter sur le rivage; *sl.* ⁓*ed up* fini, fichu; *v/i.* se laver; ⁓ *against the cliff* baigner la falaise; ⚓ ⁓ *over* balayer (*le pont*); **2.** lessive *f*, blanchissage *m*; toilette *f*; remous *m*; ⚓ sillage *m*; ✈ souffle *m* (*de l'hélice*); *peint.* lavis *m*; (*a.* colo[u]r ⁓) badigeon *m*; *péj.* lavasse *f*; ♒, *pharm.*, *vét.* lotion *f*; '**wash·a·ble** lavable; '**wash(-)and(-)wear** 'ne pas repasser'; '**wash-ba·sin** cuvette *f*, lavabo *m*; '**wash-cloth** torchon *m*; '**washed-'out** F épuisé, F lessivé; '**washed-'up** F fichu, ruiné; épuisé, F lessivé.

wash·er ['wɔʃə] laveur (-euse *f*) *m*; *machine*: laveuse *f*; ⊕ cylindre *m* à laver; '**⁓-wom·an** blanchisseuse *f*.

wash·i·ness F ['wɔʃinis] fadeur *f*, insipidité *f*.

wash·ing ['wɔʃiŋ] **1.** lavage *m*; ablution *f*; lessive *f*, blanchissage *m*; ⊕ lavée *f* (*de laine, de minerai*); ⁓*s pl.* produits *m/pl.* de lavage; ⊕ chantier *m* de lavage; **2.** *de lessive*; ⁓ *machine* machine *f* à laver; ⁓ *powder* lessive *f*; '**⁓-silk** soie *f* lavable; '**⁓-'up** (*lavage m de la*) vaisselle *f*; ⁓ *basin* cuvette *f*; ⁓ *water* eau *f* de vaisselle; *do the ⁓* faire la vaisselle.

wash...: '**⁓-'out** *sl.* fiasco *m*; raté(e *f*) *m* (*personne*); '**⁓-rag** *surt. Am.* lavette *f*, gant *m* de toilette; '**⁓-stand** lavabo *m*; '**wash·y** délavé (*couleur*); *fig.* fade, insipide.

wasp [wɔsp] guêpe *f*; '**wasp·ish** □

méchant (*a. fig.*); acerbe; acariâtre (*femme*).

wast·age ['weistidʒ] déperdition *f*, perte *f*; gaspillage *m*; *coll.* déchets *m/pl.*

waste [weist] **1.** désert, inculte; perdu (*temps*); ⊕ de rebut; *lay ⁓* dévaster, ravager; ⁓ *heat* chaleur *f* perdue; ⁓ *paper* vieux papiers *m/pl.*; papier *m* de rebut; ⁓ *products pl.* déchets *m/pl.*; ⁓ *steam* vapeur *f* perdue; ⁓ *water* eaux *f/pl.* ménagères; ⊕ eaux-vannes *f/pl.*; **2.** perte *f*; gaspillage *m*; rebut *m*; déchet *m*; région *f* inculte; *go* (*ou run*) *to ⁓* se perdre, se dissiper; s'affricher (*terrain*); **3.** *v/t.* user, consumer, gaspiller; perdre (*son temps*); *v/i.* se perdre; s'user; maigrir (*malade*); **waste·ful** □ ['⁓ful] gaspilleur (-euse *f*); prodigue; inutile; ruineux (-euse *f*); '**waste-land** terre *f* en friche; '**waste-pa·per bas·ket** corbeille *f* à papier; '**waste-pipe** trop-plein *m*; *baignoire*: écoulement *m*; '**wast·er** gaspilleur (-euse *f*) *m*; *see* wastrel.

wast·rel ['weistrəl] vaurien *m*; mauvais sujet *m*.

watch [wɔtʃ] **1.** garde *f*; † veille *f*; † *personne*: garde *m*; ⚓ quart *m*; montre *f*; *be on the ⁓ for* épier, guetter; être à l'affût de; ♀ *Committee* comité *m* municipal qui veille au maintien de l'ordre; **2.** *v/i.* veiller (sur, over); ⁓ *for* attendre (*q., qch.*); guetter (*q.*); *v/t.* veiller sur, regarder; assister à; guetter (*l'occasion*); '**⁓·boat** ⚓ (bateau *m*) patrouilleur *m*; '**⁓-brace·let** montre-bracelet (*pl.* montres-bracelets) *f*; '**⁓-case** boîte *f* de montre; '**⁓·dog** chien *m* de garde; '**watch·er** veilleur (-euse *f*) *m*; observateur (-trice *f*) *m*; **watch·ful** □ ['⁓ful] vigilant, attentif (-ive *f*).

watch...: '**⁓-mak·er** horloger *m*; '**⁓-man** gardien *m*; veilleur *m* (*de nuit*); '**⁓-tow·er** tour *f* de guet; '**⁓-word** *pol. etc.* mot *m* d'ordre.

wa·ter ['wɔːtə] **1.** eau *f*; ⁓ *supply* (provision *f* d')eau *f*; service *m* des eaux; *high* (*low*) ⁓ marée *f* haute (basse); *by* ⁓ en bateau, par eau; *drink* (*ou take*) *the* ⁓*s* prendre les eaux; *of the first* ⁓ de première eau (*diamant*); *fig.* de premier ordre; F *be in hot* ⁓ être dans le pétrin; avoir des ennuis; F *be in low* ⁓ être dans la gêne; **2.** *v/t.* arroser (*terre, route, plante, région*); abreuver (*les bêtes*); *fig.* atténuer, affaiblir; (*souv.* ~ down) mouiller, diluer; ⊕ alimenter en eau (*une machine*); *tex.* moirer; *v/i.* pleurer (*yeux*); faire provision d'eau; s'abreuver (*bêtes*); ⊕, ⚓, *mot.* faire de l'eau; *make s.o.'s mouth* ~ faire venir l'eau à la bouche de q.; '~**blis·ter** ⚕ cloque *f*; '~**borne** flottant; transporté par voie d'eau; ~ **can·non** lance-eau *m/inv.*; '~**cart** arroseuse *f* (*dans les rues*); '~**clos·et** (*usu. écrit* W.C.) cabinets *m/pl.*, F waters *m/pl.*; '~**col·o(u)r** aquarelle *f*; couleur *f* à l'eau; '~**cooled** refroidi à eau; '~**cool·ing** refroidissement *m* à eau; '~**course** cours *m* d'eau; conduite *f* d'eau; '~**cress** ⚘ cresson *m* (de fontaine); '~**fall** chute *f* d'eau; '~**fowl** gibier *m, coll.* ~s *m/pl.* d'eau; '~**front** surt. Am. quai *m*, bord *m* de l'eau; '~**gauge** ⊕ hydromètre *m*; (indicateur *m* de) niveau *m* d'eau; '~**hose** tuyau *m* d'arrosage; *qqfois* manche *f* à feu; '**wa·ter·i·ness** aquosité *f*; ⚕ sérosité *f*; *fig.* fadeur *f*.

wa·ter·ing ['wɔ:tərɪŋ] arrosage *m*; irrigation *f*; abreuvage *m* (*des bêtes*); '~**can,** '~**pot** arrosoir *m*; '~**place** abreuvoir *m*; ville *f* d'eau; plage *f*, bains *m/pl.* de mer.

wa·ter...: '~**jack·et** ⊕ chemise *f* d'eau; '~**lev·el** niveau *m* d'eau (*a.* ⊕); '~**lil·y** ⚘ nénuphar *m*; '~**logged** imbibé d'eau; ⚓ plein d'eau; '~**main** conduite *f* (principale) d'eau; '~**man** batelier *m*, marinier *m*; '~**mark** niveau *m* des eaux; ⚓ laisse *f*; *papier*: filigrane *m*; '~**part·ing** ligne *f* de partage des eaux; '~**pipe** conduite *f* d'eau; '~**plane** hydravion *m*; ~ **pol·lu·tion** pollution *f* de l'eau; '~**po·lo** water-polo *m*; '~**pow·er** force *f* ou énergie *f* hydraulique; ~ *station* centrale *f* hydraulique; '~**proof 1.** imperméable (*a. su./m*); **2.** rendre imperméable; caoutchouter; '~**re'pel·lent wool** laine *f* cirée; '~**shed** *see* waterparting; *p. ext.* bassin *m*; ~'**side 1.** riverain; **2.** bord *m* de l'eau; '~**spout** descente *f* d'eau; gouttière *f*; *météor.* trombe *f*; '~**ta·ble** niveau *m* hydrostatique; '~**tap** robinet *m*; '~**tight** étanche; *fig.* sans échappatoire, inattaquable; *fig. in* ~ compart-

ments séparé(s) par des cloisons étanches; '~**wave 1.** *cheveux*: mise *f* en plis; **2.** mettre (*les cheveux*) en plis; '~**way** voie *f* d'eau; ⚓ gouttière *f*; '~**works** *usu. sg.* usine *f* de distribution d'eau; '**wa·ter·y** aqueux (-euse *f*); larmoyant (*yeux*); *fig.* noyé *ou* plein d'eau; *fig.* peu épais (-se *f*).

watt ⚡ [wɔt] watt *m*.

wat·tle ['wɔtl] **1.** clayonnage *m*; claie *f*; *dindon*: caroncule *f*; **2.** clayonner; tresser (*l'osier*).

waul [wɔ:l] miauler.

wave [weɪv] **1.** vague *f* (*a. fig.*); *phys.* onde *f*; *cheveux*: ondulation *f*; geste *m*, signe *m* (de la main); **2.** *v/t.* agiter; brandir; onduler (*les cheveux*); faire signe de (*la main*); ~ *s.o. aside* écarter q. d'un geste; *v/i.* s'agiter; flotter; onduler; faire signe (à q., *to s.o.*); '~**length** ⚡ *radio*: longueur *f* d'onde; F *fig. be on the same* ~ être sur la même longueur d'onde(s); '~**me·ter** ondemètre *m*.

wa·ver ['weɪvə] hésiter; vaciller (*a. fig.*); ⚔ *etc.* fléchir.

wave...: '~**range** *radio*: gamme *f* de longueur d'onde; '~**trap** *radio*: ondemètre *m* d'absorption.

wav·y ['weɪvɪ] onduleux (-euse *f*); ondulé; tremblé (*ligne*).

wax¹ [wæks] **1.** cire *f*; *oreilles*: cérumen *m*; ~ *candle* bougie *f* de cire; *eccl.* cierge *m*; ~ *doll* poupée *f* de cire; **2.** cirer; mettre (*le cuir*) en cire; empoisser (*le fil*).

wax² [~] croître (*lune*); *co. devant adj.*: devenir.

wax·en ['wæksn] de *ou* en cire; *fig. a.* cireux (-euse *f*); '**wax·work** figure *f* de cire; ~s *pl.*, ~ *show* figures *f/pl.* de cire; '**wax·y** □ cireux (-euse *f*).

way [weɪ] **1.** chemin *m*, route *f*, voie *f*; direction *f*, côté *m*; façon *f*, manière *f*; genre *m*; moyen *m*; marche *f*; progrès *m*; état *m*; habitude *f*; idée *f*, guise *f*; ~ *in* entrée *f*; ~ *out* sortie *f*; *admin.* ~s *and means* voies *f/pl.* et moyens *m/pl.*; *parl.* Committee of ⊙s *and* Means Commission *f* du Budget; *right of* ~ 👮 servitude *f* ou droit *m* de passage; *surt. mot.* priorité *f* de passage; *this* ~ par ici; *in some (ou a)* ~ en quelque sorte; *in no* ~ ne … aucunement *ou* d'aucune façon; *go a great (ou some)* ~ *to-wards (gér.), go a long (ou some)* ~ *to* (inf.) contribuer de beaucoup ou quelque peu à (inf.); by the ~ en passant, à propos; by ~ of par la voie de; en guise de, à titre de; by ~ of excuse en guise d'excuse; on the (ou one's) ~ en route (pour, to); chemin faisant; out of the ~ écarté, isolé; fig. peu ordinaire; under ~ en marche (a. ♏); give ~ céder, lâcher pied; faire place; have one's ~ agir à sa guise; if I had my ~ si on me laissait faire; have a ~ with se faire bien voir de (q.); lead the ~ marcher en tête; montrer le chemin; see make 1; pay one's ~ joindre les deux bouts; se suffire; see one's ~ to juger possible de; trouver moyen de; Am.~ station petite gare f; Am. ~ train train m omnibus; 2. adv. Am. loin; là-bas; '~-bill feuille f de route; lettre f de voiture; '~·far·er voyageur (-euse f) m; ~·lay [irr. (lay)] guetter (au passage); '~-leave droit m de passage ou de survol; '~-side 1. bord m de la route; by the ~ au bord de la route; 2. au bord de la route, en bordure de route.

way·ward □ ['weiwəd] capricieux (-euse f); entêté, rebelle; 'way-ward·ness entêtement m; caractère m difficile.

we [wi:; wi] nous (a. accentué).

weak □ [wi:k] faible; léger (-ère f) (thé); 'weak·en (s')affaiblir; 'weak-ling personne f faible; 'weak·ly 1. adj. faible; 2. adv. faiblement; sans résolution; 'weak-'mind·ed faible d'esprit; qui manque de résolution; 'weak·ness faiblesse f.

weal[1] [wi:l] 1. bien(-être) m.

weal[2] [~] marque f.

wealth [welθ] richesse f, -s f/pl.; fig. abondance f; 'wealth·y □ riche, opulent.

wean [wi:n] sevrer (un enfant); fig. détourner (q.) (de from, of).

weap·on ['wepən] arme f; 'weap-on·less sans armes, désarmé; 'weap·on·ry armes f/pl.; armement(s) m (pl.).

wear [wɛə] [irr.] 1. v/t. porter (un vêtement etc.); (a. ~ away, down, off, out) user, effacer; épuiser, lasser (la patience); v/i. faire bon usage; se conserver (bien etc.) (personne); ~ away s'user; s'effacer; passer; ~ off disparaître (a. fig.), s'effacer; ~ on s'écouler (temps);

s'avancer; ~ out s'user; s'épuiser; 2. usage m; mode f; vêtements m/pl.; fatigue f; (a. ~ and tear) usure f; gentlemen's ~ vêtements m/pl. pour hommes; for hard ~ d'un bon usage; be the ~ être à la mode ou de mise; the worse for ~ usé; there is plenty of ~ in it yet il est encore portable; 'wear·a·ble portable (vêtement).

wea·ri·ness ['wiərinis] fatigue f; lassitude f; fig. dégoût m.

wea·ri·some □ ['wiərisəm] ennuyeux (-euse f); fig. ingrat, f assommant; 'wea·ri·some·ness ennui m.

wea·ry ['wiəri] 1. □ las(se f), fatigué (de, with); fig. dégoûté (de, of); fatigant, fastidieux (-euse f); 2. (se) lasser, fatiguer.

wea·sel zo. ['wi:zl] belette f.

weath·er ['weðə] 1. temps m; see permit 1; 2. météorologique; see côté du vent, au vent; 3. v/t. altérer (par les intempéries); ♏ passer au vent de; doubler (un cap); (a. ~ out) étaler (une tempête etc.), fig. survivre à; ~ed altéré par le temps ou les intempéries; v/i. s'altérer; prendre la patine (cuivre etc.); '~-beat·en battu par les tempêtes; basané (figure etc.); '~-board fenêtre: reverseau m; toit etc.: planche f à recouvrement; '~-board·ing planches f/pl. à recouvrement; '~-bound retenu par le mauvais temps; '~-bu·reau bureau m météorologique; '~-chart carte f météorologique; '~-cock girouette f; '~-fore·cast bulletin m météorologique; prévisions f/pl. du temps; '~-proof, '~-tight imperméable; étanche; '~-sta·tion station f météorologique; '~-strip bourrelet m étanche; mot. gouttière f d'étanchéité; '~-vane girouette f; '~-worn rongé par les intempéries.

weave [wi:v] 1. [irr.] tisser; fig. tramer; 2. armure f; tissage m; 'weav-er tisserand(e f) m; 'weav·ing tissage m; entrelacement m; route: zig-zags m/pl.; attr. à tisser.

wea·zen ['wi:zn] ratatiné, desséché.

web [web] tissu m (a. fig.); toile f (d'araignée); orn. plume: lame f; pattes: palmure f; ⊕ rouleau m (d'étoffe, de papier); **webbed** palmé, membrané; '**web·bing** (toile f à) sangles *f/pl.*; '**web-foot·ed** palmipède, aux pieds palmés.

wed [wed] *v/t.* épouser, se marier avec (*q.*); marier (*un couple*); *fig.* unir (à *to*, *with*); *v/i.* se marier; '**wed·ded** conjugal (-aux *m/pl.*); marié; '**wed·ding 1.** mariage *m*; noce *f*, -s *f/pl.*; **2.** de noce(s); de mariage; nuptial (-aux *m/pl.*); ~ *anniversary* anniversaire *m* de mariage; ~ *ring* alliance *f*.

wedge [wedʒ] **1.** coin *m*; *fig.* the thin end of the ~ le premier pas, un pied de pris; **2.** coincer; (*a. ~ in*) enclaver, insérer; '**~-shaped** en forme de coin; cunéiforme (*caractères, os*).

wed·lock ['wedlɔk] mariage *m*.

Wednes·day ['wenzdi] mercredi *m*.

wee *écoss.*, F [wiː] (tout) petit.

weed [wiːd] **1.** mauvaise herbe *f*; F tabac *m*; F personne *f* étique; **2.** sarcler; (*a. ~ up*, *out*) arracher les mauvaises herbes; *fig.* éliminer; '**weed·er** sarcleur (-euse *f*) *m*; *outil:* sarcloir *m*; extirpateur *m*.

weeds [wiːdz] *pl.* (*usu.* widow's ~) (vêtements *m/pl.* de) deuil *m*.

weed·y ['wiːdi] plein de mauvaises herbes; *fig.* étique; maigre.

week [wiːk] semaine *f*; *short working* ~ semaine *f* courte; *by the* ~ à la semaine; *this day* ~ d'aujourd'hui en huit; '**~-day** jour *m* de semaine; jour *m* ouvrable; '**~-'end 1.** fin *f* de semaine; week-end *m*; ~ *ticket* billet *m* valable du samedi au lundi; **2.** passer le week-end; '**~-'end·er** touriste *mf* de fin de semaine; '**week·ly 1.** hebdomadaire; **2.** (*a. ~ paper*) hebdomadaire *m*.

wee·ny F ['wiːni] tout petit, minuscule.

weep [wiːp] [*irr.*] pleurer (de *joie etc.*, *for*; qch. *for*, over *s.th.*); verser des larmes; '**weep·er** pleureur (-euse *f*) *m*; ~*s pl.* manchettes *f/pl.* de deuil; '**weep·ing 1.** qui pleure; humide; ♃ ~ *willow* saule *m* pleureur; **2.** larmes *f/pl.*, pleurs *m/pl.*

wee·vil ['wiːvil] charançon *m* (*du blé etc.*).

weft [weft] *tex.* trame *f*; *fig.* traînée *f* (*d'un nuage etc.*).

weigh [wei] **1.** *v/t.* peser (*a. fig. le pour et le contre*); *fig.* (*a. ~ up*) jauger; ⚓ ~ *anchor* lever l'ancre; ~ *down* peser plus que; ~*ed down* sur-

chargé, *fig.* accablé (de, *with*); *v/i.* peser (*a. fig.*); *fig.* avoir du poids (pour, *with*); ~ (*up*)*on* peser (lourd) sur; **2.** ⚓ *get under* ~ (*ou way*) se mettre en route; '**weigh·a·ble** pesable; '**weigh·bridge** (pont *m* à) bascule *f*; '**weigh·er** peseur (-euse *f*) *m*; '**weigh·ing-ma·chine** bascule *f*; appareil *m* de pesage.

weight [weit] **1.** poids *m*; pesanteur *f*, lourdeur *f*; force *f* (*d'un coup*); *fig.* importance *f*; *fig.* carry great ~ avoir beaucoup d'influence; avoir de l'autorité; *sp.* putting the ~ lancement *m* du poids; **2.** alourdir; attacher un poids à; *fig.* affecter d'un coefficient; '**weight·i·ness** pesanteur *f*; *fig.* importance *f*; '**weight·less** qui ne pèse rien; en état d'apesanteur; '**weight·less·ness** apesanteur *f*; '**weight·y** □ pesant, lourd; grave; sérieux (-euse *f*).

weir [wiə] barrage *m*; *étang:* déversoir *m*.

weird [wiəd] étrange; mystérieux (-euse *f*); F singulier (-ère *f*).

wel·come ['welkəm] **1.** □ bienvenu; agréable; *you are* ~ *to* (*inf.*) libre à vous de (*inf.*); *you are* ~ *to it* c'est à votre service; *iro.* grand bien vous fasse!; (*you are*) ~! soyez le bienvenu!; il n'y a pas de quoi!; **2.** bienvenue *f*; **3.** souhaiter la bienvenue à; accueillir (*a. fig.*).

weld [weld] **1.** (se) souder; (se) corroyer (*acier*); ~ *into* fondre en; **2.** (*a. ~ing seam*) (joint *m* de) soudure *f*; '**weld·ing** ⊕ soudage *m*, soudure *f*; *attr.* soudant; à souder.

wel·fare ['welfeə] bien-être *m*; ~ *centre* dispensaire *m*; ~ *work* assistance *f* sociale; ~ *worker* assistant (-e *f*) *m* social(e).

well[1] [wel] **1.** puits *m*; *fig.* source *f*; ⊕ *haut fourneau:* creuset *m*; (*a. ink-*~) encrier *m*; *ascenseur:* cage *f*; *hôtel:* cour *f*; **2.** jaillir, sourdre.

well[2] [~] **1.** *adv.* bien; *see as 1*; ~ *off* aisé, riche; bien fourni (de, *for*); *be* ~ *past fifty* avoir largement dépassé la cinquantaine; *beat s.o.* ~ battre q. à plate couture; **2.** *adj.* *préd.* en bonne santé; bon; bien; *I am not* ~ je ne me porte pas bien; *all's well* tout va bien; **3.** *int.* eh bien!; F ça alors!; '**~-ad·vised** sage; bien avisé (*personne*); '**~-'bal·anced**

(bien) equilibré; '~-'**be·ing** bien-être m; '~-'**born** de bonne famille; bien né; '~-'**bred** bien élevé; '~-**dis**'**posed** bien disposé (envers, to[wards]); '~-'**fa·vo(u)red** beau (bel devant une voyelle ou un h muet; belle f); de bonne mine; '~-**in**-'**formed** bien renseigné.

Wel·ling·tons ['weliŋtənz] pl. bottes f/pl. en caoutchouc.

well...: '~-**in**'**ten·tioned** bien intentionné; '~-'**judged** bien calculé; judicieux (-euse f); '~-'**knit** bien bâti; solide; '~-'**made** de coupe soignée (habit); bien découplé; '~-'**man·nered** bien élevé; '~-'**mean·ing** bien intentionné; '~-'**meant** fait avec de bonnes intentions; amical (-aux m/pl.) (conseil etc.); '~-**nigh** presque; '~-'**off** bien inv.; (a. ~ for money) aisé, (bien) nanti; '~-**pre**-'**served** bien conservé; '~-'**read** lettré, érudit; instruit; cultivé; '~-'**spok·en** qui soigne son élocution; cultivé; '~-'**thought-of** (bien) considéré; estimé; '~-'**timed** opportun, à propos; bien calculé; ~-**to-do** aisé; prospère; ~ **turned** fig. bien tourné; '~-'**wish·er** ami(e f) m sincère, partisan m; '~-'**worn** usé; fig. rebattu.

Welsh¹ [welʃ] **1.** gallois; **2.** ling. gallois m; the ~ les Gallois m/pl.

welsh² [~] turf: décamper avec les enjeux des parieurs; '**welsh·er** bookmaker m marron; p.ext. escroc m.

Welsh...: '~-**man** Gallois m; '~-**wom·an** Galloise f.

welt [welt] **1.** ⊕ semelle: trépointe f; chaussette, gant: bordure f; couvre-joint m; **2.** mettre des trépointes à (des souliers); border; F rosser; ~ed à trépointes (soulier).

wel·ter ['weltə] **1.** se rouler, se vautrer; fig. ~ in nager dans (son sang etc.); **2.** désordre m; '~-**weight** box. poids m mi-moyen.

wen 𝒮 [wen] kyste m sébacé; F goitre m.

wench [wentʃ] jeune fille f ou femme f.

wend [wend]: ~ one's way (vers, to) diriger ses pas; se diriger.

went went prét. de go 1.

wept [wept] prét. et p.p. de weep.

were [wɔː; wə] prét. et sbj. prét. de be.

west [west] **1.** su. ouest m; **2.** adj. de

l'ouest; occidental (-aux m/pl.); **3.** adv. à ou vers l'ouest; sl. go ~ casser sa pipe (= mourir); '~·**bound** en direction de l'ouest; allant vers l'ouest.

west·er·ly ['westəli] de ou à l'ouest ; **west·ern** ['westən] **1.** de l'ouest; occidental (-aux m/pl.); **2.** see westerner; Am. 𝒮 film m ou roman m de cowboys; western m; '**west·ern·er** occidental(e f) m; habitant(e f) m de l'ouest; '**west·ern·most** le plus à l'ouest.

west·ing ⚓ ['westiŋ] route f vers l'ouest; départ m pour l'ouest.

west·ward ['westwəd] **1.** adj. à ou de l'ouest: **2.** adv. (a. west·wards ['~dz]) vers l'ouest.

wet [wet] **1.** mouillé; humide; Am. qui permet la vente de l'alcool; see blanket 1; ⚡ ~ cell pile f à l'élément humide; ⊕~ process voie f humide; ~ steam vapeur f mouillée; ~ through trempé (jusqu'aux os); F with a ~ finger à souhait; **2.** pluie f; humidité f; **3.** [irr.] mouiller; tremper; F pleuvoir; F arroser (une affaire); ~ through tremper (jusqu'aux os).

wet·back Am. sl. ['wetbæk] immigrant m mexicain illégal.

weth·er ['weðə] bélier m châtré.

wet-nurse ['wetnəːs] nourrice f.

whack F [wæk] **1.** battre; **2.** coup m; claque f; (grand) morceau m; have (ou take) a ~ at (gér.) essayer de (inf.); '**whack·er** F chose f ou personne f énorme; gros mensonge m; '**whack·ing** F **1.** rossée f, fessée f; **2.** colossal (-aux m/pl.).

whale [weil] baleine f; F a ~ of a castle un château magnifique; F a ~ at un as à; '~-**bone** baleine f; '~-**fish·er** '~-**man**, usu. '**whal·er** baleinier m; '**whale-oil** huile f de baleine.

whal·ing ['weiliŋ] pêche f à la baleine.

whang F [wæŋ] **1.** coup m retentissant; **2.** retentir.

wharf [wɔːf] **1.** (pl. a. **wharves** [wɔːvz]) quai m; entrepôt m (pour marchandises); **2.** débarquer; déposer sur le quai; **wharf·age** ['~idʒ] débarquement m; mise f en entrepôt; quayage m; **wharf·in·ger** ['~indʒə] propriétaire m d'un quai.

what [wɔt] **1.** pron. interr. que, quoi; qu'est-ce que; qu'est-ce que; ~ about...? et ...?; ~ about (gér.)? que pensez-vous de (inf.)?; ~ for? pour-

quoi donc?; ~ of it? et alors?; ~ if
...? et si ...?; ~ though ...? qu'importe que (*sbj.*)?; F ~-d'ye-call-him
(-*her*, -*it*, -'*em*), ~'s-his-name (-*her-name*, -*its-name*), *Am.* ~-*is-it* machin *m*, chose *mf*; ~ next? et ensuite?;
iro. par exemple!; et quoi encore?;
2. *pron. rel.* ce qui, ce que; *know*
~'s ~ en savoir long; savoir son
monde; *and* ~ *not* et ainsi de suite;
~ *with* ... ~ *with* ... entre ... et ...;
3. *adj. interr.* quel, quelle, quels,
quelles; ~ *time is it?* quelle heure
est-il?; ~ *a blessing!* quel bonheur!;
~ *impudence!* quelle audace!, F quel
toupet!; (*of*) ~ *use is it?* à quoi
sert-il (*de*, *inf.*, *to inf.*)?; **4.** *adj. rel.*
que, qui; ~ *money I had* l'argent
dont je disposais; '**what-not** étagère *f*; **what**(·**so**)'**ev·er 1.** *pron.*
tout ce qui, tout ce que, quoi qui
(*sbj.*), quoi que (*sbj.*); **2.** *adj.* quelque ... qui *ou* que (*sbj.*); aucun;
quelconque.

wheat ♀ [wi:t] blé *m*; '**wheat·en**
de blé, de froment.

whee·dle ['wi:dl] cajoler; ~ *s.o. into*
(*gér.*) amener q. à (*inf.*) à force de
cajoleries; ~ *money out of s.o.*
soutirer de l'argent à q.

wheel [wi:l] **1.** roue *f*; (*a. steering-*~)
volant *m*; *Am.* F bicyclette *f*; ⊕
(*a. grinding-*~) meule *f*; *see*
*potter*²; ⚓ barre *f*; ✂ conversion *f*;
2. *v/t.* rouler, tourner; promener;
v/i. tourn(oy)er; se retourner (*per-sonne*); ✂ faire une conversion; *Am.*
aller à bicyclette; '~·**bar·row**
brouette *f*; ~ **base** ⊕ empattement
m; ~ **chair** fauteuil *m* roulant;
'**wheeled** à roues; roulant; '**wheel·ing and** '**deal·ing** F affaires *f/pl.*
louches, manigances *f/pl.*; '**wheel·man** F cycliste *m*; '**wheel-spi·der**
⊕ croisillon *m* (de roue); '**wheel·wright** charron *m*.

wheeze [wi:z] **1.** *v/i.* siffler; respirer
péniblement; corner (*cheval*); *v/t.* F
seriner (*un air*); **2.** sifflement *m*,
respiration *f* asthmatique; *cheval:*
cornage *m*; *théâ. sl.* trouvaille *f*; *sl.*
truc *m*; '**wheez·y** □ asthmatique;
cornard (*cheval*).

whelp [welp] **1.** *see* puppy; petit *m*
(*d'un fauve*); **2.** mettre bas.

when [wen] **1.** *adv.* quand?; **2.** *cj.*
quand, lorsque; et alors; (*le jour*)
où; (*un jour*) que.

whence [wens] d'où.

when(·**so**)·**ev·er** [wen(so)'evə] cha-que fois que, toutes les fois que;
quand.

where [wɛə] **1.** *adv.* où?; **2.** *cj.* (là) où;
~·**a·bout** ['wɛərə'baut] **1.** où (donc);
2. (*usu.* '~·**a·bouts** [~s]): *the* ~ *of*
le lieu *m* où (*q.*, *qch.*) se trouve; ~'**as**
puisque, vu que, attendu que;
tandis que, alors que; ⚖ considé-rant que; ~'**at** sur *ou* à *ou* de quoi;
~'**by** par où; par quoi; par lequel
(*etc.*); '~·**fore 1.** *adv.* pourquoi?;
2. *cj.* c'est pourquoi; ~'**in** en quoi;
où; dans lequel (*etc.*); ~'**of** dont, de
quoi; duquel *etc.*; ~'**on** où; sur quoi;
sur lequel (*etc.*); ~·**so**'**ev·er** partout
où; ~·**up**'**on** sur quoi; sur lequel
(*etc.*); **wher**'**ev·er** partout où;
where·with·al 1. [wɛəwi'ðɔ:l] avec
quoi; avec lequel (*etc.*); **2.** F ['~]
nécessaire *m*; moyens *m/pl.*; fonds
m/pl.

wher·ry ['weri] bachot *m*; esquif *m*.

whet [wet] **1.** aiguiser, affiler; *fig.*
stimuler; **2.** affilage *m*; *fig.* stimu-lation *f*; F stimulant *m*; petit
verre *m*.

wheth·er ['weðə] si; ~ ... *or no*
que ... (*sbj.*) ou non.

whet·stone ['wetstoun] pierre *f* à
aiguiser. [fichtre!\
whew [hwu:] ouf!; *int. par surprise:*/
whey [wei] petit lait *m*.

which [witʃ] **1.** *pron. interr.* lequel,
laquelle, lesquels, lesquelles; **2.** *pron.*
rel. qui, que; *all* ~ toutes choses qui
ou que; *in* (*by*) ~ en (par) quoi; **3.**
adj. interr. quel, quelle, quels,
quelles; **4.** *adj. rel.* lequel, laquelle,
lesquels, lesquelles; ~'**ev·er 1.** *pron.*
rel. celui qui, celui que; n'importe
lequel (*etc.*); **2.** *adj.* le ... que,
n'importe quel (*etc.*); quelque ...
que (*sbj.*).

whiff [wif] **1.** *air*, fumée, vent:
bouffée *f*; petit cigare *m*; ⚓ skiff
m; **2.** émettre des bouffées (*v/t.* de
fumée *etc.*).

whif·fle·tree ⊕ ['wifltri:] palon-nier *m*.

Whig *hist. Brit.* [wig] **1.** whig *m*
(*membre d'un parti libéral*); **2.** des
whigs; whig (*parti*); '**Whig·ism**
whiggisme *m*.

while [wail] **1.** temps *m*; espace *m*;
for a ~ pendant quelque temps; F
be worth ~ valoir la peine; **2.** (*usu.*

~ *away*) faire passer, tuer (*le temps*); **3.** (*a.* whilst [wailst]) pendant que, tandis que, en (*gér.*).

whim [wim] caprice *m*; lubie *f*; ⊕ triqueballe *m*.

whim·per ['wimpə] **1.** *v/i.* pleurnicher; pousser des petits cris plaintifs (*chien*); *v/t.* dire (*qch.*) en pleurnichant; **2.** pleurnicherie *f*; plainte *f*; petit cri *m* plaintif.

whim·si·cal □ ['wimzikl] bizarre; capricieux (-euse *f*) (*personne*); fantasque; **whim·si·cal·i·ty** [~-'kæliti], **whim·si·cal·ness** ['~klnis] bizarrerie *f*; caractère *m* fantasque.

whim·s(e)y ['wimzi] caprice *m*; boutade *f*.

whin ⚘ [win] ajonc *m*.

whine [wain] **1.** *v/i.* se plaindre; gémir; *v/t.* dire (*qch.*) d'un ton dolent; **2.** plainte *f*; cri *m* dolent.

whin·ny ['wini] hennir.

whip [wip] **1.** *v/t.* fouetter (*q.*, *qch.*, *de la crème*); *fig.* corriger; *fig.* pluie: cingler (*le visage etc.*); *fig. surt. Am.* vaincre; battre (*des œufs*); *cost.* surjeter; ⚓ surlier (*un cordage*); *avec adv. ou prp.*: mouvoir (*qch.*) vivement *ou* brusquement; ~ *away* chasser à coups de fouet; enlever vivement (à, *from*); *parl.* ~ *in* appeler; ~ *off* chasser; enlever (*qch.*) vivement; ~ *on* faire avancer à coups de fouet; *cost.* attacher à points roulés; ~ *up* stimuler; saisir vivement; *parl.* faire passer un appel urgent à (*q.*); *cuis.* ~*ped cream* crème *f* Chantilly; *v/i.* fouetter; ~ *round* se retourner vivement; **2.** fouet *m*; cocher *m*; *parl.* chef *m* de file; *parl.* appel *m* aux membres du parti; '~**cord** mèche *f* de fouet; corde *f* à fouet; '~**hand** main *f* droite (*du cocher*); *have the ~ of* avoir la haute main sur (*q.*).

whip·per ['wipə] fouetteur (-euse *f*) *m*; '~**in** *chasse*: piqueur *m*; *parl.* chef *m* de file; '~**snap·per** freluquet *m*; moucheron *m*.

whip·pet *zo.* ['wipit] *lévrier de course*: whippet *m*; ✗ char *m* léger.

whip·ping ['wipiŋ] fouettage *m*; fouettement *m*; fouettée *f*; '~**boy** F tête *f* de Turc; '~**top** *jouet*: sabot *m*.

whip-round *Brit.* F ['wipraund]: *have a ~* faire une collecte.

whip-saw ⊕ ['wipsɔ:] scie *f* à chantourner, scie *f* de long.

whirl [wə:l] **1.** (faire) tournoyer; *v/i.* tourbillonner; **2.** tourbillon(nement) *m*; **whirl·i·gig** ['~igig] tourniquet *m*; manège *m* de chevaux de bois; *fig.* tourbillon *m* (*d'eau*); '**whirl·pool** tourbillon *m*; gouffre *m*; **whirl·wind** ['~wind] trombe *f*, tourbillon *m* (*de vent*); **whirl·y·bird** ['~i'bə:d] *Am.* F helicoptère *m*, F banane *f*.

whir(r) [wə:] **1.** tourner en ronronnant; vrombir; siffler; **2.** bruissement *m* (*des ailes*); ronflement *m*; vrombissement *m*; sifflement *m*.

whisk [wisk] **1.** époussette *f*; verge(tte) *f*; *cuis.* fouet *m*; **2.** *v/t.* épousseter; agiter; *cuis.* fouetter, battre; ~ *away* enlever d'un geste rapide; *v/i.* aller comme un trait *ou* à toute vitesse; '**whisk·er** *zo.* moustache *f*; *usu.* (*a pair of*) ~*s pl.* (*des*) favoris *m/pl.*

whis·k(e)y ['wiski] whisky *m*.

whis·per ['wispə] **1.** *vt/i.* chuchoter; *v/i.* parler bas; murmurer; susurrer; **2.** chuchotement *m*; *fig.* bruit *m*; '**whis·per·er** chuchoteur (-euse *f*) *m*.

whist[1] [wist] chut!

whist[2] [~] *jeu de cartes*: whist *m*.

whis·tle ['wisl] **1.** siffler; **2.** sifflement *m*; sifflet *m*; F gorge *f*; '~**stop** *Am.* petite station *f*.

whit[1] *poét.* [wit] brin *m*; *not a ~* ne ... aucunement.

Whit[2] [~] de la Pentecôte.

white [wait] **1.** blanc(he *f*); blême, pâle *f*; F peur, innocent; *Am.* loyal (-aux *m/pl.*); ✗ ~ *arms pl.* armes *f/pl.* blanches; ⊕ ~ *bronze* métal *m* blanc; ~ *coffee* café *m* crème *ou* au lait; ~ *heat* chaude *f ou* chaleur *f* blanche; ~ *lead* blanc *m* de plomb; ~ *lie* mensonge *m* innocent; ~ *meat* viande *f* blanche; ✝ ~ *sale* exposition *f* de blanc; ~ *war* guerre *f* économique; *Am.* ~ *way* rue *f* commerçante éclairée à giorno; **2.** blanc *m*; couleur *f* blanche; *typ.* ligne *f* de blanc; '~**bait** *icht.* blanchaille *f*; ~ *book pol.* livre *m* blanc; '**white-col·lar** d'employé de bureau; ~ *job* emploi *m* dans un bureau; ~ *worker* col *m* blanc; '~**hot** chauffé à blanc; '~**liv·ered** pusillanime; '**whit·en** *v/t.* blanchir (*a. fig.*); blanchir à la chaux; ⊕ étamer (*du métal*); *v/i.* blanchir;

pâlir (*personne*); **'whit·en·er** blanchisseur *m*; **'white·ness** blancheur *f*; pâleur *f*; **'whit·en·ing** blanchiment *m*; *cheveux*: blanchissement *m*; *métal*: étamage *m*.

white...: **'~·smith** ferblantier *m*; serrurier *m*; **'~·wash 1.** blanc *m* de chaux; badigeon *m* blanc; **2.** blanchir à la chaux; *fig.* blanchir; **'~·wash·er** badigeonneur *m*; *fig.* apologiste *m*.

whith·er *poét.* ['wiðə] où.

whit·ing ['waitiŋ] blanc *m* d'Espagne; *icht.* merlan *m*.

whit·ish ['waitiʃ] blanchâtre.

whit·low ✞ ['witlou] panaris *m*.

Whit·sun ['witsn] de la Pentecôte; **~·day** ['wit'sʌndi] dimanche *m* de la Pentecôte; **~·tide** ['witsntaid] (fête *f* de) la Pentecôte *f*.

whit·tle ['witl] amenuiser; *fig.* ~ *away* (*ou* *down*) rogner, réduire petit à petit. [brun; *fig.* terne.]

whit·y-brown ['waiti'braun] gris-ƒ

whiz(z) [wiz] **1.** siffler; ~ *past* passer à toute vitesse; **2.** sifflement *m*.

who [hu:] **1.** *pron. interr.* qui (est-ce qui); quelle personne; lequel, laquelle, lesquels, lesquelles; *Who's Who* le Bottin mondain (= *annuaire des notabilités*); **2.** *pron. rel.* [*a.* hu] qui; lequel, laquelle, lesquels, lesquelles; celui (celle, ceux *pl.*) qui.

whoa [wou] ho!

who·dun·(n)it *sl.* [hu:'dʌnit] roman *m ou* film *m* policier.

who·ev·er [hu:'evə] celui qui; quiconque; qui que (*sbj.*).

whole [houl] **1.** □ entier (-ère *f*); complet (-ète *f*); tout (tous *m/pl.*); *Am.* F *made out of ~ cloth* inventé de toutes pièces; *Am. sl. go the ~ hog* aller jusqu'au bout; *pol.* **~-*hogger*** jusqu'au-boutiste *m*; ~ *milk* lait *m* entier; **2.** tout *m*, ensemble *m*; *the ~ of London* tout Londres; (*up*)*on the ~* à tout prendre; somme toute; **'~-'bound** relié pleine peau; **'~-'heart·ed** □ sincère, qui vient du cœur; **'~-'length** (*a. ~ portrait*) portrait *m* en pied; **'~-'meal** complet (-ète *f*) (*pain*); **'~·sale 1.** (*usu. ~ trade*) (vente *f* en) gros *m*; **2.** en gros; de gros; F *fig.* en masse; **'~-'sal·er** grossiste *mf*; **whole·some** □ ['~·səm] sain, salubre; **'whole-time**

de toute la journée; pour toute la semaine.

whol·ly ['houlli] *adv.* tout à fait, complètement; intégralement.

whom [hu:m; hum] *accusatif de* who.

whoop [hu:p] **1.** houp *m/inv.*; cri *m*; ✞ quinte *f*; **2.** pousser des houp *ou* cris; *Am. sl.* ~ *it up* for faire de la réclame pour, louer jusqu'aux astres; **whoop·ee** *Am.* F ['wupi:] bombe *f*, noce *f*; *make* ~ faire la bombe; faire du chahut; **whooping-cough** ✞ ['hu:piŋkɔf] coqueluche *f*.

whop *sl.* [wɔp] rosser; battre; **'whop·per** *sl.* personne *f ou* chose *f* énorme; *surt.* gros mensonge *m*; **'whop·ping** *sl.* colossal (-aux *m/pl.*), énorme.

whore V [hɔ:] prostituée *f*, putain *f*.

whorl [wə:l] ⊕ *fuseau*: volant *m*; ✿ verticille *m*; *zo.* volute *f*.

whor·tle·ber·ry ✿ ['wə:tlberi] airelle *f*; *red* ~ airelle *f* rouge.

whose [hu:z] *génitif de* who; **who-so·ev·er** [hu:sou'evə] celui qui; quiconque; qui que (*sbj.*).

why [wai] **1.** pourquoi?; pour quelle raison?; ~ *so?* pourquoi cela?; **2.** tiens!; eh bien; vraiment.

wick [wik] mèche *f*.

wick·ed □ ['wikid] mauvais, méchant; *co.* fripon(ne *f*); **'wick·ed·ness** méchanceté *f*.

wick·er ['wikə] en *ou* d'osier; ~ *basket* panier *m* d'osier; ~ *chair* fauteuil *m* en osier; ~ *furniture* meubles *m/pl.* en osier; **'~·work 1.** vannerie *f*; **2.** *see* wicker.

wick·et ['wikit] guichet *m* (*a. cricket*); barrière *f* (*d'un jardin*).

wide [waid] **1.** *adj.* (*a.* □) large; étendu, ample, vaste; répandu (*influence*); grand (*différence etc.*); loin (de, *of*); *cricket*: écarté; *3 feet ~* large de 3 pieds; **2.** *adv.* loin; à de grands intervalles; largement; ~ *awake* tout éveillé; **'~-an·gle** *phot.*: ~ *lense* (objectif *m*) grand angulaire *m*; **~-a·wake** F **1.** ['waidə'weik] averti, malin (-igne *f*); **2.** ['waidə-weik] chapeau *m* (en feutre) à larges bords; **wid·en** ['waidn] (s')élargir; (s')agrandir; **'wide·ness** largeur *f*; **'wide-'o·pen** grand ouvert; écarté (*jambes*); *Am. sl.* qui manque de discipline *ou* fermeté; **'wide-spread** répandu.

wid·ow ['widou] veuve *f*; **'wid-owed** veuf (veuve *f*); *fig.* privé (de, of); **'wid·ow·er** veuf *m*; **wid·ow-hood** ['⁓hud] veuvage *m*.

width [widθ] largeur *f*; ampleur *f*.

wield *poét.* [wi:ld] manier (*l'épée, la plume*); tenir (*le sceptre*); *fig.* exercer (*le contrôle etc.*).

wife [waif] (*pl.* **wives**) femme *f*; épouse *f*; **'wife·ly** d'épouse.

wig¹ [wig] perruque *f*; postiche *m*; *attr.* à perruque; de perruques.

wig² F [⁓] **1.** (*ou* **'wig·ging**) verte semonce *f*; **2.** laver la tête à (*q.*).

wig·gle ['wigl] agiter, remuer.

wight *co.* [wait] personne *f*, individu *m*.

wig·wam ['wigwæm] wigwam *m*.

wild [waild] **1.** □ sauvage; *p.ext.* insensé, fou (fol *devant une voyelle ou un h muet*; folle *f*); orageux (-euse *f*); effaré (*air, yeux*); run ⁓ courir en liberté; vagabonder; se dissiper; ♀ retourner à l'état sauvage; s'étendre de tous côtés; ⁓ *talk* propos *m/pl.* en l'air; *fig.* ⁓ *for* (*ou about*) passionné pour (*qch.*); **2.** (*ou* ⁓*s pl.*) *see* wilderness; **'wild·cat 1.** *zo.* chat *m* sauvage; *Am.* entreprise *f* risquée; *surt. Am.* (*ou* **'wild·cat·ting**) forage *m* dans un champ (*de pétrole*) non encore exploré; **2.** *fig.* risqué *m/pl.*); illégal (-aux *m/pl.*); ⁓ *strike* grève *f* sauvage; **wil·der·ness** ['wildənis] désert *m*; pays *m* inculte; **'wild·fire** ['waildfaiə]: *like* ⁓ comme l'éclair; **'wild-goose chase** *fig.* poursuite *f* vaine; **'wild·ing** ♀ plante *f* sauvage; **'wild·ness** état *m* sauvage; férocité *f*; folie *f*; air *m* égaré.

wile [wail] **1.** artifice *m*; *usu.* ⁓*s pl.* ruses *f/pl.*; **2.** séduire; ⁓ *away see* while 2.

wil·ful □ ['wilful] obstiné, entêté.

wil·i·ness ['wailinis] astuce *f*.

will [wil] **1.** volonté *f*; gré *m*; testament *m*; at ⁓ à volonté; at one's own free ⁓ selon son bon plaisir; with a ⁓ de bon cœur; **2.** [*irr.*] *v/aux.* (*défectif*) *usité pour former le fut.*; he ⁓ come il viendra; il viendra avec plaisir; il veut bien venir; I ⁓ do it je le ferai; je veux bien le faire; **3.** *prét. et. p.p.* **willed** *v/t.* † Dieu, souverain: vouloir, ordonner (*qch.*); ⚖ léguer; **willed**

dispose (à *inf.*, to *inf.*); strong-⁓ de forte volonté.

will·ing □ ['wiliŋ] de bonne volonté; bien disposé, prêt (à, to); I am ⁓ to believe je veux bien croire; ⁓*ly adv.* volontiers; de bon cœur; **'will·ing·ness** bonne volonté *f*; empressement *m*; complaisance *f*.

will-o'-the-wisp ['wiləðwisp] feu *m* follet.

wil·low ['wilou] ♀ saule *m*; F *cricket*: batte *f*; ⊕ effilocheuse *f*; **'⁓-herb** ♀ épilobe *m* à épi, F osier *m* fleuri; **'wil·low·y** couvert *ou* bordé de saules; *fig.* svelte, souple, élancé.

will·pow·er ['wilpauə] volonté *f*.

wil·ly-nil·ly ['wili'nili] bon gré mal gré.

wilt¹ † [wilt] *2me personne du sg. de* will 2.

wilt² [⁓] (se) flétrir; *v/i.* se faner; *fig.* languir; *sl.* se dégonfler.

Wil·ton car·pet ['wiltn'kɑ:pit] tapis *m* Wilton (=*tapis de haute laine*).

wily □ ['waili] astucieux (-euse *f*), rusé.

wim·ple ['wimpl] guimpe *f* (*de religieuse*).

win [win] **1.** [*irr.*] *v/t.* gagner; remporter (*un prix, une victoire*); acquérir; ⚔ *sl.* récupérer; amener (*q.*) (à *inf.*, to *inf.*); ⁓ *s.o. over* attirer q. à son parti; convertir q.; *v/i.* gagner; remporter la victoire; ⁓ *through* parvenir (à, to); **2.** *sp.* victoire *f*.

wince [wins] **1.** faire une grimace de douleur; sourciller; **2.** crispation *f*.

winch [wintʃ] manivelle *f*; treuil *m* (de hissage).

wind¹ [wind, *poét. a.* waind] **1.** vent *m* (*a.* ♂); *fig.* haleine *f*, souffle *m*; ♪ instruments *m/pl.* à vent; be in the ⁓ se préparer; have a long ⁓ avoir du souffle; *fig.* throw to the ⁓*s* abandonner; F raise the ⁓ se procurer de l'argent; *sl.* get the ⁓ *up* avoir la frousse; it's an ill ⁓ that blows nobody good à quelque chose malheur est bon; **2.** *chasse*: flairer (*le gibier*); faire perdre le souffle à (*q.*); essouffler; be ⁓*ed* être à bout de souffle; ♪ [waind] sonner du cor.

wind² [waind] [*irr.*] *v/t.* tourner; enrouler; ⁓ *up* enrouler; remonter (*un horloge,* † *un ressort etc.*); *fig.* terminer, finir; † liquider; clôturer *(un compte)*; *v/i.* tourner; *(a.* ~ *o.s.,* ~ one's way)* serpenter; *fig.* ~ *up* se terminer, s'achever.

wind... [wind]: '~**bag** *péj.* moulin *m* à paroles; '~**bound** ⚓ retardé par le vent; retenu par le vent; '~**cheat·er** *cost.* anorak *m*; '~**fall** fruit *m* abattu par le vent; *fig.* aubaine *f*; '~**gauge** indicateur *m* de pression du vent; '**wind·i·ness** temps *m* venteux; F verbosité *f*; *sl.* frousse *f*.

wind·ing ['waindiŋ] **1.** mouvement *m ou* cours *m* sinueux; replis *m/pl.*; *tex.* bobinage *m*; ⚡ enroulement *m*; ⊕ gauchissement *m*; **2.** □ sinueux (-euse *f*); qui serpente; ~ *staircase (ou stairs pl.)* escalier *m* tournant; '~**sheet** linceul *m*; '~'**up** remontage *m*; *fig.* fin *f*; ♰ liquidation *f*.

wind·in·stru·ment ['windinstrumənt] instrument *m* à vent.

wind·jam·mer ['winddʒæmə] ⚓ *sl.* voilier *m.*   [guindeau *m.*]

wind·lass ['windləs] ⊕ treuil *m*; ⚓}

wind·mill ['windmil] moulin *m* à vent; ~ *plane* autogire *m*.

win·dow ['windou] fenêtre *f*; ♰ vitrine *f*, devanture *f*; *mot. etc.* glace *f*; *théâ. etc.* guichet *m*; ~ *display* étalage *m*; ~ *goods* articles *m/pl.* en devanture; '~**dress·ing** art *m* de l'étalage; arrangement *m* de la vitrine; *fig.* façade *f*, camouflage *m*, trompe-l'œil *m/inv.*; ~ décor *m* de théâtre; '**win·dowed** à fenêtre(s).

win·dow...: ~ **en·ve·lope** enveloppe *f* à fenêtre; '~**frame** châssis *m* de fenêtre; '~**shade** *Am.* store *m*; '~**shop** = *go* ~*ping* faire du lèche-vitrines; '~**shut·ter** volet *m*; '~**sill** rebord *m* de fenêtre.

wind... [wind]: '~**pipe** *anat.* trachée-artère *(pl.* trachées-artères) *f*; '~**screen,** *Am.* '~**shield** pare-brise *m/inv.*; ~ *wiper* essuie-glace *m*; '~**tun·nel** ✈ tunnel *m* aérodynamique.

wind·ward ['windwəd] **1.** au vent; **2.** côté *m* au vent.

wind·y □ ['windi] venteux (-euse *f*) *(a.* ✈); exposé au vent; *fig.* vain; *sl.* qui a le trac.

wine [wain] vin *m*; '~**grow·er** viticulteur *m*; vigneron *m*; '~**mer·chant** négociant *m* en vins; '~**press** pressoir *m*; '~**vault** cave *f*, caveau *m.*

wing [wiŋ] **1.** aile *f (a. fig.,* ✕, ⚓, ✈, ✈, *mot., sp.*); vol *m*, essor *m*; F *co.* bras *m*; *foot. personne:* ailier *m*; *porte:* battant *m*; ⊕ oreille *f (d'un écrou)*; ~s *pl.* coulisse *f*; *take* ~ s'envoler; prendre son vol; *be on the* ~ voler; *fig.* partir; **2.** *v/t.* empenner; voler; blesser à l'aile *ou fig.* au bras; *v/i.* voler; '~**case,** '~**sheath** *zo.* élytre *m*; '~**chair** fauteuil *m* à oreillettes; **winged** [~d] ailé; blessé à l'aile *ou fig.* au bras; ~ *word* parole *f* ailée; '**wing·span,** '**wing·spread** envergure *f*.

wink [wiŋk] **1.** clignement *m* d'œil; clin *m* d'œil; F *not get a* ~ *of sleep* ne pas fermer l'œil de toute la nuit; F *tip s.o. the* ~ faire signe de l'œil à q., prévenir q.; **2.** *v/i.* cligner les yeux; clignoter *(lumière)*; *v/t.* cligner de *(l'œil)*; signifier *(qch.)* par un clin d'œil; ~ *at* cligner de l'œil à *(q.)*; fermer les yeux sur *(qch.).*

win·ner ['winə] gagnant(e *f*) *m*; *sp.* vainqueur *m (=homme ou femme).*

win·ning ['winiŋ] **1.** □ gagnant; *fig.* engageant; ~s *pl.* gains *m/pl. (au jeu etc.)*; '~**post** *sp.* poteau *m* d'arrivée.

win·now ['winou] vanner *(le grain)*; *fig.* examiner minutieusement.

win·ter ['wintə] **1.** hiver *m*; ~ *sports pl.* sports *m/pl.* d'hiver; **2.** hiverner; **win·ter·ize** ['~təraiz] préparer pour l'hiver; **win·try** ['wintri] d'hiver; *fig.* glacial (-als *m/pl.*).

wipe [waip] **1.** essuyer; nettoyer; ~ *off* essuyer, enlever; liquider *(une dette)*; ~ *out* essuyer; *fig.* effacer; exterminer; **2.** coup *m* de torchon *etc.*; F taloche *f (= coup)*; '**wip·er** essuyeur (-euse *f*) *m*; torchon *m.*

wire ['waiə] **1.** fil *m* (de fer); *Am.* F dépêche *f*; *attr.* en *ou* de fil de fer; **2.** *v/t.* munir d'un fil métallique; ⚡ équiper *(une maison)*; *(a. v/i.)* *tél.* télégraphier; '~**drawn** tréfilé *(métal)*; trait *(or etc.)*; '~**gauge** ⊕ jauge *f* pour fils métalliques; '~**haired** à poil dur *(chien)*; '**wire·less 1.** □ sans fil; de T.S.F., de radio; *on the* ~ à la radio; ~ *control* radioguidage *m*; ~ *(message ou telegram)* radiogramme *m*; ~ *(telegraphy)* radiotélégraphie *f*; télégraphie *f* sans fil; *(air)* ~ *operator* sans-filiste *mf*; opérateur *m* de T.S.F.; ~ *pirate radio:* auditeur *m* illicite; ~

(set) poste *m* (de radio); ~ station poste *m* émetteur; **2.** radiotélégraphier; '**wire-'net·ting** treillis *m* métallique; grillage *m*; '**wire-pull·er** *fig.* intrigant(e *f*) *m*; '**wire-'tap·ping** *téléph.* mise *f* sur écoute.

wir·ing ['waiəriŋ] grillage *m* métallique; ⚡ câblage *m*; pose *f* des fils; *radio:* montage *m*; ⚡ croisillonnage *m*; ⚡ ~ *diagram* plan *m* de pose; '**wir·y** □ raide *(cheveux)*; sec (sèche *f*) et nerveux (-euse *f*) *(personne)*.

wis·dom ['wizdəm] sagesse *f*; ~ *tooth* dent *f* de sagesse.

wise[1] □ [waiz] sage; prudent; ~ *crack* Am. F bon mot *m*, saillie *f*; *Am. sl.* ~ *guy* finaud *m*, monsieur *m* je-sais-tout; *Am.* put *s.o.* ~ mettre q. à la page; avertir q. (de *to*, on).

wise[2] † [~] façon *f*; guise *f*.

wise·a·cre ['waizeikə] prétendu sage *m*; pédant(e *f*) *m*; '**wise-crack** *Am.* F faire de l'esprit.

wish [wiʃ] **1.** vouloir, désirer; souhaiter; ~ *s.o. joy* féliciter q. (de, of); ~ *for* désirer, vouloir, souhaiter *(qch.)*; ~ *s.o. well (ill)* vouloir du bien (mal) à q.; **2.** vœu *m*, souhait *m*; désir *m*; *good* ~*es pl.* souhaits *m/pl.*, meilleurs vœux *m/pl.*; '**wish·ful** □ ['~ful] désireux (-euse *f*) (de of, to); '**wish(·ing)-bone** *volaille:* lunette *f*.

wish-wash F ['wiʃwɔʃ] lavasse *f*; mèche *f* folle *(de cheveux)*. '**wish·y-wash·y** F fade, insipide.

wisp [wisp] bouchon *m* (de paille); mèche *f* folle *(de cheveux)*.

wist·ful □ ['wistful] pensif (-ive *f*); d'envie; désenchanté.

wit [wit] **1.** *(a.* ~*s pl.)* esprit *m*; ~*s pl.* raison *f*, intelligence *f*; *personne:* homme *m ou* femme *f* d'esprit; *be at one's* ~*'s end* ne plus savoir que faire; *have one's* ~*s about one* avoir toute sa présence d'esprit; *live by one's* ~*s* vivre d'expédients *ou* d'industrie; *be out of one's* ~*s* avoir perdu la raison; **2.:** *to* ~ à savoir; c'est-à-dire.

witch [witʃ] sorcière *f*; *fig.* jeune charmeuse *f*; '**~·craft**, '**witch·er·y** sorcellerie *f*; *fig.* magie *f*; '**witch-hunt** *pol. Am. fig.* chasse *f* aux sorcières.

with [wið] avec; de; à; par; malgré; *sl.* ~ *it* dans le vent; *it is just so* ~ *me* il en va de même pour moi.

with·al † [wi'ðɔ:l] **1.** *adv.* aussi, de plus; **2.** *prp.* avec *etc.*

with·draw [wið'drɔ:] *[irr. (draw)]* (se) retirer (de, from); **with'draw·al** retraite *f*; rappel *m*; ✗ repli(ement) *m*; retrait *m (d'argent)*.

withe [wiθ] brin *m ou* branche *f* d'osier.

with·er ['wiðə] *(souv.* ~ *up, away)* (se) flétrir; (se) dessécher; *v/i.* dépérir *(personne)*; '**with·er·ing** □ *fig.* foudroyant, écrasant.

with·ers ['wiðəz] *pl.* garrot *m*.

with·hold [wið'hould] *[irr. (hold)]* retenir, empêcher (q. de *inf.*, *s.o. from* gér.); cacher, refuser (à q., *from s.o.*); *Am.* ~*ing tax* retenue *f ou* impôt *m* retenu à la source; **with'in** *poét.* **1.** *adv.* à l'intérieur, au dedans; à la maison; *from* ~ de l'intérieur; **2.** *prp.* à l'intérieur de, en dedans de; ~ *doors* à la maison; ~ *10 minutes* en moins de dix minutes; ~ *a mile* à moins d'un mille (de, of); dans un rayon d'un mille; ~ *call (ou hearing)* à (la) portée de la voix *ou* d'oreille; ~ *sight* en vue; **with'out** **1.** *adv. poét.* à l'extérieur, au dehors; *from* ~ de l'extérieur, du dehors; **2.** *prp.* sans; *poét.* en dehors de; **with'stand** *[irr. (stand)]* résister à; supporter.

with·y ['wiði] *see* withe.

wit·less □ ['witlis] sot(te *f*); faible d'esprit; sans intelligence.

wit·ling *péj.* ['witliŋ] petit *ou iro.* bel esprit *m*.

wit·ness ['witnis] **1.** témoignage *m*; *personne:* témoin *m*; *bear* ~ témoigner, porter témoignage (de *to*, of); *in* ~ *of* en témoignage de; **2.** *v/t.* être témoin de; assister à; attester *(un acte etc.)*; témoigner de; *v/i.* témoigner; ~ *for (against)* témoigner en faveur de (contre); '**~·box**, *Am.* ~ **stand** barre *f* des témoins.

wit·ted ['witid]: *quick-*~ à l'esprit vif; **wit·ti·cism** ['~tisizm] trait *m* d'esprit, bon mot *m*; '**wit·ti·ness** esprit *m*; '**wit·ting·ly** à dessein; en connaissance de cause; '**wit·ty** □ spirituel(le *f*).

wives [waivz] *pl. de* wife.

wiz *Am. sl.* [wiz], **wiz·ard** ['~əd] **1.** sorcier *m*, magicien *m*; **2.** *fig. sl.* magnifique; **wiz·ard·ry** sorcellerie *f*, magie *f*.

wiz·en(·ed) ['wizn(d)] tatatiné; parcheminé *(visage etc.)*.

wo(a) [wou] ho!
woad ♮,⊕ [woud] guède *f*.
wob·ble ['wɔbl] ballotter; trembler; chevroter (*voix*); ⊕ branler; *mot.* *wheel that* ~*s* roue *f* dévoyée.
woe *poét. ou co.* [wou] chagrin *m*; malheur *m*; ~ *is me!* pauvre de moi!; '~-**be·gone** triste, désolé; **woe·ful** ☐ *poét. ou co.* ['~ful] triste, affligé; de malheur; '**woe·ful·ness** tristesse *f*; malheur *m*.
wog *sl.* [wɔg] métèque *m*.
woke [wouk] *prét. et p.p.* de **wake**² 1.
wold [would] plaine *f* vallonnée.
wolf [wulf] **1.** (*pl.* **wolves**) *zo.* loup *m*; *sl.* coureur *m* de cotillons, tombeur *m* de femmes; ~ *call,* ~ *whistle* sifflement *m* admiratif (*au passage d'une femme attractive*); *cry* ~ crier au loup; **2.** F dévorer; '**wolf·ish** ☐ de loup; F *fig.* rapace.
wolf·ram *min.* ['wulfrəm] wolfram *m*; tungstène *m*.
wolves [wulvz] *pl.* de **wolf** 1.
wom·an ['wumən] (*pl.* **women**) femme *f*; *young* ~ jeune femme *f ou* fille *f*; ~'*s* (*ou* **women's**) *rights* pl. droits *m*/*pl.* de la femme; *attr.* femme ...; de femme(s); ~ *doctor* femme *f* médecin; ~ *student* étudiante *f*; '~-**hat·er** misogyne *m*; '**wom·an·hood** ['~hud] état *m* de femme; *coll.* les femmes *f*/*pl.*; *reach* ~ devenir femme; '**wom·an·ish** ☐ féminin; efféminé (*homme*); '**wom·an·kind** les femmes *f*/*pl.*; '**wom·an·like** **1.** *adj.* de femme; **2.** *adv.* en femme; '**wom·an·ly** féminin.
womb [wu:m] *anat.* matrice *f*; *fig.* sein *m*.
wom·en ['wimin] *pl.* de **woman**; *votes* pl. *for* ~ suffrage *m* féminin; ~'*s lib* movement *m* de libération de la femme; ~'*s rights* pl. droits *m*/*pl.* de la femme; *sp.* ~'*s team* équipe *f* féminine; ~'*s single tennis*: simple *m* dames; '**wom·en·folk** ['~fouk] *pl.*, '**wom·en·kind** les femmes *f*/*pl.* (*surt. d'une famille*).
won [wʌn] *prét. et p.p.* de **win** 1.
won·der ['wʌndə] **1.** merveille *f*, prodige *m*; étonnement *m*; **2.** s'étonner, s'émerveiller (de, *at*); se demander (si *whether*, *if*); **won·der·ful** ☐ ['~ful] merveilleux (-euse *f*), étonnant; admirable; '**won·der·ing** **1.** ☐ émerveillé, étonné; **2.** étonnement *m*; '**won·der-struck** émer-

veillé; '**won·der-work·er** faiseur (-euse *f*) *m* de prodiges.
won·drous ☐ *poét.* ['wʌndrəs] merveilleux (-euse *f*), étonnant.
won·ky *sl.* ['wɔŋki] patraque (= *branlant*).
won't [wount] = *will not*.
wont [wount] **1.** *préd.* habitué; *be* ~ *to* (*inf.*) avoir l'habitude de (*inf.*); **2.** coutume *f*, habitude *f*; '**wont·ed** accoutumé.
woo [wu:] faire la cour à; courtiser (*a. fig.*); solliciter (de *inf.*, *to inf.*).
wood [wud] bois *m*; fût *m*, tonneau *m*; ♪ bois *m*/*pl.*; *sp.* ~*s pl.* boules *f*/*pl.*; F *touch* ~! touchez du bois!; **2.** *attr. souv.* des bois; ~-**bine**, *a.* ~-**bind** ♮ ['~bain(d)] chèvrefeuille *m* des bois; *Am.* vigne *f* vierge; '~-**carv·ing** sculpture *f* sur bois; '~-**cock** *orn.* (*pl. usu.* ~) bécasse *f*; '~-**craft** connaissance *f* de la chasse à courre *ou* de la forêt; '~-**cut** gravure *f* sur bois; '~-**cut·ter** bûcheron *m*; graveur *m* sur bois; '**wood·ed** boisé; '**wood·en** en bois; de bois (*a. fig.*); *fig.* raide; '**wood-en-grav·er** graveur *m* sur bois; '**wood-en-grav·ing** gravure *f* sur bois (= *objet et art*); '**wood·i·ness** caractère *m* ligneux.
wood...: '~-**land** **1.** bois *m*, pays *m* boisé; **2.** sylvestre; des bois; '~-**lark** *orn.* alouette *f* des bois; '~-**louse** *zo.* cloporte *m*; '~-**man** garde *m* forestier; bûcheron *m*; † trappeur *m*; '~-**peck·er** *orn.* pic *m*; '~-**pile** tas *m* de bois; '~-**pulp** pâte *f* de bois; '~-**ruff** ♮ aspérule *f* odorante; '~-**shav·ings** *pl.* copeaux *m*/*pl.* de bois; '~-**shed** bûcher *m*; ~-**wind** ♪ ['~wind] (*ou* ~ *instruments pl.*) bois *m*/*pl.*; '~-**work** (*surt.* △) boiserie *f*, charpente *f*; menuiserie *f*; travail *m* (*pl. -aux*) *m* du bois; '~-**work·ing ma-chine** machine *f* à bois; '**wood·y** boisé; couvert de bois; des bois; sylvestre; ♮ ligneux (-euse *f*); *fig.* sourd, mat; '**wood·yard** chantier *m* (de bois à brûler).
woo·er ['wu:ə] prétendant *m*.
woof [wu:f] *see* **weft**.
wool [wul] laine *f* (*fig. co.* = *cheveux* crépus); *dyed in the* ~ teint en laine; *fig.* convaincu; pur sang *adj.*/*inv.*; '~-**gath·er·ing 1.** F rêvasserie *f*; *go* ~ avoir l'esprit absent, être distrait; **2.** distrait; '**wool·(l)en 1.** de laine;

2.: ⁓s *pl.* laines *f/pl.*; draps *m/pl.*; tissus *m/pl.* de laine; **'wool·(l)y 1.** laineux (-euse *f*); de laine; cotonneux (-euse *f*) (*fruit*); *peint.* flou; *fig.* mou (mol *devant une voyelle ou un h muet*; molle *f*); *fig.* imprécis (*idée*); **2.** woollies *pl.* (*vêtements m/pl.* en) tricot *m*; lainages *m/pl.*

wool...: '⁓sack *parl.* siège *m* du *ou* dignité *f* de Lord Chancelier; '⁓sta·pler négociant *m* en laine; '⁓work tapisserie *f*.

wop *Am. sl.* [wɔp] immigrant(e *f*) *m* italien(ne); Italien(ne *f*) *m*.

word [wəːd] **1.** *usu.* mot *m*; parole *f* (*a. fig.*); ordre *m*; ✗ mot *m* d'ordre; ⁓s *pl.* paroles *f/pl.*; *fig.* termes *m/pl.*; *opéra:* livret *m*; *chanson:* paroles *f/pl.*; *gramm.* ⁓ order ordre des mots; ⁓ processing traitement des mots; *by* ⁓ *of mouth* de vive voix; *eat one's* ⁓*s* se rétracter; *have* ⁓*s* se disputer (avec, *with*); *leave* ⁓ *that* faire dire que; *send* (*bring*) *s.o.* ⁓ *of s.th.* faire (venir) dire qch. à q.; *be as good as one's* ⁓ tenir sa parole; *take s.o. at his* ⁓ prendre q. au mot; **2.** rédiger; formuler par écrit; ⁓ed *as follows* ainsi conçu; '⁓book vocabulaire *m*, lexique *m*; **'word·i·ness** verbosité *f*; **'word·ing** rédaction *f*; langage *m*, termes *m/pl.*; **'word-'per·fect** *théâ.* qui connaît parfaitement son rôle (*école:* sa leçon); **'word-split·ting** ergotage *m*.

word·y □ ['wəːdi] verbeux (-euse *f*), diffus.

wore [wɔː] *prét. de* wear 1.

work [wəːk] **1.** travail *m*; tâche *f*, besogne *f*; ouvrage *m* (*a. littérature, couture, etc.*); emploi *m*; œuvre *f*; ⊕ ⁓s *usu. sg.* usine *f*, atelier *m*; *horloge:* mouvement *m*; *public* ⁓s *pl.* travaux *m/pl.* publics; ⁓ *of art* œuvre *f* d'art; ⁓s *pl. of Keats* l'œuvre *m* de Keats; *at* ⁓ au travail; en marche; *fig.* en jeu; *be in* ⁓ avoir du travail; *be out of* ⁓ chômer, être sans travail; *make sad* ⁓ *of* s'acquitter peu brillamment de; *make short* ⁓ *of* expédier (*qch.*); *put s.o. out of* ⁓ priver q. de travail; *set to* ⁓ se mettre au travail; *set s.o. to* ⁓ faire travailler q.; ⁓s *council* comité *m* de directeurs et de délégués syndicaux; **2.** [*irr.*] *v/i.* travailler; fonctionner, aller (*machine*); *fig.* réussir; se crisper (*bouche*); ⁓ *at* travailler (à); ⁓ *out*

sortir peu à peu; s'élever (à, *at*); aboutir; *v/t.* faire travailler; faire fonctionner *ou* marcher (*une machine*); diriger (*un projet*); opérer, amener, broder (*un dessin etc.*); ouvrer (*du métal*); façonner (*du bois*); faire (*un calcul*); résoudre (*un problème*); exploiter (*une mine*); ⁓ *mischief* semer le mal *ou* la discorde; ⁓ *off* se dégager de; cuver (*sa colère*); ✝ écouler (*un stock*); ⁓ *one's way* se frayer un chemin; ⁓ *out* mener à bien; élaborer, développer; résoudre; ⁓ *up* développer; se faire (*une clientèle*); exciter, émouvoir; élaborer (*une idée, un sujet*); *phot.* retoucher; préparer.

work·a·ble □ ['wəːkəbl] réalisable (*projet*); ouvrable (*bois etc.*); exploitable (*mine*); **'work·a·day** de tous les jours; *fig.* prosaïque; **work·a·hol·ic** F ['wəːkə'hɔlik] bourreau *m* de travail; **'work·bench** établi *m*; **'work·day** jour *m* ouvrable; **'work·er** travailleur (-euse *f*) *m*; ouvrier (-ère *f*) *m*; ⁓s *pl.* classes *f/pl.* laborieuses; ouvriers *m/pl.*; *social* ⁓ assistante *f* sociale; **'work·force** main-d'œuvre *f*, *les* ouvriers *m/pl.*; **'work·house** hospice *m*, asile *m* des pauvres; *Am.* maison *f* de correction; **'work·ing 1.** fonctionnement *m*; manœuvre *f*; exploitation *f*; ⁓s *pl.* mécanisme *m*; **2.** qui travaille; qui fonctionne; de travail; *in* ⁓ *order* en état de service; ⁓ *association* (*ou co-operation*) groupe *m* de travailleurs; ✝ ⁓ *capital* capital *m* d'exploitation; ⁓ *class* classe *f* ouvrière; ⁓ *committee* (*ou party*) commission *f* d'enquête; ⁓ *condition* état *m* de fonctionnement; ⁓ *day* jour *m* ouvrable; journée *f*; ⁓ *expenses pl.* frais *m/pl.* généraux; ⁓ *process* mode *m* d'opération; ⁓ *student* étudiant *m* qui travaille pour gagner sa vie.

work·man ['wəːkmən] ouvrier *m*, artisan *m*; '⁓like bien travaillé, bien fait; compétent; **'work·man·ship** exécution *f*; fini *m*; construction *f*; travail (*pl.* -aux) *m*.

work...: ⁓out *Am.* F ['wəːkaut] *usu. sp.* entraînement *m* (préliminaire); '⁓shop atelier *m*; ⁓ *place* établi *m*; '⁓-'shy **1.** qui renâcle à la besogne; paresseux (-euse *f*); **2.** fainéant *m*; ⁓-to-'rule grève *f* du zèle; '⁓wom·an ouvrière *f*.

wrangler

world [wə:ld] monde *m*; *fig. a* ~ *of* beaucoup de; *in the* ~ au monde; *what in the* ~? que diable?; *bring (come) into the* ~ mettre (venir) au monde; *be for all the* ~ *like* avoir exactement l'air de (*qch., inf.*); *a* ~ *too wide* de beaucoup trop large; *think the* ~ *of* avoir une très haute opinion de; *man of the* ~ homme *m* qui connaît la vie; mondain *m*; ~ *champion* champion *m* du monde; ~ *championship* championnat *m* du monde; ~ *record* record *m* mondial; ~ *record holder* recordman *m* du monde; *Am.* ~ *series baseball*: matches *m/pl.* entre les champions de deux ligues professionnelles; '**world·li·ness** mondanité *f*; '**world·ling** mondain(e *f*) *m*.

world·ly ['wə:ldli] du monde, de ce monde; mondain; ~ *innocence* candeur *f*; naïveté *f*; ~ *wisdom* sagesse *f* du siècle; '~-'**wise** qui connaît la vie.

world...: '~-'**pow·er** *pol.* puissance *f* mondiale; '~-'**wide** universel(le *f*); mondial (-aux *m/pl.*).

worm [wə:m] **1.** ver *m* (*a. fig.*); ⊕ *alambic*: serpentin *m*; vis *f* sans fin; ⊕ spirale *f*; **2.**: ~ *a secret out of s.o.* tirer un secret de q.; ~ *o.s.* se glisser; *fig.* s'insinuer (dans, *into*); '~-**drive** ⊕ transmission *f* par vis sans fin; '~-**eat·en** rongé des vers; vermoulu (*bois*); '~-**gear** ⊕ engrenage *m* à vis sans fin; (*ou* '~-**wheel**) ⊕ roue *f* hélicoïdale; '~-**wood** armoise *f* amère; *fig. be* ~ *to* n'être qu'absinthe pour (*q.*); '**worm·y** plein de vers.

worn [wɔ:n] *p.p. de* wear 1; '~-'**out** usé; râpé (*vêtement*); épuisé (*personne*).

wor·ri·ment F ['wʌrimənt] souci *m*; **wor·rit** V ['wʌrit] (se) tourmenter, (se) tracasser; '**wor·ry 1.** *fig.* (se) tourmenter, (se) tracasser, (s')inquiéter; *v/t.* harceler; piller (*des moutons*); **2.** ennui *m*, souci *m*, tracasserie *f*.

worse [wə:s] **1.** *adj.* pire; plus mauvais; ⚕ plus malade; *adv.* pis; plus mal; (*all*) *the* ~ *adv.* encore pis; *adj.* (encore) pire; ~ *luck!* tant pis!; *he is none the* ~ *for it* il ne s'en trouve pas plus mal; **2.** quelque chose *m* de pire; le pire; *from bad to* ~ de mal en pis; '**wors·en** empirer; (s')aggraver.

wor·ship ['wə:ʃip] **1.** culte *m*, adoration *f*; *your* ⚖ monsieur le maire *ou* juge; *place of* ~ église *f*; *religion protestante*: temple *m*; **2.** adorer; **wor·ship·ful** □ ['~ful] *titre*: honorable; '**wor·ship·(p)er** adorateur (-trice *f*) *m*; *eccl.* fidèle *mf*.

worst [wə:st] **1.** *adj.* (*le*) pire; (*le*) plus mauvais; **2.** *adv.* (le) pis, (le) plus mal; **3.** *su. le* pire *m*; *at* (*the*) ~ au pire; en tout cas; *do your* ~! faites du pis que vous pourrez!; *get the* ~ *of it* avoir le dessous; *if the* ~ *comes to the* ~ en mettant les choses au pis; **4.** *v/t.* vaincre, battre.

wor·sted ['wustid] laine *f* peignée; (*a.* ~ *yarn*) laine *f* à tricoter; tissu *m* de laine peignée; ~ *stockings* bas *m/pl.* en laine peignée.

wort[1] ♀ [wə:t] plante *f*, herbe *f*.

wort[2] [~] moût *m* (*de bière*).

worth [wə:θ] **1.** valant; *he is* ~ *a million £* il est riche d'un million de livres; ~ *reading* qui mérite d'être lu; **2.** valeur *f*; **wor·thi·ness** ['~ðinis] mérite *m*; **worth·less** □ ['~θlis] sans valeur, de nulle valeur; '**worth-'while** F *be* ~ valoir la peine; **wor·thy** □ ['wə:ði] **1.** digne (de, *of*); de mérite; **2.** personnage *m* (éminent).

would [wud] *prét. de* will 2 (*a. usité pour former le cond.*).

would-be F ['wudbi:] prétendu; soi-disant; affecté; ~ *buyer* acheteur *m* éventuel; personne *f* qui voudrait acheter; ~ *painter* personne *f* qui cherche à se faire peindre; ~ *poet* poète *m* à la manque; ~ *wit* prétendu bel esprit *m*; ~ *worker* personne *f* qui voudrait avoir du travail.

wouldn't ['wudnt] = *would not*.

wound[1] [wu:nd] **1.** blessure *f* (*a. fig.*); plaie *f*; **2.** blesser (*a. fig.*).

wound[2] [waund] *prét. et p.p. de* wind[2]. [*p.p. de* weave 1.)

wove [wouv] *prét.*, **wo·ven** ['-vn]f

wow *Am.* [wau] *théâ. sl.* grand succès *m*; *p.ext.* chose *f* épatante.

wrack[1] ♀ [ræk] varech *m*.

wrack[2] [~] *see* rack[3].

wraith [reiθ] apparition *f*.

wran·gle ['ræŋgl] **1.** se chamailler, se disputer, se quereller; **2.** dispute *f*, querelle *f*, chamaille(rie) *f*; '**wran·gler** querelleur (-euse *f*) *m*, chamailleur (-euse *f*) *m*; *Am.* (*a. horse* ~) cowboy *m*.

wrap [ræp] **1.** v/t. (souv. ~ up) envelopper (de, in) (a. fig.); fig. be ~ped up in être plongé dans; v/i. ~ up s'envelopper (dans, in); **2.** couverture f; p.ext. pardessus m, châle m; manteau m; '**wrap·per** couverture f; documents: chemise f; papier m d'emballage; cigare: robe f; cost. robe f de chambre; (ou postal ~) bande f; '**wrap·ping** enveloppe (-ment m) f; (a. ~ paper) papier m d'emballage; '**wrap-'up** Am. F résumé m.

wrath poét. ou co. [rɔ:θ] colère f; courroux m; **wrath·ful** □ ['~ful] courroucé; irrité.

wreak [ri:k] assouvir (sa haine, sa colère, sa vengeance) (sur, [up]on).

wreath [ri:θ], pl. **wreaths** [~ðz] fleurs: couronne f, guirlande f; (a. artificial ~) couronne f de perles; spirale f, volute f (de fumée); écoss. amoncellement m (de neige); **wreathe** [ri:ð] [irr.] v/t. couronner; enguirlander; tresser (des fleurs etc.); v/i. tourbillonner; s'enrouler.

wreck [rek] **1.** ♪ naufrage m (a. fig.); fig. ruine f; navire m naufragé; **2.** causer le naufrage de; faire dérailler (un train); fig. faire échouer; ♪ be ~ed faire naufrage; '**wreckage** débris m/pl.; fig. naufrage m; **wrecked** naufragé; fig. ruiné; '**wreck·er** démolisseur m (a. de bâtiments); ♪ sauveteur m (d'épaves), mot. Am. dépanneuse f, camion-grue m (pl. camions-grues); Am. marchand m de voitures délabrées; † ♪ pilleur m d'épaves; '**wreck·ing** démolition f; Am. ~ company entreprise f de démolitions; mot. ~ service (service de) dépannage m.

wren orn. [ren] roitelet m.

wrench [rentʃ] **1.** tordre; arracher (violemment) (à, from); forcer (l'épaule, le sens); ~ open forcer (un couvercle etc.); ~ out arracher; **2.** mouvement m ou effort m de torsion; effort m violent; fig. déchirement m de cœur; fig. violente douleur f; ⊕ clef f à écrous.

wrest [rest] arracher (à, from); fausser (le sens); **wres·tle** ['resl] **1.** v/i. lutter; v/t. lutter avec ou contre; **2.** (ou '**wres·tling**) lutte f; '**wres·tler** lutteur m.

wretch [retʃ] malheureux (-euse f) m; infortuné(e f) m; scélérat(e f) m;

co. fripon(ne f) m; type m; poor ~ pauvre diable m.

wretch·ed □ ['retʃid] misérable; malheureux (-euse f); lamentable; F diable de ..., sacré; '**wretch·edness** malheur m; misère f.

wrick [rik] **1.** fouler (une cheville); ~ one's neck se donner le torticolis; **2.** ♣ effort m; ~ in the neck torticolis m.

wrig·gle ['rigl] (se) tortiller, (s')agiter, (se) remuer; ~ out of se tirer de.

wright [rait] mots composés: ouvrier m, artisan m.

wring [riŋ] [irr.] **1.** tordre (les mains, le linge, le cou à une volaille); étreindre (la main de q.); déchirer (le cœur); ~ s.th. from s.o. arracher qch. à q.; ~ing wet mouillé à tordre; trempé jusqu'aux os (personne); **2.** torsion f; '**wring·er**, '**wring·ingma·chine** essoreuse f.

wrin·kle[1] ['riŋkl] **1.** figure, eau: ride f; robe: pli m; rugosité f; **2.** (se) rider; (se) froisser.

wrin·kle[2] F [~] tuyau m; bonne idée f; ruse f.

wrist [rist] poignet m; ~ watch montre-bracelet (pl. montres-bracelets) f; '**wrist·band** poignet m, manchette f; (ou **wrist·let** ['ristlit]) bracelet m; sp. bracelet m de force; ~s pl. menottes f/pl.; ~ watch see wrist watch.

writ [rit] mandat m, ordonnance f; acte m judiciaire; assignation f; Holy ⚷ Écriture f sainte; ~ for an election ordonnance f de procéder à une élection; ‡‡ ~ of attachment ordre m de saisie; ~ of execution exécutoire m.

write [rait] [irr.] v/t. écrire; rédiger (un article); ~ down coucher par écrit; noter; inscrire (un nom); ~ off écrire (une lettre etc.) d'un trait; † défalquer (une dette), réduire (un capital); ~ out transcrire; écrire en toutes lettres; remplir (un chèque); ~ up rédiger; écrire; fig. prôner; ajouter à; mettre au courant; v/i. écrire; être écrivain; ~ for faire venir, commander; ~ off to écrire à (q.); F nothing to ~ home about rien d'étonnant; '~-off annulation f par écrit.

writ·er ['raitə] écrivain m; auteur m; femme f écrivain ou auteur;

écoss. ~ to the signet notaire m; ~'s cramp (ou palsy) crampe f des écrivains.

write-up Am. F ['rait'ʌp] éloge m exagéré; compte m rendu.

writhe [raið] se tordre; se crisper.

writ·ing ['raitiŋ] écriture f; écrit m; ouvrage m littéraire; art m d'écrire; métier m d'écrivain; attr. d'écriture; à écrire; in ~ par écrit; ~ desk bureau m, secrétaire m; ~ pad sous-main m (pl. sous-mains); bloc-notes (pl. blocs-notes); ~ paper papier m à écrire ou à lettres. [(fait par) écrit.)

writ·ten ['ritn] 1. p.p. de write; 2.J

wrong [rɔŋ] 1. □ mauvais; faux (fausse f); inexact; erroné; be ~ être faux; être mal (de inf., to inf.); ne pas être à l'heure (montre); avoir tort (personne); go ~ se tromper (a. de chemin); fig. tomber dans le vice; ⊕ se détraquer; there is something ~ il y a quelque chose qui ne va pas ou qui cloche; F what's ~ with him? qu'est-ce qu'il a?; on the ~ side of sixty qui a dépassé la soixantaine; 2. mal m; tort m; ⚖ dommage m; be in the ~ avoir tort, être dans son tort; put s.o. in the ~ mettre q. dans son tort; 3. faire tort à; être injuste envers; '~'do·er méchant m; ⚖ délinquant(e f) m; '~'do·ing mal m; méfaits m/pl.; ⚖ infraction f à la loi; **wrong·ful** □ ['~ful] injuste; injustifié; préjudiciable; illégal (-aux m/pl.); '**wrong-'head·ed** (qui a l'esprit) pervers; '**wrong·ness** erreur f; inexactitude f; mal m.

wrote [rout] prét. de write.

wroth poét. [rouθ] courroucé.

wrought [rɔːt] prét. et p.p. de work 2; ~ goods produits m/pl. ouvrés; articles m/pl. apprêtés; ⊕ ~ iron fer m forgé ou ouvré.

wrung [rʌŋ] prét. et p.p. de wring 1.

wry □ [rai] tordu; de travers; pull a ~ face faire la grimace.

X

X, x [eks] X *m*, x *m*; Ⅹ, *a. fig.* Ⅹ Ⅹ *m*
(= *l'inconnue*); x(-*certificate*) *film*
film *m* interdit aux moins de 18 ans.
xen·o·pho·bi·a [zenə'foubiə] xéno-
phobie *f*   [phie *f*.⟩
xe·rog·ra·phy [ziə'rɔgrəfi] xérogra-⟩
xe·rox (*TM*) ['ziərɔks] **1.** photocopie
f; **2.** photocopier.
X·mas F ['eksməs, 'krisməs] Noël *m*;
see a. Christmas.

X-ray ['eks'rei] **1.**: ⌣*s pl.* rayons *m/pl.*
X; **2.** radiologique; **3.** radiographier.
xy·log·ra·pher [zai'lɔgrəfə] xylo-
graphe *m* (= *graveur sur bois*);
xy·lo·graph·ic, xy·lo·graph·i·cal
[⌣lə'græfik(l)] xylographique; **xy·
log·ra·phy** [⌣'lɔgrəfi] xylographie *f*
(= *gravure sur bois*).
xy·lo·phone ♪ ['zailəfoun] xylophone *m*.

Y

Y, y [wai] Y *m*, y *m*.

yacht ⚓ [jɔt] **1.** yacht *m*; **2.** faire du yachting; **'yacht·er, yachts·man** [ˈ‿smən] yachtman (*pl.* yachtmen) *m*; **'yacht·ing** yachting *m*; *attr.* en yacht; de yachtman.

ya·hoo [jəˈhuː] F brute *f*; *Am. sl.* petzouille *m*.

yam ♀ [jæm] igname *f*.

yank[1] [jæŋk] **1.** *v/t.* tirer (d'un coup sec); arracher; *v/i.* se mouvoir brusquement; **2.** coup *m* sec; secousse *f*.

Yank[2] *sl.* [‿] *see* Yankee.

Yan·kee F [ˈjæŋki] Yankee *m*; Américain(e *f*) *m* (*des É.-U.*); ‿ Doodle *chanson populaire des É.-U.*

yap [jæp] **1.** japper; F criailler; **2.** jappement *m*; *sl.* gueule *f*; *sl.* fadaises *f/pl.*; *sl.* rustre *m*.

yard[1] [jɑːd] *mesure:* yard *m* (= *0,914 m*); ⚓ vergue *f*; ⛴ ‿ goods *pl.* étoffes *f/pl.*, nouveautés *f/pl.*; mercerie *f*.

yard[2] [‿] cour *f*; chantier *m* (*de travail*); dépôt *m* (*de charbon, a.* 🚂); (*ou railway* ‿) gare *f* de triage.

yard...: '‿**arm** ⚓ bout *m* de vergue; '‿**man** manœuvre *m* de chantier; garçon *m* d'écurie; 🚂 gareur *m* de trains; '‿**stick** yard *m*; *fig.* étalon *m*; *fig.* aune *f*.

yarn [jɑːn] **1.** *tex.* fil(é) *m*; ⚓ fil *m* de caret; *spin a* ‿ débiter une histoire *ou* des histoires. [achillée *f.*)

yar·row ♀ [ˈjærou] mille-feuille *f*,)

yaw [jɔː] ⚓ faire des embardées; ✈ faire un mouvement de lacet.

yawl ⚓ [jɔːl] yole *f*.

yawn [jɔːn] **1.** bâiller; **2.** bâillement *m*.

ye † *ou poét. ou co.* [jiː] vous.

yea † *ou prov.* [jei] **1.** oui; voire; **2.** oui *m*.

year [jəː] an *m*; année *f*; ‿ of grace an(née *f*) *m* de grâce; *he bears his ‿s well* il porte bien son âge; '‿**book** annuaire *m*, almanach *m*; **year·ling** [ˈjəːliŋ] animal *m* d'un an; '**year·long** qui dure un an, d'un an;

'year·ly 1. *adj.* annuel(le *f*); **2.** *adv.* tous les ans; une fois par an.

yearn [jəːn] languir (pour, *for*; après, *after*); brûler (de *inf.*, *to inf.*); **'yearn·ing 1.** envie *f* (de, *for*); désir *m* ardent; **2.** □ ardent; plein d'envie.

yeast [jiːst] levure *f*; levain *m* (*a. fig.*); **'yeast·y** □ de levure; écumant (*mer etc.*); *fig.* enflé (*style*); emphatique (*personne*).

yegg(·man) *Am. sl.* [ˈjeg(mən)] cambrioleur *m*.

yell [jel] **1.** *vt/i.* hurler; *v/i.* crier à tue-tête; **2.** hurlement *m*; cri *m* aigu.

yel·low [ˈjelou] **1.** jaune; F lâche, poltron(ne *f*); F sensationel(le *f*), à sensation, à effet; ⊕ ‿ brass cuivre *m* jaune, laiton *m*; *Am.* ‿ dog roquet *m*; *fig.* sale type *m*; *attr.* contraire aux règlements syndicaux; ‿ fever, F‿ Jack fièvre *f* jaune; zo. *Am.*‿ jacket petite guêpe *f*; ‿ jaundice jaunisse *f*, ictère *m*; *téléph.* ‿ pages *pl.* pages *f/pl.* jaunes; ‿ press presse *f* sensationelle, journaux *m/pl.* à sensation; **2.** jaune *m*; **3.** *vt/i.* jaunir; ‿ed jauni; '‿**back** livre *m* broché; roman *m* bon marché; '‿**(h)am·mer** orn. bruant *m* jaune; '**yel·low·ish** jaunâtre.

yelp [jelp] **1.** jappement *m*; **2.** japper.

yen *Am. sl.* [jen] désir *m* (ardent).

yeo·man [ˈjoumən] yeoman (*pl.* yeomen) *m*, franc tenancier *m*; petit propriétaire *m*; ⚓ *Am.* sous-officier *m* aux écritures; ✗ ‿ of the guard soldat *m* de la Garde du corps; '**yeoman·ry** francs tenanciers *m/pl.*; ✗ garde *f* montée.

yep *Am.* F [jep] oui.

yes [jes] **1.** oui; **2.** oui *m*; ‿**man** *sl.* [ˈ‿mæn] flagorneur *m*; béni-oui-oui *m*.

yes·ter·day [ˈjestədi] hier (*a. su./m*); '**yes·ter·year** l'an *m* dernier.

yet [jet] **1.** *adv.* encore; jusqu'ici; jusque-là; déjà; malgré tout; *as ‿* jusqu'à présent; *not ‿* pas encore; **2.** *cj.* (et) cependant; tout de même.

yew ♀ [juː] if *m; attr.* en bois d'if.

Yid·dish [ˈjidiʃ] yiddish *m, adj.*

yield [jiːld] **1.** *v/t.* rendre; donner; produire; céder (*un terrain, une ville, etc.*); rapporter (*a.* ♀ *un profit*); *v/i. surt.* ✗ rendre; céder (à *to, beneath*); se rendre (*personne*); **2.** rapport *m;* rendement *m;* production *f; planche etc.:* fléchissement *m;* '**yield·ing** □ peu résistant; mou (mol *devant une voyelle ou un h muet;* molle *f); fig.* accommodant (*personne*).

yip *Am.* F [jip] aboyer; rouspéter.

yo·del, yo·dle [ˈjoudl] **1.** ioulement *m;* tyrolienne *f;* **2.** iouler; chanter à la tyrolienne.

yo·ga [ˈjougə] yoga *m.*

yog·hourt, yog·(h)urt [ˈjɔgət] [yaourt *m.*]

yo·ho [jouˈhou] oh, hisse!

yoicks! [jɔiks] taïaut!

yoke [jouk] **1.** joug *m (a. fig.);* couple *f (de bœufs);* palanche *f (pour seaux); cost.* empiècement *m;* **2.** accoupler; atteler; *fig.* unir (à, to); '**~·fel·low** compagnon (compagne *f) m* de travail; F époux (-ouse *f) m.*

yo·kel F [ˈjoukl] rustre *m.*

yolk [jouk] jaune *m* (d'œuf); suint *m (de laines).*

yon † *ou poét.* [jɔn], **yon·der** *poét.* [ˈ~də] **1.** *adj.* ce (cette *f,* ces *pl.*) -là; **2.** *adv.* là-bas.

yore [jɔː]: *of ~* (d')autrefois.

you [juː] **1.** tu; *accentué et datif:* toi; *accusatif:* te; *a.* on; **2.** vous.

young [jʌŋ] **1.** jeune; petit (*animal*); fils; *fig.* peu avancé (*nuit etc.*); **2.** jeunesse *f,* jeunes gens *m/pl.; with ~* pleine *f (animal);* '**young·ish** assez jeune; **young·ster** F [ˈjʌŋstə] jeune homme *m;* petit(e *f) m.*

your [jɔː; jə] **1.** ton, ta, tes; **2.** votre, vos; **yours 1.** le tien, la tienne, les tiens, les tiennes; à toi; **2.** le (la) vôtre, les vôtres; à vous; **your'self** toi-même; *réfléchi:* te, *accentué:* toi; **your'selves** *pl.* [~ˈselvz] vous-mêmes; *réfléchi:* vous (*a.* accentué).

youth [juːθ] jeunesse *f; coll.* jeunes gens *m/pl.; (pl.* **youths** [juːðz]) jeune homme *m,* adolescent *m; ~ hostel* auberge *f* de la jeunesse; **youth·ful** [ˈ~ful] jeune; de jeunesse; '**youth·ful·ness** (air *m* de) jeunesse *f.*

Yu·go·slav [ˈjuːgouˈslɑːv] **1.** yougoslave; **2.** *ling.* yougoslave *m;* Yougoslave *mf.*

Yule *poét.* [juːl] Noël *usu. f; ~ log* bûche *f* de Noël.

Z

Z, z [zed; *Am.* zi:] Z *m*, z *m*.
za·ny ['zeini] **1.** bouffon *m*; **2.** burlesque; loufoque.
zap *sl.* [zæp] **1.** *v/t.* descendre (*q.*); agresser, assommer; (*a.* ~ *up*) faire à la hâte; *v/i.* filer (à toute allure); **2.** vigueur *f*, énergie *f*, entrain *m*.
zeal [zi:l] zèle *m*; **zeal·ot** ['zelət] zélateur (-trice *f*) *m* (*a. eccl.*) (de, for); **'zeal·ot·ry** fanatisme *m*; *eccl.* zélotisme *m*; **'zeal·ous** □ zélé; zélateur (-trice *f*) (de, for); plein de zèle (pour, for); fanatique.
ze·bra *zo.* ['zi:brə] zèbre *m*; ~ *crossing* passage *m* clouté.
ze·bu *zo.* ['zi:bu:] zébu *m*, bœuf *m* à bosse.
ze·nith ['zeniθ] zénith *m*; *fig. a.* apogée *m*.
zeph·yr ['zefə] zéphyr *m*; ✝ laine *f* zéphire; *sp.* maillot *m*.
ze·ro ['ziərou] **1.** zéro *m* (*a. fig.*); **2.** zéro *inv.*, nul(le *f*); ~ *growth* croissance *f* zéro; ~ *hour* ✗ l'heure *f* H; *fig.* le moment décisif; ~ *option* option *f* zéro; ✂ ~ *point* point *m* zéro, *a. fig.* origine *f*; **3.** ~ *in on* ✗ régler le tir sur; *fig.* diriger son attention sur; *fig.* piquer droit sur.
zest [zest] **1.** ✝ zeste *m*; saveur *f*, goût *m*; enthousiasme *m* (pour, for); élan *m*; verve *f*; ~ *for life* entrain *m*; **2.** épicer.
zig·zag ['zigzæg] **1.** zigzag *m*; **2.** en zigzag; en lacets; **3.** zigzaguer, faire des zigzags.
zinc [ziŋk] **1.** *min.* zinc *m*; **2.** zinguer.
zi·on ['zaiən] Sion *m*; **'zi·on·ism**

sionisme *m*; **'zi·on·ist** sioniste (*a. su./mf*).
zip [zip] **1.** sifflement *m*; F énergie *f*, allant *m*, vigueur *f*; (*a.* ~ *fastener*) fermeture *f* éclair *inv.* (*TM*) *ou* à glissière; *Am.* ~ *code* code *m* postal; **2.** siffler; fermer; **'zip·per 1.** fermeture *f* éclair *inv.* (*TM*) *ou* à glissière; **2.** fermer (avec une fermeture éclair); **'zip·py** F plein d'allant, vif (vive *f*); dynamique.
zith·er ♪ ['ziθə] cithare *f*.
zo·di·ac *astr.* ['zoudiæk] zodiaque *m*; **zo·di·a·cal** [zou'daiəkl] zodiacal (-aux *m/pl.*).
zon·al □ ['zounl] zonal (-aux *m/pl.*); **zone** [zoun] zone *f*; ⚕ couche *f* (*annuelle*); *fig.* ceinture *f*.
zoo F [zu:] zoo *m* (= *jardin zoologique*).
zo·o·log·i·cal □ [zouə'lɔdʒikl] zoologique; ~ *gar·den(s pl.*) [zu-'lɔdʒikl'ga:dn(z)] jardin *m* zoologique, F zoo *m*; **zo·ol·o·gist** [zou-'ɔlədʒist] zoologiste *m*; **zo'ol·o·gy** zoologie *f*.
zoom *sl.* [zu:m] **1.** ✈ monter en chandelle; filer (à toute allure); vrombir, bourdonner; *fig.* (*a.* ~ *up*) monter en flèche; **2.** ✈ (montée *f* en) chandelle *f*; vrombissement *m*, bourdonnement *m*; *phot.* (*a.* ~ *lens*) zoom *m*.
zoot suit *Am.* ['zu:t 'sju:t] complet *m* zazou.
Zu·lu ['zu:lu:] zoulou *m*; femme *f* zoulou. [tique.⟩
zy·mot·ic *biol.* [zai'mɔtik] zymo-⟩

Proper names with pronunciation and explanation

Noms propres avec leur prononciation et notes explicatives

A

Ab·er·deen [æbə'di:n] *ville d'Écosse.*

A·bra·ham ['eibrəhæm] Abraham *m.*

Ab·ys·sin·i·a [æbi'sinjə] l'Abyssinie *f* (*ancien nom d'Éthiopie*).

A·chil·les [ə'kili:z] Achille *m* (*héros grec*).

Ad·am ['ædəm] Adam *m.*

Ad·di·son ['ædisn] *auteur anglais.*

Ad·e·laide ['ædəleid] Adélaïde *f*; ['⌣lid] Adélaïde (*ville d'Australie*).

A·den ['eidn] *ville et port d'Arabie.*

Ad·i·ron·dacks [ædi'rɔndæks] *région montagneuse de l'État de New York (É.-U.).*

Ad·olf ['ædɔlf], **A·dol·phus** [ə'dɔlfəs] Adolphe *m.*

A·dri·at·ic (Sea) [eidri'ætik('si:)] (mer *f*) Adriatique *f.*

Ae·sop ['i:sɔp] Ésope *m* (*fabuliste grec*).

Af·ghan·i·stan [æf'gænistæn] l'Afghanistan *m.*

Af·ri·ca ['æfrikə] l'Afrique *f.*

Ag·a·tha ['ægəθə] Agathe *f.*

Al·a·bam·a [ælə'ba:mə; *Am.* ælə-'bæmə] *État des É.-U.*

A·las·ka [ə'læskə] *État des É.-U.*

Al·ba·ni·a [æl'beinjə] l'Albanie *f.*

Al·ba·ny ['ɔ:lbəni] *capitale de l'État de New York (É.-U).*

Al·bert ['ælbət] Albert *m.*

Al·ber·ta [æl'bə:tə] *province du Canada.*

Al·bi·on *poét.* ['ælbjən] Albion *f*, la Grande-Bretagne *f.*

Al·der·ney ['ɔ:ldəni] Aurigny *f* (*île Anglo-Normande*).

Al·ex·an·der [ælig'za:ndə] Alexandre *m.*

Al·ex·an·dra [ælig'za:ndrə] Alexandra *f.*

Al·fred ['ælfrid] Alfred *m.*

Al·ge·ri·a [æl'dʒiəriə] l'Algérie *f.*

Al·ger·non ['ældʒənən] *prénom masculin.*

Al·giers [æl'dʒiəz] Alger *m.*

Al·ice ['ælis] Alice *f.*

Al·le·ghe·ny ['æligeini] *chaîne de montagnes des É.-U.; rivière des É.-U.*

Al·len ['ælin] Alain *m.*

Alps [ælps] *pl.* les Alpes *f/pl.*

Al·sace [æl'sæs] l'Alsace *f.*

A·me·lia [ə'mi:ljə] Amélie *f.*

A·mer·i·ca [ə'merikə] l'Amérique *f.*

A·my ['eimi] Aimée *f.*

An·chor·age ['æŋkəridʒ] *ville de l'Alaska (É.-U.).*

An·des ['ændi:z] *pl.* la Cordillère *f* des Andes, les Andes *f/pl.*

An·dor·ra [æn'dɔrə] Andorre *f.*

An·drew ['ændru:] André *m.*

An·gle·sey ['æŋglsi] *comté du Pays de Galles.*

An·nap·o·lis [ə'næpəlis] *capitale du Maryland (É.-U.), école navale.*

Ann(e) [æn] Anne *f.*

An·tho·ny ['æntəni] Antoine *m.*

An·til·les [æn'tili:z] *pl.* les Antilles *f/pl.* (*archipel entre l'Amérique du Nord et l'Amérique du Sud*).

An·to·ni·a [æn'tounjə] Antoinette *f.*

An·to·ny ['æntəni] Antoine *m.*

Ap·en·nines ['æpinainz] *pl.* les Apennins *m/pl.*

Ap·pa·lach·i·ans [æpə'leitʃiənz] *pl.* les Appalaches *m/pl.*

Ar·chi·bald ['a:tʃibəld] Archambaud *m.*

Ar·chi·me·des [a:ki'mi:di:z] Archimède *m* (*savant grec*).

Ar·den ['ɑːdn] *nom de famille anglais.*

Ar·gen·ti·na [ɑːdʒən'tiːnə], **the Ar·gen·tine** [ðiˈɑːdʒəntain] l'Argentine *f.*

Ar·gyll(·shire) [ɑːˈgail(ʃiə)] *comté d'Écosse.*

Ar·is·tot·le ['æristɔtl] Aristote *m (philosophe grec).*

Ar·i·zo·na [æri'zounə] *État des É.-U.*

Ar·kan·sas ['ɑːkənsɔː] *État des É.-U.; fleuve des É.-U.*

Ar·ling·ton ['ɑːliŋtən] *cimetière national des É.-U. près de Washington.*

Ar·thur ['ɑːθə] Arthur *m;* King ∿ le roi Arthur *(ou* Artus).

As·cot ['æskət] *ville et champ de courses d'Angleterre.*

A·sia ['eiʃə] l'Asie *f;* ∿ Minor l'Asie *f* Mineure.

Ath·ens ['æθinz] Athènes *f.*

At·kins ['ætkinz]: Tommy ∿ *sobriquet du soldat britannique.*

At·lan·tic [ət'læntik] *m* l'Atlantique *m.*

Auck·land ['ɔːklənd] *ville et port de la Nouvelle-Zélande.*

Au·drey ['ɔːdri] *prénom féminin.*

Au·gus·tus [ɔːˈgʌstəs] Auguste *m.*

Aus·ten ['ɔːstin] *femme écrivain anglaise.*

Aus·tin [∿] *capitale du Texas (É.-U.).*

Aus·tra·lia [ɔːsˈtreiljə] l'Australie *f.*

Aus·tri·a ['ɔːstriə] l'Autriche *f.*

A·von ['eivən] *rivière d'Angleterre.*

Ax·min·ster ['æksminstə] *ville d'Angleterre.*

Ayr [ɛə] *ville d'Écosse; a.* **Ayr·shire** ['∿ʃiə] *comté d'Écosse.*

A·zores [ə'zɔːz] *pl. les* Açores *f|pl.*

B

Bac·chus *myth.* ['bækəs] Bacchus *m (dieu grec du vin).*

Ba·con ['beikən] *homme d'État et philosophe anglais.*

Ba·den-Pow·ell ['beidn'pouel] *fondateur du scoutisme.*

Ba·ha·mas [bə'hɑːməz] *pl. les* Bahamas *f|pl. (archipel de l'Atlantique).*

Bai·le A·tha Cli·ath [blɔːˈkliː] *nom gaélique de Dublin.*

Bald·win ['bɔːldwin] Baudouin *m.*

Bal·mor·al [bæl'mɔrəl] *château royal en Écosse.*

Bal·ti·more ['bɔːltimɔː] *ville et port des É.-U.*

Bar·thol·o·mew [bɑːˈθɔləmjuː] Barthélemy *m.*

Bath [bɑːθ] *station thermale d'Angleterre.*

Ba·ton Rouge ['bætn'ruːʒ] *capitale de la Louisiane (É.-U.).*

Ba·var·ia [bəˈvɛəriə] la Bavière *f.*

Bea·cons·field ['biːkənzfiːld] *titre de noblesse de Disraeli.*

Beards·ley ['biədzli] *dessinateur et illustrateur anglais.*

Beck·ett ['bekit] *poète et dramaturge irlandais.*

Beck·y ['beki] *diminutif de Rebecca.*

Bed·ford ['bedfəd] *ville d'Angleterre; a.* **Bed·ford·shire** ['∿ʃiə] *comté d'Angleterre.*

Bel·fast ['belfɑːst] *capitale de l'Irlande du Nord.*

Bel·gium ['beldʒəm] la Belgique *f.*

Bel·grade [bel'greid] *capitale de la Yougoslavie.*

Bel·gra·vi·a [bel'greivjə] *quartier résidentiel de Londres.*

Ben [ben] *diminutif de Benjamin.*

Ben·e·dict ['benidikt; 'benit] Benoît *m.*

Ben·gal [beŋ'gɔːl] le Bengale *m.*

Ben·ja·min ['bendʒəmin] Benjamin *m.*

Ben Ne·vis [ben'niːvis] *point culminant de la Grande-Bretagne.*

Berke·ley ['bɑːkli] *philosophe irlandais;* ['bəːkli] *ville des É.-U. (Californie).*

Berk·shire ['bɑːkʃiə] *comté d'Angleterre;* ∿ **Hills** ['bəːkʃiə'hilz] *pl. chaîne de montagnes du Massachusetts (É.-U.).*

Ber·lin [bəːˈlin] Berlin.

Ber·mu·das [bəːˈmjuːdəz] *pl. les* Bermudes *f|pl. (archipel de l'Atlantique).*

Ber·nard ['bəːnəd] Bernard *m.*

Bern(e) [bəːn] Berne.

Ber·tha ['bəːθə] Berthe *f.*

Ber·trand ['bəːtrənd] Bertram *m.*

Ber·yl ['beril] *prénom féminin.*

Bess, Bes·sy ['bes(i)], **Bet·s(e)y** ['betsi], **Bet·ty** ['beti] Babette *f.*

Bill, Bil·ly ['bil(i)] *diminutif de William.*

Bir·ken·head ['bəːkənhed] *port et ville industrielle d'Angleterre.*

Bir·ming·ham ['bəːmiŋəm] *ville industrielle d'Angleterre;* ['∿hæm] *ville des É.-U. (Alabama).*

Bis·kay ['biskei]: *the Bay of* ~ le golfe *m* de Gascogne.

Blooms·bur·y ['blu:mzbri] *quartier d'artistes de Londres.*

Bob [bɔb] *diminutif de Robert.*

Bo·he·mia [bəu'hi:mjə] la Bohême *f.*

Boi·se ['bɔisi] *capitale de l'Idaho (É.-U.).*

Bol·eyn ['bulin]: *Anne* ~ Anne Boleyn *(femme de Henri VIII d'Angleterre).*

Bo·liv·i·a [bə'liviə] la Bolivie *f.*

Bom·bay [bɔm'bei] *ville et port de l'Inde.*

Bonn [bɔn] *capitale de la République fédérale d'Allemagne.*

Bos·ton ['bɔstən] *capitale du Massachusetts (É.-U.).*

Bourne·mouth ['bɔ:nməθ] *station balnéaire d'Angleterre.*

Brad·ford ['brædfəd] *ville industrielle d'Angleterre.*

Bra·zil [brə'zil] le Brésil *m.*

Breck·nock(·shire) ['breknɔk(ʃiə)] *comté du Pays de Galles.*

Bri·an ['braiən] *prénom masculin.*

Bridg·et ['bridʒit] Brigitte *f.*

Brigh·ton ['braitn] *station balnéaire d'Angleterre.*

Bris·tol ['bristl] *ville et port d'Angleterre.*

Bri·tan·ni·a *poét.* [bri'tænjə] la Grande-Bretagne *f.*

Brit·ta·ny ['britəni] la Bretagne *f.*

Brit·ten ['britn] *compositeur anglais.*

Broad·way ['brɔ:dwei] *rue principale de New York (É.-U.).*

Brontë ['brɔnti] *nom de trois femmes de lettres anglaises.*

Brook·lyn ['bruklin] *quartier de New York (É.-U.).*

Brus·sels ['brʌslz] Bruxelles.

Bu·cha·rest ['bju:kərest] Bucarest.

Buck [bʌk] *femme écrivain américaine.*

Buck·ing·ham ['bʌkiŋəm] *comté d'Angleterre;* ~ *Palace palais des rois de Grande-Bretagne;* **Buck·ing·ham·shire** ['bʌkiŋəmʃiə] *see Buckingham.*

Bu·da·pest ['bju:də'pest] *capitale de la Hongrie.*

Bud·dha ['budə] Bouddha.

Bul·gar·i·a [bʌl'gɛəriə] la Bulgarie *f.*

Bul·wer ['bulwə] *auteur anglais.*

Bur·ma ['bə:mə] la Birmanie *f.*

Burns [bə:nz] *poète écossais.*

By·ron ['baiərən] *poète anglais.*

C

Cae·sar ['si:zə] (Jules) César *m (général et dictateur romain).*

Cai·ro ['kaiərou] Le Caire *m.*

Cal·cut·ta [kæl'kʌtə] *capitale de l'État de Bengale-Occidental.*

Cal·i·for·nia [kæli'fɔ:njə] la Californie *f (État des É.-U.).*

Cam·bridge ['keimbridʒ] *ville universitaire anglaise; ville des É.-U. (Massachusetts), siège de l'université Harvard; a.* **Cam·bridge·shire** ['~ʃiə] *comté d'Angleterre.*

Camp·bell ['kæmbl] *nom de famille.*

Can·a·da ['kænədə] le Canada *m.*

Ca·nar·y Is·lands [kə'nɛəri'ailəndz] *les îles f/pl.* Canaries, *les* Canaries *f/pl.*

Can·ber·ra ['kænbərə] *capitale de l'Australie.*

Can·ter·bur·y ['kæntəbəri] Cantorbéry *f (ville d'Angleterre).*

Cape Town, Cape·town ['keiptaun] le Cap *m.*

Ca·pote [kə'pouti] *écrivain américain.*

Car·diff ['kɑ:dif] *capitale du Pays de Galles.*

Car·di·gan(·shire) ['kɑ:digən(ʃiə)] *comté du Pays de Galles.*

Car·lisle [kɑ:'lail] *ville d'Angleterre.*

Car·lyle [kɑ:'lail] *auteur anglais.*

Car·mar·then(·shire) [kə'mɑ:ðən(-ʃiə)] *comté du Pays de Galles.*

Car·nar·von(·shire) [kə'nɑ:vən(-ʃiə)] *comté du Pays de Galles.*

Car·neg·ie ['kɑ:negi] *industriel américain.*

Car·o·li·na [kærə'lainə]: *(North* ~, *South* ~*)* la Caroline *f (du Nord, du Sud) (États des É.-U.).*

Car·o·line ['kærəlain] Caroline *f.*

Car·pa·thi·ans [kɑ:'peiθjənz] *pl. les* Karpates *f/pl.*

Car·rie ['kæri] *diminutif de Caroline.*

Cath·e·rine ['kæθərin] Catherine *f.*

Cau·ca·sus ['kɔ:kəsəs] Caucase *m.*

Cec·il ['sesl; 'sisl] *prénom masculin.*

Ce·cil·i·a [si'siljə], **Cec·i·ly** ['sisili] Cécile *f.*

Cey·lon [si'lɔn] Ceylan *m.*

Cham·ber·lain ['tʃeimbəlin] *nom de plusieurs hommes d'État britanniques.*

Chan·nel ['tʃænl]: *the English* ~ la Manche *f.*

Char·ing Cross ['tʃæriŋ'krɔs] *carrefour de Londres.*

Charles [tʃɑ:lz] Charles *m.*

Charles·ton ['tʃɑːlstən] *capitale de la Virginie Occidentale (É.-U.).*

Char·lotte ['ʃɑːlət] Charlotte *f.*

Chat·ham ['tʃætəm] *ville et port d'Angleterre.*

Chau·cer ['tʃɔːsə] *poète anglais.*

Chel·sea ['tʃelsi] *quartier de Londres.*

Chesh·ire ['tʃeʃə] *comté d'Angleterre.*

Ches·ter·field ['tʃestəfiːld] *ville industrielle d'Angleterre.*

Chev·i·ot Hills ['tʃeviət'hilz] *pl. chaîne de montagnes qui sépare l'Écosse de l'Angleterre.*

Chi·ca·go [ʃi'kɑːgou; *Am. souv.* ʃi-'kɔːgou] *ville des États de la Prairie (É.-U.).*

Chil·e, Chil·i ['tʃili] le Chili *m.*

Chi·na ['tʃainə] la Chine *f.*

Chlo·e ['kləui] *prénom féminin.*

Chris·ti·na [kris'tiːnə] Christine *f.*

Chris·to·pher ['kristəfə] Christophe *m.*

Chrys·ler ['kraislə] *industriel américain.*

Church·ill ['tʃəːtʃil] *homme d'État britannique.*

Cin·cin·nat·i [sinsi'næti] *ville des É.-U.*

Cis·sie ['sisi] *diminutif de Cecilia.*

Clar·a ['klɛərə], **Clare** [klɛə] Claire *f.*

Clar·en·don ['klærəndən] *nom de plusieurs hommes d'État britanniques.*

Cle·o·pa·tra [kliə'pætrə] Cléopâtre *f (reine d'Égypte).*

Cleve·land ['kliːvlənd] *ville industrielle et port des É.-U.*

Clive [klaiv] *général qui fonda la puissance britannique dans l'Inde.*

Clyde [klaid] *fleuve d'Écosse.*

Cole·ridge ['koulridʒ] *poète anglais.*

Col·in ['kɔlin] *prénom masculin.*

Co·lom·bi·a [kə'lɔmbiə] la Colombie *f.*

Col·o·ra·do [kɔlə'rɑːdou] *État des É.-U.; nom de deux fleuves des É.-U.*

Co·lum·bi·a [kə'lʌmbiə] *fleuve des É.-U.; district fédéral des É.-U. (capitale Washington); capitale de la Caroline du Sud (É.-U.).*

Con·cord ['kɔŋkəd] *capitale du New Hampshire (É.-U.).*

Con·nacht ['kɔnət], **Con·naught** ['kɔnɔːt] *province de la République d'Irlande.*

Con·nect·i·cut [kə'netikət] *fleuve des É.-U.; État des É.-U.*

Con·stance ['kɔnstəns] Constance *mf.*

Coo·per ['kuːpə] *auteur américain.*

Co·pen·ha·gen [koupn'heign] Copenhague.

Cor·dil·le·ras [kɔːdi'ljɛərəz] *pl. see Andes.*

Cor·ne·lia [kɔː'niːljə] Cornélie *f.*

Corn·wall ['kɔːnwəl] la Cornouailles *f (comté d'Angleterre).*

Cos·ta Ri·ca ['kɔstə'riːkə] le Costa Rica *m.*

Cov·ent Gar·den ['kɔvənt'gɑːdn] *l'opéra de Londres.*

Cov·en·try ['kɔvəntri] *ville industrielle d'Angleterre.*

Craig [kreig] *prénom.*

Crete [kriːt] la Crète *f.*

Cri·me·a [krai'miə] la Crimée *f.*

Crom·well ['krɔmwəl] *homme d'État anglais.*

Croy·don ['krɔidn] *ancien aéroport de Londres.*

Cu·ba ['kjuːbə] (île *f* de) Cuba *m.*

Cum·ber·land ['kʌmbələnd] *comté d'Angleterre.*

Cu·pid *myth.* ['kjuːpid] Cupidon *m (dieu romain de l'Amour).*

Cyn·thi·a ['sinθiə] *prénom féminin.*

Cy·prus ['saiprəs] Chypre *f.*

Cy·rus ['sairəs] Cyrus *m.*

Czech·o·Slo·va·ki·a ['tʃekouslou-'vækiə] la Tchécoslovaquie *f.*

D

Da·ko·ta [də'koutə]: (*North* ~, *South* ~) le Dakota *m (du Nord, du Sud) (États de É.-U.).*

Dan·iel ['dænjəl] Daniel *m.*

Dan·ube ['dænjuːb] *le* Danube *m.*

Daph·ne ['dæfni] Daphne *f.*

Dar·da·nelles [dɑːdə'nelz] *pl. les* Dardanelles *f/pl.*

Dar·jee·ling [dɑː'dʒiːliŋ] *ville de l'Inde.*

Dart·moor ['dɑːtmuə] *massif cristallin d'Angleterre; prison.*

Dar·win ['dɑːwin] *naturaliste anglais.*

Da·vid ['deivid] David *m.*

Dee [diː] *fleuve d'Angleterre et d'Écosse.*

De·foe [di'fou] *auteur anglais.*

Deir·dre ['diədri] *prénom féminin.*

Del·a·ware ['deləwɛə] *fleuve des É.-U.; État des É.-U.*

Den·bigh(·shire) ['denbi(ʃiə)] *comté du Pays de Galles.*

Den·mark ['denmɑːk] le Danemark *m.*

Den·ver [ˈdenvə] *capitale du Colorado (É.-U.).*

Der·by(·shire) [ˈdɑːbi(ʃiə)] *comté d'Angleterre.*

Des Moines [dəˈmɔin] *capitale de l'Iowa (É.-U.).*

De·troit [diˈtrɔit] *ville industrielle des É.-U.*

De Va·le·ra [dəvəˈliərə] *homme d'État irlandais.*

Dev·on(·shire) [ˈdevn(ʃiə)] *comté d'Angleterre.*

Dew·ey [ˈdjuːi] *philosophe américain.*

Di·an·a [daiˈænə] *Diane f.*

Dick [dik] *diminutif de Richard.*

Dick·ens [ˈdikinz] *auteur anglais.*

Dick·in·son [ˈdikinsn] *femme poète américaine.*

Dis·rae·li [dizˈreili] *homme d'État britannique.*

Dol·ly [ˈdɔli] *diminutif de Dorothy.*

Do·min·i·can Re·pub·lic [dəˈminikən riˈpʌblik] *la République f Dominicaine.*

Don·ald [ˈdɔnld] *prénom masculin.*

Don Quix·ote [dɔnˈkwiksət] *Don Quichotte m.*

Dor·o·the·a [dɔrəˈθiə], **Dor·o·thy** [ˈdɔrəθi] *Dorothée f.*

Dor·set(·shire) [ˈdɔːsit(ʃiə)] *comté d'Angleterre.*

Dos Pas·sos [dəsˈpæsəs] *écrivain américain.*

Doug [dʌg] *diminutif de Douglas.*

Doug·las [ˈdʌgləs] *puissante famille écossaise; prénom masculin.*

Do·ver [ˈdouvə] *Douvres (port d'Angleterre, sur la Manche); capitale du Delaware (É.-U.).*

Down·ing Street [ˈdauniŋˈstriːt] *rue de Londres, résidence officielle du premier ministre.*

Drei·ser [ˈdraisə] *auteur américain.*

Dry·den [ˈdraidn] *poète anglais.*

Dub·lin [ˈdʌblin] *capitale de la République d'Irlande.*

Du·luth [dəˈluːθ] *ville des É.-U. (Minnesota).*

Dun·kirk [dʌnˈkəːk] *Dunkerque m.*

Dur·ham [ˈdʌrəm] *comté d'Angleterre.*

E·den [ˈiːdn] *Eden m, le paradis m terrestre.*

Ed·in·burgh [ˈedinbərə] *Édimbourg.*

Ed·i·son [ˈedisn] *inventeur américain.*

Ed·mund [ˈedmənd] *Edmond m.*

Ed·ward [ˈedwəd] *Édouard m.*

E·gypt [ˈiːdʒipt] *l'Égypte f.*

Ei·leen [ˈailiːn] *prénom féminin.*

Ei·re [ˈɛərə] *ancien nom de la République d'Irlande.*

Ei·sen·how·er [ˈaizənhauə] *général et 34e président des É.-U.*

E·laine [iˈlein] *prénom féminin.*

El·ea·nor [ˈelinə] *Eléonore f.*

E·li·as [iˈlaiəs] *Élie m.*

El·i·nor [ˈelinə] *Éléonore f.*

El·i·ot [ˈeljət] *femme écrivain anglaise; poète anglais, né aux É.-U.*

E·li·za [iˈlaizə] *diminutif de Elizabeth.*

E·liz·a·beth [iˈlizəbəθ] *Elisabeth f.*

El·lis Is·land [ˈelisˈailənd] *île de la baie de New York (É.-U.).*

El Sal·va·dor [elˈsælvədɔː] *El Salvador m.*

Em·er·son [ˈeməsn] *philosophie et poète américain.*

Em·i·ly [ˈemili] *Émilie f.*

Eng·land [ˈiŋglənd] *l'Angleterre f.*

E·noch [ˈiːnɔk] *Énoch m.*

Ep·som [ˈepsəm] *ville d'Angleterre, célèbre course de chevaux.*

E·rie [ˈiəri] *Lake ⁓ le lac m Érie (un des cinq grands lacs de l'Amérique du Nord).*

Er·nest [ˈəːnist] *Ernest m.*

Es·sex [ˈesiks] *comté d'Angleterre.*

Eth·el [ˈeθl] *prénom féminin.*

E·thi·o·pi·a [iːθiˈoupjə] *l'Éthiopie f.*

E·ton [ˈiːtn] *collège et ville d'Angleterre.*

Eu·clid [ˈjuːklid] *Euclide (mathématicien grec).*

Eu·gene [ˈjuːdʒiːn] *Eugène m.*

Eu·ge·ni·a [juːˈdʒiːniə] *Eugénie f.*

Eu·phra·tes [juːˈfreitiːz] *l'Euphrate m.*

Eu·rope [ˈjuərəp] *l'Europe f.*

Eus·tace [ˈjuːstəs] *Eustache m.*

Ev·ans [ˈevənz] *nom de famille anglais et gallois.*

Eve [iːv] *Ève f.*

Ev·e·lyn [ˈiːvlin] *Éveline f.*

E

Ec·ua·dor [ekwəˈdɔː] *Équateur m.*

Ed·die [ˈedi] *diminutif de Edmund, Edward.*

F

Falk·land Is·lands [ˈfɔːkləndˈailəndz] *pl. les îles f/pl. Falkland (archipel de l'Atlantique).*

Faulk·ner ['fɔːknə] *auteur américain.*

Fawkes [fɔːks] *nom de famille anglais; chef de la Conspiration des Poudres (1605).*

Fe·li·ci·a [fi'lisiə] *prénom féminin.*

Fe·lix ['fiːliks] *Félix m.*

Fin·land ['finlənd] *la Finlande f.*

Fitz·ger·ald [fits'dʒerəld] *nom de famille.*

Flan·ders ['flɑːndəz] *la Flandre f.*

Flint·shire ['flintʃiə] *comté du Pays de Galles.*

Flor·ence ['flɔrəns] *Florence f (prénom).*

Flor·i·da ['flɔridə] *la Floride f (État des É.-U.).*

Flush·ing ['flʌʃiŋ] *Flessingue.*

Folke·stone ['foukstən] *ville et port d'Angleterre sur la Manche.*

Ford [fɔːd] *industriel américain.*

France [frɑːns] *la France f.*

Fran·ces ['frɑːnsis] *Françoise f.*

Fran·cis [~] *François m.*

Frank·fort ['fræŋkfət] *capitale du Kentucky (É.-U.).*

Frank·lin ['fræŋklin] *homme d'État et auteur américain.*

Fred(·dy) ['fred(i)] *diminutif de Alfred, Frederic(k).*

Fred·er·ic(k) ['fredrik] *Frédéric m.*

Ful·bright ['fulbrait] *homme politique américain.*

Ful·ton ['fultən] *inventeur américain.*

G

Gains·bor·ough ['geinzbərə] *peintre anglais.*

Gals·wor·thy ['gælzwəːði] *auteur anglais.*

Gan·ges ['gændʒiːz] *le Gange m.*

Gaul [gɔːl] *la Gaule f.*

Ge·ne·va [dʒi'niːvə] *Genève.*

Geof·frey ['dʒefri] *Geoffroi m.*

George [dʒɔːdʒ] *Georges m.*

Geor·gia ['dʒɔːdʒiə] *la Georgie f (État des É.-U.).*

Ger·ald ['dʒerəld] *Gérard m.*

Ger·al·dine ['dʒerəldiːn] *prénom féminin.*

Ger·ma·ny ['dʒəːməni] *l'Allemagne f.*

Gersh·win ['gəːʃwin] *compositeur américain.*

Ger·trude ['gəːtruːd] *Gertrude f.*

Get·tys·burg ['getizbəːg] *ville des É.-U.*

Gha·na ['gɑːnə] *le Ghana m.*

Gi·bral·tar [dʒi'brɔːltə] *Gibraltar m.*

Giles [dʒailz] *Gilles m.*

Gill [gil] *Julie f.*

Glad·ys ['glædis] *prénom féminin.*

Glad·stone ['glædstən] *homme d'État britannique.*

Gla·mor·gan(·shire) [glə'mɔːgən (-ʃiə)] *comté du Pays de Galles.*

Glas·gow ['glɑːsgou] *ville et port d'Écosse.*

Glouces·ter ['glɔstə] *ville d'Angleterre; a.* **Glouces·ter·shire** ['~ʃiə] *comté d'Angleterre.*

Gold·smith ['gouldsmiθ] *auteur anglais.*

Gor·don ['gɔːdn] *nom de famille anglais.*

Go·tham ['gɔtəm] *village d'Angleterre.*

Gra·ham ['greiəm] *nom de famille et prénom masculin anglais.*

Grand Can·yon [grænd'kæniən] *nom des gorges du Colorado (É.-U.).*

Great Brit·ain ['greit'britən] *la Grande-Bretagne f.*

Great Di·vide ['greitdi'vaid] *les montagnes Rocheuses (É.-U.).*

Greece [griːs] *la Grèce f.*

Greene [griːn] *auteur anglais.*

Green·land ['griːnlənd] *le Groenland m.*

Green·wich ['grinidʒ] *faubourg de Londres;~ Village quartier d'artistes de New York.*

Greg·o·ry ['gregəri] *Grégoire m.*

Gros·ve·nor ['grouvnə] *place et rue de Londres.*

Gua·te·ma·la [gwæti'mɑːlə] *le Guatemala m.*

Guern·sey ['gəːnzi] *Guernesey f (île Anglo-Normande).*

Gui·a·na [gi'ɑːnə] *la Guyane f.*

Guin·ea ['gini] *la Guinée f.*

Guin·ness ['ginis; gi'nes] *nom de famille, surt. irlandais.*

Guy [gai] *Gui m, Guy m.*

Gwen·do·len, Gwen·do·lyn ['gwendəlin] *prénom féminin.*

H

Hai·ti ['heiti] *la Haïti f.*

Hague [heig]: *the ~ La Haye.*

Hal·i·fax ['hælifæks] *ville du Canada et d'Angleterre.*

Ham·il·ton ['hæmiltən] *nom de famille anglais.*

Hamp·shire ['hæmpʃiə] *comté d'Angleterre.*

Hamp·stead ['hæmpstid] *faubourg de Londres.*

Han·o·ver ['hænəvə] *Hanovre m.*

Har·lem ['hɑːləm] *quartier de New York, habité surtout par des noirs.*

Har·ri·et ['hæriət] *Henriette f.*

Har·ris·burg ['hærisbəːg] *capitale de la Pennsylvanie (É.-U.).*

Har·row ['hærou] *collège et ville d'Angleterre.*

Har·ry ['hæri] *diminutif de Henry.*

Har·vard U·ni·ver·si·ty ['hɑːvəd juːniˈvəːsiti] *université américaine.*

Har·wich ['hæridʒ] *ville et port d'Angleterre.*

Has·tings ['heistiŋz] *ville d'Angleterre; homme d'État, gouverneur de l'Inde anglaise.*

Ha·wai·i [hɑːˈwaii] *pl. les Hawaii f/pl. (archipel de la Polynésie, État des É.-U.).*

Heb·ri·des ['hebridiːz] *pl. les Hébrides f/pl. (îles d'Écosse).*

Hel·en ['helin] *Hélène f.*

Hel·sin·ki ['helsiŋki] *capitale de la Finlande.*

Hem·ing·way ['hemiŋwei] *auteur américain.*

Hen·ley ['henli] *ville d'Angleterre sur la Tamise; régates célèbres.*

Hen·ry ['henri] *Henri m.*

Her·cu·les ['həːkjuliːz] *Hercule m.*

Her·e·ford(·shire) ['herifəd(ʃiə)] *comté d'Angleterre.*

Hert·ford(·shire) ['hɑːfəd(ʃiə)] *comté d'Angleterre.*

Hil·a·ry ['hiləri] *Hilaire f.*

Hi·ma·la·ya [himəˈleiə] *l'Himalaya m.*

Hin·du·stan [hinduˈstæn] *l'Hindoustan m.*

Ho·garth ['hougɑːθ] *peintre anglais.*

Hol·born ['houbən] *quartier de Londres.*

Hol·land ['hɔlənd] *la Hollande f.*

Hol·ly·wood ['hɔliwud] *centre de l'industrie cinématographique américaine.*

Home [hjuːm]: *Sir Alec Douglas-~ homme politique anglais.*

Ho·mer ['houmə] *Homère m (poète grec).*

Hon·du·ras [hɔnˈdjuərəs] *le Honduras m.*

Ho·no·lu·lu [hɔnəˈluːlu] *capitale des Hawaii (É.-U.).*

Hoo·ver ['huːvə] *31e président des É.-U.*

Hous·ton ['(h)juːstən] *ville des É.-U. (Texas).*

Hud·son ['hʌdsn] *fleuve des É.-U., avec New York à l'embouchure; vaste golfe au nord de l'Amérique.*

Hugh [hjuː] *Hugues m.*

Hughes [hjuːz] *nom de famille.*

Hull [hʌl] *ville et port d'Angleterre.*

Hume [hjuːm] *philosophe anglais.*

Hum·phr(e)y ['hʌmfri] *prénom masculin.*

Hun·ga·ry ['hʌŋgəri] *la Hongrie f.*

Hun·ting·don(·shire) ['hʌntiŋdən (-ʃiə)] *comté d'Angleterre.*

Hu·ron ['hjuərən]: *Lake ~ le lac m Huron (un des cinq grands lacs de l'Amérique du Nord).*

Hux·ley ['hʌksli] *naturaliste anglais; zoologiste anglais; auteur anglais.*

Hyde Park ['haidˈpɑːk] *Parc de Londres.*

I

I·an ['iːən, iən] *Jean m.*

Ice·land ['aislənd] *l'Islande f.*

I·da·ho ['aidəhou] *État des É.-U.*

I·dle·wild ['aidlwaild] *ancien nom de Kennedy Airport.*

Il·li·nois [iliˈnɔi(z)] *rivière des É.-U.; État des É.-U.*

In·di·a ['indjə] *l'Inde f.*

In·di·an·a [indiˈænə] *État des É.-U.*

In·di·an Ocean ['indjənˈouʃən] *océan m Indien.*

In·dies ['indiz] *pl.: the (East, West) ~ les Indes f/pl. (orientales, occidentales).*

In·dus ['indəs] *l'Indus m.*

I·o·wa ['aiouə] *État des É.-U.*

I·rak, I·raq [iˈrɑːk] *l'Irak m, l'Iraq m.*

I·ran [iəˈrɑːn] *l'Iran m.*

Ire·land ['aiələnd] *l'Irlande f.*

I·re·ne [aiˈriːni; 'airiːn] *Irène f.*

I·ris ['aiəris] *prénom féminin.*

Ir·ving ['əːviŋ] *auteur américain.*

I·saac ['aizək] *Isaac m.*

Is·a·bel ['izəbəl] *Isabelle f.*

Isle of Man [ailəvˈmæn] *Isle f de*

Man (*île de la mer d'Irlande*).
Is·ra·el ['izrɛiəl] l'Israël *m.*
It·a·ly ['itəli] l'Italie *f.*
I·vy ['aivi] *prénom féminin.*

J

Jack [dʒæk] Jean(not) *m* (*see Jack au dictionnaire*).
Ja·mai·ca [dʒə'meikə] la Jamaïque *f.*
James [dʒeimz] Jacques *m.*
Jane [dʒein] Jeanne *f.*
Ja·net ['dʒænit] Jeanette *f.*
Ja·pan [dʒə'pæn] le Japon *m.*
Jean [dʒiːn] Jeanne *f.*
Jef·fer·son ['dʒefəsn] *3ᵉ président des É.-U.*, *auteur de la Déclaration d'Indépendance*; ~ *City capitale du Missouri* (*É.-U.*).
Jen·ny ['dʒeni] Jeanneton *f*, Jeannette *f.*
Jer·e·my ['dʒerimi] Jérémie *m.*
Jer·sey ['dʒɔːzi] *île Anglo-Normande*; ~ *City ville des É.-U.*
Je·ru·sa·lem [dʒə'ruːsələm] Jérusalem.
Jes·si·ca ['dʒesikə] Jessica *f.*
Je·sus (**Christ**) ['dʒiːzəs ('kraist)] Jésus(-Christ) *m.*
Jill [dʒil] Julie *f*; *Jack and* ~ Jeannot et Colette.
Jim(·my) ['dʒim(i)] *diminutif de James.*
Joan [dʒoun] Jeanne *f.*
Joc·e·lin(e), **Joc·e·lyn** ['dʒɔslin] *prénom féminin.*
Jo(e) [dʒou] *diminutif de Joseph.*
John [dʒɔn] Jean *m.*
John·ny ['dʒɔni] Jeannot *m.*
John·son ['dʒɔnsn] *36ᵉ président des É.-U.*; *auteur anglais.*
Jo·nah ['dʒounə] Jonas *m.*
Jon·a·than ['dʒɔnəθən] Jonathas *m.*
Jor·dan ['dʒɔːdn] la Jordanie *f.*
Jo·seph ['dʒouzif] Joseph *m.*
Josh·u·a ['dʒɔʃwə] Josué *m.*
Joyce [dʒɔis] *écrivain irlandais.*
Ju·go·sla·vi·a ['juːgou'slɑːviə] la Yougoslavie *f.*
Jul·ia ['dʒuːljə], **Ju·li·et** ['~t] Julie(tte) *f.*
Jul·ian ['dʒuːliən] *prénom masculin.*
Jul·ius ['dʒuːljəs] Jules *m.*
Ju·neau ['dʒuːnou] *capitale de l'Alaska* (*É.-U.*).

K

Kam·pu·che·a [kæmpu'tʃiə] Cambodge *m.*
Kan·sas ['kænzəs] *rivière des É.-U.*; *État des É.-U.*
Kash·mir [kæʃ'miə] le Cachemire *m* (*ancien État de l'Inde*).
Kate [keit] *diminutif de Catherine, Katharine, Katherine, Kathleen.*
Kath·a·rine, **Kath·er·ine** ['kæθərin] Catherine *f.*
Kath·leen ['kæθliːn] Catherine *f.*
Keats [kiːts] *poète anglais.*
Keith [kiːθ] *prénom masculin.*
Ken·ne·dy ['kenidi] *35ᵉ président des É.-U.*; *Cape* ~ *cap de la côte de Floride* (*lancement d'engins téléguidés et de satellites artificiels*); ~ *airport aéroport international de New York.*
Ken·neth ['keniθ] *prénom masculin.*
Ken·sing·ton ['kenziŋtən] *quartier de Londres.*
Kent [kent] *comté d'Angleterre.*
Ken·tuck·y [ken'tʌki] *rivière des É.-U.*; *État des É.-U.*
Ken·ya ['kiːnjə; 'kenjə] le Kenya *m.*
Kip·ling ['kipliŋ] *poète anglais.*
Kit·ty ['kiti] *diminutif de Catherine.*
Klon·dike ['klɔndaik] *rivière et région du Canada.*
Knox [nɔks] *réformateur écossais.*
Krem·lin ['kremlin] le Kremlin *m.*
Ku·wait [ku'weit] Koweït *m.*

L

Lab·ra·dor ['læbrədɔː] *péninsule de l'Amérique du Nord.*
Lan·ca·shire ['læŋkəʃiə] *comté d'Angleterre.*
Lan·cas·ter ['læŋkəstə] Lancastre *f* (*ville d'Angleterre*; *ville des É.-U.*); *see Lancashire.*
Lau·rence, **Law·rence** ['lɔːrəns] Laurent *m.*
Leb·a·non ['lebənən] le Liban *m.*
Leeds [liːdz] *ville industrielle d'Angleterre.*
Leg·horn ['leg'hɔːn] Livourne *f.*
Leices·ter ['lestə] *ville d'Angleterre*; *a.* **Leices·ter·shire** ['~ʃiə] *comté d'Angleterre.*
Leigh [liː; lai] *ville industrielle d'Angleterre*; *nom de famille anglais.*
Leix [liːʃ] *comté d'Irlande.*

Le·man ['lemən]: *Lake* ~ le lac *m* Léman.

Leon·ard ['lenəd] Léonard *m.*

Les·lie ['lezli] *prénom masculin.*

Lew·is ['lu:is] Louis *m*; *auteur américain*; *poète anglais.*

Lil·i·an ['liliən] *prénom féminin.*

Lim·er·ick ['limərik] *comté d'Irlande.*

Lin·coln ['liŋkən] *16ᵉ président des É.-U.*; *capitale du Nébraska (É.-U.)*; *ville d'Angleterre*; *a.* **Lin·coln·shire** ['~ʃiə] *comté d'Angleterre.*

Li·o·nel ['laiənl] *prénom masculin.*

Lis·bon ['lizbən] Lisbonne *f.*

Lit·tle Rock ['litl'rɔk] *capitale de l'Arkansas (É.-U.).*

Liv·er·pool ['livəpu:l] *ville industrielle et port d'Angleterre.*

Liz·zie ['lizi] Lisette *f.*

Lloyd [lɔid] *prénom masculin.*

Locke [lɔk] *philosophe anglais.*

Lon·don ['lʌndən] Londres.

Long·fel·low ['lɔŋfelou] *poète américain.*

Lor·raine [lɔ'rein] la Lorraine *f.*

Los An·ge·les [lɔs'ændʒili:z; *Am. a.* 'æŋgələs] *ville et port des É.-U.*

Lou·i·sa [lu:'i:zə] Louise *f.*

Lou·i·si·an·a [lu:i:zi'ænə] la Louisiane *f* (*État des É.-U.*).

Lu·cia ['lu:siə] Lucie *f.*

Lu·cius ['lu:siəs] Lucien *m.*

Lu·cy ['lu:si] Lucie *f.*

Luke [lu:k] Luc *m.*

Lux·em·b(o)urg ['lʌksəmbə:g] Luxembourg *m.*

Lyd·i·a ['lidiə] Lydie *f.*

M

Mab [mæb] *reine des fées.*

Ma·bel ['meibl] *prénom féminin.*

Ma·cau·lay [mə'kɔ:li] *historien et homme politique anglais*; *femme écrivain anglaise.*

Mac·Don·ald [mək'dɔnld] *homme d'État britannique.*

Mac·Gee [mə'gi:] *nom de famille.*

Mac·ken·zie [mə'kenzi] *fleuve du Canada.*

Ma·dei·ra [mə'diərə] Madère *f.*

Madge [mædʒ] Margot *f.*

Mad·i·son ['mædisn] *4ᵉ président des É.-U.*; *capitale du Wisconsin (É.-U.).*

Ma·dras [mə'drɑ:s] *ville et port de l'Inde.*

Ma·drid [mə'drid] *capitale de l'Espagne.*

Mag·da·len ['mægdəlin] Madeleine *f.*

Mag·gie ['mægi] Margot *f.*

Ma·hom·et [me'hɔmit] Mahomet *m.*

Maine [mein] *État des É.-U.*

Ma·lay·sia [mə'leiʒə]: *the Federation of* ~ la Fédération *f* de Malaisie.

Mal·colm ['mælkəm] *prénom masculin.*

Mal·ta ['mɔ:ltə] Malte *f.*

Man·ches·ter ['mæntʃistə] *ville industrielle d'Angleterre.*

Man·hat·tan [mæn'hætn] *île et quartier de New York (É.-U.).*

Man·i·to·ba [mæni'toubə] *province du Canada.*

Mar·ga·ret ['mɑ:gərit] Marguerite *f.*

Mar·jo·rie ['mɑ:dʒəri] *prénom féminin.*

Mark [mɑ:k] Marc *m.*

Marl·bor·ough ['mɔ:lbərə] *général anglais.*

Mar·tha ['mɑ:θə] Marthe *f.*

Mar·y ['mɛəri] Marie *f.*

Mar·y·land ['mɛərilænd; *Am.* 'merilənd] *État des É.-U.*

Mas·sa·chu·setts [mæsə'tʃu:sets] *État des É.-U.*

Ma(t)·thew ['mæθju:] Mat(t)hieu *m.*

Maud [mɔ:d] Mathilde *f.*

Maugham [mɔ:m] *auteur anglais.*

Mau·reen [mə'ri:n] *prénom féminin.*

Mau·rice ['mɔris] Maurice *m.*

May [mei] Mariette *f*, Manon *f.*

Meath [mi:ð, mi:θ] *comté d'Irlande.*

Mel·bourne ['melbən] *ville et port d'Australie.*

Mel·ville ['melvil] *auteur américain.*

Mer·e·dith ['merədiθ] *auteur anglais.*

Mer·i·on·eth(·shire) [meri'ɔniθ (-ʃiə)] *comté du Pays de Galles.*

Mex·i·co ['meksikou] le Mexique *m.*

Mi·am·i [mai'æmi] *station balnéaire de la Floride (É.-U.).*

Mi·chael ['maikl] Michel *m.*

Mich·i·gan ['miʃigən] *État des É.-U.*; *Lake* ~ le lac *m* Michigan (*un des cinq grands lacs de l'Amérique du Nord*).

Mid·dle·sex ['midlseks] *comté d'Angleterre.*

Mid·west ['mid'west] *les États m/pl. de la Prairie (É.-U.).*

Mil·dred ['mildrid] *prénom féminin.*

Mil·li·cent ['milisnt] *prénom féminin.*

Mil·ton ['miltən] *poète anglais.*

Mil·wau·kee [mil'wɔ:ki:] *ville des É.-U.*

Min·ne·ap·o·lis [mini'æpəlis] *ville des É.-U.*

Min·ne·so·ta [mini'soutə] *État des É.-U.*

Mis·sis·sip·pi [misi'sipi] *État des É.-U.; fleuve des É.-U.*

Mis·sou·ri [mi'suəri; Am. mi'zuəri] *rivière des É.-U.; État des É.-U.*

Mitch·ell ['mitʃl] *prénom; nom de famille.*

Mo·ham·med [mou'hæmed] Mohammed *m; islam:* Mahomet *m.*

Moll [mɔl] Mariette *f,* Manon *f.*

Mo·na·co ['mɔnəkou] Monaco *m.*

Mon·mouth(·shire) ['mʌnməθ(ʃiə)] *comté de Angleterre.*

Mon·roe [mən'rou] *5ᵉ président des É.-U.*

Mon·tan·a [mɔn'tænə] *État des É.-U.*

Mont·gom·er·y [mənt'gʌməri] *maréchal britannique; a.* **Mont'gom·er·y·shire** [~ʃiə] *comté du Pays de Galles.*

Mont·re·al [mɔntri'ɔ:l] Montréal *m (ville du Canada).*

Moore [muə] *sculpteur anglais.*

Mo·roc·co [mə'rɔkou] le Maroc *m.*

Mos·cow ['mɔskou] Moscou.

Mu·ri·el ['mjuəriəl] *prénom féminin.*

Mur·ray ['mʌri] *fleuve d'Australie.*

My·ra ['maiərə] *prénom féminin.*

N

Nan·cy ['nænsi] Nanette *f,* Annette *f.*

Na·ples ['neiplz] Naples.

Na·tal [nə'tæl] le Natal *m.*

Ne·bras·ka [ni'bræskə] *État des É.-U.*

Neil(1) [ni:l] *prénom; nom de famille.*

Nell, Nel·ly ['nel(i)] *diminutif de Eleanor, Helen.*

Nel·son ['nelsn] *amiral britannique.*

Ne·pal [ni'pɔ:l] le Népal *m.*

Neth·er·lands ['neðələndz] *pl.* les Pays-Bas *m/pl.*

Ne·vad·a [ne'vɑ:də] *État des É.-U.*

New Bruns·wick [nju:'brʌnzwik] *province du Canada.*

New·cas·tle ['nju:kɑ:sl] *ville et port d'Angleterre.*

New Del·hi ['nju:'deli] *capitale de l'Inde.*

New Eng·land ['nju:'iŋglənd] la Nouvelle-Angleterre *f (États des É.-U.).*

New·found·land [nju:'faundlənd; surt. ⚓ nju:fənd'lænd] Terre-Neuve *f (province du Canada).*

New Hamp·shire [nju:'hæmpʃiə] *État des É.-U.*

New Jer·sey [nju:'dʒɔ:zi] *État des É.-U.*

New Guin·ea [nju:'gini] la Nouvelle-Guinée *f.*

New Mex·i·co [nju:'meksikou] le Nouveau-Mexique *m (État des É.-U.).*

New Or·le·ans [nju:'ɔ:liənz] la Nouvelle-Orléans *f (ville des É.-U.).*

New·ton ['nju:tn] *physicien et philosophe anglais.*

New York ['nju:'jɔ:k] New York *f (ville des É.-U.);* New York *m (État des É.-U.).*

New Zea·land [nju:'zi:lənd] la Nouvelle-Zélande *f.*

Ni·ag·a·ra [nai'ægərə] *le* Niagara *m (rivière de l'Amérique du Nord, unissant les lacs Erie et Ontario).*

Nich·o·las ['nikələs] Nicolas *m.*

Ni·ger ['naidʒə] *le* Niger *m.*

Ni·ge·ri·a [nai'dʒiəriə] le *(ou* la*)* Nigeria *m(f).*

Nile [nail] *le* Nil *m.*

Nix·on ['niksn] *37ᵉ président des É.-U.*

No·el ['nouəl] *prénom masculin.*

Nor·folk ['nɔ:fək] *comté d'Angleterre; ville et port des É.-U.*

North·amp·ton [nɔ:'θæmptən] *ville d'Angleterre; a.* **North'amp·ton·shire** [~ʃiə] *comté d'Angleterre.*

North·ern Ire·land [nɔ:ðən'aiəlænd] *l'Irlande du Nord.*

North Sea ['nɔ:θ'si:] *mer f du Nord.*

North·um·ber·land [nɔ:'θʌmbələnd] *comté d'Angleterre.*

Nor·way ['nɔ:wei] la Norvège *f.*

Not·ting·ham ['nɔtiŋəm] *ville d'Angleterre; a.* **Not·ting·ham·shire** ['~ʃiə] *comté d'Angleterre.*

No·va Sco·tia ['nouvə'skouʃə] la Nouvelle-Écosse *f (province du Canada).*

O

Oak Ridge ['ouk'ridʒ] *ville des É.-U.; centre de recherches nucléaires.*

O'Ca·sey [ou'keisi] *dramaturge irlandais.*

O·ce·an·i·a [ouʃi'einiə] l'Océanie f.

O'Fla·her·ty [ou'flæ(h)əti] écrivain irlandais.

O'Har·a [əu'hɑːrə] nom de famille.

O.Hen·ry [əu'henri] écrivain américain.

O·hi·o [ou'haiou] rivière des É.-U.; État des É.-U.

O·kla·ho·ma [ouklə'houmə] État des É.-U.; ~ City capitale de l'Oklahoma (É.-U.).

Ol·i·ver ['ɔlivə] Olivier m.

O·liv·i·a [o'liviə] Olivia f, Olivie f.

O·ma·ha ['oumǝhɑː] ville des É.-U.

O'Neill [ou'niːl] auteur américain.

On·tar·i·o [ɔn'tɛəriou] province du Canada; Lake ~ le lac m Ontario (un des cinq grands lacs de l'Amérique du Nord).

Or·ange ['ɔrindʒ] l'Orange m (fleuve de l'Afrique australe).

Or·e·gon ['ɔrigən] État des É.-U.

Ork·ney Is·lands ['ɔ:kni'ailəndz] pl. les Orcades f/pl. (comté d'Écosse).

Or·well ['ɔ:wəl] auteur anglais.

Os·borne ['ɔzbən] auteur anglais.

Os·lo ['ɔzlou] capitale de la Norvège.

Ost·end [ɔs'tend] Ostende f.

O'Sul·li·van [əu'sʌlivən] nom de famille.

Ot·ta·wa ['ɔtəwə] capitale du Canada.

Ouse [uːz] nom de deux rivières d'Angleterre.

Ox·ford ['ɔksfəd] ville universitaire d'Angleterre; a. **Ox·ford·shire** ['~ʃiə] comté d'Angleterre.

O·zark Moun·tains ['ouzɑːk'mauntinz] pl. les Ozark m/pl. (massif des É.-U.).

P

Pa·cif·ic [pə'sifik] le Pacifique m.

Pad·dy ['pædi] diminutif de Patrick; sobriquet de l'Irlandais.

Pak·i·stan [pɑːkis'tɑːn] le Pakistan m.

Pall Mall ['pel'mel] rue des Londres.

Palm Beach ['pɑːm'biːtʃ] station balnéaire de la Floride (É.-U.).

Pal·mer ['pɑː(l)mə] nom de famille.

Pan·a·ma [pænə'mɑː, 'pænəmɑː] le Panama m.

Par·a·guay ['pærəgwai] le Paraguay m.

Par·is ['pæris] Paris m.

Pa·tri·cia [pə'triʃə] prénom féminin.

Pat·rick ['pætrik] Patrice m, Patrick m (patron de l'Irlande).

Paul [pɔːl] Paul m.

Pau·line [pɔː'liːn; '~] Pauline f.

Pearl Har·bor ['pɔːl'hɑːbə] port des îles Hawaii.

Peg(·gy) ['peg(i)] Margot m.

Pe·kin(g) ['piːkin (٨kiŋ)] Pékin.

Pem·broke(·shire) ['pembruk(ʃiə)] comté du Pays de Galles.

Penn·syl·va·nia [pensil'veinjə] la Pennsylvanie f (État des É.-U.).

Per·cy ['pəːsi] prénom masculin.

Pe·ru [pə'ruː] le Pérou m.

Pe·ter ['piːtə] Pierre m.

Phil·a·del·phi·a [filə'delfjə] Philadelphie f (ville des É.-U.).

Phil·ip ['filip] Philippe m.

Phil·ip·pines ['filipiːnz] pl. archipel de la mer de Chine.

Phoe·be ['fiːbi] prénom féminin.

Phoe·nix ['fiːniks] capitale de l'Arizona (É.-U).

Pic·ca·dil·ly [pikə'dili] rue de Londres.

Pierce [piəs] prénom: nom de famille.

Pin·ter ['pintə] dramatiste anglais.

Pitts·burgh ['pitsbəːg] ville des É.-U.

Pla·to ['pleitou] Platon m (philosophe grec).

Plym·outh ['plimǝθ] ville et port d'Angleterre; ville des É.-U.

Poe [pou] auteur américain.

Po·land ['poulənd] la Pologne f.

Poll [pɔl] Mariette f, Manon f.

Port·land ['pɔːtlənd] ville et port des É.-U. (Maine); ville des É.-U. (Oregon).

Ports·mouth ['pɔːtsməθ] ville et port d'Angleterre.

Por·tu·gal ['pɔːtugəl] le Portugal m.

Po·to·mac [pə'toumæk] fleuve des É.-U.

Pow·ell ['pauəl] nom de famille; prénom.

Prague [prɑːg] capitale de la Tchécoslovaquie.

Prus·sia ['prʌʃə] la Prussie f.

Pul·itz·er ['pulitsə] journaliste américain.

Pun·jab [pʌn'dʒɑːb] le Pendjab m.

Pur·cell ['pəːsl] compositeur anglais.

Q

Que·bec [kwi'bek] Québec m (ville et province du Canada).

Queens [kwi:nz] *quartier de New York.*
Quin·c(e)y ['kwinsi] *nom de famille; prénom.*

R

Ra·chel ['reitʃəl] Rachel *f.*
Rad·nor(·shire) ['rædnə(ʃiə)] *comté du Pays de Galles.*
Rae [rei] *prénom.*
Ra·leigh ['rɔ:li; 'rɑ:li; 'ræli] *navigateur anglais; capitale de la Caroline du Nord (É.-U.).*
Ralph [reif; rælf] Raoul *m.*
Ra·wal·pin·di [rɔ:l'pindi] *capitale du Pakistan.*
Ray [rei] *prénom.*
Ray·mond ['reimənd] Raymond *m.*
Read·ing ['rediŋ] *ville industrielle d'Angleterre; ville des É.-U.*
Rea·gan ['regən] *40ᵉ président des É.-U.*
Re·bec·ca [ri'bekə] Rébecca *f.*
Reg·i·nald ['redʒinld] Renaud *m.*
Rey·kja·vik ['reikjəvi:k] *capitale de l'Islande.*
Rhine [rain] *le Rhin m.*
Rhode Is·land [roud'ailənd] *État des É.-U.*
Rhodes [roudz] Rhodes *f.*
Rho·de·sia [rou'di:ziə] *la Rhodésie f.*
Rich·ard ['ritʃəd] Richard *m.*
Rich·mond ['ritʃmənd] *capitale de la Virginie (É.-U.); district de New York; faubourg de Londres.*
Rob·ert ['rɔbət] Robert *m.*
Rob·in ['rɔbin] *diminutif de Robert.*
Rock·e·fel·ler ['rɔkifelə] *industriel américain.*
Rock·y Moun·tains ['rɔki'mauntinz] *pl. les* (montagnes *f/pl.*) Rocheuses *f/pl.*
Rog·er ['rɔdʒə] Roger *m.*
Rome [roum] Rome *f.*
Roo·se·velt [*Am.* 'rouzəvelt; *angl. usu.* 'ru:svelt] *nom de deux présidents des É.-U.*
Rud·yard ['rʌdjəd] *prénom masculin.*
Rug·by ['rʌgbi] *collège et ville d'Angleterre.*
Ru·ma·ni·a [ru:'meinjə] *la Roumanie f.*
Rus·sel [rʌsl] *nom de famille anglais.*
Rus·sia ['rʌʃə] *la Russie f.*
Rut·land(·shire) ['rʌtlənd(ʃiə)] *comté de'Angleterre.*

S

Sac·ra·men·to [sækrə'mentou] *capitale de la Californie (É.-U.).*
Salis·bur·y ['sɔ:lzbəri] *ville d'Angleterre.*
Sal·ly ['sæli] *diminutif de Sarah.*
Salt Lake Cit·y ['sɔ:lt'leik'siti] *capitale de l'Utah (É.-U.).*
Sam [sæm] *diminutif de Samuel;* Uncle ~ *les États-Unis; sobriquet de l'Américain.*
Sam·u·el ['sæmjuəl] Samuel *m.*
San Fran·cis·co [sænfrən'siskou] *ville et port des É.-U.*
San Ma·ri·no [sænmə'ri:nou] Saint-Marin *m.*
Sar·ah ['sɛərə] Sarah *f.*
Sas·katch·e·wan [səs'kætʃiwən] *rivière et province du Canada.*
Sa·u·di A·ra·bi·a [sɑ'udiə'reibjə] *l'Arabie f Saoudite.*
Say·ers ['seiəz] *femme écrivain anglaise.*
Scan·di·na·vi·a [skændi'neivjə] *la Scandinavie f.*
Sche·nec·ta·dy [ski'nektədi] *ville des É.-U.*
Scot·land ['skɔtlənd] *l'Écosse f;* ~ Yard *siège de la police londonienne.*
Sean [ʃɔ:n] Jean *m.*
Scott [skɔt] *nom de famille et prénom anglais; auteur anglais.*
Se·at·tle [si'ætl] *ville et port des É.-U.*
Sev·ern ['sevə:n] *fleuve d'Angleterre.*
Sey·mour ['si:mɔ:, 'seimɔ:] *prénom; nom de famille.*
Shake·speare ['ʃeikspiə] *poète anglais.*
Shaw [ʃɔ:] *auteur anglo-irlandais.*
Shef·field ['ʃefi:ld] *ville industrielle d'Angleterre.*
Shei·la ['ʃi:lə] *prénom féminin.*
Shel·ley ['ʃeli] *poète anglais.*
Shir·ley ['ʃə:li] *prénom féminin.*
Sher·lock ['ʃə:lɔk] *prénom masculin.*
Shet·land Is·lands ['ʃetlənd'ailəndz] *pl. les îles f/pl.* (de) Shetland *(comté d'Écosse).*
Shrop·shire ['ʃrɔpʃiə] *comté d'Angleterre.*
Sib·yl ['sibil] Sibylle *f.*
Sic·i·ly ['sisili] *la Sicile f.*
Sid·ney ['sidni] *prénom et nom de famille anglais.*
Sin·clair ['siŋklɛə] *prénom masculin; auteur américain.*

Sin·ga·pore [siŋgə'pɔː] Singapour f.

Sing-Sing ['siŋsiŋ] prison de l'État de New York (É.-U.).

Snow·don ['snoudn] montagne du Pays de Galles.

So·fia ['soufjə] Sofia, capitale de la Bulgarie.

Sol·o·mon ['sɔləmən] Salomon m.

Som·er·set(·shire) ['sʌməsit(ʃiə)] comté d'Angleterre.

So·phi·a [so'faiə], **So·phy** ['soufi] Sophie f.

Sou·dan [suː'dæn] see Sudan.

South·amp·ton [sau'θæmtən] ville et port d'Angleterre.

South·wark ['sʌðək; 'sauθwək] quartier de Londres.

Spain [spein] l'Espagne f.

Staf·ford(·shire) ['stæfəd(ʃiə)] comté d'Angleterre.

Stat·en Is·land [stætn'ailənd] quartier de New York (situé dans une île).

Stein·beck ['stainbek] auteur américain.

Ste·phen, Ste·ven ['stiːvn] Stéphan m.

Ste·ven·son ['stiːvnsn] auteur anglais.

Stew·art ['st(j)uːət] prénom masculin; nom de famille.

St. Law·rence [snt'lɔːrəns] le Saint-Laurent m.

St. Lou·is [snt'luːis] ville des É.-U.

Stock·holm ['stɔkhoum] Stockholm, capitale de la Suède.

Strat·ford on A·von ['strætfədɔn-'eivən] patrie de Shakespeare.

Stu·art ['stjuət] famille royale d'Écosse et d'Angleterre.

Su·dan [su(ː)'daːn] le Soudan m.

Sue [sjuː, suː] Suzanne f.

Su·ez ['suːiz] Suez m.

Suf·folk ['sʌfək] comté d'Angleterre.

Su·pe·ri·or [sjuː'piəriə]: Lake ~ le lac m Supérieur (un des cinq grands lacs de l'Amérique du Nord).

Sur·rey ['sʌri] comté d'Angleterre.

Su·san ['suːzn] Suzanne f.

Sus·que·han·na [sʌskwə'hænə] fleuve des É.-U.

Sus·sex ['sʌsiks] comté d'Angleterre.

Swan·sea ['swɔnzi] ville et port du Pays de Galles.

Swe·den ['swiːdn] la Suède f.

Swift [swift] auteur irlandais.

Swit·zer·land ['switsələnd] la Suisse f.

Syd·ney ['sidni] capitale de la Nouvelle-Galles du Sud (Australie).

Synge [siŋ] poète et dramaturge irlandais.

Syr·i·a ['siriə] la Syrie f.

T

Ta·hi·ti [taː'hiːti] Tahiti f.

Tal·la·has·see [tælə'hæsi] capitale de la Floride (É.-U.).

Tan·gier [tæn'dʒiə] Tanger f.

Tay·lor ['teilə] nom de famille.

Ted(·dy) ['ted(i)] diminutif de Edward, Edmund, Theodore.

Ten·nes·see [tene'siː] rivière des É.-U.; État des É.-U.

Ten·ny·son ['tenisn] poète anglais.

Ter·ence ['terəns] prénom masculin.

Tex·as ['teksəs] État des É.-U.

Thack·er·ay ['θækəri] auteur anglais.

Thames [temz] la Tamise f.

The·o·dore ['θiədɔː] Théodore m.

The·re·sa [ti'riːzə] Thérèse f.

Thom·as ['tɔməs] Thomas m.

Tho·reau ['θɔːrou] philosophe américain.

Ti·gris ['taigris] le Tigre m.

Tim [tim] diminutif de Timothy.

Tim·o·thy ['timəθi] Timothée m.

Ti·ra·na [ti'raːnə] capitale de l'Albanie.

To·bi·as [tə'baiəs] Tobie m.

To·by ['toubi] diminutif de Tobias.

To·kyo ['toukjou] Tokyo.

Tol·kien ['tɔlkiːn] écrivain et philologue anglais.

Tom(·my) ['tɔm(i)] diminutif de Thomas.

To·pe·ka [to'piːkə] capitale du Kansas (É.-U.).

To·ron·to [tə'rɔntou] ville du Canada.

Tow·er ['tauə]: the ~ of London la Tour de Londres.

Tra·fal·gar [trə'fælgə] cap de la côte d'Espagne.

Trent [trent] rivière d'Angleterre.

Trol·lope ['trɔləp] auteur anglais.

Tru·man ['truːmən] 33e président des É.-U.

Tu·dor ['tjuːdə] famille royale anglaise.

Tu·ni·si·a [tjuː'niziə] la Tunisie f.

Tur·key ['təːki] la Turquie f.

Twain [twein] auteur américain.

U

Ul·ster ['ʌlstə] l'Ulster *m* (*province d'Irlande*).

U·nit·ed Ar·ab Re·pub·lic [ju:-'naitid'ærəbri'pʌblik] République *f* arabe unie.

U·nit·ed States of A·mer·i·ca [ju:'naitid'steitsəvə'merikə] les États-Unis *m/pl.* d'Amérique.

Up·dike ['ʌpdaik] *écrivain américain.*

U·ri·ah [juə'raiə] *prénom masculin.*

U·ru·guay ['urugwai] l'Uruguay *m.*

U·tah ['ju:ta:] *État des É.-U.*

V

Val·en·tine ['væləntain] Valentin *m*; Valentine *f.*

Van·cou·ver [væn'ku:və] *ville et port du Canada.*

Vat·i·can ['vætikən] *le* Vatican *m.*

Vaux·hall ['vɔks'hɔːl] *district de Londres.*

Ven·e·zue·la [vene'zweilə] *le* Venezuela *m.*

Ven·ice ['venis] Venise *f.*

Ver·mont [və:'mɔnt] *État des É.-U.*

Ver·non ['və:nən] *prénom masculin.*

Vic·to·ri·a [vik'tɔːriə] Victoire *f.*

Vi·en·na [vi'enə] Vienne *f.*

Vir·gin·ia [və'dʒinjə] *la* Virginie *f* (*État des É.-U.*).

Vi·tus ['vaitəs] Guy *m*, Gui *m.*

Viv·i·an ['viviən] Vivien *m*; Vivienne *f.*

W

Wa·bash ['wɔ:bæʃ] *rivière des É.-U.*

Wales [weilz] *le* Pays *m* de Galles.

Wal·lace ['wɔləs] *auteur anglais*; *auteur américain.*

Wall Street ['wɔ:lstriːt] *rue de New York*; *siège de la Bourse.*

Wal·pole ['wɔ:lpoul] *nom de deux écrivains anglais.*

Wal·ter ['wɔːltə] Gauthier *m.*

War·hol ['wɑːhɔ:l, 'wɑːhoul] *artiste pop américain.*

War·saw ['wɔːsɔ:] Varsovie.

War·wick(·shire) ['wɔrik(ʃiə)] *comté d'Angleterre.*

Wash·ing·ton ['wɔʃiŋtən] *1ᵉʳ président des É.-U.; État des É.-U.; capitale et siège du gouvernement des É.-U.*

Wa·ter·loo [wɔ:tə'lu:] *commune de Belgique.*

Watt [wɔt] *inventeur anglais.*

Waugh [wɔ:] *écrivain anglais.*

Wayne [wein] *nom de famille*; *acteur américain.*

Wedg·wood ['wedʒwud] *céramiste anglais.*

Wel·ling·ton ['weliŋtən] *général et homme d'État anglais*; *capitale de la Nouvelle-Zélande.*

Wells [welz] *auteur anglais.*

West·min·ster ['westminstə] *quartier de Londres, siège du parlement britannique.*

West·mor·land ['westmələnd] *comté d'Angleterre.*

West Vir·gin·ia ['westvə'dʒinjə] *la* Virginie Occidentale *f* (*État des É.-U.*).

Whit·acker, Whit·a·ker ['witəkə] *nom de famille.*

White·hall ['wait'hɔ:l] *rue de Londres, quartier des Ministères.*

White House ['wait'haus] *la* Maison-Blanche *f* (*résidence du président des É.-U. à Washington*).

Wight [wait]: *Isle of* ~ *île anglaise de la Manche.*

Wilde [waild] *écrivain et poète anglais.*

Will [wil], **Wil·liam** ['wiljəm] Guillaume *m.*

Wil·son ['wilsn] *homme politique britannique*; *28ᵉ président des É.-U.*

Wilt·shire ['wiltʃiə] *comté d'Angleterre.*

Wim·ble·don ['wimbldən] *faubourg de Londres (championnat international de tennis).*

Win·ni·peg ['winipeg] *ville du Canada.*

Win·ston ['winstən] *prénom masculin.*

Wis·con·sin [wis'kɔnsin] *rivière des É.-U.; État des É.-U.*

Wolfe [wulf] *auteur américain.*

Wol·sey ['wulzi] *cardinal et homme d'État anglais.*

Woolf [wulf] *femme écrivain anglaise.*

Worces·ter ['wustə] *ville industrielle d'Angleterre et des É.-U.; a.* **Worces·ter·shire** ['ˌ~ʃiə] *comté d'Angleterre.*

Words·worth ['wə:dzwə(:)θ] *poète anglais.*

Wren [ren] *architecte anglais.*

Wright [rait] *nom de famille*; *nom de*

deux pionniers de l'aviation améri-cains.
Wyc·lif(fe) ['wiklif] *réformateur reli-gieux anglais.*
Wy·o·ming [wai'oumiŋ] *État des É.-U.*

York [jɔːk] *ville d'Angleterre;* a. **York·shire** ['-ʃiə] *comté d'Angle-terre.*
Yo·sem·i·te [jou'semiti] *parc national des É.-U.*
Yu·go·sla·vi·a ['juːgouˈslɑːviə] *la Yougoslavie f.*

Y

Yale U·ni·ver·si·ty ['jeiljuːniˈvəːsiti] *université américaine.*
Yeats [jeits] *poète irlandais.*
Yel·low·stone ['jeloustoun] *rivière des É.-U.; parc national.*
Yem·en ['jemən] *le Yémen m.*

Z

Zach·a·ri·ah [zækəˈraiə], **Zach·a·ry** ['zækəri] *Zacharie m.*
Zam·be·zi [zæmˈbiːzi] *le Zambèze m.*
Zim·ba·bwe [zimˈbɑːbwi] *Zimbabwe m.*
Zoe ['zoui] *Zoë f.*

Common British
and American Abbreviations

Abréviations usuelles, britanniques et américaines

A

a *acre* acre *f.*

A.A. *anti-aircraft* A.A., antiaérien; *Brit. Automobile Association* Automobile Club *m*; Alcoholics Anonymous.

A.A.A. *Brit. Amateur Athletic Association* Association *f* d'athlétisme amateur; *Am. American Automobile Association* Automobile Club *m* américaine.

A.B. *able-bodied seaman* matelot *m* (de deuxième classe); *see* B.A.

abbr. *abbreviated* abrégé; *abbreviation* abréviation *f.*

abr. *abridged* abrégé; *abridg(e)ment* abrégé *m*; réduction *f.*

A.B.C. *American Broadcasting Company* radiodiffusion-télévision *f* américaine.

A.B.M. *anti-ballistic missile* missile *m* anti-balistique.

a/c *account (current)* C.C., compte *m* (courant).

A.C. *alternating current* C.A., courant *m* alternatif.

acc(t). *account* compte *m*, note *f.*

A.D. *Anno Domini (latin = in the year of our Lord)* après J.-C., en l'an du Seigneur *ou* de grâce.

A.D.A. *Brit. Atom Development Administration* Commission *f* pour le développement de l'énergie atomique.

Adm. *Admiral* amiral *m*; *admiralty* amirauté *f.*

advt. *advertisement* annonce *f.*

AEC *Atomic Energy Commission* CEA, Commission *f* de l'énergie atomique.

A.E.F. *American Expeditionary Forces* corps *m* expéditionnaire américain.

AFL-CIO *American Federation of Labor & Congress of Industrial Organizations (fédération américaine du travail).*

A.F.N. *American Forces Network (radiodiffusion-télévison des forces armées américaines).*

AIDS *acquired immunity deficiency syndrome* S.I.D.A., syndrome *m* immuno-déficitaire acquis.

Ala. *Alabama (État des É.-U.).*

Alas. *Alaska (État des É.-U.).*

Am. *America* Amérique *f*; *American* américain.

a.m. *ante meridiem (latin = before noon)* avant midi.

A.M. *amplitude modulation* modulation *f* d'amplitude; *see* M.A.

A/P *account purchase* achat *m* porté sur un compte courant.

A.P. *Associated Press (agence d'informations américaine).*

A.P.O. *Am. Army Post Office* poste *f* aux armées.

A.R.C. *American Red Cross* Croix-Rouge *f* américaine.

Ariz. *Arizona (État des É.-U.).*

Ark. *Arkansas (État des É.-U).*

A.R.P. *air-raid precautions* D.A., défense *f* aérienne.

arr. *arrival* arrivée *f.*

A/S *account sales* compte *m* de vente.

ASA *American Standards Association* association *f* américaine de normalisation.

av. *average* moyenne *f*; avaries *f/pl.*

avdp. *avoirdupois* poids *m* du commerce.

A.W.O.L. *Am. absent without leave* absent sans permission.

B

b. *born* né(e *f*).

BA *British Airways* (*compagnie aérienne britannique*).

B.A. *Bachelor of Arts* (*approx.*) L. ès L., licencié(e *f*) *m* ès lettres.

B.A.O.R. *British Army of the Rhine* armée *f* britannique du Rhin.

Bart. *Baronet* Baronet *m* (*titre de noblesse*).

B.B.C. *British Broadcasting Corporation* radiodiffusion-télévision *f* britannique.

bbl. *barrel* tonneau *m*.

B.C. *before Christ* av. J.-C., avant Jésus-Christ.

B.D. *Bachelor of Divinity* (*approx.*) licencié(e *f*) *m* en théologie.

B.E. *Bachelor of Education* (*approx.*) licencié(e *f*) *m* en pédagogie; *Bachelor of Engineering* (*approx.*) ingénieur *m* diplômé.

B/E *Bill of Exchange* lettre *f* de change.

B.E.A. *British European Airways* (*compagnie aérienne britannique*).

Beds. *Bedfordshire* (*comté d'Angleterre*).

Benelux ['beneᶦl ks] *Belgium, Netherlands, Luxemburg* Bénélux *m*, Belgique-Nederland-Luxembourg.

Berks. *Berkshire* (*comté d'Angleterre*).

b/f *brought forward* à reporter; report *m*.

B.F.A. *British Football Association* association *f* britannique du football.

B.F.N. *British Forces Network* (*radiodiffusion-télévision des forces armées britanniques*).

bl. *barrel* tonneau *m*.

B.L. *Bachelor of Law* (*approx.*) bachelier (-ère *f*) *m* en droit.

B/L *bill of lading* connaissement *m* (maritime).

bls. *bales* balles *f/pl.*, ballots *m/pl.*; *barrels* tonneaux *m/pl.*

B.M. *Bachelor of Medicine* (*approx.*) bachelier (-ère *f*) *m* en médecine.

B.M.A. *British Medical Association* association *f* médicale britannique.

B/O *Branch Office* filiale *f*.

B.O.A.C. *British Overseas Airways Corporation* (*compagnie aérienne britannique*).

bot. *bought* acheté; *bottle* bouteille *f*.

B.O.T. *Brit. Board of Trade* Ministère *m* du Commerce.

B.R. *British Railways* (*réseau national du chemin de fer britannique*).

B/R *bills receivable* effets *m/pl.* à recevoir.

B.R.C.S. *British Red Cross Society* Croix-Rouge *f* britannique.

Br(it). *Britain* la Grande-Bretagne *f*; *British* britannique.

Bros. *brothers* frères *m/pl.* (*dans un nom de société*).

B/S *bill of sale* acte *m* (*ou* contrat *m*) de vente; *Am.* facture *f*; bulletin *m* de livraison.

B.Sc. *Bachelor of Science* (*approx.*) L. ès Sc., licencié(e *f*) *m* ès sciences naturelles.

B.Sc.Econ. *Bachelor of Economic Science* (*approx.*) licencié(e *f*) *m* en économie politique.

bsh., bu. *bushel* boisseau *m*.

Bucks. *Buckinghamshire* (*comté d'Angleterre*).

B.U.P. *British United Press* (*agence d'informations britannique*).

bus(h). *bushel(s)* boisseau(x *pl.*) *m*.

C

c. *cent(s)* cent(s *pl.*) *m*; *circa* environ; *cubic* cubique, au cube; *century* siècle *m*.

C. *thermomètre:* Celsius, centigrade C, Celsius, cgr, centigrade.

C.A. *Brit. chartered accountant* expert *m* comptable.

C/A *current account* C.C., compte *m* courant.

c.a.d. *cash against documents* paiement *m* contre documents.

Cal(if). *California* (*État des É.-U*).

Cambs. *Cambridgeshire* (*comté d'Angleterre*).

Can. *Canada* Canada *m*; *Canadian* canadien.

Capt. *Captain* capitaine *m*.

C.B. (*a.* **C/B**) *cash book* livre *m* de caisse; *Companion of the Bath* Compagnon *m* de l'ordre du Bain; *Confinement to barracks* consigné au quartier.

C.B.C. *Canadian Broadcasting Corporation* radiodiffusion-télévision *f* canadienne.

C.B.I. *Confederation of British Industry* confédération *f* des industries britanniques.

C.C. *Brit. County Council* Conseil *m* de

Comté; *continuous current* C.C., courant *m* continu.

C.E. *Church of England* Église *f* Anglicane; *Civil Engineer* ingénieur *m* civil.

cert. *certificate* certificat *m*.

CET *Central European Time* H.E.C., heure *f* de l'Europe Centrale.

cf. *confer* Cf., conférez.

ch. *chain* (*approx.*) double décamètre *m*; *chapter* chapitre *m*.

Ches. *Cheshire* (*comté d'Angleterre*).

CIA *Am. Central Intelligence Agency* S.C.E., service *m* contre-espionnage.

C.I.D. *Brit. Criminal Investigation Department* (*police judiciaire*).

c.i.f. *cost, insurance, freight* C.A.F., coût, assurance, fret.

C. in C., CINC *Commander-in-Chief* commandant *m* en chef.

cl. *class* classe *f*.

Co. *Company* compagnie *f*, société *f*; *county* comté *m*.

C.O. *Commanding Officer* officier *m* commandant.

c/o *care of* aux bons soins de, chez.

C.O.D., c.o.d. *cash* (*Am. a. collect*) *on delivery* RB, (envoi *m*) contre remboursement.

Col. *Colorado* (*État des É.-U.*); *Colonel* Col., colonel *m*.

Colo. *Colorado* (*État des É.-U.*).

Conn. *Connecticut* (*État des É.-U.*).

Cons. *Conservative* conservateur *m*.

Corn. *Cornwall* (*comté d'Angleterre*).

Corp. *corporation* compagnie *f* (commerciale); *Corporal* caporal *m*.

cp. *compare* comparer.

C.P. *Canadian Press* (*agence d'informations canadienne*).

C.P.A. *Am. Certified Public Accountant* expert *m* comptable.

ct(s). *cent(s)* cent(s *pl.*) *m*.

cu(b). *cubic* cubique, au cube.

Cum(b). *Cumberland* (*comté d'Angleterre*).

c.w.o. *cash with order* payable à la commande.

cwt. *hundredweight* quintal *m*.

D

d. *penny, pence* (*pièce de monnaie britannique*); *died* m., mort.

D.A. *deposit account* compte *m* de dépôts; *Am. District Attorney approx.* procureur *m* de la République.

D.A.R. *Am. Daughters of the American*

Revolution Filles *f/pl.* de la révolution américaine (*union patriotique féminine*).

D.B. *Day Book* (livre *m*) journal *m*.

D.C. *direct current* courant *m* continu; *District of Columbia* (*district fédéral des É.-U., capitale Washington*).

D.C.L. *Doctor of Civil Law* Docteur *m* en droit civil.

d-d *damned s...*, sacré ...!

D.D. *Doctor of Divinity* Docteur *m* en théologie.

DDD *Am. direct distance dialing* service *m* automatique interurbain.

DDT *dichloro-diphenyl-trichloroethane* D.D.T., dichlorodiphényltrichloréthane *m* (*insecticide*).

dec. *deceased* déc(édé).

Del. *Delaware* (*État des É.-U.*).

dep. *departure* depart *m*.

dept. *department* dép., département *m*.

Derby. *Derbyshire* (*comté d'Angleterre*).

Devon. *Devonshire* (*comté d'Angleterre*).

dft. *draft* traite *f*.

disc. *discount* escompte *m*.

div. *dividend* div., dividende *m*.

D.I.Y. *do-it-yourself* de bricolage (*magasin etc.*).

D.J. *disc jockey*.

do. *ditto* do., dito.

doc. *document* document *m*.

Dors. *Dorsetshire* (*comté d'Angleterre*).

doz. *dozen(s)* Dzne, douzaine(s *pl.*) *f*.

d/p *documents against payment* documents *m/pl.* contre paiement.

dpt. *department* dép., département *m*.

dr. *dra(ch)m* (*poids*); *drawer* tireur *m*.

Dr. *Doctor* D^r., docteur *m*; *debtor* débiteur *m*.

d.s., d/s *days after sight* traite: jours *m/pl.* de vue.

Dur(h). *Durhamshire* (*comté d'Angleterre*).

dwt. *pennyweight* (*poids*).

dz. *dozen(s)* Dzne, douzain(s *pl.*) *f*.

E

E. *east* E., est *m*; *eastern* (de l')est; *English* anglais *m*.

E. & O.E. *errors and omissions excepted* S.E. ou O., sauf erreur ou omission.

E.C. *East Central* (*district postal de Londres*).

ECE *Economic Commission for Europe* CEE, Commission *f* économique pour l'Europe.

ECOSOC *Economic and Social Council* CES, Conseil *m* Économique et Social.

ECSC *European Coal and Steel Community* CECA, Communauté *f* européenne du charbon et de l'acier.

Ed., ed. *edition* édition *f*; *editor* éditeur *m*.

EDP *electronic data processing* informatique *f*.

EE., E./E. *errors excepted* sauf erreur.

EEC *European Economic Community* CEE, Communauté *f* économique européenne.

EFTA *European Free Trade Association* AELE, Association *f* européenne de libre échange.

e.g. *exempli gratia* (*latin = for instance*) p.ex., par exemple.

EMA *European Monetary Agreement* A.M.E., Accord *m* monétaire européen.

enc(l). *enclosure(s)* pièce(s *pl.*) *f* jointe(s).

Eng(l). *England* l'Angleterre *f*; *English* anglais.

EPU *European Payments Union* UEP, Union *f* européenne de paiements.

Esq. *Esquire* Monsieur *m* (*titre de politesse*).

ESRO *European Space-Research Organization* Organisation *f* européenne de recherches spatiales.

Ess. *Essex* (*comté d'Angleterre*).

E.T.A. *estimated time of arrival* heure *f* probable d'arrivée.

etc., &c. *et cetera, and so on* etc., et cætera, et ainsi de suite.

E.T.D. *estimated time of departure* heure *f* probable de départ.

EUCOM *Am. European Command* commandement *m* des troupes en Europe.

EURATOM *European Atomic Energy Community* EURATOM, Communauté *f* européenne de l'énergie atomique.

exam. *examination* examen *m*.

excl. *exclusive, excluding* non compris.

ex div. *ex dividend* ex D., ex-dividende.

ex int. *ex interest* sans intérêt.

F

f. *fathom* brasse *f*; *feminine* f., féminin; *foot* (*feet*) pied(s *pl.*) *m*; *following* suivant.

F. *thermomètre*: Fahrenheit F, Fahrenheit; *Fellow* agrégé(e *f*) *m*, membre *m* (*d'une société savante*).

F.A. *Football Association* Association *f* du football.

f.a.a. *free of all average* franc de toute avarie.

Fahr. *thermomètre*: Fahrenheit F, Fahrenheit.

FAO *Food and Agriculture Organization* OAA, Organisation *f* pour l'alimentation et l'agriculture.

f.a.s. *free alongside ship* F.A.S., franco à quai.

FBI *Federal Bureau of Investigation* (*service du département de la Justice des É.-U. qui est à la charge de la police fédérale*).

F.B.I. *Federation of British Industries* fédération *f* des industries britanniques.

F.C.C. *Am. Federal Communications Commission* Comité *m* fédéral des communications.

fig. *figure(s)* figure(s) *f*/(*pl.*).

Fla. *Florida* (*État des É.-U.*).

fm. *fathom* brasse *f*.

F.M. *frequency modulation* F.M., fréquence *f* modulée, modulation *f* de fréquence.

F.O. *Foreign Office* Ministère *m* britannique des Affaires étrangères.

f.o.b. *free on board* F.A.B., franco à bord.

fo(l). *folio* folio *m*, feuillet *m*.

f.o.q. *free on quay* F.O.Q., franco à quai.

f.o.r. *free on rail* F.O.R., franco sur rail.

f.o.t. *free on truck* F.O.T., franco en wagon.

f.o.w. *free on waggon* F.O.W., franco en wagon.

F.P. *fire-plug* bouche *f* d'incendie; *freezing point* point *m* de congélation.

fr. *franc(s)* franc(s) *m*/(*pl.*).

Fr. *France* la France *f*; *French* français.

Fri. *Friday* vendredi *m*.

ft. *foot* (*feet*) pied(s *pl.*) *m*.

FTC *Am. Federal Trade Commission* commission *f* du commerce fédéral.

fur. *furlong* (*mesure*).

G

g. *gauge* mesure-étalon *f*; ⚓ écartement *m*; *gramme* gr., *gramme m*; *guinea* guinée *f* (*unité monétaire anglaise*); *grain* grain *m* (*poids*).

G *Am. cin. general audiences* pour tout le monde.

Ga. *Georgia* (*État des É.-U.*).

G.A. *General Agent* agent *m* d'affaires; *General Assembly* assemblée *f* générale.

gal. *gallon* gallon *m*.

GATT *General Agreement on Tariffs and Trade* Accord *m* Général sur les Tarifs Douaniers et le Commerce.

G.B. *Great Britain* la Grande-Bretagne *f*.

G.B.S. *George Bernard Shaw*.

G.C.B. (*Knight*) *Grand Cross of the Bath* (Chevalier *m*) Grand-croix *f* de l'ordre du Bain.

GCE *Brit. General Certificate of Education* Certificat *m* général d'éducation.

GDR *German Democratic Republic* RDA, République *f* démocratique allemande.

gen. *generally* généralement.

Gen. *General* Gal, général *m*.

GFR *German Federal Republic* RFA, République *f* fédérale d'Allemagne.

gi. *gill* gill *m*.

G.I. *government issue* fourni par le gouvernement; *fig. le* soldat américain.

gl. *gill* gill *m*.

G.L.C. *Greater London Council* (*conseil municipal de Londres*).

Glos. *Gloucestershire* (*comté d'Angleterre*).

G.M.T. *Greenwich mean time* T.U., temps universel.

GNP *gross national product* PNB, produit *m* national brut.

gns. *guineas* guinées *f/pl.* (*unité monétaire anglaise*).

G.O.P. *Am. Grand Old Party* (*le parti républicain*).

Gov(t). *Government* gouvernement *m*.

G.P. *general practitioner* médecin *m* de médecine générale.

G.P.O. *General Post Office* bureau *m* central des postes.

gr. *grain* grain *m* (*poids*); *gross* brut; grosse *f*.

gr.wt. *gross weight* poids *m* brut.

gs. *guineas* guinées *f/pl.* (*unité monétaire anglaise*).

Gt.Br. *Great Britain* la Grande-Bretagne *f*.

guar. *guaranteed* avec garantie.

H

h. *hour(s)* h., heure(s *pl.*) *f*.

Hants. *Hampshire* (*comté d'Angleterre*).

H.B.M. *His* (*Her*) *Britannic Majesty* Sa Majesté *f* britannique.

H.C. *House of Commons* Chambre *f* des Communes.

H.C.J. *Brit. High Court of Justice* Haute Cour *f* de Justice.

H.E. *high explosive* explosif *m* puissant; très explosif; *His Excellency* Son Excellence *f*.

Heref. *Herefordshire* (*comté d'Angleterre*).

Herts. *Hertfordshire* (*comté d'Angleterre*).

hf. *half* demi.

H.F. *high frequency* H.F., haute fréquence *f*.

HGV *Brit. heavy goods vehicle* poids lourds *m*.

hhd. *hogshead* fût *m*.

H.I. *Hawaiian Islands* les Hawaii *f/pl.* (*État des É.-U.*).

H.L. *House of Lords* Chambre *f* des Lords.

H.M. *His* (*Her*) *Majesty* S.M., Sa Majesté *f*.

H.M.S. *His* (*Her*) *Majesty's Service* service *m* de Sa Majesté (*marque des administrations nationales, surt. pour la franchise postale*); *His* (*Her*) *Majesty's Ship* le navire *m* de guerre ...

H.O. *Head Office* bureau *m* or siège *m* central, agence *f* centrale; *Home Office* Ministère *m* britannique de l'Intérieur.

Hon. *Honorary* honoraire; *Honourable* l'honorable (*titre de politesse ou de noblesse*).

H.P., h.p. *horse-power* ch, c.v., cheval-vapeur *m*; *high pressure* haute pression *f*; *hire purchase* achat *m* or vente *f* à tempérament.

H.Q., Hq. *Headquarters* quartier *m* général, état-major *m*.

H.R. *Am. House of Representatives* Chambre *f* des Représentants.

H.R.H. *His (Her) Royal Highness*
S.A.R., Son Altesse *f* Royale.
hrs. *hours* heures *f/pl.*
H.T., h.t. *high tension* haute tension *f*.
ht *height* hauteur *f*.
Hunts. *Huntingdonshire* (*comté d'An-gleterre*).

I

I. *Island, Isle* île *f*; *Idaho* (*État des É.-U.*).
Ia. *Iowa* (*État des É.-U.*).
IAAF *International Amateur Athletic Federation* FIAA, Fédération *f* internationale d'athlétisme amateur.
IATA *International Air Transport Association* Association *f* internationale des transports aériens.
I.B. *Invoice Book* livre *m* des achats.
ib(id). *ibidem* (*latin = in the same place*) ibid., ibidem.
IC *integrated circuit* circuit *m* intégré.
ICAO *International Civil Aviation Organization* OACI, Organisation *f* de l'aviation civile internationale.
I.C.B.M. *intercontinental ballistic missile* missile *m* balistique intercontinental.
ICFTU *International Confederation of Free Trade Unions* CISL, Confédération *f* internationale des syndicats libres.
ICPO *International Criminal Police Organization* OIPC, INTERPOL, Organisation *f* internationale de police criminelle.
ICRC *International Committee of the Red Cross* CICR, Comité *m* international de la Croix-Rouge.
id. *idem* (*latin = the same author ou word*) id., idem.
I.D. *Intelligence Department* service *m* des renseignements.
Id(a). *Idaho* (*État des É.-U.*).
ID card *identification or identity card* carte *f* d'identité.
i.e. *id est* (*latin = that is to say*) c.-à-d., c'est-à-dire.
IFT *International Federation of Translators* FIT, Fédération *f* internationale des traducteurs.
I.H.P., i.h.p. *indicated horse-power* chevaux *m/pl.* indiqués.
Ill. *Illinois* (*État des É.-U.*).
ILO *International Labo(u)r Organization* OIT, Organisation *f* interna-

tionale du travail.
IMF *International Monetary Fund* FMI, Fonds *m* monétaire international.
in. *inch(es)* pouce(s *pl.*) *m*.
Inc. *Incorporated* associés *m/pl.* (*après un nom de société*), *Am.* S.A., société *f* anonyme; *inclosure* pièce *f* jointe.
incl. *inclusive, including* inclusivement; y compris; ... compris.
incog. *incognito* incognito.
Ind. *Indiana* (*État des É.-U.*).
ins. *inches* pouces *m/pl.*
I.N.S. *International News Service* agence *f* d'informations internationale.
inst. *instant* c^t, courant, de ce mois.
IOC *International Olympic Committee* CIO, Comité *m* international olympique.
I.of.M. *Isle of Man* (*île anglaise*).
I.of.W. *Isle of Wight* (*île anglaise*).
I.O.U. *I owe you* reconnaissance *f* de dette.
IPA *International Phonetic Association* API, Association *f* phonétique internationale.
I.Q. *intelligence quotient* quotient *m* intellectuel.
Ir. *Ireland* l'Irlande *f*; *Irish* irlandais.
I.R.A. *Irish Republican Army* Armée *f* républicaine d'Irlande.
IRC *International Red Cross* CRI, Croix-Rouge *f* internationale.
IRO *International Refugee Organization* OIR, Organisation *f* internationale pour les réfugiés.
ISBN *international standard book number* ISBN.
ISO *International Organization for Standardization* OIN, Organisation *f* internationale de normalisation.
ITO *International Trade Organization* OIC, Organisation *f* internationale du commerce.
IUS *International Union of Students* UIE, Union *f* internationale des étudiants.
IUSY *International Union of Socialist Youth* UIJS, Union *f* internationale de la jeunesse socialiste.
IVS(P.) *International Voluntary Service* (*for peace*) SCI, Service *m* civil international (pour la paix).
I.W.W. *Industrial Workers of the World* Confédération *f* mondiale des ouvriers industriels.
IYHF *International Youth Hostel Fede-*

ration FIAJ, Fédération *f* internationale des auberges de la jeunesse.

J

J. *judge* juge *m*; *justice* justice *f*; juge *m*.
J.C. *Jesus Christ* J.-C., Jésus-Christ.
J.I.B. *Brit. Joint Intelligence Bureau* (*service de renseignements et de sécurité*).
J.P. *Justice of the Peace* juge *m* de paix.
Jr. *junior* (*latin = the younger*) cadet; fils; jeune.
Jun(r). *junior* (*latin = the younger*) cadet; fils.

K

Kan(s). *Kansas* (*État des É.-U.*).
K.C. *Knight Commander* Chevalier *m* Commandeur; *Brit. King's Counsel* conseiller *m* du Roi (*approx.* avocat général).
K.C.B. *Knight Commander of the Bath* Chevalier *m* Commandeur de l'ordre du Bain.
kg. *kilogramme* kg, kilogramme *m*.
K.G.B. *Russian secret police* (*police secrète russe*).
K.K.K. *Ku Klux Klan* (*association secrète de l'Amérique du Nord hostile aux Noirs*).
km. *kilometre* km, kilomètre *m*.
k.o., KO *knock(ed) out* K.-O., knockout.
k.v. *kilovolt* kV, kilovolt *m*.
k.w. *kilowatt* kW, kilowatt *m*.
Ky. *Kentucky* (*État des É.-U.*).

L

l. *left* gauche; *line* ligne *f*; vers *m*; *link* (*mesure*); litre l, litre *m*.
£ *pound sterling* livre *f* sterling (*unité monétaire britannique*).
La. *Louisiana* (*État des É.-U.*).
LA *Los Angeles* (*ville des É.-U.*).
Lancs. *Lancashire* (*comté d'Angleterre*).
lat. *latitude* lat., latitude *f*.
lb. *pound* livre *f* (*poids*).
L.C. *letter of credit* lettre *f* de crédit.
l.c. *loco citato* (*latin = at the place cited*) loc. cit., loco citato.
L.C.J. *Lord Chief Justice* président *m* du Tribunal du Banc de la Reine.

Leics. *Leicestershire* (*comté d'Angleterre*).
Lincs. *Lincolnshire* (*comté d'Angleterre*).
ll. *lines* v.v., vers *m*/*pl.*, ll., lignes *f*/*pl.*
LL.D. *legum doctor* (*latin = Doctor of Laws*) Docteur *m* en Droit.
LMT *local mean time* heure *f* locale.
loc.cit. *loco citato* (*latin = at the place cited*) loc. cit., loco citato.
L of N *League of Nations* SDN, Société *f* des Nations.
lon(g). *longitude* longitude *f*.
l.p. *low pressure* BP, basse pression *f*.
L.P. *Labour Party* Parti *m* Travailliste.
LP *long-playing record, long-player* (*disque m*) microsillon *m*.
LSD *lysergic acid diethylamide* diéthylamide *m* de l'acide lysergique (*hallucinogène*).
L.S.S. *Life Saving Service* service *m* américain de sauvetage.
Lt. *Lieutenant* Lt, Lieut., lieutenant *m*.
L.T., l.t. *low tension* BT, basse tension *f*.
Lt.-Col. *Lieutenant-Colonel* Lt-Col., lieutenant-colonel *m*.
Ltd. *limited* à responsabilité limitée (*après un nom de société*).
Lt.-Gen. *Lieutenant-General* général *m* de corps d'armée.

M

m *minim* (*mesure*).
m. *masculin* m., masculin; *metre* m, mètre *m*; *mile* mille *m*; *minute* mn, minute *f*.
M.A. *Master of Arts* Maître *m* ès Arts; diplômé(e *f*) *m* d'études supérieures.
Maj. *Major* commandant *m*.
Maj.-Gen. *Major-General* général *m* de brigade.
Man. *Manitoba* (*État des É.-U.*).
Mass. *Massachusetts* (*État des É.-U.*).
M.C. *Master of Ceremonies* maître *m* des cérémonies; *Am. Member of Congress* membre *m* du Congrès.
MCH *Maternal and Child Health* PMI, Protection *f* maternelle et infantile.
M.D. *medicinae doctor* (*latin = Doctor of Medicine*) Docteur *m* en Médecine; *Managing Director* Président *m* directeur général.
Md. *Maryland* (*État des É.-U.*).
Me. *Maine* (*État des É.-U.*).
mg. *milligramme* mg, milligramme *m*.

mi. *mile* mille *m.*

MI 5 (6) *Military Intelligence, section five (six)* (*service contre-espionnage*).

Mich. *Michigan* (*État des É.-U.*).

min. *minute(s)* mn, minute(s) *f*/(*pl.*); *minimum* minimum *m.*

Minn. *Minnesota* (*État des É.-U.*).

Miss. *Mississippi* (*État des É.-U.*).

mm. *millimetre* mm, millimètre *m.*

Mo. *Missouri* (*État des É.-U.*).

M.O. *money order* mandat-poste *m*; *mail order* achat *m or* vente *f* par correspondence.

Mon. *Monday* lundi *m.*

Mont. *Montana* (*État des É.-U.*).

MP, M.P. *Member of Parliament* membre *m* de la Chambre des Communes; *Military Police* P.M., police *f* militaire.

m.p.g. *miles per gallon approx.* litres au cent (kilomètres).

m.p.h. *miles per hour* milles *m*/*pl.* à l'heure (*vitesse horaire*).

Mr. *Mister* M., Monsieur *m.*

Mrs. *Mistress* Mme, Madame *f.*

MS. *manuscript* ms, manuscrit *m.*

Ms. [miz] = *Miss or Mrs.* Madame.

M.S. *motorship* M/S, navire *m* à moteur Diesel.

MSA *Mutual Security Agency* organisation *f* américaine de sécurité mutuelle.

MSS *manuscripts* mss, manuscrits *m*/*pl.*

mt. *megaton* mégatonne *f.*

Mt. *Mount* mont *m.*

N

N. *north* N., nord *m*; *northern* (du) nord.

N.A.A.F.I. *Navy, Army and Air Force Institutes* (*cantines organisées à l'intention des troupes britanniques*).

NASA *Am. National Aeronautics and Space Administration* administration *f* des questions aéronautiques et spatiales.

NATO *North Atlantic Treaty Organization* OTAN, Organisation *f* du traité de l'Atlantique Nord.

n.b., N.B. *nota bene* (*latin* = *note well*) N.B., notez bien.

N.B.C. *National Broadcasting Corporation* (*radiodiffusion-télévision américaine*).

N.C. *North Carolina* (*État des É.-U.*).

N.C.B. *Brit. National Coal Board* Office *m* national du charbon.

n.d. *no date* s.d., sans date.

N.D(ak). *North Dakota* (*État des É.-U.*).

N.E. *northeast* N.E., nord-est *m*; *northeastern* (du) nord-est.

Neb(r). *Nebraska* (*État des É.-U.*).

Nev. *Nevada* (*État des É.-U.*).

N.F., n/f. *no funds* défaut *m* de provision.

N.H. *New Hampshire* (*État des É.-U.*).

N.H.S. *Brit. National Health Service* (*service de santé national*; *sécurité sociale*).

N.J. *New Jersey* (*État des É.-U.*).

N.M(ex). *New Mexico* (*État des É.-U.*).

No. (*a.* **no.**) *numero* N°, n°, numéro *m*; *number* nombre *m*; *north* N., nord *m.*

Norf. *Norfolk* (*comté d'Angleterre*).

Northants. *Northamptonshire* (*comté d'Angleterre*).

Northumb. *Northumberland* (*comté d'Angleterre*).

Notts. *Nottinghamshire* (*comté d'Angleterre*).

n.p. or d. *no place or date* s.l.n.d., sans lieu ni date.

N.S.P.C.A. *Brit. National Society for the Prevention of Cruelty to animals* S.P.A., Société *f* protectrice des animaux.

N.S.P.C.C. *National Society for the Prevention of Cruelty to Children* Société *f* nationale protectrice des enfants.

Nt.wt. *net weight* poids *m* net.

N.U.M. *Brit. National Union of Mineworkers* Syndicat *m* national des mineurs.

N.W. *northwest* N.O., N.W., nordouest; *northwestern* (du) nordouest.

N.Y. *New York* (*État des É.-U.*).

N.Y.C. *New York City* ville *f* de New York.

N.Z. *New Zealand* la Nouvelle-Zélande *f.*

O

O. *Ohio* (*État des É.-U.*); *order* ordre *m.*

o/a *on account* P.C., Pour-compte.

OAP *old-age-pensioner* retraité(e *f*) *m.*

O.A.S. *Organization of American States* O.E.A., Organisation *f* des États américains.

ob. *obiit* (*latin* = *died*) décédé.

OECD *Organization for Economic Co-operation and Development* OCED, Organisation *f* de coopération économique et de développement.
OEEC *Organization for European Economic Cooperation* OECE, Organisation *f* européenne de coopération économique.
O.H. *on hand* en magasin.
O.H.M.S. *On His (Her) Majesty's Service* (pour le) service *m* de Sa Majesté (*marque des administrations nationales, surt. pour la franchise postale*).
O.K. (*peut-être de*) *all correct* très bien, d'accord.
Okla. *Oklahoma* (*État des É.-U.*).
O.N.A. *Overseas News Agency* (*agence d'informations américaine*).
O.N.S. *Overseas News Service* (*agence d'informations britannique*).
OPEC *Organization of Petroleum Exporting Countries* OPEP, Organisation *f* des pays exportateurs de pétrole.
o.r. *owner's risk* aux risques et périls du propriétaire.
Ore(g). *Oregon* (*État des É.-U.*).
Oxon. *Oxfordshire* (*comté d'Angleterre*).
oz. *ounce(s)* once(s *pl.*) *f*.

P

p (*new*) *penny*, (*new*) *pence* (*pièce de monnaie britannique*).
p. *page* page *f*; *part* partie *f*.
p.a. *per annum* (*latin = yearly*) par an.
Pa. *Pennsylvania* (*État des É.-U.*).
P.A. *public address* (*system*) sonorisation *f*; *personal assistant* assistant(e *f*) *m* personnel(le).
Panam *Pan American Airways* (*compagnie aérienne américaine*).
par. *paragraph* paragraphe *m*, alinéa *m*.
P.A.Y.E. *Brit.* *pay as you earn* impôt *m* retenu à la source.
P.C. *post-card* carte *f* postale; *police constable* gardien *m* de la paix, policeman *m*; *Personal Computer* ordinateur *m* personnel.
p.c. *per cent* P.C., pour-cent.
p/c *price current* P.C., prix *m* courant.
pd *paid* payé.
P.D. *Police Department* police *f*; *a.* **p.d.** *per diem* (*latin = by the day*) par jour.
P.E.N. *usu.* **PEN Club** *Poets, Playwrights, Editors, Essayists and Novelists*

Union *f* internationale PEN (*fédération internationale d'écrivains*).
Penn(a). *Pennsylvania* (*État des É.-U.*).
per pro(c). *per procurationem* (*latin = by proxy*) par procuration.
P.f.c. *Am.* *private first class* caporal *m*.
PG *cin.* *parental guidance* (*suggested*) (*contient des scènes qui nécessitent l'explication des parents*).
Ph.D. *Philosophiae Doctor* (*latin = Doctor of Philosophy*) Docteur *m* en Philosophie.
pk. *peck* (*mesure*).
P./L. *profit and loss* profits et pertes.
PLC *public limited company* S.A., société *f* anonyme.
PLO *Palestine Liberation Organization* O.L.P., Organisation *f* de libération de la Palestine.
p.m. *post meridiem* (*latin = after noon*) de l'après-midi.
P.M. *Prime Minister* Premier ministre.
P.O. *Post Office* bureau *m* de poste; (*a.* **p.o.**) *postal order* mandat-poste *m*.
P.O.B. *Post Office Box* boîte *f* postale.
p.o.d. *pay on delivery* contre remboursement.
P.O.O. *Post Office Order* mandat-poste *m*.
P.O.S.B. *Post Office Savings Bank* caisse *f* d'épargne postale.
P.O.W. *Prisoner of War* P.G., prisonnier *m* de guerre.
p.p. *per procurationem* (*latin = by proxy*) par procuration.
P.R. *public relations* relations *f/pl.* publiques.
Pres. *President* président(e *f*) *m*.
Prof. *Professor* professeur *m*.
prox. *proximo* (*latin = next month*) du mois prochain.
P.S. *postscript* P.-S., post-scriptum *m*; *Passenger Steamer* paquebot *m*.
pt. *pint* pinte *f*.
P.T.A. *Parent-Teacher Association* Association *f* professeurs-parents.
Pte. *Private* soldat *m* de 1ère ou de 2ème classe.
P.T.O., **p.t.o.** *please turn over* T.S.V.P., tournez, s'il vous plaît.
PVC *polyvinyl chloride* chlorure *f* de polyvinyle.
Pvt. *Private* soldat *m* de 1ère ou de 2ème classe.

P.W. *Prisoner of War* P.G., prisonnier *m* de guerre.

PX *Post Exchange* (*cantines de l'armée américaine*).

Q

q. *query* question *f*.

Q.C. *Brit. Queen's Counsel* conseiller *m* de la Reine (*approx. avocat général*).

qr. *quarter* quarter *m*.

qt. *quart* (*approx.*) litre *m*.

qu. *query* question *f*.

quot. *quotation* cours *m*.

qy. *query* question *f*.

R

R *Am. cin. restricted* (*les mineurs doivent être accompagnés de leurs parents*).

R. *River* rivière *f*; fl., fleuve *m*; *Road* r., rue *f*; *thermomètre*: Réaumur R, Réaumur.

r. *right* dr., droit, à droite.

R.A. *Royal Academy* Acadèmie *f* royale.

R.A.C. *Brit. Royal Automobile Club* Automobile Club *m* royal.

RADWAR *Am. radiological warfare* guerre *f* atomique.

R.A.F. *Royal Air Force* armée *f* de l'air britannique.

R.C. *Red Cross* C.R., Croix-Rouge *f*; *Roman Catholic* catholique.

rd. *rod* (*mesure*).

Rd. *Road* r., rue *f*.

recd. *received* reçu.

ref(c). (*In*) *reference* (*to*) faisant suite à; mention *f*.

regd. *registered* déposé; *poste*: recommandé.

reg.tn. *register(ed) tonnage* tonnage *m* enregistré.

res. *residence* résidence *f*; *research* recherche(s) *f*/(*pl.*).

resp. *respective(ly)* respectif (respectivement).

ret. *retired* retraité, à la retraite.

Rev. *Reverend* Révd., Révérend.

R.I. *Rhode Island* (*État des É.-U.*).

R.L.O. *Brit. Returned Letter Office* retour *m* à l'envoyeur.

rm *room* pièce *f*, chambre *f*.

R.N. *Royal Navy* Marine *f* britannique.

R.P. *reply paid* R.P., réponse *f* payée.

r.p.m. *revolutions per minute* t.p.m., tours *m*/*pl.* par minute.

R.R. *Am. Railroad* ch.d.f., chemin *m* de fer.

R.S. *Brit. Royal Society* Société *f* royale.

R.S.V.P. répondez s'il vous plaît.

Rt.Hon. *Right Honourable le* très honorable.

Ry. *Brit. Railway* Ch.d.f., chemin *m* de fer.

S

S. *South* S., sud *m*; *Southern* (du) sud.

s. *second* s, seconde *f*; *shilling* shilling *m*.

S.A. *South Africa* l'Afrique *f* du Sud; *South America* l'Amérique *f* du Sud; *Salvation Army* Armée *f* du Salut.

SACEUR *Supreme Allied Commander Europe* Commandant *m* Suprême des Forces Alliées en Europe.

SACLANT *Supreme Allied Commander Atlantic* Commandant *m* Suprême des Forces Alliées de l'Atlantique.

s.a.e. *stamped addressed envelope* enveloppe *f* munie de timbre et d'adresse.

Salop. *Shropshire* (*comté d'Angleterre*).

Sask. *Saskatchewan* (*province du Canada*).

S.B. *Sales Book* livre *m* de(s) vente(s).

S.C. *South Carolina* (*État des É.-U.*); *Security Council* Conseil *m* de Sécurité.

S.D(ak). *South Dakota* (*État des É.-U.*).

S.E. *Southeast* S.E., sud-est *m*; *southeastern* (du) sud-est; *Stock Exchange* Bourse *f*.

SEATO *South East Asia (Collective Defense) Treaty Organisation* O.T.A.S.E., Organisation *f* du traité de (défense collective pour) l'Asie du Sud-Est.

sec. *second* s, seconde *f*.

Sec. *Secretary* secrétaire *m*; ministre *m*.

SF *science fiction* science-fiction *f*.

SG *Secretary General* SG, Secrétaire *m* général.

sen(r). *senior* (*latin = the elder*) aîné, père.

S(er)gt. *Sergeant* Sgt, sergent *m*.

sh. *shilling* shilling *m*; ✝ *share* action *f*.

SHAPE *Supreme Headquarters Allied Powers Europe* Quartiers *m*/*pl.* Généraux des Forces Alliées en Europe.

S.M. *Sergeant-Major* Sergent-major *m*.

S.N. *shipping note* note *f* d'expédition.
Soc. *society* société *f*, association *f*; *Socialist* socialiste (*a. su.*).
Som(s). *Somersetshire* (*comté d'Angleterre*).
SOS *S.O.S.* (*signal de détresse*).
sov. *sovereign* souverain *m* (*pièce de monnaie britannique*).
sp.gr. *specific gravity* gravité *f* spécifique.
S.P.Q.R. *small profits, quick returns* à petits bénéfices, vente rapide.
sq. *square* ... carré.
Sq. *Square* place *f*.
Sr. *senior* (*latin* = *the elder*) aîné, père.
S.R.N. *Brit. State Registered Nurse* infirmière *f* diplômée d'État.
S.S. *steamship* S/S, navire *m* à vapeur.
st. *stone* (*poids*).
St. *Saint* St(e*f*), saint(e*f*); *Street* r., rue *f*; *Station* gare *f*.
Sta. *station* gare *f*.
Staffs. *Staffordshire* (*comté d'Angleterre*).
S.T.D. *Brit. subscriber trunk dialling* service *m* automatique interurbain.
St. Ex. *Stock Exchange* Bourse *f*.
stg. *sterling* sterling *m* (*unité monétaire britannique*).
sub. *substitute* succédané *m*.
Suff. *Suffolk* (*comté d'Angleterre*).
Sun. *Sunday* dimanche *m*.
suppl. *supplement* supplément *m*.
Suss. *Sussex* (*comté d'Angleterre*).
S.W. *southwest* S.-O., sud-ouest; *southwestern* (du) sud-ouest.
Sy. *Surrey* (*comté d'Angleterre*).

T

t. *ton* tonne *f*.
TB *tuberculosis* TB, tuberculose *f*.
TC *Trusteeship Council of the United Nations* Conseil *m* de tutelle des Nations Unies.
T.D. *Treasury Department* Ministère *m* américain des Finances.
tel. *telephone* téléphone *m*.
Tenn. *Tennessee* (*État des É.-U.*).
Tex. *Texas* (*État des É.-U.*).
tgm. *telegram* télégramme *m*.
T.G.W.U. *Brit. Transport General Workers' Union* Confédération *f* des employés d'entreprises de transport.
Thur(s). *Thursday* jeudi *m*.
T.M.O. *telegraph money order* mandat *m* télégraphique.

tn *ton(s)* tonne(s) *f*/(*pl.*).
TNT *trinitrotoluene* trinitrotoluène *m*.
T.O. *Telegraph* (*Telephone*) *Office* bureau *m* télégraphique (téléphonique).
t.o. *turnover* chiffre *m* d'affaires.
T.P.O. *Travelling Post Office* poste *f* ambulante.
TT *teetotal(ler)* abstinent (*a. su.*).
T.U. *Trade(s) Union(s)* syndicat(s *pl.*) *m* ouvrier(s).
T.U.C. *Brit. Trade(s) Union Congress* (*approx.*) C.G.T., Confédération *f* générale du travail.
Tue(s). *Tuesday* mardi *m*.
TV. *television* T.V., télévision *f*.
T.V.A. *Tennessee Valley Authority* (*organisation pour l'exploitation de la vallée de la rivière Tennessee*).
T.W.A. *Trans World Airlines* (*compagnie aérienne américaine*).

U

U *Brit. cin. universal* pour tout le monde.
UFO *unidentified flying object* OVNI *m*, objet *m* volant non identifié.
U.H.F. *ultra-high frequency* UHF, ultra haute fréquence *f*.
U.K. *United Kingdom* Royaume-Uni *m*.
ult. *ultimo* (*latin* = *last day of the month*) dernier, du mois dernier.
UMW *Am. United Mine Workers* Syndicat *m* des mineurs.
U.N. *United Nations* Nations *f*/*pl.* Unies.
UNESCO *United Nations Educational, Scientific, and Cultural Organization* UNESCO, Organisation *f* des Nations Unies pour l'Éducation, la Science et la Culture.
UNICEF *United Nations International Children's Emergency Fund* FISE, Fonds *m* International de Secours aux Enfants.
UNO *United Nations Organization* O.N.U., Organisation *f* des Nations Unies.
U.N.S.C. *United Nations Security Council* Conseil *m* de Sécurité des Nations Unies.
UPI *United Press International* (*agence d'informations américaine*).
U.S.(A.) *United States* (*of America*) É.-U., États-Unis *m*/*pl.* (d'Amérique).

USAF(E) *United States Air Force (Europe)* armée *f* de l'air des É.-U. (en Europe).

U.S.S.R. *Union of Socialist Soviet Republics* U.R.S.S., Union *f* des Républiques Socialistes Soviétiques.

Ut. *Utah* (*État des É.-U.*).

V

v. *verse* v., vers *m*, verset *m*; *versus* (*latin = against*) contre; *vide* (*latin = see*) v., voir, voyez.

V *volt* V, volt *m*.

Va. *Virginia* (*État des É.-U.*).

V.A.T. *value-added tax* T.V.A., taxe *f* à la valeur ajoutée.

V.D. *venereal disease* M.V., maladie *f* vénérienne.

VHF *very high frequency* OTC, onde *f* très courte.

V.I.P. *very important person* personnage *m* important.

Vis. *viscount(ess)* vicomte(sse *f*) *m*.

viz. *videlicet* (*latin = namely*) à savoir; c.-à-d., c'est-à-dire.

vol. *volume* t., tome *m*, vol., volume *m*.

vols. *volumes* tomes *m*/*pl.*, volumes *m*/*pl.*

V.P., V.Pres. *Vice-President* vice-président(e *f*) *m*.

V.S. *veterinary surgeon* vétérinaire *m*.

V.S.O.P. *very superior old pale* (*cognac de qualité supérieure*).

Vt. *Vermont* (*État des É.-U.*).

V.T.O.(L.) *vertical take-off (and landing) (aircraft)* A.D.A.V., avion *m* à décollage et atterrissage vertical.

v.v *vice versa* (*latin = conversely*) vice versa, réciproquement.

W

W *watt* W, watt *m*.

W. *west* O., W., ouest *m*; *western* (de l')ouest.

War. *Warwickshire* (*comté d'Angleterre*).

Wash. *Washington* (*État des É.-U.*).

W.C. *West Central* (*district postal de Londres*); *water-closet* W.-C., water-closet *m*.

WCC *World Council of Churches* COE, Conseil *m* œcuménique des églises.

Wed(s). *Wednesday* mercredi *m*.

WFPA *World Federation for the Protection of Animals* FMPA, Fédération *f* mondiale pour la protection des animaux.

WFTU *World Federation of Trade Unions* F.S.M., Fédération *f* syndicale mondiale.

WHO *World Health Organization* OMS, Organisation *f* mondiale de la Santé.

W. I. *West Indies* Indes *f*/*pl.* occidentales.

Wilts. *Wiltshire* (*comté d'Angleterre*).

Wis. *Wisconsin* (*État des É.-U.*).

wk *week* semaine *f*.

wkly *weekly* hebdomadaire; par semaine.

wks *weeks* semaines *f*/*pl.*

W/L., w.l. *wave length* longueur *f* d'onde.

w/o *without* sans.

W.O.M.A.N. *World Organization of Mothers of All Nations* Organisation *f* mondiale des mères de famille.

Worcs. *Worcestershire* (*comté d'Angleterre*).

W.P. *weather permitting* si le temps le permet.

W.S.R. *World Students' Relief* service *m* international de secours aux étudiants.

W/T *wireless telegraphy (telephony)* T.S.F., Télégraphie *f* (Téléphonie *f*) sans Fil.

wt. *weight* poids *m*.

W. Va. *West Virginia* (*État des É.-U.*).

WW *World War* guerre *f* mondiale.

Wyo. *Wyoming* (*État des É.-U.*).

X

X *cin. adults only* interdit aux mineurs.

x.-d. *ex dividend* ex D., ex-dividende.

x.-i. *ex interest* sans intérêt.

Xmas *Christmas* Noël *f*.

Xn *christian* chrétien.

Xroads *cross roads* carrefour *m*.

Xt. *Christ* le Christ, Jésus-Christ *m*.

Y

yd. *yard(s)* yard(s *pl.*) *m*.

YMCA *Young Men's Christian Association* UCJG, Union *f* chrétienne de jeunes gens.

Yorks. *Yorkshire* (*comté d'Angleterre*).

yr(s.) *year(s)* an(s) *m*/(*pl.*).

YWCA *Young Women's Christian Association* Union *f* chrétienne féminine.

Numerals

Nombres

Cardinal Numbers — Nombres cardinaux

0 nought, zero, cipher *zéro*
1 one *un, une*
2 two *deux*
3 three *trois*
4 four *quatre*
5 five *cinq*
6 six *six*
7 seven *sept*
8 eight *huit*
9 nine *neuf*
10 ten *dix*
11 eleven *onze*
12 twelve *douze*
13 thirteen *treize*
14 fourteen *quatorze*
15 fifteen *quinze*
16 sixteen *seize*
17 seventeen *dix-sept*
18 eighteen *dix-huit*
19 nineteen *dix-neuf*
20 twenty *vingt*
21 twenty-one *vingt et un*
22 twenty-two *vingt-deux*
30 thirty *trente*
40 forty *quarante*

50 fifty *cinquante*
60 sixty *soixante*
70 seventy *soixante-dix*
71 seventy-one *soixante et onze*
72 seventy-two *soixante-douze*
80 eighty *quatre-vingts*
81 eighty-one *quatre-vingt-un*
90 ninety *quatre-vingt-dix*
91 ninety-one *quatre-vingt-onze*
100 a *ou* one hundred *cent*
101 one hundred and one *cent un*
200 two hundred *deux cents*
211 two hundred and eleven *deux cent onze*
1000 a *ou* one thousand *mille*
1001 one thousand and one *mille un*
1100 eleven hundred *onze cents*
1967 nineteen hundred and sixty-seven *dix-neuf cent soixante-sept*
2000 two thousand *deux mille*
1 000 000 a *ou* one million *un million*
2 000 000 two million *deux millions*
1 000 000 000 a *ou* one milliard, *Am.* one billion *un milliard*

Ordinal Numbers — Nombres ordinaux

1. first *le premier, la première*
2. second *le ou la deuxième, le second, la seconde*
3. third *troisième*
4. fourth *quatrième*
5. fifth *cinquième*
6. sixth *sixième*
7. seventh *septième*
8. eighth *huitième*
9. ninth *neuvième*
10. tenth *dixième*
11. eleventh *onzième*
12. twelfth *douzième*
13. thirteenth *treizième*
14. fourteenth *quatorzième*
15. fifteenth *quinzième*
16. sixteenth *seizième*

17. seventeenth *dix-septième*
18. eighteenth *dix-huitième*
19. nineteenth *dix-neuvième*
20. twentieth *vingtième*
21. twenty-first *vingt et unième*
22. twenty-second *vingt-deuxième*
30. thirtieth *trentième*
31. thirty-first *trente et unième*
40. fortieth *quarantième*
41. forty-first *quarante et unième*
50. fiftieth *cinquantième*
51. fifty-first *cinquante et unième*
60. sixtieth *soixantième*
61. sixty-first *soixante et unième*
70. seventieth *soixante-dixième*
71. seventy-first *soixante et onzième*

72. seventy-second *soixante-douzième*
80. eightieth *quatre-vingtième*
81. eighty-first *quatre-vingt-unième*
90. ninetieth *quatre-vingt-dixième*

91. ninety-first *quatre-vingt-onzième*
100. (one) hundredth *centième*
101. hundred and first *cent unième*
200. two-hundredth *deux centième*
1000. (one) thousandth *millième*

Fractions — Fractions

½ one half *(un) demi*; (the) half *la moitié*
1½ one and a half *un et demi*
⅓ one third *un tiers*
⅔ two thirds *deux tiers*
¼ one quarter *un quart*
¾ three quarters *(les) trois quarts*

⅕ one fifth *un cinquième*
⅝ five eights *(les) cinq huitièmes*
⁹⁄₁₀ nine tenths *(les) neuf dixièmes*
0.45 point four five *zéro, virgule, quarante-cinq*
17.38 seventeen point three eight *dix-sept, virgule, trente-huit*

British and American weights and measures

Mesures britanniques et américaines

Linear Measures — Mesures de longueur

1 **inch (in.)**
   = 2,54 cm
1 **foot (ft.)**
   = 12 inches = 30,48 cm
1 **yard (yd.)**
   = 3 feet = 91,44 cm
1 **link (l.)**
   = 7.92 inches = 20,12 cm

1 **rod (rd.), pole** *ou* **perch (p.)**
   = 25 links = 5,03 m
1 **chain (ch.)**
   = 4 rods = 20,12 m
1 **furlong (fur.)**
   = 10 chains = 201,17 m
1 **(statute) mile (mi.)**
   = 8 furlongs = 1609,34 m

Nautical Measures — Mesures nautiques

1 **fathom (fm.)**
   = 6 feet = 1,83 m
1 **cable's length**
   = 100 fathoms = 183 m

Am. 120 fathoms
   = 219 m
1 **nautical mile (n.m.)**
   = 10 cables' length = 1852 m

Square Measures — Mesures de surface

1 **square inch (sq. in.)**
   = 6,45 cm²
1 **square foot (sq. ft.)**
   = 144 square inches
   = 929,03 cm²
1 **square yard (sq. yd.)**
   = 9 square feet = 0,836 m²

1 **square rod (sq. rd.)**
   = 30.25 square yards = 25,29 m²
1 **rood (ro.)**
   = 40 square rods = 10,12 ares
1 **acre (a.)**
   = 4 rods = 40,47 ares
1 **square mile (sq. mi.)**
   = 640 acres = 2,59 km²

Cubic Measures — Mesures de volume

1 **cubic inch (cu. in.)**
   = 16,387 cm³
1 **cubic foot (cu. ft.)**
   = 1728 cubic inches
   = 0,028 m³

1 **cubic yard (cu. yd.)**
   = 27 cubic feet = 0,765 m³
1 **register ton (reg. tn.)**
   = 100 cubic feet
   = 2,832 m³

British Measures of Capacity — Mesures de capacité britanniques

1 **gill (gi., gl.)**
   = 0,142 l
1 **pint (pt.)**
   = 4 gills = 0,568 l

1 **quart (qt.)**
   = 2 pints = 1,136 l
1 **gallon (gal.)**
   = 4 quarts = 4,546 l

1 **peck (pk.)**
   = 2 gallons = 9,092 l
1 **bushel (bu., bsh.)**
   = 4 pecks = 36,36 l

1 **quarter (qr.)**
   = 8 bushels = 290,94 l
1 **barrel (bbl., bl.)**
   = 36 gallons = 1,636 hl

U.S. Measures of Capacity — Mesures de capacité américaines

1 **dry pint**
   = 0,550 l
1 **dry quart**
   = 2 dry pints = 1,1 l
1 **peck**
   = 8 dry quarts = 8,81 l
1 **bushel**
   = 4 pecks = 35,24 l
1 **liquid gill**
   = 0,118 l

1 **liquid pint**
   = 4 liquid gills = 0,473 l
1 **liquid quart**
   = 2 liquid pints = 0,946 l
1 **gallon**
   = 4 liquid quarts = 3,785 l
1 **barrel**
   = 31.50 gallons = 119 l
1 **barrel petroleum**
   = 42 gallons = 158,97 l

Apothecaries' Fluid Measures — Mesures pharmaceutiques

1 **minim (min., m.)**
   = 0,0006 dl
1 **fluid drachm,** *Am.* **dram (dr. fl.)**
   = 60 minims = 0,0355 dl

1 **fluid ounce (oz. fl.)**
   = 8 fluid drachms = 0,284 dl
1 **pint (pt.)**
   Brit. = 20 fluid ounces = 0,586 l
   Am. = 16 fluid ounces = 0,473 l

Avoirdupois Weight – Poids (système avoirdupois)

1 **grain (gr.)**
   = 0,0684 g
1 **drachm,** *Am.* **dram (dr. av.)**
   = 27.34 grains = 1,77 g
1 **ounce (oz. av.)**
   = 16 drachms = 28,35 g
1 **pound (lb. av.)**
   = 16 ounces = 0,453 kg
1 **stone (st.)**
   = 14 pounds = 6,35 kg
1 **quarter (qr.)**

   Brit. = 28 pounds = 12,70 kg
   Am. = 25 pounds = 11,34 kg
1 **hundredweight (cwt.)**
   Brit. = 112 pounds = 50,80 kg
   Am. = 100 pounds = 45,36 kg
1 **long ton (tn. l.)**
   Brit. = 20 hundredweights
   = 1016 kg
1 **short ton (tn. sh.)**
   Am. = 20 hundredweights
   = 907,18 kg

Troy and Apothecaries' Weight – Poids (système troy) et poids pharmaceutiques

1 **grain (gr.)**
   = 0,0684 g
1 **scruple (s. ap.)**
   = 20 grains = 1,296 g
1 **pennyweight (dwt.)**
   = 24 grains = 1,555 g

1 **drachm,** *Am.* **dram (dr. t., dr. ap.)**
   = 3 scruples = 3,888 g
1 **ounce (oz. ap.)**
   = 8 drachms = 31,104 g
1 **pound (lb. t., lb. ap.)**
   = 12 ounces = 0,373 kg

Conjugations of English verbs
Conjugaisons des verbes anglais

a) Conjugaison régulière faible

L'actif du présent de l'indicatif a la forme de l'infinitif. La 3e personne du singulier se termine par ...s. Après une consonne sonore, cet s se sonorise; p.ex. *he sends* [sendz]; après une consonne sourde, il est sourd; p.ex. *he paints* [peints]; après une sifflante, suivie d'un e muet ou non, elle se termine par ...es, prononcé [iz]; p.ex. *he catches* ['kætʃiz], *wishes* ['wiʃiz], *passes* ['pɑːsiz], *judges* ['dʒʌdʒiz], *rises* ['raiziz]. Les verbes terminés par ...o précédé d'une consonne la forment en ...es, prononcé [z]; p.ex. *he goes* [gouz].

Le prétérit et le participe passé se forment en ajoutant ...ed, ou, après e, ...d seulement, à l'infinitif; p.ex. *fetched* [fetʃt], mais *agreed* [əˈgriːd], *judged* [dʒʌdʒd]. La terminaison ...ed se prononce [d] après un radical sonore; p.ex. *arrived* [əˈraivd], *judged* [dʒʌdʒd]. Ajoutée à la fin d'un radical sourd, elle se prononce [t]; p.ex. *liked* [laikt]. Après les verbes se terminant par ...d, ...de, ...t et ...te cet ...ed se prononce [id]; p.ex. *mended* ['mendid], *glided* ['glaidid], *painted* ['peintid], *hated* ['heitid].

La terminaison du participe présent et du gérondif se rend par ...ing. Les verbes terminés par ...ie les forment en ...ying; p.ex. *lie* [lai]: *lying* ['laiiŋ].

Les verbes terminés par ...y précédé d'une consonne transforment cet y en i et prennent les terminaisons ...es, ...ed; devant ...ing, y reste inchangé; p.ex. *try* [trai]: *he tries* [traiz], *he tried* [traid], mais *trying* ['traiiŋ].

Un e muet à la fin d'un verbe tombe devant ...ed ou ...ing; p.ex. *loved* [lʌvd], *loving* ['lʌviŋ]. Des cas exceptionnels sont *dyeing* ['daiiŋ] de *dye* [dai] et *shoeing* ['ʃuːiŋ] de *shoe* [ʃuː]. Pour des raisons phonétiques *singe* [sindʒ] a *singeing* ['sindʒiŋ] comme participe présent.

Les verbes terminés par une consonne simple précédée d'une seule voyelle accentuée, ou les verbes terminés par r simple, précédé d'une seule voyelle longue, redoublent leur consonne finale devant les terminaisons ...ed et ...ing; p.ex.

to lob [lɔb]	lobbed [lɔbd]	lobbing ['lɔbiŋ]
to wed [wed]	wedded ['wedid]	wedding ['wediŋ]
to beg [beg]	begged [begd]	begging ['begiŋ]
to step [step]	stepped [stept]	stepping ['stepiŋ]
to quit [kwit]	quitted ['kwitid]	quitting ['kwitiŋ]
to compel [kəmˈpel]	compelled [kəmˈpeld]	compelling [kəmˈpeliŋ]
to bar [bɑː]	barred [bɑːd]	barring ['bɑːriŋ]
to stir [stəː]	stirred [stəːd]	stirring ['stəːriŋ]

Dans les verbes terminés par **...l** ou **...p**, précédé d'une seule voyelle simple, inaccentuée, le redouble-ment se fait si l'on écrit le mot à l'anglaise, et ne se fait pas généralement si on l'écrit à l'américaine:

to travel ['trævl]	*travelled* ['trævld]	*travelling* ['trævliŋ]
to worship ['wɔːʃip]	*worshipped* ['wɔːʃipt]	*worshipping* ['wɔːʃipiŋ]

Les verbes terminés par **...c** transforment ce **c** en **ck** devant **...ed** et **...ing**; p.ex. *to traffic* ['træfik] *trafficked* ['træfikt] *trafficking* ['træfikiŋ].

Le subjonctif présent a la même forme que l'indicatif, à l'exception de la 3e personne du singulier qui ne prend pas d's. Au prétérit il correspond à l'indicatif.

Les temps composés se forment à l'aide de l'auxiliaire *to have,* plus le participe passé.

Le passif se forme à l'aide de l'auxiliaire *to be,* plus le participe passé.

b) Liste des verbes forts et des verbes faibles irréguliers

La première forme en caractère gras indique le présent (*present*); après le premier tiret, on trouve le passé simple (*preterite*), après le deuxième tiret, le participe passé (*past participle*).

abide - abode - abode
arise - arose - arisen
awake - awoke - awoke, awaked

be (am, is, are) - was (were) - been
bear - bore - borne *porté,* born *né*
beat - beat - beaten, beat
become - became - become
beget - begot - begotten
begin - began - begun
belay - belayed, belaid - belayed, belaid
bend - bent - bent
bereave - bereaved, bereft - bereaved, bereft
beseech - besought - besought
bestead - besteaded - bested, bestead
bestrew - bestrewed - bestrewed, bestrewn
bestride - bestrode - bestridden
bet - bet, betted - bet, betted
bid - bade, bid - bidden, bid
bind - bound - bound
bite - bit - bitten
bleed - bled - bled
blow - blew - blown
break - broke - broken
breed - bred - bred
bring - brought - brought

build - built - built
burn - burnt, burned - burnt, burned
burst - burst - burst
buy - bought - bought

can - could
cast - cast - cast
catch - caught - caught
chide - chid - chid, chidden
choose - chose - chosen
cleave - clove, cleft - cloven, cleft
cling - clung - clung
clothe - clothed, *poét.* clad - clothed, *poét.* clad
come - came - come
cost - cost - cost
creep - crept - crept
cut - cut - cut

dare - dared, durst - dared
deal - dealt - dealt
dig - dug - dug
do - did - done
draw - drew - drawn
dream - dreamt, dreamed - dreamt, dreamed
drink - drank - drunk
drive - drove - driven
dwell - dwelt - dwelt

eat - ate -eaten

fall - fell - fallen
feed - fed - fed
feel - felt - felt
fight - fought - fought
find - found - found
flee - fled - fled
fling - flung - flung
fly - flew - flown
forbear - forbore - forborne
forbid - forbad(e) - forbidden
forget - forgot - forgotten
forgive - forgave - forgiven
forsake - forsook - forsaken
freeze - froze - frozen

geld - gelded, gelt - gelded, gelt
get - got - got
gild - gilded, gilt - gilded, gilt
gird - girded, girt - girded, girt
give - gave - given
go - went - gone
grave - graved - graved, graven
grind - ground - ground
grow - grew - grown

hang - hung, hanged - hung, hanged
have (has) - had - had
hear - heard - heard
heave - heaved, ⚓ hove - heaved, ⚓ hove
hew - hewed - hewed, hewn
hide - hid - hidden, hid
hit - hit - hit
hold - held - held
hurt - hurt - hurt

keep - kept - kept
kneel - knelt, kneeled - knelt, kneeled
knit - knitted, knit - knitted, knit
know - knew - known

lade - laded - laded, laden
lay - laid - laid
lead - led - led
lean - leaned, leant - leaned, leant
leap - leaped, leapt - leaped, leapt
learn - learned, learnt - learned, learnt
leave - left - left
lend - lent - lent

let - let - let
lie - lay - lain
light - lighted, lit - lighted, lit
lose - lost - lost

make - made - made
may - might
mean - meant - meant
meet - met - met
mow - mowed - mowed, mown
must - must

ought

pay - paid - paid
pen - penned, pent - penned, pent
put - put - put

read - read - read
rend - rent - rent
rid - ridded, rid - rid, ridded
ride - rode - ridden
ring - rang - rung
rise - rose - risen
rive - rived - riven
run - ran - run

saw - sawed - sawn, sawed
say - said - said
see - saw - seen
seek - sought - sought
sell - sold - sold
send - sent - sent
set - set - set
sew - sewed - sewed, sewn
shake - shook - shaken
shall - should
shave - shaved - shaved, shaven
shear - sheared - shorn
shed - shed - shed
shine - shone - shone
shoe - shod - shod
shoot - shot - shot
show - showed - shown
shred - shredded - shredded, shred
shrink - sharnk - shrunk
shut - shut - shut
sing - sang - sung
sink - sank - sunk
sit - sat - sat
slay - slew - slain
sleep - slept - slept
slide - slid - slid

sling - slung - slung
slink - slunk - slunk
slit - slit - slit
smell - smelt, smelled - smelt, smelled
smite - smote - smitten
sow - sowed - sown, sowed
speak - spoke - spoken
speed - sped, ⊕ speeded - sped, ⊕ speeded
spell - spelt, spelled - spelt, spelled
spend - spent - spent
spill - spilt, spilled - spilt, spilled
spin - spun, span - spun
spit - spat - spat
split - split - split
spoil - spoiled, spoilt - spoiled, spoilt
spread - spread - spread
spring - sprang - sprung
stand - stood - stood
stave - staved, stove - staved, stove
steal - stole - stolen
stick - stuck - stuck
sting - stung - stung
stink - stunk, stank - stunk
strew - strewed - (have) strewed, (be) strewn
stride - strode - stridden
strike - struck - struck

string - strung - strung
strive - strove - striven
swear - swore - sworn
sweep - swept - swept
swell - swelled - swollen
swim - swam - swum
swing - swung - swung

take - took - taken
teach - taught - taught
tear - tore - torn
tell - told - told
think - thought - thought
thrive - throve - thriven
throw - threw - thrown
thrust - thrust - thrust
tread - trod - trodden

wake - woke, waked - waked, woke(n)
wear - wore - worn
weave - wove - woven
weep - wept - wept
wet - wetted, wet - wetted, wet
will - would
win - won - won
wind - wound - wound
work - worked, *surt.* ⊕ wrought - worked, *surt.* ⊕ wrought
wring - wrung - wrung
write - wrote - written

Temperature Conversion Tables
Tables de conversion des températures

1. FROM − 273 °C TO + 1000 °C
1. DE − 273 °C À + 1000 °C

Celsius °C	Kelvin K	Fahrenheit °F	Réaumur °R
1000	1273	1832	800
950	1223	1742	760
900	1173	1652	720
850	1123	1562	680
800	1073	1472	640
750	1023	1382	600
700	973	1292	560
650	923	1202	520
600	873	1112	480
550	823	1022	440
500	773	932	400
450	723	842	360
400	673	752	320
350	623	662	280
300	573	572	240
250	523	482	200
200	473	392	160
150	423	302	120
100	373	212	80
95	368	203	76
90	363	194	72
85	358	185	68
80	353	176	64
75	348	167	60
70	343	158	56
65	338	149	52
60	333	140	48
55	328	131	44
50	323	122	40
45	318	113	36
40	313	104	32
35	308	95	28
30	303	86	24
25	298	77	20
20	293	68	16
15	288	59	12
10	283	50	8
+ 5	278	41	+ 4
0	273.15	32	0
− 5	268	23	− 4
− 10	263	14	− 8

Celsius °C	Kelvin K	Fahrenheit °F	Réaumur °R
− 15	258	+ 5	− 12
− 17.8	255.4	0	− 14.2
− 20	253	− 4	− 16
− 25	248	− 13	− 20
− 30	243	− 22	− 24
− 35	238	− 31	− 28
− 40	233	− 40	− 32
− 45	228	− 49	− 36
− 50	223	− 58	− 40
− 100	173	− 148	− 80
− 150	123	− 238	− 120
− 200	73	− 328	− 160
− 250	23˙	− 418	− 200
− 273.15	0	− 459.4	− 218.4

2. CLINICAL THERMOMETER
2. THERMOMÈTRE MÉDICAL

Celsius °C	Fahrenheit °F	Réaumur °R
42.0	107.6	33.6
41.8	107.2	33.4
41.6	106.9	33.3
41.4	106.5	33.1
41.2	106.2	33.0
41.0	105.8	32.8
40.8	105.4	32.6
40.6	105.1	32.5
40.4	104.7	32.3
40.2	104.4	32.2
40.0	104.0	32.0
39.8	103.6	31.8
39.6	103.3	31.7
39.4	102.9	31.5
39.2	102.6	31.4
39.0	102.2	31.2
38.8	101.8	31.0
38.6	101.5	30.9
38.4	101.1	30.7
38.2	100.8	30.6
38.0	100.4	30.4
37.8	100.0	30.2
37.6	99.7	30.1
37.4	99.3	29.9
37.2	99.0	29.8
37.0	98.6	29.6
36.8	98.2	29.4
36.6	97.9	29.3

3. RULES FOR CONVERTING TEMPERATURES
3. FORMULES DE CONVERSION DES TEMPÉRATURES

	Celsius	*Kelvin*
$x\,°C$	–	$= x + 273.15\ K$
$x\,K$	$= x - 273.15\,°C$	–
$x\,°F$	$= \dfrac{5}{9}(x - 32)\,°C$	$= \dfrac{5}{9}(x - 32) + 273.15\ K$
$x\,°R$	$= \dfrac{5}{4}\,x\,°C$	$= \left(\dfrac{5}{4}\,x\right) + 273.15\ K$
	Fahrenheit	*Réaumur*
$x\,°C$	$= \dfrac{9}{5}\,x + 32\,°F$	$= \left(\dfrac{4}{5}\,x\right)\,°R$
$x\,K$	$= \dfrac{9}{5}(x - 273.15) + 32\,°F$	$= \dfrac{4}{5}(x - 273.15)\,°R$
$x\,°F$	–	$= \dfrac{4}{9}(x - 32)\,°R$
$x\,°R$	$= \left(\dfrac{9}{4}\,x\right) + 32\,°F$	–

Phonetic Alphabets

Codes d'épellation

	Français	Anglais britannique	Anglais américain	International	Aviation civile
A	Anatole	Andrew	Abel	Amsterdam	Alfa
B	Berthe	Benjamin	Baker	Baltimore	Bravo
C	Célestin	Charlie	Charlie	Casablanca	Charlie
D	Désiré	David	Dog	Danemark	Delta
E	Eugène	Edward	Easy	Edison	Echo
É	Émile	—	—	—	—
F	François	Frederick	Fox	Florida	Foxtrot
G	Gaston	George	George	Gallipoli	Golf
H	Henri	Harry	How	Havana	Hotel
I	Irma	Isaac	Item	Italia	India
J	Joseph	Jack	Jig	Jerusalem	Juliett
K	Kléber	King	King	Kilogramme	Kilo
L	Louis	Lucy	Love	Liverpool	Lima
M	Marcel	Mary	Mike	Madagaskar	Mike
N	Nicolas	Nellie	Nan	New York	November
O	Oscar	Oliver	Oboe	Oslo	Oscar
P	Pierre	Peter	Peter	Paris	Papa
Q	Quintal	Queenie	Queen	Québec	Quebec
R	Raoul	Robert	Roger	Roma	Romeo
S	Suzanne	Sugar	Sugar	Santiago	Sierra
T	Thérèse	Tommy	Tare	Tripoli	Tango
U	Ursule	Uncle	Uncle	Upsala	Uniform
V	Victor	Victor	Victor	Valencia	Victor
W	William	William	William	Washington	Whiskey
X	Xavier	Xmas	X	Xanthippe	X-Ray
Y	Yvonne	Yellow	Yoke	Yokohama	Yankee
Z	Zoé	Zebra	Zebra	Zürich	Zulu